To better care for all surgical patients

CONTENTS

7.   TRAUMA AND THERMAL INJURY

8.   CRITICAL CARE

Resuscitation and Stabilization

Available Exclusively Online at www.acssurgery.com

ELEMENTS OF CONTEMPORARY PRACTICE

1. BASIC SURGICAL AND PERIOPERATIVE CONSIDERATIONS

3. BREAST, SKIN, AND SOFT TISSUE

See inside front cover to get started online.

CONTRIBUTORS

CAMERON M. AKBARI, M.D., F.A.C.S. Assistant Professor of Surgery, Georgetown University School of Medicine, and Director, Vascular Diagnostic Laboratory, Washington Hospital Center

ELIAS J. ANAISSIE, M.D. Professor of Medicine, Myeloma and Transplantation Research Center, University of Arkansas College of Medicine, and Director, Department of Clinical Affairs, University Hospital of Arkansas

JOHN T. ANDERSON, M.D., F.A.C.S. Associate Professor of Surgery, University of California, Davis, School of Medicine

RAFAEL S. ANDRADE, M.D. Assistant Professor of Surgery, University of Minnesota Medical School

FRANK R. ARKO, M.D. Assistant Professor, Department of Surgery, University of Texas Southwestern Medical School

STANLEY W. ASHLEY, M.D., F.A.C.S. Vice-Chairman and Frank Sawyer Professor of Surgery, Harvard Medical School, and Program Director and Senior Surgeon, Department of Surgery, Division of General and Gastrointestinal Surgery, Brigham and Women's Hospital

AHMAD S. ASHRAFI, M.D., F.R.C.S.C. Fellow in Advanced Minimally Invasive Thoracic Surgery, University of Pittsburgh Medical Center

MARVIN D. ATKINS, M.D. Clinical and Research Fellow, Department of Surgery, Harvard Medical School

JUAN AYERDI, M.D. Assistant Professor, Department of General Surgery, Wake Forest University School of Medicine

STEVEN B. BACKMAN, M.D.C.M., Ph.D. Associate Professor, Department of Anesthesia, McGill University Faculty of Medicine

SEAN M. BAGSHAW, M.D., M.Sc., F.R.C.P.C. Fellow in Critical Care Medicine, Department of Intensive Care, Austin Hospital, Heidelberg, Australia

ALAN N. BARKUN, M.D. Associate Professor, Department of Medicine, McGill University Faculty of Medicine, and Director, Division of Gastroenterology, McGill University Health Centre

JEFFREY S. BARKUN, M.D., F.A.C.S. Associate Professor and Director, Division of Gastroenterology, Department of Surgery, McGill University Faculty of Medicine, and Department of Surgery, McGill University Health Centre

ROBERT H. BARTLETT, M.D., F.A.C.S. Professor, Division of General and Thoracic Surgery, University of Michigan Medical School

NANCY N. BAXTER, M.D., Ph.D., F.R.C.S.C., F.A.S.C.R.S. Assistant Professor, Department of Surgery, University of Minnesota Medical School

DAVID E. BECK, M.D., F.A.C.S., F.A.S.C.R.S. Chairman, Department of Colon and Rectal Surgery, Ocshner Clinic Foundation of New Orleans

MICHAEL BELKIN, M.D., F.A.C.S. Associate Professor, Division of Vascular Surgery, Harvard Medical School

RINALDO BELLOMO, M.D., F.R.A.C.P., F.J.F.I.C.M. Professor of Medicine, University of Melbourne Faculty of Medicine; Director of Intensive Care Research; and Staff Specialist in Intensive Care, Austin Hospital, Heidelberg, Australia

JOHN J. BERGAN, M.D., F.A.C.S. Professor, Department of Surgery, University of California, San Diego, School of Medicine, and Staff Surgeon, Scripps Memorial Hospital

RAMON BERGUER, M.D., F.A.C.S. Clinical Professor of Surgery, University of California, Davis, School of Medicine

PALMER Q. BESSEY, M.D., F.A.C.S. Professor, Department of Surgery, Weill Medical College of Cornell University, and Associate Director, William Randolph Hearst Burn Center, New York Presbyterian Hospital-Cornell Medical Center

ROBERT R. BIES, Pharm.D., Ph.D.   Assistant Professor of Pharmaceutical Sciences, University of Pittsburgh School of Pharmacy

JOHN D. BIRKMEYER, M.D., F.A.C.S.   George D. Zuidema Professor, Department of Surgery, University of Michigan Medical School

ALBAIR B. BISHARA, M.D.   Postdoctoral Fellow, Department of Surgery, University of Arkansas College of Medicine

F. WILLIAM BLAISDELL, M.D., F.A.C.S.   Professor and Chairman Emeritus, Department of Surgery, University of California, Davis, School of Medicine, and Chief of Surgical Services, Department of Surgery, Mather Veterans Affairs Hospital, Mather, California

LESLIE H. BLUMGART, M.D., F.A.C.S., F.R.C.S.   Enid A. Haupt Chair in Surgery, and Chief, Hepatobiliary Services, Memorial Sloan-Kettering Cancer Center

RICHARD M. BONDY, M.D.C.M.   Associate Professor, Department of Anesthesia, McGill University Faculty of Medicine

JENNIFER J. BONNER, Pharm.D.   Department of Pharmacy, University of Pittsburgh Medical Center

WILBUR B. BOWNE, M.D.   Assistant Professor of Surgery, State University of New York Downstate Medical Center College of Medicine

CAROL R. BRADFORD, M.D., F.A.C.S.   Associate Professor, Department of Otolaryngology, University of Michigan Medical Center

BRUCE M. BRENNER, M.D., F.A.C.S.   Assistant Professor, Division of Surgical Oncology, Medical College of Wisconsin

JULIAN BRITTON, M.S., F.R.C.S.   Consultant Surgeon, Nuffield Department of Surgery, University of Oxford

DAVID C. BROOKS, M.D., F.A.C.S.   Associate Professor, Department of Clinical Surgery, Harvard Medical School, and Senior Surgeon, Brigham and Women's Hospital

L. MICHAEL BRUNT, M.D., F.A.C.S.   Associate Professor, Department of Surgery, Washington University School of Medicine, St. Louis

AYESHA S. BRYANT, M.D., M.S.P.H.   Resident, Department of Surgery, Emory University Hospital

RAPHAEL BUENO, M.D., F.A.C.S.   Associate Professor of Surgery, Harvard Medical School

JON M. BURCH, M.D., F.A.C.S.   Professor, Department of Surgery, University of Colorado Health Sciences Center, and Chief, Department of General and Vascular Surgery, Denver Health Medical Center

JOHN BYRNE, M.Ch., F.R.C.S.I. (GEN.)   Assistant Professor of Surgery, Albany Medical College

JOHN L. CAMERON, M.D., F.A.C.S.   Alfred Blaylock Distinguished Service Professor of Surgery, Johns Hopkins University School of Medicine

SHAMUS R. CARR, M.D.   Instructor in Surgery, University of Pennsylvania School of Medicine, and Chief Resident, Department of Surgery, Hospital of the University of Pennsylvania

KATHLEEN CASEY, M.D.   Chief, Section of Infectious Disease, Jersey Shore Medical Center, and Clinical Professor of Medicine, University of Medicine and Dentistry of New Jersey Robert Wood Johnson Medical School

SUSAN M. CERA, M.D.   Colorectal Surgeon, Cleveland Clinic Florida

ROBERT JAMES CERFOLIO, M.D., F.A.C.S., F.C.C.P.   Associate Professor of Surgery, University of Alabama at Birmingham School of Medicine, and Chief of General Thoracic Surgery, University of Alabama at Birmingham Medical Center

ARA A. CHALIAN, M.D., F.A.C.S.   Associate Professor Department of Otorhinolaryngology: Head and Neck Surgery, University of Pennsylvania School of Medicine

PROSANTO CHAUDHURY, M.D.   Assistant Professor of Surgery, McGill University Faculty of Medicine

CLIFFORD S. CHO, M.D.   Fellow, Department of Surgical Oncology, Memorial Sloan-Kettering Cancer Center

TAE CHONG, M.D.   Resident, Department of Surgery, University of Virginia Health System

NICOLAS V. CHRISTOU, M.D., Ph.D., F.A.C.S.   Professor, Department of Surgery, McGill University Faculty of Medicine, and Head, Division of General Surgery, McGill University Health Centre

ROBERT E. CILLEY, M.D., F.A.C.S.   Professor of Surgery and Pediatrics, Penn State University College of Medicine, and Chief, Division of Pediatric Surgery, Milton S. Hershey Medical Center

ROBERT R. CIMA, M.D., F.A.C.S., F.A.S.C.R.S.   Assistant Professor of Surgery, Division of Colon and Rectal Surgery, Mayo Clinic College of Medicine

CLAUDIO S. CINÀ, M.D., Sp.Chir. (It.), M.Sc., F.R.C.S.C.   Assistant Clinical Professor, Department of Surgery, McMaster University Faculty of Health Sciences

G. PATRICK CLAGETT, M.D., F.A.C.S.   Professor of Surgery and Chairman, Division of Vascular Surgery, University of Texas Southwestern Medical Center at Dallas

THOMAS E. CLANCY, M.D.   Instructor of Surgery, Harvard Medical School, and Associate Surgeon, Brigham and Women's Hospital

ORLO H. CLARK, M.D., F.A.C.S. Professor and Vice Chair, Department of Surgery, University of California, San Francisco, School of Medicine, and Chief, Department of Surgery, Mount Zion Medical Center of UC-San Francisco

CATHERINE M. CLASE, M.B., B.Chir., M.Sc. Associate Professor, Michael G. DeGroote School of Medicine, McMaster University Faculty of Medicine

JEFFREY L. COHEN, M.D., F.A.C.S., F.A.S.C.R.S. Associate Clinical Professor, University of Connecticut School of Medicine, and Adjunct Assistant Clinical Professor of Surgery, Dartmouth Medical School

CRAIG M. COOPERSMITH, M.D., F.A.C.S., F.C.C.M. Associate Professor of Surgery and Anesthesiology, Department of Surgery, Washington University School of Medicine

ARNOLD G. CORAN, M.D., F.A.C.S. Professor, Division of Pediatric Surgery, Department of Surgery, University of Michigan Medical School, and Surgeon-in-Chief, Section of Pediatric Surgery, Department of Surgery, C. S. Mott Children's Hospital

DAVID CRIPPEN, M.D., F.C.C.M. Associate Professor, Department of Critical Care Medicine, University of Pittsburgh School of Medicine

VICTOR J. D'ADDIO, M.D., F.A.C.S. Staff Vascular Surgeon, Mary Washington Hospital, Surgical Associates of Fredericksburg, Virginia

THOMAS A. D'AMICO, M.D., F.A.C.S. Associate Professor of Surgery, Duke University School of Medicine

R. CLEMENT DARLING III, M.D., F.A.C.S. Professor of Surgery and Chief, Division of Vascular Surgery, Albany Medical College

MARK G. DAVIES, M.D., Ph.D., F.A.C.S. Associate Professor of Surgery, University of Rochester School of Medicine and Dentistry, and Attending Physician, Department of Surgery, Division of Vascular Surgery, University of Rochester Medical Center

JOHN MIHRAN DAVIS, M.D., F.A.C.S. Professor, Department of Surgery, University of Medicine and Dentistry of New Jersey Robert Wood Johnson Medical School, and Surgery Program Director, Jersey Shore Medical Center

ROMANO DELCORE, M.D., F.A.C.S. Professor of Surgery, University of Kansas School of Medicine, and Medical Director, Department of Surgery, University of Kansas Medicial Center

E. PATCHEN DELLINGER, M.D., F.A.C.S. Professor and Vice Chairman, Department of Surgery, University of Washington School of Medicine, and Chief and Associate Medical Director, Department of Surgery, University of Washington Medical Center

ERIC J. DEMARIA, M.D., F.A.C.S. Professor and Vice-Chairman of Network General Surgery, Duke University School of Medicine, and Chief of Endosurgery and Duke Surgery, Durham Regional Hospital, Duke University Medical Center

ACHILLES A. DEMETRIOU, M.D., Ph.D., F.A.C.S. Chairman, Department of Surgery, Cedars-Sinai Medical Center, Los Angeles

TINA R. DESAI, M.D., F.A.C.S. Assistant Professor of Surgery, University of Chicago Pritzker School of Medicine

ALAIN DESCHAMPS, M.D., Ph.D. Assistant Professor, Department of Anesthesia, McGill University Faculty of Medicine

PETER W. DILLON, M.D., F.A.C.S. Professor of Surgery and Pediatrics, Penn State University College of Medicine; Vice Chair of Clinical Affairs, Department of Surgery; and Surgical Director, Perioperative Services, Milton S. Hershey Medical Center

JOSEPH J. DISA, M.D., F.A.C.S. Assistant Attending Surgeon, Department of Plastic and Reconstructive Surgery, Memorial Sloan-Kettering Cancer Center

MATTHEW S. EDWARDS, M.D., F.A.C.S. Assistant Professor, Department of General Surgery, Wake Forest University School of Medicine

LOREN H. ENGRAV, M.D., F.A.C.S. Professor of Surgery, University of Washington School of Medicine, and Patient Care Coordinator, Burns/Plastic Surgery Clinic, Harborview Medical Center

MARK K. ESKANDARI, M.D., F.A.C.S. Assistant Professor, Department of Surgery, Northwestern University Feinberg School of Medicine

DAVID C. EVANS, M.D., F.A.C.S. Assistant Professor, Department of Surgery, McGill University Faculty of Medicine, and Director, Trauma Unit, Montreal General Hospital

TIMOTHY C. FABIAN, M.D., F.A.C.S. Harwell Wilson Alumni Professor and Chairman, Department of Surgery, University of Tennessee Health Science Center College of Medicine

LEE D. FAUCHER, M.D., F.A.C.S. Assistant Professor, Department of Surgery, University of Iowa Carver College of Medicine

ALICIA FANNING, M.D. Laparoscopic/Endoscopic Fellow, Cleveland Clinic Foundation

LIANE S. FELDMAN, M.D., F.A.C.S. Assistant Professor, Department of Surgery, McGill University Faculty of Medicine, and Staff, Departments of Videoendoscopic Surgery and Surgery, McGill University Hospital Centre

DAVID V. FELICIANO, M.D., F.A.C.S. Professor, Department of Surgery, Emory University School of Medicine, and Chief of Surgery, Grady Memorial Hospital

DAVID M. HEIMBACH, M.D., F.A.C.S. Professor, Department of Surgery, University of Washington School of Medicine

JOHN W. HELLSTEIN, D.D.S. Professor of Oral Pathology, Radiology, and Medicine, University of Iowa College of Dentistry

W. SCOTT HELTON, M.D., F.A.C.S. Professor of Surgery, Chief of General Surgery, Director of Minimally Invasive Surgery Program, University of Illinois at Chicago College of Medicine

LEONARD R. HENRY, M.D. Instructor, Department of Surgery, Uniformed Services University of the Health Sciences

DAVID A. HIDALGO, M.D., F.A.C.S. Associate Professor, Department of Surgery, Weill Medical College of Cornell University, and Associate Professor, Division of Plastic and Reconstructive Surgery, Manhattan Eye, Ear, and Throat Hospital

HUNG S. HO, M.D., F.A.C.S. Associate Professor, Division of Gastrointestinal and Laparoscopic Surgery, Department of Surgery, University of California, Davis, School of Medicine, and Medical Director and Attending Staff, Section of Gastrointestinal and Laparoscopic Surgery, Department of Surgery, University of California, Davis, Medical Center

HENRY T. HOFFMAN, M.D., F.A.C.S. Professor, Department of Otolaryngology, University of Iowa Carver College of Medicine

JAMES W. HOLCROFT, M.D., F.A.C.S. Professor, Department of Surgery, University of California, Davis, School of Medicine

RICHARD J. HOWARD, M.D., Ph.D., F.A.C.S. Robert H. and Kathleen M. Axline Professor of Surgery, Division of General Surgery and Transplantation, Department of Surgery, University of Florida College of Medicine

ROGER D. HURST, M.D., F.A.C.S., F.R.C.S.Ed., F.C.S.H.K. Associate Professor, Department of Surgery, University of Chicago Pritzker School of Medicine

ADAM S. JACOBSON, M.D. Department of Otolaryngology, Mount Sinai School of Medicine–Mount Sinai Hospital

ROBERT C. JACOBY, M.D., F.A.C.S. Assistant Professor, Department of Surgery, University of California, Davis, School of Medicine

JENNIFER W. JANELLE, M.D. Clinical Professor of Medicine, Division of Infectious Diseases, Department of Medicine, University of Florida College of Medicine

YIXING JIANG, M.D., Ph.D. Assistant Professor of Medicine, Penn State University College of Medicine

GREGG H. JOSSART, M.D., F.A.C.S. Director of Minimally Invasive Surgery, California Pacific Medical Center, San Francisco

GREGORY J. JURKOVICH, M.D., F.A.C.S. Professor of Surgery, University of Washington School of Medicine

RENA B. KASS, M.D., F.A.C.S. Assistant Professor of Surgery, Penn State University College of Medicine

AMIR KAVIANI, M.D. Fellow in Vascular Surgery, Cleveland Clinic Foundation Lerner College of Medicine of Case Western Reserve University

HENRIK KEHLET, M.D., Ph.D., F.A.C.S. (Hon.) Professor, Section for Surgical Pathophysiology, Copenhagen University School of Medicine, and Director of Section for Surgical Pathophysiology, Rigshospitalet, Copenhagen, Denmark

JOHN A. KELLUM, M.D. Associate Professor of Critical Care Medicine, University of Pittsburgh School of Medicine

MELINA R. KIBBE, M.D., R.V.T., F.A.C.S. Assistant Professor, Department of Surgery, Northwestern University Feinberg School of Medicine

KEE D. KIM, M.D. Assistant Professor, Department of Neurological Surgery, University of California, Davis, School of Medicine

ERIC KIMCHI, M.D. Assistant Professor of Surgery, Penn State University College of Medicine

EDWARD H. KINCAID, M.D., F.A.C.S. Assistant Professor of Cardiothoracic Surgery, Wake Forest University Baptist Medical Center

DENNIS R. KLASSEN, M.D. Assistant Professor, Department of Surgery, Dalhousie University Faculty of Medicine

MATTHEW B. KLEIN, M.D. Assistant Professor, Burn Center and Division of Plastic Surgery, Department of Surgery, Harborview Medical Center, University of Washington School of Medicine

IRA J. KODNER, M.D., F.A.C.S., F.A.S.C.R.S. Solon and Bettie Gershman Professor, Division of Colon and Rectal Surgery, Department of Surgery, Washington University School of Medicine, St. Louis

MARIN H. KOLLEF, M.D. Associate Professor, Division of Pulmonary and Critical Care Medicine, Washington University School of Medicine, St. Louis

BENJAMIN D. KOZOWER, M.D. Thoracic Surgery Fellow, Washington University School of Medicine, St. Louis

DAVID N. KRAG, M.D., F.A.C.S. S. D. Ireland Professor, Department of Surgery, University of Vermont College of Medicine

PAUL R. KRAMER, JR., M.D. Assistant Professor of Obstetrics and Gynecology, Penn State University College of Medicine

JOHN C. KUCHARCZUK, M.D., F.A.C.S. Assistant Professor, Department of Surgery, University of Pennsylvania School of Medicine

CONSTANTINOS KYRIAKIDES, M.D. Senior Clinical Vascular Fellow, Regional Vascular Unit, St. Mary's Hospital, London, England

RENE LAFRENIERE, M.D., C.M., F.A.C.S. Professor and Head, Department of Surgery, University of Calgary Faculty of Medicine, and Regional Clinical Director of Surgery, Calgary Regional Health Authority

ERIC S. LAMBRIGHT, M.D. Assistant Professor of Thoracic Surgery, Vanderbilt University School of Medicine, and Chief of Thoracic Surgery, Veterans Affairs Medical Center, Nashville

BERNARD LANGER, M.D., F.A.C.S., F.R.C.S.C. Professor, Department of Surgery, University of Toronto Faculty of Medicine, and Senior Staff Surgeon, Toronto General Hospital

MIRIAM N. LANGO, M.D. Associate Member, Attending Surgeon, Head and Neck Oncology, Fox Chase Cancer Center

KEITH D. LILLEMOE, M.D., F.A.C.S. Jay L. Grosfeld Professor of Surgery, Indiana University School of Medicine

D. SCOTT LIND, M.D., F.A.C.S. Professor, Department of Surgery, University of Florida College of Medicine, and Chief of Surgical Services, North Florida, South Georgia VA System

DAVID C. LINEHAN, M.D., F.A.C.S. Assistant Professor, Department of Surgery, Washington University School of Medicine, St. Louis

FRANK W. LOGERFO, M.D., F.A.C.S. William V. McDermott Professor of Surgery, Harvard Medical School

VIVIAN G. LOO, M.D., M.Sc. Assistant Professor, Department of Medicine, McGill University Faculty of Medicine, and Director, Infection Control and Prevention Service, McGill University Health Centre

ANDREW E. LUCKEY, M.D. Senior Surgery Resident, East Bay Surgery Program, University of California, San Francisco, School of Medicine

DANA C. LYNGE, M.D., F.A.C.S. Associate Professor of Surgery, University of Washington School of Medicine

MICHAEL MADDAUS, M.D., F.A.C.S. Professor of Surgery, University of Minnesota Medical School

ROBERT D. MADOFF, M.D., F.A.C.S., F.A.S.C.R.S. Professor, Department of Surgery, University of Minnesota Medical School

MARK A. MALANGONI, M.D., F.A.C.S. Professor and Chair of Surgery, Case Western Reserve University School of Medicine

THOMAS S. MALDONADO, M.D. Assistant Professor, Department of Surgery, New York University School of Medicine

JOSEPH MAMAZZA, M.D., F.A.C.S., F.R.C.S.C. Chair, Division of General Surgery, and Professor, Department of Surgery, University of Ottawa Faculty of Medicine; and Head, Division of General Surgery, and Medical Director of Minimally Invasive Surgery, Ottawa Hospital

MALCOLM G. MAN-SON-HING, M.D., M.Sc., F.R.C.P.C. Associate Professor, Department of Medicine, University of Ottawa Faculty of Medicine

D. L. MARQUARDT, M.D. Chief Resident, Department of Surgery, University of Washington School of Medicine

JOHN C. MARSHALL, M.D., F.A.C.S., F.R.C.S.C. Professor, Department of Surgery, University of Toronto Faculty of Medicine, and Director of Research, Medical and Surgical Intensive Care Unit, and Staff Surgeon, Toronto General Hospital University Health Network

BYRON J. MASTERSON, M.D., F.A.C.S. J. Wayne Reitz Professor Emeritus, University of Florida College of Medicine, Gainesville, and Associate Dean and Chairman Emeritus, Department of Obstetrics and Gynecology, Shands Hospital, Gainesville

JON MATSUMURA, M.D., F.A.C.S. Associate Professor, Department of Surgery, Northwestern University Feinberg School of Medicine

JACQUELINE C. MCCLARAN, M.D. Assistant Medical Director, John Radcliffe Trust, University of Oxford

CHRISTOPHER R. MCHENRY, M.D., F.A.C.S. Professor of Surgery, Case Western Reserve University School of Medicine, and Vice Chairman, Department of Surgery, MetroHealth Medical Center, Cleveland

DANIEL P. MCKELLAR, M.D., F.A.C.S. Associate Clinical Professor, Department of Surgery, Wright State University School of Medicine

A. PETER MCLEAN, M.D., F.A.C.S. Associate Professor, Department of Surgery, McGill University Faculty of Medicine, and Senior Surgeon, McGill University Health Centre

JONATHAN L. MEAKINS, M.D., D.Sc., F.A.C.S., F.R.C.S.C. Nuffield Professor and Head, Nuffield Department of Surgery, University of Oxford

ANDREAS H. MEIER, M.D. Assistant Professor of Surgery and Pediatrics, Penn State University College of Medicine, and Pediatric Surgeon, Milton S. Hershey Medical Center

TERRY J. MENGERT, M.D. Professor of Medicine, University of Washington School of Medicine, and Attending Physician, Emergency Department, University of Washington Medical Center

J. WAYNE MEREDITH, M.D., F.A.C.S. Professor and Chairman, Department of General Surgery, Wake Forest University School of Medicine

BRYAN F. MEYERS, M.D., F.A.C.S. Associate Professor, Department of Surgery, Washington University School of Medicine, St. Louis

SHARI L. MEYERSON, M.D. Fellow in Cardiothoracic Surgery, Duke University Medical Center

FABRIZIO MICHELASSI, M.D., F.A.C.S. Lewis Atterbury Stimson Professor and Chairman, Department of Surgery, Weill Medical College of Cornell University

CHARLES M. MILLER, M.D., F.A.C.S. Alfred and Florence Gross Professor of Surgery, Mount Sinai School of Medicine of the City University of New York, and Director, Recanati-Miller Transplantation Institute, Mount Sinai Medical Center, New York City

JEFFREY W. MILSOM, M.D., F.A.C.S. Professor of Surgery, Joan and Sanford I. Weill Medical College of Cornell University

FREDERICK L. MOFFAT, JR., M.D., F.A.C.S. Professor, Department of Surgery, University of Miami School of Medicine

GREGORY L. MONETA, M.D., F.A.C.S. Professor, Department of Surgery, and Chief of Vascular Surgery, Oregon Health and Science University School of Medicine

BERNARD MONTREUIL, M.D., F.A.C.S. Assistant Professor, Department of Vascular Surgery, Maisonneuve-Rosemont Hospital, University of Montreal Faculty of Medicine

ANNE MOORE, M.D. Associate Professor, Department of Surgery, McGill University Faculty of Medicine

ERNEST E. MOORE, M.D., F.A.C.S. Professor and Vice Chairman, Department of Surgery, University of Colorado Health Sciences Center, and Chief, Department of Surgery, Denver Health Medical Center

FREDERICK A. MOORE, M.D., F.A.C.S. Professor and Vice Chairman, Department of Surgery, University of Texas Medical School at Houston, and Chief, Department of General Surgery, Trauma, and Critical Care, Memorial Hermann Hospital

HARVEY G. MOORE, M.D. Research Fellow, Memorial Sloan-Kettering Cancer Center

WESLEY S. MOORE, M.D., F.A.C.S. Professor, Division of Vascular Surgery, Department of Surgery, David Geffen School of Medicine, University of California, Los Angeles

J. PAUL MUIZELAAR, M.D., Ph.D. Professor and Chairman, Department of Neurological Surgery, University of California, Davis, School of Medicine

SCOTT E. MUSICANT, M.D. Fellow, Division of Vascular Surgery, Oregon Health and Science University School of Medicine

ROBERT B. NADLER, M.D., F.A.C.S. Associate Professor of Urology, Northwestern University Feinberg School of Medicine

ATTILA NAKEEB, M.D., F.A.C.S. Associate Professor of Surgery, Indiana University School of Medicine

LENA M. NAPOLITANO, M.D., F.A.C.S. Professor, Department of Surgery, University of Michigan, and Chief, Surgical Critical Care, and Associate Chair, Department of Surgery, University of Michigan Health System

AVERY B. NATHENS, M.D., Ph.D., M.P.H., F.A.C.S. Assistant Professor of Surgery, University of Washington School of Medicine

ABDELRAHMAN A. NIMERI, M.D. Assistant Clinical Professor, Department of Surgery, University of California, San Francisco, School of Medicine

PATRICK J. O'HARA, M.D., F.A.C.S. Professor, Department of Surgery, Cleveland Clinic Lerner College of Medicine of Case Western Reserve University, and Staff Vascular Surgeon, Cleveland Clinic Foundation

TERENCE O'KEEFFE, M.B., Ch.B., F.R.C.S.Ed. Assistant Professor of Surgery, University of Texas Southwestern Medical School at Dallas

BERT W. O'MALLEY, JR., M.D., F.A.C.S. Professor and Chair, Department of Otorhinolaryngology: Head and Neck Surgery, University of Pennsylvania School of Medicine

DAVID M. OTA, M.D., F.A.C.S. Group Co-Chair, American College of Surgeons Oncology Group

JOHN T. OWINGS, M.D., F.A.C.S. Professor, Department of Surgery, Chief, Surgical Critical Care, and Assistant Dean of Student Affairs, University of California, Davis, School of Medicine

VICKEN N. PAMOUKIAN, M.D., F.A.C.S. Attending Vascular Surgeon, Lenox Hill Hospital, New York

BERNARD PARK, M.D., F.A.C.S. Department of Surgery, Memorial Sloan-Kettering Cancer Center

CYRUS J. PARSA, M.D. Senior Resident, East Bay Surgery Program, University of California, San Francisco, School of Medicine

CHERIE P. PARUNGO, M.D. Department of Surgery, Brigham and Women's Hospital

LUIGI PASCARELLA, M.D. Clinical Instructor, Department of Surgery, University of California, San Diego, School of Medicine

VIVEK PATEL, M.B.B.S. Resident, Department of Surgery, University of Pennsylvania Medical Center

MARCO G. PATTI, M.D., F.A.C.S. Associate Professor, Department of Surgery, University of California, San Francisco, School of Medicine, and Director, Center for the Study of GI Motility and Secretion, University of California, San Francisco, Medical Center

PHILIP S. K. PATY, M.D., F.A.C.S. Associate Professor of Surgery, Albany Medical College

SUBROTO PAUL, M.D. Clinical Fellow in Surgery, Brigham and Women's Hospital

TAINE T. V. PECHET, M.D., F.A.C.S. Assistant Professor of Surgery, University of Pennsylvania School of Medicine, and Vice Chief, General Thoracic Surgery, Division of Thoracic Surgery, University of Pennsylvania Health System

JOHN H. PEMBERTON, M.D., F.A.C.S., F.A.S.C.R.S. Professor, Department of Surgery, Mayo Graduate School of Medicine

WILLIAM C. PEVEC, M.D., F.A.C.S. Associate Professor of Vascular Surgery, Department of Surgery, University of California, Davis, School of Medicine, and Chief of Vascular Surgery, University of California, Davis, Medical Center

EDWARD S. PODCZASKI, M.D., F.A.C.S. Professor of Obstetrics and Gynecology, Penn State University College of Medicine

K. J. PONSEN, M.D. Assistant Professor of Surgery, Academic Medical Center, University of Amsterdam

JEFFREY L. PONSKY, M.D., F.A.C.S. Professor of Surgery, Cleveland Clinic Health Sciences Center of the Ohio State University, and Director, Section of Endoscopic Surgery, Department of General Surgery, Cleveland Clinic Foundation

ERIC C. POULIN, M.D., M.Sc., F.A.C.S., F.R.C.S.C. Professor and Chair, Department of Surgery, University of Ottawa, and Surgeon-in-Chief, Ottawa Wilbert J. Keon Hospital

MARK E. P. PRINCE, M.D., F.R.C.S.C. Assistant Professor, Department of Otolaryngology, University of Michigan Medical School

JUAN CARLOS PUYANA, M.D., F.A.C.S. Associate Professor of Surgery and Critical Care, Javeriana University School of Medicine

THOMAS H. QUINN, Ph.D. Professor, Department of Biomedical Services, Creighton University School of Medicine

ALEKSANDAR RADAN, M.D., B.Sc. General Surgery Resident, Department of Surgery, McMaster University Faculty of Health Sciences

RICHARD B. REILING, M.D., F.A.C.S. Clinical Professor of Surgery, Wright State University School of Medicine, and Medical Director of the Cancer Center, Presbyterian Hospital, Charlotte

DOUGLAS S. REINTGEN, M.D., F.A.C.S. Professor, Department of Surgery, University of South Florida College of Medicine, and Program Leader, Department of Cutaneous Oncology, H. Lee Moffitt Cancer Center and Research Institute

ROBERT S. RHODES, M.D., F.A.C.S. Adjunct Professor, Department of Surgery, University of Pennsylvania School of Medicine, and Associate Executive Director and Director of Evaluation, American Board of Surgery, Philadelphia

ROCCO RICCIARDI, M.D. Colorectal Fellow, Department of Surgery, University of Minnesota Medical School

CHARLES L. RICE, M.D., F.A.C.S. Professor, Department of Surgery, and President, Uniformed Services University of Health Sciences

PRESTON B. RICH, M.D., F.A.C.S. Chief, Division of Trauma and Critical Care, Department of Surgery, University of North Carolina at Chapel Hill School of Medicine

ALAN T. RICHARDS, M.D., F.A.C.S. Professor, Department of Otolaryngology/Head and Neck Surgery, University of Nebraska College of Medicine, and Attending Surgeon, University of Nebraska Medical Center

JOHN A. RIDGE, M.D., Ph.D., F.A.C.S. Chief, Head and Neck Surgery, Department of Surgical Oncology, Fox Chase Cancer Center, Philadelphia

LAYTON F. RIKKERS, M.D., F.A.C.S. A. R. Curreri Professor and Chairman, Department of Surgery, University of Wisconsin Medical School

THOMAS S. RILES, M.D., F.A.C.S. George David Stewart Professor and Chairman, Department of Surgery, New York University School of Medicine

ROLANDO H. ROLANDELLI, M.D., F.A.C.S. Professor, Department of Surgery, Temple University School of Medicine, and Chief, Section of General Surgery, Temple University Hospital

BARRY J. ROSEMAN, M.D., F.A.C.S. Roseman and Budayr, M.D., P.C., Thompson Cancer Survival Center, Knoxville, Tennessee, and Blount Memorial Hospital Regional Cancer Center, Maryville, Tennessee

MICHAEL J. ROSEN, M.D. Department of Surgery, Cleveland Clinic Foundation

STUART ROTH, M.D., Ph.D. Orthopedic Liaison, Good Samaritan Hospital, Baltimore

DAVID A. ROTHENBERGER, M.D., F.A.C.S., F.A.S.C.R.S. Professor, Department of Surgery, University of Minnesota Medical School

RONALD RUBENSTEIN, M.D. Endourology Fellow, Department of Urology, Northwestern University Feinberg School of Medicine

VALERIE W. RUSCH, M.D., F.A.C.S. Professor, Department of Surgery, Weill Medical College of Cornell University, and William G. Cahan Chair of Surgery and Chief of Thoracic Surgery, Memorial Sloan-Kettering Cancer Center

JUAN R. SANABRIA, M.D., M.Sc., F.A.C.S. Assistant Professor of Surgery, Medical University of Ohio at Toledo

ROBERT G. SAWYER, M.D., F.A.C.S. Associate Professor of Surgery and Health Evaluation Science, University of Virginia School of Medicine, and Co-Director, Surgical Intensive Care Unit, University of Virginia Hospital

TIMOTHY A. SCHAUB, M.D. Resident, Department of Surgery, University of Michigan Medical Center

CHRISTOPHER M. SCHLACHTA, M.D., F.A.C.S. Lecturer and General Surgeon, Department of Surgery, University of Toronto Faculty of Medicine

RICHARD T. SCHLINKERT, M.D., F.A.C.S. Professor, Department of Surgery, Mayo Graduate School of Medicine, and General Surgeon, Department of Surgery, Mayo Clinic Scottsdale

THOMAS SCHRICKER, M.D., Ph.D. Assistant Professor, Department of Anesthesia, McGill University Faculty of Medicine

PATRICIA C. SEIFERT, B.A, Assoc.D., M.S.N., R.N. Adjunct Professor, Nursing, George Mason University School of Nursing

MATTHEW J. SENA, M.D. Assistant Professor, Division of Trauma and Emergency Surgery, Department of Surgery, University of California, Davis, School of Medicine

HIMANSU R. SHAH, M.D. Assistant Professor, Division of Plastic Surgery, Department of Surgery, University of Nevada School of Medicine

ASHOK R. SHAHA, M.D., F.A.C.S. Professor of Surgery, Joan and Sanford I. Weill Medical College of Cornell University, and Attending Surgeon, Memorial Sloan-Kettering Cancer Center

CYNTHIA K. SHORTELL, M.D., F.A.C.S. Chief of Vascular Surgery, Duke University School of Medicine

JOSEPH B. SHRAGER, M.D., F.A.C.S. Associate Professor of Surgery, University of Pennsylvania School of Medicine, and Chief, Section of General Thoracic Surgery, University of Pennsylvania Health System

BARBARA L. SMITH, M.D., Ph.D., F.A.C.S. Assistant Professor, Department of Surgery, Harvard Medical School; Director, Comprehensive Breast Health Center, Massachusetts General Hospital; Co-Director, Women's Cancers Program, Dana Farber/Partner's Cancer Care; and Chief of Breast Surgical Services, Gillette Center at the Dana Farber Cancer Institute

ROBERT SMITH, M.D. Surgical Research Fellow, University of Virginia School of Medicine

STEPHEN T. SMITH, M.D. Vascular and Endovascular Fellow, University of Texas Southwestern Medical School at Dallas

JOSEPH S. SOLOMKIN, M.D., F.A.C.S. Professor, Department of Surgery, and Director, Surgical Infectious Diseases Division, University of Cincinnati College of Medicine

TOYOOKI SONODA, M.D. Assistant Professor of Surgery, Joan and Sanford I. Weill Medical College of Cornell University

WILEY W. SOUBA, M.D., Sc.D., F.A.C.S. John A. and Marian T. Waldhausen Professor of Surgery and Chair, Department of Surgery, Penn State College of Medicine, and Surgeon-in-Chief, Milton S. Hershey Medical Center

DAVID I. SOYBEL, M.D., F.A.C.S. Associate Professor of Surgery, Harvard Medical School, and Senior Staff Surgeon, Division of General and Gastrointestinal Surgery, Brigham and Women's Hospital

THOMAS E. STARZL, M.D., Ph.D., F.A.C.S. Professor, Department of Surgery, and Director, Thomas E. Starzl Transplantation Institute, University of Pittsburgh School of Medicine

KEVIN STAVELEY-O'CARROLL, M.D., Ph.D., F.A.C.S. Associate Professor of Surgery, Penn State College of Medicine

RICHARD H. STERNS, M.D. Professor of Medicine, University of Rochester School of Medicine and Dentistry, and Chief of Medicine, Rochester General Hospital and the Genesee Hospital

STEVEN M. STRASBERG, M.D., F.A.C.S. Pruett Professor of Surgery, Washington University School of Medicine, St. Louis

HARVEY J. SUGERMAN, M.D., F.A.C.S. David M. Hume Professor and Head, Division of General and Trauma Surgery, Department of Surgery, Virginia Commonwealth University, Medical College of Virginia

WILLIAM D. SUGGS, M.D., F.A.C.S. Associate Professor, Department of Surgery, Albert Einstein College of Medicine of Yeshiva University

STEPHEN R. SULLIVAN, M.D. Department of Surgery, University of Washington School of Medicine

TIMOTHY M. SULLIVAN, M.D., F.A.C.S. Senior Associate Consultant, Associate Professor of Surgery, Division of Vascular Surgery, Mayo Medical School

R. SUDHIR SUNDARESAN, M.D., F.A.C.S., F.R.C.S.C. Associate Professor and Chief, Thoracic Surgery, University of Ottawa Faculty of Medicine, and Attending Staff Physician and Chief, Division of General Thoracic Surgery, Ottawa Hospital

MARK S. TALAMONTI, M.D., F.A.C.S. Professor, Surgical Oncology, Northwestern University Feinberg School of Medicine, and Chief, Division of Surgical Oncology, Northwestern Memorial Hospital

KENNETH TANABE, M.D., F.A.C.S. Associate Professor of Surgery, Harvard Medical School; Chief, Division of Surgical Oncology, Massachusetts General Hospital; and Surgeon, Gastrointestinal Cancer Center, Dana-Faber Cancer Institute

ROGER P. TATUM, M.D., F.A.C.S. Assistant Professor of Surgery, University of Washington School of Medicine

BRYCE R. TAYLOR, M.D., F.A.C.S., F.R.C.S.C. Professor and Associate Chair, Division of General Surgery, Department of Surgery, University of Toronto Faculty of Medicine, and McCutcheon Chair in Surgery, Surgeon-in-Chief, and Director of Surgical Services, University Health Network, Toronto

LLOYD M. TAYLOR, JR., M.D., F.A.C.S. Professor, Department of Surgery, Division of Vascular Surgery, Oregon Health and Science University School of Medicine

MARITA S. TENG, M.D. Clinical Fellow, University of Washington School of Medicine

ERWIN R. THAL, M.D., F.A.C.S. Professor, Department of Surgery, University of Texas Southwestern Medical Center

SETH THALLER, M.D., F.A.C.S. Professor and Chief, Department of Plastic Surgery, University of Miami School of Medicine

SAMUEL A. TISHERMAN, M.D., F.A.C.S., F.C.C.M. Associate Professor of Surgery and Critical Care Medicine, University of Pittsburgh School of Medicine

GEORGE TZIMAS, M.D. Chief of Surgical Services, Kypselis General Hospital, Athens, Greece

GILBERT R. UPCHURCH, JR., M.D., F.A.C.S. Assistant Professor, Department of Surgery, University of Michigan Medical School

MARK L. URKEN, M.D., F.A.C.S. Professor, Department of Otolaryngology, Mount Sinai School of Medicine

CAESAR URSIC, M.D., F.A.C.S. Assistant Professor, Department of Surgery, UCSF–East Bay Surgery Program, University of California, San Francisco, School of Medicine

GARTH H. UTTER, M.D., M.Sc. Assistant Professor of Surgery, Division of Trauma and Emergency Surgery, University of California, Davis, School of Medicine

O. M. VAN DELDEN, M.D., Ph.D. Associate Professor of Radiology, Academic Medical Center, University of Amsterdam

ARA VAPORCIYAN, M.D., F.A.C.S. Associate Professor of Surgery, University of Texas Medical School at Houston

FRANK J. VEITH, M.D., F.A.C.S. Professor, Department of Surgery, Albert Einstein College of Medicine of Yeshiva University

JOSEPH VIJUNGCO, M.D. Vascular Surgeon, General & Vascular Associates, Reno, Nevada

TODD R. VOGEL, M.D., M.P.H. Assistant Professor, University of Washington School of Medicine

JENNIFER A. WARGO, M.D. Instructor in Surgery, Harvard Medical School

MICHAEL T. WATKINS, M.D., F.A.C.S. Associate Professor of Surgery, Harvard Medical School

JAMES M. WATTERS, M.D., F.A.C.S. Professor, Department of Surgery, University of Ottawa Faculty of Medicine, and Attending Surgeon, Department of Surgery, Ottawa Hospital-Civic Campus

JEFFREY D. WAYNE, M.D., F.A.C.S. Assistant Professor of Surgery, Northwestern University Feinberg School of Medicine, and Staff Physician, Northwestern Memorial Hospital

ROBERT WEBER, M.S., F.A.S.H.P. Associate Professor and Chairman of Pharmacy and Therapeutics, University of Pittsburgh School of Pharmacy

JORDAN A. WEINBERG, M.D., F.R.C.S.C. Trauma Fellow, Department of Surgery, University of Tennessee Health Science Center College of Medicine

JOHN P. WELCH, M.D., F.A.C.S. Clinical Professor of Surgery, University of Connecticut School of Medicine, and Adjunct Professor of Surgery, Dartmouth Medical School

HUNTER WESSELLS, M.D., F.A.C.S. Associate Professor, Department of Urology, University of Washington School of Medicine

MARVIN J. WEXLER, M.D., F.A.C.S. Professor, Departments of Surgery and Oncology, McGill University Faculty of Medicine, and Senior Surgeon, Department of Surgery, Royal Victoria Hospital, Montreal

STEVEN D. WEXNER, M.D., F.A.C.S., F.A.S.C.R.S., F.R.C.S., F.R.C.S.Ed. Chief of Staff and Chairman, Department of Colorectal Surgery, Cleveland Clinic Hospital/Cleveland Clinic Florida

J. GRAHAM WILLIAMS, M.Ch., F.R.C.S. Consultant Surgeon, Royal Wolverhampton Hospitals NHS Trust, Wolverhampton, England

KAREN STANLEY WILLIAMS, M.D. Medical Director, St. Agnes Healthcare, Baltimore

DOUGLAS W. WILMORE, M.D., F.A.C.S. Frank Sawyer Professor, Department of Surgery, Harvard Medical School, and Senior Staff Surgeon, Department of Surgery, Brigham and Women's Hospital

DAVID H. WISNER, M.D., F.A.C.S. Professor and Chief, Division of Trauma Surgery, Department of Surgery, University of California, Davis, School of Medicine

HEATHER Y. WOLFORD, M.D. Vascular Fellow, University of Rochester School of Medicine and Dentistry and Strong Memorial Hospital, Rochester

JOHN YEE, M.D., F.R.C.S.C. Assistant Professor of Surgery, Division of Thoracic Surgery, University of British Columbia Faculty of Medicine, and Surgical Director of Transplant Surgery, Vancouver Hopital and Health Sciences Centre

TONIA YOUNG-FADOK, M.D., M.S., F.A.C.S., F.A.S.C.R.S. Associate Professor, Department of Surgery, Division of Colon and Rectal Surgery, Mayo Clinic College of Medicine, Scottsdale

CHRISTOPHER K. ZARINS, M.D., F.A.C.S. Chidester Professor of Surgery, Stanford University School of Medicine, and Chief, Division of Vascular Surgery, Stanford University Medical Center

HERBERT ZEH, M.D., F.A.C.S. Assistant Professor of Surgery, University of Pittsburgh School of Medicine

MICHAEL E. ZENILMAN, M.D., F.A.C.S. Professor and Chairman, Department of Surgery, State University of New York Downstate Medical Center College of Medicine, and Chairman, Department of Surgery, University Hospital of Brooklyn

MARIKE ZWIENENBERG-LEE, M.D. Research Fellow, Department of Neurological Surgery, University of California, Davis, School of Medicine

FOREWORD

Wiley Souba and his collaborators have continued the tradition of constant improvement that has characterized *ACS Surgery: Principles & Practice* and have put together an extraordinary new edition. Indeed, the 2007 edition is the most comprehensive to date, with several new and many updated chapters. Totaling nearly 2,000 pages, the text covers information that is most relevant to all surgeons. The book's contents are currently available in four formats: the bound book, an online version that is updated monthly, a quarterly CD-ROM, and an annual CD-ROM.

The book opens with the section "Elements of Contemporary Practice," which covers several aspects of surgical practice not found in more traditional surgical textbooks, including "Professionalism in Surgery" and "Performance Measures." Two new chapters have been added to this section in 2007: "Benchmarking Surgical Outcomes" and "Evidence-Based Surgery." These topics are well suited to the needs of surgeons practicing in a world that is gravitating more and more toward regulation of surgical practice. The section "Basic Surgical and Perioperative Conditions" provides students and residents with practical tips on all elements of perioperative management. Just as important, this section is relevant to all practitioners of surgery who wish to keep up with changes in the management of respiratory failure, practical use of ICU monitoring devices, and a number of other issues applicable to postoperative conditions.

The core of the book is organized according to body regions—head and neck; breast, skin, and soft tissue; thorax; and the abdomen and gastrointestinal tract. The section "Thorax" has eight new chapters in this edition, and several other chapters have been added to the "Gastrointestinal Tract and Abdomen" section. The last portion of the book covers vascular surgery, trauma and thermal injury, and critical care. All of these sections also contain several new or updated chapters. In addition, an entirely new section, "Care in Special Situations," has been added, making this volume more than 10% larger than the previous edition.

One aspect of this book that has been widely praised is the fact that the chapters are relatively short—most can be read in about one hour. In addition, most of the chapters are problem-based—for example, "The Diabetic Foot." Thus, a surgeon seeking advice on how to manage this condition does not have to look through an entire section on peripheral vascular disease but can read the chapter that specifically addresses the problem. Because most chapters are clinically relevant and very focused, they offer not only the scientific underpinnings of surgical problems but also real, practical day-to-day knowledge that can be tapped on relatively short notice to aid in management.

What I found particularly interesting is the online version of this book, which in my opinion makes it truly a "living" document. *What's New in ACS Surgery* is a monthly online newsletter that describes the content of the monthly updates, which rotate from topic to topic in such a way that the entire book is constantly being rewritten. In "The Best Surgical Thinking" column, an *ACS Surgery* editor expands on an aspect of surgical practice with reference to current literature. Each monthly issue provides one or more "Special Alerts," which direct the reader to a recently published article that has the potential to impact the practice of surgery. These articles are usually linked directly to their original source—another advantage of being online. The online version makes it possible for residents to print out a chapter that is relevant to their needs that particular day. The chapter can be easily carried around and read in the occasional moments of downtime during the day. In addition, subscribers to *ACS Surgery Online* can obtain 60 Category 1 CME credits per year, which meets the American Board of Surgery CME credit requirements—another reminder to the young and the not-so-young surgeon of the era of Maintenance of Certification.

As I was preparing to write this Foreword, I asked several individuals who used previous editions to tell me what made them choose this text instead of a number of other available textbooks. One resident said, "This is the official book of the American College of Surgeons...Who would you trust more than the College to provide you with information and education in surgery?" I found this statement to be simple, spontaneous, and truthful.

Carlos A. Pellegrini, M.D., F.A.C.S.

The Henry N. Harkins Professor and Chair
Department of Surgery
University of Washington School of Medicine

PREFACE

Over the past decade, evidence-based medicine (EBM), which is an attempt to more consistently apply the standards of evidence gained from the scientific method to medical practice, has come to be recognized as the most well-founded basis for making clinical decisions. Predictably, EBM has had a profound impact on surgical practice. The discipline of surgery, which once relied heavily on opinion and tradition, now increasingly requires its practitioners to weigh the best available scientific evidence when making decisions about the care of surgical patients. And what better text to function as a trusted source of evidence-based surgical information than *ACS Surgery: Principles & Practice*, the official general surgery textbook of the American College of Surgeons?

Closely tied to the movement toward evidence-based surgery are current efforts to obtain comprehensive and accurate data about surgical outcomes. Patients, their families, and health insurers are all seeking information about surgical performance to guide their choices and decisions. And surgeons themselves require information about surgical outcomes to gauge their own performance and help direct their efforts at improvement. Among the important data sources for benchmarking surgical outcomes is the National Surgical Quality Improvement Program (NSQIP), an improvement-oriented outcome registry that is currently being promoted by the American College of Surgeons. In this edition of *ACS Surgery*, you will find two new chapters that cover the topics of evidence-based surgery and the benchmarking of surgical outcomes in great detail.

Another striking characteristic of *ACS Surgery, 6th Edition*, is that, at almost 2,000 pages, it is significantly larger and more comprehensive than any previous edition. This expansion has allowed us to add more than 20 chapters that did not appear in last year's edition. For example, the new thoracic section that was introduced in 2006 has more than doubled in size this year with the addition of eight new chapters. The expanded section covers important thoracic problems such as cough and hemoptysis, pleural effusion, and solitary pulmonary nodules. We have also added several new, highly illustrated chapters that provide detailed descriptions of specific thoracic surgical techniques, including mediastinal procedures, pericardial procedures, decortication and pleurectomy, pulmonary resection, and diaphragmatic procedures. The new thoracic chapters represent the continued commitment of the ACS editorial board to a broader understanding of general surgery.

Our vascular section has seen the addition of two new chapters—one covering upper-extremity revascularization procedures and the other describing endovascular procedures for lower-extremity vascular disease. The topics of cardiovascular monitoring and clinical pharmacology have been added to the critical care section, and the head and neck section now includes discussions of parotid mass and tracheostomy. In addition, this year we have incorporated a new section—Care in Special Situations. The five chapters in this section address important issues that surgeons confront in certain patient groups, such as the elderly, children, or pregnant women, as well as specific urologic or gynecologic problems commonly encountered by the general surgeon.

And of course, as we do every year, we have revised chapters throughout the book. Compared with the 2006 edition, almost 40% of the text is either completely new or revised. And this edition also includes many beautiful new illustrations, particularly in the chapters that are appearing for the first time this year.

And still more content is available online, at www.acssurgery.com, where book-buyers receive a free 3-month trial. This year, we have added two new online features—"Special Alerts" and "Clinical Practice Guidelines"—that we believe will significantly enhance the usefulness of *ACS Surgery* for our readers. "Special Alerts" are reports on recent key studies that our editors think will have an important impact on clinical practice. "Clinical Practice Guidelines" are evidence-based guidelines designed to reduce variation in clinical practice and improve patient care. The "Alerts" and "Guidelines" are highlighted in the monthly newsletter and can be accessed online by clicking on an icon placed next to the relevant text in the appropriate chapters.

Also at www.acssurgery.com, you can learn about other great features, such as a CME program that offers 60 Category 1 credits in a convenient online format. And be sure to sign up for our free monthly email alert, *What's New in ACS Surgery*, which keeps you current on general surgery with highlights from new and updated chapters.

I am very pleased with the changes and updates that have been added to *ACS Surgery* this year, and I believe our highly referenced and up-to-date text provides an invaluable tool for surgeons who increasingly appreciate the importance of evidence-based surgery in their daily practice.

Wiley W. Souba, M.D., Sc.D., F.A.C.S.
Dean, College of Medicine
Professor of Surgery
Ohio State University
Editorial Chair
ACS Surgery
wileysoubamd@webmd.net

1 PROFESSIONALISM IN SURGERY

Wiley W. Souba, M.D., Sc.D., F.A.C.S.

Over the past decade, the American health care system has had to cope with and manage an unprecedented amount of change. As a consequence, the medical profession has been challenged along the entire range of its cultural values and its traditional roles and responsibilities. It would be difficult, if not impossible, to find another social issue directly affecting all Americans that has undergone as rapid and remarkable a transformation—and oddly, a transformation in which the most important protagonists (i.e., the patients and the doctors) remain dissatisfied.[1]

Nowhere is this metamorphosis more evident than in the field of surgery. Marked reductions in reimbursement, explosions in surgical device biotechnology, a national medical malpractice crisis, and the disturbing emphasis on commercialized medicine have forever changed the surgical landscape, or so it seems. The very foundation of patient care—the doctor-patient relationship—is in jeopardy. Surgeons find it increasingly difficult to meet their responsibilities to patients and to society as a whole. In these circumstances, it is critical for us to reaffirm our commitment to the fundamental and universal principles and values of medical professionalism.

The concept of medicine as a profession grounded in compassion and sympathy for the sick has come under serious challenge.[2] One eroding force has been the growth and sovereignty of biomedical research. Given the high position of science and technology in our societal hierarchy, we may be headed for a form of medicine that includes little caring but becomes exclusively focused on the mechanics of treatment, so that we deal with sick patients much as we would a flat tire or a leaky faucet. In such a form of medicine, healing becomes little more than a technical exercise, and any talk of morality that is unsubstantiated by hard facts is considered mere opinion and therefore carries little weight.

The rise of entrepreneurialism and the growing corporatization of medicine also challenge the traditions of virtue-based medical care. When these processes are allowed to dominate medicine, health care becomes a commodity. As Pellegrino and Thomasma remark, "When economics and entrepreneurism drive the professions, they admit only self-interest and the working of the marketplace as the motives for professional activity. In a free-market economy, effacement of self-interest, or any conduct shaped primarily by the idea of altruism or virtue, is simply inconsistent with survival."[2]

These changes have caused a great deal of anxiety and fear among both patients and surgeons nationwide. The risk to the profession is that it will lose its sovereignty, becoming a passive rather than an active participant in shaping and formulating health policy in the future. The risks to the public are that issues of cost will take precedence over issues of quality and access to care and that health care will be treated as a commodity—that is, as a privilege rather than a right.

The Meaning of Professionalism

A profession is a collegial discipline that regulates itself by means of mandatory, systematic training. It has a base in a body of technical and specialized knowledge that it both teaches and advances; it sets and enforces its own standards; and it has a service orientation, rather than a profit orientation, enshrined in a code of ethics.[3-5] To put it more succinctly, a profession has cognitive, collegial, and moral attributes. These qualities are well expressed in the familiar

sentence from the Hippocratic oath: "I will practice my art with purity and holiness and for the benefit of the sick."

The escalating commercialization and secularization of medicine have evoked in many physicians a passionate desire to reconnect with the core values, practices, and behaviors that they see as exemplifying the very best of what medicine is about. This tension between commercialism on the one hand and humanism and altruism on the other is a central part of the professionalism challenge we face today.[6] As the journalist Loretta McLaughlin once wrote, "The rush to transform patients into units on an assembly line demeans medicine as a caring as well as curative field, demeans the respect due every patient and ultimately demeans illness itself as a significant human condition."[7]

Historically, the legitimacy of medical authority is based on three distinct claims[2,8]: first, that the knowledge and competence of the professional have been validated by a community of peers; second, that this knowledge has a scientific basis; and third, that the professional's judgment and advice are oriented toward a set of values. These aspects of legitimacy correspond to the collegial, cognitive, and moral attributes that define a profession.

Competence and expertise are certainly the basis of patient care, but other characteristics of a profession are equally important [see Table 1]. Being a professional implies a commitment to excellence and integrity in all undertakings. It places the responsibility to serve (care for) others above self-interest and reward. Accordingly, we, as practicing medical professionals, must act as role models by exemplifying this commitment and responsibility, so that medical students and residents are exposed to and learn the kinds of behaviors that constitute professionalism [see Sidebar Elizabeth Blackwell: A Model of Professionalism].

The medical profession is not infrequently referred to as a vocation. For most people, this word merely refers to what one does for a living; indeed, its common definition implies income-generating activity. Literally, however, the word vocation means "calling," and the application of this definition to the medical profession yields a more profound meaning. According to *Webster's Third New International Dictionary,*[9] a profession may be defined as

> a calling requiring specialized knowledge and often long academic preparation, including instruction in skills and methods as well as in the scientific, historical, or scholarly principles underlying such skills and methods, maintaining by force of organization or concerted opinion high standards of achievement and conduct, and committing its members to continued study and to

---

Table 1 Elements of a Profession

A profession
- Is a learned discipline with high standards of knowledge and performance
- Regulates itself via a social contract with society
- Places responsibility for serving others above self-interest and reward
- Is characterized by a commitment to excellence in all undertakings
- Is practiced with unwavering personal integrity and compassion
- Requires role-modeling of right behavior
- Is more than a job—it is a calling and a privilege

---

a kind of work which has for its prime purpose the rendering of a public service[.]

Most of us went to medical school because we wanted to help and care for people who are ill. This genuine desire to care is unambiguously apparent in the vast majority of personal statements that medical students prepare as part of their application process. To quote William Osler, "You are in this profession as a calling, not as a business; as a calling which extracts from you at every turn self-sacrifice, devotion, love and tenderness to your fellow man. We must work in the missionary spirit with a breath of charity that raises you far above the petty jealousies of life."[10] To keep medicine a calling, we must explicitly incorporate into the meaning of professionalism those nontechnical practices, habits, and attributes that the compassionate, caring, and competent physician exemplifies. We must remind ourselves that a true professional places service to the patient above self-interest and above reward.

Professionalism is the basis of our contract with society. To maintain our professionalism, and thus to preserve the contract with society, it is essential to reestablish the doctor-patient relationship as the foundation of patient care.

The Surgeon-Patient Relationship

The underpinning of medicine as a compassionate, caring profession is the doctor-patient relationship, a relationship that has become jeopardized and sometimes fractured over the past decade. Our individual perceptions of what this relationship is and how it should work will inevitably have a great impact on how we approach the care of our patients.

The fundamental question to be answered is, what should the surgeon-patient relationship be governed by?[2] If this relationship is viewed solely as a contract for services rendered, it is subject to the law and the courts; if it is viewed simply as an issue of applied biology, it is governed by science; and if it is viewed exclusively as a commercially driven business transaction, it is regulated by the marketplace. If, however, our relationship with our patients is understood as going beyond basic delivery of care and as constituting a covenant in which we act in the patient's best interest even if that means providing free care, it is based on the virtue of charity. Such a perspective transcends questions of contracts, politics, economics, physiology, and molecular genetics—all of which rightly influence treatment strategies but none of which is any substitute for authentic caring.

The view of the physician-patient relationship as a covenant does not demand devotion to medicine at the exclusion of other responsibilities, and it is not inconsistent with the fact that medicine is also a science, an art, and a business.[2] Nevertheless, in our struggle to remain viable in a health care environment that has become a commercial enterprise, efforts to preserve market share cannot take precedence over the provision of care that is grounded in charity and compassion. It is exactly for this reason that medicine always will be, and should be, a relationship between people. To fracture that relationship by exchanging a covenant based on charity and compassion for a contract based solely on the delivery of goods and services is something none of us would want for ourselves. The nature of the healing relationship is itself the foundation of the special obligations of physicians as physicians.[2]

Translation of Theory into Practice

The American College of Surgeons (ACS) Task Force on Professionalism has developed a Code of Professional Conduct,[11] which emphasizes the following four aspects of professionalism:

Elizabeth Blackwell: A Model of Professionalism[17]

Elizabeth Blackwell was born in England in 1821, the daughter of a sugar refiner. When she was 10 years old, her family emigrated to New York City. Discovering in herself a strong desire to practice medicine and care for the underserved, she took up residence in a physician's household, using her time there to study using books in the family's medical library.

As a young woman, Blackwell applied to several prominent medical schools but was snubbed by all of them. After 29 rejections, she sent her second round of applications to smaller colleges, including Geneva College in New York. She was accepted at Geneva—according to an anecdote, because the faculty put the matter to a student vote, and the students thought her application a hoax. She braved the prejudice of some of the professors and students to complete her training, eventually ranking first in her class. On January 23, 1849, at the age of 27, Elizabeth Blackwell became the first woman to earn a medical degree in the United States. Her goal was to become a surgeon.

After several months in Pennsylvania, during which time she became a naturalized citizen of the United States, Blackwell traveled to Paris, where she hoped to study with one of the leading French surgeons. Denied access to Parisian hospitals because of her gender, she enrolled instead at La Maternité, a highly regarded midwifery school, in the summer of 1849. While attending to a child some 4 months after enrolling, Blackwell inadvertently spattered some pus from the child's eyes into her own left eye. The child was infected with gonorrhea, and Blackwell contracted a severe case of ophthalmia neonatorum, which later necessitated the removal of the infected eye. Although the loss of an eye made it impossible for her to become a surgeon, it did not dampen her passion for becoming a practicing physician.

By mid-1851, when Blackwell returned to the United States, she was well prepared for private practice. However, no male doctor would even consider the idea of a female associate, no matter how well trained. Barred from practice in most hospitals, Blackwell founded her own infirmary, the New York Infirmary for Indigent Women and Children, in 1857. When the American Civil War began, Blackwell trained nurses, and in 1868 she founded a women's medical college at the Infirmary so that women could be formally trained as physicians. In 1869, she returned to England and, with Florence Nightingale, opened the Women's Medical College. Blackwell taught at the newly created London School of Medicine for Women and became the first female physician in the United Kingdom Medical Register. She set up a private practice in her own home, where she saw women and children, many of whom were of lesser means and were unable to pay. In addition, Blackwell mentored other women who subsequently pursued careers in medicine. She retired at the age of 86.

In short, Elizabeth Blackwell embodied professionalism in her work. In 1889 she wrote, "There is no career nobler than that of the physician. The progress and welfare of society is more intimately bound up with the prevailing tone and influence of the medical profession than with the status of any other class."

---

1. A competent surgeon is more than a competent technician.
2. Whereas ethical practice and professionalism are closely related, professionalism also incorporates surgeons' relationships with patients and society.
3. Unprofessional behavior must have consequences.
4. Professional organizations are responsible for fostering professionalism in their membership.

If professionalism is indeed embodied in the principles discussed [see Table 1], the next question that arises is, how do we translate theory into practice? That is, what do these principles look like in action? To begin with, a competent surgeon must possess the medical knowledge, judgment, technical ability, professionalism, clinical excellence, and communication skills required for provision of high-quality patient-centered care. Furthermore, this expertise must be demonstrated to the satisfaction of the profession as a whole. The Accreditation Council on Graduate Medical Education (ACGME) has identified six competencies that must be demonstrated by the surgeon: (1) patient care, (2) medical knowledge, (3) practice-based learning and improvement, (4) interpersonal and communication skills, (5) professionalism, and (6) systems-based practice. These competencies are now being integrated into the training programs of all accredited surgical residencies.

A surgical professional must also be willing and able to take responsibility. Such responsibility includes, but is not necessarily limited to, the following three areas: (1) provision of the highest-quality care, (2) maintenance of the dignity of patients and co-workers, and (3) open, honest communication. Assumption of responsibility as a professional involves leading by example, placing the delivery of quality care above the patient's ability to pay, and displaying compassion. Cassell reminds us that a sick person is not just "a well person with a knapsack of illness strapped to his back"[12] and that whereas "it is possible to know the suffering of others, to help them, and to relieve their distress, [it is not possible] to become one with them in their torment."[13] Illness and suffering are not just biologic problems to be solved by biomedical research and technology: they are also enigmas that can serve to point out the limitations, vulnerabilities, and frailties that we want so much to deny, as well as to reaffirm our links with one another.

Most important, professionalism demands unwavering personal integrity. Regrettably, examples of unprofessional behavior exist. An excerpt from a note from a third-year medical student to the core clerkship director reads as follows: "I have seen attendings make sexist, racist jokes or remarks during surgery. I have met residents who joke about deaf patients and female patients with facial hair. [I have encountered] teams joking and counting down the days until patients die." This kind of exposure to unprofessional conduct and language can influence young people negatively, and it must change.

It is encouraging to note that many instances of unprofessional conduct that once were routinely overlooked—such as mistreating medical students, speaking disrespectfully to coworkers, and fraudulent behavior—now are being dealt with. Still, from time to time an incident is made public that makes us all feel shame. In March 2003, the *Seattle Times* carried a story about the chief of neurosurgery at the University of Washington, who pleaded guilty to a felony charge of obstructing the government's investigation and admitted that he asked others to lie for him and created an atmosphere of fear in the neurosurgery department. According to the United States Attorney in Seattle, University of Washington employees destroyed reports revealing that University doctors submitted inflated billings to Medicare and Medicaid. The department chair lost his job, was barred from participation in Medicare, and, as part of his plea bargain, had to pay a $500,000 fine, perform 1,000 hours of community service, and write an article in a med-

ical journal about billing errors. The University spent many millions in legal fees and eventually settled the billing issues with the Federal government for one of the highest Physicians at Teaching Hospitals (PATH) settlements ever.

Fortunately, such extreme cases of unprofessionalism are quite uncommon. Nevertheless, it remains our responsibility as professionals to prevent such behaviors from developing and from being reinforced. To this end, we must lead by example. A study published in 2004 demonstrated an association between displays of unprofessional behavior in medical school and subsequent disciplinary action by a state medical board.[14] The authors concluded that professionalism is an essential competency that students must demonstrate to graduate from medical school. Who could disagree?

The Future of Surgical Professionalism

It is often subtly implied—or even candidly stated—that no matter how well we adjust to the changing health care environment, the practice of surgery will never again be quite as rewarding as it once was. This need not be the case. The ongoing advances in surgical technology, the increasing opportunities for community-based surgeons to enroll their patients into clinical trials, and the growing emphasis on lifelong learning as part of maintenance of certification are factors that not only help satisfy social and organizational demands for quality care but also are in the best interest of our patients.

In the near future, maintenance of certification for surgeons will involve much more than taking an examination every decade. The ACS is taking the lead in helping to develop new measures of competence. Whatever specific form such measures may take, displaying professionalism and living up to a set of uncompromisable core values[15] will always be central indicators of the performance of the individual surgeon and the integrity of the discipline of surgery as a whole.

Although surgeons vary enormously with respect to personality, practice preferences, areas of specialization, and style of relating to others, they all have one role in common: that of healer. Indeed, it is the highest of privileges to be able to care for the sick. As the playwright Howard Sackler once wrote, "To intervene, even briefly, between our fellow creatures and their suffering or death, is our most authentic answer to the question of our humanity." Inseparable from this privilege is a set of responsibilities that are not to be taken lightly: a pledge to offer our patients the best care possible and a commitment to teach and advance the science and practice of medicine. Commitment to the practice of patient-centered, high-quality, cost-effective care is what gives our work meaning and provides us with a sense of purpose.[16] We as surgeons must participate actively in the current evolution of integrated health care; by doing so, we help build our own future.

References

1. Fein R: The HMO revolution. Dissent, spring 1998, p 29
2. Pellegrino ED, Thomasma DC: Helping and Healing. Georgetown University Press, Washington, DC, 1997
3. Brandeis LD: Familiar medical quotations. Business—A Profession. Maurice Strauss, Ed. Little Brown & Co, Boston, 1986
4. Cogan ML: Toward a definition of profession. Harvard Educational Reviews 23:33, 1953
5. Greenwood E: Attributes of a profession. Social Work 22:44, 1957
6. Souba W, Day D: Leadership values in academic medicine. Acad Med (in press)
7. McLaughlin L: The surgical express. Boston Globe,

April 24, 1995
8. Starr PD: The social transformation of American medicine. Basic Books, New York, 1982
9. Webster's Third New International Dictionary of the English Language, Unabridged. Gove PB, Ed. Merriam-Webster Inc, Springfield, Massachusetts, 1986, p 1811
10. Osler's "Way of Life" and Other Addresses, with Commentary and Annotations. Hinohara S, Niki H, Eds. Duke University Press, Durham, North Carolina, 2001
11. Gruen RI, Arya J, Cosgrove EM, et al: Professionalism in surgery. J Am Coll Surg 197:605, 2003
12. Cassell EJ: The function of medicine. Hastings Center Report 7:16, 1977

13. Cassell EJ: Recognizing suffering. Hastings Center Report 21:24, 1991
14. Papadakis M, Hodgson C, Teherani A, et al: Unprofessional behavior in medical school is associated with subsequent disciplinary action by a state medical board. Acad Med 79:244, 2004
15. Souba W: Academic medicine's core values: what do they mean? J Surg Res 115:171, 2003
16. Souba W: Academic medicine and our search for meaning and purpose. Acad Med 77:139, 2002
17. Speigel R: Elizabeth Blackwell: the first woman doctor. Snapshots of Science and Medicine, 1998 http://science-education.nih.gov/snapshots. nsf/story?openform&pds~Elizabeth_Blackwell_ Doctor

2 PERFORMANCE MEASURES IN SURGICAL PRACTICE

John D. Birkmeyer, M.D., F.A.C.S.

With the growing recognition that the quality of surgical care varies widely, there is a rising demand for good measures of surgical performance. Patients and their families need to be able to make better-informed decisions about where to get their surgical care—and from whom.[1] Employers and payers need data on which to base their contracting decisions and pay-for-performance initiatives.[2] Finally, clinical leaders need tools that can help them identify "best practices" and guide their quality-improvement efforts. To meet these different needs, an ever-broadening array of performance measures is being developed.

The consensus about the general desirability of surgical performance measurement notwithstanding, there remains considerable uncertainty about which specific measures are most effective in measuring surgical quality. The measures currently in use are remarkably heterogeneous, encompassing a range of different elements. In broad terms, they can be grouped into three main categories: measures of health care structure, process-of-care measures, and measures reflecting patient outcomes. Although each of these three types of performance measure has its unique strengths, each is also associated with conceptual, methodological, or practical problems [see Table 1]. Obviously, the baseline risk and frequency of the procedure are important considerations in weighing the strengths and weaknesses of different measures.[3] So too is the underlying purpose of performance measurement; for example, measures that work well when the primary intent is to steer patients to the best hospitals or surgeons (selective referral) may not be optimal for quality-improvement purposes.

Several reviews of performance measurement have been published in the past few years.[3-5] In what follows, I expand on these reviews, providing an overview of the measures commonly used to assess surgical quality, considering their main strengths and limitations, and offering recommendations for selecting the optimal quality measure.

Overview of Current Performance Measures

The number of performance measures that have been developed for the assessment of surgical quality is already large and continues to grow. For present purposes, it should be sufficient to consider a representative list of commonly used quality indicators that have been endorsed by leading quality-measurement organizations or have already been applied in hospital accreditation, pay-for-performance, or public reporting efforts [see Table 2]. A more exhaustive list of performance measures is available on the National Quality Measures Clearinghouse (NQMC) Web site, sponsored by the Agency for Healthcare Research and Quality (AHRQ) (http://www.qualitymeasures.ahrq.gov).

To date, the National Quality Forum (NQF), the Joint Commission on Accreditation of Healthcare Organizations (JCAHO), and the Center for Medicare and Medicaid Services (CMS) have focused primarily on preventive care and hospital-based medical care, with an emphasis on process-of-care variables. In surgery, these groups have all endorsed one process measure—appropriate and timely use of prophylactic antibiotics [see Table 2]—in partnership with the Centers for Disease Control and Prevention (CDC). In 2006, CMS, as part of its Surgical Care Improvement Program (SCIP), is also endorsing process measures related to prevention of postoperative cardiac events, venous thromboembolism, and respiratory complications.

The AHRQ has focused primarily on quality measures that take advantage of readily available administrative data. Because little information on process of care is available in these datasets, these

Table 1 Primary Strengths and Limitations of Structural, Process, and Outcome Measures

Type of Measure	Examples	Strengths	Limitations
Structural	Procedure volume Intensivist-managed ICU	Measures are expedient and inexpensive Measures are efficient—a single one may relate to several outcomes For some procedures, measures predict subsequent performance better than process or outcome measures do	Number of measures is limited Measures are generally not actionable Measures do not reflect individual performance and are considered unfair by providers
Process of care	Appropriate use of prophylactic antibiotics	Measures reflect care that patients actually receive—hence, greater buy-in from providers Measures are directly actionable for quality-improvement activities For many measures, risk adjustment is unnecessary	Many measures are hard to define with existing databases Extent of linkage between measures and important patient outcomes is variable High-leverage, procedure-specific measures are lacking
Direct outcome	Risk-adjusted mortalities for CABG from state or national registries	Face validity Measurement may improve outcomes in and of itself (Hawthorne effect)	Sample sizes are limited Clinical data collection is expensive Concerns exist about risk adjustment with administrative data

CABG—coronary artery bypass grafting

4

measures are mainly structural (e.g., hospital procedure volume) or outcome-based (e.g., risk-adjusted mortality).

The Leapfrog Group (http://www.leapfroggroup.org), a coalition of large employers and purchasers, developed perhaps the most visible set of surgical quality indicators for its value-based purchasing initiative. The organization's original (2000) standards focused exclusively on procedure volume, but these were expanded in 2003 to include selected process variables (e.g., the use of beta blockers in patients undergoing abdominal aortic aneurysm repair) and outcome measures.

Structural Measures

The term health care structure refers to the setting or system in which care is delivered. Many structural performance measures reflect hospital-level attributes, such as the physical plant and resources or the coordination and organization of the staff (e.g., the registered nurse–bed ratio and the designation of a hospital as a level I trauma center). Other structural measures reflect physician-level attributes (e.g., board certification, subspecialty training, and procedure volume).

STRENGTHS

Structural performance measures have several attractive features. A strength of such measures is that many of them are strongly related to outcomes. For example, with esophagectomy and pancreatic resection for cancer, operative mortality is as much as 10% lower, in absolute terms, at very high volume hospitals than at lower-volume centers.[6,7] In some instances, structural measures (e.g., procedure volume) are better predictors of subsequent hospital performance than any known process or outcome measures are [see Figure 1].[8]

A second strength is efficiency. A single structural measure may be associated with numerous outcomes. For example, with some types of cancer surgery, higher hospital or surgeon procedure volume is associated not only with lower operative mortality but also with lower perioperative morbidity and improved late survival.[9-11] Intensivist-staffed intensive care units are linked to shorter lengths of stay and reduced use of resources, as well as to lower mortality.[12,13]

The third, and perhaps most important, strength of structural measures is expediency. Many such measures can easily be assessed with readily available administrative data. Although some structural measures require surveying of hospitals or providers, such data are much less expensive to collect than data obtained through review of individual patients' medical records.

LIMITATIONS

Relatively few structural performance measures are strongly linked to patients and thus potentially useful as quality indicators. Another limitation is that most structural measures, unlike most process measures, are not readily actionable. For example, a small hospital can increase the percentage of its surgical patients who receive antibiotic prophylaxis, but it cannot easily make itself a high-volume center. Thus, although some structural measures may be useful for selective referral initiatives, they are of limited value for quality improvement.

Whereas some structural measures can identify groups of hospitals or providers that perform better on average, they are not adequate discriminators of performance among individuals. For example, in the aggregate, high-volume hospitals have a much lower operative mortality for pancreatic resection than lower-volume centers do. Nevertheless, some individual high-volume hospitals may have a high mortality, and some individual low-volume centers may

Table 2 Performance Measures Currently Used in Surgical Practice

Diagnosis or Procedure	Performance Measure Developer/Endorser
Critical illness	Staffing with board-certified intensivists (LF)
Any surgical procedure	Appropriate antibiotic prophylaxis (correct approach: give 1 hr preoperatively, discontinue within 24 hr) (NQF, JCAHO, CMS)
Abdominal aneurysm repair	Hospital volume (AHRQ, LF) Risk-adjusted mortality (AHRQ) Prophylactic beta blockers (LF)
Carotid endarterectomy	Hospital volume (AHRQ)
Esophageal resection for cancer	Hospital volume (AHRQ)
Coronary artery bypass grafting	Hospital volume (NQF, AHRQ, LF) Risk-adjusted mortality (NQF, AHRQ, LF) Use of internal mammary artery (NQF, LF)
Pancreatic resection	Hospital volume (AHRQ, LF) Risk-adjusted mortality (AHRQ)
Pediatric cardiac surgery	Hospital volume (AHRQ) Risk-adjusted mortality (AHRQ)
Hip replacement	Risk-adjusted mortality (AHRQ)
Craniotomy	Risk-adjusted mortality (AHRQ)
Cholecystectomy	Laparoscopic approach (AHRQ)
Appendectomy	Avoidance of incidental appendectomy (AHRQ)

AHRQ—Agency for Healthcare Research and Quality CMS—Center for Medicare and Medicaid Services JCAHO—Joint Commission on Accreditation of Healthcare Organizations LF—Leapfrog Group NQF—National Quality Forum

have a low mortality (though the latter possibility may be difficult to confirm because of the smaller sample sizes involved).[14] For this reason, many providers view structural performance measures as unfair.

Process Measures

Processes of care are the clinical interventions and services provided to patients. Process measures have long been the predominant quality indicators for both inpatient and outpatient medical care, and their popularity as quality measures for surgical care is growing rapidly.

STRENGTHS

A strength of process measures is their direct connection to patient management. Because they reflect the care that physicians actually deliver, they have substantial face validity and hence greater "buy-in" from providers. Such measures are usually directly actionable and thus are a good substrate for quality-improvement activities.

A second strength is that risk adjustment, though important for outcome measures, is not required for many process measures. For example, appropriate prophylaxis against postoperative venous thromboembolism is one performance measure in CMS's expanding pay-for-performance initiative and is part of SCIP. Because it is widely agreed that virtually all patients undergoing open abdominal procedures should be offered some form of prophylaxis, there is little need to collect detailed clinical data about illness severity for the purposes of risk adjustment.

Another strength is that process measures are generally less constrained by sample-size problems than outcome measures are. Important outcome measures (e.g., perioperative death) are relatively rare, but most targeted process measures are relevant to a much larger proportion of patients. Moreover, because process measures generally target aspects of general perioperative care, they can often be applied to patients who are undergoing numerous different procedures, thereby increasing sample sizes and, ultimately, improving the precision of the measurements.

LIMITATIONS

At present, a major limitation of process measures is the lack of a reliable data infrastructure. Administrative datasets do not have the clinical detail and specificity required for close evaluation of processes of care. Measurement systems based on clinical data, including that of the National Surgical Quality Improvement Program (NSQIP) of the Department of Veterans Affairs (VA),[15] focus on patient characteristics and outcomes and do not collect information on processes of care. Currently, most pay-for-performance programs rely on self-reported information from hospitals, but the reliability of such data is uncertain (particularly when reimbursement is at stake).

A second limitation is that at present, targeted process measures in surgery pertain primarily to general perioperative care and often relate to secondary rather than primary outcomes. Although the value of antibiotic prophylaxis in reducing the risk of superficial surgical site infection (SSI) should not be underestimated, superficial SSI is not among the most important adverse events of major surgery (including death). Thus, improvements in the use of prophylactic antibiotics will not address the fundamental problem of variation in the rates of important outcomes from one hospital to another and from one surgeon to another. Except, possibly, in the case of coronary artery bypass grafting (CABG), the processes that determine the success of individual procedures have yet to be identified.

Outcome Measures

Direct outcome measures reflect the end result of care, either from a clinical perspective or from the patient's viewpoint. Mortality is by far the most commonly used surgical outcome measure, but there are other outcomes that could also be used as qual-

ity indicators, including complications, hospital readmission, and various patient-centered measures of satisfaction or health status.

Several large-scale initiatives involving direct outcome assessment in surgery are currently under way. For example, proprietary health care rating firms (e.g., Healthgrades) and state agencies are assessing risk-adjusted mortalities by using Medicare or state-level administrative datasets. Most of the current outcome-measurement initiatives, however, involve the use of large clinical registries, of which the cardiac surgery registries in New York, Pennsylvania, and a growing number of other states are perhaps the most visible examples. At the national level, the Society for Thoracic Surgeons and the American College of Cardiology have implemented systems for tracking the morbidity and mortality associated with cardiac surgery and percutaneous coronary interventions, respectively. Although the majority of the outcome-measurement efforts to date have been procedure-specific (and largely limited to cardiac procedures), NSQIP has assessed hospital-specific morbidities and mortalities aggregated across surgical specialties and procedures. Efforts to apply the same measurement approach outside the VA are now being implemented.[16]

STRENGTHS

Direct outcome measures have at least two major strengths. First, they have obvious face validity and thus are likely to garner a high degree of support from hospitals and surgeons. Second, outcome measurement, in and of itself, may improve performance—the so-called Hawthorne effect. For example, surgical morbidity and mortality in VA hospitals have fallen dramatically since the implementation of NSQIP in 1991.[15] Undoubtedly, many surgical leaders at individual hospitals made specific organizational or process improvements after they began receiving feedback on their hospitals' performance. However, it is very unlikely that even a full inventory of these specific changes would explain such broad-based and substantial improvements in morbidity and mortality.

LIMITATIONS

One limitation of hospital- or surgeon-specific outcome measures is that they are severely constrained by small sample sizes. For the large majority of surgical procedures, very few hospitals (or surgeons) have sufficient adverse events (numerators) and cases (denominators) to be able to generate meaningful, proce-

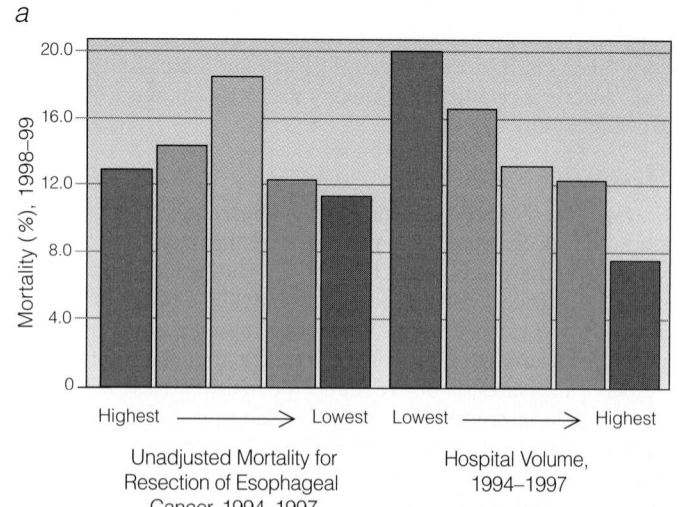
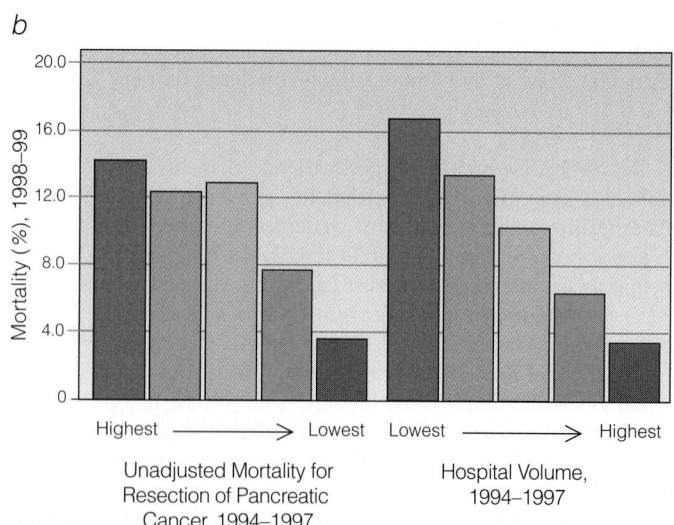

Figure 1 **Illustrated is the relative ability of historical (1994–1997) measures of hospital volume and risk-adjusted mortality to predict subsequent (1998–1999) risk-adjusted mortality in Medicare patients undergoing (a) esophageal or (b) pancreatic resection for cancer.**[8]

dure-specific measures of morbidity or mortality. For example, a 2004 study used data from the Nationwide Inpatient Sample to study seven procedures for which mortality was advocated as a quality indicator by the AHRQ.[17] For six of the seven procedures, only a very small proportion of hospitals in the United States had large enough caseloads to rule out a mortality that was twice the national average. Although identifying poor-quality outliers is an important function of outcome measurement, to focus on this goal alone is to underestimate the problems associated with small sample sizes. Distinguishing among individual hospitals with intermediate levels of performance is even more difficult.

Other limitations of direct outcome assessment depend on whether the assessment is based on administrative data or on clinical information abstracted from medical records. For outcome measures based on clinical data, the major problem is expense. For example, it costs more than $100,000 annually for a private-sector hospital to participate in NSQIP.

For outcome measures based on administrative data, a major concern is the adequacy of risk adjustment. For outcome measures to have face validity with providers, high-quality risk adjustment may be essential. It may also be useful for discouraging gaming of the system (e.g., hospitals or providers avoiding high-risk patients to optimize their performance measures). It is unclear, however, to what extent the scientific validity of outcome measures is threatened by imperfect risk adjustment with administrative data. Although administrative data lack clinical detail on many variables related to baseline risk,[18-21] the degree to which case mix varies systematically across hospitals or surgeons has not been determined. Among patients who are undergoing the same surgical procedure, there is often surprisingly little variation. For example, among patients undergoing CABG in New York State, unadjusted hospital mortality and adjusted hospital mortality (as derived from clinical registries) were nearly identical in most years (with correlations exceeding 0.90) [see Figure 2].[22] Moreover, hospital rankings based on unadjusted mortality and those based on adjusted mortality were equally useful in predicting subsequent hospital performance.

Matching the Performance Measure to the Underlying Goal

Performance measures will never be perfect. Certainly, over time, better analytic methods will be developed, and better access to higher-quality data may be gained with the addition of clinical elements to administrative datasets or the broader adoption of electronic medical records. There are, however, some problems with performance measurement (e.g., sample-size limitations) that are inherent and thus not fully correctable. Consequently, clinical leaders, patient advocates, payers, and policy makers will all have to make decisions about when imperfect measures are nonetheless good enough to act on.

A measure should be implemented only with the expectation that acting on it will yield a net improvement in health quality. In other words, the direct benefits of implementing a particular measure cannot be outweighed by the indirect harm. Unfortunately, benefits and harm are often difficult to measure. Moreover, measurement is heavily influenced by the specific context and by who—patients, payers, or providers—is doing the accounting. For this reason, the question of where to set the bar, so to speak, has no simple answer.

It is important to ensure a good match between the performance measure and the primary goal of measurement. It is particularly important to be clear about whether the underlying goal is (1) quality improvement or (2) selective referral (i.e., directing

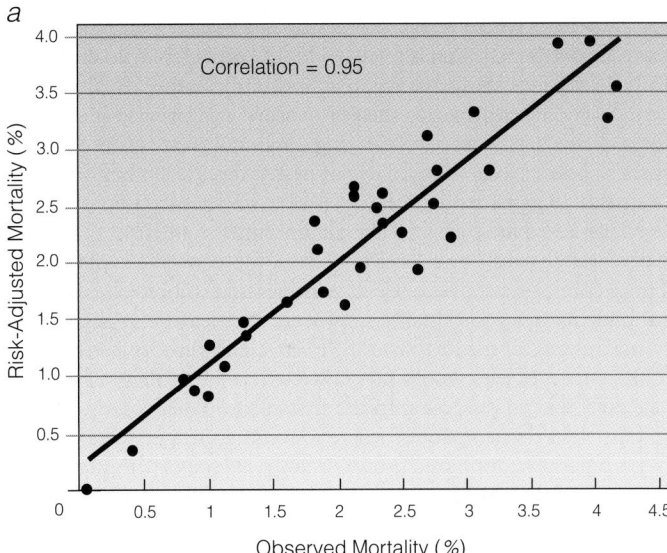

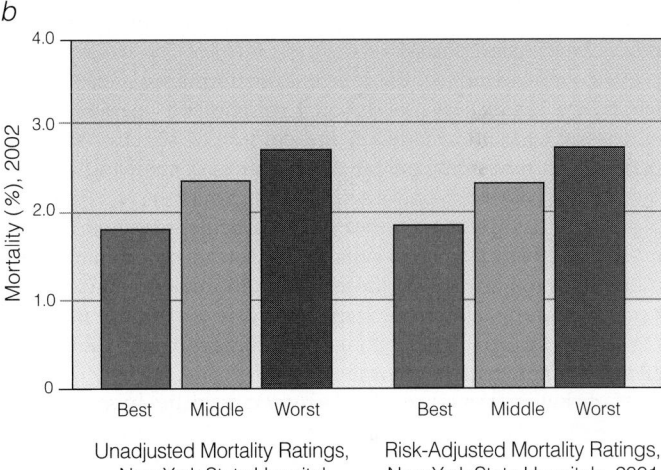

Figure 2 **Shown are mortality figures from CABG in New York State hospitals, based on data from the state's clinical outcomes registry. (*a*) Depicted is the correlation between adjusted and unadjusted mortalities for all state hospitals in 2001. (*b*) Illustrated is the relative ability of adjusted mortality and unadjusted mortality to predict performance in the subsequent year.**

patients to higher-quality hospitals or providers). Although some pay-for-performance initiatives may have both goals, one usually predominates. For example, the ultimate objective of CMS's pay-for-performance initiative with prophylactic antibiotics is to improve quality at all hospitals, not to direct patients to centers with high compliance rates. Conversely, the Leapfrog Group's efforts in surgery are primarily aimed at selective referral, though they may indirectly provide incentives for quality improvement.

For the purposes of quality improvement, a good performance measure—most often, a process-of-care variable—must be actionable. Measurable improvements in the given process should translate into clinically meaningful improvements in patient outcomes. Although quality-improvement activities are rarely actually harmful, they do have potential downsides, mainly related to their opportunity cost. Initiatives that hinge on bad performance measures siphon away resources (e.g., time and focus) from more productive activities.

For the purposes of selective referral, a good performance measure is one that steers patients toward better hospitals or physicians (or away from worse ones). For example, a measure based on previous performance should reliably identify providers who are likely to have superior performance now and in the future. At the same time, a good performance measure should not provide incentives for perverse behaviors (e.g., carrying out unnecessary procedures to meet a specific volume standard) or negatively affect other domains of quality (e.g., patient autonomy, access, and satisfaction).

Measures that work well for quality improvement may not be particularly useful for selective referral; the converse is also true. For example, appropriate use of perioperative antibiotics in surgical patients is a good quality-improvement measure: it is clinically meaningful, linked to lower SSI rates, and directly actionable. This process of care would not, however, be particularly useful for selective referral purposes. In the first place, patients are unlikely to base their decision about where to undergo surgery on patterns of perioperative antibiotic use. Moreover, surgeons with high rates of appropriate antibiotic use do not necessarily do better with respect to more important outcomes (e.g., mortality). A physician's performance on one quality indicator often correlates poorly with his or her performance on other indicators for the same or other clinical conditions.[23]

As a counterexample, the two main performance measures for pancreatic cancer surgery—hospital volume and operative mortality—are very informative in the context of selective referral: patients can markedly improve their chances of surviving surgery by selecting hospitals highly ranked on either measure [see Figure 1]. Neither of these measures, however, is particularly useful for quality-improvement purposes. Volume is not readily actionable, and mortality is too unstable at the level of individual hospitals (again, because of the small sample sizes) to serve as a means of identifying top performers, determining best practices, or evaluating the effects of improvement activities.

Many believe that a good performance measure must be capable of distinguishing levels of performance on an individual basis. From the perspective of providers in particular, a measure cannot be considered fair unless it reliably reflects the performance of individual hospitals or physicians. Unfortunately, as noted (see above), small caseloads (and, sometimes, variations in the case mix) make this degree of discrimination difficult or impossible to achieve with most procedures. Even so, information that at least improves the chances of a good outcome on average is still of real value to patients. Many performance measures can achieve this less demanding objective even if they do not reliably reflect individual performance.

For example, a 2002 study used clinical data from the Cooperative Cardiovascular Project to assess the usefulness of the Healthgrades hospital ratings for acute myocardial infarction (based primarily on risk-adjusted mortality from Medicare data).[24] Compared with the one-star (worst) hospitals, the five-star (best) hospitals had a significantly lower mortality (16% versus 22%) after risk adjustment with clinical data; they also discharged significantly more patients on appropriate aspirin, beta-blocker, and angiotensin-converting enzyme inhibitor regimens. However, the Healthgrades ratings proved not to be useful for discriminating between any two individual hospitals. In only 3% of the head-to-head comparisons did five-star hospitals have a statistically lower mortality than one-star hospitals.

Thus, some performance measures that clearly identify groups of hospitals or providers that exhibit superior performance may be limited in their ability to differentiate individual hospitals from one another. There may be no simple way of resolving the basic tension implied by performance measures that are unfair to providers yet informative for patients. This tension does, however, underscore the importance of being clear about (1) what the primary purpose of performance measurement is (quality improvement or selective referral) and (2) whose interests are receiving top priority (the provider or the patient).

References

1. Lee TH, Meyer GS, Brennan TA: A middle ground on public accountability. N Engl J Med 350:2409, 2004

2. Galvin R, Milstein A: Large employers' new strategies in health care. N Engl J Med 347:939, 2002

3. Birkmeyer JD, Birkmeyer NJ, Dimick JB: Measuring the quality of surgical care: structure, process, or outcomes? J Am Coll Surg 198:626, 2004

4. Landon BE, Normand SL, Blumenthal D, et al: Physician clinical performance assessment: prospects and barriers. JAMA 290:1183, 2003

5. Bird SM, Cox D, Farewell VT, et al: Performance indicators: good, bad, and ugly. J R Statist Soc 168:1, 2005

6. Halm EA, Lee C, Chassin MR: Is volume related to outcome in health care? A systematic review and methodologic critique of the literature. Ann Intern Med 137:511, 2002

7. Dudley RA, Johansen KL, Brand R, et al: Selective referral to high volume hospitals: estimating potentially avoidable deaths. JAMA 283:1159, 2000

8. Birkmeyer JD, Dimick JB, Staiger DO: Hospital volume and operative mortality as predictors of subsequent performance. Ann Surg (in press)

9. Bach PB, Cramer LD, Schrag D, et al: The influence of hospital volume on survival after resection for lung cancer. N Engl J Med 345:181, 2001

10. Begg CB, Reidel ER, Bach PB, et al: Variations in morbidity after radical prostatectomy. N Engl J Med 346:1138, 2002

11. Finlayson EVA, Birkmeyer JD: Effects of hospital volume on life expectancy after selected cancer operations in older adults: a decision analysis. J Am Coll Surg 196:410, 2002

12. Pronovost PJ, Angus DC, Dorman T, et al: Physician staffing patterns and clinical outcomes in critically ill patients: a systematic review. JAMA 288:2151, 2002

13. Pronovost PJ, Needham DM, Waters H, et al: Intensive care unit physician staffing: financial modeling of the Leapfrog standard. Crit Care Med 32:1247, 2004

14. Shahian DM, Normand SL: The volume-outcome relationship: from Luft to Leapfrog. Ann Thorac Surg 75:1048, 2003

15. Khuri SF, Daley J, Henderson WG: The comparative assessment and improvement of quality of surgical care in the Department of Veterans Affairs. Arch Surg 137:20, 2002

16. Fink A, Campbell DJ, Mentzer RJ, et al: The National Surgical Quality Improvement Program in non–Veterans Administration hospitals: initial demonstration of feasibility. Ann Surg 236:344, 2002

17. Dimick JB, Welch HG, Birkmeyer JD: Surgical mortality as an indicator of hospital quality: the problem with small sample size. JAMA 292:847, 2004

18. Finlayson EV, Birkmeyer JD, Stukel TA, et al: Adjusting surgical mortality rates for patient comorbidities: more harm than good? Surg 132:787, 2002

19. Fisher ES, Whaley FS, Krushat WM, et al: The accuracy of Medicare's hospital claims data: progress, but problems remain. Am J Public Health 82:243, 1992

20. Iezzoni LI, Foley SM, Daley J, et al: Comorbidities, complications, and coding bias. Does the number of diagnosis codes matter in predicting in-hospital mortality? JAMA 267:2197, 1992

21. Iezzoni LI: The risks of risk adjustment. JAMA 278:1600, 1997

22. Birkmeyer J: Unpublished data, 2005

23. Palmer RH, Wright EA, Orav EJ, et al: Consistency in performance among primary care practitioners. Med Care 34(9 suppl):SS52, 1996

24. Krumholz HM, Rathore SS, Chen J, et al: Evaluation of a consumer-oriented internet health care report card: the risk of quality ratings based on mortality data. JAMA 287:1277, 2002

3 BENCHMARKING SURGICAL OUTCOMES

Emily V. A. Finlayson, M.D., M.S., and John D. Birkmeyer, M.D., F.A.C.S.

Currently, there is growing interest in obtaining information about surgical outcomes. Patients and their families are increasingly looking for—and finding—hospital- and surgeon-specific quality data as they try to make informed decisions about where and from whom to receive surgical care.[1,2] Payers, both private and public, are also seeking information about surgical performance for their value-based purchasing initiatives. For example, the Leapfrog Group (www.leapfroggroup.org), a large coalition of health-care purchasers, is collating data on hospital volume, process, and outcome measures in an effort to steer patients to the centers likely to have the best results [*see 2 Performance Measures in Surgical Practice*]. As part of its Surgical Care Improvement Program (SCIP) and Centers of Excellence projects, the Centers for Medicare and Medicaid Services (CMS) is requiring that hospitals report outcome data for selected procedures, as well as other performance measures.

Surgeons should be just as interested in surgical outcome data as patients and payers are, for several reasons. First, it is essential that surgeons be able to provide patients with accurate, realistic information about the risks and benefits they can expect from specific procedures. Unfortunately, the medical literature is not always reliable for this purpose: it is limited by publication bias [*see 4 Evidence-Based Surgery*], and the findings tend to be skewed by case series from large, nonrepresentative referral centers, which may not reflect outcomes in the "real world." Second, as patients increasingly turn to the Internet for information, surgeons need to be aware of what data their patients are seeing and prepared to address their questions. Third, and most important, surgeons require information about surgical outcomes to benchmark their own performance against both national norms and the performance of their peers, as well to help guide their own efforts at improvement.

In this chapter, we review various data sources for benchmarking surgical outcomes, including ongoing public reporting programs, public-use administrative databases that can be analyzed for benchmarking purposes, and improvement-oriented clinical outcomes registries, such as the National Surgical Quality Improvement Program (NSQIP) now being promoted by the American College of Surgeons (ACS). In particular, we consider the strengths and weaknesses of these sources and provide representative surgical mortality data from some of them.

Public Reporting Programs

The most readily available sources of surgical outcome data are Internet-based public reporting programs. At present, the only such programs that are based on clinical data are in the field of cardiac surgery. Following the lead of New York State, which first initiated public reporting in 1989, state agencies in New Jersey, Pennsylvania, California, and Massachusetts now administer longitudinal clinical registries and regularly release (on the Internet and elsewhere) information on risk-adjusted mortality for coro-

nary artery bypass grafting (CABG). All of these states release hospital-specific performance data, but only some report surgeon-specific information.

Public reporting programs related to other surgical procedures generally rely on administrative data. A few states use data from their discharge abstract databases to determine and report volume and risk-adjusted mortalities for selected procedures, including major cancer resections. The most widely available providers of data on noncardiac surgical outcomes are proprietary rating firms, which rely primarily on public-use Medicare files. Of these rating firms, the most notable is probably Healthgrades (www.healthgrades.com), which currently allows users to select from 31 different procedures or conditions and to obtain data on hospitals in any specified geographic region. For each procedure, hospitals are given a ranking, ranging from 5 stars (best) to 1 star (worst), on the basis of risk-adjusted mortality and, in some cases, morbidity. Hospital-specific information is provided free of charge, but a small fee is charged for information on specific surgeons.

The clinical outcome data from the state cardiac surgery registries are generally considered robust. The other sources of publicly reported outcome data, however, have several important limitations, some of which pertain to the use of administrative rather than clinical data [*see* Public-Use Administrative Databases, *below*] and some of which are specific to the vendor. For example, Healthgrades is often criticized on the grounds that its methods of calculating rates and risk adjustment are insufficiently transparent.[3] It is also criticized for its reliance on categorical rankings and its failure to provide actual rates (along with numerators and denominators).

Public-Use Administrative Databases

As an alternative to relying on outside analysis, surgeons can obtain administrative data and perform the analysis themselves. Although this approach requires a certain level of data skills, it may be practical for surgeons with sufficient analytic expertise (or else access to analytic support). Public-use administrative databases [*see Table 1*] are increasingly available, remain relatively inexpensive, and no longer require special equipment for data transmission or storage.

Most of the administrative databases that are useful for benchmarking surgical outcomes consist of hospital discharge abstracts, which contain information on patients admitted to acute care hospitals. The information collected includes demographic data (e.g., name, age, sex, race/ethnicity, and place of residence), admission and discharge dates, total charges, expected payment source, admission type (elective, urgent, or emergency), and discharge disposition. In addition, the abstracts may list attending physicians and surgeons, identified by means of Unique Physician Identification Numbers (UPINs). Claims for surgical admissions contain procedure-specific codes from the International Classification of Diseases, Ninth Edition, Clinical Modification (ICD-9-CM). In addition, hospital discharge abstracts contain fields for at least 10

Table 1 Public-Use Administrative Databases and Clinical Registries

Database/Registry	Patients	Participating Hospitals	Strengths	Limitations
Medicare	Medicare recipients ≥ 65 years old undergoing inpatient surgery	All U.S. hospitals treating Medicare patients	Large sample size; population-based	Limited to elderly patients; not specific for some procedure codes; no detailed clinical information for risk adjustment
Nationwide Inpatient Sample (NIS)	Patients undergoing inpatient surgery	20% sample of all U.S. nonfederal hospitals (~ 1,000 hospitals in 37 states)	All ages; large sample size	Limited to inpatient mortality; not specific for some procedure codes; no detailed clinical information for risk adjustment
National Surgical Quality Improvement Program (NSQIP)	Patients undergoing general and vascular surgery	> 100 private sector hospitals	Prospectively acquired clinical data	Costly to participate in; not designed to assess procedure-specific performance
Society of Thoracic Surgeons (STS) National Database	Patients undergoing cardiothoracic surgery	Registry participants accounting for > 70% of all adult cardiothoracic operations performed annually in the U.S.	Prospectively acquired clinical data	Historically rather than externally audited
National Cancer Data Base (NCDB)	Patients undergoing surgery for cancer	~1,400 hospitals nationwide (~ 75% of incident cancer cases in the U.S.)	Prospectively acquired clinical data; detailed cancer-specific data	Not externally audited

diagnosis codes, which are used to record preexisting medical conditions or medical complications of surgery for billing purposes.

There are a number of different administrative databases that surgeons can use for benchmarking surgical outcomes. For example, most states maintain discharge abstract databases that are available for public use (though the accessibility of these databases and other details vary widely from state to state). Moreover, surgeons can conveniently obtain data from the Nationwide Inpatient Sample (NIS) for this purpose at relatively low cost. Developed as part of the Healthcare Cost and Utilization Project (HCUP), a federal-state-industry partnership sponsored by the Agency for Healthcare Research and Quality (www.hcup-us.ahrq.gov), the NIS is an all-payer inpatient care database that collects information from approximately 8 million hospital admissions annually. It includes all patients from a 20% sample of all nonfederal hospitals (approximately 1,000 facilities) from 37 states and is designed to provide nationally representative estimates of health care utilization and outcomes. To this end, hospitals are selected to be as representative as possible with respect to ownership/control, bed size, teaching status, rural/urban location, and geographic region. Finally, surgeons can obtain public-use Medicare data for benchmarking surgical outcomes, just as some proprietary rating firms do. The Medicare inpatient database (i.e., the Medicare Provider Analysis and Review [MEDPAR] file) is the most accessible and widely used source of such data. It contains data on all fee-for-service acute care admissions for Medicare recipients, including most Americans older than 65 years, disabled patients younger than 65 years, and patients with end-stage renal disease.

Primary analysis of administrative databases has a number of advantages for surgeons interested in benchmarking outcomes. In the absence of comparable clinical databases (except for cardiac surgery), administrative databases are currently the only source of population-based outcome data. By accessing these databases directly, surgeons can obtain information on virtually any inpatient procedure of interest to them, not just those procedures currently targeted by proprietary rating firms. Because the sample sizes are so large, surgeons can effectively analyze the outcomes even of infrequently performed procedures.

Nevertheless, reliance on administrative data for benchmarking outcomes also has certain drawbacks. Some of these drawbacks are related to the specific database under consideration. For example, Medicare data apply primarily to elderly patients and thus are not useful for evaluating the outcomes of procedures that are most commonly performed in younger patients. In addition, they miss large numbers of elderly patients in regions of the United States with a high penetration of Medicare-managed care. As another example, all-payer databases, including state-level files and the NIS, provide in-hospital mortality data but not 30-day mortality data, and unlike Medicare databases, they usually do not contain codes identifying hospitals or surgeons. Thus, these databases are useful for generating national or state-level norms for specific procedures, but not for assessing the outcomes achieved by specific providers.

The most important drawbacks of administrative databases, however, are related to problems with the accuracy, completeness, and clinical precision of the data coding.[4,5] The ICD-9-CM diagnosis codes used to identify comorbidities are often clinically imprecise, do not reflect disease severity, and cannot differentiate preadmission conditions from acute complications. For this reason, risk adjustment and measurement of postoperative complications are possible only to a limited extent when administrative databases are employed. The ICD-9-CM procedure codes, though generally much more reliable than the diagnosis codes, still lack sufficient clinical specificity, particularly in relation to the Current Procedural Terminology (CPT) codes used for physician billing. For example, they often fail to distinguish between laparoscopic and open procedures or between similar procedures that are associated with different baseline risk levels (e.g., laparoscopic antireflux surgery and repair of paraesophageal hernias).

Clinical Registries

Of course, the ideal sources of information for benchmarking surgical outcomes are clinical outcome registries containing prospectively collected data [*see Table 1*]. As noted [*see Public Reporting Programs, above*], several states administer such registries for cardiac surgery as part of their efforts at quality improvement and public reporting. In the past few years, however, a number of professional organizations, including the ACS, have launched national outcome registries in other clinical areas. Outcome data from these registries are not reported publicly but are used to provide confidential feedback on performance to hospitals and surgeons for the purposes of internal quality improvement. With one prominent exception (NSQIP), the currently available outcome registries target specific specialties, conditions, or procedures.

NATIONAL SURGICAL QUALITY IMPROVEMENT PROGRAM

Perhaps the most visible and powerful source of benchmarking information is the NSQIP. Originally developed and implemented in Veterans Affairs (VA) hospitals, the NSQIP was later applied in a consortium of large academic medical centers and private sector hospitals and subsequently marketed by the ACS to all types of hospitals. As of 2006, more than 100 non-VA hospitals had enrolled. At participating hospitals, NSQIP data are collected through review of the medical records by dedicated nurse abstractors. Preoperative risk factors, intraoperative variables, and 30-day postoperative mortality and morbidity outcomes for patients undergoing major operations are submitted. Risk-adjusted morbidity and mortality results for each hospital are calculated semiannually and are reported as observed-to-expected (O/E) ratios.

As private-sector participation grows, the NSQIP is becoming a valuable resource for benchmarking surgical outcomes. Because the clinical data are prospectively collected, robust risk adjustment is possible. In addition, participants can readily access their own outcome data on a user-friendly Web interface. Moreover, they can easily navigate through different procedures and outcomes to obtain a range of information pertaining to their own specialty and can benchmark their own results against those of community centers, academic centers, or both. Nonetheless, the NSQIP currently has several weaknesses that reduce its usefulness in benchmarking surgical outcomes. First, it is expensive to administer. Besides paying an annual fee, each center is required to hire and train a dedicated surgical clinical nurse reviewer to review and enter data. Second, the NSQIP is not designed for assessing procedure-specific performance. Risk adjustment is based on a common set of preoperative variables that apply to all procedures, not on differing sets of risk factors that are specific to individual procedures. Furthermore, the program collects data on a sample of the procedures performed at each hospital, not on all procedures. Thus, the sample sizes are relatively small, and as a result, procedure-specific outcome measures may be imprecise. Third, the NSQIP's global measures of morbidity and mortality may be limited in terms of how well they account for differences in procedure mix across hospitals.

SOCIETY OF THORACIC SURGEONS NATIONAL DATABASE

The Society of Thoracic Surgeons (STS) National Database is the best source of national data for benchmarking the outcomes of cardiac procedures.[6] This database includes clinical data on more than 70% of all cardiothoracic operations performed in adults each year in the United States. Participating hospitals receive regular feedback on mortality after adult and congenital cardiac and general thoracic surgery. The main strengths of the STS registry are the robust and procedure-specific risk adjustment and the high hospital participation rate (which suggests that the STS outcome data should be highly generalizable). Historically, its major weakness has been the lack of external auditing to ensure that the outcome data submitted by hospitals are accurate and complete.

NATIONAL CANCER DATA BASE

A joint effort of the ACS Commission on Cancer (CoC) and the American Cancer Society, the National Cancer Data Base (NCDB) is a national registry that tracks information related to the treatment and outcome of cancer patients (www.facs.org/dept/cancer/ncdb/index.html). About 1,400 hospitals participate in the NCDB, which currently captures approximately 75% of incident cancer cases in the United States. The participating centers provide data on patient characteristics, tumor stage and grade, type of treatment, disease recurrence, and survival. Health care providers at CoC-approved cancer centers are able to access benchmark reports that summarize the data from the user's own center and compare them with state, regional, or national data, as well as with data from other individual cancer centers. Although the NCDB is undoubtedly the richest source of clinical data for benchmarking the outcomes of cancer surgery, it has certain limitations. As with the STS National Database, the data are not externally audited to ensure accuracy and completeness. Moreover, unlike most clinical outcome registries, the NCDB was not originally designed for tracking outcomes related to quality; it only recently began collecting information on comorbidity (for the purposes of risk adjustment), and it provides no information on outcomes other than mortality.

NATIONAL TRAUMA DATA BANK

The ACS, along with its Committee on Trauma, also oversees the National Trauma Data Bank (NTDB) (www.facs.org/trauma/ntdb.html). At present, approximately 556 hospitals submit data to the NTDB, including 70% of level I trauma centers and 53% of level II centers. Participating hospitals submit extensive information about comorbid conditions, patient status on arrival at the hospital, procedures performed, complications, and mortality. They also have access to the primary data, so that they can perform their own analyses. Although the NTDB captures a large percentage of trauma admissions in the United States, it should be kept in mind that data submission to NTDB is voluntary and that the data are not externally audited.

REGISTRIES FOR BARIATRIC SURGERY

In the past few years, two competing programs for tracking the outcomes of bariatric procedures have been launched: the ACS Bariatric Surgery Center Network (www.facs.org/cqi/bscn) and the Surgical Review Corporation (SRC) (www.surgicalreview.org). The details of these two clinical registries have not yet been released or even fully developed, but it is clear that these programs are intended to support hospital accreditation and "center of excellence" designations in bariatric surgery. In the ACS Bariatric Surgery Network, hospitals that are participating in the NSQIP submit all their data via their Web-based portals and compare their bariatric surgery results with those of other centers, as is done with other procedures included in the NSQIP. Hospitals that are not participating in the NSQIP submit only their bariatric outcome data and receive annual summaries of their outcomes, which are not adjusted for risk or benchmarked against the outcomes of other programs. The SRC, which is closely aligned with the American Society for Bariatric Surgery, is a nonprofit organization that assesses bariatric surgery programs, analyzes outcome data, and formulates practice guidelines. Participating centers must report their outcomes annually in order to maintain their status as SRC-approved centers. In addition to access to their own data, SRC-approved centers have access to benchmark outcome data aggregated from all participating institutions.

Table 2 Operative Mortality for Selected Procedures in Two National Databases

Operation	Medicare (2003)		NIS (2003)	
	N	Mortality (%)	N	Mortality (%)
Cardiac procedures				
CABG	79,704	3.8	32,123	2.2
Aortic valve replacement	21,464	5.8	7,221	4.0
Mitral valve replacement	6,844	8.9	2,903	5.9
Vascular procedures				
Lower-extremity bypass	31,861	2.9	10,830	1.3
Elective aortic aneurysm repair	16,481	5.1	5,757	3.6
Carotid endarterectomy	67,895	0.9	21,441	0.4
Cancer procedures				
Pulmonary lobectomy	14,696	3.8	5,298	1.9
Pneumonectomy	1,184	11.7	563	8.7
Esophagectomy	2,760	7.5	1,198	5.0
Gastrectomy	5,929	6.6	2,776	3.5
Pancreaticoduodenectomy	1,424	9.1	629	5.2
Colectomy	56,669	3.5	23,074	1.5
Abdominoperineal resection	3,680	2.8	1,489	1.1
Gastric bypass	5,663	1.0	14,056	0.2

CABG—coronary artery bypass grafting   NA—not available

Additional Considerations

Although it is important to understand that the various sources of surgical benchmarking data all have their own distinct strengths and weaknesses, it is also worthwhile to keep in mind that these sources all have certain limitations in common. One such limitation has to do with sample size. Whereas the benchmark data themselves usually are based on large numbers and thus are statistically robust, the outcome data of the hospitals and surgeons assessing their own performance against these benchmarks are not, particularly at the level of individual procedures. When sample sizes are too small, it may be difficult to determine whether complication rates higher than the benchmark rate reflect genuine problems or are simply the result of chance. A 2004 study considered hypothetical hospitals with operative mortalities twice the national average and estimated how many cases these hospitals would need over a 3-year period to be reasonably confident that their higher mortality figures were real and not just statistical artifacts.[7] The estimated minimal caseloads varied by procedure, ranging from 77 for esophagectomy to 2,668 for hip replacement. According to the authors' analysis of the NIS, the only procedure for which a majority of U.S. hospitals met these caseload criteria was CABG.

Another limitation has to do with generalizability. In this regard, it is illustrative to consider the overall reported mortalities for several procedures, determined on the basis of data from two different national databases: the Medicare Inpatient File (2003) and the NIS (2003) [*see Table 2*]. These databases have their own distinct characteristics (e.g., a particular patient population or method of defining mortality), and the different datasets yield different mortality estimates. For example, the predominantly elderly Medicare population had the highest mortalities across all procedures, ranging from 0.9% for carotid endarterectomy to 11.7% for pneumonectomy. In the NIS population, operative mortalities were considerably (sometimes more than 3%) lower for all procedures than in the Medicare population (e.g., 5.2% versus 9.1% for pancreaticoduodenectomy and 3.5% versus 6.6% for gastrectomy). Although neither the Medicare estimates nor the NIS estimates are wrong, they should not be considered universally applicable. Surgeons must recognize that risk estimates derived from any given database are dependent on the distinct composition of that database and therefore may not be generalizable to their own practice.

Our primary focus in this chapter has been on sources of information about morbidity and mortality; however, there are other measures related to surgical quality that surgeons may also be interested in benchmarking. For example, information about hospital volumes can be obtained from Healthgrades, the Leapfrog Group, and a growing number of state agencies. As another example, information pertaining to selected processes of care (e.g., processes related to preventing surgical site infection, venous thromboembolism, cardiac events, and ventilator-acquired pneumonia after operation) is now being collected by CMS as part of SCIP; although this information is not currently available, there are plans for eventual public reporting. Finally, information about patient satisfaction can be obtained from several private vendors. A large number of hospitals participate in a survey measurement program administered by Press-Ganey, a health care satisfaction survey business that has created national databases of comparative satisfaction information. In addition, both HCIA Inc. (formerly called Health Care Investment Analysts) and the Medical Group Management Association offer patient satisfaction comparison services.

References

1. Schwartz LM, Woloshin S, et al: How do elderly patients decide where to go for major surgery? Telephone interview survey. BMJ 331:821, 2005
2. National Survey on Americans as Health Care Consumers: An Update on the Role of Quality Information. Kaiser Family Foundation and Agency for Healthcare Research and Quality, December 2000
3. Krumholz HM, Rathore SS, et al: Evaluation of a consumer-oriented internet health care report card: the risk of quality ratings based on mortality data. JAMA 10:1277, 2002
4. Hsia DC, Krushat WM, et al: Accuracy of diagnostic coding for Medicare patients under the prospective-payment system. N Engl J Med 318:352, 1988
5. Jollis JG, Peterson ED, et al: The relationship between the volume of coronary angioplasty procedures at hospitals treating Medicare beneficiaries and short-term mortality. N Engl J Med 331:1625, 1994
6. Grover FL, Edwards FH: Similarity between the STS and New York State databases for valvular heart disease. Ann Thorac Surg 70:1143, 2000
7. Dimick JB, Welch HG, et al: Surgical mortality as an indicator of hospital quality: the problem with small sample size. JAMA 292:847, 2004

4 EVIDENCE-BASED SURGERY

Samuel R. G. Finlayson, M.D., M.P.H., F.A.C.S.

Evidence-based surgery may be defined as the consistent and judicious use of the best available scientific evidence in making decisions about the care of surgical patients. It is not an isolated phenomenon; rather, it is one part of a broad movement—evidence-based medicine—whose aim is to apply the scientific method to all of medical practice. The historical roots of this broad movement lie in the pioneering work of the Scottish epidemiologist Archibald Cochrane (1909–1988), for whom the preeminent international organization for research in evidence-based medicine (the Cochrane Collaboration) is named. The term evidence-based medicine itself was popularized by a landmark article that appeared in the *Journal of the American Medical Association* in 1992.[1] This article advocated a new approach to medical education, urging physicians and educators to deemphasize "intuition, unsystematic clinical experience, and pathophysiologic rationale as sufficient grounds for clinical decision making." In essence, advocates of evidence-based medicine seek to demote so-called expert opinion from its previous relatively high standing, regarding it as being, in fact, the least valid basis for making clinical decisions. As a consequence of the growth of this movement, the discipline of surgery, once driven more by the eminence of tradition than by the evidence of science, now increasingly requires its students to adopt evidence-based scientific standards of practice.

The imperative that surgical care be delivered in accordance with the best available scientific evidence is only one facet of evidence-based surgery. Other facets include systematic efforts to establish standards of care supported by science and the movement to popularize evidence-based practice. Systematic reviews of the literature are often generated by independent researchers or collaborative study groups (e.g., Cochrane collaborations) and published as review articles in journals or disseminated as practice guidelines. The movement to popularize evidence-based surgical practice is a relatively recent phenomenon that is exemplified by the activities of the Surgical Care Improvement Project (SCIP) (http://www.medqic.org/scip/scip_homepage.html). Although researchers are charged with generating and disseminating scientific evidence, the greatest responsibility for the success of evidence-based surgery ultimately lies with individual surgeons, who must not only practice evidence-based surgery but also understand and appropriately interpret an immense surgical literature.

In this chapter, I provide a framework for evaluating the strength of evidence for surgical practices, examining the validity of scientific studies in surgery, and assessing the role of evidence-based surgery in measuring and improving the quality of surgical care. These are the basic conceptual and analytic tools that a modern evidence-based surgeon needs to navigate the surgical literature and implement practices that are based on sound science.

Evaluation of Strength of Evidence for Surgical Practices

GUIDELINES AND SECONDARY SOURCES OF SCIENTIFIC EVIDENCE

To meet the growing demand for evidence-based practice information, a market has developed around the process of pooling and interpreting the best scientific evidence. Scientific reviews serve as secondary sources for evidence-based practice and are increasingly found in journals, in books, and on the Internet. Prominent examples include *Clinical Evidence* (published semiannually by the *British Journal of Medicine* and continually updated online [http://www.clinicalevidence.com]) and the Cochrane Database of Systematic Reviews (http://www.cochrane.org). SCIP serves as a clearinghouse for evidence-based guidelines that specifically address surgical practices.

These efforts to summarize and disseminate information about evidence-based surgery provide a convenient means of access to the surgical literature that can be very helpful to practicing surgeons. Such aids, however, are far from complete, and new evidence emerges continually. Accordingly, modern evidence-based surgeons cannot afford to rely entirely on these sources: they must also learn to assess the quality of individual scientific studies for themselves, as well as to interpret the implications of these studies for their own practices.

LEVELS OF EVIDENCE

Evidence for surgical practices comes in many forms, with varying degrees of reliability. At one end of the spectrum is an empirical impression that a practice makes physiologic sense and seems to work well; much of what surgeons actually do falls into this category and has not been formally tested. At the other end of the spectrum is evidence accumulated from multiple carefully conducted scientific experiments that yield consistent and reproducible results. The ultimate task of the evidence-based surgeon is to select practices that conform to the best evidence available; to that end, it is essential to be able to judge the reliability of scientific evidence.

In an effort to help clinicians judge the strength of scientific evidence, researchers have attempted to create hierarchies of evidence, in which the highest places are occupied by those sources that are most reliable and the lowest places by those that are least sure. With the understanding that not all practices have been subjected to the highest levels of scientific scrutiny, clinicians are advised to base practices on evidence gleaned from studies as high on the evidence hierarchy as possible.

An oft-cited example of such an evidence hierarchy is the levels-of-evidence system popularized by the United States Preventive Medicine Task Force (USPMTF) [*see Table 1*].[2] Since the inception of this system, the terms and concepts it employs have become common parlance among clinicians—hence, for example, the frequently heard references to level 1 evidence (i.e., evidence from well-conducted, randomized, controlled trials). However, almost as soon as the USPMTF levels-of-evidence system was released, debate about its adequacy began.[3] The predominant criticism has been that the system is too simple and inflexible to provide a precise description of the strength of evidence for clinical practices. Although the system identifies the design of the study from which the evidence is drawn, it does not consider certain other important factors that influence the quality of the study. For example, in the USPMTF system, the same grade is awarded to a randomized, double-blind, placebo-controlled trial with 50,000 subjects as to a randomized, unblinded trial with 30 subjects. Furthermore, a higher grade is awarded to the latter trial than to a well-designed, well-conducted, multi-institution, prospective cohort study with 10,000 subjects.

In response to the deficiencies of the USPMTF system, numerous alternative grading systems have been developed that take into account factors other than study design, such as quality, consistency, and completeness. Nevertheless, it is widely recognized that no grading system yet developed is perfect.[4] Consequently, surgeons are often required to judge the quality and applicability of scientific evidence for themselves.

APPRAISING SCIENTIFIC EVIDENCE

Specific study designs are associated with different levels of confidence about cause and effect. The clinical study design that is considered to have the greatest potential for determining causation is the randomized, controlled clinical trial. However, even studies with this design can lead to erroneous conclusions if they are not performed properly. Therefore, in evaluating the quality of clinical evidence, it is not sufficient simply to ascertain the design of the study that produced the evidence: one must also take a close look at how the study was conceived, implemented, analyzed, and interpreted.

Scientific evidence from studies of clinical practice relies on two important inferences. The first inference is that the observed outcome is the result of the practice and cannot be attributed to some alternative explanation. When this inference is deemed to be true, the study is considered to have internal validity. The second inference is that what was observed in the clinical study is relevant to scenarios outside the study in which the surgeon seeks to implement the practice. The extent to which this inference is true is referred to as external validity or generalizability. Whereas internal validity is determined by how well the study is conducted and how accurately the results are analyzed, external validity is determined by how well the study plan reflects the real-world clinical question that inspired it and how well the study's conclusions apply to real-world scenarios outside the study [see Figure 1]. External validity can also refer to the difference between an intervention's efficacy (how well it works when applied perfectly) and its effectiveness (how well it works when applied generally in an uncontrolled environment); when this difference is substantial, the study's external validity is poor.

Assessment of Validity of Scientific Studies in Surgery

INTERNAL VALIDITY: EVALUATING STUDY QUALITY

Assessment of the internal validity of a study requires an understanding of the potential influence of three key factors: chance, bias, and confounding. Chance refers to unpredictable randomness of events that might mislead researchers. Bias refers to systematic errors in how study subjects are selected or assessed. Confounding refers to differences in the comparison groups (other than the intended difference that is the subject of the comparison) that lead to differences in outcomes.

Chance

In clinical studies that compare outcomes between two or more groups, the assumption that there is no difference in outcomes is called the null hypothesis. Erroneous conclusions with regard to the null hypothesis can sometimes occur by chance alone. There

Table 1 Levels of Evidence According to USPMTF Schema

Level of Evidence	Source of Evidence
I	At least one properly randomized, controlled trial
II-1	Well-designed controlled trials without randomization
II-2	Well-designed cohort or case-control analytic study, preferably from more than one center or research group
II-3	Multiple time-series with or without intervention or, possibly, dramatic results from uncontrolled trials (e.g., penicillin treatment in 1940s)
III	Opinions from respected authorities based on clinical experience, descriptive studies, and case reports or opinions from committees of experts

Category of Recommendation	Basis of Recommendation
Level A	Good and consistent scientific evidence
Level B	Limited or inconsistent scientific evidence
Level C	Consensus, expert opinion, or both

USPMTF–United States Preventive Medicine Task Force

are two types of chance-related errors: type I and type II. Type I error (also called α error) occurs when researchers erroneously reject the null hypothesis—that is, they infer that there is a difference in outcomes when no difference really exists. Type II error (also called β error) occurs when researchers erroneously confirm the null hypothesis—that is, they infer that there is no difference in outcomes when a difference really does exist.

Type I errors Statistical testing is used to quantify the likelihood of a type I error. A variable commonly employed for this purpose is the P value, which is a measure of the probability that observed differences between groups might be attributable to chance alone. The threshold for statistical significance is conventionally set at a P value of 0.05, which signifies that the likelihood that the observed differences would occur by chance alone is 5%. Although a P value of 0.05 falls short of absolute certainty, it is generally accepted as sufficient for scientific proof.

An alternative expression of statistical likelihood is the confidence interval, which is a measure of the probability that the observed difference would occur if the same study were repeated an infinite number of times. For example, a confidence interval of 95% indicates that the observed difference would be present in 95% of the repetitions of the study.

There are many statistical tests that can be used to calculate P values and confidence intervals. Which statistical test is most appropriate for a particular situation depends on several factors, including the number of observations in the comparison groups, the number of groups being compared, whether two or more groups are being compared to each other or one group is being compared to itself after some time interval, what kind of numerical data are being analyzed (e.g., continuous or categorical), and whether risk adjustment is required. It is likely that only a minority of surgeons will have a firm grasp of all the nuances of the more complex statistical analyses. Fortunately, however, most clinical surgical studies are designed simply enough to employ statistical tests that are within the reach of the nonstatistician.

Type II errors Type II errors often occur when the sample size is simply too small to permit detection of small but clinically important differences in outcomes between comparison groups. When a study's sample size is insufficient for identification of outcome differences, the study is said to lack sufficient statistical power. Once a study is complete, no amount of analysis can correct for insufficient statistical power. Therefore, before starting a study, researchers should perform what is known as a power calculation, which involves determining the minimum size a difference must have to be meaningful, then calculating the minimum number of observations that would be required to demonstrate such a difference statistically. Surgeons should be particularly cautious when evaluating studies with null findings, particularly when no power calculation is explicitly reported. It is wise to remember that, as the adage has it, no evidence of effect is not necessarily evidence of no effect.

Bias

The term bias refers to a systematic problem with a clinical study that results in an incorrect estimate of the differences in outcomes between comparison groups. There are two general types of bias: selection bias and information bias. The former results from errors in how study subjects are chosen, whereas the latter results from errors in how information about exposures or outcomes (or other pertinent information) is obtained.

Selection bias The term selection bias applies to any imperfection in the selection process that results in a study population containing either the wrong types of subjects (i.e., persons who are not typical of the target population) or subjects who, for some reason unrelated to the intervention being evaluated, are more likely to have the outcome of interest. As an example, paid volunteer subjects may be more motivated to comply with treatment regimens and report favorable results than unpaid subjects are, and this difference may result in overestimation of the effect of an intervention. Such overestimation may involve both the internal validity and the external validity of the study. As another example,

in a trial of medical versus surgical treatment of gastroesophageal reflux disease, selecting study subjects from a group of diners at a Szechuan Chinese restaurant might lead to results favoring medical treatment (in that consumers of Szechuan Chinese food may be more likely to have well-controlled reflux). When assessing the validity of scientific evidence, surgeons must carefully consider the characteristics of the subjects selected for study.

Information bias The term information bias applies to any problem caused by the way in which outcome data or other pertinent data are obtained. As an example, in a study of sexual function after surgical treatment of rectal cancer, subjects may report symptoms differently in an in-person interview from how they would report them in an anonymous mailed survey. As another example, in a study of hernia repair outcomes, rates of chronic postoperative pain might be incorrectly reported if surgeons assess outcomes in their own patients. Also, recall bias (i.e., selective memory of past events) is a type of information bias to which retrospective clinical studies are particularly vulnerable.

Information bias is often more subtle than selection bias; accordingly, particular attention to the reported study methods is required to control this problem. Measures employed to control information bias include blinding and prospective study design.

Confounding

The term confounding refers to differences in outcomes that occur because of differences in the respective baseline risks of the comparison groups. Confounding is often the result of selection bias. For example, a comparison of mortality after open colectomy with that after laparoscopic colectomy might be skewed because of the greater likelihood that open colectomy will be performed on an emergency basis in a critically ill patient. In other words, severity of illness might confound the observed association between mortality and surgical approach.

Confounding can be effectively addressed by means of randomization. When subjects are randomized, potentially confounding variables (both recognized and unrecognized) are likely to be evenly distributed across comparison groups. Thus, even if these variables influence the baseline rates of certain outcomes in the cohort as a whole, they are unlikely to have a significant effect on differences observed across comparison groups. When randomization is not practical, confounding can be minimized by tightly controlling the study entry criteria. For instance, in the aforementioned comparison of open and laparoscopic colectomy (see above), one might opt to include only elective colectomies. It should be kept in mind, however, that restrictive entry criteria can sometimes limit generalizability. Another way to combat confounding is to use statistical risk-adjustment techniques; the downside to these is that they can reduce statistical power.

EXTERNAL VALIDITY: INTERPRETING AND APPLYING EVIDENCE TO PRACTICE

Once one is convinced that a clinical study is internally valid (i.e., that the observed outcome is the result of the exposure or intervention and cannot be attributed to some alternative explanation), the challenge is to assess the study's external validity (i.e., to determine whether the findings are applicable to a particular clinical scenario). To make an assessment of the external validity of a clinical study, it is necessary to examine several components of the study, including the patient population, the intervention, and the outcome measure. This process can be illustrated by briefly considering the example of a large, prospective, randomized clinical

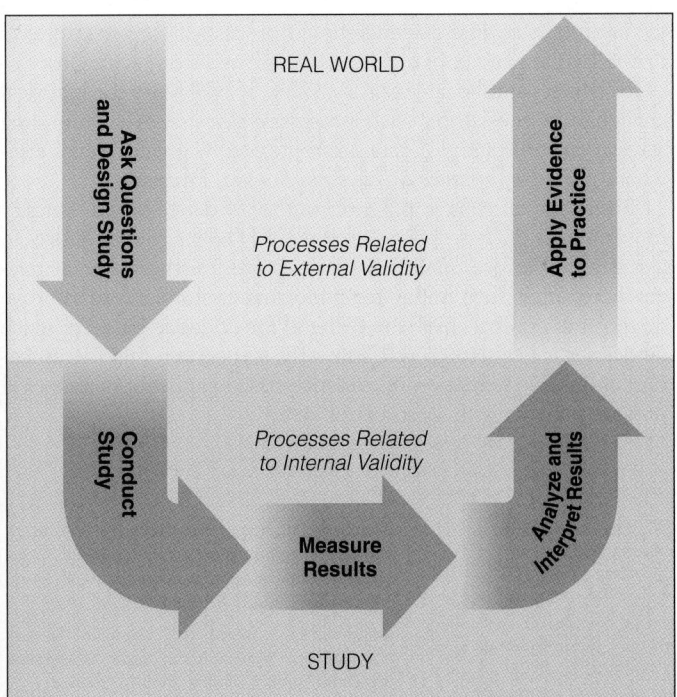

Figure 1 **Schematically depicted are processes that affect the internal and external validity of a clinical study.**

trial of laparoscopic versus open inguinal hernia repair performed in Veterans' Affairs (VA) medical centers.[5]

The VA trial concluded that the outcomes of open hernia repair were superior to those of laparoscopic repair. The trial was well designed and well conducted, but it generated substantial discussion about the generalizability of the results. As noted [see Internal Validity: Evaluating Study Quality, Bias, above], subject selection bias can adversely affect the external validity (generalizability) of a study's results: if the study population is in some important respect different from a particular population for which a surgeon is making clinical decisions, the results may not be entirely generalizable to the latter population. In the VA hernia trial, the subjects were military veterans, who tend to be, on average, older than the nonveteran general population. If older persons are more vulnerable to the risks of laparoscopic hernia repair (e.g., complications associated with general anesthesia), one might expect that any differences between open and laparoscopic herniorrhaphy with respect to morbidity outcomes would be exaggerated in a trial that included a higher number of older subjects, as the VA trial did. Accordingly, a surgeon attempting to assess the external validity of the VA trial might consider the evidence provided by the trial to be applicable to older patients but might reserve his or her judgment on the use of laparoscopy to repair hernias in younger, healthier patients.

A striking example of the potential effect of selection bias on generalizability comes from the Asymptomatic Carotid Artery Stenosis (ACAS) trial.[6] In this large, prospective, randomized study, volunteers for the trial were substantially younger and healthier than the average patient who undergoes carotid endarterectomy. As a result, the observed perioperative mortality in the ACAS trial was considerably lower than that observed in the general population—and, for that matter, lower even than the overall perioperative mortality in the very hospitals where the trial was conducted.[7] Although the results of the ACAS trial significantly changed practice, an argument could be made that the evidence provided by this trial, strictly speaking, was generalizable only to younger populations.

The external validity of a clinical study can also be affected by who provides the intervention. For example, in the VA hernia trial, surgeons had varying degrees of experience with the laparoscopic approach, and there were twofold differences in hernia recurrence rates between surgeons who had done more than 250 cases and surgeons who had less experience. Surgeons considering whether the evidence supports the use of laparoscopic repair will therefore have to examine their own experience with this approach before they can determine to what extent the results of the VA trial are generalizable to their own practices.

Furthermore, external validity can be influenced by what type of intervention is provided. For example, some have argued that one of the laparoscopic techniques commonly used in the VA trial, transabdominal preperitoneal repair (TAPP), is outmoded and more hazardous than the competing approach, totally extraperitoneal repair (TEP).[8] Surgeons who avoid using TAPP might reasonably question the generalizability of the VA study to their practices.

Finally, the type of outcome measured can affect the generalizability of clinical studies. The outcomes chosen for clinical studies may be those that are most convenient or most easily quantified rather than those that are of greatest interest to patients. In the VA hernia trial, several outcomes were studied, including operative complications, hernia recurrence, pain, and length of convalescence. Some of the outcome differences favored open repair, whereas others favored laparoscopic repair. To interpret the evidence as favoring one type of repair or the other involves making implicit value judgments regarding which outcomes are most important to patients. Surgeons interested in applying the evidence from the VA hernia trial to their own decisions about hernia repair will have to examine the specific outcomes measured before they can determine to what extent this study is generalizable to specific patients with specific values and interests.

Role of Evidence-Based Surgery in Measuring and Improving Quality of Care

In clinical studies, the efficacy of a surgical practice is measured in terms of the resulting patient outcomes. Until relatively recently, efforts to assess the quality of surgical care have focused almost exclusively on clinical outcomes. In the past few years, however, the evidence-based surgery movement has begun to promote an alternative measure of surgical quality—namely, adherence to processes of care supported by the best available scientific evidence.

The question of whether efforts to assess quality should focus on evidence-based processes of care or clinical outcomes is as much practical as philosophical. The practical argument against outcome measures is largely driven by a growing recognition that when hospitals and surgeons are considered on an individual basis, adverse outcomes generally are not numerous enough to allow identification of meaningful differences between providers.[9] In other words, outcome-based studies of the quality of care supplied by individual providers tend to have insufficient statistical power. The practical argument against evidence-based process-of-care measures is driven by the paucity of high-leverage, procedure-specific processes for which sound evidence is available, as well as by the logistical challenge of measuring such processes. The issues surrounding assessment of quality of care are discussed in greater detail elsewhere [see 2 Performance Measures in Surgical Practice].

Given its current momentum, the evidence-based surgery movement is likely to play a progressively larger role in efforts to assess and improve quality of surgical care. Furthermore, as payers increasingly turn to pay-for-performance strategies to improve quality and control costs, the demand for evidence-based practice guidelines is likely to grow. Ultimately, it is certain that identification and implementation of evidence-based surgical practices will provide patients with safer, better care.

References

1. Evidence-Based Medicine Working Group: Evidence-based medicine: a new approach to teaching the practice of medicine. JAMA 268:2420, 1992

2. Harris RP, Helfand M, Woolf SH, et al: Current methods of the US Preventive Services Task Force: a review of the process. Am J Prev Med 20(suppl 3):21, 2001

3. Woloshin S: Arguing about grades. Eff Clin Pract 3:94, 2000

4. Atkins D, Eccles M, Flottorp S, et al: Systems for grading the quality of evidence and the strength of recommendations I: critical appraisal of existing approaches—the GRADE Working Group. BMC Health Services Research 4:38, 2004

5. Neumayer L, Giobbe-Hurder O, Johansson O, et al: Open mesh versus laparoscopic mesh repair of inguinal hernia. N Engl J Med 350:1819, 2004

6. Executive Committee for the Asymptomatic Carotid Atherosclerosis Study: Endarterectomy for asymptomatic carotid artery stenosis. JAMA 273:1421, 1995

7. Wennberg DE, Lucas FL, Birkmeyer JD, et al: Variation in carotid endarterectomy mortality in the Medicare population: trial hospitals, volume, and patient characteristics. JAMA 279:1278, 1998

8. Grunwaldt LJ, Schwaitzberg SD, Rattner DW, et al: Is laparoscopic inguinal hernia repair an operation of the past? J Am Coll Surg 200:616, 2005

9. Dimick JB, Welch HG, Birkmeyer JD: Surgical mortality as an indicator of hospital quality: the problem with small sample size. JAMA 292:847, 2004

5 PREVENTION OF POSTOPERATIVE INFECTION

Jonathan L. Meakins, M.D., D.Sc., F.A.C.S., and Byron J. Masterson, M.D., F.A.C.S.

Epidemiology of Surgical Site Infection

Historically, the control of wound infection depended on antiseptic and aseptic techniques directed at coping with the infecting organism. In the 19th century and the early part of the 20th century, wound infections had devastating consequences and a measurable mortality. Even in the 1960s, before the correct use of antibiotics and the advent of modern preoperative and postoperative care, as much as one quarter of a surgical ward might have been occupied by patients with wound complications. As a result, wound management, in itself, became an important component of ward care and of medical education. It is fortunate that many factors have intervened so that the so-called wound rounds have become a practice of the past. The epidemiology of wound infection has changed as surgeons have learned to control bacteria and the inoculum as well as to focus increasingly on the patient (the host) for measures that will continue to provide improved results.

The following three factors are the determinants of any infectious process:

1. The infecting organism (in surgical patients, usually bacteria).
2. The environment in which the infection takes place (the local response).
3. The host defense mechanisms, which deal systemically with the infectious process.[1]

Wounds are particularly appropriate for analysis of infection with respect to these three determinants. Because many components of the bacterial contribution to wound infection now are clearly understood and measures to control bacteria have been implemented, the host factors become more apparent. In addition, interactions between the three determinants play a critical role, and with limited exceptions (e.g., massive contamination), few infections will be found to be the result of only a single factor [*see Figure 1*].

Definition of Surgical Site Infection

Wound infections have traditionally been thought of as infections in a surgical wound occurring between the skin and the deep soft tissues—a view that fails to consider the operative site as a whole. As prevention of these wound infections has become more effective, it has become apparent that definitions of operation-related infection must take the entire operative field into account; obvious examples include sternal and mediastinal infections, vascular graft infections, and infections associated with implants (if occurring within 1 year of the procedure and apparently related to it). Accordingly, the Centers for Disease Control and Prevention currently prefers to use the term surgical site infection (SSI). SSIs can be classified into three categories: superficial incisional SSIs (involving only skin and subcutaneous tissue), deep incisional SSIs (involving deep soft tissue), and organ/space SSIs (involving anatomic areas other than the incision itself that are opened or

manipulated in the course of the procedure) [*see Figure 2*].[2,3]

Standardization in reporting will permit more effective surveillance and improve results, as well as offer a painless way of achieving quality assurance. The natural tendency to deny that a surgical site has become infected contributes to the difficulty of defining SSI in a way that is both accurate and acceptable to surgeons. The surgical view of SSI recalls one judge's (probably apocryphal) remark about pornography: "It is hard to define, but I know it when I see it." SSIs are usually easy to identify. Nevertheless, there is a critical need for definitions of SSI that can be applied in different institutions for use as performance indicators.[4] The criteria on which such definitions must be based are, of course, more detailed than the simple apocryphal remark just cited.

STRATIFICATION OF RISK FOR SSI

The National Academy of Sciences–National Research Council classification of wounds [*see Table 1*], published in 1964, was a landmark in the field.[5] This report provided incontrovertible data to show that wounds could be classified as a function of probability of bacterial contamination (usually endogenous) in a consistent manner. Thus, wound infection rates could be validly compared from month to month, between services, and between hospitals. As surgery became more complex in the following decades, however, antibiotic use became more standardized and other risk variables began to assume greater prominence. In the early 1980s, the Study on the Efficacy of Nosocomial Infection Control (SENIC) study identified three risk factors in addition to wound class: location of operation (abdomen or chest), duration of operation, and

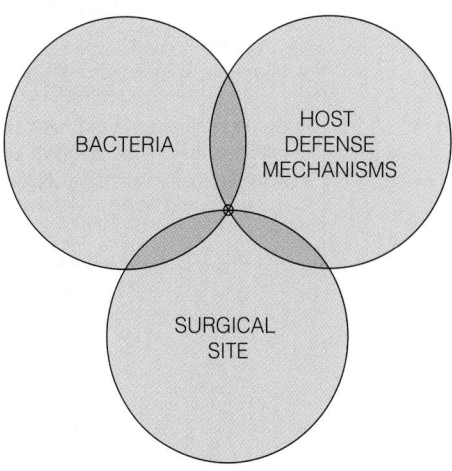

Figure 1 In a homeostatic, normal state, the determinants of any infectious process—bacteria, the surgical site, and host defense mechanisms (represented by three circles)—intersect at a point indicating zero probability of sepsis.

Epidemiology of Surgical Site Infection

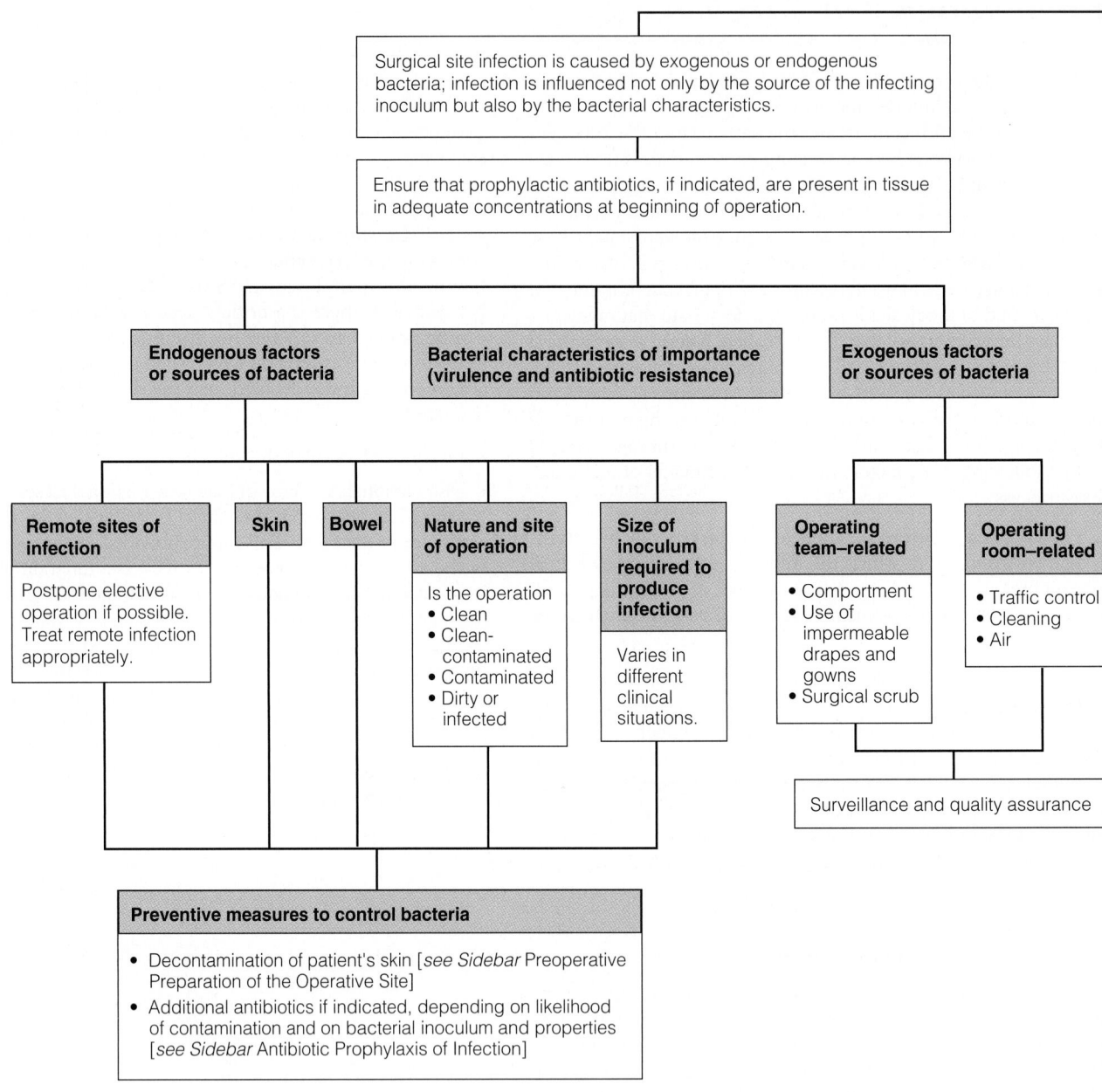

Surgical site infection is caused by exogenous or endogenous bacteria; infection is influenced not only by the source of the infecting inoculum but also by the bacterial characteristics.

Ensure that prophylactic antibiotics, if indicated, are present in tissue in adequate concentrations at beginning of operation.

Endogenous factors or sources of bacteria

Bacterial characteristics of importance (virulence and antibiotic resistance)

Exogenous factors or sources of bacteria

Remote sites of infection

Postpone elective operation if possible. Treat remote infection appropriately.

Skin

Bowel

Nature and site of operation

Is the operation
• Clean
• Clean-contaminated
• Contaminated
• Dirty or infected

Size of inoculum required to produce infection

Varies in different clinical situations.

Operating team–related

• Comportment
• Use of impermeable drapes and gowns
• Surgical scrub

Operating room–related

• Traffic control
• Cleaning
• Air

Surveillance and quality assurance

Preventive measures to control bacteria

• Decontamination of patient's skin [*see Sidebar* Preoperative Preparation of the Operative Site]
• Additional antibiotics if indicated, depending on likelihood of contamination and on bacterial inoculum and properties [*see Sidebar* Antibiotic Prophylaxis of Infection]

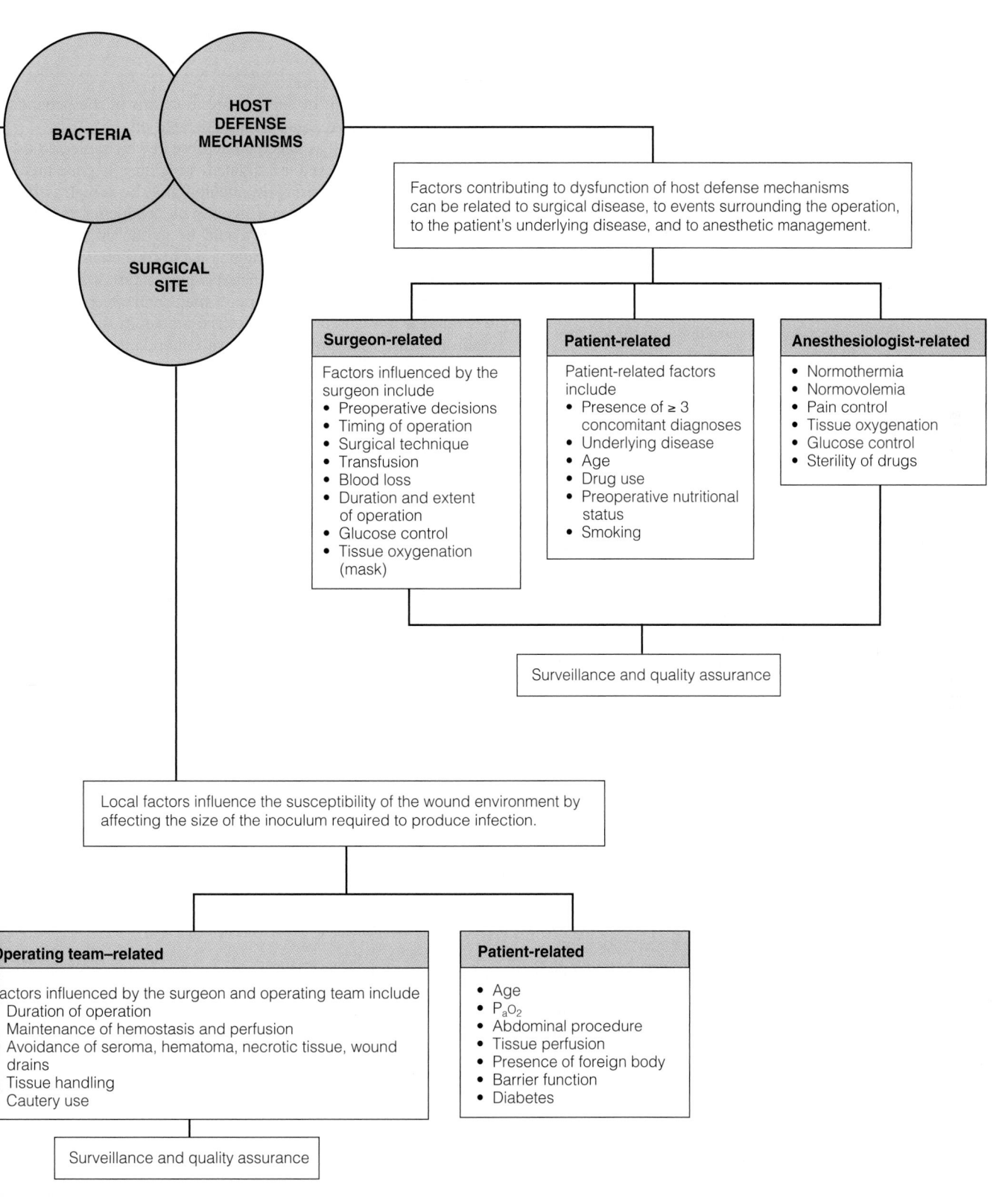

BACTERIA

HOST DEFENSE MECHANISMS

SURGICAL SITE

Factors contributing to dysfunction of host defense mechanisms can be related to surgical disease, to events surrounding the operation, to the patient's underlying disease, and to anesthetic management.

Surgeon-related

Factors influenced by the surgeon include
- Preoperative decisions
- Timing of operation
- Surgical technique
- Transfusion
- Blood loss
- Duration and extent of operation
- Glucose control
- Tissue oxygenation (mask)

Patient-related

Patient-related factors include
- Presence of ≥ 3 concomitant diagnoses
- Underlying disease
- Age
- Drug use
- Preoperative nutritional status
- Smoking

Anesthesiologist-related

- Normothermia
- Normovolemia
- Pain control
- Tissue oxygenation
- Glucose control
- Sterility of drugs

Surveillance and quality assurance

Local factors influence the susceptibility of the wound environment by affecting the size of the inoculum required to produce infection.

Operating team–related

Factors influenced by the surgeon and operating team include
- Duration of operation
- Maintenance of hemostasis and perfusion
- Avoidance of seroma, hematoma, necrotic tissue, wound drains
- Tissue handling
- Cautery use

Patient-related

- Age
- P_aO_2
- Abdominal procedure
- Tissue perfusion
- Presence of foreign body
- Barrier function
- Diabetes

Surveillance and quality assurance

19

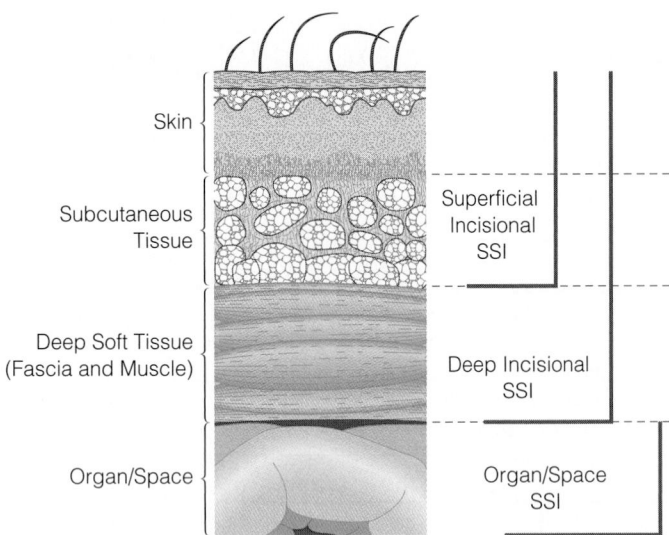

Figure 2 **Surgical site infections are classified into three categories, depending on which anatomic areas are affected.**[3]

patient clinical status (three or more diagnoses on discharge).[6] The National Nosocomial Infection Surveillance (NNIS) study reduced these four risk factors to three: wound classification, duration of operation, and American Society of Anesthesiologists (ASA) class III, IV or V.[7,8] Both risk assessments integrate the three determinants of infection: bacteria (wound class), local environment (duration), and systemic host defenses (one definition of patient health status), and they have been shown to be applicable outside the United States.[9] However, the SENIC and NNIS assessments do not integrate other known risk variables, such as smoking, tissue oxygen tension, glucose control, shock, and maintenance of normothermia, all of which are relevant for clinicians (though often hard to monitor and to fit into a manageable risk assessment).

Bacteria

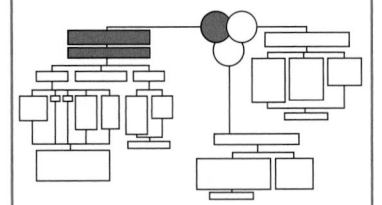

Clearly, without an infecting agent, no infection will result. Accordingly, most of what is known about bacteria is put to use in major efforts directed at reducing their numbers by means of asepsis and antisepsis. The principal concept is based on the size of the bacterial inoculum.

Wounds are traditionally classified according to whether the wound inoculum of bacteria is likely to be large enough to overwhelm local and systemic host defense mechanisms and produce an infection [*see Table 1*]. One study showed that the most important factor in the development of a wound infection was the number of bacteria present in the wound at the end of an operative procedure.[10] Another study quantitated this relation and provided insight into how local environmental factors might be integrated into an understanding of the problem [*see Figure 3*].[11] In the years before prophylactic antibiotics, as well as during the early phases of their use, there was a very clear relation between the classification of the operation (which is related to the probability of a significant inoculum) and the rate of wound infection.[5,12] This relation is now less dominant than it once was; therefore, other factors have come to play a significant role.[6,13]

CONTROL OF SOURCES OF BACTERIA

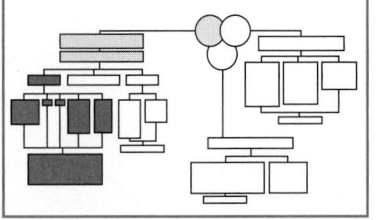

Endogenous bacteria are a more important cause of SSI than exogenous bacteria. In clean-contaminated, contaminated, and dirty-infected operations, the source and the amount of bacteria are functions of the patient's disease and the specific organs being operated on.

Operations classified as infected are those in which infected tissue and pus are removed or drained, providing a guaranteed inoculum to the surgical site. The inoculum may be as high as 10^{10} bacteria/ml, some of which may already be producing an infection. In addition, some bacteria could be in the growth phase rather than the dormant or the lag phase and thus could be more pathogenic. The heavily contaminated wound is best managed by delayed primary closure. This type of management ensures that the wound is not closed over a bacterial inoculum that is almost certain to cause a wound infection, with attendant early and late consequences.

Patients should not have elective surgery in the presence of remote infection, which is associated with an increased incidence of wound infection.[5] In patients with urinary tract infections, wounds frequently become infected with the same organism. Remote infections should be treated appropriately, and the operation should proceed only under the best conditions possible. If operation cannot be appropriately delayed, the use of prophylactic and therapeutic antibiotics should be considered [*see Sidebar Antibiotic Prophylaxis of Infection and Tables 2 through 4*].

Preoperative techniques of reducing patient flora, especially endogenous bacteria, are of great concern. Bowel preparation, antimicrobial showers or baths, and preoperative skin decontami-

Table 1 National Research Council Classification of Operative Wounds[5]

Clean (class I)	Nontraumatic No inflammation encountered No break in technique Respiratory, alimentary, or genitourinary tract not entered
Clean-contaminated (class II)	Gastrointestinal or respiratory tract entered without significant spillage Appendectomy Oropharynx entered Vagina entered Genitourinary tract entered in absence of infected urine Biliary tract entered in absence of infected bile Minor break in technique
Contaminated (class III)	Major break in technique Gross spillage from gastrointestinal tract Traumatic wound, fresh Entrance of genitourinary or biliary tracts in presence of infected urine or bile
Dirty and infected (class IV)	Acute bacterial inflammation encountered, without pus Transection of "clean" tissue for the purpose of surgical access to a collection of pus Traumatic wound with retained devitalized tissue, foreign bodies, fecal contamination, or delayed treatment, or all of these; or from dirty source

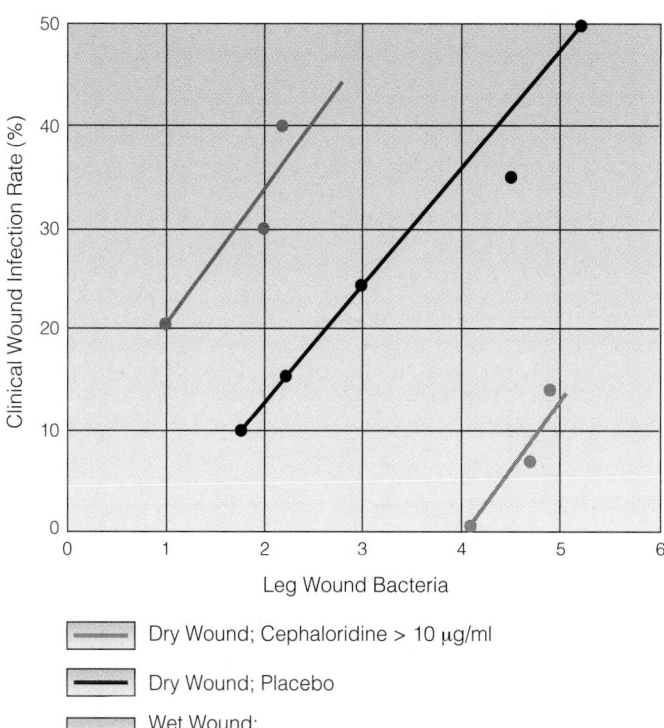

Dry Wound; Cephaloridine > 10 µg/ml

Dry Wound; Placebo

Wet Wound;
Wound Fluid Hematocrit > 8%; Placebo

Figure 3 **The wound infection rate is shown here as a function of bacterial inoculum in three different situations: a dry wound with an adequate concentration of antibiotic (cephaloridine > 10 µg/ml), a dry wound with no antibiotic (placebo), and a wet wound with no antibiotic (placebo, wound fluid hematocrit > 8%).**[11]

nation have been proposed frequently. These techniques, particularly preoperative skin decontamination [*see Sidebar* Preoperative Preparation of the Operative Site], may have specific roles in selected patients during epidemics or in units with high infection rates. As a routine for all patients, however, these techniques are unnecessary, time-consuming, and costly in institutions or units where infection rates are low.

The preoperative shave is a technique in need of reassessment. It is now clear that shaving the evening before an operation is associated with an increased wound infection rate. This increase is sec-

ondary to the trauma of the shave and the inevitable small areas of inflammation and infection. If hair removal is required,[14,15] clipping is preferable and should be done in the OR or the preparation room just before the operative procedure. Shaving, if ever performed, should not be done the night before operation.

In the past few years, the role of the classic bowel preparation [*see Table 5*] has been questioned [*see* Discussion, Infection Prevention in Bowel Surgery, *below*].[16-20] The suggestion has been made that selective gut decontamination (SGD) may be useful in major elective procedures involving the upper GI tract and perhaps in other settings. At present, SGD for prevention of infection cannot be recommended in either the preoperative or the postoperative period.

When infection develops after clean operations, particularly those in which foreign bodies were implanted, endogenous infecting organisms are involved but the skin is the primary source of the infecting bacteria. The air in the operating room and other OR sources occasionally become significant in clean cases; the degree of endogenous contamination can be surpassed by that of exogenous contamination. Thus, both the operating team—surgeon, assistants, nurses, and anesthetists—and OR air have been reported as significant sources of bacteria. In fact, personnel are the most important source of exogenous bacteria.[21-23] In the classic 1964 study by the National Academy of Sciences–National Research Council, ultraviolet light (UVL) was efficacious only in the limited situations of clean and ultraclean cases.[5] There were minimal numbers of endogenous bacteria, and UVL controlled one of the exogenous sources.

Clean air systems have very strong advocates, but they also have equally vociferous critics. It is possible to obtain excellent results in clean cases with implants without using these systems. However, clean air systems are here to stay. Nevertheless, the presence of a clean air system does not mean that basic principles of asepsis and antisepsis should be abandoned, because endogenous bacteria must still be controlled.

The use of impermeable drapes and gowns has received considerable attention. If bacteria can penetrate gown and drapes, they can gain access to the wound. The use of impermeable drapes may therefore be of clinical importance.[24,25] When wet, drapes of 140-thread-count cotton are permeable to bacteria. It is clear that some operations are wetter than others, but generally, much can be done to make drapes and gowns impermeable to bacteria. For example, drapes of 270-thread-count cotton that have been water-

Table 2   Parenteral Antibiotics Recommended
for Prophylaxis of Surgical Site Infection

	Antibiotic	Dose	Route of Administration
For coverage against aerobic gram-positive and gram-negative organisms	Cefazolin	1 g	I.V. or I.M. (I.V. preferred)
If patient is allergic to cephalosporins or if methicillin-resistant organisms are present	Vancomycin	1 g	I.V.
	Clindamycin	600 mg	I.V.
	or		
Combination regimens for coverage against gram-negative aerobes and anaerobes	Metronidazole	500 mg	I.V.
	plus		
	Tobramycin (or equivalent aminoglycoside)	1.5 mg/kg	I.V. or I.M. (I.V. preferred for first dose)
For single-agent coverage against gram-negative aerobes and anaerobes	Cefoxitin	1–2 g	I.V.
	Cefotetan	1–2 g	I.V.

Antibiotic Prophylaxis of Infection

Selection

Spectrum. The antibiotic chosen should be active against the most likely pathogens. Single-agent therapy is almost always effective except in colorectal operations, small-bowel procedures with stasis, emergency abdominal operations in the presence of polymicrobial flora, and penetrating trauma; in such cases, a combination of antibiotics is usually used because anaerobic coverage is required.

Pharmacokinetics. The half-life of the antibiotic selected must be long enough to maintain adequate tissue levels throughout the operation.

Administration

Dosage, route, and timing. A single preoperative dose that is of the same strength as a full therapeutic dose is adequate in most instances. The single dose should be given I.V. immediately before skin incision. Administration by the anesthetist is most effective and efficient.

Duration. A second dose is warranted if the duration of the operation exceeds either 3 hours or twice the half-life of the antibiotic. No additional benefit has been demonstrated in continuing prophylaxis beyond the day of the operation, and mounting data suggest that the preoperative dose is sufficient. When massive hemorrhage has occurred (i.e., blood loss equal to or greater than blood volume), a second dose is warranted. Even in emergency or trauma cases, prolonged courses of antibiotics are not justified unless they are therapeutic.[77,108]

Indications

CLEAN CASES

Prophylactic antibiotics are not indicated in clean operations if the patient has no host risk factors or if the operation does not involve placement of prosthetic materials. Open heart operation and operations involving the aorta of the vessels in the groin require prophylaxis.

Patients in whom host factors suggest the need for prophylaxis include those who have more than three concomitant diagnoses, those whose operations are expected to last longer than 2 hours, and those whose operations are abdominal.[6] A patient who meets any two of these criteria is highly likely to benefit from prophylaxis. When host factors suggest that the probability of a surgical site infection is significant, administration of cefazolin at induction of anesthesia is appropriate prophylaxis. Vancomycin should be substituted in patients who are allergic to cephalosporins or who are susceptible to major immediate hypersensitivity reactions to penicillin.

When certain prostheses (e.g., heart valves, vascular grafts, and orthopedic hardware) are used, prophylaxis is justified when viewed in the light of the cost of a surgical site infection to the patient's health. Prophylaxis with either cefazolin or vancomycin is appropriate for cardiac, vascular, or orthopedic patients who receive prostheses.

Catheters for dialysis or nutrition, pacemakers, and shunts of various sorts are prone to infection mostly for technical reasons, and prophylaxis is not usually required. Meta-analysis indicates, however, that antimicrobial prophylaxis reduces the infection rate in CSF shunts by 50%.[109] Beneficial results may also be achievable for other permanently implanted shunts (e.g., peritoneovenous) and devices (e.g., long-term venous access catheters and pacemakers); however, the studies needed to confirm this possibility will never be done, because the infection rates are low and the sample sizes would have to be prohibitively large. The placement of such foreign bodies is a clean operation, and the use of antibiotics should be based on local experience.

CLEAN-CONTAMINATED CASES

Abdominal procedures. In biliary tract procedures (open or laparoscopic), prophylaxis is required only for patients at high risk: those whose common bile duct is likely to be explored (because of jaundice, bile duct obstruction, stones in the common bile duct, or a reoperative biliary procedure); those with acute cholecystitis; and those older than 70 years. A single dose of cefazolin is adequate. In hepatobiliary and pancreatic procedures, antibiotic prophylaxis is always warranted because these operations are clean-contaminated, because they are long, because they are abdominal, or for all of these reasons. Prophylaxis is also warranted for therapeutic endoscopic retrograde cholangiopancreatography. In gastroduodenal procedures, patients whose gastric acidity is normal or high and in whom bleeding, cancer, gastric ulcer, and obstruction are absent are at low risk for infection and require no prophylaxis; all other patients are at high risk and require prophylaxis. Patients undergoing operation for morbid obesity should receive double the usual prophylactic dose[110]; cefazolin is an effective agent.

Operations on the head and neck (including the esophagus). Patients whose operation is of significance (i.e., involve entry into the oral cavity, the pharynx, or the esophagus) require prophylaxis.

Gynecologic procedures. Patients whose operation is either high-risk cesarean section, abortion, or vaginal or abdominal hysterectomy will benefit from cefazolin. Aqueous penicillin G or doxycycline may be preferable for first-trimester abortions in patients with a history of pelvic inflammatory disease. In patients with cephalosporin allergy, doxycycline is effective for those having hysterectomies and metronidazole for those having cesarean sections. Women delivering by cesarean section should be given the antibiotic immediately after cord clamping.

Urologic procedures. In principle, antibiotics are not required in patients with sterile urine. Patients with positive cultures should be treated. If an operative procedure is performed, a single dose of the appropriate antibiotic will suffice.

(*continued*)

---

proofed are impermeable, but they can be washed only 75 times. Economics plays a role in the choice of drape fabric because entirely disposable drapes are expensive. Local institutional factors may be significant in the role of a specific type of drape in the prevention of SSI.

PROBABILITY OF CONTAMINATION

The probability of contamination is largely defined by the nature of the operation [*see Table 1*]. However, other factors contribute to the probability of contamination; the most obvious is the expected duration of the operative procedure, which, whenever examined, has been significantly correlated with the wound infection rate.[6,10,12] The longer the procedure lasts, the more bacteria accumulate in a wound; the sources of bacteria include the patient, the operating team (gowns, gloves with holes, wet drapes), the OR, and the equipment. In addition, the patient undergoing a longer operation is likely to be older, to have other diseases, and to have cancer of—or to be undergoing operation on—a structure

with possible contamination. A longer duration, even of a clean operation, represents increased time at risk for contamination. These points, in addition to pharmacologic considerations, suggest that the surgeon should be alert to the need for a second dose of prophylactic antibiotics [*see Sidebar* Antibiotic Prophylaxis of Infection].

Abdominal operation is another risk factor not found in the NNIS risk assessment.[6,8] Significant disease and age are additional factors that play a role in outcome; however, because the major concentrations of endogenous bacteria are located in the abdomen, abdominal operations are more likely to involve bacterial contamination.

For some years, postoperative contamination of the wound has been considered unlikely. However, one report of SSI in sternal incisions cleaned and redressed 4 hours postoperatively clearly shows that wounds can be contaminated and become infected in the postoperative period.[26] Accordingly, use of a dry dressing for 24 hours seems prudent.

Antibiotic Prophylaxis of Infection (*continued*)

CONTAMINATED CASES

Abdominal procedures. In colorectal procedures, antibiotics active against both aerobes and anaerobes are recommended. In appendectomy, SSI prophylaxis requires an agent or combination of agents active against both aerobes and anaerobes; a single dose of cefoxitin, 2 g I.V., or, in patients who are allergic to β-lactam antibiotics, metronidazole, 500 mg I.V., is effective. A combination of an aminoglycoside and clindamycin is effective if the appendix is perforated; a therapeutic course of 3 to 5 days is appropriate but does not seem warranted unless the patient is particularly ill. A laparotomy without a precise diagnosis is usually an emergency procedure and demands preoperative prophylaxis. If the preoperative diagnosis is a ruptured viscus (e.g., the colon or the small bowel), both an agent active against aerobes and an agent active against anaerobes are required. Depending on operative findings, prophylaxis may be sufficient or may have to be supplemented with postoperative antibiotic therapy.

Trauma. The proper duration of antibiotic prophylaxis for trauma patients is a confusing issue—24 hours or less of prophylaxis is probably adequate, and more than 48 hours is certainly unwarranted. When laparotomy is performed for nonpenetrating injuries, prophylaxis should be administered. Coverage of both aerobes and anaerobes is mandatory. The duration of prophylaxis should be less than 24 hours. In cases of penetrating abdominal injury, prophylaxis with either cefoxitin or a combination of agents active against anaerobic and aerobic organisms is required. The duration of prophylaxis should be less than 24 hours, and in many cases, perioperative doses will be adequate. For open fractures, management should proceed as if a therapeutic course were required. For grade I or II injuries, a first-generation cephalosporin will suffice, whereas for grade III injuries, combination therapy is warranted; duration may vary. For operative repair of fractures, a single dose of cefazolin may be given preoperatively, with a second dose added if the procedure is long. Patients with major soft tissue injury with a danger of spreading infection will benefit from cefazolin, 1 g I.V. every 8 hours for 1 to 3 days.

DIRTY OR INFECTED CASES

Infected cases require therapeutic courses of antibiotics; prophylaxis is not appropriate in this context. In dirty cases, particularly those resulting from trauma, contamination and tissue destruction are usually so extensive that the wounds must be left open for delayed primary or secondary closure. Appropriate timing of wound closure is judged at the time of debridement. Antibiotics should be administered as part of resuscitation. Administration of antibiotics for 24 hours is probably adequate if infection is absent at the outset. However, a therapeutic course of antibiotics is warranted if infection is present from the outset or if more than 6 hours elapsed before treatment of the wounds was initiated.

Prophylaxis of Endocarditis

Studies of the incidence of endocarditis associated with dental procedures, endoscopy, or operations that may result in transient bacteremia are lacking. Nevertheless, the consensus is that patients with specific cardiac and vascular conditions are at risk for endocarditis or vascular prosthetic infection when undergoing certain procedures; these patients should receive prophylactic antibiotics.[111-113] A variety of organisms are dangerous, but viridans streptococci are most common after dental or oral procedures, and enterococci are most common if the portal of entry is the GU or GI tract. Oral amoxicillin now replaces penicillin V or ampicillin because of superior absorption and better serum levels. In penicillin-allergic patients, clindamycin is recommended; alternatives include cephalexin, cefadroxil, azithromycin, and clarithromycin. When there is a risk of exposure to bowel flora or enterococci, oral amoxicillin may be given. If an I.V. regimen is indicated, ampicillin may be given, with gentamicin added if the patient is at high risk for endocarditis. In patients allergic to penicillin, vancomycin is appropriate, with gentamicin added in high-risk patients. These parenteral regimens should be reserved for high-risk patients undergoing procedures with a significant probability of bacteremia.

In patients receiving penicillin-based prophylaxis because of a history of rheumatic fever, erythromycin rather than amoxicillin should be used to protect against endocarditis.[111] There is consensus concerning prophylaxis for orthopedic prostheses and acquired infection after transient bacteremia. In major procedures, where the risk of bacteremia is significant, the above recommendations are pertinent.

BACTERIAL PROPERTIES

Not only is the size of the bacterial inoculum important; the bacterial properties of virulence and pathogenicity are also significant. The most obvious pathogenic bacteria in surgical 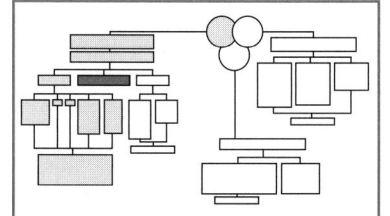 patients are gram-positive cocci (e.g., *Staphylococcus aureus* and streptococci). With modern hygienic practice, it would be expected that *S. aureus* would be found mostly in clean cases, with a wound infection incidence of 1% to 2%; however, it is in fact an increasingly common pathogen in SSIs. Surveillance can be very useful in identifying either wards or surgeons with increased rates. Operative procedures in infected areas have an increased infection rate because of the high inoculum with actively pathogenic bacteria.

The preoperative hospital stay has frequently been found to make an important contribution to wound infection rates.[12] The usual explanation is that during this stay, either more endogenous bacteria are present or commensal flora is replaced by hospital flora. More likely, the patient's clinical picture is a complex one, often entailing exhaustive workup of more than one organ system, various complications, and a degree of illness that radically changes the host's ability to deal with an inoculum, however small. Therefore, multiple factors combine to transform the hospitalized preoperative patient into a susceptible host. Same-day admission should eliminate any bacterial impact associated with the preoperative hospital stay.

Bacteria with multiple antibiotic resistance (e.g., methicillin-resistant *S. aureus* [MRSA], *S. epidermidis*, and vancomycin-resistant enterococci [VRE]) can be associated with significant SSI problems. In particular, staphylococci, with their natural virulence, present an important hazard if inappropriate prophylaxis is used.

Many surgeons consider it inappropriate or unnecessary to obtain good culture and sensitivity data on SSIs; instead of conducting sensitivity testing, they simply drain infected wounds, believing that the wounds will heal. However, there have been a number of reports of SSIs caused by unusual organisms[23,26,27]; these findings underscore the usefulness of culturing pus or fluid when an infection is being drained. SSIs caused by antibiotic-resistant organisms or unusual pathogens call for specific prophylaxis, perhaps other infection control efforts, and, if the problem persists, a search for a possible carrier or a common source.[21-23,26,27]

SURGEONS AND BACTERIA

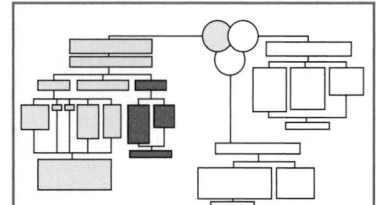

The surgeon's perioperative rituals are designed to reduce or eliminate bacteria from the operative field. Many old habits are obsolete [*see* Discussion, Hand Washing, *below*]. Nonetheless, it is clear that surgeons can exert some influence on SSI rates.[13] The refusal to use delayed primary closure or secondary closure is an example. Careful attention to the concepts of asepsis and antisepsis in the preparation and conduct of the operation is important. Although no single step in the ritual of preparing a patient for the operative procedure is indispensable, it is likely that certain critical standards of behavior must be maintained to achieve good results.

The measurement and publication of data about individuals or hospitals with high SSI rates have been associated with a diminution of those rates [*see* Table 6].[12,13,28] It is uncertain by what process the diffusion of these data relates to the observed improvements. Although surveillance has unpleasant connotations, it provides objective data that individual surgeons are often too busy to acquire but that can contribute to improved patient care. For example, such data can be useful in identifying problems (e.g., the presence of MRSA, a high SSI incidence, or clusters), maintaining quality assurance, and allowing comparison with accepted standards.

Environment: Local Factors

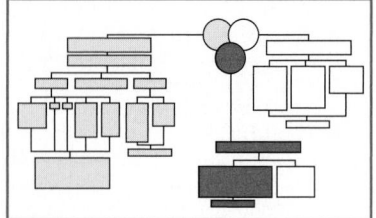

Local factors influence SSI development because they affect the size of the bacterial inoculum that is required to produce an infection: in a susceptible wound, a smaller inoculum produces infection [*see Figure 2*].

THE SURGEON'S INFLUENCE

Most of the local factors that make a surgical site favorable to bacteria are under the control of the surgeon. Although Halsted usually receives, deservedly so, the credit for having established the importance of technical excellence in the OR in preventing infection, individual surgeons in the distant past achieved remarkable results by careful attention to cleanliness and technique.[29] The Halstedian principles dealt with hemostasis, sharp dissection, fine sutures, anatomic dissection, and the gentle handling of tissues. Mass ligatures, large or braided nonabsorbable sutures, necrotic tissue, and the creation of hematomas or seromas must be avoided, and foreign materials must be judiciously used because these techniques and materials change the size of the inoculum required to initiate an infectious process. Logarithmically fewer bacteria are required to produce infection in the presence of a foreign body (e.g., suture, graft, metal, or pacemaker) or necrotic tissue (e.g., that caused by gross hemostasis or injudicious use of electrocautery devices).

The differences in inoculum required to produce wound infections can be seen in a model in which the two variables are the wound hematocrit and the presence of antibiotic [*see Figure 3*]. In the absence of an antibiotic and in the presence of wound fluid with a hematocrit of more than 8%, 10 bacteria yield a wound infection rate of 20%. In a technically good wound with no antibiotic, however, 1,000 bacteria produce a wound infection rate of 20%.[11] In the presence of an antibiotic, 10^5 to 10^6 bacteria are required.

Drains

The use of drains varies widely and is very subjective. All surgeons are certain that they understand when to use a drain. However, certain points are worth noting. It is now recognized that a simple Penrose drain may function as a drainage route but is also an access route by which pathogens can reach the patient.[30] It is important that the operative site not be drained through the wound. The use of a closed suction drain reduces the potential for contamination and infection.

Many operations on the GI tract can be performed safely without employing prophylactic drainage.[31] A review and meta-analysis from 2004 concluded that (1) after hepatic, colonic, or rectal resection with primary anastomosis and after appendectomy for any stage of appendicitis, drains should be omitted (recommendation grade A), and (2) after esophageal resection and total gastrectomy, drains should be used (recommendation grade D). Additional randomized, controlled trials will be required to determine the value of prophylactic drainage for other GI procedures, especially those involving the upper GI tract.

Table 3   Conditions and Procedures That Require Antibiotic Prophylaxis against Endocarditis[111,112]

CONDITIONS

Cardiac
Prosthetic cardiac valves (including biosynthetic valves)
Most congenital cardiac malformations
Surgically constructed systemic-pulmonary shunts
Rheumatic and other acquired valvular dysfunction
Idiopathic hypertrophic subaortic stenosis
History of bacterial endocarditis
Mitral valve prolapse causing mitral insufficiency
Surgically repaired intracardiac lesions with residual hemodynamic abnormality or < 6 mo after operation

Vascular
Synthetic vascular grafts

PROCEDURES

Dental or oropharyngeal
Procedures that may induce bleeding
Procedures that involve incision of the mucosa

Respiratory
Rigid bronchoscopy

Incision and drainage or debridement of sites of infection

Urologic
Cystoscopy with urethral dilatation
Urinary tract procedures
Catheterization in the presence of infected urine

Gynecologic
Vaginal hysterectomy
Vaginal delivery in the presence of infection

Gastrointestinal
Procedures that involve incision or resection of mucosa
Endoscopy that involves manipulation (e.g., biopsy, dilatation, or sclerotherapy) or ERCP

Table 4   Antibiotics for Prevention of Endocarditis[55,111]

Manipulative Procedure	Prophylactic Regimen*	
	Usual	In Patients with Penicillin Allergy
Dental procedures likely to cause gingival bleeding; operations or instrumentation of the upper respiratory tract	*Oral* Amoxicillin, 2.0 g 1 hr before procedure *Parenteral* Ampicillin, 2.0 g I.M. or I.V. 30 min before procedure	*Oral* Clindamycin, 600 mg 1 hr before procedure *or* Cephalexin or cefadroxil,† 2.0 g 1 hr before procedure *or* Azithromycin or clarithromycin, 500 mg 1 hr before procedure *Parenteral* Clindamycin, 600 mg I.V. within 30 min before procedure *or* Cefazolin, 1.0 g I.M. or I.V. within 30 min before procedure
Gastrointestinal or genitourinary operation; abscess drainage	*Oral* Amoxicillin, 2.0 g 1 hr before procedure *Parenteral* Ampicillin, 2.0 g I.M. or I.V. within 30 min before procedure; if risk of endocarditis is considered high, add gentamicin, 1.5 mg/kg (to maximum of 120 mg) I.M. or I.V. 30 min before procedure‡	Vancomycin, 1.0 g I.V. infused slowly over 1 hr, beginning 1 hr before procedure; if risk of endocarditis is considered high, add gentamicin, 1.5 mg/kg (to maximum of 120 mg) I.M. or I.V. 30 min before procedure‡

*Pediatric dosages are as follows: oral amoxicillin, 50 mg/kg; oral or parenteral clindamycin, 20 mg/kg; oral cephalexin or cefadroxil, 50 mg/kg; oral azithromycin or clarithromycin, 15 mg/kg; parenteral ampicillin, 50 mg/kg; parenteral cefazolin, 25 mg/kg; parenteral gentamicin, 2 mg/kg; parenteral vancomycin, 20 mg/kg. *Total pediatric dose should not exceed total adult dose.*
†Patients with a history of immediate-type sensitivity to penicillin should not receive these agents.
‡High-risk patients should also receive ampicillin, 1.0 g I.M. or I.V., or amoxicillin, 1.0 g p.o., 6 hr after procedure.

Duration of Operation

In most studies,[6,10,12] contamination certainly increases with time (see above). Wound edges can dry out, become macerated, or in other ways be made more susceptible to infection (i.e., requiring fewer bacteria for development of infection). Speed and poor technique are not suitable approaches; expeditious operation is appropriate.

Electrocautery

The use of electrocautery devices has been clearly associated with an increase in the incidence of superficial SSIs. However, when such devices are properly used to provide pinpoint coagulation (for which the bleeding vessels are best held by fine forceps) or to divide tissues under tension, there is minimal tissue destruction, no charring, and no change in the wound infection rate.[30]

PATIENT FACTORS

Local Blood Flow

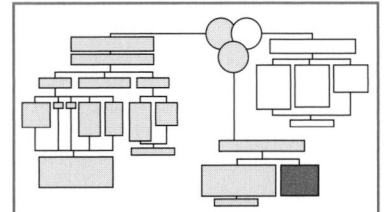

Local perfusion can greatly influence the development of infection, as is seen most easily in the tendency of the patient with peripheral vascular disease to acquire infection of an extremity. As a local problem, inadequate perfusion reduces the number of bacteria required for infection, in part because inadequate perfusion leads to decreased tissue levels of oxygen. Shock, by reducing local perfusion, also greatly enhances susceptibility to infection. Fewer organisms are required to produce infection during or immediately after shock [*see Figure 4*].

To counter these effects, the arterial oxygen tension (P_aO_2) must be translated into an adequate subcutaneous oxygen level (determined by measuring transcutaneous oxygen tension)[32]; this, together with adequate perfusion, will provide local protection by increasing the number of bacteria required to produce infection. Provision of supplemental oxygen in the perioperative period may

lead to a reduced SSI rate, probably as a consequence of increased tissue oxygen tension,[33] though the value of this practice has been questioned.[34] If the patient is not intubated, a mask, not nasal prongs, is required.[35]

Barrier Function

Inadequate perfusion may also affect the function of other organs, and the resulting dysfunction will, in turn, influence the patient's susceptibility to infection. For example, ischemia-reperfusion injury to the intestinal tract is a frequent consequence of hypovolemic shock and bloodstream infection. Inadequate perfusion of the GI tract may also occur during states of fluid and electrolyte imbalance or when cardiac output is marginal. In experimental studies, altered blood flow has been found to be associated with the breakdown of bowel barrier function—that is, the inability of the intestinal tract to prevent bacteria, their toxins, or both from moving from the gut lumen into tissue at a rate too fast to permit clearance by the usual protective mechanisms. A variety of experimental approaches aimed at enhancing bowel barrier function have been studied; at present, however, the most clinically applicable method of bowel protection is initiation of enteral feeding (even if the quantity of nutrients provided does not satisfy all the nutrient requirements) and administration of the amino acid glutamine [*see 137 Nutritional Support*]. Glutamine is a specific fuel for enterocytes and colonocytes and has been found to aid recovery of damaged intestinal mucosa and enhance barrier function when administered either enterally or parenterally.

Advanced Age

Aging is associated with structural and functional changes that render the skin and subcutaneous tissues more susceptible to infection. These changes are immutable; however, they must be evaluated in advance and addressed by excellent surgical technique and, on occasion, prophylactic antibiotics [*see Sidebar Antibiotic Prophylaxis of Infection*]. SSI rates increase with aging until the age of 65 years, after which point the incidence appears to decline.[36]

Preoperative Preparation of the Operative Site

The sole reason for preparing the patient's skin before an operation is to reduce the risk of wound infection. A preoperative antiseptic bath is not necessary for most surgical patients, but their personal hygiene must be assessed and preoperative cleanliness established. Multiple preoperative baths may prevent postoperative infection in selected patient groups, such as those who carry *Staphylococcus aureus* on their skin or who have infectious lesions. Chlorhexidine gluconate is the recommended agent for such baths.[114]

Hair should not be removed from the operative site unless it physically interferes with accurate anatomic approximation of the wound edges.[115] If hair must be removed, it should be clipped in the OR.[14] Shaving hair from the operative site, particularly on the evening before operation or immediately before wound incision in the OR, increases the risk of wound infection. Depilatories are not recommended, because they cause serious irritation and rashes in a significant number of patients, especially when used near the eyes and the genitalia.[116]

In emergency procedures, obvious dirt, grime, and dried blood should be mechanically cleansed from the operative site by using sufficient friction. In one study, cleansing of contaminated wounds by means of ultrasound debridement was compared with high-pressure irrigation and soaking. The experimental wounds were contaminated with a colloidal clay that potentiates infection 1,000-fold. The investigators irrigated wounds at pressures of 8 to 10 psi, a level obtained by using a 30 ml syringe with a 1.5 in. long 19-gauge needle and 300 ml of 0.85% sterile saline solution. High-pressure irrigation removed slightly more particulate matter (59%) than ultrasound debridement (48%), and both of these methods removed more matter than soaking (26%).[117] Both ultrasound debridement and high-pressure irrigation were also effective in reducing the wound infection rate in experimental wounds contaminated with a subinfective dose of *S. aureus*.

For nonemergency procedures, the necessary reduction in microorganisms can be achieved by using povidone-iodine (10% available povidone-iodine and 1% available iodine) or chlorhexidine gluconate both for mechanical cleansing of the intertriginous folds and the umbilicus and for painting the operative site. Which skin antiseptic is optimal is unclear. The best option appears to be chlorhexidine gluconate or an iodophor.[118] The patient should be assessed for evidence of sensitivity to the antiseptic (particularly if the agent contains iodine) to minimize the risk of an allergic reaction. What some patients report as iodine allergies are actually iodine burns. Iodine in alcohol or in water is associated with an increased risk of skin irritation,[90] particularly at the edges of the operative field, where the iodine concentrates as the alcohol evaporates. Iodine should therefore be removed after sufficient contact time with the skin, especially at the edges. Iodophors do not irritate the skin and thus need not be removed.

Host Defense Mechanisms

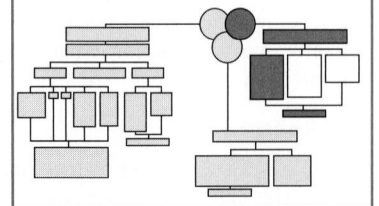

The systemic response is designed to control and eradicate infection. Many factors can inhibit systemic host defense mechanisms; some are related to the surgical disease, others to the patient's underlying disease or diseases and the events surrounding the operation.

SURGEON-RELATED FACTORS

There are a limited number of ways in which the surgeon can improve a patient's systemic responses to surgery. Nevertheless, when appropriate, attempts should be made to modify the host. The surgeon and the operation are both capable of reducing immunologic efficacy; hence, the operative procedure should be carried out in as judicious a manner as possible. Minimal blood loss, avoidance of shock, and maintenance of blood volume, tissue perfusion, and tissue oxygenation all will minimize trauma and will reduce the secondary, unintended immunologic effects of major procedures.

Diabetes has long been recognized as a risk factor for infection and for SSI in particular. Three studies from the past decade demonstrated the importance of glucose control for reducing SSI rates in both diabetic and nondiabetic patients who underwent operation,[37,38] as well as in critically ill ICU patients.[39] Glucose control is required throughout the entire perioperative period. The beneficial effect appears to lie in the enhancement of host defenses. The surgical team must also ensure maintenance of adequate tissue oxygen tension[32,33] and maintenance of normothermia.[40]

When abnormalities in host defenses are secondary to surgical disease, the timing of the operation is crucial to outcome. With acute and subacute inflammatory processes, early operation helps restore normal immune function. Deferral of definitive therapy frequently compounds problems.

PATIENT FACTORS

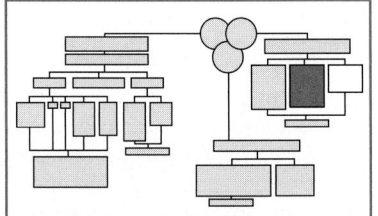

Surgeons have always known that the patient is a significant variable in the outcome of operation. Various clinical states are associated with altered resistance to infection. In all patients, but particularly those at high risk, SSI creates not only wound complications but also significant morbidity (e.g., reoperation, incisional hernia, secondary infection, impaired mobility, increased hospitalization, delayed rehabilitation, or permanent disability) and occasional mortality.[22] SENIC has proposed that the risk of wound infection be assessed not only in terms of prob-

---

Table 5 Parenteral Antibiotics Commonly Used for Broad-Spectrum Coverage of Colonic Microflora

COMBINATION THERAPY OR PROPHYLAXIS

Aerobic Coverage
(to be combined with a drug having anaerobic activity)

Amikacin	Ciprofloxacin
Aztreonam	Gentamicin
Ceftriaxone	Tobramycin

Anaerobic Coverage
(to be combined with a drug having aerobic activity)

Chloramphenicol	Metronidazole
Clindamycin	

SINGLE-DRUG THERAPY OR PROPHYLAXIS

Aerobic-Anaerobic Coverage

Ampicillin-sulbactam	Imipenem-cilastatin*
Cefotetan	Piperacillin-tazobactam
Cefoxitin	Ticarcillin-clavulanate
Ceftizoxime	

*This agent should be used *only* for therapeutic purposes; it should not be used for prophylaxis.

Table 6   Effect of Surveillance and Feedback on Wound Infection Rates in Two Hospitals[28]

		Period 1	Period 2*
Hospital A	Number of wounds	1,500	1,447
	Wound infection rate	8.4%	3.7%
Hospital B	Number of wounds	1,746	1,939
	Wound infection rate	5.7%	3.7%

*Periods 1 and 2 were separated by an interval during which feedback on wound infection rates was analyzed.

ability of contamination but also in relation to host factors.[6,7,9] According to this study, patients most clearly at risk for wound infection are those with three or more concomitant diagnoses; other patients who are clearly at risk are those undergoing a clean-contaminated or contaminated abdominal procedure and those undergoing any procedure expected to last longer than 2 hours. These last two risk groups are affected by a bacterial component, but all those patients who are undergoing major abdominal procedures or lengthy operations generally have a significant primary pathologic condition and are usually older, with an increased frequency of concomitant conditions. The NNIS system uses most of the same concepts but expresses them differently. In the NNIS study, host factors in the large study are evaluated in terms of the ASA score. Duration of operation is measured differently as well, with a lengthy operation being defined by the NNIS as one that is at or above the 75th percentile for operating time. Bacterial contamination remains a risk factor, but operative site is eliminated.[8]

Shock has an influence on the incidence of wound infection [*see Figure 4*]. This influence is most obvious in cases of trauma, but there are significant implications for all patients in regard to maintenance of blood volume, hemostasis, and oxygen-carrying capacity. The effect of shock on the risk of infection appears to be not only immediate (i.e., its effect on local perfusion) but also late because systemic responses are blunted as local factors return to normal.

Advanced age, transfusion, and the use of steroids and other immunosuppressive drugs, including chemotherapeutic agents, are associated with an increased risk of SSI.[41,42] Often, these factors cannot be altered; however, the proper choice of operation, the appropriate use of prophylaxis, and meticulous surgical technique can reduce the risk of such infection by maintaining patient homeostasis, reducing the size of any infecting microbial inoculum, and creating a wound that is likely to heal primarily.

Smoking is associated with a striking increase in SSI incidence. As little as 1 week of abstinence from smoking will make a positive difference.[43]

Pharmacologic therapy can affect host response as well. Nonsteroidal anti-inflammatory drugs that attenuate the production of certain eicosanoids can greatly alter the adverse effects of infection by modifying fever and cardiovascular effects. Operative procedures involving inhalational anesthetics result in an immediate rise in plasma cortisol concentrations. The steroid response and the associated immunomodulation can be modified by using high epidural anesthesia as the method of choice; pituitary adrenal activation will be greatly attenuated. Some drugs that inhibit steroid elaboration (e.g., etomidate) have also been shown to be capable of modifying perioperative immune responses.

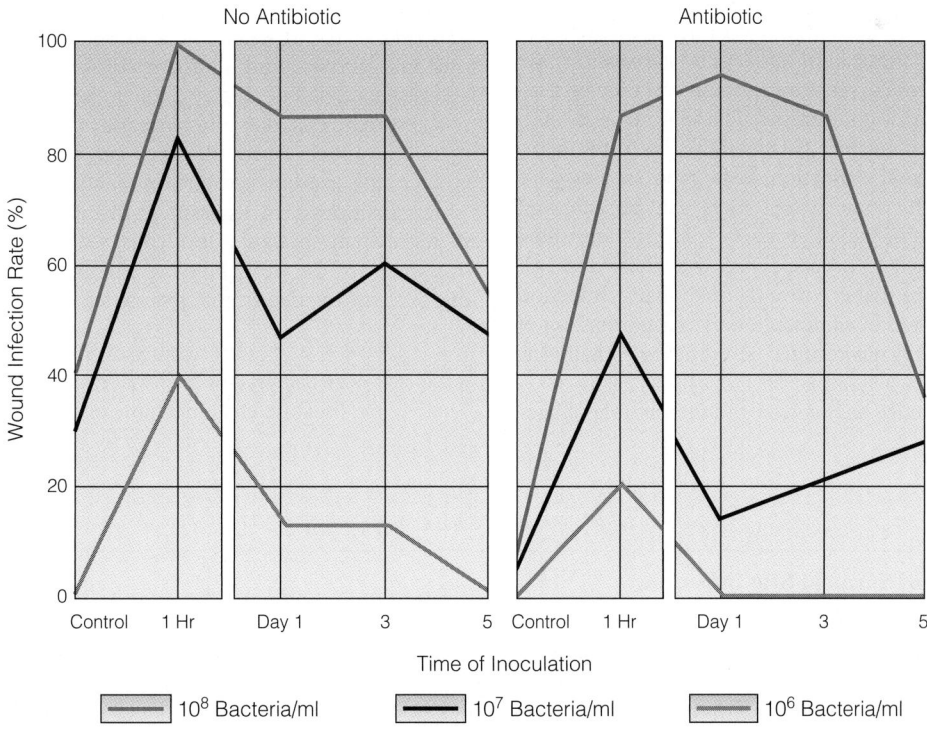

Figure 4   **Animals exposed to hemorrhagic shock followed by resuscitation show an early decreased resistance to wound infection. There is also a persistent influence of shock on the development of wound infection at different times of inoculation after shock. The importance of inoculum size (10^6/ml to 10^8/ml) and the effect of antibiotic on infection rates are evident at all times of inoculation.[103]**

Table 7 Determinants of Infection and Factors
That Influence Wound Infection Rates

Variable	Determinant of Infection		
	Bacteria	Wound Environment (Local Factors)	Host Defense Mechanisms (Systemic Factors)
Bacterial numbers in wound[10]	A		
Potential contamination[6,10,12]	A		
Preoperative shave[12]	A		
Presence of 3 or more diagnoses[6]			C
Age[10,12]		B	C
Duration of operation[6,10,12]	A	B	C
Abdominal operation[6]	A	B	C
ASA class III, IV, or V[8]			C
O₂ tension[32]		B	
Glucose control[37,38]			C
Normothermia[40]		B	C
Shock[103]		B	C
Smoking[43]		B	C

ANESTHESIOLOGIST-
RELATED FACTORS

A 2000 commentary in *The Lancet* by Donal Buggy considered the question of whether anesthetic management could influence surgical wound healing.[44] In

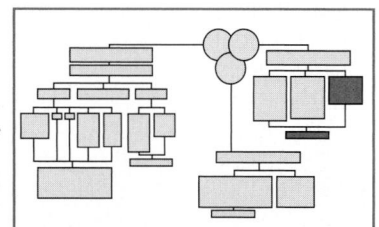

addition to the surgeon- and patient-related factors already discussed (see above), Buggy cogently identified a number of anesthesiologist-related factors that could contribute to better wound healing and reduced wound infection. Some of these factors (e.g., pain control, epidural anesthesia, and autologous transfusion) are unproven but nonetheless make sense and should certainly be tested. Others (e.g., tissue perfusion, intravascular volume, and—significantly—maintenance of normal perioperative body temperature) have undergone formal evaluation. Very good studies have shown that dramatic reductions in SSI rates can be achieved through careful avoidance of hypothermia.[40,45] Patient-controlled analgesia pumps are known to be associated with increased SSI rates, through a mechanism that is currently unknown.[46] Infection control practices are required of all practitioners; contamination of anesthetic drugs by bacteria has resulted in numerous small outbreaks of SSI.[47,48]

As modern surgical practice has evolved and the variable of bac-terial contamination has come to be generally well managed, the importance of all members of the surgical team in the prevention of SSI has become increasingly apparent. The crux of Buggy's commentary may be expressed as follows: details make a difference, and all of the participants in a patient's surgical journey can contribute to a continuing decrease in SSI. It is a systems issue.

INTEGRATION OF DETERMINANTS

As operative infection rates slowly fall, despite the performance of increasingly complex operations in patients at greater risk, surgeons are approaching the control of infection with a broader view than simply that of asepsis and antisepsis. This new, broader view must take into account many variables, of which some have no relation to bacteria but all play a role in SSI [*see Table 7 and Figure 1*].

To estimate risk, one must integrate the various determinants of infection in such a way that they can be applied to patient care. Much of this exercise is vague. In reality, the day-to-day practice of surgery includes a risk assessment that is essentially a form of logistic regression, though not recognized as such. Each surgeon's assessment of the probability of whether an SSI will occur takes into account the determining variables:

$$\text{Probability of SSI} =$$
$$x + a \text{ (bacteria)} + b \text{ (environment: local factors)}$$
$$+ c \text{ (host defense mechanisms: systemic factors)}$$

Discussion

Antibiotic Prophylaxis of Surgical Site Infection

It is difficult to understand why antibiotics have not always prevented SSI successfully. Certainly, surgeons were quick to appreciate the possibilities of antibiotics; nevertheless, the efficacy of antibiotic prophylaxis was not proved until the late 1960s.[11] Studies before then had major design flaws—principally, the administration of the antibiotic some time after the start of the operation, often in the recovery room. The failure of studies to demonstrate efficacy and the occasional finding that prophylactic antibiotics worsened rather than improved outcome led in the late 1950s to profound skepticism about prophylactic antibiotic use in any operation.

The principal reason for the apparent inefficacy was inadequate understanding of the biology of SSIs. Fruitful study of antibiotics and how they should be used began after physiologic groundwork established the importance of local blood flow, maintenance of local immune defenses, adjuvants, and local and systemic perfusion.[49]

The key antibiotic study, which was conducted in guinea pigs, unequivocally proved the following about antibiotics:

1. They are most effective when given before inoculation of bacteria.
2. They are ineffective if given 3 hours after inoculation.
3. They are of intermediate effectiveness when given in between these times [*see Figure 5*].[50]

Although efficacy with a complicated regimen was demonstrated in 1964,[51] the correct approach was not defined until 1969.[11] Established by these studies are the philosophical and practical bases of the principles of antibiotic prophylaxis of SSI in all surgical arenas[11,50]: that prophylactic antibiotics must be given preoperatively within 2 hours of the incision, in full dosage, parenterally, and for a very limited period. These principles remain essentially unchanged despite minor modifications from innumerable subsequent studies.[52-56] Prophylaxis for colorectal operations is discussed elsewhere [*see Infection Prevention in Bowel Surgery, below*].

PRINCIPLES OF PATIENT SELECTION

Patients must be selected for prophylaxis on the basis of either their risk for SSI or the cost to their health if an SSI develops (e.g., after implantation of a cardiac valve or another prosthesis). The most important criterion is the degree of bacterial contamination expected to occur during the operation. The traditional classification of such contamination was defined in 1964 by the historic National Academy of Sciences–National Research Council study.[5] The important features of the classification are its simplicity, ease of understanding, ease of coding, and reliability. Classification is dependent on only one variable—the bacterial inoculum—and the effects of this variable are now controllable by antimicrobial prophylaxis. Advances in operative technique, general care, antibiotic

use, anesthesia, and surveillance have reduced SSI rates in all categories that were established by this classification [*see Table 8*].[6,12,13,51]

In 1960, after years of negative studies, it was said, "Nearly all surgeons now agree that the routine use of prophylaxis in clean operations is unnecessary and undesirable."[57] Since then, much has changed: there are now many clean operations for which no competent surgeon would omit the use of prophylactic antibiotics, particularly as procedures become increasingly complex and prosthetic materials are used in patients who are older, sicker, or immunocompromised.

A separate risk assessment that integrates host and bacterial variables (i.e., whether the operation is dirty or contaminated, is longer than 2 hours, or is an abdominal procedure and whether the patient has three or more concomitant diagnoses) segregates more effectively those patients who are prone to an increased incidence of SSI [*see Integration of Determinants of Infection, below*]. This approach enables the surgeon to identify those patients who are likely to require preventive measures, particularly in clean cases, in which antibiotics would normally not be used.[6]

The prototypical clean operation is an inguinal hernia repair. Technical approaches have changed dramatically over the past 10 years, and most primary and recurrent hernias are now treated with a tension-free mesh-based repair. The use of antibiotics has become controversial. In the era of repairs under tension, there was some evidence to suggest that a perioperative antibiotic (in a single preoperative dose) was beneficial.[58] Current studies, however, do not support antibiotic use in tension-free mesh-based inguinal hernia repairs.[59,60] On the other hand, if surveillance indicates that there is a local or regional problem[61] with SSI after hernia surgery, antibiotic prophylaxis (again in the form of single preoperative dose) is appropriate. Without significantly more supportive data, prophylaxis for clean cases cannot be recommended unless specific risk factors are present.

Data suggest that prophylactic use of antibiotics may contribute to secondary *Clostridium difficile* disease; accordingly, caution should be exercised when widening the indications for prophylaxis is under consideration.[62] If local results are poor, surgical practice should be reassessed before antibiotics are prescribed.

ANTIBIOTIC SELECTION AND ADMINISTRATION

When antibiotics are given more than 2 hours before operation, the risk of infection is increased.[52,54] I.V. administration in the OR or the preanesthetic room guarantees appropriate levels at the time of incision. The organisms likely to be present dictate the choice of antibiotic for prophylaxis. The cephalosporins are ideally suited to prophylaxis: their features include a broad spectrum of activity, an excellent ratio of therapeutic to toxic dosages, a low rate of allergic responses, ease of administration, and attractive cost advantages. Mild allergic reactions to penicillin are not contraindications for the use of a cephalosporin.

Physicians like new drugs and often tend to prescribe newer, more expensive antibiotics for simple tasks. First-generation cephalosporins (e.g., cefazolin) are ideal agents for prophylaxis. Third-generation cephalosporins are not: they cost more, are not more effective, and promote emergence of resistant strains.[63,64]

The most important first-generation cephalosporin for surgical patients continues to be cefazolin. Administered I.V. in the OR at the time of skin incision, it provides adequate tissue levels throughout most of the operation. A second dose administered in the OR after 3 hours will be beneficial if the procedure lasts longer than that. Data on all operative site infections are imprecise, but SSIs

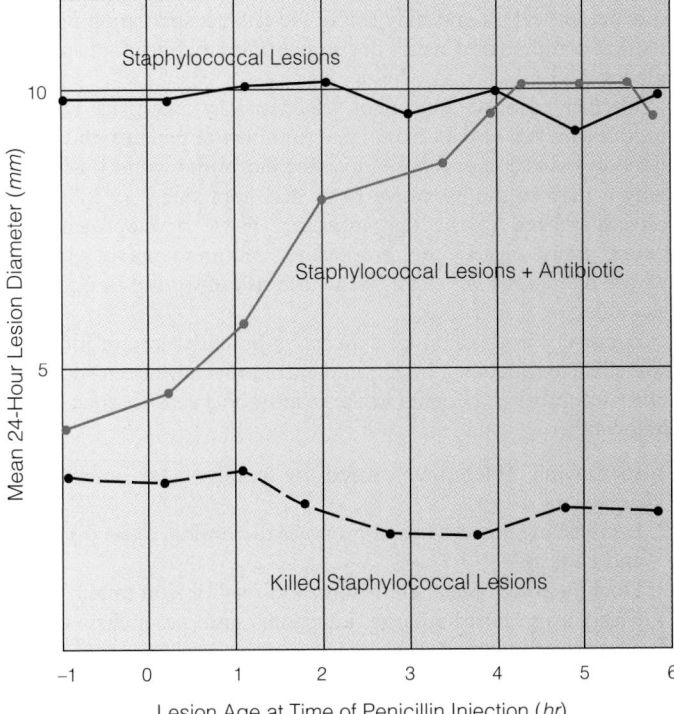

Figure 5   In a pioneer study of antibiotic prophylaxis,[50] the diameter of lesions induced by staphylococcal inoculation 24 hours earlier was observed to be critically affected by the timing of penicillin administration with respect to bacterial inoculation.

Table 8 Historical Rates of Wound Infection

Wound Classification	Infection Rate (%)				
	1960–1962[51] (15,613 patients)	1967–1977[12] (62,937 patients)	1975–1976[6] (59,353 patients)	1977–1981[13] (20,193 patients)	1982–1986[107] (20,703 patients)
Clean	5.1	1.5	2.9	1.8	1.3
Clean-contaminated	10.8	7.7	3.9	2.9	2.5
Contaminated	16.3	15.2	8.5	9.9	7.1
Dirty-infected	28.0	40.0	12.6	—	—
Overall	7.4	4.7	4.1	2.8	2.2

can clearly be reduced by this regimen. No data suggest that further doses are required for prophylaxis.

Fortunately, cefazolin is effective against both gram-positive and gram-negative bacteria of importance, unless significant anaerobic organisms are encountered. The significance of anaerobic flora has been disputed, but for elective colorectal surgery,[65] abdominal trauma,[66,67] appendicitis,[68] or other circumstances in which penicillin-resistant anaerobic bacteria are likely to be encountered, coverage against both aerobic and anaerobic gram-negative organisms is strongly recommended and supported by the data.

Despite several decades of studies, prophylaxis is not always properly implemented.[52,54,68,69] Unfortunately, didactic education is not always the best way to change behavior. Preprinted order forms[70] and a reminder sticker from the pharmacy[71] have proved to be effective methods of ensuring correct utilization.

The commonly heard decision "This case was tough, let's give an antibiotic for 3 to 5 days" has no data to support it and should be abandoned. Differentiation between prophylaxis and therapeusis is important. A therapeutic course for perforated diverticulitis or other types of peritoneal infection is appropriate. Data on casual contamination associated with trauma or with operative procedures suggest that 24 hours of prophylaxis or less is quite adequate.[72-74] Mounting evidence suggests that a single preoperative dose is good care and that additional doses are not required.

Trauma Patients

The efficacy of antibiotic administration on arrival in the emergency department as an integral part of resuscitation has been clearly demonstrated.[66] The most common regimens have been (1) a combination of an aminoglycoside and clindamycin and (2) cefoxitin alone. These two regimens or variations thereof have been compared in a number of studies.[40,67,75] They appear to be equally effective, and either regimen can be recommended with confidence. For prophylaxis, there appears to be a trend toward using a single drug: cefoxitin or cefotetan.[55] If therapy is required because of either a delay in surgery, terrible injury, or prolonged shock, the combination of an agent that is effective against anaerobes with an aminoglycoside seems to be favored. Because aminoglycosides are nephrotoxic, they must be used with care in the presence of shock.

In many of the trauma studies just cited, antibiotic prophylaxis lasted for 48 hours or longer. Subsequent studies, however, indicated that prophylaxis lasting less than 24 hours is appropriate.[73,74,76] Single-dose prophylaxis is appropriate for patients with closed fractures.[77]

COMPLICATIONS

Complications of antibiotic prophylaxis are few. Although data linking prophylaxis to the development of resistant organisms are

meager, resistant microbes have developed in every other situation in which antibiotics have been utilized, and it is reasonable to expect that prophylaxis in any ecosystem will have the same result, particularly if selection of patients is poor, if prophylaxis lasts too long, or if too many late-generation agents are used.

A rare but important complication of antibiotic use is pseudomembranous enterocolitis, which is induced most commonly by clindamycin, the cephalosporins, and ampicillin [*see 131 Nosocomial Infection*].[62] The common denominator among different cases of pseudomembranous enterocolitis is hard to identify. Diarrhea and fever can develop after administration of single doses of prophylactic antibiotics. The condition is rare, but difficulties occur because of failure to make a rapid diagnosis.

CURRENT ISSUES

The most significant questions concerning prophylaxis of SSIs already have been answered. An important remaining issue is the proper duration of prophylaxis in complicated cases, in the setting of trauma, and in the presence of foreign bodies. No change in the criteria for antibiotic prophylaxis is required in laparoscopic procedures; the risk of infection is lower in such cases.[78,79] Cost factors are important and may justify the endless succession of studies that compare new drugs in competition for appropriate clinical niches.

Further advances in patient selection may take place but will require analysis of data from large numbers of patients and a distinction between approaches to infection of the wound, which is only a part of the operative field, and approaches to infections directly related to the operative site. These developments will define more clearly the prophylaxis requirements of patients whose operations are clean but whose risk of wound or operative site infection is increased.

A current issue of some concern is potential loss of infection surveillance capability. Infection control units have been shown to offer a number of benefits in the institutional setting, such as the following:

1. Identifying epidemics caused by common or uncommon organisms.[23,26,56]
2. Establishing correct use of prophylaxis (timing, dose, duration, and choice).[52,55,72]
3. Documenting costs, risk factors, and readmission rates.[80,81]
4. Monitoring postdischarge infections and secondary consequences of infections.[82-84]
5. Ensuring patient safety.[85]
6. Managing MRSA and VRE.[86]

S. aureus—in particular, MRSA—is a major cause of SSI.[86] Cross-infection problems are a concern, in a manner reminiscent of the preantibiotic era. Hand washing (see below) is coming back into fashion, consistent with the professional behavior toward cross-infection characteristic of that era. At present, hard evidence is lacking, but clinical observation suggests that S. aureus SSIs are especially troublesome and destructive of local tissue and require a longer time to heal than other SSIs do. When S. aureus SSIs occur after cardiac surgery, thoracotomy, or joint replacement, their consequences are significant. Prevention in these settings is important. When nasal carriage of S. aureus has been identified, mupirocin may be administered intranasally to reduce the incidence of S. aureus SSIs.[87]

The benefits of infection surveillance notwithstanding, as the business of hospital care has become more expensive and financial control more rigid, the infection control unit is a hospital component that many administrators have come to consider a luxury and therefore expendable. Consequently, surveillance as a quality control and patient safety mechanism has been diminished.

It is apparent that SSIs have huge clinical and financial implications. Patients with infections tend to be sicker and to undergo more complex operations. Therefore, higher infection rates translate into higher morbidity and mortality as well as higher cost to the hospital, the patient, and society as a whole. With increasingly early discharge becoming the norm, delayed diagnosis of postdischarge SSI and the complications thereof is a growing problem.[82-84] Effective use of institutional databases may contribute greatly to identification of this problem.[83]

Clearly, the development of effective mechanisms for identifying and controlling SSIs is in the interests of all associated with the delivery of health care.[85] The identification of problems by means of surveillance and feedback can make a substantial contribution to reducing SSI rates [see Table 6].[12,85]

Hand Washing

The purpose of cleansing the surgeon's hands is to reduce the numbers of resident flora and transient contaminants, thereby decreasing the risk of transmitting infection. Although the proper duration of the hand scrub is still subject to debate, evidence suggests that a 120-second scrub is sufficient, provided that a brush is used to remove the bacteria residing in the skin folds around the nails.[88] The nail folds, the nails, and the fingertips should receive the most attention because most bacteria are located around the nail folds and most glove punctures occur at the fingertips. Friction is required to remove resident microorganisms which are attached by adhesion or adsorption, whereas transient bacteria are easily removed by simple hand washing.

Solutions containing either chlorhexidine gluconate or one of the iodophors are the most effective surgical scrub preparations and have the fewest problems with stability, contamination, and toxicity.[89] Alcohols applied to the skin are among the safest known antiseptics, and they produce the greatest and most rapid reduc-

tion in bacterial counts on clean skin.[90] All variables considered, chlorhexidine gluconate followed by an iodophor appears to be the best option [see Table 9].

The purpose of washing the hands after surgery is to remove microorganisms that are resident, that flourished in the warm, wet environment created by wearing gloves, or that reached the hands by entering through puncture holes in the gloves. On the ward, even minimal contact with colonized patients has been demonstrated to transfer microorganisms.[91] As many as 1,000 organisms were transferred by simply touching the patient's hand, taking a pulse, or lifting the patient. The organisms survived for 20 to 150 minutes, making their transfer to the next patient clearly possible.

A return to the ancient practice of washing hands between each patient contact is warranted. Nosocomial spread of numerous organisms—including C. difficile; MRSA, VRE, and other antibiotic-resistant bacteria; and viruses—is a constant threat.

Hand washing on the ward is complicated by the fact that overwashing may actually increase bacterial counts. Dry, damaged skin harbors many more bacteria than healthy skin and is almost impossible to render even close to bacteria free. Although little is known about the physiologic changes in skin that result from frequent washings, the bacterial flora is certainly modified by alterations in the lipid or water content of the skin. The so-called dry hand syndrome was the impetus behind the development of the alcohol-based gels now available. These preparations make it easy for surgeons to clean their hands after every patient encounter with minimal damage to their skin.

Infection Prevention in Bowel Surgery

At present, the best method of preventing SSIs after bowel surgery is, once again, a subject of debate. There have been three principal approaches to this issue, involving mechanical bowel preparation in conjunction with one of the following three antibiotic regimens[55,92-97]:
1. Oral antibiotics (usually neomycin and erythromycin),[20,96]
2. Intravenous antibiotics covering aerobic and anaerobic bowel flora,[16,20,55,94,95] or
3. A combination of regimens 1 and 2 (meta-analysis suggests that the combination of oral and parenteral antibiotics is best).[97]

The present controversy, triggered by a clinical trial,[16] a review,[20] and three meta-analyses, relates to the need for mechanical bowel preparation,[17-19] which has been a surgical dogma since the early 1970s. The increased SSI and leak rates noted have been attributed to the complications associated with vigorous bowel preparation, leading to dehydration, overhydration, or electrolyte abnormalities.

An observational study reported a 26% SSI rate in colorectal

Table 9 Characteristics of Three Topical Antimicrobial Agents Effective against Both Gram-Positive and Gram-Negative Bacteria[90]

Agent	Mode of Action	Antifungal Activity	Comments
Chlorhexidine	Cell wall disruption	Fair	Poor activity against tuberculosis-causing organisms; can cause ototoxicity and eye irritation
Iodine/iodophors	Oxidation and substitution by free iodine	Good	Broad antibacterial spectrum; minimal skin residual activity; possible absorption toxicity and skin irritation
Alcohols	Denaturation of protein	Good	Rapid action but little residual activity; flammable

Table 10 Comparison of Wound Classification Systems[6]

Traditional Wound Classification System	Simplified Risk Index					All from Traditional Classification
	Low Risk	Medium Risk	High Risk			
	0	1	2	3	4	
Clean	1.1	3.9	8.4	15.8		2.9
Clean-contaminated	0.6	2.8	8.4	17.7		3.9
Contaminated		4.5	8.3	11.0	23.9	8.5
Dirty-infected		6.7	10.9	18.8	27.4	12.6
All from SENIC index	1.0	3.6	8.9	17.2	27.0	4.1

SENIC—Study of the Efficacy of Nosocomial Infection Control

surgery patients.[98] Intraoperative hypotension and body mass index were the only independent predictive variables. All patients underwent mechanical bowel preparation the day before operation and received oral antibiotics and perioperative I.V. antibiotics. Half of the SSIs were discovered after discharge. Most would agree that the protocol was standard. These and other results suggest that a fresh look at the infectious complications of surgery—and of bowel surgery in particular—is required.

The recommended antibiotic regimen for bowel surgery consists of oral plus systemic agents (see above).[55] The approach to mechanical bowel preparation, however, is open. Intuition would suggest that the presence of less liquid and stool in the colon might be beneficial and perhaps that a preoperative phosphate enema with 24 hours of fluid might make sense. It is hard to throw out 30 years of apparent evidence on the basis of these three meta-analyses. These studies do, however, present data that cannot be ignored. Protocols for bowel surgery in the modern era of same-day admission, fast track surgery, and rapid discharge will require further study and clinical trials.

Integration of Determinants of Infection

The significant advances in the control of wound infection during the past several decades are linked to a better understanding of the biology of wound infection, and this link has permitted the advance to the concept of SSI.[2] In all tissues at any time, there will be a critical inoculum of bacteria that would cause an infectious process [*see Figure 3*]. The standard definition of infection in urine and sputum has been 10^5 organisms/ml. In a clean dry wound, 10^5 bacteria produce a wound infection rate of 50% [*see Figure 3*].[11] Effective use of antibiotics reduces the infection rate to 10% with the same number of bacteria and thereby permits the wound to tolerate a much larger number of bacteria.

All of the clinical activities described are intended either to reduce the inoculum or to permit the host to manage the number of bacteria that would otherwise be pathologic. One study in guinea pigs showed how manipulation of local blood flow, shock, the local immune response, and foreign material can enhance the development of infection.[99] This study and two others defined an early decisive period of host antimicrobial activity that lasts for 3 to 6 hours after contamination.[50,99,100] Bacteria that remain after this period are the infecting inoculum. Processes that interfere with this early response (e.g., shock, altered perfusion, adjuvants, or foreign material) or support it (e.g., antibiotics or total care)

have a major influence on outcome.

One investigation demonstrated that silk sutures decrease the number of bacteria required for infection.[101] Other investigators used a suture as the key adjuvant in studies of host manipulation,[102] whereas a separate study demonstrated persistent susceptibility to wound infection days after shock.[103] The common variable is the number of bacteria. This relation may be termed the inoculum effect, and it has great relevance in all aspects of infection control. Applying knowledge of this effect in practical terms involves the following three steps:

1. Keeping the bacterial contamination as low as possible via asepsis and antisepsis, preoperative preparation of patient and surgeon, and antibiotic prophylaxis.
2. Maintaining local factors in such a way that they can prevent the lodgment of bacteria and thereby provide a locally unreceptive environment.
3. Maintaining systemic responses at such a level that they can control the bacteria that become established.

These three steps are related to the determinants of infection and their applicability to daily practice. Year-by-year reductions in wound infection rates, when closely followed, indicate that it is possible for surgeons to continue improving results by attention to quality of clinical care and surgical technique, despite increasingly complex operations.[5,13,28-30] In particular, the measures involved in the first step (control of bacteria) have been progressively refined and are now well established.

The integration of determinants has significant effects [*see Figures 3 and 4*]. When wound closure was effected with a wound hematocrit of 8% or more, the inoculum required to produce a wound infection rate of 40% was 100 bacteria [*see Figure 3*]. Ten bacteria produced a wound infection rate of 20%. The shift in the number of organisms required to produce clinical infection is significant. It is obvious that this inoculum effect can be changed dramatically by good surgical technique and further altered by use of prophylactic antibiotics. If the inoculum is always slightly smaller than the number of organisms required to produce infection in any given setting, results are excellent. There is clearly a relation between the number of bacteria and the local environment. The local effect can also be seen secondary to systemic physiologic change, specifically shock. One study showed the low local perfusion in shock to be important in the development of an infection.[99,100]

One investigation has shown that shock can alter infection rates immediately after its occurrence [*see Figure 4*].[103] Furthermore, if the inoculum is large enough, antibiotics will not control bacteria. In addition, there is a late augmentation of infection lasting up to 3 days after restoration of blood volume. These early and late effects indicate that systemic determinants come into play after local effects are resolved. These observations call for further study, but obviously, it is the combined abnormalities that alter outcome.

Systemic host responses are important for the control of infection. The patient has been clearly implicated as one of the four critical variables in the development of wound infection.[6] In addition, the bacterial inoculum, the location of the procedure and its duration, and the coexistence of three or more diagnoses were found to give a more accurate prediction of the risk of wound infection. The spread of risk is defined better with the SENIC index (1% to 27%) than it is with the traditional classification (2.9% to 12.6%) [see Table 10]. The importance of the number of bacteria is lessened if the other factors are considered in addition to inoculum. The inoculum effect has to be considered with respect to both the number of organisms and the local and systemic host factors that are in play. Certain variables were found to be significantly related to the risk of wound infection in three important prospective studies [see Table 10].[6,10,12] It is apparent that the problem of SSI cannot be examined only with respect to the management of bacteria. Host factors have become much more significant now that the bacterial inoculum can be maintained at low levels by means of asepsis, antisepsis, technique, and prophylactic antibiotics.[104]

Important host variables include the maintenance of normal homeostasis (physiology) and immune response. Maintenance of normal homeostasis in patients at risk is one of the great advances of surgical critical care.[104] The clearest improvements in this regard have come in maintenance of blood volume, oxygenation, and oxygen delivery.

One group demonstrated the importance of oxygen delivery, tissue perfusion, and P_aO_2 in the development of wound infection.[105] Oxygen can have as powerful a negative influence on the development of SSI as antibiotics can.[106] The influence is very similar to that seen in other investigations. Whereas a P_aO_2 equivalent to a true fractional concentration of oxygen in inspired gas (F_IO_2) of 45% is not feasible, maintenance, when appropriate, of an increased F_IO_2 in the postoperative period may prove an elementary and effective tool in managing the inoculum effect.

Modern surgical practice has reduced the rate of wound infection significantly. Consequently, it is more useful to think in terms of SSI, which is not limited to the incision but may occur anywhere in the operative field; this concept provides a global objective for control of infections associated with a surgical procedure. Surveillance is of great importance for quality assurance. Reports of recognized pathogens (e.g., *S. epidermidis* and group A streptococci) as well as unusual organisms (e.g., *Rhodococcus [Gordona] bronchialis, Mycoplasma hominis,* and *Legionella dumoffii*) in SSIs highlight the importance of infection control and epidemiology for quality assurance in surgical departments.[21-23,26,27] (Although these reports use the term wound infection, they are really addressing what we now call SSI.) The importance of surgeon-specific and service-specific SSI reports should be clear [see Table 6],[12,13,107] and their value in quality assurance evident.

References

1. Meakins JL: Host defence mechanisms: evaluation and roles of acquired defects and immunotherapy. Can J Surg 18:259, 1975

2. Consensus paper on the surveillance of surgical wound infections. The Society for Hospital Epidemiology of America; the Association for Practitioners in Infection Control; the Centers for Disease Control; the Surgical Infection Society. Infect Control Hosp Epidemiol 13:599, 1992

3. Horan TC, Gaynes RP, Martone WJ, et al: CDC definitions of nosocomial surgical site infections, 1992: a modification of CDC definitions of surgical wound infections. Infect Control Hosp Epidemiol 13:606, 1992

4. Wilson APR, Gibbons C, Reeves BC, et al: Surgical wound infection as a performance indicator: agreement of common definitions of wound infection in 4773 patients. BMJ 329:720, 2004

5. Report of an Ad Hoc Committee of the Committee on Trauma, Division of Medical Sciences, National Academy of Sciences-National Research Council Postoperative wound infections: the influence of ultraviolet irradiation of the operating room and of various other factors. Ann Surg 160(suppl):1, 1964

6. Haley RW, Culver DH, Morgan WM, et al: Identifying patients at high risk of surgical wound infection: a simple multivariate index of patient susceptibility and wound contamination. Am J Epidemiol 121:206, 1985

7. Mangram AJ, Horan TC, Pearson ML, et al: The Hospital Infection Control Practices Advisory Committee: guideline for prevention of surgical site infection, 1999. Infect Control Hosp Epidemiol 20:247, 1999

8. Culver DH, Horan TC, Gaynes RP, et al: Surgical wound infection rates by wound class, operative procedure and patient risk index. Am J Med 91(suppl 3B):153S, 1991

9. Farias-Álvarez C, Farias C, Prieto D, et al: Applicability of two surgical-site infection risk indices to risk of sepsis in surgical patients. Infect Control Hosp Epidemiol 21:633, 2000

10. Davidson AIG, Clark C, Smith G: Postoperative wound infection: a computer analysis. Br J Surg 58:333, 1971

11. Polk HC Jr, Lopez-Mayor JF: Postoperative wound infection: a prospective study of determinant factors and prevention. Surgery 66:97, 1969

12. Cruse PJE, Foord R: The epidemiology of wound infection: a 10-year prospective study of 62,939 wounds. Surg Clin North Am 60:27, 1980

13. Olson M, O'Connor M, Schwartz ML: Surgical wound infections: a 5-year prospective study of 20,193 wounds at the Minneapolis VA Medical Center. Ann Surg 199:253, 1984

14. Alexander JW, Fischer JE, Boyajian M, et al: The influence of hair-removal methods on wound infections. Arch Surg 118:347, 1983

15. Olson MM, MacCallum J, McQuarrie DG: Preoperative hair removal with clippers does not increase infection rate in clean surgical wounds. Surg Gynecol Obstet 162:181, 1986

16. Zmora O, Mahajna A, Greenlee H, et al: Colon and rectal surgery without mechanical bowel preparation: a randomized prospective trial. Ann Surg 237:363, 2003

17. Guenaga KF, Matos D, Castro AA, et al: Mechanical bowel preparation for elective colorectal surgery. Cochrane Database Syst Rev 2:CD001544, 2003

18. Slim K, Vicaut E, Panis Y, Chipponi J: Meta-analysis of randomized clinical trials of colorectal surgery with or without mechanical bowel preparation. Br J Surg 91:1125, 2004

19. Bucher P, Mermillod B, Gervaz P, et al: Mechanical bowel preparation for elective colorectal surgery. Arch Surg 139:1359, 2004

20. Jimenez JC, Wilson SE: Prophylaxis of infection for elective colorectal surgery. Surg Infect 4:273, 2003

21. Boyce JM, Potter-Bynoe G, Opal SM, et al: A common-source outbreak of Staphylococcus epidermidis infections among patients undergoing cardiac surgery. J Infect Dis 161:493, 1990

22. Mastro TD, Farley TA, Elliott JA, et al: An outbreak of surgical-wound infections due to group A Streptococcus carried on the scalp. N Engl J Med 323:968, 1990

23. Richet HM, Craven PC, Brown JM, et al: A cluster of *Rhodococcus (Gordona) bronchialis* sternal-wound infections after coronary-artery bypass surgery. N Engl J Med 324:104, 1991

24. Moylan JA, Kennedy BV: The importance of gown and drape barriers in the prevention of wound infection. Surg Gynecol Obstet 151:465, 1980

25. Garibaldi RA, Maglio S, Lerer T, et al: Comparison of nonwoven and woven gown and drape fabric to prevent intraoperative wound contamination and postoperative infection. Am J Surg 152:505, 1986

26. Lowry PW, Blankenship RJ, Gridley W, et al: A cluster of Legionella sternal-wound infections due to postoperative topical exposure to contaminated tap water. N Engl J Med 324:109, 1991

27. Wilson ME, Dietze C: Mycoplasma hominis surgical wound infection: a case report and discussion. Surgery 103:257, 1988

28. Cruse PJE: Surgical wound sepsis. Can Med Assoc J 102:251, 1970

29. Wangensteen OH, Wangensteen SD: The Rise of Surgery: Emergence from Empiric Craft to Scientific Discipline. University of Minnesota Press, Minneapolis, 1978

30. Cruse PJE: Wound infections: epidemiology and clinical characteristics. Surgical Infectious Disease, 2nd ed. Howard RJ, Simmons RL, Eds. Appleton and Lange, Norwalk, Connecticut, 1988

31. Petrowsky H, Demartines N, Rousson V, et al: Evidence-based value of prophylactic drainage in gastrointestinal surgery: a systematic review and meta-analyses. Ann Surg 240:1074, 2004

32. Hopf HW, Hunt TK, West JM, et al: Wound tissue oxygen tension predicts the risk of wound infection in surgical patients. Arch Surg 132:997, 1997

33. Greif R, Akca O, Horn EP, et al: Supplemental perioperative oxygen to reduce the incidence of surgical-wound infection. Outcomes Research Group. N Engl J Med 342:161, 2000

34. Pryor KO, Fahey TJ, Lien CY, et al: Surgical site infection and the routine use of perioperative hyperoxia in a general surgical population: a randomized controlled trial. JAMA 291:79, 2004

35. Gottrup F: Prevention of surgical-wound infections. N Engl J Med 342:202, 2000

36. Kaye KS, Schmit K, Pieper C, et al: The effect of increasing age on the risk of surgical site infection. J Infect Dis 191:1056, 2005

37. Latham R, Lancaster AD, Covington JF, et al: The association of diabetes and glucose control with surgical-site infections among cardiothoracic surgery patients. Infect Control Hosp Epidemiol 22:607, 2001

38. Furnary AP, Zerr KJ, Grunkemeier GI, et al: Continuous intravenous insulin infusion reduces the incidence of deep sternal wound infection in diabetic patients after cardiac surgical procedures. Ann Thorac Surg 67:352, 1999

39. Van Den Berghe G, Wouters P, Weekers F, et al: Intensive insulin therapy in critically ill patients. N Engl J Med 345:1359, 2001

40. Kurz H, Sessler DI, Lenhardt R: Perioperative normothermia to reduce the incidence of surgical wound infection and shorten hospitalization. N Engl J Med 334:1209, 1996

41. Nichols RL, Smith JW, Klein DB, et al: Risk of infection after penetrating abdominal trauma. N Engl J Med 311:1065, 1984

42. Jensen LS, Andersen A, Fristup SC, et al: Comparison of one dose versus three doses of prophylactic antibiotics, and the influence of blood transfusion, on infectious complications in acute and elective colorectal surgery. Br J Surg 77:513, 1990

43. Møller AM, Villebro N, Pedersen T, et al: Effect of preoperative smoking intervention on postoperative complications: a randomised clinical trial. Lancet 359:114, 2002

44. Buggy D: Can anaesthetic management influence surgical wound healing? Lancet 356:355, 2000

45. Melling AC, Ali B, Scott EM, et al: Effects of preoperative warming on the incidence of wound infection after clean surgery: a randomised controlled trial. Lancet 358:876, 2001

46. Horn SD, Wright HL, Couperus JJ, et al: Association between patient-controlled analgesia pump use and postoperative surgical site infection in intestinal surgery patients. Surg Infect 3:109, 2002

47. Bennett SN, McNeil MM, Bland LA, et al: Postoperative infections traced to contamination of an intravenous anesthetic: propofol. N Engl J Med 333:147, 1995

48. Nichols RL, Smith JW: Bacterial contamination of an anesthetic agent. N Engl J Med 333:184, 1995

49. Miles AA, Miles EM, Burke J: The value and duration of defense reactions of the skin to the primary lodgment of bacteria. Br J Exp Pathol 38:79, 1957

50. Burke JF: The effective period of preventive antibiotic action in experimental incisions and dermal lesions. Surgery 50:161, 1961

51. Bernard HR, Cole WR: The prophylaxis of surgical infection: the effect of prophylactic antimicrobial drugs on incidence of infection following potentially contaminated wounds. Surgery 56:151, 1964

52. Classen DC, Evans RS, Pestotnik SC, et al: The timing of prophylactic administration of antibiotics and the risk of surgical-wound infection. N Engl J Med 326:282, 1992

53. Scottish Intercollegiate Guidelines Network. Antibiotic prophylaxis in surgery. http://www.show.scot.nhs.uk/sign/guidelines/fulltext/45/section1.html, accessed 12/11/2004

54. Burke JP: Maximizing appropriate antibiotic prophylaxis for surgical patients: an update from LDS Hospital, Salt Lake City. Clin Infect Dis 33(suppl):78, 2001

55. Antimicrobial prophylaxis for surgery: treatment guidelines. Med Lett 2:27, 2004

56. Kaiser AB: Surgical wound infection. N Engl J Med 324:123, 1991

57. Finland M: Antibacterial agents: uses and abuses in treatment and prophylaxis. RI Med J 43:499, 1960

58. Platt R, Zaleznik DF, Hopkins CC, et al: Perioperative antibiotic prophylaxis for herniorrhaphy and breast surgery. N Engl J Med 322:153, 1990

59. Taylor EW, Duffy K, Lee K, et al: Surgical site infection after groin hernia repair. Br J Surg 91:105, 2004

60. Aufenacker TJ, van Geldere D, Bossers AN, et al: The role of antibiotic prophylaxis in prevention of wound infection after Lichtenstein open mesh repair of primary inguinal hernia: a multicenter double-blind randomized controlled trial. Ann Surg 240:955, 2005

61. Perez AR, Roxas MF, Hilvano SS: A randomized, double-blind placebo-controlled trial to deter effectiveness of antibiotic prophylaxis for tension-free mesh herniorrhaphy. J Am Coll Surg 200:393, 2005

62. Yee J, Dixon CM, McLean APH, et al: Clostridium difficile disease in a department of surgery: the significance of prophylactic antibiotics. Arch Surg 126:241, 1991

63. Meijer WS, Schmitz PI, Jeekel J: Meta-analysis of randomized, controlled clinical trials of antibiotic prophylaxis in biliary tract surgery. Br J Surg 77:283, 1990

64. Rotman N, Hay J-M, Lacaine F, et al: Prophylactic antibiotherapy in abdominal surgery: first- vs third-generation cephalosporins. Arch Surg 124:323, 1989

65. Washington JA III, Dearing WH, Judd ES, et al: Effect of preoperative antibiotic regimen on development of infection after intestinal surgery. Ann Surg 180:567, 1974

66. Fullen WD, Hunt J, Altemeier WA: Prophylactic antibiotics in penetrating wounds of the abdomen. J Trauma 12:282, 1972

67. Gentry LO, Feliciano DV, Lea AS, et al: Perioperative antibiotic therapy for penetrating injuries of the abdomen. Ann Surg 200:561, 1984

68. Heseltine PNR, Yellin AE, Appleman MD, et al: Perforated and gangrenous appendicitis: an analysis of antibiotic failures. J Infect Dis 148:322, 1983

69. Bratzler DW, Houck PM, Richards C, et al: Use of antimicrobial prophylaxis for major surgery. Arch Surg 140:174, 2005

70. Girotti MJ, Fodoruk S, Irvine-Meek J, et al: Antibiotic handbook and pre-printed perioperative order forms for surgical prophylaxis: do they work? Can J Surg 33:385, 1990

71. Larsen RA, Evans RS, Burke JP, et al: Improved perioperative antibiotic use and reduced surgical wound infections through use of computer decision analysis. Infect Control Hosp Epidemiol 10:316, 1989

72. Stone HN, Haney BB, Kolb LD, et al: Prophylactic and preventive antibiotic therapy: timing duration and economics. Ann Surg 189:691, 1978

73. Fabian TC, Croce MA, Payne LW, et al: Duration of antibiotic therapy for penetrating abdominal trauma: a prospective trial. Surgery 112:788, 1992

74. Sarmiento JM, Aristizabal G, Rubiano J, et al: Prophylactic antibiotics in abdominal trauma. J Trauma 37:803, 1994

75. Hofstetter SR, Pachter HL, Bailey AA, et al: A prospective comparison of two regimens of prophylactic antibiotics in abdominal trauma: cefoxitin versus triple drug. J Trauma 24:307, 1984

76. Dellinger EP: Antibiotic prophylaxis in trauma: penetrating abdominal injuries and open fractures. Rev Infect Dis 13:5847, 1991

77. Boxma H, Broekhuisen T, Patka P, et al: Randomized controlled trial of single-dose antibiotic prophylaxis in surgical treatment of closed fractures: the Dutch Trauma Trial. Lancet 347:1133, 1996

78. Illig KA, Schmidt E, Cavanaugh J, et al: Are prophylactic antibiotics required for elective laparoscopic cholecystectomy? J Am Coll Surg 184:353, 1997

79. Richards C, Edwards J, Culver D, et al: Does using a laparoscopic approach to cholecystectomy decrease the risk of surgical site infection? Ann Surg 237:358, 2003

80. Kirkland KB, Briggs JP, Trivette SL, et al: The impact of surgical-site infection in 1990's: attributable mortality, excess length of hospitalisation, and extra costs. Infect Control Hosp Epidemiol 20:725, 1999

81. Gaynes RP: Surveillance of surgical-site infections: the world coming together? Infect Control Hosp Epidemiol 21:309, 2000

82. Weiss CA, Statz CL, Dahms RA, et al: Six years of surgical wound infection surveillance at a tertiary care center. Arch Surg 134:1041, 1999

83. Sands K, Vineyard G, Livingston J, et al: Efficient identification of postdischarge surgical site infections: use of automated pharmacy dispensing information, administrative data, and medical record information. J Infect Dis 179:434, 1999

84. Platt R: Progress in surgical-site infection surveillance. Infect Control Hosp Epidemiol 23:361, 2002

85. Burke JP: Infection control—a problem for patient safety. N Engl J Med 348:651, 2003

86. Simor AE, Ofner-Agostini M, Bryce E, et al: The evolution of methicillin-resistant Staphylococcus aureus in Canadian hospitals: 5 years of national surveillance. CMAJ 165:21, 2001

87. Perl TM, Cullen JJ, Wenzel RP, et al: Intranasal mupirocin to prevent postoperative Staphylococcus aureus infections. N Engl J Med 346:1871, 2002

88. Lowbury EJL, Lilly HA, Bull JP: Methods for disinfection of hands and operation sites. Br Med J 2:531, 1964

89. Aly R, Maibach HI: Comparative antibacterial efficacy of a 2-minute surgical scrub with chlorhexidine gluconate, povidone-iodine, and chloroxylenol sponge-brushes. Am J Infect Control 16:173, 1988

90. Larson E: Guideline for use of topical antimicrobial agents. Am J Infect Control 16:253, 1988

91. Casewell M, Phillips I: Hands as route of transmission for Klebsiella species. Br Med J 2:1315, 1977

92. Jagelman DG, Fabian TC, Nichols RL, et al: Single dose cefotetan versus multiple dose cefoxitin as prophylaxis in colorectal surgery. Am J Surg 155(suppl 5A):71, 1988

93. Periti P, Mazzei T, Tonelli F, et al: Single dose cefotetan versus multiple dose cefoxitin—antimicrobial prophylaxis in colorectal surgery. Dis Colon Rectum 32:121, 1989

94. Norwegian Study Group for Colorectal Surgery Should antimicrobial prophylaxis in colorectal surgery include agents effective against both anaerobic and aerobic microorganisms? A double-blind, multicenter study. Surgery 97:402, 1985

95. Song J, Glenny AM: Antimicrobial prophylaxis in colorectal surgery: a systematic review of randomized controlled trials. Br J Surg 85:1232, 1998

96. Condon RE, Bartlett JG, Greenlee H, et al: Efficacy of oral and systemic antibiotic prophylaxis in colorectal operations. Arch Surg 118:496, 1983

97. Lewis RT: Oral versus systemic antibiotic prophylaxis in elective colon surgery: a randomized study and meta-analysis send a message from the 1990's. Can J Surg 45:173, 2002

98. Smith RL, Bohl JK, McElearney ST, et al: Wound infection after elective colorectal resection. Ann Surg 239:599, 2004

99. Miles AA, Miles EM, Burke J: The value and duration of defence reactions of the skin to the primary lodgement of bacteria. Br J Exp Pathol 38:79, 1957

100. Miles AA: The inflammatory response in relation to local infections. Surg Clin North Am 60:93, 1980

101. Alexander JW, Alexander WA: Penicillin prophylaxis of experimental staphylococcal wound infections. Surg Gynecol Obstet 120:243, 1965

102. Polk HC Jr: The enhancement of host defenses against infection: search for the holy grail. Surgery 99:1, 1986

103. Livingston DH, Malangoni MA: An experimental study of susceptibility to infection after hemorrhagic shock. Surg Gynecol Obstet 168:138, 1989

104. Meakins JL: Surgeons, surgery and immunomodulation. Arch Surg 126:494, 1991

105. Knighton D, Halliday B, Hunt TK: Oxygen as an antibiotic: a comparison of the effects of inspired oxygen concentration and antibiotic administration on in vivo bacterial clearance. Arch Surg 121:191, 1986

106. Rabkin J, Hunt TK: Infection and oxygen. Problem Wounds: The Role of Oxygen. Davis JC, Hunt TK, Eds. Elsevier, New York, 1987, p 1

107. Olson MM, Lee JT Jr: Continuous, 10-year wound infection surveillance: results, advantages, and unanswered questions. Arch Surg 125:794, 1990

108. Oreskovich MR, Dellinger EP, Lennard ES, et al: Duration of preventive antibiotic administration for penetrating abdominal trauma. Arch Surg 117:200, 1982

109. Langely JM, Le Blanc JC, Drake J, et al: Efficacy of antimicrobial prophylaxis in placement of cerebrospinal fluid shunts: meta-analysis. Clin Infect Dis 17:98, 1993

110. Forse RA, Karam B, MacLean LD, et al: Antibiotic prophylaxis for surgery in morbidly obese patients. Surgery 106:750, 1989

111. Dajani AS, Taubert KA, Wilson W, et al: Prevention of bacterial endocarditis: recommendations by the American Heart Association. JAMA 277:1794, 1997

112. Durack DT: Prevention of infective endocarditis. N Engl J Med 332:38, 1995

113. Prevention of bacterial endocarditis. Med Lett Drugs Ther 43:98, 2001

114. Hayek LJ, Emerson JM, Gardner AMN: A placebo-controlled trial of the effect of two preoperative baths or showers with chlorhexidine detergent on postoperative wound infection rates. J Hosp Infect 10:165, 1987

115. Garner JS: CDC guidelines for the prevention and control of nosocomial infections: guideline for prevention of surgical wound infections, 1985. Am J Infect Control 14:71, 1986

116. Hamilton HW, Hamilton KR, Lone FJ: Preoperative hair removal. Can J Surg 20:269, 1977

117. McDonald WS, Nichter LS: Debridement of bacterial and particulate-contaminated wounds. Ann Plast Surg 33:142, 1994

118. Edwards PS, Lipp A, Holmes A: Preoperative skin antiseptics for preventing surgical wound infections after clean surgery. Cochrane Database Syst Rev 3:CD003949, 2004

Acknowledgment

Figures 3 and 4 Albert Miller.

6 INFECTION CONTROL IN SURGICAL PRACTICE

Vivian G. Loo, M.D., M.Sc., *and A. Peter McLean*, M.D., F.A.C.S.

Surgical procedures, by their very nature, interfere with the normal protective skin barrier and expose the patient to microorganisms from both endogenous and exogenous sources. Infections resulting from this exposure may not be limited to the surgical site but may produce widespread systemic effects. Prevention of surgical site infections (SSIs) is therefore of primary concern to surgeons and must be addressed in the planning of any operation. Standards of control have been developed for every step of a surgical procedure to help reduce the impact of exposure to microorganisms.[1-3] Traditional control measures include sterilization of surgical equipment, disinfection of the skin, use of prophylactic antibiotics, and expeditious operation.

The Study on the Efficacy of Nosocomial Infection Control (SENIC), conducted in United States hospitals between 1976 and 1986, showed that surgical patients were at increased risk for all types of infection. The nosocomial, or hospital-acquired, infection rate at that time was estimated to be 5.7 cases out of every 100 hospital admissions.[4] These infections included SSIs as well as bloodstream, urinary, and respiratory infections. Today, the increased use of minimally invasive surgical procedures and early discharge from the hospital necessitates postdischarge surveillance[5] in addition to in-hospital surveillance for the tracking of nosocomial infections. With the reorganization of health care delivery programs, nosocomial infections will appear more frequently in the community and should therefore be considered a part of any patient care assessment plan.

Care assessment programs designed to help minimize the risk of nosocomial infections were first introduced in 1951 by the Joint Commission on Accreditation of Healthcare Organizations (JCAHO). Since then, as medical technology has changed, JCAHO has redesigned the survey process. In its plan for infection control programs, JCAHO strongly recommends that the survey, documentation, and reporting of infections be made mandatory for the purpose of hospital accreditation.[6]

Effective infection control and prevention requires an organized, hospital-wide program aimed at achieving specific objectives. The program's purpose should be to obtain relevant information on the occurrence of nosocomial infections both in patients and in employees. The data should be documented, analyzed, and communicated with a plan for corrective measures. Such surveillance activities, combined with education, form the basis of an infection control program.

Data relating to host factors are an integral part of infection data analysis. Documentation of host factors has made for a better appreciation of the associated risks and has allowed comparative evaluation of infection rates. Development of new surgical equipment and technological advances have influenced the impact of certain risk factors, such as lengthy operation and prolonged hospital stay. Clinical investigations have helped improve the understanding of host factors and have influenced other aspects of surgical practice.[7-12] Excessive use of and reliance on antibiotics have led to problems not previously encountered in practice—for example, the emergence of drug-resistant microorganisms, such as methicillin-resistant *Staphylococcus aureus* (MRSA), glycopeptide-intermediate *S. aureus* (GISA), multidrug-resistant *Mycobacterium tuberculosis*, and multidrug-resistant *Enterococcus* strains.[13-16] Such complications reemphasize the need to focus on infection control as an essential component of preventive medicine.

Besides the impact of morbidity and mortality on patients, there is the cost of treating nosocomial infections, which is a matter of concern for surgeons, hospital administrators, insurance companies, and government planners alike. Efforts to reduce the occurrence of nosocomial infections are now a part of hospital cost-control management programs.[17,18] The challenge to clinicians is how to reduce cost while maintaining control over, and preventing spread of, infection.

The Surgical Wound and Infection Control

Nosocomial infections are defined as infections acquired in the hospital. There must be no evidence that the infection was present or incubating at the time of hospital admission. Usually, an infection that manifests 48 to 72 hours after admission is considered to be nosocomially acquired. An infection that is apparent on the day of admission is usually considered to be community acquired, unless it is epidemiologically linked to a previous admission or to an operative procedure at the time of admission.

IDENTIFICATION OF RISK FACTORS

The risk of development of an SSI depends on host factors, perioperative wound hygiene, and the duration of the surgical procedure. The risk of development of other nosocomial infections depends on these and other factors, including length of the hospital stay and appropriate management of the hospital environment [*see* Activities of an Infection Control Program, *below*]. Identification of host and operative risk factors can help determine the potential for infection and point toward measures that might be necessary for prevention and control.

Host Risk Factors

Host susceptibility to infection can be estimated according to the following variables: older age, severity of disease, physical-status classification (see below), prolonged preoperative hospitalization, morbid obesity, malnutrition, immunosuppressive therapy, smoking, preoperative colonization with *S. aureus,* and coexistent infection at a remote body site.[19]

A scale dividing patients into five classes according to their physical status was introduced by the American Society of Anesthesiologists (ASA) in 1974 and tested for precision in 1978.[20] The test results showed that the ASA scale is a workable system, although it lacks scientific definition [*see Table 1*].

Significant differences in infection rates have been shown in patients with different illnesses. In one prospective study, the severity of underlying disease (rated as fatal, ultimately fatal, or

Table 1 American Society of Anesthesiologists Physical-Status Scale

Class 1	A normally healthy individual
Class 2	A patient with mild systemic disease
Class 3	A patient with severe systemic disease that is not incapacitating
Class 4	A patient with incapacitating systemic disease that is a constant threat to life
Class 5	A moribund patient who is not expected to survive 24 hr with or without operation
E	Added for emergency procedures

nonfatal) was shown to have predictive value for endemic nosocomial infections: the nosocomial infection rate in patients with fatal diseases was 23.6%, compared with 2.1% in patients with nonfatal diseases.[21]

Operative Risk Factors

Several factors related to the operative procedure may be associated with the risk of development of an SSI [*see 5 Prevention of Postoperative Infection*]. These include method of hair removal (and likelihood of consequent skin injury), inappropriate use of antimicrobial prophylaxis, duration of the operation, and wound classification. The influence of hair removal methods on SSI has been examined by many investigators. Lower infection rates were reported with the use of depilatory agents and electric clippers than with razors.[7,8] Antimicrobial prophylaxis is used for all operations that involve entry into a hollow viscus. Antimicrobial prophylaxis is also indicated for clean operations in which an intraarticular or intravascular prosthetic device will be inserted and for any operation in which an SSI would have a high morbidity.[19] A comprehensive study determined that there is considerable variation in the timing of administration of prophylactic antibiotics, but that the administration within 2 hours before surgery reduces the risk of SSI.[9]

Operative wounds are susceptible to varying levels of bacterial contamination, by which they are classified as clean, clean-contaminated, contaminated, or dirty.[22] In most institutions, the responsibility for classifying the incision site is assigned to the operating room circulating nurse; one assessment suggests that the accuracy of decisions made by this group is as high as 88%.[23]

Composite Risk Indices

The Centers for Disease Control and Prevention (CDC) established the National Nosocomial Infections Surveillance (NNIS) system in 1970 to create a national database of nosocomial infections.[24] The NNIS system has been used to develop indices for predicting the risk of nosocomial infection in a given patient.

NNIS basic risk index NNIS developed a composite risk index composed of the following criteria: ASA score, wound class, and duration of surgery. Reporting on data collected from 44 United States hospitals between 1987 and 1990, NNIS demonstrated that this risk index is a significantly better predictor for development of SSI than the traditional wound classification system alone.[25,26] The NNIS risk index is a useful method of risk adjustment for a wide variety of procedures.

The NNIS risk index is scored as 0, 1, 2, or 3. A patient's score is determined by counting the number of risk factors present from among the following: an ASA score of 3, 4, or 5; a surgical wound that is classified as contaminated or dirty/infected;

and an operation lasting over T hours (where T represents the 75th percentile of distribution of the duration of the operative procedure being performed, rounded to the nearest whole number of hours).

Modified NNIS basic risk index for procedures using laparoscopes For cholecystectomy and colon surgery procedures, the use of a laparoscope lowered the risk of SSI within each NNIS risk index category.[27] Hence, for these procedures, when the procedure is performed laparoscopically, the risk index should be modified by subtracting 1 from the basic NNIS risk index score. With this modification, the risk index has values of M (or –1), 0, 1, 2, or 3. For appendectomy and gastric surgery, use of a laparoscope affected SSI rates only when the NNIS basic risk index was 0, thereby yielding five risk categories: 0–Yes, 0–No, 1, 2, and 3, where Yes or No refers to whether the procedure was performed with a laparoscope.[27]

Operation-specific risk factors It is likely that operation-specific logistic regression models will increasingly be used to calculate risk. For example, in spinal fusion surgery, Richards and colleagues identified diabetes mellitus, ASA score greater than 3, operation duration longer than 4 hours, and posterior surgical approach as significant independent predictors of SSI.[28] Other logistic regression models have been developed for craniotomy and cesarean section.[29,30] These models should permit more precise risk adjustment.

PREVENTIVE MEASURES

In any surgical practice, policies and procedures should be in place pertaining to the making of a surgical incision and the prevention of infection. These policies and procedures should govern the following: (1) skin disinfection and hand-washing practices of the operating team, (2) preoperative preparation of the patient's skin (e.g., hair removal and use of antiseptics), (3) the use of prophylactic antibiotics, (4) techniques for preparation of the operative site, (5) management of the postoperative site if drains, dressings, or both are in place, (6) standards of behavior and practice for the operating team (e.g., the use of gown, mask, and gloves), (7) special training of the operating team, and (8) sterilization and disinfection of instruments.

Hand Hygiene

Although hand washing is considered the single most important measure for preventing nosocomial infections, poor compliance is frequent.[31] Role modeling is important in positively influencing this behavior. One study showed that a hand-washing educational program contributed to a reduction in the rate of nosocomial infections.[32] Good hand-washing habits can be encouraged by making facilities (with sink, soap, and towel) visible and easily accessible in patient care areas [*see 5 Prevention of Postoperative Infection*].

Cleansers used for hand hygiene include plain nonantimicrobial soap, antimicrobial soaps, and waterless alcohol-based hand antiseptics. Plain soaps have very little antimicrobial activity; they mainly remove dirt and transient flora.[33] Compared with plain soaps, antimicrobial soaps achieve a greater log reduction in eliminating transient flora and have the additional advantage of sustained activity against resident hand flora.[33] Alcohol-based hand antiseptics have an excellent spectrum of antimicrobial activity and rapid onset of action, dry rapidly, and do not require the use of water or towels.[34] Therefore, they are recommended for routine decontamination of hands during patient care except when hands are visibly soiled. Emollients are often added to alcohol-based waterless hand antiseptics because of these antiseptics' tendency to cause drying of the skin.[34]

Sterilization and Disinfection

Spaulding proposed in 1972 that the level of disinfection and sterilization for surgical and other instruments be determined by classifying the instruments into three categories—critical, semicritical, and noncritical—according to the degree of infection risk involved in their use.[35]

Critical items include objects or instruments that enter directly into the vascular system or sterile areas of the body. These items should be sterilized by steam under pressure, dry heat, ethylene oxide, or other approved methods. Flash sterilization is the process by which surgical instruments are sterilized for immediate use should an emergency situation arise (e.g., to sterilize an instrument that was accidentally dropped). This is usually achieved by leaving instruments unwrapped in a container and using a rapid steam cycle.[36] Instruments must still be manually cleaned, decontaminated, inspected, and properly arranged in the container before sterilization. Implantables should not be flash sterilized. Flash sterilization is not intended to replace conventional steam sterilization of surgical instruments or to reduce the need for adequate instrument inventory.[36]

Semicritical items are those that come into contact with mucous membranes or skin that is not intact (e.g., bronchoscopes and gastroscopes). Scopes have the potential to cause infection if they are improperly cleaned and disinfected. Transmission of infection has been documented after endoscopic investigations, including infection with *Salmonella typhi*[37] and *Helicobacter pylori*.[38] Such incidents emphasize the need for sterilization of the endoscopic biopsy forceps. Semicritical items generally require high-level disinfection that kills all microorganisms except bacterial spores.[39]

Glutaraldehyde 2% is a high-level disinfectant that has been used extensively in flexible endoscopy. Before disinfection, scopes should receive a thorough manual cleaning to eliminate gross debris. To achieve high-level disinfection, the internal and external surfaces and channels should come into contact with the disinfecting agent for a minimum of 20 minutes.[39] Glutaraldehyde has certain disadvantages. In particular, it requires activation before use; moreover, it is irritating to the skin, eyes, and nasal mucosa, and thus, its use requires special ventilation or a ducted fume hood.[39]

An alternative to glutaraldehyde is orthophthaldehyde (OPA), a newer agent approved by the Food and Drug Administration (FDA) for high-level disinfection. OPA is odorless and nonirritating and does not require activation before use.[40]

Noncritical items are those that come in contact with intact skin (e.g., blood pressure cuffs). They require only washing or scrubbing with a detergent and warm water or disinfection with an intermediate-level or low-level germicide for 10 minutes.

The reuse of single-use medical devices has become a topic of interest because of the implied cost saving. The central concerns are the effectiveness of sterilization or disinfection according to category of use, as well as maintenance of the essential mechanical features and the functional integrity of the item to be reused. The FDA has issued regulations governing third-party and hospital reprocessors engaged in reprocessing single-use devices for reuse.[41] These regulations are available on the FDA's web site (www.fda.gov/cdrh/comp/guidance/1168.pdf).

Hair Removal

An infection control program should have a hair-removal policy for preoperative skin preparation [see 5 Prevention of Postoperative Infection].

Operating Room Environment

Environmental controls in the OR have been used to reduce the risk of SSI. The OR should be maintained under positive pressure of at least 2.5 Pa in relation to corridors and adjacent areas. In addition, there should be at least 15 air changes per hour, of which three should involve fresh air.[42]

HEALTH STATUS OF THE HEALTH CARE TEAM

The health care team has a primary role in the prevention of infection. Continued education and reindoctrination of policies are essential: the team must be kept well informed and up to date on concepts of infection control. Inadvertently, team members may also be the source of, or the vector in, transmission of infection. Nosocomial infection outbreaks with MRSA have been traced to MRSA carriers among health care workers.[43] Screening of personnel to identify carriers is undertaken only when an outbreak of nosocomial infection occurs that cannot be contained despite implementation of effective control measures and when a health care worker is epidemiologically linked to cases.

Protecting the health care team from infection is a constant concern. Preventive measures, such as immunizations and preemployment medical examinations, should be undertaken at an employee health care center staffed by knowledgeable personnel.[44] Preventable infectious diseases, such as chickenpox and rubella, should be tightly controlled in hospitals that serve immunocompromised and obstetric patients. It is highly recommended that a record be maintained of an employee's immunizations. Knowledge of the employee's health status on entry to the hospital helps ensure appropriate placement and good preventive care.

When exposure to contagious infections is unavoidable, susceptible personnel should be located, screened, and given prophylactic treatment if necessary. Infection control personnel should define the problem, establish a definition of contact, and take measures to help reduce panic.

Isolation Precautions

CDC guidelines have been developed to prevent the transmission of infections.[45] These isolation guidelines promote two levels of isolation precautions: standard precautions and transmission-based precautions.

Standard precautions The standard precautions guidelines—which incorporate the main features of the older universal precautions and body substance isolation guidelines—were developed to reduce the risk of transmission of microorganisms for all patients regardless of their diagnosis.[45-47] Standard precautions apply to blood, all body fluids, secretions and excretions, and mucous membranes.

Transmission-based precautions Transmission-based isolation precautions were developed for use in patients with certain epidemiologically important pathogens or clinical presentations. These precautions comprise three categories, based on the mode of transmission: airborne precautions, droplet precautions, and contact precautions.[45] These categories of precautions may be combined for certain microorganisms or clinical presentations (e.g., both contact and airborne precautions are indicated for a patient with varicella).

Airborne precautions are designed to reduce transmission of microorganisms spread via droplets that have nuclei 5 μm in size or smaller, remain suspended in air for prolonged periods of time, and have the capability of being dispersed widely.[45] Airborne precautions include wearing an N95 respirator, placing the patient in a single room that is under negative pressure of 2.5 Pa in relation to adjacent areas, keeping the door closed, providing a minimum of 6 to 12 air changes per hour, and exhausting room air outside the building and away from intake ducts or through a high-efficiency particulate air (HEPA) filter if recirculated.[45,48] Airborne precautions are indicated for patients with suspected or confirmed infectious pulmonary or laryngeal tuberculosis; measles; varicella; disseminated zoster; and Lassa, Ebola, Marburg, and other hemorrhagic fevers with pneumonia. Varicella, disseminated herpes zoster, and hemorrhagic fevers with pneumonia also call for contact precautions (see below).

Droplet precautions are designed to reduce the risk of transmission of microorganisms spread via large-particle droplets that are greater than 5 μm in size, do not remain suspended in the air for prolonged periods, and usually travel 1 m or less.[45] No special ventilation requirements are required to prevent droplet transmission. A single room is preferable, and the door may remain open. Examples of patients for whom droplet precautions are indicated are those with influenza, rubella, mumps, and meningitis caused by *Haemophilus influenzae* and *Neisseria meningitidis*.

Contact precautions are designed to reduce the risk of transmission of microorganisms by direct or indirect contact. Direct contact involves skin-to-skin contact resulting in physical transfer of microorganisms.[45] Indirect contact involves contact with a contaminated inanimate object that acts as an intermediary. Contact precautions are indicated for patients colonized or infected with multidrug-resistant bacteria that the infection control program judges to be of special clinical and epidemiologic significance on the basis of recommendations in the literature.[45]

Exposure to Bloodborne Pathogens

The risk of transmission of HIV and hepatitis B virus (HBV) from patient to surgeon or from surgeon to patient has resulted in a series of recommendations governing contact with blood and body fluids.[48] The risk of acquiring a bloodborne infection—such as with HBV, hepatitis C virus (HCV), or HIV—depends on three factors: type of exposure to the bloodborne pathogen, prevalence of infection in the population, and the rate of infection after exposure to the bloodborne pathogen.[49] Postexposure management has been discussed in CDC guidelines (www.cdc.gov/mmwr/pdf/rr/rr5011.pdf).[50]

Protection of the face and hands during operation has become important. A study of 8,502 operations found that the rate of direct blood exposure was 12.4%, whereas the rate of parenteral exposure via puncture wounds and cuts was 2.2%. Parenteral blood contacts were twice as likely to occur among surgeons as among other OR personnel.[51] These findings support the need for OR practice policies and the choice of appropriate protective garments for the OR staff. OR practice policy should give particular attention to methods of using sharp instruments and to ways of reducing the frequency of percutaneous injuries: sharp instruments should be passed in a metal dish, cautery should be used, and great care should be taken in wound closures. It is important that masks protect the operating team from aerosolized fluids. Researchers have shown that for ideal protection, a mask should be fluid-capture efficient and air resistant.[52]

For invasive surgical procedures, double gloving has become routine. However, there are recognized differences among the gloves available. Latex allergy is an important issue; nonlatex alternatives are available for those who are allergic.[53]

Table 2 CDC Recommendations for Prevention of HIV and HBV Transmission during Invasive Procedures[48]

Health care workers with exudative lesions or weeping dermatitis should cover any unprotected skin, or they should not provide patient care until the damaged skin has healed.

Hands should be washed after every patient contact.

Health care workers should wear gloves when contact with blood or body substances is anticipated; double gloves should be used during operative procedures; hands should be washed after gloves are removed.

Gowns, plastic aprons, or both should be worn when soiling of clothing is anticipated.

Mask and protective eyewear or face shield should be worn if aerosolization or splattering of blood or body substances is expected.

Resuscitation devices should be used to minimize the need for mouth-to-mouth resuscitation.

Disposable containers should be used to dispose of needles and sharp Instruments.

Avoid accidents and self-wounding with sharp instruments by following these measures:
• Do not recap needles.
• Use needleless systems when possible.
• Use cautery and stapling devices when possible.
• Pass sharp instruments in metal tray during operative procedures.

In the case of an accidental spill of blood or body substance on skin or mucous membranes, do the following:
• Rinse the site immediately and thoroughly under water.
• Wash the site with soap and water.
• Document the incident (i.e., report to Occupational Safety and Health Administration or to the Infection Control Service).

Blood specimens from all patients should be considered hazardous at all times.

Prompt attention should be given to spills of blood or body substances, which should be cleaned with an appropriate disinfectant.

Hepatitis B virus For active surgeons and other members of the health care team, HBV infection continues to pose a major risk. Hepatitis B vaccination has proved safe and protective and is highly recommended for all high-risk employees; it should be made available through the employee health care center.

Despite the efficacy of the vaccine, many surgeons and other personnel remain unimmunized and are at high risk for HBV infection.[48] HBV is far more easily transmitted than HIV and continues to have a greater impact on the morbidity and mortality of health care personnel. An estimated 8,700 new cases of hepatitis B are acquired occupationally by health care workers each year; 200 to 250 of these cases result in death.[54] The risk of seroconversion is at least 30% after a percutaneous exposure to blood from a hepatitis B e antigen–seropositive source.[50] Given that a patient's serostatus may be unknown, it is important that health care workers follow standard precautions for all patients.

With HBV infection, as with HIV (see below), the approach to prevention and control is a two-way street—that is, protection should be afforded to patients as well as health care personnel. In addition to standard precautions, the CDC has developed recommendations for health care workers that are designed to prevent transmission of HBV and HIV from health care worker to patient or from patient to health care worker during exposure-prone invasive procedures [see Table 2]. Cognizant of the CDC recommendations, the American College of Surgeons has issued additional recommendations regarding the surgeon's role in the prevention of hepatitis transmission [see Table 3].[54]

Hepatitis C virus The average incidence of seroconversion after percutaneous exposure from an HCV-positive source is 1.8% (range, 0% to 7%).[55-57] Mucous membrane exposure to blood rarely results in transmission, and no transmission has been documented from exposure of intact or nonintact skin to blood.[50,58] There is no recommended postexposure prophylaxis regimen for HCV. The use of immunoglobulin has not been demonstrated to be protective.[50] There are no antiviral medications recommended for postexposure prophylaxis.[50]

Human immunodeficiency virus Exposure to blood and body substances of patients who have AIDS or who are seropositive for HIV constitutes a health hazard to hospital employees. The magnitude of the risk depends on the degree and method of exposure [see *136 Acquired Immunodeficiency Syndrome*].

The presence of HIV infection in a patient is not always known. Because the prevalence of HIV in the North American patient population is less than 1% (range, 0.09% to 0.89%), and because a caregiver's risk of seroconversion after needlestick injury is likewise less than 1%, the CDC recommends taking standard precautions [see *135 Viral Infection*] and following in all patients the same guidelines for invasive procedures that one would use in cases of known HBV-infected patients [see *Table 2*].[48] Infection control personnel have introduced realistic control measures and educational programs to help alleviate fears that health care workers might have about coming in contact with patients infected with HIV.

Exposure to Tuberculosis

In studies of health care workers, positive results on tuberculin skin testing have ranged from 0.11% to 10%.[59,60] Health care workers who are immunocompromised are at high risk for development of disease postexposure.[59]

The CDC recommendation for tuberculosis prevention places emphasis on a hierarchy of control measures, including administrative engineering controls and personal respiratory protection

(www.cdc.gov/mmwr/pdf/rr/rr4313.pdf). The following measures should be considered:

1. The use of risk assessments and development of a written tuberculosis control protocol.
2. Early identification and treatment of persons who have tuberculosis.
3. Tuberculosis screening programs for health care workers.
4. Training and education.
5. Evaluation of tuberculosis infection control programs.[61]

Activities of an Infection Control Program

SURVEILLANCE

The cornerstone of an infection control program is surveillance. This process depends on the verification, classification, analysis, reporting, and investigation of infection occurrences, with the intent of generating or correcting policies and procedures. Five surveillance methods can be applied[62,63]:

1. Total, or hospital-wide, surveillance-collection of comprehensive data on all infections in the facility, with the aim of correcting problems as they arise. This is labor intensive.
2. Surveillance by objective, or targeted surveillance, in which a specific goal is set for reducing certain types of infection. This concept is priority-directed and can be further subdivided into two distinct activities:
   a. The setting of outcome objectives, in which the objectives for the month or year are established and all efforts applied to achieve a desired rate of infection. As with the hospital-wide approach, a short-term plan would be made to monitor, record, and measure results and provide feedback on the data.
   b. The setting of process objectives, which incorporates the patient care practices of doctors and nurses as they relate to outcome (e.g., wound infections and their control).
3. Periodic surveillance—intensive surveillance of infections and patient-care practices by unit or by service at different times of the year.
4. Prevalence survey—the counting and analysis of all active infections during a specified time period. This permits identification of nosocomial infection trends and problem areas.
5. Outbreak surveillance—the identification and control of outbreaks of infection. Identification can be made on the basis of outbreak thresholds if baseline bacterial isolate rates are available and outbreak thresholds can be developed. Problems are evaluated only when the number of isolates of a particular bacterial species exceeds outbreak thresholds.

Surveillance techniques include the practice of direct patient observation[7] and indirect observation by review of microbiology reports, nursing Kardex, or the medical record to obtain data on nosocomial infections. The sensitivity of case finding by microbiology reports was found to be 33% to 65%; by Kardex, 85%; and by total chart review, 90%.[62] These methods may be used either separately or in combination to obtain data on clinical outcomes.

One use of surveillance data is to generate information for individual surgeons, service chiefs, and nursing personnel as a reminder of their progress in keeping infections and diseases under control. This technique was used by Cruse in 1980 to show a progressive decrease in infection rates of clean surgical wounds to less than 1% over 10 years.[8] In other settings, endemic rates of bloodstream, respiratory, and urinary tract infections were cor-

---

Table 3 ACS Recommendations for Preventing Transmission of Hepatitis[54]

Surgeons should continue to utilize the highest standards of infection control, involving the most effective known sterile barriers, universal precautions, and scientifically accepted measures to prevent blood exposure during every operation. This practice should extend to all sites where surgical care is rendered and should include safe handling practices for needles and sharp instruments.

Surgeons have the same ethical obligations to render care to patients with hepatitis as they have to render care to other patients.

Surgeons with natural or acquired antibodies to HBV are protected from acquiring HBV from patients and cannot transmit the disease to patients. All surgeons and other members of the health care team should know their HBV immune status and become immunized as early as possible in their medical career.

Surgeons without evidence of immunity to HBV who perform procedures should know their HBsAg status and, if this is positive, should also know their HBeAg status. In both instances, expert medical advice should be obtained and all appropriate measures taken to prevent disease transmission to patients. Medical advice should be rendered by an expert panel composed and convened to fully protect practitioner confidentiality. The HBeAg-positive surgeon and the panel should discuss and agree on a strategy for protecting patients at risk for disease transmission.

On the basis of current information, surgeons infected with HCV have no reason to alter their practice but should seek expert medical advice and appropriate treatment to prevent chronic liver disease.

rected and reduced by routine monitoring and reporting to medical and nursing staff.[21]

The increasing practice of same-day or short-stay surgical procedures has led to the need for postdischarge surveillance. This may be done by direct observation in a follow-up clinic, by surveying patients through the mail or over the telephone, by reviewing medical records, or by mailing questionnaires directly to surgeons. The original CDC recommendation of 30 days for follow-up was used by one hospital to randomly screen post–joint arthroplasty patients by telephone. This screening identified an infection rate of 7.5%, compared with 2% for hospitalized orthopedic patients.[64] Results from another medical center suggested that 90% of cases would be captured in a 21-day postoperative follow-up program.[5] Infections that occur after discharge are more likely with clean operations, operations of short duration, and operations in obese patients and in nonalcoholic patients. The use of prosthetic materials for implants requires extending the follow-up period to 1 year.

Definition of Surgical Site Infections

The CDC defines an incisional SSI as an infection that occurs at the incision site within 30 days after surgery or within 1 year if a prosthetic implant is in place. Infection is characterized by redness, swelling, or heat with tenderness, pain, or dehiscence at the incision site and by purulent drainage. Other indicators of infection include fever, deliberate opening of the wound, culture-positive drainage, and a physician's diagnosis of infection with prescription of antibiotics. To encourage a uniform approach among data collectors, the CDC has suggested three categories of SSIs, with definitions for each category [see Table 4].[65] The category of organ or space SSI was included to cover any part of the anatomy (i.e., organs or spaces) other than the incision that might have been opened or manipulated during the operative procedure. This category would include, for example, arterial and venous infections, endometritis, disk space infections, and mediastinitis.[65]

There should be collaboration between the physician or nurse and the infection control practitioner to establish the presence of an SSI. The practitioner should complete the surveillance with a chart review and document the incident in a computer database program for later analysis. The data must be systematically recorded; many commercial computer programs are available for this purpose. One group reported that their experience with the Health Evaluation through Logical Processing system was useful for identifying patients at high risk for nosocomial infections.[66]

Verification of Infection

A complete assessment should include clinical evaluation of commonly recognized sites (e.g., wound, respiratory system, urinary tract, and intravenous access sites) for evidence of infection, especially when no obvious infection is seen at the surgical site. Microbiologic evaluation should identify the microorganism. Such evaluation, however, depends on an adequate specimen for a Gram stain and culture. For epidemiologic reasons, DNA fingerprinting may be required, especially for outbreak investigation.

A system of internal auditing should alert the infection control service to multiresistant microorganisms—for example, to the presence of MRSA or vancomycin-resistant *Enterococcus* (VRE) in a patient. Differentiation between infection and colonization is important for the decision of how to treat. Regardless of whether infection or colonization is identified, verification of MRSA or VRE should generate a discussion on control measures.

Table 4 Surgical Site Infections (SSIs)[65]
Superficial SSIs
Skin
Deep incisional SSIs
Fascia
Muscle layers
Organ or space SSIs
Body organs
Body spaces

Data Interpretation

The predictive value of data is deemed more useful when it is applied to specific situations. According to CDC experts, the scoring for infections depends on specified, related denominators to interpret the data, especially when there is to be interhospital comparison.[67]

Data Analysis

The original practice of presenting overall hospital-wide crude rates provided little means for adjustment of variables (e.g., risk related to the patient or to the operation). The following three formulas, however, are said to offer more precision than traditional methods[67]:

$$(\text{Number of nosocomial infections/Service operations}) \times 100$$

$$[\text{Number of site-specific nosocomial infections/Specific operations (e.g., number of inguinal hernias)}] \times 100$$

$$[\text{Number of nosocomial infections/Hospital admissions (patient-days)}] \times 1{,}000$$

Data on infections of the urinary tract, respiratory system, and circulatory system resulting from exposure to devices such as Foley catheters, ventilators, and intravascular lines can be illustrated as device-associated risks according to site, as follows:

$$(\text{Number of device-associated infections of a site/Number of device days}) \times 1{,}000$$

Reporting

Infection notification to surgeons has been shown by Cruse and Foord to have a positive influence on clean-wound infection rates.[7,8] In a medical setting, Britt and colleagues also reported a reduction in endemic nosocomial infection rates for urinary tract infections, from 3.7% to 1.3%, and for respiratory tract infections, from 4.0% to 1.6%, simply by keeping medical personnel aware of the rates.[21]

Outbreak Investigation

There are 10 essential components to an outbreak investigation:

1. Verify the diagnosis and confirm that an outbreak exists. This is an important step, because other factors may account for an apparent increase in infections. These factors may include a reporting artifact resulting from a change in surveillance methodology, a laboratory error or change in laboratory methodology, or an increase in the denominator of the formula used for data analysis (if this increase is proportionate to the rise in the numerator, the infection rate has not changed).

2. Formulate a case definition to guide the search for potential patients with disease.

3. Draw an epidemic curve that plots cases of the disease against time of onset of illness. This curve compares the number of cases during the epidemic period with the baseline. In addi-

tion, the epidemic curve helps to determine the probable incubation period and how the disease is being transmitted (i.e., a common source versus person to person).

4. Review the charts of case patients to determine demographics and exposures to staff, medications, therapeutic modalities, and other variables of importance.

5. Perform a line listing of case patients to determine whether there is any common exposure.

6. Calculate the infection rate. The numerator is the number of infected patients and the denominator is the number of patients at risk.

7. Formulate a tentative hypothesis to explain the reservoir and the mode of transmission. A review of the literature on similar outbreaks may be necessary.

8. Test the hypothesis, using a case-control study, cohort study, prospective intervention study, or microbiologic study. A case-control study is usually used, because it is less labor intensive. For a case-control study, control subjects should be selected from an uninfected surgical population of patients who were hospitalized at the same time as those identified during the epidemic period and matched for age, gender, service operation, operation date, and health status (ASA score). Two or three control patients are usually selected for every case patient. The cases and controls are then compared with respect to possible exposures that may increase the risk of disease. Patient, personnel, and environmental microbiologic isolates (if any) should be kept for fingerprinting (e.g., pulsed-field gel electrophoresis, random amplified polymorphic DNA polymerase chain reaction).

9. Institute infection control measures. This may be done at any time during the investigation. The control measures should be reviewed after institution to determine their efficacy and the possible need for changing them.

10. Report the incident to the infection control committee and, at the completion of the investigation, submit a report. The administrators, physicians, and nurses involved should be informed and updated as events change.[68]

ANTIMICROBIAL-RESISTANT MICROORGANISMS

Hospitals and communities worldwide are facing the challenge posed by the spread of antimicrobial-resistant microorganisms. Strains of MRSA are increasing in hospitals and are an important cause of nosocomial infections; in the United States in the year 2002, the proportion of *S. aureus* isolates resistant to methicillin or oxacillin was more than 55%.[69] MRSA strains do not merely replace methicillin-susceptible strains as a cause of hospital-acquired infections but actually increase the burden of nosocomial infections.[70] Moreover, there are reports that MRSA may be becoming a community-acquired pathogen.[71,72] A proactive approach for controlling MRSA at all levels of health care can result in decreased MRSA infection rates.[73,74]

Strains of GISA, an emerging pathogen, exhibit reduced susceptibility to vancomycin and teicoplanin. The first GISA strain was isolated in 1996 in Japan.[75] DNA fingerprinting suggests that these GISA strains evolved from preexisting MRSA strains that infected patients in the months before the GISA infection. Contact precautions are indicated for patients infected or colonized with GISA; infection control guidelines to prevent the spread of GISA are available.[76]

VRE accounts for 31% of all enterococci in the NNIS system.[70] Transmission usually occurs through contact with the contaminated hands of a health care worker. The environment is an important reservoir for VRE, but it is not clear whether the environment plays a significant role in transmission.[77] Risk factors for VRE

acquisition include length of hospital stay, liver transplantation, presence of feeding tubes, dialysis, and exposure to cephalosporins.[78] Contact precautions are indicated for patients infected or colonized with VRE.[79]

Strategies to prevent and control the emergence and spread of antimicrobial-resistant microorganisms have been developed. These include optimal use of antimicrobial prophylaxis for surgical procedures; optimizing choice and duration of empirical therapy; improving antimicrobial prescribing patterns by physicians; monitoring and providing feedback regarding antibiotic resistance; formulating and using practice guidelines for antibiotic usage; developing a system to detect and report trends in antimicrobial resistance; ensuring that caregivers respond rapidly to the detection of antimicrobial resistance in individual patients; incorporating the importance of controlling antimicrobial resistance into the institutional mission and climate; increasing compliance with basic infection control policies and procedures; and developing a plan for identifying, transferring, discharging, and readmitting patients colonized or infected with specific antimicrobial-resistant microorganisms.[80]

Severe Acute Respiratory Syndrome

The severe acute respiratory syndrome (SARS) first emerged in Guangdong Province, China, in November 2002. SARS is caused by a novel coronavirus (SARS-CoV) that may have originated from an animal reservoir.[81] It is characterized by fever, chills, cough, dyspnea, and diarrhea and radiologic findings suggestive of atypical pneumonia.[82] As of August 7, 2003, a total of 8,422 probable cases, with 916 deaths (11%), had been reported from 29 countries.[83]

The incubation period is estimated to be 10 days, and patients appear to be most infectious during the second week of illness.[83] Available evidence suggests that SARS-CoV is spread through contact, in droplets, and possibly by airborne transmission.[83] Accordingly, health care workers must adhere to contact, droplet, and airborne precautions when caring for SARS patients. Included in such precautions are the use of gloves, gowns, eye protection, and the N95 respirator.[83] A comprehensive review of SARS is available at the WHO web site (www.who.int/csr/sars/en/WHOconsensus.pdf).

ENVIRONMENTAL CONTROL

Control of the microbial reservoir of the patient's immediate environment in the hospital is the goal of an infection control program. Environmental control begins with design of the hospital's physical plant. The design must meet the functional standards for patient care and must be integrated into the architecture to provide traffic accessibility and control. Since the 1960s, the practice of centralizing seriously ill patients in intensive care, dialysis, and transplant units has accentuated the need for more careful analysis and planning of space. The primary standards for these special care units and ORs require planning of floor space, physical surfaces, lighting, ventilation, water, and sanitation to accommodate easy cleaning and disinfecting of surfaces, sterilization of instruments, proper food handling, and garbage disposal. These activities should then be governed by workable policies that are understandable to the staff. Preventive maintenance should be a basic and integral activity of the physical plant department.

Surveillance of the environment by routine culturing of operating room floors and walls was discontinued in the late 1970s. Autoclaves and sterilization systems should, however, be continuously monitored with routine testing for efficiency and performance. The results should be documented and records maintained.

Investigations of the physical plant should be reserved for specific outbreaks, depending on the organism and its potential for causing infection. This was demonstrated by the incident of a cluster outbreak of sternal wound *Legionella* infections in post–cardiovascular surgery patients after they were exposed to tap water during bathing.[84] Because outbreaks of nosocomial respiratory infections caused by *L. pneumophila* continue to be a problem,[85] the CDC includes precautionary measures for this disease in its pneumonia prevention guidelines.[86] In addition, several water-treatment measures are available to help eradicate or clear the water of these bacteria.[87]

Hospital-acquired aspergillosis is caused by another ubiquitous type of microorganism that is often a contaminant of ambient air during construction. The patients most at risk are usually immunosuppressed (i.e., neutropenic). It is recommended that preventive measures be organized for these patients when construction is being planned.[88] The provision of clean (i.e., HEPA-filtered) air in positive pressure-ventilated rooms, with up to 12 air exchanges an hour, is the basic requirement for these patients.[42]

A comprehensive review of environmental infection control in health care facilities is available at the CDC Web site (www.cdc.gov/mmwr/pdf/rr/rr5210.pdf). This review contains recommendations for preventing nosocomial infections associated with construction, demolition, and renovation.

EDUCATION

A strategy for routine training of the health care team is necessary at every professional level. The process may vary from institution to institution, but some form of communication should be established for the transmittal of information about the following:

1. Endemic infection rates.
2. Endemic bacterial trends.
3. Updates on infection prevention measures (especially during and after an outbreak).
4. Updates on preventive policies pertaining to intravenous line management, hand washing, isolation precautions, and other areas of concern.

Although members of the infection control team are the responsible resource persons in the hospital system, each member of the health care team also has a responsibility to help prevent infection in hospitalized patients. Under the JCAHO guidelines,[6] education of patients and their families should become a part of teaching plans, as well.

RESEARCH

Infection control policies are constantly being evaluated and remodeled because most traditional preventive measures are not scientifically proved but are based on clinical experience. Although infection data are useful, research in infection control requires microbiologic support to conduct realistic studies. Very few infection control programs have the personnel and resources for these activities.

PUBLIC HEALTH AND COMMUNITY HEALTH SERVICE

According to existing public health acts, certain infectious diseases must be reported by law. Differences exist between the reporting systems of one country and those of another, but on the whole, diseases such as tuberculosis and meningococcal meningitis are reported for community follow-up.

Open communication with community hospitals and other health care facilities provides for better management of patients with infections, allowing for notification and planning for additional hospitalization or convalescence as the patient moves to and from the community and hospital.

Benefits of an Infection Control Program

The establishment of an infection control program can greatly benefit a hospital. An infection control program supports patient care activities and is a means for continuous quality improvement in the care that is given, in addition to being an accreditation requirement. In Canada and the United States, the need for infection control programs is supported by all governing agents, including the Canadian Council on Hospital Accreditation, JCAHO, the American Hospital Association (AHA), the Canadian Hospital Association, the Association for Practitioners in Infection Control (APIC), the Society of Hospital Epidemiologists of America (SHEA) Joint Commission Task Force, and the Community and Hospital Infection Control Association–Canada (CHICA-Canada).

An infection control program requires a multidisciplinary committee that includes an infection control practitioner, who may be a nurse or a technician. In the original concept, Infection Control Officer was the title given to the person in charge of the program. As the practice has expanded into research and more sophisticated data analysis, physicians and nurses have had to update their epidemiologic skills, and some hospitals have acquired the services of an epidemiologist. The historical development of infection control programs in hospitals dates to the late 1970s. The SENIC project endorsed the use of nurses[89] because of their patient care expertise; the literature contains many examples of collaboration between infection control officers and nurse practitioners.

Controlling and preventing the spread of infections in health care facilities has taken many forms:

1. Prevention of cross-infection between patients.
2. Monitoring environmental systems (e.g., plumbing and ventilation).
3. Procedures for sterilization of equipment and instruments.
4. Policies and procedures for the implementation of sterile technique for surgical and other invasive procedures.
5. Procedures for nursing care activities for the postoperative patient.
6. Policies and procedures for dietary, housekeeping, and other ancillary services.
7. Policies for the control of antibiotics.
8. Policies and procedures for occupational health prevention.
9. Educational strategies for the implementation of isolation precautions.

At present, infection control practices have developed into a sophisticated network that does not allow for hospital-wide surveillance as it was once practiced. However, the use of surveillance by objective and the use of indicators to monitor select groups of patients or select situations provide information that will benefit the entire hospital. For example, monitoring bloodborne infections in an intensive care setting will provide data to support an intravenous care plan for general use. Accomplishing a high-quality infection control program requires organization and the dedicated service of all health care employees.

Organization of an Infection Control Program

INFECTION CONTROL COMMITTEE

The chair of the infection control committee should have an ongoing interest in the prevention and control of infection. Members should represent microbiology, nursing, the OR, central supply, medicine, surgery, pharmacy, and housekeeping. This multidisciplinary group becomes the advocate for the entire hospital. The members work with the infection control service to make decisions in the following areas: (1) assessing the effectiveness and pertinence of infection control policies and protocols in their areas and (2) raising infection control–related concerns.

INFECTION CONTROL SERVICE

Collecting surveillance data on nosocomial infections and taking actions to decrease nosocomial infections are the benchmarks of the infection control service. In the traditional sense, the service provides information on all types of endemic infections (e.g., wound, urinary tract, and bloodstream) to the benefit of the health care system. The cost-effectiveness of data collection was demonstrated by the SENIC study.[90] Since then, other studies have shown that there are benefits in reducing nosocomial infection.[17,18,50] Cruse and Foord presented data to show that clean-wound infection rates could be brought below 0.8%.[8] Such reductions bring multiple benefits because nosocomial infections have a substantial impact on morbidity, mortality, length of stay, and cost[90]; for example, the extra costs of treating bloodstream infections in an intensive care setting were recently estimated to be $40,000 per survivor.[91]

INFECTION CONTROL PRACTITIONERS

The reshaping of hospitals because of cost constraints will have an effect on the work of infection control practitioners. Already, some institutions have regrouped responsibilities and changed the role of these professionals. Given the accreditation mandate, the need to continue an active program may be reviewed. Many training programs are available to assist with professional and organizational development (see below), and the APIC certification program supports continuous professional improvement. A viable and useful program for surveillance and collection of data requires a computer database program networked to microbiology, the OR, and nursing units. Methods for collecting, editing, storing, and sharing data should be based on the CDC's NNIS system,[26] which promotes the use of high-quality indicators for future monitoring and comparison among health care institutions.

Training programs for infection control practitioners are available through the following organizations:

Society of Hospital Epidemiologists of America (SHEA)
19 Mantua Road, Mt. Royal, NJ 08061
Telephone: 856-423-7222; Fax: 856-423-3420
E-mail: sheamtg@talley.com
Web site: www.shea-online.org

Association for Professionals in Infection Control (APIC)
1275 K Street NW, Suite 1000
Washington, DC 20005-4006
Telephone: 202-789-1890; Fax: 202-789-1899
E-mail: APICinfo@apic.org
Web site: www.apic.org

Community and Hospital Infection Control Association–Canada (CHICA-Canada)
Web site: www.chica.org

References

1. Preparation of the operating team and supporting personnel. Manual on Control of Infection in Surgical Patients, 2nd ed. Altemeier WA, Burke JF, Pruitt BA, et al, Eds. JB Lippincott Co, Philadelphia, 1986, p 91

2. LaForce FM: The control of infections in hospitals, 1750 to 1950. Prevention and Control of Nosocomial Infections, 2nd ed. Wenzel RP, Ed. Williams & Wilkins, Baltimore, 1993, p 1

3. US Public Health Service: Disinfection and sterilization: cleaning, disinfection, and sterilization of hospital equipment. US Dept of Health and Human Services (HHS Publication No. [CDC] 3N84-19281). Centers for Disease Control, Atlanta, 1981

4. Haley RW, Culver DH, White JW, et al: The nationwide nosocomial infection rate: a new need for vital statistics. Am J Epidemiol 121:159, 1985

5. Weigelt JA, Dryer D, Haley RW: The necessity and efficiency of wound surveillance after discharge. Arch Surg 127:77, 1992

6. APIC-SHEA Joint Commission Task Force: Review of 1995 Accreditation Manual for Hospitals [Insert]. APIC News 14(January/February):1, 1995

7. Alexander W, Fischer JE, Boyajian M, et al: The influence of hair-removal methods on wound infections. Arch Surg 118:347, 1983

8. Cruse PJE, Foord R: The epidemiology of wound infection: a 10-year study of 62,939 wounds. Surg Clin North Am 60:27, 1980

9. Classen DC, Evans RS, Pestotnik SL, et al: The timing of prophylactic administration of antibiotics and the risk of surgical-wound infection. N Engl J Med 326:281, 1992

10. Clarke JS, Condon RE, Bartlett JG, et al: Preoperative oral antibiotics reduce septic complications of colon operations. Ann Surg 186:251, 1977

11. Farnell MB, Worthington-Self S, Mucha P, et al: Closure of abdominal incisions with subcutaneous catheters: a prospective randomized trial. Arch Surg 121:641, 1986

12. Miles AA, Miles EM, Burke J: The value and duration of defence reactions of the skin to the primary lodgement of bacteria. Br J Exp Pathol 38:79, 1957

13. Rao N, Jacobs S, Joyce L: Cost-effective eradication of an outbreak of methicillin-resistant Staphylococcus aureus in a community teaching hospital. Infect Control Hosp Epidemiol 9:255, 1988

14. DiPerri G, Cadeo G, Castelli F, et al: Transmission of HIV-associated tuberculosis to health-care workers. Infect Control Hosp Epidemiol 14:67, 1993

15. Sepkowitz KA: AIDS, tuberculosis, and the health care worker. Clin Infect Dis 20:232, 1995

16. Nosocomial enterococci resistant to vancomycin—United States, 1989-1993. MMWR Morb Mortal Wkly Rep 42:597, 1993

17. Miller PJ, Farr BM, Gwaltney JM: Economic benefits of an effective infection control program: case study and proposal. Rev Infect Dis 11:284, 1989

18. Haley RW: Measuring the costs of nosocomial infections: methods for estimating economic burden on the hospital. Am J Med 91(suppl 3B):32S, 1991

19. Hospital Infection Control Practices Advisory Committee Guideline for the prevention of surgical site infection, 1999. Infect Control Hosp Epidemiol 20:247, 1999

20. Owens WD, Felts JA, Spitznagel EL: ASA physical status classifications: a study of consistency of ratings. Anesthesiology 49:239, 1978

21. Britt MR, Schleupner CJ, Matsumiya S: Severity of underlying disease as a predictor of nosocomial infection: utility in the control of nosocomial infection. JAMA 239:1047, 1978

22. Manual on Control of Infection in Surgical Patients, 2nd ed. Altemeier WA, Burke JF, Pruitt BA, et al, Eds. JB Lippincott Co, Philadelphia, 1986, p 29

23. Cardo DM, Falk PS, Mayhall CG: Validation of surgical wound classification in the operating room. Infect Control Hosp Epidemiol 14:255, 1993

24. Emori GT, Culver DH, Horan TC, et al: National nosocomial infections system (NNIS): description of surveillance methods. Am J Infect Control 19:19, 1991

25. Nosocomial infection rates for interhospital comparison: limitations and possible solutions. Infect Control Hosp Epidemiol 12:609, 1991

26. Culver DH, Horan TC, Gaynes RP, et al: Surgical wound infection rates by wound class, operative procedure, and patient risk index. Am J Med 91(suppl 3B):152S, 1991

27. Gaynes RP, Culver DH, Horan TC, et al: Surgical site infection (SSI) rates in the United States, 1992-1998: the National Nosocomial Infections Surveillance System basic SSI risk index. Clin Infect Dis 33(suppl 2):S69, 2001

28. Richards C, Gaynes RP, Horan T, et al: Risk factors for surgical site infection following spinal fusion surgery in the United States. Presented at the 4th Decennial International Conference on Nosocomial and Healthcare-Associated Infections; March 5-9, 2000 Atlanta, Georgia, p 153

29. Emori TG, Edwards JR, Horan TC, et al: Risk factors for surgical site infection following craniotomy operation reported to the National Nosocomial Infections Surveillance System. Presented at the 4th Decennial International Conference on Nosocomial and Healthcare-Associated Infections, March 5–9, 2000, Atlanta, Georgia, p 153

30. Horan TC, Edwards JR, Culver DH, et al: Risk factors for endometritis after cesarean section: results of a 5-year multicenter study. Presented at the 4th Decennial International Conference on Nosocomial and Healthcare-Associated Infections; March 5-9, 2000, Atlanta, Georgia, p 151

31. Pittet D, Mourouga P, Perneger TV: Compliance with handwashing in a teaching hospital. Ann Intern Med 130:126, 1999

32. Pittet D, Hugonnet S, Harbath S, et al: Effectiveness of a hospital-wide programme to improve compliance with hand hygiene. Lancet 356:1307, 2000

33. Larson EL: APIC guideline for handwashing and hand antisepsis in health care settings. Am J Infect Control 23:251, 1995

34. Rotter ML: Hand washing and hand disinfection. Hospital Epidemiology and Infection Control, 2nd ed. Mayhall CG, Ed. Lippincott Williams & Wilkins, Philadelphia, 1999, p 1339

35. Spaulding EH: Chemical disinfection and antisepsis in the hospital. J Hosp Res 9:5, 1972

36. Association for the Advancement of Medical Instrumentation Flash sterilization: steam sterilization of patient care items for immediate use (ANSI/AAMI ST37-1996). Association for the Advancement of Medical Instrumentation, Arlington, Virginia, 1996

37. Dean AG: Transmission of Salmonella typhi by fiberoptic endoscopy. Lancet 2:134, 1977

38. Langenberg W, Rauws EAJ, Oudbier JH, et al: Patient-to-patient transmission of Campylobacter pylori infection by fiberoptic gastroduodenoscopy and biopsy. J Infect Dis 161:507, 1990

39. Rutala WA: APIC guideline for selection and use of disinfectants. Am J Infect Control 24:313, 1996

40. Rutala WA, Weber DJ: Disinfection of endoscopes: review of new chemical sterilants used for high-level disinfection. Infect Control Hosp Epidemiol 20:69, 1999

41. Enforcement priorities for single-use devices reprocessed by third parties and hospitals. United States Department of Health and Human Services, August 2000

42. The American Institute of Architects and the Facilities Guidelines Institute: Guidelines for Design and Construction of Hospital and Health Care Facilities, 2001. American Institute of Architects Press, Washington, DC, 2001

43. Sheretz RJ, Reagan DR, Hampton KD, et al: A cloud adult: the Staphylococcus aureus–virus interaction revisited. Ann Intern Med 124:539, 1996

44. Immunization of health-care workers: recommendations of the Advisory Committee on Immunization Practices (ACIP) and the Hospital Infection Control Practices Advisory Committee (HICPAC). MMWR Morb Mortal Wkly Rep 46(RR-18):1, 1997

45. Hospital Infection Control Practices Advisory Committee Guideline for isolation precautions in hospitals. Infect Control Hosp Epidemiol 17:53, 1996

46. Recommendations for preventing transmission of infection with human T-lymphotropic virus type III/lymphadenopathy-associated virus in the workplace. MMWR Morb Mortal Wkly Rep 34:681, 1985

47. Lynch P, Jackson MM, Cummings MJ, et al: Rethinking the role of isolation practices in the prevention of nosocomial infections. Ann Intern Med 107:243, 1987

48. Recommendations for preventing transmission of human immunodeficiency virus and hepatitis B virus to patients during exposure-prone invasive procedures. MMWR Morb Mortal Wkly Rep 40(RR-8):1, 1991

49. Robillard P: Epidemiology of blood borne pathogens (HIV, HBV, and HCV). Proceedings of a National Symposium on Risk and Prevention of Infectious Diseases for Emergency Response Personnel. Sept 27–28, 1994, Ottawa

50. Updated U.S. Public Health Service Guidelines for the management of occupational exposures to HBV, HCV, and HIV and recommendations for postexposure prophylaxis. MMWR Morb Mortal Wkly Rep 50(RR-11):1, 2001

51. White MC, Lynch P: Blood contact and exposure among operating room personnel: a multicenter study. Am J Infect Control 21:243, 1993

52. Chen CC, Willeke K: Aerosol penetration through surgical masks. Am J Infect Control 20:177, 1992

53. Rich P, Belozer ML, Norris P, et al: Allergic contact dermatitis to two antioxidants in latex gloves: 4,4′-thiobis(6-tert-butyl-meta-cresol) (Lowinox 44S36) and butylhydroxyanisole. J Am Acad Dermatol 24:37, 1991

54. Statement on the surgeon and hepatitis. Bull Am Coll Surg 84(4):21, 1999

55. Lanphear BP, Linnemann CC Jr, Cannon CG, et al: Hepatitis C virus infection in healthcare workers: risk of exposure and infection. Infect Control Hosp Epidemiol 15:745, 1994

56. Risk of hepatitis C seroconversion after occupational exposure in health care workers. Italian Study Group on Occupational Risk of HIV and Other Bloodborne Infections. Am J Infect Control 23:273, 1995

57. Mitsui T, Iwano K, Masuko K, et al: Hepatitis C virus infection in medical personnel after needlestick accident. Hepatology 16:1109, 1994

58. Sartori M, La Terra G, Aglietta M, et al: Transmission of hepatitis C via blood splash into conjunctiva (letter). Scand J Infect Dis 25:270, 1993

59. McKenna MT, Hutton MD, Cauthen G, et al: The association between occupation and tuberculosis: a population based survey. Am J Respir Crit Care Med 154:587, 1996

60. Menzies D, Fanning A, Yuan L, et al: Tuberculosis among health care workers. N Engl J Med 332:92, 1995

61. Guidelines for preventing the transmission of Mycobacterium tuberculosis in health-care facilities MMWR Morb Mortal Wkly Rep 43(RR-13):1, 1994

62. Pottinger JM, Herwaldt LA, Perl TM: Basics of surveillance-an overview. Infect Control Hosp Epidemiol 18:513, 1997

63. Haley RW: Surveillance by objective: a new priority-directed approach to the control of nosocomial infections. Am J Infect Control 13:78, 1985

64. Taylor S, McKenzie M, Taylor G, et al: Wound infection in total joint arthroplasty: effect of extended wound surveillance on infection rates. Can J Surg 37:217, 1994

65. Horan TC, Gaynes RP, Martone WJ: CDC definitions of nosocomial surgical site infections, 1992: a modification of CDC definitions of surgical wound infections. Infect Control Hosp Epidemiol 13:271, 1992

66. Evans RS, Burke JP, Classen DC, et al: Computerized identification of patients at high risk for hospital-acquired infection. Am J Infect Control 20:4, 1992

67. Nosocomial infection rates for interhospital comparison: limitations and possible solutions. Infect Control Hosp Epidemiol 12:609, 1991

68. Jarvis WR, Zaza S: Investigation of outbreaks. Hospital Epidemiology and Infection Control, 2nd ed. Mayhall CG, Ed. Lippincott Williams & Wilkins, Philadelphia, 1999, p 111

69. National Nosocomial Infections Surveillance (NNIS) System Report, data summary from January 1992 through June 2003, issued August 2003. Centers for Disease Control and Prevention. Am J Infect Control 31:481, 2003

70. Boyce JM, White RL, Spruill EY: Impact of methicillin-resistant Staphylococcus aureus on the incidence of nosocomial staphylococcal infections. J Infect Dis 148:763, 1983

71. Herold BC, Immergluck LC, Maranan MC, et al: Community-acquired methicillin-resistant Staphylococcus aureus in children with no identified predisposing risk. JAMA 279:593, 1998

72. Shopsin B, Mathema B, Martinez J, et al: Prevalence of methicillin-resistant and methicillin-susceptible Staphylococcus aureus in the community. J Infect Dis 182:359, 2000

73. Jans B, Suetens C, Struelens M: Decreasing MRSA rates in Belgian hospitals: results from the national surveillance network after introduction of national guidelines. Infect Control Hosp Epidemiol 21:419, 2000

74. Verhoef J, Beaujean D, Blok H, et al: A Dutch approach to methicillin-resistant Staphylococcus aureus. Eur J Clin Microbiol Infect Dis 18:461, 1999

75. Hiramatsu K, Hanaki H, Ino T, et al: Methicillin-resistant clinical strain with reduced vancomycin susceptibility. J Antimicrob Chemother 40:135, 1997

76. Interim guidelines for prevention and control of staphylococcal infection associated with reduced susceptibility to vancomycin. MMWR Morb Mortal Wkly Rep 46:626, 1997

77. Notskin GA, Stosor V, Cooper I, et al: Recovery of vancomycin-resistant enterococci on fingertips and environmental surfaces. Infect Control Hosp Epidemiol 16:577, 1995

78. Boyce JM: Vancomycin-resistant enterococcus: detection, epidemiology, and control measures. Infect Dis Clin North Am 11:367, 1997

79. Recommendations for preventing the spread of vancomycin resistance: recommendations of the Hospital Infection Control Practices Advisory Committee (HICPAC). MMWR Morb Mortal Wkly Rep 44(RR-12):1, 1995

80. Goldmann DA, Weinstein RA, Wenzel RP, et al: Strategies to prevent and control the emergence and spread of antimicrobial-resistant microorganisms in hospitals. JAMA 275:234, 1996

81. Guan Y, Zheng BJ, He YQ, et al: Isolation and characterization of viruses related to the SARS coronavirus from animals in southern China. Science 302: 276, 2003

82. Lee N, Hui D, Wu A, et al: A major outbreak of severe acute respiratory syndrome in Hong Kong. N Engl J Med 348: 1986, 2003

83. WHO: Consensus document. Global Meeting on the Epidemiology of SARS, Geneva, May 16–17, 2003. http://www.who.int/csr/sars/en/WHOconsensus.pdf

84. Lowry PW, Blankenship RJ, Gridley W, et al: A

cluster of *Legionella* sternal-wound infections due to postoperative topical exposure to contaminated tap water. N Engl J Med 324:109, 1991

85. Arnow PM, Chou T, Weil D, et al: Nosocomial Legionnaires' disease caused by aerosolized tap water from respiratory devices. J Infect Dis 146: 460, 1982

86. Guidelines for prevention of nosocomial pneumonia. MMWR Morb Mortal Wkly Rep 46(RR-1):1, 1997

87. Muraca PW, Yu VL, Goetz A: Disinfection of water distribution systems for *Legionella:* a review of application procedures and methodologies. Infect Control Hosp Epidemiol 11:79, 1990

88. Walsh TJ, Dixon DM: Nosocomial aspergillosis: environmental microbiology, hospital epidemiology, diagnosis, and treatment. Eur J Epidemiol 5:131, 1989

89. Haley RW, Culver DH, White JW, et al: The efficacy of infection surveillance and control programs in preventing nosocomial infections in US hospitals. Am J Epidemiol 121:182, 1985

90. Jarvis WR: Selected aspects of the socioeconomic impact of nosocomial infections: morbidity, mortality, cost and prevention. Infect Control Hosp Epidemiol 17:552, 1996

91. Pittet D, Tarara D, Wenzel RP: Nosocomial bloodstream infection in critically ill patients: excess length of stay, extra costs and attributable mortality. JAMA 271:1598, 1994

7 PERIOPERATIVE CONSIDERATIONS FOR ANESTHESIA

Steven B. Backman, M.D.C.M., Ph.D., Richard M. Bondy, M.D.C.M., Alain Deschamps, M.D., Ph.D., Anne Moore, M.D., and Thomas Schricker, M.D., Ph.D.

Ongoing advancements in modern surgical care are being complemented by alterations in anesthetic management aimed at providing maximum patient benefit. Since the early 1990s, anesthesia practice has changed enormously—through the proliferation of airway devices, the routine employment of patient-controlled analgesia (PCA), the wider popularity of thoracic epidural anesthesia, the development of computer-controlled devices for infusing short-acting drugs, the growing use of quickly reversible inhalational drugs and muscle relaxants, the availability of online monitoring of CNS function, and the increased application of transesophageal echocardiography, to name but a few examples. Our aim in this chapter is to offer surgeons a current perspective on perioperative considerations for anesthesia so as to facilitate dialogue between the surgeon and the anesthesiologist and thereby help minimize patient risk. The primary focus is on the adult patient: the special issues involved in pediatric anesthesia are beyond the scope of our review. In addition, the ensuing discussion is necessarily selective; more comprehensive discussions may be found elsewhere.[1,2]

Perioperative Patient Management

Preoperative medical evaluation is an essential component of preoperative assessment for anesthesia. Of particular importance to the anesthesiologist is any history of personal or family problems with anesthesia. Information should be sought concerning difficulty with airway management or intubation, drug allergy, delayed awakening, significant postoperative nausea or vomiting (PONV), unexpected hospital or ICU admission, and post–dural puncture headache (PDPH). Previous anesthetic records may be requested.

The airway must be carefully examined to identify patients at risk for difficult ventilation or intubation [*see* Special Scenarios, Difficult Airway, *below*], with particular attention paid to teeth, caps, crowns, dentures, and bridges. Patients must be informed about the risk of trauma associated with intubation and airway management. Anesthetic options [*see* Choice of Anesthesia, *below*] should be discussed, including the likelihood of postoperative ventilation and admission to the hospital or the intensive care unit. When relevant, the possibility of blood product administration should be raised [*see 8 Bleeding and Transfusion*], and the patient's acceptance or refusal of transfusion should be carefully documented. Postoperative pain management [*see 10 Postoperative Pain*] should be addressed, particularly when a major procedure is planned. The risks associated with general or regional anesthesia should be discussed in an informative and reassuring manner; a well-conducted preoperative anesthesia interview plays an important role in alleviating anxiety.

The medications the patient is taking can have a substantial impact on anesthetic management. Generally, patients should continue to take their regular medication up to the time of the operation. It is especially important not to abruptly discontinue medications that may result in withdrawal or rebound phenomena (e.g., beta blockers, alpha agonists, barbiturates, and opioids). With some medications (e.g., oral hypoglycemics, insulin, and corticosteroids), perioperative dosage adjustments may be necessary [*see 125 Endocrine Problems*]. Angiotensin-converting enzyme (ACE) inhibitors have been associated with intraoperative hypotension and may be withheld at the discretion of the anesthesiologist.[3] Drugs that should be discontinued preoperatively include monoamine oxidase inhibitors (MAOIs) and oral anticoagulants [*see Table 1*].

Many surgical patients are taking antiplatelet drugs. Careful consideration should be given to the withdrawal of these agents in the perioperative period [*see Table 1*] because of the possibility that discontinuance may lead to an acute coronary syndrome. If increased bleeding is a significant risk, longer-acting agents (e.g., aspirin, clopidogrel, and ticlopidine) can be replaced with nonsteroidal anti-inflammatory drugs (NSAIDs) that have shorter half-lives. Typically, these shorter-acting drugs are given for 10 days, stopped on the day of surgery, and then restarted 6 hours after operation. Platelet transfusion should be considered only in the presence of significant medical bleeding.[4]

The increasing use of herbal and alternative medicines has led to significant morbidity and mortality as a consequence of unexpected interactions with traditional drugs. Because many patients fail to mention such agents as part of their medication regimen during the preoperative assessment, it is advisable to question all patients directly about their use. Particular attention should be given to Chinese herbal teas, which include organic compounds and toxic contaminants that may produce renal fibrosis or failure, cholestasis, hepatitis, and thrombocytopenia. Specific recommendations for discontinuance for many of these agents have been developed [*see Table 1*].

Inpatient versus Outpatient Surgery

An ever-increasing number of operations are performed on an ambulatory basis. Operations considered appropriate for an ambulatory setting are associated with minimal physiologic trespass, low anesthetic complexity, and uncomplicated recovery.[5,6] The design of the ambulatory facility may impose limitations on the types of operations or patients that can be considered for ambulatory surgery. Such limitations may be secondary to availability of equipment, recovery room nursing expertise and access to consultants, and availability of ICU beds or hospital beds. Patients who are in class I or class II of the American Society of Anesthesiologists (ASA) physical status scale are ideally suited for ambulatory surgery; however, a subset of ASA class III patients may be at increased risk for prolonged recovery and hospital admission [*see Table 2*].

Premedication to produce anxiolysis, sedation, analgesia, amnesia, and reduction of PONV and aspiration may be considered for patients undergoing outpatient procedures, as it may for those

Table 1   Recommendations for Preoperative Discontinuance of Drugs and Medicines[51-64]

Type of Drug	Agent	Pharmacologic Effects	Adverse Effects	Discontinuance Recommendations
MAOIs	Isocarboxazid Phenelzine Pargyline Tranylcypromine Selegiline	Irreversible inhibition of mono-amine oxidase with the resultant increase in serotonin, norepineph-rine, epinephrine, dopamine, and octamine neurotransmitters	Potentiation of sympathomimetic amines, possible hypertensive crisis May prolong and intensify effects of other CNS depressants Severe idiopathic hyperpyrexic reaction with meperidine and possibly other narcotics Potential catastrophic interaction with tricyclic antidepressants, characterized by high fever and excessive cerebral excitation and hypertension	*Elective surgery:* discontinue at least 2 wk in advance; consider potential for suicidal tendency—mental health specialist should be involved *Emergency surgery:* avoid meperidine; consider regional anesthesia
Oral anticoagulants	Warfarin	Inhibition of vitamin K–dependent clotting factors II, VII, IX, X	Bleeding	*Elective surgery:* discontinue 5–7 days in advance; replace with heparin if necessary
Antiplatelet agents	*Aspirin and NSAIDs* Aspirin Fenoprofen Ibuprofen Sodium meclofenamate Tolmetin Indomethacin Ketoprofen Diflunisal Naproxen Sulindac Piroxicam	Inhibition of thromboxane A_2 80% of platelets must be inhibited for therapeutic effect Susceptibility to aspirin varies between patients	May increase intraoperative and post-operative bleeding, but not transfusion requirement Perioperative hemorrhagic complications increase with increasing half-life of drug	Primary hemostasis normalizes in 48 hr in healthy persons; platelet activity fully recovered in 8–10 days Patients on long-term aspirin therapy for coronary or cerebrovascular pathology should *not* discontinue drug in periopera-tive period unless hemorrhagic complica-tions of procedure outweigh risk of acute thrombotic event
	Thienopyridines Ticlopidine Clopidogrel	Inhibition of platelet aggregation Inhibition of platelet ADP–induced amplification	Synergistic antithrombotic effect with aspirin	Discontinue ticlopidine 2 wk in advance; discontinue clopidogrel 7–10 days in advance Patients with coronary artery stents must receive aspirin plus ticlopidine for 2–4 wk after angioplasty; stopping therapy con-siderably increases risk of coronary throm-bosis; elective surgery should be delayed for 1–3 mo
	Antiglycoprotein agents Eptifibatide Tirofiban Abciximab	Competitive inhibition of GPIIb/IIIa receptors to prevent platelet aggregation Rapid onset of action Short half-lives Often combined with aspirin and/or heparin	Literature (mainly from cardiac surgery) shows increased hemorrhagic risk if surgery undertaken < 12 hr after discontinuance of abciximab Individual variability in recovery time of platelet function	Discontinue at least 12 hr in advance Transfuse platelets only if needed to correct clinically significant bleeding

(continued)

undergoing inpatient procedures. Such premedication should not delay discharge. Fasting guidelines [*see Table 3*] and intraoperative monitoring standards for ambulatory surgery are identical to those for inpatient procedures [*see* Patient Monitoring, *below*].

A number of currently used anesthetics (e.g., propofol and des-flurane), narcotics (e.g., alfentanil, fentanyl, sufentanil, and remifentanil), and muscle relaxants (e.g., atracurium, mivacuri-um, and rocuronium) demonstrate rapid recovery profiles. Nitrous oxide also has desirable pharmacokinetic properties, but it may be associated with increased PONV. Titration of anesthet-ics to indices of CNS activity (e.g., the bispectral index) may result in decreased drug dosages, faster recovery from anesthesia, and fewer complications.[7,8] Multimodal analgesia (involving the use of local anesthetics, ketamine, α_2-adrenergic agonists, beta blockers, acetaminophen, or NSAIDs) may reduce intraoperative and post-operative opioid requirements and accelerate patient discharge. Use of a laryngeal mask airway (LMA) rather than an endotra-cheal tube is ideal in the outpatient setting because lower doses of

induction agent are required to blunt the hypertension and tachy-cardia associated with its insertion; in addition, it is associated with a decreased incidence of sore throat and does not require muscle paralysis for insertion. On the other hand, an LMA may not protect as well against aspiration.[5,9,10]

The benefits of regional anesthesia [*see* Regional Anesthesia Techniques, *below*] may include decreases in the incidence of aspi-ration, nausea, dizziness, and disorientation. Spinal and epidural anesthesia may be associated with PDPH and backache. Compared with spinal anesthesia, epidural anesthesia takes more time to perform, has a slower onset of action, and may not pro-duce as profound a block; however, the duration of an epidural block can readily be extended intraoperatively or postoperatively if necessary. Care should be exercised in choosing a local anesthetic for neuraxial blockade: spinal lidocaine may be associated with a transient radicular irritation, and bupivacaine may be associated with prolonged motor block; narcotics may produce pruritus, uri-nary retention, nausea and vomiting, and respiratory depression.

Table 1 (*continued*)

Type of Drug	Agent	Pharmacologic Effects	Adverse Effects	Discontinuance Recommendations
Herbal medicines	Garlic (*Allium sativum*)	Irreversible dose-dependent inhibition of platelet aggregation	Increased bleeding May potentiate other platelet inhibitors	Discontinue at least 7 days in advance
	Ginkgo (*Ginkgo biloba*)	Inhibition of platelet-activating factor Modulation of neurotransmitter receptor activity	Increased bleeding May potentiate other platelet inhibitors	Discontinue at least 36 hr in advance
	Ginger (*Zingiber officinale*)	Potent inhibitor of thromboxane synthase	Increased bleeding May potentiate effects of other anticoagulants	Discontinue at least 36 hr in advance
	Ginseng (*Panax ginseng*)	Inhibition of platelet aggregation, possibly irreversibly Antioxidant action Antihyperglycemic action "Steroid hormone"–like activity	Prolonged PT and PTT Hypoglycemia Reduced anticoagulation effect of warfarin Possible additive effect with other stimulants, with resultant hypertension and tachycardia	Discontinue at least 7 days in advance
	Ephedra/ma huang (*Ephedra sinica*)	Noncatecholamine sympatho-mimetic agent with α_1, β_1, and β_2 activity; both direct and indirect release of endogenous catecholamines	Dose-dependent increase in HR and BP, with potential for serious cardiac and CNS complications Possible adverse drug reactions: MAOIs (life-threatening hypertension, hyper-pyrexia, coma), oxytocin (hypertension), digoxin and volatile anesthetics (dysrhythmias), guanethedine (hypertension, tachycardia)	Discontinue at least 24 hr in advance
	Echinacea (*Echinacea purpurea*)	Immunostimulatory effect	Hepatotoxicity Allergic potential	Discontinue as far in advance as possible in any patient with hepatic dysfunction or surgery with possible hepatic blood flow compromise
	Licorice (*Glycyrrhiza glabra*)		Hypertension Hypokalemia Edema Contraindicated in chronic liver and renal insufficiency	
	Kava (*Piper methysticum*)	Dose-dependent potentiation of GABA-inhibitory neurotransmitter with sedative, anxiolytic, and antiepileptic effects	Potentiation of sedative anesthetics, including barbiturates and benzodi-azepines Possible potentiation of ethanol effects	
	Valerian (*Valeriana officinalis*)	Dose-dependent modulation of GABA neurotransmitter and receptor function	Possible potentiation of sedative anesthetics, including barbiturates and benzodiazepines	Discontinue at least 24 hr in advance
	St. John's wort (*Hypericum perforatum*)	Inhibits reuptake of serotonin, norepinephrine, and dopamine by neurons Increases metabolism of some P-450 isoforms	Possible interaction with MAOIs Evidence for reduced activity of cyclosporine, warfarin, calcium chan-nel blockers, lidocaine, midazolam, alfentanil, and NSAIDs	Discontinue on day of surgery; abrupt with-drawal in physically dependent patients may produce benzodiazepine-like with-drawal syndrome

ADP—adenosine diphosphate ETOH—ethyl alcohol GABA—γ-aminobutyric acid GP—glycoprotein MAOIs—monoamine oxidase inhibitors NSAIDs—nonsteroidal anti-inflammatory drugs PT—prothrombin time PTT—partial thromboplastin time

Various dosing regimens, including minidose spinal techniques, have been proposed as means of minimizing these side effects.[11-14]

Monitored anesthesia care [*see* Choice of Anesthesia, *below*] achieves minimal CNS depression, so that the airway and spontaneous ventilation are maintained and the patient is able to respond to verbal commands. Meticulous attention to monitoring is required to guard against airway obstruction, arterial desaturation, and pulmonary aspiration.

In the recovery room, the anesthetic plan is continued until discharge. Shorter-acting narcotics and NSAIDs are administered for pain relief, and any of several agents may be given for control of nausea and vomiting. Criteria for discharge from the recovery room have been established [*see Table 4*]. Recovery of normal muscle strength and sensation (including proprioception of the lower extremity, autonomic function, and ability to void) should be demonstrated after spinal or epidural anesthesia. Delays in discharge are usually the result of pain, PONV, hypotension, dizziness, unsteady gait, or lack of an escort.[15]

Elective versus Emergency Surgery

Surgical procedures performed on an emergency basis may range from relatively low priority (e.g., a previously cancelled case that was originally elective) to highly urgent (e.g., a case of

Table 2 Association between Preexisting
Medical Conditions and Adverse Outcomes[65]

Medical Condition	Associated Adverse Outcome
Congestive heart failure	12% prolongation of postoperative stay
Hypertension	Twofold increase in risk of intraoperative cardiovascular events
Asthma	Fivefold increase in risk of postoperative respiratory events
Smoking	Fourfold increase in risk of postoperative respiratory events
Obesity	Fourfold increase in risk of intraoperative and postoperative respiratory events
Reflux	Eightfold increase in risk of intubation-related adverse events

impending airway obstruction). For trauma, specific evaluation and resuscitation sequences have been established to facilitate patient management [*see 100 Initial Management of Life-Threatening Trauma*]. The urgency of the situation dictates how much time can be allotted to preoperative patient assessment and optimization. When it is not possible to communicate with the patient, information obtained from family members and paramedics may be crucial. Information should be sought concerning allergies, current medications, significant past medical illnesses, nihil per os (NPO) status, personal or family problems with anesthesia, and recent ingestion of alcohol or drugs. Any factor that may complicate airway management should be noted (e.g., trauma to the face or the neck, a beard, a short and thick neck, obesity, or a full stomach). When appropriate, blood samples should be obtained as soon as possible for typing and crossmatching, as well as routine blood chemistries and a complete blood count. Arrangements for postoperative ICU monitoring, if appropriate, should be instituted early.

Clear communication must be established between the surgical team and anesthesia personnel so that an appropriate anesthetic management plan can be formulated and any specialized equipment required can be mobilized in the OR. The induction of anesthesia may coincide with resuscitation. Accordingly, the surgical team must be immediately available to help with difficult I.V. access, emergency tracheostomy, and cardiopulmonary resuscitation. Patients in shock may not tolerate standard anesthetics, which characteristically blunt sympathetic outflow. The anesthetic dose must be judiciously titrated, and definitive surgical treatment must not be unduly delayed by attempts to "get a line."

Choice of Anesthesia

Anesthesia may be classified into three broad categories: (1) general anesthesia, (2) regional anesthesia, and (3) monitored anesthesia care. General anesthesia can be defined as a state of insensibility characterized by loss of consciousness, amnesia, analgesia, and muscle relaxation. This state may be achieved either with a single anesthetic or, in a more balanced fashion, with a combination of several drugs that specifically induce hypnosis, analgesia, amnesia, and paralysis.

There is, at present, no consensus as to which general anesthetic regimen best preserves organ function. General anesthesia is employed when contraindications to regional anesthesia are present or when regional anesthesia or monitored anesthesia care fails to provide adequate intraoperative analgesia. In addition, there are a few situations that specifically mandate general anesthesia and

controlled ventilation: the need for abdominal muscle paralysis, lung isolation, and hyperventilation; the presence of serious cardiorespiratory instability; and the lack of sufficient time to perform regional anesthesia. Alternatives to general anesthesia should be considered for patients who are susceptible to malignant hyperthermia (MH), for those in whom intubation is likely to prove difficult or the risk of aspiration is high, and for those with pulmonary compromise that may worsen after intubation and positive pressure ventilation.

Regional anesthesia is achieved by interfering with afferent or efferent neural signaling at the level either of the spinal cord (neuraxial blockade) or of the peripheral nerves. Neuraxial anesthesia (i.e., epidural or spinal administration of local anesthetics) is commonly employed as the sole anesthetic technique for procedures involving the lower abdomen and the lower extremities; it also provides effective pain relief after intraperitoneal and intrathoracic procedures. Combining regional and general anesthesia has become increasingly popular.[16] Currently, some physicians are using neuraxial blockade as the sole anesthetic technique for procedures such as thoracotomy and coronary artery bypass grafting, which are traditionally thought to require general anesthesia and endotracheal intubation.[17]

Neuraxial blockade has several advantages over general anesthesia, including better dynamic pain control, shorter duration of paralytic ileus, reduced risk of pulmonary complications, and decreased transfusion requirements; it is also associated with a decreased incidence of renal failure and myocardial infarction [*see 10 Postoperative Pain*].[18-21] Contrary to conventional thinking, however, the type of anesthesia used (general or neuraxial) is not an independent risk factor for long-term cognitive dysfunction.[22] Neuraxial blockade is an essential component of multimodal rehabilitation programs aimed at optimization of perioperative care and acceleration of recovery.[23,24]

For short, superficial procedures, a wide variety of peripheral nerve blocks may be considered.[25] For procedures on the upper or lower extremity, an I.V. regional (Bier) block with diluted lidocaine is often useful. Anesthesia of the upper extremity and shoulder may be achieved with brachial plexus blocks. Anesthesia of the lower extremity may be achieved by blocking the femoral, obturator, and lateral femoral cutaneous nerves (for knee surgery) or the ankle and popliteal sciatic nerves (for foot surgery). Anesthesia of the thorax may be achieved with intercostal or intrapleural nerve blocks. Anesthesia of the abdomen may be achieved with celiac

Table 3 Fasting Recommendations* to
Reduce Risk of Pulmonary Aspiration[66]

Ingested Material	Minimum Fasting Period† (hr)
Clear liquids‡	2
Breast milk	4
Infant formula	6
Nonhuman milk§	6
Light meal¶	8

*These recommendations apply to healthy patients undergoing elective procedures; they are not intended for women in labor. Following the guidelines does not guarantee complete gastric emptying.
†These fasting periods apply to all ages.
‡Examples of clear liquids include water, fruit juices without pulp, carbonated beverages, clear tea, and black coffee.
§Because nonhuman milk is similar to solids in gastric emptying time, amount ingested must be considered in determining appropriate fasting period.
¶A light meal typically consists of toast and clear liquids. Meals that include fried or fatty foods or meat may prolong gastric emptying time. Both amount and type of foods ingested must be considered in determining appropriate fasting period.

Table 4   Postanesthetic Discharge
Scoring System (PADSS)[67]

Category	Score*	Explanation
Vital signs	2	Within 20% of preoperative value
	1	Within 20% to 40% of preoperative value
	0	Within 40% of preoperative value
Activity, mental status	2	Oriented and steady gait
	1	Oriented or steady gait
	0	Neither
Pain, nausea, vomiting	2	Minimal
	1	Moderate
	0	Severe
Surgical bleeding	2	Minimal
	1	Moderate
	0	Severe
Intake/output	2	Oral fluid intake and voiding
	1	Oral fluid intake or voiding
	0	Neither

*Total possible score is 10; patients scoring ≥ 9 are considered fit for discharge home.

plexus and paravertebral blocks. Anesthesia of the head and neck may be achieved by blocking the trigeminal, supraorbital, supratrochlear, infraorbitral, and mental nerves and the cervical plexus. Local infiltration of the operative site may provide intraoperative as well as postoperative analgesia.

Unlike the data on neuraxial blockade, the data on peripheral nerve blockade neither support nor discourage its use as a substitute for general anesthesia. Generally, however, we favor regional techniques when appropriate: such approaches maintain consciousness and spontaneous breathing while causing only minimal depression of the CNS and the cardiorespiratory system, and they yield improved pain control in the immediate postoperative period.

Monitored anesthesia care involves the use of I.V. drugs to reduce anxiety, provide analgesia, and alleviate the discomfort of immobilization. This approach may be combined with local infiltration analgesia provided by the surgeon. Monitored anesthesia care requires monitoring of vital signs and the presence of an anesthesiologist who is prepared to convert to general anesthesia if necessary. Its benefits are substantially similar to those of regional anesthesia. These benefits are lost when attempts are made to overcome surgical pain with excessive doses of sedatives and analgesics.

Table 5   Benzodiazepines: Doses
and Duration of Action[68]

Benzodiazepine	Dose (for Sedation)	Elimination Half-life	Comments
Midazolam	0.5–1.0 mg, repeated	1.7–2.6 hr	Respiratory depression, excessive sedation, hypotension, bradycardia, withdrawal Anticonvulsant activity
Lorazepam	0.25 mg, repeated	11–22 hr	See midazolam Venous thrombosis
Diazepam	2.0 mg, repeated	20–50 hr	See midazolam and lorazepam

Patient Monitoring

Patient monitoring is central to the practice of anesthesia. A trained, experienced physician is the only truly indispensable monitor; mechanical and electronic monitors, though useful, are, at most, aids to vigilance. Wherever anesthesia is administered, the proper equipment for pulse oximetry, blood pressure measurement, electrocardiography, and capnography should be available. At each anesthesia workstation, equipment for measuring temperature, a peripheral nerve stimulator, a stethoscope, and appropriate lighting must be immediately available. A spirometer must be available without undue delay.

Additional monitoring may be indicated, depending on the patient's health, the type of procedure to be performed, and the characteristics of the practice setting. Cardiovascular monitoring, including measurement of systemic arterial, central venous, pulmonary arterial, and wedge pressures, is covered in detail elsewhere [*see 119 Cardiovascular Monitoring*]. Additional information about the cardiovascular system may be obtained by means of transesophageal echocardiography.[26] Practice guidelines for this modality have been developed.[27] It may be particularly useful in patients who are undergoing valvular repair or who have persistent severe hypotension of unknown etiology.

The effects of anesthesia and surgery on the CNS may be monitored by recording processed electroencephalographic activity, as in the bispectral index or the Patient State Index. These indices are used as measures of hypnosis to guide the administration of anesthetics.[28,29]

General Anesthesia Techniques

An ever-expanding armamentarium of drugs is available for premedication and for induction and maintenance of anesthesia. Selection of one agent over another is influenced by the patient's baseline condition, the procedure, and the predicted duration of hospitalization.

PREMEDICATION

Preoperative medications are given primarily to decrease anxiety, to reduce the incidence of nausea and vomiting, and to prevent aspiration. Other benefits include sedation, amnesia, analgesia, drying of oral secretions, and blunting of undesirable autonomic reflexes.

Sedatives and Analgesics

Benzodiazepines produce anxiolysis, sedation, hypnosis, amnesia, and muscle relaxation; they do not produce analgesia. They may be classified as short-acting (midazolam), intermediate-acting (lorazepam), or long-acting (diazepam). Adverse effects [*see Table 5*] may be marked in debilitated patients. Their central effects may be antagonized with flumazenil.

Muscarinic antagonists (e.g., scopolamine and atropine) were commonly administered at one time; this practice is not as popular today. They produce, to varying degrees, sedation, amnesia, lowered anesthetic requirements, diminished nausea and vomiting, reduced oral secretions, and decreased gastric hydrogen ion secretion. They blunt the cardiac parasympathetic reflex responses that may occur during certain procedures (e.g., ocular surgery, traction on the mesentery, and manipulation of the carotid body). Adverse effects include tachycardia, heat intolerance, inhibition of GI motility and micturition, and mydriasis.

Opioids are used when analgesia, in addition to sedation and anxiolysis, is required. With morphine and meperidine, the time of

Table 6 Opioids: Doses and Duration of Action[69]

Agent	Relative Analgesic Potency	Dose		Time to Peak Effect	Duration of Action	Comments
		Induction	Maintenance			
Morphine	1	1 mg/kg	For perioperative analgesia: 0.1 mg/kg I.V., I.M.	5–20 min	2–7 hr	Respiratory depression, nausea, vomiting, pruritus, constipation, urinary retention, biliary spasm, neuroexcitation ± seizure, tolerance Cough suppression, relief of dyspnea-induced anxiety (common to all opioids) Histamine release, orthostatic hypotension, prolonged emergence
Meperidine	0.1	NA	For perioperative analgesia: 0.5–1.5 mg/kg I.V., I.M., s.c.	2 hr (oral); 1 hr (s.c., I.M.)	2–4 hr	See morphine Orthostatic hypotension, myocardial depression, dry mouth, mild tachycardia, mydriasis, histamine release Attenuates shivering; to be avoided with MAOIs Local anesthetic–like effect
Remifentanil	250–300	1 µg/kg	0.25–0.4 µg/kg/min	3–5 min	5–10 min	See morphine Awareness, bradycardia, muscle rigidity Ideal for infusion; fast recovery, no postoperative analgesia
Alfentanil	7.5–25	50–300 µg/kg	1.25–8.0 µg/kg/min	1–2 min	10–15 min	See morphine Awareness, bradycardia, muscle rigidity
Fentanyl	75–125	5–30 µg/kg	0.25–0.5 µg/kg/min	5–15 min	30–60 min	See morphine and alfentanil
Sufentanil	525–625	2–20 µg/kg	0.05–0.1 µg/kg/min	3–5 min	20–45 min	See morphine and alfentanil Ideal for prolonged infusion

onset of action and the peak effect are unpredictable. Fentanyl has a rapid onset and a predictable time course, which make it more suitable for premedication immediately before operation. Adverse effects [*see Table 6*] can be reversed with full (naloxone) or partial (e.g., nalbuphine) antagonists.

The α_2-adrenergic agonists clonidine and dexmedetomidine are sympatholytic drugs that also exert sedative, anxiolytic, and analgesic effects. They reduce intraoperative anesthetic requirements, thus allowing faster recovery, and attenuate sympathetic activation secondary to intubation and surgery, thus improving intraoperative hemodynamic stability. Major drawbacks are hypotension and bradycardia; rebound hypertensive crises may be precipitated by their discontinuance.[30,31]

Prevention of Aspiration

Aspiration of gastric contents is an extremely serious complication that is associated with significant morbidity and mortality.

Fasting helps reduce the risk of this complication [*see Table 3*]. When the likelihood of aspiration is high, pharmacologic treatment may be helpful [*see Table 7*]. H_2-receptor antagonists (e.g., cimetidine, ranitidine, and famotidine) and proton pump inhibitors (e.g., omeprazole) reduce gastric acid secretion, thereby raising gastric pH without affecting gastric volume or emptying time. Nonparticulate antacids (e.g., sodium citrate) neutralize the acidity of gastric contents. Metoclopramide promotes gastric emptying (by stimulating propulsive GI motility) and decreases reflux (by increasing the tone of the esophagogastric sphincter); it may also possess antiemetic properties.

In all patients at risk for aspiration who require general anesthesia, a rapid sequence induction is essential. This is achieved through adequate preoxygenation, administration of drugs to produce rapid loss of consciousness and paralysis, and exertion of pressure on the cricoid cartilage (the Sellick maneuver) as loss of consciousness occurs to occlude the esophagus and so limit reflux of gastric con-

Table 7 Pharmacologic Prevention of Aspiration[70,71]

Agent	Dose	Timing of Administration before Operation	Comments
H_2 receptor antagonists		1–3 hr	
Cimetidine	300 mg, p.o.		Hypotension, bradycardia, heart block, increased airway resistance, CNS dysfunction, reduced hepatic metabolism of certain drugs
Ranitidine	50 mg I.V.		Bradycardia
Famotidine	20 mg I.V.		Rare CNS dysfunction
Sodium citrate	30 ml p.o.	20–30 min	Increased gastric fluid volume
Omeprazole	40 mg I.V.	40 min	Possible alteration of GI drug absorption, hepatic metabolism
Metoclopramide	10 mg I.V.	15–30 min	Extrapyramidal reactions, agitation, restlessness (large doses); to be avoided with MAOIs, pheochromocytoma, bowel obstruction

Table 8 Induction Agents: Doses and Duration of Action[68]

Agent	Induction Dose	Time to Peak Effect (sec)	Duration of Action (min)	Comments
Propofol	1.0–2.5 mg/kg	90–100	5–10	Hypotension, apnea, antiemetic (low dose), sexual fantasies and hallucinations, convulsions ± seizures (rare), pain on injection, thrombophlebitis
Thiopental	2.5–4.5 mg/kg	60	5–8	Hypotension, apnea, emergence delirium, prolonged somnolence, anaphylactoid reaction, injection pain, hyperalgesia Anticonvulsant effect Contraindicated with porphyria
Ketamine	0.5–2 mg/kg	30	10–15	Analgesia; increased BP, HR, CO; lacrimation and salivation; bronchial dilatation; elevated ICP Dreaming, illusions, excitement Preservation of respiration (apnea possible with high doses)
Etomidate	0.2–0.6 mg/kg	60	4–10	Minor effects on BP, HR, CO Adrenocortical suppression, injection pain and thrombophlebitis, myoclonus, nausea and vomiting

CO—cardiac output

tents into the pharynx. An alternative is the so-called modified rapid sequence induction, which permits gentle mask ventilation during the application of cricoid pressure (thereby potentially reducing or abolishing insufflation of gas into the stomach). The advantages of the modified approach are that there is less risk of hypoxia and that there is more time to treat cardiovascular responses to induction agents before intubation. Regardless of which technique is used, consideration should be given to emptying the stomach via an orogastric or nasogastric tube before induction.

INDUCTION

Induction of general anesthesia is produced by administering drugs to render the patient unconscious and secure the airway. It is one of the most crucial and potentially dangerous moments for the patient during general anesthesia. Various agents can be used for this purpose; the choice depends on the patient's baseline medical condition and fasting status, the state of the airway, the surgical procedure, and the expected length of the hospital stay. The agents most commonly employed for induction are propofol, sodium thiopental, ketamine, and etomidate [see Table 8]. The opioids alfentanil, fentanyl, sufentanil, and remifentanil are also used for this purpose; they are associated with a very stable hemodynamic profile during induction and operation [see Table 6].

Volatile agents [see Table 9] may be employed for induction of general anesthesia when maintenance of spontaneous ventilation is of paramount importance (e.g., with a difficult airway) or when bronchodilation is required (e.g., with severe hyperreactive airway disease). Inhalation induction is also popular for ambulatory surgery when paralysis is not required. Sevoflurane is well suited for this application because it is not irritating on inhalation, as most other volatile agents are, and it produces rapid loss of consciousness. Sevoflurane has mostly replaced halothane as the agent of choice for inhalation induction because it is less likely to cause dysrhythmias and is not hepatotoxic.

MAINTENANCE

Balanced general anesthesia is produced with a variety of drugs to maintain unconsciousness, prevent recall, and provide analgesia. Various combinations of volatile and I.V. agents may be employed to achieve these goals. The volatile agents isoflurane, desflurane, and sevoflurane are commonly used for maintenance [see Table 9]. Nitrous oxide is a strong analgesic and a weak anesthetic agent that possesses favorable pharmacokinetic properties. It cannot be used as the sole anesthetic agent unless it is adminis-

Table 9 Volatile Drugs[72,73]

Agent	Oil/Gas Coefficient*	MAC† (atm)	Blood/Gas Coefficient‡	Rank Order (F_A/F_I)§
Halothane	224	0.0074	2.5	6
Enflurane	96.5	0.0168	1.8	5
Isoflurane	90.8	0.0115	1.4	4
Desflurane	18.7	0.060	0.45	2
Sevoflurane	47.2	0.0236	0.65	3
Nitrous oxide	1.4	1.04	0.47	1

*Lipid solubility correlates closely with anesthetic potency (Meyer-Overton rule).
†Correlates closely with lipid solubility.
‡Relative affinity of an anesthetic for blood compared to gas at equilibrium. The larger the coefficient, the greater the affinity of the drug for blood and hence the greater the quantity of drug contained in the blood.
§Rise in alveolar anesthetic concentration towards the inspired concentration is most rapid with the least soluble drugs and slowest with the most soluble.
F_A/F_I—alveolar concentration of gas/inspired concentration   MAC—minimum alveolar concentration to abolish purposeful movement in response to noxious stimulation in 50% of patients

Table 10   Neuromuscular Blocking Agents: Doses and Duration of Action[74]

Agent	Dose (mg/kg)	Duration of Action[1] (min)	Metabolism	Elimination	Comments
Succinylcholine chloride	0.7–2.5	5–10	Plasma cholinesterase	Renal < 2%, hepatic 0%	Fasciculations, elevation of serum potassium, increased ICP, bradycardia, MH trigger; prolonged effect in presence of atypical pseudocholinesterase
Pancuronium	0.04–0.1	60–120	Hepatic 10%–20%	Renal 85%, hepatic 15%	Muscarinic antagonist (vagolytic), prolonged paralysis (long-term use)
Rocuronium	0.6–1.2	35–75	None	Renal < 10%, hepatic > 70%	Minimal histamine release
Vecuronium	0.08–0.1	45–90	Hepatic 30%–40%	Renal 40%, hepatic 60%	Prolonged paralysis (long-term use)
Atracurium	0.3–0.5	30–45	Hoffman elimination, nonspecific ester hydrolysis	Renal 10%–40%, hepatic 0%	Histamine release; laudanosine metabolite (a CNS stimulant)
Cisatracurium	0.15–0.2	40–75	Hoffman elimination	Renal 16%, hepatic 0%	Negligible histamine release; laudanosine metabolite
Mivacurium	0.15–0.2	15–20	Plasma cholinesterase	Renal < 5%, hepatic 0%	Histamine release; prolonged effect in presence of atypical pseudocholinesterase

tered in a hyperbaric chamber; it is usually administered with at least 30% oxygen to prevent hypoxia. Nitrous oxide is commonly used in combination with other volatile agents. All of the volatile agents can trigger malignant hyperthermia in susceptible patients.

The I.V. drugs currently used to maintain general anesthesia, whether partially or entirely, feature a short context-sensitive elimination half-life; thus, pharmacologically significant drug accumulation during prolonged infusion is avoided. Such agents (including propofol, midazolam, sufentanil, and remifentanil) are typically administered via computer-controlled infusion pumps that use population-based pharmacokinetic data to establish stable plasma (and CNS effector site) concentrations. Because of the extremely rapid hydrolysis of remifentanil, its administration may be labor intensive, necessitating frequent administration of boluses and constant vigilance. Its short half-life also limits its usefulness as an analgesic in the postoperative period and may even contribute to acute opioid intolerance. To help circumvent these problems, various dosing regimens have been proposed in which the patient is switched from remifentanil to a longer-acting narcotic.

NEUROMUSCULAR BLOCKADE

The reversible paralysis produced by neuromuscular blockade improves conditions for endotracheal intubation and facilitates surgery. Neuromuscular blocking agents are classified as either depolarizing (succinylcholine) or nondepolarizing (pancuronium,

rocuronium, vecuronium, atracurium, cisatracurium, and mivacurium) and may be further differentiated on the basis of chemical structure and duration of action [*see Table 10*]. The blocking effect of nondepolarizing muscle relaxants is enhanced by volatile drugs, hypothermia, acidosis, certain antibiotics, magnesium sulfate, and local anesthetics and is reduced by phenytoin and carbamazepine. Patients with weakness secondary to neuromuscular disorders (e.g., myasthenia gravis and Eaton-Lambert syndrome) may be particularly sensitive to nondepolarizing muscle relaxants.

EMERGENCE

General anesthesia is terminated by cessation of drug administration, reversal of paralysis, and extubation. During this period, close scrutiny of the patient is essential, and all OR personnel must coordinate their efforts to help ensure a smooth and safe emergence. In this phase, patients may demonstrate hemodynamic instability, retching and vomiting, respiratory compromise, and, occasionally, uncooperative or aggressive behavior.

Reversal of neuromuscular blockade is achieved by administering anticholinesterases such as neostigmine and edrophonium. These drugs should be given in conjunction with a muscarinic antagonist (atropine or glycopyrrolate) to block their unwanted parasympathomimetic side effects. Neostigmine is more potent than edrophonium in reversing profound neuromuscular blockade. It is imperative that paralysis be sufficiently reversed before

Table 11   Pharmacology of Anticoagulant Agents

Drug	Coagulation Tests		Time to Peak Effect	Time to Normal Hemostasis after Discontinuance
	INR	PTT		
Heparin				
I.V.	⇔	⇑	min	4–6 hr
s.c.	⇔	↑	1 hr	4–6 hr
LMWH	⇔	⇔	2–4 hr	12 hr
Warfarin	⇑	⇔	2–6 days	4–6 days
Aspirin	⇔	⇔	hr	5–8 days
Thrombolytic agents (t-PA, streptokinase)	⇔	⇑	min	1–2 days

⇑—clinically significant increase   ↑—possibly clinically significant increase   ⇔—clinically insignificant increase or no effect
LMWH—low-molecular-weight heparin   t-PA—tissue plasminogen activator

extubation to ensure that spontaneous respiration is adequate and that the airway can be protected. Reversal can be clinically verified by confirming the patient's ability to lift the head for 5 seconds. Reversal can also be assessed by measuring muscle contraction in response to electrical nerve stimulation.

Causes of failure to emerge from anesthesia include residual neuromuscular blockade, a benzodiazepine or opioid overdose, the central anticholinergic syndrome, an intraoperative cerebrovascular accident, preexisting pathophysiologic conditions (e.g., CNS disorders, hepatic insufficiency, and drug or alcohol ingestion), electrolyte abnormalities, acidosis, hypercarbia, hypoxia, hypothermia, and hypothyroidism. As noted, the effects of narcotics and benzodiazepines can be reversed with naloxone and flumazenil, respectively. Physostigmine may be given to reverse the reduction in consciousness level produced by general anesthetics. Electrolyte, glucose, blood urea nitrogen, and creatinine levels should be measured; liver and thyroid function tests should be performed; and arterial blood gas values should be obtained. Patients should be normothermic. Unexplained failure to emerge from general anesthesia warrants immediate consultation with a neurologist.

Regional Anesthesia Techniques

Neuraxial (central) anesthesia techniques involve continuous or intermittent injection of drugs into the epidural or intrathecal space to produce sensory analgesia, motor blockade, and inhibition of sympathetic outflow. Peripheral nerve blockade involves inhibition of conduction in fibers of a single peripheral nerve or plexus (cervical, brachial, or lumbar) in the periphery. Intravenous regional anesthesia involves I.V. administration of a local anesthetic into a tourniquet-occluded extremity. Perioperative pain control may be facilitated by administering local anesthetics, either infiltrated into the wound or sprayed into the wound cavity.[32,33] Procedures performed solely under infiltration may be associated with patient dissatisfaction caused by intraoperative anxiety and pain.[34]

CONTRAINDICATIONS

Strong contraindications to regional (particularly neuraxial) anesthesia include patient refusal or inability to cooperate during the procedure, elevated intracranial pressure, anticoagulation, vascular malformation or infection at the needle insertion site, severe hemodynamic instability, and sepsis. Preexisting neurologic disease is a relative contraindication.

ANTICOAGULATION AND BLEEDING RISK

Although hemorrhagic complications can occur after any regional technique, bleeding associated with neuraxial blockade is the most serious possibility because of its devastating consequences. Spinal hematoma may occur as a result of vascular trauma from placement of a needle or catheter into the subarachnoid or epidural space. Spinal hematoma may also occur spontaneously, even in the absence of antiplatelet or anticoagulant therapy. The actual incidence of spinal cord injury resulting from hemorrhagic complications is unknown; the reported incidence is estimated to be less than 1/150,000 for epidural anesthesia and 1/220,000 for spinal anesthesia.[35] With such low incidences, it is difficult to determine whether any increased risk can be attributed to anticoagulant use [see Table 11] without data from millions of patients, which are not currently available. Much of our clinical practice is based on small surveys and expert opinion.

Antiplatelet Agents

There is no universally accepted test that can guide antiplatelet therapy. Antiplatelet agents can be divided into four major classes: (1) aspirin and related cyclooxygenase inhibitors (nonsteroidal anti-inflammatory drugs, or NSAIDs); (2) ticlopidine and selective adenosine diphosphate antagonists; (3) direct thrombin inhibitors (e.g., hirudin); and (4) glycoprotein IIb/IIIa inhibitors. Only with aspirin is there sufficient experience to suggest that it does not increase the risk of spinal hematoma when given at clinical dosages.[36] Caution should, however, be exercised when aspirin is used in conjunction with other anticoagulants.[37]

Oral Anticoagulants

Therapeutic anticoagulation with warfarin is a contraindication to regional anesthesia.[38] If regional anesthesia is planned, oral warfarin can be replaced with I.V. heparin (see below).

Heparin

There does not seem to be an increased risk of spinal bleeding in patients receiving subcutaneous low-dose (5,000 U) unfractionated heparin [see 85 Venous Thromboembolism] if the interval between administration of the drug and initiation of the procedure is greater than 4 hours.[39] Higher doses, however, are associated with increased risk. If neuraxial anesthesia or epidural catheter removal is planned, heparin infusion must be discontinued for at least 6 hours, and the partial thromboplastin time (PTT) should be measured. Recommendations for standard heparin cannot be extrapolated to low-molecular-weight heparin (LMWH), because the biologic actions of LMWH are different and the effects cannot be monitored by conventional coagulation measurements. After the release of LMWH for general use in the United States in 1993, more than 40 spinal hematomas were reported during a 5-year period. LMWH should be stopped at least 24 hours before regional blockade, and the first postoperative dose should be given no sooner than 24 hours afterward.[37]

COMPLICATIONS

Drug Toxicity

Systemic toxic reactions to local anesthetics primarily involve the CNS and the cardiovascular system [see Table 12]. The initial symptoms are light-headedness and dizziness, followed by visual and auditory disturbances. Convulsions and respiratory arrest may ensue and necessitate treatment and resuscitation.

The use of neuraxial analgesic adjuncts (e.g., opioids, clonidine, epinephrine, and neostigmine) decreases the dose of local anesthetic required, speeds recovery, and improves the quality of analgesia. The side effects of such adjuncts include respiratory depression (with morphine), tachycardia (with epinephrine), hypotension (with clonidine), and nausea and vomiting (with neostigmine and morphine).

Neurologic Complications

The incidence of neurologic complications ranges from 2/10,000 to 12/10,000 with epidural anesthesia and from 0.3/10,000 to 70/10,000 with spinal anesthesia.[40] The most common serious complication is neuropathy, followed by cranial nerve palsy, epidural abscess, epidural hematoma, anterior spinal artery syndrome, and cranial subdural hematoma. Vigilance and routine neurologic testing of sensory and motor function are of paramount importance for early detection and treatment of these potentially disastrous complications.

Table 12   Local Anesthetics for Infiltration Anesthesia:
Maximum Doses* and Duration of Action

Drug	Without Epinephrine		With Epinephrine (1:200,000)	
	Maximum Dose (mg)	Duration of Action (min)	Maximum Dose (mg)	Duration of Action (min)
Chloroprocaine	800	15–30	1,000	3–90
Lidocaine	300	30–60	500	120–360
Mepivacaine	300	45–90	500	120–360
Prilocaine	500	30–90	600	120–360
Bupivacaine	175	120–240	225	180–420
Etidocaine	300	120–180	400	180–420

*Recommended maximum dose can be given to healthy, middle-aged, normal-sized adults without toxicity.
Subsequent doses should not be given for at least 4 hr. Doses should be reduced during pregnancy.

Transient neurologic symptoms   The term transient neurologic symptoms (TNS) refers to backache with pain radiating into the buttocks or the lower extremities after spinal anesthesia. It occurs in 4% to 33% of patients, typically 12 to 36 hours after the resolution of spinal anesthesia, and lasts for 2 to 3 days.[41] TNS has been described after intrathecal use of all local anesthetics but is most commonly noted after administration of lidocaine, in the ambulatory surgical setting, and with the patient in the lithotomy position during operation. Discomfort from TNS is self-limited and can be effectively treated with NSAIDs.

Post–Dural Puncture Headache

Use of small-gauge pencil-point needles for spinal anesthesia is associated with a 1% incidence of PDPH. The incidence of PDPH after epidural analgesia varies substantially because the risk of inadvertent dural puncture with a Tuohy needle is directly dependent on the anesthesiologist's training. PDPH is characteristically aggravated by upright posture and may be associated with photophobia, neck stiffness, nausea, diplopia, and tinnitus. Meningitis should be considered in the differential diagnosis. Although PDPH is not life-threatening, it carries substantial morbidity in the form of restricted activity. Medical treatment with bed rest, I.V. fluids, NSAIDs, and caffeine is only moderately effective. An epidural blood patch is the treatment of choice: the success rate is approximately 70%.

Recovery

Admission to the postanesthetic care unit (PACU) is appropriate for patients whose vital signs are stable and whose pain is adequately controlled after emergence from anesthesia. Patients requiring hemodynamic or respiratory support may be admitted to the PACU if rapid improvement is expected and appropriate monitoring and personnel are available. Hemodynamic instability, the need for prolonged respiratory support, and poor baseline condition mandate admission of the patient to the ICU. Common complications encountered in the PACU include postoperative pulmonary insufficiency, cardiovascular instability, acute pain, and nausea and vomiting [*see Table 13*]. These complications are discussed in greater detail elsewhere [*see 120 Pulmonary Insufficiency, 117 Acute Cardiac Dysrhythmia, and 10 Postoperative Pain*].

Special Scenarios

DIFFICULT AIRWAY

Airway management is a pivotal component of patient care because failure to maintain airway patency can lead to permanent disability, brain injury, or death. The difficult airway should be managed in accordance with contemporary airway guidelines, such as the protocols established by the ASA, to reduce the risk of adverse outcomes during attempts at ventilation and intubation. (The ASA protocols may be accessed on the organization's Web site: http://www.asahq.org/publicationsandservices/difficult%20airway.pdf.) The emphasis on preserving spontaneous ventilation and the focus on awake intubation options are central themes whose importance cannot be overemphasized.

It is crucial that all patients who are undergoing difficult or prolonged airway instrumentation be appropriately treated with topical anesthesia, sedation, and monitoring so as to ensure adequate ventilation and to attenuate, detect, and treat harmful neuroendocrine responses that can cause myocardial ischemia, bronchospasm, and intracranial hypertension. Extubation is stressful as well and may be associated with intense mucosal stimulation and exaggerated glottic closure reflexes resulting in laryngospasm and, possibly, pulmonary edema secondary to vigorous inspiratory efforts against an obstructed airway. Laryngeal incompetence and aspiration can also occur after extubation. Removal of an endotracheal tube from a known or suspected difficult airway should ideally be performed over a tube exchanger so as to facilitate emergency reintubation.

Alternatives to standard oral airways, masks, introducers, exchangers, laryngoscopes, and endotracheal tubes now exist that offer more options, greater safety, and better outcomes. It would be naive to believe that any single practitioner could master every new airway protocol and device. To keep up with technical and procedural advances, university hospital program directors should consider incorporating technical skill laboratories and simulator training sessions into their curricula.

MORBID OBESITY

Morbid obesity represents the extreme end of the overweight spectrum and is usually defined as a body-mass index higher than 40 kg/m² [*see 49 Morbid Obesity*].[42] It poses a formidable challenge to health care providers in the OR, the postoperative recovery ward, and the ICU. The major concerns in the surgical setting are the possibility of a difficult airway, the increased risk of known or occult cardiorespiratory compromise, and various serious technical problems related to positioning, monitoring, vascular access, and transport. Additional concerns are the potential for underlying hepatic and endocrine disease and the effects of altered drug pharmacokinetics and pharmacodynamics. For the morbidly obese patient, there is no such thing as minor surgery.

Initial management should be based on the assumptions that (1) a difficult airway is likely, (2) the patient will be predisposed to hiatal hernia, reflux, and aspiration, and (3) rapid arterial desaturation will occur with induction of anesthesia as a consequence of decreased functional residual capacity and high basal oxygen consumption. Often, the safest option is an awake fiberoptic intubation with appropriate topical anesthesia and light sedation.[43] In expert hands, this technique is extremely well tolerated and can usually be performed in less than 10 minutes. Morbidly obese patients often are hypoxemic at rest and have an abnormal alveolar-arterial oxygen gradient caused by ventilation-perfusion mismatching. The combination of general anesthesia and the supine position exacerbates alveolar collapse and airway closure. Mechanical ventilation, weaning, and extubation may be difficult and dangerous, especially in the presence of significant obstructive sleep apnea. Postoperative pulmonary complications (e.g., pneumonia, aspiration, atelectasis, and emboli) are common.

Morbid obesity imposes unusual loading conditions on both sides of the heart and the circulation, leading to the progressive development of insulin resistance, atherogenic dyslipidemias, systemic and pulmonary hypertension, ventricular hypertrophy, and a high risk of premature coronary artery disease and biventricular heart failure. Perioperative cardiac morbidity and mortality are therefore significant problems. Untoward events can happen suddenly, and resuscitation is extremely difficult. Cardiorespiratory compromise may be attenuated by effective postoperative pain control that permits early ambulation and effective ventilation. Surgical site infection and dehiscence may result in difficult reoperation and prolonged hospitalization.

MALIGNANT HYPERTHERMIA

MH is a rare but potentially fatal genetic condition characterized by life-threatening hypermetabolic reactions in susceptible individuals after the administration of volatile anesthetics or depolarizing muscle relaxants.[44] Abnormal function of the sarcoplasmic reticulum calcium release channel in skeletal muscle has been identified as a possible underlying cause.

In making the diagnosis of MH, it is important to consider other possible causes of postoperative temperature elevation. Such causes include inadequate anesthesia, equipment problems (e.g., misuse or malfunction of heating devices, ventilators, or breathing circuits), local or systemic inflammatory responses (either related or unrelated to infection), transfusion reaction, hypermetabolic endocrinopathy (e.g., thyroid storm or pheochromocytoma), neurologic catastrophe (e.g., intracranial hemorrhage), and reaction to or abuse of a drug.

Immediate recognition and treatment of a fulminant MH episode are essential for preventing morbidity and mortality. Therapy consists of discontinuing all triggers, instituting aggressive cooling measures, giving dantrolene in an initial dose of 2.5 mg/kg, and administering 100% oxygen to compensate for the tremendous increase in oxygen utilization and carbon dioxide production. An indwelling arterial line, central venous access, and bladder catheterization are indispensable for monitoring and resuscitation. Acidosis, hyperkalemia, and malignant dysrhythmias must be rapidly treated, with the caveat that calcium channel blockers are contraindicated in this setting. Maintenance of adequate urine output is of paramount importance and may be facilitated by the clinically significant amounts of mannitol contained in commercial dantrolene preparations. When the patient is stable and the surgical procedure is complete, monitoring and support are continued in the ICU, where repeat doses of dantrolene may be needed to prevent or treat recrudescence of the disease.

MASSIVE TRANSFUSION

Massive blood transfusion, defined as the replacement of a patient's entire circulating blood volume in less than 24 hours, is associated with significant morbidity and mortality. Management of massive transfusion requires an organized multidisciplinary team approach and a thorough understanding of associated hematologic and biochemical abnormalities and subsequent treatment options.

Patients suffering from shock as a result of massive blood loss often require transfusions of packed red blood cells, platelets, fresh frozen plasma, and cryoprecipitate to optimize oxygen-carrying capacity and address dilutional and consumptive loss of platelets and clotting factors [see 118 Shock and 8 Bleeding and Transfusion]. Transfusion of large amounts of blood products into a critically ill patient can lead to coagulopathies, hyperkalemia, acidosis, citrate intoxication, fluid overload, and hypothermia.[45] Therapy should be

Table 13 Pharmacologic Treatment of PONV[5]

Agent	Dose	Comments
Propofol	10 mg I.V., repeated dose	[See Table 8]
Ondansetron	4.0–8.0 mg I.V.	Highly effective, costly; headache, constipation, transiently increased LFTs
Dexamethasone	4.0–8.0 mg I.V.	Adrenocortical suppression, delayed wound healing, fluid retention, electrolyte disturbances, psychosis, osteoporosis
Droperidol	0.5–1.0 mg I.V.	Sedation, restlessness, dysphoria, ?dysrhythmia
Metoclopramide	10–20 mg I.V.	Avoid in bowel obstruction, extrapyramidal reactions
Scopolamine	0.1–0.6 mg s.c., I.M., I.V.	Muscarinic side effects, somnolence
Dimenhydrinate	25–50 mg I.V.	Drowsiness, dizziness

LFTs—liver function tests

guided by vital signs, urine output, pulse oximetry, electrocardiography, capnography, invasive hemodynamic monitoring, serial arterial blood gases, biochemical profiles, and bedside coagulation screens. Fluids should be administered through large-bore cannulas connected to modern countercurrent warming devices. Shed blood should be salvaged and returned to the patient whenever possible. In refractory cases, transcatheter angiographic embolization techniques should be considered for control of bleeding.

Newer hemostatic agents, such as aprotinin and recombinant factor VIIa, should also be considered [see 8 Bleeding and Transfusion]. Aprotinin is a serine protease inhibitor with unique antifibrinolytic and hemostatic properties. It is used during surgery to decrease blood loss and transfusion requirements as well as to attenuate potentially harmful inflammatory responses and minimize reperfusion injury. Recombinant factor VIIa was originally approved for hemophiliacs who developed antibodies against either factor VIII or factor IX; it may prove useful for managing uncontrolled hemorrhage deriving from trauma or surgery.

HYPOTHERMIA

Significant decreases in core temperature are common during anesthesia and surgery as a consequence of exposure to a cold OR environment and of disturbances in normal protective thermoregulatory responses. Patients lose heat through conduction, convection, radiation, and evaporation, especially from large wounds and during major intracavitary procedures. Moreover, effective vasoconstrictive reflexes and both shivering and nonshivering thermogenesis are severely blunted by anesthetics.[46] Neonates and the elderly are particularly vulnerable.

Hypothermia may confer some degree of organ preservation during ischemia and reperfusion. For example, in cardiac surgery, hypothermic cardiopulmonary bypass is a common strategy for protecting the myocardium and the CNS. Intentional hypothermia has also been shown to improve neurologic outcome and survival in comatose victims of cardiac arrest. Perioperative hypothermia can have significant deleterious effects as well, however, including myocardial ischemia, surgical site infection, increased blood loss and transfusion requirements, and prolonged anesthetic recovery and hospital stay.

The sensation of cold is highly uncomfortable for the patient, and shivering impedes monitoring, raises plasma catecholamine levels, and exacerbates imbalances between oxygen supply and demand by consuming valuable energy for involuntary muscular activity. It is therefore extremely important to measure the patient's temperature and maintain thermoneutrality. Increasing the ambient temperature of the OR and applying modern forced-air warming systems are the most effective techniques available. In addition, all I.V. and irrigation fluids should be heated. After the patient has been transferred from the OR, aggressive treatment of hypothermia with these techniques should be continued as necessary. Shivering may also be reduced by means of drugs such as meperidine, nefopam, tramadol, physostigmine, ketamine, methylphenidate, and doxapram.[47]

INTRAOPERATIVE AWARENESS

One of the goals of anesthesia is to produce a state of unconsciousness during which the patient neither perceives nor recalls noxious surgical stimuli. When this objective is not met, awareness occurs, and the patient will have explicit or implicit memory of intraoperative events. In some instances, intraoperative awareness develops because human error, machine malfunction, or technical problems result in an inappropriately light level of anesthesia. In others (e.g., when the patient is severely hemodynamically unstable

or efforts are being made to avoid fetal depression during cesarean section), the light level of anesthesia may have been intentionally chosen. Regardless of the cause, intraoperative awareness is a terrifying experience for the patient and has been associated with serious long-term psychological sequelae.[48] Prevention of awareness depends on regular equipment maintenance, meticulous anesthetic technique, and close observation of the patient's movements and hemodynamic responses during operation. CNS monitoring may reduce the risk of intraoperative awareness.

ANAPHYLAXIS

Allergic reactions range in severity from mild pruritus and urticaria to anaphylactic shock and death. Inciting agents include antibiotics, contrast agents, blood products, volume expanders, protamine, aprotinin, narcotics, induction agents, muscle relaxants, latex,[49] and, rarely, local anesthetic solutions. Many drug additives and preservatives have also been implicated.

True anaphylaxis presents shortly after exposure to an allergen and is mediated by chemicals released from degranulated mast cells and basophils. Manifestations usually include dramatic hypotension, tachycardia, bronchospasm, arterial oxygen desaturation, and cutaneous changes. Laryngeal edema can occur within minutes, in which case the airway should be secured immediately. Anaphylaxis can mimic heart failure, asthma, pulmonary embolism, and tension pneumothorax. Treatment involves withdrawing the offending substance and administering oxygen, fluids, and epinephrine, followed by I.V. steroids, bronchodilators, and histamine antagonists. Prolonged intubation and ICU monitoring may be required until symptoms resolve. Appropriate skin and blood testing should be done to identify the causative agent.

PERIOPERATIVE DYSRHYTHMIAS

In 2005, current scientific developments in the acute treatment of cerebrovascular, cardiac, and pulmonary disease were merged with the evolving discipline of evidence-based medicine to produce the most comprehensive set of resuscitation standards ever created: a 14-part document from the American Heart Association entitled "2005 American Heart Association Guidelines for Cardiopulmonary Resuscitation and Emergency Cardiovascular Care."[50] This document addresses a wide array of key issues in both in-hospital and out-of-hospital resuscitation, including a recommendation for confirmation of tube position after endotracheal intubation and a warning about the danger associated with unintentional massive auto-PEEP.

As regards the impact the new guidelines have on the management of cardiopulmonary resuscitation, an increase in compression:ventilation ratios (to 30:2) and an emphasis on effective chest compressions ("push hard, push fast") are suggested. In addition, early chest compressions before defibrillation, a one-shock sequence for defibrillation as opposed to a three-shock sequence, and avoidance of prolonged interruption of chest compressions are recommended. For wide QRS dysrhythmias, amiodarone continues to be the drug of choice. It may also be administered for ventricular fibrillation or for pulseless ventricular tachycardia that does not respond to cardiopulmonary resuscitation, cardioversion, and a vasopressor.

Amiodarone is a complex, powerful, and broad-spectrum agent that inhibits almost all of the drug receptors and ion channels conceivably responsible for the initiation and propagation of cardiac ectopy, irrespective of underlying ejection fraction, accessory pathway conduction, or anatomic substrate. It does, however, have potential drawbacks, such as its relatively long half-life, its toxicity to multiple organs, and its complicated administration scheme.

Furthermore, amiodarone is a potent noncompetitive alpha and beta blocker, which has important implications for anesthetized, mechanically ventilated patients who may be debilitated and experiencing volume depletion, abnormal vasodilation, myocardial depression, and fluid, electrolyte, and acid-base abnormalities. That said, no other drug in its class has ever demonstrated a significant benefit in randomized trials addressing cardiac arrest in humans.

Amiodarone is effective in both children and adults, and it can be used for prophylaxis as well as treatment. The recommended cardiac arrest dose is a 300 mg I.V. bolus. In less acute situations (e.g., wide-complex tachycardia), an initial 150 mg dose should be administered slowly over 10 minutes, and one or two additional boluses may be given similarly. A loading regimen is then initiated, first at 1 mg/min for 6 hours and then at 0.5 mg/min for 18 hours.

Vasopressin (antidiuretic hormone) continues to be listed as an alternative to epinephrine in the ventricular tachycardia/ventricular fibrillation protocol. Vasopressin is an integral component of the hypothalamic-pituitary-adrenal axis and the neuroendocrine stress response. The recommended dose for an adult in fibrillatory arrest is 40 units in a single bolus. For vasodilatory shock states associated with sepsis, hepatic failure, or vasomotor paralysis after cardiopulmonary bypass, infusion at a rate of 0.01 to 0.04 units/min may be particularly useful. Vasopressin is neither recommended nor forbidden in cases of pulseless electrical activity or asystolic arrest, and it may be substituted for epinephrine.

References

1. Clinical Anesthesia, 3rd ed. Barash PG, Cullen BF, Stoelting RK, Eds. Lippincott-Raven, Philadelphia, 2000

2. Anesthesia, 5th ed. Miller RD, Ed. Churchill Livingstone Inc, Philadelphia, 2000

3. Licker M, Neidhart P, Lustenberger S, et al: Long-term angiotensin-converting enzyme inhibitor attenuates adrenergic responsiveness without altering hemodynamic control in patients undergoing cardiac surgery. Anethesiology 84:789, 1996

4. Antiplatelet agents in the perioperative period: expert recommendations of the French Society of Anesthesiology and Intensive Care (SFAR) 2001—summary statement. Can J Anaesth 49:S26, 2002

5. Van Vlymen JM, White PF: Outpatient anesthesia. Anesthesia, 5th ed. Miller RD, Ed. Churchill Livingstone Inc, Philadelphia, 2000, p 2213

6. Dexter F, Macario A, Penning DH, et al: Development of an appropriate list of surgical procedures of a specified maximim anesthetic complexity to be performed at a new ambulatory surgery facility. Anesth Analg 95:78, 2002

7. Nelskyla KA, Yli-Hankala AM, Puro PH, et al: Sevoflurane titration using bispectral index decreases postoperative vomiting in phase II recovery after ambulatory surgery. Anesth Analg 93:1165, 2001

8. Song D, van Vlymen J, White PF: Is the bispectral index useful in predicting fast-track eligibility after ambulatory anesthesia with propofol and desflurane? Anesth Analg 87:1245, 1998

9. Brimacombe J, Brain AIJ, Berry A: The Laryngeal Mask Airway: Review and Practical Guide. WB Saunders Co, London, 1997

10. Joshi GP, Inagaki Y, White PF, et al: Use of the laryngeal mask airway as an alternative to the tracheal tube during ambulatory anesthesia. Anesth Analg 85:573, 1997

11. Tsen LC, Schultz R, Martin R, et al: Intrathecal low-dose bupivicaine versus lidocaine for in vitro fertilization procedures. Reg Anesth Pain Med 26:52, 2001

12. Frey K, Holman S, Mikat-Stevens M, et al: The recovery profile of hyperbaric spinal anesthesia with lidocaine, tetracaine, and bupivicaine. Reg Anesth Pain Med 23:159, 1998

13. Liguori GA, Zayas VM, Chisolm MF: Transient neurologic symptoms after spinal anesthesia with mepivacaine and lidocaine. Anesthesiology 88:619, 1998

14. Liu SS: Optimizing spinal anesthesia for ambulatory surgery. Reg Anesth 22:500, 1997

15. Chung F, Mezei G: Factors contributing to a prolonged stay after ambulatory surgery. Anesth Analg 89:1352, 1999

16. Kehlet H, Nolte K: Effect of postoperative analgesia on surgical outcome. Br J Anaesth 87:62, 2001

17. Kessler P, Neidhart G, Bremerich DH, et al: High thoracic epidural anesthesia for coronary artery bypass grafting using two different surgical approaches in conscious patients. Anesth Analg 95:791, 2002

18. Nolte K, Kehlet H: Postoperative ileus: a preventable event. Br J Surg 87:1480, 2000

19. Rodgers A, Walker N, Schug S, et al: Reduction of postoperative mortality and morbidity with epidural or spinal anaesthesia: results from overview of randomised trials. BMJ 321:1493, 2000

20. Beattie WS, Badner NH, Choi P: Epidural analgesia reduces postoperative myocardial infarction: a meta-analysis. Anesth Analg 93:853, 2001

21. Ballantyne JC, Carr DB, deFerranti S, et al: The comparative effects of postoperative analgesic therapies on pulmonary outcome: cumulative meta-analyses of randomized controlled trials. Anesth Analg 86:598, 1998

22. Moller JT, Cluitmans P, Houx P, et al: Long-term postoperative cognitive dysfunction in the elderly: ISPOCD1 study. Lancet 51:857, 1998

23. Kehlet H, Mogensen T: Hospital stay of 2 days after open sigmoidectomy with a multimodal rehabilitation programme. Br J Surg 86:227, 1999

24. Basse L, Jakobsen DH, Billesbolle P, et al: A clinical pathway to accelerate recovery after colonic resection. Ann Surg 232:51, 2000

25. Wedel DJ: Nerve blocks. Anesthesia, 5th ed. Miller RD, Ed. Churchill Livingstone Inc, Philadelphia, 2000, p 520

26. Cahalan MK: Transesophageal echocardiography. Anesthesia, 5th ed. Miller RD, Ed. Churchill Livingstone Inc, Philadelphia, 2000, p 1207

27. Practice Guidelines for Perioperative Transesophageal Echocardiography: a report by the American Society of Anesthesiologists and the Society of Cardiovascular Anesthesiologists Task Force on Transesophageal Echocardiography. Anesthesiology 84:986, 1996

28. Lehmann A, Boldt J, Thaler E, et al: Bispectral index in patients with target-controlled or manually controlled infusion of propofol. Anesth Analg 95:639, 2002

29. Drover DR, Lemmens HJ, Pierce ET, et al: Patient state index: titration of delivery and recovery from propofol, alfentanil and nitrous oxide anesthesia. Anesthesiology 97:82, 2002

30. Maze M, Tranquilli W: Alpha-2 adrenoceptor agonists: defining the role in clinical anesthesia. Anesthesiology 74:581, 1991

31. Peden CJ, Prys-Roberts C: Dexmedetomidine: a powerful new adjunct to anaesthesia? Br J Anaesth 68:123, 1992

32. Dahl JB, Moiniche S, Kehlet H: Wound infiltration with local anaesthetics for postoperative pain relief. Acta Anaesthesiol Scand 38:7, 1994

33. Labaille T, Mazoit JX, Paqueron X, et al: The clinical efficacy and pharmacokinetics of intraperitoneal ropivacaine for laparoscopic cholecystectomy. Anesth Analg 94:100, 2002

34. Callesen T, Bech K, Kehlet H: One-thousand consecutive inguinal hernia repairs under unmonitored local anesthesia. Anesth Analg 93:1373, 2001

35. Horlocker TT, Wedel DJ: Anticoagulation and neuraxial block: historical perspective, anesthetic implications, and risk management. Reg Anesth Pain Med 23:129, 1998

36. Horlocker TT, Wedel DJ, Schroeder DR, et al: Preoperative antiplatelet therapy does not increase the risk of spinal hematoma associated with regional anesthesia. Anesth Analg 80:303, 1995

37. Tryba M, Wedel DJ: Central neuraxial blockade and low molecular weight heparin (enoxaparine): lessons learned from different dosage regimes in two continents. Acta Anaesthesiol Scand 41:100, 1997

38. Tryba M: European practice guidelines: thromboembolism prophylaxis and regional anesthesia. Reg Anesth Pain Med 23:178, 1998

39. Horlocker TT, Wedel DJ: Neurological complications of spinal and epidural anesthesia. Reg Anesth Pain Med 25:83, 2000

40. Loo CC, Dahlgren G, Irestedt L: Neurological complications in obstetric regional anesthesia. Int J Obstet 9:99, 2000

41. Freedman JM, Li DK, Drasner K, et al: Transient neurologic symptoms after spinal anesthesia: an epidemiologic study of 1,863 patients. Anesthesiology 89:633, 1998

42. Yanovski SZ: Obesity. N Engl J Med 346:591, 2002

43. Simmons ST, Schleich AR: Airway regional anesthesia for awake fiberoptic intubation. Reg Anesth Pain Med 27:180, 2002

44. Hopkins PM: Malignant hyperthermia. Br J Anaesth 85:118, 2000

45. Desjardins G: Management of massive hemorrhage and transfusion. Semin Anesth 20:60, 2001

46. Sessler DI: Perioperative heat balance. Anesthesiology 92:578, 2000

47. de Witte J, Sessler DI: Perioperative shivering. Anesthesiology 96:467, 2002

48. Ghoneim MM: Awareness during anesthesia. Anesthesiology 92:597, 2000

49. Zucker-Pinchoff B: Latex allergy. Mt Sinai J Med 69:88, 2002

50. 2005 American Heart Association guidelines for cardiopulmonary resuscitation and emergency cardio-

vascular care. Circulation 112(24 suppl):IV-1, 2005 http://circ.ahajournals.org/content/vol112/24_suppl

51. Baldessarini RJ: Drugs and the treatment of psychiatric disorders: depression and anxiety disorders. Goodman & Gilman's The Pharmacological Basis of Therapeutics, 10th ed. Hardman JG, Limbird LE, Gilman AG, Eds. McGraw-Hill, New York, 2001, p 447

52. Kearon C, Hirsh J: Management of anticoagulation before and after elective surgery. N Engl J Med 336:1506, 1997

53. Connelly CS, Panush RS: Should nonsteroidal anti-inflammatory drugs be stopped before elective surgery? Arch Intern Med 151:1963, 1991

54. Sonksen JR, Kong KL, Holder R: Magnitude and time course of impaired primary hemostasis after stopping chronic low and medium dose aspirin in healthy volunteers. Br J Anaesth 82:360, 1999

55. Gammic JS, Zenate M, Kormos RL, et al: Abciximab and excessive bleeding in patients undergoing emergency cardiac operations. Ann Thorac Surg 65:465, 1998

56. Hardy JF: Anticipated agents on perioperative bleeding. Anesthesiology Rounds 1(1):1, 2002

57. Majerus PW, Broze GJ Jr, Miletich JP, et al: Anticoagulant, thrombolytic, and antiplatelet drugs. Goodman & Gilman's The Pharmacological Basis of Therapeutics, 9th ed. Hardman JG, Limbird LE, Molinoff PB, et al, Eds. McGraw-Hill, New York, 1996, p 1341

58. Eisenberg DM, Davis RB, et al: Trends in alternative medicine use in the United States, 1990–1997: results of a follow-up national survey. JAMA 280: 1569, 1998

59. Kaye AD, Clarke RC, Sabar R, et al: Herbal medicines: current trends in anesthesiology practice—a hospital survey. J Clin Anesth 12:468, 2000

60. Ang-Lee MK, Moss J, Yvan CS: Herbal medicines and perioperative care. JAMA 286:208, 2001

61. Vanderweghem JL, Depurreux M, Tielmans CH, et al: Rapidly progressive interstitial renal fibrosis in young women: association with summing regimen including Chinese herbs. Lancet 341:387, 1993

62. Jadont M, Plaen JF, Cosyns JP, et al: Adverse effects from traditional Chinese medicine. Lancet 347:892, 1995

63. Kao WF, Hung DZ, Lin KP: Podophylotoxin intoxication: toxic effect of Bajiaolian in herbal therapeutics. Hum Exp Toxicol 11:480, 1992

64. Edzard E: Harmless herbs? A review of the recent literature. Am J Med 104:170, 1998

65. Chung F, Mezei G: Adverse outcomes in ambulatory anesthesia. Can J Anesth 46:R18, 1999

66. ASA Task Force on Preoperative Fasting. Practice guidelines for preoperative fasting and the use of pharmacologic agents to reduce the risk of pulmonary aspiration: application to healthy patients undergoing elective procedures. Anesthesiology 90:896, 1999

67. Chung F: A post-anesthetic discharge scoring system for home readiness after ambulatory surgery. J Clin Anesth 7:500, 1995

68. Reves JG, Glass PSA, Lubarsky DA: Nonbarbiturate intravenous anesthetics. Anesthesia, 5th ed. Miller RD, Ed. Churchill Livingstone Inc, Philadelphia, 2000, p 228

69. Bailey PL, Egan TD, Stanley TH: Intravenous opioid anesthetics. Anesthesia, 5th ed. Miller RD, Ed. Churchill Livingstone Inc, Philadelphia, 2000, p 273

70. Stoelting RK: Histamine and histamine receptor antagonists. Pharmacology and Physiology in Anesthetic Practice, 3rd ed. Stoelting RK, Ed. Lippincott Williams & Wilkins, Philadelphia, p 385

71. Compendium of Pharmaceuticals and Specialties, Canadian Pharmacists Association. Webcom Limited, Toronto, 2002

72. Koblin DD: Mechanisms of action. Anesthesia, 5th ed. Miller RD, Ed. Churchill Livingstone Inc, Philadelphia, 2000, p 48

73. Eger EE II: Uptake and distribution. Anesthesia, 5th ed. Miller RD, Ed. Churchill Livingstone Inc, Philadelphia, 2000, p 74

74. Savarese JJ, Caldwell JE, Lien CA, et al: Pharmacology of muscle relaxants and their antagonists. Anesthesia, 5th ed. Miller RD, Ed. Churchill Livingstone Inc, Philadelphia, 2000, p 412

8 BLEEDING AND TRANSFUSION

John T. Owings, M.D., F.A.C.S., Garth H. Utter, M.D., M.Sc., and Robert C. Gosselin, M.T.

Approach to the Patient with Ongoing Bleeding

A surgeon is often the first person to be called when a patient experiences ongoing bleeding. To treat such a patient appropriately, the surgeon must identify the cause or source of the bleeding. Causes fall into two main categories: (1) conditions leading to loss of vascular integrity, as in a postoperative patient with an unligated vessel that is bleeding or a trauma patient with a ruptured spleen, and (2) conditions leading to derangement of the hemostatic process. In this chapter, we focus on the latter category, which includes a broad spectrum of conditions, such as aspirin-induced platelet dysfunction, von Willebrand disease (vWD), disseminated intravascular coagulation (DIC), and even hemophilia.

Coagulopathies are varied in their causes, treatments, and prognoses. Our aim is not to downplay the usefulness of the specialized hematologic tests required for identification of rare congenital or acquired clotting abnormalities but to outline effective management approaches to the coagulopathies surgeons see most frequently. The vast majority of these coagulopathies can be diagnosed by means of a brief patient and family history, a review of medications, physical examination, and commonly used laboratory studies—in particular, activated partial thromboplastin time (aPTT), prothrombin time (PT, commonly expressed as an international normalized ratio [INR]), complete blood count (CBC), and D-dimer assay.

Exclusion of Technical Causes of Bleeding

It is critical for the surgeon to recognize that the most common causes of postoperative bleeding are technical: an unligated vessel or an unrecognized
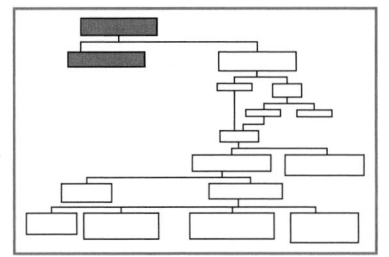
injury is much more likely to be the cause of a falling hematocrit than either a drug effect or an endogenous hemostatic defect. Furthermore, if an unligated vessel is treated as though it were an endogenous hemostatic defect (i.e., with transfusions), the outcome is likely to be disastrous. For these reasons, in all cases of ongoing bleeding, the first consideration must always be to exclude a surgically correctable cause.

Ongoing bleeding may be surprisingly difficult to diagnose. Healthy young patients can usually maintain a normal blood pressure until their blood loss exceeds 40% of their blood volume (roughly 2 L). If the bleeding is from a laceration to an extremity, it will be obvious; however, if the bleeding is occurring internally (e.g., from a ruptured spleen or an intraluminal GI source), there may be few physiologic signs [*see 8:3 Shock*]. For the purposes of the ensuing discussion, we assume that bleeding is known to have occurred or to be occurring.

Even when a technical cause of bleeding has seemingly been excluded, the possibility often must be reconsidered periodically throughout assessment. Patients who are either unresuscitated or underresuscitated undergo vasospasm that results in decreased bleeding.[1] As resuscitation proceeds, the catecholamine-induced vasospasm subsides and the bleeding may recur. For this reason, repeated reassessment of the possibility of a technical cause of bleeding is appropriate. Only when the surgeon is confident that a missed injury or unligated vessel is not the cause of the bleeding should other potential causes be investigated.

Initial Assessment of Potential Coagulopathy

The first step in assessment of a patient with a potential coagulopathy is to draw a blood sample. The blood should be drawn into a tube containing ethylene-
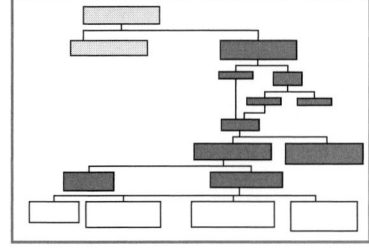
diaminetetraacetic acid (EDTA) for a CBC and into a citrated tube for coagulation analysis (at most centers, these tubes have purple and blue tops, respectively).

At the same time, the patient's temperature should be noted. Because coagulation is a chemical reaction, it slows with decreasing temperature.[2] Thus, a patient with a temperature lower than 35° C (95° F) clots more slowly and less efficiently than one with a temperature of 37° C (98.6° F).[3] The resulting coagulatory abnormality is what is known as a hypothermic coagulopathy. Upon receipt of the drawn specimen, the laboratory warms the sample to 37° C to run the coagulation assays (aPTT and INR). In a patient with a purely hypothermic coagulopathy, this step results in normal coagulation parameters. Hypothermic patients should be actively rewarmed.[4] Typically, such patients cease to bleed after rewarming, and no further treatment is required. If the patient is normothermic and exhibits normal coagulation values but bleeding continues, attention should again be focused on the possibility of an unligated bleeding vessel or an uncontrolled occult bleeding source (e.g., the GI tract).

Ongoing bleeding in conjunction with abnormal coagulation parameters may have any of several underlying causes. In this setting, one of the most useful pieces of information to obtain is a personal and family history. A patient who has had dental extractions without major problems or who had a normal adolescence without any history of bleeding dyscrasias is very unlikely to have a congenital or hereditary bleeding disorder.[5] If there is a personal or family history of a specific bleeding disorder, appropriate steps should be taken to diagnose and treat the disorder [*see Discussion, Bleeding Disorders, below*].

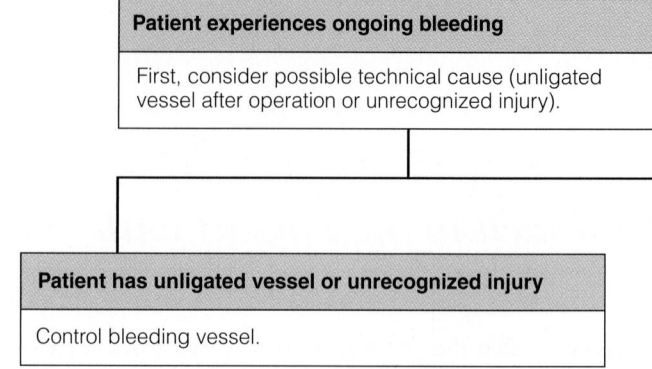

Patient experiences ongoing bleeding

First, consider possible technical cause (unligated vessel after operation or unrecognized injury).

Patient has unligated vessel or unrecognized injury

Control bleeding vessel.

Approach to the Patient with Ongoing Bleeding

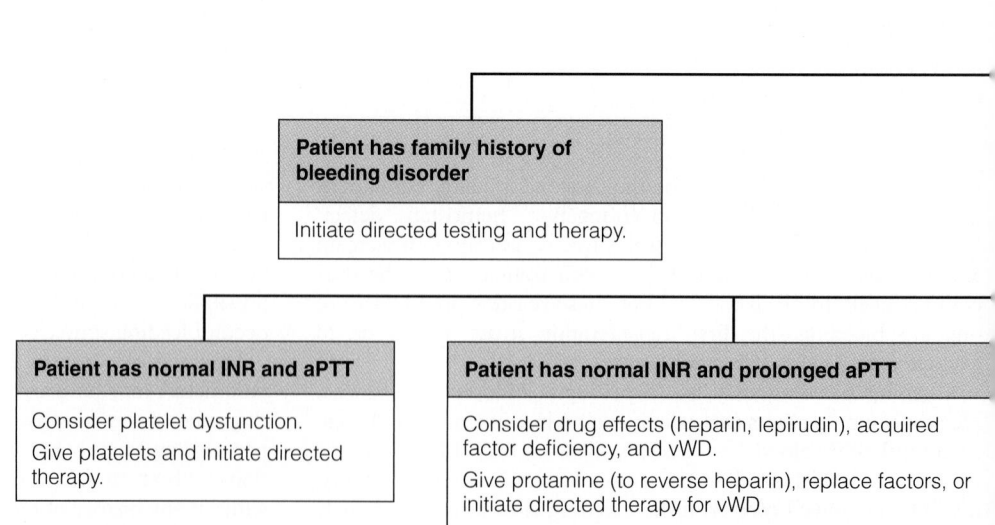

Patient has family history of bleeding disorder

Initiate directed testing and therapy.

Patient has normal INR and aPTT

Consider platelet dysfunction.
Give platelets and initiate directed therapy.

Patient has normal INR and prolonged aPTT

Consider drug effects (heparin, lepirudin), acquired factor deficiency, and vWD.
Give protamine (to reverse heparin), replace factors, or initiate directed therapy for vWD.

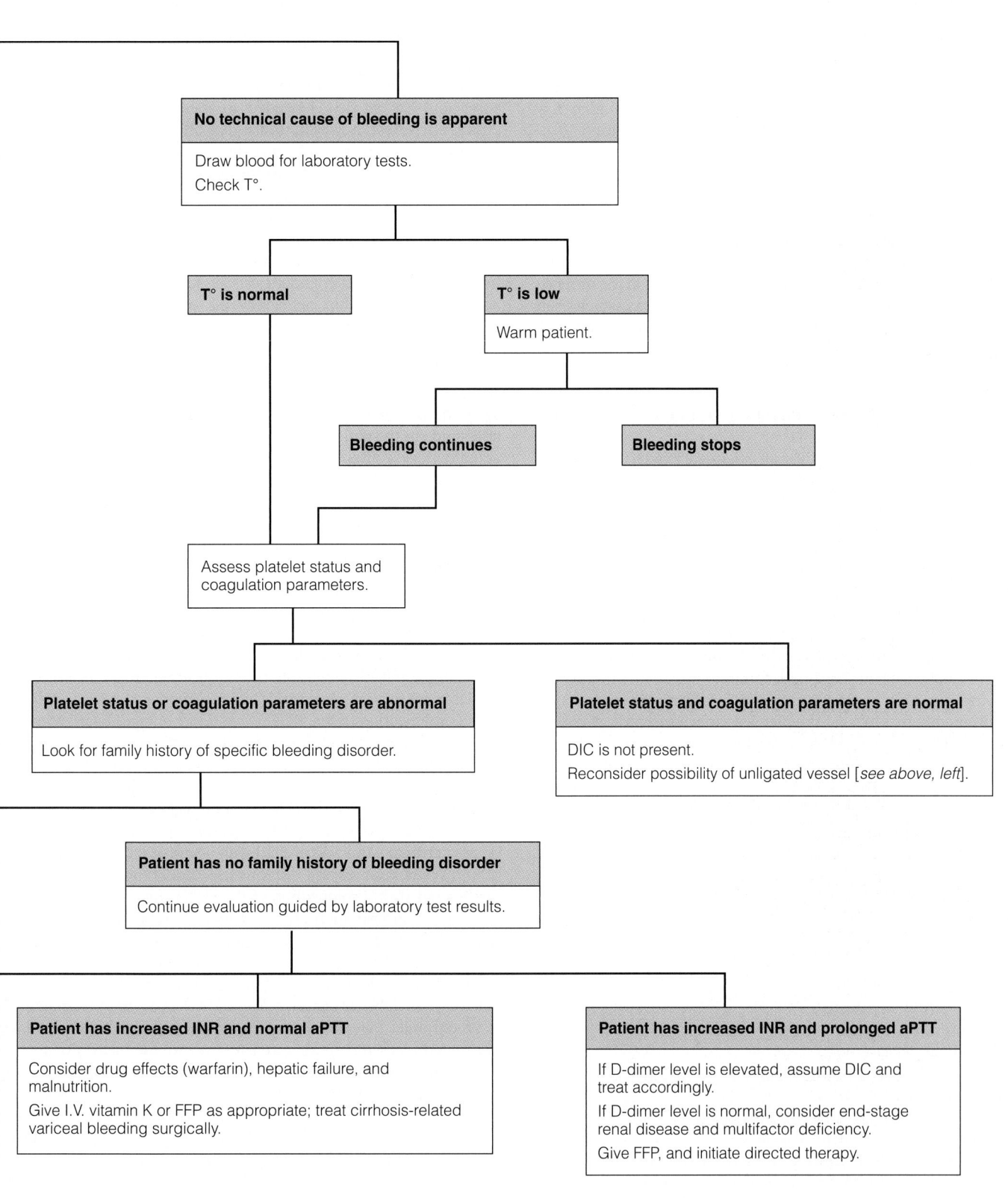

No technical cause of bleeding is apparent

Draw blood for laboratory tests.
Check T°.

T° is normal

T° is low

Warm patient.

Bleeding continues

Bleeding stops

Assess platelet status and
coagulation parameters.

Platelet status or coagulation parameters are abnormal

Look for family history of specific bleeding disorder.

Platelet status and coagulation parameters are normal

DIC is not present.
Reconsider possibility of unligated vessel [*see above, left*].

Patient has no family history of bleeding disorder

Continue evaluation guided by laboratory test results.

Patient has increased INR and normal aPTT

Consider drug effects (warfarin), hepatic failure, and
malnutrition.
Give I.V. vitamin K or FFP as appropriate; treat cirrhosis-related
variceal bleeding surgically.

Patient has increased INR and prolonged aPTT

If D-dimer level is elevated, assume DIC and
treat accordingly.
If D-dimer level is normal, consider end-stage
renal disease and multifactor deficiency.
Give FFP, and initiate directed therapy.

Measurement of Coagulation Parameters

NORMAL INR, NORMAL aPTT

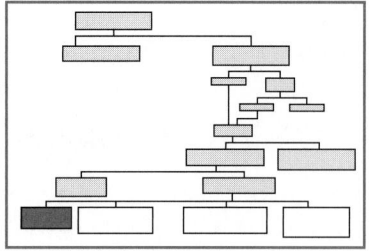

Patients with a normal INR and aPTT who exhibit ongoing bleeding may have impaired platelet activity. Inadequate platelet activity is frequently manifested as persistent oozing from wound edges or as low-volume bleeding. Such bleeding is rarely the cause of exsanguinating hemorrhage, though it may be life-threatening on occasion, depending on its location (e.g., inside the cranium or the pericardium). Inadequate platelet activity may be attributable either to an insufficient number of platelets or to platelet dysfunction. In the absence of a major surgical insult or concomitant coagulopathy, a platelet count of 20,000/mm³ or higher is usually adequate for normal coagulation.[6,7] There is some disagreement regarding the absolute level to which the platelet count must fall before platelet transfusion is justified in the absence of active bleeding. Patients undergoing procedures in which even capillary oozing is potentially life-threatening (e.g., craniotomy) should be maintained at a higher platelet count (i.e., > 20,000/mm³). Patients without ongoing bleeding who are not specifically at increased risk for major complications from low-volume bleeding may be safely watched with platelet counts lower than 20,000/mm³.

Oozing in a patient who has an adequate platelet count and normal coagulation parameters may be a signal of platelet dysfunction. The now-routine administration of aspirin to reduce the risk of myocardial infarction and stroke has led to a rise in the incidence of aspirin-induced platelet dysfunction. Aspirin causes irreversible platelet dysfunction through the cyclooxygenase pathway; the effect of aspirin can thus be expected to last for approximately 10 days. The platelet dysfunction caused by other nonsteroidal anti-inflammatory drugs (e.g., ibuprofen) is reversible and consequently does not last as long as that caused by aspirin. Newer platelet-blocking agents have been found to be effective in improving outcome after coronary angioplasty.[8] These drugs function predominantly by blocking the platelet surface receptor glycoprotein (GP) IIb-IIIa, which binds platelets to fibrinogen.

In patients with platelet dysfunction caused by an inhibitor of platelet function, such as an elevated blood urea nitrogen (BUN) level or aspirin, 1-desamino-8-D-arginine vasopressin (DDAVP) is capable of significantly reversing the platelet dysfunction.[9]

Less common causes of bleeding in patients with a normal INR and a normal aPTT include factor XIII deficiency, hypofibrinogenemia or dysfibrinogenemia, and derangements in the fibrinolytic pathway [see Discussion, Mechanics of Hemostasis, below].

NORMAL INR, PROLONGED aPTT

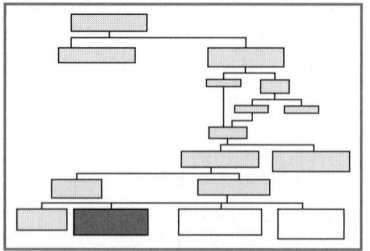

Patients with a normal INR and an abnormal aPTT are likely to have a drug-induced coagulation defect. The agent most commonly responsible is unfractionated heparin. Reversal of the heparin effect, if desired, can be accomplished by administering protamine sulfate. Protamine should be given with caution, however, because it has been reported to induce a hypercoagulable state[10] (though many of the thrombotic complications may simply be related to reversal of a needed anticoagulant state). Protamine should also be used with caution in diabetic patients. These persons sometimes become sensitized to impurities in protamine through their exposure to similar impurities in protamine-containing insulin formulations, and this sensitization may result in an anaphylactic reaction.[11]

It should be remembered that the aPTT does not accurately measure the anticoagulant activity of low-molecular-weight heparins (LMWHs). Because such heparins exert the greater proportion of their anticoagulant effect by potentiating antithrombin to inactivate factor Xa rather than factor IIa, an assay that measures anti-Xa activity is needed to measure the anticoagulant effect. This effect, however, unlike that of unfractionated heparin, is not effectively reversed by protamine.

It should also be noted that the anti-Xa laboratory assay does not truly measure the degree of anticoagulation in vivo; rather, it measures only the LMWH concentration in plasma. Because heparins (including LMWHs) function almost exclusively by catalyzing the activity of antithrombin, the therapeutic effect of heparin is critically dependent on adequate antithrombin levels; acquired antithrombin deficiency (as occurs with trauma and other critical illnesses) is the most common reason for LMWH to have an inadequate effect. The anti-Xa laboratory assay does not account for in vivo antithrombin levels, because it involves the addition of antithrombin itself to the plasma sample as a reagent. Consequently, the results of this assay cannot be taken as a reliable guide to the patient's coagulation status. In effect, all the assay actually does is give the physician some idea of the concentration of circulating LMWH, which is dependent on the dosing, renal clearance, and the time since LMWH was last administered.

An additional crucial point is that the administration of fresh frozen plasma (FFP) will not correct the anticoagulant effect of either unfractionated heparin or LMWHs. In fact, given that plasma contains antithrombin and that both unfractionated heparin and LMWHs act by potentiating antithrombin, administration of FFP could actually enhance the heparins' anticoagulant effect.

A variety of direct thrombin inhibitors (e.g., bivalirudin [Hirulog], lepirudin, argatroban, and ximelagatran) are currently available in Europe, Asia, and North America.[12] Many of them cause prolongation of the aPTT. One disadvantage shared by most of the direct thrombin inhibitors is that the effects are not reversible; if thrombin inhibition is no longer desired, FFP must be given to correct the aPTT. Because the inhibitor that is circulating but not bound at the time of FFP administration will bind the prothrombin in the FFP, the amount of FFP required to correct the aPTT may be greater than would be needed with a simple factor deficiency.

Von Willebrand disease is frequently, though not always, associated with a slight prolongation of the aPTT. Its clinical expression is variable. Confirmation of the diagnosis can be obtained by testing for circulating factor levels. Platelet function analysis will also show abnormal function. Correction is accomplished by administering directed therapy (von Willebrand factor [vWF]) [see Discussion, Bleeding Disorders, below], DDAVP, or cryoprecipitate.

Hemophilia may either cause spontaneous bleeding or lead to prolonged bleeding after a surgical or traumatic insult. As noted, hemophilia is rare in the absence of a personal or family history of the disorder. The most common forms of hemophilia involve deficiencies of factors VIII, IX, and XI (hemophilia A, hemophilia B, and hemophilia C, respectively). In contrast to depletion of natural anticoagulants such as antithrombin and protein C [see 85 Venous Thromboembolism], depletion of procoagulant factors rarely gives rise to significant manifestations until it is relatively severe. Typically, no laboratory abnormalities result from depletion of

Table 1 Preparations Used in Directed Therapy for Hemophilia

Product (Manufacturer)	Origin	Used to Compensate for Depletion of Factors		
		Factor VIII	Factor IX	vWF
Alphanate (Alpha Therapeutic)	Plasma	Yes	—	Yes
Monarc-M (American Red Cross)	Plasma	Yes	—	Yes
Hemofil M (Baxter Healthcare)	Plasma	Yes	—	Yes
Humate-P (Centeon)	Plasma	Yes	—	Yes
Koāte-HP (Bayer)	Plasma	Yes	—	Yes
Monoclate-P (Centeon)	Plasma	Yes	—	Yes
Recombinate (Baxter Healthcare)	Recombinant	Yes	—	—
Kogenate (Bayer)	Recombinant	Yes	—	—
Bioclate (Baxter Healthcare), Helixate (Centeon)	Recombinant	Yes	—	—
Hyate:C (Speywood)	Porcine plasma	Yes	—	—
Autoplex T (prothrombin complex concentrate) (NABI)	Plasma	—	Yes	—
Feiba VH Immuno (prothrombin complex concentrate) (Immuno-US)	Plasma	—	Yes	—
Mononine (Centeon)	Plasma	—	Yes	—
AlphaNine-SD (Alpha Therapeutic)	Plasma	—	Yes	—
Bebulin VH Immuno (Immuno-US)	Plasma	—	Yes	—
Proplex T (Baxter Healthcare)	Plasma	—	Yes	—
Konȳne 80 (Bayer)	Plasma	—	Yes	—
Profilnine SD (Alpha Therapeutic)	Plasma	—	Yes	—
BeneFix (Genetics Institute)	Recombinant	—	Yes	—
Novo Seven (Novo Nordisk)	Recombinant	Yes	Yes	—

procoagulant factors until factor activity levels fall below 40% of normal, and clinical abnormalities are frequently absent even when factor activity levels fall to only 10% of normal. This tolerance for subcritical degrees of depletion is a reflection of the built-in redundancies in the procoagulant pathways.

If hemophilia is suspected, specific factor analysis is indicated. Appropriate therapy involves administering the deficient factor or factors [*see Table 1*]. Hemophiliac patients who have undergone extensive transfusion therapy may pose a particular challenge: massive transfusions frequently lead to the development of antibodies that make subsequent transfusion or even directed therapy impossible. Accordingly, several alternatives to transfusion or directed factor therapy (e.g., recombinant activated factor VII [rVIIa]) have been developed for use in this population.

INCREASED INR, NORMAL aPTT

An increased INR in association with a normal aPTT is a more ominous finding in a patient with a coagulopathy. Any of a number of causes, all centering on factor deficiency, may be responsible.

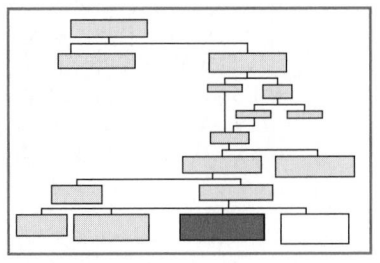

Cirrhosis is arguably the most serious of the causes of an elevated INR. It is a major problem not so much because of the coagulopathy itself but because of the associated deficits in wound healing and immune function that result from the synthetic dysfunction and the loss of reticuloendothelial function. In all cases, factor replacement should be instituted with FFP. If the bleeding is a manifestation of the cirrhosis (as in variceal bleeding), emergency portal decompression should be accomplished before the coagulopathy worsens. Management of cirrhotic patients who have sustained injuries is particularly troublesome because such patients are at disproportionately high risk for subdural hematoma. The reason this risk is so high is that in addition to their pathologic autoanticoagulation, these patients often have some degree of cerebral atrophy as a result of one of the more frequent causes of cirrhosis—namely, alcoholism. As a result, the bridging intracranial veins are more vulnerable to tears and more likely to bleed. For patients with life-threatening intracranial bleeding and an elevated INR, off-label use of activated factor VII has become widespread. Although to date, no prospective randomized studies have demonstrated that this practice confers a survival advantage, the administration of activated factor VII, 20 to 40 µg/kg, does appear promising.[13] Modest elevations of the INR in patients who are not actively bleeding, have not recently undergone operation, and are not specifically at increased risk for life-threatening hemorrhage may be observed without correction.

An elevated INR with a normal aPTT may also be a consequence of warfarin administration. Such a coagulopathy is the
result of a pure factor deficiency, and its degree is proportional to
the prolongation of the INR. Because warfarin acts by disrupting
vitamin K metabolism, the coagulopathy may be corrected by giving vitamin K [*see Table 2*].[14] If the patient is actively bleeding, vitamin K should still be given, but the primary corrective measure
should be to administer FFP in an amount proportional to the
patient's size and the relative increase in the INR. The INR should
subsequently be rechecked to ensure that replacement therapy is
adequate. Vitamin K replacement therapy has two main potential
drawbacks: (1) if the patient is to be reanticoagulated with warfarin in the near future, dosing will be difficult because the patient
will exhibit resistance to warfarin for a variable period; and (2) anaphylactic reactions have been reported when vitamin K is given I.V.

INCREASED INR, PRO-
LONGED aPTT

Increases in both the INR
and the aPTT may be the
most problematic finding of
all. When both assays show
increases, the patient is likely to have multiple factor
deficiencies; possible causes

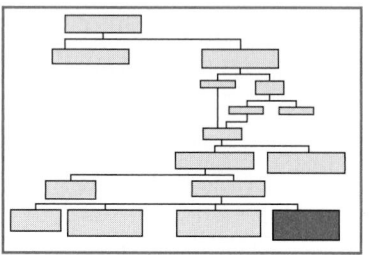

include DIC, severe hemodilution, and renal failure with severe
nephrotic syndrome. However, when dramatic elevations of the
aPTT and the INR are observed in a seemingly asymptomatic
patient, the problem may lie not in the patient's condition but in
the laboratory analysis. If the tube in which the blood sample was
drawn for these tests was not adequately filled, the results of the
coagulation assays may be inaccurate. In such cases, the blood
sample should be redrawn and the tests repeated.

Hemodilution and nephrotic syndrome result in a coagulopathy
that is attributable to decreased concentration of coagulation proteins. Dilutional coagulopathy may occur when a patient who is
given a large volume of packed red blood cell (RBC) units is not
also given coagulation factors.[15] Because of the tremendous
redundancy of the hemostatic process, pure dilutional coagulopathy is rare. It is considered an unlikely diagnosis until after one full
blood volume has been replaced (as when a patient requires 10
units of packed RBCs to maintain a stable hematocrit). Nephrotic
syndrome is associated with loss of protein (coagulation proteins
as well as other body proteins) from the kidneys.

Both hemodilution and nephrotic syndrome should be distinguished from DIC (which is a consumptive rather than a dilutional process[16]), though on occasion this distinction is a difficult one
to make. A blood sample should be sent for D-dimer assay. If the
D-dimer level is low (< 1,000 ng/ml), DIC is unlikely; if it is very
high (> 2,000 ng/ml) and there is no other clear explanation (e.g.,
a complex unstable pelvic fracture), the diagnosis of DIC rather
than dilution should be made. Treatment of dilutional coagulopathy should be directed at replacement of lost factors. FFP should
be given first, followed by cryoprecipitate, calcium, and platelets.
Transfusion should be continued until the coagulation parameters
are corrected and the bleeding stops.

DIC is a diffuse, disorganized activation of the clotting cascade
within the vascular space. It may result either from intravascular
presentation of an overwhelming clotting stimulus (e.g., massive
crush injury, overwhelming infection, or transfusion reaction) or
from presentation of a moderate clotting stimulus in the context of
shock. Different degrees of severity have been described. In the
mildest form of DIC, acceleration of the clotting cascade is seen,

Table 2 Management of the Patient
with an Increased INR[14]

Indication	Recommended Treatment
INR above therapeutic range but < 5.0	If no bleeding is present or surgery is indicated, lower or hold next dose
INR > 5.0 but < 9.0 Patient has no significant bleeding	In the absence of additional risk factors for bleeding, withhold next 1–2 doses; alternatively, withhold next dose and give vitamin K, 1.0–2.5 mg (oral route is acceptable)
Rapid reduction of INR is required	Give vitamin K, 2.0–4.0 mg p.o.; expected reduction of INR should occur within 24 hr
INR > 9.0 Patient has no significant bleeding	Give vitamin K, 3.0–5.0 mg p.o.; expected reduction of INR should occur within 24 hr
Patient has serious bleeding or is overly anticoagulated (INR > 20.0)	Give vitamin K, 10 mg I.V., and FFP; further vitamin K supplementation may be required every 12 hr
Patient has life-threatening bleeding or is seriously overanticoagulated	Prothrombin complexes may be indicated, along with vitamin K, 10 mg I.V.

and microthrombi are formed in the vascular space but are cleared
effectively. Thus, mild DIC may be little more than an acceleration
of the clotting cascade that escapes recognition. In the moderate
form of DIC, the microthrombi are ineffectively lysed and cause
occlusion of the microcirculation. This process is clinically manifested in the lungs as the acute respiratory distress syndrome (ARDS),
in the kidneys as renal failure, and in the liver as hepatic failure.

Neither mild DIC nor moderate DIC is what surgeons traditionally think of as DIC. Severe DIC arises when congestion of the
microvasculature with thrombi occurs, resulting in large-scale activation of the fibrinolytic system to restore circulation. This fibrinolytic activity results in breakdown of clot at previously hemostatic sites of microscopic injury (e.g., endothelial damage) and macroscopic injury (e.g., I.V. catheter sites, fractures, or surgical wounds).
Bleeding and reexposure to tissue factor stimulate activation of
factor VII with increased coagulation activity; thus, microthrombi
are formed, and the vicious circle continues. The ultimate manifestation of severe DIC is bleeding from (1) fibrinolysis and (2)
depletion (consumption) of coagulation factors.

Several scoring systems have been devised to assess the severity
of DIC. In the absence of any specific treatment for this condition,
these scoring systems are currently most useful for distinguishing
DIC from other causes of coagulopathy (e.g., hypothermia, dilution, and drug effects) [*see Table 3*].[17]

DIC is a diagnosis of exclusion, largely because none of the various treatment strategies tried to date have been particularly suc-

Table 3 Coagulopathy (DIC) Score

Score	INR (sec)	aPTT (sec)	Platelets (1,000/mm³)	Fibrinogen (mg/dl)	D-dimer (ng/ml)
0	< 1.2	< 34	> 150	> 200	< 1,000
1	> 1.2	> 34	< 150	< 200	< 2,000
2	> 1.4	> 39	< 100	< 150	< 4,000
3	> 1.6	> 54	< 60	< 100	> 4,000

aPTT—activated partial thromboplastin time   DIC—disseminated intravascular
coagulopathy   INR—international normalized ratio

cessful. Heparin has been given in large doses in an attempt to break the cycle by stopping the clotting, thus allowing clotting factor levels to return to normal. Antifibrinolytic agents (e.g., ε-aminocaproic acid) have also been tried in an attempt to reduce fibrinolytic activity and thus slow the bleeding that stimulates subsequent clot formation. Antithrombotics (e.g., antithrombin and protein C) have been used as well; improvements have been noted in laboratory measures of DIC but not in survival. At present, interest is focused on activated factor VII, though as yet, the available data are insufficient to validate its use.

Currently, the most appropriate way of treating a patient with severe DIC is to follow a multifaceted approach. First, the clotting stimulus, if still present, should be removed: dead or devitalized tissue should be debrided, abscesses drained, and suspect transfusions discontinued. Second, hypothermia, of any degree of severity, should be corrected. Third, both blood loss (as measured by the hematocrit) and clotting factor deficits (as measured by the INR) should be aggressively corrected (with blood and plasma, respectively). This supportive approach is only modestly successful. For certain groups of patients in whom DIC develops (e.g., those who have sustained head injuries), mortality approaches 100%. This alarmingly high death rate is probably related more to the underlying pathology than to the hematologic derangement.

An increased INR with a prolonged aPTT may also be caused by various isolated factor deficiencies of the common pathway. Congenital deficiencies of factors X, V, and prothrombin are very rare. Acquired factor V deficiencies have been observed in patients with autoimmune disorders. Acquired hypoprothrombinemia has been documented in a small percentage of patients with lupus anticoagulants who exhibit abnormal bleeding. Factor X deficiencies have been noted in patients with amyloidosis.

Stabilized warfarin therapy will increase both the INR and the aPTT. Several current rodenticides (e.g., brodifacoum) exert the same effect on these parameters that warfarin does; however, because they have a considerably longer half-life than warfarin, the reversal of the anticoagulation effect with vitamin K or FFP may be correspondingly longer.[18] Animal venoms may also increase the INR and the aPTT.

Management of Anemia and Indications for Transfusion

Anemia is common among hospitalized surgical patients. In two large prospective cohort studies, the average hemoglobin level in surgical ICU patients was 11.0 g/dl,[19] and 55% of surgical ICU patients received transfusions.[20] Anemia results from at least three factors: (1) blood loss related to the primary condition or to the operation, (2) serial blood draws (totaling, on average, approximately 40 ml/day in the ICU),[19] and (3) diminished erythropoiesis related to the primary illness.

Treatment of anemia has changed substantially since the early 1990s. Blood cell transfusions have been shown to have significant immunosuppressive potential, and transmission of fatal diseases through the blood supply has been extensively documented. Although the blood-banking community has systematically reduced the risk of transmission of infection by restricting the eligible donor pool and routinely testing blood products for serologic and nucleic acid evidence of pathogens,[21] comparatively little progress has been made in defining and controlling the immunomodulatory effects of transfusion [see Discussion, Mechanism and Significance of Transfusion-Related Immunomodulation, below]. Moreover, at least one large trial, the Transfusion Requirements in Critical Care (TRICC) study, found that using a restrictive RBC

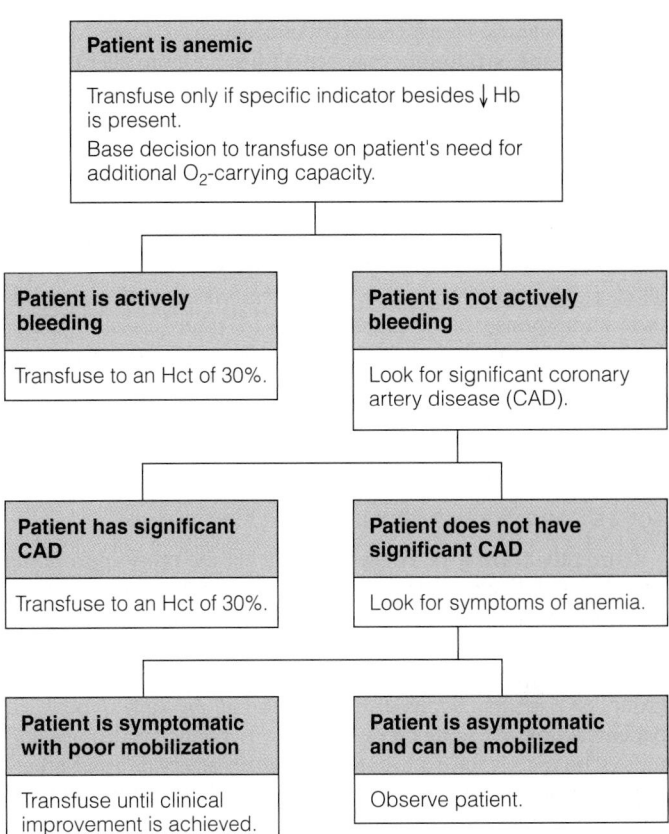

Figure 1 Algorithm depicts decision-making process for transfusion in anemic patients.

transfusion protocol (aimed at maintaining a hemoglobin concentration of 7.0 to 9.0 g/dl) in place of a more traditional protocol (aimed at maintaining a hemoglobin concentration of 10.0 to 12.0 g/dl) did not harm critically ill patients and even appeared to improve survival for younger or less severely ill patients.[22] These findings have encouraged a paradigm shift with respect to RBC transfusion: whereas the traditional view was that anemia by itself was a sufficient indication for transfusion, the current consensus is that the threshold for transfusion should be determined by taking into account additional clinical factors besides the hemoglobin concentration.[23]

The decision whether to transfuse should be based on the patient's current and predicted need for additional oxygen-carrying capacity [see Figure 1]. A major component of this decision is to determine as promptly as possible whether significant hypovolemia or active bleeding is present. In a hypovolemic or actively bleeding patient, liberal transfusion is indicated as a means of increasing intravascular volume and preventing the development of profound deficits in oxygen-carrying capacity. Coagulation factors must also be replaced as necessary [see Measurement of Coagulation Parameters, Increased INR, Prolonged aPTT, above]. In a hemodynamically stable patient without evidence of active hemorrhage, it is appropriate to take a more restrictive approach to transfusion, one that is tailored to the symptoms observed and to the specific anticipated risks. Thus, there is no specific hemoglobin concentration or hematocrit (i.e., transfusion trigger) at which all patients should receive transfusions.

There are two groups of patients for whom a more aggressive RBC transfusion policy should be considered. Patients who are at high risk for active bleeding and patients who have acute coronary artery ischemic syndromes may benefit from a more liberal transfusion protocol than that applied to the general patient population.

HIGH RISK FOR ACTIVE BLEEDING

Patients who are at high risk for active bleeding (e.g., those with a massive liver injury or recurrent GI hemorrhage) should receive transfusions up to a level at which, should bleeding occur or recur, enough reserve oxygen-carrying capacity would be available to allow diagnosis and correction of the hemorrhage without significant compromise of oxygen delivery. In acute cases of major injury, we advocate an initial target hematocrit of 30%; however, this is not a fixed value but a rule-of-thumb figure that may be increased or decreased as appropriate, depending on the individual patient's reserves and the individual surgical team's ability to diagnose and correct the underlying problem.

ACUTE CORONARY ARTERY ISCHEMIC SYNDROMES

Currently, there is no consensus on what the most appropriate transfusion strategy is for patients with acute coronary artery ischemic syndromes, such as active myocardial infarction and unstable angina. The results of observational studies have been mixed,[24,25] and no clinical trial has yet addressed this specific subgroup of patients. Some distinction should be drawn between patients who have acute coronary artery ischemic syndromes and those who merely have a history of coronary artery or other atherosclerotic disease. Although the TRICC trial apparently did not enroll many patients with severe cardiovascular morbidity,[22] it included enough patients with cardiovascular disease to allow a sizable subgroup analysis.[26] This post hoc analysis suggested that in patients with cardiovascular disease as a primary diagnosis or an important comorbid condition, survival was essentially the same regardless of whether a liberal transfusion protocol or a restrictive one was followed. In patients with confirmed ischemic heart disease, however, a nonsignificant decrease in survival was noted, generating some concern that adverse cardiovascular events (e.g., myocardial infarction and stroke) might increase in frequency at lower hematocrits. Consequently, a target hematocrit of 30% is generally considered acceptable for patients with acute coronary artery ischemic syndromes or significant coronary artery disease.

NEUROLOGIC CONDITIONS

Some have argued that just as the heart may be sensitive to decreases in oxygen-carrying capacity, the injured central nervous system may be vulnerable to further damage from anemia because anemia may limit the delivery of oxygen to damaged tissue. According to this view, patients with traumatic brain injury, stroke, or spinal cord injury may be vulnerable to anemia-related damage; however, as yet, the clinical evidence is insufficient either to support or to refute this notion.

SYMPTOMATIC ANEMIA

An additional consideration in the decision to transfuse blood is the oxygen-carrying capacity that is necessary to prevent patient fatigue or discomfort. Typical symptoms of anemia include light-headedness, tachycardia, and tachypnea either during activity or at rest. Clearly, some degree of tachycardia is to be expected in any patient who has undergone a major operation or sustained a serious injury. The key judgment to make in deciding whether to treat symptomatic anemia with transfusion is whether the anemia is truly compromising the patient's health or recovery. It is not always easy, however, to determine whether the patient will actually benefit from transfusion. For example, a lib-

eral transfusion approach does not seem to lead to earlier liberation from mechanical ventilation.[27] Moreover, although some studies support the notion that transfusion speeds wound healing,[28] others suggest that transfusion may also increase the incidence of infection and impaired wound healing.[29] A major randomized trial, the Functional Outcomes in Cardiovascular Patients Undergoing Surgical hip fracture repair (FOCUS) study, is currently being conducted to address the issue of functional recovery. Its primary aim is to determine whether liberal transfusion improves walking ability among anemic patients with a history of cardiovascular disease who undergo operative repair of a hip fracture.[30]

OBSERVATION OF ANEMIA

It is now standard practice to observe patients with low hemoglobin concentrations that in the past would have triggered transfusion. For most acutely anemic patients, the data currently available support this approach down to a hemoglobin concentration of 6 to 7 g/dl; however, below 6 g/dl, the data suggest that the benefits of transfusion outweigh the risks.

For all patients, if the hemoglobin level drops low enough, cellular metabolism cannot be sustained and death becomes a certainty. Followers of certain religious faiths have frequently declined blood transfusion even when death is the probable or certain consequence. Such situations have challenged the medical community to find techniques for supporting life at extremely low hemoglobin concentrations, and they have helped to define the limits beyond which a restrictive transfusion protocol may be fatal. Reviews of patients who have refused transfusion suggest that a hemoglobin below 5 g/dl results in substantial increases in mortality, especially in elderly persons and patients with cardiovascular disease.[31]

When RBC transfusion is not possible (whether because the patient declines transfusion or because compatible blood is unavailable), there are a number of temporizing measures that can be used to support life. First, steps should be taken to minimize additional iatrogenic blood loss. Laboratory tests should be restricted to those that are most likely to benefit the patient, and they should be conducted with the smallest amount of blood possible (e.g., the volume contained in pediatric specimen tubes). Non-emergency operations that are likely to involve appreciable blood loss should be postponed if possible. Second, any impediments to native erythropoiesis should be removed: iron should be supple-

Table 4 Blood Substitutes[99]

Product (Manufacturer)	Source
PHP (Apex Bioscience)	Pyridoxylated human hemoglobin conjugated to polyoxyethylene
PEG-hemoglobin (Enzon)	Bovine hemoglobin conjugated to polyethylene glycol
PolyHeme (Northfield Laboratories)	Glutaraldehyde-polymerized pyridoxylated human hemoglobin
Hemopure (Biopure)	Glutaraldehyde-polymerized bovine hemoglobin
Hemolink (Hemosol)	Oxidized raffinose–cross-linked human hemoglobin from expired stored blood
Oxygent (Alliance Pharmaceutical)	Emulsified perflubron

mented orally if possible, and the administration of recombinant erythropoietin should be considered. Third, in extreme cases, consideration should be given to decreasing oxygen demand. Oxygen demand is directly proportional to metabolic activity; that is, as metabolic rate increases, so too does oxygen demand. Once the patient is immobile, respiration becomes a significant contributor to metabolic requirements. Mechanical ventilation reduces the work of breathing and with it the oxygen requirements of the respiratory muscles. Respiratory efforts can be fully eliminated with neuromuscular blocking agents, which will reduce oxygen demand in essentially all skeletal muscle, and the metabolic rate can be further reduced by inducing hypothermia.

A completely different approach to the issue of the unacceptability or unavailability of RBC transfusion involves the use of RBC substitutes to augment oxygen-carrying capacity. Various different substitutes are currently under investigation [see Table 4].[32] None have been approved for routine use by the United States Food and Drug Administration, but several have demonstrated promise in clinical trials. Without modification, the hemoglobin molecule is nephrotoxic. Accordingly, virtually all of the products now being studied depend on techniques for making an acellular hemoglobin molecule nontoxic for I.V. administration.

Acellular blood substitutes clearly possess a number of advantages, including greatly increased shelf life, reduced risk of viral transmission, availability that is not limited by donor supply, reduced or eliminated risk of incompatibility reactions, and potentially greater acceptance among patients who decline blood transfusions.[33] To what extent this approach is suited to the treatment of anemia in surgical patients should be clarified when the results of the trials now under way are published.

Discussion

Mechanics of Hemostasis

Hemostasis is the term for the process by which cellular and plasma components interact in response to vessel injury in order to maintain vascular integrity and promote wound healing. The initial response to vascular injury (primary hemostasis) involves the recruitment and activation of platelets, which then adhere to the site of injury. Subsequently, plasma proteins, in concert with cellular components, begin to generate thrombin, which causes further activation of platelets and converts fibrinogen to fibrin monomers that polymerize into a fibrin clot. The final step is the release of plasminogen activators that induce clot lysis and tissue repair.

The cellular components of hemostasis include endothelium, white blood cells (WBCs), RBCs, and platelets. The plasma components include a number of procoagulant and regulatory proteins that, once activated, can accelerate or downregulate thrombin formation or clot lysis to facilitate wound healing. In normal individuals, these hemostatic components are in a regulatory balance; thus, any abnormality involving one or more of these components can result in a pathologic state, whether of uncontrolled clot formation (thrombosis) or of excessive bleeding (hemorrhage). These pathologies can result from either hereditary defects of protein synthesis or acquired deficiencies attributable to metabolic causes.

CELLULAR COMPONENTS

Endothelium

The endothelium has both procoagulant and anticoagulant properties. When vascular injury occurs, the endothelium serves as a nidus for recruitment of platelets, adhesion of platelets to the endothelial surface, platelet aggregation, migration of platelets across the endothelial surface, generation of fibrin, and expression of adhesion molecule receptors (E-selectin and P-selectin). Exposure of collagen fibrils and release of vWF from the Weibel-Palade bodies cause platelets to adhere to the cellular surface of the endothelium. The presence of interleukin-1β (IL-1β), tissue necrosis factor (TNF), interferon gamma (IFN-γ), and thrombin promotes expression of tissue factor (TF) on the endothelium.[34,35] TF activates factors X and VII, and these activated factors generate additional thrombin, which increases both fibrin formation and platelet aggregation.

The endothelium also acts in numerous ways to downregulate coagulation.[36] Heparan sulfate and thrombomodulin are both down-regulators of thrombin formation. In the presence of thrombin, the endothelium responds by (1) releasing thrombomodulin, which forms a complex with thrombin to activate protein C; (2) producing endothelium-derived relaxing factor (i.e., nitric oxide[37]) and prostacyclin, which have vasodilating and platelet aggregation-inhibiting effects, respectively; and (3) releasing tissue plasminogen activator (t-PA) or urokinase-type plasminogen activator (u-PA), either of which converts the zymogen plasminogen to an active form (i.e., plasmin) that degrades fibrin and fibrinogen.[34,38] Heparan sulfate, on the endothelium wall, forms a complex with plasma antithrombin to neutralize thrombin. The endothelium is also the source of tissue factor pathway inhibitor (TFPI), which downregulates TF-VIIa-Xa complexes.

Erythrocytes and Leukocytes

The nonplatelet cellular components of blood play indirect roles in hemostasis. RBCs contain thromboplastins that are potent stimulators of various procoagulant proteins. In addition, the concentration of RBCs within the bloodstream (expressed as the hematocrit) assists in primary hemostasis by physically forcing the platelets toward the endothelial surfaces. When the RBC count is low enough, the absence of this force results in inadequate endothelium-platelet interaction and a bleeding diathesis.

Leukocytes have several functions in the hemostatic process. The interaction between the adhesion molecules expressed on both leukocytes and endothelium results in cytokine production, initiation of inflammatory responses, and degradation of extracellular matrix to facilitate tissue healing. In the presence of thrombin, monocytes express TF, which is an integral procoagulant for thrombin generation. Neutrophils and activated monocytes bind to stimulated platelets and endothelial cells that express P-selectin. Adhesion and rolling of neutrophils, mediated by fibrinogen and selectins on the endothelium, appear to help restore vessel integrity but may also lead to inflammatory responses.[39,40] Lymphocytes also adhere to endothelium via adhesion molecule receptors and appear to be responsible for cytokine production and inflammatory responses.

Platelets

The roles platelets play in hemostasis and subsequent fibrin formation rest on providing a phospholipid surface for localizing procoagulant activation. Activation of platelets by agonists such as adenosine triphosphate (ATP), adenosine diphosphate (ADP), epinephrine, thromboxane A$_2$, collagen, and thrombin causes platelets to undergo morphologic changes and degranulation. Degranulation of platelets results in the release of procoagulants that promote further platelet adhesion and aggregation (e.g., thrombospondin, vWF, fibrinogen, ADP, ATP, and serotonin), and surface expression of P-selectin, which induces cellular adhesion. Platelet degranulation also results in the release of β-thromboglobulin, platelet factor 4 (which has antiheparin properties), various growth factors, coagulation procoagulants, and calcium as well as the formation of platelet microparticles. Plasminogen activator inhibitor-1 (PAI-1) released from degranulated platelets neutralizes the fibrinolytic pathway by forming a complex with t-PA.

Upon exposure to vascular injury, platelets adhere to the exposed endothelium via binding of vWF to the GPIb-IX-V complex.[41] Conformational changes in the GPIIb-IIIa complex on the activated platelet surface enhance fibrinogen binding, which results in platelet-to-platelet interaction (i.e., complex morphologic changes and aggregation). The phospholipid surface of the platelet membranes anchors activated IXa-VIIIa and Xa-Va complexes, thereby localizing thrombin generation.[42]

PLASMA COMPONENTS

Procoagulants

Traditional diagrams of the coagulation cascade depict two distinct pathways for thrombin generation: the intrinsic pathway and the extrinsic pathway. The premise for the distinction between the two is that the intrinsic pathway requires no extravascular source for initiation, whereas the extrinsic pathway requires an extravascular component (i.e., TF). This traditional depiction is useful in interpreting coagulation tests, but it is not an accurate reflection of the hemostatic process in vivo. Accordingly, our focus is not on this standard view but rather on the roles contact factors (within the intrinsic cascade) and TF play in coagulation. As noted, circulating plasma vWF is necessary for normal adhesion of platelets to the endothelium. Plasma vWF also serves as the carrier protein for factor VIII, preventing its neutralization by the protein C regulatory pathway.

Even in patients in whom laboratory tests strongly suggest a severe clotting abnormality (i.e., the aPTT is markedly prolonged), contact factors do not play a significant role in the generation of thrombin. However, contact factor activation does appear to play secondary roles that are essential to normal hemostasis and tissue repair. Factor XII, prekallikrein, and high-molecular-weight kininogen are bound to the endothelium to activate the bradykinin (BK) pathway. The BK pathway exerts profibrinolytic effects by stimulating endothelial release of plasminogen activators. It also stimulates endothelial production of nitric oxide and prostacyclin, which play vital regulatory roles in vasodilation and regulation of platelet activation.[43]

The key initiator of plasma procoagulant formation is the expression of TF on cell surfaces.[35,44] TF activates factor VII and binds with it to form the TF-VIIa complex, which activates factors X and IX. Factor Xa also enhances its own production by activating factor IX, which in turn activates factor X to form factor Xa. Factor Xa also produces minimal amounts of thrombin by cleaving the prothrombin molecule. The thrombin generated from this process cleaves the coagulation cofactors V and VIII to enhance production of the factor complexes IX-VIIIa (intrinsic tenase) and Xa-Va (prothrombinase), which catalyze conversion of prothrombin to thrombin [see Figure 2].[45]

Thrombin has numerous functions, including prothrombotic and regulatory functions. Its procoagulant properties include cleaving fibrinogen, activating the coagulation cofactors V and VIII, inducing platelet aggregation, inducing expression of TF on cell surfaces, and activating factor XIII. In cleaving fibrinogen, thrombin causes the release of fibrinopeptides A and B (fibrin monomer). The fibrin monomer undergoes conformational changes that expose the α and β chains of the molecule, which then polymerize with other fibrin monomers to form a fibrin mesh. Activated factor XIII cross-links the polymerized fibrin (between the α chains and the γ chains) to stabilize the fibrin clot and delay fibrinolysis.

Fibrin(ogen)olysis

Plasminogen is the primary fibrinolytic zymogen that circulates in plasma. In the presence of t-PA or u-PA (released from the endothelium), plasminogen is converted to the active form, plasmin. Plasmin cleaves fibrin (or fibrinogen) between the molecule's D and E domains, causing the formation of X, Y, D, and E fragments. The secondary function of the fibrinolytic pathway is the activation by u-PA of matrix metalloproteinases that degrade the extracellular matrix.[46]

Regulatory Factors

In persons with normal coagulation status, downregulation of hemostasis occurs simultaneously with the production of procoagulants (e.g., activated plasma factors, stimulated endothelium, and stimulated platelets). In addition to their procoagulant activity, both thrombin and contact factors stimulate downregulation of the coagulation process. Thrombin forms a complex with endothelium-bound thrombomodulin to activate protein C, which inhibits factors Va and VIIIa. The thrombin-thrombomodulin complex also regulates the fibrinolytic pathway by activating a circulating plasma protein known as thrombin-activatable fibrinolysis inhibitor (TAFI), which appears to suppress conversion of plasminogen to plasmin.[47] Contact factors are known to be required for normal surface-dependent fibrinolysis, and there is some evidence that contact factor deficiencies can lead to thromboembolism. Another plasma protein responsible for regulation of fibrinolysis is α$_2$-antiplasmin, which binds to circulating and bound plasmin to limit breakdown of fibrin.

Circulating downregulating proteins include antithrombin (a serine protease inhibitor of activated factors—especially factors IXa, Xa, and XIa—and thrombin[45]), proteins C and S (regulators of factors VIIIa and Va[48]), C1 inhibitor (a regulator of factor XIa), TFPI (a regulator of the TF-VIIa-Xa complex[49]), and α$_2$-macroglobulin (a thrombin inhibitor—the primary thrombin inhibitor in neonates[50]). Limitation of platelet activation occurs secondarily as a result of decreased levels of circulating agonists and endothelial release of prostacyclin [see Figure 2].

Bleeding Disorders

INHERITED COAGULOPATHIES

Numerous congenital abnormalities of the coagulation system have been identified. In particular, various abnormalities involving plasma proteins (e.g., hemophilia and vWD), platelet receptors (e.g., Glanzmann thrombasthenia and Bernard-Soulier syndrome), and endothelium (e.g., telangiectasia) have been described in detail. For the sake of brevity, we will refer to abnormal protein synthesis resulting in a dysfunctional coagulation protein as a defect and to abnormal protein synthesis resulting in decreased protein production as a deficiency.

Most of the coagulation defects associated with endothelium are closely related to thrombosis or atherosclerosis. Defects or

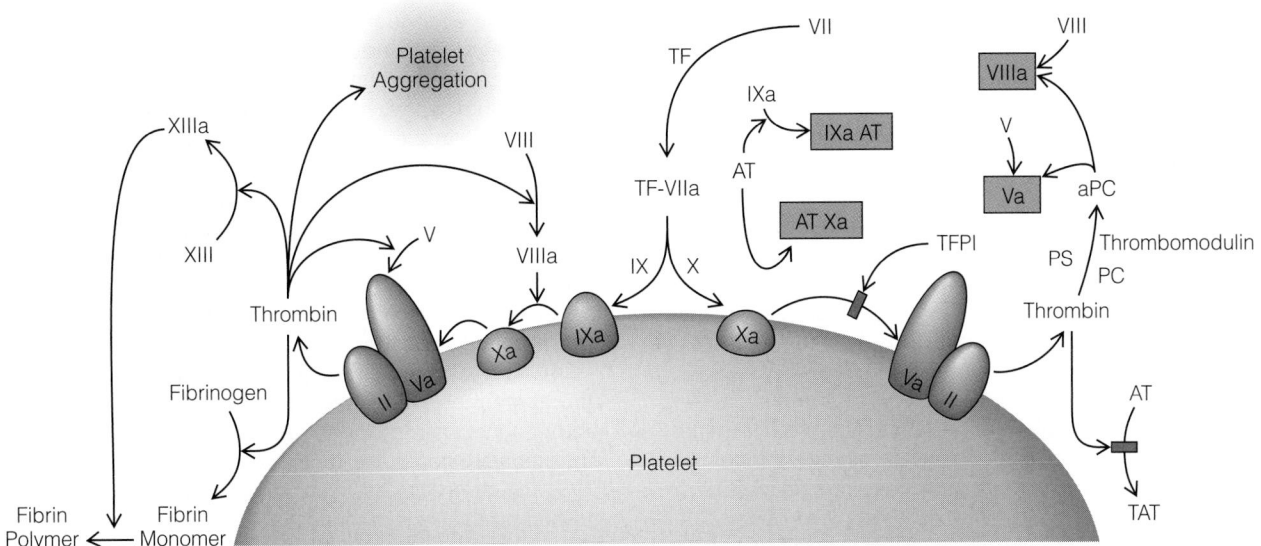

Figure 2 **Shown is a schematic representation of the procoagulant pathways.**

deficiencies of thrombomodulin, TFPI, and t-PA, albeit rare, are associated with thrombosis.[51,52] Vascular defects (e.g., hemorrhagic telangiectasias) may carry an increased risk of bleeding as a consequence of dysfunctional fibrinolysis, concomitant platelet dysfunction, or coagulation factor deficiencies.[53]

Defects or deficiencies of RBCs and WBCs have other primary clinical manifestations that are not related to hemostasis. Alterations in the physical properties of blood (e.g., decreased blood flow from increased viscosity, polycythemia vera, leukocytosis, and sickle-cell anemia) have been reported to lead to thrombosis but usually not to major bleeding.

Inherited platelet membrane receptor defects are relatively common. Of these, vWD is the one that most frequently causes bleeding.[54] The condition is characterized by vWF abnormalities, which may take three forms: vWF may be present in a reduced concentration (type I vWD), dysfunctional (type II vWD), or absent altogether (type III). Diagnosis of vWD is based on a combination of the patient history (e.g., previous mucosal bleeding) and laboratory parameters [*see* Laboratory Assessment of Bleeding, *below*]. It is necessary to identify the correct type or subtype of vWD: some treatments (e.g., DDAVP) are contraindicated in patients with type IIb vWD.[55]

Less common receptor defects include Glanzmann thrombasthenia (a defect in the GPIIb-IIIa complex), Bernard-Soulier syndrome (a defect in the GPIb-IX complex), and Scott syndrome (a defect in the platelet's activated surface that promotes thrombin formation); other agonist receptors on the platelet membrane may be affected as well.[56,57] Intracellular platelet defects are relatively rare but do occur; examples are gray platelet syndromes (e.g., alpha granule defects), Hermansky-Pudlak syndrome, dense granule defects, Wiskott-Aldrich syndrome, and various defects in intracellular production and signaling (involving defects of cyclooxygenase synthase and phospholipase C, respectively).[57]

Numerous pathologic states are also associated with deficiencies or defects of plasma procoagulants. Inherited sex-linked deficiencies of factor VIII (i.e., hemophilia A) and factor IX (i.e., hemophilia B and Christmas disease) are relatively common.[58-60] The clinical presentations of hemophilia A and hemophilia B are similar: hemarthroses are the most common clinical manifestations, ultimately leading to degenerative joint deformities.

Spontaneous bleeding may also occur, resulting in intracranial hemorrhage, large hematomas in the muscles of extremities, hematuria, and GI bleeding. Factor XI deficiency is relatively common in Jewish persons but rarely results in spontaneous bleeding.[61,62] Such deficiency may result in bleeding after oral operations and trauma; however, there are a number of major procedures (e.g., cardiac bypass surgery) that do not result in postoperative bleeding in this population.[63]

Inherited deficiencies of the other coagulation factors are very rare. Factor XIII deficiencies result in delayed postoperative or posttraumatic bleeding. Congenital deficiencies of factor V, factor VII, factor X, prothrombin, and fibrinogen may become apparent in the neonatal period (presenting, for example, as umbilical stump bleeding); later in life, they result in clinical presentations such as epistaxis, intracranial bleeding, GI bleeding, deep and superficial bruising, and menorrhagia.

Defects or deficiencies in the fibrinolytic pathway are also rare and are most commonly associated with thromboembolic events. α_2-Antiplasmin deficiencies and primary fibrin(ogen)olysis are rare congenital coagulopathies with clinical presentations similar to those of factor deficiencies. In primary fibrin(ogen)olysis, failure of regulation of t-PA and u-PA leads to increases in circulating plasmin levels, which result in rapid degradation of clot and fibrinogen.[64,65]

ACQUIRED COAGULOPATHIES

A wide range of clinical conditions may cause deficiencies of the primary, secondary, or fibrinolytic pathways. Acquired coagulopathies are very common, and most do not result in spontaneous bleeding. (DIC is an exception [*see* Disseminated Intravascular Coagulation, *below*].)

As noted, coagulopathies related to the endothelium are primarily associated with thrombosis rather than bleeding. There are a number of disorders that may cause vascular injury, including sickle-cell anemia, hemolytic-uremic syndrome, and thrombotic thrombocytopenic purpura.

Acquired platelet abnormalities, both qualitative (i.e., dysfunction) and quantitative (i.e., decreases in absolute numbers), are common occurrences. Many acquired thrombocytopathies are attributable to either foods (e.g., fish oils, chocolate, red wine, garlic, and herbs) or drugs (e.g., aspirin, ibuprofen, other nonsteroidal anti-inflammatory drugs, ticlopidine, various antibiotics, certain antihistamines, and phenytoin).[66-70] Direct anti–platelet receptor drugs (e.g., abciximab and eptifibatide) block the GPIIb-IIIa complex, thereby preventing platelet aggregation.[71] Thrombocytopenia can be primary or secondary to a number of clinical conditions. Primary bone disorders (e.g., myelodysplastic or myelophthisic syndromes) and spontaneous bleeding may arise when platelet counts fall below 10,000/mm³.

Thrombocytopenia can be associated with immune causes (e.g., immune thrombocytopenic purpura or thrombotic thrombocytopenic purpura) or can occur secondary to administration of drugs (e.g., heparin). Acquired platelet dysfunction (e.g., acquired vWD) that is not related to dietary or pharmacologic causes has been observed in patients with immune disorders or cancer.

Acquired plasma factor deficiencies are common as well. Patients with severe renal disease typically exhibit platelet dysfunction (from excessive amounts of uremic metabolites), factor deficiencies associated with impaired synthesis or protein loss (as with increased urinary excretion), or thrombocytopenia (from diminished thrombopoietin production).[72,73] Patients with severe hepatic disease commonly have impairment of coagulation factor synthesis, increases in circulating levels of paraproteins, and splenic sequestration of platelets.

Hemodilution from massive RBC transfusions can occur if more than 10 packed RBC units are given within a short period without plasma supplementation. Immunologic reactions to ABO/Rh mismatches can induce immune-mediated hypercoagulation. Acquired multifactorial deficiencies associated with extracorporeal circuits (e.g., cardiopulmonary bypass, hemodialysis, and continuous venovenous dialysis) can arise as a consequence of hemodilution from circuit priming fluid or activation of procoagulants after exposure to thrombogenic surfaces.[74-76] Thrombocytopenia can result from platelet destruction and activation caused by circuit membrane exposure, or it can be secondary to the presence of heparin antibody.

Animal venoms can be either procoagulant or prothrombotic. The majority of the poisonous snakes in the United States (rattlesnakes in particular) have venom that works by activating prothrombin, but cross-breeding has produced a number of new venoms with different hemostatic consequences. The clinical presentation of coagulopathies associated with snakebites generally mimics that of consumptive coagulopathies.[77]

Drug-induced factor deficiencies are common, particularly as a result of anticoagulant therapy. The most commonly used anticoagulants are heparin and warfarin. Heparin does not cause a factor deficiency; rather, it accelerates production of antithrombin, which inhibits factor IXa, factor Xa, and thrombin, thereby prolonging clot formation. Warfarin reduces procoagulant potential by inhibiting vitamin K synthesis, thereby reducing carboxylation of factor VII, factor IX, factor X, prothrombin, and proteins C and S. Newer drugs that may also cause factor deficiencies include direct thrombin inhibitors (e.g., lepirudin and bivalirudin[78]) and fibrinogen-degrading drugs (e.g., ancrod[79]).

Isolated acquired factor deficiencies are relatively rare. Clinically, they present in exactly the same way as inherited factor deficiencies, except that there is no history of earlier bleeding. In most cases, there is a secondary disease (e.g., lymphoma or an autoimmune disorder) that results in the development of antibody to a procoagulant (e.g., factor V, factor VIII, factor IX, vWF, prothrombin, or fibrinogen).[80-82]

Disseminated Intravascular Coagulation

DIC is a complex coagulation process that involves activation of the coagulation system with resultant activation of the fibrinolytic pathway and deposition of fibrin; the eventual consequence is the multiple organ dysfunction syndrome (MODS).[83] The activation occurs at all levels (platelets, endothelium, and procoagulants), but it is not known whether this process is initiated by a local stimulus or a systemic one. It is crucial to emphasize that DIC is an acquired disorder that occurs secondary to an underlying clinical event (e.g., a complicated birth, severe gram-negative infection, shock, major head injury, polytrauma, severe burns, or cancer). As noted [*see* Measurement of Coagulation Parameters, Increased INR, Prolonged aPTT, *above*], there is some controversy regarding the best approach to therapy, but there is no doubt that treating the underlying cause of DIC is paramount to patient recovery.

DIC is not always clinically evident: low-grade DIC may lack clinical symptoms altogether and manifest itself only through laboratory abnormalities, even when thrombin generation and fibrin deposition are occurring. In an attempt to facilitate recognition of DIC, the disorder has been divided into three phases, distinguished on the basis of clinical and laboratory evidence. In phase I DIC, there are no clinical symptoms, and the routine screening tests (i.e., INR, aPTT, fibrinogen level, and platelet count) are within normal limits.[84] Secondary testing (i.e., measurement of antithrombin, prothrombin fragment, thrombin-antithrombin complex, and soluble fibrin levels) may reveal subtle changes indicative of thrombin generation. In phase II DIC, there are usually clinical signs of bleeding around wounds, suture sites, I.V. sites, or venous puncture sites, and decreased function is noted in specific organs (e.g., lung, liver, and kidneys). The INR is increased, the aPTT is prolonged, and the fibrinogen level and platelet count are decreased or decreasing. Other markers of thrombin generation and fibrinolysis (e.g., D-dimer level) show sizable elevations. In phase III DIC, MODS is observed, the INR and the aPTT are markedly increased, the fibrinogen level is markedly depressed, and the D-dimer level is dramatically increased. A peripheral blood smear would show large numbers of schistocytes, indicating RBC shearing resulting from fibrin deposition.

The activation of the coagulation system seen in DIC appears to be primarily caused by TF. The brain, the placenta, and solid tumors are all rich sources of TF. Gram-negative endotoxins also induce TF expression. The exposure of TF on cellular surfaces causes activation of factors VII and IX, which ultimately leads to thrombin generation. Circulating thrombin is rapidly cleared by antithrombin. Moreover, the coagulation pathway is downregulated by activated protein C and protein S. However, constant exposure of TF (as a result of underlying disorders) results in constant generation of thrombin, and these regulator proteins are rapidly consumed. TAFI and PAI also contribute to fibrin deposition by restricting fibrinolysis and subsequent fibrin degradation and clearance. Finally, it is likely that release of cytokines (e.g., IL-6, IL-10, and TNF) may play some role in causing the sequelae of DIC by modulating or activating the coagulation pathway.

Laboratory Assessment of Bleeding

Laboratory testing is an integral part of the diagnostic algorithm used in assessing the bleeding patient. It may not be prudent to wait for laboratory values before beginning treatment of acute bleeding, but it is imperative that blood samples for coagulation testing be drawn before therapy. The development of microprocessor technology has made it possible to perform diagnostic laboratory testing outside the confines of the clinical laboratory (so-called near-care testing). Whether near-care testing or clinical laboratory testing is employed, it is important to recognize that valuable as such testing is, it does not provide all of the needed diagnostic information.

In particular, the value of a careful patient history must not be underestimated. Previous bleeding events and a familial history of bleeding are both suggestive of a congenital coagulopathy. A thorough medication inventory is necessary to assess the possible impact of drugs on laboratory and clinical presentations. In the patient history query, it is advisable to ask explicitly about nonprescription drugs—using expressions such as "over-the-counter drugs," "cold medicines," and "Pepto-Bismol"—because unless specifically reminded, patients tend to equate the term medications with prescription drugs. If this is not done, many drugs that are capable of influencing hemostasis in vivo and in vitro (e.g., salicylates, cold and allergy medicines, and herbal supplements) may be missed. Mucosal and superficial bleeding is suggestive of platelet abnormalities, and deep bleeding is suggestive of factor deficiency.

It is important to be clear on the limitations of coagulation testing. At present, there are no laboratory or ex vivo methods capable of directly measuring the physiologic properties of the endothelium. Indirect assessments of endothelial damage can be obtained by measuring levels of several laboratory parameters (e.g., vWF, the soluble cytokines endothelin-1 and E-selectin, and thrombomodulin), but such measurements have no clinical utility in the assessment of a bleeding patient.

Another issue is that of bias resulting from technical factors. PT (i.e., INR) and aPTT testing involves adding activators, phospholipids, and calcium to plasma in a test tube (or the equivalent) and determining the time to clot formation. Time to clot formation is a relative value, in that it is compared with the time in a normal population. A perturbation within the coagulation cascade, an excess of calcium, or poor sampling techniques (e.g., inadequately filled coagulation tubes, excessive tourniquet time, and clotted or activated samples) can bias the results. Hemolysis from the drawing of blood can also bias results via the effects of thromboplastins released from RBC membranes to initiate the coagulation process. In addition, many coagulation factors are highly labile, and failure to process and run coagulation samples immediately can bias test results.

Finally, not all coagulation tests are functionally equivalent: different laboratory methods may yield differing results.[85] Coagulation reagents have been manufactured in such a way as to ensure that the coagulation screening tests are sensitive to factor VIII and IX deficiencies and the effects of anticoagulation with warfarin or heparin. Thus, a normal aPTT in a patient with an abnormal INR may not exclude the possibility of common pathway deficiencies (e.g., deficiencies of factors X, V, and II), and most current methods of determining the INR and the aPTT do not detect low fibrinogen levels. The approach we use assumes that the methods used to assess INR and aPTT can discriminate normal factor activity levels from abnormal levels (< 0.4 IU/ml).

The CBC (including platelet count and differential count), the INR, and the aPTT tests should be the primary laboratory tests for differentiating coagulopathies [see Figure 3].

Platelet count and platelet function should be considered as independent values [see Figure 4]. Patients with congenital thrombocytopathies often have normal platelet counts; therefore, assessment of platelet function is required as well. Historically, the bleeding time has been used to assess platelet function. This test is grossly inadequate, in that it may yield normal results in as many as 50% of patients with congenital thrombocytopathies.[86,87] Numerous rapid tests of platelet function are currently available that can be used to screen for platelet defects; these tests should be considered in the diagnostic approach to the bleeding patient [see Table 5].[87-89]

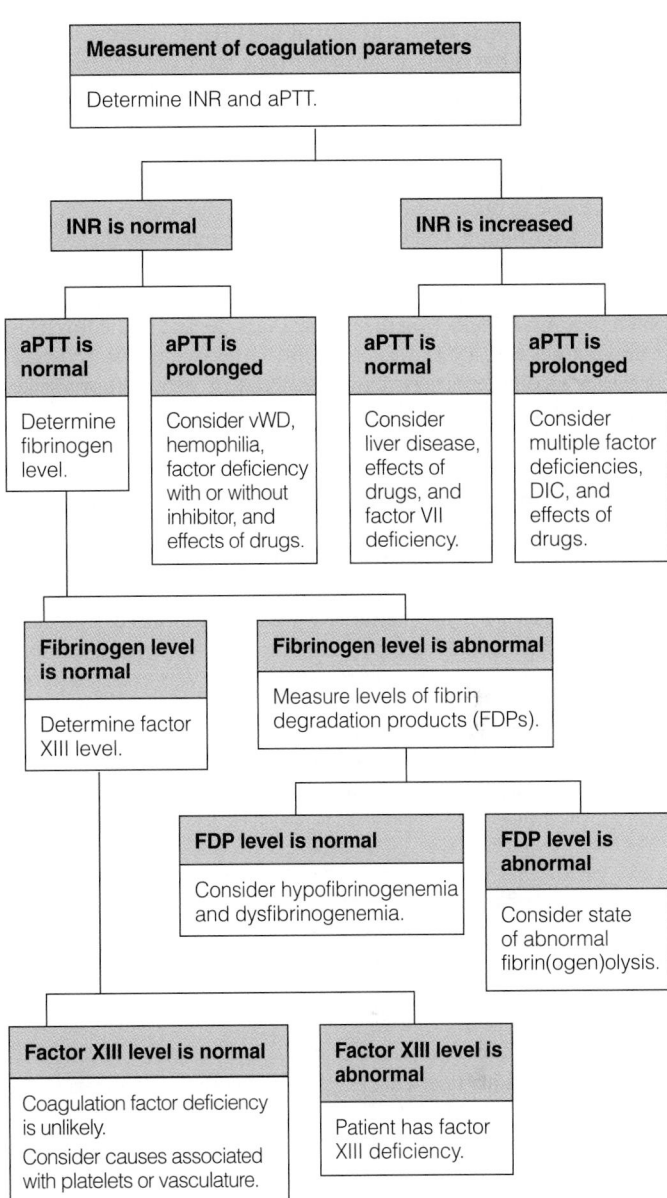

Figure 3 **Algorithm depicts use of coagulation parameters in assessment of coagulopathies.**

Novel and Experimental Therapies for Bleeding

Novel approaches to controlling bleeding have been developed for use in two specific patient groups: (1) patients with uncontrolled exsanguinating hemorrhage and (2) elderly patients on warfarin therapy who have a therapeutic INR and who present with intracranial bleeding.

As noted [see Measurement of Coagulation Parameters, Normal INR, Prolonged aPTT, *above*], recombinant factor VIIa is currently used for control of bleeding in hemophilia A patients with antibodies to factors VIII as well as in hemophilia B patients with antibodies to factor IX, and it has received FDA approval for this indication. The remarkable success of rVIIa in this setting led many investigators to consider the possibility that giving this agent to actively bleeding patients would enhance the normal clotting mechanism and provide nonsurgical control or reduction of traumatic bleeding. Accordingly, rVIIa has been advocated for early use in injured patients with uncontrolled hemorrhage.[90]

One international randomized trial of rVIIa in severely injured trauma patients has been performed.[91] The results of this trial suggested that there was a decreased requirement for blood transfusions and a trend toward decreased organ failure among blunt trauma patients who received rVIIa, but no reduction in mortality was demonstrated. It is to be hoped that the trauma surgery community will be able to organize a more robust trial that will be capable of formally determining whether the putative benefits of rVIIa are outweighed by the potential risks.[92] In the absence of such a formal determination, surgeons will continue to encounter situations in which they must decide whether to use rVIIa despite its incompletely understood efficacy and safety profile in this setting. Accordingly, consensus recommendations have attempted to define appropriate usage in the light of insufficient evidence.[93]

In elderly patients receiving therapeutic warfarin therapy, head injuries that would normally be inconsequential can result in life-threatening intracranial bleeding. Correction of the INR with either FFP or vitamin K may take so long that the patient becomes vegetative before the hemorrhage is controlled. Prothrombin complex concentrate appears to correct the INR more rapidly and effectively than FFP or vitamin K.[94] One randomized trial that included nonanticoagulated patients who had sustained a hemorrhagic stroke suggested that administration of rVIIa reduces hemorrhage volume and may improve survival as well.[95] With both prothrombin complex and rVIIa, additional trials will have to be done before routine use of these agents to correct elevated INRs in this patient population can be recommended.

Table 5 Tests of Platelet Function

Product (Manufacturer)	Method
PFA-100 (Dade Behring)	Measures time required to occlude aperture after exposure to platelet agonists at shear rates
hemoSTATUS (Medtronic)	Measures activated clotting time; platelet-activating factor is the platelet agonist
AggreStat (Centocor)	Measures changes in voltage (impedance) after addition of platelet agonist
Thromboelastograph (Haemascope)	Measures changes in the viscoelastic properties of clotting blood induced by a rotating piston
Sonoclot Analyzer (Sienco)	Measures changes in the viscoelastic properties of clotting blood induced by a vibrating probe
Clot Signature Analyzer (Xylum)	Measures changes in platelet function at shear rates
Ultegra Analyzer (Accumetrics)	Used primarily for measuring the effect of platelet glycoprotein blockers (e.g., abciximab and eptifibatide); thrombin receptor activator peptide is the agonist

Another novel agent that has been assessed as a means of achieving hemostasis in military settings is QuikClot (Z-Medica, Wallingford, Connecticut), a granular substance containing the mineral zeolite. To date, however, the use of this contact agent has generally been restricted to the extremities, and the available data are not sufficient to determine its efficacy.

Mechanism and Significance of Transfusion-Related Immunomodulation

Although a unit of packed RBCs is an exceedingly complex biologic substance, blood is used frequently and somewhat casually, compared with many pharmaceutical agents that have undergone extensive regulatory review. A unit of allogeneic transfused blood contains antigenic RBCs, WBCs, and platelets; an array of antigenic or immunologically active substances in plasma (including both substances from donor plasma and substances that accumulate during storage); and, potentially, viral, bacterial, and parasitic pathogens. However, the specific transfusion-related factors that result in dysregulation of the innate or adaptive immune responses, as well as the clinical consequences of this immunomodulation, remain inadequately defined.

Interest in the immunosuppressive effect of blood transfusion stems from the observation by Opelz and associates in 1973 that recipients of cadaveric renal transplants experienced longer graft survival if they had undergone allogeneic blood transfusion before transplantation.[96] A subsequent randomized trial showed that even with concomitant use of cyclosporine-based immunosuppressive regimens, pretransplantation transfusion resulted in improved renal allograft survival at 5 years after operation.[97]

A number of different strategies for mitigating this immunosuppressive effect have been considered, including the use of more restrictive criteria for transfusion and the administration of autologous blood products. Besides these two strategies, the approach that has attracted the most interest is to decrease the number of donor leukocytes in units of blood. In Europe, before the adoption of leukoreduction, buffy-coat reduction was employed to remove 70% to 80% of donor leukocytes. The concept was taken one step

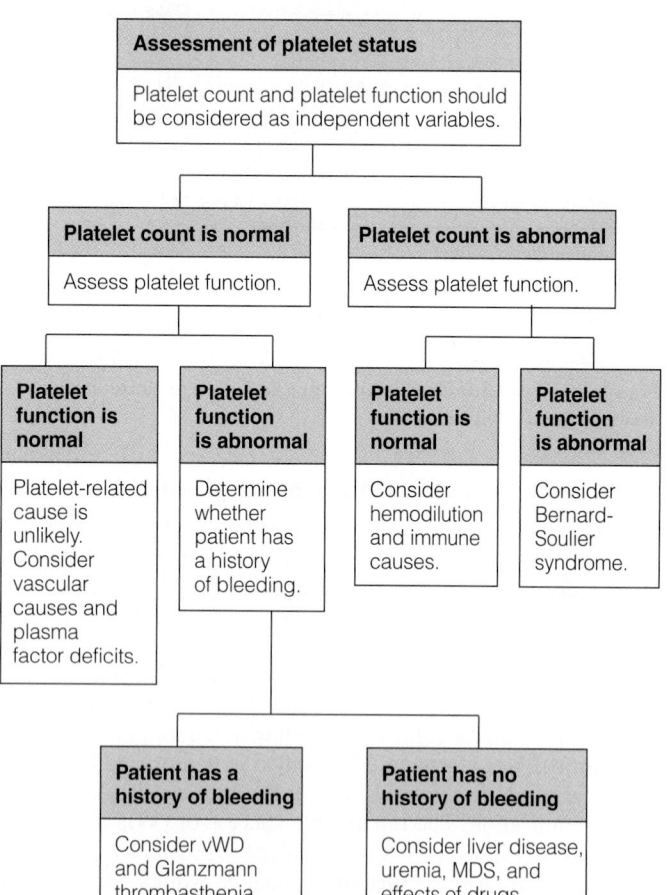

Figure 4 **Algorithm depicts use of platelet count and platelet functional status in assessment of coagulopathies. (MDS—myelodysplastic syndrome)**

further by the development of leukoreduction, which typically involves the use of prestorage filtration techniques to remove more than 99.9% of donor leukocytes. Although leukoreduction has been adopted by Canada and several European countries, the FDA has stopped short of mandating universal leukoreduction in the United States.

As an alternative to reducing the number of donor leukocytes, some have advocated controlling the storage time of blood products so that either fresher or older blood can be provided if desired. Fresh units of blood may contain fewer deformed erythrocytes that could impair the capillary microcirculation; older units of blood may contain fewer viable donor leukocytes, which may be the most harmful agents immunologically. Others have advocated restricting blood donations from previously pregnant women, who, by virtue of greater alloimmunization, may have more immunologically active leukocytes.

Since the initial report on the immunosuppressive effect of blood transfusion,[96] a plethora of observational studies and some randomized trials have attempted to evaluate the role of blood transfusion in the recurrence of resected malignancies and postoperative infection. Most of the observational studies have compared the outcomes of transfused cohorts with those of nontransfused cohorts. The randomized trials, however, have mostly evaluated different kinds of blood transfusions against one another (e.g. autologous versus allogeneic and leukoreduced versus nonleukoreduced). The literature is extensive, but many methodologic issues have been identified that limit the validity of the studies.[98] Accordingly, the evidence appears to be insufficient to establish a causal connection between allogeneic blood transfusion and either increased cancer recurrence or postoperative infection. Nonetheless, the heterogeneity of the study results and the finding of the TRICC trial that a restrictive transfusion policy may improve survival in some patients continue to fuel debate over whether the avoidance or modification of allogeneic blood transfusion may improve patient outcomes.

References

1. Bickell WH, Wall MJ Jr, Pepe PE, et al: Immediate versus delayed fluid resuscitation for hypotensive patients with penetrating torso injuries. N Engl J Med 331:1105, 1994
2. Gubler KD, Gentilello LM, Hassantash SA, et al: The impact of hypothermia on dilutional coagulopathy. J Trauma 36:847, 1994
3. Watts DD, Trask A, Soeken K, et al: Hypothermic coagulopathy in trauma: effect of varying levels of hypothermia on enzyme speed, platelet function, and fibrinolytic activity. J Trauma 44:846, 1998
4. Gentilello LM, Jurkovich GJ, Stark MS, et al: Is hypothermia in the victim of major trauma protective or harmful? A randomized, prospective study. Ann Surg 226:439, 1997
5. Rapaport SI: Blood coagulation and its alterations in hemorrhagic and thrombotic disorders. West J Med 158:153, 1993
6. Practice guidelines for blood component therapy: a report by the American Society of Anesthesiologists Task Force on Blood Component Therapy. Anesthesiology 84:732, 1996
7. Heckman KD, Weiner GJ, Davis CS, et al: Randomized study of prophylactic platelet transfusion threshold during induction therapy for adult acute leukemia: 10,000/μL versus 20,000/μL. J Clin Oncol 15:1143, 1997
8. Dyke CM, Bhatia D, Lorenz TJ, et al: Immediate coronary artery bypass surgery after platelet inhibition with eptifibatide: results from PURSUIT. Platelet Glycoprotein IIb/IIIa in Unstable Angina: Receptor Suppression Using Integrelin Therapy. Ann Thorac Surg 70:866, 2000
9. Despotis GJ, Levine V, Saleem R, et al: Use of point-of-care test in identification of patients who can benefit from desmopressin during cardiac surgery: a randomised controlled trial. Lancet 354:106, 1999
10. Levy JH, Schwieger IM, Zaidan JR, et al: Evaluation of patients at risk for protamine reactions. J Thorac Cardiovasc Surg 98:200, 1989
11. Stewart WJ, McSweeney SM, Kellet MA, et al: Increased risk of severe protamine reactions in NPH insulin-dependent diabetics undergoing cardiac catheterization. Circulation 70:788, 1984
12. Fenton JW 2nd, Ofosu FA, Brezniak DV, et al: Thrombin and antithrombotics. Semin Thromb Hemost 24:87, 1998
13. Sorensen B, Johansen P, Nielsen GL, et al: Reversal of the International Normalized Ratio with recombinant activated factor VII in central nervous system bleeding during warfarin thromboprophylaxis: clinical and biochemical aspects. Blood Coagul Fibrinolysis 14:469, 2003

14. Hirsh J, Dalen JE, Anderson DR, et al: Oral anticoagulants: mechanism of action, clinical effectiveness, and optimal therapeutic range. Chest 114(5 suppl):445S, 1998
15. Murray DJ, Pennell BJ, Weinstein SL, et al: Packed red cells in acute blood loss: dilutional coagulopathy as a cause of surgical bleeding. Anesth Analg 80:336, 1995
16. Holcroft JW, Blaisdell FW, Trunkey DD, et al: Intravascular coagulation and pulmonary edema in the septic baboon. J Surg Res 22:209, 1977
17. Owings JT, Bagley M, Gosselin R, et al: Effect of critical injury on plasma antithrombin activity: low antithrombin levels are associated with thromboembolic complications. J Trauma 41:396, 1996
18. Weitzel JN, Sadowski JA, Furie BC, et al: Surreptitious ingestion of a long-acting vitamin K antagonist/rodenticide, brodifacoum: clinical and metabolic studies of three cases. Blood 76:2555, 1990
19. Vincent JL, Baron JF, Reinhart K, et al: Anemia and blood transfusion in critically ill patients. JAMA 288:1499, 2002
20. Corwin HL, Gettinger A, Pearl RG, et al: The CRIT Study: Anemia and blood transfusion in the critically ill—current clinical practice in the United States. Crit Care Med 32:39, 2004
21. Busch MP, Kleinman SH, Nemo GJ: Current and emerging infectious risks of blood transfusions. JAMA 289:959, 2003
22. Hébert PC, Wells G, Blajchman MA, et al: A multicenter, randomized, controlled clinical trial of transfusion requirements in critical care. Transfusion Requirements in Critical Care Investigators, Canadian Critical Care Trials Group. N Engl J Med 340:409, 1999
23. Consensus conference. Perioperative red blood cell transfusion. JAMA 260:2700, 1988
24. Wu WC, Rathore SS, Wang Y, et al: Blood transfusion in elderly patients with acute myocardial infarction. N Engl J Med 345:1230, 2001
25. Rao SV, Jollis JG, Harrington RA, et al: Relationship of blood transfusion and clinical outcomes in patients with acute coronary syndromes. JAMA 292:1555, 2004

26. Hebert PC, Yetisir E, Martin C, et al: Is a low transfusion threshold safe in critically ill patients with cardiovascular diseases? Crit Care Med 29:227, 2001
27. Hebert PC, Blajchman MA, Cook DJ, et al: Do blood transfusions improve outcomes related to mechanical ventilation? Chest 119:1850, 2001
28. Jurkiewicz MJ, Garrett LP: Studies on the influence of anemia on wound healing. Am Surg 30:23, 1964
29. Weber EWG, Slappendel R, Prins MH, et al: Perioperative blood transfusions and delayed wound healing after hip replacement surgery: effects on duration of hospitalization. Anesth Analg 100:1416, 2005
30. U.S. National Library of Medicine Clinical Trials.gov website. Available at http://www.clinicaltrials.gov/ct, accessed March 2006
31. Carson JL, Noveck H, Berlin JA, et al: Mortality and morbidity in patients with very low postoperative Hb levels who decline blood transfusion. Transfusion 42:812, 2002
32. Maxwell RA, Gibson JB, Fabian TC, et al: Resuscitation of severe chest trauma with four different hemoglobin-based oxygen-carrying solutions. J Trauma 49:200, 2000
33. Creteur J, Sibbald W, Vincent JL: Hemoglobin solutions—not just red blood cell substitutes. Crit Care Med 28:3025, 2000
34. Mantovani A, Sozzani S, Vecchi A, et al: Cytokine activation of endothelial cells: new molecules for an old paradigm. Thromb Haemost 78:406, 1997
35. Edington TS, Mackman N, Brand K, et al: The structural biology of expression and function of tissue factor. Thromb Haemost 66:67, 1991
36. Vane JR, Anggard EE, Botting RM: Regulatory function of the vascular endothelium. N Engl J Med 323:27, 1990
37. Ignarro LJ, Buga GM, Wood KS, et al: Endothelium-derived relaxing factor produced and released from artery and vein is nitric oxide. Proc Natl Acad Sci 84:9265, 1987
38. ten Cate JW, van der Poll T, Levi M, et al: Cytokines: triggers of clinical thrombotic disease. Thromb Haemost 78:415, 1997
39. Cerletti C, Evangelista V, de Gaetano G: P-selectin-β2-integrin cross-talk: a molecular mechanism for polymorphonuclear leukocyte recruitment at the site of vascular damage. Thromb Haemost 82:787, 1999

40. Brunetti M, Martelli N, Manarini S, et al: Polymorphonuclear apoptosis is inhibited by platelet mediated-released mediators, role of TGFb-1.Thromb Haemost 84:478, 2000

41. Stel HV, Sakariassen KS, de Groot PG, et al: VonWillebrand factor in the vessel wall mediates platelet adherence. Blood 65:85, 1985

42. Michelson AD, Barnard MR: Thrombin-induced changes in platelet membrane glycoproteins Ib, IX, and IIb-IIIa complex. Blood 70:1673, 1987

43. Motta G, Rojkjaer R, Hasan AA, et al: High molecular weight kininogen regulates prekallikrein assembly and activation on endothelial cells: a novel mechanism for contact activation. Blood 91:516, 1998

44. Osterud B, Rappaport SI: Activation of factor IX by the reaction product of tissue factor and factor VII: additional pathway for initiating blood coagulation. Proc Natl Acad Sci USA 74:5260, 1997

45. Mann KG: Biochemistry and physiology of blood coagulation. Thromb Haemost 82:165, 1999

46. Collen D, Lijnen HR: Basic and clinical aspects of fibrinolysis and thrombolysis. Blood 78:3114, 1991

47. Chetaille P, Alessi MC, Kouassi D, et al: Plasma TAFI antigen variations in healthy subjects. Thromb Haemost 83:902, 2000

48. Esmon CT, Owen WG: Identification of an endothelial cell cofactor for thrombin-catalyzed activation of protein C. Proc Natl Acad Sci USA 78:2249, 1981

49. Broze GJ, Warren LA, Novotny WF, et al: The lipo-protein-associated coagulation inhibitor that inhibits factor Xa: insight into its possible mechanism of action. Blood 71:335, 1988

50. Schmidt B, Mitchell L, Ofosu FA, et al: Alpha-2-macroglobulin is an important progressive inhibitor of thrombin in neonatal and infant plasma. Thromb Haemost 62:1074, 1989

51. Juhan-Vague I, Valadier J, Alessi MC, et al: Deficient tPA release and elevated PA inhibitor levels on patients with spontaneous recurrent DVT. Thromb Haemost 57:67, 1987

52. Korninger C, Lechner K, Niessner H, et al: Impaired fibrinolytic capacity predisposes for recurrence of venous thrombosis. Thromb Haemost 52:127, 1984

53. Shovlin CL: Molecular defects in rare bleeding disorders: hereditary hemorrhagic telangiectasia. Thromb Haemost 78:145, 1997

54. Sadler JE, Mannucci PM, Berntop E, et al: Impact, diagnosis, and treatment of von Willebrand's disease. Thromb Haemost 84:160, 2000

55. Mannucci PM: Desmopressin: a nontransfusional form of treatment for congenital and acquired bleeding disorders. Blood 72:1449, 1988

56. Weiss HJ: Congenital disorders of platelet function. Semin Thromb Hemost 17:228, 1980

57. Nurden AT: Inherited abnormalities of platelets. Thromb Haemost 82:468, 1999

58. Ljung RC: Prenatal diagnosis of haemophilia. Haemophilia 5:84, 1999

59. Lillicrap D: Molecular diagnosis of inherited bleeding disorders and thrombophilia. Semin Hematol 36:340, 1999

60. Cawthern KM, van't Veer C, Lock JB, et al: Blood coagulation in hemophilia A and hemophilia C. Blood 91:4581, 1998

61. Rodriguez-Merchan EC: Common orthopaedic problems in haemophilia. Haemophilia 5[suppl 1]:53, 1999

62. Mannucci PM, Tuddenbam EG: The hemophil-
ias: progress and problems. Semin Hematol 36(4 suppl 7):104, 1999

63. Bolton-Maggs PH: The management of factor XI deficiency. Haemophilia 4:683, 1998

64. Minowa H, Takahashi Y, Tanaka T, et al: Four cases of bleeding diathesis in children due to congenital plasminogen activator inhibitor-1 deficiency. Haemostasis 29:286, 1999

65. Lind B, Thorsen S: A novel missense mutation in the human plasmin inhibitor (alpha2-antiplasmin) gene associated with a bleeding tendency. Br J Haematol 107:317, 1999

66. Turpeinen AM, Mutanen M: Similar effects of diets high in oleic or linoleic acids on coagulation and fibrinolytic factors in healthy humans. Nutr Metab Cardiovasc Dis 9(2):65, 1999

67. Li D, Sinclair A, Mann N, et al: The association of diet and thrombotic risk factors in healthy male vegetarians and meat-eaters. Eur J Clin Nutr 53:612, 1999

68. Temme EH, Mensink RP, Hornstra G: Effects of diets enriched in lauric, palmitic or oleic acids on blood coagulation and fibrinolysis. Thromb Haemost 81:259, 1999

69. Rein D, Paglieroni T, Wun T, et al: Cocoa inhibits platelet activation and function. Am J Clin Nutr 72:30, 2000

70. Rein D, Paglieroni T, Wun T, et al: Cocoa and wine polyphenols modulate platelet activation and function. J Nutr 130:2120S, 2000

71. Bhatt DL, Topol EJ: Current role of platelet glycoprotein IIb/IIIa inhibitors in acute coronary syndromes. JAMA 284:1549, 2000

72. Humphries JE: Transfusion therapy in acquired coagulopathies. Hematol Oncol Clin North Am 8:1181, 1994

73. Zachee P, Vermylen J, Boogaerts MA: Hematologic aspects of end-stage renal failure. Ann Hematol 69:33, 1994

74. Peek GJ, Firmin RK: The inflammatory and coagulative response to prolonged extracorporeal membrane oxygenation. ASAIO J 45:250, 1999

75. Hobisch-Hagen P, Wirleitner B, Mair J, et al: Consequences of acute normovolaemic haemodilution on haemostasis during major orthopaedic surgery. Br J Anaesth 82:503, 1999

76. Konrad C, Markl T, Schuepfer G, et al: The effects of in vitro hemodilution with gelatin, hydroxyethyl starch, and lactated Ringer's solution on markers of coagulation: an analysis using SONOCLOT. Anesth Analg 88:483, 1999

77. Boyer LV, Seifert SA, Clark RF, et al: Recurrent and persistent coagulopathy following pit viper envenomation. Arch Intern Med 159:706, 1999

78. Eriksson BI, Kalebo P, Ekman S, et al: Direct thrombin inhibition with rec-hirudin CGP 39393 as prophylaxis of thromboembolic complications after total hip replacement. Thromb Haemost 72:227, 1994

79. Sherman DG, Atkinson RP, Chippendale T, et al: Intravenous ancrod for treatment of acute ischemic stroke: the STAT study: a randomized controlled trial. Stroke Treatment with Ancrod Trial. JAMA 282:2395, 2000

80. Oleksowicz L, Bhagwati N, DeLeon-Fernandez M: Deficient activity of von Willebrand's factor-cleaving protease in patients with disseminated malignancies. Cancer Res 59:2244, 1999

81. Francis JL, Biggerstaff J, Amirkhosravi A: Hemostasis and malignancy. Semin Thromb Hemost 24:93, 1998

82. Amirkhosravi M, Francis JL: Coagulation activation by MC28 fibrosarcoma cells facilitates lung
tumor formation. Thromb Haemost 73:59, 1995

83. Williams EC, Moshen DF: Disseminated intravascular coagulation. Hematology: Basic Principles and Practice. Hoffman R, Benz EJ Sr, Shattil SJ, et al, Eds. Churchill-Livingstone, New York, 1995 , p 1758

84. Muller-Berghaus G, ten Cate H, Levi M: Disseminated intravascular coagulation: clinical spectrum and established as well as new diagnostic approaches. Thromb Haemost 82:706, 1999

85. Lawrie AS, Kitchen S, Purdy G, et al: Assessment of Actin FS and Actin FSL sensitivity to specific clotting factor deficiencies. Clin Lab Haematol 20:179, 1998

86. Lind SE: The bleeding time does not predict surgical bleeding. Blood 77:2547, 1991

87. Mammen EF, Comp PC, Gosselin R, et al: PFA-100 System: A new method for assessment of platelet dysfunction. Semin Thromb Hemost 24:195, 1998

88. Speiss BD: Coagulation function in the operating room. Anesth Clin North Am 8:481, 1990

89. LeForce WR, Bruno DS, Kanot WP, et al: Evaluation of the Sonoclot analyzer for the measurement of platelet function in whole blood. Am Clin Lab Sci 22:30, 1992

90. Martinowitz U, Kenet G, Segal E, et al: Recombinant activated factor VII for adjunctive hemorrhage control in trauma. J Trauma 51:431, 2001

91. Boffard KD, Riou B, Warren B, et al: Recombinant factor VIIa as adjunctive therapy for bleeding control in severely injured trauma patients: two parallel randomized, placebo-controlled, double-blind clinical trials. J Trauma 59:8, 2005

92. O'Connell KA, Wood JJ, Wise RP, et al: Thromboembolic adverse events after use of recombinant human coagulation factor VIIa. JAMA 295:293, 2006

93. Shander A, Goodnough LT, Ratko T, et al: Consensus recommendations for the off-label use of recombinant human factor VIIa (NovoSeven) therapy. Pharmacy and Therapeutics 30:644, 2005

94. Cartmill M, Dolan G, Byrne JL, et al: Prothrombin complex concentrate for oral anticoagulant reversal in neurosurgical emergencies. Br J Neurosurg 14:458, 2000

95. Mayer SA, Brun NC, Begtrup K, et al: Recombinant activated factor VII for acute intracerebral hemorrhage. N Engl J Med 352:777, 2005

96. Opelz G, Sengar DP, Mickey MR, et al: Effect of blood transfusions on subsequent kidney transplants. Transplant Proc 5:253, 1973

97. Opelz G, Vanrenterghem Y, Kirste G, et al: Prospective evaluation of pretransplant blood transfusions in cadaver kidney recipients. Transplantation 63:964, 1997

98. Vamvakas EC, Blajchman MA: Deleterious effects of transfusion-associated immunomodulation: fact or fiction? Blood 97:1180, 2001

99. Winslow RM: Blood substitutes. Adv Drug Deliv Rev 40:131, 2000

Acknowledgments

Figures 1, 3, and 4   Marcia Kammerer.

Figure 2   Seward Hung.

9 POSTOPERATIVE MANAGEMENT OF THE HOSPITALIZED PATIENT

Deborah L. Marquardt, M.D., Roger P. Tatum, M.D., F.A.C.S., and Dana C. Lynge, M.D., F.A.C.S.

At the beginning of the modern era of surgery, operative procedures commonly took place in an operating theater, performed by plainclothes surgeons in aprons for audiences of students and other onlookers. Afterward, patients were typically cared for at home or in a hospital ward, with scarcely any monitoring and little to help them toward recovery besides their own strength and physiologic reserve. In the current era, surgery is a high-tech, rapid-paced field, with new knowledge and technological advances seemingly appearing around every corner. Many of these new discoveries have allowed surgeons to work more efficiently and safely, and as a result, a number of operations have now become same-day procedures. In addition, some very complex operations that were once thought to be impossible or to be associated with unacceptably high morbidity and mortality have now become feasible, thanks to advances in surgical technique, anesthesia, postoperative management, and critical care. The focus of our discussion is on the postoperative considerations that have become essential for successful recovery from surgery.

Each patient is unique, and each patient's case deserves thoughtful attention; no two patients can be managed in exactly the same way. Nevertheless, there are certain basic categories of postoperative care that apply to essentially all patients who undergo surgical procedures. Many of these categories are discussed in greater detail elsewhere in *ACS Surgery*. Our objective in this chapter is to provide a complete yet concise overview of each pertinent topic.

Disposition

The term disposition refers to the location and level of care and monitoring to which the patient is directed after the completion of the operative procedure. Although disposition is not often discussed as a topic in its own right, it is an essential consideration that takes into account many important factors. It may be classified into four general categories, as follows:

1. Home or same-day surgery via the recovery room.
2. The intensive care unit, with or without a stay in the recovery room.
3. The surgical floor via the recovery room.
4. The telemetry ward via the recovery room.

The disposition category that is appropriate for a given patient is determined by considering the following four factors:

1. The patient's preoperative clinical status (including both the condition being treated and any comorbid conditions), as indicated by the history, the physical examination, and the input of other medical practitioners.
2. The operative procedure to be performed.
3. The course and duration of the operative procedure.
4. The patient's clinical status at the completion of the procedure, as managed with the help of anesthesia colleagues.

The initial phase of disposition planning begins preoperatively. After a full history has been obtained and a complete physical examination carried out, the procedure to be performed is decided on. This decision then initiates a discussion of the complexity and potential complications associated with the procedure, as well as of the concerns and special needs related to any comorbid conditions that may be present. If, as is often the case, the surgeon requires some assistance with planning the operation around the patient's other health problems, input from appropriate medical and surgical colleagues can be extremely helpful. Key factors to take into consideration include the potential complications related to the procedure and the urgency of their treatment; the level of monitoring the patient will require with respect to vital signs, neurologic examination, and telemetry; and the degree of care that will be necessary with respect to treatments, use of drains, and wound care. There are relatively few published references describing specific criteria for the various disposition categories; however, most hospitals and surgery centers will have developed their own policies specifying a standard of care to be provided for each category.

SAME-DAY SURGERY

Same-day surgery is appropriate for patients who (1) have few or no comorbid medical conditions and (2) are undergoing a procedure that involves short-duration anesthesia or local anesthesia plus sedation and that carries a low likelihood of urgent complications. Operations commonly performed on a same-day basis include inguinal or umbilical hernia repair, simple laparoscopic cholecystectomy, breast biopsy, and small subcutaneous procedures.

The growth in the performance of minor and same-day procedures has led to the development of various types of short-stay units or wards. The level of care provided by a short-stay ward is generally equivalent to that provided by a regular nursing ward; however, the anticipated duration of care is substantially shorter, typically ranging from several hours to a maximum of 48 hours. Short-stay wards also undergo some modifications to facilitate the use of streamlined teaching protocols designed to prepare patients for home care. Many hospitals now have short-stay units, as do some independent surgery centers.

SURGICAL FLOOR

The vast majority of patients receive the postoperative care they require on the surgical floor (or regular nursing ward). Assessment of vital signs, control of pain, care of wounds, management of tubes and drains, and monitoring of intake and output are addressed every 2 to 8 hours (depending on the variable). Assignment of the patient to the regular nursing ward presupposes that he or she is hemodynamically stable and does not need continuous monitoring.

The telemetry ward is a variant of the regular nursing ward. The care provided in the telemetry ward is generally equivalent to that provided on other floor wards, except that patients undergo continuous cardiac monitoring. Patients commonly assigned to the telemetry ward after operation include (1) those with a known medical history of arrhythmias that may necessitate intervention, (2) those with intraoperative arrhythmias or other electrocardiographic (ECG) changes who are not believed to require ICU monitoring but who do need this form of cardiac follow-up, and (3) those making the transition from the ICU to a regular ward who are hemodynamically stable but who require ongoing follow-up of a cardiac issue.

INTENSIVE CARE UNIT

When early postoperative complications may necessitate urgent intervention and close observation is therefore essential, patients should be admitted to the ICU for postoperative care. Postoperative ICU admission may also be appropriate for patients who are clinically unstable after the procedure; these patients often require ongoing resuscitation, intravenous administration of vasoactive agents, ventilatory support, or continuous telemetry monitoring for dysrrhythmias. In addition, admission to the ICU should be considered for patients in whom the complexity of drain management, wound care, or even pain control may necessitate frequent postoperative monitoring that is not available on a regular nursing ward. At present, there is no single set of accepted guidelines directing ICU admission. There are, however, published sources that can provide some guidance. For example, a 2003 article supplied recommendations for the various services to be provided by differing levels of ICUs.[1] Published recommendations of this sort may be adopted or modified by individual hospitals and surgery centers as necessary.

Care Orders

Nurses and other ancillary personnel provide the bulk of the care received by patients after a surgical procedure; accordingly, it is essential that they receive clear and ample instructions to guide their work. Such instructions generally take the form of specific postoperative orders directed to each ancillary service. Services for which such orders may be appropriate include nursing, respiratory therapy, physical therapy (PT), occupational therapy (OT), and diet and nutrition. In what follows, we briefly outline some of the common tasks that require orders to be directed toward these services.

NASOGASTRIC TUBES

Nasogastric (NG) tubes are commonly placed after gastrointestinal operations, most frequently for drainage of gastric secretions when an ileus is anticipated or offloading of the upper GI tract when a fresh anastomosis is located close by. Although NG tubes have often been placed routinely after abdominal surgery, the current literature cites a number of reasons why routine use is inadvisable and selective use is preferable. For example, significantly earlier return of bowel function, a trend toward less pulmonary complications, and enhanced patient comfort and decreased nausea are reported when NG tubes are not routinely placed or when they are removed within 24 hours after operation.[2]

When postoperative placement of an NG tube is considered appropriate, an order from a physician is required, along with direction regarding the method of drainage. Sometimes, NG tubes are placed to low continuous suction; more often, however, they are placed to low intermittent suction to eliminate the chance of continuous suction against a visceral wall and to promote generalized drainage. If large volumes of secretions are not expected, continuous gravity may be used instead of suction. A key concern with NG tubes is maintenance of the patency of both the main port and the sump port. Should either port become blocked, the tube will be rendered ineffective. This concern should be discussed with the nursing staff. At times, it may be necessary to issue specific orders to ensure that this concern is appropriately addressed. As a rule, surgical nurses are well acquainted with tube maintenance; however, if thick secretions are expected, orders for routine flushing may be indicated. When the tube is no longer indicated, its removal may be ordered.

URINARY CATHETERS

Urinary catheters can serve a large variety of purposes. In the setting of bladder or genitourinary surgery, they are often employed to decompress the system so that it will heal more readily. After general surgical procedures—and many other surgical procedures as well—they are used to provide accurate measurements of volume output and thus, indirectly, to give some indication of the patient's overall volume and resuscitation status. Furthermore, after many procedures, patients initially find it extremely difficult or impossible to mobilize for urination, and a urinary catheter may be quite helpful during this time.

Their utility and importance notwithstanding, urinary catheters are associated with the development of nosocomial urinary tract infections (UTIs). As many as 40% of all hospital infections are UTIs, and 80% to 90% of these UTIs are associated with urinary catheters [see Complications, below]. Accordingly, when catheterization is no longer deemed necessary, prompt removal is indicated. As a rule, orders specifically pertaining to urinary catheter care are few, typically including gravity drainage, flushing to maintain patency (if warranted), and removal when appropriate. At times, irrigation is employed after urologic procedures or for the management of certain infectious agents.

OXYGEN THERAPY

Supplemental administration of oxygen is often necessary after a surgical procedure. Common indicators of a need for postoperative oxygen supplementation include shallow breathing and pain, atelectasis, operative manipulation in the chest cavity, and postoperative impairment of breathing mechanics. Because supplemental oxygen is considered a medication, a physician's order is required before it can be administered. In many cases, oxygen supplementation is ordered on an as-needed basis with the aim of enabling the patient to meet specific peripheral oxygen saturation criteria. In other cases, it is ordered routinely in the setting of known preoperative patient oxygen use.

An important factor to keep in mind is that oxygen supplementation protocols may vary from one nursing unit to another. Different units may place different limitations on the amount of supplemental oxygen permitted, depending on their specific monitoring and safety guidelines. Another important factor is that patients with known obstructive pulmonary disease and carbon dioxide retention are at increased risk for respiratory depression with hyperoxygenation; accordingly, particular care should be exercised in ordering supplemental oxygen for these patients.

DRAINS

Drains and tubes are placed in a wide variety of locations for a number of different purposes—in particular, drainage of purulent materials, serum, or blood from body cavities. Several types are commonly used, including soft gravity drains (e.g., Penrose), closed suction drains (e.g., Hemovac, Jackson-Pratt, and Blake), and sump drains, which draw air into one lumen and extract fluid via a companion lumen. Traditionally, surgeons have often made the decision to place a drain on the basis of their surgical training and practice habits rather than of any firm evidence that drainage is warranted. Multiple randomized clinical trials have now demonstrated that routine use of drains after elective operations—

including appendectomies and colorectal, hepatic, thyroid, and parathyroid procedures—does not prevent anastomotic and other complications (though it does reduce seroma formation). Consequently, it is recommended that drains, like NG tubes, be employed selectively.[3-5] Once a drain is in place, specific orders must be issued for its maintenance. These include use of gravity or suction (and the means by which suction is to be provided if ordered), management and measurement of output, stripping, and care around the drain exit site.

Biliary tract drains include T tubes, cholecystostomy tubes, percutaneous drains of the biliary tree, and nasobiliary drains. Daily site maintenance, flushing, and output recording are performed by the nursing staff. Most biliary tract drains are removed by the practitioner or other trained midlevel staff members.

T tubes are generally placed after operative exploration or repair of the common bile duct (CBD). The long phalanges are left within the CBD, and the long portion of the tube is brought out to the skin for drainage. The tube is left in place until the CBD is properly healing and there is evidence of adequate distal drainage (signaled by a decrease in external drainage of bile). Before the T tube is removed, a cholangiogram is recommended to document distal patency and rule out retained gallstones or leakage.[6]

Cholecystostomy tubes are placed percutaneously—typically under ultrasonographic guidance and with local anesthesia—to decompress the gallbladder. Generally, they are used either (1) when cholecystectomy cannot be performed, because concomitant medical problems make anesthesia or the stress of operation intolerable, or (2) when the presence of severe inflammation leads the surgeon to conclude that dissection poses too high an operative risk. Particularly in the latter setting, delayed elective cholecystectomy may be appropriate; if so, the cholecystostomy tube may be removed at the time of the operation.

Nasobiliary tubes are placed endoscopically in the course of biliary endoscopy. They are used to decompress the CBD in some settings. They usually are placed to gravity and otherwise are managed in much the same way as NG tubes.[7]

WOUND CARE

The topic of wound care is a broad one. Here, we focus on initial postoperative dressing care, traditional wet-to-dry dressings, and use of a vacuum-assisted closure device (e.g., VAC Abdominal Dressing System; Kinetic Concepts, Inc., San Antonio, Texas). These and other components of wound care are discussed in more detail elsewhere [see 11 Acute Wound Care and 23 Open Wound Requiring Reconstruction].

Initial wound management after an operative procedure generally entails placement of a sterile dressing to cover the incision. The traditional recommendation has been to keep this dressing in place and dry for the first 48 hours after operation; because epithelialization is known to take place within approximately this period, the assumption is that this measure will reduce the risk of wound infection. Although most surgeons still follow this practice, especially in general surgical cases, supporting data from randomized clinical studies are lacking. In addition, several small studies that evaluated early showering with closed surgical incisions found no increases in the rate of infection or dehiscence.[8,9] It should be kept in mind, however, that these small studies looked primarily at soft tissue and other minor skin incisions that did not involve fascia. Thus, even though the traditional approach to initial dressing management is not strongly supported, the data currently available are insufficient to indicate that it should be changed.

Wet-to-dry dressings are used in a variety of settings. In a surgical context, they are most often applied to a wound that cannot be closed primarily as a consequence of contamination or inability to approximate the skin edges. Wet-to-dry dressings provide a moist environment that promotes granulation and wound closure by secondary intention. Moreover, their removal and replacement causes debridement of excess exudate or unhealthy superficial tissue. Postoperative orders should specify the frequency of dressing changes, as well as the solution used to provide dampness. For most clean open incisions, twice-daily dressing changes using normal saline solution represent the most common approach. If there is excess wound exudate to be debrided, dressing changes may be performed more frequently. If there is particular concern about wound contamination or superficial colonization of organisms, substitution of dilute Dakin solution for normal saline may be considered.

A new era of wound management arrived in the late 1990s with the introduction of negative-pressure wound therapy (NPWT). In NPWT, a vacuum-assisted wound closure device places the wound under subatmospheric pressure conditions, thereby encouraging blood flow, decreasing local wound edema and excess fluid (and consequently lowering bacterial counts and encouraging wound granulation), and increasing wound contraction.[10,11] Since the first published animal studies, NPWT has been successfully employed for a multitude of wound types, including complex traumatic and surgical wounds, skin graft sites, and decubitus wounds. Before vacuum-assisted closure is used, however, it is necessary to consider whether and to what extent the wound is contaminated, the proximity of the wound to viscera or vascular structures, and the potential ability of the patient to tolerate dressing changes. Wounds that are grossly contaminated or contain significant amounts of nonviable tissue probably are not well suited to an occlusive dressing system of this type, given that frequent evaluation and possibly debridement may be needed to prevent ongoing tissue infection and death. Furthermore, the suction effect of the standard vacuum sponge may cause serious erosion of internal viscera or exposed major blood vessels. Some silicone-impregnated nonadherent sponges are available that may be suitable in this setting, but caution should be exercised in using them. Finally, because of the adherence of the sponge and the occlusive adhesive dressing, some patients may be unable to tolerate dressing changes without sedation or anesthesia.

Nutrition

The patient's nutritional status has a significant effect on postoperative morbidity and even mortality. After most operative procedures that do not involve the alimentary tract or the abdomen and do not affect swallowing and airway protection, the usual practice is to initiate the return to full patient-controlled oral nutrition as soon as the patient is fully awake. In these surgical settings, therefore, it is rarely necessary to discuss postoperative nutrition approaches to any great extent.

After procedures that do involve the alimentary tract or the abdomen, however, the situation is different. The traditional practice has been to institute a nihil per os (NPO) policy, with or without nasogastric drainage, after all abdominal or alimentary tract procedures until the return of bowel function, as evidenced by flatus or bowel movement, is confirmed. The routine application of this practice has been challenged, however, especially over the past 15 years. Data from prospective studies of high statistical power are lacking, but many smaller studies evaluating early return to enteral nutrition after alimentary tract procedures have yielded evidence tending to favor more routine use of enteral intake within 48 hours after such procedures.

Issues related to postoperative nutritional support are discussed further and in greater detail elsewhere [see *137 Nutritional Support*].

NPO STATUS

In the setting of elective colorectal surgery, it is well-accepted practice to initiate a return to patient-controlled enteral-oral feeding within 24 to 48 hours after operation; this practice yields no increase in the incidence of postoperative complications (e.g., anastomotic leakage, wound and intra-abdominal infection, and pneumonia) or the length of hospital stay and, according to some reports, may even decrease them.[12] In the setting of upper GI surgery (specifically, gastric resection, total gastrectomy, and esophagectomy), the situation is less clear-cut. Traditional concerns—in particular, the need to avoid distention stress on gastric or gastrojejunal anastomoses after gastric resection, the more tenuous nature of a esophagojejunostomy after total gastrectomy, and the delayed gastric conduit emptying, aspiration risk, and anastomotic stress seen after esophagectomy or resection—have led to the current practice of instituting nasogastric drainage and placing the patient on NPO status postoperatively until evidence of the return of bowel function is apparent, as well as, in some cases, investigating the anastomosis for possible leakage by means of contrast fluoroscopy. There are no clinical trial data to support this approach. In fact, many surgeons routinely remove the NG tube within 24 hours after gastric resection and early feeding without incurring increased complications. However, there are also no clinical trial data indicating that the current approach is potentially ineffective or harmful. Consequently, traditional management methods after upper GI procedures still are often endorsed in the literature.[13,14]

ENTERAL NUTRITION

Enteral nutrition may be delivered via several routes. Most patients who have undergone an operation are able to take in an adequate amount of calories orally. When they are unable to do so, whether because of altered mental status, impaired pulmonary function, or some other condition, the use of enteral feeding tubes may be indicated. In the acute setting, nasogastric and nasojejunal feeding tubes are the types most commonly employed to deliver enteral solutions into the GI tract. Either type is appropriate for this purpose; the two types are equivalent overall as regards their ability to provide adequate nutrition, and there are no significant differences in outcome or complications. In cases where prolonged inability to take in adequate calories orally is expected, the use of an indwelling feeding tube, such as a gastrostomy or jejunostomy tube, may be indicated. These tubes must be placed either at the time of operation or subsequently via surgical or percutaneous means, and there is some potential for complications. The specific indications for the use of such tubes are patient derived; they are not routinely associated with the performance of specific procedures.

TOTAL PARENTERAL NUTRITION

Total parenteral nutrition (TPN) is a surrogate form of nutrition in which dextrose, amino acids, and lipids are delivered via a central venous catheter. It is a reliable method, in that it delivers nutrients and calories regardless of whether the patient's gut is functioning or not. Nevertheless, multiple studies over the past 20 years have shown that when the patient has a functioning intestinal tract, enteral feeding is clearly preferable to TPN. Although the specific mechanisms are not fully understood, enteral nutrition is known to foster gut mucosal integrity, to support overall immune function, and to be associated with lower complication rates and shorter hospital stays. In contrast, TPN is known to be associated with altered immune function, an increased rate of infectious complications, and, in some studies, a higher incidence of anastomotic complications after GI surgery. Moreover, there are as yet no data to indicate that acute utilization of TPN during short periods of starvation benefits patients who are adequately nourished preoperatively. TPN may, however, be lifesaving in patients who are malnourished and who do not have functioning GI tracts (e.g., those with short gut syndrome, severe gut dysmotility or malabsorption, mesenteric vascular insufficiency, bowel obstruction, high-output enteric fistulas, or bowel ischemia).[15]

CALORIC GOALS

Once a route of nutritional support has been decided on, overall goals for caloric and protein intake may be established on the basis of the patient's ideal body weight (IBW) and expected postoperative metabolic state. One approach is to rely on a general estimate; a commonly used formula is 25 kcal/kg IBW. Another approach is to calculate a basal energy requirement by using the Harris-Benedict equation. This calculation is separate from the calculation of protein needs. A daily protein intake goal may be calculated on the basis of the patient's estimated level of physical stress. A well-nourished unstressed person requires a protein intake of approximately 1.0 g/kg IBW/day. A seriously ill patient under ongoing severe physical stress, however, may require 2.0 g/kg IBW/day; in some settings (e.g., extensive burns), a protein intake as high as 3.0 g/kg IBW/day may be recommended. Once the patient's needs specific needs have been calculated, the amount and type of nutrient solution to be provided enterally or via TPN is determined. If the patient is on a full oral diet, a calorie count or recording of the percentage of items eaten at each meal or snack may be made by the nursing staff and used to estimate the patient's intake, with nutritional supplementation provided as needed.[16]

Patients who require assistance with nutritional intake should be monitored to determine whether the interventions being carried out are having the desired effect. The most common method of monitoring patients' nutritional status with nutritional supplementation is to measure the serum albumin and prealbumin (transthyretin) concentrations. Albumin has a half life of approximately 14 to 20 days and thus serves as a marker of longer-term nutritional status. A value lower than 2.2 g/dl is generally considered to represent severe malnutrition, but even somewhat higher values (< 3.0 g/dl) have been associated with poorer outcomes after elective surgery. Although the serum albumin concentration is a commonly used marker, it is not always a reliable one. Because of albumin's relatively long half-life, the serum concentration does not reflect the patient's more recent nutritional status. In addition, the measured concentration can change quickly in response to the infusion of exogenous albumin or to the development of dehydration, sepsis, and liver disease despite adequate nutrition. Prealbumin is a separate serum protein that has a half-life of approximately 24 to 48 hours and thus can serve as a marker of current and more recent nutritional status. Like the albumin concentration, the prealbumin concentration can be affected by liver and renal disease. Overall, however, it is more immediately reliable in following the effects of nutritional intervention.

Fluid Management

Intravenous fluids may be classified into two main categories: resuscitation and maintenance. Supplemental fluids constitute a third category.

RESUSCITATION FLUIDS

Resuscitation fluids maintain tissue perfusion in the setting of hypovolemia by restoring lost volume to the intravascular space. They may be further classified into two subcategories: crystalloids and colloids.

Crystalloids

Crystalloid solutions are water-based solutions to which electrolytes (and, sometimes, organic molecules such as dextrose) have been added. The crystalloid solutions used for resuscitation are generally isotonic to blood plasma and include such common examples as 0.9% sodium chloride, lactated Ringer solution, and Plasma-Lyte (Baxter Healthcare, Round Lake, Illinois). The choice to use one solution over another is usually inconsequential, but there are a few notable exceptions. For example, in the setting of renal dysfunction, there is a risk of hyperkalemia when potassium-containing solutions such as lactated Ringer solution and Plasma-Lyte are used. As another example, the administration of large volumes of 0.9% sodium chloride, which has a pH of 5.0 and a chloride content of 154 mmol/L, can lead to hyperchloremic metabolic acidosis. Regardless of which crystalloid solution is used, large volumes may have to be infused to achieve a significant increase in the circulating intravascular volume. Only one third to one quarter (250 to 330 ml/L) of the fluid administered stays in the intravascular space; the rest migrates by osmosis into the interstitial tissues, producing edema and potential impairment of tissue perfusion (the latter is a theoretical consequence whose existence has not yet been directly demonstrated).[17]

Colloids

Colloid solutions are composed of microscopic particles dispersed in a second substance in such a way that they are suspended and do not separate out by normal filtration. Colloids are derived from three main forms of semisynthetic molecules: gelatins, dextrans, and hytroxyethyl starches. All of the commonly used synthetic colloids are dissolved in crystalloid solution. Nonsynthetic colloids also exist, including human albumin solutions, fresh frozen plasma, plasma-protein fraction, and immunoglobulin solutions. Compared with crystalloid solutions, colloid solutions increase the circulating intravascular volume to a much greater degree per unit of volume infused. In this respect, the various colloids may be thought of as a single group; however, in practice, they are most often given selectively on the basis of secondary characteristics other than their volume-increasing action, such as effect on hemostasis, risk of allergic reaction, and cost.

Crystalloids versus Colloids

The debate over whether crystalloids or colloids are superior for resuscitation has been going on for at least 30 years. Although multiple randomized, controlled trials have compared the two types of solutions in a variety of settings, including sepsis, trauma, burns, and surgery, the evidence accumulated to date has not established that one is clearly better than the other in terms of overall outcome. Supporters of crystalloid resuscitation cite the risk of altered hemostasis, the increased likelihood of drug interactions and allergic reactions, the potential for volume overload, and the relatively high cost as factors arguing against the use of colloids. Supporters of colloid resuscitation cite the large volume of crystalloid needed to produce significant volume effects, the subsequent tissue edema, and for the potential for impaired tissue perfusion and oxygenation as factors arguing against the use of crystalloids. Current recommendations favor crystalloid for resuscitation, with colloid an acceptable substitute when its secondary effects are desired in specific situations.[17,18]

MAINTENANCE FLUIDS

Maintenance fluids provide required daily amounts of free water and electrolytes (e.g., sodium, potassium, and chloride) in order to balanced expected daily losses and maintain homeostasis. A basic rule of thumb used by many practitioners to calculate the infusion rate for maintenance I.V. fluids is the so-called 4, 2, 1 rule:

- 4 ml/kg/hr for the first 10 kg of body weight;
- 2 ml/kg/hr for the next 10 kg of body weight; and
- 1 ml/kg/hr for every 1 kg of body weight above 20 kg.

Generally accepted maintenance requirements include 30 to 35 ml/kg/day for free water, 1.5 mEq/kg/day for chloride, 1 mEq/kg/day for sodium, and 1 mEq/kg/day for potassium. In the setting of starvation or poor oral intake, dextrose 5% is often added to maintenance fluids to inhibit muscle breakdown. In regular practice, however, these specific values are not commonly used: more often, a rough estimate is made of expected daily fluid requirements, and solutions are ordered in accordance with this estimate. Although this practice is unlikely to cause noticeable harm in the majority of postoperative patients, there are situations where inaccurate calculations can lead to dehydration and volume overload. Three studies from the early 2000s evaluated patients undergoing elective colorectal surgery with the aim of determining whether providing higher volumes of fluid perioperatively had an impact on outcome.[19-21] In all three, the data supported the use of smaller fluid volumes perioperatively, which was shown to result in earlier return of gut function after operation, shorter hospital stays, and overall decreases in cardiopulmonary and tissue-healing complications.

SUPPLEMENTAL FLUIDS

Supplemental fluids are given to replace any ongoing fluid loss beyond what is expected to occur via insensible loss and excretion in urine and stool. They are most commonly required by patients with prolonged NG tube output, enterocutaneous fistulas, diarrhea, high-output ileostomies, or large open wounds associated with excessive insensible fluid loss. In each case, the amount of fluid lost daily should be calculated, and replacement fluid should be given in a quantity determined by this measurement (either as a whole or in part) and by the patient's overall intravascular volume status. The particular solution to be used depends on the characteristics of the fluid loss. The components and volume of the fluids produced in the GI tract are different at different sites [see Table 1].

Pain Control

The topic of postoperative pain control covers a broad spectrum of possible interventions that serve a wide range of purposes. The most obvious purpose is simply to relieve the suffering and stress associated with postoperative pain. Another is to improve the patient's overall postoperative status. Bringing the patient closer to the baseline sensory state by reducing pain allows him or her to engage in activities that promote healing and prevent complications, including mobilization to help prevent deep vein thrombosis (DVT) and deep breathing and coughing to help prevent pneumonia. Common methods of pain relief include intravenous infusion of narcotics, epidural analgesia using local anesthetics with or without narcotics, oral administration of narcotics, and the use of

Table 1 Electrolyte Content and Rate of Production of Fluids Secreted in the Gastrointestinal Tract

Source of Secretion	Electrolyte Concentration (mEq/L)					Rate of Production (ml/day)
	Na^+	K^+	Cl^-	HCO_3^-	H^+	
Salivary glands	50	20	40	30		100–1,000
Stomach						
Basal	100	10	140		30	1,000
Stimulated	30	10	140		100	4,000
Bile	140	5	100	60		500–1,000
Pancreas	140	5	75	100		1,000
Duodenum	140	5	80			100–2,000
Ileum	140	5	70	50		100–2,000
Colon	60	70	15	30		

nonnarcotic oral medications such as nonsteroidal anti-inflammatory drugs (NSAIDs) and acetaminophen (see below). These and other issues related to postoperative pain control are discussed in greater detail elsewhere [*see 10 Postoperative Pain*].

I.V. NARCOTIC ANALGESIA

Intravenous narcotics may be administered either by the medical staff or, if patient-controlled analgesia (PCA) is feasible, by the patient. In most cases, with the exception of brief hospital stays (< 48 hours) and ICU settings where the patient may not be alert enough to manage a patient-controlled system, PCA is now generally considered preferable to as-needed nurse-administered I.V. narcotic analgesia. Numerous studies and reviews have shown that PCA is safe and is no more likely to cause side effects (e.g., oversedation, overdose, itching, and nausea) than nurse-administered I.V. narcotic analgesia is. In addition, the use of PCA improves patients' subjective perceptions of the efficacy of pain relief and the timeliness of drug administration.[22]

EPIDURAL ANALGESIA

Epidural analgesia usually makes use of a local anesthetic (e.g., bupivicaine), with or without the addition of a narcotic (e.g., fentanyl). The anesthetic solution is instilled into the epidural space, bathing the nerve roots in a given region and thereby providing pain relief. Until the past decade or so, epidural analgesia was considered a more dangerous method of pain relief and was not routinely employed outside the ICU. With time and further observation has come the recognition that epidural analgesia is safe and effective for postoperative pain control in a routine floor setting if managed by the proper supporting team of physicians.

There has been some debate regarding whether epidural analgesia leads to earlier return of bowel function after GI surgery or reduces the incidence of pulmonary complications; at present, this debate remains unresolved. There is clear evidence, however, that patients subjectively experience less pain with epidural analgesia, both at rest and in the course of activities such as mobilization and coughing. Moreover, in patients who have sustained traumatic rib fractures, early use of epidural analgesia in place of I.V. narcotic analgesia has been shown to reduce the incidence of associated pneumonia and shorten the time for which mechanical ventilation is required.[23] Epidural analgesia does have certain drawbacks, including an increased incidence of orthostatic episodes and a need for more frequent adjustments of the medication dosage. Nevertheless, it can be highly effective and can be a reasonable option when judged appropriate by the anesthesiologist and agreed to by the patient.[24,25]

ORAL ADMINISTRATION OF NARCOTICS

Oral administration of narcotics is one of the oldest methods of providing postoperative pain relief. Numerous different narcotic agents are now available for use in this setting. When deciding which narcotic to prescribe, however, physicians typically do not select freely from the entire available range; rather, they tend to choose from a small subset of agents that they know well and are comfortable with. A key point to keep in mind is that in some formulations, narcotics are combined with other compounds (e.g., acetaminophen or aspirin), and these added medications can have side effects of their own if taken in excessively high doses. Such formulations may require more careful titration than narcotics alone would. Another key point is that many narcotics are available in both short-acting and long-acting versions. In patients who are experiencing substantial postoperative pain, a combination of long-acting agents and short-acting agents may yield more sustained and predictable pain relief than either type alone would.

Finally, for patients who have a history of chronic pain conditions and who regularly used pain medications preoperatively, the assistance of an acute pain service management team may be invaluable in treating pain postoperatively.

NSAIDS AND ACETAMINOPHEN

NSAIDs are available both by prescription and over the counter. They not only provide effective analgesia for pain from minor procedures but also may be a powerful adjunct to narcotics in more acute hospital settings. Their major disadvantages, which in some contexts are substantial enough to limit their use, include their propensity to cause gastric irritation and ulceration; their antiplatelet effects, which increase the tendency toward bleeding; and their potential nephrotoxic effects in some formulations. When employed in settings where these disadvantages are not considered to pose a high risk, NSAIDs can be a useful addition to narcotics, both by providing further pain relief and by reducing the required narcotic doses (and thus the incidence of narcotic-related side effects).

Like the NSAIDs, acetaminophen provides minor pain relief and is an antipyretic, but unlike the NSAIDs, it has no anti-inflammatory effect. Acetaminophen also is often added to narcotic regimens or formulations to reduce the need for narcotics. Its greatest potential side effect is hepatic toxicity with excessive use. Accordingly, the dosage should be less than 2 g/day in patients with normal hepatic function and even lower in those with impaired hepatic function. It is particularly important to keep these dose limits in mind when narcotic-acetaminophen combinations are prescribed on an as-needed basis; in this situation, safe dosage limits may well be exceeded if sufficient care is not taken.

Glycemic Control

Over the last decade, blood glucose control in the postoperative period has become a topic of great interest. Many studies, beginning with that of Van den Berghe and associates in 2001,[26] have found that strict glucose control reduces morbidity and mortality in critically ill surgical ICU patients. Although most of the data currently available are derived from ICU patients rather than from the surgical population as a whole, the principle of tight glycemic control has been generalized to apply to most postoperative patients.

The target glucose range has been the subject of debate, with most institutions using a range of 80 to 140 mg/dl. The ability to achieve this target range and the means of achieving it vary according to the level of nursing care that is provided. Options include continuous I.V. insulin infusion and combinations of subcutaneous injections that utilize various long- and short-acting insulin formulations. Episodes of hypoglycemia are an ever-present risk with tight glucose control; accordingly, the use of standard dosage regimens and careful monitoring are recommended to reduce the risk of such episodes.

The debate over the specifics of glycemic control notwithstanding, it is generally well accepted that this issue should be addressed in all patients who have undergone major operative procedures, regardless of whether they carry a preoperative diagnosis of diabetes mellitus.[26,27]

Postoperative Complications

There are numerous complications that may arise in the postoperative period. Many of these are specific to particular operative procedures and hence are best discussed in connection with those procedures. Many others, however, may develop after virtually any operation and thus warrant a general discussion in this chapter (see below). Prompt discovery and treatment of these latter complications relies heavily on a sufficiently high index of suspicion.

POSTOPERATIVE FEVER

Postoperative temperature elevations are quite common, occurring in nearly one third of patients after surgery. Only a relatively small number of these are actually caused by infection. Fevers that are caused by infections (e.g., pneumonias, wound infections, or urinary tract infections) tend to reach higher temperatures (> 38.5°C), usually are associated with moderate elevation of the white blood cell (WBC) count 3 or more days after operation, and typically extend over consecutive days. Noninfectious causes of postoperative fevers include components of the inflammatory response to surgical intervention, reabsorption of hematomas, and (possibly) atelectasis.[28]

Beyond checking the WBC count, a shotgun approach to the workup of postoperative fever probably is not warranted. A focused approach based on well-directed questioning and a careful physical examination is more likely to obtain the highest diagnostic yield. Coughing, sputum production, and respiratory effort should be noted, and the lungs should be auscultated for rales. All incisions should be inspected for erythema and drainage, and current and recent I.V. sites should be checked for evidence of cellulitis. If a central line has been placed, particularly if it has been in place for several days, the possibility of a line infection should be considered. Patients who have undergone prolonged nasogastric intubation may have sinusitis, which is most readily diagnosed through computed tomography of the sinuses. Further workup for fever may include, as indicated, chest x-ray, sputum cultures, urinalysis, blood cultures, or CT of the abdomen (after procedures involving laparotomy—especially bowel resections—where intra-abdominal abscess is a possible complication).

PNEUMONIA

Respiratory infections in the postoperative period are generally considered nosocomial pneumonias and, as such, are potentially serious complications [see 131 Nosocomial Infection]. The estimated incidence of postoperative pneumonia varies significantly, with many estimates tending to run high. A 2001 study of more than 160,000 patients undergoing major noncardiac surgery provided what may be a reasonable overall figure, finding the incidence of postoperative pneumonia to be approximately 1.5%.[29] In the 2,466 patients with pneumonia, the 30-day mortality was 21%. Thoracic procedures, upper abdominal procedures, abdominal aortic aneurysm repair, peripheral vascular procedures, and neurosurgical procedures were all identified as placing patients at significantly increased risk for pneumonia. Patient-specific risk factors included age greater than 60 years, recent alcohol use, dependent functional status, long-term steroid use, and a 10% weight loss in the 6 months preceding the operation.[29]

The diagnosis of postoperative pneumonia is based on the usual combination of index of suspicion, findings from the history and physical examination (e.g., fever, shortness of breath, hypoxia, productive cough, and rales on lung auscultation), imaging, and laboratory evaluation [see 132 Postoperative and Ventilator-Associated Pneumonia]. Appropriate workup, directed by the clinical findings, typically starts with chest x-rays (preferably in both posteroanterior and lateral views, if possible) and sputum cultures, sometimes accompanied by CT scanning of the chest and, possibly, bronchoscopy with bronchoalveolar lavage (which may be useful in directing antibiotic therapy when sputum cultures are nondiagnostic). Empirical broad-spectrum antibiotic therapy is typically initiated before the causative organism is identified; this practice has been shown to reduce mortality. Piperacillin-tazobactam, which is effective against Pseudomonas aeruginosa, is commonly used for this purpose; however, when Gram's staining of the sputum identifies gram-positive cocci, vancomycin or linezolid may be used initially instead.[30] Once the causative organism is identified, specific antibiotic therapy directed at that organism is indicated, as in treatment of other infectious processes. Drainage of parapneumonic effusions may also be necessary, and this measure may be helpful in diagnosing or preventing the development of empyema.

SURGICAL SITE INFECTION

Surgical site infection (SSI) is one of the most common postoperative complications and may occur after virtually any type of procedure [see 5 Prevention of Postoperative Infection]. Rates of infection vary widely (from less than 1% to approximately 20%), depending on the procedure performed, the classification of the operative wound (clean, clean-contaminated, contaminated, or dirty), and a host of patient-related and situation-specific factors. The majority of SSIs, regardless of site, are caused by skin-based flora, most commonly gram-positive cocci (e.g., staphylococci). Gram-negative infections are also commonly seen after GI procedures, and anaerobes may be present after pharyngoesophageal procedures.[31] With SSI, as with other postoperative infectious complications, prompt recognition of the signs and symptoms is the key to successful management. Hence, regular examination of the wound, particularly in the setting of postoperative fever, is critical. Erythema and induration (indicative of cellulitis) are obvious signs of SSI, as is active drainage of pus from the wound. A more subtle sign is pain that is greater than expected, especially when the pain seems to be increasing several days after operation.

In most cases, it is necessary to open and drain the wound (which is easily done at the bedside or in the clinic in most cases) and allow it to heal via secondary intention. Generally, wet-to-dry dressing changes with saline are employed; however, larger wounds may benefit from NPWT [see Care Orders, Wound Care, above]. Success with NPWT has been widely reported, and this technique has been used to treat such difficult wounds as exposed vascular grafts and sternotomy infections.[32,33] The use of antibiotics depends on the presence and degree of cellulitis. The initial choice of an agent should be guided by the likelihood that particular organisms will be present, which is estimated on the basis of the site of the operation and the type of procedure being performed. Whenever possible, any purulent material in the SSI should be cultured; this step may permit more targeted antimicrobial therapy.

DEEP VEIN THROMBOSIS AND PULMONARY EMBOLISM

In the absence of appropriate prophylaxis, the incidence of DVT may be as high as 30% in abdominal and thoracic surgery patients, and that of fatal pulmonary embolism (PE) may be as high as 0.9%. Thus, prophylaxis against thromboembolism is clearly of high importance in the postoperative care of many patients [see 85 Venous Thromboembolism]. Major risk factors for DVT and PE in this setting include the operation itself, physical immobility, advanced age, the presence of a malignancy, obesity, and a history of smoking.[34]

DVT should be suspected postoperatively whenever a patient complains of lower-extremity pain or one leg is noticeably more swollen than the other. The gold standard for diagnosis remains a venous duplex examination, which has a sensitivity of 97% for detecting DVT of the femoral and popliteal veins.[35] In most cases, treatment involves starting a heparin infusion (typically without a loading bolus in the postoperative setting), targeting a partial thromboplastin time (PTT) that is double to triple the normal PTT (i.e., approximately 60 to 80 seconds), and then switching to warfarin therapy when the patient is stable and able to tolerate oral medications.

PE should be suspected whenever a postoperative patient experiences a decrease in oxygen saturation or shortness of breath; this decrease may be accompanied by chest pain, tachycardia, and diaphoresis, all of which may also be seen in the setting of myocardial infarction (MI). When PE is suspected, it may be appropriate to start heparin therapy even before the diagnosis has been confirmed, depending on the degree of suspicion and the relative risk anticoagulation may pose to the patient. Currently, the principal means of diagnosing acute PE is spiral CT. This modality has relatively wide availability, can be performed fairly rapidly, and has a sensitivity of 53% to 100% and a specificity of 81% to 100%. In addition, it is readily usable in most critically ill patients, including those undergoing mechanical ventilation (though the amount of I.V. contrast material it requires may limit its use in patients with renal insufficiency). Greater diagnostic yield may be obtained by combining spiral CT with a lower-extremity venous duplex examination.[36] For most patients with postoperative PE, anticoagulation is administered in the form of heparin. Low-molecular-weight heparins (LMWHs) are also generally safe and effective; however, because their effect cannot be turned off in the same way as that of I.V. unfractionated heparin, they may be less useful in the period after operation.[37] In patients with massive PE, surgical embolectomy or suction-catheter embolectomy may be considered, as conditions warrant. Thrombolytic therapy is generally contraindicated in the postoperative setting.

CARDIAC COMPLICATIONS

Cardiac dysrhythmias may occur after a wide variety of surgical procedures; as one might imagine, they are most common after cardiac operations. Predisposing factors and possible causes are numerous and various, including underlying cardiac disease, perioperative systemic stress, electrolyte and acid-base imbalances, hypoxemia, and hypercarbia. Thus, controlling such conditions to the extent possible both preoperatively and postoperatively is an important part of preventing and managing postoperative cardiac dysrhythmias. Treatment generally involves first achieving hemodynamic stability and then converting the rhythm back to sinus if possible.

Supraventricular tachycardias (SVTs) are the dysrhythmias most commonly seen in the postoperative period, occurring after approximately 4% of noncardiac major operations. Atrial fibrillation and atrial flutter account for the majority of SVTs.[38] Ventricular rate control may be achieved pharmacologically by infusing diltiazem. Digoxin has long been used for this purpose, but it is less effective in acute settings than diltiazem is. Amiodarone, which is used to treat ventricular dysrhythmias [see 117 Acute Cardiac Dysrhythmia], may also be used to restore sinus rhythm postoperatively in some cases, especially after cardiac procedures.[39] When pharmacologic rate control is not possible, particularly in hypotensive patients, cardioversion is indicated.

Approximately one third of patients who undergo noncardiac surgery in the United States have some degree of coronary artery disease and thus are at increased risk for perioperative MI. The incidence of coronary artery disease is even higher in certain subpopulations, such as patients who undergo major vascular procedures.[40,41] In the perioperative setting, however, the pathophysiology of coronary ischemia is different from that in nonsurgical settings, where plaque rupture is the most common cause of MI. Approximately 50% of all MIs occurring in surgical patients are caused by increased myocardial oxygen demand in the face of inadequate supply resulting from factors such as fluid shifts, physiologic stress, hypotension, and the effects of anesthesia. The majority of cardiac ischemic events occur in the first 4 days of the postoperative period.[41]

Perioperative beta blockade for patients at risk for MI is now routine. Multiple trials and meta-analyses have demonstrated that this practice yields significant risk reductions in terms of both cardiac morbidity and mortality[42,43] and that these risk reductions are achieved regardless of the type of surgery being performed. Although there has been some variation in the protocols used by these trials and the results reported, there is general agreement that beta blockade should be initiated preoperatively, delivered at the time of surgery, and continued postoperatively for up to 1 week.[42]

Diagnosis of postoperative MI is complicated by the fact that as many as 95% of patients who experience this complication may not present with classic symptoms (e.g., chest pain). Identification of MI may be further hindered by the ECG changes brought on by the stress of the perioperative period (including dysrhythmias). Ultimately, the most useful signal of an ischemic cardiac event in the postoperative period is a rise in the levels of cardiac enzymes, particularly troponin-I. Accordingly, cardiac enzyme activity should be assessed whenever there is a high index of suspicion for MI or a patient is considered to be at significant perioperative risk for MI.[40]

Treatment of postoperative MI focuses on correcting any factors contributing to or exacerbating the situation that led to the event (e.g., hypovolemia or hypotension). Typically, although antiplatelet agents (e.g., aspirin) are sometimes given, thrombolytic therapy is avoided because of concerns about postoperative bleeding. Acute percutaneous coronary intervention is also associated with an increased risk of bleeding, but it has nonetheless been used successfully in the perioperative setting and is recommended by some physicians.[44] Beta blockade is often advocated as a means of treating postoperative MI, though it is probably more effective when used both preoperatively and perioperatively as a means of preventing MI.[40]

Discharge

Planning for discharge from the hospital is clearly an essential part of perioperative care. In the best of circumstances, discharge planning starts before admission for elective surgery and is discussed with the patient and family as part of preoperative patient education. Starting the process early enables the provider to estimate the patient's probable needs at the end of acute hospitalization and thus to make preliminary arrangements as needed. For example, if it appears likely that the patient will have to stay in a skilled nursing or extended care facility or will require prolonged physical therapy and rehabilitation, these matters can be addressed to the mutual satisfaction of both patient and physician in advance of hospital discharge. In this way, delays in discharge and unnecessary days of acute hospitalization can be avoided, at least in some instances.

Criteria for discharge or transfer from acute hospital care vary widely, depending on the procedure, the provider, and the patient; rarely are they codified. For example, in a 2005 survey of 16 surgeons performing open colorectal resections within one hospital, only two factors—absence of complications and reported postoperative bowel movement—were considered criteria for early discharge by most (but not all) of the surgeons.[45] There was wide disagreement on all other criteria, including postoperative mobility and the ability to tolerate a general diet. Given such variation in discharge criteria for even one category of procedure, it is clear that a discussion of specific criteria for each type of surgery is well beyond the scope of this chapter. It is worth pointing out, however, that the various discharge criteria now in use, despite their differences, have a common basis—namely, the idea that at discharge, the patient should ideally be able to manage basic self-care activities (e.g., feeding, wound care, and mobility) without advanced assistance and that the likelihood of readmission should be minimized to the extent possible. Identification, investigation, and control of factors such as nausea, pain, fever, deconditioning, and fatigue are important in determining whether a patient is at risk for a return to the hospital in the postoperative period.[46]

Over the past two decades, critical pathways, which are organized plans that outline the sequence of patient care and discharge, have been increasingly used in managing postoperative care after a variety of procedures from all disciplines. They have been shown to reduce hospital stays and maintain safety in patients undergoing common procedures (e.g., colectomy), patients undergoing complex procedures (e.g., esophagectomy),[47] and patients with high comorbidity.[48] Individual pathways are typically specific to a hospital or health care system; thus, the discharge criteria are those agreed on by the providers involved in the care of eligible patients at that particular institution. Critical pathways can be helpful not only by standardizing care and improving the relative appropriateness of postoperative discharge but also, in many cases, by decreasing the overall length of postoperative hospitalization.[46] In a 2003 study of 27 postoperative critical pathways used at the Johns Hopkins Hospital, the authors found that seven (27%) of the pathways were associated with significant (5% to 45%) decreases in length of stay.[49]

Regardless of whether critical pathways are implemented, if discharge planning is not addressed preoperatively, addressing it as early as possible in the postoperative period is extremely valuable not only for ensuring an appropriate length of stay but also for maintaining the satisfaction and comfort of both patient and family. Specific issues should be addressed at this point as needed, including the home resources and support available to the patient, wound care, ostomy care, management of feeding tubes and drains, I.V. antibiotic therapy, and physical rehabilitation. Thus, as soon as it appears that a patient is on track either for discharge home or for transfer to a rehabilitation or skilled nursing facility, a discussion with the appropriate social work or discharge planning personnel should be scheduled. Physical therapy and occupational therapy (PT/OT) evaluations early in the postoperative course can also be of great assistance in determining a patient's needs upon discharge, and such evaluations are essential for any patient who may need a stay in an inpatient rehabilitation facility. Typically, it requires at least 1 day to set up services such as home health care and outpatient physical therapy, and it may take this long or longer to obtain a bed at an appropriate rehabilitation or skilled nursing facility. Consequently, the earlier these plans are made, the better. For many surgical patients, formal discharge planning and PT/OT evaluations are not actually necessary. Brief discussions with the patient, the family, or the nursing staff caring for the patient will assist in determining which surgical patients are most likely to benefit from this approach.

References

1. Haupt M, Bekes C, Brilli R, et al: Guidelines on critical care services and personnel: Recommendations based on a system of categorization of three levels of care. Crit Care Med 31:2677, 2003

2. Nelson R, Edwards S, Tse B: Prophylactic nasogastric decompression after abdominal surgery (review). Cochrane Database Syst Rev (3):1, 2006

3. Pothier DD: The use of drains following thyroid and parathyroid surgery: a meta-analysis. J Laryngol Otol 119: 669, 2005

4. Petrowsky H, Demartines N, Rousson V, et al: Evidence-based value of prophylactic drainage in gastrointesinal surgery. Ann Surg 240:1074, 2004

5. Jesus EC, Karliczek A, Matos D, et al: Prophylactic anastamotic drainage for colorectal surgery. Cochrane Database Syst Rev (18):1, 2006

6. Halpin V, Soper N: The management of common bile duct stones. Current Surgical Therapy, 7th ed. Cameron J, Ed. CV Mosby, Inc, St Louis, 2001

7. Fakhry SM, Rutherford EJ, Sheldon GF: Routine postoperative management of the hospitalized patient. ACS Surgery: Principles and Practice 2006. Souba WW, Jurkovich GJ, Fink MP, et al, Eds. WebMD Inc, New York, 2006, p 90

8. Heal C, Buettner P, Raasch B, et al: Can sutures get wet? Prospective randomized controlled trial of wound management in general practice. BMJ 332:1053, 2006

9. Noe JM, Keller M: Can stitches get wet? Plast Reconstr Surg 81:82, 1988

10. Morykwas MF, Argenta LC, Shelton-Brown ET, et al: Vacuum-assisted closure: a new method for wound treatment: animal studies and basic foundation. Ann Plast Surg 38:553, 1997

11. Venturi ML, Attinger CE, Mesbahi AN, et al: Mechanisms and clinical application of the vacuum assisted closure (VAC) device. Am J Clin Dermatol 6:185, 2005

12. Lewis SJ, Egger M, Sylvester PA, et al: Early enteral feeding vs "nil by mouth" after gastrointestinal surgery: systematic review and meta-analysis of controlled trials: BMJ 323:1, 2001

13. Lassen K, Revhaug A: Early oral nutrition after major upper gastrointestinal surgery: why not? Curr Opin Clin Nutr Metab Care 9:613, 2006

14. Ward N: Nutrition support to patients undergoing gastrointestinal surgery. Nutr J 2:18, 2003

15. Zaloga G: Parenteral nutrition in adult inpatients with functioning gastrointestinal tracts: assessment of outcomes. Lancet 367:1101, 2006

16. Heyland DK, Dhaliwal R, Drover JW, et al: Canadian clinical practice guidelines for nutritional support in mechanically ventilated patients. JPEN J Parenter Enteral Nutr 27:355, 2003

17. Grocott MPW, Hamilton MA: Resuscitation fluids. Vox Sanguinis 82:1, 2002

18. Roberts I, Alderson P, Bunn F, et al: Colloids versus crystalloids for fluid resuscitation in critically ill patients (review). Cochrane Database Syst Rev (3):1, 2006

19. Tambyraja AL, Sengupta F, MacGregor AB, et al: Patterns and clinical outcomes associated with routine intravenous fluid administration after colorectal resection. World J Surg 28:1046, 2004

20. Brandstrup B, Tennesen H, Beier-Holgersen R: Effects of intravenous fluid restriction on postoperative complications: comparison of two perioperative fluid regimens. Ann Surg 238:641, 2003

21. Lobo DN, Bostock KA, Neal KR, et al: Effect of salt and water balance on recovery of gastrointestinal function after elective colonic resection: a randomized controlled trial. Lancet 359:1812, 2002

22. Macintyre PE: Safety and efficacy of patient-controlled analgesia. Br J Anaesth 87:36, 2001

23. Bulger EM, Edwards T, Klotz P, et al: Epidural analgesia improves outcome after multiple rib fractures. Surgery 136:426, 2004

24. Mann C, Pouzeratte Y, Boccara B, et al: Comparison of intravenous or epidural patient-controlled analgesia in the elderly after major abdominal surgery. Anesthesiology 92:433, 2000

25. Flisburg P, Rudin A, Linner R, et al: Pain relief and safety after major surgery: a prospective study of epidural and intravenous analgesia in 2696 patients. Acta Anaesthesiol Scand 47:457, 2003

26. Van den Berghe G, Wouters P, Weekers F, et al: Intensive insulin therapy in critically ill patients. N Engl J Med 345:1345, 2001

27. Hammer L, Dessertaine G, Timsit JF, et al: Intensive insulin therapy in the medical ICU (letter). N Engl J Med 354: 2069, 2006

28. De la Torre S, Mandel L, Goff BA: Evaluation of postoperative fever: usefulness and cost effectiveness of routine workup. Am J Obstet Gynecol 188:1642, 2003

29. Arozullah AM, Khuri SF, Henderson WG, et al: Development and validation of a multifactorial risk index for predicting postoperative pneumonia after major noncardiac surgery. Ann Intern Med 135:847, 2001

30. Mehta RM, Niederman MS: Nosocomial pneumonia. Curr Opin Infect Dis 15:387, 2002

31. Barie PS, Eachempati SR: Surgical site infections. Surg Clin North Am 85:1115, 2005

32. Dosluoglu HH, Schimpf DK, Schultz R, et al: Preservation of infected and exposed vascular grafts using vacuum assisted closure without muscle flap coverage. J Vasc Surg 42:989, 2005

33. Cowan KN, Teague L, Sue SC, et al: Vacuum-assisted wound closure of deep sternal infections in high-risk patients after cardiac surgery. Ann Thorac Surg 80:2205, 2005

34. Anaya DA, Nathens AB: Thrombosis and coagulation: deep vein thrombosis and pulmonary embolism prophylaxis. Surg Clin North Am 85:1163, 2005

35. Michiels JJ, Gadisseur A, van der Planken M, et al: Screening for deep vein thrombosis and pulmonary embolism in outpatients with suspected DVT or PE by the sequential use of clinical score: a sensitive quantitative D-dimer test and noninvasive diagnostic tools. Semin Vasc Med 5:351, 2005

36. Cook D, Douketis J, Crowther MA, et al: The diagnosis of deep vein thrombosis and pulmonary embolism in medical-surgical intensive care unit patients. J Crit Care 20:314, 2005

37. Piazza G, Goldhaber SZ: Acute pulmonary embolism: part II: treatment and prophylaxis. Circulation 114:42, 2006

38. Heintz KM, Hollenberg SM: Perioperative cardiac issues: postoperative arrhythmias. Surg Clin North Am 85:1103, 2005

39. Samuels LE, Holmes EC, Samuels FL: Selective use of amiodarone and early cardioversion for postoperative atrial fibrillation. Ann Thorac Surg 79:113, 2005

40. Akhtar S, Silverman DG: Assessment and management of patients with ischemic heart disease. Crit Care Med 32:S126, 2004

41. Grayburn PA, Hillis DL: Cardiac events in patients undergoing noncardiac surgery: shifting the paradigm from noninvasive risk stratification to therapy. Ann Intern Med 138:506, 2003

42. Schouten O, Shaw LJ, Boersma E, et al: A meta-analysis of safety and effectiveness of perioperative beta-blocker use for the prevention of cardiac events in different types of noncardiac surgery. Coron Artery Dis 17:173, 2006

43. McGory ML, Maggard MA, Ko CY: A meta-analysis of perioperative beta blockade: what is the actual risk reduction? Surgery 138:171, 2005

44. Obal D, Kindgen-Milles D, Schoebel F, et al: Coronary artery angioplasty for treatment of perioperative myocardial ischaemia. Anaesthesia 60:194, 2005

45. Nascimbeni R, Cadoni R, Di Fabio F, et al: Hospitalization after open colectomy: expectations and practice in general surgery. Surg Today 35:371, 2005

46. Kiran RP, Delaney CP, Senagore AJ, et al: Outcomes and prediction of hospital readmission after intestinal surgery. J Am Coll Surg 198:877, 2004

47. Cerfolio RJ, Bryant AS, Bass C, et al: Fast tracking after Ivor-Lewis esophagogastrectomy. Chest 126:1187, 2004

48. Delaney CP, Fazio VW, Senagore AJ, et al: 'Fast track' postoperative management protocol for patients with high co-morbidity undergoing complex abdominal and pelvic colorectal surgery. Br J Surg 88:1533, 2001

49. Dy SM, Garg PP, Nyberg D, et al: Are critical pathways effective for reducing postoperative length of stay? Med Care 41:637, 200

10 POSTOPERATIVE PAIN

Henrik Kehlet, M.D., Ph.D., F.A.C.S. (Hon.)

Approach to the Patient with Postoperative Pain

Pain may usefully be classified into two varieties: acute and chronic. As a rule, postoperative pain is considered a form of acute pain, though it may become chronic if it is not effectively treated.

Postoperative pain consists of a constellation of unpleasant sensory, emotional, and mental experiences associated with autonomic, psychological, and behavioral responses precipitated by the surgical injury. Despite the considerable progress that has been made in medicine during the past few decades, the apparently simple problem of how to provide total or near total relief of postoperative pain remains largely unsolved. Pain management does not occupy an important place in academic surgery. However, government agencies have attempted to foster improved postoperative pain relief, and guidelines have been published.[1-3] In 2001, the Joint Commission on Accreditation of Healthcare Organizations (JCAHO) introduced standards for pain management,[4] stating that patients have the right to appropriate evaluation and management and that pain must be assessed.

Postoperative pain relief has two practical aims. The first is provision of subjective comfort, which is desirable for humanitarian reasons. The second is inhibition of trauma-induced nociceptive impulses to blunt autonomic and somatic reflex responses to pain and to enhance subsequent restoration of function by allowing the patient to breathe, cough, and move more easily. Because these effects reduce pulmonary, cardiovascular, thromboembolic, and other complications, they may lead secondarily to improved postoperative outcome.

Inadequate Treatment of Pain

A common misconception is that pain, no matter how severe, can always be effectively relieved by opioid analgesics. It has repeatedly been demonstrated, however, that in a high proportion of postoperative patients, pain is inadequately treated.[5,6] This discrepancy between what is possible and what is practiced can be attributed to a variety of causes [*see Table 1*], which to some extent can be ameliorated by increased teaching efforts. In general, however, the scientific approach to postoperative pain relief has not been a great help to surgical patients in the general ward, where intensive surveillance facilities may not be available.

Guidelines for Postoperative Pain Treatment

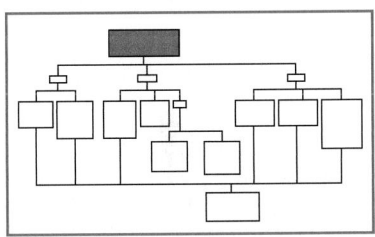

The recommendations provided below are aimed at surgeons working on the general surgical ward; superior regimens have been constructed by specialized groups interested in postoperative pain research, but these regimens are not currently applicable to the general surgical population, unless an acute pain service is available. Consideration is given to the efficiency of each analgesic technique, its safety versus its side effects, and the cost-efficiency problems arising from the need for intensive surveillance. For several analgesic techniques, evidence-based recommendations are now available.[7] For many others, however, there are not sufficient data in the literature to form a valid scientific database; accordingly, recommendations regarding their use are made on empirical grounds only.

In the past few years, efforts have been made to develop procedure-specific perioperative pain management guidelines. The impetus for these efforts has been the realization that the analgesic efficacy may be procedure dependent and that the choice of analgesia in a given case must also depend on the benefit-to-risk ratio, which varies among procedures. In addition, it is clear that some analgesic techniques will only be considered for certain specific operations (e.g., peripheral nerve blocks, cryoanalgesia, and intraperitoneal local anesthesia).[8-10] At present, these procedure-specific guidelines are still largely in a developmental state and are available only for laparoscopic cholecystectomy, colon surgery, hysterectomy, and hip replacement.[10-12]

THORACIC PROCEDURES

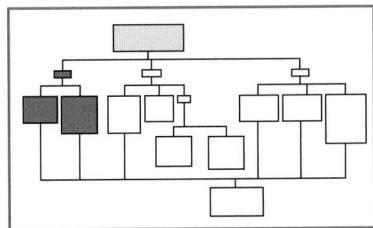

Pain after thoracotomy is severe, and pain therapy should therefore include a combination regimen, preferably comprising epidural local anesthetics and opioids plus systemic nonsteroidal anti-inflammatory drugs (NSAIDs) or cyclooxygenase-2 (COX-2) inhibitors (depending on risk factors). If the epidural regimen is not available, NSAIDs and systemic opioids should be

---

Table 1   Contributing Causes of Inadequate Pain Treatment

Insufficient knowledge of drug pharmacology among surgeons and nurses

Uniform (p.r.n.) prescriptions

Lack of concern for optimal pain relief

Failure to give prescribed analgesics

Fear of side effects

Fear of addiction

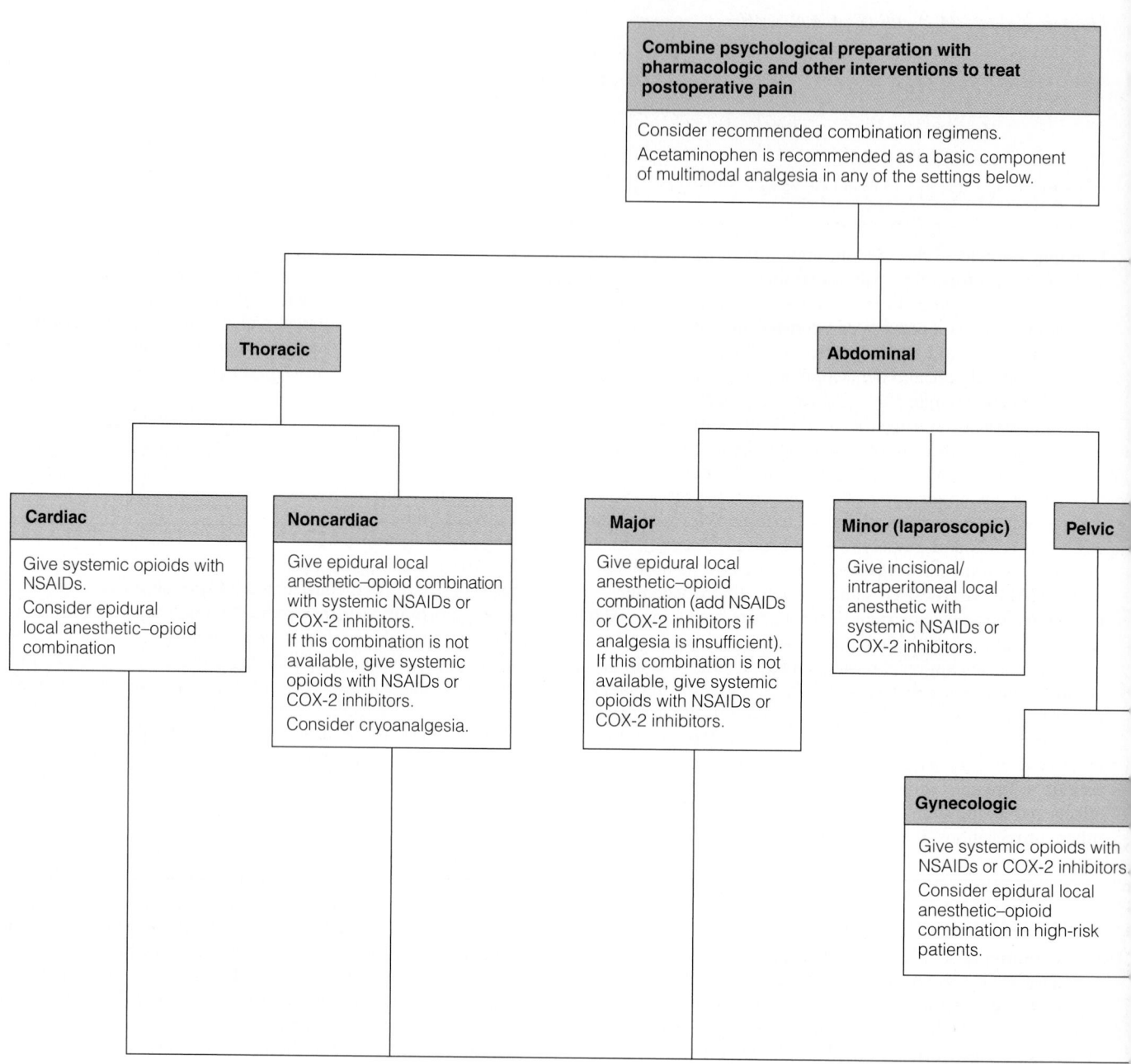

Combine psychological preparation with pharmacologic and other interventions to treat postoperative pain

Consider recommended combination regimens.
Acetaminophen is recommended as a basic component of multimodal analgesia in any of the settings below.

Thoracic

Abdominal

Cardiac

Give systemic opioids with NSAIDs.

Consider epidural local anesthetic–opioid combination

Noncardiac

Give epidural local anesthetic–opioid combination with systemic NSAIDs or COX-2 inhibitors.
If this combination is not available, give systemic opioids with NSAIDs or COX-2 inhibitors.

Consider cryoanalgesia.

Major

Give epidural local anesthetic–opioid combination (add NSAIDs or COX-2 inhibitors if analgesia is insufficient).
If this combination is not available, give systemic opioids with NSAIDs or COX-2 inhibitors.

Minor (laparoscopic)

Give incisional/intraperitoneal local anesthetic with systemic NSAIDs or COX-2 inhibitors.

Pelvic

Gynecologic

Give systemic opioids with NSAIDs or COX-2 inhibitors.
Consider epidural local anesthetic–opioid combination in high-risk patients.

88

pproach to the Patient with Postoperative Pain

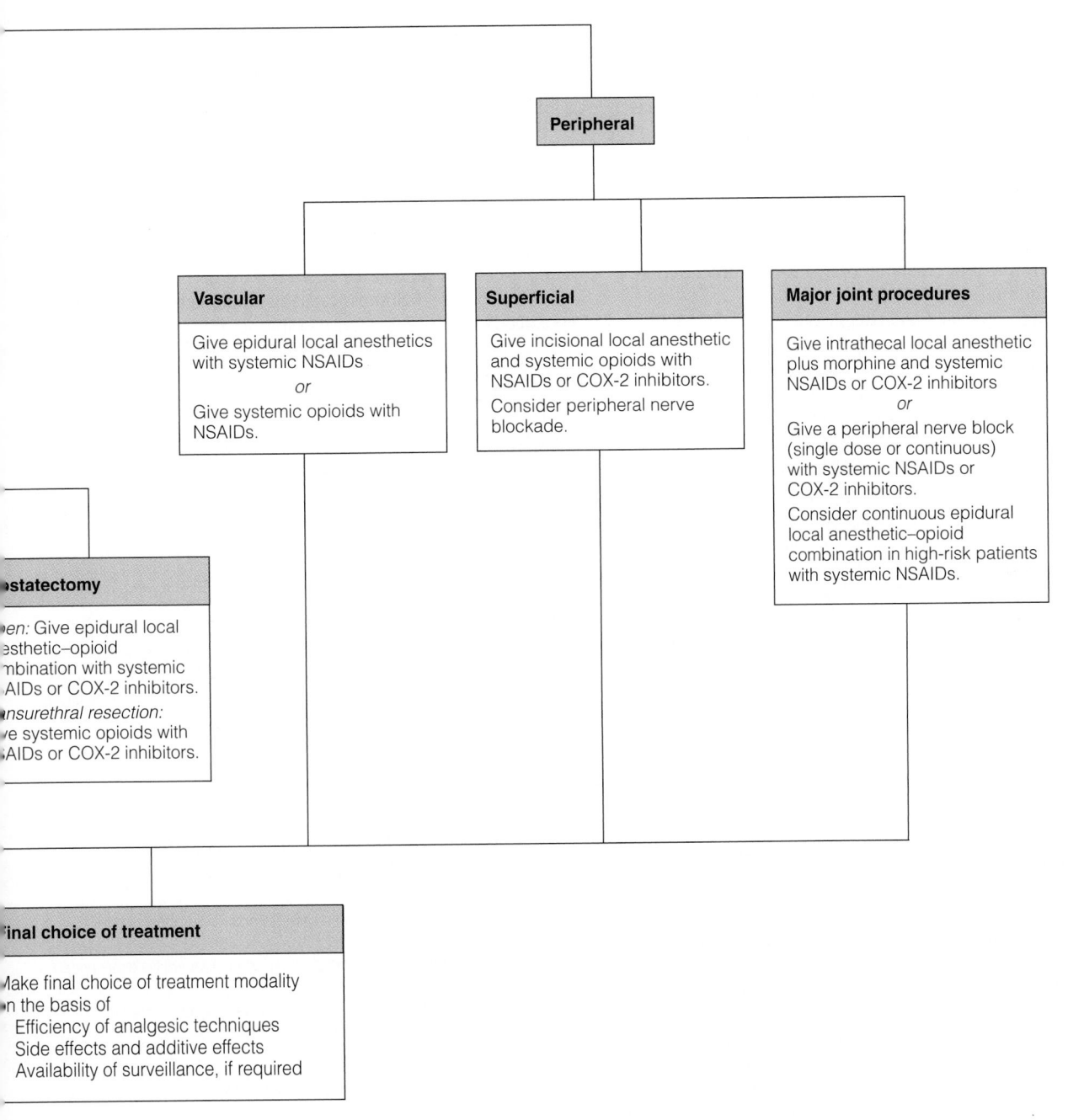

Peripheral

Vascular

Give epidural local anesthetics with systemic NSAIDs
or
Give systemic opioids with NSAIDs.

Superficial

Give incisional local anesthetic and systemic opioids with NSAIDs or COX-2 inhibitors.
Consider peripheral nerve blockade.

Major joint procedures

Give intrathecal local anesthetic plus morphine and systemic NSAIDs or COX-2 inhibitors
or
Give a peripheral nerve block (single dose or continuous) with systemic NSAIDs or COX-2 inhibitors.
Consider continuous epidural local anesthetic–opioid combination in high-risk patients with systemic NSAIDs.

ostatectomy

en: Give epidural local
esthetic–opioid
mbination with systemic
AIDs or COX-2 inhibitors.
nsurethral resection:
e systemic opioids with
AIDs or COX-2 inhibitors.

inal choice of treatment

Make final choice of treatment modality
n the basis of
  Efficiency of analgesic techniques
  Side effects and additive effects
  Availability of surveillance, if required

89

given to obtain the documented synergistic-additive effect. Cryoanalgesia is useful because it is moderately effective, easy to perform, free of significant side effects, and relatively inexpensive. Paravertebral blocks are also effective but necessitate continuous infusion. Acetaminophen is recommended as a basic analgesic for multimodal analgesia.

Pain after cardiac operation with sternotomy is less severe, and systemic opioids plus NSAIDs are recommended. The combined regimen of epidural local anesthetics and opioids is recommended when more effective pain relief is necessary, and it may reduce cardiopulmonary morbidity.[13]

ABDOMINAL
PROCEDURES

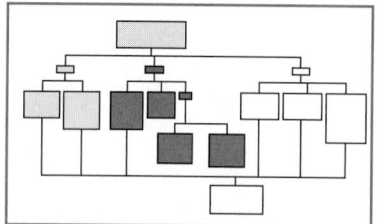

Pain after major and upper abdominal operations is severe, and a combined regimen of epidural local anesthetics and opioids is recommended because it has proved to be very effective and to have few and acceptable side effects.[11,12,14] Furthermore, the epidural regimen will reduce postoperative pulmonary complications and ileus, as compared with treatment with systemic opioids. Systemic NSAIDs or COX-2 inhibitors are added when needed. Acetaminophen is recommended as a basic analgesic for multimodal analgesia.

After gynecologic operations,[12] systemic opioids plus NSAIDs or COX-2 inhibitors are recommended except in patients in whom more effective pain relief is desirable. In such patients, the combined regimen of epidural local anesthetics and opioids is preferable. Acetaminophen is recommended as a basic analgesic for multimodal analgesia.

Pain following prostatectomy is usually not severe and may be treated with systemic opioids combined with NSAIDs or COX-2 inhibitors and acetaminophen. However, blood loss and thromboembolic complications are reduced when epidural local anesthetics are administered. This method is therefore recommended intraoperatively and continued in selected high-risk patients for pain relief after open prostatectomy and transurethral resection. In low-risk patients, systemic opioids with NSAIDs or COX-2 inhibitors and acetaminophen alleviate postoperative pain.

PERIPHERAL
PROCEDURES

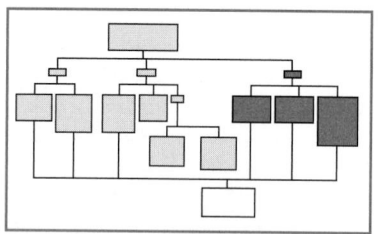

After vascular procedures, postoperative pain control is probably best achieved with epidural local anesthetic–opioid mixtures, combined with systemic NSAIDs or COX-2 inhibitors. Acetaminophen is recommended as a basic analgesic for multimodal analgesia. This regimen will be effective, and the increase in peripheral blood flow that is documented to occur with epidural local anesthetics may lower the risk of graft thrombosis.

Pain relief after major joint procedures (e.g., hip and knee operations)[12] may involve an epidural regimen in high-risk patients because such regimens have been shown to reduce thromboembolic complications and intraoperative blood loss and to facilitate rehabilitation. The severe pain noted after knee replacement is probably best treated with epidural local anesthetics combined with opioids. Otherwise, for routine management, a single intrathecal dose of a local anesthetic–low-dose

morphine combination will provide effective analgesia for the first 8 to 16 hours, after which NSAIDs or COX-2 inhibitors may be added. The use of peripheral nerve blocks is gaining more popularity and may be continued postoperatively.[15,16] Acetaminophen is provided as a basic analgesic for multimodal analgesia. After arthroscopic joint procedures, instillation of a local anesthetic and an opioid analgesic (e.g., morphine) provides effective early postoperative pain relief.

During superficial procedures, systemic opioids combined with NSAIDs or COX-2 inhibitors should suffice. Acetaminophen is provided as a basic analgesic for multimodal analgesia.

Treatment Modalities

PSYCHOLOGICAL
INTERVENTIONS

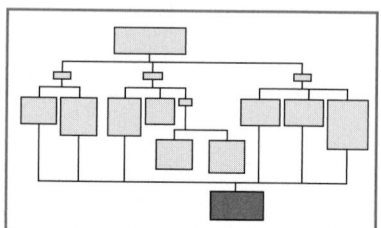

Individuals differ considerably in how they respond to noxious stimuli; much of this variance is accounted for by psychological factors. Cognitive, behavioral, or social interventions should be used in combination with pharmacologic therapies to prevent or control acute pain, with the goal of such interventions being to guide the patient toward partial or complete self-control of pain.[17,18] Sophisticated psychological techniques, such as biofeedback and hypnosis therapy, are not applicable to a busy surgical unit, but simple psychological techniques are a valuable part of good medical practice.

Psychological preparation in patients with postoperative pain has been demonstrated to shorten hospital stay and reduce postoperative narcotic use [see Table 2].[19] Psychological techniques should be combined with pharmacologic or other interventions, but care must be taken to ensure that the pharmacologic treatment does not compromise the mental function necessary for the success of the planned psychological intervention.

SYSTEMIC OPIOIDS

The terminology associated with the pharmacology of the opioids is confusing, to say the least. Opiate is an appropriate term for any alkaloid derived from the juice of the plant (i.e., from opium). The proper term for the class of agents, whether exogenous, endogenous, natural, or synthetic, is opioid.

Table 2 Psychological Preparation
of Surgical Patients

Procedural information   Give a careful and relevant description of what will take place

Sensory information   Describe the sensations that will be experienced either during or after the operation

Pain treatment information   Outline the plan for administering sedative and analgesic medication, and encourage patients to communicate concerns and discomforts

Instructional information   Teach patients postoperative exercises, such as leg exercises, and show them how to turn in bed or move so that pain is minimal

Reassurance   Reassure those who are mentally, emotionally, or physically unable to cooperate that they are not expected to take an active role in coping with pain and will still receive sufficient analgesic treatment

Table 3 Opioid Receptor Types and Physiologic Actions

Receptor Type	Prototypical Ligand		Physiologic Actions
	Endogenous	Exogenous	
Mu$_1$	β-Endorphin	Morphine	Supraspinal analgesia
Mu$_2$	β-Endorphin	Morphine	Respiratory depression
Delta	Enkephalin	—	Spinal analgesia
Kappa	Dynorphin	Ketocyclazocine	Spinal analgesia, sedation, ?visceral analgesia
Epsilon	β-Endorphin	—	?Hormone
Sigma	—	N-Allylnormetazocine	Psychotomimetic effect, dysphoria

Mechanisms of Action

Opioids produce analgesia and other physiologic effects by binding to specific receptors in the peripheral and central nervous system [see Table 3]. These receptors normally bind a number of endogenous substances called opioid peptides. These receptor-binding interactions mediate a wide array of physiologic effects.[20] Five types of opioid receptors and their subtypes have been discovered: mu, delta, kappa, epsilon, and sigma receptors. Most commonly used opioids bind to mu receptors. The mu$_1$ receptor is responsible for the production of opioid-induced analgesia, whereas the mu$_2$ receptor appears to be related to the respiratory depression, cardiovascular effects, and inhibition of GI motility commonly seen with opioids. In studies from 2001 and 2004, investigators were able to obtain a reduction in the GI side effects of morphine with a specific peripherally acting mu antagonist without interfering with analgesia.[21,22]

The demonstration of the existence of peripheral opioid receptors has given rise to studies investigating the effect of administering small opioid doses at the surgical site. Unfortunately, incisional opioid administration has no significant beneficial effect[23]; however, intra-articular administration does yield a modest benefit.[24]

The relation between receptor binding and the intensity of the resultant physiologic effect is known as the intrinsic activity of an opioid. Most of the commonly used opioid analgesics are agonists. An agonist produces a maximal biologic response by binding to its receptor. Other opioids, such as naloxone, are termed antagonists because they compete with agonists for opioid receptor binding sites. Still other opioids are partial agonists because they produce a submaximal response after binding to the receptor. (An excellent example of a submaximal response produced by partial agonists is buprenorphine's action at the mu receptor.)

Drugs such as nalbuphine, butorphanol, and pentazocine are known as agonist-antagonists or mixed agonist-antagonists.[20] These opioids simultaneously act at different receptor sites: their action is agonistic at one receptor and antagonistic at another [see Table 4]. The agonist-antagonists have certain pharmacologic properties that are distinct from those of the more common mu agonists: (1) they exhibit a ceiling effect and cause only submaximal analgesia as compared with mu agonists, and (2) administration of an agonist-antagonist with a complete agonist may cause a reduction in the effect of the complete agonist.[20]

Agents

Morphine Morphine is the opioid with which the most clinical experience has been gained. Sufficient pharmacokinetic and pharmacodynamic data are available. Use of this agent is recommended; it may be given orally, intravenously, or intramuscularly [see Table 5].

Meperidine Detailed and sufficient pharmacokinetic and pharmacodynamic data on meperidine are available. It is less suitable than morphine as an analgesic because its active metabolite, normeperidine, can accumulate, even in patients with normal renal clearance, and this accumulation can result in CNS excitation and seizures.[20] Other agents should be used before meperidine is considered. Like morphine, meperidine can be given orally, intravenously, or intramuscularly.

Side Effects

By depressing or stimulating the CNS, opioids cause a number of physiologic effects in addition to analgesia. The depressant effects of opioids include analgesia, sedation, and altered respiration and mood; the excitatory effects include nausea, vomiting, and miosis.

All mu agonists produce a dose-dependent decrease in the responsiveness of brain-stem respiratory centers to increased carbon dioxide tension (Pco_2). This change is clinically manifested as an increase in resting Pco_2 and a shift in the CO_2 response curve. Agonist-antagonist opioids have a limited effect on the brain stem and appear to elicit a ceiling effect on increases in Pco_2.

Opioids also have effects on the GI tract. Nausea and vomiting are caused by stimulation of the chemoreceptor trigger zone of the medulla. Opioids enhance sphincteric tone and reduce peristaltic contraction. Delayed gastric emptying is caused by decreased motility, increased antral tone, and increased tone in the first part of the duodenum. Delay in passage of intestinal contents because of decreased peristalsis and increased sphincteric tone leads to greater absorption of water, increased viscosity, and desiccation of bowel contents, which cause constipation and contribute to postoperative ileus. Opioids also increase biliary tract pressure. Finally, opioids may inhibit urinary bladder function, thereby increasing the risk of urinary retention.

Several long-acting, slow-release oral opioids are currently available, but their role (in particular, their safety) in the setting of moderate to severe postoperative pain remains to be established. In addition, modern principles of treatment increasingly emphasize the use of opioid-sparing analgesic approaches to enhance recovery (see below).

EPIDURAL AND SUBARACHNOID OPIOIDS

Opioids were first used in the epidural and subarachnoid space

Table 4 Intrinsic Activity of Opioids

Opioid	Receptor Type			
	Mu	Kappa	Delta	Sigma
Agonists				
Morphine	Agonist	—	—	—
Meperidine (Demerol)	Agonist	—	—	—
Hydromorphone (Dilaudid)	Agonist	—	—	—
Oxymorphone (Numorphan)	Agonist	—	—	—
Levorphanol (Levo-Dromoran)	Agonist	—	—	—
Fentanyl (Duragesic)	Agonist	—	—	—
Sufentanil (Sufenta)	Agonist	—	—	—
Alfentanil (Alfenta)	Agonist	—	—	—
Methadone (Dolophine)	Agonist	—	—	—
Agonist-Antagonists				
Buprenorphine (Buprenex)	Partial agonist	—	—	—
Butorphanol (Stadol)	Antagonist	Agonist	Agonist	—
Nalbuphine (Nubain)	Antagonist	Partial agonist	Agonist	—
Pentazocine (Talwin)	Antagonist	Agonist	Agonist	—
Dezocine (Dalgan)	Partial agonist	—	—	Agonist
Antagonists				
Naloxone (Narcan)	Antagonist	Antagonist	Antagonist	Antagonist

in 1979. Since that time, they have become the mainstay of post-operative management for severe pain. Epidural opioids may be administered in a single bolus or via continuous infusions. They are usually combined with local anesthetics in a continuous epidural infusion to enhance analgesia.[14]

Mechanisms of Action

Opioids injected into the epidural or subarachnoid space cause segmental (i.e., selective, spinally mediated) analgesia by binding to opioid receptors in the dorsal horn of the spinal cord.[25] The lipid solubility of an opioid, described by its partition coefficient, predicts its behavior when introduced into the epidural or sub-arachnoid space. Opioids with low lipid solubility (i.e., hydrophilic opioids) have a slow onset of action and a long duration of action. Opioids with high lipid solubility (i.e., lipophilic opioids) have a quick onset of action but a short duration of action. Thus, the lipid

solubility of an opioid determines its access to the dorsal horn via (1) diffusion through the arachnoid granulations and (2) diffusion into spinal radicular artery blood flow.

Subarachnoid opioids should be used when the required duration of analgesia after surgery is relatively short. When protracted analgesia is required, epidural administration is preferred; repeated injections may be given through epidural catheters, or continuous infusions may be used. Smaller doses of subarachnoid opioids are generally required to produce analgesia. Ordinarily, no more than 0.1 to 0.25 mg of morphine should be used. These doses, which are about 10% to 20% of the size of comparably effective epidural doses, provide reliable pain relief with few side effects.[26] Fentanyl has also been extensively used in the subarachnoid space in a dose range of 6.25 to 50 µg. Pain relief after administration of subarachnoid fentanyl is as potent but not as prolonged as analgesia after administration of morphine.

Table 5 Suggested Regimens for Systemic Morphine Administration

	Intermittent Administration (Suggested Initial Dose)*			
	p.o.	I.M.	I.V.	Duration (hr)
Morphine	30–50 mg	10 mg	5–10 mg	3–4

	Continuous I.V. Infusion†
Morphine	≈ 3 mg/hr (loading dose: 5–10 mg)

*Number of doses to be given is calculated with the following formula:

$$\frac{24 \text{ hr}}{\text{actual duration of single effective dose (hr)}}$$

Single doses should be given at calculated fixed intervals approximately 30 min before expected recurrence of pain. Single dose should be readjusted daily. Elderly patients may be more susceptible to opioids.

†Dose should be adjusted according to effect and side effects.

Regimens for Acute Pain Relief

It is generally agreed that at least 2 mg of epidural morphine is needed to achieve a significant analgesic response, but the criteria used to assess this response have varied greatly in reported studies, and no firm conclusion can be derived from them.[25,27] Epidural opioids are less efficient in the earliest stages of the acute pain state than on subsequent days; moreover, they appear to be more successful at alleviating pain after procedures in the lower half of the body than at alleviating upper abdominal and thoracic pain. In general, 2 to 4 mg of morphine administered epidurally is sufficient after minor procedures, whereas about 4 mg is needed after vascular and gynecologic procedures and after major upper abdominal and thoracic procedures.[20,25,27] On postoperative day 1, however, such a regimen, even when repeated as many as three times, relieves pain completely in fewer than 50% of patients; on subsequent days, the success rate is substantially higher. The efficiency of this approach is lowest after major procedures.

There is evidence to suggest that continuous epidural administration of low-dosage morphine (0.1 to 0.3 mg/hr) or fentanyl (10 to 20 μg/hr) may lower the risk of late respiratory depression and may be more efficient than intermittent administration of higher dosages of morphine.[27] The continuous low-dosage approach is therefore recommended.

Side Effects

The chief side effects associated with epidural and subarachnoid opioids are respiratory depression, nausea and vomiting, pruritus, and urinary retention.[25-27] The poor lipid solubility of morphine is responsible for its protracted duration of action but also allows morphine to undergo cephalad migration in the cerebrospinal fluid. This migration can cause delayed respiratory depression, with a peak incidence 3 to 10 hours after an injection. The high lipid solubility of lipophilic opioids such as fentanyl allows them to be absorbed into lipids close to the site of administration. Consequently, the lipophilic opioids do not migrate rostrally in the CSF and cannot cause delayed respiratory depression. Of course, the high lipid solubility of lipophilic opioids allows them to be absorbed into blood vessels, which may cause early respiratory depression, as is commonly seen with systemic administration of opioids.

Naloxone reverses the depressive respiratory effects of spinal opioids. In an apneic patient, 0.4 mg I.V. will usually restore ventilation. If a patient has a depressed respiratory rate but is still breathing, small aliquots of naloxone (0.2 to 0.4 mg) can be given until the respiratory rate returns to normal.

Nausea and vomiting are caused by transport of opioids to the vomiting center and the chemoreceptor trigger zone in the medulla via CSF flow or the systemic circulation. Nausea can usually be treated with antiemetics or, if severe, with naloxone (in 0.2 mg increments, repeated if necessary).

Pruritus is probably the most common side effect of the spinal opioids. Histamine is released by certain opioids, but this mechanism probably plays a negligible role in the genesis of itching. Treatment of pruritus is similar to that of nausea.

The mechanism of spinal opioid–induced urinary retention involves inhibition of volume-induced bladder contractions and blockade of the vesical reflex. Naloxone administration is the treatment of choice, though bladder catheterization is sometimes required.

EPIDURAL LOCAL ANESTHETICS AND OTHER REGIONAL BLOCKS

Local anesthetics have become increasingly popular because of the growing familiarity with both epidural catheterization and regional nerve blockade. In addition, there is a great deal of experimental evidence that documents the benefits of blocking noxious impulses.[28] Local anesthetic neural blockade is unique among available analgesic techniques in that it may offer sufficient afferent neural blockade, resulting in relief of pain; avoidance of sedation, respiratory depression, and nausea; and, finally, efferent sympathetic blockade, resulting in increased blood flow to the region of neural blockade.[28] Despite the considerable scientific data documenting these beneficial effects, the place of epidural local anesthesia as a method of pain relief remains somewhat controversial in comparison with that of other analgesic techniques. Its side effects (e.g., hypotension, urinary retention, and motor blockade) and the need for trained staff for surveillance argue against its use; however, these side effects can be reduced by using combination regimens (see below).[27]

Mechanism of Action

Local anesthetic neural blockade is a nondepolarizing block that reduces the permeability of cell membranes to sodium ions.[29] Whether different local anesthetics have different effects on different nerve fibers is debatable.

Choice of Drug

For optimal management of postoperative pain, the anesthetic agent should provide excellent analgesia of rapid onset and long duration without inducing motor blockade. The various local anesthetic agents all meet one or more of these criteria; however, the ones that come closest to meeting all of the criteria are bupivacaine, ropivacaine, and levobupivacaine. This should not preclude the use of other agents, because their efficacy has also been demonstrated. Ropivacaine and levobupivacaine may have a better safety profile, but the improvement may be relevant only when high intraoperative doses are given.[29]

Continuous Epidural Analgesia

No regimen has been found that provides complete analgesia in all patients all of the time, and it is unlikely that one ever will be

Table 6 **Regimen for Pain Relief with Continuous Epidural Bupivacaine during Initial 24 Postoperative Hours**

Type of Operation	Interspace for Catheter Insertion	Concentration (%)	Volume (ml/hr)
Thoracic procedures	T4–6	0.250–0.125	5–10
Upper laparotomy	T7–8	0.250–0.125	4–12
Gynecologic laparotomy	T10–12	0.250–0.125	4–10
Hip procedures	L2	0.125–0.0625	4–8
Vascular procedures	T10–12	0.250–0.125	4–10

Note: indications for postoperative epidural bupivacaine may be strengthened if this method is also indicated for intraoperative analgesia. Dosage requirements may vary and should be assessed 3 hr after the start of treatment, every 6 hr thereafter on the first day, and then every 12 hr (more often if pain occurs). The duration of treatment is 1–4 days, depending on the intensity of the pain. The concentration of bupivacaine employed should be the lowest possible and should be decreased with time postoperatively. Some patients, especially those who have undergone major upper abdominal operation, require 0.5% bupivacaine initially.

Table 7 Procedures for Maintenance of Epidural Anesthesia for Longer Than 24 Hours

1. Administer appropriate drug in appropriate dosage at selected infusion rate as determined by physician.
2. Nurse evaluates vital signs and intake and output as required for a postoperative patient.
3. Nurse checks infusion pump hourly to ensure that it is functioning properly, that infusion rate is proper, and that alarm is on.
4. Nurse also assesses
   - Bladder—for distention, if patient is not catheterized
   - Lower extremities—for status of motor function
   - CNS—for signs of toxicity or respiratory depression
   - Relief of pain (drug dosage may require modification)
   - Skin integrity on back (breakdown may occur if motor function is not present)
   - Tubing and dressing (disconnection of tubing or dislodgment of catheter may occur)
5. Every 48 hr, the catheter dressing should be removed, the catheter entrance site cleaned, and topical antibiotic applied (much as in care of a central venous catheter).

found. As a rule, the block should be limited to the area in which pain is felt. Care should be taken to avoid motor blockade and to spare autonomic function to the urinary bladder, as well as to formulate a regimen that requires only minimal attention from staff members and carries no significant toxicity. Given these requirements, continuous infusion [*see Table 6*] is more effective and reliable than intermittent injection.[27] Whether low hourly volume and high concentration approaches are preferable to high hourly volume and low concentration approaches remains to be determined.[27] The weaker solutions may produce less motor blockade while continuing to block smaller C and A-delta pain fibers and are recommended in lumbar epidural analgesia as a means of reducing the risk of orthostatic hypotension and lower-extremity motor blockade.[27]

Specific indications for continuous epidural analgesia that are supported by data from controlled morbidity studies include (1) pain relief and reduction of deep vein thrombosis, pulmonary embolism, and hypoxemia after total hip replacement and prostatectomy; (2) pain relief, facilitation of coughing, and reduction of chest infections after thoracic, abdominal, and orthopedic procedures; (3) pain relief, control of hypertension, and enhancement of graft flow after major vascular operations; and (4) pain relief and reduction of paralytic ileus after abdominal procedures.[30,31]

Side Effects

The main side effects of epidural local anesthesia are hypotension caused by sympathetic blockade, vagal overactivity, and decreased cardiac function (during a high thoracic block). Under no circumstances should epidural local anesthetics be used before a preexisting hypovolemic condition is treated. Hypotension may be treated with ephedrine, 10 to 15 mg I.V., and fluids, with the patient tilted in a head-down position. Atropine, 0.5 to 1.0 mg I.V., may be effective during vagal overactivity.

Urinary retention occurs in 20% to 100% of patients. Fortunately, urinary catheterization for only 24 to 48 hours in the course of a high-dose regimen probably has no important side effects, and many patients for whom epidural analgesia is indicated need an indwelling catheter for other reasons in any case. The incidence of urinary retention is probably below 10% when

epidural local anesthetics are used in weak solutions.[32] Motor blockade may delay mobilization; however, its incidence can be reduced by using the weakest concentration of local anesthetic that is compatible with adequate sensory blockade. Cerebral and epidural analgesia should not be employed in patients already receiving anticoagulant therapy, but it may be started with catheter insertion before vascular or other procedures in which controlled heparin therapy is used. Epidural analgesia has been used in patients receiving thromboembolic prophylaxis with low-dose heparin and low-molecular-weight heparin without significant risk,[27] provided that current guidelines are followed.[33,34] It should be emphasized that the heparin doses commonly employed in the United States are higher than those recommended in Europe; the higher doses may pose a risk when heparin prophylaxis is combined with epidural analgesia.[33,34] The complications associated with the epidural catheter are minimal when proper nursing protocols are followed [*see Table 7*].[27] The decision to employ epidural local anesthetics in such patients should be made only after the risks[33,34] are carefully compared with the documented advantages of such anesthetics.[27,31] It is important that the level of insertion into the epidural space correspond with the level of incision.

Other Nerve Blocks

The popularity of single-dose intercostal block and intrapleural regional analgesia has decreased in comparison with that of continuous epidural treatment. Intermittent or continuous administration of local anesthetics through a catheter inserted into the paravertebral space seems to be a promising approach to providing analgesia after thoracic and abdominal procedures,[35] but further data are needed. Intravenous and intraperitoneal administration of local anesthetics cannot be recommended for postoperative analgesia, because they are not efficacious,[36] except in laparoscopic cholecystectomy.[12,37] Intraincisional administration of bupivacaine, which has negligible side effects and demands little or no surveillance, is recommended for patients undergoing relatively minor procedures.[38]

Several studies have now reported that continuous administration of local anesthetics into the wound improves postoperative analgesia in a variety of procedures[38-44]; however, there is still a need for more procedure-specific data before general recommendations can be made. Continuous peripheral nerve blocks are growing in popularity, and the analgesic treatment may be continued after discharge.[15,16,45] Before general recommendations for continuous peripheral blockade can be formulated, however, further safety data are required.

More detailed information on special blocks can be found in the anesthesiology literature. In general, despite its disadvantages, neural blockade with local anesthetics is recommended for relief of

Table 8 Recommended Dosages of NSAIDs or COX-2 Inhibitors for Relief of Postoperative Pain

NSAID	Dosage
Acetylsalicylic acid	500–1,000 mg q. 4–6 hr
Acetaminophen	500–1,000 mg q. 4–6 hr
Indomethacin	50–100 mg q. 6–8 hr
Ibuprofen	200–400 mg q. 4–6 hr
Ketorolac	30 mg q. 4–6 hr
Celecoxib	200–400 mg q. 12 hr
Rofecoxib	12–25 mg q. 12 hr

moderate to severe postoperative pain because of the advantageous physiologic effects it exerts and the reduction in postoperative morbidity it brings about.

CONVENTIONAL NSAIDS AND COX-2 INHIBITORS

NSAIDs are minor analgesics that, because of their anti-inflammatory effect, may be suitable for management of postoperative pain associated with a significant degree of inflammation (e.g., bone or soft tissue damage).[46] They may, however, have central analgesic effects as well and thus may have analgesic efficacy after all kinds of operations. Conventional NSAIDs inhibit both COX-1 and COX-2. Selective COX-2 inhibitors, which do not inhibit COX-1, have the potential to achieve analgesic efficacy comparable to that of conventional NSAIDs but with fewer side effects [*see Table 8*].[47-49]

Only a few of the NSAIDs may be given parenterally. The data now available on the use of NSAIDs for postoperative pain are insufficient to allow definitive recommendation of any agent or agents over the others, and selection therefore may depend on convenience of delivery, duration, and cost.[46] It is clear, however, that these agents may play a valuable role as adjuvants to other analgesics; accordingly, they have been recommended as basic analgesics for all operations in low-risk patients. All of the NSAIDs have potentially serious side effects: GI and surgical site hemorrhage, renal failure, impaired bone healing and asthma. The endoscopically verified superficial ulcer formation seen within 7 to 10 days after the initiation of NSAID therapy is not seen with selective COX-2 inhibitor treatment in volunteers. The clinical relevance of these findings for perioperative treatment remains to be established, however, given that acute severe GI side effects (bleeding, perforation) are extremely rare in elective cases.

Because prostaglandins are important for regulation of water and mineral homeostasis by the kidneys in the dehydrated patient, perioperative treatment with NSAIDs, which inhibit prostaglandin synthesis, may lead to postoperative renal failure. So far, specific COX-2 inhibitors have not been demonstrated to be less nephrotoxic than conventional NSAIDs.[48-51] Although little systematic evaluation has been done, extensive clinical experience with NSAIDs suggests that the renal risk is not substantial.[51] Nonetheless, conventional NSAIDs and COX-2 inhibitors should be used with caution in patients who have preexisting renal dysfunction.

Although conventional NSAIDs prolong bleeding time and inhibit platelet aggregation, there generally does not seem to be a clinically significant risk of increased bleeding. However, in some procedures for which strict hemostasis is critical (e.g., tonsillectomy, cosmetic surgery, and eye surgery), these drugs have been shown to increase the risk of bleeding complications and should therefore be replaced with COX-2 inhibitors, which do not inhibit platelet aggregation.[52,53] The observation that prostaglandins are involved in bone and wound healing has given rise to concern about potential side effects in surgical patients. Although there is experimental evidence that both conventional NSAIDs and COX-2 inhibitors can impair bone healing,[54-57] the clinical data available at present are insufficient to document wound or bone healing failure with these drugs. This is a particularly important issue for future study, in that many orthopedic surgeons remain reluctant to use NSAIDs.

Currently, there is widespread concern about the increased risk of cardiovascular complications associated with long-term treatment with selective COX-2 inhibitors. Generally, such side effects have appeared after 1 to 2 years of treatment. In the past few years, however, two studies of patients undergoing coronary artery bypass grafting (CABG) found that the risk of cardiovascular complications was increased significantly (two- to threefold) in

this setting,[58,59] and the investigators concluded that these drugs were therefore contraindicated in CABG patients. The larger question is whether these drugs should also be contraindicated for perioperative use, or at least used with caution, in high-risk cardiovascular patients who are undergoing procedures other than CABG. At present, the data are insufficient to allow any conclusions, but in my view, until more information is available, it may be prudent to avoid perioperative use of COX-2 inhibitors in all high-risk cardiovascular patients (i.e., those with uncontrolled hypertension, previous myocardial infarction, heart failure, or previous cerebral vascular disorders). In other patients, however, perioperative administration of selective COX-2 inhibitors may be justified if the advantageous effects appear to outweigh the potential (low) risk of complications.

Finally, the already quite low risk of NSAID-induced asthma may be further reduced by the use of selective COX-2 inhibitors.[48,49]

Peripheral (i.e., surgical site) administration of NSAIDs may have a slight additional analgesic effect in comparison with systemic administration,[60] but further data on safety are required.

Acetaminophen also possesses anti-inflammatory capability, both peripherally and centrally. Its analgesic effect is somewhat (about 20% to 30%) weaker than those of conventional NSAIDs and COX-2 inhibitors; however, it lacks the side effects typical of these agents.[61-63] Combining acetaminophen with NSAIDs may improve analgesia, especially in smaller and moderate-sized oper-

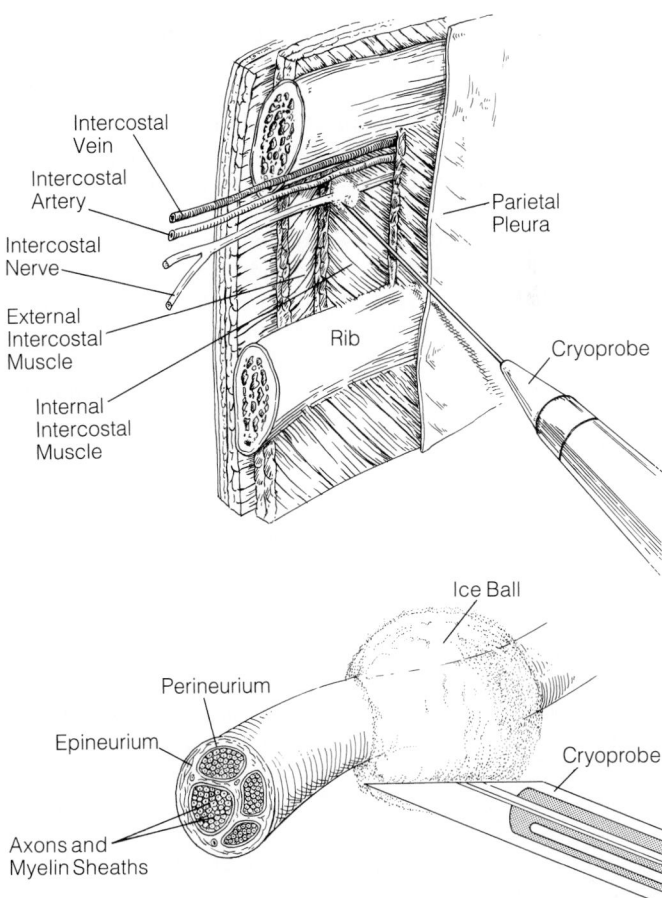

Figure 1 Illustrated is the procedure for performing cryoanalgesia in a thoracotomy. The intercostal nerve in the thoracotomy space is isolated, together with the two intercostal nerves above the space and the two below it, and the cryoprobe is applied to the nerves for 45 seconds. The probe is then defrosted and reapplied to the nerves for 45 seconds. The analgesia obtained lasts about 30 days.

ations[61-62]; accordingly, this agent is recommended as a basic component of multimodal analgesia in all operations.

Despite the gaps in our current understanding of the workings and differential effects of NSAIDs and COX-2 inhibitors, what is known is sufficiently encouraging to suggest that they should be recommended for baseline analgesic treatment after most operative procedures, with the exceptions already mentioned (see above). This recommendation is based not only on their analgesic efficacy but also on their opioid-sparing effect, which may enhance recovery (see below).

Glucocorticoids are powerful anti-inflammatory agents and have proven analgesic value in less extensive procedures,[64] especially dental, laparoscopic, and arthroscopic operations. In addition, they have profound antiemetic effects. Concerns about possible side effects in the setting of perioperative administration have not been borne out by the results of randomized studies.[64]

OTHER ANALGESICS

Tramadol is a weak analgesic that has several relatively minor side effects (e.g., dizziness, nausea, and vomiting).[65] It can be combined with acetaminophen to yield analgesic activity comparable to that of NSAIDs.[66]

Several systematic reviews have suggested that some analgesic and perioperative opioid-sparing effects can be achieved by adding an N-methyl-D-aspartate receptor antagonist (e.g., ketamine),[67-69] gabapentin, or pregabalin[70] [see Combination Regimens, below].

CRYOANALGESIA

Cryoanalgesia is the application of low temperatures ($-20°$ to $-29°$ C) to peripheral nerves with the goal of producing axonal degeneration and thus analgesia [see Figure 1]. Axonal regeneration takes place at a rate of 1 to 3 mm/day, which means that analgesia after intercostal blocks lasts about 30 days. Cryoanalgesia has no cardiac, respiratory, or cerebral side effects, and local side effects (e.g., neuroma formation) are extremely rare. In this context, it should be emphasized that postthoracotomy patients are at substantial risk (~30%) for chronic neuropathic pain without the use of cryoanalgesia[71]; however, this technique can be used only on sensory nerves or on nerves supplying muscles of no clinical importance.

At present, no information is available on the use of cryoanalgesia in operative procedures other than herniotomy and thoracotomy.[72] Cryoanalgesia is not efficacious after herniotomy.[73] The data on postthoracotomy cryoanalgesia, however, suggest improved pain alleviation and a concomitant reduction in the need for narcotics, which, in conjunction with the simplicity and low cost of the modality and the absence of side effects, present a strong argument for more extensive use of cryoanalgesia.

TRANSCUTANEOUS ELECTRICAL NERVE STIMULATION

Transcutaneous electrical nerve stimulation (TENS) is the application of a mild electrical current through the skin surface to a specific area, such as a surgical wound, to achieve pain relief; the exact mechanism whereby it achieves this effect is yet to be explained. Many TENS devices are available for clinical use, but the specific values and the proper uses of the various stimulation frequencies, waveforms, and current intensities have not been determined. Unfortunately, the effect of TENS on acute pain is too small to warrant a recommendation for routine use.[74]

PATIENT-CONTROLLED ANALGESIA

Patient-controlled administration of opioids has experienced a dramatic increase in use. This increase may be attributed to (1) awareness of the inadequacy of traditional I.M. opioid regimens, (2) the development of effective and safe biotechnology, and (3)

Table 9 Prescription Guidelines for Intravenous Patient-Controlled Analgesia

Drug (Concentration)	Demand Dose	Lockout Interval (min)
Morphine (1 mg/ml)	0.5–3.0 mg	5–12
Meperidine (10 mg/ml)	5–30 mg	5–12
Fentanyl (10 µg/ml)	10–20 µg	5–10
Hydromorphone (0.2 mg/ml)	0.1–0.5 mg	5–10
Oxymorphone (0.25 mg/ml)	0.2–0.4 mg	8–10
Methadone (1 mg/ml)	0.5–2.5 mg	8–20
Nalbuphine (1 mg/ml)	1–5 mg	5–10

the widespread patient satisfaction with patient-controlled analgesia (PCA).[75,76] It must be emphasized, however, that the effect of PCA on movement-associated pain is limited in comparison with that of epidural local anesthesia.[14]

Mechanisms of Action

Traditional I.M. dosing of opioids does not result in consistent blood levels,[75,76] because opioids are absorbed at a variable rate from the vascular bed of muscle. Moreover, administration of traditional I.M. regimens results in opioid concentrations that exceed the concentrations required to produce analgesia only about 30% of the time during any 4-hour dosing interval. PCA avoids these pitfalls by allowing repeated dosing on demand. PCA yields more constant and consistent plasma opioid levels and therefore provides better analgesia.[75,76]

Modes of Administration and Dosing Parameters

There are several modes by which opioids can be administered under patient control. Intermittent delivery of a fixed dose is known as demand dosing. Background infusions have been used to supplement patient-administered doses, but this practice increases the risk of respiratory depression and should therefore be avoided.[75,76]

There are several basic prescription parameters for PCA: loading dose, demand dose, lockout interval, and 4-hour limits [see Table 9].[75,76] When PCA is used for postoperative care, it is usually initiated in the recovery room. The patient is made comfortable by administering as much opioid as is needed (i.e., a loading dose). When the patient is sufficiently recovered from the anesthetic, he or she may begin to use the infuser.

Side Effects

Minor side effects associated with PCA include nausea, vomiting, sweating, and pruritus. Clinically significant respiratory depression with PCA is rare. There is no evidence to suggest that PCA is associated with a higher incidence of side effects than are other routes of systemic opioid administration.[75,76] Side effects are the result of the pharmacologic properties of opioids, not the method of administration.[75,76]

COMBINATION REGIMENS

Because no single pain treatment modality is optimal, combination regimens (e.g., balanced analgesia or multimodal treatment) offer major advantages over single-modality regimens, whether by maintaining or improving analgesia, by reducing side effects, or by doing both.[77,78] Combinations of epidural local anesthetics and morphine,[14,27] of NSAIDs and opioids,[46,77,78] of NSAIDs and acetaminophen,[61,62] of acetaminophen and opioids,[63] of acetaminophen and tramadol,[66] and of a selective COX-2 inhibitor and gabapentin[79] have been reported to have additive effects. At present, information on other combinations (involving ketamine, clonidine, glucocorticoids, and other agents) is too sparse to allow firm recommendations; however, multimodal analgesia is undoubtedly promising, and multidrug combinations should certainly be explored further.

The potential of combination regimens is especially intriguing with respect to the concept of perioperative opioid-sparing analgesia. The use of one or several nonopioid analgesics in such regimens may enhance recovery, in that the concomitant reduction in the opioid dosage will lead to decreased nausea, vomiting, and sedation.[80-84] Both the adverse events associated with postoperative opioid analgesia and the relatively high costs of such analgesia argue for an opioid-sparing approach.[85,86] Another argument that has been advanced is that the introduction of the JCAHO pain initiative may precipitate increased use of opioids (and thereby an increased risk of side effects), though it is not certain that this will be the case.[87,88]

Perception of Pain

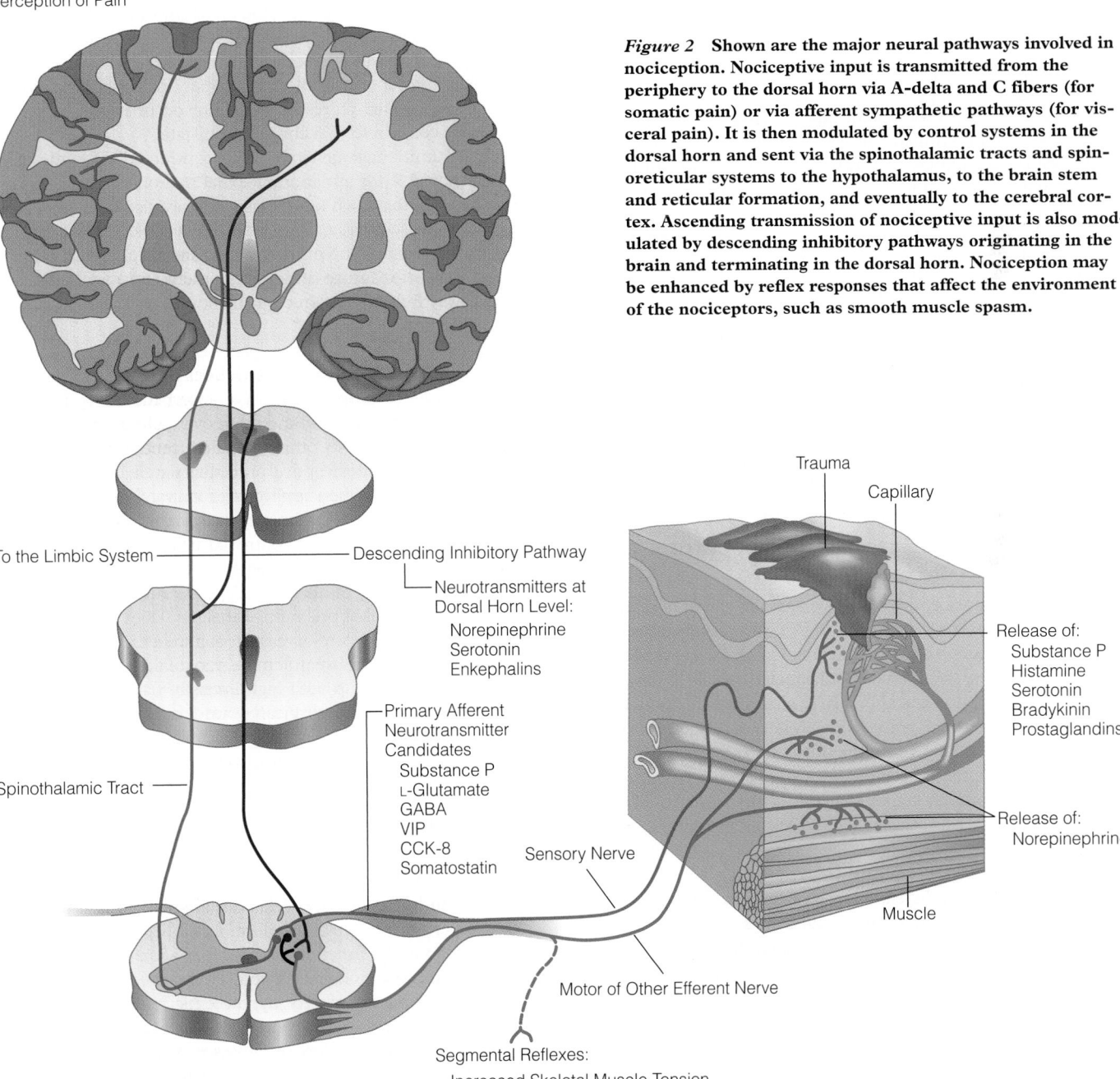

To the Limbic System

Spinothalamic Tract

Descending Inhibitory Pathway
Neurotransmitters at
Dorsal Horn Level:
Norepinephrine
Serotonin
Enkephalins

Primary Afferent
Neurotransmitter
Candidates
Substance P
L-Glutamate
GABA
VIP
CCK-8
Somatostatin

Sensory Nerve

Motor of Other Efferent Nerve

Segmental Reflexes:
Increased Skeletal Muscle Tension
Decreased Chest Compliance
More Nociceptive Input
Increased Sympathetic Tone
Decreased Gastric Mobility
Ileus, Nausea, Vomiting

Trauma
Capillary

Release of:
Substance P
Histamine
Serotonin
Bradykinin
Prostaglandins

Release of:
Norepinephrine

Muscle

Figure 2 Shown are the major neural pathways involved in nociception. Nociceptive input is transmitted from the periphery to the dorsal horn via A-delta and C fibers (for somatic pain) or via afferent sympathetic pathways (for visceral pain). It is then modulated by control systems in the dorsal horn and sent via the spinothalamic tracts and spinoreticular systems to the hypothalamus, to the brain stem and reticular formation, and eventually to the cerebral cortex. Ascending transmission of nociceptive input is also modulated by descending inhibitory pathways originating in the brain and terminating in the dorsal horn. Nociception may be enhanced by reflex responses that affect the environment of the nociceptors, such as smooth muscle spasm.

Discussion

Physiologic Mechanisms of Acute Pain

The basic mechanisms of acute pain are (1) afferent transmission of nociceptive stimuli through the peripheral nervous system after tissue damage, (2) modulation of these injury signals by control systems in the dorsal horn, and (3) modulation of the ascending transmission of pain stimuli by a descending control system originating in the brain [see Figure 2].[89-92]

PERIPHERAL PAIN RECEPTORS AND NEURAL TRANSMISSION TO SPINAL CORD

Peripheral pain receptors (nociceptors) can be identified by function but cannot be distinguished anatomically. The responsiveness of peripheral pain receptors may be enhanced by endogenous analgesic substances (e.g., prostaglandins, serotonin, bradykinin, nerve growth factor, and histamine), as well as by increased efferent sympathetic activity.[89] Antidromic release of substance P may amplify the inflammatory response and thereby increase pain transmission. The peripheral mechanisms of visceral pain still are not well understood[90]—for example, no one has yet explained why cutting or burning may provoke pain in the skin but not provoke pain in visceral organs. Peripheral opioid receptors have been demonstrated to appear in inflammation on the peripheral nerve terminals, and clinical studies have demonstrated that there are analgesic effects from peripheral opioid administration during arthroscopic knee surgery.[93]

Somatic nociceptive input is transmitted to the CNS through A-delta and C fibers, which are small in diameter and either unmyelinated or thinly myelinated. Visceral pain is transmitted through afferent sympathetic pathways; the evidence that afferent parasympathetic pathways play a role in visceral nociception is inconclusive.[90]

DORSAL HORN CONTROL SYSTEMS AND MODULATION OF INCOMING SIGNALS

All incoming nociceptive traffic synapses in the gray matter of the dorsal horn (Rexed's laminae I to IV). Several substances may be involved in primary afferent transmission of nociceptive stimuli in the dorsal horn: substance P, enkephalins, somatostatin, neurotensin, γ-aminobutyric acid (GABA), glutamic acid, angiotensin II, vasoactive intestinal polypeptide (VIP), and cholecystokinin octapeptide (CCK-8).[91] From the dorsal horn, nociceptive information is transmitted through the spinothalamic tracts to the hypothalamus, through spinoreticular systems to the brain stem and reticular formation, and finally to the cerebral cortex.

DESCENDING PAIN CONTROL SYSTEM

A descending control system for sensory input originates in the brain stem and reticular formation and in certain higher brain areas. The main neurotransmitters in this system are norepinephrine, serotonin, and enkephalins. Epidural-intrathecal administration of alpha-adrenergic agonists (e.g., clonidine) may therefore provide pain relief.[91]

SPINAL REFLEXES

Nociception may be enhanced by spinal reflexes that affect the environment of the nociceptive nerve endings. Thus, tissue damage may provoke an afferent reflex that causes muscle spasm in the vicinity of the injury, thereby increasing nociception. Similarly, sympathetic reflexes may cause decreased microcirculation in injury tissue, thereby generating smooth muscle spasm, which amplifies the sensation.

POSTINJURY CHANGES IN PERIPHERAL AND CENTRAL NERVOUS SYSTEMS

After an injury, the afferent nociceptive pathways undergo physiologic, anatomic, and chemical changes.[91,92] These changes include increased sensitivity on the part of peripheral nociceptors, as well as the growth of sprouts from damaged nerve fibers that become sensitive to mechanical and alpha-adrenergic stimuli and eventually begin to fire spontaneously. Moreover, excitability may be increased in the spinal cord, which leads to expansion of receptive fields in dorsal horn cells. Such changes may lower pain thresholds, may increase afferent barrage in the late postinjury state, and, if normal regression does not occur during convalescence, may contribute to a chronic pain state.[91]

Neural stimuli have generally been considered to be the main factor responsible for initiation of spinal neuroplasticity; however, it now appears that such neuroplasticity may also be mediated by cytokines released as a consequence of COX-2 induction.[92] Improved understanding of the mechanisms of pain may serve as a rational basis for future drug development and may help direct therapy away from symptom control and toward mechanism-specific treatment.[94]

In experimental studies, acute pain behavior or hyperexcitability of dorsal horn neurons may be eliminated or reduced if the afferent barrage is prevented from reaching the CNS. Preinjury neural blockade with local anesthetics or opioids can suppress excitability of the CNS; this is called preemptive analgesia. Because similar antinociceptive procedures were less effective in experimental studies when applied after injury, timing of analgesia seems to be important in the treatment of postoperative pain; however, a critical analysis of controlled clinical studies that compared the efficacy of analgesic regimens administered preoperatively with the efficacy of the same regimens administered postoperatively concluded that preemptive analgesia does not always provide a clinically significant increase in pain relief.[95,96] Nonetheless, it is important that pain treatment be initiated early to ensure that patients do not wake up with high-intensity pain. As long as the afferent input from the surgical wound continues, continuous treatment with multimodal or balanced analgesia may be the most effective method of treating postoperative pain.[95,97]

Effects of Pain Relief

METABOLIC RESPONSE TO OPERATION

It still is not generally appreciated that acute pain in the postoperative period or after hospitalization for accidental injury not only serves no useful function but also may actually exert harmful physiologic and psychological effects. Therefore, except in the initial stage in acutely injured hypovolemic patients for whom increased sympathetic activity may provide cardiovascular support, the pain-induced reflex responses that may adversely affect respiratory function, increase cardiac demands, decrease intestinal motility, and initiate skeletal muscle spasm (thereby impairing mobilization) should be counteracted by all available means.

The traditional view of the physiologic role of the stress response to surgical injury is that it is a homeostatic defense mechanism that helps the body heal tissue and adapt to injury. However, the necessity for the stress response in modern anesthesiology and surgery has been questioned.[28] Thus, concern about the detrimental effects of operative procedures (e.g., myocardial infarction, pulmonary complications, and thromboembolism) that cannot be attributed solely to imperfections in surgical technique has led to the hypothesis that the unsupported continuous injury response may instead be a maladaptive response that erodes body mass and physiologic reserve.[28,98] Because neural stimuli play an important role in releasing the stress response to surgical injury, pain relief may modify this response, but this modulation is dependent on the mechanism of action of the pain treatment modality employed.[28]

Alleviation of pain through antagonism of peripheral pain mediators (i.e., through use of NSAIDs) has no important modifying effect on the response to operation.[22,30] The effects of blockade of afferent and efferent transmission of pain stimuli by means of regional anesthesia have been studied in detail.[22,31] Spinal or epidural analgesia with local anesthetics prevents the greater part of the classic endocrine metabolic response to operative procedures in the lower region of the body (e.g., gynecologic and urologic procedures and orthopedic procedures in the lower limbs) and improves protein economy; however, this effect is considerably weaker in major abdominal and thoracic procedures, probably because of insufficient afferent neural blockade. The modifying effect of epidural analgesia on the stress response is most pronounced if the neural blockade takes effect before the surgical insult. The optimal duration of neural blockade for attenuating the hypermetabolic response has not been established, but it should include at least the initial 24 to 48 hours.[22,31]

Alleviation of postoperative pain through administration of epidural-intrathecal opioids has a smaller modifying effect on the surgical stress response, in comparison with the degree of pain relief it provides[22,31]; furthermore, it does not provide efferent sympathetic blockade. Systemic administration of opioids, either according to a fixed administration regimen or according to a demand-based regimen, has no important modifying effect on the stress response.[22] The effects of pain relief by acetaminophen, tramadol, cryoanalgesia, or TENS on the stress response have not been established but probably are of no clinical significance. Further studies aimed at defining the effects of multimodal analgesia on the surgical stress response are required.

POSTOPERATIVE MORBIDITY

The effects of nociceptive blockade and pain relief on postoperative morbidity remain to be defined, except with respect to intraoperative spinal or epidural local anesthetics in lower-body procedures, about which the following four conclusions can be made.[22,99] First, intraoperative blood loss is reduced by about 30%. Second, thromboembolic and pulmonary complications are reduced by about 30% to 40%. Third, when epidural local anesthetics are continuously administered (with or without small doses of opioids) to patients undergoing abdominal or thoracic procedures, pulmonary infectious complications appear to be reduced by about 40%.[30] Fourth, the duration of postoperative ileus is reduced[14,31]; this effect may be of major significance, in that reduction of ileus allows earlier oral nutrition,[31] which has been demonstrated to improve outcome.

The impact of continuous epidural analgesia on postoperative outcome after major operations remains the subject of some debate. Three large randomized trials from 2001 and 2002 found no positive effects except for improved pulmonary outcome.[100-102] One explanation for these negative findings may be the use of a predominantly opioid-based epidural analgesic regimen, which would hinder the normal physiologic responses supporting recovery to a greater extent than a local anesthetic regimen would.[22] Another explanation may be inadequate study design in some cases: most studies to date have focused on the effects of a single factor (i.e., epidural analgesia) on overall postoperative morbidity, which is probably too simplistic an approach, given that overall postoperative outcome is known to be determined by multiple factors.[103,104] Besides postoperative pain relief, reinforced psychological preparation of the patient, reduction of stress by performing neural blockade or opting for minimal invasive procedures, and enforcement of early oral postoperative feeding and mobilization may all play a significant role in determining outcome.[103,104] Prevention of intraoperative hypothermia, avoidance of fluid overloading, and avoidance of hypoxemia may be important as well.[103,104]

Therefore, although adequate pain relief is obviously a prerequisite for good outcome, the best results are likely to be achieved by combining analgesia with all the aforementioned factors in a multimodal rehabilitation effort.[103,104] Observations from patients undergoing a variety of surgical procedures suggest that such a multimodal approach may lead to significant reductions in hospital stay, morbidity, and convalescence.[103,104] Admittedly, these preliminary observations require confirmation by randomized or multicenter trials. The role of the acute pain service[105] and the effect of establishing a postoperative rehabilitation unit should be assessed as well.

TOLERANCE, PHYSICAL DEPENDENCE, AND ADDICTION

Continued exposure of an opioid receptor to high concentrations of opioid will cause tolerance. Tolerance is the progressive decline in an opioid's potency with continuous use, so that higher and higher concentrations of the drug are required to cause the same analgesic effect. Physical dependence refers to the production of an abstinence syndrome when an opioid is withdrawn. It is defined by the World Health Organization as follows[106]:

> A state, psychic or sometimes also physical, resulting from interactions between a living organism and a drug, characterized by behavioural and other responses that always include a compulsion to take the drug on a continuous or periodic basis in order to experience its psychic effects, and sometimes to avoid discomfort from its absence.

This definition is very close to the popular conception of addiction. It is important, however, to distinguish addiction (implying compulsive behavior and psychological dependence) from tolerance (a pharmacologic property) and from physical dependence (a characteristic physiologic effect of a group of drugs). Physical dependence does not imply addiction. Moreover, tolerance can occur without physical dependence; the converse does not appear to be true.

The possibility that the medical administration of opioids could result in a patient's becoming addicted has generated much debate about the use of opioids. In a prospective study of 12,000 hospitalized patients receiving at least one strong opioid for a protracted period, there were only four reasonably well documented cases of subsequent addiction, and in none of these was there a history of previous substance abuse.[107] Thus, the iatrogenic production of opioid addiction may be very rare.

CONCLUSION

The choice of therapeutic intervention for acute postoperative pain is determined largely by the nature of the patient's problem, the resources available, the efficacy of the various treatment techniques, the risks attendant on the procedures under consideration, and the cost to the patient.[108] Whereas trauma has been the subject of intensive research, the mechanisms of the pain associated with trauma and surgical injury and the optimal methods of relieving such pain have received comparatively little attention from surgeons. It is to be hoped that our growing understanding of basic pain mechanisms and appropriate therapy, combined with the promising data supporting the idea that adequate inhibition of surgically induced nociceptive stimuli may reduce postoperative morbidity, will stimulate more surgeons to turn their attention to this area. Effective control of postoperative pain, combined with a high degree of surgical expertise and the judicious use of other perioperative therapeutic interventions within the context of multimodal postoperative rehabilitation, is certain to improve surgical outcome.

References

1. American Pain Society Quality of Care Committee: Quality improved guidelines for the treatment of acute pain and cancer pain. JAMA 274:1874, 1995

2. Warfield CA, Kahn C: Acute pain management: programs in U.S. hospitals and experiences and attitudes among U.S. adults. Anesthesiology 83:1090, 1995

3. Ashburn MA, Caplan RA, Carr DB, et al: Practice guidelines for acute pain management in the perioperative setting. Anesthesiology 100:1573, 2004

4. Joint Commission on Accreditation of Health-care Organizations: Pain management standards. www.jcaho.org/accredited+organizations/hospitals/standards/revisions/2001/pain+management1.htm

5. Huang N, Cunningham F, Laurito CE, et al: Can we do better with postoperative pain management? Am J Surg 182:440, 2001

6. Apfelbaum JL, Chen C, Shilpa S et al: Postoperative pain experience: results from a national survey suggest postoperative pain continues to be undermanaged. Anesth Analg 97:534, 2003

7. Moore A, Edwards J, Barden J, et al: Bandolier's Little Book of Pain. Oxford University Press, Oxford, England, 2003

8. Kehlet H: Procedure-specific postoperative pain management. Anesthesiol Clin North Am 23:203, 2005

9. Gray A, Kehlet H, Bonnet F, et al: Predictive postoperative analgesia outcomes: NNT league tables or procedure-specific evidence? Br J Anaesth 94:710, 2005

10. Rosenquist RW, Rosenberg J: Postoperative pain guidelines. Reg Anesth Pain Med 28:279, 2003

11. Liu SS: Anesthesia and analgesia for colon surgery. Reg Anesth Pain Med 29:52, 2004

12. Prospect Working Group Guidelines available at: www.postoppain.org

13. Liu SS, Block BM, Wu CL: Effects of perioperative central neuraxial analgesia on outcome after coronary artery bypass surgery. Anesthesiology 101:153, 2004

14. Jørgensen H, Wetterslev J, Møiniche S, et al: Epidural local anesthetics versus opioid-based analgesic regimens on postoperative gastrointestinal paralysis, PONV and pain after abdominal surgery. Cochrane Database Syst Rev (4):1, 2000

15. Liu SS, Salinas FV: Continuous plexus and peripheral nerve block for postoperative analgesia. Anesth Analg 96:263, 2003

16. Klein S: Introduction: ambulatory continuous regional anesthesia. Tech Reg Anesth Pain Manage 8:57, 2004

17. Chapman CR: Psychological factors in postoperative pain. Acute Pain. Smith G, Covino BG, Eds. Butterworth Publishers, Stoneham, Massachusetts, 1985, p 22

18. Peck CL: Psychological factors in acute pain management. Acute Pain Management. Cousins MJ, Phillips GD, Eds. Churchill Livingstone, New York, 1986, p 251

19. Egbert LD, Battit GE, Welch SE, et al: Reduction of postoperative pain by encouragement and instruction of patients: a study of doctor-patient rapport. N Engl J Med 170:825, 1964

20. Austrup ML, Korean G: Analgesic agents for the postoperative period: opioids. Surg Clin North Am 79:253, 1999

21. Taguchi A, Sharma N, Saleem RM, et al: Selective postoperative inhibition of gastrointestinal opioid receptors. N Engl J Med 345:935, 2001

22. Wolff BG, Michelassi F, Gerkin TM, et al: Alvimopan, a novel, peripherally acting mu opioid antagonist: results of a multicenter, randomized, double-blind, placebo-controlled, phase III trial of major abdominal surgery and postoperative ileus. Ann Surg 240:728, 2004

23. Picard PR, Tramèr MR, McQuay HJ, et al: Analgesic efficacy of peripheral opioids (all except intra-articular): a qualitative systematic review of randomized controlled trials. Pain 72:309, 1997

24. Gupta A, Bodin L, Holmström B, et al: A systematic review of the peripheral analgesic effects of intraarticular morphine. Anesth Analg 93:761, 2001

25. Rawal N: Epidural and spinal agents for postoperative analgesia. Surg Clin North Am 79:313, 1999

26. Dahl JB, Jeppesen IS, Jørgensen H, et al: Intraoperative and postoperative analgesic efficacy and adverse effects of intrathecal opioids in patients undergoing cesarean section with spinal anesthesia: a qualitative and quantitative systematic review of randomized controlled trials. Anesthesiology 91:1919, 1999

27. Wheatley RG, Schug SA, Watson D: Safety and efficacy of postoperative epidural analgesia. Br J Anaesth 87:47, 2001

28. Kehlet H: Modification of responses to surgery by neural blockade: clinical implications. Cousins MJ, Bridenbaugh, Eds. Neural Blockade in Clinical Anesthesia and Management of Pain, 3rd ed. Lippincott-Raven, Philadelphia, 1998, p 129

29. Whiteside JB, Wildsmith JAW: Developments in local anaesthetic drugs. Br J Anaesth 87:27, 2001

30. Kehlet H, Holte K: Effect of postoperative analgesia on surgical outcome. Br J Anaesth 87:62, 2001

31. Holte K, Kehlet H: Epidural anaesthesia and analgesia: effects on surgical stress responses and implications for postoperative nutrition. Clin Nutr 21:199, 2002

32. Basse L, Werner M, Kehlet H: Is urinary drainage necessary during continuous epidural analgesia? Reg Anesth Pain Med 25:498, 2000

33. Horlocker TT, Wedel DJ, Benzon H, et al: Regional anesthesia in the anticoagulated patient: Defining the risks. Reg Anesth Pain Med 29(suppl 1):1, 2004

34. Geerts WH, Pineo GF, Heit JA, et al: Prevention of venous tromboembolism. Chest 126:338S, 2004

35. Peng PWH, Chan VWS: Local and regional block in postoperative pain control. Surg Clin North Am 79:345, 1999

36. Møiniche S, Jørgensen H, Wetterslev J, et al: Local anesthetic infiltration for postoperative pain relief after laparoscopy: a qualitative and quantitative systematic review of intraperitoneal, port-site infiltration and mesosalpinx block. Anesth Analg 90:899, 2000

37. Kehlet H, Gray W, Bonnet F, et al: A procedure-specific systematic review and consensus recommendations for postoperative analgesia following laparoscopic cholecystectomy. Surg Endosc (in press)

38. Møiniche S, Mikkelsen S, Wetterslev J, et al: A qualitative systematic review of incisional local anaesthesia for postoperative pain relief after abdominal operations. Br J Anaesth 81:377, 1998

39. LeBlanc KA, Bellanger D, Rhynes K, et al: Evaluation of continuous infusion of 0.5% bupivacaine by elastomeric pump for postoperative pain management after open inguinal hernia repair. J Am Coll Surg 200:198, 2005

40. White PF, Rawal S, Latham P, et al: Use of a continuous local anesthetic infusion for pain management after median sternotomy. Anesthesiology 99:918, 2003

41. Schurr MJ, Gordon DB, Pellino TA, et al: Continuous local anesthetic infusion for pain management after outpatient inguinal herniorrhaphy. Surgery 136:761, 2004

42. McDonald SB, Jacobsohn E, Kopacz DJ, et al: Parasternal block and local anesthetic infiltration with levobupivacaine after cardiac surgery with desflurane: the effect on postoperative pain, pulmonary function, and tracheal extubation times. Anesth Analg 100:25, 2005

43. Bianconi M, Ferraro L, Ricci R, et al: The pharmacokinetics and efficacy of ropivacaine continuous wound infiltration after spine fusion surgery. Anesth Analg 98:166, 2004

44. Bianconi M, Ferraro L, Traina GC, et al: Pharmacokinetics and efficacy of ropivacaine continuous wound instillation after joint replacement surgery. Br J Anaesth 91:830, 2003

45. Ilfeld B, Morey T, Enneking F: Continuous infraclaviculabrachial plexus block for postoperative pain control at home: a randomized, double-blinded placebo-controlled study. Anesthesiology 96:1297, 2002

46. Power I, Barratt S: Analgesic agents for the postoperative period: nonopioids. Surg Clin North Am 79:275, 1999

47. Rømsing J, Møiniche S: A systematic review of Cox-2 inhibitors compared with traditional NSAIDs, or different Cox-2 inhibitors for post-operative pain. Acta Anesthesiol Scand 48:525, 2004

48. Gilron I, Milne B, Hong M: Cyclooxygenase-2 inhibitors in postoperative pain management. Anesthesiology 99:1198, 2003

49. Gajraj NM: Cyclooxygenase-2 inhibitors. Anesth Analg 96:1720, 2003

50. Gambaro G, Perazella MA: Adverse renal effects of anti-inflammatory agents: evaluation of selective and nonselective cyclooxygenase inhibitors. J Intern Med 253:643, 2003

51. Lee A, Cooper MG, Craig JC, et al: The effects of non-steroidal anti-inflammatory drugs (NSAIDs) on postoperative renal function: a meta-analysis. Anesth Intensive Care 27:574, 1999

52. Møiniche S, Rømsing J, Dahl JB, et al: Non-steroidal anti-inflammatory drugs and the risk of operative site bleeding after tonsillectomy: a quantitative, systematic review. Anesth Analg 96:68, 2003

53. Marret E, Flahault A, Samama CM, et al: Effects of postoperative, nonsteroidal, anti-inflammatory drugs on bleeding risk after tonsillectomy. Anesthesiology 98:1497, 2003

54. Einhorn TA: Do inhibitors of cyclooxygenase-2 impair bone healing? J Bone Mineral Res 17:977, 2002

55. Gajraj NM: The effect of cyclooxygenase-2 inhibitors on bone healing. Reg Anesth Pain Med 28:456, 2003

56. Reuben SS: The effects of non-steroidal anti-inflammatory drugs on spinal fusion. Acute Pain 6:41, 2004

57. Reuben SS, Ekman EF: The effect of cyclooxygenase-2 inhibitor on analgesia and spinal fusion. J Bone Joint Surg 87:536, 2005

58. Ott E, Nussmeier NA, Duke PC, et al: Efficacy and safety of the cyclooxygenase-2 inhibitors parecoxib and valdecoxib in patients undergoing coronary artery bypass surgery. J Thorac Cardiovasc Surg 125: 1481, 2003

59. Nussmeier NA, Whelton AA, Brown MT, et al: Complications of the Cox-2 inhibitors parecoxib and valdecoxib after cardiac surgery. N Engl J Med 352:1081, 2005

60. Rømsing J, Møiniche S, Østergaard D, et al: Local infiltration with NSAIDs for postoperative analgesia: evidence for a peripheral analgesic action. Acta Anaesthesiol Scand 44:672, 2000

61. Rømsing J, Møiniche S, Dahl JB: Rectal and parenteral paracetamol, and paracetamol in combination with NSAID's for postoperative analgesia. Br J Anaesth 88:215, 2002

62. Hyllested M, Jones S, Pedersen JL, et al: Comparative effect of paracetamol, NSAID's or their combination in postoperative pain management: a qualitative review. Br J Anaesth 88:199, 2002

63. Moore A, Collins S, Carroll D, et al: Paracetamol with and without codeine in acute pain: a quantitative systematic review. Pain 70:193, 1997

64. Holte K, Kehlet H: Perioperative single-dose glucocorticoid administration: pathophysiological effects and clinical implications. J Am Coll Surg 195:694, 2002

65. Scott LJ, Perry CM: Tramadol: a review of its use in perioperative pain. Drugs 60:139, 2000

66. Edwards JE, McQuay HJ, Moore RA: Combination analgesic efficacy: individual patient data meta-analysis of single-dose oral tramadol plus acetaminophen in acute postoperative pain. J Pain Symptom Manage 23:121, 2002

67. Himmelseher S, Durieux ME: Ketamine for perioperative pain management. Anesthesiology 102:211, 2005

68. Elia N, Tramèr MR: Ketamine and postoperative pain—a quantitative systematic review of randomized trials. Pain 113:61, 2005

69. McCartney CJL, Sinha A, Katz J: A qualitative systematic review of the role of N-Methyl-D-aspartate receptor antagonists in preventive analgesia. Anesth Analg 98:1385, 2004

70. Dahl JB, Mathiesen O, Møiniche S: Prospective premedication: an option with gabapentin and related drugs? Acta Anaesthesiol Scand 48:1130, 2004

71. Perkins FM, Kehlet H: Chronic pain as an outcome of surgery. Anesthesiology 93:1123, 2000

72. Kruger M, McRae K: Pain management in cardiothoracic practice. Surg Clin North Am 79:387, 1999

73. Callesen T, Bech K, Thorup J, et al: Cryoanalgesia: effect on posthherniorrhaphy pain. Anesth Analg 87:896, 1998

74. Carroll D, Tramèr M, McQuay H, et al: Randomization is important in studies with pain outcomes: systematic review of transcutaneous electrical nerve stimulation in acute postoperative pain. Br J Anaesth 77:798, 1996

75. Etches RC: Patient-controlled analgesia. Surg Clin North Am 79:297, 1999

76. Macintyre PE: Safety and efficacy of patient-controlled analgesia. Br J Anaesth 87:36, 2001

77. Kehlet H, Werner M, Perkins F: Balanced analgesia: what is it and what are its advantages in postoperative pain? Drugs 58:793, 1999

78. Jin F, Chung F: Multimodal analgesia for postoperative pain control. J Clin Anesth 13:524, 2001

79. Gilron I, Orr E, Dongsheng T, et al: A placebo-controlled randomized clinical trial of perioperative administration of gabapentin, rofecoxib and their combination for spontaneous and movement-evoked pain after abdominal hysterectomy. Pain 113:191, 2005

80. Marret E, Kurdi O, Zufferey P, et al: Effects of nonsteroidal anti-inflammatory drugs on patient-controlled analgesia morphine side effects: meta-analysis of randomized controlled trials. Anesthesiology 102:1249, 2005

81. Kehlet H: Postoperative opioid-sparing to hasten recovery—what are the issues? Anesthesiology 102: 1083, 2005

82. Gan TJ, Joshi GP, Zhao SZ, et al: Presurgical intravenous parecoxib sodium and follow-up oral valdecoxib for pain management after laparoscopic cholecystectomy surgery reduces opioid requirements and opioid-related adverse effects. Acta Anaesthesiol Scand 48:1194, 2004

83. Zhao SZ, Chung F, Hanna DB, et al: Dose-response relationship between opioid use and adverse effects after ambulatory surgery. J Pain Sympt Manage 28:35, 2004

84. Rømsing J, Møiniche S, Mathiesen O et al: Reduction of opioid-related adverse events using opioid-sparing analgesia with Cox-2 inhibitors lacks documentation: a systematic review. Acta Anaesthesiol Scand 49:133, 2005

85. Wheeler M, Oderda GM, Ashburn MA, et al: Adverse events associated with postoperative opioid analgesia: a systematic review. J Pain 3:159, 2002

86. Philip BK, Reese PR, Burch SP: The economic impact of opioids on postoperative pain management. J Clin Anesth 14:354, 2002

87. Frasco PE, Sprung J, Trentman TL: The impact of the Joint Commission for Accreditation of Healthcare Organisations pain initiative on perioperative opiate consumption and recovery room length of stay. Anesth Analg 100:162, 2005

88. Taylor S, Voytovich AE, Kozol RA: Has the pendulum swung too far in postoperative pain control? Am J Surg 186:472, 2003

89. Kidd BL, Urban LA: Mechanisms of inflammatory pain. Br J Anaesth 87:3, 2001

90. Cervero F, Laird JMA: Visceral pain. Lancet 353:2145, 1999

91. Carr DB, Goudas LC: Acute pain. Lancet 353:2051, 1999

92. Woolf CJ, Salter MW: Neural plasticity: increasing the gain in pain. Science 288:1765, 2000

93. Stein C, Schäfer M, Machelska H: Attacking pain at its source: new perspectives on opioids. Nature Med 9:1003, 2003

94. Woolf CJ: Pain: moving from symptom control toward mechanism-specific pharmacologic management. Ann Intern Med 140:441, 2004

95. Møiniche S, Kehlet H, Dahl JB: A qualitative and quantitative systematic review of preemptive analgesia for postoperative pain relief. Anesthesiology 96:725, 2002

96. Ong CKS, Lirk P, Seymour RA, et al: The efficacy of preemptive analgesia for acute postoperative pain management: a meta-analysis. Anesth Analg 100:757, 2005

97. Kissin I: Preemptive analgesia at the crossroad. Anesth Analg 100:754, 2005

98. Wilmore DW: Metabolic response to severe surgical illness: overview. World J Surg 24:705, 2000

99. Rodgers A, Walker N, Schug S, et al: Reduction of postoperative mortality and morbidity with epidural or spinal anaesthesia: results from overview of randomized trials. BMJ 321:1493, 2000

100. Effect of epidural anesthesia and analgesia on perioperative outcome: a randomized, controlled Veterans Affairs Cooperative study. Department of Veterans Affairs Cooperative Study #345 Study Group. Ann Surg 234:560, 2001

101. Norris EJ, Beattie C, Perler BA, et al: Double-masked randomized trial comparing alternate combinations of intraoperative anesthesia and postoperative analgesia in abdominal aortic surgery. Anesthesiology 95:1054, 2001

102. Epidural anaesthesia and analgesia and outcome of major surgery: a randomized trial. MASTER Anaesthesia Trial Study Group. Lancet 359:1276, 2002

103. Kehlet H, Wilmore DW: Multimodal strategies to improve surgical outcome. Am J Surg 183:630, 2002

104. Kehlet H, Dahl JB: Anaesthesia, surgery, and challenges in postoperative recovery. Lancet 362:1921, 2003

105. Werner M, Søholm L, Rotbøll P, et al: Does an acute pain service improve postoperative outcome? Anesth Analg 95:1361, 2002

106. World Health Organization: Expert committee on drug dependence, 16th report. Technical Report Series No. 407. World Health Organization, Geneva, 1969

107. Porter J, Jick H: Addiction is rare in patients treated with narcotics (letter). N Engl J Med 302:123, 1980

108. Dahl JB, Kehlet H: Postoperative pain and its management. Wall & Melzack's Textbook of Pain, 5th ed. McMahon S, Koltzenburg M, Eds. Elsevier, London, 2005

Acknowledgments

Figure 1 Carol Donner.
Figure 2 Dana Burns Pizer.

11 ACUTE WOUND CARE

Stephen R. Sullivan, M.D., Loren H. Engrav, M.D., F.A.C.S., and Matthew B. Klein, M.D.

Approach to Acute Wound Management

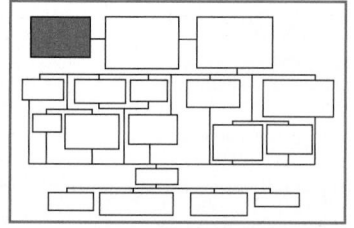

Acute wounds are the result of local trauma and may be associated with severe life-threatening injuries. The approach to a patient with an acute wound begins with assessment of the ABCs (*A*irway, *B*reathing, and *C*irculation). Management of any life-threatening injuries present is addressed first; only after more urgent problems have been ruled out or corrected is management of the wound itself addressed. A complete history is obtained and a thorough physical examination performed, with special attention paid to both local and systemic wound environment factors that may affect healing. Information about the cause of injury is sought. In the case of a hand injury, the patient's hand dominance and occupation are determined. All patients with acute wounds should be assessed for malnutrition, diabetes, peripheral vascular disease, neuropathy, obesity, immune deficiency, autoimmune disorders, connective tissue diseases, coagulopathy, hepatic dysfunction, malignancy, smoking practices, medication use that could interfere with healing, and allergies. The local wound environment should be evaluated to determine the extent and complexity of injury, the tissues involved, the presence or absence of contamination by microorganisms or foreign bodies, and the degree of any damage related to previous irradiation or injury to surrounding tissues.

Gloves and a shielded mask are worn to protect the practitioner from exposure to body fluids. Gloves must be powder free, as well as latex free (to prevent allergic reactions to latex).[1] The wound is carefully examined, with particular attention paid to size, location, bleeding, arterial or venous insufficiency, tissue temperature, tissue viability, and foreign bodies. The possibility of damage to vessels, nerves, ducts, cartilage, muscles, or bones in proximity to the injury is assessed. X-rays and a careful motor and sensory examination may be required to rule out such coexisting injuries. While these tests are being performed, moist gauze should be applied to wounds. For thorough assessment of injuries, it may be necessary to probe ducts (e.g., the parotid duct or the lacrimal duct).

At this point, decisions must be made about acute wound care. The goal of acute wound management is a closed, healing wound that will result in the best functional and aesthetic outcome. In what follows, we address the key considerations in management of the acute wound, including anesthesia, choice of repair site (i.e., operating room or emergency department), debridement, irrigation, hemostasis, closure materials, timing and methods of closure, appropriate closure methods for specific wound types, dressings, adjunctive treatment (e.g., tetanus and rabies prophylaxis, antibiotics, and nutritional supplementation), postoperative wound care, and potential disturbances of wound healing. Finally, we briefly review the physiology of wound healing.

Wound Preparation

ANESTHESIA

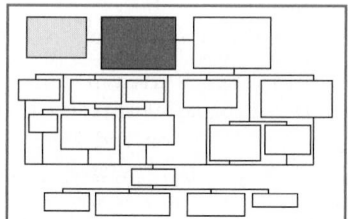

Adequate general or local anesthesia, preceded by careful motor and sensory examination, must be instituted before examination and treatment of the wound can begin. General anesthesia in the OR is employed if the patient is unable to tolerate local anesthesia; adequate pain control cannot be achieved with a local block; the wound requires significant debridement, exploration, or repair; bleeding is difficult to control; or the local anesthetic dose required for adequate pain control exceeds the maximum dose that can be safely delivered. Local anesthesia is usually sufficient for debridement and closure of most small traumatic wounds. Often, the local anesthetic may be injected directly into wounded tissue. However, direct wound injection may be less reliable in inflamed or infected tissue or may distort important anatomic landmarks used to align wound edges. In these situations, regional nerve blocks directed at specific sensory nerves outside the injured field may be employed instead.

The main injectable anesthetics can be broadly divided into amides and esters [*see Table 1*]. (An easy way of remembering which category an agent belongs to is to recall that the amides all have two *I*s in their generic name, whereas the esters have only one.) Lidocaine, an amide, is the most commonly used local anesthetic. Its advantages include its rapid onset of action (< 2 minutes), its extended duration of action (60 to 120 minutes), its relative safety in comparison with more potent anesthetics (e.g., bupivacaine), and its availability in multiple forms (e.g., liquid, jelly, and ointment) and concentrations (e.g., 0.5%, 1.0%, and 2.0%). In addition, lidocaine rarely causes allergic reactions, whereas ester anesthetics (e.g., tetracaine) are metabolized to para-aminobenzoic acid, to which some persons are allergic. Cocaine, an ester, is an excellent local anesthetic for wounds in

Table 1 Common Injectable Anesthetics[3]

Amides	Esters
Lidocaine (Xylocaine)	Procaine (Novocain)
Bupivacaine (Marcaine)	Chloroprocaine (Nesacaine)
Mepivacaine (Carbocaine)	Tetracaine (Pontocaine)
Prilocaine (Citanest)	Benzocaine (multiple brands)
Etidocaine (Duranest)	Propoxycaine (Ravocaine)
Phenocaine	Cocaine
Dibucaine (Nupercainal)	
Ropivacaine (Naropin)	
Levobupivacaine (Chirocaine)	

mucous membrane (e.g., those in the nose or the throat). It is unique among local anesthetics in that it causes vasoconstriction, which helps reduce hemorrhage. Typically, cocaine is applied topically by soaking gauze or pledgets in a solution.

Vasoconstriction can also be produced by adding epinephrine to a local anesthetic, usually in a dilution of 1:100,000 or 1:200,000 (5 to 10 μg/ml). Through vasoconstriction, epinephrine prolongs the anesthetic agent's duration of action, allows a larger dose to be safely administered, and aids in hemostasis.[2] Traditionally, local anesthetics with epinephrine have not been used in finger and toe wounds, because of the theoretical risk of ischemia and tissue loss; however, these adverse effects have not yet been reported clinically or documented by any prospective studies.[3]

Local anesthetics can cause systemic toxicity when injected intravascularly or given in excessive doses. Manifestations of systemic toxicity begin with central nervous system effects (e.g., vertigo, tinnitus, sedation, and seizures) and may progress to cardiovascular effects (e.g., hypotension, cardiac conduction abnormalities, and cardiovascular collapse). Treatment for systemic toxicity is supportive, with oxygen, airway support, and cardiovascular bypass (if necessary) provided until the anesthetic has been metabolized by the liver. The maximum safe dose of lidocaine is 3 to 5 mg/kg without epinephrine and 7 mg/kg with epinephrine. Doses as high as 55 mg/kg have been used without toxicity for tumescent anesthesia in patients undergoing liposuction[4]; however, in this scenario, some of the anesthetic is aspirated by the liposuction, which means that the effective dose is lower. The lidocaine doses used for local wound injection should be substantially smaller than those used in liposuction. The maximum safe dose of cocaine is 2 to 3 mg/kg. To prevent local anesthesia from causing systemic toxicity, the recommended safe doses of the anesthetics should not be exceeded, and aspiration should be performed before injection into the wound to ensure that the agent will not be injected intravascularly.

The pain associated with injection of the local anesthetic can be minimized by using a small-caliber needle (27 to 30 gauge), warming the anesthetic, injecting the agent slowly, using a subcutaneous rather than an intradermal injection technique,[5] providing counterirritation, buffering the anesthetic with sodium bicarbonate to reduce acidity (in a 1:10 ratio of sodium bicarbonate to local anesthetic),[6] and applying a topical local anesthetic before injection. Topical local anesthetics (e.g., TAC [tetracaine, adrenaline (epinephrine), and cocaine] and EMLA [a eutectic mixture of lidocaine and prilocaine]) are as effective as injectable anesthetics when applied to an open wound.[7] EMLA requires approximately 60 minutes to induce sufficient anesthesia for open wounds; TAC requires approximately 30 minutes.[8] EMLA is more effective than TAC for open wounds of the extremity. Benzocaine 20% (in gel, liquid, or spray form) can also be used for topical anesthesia and is frequently employed before endoscopic procedures. It is poorly absorbed through intact skin but well absorbed through mucous membranes and open wounds. A 0.5- to 1-second spray is usually recommended, though even with a standardized spray duration, the delivered dose can vary considerably.[9] A 2-second spray results in a statistically, though not clinically, significant increase in methemoglobin levels.[10] Methemoglobinemia is a rare but life-threatening complication of benzocaine spray use. If symptoms of methemoglobinemia develop (e.g., cyanosis or elevated methemoglobin levels on cooximetry), prompt treatment with intravenous methylene blue, 1 to 2 mg/kg, is indicated.[9]

DEBRIDEMENT

Normal healing can proceed only if tissues are viable, if the wound contains no foreign bodies, and if tissues are free of excessive bacterial contamination. To reduce the risk of infection in an acute wound, necrotic tissue and foreign bodies must be removed.[11] The wound and the surrounding local tissue must be exposed so that necrotic tissue can be identified and debrided. Hair may be trimmed with scissors or an electric clipper or retracted with an ointment or gel to facilitate exposure, debridement, and wound closure. Close shaving with a razor should be avoided, however, because it potentiates wound infections.[12] Clipping of eyebrows should also be avoided, both because the eyebrows may not grow back and because the hair is necessary for proper alignment.

Some wounds contain a significant amount of questionably viable tissue. If there is enough questionably viable tissue to preclude acute debridement, dressing changes may be initiated. When all tissue has been declared to be either viable or necrotic and when the necrotic tissue has been debrided surgically or by means of dressing changes, the wound can be closed.

Most foreign bodies are easily removed from wounds either by hand or via surgical debridement. Abrasion injuries or gunpowder explosions can cause small foreign body fragments to be embedded in and beneath the skin. These small foreign bodies are often difficult to extract but should be removed as soon after the injury as possible. Irrigation usually suffices for removal of loose foreign bodies, but surgical debridement with a small drill, a sharp instrument, or a brush may be required for removal of more firmly embedded foreign material. If the interval between injury and treatment exceeds 1 to 2 days, the wounds will begin to epithelialize and the embedded material will be trapped in the skin, resulting in traumatic tattooing.

IRRIGATION

After debridement of necrotic tissue and foreign bodies, the next step is irrigation of the wound. This may be accomplished by means of several different methods, including bulb syringe irrigation, gravity flow irrigation, and pulsatile lavage. These methods can be further divided into high-pressure (35 to 70 psi) and low-pressure (1 to 15 psi) delivery systems. High-pressure pulsatile lavage reduces bacterial concentrations in the wound more efficiently than low-pressure and bulb syringe irrigation do,[13] but it also causes considerable disruption to soft tissue structure[14] and results in deeper penetration and greater retention of bacteria in soft tissue than low-pressure lavage does.[15] In general, low-pressure systems should be employed for acute wound irrigation, though merely running saline over a wound is of little value. To obtain continuous irrigation with pressures as low as 5 to 8 psi, one group recommended using a saline bag in a pressure cuff inflated to 400 mm Hg and connected to I.V. tubing with a 19-gauge angiocatheter.[16]

Only nontoxic solutions (e.g., 0.9% sterile saline, lactated Ringer solution, sterile water, and tap water) should be used for wound irrigation.[17] Irrigation with an antibiotic solution appears to offer no advantages over irrigation with a nonsterile soap solution, and the antibiotic solution may increase the risk of wound-healing problems.[18] Strong antiseptics (e.g., povidone-iodine, chlorhexidine, alcohol, sodium hypochlorite, and hydrogen peroxide) should not be placed directly into the wound, because they are toxic to the tissues and impede healing. The surrounding skin should be prepared with an antibacterial solution, and a sterile field created to limit contamination.

HEMOSTASIS

In most wounds, hemorrhage can be readily controlled with pressure, cauterization, or ligation of vessels. Lacerated arteries

Patient presents with acute wound

Obtain complete history, and perform thorough physical examination. Life-threatening conditions take priority over wound care.

Examine local wound environment, look for local and systemic factors that may impair healing, and identify wounded structures.

Consider antibiotic prophylaxis for clean or clean-contaminated wounds if factors likely to impair wound healing [*see Table 7*] are present. Initiate antibiotic prophylaxis for contaminated and dirty wounds and for wounds with extensive devitalized tissue.

Initial measures are complete, and wound care is initiated

Prepare wound:
- *Anesthesia:* use local anesthesia in most cases. Use general anesthesia if local anesthesia cannot be tolerated, if pain cannot be controlled with local anesthesia, if wound requires significant repair, if bleeding is hard to control, or if local anesthetic dose needed would be unsafe.
- *Debridement:* debride necrotic tissue, and remove foreign bodies. If there is significant questionably viable tissue, defer debridement until status is clarified, and initiate dressing changes.
- *Irrigation:* use only nontoxic irrigants, avoiding antibiotics and strong antiseptics. Low pressure is preferable to high pressure (but bulb syringe is inadequate).
- *Hemostasis:* use pressure, cauterization, or ligation (but do not ligate lacerated arteries proximal to amputated part). Place drain if there is risk of hematoma or fluid collection.

Abrasion

Remove foreign bodies to prevent traumatic tattooing.

Allow healing by secondary closure. Tape or glue may be used.

Laceration

Close immediately if patient presents with clean wound within 8 hr of injury (or 24 hr for simple facial injury). Otherwise, delay closure or allow wound to heal without closure.

Close deep laceration in layers.

Crush injury

Severity of injury is not always apparent.

Monitor for compartment syndrome, and treat on urgent basis.

Puncture wound

Leave wound open, and allow healing by secondary closure.

Complex wound

Inform patient of potential for poor aesthetic outcome, and discuss alternatives.

Close immediately if wound is clean and tissue viable. Delay closure if wound is contaminated or there is significant nonviable or questionably viable tissue.

Perform primary closure if possible. Severe injury may necessitate delayed primary closure, secondary closure, skin grafting, or tissue transfer.

Extravasation injury

Conservative management (i.e., elevation, ice, and monitoring) suffices in most cases. Injury involving high volume, high osmolarity, or chemotherapeutic agent may necessitate additional measures (e.g., hydrocortisone, incision and drainage, hyaluronidase, saline, or aspiration).

Consider tetanus treatment, antibiotic prophylaxis, or both.

Apply dressings as appropriate for individual wound type.

Abrasion

Use occlusive dressings (impregnated gauze may be used for small superficial wounds). Avoid dry dressings.

Laceration, complex wound closed primarily, injection injury, high-velocity wound, bite wound, or sting

Consider three-layer dressings for open draining wound, with inner nonadherent layer, middle absorbent layer, and outer binding layer.

Consider ointment if there is minimal drainage.

Wound is ready for closure

Select closure materials: sutures, tapes, staples, or adhesives.
Determine timing and methods of closure:
- *Immediate primary closure:* clean wound without contraindications to closure
- *Delayed primary closure:* contaminated wound, wound with questionably viable tissue, or patient who cannot tolerate immediate closure
- *Secondary closure (allowing wound to heal by itself):* wound with contamination or contraindication to closure, patient who cannot tolerate closure, or wound for which closure is not needed for aesthetic result
- *Skin grafting:* large superficial wound
- *Tissue transfer:* large wound with exposed vital structure

Formulate specific closure approach suitable for individual wound type.

Approach to Acute Wound Management

...jection injury

...ound appearance is often deceptively benign.
...amine wound area carefully and obtain
...propriate radiographs.
...eat aggressively with incision, wide exposure,
...bridement, and removal of foreign bodies.
...ow healing by secondary closure.

Bite wound

Take into account risks of rabies, bacterial and other viral infections, and envenomation.

Treat with exploration, irrigation, and debridement.

Close immediately if wound is clean and tissue viable. Delay closure if wound is contaminated or there is significant nonviable or questionably viable tissue.

Perform primary closure if possible. Severe injury may necessitate secondary closure, skin grafting, or tissue transfer.

Consider rabies treatment, rabies prophylaxis, or both.

High-velocity wound

Wound appearance is often deceptively benign; foreign bodies are frequently present. Examine wound area carefully and obtain appropriate radiographs.

Debride wound extensively and identify all injured tissue.

Avoid immediate primary closure. Perform delayed primary closure or allow healing by secondary closure.

Sting

Take into account risk of envenomation.

Symptoms may be local or systemic. Treatment is usually directed toward local symptoms. For systemic reactions, epinephrine, diphenhydramine, and supportive airway and BP care may be required.

...mplex wound left open or closed after delay

...erally, use wet-to-dry dressings; use wet-to-wet
...sings if wound bed contains tendons, arteries,
...es, or bone. Avoid compression dressings.
...sider NPWT for large open wound.

Extravasation injury or crush injury

Avoid compression dressings.

proximal to amputated parts such as fingers or ears, however, should not be ligated, because an intact vessel is necessary for microsurgical replantation. Packing, wrapping, and elevating can help control hemorrhage temporarily. If necessary (though the need should be rare), a tourniquet may be applied to an injured extremity. Hemostasis prevents hematoma formation, which increases the risk of infection and wound inflammation. If there appears to be a potential risk of hematoma or fluid collection, drains should be placed. Although drains may help prevent accumulation of blood or serum in the wound, they are not a replacement for meticulous hemostasis. Drains facilitate approximation of tissues, particularly under flaps; however, they also tend to potentiate bacterial infections and should therefore be removed from the wound as soon as possible.[19]

As a rule, drains can be safely removed when drainage reaches levels of 25 to 50 ml/day. If a hematoma or seroma forms, the subsequent course of action depends on the size of the fluid collection. Small hematomas and seromas usually are reabsorbed and thus can be treated conservatively. Larger hematomas and seromas provide a significant barrier to healing, and treatment may require reopening the wound and placing drains. Intermittent sterile aspirations, followed by application of a compressive dressing, may be indicated for seromas. If this approach fails to eliminate the seroma, a drain may be reintroduced.

Wound Closure

MATERIALS

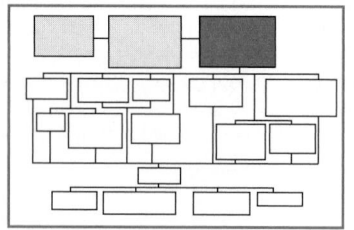

Once the appropriate preparatory measures have been taken (see above), the wound is ready to be closed. The first step is to choose the material to be used for wound closure. The materials currently available for this purpose include sutures, staples, tapes, and glues. Selection of the appropriate material is based on the type and location of the wound, the potential for infection, the patient's ability to tolerate closure, and the degree of mechanical stress imposed by closure. The selected material must provide wound edge approximation until the tensile strength of the wound has increased to the point where it can withstand the stress present.

The majority of wounds are closed with sutures. A suture is a foreign body by definition, and as such, it may generate an inflammatory response, interfere with wound healing, and increase the risk of infection. Accordingly, the number and diameter of sutures used to close a wound should be kept to the minimum necessary for coaptation of the edges.

Sutures are categorized on the basis of material used, tensile strength, configuration, absorbability, and time to degradation [see Table 2]. Suture material may be either natural or synthetic; natural fibers (e.g., catgut and silk) cause more intense inflammatory reactions than synthetic materials (e.g., polypropylene) do.[20] The tensile strength of suture material is defined as the amount of weight required to break a suture divided by the suture's cross-sectional area. It is typically expressed in an integer-hyphen-zero form, whereby larger integers correspond to smaller suture diameters (e.g., 3-0 sutures have a greater diameter and more tensile strength than 5-0 sutures do).[21] Closure of acute wounds rarely requires sutures larger than 4-0. In terms of configuration, suture material may be composed either of a single filament or of multiple filaments. Multifilament suture material may be twisted or braided, and the interstices created by braiding may harbor organisms and

increase the risk of infection. Monofilament sutures hold knots less well than multifilament sutures, requiring five knots for security; multifilament sutures are easier to handle and require only three knots. With all sutures, the knots must be square to be secure and must be only tight enough to coapt the wound edges. To minimize foreign body bulk, buried suture knot ends should be cut right on the knot. In terms of absorbability, either absorbable or nonabsorbable sutures may be appropriate, depending on the situation. Absorbable sutures are generally used for buried sutures to approximate deep tissues (e.g., dermis, muscle, or fascia). Absorption of synthetic suture material occurs by hydrolysis and causes less tissue reaction than absorption of natural suture material, which occurs by proteolysis. Nonabsorbable sutures (e.g., those made of silk, nylon, polyester, or polybutester) are most commonly used for wounds in the skin, from where they will eventually be removed, or for wounds in deeper structures that require prolonged support (e.g., abdominal wall fascia, tendons, nerves, and blood vessels).

Staple closure is less expensive and significantly faster than suture closure, and it offers a slightly, though not significantly, better cosmetic outcome when used to close scalp wounds.[22,23] Contaminated wounds closed with staples have a lower incidence of infection than those closed with sutures.[24] In addition, staple closure eliminates the risk that a health care provider will experience a needle stick, which is a particularly important consideration in caring for a trauma patient with an unknown medical history.

The tapes used for wound closure either are rubber-based or employ an acrylate adhesive. Rubber-based tapes (e.g., athletic tape) are a potential irritant to skin, degrade with exposure to heat, light, and air, and are occlusive, thereby preventing transepidermal water loss. Tapes that include acrylate adhesives (e.g., Micropore and Steri-Strip), however, are hypoallergenic, have a long shelf life, and are porous, thereby allowing water to evaporate.[25] Linear wounds in areas with little tension are easily approximated with tape alone, whereas wounds in areas where the skin is more taut (e.g., the extremities) generally require that tape skin closure be supplemented by dermal sutures. The use of tape alone is desirable when feasible, in that it spares the patient the discomfort associated with suture removal, prevents suture puncture scars, and avoids the emotional upset that may attend suture closure of small facial wounds on children.[25] Tape closure has some significant advantages: it immobilizes wound edges, permits early suture removal, is easy to perform and comfortable for the patient, leaves no marks on the skin, and yields a lower infection rate in contaminated wounds than suture closure does.[26] It also has a few disadvantages: patients may inadvertently remove the tapes, and wound edge approximation is less precise with tapes alone than with sutures. In addition, tape will not adhere to mobile areas under tension (e.g., the plantar aspects of the feet) or to moist areas (e.g., mucous membranes and groin creases), and wound edema can lead to blistering at the tape margins and to inversion of taped wound edges.

The use of tissue adhesives (e.g., octylcyanoacrylate) is a fast, strong, and flexible method of approximating wound edges. Compared with sutures, staples, and tapes, adhesives provide a faster closure and are essentially equivalent in terms of cosmetic outcome, infection rate, and dehiscence rate.[27] Adhesives can be used on most parts of the body and have been employed to close wounds ranging from 0.5 to 50 cm in length. Their advantages include reduced cost, ease of application, and the absence of any need for needles or suture removal; their major disadvantage is lack of strength.[28] They must not be applied to tissues within wounds but, rather, should be applied to intact skin at wound edges, where they serve to hold injured surfaces together. In addi-

Table 2 Types and Characteristics of Suture Material Used for Wound Closure

Suture Type	Material	Comment	Configuration	Method of Absorption	Tensile Strength at 2 Wk	Time to Degradation
Absorbable	Plain catgut (bovine intestinal serosa)	Natural; high tissue reactivity	Monofilament	Proteolysis	0%	10–14 days
	Chromic catgut (bovine intestinal serosa treated with chromic acid)	Natural; stronger, less reactive, and longer-lasting than plain catgut	Monofilament	Proteolysis	0%	21 days
	Fast-absorbing catgut	Natural	Monofilament	Proteolysis	0%	7–10 days
	Polyglytone 6211 (Caprosyn)	Synthetic	Monofilament	Hydrolysis	10%	56 days
	Glycomer 631 (Biosyn)	Synthetic	Monofilament	Hydrolysis	75%	90–110 days
	Polyglycolic acid (Dexon)	Synthetic	Monofilament/ multifilament	Hydrolysis	20%	90–120 days
	Polyglactic acid (Vicryl)	Synthetic	Multifilament	Hydrolysis	20%	60–90 days
	Polyglyconate (Maxon)	Synthetic	Monofilament	Hydrolysis	81%	180–210 days
	Polyglycolide (Polysorb)	Synthetic	Multifilament	Hydrolysis	80%	56–70 days
	Polydioxanone (PDS)	Synthetic	Monofilament	Hydrolysis	74%	180 days
	Polyglecaprone 25 (Monocryl)	Synthetic	Monofilament	Hydrolysis	25%	90–120 days
	Polyglactin 910 (Vicryl RAPIDE)	Synthetic	Multifilament	Hydrolysis	0%	7–14 days
Nonabsorbable	Polybutester (Novafil)	Synthetic; low tissue reactivity; elastic; good knot security	Monofilament	—	High	—
	Nylon (Monosof, Dermalon, Ethilon)	Synthetic; low tissue reactivity; memory effect necessitates more knots	Monofilament	—	High	—
	Nylon (Nurolon)	Synthetic; low tissue reactivity	Multifilament	—	High	—
	Nylon (Surgilon)	Synthetic; silicon coated; low tissue reactivity	Multifilament	—	High	—
	Polypropylene (Prolene, Surgilene, Surgipro)	Synthetic; low tissue reactivity; slippery	Monofilament	—	High	—
	Polyethylene (Dermalene)	Synthetic	Monofilament	—	High	—
	Stainless steel	Lowest tissue reactivity of all sutures; poor handling; creates artifact on CT scan; moves with MRI	Monofilament/ multifilament	—	Highest	—
	Cotton	Natural	Multifilament	—	—	—
	Silk (Sofsilk)	Natural; high tissue reactivity; good knot security	Multifilament	—	Poor	—
	Polyester (Dacron, Mersilene, Surgidac)	Synthetic; uncoated; high friction; low tissue reactivity; poor knot security	Multifilament	—	High	—
	Polyester (Ticron)	Synthetic; silicon coated; low tissue reactivity; good knot security	Multifilament	—	High	—
	Polyester (Ethibond)	Synthetic; polybutylate coated; low tissue reactivity; good knot security	Multifilament	—	High	—
	Polyester (Ethiflex, Tevdek)	Synthetic; Teflon coated; low tissue reactivity; good knot security	Multifilament	—	High	—

tion, they should not be used for wounds in mucous membranes, contaminated wounds, deep wounds, or wounds under tension. Adhesives are particularly useful for superficial wounds or wounds in which the deep dermis has been closed with sutures.

TIMING AND METHODS

Appropriate materials having been selected, the next issue to address is the timing of wound closure. The choices are (1) to close the wound at the time of initial presentation, (2) to delay closure until after a period of healing or wound care, and (3) to allow the wound to heal on its own. The best choice in a given situation depends whether the patient is stable and able to undergo wound repair, whether hemorrhage is under control, whether necrotic material has been adequately debrided and foreign bodies removed, whether and to what degree bacterial contamination is present, and what the expected aesthetic outcome of immediate closure might be in comparison with that of delayed closure or secondary healing.

The timing of wound closure determines the method that will be employed. The closure methods available include (1) primary closure by direct approximation; (2) delayed primary closure, in which the wound is closed after a healing period; (3) secondary closure, in which the wound is allowed to heal on its own; (4) skin grafting; and (5) the use of local or distant flaps. The ideal wound closure method would support the wound until it has nearly reached full strength (i.e., about 6 weeks), would not induce inflammation, would not induce ischemia, would not penetrate the epidermis and predispose to additional scars, and would not interfere with the healing process. Unfortunately, no existing method accomplishes all of these goals in all cases; some sort of compromise is virtually always necessary. In the acute wound setting, the simplest method that will achieve a good closure is preferred.

Primary closure provides optimal wound healing when two perpendicular, well-vascularized wound edges are approximated without tension. Closure should proceed from deep to superficial. The initial step is to identify landmarks and line up tissues, using skin hooks or fine forceps to keep from causing wound edge trauma. Although wound closure is usually a straightforward process, situations occasionally arise in which special caution is necessary. For instance, when a wound crosses tissues with different characteristics (e.g., at the vermilion border of the lip, the eyebrow, or the hairline of the scalp), particular care must be taken to align the damaged structures accurately. In the repair of soft tissue, it is critical to handle tissue gently with atraumatic surgical technique, to place sutures precisely, and to minimize tension and contamination.

The next step is tissue-specific repair, which may require the consultation of an experienced surgeon. Bone fractures are reduced and repaired with plates, rods, or external fixation devices. Muscle lacerations should be repaired because muscle is capable of a significant degree of regeneration. A completely lacerated muscle that is properly repaired recovers approximately 50% of its ability to produce tension and 80% of its ability to shorten, whereas a partially lacerated muscle that is properly repaired recovers approximately 60% of its ability to produce tension and 100% of its ability to shorten.[29] Tendon lacerations should be meticulously approximated to allow gliding and restore tensile strength. Either 4-0 multifilament polyester or monofilament polypropylene is a reasonable choice for muscle and tendon repair.[30] Early active mobilization promotes the restoration of tensile strength in muscles and tendons. Penetrating nerve trauma is treated with tension-free coaptation at the time of wound closure by primary repair or repair with a nerve graft or nerve tube. Epineurial coaptation is typically achieved by placing 8-0 to 10-0 monofilament

nylon sutures under loupe or microscope magnification. For ischemic or amputated tissues (e.g., an ear, a digit, or a limb), vessel repair is performed with 8-0 to 10-0 monofilament nylon sutures under magnification.

In subcutaneous fat, suture placement should be avoided whenever possible; if sutures in this location are absolutely necessary, they should be placed at the fat-fascia junction or the fat-dermis junction, not in fat alone. Fat cannot hold sutures by itself, and because it has a poor blood supply, suturing may lead to fat necrosis. The deeper fascial layers that contribute to the structural integrity of areas such as the abdomen, the chest, and the galea should be closed as a separate layer to prevent hernias, structural deformities, and hematomas.

At the skin level, the deep dermis is responsible for the strength of the acute wound closure. Deep dermal repair is performed with 4-0 absorbable suture material (e.g., polyglactin 910) and a cutting needle. The sutures are buried and placed 5 to 8 mm apart, with care taken to evert the skin edges. Buried dermal sutures are often used in conjunction with tapes (e.g., Steri-Strips), fine epidermal sutures, or adhesives to facilitate precise alignment. Skin edges should be coapted and everted with 4-0 to 6-0 nylon or polypropylene sutures placed in the superficial dermis and the epidermis. The distance between the sutures and the distance between the wound edge and the suture insertion point should be equal to the thickness of the skin (epidermis and dermis combined).

Several different skin suturing methods may be used, depending on the nature of the wound. Simple interrupted sutures are useful for irregular wounds. Vertical mattress sutures are good for either thick (e.g., scalp) or thin (e.g., eyelid) skin. Horizontal mattress sutures can lead to ischemia and thus must be applied loosely; they may look untidy early after repair, but they generally achieve good wound-edge eversion and long-term healing. Half-buried horizontal and vertical mattress sutures are used for flap edges to minimize ischemia. A continuous intradermal or subcuticular suture is easy to remove and relatively inconspicuous visually. A simple continuous suture should be used only for linear wounds; it is quick to place but tends to invert the wound edges. Flap tips should be sutured with a three-point method to prevent strangulation [see Figure 1]. For children, suture removal can be both emotionally and physically traumatic; accordingly, when suturing is employed for skin closure in a pediatric patient, the use of fast-absorbing suture material (e.g., plain catgut) or a pullout continuous subcuticular suturing method should be considered.

Primary direct approximation of wounds is not always indicated. In cases where obvious bacterial contamination is present, there is a substantial amount of questionably necrotic tissue, or the patient is unstable and unfit to undergo primary repair at the time of presentation, delayed primary closure is performed. Delayed primary closure involves direct approximation of wound edges after a period (usually 4 to 5 days) of wound hygiene. This closure method markedly diminishes the incidence of wound infection in patients with contaminated wounds.

Secondary closure, in which the wound is left open and allowed to heal on its own, is also sometimes chosen. Secondary closure depends on contraction of the surrounding tissue and epithelialization from the wound margins. When this approach is followed, caution and close observation are essential because the process of tissue contraction can sometimes lead to contracture, a pathologic scar deformity. Secondary closure can, however, yield acceptable results with specific wound types and at specific anatomic sites. With puncture wounds, for example, secondary closure is preferred because it diminishes the likelihood of infection. For both abrasions and puncture wounds, the functional and aesthetic

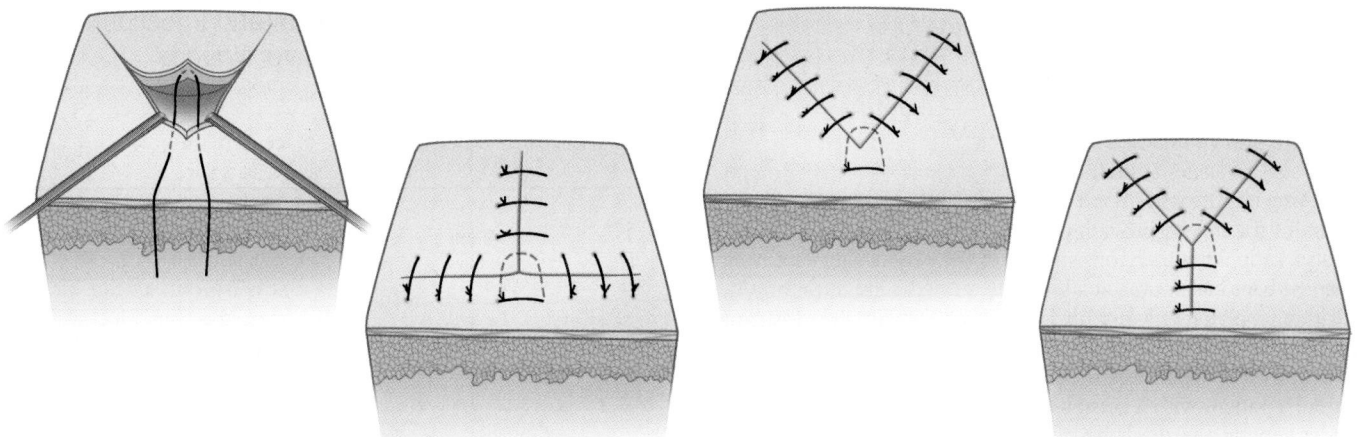

Figure 1 **Shown is the method for inserting three-point sutures, along with three different applications of this method.**

results of secondary closure are generally as good as or better than those obtained by primary or delayed primary closure. For wounds on anatomically concave surfaces (e.g., the medial canthal region, the nasolabial region, or the perineum), secondary wound healing generally yields excellent results.[31] Secondary closure should also be considered for severely contaminated wounds, infected wounds, wounds with significant amounts of devitalized tissue, wounds with foreign bodies, lacerations older than 24 hours, wounds in patients who are in shock, and high-velocity wounds.[32]

Occasionally, an acute wound is so large that neither primary nor secondary closure will suffice. Such wounds must be covered with skin grafts or transferred tissue (i.e., flaps) [*see 23 Open Wound Requiring Reconstruction and 27 Surface Reconstruction Procedures*]. Local or distant flaps must be considered for wounds that involve exposed bone denuded of periosteum, cartilage denuded of perichondrium, tendon denuded of paratenon, or nerve denuded of perineurium.

CLOSURE OF SPECIFIC TYPES OF WOUNDS

Wounds may be divided into 10 main types: abrasions, puncture wounds, lacerations, complex wounds, crush injuries, extravasation injuries, injection injuries, high-velocity wounds, bite wounds, and stings. In addition, the American College of Surgeons (ACS) has divided wounds into four major categories: clean, clean-contaminated, contaminated, and dirty [*see Table 3*]. The likelihood of infection after any surgical procedure is correlated with the ACS wound category: class I and II wounds have infection rates lower than 11%, whereas wounds in class IV have infection rates as high as 40%.[33]

Abrasions

Abrasions are superficial wounds caused by scraping. They involve only the epidermis and a portion of the dermis and frequently heal secondarily within 1 to 2 weeks. If an abrasion is to be closed primarily, tape or glue may be used for epidermal approximation to prevent suture mark scars (which could be worse than the actual wound scar). In some patients who have experienced abrasion injuries (e.g., motorcycle accidents in which victims slide along asphalt) or blast injuries (e.g., firework explosions), small foreign body fragments become embedded in and beneath the skin, often

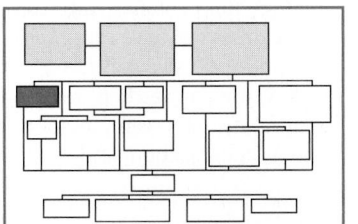

proving quite difficult to remove. Complete debridement of these embedded foreign bodies within 24 to 48 hours of injury is crucial in preventing so-called traumatic tattooing. In the early postinjury period, surgical debridement with a small drill, a sharp instrument, or a scrub brush may suffice for removal of the foreign material causing the traumatic tattoo; later, dermabrasion will be necessary.[34,35] Once the wound is adequately debrided, semiocclusive dressings should be applied to optimize epithelialization.

Puncture Wounds

Puncture wounds should be examined for foreign bodies, which must be removed when found. They are typically left open, treated with wound care, and allowed to heal by secondary intention. With

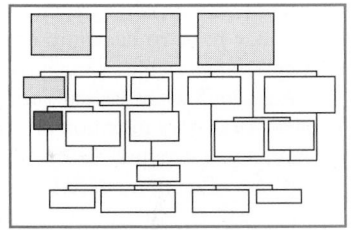

puncture wounds, secondary closure reduces the risk of infection and generally yields excellent aesthetic results.

Lacerations

The type of wound most commonly encountered by surgeons is a superficial or deep acute traumatic or surgical wound that is suitable for primary closure by direct approximation of the wound

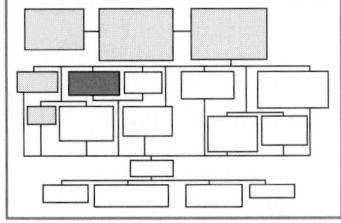

edges. In this setting, the goal is to provide the best possible chance for uncomplicated healing. If the wound is to be closed, primary closure at the time of evaluation is preferred if it is feasible. As a rule, closure should be completed within 6 to 8 hours of the injury, though simple noncontaminated wounds of the face can be safely closed as long as 24 hours after the injury. Primary closure is generally desirable in that it eliminates the need for extensive wound care, allows the wound to heal more quickly, and minimizes patient discomfort. However, lacerations containing foreign bodies or necrotic tissue that cannot be removed by irrigation or debridement and lacerations with excessive bacterial contamination should not be closed primarily, nor should wounds in which hemostasis is incomplete. Hematomas,[36] necrotic tissue,[37] and foreign bodies[38] all promote bacterial growth and place a mechanical barrier between healing tissues.

Complex Wounds

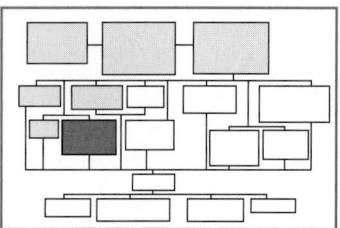

The term complex wounds includes stellate wounds and those caused by degloving, avulsion, and mutilation. The goals of treatment include achieving closure within 6 to 8 hours of the injury, providing treatment in a manner consistent with the patient's general health, keeping bacterial counts at a low level, protecting tissues from desiccation, applying only nonnoxious agents, and supplying adequate permanent coverage. In addition, it is important to discuss with the patient the particular treatment difficulties posed by these wounds. Often, a patient with a complex wound must be treated in the OR under general anesthesia because the injury is extensive or because there is a need for exploration of tissues, removal of foreign bodies, and debridement of nonviable tissue.

Stellate wounds can be approximated with careful placement of interrupted and three-point sutures. Severely injured tissue may have to be removed as an ellipse, with the resulting defect closed.

Degloving refers to circumferential elevation of skin and fat from muscle; the skin flap created by this process rarely survives. In the acute setting, questionably viable flaps of tissue may be evaluated by administering fluorescein, up to 15 mg/kg I.V., and observing the flap for fluorescence under an ultraviolet lamp after 10 to 15 minutes have elapsed.[39] Viable flap tissue fluoresces green. Tissue that is determined to be devascularized, on the basis of either physical examination or fluorescein testing, should be debrided. If the viability of a tissue segment is in doubt, the segment may be sewn back into its anatomic location and allowed to define itself as viable or nonviable over time.

Large open wounds resulting from avulsion can be either left to heal by secondary intention or treated with delayed skin grafting.[32]

Mutilating wounds caused by machinery (e.g., farm equipment) are often contaminated by a mixture of gram-positive and gram-negative organisms, though not always excessively so.[40] When such a wound is grossly contaminated, antibiotic therapy (preferably with an agent or combination of agents that offers broad-spectrum coverage) is indicated. Contaminated wounds closed with either tape or staples have a lower incidence of infection than those closed with sutures.[24,26]

Crush Injuries

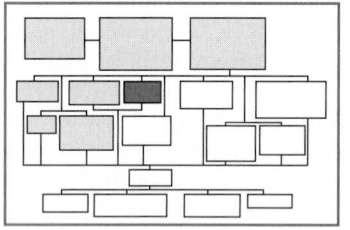

A notable feature of crush injury is that the severity of the wound is not always readily apparent. In many cases, no external laceration can be seen, even though deep tissue damage may be extensive. Ultrasonography or magnetic resonance imaging may help identify a hematoma that is amenable to evacuation.[32] Deep tissue injury can lead to compartment syndrome and subsequent extremity loss. Early diagnosis is the key to successful treatment. Generally, the diagnosis can be made on the basis of physical signs and symptoms, including increasing pain that is out of proportion to the stimulus, altered sensation, pain on passive stretching of the affected muscle compartment, muscle weakness, and palpable tenseness of the compartment.[41]

If compartment syndrome is suspected, the intracompartmental pressure should be measured.[42] If the intracompartmental pressure exceeds 30 mm Hg or if the so-called delta pressure (i.e., the diastolic blood pressure minus the intracompartmental pres-

Table 3 Classification and Infection Rates of Operative Wounds

Classification	Infection Rate (%)	Wound Characteristics
Clean (class I)	1.5–5.1	Atraumatic, uninfected; no entry of GU, GI, or respiratory tract
Clean-contaminated (class II)	7.7–10.8	Minor breaks in sterile technique; entry of GU, GI, or respiratory tract without significant spillage
Contaminated (class III)	15.2–16.3	Traumatic wounds; gross spillage from GI tract; entry into infected tissue, bone, urine, or bile
Dirty (class IV)	28.0–40.0	Drainage of abscess; debridement of soft tissue infection

sure) is less than or equal to 30 mm Hg, compartment syndrome is considered to be present. If clinical symptoms develop or the delta pressure is below 30 mm Hg, appropriate therapeutic measures should be taken, including restoration of normal blood pressure in the hypotensive patient, removal of all constrictive dressings, and maintenance of the limb at heart level.[1] If the delta pressure remains below 30 mm Hg, clinical symptoms and signs persist despite conservative measures, or both, fasciotomies should be performed within 6 hours.[41] Hyperbaric oxygen therapy may also be beneficial in cases of crush injury with compartment syndrome in an extremity.[43] Compartment syndrome with muscle damage can also lead to rhabdomyolysis and renal failure. If an elevated serum creatine kinase concentration is reported, intravascular volume is stabilized, and urine flow is confirmed, a forced mannitol-alkaline diuresis should be initiated as prophylaxis against hyperkalemia and acute renal failure.[44]

Extravasation Injuries

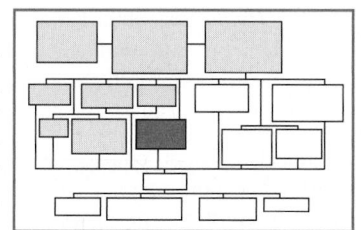

In some patients with arterial or venous catheters in place, a vessel may become occluded or a catheter dislodged from the intravascular space, leading to extravasation injury, whereby solutions or medicines are delivered into the interstitial space. The majority of acute extravasation injuries are quickly diagnosed and heal without complications, and in most cases, conservative management (i.e., elevation of the limb, application of ice packs, and careful monitoring) is adequate.[45] However, extravasation injuries involving high fluid volumes, high-osmolar contrast agents, or chemotherapeutic drugs can have more serious effects, resulting in skin ulceration and extensive soft tissue necrosis. Treatment of these injuries is not standardized; it may include conservative management, hydrocortisone cream, incision and drainage, hyaluronidase injection, saline injection, and aspiration by means of liposuction.[45-47]

Injection Injuries

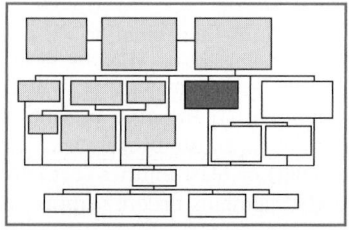

Wounds caused by injection of foreign materials (e.g., paint, oil, grease, or dirty water) can be severe. Injection injuries usually result from the use of high-pressure spray guns (600 to

12,000 psi) and often occur on the nondominant hand.[48,49] On initial examination, the injury may appear deceptively benign, with only a punctate entry wound visible; however, foreign material is often widely distributed in the deeper soft tissues. Radiographs are obtained to identify any fractures present and, in some cases, to determine the extent to which the injected material is distributed. Injection wounds must be treated aggressively with incision, wide exposure, debridement, and removal of foreign bodies to prevent extensive tissue loss and functional impairment. The functional outcome is determined by the time elapsed between injury and treatment and by the type of material injected. Oil-based paint is more damaging to tissues than water-based paint, oil, grease, water, or air.[50,51]

High-Velocity Wounds

High-velocity wounds from explosions or gunshots cause extensive tissue damage as a consequence of the release of kinetic energy. Small entry wounds are common, but the

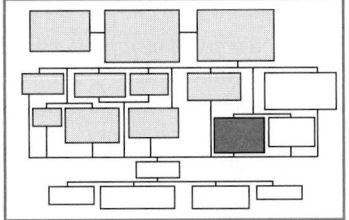

seemingly benign appearance of such a wound often belies the actual severity of injury: the exit wound and interspace may contain large areas of ischemic and damaged tissue that affect critical structures (e.g., bone and blood vessels). Clothing and dirt may also be transmitted into the deep spaces. Radiographs may identify radiopaque foreign bodies (e.g., metal objects or pieces of leaded glass).[52] Treatment of wounds created by high-velocity missiles involves extensive debridement and identification of injured tissue. Wounds should be left open to heal by secondary or delayed primary closure.[32]

Bite Wounds

Treatment of bite wounds involves thorough exploration, irrigation, and debridement. X-rays must be obtained and wounds explored to evaluate the patient for fractures or open

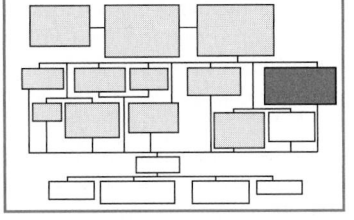

joint injuries. If a joint capsule has been violated, the joint must be thoroughly cleaned. Because of the infection risk, wounds may be allowed to heal by secondary or delayed primary closure; primary closure is also possible if thorough debridement is performed.[32] Rabies prophylaxis treatment should be considered for patients who have been bitten by wild animals [see Adjunctive Wound Treatment, Rabies Prophylaxis, below].

Humans and nonvenomous animals   Most human bite wounds are clenched fist wounds sustained by young men.[53] Human bite wounds are considered infected from the moment of infliction and must be treated with antibiotics.[54,55] The antibiotic regimen should be selected on the basis of the bacterial species believed to be present. Common isolates from bite wounds includes *Streptococcus anginosus, Staphylococcus aureus, Eikenella corrodens, Fusobacterium nucleatum, Prevotella melaninogenica,* and *Candida* species.[53] To cover these species, a broad-spectrum antibiotic or combination of antibiotics (e.g., amoxicillin-clavulanate or moxifloxacin) should be administered.[53]

Nonhuman primates can cause viral infection, most commonly with cercopithecine herpesvirus type 1. If left untreated, such infection can lead to meningoencephalitis, which carries a 70% mortality. Accordingly, acyclovir prophylaxis is recommended.[56]

Wounds caused by cat bites or scratches are at high (80%) risk

for infection, usually attributable to *Pasteurella multocida*. The aerobic and anaerobic organisms commonly found in cat-bite wounds are similar to those found in dog-bite wounds, and antibiotic prophylaxis with amoxicillin-clavulanate is appropriate.[57] Acute regional lymphadenitis after a cat scratch is known as cat-scratch disease and is caused by *Bartonella henselae*[58]; it is treated by administering azithromycin.[59]

Dog-bite wounds are at lower (16%) risk for infection than human-bite or cat-bite wounds and tend to be less severely contaminated with bacteria. The aerobic species commonly isolated from such wounds include *Pasteurella (P. canis), Streptococcus, Staphylococcus, Moraxella,* and *Neisseria;* common anaerobic isolates include *Fusobacterium, Bacteroides, Porphyromonas,* and *Prevotella*.[57] Prophylactic treatment with a combination of a β-lactam antibiotic with a β-lactamase inhibitor (e.g., amoxicillin-clavulanate) is appropriate.[57,60]

Venomous animals   *Snake bites.* Four types of poisonous snakes are native to the United States: the coral snakes (*Micrurus* and *Micruroides* species), from the family Elapidae, and three species of pit vipers, from the family Viperidae (rattlesnakes [*Crotalus* species], copperheads [*Agkistrodon tortortrix*], and cottonmouths or water moccasins [*Agkistrodon piscivorus*]).[61-63] Pit vipers can be identified by the pit between the eye and the nostril on each side of the head, the vertical elliptical pupils, the triangle-shaped head, the single row of subcaudal plates distal to the anal plate, and the two hollow fangs protruding from the maxillae that produce the characteristic fang marks.[64] Coral snakes have rounder heads and eyes and lack fangs; they are identified by their characteristic color pattern, consisting of red, yellow, and black vertical bands.

Patients bitten by any of the pit vipers must be examined for massive swelling and pain, which, in conjunction with fang marks, suggest envenomation. Local pain and swelling typically develops within 30 minutes of the bite, though in some cases, these manifestations may take up to 4 hours to appear. Erythema, petechiae, bullae, and vesicles are sometimes seen. Severe envenomation may induce systemic reactions, including disseminated intravascular coagulation (DIC), bleeding, hypotension, shock, acute respiratory distress syndrome (ARDS), and renal failure. Patients bitten by coral snakes, on the other hand, show no obvious local signs when envenomation has occurred. Consequently, the physician must look for systemic signs, such as paresthesias, increased salivation, fasciculations of the tongue, dysphagia, difficulty in speaking, visual disturbances, respiratory distress, convulsions, and shock. These symptoms may not develop until several hours after the bite.

If signs or symptoms suggestive of envenomation are found, appropriate laboratory tests (hematocrit, fibrinogen level, coagulation studies, platelet count, urinalysis, and serum chemistries) should be ordered. Laboratory tests should be repeated every 8 to 24 hours for the first 1 to 3 days to determine whether envenomation is progressing. Severe envenomation can cause decreased fibrinogen levels, coagulopathy, bleeding, and myoglobinuria.

Treatment of venomous snake bites includes immobilization and elevation. If envenomation is suspected or confirmed, antivenin should be administered intravenously and as early as possible. Antivenins commonly used in the United States include Antivenin (Crotalidae) Polyvalent (ACP) (Wyeth Pharmaceuticals, Collegeville, Pennsylvania) and Crotalidae Polyvalent Immune Fab (Ovine) (CroFab; Protherics Inc., Nashville, Tennessee).[65] Fab antivenom (FabAV) is less allergenic and more potent than ACP and thus has largely supplanted it in the United States.[65,66] Patients are treated with a loading dose of four to six vials of FabAV, followed by three two-vial maintenance doses at 6, 12, and

18 hours to prevent recurrence of symptoms. If symptoms progress despite antivenin treatment, an additional four to six vials of FabAV are given twice more; if symptoms continue to progress, consideration should be given to using ACP. ACP remains the most effective antivenin for patients with coral snake bites and those who do not respond to FabAV. Before ACP is administered, the patient must be tested for sensitivity. The major complication of antivenin therapy is serum sickness. This complication occurs in approximately 50% to 75% of patients treated with ACP but in only 16% of those treated with FabAV.[65,67]

Compartment syndrome is a rare but severe complication of a snake bite. Fasciotomy is sometimes required to relieve extremity compartment syndrome, but it is not necessary for prophylactic purposes. Tourniquets, incision and suction, cryotherapy, and electric shock treatment are of little value for snake bites and may increase complication rates. There is no clear evidence to support antibiotic prophylaxis in this setting.[64]

Spider bites. The bites of most spiders found in the United States cause little to no wound or local reaction; however, there are three types that are capable of injecting venom with skin-penetrating bites. Brown recluse spiders (*Loxosceles reclusa*) can be identified by a violin-shaped dorsal mark. They are nocturnal, live in dark and dry places, and are found in the central and southern United States. The venom is a phospholipase enzyme that acts as a dermal toxin and almost always causes a local reaction.[68] Local signs and symptoms may be limited to minor irritation, though they may also progress to extreme tenderness, erythema, and edema. The onset of local signs and symptoms may be delayed for as long as 8 hours after a bite, and tissue necrosis may then develop over the following days to weeks. Systemic reactions may include mild hemolysis, mild coagulopathy, and DIC, though severe intravascular hemolytic syndrome and death have also been reported.[68,69] Oral administration of dapsone (50 to 100 mg/day) to minimize tissue necrosis has been advocated by some[70]; however, this treatment is of uncertain efficacy, and no prospective data currently support its use. Moreover, dapsone can cause a serious unwanted side effect, hemolytic anemia.[69] If systemic symptoms develop, systemic corticosteroid therapy and supportive measures are indicated. Brown recluse antivenin is not available in the United States.

Black widow spiders (*Latrodectus mactans*) can be identified by a red-hourglass ventral mark.[63] They live in dark, dry, and protected areas and are distributed widely throughout the continental United States. The venom is a neurotoxin that produces immediate and severe local pain. Local signs and symptoms include two fang marks, erythema, swelling, and piloerection.[68] Systemic reactions with neurologic signs may develop within 10 minutes and may include muscle pain and cramps starting in the vicinity of the bite, abdominal pain, vomiting, tremors, increased salivation, paresthesias, hyperreflexia, and, with severe envenomation, shock. Systemic symptoms may last for days to weeks. High-risk persons (e.g., those who are younger than 16 years, the elderly, pregnant women, hypertensive patients, or persons who continue to show symptoms despite treatment) may experience paralysis, hemolysis, renal failure, or coma. Treatment includes 10% calcium gluconate I.V. for relief of muscle spasm, methocarbamol or diazepam for muscle relaxation, and a single dose of antivenin. Antivenin causes serum sickness in as many as 9% of patients; consequently, its use is controversial except in cases where the patient is at high risk.[71]

Hobo spiders (*Tegenaria agrestis*) can be identified by their long hairy legs and a cephalothorax that is marked by two stripes and butterfly markings dorsally and two stripes ventrally. Found throughout the northwestern United States, they live in low places and build funnel-shaped webs in dark spaces. Hobo spiders have been reported to inflict painful bites that lead to wound ulceration, dermonecrosis, and a persistent headache, though the accuracy of such reports has been debated.[69,72,73] A slow-healing ulcer that leaves a central crater has been described. Treatment consists of local wound care.

Stings

Scorpions Stings from most of scorpion species found in the United States cause only limited local reactions that can be managed conservatively; however, stings from *Centruroides sculpturatus*, which is 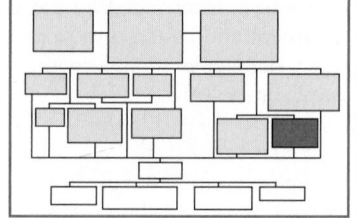 found in California and many southern states, may be more severe. *Centruroides* has a sting that causes envenomation with a neurotoxin. Erythema, edema, and ecchymosis at the site of the sting are evidence that envenomation did not take place. Instead, envenomation is indicated by an immediate and intense burning pain at the wound site.[74] The initial local pain may then be followed by systemic symptoms such as muscle spasm, excess salivation, fever, tachycardia, slurred speech, blurry vision, convulsions, or death.[68] Treatment consists of icing and elevation of the wounded area, followed by administration of barbiturates for control of neuromuscular activity and institution of supportive therapy with antihistamines, corticosteroids, and analgesics.[74]

Centipedes Centipedes are slender, multisegmented, and multilegged arthropods that range in size from 1 to 30 cm and in color from bright yellow to brownish black. The first pair of legs are modified into sharp stinging structures that are connected to venom glands. Centipedes prefer dark, damp environments and may be found throughout the southern United States. Local symptoms associated with centipede stings include pain, erythema, edema, lymphangitis, lymphadenitis, weakness, and paresthesia. Skin necrosis may occur at the envenomation site. Systemic symptoms may include anxiety, fever, dizziness, palpitations, and nausea.[75] Treatment consists of symptomatic pain control, infiltration of local anesthetics, administration of antihistamines, and local wound care.[75]

Hymenoptera The order Hymenoptera includes wasps, bees, and ants. Wasps, which are found across the United States, live in small colonies and may attack in groups when provoked. Honeybees (*Apis mellifera*) and bumblebees (*Bombus* species), also found across the United States, are generally docile and rarely sting unless provoked. Africanized honeybees (*Apis mellifera scutellata*, also referred to as killer bees), found primarily in the southwestern states, are far more aggressive than other bees. Fire ants (*Solenopsis invicta* and *Solenopsis richteri*) are wingless, ground-dwelling arthropods that are found in many southern states and that attack in an aggressive swarm.

Although Hymenoptera stingers are small, they can evoke severe local and systemic reactions. The local response to a Hymenoptera sting is a painful, erythematous, and edematous papule that develops within seconds and typically subsides in 4 to 6 hours. Some stingers are barbed and must be removed with a scraping, rather than pinching, motion to prevent the injection of more venom. Systemic reactions occur in about 5% of the population and may lead to anaphylaxis with syncope, bronchospasm, hypotension, and arrhythmias. Wounds and local reactions are treated with ice, elevation, and analgesics. Systemic reactions are treated with subcutaneous epinephrine, diphenhydramine, and supportive airway and blood pressure care.[68] Persons with a history of systemic reactions to insect stings should carry epinephrine kits.

DRESSINGS FOR SPECIFIC TYPES OF WOUNDS

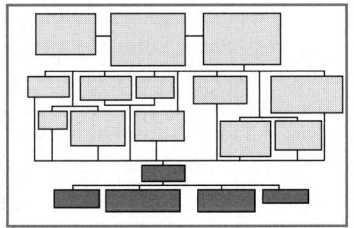

Generally, the functions of a wound dressing include protection, antisepsis, pressure, immobilization, debridement, provision of a physiologic environment, absorption, packing, support, information, comfort, and aesthetic appearance. More specifically, the functions of a dressing should be tailored to the wound type, and the purpose of the dressing must be carefully considered before application.

Abrasions

Abrasions heal by epithelialization, which is accelerated by the warm, moist environment created by an occlusive dressing.[76,77] Such an environment not only promotes epithelialization but also enhances healing, both because of the moisture itself and because of the low oxygen tension that promotes the inflammatory phase.[78] A variety of dressings are suitable for treatment of abrasions, including biologic dressings, hydrogels, hydrocolloids, and semipermeable films. These dressings need not be changed as long as they remain adherent. Small, superficial wounds also heal readily when dressed with impregnated gauze dressings (e.g., Xeroform and Scarlet Red [Kendall, Mansfield, Massachusetts]), which allow exudates to pass through while maintaining a moist wound bed.[78] These less adherent dressings must be changed more regularly.[79]

Dry dressings (e.g., gauze) should be avoided with abrasions because they facilitate scab formation. Scabs slow epithelialization, in that advancing cells must enzymatically debride the scab-wound interface in order to migrate.[80] Wounds covered with a scab also tend to cause more discomfort than wounds covered with occlusive dressings.

Lacerations

For sutured deep wounds, the specific purposes of a dressing are to prevent bacterial contamination, to protect the wound, to manage drainage, and to facilitate epithelialization. Dressings used on such wounds usually consist of three basic layers. The inner (contact) layer is chosen to minimize adherence of the dressing to the wound and to facilitate drainage through itself to the overlying layers. Common choices for this layer include fine-mesh gauze, petrolatum gauze, Xeroform or Xeroflo (Kendall, Mansfield, Massachusetts) gauze, and Adaptic (Johnson & Johnson, New Brunswick, New Jersey). These substances should be applied only as a single layer; in multiple layers, they become occlusive. The middle layer is chosen for absorbency and ability to conform to shape of the wound area. It is usually composed of fluffs, Kerlix (Kendall, Mansfield, Massachusetts), or wide-mesh gauze, all of which facilitate capillary action and drainage.[81] The middle layer must not be allowed to become soaked, because if it is, exudate will collect on the wound surface, and maceration and bacterial contamination may occur. The outer (binding) layer serves to secure the dressing. Common choices for this layer include Kling (Johnson & Johnson, New Brunswick, New Jersey), ACE bandages (BD Medical, Franklin Lakes, New Jersey), and Coban (3M, St. Paul, Minnesota).

With sutured wounds, dressings are required only until drainage from the wound ceases. With nondraining wounds, dressings may be removed after 48 hours, by which time epithelial cells will have sealed the superficial layers of the wound. An alternative method of treating minimally draining incisional wounds is to apply an antibacterial ointment [see Adjunctive Wound Treatment, Topical Antimicrobials, below]. Such ointments are occlusive and maintain a sterile, moist environment for the 48 hours required for epithelialization. In anatomic areas that are difficult to dress (e.g., the scalp), it may be reasonable to forgo a dressing and simply apply ointments or allow a scab to form on the wound surface. Operative incisional wounds are also sometimes covered with an occlusive dressing to optimize epithelialization [see Abrasions, above]. Some of these dressings are transparent, allowing observation of the wound. The disadvantage of occlusive dressings is their limited absorptive capacity, which allows drainage from the wound to collect underneath.

Complex Wounds

For complex wounds containing questionably necrotic tissue, foreign bodies, or other debris that cannot be removed sharply, wet-to-dry dressings are effective, simple, and inexpensive. A single layer of coarse wet gauze is applied to a wound, allowed to dry over a period of 6 hours, and removed. Necrotic tissue, granulation tissue, debris, and wound exudate become incorporated within the gauze and are removed with the dressing. The disadvantages of wet-to-dry dressings are pain and damage to or removal of some viable tissue. If the wound bed contains tendons, arteries, nerves, or bone, wet-to-wet dressings should be used to prevent desiccation of these critical structures.

Wet-to-wet dressings, which are not allowed to dry, cause less tissue damage than wet-to-dry dressings but do not produce as much debridement. Most wet-to-wet dressings are kept moist with saline. Wounds with significant bacterial contamination may be treated with dressings that contain antibacterial agents (e.g., mafenide, silver sufadiazine, silver nitrate, or iodine).

Biologic and semipermeable films also maintain a moist wound bed, but they are difficult to use on deep or irregular wounds and wounds with a great deal of drainage. Consequently, wet-to-wet dressings with agents such as silver sulfadiazine are often used for these types of wounds. Enzymatic agents can debride wounds effectively and are a reasonable alternative to wet-to-dry or wet-to-wet dressings for wounds that contain necrotic tissue.[82]

Table 4 Recommendations for Tetanus Immunization[89,90]

Tetanus Immunization History	Tt*	TIG
Unknown	Yes	Yes
> 10 yr since last booster	Yes	Yes
5 and 10 yr since last booster	Yes	No
< 5 yr since last booster	No	No

Note: Tetanus toxoid (Tt) and tetanus immune globulin (TIG) should be administered with separate syringes at different anatomic sites. Tetanus and diphtheria toxoids are contraindicated for the wounded patient if there is a history of a neurologic or severe hypersensitivity reaction after a previous dose. Local side effects alone do not preclude continued use. If a systemic reaction is suspected of representing allergic hypersensitivity, immunization should be postponed until appropriate skin testing is performed. If a contraindication to a Tt-containing preparation exists, TIG alone should be used.
*For patients younger than 7 years, diphtheria-tetanus-pertussis vaccine (DTP) (or tetanus and diphtheria toxoids, if pertussis vaccine is contraindicated) is preferable to Tt alone. For patients 7 years of age or older, Tt alone may be given.

Some wounds are difficult to dress and require special consideration. For wounds with flaps or questionably viable tissue, compression dressings should not be used, because they may cause ischemia. Wounds that cross joints are best dressed with plaster splints for temporary immobilization; semipermeable films are flexible and may also be used in this setting. Wounds with high levels of exudates may be dressed with hydrocolloids, hydrogels, or alginates.[78] For large or irregular wounds, negative-pressure wound therapy (NPWT) with the VAC system (Kinetic Concepts Inc., San Antonio, Texas) is recommended; VAC dressings conform well and remain adherent. Additionally, NPWT uses subatmospheric pressure to remove excess wound fluid, stimulates the formation of granulation tissue, improves peripheral blood flow and tissue oxygenation, and reduces the size of the wound.[83,84] Use of the VAC system is contraindicated in wounds with exposed blood vessels or bowel.

Adjunctive Wound Treatment

PROPHYLACTIC SYSTEMIC ANTIBIOTICS

For most wounds, antibiotic prophylaxis is not indicated. When it is called for, the agent or agents to be used should be selected on the basis of the bacterial species believed to be present. The anatomic location of a wound may also suggest whether oral flora, fecal flora, or some less aggressive bacterial contaminant is likely to be present. Gram staining can provide an early clue to the nature of the contamination. Ultimately, the choice of a prophylactic antibiotic regimen is based on the clinician's best judgment regarding which agent or combination of agents will cover the pathogens likely to be present in the wound on the basis of the information available.

As a rule, clean and clean-contaminated wounds are adequately treated with irrigation and debridement. There are, however, some local factors (e.g., impaired circulation and radiation injury) and systemic factors (e.g., diabetes, AIDS, uremia, and cancer) that increase the risk of wound infection; in the presence of any of these factors, prophylactic antibiotics should be considered. In addition, prophylactic antibiotics should be given to patients with extensive injuries to the central area of the face (to prevent spread of infection through the venous system to the meninges), patients with valvular disease (to prevent endocarditis), and patients with prostheses (to reduce the risk of bacterial seeding of the prosthesis). Lymphedematous extremities are especially prone to cellulitis, and antibiotics are indicated whenever such extremities are wounded.

Contaminated and dirty wounds are associated with a higher risk of infection and are therefore more likely to necessitate antibiotic prophylaxis. Human bite wounds, mammalian bite wounds, and wounds contaminated with dirt, bodily fluids, or feces are all prone to infection and must be treated with antibiotics.[54,55] Prophylactic administration of a combination of a β-lactam antibiotic with a β-lactamase inhibitor (e.g., amoxicillin-clavulanate) is appropriate.[57,60] Antibiotic prophylaxis is also indicated for mutilating wounds with extensive amounts of devitalized tissue. Such wounds are often contaminated by a mixture of gram-positive organisms and gram-negative organisms.[40] When antibiotics are indicated for these injuries, broad-spectrum coverage is appropriate.

TOPICAL ANTIMICROBIALS

Topical antimicrobials (e.g., antibiotic ointments, iodine preparations, and silver agents) are commonly used to prevent wound infection. Application of mupirocin ointment to a clean surgical wound before an occlusive dressing does not reduce the infection rate and may promote antibiotic resistance.[85] For uncomplicated traumatic wounds, however, application of bacitracin and neomycin ointment results in a significantly lower infection rate than application of petrolatum.[86] Neomycin-containing ointments reduce bacterial counts in partial-thickness wounds in animals, but many other over-the-counter antibiotic ointments are not effective at reducing bacterial counts in wounds.[87]

Wounds contaminated by bacteria can be treated with dressings that contain antibacterial agents such as mafenide, silver nitrate, silver sulfadiazine, or iodine. Mafenide penetrates eschar well, but it can cause pain and has the potential to induce metabolic acidosis through inhibition of carbonic anhydrase. Silver has microbicidal effects on common wound contaminants and may also be affective against methicillin-resistant S. aureus (MRSA).[84] Silver nitrate does not cause pain, but it can cause hypochloremia, and it stains fingernails and toenails black. Silver sulfadiazine is frequently used because of its broad antibacterial spectrum, its relatively low side effect profile (transient leukopenia is occasionally seen), and its ability to maintain a moist wound environment (thereby speeding healing and epithelialization).[88]

TETANUS PROPHYLAXIS

Tetanus is a nervous system disorder that is caused by Clostridium tetani and is chacracterized by muscle spasm. In the past, wounds were classified as either tetanus-prone or non–tetanus-prone on the basis of their severity. It is now clear, however, that wound severity is not directly correlated with tetanus susceptibility; tetanus has been associated with a wide variety of injury types over a broad spectrum of wound severity.[89] Accordingly, all wounds, regardless of cause or severity, must be considered tetanus prone, and the patient's tetanus immunization status must always be considered. Tetanus wound prophylaxis should be provided as appropriate [see Table 4].[89,90]

RABIES PROPHYLAXIS

Rabies is an acute progressive encephalitis that is caused by viruses from the family Rhabdoviridae. The rabies virus can be transmitted by any mammal, but viral reservoirs are found only in carnivores and bats. In North America, raccoons, skunks, bats, and foxes are the animals most commonly responsible for transmission.[91] Bite wounds in which the animal's saliva penetrates the dermis are the most common cause of exposure.

Postexposure treatment consists of wound care, infiltration of rabies immune globulin into the wound, and administration of vaccine.[91,92] Wound care involves washing with soap and water, as well as the use of iodine- or alcohol-based virucidal agents.[93] Guidelines for postexposure prophylaxis have been established [see Table 5]. The vaccination regimen is determined by the patient's previous vaccination status [see Table 6].

Postoperative Wound Care

Closed wounds should be kept clean and dry for 24 to 48 hours after repair. Epithelialization begins within hours after wound approximation and forms a barrier to contamination. Gentle cleansing with running water will help remove bacteria and crusting. The patients should not place tension on the wound or engage in strenuous activity until the wound has regained sufficient tensile strength. In the first 6 weeks after repair, the wound's tensile strength increases rapidly; after this period, tensile strength increases more slowly, eventually reaching a maximum of 75% to 80% of normal skin strength [see Figure 2].

Table 5 Recommendations for Postexposure Rabies Prophylaxis[91-93]

Animal Type	Animal Disposition and Evaluation	Prophylaxis
Dogs, cats, ferrets	If animal is healthy and available, it is confined for 10 days of observation	Start vaccination if animal exhibits rabies symptoms*
	If animal is rabid or suspected of being rabid, no observation is indicated	Provide immediate vaccination
	If animal's rabies status is unknown, consultation is indicated	Consult public health official
Bats, skunks, raccoons, foxes, bobcats, coyotes, mongooses, and most carnivores	Animal is regarded as rabid unless brain laboratory tests are negative	Provide immediate vaccination unless brain laboratory tests are negative
Livestock, small rodents (e.g., squirrels, chipmunks, rats, hamsters, gerbils, guinea pigs, and mice), large rodents (e.g., woodchucks and beavers), rabbits, hares, and other mammals	Each case is considered indivdually; rabies reported in large rodents in some areas	Consult public health officials; almost never require antirabies treatment

*If the isolated animal shows symptoms of rabies, postexposure prophylaxis is started immediately, and the animal is euthanized for laboratory testing. Vaccination prophylaxis is stopped if laboratory tests are negative for rabies.

Wounds at risk for infection should be assessed by a medical provider within 48 hours of care. In addition, the patient should be taught to look for signs of infection (e.g., erythema, edema, pain, purulent drainage, and fever).

The timing of suture or staple removal is determined by balancing the requirements for optimal cosmesis against the need for wound support. On one hand, it is clear that for optimal cosmesis, sutures should be removed early, before inflammation and epithelialization of suture tracts. An epithelialized tract will develop around a suture or staple that remains in the skin for longer than 7 to 10 days; once the suture or staple is removed, the tract will be replaced by scar.[94] On the other hand, it takes a number of weeks for the wound to gain significant tensile strength, and early removal of wound support can lead to dehiscence of wounds that are under substantial tension. Early suture removal is warranted for some wounds. For example, sutures in aesthetically sensitive areas (e.g., the face) may be removed on day 4 or 5, and sutures in areas under minimal tension (e.g., in wounds parallel to skin tension lines) may be removed on day 7. Sutures in wounds subject to greater stress (e.g., wounds in the lower extremities or the trunk) should remain in place longer, as should sutures in wounds sustained by patients who have a condition that hinders healing (e.g., malnutrition). In such cases, suture-mark scars are considered acceptable. The appropriate method of removing a suture is first to cut it, then to pull on the knot parallel to or toward, rather than away from, the wound.

After suture removal, numerous methods are employed to minimize unsightly scar formation. The cosmetic outcome of a scar is largely determined by the nature and severity of the wound, which are outside the surgeon's control. The greatest impact a surgeon can have on cosmetic outcome is derived from providing meticulous care when the acute wound is initially encountered. Postoperative wound care measures employed to optimize cosmetic outcome include massage, the use of silicone bandages or pressure garments, and the application of lotions. These interventions appear to help, but prospective trials are needed to confirm their efficacy and establish treatment guidelines. The healing wound is fragile, and topical application of ointments to achieve an improved scar appearance may actually achieve the opposite result. For example, vitamin E, which is commonly applied to healing wounds, can induce contact dermatitis and cause scars to look worse.[95]

Table 6 Recommendations for Postexposure Rabies Vaccination[91-93]

Vaccine	Dosage	
	No Previous Vaccination	Previous Vaccination
Human rabies immune globulin (HRIG)	Full dose of 20 IU/kg infiltrated around wound(s) at initial presentation; use separate syringe and anatomic site from vaccine	Not administered
Human diploid cell vaccine (HDCV), rabies vaccine adsorbed (RVA), or purified chick embryo cell vaccine (PCECV)	1.0 ml IM on days 0, 3, 7, 14, and 28*	1.0 ml IM on days 0 and 3*

*Vaccine administration site for adults is the deltoid; for children, the anterolateral thigh may be used. To prevent sciatic nerve injury and reduce adipose depot delivery, the gluteus is never used.

Factors That May Hinder Wound Healing

Despite a surgeon's best efforts, healing does not always occur in an undisturbed fashion: sometimes, a closed wound dehisces. If the dehiscence is sudden, the wound is clean, and only skin and superficial tissues are involved, then the wound should be reclosed, and the cause of the dehiscence should be corrected if possible. If the dehiscence is slow and the wound is contaminated or infected, then the wound should be allowed to heal secondarily, with dressing changes and scar revision to be performed at a later date.

There are a number of local and systemic factors [see Table 7] that can interfere with wound healing (see below). Accordingly, it is essential for clinicians to be aware of and knowledgeable about these factors and, whenever possible, to take appropriate measures to improve the chances for optimal healing. The use of nutrients and growth factors to stimulate wound healing may be considered; this measure is currently the subject of extensive research.

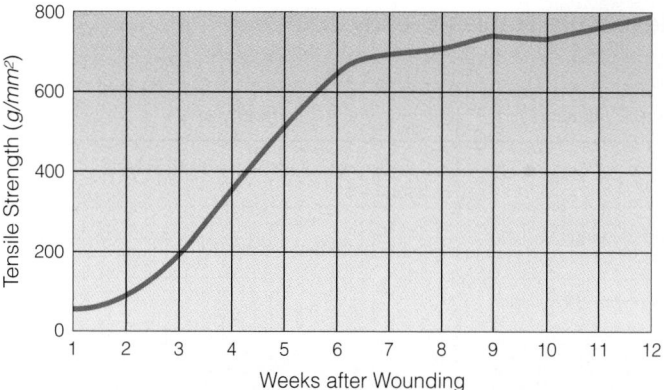

Figure 2 **The tensile strength of skin wounds increases rapidly for approximately 6 weeks after wounding; it then continues to increase slowly for 6 to 12 months after wounding, though it never reaches the tensile strength of unwounded tissue. Collagen is remodeled and replaced with highly cross-linked collagen along tissue stress lines. The process of collagen replacement and scar remodeling continues for years.**

LOCAL FACTORS

Tension

Tension—whether from inherent skin tension, poor surgical technique, movement of joints, or inadequate wound support—may lead to separation of wound edges. It should be minimized by undermining the wound edges during closure to allow easy coaptation. Tissue ellipses from complex wound edges should be kept as narrow as possible and should be created along relaxed skin tension lines. Adequate support of the wound after suture removal is critical; many surgeons keep tapes (e.g., Steri-Strips) over a wound for 3 weeks, until the strength of the wound equals that of the deep sutures and tapes. Wounds over joints should be splinted to reduce tension.

Foreign Body

All foreign bodies that contaminate a wound should be removed at the time of initial debridement and before wound closure. Retained foreign bodies may cause failed healing, infection, or traumatic tattooing. Iatrogenic foreign bodies may also interfere with wound healing and promote infection. Suture material is a foreign body; thus, the number and size of sutures placed in a wound should be kept to the minimum necessary for coaptation of the wound edges.

Infection

All traumatic wounds are contaminated and should therefore be irrigated to remove organisms. Infection occurs when bacteria are too numerous (>10^5 organisms/g tissue) or virulent for local tissue defenses to be able to control them.[96] As noted [*see* Adjunctive Wound Care, Prophylactic Antibiotics, *above*], local factors (e.g., impaired circulation and radiation injury) increase the risk of infection, as do various systemic diseases (e.g., diabetes, AIDS, uremia, and cancer). Wound cultures should be obtained, and broad-spectrum antibiotic therapy should be started when infection is diagnosed. The antibiotic regimen is adjusted on the basis of culture results and sensitivities.

Ischemia

Ischemic wound tissue readily becomes infected and therefore must be debrided. Tissue with dermal edges that do not bleed or

that show no perfusion on fluorescein testing is ischemic. Questionably viable tissue should be monitored closely and debrided when declared nonviable.

Hematoma and Seroma

Hematomas and seromas increase the risk of infection and the likelihood of wound dehiscence. To prevent their formation, hemostasis at the time of wound closure must be meticulous, and bleeding diatheses must be corrected. Because the rubbing of wound edges against one another is associated with the formation of hematomas and seromas, wound edge movement should be minimized and immobilization employed as necessary. Wounds at significant risk for hematoma or seroma formation should be closed over a drain.

Large hematomas or seromas that are recognized early, before infection develops, should be evacuated, and the wound should be reclosed. Small hematomas or seromas can usually be treated conservatively until they are reabsorbed, but close observation is required. If a hematoma or seroma is not recognized until late, when infection has already set in, the wound should be opened, drained, and allowed to heal secondarily; scar revision may be carried out at a later point.

Trauma

Tissue injury is obviously associated with external trauma, but it can also be iatrogenic. Rough handling of tissue edges with forceps produces minute crush injuries, which promote wound infection. It is preferable to handle wound edges with hooks, using gentle surgical technique.

Edema

Edema results from the accumulation of fluid in the interstitial space. It may occur as an acute process, in which tissue injury leads to histamine release, leaky capillaries, and inflammation, or as a chronic process, in which venous insufficiency, lymphatic insufficiency, and a low plasma oncotic pressure may cause fluid to collect in the interstitium. In both cases, edema raises tissue pressure and inhibits perfusion and healing. The proteinaceous and fibrin-rich fluid also forms clot and fibrous tissue, which hinder the supply of oxygen and inflammatory cells.[97] Clearance of wound edema is necessary for healing and may be successfully accomplished by means of compression therapy[98] or NPWT with a VAC device.[83]

Table 7 Local and Systemic Factors That Impair Wound Healing

Local Factors	Systemic Factors
Tension	Inherited connective tissue disorders
Foreign body	Hypothermia
Infection	Oxygen
Ischemia	Tobacco smoking
Hematoma and seroma	Malnutrition
Edema	Jaundice
Irradiation	Age
	Diabetes mellitus
	Uremia
	Steroids
	Chemotherapeutic agents
	Other drugs

Irradiation

Irradiation damages the skin and can cause wounds to heal slowly. It also induces chronic skin changes: previously irradiated tissues demonstrate delayed healing when wounded.[99] Irradiated tissue is characterized by a thickened and fibrotic dermis, a thin epidermis, pigment changes, telangiectasia, decreased hair, and increased dryness (as a consequence of damage to sebaceous and sweat glands). The microvasculature of the skin is obliterated, leading to tissue ischemia and impaired healing. Keratinocytes, which are necessary for wound epithelialization, exhibit impaired mitotic ability and slow progressive desquamation (as a consequence of their superficial location and high replication rate).[97] Collagen bundles become edematous and fibrotic. Fibroblasts, which are necessary for collagen synthesis, also show diminished migration and proliferation.[100]

Because irradiated skin is irreversibly damaged, tissue transfer may be required for repair of wounds in areas subjected to radiation. Vitamin A supplementation can lessen the adverse effects of irradiation on wound healing.[101]

SYSTEMIC FACTORS

Inherited Connective Tissue Disorders

Several inherited connective tissue disorders are known to interfere with normal wound healing. Ehlers-Danlos syndrome exists as multiple types that exhibit certain differences, but in general, the syndrome leads to deficient collagen cross-linking, which results in lax and fragile skin, lax joints, and impaired wound healing. For example, an Ehlers-Danlos patient who undergoes an elective hernia repair or facelift may have a poor outcome as a consequence of deficient collagen formation and poor wound healing.[102,103] Osteogenesis imperfecta is a procollagen formation disorder that is clinically manifested by brittle bones, increased laxity of ligaments and skin, bone deformities, and impaired wound healing.[104] Marfan syndrome is an autosomal dominant disorder characterized by deficient synthesis of fibrillin, which is a key component in elastin formation. Patients with this syndrome have long extremities and hyperextendable joints; those who are seriously affected have lax ligaments, dissecting aneurysms, dislocated eye lenses, pectus excavatum, and scoliosis. Surgical repair of aneurysms and hernias is usually successful in this population, though healing difficulties may be encountered.[103] Cutis laxa is a disease in which an elastase inhibitor deficiency gives rise to defective elastic tissue. Patients with this disease have thick, coarse, and drooping skin, along with hernias, aneurysms, heart disease, and emphysema. Unlike patients with the other heritable diseases mentioned, cutis laxa patients often show no impairment of wound healing.[105]

Hypothermia

Hypothermia may develop as a consequence of administration of anesthetic drugs, exposure to cold, or redistribution of body heat; it leads to peripheral vasconstriction and impaired wound oxygen delivery.[106] Wound tensile strength increases more slowly when healing occurs in a cold environment. Prevention or correction of hypothermia reduces the wound infection rate and increases collagen deposition in patients undergoing abdominal surgery.[107] Preoperative systemic and local warming also reduces the wound infection rate in patients undergoing elective operations.[108] A warm body temperature must be maintained in all wounded patients to reduce subcutaneous vasoconstriction and maximize wound healing potential.

Oxygen

Tissue oxygenation is necessary for aerobic metabolism, fibroblast proliferation, collagen synthesis, and the antimicrobial oxidative burst of inflammatory cells. Transcutaneous oxygen tension is directly correlated with wound healing.[109] Wound tissue oxygenation is determined by blood perfusion, hemoglobin dissociation, local oxygen consumption, fraction of inspired oxygen (F_IO_2), oxygen-carrying capacity (as measured by hemoglobin content), arterial oxygen tension (P_aO_2), circulating blood volume, cardiac function, arterial inflow, and venous drainage.[106,110] Each of these variables should be addressed in promoting wound healing.

Supplemental administration of oxygen (inspired or hyperbaric) has beneficial effects on wound healing. The incidence of infection in surgical wounds can be reduced by improving the F_IO_2 with supplemental oxygen.[111] In a study of patients undergoing colon surgery, for example, the wound infection rate was 50% lower when an F_IO_2 of 0.8 was maintained intraoperatively and for 2 hours postoperatively than when an F_IO_2 of 0.3 was maintained.[112] Hyperbaric oxygen therapy (i.e., the delivery of oxygen in an environment of increased ambient pressure) has been used for treatment of many types of wounds in which tissue hypoxia may impair healing.[43] It increases tissue oxygen concentrations tenfold while also causing vasoconstriction, which results in decreased posttraumatic edema and decreased compartment pressures.[113] The elevated pressure and hyperoxia induced by hyperbaric oxygen therapy may promote wound healing; for patients with an acute wound, this modality may be a useful adjunct in treating limb-threatening injury, crush injury, and compartment syndrome.[43]

Circulating volume can be improved by administering crystalloids or blood. However, anemia alone is not associated with impaired wound healing unless it is severe enough to limit circulating blood volume.[114] The vasculature may be compromised either systemically (e.g., by diabetes mellitus or peripheral vascular disease) or locally (e.g., by trauma or scar). Vascular bypasss may be necessary to improve tissue oxygenation in patients with poor arterial inflow.[97]

Tobacco Smoking

Tobacco smoking reduces tissue oxygen concentrations, impairs wound healing, and contributes to wound infection and dehiscence.[115,116] The effects of smoking are attributable to vasoconstriction (caused by nicotine), displacement of oxygen binding (resulting from the high affinity of carbon monoxide for hemoglobin), increased platelet aggregation,[117] impairment of the inflammatory cell oxidative burst,[118] endothelial damage, and the development of atherosclerosis.[115,116,119] All acutely injured patients should stop smoking, and ideally, all noninjured patients scheduled to undergo surgery should stop smoking at least 3 weeks before an elective surgical wound is made.[118,120] Like smoked tobacco, transcutaneous nicotine patches alter the inflammatory cell oxidative burst and cause vasoconstriction; accordingly, they too should not be used when a wound is present.[118]

Malnutrition

On average, hospitalized patients show a 20% increase in energy expenditure, and this increase calls for appropriate nutritional compensation.[97] Good nutritional balance and adequate caloric intake (including sufficient amounts of protein, carbohydrates, fatty acids, vitamins, and other nutrients) are necessary for normal wound healing.[121]

All patients who have sustained wounds should undergo nutritional assessment,[122] which typically includes measuring serum levels of albumin, protein, prealbumin, transferrin, and insulinlike growth factor–1 (IGF-1).[97] The serum albumin level is one of the best predictors of operative mortality and morbidity.[123] A value lower than 2.5 g/dl is considered severely depressed, and a value lower than 3.4 g/dl is associated with higher perioperative mortality.[124,125] Protein provides an essential supply of the amino acids used in collagen synthesis, and hypoproteinemia results in impaired healing; consequently, it is not surprising that protein replacement and supplementation can improve wound healing.[126,127] In particular, supplementation specifically with the amino acids arginine, glutamine, and taurine (which are essential for anabolic processes and collagen synthesis) is known to enhance wound healing.[128-130] Glutamine is the most abundant free amino acid in the body, and under catabolic conditions, it is released from muscle unless provided as a supplement.

Vitamins C, A, K, and D are essential for normal healing. Vitamin C (ascorbic acid) hydroxylates the amino acids lysine and proline during collagen synthesis and cross-linking. A deficiency of this vitamin causes scurvy, marked by failed healing of new wounds and dehiscence of old wounds. Vitamin C supplementation (100 to 1,000 g/day) can improve wound healing.[97,130] Vitamin A (retinoic acid) is essential for normal epithelialization, proteoglycan synthesis, and normal immune function.[131-133] Retinoids and topical tretinoin may help foster acute wound healing by accelerating epithelialization of full- and partial-thickness wounds, activating fibroblasts, increasing type III collagen synthesis, and decreasing metalloprotease activation.[134,135] Oral retinoid treatment significantly increases the decreased hydroxyproline content, tumor growth factor–β (TGF-β) level, and IGF-1 concentration associated with corticosteroids.[134] In addition, all aspects of corticosteroid-impaired healing—other than wound contraction—can be reversed by providing supplemental oral vitamin A at a recommended dosage of 25,000 IU/day.[136] The retinoic acid derivative isotretinoin (13-*cis*-retinoic acid), however, impairs wound epithelialization and delays wound healing.[137] Vitamin K is a cofactor in the synthesis of coagulation factors II, VII, IX, and X, as well as thrombin. Consequently, vitamin K is necessary for clot formation and hemostasis, the first step in acute wound healing. Vitamin D is required for normal calcium metabolism and therefore plays a necessary role in bone healing.

Dietary minerals (e.g., zinc and iron) are also essential for normal healing. Zinc is a necessary cofactor for DNA and RNA synthesis. A deficiency of this mineral can lead to inhibition cell proliferation, deficient granulation tissue formation,[138] and delayed wound healing.[139] Zinc replacement and supplementation can improve wound healing.[130] However, daily intake should not exceed 40 mg of elemental zinc, because excess zinc can immobilize macrophages, bind copper, and depress wound healing.[140] Iron is also a cofactor for DNA synthesis, as well as for hydroxylation of proline and lysine in collagen synthesis.[97] However, iron deficiency anemia does not appear to affect wound strength.[141]

Jaundice

The effect of jaundice on wound healing is controversial. Jaundiced patients appear to have a higher rate of postoperative wound healing complications,[142] as well as a lower level of collagen synthesis.[143] However, obstructive jaundice does not affect healing of blister wounds in humans.[143] Jaundiced animals show a significant delay in collagen accumulation within the wound, but no significant reduction in the mechanical strength of the wound.[144] Biliary drainage may be considered in jaundiced patients with wounds; this measure will improve collagen synthesis, though it may not have any appreciable effect on the healing rate.[143]

Age

Aging has a deleterious effect on the capacity for wound healing.[145] Increasing age is associated with an altered inflammatory response, impaired macrophage phagocytosis, and delayed healing.[146] Nevertheless, even though the wound healing phases begin later in elderly persons, proceed more slowly, and often do not reach the same level that they would in younger persons, elderly patients are still able to heal most wounds with ease.[147]

Diabetes Mellitus

Diabetes mellitus is associated with poor wound healing and an increased risk of infection. Diabetic neuropathy leads to sensory loss (typically in the extremities) and diminished ability to detect or prevent injury and wounding. Once present, wounds in diabetic patients heal slowly. The etiology of this healing impairment is multifactorial. Diabetes is associated with impaired granulocyte function and chemotaxis, depressed phagocytic function, altered humoral and cellular immunity, peripheral neuropathy, peripheral vascular disease, and various immunologic disturbances, any of which may hinder wound healing.[148-151] In addition, it is associated with a microangiopathy that can limit perfusion and delivery of oxygen, nutrients, and inflammatory cells to the healing wound.[152] Diabetes-induced impairment of healing, as well as the attendant morbidity and mortality, may be reduced by tightly controlling blood sugar levels with insulin.[153] Diabetic patients must also closely monitor themselves for wounds and provide meticulous care for any wounds present.

Uremia

Uremia and chronic renal failure are associated with weakened host defenses, an increased risk of infection, and impaired wound healing.[154] Studies using uremic animal models show delayed healing of intestinal anastomoses and abdominal wounds.[155] Uremic serum also interferes with the proliferation of fibroblasts in culture.[103,155] Treatment of this wound healing impairment includes dialysis.

Uremic patients with wounds may experience bleeding complications. In this situation, appropriate evaluation includes determining the prothrombin time (PT), the activated partial thromboplastin time (aPTT), the platelet count, and the hematocrit. Treatment includes dialysis without heparin; administration of desmopressin (0.3 μg/kg), cryoprecipitate, conjugated estrogens (0.6 mg/kg/day I.V. for 5 days),[156] and erythropoietin; and transfusion of red blood cells to raise the hematocrit above 30%.[157,158]

Uremic patients with hyperparathyroidism may also exhibit the uremic gangrene syndrome (calciphylaxis), which involves the spontaneous and progressive development of skin and soft tissue wounds, usually on the lower extremities. Patients with this syndrome typically are dialysis dependent and have secondary or tertiary hyperparathyroidism. Wound biopsies demonstrate fat necrosis, tissue calcification, and microarterial calcification.[159] Treatment includes local wound care, correction of serum phosphate levels with oral phosphate binders,[160] correction of calcium levels with dialysis, and subtotal parathyroidectomy.[159]

Drugs

Steroids Corticosteroids are anti-inflammatory agents that inhibit all aspects of healing, including inflammation, macrophage migration, fibroblast proliferation, protein and collagen synthesis, development of breaking strength, wound contraction, and epithelialization.[103,136,161] In the setting of an acute wound that fails to heal, corticosteroid doses may be reduced, vitamin A administered topically or systemically, and anabolic steroids given to restore steroid-retarded inflammation.[103,136]

Unlike corticosteroids, anabolic steroids accelerate normal collagen deposition and wound healing. Oxandrolone is an oral anabolic steroid and testosterone analogue that is employed clinically to treat muscle wasting, foster wound healing, and mitigate the catabolism associated with severe burn injury. Supplementation with this agent leads to significant improvements in the wound healing rate.[162] In burn patients treated with oral oxandrolone, hospital length of stay is significantly reduced, and the number of necessary operative procedures is decreased.[163] In ventilator-dependent surgical patients receiving oxandrolone, however, the course of mechanical ventilation is longer than in those not treated with oxandrolone. It has been suggested that the very ability of oxandrolone to enhance wound healing may increase collagen deposition and fibrosis in the later stages of ARDS and thereby prolong recovery.[164] Acute elevation of liver enzyme levels has been seen in some patients treated with oxandrolone; accordingly, hepatic transaminase concentrations should be intermittently monitored in all patients treated with this agent.[163]

Chemotherapeutic agents   Both wound healing and tumor growth depend on metabolically active and rapidly dividing cells. Consequently, chemotherapeutic anticancer drugs that hinder tumor growth can also impair wound healing. These agents (which include adrenocorticosteroids, alkylating agents, antiestrogens, antimetabolites, antitumor antibodies, estrogen, progestogens, nitroureas, plant alkaloids, and random synthetics) attenuate the inflammatory phase of wound healing, decrease fibrin deposition, reduce the synthesis of collagen by fibroblasts, and delay wound contraction.[97] Some cytotoxic drugs (e.g., methotrexate and doxorubicin) substantially attenuate the early phases of wound repair and reduce wound tear strength.[165] The magnitude of these effects is influenced by the timing of the chemotherapeutic agent's delivery in relation to the time when the wound is sustained. Preoperative delivery has a greater adverse effect on healing; for example, doxorubicin impairs wound healing to a greater extent if given before operation than if treatment is delayed until 2 weeks after operation.[166] Chemotherapy also results in myelosuppression and neutropenia that can decrease resistance to infection, allowing small wounds to progress to myonecrosis and necrotizing soft tissue infections.[167] In all acutely wounded patients who have recently been treated with, are currently taking, or will soon begin to take chemotherapeutic agents, the wounds must be closely observed for poor healing and complications.

Other drugs   Many other commonly used drugs affect wound healing and thus should be avoided in the setting of an acute wound. Nicotine, cocaine, ergotomine, and epinephrine all cause vasocontriction and tissue hypoxia. Nonsteroidal anti-inflammatory drugs (e.g., ibuprofen and ketorolac) inhibit cyclooxygenase production and reduce wound tensile strength. Colchicine decreases fibroblast proliferation and degrades newly formed extracellular matrix. Antiplatelet agents (e.g., aspirin) inhibit platelet aggregation and arachidonic acid–mediated inflammation. Heparin and warfarin impair hemostasis by virtue of their effects on fibrin formation.[84,168,169] As noted [see Malnutrition, above], isotretinoin inhibits wound epithelialization and delays wound healing.[137] Vitamin E (α-tocopherol) impairs collagen formation, inflammation, and wound healing[170]; topical application of this agent can causes contact dermatitis and worsen the cosmetic appearance of scars.[95]

Discussion

Physiology of Wound Healing

Wound healing is not a single event but a continuum of processes that begin at the moment of injury and continue for months. These processes take place in much the same way throughout the various tissues of the body and, for the purposes of description, may be broadly divided into three phases: (1) inflammation, (2) migration and proliferation, and (3) maturation [see Figure 3]. Humans, unlike (for instance) salamanders, lack the ability to regenerate specialized structures; instead, they heal by forming a scar that lacks the complex and important skin structures seen in unwounded skin [see Figure 4].

INFLAMMATORY PHASE

The inflammatory phase of wound healing begins with hemostasis, followed by the arrival first of neutrophils and then of macrophages. This response is most prominent during the first 24 hours after a wound is sustained. Signs of inflammation (i.e., erythema, edema, heat, and pain) are apparent, generated primarily by changes in the venules on the distal side of the capillary bed. In clean wounds, signs of inflammation dissipate relatively quickly, and few if any inflammatory cells are seen after 5 to 7 days. In contaminated wounds, inflammation may persist for a prolonged period.

Because wounds bleed when blood vessels are injured, hemostasis is essential. In the first 5 to 10 minutes after wounding, vasoconstriction contributes to hemostasis, and the skin blanches as a result. Vasoconstriction is mediated by catecholamines (e.g., epinephrine and norepinephrine) and prostaglandins (e.g., prostaglandin $F_{2\alpha}$ [$PGF_{2\alpha}$] and thromboxane A_2 [TXA_2]). As vessels contract, platelets aggregate and adhere to the blood vessel collagen exposed by the injury. Aggregating platelets release alpha-granule proteins, resulting in further platelet aggregation and triggering cytokine release. The cytokines involved in cutaneous wound healing include epidermal growth factors, fibroblast growth factors, transforming growth factor–β, platelet-derived growth factor, vascular endothelial growth factor (VEGF), tumor necrosis factor–α (TNF-α), interleukin-1 (IL-1), IGF-1, granulocyte colony-stimulating factor, and granulocyte-macrophage colony-stimulating factor.[171] Some of these cytokines have direct effects early in the healing process; others are bound locally and play critical roles in later healing phases. The use of specific cytokines to reverse healing deficits or promote wound healing appears to be a promising clinical tool and is currently the subject of ongoing basic scientific and clinical research.[172]

The coagulation cascade also contributes to hemostasis. The extrinsic pathway is essential to hemostasis and is stimulated by the release of tissue factor from injured tissue; the intrinsic cascade is not essential and is triggered by exposure to factor XII. Both coagulation pathways lead to the generation of fibrin, which acts with platelets to form a clot in the injured area [see 8 Bleeding and Transfusion]. Fibrin both contributes to hemostasis and is the primary component of the provisional matrix [see Migratory and Proliferative Phase, Provisional Matrix Formation, below].

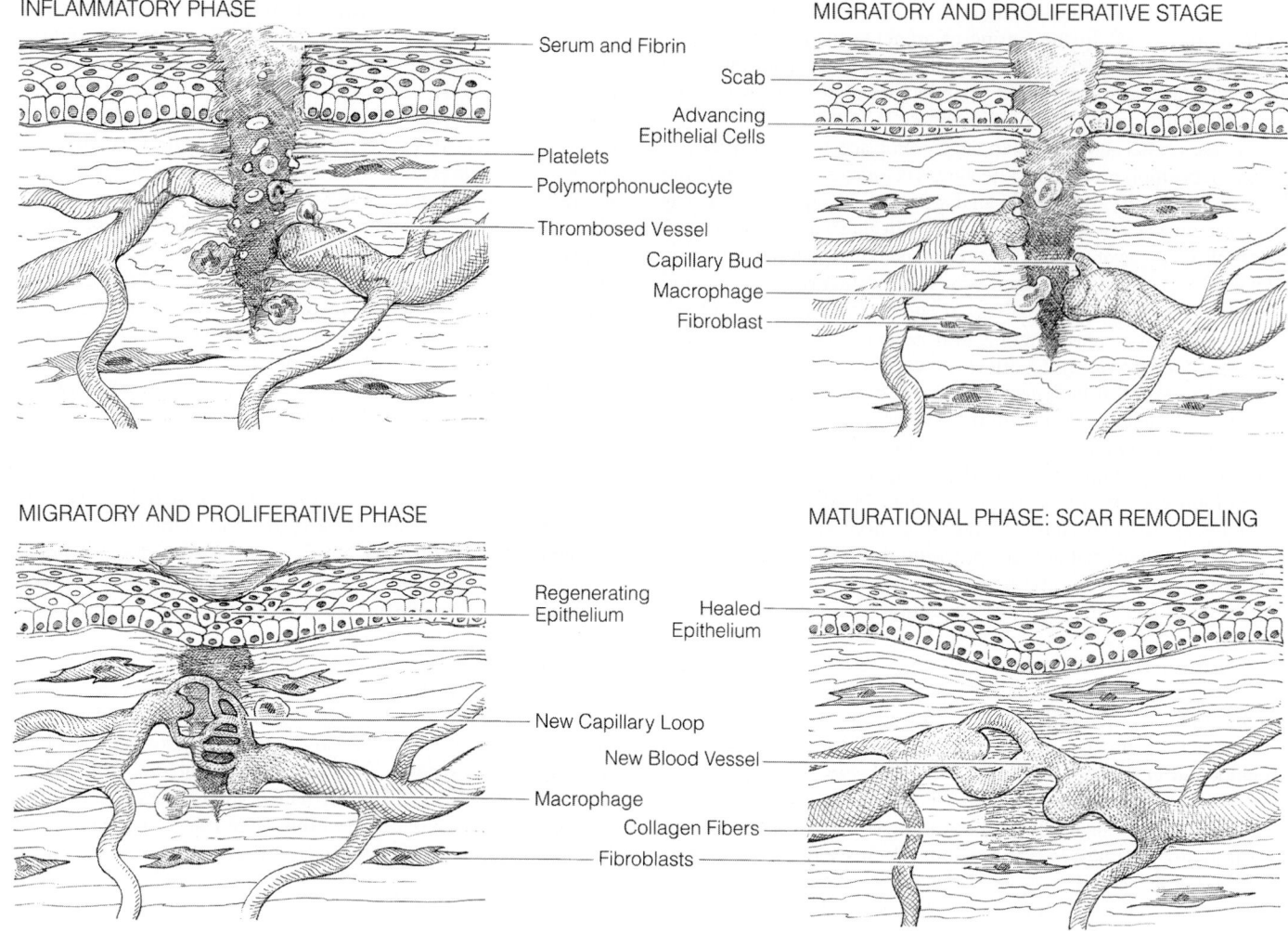

INFLAMMATORY PHASE

- Serum and Fibrin
- Platelets
- Polymorphonucleocyte
- Thrombosed Vessel

MIGRATORY AND PROLIFERATIVE STAGE

- Scab
- Advancing Epithelial Cells
- Capillary Bud
- Macrophage
- Fibroblast

MIGRATORY AND PROLIFERATIVE PHASE

- Regenerating Epithelium
- New Capillary Loop
- Macrophage
- Fibroblasts

MATURATIONAL PHASE: SCAR REMODELING

- Healed Epithelium
- New Blood Vessel
- Collagen Fibers

Figure 3 **Depicted are the phases of wound healing. In the inflammatory phase (top, left), platelets adhere to collagen exposed by damage to blood vessels to form a plug. The intrinsic and extrinsic pathways of the coagulation cascade generate fibrin, which combines with platelets to form a clot in the injured area. Initial local vasoconstriction is followed by vasodilatation mediated by histamine, prostaglandins, serotonin, and kinins. Neutrophils are the predominant inflammatory cells (a polymorphonucleocyte is shown here). In the migratory and proliferative phase (top, right; bottom, left), fibrin and fibronectin are the primary components of the provisional extracellular matrix. Macrophages, fibroblasts, and other mesenchymal cells migrate into the wound area. Gradually, macrophages replace neutrophils as the predominant inflammatory cells. Angiogenic factors induce the development of new blood vessels as capillaries. Epithelial cells advance across the wound bed. Wound tensile strength increases as collagen produced by fibroblasts replaces fibrin. Myofibroblasts induce wound contraction. In the maturational phase (bottom, right), scar remodeling occurs. The overall level of collagen in the wound plateaus; old collagen is broken down as new collagen is produced. The number of cross-links between collagen molecules increases, and the new collagen fibers are aligned so as to yield an increase in wound tensile strength.**

Vasoconstriction and hemostasis are followed by vasodilatation, which is associated with the characteristic signs of erythema, edema, heat, and pain. Vasodilatation is mediated by prostaglandins (e.g., PGE_2 and PGI_2 [prostacyclin]), histamine, serotonin, and kinins.[173,174] As the blood vessels dilate, the endothelial cells separate from one another, thereby increasing vascular permeability. Inflammatory cells initially roll along the endothelial cell lining, subsequently undergo integrin-mediated adhesion, and finally transmigrate into the extravascular space.[175]

For the first 48 to 72 hours after wounding, neutrophils are the predominant inflammatory cells in the wound. About 48 to 96 hours after wounding, however, monocytes migrate from nearby tissue and blood and transform into macrophages, and eventually, macrophages become the predominant inflammatory cells in the wound. Both neutrophils and macrophages engulf damaged tissue and bacteria and digest them. After neutrophils phagocytose damaged material, they cease to function and often release lysosomal contents, which can contribute to tissue damage and a prolonged inflammatory response. Macrophages, however, are essential to wound healing and do not cease to function after phagocytosing bacteria or damaged material.[176] In the wound environment, macrophages also secrete collagenase, elastase, and matrix metalloproteinases (MMPs) that break down damaged tissue. Macrophages also produce cytokines that mediate wound-healing processes, as well as IL-1 (which can lead to a systemic response, including fever) and TNF-α.[171]

MIGRATORY AND PROLIFERATIVE PHASE

The migratory and proliferative phase is marked by the attraction of epidermal cells, fibroblasts, and endothelial cells to the

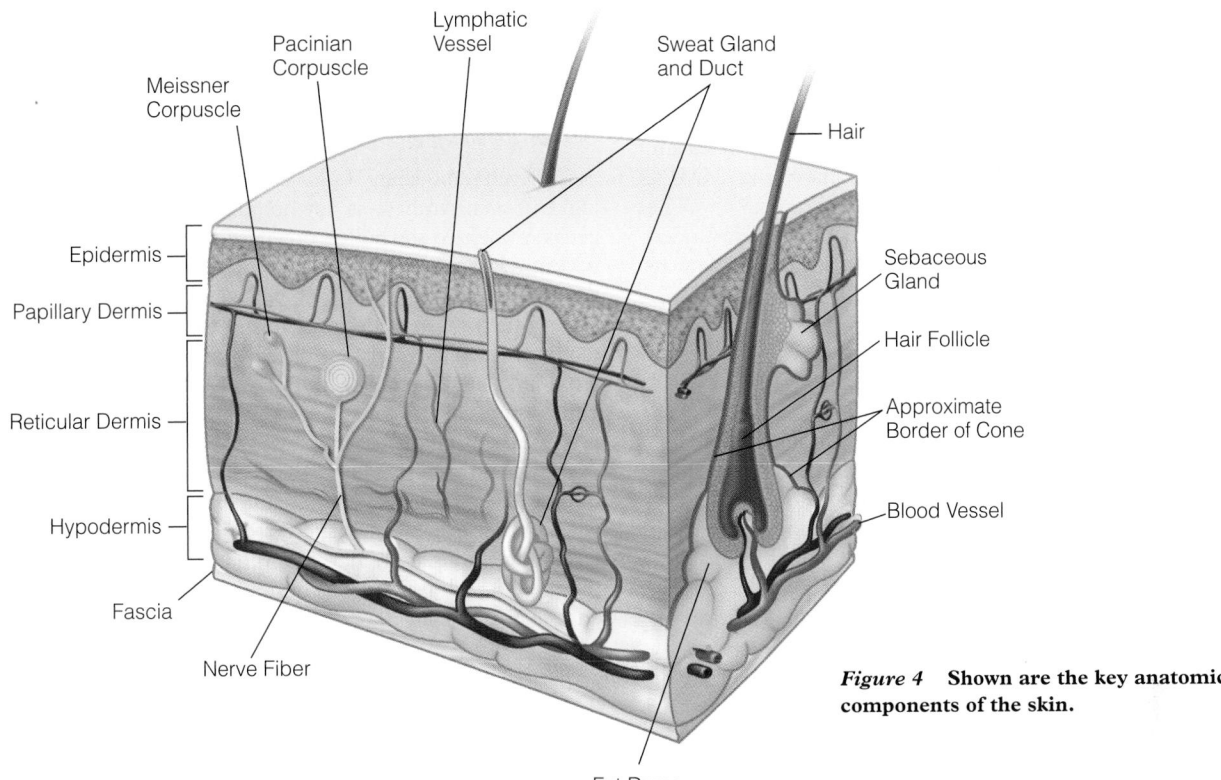

Meissner
Corpuscle

Pacinian
Corpuscle

Lymphatic
Vessel

Sweat Gland
and Duct

Hair

Epidermis

Papillary Dermis

Reticular Dermis

Hypodermis

Fascia

Nerve Fiber

Sebaceous
Gland

Hair Follicle

Approximate
Border of Cone

Blood Vessel

Fat Dome

Figure 4   **Shown are the key anatomic components of the skin.**

wound. Cells migrate along the scaffolding of fibrin and fibronectin. This process involves the upregulation of integrin receptor sites on the cell membranes, which allows the cells to bind at different sites in the matrix and pull themselves through the scaffolding. Migration through the provisional matrix is facilitated by proteolytic enzymes. Cytokines and growth factors then stimulate the proliferation of these cells.[171,176]

Epithelialization

Within approximately 24 hours of injury, epidermal cells from the wound margin and skin appendages begin to migrate into the wound bed. These migrating epidermal cells dissect the wound, separating desiccated eschar from viable tissue.[80] At 24 to 48 hours after wounding, epidermal cells at the wound margin begin to proliferate, producing more migrating cells.[171] As epidermal migration is initiated, the desmosomes that link epidermal cells together and the hemidesmosomes that link the epidermal cells to the basement membrane disappear.[177] Migrating epidermal cells express integrin receptors that allow interaction with extracellular matrix proteins, laminin, collagen, and fibrin clot.[178] When epidermal cells migrating from two areas meet, contact inhibition prevents further migration. The cells making up the epidermal monolayer then differentiate, divide, and form a multilayer epidermis.

Provisional Matrix Formation

Formation of the provisional matrix and granulation tissue begins approximately 3 to 4 days after wounding. Fibroblasts synthesize an extracellular matrix of fibrin, fibronectin, and proteoglycans that supports epidermal and endothelial cell migration and proliferation.[178,179] Proteoglycans (e.g., dermatan sulfate, heparin, heparan sulfate, keratan sulfate, and hyaluronic acid) consist of a protein core that is linked to one or more glycosaminoglycans; they anchor proteins and facilitate the alignment of collagen into fibrils.

Fibrin becomes coated with vitronectin and fibronectin, which are glycoproteins that facilitate the adhesion of migrating fibro-

blasts and other cells to the provisional extracellular matrix.[180] By influencing cellular attachment, fibronectin helps modulate cell migration into the wound.[181] In addition, the fibrin-fibronectin lattice binds various cytokines that are released at the time of injury and serves as a reservoir for these factors in the later stages of healing.[182]

Fibroblasts then replace the provisional extracellular matrix with a collagen matrix, and the wound gains strength. The rate of collagen synthesis increases greatly after the initial 3 to 5 days and continues at an increased rate for 21 days before gradually declining.[183] Of the many types of collagen, the ones that are of primary importance in the skin are types I and III. Approximately 80% to 90% of the collagen in the skin is type I collagen; the remaining 10% to 20% is type III. The percentage of type III collagen is higher in embryonic skin and in skin that is in the early stages of wound healing.

Collagen molecules are synthesized by fibroblasts. Lysine and proline residues within the collagen molecule become hydroxylated after being incorporated into polypeptide chains. This process requires specific enzymes, as well as various cofactors (i.e., oxygen, vitamin C, α-ketoglutarate, and ferrous iron). The result is procollagen, which is released into the extracellular space. Individual collagen molecules then align and associate with one another to form fibrils. Covalent cross-links form between various combinations of the hydroxylated residues (lysine and hydroxylysine) in aligned collagen fibrils, with the strongest links occurring between hydroxylysine and hydroxylysine. These cross-links are essential to the tensile strength of the wound. Cofactor deficiencies (e.g., vitamin C deficiency in scurvy) and the use of corticosteroids can lead to the synthesis of weak, underhydroxylated collagen that is incapable of generating strong cross-links.

Angiogenesis

The growth of new blood vessels, which is necessary to support the wound tissue, begins 2 to 3 days after wounding. This process of angiogenesis may be stimulated by the hypoxic and acidic wound microenvironment, as well as by cytokines (e.g., VEGF) derived from epidermal cells and macrophages.[171,184] Endothelial cells from surrounding vessels express fibronectin receptors and grow into the provisional matrix. These migrating endothelial cells create paths in the matrix for developing capillaries by releasing plasminogen activator, procollagenase, heparanase, and MMPs, which break down fibrin and basement membranes.[171,185] The budding capillaries join and initiate blood flow. As the wounded area becomes better vascularized, the capillaries consolidate to form larger blood vessels or undergo apoptosis.[186]

MATURATIONAL PHASE

Wound Contraction

Myofibroblasts are specialized fibroblasts containing alpha–smooth muscle actin microfilaments that contribute to wound contraction.[187,188] The wound edges are pulled together by the contractile forces supplied by the myofibroblast. Wound contraction generally begins in the 4- to 5-day period after wounding and continues for 12 to 15 days or until the wound edges meet. The rate at which contraction occurs varies with the laxity of the tissue and is highest at anatomic sites with redundant tissue. Excessive contraction can lead to contracture, a pathologic scarring that impairs the function and appearance of the scar.

Scar Remodeling

Collagen remodeling begins approximately 3 weeks after wounding. Collagen synthesis is downregulated, the rates at which collagen is synthesized and broken down reach equilibrium, and the wound becomes less cellular as apoptosis occurs. During this process, the extracellular matrix, including collagen, is continually remodeled and synthesized in a more organized fashion along stress lines.[183] Collagen breakdown is mediated by MMPs.[189] The number of cross-links between collagen fibers increases,[183] and the realigned, highly cross-linked collagen is much stronger than the collagen produced during the earlier phases of healing. The tensile strength of the wound increases rapidly for 6 weeks after injury; accordingly, during this period, heavy lifting and any other activity that applies stress across the wound should be avoided. After the initial 6 weeks, tensile strength increases more slowly for a further 6 to 12 months, though it never reaches the tensile strength of unwounded tissue [*see Figure 2*].

References

1. Edlich RF, Reddy VR: 5th Annual David R. Boyd, MD Lecture: revolutionary advances in wound repair in emergency medicine during the last three decades: a view toward the new millennium. J Emerg Med 20:167, 2001

2. Siegel RJ, Vistnes LM, Iverson RE: Effective hemostasis with less epinephrine: an experimental and clinical study. Plast Reconstr Surg 51:129, 1973

3. Wilhelmi BJ, Blackwell SJ, Miller JH, et al: Do not use epinephrine in digital blocks: myth or truth? Plast Reconstr Surg 107:393, 2001

4. Ostad A, Kageyama N, Moy RL: Tumescent anesthesia with a lidocaine dose of 55 mg/kg is safe for liposuction. Dermatol Surg 22:921, 1996

5. Arndt KA, Burton C, Noe JM: Minimizing the pain of local anesthesia. Plast Reconstr Surg 72:676, 1983

6. Christoph RA, Buchanan L, Begalla K, et al: Pain reduction in local anesthetic administration through pH buffering. Ann Emerg Med 17:117, 1988

7. Anderson AB, Colecchi C, Baronoski R, et al: Local anesthesia in pediatric patients: topical TAC versus lidocaine. Ann Emerg Med 19:519, 1990

8. Zempsky WT, Karasic RB: EMLA versus TAC for topical anesthesia of extremity wounds in children. Ann Emerg Med 30:163, 1997

9. Moore TJ, Walsh CS, Cohen MR: Reported adverse event cases of methemoglobinemia associated with benzocaine products. Arch Intern Med 164:1192, 2004

10. Guertler AT, Pearce WA: A prospective evaluation of benzocaine-associated methemoglobinemia in human beings. Ann Emerg Med 24:626, 1994

11. Haury B, Rodeheaver G, Vensko J, et al: Debridement: an essential component of traumatic wound care. Am J Surg 135:238, 1978

12. Alexander JW, Fischer JE, Boyajian M, et al: The influence of hair-removal methods on wound infections. Arch Surg 118:347, 1983

13. Brown LL, Shelton HT, Bornside GH, et al: Evaluation of wound irrigation by pulsatile jet and conventional methods. Ann Surg 187:170, 1978

14. Boyd JI 3rd, Wongworawat MD: High-pressure pulsatile lavage causes soft tissue damage. Clin Orthop Relat Res 427:13, 2004

15. Hassinger SM, Harding G, Wongworawat MD: High-pressure pulsatile lavage propagates bacteria into soft tissue. Clin Orthop Relat Res 439:27, 2005

16. Singer AJ, Hollander JE, Subramanian S, et al: Pressure dynamics of various irrigation techniques commonly used in the emergency department. Ann Emerg Med 24:36, 1994

17. Dulecki M, Pieper B: Irrigating simple acute traumatic wounds: a review of the current literature. J Emerg Nurs 31:156, 2005

18. Anglen JO: Comparison of soap and antibiotic solutions for irrigation of lower-limb open fracture wounds: a prospective, randomized study. J Bone Joint Surg Am 87:1415, 2005

19. Magee C, Rodeheaver GT, Golden GT, et al: Potentiation of wound infection by surgical drains. Am J Surg 131:547, 1976

20. Postlethwait RW, Willigan DA, Ulin AW: Human tissue reaction to sutures. Ann Surg 181:144, 1975

21. Moy RL, Lee A, Zalka A: Commonly used suture materials in skin surgery. Am Fam Physician 44: 2123, 1991

22. Kanegaye JT, Vance CW, Chan L, et al: Comparison of skin stapling devices and standard sutures for pediatric scalp lacerations: a randomized study of cost and time benefits. J Pediatr 130:808, 1997

23. Khan AN, Dayan PS, Miller S, et al: Cosmetic outcome of scalp wound closure with staples in the pediatric emergency department: a prospective, randomized trial. Pediatr Emerg Care 18:171, 2002

24. Stillman RM, Marino CA, Seligman SJ: Skin staples in potentially contaminated wounds. Arch Surg 119:821, 1984

25. Edlich RF, Becker DG, Thacker JG, et al: Scientific basis for selecting staple and tape skin closures. Clin Plast Surg 17:571, 1990

26. Conolly WB, Hunt TK, Zederfeldt B, et al: Clinical comparison of surgical wounds closed by suture and adhesive tapes. Am J Surg 117:318, 1969

27. Singer AJ, Quinn JV, Clark RE, et al: Closure of lacerations and incisions with octylcyanoacrylate: a multicenter randomized controlled trial. Surgery 131:270, 2002

28. Singer AJ, Thode HC Jr: A review of the literature on octylcyanoacrylate tissue adhesive. Am J Surg 187:238, 2004

29. Garrett WE Jr, Seaber AV, Boswick J, et al: Recovery of skeletal muscle after laceration and repair. J Hand Surg 9:683, 1984

30. Trail IA, Powell ES, Noble J: An evaluation of suture material used in tendon surgery. J Hand Surg Br 14:422, 1989

31. Zitelli JA: Wound healing by secondary intention. A cosmetic appraisal. J Am Acad Dermatol 9:407, 1983

32. Leaper DJ, Harding KG: Traumatic and surgical wounds. BMJ 332:532, 2006

33. Cruise PJE, Foord R: The epidemiology of wound infection: a 10-year prospective study of 62,939 wounds. Surg Clin North Am 60:27, 1980

34. Iverson PC: Surgical removal of traumatic tattoos of the face. Plast Reconstr Surg 2:427, 1947

35. Agris J: Traumatic tattooing. J Trauma 16:798, 1976

36. Krizek TJ, Davis JH: The role of the red cell in subcutaneous infection. J Trauma 147:85, 1965

37. Howe CW: Experimental studies on determinants of wound infection. Surg Gynecol Obstet 123:507, 1966

38. Elek SD: Experimental staphylococcal infections in the skin of man. Ann NY Acad Sci 65:85, 1956

39. Myers MB, Brock D, Cohn I Jr: Prevention of skin slough after radical mastectomy by the use of a vital dye to delineate devascularized skin. Ann Surg 173:920, 1971

40. Fitzgerald RH Jr, Cooney WP 3rd, Washington JA 2nd, et al: Bacterial colonization of mutilating hand injuries and its treatment. J Hand Surg [Am] 2:85, 1977

41. Elliott KG, Johnstone AJ: Diagnosing acute compartment syndrome. J Bone Joint Surg Br 85:625, 2003

42. Matsen FA 3rd: Compartment syndrome: a unified approach. Clin Orthop113:8, 1975

43. Roth RN, Weiss LD: Hyperbaric oxygen and wound healing. Clin Dermatol 12:141, 1994

44. Malinoski DJ, Slater MS, Mullins RJ: Crush injury and rhabdomyolysis. Crit Care Clin 20:171, 2004

45. Bellin MF, Jakobsen JA, Tomassin I, et al: Contrast medium extravasation injury: guidelines for prevention and management. Eur Radiol 12:2807, 2002

46. Khan MS, Holmes JD: Reducing the morbidity from extravasation injuries. Ann Plast Surg 48:628, 2002

47. Vandeweyer E, Heymans O, Deraemaecker R: Extravasation injuries and emergency suction as treatment. Plast Reconstr Surg 105:109, 2000

48. Ramos H, Posch JL, Lie KK: High-pressure injection injuries of the hand. Plast Reconstr Surg 45:221, 1970

49. Gelberman RH, Posch JL, Jurist JM: High-pressure injection injuries of the hand. J Bone Joint Surg Am 57:935, 1975

50. Weltmer JB Jr, Pack LL: High-pressure water-gun injection injuries to the extremities: a report of six cases. J Bone Joint Surg Am 70:1221, 1988

51. Christodoulou L, Melikyan EY, Woodbridge S, et al: Functional outcome of high-pressure injection injuries of the hand. J Trauma 50:717, 2001

52. Lammers RL: Soft tissue foreign bodies. Ann Emerg Med 17:1336, 1988

53. Talan DA, Abrahamian FM, Moran GJ, et al: Clinical presentation and bacteriologic analysis of infected human bites in patients presenting to emergency departments. Clin Infect Dis 37:1481, 2003

54. Peeples E, Boswick JA Jr, Scott FA: Wounds of the hand contaminated by human or animal saliva. J Trauma 20:383, 1980

55. Edlich RF, Rodeheaver GT, Morgan RF, et al: Principles of emergency wound management. Ann Emerg Med 17:1284, 1988

56. Brown DW: Threat to humans from virus infections of non-human primates. Rev Med Virol 7:239, 1997

57. Talan DA, Citron DM, Abrahamian FM, et al: Bacteriologic analysis of infected dog and cat bites. Emergency Medicine Animal Bite Infection Study Group. N Engl J Med 340:85, 1999

58. Giladi M, Avidor B: Images in clinical medicine. Cat scratch disease. N Engl J Med 340:108, 1999

59. Bass JW, Freitas BC, Freitas AD, et al: Prospective randomized double blind placebo-controlled evaluation of azithromycin for treatment of cat-scratch disease. Pediatr Infect Dis J 17:447, 1998

60. Cummings P: Antibiotics to prevent infection in patients with dog bite wounds: a meta-analysis of randomized trials. Ann Emerg Med 23:535, 1994

61. Kurecki BA 3rd, Brownlee HJ Jr: Venomous snakebites in the United States. J Fam Pract 25:386, 1987

62. Sprenger TR, Bailey WJ: Snakebite treatment in the United States. Int J Dermatol 25:479, 1986

63. Pennell TC, Babu SS, Meredith JW: The management of snake and spider bites in the southeastern United States. Am Surg 53:198, 1987

64. Lawrence WT, Giannopoulos A, Hansen A: Pit viper bites: rational management in locales in which copperheads and cottonmouths predominate. Ann Plast Surg 36:276, 1996

65. Gold BS, Dart RC, Barish RA: Bites of venomous snakes. N Engl J Med 347:347, 2002

66. Dart RC, Seifert SA, Boyer LV, et al: A randomized multicenter trial of crotalinae polyvalent immune Fab (ovine) antivenom for the treatment for crotaline snakebite in the United States. Arch Intern Med 161:2030, 2001

67. Jurkovich GJ, Luterman A, McCullar K, et al: Complications of Crotalidae antivenin therapy. J Trauma 28:1032, 1988

68. Kemp ED: Bites and stings of the arthropod kind: treating reactions that can range from annoying to menacing. Postgrad Med 103:88, 1998

69. Swanson DL, Vetter RS: Bites of brown recluse spiders and suspected necrotic arachnidism. N Engl J Med 352:700, 2005

70. Rees RS, Altenbern DP, Lynch JB, et al: Brown recluse spider bites: a comparison of early surgical excision versus dapsone and delayed surgical excision. Ann Surg 202:659, 1985

71. Zukowski CW: Black widow spider bite. J Am Board Fam Pract 6:279, 1993

72. Centers for Disease Control and Prevention (CDC): Necrotic arachnidism—Pacific Northwest, 1988–1996. MMWR Morb Mortal Wkly Rep 45:433, 1996

73. Vetter RS, Isbister GK: Do hobo spider bites cause dermonecrotic injuries? Ann Emerg Med 44:605, 2004

74. Carbonaro PA, Janniger CK, Schwartz RA: Scorpion sting reactions. Cutis 57:139, 1996

75. Bush SP, King BO, Norris RL, et al: Centipede envenomation. Wilderness Environ Med 12:93, 2001

76. Gimbel NS, Farris W: Skin grafting: the influence of surface temperature on the epithelization rate of split thickness skin donor sites. Arch Surg 92:554, 1966

77. Alvarez OM, Mertz PM, Eaglstein WH: The effect of occlusive dressings on collagen synthesis and re-epithelialization in superficial wounds. J Surg Res 35:142, 1983

78. Jones V, Grey JE, Harding KG: Wound dressings. BMJ 332:777, 2006

79. Salomon JC, Diegelmann RF, Cohen IK: Effect of dressings on donor site epithelialization. Surg Forum 25:516, 1974

80. Pilcher BK, Dumin JA, Sudbeck BD, et al: The activity of collagenase-1 is required for keratinocyte migration on a type I collagen matrix. J Cell Biol 137:1445, 1997

81. Noe JM, Kalish S: The mechanism of capillarity in surgical dressings. Surg Gynecol Obstet 143:454, 1976

82. Varma AO, Bugatch E, German FM: Debridement of dermal ulcers with collagenase. Surg Gynecol Obstet 136:281, 1973

83. Argenta LC, Morykwas MJ: Vacuum-assisted closure: a new method for wound control and treatment: clinical experience. Ann Plast Surg 38:563, 1997

84. Enoch S, Grey JE, Harding KG: ABC of wound healing: non-surgical and drug treatments. BMJ 332:900, 2006

85. Dixon AJ, Dixon MP, Dixon JB: Randomized clinical trial of the effect of applying ointment to surgical wounds before occlusive dressing. Br J Surg 93:937, 2006

86. Dire DJ, Coppola M, Dwyer DA, et al: Prospective evaluation of topical antibiotics for preventing infections in uncomplicated soft-tissue wounds repaired in the ED. Acad Emerg Med 2:4, 1995

87. Davis SC, Cazzaniga AL, Eaglstein WH, et al: Over-the-counter topical antimicrobials: effective treatments? Arch Dermatol Res 297:190, 2005

88. Kucan JO, Robson MC, Heggers JP, et al: Comparison of silver sulfadiazine, povidone-iodine and physiologic saline in the treatment of chronic pressure ulcers. J Am Geriatr Soc 29:232, 1981

89. Rhee P, Nunley MK, Demetriades D, et al: Tetanus and trauma: a review and recommendations. J Trauma 58:1082, 2005

90. Centers for Disease Control and Prevention: General recommendation on immunization: recommendations of the Advisory Committee on Immunization Practices (ACIP). MMWR 43:1, 1994

91. Rupprecht CE, Gibbons RV: Prophylaxis against rabies. N Engl J Med 351:2626, 2004

92. Centers for Disease Control and Prevention: Human rabies prevention—United States, 1999: recommendations of the Advisory Committee on Immunization Practices (ACIP). MMWR 48(RR-1):1, 1999

93. Warrell MJ, Warrell DA: Rabies and other lyssavirus diseases. Lancet 363:959, 2004

94. Ordman LJ, Gillman T: Studies in the healing of cutaneous wounds: II. The healing of epidermal, appendageal, and dermal injuries inflicted by suture needles and by the suture material in the skin of pigs. Arch Surg 93:883, 1966

95. Baumann LS, Spencer J: The effects of topical vitamin E on the cosmetic appearance of scars. Dermatol Surg 25:311, 1999

96. Krizek TJ, Robson MC: Evolution of quantitative bacteriology in wound management. Am J Surg 130:579, 1975

97. Burns JL, Mancoll JS, Phillips LG: Impairments to wound healing. Clin Plast Surg 30:47, 2003

98. Macdonald JM, Sims N, Mayrovitz HN: Lymphedema, lipedema, and the open wound: the role of compression therapy. Surg Clin North Am 83:639, 2003

99. Rudolph R: Complications of surgery for radiotherapy skin damage. Plast Reconstr Surg 70:179, 1982

100. Miller SH, Rudolph R: Healing in the irradiated wound. Clin Plast Surg 17:503, 1990

101. Levenson SM, Gruber CA, Rettura G, et al: Supplemental vitamin A prevents the acute radiation-induced defect in wound healing. Ann Surg 200:494, 1984

102. Guerrerosantos J, Dicksheet S: Cervicofacial rhytidoplasty in Ehlers-Danlos syndrome: hazards on healing. Plast Reconstr Surg 75:100, 1985

103. Hunt TK: Disorders of wound healing. World J Surg 4:271, 1980

104. Woolley MM, Morgan S, Hays DM: Heritable disorders of connective tissue: surgical and anesthetic problems. J Pediatr Surg 2:325, 1967

105. Nahas FX, Sterman S, Gemperli R, et al: The role of plastic surgery in congenital cutis laxa: a 10-year follow-up. Plast Reconstr Surg 104:1174, 1999

106. Ueno C, Hunt TK, Hopf HW: Using physiology to improve surgical wound outcomes. Plast Reconstr Surg 117(7 suppl):59S, 2006

107. Kurz A, Sessler DI, Lenhardt R: Perioperative normothermia to reduce the incidence of surgical-wound infection and shorten hospitalization. Study of Wound Infection and Temperature Group. N Engl J Med 334:1209, 1996

108. Melling AC, Ali B, Scott EM, et al: Effects of preoperative warming on the incidence of wound infection after clean surgery: a randomised controlled trial. Lancet 358:876, 2001

109. Hauser CJ: Tissue salvage by mapping of skin surface transcutaneous oxygen tension index. Arch Surg 122:1128, 1987

110. Hunt TK, Zederfeldt BH, Goldstick TK, et al: Tissue oxygen tensions during controlled hemorrhage. Surg Forum 18:3, 1967

111. Hopf HW, Hunt TK, Rosen N: Supplemental oxygen and risk of surgical site infection. JAMA 291:195, 2004

112. Greif R, Akca O, Horn EP, et al: Supplemental perioperative oxygen to reduce the incidence of surgical-wound infection. Outcomes Research Group. N Engl J Med 342:161, 2000

113. Bird AD, Telfer AB: Effect of hyperbaric oxygen on limb circulation. Lancet 13:355, 1965

114. Heughan C, Grislis G, Hunt TK: The effect of anemia on wound healing. Ann Surg 179:163, 1974

115. Jensen JA, Goodson WH, Hopf HW, et al: Cigarette smoking decreases tissue oxygen. Arch Surg 126:1131, 1991

116. Silverstein P: Smoking and wound healing. Am J Med 93:22S, 1992

117. Birnstingl MA, Brinson K, Chakrabarti BK: The effect of short-term exposure to carbon monoxide on platelet stickiness. Br J Surg 58:837, 1971

118. Sorensen LT, Nielsen HB, Kharazmi A, et al: Effect of smoking and abstention on oxidative burst and reactivity of neutrophils and monocytes. Surgery 136:1047, 2004

119. Sackett DL, Gibson RW, Bross ID, et al: Relation between aortic atherosclerosis and the use of cigarettes and alcohol: an autopsy study. N Engl J Med 279:1413, 1968

120. Kuri M, Nakagawa M, Tanaka H, et al: Determination of the duration of preoperative smoking cessation to improve wound healing after head and neck surgery. Anesthesiology 102:892, 2005

121. Howes EL, Briggs H, Shea R, et al: Effect of complete and partial starvation on the rate of fibroplasia in the healing wound. Arch Surg 27:846, 1933

122. Gray D, Cooper P: Nutrition and wound healing: what is the link? J Wound Care 10:86, 2001

123. Gibbs J, Cull W, Henderson W, et al: Preoperative serum albumin level as a predictor of operative mortality and morbidity: results from the National VA Surgical Risk Study. Arch Surg 134:36, 1999

124. Reinhardt GF, Myscofski JW, Wilkens DB, et al: Incidence and mortality of hypoalbuminemic patients in hospitalized veterans. JPEN J Parenter Enteral Nutr 4:357, 1980

125. Stack JA, Babineau TJ, Bistrian BR: Assessment of nutritional status in clinical practice. Gastroenterologist 4:S8, 1996

126. Jeschke MG, Herndon DN, Ebener C, et al: Nutritional intervention high in vitamins, protein, amino acids, and omega3 fatty acids improves protein metabolism during the hypermetabolic state after thermal injury. Arch Surg 136:1301, 2001

127. Chernoff R: Physiologic aging and nutritional status. Nutr Clin Pract 5:8, 1990

128. Soeters PB, van de Poll MC, van Gemert WG, et al: Amino acid adequacy in pathophysiological states. J Nutr 134(6 suppl):1575S, 2004

129. Williams JZ, Abumrad N, Barbul A: Effect of a specialized amino acid mixture on human collagen deposition. Ann Surg 236:369, 2002

130. Desneves KJ, Todorovic BE, Cassar A, et al: Treatment with supplementary arginine, vitamin C and zinc in patients with pressure ulcers: a randomised controlled trial. Clin Nutr 24:979, 2005

131. Freiman M, Seifter E, Connerton C, et al: Vitamin A deficiency and surgical stress. Surg Forum 21:81, 1970

132. Shapiro SS, Mott DJ: Modulation of glycosaminoglycan biosynthesis by retinoids. Ann NY Acad Sci 359:306, 1981

133. Cohen BE, Gill G, Cullen PR, et al: Reversal of postoperative immunosuppression in man by vitamin A. Surg Gynecol Obstet 149:658, 1979

134. Wicke C, Halliday B, Allen D, et al: Effects of steroids and retinoids on wound healing. Arch Surg 135:1265, 2000

135. Leyden JJ: Treatment of photodamaged skin with topical tretinoin: an update. Plast Reconstr Surg 102:1667, 1998

136. Hunt TK, Ehrlich HP, Garcia JA, et al: Effect of vitamin A on reversing the inhibitory effect of cortisone on healing of open wounds in animals and man. Ann Surg 170:633, 1969

137. Zachariae H: Delayed wound healing and keloid formation following argon laser treatment or dermabrasion during isotretinoin treatment. Br J Dermatol 118:703, 1988

138. Fernandez-Madrid F, Prasad AS, Oberleas D: Effect of zinc deficiency on nucleic acids, collagen, and noncollagenous protein of the connective tissue. J Lab Clin Med 82:951, 1973

139. Andrews M, Gallagher-Allred C: The role of zinc in wound healing. Adv Wound Care 12:137, 1999

140. Posthauer ME: Do patients with pressure ulcers benefit from oral zinc supplementation? Adv Skin Wound Care 18:471, 2005

141. Macon WL, Pories WJ: The effect of iron deficiency anemia on wound healing. Surgery 69:792, 1971

142. Grande L, Garcia-Valdecasas JC, Fuster J, et al: Obstructive jaundice and wound healing. Br J Surg 77:440, 1990

143. Koivukangas V, Oikarinen A, Risteli J, et al: Effect of jaundice and its resolution on wound re-epithelization, skin collagen synthesis, and serum collagen propeptide levels in patients with neoplastic pancreaticobiliary obstruction. J Surg Res 124:237, 2005

144. Greaney MG, Van Noort R, Smythe A, et al: Does obstructive jaundice adversely affect wound healing? Br J Surg 66:478, 1979

145. Lindstedt E, Sandblom P: Wound healing in man: tensile strength of healing wounds in some patient groups. Ann Surg 181:842, 1975

146. Swift ME, Burns AL, Gray KL, et al: Age-related alterations in the inflammatory response to dermal injury. J Invest Dermatol 117:1027, 2001

147. Eaglstein WH: Wound healing and aging. Clin Geriatr Med 5:183, 1989

148. Nolan CM, Beaty HN, Bagdade JD: Further characterization of the impaired bactericidal function of granulocytes in patients with poorly controlled diabetes. Diabetes 27:889, 1978

149. Fahey TJ 3rd, Sadaty A, Jones WG 2nd, et al: Diabetes impairs the late inflammatory response to wound healing. J Surg Res 50:308, 1991

150. Bagdade JD, Root RK, Bulger RJ: Impaired leukocyte function in patients with poorly controlled diabetes. Diabetes 23:9, 1974

151. Greenhalgh DG: Wound healing and diabetes mellitus. Clin Plast Surg 30:37, 2003

152. Duncan HJ, Faris IB: Skin vascular resistance and skin perfusion pressure as predictors of healing of ischemic lesion of the lower limb: influences of diabetes mellitus, hypertension, and age. Surgery 99:432, 1986

153. Van den Berghe G, Wouters P, Weekers F, et al: Intensive insulin therapy in the critically ill patients. N Engl J Med 345:1359, 2001

154. Cheung AH, Wong LM: Surgical infections in patients with chronic renal failure. Infect Dis Clin North Am 15:775, 2001

155. Colin JF, Elliot P, Ellis H: The effect of uraemia upon wound healing: an experimental study. Br J Surg 66:793, 1979

156. Vigano G, Gaspari F, Locatelli M, et al: Dose-effect and pharmacokinetics of estrogens given to correct bleeding time in uremia. Kidney Int 34:853, 1988

157. Mannucci PM: Hemostatic drugs. N Engl J Med 339:245, 1998

158. DeLoughery TG: Management of bleeding with uremia and liver disease. Curr Opin Hematol 6:329, 1999

159. Kane WJ, Petty PM, Sterioff S, et al: The uremic gangrene syndrome: improved healing in spontaneously forming wounds following subtotal parathyroidectomy. Plast Reconstr Surg 98:671, 1996

160. Gipstein RM, Coburn JW, Adams DA, et al: Calciphylaxis in man: a syndrome of tissue necrosis and vascular calcification in 11 patients with chronic renal failure. Arch Intern Med 136:1273, 1976

161. Stephens FO, Dunphy JE, Hunt TK: Effect of delayed administration of corticosteroids on wound contraction. Ann Surg 173:214, 1971

162. Demling RH, Orgill DP: The anticatabolic and wound healing effects of the testosterone analog oxandrolone after severe burn injury. J Crit Care 15:12, 2000

163. Wolf SE, Edelman LS, Kemalyan N, et al: Effects of oxandrolone on outcome measures in the severely burned: a multicenter prospective randomized double-blind trial. J Burn Care Res 27:131, 2006

164. Bulger EM, Jurkovich GJ, Farver CL, et al: Oxandrolone does not improve outcome of ventilator dependent surgical patients. Ann Surg 240:472, 2004

165. Bland KI, Palin WE, von Fraunhofer JA, et al: Experimental and clinical observations of the effects of cytotoxic chemotherapeutic drugs on wound healing. Ann Surg 199:782, 1984

166. Lawrence WT, Talbot TL, Norton JA: Preoperative or postoperative doxorubicin hydrochloride (adriamycin): which is better for wound healing? Surgery 100:9, 1986

167. Johnston DL, Waldhausen JH, Park JR: Deep soft tissue infections in the neutropenic pediatric oncology patient. J Pediatr Hematol Oncol 23:443, 2001

168. Karukonda SR, Flynn TC, Boh EE, et al: The effects of drugs on wound healing—part II. Specific classes of drugs and their effect on healing wounds. Int J Dermatol 39:321, 2000

169. Karukonda SR, Flynn TC, Boh EE, et al: The effects of drugs on wound healing: part 1. Int J Dermatol 39:250, 2000

170. Ehrlich HP, Tarver H, Hunt TK: Inhibitory effects of vitamin E on collagen synthesis and wound repair. Ann Surg 175:235, 1972

171. Singer AJ, Clark RA: Cutaneous wound healing. N Engl J Med 341:738, 1999

172. Robson MC: Cytokine manipulation of the wound. Clin Plast Surg 30:57, 2003

173. Williams TJ, Peck MJ: Role of prostaglandin-mediated vasodilatation in inflammation. Nature 270(5637):530, 1977

174. Ryan GB, Majno G: Acute inflammation: a review. Am J Pathol 86:183, 1977

175. Ley K: Leukocyte adhesion to vascular endothelium. J Reconstr Microsurg 8:495, 1992

176. Leibovich SJ, Ross R: The role of the macrophage in wound repair: a study with hydrocortisone and antimacrophage serum. Am J Pathol 78:71, 1975

177. Gipson IK, Spurr-Michaud SJ, Tisdale AS: Hemidesmosomes and anchoring fibril collagen appear synchronously during development and wound healing. Dev Biol 126:253, 1988

178. Clark RA, Lanigan JM, DellaPelle P, et al: Fibronectin and fibrin provide a provisional matrix for epidermal cell migration during wound reepithelialization. J Invest Dermatol 79:264, 1982

179. Greiling D, Clark RA: Fibronectin provides a conduit for fibroblast transmigration from collagenous stroma into fibrin clot provisional matrix. J Cell Sci 110:861, 1997

180. Grinnell F, Billingham RE, Burgess L: Distribution of fibronectin during wound healing in vivo. J Invest Dermatol 76:181, 1981

181. Clark RA, Folkvord JM, Wertz RL: Fibronectin, as well as other extracellular matrix proteins, mediate human keratinocyte adherence. J Invest Dermatol 84:378, 1985

182. Wysocki AB, Grinnell F: Fibronectin profiles in normal and chronic wound fluid. Lab Invest 63:825, 1990

183. Madden JW, Peacock EE Jr: Studies on the biology of collagen during wound healing: 3. Dynamic

metabolism of scar collagen and remodeling of dermal wounds. Ann Surg 174:511, 1971

184. Detmar M, Brown LF, Berse B, et al: Hypoxia regulates the expression of vascular permeability factor/vascular endothelial growth factor (VPF/VEGF) and its receptors in human skin. J Invest Dermatol 108:263, 1997

185. Nadav L, Eldor A, Yacoby-Zeevi O, et al: Activation, processing and trafficking of extracellular heparanase by primary human fibroblasts. J Cell Sci 115:2179, 2002

186. Ilan N, Mahooti S, Madri JA: Distinct signal transduction pathways are utilized during the tube formation and survival phases of in vitro angiogenesis. J Cell Sci 111:3621, 1998

187. Gabbiani G, Ryan GB, Majne G: Presence of modified fibroblasts in granulation tissue and their possible role in wound contraction. Experientia 27:549, 1971

188. Desmouliere A, Chaponnier C, Gabbiani G: Tissue repair, contraction, and the myofibroblast. Wound Repair Regen 13:7, 2005

189. Riley WB Jr, Peacock EE Jr: Identification, distribution, and significance of a collagenolytic enzyme in human tissues. Proc Soc Exp Biol Med 124:207, 1967

Acknowledgments

Figures 1 and 4 Thom Graves, CMI.

Figure 2 Janet Betries.

Figure 3 Carol Donner.

12 ORAL CAVITY LESIONS

David P. Goldstein, M.D., Henry T. Hoffman, M.D., F.A.C.S., John W. Hellstein, D.D.S., and Gerry F. Funk, M.D., F.A.C.S.

Approach to Oral Cavity Lesions

The oral cavity is a complex structure that plays a role in many important functions, including mastication, swallowing, speech, and respiration. It extends from the vermilion border of the lips to the oropharynx and is separated from the oropharynx by the anterior tonsillar pillars, the junction of the hard and soft palates, and the junction between the base of the tongue and the oral tongue at the circumvallate papillae.

In most cases, lesions of the oral cavity reflect locally confined processes, but on occasion, they are manifestations of systemic disease. The cause of an oral cavity lesion can usually be identified by the history and the physical examination; however, it is most often determined definitively by either a response to a therapeutic trial or a biopsy. A systematic classification of oral cavity lesions facilitates the development of a differential diagnosis. One approach to classification is based on the appearance of the lesion (e.g., white, red, pigmented, ulcerative, vesiculobullous, raised, or cystic). Another approach is first to categorize the lesion as either neoplastic or nonneoplastic and then to further divide the non-neoplastic lesions into various subcategories (e.g., infectious, inflammatory, vascular, traumatic, and tumorlike) [*see Table 1*]. In the following discussion, we adopt the second approach.

Clinical Evaluation

HISTORY

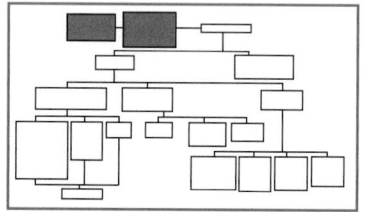

The onset, duration, and growth rate of the oral lesion should be determined. Inflammatory lesions usually have an acute onset and are self-limited, and they may be recurrent. Neoplasms tend to exhibit progressive enlargement; a rapid growth rate is suggestive of malignancy. It is often possible to identify specific events (e.g., upper respiratory tract infection, oral trauma, or medications) that precipitated the lesions. Both malignancies and inflammatory conditions may be associated with various nonspecific symptoms, including pain and dysphagia. Symptoms suggestive of malignancy include trismus, bleeding, a change in denture fit or occlusion, facial sensory changes, and referred otalgia. Fever, night sweats, and weight loss may occur in various settings but are particularly associated with lymphomas and systemic inflammatory conditions. Some oral lesions are identified without presenting signs or symptoms as incidental findings noted during a general dental or medical examination.[1]

A review of systems may uncover signs (e.g., rashes or arthritis) that suggest a possible autoimmune disorder. The medical history should always address previous or current connective tissue diseases, malignancies, radiation therapy, chemotherapy, and HIV infection. It is especially important to elicit a medication history because many classes of medications cause drug eruptions that involve the oral mucosa: for instance, well over 100 medications are associated with lichenoid drug reaction, and even more are associated with xerostomia. Use of alcohol or tobacco is a notable risk factor for the development of oral cavity carcinoma, as is a previous head and neck carcinoma. The quantity of alcohol or tobacco consumed should be determined because a dose-response relationship exists between the level of use and the risk of cancer. Other risk factors for oral cavity carcinoma include sun exposure (lip cancer), human papillomavirus infection, and nutritional deficiencies. Radiation exposure is a risk factor for soft tissue sarcoma, lymphoma, and minor salivary gland tumors, and HIV infection is a risk factor for Kaposi sarcoma.

PHYSICAL EXAMINATION

The head and neck should be examined in an organized and systematic manner. Illumination with a headlight or a reflecting mirror facilitates oral examination by freeing the examiner's hands for use in retracting the cheeks and the tongue.

The mucosa of the oral cavity is evaluated at each of the oral subsites [*see Figure 1*]. Any trismus should be noted, as should the general health of the teeth and the gingiva. Percussion of carious teeth with pulpitis often elicits pain, though this is not always the case if caries is shallow or pulpal necrosis is present. Palpation of the tongue, the floor of the mouth, and the oral vestibule is an essential component of oral examination. Palpation of the submandibular and submental regions is best performed bimanually.

Oral lesions should be characterized in terms of color, depth, location, texture, fixation, and other applicable attributes. When cancer is present, tenderness, induration, and fixation are common. Invasion of surrounding structures (e.g., the mandible, the parotid duct, or the teeth) by a malignant lesion should be noted. Physical examination is not a definitive means of detecting mandibular invasion, because tumor fixation can be secondary to other factors and cortical invasion can occur with minimal fixation.[2] In addition, lesions in some areas of the oral cavity (e.g., the hard palate and the attached gingiva) almost always appear to be fixed.

A history of otalgia warrants otoscopic examination. Otalgia in the absence of any identifiable pathologic condition of the ear often represents referred pain from a malignancy of the upper aerodigestive tract. The presence of otalgia in a middle-aged person should always trigger a search for an underlying cause. The nasal cavity should be examined with a speculum to rule out tumor extension in lesions of the hard palate, and transnasal fiberoptic pharyngoscopy and laryngoscopy should be done if a malignant neoplasm is a possibility or if a systemic condition is suspected that may also affect the nasal or pharyngeal mucosa.

Examination of the neck may reveal enlarged lymph nodes. Lymphadenopathy in an adult should be considered to represent metastatic cancer until proved otherwise. A benign ulcer in the oral cavity may cause a reactive adenopathy as a consequence of the associated inflammation, but in the setting of cervical lymphadenopathy, the initial diagnostic assumptions should emphasize the strong possibility of a primary oral cancer with metastases to the neck. Asymmetrical enlargement of the parotid or submandibular glands may result either from obstruction of the ducts by an oral cavity mass or from enlargement of nodes intimately associated with the glands. Symmetrical enlargement suggests a systemic process (e.g., Sjögren syndrome or HIV infection). The

Table 1 **Differential Diagnosis of Oral Cavity Lesions Based on Etiology**

Inflammatory lesions	Infectious
	  Viral
	    Herpes simplex
	    Herpes zoster
	    Cytomegalovirus
	    Herpangina
	    Hand, foot, and mouth disease
	    Oral hairy leukoplakia (Epstein-Barr virus)
	  Bacterial
	    Mycobacterial infection
	    Syphilis
	    Gingivostomatitis
	  Fungal
	    Candidiasis
	    Coccidioidomycosis
	Noninfectious
	    Recurrent aphthous stomatitis
	    Traumatic ulcer
	    Autoimmune disorders
	    Behçet syndrome
	    SLE
	    Wegener granulomatosis
	    Sarcoidosis
	    Amyloidosis
	    Pemphigus and pemphigoid
	    Pyogenic granuloma
	    Necrotizing sialometaplasia
	    Lichen planus

Tumorlike lesions	Mucocele Ranula Tori Fibroma Odontogenic cysts

Neoplasms	Benign
	  Squamous papilloma
	  Minor salivary gland neoplasms
	  Ameloblastoma
	  Hemangioma
	  Granular cell tumor
	  Brown tumor
	  Neuroma, schwannoma, neurofibroma
	  Osteoma, chondroma
	Malignant
	  Squamous cell carcinoma
	  Verrucous carcinoma
	  Minor salivary gland malignancies
	  Mucoepidermoid carcinoma
	  Adenoid cystic carcinoma
	  Polymorphous low-grade adenocarcinoma
	  Mucosal melanoma
	  Kaposi sarcoma
	  Lymphoma
	  Osteosarcoma

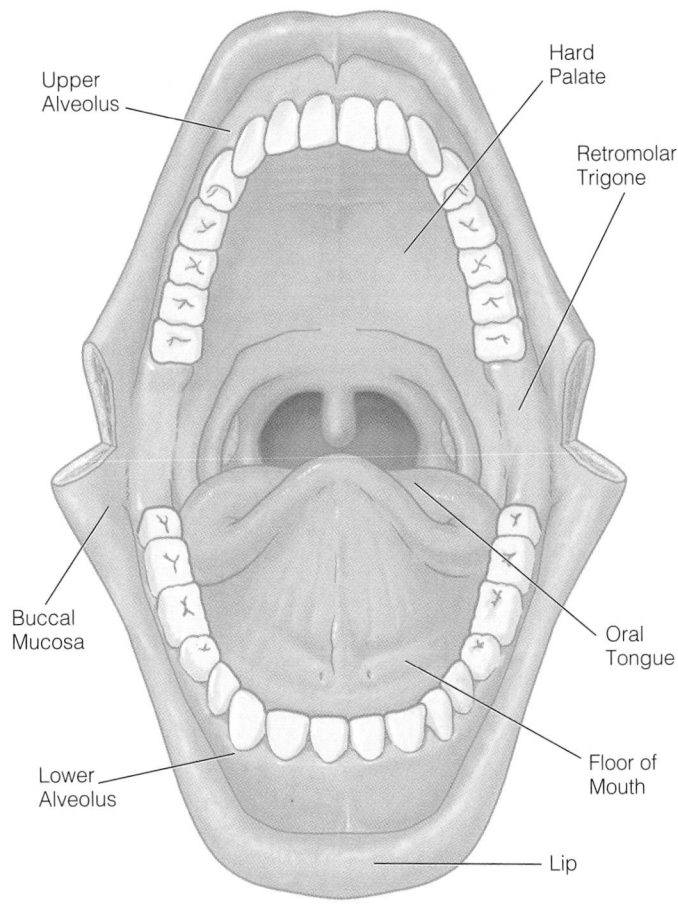

Figure 1 **Depicted are the major anatomic subsites of the oral cavity.**

cranial nerves should be examined, with particular attention focused on the trigeminal, facial, and hypoglossal nerves.

Investigative Studies

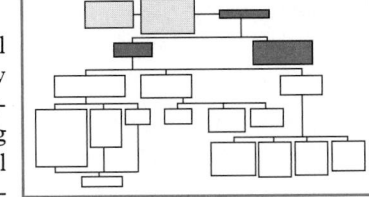

The history and physical examination should narrow down the differential diagnosis and lead to a working diagnosis. If a benign local process (e.g., aphthous stomatitis, traumatic ulcer, or viral infection) is suspected, no further investigation, other than reevaluation, may be needed. If the lesion persists or progresses, further investigation is warranted.

LABORATORY TESTS

Laboratory studies are usually not beneficial in the initial workup of oral cavity lesions. If a connective tissue disease is suspected, serologic tests [*see Table 2*] and referral to a rheumatologist or another appropriate specialist may be considered.

IMAGING

The value of advanced imaging with computed tomography, magnetic resonance imaging, or both in the management of oral cavity lesions has not been firmly established. Accordingly, judgment must be exercised. There is evidence to suggest that early oral cavity malignancies can be managed without either CT or MRI. Nevertheless, many clinicians obtain these studies in all

Approach to Oral Cavity Lesions

Patient presents with oral cavity lesion

Obtain clinical history.
- Onset, duration, progression, precipitating events, previous oral lesions
- Associated symptoms
- Review of systems
- Risk factors for malignancy

Perform head and neck exam.
- Visual assessment of mucosa of oral cavity subsites
- Color, depth, location, texture, and fixation of lesions
- Ear exam, especially for otalgia
- Neck exam for adenopathy
- Nasal exam for palatal or upper alveolar lesions or systemic diseases
- Exam of oropharynx, larynx, and hypopharynx if malignancy suspected

Diagnosis is probable

Estimate likelihood of malignancy.

Index of suspicion for malignancy is low

Further investigation with culture and sensitivity, lab tests, or imaging may be warranted, depending on working diagnosis.
Generally, these conditions can be managed with observation, symptomatic treatment, or therapeutic trial.

Lesion is suspected of being premalignant (leukoplakia or erythroplakia)

- *Small lesions:* perform excisional biopsy.
- *Larger lesions:* perform incisional biopsy.
Treat specific lesion.

Inflammatory lesion

Infectious
- *Viral:* symptomatic treatment, antivirals if patient is immunocompromised
- *Bacterial:* antibiotics
- *Fungal:* antifungals, usually topical (systemic for persistent infection)
- *Oral hairy leukoplakia or unusual infection:* rule out HIV infection, refer patient to infectious disease specialist

Noninfectious
- *Aphthous ulcer:* symptomatic treatment, topical anti-inflammatories
- *Traumatic ulcer:* symptomatic treatment
- *Autoimmune:* symptomatic treatment, topical or systemic steroids
- *Necrotizing sialometaplasia:* observation, biopsy to rule out cancer

Tumorlike lesion

- *Torus:* intervention only if denture fit affected
- *Cyst:* observation or excision
- *Fibroma:* observation or excision
- *Odontogenic cyst:* excision or debridement; tooth extraction for dentigerous cyst

Benign neoplasm

Treat with local excision.

Hyperkeratosis

Observe; repeat biopsy if changes noted.

If lesion persists or therapeutic trial fails, perform biopsy.

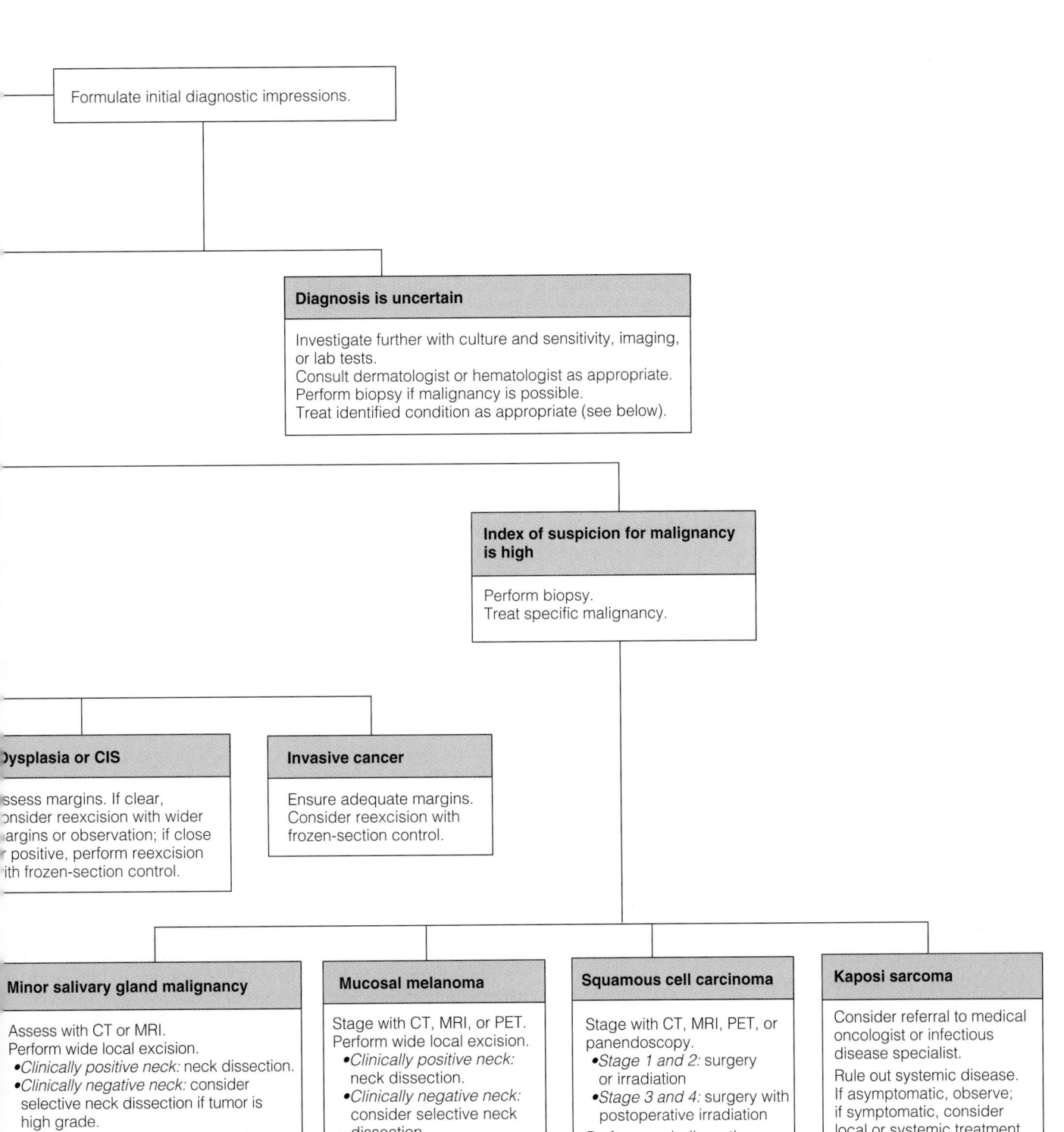

Formulate initial diagnostic impressions.

Diagnosis is uncertain

Investigate further with culture and sensitivity, imaging, or lab tests.
Consult dermatologist or hematologist as appropriate.
Perform biopsy if malignancy is possible.
Treat identified condition as appropriate (see below).

Index of suspicion for malignancy is high

Perform biopsy.
Treat specific malignancy.

Dysplasia or CIS

Assess margins. If clear, consider reexcision with wider margins or observation; if close or positive, perform reexcision with frozen-section control.

Invasive cancer

Ensure adequate margins.
Consider reexcision with frozen-section control.

Minor salivary gland malignancy

Assess with CT or MRI.
Perform wide local excision.
• *Clinically positive neck:* neck dissection.
• *Clinically negative neck:* consider selective neck dissection if tumor is high grade.
Consider postoperative irradiation for high-grade tumor or perineural spread.

Mucosal melanoma

Stage with CT, MRI, or PET.
Perform wide local excision.
• *Clinically positive neck:* neck dissection.
• *Clinically negative neck:* consider selective neck dissection.
Consider postoperative irradiation.

Squamous cell carcinoma

Stage with CT, MRI, PET, or panendoscopy.
• *Stage 1 and 2:* surgery or irradiation
• *Stage 3 and 4:* surgery with postoperative irradiation
Perform neck dissection as indicated.

Kaposi sarcoma

Consider referral to medical oncologist or infectious disease specialist.
Rule out systemic disease. If asymptomatic, observe; if symptomatic, consider local or systemic treatment.

cases of malignancy and in most cases of suspected malignancy. CT and MRI can help assess the size and location of the lesion and determine the degree to which surrounding structures are involved. In patients with oral cavity carcinoma, imaging facilitates the staging of tumors and the planning of treatment. In patients with cervical metastases, physical examination augmented by MRI and CT has a better diagnostic yield than physical examination alone. Bone-window CT scans are particularly helpful for assessing invasion of the mandible, the maxilla, the cervical spine, and the base of the skull. CT scans are highly sensitive and specific for detecting mandibular invasion.[2,3] MRI provides better soft tissue delineation than CT, with fewer dental artifacts, and therefore is particularly valuable for assessing malignancies of the tongue, the floor of the mouth, and the salivary glands. Loss of the usual marrow enhancement on T_1-weighted MRI images suggests bone invasion, though this is not a specific finding. Chest x-ray, CT, or both may be employed to search for lung metastases or a second primary tumor.

Positron emission tomography (PET) is playing an increasingly important role in the workup of patients with head and neck carcinoma or mucosal melanoma. PET is useful for confirming the presence of a malignancy, as well as for assessing cervical and distant metastases[4-6]; it is particularly valuable for detecting recurrent or persistent disease.[7] Drawbacks include frequent false positive results with active inflammation, high cost, and limited availability. In addition, the quality of the PET images obtained and the level of technical experience available vary considerably among institutions. Although broad guidelines have been developed for certifying physicians in the use of PET, the specific expertise needed for optimal imaging of the complexities of the head and neck is not easily acquired.

BIOPSY

For oral cavity lesions that are suggestive of malignancy or are probably of neoplastic origin, biopsy is usually required. A brief observation period to allow reevaluation, with biopsy withheld, may be warranted if a response to therapy or spontaneous resolution is possible. The potential morbidity associated with a biopsy done in a previously irradiated region should be considered in deciding whether biopsy is advisable. Specimens are usually sent to the pathologist in 10% buffered formalin, but there are notable exceptions. If a lymphoma is suspected, specimens should be sent without formalin for genetic testing and flow cytometry. If an autoimmune disease is suspected, special tests requiring immunofluorescence are indicated, and specimens should be sent either fresh or in Michel solution. In addition, if fungal, mycobacterial,

Table 2 Serologic Tests for Diagnosing Connective Tissue Disease

Connective Tissue Disease	Serologic Tests
SLE	CBC, antinuclear antibody, anti–double-stranded DNA antibody, anti-Smith antibody
Sjögren syndrome	Antinuclear antibody, rheumatoid factor, anti-Ro (SS-A), and anti-La (SS-B) antibodies
Wegener granulomatosis	cANCA, serum creatinine level, urine microscopy
Sarcoidosis	Serum calcium and ACE levels

ACE—angiotensin-converting enzyme cANCA—cytoplasmic antineutrophil cytoplasmic antibodies CBC—complete blood count SLE—systemic lupus erythematosus

bacterial, or viral infection is suspected, a small portion of a specimen may be sent separately for culture. If there is an associated neck mass [see 14 Neck Mass], fine-needle aspiration (FNA) may be performed to rule out metastatic disease. In general, FNA is not useful for biopsy of oral lesions: incisional biopsy is often technically easier and provides more tissue.

EXAMINATION UNDER ANESTHESIA AND PANENDOSCOPY

In patients with oral carcinoma, examination under anesthesia (EUA) and panendoscopy may be performed either before or during operation to assess the extent of the primary tumor and identify any synchronous tumors. Both EUA and panendoscopy are commonly performed in the operating room with the patient under general anesthesia. Panendoscopy involves endoscopic examination of the larynx, the oropharynx, the hypopharynx, the esophagus, and, occasionally, the nasopharynx. As a rule, assessment of the tumor and neck is more accurately performed when the patient is relaxed under a general anesthetic. With improved imaging techniques and the wider availability of office endoscopes, the role of panendoscopy is decreasing.

Diagnosis and Management of Specific Oral Cavity Lesions

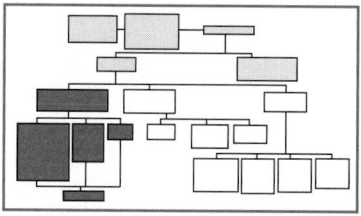

INFLAMMATORY LESIONS

Infectious

Viral stomatitis may be caused by a number of different viruses, including herpes simplex virus (type 1 or type 2), varicella-zoster virus, and coxsackievirus [see Figures 2a and 2b].[8] It is most common in children and immunocompromised patients. The lesions of viral stomatitis are generally vesicular, occur in the oral cavity and the oropharynx, and erupt over the course of several days to form painful ulcers. Eruption may be preceded by local symptoms (e.g., burning, itching, or tingling) or systemic symptoms (e.g., fever, rash, malaise, or lymphadenopathy). The diagnosis is usually established by the history and the physical examination and may be confirmed by means of biopsy or viral culture.

Treatment of viral stomatitis primarily involves managing symptoms with oral rinses, topical anesthetics, hydration, and antipyretics. Systemic antiviral medications may shorten the course of herpetic stomatitis and are indicated in immunocompromised patients.[9]

Candidiasis is a common fungal infection of the oral cavity [see Figures 2c and 2d]. Candida albicans is the species most commonly responsible; however, other Candida species can cause this condition as well, with C. glabrata emerging as a growing problem in immunocompromised hosts. Factors predisposing to oral candidal infection include immunosupression, use of broad-spectrum antibiotics, diabetes, prolonged use of local or systemic steroids, and xerostomia.[10] Oral candidiasis presents in several different forms [see Table 3], of which pseudomembranous candidiasis (thrush) is the most common. This form is characterized by white, curdlike plaques on the oral mucosa that may be wiped off (with difficulty) to leave an erythematous, painful base (the Auspitz sign). Widespread oral and pharyngeal involvement is common. The diagnosis is based on the clinical appearance of the lesion and on evaluation of scrapings with the potassium hydroxide (KOH) test. Culture is generally not useful, because Candida is a common commensal oral organism.[11]

Ideally, initial management of oral candidiasis is aimed at

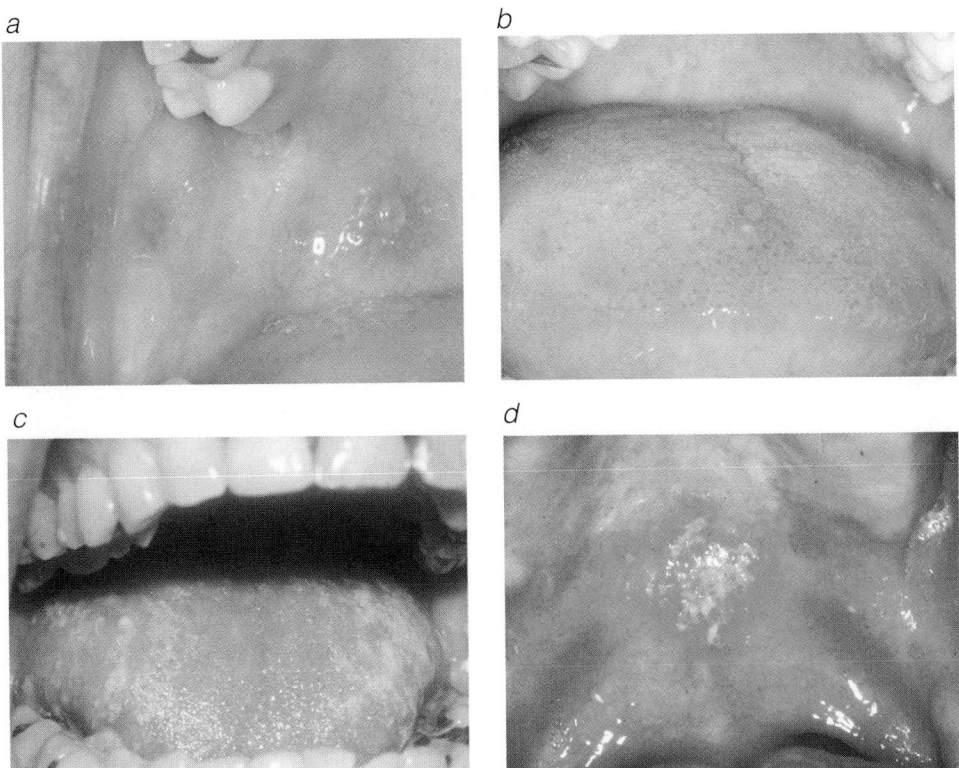

Figure 2 Shown are infectious lesions of the oral cavity: (*a*) primary herpes stomatitis of the buccal mucosa and soft palate; (*b*) primary herpes stomatitis of the tongue (in the same patient as in frame *a*); (*c*) oral candidiasis (pseudomembranous form); and (*d*) oral candidiasis (erythematous form).

reversing the underlying condition, though this is not always possible. Treatment typically involves either topically administered antifungal agents or, if infection is severe or topical therapy fails, systemically administered antifungals. Patients who are immunocompromised or have xerostomia may benefit from long-term prophylaxis.

Noninfectious

Recurrent aphthous stomatitis Aphthous stomatitis is a common idiopathic ulcerative condition of the oral cavity [*see Figures 3a and 3b*]. The ulcers are typically painful and may occur anywhere in the oral cavity and the oropharynx but are rarely found on the hard palate, the dorsal tongue, and the attached gingiva.[9] Affected patients often have a history of lesions, beginning before adolescence. There are three different clinical presentations of recurrent aphthous stomatitis, of which minor aphthous

ulcers are the most common [*see Table 4*].[9] The diagnosis is made on the basis of the history and the physical examination; biopsy is reserved for lesions that do not heal or that grow in size.

Numerous therapies have been tried for recurrent aphthous stomatitis, most with only minimal success. The majority of aphthous ulcers heal within 10 to 14 days and require no treatment; however, patients with severe symptoms may require medical intervention. Temporary pain relief can be obtained with topical anesthetic agents (e.g., viscous lidocaine). Tetracycline oral suspension and antiseptic mouthwashes have also been used, with varying success.[9] Topical steroids are the mainstay of therapy and may shorten the duration of the ulcers if applied during the early phase.[11] These agents may be applied either in a solution (e.g., dexamethasone oral suspension, 0.5 mg/5 ml) or in an ointment (e.g., fluocinolone or clobetasol). Ointments work much better in the oral cavity than creams or gels do. Systemic steroids are indicated when the number of ulcers is large or when the outbreak has persisted for a long time.

Necrotizing sialometaplasia Necrotizing sialometaplasia is a rare benign inflammatory lesion of the minor salivary glands that resembles carcinoma clinically and histologically and is readily mistaken for it [*see Figure 3c*].[12] This condition most commonly develops in white males in the form of a deep, sudden ulcer of the hard palate. The presumed cause is ischemia of the minor salivary glands resulting from infection, trauma, surgery, irradiation, or irritation caused by ill-fitting dentures.[9] Biopsy is usually necessary to rule out squamous cell carcinoma or a minor salivary gland malignancy. Review of the tissue by a pathologist well versed in head and neck pathology is essential. Characteristic histologic findings include coagulation necrosis of the salivary gland acini,

Table 3 Clinical Presentation of Oral Candidiasis

Type of Oral Candidiasis	Presentation
Pseudomembranous	White, curdlike plaques on oral mucosa that when wiped off (with difficulty) leave erythematous, painful base
Hyperplastic	Thick white plaques on oral mucosa that cannot be rubbed off
Erythematous	Red, atrophic areas on palate or dorsum of tongue
Angular cheilitis	Cracking and fissuring at oral commissures

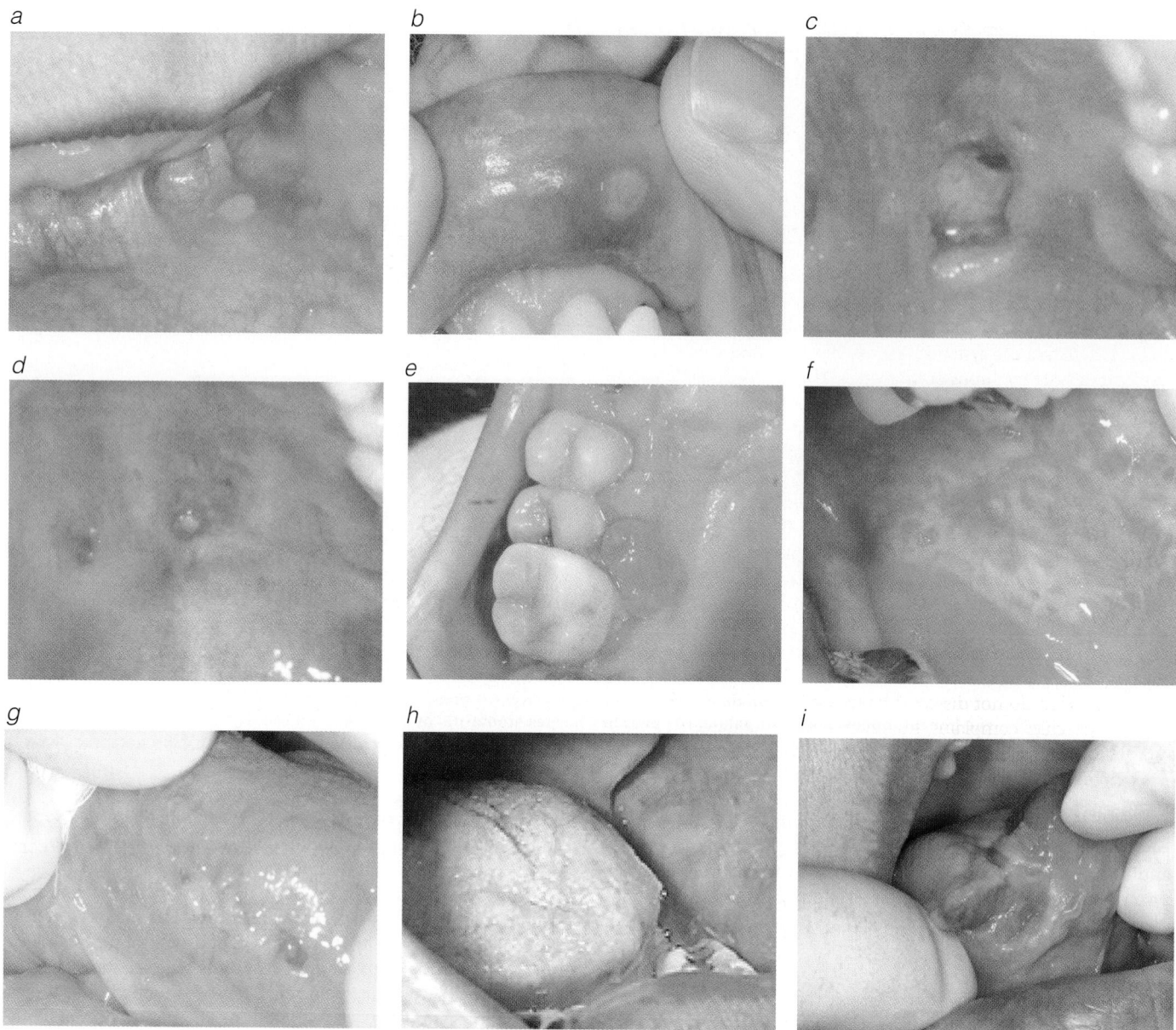

Figure 3 Shown are noninfectious inflammatory lesions of the oral cavity: (*a*) minor aphthous ulcer of the lower lip; (*b*) minor aphthous ulcer of the upper lip; (*c*) necrotizing sialometaplasia of the hard palate; (*d*) resolution of necrotizing sialometaplasia without treatment (in the same patient as in frame *c*); (*e*) pyogenic granuloma of the upper alveolus; (*f*) reticular lichen planus involving the buccal mucosa; (*g*) lichen planus of the lateral tongue; (*h*) pemphigus vulgaris of the oral cavity, with an erythematous base after rupture of bullae (involving the left lateral tongue, the buccal mucosa, and the lip); and (*i*) traumatic ulcer of the tongue secondary to dental trauma.

ductal squamous metaplasia, preservation of the lobular architecture, and a nonmalignant appearance of squamous nests.[12,13]

Lesions resolve without treatment within 6 to 10 weeks [*see Figure 3d*].

Pyogenic granuloma   A pyogenic granuloma is an aggregation of proliferating endothelial tissue [*see Figure 3e*] that occurs in response to chronic persistent irritation (e.g., from a calculus or a foreign body) or trauma.[10] The lesion appears as a raised, soft, sessile or pedunculated mass with a smooth, red surface that bleeds easily and can grow rapidly.[14] Surface ulceration may occur, but the ulcers are not invasive. The gingiva is the most common location, but any of the oral tissues may be involved.

Conservative excision with management of the underlying irri-

tant is the recommended treatment. The classic presentation is in a pregnant woman, and hormonal influences may have an additional influence on recurrence.

Lichen planus   Lichen planus is a common immune-mediated inflammatory mucocutaneous disease [*see Figures 3f and 3g*].[15] Clinically, idiopathic lichen planus is indistinguishable from lichenoid drug reaction. The reticular form of lichen planus is the most common one and presents as interlacing white keratotic striae on the buccal mucosa, the lateral tongue, and the palate.[15] Lichen planus is usually bilateral, symmetrical, and asymptomatic.[16] The symptomatic phases may wax and wane, with erythematous and ulcerative changes being the primary signs. Cutaneous lesions occur less frequently and appear as small, violaceous, pruritic papules. The diagnosis is generally made on the basis of the history and the physical examination; biopsy is not always necessary.

For asymptomatic lesions, no treatment is required other than observation.[17] For painful lesions, which are more common with the erosive form of the disease, either topical or systemic steroids are appropriate.[17] There is some controversy regarding the risk of malignant transformation; however, long-term follow-up is still recommended.[16,18] The main risk posed by lichen planus may be the masking effect that the white striae cause, which can prevent the clinician from observing the early leukoplakic and erythroplakic changes associated with epithelial dysplasia.

Ulcer from autoimmune disease Oral ulcers may be the first manifestation of a systemic illness. The most common oral manifestation of systemic lupus erythematosus (SLE) is the appearance of painful oral ulcers in women of childbearing age. Patients with Behçet disease present with the characteristic triad of painful oral ulcers, genital ulcers, and associated iritis or uveitis. Patients with Crohn disease or Wegener granulomatosis frequently manifest oral ulceration during the course of the illness. These disorders should be managed in conjunction with a rheumatologist.

Mucous membrane pemphigoid and pemphigus vulgaris are chronic vesiculobullous autoimmune diseases that frequently affect the oral mucosa [see Figure 3h]. In mucous membrane pemphigoid, the antibodies are directed at the mucosal basement membrane, resulting in subepithelial bullae.[16] These bullae rupture after 1 to 2 days to form painful ulcers, which may heal over a period of 1 to 2 weeks but often do not display a predictable periodicity. Oral pain is often the chief complaint, but there may be undetected ocular involvement that can lead to entropion and blindness.

Pemphigus vulgaris is a more severe disease than mucous membrane pemphigoid. In this condition, the antibodies are directed at intraepithelial adhesion molecules, leading to the formation of intraepithelial bullae.[9] The blisters are painful and easily ruptured and tend to occur throughout the oral cavity and the pharynx.[19] The Nikolsky sign (i.e., vesicle formation or sloughing when a lateral shearing force is applied to uninvolved oral mucosa or skin) is present in both pemphigus and pemphigoid. In most cases, biopsy with pathologic evaluation (including immunofluorescence studies) is

helpful in establishing the diagnosis. Circulating antibodies may be present in either condition but are more common in pemphigus. Serologic tests may suffice to establish the diagnosis, without any need for biopsy. Management involves administration of immunosuppressive agents, often in conjunction with a dermatologist.

Traumatic ulcer Trauma (e.g., from tooth abrasion, tooth brushing, poor denture fit, or burns) is a common cause of oral mucosal ulceration [see Figure 3i]. The ulcers usually are painful but typically are self-limited and resolve without treatment. Topical anesthetic agents may be beneficial if pain is severe enough to limit oral intake.

Tumorlike Lesions

TORUS MANDIBULARIS AND TORUS PALATINUS

Palatal and mandibular tori are benign focal overgrowths of cortical bone [see Figures 4a and 4b].[10] They appear as slow-growing, asymptomatic, firm, submucosal bony masses developing on the lingual surface of the mandible or the midline of the hard palate.[14] When these lesions occur on the labial or buccal aspect of the mandible and the maxilla, they are termed exostosis.[20] Torus mandibularis tends to occur bilaterally, whereas torus palatinus arises as a singular, often lobulated mass in the midline of the hard palate. Surgical management is required only if the tori are interfering with denture fit.

MUCOCELE AND MUCOUS RETENTION CYST

A mucocele is a pseudocyst that develops when injury to a minor salivary gland duct causes extravasation of mucous, surrounding inflammation, and formation of a pseudocapsule [see Figures 4c and 4d].[14] Mucoceles are soft, compressible, bluish or translucent masses that may fluctuate in size. They are most commonly seen on the lower lip but also may develop on the buccal mucosa, anterior ventral tongue, and floor of the mouth. Only very rarely do they involve the upper lip; masses in the upper lip, even if they are fluctuant, should be assumed to be neoplastic, developmental, or infectious. Treatment involves excision of the mucocele and its associated minor salivary gland.

A ranula (from a diminutive form of the Latin word for frog) is a mucocele that develops in the floor of the mouth as a consequence of obstruction of the sublingual duct,[16] secondary either to trauma or to sublingual gland sialoliths. If the ranula extends through the mylohyoid muscle into the neck, it is referred to as a plunging ranula. A plunging ranula may present as a submental or submandibular neck mass. Imaging helps delineate the extent of the mass and may confirm the presence of a sialolith. The recommended treatment is excision of the ranula with removal of the sublingual gland and often the adjacent submandibular gland. Marsupialization is an option but is associated with a relatively high recurrence rate.[21]

A mucous retention cyst (salivary duct cyst) is usually the result of partial obstruction of a salivary gland duct accompanied by mucous accumulation and ductal dilatation [see Figure 4e].[21] It is a soft, compressible mass that may occur at any location in the oral cavity where minor salivary glands are present. Treatment involves surgical excision with removal of the associated minor salivary gland.

FIBROMA

A fibroma is a hyperplastic response to inflammation or trauma [see Figures 4f and 4g].[22] It is a pedunculated soft or firm mass

Table 4 Clinical Presentation of Aphthous Stomatitis

Type of Aphthous Ulcer	Presentation	Time to Resolution
Minor	Multiple painful, well-demarcated ulcers, < 1.0 cm in diameter, are noted, with yellow fibrinoid base and surrounding erythema; typically involve mobile mucosa, with tongue, palate, and anterior tonsillar pillar the most common sites	7–10 days, without scarring
Major (Sutton disease)	Ulcers, often multiple, may range in size from a few millimeters to 3 cm and may penetrate deeply with elevated margins; typically involve mobile mucosa, with tongue, palate, and anterior tonsillar pillar the most common sites	4–6 wk, with scarring
Herpetiform	Small (1–3 mm) ulcers occur in "crops" but are still limited to movable mucosal surfaces; gingival involvement, if present, is caused by extension from nonkeratinizing crevicular epithelium	1–2 wk

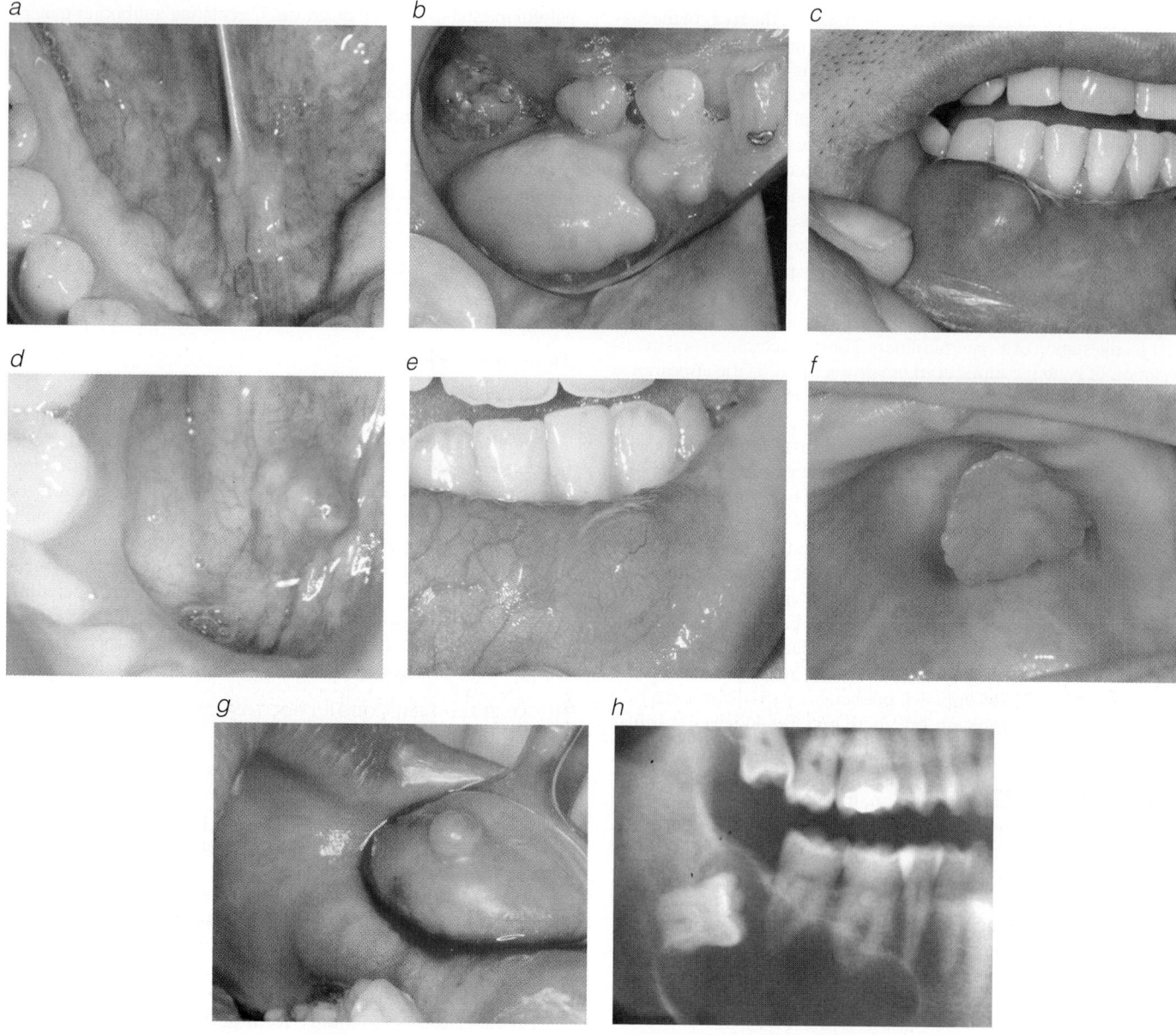

Figure 4 Shown are tumorlike lesions of the oral cavity: (*a*) torus mandibularis, with bilateral bony protuberances on the lingual surface of the mandible; (*b*) mandibular exostosis, with a unilateral bony protuberance on the labial-buccal surface of the mandible; (*c*) mucocele of the lip (note the bluish hue of the cystic lesion; cf. frame *e*); (*d*) mucocele of the floor of the mouth associated with the sublingual gland (ranula); (*e*) mucous retention cyst of the lower lip (presenting much like mucocele, but appearing more transparent); (*f*) fibroma of the hard palate resulting from denture trauma; (*g*) fibroma of the lower lip; and (*h*) dentigerous cyst (a unilocular radiolucency surrounding the crown of an unerupted tooth, with no bone destruction).

with a smooth mucosal surface that may be located anywhere in the mouth. Such lesions are managed with either observation or local excision.

ODONTOGENIC CYST

A dentigerous cyst is an epithelium-lined cyst that, by definition, is associated with the crown of an unerupted tooth [*see Figure 4h*]. Such cysts cause painless expansion of the mandible or the maxilla. Treatment involves enucleation of the cyst and its lining and extraction of the associated tooth.[23]

An odontogenic keratocyst is a squamous epithelium–lined cyst that produces keratin. Bone resorption occurs secondary to

pressure resorption and to inflammation caused by retained keratin. Management involves either excision or debridement and creation of a well-ventilated and easily maintained cavity.[24]

Neoplastic Lesions

BENIGN

Squamous Papilloma

Squamous papilloma is one of the most common benign neoplasms of the oral cavity [*see Figures 5a and 5b*].[13] It usually presents as a solitary, slow-growing, asymptomatic lesion, typically

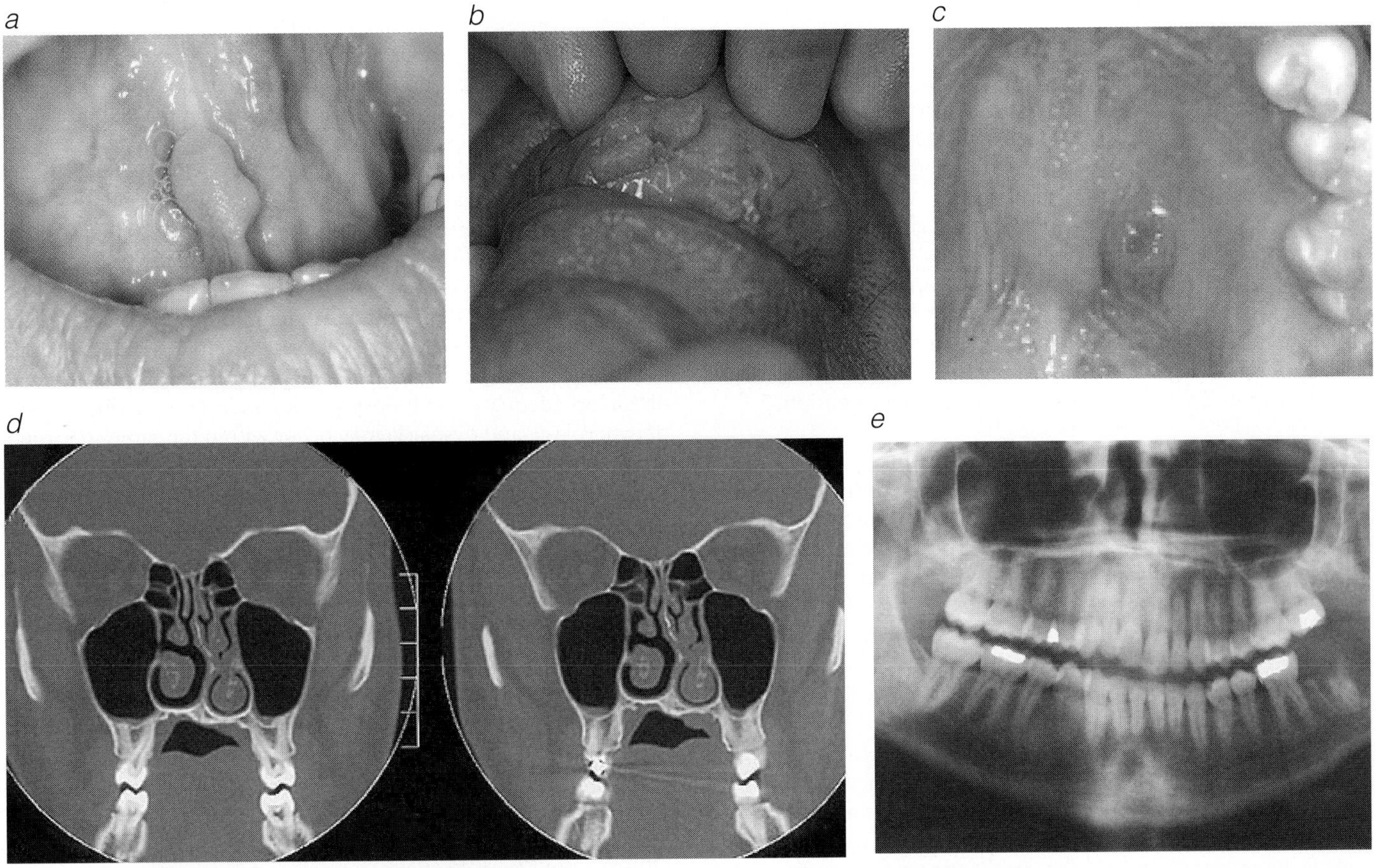

a *b* *c*

d *e*

f

Figure 5 Shown are benign neoplasms of the oral cavity: (*a*) squamous papilloma of the frenulum; (*b*) squamous papilloma of the ventral tongue; (*c*) pleomorphic adenoma of the hard palate; (*d*) pleomorphic adenoma of the hard palate on coronal CT (note the soft tissue thickening along the left hard palate, with no bone erosion or destruction); (*e*) ameloblastoma of the left angle and ramus of the mandible (a multilocular radiolucency); and (*f*) ameloblastoma on CT, with a soft tissue mass in the left mandible and erosion of the lingual plate of the mandible.

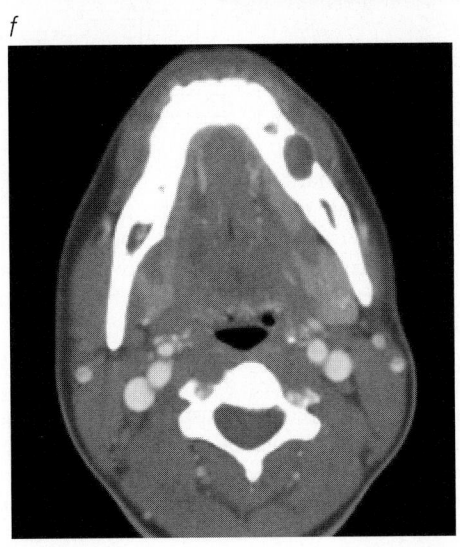

less than 1 cm in diameter. It is well circumscribed and pedunculated and has a warty appearance.[16] The palate and tongue are the sites most frequently affected[13]; occasionally, multiple sites are involved. The presumed cause is a viral infection, most likely human papillomavirus.[25]

Papillomas are managed with complete excision, including the base of the stalk.

Giant Cell Lesions

Central giant cell granulomas, brown tumors of hyperparathyroidism, aneurysmal bone cysts, and lesions associated with genetic diseases (e.g., cherubism) may all be seen in the jaws. Of particular note is the aneurysmal bone cyst that may occur at sites of trauma, which, in theory, is the consequence of an organizing

hematoma that leads to bony expansion and giant cell proliferation.[26] Eventually, erosion of the buccal cortex may occur with the development of facial swelling.

Management involves enucleation and curettage.[26] The surgeon should be prepared for bleeding during treatment. The use of calcitonin or intralesional steroid injections is gaining popularity.

Minor Salivary Gland Neoplasms

The minor salivary glands are small mucus-secreting glands that are distributed throughout the upper aerodigestive tract, with the largest proportion concentrated in the oral cavity. Minor salivary gland neoplasms are uncommon, but when they do occur, they are most likely to develop in the oral cavity. Within the oral cavity, the hard palate and the soft palate are the most common sites of minor salivary gland neoplasms; however, tumors involving the tongue, the lips, the buccal mucosa, and the gingivae have been described. Approximately 30% of minor salivary gland neoplasms are benign. Of these benign lesions, the most common is pleomorphic adenoma, which presents as a painless, slow-growing submucosal mass [*see Figures 5c and 5d*].[13,27]

Pleomorphic adenoma is managed with complete surgical excision to clear margins. This tumor exhibits small pseudopodlike extensions that may persist and cause recurrence if enucleation around an apparent capsule is attempted.

Granular Cell Tumor

A granular cell tumor is a benign neoplasm that is thought to arise from Schwann cells.[13] It usually presents as a small, asymptomatic, solitary submucosal mass. The lateral border and the dorsal surface of the tongue are the sites where this tumor is most frequently found in the oral cavity.[28] Pathologic examination may reveal pseudoepitheliomatous hyperplasia, which is similar in appearance to well-differentiated squamous cell carcinoma.[29] This similarity has led to reports of misdiagnosis on histopathologic evaluation. Accordingly, given the known rarity of squamous cell carcinoma of the dorsal surface of the anterior two thirds of the tongue, it may be prudent to obtain a second histopathologic opinion whenever a diagnosis of squamous cell carcinoma is rendered in this location. Treatment consists of conservative excision.[28]

Ameloblastoma

Ameloblastoma is a neoplasm that arises from odontogenic (dental) epithelium, most frequently in the third and fourth decades of life [see Figures 5e and 5f].[22] It often presents as a painless swelling with bony enlargement. Approximately 80% of ameloblastomas involve the mandible and 20% the maxilla[30]; the mandibular ramus is the most common site.[30] Ameloblastomas are usually benign but are often locally aggressive and infiltrative. Malignant ameloblastomas are rare but are notable for being associated with pain, rapid growth, and metastases.[11]

On CT and panoramic jaw films, ameloblastomas typically appear as multilocular radiolucent lesions with a honeycomb appearance and scalloped borders.[31] These tumors are often associated with an unerupted third molar tooth and, with the exception of the desmoplastic variant, rarely appear radiopaque. They may also appear unilocular on radiographic imaging.[32] Histologic examination shows proliferating odontogenic epithelium with palisading peripheral cells that display reverse polarization of the nuclei.[13]

Appropriate management of ameloblastomas involves resection to clear margins. For mandibular ameloblastomas, either a marginal or a segmental mandibulectomy is done, depending on the relation of the lesion to the inferior cortical border. Curettage is associated with a high recurrence rate.[33] The prognosis for maxillary multicystic ameloblastoma is relatively poor because of the higher recurrence rate and the greater frequency of invasion of local adjacent structures (e.g., the skull base).[34]

Most types of mesenchymal neoplasms may be found also in the oral region. Benign mesenchymal neoplasms known to occur in the oral cavity include (but are not limited to) hemangiomas, lipomas, schwannomas, neuromas, and neurofibromas. These are relatively rare lesions but should nonetheless be included in the differential diagnosis of intraoral masses. The diagnosis is usually made on the basis of histopathologic examination of biopsy specimens. Benign bone tumors, though uncommon, are not unknown. Chondromas, hemangiomas, ossifying fibromas, and osteomas may all present as intraoral masses with bony expansion and normal overlying mucosa.

PREMALIGNANT

Leukoplakia

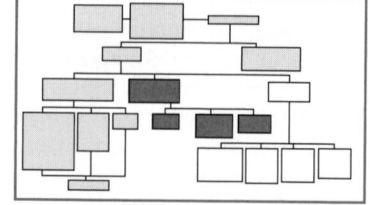

Leukoplakia is defined by the World Health Organization as a whitish patch or plaque that cannot be characterized clinically or pathologically as any other disease and that is not associated with any physical or chemical causative agent (except tobacco).[35] It is often considered a potentially premalignant lesion. Leukoplakic lesions vary in size, shape, and consistency; there is usually no relationship between morphologic appearance and histologic diagnosis. Histologic examination may reveal hyperkeratosis, dysplasia, carcinoma in situ (CIS), or invasive squamous cell carcinoma, or other pathologic processes.[16] Dysplasia occurs in as many as 30% of leukoplakic lesions.[8] Whereas a small percentage of lesions show invasive squamous cell carcinoma on pathologic examination,[14] 60% of oral mucosa carcinomas present as white, keratotic lesions.[16]

All leukoplakic lesions should undergo biopsy. For small areas of leukoplakia, excisional biopsy is usually appropriate. For larger lesions, incisional biopsy is generally preferable: it is important to obtain an adequate-size biopsy specimen, in that varying degrees of hyperplasia and dysplasia may occur within the same specimen. Hyperkeratotic lesions may be followed on a long-term basis, with rebiopsy performed if there are any changes in size or appearance. Lesions characterized by dysplasia and CIS should be completely excised to clear margins when possible.

Erythroplakia

Erythroplakia is defined as a red or erythematous patch of the oral mucosa. It is associated with significantly higher rates of dysplasia, CIS, and invasive carcinoma than leukoplakia is.[8] Erythroplakia is managed in much the same fashion as leukoplakia, with biopsy performed to rule out a malignant or premalignant lesion. Complete surgical excision is indicated if either a malignancy or a premalignancy is confirmed, and frequent follow-up is necessary.

MALIGNANT

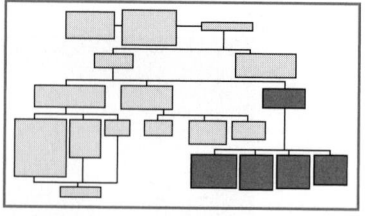

Minor Salivary Gland Malignancies

The majority (60% to 70%) of minor salivary gland neoplasms are malignant, with adenoid cystic carcinoma, mucoepidermoid carcinoma, and adenocarcinoma [see Figure 6a] being the most commonly encountered cancers.[27,36] As with benign minor salivary gland neoplasms, the hard and soft palates are the most common sites.[36]

A minor salivary gland malignancy usually appears as a painless, slow-growing intraoral mass.[37] Nodal involvement at presentation is uncommon.[27] Treatment usually involves surgical excision; adequate margins should be obtained with frozen-section control. Because these malignancies—particularly adenoid cystic carcinoma and polymorphous low-grade adenocarcinoma—have a propensity for perineural spread, frozen-section analysis of the nerves within the field of resection is usually obtained at the time of operation. If perineural spread occurs, postoperative irradiation is usually indicated, and distant metastases are likely to develop despite surgery and locoregional radiotherapy. As a result, it is usually best to limit the extent of the operation if major morbidity is anticipated from a radical resection.

Neck dissection is warranted in the treatment of minor salivary gland malignancies only if there is clinical or radiographic evidence of cervical metastases. Postoperative irradiation is indicated for most patients with high-grade malignancies, positive or close surgical margins, cervical metastases, or pathologic evidence of perineural spread or bone invasion.[37] Studies suggest that postoperative radiotherapy allows improved local control and may lead to longer disease-free survival.[38,39]

Local recurrence and distant metastases are common, often

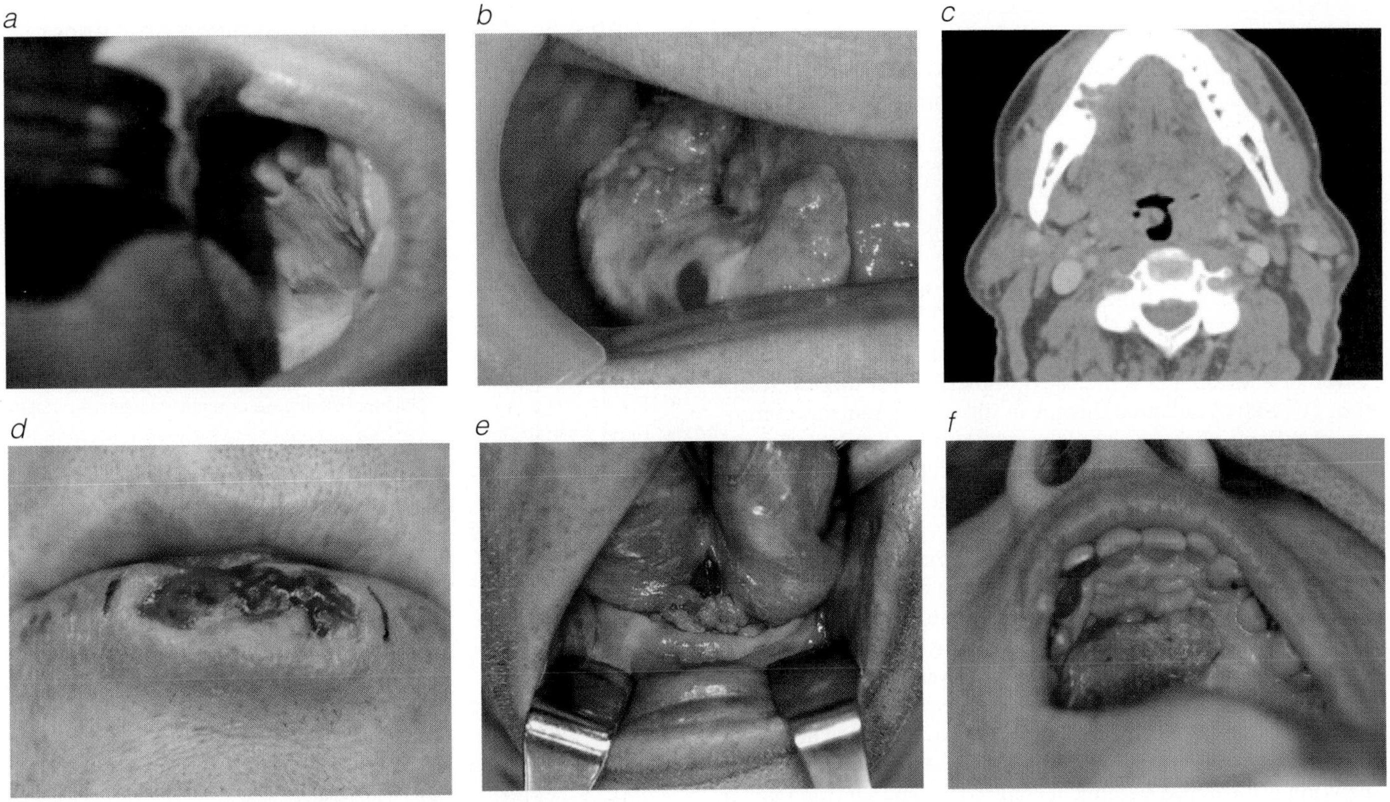

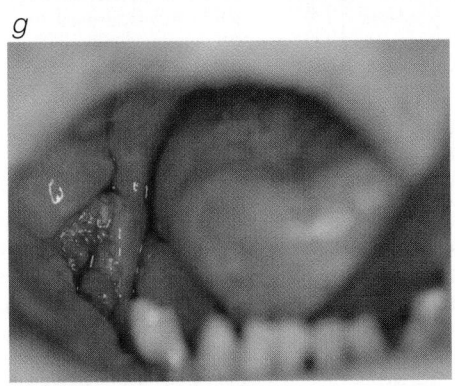

Figure 6 **Shown are malignant lesions of the oral cavity: (*a*) polymorphous low-grade adenocarcinoma of the hard palate (raised, erythematous lesion); (*b*) extensive squamous cell carcinoma of the tongue, the alveolar ridge, and the floor of the mouth; (*c*) squamous cell carcinoma of the right floor of the mouth, with mandibular invasion on CT scan; (*d*) squamous cell carcinoma of the lip (ulcerative lesion); (*e*) squamous cell carcinoma of the floor of the mouth (exophytic lesion); (*f*) squamous cell carcinoma of the hard palate; and (*g*) squamous cell carcinoma of the retromolar trigone.**

developing many years later; regional recurrence is uncommon.[36] The survival rate for adenoid cystic carcinoma is relatively high (approximately 80%) at 5 years but decreases dramatically over the subsequent 10 to 15 years.[36,40] Various factors predictive of poor survival have been identified [*see Table 5*].[40]

Mucosal Melanoma

After the sinonasal region, the oral cavity is the site at which mucosal melanoma most often occurs in the head and neck.[41] Within the oral cavity, mucosal melanoma is most frequently found involving the upper alveolus and the hard palate.[42] It is most common in men, usually developing in the sixth decade of life.[42] No specific risk factors or premalignant lesions have been identified. There may, however, be an increased risk among certain subsets of East Asian patients.

Oral mucosal melanoma typically appears as a flat or nodular pigmented lesion, frequently associated with ulceration. Amelanotic melanoma is, fortunately, rare.[43] Patients usually seek medical attention at an advanced stage of the disease, when pain develops or when they notice a change in the fit of their dentures. Early asymptomatic lesions are usually identified incidentally by either a physician or a dentist. Approximately 25% of patients

have nodal metastases at presentation.[42] Tumors thicker than 5 mm are associated with an increased likelihood of nodal metastases at presentation.[44]

No formal staging system has been developed for mucosal melanoma. The diagnosis is made by means of biopsy and immunohistochemical staining (e.g., for HMB-45 antigen, Melan-A, or S-100 protein). Any suspicious pigmented lesion in the oral cavity should undergo biopsy to rule out melanoma. Amalgam tattoos are common in the oral cavity and can often be diagnosed on the basis of

---

Table 5 Poor Prognostic Factors for Minor Salivary Gland Malignancies

Advanced disease at time of diagnosis
Positive nodes
High-risk histologic type (i.e., high-grade malignancies such as high-grade mucoepidermoid carcinoma, adenocarcinoma, carcinoma ex pleomorphic adenoma, and adenoid cystic carcinoma)
Positive margins
Male sex

Table 6 Poor Prognostic Factors for Mucosal Melanoma

Amelanotic melanoma
Advanced stage at presentation
Tumor thickness > 5 mm
Presence of vascular invasion
Distant metastases

---

the presence of metallic fragments on dental radiographs.

Mucosal melanoma is managed primarily with surgical resection. The role of radiation therapy in this setting remains controversial.[41] Some clinicians recommend postoperative radiotherapy for all cases of mucosal melanoma; others recommend it only for patients with close or positive margins. The role of lymph node mapping [see 26 Lymphatic Mapping and Sentinel Lymph Node Biopsy] has not been defined for mucosal melanoma. Because of the high incidence of nodes at presentation and the high regional recurrence rates reported in some studies, consideration should be given to treating the neck prophylactically by extending the postoperative radiation fields to cover this region.[41,42]

The poor prognosis of mucosal melanoma with conventional treatment employing surgery and irradiation is a strong argument for referring patients to a medical oncologist for potential enrollment in postoperative systemic therapy trials. The survival rate for oral mucosal melanomas at 5 years ranges from 15% to 45%,[42,43,45] with most patients dying of distant disease. Nodal involvement further reduces survival.[43] Melanoma of the gingiva has a slightly better prognosis than melanoma of the palate.[43] Several factors predictive of poor survival have been identified [see Table 6].[42] The relation between lesion depth and prognosis is not as clearly defined for oral mucosal melanoma as it is for cutaneous melanoma.

Squamous Cell Carcinoma

The incidence of squamous cell carcinoma increases with age, with the median age at diagnosis falling in the seventh decade of life,[46,47] and is higher in men than in women. This cancer may be found at any of a number of oral cavity subsites [see Figures 6b through 6g]. Lip carcinoma is the most common oral cavity cancer; 80% to 90% of these lesions occur on the lower lip.[13] After the lip, the most common sites for oral cavity carcinoma are the tongue and the floor of the mouth. When the primary lesion is on the tongue, the lateral border is the most common location, followed by the anterior tongue and the dorsum.[8] Approximately 75% of

---

Table 7 Growth Patterns of Squamous Cell Carcinoma of Oral Cavity[55]

Growth Pattern	Characteristics
Ulceroinfiltrative	Most common pattern; appears as ulcerated lesion that penetrates deep into underlying structures with surrounding induration
Exophytic	Common on lip and buccal mucosa; appears as papillary mass that may ulcerate when large
Endophytic	Uncommon; extends deep into soft tissue, with only small surface area involved
Superficial	Flat, superficial appearance; may be either a white patch or a red/velvety patch

---

Table 8 American Joint Committee on Cancer TNM Classification of Head and Neck Cancer

Primary tumor (T)	TX	Primary tumor cannot be assessed
	T0	No evidence of primary tumor
	Tis	Carcinoma in situ
	T1	Tumor 2 cm or less in greatest dimension
	T2	Tumor more than 2 cm but not more than 4 cm in greatest dimension
	T3	Tumor more than 4 cm in greatest dimension
	T4a	Tumor invades adjacent structures, extending through cortical bone into deep (extrinsic) muscles of tongue, maxillary sinus, or facial skin
	T4b	Tumor invades masticator space, pterygoid plates, or skull base or encases internal carotid artery
Regional lymph nodes (N)	NX	Regional lymph nodes cannot be assessed
	N0	No regional lymph node metastases
	N1	Metastases in a single ipsilateral lymph node ≤ 3 cm in greatest dimension
	N2a	Metastases in a single ipsilateral lymph node > 3 cm but ≤ 6 cm in greatest dimension
	N2b	Metastases in multiple ipsilateral lymph nodes, none > 6 cm in greatest dimension
	N2c	Metastases in bilateral or contralateral lymph nodes, none > 6 cm in greatest dimension
	N3	Metastases in lymph node > 6 cm in greatest dimension
Distant metastases (M)	MX	Distant metastases cannot be assessed
	M0	No distant metastases
	M1	Distant metastases

---

cases of oral cavity squamous cell carcinoma arise from a specific 10% of the mucosal surface of the mouth,[11] an area extending from the anterior floor of the mouth along the gingivobuccal sulcus and the lateral border to the retromolar trigone and the anterior tonsillar pillar.[11] Verrucous carcinoma is a subtype of squamous cell carcinoma and occurs most frequently on the buccal mucosa, appearing as a papillary mass with keratinization.

Between 80% and 90% of patients with oral cavity carcinoma have a history of either tobacco use (cigarette smoking or tobacco chewing) or excessive alcohol intake.[48] A synergistic effect is created when alcohol and tobacco are frequently used together.[48] In Asia, the practice of reverse smoking is associated with a high incidence of palatal carcinoma; betel nut chewing is associated with a high incidence of buccal carcinoma.

Small lesions tend to be asymptomatic. Larger lesions are often associated with pain, bleeding, poor denture fit, facial weakness or sensory changes, dysphagia, odynophagia, and trismus. Oral intake may worsen the pain, leading to malnutrition and dehydration.

Squamous cell carcinoma of the oral cavity has four different possible growth patterns: ulceroinfiltrative, exophytic, endophytic, and superficial [see Table 7].[49] Lip and buccal carcinomas tend to appear as exophytic masses. Ulceration is less common early in the course of cancers arising at these sites, but it may develop as the lesion enlarges. Cancers of the floor of the mouth may be associated with invasion of the tongue and the mandible. Decreased tongue mobility as a result of fixation is an indicator of an advanced tumor.[8,50] Mandibular invasion occurs frequently in carcinomas of the floor of the mouth, the retromolar trigone, and the alveolar ridge as a consequence of the tight adherence of the mucosa to the periosteum in these regions.[2] The risk of mandibular invasion increases with higher tumor stages. The majority

Table 9   American Joint Committee on Cancer Staging System for Head and Neck Cancer

Stage	T	N	M
Stage 0	Tis	N0	M0
Stage I	T1	N0	M0
Stage II	T2	N0	M0
Stage III	T3 T1, T2, T3	N0 N1	M0 M0
Stage IVA	T4a T1, T2, T3, T4a	N0, N1 N2	M0 M0
Stage IVB	Any T T4b	N3 Any N	M0 M0
Stage IVC	Any T	Any N	M1

Table 11   Five-Year Carcinoma Survival Rates for Oral Cavity Subsites

Oral Cavity Subsite	Survival Rate
Lip	80%; > 90% for early-stage disease
Tongue	30%–35% (advanced-stage disease); > 80% (early-stage disease)
Floor of mouth	85% for stages I and II (T1 lesions > 95%); 20%–52% for stages III and IV
Alveoli	50%–60%
Retromolar trigone	75% for T1 and T2 lesions; approximately 20%–50% for T3 and T4 lesions
Buccal mucosa	49%–68%
Palate	85% for T1 lesions; 30% for T4 lesions

(70%–80%) of alveolar ridge carcinomas occur on the lower alveolus, often in areas of leukoplakia.[51]

Oral cavity carcinoma is generally classified according to the staging system developed by the American Joint Committee on Cancer [see Tables 8 and 9].[52] Staging is based on clinical examination and diagnostic imaging. The diagnosis is made on the basis of biopsy and immunohistochemical staining (e.g., for cytokeratin and epithelial membrane antigen).

Squamous cell carcinoma of the oral cavity is usually managed with surgery, radiation therapy, or a combination of the two; chemotherapy is used primarily for palliation of incurable disease. For localized disease without bone invasion, the cure rate for radiation therapy is comparable to that of surgery.[48] Advanced tumors of the oral cavity are best managed with both surgery and irradiation. Traditionally, in North America, oral cavity cancer is treated primarily with surgery, and postoperative radiotherapy is added if the disease is advanced or if there are pathologic features indicative of a high risk of recurrence (i.e., positive margins on microscopy; extensive perineural or intravascular invasion; two or more positive nodes or positive nodes at multiple levels; or nodal capsular extension). North American practice is reflected in the guidelines developed by the American Head and Neck Society (www.headandneckcancer.org/clinicalresources/docs/oralcavity.php).

Postoperative radiation, if indicated, should be started 4 to 6 weeks after surgery. The total radiation dose depends on the clinical and pathologic findings; the usual range is between 50 and 70 Gy, administered over 5 to 8 weeks. Brachytherapy can be used as an adjunct when close or positive margins are noted. Advances in

Table 10   Incidence of Nodal Metastases* at Presentation in Oral Cavity Subsites

Oral Cavity Subsite	Incidence of Metastases
Lip	10%
Tongue	30%–40%
Floor of mouth	50%
Alveoli	28%–32%
Buccal mucosa	40%–52%

*Clinically detectable or occult.

treatment planning and conformal radiotherapy have led to improved dosimetry with external beam radiotherapy, which has limited the perceived value of brachytherapy in our practice.

The decision regarding which treatment is presented to a patient as the first option is often determined by factors other than the extent of the tumor. Patient factors to be considered include desires and wishes, age, medical comorbidities, and performance status. Disease factors to be considered include tumor grade and stage; extent of invasion; primary site; the presence and degree of nodal or distant metastasis; and previous treatment. It is often helpful to discuss each case at a multidisciplinary treatment planning conference in order to develop a ranked list of options.

Squamous cell carcinoma of the oral cavity tends to spread to regional lymph nodes in a relatively predictable fashion. The primary levels of metastatic spread from oral cavity carcinoma includes level I through III nodes and, less frequently, level IV nodes[53-55]; metastases to level V are infrequent.[53,55] The likelihood that cervical node metastases will develop varies depending on the location of the primary tumor in the oral cavity and on the stage of the tumor. Cervical metastases from carcinomas of the lip or the hard palate usually occur only in advanced disease[8]; however, cervical metastases from carcinomas of any of the other oral cavity subsites are common at presentation [see Table 10].[8,11,48,50,51,53,56,57] Larger tumors carry a higher risk of cervical metastasis.

The clinically positive neck is usually managed with either a radical or a modified radical neck dissection, depending on the extent of the disease. Some studies have found that for N1 and some N2a patients, a comparable control rate can be achieved with a selective neck dissection encompassing levels I through IV, with postoperative radiation therapy added when indicated.[58,59]

The clinically negative neck can occasionally be managed with observation alone, with treatment initiated only when nodal metastases develop. Alternatively, the nodal basins at risk can be managed prophylactically by means of either surgery or radiation therapy (involving levels I through III and, possibly, IV). The rationale for prophylactic neck management is that treatment initiated while metastases are still occult is thought to be more effective than treatment initiated after the disease has progressed to the point where it is clinically detectable. For this reason, many clinicians advocate prophylactic neck dissection for patients with oral cavity carcinomas who are at moderate

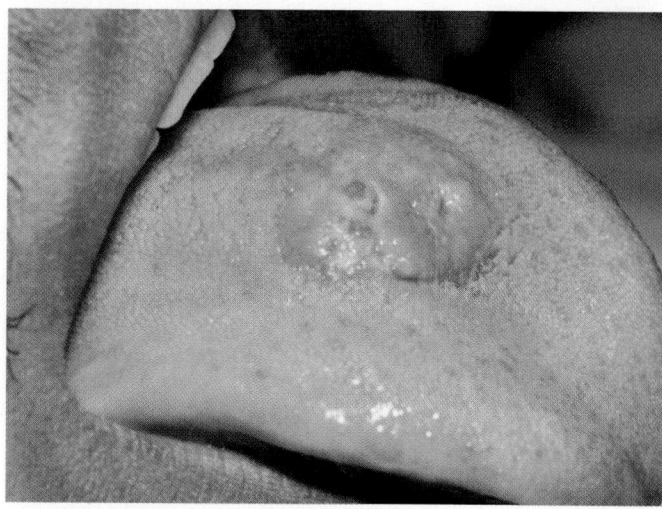

Figure 7 **Shown is coccidioidomycosis of the tongue in an HIV-positive patient.**

(15%–20%) risk for occult metastases at presentation. The selective neck dissection not only addresses any occult metastatic nodes but also functions as a staging procedure that helps in determining the prognosis and assessing the need for postoperative radiotherapy.[60,61] In general, elective neck management is recommended for T2 and higher-stage carcinomas of the tongue, the floor of the mouth, the buccal mucosa, the alveolus, and the retromolar trigone, as well as for advanced (T3 or T4) carcinomas of the lip and the hard palate.[8,11,48,57,62,63] Most surgeons now emphasize the depth of invasion of the primary tumor as a critical determinant of the risk of occult nodal metastases. It has been suggested that elective treatment of the neck with surgery or radiation therapy should be considered on the basis of the depth of tumor invasion rather than the surface diameter of the lesion. The tumor depth that is held to warrant investigation varies among published studies, ranging from 2 to 5 mm.[64-66] Bilateral neck dissection may be indicated for midline oral cavity cancers.

Radiation may be delivered to an oral cavity carcinoma via either external beam radiotherapy or brachytherapy, with the former being more commonly employed. Primary radiation therapy is indicated for patients with stage I and selected stage II oral cavity carcinomas, patients who refuse surgery or in whom surgery is contraindicated, and patients with incurable lesions who require palliative treatment. The total radiation dose for primary treatment ranges from 65 to 75 Gy. Radiation therapy is less effective against large or deeply invasive tumors, especially those that are invading bone, and therefore generally is not used alone for curative management of T3 and T4 lesions. For advanced-stage tumors of the oral cavity, surgery with postoperative radiotherapy is performed to decrease recurrence rates.

The prognosis depends on the location of the tumor in the oral cavity. Overall, if all of the oral cavity subsites are considered together, the presence of cervical metastases decreases survival by approximately 50%. Varying 5-year survival rates have been reported for the different subsites of the oral cavity [*see Table 11*].[8,11,48,50,51,56,67]

Oral Cavity Manifestations of HIV Infection

Infectious and neoplastic oral cavity lesions are often the first manifestation of HIV infection or the first indication of the progression to AIDS.

INFECTIONS

The same organisms that affect the general population cause most of the oral infections seen in the HIV population; however, oral infections in HIV patients tend to be recurrent, comparatively severe, and relatively resistant to treatment.[68] Oral hairy leukoplakia, caused by Epstein-Barr virus, is a common oral infection seen almost exclusively in the HIV population. It presents as an asymptomatic, corrugated, whitish, nonremovable, slightly raised patch on the lateral borders of the tongue. The finding of such a lesion on clinical examination of an HIV patient is suggestive of the diagnosis, but confirmation of the diagnosis requires biopsy. Treatment usually is not necessary. High-dose acyclovir may be given if the patient requests treatment.

Several rare infections of the oral cavity are being seen with increasing frequency in the HIV population, including tuberculosis, syphilis, *Rochalimaea henselae* infection (bacillary angiomatosis), *Borrelia vincentii* infection (acute necrotizing ulcerative gingivitis), cryptococcosis, histoplasmosis, coccidioidomycosis [*see Figure 7*], and human papillomavirus infection.

NEOPLASMS

The two most common intraoral neoplasms in the HIV population are Kaposi sarcoma and non-Hodgkin lymphoma. Kaposi sarcoma occurs most commonly in patients with HIV, though it is not exclusive to this population. It frequently involves the oral cavity, showing a predilection for the attached mucosa of the palate or the gingiva.[68] The characteristic lesions are blue, brown, purple, or red exophytic masses that may be either confined to the oral mucosa or systemic. They are usually asymptomatic but may become painful or obstructive with growth or ulceration. Treatment is aimed at palliation of symptoms and may involve sclerotherapy, intralesional chemotherapy, laser ablation, cryotherapy, surgical excision, or radiation therapy.[69] Systemic chemotherapy may be provided if the disease is systemic.

The risk of non-Hodgkin lymphoma is much higher in the HIV population than in the general population.[69] It should be suspected in any HIV patient who presents with an intraoral mass or an ulcerated lesion. Non-Hodgkin lymphoma appears as painful lesions that show a predilection for the palate, the retromolar trigone, and the tongue. Associated symptoms include facial paresthesias, loose dentition, fever, night sweats, and weight loss. Local disease is managed with radiation, systemic disease with chemotherapy.

References

1. Rubright WC, Hoffman HT, Lynch CF, et al: Risk factors for advanced-stage oral cavity cancer. Arch Otolaryngol Head Neck Surg 122:621, 1996

2. Tsue TT, McCulloch TM, Girod DA, et al: Predictors of carcinomatous invasion of the mandible. Head Neck 16:116, 1994

3. Bahadur S: Mandibular involvement in oral cancer. J Laryngol Otol 104:968, 1990

4. Sigg MB, Steinert H, Gratz K, et al: Staging of head and neck tumors: fluorodeoxyglucose positron emission tomography compared with physical examination and conventional imaging modalities. J Oral Maxillofac Surg 61:1022, 2003

5. Nakasone Y, Inoue T, Oriuchi N, et al: The role of whole body FDG-PET in preoperative assessment of tumor staging in oral cancers. Ann Nucl Med 15:505, 2001

6. Goeress GW, Stoeckli SJ, von Schulthess GK, et al: FDG PET for mucosal melanoma of the head and neck. Laryngoscope 112:381, 2002

7. Lonneux M, Lawson G, Ide C, et al: Positron emission tomography with fluorodeoxyglucose for suspected head and neck tumor recurrence in the symptomatic patient. Laryngoscope 110:1493, 2000

8. Cummings CW, Fredrickson JM, Harker LA, et al: Otolaryngology Head and Neck Surgery, 3rd ed. Mosby, St Louis, 1998

9. Murray N, Muller S, Amedee RC: SIPAC: Ulcerative Lesions of the Oral Cavity. American Academy of Otolaryngology–Head and Neck Surgery Foundation, 2000

10. Sciubba J, Regezei J, Rogers R III: PDQ Oral Disease Diagnosis and Treatment. BC Decker, Hamilton, Ontario, 2002

11. Bailey BJ, Calhoun KH: Head and Neck Surgery–Otolaryngology, 3rd ed. Lippincott-Raven, Philadelphia, 2002

12. Sandmeier D, Bouzourene H: Necrotizing sialometaplasia: a potential diagnostic pitfall. Histopathology 40:200, 2002

13. Fu YS, Wenig BM, Abemayor E, et al: Head and Neck Pathology: With Clinical Correlations. Churchill Livingstone, New York, 2001

14. Lumerman H: Essentials of Oral Pathology. JB Lippincott, Philadelphia, 1975

15. Mollaoglu N: Oral lichen planus: a review. Br J Oral Maxillofac Surg 38:370, 2000

16. Giunta JL: Oral Pathology, 3rd ed. BC Decker, Toronto, 1989

17. Sugerman PB, Savage NW, Zhou X, et al: Oral lichen planus. Clin Dermatol 18:533, 2000

18. Silverman S: Oral lichen planus: a potentially premalignant lesion. J Oral Maxillofac Surg 58:1286, 2000

19. Casiglia J, Woo S, Ahmed AR: Oral involvement in autoimmune blistering diseases. Clin Dermatol 19:737, 2001

20. Jainkittivong A, Langlais RP: Buccal and palatal exostosis: prevalence and concurrence with tori. Oral Surg Oral Med Oral Pathol Oral Radiol Endod 90:48, 2000

21. Baurmash HD: Mucoceles and ranulas. J Oral Maxillofac Surg 61:369, 2003

22. Chow J, Skolnik E: Nonsquamous tumors of the oral cavity. Otolaryngol Clin North Am 19:573, 1986

23. Williams T, Hellstein JW: Odontogenic cysts of the jaws and other selected cysts. Oral and Maxillofacial Surgery, vol 5: Surgical Pathology. Fonseca R, Ed. WB Saunders, Philadelphia, 2000, p 297

24. Bataineh A, al Qudah M: Treatment of mandibular odontogenic keratocysts. Oral Surg Oral Med Oral Pathol Oral Radiol Endod 86:42, 1998

25. Praetorius F: HPV-associated diseases of the oral mucosa. Clin Dermatol 15:399, 1997

26. Auclair P, Arendt D, Hellstein J: Giant cell lesions of the jaws. Oral Maxillofac Surg Clin North Am 9:655, 1997

27. Lopes MA, Kowalski LP, da Cunha Santos G, et al: A clinicopathologic study of 196 intraoral minor salivary gland tumors. J Oral Pathol Med 28:264, 1999

28. Alessi DM, Zimmerman MC: Granular cell tumors of the head and neck. Laryngoscope 98:810, 1998

29. Kershisnik M, Batsakis JG, Mackay B: Pathology consultation: granular cell tumors. Ann Otol Rhinol Laryngol 103:416, 1994

30. Kim S, Jang HS: Ameloblastoma: a clinical, radiographic and histopathologic analysis of 71 cases. Oral Surg Oral Med Oral Pathol Oral Radiol Endod 91:649, 2001

31. Katz JO, Underhill TE: Multilocular radiolucencies. Dent Clin North Am 38:63, 1994

32. Wenig B: Atlas of Head and Neck Pathology. WB Saunders, Philadelphia, 1993

33. Sampson DE, Pogrel MA: Management of mandibular ameloblastoma: the clinical basis for a treatment algorithm. J Oral Maxillofac Surg 57:1074, 1999

34. Zwahlen RA, Gratz KW: Maxillary ameloblastomas: a review of the literature and of a 15-year database. J Craniomaxillofac Surg 30:273, 2002

35. Fischman SL, Ulmansky M, Sela J, et al: Correlative clinico-pathological evaluation of oral premalignancy. J Oral Pathol 11:283, 1982

36. Jones AS, Beasley NP, Houghton DJ, et al: Tumors of the minor salivary glands. Clin Otolaryngol 22:27, 1997

37. Spiro RH: Salivary neoplasms: overview of a 35 year experience with 2807 patients. Head Neck Surg 8:177, 1986

38. Le QT, Birdwell S, Terris DJ, et al: Postoperative irradiation of minor salivary gland malignancies of the head and neck. Radiother Oncol 52:165, 1999

39. Garden AS, Weber RS, Ang KK, et al: Postoperative radiation therapy for malignant tumors of minor salivary glands: outcome and patterns of failure. Cancer 73:2563, 1994

40. Lopes MA, Santos GC, Kowalski LP: Multivariate survival analysis of 128 cases of oral cavity minor salivary gland carcinomas. Head Neck 20:699, 1998

41. Medina JE, Ferlito A, Pellitteri PK, et al: Current management of mucosal melanoma of the head and neck. J Surg Oncol 83:116, 2003

42. Patel SG, Prasad ML, Escrig M, et al: Primary mucosal malignant melanoma of the head and neck. Head Neck 24:247, 2002

43. Hicks MJ, Flaitz CM: Oral mucosal melanoma: epidemiology and pathobiology. Oral Oncol 36:152, 2000

44. Umeda M, Shimada K: Primary malignant melanoma of the oral cavity: its histological classification and treatment. Br J Oral Maxillofac Surg 32:39, 1994

45. Nandapalan V, Roland NJ, Helliwell TR, et al: Mucosal melanoma of the head and neck. Clin Otolaryngol 23:107, 1998

46. Funk GF, Hynds Karnell L, Robinson RA, et al: Presentation, treatment, and outcome of oral cavity cancer: a National Cancer Data Base Report. Head Neck 24:165, 2002

47. Teresa Canto M, Devesa SS: Oral cavity and pharynx cancer incidence rates in the United States, 1975-1988. Oral Oncol 38:610, 2002

48. Rhys Evans PH, Montgomery PQ, Gullane PJ: Principles and Practice of Head and Neck Oncology. Martin Dunitz, London, 2003

49. Shah JP, Patel SG: Head and Neck Surgery and Oncology, 3rd ed. Mosby, London, 2003

50. Hicks WL Jr, Loree TR, Garcia RI, et al: Squamous cell carcinoma of the floor of mouth: a 20 year review. Head Neck 19:400, 1997

51. Soo KC, Spiro RH, King W, et al: Squamous carcinoma of the gums. Am J Surg 156:281, 1998

52. Greene FL, Page DL, Fleming ID, et al: AJCC Cancer Staging Manual, 6th ed. Springer, New York, 2002

53. Shah JP: Patterns of cervical lymph node metastasis from squamous carcinomas of the upper aerodigestive tract. Am J Surg 160:405, 1990

54. Khafif A, Lopez-Garza JR, Medina JE: Is dissection of level IV necessary in patients with T1-T3 N0 tongue cancer? Laryngoscope 111:1088, 2001

55. Shah JP, Candela FC, Poddar AK: The patterns of cervical lymph node metastases from squamous carcinoma of the oral cavity. Cancer 66:109, 1990

56. Byers RM, Anderson B, Schwartz EA, et al: Treatment of squamous carcinoma of the retromolar trigone. Am J Clin Oncol 7:647, 1984

57. Diaz EM, Holsinger FC, Zuniga ER, et al: Squamous cell carcinoma of the buccal mucosa: one institution's experience with 119 previously untreated patients. Head Neck 25:267, 2003

58. Kolli VR, Datta RV, Orner JB, et al: The role of supraomohyoid neck dissection in patients with positive nodes. Arch Otolaryngol Head Neck Surg 126:413, 2000

59. Majoufre C, Faucher A, Laroche C, et al: Supraomohyoid neck dissection in cancer of the oral cavity. Am J Surg 178:73, 1999

60. Tankere F, Camproux A, Barry B, et al: Prognostic value of lymph node involvement in oral cancers: a study of 137 cases. Laryngoscope 110:2061, 2000

61. Hao S, Tsang N: The role of the supraomohyoid neck dissection in patients of oral cavity carcinoma. Oral Oncol 38:309, 2002

62. Haddadin KJ, Soutar DS, Oliver RJ, et al: Improved survival for patients with clinically T1/T2, N0 tongue tumors undergoing a prophylactic neck dissection. Head Neck 21:517, 1999

63. Zitsch RP, Lee BW, Smith RB: Cervical lymph node metastases and squamous cell carcinoma of the lip. Head Neck 21:447, 1999

64. Spiro RH, Huvos AG, Wong GY, et al: Predictive value of tumor thickness in squamous carcinoma confined to the tongue and floor of the mouth. Am J Surg 152:345, 1986

65. Kurokawa H, Yamashita Y, Takeda S, et al: Risk factors for late cervical lymph node metastases in patients with stage 1 or 2 carcinoma of the tongue. Head Neck 24:731, 2002

66. Jones KR, Lodge-Rigal RD, Reddick RL, et al: Prognostic factors in the recurrence of stage I and II squamous cell cancer of the oral cavity. Arch Otolaryngol Head Neck Surg 5:483, 1992

67. Gomez D, Faucher A, Picot V, et al: Outcome of squamous cell carcinoma of the gingiva: a follow-up study of 83 cases. J Craniomaxillofac Surg 28:331, 2000

68. Laskaris G: Oral manifestations of HIV disease. Clin Dermatol 18:447, 2000

69. Casiglia JW, Woo S: Oral manifestations of HIV infection. Clin Dermatol 18:541, 2000

Acknowledgment

Figure 1 Tom Moore.

13 PAROTID MASS

Ashok R. Shaha, M.D., F.A.C.S.

Approach to Evaluation of a Parotid Mass

There are three major salivary glands in the human body—the parotid gland, the submandibular gland, and the sublingual gland—of which the parotid gland is the largest. In addition, there are approximately 600 to 800 minor salivary glands distributed throughout the entire upper aerodigestive tract, starting from the lip and extending to the lower end of the esophagus and up to the pulmonary alveoli. Almost half of these minor salivary glands are on the hard palate. Accordingly, any mass on the hard palate should be considered a minor salivary gland tumor until proved otherwise.[1]

The majority of salivary gland tumors originate in the parotid gland. Approximately 75% to 80% of parotid tumors are benign.[2,3] In the evaluation and surgical treatment of parotid tumors, it is essential to maintain awareness of the possibility of temporary or permanent facial nerve injury [*see* Discussion, Principles of Facial Reanimation, *below*]. Because surgery necessarily entails some risk of an injury to this structure or its branches, as well as because most parotid masses do not give rise to significant symptoms, many patients with parotid tumors may find the prospect of surgical therapy difficult to accept.

Clinical Evaluation

HISTORY

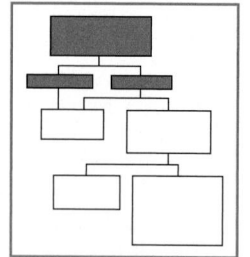

Evaluation of a parotid mass begins with a good clinical history. The most important question is, how long has the mass been present? If local pain and swelling of recent onset (i.e., within the past few days) are reported, infection or obstruction is the likely cause. If the mass has been present for a longer period (i.e., weeks to months), a neoplasm is more likely. Unfortunately, the presentations of some nonneoplastic conditions resemble those of neoplasms, and distinguishing one type of condition from the other can be challenging. Thus, the history should continue with further questions focusing on local or systemic signs and symptoms, the presence of swelling or other masses in the salivary glands, and previous medical conditions (including skin cancer).

Classification

Major salivary gland masses can be classified as nonneoplastic, lymphoepithelial, or neoplastic.[4]

Nonneoplastic The causes of nonneoplastic masses include congenital, granulomatous, infectious or inflammatory, and noninflammatory conditions. Some congenital lesions (e.g., hemangioma or vascular malformation) present as a vague swelling in the parotid region that has been present since childhood. One congenital lesion, a first branchial cleft cyst, presents as a mass inferior to the cartilaginous ear canal, with a cyst tract that can be either medial or lateral to the facial nerve and may even divide the trunk of the nerve. This cyst is most commonly noted in the second through fourth decades in life.

Granulomatous diseases are frequently manifested by an asymptomatic, gradual enlargement of a lymph node within the gland; often, they cannot be readily distinguished from neoplasms. In sarcoidosis, salivary gland involvement may cause duct obstruction, pain associated with the duct, xerostomia, or enlargement of the gland. The diagnosis is supported by chest x-rays that show bilateral hilar adenopathy and by elevated levels of angiotensin-converting enzyme (ACE).

As noted (see above), infectious or inflammatory diseases involving the parotid, unlike neoplasms, tend to give rise to pain in their early stages. Most such inflammatory conditions begin with diffuse enlargement of one or more salivary glands. Although parotitis is generally unilateral, it may be bilateral if a systemic causative condition is involved, and other salivary glands may be affected as well. The pain reported may be related to the presence of a stone in the salivary duct or to diffuse obstructive parotitis. Chronic parotitis may lead to recurrent infection and inflammation. When recurrent swelling of the salivary gland does occur, it is directly related to eating and increased salivation.

Sialadenosis is a noninflammatory, nonneoplastic condition of unknown origin that is characterized by diffuse enlargement of the salivary gland, with no discrete mass or inflammation.

Lymphoepithelial Lymphoepithelial lesions may be divided into lymphocytic infiltrative diseases and lymphomas. In many cases, patients with lymphocytic infiltrative diseases (e.g., Mikulicz disease, sicca complex, and Sjögren syndrome) have had their conditions for long periods, and they may feel that they have always been chubby, when in fact they have had chronic enlargement of both parotid glands. In patients with Sjögren syndrome, malignant transformation to high-grade lymphoma is known to occur. Lymphoepithelial cysts are benign cystic lesions that may arise from lymph nodes or from lymphoid aggregates in the salivary gland. These lesions may be associated with HIV infection.

Approach to Evaluation of a Parotid Mass

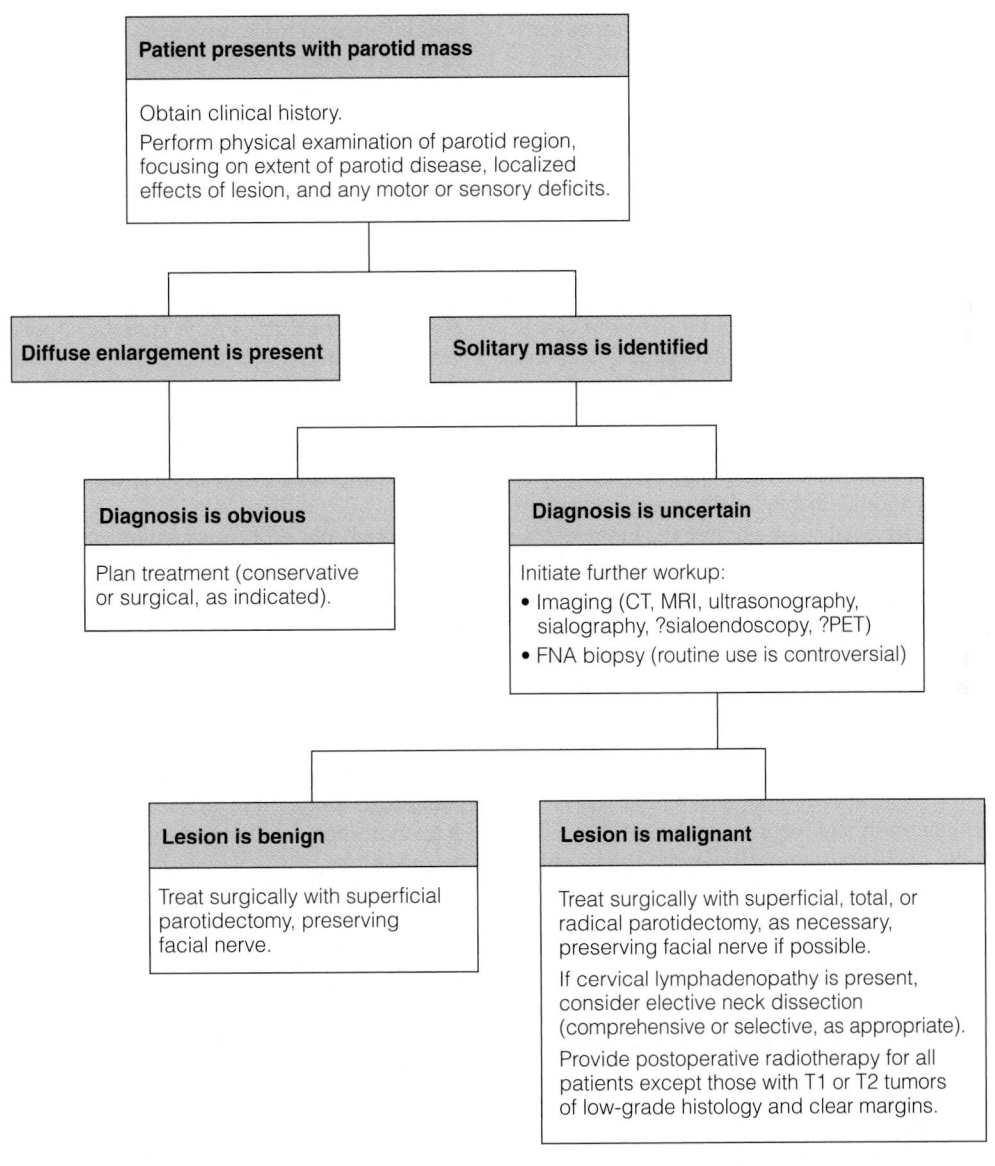

Patient presents with parotid mass

Obtain clinical history.
Perform physical examination of parotid region, focusing on extent of parotid disease, localized effects of lesion, and any motor or sensory deficits.

Diffuse enlargement is present

Solitary mass is identified

Diagnosis is obvious

Plan treatment (conservative or surgical, as indicated).

Diagnosis is uncertain

Initiate further workup:
- Imaging (CT, MRI, ultrasonography, sialography, ?sialoendoscopy, ?PET)
- FNA biopsy (routine use is controversial)

Lesion is benign

Treat surgically with superficial parotidectomy, preserving facial nerve.

Lesion is malignant

Treat surgically with superficial, total, or radical parotidectomy, as necessary, preserving facial nerve if possible.

If cervical lymphadenopathy is present, consider elective neck dissection (comprehensive or selective, as appropriate).

Provide postoperative radiotherapy for all patients except those with T1 or T2 tumors of low-grade histology and clear margins.

Primary lymphoma of the salivary gland is uncommon, occurring in fewer than 5% of patients with parotid masses.[5] Suggestive clinical features include (1) the development of a parotid mass in a patient with a known history of malignant lymphoma, (2) the occurrence of a parotid mass in a patient with an immune disorder (e.g., Sjögren syndrome, rheumatoid arthritis, or AIDS), (3) the presence of a parotid mass in a patient with a previous diagnosis of benign lymphoepithelial lesion, (4) the finding of multiple masses in one parotid gland or of masses in both parotid glands, and (5) the association of a parotid mass with multiple enlarged cervical lymph nodes unilaterally or bilaterally.[6]

Neoplastic Neoplastic masses may be present for years without causing any symptoms. Benign salivary tumors are more common in younger persons, whereas malignant parotid lesions are more common in the fifth and sixth decades of life.[7] The classic presentation of a benign parotid tumor is that of an asymptomatic parotid mass that has been present for months to years. Benign neoplasms of the parotid include pleomorphic adenoma, basal cell adenoma, myoepithelioma, Warthin tumor, oncocytoma, and cystadenoma. The observation of rapid growth in a long-standing pleomorphic adenoma is suggestive of malignant transformation. In a 2005 study of 94 patients with pleomorphic adenoma, malignant transformation to carcinoma was documented in 8.5% of cases.[8] Rapid tumor growth, metastasis to lymph nodes, deep fixation, and facial nerve weakness are all strongly suggestive of malignant disease and are indicators of a poor prognosis.[9] Although pain is more often experienced by patients with benign conditions, it is also reported by some patients with infiltrative malignant tumors. In the latter patients, pain is another indicator of a poor prognosis.[10]

The presence of facial nerve palsy should raise the index of suspicion for malignancy. Occasionally, patients present with classic Bell palsy. This condition is usually of viral origin, and most patients recover over time. If Bell palsy persists, however, further investigation is required, including imaging studies to rule out any obvious parotid lesion. Facial palsy occurring in association with parotitis and anterior uveitis is known as Heerfordt syndrome and is often seen in patients with sarcoidosis.

PHYSICAL EXAMINATION

The physical examination should focus on the extent of the disease in the parotid, the neck, and the parapharynx; the localized effects of the tumor (including trismus); and the motor or sensory deficits resulting from neural invasion.

The mass is palpated to determine whether it is painless or painful; whether it is soft, firm, hard, or cystic; and whether it is mobile or fixed to deep tissue or skin. The skin of the scalp, the ear, and the face is examined for lesions. The neck is palpated for adenopathy. In the oral cavity, the ducts are examined for discharge or saliva after the glands are milked. The pharyngeal wall is examined for deviation, and the jaw is examined for trismus.

The parotid occupies a large area, starting from the zygoma and extending to the upper portion of the neck and behind the mandible to what is commonly called the tail of the parotid. Occasionally, the parotid tissue extends behind the earlobe, in which case it may be misdiagnosed preoperatively as a nonsalivary pathologic condition. Accessory parotid tissue is present along Stenson's duct in approximately 21% of persons.[11] Patients sometimes present with a tumor (most commonly, a benign mixed tumor) of this accessory tissue.[12] Attempts to excise such masses locally must be avoided, because of the high risk of injury to branches of the facial nerve.

The most common presentation of a parotid mass, whether benign or malignant, is an asymptomatic swelling in the preauricular or retromandibular region. Occasionally, patients present with metastases to the intraparotid or periparotid lymph nodes. There are approximately 17 to 20 lymph nodes in the substance of the parotid and along its tail, and there may be a smaller number of lymph nodes within the deep lobe of the gland. These lymph nodes may be directly affected by metastatic tumors originating from the anterior scalp or the temporal, periocular, or malar regions. Especially with elderly patients, it is extremely crucial to obtain a detailed history of any previously excised skin lesions, some of which may have been squamous cell carcinomas (SCCs) that metastasized to the periparotid nodes. Generally, such metastasis involves multiple superficial lymph nodes and presents as diffuse enlargement of the parotid parenchyma. With the massive involvement of the parotid gland, facial nerve palsy is not uncommon in this setting. The majority of metastases to the parotid gland derive from cutaneous SCC or melanoma; however, metastatic spread from the lung, the breast, and the kidney also is known to occur.[13]

The location of the parotid mass is a very important diagnostic factor. The classic presentation of a benign mixed tumor is as a marblelike lesion in the parotid gland—a firm, mobile mass that commonly originates in the superficial portion of the gland and generally is not fixed to the deeper structures or to the skin. Parotid tumors that originate in the deep lobe may present as a vague, diffuse swelling behind the angle of the mandible; more often, however, they present as a swelling of the parapharyngeal area accompanied by medial displacement of the tonsil or the soft palate.

Although physical examination of a parotid mass is a simple process in itself, it should be accompanied by a thorough evaluation of the head and neck that includes a detailed examination of the oral cavity and the oropharyngeal, nasopharyngeal, hypopharyngeal, and laryngopharyngeal areas. Occasionally, a tumor of the oropharynx presents as cervical lymphadenopathy or as metastatic disease in the tail of the parotid. In such cases, it may be difficult to determine whether the patient has a primary salivary gland tumor or a metastatic lesion. The presence of any suspicious pathologic condition in the oropharynx or the base of the tongue is an indication for appropriate endoscopy and biopsy of the suspected primary site.

Physical findings suggestive of malignancy include a large and fixed mass, facial nerve weakness, lymph node metastasis, and skin involvement; patients with advanced parotid malignancies may present with trismus. Whereas patients with benign parotid tumors rarely exhibit facial nerve weakness, approximately 12% to 15% of patients with parotid malignancies have facial nerve dysfunction at presentation.[14] The most common causes of facial nerve weakness in this setting are adenoid cystic carcinoma, poorly differentiated carcinoma, and SCC. Primary SCC of the parotid is quite rare, and a diagnosis of SCC in the gland should lead one to suspect that a tumor has metastasized to the parotid lymph nodes. Before the diagnosis of primary SCC of the parotid is made, high-grade mucoepidermoid carcinoma and metastatic SCC must be excluded.

The presence of cervical lymph node metastasis may direct one's attention to the parotid mass, though only about 20% of persons with parotid malignancies actually have clinically apparent cervical lymph node metastases at the time of initial presentation.[10] The parotid tumors most commonly associated with metastatic disease to the lymph nodes at presentation are high-grade mucoepidermoid carcinoma, poorly differentiated carcinoma, and SCC. Lymph node metastases may also derive from high-grade adenocarcinomas or malignant mixed tumors.

Some patients are totally asymptomatic, with the only significant physical finding being a mass visible through the open mouth, which is suggestive of either a deep-lobe parotid tumor or a parapharyngeal tumor. The majority of parotid tumors develop within the superficial lobe of the parotid—not surprisingly, given that between 80% and 90% of the parotid tissue is superficial to the facial nerve. However, a significant minority of parotid masses—about 10%—are found within the deep lobe. Most deep-lobe parotid tumors are benign, in which case surgical treatment generally consists of a superficial parotidectomy with dissection and preservation of the facial nerve, followed by removal of the tumor. Occasionally, however, malignant deep-lobe parotid tumors do occur. Such tumors frequently involve the facial nerve, and surgical treatment may require sacrifice of the facial nerve in select circumstances. Most patients who have undergone surgical treatment of a malignant deep-lobe tumor will require postoperative radiation therapy.

Investigative Studies

The majority of parotid masses can easily be evaluated with a careful history and a thorough physical examination. Nevertheless, it sometimes happens that even after these measures have been carried out, there remains some clinical uncertainty regarding whether the pathologic process is of parotid or of nonsalivary origin. A number of nonsalivary tumors (e.g., neurofibromas, lipomas, lymphadenopathies, metastatic cutaneous lesions, and lymphomas) are known to present in the parotid region on occasion. These tumors may be difficult to evaluate clinically, and further diagnostic studies may therefore be required.

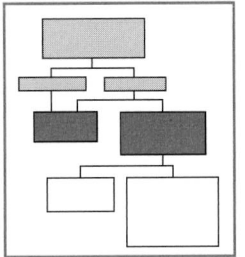

IMAGING

Generally, parotid masses are imaged with either computed tomography or magnetic resonance imaging.[15] CT is superior to MRI for evaluation of the bony structures, whereas MRI may be more helpful in distinguishing between inflammatory conditions and salivary neoplasms. CT scanning is indicated in patients with diffuse enlargement of the parotid gland, tumor extension beyond the superficial lobe, facial nerve weakness, trismus, or deep-lobe parotid tumors that are difficult to evaluate clinically. If the parotid mass appears to be fixed to the deeper structures, it is appropriate to proceed with CT to evaluate the extent and parapharyngeal extension of the disease. MRI is indicated in patients with facial nerve paralysis. Occasionally, it may be necessary to perform both CT and MRI. Both imaging methods are helpful and accurate in distinguishing deep-lobe parotid tumors from other parapharyngeal masses. They are also useful for evaluating suspicious lymph nodes and the periphery of the mass (specifically with respect to determining whether the lesion is encapsulated or has irregular borders).

Ultrasonography can be useful for determining the location of the lesion and for guiding fine-needle aspiration (FNA) biopsy. In the past, technetium-99m scanning was commonly employed for the diagnosis of oncocytoma and Warthin tumor.[16]

Various other diagnostic studies are available for evaluation of parotid masses. At one time, sialography was commonly employed to assess patients with suspected salivary stones, as well as to eval-uate the ductal arrangements in patients with chronic sialoadenitis. Currently, however, sialography is rarely used, both because there is a significant possibility of an infectious flare-up and because the study actually yields only minimal information. In the early 1980s, CT sialography became popular for a time; however, it was quite a complicated procedure, and clinicians eventually found that the information it yielded could easily be obtained from spiral (helical) CT. Occasionally, surface-coil MRI may be helpful for evaluating parotid masses deriving from subcutaneous processes. Sialoendoscopy has generated considerable interest, especially in Europe and Germany[17]; however, this sophisticated technology has not yet entered everyday practice. Although sialoendoscopy may be of some value in the assessment of salivary stone disease or chronic sialectasis, it is rarely performed in the United States at present, and its eventual role in the evaluation of parotid masses remains to be determined.

For a classic benign mixed tumor presenting in the form of a small nodule in the superficial lobe of the parotid gland, imaging is not required.

Currently, the role of positron emission tomography (PET) in the initial evaluation of a parotid mass remains undefined. This modality may, however, be of some value in the evaluation of suspected recurrent parotid cancers, lymph node metastases, or distant metastases.

FINE-NEEDLE ASPIRATION BIOPSY

Routine use of FNA biopsy in the evaluation of a parotid mass [see Table 1] continues to be controversial. One reason for the controversy is that cytologic evaluation is difficult. Another is that the extent of surgical treatment can easily be defined by means of the clinical assessment. The main argument against routine use of FNA biopsy is based on the standard approach to most parotid masses, which is a superficial parotidectomy that includes identification and preservation of the facial nerve. Nevertheless, FNA biopsy can be quite helpful, especially for the purposes of preoperative consultation with patients regarding the suspected pathologic process and the extent of surgical therapy. FNA biopsy has an overall accuracy that exceeds 90%,[18,19] and it is considered a good investigational tool as long as it is used in the appropriate clinical context.

In the case of a classic benign mixed tumor, which presents as a mobile, confined, superficial nodule in the parotid gland, FNA biopsy is not required for further treatment. However, in cases where the clinical picture is not definitive and one cannot determine whether the pathologic process is of parotid origin or not, FNA biopsy is extremely important. Besides distinguishing between benign and malignant conditions, FNA biopsy can also distinguish between salivary and nonsalivary processes [see Table

---

Table 1 **Uses of FNA Biopsy in Evaluation of Parotid Mass**

To identify suspected malignancy
To diagnose metastatic carcinoma
To identify suspected lymphoma
To distinguish between salivary and nonsalivary lesions
To facilitate conservative management of Warthin tumor or pleomorphic adenoma in a poor-risk patient
To confirm preoperatively suspected malignancy in a patient with facial palsy
To evaluate bilateral tumors

Table 2 Salivary and Nonsalivary Pathologic Processes Distinguished by FNA Biopsy

Salivary processes	Benign
	    Mixed tumor
	    Warthin tumor
	Malignant
	    Primary salivary gland cancer
	    Metastatic disease in salivary gland
	    Cystic adenoma
	    SCC
	    Adenocarcinoma
	    Melanoma

Nonsalivary processes	Lipoma
	Sebaceous cyst
	Lymph node pathology
	    Benign melanoma
	    Metastatic cancer
	    Lymphoma

2].[20] A variety of different lymph node pathologies, benign parotid tumors, and even suspected malignant parotid tumors can be differentiated by means of FNA biopsy. Furthermore, lymphoepithelial lesions of the parotid, benign mixed tumors, and Warthin tumors are easily diagnosed with this procedure. FNA biopsy is particularly useful when a parotid mass is likely to be the result of metastasis.

Occasionally, in an elderly person whose overall physical condition is poor, a conservative approach can be taken when a Warthin tumor is diagnosed by means of FNA biopsy. Similarly, in a person with a long-standing benign mixed tumor, observation may be appropriate if the patient is not a candidate for surgical intervention and if FNA biopsy confirms that the lesion is benign.

FNA biopsy findings that suggest lymphoma may help one avoid unnecessary parotidectomy and risk to the facial nerve. Often, it is hard to achieve a definitive diagnosis of lymphoma by means of FNA biopsy alone. In such cases, core biopsy or open biopsy can be performed to establish the diagnosis. Core biopsy of a parotid mass is a difficult procedure (unless the mass is very large and very superficial), and it is generally contraindicated on the grounds that it may cause bleeding or facial nerve injury. Nevertheless, if core biopsy can be performed safely, it can be a good choice in cases where lymphoma is suspected on the basis of FNA biopsy.[21] Open incisional biopsy can also be performed safely when done in conjunction with continuous monitoring of the facial nerve.[22]

Benign lymphoepithelial lesions related to HIV disease are readily diagnosed by means of FNA biopsy, especially if they are multiply recurrent cystic lesions in the tail of the parotid or if they occur bilaterally. In general, HIV-related pathology is quite easy to diagnose with FNA; HIV-infected patients with benign lymphoepithelial lesions may be treated by providing appropriate management of the underlying illness.

The crucial points for clinicians with respect to FNA biopsy in the setting of a parotid mass are (1) that this investigative study will not make a definitive diagnosis of parotid malignancy and (2) that one therefore should not make decisions about how to manage the facial nerve solely on the basis of an FNA-suggested malignant diagnosis. Any decisions regarding the approach to the facial nerve should also be based on preoperative assessment of facial nerve function and intraoperative evaluation of the nerve in relation to the tumor.

Table 3 American Joint Committee on Cancer TNM Clinical Classification of Major Salivary Gland Tumors

Primary tumor (T)	TX: Primary tumor cannot be assessed T0: No evidence of primary tumor T1: Tumor ≤ 2 cm in greatest dimension without extraparenchymal extension T2: Tumor > 2 cm but ≤ 4 cm in greatest dimension without extraparenchymal extension T3: Tumor having extraparenchymal extension without seventh nerve involvement and/or > 4 cm but ≤ 6 cm in greatest dimension T4: Tumor invades base of skull, seventh nerve, and/or > 6 cm in greatest dimension
Regional lymph nodes (N)	NX: Regional lymph nodes cannot be assessed N0: No regional lymph node metastasis N1: Metastasis in a single ipsilateral lymph node, ≤ 3 cm in greatest dimension N2: Metastasis in a single ipsilateral lymph node, > 3 cm but ≤ 6 cm in greatest dimension; or in multiple ipsilateral lymph nodes, none > 6 cm in greatest dimension; or in bilateral or contralateral lymph nodes, none > 6 cm in greatest dimension 　N2a: Metastasis in a single ipsilateral lymph node > 3 cm but ≤ 6 cm in greatest dimension 　N2b: Metastasis in multiple ipsilateral lymph nodes, none > 6 cm in greatest dimension 　N2c: Metastasis in bilateral or contralateral lymph nodes, none > 6 cm in greatest dimension N3: Metastasis in a lymph node > 6 cm in greatest dimension
Distant metastasis (M)	MX: Distant metastasis cannot be assessed M0: No distant metastasis M1: Distant metastasis

Staging and Prognosis

For cancers of the parotid gland (as well as those of other major salivary glands), staging is accomplished by means of the familiar tumor-node-metastasis (TNM) system developed by the American Joint Committee on Cancer (AJCC) and the International Union Against Cancer (UICC) [*see Tables 3 and 4*].[23]

The prognostic factors in the management of parotid gland tumors must be understood in relation to the stage the disease has reached, the need for postoperative radiation therapy, and the overall long-term outcome [*see Table 5*]. Such factors include age

Table 4 American Joint Committee on Cancer Staging System for Major Salivary Gland Tumors

Stage	T	N	M
Stage I	T1, T2	N0	M0
Stage II	T3	N0	M0
Stage III	T1, T2	N1	M0
Stage IV	T4 T3, T4 Any T Any T	N0 N1 N2, N3 Any N	M0 M0 M0 M1

Table 5 Prognostic Factors for Salivary Gland Tumors	
Age at diagnosis	Facial nerve dysfunction
Pain at presentation	Perineural growth
T stage	Positive surgical margins
N stage	Soft tissue invasion
Skin invasion	Treatment type

at diagnosis, pain at presentation, TNM staging, skin invasion, facial nerve dysfunction, perineural growth of the primary tumor, positive surgical margins in the final pathology report, soft tissue invasion by the primary tumor, treatment type, and extranodal spread of the metastatic disease in the neck. To make definitive decisions regarding treatment, it is necessary to analyze these prognostic factors critically in individual patients. An example of such critical analysis is the prognostic index devised by the Dutch Head and Neck Cooperative Group for patients with parotid cancer.[24,25] In this index, a weighted combination of the parameters of age, pain, tumor size, nodal stage, skin invasion, facial nerve dysfunction, perineural growth, and positive surgical margins is employed to compute a prognostic score. The score is then used to assign patients to one of four groups, each of which is associated with an expected recurrence-free percentage.

Management

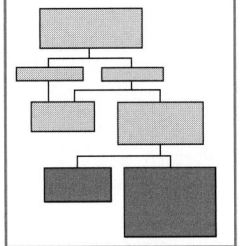

Treatment of a parotid mass depends on the nature and extent of the lesion [see Table 6]. Malignant parotid masses are treated surgically according to established oncologic principles [see Surgical Therapy, below], with postoperative radiation therapy added as necessary [see Radiation Therapy, below]. Generally, benign parotid masses are managed surgically as well, with exploration of the parotid gland, evaluation of the neoplasm, and appropriate parotidectomy with identification and preservation of the facial nerve and its branches. In the case of a suspected benign mixed tumor, enucleation is contraindicated because of the possibility of tumor spillage, incomplete removal of the tumor, injury to the capsule and resultant seeding of the tumor into the parotid tissue, or inadvertent injury to the branches of the facial nerve. Enucleation of such a tumor is very likely to result in local recurrence, which invariably is much more difficult to manage than the original lesion was and poses a high risk of injury to the facial nerve.

SURGICAL THERAPY

Parotidectomy with or without Facial Nerve Reconstruction

The minimum surgical procedure for a parotid mass is superficial parotidectomy with identification and preservation of the facial nerve [see 17 Parotidectomy]. Subtotal parotidectomy may be required for larger tumors that involve the deep lobe of the parotid gland; however, true total parotidectomy with preservation of the facial nerve is almost impossible, because of the parotid gland tissues surrounding the nerve. If the tumor involves the facial nerve and is directly infiltrating into it, a diagnosis of malignancy should be explored, and only if the diagnosis is confirmed should the facial nerve be sacrificed. Preoperative facial nerve weakness generally indicates that the tumor is involving the nerve, in which case

due consideration should be given to the sacrifice and subsequent reconstruction of this structure.

Reconstruction of the facial nerve can be performed with a nerve graft from the greater auricular nerve, from the sural nerve in the leg, or from the ansa hypoglossi. In view of the technical complexity of nerve grafting, preoperative consultation with a plastic surgeon may be necessary. The functional results of nerve grafting vary considerably, depending on the age of the patient, the extent of the disease, and the identification of and appropriate anastomosis to the peripheral branches of the facial nerve. If postoperative radiation therapy is envisioned, its potential deleterious effects on nerve regeneration should be kept in mind.

If the tumor involves only an isolated branch of the facial nerve, one may opt for selective sacrifice of that branch, along with nerve grafting. If the tumor extends beyond the parotid gland and involves the infratemporal fossa, the ascending ramus of the mandible, or the mastoid process, a much more extensive surgical procedure (e.g., composite resection, lateral temporal bone resection, or radical parotidectomy with sacrifice of the entire facial nerve) becomes necessary. Such patients invariably require postoperative radiation therapy [see Radiation Therapy, below]. However, in the majority of patients who present with an isolated parotid mass and a functioning facial nerve, every attempt should be made to preserve the nerve.[26] It is rarely necessary to sacrifice a functioning facial nerve: the only indication for doing so is a situation in which the entire tumor cannot be resected without sacrifice of the main trunk or the branches of the facial nerve and there is concern about leaving any gross tumor behind.

Intraoperative Frozen-Section Examination

The role of intraoperative frozen-section examination in the evaluation of a parotid mass, like that of FNA biopsy, is the subject of considerable debate. Nevertheless, frozen-section examination has been found to be useful for distinguishing salivary processes from nonsalivary processes and benign disease from malignant disease. In 80% to 90% of cases, the findings from intraoperative frozen-section examination correlate with the final pathologic diagnosis.[27] This study is also helpful in making a definitive diagnosis of Warthin tumor. If frozen-section examination shows a benign mixed tumor and this finding agrees with one's clinical judgment, lateral superficial parotidectomy should be sufficient. If frozen-section examination shows high-grade mucoepidermoid carcinoma, selective neck dissection may be considered (mainly for staging purposes, to determine whether any of the deep jugular nodes are positive). If frozen-section examination provides a definitive diagnosis of malignancy, further decisions about the extent of parotidectomy and possible selective neck dissection can be made accordingly; if not, the procedure originally planned can be performed, with any further interventions (if required) dictated by the final pathologic diagnosis. Obviously, the decision whether to sacrifice the facial nerve must not be based solely on whether the frozen section shows a benign or a malignant process.

Table 6 Principles of Treatment of Parotid Tumors
Adequate local excision of tumor, based on extent of primary lesion
Preservation of facial nerve if possible
Elective neck dissection reserved for selected patients
Postoperative radiotherapy when indicated (in appropriate fields)
Prognosis determined primarily by stage and grade of tumor

Table 7 Indications for Postoperative Radiation Therapy for Parotid Cancer

Aggressive, highly malignant tumor
Invasion of adjacent tissues outside parotid capsule
Regional lymph node metastases
Deep-lobe cancer
Gross residual tumor after resection
Recurrent tumor after resection
Invasion of facial nerve by tumor

Neck Dissection

Overall, about 20% of patients with malignant parotid tumors present with clinically detectable cervical lymphadenopathy (cN+).[10] There is wide agreement that these patients require either a comprehensive or a modified neck dissection [see 2:6 Neck Dissection], depending on the extent of the disease, but there continues to be controversy regarding the management of patients with salivary malignancies who have no clinically detectable cervical lymphadenopathy (cN0). In one study, approximately 14% of the patients were in cN+ status; however, approximately 12% were in cN0 status but presented with pathologically positive nodes (pN+).[28] In view of the low frequency of occult metastasis in the group as a whole, the investigators generally did not recommend routine elective treatment of the neck. They did find that certain histologic grades were associated with a higher incidence of metastatic disease to the neck nodes: the incidence of occult metastasis was about 49% in patients with high-grade lesions, compared with 7% in those with intermediate-grade or low-grade lesions. In addition, the incidence of having occult metastatic disease was more than 20% in patients with tumors larger than 4 cm, compared with 4% in those with smaller tumors.

The incidence of lymph node metastasis is affected not only by the size and histologic grade of the tumor but also by the histologic type, the primary tumor stage, the presence of facial nerve palsy, the patient's age, the extraparotid extension of the disease, and the degree of perilymphatic invasion.[29] In a multivariate analysis, the variables that showed the highest correlation with the incidence of lymph node metastasis were the histologic type (i.e., adenocarcinoma, undifferentiated carcinoma, high-grade mucoepidermoid carcinoma, SCC, or salivary duct carcinoma) and the T stage.[30]

Thus, elective neck dissection may be considered in patients with advanced-stage primary tumors, those whose tumors are of high histologic grades, and those whose tumors are of certain specific histologic types. A selective neck dissection may be performed to remove the lymph nodes of the submandibular triangle, level II, level III, and the upper part of level V for the purposes of staging.[29] However, a comprehensive neck dissection that encompasses levels I through V may be necessary in patients who present with clinically obvious cervical metastases.

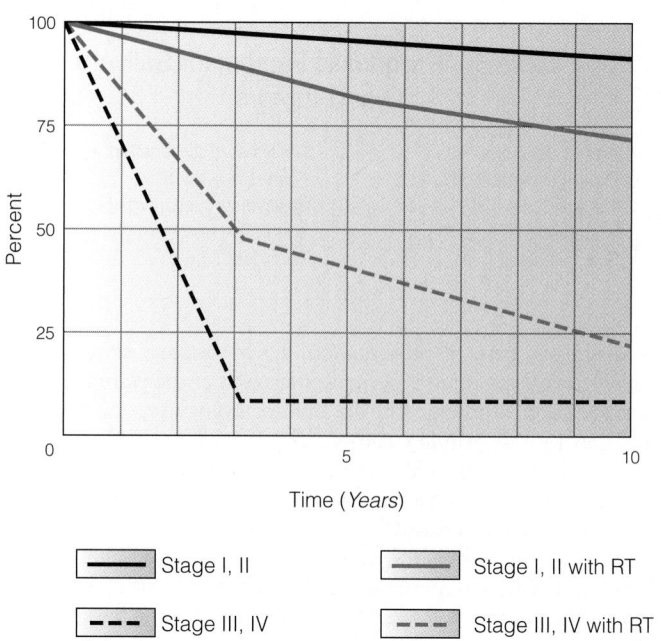

Figure 1 **Depicted is the impact of postoperative radiation therapy (RT) on overall outcome for patients with stage I or II tumors and patients with stage III or IV tumors.**

RADIATION THERAPY

Patients who present with advanced-stage (stage III or IV) disease, a large primary tumor, close margins, perineural spread, soft tissue extension, facial nerve dysfunction, or cervical lymph node metastasis invariably require postoperative radiation therapy [see Table 7].[31,32] In general, this means that postoperative radiation therapy is indicated for all patients except those with T1 or T2 malignant tumors of low-grade histology and clear margins. Thus, the decision whether to employ such therapy depends largely on the intraoperative findings and the final pathology report. A 1990 analysis showed that postoperative radiation therapy had a major impact on overall outcome in patients with stage III or IV tumors but conferred no statistically significant benefit on patients with stage I or II tumors [see Figure 1].[33]

Currently, there is substantial interest in the potential role of neutron therapy as a primary treatment modality for parotid malignancies, especially advanced inoperable parotid cancers and adenoid cystic carcinomas. A group from the University of Washington demonstrated that neutron therapy exerted a beneficial effect when used as the sole treatment of advanced parotid cancers.[34] Although these results are extremely promising, the patients treated with this modality clearly experienced an increased incidence of complications. Nevertheless, for patients with inoperable parotid cancer, neutron therapy may be the best option currently available.

Discussion

Implications of Histopathologic Classification of Parotid Gland Cancer

Alhough considerable controversy and debate continue to surround the histopathologic classification of malignant parotid tumors, most clinicians currently prefer either the classification system of the Armed Forces Institute of Pathology[35] or that of the World Health Organization.[36] The most common types of parotid tumor are mucoepidermoid carcinoma, adenoid cystic carcinoma, adenocarcinoma, malignant mixed tumor, acinic cell carcinoma, and primary SCC [see Figure 2].

As noted (see above), primary SCC of the parotid gland is quite rare, and most diagnoses of parotid SCC represent skin cancer

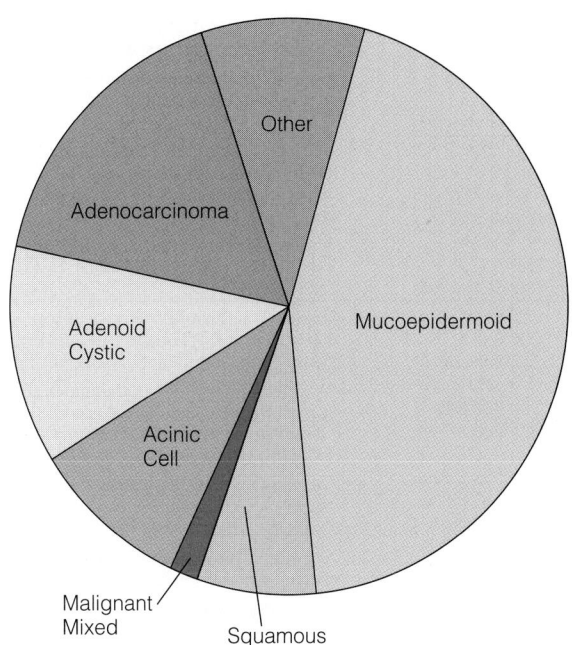

Figure 2 **Shown are the approximate relative frequencies of the most common types of parotid gland tumors.**

cystic carcinoma is low; however, the incidence of distant metastasis (especially pulmonary metastasis) appears to be high.[41] It is noteworthy that even when adenoid cystic carcinoma patients have pulmonary metastases, they tend to do remarkably well. Quite often, the metastatic disease in the lungs remains dormant for months or even years. At present, the role of chemotherapy in the management of adenoid cystic carcinoma and parotid tumors is supported only by anecdotal evidence and remains investigational.

Principles of Facial Reanimation

Every surgeon who performs parotid surgery, especially surgery for parotid cancer, should be familiar with the principles of facial reanimation. If the facial nerve dysfunction is recognized before the operation, appropriate arrangements may be made for plastic surgical consultation and facial nerve grafting. If the proximal stump of the facial nerve can be identified and the peripheral branches detected at the time of the operation, a nerve graft repair can be performed. The main donor nerves used in facial nerve grafting are the greater auricular nerve, the ansa hypoglossi, and the sural nerve. Of these, the greater auricular nerve is the preferred source for a graft: harvesting is relatively easy, the diameter matches that of the facial nerve, and the arborization of the distal branches allows for a greater number of facial nerve grafts.[42] The use of loupes or a microscope helps in the placement of the 9-0 nylon stitches employed in facial nerve grafting.

Regeneration of the facial nerve may take 3 to 6 months. There is some controversy regarding whether postoperative radiation therapy has a beneficial effect on functional outcome after nerve grafting: some studies cite detrimental effects,[43] whereas others report adequate functional outcomes.[42,44] In any case, if it is feasible to perform nerve grafting, every attempt should be made to do so. Currently, hypoglossal nerve transfer is rarely performed,[45] because various effective alternatives (e.g., fascia lata slings and Gore-Tex slings) are available. A consultation with a facial plastic surgeon may be quite helpful in the management of patients with total facial nerve palsy.

One of the most important considerations in addressing facial nerve paralysis is how to prevent exposure keratopathy and other ocular complications. Placement of a gold weight or a palpebral spring on the upper eyelid may be considered as a primary rehabilitative measure aimed at preventing corneal ulceration and opacification.[46] In the past, lateral tarsorrhaphy was commonly employed for this purpose, but currently, as a consequence of the superior results obtained with the gold weight and the palpebral spring, it is rarely performed. Other, simpler measures for preventing or minimizing ocular complications include the use of artificial tears and an eye patch during the day and the use of ointment with proper taping to keep the eyelid closed at night.

that has metastasized to the periparotid lymph nodes. Primary SCC has a high malignant potential, and radical surgical extirpation (with preservation of the facial nerve when possible), followed by planned postoperative radiotherapy, is the treatment of choice.[37]

Mucoepidermoid carcinomas are best divided into low-grade, intermediate-grade, and high-grade tumors.[38] For high-grade tumors, selective node dissection may be appropriate, with due consideration given to postoperative radiation therapy. For the majority of low-grade tumors—provided that they are properly excised with appropriate superficial parotidectomy—postoperative radiation therapy is unnecessary, because the incidence of local recurrence is lower than 5%.

Adenoid cystic carcinoma is a unique salivary gland tumor with a classic Swiss-cheese appearance under the microscope. There is a very high incidence of perineural spread with skip metastasis along the facial nerve and its branches, and the incidence rises with higher T stages.[39] The incidence of local recurrence is also very high, and thus, postoperative radiation therapy should be provided to patients who are at high risk for relapse (i.e., those with close or positive margins and those with perineural invasion). Such therapy appears to reduce the incidence of local recurrence.[40] The incidence of cervical lymph node metastasis in patients with adenoid

References

1. Beckhardt RN, Weber RS, Zane R, et al: Minor salivary gland tumors of the palate: clinical and pathologic correlates of outcome. Laryngoscope 105:1155, 1995
2. Eneroth CM: Salivary gland tumors in the parotid gland, submandibular gland and the palate region. Cancer 27:1415, 1971
3. Spiro RH: Salivary neoplasms: overview of a 35-year experience with 2,807 patients. Head Neck Surg 8:177, 1986
4. Fu YS, Wenig BM, Abemayor E, et al: Head and Neck Pathology With Clinical Correlations. Churchill Livingstone, New York, 2001, p 234
5. Batsakis JG: Primary lymphomas of the major salivary glands. Ann Otol Rhinol Laryngol 95:107, 1986
6. Barnes L, Myers EN, Prokopakis EP: Primary malignant lymphoma of the parotid gland. Arch Otolaryngol Head Neck Surg 124:573, 1988
7. Kane WJ, McCaffrey TV, Olsen KD, et al: Primary parotid malignancies. A clinical and pathologic review. Arch Otolaryngol Head Neck Surg 117:307, 1991
8. Friedrich RE, Li L, Knop J, et al: Pleomorphic adenoma of the salivary glands: analysis of 94 patients. Anticancer Res 25:1703, 2005
9. Wong DS: Signs and symptoms of malignant parotid tumours: an objective assessment. J R Coll Surg Edinb 46:91, 2001
10. Spiro RH, Huvos AG, Strong EWL: Cancer of the parotid gland: a clinicopathologic study of 288 primary cases. Am J Surg 130:452, 1975
11. Frommer J: The human accessory parotid gland: its incidence, nature, and significance. Oral Surg Oral Med Oral Pathol 43:671, 1977
12. Rodino W, Shaha AR: Surgical management of accessory parotid tumors. J Surg Oncol 54:153, 1993

13. Batsakis JG, Bautina E: Metastases to major salivary glands. Ann Otol Rhinol Laryngol 99:501, 1990

14. O'Brien CJ, Fracs MS, Adams JR: Surgical management of the facial nerve in the presence of malignancy about the face. Curr Opin Otolaryngol Head Neck Surg 9:90, 2001

15. Rabinov JD: Imaging of salivary gland pathology. Radiol Clin North Am 38:1047, 2000

16. Higashi T, Murahashi H, Ikuta H, et al: Identification of Warthin's tumor with technetium-99m pertechnetate. Clin Nucl Med 12:796, 1987

17. Gundlach P, Hopf J, Linnarz M: Introduction of a new diagnostic procedure: salivary duct endoscopy (sialendoscopy) clinical evaluation of sialendoscopy, sialography, and x-ray imaging. Endosc Surg Allied Technol 2:294, 1994

18. Qizilbash AH, Sianos J, Young JE, et al: Fine needle aspiration biopsy cytology of major salivary glands. Acta Cytol 29:503, 1985

19. Stewart CJ, MacKenzie K, McGarry GW, et al: Fine-needle aspiration cytology of salivary gland: a review of 341 cases. Diagn Cytopathol 22:139, 2000

20. Shaha AR, Webber C, DiMaio T, et al: Needle aspiration biopsy in salivary gland lesions. Am J Surg 160:373, 1990

21. Kesse KW, Manjaly G, Violaris N, et al: Ultrasound-guided biopsy in the evaluation of focal lesions and diffuse swelling of the parotid gland. Br J Oral Maxillofac Surg 40:384, 2002

22. Gross M, Ben-Yaacov A, Rund D, et al: Role of open incisional biopsy in parotid tumors. Acta Otolaryngol 124:758, 2004

23. AJCC Cancer Staging Manual, 6th edition. Springer-Verlag, New York, 2002

24. Vander Poorten VL, Balm AJ, Hilgers FJ, et al: The development of a prognostic score for patients with parotid carcinoma. Cancer 85:2057, 1999

25. Vander Poorten VL, Hart AA, van der Laan BF, et al: Prognostic index for patients with parotid carcinoma: external validation using the nationwide 1985–1994 Dutch Head and Neck Oncology Cooperative Group database. Cancer 97:1453, 2003

26. Nussbaum M, Bortikner D: Facial nerve preservation in parotid carcinoma. Bull NY Acad Med 62:862, 1986

27. Heller KS, Attie JN, Dubner S: Accuracy of frozen section in the evaluation of salivary tumors. Am J Surg 166:424, 1993

28. Armstrong JG, Harrison LB, Thaler HT, et al: The indications for elective treatment of the neck in cancer of the major salivary glands. Cancer 69:615, 1992

29. Ferlito A, Shaha AR, Rinaldo A, et al: Management of clinically negative cervical lymph nodes in patients with malignant neoplasms of the parotid gland. ORL J Otorhinolaryngol Relat Spec 63:123, 2001

30. Regis De Brito Santos I, Kowalski LP, Cavalcante De Araujo V, et al: Multivariate analysis of risk factors for neck metastases in surgically treated parotid carcinomas. Arch Otolaryngol Head Neck Surg 127:56, 2001

31. Tullio A, Marchetti C, Sesenna E, et al: Treatment of carcinoma of the parotid gland: the results of a multicenter study. J Oral Maxillofac Surg 59:263, 2001

32. Harrison LB, Armstrong JG, Spiro RH, et al: Postoperative radiation therapy for major salivary gland malignancies. J Surg Oncol 45:52, 1990

33. Armstrong JG, Harrison LB, Spiro RH, et al: Malignant tumors of major salivary gland origin: a matched-pair analysis of the role of combined surgery and postoperative radiotherapy. Arch Otolaryngol Head Neck Surg 116:290, 1990

34. Laramore GE, Krall JM, Griffin TW, et al: Neutron versus photon irradiation for unresectable salivary gland tumors: final report of an RTOG-MRC randomized clinical trial. Radiation Therapy Oncology Group. Medical Research Council. Int J Radiat Oncol Biol Phys 27:235, 1993

35. Ellis GL, Auclair PL: Tumors of the Salivary Glands. Atlas of Tumor Pathology, series 3, fascicle 17. Armed Forces Institute of Pathology, Washington, DC, 1996

36. Seifert G, Sobin LH: The World Health Organization's histological classification of salivary gland tumors: a commentary on the second edition. Cancer 70:379, 1992

37. Shemen LJ, Huvos AG, Spiro RH: Squamous cell carcinoma of salivary gland origin. Head Neck Surg 9:235, 1987

38. Batsakis JG, Luna MA: Histopathologic grading of salivary gland neoplasms: I. Mucoepidermoid carcinomas. Ann Otol Rhinol Laryngol 99:835, 1990

39. Vrielinck LJ, Ostyn F, van Damme B, et al: The significance of perineural spread in adenoid cystic carcinoma of the major and minor salivary glands. Int J Oral Maxillofac Surg 17:190, 1988

40. Vikram B, Strong EW, Shah JP, et al: Radiation therapy in adenoid-cystic carcinoma. Int J Radiat Oncol Biol Phys 10:221, 1984

41. Spiro RH: Distant metastasis in adenoid cystic carcinoma of salivary origin. Am J Surg 174:495, 1997

42. Reddy PG, Arden RL, Mathog RH: Facial nerve rehabilitation after radical parotidectomy. Laryngoscope 109:894, 1999

43. Pillsbury HC, Fisch U: Extratemporal facial nerve grafting and radiotherapy. Arch Otolaryngol 105:441, 1979

44. McGuirt WF, McCabe BF: Effect of radiation therapy on facial nerve cable autografts. Laryngoscope 87:415, 1977

45. Conley J, Baker DC: Hypoglossal-facial nerve anastomosis for reinnervation of the paralyzed face. Plast Reconstr Surg 63:63, 1979

46. Levine RE, Shapiro JP: Reanimation of the paralyzed eyelid with the enhanced palpebral spring or the gold weight: modern replacements for tarsorrhaphy. Facial Plast Surg 16:325, 2000

14 NECK MASS

Barry J. Roseman, M.D., and Orlo H. Clark, M.D., F.A.C.S.

Assessment of a Neck Mass

Clinical Evaluation

HISTORY

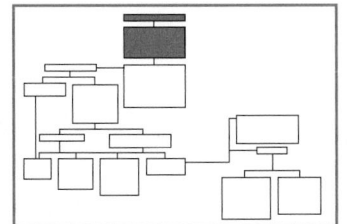

The evaluation of any neck mass begins with a careful history. The history should be taken with the differential diagnosis in mind [*see Table 1*] because directed questions can narrow down the diagnostic possibilities and focus subsequent investigations. For example, in younger patients, one would tend to look for congenital lesions, whereas in older adults, the first concern would always be neoplasia.

The duration and growth rate of the mass should be determined: malignant lesions are far more likely to exhibit rapid growth than benign ones, which may grow and shrink. Next, the location of the mass in the neck should be determined. This is particularly important for differentiating congenital masses from neoplastic or inflammatory ones because each type usually occurs consistently in particular locations. In addition, the location of a neoplasm has both diagnostic and prognostic significance. The possibility that the mass reflects an infectious or inflammatory process should also be assessed. One should check for evidence of infection or inflammation (e.g., fever, pain, or tenderness); a recent history of tuberculosis, sarcoidosis, or fungal infection; the presence of dental problems; and a history of trauma to the head and neck. Masses that appear inflamed or infected are far more likely to be benign.

Finally, factors suggestive of cancer should be sought: a previous malignancy elsewhere in the head and neck (e.g., a history of skin cancer, melanoma, thyroid cancer, or head and neck cancer); night sweats (suggestive of lymphoma); excessive exposure to the sun (a risk factor for skin cancer); smoking or excessive alcohol consumption (risk factors for squamous cell carcinoma of the head and neck); nasal obstruction or bleeding, otalgia, odynophagia, dysphagia, or hoarseness (suggestive of a malignancy in the upper aerodigestive tract); or exposure to low-dose therapeutic radiation (a risk factor for thyroid cancer).

PHYSICAL EXAMINATION

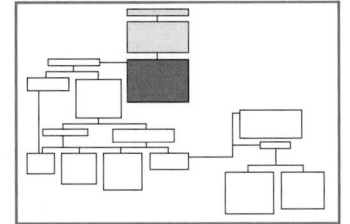

Examination of the head and neck is challenging in that much of the area to be examined is not easily visualized. Patience and practice are necessary to master the special instruments and techniques of examination. A head and neck examination is usually performed with the patient sitting in front of the physician. Constant repositioning of the head is necessary to obtain adequate visualization of the various areas. Gloves must be worn during the examination, particularly if the mucous membranes are to be examined. Good illumination is essential. The time-honored but cumbersome head mirror has been largely supplanted by the headlight (usually a high-intensity halogen lamp). Fiberoptic endoscopy with a flexible laryngoscope and a nasopharyngoscope has become a common component of the physical examination for evaluating the larynx, the nasopharynx,

Table 1 Etiology of Neck Mass

Inflammatory and infectious disorders	Acute lymphadenitis (bacterial or viral infection)
	Subcutaneous abscess (carbuncle)
	Infectious mononucleosis
	Cat-scratch fever
	AIDS
	Tuberculous lymphadenitis (scrofula)
	Fungal lymphadenitis (actinomycosis)
	Sarcoidosis
Congenital cystic lesions	Thyroglossal duct cyst
	Branchial cleft cyst
	Cystic hygroma (lymphangioma)
	Vascular malformation (hemangioma)
	Laryngocele
Benign neoplasms	Salivary gland tumor
	Thyroid nodules or goiter
	Soft tissue tumor (lipoma, sebaceous cyst)
	Chemodectoma (carotid body tumor)
	Neurogenic tumor (neurofibroma, neurilemoma)
	Laryngeal tumor (chondroma)
Malignant neoplasms	*Primary*
	Salivary gland tumor
	Thyroid cancer
	Upper aerodigestive tract cancer
	Soft tissue sarcoma
	Skin cancer (melanoma, squamous cell carcinoma, and basal cell carcinoma)
	Lymphoma
	Metastatic
	Upper aerodigestive tract cancer
	Skin cancer (melanoma, squamous cell carcinoma)
	Salivary gland tumor
	Thyroid cancer
	Adenocarcinoma (breast, GI tract, GU tract, lung)
	Unknown primary

Assessment of a Neck Mass

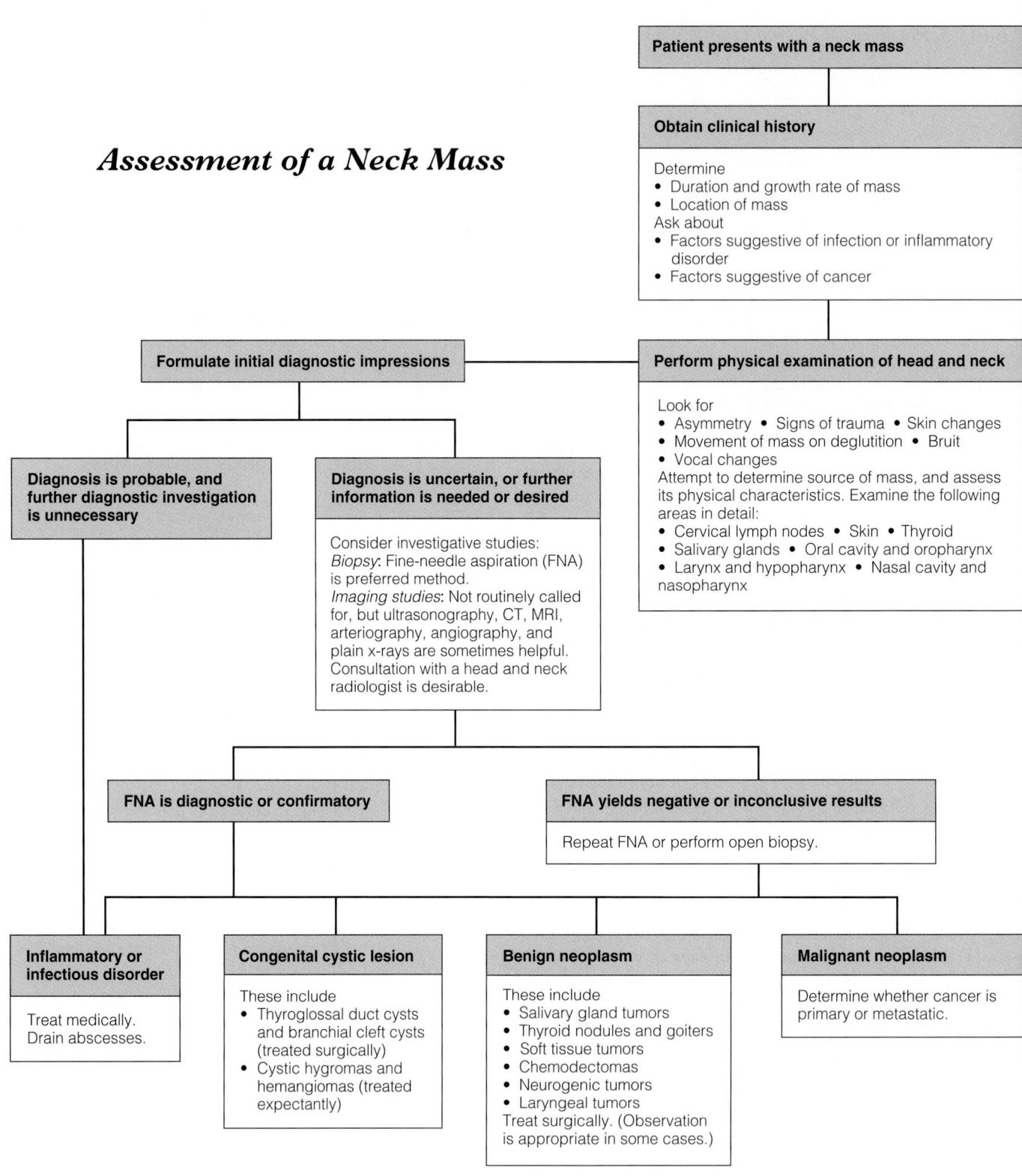

Patient presents with a neck mass

Obtain clinical history

Determine
- Duration and growth rate of mass
- Location of mass

Ask about
- Factors suggestive of infection or inflammatory disorder
- Factors suggestive of cancer

Perform physical examination of head and neck

Look for
- Asymmetry • Signs of trauma • Skin changes
- Movement of mass on deglutition • Bruit
- Vocal changes

Attempt to determine source of mass, and assess its physical characteristics. Examine the following areas in detail:
- Cervical lymph nodes • Skin • Thyroid
- Salivary glands • Oral cavity and oropharynx
- Larynx and hypopharynx • Nasal cavity and nasopharynx

Formulate initial diagnostic impressions

Diagnosis is probable, and further diagnostic investigation is unnecessary

Diagnosis is uncertain, or further information is needed or desired

Consider investigative studies:
Biopsy: Fine-needle aspiration (FNA) is preferred method.
Imaging studies: Not routinely called for, but ultrasonography, CT, MRI, arteriography, angiography, and plain x-rays are sometimes helpful. Consultation with a head and neck radiologist is desirable.

FNA is diagnostic or confirmatory

FNA yields negative or inconclusive results

Repeat FNA or perform open biopsy.

Inflammatory or infectious disorder

Treat medically.
Drain abscesses.

Congenital cystic lesion

These include
- Thyroglossal duct cysts and branchial cleft cysts (treated surgically)
- Cystic hygromas and hemangiomas (treated expectantly)

Benign neoplasm

These include
- Salivary gland tumors
- Thyroid nodules and goiters
- Soft tissue tumors
- Chemodectomas
- Neurogenic tumors
- Laryngeal tumors

Treat surgically. (Observation is appropriate in some cases.)

Malignant neoplasm

Determine whether cancer is primary or metastatic.

Primary neoplasm

These include
- Lymphoma • Thyroid cancer • Upper aerodigestive tract cancer • Soft tissue sarcoma
- Skin cancer

Treat with surgery, radiation therapy, and/or chemotherapy, as appropriate.

Metastatic tumor

Primary is known

Metastatic squamous cell carcinoma: Perform selective neck dissection, and consider adjuvant radiation therapy.
Metastatic adenocarcinoma: Perform neck dissection (selective or other), and consider adjuvant radiation therapy.
Metastatic melanoma: Perform full-thickness excision and SLN biopsy; if there are positive SLNs or lymph nodes are palpable, perform modified neck dissection.

Primary is unknown

Evaluate nasopharynx, larynx, esophagus, hypopharynx, and tracheobronchial tree endoscopically.
Biopsy nasopharynx, tonsils, and hypopharynx.
Perform unilateral neck dissection followed by irradiation of neck, entire pharynx, and nasopharynx.

Table 2 Classification of Cervical Lymph Nodes

Level	Nodes
I	Submental nodes Submandibular nodes
II	Upper internal jugular chain nodes
III	Middle internal jugular chain nodes
IV	Lower internal jugular chain nodes
V	Spinal accessory nodes Transverse cervical nodes
VI	Tracheoesophageal groove nodes

and the paranasal sinuses, especially when these areas cannot be adequately visualized with more standard techniques.

The examination should begin with inspection for asymmetry, signs of trauma, and skin changes. One should ask the patient to swallow to see if the mass moves with deglutition. Palpation should be done both from the front and from behind. Auscultation is performed to detect audible bruits. One should also ask about the patient's voice, changes in which may suggest either a laryngeal tumor or recurrent nerve dysfunction from locally invasive thyroid cancer.

During the physical examination, one should be thinking about the following questions: What structure is the neck mass arising from? Is it a lymph node? Is the mass arising from a normally occurring structure, such as the thyroid gland, a salivary gland, a nerve, a blood vessel, or a muscle? Or is it arising from an abnormal structure, such as a laryngocele, a branchial cleft cyst, or a cystic hygroma? Is the mass soft, fluctuant, easily mobile, well-encapsulated, and smooth? Or is it firm, poorly mobile, and fixed to surrounding structures? Does it pulsate? Is there a bruit? Does it appear to be superficial, or is it deeper in the neck? Is it attached to the skin? Is it tender?

The following areas of the head and neck are examined in some detail.

Cervical Lymph Nodes

Enlarged lymph nodes are by far the most common neck masses encountered. The cervical lymphatic system consists of interconnected groups or chains of nodes that parallel the major neurovascular structures in the head and neck. The skin and mucosal surfaces of the head and neck all have specific and predictable nodes associated with them. The classification of cervical lymph nodes has been standardized to comprise six levels [*see Table 2 and Figure 1*]. Accurate determination of lymph node level on physical examination and in surgical specimens not only helps establish a common language among clinicians but also permits comparison of data among different institutions.

The location, size, and consistency of lymph nodes furnish valuable clues to the nature of the primary disease. Other physical characteristics of the adenopathy should be noted as well, including the number of lymph nodes affected, their mobility, their degree of fixation, and their relation to surrounding anatomic structures. One can often establish a tentative diagnosis on the basis of these findings alone. For example, soft or tender nodes are more likely to derive from an inflammatory or infectious condition, whereas hard, fixed, painless nodes are more likely to rep-

resent metastatic cancer. Multiple regions of enlarged lymph nodes are usually a sign of systemic disease (e.g., lymphoma, tuberculosis, or infectious mononucleosis), whereas solitary nodes are more often due to malignancy. Firm, rubbery nodes are typical of lymphoma. Low cervical nodes are more likely to contain metastases from the thyroid or a primary source other than the head and neck, whereas upper cervical nodes are more likely to contain metastases from the head and neck.

The submental and submandibular nodes (level I) are palpated bimanually. Metastases to level I are commonly from the lips, the oral cavity, or the facial skin. The three levels of internal jugular chain nodes (levels II, III, and IV) are best examined by gently rolling the sternocleidomastoid muscle between the thumb and the index finger. Level II and level III lymph nodes are common sites for lymph node metastases from primary cancers of the oropharynx, the larynx, and the hypopharynx. Metastases in level IV lymph nodes can arise from cancers of the upper aerodigestive tract, cancers of the thyroid gland, or cancers arising below the clavicle (Virchow's node). Nodal metastases in the posterior triangle (level V) can arise from nasopharyngeal and thyroid cancers as well as from squamous cell carcinoma or melanoma of the posterior scalp and the pinna of the ear. The tracheoesophageal groove nodes (level VI) or control nodes are then palpated.

Skin

Careful examination of the scalp, the ears, the face, the oral cavity, and the neck will identify potentially malignant skin lesions, which may give rise to lymph node metastases.

Thyroid Gland

The thyroid gland is first observed as the patient swallows; it is then palpated and its size and consistency assessed to determine whether it is smooth, diffusely enlarged, or nodular and whether one nodule or several are present. If it is unclear whether the mass is truly thyroid, one can clarify the point by asking the patient to swallow and watching to see whether the mass moves. Signs of superior mediastinal syndrome (e.g., cervical venous engorgement and facial edema) suggest retrosternal extension of a thyroid goiter. Elevation of the arms above the head often causes such signs in a patient with a substernal goiter (a positive Pemberton sign). The larynx and trachea are examined, with special attention to the cricothyroid membrane, over which Delphian nodes can be palpated. These nodes can be a harbinger of thyroid or laryngeal cancer.

Major Salivary Glands

Examination of the paired parotid and submandibular glands involves not only palpation of the neck but also an intraoral examination to inspect the duct openings. The submandibular glands are best assessed by bimanual palpation, with one finger in the mouth and one in the neck. They are normally lower and more prominent in older patients. The parotid glands are often palpable in the neck, though the deep lobe cannot always be assessed. A mass in the region of the tail of the parotid must be distinguished from enlarged level II jugular nodes. The oropharynx is inspected for distortion of the lateral walls. The parotid (Stensen's) duct may be found opening into the buccal mucosa, opposite the second upper molar.

Oral Cavity and Oropharynx

The lips should be inspected and palpated. Dentures should be removed before the mouth is examined. The buccal mucosa, the teeth, and the gingiva are then inspected. The patient should be

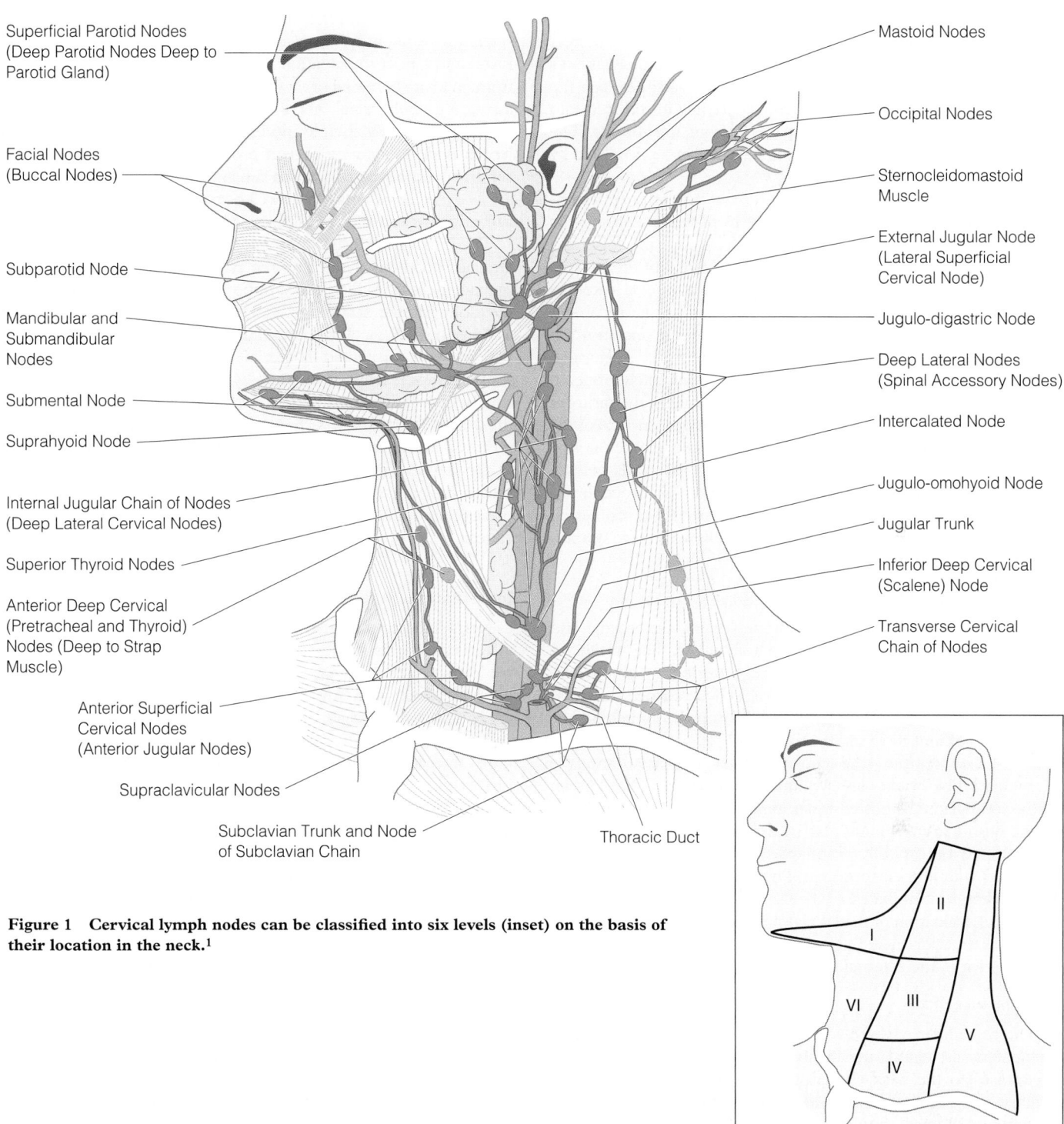

Superficial Parotid Nodes (Deep Parotid Nodes Deep to Parotid Gland)

Facial Nodes (Buccal Nodes)

Subparotid Node

Mandibular and Submandibular Nodes

Submental Node

Suprahyoid Node

Internal Jugular Chain of Nodes (Deep Lateral Cervical Nodes)

Superior Thyroid Nodes

Anterior Deep Cervical (Pretracheal and Thyroid) Nodes (Deep to Strap Muscle)

Anterior Superficial Cervical Nodes (Anterior Jugular Nodes)

Supraclavicular Nodes

Subclavian Trunk and Node of Subclavian Chain

Mastoid Nodes

Occipital Nodes

Sternocleidomastoid Muscle

External Jugular Node (Lateral Superficial Cervical Node)

Jugulo-digastric Node

Deep Lateral Nodes (Spinal Accessory Nodes)

Intercalated Node

Jugulo-omohyoid Node

Jugular Trunk

Inferior Deep Cervical (Scalene) Node

Transverse Cervical Chain of Nodes

Thoracic Duct

Figure 1   Cervical lymph nodes can be classified into six levels (inset) on the basis of their location in the neck.[1]

asked to elevate the tongue so that the floor of the mouth can be examined and bimanual inspection performed. The tongue should be inspected both in its normal position in the mouth and during protrusion.

Most of the oropharyngeal contents are easily visualized if the tongue is depressed. Only the anterior two thirds of the tongue is clearly visible on examination, however. The base of the tongue is best visualized by using a mirror. In most persons, the tongue base can be palpated, at the cost of some discomfort to the patient. The ventral surface of the tongue must also be care-

fully inspected and palpated.

The hard palate is examined by gently tilting the patient's head backward, and the soft palate is inspected by gently depressing the tongue with a tongue blade. The movement of the palate is assessed by having the patient say "ahh."

The tonsils are then examined. They are usually symmetrical but may vary substantially in size. For example, in young patients, hyperplastic tonsils may almost fill the oropharynx, but in adult patients, this is an uncommon finding. Finally, the posterior pharyngeal wall is inspected.

Larynx and Hypopharynx

The larynx and the hypopharynx are best examined by indirect or direct laryngoscopy. A mirror is warmed, and the patient's tongue is gently held forward to increase the space between the oropharyngeal structures. The mirror is carefully introduced into the oropharynx without touching the base of the tongue. The oropharynx, the larynx, and the hypopharynx can be visualized by changing the angle of the mirror.

The lingual and laryngeal surfaces of the epiglottis are examined. Often, the patient must be asked to phonate to bring the endolarynx into view. The aryepiglottic folds and the false and true vocal cords should be identified. The mobility of the true vocal cords is then assessed: their resting position is carefully noted, and their movement during inspiration is recorded. Normally, the vocal cords abduct during breathing and move to the median position during phonation. The larynx is elevated when the patient attempts to say "eeeee"; this allows one to observe vocal cord movement and to better visualize the piriform sinuses, the postcricoid hypopharynx, the laryngeal surface of the epiglottis, and the anterior commissure of the glottic larynx. Passage of a fiberoptic laryngoscope through the nose yields a clear view of the hypopharynx and the larynx. This procedure is well tolerated by almost all patients, particularly if a topical anesthetic is gently sprayed into the nose and swallowed, thereby anesthetizing both the nose and the pharynx.

Nasal Cavity and Nasopharynx

The nasopharynx is examined by depressing the tongue and inserting a small mirror behind the soft palate. The patient is instructed to open the mouth widely and breathe through it to elevate the soft palate. With the patient relaxed, a warmed nasopharyngeal mirror is carefully placed in the oropharynx behind the soft palate without touching the mucosa.

The nasal septum, the choanae, the turbinates, and the eustachian tube orifices are systematically assessed. The dorsum of the soft palate, the posterior nasopharyngeal wall, and the vault of the nasopharynx should also be assessed. The exterior of the nose should be carefully examined, and the septum should be inspected with a nasal speculum. Polyps or other neoplasms can be mistaken for turbinates.

Careful evaluation of the cranial nerves is essential, as is examination of the eyes (including assessment of ocular movement and visual activity), the external ear, and the tympanic membrane.

Additional Areas

The remainder of the physical examination is also important, particularly as regards the identification of a possible source of metastases to the neck. Other sets of lymph nodes—especially axillary and inguinal nodes—are examined for enlargement or tenderness. Women should undergo complete pelvic and rectal examinations. Men should undergo rectal, testicular, and prostate examinations; tumors from these organs may metastasize to the neck, albeit rarely.

Initial Diagnostic Impressions

Having obtained a comprehensive history and performed a physical examination, one is likely to have a better idea of whether the neck mass is inflammatory, benign, or malignant. In

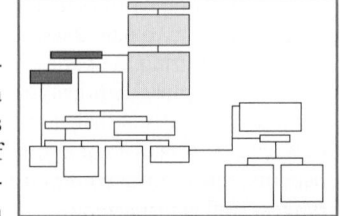

some patients, the findings are clear enough to strongly suggest a specific disease entity. For example, a rapidly developing mass that is soft and tender to palpation is most likely a reactive lymph node from an acute bacterial or viral illness. A slow-growing facial mass associated with facial nerve deficits is probably a malignant parotid tumor. A thyroid nodule with an adjacent abnormal lymph node in a young patient probably represents thyroid cancer. In an elderly patient with a substantial history of smoking and alcohol use, a neck mass may well be a metastasis from squamous cell carcinoma in the aerodigestive tract.

The initial diagnostic impressions and the degree of certainty attached to them determine the next steps in the workup and management of a neck mass; options include empirical therapy, ultrasonographic scanning, computed tomography, fine-needle aspiration (FNA), and observation alone. For example, in a patient with suspected bacterial lymphadenitis from an oral source, empirical antibiotic therapy with close follow-up is a reasonable approach. In a patient with a suspected parotid tumor, the best first test is a CT scan: the tumor probably must be removed, which means that one will have to ascertain the relation of the mass to adjacent structures. In a patient with suspected metastatic cancer, FNA is a sensible choice: it will confirm the presence of malignancy and may suggest a source of the primary cancer.

Investigative Studies

Neck masses of suspected infectious or inflammatory origin can be observed for short periods. Most neck masses in adults, however, are abnormal, and they are often manifestations of serious underlying conditions. In most cases, therefore, further diagnostic evaluation should be rigorously pursued.

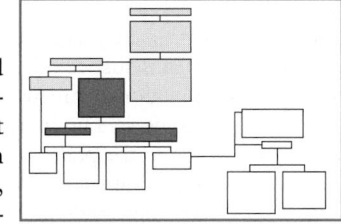

BIOPSY

Whether or not the history and the physical examination strongly suggest a specific diagnosis, the information obtained by sampling tissue from the neck mass is often highly useful. In many cases, biopsy establishes the diagnosis or, at least, reduces the diagnostic possibilities. At present, the preferred method of obtaining biopsy material from a neck mass is FNA, which is generally well tolerated and can usually be performed without local anesthesia. Although FNA is, on the whole, both safe and accurate, it is an invasive diagnostic procedure and carries a small but definable risk of potential problems (e.g., bleeding and sampling error). Accordingly, FNA should be done only when the results are likely to influence treatment.

FNA reliably distinguishes cystic from solid lesions and can often diagnose malignancy. It has in fact become the standard for making treatment decisions in patients with thyroid nodules and for confirming the clinical suspicion of a cystic lesion. FNA is also useful in patients with a known distant malignancy in whom confirmation of metastases is needed for staging and for planning therapy, as well as in patients with a primary tumor of the head and neck who are not candidates for operation but in whom a tissue diagnosis is necessary for appropriate nonsurgical therapy to be initiated. In addition, FNA is helpful in dealing with overly anxious patients in whom the clinical index of suspicion for a neoplasm is low and the head and neck examination is negative: negative biopsy results tend to reassure these patients and allow the surgeon time to follow the mass more confidently. (Of course, negative FNA results should not be considered the end point of any search and do not rule out cancer.)

Several studies have shown FNA to be approximately 90% accurate in establishing a definitive diagnosis. Lateral cystic neck masses that collapse on aspiration usually represent hygromas, branchial cleft cysts, or cystic degeneration of a metastatic papillary thyroid cancer. Fluid from these masses is sent for cytologic examination. If a palpable mass remains after cyst aspiration, a biopsy of the solid component should be done; the morphology of the cells will be better preserved.

If an extensive physical examination has been completed and the FNA is not diagnostic, one may have to perform an open biopsy to obtain a specimen for histologic sections and microbiologic studies. It is estimated that open biopsy eventually proves necessary in about 10% of patients with a malignant mass. In an open biopsy, it is important to orient skin incisions within the boundaries of a neck dissection; the incisions can then, if necessary, be extended for definitive therapy or reexcised if reoperation subsequently proves necessary. Crossing incisions should never be situated over vessels.

A case in which lymphoma and metastatic squamous cell carcinoma are diagnostic possibilities constitutes a special situation. FNA alone is often incapable of determining the precise histologic subtype for lymphoma, but it is usually capable of distinguishing a lymphoproliferative disease from metastatic squamous cell carcinoma. This is a crucial distinction, in that the two neoplasms are treated in drastically different ways.

If a lymphoma is suspected, FNA is typically followed by open biopsy, frozen-section confirmation, and submission of fresh tissue to the pathologist. The intact node is placed in normal saline and sent directly to the pathologist for analysis of cellular content and nodal architecture and identification of lymphocyte markers. If, however, metastatic squamous cell carcinoma is suspected, FNA usually suffices for establishing the diagnosis and formulating a treatment plan, which often includes chemotherapy and radiation initially. In this setting, performing an open biopsy can lead to significant wound healing complications; there is no need to incur this risk when FNA is all that is necessary to initiate treatment.

IMAGING

Diagnostic imaging should be used selectively in the evaluation of a neck mass; imaging studies should be performed only if the results are likely to affect subsequent therapy. Such studies often supply useful information about the location and characteristics of the mass and its relation to adjacent structures. Diagnostic imaging is particularly useful when a biopsy has been performed and a malignant tumor identified. In such cases, these studies can help establish the extent of local disease and the presence or absence of metastases.

Ultrasonography of the neck reliably differentiates solid masses from cystic ones and is especially useful in assessing congenital and developmental cysts. It is a valuable noninvasive technique for vascular lesions and clearly delineates thyroid and parathyroid abnormalities. CT is also useful for differentiating cysts from solid neck lesions and for determining whether a mass is within or outside a gland or nodal chain. In addition, CT scanning can delineate small tongue-base or tonsillar tumors that have a minimal mucosal component. MRI provides much the same information as CT. T_2-weighted gadolinium-enhanced scans are particularly useful for delineating the invasion of soft tissue by tumor: endocrine tumors are often enhanced on such scans. PET scanning is useful in the staging of many cancers, as well as in searching for the primary site in metastatic disease from an unknown source.

Arteriography is useful mainly for evaluating vascular lesions and tumors fixed to the carotid artery. Angiography is helpful for evaluating the vascularity of a mass, its specific blood supply, or the status of the carotid artery, but it provides very little information about the physical characteristics of the mass. Plain radiographs of the neck are rarely helpful in differentiating neck masses, but a chest x-ray can often confirm a diagnosis (e.g., in patients with lymphoma, sarcoidosis, or metastatic lung cancer). A chest x-ray is also important in any patient with a new diagnosis of cancer to determine if pulmonary metastases are present. It is also an essential component of preoperative evaluation for any patient older than 40 years.

It is important to communicate with the radiologist: an experienced head and neck radiologist may be able to offer the surgeon valuable guidance in choosing the best diagnostic test in a specific clinical scenario. Furthermore, providing the radiologist with a detailed clinical history facilitates interpretation of the images.

Management of Specific Disorders

INFLAMMATORY AND INFECTIOUS DISORDERS

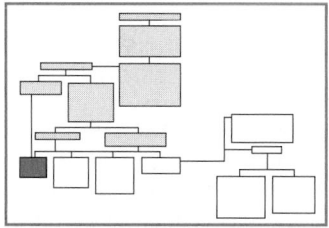

Acute infection of the neck (cervical adenitis) is most often the result of dental infection, tonsillitis, pharyngitis, viral upper respiratory tract infection, or skin infection. Lymph node enlargement is a frequent finding that may reflect any of a number of infectious disorders. The most common cause of this symptom is an acute infection of the mouth or pharynx. In this situation, the enlarged lymph nodes are usually just posterior and inferior to the angle of the mandible. Signs of acute infection (e.g., fever, malaise, and a sore mouth or throat) are usually present. A constitutional reaction, tenderness of the cervical mass, and the presence of an obvious infectious source confirm the diagnosis. Treatment should be directed toward the primary disease and should include a monospot test for infectious mononucleosis.

Neck masses may also derive from subcutaneous abscesses, infected sebaceous or inclusion cysts, or multiloculated carbuncles (most often occurring in the back of the neck in a patient with diabetes mellitus). The physical characteristics of abscesses make recognition of these problems relatively straightforward.

On occasion, primary head and neck bacterial infections can lead to infection of the fascial spaces of the neck. A high index of suspicion is required in this situation: such infections are sometimes difficult to diagnose. Aggressive treatment with antibiotics and drainage of closed spaces is indicated to prevent overwhelming fasciitis.

Various chronic infections (e.g., tuberculosis, fungal lymphadenitis, syphilis, cat-scratch fever, and AIDS) may also involve cervical lymph nodes. Certain chronic inflammatory disorders (e.g., sarcoidosis) may present with cervical lymphadenopathy as well. Because of the chronic lymph node involvement, these conditions are easily confused with neoplasms, especially lymphomas. Biopsy is occasionally necessary; however, skin tests and serologic studies are often more useful for establishing a diagnosis. Treatment of these conditions is primarily medical; surgery is reserved for complications.

CONGENITAL CYSTIC LESIONS

Thyroglossal Duct Cysts

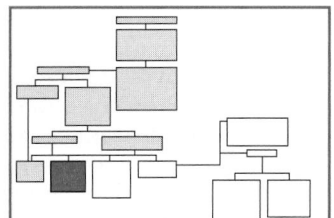

Thyroglossal duct cysts are remnants of the tract along which the thyroid gland descended into the neck from the foramen cecum [see Figure 2]. They account for about 70% of all congenital abnormalities of the neck. Thyroglossal duct cysts may be found in patients of any age but are most common in the first decade of life. They may take the form of a lone cyst, a cyst with a sinus tract, or a solid core of thyroid tissue. They may be so small as to be barely perceptible, as large as a grapefruit, or anything in between. Thyroglossal duct cysts are almost always found in the midline, at or below the level of the hyoid bone; however, they may be situated anywhere from the base of the tongue to the suprasternal notch. They occasionally present slightly lateral to the midline and are sometimes associated with an external fistula to the skin of the anterior neck. They are often ballotable and can usually be moved slightly from side to side but not up or down; however, they do move up and down when patients swallow or protrude the tongue.

Thyroglossal duct cysts must be differentiated from dermoid cysts, lymphadenomegaly in the anterior jugular chain, and cutaneous lesions (e.g., lipomas and sebaceous cysts). Operative treatment is almost always required, not only because of cosmetic considerations but also because of the high incidence of recurrent infection, including abscess formation. About 1% of thyroglossal duct cysts contain cancer; papillary cancer is the neoplasm most commonly encountered, followed by squamous cell carcinoma. About 25% of patients with papillary thyroid cancer in thyroglossal duct cysts have papillary thyroid cancer in other parts of the thyroid gland as well. About 10% have nodal metastases, which in some cases are bilateral.

Branchial Cleft Cysts

Branchial cleft cysts are vestigial remnants of the fetal branchial apparatus from which all neck structures are derived. Early in embryonic development, there are five branchial arches and four grooves (or clefts) between them. The internal tract or opening of a branchial cleft cyst is situated at the embryologic derivative of the corresponding pharyngeal groove, such as the tonsil (second arch) or the piriform sinus (third and fourth arches). The second arch is the most common area of origin for such cysts. The position of the cyst tract is also determined by the embryologic relation of its arch to the derivatives of the arches on either side of it.

The majority of branchial cleft cysts (those that develop from the second, third, and fourth arches) tend to present as a bulge along the anterior border of the sternocleidomastoid muscle, with or without a sinus tract. Branchial cleft cysts may become symptomatic at any age, but most are diagnosed in the first two decades of life. They often present as a smooth, painless, slowly enlarging mass in the lateral neck. Frequently, there is a history of fluctuating size and intermittent tenderness. The diagnosis is more obvious when there is an external fistulous tract and there is a history of intermittent discharge. Infection of the cyst may be the reason for the first symptoms.

Treatment consists of complete surgical removal of the cyst and the sinus tract. Any infection or inflammation should be treated and allowed to resolve before the cyst and the tract are removed.

Cystic Hygromas (Lymphangiomas)

A cystic hygroma is a lymphangioma that arises from vestigial lymph channels in the neck. Almost always, this condition is first noted by the second year of life; on rare occasions, it is first diagnosed in adulthood. A cystic hygroma may present as a relatively simple thin-walled cyst in the floor of the mouth or may involve all the tissues from the floor of the mouth to the mediastinum. About 80% of the time, there is only a painless cyst in the posterior cervical triangle or in the supraclavicular area. A cystic hygroma can also occur, however, at the root of the neck, in the angle of the jaw (where it may involve the parotid gland), and in the midline (where it may involve the tongue, the floor of the mouth, or the larynx).

The typical clinical picture is of a diffuse, soft, doughy, irregular mass that is readily transilluminated. Cystic hygromas look and feel somewhat like lipomas but have less well defined margins. Aspiration of cystic hygromas yields straw-colored fluid. They may be confused with angiomas (which are compressible), pneumatoceles from the apex of the lung, or aneurysms. They can be distinguished from vascular lesions by means of arteriography. On occasion, a cystic hygroma grows suddenly as a result of an upper respiratory tract infection, infection of the hygroma itself, or hemorrhage into the tissues. If the mass becomes large enough, it can compress the trachea or hinder swallowing.

In the absence of pressure symptoms (i.e., obstruction of the airway or interference with swallowing) or gross deformity, cystic hygromas may be treated expectantly. They tend to regress spontaneously; if they do not, complete surgical excision is indicated. Excision can be difficult because of the numerous satellite extensions that often surround the main mass and because of the association of the tumor with vital structures such as the cranial nerves. Recurrences are common; staged resections for complete excision are often necessary.

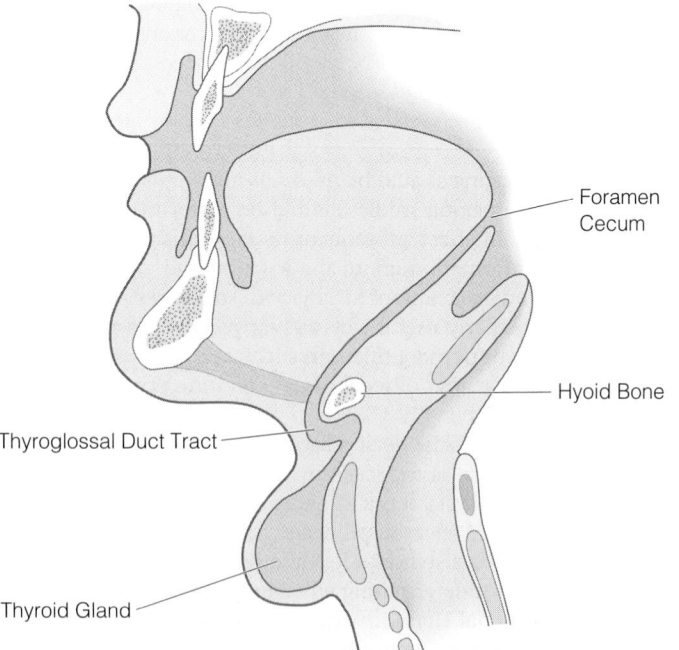

Foramen Cecum

Hyoid Bone

Thyroglossal Duct Tract

Thyroid Gland

Figure 2 Shown is the course of the thyroglossal duct tract from its origin in the area of the foramen cecum to the pyramidal lobe of the thyroid gland.[2] In the operative treatment of a thyroglossal duct cyst, the central portion of the hyoid bone must be removed to ensure complete removal of the tract and to prevent recurrence.

Vascular Malformation (Hemangiomas)

Hemangiomas are usually considered congenital because they either are present at birth or appear within the first year of life. A number of characteristic findings—bluish-purple coloration, increased warmth, compressibility followed by refilling, bruit, and thrill—distinguish them from other head and neck masses. Angiography is diagnostic but is rarely indicated.

Given that most of these congenital lesions resolve spontaneously, the treatment approach of choice is observation alone unless there is rapid growth, thrombocytopenia, or involvement of vital structures.

BENIGN NEOPLASMS

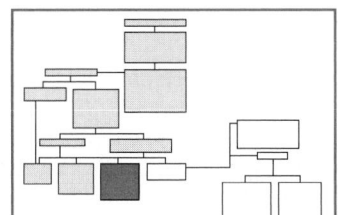

Salivary Gland Tumors

The possibility of a salivary gland neoplasm must be considered whenever an enlarging solid mass lies in front of and below the ear, at the angle of the mandible, or in the submandibular triangle. Benign salivary gland lesions are often asymptomatic; malignant ones are often associated with seventh cranial nerve symptoms or skin fixation. Diagnostic radiographic studies (CT or MRI) indicate whether the mass is salivary in origin but do not help classify it histologically. The diagnostic test of preference is open biopsy in the form of complete submandibular gland removal or superficial parotidectomy.

With any mass in or around the ear, one should be prepared to remove the superficial lobes of the parotid, the deep lobes, or both and to perform a careful facial nerve dissection. Any less complete approach reduces the chances of a cure: there is a high risk of implantation and seeding of malignant tumors. Benign mixed tumors make up two thirds of all salivary tumors; these must also be completely removed because recurrence is common after incomplete resection.

Benign Thyroid Nodules and Nodular Goiters

Thyroid disease is a relatively common cause of neck masses: in the United States, about 4% of women and 2% of men have a palpable thyroid nodule. Patients should be questioned about local symptoms (pain, dysphagia, pressure, hoarseness, or a change in the voice), about the duration of the nodule, and about systemic symptoms (from hyperthyroidism, hypothyroidism, or any other illness). Although most nodules are benign, malignancy is a significant concern. Nodules in children, young men, older persons, pregnant women, or persons with a history of radiation exposure or a family history of thyroid cancer are more likely to be malignant. Nodules that are truly solitary, feel firm or hard on examination, are growing rapidly, or are nonfunctional on scans are more likely to be malignant.

If physical examination suggests a discrete thyroid nodule, FNA should be done to ascertain whether malignancy is present within the nodule. If malignancy is confirmed or suspected, surgery is indicated. If the nodule is histologically benign or disappears with aspiration, thyroid suppression and observation are often sufficient. FNA often yields unrepresentative results in patients with a history of radiation exposure, in whom there is approximately a 40% chance that one of the nodules present contains cancer.

Surgery for thyroid nodules involves excisional biopsy consisting of at least total lobectomy [see 20 Thyroid and Parathyroid Procedures]; enucleation is almost never indicated. The surgical approach of choice for most patients with Graves disease or multinodular goiter is subtotal or total thyroidectomy or total lobectomy on one side and subtotal lobectomy on the other (Dunhill's operation). Treatment of thyroid cancer is discussed elsewhere [see Primary Malignant Neoplasms, Thyroid Cancer, below].

Soft Tissue Tumors (Lipomas, Sebaceous Cysts)

Superficial intracutaneous or subcutaneous masses may be sebaceous (or epidermal inclusion) cysts or lipomas. Final diagnosis and treatment usually involves simple surgical excision, often done as an office procedure with local anesthesia.

Chemodectomas (Carotid Body Tumors)

Carotid body tumors belong to a group of tumors known as chemodectomas (or, alternatively, as glomus tumors or nonchromaffin paragangliomas), which derive from the chemoreceptive tissue of the head and neck. In the head and neck, chemodectomas most often arise from the tympanic bodies in the middle ear, the glomus jugulare at the skull base, the vagal body near the skull base along the inferior ganglion of the vagus, and the carotid body at the carotid bifurcation. They are occasionally familial and sometimes occur bilaterally.

A carotid body tumor presents as a firm, round, slowly growing mass at the carotid bifurcation. Occasionally, a bruit is present. The tumor cannot be separated from the carotid artery by palpation and can usually be moved laterally and medially but not in a cephalocaudal plane. The differential diagnosis includes a carotid aneurysm, a branchial cleft cyst, a neurogenic tumor, and nodal metastases fixed to the carotid sheath. The diagnosis is made by means of CT scanning or arteriography, which demonstrate a characteristic highly vascular mass at the carotid bifurcation. Neurofibromas tend to displace, encircle, or compress a portion of the carotid artery system, events that are readily demonstrated by carotid angiography.

Biopsy should be avoided. Chemodectomas are sometimes malignant and should therefore be removed in most cases to prevent subsequent growth and pressure symptoms. Fortunately, even malignant chemodectomas are usually low grade; long-term results after removal are excellent on the whole. Vascular surgical experience is desirable, in that bleeding may occur and clamping of the carotid artery may result in a stroke. Expectant treatment may be indicated in older or debilitated individuals. Radiotherapy may be appropriate for patients with unresectable tumors.

Neurogenic Tumors (Neurofibromas, Neurilemomas)

The large number of nerves in the head and neck renders the area susceptible to neurogenic tumors. The most common of such tumors, neurilemomas (schwannomas) and neurofibromas, arise from the neurilemma and usually present as painless, slowly growing masses in the lateral neck. Neurilemomas can be differentiated from neurofibromas only by means of histologic examination.

Given the potential these tumors possess for malignant degeneration and slow but progressive growth, surgical resection is indicated. This may include resection of the involved nerves, particularly with neurofibromas, which tend to be more invasive and less encapsulated than neurilemomas.

Laryngeal Tumors

In rare cases, a chondroma may arise from the thyroid cartilage or the cricoid cartilage. It is firmly fixed to the cartilage and may present as a mass in the neck or as the cause of a progressively compromised airway. Surgical excision is indicated.

PRIMARY MALIGNANT NEOPLASMS

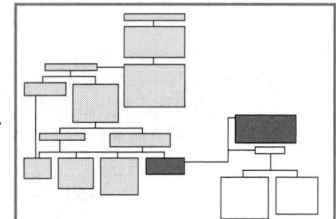

Lymphomas

Cervical adenopathy is one of the most common presenting symptoms in patients with Hodgkin and non-Hodgkin lymphoma. The nodes tend to be softer, smoother, more elastic, and more mobile than nodes containing metastatic carcinoma would be. Rapid growth is not unusual, particularly in non-Hodgkin lymphoma. Involvement of extranodal sites, particularly Waldeyer's tonsillar ring, is often seen in patients with non-Hodgkin lymphoma; enlargement of these sites may provide a clue to the diagnosis. The diagnosis is usually suggested by FNA, then confirmed via excisional biopsy of an intact lymph node. The precise histologic subtype cannot be determined by FNA alone. Open biopsy must ultimately be done and fresh tissue must be submitted for analysis by histology, immunochemistry, and electron microscopy.

Lymphoma is treated by means of radiation therapy, chemotherapy, or both, depending on the disease's pathologic type and clinical stage.

Thyroid Cancer

The approach to suspected thyroid cancer differs in some respects from the approach to benign thyroid disease. The operation of choice for papillary thyroid cancer that is occult (< 1 cm in diameter) and confined to the thyroid gland and for follicular thyroid cancer that is minimally invasive (i.e., exhibiting only capsular invasion) is thyroid lobectomy; the prognosis is excellent. The procedure of choice for papillary, follicular, Hürthle cell, and medullary thyroid cancer is total or near-total thyroidectomy (when it can be done safely) [see 20 Thyroid and Parathyroid Procedures]. Patients who present with thyroid nodules and have a history of radiation exposure or a family history of thyroid cancer should also undergo total or near-total thyroidectomy because about 40% of them will have at least one focus of papillary thyroid cancer. Total thyroidectomy decreases recurrence and permits the use of iodine-131 (^{131}I) to scan for and treat residual disease; it also makes serum thyroglobulin and calcitonin assays more sensitive for diagnosing recurrent or persistent differentiated thyroid tumors of follicular or parafollicular cell origin.

Patients with medullary thyroid cancer should undergo meticulous elective (prophylactic) or therapeutic bilateral central neck dissection. All patients with medullary thyroid cancer should be screened for *ret* proto-oncogene mutations on chromosome 10, as well as for pheochromocytoma. Therapeutic modified neck dissection is indicated for all patients with thyroid cancer and palpable nodes laterally. Prophylactic modified neck dissection is indicated for patients with medullary thyroid cancer and either primary tumors larger than 1.5 cm or evidence of central neck node involvement.

Patients with anaplastic thyroid cancer are probably best treated with a combination of chemotherapy and radiation therapy, in conjunction with the removal of as much of the neoplasm as can safely be excised. Most patients with thyroid lymphoma should receive chemotherapy, radiation therapy, or both.

Upper Aerodigestive Tract Cancer

Deciding on the optimal therapeutic approach to tumors of the aerodigestive tract (i.e., surgery, radiation therapy, or some combination of the two) generally requires expertise beyond that of most general surgeons. Therefore, cancers involving the nose, the paranasal sinuses, the nasopharynx, the floor of the mouth, the tongue, the palate, the tonsils, the piriform sinus, the hypopharynx, or the larynx are best managed by an experienced head and neck oncologic surgeon in conjunction with a radiation therapist and a medical oncologist.

Soft Tissue Sarcomas

Malignant sarcomas are not common in the head and neck. The sarcomas most frequently encountered include the rhabdomyosarcoma seen in children, fibrosarcoma, liposarcoma, osteogenic sarcoma (which usually arises in young adults), and chondrosarcoma. The most common head and neck sarcoma, however, is malignant fibrous histiocytoma (MFH). MFH is seen most frequently in the elderly and extremely rarely in children, but it can arise at any age. It is often difficult to differentiate pathologically from other entities (e.g., fibrosarcoma). MFH can occur in the soft tissues of the neck or involve the bone of the maxilla or the mandible. The preferred treatment is wide surgical resection; adjuvant radiation therapy and chemotherapy are being studied in clinical trials.

Rhabdomyosarcoma, usually of the embryonic form, is the most common form of sarcoma in children. It generally occurs near the orbit, the nasopharynx, or the paranasal sinuses. The diagnosis is confirmed by biopsy. A thorough search for distal metastases is made before treatment—consisting of a combination of surgical resection, radiation therapy, and chemotherapy—is begun.

Skin Cancer

Basal cell carcinomas are the most common of the skin malignancies [see 24 Malignant Skin Lesions]. These lesions arise in areas that have been extensively exposed to sunlight (e.g., the nose, the forehead, the cheeks, and the ears). Treatment consists of local resection with adequate clear margins. Metastases are rare, and the prognosis is excellent. Inadequately excised and neglected basal cell carcinomas may ultimately spread to regional lymph nodes and can cause extensive local destruction of soft tissue and bone. For example, basal cell carcinoma of the medial canthus may invade the orbit, the ethmoid sinus, and even the brain. Periauricular basal cell carcinoma can spread across the cartilage of the ear canal or into the parotid gland.

Squamous cell carcinoma also arises in areas associated with extensive sunlight exposure; the lower lip and the pinna are the most common sites. Unlike basal cell carcinoma, however, squamous cell carcinoma tends to metastasize regionally and distally. This tumor must also be excised with an adequate margin.

Melanoma is primarily classified on the basis of depth of invasion (as quantified by Clark level or Breslow thickness), location, and histologic subtype, although the prognosis is closely related to the thickness of the tumor [see Metastatic Tumors, Metastatic Melanomas, below]. In addition to the typical pigmented, irregularly shaped skin lesions [see 24 Malignant Skin Lesions], malignant melanoma may also arise on the mucous membranes of the nose or the throat, on the hard palate, or on the buccal mucosa. The treatment of choice is wide surgical resection. Radiation therapy, chemotherapy, and immunotherapy may also be considered.

METASTATIC TUMORS

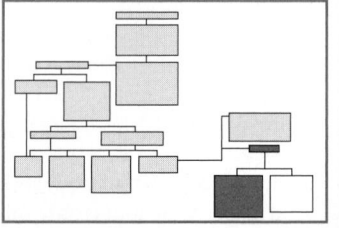

Any surgeon who is managing patients with head and neck cancers must have a thorough understanding of neck dissections and should have sufficient training and experience to perform these operations in the appropriate clinical circumstances.

Classification of Neck Dissections

There are two classification systems for neck dissections. The first is based on the indications and goals of surgery. An *elective* (or *prophylactic*) neck dissection is done when the neck is clinically negative (that is, when no abnormal lymph nodes are palpable or visible on radiographic imaging). A *therapeutic* neck dissection is done to remove all palpable and occult disease in patients with suspicious lymph nodes discovered via physical examination or CT scanning.

The second system is based on the extent and type of dissection. *Comprehensive* neck dissections include the classic radical neck dissection, as well as the modified radical (or functional) neck dissection [*see Figure 3*]. In a radical neck dissection, the sternocleidomastoid muscle, the internal and external jugular veins, the spinal accessory nerve, and the submaxillary gland are removed, along with all lymph node–bearing tissues. The modified radical or functional neck dissection is a modification of the radical neck dissection in which the lymphatic tissue from these areas is removed but the functional structures are preserved. *Selective* neck dissections involve the removal of specific levels of lymph nodes [*see Figure 1*]. The rationale for selective dissections is that several head and neck cancers consistently metastasize to specific localized lymph node regions. The following are examples of selective neck dissections: suprahyoid neck dissection (levels I and II); supraomohyoid neck dissection (levels I, II, and III); lateral neck dissection (levels II, III, and IV); and posterolateral neck dissection (levels II, III, IV, and V).

Metastatic Squamous Cell Carcinomas

The basic principle in the management of metastatic squamous cell carcinoma is to treat all regional lymph node groups at highest risk for metastases by means of surgery or radiation therapy, depending on the clinical circumstances. Selective lymph node dissection can be performed along with wide excision of the primary tumor at the time of initial operation. For example, carcinomas of the oral cavity are treated with supraomohyoid neck dissection, and carcinomas of the oropharynx, the hypopharynx, and the larynx are treated with lateral neck dissection. If extranodal extension or the presence of multiple levels of positive nodes is confirmed by the pathologic findings, the patient should receive adjuvant bilateral neck radiation for 4 to 6 weeks after operation.

Metastatic Adenocarcinomas

Adenocarcinoma in a cervical node most frequently represents a metastasis from the thyroid gland, the salivary glands, or the GI tract. The primary tumor must therefore be sought through endoscopic and radiologic study of the bronchopulmonary tract, the GI tract, the genitourinary tract, the salivary glands, and the thyroid gland. Other possible primary malignancies to be considered include breast and pelvic tumors in women and prostate cancer in men.

If the primary site is controlled and the patient is potentially curable or if the primary site is not found and the neck disease is the only established site of malignancy, neck dissection is the appropriate treatment. Postoperative adjuvant radiation may also be considered. If the patient has thyroid cancer and palpable nodes, lateral neck dissection and ipsilateral central neck dissection are recommended.

Overall survival is low—about 20% at 2 years and 9% at 5 years—except for patients with papillary or follicular thyroid cancer, who have a good prognosis. Two factors associated with a better prognosis are unilateral neck involvement and limitation of disease to lymph nodes above the cricoid cartilage.

Metastatic Melanomas

If the patient has a thin melanoma (Breslow thickness < 1 mm; Clark level I, II, or III), full-thickness excision with 1 cm margins should be done. Intermediate-thickness melanomas (Breslow thickness 1 to 4 mm; Clark level IV) have a definable risk of lymph-node spread and thus are staged with lymphatic mapping and sentinel lymph node (SLN) biopsy [*see 26 Lymphatic Mapping and Sentinel Lymph Node Biopsy*] in addition to wide excision with at least 1.5 to 2 cm margins. All patients with intermediate-thickness melanomas and positive SLNs and all melanoma patients with palpable lymph nodes should undergo modified neck dissection for adequate local disease control. Because these tumors may metastasize to nodes in the parotid region, superficial parotidectomy is often included in the neck dissection, particularly in the case of melanoma located on the upper face or the anterior scalp. Consultation with a medical oncologist is indicated for all patients with intermediate-thickness or thick (Breslow thickness > 4 mm; Clark level V) melanomas; immunotherapy or chemotherapy may be considered. Radiation therapy is often considered in patients with extensive local or nodal disease.

Metastases from an Unknown Primary Malignancy

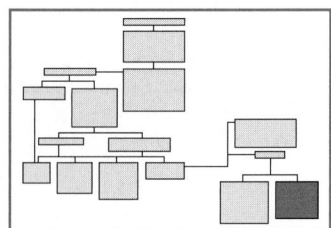

Management of patients with an unknown primary malignancy is challenging for the surgeon. It is helpful to know that when cervical lymph nodes are found to contain metastatic squamous cell carcinoma, the primary tumor is in the head and neck about 90% of the time. Typically, such patients are found to have squamous cell carcinoma on the basis of FNA of an abnormal cervical lymph node; this finding calls for an exhaustive review of systems as well as a detailed physical examination of the head and neck.

If no primary tumor is identified, the patient should undergo endoscopic evaluation of the nasopharynx, the hypopharynx, the

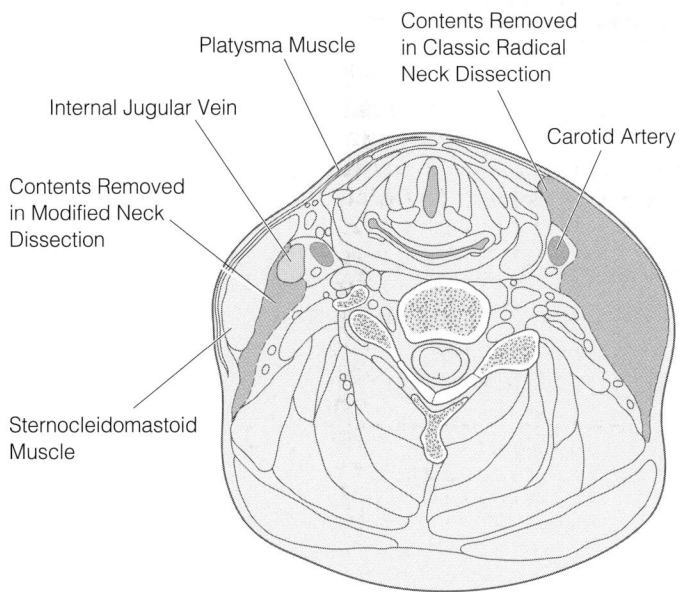

Figure 3 Cross section of the neck shows the structures removed in a classic radical neck dissection (right) and in a modified radical neck dissection (left).[3]

esophagus, the larynx, and the tracheobronchial tree under general anesthesia. Biopsies of the nasopharynx, the tonsils, and the hypopharynx often identify the site of origin (though there is some debate on this point). If the biopsies do not reveal a primary source of cancer, the preferred treatment is unilateral neck dissection, followed by radiation therapy directed toward the neck, the entire pharynx, and the nasopharynx. In 15% to 20% of cases, the primary cancer is ultimately detected. Overall 5-year survival in such cases ranges from 25% to 50%.

If a malignant melanoma is found in a cervical lymph node but no primary tumor is evident, the patient should be asked about previous skin lesions, and a thorough repeat head and neck examination should be done, with particular attention to the scalp, the nose, the oral cavities, and the sinuses. An ophthalmologic examination is also required. If physical examination and radiographic studies find no evidence of metastases, modified neck dissection should be performed on the involved side.

Metastatic adenocarcinoma in a cervical lymph node with no known primary tumor is discussed elsewhere [see Metastatic Adenocarcinomas, above]. The most common primary sites in the head and neck are the salivary glands and the thyroid gland. The possibility of an isolated metastasis from the breast, the GI tract, or the genitourinary tract must also be rigorously investigated. If no primary site is identified, the patient should be considered for protocol-based chemotherapy and radiation therapy, directed according to what the primary site is most likely to be in that patient.

References

1. Fabian RL: Benign and malignant diseases of the head and neck. Current Practice of Surgery. Levine BA, Copeland EM III, Howard RJ, et al, Eds. Churchill Livingstone, New York, 1993, vol 2, sect VII, chap 1

2. Cohen JI: Benign neck masses. Boie's Fundamentals of Otolaryngology: A Textbook of Ear, Nose and Throat Disease, 6th ed. Adams GL, Boie LR Jr, Hilger PA, Eds. WB Saunders Co, Philadelphia, 1989

3. Coleman JJ III, Sultan MR: Tumors of the head and neck. Principles of Surgery, 6th ed. Schwartz SI, Shires GT, Spencer FC, Eds. McGraw-Hill Book Co, New York, 1994, p 595

Recommended Reading

Beenken SW, Maddox WA, Urist MM: Workup of a patient with a mass in the neck. Adv Surg 28:371, 1995

Byers RM: Neck dissection: concepts, controversies and technique. Semin Surg Oncol 7:9, 1991

Chandler JR, Mitchell B: Branchial cleft cysts, sinuses and fistulas. Otolaryngol Clin North Am 14:175, 1981

Clark O, Duh QY: Textbook of Endocrine Surgery. WB Saunders Co, Philadelphia, 1997

Clark O, Duh QY, Perrier N, et al: Endocrine Tumors. BC Decker Inc, Hamilton, Ontario, Canada, 2003

Clark OH, Noguchi S: Thyroid Cancer Diagnosis and Treatment. Quality Medical Publishing, St Louis, 2000

Davidson BJ, Spiro RH, Patel S, et al: Cervical metastases of occult origin: the impact of combined modality therapy. Am J Surg 168:195, 1994

Delbridge L, Guinea AL, Reeve TS: Total thyroidectomy for bilateral benign multinodular goiter: effect of changing practice. Arch Surg 134:1385, 1999

Hainsworth JD: Poorly differentiated carcinoma and poorly differentiated adenocarcinoma of unknown primary tumor site of the neck. Semin Oncol 20:279, 1993

Hoffman HT, Karnell LH, Funk GF, et al: The National Cancer Database report on cancer of the head and neck. Arch Otolaryngol Head Neck Surg 124:951, 1998

Jossart GH, Clark OH: Well-differentiated thyroid cancer. Curr Probl Surg 31:933, 1994

Lee NK, Byers RM, Abbruzzese JL, et al: Metastatic adenocarcinoma to the neck from an unknown primary source. Am J Surg 162:306, 1991

McGuirt WF: Diagnosis and management of masses in the neck, with special emphasis on metastatic disease. Oncology 4:85, 1990

Moley JF, De Beneditti MK: Patterns of nodal metastases in palpable medullary thyroid carcinoma: recommendations for extent of node dissection. Ann Surg 225:880, 1999

Montgomery WW: Surgery of the neck. Surgery of the Upper Respiratory System, 2nd ed. Lea & Febiger, Philadelphia, 1989, p 83

Nguyen TD, Malissard L, Theobald S, et al: Advanced carcinoma of the larynx: results of surgery and radiotherapy without induction chemotherapy (1980–1985): a multivariate analysis. Int J Radiat Oncol Biol Phys 36:1013, 1996

Shah JP, Medina JE, Shaha AR, et al: Cervical lymph node metastasis. Curr Probl Surg 30:1, 1993

Spiro RH: Management of malignant tumor of the salivary glands. Oncology 12:671, 1998

Van den Brekel MW, Castelijns JA: Surgery of lymph nodes in the neck. Semin Roentgenol 35:42, 2000

Wu HS, Young MT, Ituarte P, et al: Death from thyroid cancer of follicular cell origin. J Am Coll Surg 191:600, 2000

Acknowledgment

Figures 1 through 3   Tom Moore.

15 HEAD AND NECK DIAGNOSTIC PROCEDURES

Adam S. Jacobson, M.D., Mark L. Urken, M.D., F.A.C.S., and Marita S. Teng, M.D.

Head and neck surgery deals with a wide range of pathologic conditions affecting the upper aerodigestive tract and the endocrine organs of the head and neck. As in other areas of the body, the causes of these conditions can be inflammatory, infectious, congenital, neoplastic, or traumatic. This chapter discusses the diagnostic approach to head and neck disorders, with particular attention to cancer.

Anatomic Considerations

The head and neck can be conceptualized by dividing it into the following segments: (1) nasal cavity and paranasal sinuses, (2) oral cavity, (3) pharynx, (4) larynx, (5) salivary glands, and (6) thyroid [*see Figure 1*].

NASAL CAVITY AND PARANASAL SINUSES

The nasal vault and paranasal sinuses are a complex labyrinth of interconnected cavities. These cavities are lined with mucous membranes and are normally well aerated. The nasal vault itself is divided into two equal halves by the nasal septum. There are three paired turbinates in the nasal cavity, which further subdivide the nasal vault from cephalad to caudal, creating the superior, middle, and inferior meatuses.

The ethmoid sinus is the most complicated of the paranasal sinuses; it is also known as the ethmoid labyrinth [*see Figure 2*]. The maxillary sinus lies within the body of the maxilla and is the largest of the paranasal sinuses. The frontal sinus lies within the frontal bone and is divided into two asymmetrical halves by an intersinus septum. The sphenoid sinus lies posterior to the nasal cavity and superior to the nasopharynx. It too is an asymmetrically paired structure that is divided by an intersinus septum. The sphenoid sinus remains the most dangerous sinus to manipulate surgically because of the surrounding vital structures (i.e., the carotid artery, the optic nerve, the trigeminal nerve, and the vidian nerve).

Tumors within the nasal vault or the paranasal sinuses present as nasal airway obstruction, epistaxis, pain, and nasal discharge. They can originate in any of the paranasal sinuses or the nasal cavity proper and often remain silent or are mistakenly treated as an infectious or inflammatory condition, with a consequent delay in the diagnosis.

ORAL CAVITY

Anatomically, the oral cavity extends from the vermilion border to the junction of the hard and soft palates and the circumvallate papillae. It includes the lips, the buccal mucosa, the upper and lower alveolar ridges, the retromolar trigones, the oral tongue (anterior to circumvallate papillae), the hard palate, and the floor of the mouth.

PHARYNX

The pharynx is a tubular structure extending from the base of the skull to the esophageal inlet. Superiorly, it opens into the nasal and oral cavities; inferiorly, it opens into the larynx and the esophagus. The pharynx is subdivided into the nasopharynx, the oropharynx, and the hypopharynx.

Nasopharynx

The nasopharynx extends from the posterior choanae to the inferior surface of the soft palate. Malignancies of the nasopharynx can present as nasal obstruction, epistaxis, tinnitus, headache, diminished hearing, and facial pain.

Oropharynx

The oropharynx extends from the junction of the hard and soft palates and the circumvallate papillae to the valleculae. It includes the soft palate and uvula, the base of the tongue, the pharyngoepiglottic and glossoepiglottic folds, the palatine arch (which includes the tonsils and the tonsillar fossae and pillars), the valleculae, and the lateral and posterior oropharyngeal walls. Carcinomas of the oropharynx can present as pain, sore throat, dysphagia, and referred otalgia.

Hypopharynx

The hypopharynx extends from the superior border of the hyoid bone to the inferior border of the cricoid cartilage. It includes the pyriform sinuses, the hypopharyngeal walls, and the postcricoid region (i.e., the area of the pharyngoesophageal junction). Malignancies of the hypopharynx can present as odynophagia, dysphagia, hoarseness, referred otalgia, and excessive salivation.

LARYNX

The larynx is subdivided into the supraglottis, the glottis, and the subglottis [*see Figure 3*]. It consists of a framework of cartilages that are held together by extrinsic and intrinsic musculature and lined with a mucous membrane that is topographically arranged into two characteristic folds (the false and true vocal cords). Neoplasms of the larynx can present as hoarseness, dyspnea, stridor, hemoptysis, odynophagia, dysphagia, and otalgia.

Supraglottis

The supraglottis extends from the tip of the epiglottis to the junction between respiratory and squamous epithelium on the floor of the ventricle (the space between the false and true cords). Carcinomas of the supraglottis can present as sore throat, odynophagia, dysphagia, and otalgia.

Glottis

The space between the free margin of the true vocal cords is the glottis. This structure is bounded by the anterior commissure, the true vocal cords, and the posterior commissure. The most common symptom of carcinoma of the glottis is hoarseness.

Subglottis

The subglottis extends from the junction of squamous and respiratory epithelium on the undersurface of the true vocal cords (approximately 5 to 10 mm below the true vocal cords) to the inferior edge of the cricoid cartilage. The most common symptom of carcinoma of the subglottis is hoarseness.

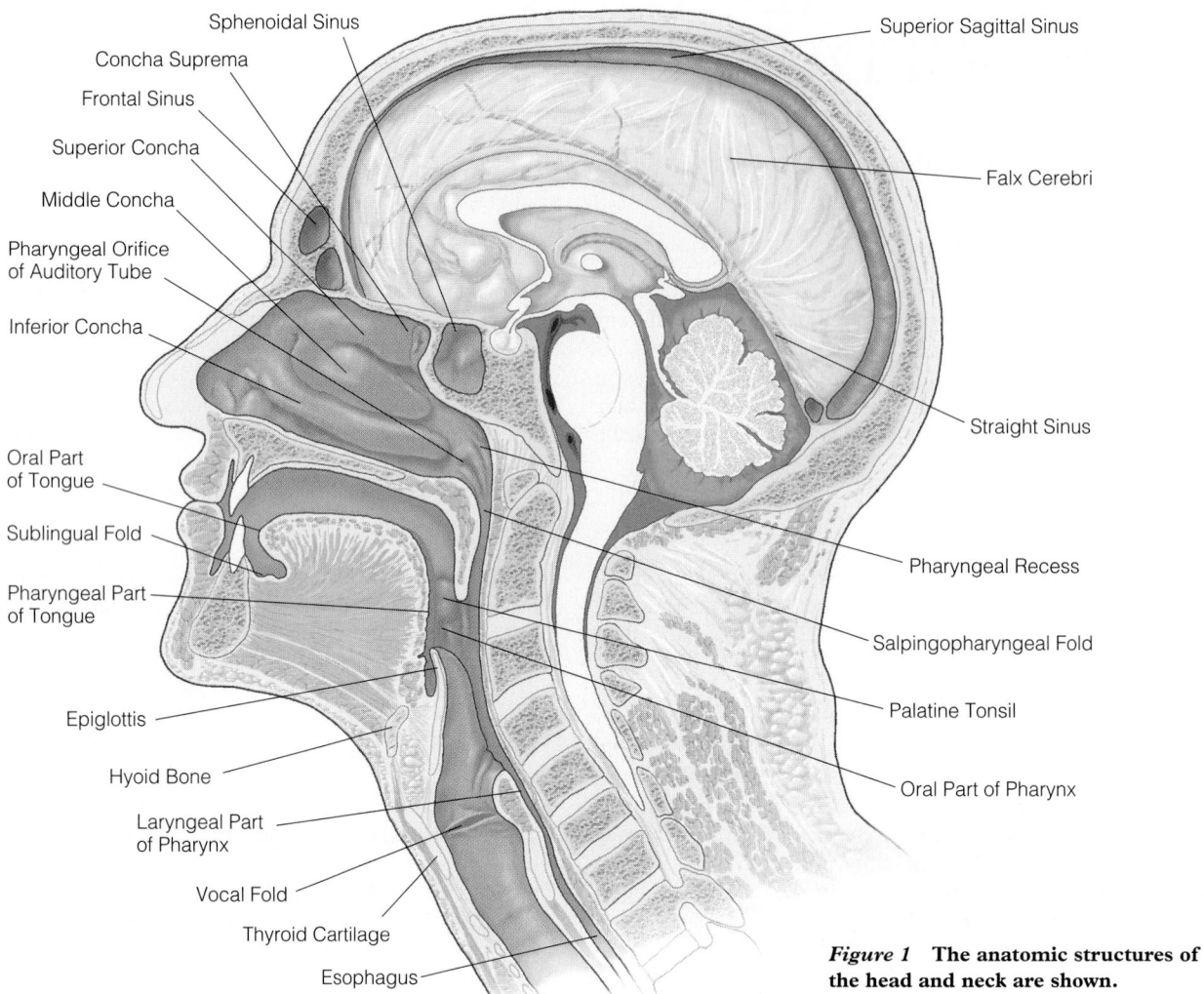

Sphenoidal Sinus
Concha Suprema
Frontal Sinus
Superior Concha
Middle Concha
Pharyngeal Orifice of Auditory Tube
Inferior Concha
Oral Part of Tongue
Sublingual Fold
Pharyngeal Part of Tongue
Epiglottis
Hyoid Bone
Laryngeal Part of Pharynx
Vocal Fold
Thyroid Cartilage
Esophagus

Superior Sagittal Sinus
Falx Cerebri
Straight Sinus
Pharyngeal Recess
Salpingopharyngeal Fold
Palatine Tonsil
Oral Part of Pharynx

Figure 1 **The anatomic structures of the head and neck are shown.**

SALIVARY GLANDS

Salivary glands are subdivided into major and minor salivary glands. The major salivary glands consist of the parotid glands, the submandibular glands, and the sublingual glands. The minor salivary glands are dispersed throughout the submucosa of the upper aerodigestive tract. Classically, benign neoplasms present as painless, slow-growing masses. A sudden increase in size is usually the result of infection, cystic degeneration, hemorrhage into the mass, or malignant transformation. Malignant neoplasms also usually present as a painless swelling or mass. However, certain features are strongly suspicious for a malignancy, such as overlying skin involvement, fixation of the mass to the underlying structures, pain, facial nerve paralysis, ipsilateral weakness or numbness of the tongue, and cervical lymphadenopathy.

THYROID

The thyroid gland performs a vital role in regulating metabolic function. It is susceptible to benign conditions (e.g., nodule, goiter, and cyst), inflammatory disease (e.g., thyroiditis), and malignancies. Additionally, congenital anomalies of the thyroid, such as a thyroglossal duct cyst, can present later in life. Thyroid lesions can present as pain, hoarseness, dyspnea, or dysphagia.

On the posterior aspect of the thyroid gland reside the four parathyroid glands. These glands play a vital role in maintaining calcium balance. Parathyroid adenomas and, rarely, carcinomas can develop.

Clinical Evaluation

The diagnostic approach to the upper aerodigestive tract begins with a thorough history, starting with a detailed evaluation of the chief complaint. Once the chief complaint has been defined (e.g., neck mass, hoarseness, hemoptysis, or nasal obstruction), it must be further characterized. The physician must determine how long the problem has been present and whether the patient has any associated symptoms (e.g., pain, paresthesias, discharge, change in voice, dyspnea, hemoptysis). In addition, it is important to ask about recent infection (e.g., of the ear, mouth, teeth, or lungs) and previous medical treatment. Once a complete history of the chief complaint has been obtained, the physician should elicit a more comprehensive general medical history from the patient, including pertinent past medical history, past surgical history, medications, allergies, social history (tobacco, ethanol, I.V. drug use), and family history.

After completion of the history, the next step is to perform a comprehensive physical examination. This begins with a thorough inspection of the entire surface of the head and neck, with a focus on gross lesions, areas that are topographically abnormal, and old scars from previous injuries or procedures. The examination should proceed in an orderly fashion from superior to inferior. Next, the inspection focuses on the mucosal surfaces of the upper aerodigestive tract.

Although an accurate history and careful physical examination of the head, neck, and mucosal surfaces are the most important steps in evaluating a lesion in this part of the body, this clinical evaluation

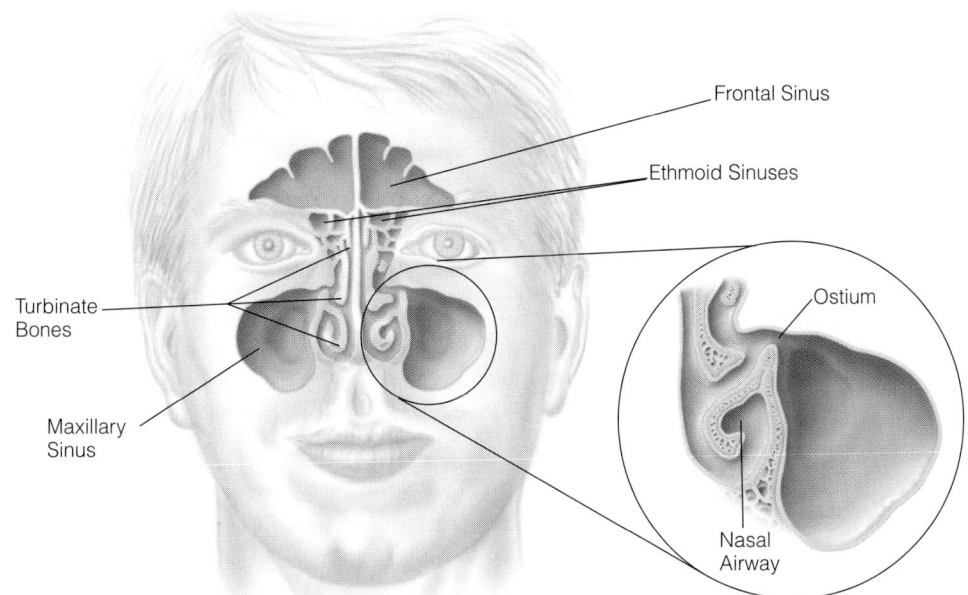

Figure 2 **The paranasal sinuses are shown.**

usually provides only a working diagnosis. The head and neck surgeon must then proceed in a stepwise fashion to further clarify the diagnosis and, in the case of neoplasm, to perform an accurate staging.

Radiographic techniques allow the head and neck surgeon to visualize the mass and determine its characteristics (i.e., to differentiate between solid and cystic lesions), as well as determine its anatomic associations. Ultrasonography, magnetic resonance imaging, and computed tomography each provides a unique view of the pathology in question and thereby helps narrow the differential diagnosis. Acquisition of a tissue specimen for cytologic or histologic analysis, or both, is the next step. Fine-needle aspiration (FNA) is often utilized at this stage in the workup, provided that the location of the mass lends itself to a safe procedure. If the lesion is located deep in the neck near vital structures, image-guided FNA can be attempted before resorting to an open biopsy. If the lesion is on a mucosal surface of the upper aerodigestive tract, an endoscopic biopsy is performed. Often, a panendoscopic procedure is performed at this point to accurately map the lesion, obtain a tissue specimen, and, in patients with cancer, assess the rest of the upper aerodigestive tract for a synchronous primary tumor.

After a histologic diagnosis has been made and correlated with the imaging information, the patient and physician can have a comprehensive discussion of the pathology, the stage of the disease, and the selection of therapy.

Nasal Diagnostic Procedures

ANTERIOR RHINOSCOPY

Using a variety of different light sources that provide both illumination and coaxial vision, the head and neck surgeon can view the nasal vault through a nasal speculum [*see Figure 4*]. This technique is performed both before and after nasal decongestion, with particular attention to mucosal color, edema, and discharge and the effect of vasoconstriction. Limited visualization of the nasal septum, the turbinates, and the vault is also possible with this technique.

RIGID NASAL ENDOSCOPY

The rigid nasal endoscope comes with a variety of lens angles (0°,

60°, and 90°), which allow for visualization of structures that are inaccessible by simple anterior rhinoscopy. Rigid nasal endoscopy is especially useful for visualizing deeper structures and structures that are not in a straight axis from the nasal aperture.

Indirect Laryngoscopy

Indirect laryngoscopy has been used since the 1800s for visualizing the pharynx and larynx. In this technique, the head light source illuminates the mirror, which in turn illuminates the laryngopharynx [*see Figure 5*]. The patient is seated in the sniffing position and protrudes the tongue while a warmed laryngeal mirror is introduced firmly against the soft palate in the midline to elevate the uvula out of the field (gently, so as not to elicit the gag reflex). The image seen on the mirror can be used to assess vocal cord mobility, as well as to inspect for a mass or foreign body of the larynx or pharynx. This technique can be performed rapidly and is inexpensive.

Endoscopic Procedures

Endoscopic evaluation of the upper aerodigestive tract is crucial in establishing a definitive diagnosis. The equipment used consists of both rigid and flexible laryngoscopes, bronchoscopes, and esophagoscopes. Many of these techniques can be performed in the office setting, providing the surgeon with an array of methods for gaining the information necessary for a working diagnosis and, in some cases, for performing a therapeutic intervention. Operative endoscopy is performed to obtain a definitive diagnosis, to stage tumors, and to rule out synchronous lesions. There is no substitute for thorough examination and biopsy of a lesion with the patient under general anesthesia. Regardless of the endoscopic method used, an adequate biopsy specimen must be obtained for a histologic diagnosis.

FLEXIBLE RHINOLARYNGOSCOPY

Flexible rhinolaryngoscopy is currently one of the most commonly used techniques for visualizing the nasal cavity, the sinuses, the pharynx, and the larynx. The technique utilizes a small-caliber flexible endoscope and can be performed in an office setting [*see Figure 6*]. Before the procedure, the patient's nasal cavity

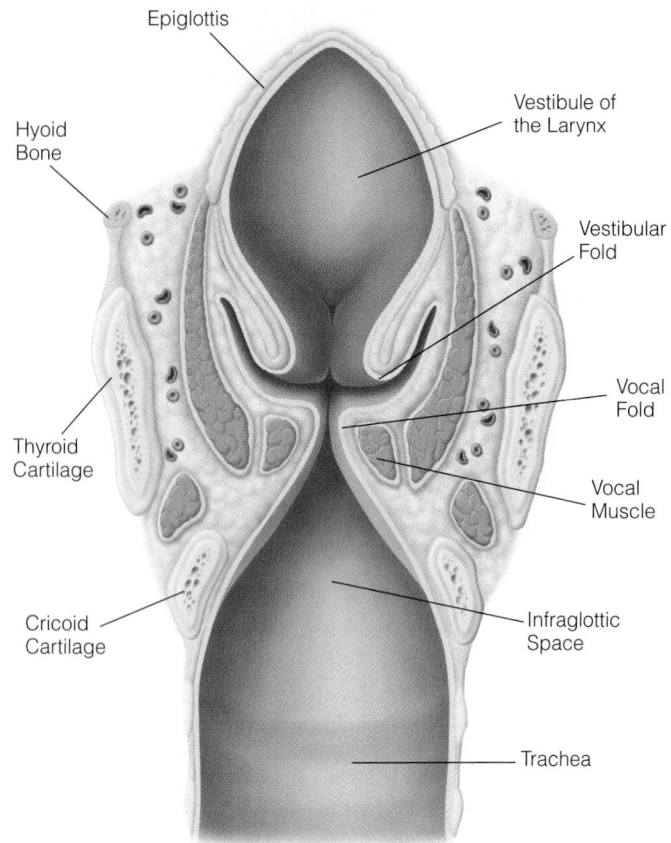

Epiglottis

Hyoid Bone

Vestibule of the Larynx

Vestibular Fold

Thyroid Cartilage

Vocal Fold

Vocal Muscle

Cricoid Cartilage

Infraglottic Space

Trachea

Figure 3   **Cross-sectional anatomy of the larynx is shown.**

is decongested and anesthetized for maximum visualization and minimal discomfort. In the procedure, the examiner threads the end of the scope into the nasal aperture along the floor of the nasal cavity. As the scope is advanced, the examiner can visualize the nasal cavity proper for any evidence of lesions or masses. Once the scope approaches the nasopharynx, it is directed inferiorly and advanced slowly, allowing direct visualization of the entire pharynx and larynx.

DIRECT LARYNGOSCOPY

Direct laryngoscopy has the advantage of permitting both diagnostic and therapeutic intervention [*see Figure 7*]. It is performed with the patient under general anesthesia and intubated. The procedure allows for direct visualization of the pharynx and the larynx and permits the surgeon to perform biopsies and remove small lesions. At the same time, the surgeon has the opportunity to palpate the structures of the oral cavity, the oropharynx, and the hypopharynx, which cannot be properly palpated in an awake patient.

The laryngoscope can also be suspended from a table-mounted Mayo stand (for hands-free use), and a microscope can be maneuvered into focal distance to allow magnified visualization of the glottis and subglottis. During a microscopic direct laryngoscopy, small lesions or topographic abnormalities can be better characterized and removed if desired. Some examples of lesions that can be diagnosed by direct laryngoscopy are vocal cord polyps, leukoplakia, intubation granulomas, contact ulcers, webs, nodules, hematomas, and papillomatosis. Additionally, small malignant lesions of the vocal cords can be examined and ablated or extirpated by using a CO_2 laser under direct microlaryngoscopic guidance.

ESOPHAGOSCOPY

Esophagoscopy plays an important role in the evaluation of patients with dysphagia, odynophagia, caustic ingestion, trauma, ingested foreign bodies, suspected anomalies, and upper aerodigestive tract malignancies. This procedure may be performed with either a flexible or a rigid scope.

Flexible Esophagoscopy

The primary application for flexible esophagoscopy is diagnosis. The procedure is particularly useful in elderly patients with limited spinal mobility and in patients with short, thick necks.

The flexible esophagoscope is used with local anesthesia and sedation in a monitored setting. To facilitate control of secretions and the passage of the instrument, the patient is placed in a flexed position and lying on one side. Using insufflation, the surgeon visualizes and enters the cricopharyngeus and carries out a safe and detailed visual study of the esophagus. If a malignancy is suspected, either a brush specimen is sent for cytology or a cup forceps is used to acquire a specimen for histologic analysis.

Rigid Esophagoscopy

Rigid esophagoscopy can be used to treat a variety of problems, including foreign bodies, hemorrhage (e.g., from esophageal varices), and endobronchial tumors. Rigid esophagoscopes [*see Figure 8*] are used with the patient under general anesthesia. The patient is placed in the supine position with the neck extended. The esophagoscope is then passed along the right side of the tongue, with the endoscopist using the left hand to cradle the instrument. The right hand is used for stabilization of the proximal end of the scope, suctioning, and insertion of instruments through the lumen of the esophagoscope. The lip of the esophagoscope is positioned anteriorly for manipulation of the epiglottis and visualization of the pyriform sinus and the arytenoids. The scope is then passed along the pyriform sinus into the cricopharyngeus (i.e., the superior esophageal valve). The left thumb is then used to advance the instrument down the esophagus. If no major lesions are noted on insertion of the esophagoscope, a careful inspection of the mucosa should be made during withdrawal of the instrument.

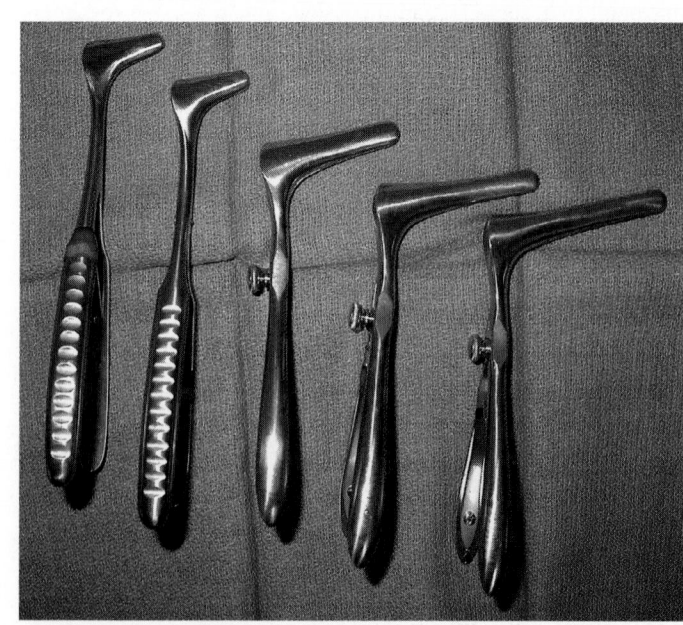

Figure 4   **Shown is an assortment of nasal specula.**

Figure 5   **Shown is a laryngeal mirror. Such an instrument is used for indirect laryngoscopy.**

BRONCHOSCOPY

Bronchoscopy provides clinically useful information by direct inspection of the tracheobronchial tree. Like esophagoscopes, bronchoscopes come in both flexible and rigid forms. The flexible bronchoscope is used primarily for diagnosis. The value of the rigid bronchoscope lies in its therapeutic applications, which include foreign-body removal, removal of bulky tumors, introduction of radioactive materials, and placement of stents.

Flexible Bronchoscopy

The flexible fiberoptic bronchoscope is usually used with local anesthesia and sedation in a monitored setting (e.g., an operating suite). After local anesthesia and decongestion of the nasal vault with topical tetracaine and 1% phenylephrine, the flexible scope is gently passed along the nasal floor into the nasopharynx, where the tip of the scope is angled inferiorly to permit visualization of the pharynx. The instrument is then advanced slowly into the glottis (between the true vocal folds) and into the tracheobronchial tree. After a visual inspection of the airway has been completed, a specimen can be retrieved by means of brush biopsy, bronchoalveolar lavage, or a biopsy forceps.

Rigid Bronchoscopy

Rigid bronchoscopy [*see Figure 9*] is performed with the patient under general anesthesia. The patient is placed in the supine position with the neck hyperextended. The bronchoscope is then passed along the right side of the tongue, with the endoscopist using the left hand to cradle the instrument. The instrument is initially held almost vertically until it reaches the posterior pharyngeal wall, at which point it is slowly guided into a more horizontal position. While advancing the scope, the endoscopist cradles the instrument with the fingers of the left hand, providing guidance and protecting the patient's lips and teeth. Once the tip of the epiglottis is

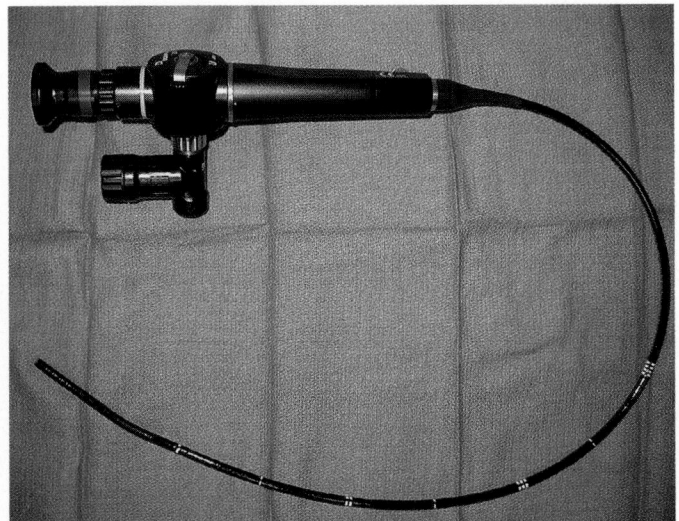

Figure 6   **A small-caliber flexible laryngoscope is used for rhino-laryngoscopy.**

visualized, the instrument is threaded anteriorly to allow visualization of the glottis. The bronchoscope is then passed between the vocal cords and into the trachea. At this point, ventilation may be resumed either by positive pressure or by jet ventilation techniques (ventilating bronchoscopes have a side port for attachment of the tubing from the ventilator). The patient's head is manipulated with the endoscopist's right hand so as to direct the tip of the bronchoscope and permit bilateral exploration of the major airways.

PANENDOSCOPY

The term panendoscopy refers to the combination of direct laryngoscopy (with or without microscopic assistance), esophagoscopy, and bronchoscopy. Together, these three procedures provide a complete examination of the entire upper aerodigestive tract. In cancer patients, this combination of procedures allows the examiner to create a detailed map of the tumor, as well as to rule out synchronous primary tumors.

Biopsy Procedures

FINE-NEEDLE ASPIRATION

FNA is often used to make an initial tissue diagnosis of a neck mass. The advantages of this technique include high sensitivity and specificity; however, 5% to 17% of FNAs are nondiagnostic. Another advantage of FNA is speed: If a cytologist or a pathologist is available, diagnosis can often be made within minutes of the biopsy.

FNA is performed with a 10 ml syringe with an attached 21- to 25-gauge needle. Larger needles are more likely to result in tumor seeding. The patient is positioned to allow for optimal palpation of the mass. The skin overlying the mass is prepared with a sterile alcohol prep sponge. Local anesthesia is not necessary. The mass is grasped and held in a fixed and stable position. The needle is introduced just under the skin surface. As the needle is advanced, the plunger of the syringe is pulled back, to create suction. Once the mass is entered, multiple passes are made without exiting the skin surface; this maneuver is critical in maximizing specimen yield. After the final pass is completed, the suction on the syringe is released and the needle withdrawn from the skin. If a cyst is encountered, it should be completely evacuated and the fluid sent for cytologic analysis.

A drop of aspirated fluid is placed on a glass slide. A smear is made by laying another glass slide on top of the drop of fluid and pulling the slides apart to spread the fluid. Fixative spray is then applied. Alternatively, wet smears are placed in 95% ethyl alcohol and treated with the Papanicolaou technique and stains.

FNA has several advantages over excisional biopsy. An FNA requires only an office visit, with minimal loss of time from work for the patient. In contrast, excisional biopsy is commonly performed in an operating room, so the patient must undergo preoperative testing. Patients with a significant medical history may require formal medical clearance. An excisional biopsy exposes the patient to the risks of anesthesia, postoperative wound infection, and tumor seeding.

a *b*

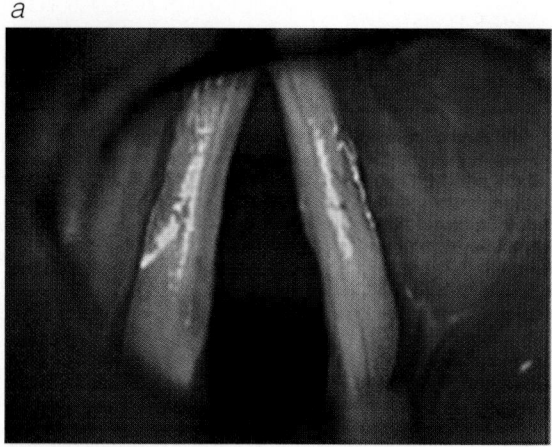 

Figure 7 **Shown are (*a*) normal vocal folds directly visualized via (*b*) a rigid laryngoscope.**

ULTRASOUND-GUIDED FNA

Ultrasonographic guidance of FNA enables the surgeon to obtain a cytologic specimen of deeper or nonpalpable masses that are not amenable to standard FNA. Real-time imaging of the needle's passage allows the surgeon to plot a more accurate trajectory and avoid underlying vital structures. Furthermore, it provides an image of the mass, allowing its characterization as solid, cystic, or heterogeneous. With cystic or complex masses, it is imperative to place the tip of the needle into the wall to increase specimen yield.

CT-GUIDED FNA

CT-guided FNA is most commonly employed to diagnose poorly accessible or deep-seated lesions of the head and neck. Like ultrasound-guided FNA, CT-guided FNA provides visualization of the needle as it is passed through the tissue and into the underlying structures, thus allowing a more accurate needle trajectory and avoidance of underlying vital structures. Additionally, visual guidance of the needle greatly increases the likelihood of obtaining a specimen from the mass rather than the surrounding tissues.

Imaging Procedures

Because many of the deep structures of the head and neck are inaccessible to either direct evaluation by palpation or indirect evaluation via endoscopy, further information must be obtained by radiography. Imaging procedures such as CT, MRI, ultrasound, and positron emission tomography (PET) scanning permit the diagnosis and analysis of pathologic conditions affecting these deep structures, including the temporal bone, skull base, paranasal sinuses, soft tissues of the neck, and larynx.

ULTRASONOGRAPHY

Ultrasonography is a safe and inexpensive method of gaining high-resolution real-time images of the structures of the head and neck. Palpable masses in the neck [see *14 Neck Mass*] can be assessed for changes in size, for association with other local structures, and for character (i.e., solid, cystic, or complex). Applications of ultrasonography include assessment of masses such as thyroglossal duct cysts, branchial cleft cysts, cystic hygromas, salivary gland tumors, abscesses, carotid body tumors, vascular tumors, and thyroid masses. Additionally, ultrasonography combined with FNA and cytologic evaluation can provide both a detailed visual description and an accurate cytologic evaluation of masses in the neck [see Ultrasound-Guided FNA, *above*].

COMPUTED TOMOGRAPHY

A CT scan with intravenous contrast is often the first-line imaging technique used to evaluate a mass of the neck and to assess for pathologic adenopathy. CT has proved to be an effective method for primary staging of tumors and lymph nodes. Additionally, it has been shown to be effective in studying capsular penetration and extranodal extension. It is clearly superior to MRI in evaluating bone cortex erosion, given that MRI cannot assess bone cortex status at all. CT scans are also widely used for posttreatment surveillance in cancer patients.

MAGNETIC RESONANCE IMAGING

MRI avoids exposing the patient to radiation and provides the investigator with superior definition of soft tissue. For example, MRI can differentiate mucous membrane from tumor, as well as detect neoplastic invasion of bone marrow. In patients with nasal cavity tumors, MRI can distinguish between neoplastic, inflammatory, and obstructive processes. MRI is also valuable in assessing the superior extent of metastatic cervical lymphadenopathy (i.e., intracranial extension). A disadvantage of MRI is its limited ability to show bone detail; it therefore cannot detect invasion of bone cortex by a neoplasm. Furthermore, an MRI scan is significantly more expensive than a CT scan.

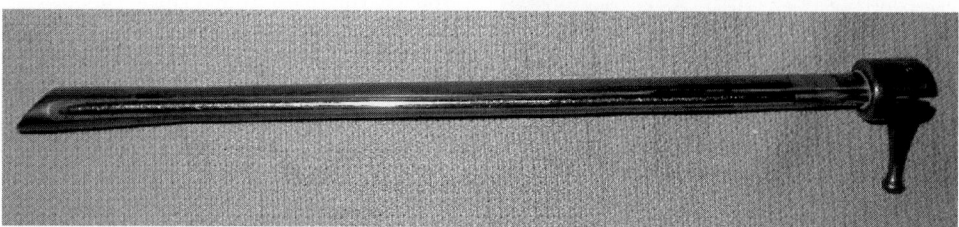

Figure 8 **Shown is a rigid endoscope.**

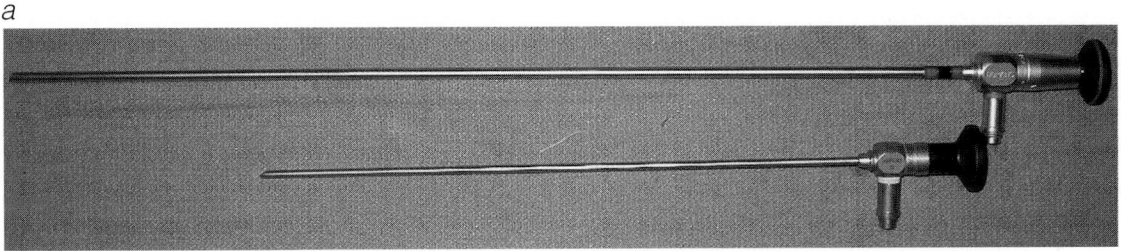

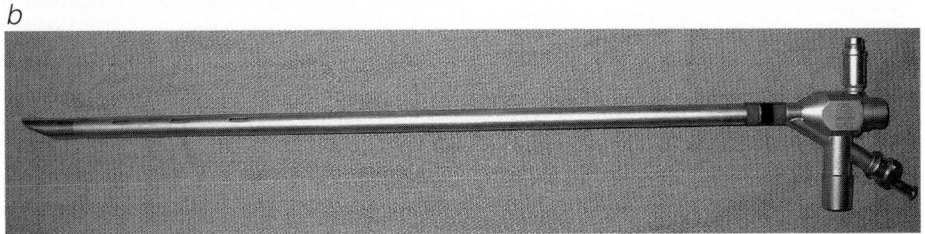

Figure 9   (*a*) **Rigid bronchoscopes incorporate stainless-steel tubes of varying length and diameter. The beveled distal end of this Hopkins bronchoscope facilitates mobilization of the epiglottis during intubation; the side ports permit ventilation and use of suction catheters. (*b*) Illumination is provided by fiberoptic rods that are inserted into the bronchoscope.**

POSITRON EMISSION TOMOGRAPHY

PET scanning is a functional imaging technique that measures tissue metabolic activity through the use of radioisotopically tagged cellular building blocks, such as glucose precursors. A range of physiologic tracers has been developed for PET imaging, with the glucose analogue 2-deoxy-2-[(18)F]fluoro-D-glucose (FDG) the most commonly used. FDG has a half-life of 110 minutes. Once given to the patient, FDG is taken up by glucose transporters and is phosphorylated by hexokinase to become FDG-6-phosphate (FDG-6-P). Further metabolism of FDG-6-P is blocked by the presence of an extra hydroxyl moiety, which allows FDG-6-P to accumulate in the cell and serve as a marker for glucose metabolism and utilization.

Because neoplastic cells have higher rates of glycolysis, localized areas of increased cellular activity on PET scans may represent neoplastic tissue. In this respect, PET is very different from CT and MRI, which depict tissue structure rather than tissue metabolic activity.

Because FDG is nonspecifically accumulated in glycolytically active cells, it demarcates areas of inflammation as well as neoplastic tissue, which can lead to a false positive scan. Muscular activity during the scan can also lead to areas of increased uptake in nonneoplastic tissue. Furthermore, healing bone, foreign body granulomas, and paranasal sinus inflammation can produce false positive results.

False negative scans occur when tumor deposits are very small (i.e., 3 to 4 mm or less in diameter). Thus, micrometastases are not reliably detected using an FDG-PET image. Furthermore, a false negative scan can occur if the PET scan is performed too soon after radiation therapy.

The role of PET imaging in head and neck oncology is rapidly expanding. Currently, the majority of PET imaging used in head and neck oncology is FDG based. FDG-PET is actively being used to look for unknown primary lesions and second primaries, to stage disease before therapy, to detect residual or recurrent disease after surgery or radiation therapy, to assess the response to organ preservation therapy, and to detect distant metastases. Because false positive and false negative PET scans do occur, accurate interpretation of PET scans requires a thorough understanding of the potential confounding factors.

PET/CT

PET/CT is essentially an FDG-PET scan that has been coregistered with a simultaneous CT scan to allow the radiologist to precisely correlate the area of increased cellular activity with the anatomic structure. This technique removes some of the guesswork involved with interpreting an area of increased activity on a simple PET scan and provides the physician with a morphologic correlate for the area of increased uptake.

Recommended Reading

AJCC Cancer Staging Manual, 5th ed. Lippincott Raven, Philadelphia, 1997

Bailey B: Head and Neck Surgery – Otolaryngology, 3rd ed. Lippincott Williams & Wilkins, Philadelphia, 2001

Cummings C: Otolaryngology Head and Neck Surgery, 3rd ed. Mosby – Year Book St. Louis, 1998

Som P: Head and Neck Imaging, 4th ed. Mosby, St. Louis, 2003

Surveillance Epidemiology and End Results. National Cancer Institute, National Institutes of Health, 2004. http://seer.cancer.gov/

Acknowledgments

Figure 1   Tom Moore.

Figures 2 and 3   Alice Y. Chen.

16 ORAL CAVITY PROCEDURES

Carol R. Bradford, M.D., F.A.C.S., and Mark E. P. Prince, M.D., F.R.C.S.C.

Preoperative Evaluation

Oral cavity procedures are commonly performed to treat malignancies. Tumors should be assessed preoperatively to allow accurate staging of the disease and to facilitate planning of definitive treatment. In most cases, an examination under anesthesia with endoscopy and biopsy is required to stage the primary tumor and to look for synchronous second primary tumors. Except in the case of very superficial lesions, computed tomography plays an important role in preoperative planning. In selected cases, plain radiographs (e.g., Panorex views) may be useful in evaluating the mandible. When the lesion is located in the tongue, magnetic resonance imaging may provide additional information about the extent of the primary tumor.

Wide surgical margins are necessary for adequate treatment of primary squamous cell carcinoma of the head and neck. A margin of 1 to 2 cm should be achieved whenever possible, ideally with frozen-section control. Current evidence clearly indicates that overall patient outcome improves when clear margins are obtained.

Nodal metastases are common with oral cavity tumors. Accordingly, patients should be assessed for cervical adenopathy both clinically and radiographically. A chest x-ray should be obtained in all cases. CT or MRI can provide valuable information regarding the nodal status of the neck. In patients with advanced disease, a more extensive search for distant metastases should be conducted, including a CT scan of the chest. In some circumstances, combining CT with positron emission tomography (PET) may be useful.

Operative Planning

Surgical management of the neck is an evolving field. In general, if the risk of occult metastasis is greater than 20% to 25%, a selective neck dissection [see 18 Neck Dissection] is recommended, particularly if postoperative radiation therapy is not planned. Whenever there is clinical evidence of nodal disease, treatment of the neck must be included in operative planning.

The oral cavity is a major component of a number of important functions, including speech and swallowing. Reconstruction of the anticipated surgical defect must be carefully planned to achieve the best results. Several basic considerations must be kept in mind. Tongue mobility and sensation must be maintained to the extent possible. Maintenance of mandibular continuity (especially in the anterior segment of the mandible) is vital for ensuring postoperative oral competence. Separation of the nasal cavity from the oral cavity is critical for the oral phase of swallowing and speech. Maintenance of the gingivobuccal and gingivolabial sulcus is important for oral function and the fitting of dentures.

As a rule, oral cavity defects should be closed primarily whenever possible. Primary closure has the advantage of using sensate tissue similar in form to the tissue that was excised. With experience and careful judgment, the surgeon can usually determine when a defect is too large for primary closure or when primary closure is likely to cause distortion and tethering of adjacent tis-

sues and result in a significant functional disturbance. In such cases, a flap reconstruction must be considered. In select cases, pedicled flaps may be appropriate. Often, particularly with larger or more complicated defects, free flaps provide the best reconstructive result. Free tissue reconstruction has the advantage of allowing the surgeon to reconstruct the defect with the exact tissue components that were excised, including bone and skin. In addition, free flaps can be reinnervated to achieve a sensate reconstruction.

If the planned surgical procedure involves resection of part of the maxilla or the mandible, appropriate dental consultation should be obtained. If a postoperative splint, obturator, or dental prosthesis is to be placed, it is critical that dental impressions be obtained before operation. Thyroid function should be tested in all patients who have a history of radiation therapy to the neck to confirm that they are euthyroid.

In cooperative patients, small primary lesions of the oral cavity can sometimes be excised with local anesthesia; however, general anesthesia with adequate relaxation is required in the majority of cases. The route of intubation must be carefully considered for each patient. When the planned resection is extensive and when significant postoperative edema is anticipated, a tracheostomy should be performed. Patients with bulky lesions should undergo tracheostomy under local anesthesia before general anesthesia is induced. When a tracheostomy is not planned, nasotracheal intubation is often desirable.

When the excision is limited to the oral cavity, perioperative antibiotics are generally unnecessary. When a graft, a flap, or packing is employed, however, perioperative I.V. administration of antibiotics is advisable. In all cases in which the neck is entered, perioperative antibiotics are recommended. The oral cavity can be prepared preoperatively with chlorhexidine and a toothbrush.

A nasogastric feeding tube should be inserted whenever it is believed that the patient may have a problem maintaining oral nutrition postoperatively. Patients who undergo primary closure or split-thickness skin grafting or whose surgical wound is allowed to heal by secondary intention may be allowed clear liquids in 24 to 48 hours and a pureed diet by postoperative day 3; they can often tolerate a soft diet within 1 week. Patients who undergo flap reconstruction will have to be fed via a nasogastric tube until they have healed to the point where they can resume oral intake.

Patients should be advised to maintain oral hygiene postoperatively by means of frequent irrigation and rinses with either normal saline or half-strength hydrogen peroxide. Teeth may be gently cleaned with a soft toothbrush until healing has occurred.

Anterior Glossectomy

OPERATIVE PLANNING

Either orotracheal or nasotracheal intubation may be appropriate, depending on the surgical approach and the extent of the planned resection. A tracheostomy should be performed whenever significant postoperative swelling or airway compromise is anticipated.

The depth of the excision and the size of the anticipated defect determine the optimal reconstructive approach. Defects that connect to the neck, unless they are small and can easily be closed primarily, usually necessitate creation of a flap for optimal reconstruction. When the excision extends down to the underlying musculature but there is no connection to the neck, a skin graft may be used. If a postoperative dental splint is planned to hold a skin graft in place, a dental consultation must be obtained before operation.

The patient should be supine in a 20° reverse Trendelenburg position. Turning the table 180° may facilitate access and positioning for the surgeon.

OPERATIVE TECHNIQUE

Step 1: Surgical Approach

Small anterior lesions up to 2 cm in diameter may be approached transorally, as may certain carefully selected larger lesions. Exposure of the tongue is usually achieved with the help of an appropriately sized bite block; alternatively, a specialized retractor (e.g., a Molt retractor) may be used. Retraction of the tongue is facilitated by the use of a piercing towel clip or a heavy silk suture placed through the tip of the tongue.

Access to posterior lesions and most larger lesions is obtained by performing a mandibulotomy through a lip-splitting incision [see Figure 1]. A stair-step incision is made in the lip and extended downward straight through the mentum, and a Z-plasty is done at the mental crease. Alternatively, the incision may be carried around the mental subunit.

The mandibular periosteum is elevated and a plate contoured to the mandible before the mandible is divided; this measure ensures exact realignment of the cut ends of the mandible. When possible, the mandibulotomy should be made anterior to the mental foramen to preserve sensation throughout the distribution of the mental nerve. Repair of the mandibulotomy is greatly facilitated by making a stair-step or chevron-type mandibulotomy [see Figure 2]. A paralingual mucosal incision is made to allow retraction of the mandible and exposure of the posterior oral cavity.

As an alternative, a visor flap may be created [see Figure 3]. Such a flap allows the surgeon to avoid making a lip-splitting incision and provides adequate exposure of small lesions of the anterior oral cavity; however, it is inadequate for exposure of lesions posterior to the middle third of the tongue or in the area of the retromolar trigone. Furthermore, creation of a visor flap results in anesthesia of the lower lip because of the necessity of dividing both mental nerves.

To create a visor flap, an incision is made from mastoid to mastoid along a skin crease in the neck, with care taken to remain below the marginal mandibular nerves. The skin flap is elevated in the subplatysmal plane to the level of the mandible. The marginal mandibular nerves are preserved. The flap is elevated from the lateral surface of the mandible, and the two mental nerves are divided. An incision is made in the oral cavity mucosa along the gingivolabial sulcus and continued so that it connects to the skin incision. The flap is then retracted superiorly to expose the anterior mandible and the oral cavity.

Step 2: Resection

The excision should include a generous mucosal margin around the visible lesion. A significant amount of the tongue musculature surrounding the lesion should be resected as well.

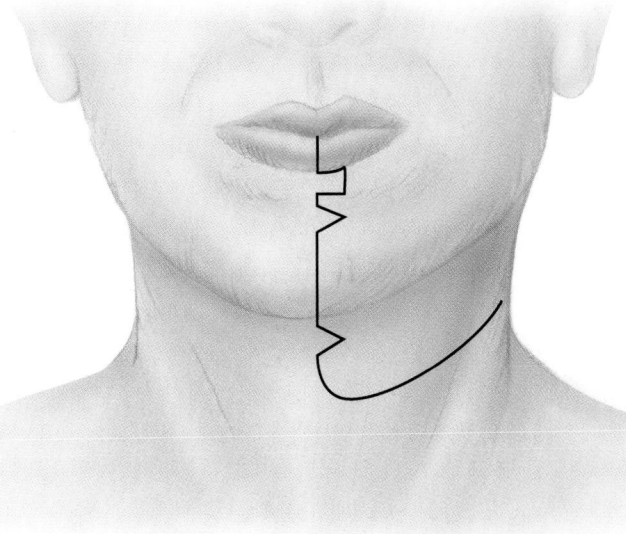

Figure 1 **Anterior glossectomy. A lip-splitting incision is made that extends downward straight through the mentum.**

Palpation of the lesion is critical for obtaining adequate deep surgical margins.

Resection may be performed with a monopolar electrocautery, with the cutting current used to incise the mucosa and the coagulation current used to cut the muscle. Alternatively, resection may be performed with a scalpel and a scissors. Hemostasis is achieved with a monopolar or bipolar electrocautery. Larger vessels are ligated with chromic catgut or Vicryl ties.

Lesions of the lateral tongue should be wedge-excised in a transverse (rather than horizontal) fashion to facilitate closure and enhance postoperative function. With larger lesions, for which either flap reconstruction or healing by secondary intention is typically indicated, the shape of the defect is contoured so as to obtain wide margins around the lesion, and the flap is designed to fill the contoured defect.

Step 3: Reconstruction

After negative margins are confirmed by frozen section examination, repair of the surgical defect is initiated. Careful preoperative assessment of the anticipated defect lays the groundwork for optimal reconstruction. Many defects can be either repaired primarily or allowed to heal by secondary intention. Free tissue transfer is an excellent reconstructive option in many cases, allowing the maintenance of tongue mobility and the separation of the tongue from the mandible and making sensate reconstruction possible.

In many patients with wedge-excised lateral tongue lesions, primary closure of the defect yields good results. The deep muscle is carefully reapproximated with long-lasting absorbable sutures. The mucosa is also closed with absorbable sutures. Care should be taken not to strangulate tissues by making the sutures too tight. When complete primary closure is not possible or desirable, the tongue may be allowed to granulate and heal by secondary intention. Split-thickness skin grafts, though useful for relining the floor of the mouth, generally do not take well on the tongue.

For large defects of the tongue and those involving the floor of the mouth, flap reconstruction is appropriate. Defects that connect to the neck, unless they are small and can be closed primarily, should also be closed with a flap. Free tissue transfer is frequently the optimal reconstructive approach. Free fasciocuta-

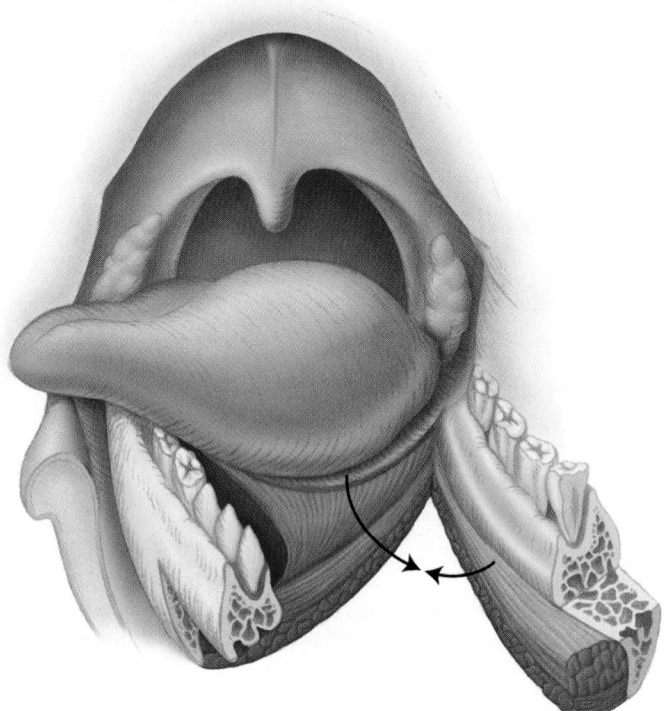

Figure 2 **Anterior glossectomy. A stair-step mandibulotomy is made.**

neous flaps from the radial forearm, the anterior lateral thigh, or the lateral arm are well suited to reconstruction in this area. Pedicled flaps (e.g., myocutaneous flaps from the pectoral muscle) are also used in this setting, but they are bulkier and harder to contour to the defects.

If a mandibulotomy was made, it is repaired with the previously contoured plate. The lip-splitting incision is closed in three layers (mucosa, muscle, and skin). Great care must be taken to ensure accurate realignment of the vermilion border and the orbicularis oris muscle.

Alternative Procedure: Laser Vaporization

Very superficial and premalignant lesions of the tongue may be vaporized by using a CO_2 laser. The desired depth of tissue destruction for leukoplakia is approximately 1 to 2 mm.

TROUBLESHOOTING

Larger excisions may lead to airway edema. Whenever this possibility is a concern, a tracheostomy should be performed. A single intraoperative dose of steroids may reduce postoperative tongue edema without adversely affecting wound healing. Using a stair-step incision for the lip-splitting incision facilitates accurate reapproximation of the vermilion border. Excessive tongue movement may result in dehiscence of the closure. Voice rest for 3 to 5 days after operation may be beneficial.

POSTOPERATIVE CARE

Patients who undergo primary closure of the tongue may begin a fluid diet on the day after operation; they should remain on a liquid diet for 7 to 10 days. Patients who undergo skin grafting may also begin a liquid diet on postoperative day 1. If a flap was used to close the defect or if there is some question whether the patient will be capable of adequate oral intake, a nasogastric feeding tube should be inserted and maintained until the suture lines heal.

Bolster dressings may be removed and skin grafts inspected

after 7 to 10 days. Patients with skin grafts should stay on a soft diet for 2 weeks. If a tracheotomy was performed, the patient may be decannulated when postoperative edema has settled.

Meticulous and frequent oral hygiene is essential. Mouth rinses and irrigation with normal saline or half-strength hydrogen peroxide should be done at least four times a day and after every meal. Teeth may be gently cleaned with a soft toothbrush.

COMPLICATIONS

The main complications of anterior glossectomy are as follows:

1. Injury to the lingual nerve, which causes numbness and loss of the sense of taste in the ipsilateral tongue.
2. Injury to the submandibular and sublingual gland ducts, which causes obstruction of the glands, pain and swelling, and possibly ranula formation.
3. Injury to the hypoglossal nerve, portions of which are resected with the lesion. Injury to the main trunk of this nerve leads to paralysis and atrophy of the remaining ipsilateral tongue.
4. Tethering and scarring of the tongue, which can lead to difficulties with speech and swallowing. This problem can usually be avoided by careful preoperative planning of reconstruction.

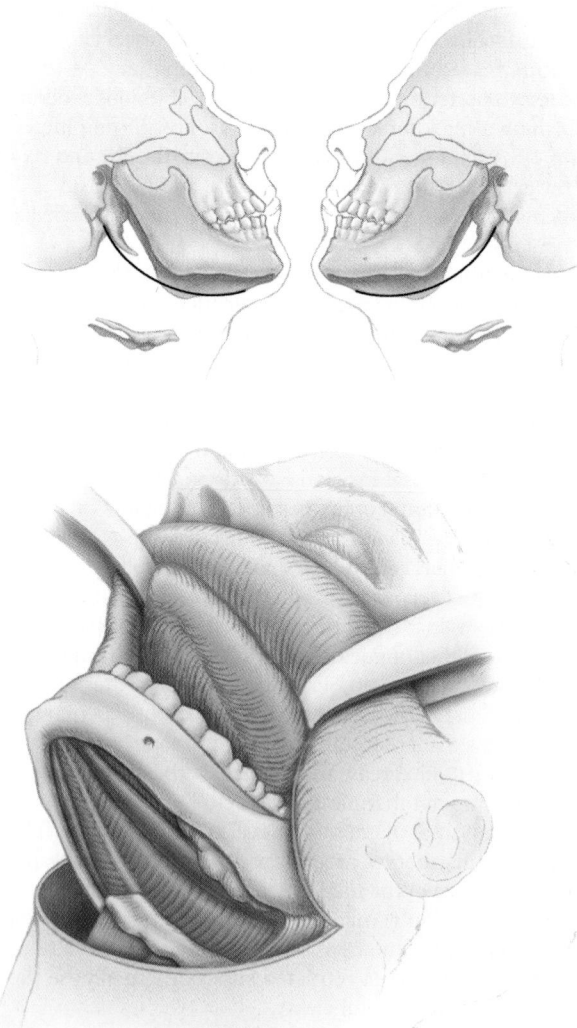

Figure 3 **Anterior glossectomy. As an alternative to a lip-splitting incision with mandibulotomy, a visor flap may be employed for exposure.**

Excision of Floor-of-Mouth Lesions

OPERATIVE PLANNING

Planning for excision of a lesion from the floor of the mouth is essentially the same as that for anterior glossectomy [*see* Anterior Glossectomy, Operative Planning, *above*]. If either or both of Wharton's ducts are to be transected without excision of the submandibular glands, consideration must be given to the management of these glands.

OPERATIVE TECHNIQUE

Step 1: Surgical Approach

The surgical approach is the same as that described for glossectomy [*see* Anterior Glossectomy, Operative Technique, Step 1, *above*].

Step 2: Resection

The area to be excised, including adequate margins, is marked. The lesion is then excised with a monopolar electrocautery; as in a glossectomy, the cutting current is used to cut the mucosa, the coagulation current to cut the deeper tissues. Palpation is important for obtaining adequate deep surgical margins.

If the excision cuts across Wharton's duct, the duct should be identified and transected obliquely so as to create a wider opening. The transected stump is held with a 4-0 chromic catgut suture. Once the resection is complete, the duct is transposed posteriorly to the cut edge of the mucosa of the floor of the mouth and sutured in place with two or three 4-0 chromic sutures. During subsequent reconstruction, care should be taken not to obstruct the orifice of the duct.

Step 3: Reconstruction

After clean surgical margins have been verified by frozen section examination, repair of the surgical defect is initiated. Small superficial defects of the floor of the mouth may be allowed to heal by secondary intention.

For small defects that do not connect to the neck, reconstruction with a 0.014 to 0.016 in.–thick split-thickness skin graft is appropriate. The graft is cut to size and sutured in place with 4-0 chromic sutures. Several perforations should be made in the graft to allow the egress of blood and serum. A Xeroform gauze bolster is fashioned to fit over the skin graft and sutured in place with 2-0 silk tie-over bolster stitches; alternatively, it may be held in place by a prefabricated dental prosthesis.

For larger defects, particularly those involving the tongue, a flap reconstruction typically yields the best functional results. In select cases, a platysma flap may be used for reconstruction of defects in the floor of the mouth. Other regional flaps tend to be bulky and difficult to shape to the contours of the defect. Free tissue transfer frequently provides the most suitable reconstructive tissue characteristics and the most favorable postoperative results. A free fasciocutaneous radial forearm flap is usually the optimal choice for reconstruction of floor-of-mouth defects when a flap is required.

TROUBLESHOOTING

Special care should be taken to identify the lingual nerve and artery so that these structures are not inadvertently divided. Meticulous hemostasis should be obtained in all cases. Any skin grafts used should be adequately sized and should not "tent up." Generally, skin grafting and bolsters do not work well on mobile structures. Quilting grafts to the underlying tissues with multiple absorbable sutures can eliminate the need for a bolster and result in acceptable graft take.

POSTOPERATIVE CARE

Postoperative care of patients undergoing excision of floor-of-mouth lesions is virtually identical to that of patients undergoing anterior glossectomy [*see* Anterior Glossectomy, Postoperative Care, *above*].

COMPLICATIONS

Excision of floor-of-mouth lesions is associated with the same complications as anterior glossectomy [*see* Anterior Glossectomy, Complications, *above*].

Excision of Superficial or Plunging Ranulas

OPERATIVE PLANNING

Planning for excision of a superficial or plunging ranula resembles that for glossectomy. A Ring-Adair-Elwyn (RAE) tube is inserted orally and taped to the contralateral cheek. Cervical exploration is usually unnecessary, because the cervical component of the ranula resolves after removal of the ipsilateral sublingual gland. In select cases, especially those involving disease recurrence after a previous attempt at excision, a transcervical approach should be considered.

OPERATIVE TECHNIQUE

Step 1: Surgical Approach

Ranulas are resected via the transoral approach. A bite block or a Molt retractor is used to gain exposure.

Step 2: Resection

A local anesthetic preparation with epinephrine is infiltrated into the area of the mucosal incisions. A small superficial ranula may be marsupialized and packed with gauze. The ranula is widely unroofed and the contents removed with suction. The margins of the cyst are sutured to the mucosa with 4-0 chromic sutures, and the cavity is packed with iodoform strip gauze. The gauze may be removed in 5 to 7 days.

A plunging ranula is treated with complete surgical excision of the cyst and the sublingual gland [*see Figure 4*]. A mucosal incision is made directly over the cyst. Careful dissection is carried out around the cyst and the associated gland. Hemostasis is achieved with a bipolar electrocautery, with care taken not to injure the adjacent lingual nerve. The submandibular gland duct is cannulated with a lacrimal probe to help guard against inadvertent injury to this structure. The incision is closed with 4-0 chromic suture.

TROUBLESHOOTING

Efforts should be made to identify the lingual nerve and artery so as to prevent inadvertent division of these structures. Meticulous hemostasis should be obtained in all cases. If the submandibular gland duct is injured, it should be transected and the cut end sutured to the adjacent floor-of-mouth mucosa (sialodochoplasty).

COMPLICATIONS

The three main complications of the procedure for excising a ranula are among those that are also associated with anterior glossectomy and excision of floor-of-mouth lesions: injury to the lingual nerve, injury to the submandibular gland duct, and injury to the hypoglossal nerve [*see* Anterior Glossectomy, Complications, *above*].

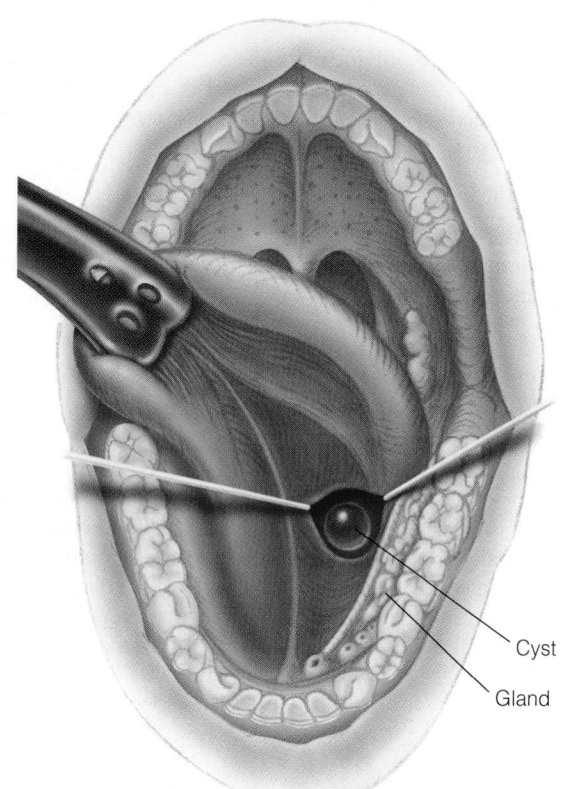

Cyst

Gland

Figure 4 **Excision of plunging ranula. A mucosal incision is made over the cyst, dissection is done around the cyst and the associated sublingual gland, and cyst and gland are completely excised.**

Removal of Submandibular Gland Duct Stones

OPERATIVE PLANNING

When a submandibular gland duct stone is readily palpable in the floor of the mouth, a transoral approach is appropriate. When the stone is within the hilum of the gland, however, it generally cannot be removed transorally and often must be treated by excising the submandibular gland.

OPERATIVE TECHNIQUE

Step 1: Surgical Approach

The procedure is easily accomplished with local anesthesia in a cooperative patient. The patient is seated upright in the examining chair, and a topical anesthetic is applied to the oral cavity.

Step 2: Resection

A local anesthetic preparation with epinephrine is infiltrated into the floor of the mouth and around the duct in which the stone is palpated. A 2-0 silk suture may be placed around the duct behind the stone to prevent it from migrating back into the hilum of the gland.

A lacrimal probe is inserted into the duct and advanced to the stone in a retrograde manner. A mucosal incision is then made directly over the stone and extended downward to the duct, with the stone and the lacrimal probe serving as guides. The duct is incised and the stone delivered. As a rule, repair of the duct is not required.

TROUBLESHOOTING

Careful dissection directly onto the duct and stone usually serves to prevent inadvertent injury to the lingual nerve.

COMPLICATIONS

The main complications of the procedure are as follows:

1. Injury to the lingual nerve, resulting in numbness and loss of the sense of taste to the ipsilateral tongue.
2. Stricture of the submandibular gland duct. This is an unusual complication that can be corrected by transecting the duct posterior to the stricture and suturing it to the mucosa of the floor of the mouth.

Resection of Hard Palate

OPERATIVE PLANNING

Careful evaluation is required to determine whether resection of part of the hard palate will suffice or whether a more extensive dissection (e.g., maxillectomy) will be required. If it is anticipated that a dental prosthesis will be required, a dental consultation should be obtained before operation. When the lesion to be resected is superficial or only a limited amount of the bony hard palate must be resected, the procedure may be performed via the transoral approach.

OPERATIVE TECHNIQUE

Step 1: Surgical Approach

The patient is supine, with the bed turned 180° to facilitate the surgeons' access to the operative site. An oral RAE tube is inserted and taped in the midline. The lesion is approached transorally, and a Dingman or Crowe-Davis retractor is used to obtain exposure.

Step 2: Resection

An incision is made around the periphery of the lesion in such a way as to maintain adequate margins; a monopolar electrocautery with a needle tip is ideal for this purpose. The periosteum is elevated away from the underlying bone, and the lesion is removed [*see Figure 5*].

When bone must be resected, the periosteum is elevated away from the incision site. A high-speed oscillating saw or an osteotome is used to make the cuts in the bone, after which the specimen is rocked free and removed.

Step 3: Reconstruction

After surgical margins have been verified by frozen-section review, repair of the surgical defect is initiated. Small mucosal defects may be allowed to heal by secondary intention. Small through-and-through resections may be closed by placing relaxing incisions laterally and advancing the mucosa to permit primary closure. Larger defects may be closed with palatal mucosal flaps. Many through-and-through defects can be closed quite satisfactorily with a dental obturator.

POSTOPERATIVE CARE

The patient should be maintained on a soft diet postoperatively. Meticulous oral hygiene is important. Oral rinses and flushes with normal saline or half-strength hydrogen peroxide should be performed at least four times daily and after meals.

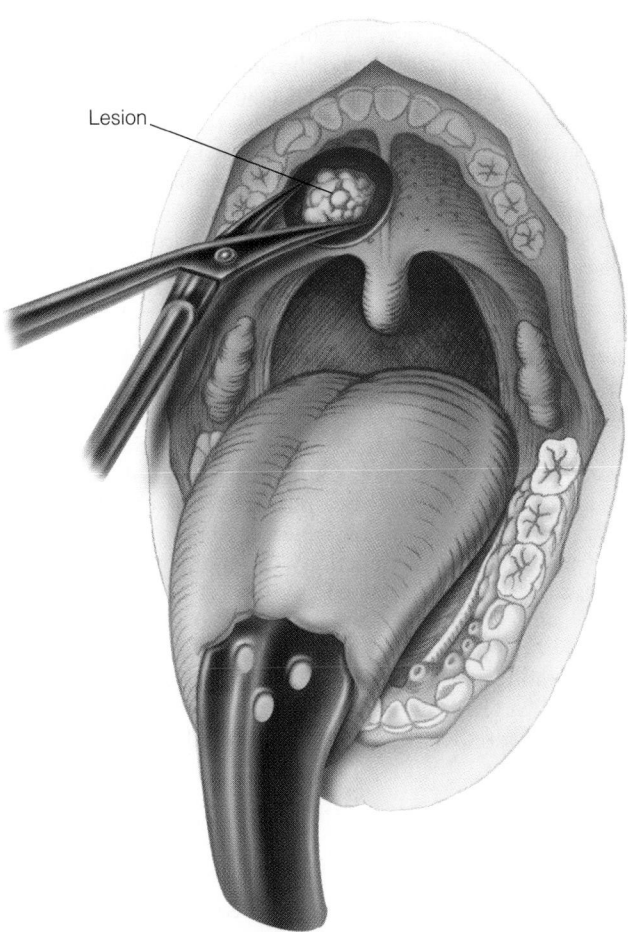

Lesion

Figure 5 Resection of hard palate. An incision is made around the lesion, with adequate margins maintained, the periosteum is lifted off the bone, and the lesion is removed.

COMPLICATIONS

The most significant potential complication of hard palate resection is oral antral or oronasal fistula; careful tissue reconstruction and the use of an obturator can prevent this complication.

Maxillectomy

OPERATIVE PLANNING

General anesthesia with muscle relaxation is essential for all types of maxillectomy. Either orotracheal or nasotracheal intubation may be appropriate, depending on the surgical approach. Skin incisions should be marked before the endotracheal tube is taped in place to avoid distortion of facial structures and skin lines. The patient should be supine in a 20° reverse Trendelenburg position. The eyes should be protected carefully (e.g., with a corneal shield or a temporary nylon tarsorrhaphy suture).

Radiographic evaluation plays a vital role in planning the surgical approach and determining the extent of resection required [see Figure 6]. Lesions of the infrastructure of the maxilla can be excised by means of partial maxillectomy via the transoral route. More extensive lesions usually must be accessed via facial incisions in conjunction with the transoral approach.

In all cases, a dental consultation should be obtained preoperatively so that a dental impression can be taken and an obturator fashioned for intraoperative use. Antibiotics should be given perioperatively and continued until nasal packing is removed.

OPERATIVE TECHNIQUE

Step 1: Surgical Approach

In addition to the transoral approach, maxillectomy usually requires exposure of the anterior face of the maxilla. There are several options for achieving such exposure, including a Weber-Ferguson incision and midface degloving. Midface degloving has the advantage of eliminating the need for visible facial incisions, but it yields limited exposure in the ethmoid region. The choice of surgical approach is determined by the extent of the planned resection and by the preferences of the patient and the surgeon.

In the Weber-Ferguson approach, the first step is to mark the path of the incision, which begins in the midline of the upper lip; extends through the philtrum; curves around the nasal vestibule and the ala; continues upward along the lateral nasal wall, just medial to the junction of the nasal sidewall and the cheek; and ends near the medial canthus. For added exposure in the ethmoid region, a Lynch extension, in which the incision is continued superiorly up to the medial eyebrow, may be performed. Alternatively, the Weber-Ferguson incision may be continued laterally in the subciliary crease along the inferior eyelid to the lateral canthus of the eye; this extension yields added exposure of the posterolateral aspect of the maxilla.

The skin incisions should initially be made with a scalpel and then continued with an electrocautery. The upper lip is divided through its full thickness, and the incision is continued in the gingivolabial sulcus laterally until the posterolateral aspect of the sinus is exposed. When possible, the infraorbital nerve is identified and preserved. The soft tissues are elevated from the anterior wall of the maxillary sinus; if access to the pterygomaxillary fissure is desired, elevation should be continued up to the zygoma.

In a midface degloving, the skin of the lower face and nose is mobilized and retracted superiorly. A standard transfixion incision is made, transecting the membranous septum. Intercartilaginous incisions are then made bilaterally and connected to the transfixion incision. The incision is then continued laterally along the cephalic border of the lower lateral cartilage and across the floor of the nose. To prevent stenosis, a small Z-plasty [see 27 Surface Reconstruction Procedures] or triangle is incised medially just before the transfixion incision is joined. The soft tissues are elevated over the nasal dorsum and the nasal tip with Joseph scissors. An incision is made in the gingivolabial sulcus with the monopolar cautery, and this incision is connected to the floor-of-nose incisions by means of gentle dissection. The soft tissues are then elevated from the anterior maxilla as far as the infraorbital rims and laterally as far as the zygoma.

Step 2: Resection

A Molt retractor is placed on the side opposite the side of the planned excision and opened as wide as possible to expose the hard palate and the alveolus.

The infraorbital rim should be preserved if it is possible to do so safely. Often, a thin strip of the rim can be preserved even when the rest of the bone must be resected. If the orbital floor must be resected but the orbital contents can be preserved, the periorbita can be dissected away from the bone of the orbital floor and preserved. If the orbital contents are involved, an orbital exenteration must be performed in conjunction with the maxillectomy.

The cut along the infraorbital rim and superior anterior maxillary wall is made with a high-speed oscillating saw with a fine blade. The level at which this superior cut is made is determined by the extent of the resection. Lesions that are confined to the alveolus or the palate and do not invade the maxilla typically can be removed by excising the infrastructure of the maxilla. The line of transection is continued through the nasal process of the maxilla medially and downward through the piriform aperture. Laterally, the cut extends to the zygomatic process of the maxilla and around the posterolateral aspect of the sinus.

If the pterygoid plates are to be preserved, they are cut free by placing a curved osteotome along the posterior wall of the sinus and sharply dividing the plates from the sinus wall. If the pterygoid plates, part of the pterygoid musculature, or both are to be resected, the soft tissue attachments are cut sharply with curved Mayo scissors once the entire maxillary specimen has been mobilized.

The line of transection in the maxillary alveolus can run between two teeth if a suitable gap is evident. In the majority of cases, however, it is advisable to extract a tooth and make the cut through the extraction site. A power saw is used, and the cut is connected to the transection line through the nasal process of the maxilla and the piriform aperture. The hard palate mucosa is then incised lateral to the proposed cut in the hard palate bone to preserve a flap of mucosa that can be used to cover the raw cut bony edge of the palate. This incision is made with a needle-tip electrocautery and carried down to the bone of the hard palate. It should extend from the maxillary tuberosity posteriorly to the cut bone in the maxillary alveolus anteriorly, with care taken to obtain adequate mucosal margins. The mucosa is elevated for a short distance over the hard palate bone to create a short muco-

sal flap that is wrapped over the cut bony edge of the palate. The mucosal cut is connected around the maxillary tuberosity to the gingivolabial sulcus incision that was made earlier.

The hard palate is then cut with a power saw. Once all the bone cuts are complete, an osteotome may be used to connect them if necessary. The remaining soft tissue attachments are divided along the posterior hard palate with curved Mayo scissors. The surgical defect is packed to control bleeding. Bleeding from the internal maxillary artery is controlled by ligatures or ligating clips.

Step 3: Reconstruction

All sharp spicules of bone are debrided. The flap of hard palate mucosa is brought up over the cut bony edge of the palate and held in place with several Vicryl sutures. The anterior and posterior cut edges of the soft palate are reapproximated with absorbable sutures.

A split-thickness skin graft, 0.014 to 0.016 in. thick, is harvested and used to line the raw undersurface of the cheek flap. The skin graft is sutured to the mucosal edge of the cheek flap with 3-0 chromic sutures. Superiorly, the graft is not sutured but draped into position and retained by a layer of Xeroform packing and strip gauze coated with antibiotic ointment. Gentle pressure is applied to the packing so that it conforms to the defect. The previously fabricated dental obturator is placed to support the packing and to close the oral cavity from the nasal cavity. In a dentulous patient, the obturator may be wired to the remaining

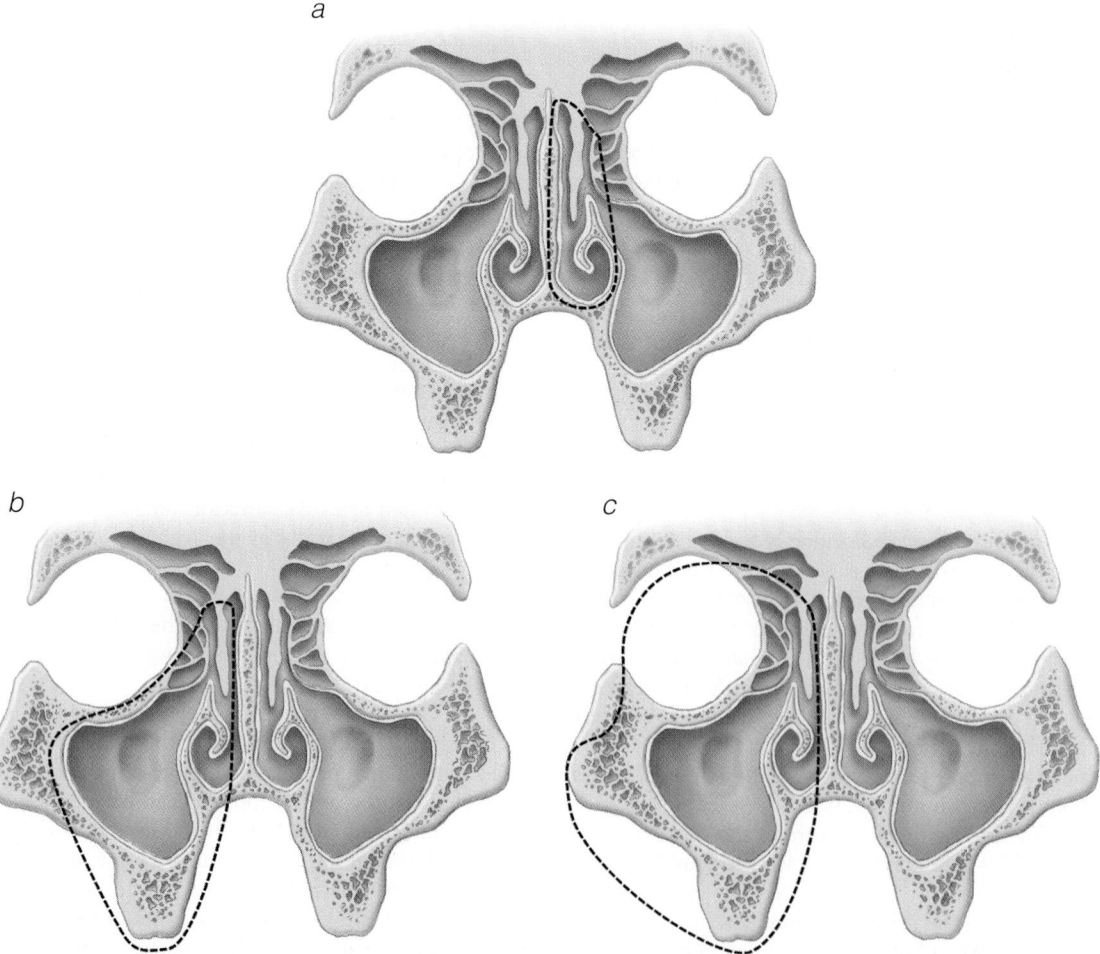

Figure 6 **Maxillectomy. Radiographic assessment helps determine the required extent of resection. Depicted are (*a*) medial maxillectomy, (*b*) subtotal maxillectomy without orbital exenteration, and (*c*) total maxillectomy with orbital exenteration.**

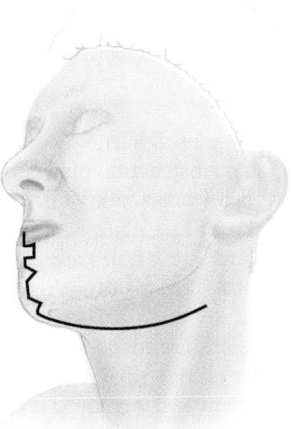

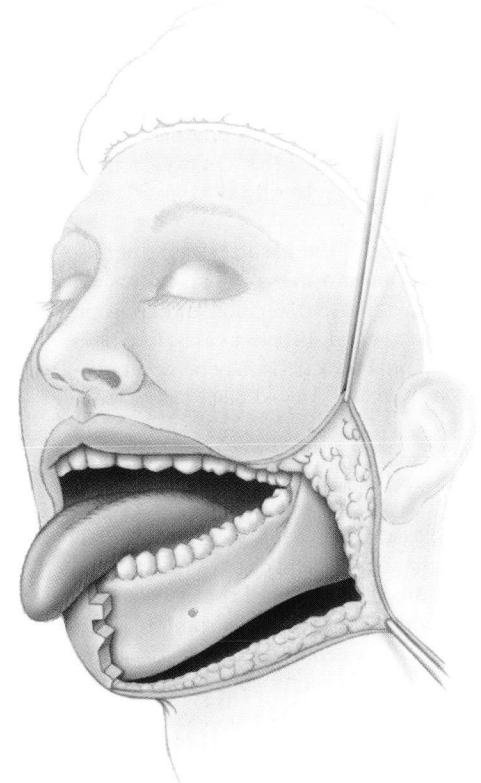

Figure 7 **Mandibulectomy. A cheek flap is created by making a lip-splitting incision and extending it down to the level of the thyrohyoid membrane, then laterally to the mastoid along a skin crease.**

teeth; in an edentulous patient, it may be temporarily fixed in place with two screws placed in the remaining hard palate.

The skin incisions are closed in two layers, with interrupted absorbable sutures used for the deep layers and nonabsorbable monofilament sutures for the skin. If a lip-splitting incision was made, care must be taken to ensure exact reapproximation of the orbicularis oris and the vermilion border.

If the infraorbital rim was resected, it should be reconstructed to yield good aesthetic results. A split calvarial bone graft may be used for this purpose when there is adequate soft tissue coverage for the bone grafts available. When soft tissue coverage is inadequate or the orbital floor must be reconstructed, an osteocutaneous radial forearm or scapular flap may be employed with excellent results.

Alternative Procedure: Peroral Partial Maxillectomy

The oral cavity is exposed with cheek retractors. An incision is made in the gingivobuccal sulcus and the mucosa of the hard palate, with care taken to maintain adequate margins; a monopolar electrocautery, set to use the cutting current, is suitable for this purpose. Incisions are made circumferentially through all the soft tissues up to the anterior wall of the maxilla and the hard palate. The infraorbital nerve should be preserved if it is not involved with the disease process.

The cut in the hard palate mucosa should be made lateral to the planned cuts in the hard palate bone to create a mucosal flap, which will be used to cover the cut bony edge of the hard palate. If necessary, teeth may be extracted to allow the surgeon to make bone cuts through tooth sockets while preserving adjacent teeth. The bone is cut with a high-speed power saw, and an osteotome is used to divide any remaining bony attachments and deliver the specimen. If the mucosa remaining in the maxillary antrum is not diseased, it need not be removed.

A split-thickness skin graft, 0.014 to 0.016 in. thick, is harvested from the anterolateral thigh and used to reline the raw buccal mucosa area. The graft is sutured to the cut edge of the buccal mucosa with 4-0 chromic catgut. Xeroform and strip gauze coated with antibiotic ointment are gently packed into the defect to secure the skin graft. The previously fabricated dental obturator is wired to the remaining teeth to hold the packing in place.

TROUBLESHOOTING

If a lip-splitting incision is planned, lip contraction can be reduced and vermilion border realignment improved by employing a stair-step lip incision and a Z-plasty. A single intraoperative steroid dose reduces facial edema without compromising wound healing. Retention of the obturator is aided by the band of scar tissue that forms at the junction of the mucosa and the skin graft. Covering the cut edge of the hard palate bone with mucosa eliminates pain caused by pressure from the obturator on thinly covered bone.

If more than a small area of the floor of the orbit is resected, it should be repaired to prevent enophthalmos. Epiphoria is uncommon; when it occurs, it is related to scarring of the nasolacrimal duct. Identifying the duct and transecting it obliquely should reduce the incidence of this complication.

POSTOPERATIVE CARE

A nasogastric tube is placed at the end of the procedure. Many patients are able to begin a liquid diet and advance to a soft diet within a few days after operation. A soft diet should be continued for at least 2 weeks. Oral rinses and flushes with normal saline or half-strength hydrogen peroxide should be performed at least four times daily and after meals.

The obturator and the packing may be removed from the cavity in 7 to 10 days. The obturator should be replaced to maintain oral competence. The prosthodontist makes a final obturator once healing is complete and the cavity has stabilized. Facial incisions are cleaned twice daily and coated with antibiotic ointment. Facial sutures are removed 5 to 7 days after operation.

COMPLICATIONS

The main complications of maxillectomy are as follows:

1. Enophthalmos and hypophthalmos, which create a cosmetic deformity.
2. Infraorbital nerve injury, which results in anesthesia or paresthesia of the ipsilateral cheek and upper lip. On occasion, the infraorbital nerve may have to be sacrificed as part of the planned resection.
3. Epiphoria, caused by scarring of the nasolacrimal duct.
4. Difficult retention of the dental prosthesis, which can usually be prevented by careful preoperative evaluation and appropriate choice of reconstructive method. In select cases, free tissue reconstruction without a dental prosthesis may be optimal.

Mandibulectomy

OPERATIVE PLANNING

General anesthesia with muscle relaxation is essential for all types of mandibulectomy. Either orotracheal or nasotracheal intubation is appropriate, depending on the surgical approach and the extent of the planned resection. A tracheostomy should be performed whenever significant postoperative swelling or airway compromise is anticipated. Skin incisions should be marked before the endotracheal tube is taped in place.

Preoperative radiographic evaluation is essential for planning the surgical approach and determining the extent of the proposed resection. For lesions without radiographic or clinical evidence of bone invasion, a marginal mandibulectomy is often appropriate. This procedure may also be performed to obtain adequate surgical margins for lesions that are in close proximity to the mandible. When the lesion is small, it is occasionally possible to perform marginal mandibulectomy via the transoral route. For more extensive lesions and those that show evidence of bone invasion, a segmental mandibulectomy is required.

The patient should be supine in a 20° reverse Trendelenburg position. Perioperative antibiotics should be administered.

OPERATIVE TECHNIQUE

Step 1: Exposure

Wide exposure for access to primary tumors of the oral cavity and the mandible may be achieved by means of either a lower-cheek flap or a visor flap. The former is often preferable, in that it allows resection of the primary and ipsilateral lymph nodes.

To create a lower-cheek flap, a lip-splitting incision is made through the full thickness of the lower lip and carried down through the chin tissues to the periosteum of the anterior mandible [see Figure 7]. This incision may be made straight through the mental subunit with a Z-plasty placed at the mental crease; alternatively, it may be made around the mental subunit. The incision is continued vertically to approximately the level of the thyrohyoid membrane, then extended laterally to the mastoid along a skin crease. The transverse component of the incision should be made at least two fingerbreadths below the mandible to prevent injury to the marginal mandibular nerve. The cheek flap is fully developed by incising the oral mucosa along the gingivolabial sulcus while maintaining adequate surgical margins around the lesion. The periosteum of the mandible is then elevated and the cheek flap retracted to expose the mandible.

A visor flap [see Figure 3] has the advantage of not requiring a lip-splitting incision, and it provides adequate exposure for lesions of the anterior oral cavity. However, it is inadequate for exposing lesions posterior to the middle third of the tongue or in the area of the retromolar trigone, and it may lead to anesthesia of the lower lip as a consequence of the need to divide both mental nerves. Technical aspects of visor flap creation are summarized elsewhere [see Anterior Glossectomy, Operative Technique, Step 1, above].

Step 2: Resection

If a plate is to be used in the reconstruction of the mandible, a template and a reconstruction plate are shaped and conformed to the mandible before resection. The segment of mandible to be resected is marked. The plate is applied to the buccal cortex of the mandible, and screw holes are predrilled in the mandible for gauging of depth. The plate is then set aside until needed for reconstruction.

Mucosal incisions are made around the lesion with the electrocautery, with care taken to maintain adequate surgical margins. The mandibular segment to be removed is cut with a high-speed sagittal saw. The lingual nerve and the hypoglossal nerve are preserved if possible. Muscle attachments to the resected mandibular segment are sharply divided, allowing the surgical specimen to be delivered [see Figure 8].

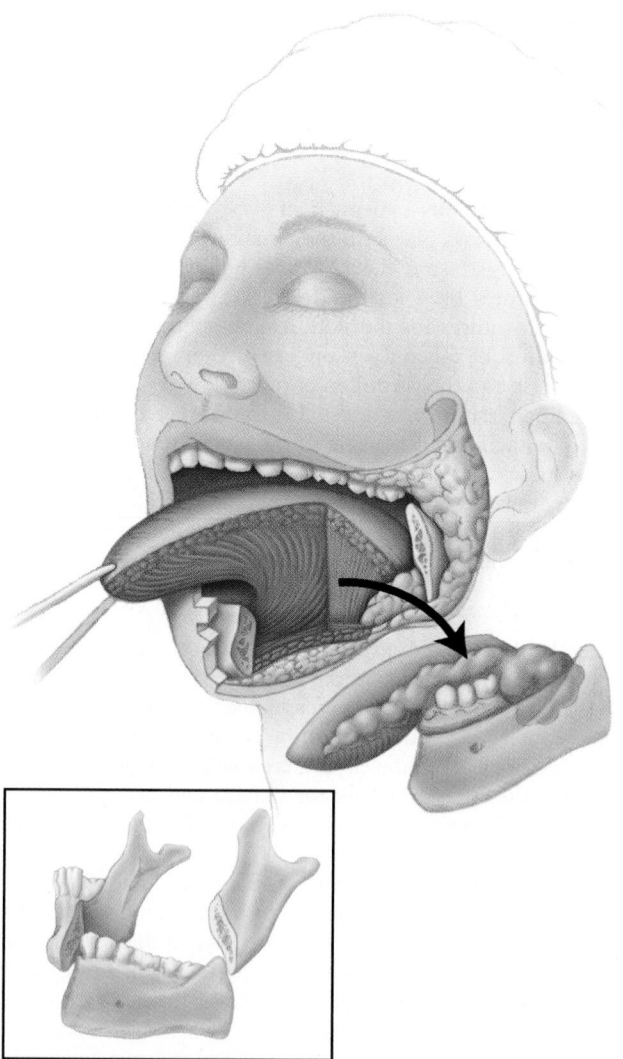

Figure 8 **Mandibulectomy. The segment to be removed is cut with a high-speed saw, with care taken to preserve the lingual and hypoglossal nerves if possible, and the muscle attachments to the segment are sharply divided to free the surgical specimen.**

In some cases, only a marginal mandibulectomy of the lingual or alveolar cortex of the mandible is necessary. The bone is cut with a high-speed saw in such a way that the cuts are rounded off and lack sharp angles, which are prone to fracturing. Once the bone cuts are made, an osteotome may be used to free the specimen.

Step 3: Reconstruction

When a marginal mandibulectomy has been performed, a plate is sometimes needed to support the mandible. This is especially likely to be the case for a patient with a thin edentulous mandible, in which the remaining bone cannot withstand the forces of mastication.

When the anterior mandible has been resected, it must be reconstructed with vascularized bone. Any of several free flaps may be employed, depending on the tissue requirements for the planned reconstruction. Free tissue flaps from the fibula, the scapula, or the iliac crest can provide bone that is suitable for mandibular reconstruction, as well as soft tissue that is suitable for reconstruction of accompanying mucosal and cutaneous defects.

After lateral mandibular resections, good results can be achieved by using mandibular reconstruction plates with suitable soft tissue reconstruction. There is a significant risk of plate failure, however, especially in dentulous patients. In many cases, replacing the resected portion of the mandible with vascularized bone—especially if the defect is longer than a few centimeters—yields better long-term results than using a reconstruction plate alone.

POSTOPERATIVE CARE

A nasogastric tube is placed at the end of the surgical procedure; most patients will need to be fed through this tube until their incisions are healed. A soft diet should be continued for 6 weeks. Oral rinses and flushes with normal saline or half-strength hydrogen peroxide should be performed at least four times a day and after meals.

Facial incisions are cleaned twice a day and coated with antibiotic ointment. Facial sutures are removed 5 to 7 days after operation.

TROUBLESHOOTING

Contouring the reconstruction plate to the mandible before resecting the mandibular segment will prevent malocclusion and enhance cosmetic results. Preserving the lingual nerve and the hypoglossal nerve, when possible, will improve postoperative swallowing and speech. The marginal mandibular nerve should be identified and protected as well. If a lip-splitting incision is used, performing a stair-step lip incision and a Z-plasty reduces lip contraction and improves vermilion border realignment.

COMPLICATIONS

The main complications of mandibulectomy are as follows:

1. Malocclusion, caused by inaccurate repair of the resected mandibular segment.
2. Plate failure or fracture, which can be reduced by reconstructing bony defects larger than 1 to 2 cm with revascularized bone.
3. Oral incompetence, caused by inadequate reconstruction of anterior mandibular defects.

Selected Readings

Baurmash H: Submandibular salivary stones: current management modalities. J Oral Maxillofac Surg 62:369, 2004

Brown JD: The midface degloving procedure for nasal, sinus and nasopharyngeal tumors. Otolaryngol Clin North Am 34:1095, 2001

Brown JS, Kalavrezos N, D'Sousa J, et al: Factors that influence the method of mandibular resection in the management of oral squamous cell carcinoma. Br J Oral Maxillofac Surg 40:275, 2002

Galloway RH, Gross PD, Thompson SH, et al: Pathogenesis and treatment of ranula: report of three cases. J Oral Maxillofac Surg 47:299, 1989

Hussain A, Hilmi OJ, Murray DP: Lateral rhinotomy through nasal aesthetic subunits: improved cosmetic outcome. J Laryngol Otol 116:703, 2002

Johnson JT, Leipzig B, Cummings CW: Management of T1 carcinoma of the anterior aspect of the tongue. Arch Otolaryngol 106:249, 1980

Lanier DM: Carcinoma of the hard palate. Surgery of the Oral Cavity. Bailey BJ, Ed. Year Book Medical Publishers, Chicago, 1989, p 163

Leipzig B, Cummings CW, Chung CT, et al: Carcinoma of the anterior tongue. Ann Otol Rhinol Laryngol 91:94, 1982

Osguthorpe JD, Weisman RA: "Medial maxillectomy" for lateral nasal neoplasms. Arch Otolaryngol Head Neck Surg 117:751, 1991

Schramm VL, Myers EN, Sigler BA: Surgical management of early epidermoid carcinoma of the anterior floor of the mouth. Laryngoscope 90:207, 1980

Spiro RH, Gerold FP, Strong EW: Mandibular "swing" approach for oral and oropharyngeal tumors. Head Neck 3:371, 1981

Stern SJ, Geopfert H, Clayman G, et al: Squamous cell carcinoma of the maxillary sinus. Arch Otolaryngol Head Neck Surg 119:964, 1993

Wald RM, Calcaterra TC: Lower alveolar carcinoma: segmental v. marginal resection. Arch Otolaryngol 109:578, 1983

Acknowledgment

Figures 1 through 8 Alice Y. Chen.

17 PAROTIDECTOMY

Leonard R. Henry, M.D., and John A. Ridge, M.D., Ph.D., F.A.C.S.

Anatomic Considerations

The parotid ("near the ear") gland, the largest of the salivary glands, occupies the space immediately anterior to the ear, overlying the angle of the mandible. It drains into the oral cavity via Stensen's duct, which enters the oral vestibule opposite the upper molars. The gland is invested by a strong fascia and is bounded superiorly by the zygomatic arch, anteriorly by the masseter, posteriorly by the external auditory canal and the mastoid process, and inferiorly by the sternocleidomastoid muscle. The masseter muscle, the styloid muscles, the posterior belly of the digastric muscle, and a portion of the sternocleidomastoid muscle lie deep to the parotid. Terminal branches of the external carotid artery, the facial vein, and the facial nerve are found within the gland. Parasympathetic innervation to the parotid is via the otic ganglion, which gives fibers to the auriculotemporal branch of the trigeminal nerve. Sympathetic innervation to the gland originates in the sympathetic ganglia and reaches the auriculotemporal nerve by way of the plexus around the middle meningeal artery.[1]

The facial nerve trunk exits the stylomastoid foramen and courses toward the parotid. Once inside the gland, it commonly bifurcates into superior (temporal-frontal) and inferior (cervico-marginal) divisions before giving rise to its terminal branches. The nerve branching within the parotid can be quite complex, but the common patterns are well known and their relative frequencies well established.[2,3] The portion of the parotid gland lateral to the facial nerve (about 80% of the gland) is designated as the superficial lobe; the portion medial to the facial nerve (the remaining 20%) is designated as the deep lobe. Deep-lobe tumors often present clinically as retromandibular or parapharyngeal masses, with displacement of the tonsil or soft palate appreciated in the throat.

Operative Planning

Obtaining informed consent for parotidectomy entails discussing both the features and the potential complications of the procedure. It is appropriate to address the possibility of facial nerve injury, but in doing so, the surgeon should not neglect other, far more common sequelae, such as cosmetic deformity, earlobe numbness, and Frey syndrome. Even conditions that are expected beforehand may prove distressing or debilitating for the patient. The risk of complications such as nerve injury is greater in cases involving reoperation or resection of malignant or deep-lobe tumors. The overwhelming majority of parotid tumors, however, are benign and lateral to the facial nerve. Accordingly, in what follows, we focus primarily on superficial parotidectomy, referring to variants of the procedure where relevant.

Excellent lighting, correctly applied traction and countertraction, adequate exposure, and clear definition of the surgical anatomy are essential in parotid surgery. The use of magnifying loupes and headlights is recommended. General anesthesia without muscle relaxation should be employed.

The patient is placed in the supine position, with the head elevated and turned away from the side undergoing operation and with the neck slightly extended. The table is positioned to allow the first assistant to stand directly above the patient's head, while the surgeon faces the operative field. A small cottonoid sponge is placed in the external auditory canal, where it remains for the duration of the procedure to prevent otitis externa from blood clots in the external auditory canal. The skin is painted with an antiseptic agent. A single perioperative dose of an antibiotic is administered.

The patient is draped in a fashion that permits the operating team to see all of the muscle groups innervated by the facial nerve. To this end, we employ a head drape that incorporates the endotracheal tube and hose. This drape secures the airway, keeps the tube from interfering with the surgeon, and permits rotation of the head without tension on the endotracheal tube. The skin of the upper chest and neck is widely painted and draped with a split sheet to allow additional exposure in the unlikely event that a neck dissection or a tracheostomy becomes necessary. The nose, the lips, and the eyes are covered with a sterile transparent drape that allows observation of movement during the procedure and permits access to the oral cavity (if desired) [*see Figure 1*].

Operative Technique

STEP 1: INCISION AND SKIN FLAPS

The incision is planned so as to permit excellent exposure with good cosmetic results. It begins immediately anterior to the ear, continues downward past the tragus, curves back under the ear (staying close to the earlobe), and finally turns downward to descend along the sternocleidomastoid muscle [*see Figure 1*]. Either all or part of this incision may be used, depending on circumstances. The incision is marked before draping. Skin creases typically help conceal the resulting scar.

Skin flaps are then created to expose the parotid gland. A tacking suture is placed within the dermis of the earlobe so that it can be retracted posteriorly. Skin hooks are used to apply vertical traction. The anterior flap is created superficial to the parotid fascia to afford access to the appropriate dissection plane. Vertically oriented blunt dissection minimizes the risk of injury to the distal branches of the facial nerve [*see Figure 2*]. The face is observed for muscle motion. The flap is raised until the anterior border of the gland is identified. The facial nerve branches are rarely encountered during flap elevation until they emerge from the parenchyma of the parotid. If muscle movement occurs, the flap has been more than adequately developed. The anterior flap is retracted with a suture through the dermis.

The posterior-inferior skin flap is then elevated in a similar manner. Careful dissection is performed to define the relationship of the parotid tail to the anterior border of the sternocleidomastoid. During this portion of the procedure, the great auricular nerve is identified coursing cephalad and superficial to the sternocleidomastoid muscle. Uninvolved branches of this nerve should be preserved if possible to prevent postoperative numbness of the earlobe.[4,5] The parotid tail is dissected away from the sternocleidomastoid muscle. Vertical traction is applied to the gland surface with clamps to facilitate exposure.

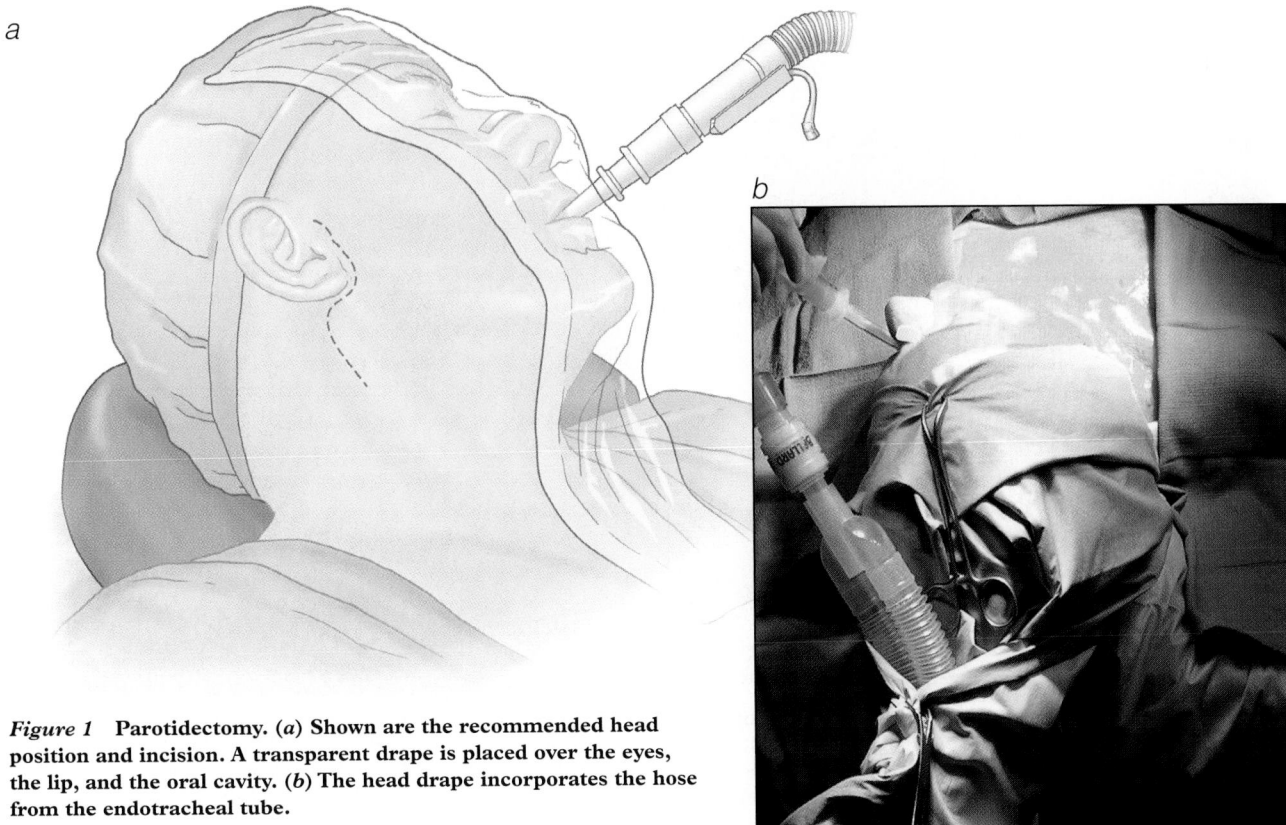

a

b

Figure 1 Parotidectomy. (*a*) Shown are the recommended head position and incision. A transparent drape is placed over the eyes, the lip, and the oral cavity. (*b*) The head drape incorporates the hose from the endotracheal tube.

Troubleshooting

A favorable skin crease, if available, may be used for the incision to improve the postoperative cosmetic result; however, it is important to keep the incision a few millimeters from the earlobe itself. A wound at the junction of the earlobe with the facial skin will distort the earlobe and create a visible contour change. An incision behind the tragus may lead to similar problems.

STEP 2: IDENTIFICATION OF FACIAL NERVE

Once the flaps have been developed and retracted, the next step is to identify the facial nerve. Usually, the nerve may be identified either at its main trunk (the antegrade approach) or at one of the distal branches, with subsequent dissection back toward the main trunk (the retrograde approach). For a lateral parotidectomy, our preference is to identify the main trunk first (unless it is thoroughly obscured by tumor or scar).

Antegrade Approach

The dissection plane is immediately anterior to the cartilage of the external auditory canal. The gland is mobilized anteriorly by means of blunt dissection. To reduce the risk of a traction injury, tissue is spread in a direction that is perpendicular to the incision and thus parallel to the direction of the main trunk of the nerve [*see Figure 3*]. The nerve trunk can usually be located underlying a point about halfway between the tip of the mastoid process and the ear canal. In addition, there are several anatomic landmarks that facilitate identification of the nerve, including the tragal pointer, the posterior belly of the digastric muscle, and the tympanomastoid suture. Of these, the tympanomastoid suture is closest to the main trunk of the facial nerve.[6] The clinical utility of this landmark is limited, however, because the tympanomastoid suture is not easily appreciated in every case. In addition, deep-lobe tumors may displace the nerve from its normal location. For appropriate and safe exposure of the nerve trunk, it is necessary to mobilize several centimeters of the parotid, thereby creating a trough rather than a deep hole. Small arteries run superficial and parallel to the facial nerve; these must be divided. Use of the electrocautery this close to the nerve is potentially hazardous. Bleeding is typically minor but nonetheless must be controlled.

Retrograde Approach

As noted, when the main trunk cannot be exposed, the most common alternative method of identifying the facial nerve is to find a peripheral branch and then dissect proximally toward the main trunk. Which branch is sought may depend on factors such as the surgeon's level of comfort with the relevant anatomy and known consistency or inconsistency of the nerve branch's location. Often, in this setting, tumor bulk is the deciding factor.

The anatomic relationships between the nerve branches and various landmarks can be exploited for more efficient identification. For example, the marginal mandibular branch of the facial nerve characteristically lies below the horizontal ramus of the mandible.[7] Often, the facial vein can be traced toward the parotid or the submandibular gland; the nerve branch can then be found coursing perpendicular and superficial to the vein. The buccal branch of the facial nerve has a typical location in the so-called buccal pocket—the area inferior to the zygoma and deep to the superficial musculoaponeurotic layer, which contains the buccal fat pad and Stensen's duct in addition to the buccal branch.[7] The zygomatic branch of the facial nerve lies roughly 3 cm anterior to the tragus, and the temporal-frontal branch lies at the midpoint between the outer canthus of the eye and the junction of the ear's helix with the preauricular skin.[7] Nerve branches to the eye should be dissected with particular care: even transient

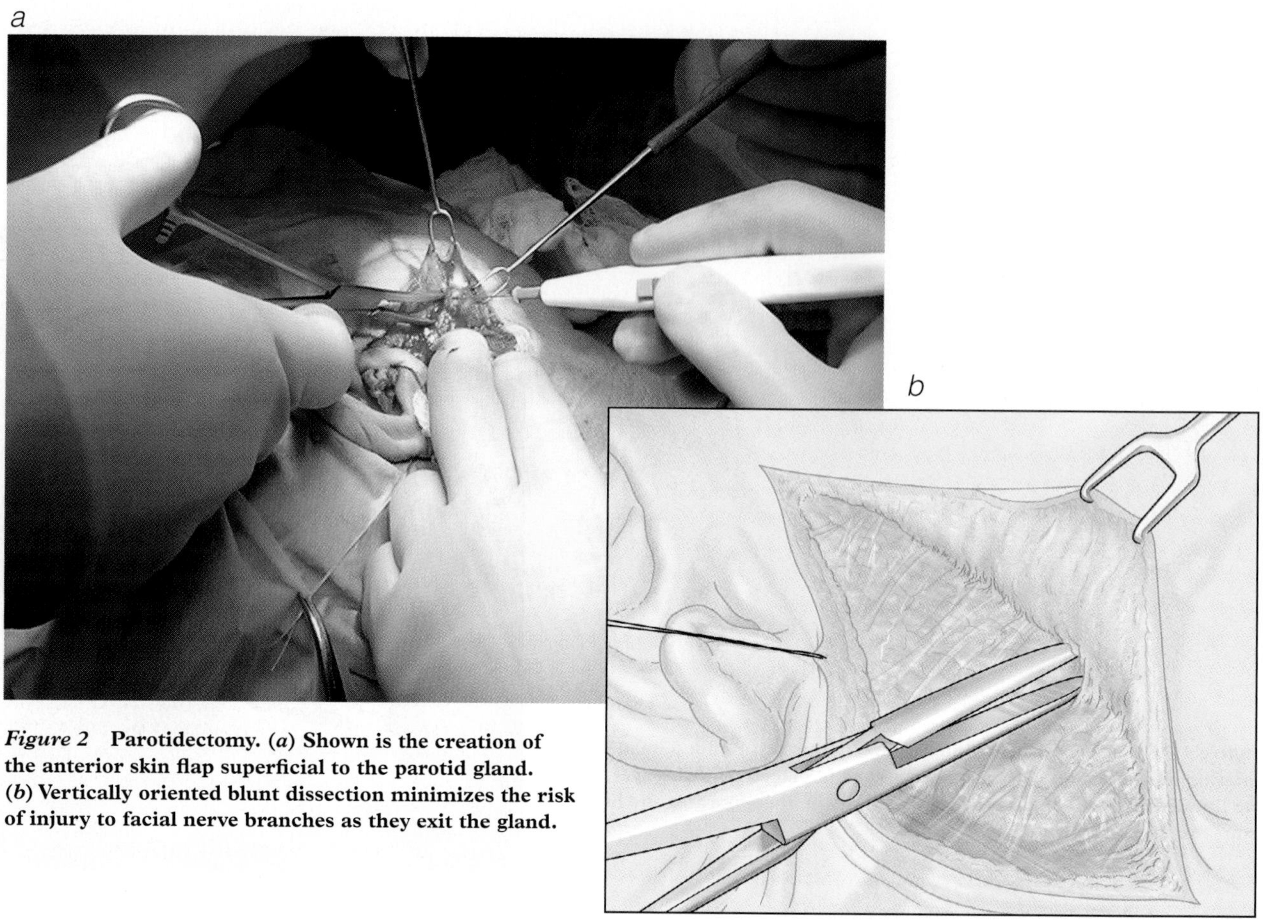

a

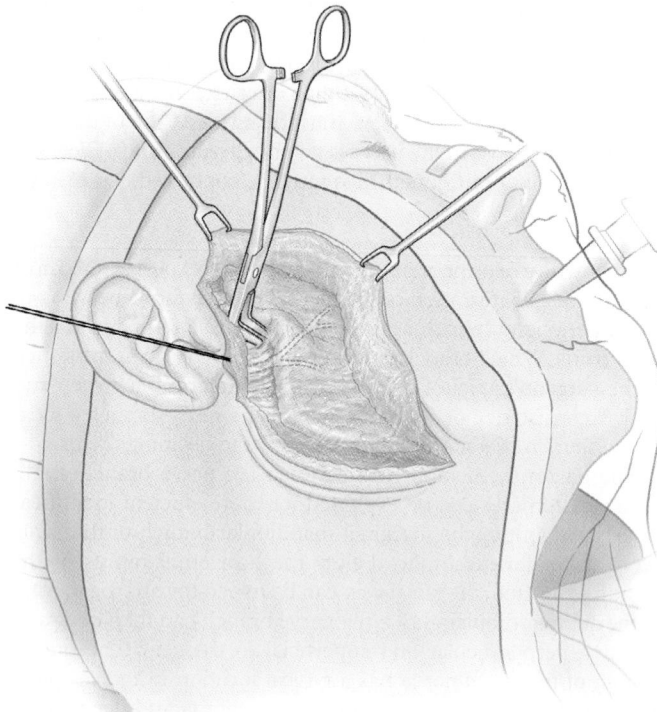

Figure 2 **Parotidectomy. (*a*) Shown is the creation of the anterior skin flap superficial to the parotid gland. (*b*) Vertically oriented blunt dissection minimizes the risk of injury to facial nerve branches as they exit the gland.**

b

Figure 3 **Parotidectomy. Depicted is identification of the facial nerve at its trunk. A wide trough is created anterior to the external auditory canal and deepened by spreading a blunt curved instrument in a direction perpendicular to the incision and parallel to the nerve trunk. Anatomic landmarks assist in identification of the nerve.**

weakness of these branches may have a significant impact on morbidity.

Troubleshooting

Special efforts should be made to ensure that the cartilage of the ear canal is not injured during exposure of the facial nerve trunk. Any injury to this cartilage must be repaired, or else an intense whistling will be heard from the closed suction drain after operation.

The anxiety associated with isolation of the nerve trunk may be alleviated somewhat by keeping in mind that the nerve typically lies deeper than one might expect. In a study of 46 cadaver dissections, the facial nerve was found to lie at a median depth of 22.4 mm from the skin at the stylomastoid foramen (range, 16 to 27 mm). The diameter of the nerve trunk was found to range from 1.1 to 3.4 mm.[8] In our experience, the facial nerve trunk is slightly larger than the nearby deep vessels.

Some surgeons advocate the use of a nerve stimulator to aid in identifying the facial nerve trunk or its branches; however, we have substantial reservations about whether this measure should be employed on a regular basis [*see* Complications, Facial Nerve Injury, *below*]. Knowledge of the anatomy and sound surgical technique are the keys to a safe parotidectomy; it may be hazardous to rely too much on practices that may diminish them.

STEP 3: PARENCHYMAL DISSECTION

Once identified, the plane of the facial nerve remains uniform throughout the gland (unless the nerve is displaced by a tumor) and serves to guide the parenchymal dissection. We divide the substance of the parotid gland sharply, using ligatures as appro-

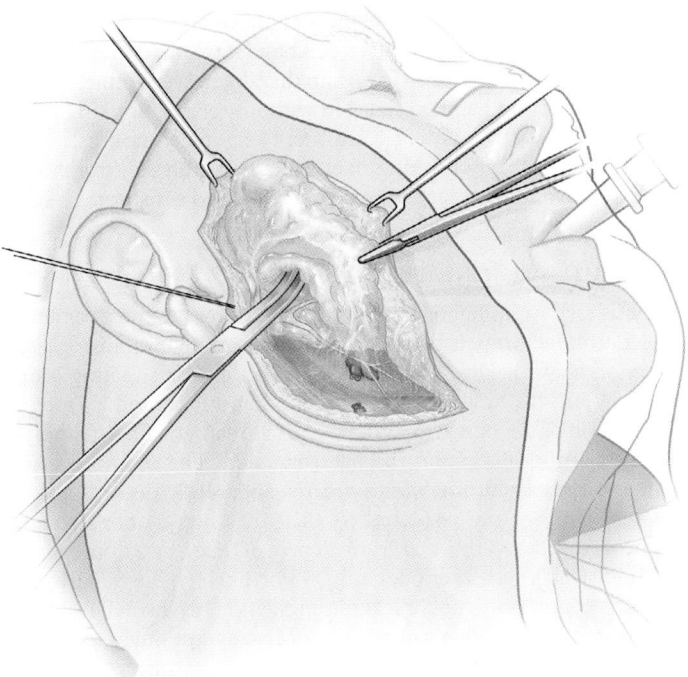

Figure 4 **Parotidectomy. Dissection of the gland parenchyma is carried out over the branches of the facial nerve to minimize the risk of nerve injury. Each division of the substance of the gland should reveal more of the facial nerve.**

priate when bleeding is encountered. Usually, there is no significant hemorrhage: loss of more than 30 ml of blood is rare.

The parenchymal dissection proceeds directly over the facial nerve. We favor using fine curved clamps for this portion of the procedure. To prevent trauma to the nerve, care must be taken to resist the tendency to rest the blades of the clamp on the nerve during dissection. Each division of the gland should reveal more of the facial nerve [*see Figure 4*]. When this is the case, the surgeon can continue the parenchymal dissection with confidence that the nerve will not be injured. As a rule, if a parenchymal division does not immediately show more of the facial nerve, it is in an improper plane.

We do not regularly resect the entire lateral lobe of the parotid unless the tumor is large and such resection is required on oncologic grounds. The goal in resecting the substance of the parotid gland is to obtain sound margins while preserving the remainder of the gland. This so-called partial superficial parotidectomy has been shown to reduce the incidence of Frey syndrome without increasing the rate of recurrence of pleomorphic adenoma.[9] The plane of dissection is developed along facial nerve branches until the lateral margins have been secured. This is the portion of the procedure during which the risk of nerve injury is highest. Once the lateral margins have been secured, the parenchymal dissection can proceed from deep to superficial for the excision of the tumor. The vertical portion of the dissection seldom poses a threat to the integrity of the facial nerve, but care must be taken to maintain appropriate margins. If division of Stensen's duct is required, the distal remnant may be either left open[10] or ligated.

Caution is appropriate in the resection of deep-lobe tumors. Tumors medial to the facial nerve may displace this structure laterally. Thus, after establishing the plane of the facial nerve, the surgeon must remain careful when dissecting near the tumor to keep from injuring the nerve. Once the substance of the gland obscuring the tumor has been removed, the nerve branches in the

area of the tumor are retracted to allow exposure of the deep portion of the gland and facilitate resection. Traction injury to the nerve may still result in transient facial weakness.

Troubleshooting

Complete superficial parotidectomy with full dissection of all facial nerve branches is seldom necessary, though in some cases, it is mandated by tumor size or histologic findings. Removal of the entire superficial lobe with the intention of gaining a larger lateral margin is rarely useful, because the closest margin is usually where the tumor is nearest the facial nerve. Even temporary paresis of the temporal-frontal branch of the facial nerve may have devastating consequences, and dissection near this branch is usually unnecessary in treating a benign tumor in the parotid tail. Any close margins remaining after nerve-preserving cancer treatment can be addressed by means of postoperative radiation therapy, usually with excellent results.[11]

The question of whether to sacrifice the facial nerve almost invariably arises in the setting of malignancy. In our view, this measure is seldom necessary. Benign tumors tend to displace the nerve, not invade it. Sacrifice of the nerve probably does not enhance survival.[12,13] Although the issue remains the subject of debate, it is our practice, like that of others,[14] to sacrifice only those branches intimately involved with tumor. Repair, if feasible, should be performed [*see Complications, Facial Nerve Injury, below*].

STEP 4: DRAINAGE AND CLOSURE

Before closure, absolute hemostasis is confirmed; the Valsalva maneuver is approximated by transiently increasing airway pressure to 30 cm H_2O. We may then assess the integrity of the facial nerve with a nerve stimulator. A 5 mm closed suction drain is placed through a stab incision posterior to the inferior aspect of the ear in a hair-bearing area. The tip of the drain is loosely tacked to the sternocleidomastoid muscle, with care taken to avoid direct contact with the facial nerve. The wound is closed with the drain placed on continuous suction. The skin is closed with interrupted 5-0 nylon sutures. Bacitracin is applied to the wound. No additional dressing is necessary or desirable [*see Figure 5*].

Troubleshooting

The use of interrupted skin sutures instead of a continuous suture allows the surgeon to perform directed suture removal to drain the rare postoperative hematoma or fluid collection instead of reopening the entire wound.

Postoperative Care

The patient is evaluated for facial nerve function in the recovery room, with particular attention paid to whether the patient is able to close the eyelid. The patient resumes eating when nausea (if any) abates. Pain is generally well controlled by means of oral agents. At discharge, the patient should be warned to protect the numb earlobe against cold injury. The closed suction drain is kept in place for 5 to 7 days (until the first postoperative visit) to minimize the risk of salivary fistula.

Complications

FACIAL NERVE INJURY

Studies have found that transient paralysis of all or part of the facial nerve occurs in 17% to 100% of patients undergoing parotidectomy,[15-18] depending on the extent of the resection and the location of the tumor. Fortunately, permanent paralysis is uncommon, occurring in fewer than 5% of cases.[17,19]

Nerve monitoring has been advocated to reduce the incidence of facial nerve injury. To date, however, no randomized trial has demonstrated that intraoperative facial nerve monitoring or nerve stimulators yield any significant reduction in the incidence of facial nerve paralysis. Indeed, indiscriminate use of nerve monitoring and nerve stimulators may imbue the surgeon with a false sense of security and cause him or her to pay insufficient attention to the appearance of nerve tissue. Transient nerve dysfunction may follow inappropriate (or even appropriate and unavoidable) trauma to or traction and pressure on nerve trunks. Nerve monitoring does not prevent such problems; moreover, it adds to the cost of the procedure and increases operating time.[20] Some, in fact, have suggested that nerve stimulators may actually increase transient dysfunction. Accordingly, our use of nerve stimulators is selective.

The management of facial nerve injury depends on when the injury is discovered and on how sure the surgeon is of the anatomic integrity of the nerve. If the injury is discovered intraoperatively, it should be repaired if possible. Primary repair—performed with interrupted fine permanent monofilament sutures under magnification[21]—is preferred if sufficient nerve is available for a tension-free anastomosis. If both transected nerve ends are identified but tension-free repair is not feasible, interposition nerve grafts may be used. Sensory nerves harvested from the neck (e.g., the great auricular nerve) are often employed for this purpose. If the nerve is injured (or deliberately sacrificed) in conjunction with treatment of malignancy, use of nerve grafts from distant sites may be indicated.[21]

If unexpected facial nerve dysfunction is identified in the postanesthesia care unit and if the surgeon is unsure of the anatomic integrity of the nerve (ideally, a rare occurrence), the patient should be returned to the operating room for wound exploration so that either the continuity of the nerve can be confirmed or the injury to the nerve can be identified and repaired if possible. When the surgeon is certain that the nerve is intact, facial nerve dysfunction can be managed without reoperation, in anticipation of recovery[21]; however, this may take many months.

Management of enduring facial nerve paralysis (from any cause) is beyond the scope of our discussion and constitutes a surgical subspecialty in itself.[21]

GUSTATORY SWEATING (FREY SYNDROME)

Gustatory sweating, or Frey syndrome, occurs in most patients after parotidectomy; it has been seen after submandibular gland resection as well. The symptom complex includes sweating, skin warmth, and flushing after chewing food and is caused by cross-innervation of the parasympathetic and sympathetic fibers supplying the parotid gland and the overlying skin. The reported incidence of Frey syndrome varies greatly, apparently depending on the sensitivity of the test used to elicit it. When Minor's starch iodine test is employed, the incidence of Frey syndrome may reach 95% at 1 year after operation.[22] Fortunately, the majority of patients exhibit only subclinical findings, and only a small fraction complain of debilitating symptoms.[22] Most symptomatic patients are adequately treated with topical antiperspirants; eventually, however, they tend to become noncompliant with such measures, preferring simply to dab the face with a napkin while eating.[22] Despite the relatively low incidence of clinically significant Frey syndrome, there is an extensive literature addressing prevention and treatment of this condition.[9,19,23-30]

SIALOCELE (SALIVARY FISTULA)

Sialocele, or salivary fistula, has been reported to occur after 1% to 15% of parotidectomies.[9,31] Although this condition is generally minor and self-limited, it may nonetheless be embarrassing for the patient. We believe that the incidence of sialocele can be reduced by maintaining closed suction drainage for 5 to 7 days (to

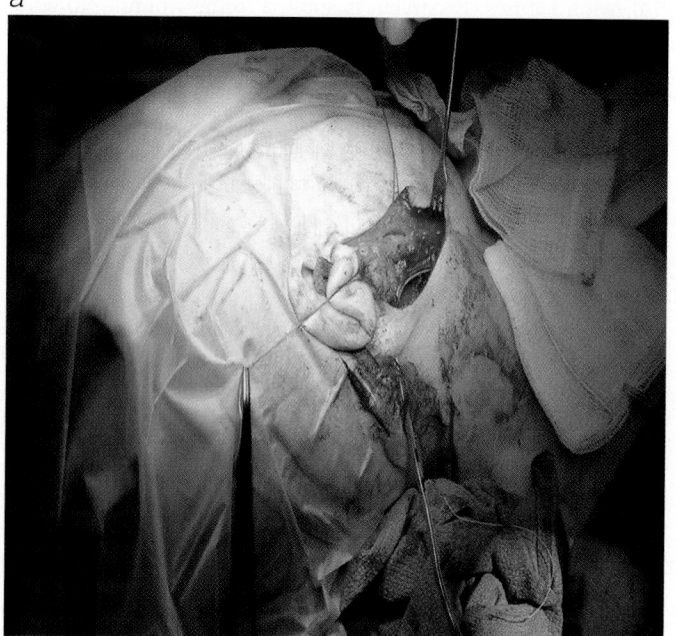 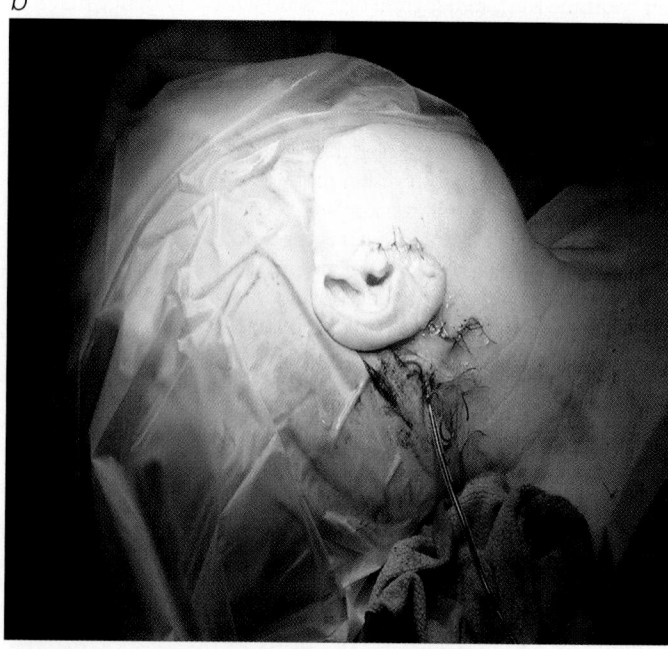

Figure 5 **Parotidectomy. Shown is drainage and closure after parotidectomy. (*a*) A closed suction drain is placed in the operative bed and loosely tacked to the sternocleidomastoid muscle. (*b*) Interrupted monofilament sutures are used for the skin. Bacitracin is applied. No additional dressings are used.**

facilitate adhesion of the skin flaps to the underlying parotid parenchyma). Postparotidectomy salivary fistula is usually attributable to gland disruption rather than to duct transection and therefore tends to resolve without difficulty.[32] Compression dressings are generally effective.[31] Anticholinergic agents have been used in this setting as well.[33-36] Low-dose radiation,[37] completion parotidectomy, and tympanic neurectomy[38] have all been employed in refractory cases.

COSMETIC CHANGES

Parotidectomy creates a hollow anterior and inferior to the ear, which may extend behind the mandible and may reach a significant size in patients with large or recurrent tumors. This cosmetic change is a necessary feature of the procedure, not a complication; nonetheless, it should be discussed with the patient before operation. Many augmentation methods, using a wide variety of techniques, have been devised for improving postoperative appearance (as well as alleviating Frey syndrome).[24-28,39,40] All of these methods have limitations or drawbacks that have kept them from being widely applied and accepted.

Outcome Evaluation

With proper surgical technique, superficial or partial superficial parotidectomy can be performed safely and within a reasonable operating time. Blood transfusions should be required only in very rare cases. Given adequate exposure, good knowledge of the relevant anatomy, limited trauma to the nerve, and appropriate use of closed suction drains (see above), complications should be uncommon. Although patients may tolerate parotidectomy on an outpatient basis, we prefer to keep them in the hospital overnight. Patients should be able to leave the hospital with minimal pain, comfortable with their drain care, by the morning of postoperative day 1.

References

1. Berkovitz BKG, Moxham BJ: A Textbook of Head and Neck Anatomy. Year Book Medical Publishers, Inc, Chicago, 1988

2. Davis BA, Anson BJ, Budinger JM, et al: Surgical anatomy of the facial nerve and the parotid gland based upon a study of 350 cervico-facial halves. Surg Gynecol Obstet 102:385, 1956

3. Bernstein L, Nelson RH: Surgical anatomy of the extraparotid distribution of the facial nerve. Arch Otolaryngol 110:177, 1984

4. Hui Y, Wong DSY, Wong LY, et al: A prospective controlled double-blind trial of great auricular nerve preservation at parotidectomy. Am J Surg 185:574, 2003

5. Christensen NR, Jacobsen SD: Parotidectomy: preserving the posterior branch of the great auricular nerve. J Laryngol Otol 111:556, 1997

6. De Ru JA, van Benthem PPG, Bleys RLAW, et al: Landmarks for parotid gland surgery. J Laryngol Otol 115:122, 2001

7. Peterson RA, Johnston DL: Facile identification of the facial nerve branches. Clin Plast Surg 14:785, 1987

8. Salame K, Ouaknine GER, Arensburg B, et al: Microsurgical anatomy of the facial nerve trunk. Clin Anat 15:93, 2002

9. Leverstein H, van der Wal JE, Tiwari RM, et al: Surgical management of 246 previously untreated pleomorphic adenomas of the parotid gland. Br J Surg 84:399, 1997

10. Woods JE: Parotidectomy: points of technique for brief and safe operation. Am J Surg 145:678, 1983

11. Garden AS, El-Naggar AK, Morrison WH, et al: Postoperative radiotherapy for malignant tumors of the parotid gland. Int J Radiat Oncol Biol Phys 37:79, 1997

12. Renehan AG, Gleave EN, Slevin NJ, et al: Clinicopathological and treatment-related factors influencing survival in parotid cancer. Br J Cancer 80:1296, 1999

13. Magnano M, Gervasio CF, Cravero L, et al: Treatment of malignant neoplasms of the parotid gland. Otolaryngol Head Neck Surg 121:627, 1999

14. Spiro JD, Spiro RH: Cancer of the parotid gland: role of 7th nerve preservation. World J Surg, 27:863, 2003

15. Witt RL: Facial nerve monitoring in parotid surgery: the standard of care? Otolaryngol Head Neck Surg 119:468, 1998

16. Reilly J, Myssiorek D: Facial nerve stimulation and postparotidectomy facial paresis. Otolaryngol Head Neck Surg 128:530, 2003

17. Dulguerov P, Marchal F, Lehmann W: Postparotidectomy facial nerve paralysis: possible etiologic factors and results with routine facial nerve monitoring. Laryngoscope 109:754, 1999

18. Bron LP, O'Brien CJ: Facial nerve function after parotidectomy. Arch Otolaryngol Head Neck Surg 123:1091, 1997

19. Debets JMH, Munting JDK: Parotidectomy for parotid tumours: 19-year experience from the Netherlands. Br J Surg 79:1159, 1992

20. Terrell JE, Kileny PR, Yian C, et al: Clinical outcome of continuous facial nerve monitoring during primary parotidectomy. Arch Otolaryngol Head Neck Surg 123:1081, 1997

21. Shindo M: Management of facial nerve paralysis. Otolaryngol Clin North Am 32:946, 1999

22. Linder TE, Huber A, Schmid S: Frey's syndrome after parotidectomy: a retrospective and prospective analysis. Laryngoscope 107:1496, 1997

23. Bonanno PC, Palaia D, Rosenberg M, et al: Prophylaxis against Frey's syndrome in parotid surgery. Ann Plast Surg 44:498, 2000

24. Ahmed OA, Kolhe PS: Prevention of Frey's syndrome and volume deficit after parotidectomy using the superficial temporal artery fascial flap. Br J Plast Surg 52:256, 1999

25. Bugis SP, Young JEM, Archibald SD: Sternocleidomastoid flap following parotidectomy. Head Neck 12:430, 1990

26. Jeng SF, Chien CS: Adipofascial turnover flap for facial contour deformity during parotidectomy. Ann Plast Surg 33:439, 1994

27. Govindaraj S, Cohen M, Genden EM, et al: The use of acellular dermis in the prevention of Frey's syndrome. Laryngoscope 111:1993, 2001

28. Nosan DK, Ochi JW, Davidson TM: Preservation of facial contour during parotidectomy. Otolaryngol Head Neck Surg 104:293, 1991

29. Sinha UK, Saadat D, Doherty CM, et al: Use of AlloDerm implant to prevent Frey syndrome after parotidectomy. Arch Facial Plast Surg 5:109, 2003

30. Beerens AJ, Snow GB: Botulinum toxin A in the treatment of patients with Frey syndrome. Br J Surg 89:116, 2002

31. Wax M, Tarshis L: Post-parotidectomy fistula. J Otolaryngol 20:10, 1991

32. Ananthakrishnan N, Parkash S: Parotid fistulas: a review. Br J Surg 69:641, 1982

33. Cavanaugh K, Park A: Postparotidectomy fistulas: a different treatment for an old problem. Int J Pediatr Otorhinolaryngol 47:265, 1999

34. Vargas H, Galati LT, Parnes SM: A pilot study evaluating the treatment of postparotidectomy sialoceles with botulinum toxin type A. Arch Otolaryngol Head Neck Surg 126:421, 2000

35. Guntinas-Lichius O, Sittel C: Treatment of postparotidectomy salivary fistula with botulinum toxin. Ann Otol Rhinol Laryngol 110:1162, 2001

36. Chow TL, Kwok SP: Use of botulinum toxin type A in a case of persistent parotid sialocele. Hong Kong Med J 9:293, 2003

37. Shimms DS, Berk FK, Tilsner TJ, et al: Low-dose radiation therapy for benign salivary disorders. Am J Clin Oncol 15:76, 1992

38. Davis WE, Holt GR, Templer JW: Parotid fistula and tympanic neurectomy. Am J Surg 133:587, 1977

39. Kerawala CJ, McAloney N, Stassen LF: Prospective randomized trial of the benefits of a sternocleidomastoid flap after superficial parotidectomy. Br J Oral Maxillofac Surg 40:468, 2002

40. Chao C, Friedman DC, Alford EL, et al: Acellular dermal allograft prevents post-parotidectomy soft tissue defects: a preliminary experience. Int Online J Otorhinolaryngol Head Neck Surg 2(5):1, 1999

Acknowledgment

The authors wish to thank Veronica Levin for her assistance in the preparation of this chapter.
Figures 1a, 2b, 3, 4 Tom Moore.

Miriam N. Lango, M.D., Bert W. O'Malley, Jr., M.D., F.A.C.S., and Ara A. Chalian, M.D., F.A.C.S.

Preoperative Evaluation

In the majority of cases, cancer in the neck is a metastasis from a primary lesion in the upper aerodigestive tract, though metastases from skin, thyroid, and salivary gland neoplasms are also encountered. Lymphomas often present as cervical lymphadenopathy.

When a patient presents with a suspicious lesion in the neck, a careful history and physical examination should be performed, along with a thorough evaluation of the aerodigestive tract aimed at locating the source of possible metastatic disease. Fine-needle aspiration (FNA) of the neck mass should then be done to determine whether the mass is malignant. FNA can often differentiate between epithelial and lymphoid malignancies, and this differentiation will guide subsequent workup. The reported sensitivity of FNA ranges from 92% to 98%; the reported specificity, from 94% to 100%.[1,2]

If FNA reveals the presence of atypical lymphoid cells, an excisional lymph node biopsy should be performed to supply the pathologist with a large enough sample to allow full typing of the tissue. An excisional biopsy may also be performed if the FNA is negative or indeterminate, the surgeon suspects a malignancy, and the rest of the physical examination yields negative results. Routine excisional biopsy of neck masses for diagnostic purposes is not recommended, however, because it may result in tumor spillage into the wound and complicate subsequent definitive resection.

Once the presence of an epithelial malignancy is established, the primary site of the lesion must be determined if it is not apparent on initial physical examination. Imaging studies (e.g., computed tomography and magnetic resonance imaging) may be helpful in locating the source of a cervical metastasis. Positron emission tomography (PET) detects lesions with increased metabolic activity but has the limitation of being unable to detect lesions smaller than 1 cm in diameter. Primary lesions greater than 1 cm in diameter usually are easily identified on physical examination and other imaging studies; thus, PET scans are of limited value in this setting. In any patient with metastatic cervical adenopathy thought to originate in the upper aerodigestive tract, panendoscopy and biopsy with general anesthesia are mandatory for locating and characterizing the primary source of the tumor and ruling out the presence of synchronous lesions. The most common occult primary sites are the base of the tongue, the tonsils, and the nasopharynx. In 5% to 10% of patients who present with a metastatic node, the primary lesion is never found despite extensive workup.

INCIDENCE AND IMPACT OF NECK METASTASES

Cutaneous Squamous Cell Carcinoma

The incidence of cervical metastases is governed by many factors. Cervical metastases from cutaneous squamous cell carcinomas are rare, occurring in 2% to 10% of cases. However, certain lesions—those that are greater than 2 cm in diameter; are recur-

rent; are deeper than 6 mm; involve the ear, the temple, or the classic H zone; occur in an immunocompromised patient; or are poorly differentiated—have a significant occult metastatic rate, ranging from 20% to 60%. The presence of cervical metastases reduces 5-year survival to about 32%,[3] which suggests that early intervention for high-risk cutaneous lesions, involving regional lymphadenectomy, sentinel lymph node (SLN) biopsy, or irradiation of at-risk lymph node basins, may be warranted.

Salivary Gland Neoplasms

With salivary gland neoplasms [see 12 Oral Cavity Lesions], the incidence of cervical metastases is related to the histopathology as well as the size of the tumor. The most aggressive salivary gland lesions are squamous cell carcinoma, carcinoma ex pleomorphic adenoma, adenocarcinoma, and salivary ductal carcinoma. Patients with these lesions often have cervical metastases at presentation that warrant a therapeutic neck dissection [see Table 1]. How best to manage occult cervical salivary gland metastatic disease is controversial. The occult metastatic rate for aggressive lesions ranges from 25% to 45%. For such lesions, a selective neck dissection is typically incorporated into the surgical approach.[4]

Metastatic Well-Differentiated Thyroid Cancer

Cervical lymph node metastases are present in 10% to 15% of patients with well-differentiated thyroid carcinoma. The impact of nodal metastases on local recurrence and survival has not been established. Other factors (e.g., age, sex, tumor extent, and distant metastases) appear to have a greater effect on prognosis. Nevertheless, in the presence of clinically apparent nodal disease, a formal neck dissection is advised: so-called cherry-picking operations or limited lymph node excisions result in higher rates of recurrence.[5]

Squamous Cell Carcinoma of the Upper Aerodigestive Tract

With upper aerodigestive tract squamous cell carcinomas, the incidence of cervical metastases is related to the site of the primary lesion, the size of the tumor, the degree of differentiation, the depth of invasion, and a number of other factors. A significant proportion of head and neck cancer patients who harbor clinically silent primary tumors of the base of the tongue, the tonsils, or the nasopharynx initially present with cervical adenopathy [see Table 1]. These sites lack anatomic barriers that limit tumor spread and are supplied by rich lymphatic networks that facilitate metastasis. In contrast, patients with glottic and lip cancers are more likely to present early, without clinical adenopathy.

The presence of cervical metastases negatively affects prognosis and has been associated with increased recurrence rates and reduced disease-free and overall survival. The presence of clinical adenopathy decreases survival by 50%. Metastatic tumors that rupture the lymph node capsule—a process known as extracapsular spread (ECS)—are biologically more aggressive. Patients

Table 1 Incidence of Cervical Metastases in Selected Head and Neck Cancers

Tumor	Incidence of Cervical Adenopathy
Cutaneous squamous cell carcinoma	2%–10%
Salivary gland malignancies	
Mucoepidermoid carcinoma (high-grade)	30%–70%
Adenoid cystic carcinoma	8%
Malignant mixed tumor	25%
Squamous cell carcinoma	46%
Salivary duct carcinoma	50%
Acinic cell carcinoma	40%
Metastatic well-differentiated thyroid cancer	10%–15%
Squamous cell carcinoma of upper aerodigestive tract	
Alveolar ridge	30%
Hard palate	10%
Oral tongue	30%
Anterior pillar/retromolar trigone	45%
Floor of mouth	30%
Soft palate	44%
Tonsillar fossa	76%
Tongue base	78%
Bilateral	20%

who have palpable cervical lymphadenopathy with ECS manifest a 50% decrease in survival compared with those who have palpable cervical lymphadenopathy without ECS.[6] In addition, about 50% of clinically negative, pathologically positive neck specimens exhibit ECS. Clinically negative, pathologically positive, and ECS-positive specimens are associated with a high risk of regional recurrence and distant metastases.[7-9] The presence of ECS in lymph node metastases may in fact be the single most important prognostic factor in patients with head and neck cancer. Identification of this patient subset may be the most important benefit of elective neck dissection, in that it allows these patients to be offered adjuvant therapy. Nonrandomized studies have found that both disease-specific and overall survival are significantly improved when these high-risk patients are treated with adjuvant postoperative chemoradiation.[10] However, randomized clinical trials are needed to confirm the clinical benefits of adjuvant chemoradiation in this setting.

Whereas anatomic and pathologic factors (e.g., ECS) have long been known to predict tumor behavior, it is only comparatively recently that the impact of comorbidity has been well characterized. When patients are stratified by tumor stage, those with comorbidities fare worse. In fact, the impact of comorbidity on overall survival is greater than that of tumor stage or treatment type.[10,11] In addition, comorbidity is associated with both increased frequency and increased severity of surgical complications. These factors may be important in treatment selection and patient counseling. To date, comorbidity has not been incorporated into clinical staging of head and neck cancer patients.

STAGING OF NECK CANCER

Staging of the neck for metastatic squamous cell carcinomas of the head and neck is based on the TNM classification formulated by the American Joint Committee on Cancer (AJCC) [*see 12 Oral Cavity Lesions*]. The N classification applies to cervical metastases from all upper aerodigestive tract mucosal sites except the nasopharynx; it also applies to metastases from major salivary gland and sinonasal malignancies but not to metastases from cutaneous or thyroid malignancies, which use an alternate staging system.

The purpose of staging is to characterize the tumor burden of an individual patient. Accordingly, an effective staging system should incorporate factors known to have prognostic and therapeutic significance, thereby facilitating planning of therapy and appropriate patient counseling. In addition, it should attempt to standardize reporting so that meaningful cross-institutional comparisons can be obtained. A staging system ideally should also be simple to apply while still incorporating biologically important factors that permit accurate patient stratification in prospective clinical trials. Precise characterization and differentiation of tumors facilitate identification of those patients who are most likely to benefit from treatment.

The TNM staging system does not include a number of factors that are known to have an impact on prognosis, such as the presence or absence of ECS and the pattern of lymphatic spread. Nonanatomic factors (e.g., comorbidity, immune status, and nutritional status) have a strong impact on survival as well but are also not incorporated in the current staging system. In general, TNM staging has been found inadequate for use in clinical trials.[12]

The limitations of clinical staging of the neck are well described. The addition of imaging to clinical examination improves diagnostic sensitivity but not specificity. Imaging is particularly useful after chemoradiation because of the difficulty of clinical examination in this setting. Pathologic review of neck specimens remains the gold standard for anatomic staging. The addition of ultrasound-guided FNA of neck nodes yields enhanced diagnostic accuracy in cases where the neck is clinically negative but the radiologic findings are positive. This approach is employed to select patients for neck dissection in a number of centers, particularly in Europe; whether it provides more accurate staging than alternative methods, such as SLN biopsy, remains to be determined. Results from the First International Conference on Sentinel Node Biopsy in Mucosal Head and Neck Cancer revealed that SLN biopsy of the clinically negative neck has a sensitivity comparable to that of a staging neck dissection.[13] In general, imaging modalities appear to be neither sufficiently sensitive nor sufficiently specific in the evaluation of the clinically negative neck. Uptake of 2-deoxy-3 [^{18}F] fluoro-D-glucose, as measured by PET scans, is undetectable in small foci of cancer in the clinically negative neck.[14]

Proper staging is important for stratification of patients into risk categories on the basis of tumor biology, so that high-risk patients may be appropriately selected for clinical trials or offered adjuvant therapy and other patients may be spared unnecessary treatment. Until accurate methods of assessing the clinically negative neck are developed, selective neck dissection will be performed to treat the neck when the occult metastatic rate is expected to be higher than 20%.

INDICATIONS FOR NECK DISSECTION

The classic indication for neck dissection is for treatment of metastatic carcinoma in the neck, most frequently deriving from a mucosal site in the upper aerodigestive tract. Over time, the indications for neck dissection have changed. With wider use of chemoradiation therapy for head and neck cancer, treatment of metastatic disease in the neck has become increasingly nonsurgical. Currently, neck dissections are considered either therapeutic (performed to treat palpable disease in the neck) or elective (per-

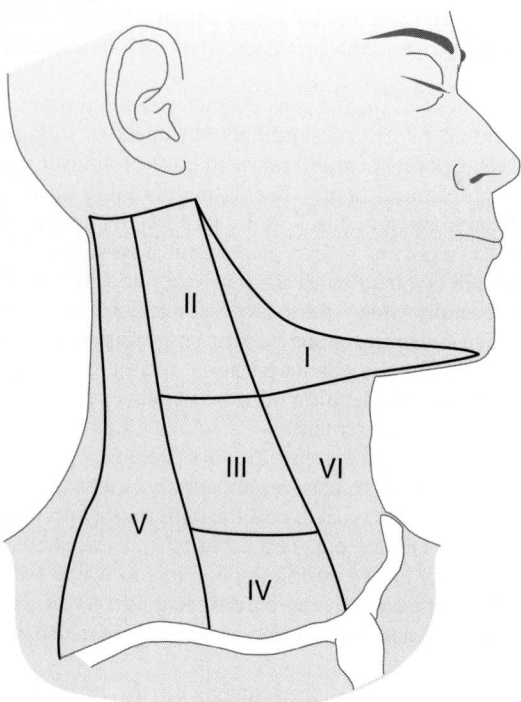

Figure 1 **Cervical lymph nodes are divided into six levels on the basis of their location in the neck.**

formed when the expected incidence of occult metastases from a lesion exceeds 20%). Technically, neck dissections are classified as comprehensive dissections, which incorporate five levels of the neck, or selective dissections, in which only selected lymph node levels are removed according to predicted drainage patterns from specific primary sites. There is also a third technical classification, extended neck dissections, which can be combined with selective or comprehensive neck dissections for removal of additional nodal basins [see Operative Planning, Choice of Procedure, below]. Six lymph node drainage basins in the neck are recognized [see Figure 1].

CONTRAINDICATIONS TO NECK DISSECTION

The only absolute contraindication to neck dissection is surgical unresectability. The determination of unresectability is made by the operating surgeon either preoperatively, on the basis of imaging studies, or in the operating room. Typically, the presence of Horner syndrome, paralysis of the vagus nerve or the phrenic nerve, or invasion of the brachial plexus or the prevertebral muscles indicates that the tumor is unresectable. The involvement of the carotid artery may be predicted on the basis of imaging studies. Encasement of the carotid artery by tumor suggests direct invasion of the vessel; however, studies correlating imaging characteristics and pathologic invasion of the carotid have shown that tumors surrounding 180° or more of the carotid's circumference have a higher incidence of carotid invasion than tumors surrounding less than 180° (75% versus 50%). In the absence of direct invasion of the vessel wall, tumor may be peeled off by means of subadventitial surgical dissection. Tumors surrounding 270° of the vessel have an 83% incidence of carotid invasion, necessitating sacrifice of the artery.[15] However, sacrifice of the carotid artery, with or without reconstruction with a vein graft, has been associated with significant morbidity and confers no survival benefit.[16]

Operative Planning

CHOICE OF PROCEDURE

Comprehensive Dissection: Radical and Modified Radical Neck Dissection

The radical neck dissection was first described in 1906 by George Crile, who based his approach on the Halstedian principle of en bloc resection. The procedure was subsequently standardized by Hayes Martin at Memorial Hospital in New York in the 1930s and 1940s. In this latter version of the procedure, lymphatic structures from the strap muscles anteriorly, the trapezius posteriorly, the mandible superiorly, and the clavicle inferiorly are removed. Nonlymphatic structures in this space are also sacrificed, including the spinal accessory nerve, the sternocleidomastoid muscle, the internal and external jugular veins, the submandibular gland, and sensory nerve roots. The routine sacrifice of the spinal accessory nerve, the internal jugular vein, and the sternocleidomastoid muscle contributes to the significant morbidity associated with radical neck dissection.

Since the 1970s, the necessity of en bloc resection for oncologic cure has been reexamined. Structures once routinely sacrificed are now routinely preserved unless they are grossly involved with cancer. The various functional, or modified, radical neck dissections are classified according to which structures are preserved. Type I dissections preserve the spinal accessory nerve; type II, the spinal accessory nerve and the internal jugular vein; type III, both of these structures along with the sternocleidomastoid muscle. Modified radical neck dissections have proved to be as effective in controlling metastatic disease to the neck as the classic radical neck dissection.[17]

Selective Neck Dissection

In a selective neck dissection, at-risk lymph node drainage basins are selectively removed on the basis of the location of the primary tumor in a patient with no clinical evidence of cervical lymphadenopathy. Cancers in the oral cavity, for example, typically metastasize to levels I through III and, occasionally, IV; laryngeal cancers typically metastasize to levels II through IV. The rationale for selective neck dissection is based on retrospective pathologic reviews of radical neck dissection specimens from patients without palpable lymphadenopathy. These reviews revealed that lymph node micrometastases were confined to specific neck levels for a given aerodigestive tract site.[18]

The advantages of selective neck dissection over radical and modified radical neck dissection are both cosmetic and functional. A selective neck dissection involves less manipulation (and thus less risk of devascularization) of the spinal accessory nerve, thereby decreasing the incidence of postoperative shoulder dysfunction. Preservation of the sternocleidomastoid muscle alleviates the cosmetic deformity seen with a radical neck dissection and provides some protection for the carotid artery.

Preservation of the internal jugular vein decreases venous congestion of the head and neck and is necessary if the contralateral internal jugular vein is sacrificed. With primary lesions located in the midline in the base of the tongue, the supraglottic larynx, or the medial wall of the piriform sinus, bilateral regional metastases are common, and bilateral neck dissections are therefore indicated. Sacrifice of both internal jugular veins is associated with significant morbidity, including increased intracranial pressure, syndrome of inappropriate antidiuretic hormone secretion, airway edema, and death. Bilateral internal jugular sacrifice is managed by staging the neck dissections or by carrying out vascular repair.

In the presence of multiple pathologically positive lymph nodes or evidence of ECS, adjuvant therapy is indicated.[19] Accordingly, selective neck dissection may be viewed as a diagnostic as well as a therapeutic procedure. To date, however, no randomized clinical trials have demonstrated that selective neck dissection with adjuvant treatment as needed is better than so-called watchful waiting with regard to prolonging survival in patients who present without evidence of cervical metastatic disease. Therefore, it is not yet possible to justify the added cost and morbidity of elective neck dissection in patients without evidence of metastatic disease. SLN mapping may facilitate pathologic staging in this setting and spare low-risk patients from unnecessary interventions; however, its sensitivity and specificity for this purpose are still under investigation.

The growing focus on preservation of function and limitation of morbidity has led some surgeons to promote the use of selective neck dissection to treat node-positive neck tumors. Although retrospective studies have suggested that a selective neck dissection may be adequate in carefully selected node-positive patients,[20] the effectiveness of this approach is still unproven, and its application remains subject to individual surgical judgment.

Extended Neck Dissection

Extended neck dissections can be combined with selective or comprehensive neck dissections to remove additional nodal basins, such as the suboccipital and retroauricular nodes. These groups of nodes, which are located in the upper posterior neck, are the first-echelon nodal basins for posterior scalp skin cancers. The retroauricular nodes lie just posterior to the mastoid process, and the suboccipital nodes lie near the insertion of the trapezius muscle into the inferior nuchal line. Cancers of the anterior scalp, the temple, and the preauricular skin drain to periparotid lymph nodes; these lymph nodes are removed in conjunction with a parotidectomy [see 17 Parotidectomy]. Retropharyngeal nodes may be removed in the treatment of selected cancers originating in the posterior pharynx, the soft palate, or the nasopharynx. A mediastinal lymph node dissection may be combined with a neck dissection in the treatment of metastatic thyroid carcinomas.

NECK DISSECTION AFTER CHEMORADIATION

The indications for neck dissection have been significantly affected by the increasing use of organ preservation protocols for the treatment of head and neck cancer. Nasopharyngeal carcinomas, which are uniquely radiosensitive, are generally treated with irradiation, with or without chemotherapy; neck dissection is reserved for patients who experience an incomplete response and for patients with bulky cervical lesions. Similarly, patients with early nodal disease (N0 or N1) treated according to organ preservation protocols may undergo nonsurgical therapy. For patients who have advanced neck disease (N2 or N3) or who respond incompletely to therapy, a planned posttreatment neck dissection is recommended because surgical salvage of so-called neck failures is rarely successful.[21] As a rule, the planned neck dissection should be done within 6 weeks of the completion of chemoradiation therapy: if it is delayed past the 6-week point, progressive soft tissue fibrosis may develop, resulting in difficult surgical dissection, increased postoperative morbidity, and, potentially, tumor progression.

A 2003 study highlighted the need for planned neck dissection after definitive chemoradiation for N2 or N3 nodal disease.[22] In this study, 76 patients presenting with N2 or N3 disease underwent a planned neck dissection. Tumor cells were present in the neck specimens of 25% of patients with complete and 39% of patients with incomplete clinical responses. No patients with complete pathologic responses experienced regional recurrence, whereas 20% of patients with pathologically positive neck dissection specimens experienced nonsalvageable regional recurrences. In addition, planned neck dissection led to reduced rates of regional recurrence in patients treated with chemoradiation. The authors suggested that all patients presenting with N2 or N3 cervical lymphadenopathy should undergo planned neck dissection, regardless of clinical response to chemoradiation therapy.

The required extent of planned neck dissection after chemoradiation is still under investigation. Neck dissection after chemoradiation carries significant morbidity in the form of severe soft tissue fibrosis and increased spinal accessory nerve injury. Pathologic review of comprehensive neck specimens after chemoradiation reveals that in patients with oropharyngeal cancer, levels I and V are rarely involved in the absence of radiographic abnormalities,[23] which suggests that a planned selective dissection involving levels II through IV may be sufficient for cases of oropharyngeal cancer treated with chemoradiation. This more limited approach undoubtedly causes less morbidity, but additional data are required to assess its oncologic efficacy.

Typically, management of the neck is determined in part by management of the primary tumor. Early neck dissection for bulky nodal disease before nonsurgical treatment of the primary lesion is a controversial practice. Bulky cervical adenopathy is unlikely to exhibit a complete pathologic response to nonsurgical treatment. A patient who requires dental extractions before radiation therapy may undergo a neck dissection at the same time, proceeding to radiation therapy 7 to 10 days after operation. Early neck dissection decreases the tumor burden, thereby allowing lower adjunctive doses of radiation to be delivered to the neck. Thus, it is possible that early neck dissection for bulky resectable cervical adenopathy can reduce the expected morbidity of planned postchemoradiation neck dissection. There is limited evidence in the literature that such an approach is feasible in certain circumstances[24]; however, it is recommended that significant delays in initiating treatment to the primary site be avoided because such delays may ultimately have a negative impact on survival.

RECONSTRUCTION AND RECURRENCE AFTER NECK DISSECTION

The use of microvascular free tissue transfer to reconstruct surgical defects in the head has allowed surgeons to resect large tumors with large margins while simultaneously achieving improved functional results. Preservation of vascular—and, occasionally, neural—structures during neck dissection may facilitate the reconstructive process. Typically, several vessels, including an artery and one or two veins, are required for inflow and outflow into a free flap. The facial artery, the retromandibular vein, and the external jugular vein, which are preserved during level I and level II dissection, are the vessels that are most frequently used for flap revascularization. If these vessels are unavailable as a consequence of high-volume neck disease, the superior thyroid artery and the transverse artery, with companion veins, are suitable substitutes. To date, there is no evidence in the literature that preservation of vascular structures in the neck predisposes patients to regional recurrence. Caution must, however, be exercised in the setting of pathologic lymphadenopathy.

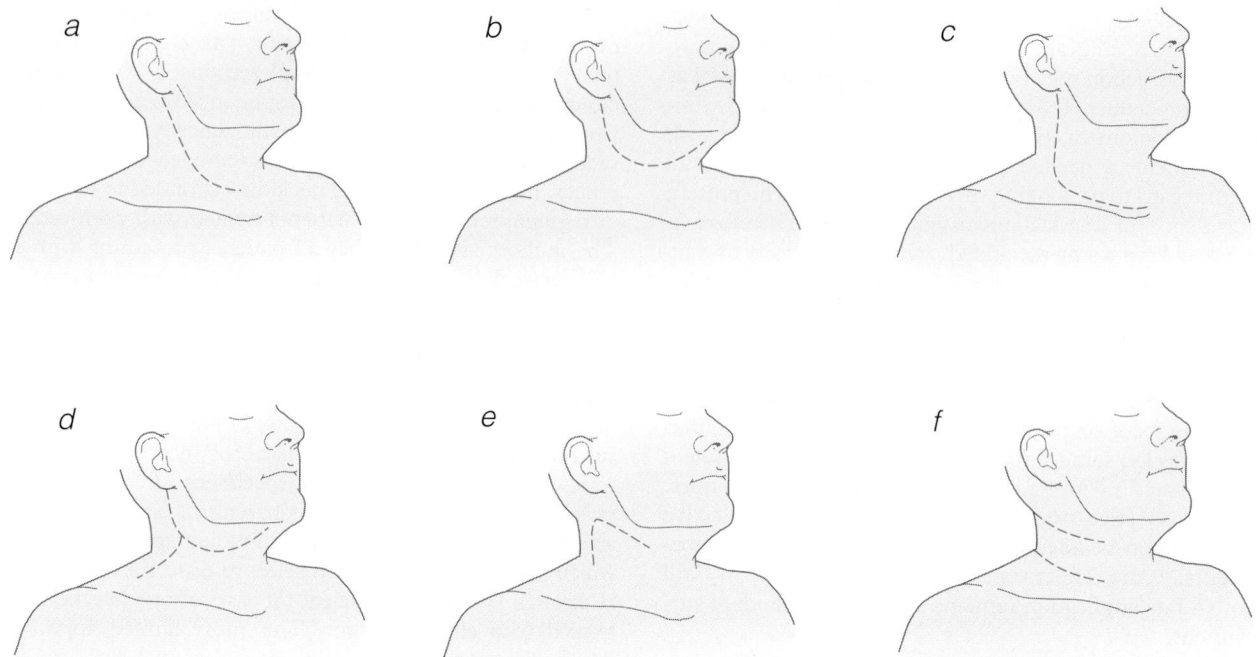

Figure 2 Illustrated are incisions used for neck dissections. Incision design is a critical element of operative planning. Incisions are chosen with the aims of optimizing exposure of relevant neck levels and minimizing morbidity. The incisions depicted in (*a*) and (*b*) are useful for selective neck dissections. For the more extensive exposure required in a radical or modified radical neck dissection, a deeper half-apron style incision (*c*) may be used, or a vertical limb may be dropped from a mastoid-submental incision (*d*); the latter incision is less reliable and may break down, exposing vital structures such as the carotid. The incision depicted in (*e*) is also useful for selective neck dissections. The Macfee incision (*f*) provides limited exposure and results in persistent lymphedema in the bipedicled skin flap.

Operative Technique

RADICAL NECK DISSECTION

Step 1: Incision and Flap Elevation

When a radical or modified radical neck dissection is indicated, appropriate neck incisions must be designed so as to facilitate exposure while preserving blood flow to the skin flaps [*see Figure 2*]. The incision provides access to the relevant levels of the neck, affects cosmesis, and determines the extent of lymphedema and postoperative fibrosis ("woody" neck), especially in previously irradiated areas. If a biopsy was previously performed, the tract should be excised and incorporated into the new incision. When a total laryngectomy is done, the stoma is fashioned separately from the neck incision; in the event of a pharyngocutaneous fistula, the salivary flow will be diverted away from the stoma.

Once the incision is made, subplatysmal flaps are raised. If there is extensive lymphadenopathy or extension of tumor into the soft tissues of the neck, skin flaps may be raised in a supraplatysmal plane to ensure negative surgical margins. Such flaps, however, are not as reliably vascularized as subplatysmal flaps. Clinical judgment must be exercised in these situations. The flaps are raised to the mandible superiorly, the clavicle inferiorly, the omohyoid muscle and the submental region anteriorly, and the trapezius posteriorly. Typically, radical neck dissections are performed in patients with clinically positive lymphadenopathy, and adequate exposure of levels I through V is required. If a vertical limb is used, it must not be centered over the carotid artery, because of the risk of potentially catastrophic dehiscence. Deep utility-type incisions yield more limited exposure of level I but provide reliable vascular inflow to skin flaps.

Step 2: Dissection of Anterior Compartment

Embedded within the fascia overlying the submandibular gland is the marginal mandibular branch of the facial nerve, which must be elevated and retracted to prevent lower-lip weakness. The submental fat pad is then grasped, retracted posteriorly and laterally, and mobilized away from the floor of the submental triangle. The omohyoid muscle is identified inferior to the digastric tendon and skeletonized to its intersection with the sternocleidomastoid muscle posteriorly. The omohyoid muscle forms the anteroinferior limit of the dissection.

Fat and lymphatic structures are dissected away from the digastric muscle and the mylohyoid muscle. The hypoglossal and lingual nerves lie just deep to the mylohyoid muscle and are protected by it [*see Figure 3*]. In this region, the distal end of the facial artery can be identified and preserved as needed for reconstructive purposes. Once the posterior edge of the mylohyoid muscle is visualized, an Army-Navy retractor is inserted beneath the muscle to expose the submandibular duct, the lingual nerve with its attachment to the submandibular gland, and the hypoglossal nerve. The submandibular duct and the submandibular ganglion, with its contributions to the gland, are ligated, and the submandibular gland is retracted out of the submandibular triangle.

The posterior belly of the digastric muscle is then identified inferior to the submandibular gland and skeletonized to the sternocleidomastoid muscle posteriorly, where it inserts on the mastoid tip. The specimen must be mobilized off structures just inferior to the digastric muscle. To prevent inadvertent injury, it is essential to understand the relationships among these structures [*see Figure 3*]. The hypoglossal nerve emerges from beneath the mylohyoid muscle and passes into the neck under the digastric

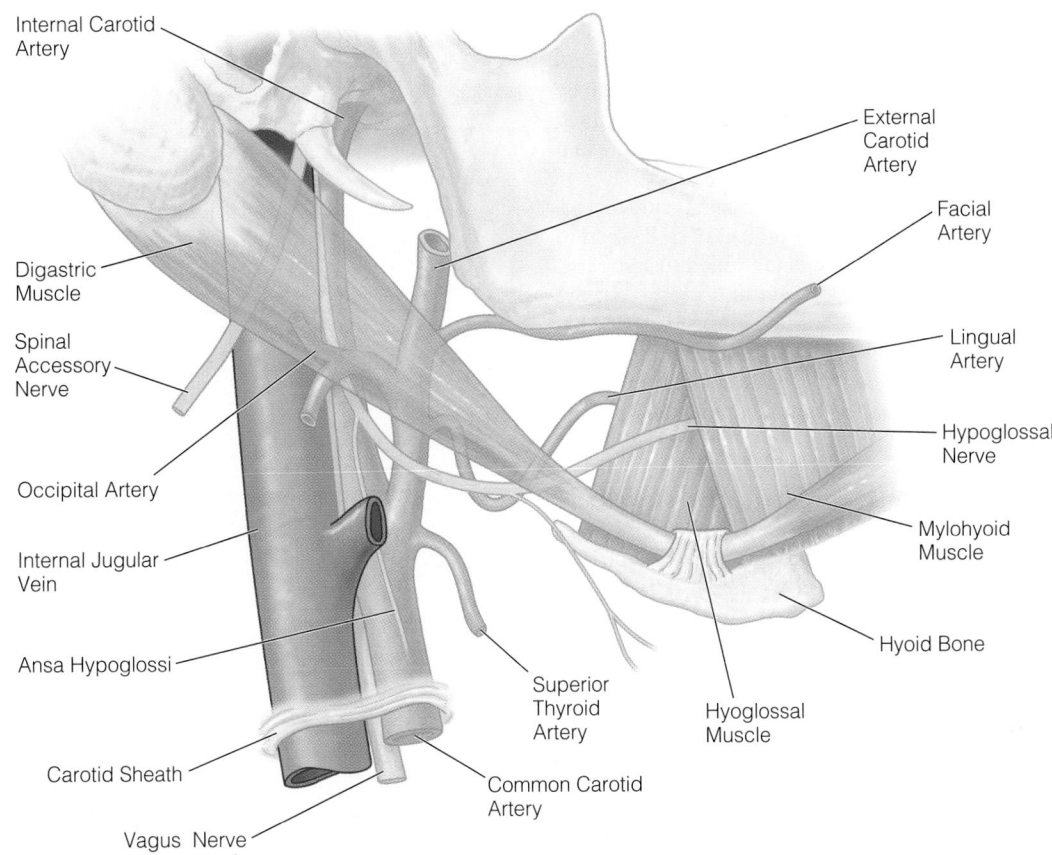

Internal Carotid
Artery

External
Carotid
Artery

Facial
Artery

Digastric
Muscle

Lingual
Artery

Spinal
Accessory
Nerve

Hypoglossal
Nerve

Occipital Artery

Mylohyoid
Muscle

Internal Jugular
Vein

Hyoid Bone

Ansa Hypoglossi

Superior
Thyroid
Artery

Hyoglossal
Muscle

Carotid Sheath

Common Carotid
Artery

Vagus Nerve

Figure 3 Depicted are the key anatomic relationships in levels I and II that must be kept in
mind in performing a neck dissection. View is of the right neck.

muscle. It then loops around the external carotid artery at the origin of the occipital artery and ascends to the skull base between the external carotid artery and the internal jugular vein. Often, the hypoglossal nerve is surrounded by a plexus of small veins, branching off the common facial vein. Bleeding in this region places the hypoglossal nerve at risk. The jugular vein, located just posterior to the external carotid artery and the hypoglossal nerve, may be isolated and doubly suture-ligated at this point. Frequently, the spinal accessory nerve is identified just lateral and posterior to the internal jugular vein, proceeding posteriorly into the sternocleidomastoid muscle.

In a radical neck dissection, the sternocleidomastoid muscle and the spinal accessory nerve are transected at this point and elevated off the splenius capitis and the levator scapulae to the trapezius posteriorly. The anterior edge of the trapezius is skeletonized from the occiput to the clavicle. The accessory nerve is again transected where it penetrates the trapezius.

Step 3: Control of Internal Jugular Vein Inferiorly; Ligation of Lymphatic Pedicle

The sternal and clavicular heads of the sternocleidomastoid muscle are transected and elevated to expose the anterior belly of the omohyoid muscle. The soft tissue overlying the posterior belly of the omohyoid muscle is dissected, clamped, and ligated as necessary. The omohyoid muscle is then transected, and the jugular vein, the carotid artery, and the vagus nerve are exposed. The jugular vein is isolated and doubly suture-ligated. Care is taken not to transect the adjacent vagus nerve and carotid artery. The lymphatic tissues in the base of the neck adjacent to the internal jugular vein are clamped and suture-ligated 1 cm superior to the clavicle. If a chyle leak is encountered, a figure-eight stitch is

placed along the lymphatic pedicle until there is no evidence of clear or turbid fluid on the Valsalva maneuver. Care is taken to avoid inadvertent injury to the vagus nerve or the phrenic nerve, which course through this region.

Step 4: Mobilization of Supraclavicular Fat Pad ("Bloody Gulch")

The fascia overlying the supraclavicular fat pad is incised, and the supraclavicular fat pad is bluntly retracted superiorly so as to free the tissues from the supraclavicular fossa. If transverse cervical vessels are encountered, they are clamped and ligated as necessary. Fascia is left on the deep muscles of the neck, which also envelop the brachial plexus and the phrenic nerve.

Step 5: Dissection and Removal of Specimen

Attention is then turned to the posterior aspect of the neck. Fat and lymphatic tissues are retracted anteriorly with Allis clamps, and the specimen is dissected off the deep muscles of the neck with a blade. Again, a layer of fascia is left on the deep cervical musculature: stripping fascia off the deep cervical musculature results in denervation of these muscles, which adds to the morbidity associated with accessory nerve sacrifice. Once the specimen is mobilized beyond the phrenic nerve, the cervical nerves (C1–C4) may be divided. The specimen is peeled off the carotid artery and removed.

Step 6: Closure

The neck incision is closed in layers over suction drains.

MODIFIED RADICAL NECK DISSECTION

The incision is made and flaps elevated as in a radical neck dissection. Care must be exercised in elevating the posterior skin flap. Typically, the platysma is deficient in this area, and often, no natural plane exists. Dissection deep in the posterior triangle may result in inadvertent injury to the spinal accessory nerve, which travels inferiorly and posteriorly across the posterior triangle in a relatively superficial plane to innervate the trapezius.

A type I modified radical neck dissection begins with dissections of levels I and II, as described for a radical neck dissection (see above). The spinal accessory nerve is identified just superficial or posterior to the internal jugular vein and preserved; the distal spinal accessory nerve is then identified in the posterior triangle. Typically, the spinal accessory nerve can be identified 1 cm superior to the cervical plexus along the posterior border of the sternocleidomastoid muscle. Provided that the patient is not fully paralyzed, the surgeon can distinguish this nerve from adjacent sensory branches by using a nerve stimulator.

Once the spinal accessory nerve is identified, it is dissected and mobilized distally to the point at which it penetrates the trapezius. Proximally, the nerve is dissected through the sternocleidomastoid muscle, which is transected over the nerve. The branch to the sternocleidomastoid muscle is divided with Metz scissors, and the nerve is fully mobilized from the trapezius posteroinferiorly to the posterior belly of the digastric muscle anterosuperiorly, then gently retracted out of the way.

The rest of the neck dissection proceeds as described for a radical neck dissection. If the tumor does not involve the internal jugular vein, it may also be preserved; this constitutes a type II modified radical neck dissection. If the spinal accessory nerve, the internal jugular vein, and the sternocleidomastoid muscle are all preserved, the procedure is a type III modified radical neck dissection. In a type III dissection, the sternocleidomastoid muscle is fully mobilized and retracted with two broad Penrose drains, and the contents of the neck are exposed. The spinal accessory nerve is preserved thoughout its entire course, including the branch to the sternocleidomastoid muscle. The remainder of the neck dissection proceeds as previously described (see above).

SELECTIVE NECK DISSECTION

Levels I to IV

In a selective neck dissection, the posterior triangle is not removed; thus, there is no need to elevate skin flaps posterior to the sternocleidomastoid muscle. Limited elevation of skin flaps is beneficial, particularly for patients who have previously undergone chemoradiation therapy, in whom extensive flap elevation may contribute to significant persistent lymphedema after operation. Subplatysmal skin flaps are raised sufficiently to expose the neck levels to be dissected, with the central compartment left undisturbed. If level I dissection is planned, the fascia overlying the submandibular gland is raised and retracted so as to preserve the marginal nerve. The submental fat pad is grasped and mobilized away from the floor of the submental triangle (composed of the anterior belly of the digastric muscle and the mylohyoid muscle). Inferiorly, the lymphatic tissues are mobilized off the posterior aspect of the omohyoid muscle, which forms the anteroinferior limit of the neck dissection.

Once the digastric tendon and the posterior edge of the mylohyoid muscle are visualized, the mylohyoid is retracted with an Army-Navy retractor so that the submandibular duct, the lingual nerve with its attachment to the submandibular gland, and the hypoglossal nerve are visualized. The submandibular duct and ganglion are ligated, and the submandibular gland is retracted out of the submandibular triangle.

At this point, the facial artery is encountered and suture-ligat-

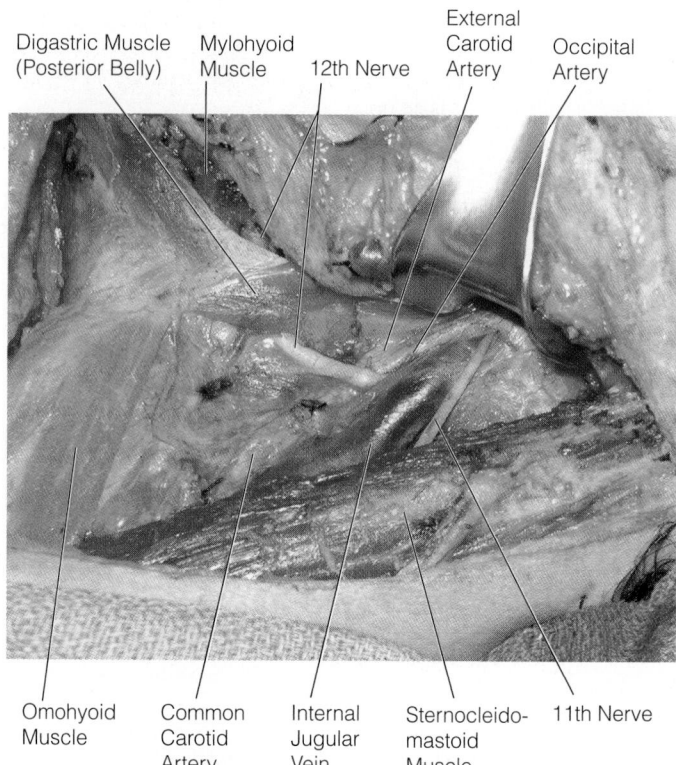

Digastric Muscle (Posterior Belly) — Mylohyoid Muscle — 12th Nerve — External Carotid Artery — Occipital Artery

Omohyoid Muscle — Common Carotid Artery — Internal Jugular Vein — Sternocleidomastoid Muscle — 11th Nerve

Figure 4 **Selective neck dissection. The posterior belly of the digastric muscle is identified inferior to the submandibular gland. This muscle protects several critical structures just deep to it (the hypoglossal nerve, the carotid artery, the internal jugular vein, and the spinal accessory nerve). View is of a left neck dissection.**

ed. Because the artery curves around the submandibular gland, the facial artery, if not preserved, must be ligated twice (proximally and distally). If the neck dissection is part of a large extirpative procedure involving free-flap reconstruction, the facial artery is preserved for use in microvascular anastomosis.

The posterior belly of the digastric muscle is then identified inferior to the submandibular gland. This muscle has been referred to as one of several "resident's friends" in the neck because it serves to protect several critical structures that lie just deep to it, including the hypoglossal nerve, the external carotid artery, the internal jugular vein, and the spinal accessory nerve [*see Figure 4*]. The posterior belly of the digastric muscle is skeletonized to the sternocleidomastoid muscle, where it inserts on the mastoid tip. The specimen is then mobilized away from structures just inferior to the digastric muscle. The hypoglossal nerve emerges from beneath the mylohyoid muscle and passes into the neck just below the digastric muscle, looping around the external carotid artery at the origin of the occipital artery and ascending to the skull base between the external carotid artery and the internal jugular vein. Bleeding from small branches of the common facial vein that envelop the hypoglossal nerve place this structure at risk for injury. The spinal accessory nerve is often visualized just superficial or posterior to the internal jugular vein, extending posteriorly to innervate the sternocleidomastoid muscle.

Next, the fascia overlying the sternocleidomastoid muscle is grasped and unrolled medially throughout its length, starting at the anterior edge of the muscle. The fascia is removed until the spinal accessory nerve is identified at the point where it penetrates the muscle. This nerve is dissected and mobilized superiorly through fat and lymphatic tissues to the digastric muscle. Care must be taken not to inadvertently injure the internal jugular vein, which lies in close proximity to the nerve superiorly. Tissue posterior to the accessory nerve is grasped and freed from the deep muscles of the neck, the digastric muscle superiorly, and the sternocleidomastoid muscle posteriorly. The tissue included in so-called level IIb is passed beneath the spinal accessory nerve and incorporated into the main specimen.

The sternocleidomastoid muscle is retracted, and the fascia posterior to the internal jugular vein is incised. Dissection is carried down to the deep cervical musculature and cervical nerves, which form the floor of the dissection. The specimen is retracted anteriorly. A layer of fascia is left on the deep cervical musculature and the cervical nerves to preserve innervation of the deep muscles of the neck and protect the phrenic nerve as it courses over the anterior scalene muscle.

The specimen is peeled off the internal jugular vein and removed. Dissection too far posteriorly behind the vein may result in injury to the vagus nerve or the sympathetic trunk and predisposes to postoperative thrombosis of the vein. Ligation of internal jugular vein branches should be done without affecting the caliber of the vein or giving the vessel a "sausage link" appearance, which would create turbulent flow patterns predisposing to thrombosis. Overall, gentle dissection around all vessels, with care taken to avoid pulling-related trauma, minimizes the risk of endothelial injury. Dissection behind the internal jugular vein may result in injury to the vagus nerve or the sympathetic trunk.

A level IV dissection may be facilitated by retracting the omohyoid muscle inferiorly or by dividing it for additional exposure. The tissue inferior to the omohyoid is mobilized and delivered with the main specimen. The lymphatic pedicle is clamped and ligated. Care is taken to look for leakage of chyle, particularly when a level IV dissection is performed on the left.

Levels II to IV

When level I is spared, a smaller incision suffices for exposure. Subplatysmal flaps are raised superiorly to the level of the submandibular gland. The inferior flap is raised, exposing the anterior edge of the sternocleidomastoid muscle. Dissection proceeds just inferior to the submandibular gland until the posterior belly of the digastric muscle is identified. The digastric muscle is skeletonized posteriorly to the sternocleidomastoid muscle and anteriorly to the omohyoid muscle, which forms the anterior limit of the dissection. The rest of the neck dissection proceeds as described for a selective neck dissection involving levels I through IV.

Complications

INTRAOPERATIVE

Most intraoperative complications may be prevented by means of careful surgical technique, coupled with a thorough understanding of head and neck anatomy. Injury to the internal jugular vein may occur either proximally or distally. Uncontrolled proximal bleeding endangers adjacent critical structures, such as the carotid artery and the hypoglossal nerve. The bleeding may be initially controlled with pressure, followed by a methodical search for the bleeding source. Internal jugular vein lacerations can often be repaired with 5-0 nylon sutures; if a laceration cannot be repaired, the vein must be ligated. Occasionally, a laceration extends up to the skull base, and the vessel cannot be controlled with clamping and ligation. In these cases, it is acceptable to pack the jugular foramen for hemostasis.

It is important to gain distal control of the internal jugular vein before repair to prevent air embolism. Harbingers of air embolism include the presence of a sucking sound in the neck, a mill-wheel murmur over the precordium, ECG changes, and hypotension. Predisposing factors include elevation of the head of the bed and spontaneous breathing, which increase negative intrathoracic pressure and thus promote entry of air into the venous system. Injury to the internal jugular vein is more difficult to control when it occurs distally in the neck or chest at the junction with the subclavian vein. For this reason, ligation of the internal jugular vein in radical and modified radical neck dissections is typically performed 1 cm superior to the clavicle.

Opalescent or clear fluid in the inferior neck suggests the presence of a chyle fistula. Chyle fistulas generally can be prevented by clamping and ligating the lymphatic pedicle at the base of the neck. Those fistulas that occur are repaired at the time of the neck dissection. There is no benefit in isolating individual lymphatic vessels, because these structures are fragile, do not hold stitches, and are prone to tearing. A figure-eight stitch is placed along the lymphatic pedicle until there is no evidence of clear or turbid fluid on the Valsalva maneuver. Care must be taken not to inadvertently injure the vagus nerve or the phrenic nerve during repair of a chyle leak.

POSTOPERATIVE

The best treatment of postoperative complications such as hematoma and chyle leak is prevention. Hematomas, once present, are best managed by promptly returning the patient to the OR for evacuation. Management of postoperative leakage of chyle depends on the volume of the leak. Low-volume leaks may be managed with packing, wound care, and nutritional supplementation with medium-chain triglycerides.

Wound complications (e.g., infection, flap necrosis, and carotid artery exposure or rupture) share certain interrelated causative factors. Poor nutritional status, advanced tumor stage at presentation, hypothyroidism, and preoperative radiation therapy have all been associated with wound complications. After chemoradiation therapy, the use of smaller incisions and more limited dissection of soft tissues may lower the incidence of postoperative wound problems, including persistent lymphedema and soft tissue fibrosis. Conversely, poor planning of skin incisions may increase the likelihood of wound complications such as wound breakdown, skin flap loss, and exposure of vital structures. Wound complications predispose to carotid artery rupture, the most catastrophic complication of neck dissection.

In some case, severe edema after planned neck dissections in patients previously treated with chemoradiation may cause respiratory decompensation that necessitates tracheotomy. Postoperative internal jugular vein thrombosis is not uncommon despite preservation at the time of surgery,[25] and it may exacerbate edema. Impaired venous outflow predisposes to increased intracranial pressure.[26] This may be a greater concern in patients who require bilateral neck dissections. If a radical neck dissection is performed on one side, the internal jugular vein must be preserved on the other, or else the neck dissections must be staged. These problems are further exacerbated when the patient has undergone chemoradiation therapy before operation.

Most neck dissections result in some degree of temporary shoulder dysfunction. Patients in whom nerve-sparing procedures are performed can expect function to return within 3 weeks to 1 year, depending on the procedure performed. Shoulder dysfunction and pain are exacerbated when nerves supplying the deep muscles of the neck are also sacrificed. All patients benefit from physical therapy, which preserves full range of motion in the shoulder while function returns.

References

1. Wakely PE Jr, Kneisl JS: Soft tissue aspiration cytopathology. Cancer 90:292, 2000

2. Carroll CM, Nazeer U, Timon CI: The accuracy of fine-needle aspiration biopsy in the diagnosis of head and neck masses. Ir J Med Sci 167:149, 1998

3. Kraus DH, Carew JF, Harrison LB: Regional lymph node metastasis from cutaneous squamous cell carcinoma. Arch Otolaryngol Head Neck Surg 124:582, 1998

4. Spiro RH: Management of malignant tumors of the salivary glands. Oncology (Huntingt) 12:671, 1998

5. Shaha AR: Management of the neck in thyroid cancer. Otolaryngol Clin North Am 31:823, 1998

6. Alvi A, Johnson JT: Extracapsular spread in the clinically negative neck (N0): implications and outcome. Otolaryngol Head Neck Surg 114:65, 1996

7. Myers JN, Greenberg JS, Mo V, et al: Extracapsular spread: a significant predictor of treatment failure in patients with squamous cell carcinoma of the tongue. Cancer 92:3030, 2001

8. Johnson JT, Wagner RL, Myers EN: A long-term assessment of adjuvant chemotherapy on outcome of patients with extracapsular spread of cervical metastases from squamous carcinoma of the head and neck. Cancer 77:181, 1996

9. Jose J, Coatesworth AP, Johnston C, et al: Cervical node metastases in squamous cell carcinoma of the upper aerodigestive tract: the significance of extracapsular spread and soft tissue deposits. Head Neck 25:451, 2003

10. Hathaway B, Johnson JT, Piccirillo JF, et al: Chemoradiation for metastatic SCCA: role of comorbidity. Laryngoscope 111(11 pt 1):1893, 2001

11. Chen AY, Matson LK, Roberts D, et al: The significance of comorbidity in advanced laryngeal cancer. Head Neck 23:566, 2001

12. Weymuller EA Jr: Clinical staging and operative reporting for multi-institutional trials in head and neck squamous cell carcinoma. Head Neck 19:650, 1997

13. Ross GL, Shoaib T, Soutar DS, et al: The First International Conference on Sentinel Node Biopsy in Mucosal Head and Neck Cancer and adoption of a multicenter trial protocol. Ann Surg Oncol 9:406, 2002

14. Civantos FJ, Gomez C, Duque C, et al: Sentinel node biopsy in oral cavity cancer: correlation with PET scan and immunohistochemistry. Head Neck 25:1, 2003

15. Jacobs JR, Arden RL, Marks SC, et al: Carotid artery reconstruction using superficial femoral arterial grafts. Laryngoscope 104(6 pt 1):689, 1994

16. Adams GL, Madison M, Remley K, et al: Preoperative permanent balloon occlusion of internal carotid artery in patients with advanced head and neck squamous cell carcinoma. Laryngoscope 109:460, 1999

17. Bocca E, Pignataro O, Oldini C, et al: Functional neck dissection: an evaluation and review of 843 cases. Laryngoscope 94:942, 1984

18. Shah JP, Candela FC, Poddar AK: The patterns of cervical lymph node metastases from squamous carcinoma of the oral cavity. Cancer 66:109, 1990

19. Pitman KT, Johnson JT, Myers EN: Effectiveness of selective neck dissection for management of the clinically negative neck. Arch Otolaryngol Head Neck Surg 123:917, 1997

20. Andersen PE, Warren F, Spiro J, et al: Results of selective neck dissection in management of the node-positive neck. Arch Otolaryngol Head Neck Surg 128:1180, 2002

21. Narayan K, Crane CH, Kleid S, et al: Planned neck dissection as an adjunct to the management of patients with advanced neck disease treated with definitive radiotherapy: for some or for all? Head Neck 21:606, 1999

22. McHam SA, Adelstein DJ, Rybycki LA, et al: Who merits a neck dissection after definitive chemoradiotherapy for N2-N3 squamous cell head and neck cancer? Head Neck 25:791, 2003

23. Doweck I, Robbins KT, Mendenhall WM, et al: Neck level-specific nodal metastases in oropharyngeal cancer: is there a role for selective neck dissection after definitive radiation therapy? Head Neck 25:960, 2003

24. Sohn HG, Har-El G: Neck dissection prior to radiation therapy for squamous cell carcinoma of tongue base. Am J Otolaryngol 23:138, 2002

25. Leontsinis TG, Currie AR, Mannell A: Internal jugular vein thrombosis following functional neck dissection. Laryngoscope 105:169, 1995

26. Lydiatt DD, Ogren FP, Lydiatt WM, et al: Increased intracranial pressure as a complication of unilateral radical neck dissection in a patient with congenital absence of the transverse sinus. Head Neck 13:359, 1991

Acknowledgment

Figures 1 through 3   Tom Moore.

Ara A. Chalian, M.D., F.A.C.S.

Strictly speaking, the term tracheostomy refers to the surgical creation of an opening into the trachea, whereas the term tracheotomy refers to an incision of the trachea. However, many surgeons use these terms virtually interchangeably; in particular, they commonly refer to more temporary openings, in which cutaneous flaps are not sutured to the trachea, as tracheotomies. Other surgeons prefer to observe a more formal distinction between the two words. In this chapter, I use the term tracheostomy to refer to the process of creating an opening in the trachea, reserving the term tracheotomy for the actual tracheal incision.

Initially, tracheostomy was performed primarily as a life-saving intervention to secure and establish an airway in patients with life-threatening airway obstruction as a consequence of infection or neoplastic disease. Currently, it is most commonly done to facilitate prolonged ventilator-based respiration in patients with respiratory failure. Tracheostomy has become an integral part of complex head and neck tumor resections for cancer involving the larynx, the base of the tongue, the pharynx, and, in some cases, the base of the skull. In addition, it is performed to provide airway diversion in patients with laryngeal stenosis or bilateral vocal cord paralysis.

Preoperative Evaluation

Patients scheduled for elective tracheostomy undergo the standard preoperative assessments. Because the surrounding tissues are highly vascular, anticoagulants and aspirin should be discontinued before operation in nonemergency settings, as should antiplatelet medications. The cervical and tracheal anatomy should be assessed; in rare instances, an extra-long tracheotomy tube will be required. Any lesions, scars, or masses in the central thyrotracheal compartment of the neck should be noted. If there is a mass in the thyroid gland (especially in the isthmus), workup or simple resection should be considered. Previous operations on the thyroid, the larynx, the trachea, or the cervical spine can alter the anatomy and present additional difficulties to the surgeon. A low-lying larynx or cricoid resulting from kyphosis or another cause is particularly troublesome. In some patients, the cricoid is at the sternal notch or even lower.

In this last situation, if it is determined that a tracheostomy is absolutely necessary, the potential problems must be considered. Although it is logical to assume that the trachea can be pulled superiorly, it is important to remember that after the procedure, the position of this structure will tend to drift down toward the mediastinum, presenting the problem of an incorrectly positioned tracheostomy tube that may "kick out" from the anterior tracheal wall opening or press against a mucosal surface. Often, this tube will pivot against the anterior wall or the trachea cephalad to the opening, thereby potentially contributing to cartilage injury with subsequent malacia or stenosis.

If the trachea is inferiorly displaced to a substantial degree, resection of the manubrium should be considered. This measure very rarely proves necessary, however, and is mentioned only for the sake of completeness.

Operative Planning

COUNSELING AND INFORMED CONSENT

The patient, the family, or both should receive counseling on the risks and benefits of the procedure. Commonly discussed issues include pain, mortality, and the range of possible early and late complications [see Complications, below]. In my experience, many families are intimidated or upset by the consideration of tracheostomy. To address their concerns, I offer the option of removing the oral or nasal tube from the areas that most affect patient comfort and ability to interact with the family. When this is done, oral alimentation and mouth care become much more feasible, and the patient's ability to speak (or at least mouth) words is often greatly improved. In patients with significant central nervous system injuries or other conditions that alter mental status, it may be advisable to secure the tracheotomy tube to the neck to maintain safety and prevent unintentional extubation.

SITE OF PROCEDURE

A tracheostomy may be performed in an intensive care unit, a shock trauma bay, or an operating room. Emergency tracheostomies are often performed in these areas, and thus, the surgical equipment is most often kept there. In elective situations, however, a tracheostomy may be performed virtually anywhere. The most commonly required equipment is portable. An electrocautery should be available, and good lighting (whether from overhead lights, headlights, or portable OR lights) is critical. OR personnel usually are more familiar with the procedure than ICU or trauma bay personnel; accordingly, many teams request a scrub nurse or a technician, then train team members in the alternative environments.

ANESTHESIA

The patient's comfort can be optimized with conscious sedation or, possibly, with local anesthesia alone. Communication and cooperation with the anesthesiologist (including specific discussion of the role of sedation and analgesia) can be critical to a successful outcome and should therefore be key components of preparation for emergency tracheostomy. In a decompensating patient, the effect of suppression of the respiratory drive is potentially catastrophic.

Operative Technique

SURGICAL TRACHEOSTOMY

The patient is positioned with a shoulder roll and a foam pad (doughnut) under the head. If cervical spine precautions are in force, the posterior portion of the cervical collar should remain in place, and the head should be stabilized by a team member. The procedure may be more difficult to execute in this setting, but otherwise, the surgical technique is the same.

The position of the patient can also be optimized by extending the headrest of the surgical bed. This measure permits better palpation of landmarks if soft tissues are thick. For patients with cervical stenosis or symptoms related to cervical spine pathology, a larger incision or so-called neutral-position tracheotomy may be considered; such problems do not necessarily preclude the procedure.

Step 1: Incision of Skin

Before the incision is made, the patient should also be assessed for a high-riding innominate artery or medially placed carotid arteries. These anatomic variants are rare, but when they are present, additional care may have to be exercised.

The cutaneous incision may be made either vertically or horizontally. Either incision leaves a well-healed scar once the tracheotomy tube is removed. The level and location of the incision may vary, depending on individual surgeons' preferences. In general, a good placement is 1 cm below the cricoid or halfway between the cricoid and the sternal notch [see Figure 1]. The size of the incision is also, to an extent, a matter of individual preference. Given the current emphasis on minimizing scars, I strive to use the smallest possible safe incision. For transverse incisions, 2 to 2.5 cm is often adequate. In an emergency setting, a longer incision—often vertical—may facilitate exposure and help the surgeon avoid large subplatysmal anterior jugular veins. The skin incision may be accompanied by excision of some of the subcutaneous fat in the immediate area.

It should be kept in mind that these recommendations regarding the size of the incision are only suggestions, not hard-and-fast rules. Each case should be considered individually, and each incision should be designed so as to allow the safest exposure in a given patient.

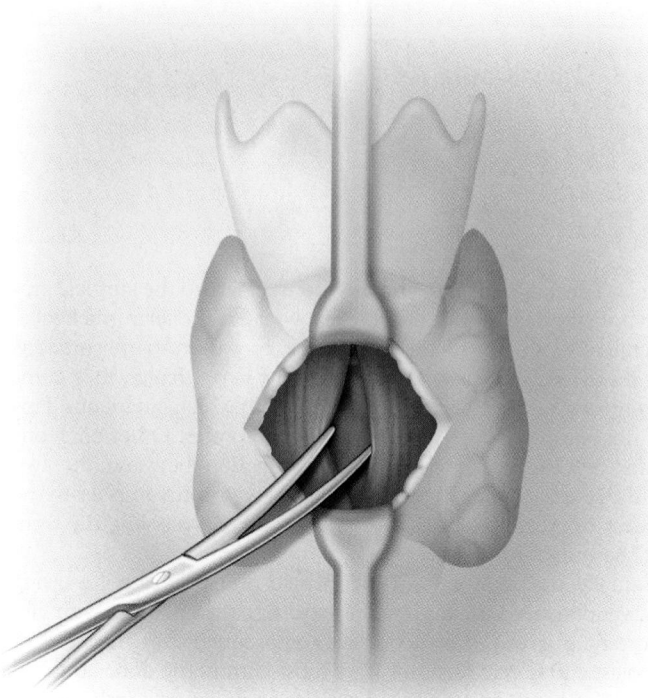

Figure 2 Surgical tracheostomy. Retractors are placed, the skin is retracted, and the strap muscles are visualized in the midline. The muscles are divided along the raphe, then retracted laterally.

Step 2: Retraction of Strap Muscles

The strap muscles are identified, and the midline raphe is divided. The muscles are then retracted laterally by the assistant with Senn or Army-Navy retractors [see Figure 2]. Undermining should be limited to minimize the potential creation of avenues for the passage of air, secretions, or instruments (including the tracheostomy tube). When there is a malignant neoplasm in the soft tissue or the thyroid compartment, anatomic landmarks may be difficult to identify. In such cases, dissection to the notch of the thyroid cartilage helps one identify the midline and work inferiorly [see Step 5, below].

Step 3: Dissection of Thyroid Gland

The thyroid isthmus lies in the field of the dissection [see Figure 3]. Its size and thickness may vary greatly. Typically, the isthmus is 5 to 10 mm in its vertical dimension. If the organ is within this size range, one can often mobilize it away from the trachea and retract it superiorly (or inferiorly), then place the tracheal incision in the second or third tracheal interspace [see Figure 4]. If the isthmus is large enough that it may block the tracheostomy site, one may divide it and ligate the edges. In the instance of an isthmus nodule, removal of the isthmus and the nodule is reasonable for diagnostic and therapeutic purposes. Although the recurrent nerves are in the surgical field, they typically are not at great risk for injury during tracheostomy; however, they may be subjected to trauma if dissection or even a retractor extends into the tracheoesophageal groove. The blood supply to the trachea is laterally based, which is another reason for avoiding significant lateral exposure of the trachea.

Step 4: Incision of Trachea

The tracheotomy should be performed with a knife. If one desires, the pretracheal tissues may be coagulated with a bipolar (or, cau-

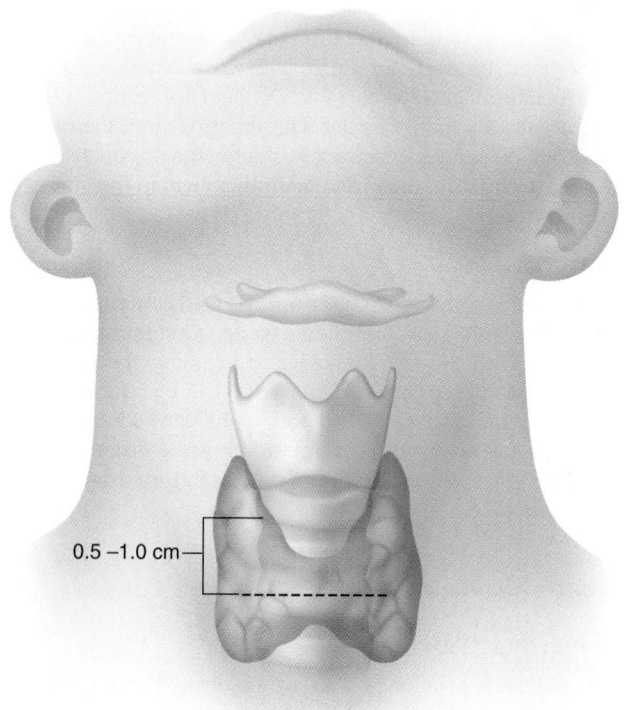

0.5 –1.0 cm

Figure 1 Surgical tracheostomy. A transverse cutaneous incision is made that is approximately 2 to 3 cm long (or as long as is necessary for adequate exposure). The extent of flap elevation may be 1 cm or less.

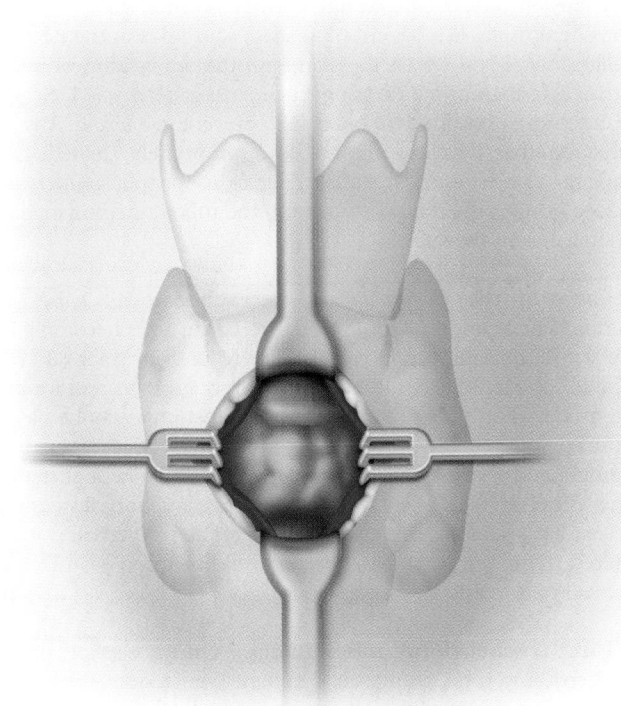

Figure 3 **Surgical tracheostomy. With the strap muscles retracted, the thyroid isthmus is visualized, and the inferior (or superior) edge of the isthmus is dissected down to the trachea. The isthmus is then retracted superiorly (or inferiorly) or divided to permit visualization of the trachea before the tracheal incision is made.**

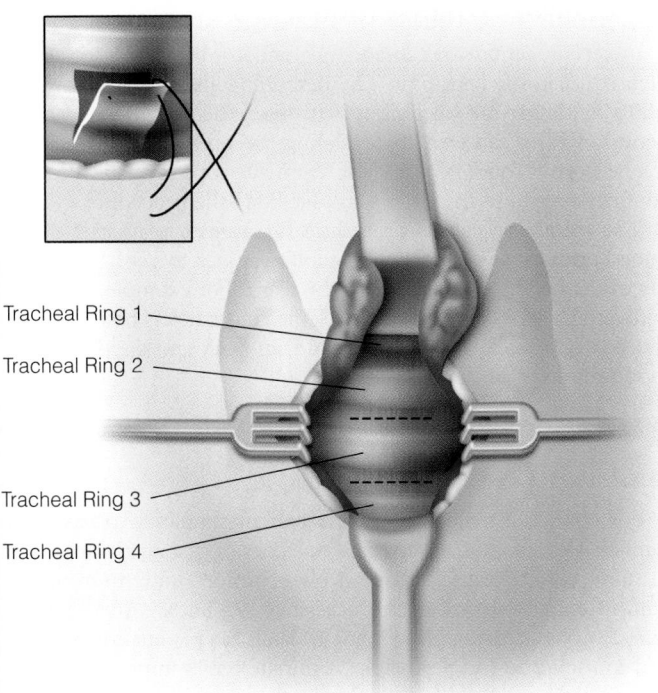

Tracheal Ring 1
Tracheal Ring 2
Tracheal Ring 3
Tracheal Ring 4

Figure 4 **Surgical tracheostomy. A tracheotomy is made either between the second and third tracheal rings or between the third and fourth rings. A Bjork flap (inset) may be created by extending the ends of the tracheotomy downward through the next lower tracheal ring in an inverted U shape.**

tiously, with a monopolar) electrocautery. The opening of the airway will bring volatile, flammable gases into the operative field; accordingly, the use of a monopolar electrocautery must be limited (or avoided if possible). The choice of a tracheal incision will not make a significant difference to the execution of the procedure.

Linear incision A linear incision is probably the simplest choice and the one that is least traumatic to the cartilage. Typically, it is made through either the interspace between the second and third tracheal rings or that between the third and fourth.

Tracheal window Instead of a simple incision, one may opt to remove the midportion of the third or fourth tracheal ring to create a window. The theoretical rationale for the tracheal window is that it minimizes trauma to the remaining cartilage resulting from passage of the tracheostomy tube.

Bjork flap A Bjork flap is an inferiorly based U-shaped flap that incorporates the ring below the tracheal incision. It is sewn to the skin at the inferior margin of the tracheotomy. The theoretical justification for the use of the Bjork flap is that it helps keep the tracheal incision close to the skin edge and facilitates tube replacement if the tube is accidentally dislodged or removed. The flap suture can be released after 3 to 5 days, once the tract has started to mature.

Stay sutures Many surgeons place lateral, inferior, or superior stay sutures (often, though not always, made of silk) in the trachea to help stabilize this structure during the procedure. For optimal stabilization of the exposure during subsequent manipulations or possible emergencies, they generally leave the sutures in situ until the first tracheostomy tube change. These sutures are taped to the patient's chest and should be labeled for easy identification in emergency situations. The use of stay sutures in tracheostomies is now a well-established (though not universal) practice, particularly in children and neonates.

Step 5 (optional): Division of Tumor to Facilitate Tube Placement

In the case of a neoplasm involving the thyroid, the tumor may have to be resected in the midline to allow placement of the tube. Often, the airway cannot be palpated. To identify the airway, the dissection should begin at the level of the thyroid cartilage—possibly, as high as the thyroid notch—and continue inferiorly until the cricoid and the trachea are identifiable. In these situations, the depth of the wound that must be created before the trachea is reached can be a problem. A standard tracheostomy tube may be too short for its intended use, in which case a custom tube will have to be ordered. With a custom tube, it is possible to specify both the distance from the tube faceplate to the turn entering the airway and the length of the segment going into the airway. If there is not enough time to order a custom tracheostomy tube, an endotracheal tube can be placed as a temporizing measure to provide an airway. To help set the length of the tube segment that will enter the airway, the endotracheal tube can be bivalved (i.e., split) along its proximal extent.

Step 6: Removal or Withdrawal of Endotracheal Tube and Placement of Tracheostomy Tube; Management of Anesthesia and Oxygenation

During the transition to tracheostomy tube ventilation, the endotracheal tube either is removed or is withdrawn and kept in position at the level of the vocal cords until the tracheostomy tube is secured. Preoxygenation is important to allow adequate apnea time for incision, withdrawal of the endotracheal tube, and place-

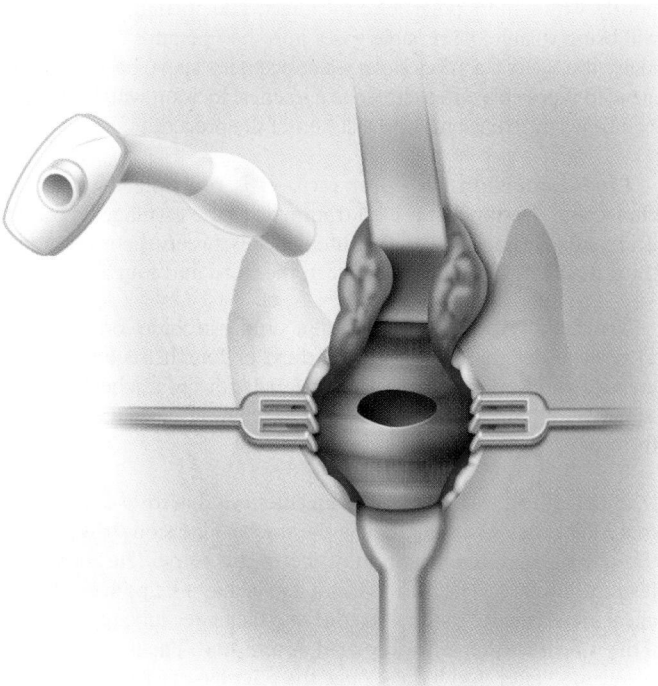

Figure 5 **Surgical tracheostomy. The tracheostomy tube is inserted into the tracheal opening from the side, with the faceplate rotated 90° so that the tube's entry into the airway can be well visualized.**

ment of the tracheostomy tube. To optimize oxygen tension, administration of nitrous oxide is often stopped before the airway is entered.

Some surgeons prepare and drape the endotracheal tube into the operative field, preferring to withdraw it themselves gradually as the changeover to the tracheostomy tube is occurring. Often, the anesthesiologist or another team member is assigned to manage the release and withdrawal of the endotracheal tube. I prefer to advance the endotracheal tube before the tracheal incision is made so that the cuff lies deep (distal) to the tracheostomy site. This measure delays the start of apnea and potentially minimizes its duration, permitting ventilation to continue even though the airway has been entered. Delivery of the volatile anesthetic, ventilation, and oxygenation can be performed actively during the first step of entry into the airway and preparation for tube changeover.

The size of the tracheostomy tube is chosen on the basis of the length and diameter required to achieve adequate respiration and correct positioning in a given patient. A No. 6 tube is appropriate for most adults. If frequent suction bronchoscopy is required, many intensivists will request a larger tube, such as a No. 8; the No. 8 tube allows passage of a standard suction bronchoscope and permits ventilation to continue.

The placement of the tracheostomy tube [*see Figure 5*] should be confirmed with auscultation or, in cases where capnography is unavailable, with visualization of chest movement; alternatively, in cases involving end-tidal CO_2 monitoring, it may be confirmed visually with the capnograph.

The fresh tracheostomy tube should be secured with sutures from the faceplate to the skin and with tracheostomy ties. (If the patient has had a microvascular flap and the tracheostomy tube was placed concurrently, the ties are not used, so as to ensure that the veins providing outflow are not compressed.) If the patient has a long-term need for a tracheostomy, the use of a soft foam collar band with hook-and-loop fasteners is recommended, once the first

tracheostomy tube change has been performed and the tract is considered safe. If a patient has excess skin folds in the neck, any collar is likely to irritate the skin, and the application of a semipermeable membrane dressing, such as Tegaderm (3M, St. Paul, Minnesota), may be advisable to help prevent ulceration. Any local infection that develops should be appropriately treated. Some patients, nurses, and surgeons prefer to use a split gauze swatch placed around the tracheostomy and the tube to help manage the drainage from the site.

Care of the patient with a tracheostomy tube Humidified air or oxygen should be delivered via a tracheostomy tube collar; the humidification is necessary to prevent tracheal crusts. The inner cannula should be cleaned frequently to remove built-up mucus. The skin and area around the stoma may be cleaned with half-strength hydrogen peroxide and water. A spare inner cannula and a spare tracheostomy tube are often kept at the bedside. Flexible tracheal suction catheters and suction devices must be readily available. Because patients' ability to verbalize will be altered (temporarily, at least), they should be given easy access to the call button and be taught its use.

First tracheostomy tube change On my service, the first tracheostomy tube change in a patient who requires ventilatory support is performed approximately 1 week after operation. In a patient with a neoplasm who does not need a cuffed tube, the initial tube is exchanged for a cuffless tube at an earlier point if possible (i.e., if the anatomy is favorable).

I do not use fenestrated tracheostomy tubes. These tubes are more often associated with suprastomal granulation (resulting from irritation of the mucosa by the fenestrae) and with the development of crusting on the fenestrae. Moreover, fenestrated inner cannulae are often difficult to find.

PERCUTANEOUS TRACHEOSTOMY

In certain centers, percutaneous tracheostomy has largely supplanted open tracheostomy. The percutaneous approach involves using Seldinger-like techniques to enter the trachea transcutaneously with a catheter, then dilating the opening and placing a tracheostomy tube. A fiberoptic bronchoscope may be used to confirm entry into the airway and facilitate the procedure.

The suitability of this procedure for a given patient is determined primarily by the patient's stability or lack thereof, the anatomy of the neck, and the skills of the team. For example, a patient with a thick neck and unclear anatomic landmarks is not a suitable candidate, whereas a patient with a thin neck and good range of motion is an ideal candidate.

AWAKE TRACHEOSTOMY

Anesthetic Considerations

For an awake tracheostomy, the patient should be placed in a semi-Fowler position to give the anesthesiologist ready access to the airway, to optimize his or her own comfort, and, most important, to enhance primary and accessory respiratory muscle function. Every effort should be made to keep the patient comfortable and to minimize (or, if possible, eliminate) environmental stimuli, especially the work noise generated by the surgical team. Generally, sedatives are contraindicated, because they can diminish or even abolish respiratory drive and protective mechanisms.

Clear communication with the anesthesiologist must be ensured before the patient even enters the room; life-threatening emergencies may arise that necessitate close collaboration. The same is true for the scrub and circulating nurses and technicians. Their instrument tray should contain the most essential equipment, along with an appropriate selection of tracheostomy tubes prepared for use.

Tracheal Stents and T Tubes

As tracheobronchial airway stenting becomes more common, tracheostomy tubes may be increasingly required for definitive or end-of-life care. The position of the airway stent must be known with some precision because the tracheostomy tube may have to interface exactly with the end of the stent. Alternatively, the stent may have to be incised to afford entry into the airway. If the stent is metal, incision may not be possible.

Complications

EARLY

Soft Tissue Placement (False Passage) of Tracheostomy Tube Adjacent to Trachea

If the tracheostomy tube is inadvertently misplaced in soft tissue during the procedure, the endotracheal tube should be advanced from its intermediate position in the larynx back into the airway. The patient should undergo ventilation, and when oxygenation and ventilation are adequate, the endotracheal tube should be withdrawn and the tracheostomy tube replaced. If the tracheostomy tube cannot be placed directly, a guide tube may be employed (via the Seldinger technique) to help guide the tube into the airway; alternatively, a flexible bronchoscope may be used for this purpose. If the tracheostomy tube cannot be properly or effectively placed, transoral intubation is the safest way of resecuring the airway.

Decannulation

If the tracheostomy tube becomes decannulated on an acute basis, the protocol for reestablishing the airway is to intubate the patient via standard transoral approaches. Although it is theoretically possible to replace the tracheostomy tube directly into the tracheostomy site, it is safer to take an endolaryngeal approach, which allows the tube to be replaced into the tracheostomy site with good lighting and retraction and with the patient stable.

Pneumomediastinum

Pneumomediastinum is a potential complication if the tube is placed in a false passage or if the patient requires ventilation with the trachea incised.

Pneumothorax

Pneumothorax is an uncommon complication of tracheostomy—so uncommon that most protocols do not require chest x-rays after routine tracheostomies.

Bleeding

Bleeding may occur after tracheostomy, usually related either to the vasculature in the field (in particular, the thyroid vessels) or to the gland itself. If the bleeding is minor, it can generally be treated by applying absorptive gauze or a collagen-type dressing to the site; if it is coming from vessels of significant size, exploration and ligation or cauterization may be required. In rare cases, early bleeding from a major vessel may become apparent through the tracheostomy site. When this occurs, it is managed with the techniques used to treat tracheoinnominate or tracheoesopahgeal fistula [see Late, Tracheoinnominate or Tracheoesophageal Fistula, below].

Infection

Impaired handling of tracheal secretions may facilitate the development of local site infection. Such infection can generally be treated with antibiotics and local wound care.

Crusting or Mucous Plug

Mucus and blood, individually or in combination, can create difficult management problems. Accordingly, a fresh tracheostomy should be carefully supported with humidified oxygen or air. Tracheal suction should be available, and the nurses caring for the patient should be comfortable with using it. The patient and the family should also learn how to employ tracheal suction. With some mucous plugs, suction bronchoscopes may be required for removal.

Negative Pressure Pulmonary Edema

This complication may develop when an awake tracheostomy is done in the setting of significant airway obstruction. The patient's negative inspiratory pressures and effort are initially high, then suddenly drop to normal after the trachea is incised. A frothy pulmonary edema will be apparent. The standard treatment is positive pressure ventilatory support, often including positive end-expiratory pressure (PEEP).

LATE

Granulation

Granulation tissue may develop at the suprastomal region as a consequence of irritation by the tracheostomy tube. Symptoms related to speech or airway function may be seen when the tracheostomy tube is capped or fitted with Passy-Muir valves, which allow inspiration via the tube and exhalation via the native airway. In some cases, granulation at the tip of the tracheostomy tube may lead to bleeding or airway symptoms (e.g., dyspnea). When these accumulations of granulation tissue give rise to symptoms, removal should be considered.

Tracheomalacia

Tracheomalacia, defined as the loss of cartilage structure in the trachea, can cause a dynamic collapse with partial or complete blockade of the trachea during inspiration. Fortunately, it is a rare complication; typically, it is manifested as inspiratory noise and, potentially, as dyspnea after decannulation. It may be related less to the placement or presence of the tracheostomy tube than to the loss of tracheal cartilage at the site of the endotracheal tube balloon as a result of previous intubation, infection, or even pressure (e.g., the pressure that can be generated by large thyroid goiters).

Stenosis

Tracheal stenosis may be seen at the site of the tracheostomy or at any site along the trachea where trauma caused by cuffs or tubes has occurred. Laryngeal stenosis, though rare, may develop after placement of the tracheostomy tube or after decannulation. Like tracheal stenosis, laryngeal stenosis is most often related to endolaryngeal or endotracheal intubation, infection, or neoplastic disease. In rare instances, stenosis can be a manifestation of conditions such as gastroesophageal reflux disease or sarcoidosis.

Tracheoinnominate or Tracheoesophageal Fistula

Moderate to heavy bleeding, though uncommon, sometimes develops. It may herald an erosion of the anterior tracheal wall into the innominate artery and may be fatal if this vessel ruptures. Such bleeding is a result either of injury caused by the tip of the tracheostomy tube or of other types of injuries associated with endotracheal intubation. Diagnostic assessment should include partial or total withdrawal of the tube to allow flexible assessment of the anterior tracheal wall for erosions, clot, or cartilage breakdown and defects and to permit visualization of the mediastinal tissues.

Supportive management includes preparation for transfusion if the patient is anemic and formulation of a plan to manage the airway if hemorrhage is occurring. In the event of hemorrhage, the tracheostomy tube usually will have to be removed, and an endotracheal tube will have to be placed through the tracheostomy and advanced deeper so that the inflated cuff is distal to the bleeding site. To tamponade the bleeding, one should try to place the tip of a finger into the tracheostomy site and compress the trachea against the manubrium; this must be done with the tube in the airway as well. Alternatively, one may pass a rigid bronchoscope into the tracheostomy, provide ventilation through the scope, and then press the scope anteriorly against the manubrium to achieve hemostasis. For salvage in cases where the bleeding is immediately life-threatening, emergency operative intervention with the appropriate cardiovascular or vascular teams is required.

Tracheocutaneous Fistula

Tracheocutaneous fistula is not a common side effect of tracheostomy. If a cutaneous-lined tract persists, repair is indicated (see below). The key differential point to consider when a fistula persists is whether there is a stenosis in the endolaryngeal or endotracheal airway that is causing the condition.

Planned Decannulation Protocols

If there is any doubt about the patient's respiratory drive, level of consciousness, or airway protective mechanisms, the airway may be sequentially downsized. If there is no real doubt, flexible laryngoscopy and tracheoscopy may be done to confirm the presence of an intact airway. If the airway is adequate, the tracheostomy tube may be withdrawn and the wound managed with local cleaning and dry compressive dressings. The wound should heal by secondary intention. If a fistula forms, the cutaneous tract should be freshened or excised, after which the wound typically heals by secondary intention. Some surgeons prefer to close the wound in three layers, including the trachea. If this approach is followed, there is a potential for cervical emphysema or for dissection into the chest and pneumomediastinum.

Recommended Reading

Goldenberg D, Ari EG, Golz A, et al: Tracheotomy complications: a retrospective study of 1130 cases. Otolaryngol Head Neck Surg 123:495, 2000

Gysin C, Dugluerov P, Guyot JP, et al: Percutaneous versus surgical tracheostomy: a double blind randomized trial. Ann Surg 230:708, 1999

Massick DD, Yao S, Powell DM, et al: Bedside tracheostomy in the intensive care unit: a prospective randomized trial comparing open surgical tracheostomy with endoscopically guided percutaneous dilational tracheotomy. Laryngoscope 111:494, 2001

Pryor JP, Reilly PM, Shapiro MB: Surgical airway management in the intensive care unit. Crit Care Clin 16:473, 2000

Walts PA, Murth SC, DeCamp MM: Techniques of surgical tracheostomy. Clin Chest Med 24:413, 2003

Acknowledgment

Figures 1 through 5   Thom Graves.

20 THYROID AND PARATHYROID PROCEDURES

Gregg H. Jossart, M.D., F.A.C.S., and Orlo H. Clark, M.D., F.A.C.S.

Thyroidectomy

OPERATIVE PLANNING

If the patient has had any hoarseness or has undergone a neck operation before, indirect or direct (ideally, fiberoptic) laryngoscopy is essential to determine whether the vocal cords are functioning normally. All patients scheduled for thyroidectomy should be euthyroid at the time of operation; in all other respects, they should be prepared as they would be for any procedure calling for general anesthesia.

Optimum exposure of the thyroid is obtained by placing a sandbag between the scapula and a foam ring under the occiput; in this way, the neck is extended, and the thyroid can assume a more anterior position. The head must be well supported to prevent postoperative posterior neck pain. The patient is placed in a 20° reverse Trendelenburg position. The skin is prepared with 1% iodine or chlorhexidine.

OPERATIVE TECHNIQUE

General Troubleshooting

Thyroid and parathyroid operations should be performed in a blood-free field so that vital structures can be identified. Operating telescopes (magnification: ×2.5 or ×3.5) are also recommended because they make it easier to identify the normal parathyroid glands and the recurrent laryngeal nerve. If bleeding occurs, pressure should be applied. The vessel should be clamped only if (1) it can be precisely identified or (2) the recurrent laryngeal nerve has been identified and is not in close proximity to the vessel.

As a rule, dissection should always be done first on the side where the suspected tumor is; if there is a problem with the dissection on this side, a less than total thyroidectomy can be performed on the contralateral side to prevent complications. There is, however, one exception to this rule: if the tumor is very extensive, the surgeon will sometimes find it easier to do the dissection on the "easy" side first to facilitate orientation with respect to the trachea and the esophagus.

Step 1: Incision and Mobilization of Skin Layers

A Kocher transverse incision paralleling the normal skin lines of the neck is made 1 cm caudad to the cricoid cartilage [*see Figure 1*]. As a rule, the incision should be about 4 to 6 cm long and should extend from the anterior border of one sternocleidomastoid muscle to the anterior border of the other and through the platysma. Five straight Kelly clamps are placed on the dermis to facilitate dissection, which proceeds first cephalad in a

subplatysmal plane anterior to the anterior jugular veins and posterior to the platysma to the level of the thyroid cartilage notch and then caudad to the suprasternal notch. Skin towels and a self-retaining retractor are then applied.

Troubleshooting Placing the incision 1 cm below the cricoid locates it precisely over the isthmus of the thyroid gland. The course of the incision should conform to the normal skin lines or creases. The length of the incision should be modified as necessary for good exposure. Patients with short, thick necks, low-lying thyroid glands, or large thyroid tumors require longer incisions than those with long, thin necks and small tumors. Patients whose necks do not extend also require longer incisions for adequate exposure. A sterile marking pen should be used to mark the midline of the neck, the level at which the incision should be made (i.e., 1 cm below the cricoid), and the lateral margins of the incision (which should be at equal distances from the midline so that the incision will be symmetrical). A scalpel should never be used to mark the neck: doing so will leave an unsightly scar in some patients. To mark the incision site itself, a 2-0 silk tie should be pressed against the neck [*see Figure 1*].

The upper flap is dissected first by placing five straight Kelly clamps on the dermis and retracting anteriorly and superiorly. Lateral traction with a vein retractor or an Army-Navy retractor

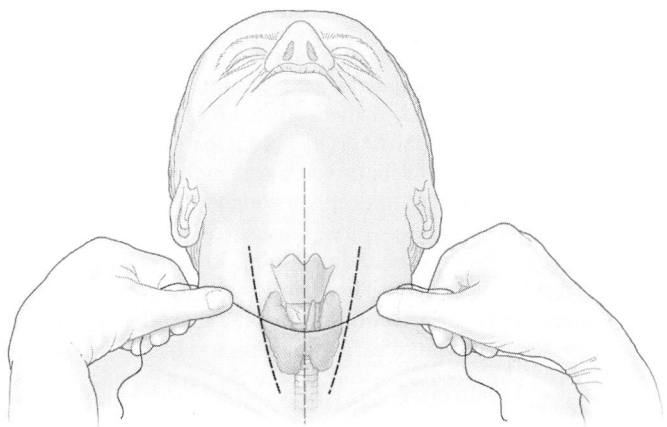

Figure 1 The initial incision in a thyroidectomy is made 1 cm below the cricoid cartilage and follows normal skin lines. A sterile marking pen is used to mark the midline of the neck, the level of the incision, and the lateral borders of the incision. A 2-0 silk tie is pressed against the neck to mark the incision site itself.[2]

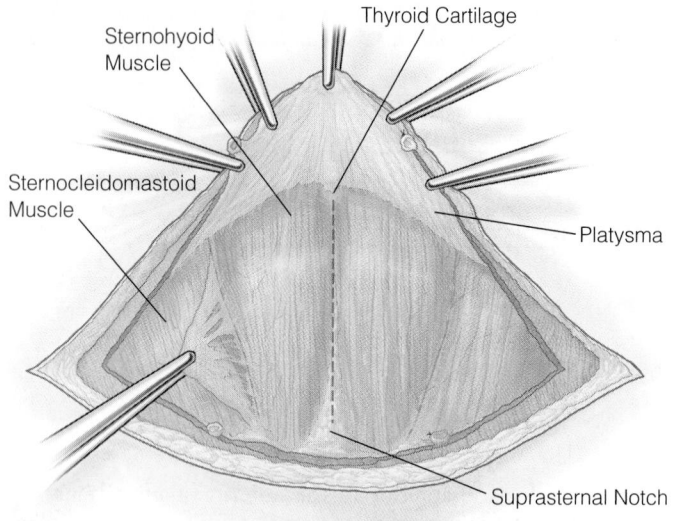

Figure 2 To expose the thyroid, a midline incision is made through the superficial layer of deep cervical fascia between the strap muscles. The incision is begun at the suprasternal notch and extended to the thyroid cartilage.[3]

helps identify the semilunar plane for dissection. This blood-free plane is deep to the platysma and superficial to the anterior jugular veins. Cephalad dissection can be done quickly with the electrocautery or a scalpel, and lateral dissection can be done bluntly. The same principles are applied to dissection of the lower flap. In thin patients, the surgeon must be careful not to dissect through the skin from within, especially at the level of the thyroid cartilage.

Step 2: Midline Dissection and Mobilization of Strap Muscles

The thyroid gland is exposed via a midline incision through the superficial layer of deep cervical fascia between the strap muscles. Because the strap muscles are farthest apart just above the suprasternal notch, the incision is begun at the notch and extended to the thyroid cartilage [*see Figure 2*].

On the side where the thyroid nodule or the suspected parathyroid adenoma is located, the more superficial sternohyoid muscle is separated from the underlying sternothyroid muscle by blunt dissection, which is extended laterally until the ansa cervicalis becomes visible on the lateral edge of the sternothyroid muscle and on the medial side of the internal jugular vein. The sternothyroid muscle is then dissected free from the thyroid and the prethyroidal fascia by blunt or sharp dissection until the middle thyroid vein or veins are encountered laterally.

A 2-0 silk suture is placed deeply through the thyroid lobe for retraction to facilitate exposure. This stitch should never be placed through the thyroid nodule: doing so could cause seeding of thyroid cancer cells. The thyroid is retracted anteriorly and medially and the carotid sheath laterally; this retraction places tension on the middle thyroid veins and helps expose the area posterolateral to the thyroid, where the parathyroid glands and the recurrent laryngeal nerves are situated. The middle thyroid veins are divided to give better exposure behind the superior portion of the thyroid lobe [*see Figure 3*].

Troubleshooting As a rule, it is not necessary to divide the strap muscles; however, if they are adherent to the underlying thyroid tumor, the portion of the muscle that is adhering to the

tumor should be sacrificed and allowed to remain attached to the thyroid. Separation of the sternohyoid muscle from the sternothyroid muscle provides better exposure of the operative field. The middle thyroid veins should be cleaned of adjacent tissues to prevent any injury to the recurrent laryngeal nerve when these veins are ligated and divided. It is always safest to mobilize tissues parallel to the recurrent laryngeal nerve.

Step 3: Division of Isthmus

When a thyroid lobectomy is to be performed, the isthmus of the thyroid gland is usually divided with Dandy or Colodny clamps at an early point in dissection to facilitate the subsequent mobilization of the thyroid gland. The thyroid tissue that is to remain is oversewn with a 2-0 silk ligature. To minimize the chance of invasion into the trachea or to avoid a visible mass in patients with compensatory thyroid hypertrophy, thyroid tissues should not be left anterior to the trachea.

Troubleshooting With larger glands, we divide the isthmus first. This step facilitates the lateral dissection by making the gland more mobile.

Step 4: Mobilization of Thyroid Gland and Identification of Upper Parathyroid Glands

Once the isthmus has been divided, dissection is continued superiorly, laterally, and posteriorly with a small peanut sponge on a clamp. The superior thyroid artery and veins are identified by retracting the thyroid inferiorly and medially. The tissues lateral to the upper lobe of the thyroid and medial to the carotid sheath can be mobilized caudally to the cricothyroid muscle; the recurrent laryngeal nerve enters the cricothyroid muscle at the level of the cricoid cartilage, first passing through Berry's ligament [*see Figure 4*]. The superior pole vessels are individually identified, skeletonized, double- or triple-clamped, ligated, and divided low on the thyroid gland [*see Figure 5*]. To prevent injury to the external laryngeal nerve, the vessels are divided and ligated on the thyroid surface, the thyroid is retracted laterally and caudally, and dissection is carried out on the medial edge of the thyroid gland and lateral to the cricothyroid muscle. As alternatives to

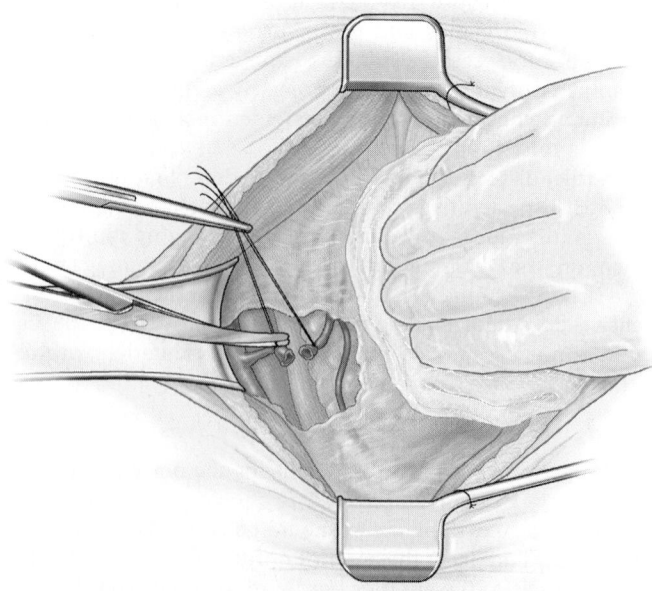

Figure 3 The middle thyroid veins are divided to give better exposure behind the superior portion of the thyroid lobe.[2]

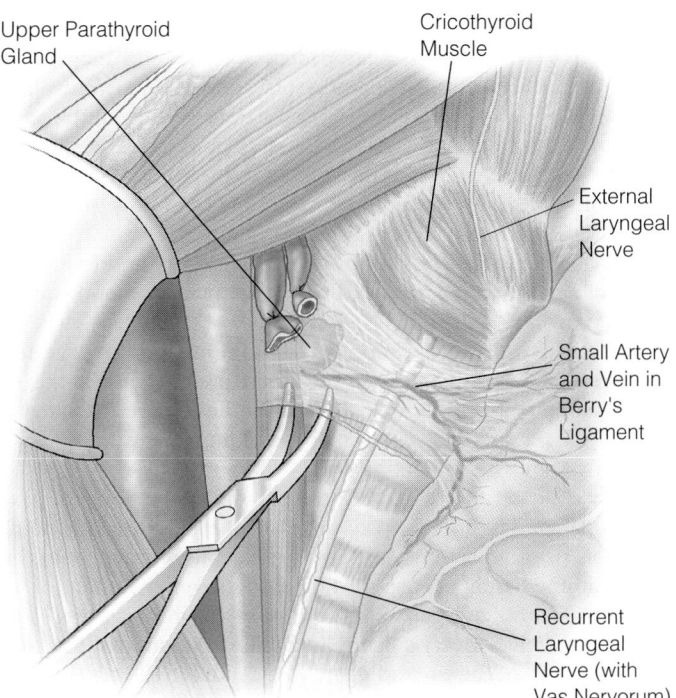

Figure 4 **The recurrent laryngeal nerve enters the cricothyroid muscle at the level of the cricoid cartilage, first passing through Berry's ligament.**[2]

sutures, devices such as the Harmonic Scalpel (Ethicon Endo-Surgery, Inc.), the Ligasure Precise (Valleylab), and the Hem-o-lok clip (Weck Closure Systems) may be used to control vessels.

The tissues posterior and lateral to the superior pole that have not already been mobilized can now be easily swept by blunt dissection away from the thyroid gland medially and anteriorly and away from the carotid sheath laterally. The upper parathyroid gland is often identified at this time at the level of the cricoid cartilage.

Troubleshooting It is essential to keep from injuring the external laryngeal nerve. This nerve is the motor branch of the superior laryngeal nerve and is responsible for tensing the vocal cords; it is also known as the high note nerve or the Amelita Galli-Curci nerve. In about 80% of patients, the external laryngeal nerve runs on the surface of the cricothyroid muscle; in about 10%, it runs with the superior pole vessels; and in the remaining 10%, it runs within the cricothyroid muscle. Given that this nerve is usually about the size of a single strand of a spider web, one should generally try to avoid it rather than to identify it. Injury to the external laryngeal nerve occurs in as many as 10% of patients undergoing thyroidectomy. The best ways of preventing such injury are (1) to provide gentle traction on the thyroid gland in a caudal and lateral direction and (2) to ligate the superior pole vessels directly on the capsule of the upper pole individually and low on the thyroid gland rather than to cross-clamp the entire superior pole pedicle.

The internal laryngeal nerve is the sensory branch of the superior laryngeal nerve; it provides sensory innervation to the posterior pharynx. Injury to this nerve can result in aspiration. Because the internal laryngeal nerve typically is cephalad to the area of dissection during thyroidectomy and runs cephalad to the lateral portion of the thyroid cartilage, it usually is at risk only when the surgeon dissects cephalad to the thyroid carti-

lage. Such dissection is necessary only when laryngeal mobilization is performed to relieve tension on the tracheal anastomosis after tracheal resection.

Step 5: Identification of Recurrent Laryngeal Nerves and Lower Parathyroid Glands

When the thyroid lobe is further mobilized, the lower parathyroid gland is usually seen; this gland is almost always located anterior to the recurrent laryngeal nerve and is usually located inferior to where the inferior thyroid artery crosses the recurrent laryngeal nerve [*see Figure 6*]. The carotid sheath is retracted laterally, and the thyroid gland is retracted anteriorly and medially. This retraction puts tension on the inferior thyroid artery and consequently on the recurrent laryngeal nerve, thereby facilitating the identification of the nerve. The recurrent laryngeal nerve is situated more medially on the left (running in the tracheoesophageal groove) and more obliquely on the right. Dissection should proceed cephalad along the lateral edge of the thyroid. Fatty and lymphatic tissues immediately adjacent to the thyroid gland are swept from it with a peanut sponge on a clamp, and small vessels are ligated. No tissue should be transected until one is sure that it is not the recurrent laryngeal nerve.

Troubleshooting The upper parathyroid glands are usually situated on each side of the thyroid gland at the level where the recurrent laryngeal nerve enters the cricothyroid muscle [*see Figure 6*]. Because the recurrent laryngeal nerve enters the cricothyroid muscle at the level of the cricoid cartilage, the area cephalad to the cricoid cartilage is relatively safe.

The right and left recurrent laryngeal nerves must be preserved during every thyroid operation. Although both nerves enter at the posterior medial position of the larynx in the cricothyroid muscle, their courses vary considerably. The right recurrent laryngeal nerve takes a more oblique course than the left recurrent laryngeal nerve and may pass either anterior or

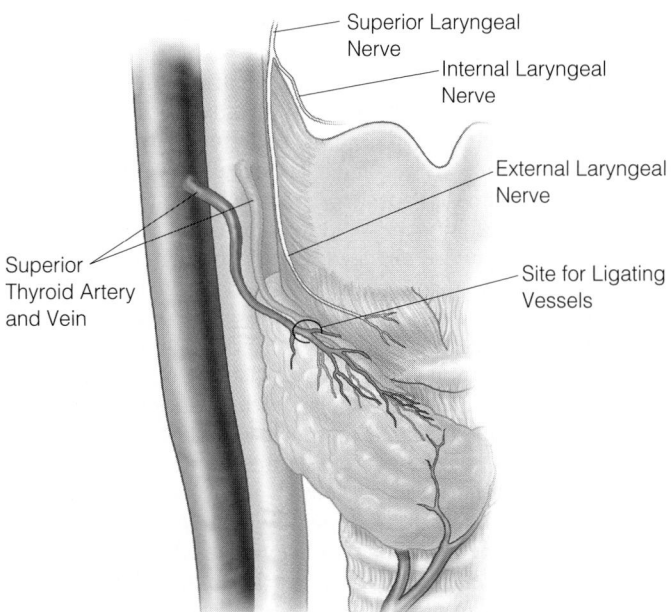

Figure 5 **The superior pole vessels should be individually identified and ligated low and laterally on the thyroid gland to minimize the chances of injury to the external laryngeal nerve.**[2]

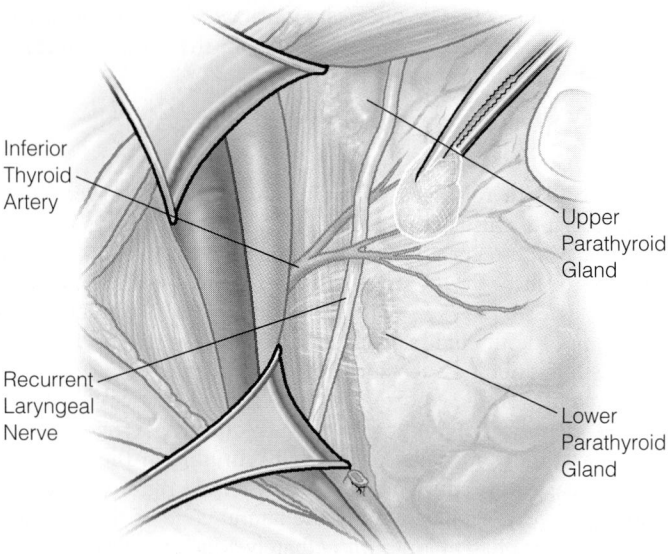

Inferior
Thyroid
Artery

Recurrent
Laryngeal
Nerve

Upper
Parathyroid
Gland

Lower
Parathyroid
Gland

Figure 6 **The upper parathyroid glands are usually situated on either side of the thyroid at the level where the recurrent laryngeal nerve enters the cricothyroid muscle. The lower parathyroid glands are usually anterior to the recurrent laryngeal nerve and inferior to where the inferior thyroid artery crosses this nerve.**[2]

posterior to the inferior thyroid artery. In about 0.5% of persons, the right recurrent laryngeal nerve is in fact nonrecurrent and may enter the thyroid from a superior or lateral direction.[1] On rare occasions, both a recurrent and a nonrecurrent laryngeal nerve may be present on the right. The left recurrent laryngeal nerve almost always runs in the tracheoesophageal groove because of its deeper origin within the thorax as it loops around the ductus arteriosus. Either recurrent laryngeal nerve may branch before entering the larynx; the left nerve is more likely to do this. Such branching is important to recognize because all of the motor fibers of the recurrent laryngeal nerve are usually in the most medial branch.

In identifying the recurrent laryngeal nerves, it is helpful to remember that they are supplied by a small vascular plexus and that a tiny vessel runs parallel to and directly on each nerve [see *Figures 4 and 6*]. In young persons, the artery usually is readily distinguished from the recurrent laryngeal nerve; however, in older persons with arteriosclerosis, the white-appearing artery may be mistaken for a nerve, and thus the nerve may be injured as a result of the misidentification. Lateral traction on the carotid sheath and medial and anterior traction on the thyroid gland place tension on the inferior thyroid artery; this maneuver often helps identify the recurrent laryngeal nerve where it courses lateral to the midportion of the thyroid gland. One should, however, be careful not to devascularize the inferior parathyroid glands by dividing the lateral vascular attachments: to remove the thyroid lobe, it is best to divide the vessels directly on the thyroid capsule to preserve the blood supply to the parathyroid glands. It is usually safest to identify the recurrent laryngeal nerve low in the neck and then to follow it to where it enters the cricothyroid muscle through Berry's ligament. The recurrent laryngeal nerves can usually be palpated through the surrounding tissue in the neck; they feel like a taut ligature of approximately 2-0 gauge.

Parathyroid glands should be swept from the thyroid gland on as broad a vascular pedicle as possible to prevent devascu-

larization. When it is unclear whether a parathyroid gland can be saved on its own vascular pedicle, one should biopsy the gland to confirm that it is parathyroid and then autotransplant it in multiple 1 × 1 mm pieces into separate pockets in the sternocleidomastoid muscle. At times, it is preferable to clip the blood vessels running from the thyroid to the parathyroid glands rather than to clamp and tie them. Clipping not only marks the parathyroid gland (which is useful if another operation subsequently becomes necessary) but also enables the gland to remain with minimal manipulation and with its remaining blood supply preserved.

In patients who have extensive thyroid tumors or who require reoperation, extensive scarring is often present. For some of these patients, it is preferable to identify the recurrent laryngeal nerve from a medial approach by dividing the isthmus with Colodny clamps and ligating and dividing the superior thyroid vessels. By carefully dissecting the thyroid away from the trachea, one can identify the recurrent laryngeal nerve at the point where its position is most consistent (i.e., at its entrance into the larynx immediately posterior to the cricothyroid muscle).

The most difficult part of dissection in a thyroidectomy is the part that involves Berry's ligament, which is situated at the posterior portion of the thyroid gland just caudal to the cricoid cartilage [see *Figure 4*]. A small branch of the inferior thyroid artery traverses the ligament, as do one or more veins from the thyroid gland. If bleeding occurs during this part of the dissection, it should be controlled by applying pressure with a gauze pad. Nothing should be clamped in this area until the recurrent laryngeal nerve is identified. In some patients (about 15%), the peduncle of Zuckerkandl, a small protuberance of thyroid tissue on the right, tends to obscure the recurrent laryngeal nerve at the level of Berry's ligament.

Step 6: Mobilization of Pyramidal Lobe

The pyramidal lobe is found in about 80% of patients. It extends in a cephalad direction, often through the notch in the thyroid cartilage to the hyoid bone. One or more lymph nodes are frequently found just cephalad to the isthmus of the thyroid gland over the cricothyroid membrane (so-called Delphian nodes) [see *Figure 7*]. The pyramidal lobe is mobilized by retracting it caudally and by dissecting immediately adjacent to it in a cephalad direction. Small vessels are coagulated or ligated.

Step 7: Thyroid Resection

Once the parathyroid glands have been carefully swept or dissected from the thyroid gland and the recurrent nerve has been identified, the thyroid lobe can be quickly resected. For total thyroidectomy, the same operation is done again on the other side.

Troubleshooting The thyroid lobe or gland should be carefully examined after removal. If a parathyroid gland is identified, a biopsy of it should be performed to confirm that it is parathyroid and then autotransplanted. In a thyroid procedure, every parathyroid gland should be treated as if it is the last one, and at least one parathyroid gland should be definitely identified. As a rule, biopsies should not be performed on normal parathyroid glands during a thyroid procedure.

Step 8: Closure

The sternothyroid muscles are approximated with 4-0 absorbable sutures, and a small opening is left in the midline at the suprasternal notch to make any bleeding that occurs more evident and to allow the blood to exit. The sternohyoid muscles are reapproximated in a similar fashion, as is the platysma. The skin is then closed with butterfly clips, which are hemostatic and inexpensive and permit precise alignment of the skin edges. In children, the skin is usually closed with a subcuticular stitch or a tissue adhesive (e.g., Indermil; Tyco Healthcare), or both, instead. A sterile pressure dressing is applied.

Special Concerns

Invasion of the trachea or the esophagus   On rare occasions, thyroid or parathyroid cancers may invade the trachea or the esophagus. As much as 5 cm of the trachea can be resected safely, without impairment of the patient's voice. If the invasion is not extensive and is confined to the anterior portion of the trachea, a small section of the trachea that contains the tumor should be excised, and a tracheostomy may be placed at the site of resection. If the invasion is more extensive or occurs in the lateral or posterior portion of the trachea, a segment of the trachea measuring several centimeters long is resected, and the remaining segments are reanastomosed. To prevent tension on the anastomosis, the trachea should be mobilized before resection, the recurrent laryngeal nerves should be preserved and mobilized from the trachea, and the mylohyoid fascia and muscles should be divided above the thyroid cartilage to drop the cartilage. Care must be taken not to injure the internal laryngeal nerves during this dissection, given that these nerves course from lateral to medial just above the lateral aspects of the thyroid cartilage. After resection, the trachea is reapproximated with 3-0 Maxon sutures. One or two Penrose drains should be left near the resection site to allow air to exit. The drains are removed after several days, when there is no more evidence of air leakage.

If the esophagus is invaded by tumor, the muscular wall of the esophagus can be resected along with the tumor, with the inner esophageal layer left in place.

Neck dissection for nodal metastases   Lymph nodes in the central neck (medial to the carotid sheath) are frequently involved in patients with papillary, medullary, and Hürthle cell cancer. These nodes should be removed without injury to the parathyroid glands or the recurrent laryngeal nerves. In most patients, it is relatively easy to remove all tissue between the carotid sheath and the trachea. In some patients with extensive lymphadenopathy, it is necessary to remove the parathyroids, perform biopsies on them to confirm that they are in fact parathyroid, and autotransplant them into the sternocleidomastoid muscle.

When lymph nodes are palpable in the lateral neck, a modified neck dissection is performed through a lateral extension of the Kocher collar incision to the anterior margin of the trapezius muscle (a MacFee incision). The jugular vein, the spinal accessory nerve, the phrenic nerve, the vagus nerve, the cervical sympathetic nerves, and the sternocleidomastoid muscle are preserved unless they are directly adherent to or invaded by tumor.

In patients with medullary thyroid cancer, a meticulous and thorough central neck dissection is necessary. When a primary medullary tumor is larger than 1 cm or the central neck nodes are obviously involved, these patients will also benefit from a lateral modified radical neck dissection (with the structures just mentioned preserved). During the dissection, all fibrofatty lymph node tissues should be removed from the level of the clavicle to the level of the hyoid bone. The deep dissection plane is developed anterior to the scalenus anticus muscle, the brachial plexus, and the scalenus medius muscle. The phrenic nerve runs obliquely on the scalenus anticus muscle. The cervical sensory nerves can usually be preserved unless there is extensive tumor involvement.

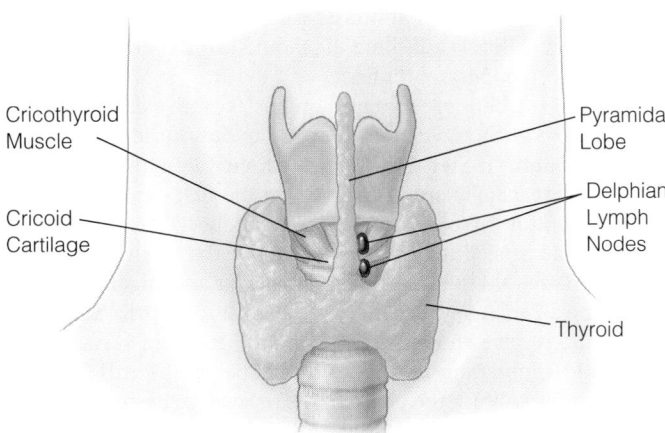

Figure 7   **Delphian lymph nodes may be found just cephalad to the isthmus over the cricothyroid membrane.**

Median sternotomy   A median sternotomy is rarely necessary for removal of the thyroid gland because the blood supply to the thyroid gland, the thymus, and the lower parathyroid glands derives primarily from the inferior thyroid arteries in the neck. Metastatic lymph nodes frequently extend inferiorly in the tracheoesophageal groove into the superior mediastinum; these nodes can almost always be removed through a cervical incision without any need for a sternotomy. On rare occasions, metastatic nodes spread to the aortic pulmonary window and can be identified preoperatively on CT or MRI. If a median sternotomy proves necessary, the sternum should be divided to the level of the third intercostal space and then laterally on one side at the space between the third rib and the fourth. Median sternotomy provides excellent exposure of the upper anterior mediastinum and the lower neck.

POSTOPERATIVE CARE

The duration of a thyroid operation is 1 to 3 hours, depending on the size and invasiveness of the tumor, its vascularity, and the location of the parathyroid glands. Postoperatively, the patient is kept in a low Fowler position with the head and shoulders elevated 10° to 20° for 6 to 12 hours to maintain negative pressure in the veins. The patient typically resumes eating within 3 to 4 hours, and an antiemetic is ordered as needed (many patients experience postoperative nausea and emesis).

The serum calcium level is measured approximately 5 to 8 hours after operation in patients who have undergone bilateral procedures; no tests are required in those who have undergone unilateral procedures. On the first morning after the thyroidectomy, the serum calcium and serum phosphate levels are measured. If the patient is still hospitalized on postoperative day 2, these tests are repeated on the second morning as well. Oral calcium supplements are given if the serum calcium is below 7.5 mg/dl or if the patient experiences perioral numbness or tingling. A low serum phosphate level (< 2.5 mg/dl) usually is a sign of so-called bone hunger and suggests that there is little reason to be concerned about permanent hypoparathyroidism, whereas a high level (> 4.5 mg/dl) should prompt concern about permanent hypoparathyroidism.

The surgical clips are removed on postoperative day 1, and tissue adhesive or Steri-Strips are applied to prevent tension on the healing wound. (If Steri-Strips are used, they are removed on day 10.) Patients usually are discharged on the first day, are given a prescription for thyroid hormone (L-thyroxine, 0.1 to 0.2 mg/day orally) if the procedure was more extensive than a thyroid lobectomy, and are told to take calcium tablets for any tingling or muscle cramps. Patients with papillary, follicular, or Hürthle cell cancer should receive enough L-thyroxine to keep their serum levels of thyroid-stimulating hormone (TSH) below 0.1 mIU/ml. On postoperative day 10, the pathology is reviewed, and further management is discussed in the light of the pathologic findings. In patients with thyroid cancer, values for serum calcium, TSH, and thyroglobulin are obtained; in patients with coexisting hyperparathyroidism, values for serum calcium, phosphorus, and parathyroid hormone (PTH) are obtained.

COMPLICATIONS

The following are the most significant complications of thyroidectomy.

1. Injury to the recurrent laryngeal nerve. Bilateral injury to the recurrent laryngeal nerve may result in vocal cord paresis and stridor and may have to be treated with a tracheostomy.
2. Hypoparathyroidism. This complication may arise as the result of removal of, injury to, or devascularization of the parathyroid glands. As noted [see Operative Technique, above], we recommend leaving parathyroid glands on their own vascular pedicle; however, if one is concerned about possible devascularization of a parathyroid, biopsy should be performed on the gland to confirm its identity and then autotransplanted in 1 × 1 mm pieces into separate pockets in the sternocleidomastoid muscle.
3. Bleeding. Postoperative bleeding can be life threatening in that it can compromise the airway. Any postoperative respiratory distress can be thought of as attributable to a neck hematoma until proved otherwise. Most bleeding occurs within four hours of operation, and virtually all occurs within 24 hours.
4. Injury to the external laryngeal nerve [see Operative Technique, above].
5. Infection. This complication is quite rare after thyroidectomy. Any patient with acute pharyngitis should not undergo this procedure.
6. Seroma. Most seromas are small and resorb spontaneously; some must be aspirated.
7. Keloid. Keloid formation after thyroidectomy is most common in African-American patients and in patients with a history of keloids.
8. There are a number of miscellaneous complications that are somewhat less common.

OUTCOME EVALUATION

Most patients can return to work or full activity in 1 to 2 weeks. Patients with benign lesions who have undergone hemithyroidectomy may or may not require thyroid hormone; those with multinodular goiter, thyroiditis, or occult papillary cancer typically do, whereas those with follicular adenoma typically do not. Patients who have undergone total or near-total thyroidectomy will require thyroid hormone. Patients with papillary or follicular cancer who have undergone total or near-total thyroidectomy appear to benefit from radioactive iodine scanning and therapy. (It is necessary to discontinue L-thyroxine for 6 to 8 weeks and L-triiodothyronine for 2 weeks before scanning.) Those considered to be at low risk (age < 45 years, tumor confined to the thyroid and not invasive, and tumor diameter < 4 cm) may receive radioactive iodine on an outpatient basis in a dose of approximately 30 mCi. Those who are considered to be at high risk should receive approximately 100 to 150 mCi. Long-term (20-year) mortality is about 4% in low-risk patients and about 40% in high-risk patients. Serum thyroglobulin levels should be determined before and after discontinuance of thyroid hormone; such levels are very sensitive indicators of persistent thyroid disease after total thyroidectomy.

Parathyroidectomy

OPERATIVE PLANNING

The preparation for parathyroidectomy is the same as that for thyroidectomy. Patients who have profound hypercalcemia (serum calcium ≥ 12.5 mg/dl) or mild to moderate renal failure should be vigorously hydrated and given furosemide before operation. On rare occasions, such patients require additional treatment—for example, administration of diphosphonates, mithramycin, or calcitonin. Any electrolyte abnormalities (e.g., hypokalemia) should be corrected.

We recommend either bilateral exploration or focused exploration with intraoperative PTH assay for most patients undergoing initial operations for primary sporadic hyperparathyroidism. The latter approach can be taken only when the abnormal gland has been identified by sestamibi scanning. For patients with familial primary hyperparathyroidism or secondary hyperparathyroidism, bilateral exploration is recommended because most of these patients have multiple abnormal parathyroid glands.

Preoperative localization studies (e.g., ultrasonography, MRI, sestamibi scanning, and CT scanning) are generally unnecessary: they provide useful information in about 75% of patients, but they are often not considered cost-effective, because an experienced surgeon can treat hyperparathyroidism successfully 95% to 98% of the time. Such studies are, however, essential when reoperation for persistent or recurrent hyperparathyroidism is indicated and when a focused approach with intraoperative PTH assay is to be used. We do not believe that using the gamma probe is any better than preoperative sestamibi scanning. All patients requiring reoperation should undergo direct or indirect laryngoscopy before operation for evaluation of vocal cord function.

OPERATIVE TECHNIQUE

Steps 1 through 4

Steps 1, 2, 3, and 4 of a parathyroidectomy are virtually identical to steps 1, 2, 4, and 5 of a thyroidectomy (see above), and essentially the same troubleshooting considerations apply.

Troubleshooting About 85% of people have four parathyroid glands, and in about 85% of these persons, the parathyroids are situated on the posterior lateral capsule of the thyroid. Normal parathyroid glands measure about 3 × 3 × 4 mm and are light brown in color. The upper parathyroid glands are more posterior (i.e., dorsal) and more constant in position (at the level of the cricoid cartilage) than the lower parathyroid glands, which typically are more anteriorly placed (on the posterior-lateral surface of the thyroid gland). Both the upper and the lower parathyroid glands are supplied by small branches of the inferior and superior thyroid arteries in most patients. About 15% of parathyroid glands are situated within the thymus gland, and about 1% are intrathyroidal. Other abnormal sites for the parathyroid glands are (1) the carotid sheath, (2) the anterior and posterior mediastinum, and (3) anterior to the carotid bulb or along the pharynx (undescended parathyroids).

The upper parathyroid glands are usually lateral to the recurrent laryngeal nerve at the level of Berry's ligament; their position makes them generally easier to preserve during thyroidectomy and easier to find during both parathyroid and thyroid surgery. When the upper parathyroids are not found at this site, they often can be found in the tracheoesophageal groove or in the posterior mediastinum along the esophagus. The lower parathyroid glands are almost always situated anterior to the recurrent laryngeal nerves and caudal to where the recurrent laryngeal nerve crosses the inferior thyroid artery; they may be surrounded by lymph nodes. When the lower parathyroids are not found at this site, they usually can be found in the anterior mediastinum (typically in the thymus or the thymic fat).

Step 5: Parathyroid Resection

Abnormal parathyroid glands are removed. In about 80% of patients with primary hyperparathyroidism, one parathyroid gland is abnormal; in about 15%, all glands are abnormal (diffuse hyperplasia); and in about 5%, two or three glands are abnormal and one or two normal. Parathyroid cancer occurs in about 1% of patients with primary hyperparathyroidism. About 50% of patients with parathyroid cancer have a palpable tumor, and most exhibit profound hypercalcemia (serum calcium ≥ 14.0 mg/dl).

Troubleshooting   In some patients, parathyroid tumors and hyperplastic parathyroid glands are difficult to find. If this is the case, the first step is to explore the sites where parathyroids are usually located, near the posterolateral surface of the thyroid gland. (About 80% of parathyroid glands are situated within 1 cm of the point where the inferior thyroid artery crosses the recurrent laryngeal nerve.) When a lower gland is missing from the usual location, it is likely to be found in the thymus; this possibility can be confirmed by mobilizing the thymus from the anterior-superior mediastinum. In all, about 15% of parathyroid glands are found within the thymus. If an upper parathyroid gland cannot be located, one should look not only far behind the thyroid gland superiorly but also in a paraesophageal position down into the posterior mediastinum. A thyroid lobectomy or thyroidotomy should be done on the side where fewer than two parathyroid glands have been located and no abnormal parathyroid tissue has been identified. The carotid sheath and the area posterior to the carotid, as well as the retroesophageal area, should also be explored. In rare cases, there may be an undescended parathyroid tumor anterior to the carotid bulb.

Although we do not recommend routine biopsy of more than one normal-appearing parathyroid gland, we do recommend biopsy (not removal) and marking of all normal parathyroid glands that have been identified when no abnormal parathyroid tissue can be found. When four normal parathyroid glands are found in the neck, the fifth (abnormal) parathyroid gland is usually in the mediastinum. The surgeon's responsibility is to make sure during parathyroidectomy that the elusive parathyroid adenoma is not in or removable through the cervical incision used for the initial operation and to minimize complications. The risk of permanent hypoparathyroidism or injury to the recurrent nerve should be less than 2%.

Step 6: Closure

Closure is essentially the same for parathyroidectomy as for thyroidectomy.

COMPLICATIONS

The complications of parathyroidectomy are similar to those of thyroidectomy but occur less often. Patients with a very high serum alkaline phosphatase level and osteitis fibrosa cystica are prone to profound hypocalcemia after parathyroidectomy. In such patients, both serum calcium and serum phosphorus levels are low. In contrast, patients with hypoparathyroidism exhibit low serum calcium levels but high serum phosphorus levels.

OUTCOME EVALUATION

Outcome considerations are essentially the same as for thyroidectomy. The patient should have a normal voice and be normocalcemic. The overall complication rate should be less than 2%.

References

1. Henry JF, Audiffret J, Denizot A, et al: The nonrecurrent inferior laryngeal nerve: review of 33 cases, including two on the left side. Surgery 104:977, 1988

2. Clark OH: Endocrine Surgery of the Thyroid and Parathyroid Glands. WB Saunders Co, Philadelphia, 2003

3. Cady B, Rossi R: Surgery of thyroid gland. Surgery of the Thyroid and Parathyroid Glands. Cady B, Rossi R, Eds. WB Saunders Co, Philadelphia, 1991

Acknowledgment

Figures 1 through 7   Tom Moore.

Recommended Reading

Chen H, Sokol LJ, Udelsman R: Outpatient minimally invasive parathyroidectomy: a combination of sestamibispect localization, cervical block anesthesia, and intraoperative parathyroid hormone assay. Surgery 126:1016, 1999

Clark OH: Total thyroidectomy and lymph node dissection for cancer of the thyroid. Mastery of Surgery, 2nd ed. Nyhus LM, Baker RJ, Eds. Little, Brown and Co, Boston, 1992, p 204

Clark OH: Total thyroid lobectomy. Atlas of Surgical Oncology. Daly JM, Cady B, Low DW, Eds. CV Mosby Co, St. Louis, 1993, p 41

Gordon LL, Snyder WH, Wians JR, et al: The validity of quick intraoperative hormone assay: an evaluation of seventy-two patients based on gross morphology criteria. Surgery 126:1030, 1999

Irvin GL, Molinari AS, Figuero C, et al: Improved success rate in reoperative parathyroidectomy with intraoperative PTH assay. Ann Surg 229:874, 1999

Tezelman S, Shen W, Shaver JK, et al: Double parathyroid adenomas: clinical and biochemical characteristics before and after parathyroidectomy. Ann Surg 218:300, 1993

21 BREAST COMPLAINTS

D. Scott Lind, M.D., F.A.C.S., *Barbara L. Smith,* M.D., Ph.D., F.A.C.S., *and Wiley W. Souba,* M.D., Sc.D., F.A.C.S.

Assessment and Management of Breast Complaints

Given that approximately one of every two women will consult a health care provider for a breast-related complaint during her lifetime,[1] all clinicians should have a fundamental understanding of the evaluation and management of breast disorders. Although most breast complaints do not result in a diagnosis of cancer, the heightened public awareness of breast cancer—currently, the most common malignancy affecting women in the United States[2]—can induce significant anxiety and a sense of urgency in women who present with symptoms suggestive of a breast disorder. Accordingly, any woman presenting with a breast complaint should receive a comprehensive evaluation.

Unfortunately, it is becoming more and more difficult for practitioners to stay current with the increasingly complex management of breast disease. Breast problems still are often written about in a manner that is more disease-focused than patient management–focused—an approach that we believe is of limited clinical utility. In this chapter, we outline the evaluation and management of the most common clinical presentations of breast disease, and we discuss specific breast disease problems in a manner clinically relevant to the practicing surgeon.

Most breast problems encountered by practicing surgeons fall into six general categories, which are associated with varying degrees of risk for breast cancer [*see Table 1*]. With some presentations, such as a dominant mass in a postmenopausal woman, the 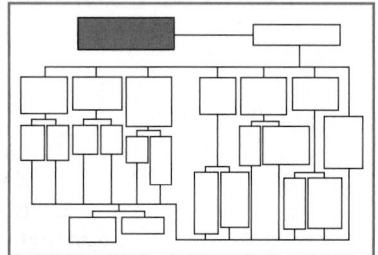 index of suspicion for malignancy is high and the workup should be prompt and relatively straightforward. With other breast presentations, such as a tender breast thickening in a premenopausal woman, benign disease is much more likely. It is important to recognize, however, that any of these presentations can be associated with a malignancy, and thus, all of them warrant a complete evaluation. In fact, it is the evaluation of the usually benign symptoms that places the greatest demands on the physician's clinical judgment. When such symptoms are the main presenting complaint of a breast cancer, their seemingly benign nature may be misleadingly reassuring and delay the diagnosis of malignancy. Missed or delayed diagnosis of breast cancer is currently a major cause of malpractice claims and plaintiff awards.[3]

Risk Factors for Breast Cancer

The fundamental task facing a physician seeing a patient with a breast complaint is to determine whether the abnormality is benign or malignant. To this end, knowledge of the main risk factors for breast cancer is essential: prompt identification of the patients at highest risk for malignancy allows the physician to take an appropriately vigorous approach from the beginning of the diagnostic workup.

Various factors that place women at increased risk for breast carcinoma have been identified [*see Table 2*].[4] These risk factors include increasing age; mutations in breast cancer risk genes (including *BRCA1* and *BRCA2, PTEN,* and *p53*) and other factors related to a family history of breast cancer[5]; hormonal and reproductive factors, including early menarche, late menopause, nulliparity, the absence of lactation,[6] and the use of exogenous hormones[4,7-12]; environmental factors, including diet and the lifestyle characteristic of developed Western nations[13-15]; certain pathologic findings within breast tissue, including previous breast cancer and various premalignant lesions[16-18]; and certain non-breast malignancies, including ovarian and endometrial carcinomas. There are also a number of molecular markers that can be correlated with prognosis, including estrogen receptor (ER) status and HER-2/*neu* gene amplification.[19]

Recognition of risk factors facilitates appropriate screening and clinical management of individual patients. It must be recognized, however, that in many women in whom breast cancer develops, known risk factors for breast carcinoma are entirely absent. The absence of these risk factors should not prevent full evaluation or biopsy of a suspicious breast lesion.

BREAST CANCER SCREENING

In the absence of a specific breast complaint, patients at risk for breast cancer may be identified through screening. The three main methods of breast cancer screening are breast self-examination (BSE), clinical breast examination (CBE), and screening

Table 1 Common Presenting Symptoms of Breast Disease

Symptom	Likelihood of Malignancy	Risk of Missed Malignancy
Palpable mass	Highest	Lowest
Abnormal mammogram with normal breast examination		
Vague thickening or nodularity		
Nipple discharge		
Breast pain		
Breast infection	Lowest	Highest

Table 2 Risk Factors for Breast Cancer

Increasing age

White race

Age at menarche ≤ 11 years

Age at menopause ≥ 55 years

Nulliparity

Age at first pregnancy ≥ 30 years

Absence of history of lactation

? Prolonged use of oral contraceptives before first pregnancy

Use of postmenopausal estrogen replacement, especially if prolonged

Use of other hormones, fertility regimens, or diethylstilbestrol

Mutations in breast cancer risk genes, including *BRCA1* and *BRCA2, PTEN,* and *p53*

Family history of breast cancer: multiple affected relatives, early onset, bilaterality

Family history of ovarian cancer: multiple affected relatives, early onset

Pathologic findings that indicate increased risk (e.g., atypical hyperplasia, lobular carcinoma in situ, proliferative fibrocystic disease)

Previous breast cancer

Previous breast problems

Previous breast operations

Previous exposure to radiation

mammography.[20] American Cancer Society screening guidelines for women aged 40 years and older specify that mammography and CBE should be included as part of an annual health examination.[21] In addition, health care providers should tell women about the benefits and limitations of BSE, stressing the importance of promptly reporting any new breast symptoms.

Breast Self-Examination

In BSE, the patient herself inspects and palpates the complete breast and the axilla. Given that women themselves detect many breast tumors, one might reasonably assume that BSE instruction would improve breast cancer detection. There is, however, no conclusive evidence that BSE is of significant value in this regard. Many self-detected tumors are in fact found incidentally, not during BSE. In addition, the best technique for BSE and the optimal frequency have not been established. The American Cancer Society recommends monthly self-examination as part of a breast cancer screening process that includes mammography and CBE.[21]

Clinical Breast Examination

In CBE, a qualified health care professional carries out a complete examination of the breast and axilla. As with BSE, there is little conclusive evidence indicating that annual or semiannual CBE increases breast cancer detection rates.[22] Nevertheless, we believe that it is prudent for the clinician to include CBE as part of the physical examination performed on every female patient.

Screening Mammography

There has been considerable debate regarding the value of screening mammography. The studies done to date suffer from flaws in the conduct of the trials and in the methods used to analyze the data. This state of affairs has led not only to uncertainty among practitioners but also to confusion among patients. Nevertheless, screening mammography is recommended by several professional societies, including both the American Cancer Society and the National Cancer Institute (NCI). The NCI continues to

evaluate data from ongoing studies and to promote and fund research aimed at developing more effective screening tools and strategies. In a statement from January 31, 2002, the NCI made the following recommendations[23]:

1. Women in their 40s should be screened every 1 to 2 years with mammography.
2. Women 50 years of age and older should be screened every 1 to 2 years.
3. Women who are at higher than average risk of breast cancer should seek expert medical advice about whether they should begin screening before 40 years of age and about the frequency of screening.

A woman should continue to undergo screening mammography as long as she is in reasonably good health and would be a candidate for treatment if cancer were detected. Thus, although no specific age has been established as a definitive cutoff point beyond which screening yields no benefit,[24] patients with comorbidities whose life expectancy is shorter than 5 years would not be expected to benefit from routine mammography.

The increased use of screening mammography has led to a dramatic rise in the number of nonpalpable breast lesions that call for tissue acquisition [*see* Investigative Studies, Biopsy, *below*]. Because primary care practitioners are the clinicians who order most screening mammograms, it is vital that they be capable of evaluating women who have abnormal results [*see* Management of Specific Breast Problems, Abnormal Mammogram, *below*].

Clinical Evaluation

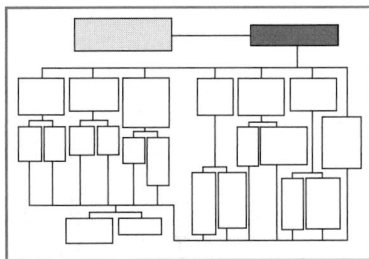

HISTORY

The first step in the evaluation of any breast complaint is a complete history. Questions should be asked regarding how long the breast complaint has been present, whether any change has been observed, and whether there are any associated symptoms. In particular, any changes in the size or tenderness of any palpable abnormalities since their initial discovery should be recorded, with special attention paid to any changes that occurred during the menstrual cycle. Previous breast problems or breast operations should also be documented, and pathology reports from any such operations should be obtained. All imaging studies or medical evaluations that have already been performed should be reviewed.

Next, the clinician should identify any risk factors for breast cancer that may be present. A reproductive history should be obtained that notes age at menarche, age at menopause, parity, and age at first full-term pregnancy. A personal or family history of breast, ovarian, or endometrial cancer and the use of oral contraceptives, fertility hormones, or postmenopausal estrogen are significant risk factors.

Approximately 10% of all breast cancers are hereditary, accounting for roughly 20,000 cases of breast cancer yearly in the United States.[25] Hereditary breast cancer is characterized by early age at onset, bilaterality, vertical transmission through both the maternal and the paternal line, and familial association with tumors of other organs, particularly the ovary and the prostate gland. Therefore, an accurate and complete family history is essential for quantifying a woman's genetic predisposition to breast cancer. Questions about breast cancer in family members should go back several generations and should extend to third-degree rela-

Assessment and Management of Breast Complaints

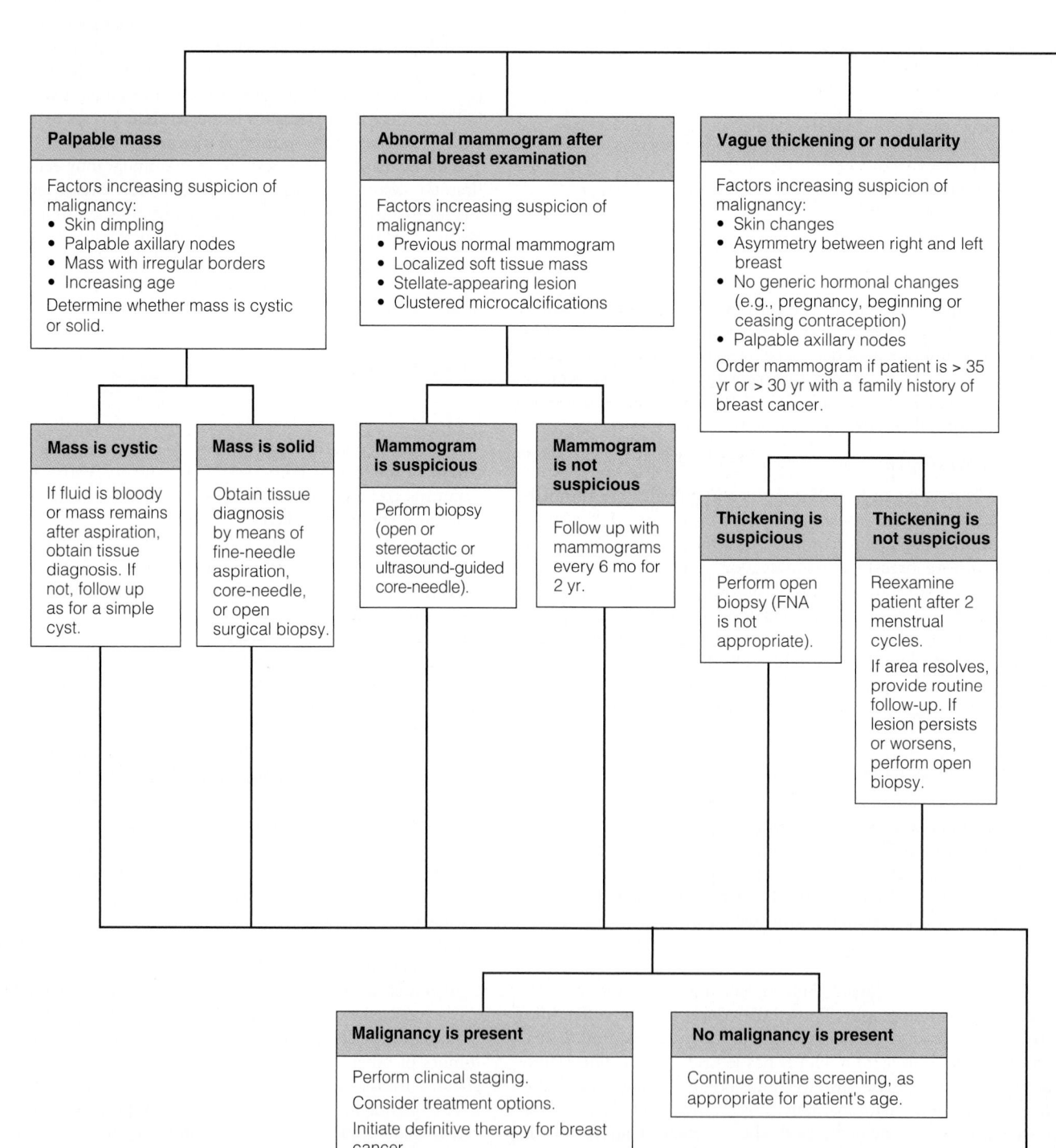

Patient presents with breast complaint

The most common presenting problems are
- Palpable mass • Normal physical examination with abnormal mammogram
- Vague thickening or nodularity • Nipple discharge • Breast pain
- Breast infection or inflammation

Evaluate likelihood that lesion reflects cancer [*see Table 1*], and be aware of patient risk factors for cancer [*see Table 2*].

Palpable mass

Factors increasing suspicion of malignancy:
- Skin dimpling
- Palpable axillary nodes
- Mass with irregular borders
- Increasing age

Determine whether mass is cystic or solid.

Abnormal mammogram after normal breast examination

Factors increasing suspicion of malignancy:
- Previous normal mammogram
- Localized soft tissue mass
- Stellate-appearing lesion
- Clustered microcalcifications

Vague thickening or nodularity

Factors increasing suspicion of malignancy:
- Skin changes
- Asymmetry between right and left breast
- No generic hormonal changes (e.g., pregnancy, beginning or ceasing contraception)
- Palpable axillary nodes

Order mammogram if patient is > 35 yr or > 30 yr with a family history of breast cancer.

Mass is cystic

If fluid is bloody or mass remains after aspiration, obtain tissue diagnosis. If not, follow up as for a simple cyst.

Mass is solid

Obtain tissue diagnosis by means of fine-needle aspiration, core-needle, or open surgical biopsy.

Mammogram is suspicious

Perform biopsy (open or stereotactic or ultrasound-guided core-needle).

Mammogram is not suspicious

Follow up with mammograms every 6 mo for 2 yr.

Thickening is suspicious

Perform open biopsy (FNA is not appropriate).

Thickening is not suspicious

Reexamine patient after 2 menstrual cycles.

If area resolves, provide routine follow-up. If lesion persists or worsens, perform open biopsy.

Malignancy is present

Perform clinical staging.

Consider treatment options.

Initiate definitive therapy for breast cancer.

No malignancy is present

Continue routine screening, as appropriate for patient's age.

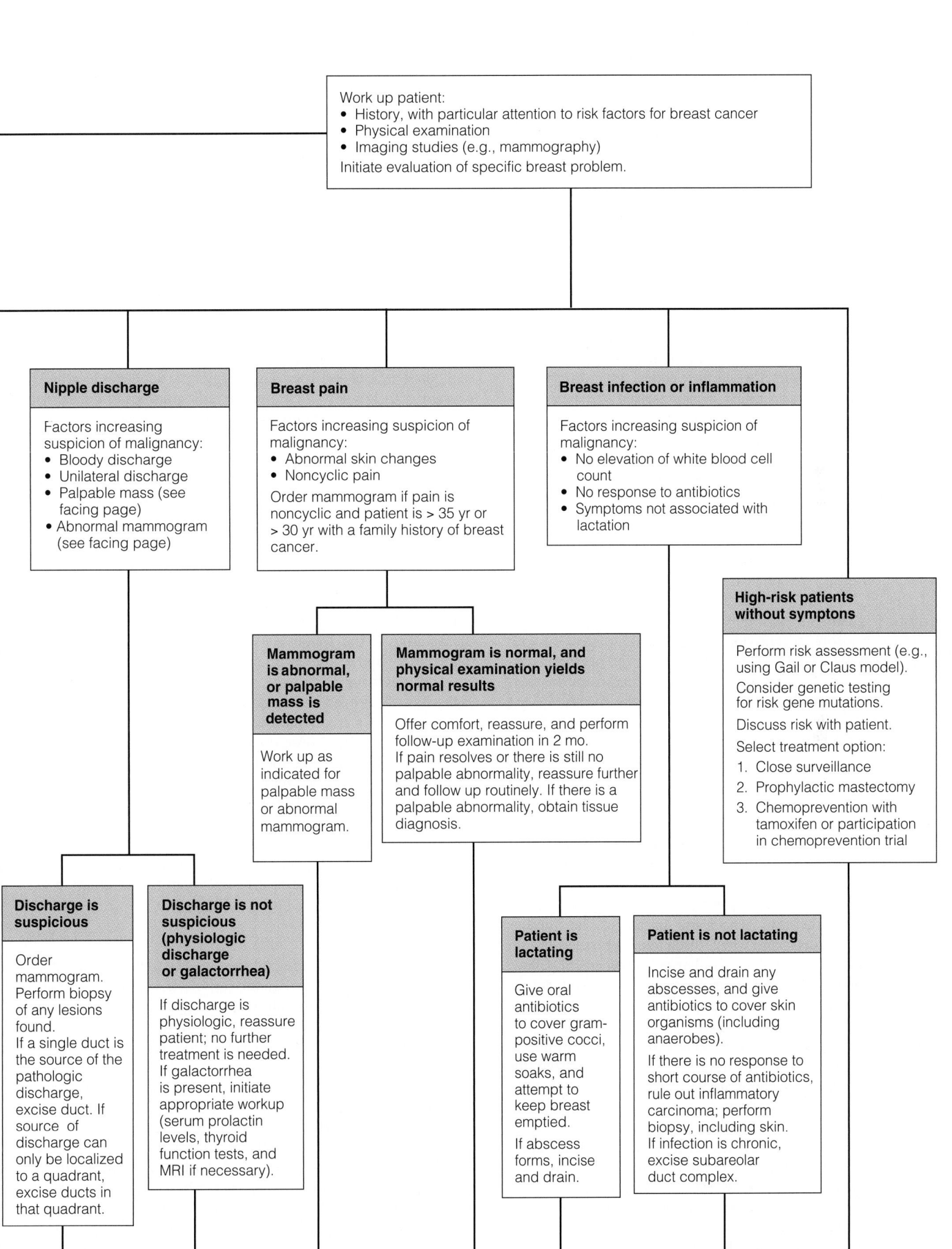

Work up patient:
- History, with particular attention to risk factors for breast cancer
- Physical examination
- Imaging studies (e.g., mammography)

Initiate evaluation of specific breast problem.

Nipple discharge

Factors increasing suspicion of malignancy:
- Bloody discharge
- Unilateral discharge
- Palpable mass (see facing page)
- Abnormal mammogram (see facing page)

Breast pain

Factors increasing suspicion of malignancy:
- Abnormal skin changes
- Noncyclic pain

Order mammogram if pain is noncyclic and patient is > 35 yr or > 30 yr with a family history of breast cancer.

Breast infection or inflammation

Factors increasing suspicion of malignancy:
- No elevation of white blood cell count
- No response to antibiotics
- Symptoms not associated with lactation

Mammogram is abnormal, or palpable mass is detected

Work up as indicated for palpable mass or abnormal mammogram.

Mammogram is normal, and physical examination yields normal results

Offer comfort, reassure, and perform follow-up examination in 2 mo. If pain resolves or there is still no palpable abnormality, reassure further and follow up routinely. If there is a palpable abnormality, obtain tissue diagnosis.

High-risk patients without symptons

Perform risk assessment (e.g., using Gail or Claus model).

Consider genetic testing for risk gene mutations.

Discuss risk with patient.

Select treatment option:
1. Close surveillance
2. Prophylactic mastectomy
3. Chemoprevention with tamoxifen or participation in chemoprevention trial

Discharge is suspicious

Order mammogram. Perform biopsy of any lesions found. If a single duct is the source of the pathologic discharge, excise duct. If source of discharge can only be localized to a quadrant, excise ducts in that quadrant.

Discharge is not suspicious (physiologic discharge or galactorrhea)

If discharge is physiologic, reassure patient; no further treatment is needed. If galactorrhea is present, initiate appropriate workup (serum prolactin levels, thyroid function tests, and MRI if necessary).

Patient is lactating

Give oral antibiotics to cover gram-positive cocci, use warm soaks, and attempt to keep breast emptied.

If abscess forms, incise and drain.

Patient is not lactating

Incise and drain any abscesses, and give antibiotics to cover skin organisms (including anaerobes).

If there is no response to short course of antibiotics, rule out inflammatory carcinoma; perform biopsy, including skin. If infection is chronic, excise subareolar duct complex.

tives, with age at diagnosis recorded if available. Similarly, any family history of ovarian or other cancers (particularly those that developed when the relative was young) should be recorded, along with age at diagnosis. Any personal history of cancer should be recorded, with particular attention paid to breast, ovarian, and endometrial cancers. Previous exposure to radiation, especially in the area of the chest wall, should be noted. Admittedly, it is not always possible to obtain complete and precise family history data, whether because of time constraints or because of family issues such as premature deaths, small family size, and distant or broken families.

It is difficult for practicing surgeons to stay current with the explosive growth of knowledge related to the genetics of breast cancer. Researchers have identified two genes—*BRCA1* and *BRCA2*—that are associated with an inherited predisposition to breast and ovarian cancers. Specific founder mutations in *BRCA1* and *BRCA2* are found within certain ethnic groups (e.g., Ashkenazi Jews).[26] Tests are commercially available that detect mutations in these genes. Whether to pursue genetic testing and how to interpret the results are complex issues. Accordingly, clinicians should consider consulting a professional genetics counselor if the option is available.

Finally, as with any surgical patient, an overview of the general medical history should be obtained that includes current medications, allergies, tobacco and alcohol use, previous surgical procedures, medical problems, and a brief social history.

PHYSICAL EXAMINATION

A thorough physical examination is an essential second step in the evaluation of any patient with a breast complaint. First, the breast should be inspected for any asymmetry, skin or nipple retraction, erythema, or *peau d'orange* (orange-peel appearance). Skin dimpling can be accentuated by having the patient sit with her hands pushing against her hips to contract the pectoral muscles. Each breast should then be carefully palpated from the clavicle to below the inframammary fold and from the sternum to the posterior axillary line, with careful attention to the subareolar area. This is done with the patient both supine and sitting. If an abnormal area is identified, its location, size, consistency, contour, tenderness, and mobility should be described; a diagram of the lesion is extremely useful for future reference. Although certain physical findings (e.g., skin changes, irregular borders, firmness, irregular margins, and immobility) are associated with a greater likelihood of cancer, the absence of these findings does not exclude the diagnosis of cancer.

Next, the nipples and the areolae are inspected for skin breakdown and squeezed gently to check for discharge. The number and position of any ducts from which discharge is obtained should be recorded, and the color of the discharge (milky, green, yellow, clear, brown, or bloody) and its consistency (watery, sticky, or thick) should be noted. Discharge on one side calls for a careful search for discharge on the other side because unilateral, single-duct discharge is much more suspicious than bilateral, multiple-duct discharge. Any discharge obtained should be tested for occult blood. Cytologic study of nipple discharge generally is not indicated: it adds expense and rarely contributes significantly to the decision whether biopsy is needed.

Finally, the axillary, supraclavicular, and infraclavicular areas are palpated bilaterally for suspicious adenopathy. If enlarged nodes are discovered, their size, mobility, and number should be recorded. Any matting of nodes or fixation of nodes to the chest walls should also be recorded. Tenderness of enlarged nodes may suggest a reactive process and should therefore be recorded as well.

Investigative Studies

IMAGING

Mammography

Diagnostic mammography is the first imaging study employed to evaluate breast abnormalities. Diagnostic, as opposed to screening, mammography is performed when a breast abnormality is already present; it is a more comprehensive examination and consists of multiple specialized images (e.g., magnification views or spot compression views). Diagnostic mammography includes a mammogram of the contralateral breast to rule out synchronous, nonpalpable lesions whenever a woman older than 35 years presents with a palpable breast mass or other specific symptoms. Approximately 4% to 5% of breast cancers occur in women younger than 40 years, and about 25% occur in women younger than 50 years.

Mammography fails to detect 10% to 15% of all palpable malignant lesions, and its sensitivity is particularly decreased in women with lobular carcinoma or radiographically dense breast tissue. Therefore, a negative mammogram should not influence the decision to perform a biopsy of a clinically palpable lesion. The purpose of mammography is to look for synchronous lesions or nonpalpable calcifications surrounding the palpable abnormality, not to determine whether to perform a biopsy of the palpable lesion.

Ultrasonography

The main value of ultrasonography is in distinguishing cystic from solid lesions. If the lesion is palpable, this distinction is best made by direct needle aspiration, which is both diagnostic and therapeutic; if the lesion is not palpable, ultrasonography can determine whether the lesion is cystic and thus potentially eliminate the need for additional workup or treatment. Ultrasonography has not proved useful for screening: it fails to detect calcifications, misses a large number of malignancies, and identifies a great deal of normal breast texture as potential nodules. It is useful, however, for directing fine-needle or core-needle biopsy of the lesions that it does visualize: it permits real-time manipulation of the needle and direct confirmation of the position of the needle within the lesion. In the operating room, ultrasonography can assist in localizing and excising nonpalpable breast lesions and achieving negative lumpectomy margins.[27] It has also been used to guide the performance of investigational tumor-ablating techniques [*see 25 Breast Procedures*].

Magnetic Resonance Imaging

Magnetic resonance imaging after injection of gadolinium contrast enhances many malignant lesions in relation to normal breast parenchyma. Although some benign lesions (e.g., fibroadenomas) are also enhanced by gadolinium, the contrast agent appears to enhance malignant lesions more rapidly and often to a greater extent.

The sensitivity and specificity of MRI in distinguishing benign from malignant lesions are still being assessed. The main approved use of MRI in breast disease is for identification of leaks in silicone breast implants, because MRI can detect the ruptured silicone membrane within the silicone gel. MRI is also useful in identifying occult primary tumors in women who have palpable axillary nodes but no palpable or mammographically identified primary breast lesion. MRI appears to be effective for assessing the extent of vaguely defined tumors, identifying unsuspected multifocal disease, and helping identify patients who are not eligible for breast-conserving surgery. In addition, it appears that MRI can distinguish between a locally recurrent tumor and surgical scarring or radiation-induced change after lumpectomy and radiation, though the technology may not provide reliable readings until 18 months or more after surgery or the completion of radiation therapy. The utility of MRI for screening of young high-risk women with mammographically dense breast tissue is being explored.[28]

Nuclear medicine studies, such as sestamibi scintimammography and positron emission tomography (PET), remain primarily investigational tools. At present, there is no proven role for thermography or xerography in the evaluation of breast problems.

BIOPSY

In the past, the preferred biopsy method for nonpalpable mammographically detected lesions was needle-localized surgical biopsy. This procedure is initially performed in the breast imaging suite, where a wire is placed in the breast adjacent to the imaged abnormality. The patient is then transferred to the OR, where the surgeon uses the wire as a guide to removal of the abnormality. A mammogram of the excised lesion is performed to confirm its removal. Wire-guided diagnostic surgical procedures have now been largely supplanted by stereotactic and ultrasound-guided percutaneous core biopsy techniques, which are less invasive, less expensive, and more expedient. With any of these approaches, however, it is important to verify that the interpretation of the imaging abnormality is in concordance with the pathologic analysis of the specimen. Follow-up should be based on the pathologic findings and on the appearance of the abnormality on breast imaging.

Management of Specific Breast Problems

PALPABLE MASS

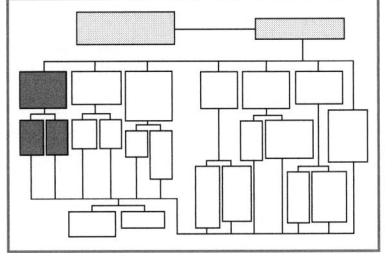

The workup and management of a discrete breast mass are governed by the age of the patient, the physical characteristics of the palpable lesion, and the patient's medical history. The likelihood of malignancy is greater when the patient is 40 years of age or older, when the mass has irregular borders, or when skin dimpling or enlarged axillary nodes are present. A prebiopsy mammogram is indicated for women older than 35 years and for those younger than 35 years who have a strong family history of premenopausal breast cancer.

Cystic Masses

Cysts are a common cause of dominant breast lumps, particularly in premenopausal women. Ultrasonography is useful in differentiating cystic from solid lesions. Sonographically, simple cysts tend to be oval or lobulated and anechoic, with well-defined borders. For asymptomatic simple cysts, no further intervention is required. For symptomatic cysts, fine-needle aspiration (FNA) is appropriate. If the aspirate is not bloody, the fluid should not be sent for cytologic analysis, because it is unlikely to yield a diagnosis of cancer. If the aspirate is bloody, it should be sent for cytologic examination. Women should be followed for 4 to 6 weeks after FNA to determine whether the cyst has recurred. If a simple cyst recurs after aspiration, it should be excised. Fewer than 20% of simple cysts recur after a single aspiration, and fewer than 9% recur after two or three aspirations.[29] Additional cysts subsequently develop in more than 50% of patients.[30] Complex cysts

with indistinct walls or intracystic solid components are more likely to be associated with carcinoma, and therefore, either image-guided or excisional biopsy is warranted.

Solid Masses

If a discrete mass in the breast is believed to be solid, either on the basis of ultrasonographic findings or because attempts at aspiration yield no fluid, a tissue diagnosis is necessary to rule out malignancy. Physical examination alone is insufficient: it correctly identifies masses as malignant in only 60% to 85% of cases.[29] Furthermore, experienced examiners often disagree on whether biopsy is needed for a particular lesion: in one study, four surgeons unanimously agreed on the necessity of biopsy for only 11 (73%) of 15 palpable masses that were later shown by biopsy to be malignant. Tissue diagnosis may be accomplished by means of FNA biopsy, core-needle biopsy, or open surgical biopsy [see 3:5 Breast Procedures].

Phyllodes tumor   The phyllodes tumor is a rare fibroepithelial breast lesion that clinically mimics a fibroadenoma. Most phyllodes tumors present as palpable, solitary, well-defined, mobile, and painless breast masses. With the widespread availability of screening mammography, an increasing number of these tumors are being discovered mammographically. Large phyllodes tumors may be associated with visible venous dilation in the skin overlying the tumor. Palpable axillary lymph nodes are encountered in 20% of patients with phyllodes tumors, but histologic evidence of malignancy is encountered in fewer than 5% of axillary lymph node dissections for clinically positive nodes. The non–tumor-containing palpable nodes are enlarged as a result of necrosis of the primary tumor.

Tumors are classified histologically as low, intermediate, or high grade on the basis of five criteria: stromal cellularity, stromal atypia, the microscopic appearance of the tumor margin (infiltrating, effacing, or bulging), mitoses per 10 high-power fields, and the macroscopic size of the tumor. Structural[31] and cytogenetic[32] studies of constituent cells have demonstrated similarities between fibroadenomas and phyllodes tumors, and there is evidence that certain fibroadenomas develop into phyllodes tumors. FNA is usually nondiagnostic, primarily because of the difficulty of obtaining adequate numbers of stromal cells for cytogenic analysis. Although most phyllodes tumors have minimal metastatic potential, they have a proclivity for local recurrence and should be excised with at least a 1 cm margin. Local recurrence has been correlated with excision margins but not with tumor grade or size.[33] The most common site of metastasis from malignant phyllodes tumors is the lungs (via the hematogenous route).

The diagnosis of phyllodes tumor should be considered in all patients with a history of a firm, rounded, well-circumscribed, solid (i.e., noncystic) lesion in the breast. Simple excisional biopsy should be performed if aspiration fails to return cyst fluid or if ultrasonography demonstrates a solid lesion. Because phyllodes tumors mimic fibroadenomas, they are often enucleated or excised with a close margin. If an adequate margin is not obtained after examination of the permanent section, the patient should undergo reexcision to obtain wider margins and avoid a 15% to 20% recurrence rate. If a simple excision cannot be accomplished without gross cosmetic deformity or if the tumor burden is too large, a simple mastectomy should be performed. Radiation therapy may have a role in the management of patients with chest wall invasion. Chemotherapy, which is reserved for patients with metastatic disease, is based on guidelines for the treatment of sarcomas, rather than breast adenocarcinomas.

ABNORMAL SCREENING MAMMOGRAM

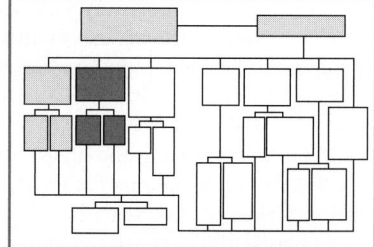

The increased use of screening mammography has led to a dramatic rise in the number of nonpalpable breast lesions that call for tissue acquisition. Generally, 5% to 10% of all screening mammograms are abnormal, and 10% of women with abnormal mammograms have breast cancer.[34] Currently, an abnormal screening mammogram is the most common initial presentation for women with breast cancer. In the Breast Imaging Reporting and Data System (BIRADS), developed by the American College of Radiology, six different assessments (numbered 0 through 5) are used in the interpretation of a screening mammogram [see Table 3].[35] Women with either a negative or a benign assessment (category 1 or 2) should undergo routine screening mammography in 1 to 2 years. Women with a possibly benign assessment (category 3) should undergo a repeat study in 6 months, at which time the mammographic abnormality is assessed for stability.

In general, whenever the radiologist states that a lesion identified on mammography is suspicious, a tissue diagnosis should be obtained by means of either open needle-localized biopsy or mammographically guided stereotactic core-needle biopsy [see 25 Breast Procedures]. Findings especially suggestive of malignancy include the presence of a localized soft tissue mass within the breast that either is new or has changed in size or appearance, architectural distortion with irregular borders producing a stellate-appearing lesion, and clustered microcalcifications, with or without a new or changed mass or architectural distortion.

VAGUE THICKENING OR NODULARITY

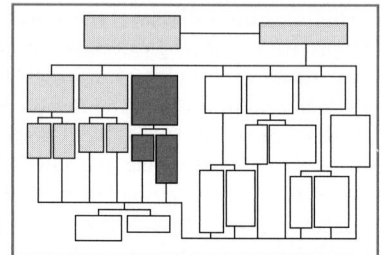

Normal breast texture is often heterogeneous, particularly in premenopausal women. Consequently, vague thickenings or tender or nontender areas of nodularity are frequently detected by the patient or the clinician. It is important to distinguish this vague breast thickening or nodularity from a discrete or dominant breast mass. A dominant breast mass is defined as a discrete lump that is distinctly different from the surrounding breast tissue. Overall, approximately 10% of dominant breast masses are malignant. The incidence of cancer in a dominant breast mass increases with age: in women 55 years of age or older, more than 30% of masses are malignant.[36]

In clinical practice, the first step in evaluating a nodular area is to compare it with the corresponding area of the opposite breast. Symmetrical tender nodularity—for example, in the upper outer quadrant of both breasts—is rarely pathologic. These areas often represent fibrocystic changes that may resolve with time and thus should be followed clinically. Asymmetrical areas of vague thickening in premenopausal women should be reexamined after one or two menstrual cycles. If the asymmetrical thickening persists, the possibility of malignancy is increased, and biopsy should be performed. Women 35 years of age or older who have not had a mammogram in the past 6 months should undergo mammography to rule out synchronous lesions. The accuracy of a negative FNA biopsy in the presence of a vague thickening (as opposed to a discrete mass) is questionable; therefore, open biopsy is generally required for adequate sampling.

Table 3 American College of Radiology Breast Imaging Reporting and Data System (BIRADS)

Category	Assessment	Description/Recommendation
0	Additional imaging evaluation required	Additional imaging recommended
1	Negative finding	Nothing to comment on; routine screening recommended
2	Benign finding	Negative mammogram, but interpreter may wish to describe a finding; routine screening recommended
3	Probably benign finding	Very high probability of benignity; short-interval follow-up suggested to establish stability
4	Suspicious abnormality	Probability of malignancy; biopsy should be considered
5	Abnormality highly suggestive of malignancy	High probability of cancer; appropriate action should be taken

NIPPLE DISCHARGE

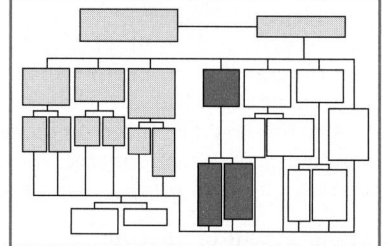

Nipple discharge is a common breast complaint, occurring in approximately 20% to 25% of women.[37] It may be classified as physiologic discharge, pathologic discharge, or galactorrhea. Although the actual incidence of malignancy in women with nipple discharge is low, this complaint produces significant anxiety among women because of the fear that it may be a harbinger of breast cancer. Galactorrhea can be a complex diagnostic challenge for the clinician; a thorough history, a focused physical examination, and appropriately chosen investigative studies are required for diagnosis.

Nipple discharge should be evaluated with respect to its duration, character (i.e., bloody, nonbloody, or milky), location (i.e., unilateral or bilateral), and precipitating factors (i.e., whether it is spontaneous or expressed). Because endocrine disorders (e.g., hypothyroidism and hyperprolactinemia) can produce galactorrhea, symptoms indicative of these conditions (e.g., lethargy, constipation, cold intolerance, and dry skin) should be looked for. The patient should also be questioned about symptoms of an intracranial mass, such as headache, visual field disturbances, and amenorrhea.

Numerous medications are associated with galactorrhea, including various antidepressants (e.g., fluoxetine, buspirone, alprazolam, and chlorpromazine). Other classes of drugs associated with nipple discharge include antihypertensives, H_2-receptor antagonists, and antidopaminergic medications (e.g., metoclopramide).

A focused physical examination is the next step in the evaluation of nipple discharge; obviously, a detailed breast examination is essential. If nipple discharge is not immediately apparent, the clinician should attempt to elicit the discharge by gently squeezing the nipple. The clinician should then attempt to determine whether the discharge is limited to a single duct or involves multiple ducts. Attention should also be paid to any physical findings suggestive of endocrine imbalance, such as thyromegaly (hypothyroidism) or visual field deficits (prolactinoma).

Nipple discharge is physiologic during pregnancy, developing as early as the second trimester and sometimes continuing for as long as 2 years post partum. Therefore, evaluation of nipple discharge in women of childbearing years should include a pregnancy test. Elevated thyroid stimulating hormone (TSH) levels associated with hypothyroidism can increase prolactin secretion and produce galactorrhea. Accordingly, women with nipple discharge should undergo thyroid function testing. When the level of suspicion for a prolactinoma is sufficiently high, the serum prolactin level should be checked. If the serum prolactin level is elevated, MRI of the head (i.e., of the sella turcica) is indicated to determine whether a prolactin-secreting pituitary tumor is present.

Mammography is the first imaging study performed to evaluate nipple discharge. It may reveal nonpalpable masses or microcalcifications that necessitate biopsy. Because most pathologic causes of nipple discharge are located close to the nipple, magnification views of the retroareolar region may help identify the underlying condition. The absence of any mammographic abnormalities, however, should not lead to a false sense of security; further evaluation is still required.

The role of exfoliative cytology in the management of nonlactational galactorrhea is unclear. Although cytology can be diagnostic of cancer, its utility is limited by its low sensitivity. The high false negative rate mandates further evaluation when the findings from cytology are negative or nondiagnostic. Discharge that is bloody, unilateral, and spontaneous is more likely to yield a diagnosis of cancer.

Ductography, or galactography, consists of mammography performed after the offending lactiferous duct has been cannulated and filled with a contrast agent. It can be performed only when active discharge is present and when the secreting duct can be identified and accessed. Not infrequently, ductography is technically impossible, or else the images are uninterpretable as a consequence of incomplete ductal filling or contrast extravasation. Solitary papillomas, the most common cause of abnormal nipple discharge, typically appear as a ductal cutoff or filling defect on ductography. Unfortunately, a normal ductogram does not exclude a pathologic condition, and as with a normal mammogram, further evaluation is still required.

Advances in endoscopic technology have made visualization and biopsy of the mammary ducts possible.[38] Flexible fiberoptic ductoscopy [see 25 Breast Procedures] may permit direct identification and treatment of pathologic conditions affecting the ducts. At present, this technology is available only at a few centers, and as with all new technologies, there is a learning curve associated with its use. Further experience with ductoscopy is required to determine its precise role in the evaluation and management of nipple discharge.

After a thorough history, a focused physical examination, and appropriate diagnostic studies, pathologic nipple discharge that persists should be treated surgically. Operative therapy can resolve the discharge and provide a diagnosis. Excision of a duct or ducts can usually be performed with the patient under local anesthesia supplemented with intravenous sedation (so-called monitored anesthesia care [MAC]). The traditional surgical management of pathologic nipple discharge is a central duct excision, which effectively removes all of the central lactiferous ducts and sinuses, thereby preventing further discharge [see 25 Breast Procedures]. Single-duct excision, or microdochectomy, can be performed when the offending duct is clearly identified. The advantage of this latter procedure is that it conserves breast tissue and causes only minimal deformity; the nipple-areola complex remains intact, so that the patient retains the ability to breast-feed. The main disadvantage of single-duct excision is that the discharge may be more likely to recur than it would be after central duct excision.

BREAST PAIN

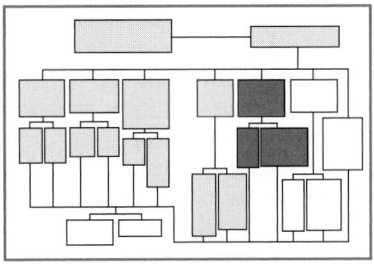

Breast pain, or mastalgia, is one of the most common symptoms for which women seek medical attention. At present, the causes of breast pain are poorly understood. Although pain is not usually a presenting symptom for breast cancer, it still warrants a comprehensive evaluation. The elements of the history that are important in the evaluation of breast pain are the location, character, severity, and timing of the pain. Breast pain occurring in a predictable pattern just before the menstrual cycle is called cyclical mastalgia and is probably hormonally mediated. Notably, however, several studies have shown no differences in circulating estrogen levels between women with mastalgia and pain-free control subjects. It has been postulated that in women with breast pain, progesterone levels may be decreased or prolactin release may be increased in response to thyrotropin-releasing factor hormone.[39] Although histologic findings consistent with cysts, apocrine metaplasia, and ductal hyperplasia have been noted in the breasts of women with mastalgia, there is no convincing evidence that any of these pathologic changes actually cause breast pain.

Mammography and physical examination usually yield normal results in patients with breast pain. The likelihood of malignancy is increased when a patient with mastalgia is postmenopausal and not taking estrogens or when the pain is associated with skin changes or palpable abnormalities; however, these situations are uncommon.

For most women with breast pain, treatment consists of relieving symptoms and reassuring the patient that the workup has not identified an underlying breast carcinoma. Nonsteroidal anti-inflammatory drugs and supportive bras are helpful. Several lifestyle interventions have been proposed as effective breast pain treatments. Dietary recommendations, such as avoidance of methylxanthines (found in coffee, tea, and sodas), are not evidence based.[40] However, oral ingestion of evening primrose oil has been reported to produce significant or complete pain relief in about 50% of women with cyclic mastalgia.[41]

For the rare patients who have severe pain that does not respond to conservative measures, administration of hormones or drugs may be appropriate. Danazol has been successful against breast pain and should be considered the first-line agent, though its androgenic effects may be troubling to many women.[42] Bromocriptine (a prolactin antagonist) and tamoxifen have also been used to treat mastalgia.[43] Pharmacotherapy for mastalgia is contraindicated in patients who are trying to become pregnant.

BREAST INFECTION OR INFLAMMATION

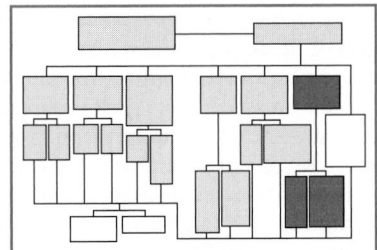

Breast infections can be divided into two general categories: (1) lactational infections and (2) chronic subareolar infections associated with duct ectasia. Both cellulitis and abscesses may occur in lactating women, either during weaning or when engorgement occurs. In the absence of an abscess, breast infections are treated by (1) giving oral antibiotics that cover gram-positive cocci, (2) applying warm packs to the breast, and (3) keeping the breast emptied. Weaning is not necessary, because the infant is not adversely affected by nursing from an infected breast.[44] A diagnosis of mastitis in a nonlactating woman must be viewed with suspicion, and the possibility of inflammatory breast cancer must be excluded. Inflammatory breast cancer is a clinicopathologic variant of breast cancer that is clinically characterized by the rapid onset of an erythema, edema, and increased temperature in the breast, with or without a palpable mass. The diagnosis is made by means of a skin biopsy; the pathologic hallmark is tumor cell invasion of the dermal lymphatics.

Once a breast abscess forms, however, surgical drainage is necessary. Because of the network of fibrous septa within the breast, breast abscesses in lactating women rarely form fluctuant masses. The clinical picture of breast erythema, tenderness, fever, and leukocytosis establishes the diagnosis. General anesthesia is usually required for optimal abscess drainage because of the tenderness of the affected area and the amount of manipulation necessary to break up the loculated abscess cavity. As with any abscess, a culture should be performed and the cavity should be packed open.

Nonlactational infections of the breast often present as chronic relapsing infections of the subareolar ducts associated with periductal mastitis or duct ectasia. These infections usually involve multiple organisms, including skin anaerobes.[45] Retraction or inversion of the nipple, subareolar masses, recurrent periareolar abscesses, or a chronic fistula to the periareolar skin may result, as may palpable masses and mammographic changes that mimic carcinoma. In the acute phase of infection, treatment entails incision, drainage, and administration of antibiotics that cover skin organisms, including anaerobes. In cases of repeated infection, the entire subareolar duct complex should be excised after the acute infection has completely resolved, with antibiotic coverage provided during the perioperative period. Whether drain placement is necessary remains debatable. Even after wide excision of the subareolar duct complex and intravenous antibiotic coverage, infections recur in some patients; excising the nipple and the areola can treat these.[46]

HIGH-RISK PATIENTS

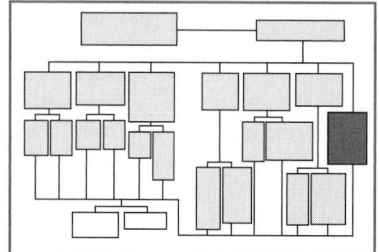

Despite significant progress in management, at least one third of women with breast cancer will ultimately die of their disease. This harsh reality has led to efforts aimed at providing primary prevention to high-risk women. Genetic testing and the use of mathematical models have significantly improved our ability to define breast cancer risk. The Gail model,[47] which relies on data from the Breast Cancer Detection Demonstration Project, and the Claus model,[48] which relies on data from the Cancer and Steroid Hormone Project, are two of the tools that have been used to make this determination. At present, there are three treatment options for women at high risk for breast cancer: (1) close surveillance, (2) prophylactic mastectomy, and (3) chemoprevention with tamoxifen or other agents in the setting of a clinical trial. Currently, no evidence-based conclusions can be made as to which of these management strategies is superior. Research involving high-risk women includes few randomized controlled trials, and many reports are based on uncontrolled studies of selected populations with varying degrees of breast cancer risk. Although most women at high risk choose the option of close surveillance, the growing body of data on chemoprevention and prophylactic mastectomy may increase selection of the other two options.

For women with a previous diagnosis of breast cancer, surveillance protocols are described elsewhere [see Management of the Patient with Breast Cancer, Follow-up after Treatment, below]. For women with lobular carcinoma in situ (LCIS) or a family history of breast carcinoma, surveillance should include twice-yearly physical examinations. Mammography should be performed annually after the diagnosis of LCIS or atypical hyperplasia. For women with a family history of breast cancer, mammography should be performed annually, beginning at least 5 years before the earliest age at which cancer was diagnosed in a relative and in any case no later than the age of 35 years.[49] For women who carry BRCA1 or BRCA2 mutations and other women from families with an autosomal dominant pattern of breast cancer transmission, annual mammographic screening should begin at least 10 years before the earliest age at which the cancer was diagnosed in a relative and no later than 25 years of age.[49]

Long-term results of prophylactic mastectomy in high-risk women indicate that breast cancer risk was reduced by at least 90% in women at high or very high risk who underwent this procedure, compared with women who did not, with risk predicted by the Gail model.[50] Mathematical modeling suggests that prophylactic mastectomy could translate into improved survival for women at very high risk if it confers a 90% reduction in risk.[51] There is, however, no clear consensus on the indications for risk reduction surgery; the benefits of prophylactic mastectomy must be weighed against the irreversibility and psychosocial consequences of the procedure.

Chemoprevention may be defined as the use of nutrients or pharmacologic agents to augment physiologic mechanisms that protect against the development of malignancy. Chemopreventive strategies are designed either to block the initiation of the carcinogenic process or to prevent (or reverse) the progression of the premalignant cell to an invasive cancer.[52] Chemoprevention began with the development of the antiestrogen tamoxifen. The efficacy of tamoxifen in ER-positive breast cancer patients was recognized early on, but its chemopreventive potential was not established until some time later.

The first—and still the most extensive—study to be published on breast cancer chemoprevention was the National Surgical Adjuvant Breast and Bowel Project (NSABP) P-1 trial, in which women at increased risk for breast cancer were randomly assigned to receive either tamoxifen, 20 mg/day, or placebo.[53] Increased risk was determined on the basis of (1) age greater than 60 years, (2) a 5-year predicted incidence of breast cancer of at least 1.66% (determined according to Gail's criteria), or (3) a personal history of lobular carcinoma in situ. After a median follow-up of 55 months, the overall risk of breast cancer was decreased by 49% in the tamoxifen group, and the risk of noninvasive breast cancer was decreased by 50%. The reduction in breast cancer risk was limited to ER-positive breast cancers. Several adverse side effects were noted in the tamoxifen group, the most worrisome of which were a threefold increase in the incidence of endometrial cancer, a higher incidence of deep vein thrombosis and pulmonary embolism, and a higher incidence of stroke. Although two subsequent trials, one from the United Kingdom[54] and one from Italy,[55] did not confirm these findings, the Food and Drug Administration (FDA) found the results of the NSABP P-1 trial to be compelling enough to warrant approval of tamoxifen as a chemopreventive agent in high-risk women.

Concerns about the side effects of tamoxifen have generated interest in the use of selective estrogen receptor modulators (SERMs) as chemopreventive agents.[56] It appears possible that such so-called designer estrogens may have fewer side effects than tamoxifen while reducing the rate of new breast cancers and lowering the incidence of osteoporosis and cardiovascular disease. One of the SERMs, raloxifene, has been approved by the FDA for the treatment of postmenopausal osteoporosis and is known also to exert beneficial effects on lipid profiles. Unlike tamoxifen, raloxifene appears not to have stimulatory effects on the endometrium. Moreover, the Multiple Outcomes of Raloxifene Evaluation (MORE) trial found that fewer breast cancers were noted in women treated with raloxifene than would have been expected without such treatment.[57]

On the basis of findings from osteoporosis trials, the NSABP incorporated raloxifene into an extensive multi-institutional chemoprevention trial that began enrolling patients in 1999. The Study of Tamoxifen and Raloxifene (STAR) trial is a randomized, double-blind trial whose purpose is to compare the effectiveness of raloxifene with that of tamoxifen in postmenopausal women at increased risk for breast cancer. Entry criteria are similar to those for the NSABP P-1 study. A total of 22,000 postmenopausal high-risk women will be randomly assigned to receive either tamoxifen, 20 mg/day orally, or raloxifene, 60 mg/day orally, for 5 years.

A number of newer agents may possess some capacity for breast cancer chemoprevention. Aromatase inhibitors, which have been used as second-line therapies after tamoxifen in cases of advanced breast cancer, may exert chemopreventive effects by inhibiting parent estrogens and their catechol metabolites, thereby preventing cancer initation.[58] In addition, gonadotropin-releasing hormone agonists, monoterpenes, isoflavones, retinoids, rexinoids, vitamin D derivatives, and inhibitors of tyrosine kinase are all undergoing evaluation in clinical or preclinical studies with a view to assessing their potential chemopreventive activity. Whether any of these compounds will play a clinically useful role in preventing breast cancer remains to be seen.

Management of Breast Cancer

STAGING

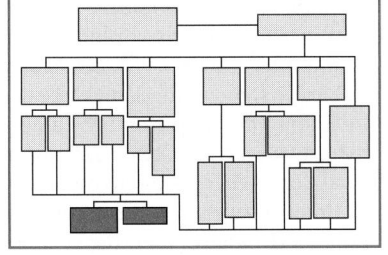

In patients with newly diagnosed breast cancer, it is important to determine the overall extent of disease before embarking on definitive therapy. This process, referred to as clinical staging, includes (1) physical examination to identify any areas of palpable disease in the breasts or the axillary and supraclavicular nodes, along with a detailed clinical history to identify symptoms that may suggest metastatic disease; (2) imaging studies, including mammography, chest x-ray, and sometimes bone scans or CT scans of the chest, the abdomen, or the head; and (3) laboratory studies, including a complete blood count (CBC) and liver function tests.

The extent of preoperative staging should be guided by the size and other characteristics of the primary tumor and by the patient's history and physical examination. The majority of patients with breast cancer present with early stage I or II disease and a low probability of metastatic disease; therefore, extensive testing adds cost without offering much benefit. For patients with stage I or II disease, mammography and routine preoperative blood work should be performed before definitive surgical therapy is initiated; further imaging studies should be reserved for patients who have abnormal test results or clinical symptoms that suggest metastatic disease (e.g., bone pain). For patients with

Table 4 American Joint Committee on Cancer TNM Clinical Classification of Breast Cancer

Primary tumor (T)	TX	Primary tumor cannot be assessed
	T0	No evidence of primary tumor
	Tis	Carcinoma in situ; intraductal carcinoma, lobular carcinoma in situ, or Paget disease of nipple with no associated tumor*
	T1	Tumor ≤ 2.0 cm in greatest dimension
		T1mic: microinvasion ≤ 0.1 cm in greatest dimension
		T1a: tumor > 0.1 cm but ≤ 0.5 cm in greatest dimension
		T1b: tumor > 0.5 cm but ≤ 1.0 cm in greatest dimension
		T1c: tumor > 1.0 cm but ≤ 2.0 cm in greatest dimension
	T2	Tumor > 2.0 cm but ≤ 5.0 cm in greatest dimension
	T3	Tumor > 5.0 cm in greatest dimension
	T4	Tumor of any size with direct extension to (a) chest wall† or (b) skin
		T4a: extension to chest wall
		T4b: edema (including *peau d'orange*) or ulceration of the skin of the breast or satellite skin nodules confined to the same breast
		T4c: both of the above (T4a and T4b)
		T4d: inflammatory carcinoma‡
Regional lymph nodes (N)	NX	Regional lymph nodes cannot be assessed (e.g., previously removed)
	N0	No regional lymph node metastasis
	N1	Metastasis to movable ipsilateral axillary lymph node(s)
	N2	Metastasis to ipsilateral axillary lymph node(s) fixed to each other or to other structures
	N3	Metastasis to ipsilateral internal mammary lymph node(s)
Pathologic classification of lymph nodes (pN)	pNX	Regional lymph nodes cannot be assessed (not removed for pathologic study or previously removed)
	pN0	No regional lymph node metastasis
	pN1	Metastasis to movable ipsilateral axillary lymph node(s)
		pN1a: only micrometastasis (none > 0.2 cm in greatest dimension)
		pN1b: metastasis to lymph node(s), any > 0.2 cm in greatest dimension
		pN1bi: metastasis in 1 to 3 lymph nodes, any > 0.2 cm and all < 2.0 cm in greatest dimension
		pN1bii: metastasis to 4 or more lymph nodes, any > 0.2 cm and all < 2.0 cm in greatest dimension
		pN1biii: extension of tumor beyond the capsule of a lymph node metastasis < 2.0 cm in greatest dimension
		pN1biv: metastasis to a lymph node ≥ 2.0 cm in greatest dimension
	pN2	Metastasis to ipsilateral axillary lymph node(s) fixed to each other or to other structures
	pN3	Metastasis to ipsilateral internal mammary lymph node(s)
Distant metastasis (M)	MX	Presence of distant metastasis cannot be assessed
	M0	No distant metastasis
	M1	Distant metastasis present (includes metastasis to ipsilateral supraclavicular lymph nodes)

* Paget disease associated with a tumor is classified according to the size of the tumor.
†The chest wall includes ribs, the intercostal muscles, and the serratus anterior, but not the pectoral muscle.
‡Inflammatory carcinoma is a clinicopathologic entity characterized by diffuse brawny induration of the skin of the breast with an erysipeloid edge, usually without an underlying palpable mass. Radiologically, there may be a detectable mass and characteristic thickening of the skin over the breast. This clinical presentation is attributable to tumor embolization of dermal lymphatics with engorgement of superficial capillaries.

higher-stage disease at presentation, the use of additional staging studies should be guided by the patient's clinical situation.

Changes in American Joint Committee on Cancer Breast Cancer Staging System

A number of evidence-based changes to the sixth edition of the American Joint Committee on Cancer (AJCC) TNM staging system for breast cancer were adopted for use in tumor registries in January 2003 [see Tables 4 and 5].[59] These changes reflected growing use of sentinel lymph node (SLN) biopsy and of immunohistochemical and molecular technologies to detect nodal metastases. They also included quantitative criteria for distinguishing micrometastases from isolated tumor cells and specific identifiers for recording the use of SLN biopsy, immunohistochemical staining, and molecular biologic techniques. In addition, the classification of lymph node status was modified to include the number of affected axillary lymph nodes, and changes were made to the classification of level III axillary lymph nodes and lymph nodes outside of the axilla. These modifications of the staging system should bring standardization to the collection of important clinicopathologic information.

TREATMENT OPTIONS

Mastectomy versus Limited Surgery

Several randomized prospective studies have documented that segmental resection (lumpectomy), axillary dissection, and postoperative irradiation of an intact breast result in disease-free and overall survival rates equal to those of modified radical mastectomy.[60-63] Although most women with stage I and II breast cancers—indeed, most women with breast cancer—are candidates for breast conservation therapy [see Table 6], some still require or desire mastectomy. When a patient is eligible for limited surgery, the decision between mastectomy and breast conservation with radiation therapy is made on the basis of patient and physician preference, access or lack of access to radiation therapy, and the presence or absence of contraindications to breast conservation.

Contraindications to breast conservation Patients for whom mastectomy is still clearly the treatment of choice fall into four broad categories: (1) those in whom radiation therapy is contraindicated, (2) those in whom lumpectomy would have an unacceptable cosmetic result, (3) those for whom local recurrence is a concern, and (4) those high-risk patients in whom surgical prophylaxis is appropriate [see Management of Specific Breast Problems, High-Risk Patients, above].

Radiation therapy may be contraindicated for any of several reasons. Some patients choose not to undergo radiation therapy, either because it is inconvenient or because they are concerned about potential complications (including the induction of second malignancies). Some patients simply do not have access to radiation therapy, either because they live in a rural area or because they have physical conditions that make daily trips for therapy onerous. Time and travel issues related to weeks-long courses of conventional radiotherapy have led to studies investigating partial-breast or limited-field irradiation after breast-conserving surgery.[64] Data from randomized prospective trials are required before this technique can be recommended in women with early-stage breast cancer. Other patients have medical or psychiatric disorders that would make it extremely difficult for them to comply with the daily treatment schedule. Still others have specific medical contraindications to radiation therapy, including pregnancy, collagen vascular disease, or previous irradiation of the

Table 5 American Joint Committee on Cancer Staging System for Breast Cancer

Stage	T	N	M
Stage 0	Tis	N0	M0
Stage I	T1	N0	M0
Stage IIA	T0	N1	M0
	T1	N1	M0
	T2	N0	M0
Stage IIB	T2	N1	M0
	T3	N0	M0
Stage IIIA	T0	N2	M0
	T1	N2	M0
	T2	N2	M0
	T3	N1, N2	M0
Stage IIIB	T4	N0, N1, N2	M0
Stage IIIC	Any T	N3	M0
Stage IV	Any T	Any N	M1

chest wall (as in a woman with a local recurrence of a breast carcinoma that was treated with radiation therapy). Although there are some clinical data supporting the use of repeat local excision without further irradiation to treat local recurrence after radiation therapy, most authorities favor mastectomy.[65]

When resection of the primary tumor to clean margins would render the appearance of the remaining breast tissue cosmetically unacceptable, mastectomy may be preferable. This is likely to be the case, for example, in patients with large primary tumors relative to their breast size: resection of the primary tumor would remove a substantial portion of the breast tissue. Another example is patients with multiple primary tumors, who would have not only an increased risk of local recurrence but also poor cosmetic results after multiple wide excisions. Patients with superficial central lesions, including Paget disease, are eligible for wide excision (including the nipple and the areola) followed by radiation therapy, provided that clean margins are obtained. The survival and local recurrence rates in these patients are equivalent to those in other groups of patients undergoing lumpectomy and radiation.[66-68] In many cases, the cosmetic results of this procedure are preferable to those of immediate reconstruction, and there is always the option to reconstruct the nipple and areola later.

Patients who are at high risk for local recurrence often choose mastectomy as primary therapy. Features of primary tumors that are associated with higher local recurrence rates after limited

---

Table 6 Determinants of Patient Eligibility for Lumpectomy and Radiation Therapy

Primary tumor ≤ 5 cm (may be larger in selected cases)

Tumor of lobular or ductal histology

Any location of primary within breast if lumpectomy to clean margins (including central lesions) will yield acceptable cosmetic results

Clinically suspicious but mobile axillary nodes

Tumor either positive or negative for estrogen and progesterone receptors

Any patient age

surgery and radiation include gross residual disease after lumpectomy, multiple primary tumors within the breast, an extensive intraductal component, large tumor size, lymphatic vessel invasion, and lobular histologic findings.[69]

In practice, obtaining tumor-free margins is probably the most critical factor in decreasing the risk of local recurrence. The difficulty of obtaining microscopically clean margins in tumors with an extensive intraductal component and in lobular carcinomas may account for the higher local recurrence rates sometimes seen with these tumors. Histologic analysis of mastectomy specimens from patients with tumors with an extensive intraductal component has shown a high rate of multifocality within ipsilateral breast tissue; this residual disease is thought to be the nidus for local recurrence.[70]

The long-term benefits of choosing mastectomy to reduce local recurrences are not clear. Whereas the appearance of distant metastases typically heralds incurable and ultimately fatal disease, local recurrence after breast conservation appears to have little, if any, impact on overall survival. Prospective, randomized trials have had difficulty showing a statistically significant reduction in survival in women who have had a local recurrence after limited surgery and radiation. It has been suggested that additional follow-up may eventually confirm reduced survival in some patients with local recurrences. Still, most of the evidence suggests that local recurrences are not the source of subsequent distant metastases. It is worthwhile to keep in mind, however, that even if mastectomy to prevent local recurrence does not actually improve survival, it may nevertheless provide significant benefit by reducing patient anxiety, the amount of follow-up testing required, and the need for subsequent treatment.

Options for axillary staging   The histologic status of the axillary nodes is the single most important predictor of outcome in breast cancer. Traditionally, axillary dissection has been a routine part of the management of breast cancer. It has been used to guide subsequent adjuvant therapy and provide local control, and it may have contributed a small overall benefit in terms of survival.[71] Unfortunately, axillary dissection can be associated with sensory morbidities and lymphedema.

SLN biopsy is a minimally invasive, less morbid, and quite accurate method of detecting or ruling out occult lymph node metastasis [see 26 Lymphatic Mapping and Sentinel Lymph Node Biopsy]. It is based on the principle that the SLN is the first node to which the tumor spreads; thus, if the SLN is tumor free, the patient can be spared the morbidity of an axillary dissection. There is a learning curve associated with this technique, however, and discussion continues as to the most appropriate way of integrating it into general practice.[72] SLN biopsy identifies an increased number of patients with micrometastases, with some identified by immunohistochemical staining alone. Treatment of patients who have only micrometastases to axillary nodes remains a topic of debate, addressed in an ongoing clinical trial of SLN biopsy by the American College of Surgeons Oncology Group.

Breast reconstruction after mastectomy   Advances in reconstructive techniques have made breast reconstruction increasingly popular [see 25 Breast Procedures]. Reconstruction may be done either at the time of the mastectomy (immediate reconstruction) or later (delayed reconstruction). In the past, reconstruction was generally delayed for 1 to 2 years after mastectomy; now, it is most often performed immediately after mastectomy. In general, immediate reconstruction should be reserved for patients who are not likely to require postoperative adjuvant therapies,

because radiation can produce capsular contracture in patients undergoing prosthetic reconstruction.

Prosthetic reconstruction involves the use of an implant to restore the breast contour. It is technically the simplest type of reconstruction but can still result in complications such as contracture, infection, and rupture, which may necessitate further surgery. Autologous reconstruction involves the transfer of the patient's own tissue to reconstruct the breast. Tissue from various sites (e.g., the transverse rectus abdominis and the latissimus dorsi) has been used for breast reconstruction. Skin-sparing mastectomy with immediate reconstruction consists of resection of the nipple-areola complex, any existing biopsy scar, and the breast parenchyma, followed by immediate reconstruction. The generous skin envelope that remains optimizes the cosmetic result after breast reconstruction. The procedure is oncologically safe and does not lead to an increase in the incidence of local recurrence.[73]

Radiation Therapy

Current radiation therapy regimens consist of the delivery of approximately 5,000 cGy to the whole breast at a dosage of approximately 200 cGy/day, along with, in most cases, the delivery of an additional 1,000 to 1,500 cGy to the tumor bed, again at a dosage of 200 cGy/day. Axillary node fields are not irradiated unless there is evidence that the patient is at high risk for axillary relapse—namely, multiple (generally more than four) positive lymph nodes, extranodal extension of tumor, or bulky axillary disease (i.e., palpable nodes several centimeters in diameter). Because the combination of surgical therapy and radiation therapy increases the risk of lymphedema of the arm, it is appropriate only when there is sufficient risk of axillary relapse to justify the increased complication rate. As a rule, supraclavicular node fields are irradiated only in patients with multiple positive axillary nodes, who are at increased risk for supraclavicular disease. The role of prophylactic irradiation of the internal mammary nodes remains controversial.

Postmastectomy radiation therapy involves the delivery of radiation to the chest wall after mastectomy; it is mainly reserved for patients with T3 or T4 primary tumors or multiple positive lymph nodes. Such therapy is recommended particularly when there are multiple positive axillary lymph nodes: significant axillary disease predicts higher rates of chest wall recurrence after mastectomy. Two series[74,75] have suggested that postmastectomy radiation therapy significantly improves survival in premenopausal women with any positive axillary nodes.

Irradiation of the breast or chest wall is generally well tolerated: most women experience only minor side effects, such as transient skin erythema, mild skin desquamation, and mild fatigue. Because a small amount of lung volume is included in the irradiated fields, there is usually a clinically insignificant but measurable reduction in pulmonary function. In addition, because the heart receives some radiation when the left breast or left chest wall is treated, there may be a slightly increased risk of future myocardial infarction. There is also a 1% to 2% chance that the radiation will induce a second malignancy (sarcoma, leukemia, or a second breast carcinoma). These radiation-induced malignancies appear after a long lag time, generally 7 to 15 years or longer.

Systemic Drug and Hormone Therapy

Despite the success of surgical treatment and radiation therapy in achieving local control of breast cancer, distant metastases still develop in many patients. Various drugs and hormones have therefore been used to treat both measurable and occult metastatic disease. Now that many clinical trials have demonstrated a survival benefit, more and more women are receiving adjuvant cytotoxic chemotherapy. It became clear in early trials that multiple-agent (or combination) chemotherapy was superior to single-agent chemotherapy.[76,77] It also became clear that chemotherapy and hormone therapy were limited in their ability to control large tumor masses, though on occasion, patients with large tumor masses showed dramatic partial responses or even complete responses to therapy.

With the goal of eradicating breast cancer metastases while they are still microscopic, systemic therapy is now administered in a so-called adjuvant setting—that is, when there is no evidence of distant metastases but there is sufficient suspicion that metastasis may have occurred. Until the late 1980s, adjuvant chemotherapy was given primarily to women who had axillary node metastases but no other evidence of disease. In node-positive premenopausal women, adjuvant chemotherapy appeared to be significantly more beneficial than adjuvant hormone therapy. In node-positive postmenopausal women, on the other hand, hormone therapy appeared to be as beneficial as chemotherapy and less toxic.

This approach to adjuvant systemic therapy changed in 1988, when the NCI issued a clinical alert stating that there was sufficient evidence of benefit to allow recommendation of adjuvant chemotherapy or hormone therapy for even node-negative breast cancer patients.[78] By that time, a number of studies had shown that adjuvant chemotherapy could improve survival in node-negative breast cancer patients.[79-81] A consensus conference of experts in the field suggested that such therapy be reserved for node-negative women with primary tumors larger than 1 cm in diameter.[82] In 1992, a meta-analysis that reviewed the treatment of 75,000 women in 133 randomized clinical trials of adjuvant therapy for breast cancer concluded that in node-negative premenopausal women, overall long-term survival was 20% to 30% higher in those who received chemotherapy than in those who did not.[83] This benefit also appeared to extend to postmenopausal women between 50 and 60 years of age. A 1998 overview of the use of adjuvant tamoxifen in randomized trials demonstrated that in women with ER-positive tumors, those given tamoxifen for 5 years had a 47% reduction in tumor recurrence and a 26% reduction in mortality, compared with those women who were given placebo.[84] In this analysis, the effects of tamoxifen on recurrence and survival were independent of age and menopausal status. Tamoxifen did not appear to improve survival, however, in women with ER-negative tumors. These results, together with data on the efficacy of tamoxifen for chemoprevention, have led to increased use of tamoxifen for premenopausal women and for women with small tumors.

TREATMENT OF NONINVASIVE CANCER

Ductal Carcinoma in Situ

Before mammographic screening was widely practiced, ductal carcinoma in situ (DCIS) was generally identified either as a palpable lesion (usually with comedo histology) or as an incidental finding on a biopsy performed for another lesion. With the increasing use of mammography, DCIS is accounting for a growing proportion of breast cancer cases. The diagnosis of DCIS is now made in 6.6% of all needle-localized breast biopsies and 1.4% of breast biopsies for palpable lesions. About 30% of all mammographically detected malignancies are DCIS.[17]

It was recognized early on that DCIS had a very favorable prognosis compared with other forms of breast cancer: long-term survival approached 100% after treatment with mastectomy. Axillary lymph nodes were positive in only 1% to 2% of patients,

most of whom had large or palpable lesions or comedo histology. The prognosis for DCIS continues to be very favorable in relation to that for invasive breast cancers. In theory, there is no potential for metastatic disease with a purely in situ lesion. In practice, however, axillary node metastases continue to be found in 1% to 2% of patients thought to have pure DCIS, presumably arising from a small area of invasion that was missed on pathologic evaluation.

DCIS is believed to be a true anatomic precursor of invasive breast cancer. There are at least two lines of evidence that support this conclusion. First, when DCIS is treated with biopsy alone (usually because it was missed on the initial biopsy and not found until subsequent review), invasive carcinoma develops in 25% to 50% of patients at the site of the initial biopsy; all these tumors appear within 10 years and are of ductal histology. Second, when DCIS recurs locally after breast conservation, invasive ductal carcinoma appears in about 50% of patients. The true relationship between DCIS and invasive ductal carcinoma awaits a better understanding of the molecular biology of breast cancer development.

The consequence of the view that DCIS is a precursor of invasive cancer is that treatment is required once the diagnosis is made. Treatment options for DCIS are similar to those for invasive breast cancer [*see Figure 1*]; however, it should be remembered that although the risk of local recurrence is greater after breast conservation for DCIS than after mastectomy, the likelihood of metastatic disease is very small. Wide excision to microscopically clean margins followed by radiation therapy has become an accepted alternative to mastectomy. Smaller areas of DCIS, particularly of low to intermediate nuclear grade, are increasingly treated with wide excision without radiation.[85] If clean margins cannot be obtained or if the cosmetic result is expected to be poor after excision to clean margins, mastectomy should be performed. The NSABP B-17 study,[86] which examined the role of radiation in the treatment of DCIS, found that the addition of radiation therapy to wide excision reduced the recurrence rate at 43 months after operation by approximately half, from 16.4% with wide excision alone to 7.0% with wide excision and radiation. The report also suggested that the addition of radiation therapy might reduce the incidence of invasive recurrences.

Most patients in whom DCIS is identified mammographically can choose between mastectomy and wide excision with or without radiation, either of which yields excellent long-term survival. Given the lack of any significant difference in survival between the two options, the patient must weigh her feelings about the risk of a local, possibly invasive, recurrence after breast conservation against her feelings about the cosmetic and psychological effects of mastectomy. Mastectomy remains a reasonable treatment even for patients with very small DCIS lesions if the primary concern is to maximize local control of the cancer. Breast reconstruction after mastectomy for DCIS is an option that is open to most such patients.

Axillary dissection is not usually performed in conjunction with lumpectomy for DCIS, because the probability of positive nodes is low: it increases morbidity and expense while providing little prognostic information. On the other hand, low axillary dissection is often included in mastectomy for DCIS: a level I axillary dissection adds little morbidity to a mastectomy, and many surgeons believe that dissection must be carried into the low axilla to ensure that the entire axillary tail of the breast is removed.

In some patients with areas of mammographically detected DCIS lesions measuring less than 2.5 cm in diameter, it may be possible to omit radiation therapy, particularly if the lesions do

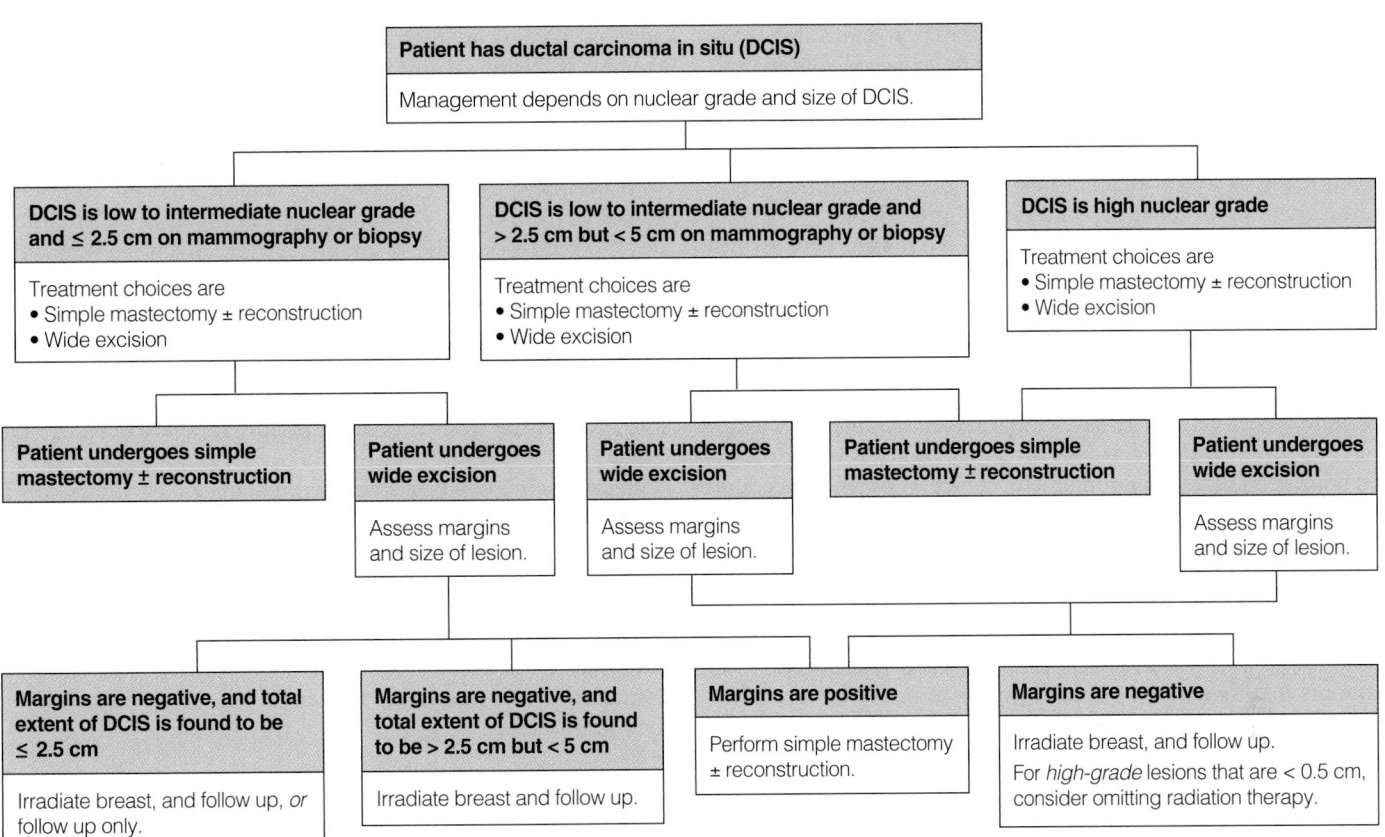

Figure 1   **Algorithm illustrates the approach to managing ductal carcinoma in situ.**

not have comedo histology. Omission of radiation therapy is a complex decision that should be based on the individual patient's histology, the presence or absence of other risk factors, the presence or absence of contraindications to radiation therapy, and the degree to which the patient is willing to accept a higher local recurrence rate. This option is probably best pursued in the context of a clinical trial.

There are certain patients with DCIS for whom mastectomy remains the preferred treatment, such as those who have lesions larger than 5 cm in diameter. Some surgeons would also include in this category those who have comedo lesions larger than 2.5 cm and those who present with palpable DCIS. In these patients, the local recurrence rate after breast conservation, even in conjunction with radiation therapy, remains high. As many as half of these recurrences will contain invasive cancer with metastatic potential. These also are the DCIS patients who are at highest risk for positive axillary nodes. For this reason, an axillary node sampling is often performed in conjunction with the mastectomy.

Lobular Carcinoma in Situ

LCIS, also referred to as lobular neoplasia, does not have the same clinical implications as DCIS, invasive ductal carcinoma, or invasive lobular carcinoma. It is now generally accepted that LCIS is a predictor of increased risk of subsequent invasive breast carcinoma rather than a marker of the site at which the subsequent carcinoma will arise. Most of the carcinomas that develop after a biopsy showing LCIS are of ductal histology.[87] The increased risk of subsequent carcinoma is equally distributed between the breast undergoing biopsy and the contralateral breast and is thought to be between 20% and 25% in patients with LCIS and no other risk

factors; it may be additive with other risk factors [*see* Risk Factors for Breast Cancer, *above*]. Because the two breasts are at equal risk for future carcinoma, unilateral mastectomy is inappropriate. Appropriate treatment options include (1) careful observation coupled with physical examination two or three times annually and mammograms annually, (2) prophylactic bilateral simple mastectomies with or without reconstruction, and (3) chemoprevention with tamoxifen or participation in chemoprevention trials with other agents. Most patients choose the first option, but there are some patients for whom prophylactic mastectomy is still preferable, either because of anxiety or because of concurrent risk factors.

Management of tumors that contain LCIS mixed with invasive carcinoma of either lobular or ductal histology is dictated primarily by the features of the invasive carcinoma. Staging is not affected by the presence of LCIS.

TREATMENT OF INVASIVE CANCER

Although the optimal treatment regimen for breast cancer continues to be the subject of active investigation, there is at least a partial consensus regarding current treatment options for the various stages of breast cancer.

Early-Stage Invasive Cancer

Local treatment   In patients with stage I or II breast cancer, lumpectomy to microscopically clean margins combined with axillary dissection and radiation therapy [*see Figure 2*] appears to yield approximately the same long-term survival rates as mastectomy. Patients undergoing lumpectomy and radiation are, however, at risk for local recurrence in the treated breast, as well as for the development of a new primary tumor in the remaining breast tissue. Local recurrences can generally be managed with mastectomy; overall survival is equivalent to that of women who underwent mastectomy at the time of initial diagnosis. There may, however, be a significant cost to the patient in terms of anxiety about recurrence, as well as the morbidity and potential mortality associated with undergoing a second surgical procedure.

On the other hand, patients who choose mastectomy as their initial surgical treatment face the psychological consequences of losing a breast. Although they are at lower risk for local recurrence than patients who choose lumpectomy, axillary node dissection, and radiation, their overall survival does not seem to be significantly improved. Each physician and each patient must weigh the inconvenience and potential complications of radiation therapy and the risk of local recurrence against the value of breast preservation, keeping in mind that the choice between procedures appears to have no significant effect on survival.

Adjuvant therapy It is generally agreed that adjuvant chemotherapy, adjuvant hormone therapy, or both should be considered for all women with tumors larger than 1 cm in diameter, even those with negative axillary lymph nodes. For patients with tumors that have a very favorable prognosis (i.e., that are smaller than 1 cm or have a favorable histology), the potential benefits of adjuvant therapy are probably outweighed by its risks. Tamoxifen therapy is being reconsidered for women with such low-risk tumors, given the data on the efficacy of this agent for both treatment and prevention of breast cancers. In premenopausal women, adjuvant therapy should consist of combination chemotherapy, with hormone therapy reserved for clinical trials; in postmenopausal women, hormone therapy (generally consisting of tamoxifen, 10 mg twice daily) is the first-line treatment. However, the idea that menopause should be an absolute cutoff point for consideration of chemotherapy is being reassessed. For healthy postmenopausal women, particularly those between 50 and 60 years of age, the decision between hormone therapy and chemotherapy plus hormone therapy is made on an individual basis and takes into account the woman's overall health and the specifics of her tumor.

In cases of node-positive disease, combination chemotherapy is used for premenopausal women and for healthy postmenopausal women up to 60 years of age or even older. Hormone therapy is generally the treatment of choice in postmenopausal women who are older than 60 years and in poor health, particularly those with ER-positive tumors. Renewed interest is being expressed in other hormonal manipulations, such as oophorectomy and chemical castration, for premenopausal women who are at high risk for metastatic disease.[88]

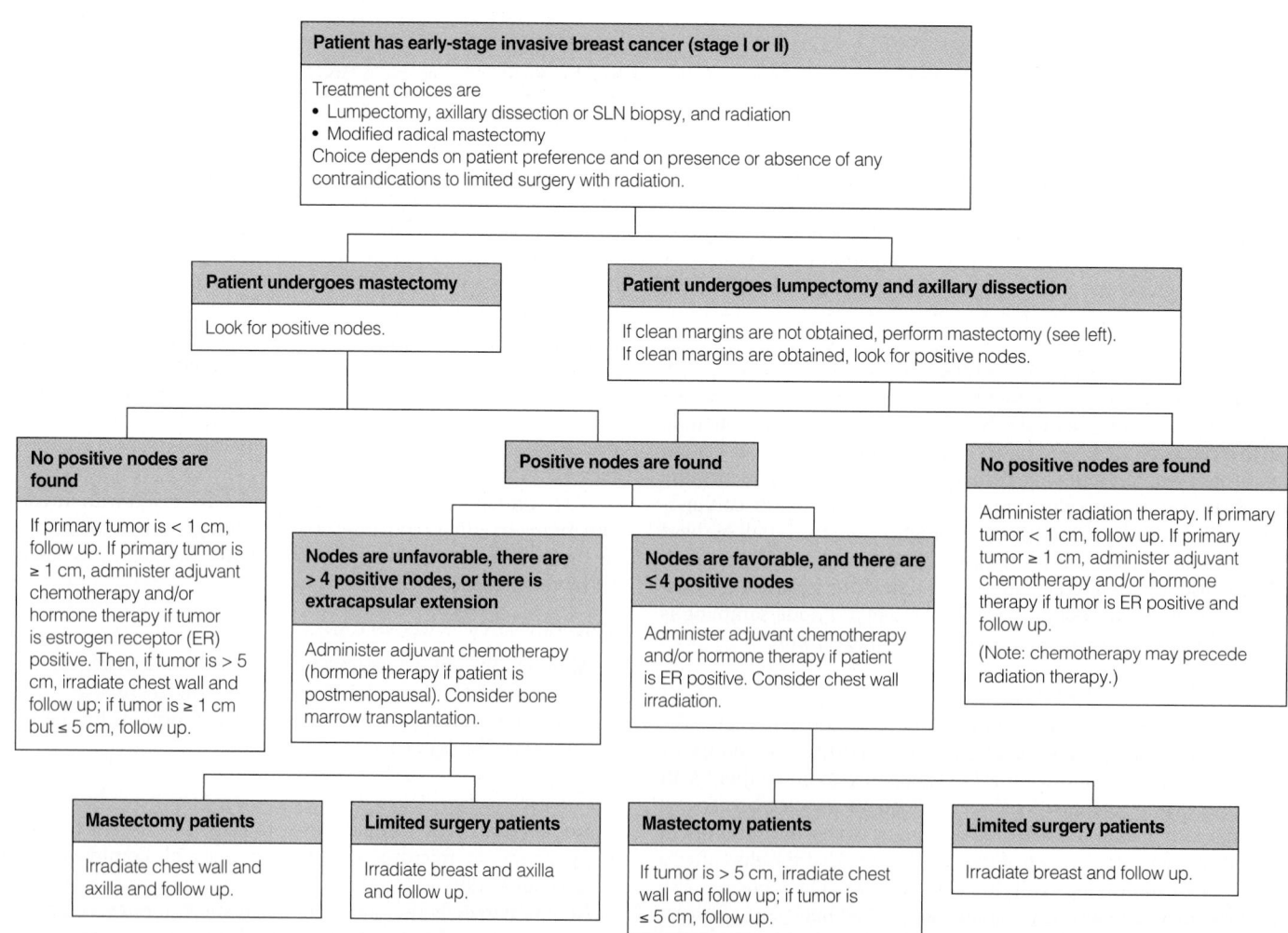

Figure 2 **Algorithm illustrates the approach to managing early-stage invasive breast cancer.**

Patient has locally advanced breast cancer (stage III or inflammatory carcinoma)
Perform needle or incisional biopsy to obtain tissue diagnosis and hormone receptor data. Administer "neoadjuvant" chemotherapy. Restage to identify distant metastases.

Metastases are identified on restaging	No metastases are identified on restaging
Initiate appropriate management [*see Figure 4*].	Determine whether tumor is operable.

Tumor is inoperable	Tumor is operable
Administer a different chemotherapy or hormone therapy regimen. Restage to assess operability.	Perform modified radical mastectomy. Lumpectomy with axillary dissection is an option for some patients. Consider radiation to the chest wall and axilla. (Most patients require both surgery and radiation in addition to chemotherapy.) Follow up.

Figure 3 **Algorithm illustrates the approach to managing locally advanced breast cancer.**

Locally Advanced Cancer

Patients with locally advanced breast cancer include those with primary tumors larger than 5 cm (particularly those with palpable axillary lymph nodes), those with fixed or matted N2 axillary nodes, and those with inflammatory breast carcinoma. These patients are at high risk for systemic disease, as well as for local failure after standard local therapy. Current practice is to administer multimodality therapy, with chemotherapy as the first treatment modality [*see Figure 3*]. This so-called neoadjuvant chemotherapy often has the effect of downstaging local disease, in some cases making inoperable tumors amenable to surgical resection. Patients are treated with FNA, core-needle, or open incisional biopsy to obtain a tissue diagnosis, hormone receptor data, and HER-2/*neu* status; they then undergo careful restaging after systemic therapy to identify any distant metastases. If the tumor responds to chemotherapy, the patient may then undergo radiation therapy, surgery, or both. Most patients require all three modalities for optimum local and systemic control.

The optimum treatment of patients with stage IIIa breast cancer remains controversial. Some practitioners favor neoadjuvant chemotherapy, whereas others favor surgery followed by chemotherapy and radiation therapy. The choice of surgical procedure for women with locally advanced breast cancer is also controversial. Whereas many surgeons favor mastectomy for all tumors larger than 5 cm, others offer wide excision with axillary dissection to patients in whom excision to clean margins will leave a cosmetically acceptable breast.

Stage IV Cancer

Patients with distant metastases, whether at their initial presentation or after previous treatment for an earlier-stage breast cancer, are rarely cured. Before treatment begins, a tissue diagnosis consistent with breast cancer must be obtained from the primary lesion

(at the initial presentation of the disease) or from a metastasis (if there is any doubt about the metastatic nature of the lesion or the source of the metastatic disease). Any tissue samples obtained should be sent for estrogen and progesterone receptor assays.

The usual first-line treatment for metastatic breast cancer is cytotoxic chemotherapy or hormone therapy [*see Figure 4*]. Radiation therapy may be used to relieve pain from bone metastases or to avert a pathologic fracture at a site of metastatic disease. There is also occasionally a role for so-called toilet mastectomy for patients who have metastatic disease and a locally advanced and ulcerated primary tumor if the condition of the primary tumor prevents the administration of needed chemotherapy.

Treatment for stage IV breast cancer should be on protocol whenever possible. For patients who are ineligible for therapy on protocol, palliative chemotherapy or hormone therapy may be the best treatment option.

TREATMENT OF MALE BREAST CANCER

Fewer than 1% of all breast carcinomas occur in men. Predisposing risk factors include conditions associated with increased estrogen levels (e.g., cirrhosis and Klinefelter syndrome) and radiation therapy.[89] In addition, an increased incidence of male breast cancer has been reported in families in which the *BRCA2* mutation has been identified. As with breast cancer in women, the most common tumor type is infiltrating ductal cancer. Because breast cancer tends to be detected at a later stage in men than in women, there is a misconception that male breast cancer has a worse prognosis. Stage for stage, however, the prognosis for men with breast cancer is similar to that for women with breast cancer. To prevent late detection, men with a breast mass must be evaluated with the same degree of suspicion as women with a breast mass are.

Surgical treatment includes mastectomy. In the absence of clinically palpable nodes, SLN biopsy is appropriate for staging the axilla. A large majority of male breast cancers are ER positive, and decisions regarding adjuvant systemic treatment should be made on the same basis as for breast cancer in women.

FOLLOW-UP AFTER TREATMENT

Patients who have been treated for breast cancer remain at risk for both the recurrence of their original tumor and the development of a new primary breast cancer. The rate of recurrence of

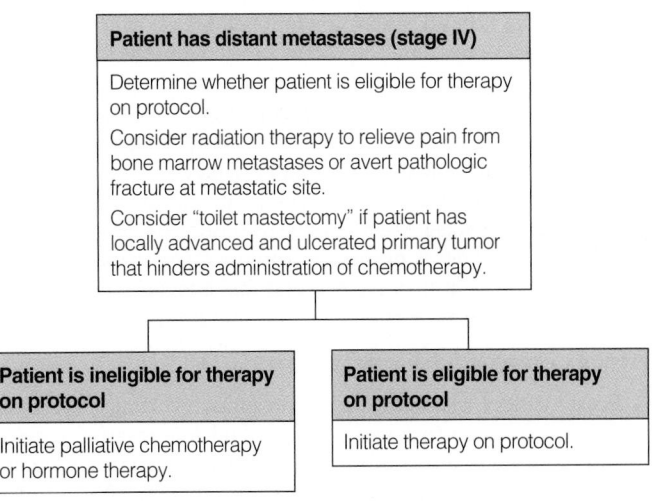

Patient has distant metastases (stage IV)
Determine whether patient is eligible for therapy on protocol. Consider radiation therapy to relieve pain from bone marrow metastases or avert pathologic fracture at metastatic site. Consider "toilet mastectomy" if patient has locally advanced and ulcerated primary tumor that hinders administration of chemotherapy.

Patient is ineligible for therapy on protocol	Patient is eligible for therapy on protocol
Initiate palliative chemotherapy or hormone therapy.	Initiate therapy on protocol.

Figure 4 **Algorithm illustrates the approach to managing stage IV breast cancer.**

breast cancer is nearly linear over the first 10 years after treatment. Recurrence becomes less likely after the first decade, but it continues at a significant rate through the second decade and beyond. In patients who have undergone limited surgery and radiation therapy, radiation-induced breast and chest wall malignancies begin to appear 7 or more years after treatment and continue to appear for at least 20 years after treatment.

Unfortunately, there is little in the way of evidence-based guidance to help the clinician determine the optimal posttreatment surveillance strategy for breast cancer patients. As a result, practice patterns vary considerably with respect to the use of follow-up tests in this population. Exhaustive posttreatment testing does not seem warranted in early-stage breast cancer patients. There is no evidence to support the use of routine bone scans, CT, PET brain imaging, and serum tumor markers in asymptomatic patients after treatment for early-stage disease. The use of such intensive surveillance is based on the presumption that detecting disease recurrence at its earliest stage would offer the best chance of cure, improved survival, or, at least, improved quality of life. Given that the majority of recurrences are detected by patients themselves, educating patients about the symptoms of recurrent disease is likely to be a more effective strategy.

Follow-up of early stage breast cancer patients should include a thorough history and physical examination and mammography. For patients treated with breast conservation, annual mammography is appropriate, beginning after any acute radiation reaction has resolved (generally 6 to 9 months after completion of radiation therapy). For patients treated with mastectomy, mammography should be continued on an annual basis for the contralateral breast. Physical examination and review of symptoms are generally performed at 3- to 6-month intervals for the first 5 years after completion of therapy, though these intervals have not yet been tested in a prospective fashion.

Although there has been little debate about the value of early detection of a local recurrence within the treated breast or of a new primary tumor in either breast, there has been a great deal of debate about the value of early detection of metastatic disease. Two prospective, randomized trials addressed this issue. In one, a group of breast cancer patients was intensively followed with blood tests every 3 months and with chest x-rays, bone scans, and liver ultrasonography annually.[90] There was no difference in survival or quality of life between this group and the control group, and metastatic disease was diagnosed, on average, less than 1 month earlier in the intensively followed group than in the control group. In the second study, a group of breast cancer patients received chest x-rays and bone scans every 6 months for 5 years.[91] Pulmonary and bone metastases were detected significantly earlier in this group than in the control group, but there was no improvement in survival. This study demonstrated that early detection of metastatic disease could be achieved with short-interval screening, but given current therapeutic options, early detection had no beneficial effect on survival. Both studies concluded that at present, there is no role for routine imaging studies in the follow-up of breast cancer patients and that imaging studies should be ordered only as prompted by clinical findings.

FUTURE DIRECTIONS IN TREATMENT

Breast cancer management is constantly evolving. The trend continues to be toward less extensive and less invasive surgical interventions, without compromising patient outcomes. Ongoing trials are examining the need for radiation therapy after lumpectomy for tumors in elderly women or tumors consisting of pure DCIS. In addition, the use of percutaneous extirpative and ablative local therapies in the management of highly selected patients with breast cancer is being investigated. The need for axillary dissection continues to be questioned, and more and more, the features of the primary tumor, rather than axillary node status, are being used to establish the prognosis and determine the need for adjuvant therapy. Trials of SLN biopsy are under way. Data are also being accumulated on the clinical significance of micrometastatic and molecular amounts of tumor in the SLN.

Many ongoing trials of chemotherapy for breast cancer focus on increasing the efficacy of treatment through dose intensification. Very high dose chemotherapy, in conjunction with administration of growth factor or autologous bone marrow transplantation, is being assessed in the hope that higher-dose chemotherapeutic regimens will improve response rates and duration of response.

The early results from studies of bone marrow transplantation have been somewhat disappointing: median survival is prolonged by only 7 to 10 months beyond what is achievable with more standard chemotherapy.[92] There is, however, a small but significant group of long-term survivors who remain free of disease for more than 5 years after undergoing bone marrow transplantation to treat breast cancer with 10 or more positive lymph nodes at initial presentation. Trials of improved bone marrow transplantation regimens continue in the hope that the toxicity and cost of the treatment can be reduced and the number of long-term survivors increased.

Immune therapy using antibodies to HER-2/*neu* protein, alone or in conjunction with chemotherapy, is being evaluated for tumors that overexpress the oncogene HER-2/*neu*. As of June 2004, there was no definitive evidence that the available biologic therapies and immune therapies were of significant value in the treatment of breast cancer. These types of therapy continue to be actively explored.

Even more exciting than the prospect of improved therapy is the concept of chemoprevention [*see* Management of Specific Breast Problems, High-Risk Patients, *above*]. Positive results of trials using tamoxifen for chemoprevention have raised hopes that many breast cancers can be prevented and have increased interest in identifying additional agents that can reduce breast cancer risk with minimal side effects. These results underscore the importance of understanding breast cancer risk factors (including gene mutations) for better identification of women who might benefit from chemoprevention. Ultimately, improved comprehension of the pathophysiologic mechanisms of breast carcinogenesis is essential to the development of biologically based methods for the prevention and treatment of breast cancer.

MULTIDISCIPLINARY BREAST CANCER CARE

Contemporary management of breast cancer demands a multidisciplinary approach involving several specialists, including surgeons, radiation oncologists, medical oncologists, radiologists, and pathologists. It is essential that each specialist have a working knowledge of the others' disciplines as they relate to breast cancer care. This team of physicians, in consultation with the patient, determines the selection and timing of individual treatments. This process is greatly simplified when the physicians concerned are able to coordinate their visits with the patient, thereby both saving time for the patient and facilitating decision making among the various specialists. A number of centers have established multidisciplinary breast centers that allow a patient to see all the specialists in a single visit while also allowing the physicians to consult with each other in reviewing the clinical data, imaging studies, and pathology and in determining treatment options.

Patient education is also becoming more and more critical in the management of breast cancer. Patients are increasingly being asked to participate in decision making, and as hospital stays for breast cancer treatments become shorter, patients are also being asked to participate more actively in their own care. To participate effectively, patients must be educated about the advantages and disadvantages of the various aspects of cancer management. The shifting of a larger proportion of cancer care to the outpatient setting also necessitates the use of other support services, such as visiting nurses, social workers, and outpatient infusion services. How best to coordinate these complex services while maintaining a focus on the problems and needs of the individual patient remains one of the major challenges faced by physicians caring for patients with breast cancer.

References

1. Seltzer MH: Breast complaints, biopsies, and cancer correlated with age in 10,000 consecutive new surgical referrals. Breast J 10:111, 2004

2. Jemal A, Tiwari RC, Murray T, et al; American Cancer Society: Cancer statistics, 2004. CA Cancer J Clin 54:8, 2004

3. Andrews BT, Bates T: Delay in the diagnosis of breast cancer: medico-legal implications. Breast 9:223, 2000

4. Henderson IC: Risk factors for breast cancer development. Cancer 71(suppl):2127, 1993

5. Slattery ML, Kerber RA: A comprehensive evaluation of family history and breast cancer risk. JAMA 270:1563, 1993

6. Newcomb PA, Storer BE, Longnecker MP, et al: Lactation and a reduced risk of premenopausal breast cancer. N Engl J Med 330:81, 1994

7. Marchant DJ: Estrogen-replacement therapy after breast cancer: risk versus benefits. Cancer 71(suppl): 2169, 1993

8. Squitieri R, Tartter PI, Ahmed S, et al: Carcinoma of the breast in postmenopausal hormone user and nonuser control groups. J Am Coll Surg 178:167, 1994

9. Steinberg KK, Thacker SB, Smith SJ, et al: A meta-analysis of the effect of estrogen replacement therapy. JAMA 265:1985, 1991

10. Wingo PA, Lee NC, Ory H, et al: Age specific differences in the relationship between oral contraceptive use and breast cancer. Obstet Gynecol 78:161, 1991

11. Colditz GA, Stampfer MJ, Willett WC: Prospective study of estrogen replacement therapy and risk of breast cancer in post-menopausal women. JAMA 264:2648, 1990

12. Dupont WD, Page DL: Menopausal estrogen-replacement therapy and breast cancer. Arch Intern Med 151:67, 1991

13. Hunter DJ, Manson JE, Colditz GA, et al: A prospective study of the intake of vitamins C, E, and A and the risk of breast cancer. N Engl J Med 329:234, 1993

14. Willett WC, Hunter DJ, Stampfer MJ, et al: Dietary fat and fiber in relation to risk of breast cancer: an 8-year follow-up. JAMA 268:2037, 1992

15. McTiernan A: Behavioral risk factors in breast cancer: can risk be modified? Oncologist 8:326, 2003

16. Page DL, Jensen RA: Evaluation and management of high risk and premalignant lesions of the breast. World J Surg 18:32, 1994

17. Frykberg ER, Bland KI: Management of in situ and minimally invasive breast carcinoma. World J Surg 18:45, 1994

18. Jacobs TJ, Byrne C, Colditz G, et al: Radial scars in benign breast-biopsy specimens and the risk of breast cancer. N Engl J Med 340:430, 1999

19. Hayes DF, Thor AD: c-erbB-2 in breast cancer: development of a clinically useful marker. Semin Oncol 29:231, 2002

20. Vahabi M: Breast cancer screening methods: a review of the evidence. Health Care Women Int 24:773, 2003

21. Smith RA, Saslow D, Sawyer KA, et al; American Cancer Society High-Risk Work Group; American Cancer Society Screening Older Women Work Group; American Cancer Society Mammography Work Group; American Cancer Society Physical Examination Work Group; American Cancer Society New Technologies Work Group; American Cancer Society Breast Cancer Advisory Group: American Cancer Society guidelines for breast cancer screening: update 2003. CA Cancer J Clin 53:141, 2003

22. Jatoi I: Screening clinical breast examination. Surg Clin North Am 83:789, 2003

23. National Cancer Institute Statement on Mammography Screening, Jan 31, 2002 www.nci.nih.gov/newscenter/mammstatement 31jan02

24. Harris R, Leininger L: Clinical strategies for breast cancer screening: weighing and using the evidence. Ann Intern Med 122:539, 1995

25. Quan ML, Petrek JA: Clinical implications of hereditary breast cancer. Adv Surg 37:197, 2003

26. Greene MH: Genetics of breast cancer. Mayo Clin Proc 72:54, 1997

27. Kaufman CS, Jacobson L, Bachman B, et al: Intraoperative ultrasound facilitates surgery for early breast cancer. Ann Surg Oncol 9:988, 2002

28. Kristoffersen Wiberg M, Aspelin P, Perbeck L, et al: Value of MR imaging in clinical evaluation of breast lesions. Acta Radiol 43:275, 2002

29. Leis HP Jr: Gross breast cysts: significance and management. Contemp Surg 39(2):13, 1991

30. Hughes LE, Bundred NJ: Breast macrocysts. World J Surg 13:711, 1989

31. Silverman JS, Tameness A: Mammary fibroadenoma and some phyllodes tumor stroma are composed of CD34+ fibroblasts and factor XIIIa+ dendrophages. Histopathology 29:411, 1996

32. Dietrich CU: Karyotypic changes in phyllodes tumors of the breast. Cancer Genet Cytogenet 78:200, 1994

33. Mangi AA, Smith BL, Gadd MA, et al: Surgical management of phyllodes tumors. Arch Surg 134:487, 1999

34. Hall FM, Storella JM, Silverstone DZ, et al: Nonpalpable breast lesions: recommendations for biopsy based on suspicion of carcinoma at mammography. Radiology 167:353, 1988

35. Lacquement MA, Mitchell D, Hollingsworth AB: Positive predictive value of the Breast Imaging Reporting and Data System. J Am Coll Surg 189:34, 1999

36. Boyd NF, Sutherland HJ, Fish EB, et al: Prospective evaluation of physical examination of the breast. Am J Surg 142:331, 1981

37. Falkenberry SS: Nipple discharge. Obstet Gynecol Clin North Am 29:21, 2002

38. Mokbel K, Elkak AE: The evolving role of mammary ductoscopy. Curr Med Res Opin 18:30, 2002

39. Watt-Boolsen S, Eskildsen P, Blaehr H: Release of prolactin, thyrotropin and growth hormone in women with cyclical mastalgia and fibrocystic disease of the breast. Cancer 56:500, 1985

40. Bundred N: Breast pain. Clin Evid (7):1631, 2002

41. Pashby NL, Mansel RE, Hughes LE, et al: A clinical trial of evening primrose oil in mastalgia. Br J Surg 68:801, 1981

42. Harrison BJ, Maddox PR, Mansel RE: Maintenance therapy of cyclical mastalgia using low-dose danazol. J R Coll Surg Edinb 34:79, 1989

43. Smith RL, Pruthi S, Fitzpatrick LA: Evaluation and management of breast pain. Mayo Clin Proc 79:353, 2004

44. Benson EA: Management of breast abscesses. World J Surg 13:753, 1989

45. Brook I: Microbiology of non-puerperal breast abscesses. J Infect Dis 157:377, 1988

46. Meguid MM, Oler A, Numann PJ, et al: Pathogenesis-based treatment of recurring subareolar breast abscesses. Surgery 118:775, 1995

47. Gail MG, Brinton LA, Byar DP, et al: Projecting individualized probabilities of developing breast cancer for white females who are being examined annually. J Natl Cancer Inst 81:1879, 1989

48. Claus EB, Risch N, Thompson WD: Autosomal dominant inheritance of early-onset breast cancer: implications for risk prediction. Cancer 73:643, 1994

49. Dershaw DD: Mammographic screening of the high-risk woman. Am J Surg 180:288, 2000

50. Hartmann LC, Schaid DJ, Woods JE, et al: Efficacy of bilateral prophylactic mastectomy in women with a family history of breast cancer. N Engl J Med 340:77, 1999

51. Schrag D, Kuntz KM, Garber JE, et al: Decision analysis: effects of prophylactic mastectomy and oophorectomy on life expectancy among women with BRCA1 or BRCA2 mutations. N Engl J Med 336:1465, 1997

52. Zujewski J: Selective estrogen receptor modulators (SERMS) and retinoids in breast cancer chemoprevention. Environ Mol Mutagen 39:264, 2002

53. Fisher B, Costantino JP, Wickerham DL, et al: Tamoxifen for prevention of breast cancer: report of the National Surgical Adjuvant Breast and Bowel Project P-1 Study. J Natl Cancer Inst 90:1371, 1998

54. Powles T, Eeles R, Ashley S, et al: Interim analysis of the incidence of breast cancer in the Royal Marsden Hospital tamoxifen randomised chemoprevention trial. Lancet 352:98, 1998

55. Veronesi U, Maisonneuve P, Costa A, et al: Prevention of breast cancer with tamoxifen: preliminary findings from the Italian randomised trial among hysterectomised women. Lancet 352:93, 1998

56. Dalton R, Kallab A: Chemoprevention of breast cancer. South Med J 94:7, 2001

57. Cummings S, Eckert S, Kreuger K, et al: The effect of raloxifene on risk of breast cancer in post-

menopausal women: results from the MORE randomized trial. Multiple Outcomes of Raloxifene Evaluation. JAMA 281:2189, 1999

58. Goss P, Strasser K: Chemoprevention with aromatase inhibitors—trial strategies. J Steroid Biochem Mol Biol 79:143, 2001

59. Woodward WA, Strom EA, Tucker SL, et al: Changes in the 2003 American Joint Committee on Cancer staging for breast cancer dramatically affect stage-specific survival. J Clin Oncol 21:3244, 2003

60. Veronesi U, Banfi A, DelVecchio M, et al: Comparison of Halstead mastectomy with quadrantectomy, axillary dissection and radiotherapy in early breast cancer: long term results. Eur J Cancer Clin Oncol 22:1085, 1986

61. Fisher B, Bauer M, Margolese R, et al: Five-year results of a randomized clinical trial comparing total mastectomy and segmental mastectomy with or without radiation in the treatment of breast cancer. N Engl J Med 312:665, 1985

62. Fisher B, Redmond C, Poisson R, et al: Eight year results of a randomized clinical trial comparing total mastectomy and lumpectomy with or without irradiation in the treatment of breast cancer. N Engl J Med 320:822, 1989

63. Fisher B, Anderson S, Bryant J, et al: Twenty-year follow-up of a randomized trial comparing total mastectomy, lumpectomy, and lumpectomy plus irradiation for the treatment of invasive breast cancer. N Engl J Med 347:1233, 2002

64. Wallner P, Arthur D, Bartelink H, et al; workshop participants: Workshop on partial breast irradiation: state of the art and the science. Bethesda, MD, December 8–10, 2002. J Natl Cancer Inst 96:175, 2004

65. Newman LA, Washington TA: New trends in breast conservation therapy. Surg Clin North Am 83:841, 2003

66. Harris JR, Hellman S, Kinne DW: Limited surgery and radiotherapy for early breast cancer. N Engl J Med 313:1365, 1985

67. Clarke DH, Le M, Sarrazin D, et al: Analysis of local regional relapses in patients with early breast cancers treated by excision and radiotherapy: experience of the Institut Gustave Roussy. Int J Radiat Oncol Biol Phys 11:137, 1985

68. Fisher B, Wolmark N: Limited surgical management for primary breast cancer: a commentary on the NSABP reports. World J Surg 9:682, 1985

69. Schnitt SJ: Risk factors for local recurrence in patients with invasive breast cancer and negative surgical margins of excision: where are we and where are we going? Am J Clin Pathol 120:485, 2003

70. Holland R, Connolly JL, Gelman R, et al: The presence of an extensive intraductal component following a limited excision correlates with prominent residual disease in the remainder of the breast. J Clin Oncol 8:113, 1990

71. Morrow M: A survival benefit from axillary dissection: was Halsted correct? Ann Surg Oncol 6:17, 1999

72. Cox CE, Salud CJ, Cantor A, et al: Learning curves for breast cancer sentinel lymph node mapping based on surgical volume analysis. J Am Coll Surg 193:593, 2001

73. Simmons RM, Adamovich TL: Skin-sparing mastectomy. Surg Clin North Am 83:885, 2003

74. Overgaard M, Hansen PS, Overgaard J, et al: Postoperative radiotherapy in high-risk premenopausal women with breast cancer who receive adjuvant chemotherapy. N Engl J Med 337:949, 1997

75. Ragaz J, Jackson SM, Le N, et al: Adjuvant radiotherapy and chemotherapy in node-positive premenopausal women with breast cancer. N Engl J Med 337:956, 1997

76. Bonadonna G, Valagussa P, Tancini G, et al: Current status of Milan adjuvant chemotherapy trials for node-positive and node-negative breast cancer. J Natl Cancer Inst Monogr 1:45, 1986

77. Fisher B, Redmond C, Fisher E, et al: Systemic adjuvant therapy in treatment of primary operable breast cancer: NSABP experience. J Natl Cancer Inst Monogr 1:35, 1986

78. Clinical Alert from the National Cancer Institute. Department of Human Services, National Cancer Institute, National Institutes of Health, May 16, 1988

79. Fisher B, Costantino J, Redmond C, et al: A randomized trial evaluating tamoxifen in the treatment of patients with node-negative breast cancer who have estrogen-receptor-positive tumors. N Engl J Med 320:479, 1989

80. Fisher B, Redmond C, Dimitrov NV, et al: A randomized clinical trial evaluating sequential methotrexate and fluorouracil in the treatment of patients with node-negative breast cancer who have estrogen-receptor-negative tumors. N Engl J Med 320:473, 1989

81. Mansour EG, Gray R, Shatila NH, et al: Efficacy of adjuvant chemotherapy in high-risk node-negative breast cancer. N Engl J Med 320:485, 1989

82. NIH Consensus Conference: Treatment of early-stage breast cancer. JAMA 265:391, 1991

83. Early Breast Cancer Trialists' Collaborative Group: Systemic treatment of early breast cancer by hormonal, cytotoxic, or immune therapy: 133 randomised trials involving 31,000 recurrences and 24,000 deaths among 75,000 women. Lancet 339:71, 1992

84. Tamoxifen for early breast cancer: an overview of the randomised trials. Early Breast Cancer Trialists' Collaborative Group. Lancet 351:1451, 1998

85. Silverstein MJ, Lagios MD, Groshen S, et al: The influence of margin width on local control of ductal carcinoma in situ of the breast. N Engl J Med 340: 1455, 1999

86. Fisher B, Costantino J, Redmond C, et al: Lumpectomy compared with lumpectomy and radiation therapy for the treatment of intraductal breast cancer. N Engl J Med 328:1581, 1993

87. Simpson PT, Gale T, Fulford LG, et al: The diagnosis and management of pre-invasive breast disease: pathology of atypical lobular hyperplasia and lobular carcinoma in situ. Breast Cancer Res 5: 258, 2003

88. Scottish Cancer Trials Breast Group: Adjuvant ovarian ablation versus CMF chemotherapy in premenopausal women with pathological stage II breast carcinoma: the Scottish trial. Lancet 341:1293, 1993

89. Buzdar AU: Breast cancer in men. Oncology (Huntingt) 17:1361, 2003

90. GIVIO Investigators: Impact of follow-up testing on survival and health-related quality of life in breast cancer patients. JAMA 271:1587, 1994

91. Del Turco MR, Palli D, Cariddi A, et al: National Research Council Project on Breast Cancer Follow-up. Intensive diagnostic follow-up after treatment of primary breast cancer: a randomized trial. JAMA 271:1593, 1994

92. Peters WP: High-dose chemotherapy and autologous bone marrow support for breast cancer. Important Advances in Oncology. DeVita VT Jr, Hellman S, Rosenberg SA, Eds. JB Lippincott Co, Philadelphia, 1991, p 135

Acknowledgments

Figure 1   Marcia Kammerer.

Figures 2 through 4   Talar Agasyan.

22 SOFT TISSUE INFECTION

Mark A. Malangoni, M.D., F.A.C.S., and Christopher R. McHenry, M.D., F.A.C.S.

Soft tissue infections are a diverse group of diseases that involve the skin and underlying subcutaneous tissue, fascia, or muscle. Such infections may be localized to a small area or may involve a large portion of the body. They may affect any part of the body, though the lower extremities, the perineum, and the abdominal wall are the most common sites of involvement. Some soft tissue infections are relatively harmless if treated promptly and adequately; others can be life-threatening even when appropriately treated. The symptoms and signs range from subtle or nonspecific indicators (e.g., pain, localized tenderness, and edema without fever) to obvious features (e.g., necrosis, blistering, and crepitus associated with systemic toxicity).

Soft tissue infections were first defined as such slightly more than a century ago. In 1883, Fournier described a gangrenous infection of the scrotum that continues to be associated with his name.[1] In 1924, Meleney documented the pathogenic role of streptococci in soft tissue infection.[2] Shortly thereafter, Brewer and Meleney described progressive polymicrobial postoperative infection of the muscular fascia with necrosis[3] (though the term necrotizing fasciitis was not introduced until more than 25 years later[4]). The association between toxic-shock syndrome and streptococcal soft tissue infection was delineated as this disease reemerged in the 1980s.[5]

Various classification systems and eponyms are used to describe specific forms of soft tissue infection [see Discussion, Etiology and Classification of Soft Tissue Infection, *below*]. In our view, however, it is more important to develop a common approach to the diagnosis and treatment of these conditions than to refine the minor details of classification. For therapeutic purposes, the primary consideration is to distinguish between necrotizing soft tissue infections and nonnecrotizing infections. Nonnecrotizing soft tissue infections involve one or both of the superficial layers of the skin (epidermis and dermis) and the subcutaneous tissue, and they usually respond to antibiotic therapy alone. Necrotizing soft tissue infections may involve not only the skin, the subcutaneous tissue, and the superficial fascia but also the deep fascia and muscle, and they must be treated with urgent surgical debridement. At times, it is difficult to distinguish between these two categories of infection, especially when obvious clinical signs of necrotizing soft tissue infection are absent.

In this chapter, we review diagnosis and management of the main soft tissue infections seen by surgeons, including both superficial infections (e.g., pyoderma, animal and human bites, and cellulitis) and necrotizing infections involving superficial and deep tissues [see Table 1].

Clinical Evaluation

The diagnosis of soft tissue infection is usually made on the basis of the history and the physical examination. Patients typically seek medical attention because of pain, tenderness, and erythema of recent onset. They should be asked about environmental factors that may have disrupted the normal skin barrier [see Table 2], as well as about any host factors that may increase their susceptibility to infection and limit their ability to contain it. It is particularly important that they be questioned about specific clinical scenarios associated with unusual pathogens, such as an animal bite (associated with *Pasteurella multocida*), a human bite (*Eikenella corrodens*), chronic skin disease (*Staphylococcus aureus*), saltwater exposure (*Vibrio vulnificus*), and freshwater exposure (*Aeromonas hydrophila*).

Physical examination usually reveals erythema, tenderness, and induration. Vesicular lesions and honey-colored crusted plaques are seen in patients with impetigo. Intense, sharply demarcated erythema is characteristic of erysipelas. A tender, swollen erythematous papule, often containing a visible hair shaft, is indicative of folliculitis. A single painful, tender, indurated, erythematous skin nodule suggests a furuncle, and the presence of multiple inflammatory nodules with sinus tracts is consistent with a carbuncle. Cellulitis in association with a decubitus ulcer or an ischemic leg ulcer frequently signals a polymicrobial infection with gram-negative organisms. An erythematous linear streak, characteristic of lymphangitis, usually indicates a superficial infection secondary to *Streptococcus pyogenes;* associated lymphadenopathy may be present as well.

Patients with necrotizing soft tissue infections often complain of severe pain that is out of proportion to their physical findings. Compared with patients who have nonnecrotizing infections, they are more likely to have fever, bullae, or blebs [see Figure 1]; signs of systemic toxicity; hyponatremia; and leukocytosis with a shift in immature forms. Physical findings characteristic of a necrotizing infection include tenderness beyond the area of erythema, crepitus, cutaneous anesthesia, and cellulitis that is refractory to antibiotic therapy.[6] Tenderness beyond the borders of the erythematous area is an especially important clinical clue that develops as the infection in the deeper cutaneous layers undermines the skin.

Table 1 Common Soft Tissue Infections

Superficial infections	Pyoderma
	  Impetigo
	  Erysipelas
	  Folliculitis
	  Furuncles and carbuncles
	Infections developing in damaged skin
	  Animal bites
	  Human bites
	Cellulitis
	  Nonnecrotizing
	  Necrotizing

Deep necrotizing cutaneous infections	Necrotizing fasciitis
	Myonecrosis
	  Gas gangrene
	  Metastatic gas gangrene

Table 2 Environmental Factors That Disrupt Skin and Alter Normal Barrier Function

Cuts, lacerations, or contusions

Injections from contaminated needles

Animal, human, or insect bites

Burns

Skin diseases (e.g., atopic dermatitis, tinea pedis, eczema, scabies, varicella infection, or angular cheilitis)

Decubitus, venous stasis, or ischemic ulcers

Contaminated surgical incisions

Early in the course of a necrotizing soft tissue infection, skin changes may be minimal despite extensive necrosis of the deeper cutaneous layers. Bullae, blebs, cutaneous anesthesia, and skin necrosis occur as a result of thrombosis of the nutrient vessels and destruction of the cutaneous nerves of the skin, which typically occur late in the course of infection.

Clinicians should be mindful of certain diagnostic barriers that may delay recognition and treatment of necrotizing soft tissue infections.[7] In particular, such infections may have a variable clinical presentation. Although most patients present with an acute, rapidly progressive illness and signs of systemic toxicity, a subset of patients may present with a more indolent, slowly progressive infection. Patients with postoperative necrotizing infections often have a more indolent course. Moreover, in the early stages, underlying necrosis may be masked by normal-appearing overlying skin. As many as 20% of necrotizing soft tissue infections are primary (idiopathic) and occur in previously healthy patients who have no predisposing factors and no known portal of entry for bacterial inoculation. Finally, crepitus is noted in only 30% of patients with necrotizing soft tissue infections.

Investigative Studies

Diagnostic studies have a low yield in patients with superficial soft tissue infections. They are rarely necessary and are used only in specific clinical circumstances. Either needle aspiration at the

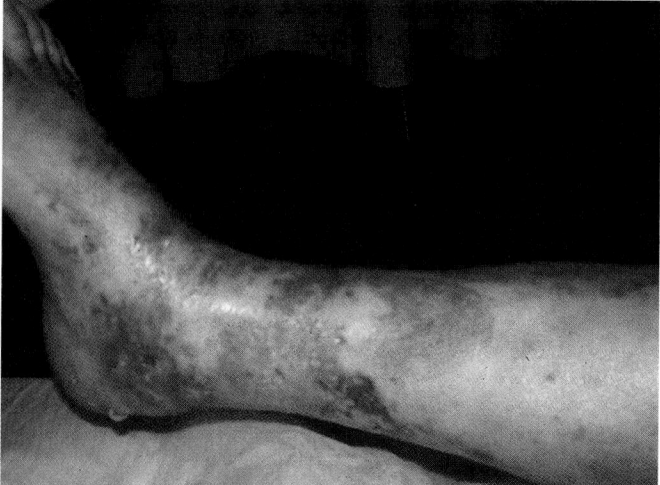

Figure 1 **Lower-extremity necrotizing fasciitis is characterized by bullae, blebs, and discolored skin.**

advancing edge of erythema with Gram staining and culture or full-thickness skin biopsy and culture may be helpful when cellulitis is refractory to antibiotic therapy or when an unusual causative organism is suspected. Because of their low yield, blood cultures are obtained only in patients with signs of systemic toxicity, those with buccal or periorbital cellulitis, and those with infection suspected of being secondary to saltwater or freshwater exposure; these clinical situations are associated with a higher likelihood of a positive culture.

When the characteristic clinical features of necrotizing soft tissue infection are absent, diagnosis may be difficult. In this setting, laboratory and imaging studies become important [see Figure 2]. In one study, logistic regression analysis showed that a white blood cell (WBC) count equal to or greater than 15,400/mm³ and a serum sodium level lower than 135 mmol/L at the time of hospital admission were predictive of a necrotizing soft tissue infection.[8] A WBC count lower than 15,400/mm³ and a serum sodium level equal to or greater than 135 mmol/L in a patient without obvious clinical signs of a necrotizing soft tissue infection had a negative predictive value of 99%. A normal serum creatine kinase (CK) level rules out muscle necrosis.

A plain x-ray of the involved area demonstrates soft tissue gas in only 15% to 30% of patients with necrotizing infections [see Figure 3].[6] Computed tomography is more sensitive in identifying soft tissue gas, but other CT findings are seldom diagnostic.

Magnetic resonance imaging is currently the preferred imaging study for documenting deep necrotizing infections [see Figure 4]. The presence of soft tissue gas on MRI is diagnostic of a necrotizing soft tissue infection. Edema and inflammatory changes of the deep soft tissues identified by MRI are suggestive of necrotizing soft tissue infection. High signal intensity on T_2-weighted images and tissue enhancement after gadolinium administration are indicative of inflamed soft tissue. The absence of gadolinium enhancement on T_1-weighted images is indicative of nonperfused tissue and necrosis.[9,10] The sensitivity of MRI in this setting is 89% to 100%, and the specificity is 46% to 86%.[9,11]

The finding of soft tissue gas on diagnostic imaging warrants immediate operative exploration and debridement. Because of the high sensitivity of MRI, necrotizing infection can be excluded when no involvement of the superficial fascia, subcutaneous tissue, or the deeper cutaneous layers is demonstrated. However, the inflammatory changes seen on MRI when necrotizing soft tissue infection is present may also be seen in patients with non-necrotizing infections, as well as in those with other inflammatory conditions affecting the deep soft tissues. Because of the relatively low specificity of this study, biopsy of the deeper cutaneous layers, with frozen-section examination and culture, may be needed to diagnose or rule out soft tissue infection [see Figure 2]. This procedure may be performed at the bedside with local anesthesia. The observation of necrotic or infected tissue through the biopsy incision indicates that immediate debridement is needed.

General Management of Nonnecrotizing and Necrotizing Soft Tissue Infection

NONNECROTIZING INFECTION

Antibiotic therapy is the cornerstone of treatment for patients with nonnecrotizing infections. Such patients usually require antibiotics that are effective against group A streptococci or *S. aureus.* Topical, oral, or intravenous preparations may be employed, depending on the nature and severity of the disease process [see Management of Specific Soft Tissue Infections, *below*]. If polymi-

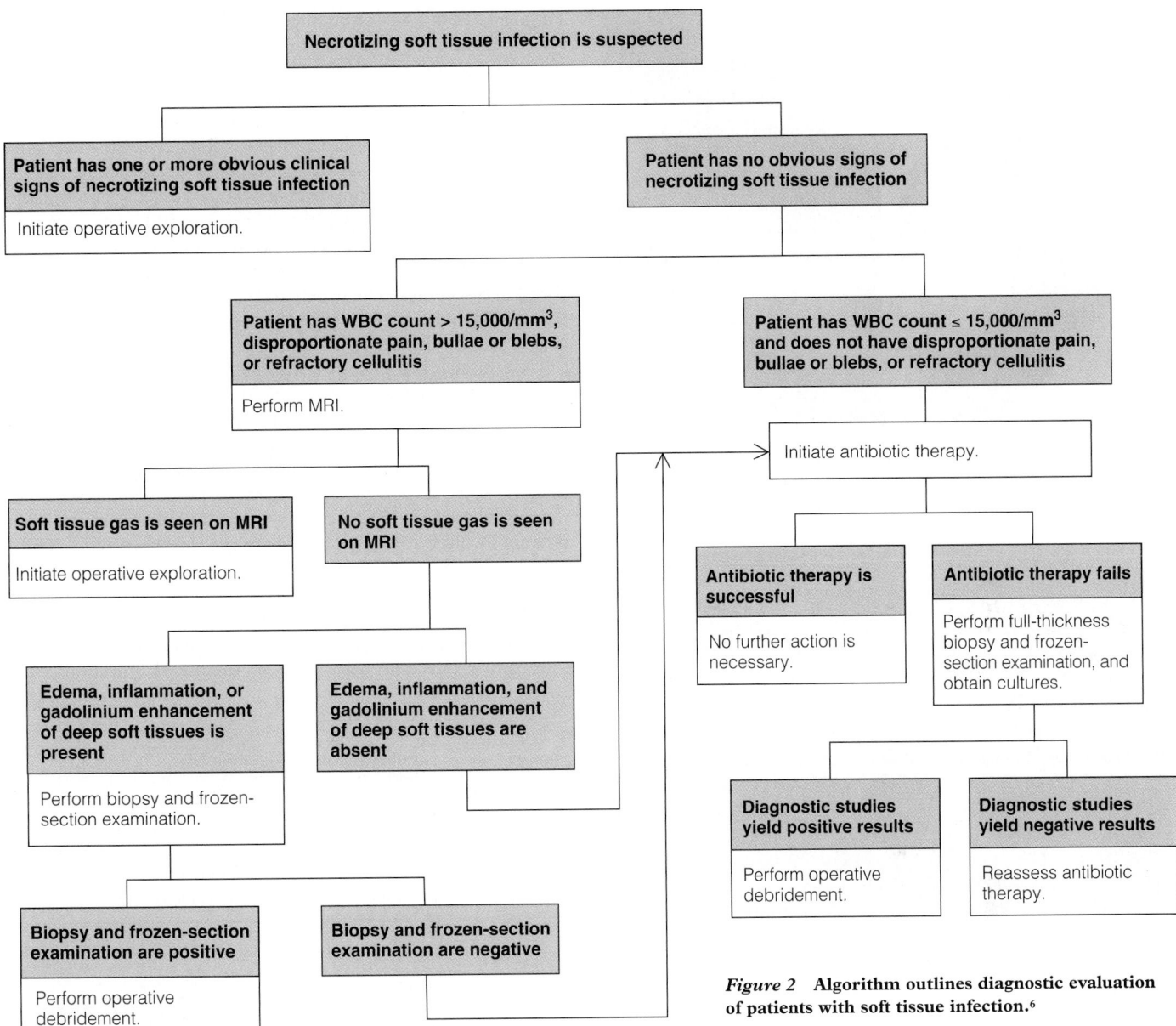

Figure 2 Algorithm outlines diagnostic evaluation of patients with soft tissue infection.[6]

crobial infection is suspected, broad-spectrum antimicrobial agents should be given, either alone or in combination.

NECROTIZING INFECTION

Management of necrotizing soft tissue infections is predicated on early recognition of symptoms and signs and on emergency operative debridement. Once the diagnosis of necrotizing soft tissue infection is established, patient survival and limb salvage are best achieved by means of prompt operation; precise identification of the causative bacteria and correct assignment of the patient to a specific clinical syndrome are unnecessary. The delay between hospital admission and initial debridement is the most critical factor influencing morbidity and mortality: a number of reports have demonstrated a strong correlation between survival and the interval between onset of symptoms and initial operation.[12-15]

The components of treatment of necrotizing soft tissue infection are (1) resuscitation and correction of fluid and electrolyte disorders, (2) physiologic support, (3) broad-spectrum antimicrobial therapy, (4) urgent and thorough debridement of necrotic tissue, and (5) supportive care [see Figure 5].

Nonoperative Measures

Patients with necrotizing soft tissue infections frequently present with tachycardia and hypotension, reflecting depleted intravascular volume and possible septic shock. Such patients often exhibit extensive extracellular fluid sequestration within the affected area, as well as more generalized sequestration resulting from sepsis. A balanced isotonic electrolyte solution, such as lactated Ringer solution (or 0.9% normal saline, for patients with renal dysfunction), is administered to replace these fluid deficits. The adequacy of intravascular volume repletion is often assessed by monitoring urinary output; however, it sometimes proves necessary to use a central venous catheter to monitor central venous or pulmonary arterial pressure in patients with associated myocardial dysfunction, septic shock, chronic pulmonary disease, renal insufficiency, or other severe chronic illnesses.

Hyponatremia is usually corrected by infusing isotonic fluids. Hypocalcemia, which can result from calcium precipitation in patients with extensive fat necrosis, is usually corrected by administering I.V. calcium gluconate. Hyperglycemia is corrected with insulin, given via either subcutaneous injection or, for patients with

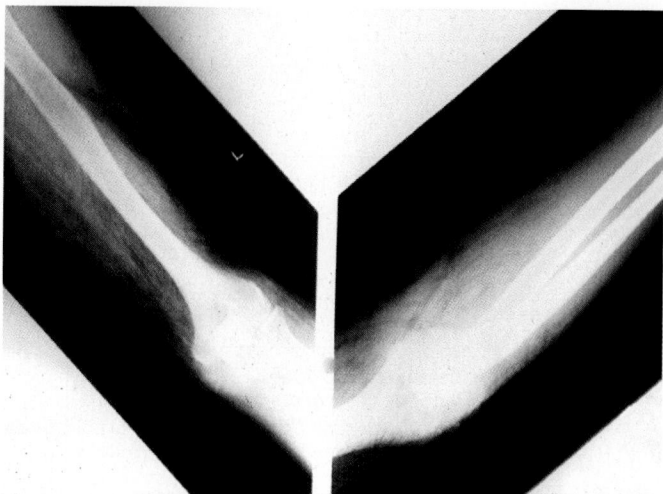

Figure 3 **Upper-extremity x-ray of a patient with necrotizing soft tissue infection demonstrates soft tissue gas outlining the muscles.**

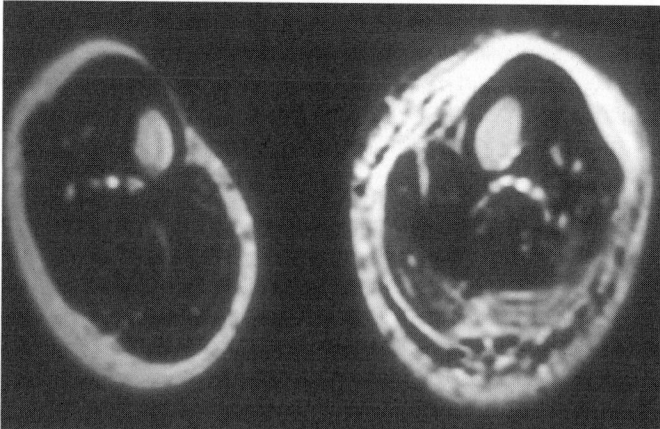

Figure 4 **Lower-extremity MRI of a patient with necrotizing fasciitis of the left leg demonstrates inflammatory changes typical of necrosis.**

more severe abnormalities, via I.V. infusion. Lactic acidosis generally responds to fluid administration. Renal function is assessed by measuring blood urea nitrogen (BUN) and serum creatinine concentrations. CK levels should be monitored and a qualitative evaluation of urine myoglobin done if muscle necrosis is suspected or renal failure is present. Myoglobinuria and elevated CK levels are suggestive of myonecrosis. Anemia is treated with packed red blood cell transfusions.

Patients whose hypotension does not resolve with appropriate intravascular fluid resuscitation often experience septic shock. In these circumstances, low dosages of I.V. dopamine (5 to 10 µg/kg/min), vasopressin (0.1 to 0.4 IU/min), or norepinephrine (0.02 to 0.08 µg/kg/min) are useful for raising blood pressure and improving myocardial function.

Patients with traumatic wounds or other contaminated sites should receive tetanus toxoid or human tetanus immunoglobulin, depending on their immunization status.

Hyperbaric oxygen has been advocated as adjunctive therapy for extensive necrotizing infections, particularly those caused by clostridia.[16] The beneficial properties of hyperbaric oxygen include inhibition of bacterial exotoxin production [see Discussion,

Pathogenesis of Soft Tissue Infections, *below*], improved leukocyte function, and attainment of tissue oxygen levels that are bactericidal for *Clostridium perfringens* and bacteriostatic for other anaerobic bacteria. Hyperbaric oxygen does not, however, neutralize exotoxin that has already been released.[16] At present, except for some data from retrospective studies, there is little evidence supporting the benefits of hyperbaric oxygen therapy. Such therapy has not been demonstrated to improve survival or to bring about earlier resolution of necrotizing soft tissue infection, and it has been associated with barotrauma, pneumothorax, and oxygen toxicity. Accordingly, we believe that operative debridement should not be delayed to accommodate hyperbaric oxygen therapy and that such therapy should not be considered a substitute for complete debridement of infected nonviable tissues.

I.V. antimicrobial therapy is indicated in all patients with necrotizing soft tissue infections [see Table 3]. Such therapy is important, but it is not a substitute for prompt and adequate operative debridement. Necrotizing soft tissue infections are usually caused by a mixed polymicrobial bacterial flora [see Table 4]. Approximately 25% to 30% of necrotizing soft tissue infections are monomicrobial. Although *S. pyogenes* is the bacterium most frequently involved, the microbiology of the infections often cannot be accurately predicted before final identification of organisms on culture. Thus, the empirical antibiotic regimen chosen should be effective against a diverse group of potential pathogens.[17] In addition, because these patients have a high incidence of associated nosocomial infections and even of metastatic infections, it is

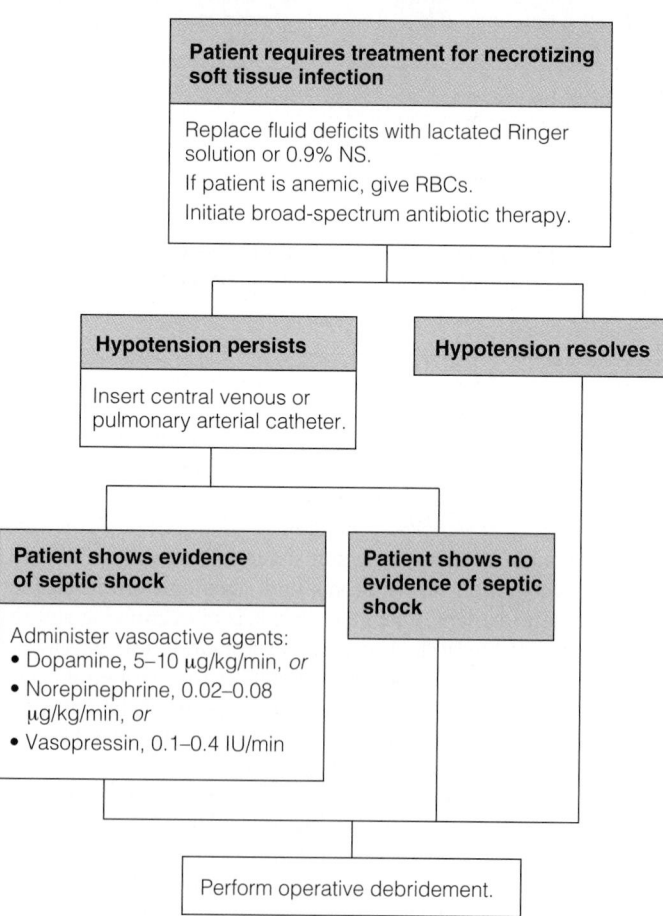

Figure 5 **Algorithm outlines treatment of necrotizing soft tissue infection.**

Table 3   I.V. Antibiotic Dosages for Adult Patients with Necrotizing Soft Tissue Infection and Normal Renal Function

Single agents	Ampicillin-sulbactam	3 g q. 6 hr
	Imipenem-cilastatin	500–1,000 mg q. 6 hr
	Meropenem	1 g q. 8 hr
	Piperacillin-tazobactam	3.375 g q. 6 hr
	Ticarcillin-clavulanate	3.1 g q. 6 hr
Agents used in combination regimens	Aerobic/facultative coverage	
	Ampicillin	2 g q. 6 hr
	Cefotaxime	1–2 g q. 8 hr
	Ceftazidime	1 g q. 8 hr
	Cefuroxime	1.5 g q. 8 hr
	Ciprofloxacin	400 mg q. 12 hr
	Gentamicin	1.7 mg/kg q. 8 hr
	Vancomycin	1 g q. 12 hr
	Anaerobic coverage	
	Clindamycin	900 mg q. 8 hr
	Metronidazole	500 mg q. 6 hr

important to ensure that the dosage is high enough to achieve adequate serum concentrations.[13,14] Once the results of intraoperative culture and antimicrobial sensitivity testing become available, antibiotic therapy is adjusted accordingly. This adjustment can be challenging, in that all of the pathogens identified must be treated.

I.V. antimicrobial therapy is continued until operative debridement is complete, there is no further evidence of infection in the involved tissues, and signs of systemic toxicity have resolved. Topical antiseptic agents (e.g., Dakin solution and Burrow solution) may help control infection that progresses despite adequate debridement and I.V. antibiotics. Topical application of mycostatin powder may help control progressive fungal infection. When patients are able to resume oral intake, they can often be switched from I.V. to oral antimicrobial therapy.

Operative Treatment

The most critical factors for reducing mortality from necrotizing soft tissue infections are early recognition and urgent operative debridement.[12,13,15,18] The extent of debridement depends on intraoperative findings and cannot be accurately predicted before operation. Operative intervention serves to limit tissue damage by removing necrotic tissue, which serves as a nidus for infection.

Thorough exploration is necessary to confirm the diagnosis of necrotizing soft tissue infection and determine the degree of involvement. Aggressive, widespread debridement of all apparent necrotic, infected tissue is essential; antibiotics will not penetrate dead tissues. The underlying necrosis of subcutaneous tissues, fascia, and muscle typically extends beyond the obvious limits of cutaneous involvement. Operative debridement should therefore be continued until viable tissue is reached. The presence of arterial bleeding generally indicates that tissues are viable; in the absence of arterial bleeding, tissues are nonviable even if venous bleeding is present. With deep necrotizing infections, debridement of the necrotic fascia and muscle may create large skin flaps that are poorly perfused. It is best to preserve as much viable skin and subcutaneous tissue as possible because these tissues can be essential for later coverage of the wound. Nonviable skin, however, should be resected.

Wound drainage or exudate should be submitted for Gram staining, as well as for aerobic, anaerobic, and fungal cultures and antimicrobial sensitivity testing. Fasciotomy is rarely required. The presence of subcutaneous gas extending beyond areas of nonviable tissue does not necessitate debridement if the surrounding tissues are viable. It is sometimes helpful to perform an exploratory incision over an area beyond the limits of debridement when it is uncertain whether necrosis is undermining viable skin. If no necrotizing infection is found, the incision may be closed primarily.

Reexploration should be routinely performed within 24 to 36 hours to ensure that all necrotic tissue has been debrided. Debridement is repeated as necessary until the infection is controlled. If repeated debridement does not control infection, if there are persistent, fulminant infections of the extremities, or if an extremity remains nonfunctional after debridement has been completed, amputation can be lifesaving. Amputation is most often required for patients with clostridial myonecrosis and for diabetic patients with necrotizing fasciitis.[15] In two large series of patients with necrotizing soft tissue infections, the incidence of amputation was approximately 15% to 25%.[12,13]

Patients with necrotizing soft tissue infections involving the perineum and perirectal areas may need a diverting colostomy to prevent tissue contamination resulting from defecation and to control local infection. Overall, this measure is required in fewer than 25% of cases.[13]

After debridement, the exposed areas should be treated with 0.9% normal saline wet-to-dry dressings. Once the initial infection has been controlled and debridement is no longer necessary, dressing changes can often be performed at the bedside after sufficient analgesics have been given to achieve adequate pain management. Patient-controlled analgesia is frequently useful early in the course of treatment. Propofol or ketamine can be given in the intensive care unit to facilitate pain control during dressing changes.

Early enteral or parenteral nutritional support should be instituted to optimize recovery. Nutritional support should begin once resuscitation is complete, the infection is adequately controlled, and the signs of sepsis have resolved. Because it frequently proves necessary to return the patient to the operating room, enteral feeding tubes should be placed beyond the pylorus so that enteral nutrition can be provided without interruption. Alternatively, parenteral nutrition may be employed.

Once the localized infection is under control and the patient is recovering, the exposed soft tissues should be covered. This is

Table 4   Organisms Causing Necrotizing Soft Tissue Infection

Aerobes	Gram-positive
	Group A *Streptococcus*
	Enterococcus species
	Staphylococcus aureus
	Group B *Streptococcus*
	Bacillus species
	Gram-negative
	Escherichia coli
	Pseudomonas aeruginosa
	Enterobacter cloacae
	Klebsiella species
	Serratia species
	Acinetobacter calcoaceticus
	Vibrio vulnificus
Anaerobes	*Bacteroides* species
	Clostridium species
	Peptostreptococcus species

most commonly done with split-thickness skin grafting, though other reconstructive procedures (e.g., rotational flaps) [see 27 Surface Reconstruction Procedures] can be effective in this setting as well. Vacuum-assisted closure devices can reduce the exposed surface area and lessen the need for skin graft coverage. Exposed tendons, nerves, or bone often should be covered with full-thickness skin to prevent desiccation and preserve limb function. Premature closure of highly contaminated or persistently infected sites usually fails and leads to recurrence of infection and a greater likelihood of death.

When the abdominal or chest wall has been excised to control infection, reconstruction is necessary. Polypropylene prosthetic mesh is useful for restoring continuity of the abdomen or the chest wall, and overlying moist dressings can help prevent desiccation of underlying viscera. Some have advocated using absorbable mesh for restoration of abdominal wall continuity; however, we prefer to use permanent mesh in most circumstances.[13]

Mortality from necrotizing soft tissue infection ranges from 21% to 29%.[12,13,15,18,19] Risk factors for mortality include age greater than 60 years, the presence of associated chronic illnesses, a relatively high percentage of total body surface area involved, and, most important, delays in recognition and treatment.[12,13,15] Patients with truncal involvement or positive blood cultures also have a higher mortality.[12,19]

Management of Specific Soft Tissue Infections

Normal skin functions as a protective barrier that prevents microorganisms from causing soft tissue infection. The skin, or cutis, is made up of two layers, the epidermis and the dermis [see Figure 6]. The epidermis, the outer avascular epithelial layer, functions as a permeability barrier for the rest of the body. The dermis, the inner layer, contains blood vessels, lymphatic vessels, sweat and sebaceous glands, and hair follicles. The subcutaneous tissue separates the skin from the deep fascia, muscle, and bone. Typically, soft tissue infections result from disruption of the skin by some exogenous factor; less commonly, they result from extension of a subjacent infection or hematogenous spread from a distant site of infection.

SUPERFICIAL INFECTIONS

Superficial infections constitute the majority of soft tissue infections. They primarily involve the epidermis or dermis (pyoderma) or the subcutaneous tissue (cellulitis) and secondarily occur in skin damaged by animal or human bites. Nonnecrotizing superficial soft tissue infections are principally treated with antibiotics. Necrosis is rare but may develop in superficial infections that are inadequately treated or neglected.

Pyoderma

Pyoderma is a general term referring to a bacterial infection of the skin. It may be divided into several subcategories, such as impetigo, erysipelas, folliculitis, and furuncles and carbuncles.

Impetigo Impetigo is a highly contagious bacterial infection that is confined to the epidermis and that usually involves the face or the extremities. It is most common in infants and preschool children and is seen more frequently in patients with preexisting skin conditions (e.g., eczema, atopic dermatitis, varicella infection, angular cheilitis, and scabies). Warm and humid weather, crowded living conditions, and poor hygiene can all contribute to the development of impetigo.[20] The dominant pathogen is *S. aureus*, which causes either a bullous or a nonbullous form of the

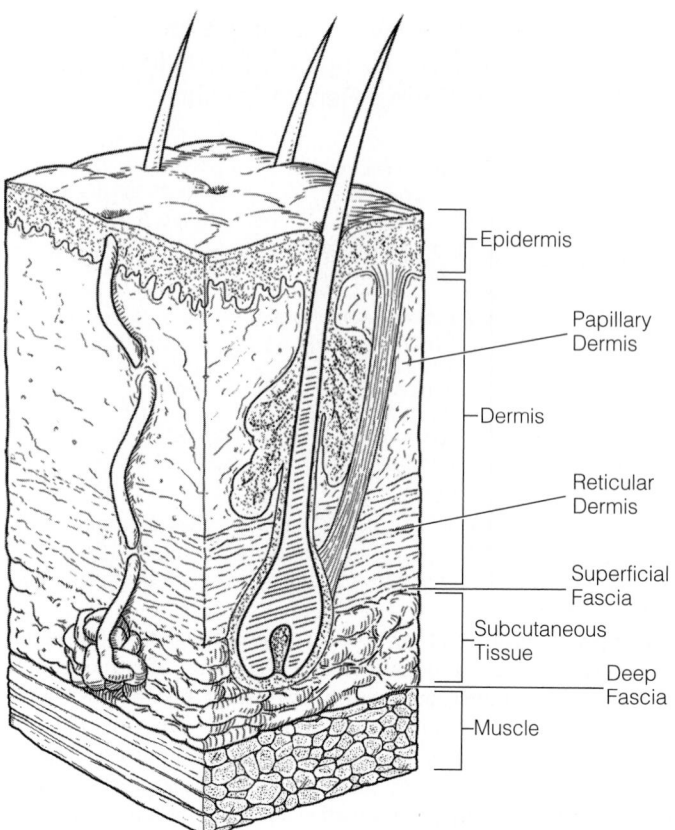

Figure 6 **Depicted is the normal anatomy of the skin and the deeper cutaneous layers.**[6]

disease; a less common pathogen is *S. pyogenes*, which causes a nonbullous form.[21]

Impetigo usually occurs in areas of skin breakdown, though *S. aureus* may give rise to de novo infection in normal skin. Bullous impetigo is manifested by numerous blisters or bullae that rapidly become pustules, then rupture within 1 to 2 days to form a thick, honey-colored, crusted plaque that remains for days to weeks. Nonbullous impetigo is characterized by erythema and tiny, less prominent vesicles that progress to crusted erosions in the skin. The skin lesions are intensely pruritic, and local spread may occur as a result of scratching and release of infected fluid from the blisters, bullae, or vesicles. Associated regional lymphadenopathy is common. Glomerulonephritis may complicate streptococcal-induced impetigo.[21,22]

The diagnosis is established by Gram stain and culture of the vesicular fluid or the crusted plaque. The skin lesions usually resolve spontaneously within 2 to 3 weeks.[22] Antibiotic therapy accelerates the resolution of these lesions. Mupirocin ointment (2%) is applied topically three times a day until the lesions clear. This agent possesses excellent in vitro activity against both staphylococci and streptococci and achieves high rates of cure in patients with localized disease. Erythromycin and clindamycin ointments are acceptable alternatives [see Table 5]. For patients who have disseminated impetigo or impetigo of the scalp or mouth and those in whom topical therapy fails, an oral antibiotic (e.g., dicloxacillin, cephalexin, cefadroxil, erythromycin, or clindamycin) may be used [see Table 5]. A 7-day course of oral antibiotic therapy is usually sufficient.[22]

Erysipelas Erysipelas is an acute bacterial infection that principally involves the dermis. It is almost invariably caused by *S. pyo-*

genes. Most cases are preceded by influenzalike symptoms. Infection extends through the dermal lymphatic vessels and is typically manifested by a tender, pruritic, intensely erythematous, sharply demarcated, and raised plaque. Patients complain of pain, often in conjunction with high fever, increased skin warmth, and leukocytosis. Lymphangitis and lymphadenopathy are sometimes present as well. The leg is the most common site of involvement, but erysipelas may also occur on the face, the arms, and the upper thighs.

The factors predisposing to the development of erysipelas of the extremity include local conditions such as tinea pedis (athlete's foot), leg ulcers, and venous stasis dermatitis.[23] Erysipelas tends to be more common in the presence of associated conditions such as lymphedema, diabetes mellitus, alcoholism, immunocompromise, and obesity,[21,23] and it is more likely to recur in patients with these associated diseases and in those whose underlying skin conditions are inadequately treated. Erysipelas recurs in 10% of patients within 6 months of their first episode and in 30% within 3 years.[23]

The standard antibiotic treatment for uncomplicated erysipelas is penicillin, which is effective in at least 80% of cases. Oral and intravenous antibiotic regimens are equally efficacious. Amoxicillin appears to work as well as penicillin. Patients with erysipelas of the lower extremity should be placed on bed rest, and the involved leg should be elevated to reduce edema and pain. Once the patient is able to resume normal activities, he or she should be fitted with elastic stockings, which help reduce the recurrence of edema and lower the risk of lymphedema. For patients with tinea pedis, a topical antifungal agent is used to treat the infection and prevent recurrence.

Table 5 Topical and Oral Antibiotic Agents Used for Superficial Soft Tissue Infections*

Mupirocin ointment (2%), applied to affected area t.i.d.†

Erythromycin ointment (2%), applied to affected area b.i.d.†

Clindamycin gel or lotion (1%), applied to affected area b.i.d.†

Gentamicin cream or ointment (0.1%), applied to affected area t.i.d. or q.i.d.

Penicillin V, 250–500 mg q.i.d. (pediatric: 25–50 mg/kg in divided doses q.i.d.)

Amoxicillin, 250–500 mg t.i.d. (pediatric: 20–30 mg/kg/day p.o. in divided doses t.i.d.)

Dicloxacillin, 250–500 mg q.i.d. (pediatric: 12.5–25.0 mg/kg/day in divided doses q.i.d.)

Cephalexin, 250–500 mg q.i.d. (pediatric: 25–100 mg/kg/day in divided doses q.i.d.)

Cefadroxil, 500–1,000 mg b.i.d. (pediatric: 30 mg/kg/day in divided doses b.i.d.)

Erythromycin, 250–500 mg q. 6 hr (pediatric: erythromycin ethyl succinate, 40 mg/kg in divided doses q.i.d.)

Clindamycin, 150–450 mg q.i.d. (pediatric: 20 mg/kg/day in divided doses t.i.d. or q.i.d.)

Trimethoprim-sulfamethoxazole, 160/800 mg b.i.d.

Amoxicillin-clavulanate, 500 mg t.i.d. (pediatric: 40 mg/kg/day in divided doses t.i.d.)

Ciprofloxacin, 500 mg p.o., b.i.d.

---

*All dosages are for patients with normal renal function.

†Adult dosage and pediatric dosage are the same.

Folliculitis Folliculitis is an infection of the hair follicle that is typically caused by S. aureus. It is characterized by a painful, tender, erythematous papule with a central pustule. A shaft of hair is often seen in the center of the pustule. Shaving, plucking, waxing, heat and humidity, the use of corticosteroids or antibiotics, immunosuppression, and occlusion of the skin by clothing, adhesives, or plastics may predispose to folliculitis.[20] Single or multiple lesions may occur in the skin of any hair-bearing area. If the pustule ruptures, superficial erosion often ensues. Infection that principally involves the deeper part of the hair follicle is characterized by a tender, swollen papule without an associated pustule at the skin surface.

In rare cases, folliculitis is caused by pathogens other than S. aureus, such as Pseudomonas aeruginosa, Klebsiella species, Enterobacter species, Proteus species, yeasts, and fungi. Pseudomonas folliculitis usually results from exposure to inadequately chlorinated water in swimming pools, hot tubs, or whirlpools. Patients with this infection have multiple papular or pustular lesions on the back, the buttocks, and the extremities, along with fever and malaise appearing 6 hours to 3 days after exposure.[22,24] Organisms may be cultured either from the pustules or from the infected water. Klebsiella, Enterobacter, and Proteus species can cause folliculitis in patients receiving long-term antibiotic therapy for acne vulgaris.[21] Yeast folliculitis and fungal folliculitis tend to occur in immunocompromised patients.[21]

In most patients, folliculitis resolves spontaneously within 7 to 10 days.[22] Topical therapy with clindamycin, erythromycin, or mupirocin ointments or benzoyl peroxide in combination with warm soaks may accelerate resolution [see Table 5]. Isotretinoin can be used to treat gram-negative folliculitis. Gentamicin cream may be helpful in drying out the pustular lesions in patients with Pseudomonas folliculitis.

In patients with refractory or disseminated follicular infections, oral antibiotic therapy is indicated. When S. aureus is considered the most likely pathogen, dicloxacillin, erythromycin, cephalexin, cefadroxil, or clindamycin may be given; oral ciprofloxacin is indicated for the treatment of gram-negative folliculitis [see Table 5]. Elimination of predisposing factors is important for reducing the likelihood of recurrence.

Furuncles and carbuncles Furuncles and carbuncles are deeper infections of the hair follicle that extend beyond the hair follicle to involve the subcutaneous tissue. For both, S. aureus is the usual causative organism.

A furuncle, or boil, is a small abscess, manifested as a firm, tender, erythematous nodule that tends to occur in skin areas exposed to friction (e.g., the inner thighs and the axilla). Furuncles also may occur on the face, the neck, the upper back, and the buttocks. Possible predisposing factors include increased friction and perspiration (as seen in obese individuals or athletes), corticosteroid use, diabetes mellitus, and inherited or acquired defects in neutrophil function.[20,22]

Initial treatment consists of applying warm compresses to help promote drainage and administering an oral antimicrobial agent that is effective against S. aureus (e.g., dicloxacillin, cephalexin, cefadroxil, erythromycin, or clindamycin) [see Table 5]. With time, the furuncle becomes fluctuant, and the pus coalesces at the skin surface. An incision-and-drainage procedure is necessary when these lesions do not drain spontaneously. This procedure should be performed with local anesthesia, and care should be taken to open the abscess cavity completely. Lesions that have drained spontaneously should be examined to confirm that the cavity has been opened sufficiently. Failure to drain these lesions adequately may result in recurrence, as well as in progression to a more serious infection.

A carbuncle is a deep cutaneous infection involving multiple hair follicles that is characterized by destruction of fibrous tissue septa and consequent formation of a series of interconnected abscesses. It is typically manifested by a painful, red, tender, indurated area of skin with multiple sinus tracts. Systemic manifestations (e.g., fever and malaise) are common. Carbuncles occur most frequently on the nape of the neck, the upper part of the back, or the posterior thigh. The thickness of the overlying skin in these areas leads to lateral extension of the infection and loculation. Patients commonly present with relatively large skin lesions that represent a confluence of inflammatory nodules. These lesions are associated with chronic drainage, sinus tracts, and scarring.

An incision-and-drainage procedure is recommended when a fluctuant carbuncle is present. A thorough search for loculated areas should be undertaken to facilitate drainage of deeper accumulations of pus and to ensure adequate treatment. Wide local excision of the involved skin and subcutaneous fat is often necessary to prevent recurrent disease. An oral antistaphylococcal agent should be given. All patients with hair follicle infections should cleanse the site with chlorhexidine or an iodine-containing solution.

Infections Developing in Damaged Skin

Damage to skin as a result of animal or human bites predisposes patients to soft tissue infection. An estimated 50% of all Americans will be bitten by an animal or by another human being during their lifetime.[25] Animal and human bites account for approximately 1% of all emergency department visits.[25] Soft tissue infection is the most common complication of such bites. The risk of infection depends on the type of bite, the site of injury, the time elapsed from the bite until presentation, host factors, and the management of the wound [see Table 6].

Most animal and human bites produce minor injuries for which patients do not seek medical attention. The overall risk of infection after a bite is estimated to be 5% to 15%[26]; however, among the subset of patients who seek medical attention, estimated infection rates range from 2% to 20% for dog bites, from 30% to more than 50% for cat bites, and from 10% to 50% for human bites.[27] Most patients with an infected bite can be managed on an outpatient basis with oral antibiotic therapy and elevation of the involved site.

Animal bites   In the United States, dog bites account for 80% to 90% of all animal bites, cat bites for 3% to 15%.[27,28] Nondomestic animals are responsible for only 1% to 2% of all animal bites. Patients with infections resulting from animal bites typically present with significant pain, soft tissue swelling, and tenderness; they may also have associated injuries to nerves, tendons, bones, joints, or blood vessels. Bites involving the hand are associated with an increased risk of tenosynovitis, septic arthritis, and abscess formation.[27]

Infections that occur after a dog or cat bite are usually polymicrobial, involving a mixture of aerobes and anaerobes [see Table 7]. *P. multocida* is the major pathogen, isolated from 50% to 80% of infections related to cat bites and from 25% of those related to dog bites.[25,27] Infection with *P. multocida* is characterized by the acute onset of severe pain, tenderness, and swelling, usually within 12 to 18 hours of the bite. In rare cases (usually involving immunocompromised patients), *Capnocytophaga canimorsus* causes soft tissue infection after a dog or cat bite. *C. canimorsus* infection can be quite serious, leading to overwhelming sepsis; the associated mortality is 25% to 30%.[27-29]

Table 6   **Risk Factors for Soft Tissue Infection Complicating Animal or Human Bite**

Location on the hand or the foot or over a major joint	Immunosuppression
Location on the scalp or the face of an infant	Chronic alcoholism
	Diabetes mellitus
Puncture wound	Corticosteroid use
Delay in treatment lasting longer than 12 hr	Preexisting edema in an affected extremity

Wounds resulting from animal bites should immediately be washed with soap and water. When seen early, dog bites should be copiously irrigated, debrided, and, in most circumstances, closed. Infected wounds, wounds older than 12 hours, cat bites, and bites on the hand should be left open. In all cases of infection related to an animal bite, aerobic and anaerobic cultures should be obtained from the site of infection. Tetanus immune status should be determined, and immunization against tetanus should be provided when appropriate. In cases of bites from nondomestic carnivores (e.g., bats, skunks, raccoons, foxes, or coyotes), wounds should be irrigated with povidone-iodine to reduce the transmission of rabies, and immunization against rabies should be provided.

Patients with established soft tissue infection and patients with noninfected bites who have risk factors for infection should receive antibiotic therapy [see Table 6]. A broad-spectrum antibiotic effective against aerobic and anaerobic organisms should be chosen [see Table 5]. Amoxicillin-clavulanate is the antibiotic of choice because of its broad spectrum of activity against common pathogens; trimethoprim-sulfamethoxazole, doxycycline, and ciprofloxacin are also used [see Table 5]. Infections secondary to *P. multocida* respond to oral treatment with penicillin V, amoxicillin, cefuroxime, or ciprofloxacin.[27] Infections secondary to *C. canimorsus* respond to penicillin, ampicillin, ciprofloxacin, erythromycin, or doxycycline. Whether antibiotics are indicated for a fresh animal bite in a patient with a low risk of infection is controversial. Because it is difficult to predict which bite wounds will become infected, some experts advocate routine antibiotic treatment of all dog bites for at least 3 to 5 days.[25]

Human bites   Human bites may be classified as either occlusional bites (in which teeth puncture the skin) or clenched-fist injuries (in which the hand is injured after contact with teeth).[27,29]

Table 7   **Organisms Most Frequently Isolated from Dog- and Cat-Bite Wounds**

Aerobes	*Pasteurella multocida* *Corynebacterium* species *Staphylococcus* species *Streptococcus* species *Capnocytophaga canimorsus* (rare)
Anaerobes	*Bacteroides* species *Prevotella* species *Porphyromonas* species Peptostreptococci *Fusobacterium* species *Bacteroides fragilis* *Veillonella parvula*

Occlusional bites carry roughly the same risk of infection as animal bites, except when they occur on the hand. Clenched-fist injuries and all hand injuries are associated with a higher risk of infection. Clenched-fist injuries typically occur at the third metacarpophalangeal joint. Penetration of the metacarpophalangeal joint capsule may occur, with subsequent development of septic arthritis and osteomyelitis.[25]

Soft tissue infections resulting from human bites are polymicrobial, involving a mixture of aerobes and anaerobes. On average, five different microorganisms are isolated from a human-bite wound[27]—significantly more than are usually isolated from an animal-bite wound. In addition, the concentration of bacteria in the oral cavity is higher in humans than in animals. The anaerobic bacteria isolated from human-bite wounds are similar to those that cause infection after dog and cat bites, except that *Bacteroides* species are more common [see Table 7]. Unlike the anaerobic pathogens in dog and cat bites, however, those involved in human-bite infections often produce β-lactamases.[27] The predominant aerobic organisms in human-bite infections are *S. aureus*, *Staphylococcus epidermidis*, α- and β-hemolytic streptococci, *Corynebacterium* species, and *E. corrodens*. *E. corrodens* is a fastidious facultative aerobic gram-negative rod that is cultured from approximately 25% of clenched-fist injuries and frequently causes a chronic indolent infection.[27] It typically is susceptible to amoxicillin-clavulanate, trimethoprim-sulfamethoxazole, doxycycline, and ciprofloxacin but resistant to dicloxacillin, nafcillin, first-generation cephalosporins, clindamycin, and erythromycin. Other pathogens may also be transmitted as a result of contact with blood or saliva, including hepatitis B and C viruses, *Mycobacterium tuberculosis*, and, possibly, HIV.

Management of human-bite wounds is similar to that of animal-bite wounds. The wound must be thoroughly irrigated, preferably with 1% povidone-iodine, which is both bactericidal and viricidal. Puncture bite wounds should be irrigated with a small catheter to achieve high-pressure irrigation. If the wound appears infected, aerobic and anaerobic cultures are obtained. Devitalized tissue should be debrided, and the wound should be left open, whether infected or not. The injured extremity should be immobilized and elevated.

Because of the high degree of contamination and local tissue damage associated with human-bite wounds to the hand, antimicrobial therapy is indicated for all such injuries. A prospective, randomized study of 45 patients with human bites to the hand seen within 24 hours after injury and without evidence of infection, tendon injury, or joint capsule penetration demonstrated that infection developed in 47% of the patients who did not receive antibiotics but in none of those who did.[30] Patients with an uncomplicated human bite to the hand should receive a broad-spectrum oral antimicrobial agent, such as amoxicillin-clavulanate (or doxycycline if they are allergic to penicillins).

Patients with human-bite wounds at sites other than the hand who have risk factors for infection [see Table 6] should also receive antimicrobial therapy. However, minor bite wounds in patients who have no risk factors for infection do not call for antibiotic therapy. As with animal-bite wounds, tetanus immunization status should be determined, and tetanus toxoid, tetanus immunoglobin, or both should be administered as indicated.

Patients with systemic manifestations of infection (e.g., fever or chills); severe cellulitis; compromised immune status; diabetes mellitus; significant bites to the hand; associated joint, nerve, bone, or tendon involvement; or infection refractory to oral antibiotic therapy should be admitted to the hospital for I.V. antibiotic therapy.[27] Appropriate choices for I.V. treatment include cefoxitin,

cefotetan, and piperacillin-tazobactam. Tenosynovitis, joint infections, and associated injuries to deep structures must also be treated if present.

Cellulitis

Cellulitis is an acute bacterial infection of the dermis and the subcutaneous tissue that primarily affects the lower extremities, though it can affect other areas as well (e.g., the periorbital, buccal, and perianal regions; the areas around incisions; and sites of body piercing).[31] The most common causes of cellulitis are (1) soft tissue trauma from injection of illicit drugs, puncture wounds from foreign bodies or bites (animal, human, or insect), or burns; (2) surgical site infection; and (3) secondary infection of preexisting skin lesions (e.g., eczema; tinea pedis; and decubitus, venous stasis, or ischemic ulcers). Less common causes include extension of a subjacent infection (e.g., osteomyelitis) and bacteremia from a remote site of infection. Predisposing factors for the development of cellulitis include lymphatic disruption or lymphedema, interstitial edema, previous irradiation of soft tissue, diabetes mellitus, immunocompromise, and peripheral vascular disease.

Nonnecrotizing The overwhelming majority of patients with cellulitis have a nonnecrotizing form of the disease. Patients typically present for medical attention because of pain and soft tissue erythema, and they often have constitutional symptoms (e.g., fever, chills, or malaise). Physical examination reveals erythema with advancing borders, increased skin warmth, tenderness, and edema. Lymphangitis may also be present, manifested as an erythematous linear streak that often extends to a draining lymph node basin; associated lymphadenopathy, fever, and leukocytosis with a shift to immature forms may be apparent.

Cellulitis is usually caused by a single aerobic pathogen. The organisms most frequently responsible for cellulitis in otherwise healthy adults are *S. pyogenes* and *S. aureus*. Of the two, *S. pyogenes* is the more common and is the usual pathogen in patients with associated lymphangitis. *S. aureus* is usually present in patients with underlying chronic skin disease. Other microorganisms may cause cellulitis on rare occasions but usually only in specific clinical circumstances. *Haemophilus influenzae* sometimes causes cellulitis in children or adults infected with HIV.[32] *Streptococcus pneumoniae* may cause this condition in patients with diabetes mellitus, alcoholism, nephrotic syndrome, systemic lupus erythematosus, or hematologic malignancies.[33] *P. multocida* may cause cellulitis as a complication of dog or cat bites. *S. epidermidis* is a recognized cause of cellulitis among immunocompromised patients, including those with HIV infection and those receiving organ transplants.[34] *V. vulnificus* occasionally causes cellulitis in patients who have ingested raw seafood or who have experienced minor soft tissue trauma and are exposed to sea water.[31] *A. hydrophila* may cause cellulitis in patients with soft tissue trauma who are exposed to fresh water.[31] Cellulitis that complicates decubitus or other nonhealing ulcers is usually a mixed infection that includes gram-negative organisms.

In most situations, cellulitis is treated with empirical antibiotic regimens that include agents effective against *S. pyogenes* and *S. aureus*. Attempts to isolate a causative pathogen are usually unsuccessful; needle aspiration and skin biopsy at an advancing margin of erythema are positive in only 15% and 40% of cases, respectively.[35] Bacteremia is uncommon, and as a result, blood cultures are positive in only 2% to 4% of patients with cellulitis.[31,36] Blood cultures are obtained selectively when the patient has high fever and chills, preexisting lymphedema, or buccal or periorbital cellulitis or when a saltwater or freshwater source of infection is suspected. In all of these clinical situations, the prevalence of bacteremia is higher.[36] Radiologic examination should be reserved for patients in whom it is difficult to exclude a deep necrotizing infection.

In an otherwise healthy adult, uncomplicated cellulitis without systemic manifestations can be treated with an oral antibiotic on an outpatient basis. Because the vast majority of cellulitides are caused either by *S. pyogenes* or by a penicillinase-producing *S. aureus*, one of the following agents is usually given: dicloxacillin, cephalexin, cefadroxil, erythromycin, or clindamycin [*see Table 5*]. The margins of the erythema should be marked with ink to facilitate assessment of the response to treatment. For lower-extremity cellulitis, reduced activity and elevation are important ancillary measures. Appropriate analgesic agents should be given.

Patients who are diabetic or immunocompromised and those who have high fever and chills, rapidly spreading cellulitis, or cellulitis that is refractory to oral antibiotic therapy should be admitted to the hospital for I.V. antibiotic therapy [*see Table 8*]. Nafcillin is the preferred I.V. agent. Cefazolin or ampicillin-sulbactam is recommended if gram-negative organisms are suspected pathogens, as when cellulitis complicates a decubitus or a diabetic foot ulcer. Clindamycin is recommended for patients with infections caused by methicillin-resistant *S. aureus* (MRSA) and those with serious penicillin allergies. Vancomycin is reserved for patients in these subgroups who are intolerant of or allergic to clindamycin.

Necrotizing Necrotizing cellulitis is similar to nonnecrotizing cellulitis in etiology and pathogenesis but is more serious and progressive. Necrosis generally occurs when the infection is neglected or inadequately treated. The microbiology of necrotizing cellulitis is also similar to that of nonnecrotizing cellulitis, except that *C. perfringens* and other clostridial species may be involved when necrosis is present. In addition to antimicrobial therapy [*see Table 8*], urgent operative debridement is indicated. In other respects, necrotizing cellulitis is treated in much the same way as deep necrotizing infections are (see below). In some patients with necrotizing fasciitis, the skin is involved secondarily.

DEEP NECROTIZING INFECTIONS

Infections that involve the soft tissues deep to the skin tend to become apparent after necrosis has developed. It is possible that deep necrotizing infections begin without necrosis but progress rapidly as a result of intrinsic factors. Alternatively, such infections may develop as a result of delayed recognition attributable to the tissue depth at which the process takes place and the lack of specific early signs and symptoms. The relatively poor blood supply to subcutaneous fat makes this tissue more susceptible to microbial invasion. Contamination of the deep soft tissues occurs either through neglect or inadequate treatment of cutaneous or subcutaneous infections or through hematogenous seeding of microorganisms in an area of injury.

Most deep necrotizing soft tissue infections are polymicrobial and occur on the extremities, the abdomen, and the perineum.[12,13,15] Necrotizing infections that involve only muscle are uncommon; therefore, necrotizing fasciitis can be considered the paradigm for these infectious processes.

The early signs and symptoms of deep necrotizing soft tissue infection are localized pain, tenderness, mild edema, and erythema of the overlying skin. These characteristics may be subtle, and this diagnosis may not readily come to mind. Sometimes, there is a history of previous injury to the area of suspected infection, which can lead to confusion about the diagnosis. The more clas-

Table 8 Suggested Parenteral Antibiotic Regimens for Treatment of Cellulitis in Adults

Agent	I.V. Dosage
Nafcillin	2 g q. 4 hr
Cefazolin	1–2 g q. 8 hr
Clindamycin	900 mg q. 8 hr
Vancomycin	500–1,000 q. 12 hr
Ampicillin-sulbactam	3 g q. 6 hr

sic findings associated with these infections—skin discoloration, the formation of bullae, and intense erythema—occur much later in the process. It is important to understand this point so that an early diagnosis can be made and appropriate treatment promptly instituted.

Necrotizing Fasciitis

Necrotizing fasciitis is characterized by angiothrombotic microbial invasion and liquefactive necrosis.[6] Progressive necrosis of the superficial fascia develops, and the deep dermis and fascia are infiltrated by polymorphonuclear leukocytes, with thrombosis of nutrient vessels and occasional suppuration of the veins and arteries coursing through the fascia; bacteria then proliferate within the destroyed fascia. Initially, tissue invasion proceeds horizontally, but as the condition progresses, ischemic necrosis of the skin develops, along with gangrene of the subcutaneous fat and dermis (characterized by progressive skin necrosis, the formation of bullae and vesicles, and occasional ulceration [*see Figure 1*]).

Myonecrosis

Myonecrosis is a rapidly progressive life-threatening infection of skeletal muscle that is primarily caused by *Clostridium* species. The classic example of myonecrosis is clostridial gas gangrene, a disease that was common in World War I soldiers who sustained extremity injuries that were contaminated with soil. Delays in definitive treatment and the use of primary closure for these contaminated wounds contributed to the severity and mortality of these infections.[37] Clostridial myonecrosis may also occur as a deep surgical site infection after contaminated operations, particularly those involving the GI tract or the biliary tract. Devitalized tissue is a perfect environment for clostridial proliferation. A rare form of this disease occurs in patients with colon cancer in whom myonecrosis caused by *Clostridium septicum* develops in the absence of tissue damage. Myonecrosis may also result from the spread of contiguous fascial infections.

Clostridial myonecrosis has a notably short incubation period: severe progressive disease can develop within 24 hours of contamination. This condition is characterized by acute catastrophic pain in the area of infection, with minimal associated physical findings. Systemic signs of toxicity (e.g., confusion, incontinence, and delirium) often precede the physical signs of localized infection. The skin initially is pale, then gradually becomes yellowish or bronze. Blebs, bullae, and skin necrosis do not appear until late in the course of the disease. Edema and tenderness occur early, and the absence of erythema distinguishes clostridial infections from streptococcal infection. A thin serosanguineous discharge is present in involved areas and may emanate from an involved incision. Gram stain reveals gram-positive coccobacilli with few leukocytes.

When clostridial myonecrosis is suspected or confirmed, penicillin G, 2 to 4 million U every 4 hours, should be given immediately; clindamycin, 900 mg every 8 hours, should be added. When *C. septicum* is identified on culture, a search for an occult GI tract malignancy should be made. Clostridial myonecrosis is the one soft tissue infection for which hyperbaric oxygen is recommended, though as yet, there is little evidence that this modality improves outcomes. If hyperbaric oxygen therapy is to be used, it should not be given before operative debridement.

Discussion

Etiology and Classification of Soft Tissue Infection

Soft tissue infection commonly results from inoculation of bacteria through a defect in the epidermal layer of the skin, such as may occur with injury, preexisting skin disease, or vascular compromise. Less commonly, soft tissue infection may be a consequence of extension from a subjacent site of infection (e.g., osteomyelitis) or of hematogenous spread from a distant site (e.g., diverticulitis or *C. septicum* infection in patients with colonic carcinoma). It may also occur de novo in healthy patients with normal-appearing skin, often as a result of virulent pathogenic organisms.[38]

Conditions that disrupt the skin and alter its normal barrier function [see Table 2] predispose patients to bacterial contamination. Host factors may increase susceptibility to infection and limit the patient's ability to contain the bacterial inoculum. Clinically occult infection or inadequate treatment of other conditions may also lead to secondary development of soft tissue infection (as is sometimes seen in patients with diverticulitis; perirectal, pilonidal, or Bartholin's cyst abscesses; strangulated hernias; or panniculitis). Delayed or inadequate treatment of superficial infections (e.g., folliculitis, furuncles, carbuncles, cellulitis, and surgical site infections) may lead to more severe necrotizing infections.

Soft tissue infections may be classified as superficial or deep, as nonnecrotizing or necrotizing, as primary (idiopathic) or secondary, and as monomicrobial or polymicrobial. Superficial infections involve the epidermis, dermis, superficial fascia, or subcutaneous tissue, whereas deep infections involve the deep fascia or muscle [see Figure 6]. Necrotizing soft tissue infections are distinguished by the presence of extensive, rapidly progressing necrosis and high mortality. Such infections are termed necrotizing cellulitis, necrotizing fasciitis, or myonecrosis according to whether the deepest tissue layer affected by necrosis is subcutaneous tissue, deep fascia, or muscle, respectively.

Primary (idiopathic) soft tissue infections occur in the absence of a known causative factor or portal of entry for bacteria. Such infections are uncommon and are believed to result from hematogenous spread or bacterial invasion through small unrecognized breaks in the epidermis.[38,39] Soft tissue infection caused by *V. vulnificus* is an example of a primary soft tissue infection: it is attributed to bacteremia developing after the ingestion of contaminated raw seafood. Only 10% to 15% of all necrotizing soft tissue infections are idiopathic; the remaining 85% to 90% are secondary infections, developing as a consequence of some insult to the skin that predisposes to infection. Secondary soft tissue infections may be further categorized as posttraumatic, postoperative, or complications of preexisting skin conditions.

Soft tissue infections are classified as monomicrobial when they are caused by a single organism and as polymicrobial when they are caused by multiple organisms. Most superficial soft tissue infections are caused by a single aerobe, usually *S. pyogenes* or *S. aureus*. Exceptions to this general rule include infections associated with skin damaged by animal or human bites, cellulitis associated with decubitus or other nonhealing ulcers, and infections in immunocompromised patients. These infections are typically polymicrobial, often involving aerobic or facultative gram-negative organisms and anaerobes in addition to aerobic gram-positive bacteria.

Deep necrotizing soft tissue infections are polymicrobial 70% to 75% of the time. They are caused by the synergistic activity of facultative aerobes and anaerobes [see Figure 7].[40,41] *S. aureus*, *S. pyogenes*, and enterococci are the most common gram-positive aerobes. *Escherichia coli* is the most common gram-negative enteric organism. *Bacteroides* species and peptostreptococci are the most common anaerobes.[13,18,41] The remaining 25% to 30% of deep necrotizing infections are monomicrobial. Most primary necrotizing soft tissue infections are monomicrobial.[38] These infections are more fulminant and are notable for their acute onset, rapid progression, and systemic toxicity. Their characteristic clinical manifestations are related to exotoxin production by the pathogen involved [see Table 9 and Pathogenesis of Soft Tissue Infections, below]. *S. pyogenes* is the pathogen in more than half of monomicrobial infections; *S. aureus*, *C. perfringens*, *V. vulnificus*, and *P. aeruginosa* are less common.

Pathogenesis of Soft Tissue Infections

Soft tissue infections generally induce localized inflammatory changes in the involved tissues, regardless of the species of bacteria involved. As the infection progresses, tissue necrosis occurs as a result of (1) direct cellular injury from bacterial toxins, (2) significant inflammatory edema within a closed tissue compartment, (3) thrombosis of nutrient blood vessels, and (4) tissue ischemia.

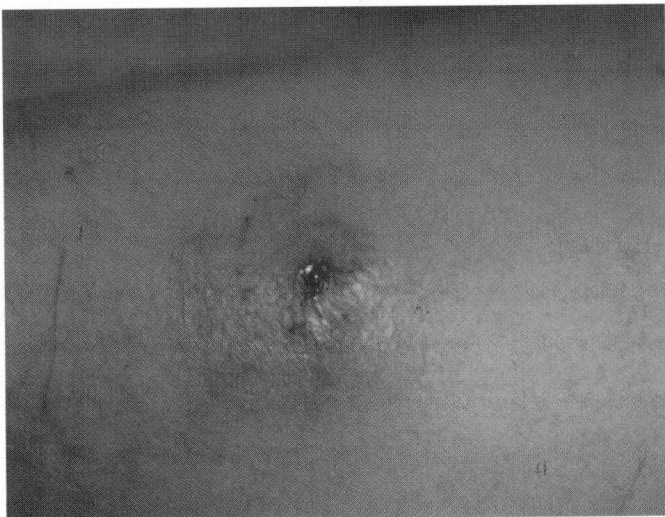

Figure 7   Meleney's ulcer is characterized by central necrosis, erythema, and edema.

Table 9 Major Exotoxins Associated with Organisms Causing Monomicrobial Necrotizing Soft Tissue Infection

Bacterium	Exotoxins
Streptococcus pyogenes	Pyrogenic exotoxins A and B, hemolysin, fibrinolysin, hyaluronidase, streptokinase
Staphylococcus aureus	Hemolysins (intravascular hemolysis and local tumor necrosis), coagulase
Pseudomonas aeruginosa	Collagenase (local tissue damage and necrosis)
Clostridium perfringens	α-Toxin (lecithinase causing tissue necrosis, intravascular hemolysis, hemoglobinemia, and acute renal failure)

The exotoxins produced by gram-positive cocci and some gram-negative bacteria are powerful proteolytic enzymes. *S. pyogenes* produces hemolysins, fibrinolysins, hyaluronidases, and streptolysins. *S. aureus* and *P. aeruginosa* produce coagulases that result in local tissue damage and necrosis. *C. perfringens* produces numerous exotoxins. The α-toxin, a lecithinase enzyme, is highly lethal: it destroys cell membranes, causes hemolysis, and alters capillary permeability. Other clostridial toxins lyse red blood cells and have direct cardiotoxic effects. These toxins also cause platelet aggregation and fibrin deposition, with resultant vascular thrombosis and necrosis. Production of the θ-toxin leads to intravascular leukostasis and inhibits diapedesis of white blood cells into infected tissue. This unique collection of bacterial toxins accounts for the rapid progression of *C. perfringens* infection in a setting of minimal inflammatory changes.

That most necrotizing soft tissue infections involve multiple bacterial species strongly suggests that bacterial synergy plays an important role in their pathogenesis. Toxin-induced cellular necrosis establishes an anaerobic environment that facilitates the growth of both facultative and anaerobic bacteria. These anaerobes elaborate additional enzymes and other by-products that facilitate tissue invasion and destruction.

Preexisting local tissue damage frequently serves as a nidus for soft tissue infection. The reduced oxygen tension of this abnormal environment allows pathogens to proliferate. In addition, various patient factors predispose susceptible individuals to these infections. Chronic illnesses can contribute to a diminished immunologic response. Peripheral vascular disease impairs the local blood and oxygen supply. Diabetes mellitus inhibits white blood cell function. Chronic pulmonary disease can result in systemic hypoxemia. Patients with congestive heart failure or significant coronary artery disease may be unable to increase their cardiac output in response to infection. Malnutrition can result in a lack of nutrients and critical enzymatic cofactors involved in the normal cellular response to infection. Each of these patient factors impairs the host response and thereby increases the likelihood that infection will develop.

In the 1920s, Meleney demonstrated that injection of animals with pathogens isolated from patients with infectious gangrene reproduced the characteristics of infection.[2] Decades later, the importance of bacterial synergy and exotoxins was demonstrated in experiments performed by Seal and Kingston,[42] who showed that a spreading infection developed in 12% of animals that received an intradermal injection of group A β-hemolytic streptococci. When *S. aureus* was coinjected with β-hemolytic streptococci, spreading infections developed in 50% of animals, and when the α-lysin of *S. aureus* was coinjected with streptococci, spreading infections developed in 75%.

Streptococcal Toxic-Shock Syndrome

Hemolytic streptococci were originally described by Meleney as the cause of a "synergistic gangrene."[2] The current resurgence of necrotizing soft tissue infections attributed to so-called flesh-eating bacteria probably represents an adaptation of group A streptococci to the contemporary environment.[43] Streptococcal toxic-shock syndrome (STSS) is defined as the isolation of group A streptococci from a normally sterile body site in conjunction with hypotension and either renal impairment, acute respiratory distress syndrome, abnormal hepatic function, coagulopathy, extensive tissue necrosis, or an erythematous rash.[35] STSS is considered the probable diagnosis when these abnormalities occur in conjunction with isolation of group A streptococci from nonsterile body sites. More than 60% of patients with STSS have bacteremia.

Population-based studies in North America and Europe documented a nearly fivefold increase in group A streptococcal infections between the late 1980s and 1995.[44] The current incidence of group A streptococcal infections in the population of Ontario, Canada, is estimated to be 1.5 per 100,000.[44] STSS develops in approximately 10% to 15% of these patients, necrotizing fasciitis in about 6%.[45] It is likely that the rise in serious group A streptococcal infections reflects an antigenic shift that has increased the virulence of these organisms.

Soft tissue infections associated with STSS typically involve an extremity. Approximately 70% of patients will progress to necrotizing fasciitis or myositis and will require operative treatment. Only about 50% of patients with streptococcal soft tissue infections have a demonstrable portal of entry for bacteria.[38,46]

Severe pain is the most common initial symptom of STSS. It is of sudden onset and generally precedes tenderness or other physical findings. Fever is another common early sign. About 80% of STSS patients show clinical signs of soft tissue infection (e.g., localized swelling, erythema, and tenderness) [*see Figure 8*]. In approximately 50%, blood pressure is initially normal, but hypotension invariably develops within 4 to 8 hours after presentation.

Hemoglobinuria and an elevated serum creatinine concentra-

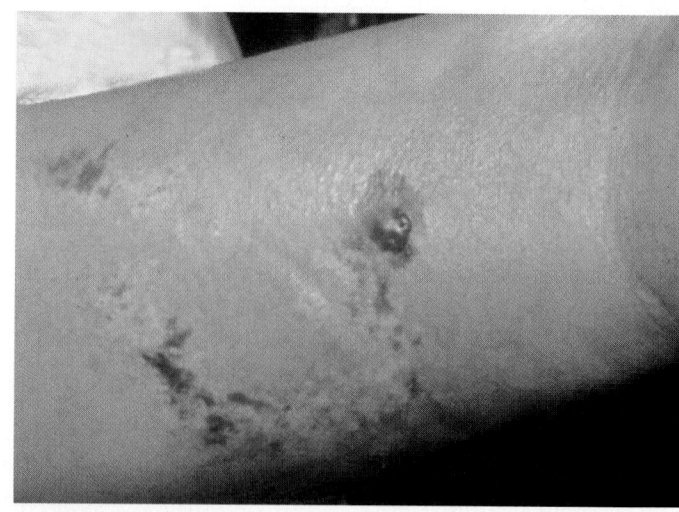

Figure 8 Shown is the superficial appearance of streptococcal gangrene of the posterior thigh.

tion are hallmarks of renal involvement. Even when adequate resuscitation is provided and antibiotics and vasopressors are given, hypotension persists in the overwhelming majority of patients. Renal dysfunction can persist or progress for 48 to 72 hours despite treatment. Hypoalbuminemia and hypocalcemia are common. Mild leukocytosis is present initially; however, the percentage of immature neutrophils is generally 40% or higher.

S. pyogenes can be classified into more than 80 different strains, or M types, on the basis of the M proteins expressed. M proteins impede phagocytosis of streptococci and induce vascular leakage by forming complexes with fibrinogen.[47] They also cleave nicotinic acid dinucleotide (NAD), thereby interrupting elemental cellular processes. The M proteins M1 and M3 are associated with the majority of streptococcal necrotizing soft tissue infections.[43] Streptococcal pyrogenic exotoxins (SPEs) are produced by most streptococci that cause severe soft tissue infection and can be transmitted by bacteriophages to different M types. They are the cause of the fever, shock, and tissue injury associated with these infections. SPE-A and SPE-B induce the synthesis of tumor necrosis factor–α (TNF-α), interleukin-1β (IL-1β), and IL-6. Peptidoglycan, lipoteichoic acid, and killed organisms also are capable of inducing TNF-α production.

It has been proposed that M proteins or SPEs act as superantigens. These exotoxins, along with certain staphylococcal toxins (e.g., toxic-shock syndrome toxin–1 [TSST-1] and staphylococcal enterotoxins), can stimulate T cell responses through conventional antigen-presenting cells, as well as through direct binding to the Vβ region of the T cell receptor. Conventional T cell activation through antigen-presenting cells is a multistage process that stimulates a relatively small percentage of T cells and limits the magnitude of the resultant cytokine response. In contrast, superantigens bypass the normal antigen presentation pathway and do not undergo phagocytosis. The superantigen processing pathway can stimulate more than a thousand times more T cells than the conventional antigen pathway and thus can trigger a massive release of cytokines. The idea that T cell stimulation by superantigens can explain the severe degree of illness and exaggerated response seen in these patients is attractive, but at present, there is no definitive proof that this process occurs in humans.

Although *S. pyogenes* is susceptible to penicillin and other β-lactam antibiotics in vitro, clinical treatment failure sometimes occurs when penicillin is used alone against *S. pyogenes* infections.[43] Such failure is a particular problem with more aggressive group A streptococcal infections and may be attributable to the large inoculum size (the so-called Eagle effect). These large inocula reach the stationary growth phase very quickly. Penicillin and other β-lactam antibiotics are ineffective in the stationary growth phase because of the reduced expression of penicillin-binding proteins in this phase. Moreover, toxin production is not inhibited by β-lactam antibiotics during the stationary growth phase. In contrast, antibiotics that inhibit protein synthesis have been associated with improved survival after serious group A streptococcal infections.

Clindamycin is more effective than β-lactam agents in managing experimental and clinical infections caused by group A streptococci, particularly when necrosis is present.[48] Clindamycin inhibits protein synthesis, and its efficacy is unaffected by inoculum size or the stage of bacterial growth. In particular, it suppresses bacterial toxin synthesis and inhibits M-protein synthesis, thus facilitating phagocytosis of *S. pyogenes*. Clindamycin also suppresses synthesis of penicillin-binding proteins, and it can act synergistically with penicillin.

References

1. Eke N: Fournier's gangrene: a review of 1726 cases. Br J Surg 87:718, 2000

2. Meleney FL: Hemolytic streptococcus gangrene. Arch Surg 9:317, 1924

3. Brewer GE, Meleney FL: Progressive gangrenous infection of the skin and subcutaneous tissues, following operation for acute perforative appendicitis. Ann Surg 84:438, 1926

4. Wilson B: Necrotizing fasciitis. Am Surg 18:416, 1952

5. Greenberg RN, Willoughby BG, Kennedy DJ, et al: Hypocalcemia and "toxic" syndrome associated with streptococcal fasciitis. South Med J 76:916, 1983

6. McHenry CR, Compton CN: Soft tissue infections. Problems in General Surgery. Malangoni MH, Soper NJ, Eds. Lippincott Williams & Wilkins, Philadelphia, 2002, p 7

7. McHenry CR: Necrotizing skin and soft tissue infections. Conn's Current Therapy 2005. Rakel RE, Bope ET, Eds. WB Saunders Co, Philadelphia, 2005

8. Wall DB, Klein SR, Black S, et al: A simple model to help distinguish necrotizing fasciitis from non-necrotizing soft tissue infection. J Am Coll Surg 191:227, 2000

9. Hopkins KL, King CP, Bergman G: Gadolinium-DTPA-enhanced magnetic resonance imaging of musculoskeletal infectious processes. Skeletal Radiol 24:325, 1995

10. Schmid MR, Kossman T, Duewell S: Differentiation of necrotizing fasciitis and cellulitis using MR imaging. AJR Am J Roentgenol 170:615, 1998

11. Brothers TE, Tagge DU, Stutley JE, et al: Magnetic resonance imaging differentiates between necrotizing and non-necrotizing fasciitis of the lower extremity. J Am Coll Surg 187:416, 2000

12. Wong CH, Chang HW, Pasupathy S, et al: Necrotizing fasciitis: clinical presentation, microbiology, and determinants of mortality. J Bone Joint Surg 85A:1454, 2003

13. McHenry CR, Pitrowski JJ, Petrinic D, et al: Determinants of mortality for necrotizing soft tissue infections. Ann Surg 221:558, 1995

14. Rouse TM, Malangoni MA, Schulte WJ: Necrotizing fasciitis: a preventable disaster. Surgery 92:765, 1981

15. Elliott DC, Kufera JA, Myers RAM: Necrotizing soft tissue infections: risk factors for mortality and strategies for management. Ann Surg 224:672, 1996

16. Brown DR, Davis NL, Lepawsky M, et al: A multicenter review of the treatment of major truncal necrotizing infections with and without hyperbaric oxygen therapy. Am J Surg 167:485, 1994

17. Elliott D, Kufera JA, Myers RAM: The microbiology of necrotizing soft tissue infections. Am J Surg 179:361, 2000

18. Childers BJ, Potyondy LD, Nachreiner R, et al: Necrotizing fasciitis: a fourteen-year retrospective study of 163 consecutive patients. Am Surg 68:109, 2002

19. Bosshardt TL, Henderson VJ, Organ CH: Necrotizing soft-tissue infections. Arch Surg 131:846, 1996

20. Trent JT, Federman D, Kirsner RS: Common bacterial skin infections. Ostomy Wound Manage 47:30, 2001

21. Stulberg DL, Penrod MA, Blatny RA: Common bacterial skin infections. Am Fam Phys 66:119, 2002

22. Sadick NS: Current aspects of bacterial infections of the skin. Dermatol Clin 15:341, 1997

23. Bonnetblanc JM, Bédane C: Erysipelas: recognition and management. Am J Clin Dermatol 4:157, 2003

24. Shirtcliffe P, Robinson GM: A case of severe *Pseudomonas* folliculitis from a spa pool. N Z Med J 139:30, 1998

25. Goldstein EJC: Bite wounds and infections. Clin Infect Dis 14:633, 1992

26. Weber DJ, Hansen AR: Infections resulting from animal bites. Infect Dis Clin North Am 5:663, 1991

27. Griego RD, Rosen T, Orengo IF, et al: Dog, cat and human bites: a review. J Am Acad Dermatol 33:1019, 1995

28. Tan JS: Human zoonotic infections transmitted by dogs and cats. Arch Intern Med 157:1933, 1997

29. Presutti RJ: Bite wounds: Early treatment and prophylaxis against infectious complications. Postgrad Med 101:243, 1997

30. Zubowicz VN, Gravier M: Management of early human bites of the hand: a prospective randomized study. Plast Reconstr Surg 88:111, 1991

31. Swartz MN: Cellulitis. N Engl J Med 350:904, 2004

32. Ginsberg CM, Hurwitz RM: *Haemophilus influenzae* type B is an unusual organism causing cellulitis in children and patients with HIV infection. Arch Dermatol 4:661, 1980

33. Parada JP, Maslow JN: Clinical syndromes associated with adult pneumococcal cellulitis. Scand J Infect Dis 32:133, 2000

34. Sadick NS: Bacterial disease of the skin. Conn's Current Therapy. Rakel RE, Ed. WB Saunders Co, Philadelphia, 1997, p 823

35. Stevens DL: Streptococcal infections. Cecil Textbook of Medicine, 20th ed. Bennet JC, Plum F, Eds. WB Saunders Co, Philadelphia, 1996, p 1585

36. Perl B, Gottehrer NP, Ravek D, et al: Cost-effectiveness of blood cultures for adult patients with cellulitis. Clin Infect Dis 29:1483, 1999

37. Altemeier WA, Fullen WD: Prevention and treatment of gas gangrene. JAMA 217:806, 1971

38. McHenry CR, Brandt CP, Piotrowski JJ, et al: Idiopathic necrotizing fasciitis: recognition, incidence and outcome of therapy. Am Surg 60:490, 1994

39. McHenry CR, Azar T, Ramahi AJ, et al: Monomicrobial necrotizing fasciitis complicating pregnancy and puerperium. Obstet Gynecol 87:823, 1996

40. McHenry CR, Malangoni M: Necrotizing soft tissue infections. Surgical Infections. Fry DE, Ed. Little, Brown & Co, Boston, 1995, p 161

41. Giuliano A, Lewis F Jr, Hadley K, et al: Bacteriology of necrotizing fasciitis. Am J Surg 134:52, 1977

42. Seal DV, Kingston D: Streptococcal necrotizing fasciitis: development of an animal model to study its pathogenesis. Br J Exp Pathol 69:813, 1988

43. Stevens DL: Streptococcal toxic-shock syndrome: spectrum of disease, pathogenesis and new concepts in treatment. Emerg Infect Dis 1:69, 1995

44. Kaul R, McGeer A, Low DE, et al: Population-based surveillance for group A streptococcal necrotizing fasciitis: clinical features, prognostic indicators and microbiologic analysis of seventy-seven cases. Am J Med 103:18, 1997

45. Davies HD, McGeer A, Schwartz B, et al: Invasive group A streptococcal infections in Ontario, Canada. N Engl J Med 335:547, 1996

46. Bisno AL, Stevens DL: Streptococcal infections of the skin and soft tissues. N Engl J Med 334:240, 1996

47. Herwald H, Cramer H, Orgelin M, et al: M protein, a classical bacterial virulence determinant, forms, complexes with fibrinogen that induce vascular leakage. Cell 116:367, 2004

48. Mulla ZO, Leaverton PE, Wiersman ST: Invasive group A streptococcal infections in Florida. South Med J 96:968, 2003

Acknowledgment

Figure 6   Tom Moore.

OPEN WOUND REQUIRING
RECONSTRUCTION

Joseph J. Disa, M.D., F.A.C.S., Eric G. Halvorson, M.D., and David A. Hidalgo, M.D., F.A.C.S.

Approach to Surgical Reconstruction

Acute Reconstruction

EVALUATION AND INITIAL
TREATMENT OF OPEN
WOUND

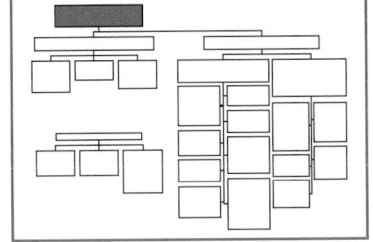

Problem wounds are characterized by one of the following: large size that precludes direct primary closure, gross infection or uncertain bacteriologic status, or threatened loss of critical structures exposed as a result of insufficient soft tissue coverage. Surgically created wounds, which generally pose less of a problem from a bacteriologic standpoint than traumatic wounds, are best managed by an immediate coverage procedure when direct closure is impossible.

Traumatic wounds are more difficult to evaluate than surgical wounds for several reasons. First, the potential for infection is high because of the environment in which the wound is created, the mechanism of injury, and the time that elapses before operative intervention. Second, the mechanism of injury (e.g., crush, avulsion, or gunshot) may extend the zone of injury beyond what is immediately apparent [*see Figure 1*]. Serious postoperative infection may develop in these cases if definitive wound coverage is provided in the absence of adequate debridement. Third, whereas accurate assessment of the chances for recovery of specific structures within the wound is vital for selecting the optimal method of acute treatment, such assessment is often difficult immediately after injury.

Evaluation

The initial step in the management of problem wounds is to decide whether the wound is suitable for immediate soft tissue coverage. Wounds that are surgically created during the course of an elective procedure are almost always best treated with primary definitive coverage. Traumatic wounds that present within 1 or 2 hours of injury and have a minimal crush component are also best treated with a primary definitive coverage procedure after thorough operative debridement (if the patient's hemodynamic status permits).

Injuries with a significant crush component and exposure of critical structures (e.g., nerves, vessels, tendons, or bone) are best treated more aggressively. In these cases, thorough debridement requires considerable surgical experience because the tendency is to debride inadequately. The accuracy with which tissue viability can be assessed varies from one type of tissue to another. For example, skin can be evaluated by its color, the nature of its capillary refill, the quality of its dermal bleeding, or its bleeding response to pinprick. After I.V. fluorescein injection, skin viability can also be assessed qualitatively, with a Wood light, or quantitatively, with a dermofluorometer. Muscle is the most difficult tissue to evaluate. Color, capillary bleeding, and contractile response to stimulation are not always reliable indicators of muscle viability. In severe injuries, they can be misleading. Inadequate debridement may lead to severe consequences resulting from infection. Therefore, serial debridement at 24- to 48-hour intervals is essential for accurately establishing the limits of muscle injury. Efforts should be made during debridement to preserve tissues such as major nerves and blood vessels unless they are severely contused. These structures are vital for function

a
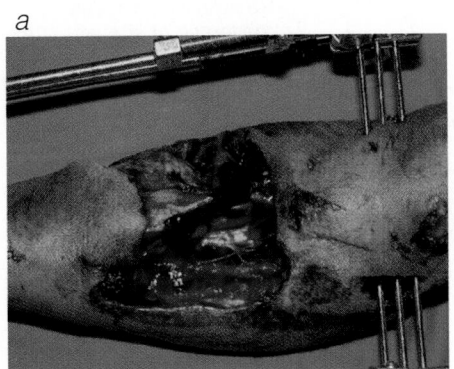

b
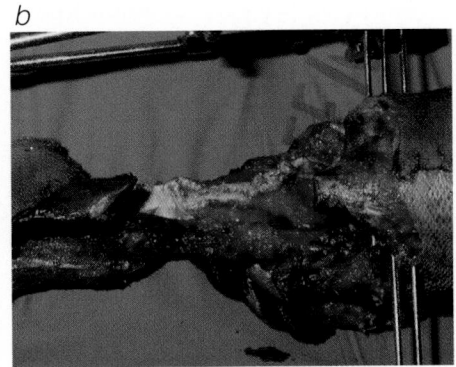

c
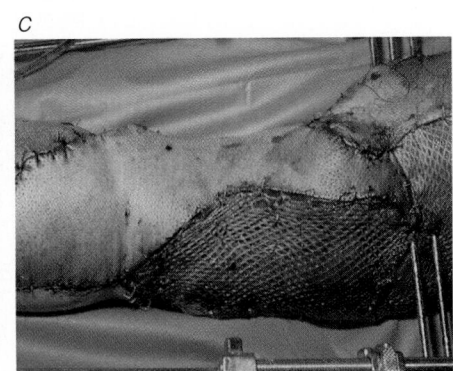

Figure 1 (*a*) **A so-called bumper injury of the leg is shown after initial debridement and bony stabilization (2 days after injury). (*b*) After the second debridement, the true extent of devitalization of bone and soft tissue is apparent (4 days after injury). (*c*) A latissimus dorsi free flap has been used to reconstruct the soft tissue defect (5 days after injury).**

Acute reconstruction is indicated

Evaluate and treat open wound. Use wet-to-dry dressings or negative-pressure wound therapy until infection is cleared and wound is healing.

Select coverage procedure to achieve healed wound and avoid infection.

Defer treatment of functional problems for secondary reconstruction.

Wound does not contain exposed bone, cartilage, nerve, or tendon but cannot be closed directly

Apply a skin graft.

Wound is a small defect but is in an area where graft contracture is not desirable (e.g., face, hand, or flexion crease)

Apply full-thickness skin graft; donor sites include the ear, upper eyelid, neck, and groin.

Wound has a large surface area or is a small wound in a noncritical area

Apply split-thickness skin graft.

Wound is clean but in an area prone to contamination

Apply meshed split-thickness skin graft. Reinstitute early dressing changes if infection develops.

Secondary reconstruction of chronic defect is indicated

Defect is a small localized scar or a focal scar contracture

Revise with Z-plasty or other local tissue rearrangement procedure.

There is a shortage of skin and subcutaneous tissue only, but skin graft coverage is not desirable

Use tissue expanders (except on hand or foot).

One or more of the following conditions is present:
- **Composite defect**
- **Functional defect of muscle or bone**
- **Contour deformity**
- **Unstable soft tissue coverage of vital structure**
- **Inadequate soft tissue coverage for bone or nerve grafting**

Repair with free or local flap.

Approach to Surgical Reconstruction

Bone, cartilage, nerve, or tendon is exposed and cannot be covered by direct wound closure

Perform flap coverage procedure.

Local donor site meets needs and is not involved in the primary process

Use local flap.
- *Small or clean wound:* use local skin flap if possible.
- *Large or contaminated wound:* use regional myocutaneous flap.

Local flap is not possible or would not provide appropriate tissue

Use free flap.
- If wound is clean and thin flap is desired, apply skin or fascial free flap.
- If wound is large or contaminated, apply muscle or myocutaneous free flap.

Muscle flaps require coverage with a meshed split-thickness skin graft.

Head or neck defect

- *Small facial defect with no facial features involved:* use Z-plasty, Limberg flap, or other advancement flap of cheek or forehead.
- *Large defect of neck or lower head:* use regional myocutaneous flap of trapezius, latissimus dorsi, or pectoralis major, or use anterolateral thigh flap.

Chest or back defect

In most cases, use regional myocutaneous flap (e.g., pectoralis major, rectus abdominis, latissimus dorsi, or trapezius).

Arm defect

Cover large wounds above the elbow with latissimus dorsi muscle transposed as a pedicled flap.

Hand defect

Free flaps are preferred, but pedicled distant skin flaps from the chest or abdomen are also acceptable. Defects of the digits can be covered with cross-finger flaps or, for tip injuries, with thenar flaps.

Abdominal defect

Use regional flap (e.g., tensor fasciae latae, rectus femoris, or rectus abdominis), or employ component separation technique.

Gluteal or perineal defect

Use regional myocutaneous flap (e.g., gluteus maximus, gracilis, tensor fasciae latae, or biceps femoris).

Thigh, knee, or leg defect

- *Thigh defect:* use regional muscle flap (e.g., tensor fasciae latae, rectus femoris, vastus lateralis, or vastus medialis).
- *Defect of knee or proximal leg:* use gastrocnemius muscle flap.
- *Proximal or midleg defect:* use soleus muscle flap.

Foot defect

- *Plantar:* close defect of weight-bearing heel or midsole with medially based skin rotation flap raised superficial to plantar fascia or with other myocutaneous or fasciocutaneous plantar flap. Cover limited defect of distal plantar surface with toe flap.
- *Posterior heel, Achilles tendon, malleoli:* use either extensor digitorum brevis muscle as pedicled flap or lateral calcaneal artery flap.

Head or neck defect

- *Large defect of scalp or upper face:* cover with latissimus dorsi, scapular, or rectus abdominis free flap, or use anterolateral thigh flap.
- *Floor of the mouth:* replace with forearm free flap.
- *Mandible:* reconstruct with various composite free flaps of bone and skin.
- *Oropharynx or cervical esophagus:* use jejunum free flap or forearm flap, or use anterolateral thigh flap.

Forearm defect

Cover large forearm wound with free flap of rectus abdominis, scapular, or latissimus dorsi muscle.

Hand defect

- *Exposed tendons on the dorsum:* cover with temporalis fascia free flap.
- *Defect of the web space:* correct with lateral arm free flap.

Knee or leg defect

- *Major wound of the popliteal fossa:* use free flap if blood supply to gastrocnemius is compromised.
- *Defect of the lower third of the leg:* use latissimus dorsi, rectus abdominis, scapular, or gracilis free flap.

Foot defect

- *Plantar:* repair very large defect with muscle free flap covered with a skin graft.
- *Dorsum:* use fascial free flap and overlying skin graft, or use thin skin free flap.

and are of small mass compared with other tissues (e.g., skin, fat, and muscle) at risk for necrosis and subsequent infection.

Wound debridement, therefore, should involve careful analysis of the injury from an anatomic point of view; debridement should not consist of indiscriminate excision of blocks of tissue. Between debridement procedures, the wound should be treated with sterile dressings but in an open manner, with either dressing changes or negative-pressure wound therapy (NPWT) if conditions permit. A definitive soft tissue coverage procedure should then be performed as soon after the initial injury as wound conditions permit. When thorough debridement and definitive coverage can be completed within less than 1 week, the wound will generally heal uneventfully. Inadequate debridement frequently results in the loss of any additional tissue invested to achieve acute soft tissue coverage. The wound becomes grossly infected, and important functional structures within the wound are reexposed.

Infected surgical wounds, neglected wounds, or other complex wounds in which initial wound management fails should be debrided and then treated by open methods. Proper care of these wounds is achieved by a multifaceted approach aimed at converting established gross infection to a much lower level of bacterial contamination, which is then compatible with successful secondary wound closure. For example, advances in the use of NPWT [see Initial Treatment, Negative-Pressure Wound Therapy, below] have simplified the management of complex lower-extremity traumatic wounds, reducing the use of free tissue transfer.[1]

Initial Treatment

Debridement Devitalized tissue provides an ideal culture medium for bacteria and isolates them from host defense mechanisms. Surgical debridement must be performed aggressively—and on a serial basis if necessary—to remove all necrotic tissue.

High-pressure irrigation A useful adjunct to debridement is high-pressure irrigation, which has been shown experimentally to reduce wound infection rates significantly.[2,3] The necessary pressure of 8 psi can be achieved by forceful irrigation through a 35 ml syringe fitted with a 19-gauge needle. Low-pressure irrigation with a bulb-type syringe, for example, has not proved to be beneficial. An antibiotic-containing solution is commonly employed.

Quantitative bacteriology The degree of bacterial wound contamination can be accurately quantified. The standard technique of quantitative bacteriology requires several days to complete and is therefore of somewhat limited utility in the management of acute wounds. In addition to a count, it provides identification and antibiotic sensitivities of the organism. As an alternative, quantitative bacteriology can be performed by using the rapid slide technique, which provides valuable information about the wound within 20 minutes.[4,5] The level of bacterial contamination has been shown to be a significant predictor of outcome in wound closure by either skin-graft or flap-coverage techniques. According to the golden-period principle of wound closure, a minimum time interval is necessary for bacteria to proliferate to a certain threshold level. Contaminated wounds take a mean time of about 5 hours to reach a bacterial count of 10^5/g of tissue. Attempts to close wounds that have counts higher than 10^5/g of tissue will fail 75% to 100% of the time, whereas attempts to close wounds with lower counts are successful more than 90% of the time.[6] β-Hemolytic streptococci are an exception in that much lower concentrations of these organisms consistently result in failure of wound closure. When a β-hemolytic streptococcus is the dominant isolate, the wound should generally be treated openly until cultures become negative.

Systemic antibiotics The role of systemic antibiotics in wound management is not clearly defined. Broad-spectrum antibiotics should be given in cases of severe trauma or established, uncontrolled infection. They may also be useful for minor wounds that cannot be closed within 3 hours of injury.

Topical antibiotics Certain antibiotics provide broad-spectrum activity when applied topically. Neomycin, 10 mg/ml, or a combination of bacitracin, 50 U/ml, and polymyxin B, 0.05 mg/ml, kills most common wound pathogens. These solutions can be used when wet dressings are indicated. In the past few years, numerous antibacterial dressings have been developed, including an antibacterial NPWT sponge. Such dressings may prove useful in the treatment of open, contaminated wounds; however, discussion of these products is outside the scope of this chapter.

Topical antiseptics A variety of topical antiseptics have been used empirically in wound care. In the concentrations usually recommended, however, these solutions are detrimental to wound healing. Povidone-iodine (1%), hydrogen peroxide (3%), acetic acid (0.25%), and sodium hypochlorite (0.5%) all have been shown to be lethal to fibroblasts, as well as to bacteria. More dilute concentrations of povidone-iodine (0.001%) and sodium hypochlorite (0.005%) are effective against bacteria while being safe for fibroblasts.[7] A number of these agents also inhibit normal white blood cell function in the wound.

Wet dressings Open wounds can be treated with wet dressings, generally consisting of gauze soaked in saline or an acceptable topical antiseptic. Wet-to-wet dressings prevent desiccation of exposed vital structures or freshly placed skin grafts. Wet-to-dry dressings are useful for assisting in daily wound debridement. These dressings are allowed to dry on the wound; when they are removed, adherent fibrinous debris is removed with the dressing. Wet dressings of either type should be changed at least twice a day.

Small wounds can be expected to close by contraction and secondary epithelialization after appropriate open management with the techniques described. Large wounds will improve with aggressive open care but will then stabilize into a chronic state of wound colonization of varying degrees. A soft tissue coverage procedure may then be necessary to complete closure in these cases.

Negative-pressure wound therapy In the past 10 years, the vacuum-assisted closure device (VAC Abdominal Dressing System; Kinetic Concepts Inc., San Antonio, Texas) has gained widespread acceptance for the treatment of open wounds. Because this device does not accomplish debridement to any significant degree, it should be applied only to a clean wound that has no necrotic debris. If any significant necrotic tissue remains after sharp debridement, wet-to-dry dressings may be employed until the wound is clean and granulating. Dressing changes are typically carried out every 2 or 3 days; this is a significant advantage, given that conventional dressing changes are generally done at least twice daily. Exudate is removed and quantified by the suction device, and more robust wound granulation and contraction can be observed. After treatment with a VAC device, wound closure can be accomplished secondarily with a skin graft, local flaps, or free tissue transfer, depending on the clinical situation. The disadvantages of NPWT include the need for specialized equipment and training and the increased cost.

SELECTION OF COVERAGE PROCEDURE

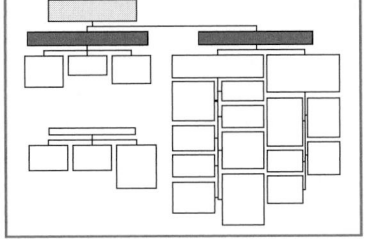

The main goals of coverage procedures [*see 27 Surface Reconstruction Procedures*] in the management of both acute and chronic wounds are (1) to achieve a healed wound and (2) to avoid infection. The treatment of functional problems is generally deferred for secondary reconstruction.

The method of coverage depends on whether vital structures (e.g., vessels, tendons, nerves, and bone) are exposed in the wound. If no vital structures are exposed, skin-graft coverage is indicated. Skin grafts can also be used over tendon if the paratenon is intact, over nerve if the epineurium is intact, and over bone if the periosteum is intact. Skin grafts are the most expendable type of soft tissue available for the coverage of open wounds. They allow the wound to heal completely and set the stage for secondary reconstruction, during which more valuable tissue can be used to achieve other goals at minimal risk. When vital structures are exposed in the wound, a flap is preferred because it provides more substantial soft tissue coverage of the structure. The choice of flap depends on the location of the wound and on its overall size, depth, and topographic configuration (see below).

Skin Grafts

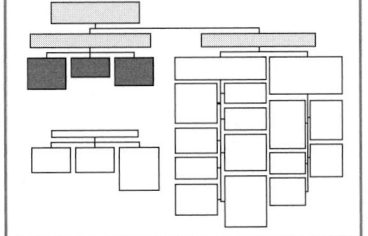

Skin grafts may be either partial thickness (i.e., split thickness) or full thickness [*see 27 Surface Reconstruction Procedures*]. Split-thickness grafts are preferred for wounds with a large surface area. Full-thickness grafts are suitable only for small defects because their donor sites must be closed primarily; the most common donor sites for full-thickness grafts are the ears, upper eyelids, neck, and groin. Full-thickness grafts contract less with time than split-thickness grafts and are therefore particularly suitable for wounds of the hands, extremity flexion creases, nose, eyelids, and other areas of the face.

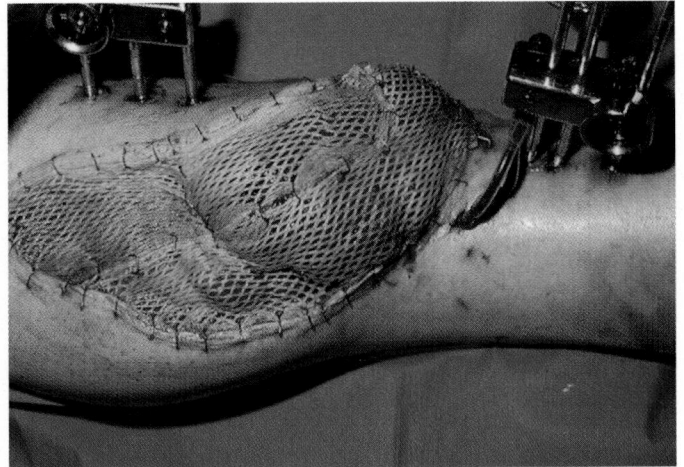

Figure 2 **A meshed (1.5:1 ratio) skin graft has been secured to the irregular contour of a muscle free flap with staples. No additional immobilization of the graft is needed. The interstices of the graft allow free drainage of serous exudate from the muscle.**

Successful healing of skin grafts requires immobilization of the recipient site to prevent shearing in the plane between the graft and the wound bed. Although complete immobilization is desirable, the required dressings may preclude observation of a wound that is known to be significantly contaminated. In such cases, a meshed split-thickness graft is indicated, and the wound should be treated in an open fashion. A meshed graft can be placed directly over the muscle of a flap and secured over its irregular contour with staples [*see Figure 2*]. Because the graft is meshed, serum can escape between the interstices and there is little risk of separation from the underlying tissue. A meshed graft is also less vulnerable to disruption by shear forces. An additional advantage of a meshed graft is that it permits the wound to be treated with wet dressings if there is still risk for infection. A mesh expansion ratio of 1.5:1 is generally preferred, except when the surface area of the wound is very large and the availability of donor sites is limited.

Flaps

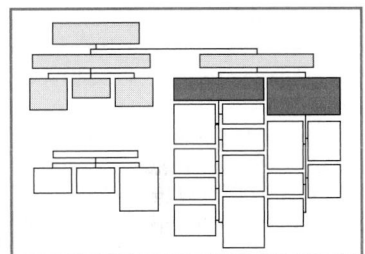

Flaps consist of tissues that have a self-contained vascular system [*see 27 Surface Reconstruction Procedures*]. They permit a more substantial transfer of tissue bulk than do skin grafts and may consist of skin and subcutaneous tissue, of fascia, of muscle, of bone, or of a combination of several of these tissue types. Local flaps consist of tissue that is mostly detached from surrounding tissue but retains enough connection to preserve an adequate blood supply to the entire flap. Local flaps are either transposed, rotated, or advanced into adjacent defects for purposes of reconstruction. Island flaps are local flaps that are based only on their skeletonized axial blood supply. Once created, an island flap is transferred through a subcutaneous tunnel into the defect. The skeletonized pedicle remains in the subcutaneous space while the cutaneous portion of the flap fills the defect. Free flaps, in contrast, are totally detached; their blood supply is reconnected at the recipient site by means of surgically performed microvascular anastomoses between recipient-site blood vessels and the major vessels that supply the flap.

Local flaps versus free flaps　The choice between a local flap and a free flap is determined by the amount and the type of tissue needed, as well as by the availability of flaps in the immediate area of the wound [*see Figure 3*]. The availability of local flaps, in turn, is determined by the nature of the regional blood supply. The vascular anatomy of a particular area determines the availability of arterialized skin flaps, fasciocutaneous flaps, myocutaneous flaps, and other forms of composite flaps. Local flaps can be grouped regionally by the types of tissue that they provide [*see Table 1*].

A local flap is generally preferred over a free flap if the two provide similar tissue, primarily because of the additional effort required to transfer a free flap. A free-flap procedure commonly takes twice as long as a local-flap procedure.

Free flaps are indicated in areas where local flaps are unavailable (e.g., the distal third of the leg) or when an extremely large flap is needed but cannot be obtained locally. When regional donor sites are affected by the primary process, free tissue transfer allows healthy, well-vascularized tissue to be brought into the compromised area. Moreover, if free tissue is transferred, the size of the wound is not extended, because the donor site is not contiguous but instead is located at a distance from the wound.

If expertise in microvascular surgery is available, free flaps are frequently a first-line choice. Free flaps allow selection of the appropri-

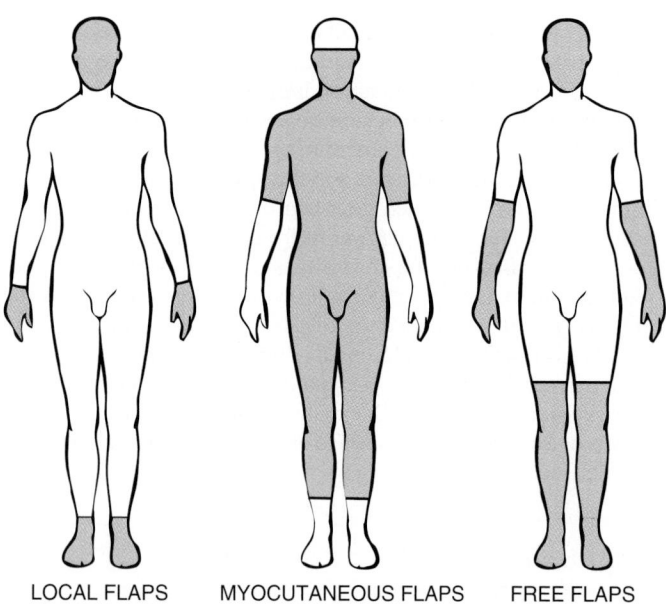

LOCAL FLAPS   MYOCUTANEOUS FLAPS   FREE FLAPS

Figure 3 **Regional alternatives in flap selection are illustrated. Defects in the central portion of the body are treated with myocutaneous flaps primarily; defects of the peripheral areas are treated with either local flaps or free flaps. In some areas, several options exist, and the choice is influenced by the size of the defect and the specific tissue requirements.**

most wounds can be met by so-called workhorse free flaps. These flaps typically have the advantages of large size, ease of dissection, and a vascular pedicle that is long and of large diameter. The disadvantages, such as awkward patient positioning for flap harvest, are minor. Most workhorse flaps consist of muscle with an optional skin component; they are the flaps of choice for contaminated wounds [*see Figure 4*]. A second group of free flaps is useful for acute reconstruction of unusually large wounds. These flaps consist of combined vascular territories supplied by a single vascular pedicle. A third category consists of smaller free flaps that provide tissue that is superior in either amount or type to the local flaps that are otherwise available. An additional advantage of these flaps is that they tend not to be bulky. They are frequently used in areas such as the head, hands, distal third of the leg, and feet [*see Figure 5*].

Flap coverage procedures are illustrated in greater detail elsewhere [*see 27 Surface Reconstruction Procedures*].

Regional alternatives in flap selection *Head, neck.* Facial defects of small to moderate size are best treated with local skin flaps. A variety of flaps are available for reconstruction of limited defects of the eyelids, cheeks, nose, and mouth.[8-10] Small 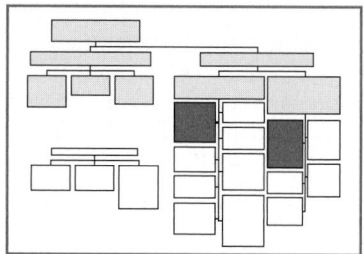 facial defects that do not directly involve the facial features can often be closed with any of several types of flaps that rearrange the existing tissue in the area—for example, a Z-plasty or a Limberg flap. Tissues that are difficult to match (e.g., those of the eyelids or lips) can often be reconstructed with flaps that borrow tissue from their opposite, intact counterparts (e.g., the Abbe lip flap).

For coverage of some large defects in the head and neck region, the trapezius, the latissimus dorsi, and the pectoralis major can be used. Each muscle can be raised with an optional skin island. These flaps are generally too bulky to be used on the face, and their reach

ate type of tissue in the most suitable size and configuration for the specific reconstructive problem. Compared with free flaps, local flaps are inefficient ways of moving tissue because only a small portion of a local flap actually reaches the defect itself. The choice of donor site is greater with free flaps because the limitations imposed by local availability are avoided.

Free flaps used in acute reconstruction can be grouped into three major types [*see Table 2*]. The soft tissue coverage requirements of

Table 1   Selection of Local Flaps by Region and Tissue Type

Site	Skin Flaps	Muscle and Myocutaneous Flaps	Fascial and Fasciocutaneous Flaps
Head and neck	Scalp; forehead; nasolabial; cervico-facial; Mustardé; eyelid; lip	Trapezius; latissimus dorsi; pectoralis major	Superficial and deep temporal fascia
Chest and back	Lateral thoracic; deltopectoral	Trapezius; pectoralis major; latissimus dorsi; rectus abdominis (superiorly based)	Scapular
Arm	Medial arm (Tagliacozzi)	Latissimus dorsi; pectoralis major	Lateral arm; forearm
Hand	Cross-finger; thenar; neurovascular island; fingertip advancement	—	Forearm
Abdomen and perineum	Groin	Rectus abdominis (inferiorly based); tensor fasciae latae; rectus femoris; gracilis	Medial thigh
Gluteal area	Sacral; thoracolumbar	Gluteus maximus; gracilis; tensor fasciae latae; biceps femoris	Gluteal thigh
Thigh	—	Tensor fasciae latae; rectus femoris; vastus lateralis; vastus medialis; gracilis; biceps femoris; rectus abdominis	Anterior thigh; anteromedial thigh; posterior thigh; anterolateral thigh
Knee and proximal leg	—	Gastrocnemius	Saphenous artery; posterior calf
Midleg	—	Soleus; tibialis anterior	Anterior leg; lateral leg; posterior leg
Distal leg	—	—	—
Foot	Dorsalis pedis; plantar rotation; lateral calcaneal artery; plantar V-Y	Flexor digitorum brevis; abductor hallucis; abductor digiti minimi; extensor digitorum brevis	—

Table 2 Free Flap Selection for Soft Tissue Coverage*

Requirement	Specific Flap	Advantages	Disadvantages
Reliable workhorse flaps	Latissimus dorsi	Ideal pedicle[†]; ease of dissection	Awkward patient positioning
	Rectus abdominis	Ideal pedicle; supine position; ease of dissection	No major disadvantages
	Scapular	Ideal pedicle; skin flap only	Awkward patient positioning
Flaps of very large surface area	Combined latissimus dorsi and scapular	Independent component inset[‡]; primary donor-site closure possible; ideal pedicle	Awkward patient positioning
	Extended tensor fasciae latae and partial quadriceps	Supine position; large skin flap component	Donor-site healing[§]; pedicle configuration[‖]
Small flaps	Gracilis	Small muscle	Small vessels
	Lateral arm	Thin, sensate; convenient for hand trauma	Small vessels; donor-site scar
	Forearm	Thin skin flap; ideal pedicle	Minor hand morbidity; poor donor-site appearance
	Temporalis fascia	Thinnest flap; ideal coverage for exposed tendons[¶]; can transfer hair-bearing scalp	Variable donor-site scar alopecia
	Anterolateral thigh	Thin; moderate surface area available for harvest; minimal donor-site morbidity	Variable anatomy; possible requirement for perforator dissection

*Includes only the more commonly used free flaps for purposes of comparison.
[†]Characterized by large-diameter vessels and long pedicle length.
[‡]Each part can be arranged and sewn into the wound separately.

[§]Donor-site closure requires a skin graft, which may result in delayed healing.
[‖]Pedicle enters middle of undersurface of flap.
[¶]Permits tendon gliding underneath if used on dorsum of the hand or of the foot.

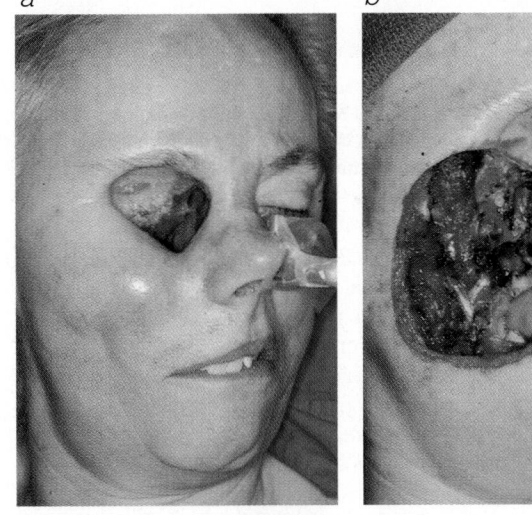

a   *b*

is limited when used as pedicled flaps: none of them can cover major portions of the scalp or comfortably reach the upper face.

Latissimus dorsi, scapular, and rectus abdominis free flaps are useful for very large defects of the scalp or upper face. Smaller defects of the scalp are best treated with local scalp flaps.

Other free flaps of a specialized nature are superior for reconstruction of the floor of the mouth and mandible, even though local myocutaneous flaps will reach this area. For example, the forearm free flap based on the radial artery is quite thin and pliable and therefore provides an ideal replacement for the floor of the mouth. Composite free flaps that contain both bone and skin (e.g., those taken from the scapula, the ilium, the radius, and the fibula) provide tissue of the appropriate type and proper configuration for defects of the lower face in which the mandible must be reconstructed along with the intraoral lining, the external skin, or both.

Chest, back. Most clean defects of the chest and back are amenable to treatment with local myocutaneous flaps because of the wide arc of rotation of muscles located in these areas.[11] In the presence of contamination, open wound management is indicated. Traditionally, this has

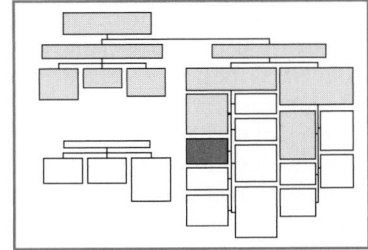

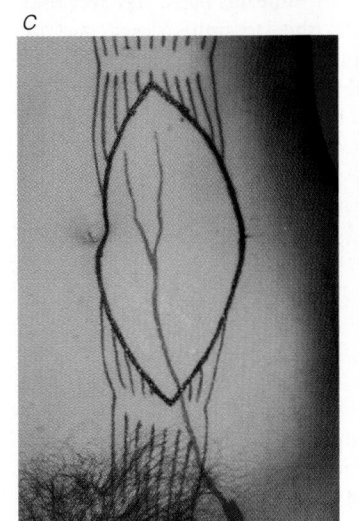

c   *d*

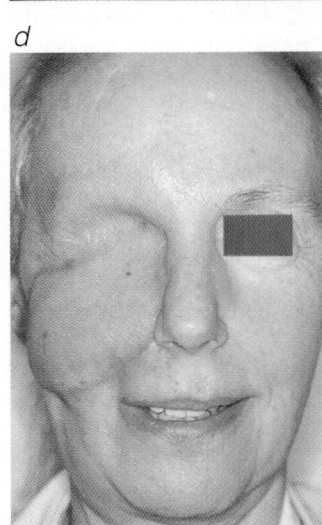

Figure 4 (*a*) Shown is a facial tumor that has recurred after previous orbital exenteration. (*b*) The defect has been resected. Local flaps and regional myocutaneous flaps are not available for this defect. (*c*) A rectus abdominis myocutaneous free flap is designed. This flap can be designed in other sizes and configurations depending on specific needs. The vascular pedicle is long and of large diameter, and the flap is easily accessible in the supine patient. (*d*) After surgery, soft tissue coverage with a reasonable restoration of facial contour has been achieved.

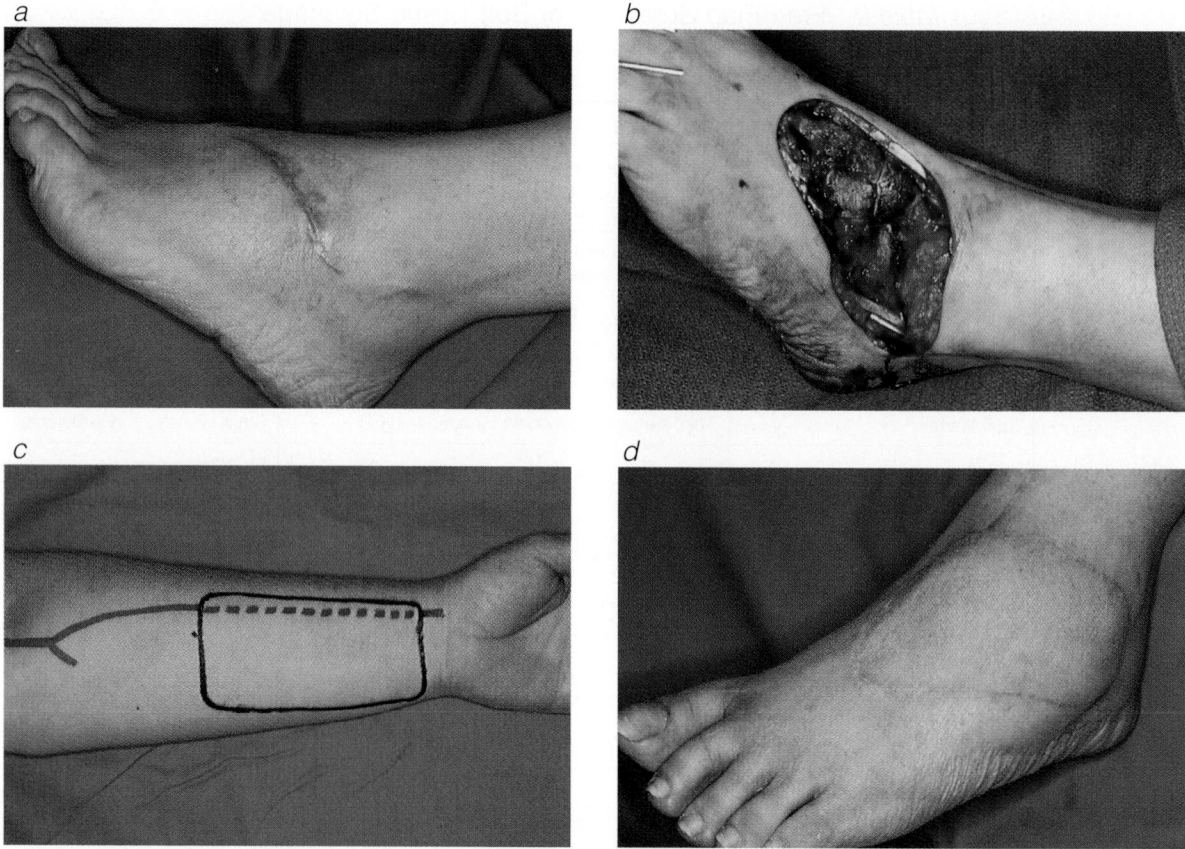

Figure 5 (*a*) A soft tissue sarcoma has recurred in the scar of a previous excision. (*b*) Reexcision of the defect has exposed bone and tendons. No regional flaps are available for satisfactory coverage of this defect. (*c*) The forearm is a source of small, thin free flaps. (*d*) Flap transfer is complete. The radial artery and venae comitantes have been anastomosed to their dorsalis pedis counterparts.

been accomplished with wet-to-dry dressing changes, which are especially effective for superficial debridement. Currently, these wounds are increasingly being managed with NPWT after all necrotic tissue is debrided. A common example is the wound resulting from the treatment of poststernotomy mediastinitis. After sepsis is eliminated and the wound is granulating, definitive flap closure can be performed.[12,13] Midline sternal wounds can be covered with either pectoralis major or rectus abdominis flaps; lateral chest defects with latissimus dorsi or pectoralis major flaps; and midline back defects with latissimus dorsi or trapezius flaps. To cover midline defects, the pectoralis major, the latissimus dorsi, and the trapezius can be divided from their primary vascular supply and folded over as local flaps based on their medial intercostal secondary blood supply.

Arm, forearm. Large wounds above the elbow can be covered with a latissimus dorsi myocutaneous flap transposed as a pedicled flap, provided that the vascular pedicle of the muscle has not been affected by the injury. Forearm wounds that require flap closure are best treated with free flaps. A rectus abdominis, scapular, anterolateral thigh, or latissimus dorsi muscle flap can be used for large defects of the arm or forearm. Although soft tissue coverage with simultaneous functional forearm muscle replacement

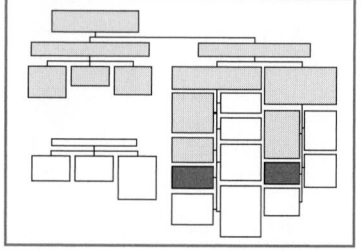

can be achieved with a single flap (e.g., a gracilis muscle flap), this procedure is not generally recommended; rather, a skin flap (e.g., a scapular free flap) is preferred as a first stage of reconstruction to achieve wound healing.

Hand. Both free flaps and pedicled skin flaps are useful for soft tissue coverage of hand wounds. A temporalis fascia free flap is particularly thin and is ideal for coverage of exposed tendons on the dorsum of the hand. A lateral arm free flap is ideal for reconstruction of a large defect of the first web space; it has sensory potential because it contains a large sensory nerve. Both of these free flaps are small. Pedicled distant skin flaps from the chest or abdomen are available as an alternative form of coverage of sizable hand defects. However, pedicled skin flaps have major disadvantages: wound care is difficult, edema persists because elevation and movement of the hand are seldom possible while it is attached to the trunk, and a second procedure is needed to divide these flaps.

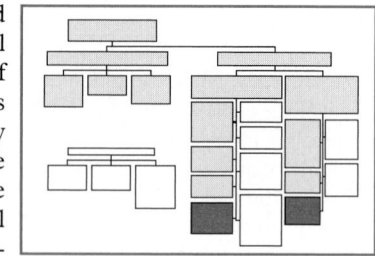

Digital injuries with exposed tendons can be closed with a variety of cross-finger flaps of skin and subcutaneous tissue raised from either the volar or extensor aspect of an adjacent digit. Because these flaps do not contain a great deal of subcutaneous tissue, they are preferred for coverage of digits proximally, where a thick subcutaneous pad is not essential. A thenar flap is useful for fingertip injuries in which the soft tissue pad of the fingertip is lost and bone is exposed. This flap provides an ideal pulp replacement, as well as better sensory recovery than skin grafts. Fingertip injuries can also be closed with several types of V-Y advancement flaps that can be raised from either the volar surface or the lateral surfaces of the end of the finger.

Abdomen. Clean defects of the abdominal wall that require flap closure are best treated with local muscle flaps such as the tensor fasciae latae and the rectus femoris from the thigh. The rectus abdominis also can occasionally be transposed to 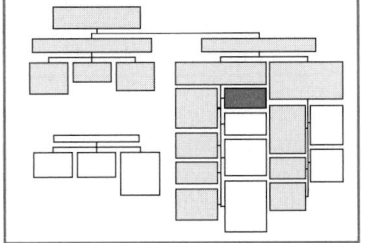 cover an abdominal defect. Each of these flaps is harvested along with skin, although a large tensor fasciae latae flap will probably necessitate skin-graft closure of the donor site. The tensor fasciae latae flap has the advantage of including the thickened deep fascia (iliotibial band) of the thigh, which can provide additional strength for abdominal wall closure. Midline defects resulting from previous operation or trauma can often be closed by means of the component separation method. The external oblique fascia is divided lateral to the lateral edge of the rectus sheath, and the bloodless plane between the external and internal oblique muscles is developed. This maneuver mobilizes the recti toward the midline, usually allowing primary closure.

As a consequence of the growing realization of the benefits of the open abdomen, increasing numbers of patients treated for abdominal trauma, sepsis, and compartment syndrome are presenting for management and closure. With contaminated wounds, the use of permanent meshes for reconstruction is contraindicated, and definitive flap closure is best delayed. In these difficult situations, the wound must be treated in an open manner, with close attention paid to the unique vulnerability of the intestines to fistula formation. Many treatment options are currently available for the open abdomen [*see 105 Operative Exposure of Abdominal Injuries and Closure of the Abdomen*]. Important considerations for any treatment modality include whether the method controls abdominal contents, whether it avoids promoting fistula formation, whether it achieves skin and fascial closure, whether it removes and quantifies exudate, whether it controls infection, and whether it promotes wound healing. The VAC device performs well with respect to all of these considerations, perhaps because of reverse tissue expansion and full-thickness wound contraction.[14,15] Once all acute problems have been addressed and recovery is well under way, an absorbable mesh is commonly applied, followed by dressing changes or NPWT. To protect the underlying bowel, a layer of nonstick gauze should be applied before dressings or NPWT sponges. Once granulation is achieved, a skin graft can be placed. Chronic hernia formation is the rule; the hernia can generally be treated as a stable chronic ventral hernia, provided that the wound is closed and free of infection.

Gluteal area, perineum. Local muscle flaps with or without skin are indicated for defects in the gluteal area or the perineum. Such flaps are preferable to large, random-pattern advancement skin flaps from the posterior thigh and thoracolumbar ro-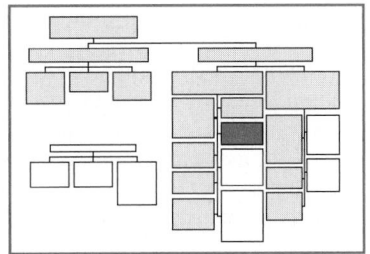

tation skin flaps. The gluteus maximus, for example, can be used as a rotation flap, a V-Y advancement flap, or a turnover flap in the treatment of pressure sores. As a turnover flap, it can be proximally or distally based, or it can be split along its longitudinal axis so that only a portion of it is used. Also useful for covering defects in the gluteal area and the perineum is the myofasciocutaneous gluteal-thigh flap, which is a combination of a gluteus muscle flap and a fasciocutaneous flap from the posterior thigh that is supplied by an extension of the inferior gluteal artery. Because of its size and location, the gracilis muscle is well suited for coverage of defects of the perineum. The gracilis and the biceps femoris are generally secondary choices for the treatment of pressure sores over the ischium. The tensor fasciae latae is frequently used for treating open wounds over the greater trochanter. The entire quadriceps can be used to close defects resulting from hemipelvectomy.

Thigh. Flaps are rarely required for soft tissue coverage in the thigh area, because critical vital structures are located deep within the thigh and are rarely exposed by injury or by surgical procedures. A number of regional muscle flaps are available for coverage in this region, however, including the tensor fasciae latae, the rectus femoris, the vastus lateralis, and the vastus medialis. The gracilis and posterior thigh muscles are rarely used in this area. An anterior defect that involves exposure of the femoral vessels can be covered with either an ipsilateral or a contralateral rectus abdominis myocutaneous flap. The rectus femoris may also be divided distally and turned over to provide coverage of exposed femoral vessels or grafts. A number of smaller local skin flaps that are supplied with blood from the deep fascia can be raised over portions of the thigh. The anterolateral thigh flap is the most commonly employed thigh flap; however, it is typically used for free tissue transfer to distant areas.

Knee, proximal leg, midleg. The two heads of the gastrocnemius can be used either together or independently to cover defects of the knee and the proximal third of the leg. The soleus is useful for coverage of defects of the proximal and middle 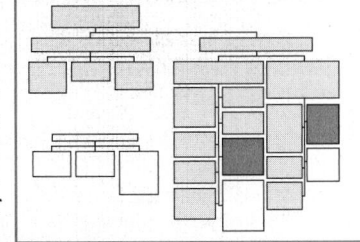 thirds of the leg. Local flaps should not be used for major leg wounds if the extent of the injury suggests involvement of the muscle donor site. Instead, a free flap should be used to bring healthy tissue into the area. Therefore, free flaps are a first choice, for example, for coverage of major wounds of the popliteal fossa, knee, and proximal leg that involve the sural artery blood supply to the gastrocnemius; they are also highly useful for coverage of defects in the distal third of the leg. Traumatic wounds of the distal lower extremity can also be managed with NPWT. Increased use of this modality has been associated with the performance of fewer free tissue transfers and more delayed local flap procedures for definitive closure.[1]

Skin flaps fed by the fascial blood supply can also be raised over the leg.[16] A number of fasciocutaneous flaps have been described in this area, but they tend to be smaller than muscle flaps and generally less reliable. These flaps are longitudinally oriented over the course of the anterior tibial artery or the peroneal artery. The maximum length at which such fasciocutaneous flaps are safe and their specific applications have not been well established.

Foot. The foot is as complex as the hand and the face in that it is composed of separate regions, each of which has a unique set of alternatives for reconstruction. These regions include the plantar surface; the dorsum; and the posterior (non–weight-bearing) heel, Achilles tendon, and malleoli.

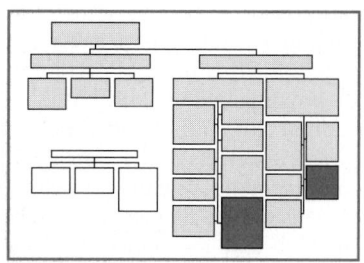

Superficial defects that lie completely within the non–weight-bearing portion of the midsole do not need flap coverage. Defects of the weight-bearing heel and midsole area that are less than 6 cm in diameter can be closed with a medially based skin rotation flap that is raised superficial to the plantar fascia.[17] This flap maintains plantar sensation. Limited defects of the distal plantar surface can be treated with local toe flaps that also maintain sensation. Very large plantar defects are best resurfaced with a muscle free flap (e.g., latissimus dorsi or rectus abdominis) covered with a skin graft. Although this type of flap lacks sensation, it appears to provide the most durable form of coverage because it resists shear forces well.[18]

Defects of the dorsum that require flap coverage are best covered either with a fascial free flap (e.g., temporalis fascia) and an overlying skin graft or with a skin free flap that is thin (e.g., from the forearm or the anterolateral thigh). The extensor digitorum brevis can be raised from the dorsum as a pedicled flap fed by the dorsalis pedis artery. This flap, which measures approximately 5 × 6 cm, has an arc of rotation that makes it useful for the coverage of defects of the malleolus or the Achilles tendon area. A narrow transposition skin flap fed by the lateral calcaneal artery is useful for coverage of defects approximately 3 cm in diameter that lie over the Achilles tendon or the non–weight-bearing posterior heel. A distally based reverse sural artery flap transfers skin, subcutaneous fat, and fascia from the proximal posterior calf and can also be used for defects of the ankle; however, this flap is prone to venous congestion.

Secondary Reconstruction

Selection of the proper method for secondary reconstruction requires analysis of the type and extent of tissue deficiency that is present and consideration of the functional goals that are involved. Superficial defects may require re-

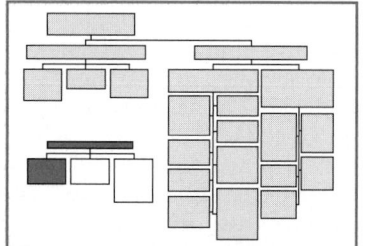

placement or supplementation of only skin and subcutaneous tissue, whereas more complex defects may require replacement of several types of tissue. Specialized tissue, such as vascularized nerve (i.e., a nerve free flap) or intestine, may be necessary to provide a functional reconstruction in some cases (see below).

SMALL LOCALIZED SCAR

When reconstruction is indicated for a small localized scar, soft tissue coverage is generally sufficient and poses no threat of breakdown leading to exposure of important structures. Instead, the reconstructive problem is generally functional in nature. An example is a tight scar band across a flexion crease, which is commonly seen after a burn injury. A local procedure that rearranges the existing tissue can relieve the tension by making more tissue available in one direction, though the amount of tissue in the area is not actually increased.

The Z-plasty is an example of such tissue rearrangement [*see 27 Surface Reconstruction Procedures*]. Multiple Z-plasties or other procedures, such as W-plasty, may be useful for some localized scars.

SHORTAGE OF SKIN AND SUBCUTANEOUS TISSUE

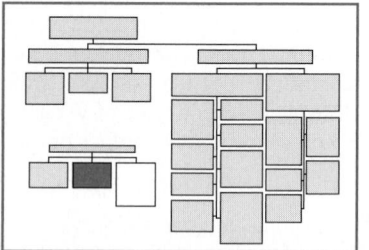

A shortage of skin and subcutaneous tissue may result from excision of a large scar or a large congenital defect (e.g., a nevus). Mastectomy commonly leaves a shortage of skin that prevents creation of a breast mound. In these cases, extra tissue can be created locally with the use of tissue expanders. These devices are inflatable plastic reservoirs of various shapes and volumes that are implanted under the skin. The skin over the expander is stretched during a period of several weeks as the expander is gradually filled by percutaneously injecting saline into an incorporated or remote fill port. The expander is then removed as a second procedure, and the expanded area of skin is advanced to cover the defect. The process of tissue expansion results in thinning of all layers of tissue overlying the expander—except for the epidermis, which actually thickens.

A number of important principles govern the use of tissue expanders. The expanders must be placed so as to allow expansion only in normal skin adjacent to the defect, not in the defect itself. To ensure adequate expansion, a sufficiently large expander or multiple expanders must be used. Complications associated with the use of tissue expanders include infection, extrusion, deflation, flipped ports (remote type), and hematoma formation.[19]

Tissue expanders are used in secondary reconstruction only; they play no role in acute wound management. They are not indicated for contour defects (see below), because the tissue they provide is two-dimensional and lacking in bulk. Nor is expanded tissue adequate for coverage of chronically exposed structures (e.g., bone). Tissue expanders do not provide adequate replacement tissue to establish a suitable bed for nerve or bone grafting. Therefore, they are not a substitute for flaps in general.

The scalp is an ideal location for the use of tissue expanders because no equivalent substitute for this type of hair-bearing tissue exists. Expanders work effectively when implanted over the hard calvarium and are useful in cases of burn alopecia and large nevi involving the scalp. Expanders are also useful for breast reconstruction, for carefully selected large lesions of the face, and for certain scars of the limbs. They are generally not indicated for use in the hands or feet. Although some local flap donor sites (e.g., the forehead) can be expanded before flap transfer, there is a loss of tissue pliability that appears to limit the usefulness of this particular application.

COMPLEX DEFECTS

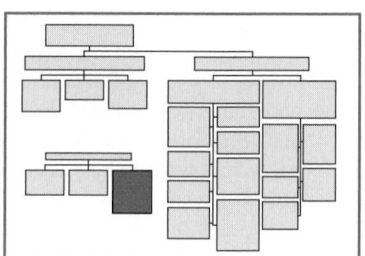

Certain reconstructive problems require substantial amounts of tissue of one or more types or of a very specialized type. Either local or free flaps are used to meet these tissue requirements.

Composite Defect

A composite defect may result from resection of an intraoral carcinoma with loss of the mandible and either the lining of the mouth or external skin. Another example is a crush injury of the leg with loss of soft tissue and a segment of weight-bearing bone. These defects require that a composite flap be brought to the area to meet more than one type of tissue deficiency. Local flaps generally do not provide the necessary types of tissue or permit the freedom of design possible with free flaps. The wide variety of free flap donor sites that exists allows selection of tissue in the appropriate quantity and configuration for a particular defect [*see Figure 6*].

Functional Defect

Functional defects require repair with specialized flaps. Free flaps are frequently used because the specific tissue requirements usually cannot be satisfied by a local flap. A functional defect may result, for example, in the cervical esophagus from tumor resection or in the forearm from Volkmann's contracture. A segment of small intestine can repair the esophageal defect; transfer of a vascularized and innervated muscle (e.g., the gracilis) can replace forearm muscle.[20]

Contour Defect

Contour defects, such as those that result from mastectomy or from trauma to the lower extremity, can be reconstructed with either local or free flaps. A mastectomy defect, because of its location on the chest, is suitable for reconstruction with one of several myocutaneous flaps from either the back or the abdomen [*see 25 Breast*

Procedures]. A free flap from the abdomen or the gluteal area is another alternative. The best reconstructive solution for a particular person is determined by variables such as body habitus and the size and configuration of the contralateral breast.

A contour defect of the lower extremity is best reconstructed with a large myocutaneous free flap that provides tissue of sufficient quantity and flexibility to allow sculpting into the appropriate shape. An excellent example is the latissimus dorsi free flap, which provides a large volume of thin, pliable muscle, which can be wrapped around orthopedic hardware.

Unstable Soft Tissue Coverage

Marginal soft tissue coverage (e.g., skin grafts) may break down after repeated minor trauma. Bones may become exposed and are then at risk for osteomyelitis. This situation can be avoided by elective replacement of the tissue at risk with a more substantial soft tissue covering. As in acute reconstruction, local flaps are the first choice for lesions of the trunk or the proximal ex-

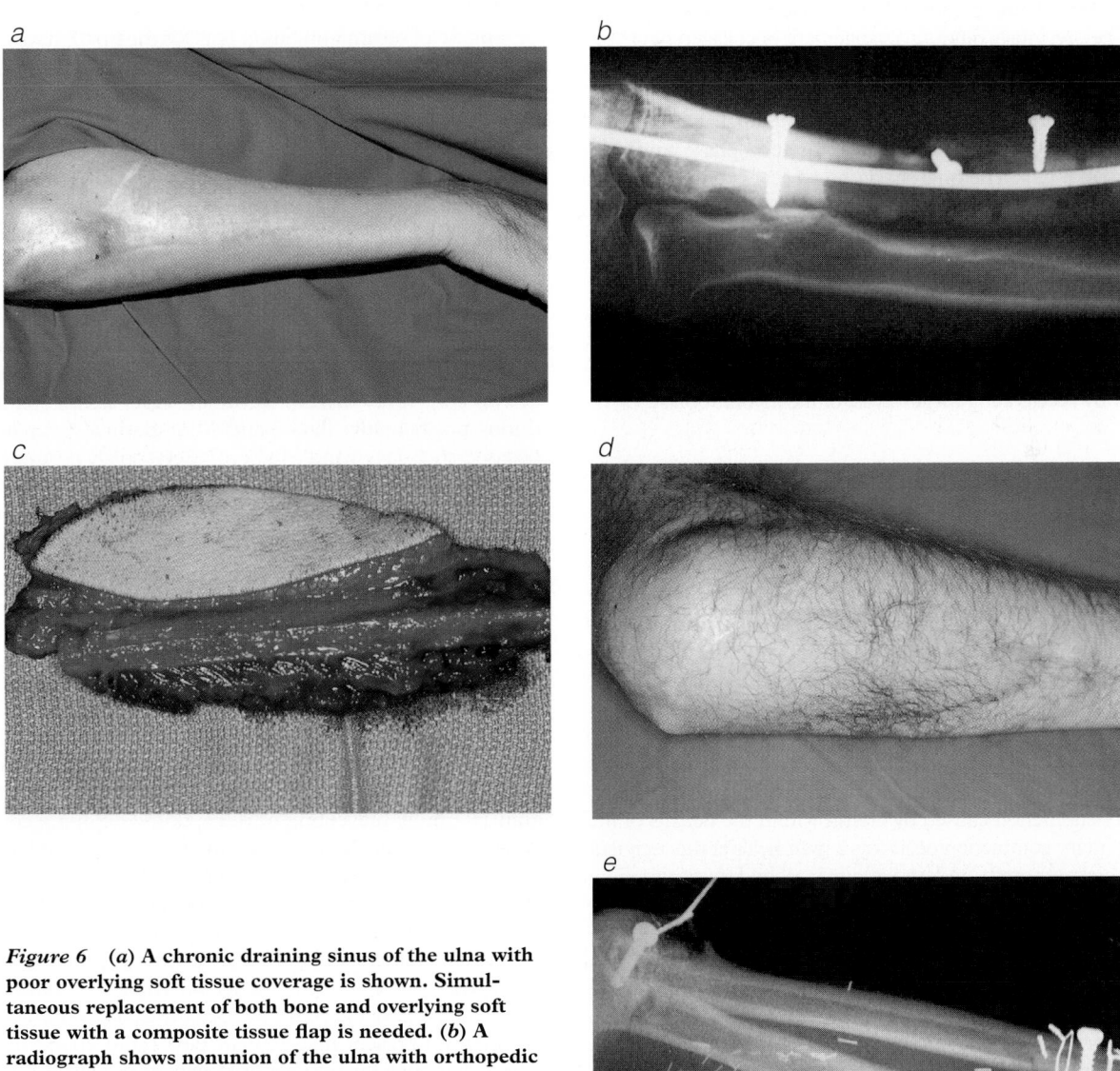

Figure 6 (*a*) **A chronic draining sinus of the ulna with poor overlying soft tissue coverage is shown. Simultaneous replacement of both bone and overlying soft tissue with a composite tissue flap is needed. (*b*) A radiograph shows nonunion of the ulna with orthopedic hardware. (*c*) A fibular free flap provides bone and skin in the appropriate amount and configuration for replacement of the affected tissues in a single stage. (*d*) The segment of ulna and overlying skin has been replaced. (*e*) A radiograph shows the vascularized fibula in place.**

tremities, whereas free flaps are often more appropriate for lesions of the distal extremities.

Soft tissue coverage is sometimes inadequate even in a healed wound. For example, certain procedures (e.g., nerve or bone grafting) require an ideal soft tissue bed to promote adequate graft revascularization. In some cases, it may initially be necessary to replace the existing soft tissue coverage as a first-stage procedure before grafting a bone or nerve gap. A skin or muscle flap is most commonly used in such cases. This problem is most common in areas such as the distal extremities, where native soft tissue coverage is not overly abundant and is easily lost as a consequence of trauma or tumor resection. Free flaps are usually chosen to provide a healthy, well-vascularized soft tissue bed before further functional reconstruction is undertaken.

Discussion

Wound Healing

The wound healing process consists of several identifiable phases [see 11 Acute Wound Care]. The first phase is an inflammatory response that includes both vascular and cellular components. The second stage is fibroplasia, during which collagen deposition by fibroblasts increases the tensile strength of the wound. The maturation phase of wound healing begins at about 3 weeks, when the rate of collagen degradation begins to balance the rate of collagen production. The previously random arrangement of collagen fibers becomes more organized, and the ratio of type I to type III collagen returns to normal. The wound gradually progresses from a raised, indurated, red scar to a mature form that is flat, soft, lighter in color, and of increased tensile strength. The maturation phase continues for more than a year. The final strength of a scar is typically about 80% of the normal strength of the skin.

Contraction of open granulating wounds is caused by myofibroblasts, which are modified fibroblasts that have smooth muscle characteristics. The number of myofibroblasts within the wound is proportional to the rate at which the wound contracts.[21,22] These cells are scattered throughout the wound and pull the edges of the wound toward the center. Skin grafts inhibit wound contraction, apparently by accelerating the life cycle of the myofibroblast.

Postoperative Management Issues

SKIN GRAFTS

Contraction and Reinnervation

Split-thickness skin grafts include the epidermis and only a portion of the dermis, whereas full-thickness skin grafts include the entire dermis. Skin grafts contract to a degree that is related to their thickness. After their harvest from donor sites, full-thickness grafts contract to a surface area as small as 40% of their original surface area, whereas split-thickness grafts contract only about half as much. This reduction in area, referred to as primary contraction, is a passive phenomenon caused by elastin within the dermis of the graft. Secondary contraction occurs as a graft heals at the recipient site. Full-thickness grafts undergo minimal secondary contraction, whereas split-thickness grafts contract to a degree that is inversely proportional to their dermal content. In other words, thick split-thickness grafts contract less than thin split-thickness grafts.

Skin grafts gradually regain sensation through reinnervation from the wound bed. Thick grafts and healthy wound beds contribute to greater sensory recovery; however, even after healing is complete, the degree of sensation in the graft does not equal that of normal skin. Graft thickness also affects recovery of certain other functions of normal skin, such as secretion from sweat glands and sebaceous glands, and of hair growth. These processes will be active only in full-thickness and thick split-thickness grafts. Secretion from sweat glands depends on sympathetic reinnervation of the graft and follows the sweat pattern of the recipient site. Sebaceous glands, on the other hand, secrete independently of graft reinnervation by the recipient bed. Thin split-thickness skin grafts tend to be quite dry because they contain inadequate numbers of functioning sebaceous glands, which are more abundant in thicker grafts. For this reason, such grafts may require application of a moisturizer for an indefinite period.

Revascularization

A phase of serum imbibition lasts for the first 2 days after placement of a skin graft. During this period, the graft is nourished by passive absorption of nutrients from serum in the recipient bed, not by direct vascular perfusion. Absorption of fluid causes the graft to increase in weight by as much as 40%. Vessels within the graft gradually dilate and fill with static columns of blood. A fibrin network in the wound bed causes graft adherence during this early phase.

The next phase in revascularization is a period of inosculation, during which anastomoses are formed between vessels in the graft and those in the wound bed. It is not clear, however, whether connections are established between existing vessels in the recipient bed and graft or whether new vessels grow into the graft from the recipient bed. Both processes may occur, and both may be important in graft revascularization. In any case, circulation is sluggish during postoperative days 3 and 4 but gradually increases during postoperative days 5 and 6 to become essentially normal by day 7.[23]

Lymphatic drainage from the graft is established at approximately the same rate as the circulation of blood. Lymphatic flow is present by postoperative day 5 or 6, and the graft starts losing the extra fluid weight it has gained. The graft begins to resume its normal weight by postoperative day 9.

Factors Affecting Graft Survival

Hematoma formation beneath a skin graft is the most common cause of graft failure. Blood accumulation interferes with graft adherence, as well as with both imbibition and inosculation. Early evacuation of blood from beneath a skin graft can result in graft survival. Shear forces that result from inadequate immobilization cause graft failure by preventing or disrupting developing communications between vessels of the graft and the recipient bed. Infection of the recipient bed makes the bed unsuitable for grafting, and such infection is another major cause of graft failure. Proteolytic enzymes produced by microorganisms destroy the fibrin bond between the graft and the recipient bed. Bacteria such as β-hemolytic streptococci and Pseudomonas are particularly virulent because they produce high levels of plasmin and other proteolytic enzymes. The type of organism present may actually be a more important factor in graft failure than the number of organisms present.[24]

Healing of Donor Sites

Donor sites for split-thickness grafts heal by reepithelialization. Epithelial cells from remaining portions of skin appendages (e.g., hair follicles, sebaceous glands, and sweat glands) migrate across the exposed dermis to establish a new epidermis. Donor sites for thin grafts heal more rapidly and leave less of a scar than those for thick grafts, which take longer to heal and can be associated with significant scarring. The epidermis of a healed donor site is fully differentiated within 3 to 4 weeks; however, the dermis shows little evidence of regeneration. An occlusive dressing such as OpSite (Smith & Nephew, Hull, United Kingdom) promotes more rapid healing of the donor site than coverage with fine mesh gauze and is potentially less painful.[25]

FLAPS

Resistance to Infection

In experimental settings, skin flaps, myocutaneous flaps, and fasciocutaneous flaps have been shown to vary in their resistance to bacterial infection.[26] Random-pattern skin flaps are not as resistant as myocutaneous flaps. The cutaneous portions of myocutaneous and of fasciocutaneous flaps have similar levels of resistance, but the muscle component of myocutaneous flaps is more resistant than the fascial component of fasciocutaneous flaps in situations where the flap lies over a focus of infection within the wound. Muscle therefore appears to be the type of flap that is most resistant to infection. Such resistance is of clinical significance in cases of exposed bone with chronic osteomyelitis, for example. This condition can be successfully treated by debridement and immediate coverage with a muscle flap.

Free Flaps and Concept of No-Reflow

Free tissue transfer is unique in that the flap is completely ischemic for a given period. How long ischemia can be tolerated without resultant flap failure (despite technically satisfactory microvascular anastomoses) is an important clinical question. An increasing duration of ischemia has been associated experimentally with obstruction to blood flow in the microcirculation.[27,28] This obstruction results from cellular edema, increased interstitial fluid pressure, and sludging of blood and thrombus formation. This phenomenon is initially reversible but becomes irreversible as the duration of ischemia increases. After 12 hours of ischemia under experimental conditions, obstruction to blood flow has been demonstrated to be complete, preventing successful reperfusion of the flap. How long uninterrupted ischemia can safely continue in a clinical setting is not precisely known, and evidence suggests that different types of tissue have different levels of tolerance for ischemia. For example, flaps that are primarily bone are more durable than muscle or bowel flaps. Evidence gained by clinical experience indicates that most free flaps can safely tolerate up to 4 hours of ischemia.

Tissue Expansion

Histologic changes noted in expanded skin include thinning of the dermis but not of the epidermis,[29] suggesting a permanent net gain in epidermal tissue only. The mitotic rate in the epidermis has been shown to increase with expansion, but the mechanism for this increase is unclear.[30]

The circulation of expanded skin also changes. The increase in vascularity observed in expanded tissue is partially explained by the fact that tissue expansion is a form of delay procedure. Experimental studies suggest, however, that an increased potential for flap survivability is directly attributable to the expansion process and not merely to its delay component.[31-33] The fibrous capsule that forms around the prosthesis during expansion appears to contribute to the increased vascularity of these flaps, and the increased pressure around the expander may stimulate angiogenesis.

References

1. Parrett BM, Matros E, Pribaz JJ, et al: Lower extremity trauma: trends in the management of soft-tissue reconstruction of open tibia-fibula fractures. Plast Reconstr Surg 117:1315, 2006

2. Edlich RF, Jones KC Jr, Buchanan L, et al: A disposable emergency wound treatment kit. J Emerg Med 10:463, 1992

3. Stevenson TR, Thacker JG, Rodeheaver GT, et al: Cleansing the traumatic wound by high pressure syringe irrigation. JACEP 5:17, 1976

4. Hollander JE, Singer AJ, Valentine SM, et al: Risk factors for infection in patients with traumatic lacerations. Acad Emerg Med 8:716, 2001

5. Edlich RF, Rodeheaver GT, Thacker JG: Technical factors in the prevention of wound infection. Surgical Infectious Diseases. Simmons R, Howard R, Eds. Appleton-Century-Croft, East Norwalk, Connecticut, 1981

6. Robson MC, Heggers JP: Delayed wound closures based on bacterial counts. J Surg Oncol 2:379, 1970

7. Teepe RG, Koebrugge EJ, Lowik CW, et al: Cytotoxic effects of topical antimicrobial and antiseptic agents on human keratinocytes in vitro. J Trauma 35:8, 1993

8. Jackson IT: Local Flaps in Head and Neck Reconstruction. CV Mosby, St Louis, 1985

9. Spinelli HM, Forman DL: Current treatment of post-traumatic deformities: residual orbital, adnexal, and soft-tissue abnormalities. Clin Plast Surg 24:519, 1997

10. Luce EA: Reconstruction of the lower lip. Clin Plast Surg 22:109, 1995

11. Mathes SJ, Nahai F: Reconstructive Surgery: Principles, Anatomy, Technique, Vol 1. Churchill Livingstone, New York, 1997, p 37

12. Orgill DP, Austen WG, Butler CE, et al: Guidelines for treatment of complex chest wounds with negative pressure wound therapy. Wounds 16(12 suppl B):1, 2004

13. Domkowski PW, Smith ML, Gonyon DL Jr, et al: Evaluation of vacuum-assisted closure in the treatment of post-sternotomy mediastinitis. J Thorac Cardiovasc Surg 126:386, 2003

14. Kaplan M, Banwell P, Orgill DP, et al: Guidelines for the management of the open abdomen: recommendations from a multidisciplinary expert advisory panel. Wounds 17(10 suppl):1, 2005

15. Miller PR, Thompson JT, Faler B, et al: Late fascial closure in lieu of ventral hernia: the next step in open abdomen management. J Trauma 53:843, 2002

16. Taylor GI, Giantoutsos MP, Morris SF: The neurovascular territories of the skin and muscles: anatomic study and clinical implications. Plast Reconstr Surg 94:1, 1994

17. Hidalgo DA, Shaw WW: Reconstruction of foot injuries. Clin Plast Surg 13:663, 1986

18. May JW Jr, Halls MJ, Simon SR: Free microvascular muscle flaps with skin graft reconstruction of extensive defects of the foot: a clinical and gait analysis study. Plast Reconstr Surg 75:627, 1985

19. Bennett RG, Hirt M: A history of tissue expansion: concepts, controversies, and complications. J Dermatol Surg Oncol 19:1066, 1993

20. Hidalgo DA, Disa JJ, Cordeiro PG: A review of 716 consecutive free flaps for oncologic surgical defects: refinement in donor site selection and technique. Plast Reconstr Surg 102:722, 1998

21. McGrath MH, Hundahl SA: The spatial and temporal quantification of myofibroblasts. Plast Reconstr Surg 69:975, 1982

22. Rudolph R: Inhibition of myofibroblasts by skin grafts. Plast Reconstr Surg 63:473, 1979

23. Angel MF, Giesswein P, Hawner P: Skin grafting. Operative Plastic Surgery. Evans GRD, Ed. McGraw-Hill, New York, 2000, p 59

24. Teh BT: Why do skin grafts fail? Plast Reconstr Surg 63:323, 1979

25. Smith DJ Jr, Thomson PD, Bolton LL: Microbiology and healing of the occluded skin-graft donor site. Plast Reconstr Surg 91:1094, 1993

26. Gosain A, Chang N, Mathes S, et al: A study of the relationship between blood flow and bacterial inoculation in musculocutaneous and fasciocutaneous flaps. Plast Reconstr Surg 86:1152, 1990

27. Kerrigan CL, Stotland MA: Ischemia reperfusion injury: a review. Microsurgery 14:165, 1993

28. Kirschner RE, Fyfe BS, Hoffman LA, et al: Ischemia-reperfusion injury in myocutaneous flaps: role of leukocytes and leukotrienes. Plast Reconstr Surg 99:1485, 1997

29. Johnson TM, Lowe L, Brown MD, et al: Histology and physiology of tissue expansion. J Dermatol Surg Oncol 19:1074, 1993

30. Olenius M, Johansson O: Variations in epidermal thickness in expanded human breast skin. Scand J Plast Reconstr Hand Surg 29:15, 1995

31. Babovic S, Angel MF, Im MJ, et al: Effects of tissue expansion on secondary ischemic tolerance in experimental free flaps. Ann Plast Surg 34:593, 1995

32. Matturri L, Azzolini A, Riberti C, et al: Long-term histopathologic evaluation of human expanded skin. Plast Reconstr Surg 90:636, 1992

33. Olenius M, Dalsgaard CJ, Wickman M: Mitotic activity in expanded human skin. Plast Reconstr Surg 91:213, 1993

Acknowledgment

Figure 3 Carol Donner.

24 MALIGNANT SKIN LESIONS

Jennifer A. Wargo, M.D., and Kenneth Tanabe, M.D., F.A.C.S.

Given the variable natural history and prognosis of skin malignancies, clinical assessment and management of these lesions can be challenging. Malignant skin lesions have become increasingly prevalent over the past several years. In the United States, approximately 1.2 million cases of nonmelanoma skin cancer are diagnosed annually.[1] More alarming is the observation that approximately 80,000 cases of melanoma are now diagnosed each year[2]—a figure that that has been steadily rising,[3] to the point where the current lifetime risk for the development of melanoma is 1 in 75.[2] This disturbing increase in the incidence of both nonmelanoma skin cancer and melanoma can largely be attributed to prevailing social attitudes toward sun exposure.[4]

Given the increasing prevalence of skin cancers and the pivotal role surgeons play in their treatment, it is critical that surgeons be well informed about the recognition, workup, and management of these conditions. Accordingly, in what follows, we address evaluation and management of malignant skin lesions in detail; management of benign skin lesions is beyond the scope of this chapter.

Assessment of Potentially Malignant Skin Lesions

CLINICAL EVALUATION

History

A careful history should be obtained, with particular attention paid to the extent of previous sun exposure. A history of blistering sunburn in childhood or adolescence is a significant risk factor and is reported by virtually all white persons with melanomas.[5] A personal or family history of skin cancer is also a risk factor: the likelihood that melanoma will develop is increased eight- to 12-fold when a first-degree relative has a history of melanoma.[6] Previous immunosuppression or transplantation should be inquired about as well; both place the patient at higher risk for the development of skin cancer.

A detailed history of the lesion's development, starting with the time when it was first noted and including any changes in its size or appearance, should be elicited. Such a history will help the clinician make the initial judgment regarding whether the lesion is suspicious or nonsuspicious. Generally speaking, lesions are considered nonsuspicious if they remain stable and uniform in terms of their physical characteristics (e.g., size, shape, color, profile, and texture). An example of a nonsuspicious lesion is a simple nevus, which typically becomes apparent at 4 to 5 years of age, darkens with puberty, and fades in the seventh to eighth decades of life. Pigmented lesions that have an irregular border or demonstrate a change in size, color, or texture are considered suspicious. Careful attention should also be paid to constitutional symptoms. Patients who present with metastatic disease may have systemic or focal complaints, such as headaches or, in the case of melanoma that has metastasized to the brain, visual changes.

Physical Examination

Physical examination should include a complete skin examination, as well as examination of mucosal membranes. In the case of a possible melanoma, particular attention should be paid to the presence or absence of surrounding nodules or nodules between the skin lesion and the closest nodal basins that may represent in-transit metastases. Attention should be paid to the draining nodal basins because lymph node metastases are known to occur in both squamous cell carcinoma (SCC) and melanoma.

If the lesion is not clinically suspicious, conservative monitoring through patient self-examination and regular follow-up with a healthcare provider is appropriate.

INVESTIGATIVE STUDIES

Biopsy

Any clinically suspicious lesion should undergo either excisional biopsy (if the lesion is small) or incisional biopsy (if the lesion is large). Excisional biopsy typically incorporates a 1 to 4 mm margin of normal skin, depending on the clinical characteristics of the lesion. With some types of lesions (e.g., a dysplastic nevus), the use of this margin may eliminate the need for subsequent reexcision if the lesion proves to contain high-grade cytologic atypia. In any case, no attempt should be made to perform a definitive radical excision until a diagnosis is established by means of biopsy.

A full-thickness excision that extends into the subcutaneous fat should be performed, and the specimen should be marked for orientation to help the pathologist evaluate the margins for possible microscopic involvement with tumor cells. As a rule, electrocauterization should not be employed to remove the specimen, because it creates artifacts that can substantially distort cells at the margins. Shave biopsy is discouraged for evaluation of pigmented lesions because it may create a positive deep margin, thereby compromising determination of the true depth of penetration of a melanoma. In the case of an elliptically shaped excisional biopsy on an extremity, the long axis of the specimen should be oriented along the long axis of the extremity to facilitate subsequent reexcision if necessary.

EXCISION OF MALIGNANCY

If the lesion proves to be benign, no further treatment is usually required. If it proves to be malignant, further excision with appropriate margins is usually necessary, and tumor staging becomes an important concern. Appropriate excision margins for different skin cancers are discussed in more detail elsewhere [see Management of Specific Types of Skin Cancer, *below*].

For lesions excised in an ellipse of skin and fat, the length of the ellipse should be approximately 3.5 to 4 times the width to allow tension-free closure without dog-ears. If an area cannot be closed primarily, skin grafting may be necessary [see *27 Surface Reconstruction Procedures*]. For very large lesions or lesions in difficult areas (e.g., the face), specialized flaps may be required.

Management of Specific Types of Skin Cancer

BASAL CELL CARCINOMA

Incidence and Epidemiology

Basal cell carcinoma (BCC) is the most common malignancy in white persons[7] and the most prevalent type of skin cancer overall. The incidence varies widely across the globe (e.g., 146/100,000 in the United States, compared with 726/100,000 in Australia).[8] The lifetime risk of BCC for a white person in the United States is approximately 30%.[1] Although BCCs have a very low metastatic potential, they impose heavy economic and social burdens on patients and society.

The vast majority of BCCs are found on the head and neck. There is no known precursor lesion. The risk of development of BCC seems to be most closely related to exposure to ultraviolet radiation. Whereas substantial sun exposure during childhood and adolescence increases the risk of BCC, no studies have demonstrated any significant correlation between the development of BCC and cumulative exposure to ultraviolet light in adulthood.[9] Several heritable conditions are associated with an increased risk of BCC, including albinism, xeroderma pigmentosum, and Gorlin syndrome. Patients with Gorlin syndrome typically have multiple BCCs, as well as anomalies of the spine and the ribs, jaw cysts, pitting of the palms and the soles, and calcification of the falx cerebri. This syndrome is inherited in an autosomal-dominant fashion.[10]

Histologic Subtypes

Several subtypes of BCC have been identified. Typical patterns seen in more mature lesions include nodular or cystic BCC, superficial BCC, morpheaform BCC, and pigmented BCC. Nodular BCC, also known as rodent ulcer, is the classic type. Nodular BCCs typically present as solitary lesions, often on the face, and are usually shiny and red with central telangectasias [see Figure 1a], an indurated edge, and an ulcerated center. If the contents of the lesion are soft and can be expressed, the condition is referred to as cystic BCC. Superficial BCC is typically found on the trunk and appears as a slow-growing erythematous patch that is often mistaken for eczema or psoriasis.[10] Morpheaform BCC [see Figure 1b] accounts for only a minority of these lesions, but it exhibits clinical features that are especially noteworthy for surgeons. In particular, morpheaform BCCs often turn out to be larger than they appear clinically, and they generally have a more aggressive natural history than other BCCs; as a result, complete excision can be highly challenging.

Treatment

Surgical excision remains the mainstay of treatment for primary BCCs. Typically, a surgical margin of 4 mm is recommended when possible.[11] With small defects, primary closure is generally feasible; with larger defects, rotation flaps or skin grafting may be necessary. Lymphatic spread identified in the primary tumor, though present only in extraordinarily rare cases, may be an indication for lymphatic mapping.[12]

Other surgical techniques used to treat BCC include cryosurgery, curettage and cauterization, and Mohs' micrographic surgery. Cryosurgery and curettage are generally contraindicated for large or morpheaform BCCs or tumors in high-risk areas (e.g., the central face), because surgical margins cannot be assessed. Mohs' micrographic surgery involves excision of serial sections with intraoperative histologic examination of frozen sections to control surgical margins. It is particularly useful in treating morpheaform BCCs, recurrent BCCs, and BCCs in high-risk sites (with 5-year cure rates approaching 95%).[13]

Nonsurgical modalities available for treatment of BCC include radiotherapy, photodynamic therapy, and the application of topical agents (e.g., 5-fluorouracil [5-FU], imiquimod, and intralesional interferon alfa [IFN-α]). Radiation therapy is generally reserved for elderly patients with extensive lesions that preclude excision; 5-year cure rates in this population approach 90%.[14] Photodynamic therapy involves the application of a 20% emulsion of δ-aminolevulinic acid to the lesion, followed by exposure to light in the wavelength range of 620 to 640 nm. This therapy is based on the uptake of the porphyrin metabolite by the tumor with subsequent conversion to protoporphyrin IX, which results in destruction of the tumor in the presence of light.[10] The response rates observed with photodynamic therapy are somewhat lower than those observed with other therapies: the overall clearance rate is 87%, but the clearance rate for nodular BCC is only 53%.[15] 5-FU, in the form of a 5% cream, may be used in the management of multiple BCCs of the trunk and limbs. Imiquimod is also given in a 5% cream to treat BCCs, with clearance rates ranging from 70% to 100%.[16] INF-α may be administered directly into the lesion; in a series of 140 patients treated in this manner, a 67% cure rate was reported.[17]

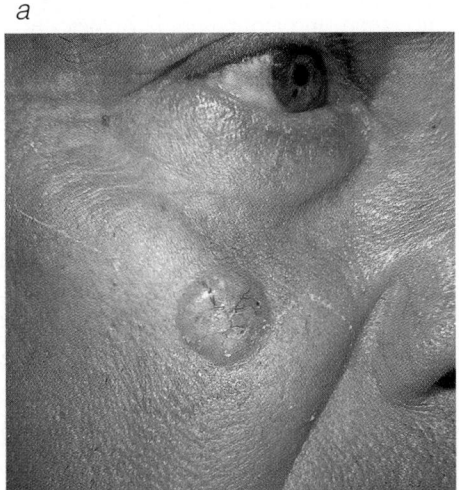
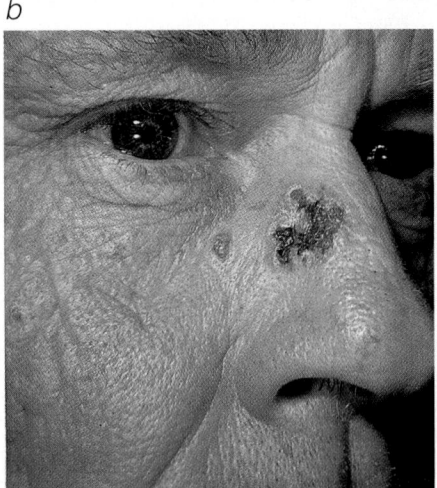

Figure 1 Shown are (*a*) a typical basal cell carcinoma and (*b*) a morpheaform basal cell carcinoma.

a

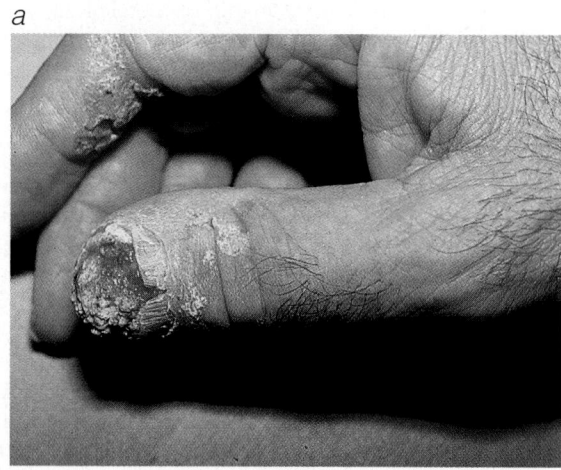

b

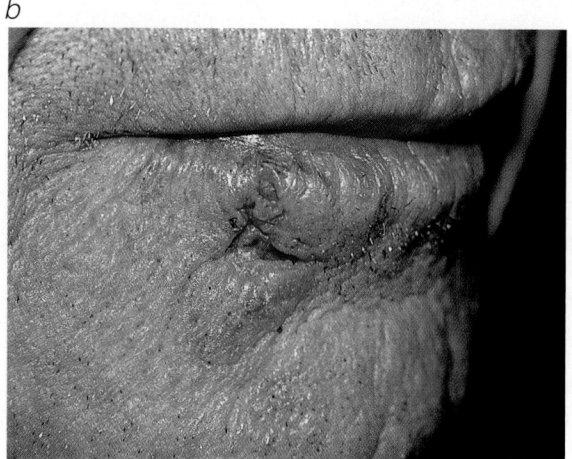

Figure 2 **Shown are squamous cell carcinomas related to (*a*) radiation exposure and (*b*) sun exposure.**

Patients who have been treated for any skin cancer, including BCC, are at higher risk for the development of additional skin cancers and should therefore perform self-examinations at frequent intervals to check for suspicious lesions. Such patients should also receive counselling to reduce sun exposure, with the aim of limiting further damage from ultraviolet irradiation. High-risk patients (e.g., those with Gorlin syndrome and those who are receiving immunosuppressive therapy after renal transplantation) should be offered oral retinoid therapy in an effort to prevent the development of other nonmelanoma skin cancers.[17]

SQUAMOUS CELL CARCINOMA

Incidence and Epidemiology

SCC of the skin is the second most common form of non-melanoma skin cancer overall. It is the most common tumor in elderly patients, probably as a consequence of cumulative doses of sun exposure over the course of their lifetimes. In white persons, the lifetime risk for the development of SCC is nearly 10%.

The majority (50% to 60%) of cutaneous SCCs are found on the head and neck. In one series, nearly 50% of fatal cases of SCC occurred in patients in whom the lesion arose on the ear.[18] The mortality associated with SCC is estimated to be approximately 1/100,000.[19]

Precursor Lesions

Unlike BCCs, SCCs often arise in precursor lesions, such as actinic keratoses.[20] Actinic keratoses, sometimes referred to as solar keratoses, develop in chronically sun-damaged areas of the body. These lesions are often multiple, are generally ill-defined and irregular, and may range in size from about 1 mm to a few centimeters. They have a scaly appearance and exhibit a wide variety of colors, from dark brown to flesh-pink. Biopsy may be necessary to rule out the presence of a SCC. Although the rate at which actinic keratosis undergoes malignant transformation to SCC is less than 0.1% per year,[21] lesions should nevertheless be treated to reduce the chances of progression. Treatment options include cryotherapy, curettage, and topical therapy. Surgical excision of actinic keratoses is rarely necessary but may be indicated if there is a high level of suspicion for concurrent SCC.

Intraepithelial SCC (carcinoma in situ), also known as Bowen disease, is thought to be the next step in the progression from actinic

keratosis to invasive SCC. The lesions are typically located on sun-exposed areas of the head, neck, trunk, or legs; when they are located on the genitalia, the condition is referred to as erythroplasia of Queyrat. Lesions that develop on non–sun-exposed areas may be associated with internal malignancy.[22] Intraepithelial SCCs typically appear as erythematous, slightly keratotic plaques and are usually larger than the lesions of actinic keratosis. They should be excised with a 5 mm to 1 cm margin.

Diagnosis

As noted (see above), SCCs are most often associated with sun exposure, though they may also be seen in patients with old scars, radiation-damaged skin [*see Figure 2a*], or chronic open wounds.[23] Chronic inflammation and irritation appear to be the common denominators. SCC that arises in a burn scar or a chronic, open wound overlying osteomyelitis is often referred to as a Marjolin ulcer. SCCs that develop from Marjolin ulcers are characterized by aggressive regrowth after incomplete biopsy.

SCCs typically appear as reddish-brown, pink, or flesh-colored keratotic papules [*see Figure 2b*]; ulceration is sometimes, though not always, present. If there is extensive hyperkeratosis, a cutaneous "horn" may be evident.[18] Symptoms that may suggest malignant transformation of actinic keratosis into SCC include pain, erythema, ulceration, and induration. Histologically, SCCs are characterized by nests of atypical keratinocytes that have invaded into the dermis, which may be either well or poorly differentiated.

Once the diagnosis of SCC is suspected, careful attention should be paid to the draining nodal basins with the aim of detecting possible lymph node metastasis. The risk of such metastasis is between 2% and 4% overall but is somewhat higher in patients with relatively large and poorly differentiated lesions and in patients with lesions located on the scalp, the nose, the ears, the lips, or the extremities. The most common sites of metastasis are regional lymph nodes, the lungs, and the liver. When metastasis or recurrence develops, it is typically within 3 years after treatment of the index lesion.

Treatment

For primary SCC, as for BCC, surgical excision remains the mainstay of treatment; however, the recommended margin of excision for SCCs is generally larger than that for BCCs, ranging from 0.5 to 2 cm. Smaller lesions can often be closed primarily; larger lesions may require rotation flaps or skin grafting.

Nonexcisional therapeutic options for SCC are similar to those for BCC. Surgical choices include cryosurgery, curettage and cauterization, and Mohs' micrographic surgery. Nonsurgical choices include radiotherapy, photodynamic therapy, and topical therapy with agents such as 5-FU, imiquimod, and intralesional IFN-α.

Posttreatment recommendations for SCC patients are essentially the same as for BCC patients [see Basal Cell Carcinoma, Treatment, above]: frequent self-examination to look for suspicious lesions, counseling to reduce sun exposure, and the offer of oral retinoid therapy for high-risk patients.[17]

MELANOMA

Incidence and Epidemiology

Although melanoma is less common than BCC or SCC, it is clearly more deadly than either. It is currently the sixth leading cause of cancer-related death in the United States, and its incidence is increasing faster than the incidence of any other malignancy. Melanoma is slightly more common in men than in women, and the median age at diagnosis is 57 years.[6] An average of 18.8 life-years are lost for each melanoma death,[24] and it is estimated that one United States citizen dies of melanoma every hour.[25]

Melanoma results from the malignant transformation of melanocytes, which are responsible for pigment production. The genetic factors implicated in this transformation have not been well characterized. As noted [see Assessment of Potentially Malignant Skin Lesions, Clinical Evaluation, History, above], patients with a family history of melanoma are at substantially higher risk for the development of melanoma.[6] Somatic mutations in the *p16* tumor suppressor gene have been identified in both familial and sporadic cases of melanoma.[26] Environmental factors—specifically, exposure to ultraviolet radiation—are also implicated in the maligant transformation of melanocytes. Increased risk of melanoma is associated with intermittent intense sun exposure rather than with the cumulative effect of long-term mild exposure, though the exact mechanism behind the pathogenesis remains unknown.

Screening and Diagnosis

In one study, multivariate analysis identified the following six risk factors as important in the development of malignant melanoma[27]:

1. A family history of melanoma;
2. A history of three or more blistering sunburns before the age of 20;
3. Blonde or red hair;
4. The presence of actinic keratosis;

Table 1 ABCD Guidelines for Pigmented Lesions

Characteristic	Comments
Asymmetry	Most early lesions grow at uneven rate, resulting in an asymmetrical appearance
Border irregularity	Uneven growth rate also results in irregular border
Color variegation	Irregular growth also causes new shades of black and of light and dark brown
Diameter	Lesions with ABC features and diameter > 6 mm should be considered suspicious for melanoma

5. A history of 3 or more years of an outdoor summer job as a teenager; and
6. Marked freckling on the upper part of the back.

For a person with one or two of these factors, the risk of melanoma is increased 3.5-fold; for a person with three or more, the risk is increased 20-fold.

The recommended frequency for melanoma screening should be based on these six risk factors. Routine screening of low-risk patients through total body skin examinations performed by healthcare providers is not a supported practice. Self-screening, however, is clearly recommended, and excellent educational materials on this subject are available from the American Academy of Dermatology and the American Cancer Society. Nevertheless, physicians should take every opportunity to screen patients as the occasion arises; in general, the lesions found by physicians are significantly thinner than those detected by patients or their spouses.[28]

For effective treatment of melanomas, early recognition is critical. The ABCD (*A*symmetry, *B*order irregularity, *C*olor variegation, *D*iameter) guidelines for pigmented lesions are frequently used as aids to melanoma identification [see Table 1].[29] Melanomas often occur on sun-exposed areas of the upper trunk and the extremities, and they are typically asymmetric, with irregular borders and variegated pigmentation [see Figure 3a]. Occasionally, they lack pigmentation or are associated with significant gross ulceration. Any lesion that appears suspicious for melanoma should undergo biopsy. Histologically, melanomas are characterized by atypical melanocytes with mitotic figures. Special staining, most commonly with HMB-45 or S100, may also be performed.

Histologic Subtypes

Melanoma may be classified into histologic subtypes on the basis of growth pattern and anatomic location. It should be kept in mind,

a

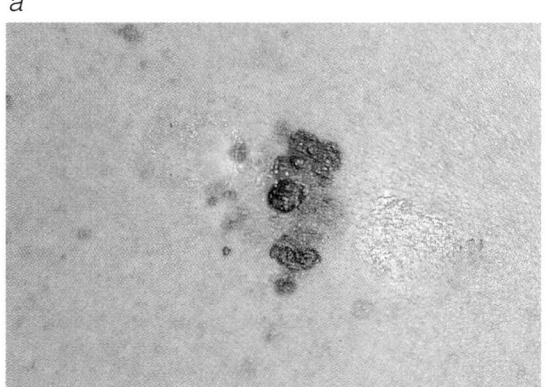

b

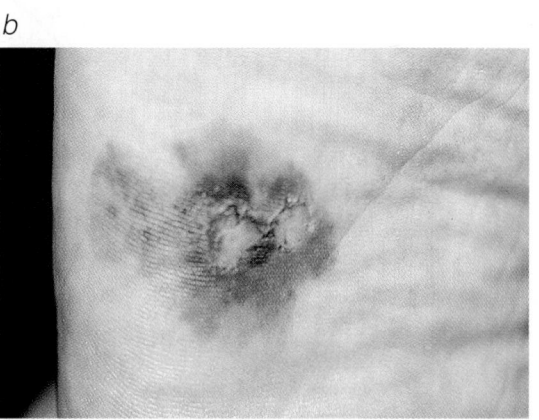

Figure 3 **Shown are (*a*) a typical melanoma and (*b*) an acral lentiginous melanoma.**

Table 2 Clark System for Staging Melanoma

Clark Level	Degree of Tumor Invasion	5-Year Survival (%)
Level I	Malignant melanocytes are confined to epidermis	99
Level II	Malignant melanocytes infiltrate papillary dermis singly or in small nests	95
Level III	Malignant melanocytes fill and expand papillary dermis, with extension of tumor to papillary-reticular dermal interface (usually signifying vertical growth phase)	82
Level IV	Malignant melanocytes infiltrate reticular dermis in significant fashion	71
Level V	Malignant melanocytes infiltrate subcutaneous fat	49

however, that the specific subtype a tumor falls into, in itself, is not as important as the pattern of growth (i.e., radial versus vertical) and the depth of penetration.[30] The main subtypes are lentigo maligna melanoma, superficial spreading melanoma, acral lentiginous melanoma, and nodular melanoma. Of these, superficial spreading melanoma is the most common, accounting for more than 70% of melanomas. These lesions occur most frequently in white adults, typically on the back or the legs. Nodular melanoma is the second most common subtype, accounting for between 15% and 30% of all melanomas. These lesions often appear dome-shaped and may occur anywhere on the body. They typically manifest an early vertical growth phase and thus tend to invade the dermis early in their natural history. Lentigo maligna melanoma accounts for approximately 5% of all melanomas and is believed to arise in a focus of lentigo maligna (Hutchinson freckle). These lesions demonstrate a prolonged radial growth phase before exhibiting an invasive component. Acral lentiginous melanoma occurs on the hands or the feet [*see Figure 3b*], often under the nailbed, where the dermis is thinner (subungual melanoma). There also exists a relatively rare histologic subtype known as desmoplastic melanoma, which typically occurs in areas of sun damage and tends to recur locally more often than other subtypes do.

Staging and Prognosis

An important variable in the prognosis of melanoma is the thickness of the primary tumor, as assessed by means of either the Breslow system or the Clark system [*see Table 2*]. In the Breslow system, a calibrated ocular micrometer is employed to measure tumor thickness from the epidermal surface to the deepest point of the tumor's extension into tissue.[31] In the Clark system, the levels are defined by the presence or absence of malignant melanocytes in each of the following layers: epidermis, papillary dermis, reticular dermis, and subcutaneous fat [*see Figure 4*].[32]

Over the past several years, extensive research has been conducted on factors that affect prognosis in both early-stage and late-stage melanoma. Clinical factors that have been shown to possess significant prognostic value include age, sex, the location of the melanoma, the number of lymph nodes involved, the presence of distant metastasis, and the serum lactate dehydrogenase (LDH) level.[33] In general, the prognosis is better when the patient is younger than 65 years of age, when the patient is female, when the tumor is located on an extremity, when no lymph nodes are involved, when there is no evidence of distant metastasis, and when the serum LDH level is normal.

Melanomas are usually staged according to the system developed by the American Joint Committee on Cancer (AJCC), the latest version of which was approved in 2002 [*see Tables 3 and 4*].[34] The AJCC stage correlates well with the 5-year survival rate [*see Table 5*].[34]

Stage I and II melanoma The vast majority of melanoma patients have a clinically localized form of the disease (i.e., stage I or II). Several clinical factors have been identified and employed for risk stratification and prognosis in this heterogeneous group. The most important prognostic factors in early-stage melanoma are tumor thickness (T1 through T4) and the presence or absence of ulceration: 5-year survival in patients with stage I and II melanomas falls significantly as tumor thickness increases and is substantially reduced (from 80% to 55%) in the presence of ulceration.[30] In the past few years, the mitotic rate in the primary tumor has also been identified as an important prognostic factor, one that may eventually prove more important than the presence or absence of ulceration in this population.[35] Accordingly, it is likely that tumor mitotic rate will be incorporated into the next iteration of the AJCC's melanoma staging system.

Study of thin (< 1 mm) melanomas, in particular, has led to further refinement of risk stratification. The Clark level has prognostic implications for these lesions, in that tumors extending to Clark level IV are considered T1b regardless of their actual thickness and are associated with a worse prognosis. A 2004 report from the University of Pennsylvania described a prognostic model that made use of a

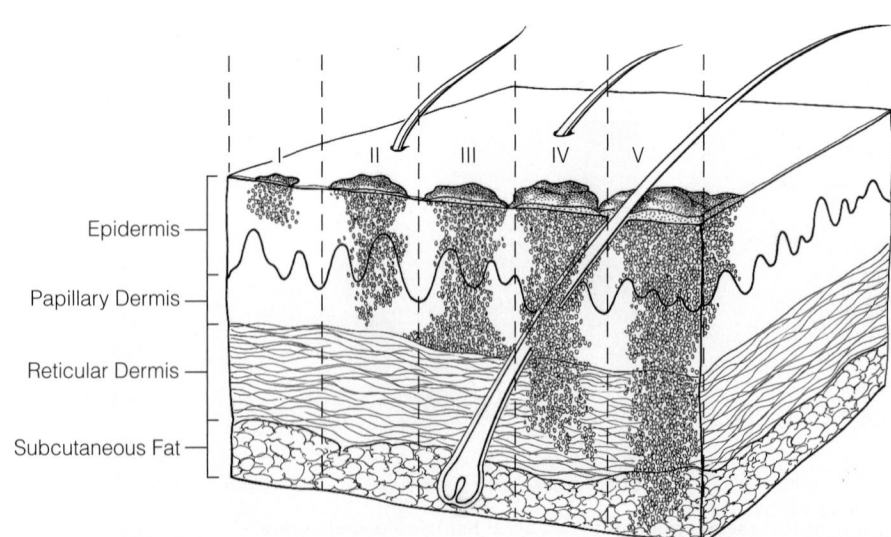

Figure 4 The Clark system classifies skin tumors according to the level of invasion, determined by the presence or absence of malignant melanocytes in the epidermis, papillary dermis, reticular dermis, and subcutaneous fat.

Table 3 American Joint Committee on Cancer TNM Clinical Classification of Melanoma[85]

Primary tumor (T)	TX Primary tumor cannot be assessed (e.g., shave biopsy or regressed melanoma)
	Tis Melanoma in situ
	T0 No evidence of primary tumor
	T1 Lesion thickness 1.0 mm
	    T1a: ulceration absent and Clark level II or III
	    T1b: ulceration present or Clark level IV or V
	T2 Lesion thickness 1.01–2.0 mm
	    T2a: ulceration absent
	    T2b: ulceration present
	T3 Lesion thickness 2.01–4.0 mm
	    T3a: ulceration absent
	    T3b: ulceration present
	T4 Lesion thickness > 4.0 mm
	    T4a: ulceration absent
	    T4b: ulceration present

Regional lymph nodes (N)	NX Regional lymph nodes cannot be assessed
	N0 No regional lymph node metastasis
	N1 1 metastatic lymph node
	    N1a: micrometastases present
	    N1b: macrometastases present
	N2 2 or 3 metastatic lymph nodes
	    N2a: micrometastases present
	    N2b: macrometastases present
	    N2c: in-transit metastases or satellite metastases present without metastatic lymph nodes
	N3 4 metastatic lymph nodes; matted lymph nodes; or combinations of in-transit metastases, satellite metastases, or ulcerated melanoma and metastatic lymph nodes

Distant metastases (M)	MX Distant metastases cannot be assessed
	M0 No distant metastasis
	M1 Distant metastases
	    M1a: metastases to skin, subcutaneous tissues, or distant lymph nodes
	    M1b: metastases to lung
	    M1c: metastases to all other visceral sites or distant metastases at any site associated with elevated serum LDH

LDH—lactic dehydrogenase

risk-stratification algorithm based on four factors: (1) mitotic rate (0% versus ≥ 1%), (2) growth pattern (radial or vertical), (3) gender, and (4) tumor-infiltrating lymphocyte (TIL) activity (brisk, non-brisk, or absent).[36] For minimal-risk and low-risk patients, the predicted risk for metastasis was less than 4%, whereas for moderate-risk and high-risk patients, the predicted risk for metastasis was 12% and 30%, respectively.[36]

Intermediate-thickness (1 to 4 mm) melanomas are clearly associated with a worse prognosis than thin melanomas: the 5-year survival rate is 89% for patients with nonulcerated T2 lesions and 77.4% for those with ulcerated lesions. For patients with ulcerated T3 lesions, the predicted 5-year survival rate is 63%.

For node-negative patients with thick (> 4 mm) lesions, the 5-year survival rate is 67.4%; this figure drops to 45.1% if the lesion is ulcerated.[34]

Stage III melanoma Stage III melanoma is characterized by the presence of nodal metastases (micrometastases or macrometas-

tases), with or without in-transit or satellite lesions. The presence of lymph node metastases is associated with a substantially worse prognosis, with fewer than 50% of node-positive patients surviving for 5 years.[34] The number of involved nodes is also a significant prognostic factor and is included as such in the current version of the AJCC melanoma staging system.

Four prognostic factors have been identified that influence survival in patients with stage III melanoma: (1) the number of lymph nodes with metastases; (2) the presence of microscopic tumor deposits in lymph nodes, as opposed to macroscopic deposits; (3) the presence of in-transit or satellite metastases; and (4) the presence of ulceration in the primary lesion.[34] At one time, the size of the involved lymph node was believed to be a significant prognostic factor, and it was included in earlier staging systems; currently, it is understood that this variable does not in fact exhibit a significant correlation with survival.[37] However, macroscopic disease (i.e., disease that is identified clinically and confirmed histologically) does have a significant impact: the survival rate is much poorer in patients with macroscopic disease than in those with microscopic disease.[34]

In-transit and satellite metastases represent dissemination of tumor via lymphatic channels. The 5-year survival rates observed in patients with these findings are similar to those observed in patients with lymph node metastases. If in-transit or satellite metastases are present in association with lymph node metastases (N3), the survival rate is markedly reduced.[34]

Stage IV melanoma For stage IV melanoma, the most important prognostic factors appear to be (1) the site at which a distant metastasis occurs and (2) the serum LDH level. Within this group, patients with cutaneous metastases and normal serum LDH levels have by far the most favorable prognosis. There are significant differences in 1-year survival between patients who have cutaneous, subcutaneous, or distant nodal metastases (M1), those who have lung metastases (M2), and those who have any other visceral metastases or who have any metastases in association with an elevated serum LDH level (M3). The predicted 1-year survival rates for M1, M2, and M3 patients are 59%, 57%, and 41%, respectively.[34]

Table 4 American Joint Committee on Cancer Staging System for Melanoma

Stage	T	N	M
0	Tis	N0	M0
IA	T1a	N0	M0
IB	T1b, T2a	N0	M0
IIA	T2b, T3a	N0	M0
IIB	T3b, T4a	N0	M0
IIC	T4b	N0	M0
IIIA	T1–4a	N1a, N2a	M0
IIIB	T1–4b T1–4a Any T	N1a, N2a N1b, N2b N2c	M0 M0 M0
IIIC	T1–4b Any T	N1b, N2b N3	M0 M0
IV	Any T	Any N	M1

Table 5 5-Year Melanoma Survival Correlated with AJCC Stage

Stage	TNM	5-Year Survival (%)
IA	T1a N0 M0	95.3
IB	T1b N0 M0	90.9
	T2a N0 M0	89.0
IIA	T2b N0 M0	77.4
	T3a N0 M0	78.7
IIB	T3b N0 M0	63.0
	T4a N0 M0	67.4
IIC	T4b N0 M0	45.1
IIIA	T1–4a N1a M0	69.5
	T1–4a N2a M0	63.3
IIIB	T1–4b N1a M0	52.8
	T1–4b N2a M0	49.6
	T1–4a N1b M0	59.0
	T1–4a N2b M0	46.3
IIIC	T1–4b N1b M0	29.0
	T1–4b N2b M0	24.0
	Any T N3 M0	26.7
IV	Any T any N M1a	18.8
	Any T any N M1b	6.7
	Any T any N M1c	9.5

Initial Evaluation

For initial evaluation of patients with thin melanomas (< 1 mm), no routine laboratory or radiologic tests are recommended. For patients with thicker melanomas (≥ 1 mm), some clinicians recommend a chest x-ray. For patients with stage III disease, chest radiography or computed tomography of the chest, the abdomen, and the pelvis may be performed and are indicated for any signs or symptoms of metastases. If inguinal lymphadenopathy is apparent, pelvic CT should be performed to assess the iliac lymph nodes.[38] For patients with stage IV disease, chest radiography should be performed and serum LDH levels obtained. Magnetic resonance imaging of the brain and CT of the chest, the abdomen, and the pelvis should be performed to address any signs or symptoms of metastases and before any therapy is initiated. Any other imaging done will be guided by protocol if the patient is enrolled in a clinical trial.[38]

Treatment

Surgical treatment of stage I and II melanoma *Margins of excision.* Surgical excision remains the mainstay of treatment for melanoma. The width of the recommended surgical margin depends on the thickness of the lesion and has been well defined by a series of prospective randomized clinical trials.[39] According to most current recommendations, a 0.5 cm margin is adequate for melanoma in situ, a 1 cm margin is suggested for melanomas thinner than 1.0 mm, a 1 or 2 cm margin should be obtained for melanomas between 1 and 2 mm thick, and a 2 cm margin is required for melanomas thicker than 2 mm.[39]

Sentinel lymph node biopsy. An important issue in the surgical management of melanoma is the use of sentinel lymph node biopsy (SLNB) [*see 26 Lymphatic Mapping and Sentinel Lymph Node Biopsy*], which has essentially replaced elective lymph node dissection. Sentinel lymph node (SLN) status is the single most important predictor of survival in patients with melanoma[40] and is now considered a standard approach in the United States. A positive result is defined as the presence of identifiable melanoma cells on routine hematoxylin-eosin staining, immunohistochemical staining with S100 or HMB-45, or both. Preoperative lymphatic mapping via lymphoscintigraphy is often quite helpful, in that many lesions have variable drainage basins that cannot be predicted clinically, and some lesions even drain to contralateral nodes.[41] The greatest accuracy is achieved with SLNB when both radioactive colloid and blue dye are used.[42]

SLNB should not be performed in patients with clinically positive nodes or in those who would otherwise not be considered for lymphadenectomy. It is generally recommended for patients who are at moderate or high risk for harboring occult regional node metastases. In patients with T1 primary tumors, SLNB may be considered in selected scenarios (i.e., primary tumor ulceration or extensive regression, a high mitotic rate, a Clark level IV lesion, or a positive deep margin).[38]

The impact of SLNB on the management of melanoma has been impressive. The results greatly facilitate accurate staging and play an important role in helping the clinician decide whether to perform completion lymph node dissection (CLND) or to offer adjuvant therapy. Several studies have demonstrated significant differences in survival and disease-free interval between SLN-negative patients and SLN-positive patients.[43,44] One such study reported a 3-year disease-free survival rate of 88.5% in SLN-negative patients, compared with 55.8% in SLN-positive patients.[43]

Surgical treatment of stage III melanoma *Completion lymph node dissection.* At present, CLND is recommended for management of the regional lymph node drainage basin in the presence of a positive SLN. Some clinical trial results do not appear to support this recommendation. For example, four randomized trials failed to demonstrate any overall survival benefit for patients randomly assigned to undergo elective lymph node dissection.[45-48] It should be noted, however, that most of the patients in these studies did not have lymph node metastases, and thus, the trials did not have sufficient statistical power to detect a small survival benefit.[49] Other trial results, however, do support the recommendation for CLND in node-positive patients, including those of the World Health Organization Program Trial No. 14, which demonstrated that the 5-year survival rate in patients with occult nodal metastases detected at elective lymph node dissection was significantly better than that in patients who underwent delayed lymphadenectomy at the time when palpable nodal metastases developed (48% versus 27%).[47]

Nonetheless, the impact of CLND on overall survival is still a matter for debate. The results of the first Multicenter Selective Lymphadenectomy Trial (MSLT-I) suggest that SLNB with immediate CLND if the SLN is positive improves disease-free survival but not overall survival.[50] In this trial, 1,973 patients were randomly assigned in a 4:6 ratio to undergo either (1) wide excision (WE) followed by nodal observation or (2) WE plus lymphatic mapping and sentinel lymph node biopsy (LM/SLNB) with immediate CLND if the SLN was positive. The two groups were comparable in regard to both patient variables (i.e., age and gender distribution) and lesion variables (i.e., location, thickness, and ulceration status). SLNs were analyzed by means of hematoxylin-eosin staining and immunohistochemical staining. The incidence of wound complications at the primary site was comparable in the two groups, though surgical morbidity was significantly greater when SLNB was followed by CLND.[50] A planned interim analysis presented at the American Society of Clinical Oncology in 2005 demonstrated a significant difference in disease-free survival between the two groups (73% for WE followed by nodal observation versus 78% for WE plus LM/SLNB); however, the difference in overall survival was not statistically significant (86% for WE followed by nodal observation versus 87% for WE plus LM/SLNB).[51] These data led some to suggest that a survival benefit might be gained by performing LM/SLNB followed by CLND in the event of a positive SLN, but this suggestion has not been widely accepted.[52] A study now under way, the second Multicenter Selective Lymphadenectomy Trial (MSLT-II), will assess the therapeutic value of CLND against that of SLNB alone in patients who have a positive SLN.[51]

An important factor in considering whether to perform CLND after a positive SLNB is the likelihood of finding metastases in the remaining non-SLNs. In one series, 90 (14%) of 658 patients had a positive SLN, and only 18 (20%) of the 90 showed evidence of metastases in additional non-SLNs removed during CLND.[53] The number of positive nodes clearly has an impact on prognosis (as reflected by its inclusion in the current version of the AJCC's melanoma staging system[34]), and this fact lends support to the argument for performing a CLND after a positive SLNB.

Another issue that has not yet been resolved is the extent of lymph node dissection required. One group, reviewing their experience with lymph node dissection before the use of SLNB, concluded that the extent of lymph node dissection was a more important concern with higher tumor burdens and a less important one with lower tumor burdens.[54] Patients with micrometastatic disease in an SLN are clearly different from patients with bulky nodal disease, and the potential benefits of aggressive lymph node dissection in either group must be carefully weighed against the morbidity of the procedure. Several studies are under way that should help address this issue, including MSLT-II.[55] The roles of lymphadenectomy and adjuvant interferon alfa-2b (IFN-α2b) may be addressed by results from the Sunbelt Melanoma Trial.[56]

Therapeutic lymph node dissection.   Therapeutic lymph node dissection is performed in patients who show evidence of lymph node metastases on physical examination. Some of these patients will survive for extended periods; most will at least be rendered free of the signs and symptoms of nodal metastases.[57]

Isolated limb perfusion.   Most patients with in-transit metastases experience unfavorable outcomes, with 5-year survival rates ranging from 25% to 30%. Surgical excision to clear margins is the mainstay of therapy when the size and number of the lesions permit. Amputation is rarely necessary.

A therapeutic alternative to surgical excision for patients who have extensive in-transit metastases in an extremity is the technique known as isolated limb perfusion (ILP). The prime advantage of ILP is that it can achieve high regional concentrations of therapeutic agents while minimizing systemic side effects.[58] The arterial supply and the venous drainage are isolated, and a tourniquet may also be used to occlude superficial collateral veins. An oxygenated extracorporeal circuit is employed to circulate a chemotherapeutic agent (typically melphalan) for 1 to 1.5 hours. The temperature of the limb is usually elevated to 39° to 40° C.[59] In patients who have clinically positive nodes, therapeutic lymph node dissection is performed in the same setting, just before limb perfusion. The effect of ILP can be dramatic; for example, the rate of complete response with melphalan

is 54%.[60] Unfortunately, the beneficial effect is often short-lived, with recurrence rates reaching 50% within 1 to 1.5 years after ILP.[61] In a 2004 series, the overall 5-year survival rate after ILP was 32%.[61] Recurrence after ILP may be treated with surgical excision, though it has also been successfully treated with repeat ILP in patients with extensive disease.[62]

Adjuvant therapy for stage IIB and III melanoma   *Radiotherapy.*   Radiotherapy has been used with some success after therapeutic lymph node dissection in patients with high-risk lesions, resulting in a decreased local recurrence rate[63] and a modest survival benefit[64] in comparison with historic controls. This modality is typically employed in stage III patients who have poor prognostic pathologic factors (e.g., positive surgical margins, multiple positive nodes, extracapsular spread, or vascular or perineural involvement).[65]

Interferon therapy.   Perhaps the most efficacious adjuvant agent tested to date is IFN-α2b, which is currently approved by the United States Food and Drug Administration for adjuvant treatment of stage IIB and stage III melanoma. Although a trial reported in 1996 found that 1 year of high-dose IFN-α2b therapy led to a prolonged relapse-free interval and improved overall survival,[66] subsequent trials and a meta-analysis did not confirm this overall survival benefit.[67] Furthermore, nearly all patients experience adverse effects (e.g., fatigue, neutropenia, headache, fever, and chills) with interferon therapy.[66]

Treatment of stage IV melanoma   *Metastasectomy.*   There is a large body of literature supporting resection of metastases from melanoma. The following five factors are commonly cited as predictive of survival after metastasectomy: (1) the initial disease stage, (2) the disease-free interval after treatment of the primary melanoma, (3) the initial site of metastasis, (4) the extent of metastatic disease (single versus multiple sites), and (5) the ability to achieve complete resection.[57] In well-selected patients, this procedure can yield a reasonable likelihood of survival: a 1995 series reported a 5-year survival rate of 27% in all patients after pulmonary metastasectomy and a rate of 39% in patients with a single metastatic lesion.[68] More modest benefits have been observed after resection of metastases to the GI tract: a 1996 series reported a median survival of 44.5 months in patients in whom a complete resection was achieved, compared with a median survival of 4 weeks in those in whom complete resection could not be achieved.[69]

The five aforementioned factors are of critical importance in patient selection for metastasectomy. To improve patient selection for curative procedures, surgeons often treat patients with a single-site asymptomatic metastasis by administering chemotherapy for 2 to 3 months before considering resection, the aim being to see whether the disease stabilizes or additional metastases develop.[57] If there is a response to treatment or the disease stabilizes with no evidence of further metastases, they proceed with resection.[57]

It is extremely important to perform high-quality imaging before considering resection of metastases. The use of 18-fluorodeoxyglucose positron emission tomography (FDG-PET) may help detect occult metastatic disease more accurately. A 2004 comparison of FDG-PET with conventional imaging in patients with stage IV melanoma reported a sensitivity and specificity of 76% and 87% for conventional imaging, 79% and 87% for FDG-PET, and 88% and 91% for conventional imaging combined with FDG-PET.[70] With FDG-PET, as with any other imaging modality, appropriate use depends on a clear understanding of its capabilities and limitations.

Another important indication for metastasectomy is palliation; the vast majority of patients with stage IV melanoma will not be candidates for curative-intent metastasectomy. The goal of a palliative procedure is to control identifiable symptoms (e.g., GI bleeding or pain) caused by an advanced malignancy while minimizing morbidity.[57] A thorough discussion should be held among the surgeon, the patient, and the family to address the goals and expected outcomes of the procedure, as well as its potential morbidity.[71]

Chemotherapy. To date, the rates of objective response to chemotherapy for melanoma have been somewhat disappointing. Darcarbazine (DTIC) is the only currently approved chemotherapeutic agent for melanoma, and it offers no more than marginal therapeutic benefit, with moderate side effects.[72] Various combination regimens—including BOLD (bleomycin, vincristine, lomustine [CCNU], DTIC), CVT (cisplatin, vincristine, DTIC), and CBDT (cisplatin, carmustine [BCNU], DTIC, tamoxifen)—have been employed, with response rates ranging from 9% to 55%.[72] The oral alkylating agent temozolamide has been studied in stage IV melanoma patients; compared with DTIC, it yields a modest prolongation of survival, with an acceptable side-effect profile.[73]

Melanoma vaccines. Several experimental melanoma vaccines are being investigated for possible use in advanced-stage melanoma. These agents use a variety of modalities to present melanoma antigens to host immune cells in an immunostimulatory context.[74-76] There was considerable initial optimism regarding this approach, but a 2004 review of the experience at the National Cancer Institute found that the response rate for cancer vaccines was only 2.6%[77] (a figure comparable to the results obtained by others). The authors concluded that the use of cancer vaccines may still prove to be a viable strategy, but profound changes will be required to enhance the efficacy of these agents.

Immunotherapy. At present, immunotherapy is perhaps the most promising area of investigation with respect to the treatment of advanced melanoma. Immunotherapy has been defined in various ways, but in general, it can be thought of as a form of treatment based on the concept of modulating the immune system to achieve a therapeutic goal.[78] There are several different modalities that can be considered immunotherapy, including monoclonal antibody therapy and interferon-based therapy. For present purposes, we will focus on two modalities that are currently under active investigation: high-dose interleukin-2 (IL-2) therapy and adoptive cell transfer.

In initial studies, the response rates after high-dose IL-2 therapy for melanoma have ranged from 15% to 20%, with about half of the responding patients experiencing complete regression.[79] In those patients who do achieve a complete response, the effect is often durable.[80] Unfortunately, IL-2 immunotherapy is associated with severe side effects.

Adoptive cell transfer involves the administration of activated cytotoxic T lymphocytes (CTLs) that are generated against specific tumor types. These CTLs can be generated either by using specific tumor-associated antigens or by culturing lymphocytes with tumor cells. The objective is to encourage the selection of tumor-specific T lymphocytes that are capable of generating a strong immunologic response and thereby help break the body's immunologic tolerance of the tumor. Unfortunately, initial clinical trials of activated T cell transfer for other types of malignancy found that the transferred cells did not remain present in sufficient concentrations to yield a significant clinical effect.[81] However, the addition of nonmyeloablative lymphodepleting chemotherapy, followed by autologous transfer of tumor-specific CTLs in conjunction with IL-2 administration, was shown to result in rapid clonal expansion of tumor-specific T lymphocytes in vivo, which was associated with a significant clinical response.[82] In a 2005 study, transfer of a T cell receptor gene from a

patient with a significant antitumor response conferred impressive T cell responses.[83]

Despite some advances in therapy, overall survival for patients with stage IV melanoma has not improved over the past 20 years. Overall 5-year survival remains lower than 5%, with a median survival of only 7.5 months.[84] The best hope for future improvements probably lies in the treatment of micrometastatic disease by means of targeted chemotherapy and immunotherapy.

Operative Technique

The inguinal nodes drain the anterior and inferior abdominal wall, the perineum, the genitalia, the hips, the buttocks, and the thighs. A superficial groin dissection removes the inguinal nodes, whereas a deep groin dissection incorporates the iliac and obturator nodes. Palpable nodes can be marked on the patient before operation.

SUPERFICIAL GROIN DISSECTION

The patient is placed in a supine position on the operating table, with the hip slightly abducted and with the hip and knee slightly flexed and supported by a pillow. A Foley catheter is inserted, and the skin is prepared and draped.

The femoral artery, the anterior superior iliac spine, the pubic tubercle, and the apex of the femoral triangle are marked. A diagonally oriented skin incision is made that extends from a point medial to

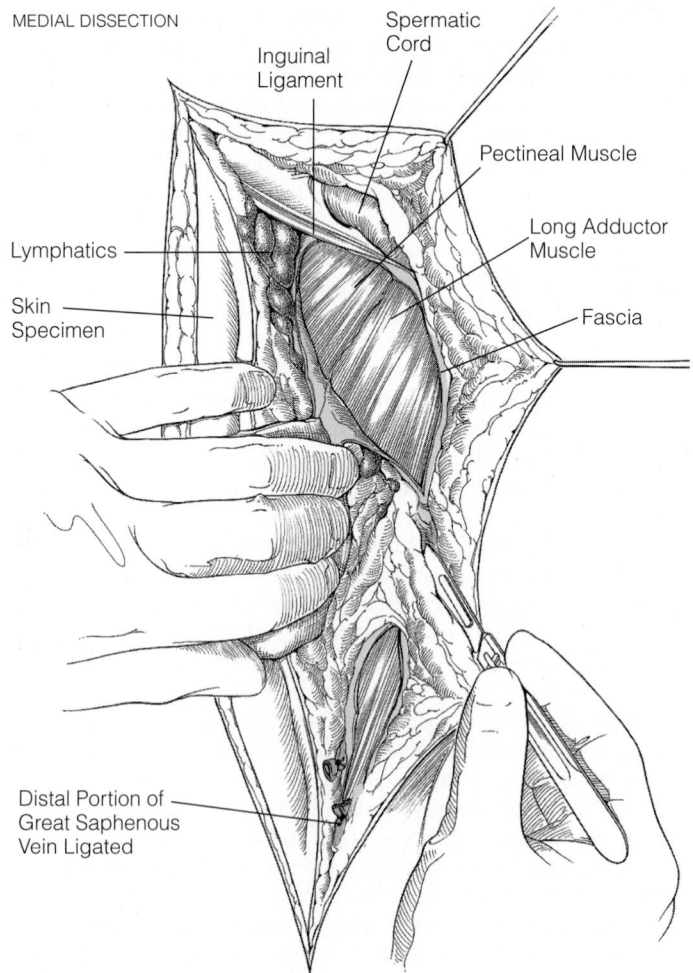

Figure 5 **Superficial groin dissection. The incision is deepened to include the deep muscular fascia.**

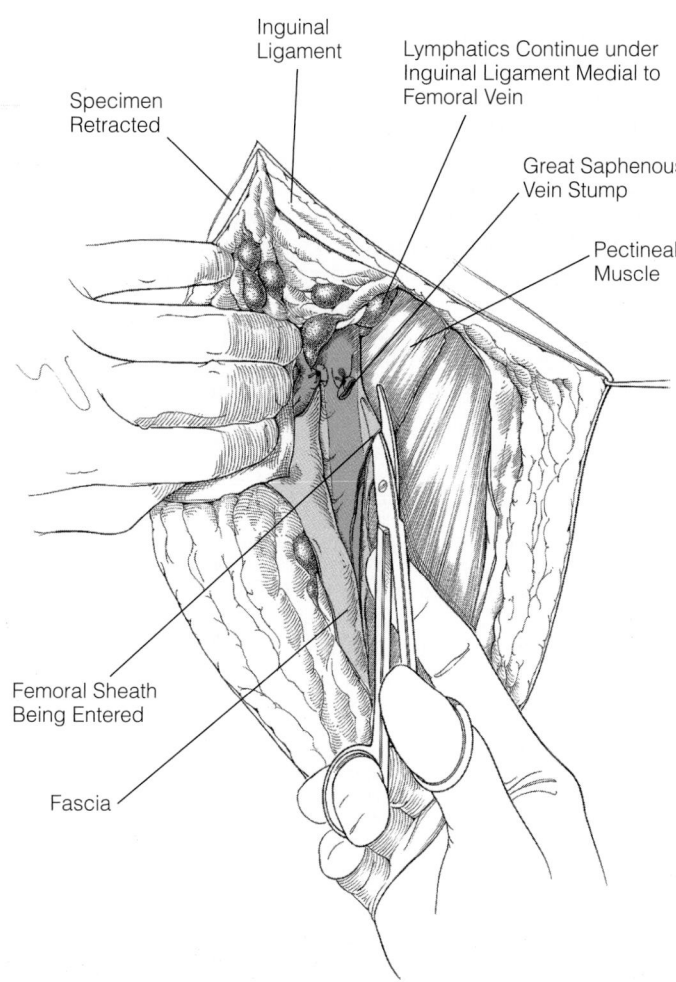

Figure 6 Superficial groin dissection. The investing fascia overlying the femoral nerve and vessels is removed.

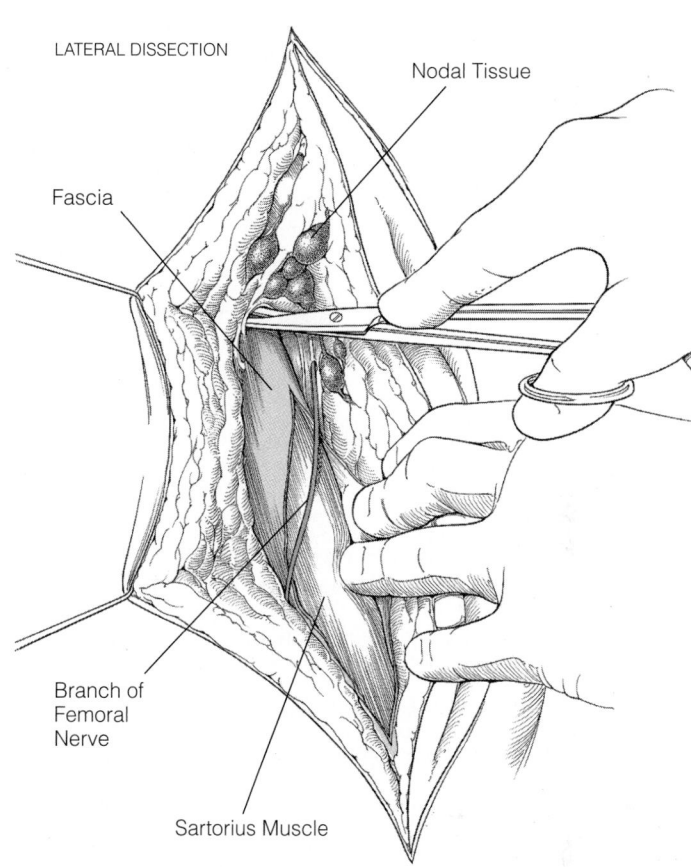

Figure 7 Superficial groin dissection. The groin dissection is continued on the lateral side.

the anterior superior iliac spine down to the apex of the femoral triangle; the incision is formed in the shape of an S so as not to cross the thigh flexion crease at a right angle. An incision oriented and shaped in this manner will cause the least possible interference with the musculocutaneous and cutaneous vascular territories of the skin, will minimize ischemia to the skin flaps, and will avoid a flexion contracture. Flaps are raised to allow identification of the medial border of the sartorius, the lateral border of the adductor longus, and the external oblique fascia on the lower abdominal wall.

Fat and nodal tissue are swept inferiorly off the external oblique aponeurosis, the spermatic cord, and the inguinal ligament [*see Figure 5*] and are reflected inferiorly. The fat and lymph nodes are then dissected from the femoral triangle, starting medially at the lateral edge of the adductor longus and proceeding laterally [*see Figures 6 and 7*]. The femoral vessels are left undisturbed. The saphenous vein is ligated and divided at the fossa ovalis [*see Figure 8*]; it is also ligated and divided as it exits the femoral triangle distally. The specimen is then dissected free from the femoral nerve. This step usually entails sacrificing branches of the lateral femoral cutaneous nerve, thereby resulting in numbness of the anterolateral thigh.

Cloquet's lymph nodes are located medial to the femoral vein under the inguinal ligament. These nodes are dissected out and submitted as a separate specimen. If Cloquet's nodes contain melanoma, the risk that iliac nodes will harbor melanoma is high, and a deep groin dissection should be performed (see below).

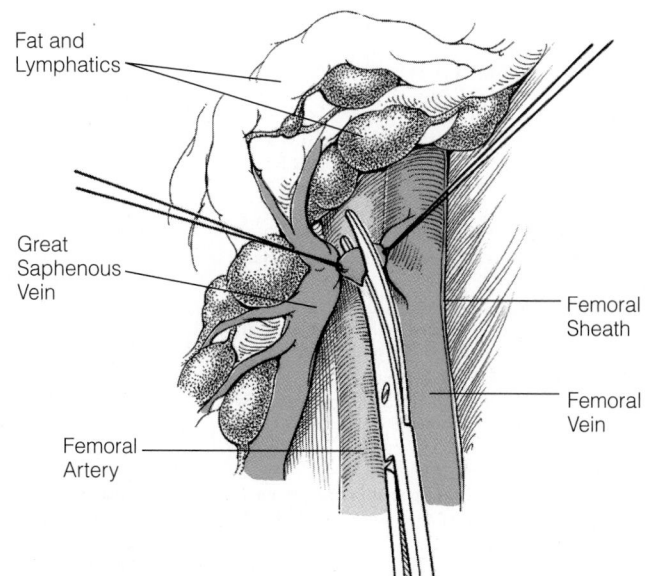

Figure 8 Superficial groin dissection. The great saphenous vein is ligated and divided.

DEEP GROIN DISSECTION

The inguinal ligament is divided, and the inguinal canal is further exposed by releasing the internal oblique abdominal muscle, the transversus abdominis, and the fascia transversalis and dissecting into the retroperitoneal space. The deep circumflex iliac vessels are ligated, and the peritoneum is separated from the preperitoneal fat and nodes by means of blunt finger dissection. Alternatively, rather than dividing the inguinal ligament, one may make a separate incision in the external oblique fascia parallel to and above the inguinal ligament.

Retractors are inserted to widen the retroperitoneal space, and the peritoneum and the abdominal viscera are retracted medially. The chain of lymph nodes, areolar tissue, and adventitial tissues along the external iliac vessels is dissected; the dissection proceeds proximally to the origins of the internal iliac vessels (avoiding the ureter) and incorporates the nodes overlying the obturator foramen while carefully avoiding injury to the obturator nerve. The deep epigastric vessels are usually ligated at their origins from the external iliac artery and vein. The lymph node–bearing specimen is then removed as a unit, oriented, and marked with sutures for orientation and identification. The inguinal canal is reconstructed to prevent a hernia. Any defect medial to the femoral vessels under the ligament is sutured closed with Cooper's ligament. The sartorius is detached from the anterior superior iliac spine and is sutured to the midportion of the inguinal ligament to cover the femoral vessels. The skin and the subcutaneous tissues are then closed in layers over a soft suction drain.

References

1. Miller DL, Weinstock MA: Nonmelanoma skin cancer in the United States: incidence. J Am Acad Dermatol 30:774. 1994

2. Rigel DS, Friedman RJ, Kopf AW: The incidence of malignant melanoma in the United States: issues as we approach the 21st century. J Am Acad Dermatol 34:839, 1996

3. Hall HI, Miller DR, Rogers JD, et al: Update on the incidence and mortality from melanoma in the United States. J Am Acad Dermatol 40:35, 1999

4. Urbach F: Incidence of nonmelanoma skin cancer. Dermatol Clin 9:751, 1991

5. English DR, Armstrong BK, Kricker A: How much melanoma is caused by sun exposure? Melanoma Res 3:395, 1993

6. Rager EL, Bridgeford EP, Ollila DW: Cutaneous melanoma: update on prevention, screening, diagnosis, and treatment. Am Fam Physician 72:269, 2005

7. Miller SJ: Aetiology and pathogenesis of basal cell carcinoma. Clin Dermatol 13:527, 1995

8. Marks R, Staples M, Giles G: Trends in nonmelanoma skin cancer treated in Australia: the second national survey. Int J Cancer 53:585, 1993

9. Vitasa BC, Taylor HR, Strickland PT, et al: Association of nonmelanoma skin cancer and actinic keratosis with cumulative solar ultraviolet exposure in Maryland watermen. Cancer 65:2811, 1990

10. Wong CSM, Strange RC, Lear JT: Basal cell carcinoma. BMJ 327:794, 2003

11. Telfer NR, Colver GB, Bowers PW: Guidelines for the management of basal cell carcinoma. Br J Dermatol 141:415, 1999

12. Harwood M, Wu H, Tanabe K, et al: Metastatic basal cell carcinoma diagnosed by sentinel lymph node biopsy. J Am Acad Dermatol 53:475, 2005

13. Rowe DE, Carroll RJ, Day CL Jr: Mohs surgery is the treatment of choice for recurrent (previously treated) basal cell carcinoma. J Dermatol Surg Oncol 15:424. 1989

14. Silverman MK, Kopf AW, Gladstein AH, et al: Recurrence rates of treated basal cell carcinomas. Part 4: x-ray therapy. J Dermatol Surg Oncol 18:549, 1992

15. Peng Q, Warloe T, Berg K, et al: 5-Aminolevulinic acid-based photodynamic therapy. Cancer 79:2282, 1997

16. Chimenti S, Peris K, Cristofaro S, et al: Use of recombinant interferon alpha-2b in the treatment of basal cell carcinoma. Dermatology 190:214, 1995

17. Hodak E, Ginzburg A, David M, et al: Etretinate treatment of the naevoid basal cell cancinoma syndrome. Int J Dermatol 26:606, 1987

18. Shelton RM: Skin cancer: a review and atlas for the medical provider. Mt Sinai J Med 68:243, 2001

19. Weinstock MA, Bogaars HA, Ashley M, et al: Nonmelanoma skin cancer mortality: a population-based study. Arch Dermatol 127:1194, 1991

20. Goldman GD: Squamous cell cancer; a practical approach. Semin Cutan Med Surg 17:80, 1998

21. Marks R: Squamous cell carcinoma. Lancet 347:735, 1996

22. Miki Y, Kawatsu T, Matsuda K, et al: Cutaneous and pulmonary cancers associated with Bowen's disease. J Am Acad Dermatol 6:26, 1982

23. Brownstein MH, Rabinowitz AD: The precursors of cutaneous squamous cell carinoma. Int J Dermatol 18:1, 1979

24. SEER cancer statistics review, 1973–1999. Ries LA, Eisner MP, Kosary CL, et al, Eds. National Cancer Institute, Bethesda, Maryland, 2002. http://seer.cancer.gov/csr/1973_1999, accessed June 2006

25. Greenlee RT, Hill-Harmon MB, Murray T, et al: Cancer statistics 2001. CA Cancer J Clin 51:15, 2001

26. Hashemi J, Linder S, Platz A, et al: Melanoma development in relation to non-functional p16/INK4A protein and dysplastic nevus syndrome in Swedish melanoma kindred. Melanoma Res 9:21, 1999

27. American Academy of Dermatology: Melanoma Net. http://www.skincarephysicians.com/melanomanet, accessed June 2006

28. Schwartz JL, Wang TS, Hamilton TA, et al: Thin primary cutaneous melanomas: associated detection patterns, lesion characteristics, and patient characteristics. Cancer 95:1562, 2002

29. Friedman RJ, Rigel DS, Silverman MK, et al: Malignant melanoma in the 1990s: the continued importance of early detection and the role of the physician examination and self-examination of the skin. CA Cancer J Clin 41:201, 1991

30. Crowson AN, Magro CM, Mihm MC Jr: Prognosticators of melanoma, the melanoma report, and the sentinel lymph node. Mod Pathol 19:S71, 2006

31. Breslow A: Thickness, cross-sectional areas and depth of invasion in the prognosis of cutaneous melanoma. Ann Surg 172:902, 1970

32. Clark WH Jr, From L, Bernardino EA, et al: Histogenesis and biologic behavior of primary human malignant melanomas of the skin. Cancer Res 29:705, 1969

33. Homsi J, Kashani-Sabet M, Messina JL, et al: Cutaneous melanoma: prognostic factors. Cancer Control 12:223, 2005

34. Balch CM, Soong SJ, Gershenwald JE, et al: Prognostic factors analysis of 17,600 melanoma patients: validation of the American Joint Committee on cancer staging system for cutaneous melanoma. J Clin Oncol 19:3622, 2001

35. Francken AB, Shaw HM, Thompson JF, et al: The prognostic importance of tumor mitotic rate confirmed in 1317 patients with primary cutaneous melanoma and long follow-up. Ann Surg Oncol 11:426, 2004

36. Gimotty PA, Guerry D, Ming ME, et al: Thin primary cutaneous malignant melanoma: a prognostic tree for 10-year metastasis is more accurate than American Joint Committee on Cancer staging. J Clin Oncol 22:3668, 2004

37. Buzaid AC, Tinoco LA, Jendiroba D, et al: Prognostic value of size of lymph node metastases in patients with cutaneous melanoma. J Clin Oncol 13:2361, 1995

38. Johnson TM, Bradford CR, Gruber SB, et al: Staging workup, sentinel node biopsy, and follow-up tests for melanoma. Arch Dermatol 140:107, 2004

39. Riker AI, Glass F, Perez I, et al: Cutaneous melanoma: methods of biopsy and definitive surgical excision. Dermatol Ther 18:387, 2005

40. Gershenwald JE, Colome MI, Lee JE, et al: Patterns of recurrence following a negative sentinel lymph node biopsy in 243 patients with stage I or II melanoma. J Clin Oncol 16:2253, 1998

41. Thompson JF, Uren RF: Lymphatic mapping in management of patients with primary cutaneous melanoma. Lancet Oncol 6:877, 2005

42. Morton DL, Thompson JF, Nieweg OE: The sentinel lymph node biopsy procedure: identification with blue dye and a gamma probe. Textbook of Melanoma. Thompson JF, Morton DL, Kroon BB, Eds. Martin Dunitz, London, 2004, p 323

43. Gershenwald JE, Mansfield PF, Lee JE, et al: Role of lymphatic mapping and sentinel lymph node biopsy in patients with thick (> 4 mm) primary melanoma. Ann Surg Oncol 7:160, 2000

44. Gershenwald JE, Thompson W, Mansfield PF, et al: Multi-institutional melanoma lymphatic mapping experience: the prognostic value of sentinel lymph node status in 612 stage I or II melanoma patients. J Clin Oncol 17:976, 1999

45. Sim FH, Taylor WF, Pritchard DJ, et al: Lymphadenectomy in the management of stage I malignant melanoma: a prospective randomized study. Mayo Clin Proc 61:697, 1986

46. Veronesi U, Adamus J, Bandiera DC, et al: Delayed regional lymph node dissection in stage I melanoma of the skin of the lower extremities. Cancer 49:2420, 1982

47. Cascinelli N, Morabito A, Santinami M, et al: Immediate or delayed dissection of regional nodes in patients with melanoma of the trunk: a randomized trial. WHO Melanoma Programme. Lancet

351:793, 1998

48. Balch DM, Soong S, Ross MI, et al: Long-term results of a multi-institutional randomized trial comparing prognostic factors and surgical results for intermediate thickness melanomas (1.0 to 4.0 mm). Intergroup Melanoma Surgical Trial. Ann Surg Oncol 7:87, 2000

49. McMasters KM, Reintgen DS, Ross MI, et al: Sentinel lymph node biopsy for melanoma: controversy despite widespread agreement. J Clin Oncol 19:2851, 2001

50. Morton D, Thompson JF, Cochran AJ: Sentinel node biopsy for early-stage melanoma: accuracy and morbidity in MSLT-I: an international multicenter trial. Ann Surg 242:302, 2005

51. Morton DL: Interim results of the Multicenter Selective Lymphadenectomy Trial (MSLT-I) in clinical stage I melanoma. http://www.asco.org/ac/1,1003,_12-002511-00_18-0034-00_19-003013,00.asp, accessed July 31, 2006

52. Thomas JM: Time for comprehensive reporting of MSLT-1. Lancet Oncol 7:9, 2006

53. Clinical Practice Guidelines for the Management of Cutaneous Melanoma. National Health and Medical Research Council, Canberra, 1999

54. Chan AD, Essner R, Wanek LA, et al: Judging the therapeutic value of lymph node dissections for melanoma. J Am Coll Surg 191:16, 2000

55. Morton DL, Thompson JF, Essner R, et al: Validation of the accuracy of intraoperative lymphatic mapping and sentinel lymphadenectomy for early-stage melanoma: a multicenter trial. Multicenter Selective Lymphadenectomy Trial Group. Ann Surg 230:453, 1999

56. McMasters KM: The Sunbelt Melanoma Trial. Ann Surg Oncol 8:41S, 2001

57. Wong SL, Coit DG: Role of surgery in patients with stage IV melanoma. Curr Opin Oncol 16:155, 2004

58. Benckhuijsen C, Kroon BB, van Geel AN, et al: Regional perfusion treatment with melphalan for melanoma in a limb: an evaluation of drug kinetics. Eur J Surg Oncol 14:157, 1988

59. Lingam MK, Byrne DS, Aitchison T, et al: A single center's 10-year experience with isolated limb perfusion in the treatment of recurrent malignant melanoma of the limb. Eur J Cancer 32A:1668, 1996

60. Vrouenraets BC, Nieweg OE, Kroon BB: Thirty-five years of isolated limb perfusion for melanoma: indications and results. Br J Surg 83:1319, 1996

61. Grunhagen DJ, Brunstein F, Graveland WJ, et al: One hundred consecutive isolated limb perfusions with TNF-alpha and Melphalan in melanoma patients with multiple in-transit metastases. Ann Surg 240:939, 2004

62. Feldman AL, Alexander HR Jr, Bartlett DL, et al: Management of extremity recurrences after complete responses to isolated limb perfusion in patients with melanoma. Ann Surg Oncol 6:562, 1999

63. Stevens G, Thompson JF, Firth I, et al: Locally advanced melanoma: results of postoperative hypofractionated radiation therapy. Cancer 88:88, 2000

64. Ang KK, Byers RM, Peters LJ, et al: Regional radiotherapy as adjuvant treatment for head and neck malignant melanoma. Arch Otolaryngol Head Neck Surg 116:169, 1990

65. Morris KT, Marquez CM, Holland JM, et al: Prevention of local recurrence after surgical debulking of nodal and subcutaneous melanoma deposits by hypofractionated radiation. Ann Surg Oncol 7:680, 2000

66. Kirkwood JM, Strawderman MH, Ernstoff MS, et al: Interferon alfa-2b adjuvant therapy of high risk resected cutaneous melanoma: The Eastern Cooperative Oncology Group Trial EST 1684. J Clin Oncol 14:7, 1996

67. Wheatley K, Ives N, Hancock B, et al: Does adjuvant interferon-alpha for high-risk melanoma provide a worthwhile benefit? A meta-analysis of the randomised trials. Cancer Treat Rev 29:241, 2003

68. Tafra L, Dale PS, Wanek LA, et al: Resection and adjuvant immunotherapy for melanoma metastatic to the lung and thorax. J Thorac Cardiovasc Surg 110:119, 1995

69. Ollila DW, Essner R, Wanek LA, et al: Surgical resection for melanoma metastatic to the gastrointestinal tract. Arch Surg 131:975, 1996

70. Finkelstein SE, Carrasquillo JA, Hoffman JM, et al: A prospective analysis of positron emission tomography and conventional imaging for detection of stage IV metastatic melanoma in patients undergoing metastasectomy. Ann Surg Oncol 11:731, 2004

71. Miner TJ, Jaques DP, Shriver CD: A prospective evaluation of patients undergoing surgery for the palliation of an advanced malignancy. Ann Surg Oncol 9:696, 2002

72. Cohen GL, Falkson CI: Current treatment options for malignant melanoma. Drugs 55:791, 1998

73. Middleton MR, Grob JJ, Aaronson N, et al: Randomized phase III study of temozolamide versus dacarbazine in the treatment of patients with advanced metastatic malignant melanoma. J Clin Oncol 18:158, 2000 [erratum, J Clin Oncol 18:2351, 2000]

74. Morton DL, Foshag IJ, Hoon DS, et al: Prolongation of survival in metastatic melanoma after active specific immunotherapy with a new polyvalent melanoma vaccine. Ann Surg 216:463, 1992

75. Butterfield LH, Ribas A, Dissette VB, et al: Determinant spreading associated with clinical response in dendritic cell-based immunotherapy for malignant melanoma. Clin Cancer Res 9:998, 2003

76. Soiffer R, Hodi FS, Haluska F, et al: Vaccination with irradiated, autologous melanoma cells engineered to secrete granulocyte-macrophage colony-stimulating factor by adenoviral-mediated gene transfer augments antitumor immunity in patients with metastatic melanoma. J Clin Oncol 21:3343, 2003

77. Rosenberg SA, Yang JC, Restifo NP: Cancer immunotherapy: moving beyond current vaccines. Nature Med 10:909, 2004

78. Immunotherapy. Wikipedia, The Free Encyclopedia. http://en.wikipedia.org/wiki/Immunotherapy, accessed August 2, 2006

79. Rosenberg SA, Yang JC, Topalian SL, et al: Treatment of 283 consecutive patients with metastatic melanoma or renal cell cancer using high-dose bolus interleukin-2. JAMA 271:907, 1994

80. Atkins MB, Kunzel L, Sznol M, et al: High-dose recombinant IL-2 therapy in patients with metastatic melanoma: long-term survival update. Cancer J Sci Am 6S:11, 2000

81. Dudley ME, Wunderlich J, Nishimura MI, et al: Adoptive transfer of cloned melanoma-reactive T lymphocytes for the treatment of patients with metastatic melanoma. J Immunother 24:363, 2001

82. Dudley ME, Wunderlich JR, Robbins PF, et al: Cancer regression and autoimmunity in patients after clonal repopulation with antitumor lymphocytes. Science 298:850, 2002

83. Hughes MS, Yu YY, Dudley ME, et al: Transfer of a TCR gene derived from a patient with marked antitumor response conveys highly active T cell effector functions. Hum Gene Ther 16:457, 2005

84. Barth A, Wanek LA, Morton DL: Prognostic factors in 1,521 melanoma patients with distant metastases. J Am Coll Surg 181:193, 1995

85. Balch CM, Buzaid AC, Soong SJ, et al: Final version of the American Joint Committee on Cancer staging system for cutaneous melanoma. J Clin Oncol 19:3635, 2001

Acknowledgment

Figures 5 through 8 Susan E. Brust, C.M.I.

25 BREAST PROCEDURES

Rena B. Kass, M.D., F.A.C.S., D. Scott Lind, M.D., F.A.C.S., and Wiley W. Souba, M.D., Sc.D., F.A.C.S.

The procedures used to diagnose, stage, and treat breast disease are rapidly becoming less invasive and more cosmetically satisfying while remaining oncologically sound. In particular, percutaneous core biopsy has largely replaced excisional breast biopsy for both palpable and nonpalpable breast lesions and has proved to be an equally accurate, less invasive, and less costly means of pathologic diagnosis.[1] Moreover, in clinically appropriate patients, sentinel lymph node biopsy (SLNB) has proved to be an accurate method of staging the axilla that reduces the incidence of many of the complications associated with traditional axillary node dissection.[2] Furthermore, breast conservation has largely supplanted mastectomy for definitive surgical treatment of breast cancer; randomized trials continue to demonstrate equivalent survival rates for the two therapies.[3] Even in those cases where mastectomy is either required or preferred, advances in reconstructive techniques have been made that yield significantly improved outcomes after breast reconstruction.[4] Finally, in an effort to eliminate the need for open surgical treatment of breast cancer, various percutaneous extirpative and ablative local therapies have been developed and are being evaluated for potential use in managing breast cancer in carefully selected patients.[5]

A more minimally invasive approach to breast disease will depend to a substantial extent on the availability of accurate and efficient imaging modalities. Adeptness with such modalities is rapidly becoming an essential part of the general surgeon's skill set. In this chapter, we describe selected standard, novel, and investigational procedures employed in the diagnosis and management of breast disease. The application of these procedures is a dynamic process that is shaped both by technological advances and by physicians' evolving understanding of the biology of breast diseases.

Breast Ultrasonography

Breast ultrasonography can be useful for evaluating palpable breast masses or mammographically indeterminate lesions; for carrying out postoperative and oncologic follow-up; for guiding aspiration and biopsy of lesions; and for facilitating intraoperative tumor localization, margin assessment, placement of catheters for partial-breast irradiation, and investigational tumor-ablating techniques.

In the office, breast ultrasonography has become a useful adjunct to the clinical breast examination, particularly in patients with radiographically dense mammograms: it defines breast lesions more clearly than physical examination does and thus can potentially reduce the number of unnecessary biopsies done for simple cysts or fibroglandular tissue presenting as a palpable nodularity. Whole-breast ultrasonography is not an effective screening tool and therefore should not be a substitute for annual mammography. The American College of Surgeons (ACS) and various surgical subspecialty organizations offer a multitude of courses, at varying skill levels, geared toward training general surgeons in the use of breast ultrasonography.

TECHNIQUE

Most real-time ultrasound imaging is performed with handheld probes generating frequencies between 7.5 and 12 MHz. The procedure is conducted with the patient supine, a pillow behind the shoulder, and the ipsilateral arm extended over the head for maximal spreading of the breast. Sonographic transmission gel is applied between the transducer and the skin to reduce air artifacts, and the transducer is pressed slightly against the skin to improve image quality. The selected breast area is imaged from the nipple outward in a radial pattern.

All lesions should be sonographically characterized with respect to margins, effect on adjacent tissue, internal echo pattern, compressibility, height-width ratio, and presence of shadowing versus posterior enhancement. Classically, simple cysts tend to be oval or lobulated, anechoic, and sharply demarginated; they typically demonstrate posterior enhancement. Benign solid lesions tend to be well circumscribed, hypoechoic, and wider than they are tall; they show homogeneous internal echoes and edge shadowing. Carcinomas are also hypoechoic masses, but they cross tissue planes and therefore tend to be taller than they are wide, with irregular borders; in addition, they can demonstrate heterogeneous interior patterns and broad acoustic shadowing [*see Figure 1*]. A lesion that has a single indeterminate characteristic on ultrasonography or that is clinically suspicious despite appearing benign on ultrasonography is an indication for core or open biopsy. Lesions should be characterized in at least two orthogonal planes, and the image should be saved for future reference.

Ductal Lavage

The majority of breast cancers originate from the epithelium of the mammary ducts. Ductal lavage is a method of recovering breast duct epithelial cells for cytologic analysis via a microcatheter that is inserted into the duct. Potential applications include identifying high-risk women, predicting risk with molecular markers, monitoring the effectiveness of chemopreventive agents, and delivering drugs directly into the ducts. At present, however, ductal lavage remains investigational, and its predictive value and clinical utility await further definition.[6]

TECHNIQUE

The breast duct epithelium may be sampled by means of either nipple fluid aspiration or ductal lavage. For the aspiration of nipple fluid, a topical anesthetic is first applied to the nipple, followed by a mild scrub with a dekeratinizing gel. Suction is then applied to the nipple while the breast is gently massaged. Aspirated fluid is sent for analysis. In ductal lavage, the breast and nipple are similarly prepared. The nipple duct orifice that yields fluid spontaneously or as a result of suction is cannulated, the duct is irrigated with saline, and the effluent is collected for cytologic analysis. Cannulation of the duct is possible in the majority of women. Both nipple fluid aspiration and ductal lavage are generally well tolerated. The former is simpler and less expensive, but the latter retrieves more cells.[7]

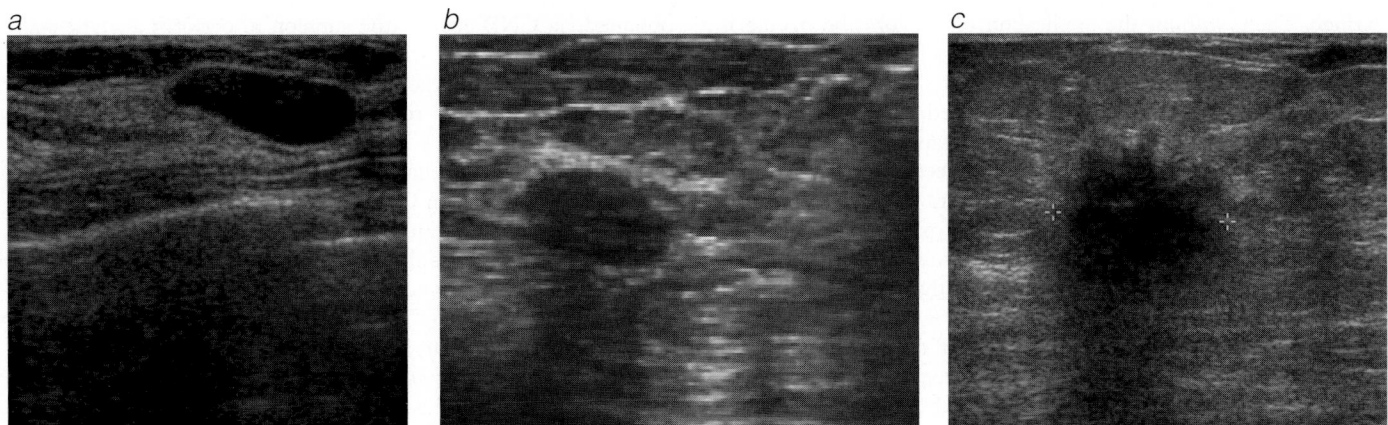

a *b* *c*

Figure 1 **Breast ultrasonography. Shown are (*a*) a simple cyst that has smooth margins, is anechoic, and shows posterior enhancement; (*b*) a fibroadenoma that has smooth margins, is hypoechoic, and shows posterior shadowing; and (*c*) a mammary carcinoma that has irregular borders, is hypoechoic, and shows irregular posterior shadowing.**

Ductoscopy

Advances in endoscopic technology have made visualization and biopsy of the mammary ducts possible. Mammary ductoscopy is a procedure in which a 0.9 mm microendoscope is employed to visualize the lining of the ductal system directly. It is currently being evaluated for use in three main areas: (1) evaluation of patients with pathologic nipple discharge,[8] (2) evaluation of high-risk patients, and (3) evaluation of breast cancer patients to determine the extent of intraductal disease and perhaps reduce the rate of positive margins.[9] At present, this investigational technology is available at only a few centers, and further study will be required to determine its precise role in the evaluation and management of breast disease.

TECHNIQUE

Ductoscopy can be performed either in the office or in the operating room with minimal discomfort. Before the procedure, a nipple block is usually performed with topical lidocaine cream, supplemented (if necessary) by intradermal injection of 1% lidocaine around the nipple-areola complex or intraductal instillation of lidocaine (or both). The breast is massaged to promote expression of nipple aspirate fluid, which facilitates identification of a ductal orifice. The duct is then gently dilated, and the ductoscope is advanced with the help of insufflation under direct visualization. Most ducts with pathologic discharge can readily be identified and dilated sufficiently to allow passage of the ductoscope.[10] An outer air channel on the fiberscope permits instillation and collection of saline solution so that cells can be retrieved for ductal lavage.[11] Intraductal lesions can be percutaneously localized under direct endoscopic visualization for subsequent biopsy; alternatively, they may be amenable to endoscopic cytologic brushing or to the newly described technique of intraductal breast biopsy.[10]

The procedure is usually well tolerated. It should be noted that duct excision is still regarded as standard practice for pathologic discharge, regardless of endoscopic findings.

Breast Biopsy

Cytologic or tissue diagnosis of a palpable breast mass may be obtained by means of fine-needle aspiration (FNA) biopsy, core-needle biopsy (CNB), or open incisional or excisional biopsy. Currently, most solid lesions are initially diagnosed by means of CNB, which is less invasive, less costly, and more expeditious than open biopsy while achieving comparable accuracy. In select circumstances, however, FNA biopsy and open biopsy may remain suitable options. All minimally invasive biopsy techniques are facilitated when guided by imaging modalities; such guidance enables the physician to perform a more directed biopsy that targets the lesion precisely while avoiding benign-appearing tissue, necrotic tissue, and adjacent structures (e.g., the chest wall, skin, and axillary vessels). Therefore, even when a lesion is palpable, ultrasound-directed biopsy is preferable to blind biopsy (though not absolutely necessary) and is recommended if the surgeon has a suitable ultrasound device in the office.

The choice of a specific biopsy technique should be individualized on the basis of the clinical and radiographic features of the lesion, the experience of the clinician, and the patient's condition and preference.

FINE-NEEDLE ASPIRATION BIOPSY

FNA biopsy permits the sampling of cells from the breast or the axillary region for cytologic analysis. It is particularly useful for sampling a clinically or sonographically suspicious axillary node and for evaluating cyst fluid that is bloody or that comes from an incompletely collapsed or recurrent cyst. In patients receiving anticoagulants, FNA biopsy is a reasonable alternative to CNB for evaluation of a solid lesion, in that there is less potential for hemorrhage if anticoagulation cannot be discontinued. Discrete masses discovered on physical examination may be either cystic or solid. A lesion that is shown by ultrasonography to be a simple cyst need not undergo FNA biopsy unless it is symptomatic.

Technique

The skin of the breast or axilla is prepared, and a local anesthetic is injected superficially via a 25-gauge needle. Although smaller needles may be used, a 21-gauge needle is optimal for FNA biopsy because it can be effectively used both for aspiration of potentially viscous fluid and for procurement of sufficient cellular material from solid masses. To generate adequate suction, a 10 ml or larger syringe should be used. As noted (see above), FNA biopsy ideally is performed under ultrasonographic guidance. If such guidance is unavailable, the lesion is held steady between the thumb and the index finger of the nondominant hand. Before the needle enters the skin, 1 ml of air is introduced into the biopsy syringe. Then, without the application of suction, the needle is advanced into the lesion. Once the needle is in place, strong suction is applied.

If the lesion is cystic, all fluid is aspirated, at which point the mass should disappear. Ultrasonography can confirm the complete collapse of a cyst or help direct the needle to an undrained portion of the cyst. The fluid need not be sent for analysis unless it is bloody or is associated with a residual palpable mass or an incompletely collapsed cyst as seen on ultrasonography. If the fluid is to be sent for analysis, it is injected directly into the pathologic preservative. The patient is reexamined 4 to 8 weeks after successful aspiration. If the same cyst has recurred, aspiration should be repeated and the new aspirate sent for cytologic analysis.

If the lesion is solid, the needle is moved back and forth within the lesion along a 5 to 10 mm tract until tissue is visualized in the hub of the needle. (This oscillation of the needle along the same tract is the most effective way of obtaining a cellular, diagnostic specimen). Suction is released while the needle is still within the lesion, and the needle is then withdrawn. The contents of the needle are expelled onto prepared glass slides, spread into a thin smear, and fixed according to the preferences of the cytology laboratory. The syringe may be rinsed so that a cellblock can be prepared for further analysis. The lesion should be sampled twice to ensure that a sufficiently cellular sample has been obtained.

Interpretation of Results

Accurate interpretation of FNA requires substantial experience on the part of both the operator and the cytopathologist; only in a few select centers with expert breast cytopathologists has it remained the diagnostic procedure of choice for solid breast masses. Consequently, one must exercise considerable caution about using FNA biopsy rather than CNB as the sole means of confirming a cancer diagnosis before the initiation of definitive operative management or neoadjuvant therapy. FNA biopsy is unable to discriminate carcinoma in situ from invasive carcinoma and therefore incapable of establishing whether axillary node staging is needed. Furthermore, because of the smaller quantity of tissue extracted, FNA biopsy is a less reliable means of assessing receptor status than CNB is. Finally, in 1% to 2% of cases, FNA biopsy may yield false positive results,[12] potentially leading to an unnecessary cancer operation. For these reasons, it is recommended that malignancies identified by FNA biopsy be confirmed by means of CNB or open biopsy (preferably the former) before definitive therapy is provided.

Cytologic analysis that is diagnostic of a specific benign lesion (e.g., a fibroadenoma) may generally be relied on if it is in concordance with the clinical features of the lesion. However, a negative result from FNA biopsy does not exclude cancer: this procedure fails to diagnose as many as 40% of breast malignancies.[12] Cellular atypia, pathologic discordance, or a nondiagnostic FNA is an indication for tissue diagnosis.

CORE-NEEDLE BIOPSY

As noted (see above), CNB is the diagnostic procedure of choice for breast lesions. Like FNA biopsy, it is easily performed in an outpatient setting. Unlike FNA biopsy, CNB removes a narrow cylinder of tissue that is submitted for pathologic rather than cytologic analysis. Whenever feasible, CNB of both palpable and nonpalpable lesions is performed under ultrasonographic guidance, which permits real-time documentation of the needle's position within the lesion. For lesions not visualized on ultrasonography or for suspicious microcalcifications, stereotactic guidance may be employed instead. A preoperative diagnosis of malignancy

obtained via CNB enables the surgeon to perform a single-stage operative procedure. It may also help lower the positive margin rate for patients undergoing breast-conserving therapy, thereby reducing the need for reexcision and improving the cosmetic outcome.[13]

Various automatic, rotational, and vacuum-assisted devices may be employed to perform CNB; in what follows, we briefly discuss these devices [see Technique, below]. When CNB is performed with a 14-gauge needle, as is the case with Tru-Cut (Cardinal Health, Dublin, Ohio) devices and spring-loaded guns, up to 30% pathologic upgrading may be seen on subsequent surgical excision.[1] When CNB is done with a larger needle (8 to 11 gauge), as is the case with image-guided vacuum-assisted and rotational devices, a greater volume of tissue is delivered, and consequently, less pathologic upgrading is seen.[14] With the vacuum-assisted core biopsy (VACB) devices currently available, it is possible to remove all radiographic evidence of the lesion. It is therefore common practice with all core biopsies to place a titanium clip or another surrogate marker at the biopsy site to facilitate future localization procedures. In addition, a clip should be placed at the biopsy site if the patient has a larger cancer for which neoadjuvant chemotherapy is required; some such lesions exhibit a complete clinical response to chemotherapy and thus are no longer radiographically visible at the time of definitive operative treatment. Two-view postbiopsy mammography should be performed to confirm accurate placement of the clip and adequate sampling of the lesion at the time of biopsy.

Technique

Palpation-guided biopsy In this setting, a manual Tru-Cut–type device or, more commonly, a spring-loaded semiautomatic biopsy gun is used to obtain the specimen. The skin is prepared, and a local anesthetic is infiltrated superficially via a 25-gauge needle. A nick is made in the skin with a No. 11 blade to permit easy entry of the biopsy needle (usually a 14-gauge needle). As with FNA biopsy (see above), the lesion is held steady in the nondominant hand while the biopsy needle is advanced into the periphery of the lesion. Next, the needle is manually advanced through the center of the lesion (if a manual device is used), or the gun is fired (if a spring-loaded device is used). Finally, the needle is withdrawn to retrieve the core. Four to five cores, each from a separate pass, should be obtained to ensure that the lesion is not undersampled. Pressure is applied over the lesion and the biopsy tract for 10 to 15 minutes to ensure adequate hemostasis. The nick in the skin is closed with an adhesive strip (e.g., Steri-Strip; 3M, St. Paul, Minnesota).

Ultrasound-guided biopsy This technique may be employed for both palpable and nonpalpable lesions. The lesion that is to undergo biopsy is centered on the screen of the ultrasound device. A local anesthetic is injected superficially, first along the anticipated biopsy tract and then both anterior and posterior to the lesion; this latter maneuver helps ensure that there is a safe distance between the lesion and the skin or the chest wall. A nick is made in the skin with a No. 11 blade. The biopsy needle is then inserted through the skin, with care taken to keep it in a plane parallel to the footplate of the ultrasound probe as it passes through the breast tissue. The biopsy itself can be either performed in a freehand manner or directed with a needle guide attached to the probe. The ideal final positions of the tip and shaft vary, depending on the particular biopsy device selected for the procedure [see Figure 2]. Regardless of which device is used, the tip and shaft of the needle should be visualized throughout the entire approach to

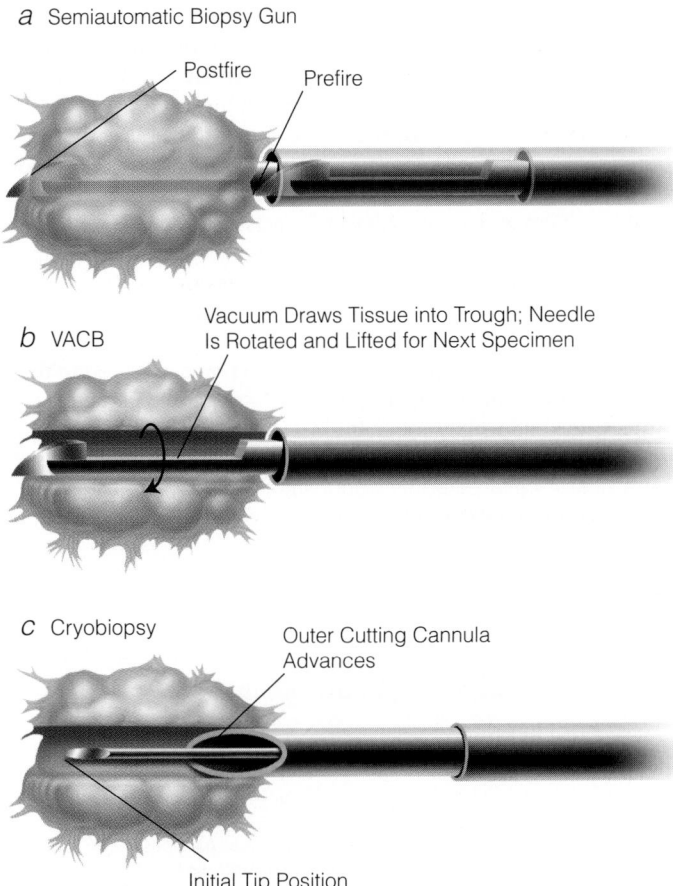

a Semiautomatic Biopsy Gun

Postfire   Prefire

b VACB

Vacuum Draws Tissue into Trough; Needle
Is Rotated and Lifted for Next Specimen

c Cryobiopsy

Outer Cutting Cannula
Advances

Initial Tip Position

Figure 2 **Core-needle biopsy. The positioning of the needle shaft
and tip varies with the particular biopsy device being used. (*a*)
For manual or semiautomatic guns that fire through the lesion,
the position of the tip before firing should be at the edge of the
lesion. Keeping the needle shaft parallel to the chest wall or the
skin keeps these structures from being injured when the gun is
fired or the core is manually obtained. (*b*) For most vacuum-
assisted devices, multiple cores can be obtained through a single
placement of the device within the breast. For diagnostic biopsies
performed under ultrasonographic or stereotactic guidance, the
needle may be placed in the center of the lesion and rotated up to
360° in specified intervals. (*c*) For cryobiopsy, the tip of the needle
should be advanced through the center of the lesion toward the
far edge of the lesion before firing. This step stabilizes the lesion.
The outer cutting and rotating cannula is then fired over the
inner needle.**

and biopsy of the lesion. Prefire and postfire images should be
obtained that show the needle in proximity to and within the
lesion, respectively. Four to five good cores are required for adequate sampling. Once the biopsy is complete, pressure is applied
over the lesion and the biopsy tract, and a Steri-Strip is placed. To
facilitate closure of larger entry sites, a single subcuticular stitch
may be used.

Brisk bleeding may occur during and immediately after the procedure, but it usually can be controlled by the application of direct
pressure. Patients are restricted from engaging in strenuous activity for 24 hours after biopsy. Bruising may result, but it typically
resolves within days. Other potential complications include
hematoma, fat necrosis, a palpable lump, and infection; however,
such events are uncommon. Most patients receiving oral anticoagulants can be switched to a subcutaneous alternative that can be
stopped on the morning of the procedure.

Semiautomated gun biopsy. When a spring-loaded semiautomatic biopsy gun is used, the tip of the needle should abut the
lesion in such a way that the biopsy trough will be in the lesion
after the device is fired. Ideally, the repeat passes should sample
different portions of the lesion and avoid any necrotic areas that
have been visualized.

Vacuum-assisted core biopsy. Vacuum-assisted rotational cutting
devices employ a 7- to 11-gauge probe with a distal sampling
trough and an inner rotating cutter. The sampling trough can be
placed either in the center of the lesion or directly under it. The
probe is attached to a vacuum system, which draws the target tissue into the trough. Once the tissue has been drawn into the
trough, the inner rotating cutter is advanced and cuts a core from
it. The tissue core is then delivered by the vacuum system through
the barrel of the probe and into a proximal collection chamber.
The probe can be rotated up to 360° and can retrieve multiple
samples through a single insertion in the skin. The larger tissue volumes obtained with these rotational VACB devices have reduced
the incidence of atypical ductal hyperplasia or ductal carcinoma in
situ (DCIS) upgrades on subsequent excisional biopsies.[5]

Cryoassisted core biopsy. In a cryobiopsy, a thin (19-gauge)
solid needle is placed in the middle of the targeted tissue. The tip
is then cooled to approximately –10° C, a temperature that freezes
the tissue to the needle but does not cause tissue necrosis. An
outer rotating cutting cannula (10 gauge) is then advanced over
the inner localizing needle. The device is removed from the breast,
and the single specimen is removed. As with the semiautomatic
biopsy gun, multiple passes into the breast are still required.
However, the local anesthetic effect of the cooling process, the
ability of the device to spear and stabilize a lesion, and the absence
of a firing gun–type action make cryobiopsy advantageous, particularly for a mobile lesion that lies close to the skin or the chest wall.

Stereotactic-guided biopsy Lesions that are visible only on
mammography—including small solid lesions, asymmetric densities, and suspicious groups of microcalcifications—can often be
targeted and subjected to core biopsy under stereotactic guidance.[15] This outpatient procedure commonly makes use of a
mounted VACB gun, similar to the handheld VACB device previously described (see above). Stereotactic biopsy is appropriate for
lesions that are clearly visible on digital images and identifiable on
stereotactic projections. Lesions that lie close to the chest wall or
in the subareolar region may not be amenable to stereotactic biopsy and are often best approached via open biopsy with needle
localization (see below). Likewise, lesions in thinly compressible
breasts may not be amenable to stereotactic biopsy, because firing
of the needle may result in a through-and-through injury to the
breast. Certain stereotactic systems may not be suitable for
patients who are unable to lie prone or are morbidly obese. It
should be kept in mind that stereotactic biopsy is a diagnostic procedure and is not intended for therapeutic purposes. On the
whole, it is safe, and the complication rate is acceptably low.

Depending on the system being employed, the patient either lies
prone on the stereotactic table or sits upright. With the breast compressed craniocaudally or mediolaterally, stereotactic digital imaging is then performed to visualize the targeted lesion and calculate
its location in three dimensions, and a suitable probe insertion site
is identified. The skin is prepared, and a small amount of buffered
1% lidocaine with epinephrine is administered. The skin at the
insertion site is punctured with a No. 11 blade, the probe is manually advanced to the prefire site, and the position of the probe is

confirmed by means of stereotactic imaging. The device is then fired, repeatedly cutting, rotating, and retrieving samples until the desired amount has been removed. Targeted removal of suspicious microcalcifications is confirmed with specimen mammography.

Once the biopsy is complete, an inert metallic clip is deployed into the biopsy site through the probe for future localization; deployment and positioning are initially confirmed by stereotactic imaging. The biopsy device is then removed, the edges of the skin incision are approximated with Steri-Strips, and a compressive bandage is applied. Typically, 1 g of tissue (equivalent to approximately 10 to 12 samples with an 11-gauge probe) is sufficient for diagnosis. Once the procedure is over and the breast has been released from compression, a two-view mammography should be obtained to verify that the clip was accurately placed and to document that the targeted lesion was adequately sampled.

Interpretation of Results

CNB is a highly accurate diagnostic tool: the false-negative rate is only 1% to 2%,[16] which is comparable to that of open wire-localized biopsy. When pathologic evaluation reveals fibroadenoma, microcalcifications within benign fibrocystic tissue, or other comparably benign pathologic conditions, there is no need for any special follow-up, and routine screening mammography may be resumed. However, when biopsy of the targeted mass lesion fails to yield a mass diagnosis or a biopsy specimen from group of clustered calcifications is devoid of microcalcifications on pathologic review, the discordant result should be viewed with some suspicion and should be considered an indication for open biopsy. Subsequent excisional biopsy is also indicated when CNB reveals atypical hyperplasia, radial scar, lobular carcinoma in situ (LCIS), or papilloma. The rationale is that the excisional biopsy may result in a pathologic upgrade to cancer. For example, open biopsy after a CNB indicative of atypical ductal hyperplasia may reveal DCIS in approximately 40% of patients when CNB was performed with a 14-gauge automated gun. The use of larger (e.g., 11-gauge) core biopsy devices has reduced the frequency of this finding to approximately 20%,[17] but it has not eliminated the need for excision. False positive results are rare with CNB; therefore, a diagnosis of malignancy may be believed, and a one-stage definitive surgical procedure may then be planned without further biopsy.

Touch Preparation of Cores

For an immediate but preliminary diagnosis, cytologic touch preparation of fresh cores may be performed in the office.[18] The tissue is blotted to remove any gross blood, the core is gently smeared along a glass slide, and the slide is then immediately fixed in 70% ethanol. A layer of cells is left on the surface of the slide for cytologic evaluation, while the core is preserved for permanent evaluation. This procedure has a diagnostic accuracy of nearly 90%. Although the false-negative rate is approximately 25%, an immediate diagnosis is obtained in 75% of patients.[18] Like all preliminary diagnoses, touch preparation diagnoses should be treated with caution until the final results of histopathologic evaluation are available.

PERCUTANEOUS EXCISIONAL BIOPSY

In some instances, patient preference may dictate complete removal of a mass regardless of its benign appearance. As an alternative to open biopsy (see below), percutaneous excision of small masses may be performed.[19-21] This procedure can be performed in an outpatient setting with the patient under local anesthesia. Some of the devices used for percutaneous excision are vacuum assisted and remove the mass as multiple cores, whereas others

deliver large intact samples in a single pass [*see Figure 3*]. Although such approaches clearly show promise for future surgical treatment of breast cancer, these percutaneous devices are currently approved by the U.S. Food and Drug Administration (FDA) only for excision of benign masses. Lesions found to be harboring cancer should undergo subsequent open surgical reexcision. Excision of lesions that are close to the skin or the chest wall or are larger than 2 to 3 cm in diameter may prove technically challenging with percutaneous techniques; open excisional biopsy [*see* Open Biopsy, *below*] may be preferable for such lesions.

CRYOABLATION

Patients with a biopsy-proven fibroadenoma who want their mass removed but desire an alternative to open or percutaneous surgical excision may be candidates for cryoablation, which destroys targeted tissue by alternately freezing and thawing it. Intracellular ice formation, osmotic injury, and ischemic injury are all believed to contribute to the mechanism of tissue destruction.

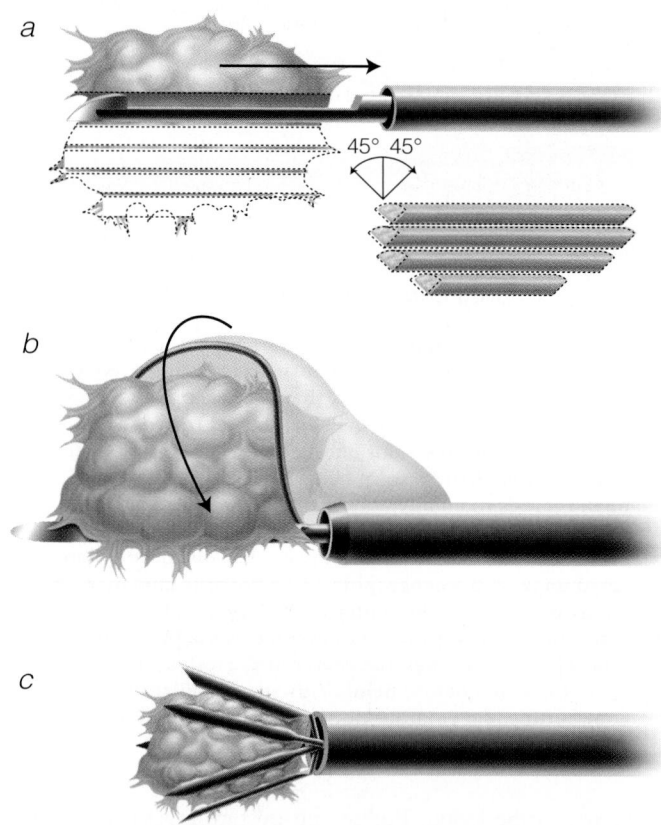

Figure 3 **Percutaneous excisional biopsy. This procedure may be performed by means of several different methods. (*a*) One approach is to employ a vacuum-assisted device, which is placed with the trough under the lesion and the shaft parallel to the posterior aspect of the lesion. The needle is then lifted anteriorly as it is rotated first 45° degrees clockwise, then back to the center position (0°), and finally 45° counterclockwise to remove the entire lesion in multiple cores. (*b*) Another option is to employ an electrosurgical device such as the Ovation (Rubicor Medical, Inc., Redwood City, California), which circumscribes the mass with a cutting wire loop while concurrently deploying a retractable plastic bag that encapsulates the lesion and retracts it through the skin en bloc. (*c*) A third option is to employ a device such as the Intact Breast Lesion Excision System (Intact Medical Corp., Natick, Massachusetts), which circumscribes the mass with radiofrequency wand and delivers it en bloc.**

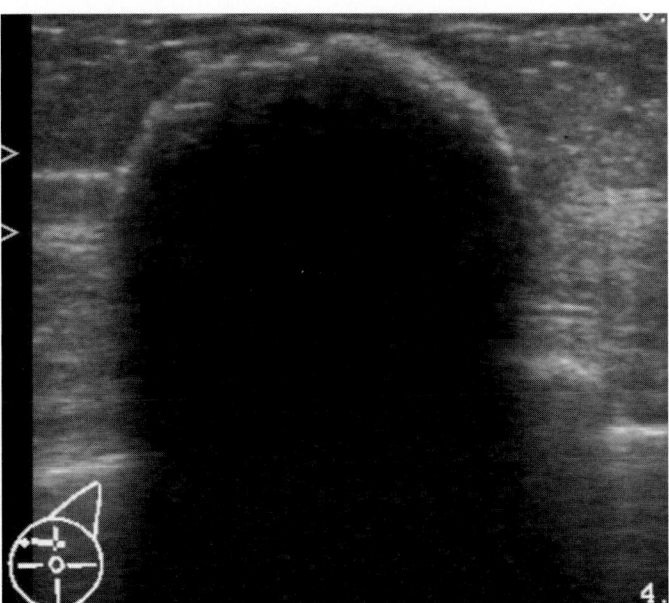

Figure 4 **Cryoablation. The needle is placed through the center of the lesion, and argon gas is delivered to create a local temperature of –40° C. The resulting iceball is well visualized by ultrasonography.**

Because of the natural analgesic effect of cold, cryoablation is generally a well-tolerated procedure that can be performed in an outpatient setting. Clinically, resorption of the fibroadenoma increases over time, with 12-month follow-up studies reporting 73% to 97% reductions in lesion volume. Despite the occasional residual disease noted when cryoablation is used to treat larger masses, both hospital-based and community-based studies have reported that patient satisfaction rates are higher than 90% with this procedure.[22]

Technique

A 12-gauge cryoprobe is inserted into the center of the lesion under ultrasonographic guidance. If the lesion is in close proximity to the chest wall or the skin, it should first be isolated by injecting normal saline. To freeze the lesion, inert argon gas is delivered through the tip of the probe in such a way as to create a local temperature of –40° C or lower. An iceball is thereby formed that is well visualized by ultrasonography [see Figure 4]. In a tightly coupled system, helium is then delivered to thaw the lesion. For adequate necrosis to occur, two freeze-thaw cycles must be performed; the exact specifications of these cycles depend on the size of the lesion.

OPEN BIOPSY

The vast majority of open breast biopsies are now performed with either local anesthesia alone or local anesthesia with I.V. sedation.

Technique

Various options for incisions are available [see Figure 5]. If the pathology is unclear, the incision is placed directly over the lesion to minimize tunneling through breast tissue. The incision should be long to ensure that the mass, together with a small rim of grossly normal tissue, can be excised as a single specimen and be oriented so that it can be included within any future lumpectomy or mastectomy incision should the lesion prove malignant. Resection of overlying skin is not necessary unless the lesion is extremely superficial. Historically, surgeons performing open biopsies have generally employed curvilinear incisions placed within the resting lines of skin tension [see Figure 5a, 5b]. Currently, however, some surgeons are advocating the use of radial incisions, particularly for medial, lateral, and inferior lesions.[13] If a previous CNB proved the lesion to be benign (e.g., fibroadenoma) but the patient still favors excision, it is acceptable to move the incision to a circumareolar position or another less visible site.

For diagnostic biopsies, the surgeon should orient the specimen, and the pathologist should ink all margins. Meticulous hemostasis should be achieved before closure to prevent the formation of hematomas that could complicate subsequent definitive oncologic resection. A cosmetic subcuticular skin closure is preferred.

NEEDLE (WIRE)-LOCALIZATION BREAST BIOPSY

Lesions that are not amenable to stereotactic core biopsy may be excised by means of needle (wire)-localization breast biopsy (NLBB). Such lesions include those that are close to the chest wall or under the nipple, as well as those occurring in a thin breast, where firing the needle may cause it to pass through the opposite side of the breast. Radiographic evidence of a radial scar is also an indication for NLBB: a core pathologic diagnosis of such a scar would ultimately necessitate open excision. Finally, reexcision is required when stereotactic or ultrasound-guided CNB reveals lesions determined to be high risk on pathologic evaluation (e.g., atypical hyperplasia, LCIS, papilloma, carcinoma, or lesion whose pathologic status is discordant with radiographic findings). In these circumstances, wire localization may be performed on the residual lesion, a clip placed at the time of CNB, or another surrogate marker (see below). To bracket a more extensive area of calcifications, multiple wires may be placed, especially if previous CNB revealed atypia or malignancy in the area.

Technique

The lesion to be excised is localized by inserting a thin needle and a fine wire under mammographic or ultrasonographic guidance immediately before operation. To facilitate incision placement, images should be sent to the OR with the wire entry site indicated on them. The incision is placed as directly as possible over the mass to minimize tunneling through breast tissue. With superficial lesions, the wire entry site is usually close to the lesion and thus may be included in the incision. With some deeper lesions, the wire entry site is on the shortest path to the lesion and so may still be included in the incision. Once the incision is made, a block of tissue is excised around and along the wire in such a way as to include the lesion [see Figure 6a, b]. This process is easier and involves less excision of tissue if the localizing wire has a thickened segment several centimeters in length that is placed adjacent to or within the lesion. The wire itself can then be followed into breast tissue until the thick segment is reached, at which point the excision can be extended away from the wire to include the lesion in a fairly small tissue fragment.

With many lesions, the wire entry site is in a fairly peripheral location relative to the position of the lesion, which means that including the wire entry site in the incision would result in excessive tunneling within breast tissue. In such cases, the incision is placed over the expected position of the lesion [see Figure 6c], the dissection is extended into breast tissue to identify the wire a few centimeters away from the lesion itself, and the free end of the wire is pulled up into the incision. A generous block of tissue is then excised around the wire. Intraoperative ultrasonography may be useful for identifying the tip of the needle and facilitating excision, particularly in the case of a deep lesion or biopsy site in a large breast.

Radiography should be performed intraoperatively on all wire-localized biopsy specimens to confirm excision of the lesion. If the

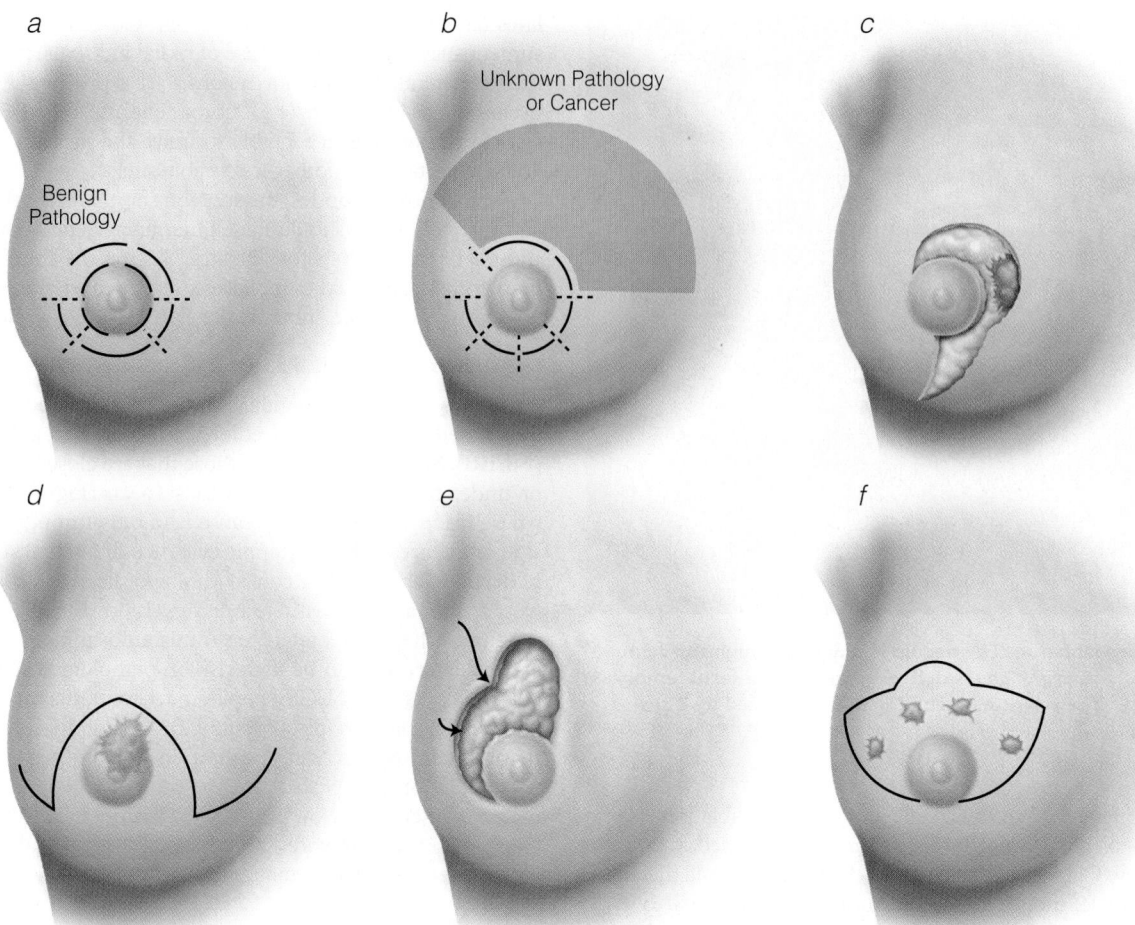

Figure 5 Open biopsy. (*a*) For biopsy-proven benign masses, a circumareolar incision generally provides excellent cosmesis and a well-hidden scar. If the lesion is too far from the nipple, curvilinear incisions are traditionally employed instead. Alternatively, medial, lateral, and inferior incisions may be placed in a radial fashion. (*b*) For lesions of unknown pathology, incisions should be placed directly over the lesion and should be oriented so that they will be included within a subsequent mastectomy incision if margins prove positive and mastectomy is indicated. As with benign lesions, either curvilinear incisions or radial incisions may be employed. Circumareolar incisions should be avoided in this setting because reexcision to provide clear margins, as is indicated in the case of malignancy, can necessitate excision of a portion of the nipple-areola complex and can commit the surgeon to a mastectomy. In cases where reexcision is indicated, avoidance of incisions in the so-called no man's land may improve cosmesis, in that it allows future reconstructive efforts to include advancement of the nipple-areola complex if desired. Various oncoplastic incisions may be employed as alternatives for (*c*) medial, (*d*) central, or (*e, f*) superior lesions.

lesion was missed, another tissue sample may be excised if the surgeon has some idea of the likely location of the missed lesion. If, however, the surgeon suspects that the wire was dislodged before or during the procedure, then the incision should be closed, and repeat localization and biopsy should be performed later. In addition to wire dislocation or transection, wire localization is occasionally associated with vasovagal reactions. Alternatives to wire localization include hematoma ultrasound-guided (HUG) excision (see below), carbon marking,[23] use of methylene blue dye,[24] and placement of radioactive seeds.[25]

Hematoma ultrasound-guided excision In patients who have undergone CNB, particularly those who have undergone VACB, the hematoma at the biopsy site can often serve as a physiologic marker that accurately guides intraoperative localization [*see Figure 7*].[26,27] This procedure, referred to as HUG excision, renders wire placement unnecessary and can facilitate operative schedul-

ing. The hematoma is localized in two planes, and 1 cm margins are marked off around the lesion; dissection is then continued down toward the chest wall in a block fashion. Excision of the hematoma can be confirmed by ultrasonography of the specimen ex vivo, as well as direct visualization of the hematoma in the gross specimen.

Terminal Duct Excision

Terminal duct excision is the procedure of choice in the surgical treatment of pathologic nipple discharge.[28] The goal is to excise the discharging duct with as little additional tissue as possible. To this end, the surgeon should carefully note the precise position of the offending duct at the time of the initial examination.

OPERATIVE TECHNIQUE

The patient is instructed to refrain from manually expressing her discharge for several days before operation. After local anes-

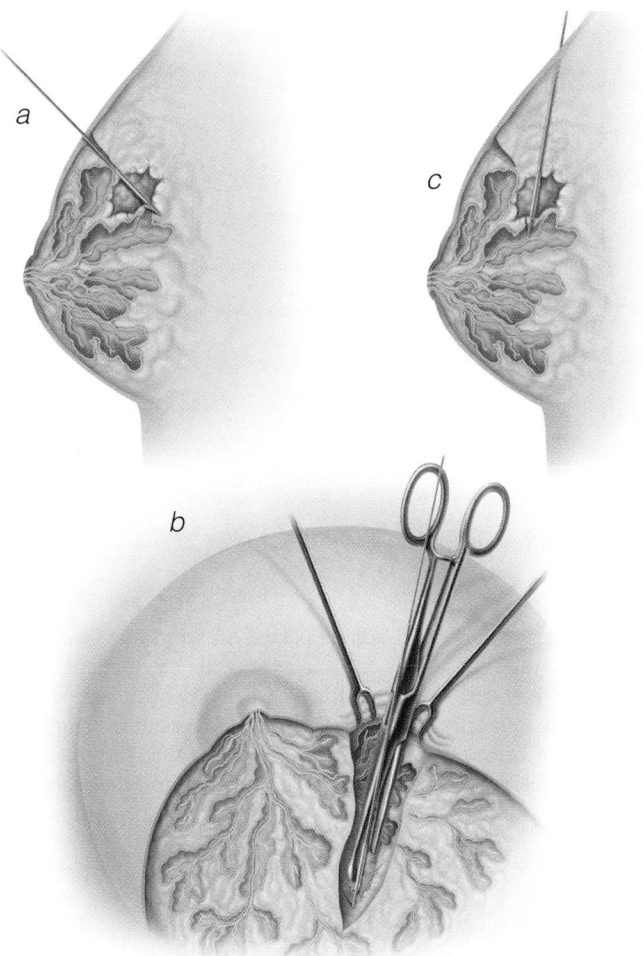

Figure 6 **Needle-localization breast biopsy. (a) The mammographic abnormality is localized preoperatively. The relation between the wire, the skin entry site, and the lesion is noted by the surgeon. The skin incision is placed over the expected location of the mammographic abnormality. (b) The tissue around the wire is removed en bloc with the wire and sent for specimen mammography. Tunneling and piecemeal removal are to be avoided. (c) It is sometimes necessary to insert the localizing wire from a peripheral site to localize a deep or central lesion. The incision should be placed directly over the expected location of the lesion, not over the wire entry site. The dissection is extended into breast tissue to identify the wire a short distance from the lesion. The free end of the wire is pulled into the wound, and the biopsy is performed as previously described.[56]**

thesia (with or without sedation) is administered, the surgeon attempts to express the discharge. If this attempt is successful, the edge of the nipple is grasped with a forceps, and a fine lacrimal duct probe (000 to 0000) is gently inserted into the discharging duct. A radial incision is made within the areola at the same clock position as is occupied by the draining duct [*see Figure 8*]; this incision is preferred to a circumareolar incision because it is believed to preserve more nipple sensation and function.[29] The nipple skin flap is raised, and the duct containing the wire is excised with a margin of surrounding tissue from just below the nipple dermis to a depth of 4 to 5 cm within the breast tissue. The electrocautery should be employed with particular caution in the superficial portions of the dissection to prevent devascularization of the nipple-areola complex. If it is not possible to pass the lacrimal duct probe into the discharging duct or it is unclear which duct has resulted

in the pathologic discharge, the entire subareolar duct complex must be excised from immediately beneath the nipple dermis to a depth of 4 to 5 cm within the breast tissue. The breast tissue should be reapproximated beneath the nipple to prevent retraction of the nipple or indentation of the areola.

Surgical Options for Breast Cancer

There are several surgical options for primary treatment of breast cancer; indications for selecting among them are reviewed elsewhere [*see 21 Breast Complaints*]. It should be emphasized that for most patients, partial mastectomy (lumpectomy) to microscopically clear margins coupled with axillary staging and radiation therapy yields long-term survival equivalent to that associated with mastectomy and axillary staging. Currently, indications for mastectomy include patient preference, the inability to achieve clean margins without unacceptable deformation of the breast, the presence of disease in multiple quadrants (multicentric disease), previous chest wall irradiation, pregnancy, the presence of severe collagen vascular disease (e.g., scleroderma), and the lack of access to a radiation therapy facility.

Partial Mastectomy

Partial mastectomy—also referred to as wide local excision or lumpectomy—involves excision of all cancerous tissue to microscopically clear margins. Although 1 cm margins are the goal, many surgeons consider 2 mm margins to be adequate for reducing the risk of local recurrence.[30] Hence, reexcision is indicated whenever margins are either positive or too close (< 2 mm). Partial mastectomy is commonly performed with the patient under local anesthesia, with or without sedation. The addition of an axillary staging procedure (a common event) usually necessitates general anesthesia, but in select circumstances, local or epidural anesthesia may suffice.

OPERATIVE TECHNIQUE

An incision is placed directly over the lesion to minimize tunneling through breast tissue; it should be oriented so as to be included within a subsequent mastectomy incision if margins prove positive. As with open biopsy (see above), curvilinear incisions have been the standard, but radial incisions are now being advocated by some surgeons, particularly for upper outer, medial, lateral, and inferior lesions. A radial incision facilitates excision of tumors that extend in a ductal distribution, preserves the contour of the breast, and permits easier reexcision if margins prove positive [*see Figure 5b*]. With current oncoplastic techniques,[31,32] lesions in the central, medial, or superior portions of the breast can be resected with minimal cosmetic deformity [*see Figure 5c, d, e, f*]. Resection of a portion of the overlying skin is not necessary unless the lesion is extremely superficial.

To obtain clear margins, a 1 to 1.5 cm margin of normal-appearing tissue should be removed beyond the edge of the palpable tumor or, if excisional biopsy has already been performed, around the biopsy cavity. In the case of nonpalpable lesions diagnosed by means of CNB, wire localization is performed, and 2 to 3 cm of tissue should be excised around the wire to obtain an adequate margin. Intraoperative ultrasonography may reduce the rate of positive margins by allowing visualization of the tumor edge or the previous biopsy site.[33]

The specimen should be oriented by the surgeon and the margins inked by the pathologist; this orientation is useful if reexcision is required to achieve clean margins. Reexcision of any close (< 2

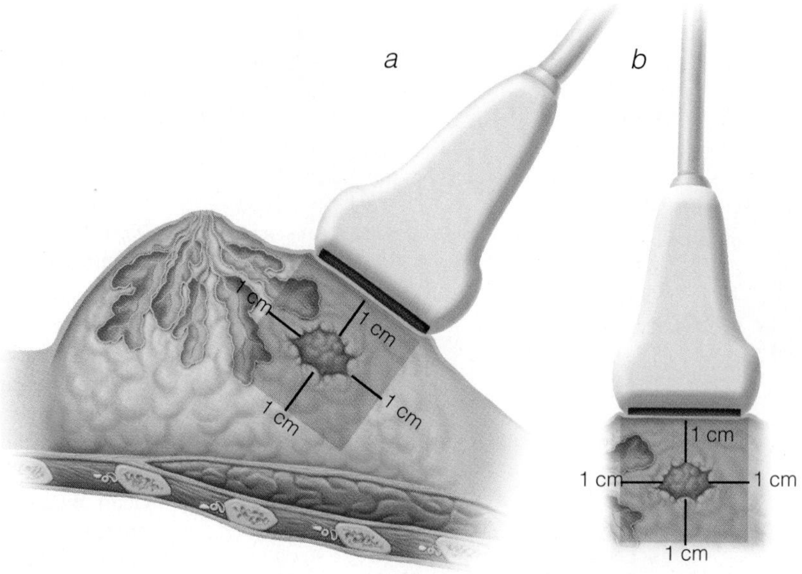

Figure 7 **Hematoma ultrasound-guided excision. (*a*) The hematoma is localized in two planes with intraoperative ultrasonography, and 1 cm margins are marked off around it. Dissection then proceeds down toward the chest wall in a block fashion. Excision of the hematoma is confirmed by ultrasonography of the specimen ex vivo (*b*), as well as by direct visualization of the hematoma in the gross specimen.**[26,27]

mm) margins may be performed during the same surgical procedure if the specimen margins are assessed immediately by the pathologist. If the specimen was not oriented, the entire biopsy cavity should be reexcised. Surgical clips may be left in the lumpectomy site to help the radiation oncologist plan the radiation

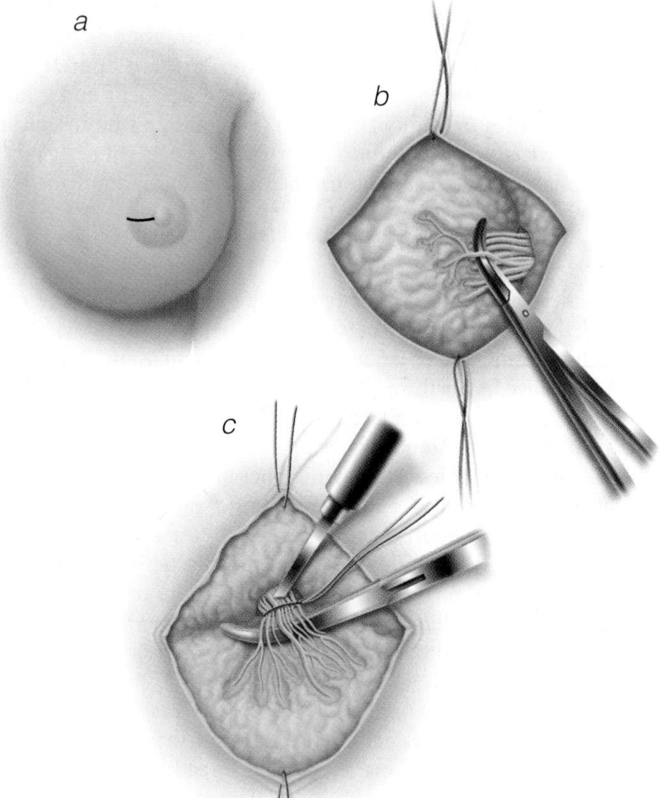

Figure 8 **Terminal duct excision. (*a*) A radial incision is made within the areola. (*b*) The involved duct is identified by means of blunt dissection and removed along with a core of breast tissue. (*c*) If no single duct is identified, the entire subareolar ductal complex is excised from immediately beneath the nipple dermis to a depth of 4 to 5 cm within breast tissue.**[28,29]

boost to the tumor bed or to direct partial-breast irradiation. In the closure of the incision, hemostasis should be meticulous: a hematoma may delay adjuvant therapy. Deep breast tissue should be approximated only if such closure does not result in significant deformity of breast contours. A cosmetic subcuticular closure is preferred. Wearing a support bra during the day and the night can reduce shearing of fragile vessels.[13]

ACCELERATED PARTIAL-BREAST IRRADIATION WITH BALLOON CATHETER

Historically, whole-breast irradiation has been the standard treatment to reduce the risk of local recurrence after breast-conserving therapy (BCT). Long-term follow-up of patients who have received BCT demonstrates, however, that only 1% to 3% of recurrences within the breast arise at a significant distance from the primary cancer site (i.e., in other breast quadrants); the remainder develop near the original biopsy site.[30,34] This approach provides the rationale for the approach known as accelerated partial-breast irradiation (APBI), in which a shortened course of high-dose radiation is delivered to the tissue surrounding the lumpectomy cavity (the region theoretically at greatest risk). Several different APBI techniques have been developed, including placement of interstitial catheters, use of a localized external beam, single-dose intraoperative treatment, implantation of radioactive beads or seeds, and insertion of a balloon catheter into the lumpectomy site. Although long-term follow-up has not been carried out, the short-term results reported for some APBI techniques indicate that in most centers, recurrence rates have been low, with good cosmesis and only mild chronic toxicity.[35]

The technique of APBI can be illustrated by considering the MammoSite Radiation Therapy System (Cytyc Corp., Palo Alto, California), in which a balloon catheter is inserted into the surgical cavity after lumpectomy to provide partial-breast irradiation (see below). Although the catheter may also be inserted at the time of the original operation, it is preferable to wait for final pathologic evaluation to confirm clear margins; if the catheter is inserted and margins are found to be positive, it will have to be replaced (a costly process). Postoperative insertion may be done either percutaneously under ultrasonographic guidance or by means of an open technique. Once the catheter is in place, a radiation source (iridium 192) is delivered into the balloon via a high–dose rate remote afterloader.

Technique

For safe and effective delivery of radiotherapy through the MammoSite balloon catheter, the lumpectomy cavity must be able to conform its shape to that of an ovoid or spherical catheter without significant air pockets, able to accommodate a volume of at least 30 ml (the volume of the smallest available balloon), and able to maintain a minimum distance of 7 mm from the skin with the catheter in place. In addition, if a percutaneous technique is being considered, the surgeon should be comfortable with ultrasonography (which will be employed for initial visualization of the lumpectomy cavity). If the above criteria seem reasonably attainable, one may proceed with a percutaneous approach [see Figure 9].

Percutaneous approach A site peripheral to the scar is chosen as the entry site for the balloon catheter, and a local anesthetic is injected along the proposed catheter tract. A trocar (supplied with the insertion kit) is inserted into the cavity via the peripheral entry site, then removed. The shape of the cavity is visualized by means of ultrasonography, and a catheter of appropriate shape (ovoid or spherical) and volume (30 to 65 ml) is advanced through the newly formed tract. Saline is then infiltrated to inflate the catheter balloon to the maximum volume that the cavity can accommodate. The cavity is then reimaged to confirm that the catheter is an adequate distance (7 mm) from the skin. If the distance is inadequate, the balloon volume is reduced. If it is not possible to keep the catheter at least 7 mm from the skin while maintaining a balloon volume of at least 30 ml, conversion to an open approach is indicated.

Open approach The cavity is reopened through the original skin incision. Occasionally, a thick rind may form around the residual seroma; this rind may be excised to reduce tension and increase the volume of the cavity. If necessary, the anterior skin may be excised in the form of an ellipse to provide improved anterior coverage of the catheter, and the subcutaneous tissue may be pulled together over the catheter and the cavity to help ensure adequate coverage and sufficient distance from the skin. A peripheral site is chosen for insertion of the catheter. After the skin is closed, ultrasonography is employed to confirm that the distance from the skin is adequate. A topical antibiotic is applied at the insertion site; no anchoring stitch is necessary. Correct positioning of the catheter is confirmed by a postplacement treatment-planning CT scan that is evaluated by the radiation oncologist.

Minimally Invasive Tumor-Ablating Techniques

The next step in the evolving application of minimally invasive techniques to breast cancer is to determine whether ablative local therapies can safely substitute for standard surgical extirpation. Cryotherapy, laser ablation, radiofrequency ablation (RFA), and focused ultrasound ablation have all been studied as means of eradicating small breast cancers.[36] In most of these techniques, a probe is placed percutaneously into the breast lesion under imaging guidance, and tumor cell destruction is achieved by means of either heat or cold.

Cryotherapy has been successfully used in the treatment of nonresectable liver tumors. It kills tumor cells by disrupting the cellular membrane during multiple freeze ($-40°$ C)/thaw cycles. Unfortunately, early study results reveal that in the treatment of breast cancer, the degree of tumor destruction achieved with cryotherapy is inconsistent.

Laser ablation causes hyperthermic cell death by delivering energy through a fiberoptic probe. Because of the precise targeting required, it has proved difficult to ensure complete tumor destruction with this technique as well.

RFA is a minimally invasive thermal ablation technique in which frictional heat is generated by intracellular ions moving in response to alternating current. It appears to be the most promising ablative method for small breast cancers. Like cryotherapy, RFA has also been extensively used to treat liver tumors. The RFA probe is percutaneously placed in the tumor under imaging guidance, and a star-shaped set of electrodes is deployed from the tip of the probe to deliver heat at a temperature of $95°$ C. Postprocedural MRI may help confirm complete tumor destruction after RFA and other ablative techniques.

To date, experience with ablative breast therapies has been limited, and long-term follow-up has not been carried out. There is some evidence that patients who have small, well-defined, unifocal cancers without extensive intraductal components may have greater success with these techniques.[36] Most of the initial studies of ablative breast therapies involved subsequent surgical excision to obtain histologic evidence of cell death. Unfortunately, when ablative therapies are used alone, the benefits of pathologic assessment of the specimen, including evaluation of margin status, are lost. Clearly, minimally invasive ablative approaches to breast cancer are technically feasible, and they do appear to offer some potential advantages; however, it remains to be determined to what extent they are oncologically appropriate.

Lymphatic Mapping and SLN Biopsy

The pathologic status of the axillary nodes is the single most important prognostic factor for outcome after treatment of breast cancer. The growing recognition of the morbidity of traditional axillary dissection (lymphedema and sensory deficits), together with the increased capability of mammography to detect smaller, potentially node-negative invasive breast cancers, has given rise to the development of SLNB as an axillary staging procedure. SLNB is a minimally invasive means of identifying the first node or nodes draining the breast and hence the first node or nodes to which tumor may spread. In experienced hands, a negative SLNB reliably predicts a tumor-free axilla (false-negative rate, 5% to 9%); therefore, when such a result is obtained, no further nodes need be removed and the patient can spared the morbidity of a traditional axillary node dissection.[37-39] Surgeons competent in SLNB should be able to identify the sentinel lymph node (SLN) with at least 90% accuracy and a false-negative rate lower than 5%.[40] It is recommended that surgeons first learning the technique use axillary dissection as a backup for the first 20 procedures to gain experience in identifying the SLN. Currently, axillary dissection is recommended for patients who have a positive SLN; however, prospective, randomized trials are required to determine the extent to which this step is necessary in SLN-positive patients.

The most common method of identifying the SLN involves injection of both a vital blue dye and a radionuclide.[41-44] The radionuclide is first injected into the subareolar lymphatic plexus, either preoperatively or, in some centers, intraoperatively.[41] Because the breast and its overlying skin drain to the same few SLNs,[43] peritumoral, intradermal, and subareolar injection are all acceptable approaches; subareolar injection has the advantage of being expeditious and accurate in cases of multicentric (as well as unicentric) disease.[44] The vital blue dye is then injected, commonly in the subareolar plexus, and the breast is massaged for 5 minutes to stimulate lymphatic flow. Lymph nodes that are "hot" (i.e., radioactive), blue, or both, as well as palpable nodes, are removed

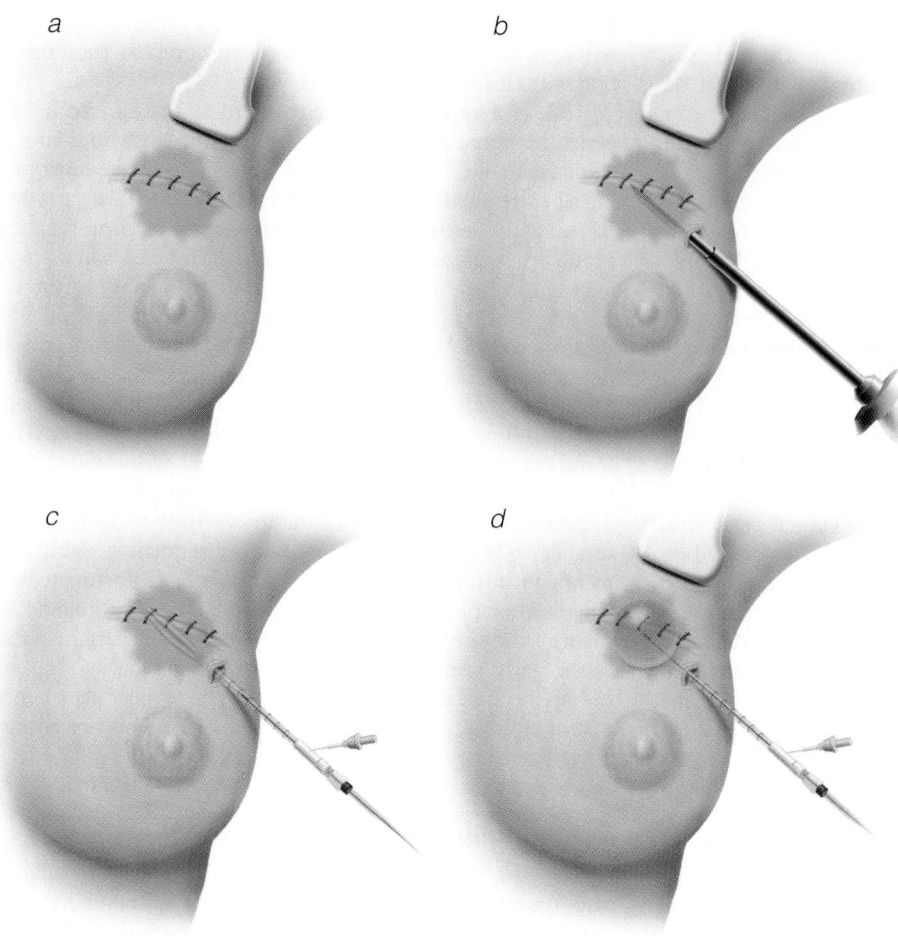

a

b

c

d

Figure 9 **Accelerated partial-breast irradiation with balloon catheter.** (*a*) **The lumpectomy cavity is evaluated by means of ultrasonography.** (*b*) **The trocar is inserted through a separate entry site under ultrasonographic guidance.** (*c*) **The uninflated balloon catheter is advanced through the trocar path.** (*d*) **Under ultrasonographic visualization, the balloon is inflated with saline or contrast material. An anterior distance of at least 7 mm between the catheter and the chest wall or skin is confirmed.**

for evaluation by frozen-section analysis or touch-print cytology. The technique of SLNB is described in greater detail elsewhere [*see 26 Lymphatic Mapping and Sentinel Lymph Node Biopsy*].

SLNB has also been employed in DCIS patients, but in general, its use should be limited to patients with extensive DCIS who are undergoing mastectomy (in the event of occult invasive disease). Some investigators recommend SLNB for patients with extensive DCIS who are undergoing BCT (in whom CNB may have missed an area of invasion),[45] though others caution against this practice.[46,47] Results from the National Surgical Adjuvant Breast and Bowel Project (NSABP) B-27 trial suggest that in patients undergoing neoadjuvant therapy, SLNB may be performed either before or after therapy, with no significant differences in identification and false-negative rates[48]; however, this suggestion is not universally accepted.[49] Contraindications to SLNB include the presence of clinically positive axillary nodes, previous axillary surgery, and pregnancy or lactation. Large or locally advanced breast cancers commonly give rise to a positive SLN but are not a contraindication to the procedure, in that some patients may still be spared the morbidity of a full axillary dissection.

Axillary Dissection

Before the advent of SLNB, axillary dissection was routinely performed in breast cancer patients: it provided prognostic information that guided subsequent adjuvant therapy, it afforded excellent local control, and it may have contributed a small overall survival benefit.

Axillary dissection includes resection of level I and level II lymph nodes [*see Figure 10a*].[50] The superior border of the dissec-tion is formed by the axillary vein; the lateral border of the dissection is formed by the latissimus dorsi; the medial border is formed by the pectoral muscles and the anterior serratus muscle; and the inferior border is formed by the tail of the breast. Level II nodes are easily removed by retracting the pectoralis major and the pectoralis minor medially; it is not necessary to divide or remove the pectoralis minor. Level III nodes are not removed unless palpable disease is present.

Axillary dissection, either alone or in conjunction with lumpectomy or mastectomy, usually calls for general anesthesia, but it may be performed with thoracic epidural anesthesia. To facilitate identification and preservation of motor nerves within the axilla, the anesthesiologist should refrain from using neuromuscular blocking agents. In the absence of neuromuscular blockade, any clamping of a motor nerve or too-close approach to a motor nerve with the electrocautery will be signaled by a visible muscle twitch.

STRUCTURES TO BE PRESERVED

There are a number of vascular structures and nerves passing through the axilla that must be preserved during axillary dissection [*see Figure 10b*]. These structures include the axillary vein and artery; the brachial plexus; the long thoracic nerve, which innervates the anterior serratus muscle; the thoracodorsal nerve, artery, and vein, which supply the latissimus dorsi; and the medial pectoral nerve, which innervates the lateral portion of the pectoralis major.

The axillary artery and the brachial plexus should not be exposed during axillary dissection. If they are, the dissection has been carried too far superiorly, and proper orientation at a more inferior position should be established. In some patients, there

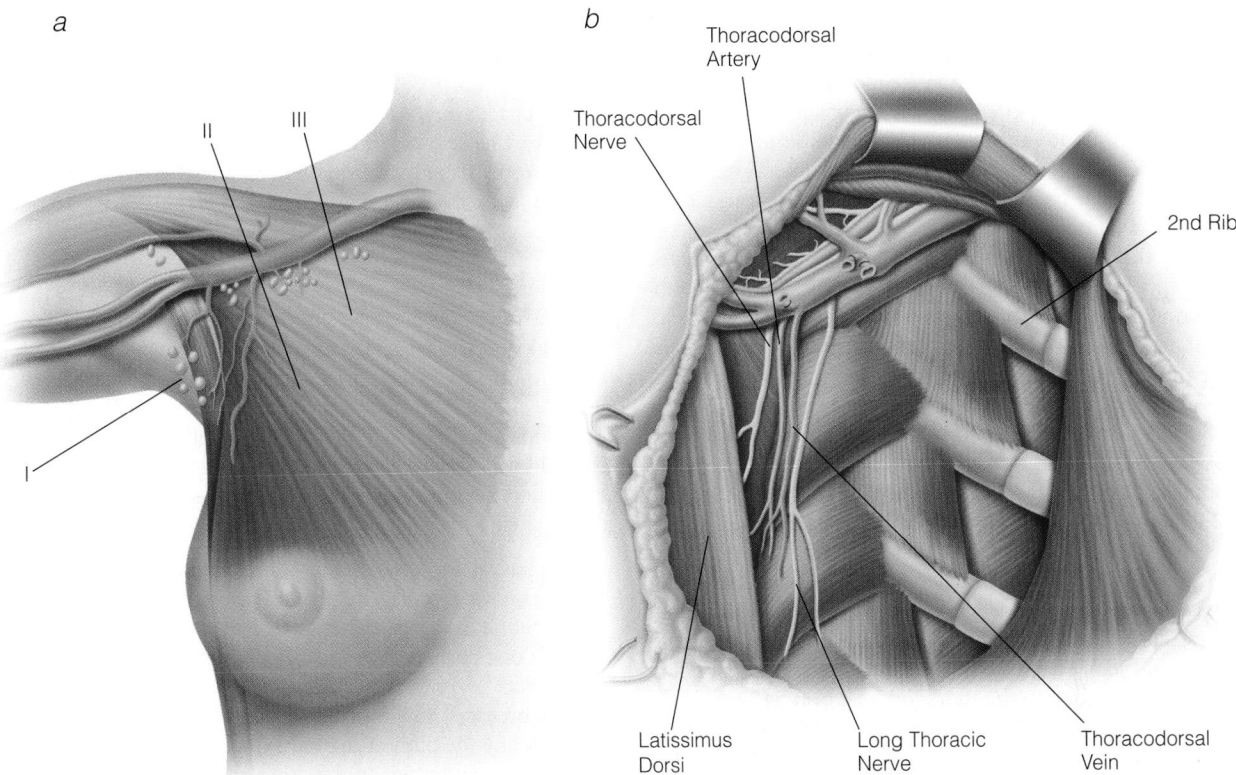

a

II   III

I

b

Thoracodorsal
Artery

Thoracodorsal
Nerve

2nd Rib

Latissimus
Dorsi

Long Thoracic
Nerve

Thoracodorsal
Vein

Figure 10 Axillary dissection.[50] (*a*) Shown are axillary lymph node levels in relation to the axillary vein and the muscles of the axilla (I = low axilla, II = midaxilla, III = apex of axilla). (*b*) Shown is a view of the structures of the axilla after completion of axillary dissection.

may be sensory branches of the brachial plexus superficial (and, rarely, inferior) to the axillary vein laterally near the latissimus dorsi; injury to these nerves results in numbness extending to the wrist. To prevent this complication, the axillary vein should initially be identified medially, under the pectoralis major. Medial to the thoracodorsal nerve and adherent to the chest wall is the long thoracic nerve of Bell. The medial pectoral nerve runs from superior to the axillary vein to the undersurface of the pectoralis major, passing through the axillary fat pad and across the level II nodes; it has an accompanying vein whose blue color may be used to identify the nerve. If a submuscular implant reconstruction [*see* Breast Reconstruction after Mastectomy, *below*] is planned, preservation of the medial pectoral nerve is especially important to prevent atrophy of the muscle.

The intercostobrachial nerve provides sensation to the posterior portion of the upper arm. Sacrificing this nerve generally leads to numbness over the triceps region. In many women, the intercostobrachial nerve measures 2 mm in diameter and takes a fairly cephalad course near the axillary vein; when this is the case, preservation of the nerve will not interfere with node dissection. Sometimes, however, the nerve is tiny, has multiple branches, and is intermingled with nodal tissue that should be removed; when this is the case, one should not expend a great deal of time on attempting to preserve the nerve. If the intercostobrachial nerve is sacrificed, it should be transected with a knife or scissors rather than with the electrocautery, and the ends should be buried to reduce the likelihood of postoperative causalgia.

OPERATIVE TECHNIQUE

The incision for axillary dissection should be a transverse or curvilinear one made in the lower third of the hair-bearing skin of the axilla. For cosmetic reasons, it should not extend anteriorly

onto the pectoralis major; however, it may be extended posteriorly onto the latissimus dorsi as necessary for exposure. Skin flaps are raised to the level of the axillary vein and to a point below the lowest extension of hair-bearing skin, either as an initial maneuver or after the initial identification of key structures.

The key to axillary dissection is obtaining and maintaining proper orientation with respect to the axillary vein, the thoracodorsal bundle, and the long thoracic nerve. After the incision has been made, the dissection is extended down into the true axillary fat pad through the overlying fascial layer. The fat of the axillary fat pad may be distinguished from subcutaneous fat on the basis of its smoother, lipomalike texture. There may be aberrant muscle slips from the latissimus dorsi or the pectoralis major; in addition, there may be an extremely dense fascial encasement around the axillary fat pad. It is important to divide these layers early in the dissection. The borders of the pectoralis major and the latissimus dorsi are then exposed, which clears the medial and lateral borders of the dissection.

The axillary vein and the thoracodorsal bundle are identified next. As discussed (see above), the initial identification of the axillary vein should be made medially, under the pectoralis major, to prevent injury to low-lying branches of the brachial plexus. Sometimes, the axillary vein takes the form of several small branches rather than a single large vessel. If this is the case, all of the small branches should be preserved.

The thoracodorsal bundle may be identified either distally at its junction with the latissimus dorsi or at its junction with the axillary vein. The junction with the latissimus dorsi is within the axillary fat pad at a point two thirds of the way down the hair-bearing skin of the axilla, or approximately 4 cm below the inferior border of the axillary vein. Occasionally, the thoracodorsal bundle is bifurcated, with separate superior and inferior branches entering the latissimus dorsi; this is particularly likely if the entry point appears very high. If the bundle is bifurcated, both branches should be preserved. The thoracodorsal bundle may be identified at its junction with the latissimus dorsi by spreading within axillary fat parallel to the border of the muscle and looking for the blue of the thoracodorsal vein. Identification is also facilitated by lateral retraction of the latissimus dorsi. The long thoracic nerve lies just medial to the thoracodorsal bundle on the chest wall at this point and at approximately the same anterior-posterior position. It may be identified by spreading tissue just medial to the thoracodorsal bundle, then running the index finger perpendicular to the course of the long thoracic nerve on the chest wall to identify the cordlike nerve as it moves under the finger. Once the nerve is identified, axillary tissue may be swept anteriorly away from the nerve by blunt dissection along the anterior serratus muscle; there are no significant vessels in this area.

The junction of the thoracodorsal bundle with the axillary vein is 1.5 to 2.0 cm medial to the point at which the axillary vein crosses the latissimus dorsi. The thoracodorsal vein enters the posterior surface of the axillary vein, and the nerve and the artery pass posterior to the axillary vein. There are generally one or two scapular veins that branch off the axillary vein medial to the junction with the thoracodorsal vein. These are divided during the dissection and should not be confused with the thoracodorsal bundle.

The axillary vein and the thoracodorsal bundle having been identified, the pectoralis major is retracted medially at the level of the axillary vein, and the latissimus dorsi is retracted laterally to place tension on the thoracodorsal bundle. Once this exposure is achieved, the axillary fat and the nodes are cleared away superficial and medial to the thoracodorsal bundle to the level of the axillary vein. Superiorly, dissection proceeds medially along the axillary vein to the point where the fat containing level II nodes crosses the axillary vein. To improve exposure, the fascia overlying the level II extension of the axillary fat pad should be incised to release tension and expose the lipomalike level II fat. As noted [see Structures to Be Preserved, *above*], the medial pectoral nerve passes onto the underside of the pectoralis major in this area and should be preserved. One or more small venous branches may pass inferiorly from the medial pectoral bundle; particular attention should be paid to preserving the nerve when ligating these venous branches.

The next step in the dissection is to reflect the axillary fat pad inferiorly by dividing the medial attachments of the axillary fat pad along the anterior serratus muscle. Care must be taken to preserve the long thoracic nerve. Because there are no significant vessels or structures in the tissue anterior to the long thoracic nerve, this tissue may be divided sharply, with small perforating vessels either tied or cauterized. Finally, the axillary fat is freed from the tail of the breast with the electrocautery or a knife.

There is no need to orient the axillary specimen for the pathologist, because treatment is not affected by the anatomic level of node involvement. A closed suction drain is placed through a separate stab wound. (Some practitioners prefer not to place a drain and simply aspirate postoperative seromas as necessary.) A long-acting local anesthetic may be instilled into the axilla—a particularly helpful practice if the dissection was done as an outpatient procedure.

Mastectomy

The goal of a mastectomy is to remove all breast tissue—including the nipple, the areola, and the pectoral fascia—while leaving viable skin flaps and a smooth chest wall for application of prosthesis. This should be the objective whether the mastectomy is performed for cancer treatment or for prophylaxis. Skin-sparing mastectomy (SSM) performed in conjunction with immediate reconstruction is discussed elsewhere [see Breast Reconstruction after Mastectomy, *below*]. Proper skin incisions and good exposure are the key components of a well-performed mastectomy. Mastectomy usually calls for general anesthesia, but it may be performed with thoracic epidural anesthesia or local anesthesia in select circumstances.

OPERATIVE TECHNIQUE

The traditional mastectomy incision is an elliptical one that is placed either transversely across the chest wall or at an upward angle toward the axilla. It should be fashioned in such a way as to include the nipple-areola complex and any incision from a previous biopsy [see Figure 11a]. Ideally, the upper and lower skin flaps should be of similar length so that there is no redundant skin on either flap. The outline of the incision may be established by using the following five steps.

1. The lateral and medial end points are marked.
2. The breast is pulled firmly downward.
3. To define the path of the upper incision, a straight line is drawn from one end point to the other across the upper surface of the breast.
4. The breast is pulled firmly upward.
5. To define the path of the lower incision, a straight line is drawn from one end point to the other across the lower surface of the breast.

The outlined incision is then checked to confirm that it can be closed without either undue tension or redundant skin. Dog-ears or lateral skin folds can be prevented by extending the incision medially or laterally to remove all the skin that contributes to the forward projection of the breast. The closure should be fairly snug intraoperatively while the arm is extended; significant slack will be created when the arm is returned to the patient's side. The medial and lateral end points of the incision may be adjusted upward or downward to include any previous biopsy incisions.

As noted [see Partial Mastectomy, *above*], there is increasing acceptance of the use of radial and oncoplastic incisions for BCT. In a small percentage of women, persistently positive margins may dictate conversion from BCT to mastectomy. In large-breasted women with excess breast skin, traditional elliptical incisions can easily incorporate any previous radial or superior-pole oncoplastic incisions that may have been performed [see Figure 11b]. In smaller-breasted women, however, sigmoid, modified Wise, or other oncoplastic mastectomy incisions may be needed to incorporate previous lumpectomy incisions [see Figure 11c].

Once the incision is made, the next step is to create even and viable flaps. In most patients, there is a fairly well defined avascular plane between subcutaneous fat and breast tissue. This plane is identified by pulling the edges of the incision upward with skin hooks and beginning a flap that is 8 to 10 mm thick. After an initial release of the skin edge, the desired plane is developed by applying firm tension downward on the breast tissue and away from the skin at a 45° angle. The fine fibrous attachments between breast tissue and subcutaneous fat (Cooper's ligaments) are then divided with the electrocautery or a blade, and crossing vessels are coagulated or ligated as they appear. To protect both arterial supply to and venous drainage from the skin flap, one must refrain from excessive ligation or cauterization of vessels on the flap. For most women, flap viability is not an issue. For diabetics, smokers, and other patients with diffuse small vessel disease, however, it is a serious consideration. In such patients, flaps should be no longer than necessary with no

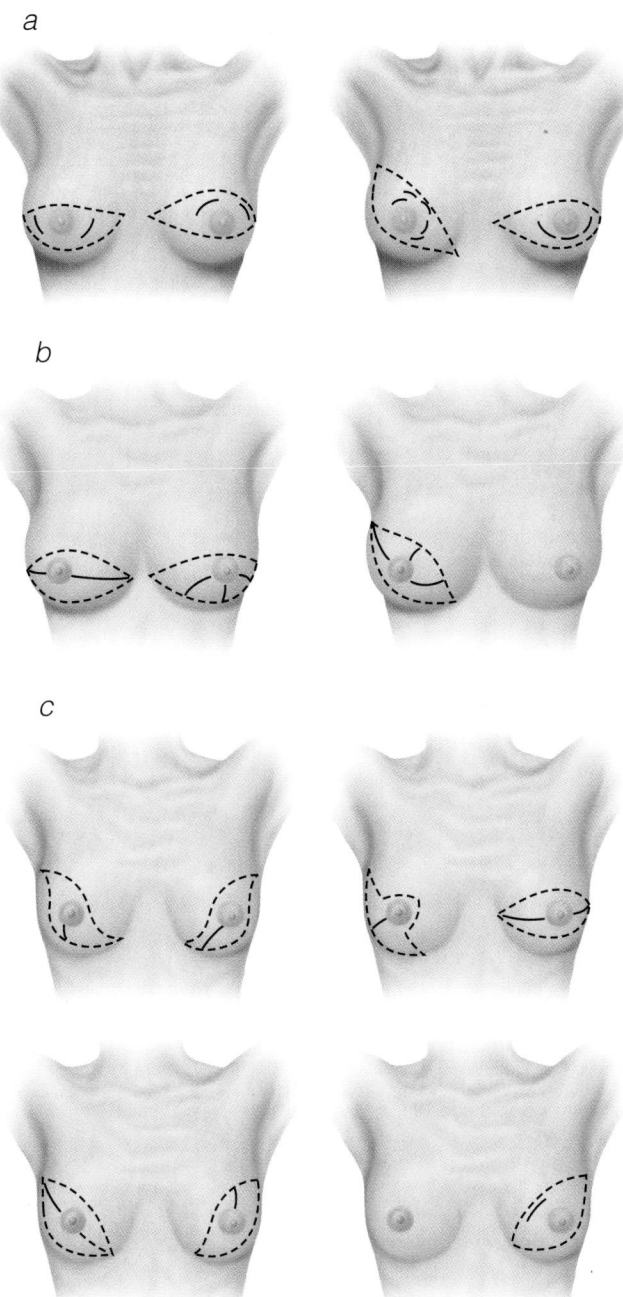

Figure 11 **Mastectomy incisions. (a) Elliptical incisions incorporate traditional lumpectomy incisions. (b) In large-breasted women with excess breast skin, traditional ellipses can easily incorporate previous radial and superior-pole oncoplastic incisions. (c) In smaller-breasted women, sigmoid, modified Wise, or other oncoplastic mastectomy incisions may be needed to incorporate previous radial lumpectomy incisions.**

excess tension, and extra care should be taken to preserve flap vessels. Patients should be warned that even with these measures, there may be some skin necrosis along the incision. Such necrosis is best treated with gradual debridement of the eschar.

Flaps are raised superiorly to the clavicle, medially to the sternum, inferiorly to the inframammary fold, and laterally to the border of the latissimus dorsi. The pectoral fascia is incised both superiorly and medially. Inferiorly, the fascia of the abdominal muscles is not divided. The pectoralis major, the abdominal muscles, and the anterior serratus muscle form the deep border of the dissection. The

pectoral fascia is removed with the breast specimen and may be separated from the muscle with either the electrocautery or a blade.

In a simple mastectomy, the dissection proceeds around the lateral edge of the pectoralis major but stops before entering the axillary fat pad (unless the procedure is being done in conjunction with SLNB). A single closed suction drain is placed through a separate lateral stab wound in such a way that it extends under the lower flap and a short distance upward along the sternal border of the dissection.

A modified radical mastectomy essentially consists of an axillary node dissection added to a simple mastectomy. At the lateral edge of the dissection, the border of the latissimus dorsi is exposed, as is the lateral border of the pectoral muscle. Retraction of these two muscles provides excellent exposure for the axillary dissection [*see* Axillary Dissection, *above*]. Some surgeons prefer to remove the breast from the chest wall first, wheareas others leave the breast attached to provide tension for the axillary dissection. Upon completion of the procedure, two closed suction drains are placed, one in the axilla and another under the lower flap and extending to the midline.

After either a simple or a modified radical mastectomy, the skin is closed and a dressing applied according to the surgeon's preference. Early arm mobilization is encouraged.

Breast Reconstruction after Mastectomy

The vast majority of women undergoing mastectomy are candidates for breast reconstruction and should be offered a plastic surgery consultation before undergoing definitive surgical treatment. Reconstruction is covered by insurance and may be done either at the time of the mastectomy (immediate reconstruction) or as a delayed procedure (delayed reconstruction). Regardless of when it is done, reconstruction does not interfere with detection of recurrent disease. Immediate breast reconstruction does not significantly delay subsequent adjuvant therapy, and if it is done through a skin-sparing incision (see below), it may contribute to a more natural cosmetic outcome. Options for reconstruction include implants with tissue expansion, the transverse rectus abdominis myocutaneous (TRAM) flap, the latissimus dorsi myocutaneous flap, and various free flaps. Patient preference and lifestyle, the availability of suitable autologous tissue, and the demands imposed by additional cancer therapies are variables that can influence the timing and choice of the optimal reconstructive technique [*see Figure 12*].

Patients who definitely need radiation therapy after mastectomy are at higher risk for complications after reconstruction. Whereas most physicians recommend delayed reconstruction in such cases, a small percentage of these patients undergo immediate reconstruction, incurring higher risk in the process. If the need for postmastectomy radiation therapy is unclear at the time of mastectomy (i.e., final pathology results are not available), a delayed-immediate reconstruction may be performed. An expander is placed at the time of SSM to preserve the breast skin envelope, and the definitive reconstructive plan is formulated once the final pathologic results have become available and the need for radiation therapy has been determined.[51]

SKIN-SPARING MASTECTOMY

SSM, which consists of resection of the nipple-areola complex, any existing biopsy scar, and the breast parenchyma, followed immediately by breast reconstruction, has become an increasingly popular approach for women requiring mastectomy.[52] With this approach, the inframammary fold is preserved, and a generous skin envelope remains after reconstruction; cosmetic results are thereby optimized. In addition, SSM is oncologically safe and is

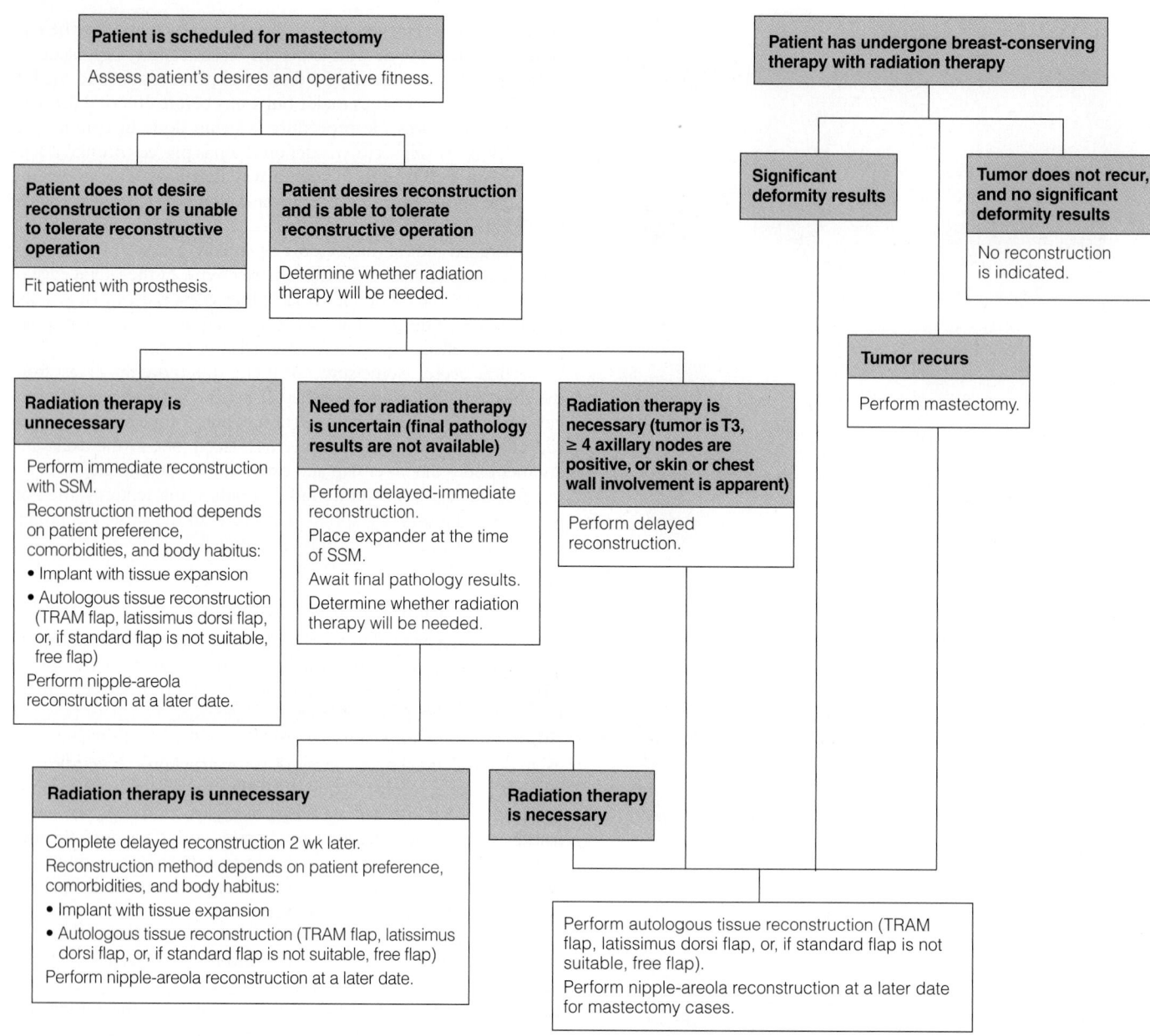

Patient is scheduled for mastectomy

Assess patient's desires and operative fitness.

Patient does not desire reconstruction or is unable to tolerate reconstructive operation

Fit patient with prosthesis.

Patient desires reconstruction and is able to tolerate reconstructive operation

Determine whether radiation therapy will be needed.

Radiation therapy is unnecessary

Perform immediate reconstruction with SSM.
Reconstruction method depends on patient preference, comorbidities, and body habitus:
• Implant with tissue expansion
• Autologous tissue reconstruction (TRAM flap, latissimus dorsi flap, or, if standard flap is not suitable, free flap)
Perform nipple-areola reconstruction at a later date.

Need for radiation therapy is uncertain (final pathology results are not available)

Perform delayed-immediate reconstruction.
Place expander at the time of SSM.
Await final pathology results.
Determine whether radiation therapy will be needed.

Radiation therapy is necessary (tumor is T3, ≥ 4 axillary nodes are positive, or skin or chest wall involvement is apparent)

Perform delayed reconstruction.

Patient has undergone breast-conserving therapy with radiation therapy

Significant deformity results

Tumor does not recur, and no significant deformity results

No reconstruction is indicated.

Tumor recurs

Perform mastectomy.

Radiation therapy is unnecessary

Complete delayed reconstruction 2 wk later.
Reconstruction method depends on patient preference, comorbidities, and body habitus:
• Implant with tissue expansion
• Autologous tissue reconstruction (TRAM flap, latissimus dorsi flap, or, if standard flap is not suitable, free flap)
Perform nipple-areola reconstruction at a later date.

Radiation therapy is necessary

Perform autologous tissue reconstruction (TRAM flap, latissimus dorsi flap, or, if standard flap is not suitable, free flap).
Perform nipple-areola reconstruction at a later date for mastectomy cases.

Figure 12 **Algorithm outlines the major steps in breast reconstruction after mastectomy.**

not associated with an increased incidence of local recurrence.[53] The recurrences that do occur typically develop below the skin flaps and thus are easily detectable; deep recurrences beneath the reconstruction are comparatively uncommon.

The incision for SSM with immediate reconstruction should be planned in collaboration with the plastic surgeon [*see Figure 13*], and the inframammary fold should be marked preoperatively with the patient in a sitting position. Several options are available for SSM. For CNB-diagnosed tumors that are not superficial, a circumareolar incision may be employed, with a lateral extension for exposure if necessary. Different incisions may be used if it proves necessary to incorporate previous incisions or to remove skin anterior to superficial tumors. A separate axillary incision may be useful when axillary dissection or SLNB is being performed. Select patients may be candidates for newer techniques that spare the nipple, the areola, or both; however, these techniques are still under investigation, and long-term follow-up is required to determine their utility and applicability. CNB sites generally are not

included in the excised skin segment, the surgeon may opt to excise them through a separate skin ellipse. Intraoperatively, flaps are created in a circular fashion to optimize exposure. Although optimal cosmesis is part of the rationale for SSM, cosmetic considerations should never be allowed to compromise the extent of the dissection in any way.

RECONSTRUCTION OPTIONS

Prosthetic Implants

The simplest method of reconstruction is to place a saline- or silicone-filled implant beneath the pectoralis major. Even after SSM, the pectoralis major is usually so tight that expansion of this muscle and the skin is necessary before an implant that matches the opposite breast can be inserted. Serial expansions are performed on an outpatient basis until an appropriate size has been attained. A second operative procedure is then required to exchange the expander for a permanent implant. A nipple and an areola are constructed at

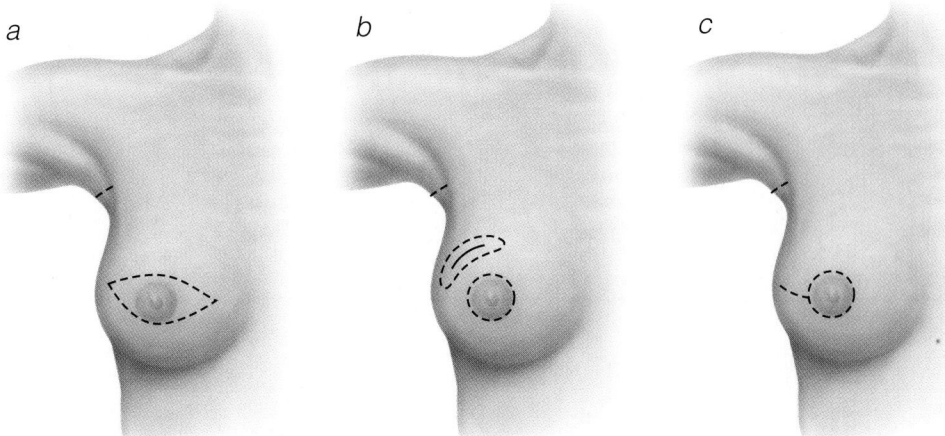

Figure 13 **Skin-sparing mastectomy. Shown is the recommended placement of a circumareolar incision for SSM. A lateral extension can provide further exposure for flap development or axillary staging. Separate incisions may be used to excise previous lumpectomy incisions or to gain access to the axilla.**

a later date. AlloDerm (LifeCell Corp., Branchburg, New Jersey), an acellular dermal matrix derived from human cadaver skin, may be sewn to the pectoralis muscle and the inframammary fold to reinforce the lower pole of the breast.[54] This measure may reduce postoperative pain and improve cosmesis, as well as facilitate immediate implant placement in smaller-breasted women.

The major advantages of implant reconstruction are reduced operating time, faster recuperation, and a reasonably good cosmetic outcome. The cosmetic result may deteriorate over time as a consequence of capsule formation or implant migration, and the implant may have to be replaced after each decade of use.

Autologous Tissue

An alternative approach to reconstruction is to transfer vascularized muscle, skin, and fat from a donor site to the mastectomy defect. The most commonly used myocutaneous flaps are the TRAM flap [*see Figure 14*] and the latissimus dorsi flap [*see Figure 15*]. Use of the free TRAM flap is advocated by certain centers and may be a preferred option for patients who smoke or are diabetic or obese.

The major advantage of autologous tissue reconstruction is that it generally yields a superior cosmetic result that remains stable over time; in addition, the reconstructed breast has a softer, more natural texture than a breast that has undergone implant recon-

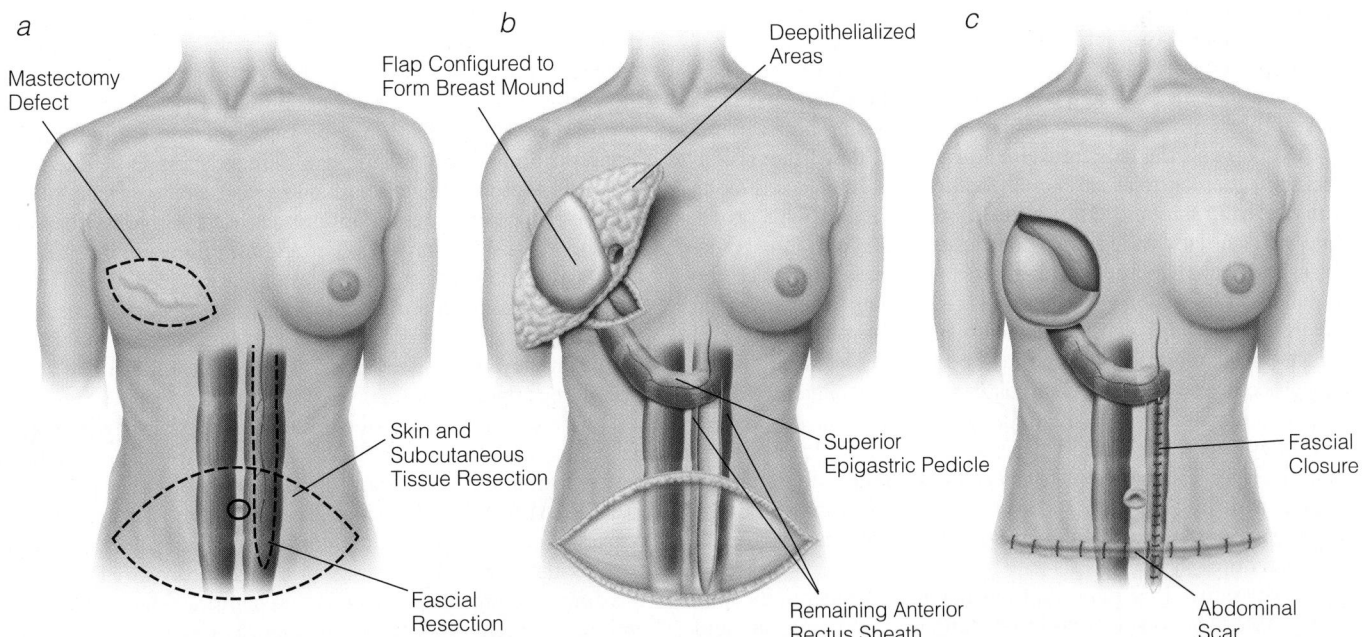

Figure 14 **Breast reconstruction after mastectomy: TRAM flap. (*a*) The infraumbilical flap is designed. The TRAM flap is tunneled subcutaneously into the chest wall cavity. Blood supply to the flap is maintained from the superior epigastric vessels of the rectus abdominis. (*b*) Subcutaneous fat and deepithelialized skin are positioned under the mastectomy flaps as needed to reconstruct the breast mound. (*c*) The fascia of the anterior rectus sheath is approximated to achieve a tight closure of the abdominal wall defect and to prevent hernia formation. The umbilicus is sutured into its new position.**

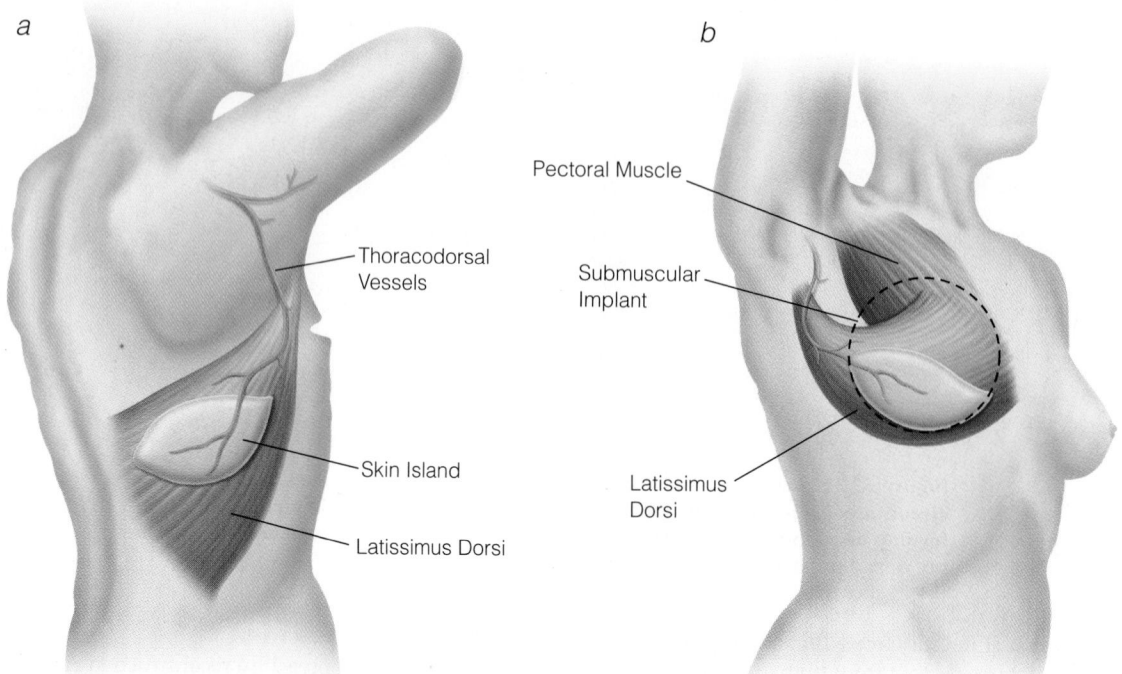

Figure 15 **Breast reconstruction after mastectomy: latissimus dorsi myocutaneous flap with submuscular implant. With this flap, addition of an implant is often required to provide the reconstructed breast with adequate volume and projection. (*a*) The myocutaneous flap is elevated; it is important to maintain the blood supply to the flap from the thoracodorsal vessels. The flap is tunneled subcutaneously to the mastectomy defect. (*b*) The latissimus dorsi is sutured to the pectoralis major and the skin of the inframammary fold, so that the implant is completely covered by muscle.**

struction. The main drawbacks are the magnitude of the surgical procedure (involving both a prolonged operating time and longer inpatient hospitalization), the potential need for blood transfusion, and the pain and loss of muscle function that arise at the donor site. Smokers and patients with significant vascular disease may not be ideal candidates for autologous tissue reconstruction. Partial necrosis of the transferred flap may create firm areas; on rare occasions, complete necrosis and consequent loss of the flap can occur.

A number of factors are considered in choosing between the TRAM flap and the latissimus dorsi flap. In a TRAM flap reconstruction, the contralateral rectus abdominis is transferred along with overlying skin and fat to create a breast mound. This procedure yields a flatter abdominal contour but calls for a long transverse abdominal incision and necessitates repositioning of the umbilicus. The major advantages of TRAM flap reconstruction are that it provides enough tissue to match most contralateral breasts and that it offers the option of performing bilateral TRAM flap procedures in healthy candidates who want bilateral reconstruction. Patients who have undergone abdominal procedures that compromise the TRAM flap's vascular supply are not ideal candidates for TRAM reconstruction. Postoperative discomfort is greater with TRAM flap reconstruction than with other flap reconstructions because of the extent of the abdominal portion of the procedure.

In a latissimus dorsi myocutaneous flap reconstruction, the ipsilateral latissimus dorsi is transferred along with overlying skin and fat to create a breast mound. The operative technique for the latissimus dorsi flap reconstruction is complex, requiring intraoperative changes in patient position (unless the oncologic surgeon is willing to perform the mastectomy with the patient in a lateral decubitus position). Patients who have undergone irradiation of the breast, the chest wall, or the axilla (including irradiation of the thoracodorsal vessels) may not be eligible for this procedure. A major advantage of the latissimus dorsi flap is that its donor site is associated with less postoperative discomfort than the abdominal donor site of the TRAM flap. In addition, transfer of the latissimus dorsi results in substantially less functional impairment than transfer of the rectus abdominis. One major drawback is that in many women, the latissimus dorsi is not bulky enough to provide symmetry with the contralateral breast; consequently, to match the size of the opposite breast, the flap must be supplemented with an implant. Thus, the drawback of the implant's limited lifespan is added to the drawbacks associated with autologous tissue reconstruction.

Free-flap reconstruction options are used primarily when other autologous and implant reconstruction options are not available, do not provide sufficient tissue volume, or have failed. They are more complex procedures, requiring microvascular anastomoses and carrying a higher risk of total flap loss. The two most commonly employed free-flap options are the free TRAM flap and the free gluteus flap.

Donor-site morbidity—including postoperative pain, wound-healing complications, decreased abdominal muscle strength, and hernia formation—is a prime disadvantage of either pedicled or free TRAM flap reconstruction. As a result, muscle-sparing alternatives to autogenous breast reconstruction have been developed, such as the deep inferior epigastric perforator (DIEP) flap.[55] In this approach, free flaps are used that comprise skin and fat alone, without the rectus abdominis. Avoidance of muscle sacrifice in the abdomen ultimately translates into greater patient satisfaction, but careful patient selection is essential to optimize outcomes. The disadvantages of the DIEP flap include the considerable technical expertise and long operating time required, as well as the greater potential for flap loss (because this flap has a more tenuous blood supply than the standard TRAM flap).

References

1. Liberman L: Percutaneous image-guided core breast biopsy. Radiol Clin North Am 40:483, 2002

2. Shoher A, Lucci A: Emerging patterns of practice in the implementation and application of sentinel lymph node biopsy in breast cancer patients in the United States. J Surg Oncol 83:65, 2003

3. Fisher B, Anderson S, Redmond CK, et al: Reanalysis and results after 12 years of follow-up in a randomized clinical trial comparing total mastectomy with lumpectomy with or without irradiation in the treatment of breast cancer. N Engl J Med 333:1456, 1995

4. Shons AR, Mosiello G: Postmastectomy breast reconstruction: current techniques. Cancer Control 8:419, 2001

5. Dowlatshahi K, Francescatti DS, Bloom KJ, et al: Image-guided surgery of small breast cancers. Am J Surg 182:419, 2001

6. Newman LA, Blake C: Ductal lavage for breast cancer risk assessment. Cancer Control 9:473, 2002

7. Dooley WC, Ljung BM, Veronesi U, et al: Ductal lavage for detection of cellular atypia in women at high risk for breast cancer. J Natl Cancer Inst 93:1624, 2001

8. Moncrief RM, Nayar R, Diaz, LK, et al: A comparison of ductoscopy-guided and conventional surgical excision in women with spontaneous nipple discharge. Ann Surg 241:575, 2005

9. Dooley WC: Routine operative breast endoscopy during lumpectomy. Ann Surg Oncol 10:38, 2003

10. Escobar PF, Crowe JP, Matsunaga T, et al: The clinical applications of mammary ductoscopy. Am J Surg 191:211, 2006

11. Mokbel K, Elkak AE: The evolving role of mammary ductoscopy. Curr Med Res Opin 18:30, 2002

12. Stanley MW, Sidawy MK, Sanchez MA, et al: Current issues in breast cytopathology. Am J Clin Pathol 113(5 suppl 1):S49, 2000

13. Choi JY, Alderman AK, Newman LA: Aesthetic and reconstruction considerations in oncologic breast surgery. J Am Coll Surg 202:943, 2006

14. Burbank F: Stereotactic breast biopsy of atypical ductal hyperplasia and ductal carcinoma in situ lesions: improved accuracy with directional, vacuum-assisted biopsy. Radiology 202:843, 1997

15. Hoorntje LE, Peeters PH, Mali WP, et al: Vacuum-assisted breast biopsy: a critical review. Eur J Cancer 39:1676, 2003

16. King TA, Fuhrman GM: Image-guided breast biopsy. Semin Surg Oncol 20:197, 2001

17. Jacobs TW, Connolly JL, Schnitt SJ: Nonmalignant lesions in breast core needle biopsies: to excise or not to excise? Am J Surg Pathol 26:1095, 2002

18. Kass R, Henry-Tillman RS, Nurko J, et al: Touch preparation of breast core needle specimens is a new method for same-day diagnosis. Am J Surg 186:737, 2003

19. Johnson AT, Henry-Tillman RS, Smith LF, et al: Percutaneous excisional breast biopsy. Am J Surg 184:550, 2002

20. Fine RE, Boyd BA, Whitworth PW, et al: Percutaneous removal of benign breast masses using a vacuum-assisted hand-held device with ultrasound guidance. Am J Surg 184:332, 2002

21. Bloom K, Fine RE, Lerner AG, et al: Intact specimen capture and collection of image-detected breast lesions via percutaneous radiofrequency device. American Society of Breast Surgeons, Las Vegas, Nevada, March 31–April 4, 2004

22. Whitworth PW, Rewcastle JC: Cryoablation and cryolocalization in the management of breast disease. J Surg Oncol 90:1, 2005

23. Mullen DJ, Eisen RN, Newman RD, et al: The use of carbon marking after stereotactic large-core-needle breast biopsy. Radiology 218:255, 2001

24. Marx M, Bernstein RM, Wack JP: Xylocaine plus methylene blue vs methylene blue alone for marking breast tissue preoperatively. AJR Am J Roentgenol 160:896, 1993

25. Gray RJ, Salud C, Nguyen K, et al: Randomized prospective evaluation of a novel technique for biopsy or lumpectomy of nonpalpable breast lesions: radioactive seed versus wire localization. Ann Surg Oncol 8:711, 2001

26. Smith LF, Henry-Tillman R, Harms S, et al: Hematoma-directed ultrasound-guided breast biopsy. Ann Surg 233:669, 2001

27. Smith LF, Henry-Tillman R, Rubio IT, et al: Intraoperative localization after stereotactic breast biopsy without a needle. Am J Surg 182:584, 2001

28. Morrow M: Management of common breast disorders. Breast Diseases, 2nd ed. Hellman S, Harris JR, Henderson IC, et al, Eds. JB Lippincott Co, Philadelphia, 1991

29. Smith J: Ductal exploration for nipple discharge. Contemp Surg 59:518, 2003

30. Kunos C, Latson L, Overmoyer B, et al: Breast conservation surgery achieving > or = 2 mm tumor-free margins results in decreased local-regional recurrence rates. Breast J 12:28, 2006

31. Silverstein M: Ductal carcinoma in situ: basics, treatment controversies, and an oncoplastic approach. Surgery of the Breast. Spear S, Ed. Lippincott Williams & Wilkins, Philadelphia, 2006, p 92

32. Grisotti A: Conservative treatment of breast cancer: reconstructive problems. Surgery of the Breast. Spear S, Ed. Lippincott Williams & Wilkins, Philadelphia, 2006, p 147

33. Smith LF, Rubio IT, Henry-Tillman R, et al: Intraoperative ultrasound-guided breast biopsy. Am J Surg 180:419, 2000

34. Kuerer HM: The case for accelerated partial-breast irradiation for breast cancer—M.D. Anderson Cancer Center telemedicine symposium. Contemp Surg 59:508, 2003

35. Wallner P, Arthur D, Bartelink H, et al: Workshop on partial breast irradiation: state of the art and the science, Bethesda, Maryland, December 8–10, 2002. J Natl Cancer Inst 96:175, 2004

36. Simmons RM: Ablative techniques in the treatment of benign and malignant breast disease. J Am Coll Surg 197:334, 2003

37. Turner RR, Ollila DW, Krasne DL, et al: Histopathologic validation of the sentinel lymph node hypothesis for breast carcinoma. Ann Surg 226:271, 1997

38. Krag D, Weaver D, Ashikaga T, et al: The sentinel node in breast cancer—a multicenter validation study. N Engl J Med 339:941, 1998

39. Sabel MS, Schott AF, Kleer CG, et al: Sentinel node biopsy prior to neoadjuvant chemotherapy. Am J Surg 186:102, 2003

40. Schwartz G, Giuliano A: Proceeding of the consensus conference of the role of sentinel lymph node biopsy in carcinoma or the breast April 19–22, 2001, Philadelphia, PA, USA. Breast J 8:124, 2002

41. Layeeque R, Kepple J, Henry-Tillman RS, et al: Intraoperative subareolar radioisotope injection for immediate sentinel lymph node biopsy. Ann Surg 239:841, 2004

42. Ozmen V, Cabioglu N: Sentinel lymph node biopsy for breast cancer: current controversies. Breast J 12(5 suppl 2):S134, 2006

43. Rubio IT, Klimberg VS: Techniques of sentinel lymph node biopsy. Semin Surg Oncol 20:214, 2001

44. Layeeque R, Henry-Tillman R, Korourian S, et al: Subareolar sentinel node biopsy for multiple breast cancers. Am J Surg 186:730, 2003

45. Camp R, Feezor R, Kasraeian A, et al: Sentinel lymph node biopsy for ductal carcinoma in situ: an evolving approach at the University of Florida. Breast J 11:394, 2005

46. Lagios MD, Silverstein MJ: Sentinel node biopsy for patients with DCIS: a dangerous and unwarranted direction. Ann Surg Oncol 8:275, 2001

47. Farkas EA, Stolier AJ, Teng SC, et al: An argument against routine sentinel node mapping for DCIS. Am Surg 70:13, 2004

48. Mamounas EP, Brown A, Anderson S, et al: Sentinel node biopsy after neoadjuvant chemotherapy in breast cancer: results from National Surgical Adjuvant Breast and Bowel Project Protocol B-27. J Clin Oncol 23:2694, 2005

49. Jones JL, Zabicki K, Christian RL, et al: A comparison of sentinel node biopsy before and after neoadjuvant chemotherapy: timing is important. Am J Surg 190:517, 2005

50. Kinne DW: Primary treatment of breast cancer. Breast Diseases, 2nd ed. Hellman S, Harris JR, Henderson IC, et al, Eds. JB Lippincott Co, Philadelphia, 1991

51. Kronowitz SJ, Robb GL: Controversies regarding immediate reconstruction: aesthetic risks of radiation. Surgery of the Breast. Spear S, Ed. Lippincott Williams & Wilkins, Philadelphia, 2006, p 679

52. Hultman CS, Daiza S: Skin-sparing mastectomy flap complications after breast reconstruction: review of incidence, management, and outcome. Ann Plast Surg 50:249, 2003

53. Carlson G: Invasive carcinoma skin sparing mastectomy. Surgery of the Breast. Spear S, Ed. Lippincott Williams & Wilkins, Philadelphia, 2006, p 140

54. Spear S: Immediate breast reconstruction with tissue expanders and AlloDerm. Surgery of the Breast. Spear S, Ed. Lippincott Williams & Wilkins, Philadelphia, 2006, p 484

55. Craigie JE, Allen RJ, DellaCroce FJ, et al: Autogenous breast reconstruction with the deep inferior epigastric perforator flap. Clin Plast Surg 30:359, 2003

56. Urist MM, Bland KI: Indications and techniques for biopsy. The Breast: Comprehensive Management of Benign and Malignant Diseases. Bland KI, Copeland EM III, Eds. WB Saunders Co, Philadelphia, 2004, p 791

Acknowledgment

Figures 2, 3, 5-11, and 13-15   Alice Y. Chen.

LYMPHATIC MAPPING AND SENTINEL LYMPH NODE BIOPSY

Seth P. Harlow, M.D., David N. Krag, M.D., F.A.C.S., Douglas S. Reintgen, M.D., F.A.C.S., Frederick L. Moffat, Jr., M.D., F.A.C.S., and Thomas G. Frazier, M.D., F.A.C.S.

Breast cancer and melanoma are among the most common malignancies treated by U.S. surgeons. In 2003, it was estimated that there were 54,200 new cases of melanoma and 212,600 new cases of breast cancer in the United States.[1] The incidence of melanoma has been rising rapidly in the past few decades, and the incidence of breast cancer is also likely to keep rising as the baby-boomer generation ages.

Over the past 20 years, significant strides have been made in the management of these two diseases from the standpoint of both surgical and adjuvant treatment. For both patients with melanoma and those with breast cancer, adjuvant therapies for high-risk lesions have been shown to have a positive impact on recurrence rates and overall survival. In melanoma, the administration of adjuvant interferon alfa-2b to patients with T4 (> 4.0 mm deep) primary tumors or nodal metastases has led to lower recurrence rates and longer overall survival.[2] In breast cancer, there is a much more extensive body of experience with adjuvant chemotherapy and hormone therapy for optimization of survival in high-risk patients.[3,4] In both diseases, the presence or absence of lymph node metastases is highly predictive of patient outcome and is the most important prognostic factor for disease recurrence and cancer-related mortality. Surgical management of the regional lymph nodes will continue to be an important component of therapy for patients with these malignancies.

Progress in the management of regional lymph nodes in melanoma and in breast cancer has taken different routes to what is likely to be the same destination—namely, the use of lymphatic mapping and sentinel lymph node (SLN) biopsy in clinically node-negative patients. The development of intraoperative lymphatic mapping and selective lymphadenectomy has made it possible to map lymphatic flow from a primary tumor to the initial draining node or nodes (i.e., the SLN or SLNs) in the regional nodal basin. The pathologic status of the SLN is known to be concordant with the pathologic status of the nodal basin as a whole. Integration of these techniques, along with increasingly detailed and sophisticated pathologic examination of the SLN, into the surgical treatment of melanoma and breast cancer offers the potential for more conservative operations, lower morbidity, and more accurate disease staging.

Lymphatic Mapping and SLN Biopsy for Melanoma

RATIONALE

Assessment of Nodal Status

There are several established factors for predicting the risk of metastatic disease in melanoma patients. These factors must be taken into account to ensure that patients are appropriately stratified into different risk groups and hence can receive appro-

priate treatment. The presence of lymph node metastases is the single most powerful predictor of recurrence and survival in melanoma patients: 5-year survival is approximately 40% lower in patients who have lymph node metastases than in those who do not. This finding suggests that many melanoma patients are likely to benefit from accurate nodal staging.

Elective lymph node dissection Until the latter part of the 1990s, elective lymph node dissection (ELND) was the mainstay of the surgeon's armamentarium for nodal staging of melanoma patients. ELND removes clinically negative nodes, as opposed to therapeutic node dissections, which are done for nodes with gross tumor involvement. Opinions are divided as to whether ELND actually extends survival or whether it is solely a staging procedure. Two prospective, randomized trials failed to demonstrate better survival in melanoma patients treated with ELND than in patients undergoing wide local excision (WLE) alone as primary surgical therapy.[5,6] Retrospective studies from large databases, however, suggested that there may be subpopulations of patients who do benefit from ELND. The Intergroup Melanoma Trial was the first randomized study to show enhanced survival in patient subgroups after surgical treatment of clinically occult metastatic melanoma.[7] The benefit was found in patients with melanomas 1.1 to 2.0 mm thick and patients younger than 60 years.[8]

Adjuvant therapy for high-risk melanoma Three national prospective, randomized trials sponsored by the Eastern Cooperative Oncology Group (ECOG) investigated the use of adjuvant interferon alfa-2b in patients with high-risk melanoma. The first trial, ECOG 1684,[2] was the impetus for the Food and Drug Administration's approval of interferon alfa-2b, in that it was the first study to demonstrate that this agent was an effective adjuvant therapy for patients with high-risk melanoma. Patients eligible for ECOG 1684 had either thick primary melanomas (> 4.0 mm thick) or nodal metastases. ECOG 1684 and a subsequent trial, ECOG 1694,[9] reported significant overall survival benefits for patients receiving adjuvant interferon alfa-2b; a third trial, ECOG 1690,[10] did not, though it did show an improvement in disease-free survival for the treated group.

Given the results from the Intergroup Melanoma Trial and the three ECOG trials, one can make a strong argument that when the risk of nodal metastases reaches a certain defined level, a nodal staging procedure should be performed. Because of the morbidity associated with a negative ELND, lymphatic mapping and SLN biopsy has become the de facto procedure of choice for nodal staging in melanoma patients.

Lymphatic mapping and selective lymphadenectomy SLN biopsy in melanoma was first described in 1992 by Morton and associates,[11] who outlined a procedure of intraoperative lymphatic mapping and selective lymphadenectomy in which a vital blue dye was injected into the skin around the site of the primary melanoma. These investigators showed that the SLN is the first node in the lymphatic basin into which the primary melanoma consistently drains (though not necessarily the closest to the primary lesion). They harvested the SLN separately from the remainder of the regional nodes, and they found that the pathologic status of the SLN was highly accurate at predicting the pathologic status of the entire nodal basin, which was surgically removed in all of the patients studied. These findings suggested that melanoma patients could be accurately staged with procedures that were far less extensive than complete nodal dissections.

PREOPERATIVE EVALUATION

Selection of Patients

The risk of nodal metastases in melanoma patients depends on a number of factors, including primary tumor thickness, presence of ulceration, primary tumor location, and patient sex. Any patient with invasive melanoma (Clark level II or higher) is at some risk for nodal metastasis; however, before recommending SLN biopsy, the surgeon should determine what the relative risk of nodal metastasis is with respect to the cost and morbidity of the procedure.

Patients with intermediate-thickness melanomas (1.0 to 4.0 mm) are the ones likely to gain most from SLN biopsy: the risk of nodal metastases in the absence of systemic disease is believed to be highest in this group. In patients with melanomas between 0.76 and 1.0 mm thick, the risk of nodal metastasis is less than 6%, but the procedure can certainly be justified in this population on the basis of its low morbidity. In patients with thin melanomas (< 0.76 mm), several prognostic factors have been shown to identify higher risk, including primary tumor depth of Clark level III or higher, ulceration, the presence of regression, male sex, and axial location.[12] Patients with thin melanomas and multiple risk factors may be at high enough risk to warrant SLN biopsy.

In patients with thick melanomas (> 4.0 mm), the risk of occult systemic metastases is as high as 70%, and that of occult nodal metastases ranges from 60% to 70%. The high risk of systemic disease was the main reason why ELND was not recommended for such patients in the past. Now that these patients have access to effective adjuvant therapy, however, they should be offered lymphatic mapping and SLN biopsy as a staging procedure. Among patients with thick melanomas, those with negative nodes survive longer than those with microscopic nodal dis-

Choice of Radiocolloid and Vital Blue Dye for Lymphatic Mapping

Choice of Radiocolloid

Little work has been done to determine which radiocolloid is best suited to either preoperative or intraoperative mapping. The ideal radiocolloid for intraoperative SLN mapping would have small particles (< 100 nm) that are uniformly dispersed, would be highly stable, and would have a short half-life that would not complicate the handling of the excised specimen. Technetium-99m (^{99m}Tc)–labeled compounds, being gamma emitters, satisfy most of these requirements. In a direct comparison between filtered (0.1 μm filter) ^{99m}Tc-labeled sulfur colloid (TSC) and ^{99m}Tc-labeled antimony trisulfide colloid (T-ATC), which has a particle size of 3 to 30 nm, filtered TSC was transported more quickly to the nodal basin and emitted less radiation to the liver, the spleen, and the whole body.[98] Unfiltered TSC contains relatively large particles (100 to 1,000 nm), and some investigators have found it to migrate more slowly from the injection site; however, other investigators have found it to be slow to flow through the first SLN to higher secondary nodes, which is actually an advantage.

A comparison between Tc-labeled human serum albumin (T-HSA), Tc-labeled stannous phytate, and T-ATC with respect to lymphoscintigram quality showed that T-ATC provided the best images for preoperative lymphoscintigraphy.[99] In an animal study comparing T-HSA with TSC, TSC was actually concentrated in the SLN over a period of 1 to 2 hours, whereas T-HSA passed rapidly through the SLN.[100] As a result, TSC yielded higher activity ratios at intraoperative mapping, improved the success rate of localization, made the technique easier, and thus was a superior reagent for this application.

The Sydney Melanoma Unit (SMU) prefers the use of T-ATC because this agent seems to have smaller, more uniform particles that rapidly migrate into the lymphatic channels but still are appropriately trapped and retained by the SLN. At SMU, use of T-ATC allows injection of the radiocolloid and imaging to be performed on the day before operation. SMU investigators find that hot spots in the regional basin are maintained even when 24 hours have elapsed from the time of injection. The radioactivity in the basin over the hot spot (i.e., the SLN) is decreased because four half-lives of technetium have been expended and because some of the radiocolloid has passed through, but the ex vivo activity ratio is not substantially affected. In the United States, T-ATC has been removed from the market and is unavailable for clinical use. Currently, TSC (filtered or unfiltered) is the agent favored by most surgeons in the United States.

Choice of Vital Blue Dye

Several vital blue dyes have been investigated with an eye to their potential applicability to cutaneous lymphatic mapping. Among these are methylene blue (American Regent, Shirley, NY); isosulfan blue, 1% in aqueous solution (Lymphazurin; United States Surgical Corp., Norwalk, CT); patent blue-V (Laboratoire Guerbet, France); Cyalume (American Cyanamid Co., Bound Brook, NJ); and fluorescein dye. All substances tested were known to be nontoxic in vivo and were injected intradermally as provided by the supplier. In a feline study, patent blue-V and isosulfan blue were the most accurate in identifying the regional lymphatic drainage pattern.[101] These dyes entered the lymphatics rapidly, with minimal diffusion into the surrounding tissue. Their bright-blue color was readily visible and allowed easy identification of the exposed lymphatics.

Isosulfan blue has worked extremely well for intraoperative SLN mapping. In some patients with thin skin, the afferent lymphatics can be seen through the skin after the injection of isosulfan blue. In addition, when the dye enters the SLN, it stains the node a pale blue, thus clearly distinguishing the SLN from the surrounding non-SLNs. The other dyes have largely been abandoned as unsatisfactory because they diffuse too rapidly into surrounding tissue and are not retained by the lymphatic channels in sufficient concentrations to stain the SLN. The fluorescent dyes fluorescein and Cyalume are readily visualized, but a dark room is necessary for optimal visualization; moreover, because of the diffusion of these dyes into surrounding tissue, the background fluorescence is unacceptably high. Methylene blue is relatively poorly retained by the lymphatic vessels and thus stains the SLN too lightly.

Use of vital blue dyes rarely causes complications but has been associated with severe allergic reactions in the literature.[19] Blue dye can be retained at the primary tumor site for more than 1 year. The color gradually fades with time; however, the patient can be left with a permanent tattoo if the injected dye is not removed with the wide excision or the lumpectomy. Fortunately, in the head and neck area, where a permanent tattoo would be unacceptable, the richness of the cutaneous lymphatics allows rapid clearance of the blue dye from the skin and subcutaneous tissues. A small amount of residual blue dye may be left behind after wide excision, but this typically disappears rapidly and poses no real problem. All patients report the presence of dye in the urine and stool during the first 24 hours. In some cases, the dye can interfere with transcutaneous oxygen monitoring during anesthesia.

ease.[13] Accordingly, some medical oncologists simply observe T4 patients unless nodal disease is documented.

The extent of any operation done at the primary site before SLN biopsy may affect the success of the biopsy procedure. In patients who have had large areas of tissue undermining or have undergone reconstruction with a rotational flap or Z-plasty, the normal lymphatic channels may be disrupted, and such disruption may render SLN biopsy inaccurate. Nevertheless, there have been reports of SLN biopsy being performed successfully after previous WLE, which suggests that many of these patients may be salvageable for accurate nodal staging if their primary tumors have been widely excised.[14] These patients may have more SLNs in more regional nodal basins than patients in whom the primary tumor has not been resected with curative intent, but at present, there is no unequivocal evidence that previous WLE of the primary lesion increases the risk of postoperative nodal relapse.[15,16]

OPERATIVE PLANNING

Positioning and Anesthesia

Patients should be prepared to undergo wide excision of the primary melanoma site (where indicated) and SLN biopsy during the same operative session. Depending on the location of the primary lesion, it may be possible to perform the two procedures with the patient in a single position; however, it often happens that the patient must be moved to a different position to afford the surgeon adequate access to the different locations. The choice of anesthesia varies, depending on the size and location of the wide excision and the likely depth of the SLNs. In selected cases, local anesthesia may be appropriate, but for many lesions, general or regional anesthesia is preferable.

OPERATIVE TECHNIQUE

Although the technical details of lymphatic mapping and SLN biopsy for melanoma vary from institution to institution, the reported results of the different approaches have been very similar. Proper performance of these procedures requires close collaboration between the surgeon, the nuclear radiologist, and the pathologist, with each member playing a critical role in the process.

Step 1: Injection of Radiolabeled Tracer and Lymphoscintigraphy

On the day of the procedure, patients report to the nuclear medicine suite for injection of the radiolabeled tracer and preoperative lymphoscintigraphy. It is crucial to have a mechanism in place by which the location of the primary melanoma site and the desired dose of the tracer can be reliably communicated to the nuclear radiologist. Some melanoma biopsy sites are difficult to locate, particularly if multiple skin biopsies have already been performed.

A radiolabeled agent is then selected; the most common choices are technetium-99m(^{99m}Tc)–labeled sulfur colloid (TSC) and ^{99m}Tc-labeled antimony trisulfide colloid (T-ATC) [*see Sidebar* Choice of Radiocolloid and Vital Blue Dye for Lymphatic Mapping]. The dose of the tracer and the volume of the injectate are largely determined by the location and size of the primary tumor site but generally can be kept to 0.5 mCi or less and 1 ml or less, respectively. Injections are made intradermally around the circumference of the lesion or biopsy site, and dynamic scans are taken 5 to 10 minutes after injection. The location of the SLN can be marked on the skin by the radiologist to assist the surgeon; however, this location may vary slightly with changes in patient position and should therefore be confirmed by the surgeon with the gamma probe in the operating room. All regional basins at risk should be marked, along with any in-transit nodes

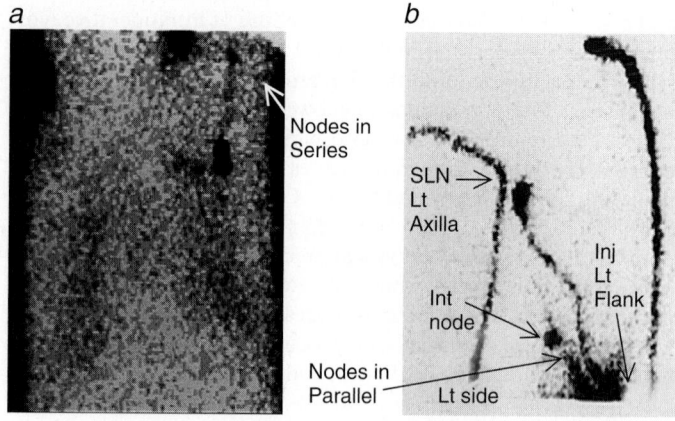

a

b

Lt Lat Chest W/M

Figure 1 Lymphatic mapping and SLN biopsy for melanoma. In-transit nodal areas are identified in 5% of melanoma patients; this is the reason why preoperative lymphoscintigraphy is performed for primary sites on either the upper or the lower extremity. In a patient with a melanoma on the left hand (*a*), the injection site and the left hand are raised above the head, and cutaneous lymphatic flow into an epitrochlear node can be seen. This in-transit node then emits a lymphatic vessel flowing to the left axilla. By definition, the SLN is the first node in the chain that receives primary lymphatic flow. The epitrochlear node and any axillary nodes are nodes in series. Hence, the epitrochlear node is the SLN and thus is the only node that must be harvested. In a patient with a primary melanoma on the left flank (*b*), there are two separate afferent lymphatics, one leading to an SLN in the left axilla and the other leading to an in-transit node on the left flank. These are nodes in parallel in that they both receive primary lymphatic flow from the skin site. Hence, the two nodes are equally at risk for metastatic disease, and both are considered SLNs and must be harvested.

that are identified [*see Figure 1*], to allow accurate nodal staging. Lymphoscintigraphy is also useful in that it provides a good estimate of the number of SLNs the surgeon can expect to find at operation.

The timing of tracer injection in relation to the surgical procedure is not critically important. Activity in the SLNs usually reaches its maximum 2 to 6 hours after injection; waiting longer to carry out the procedure may increase the labeling of secondary nodes. There have, however, been several reports of SLN procedures being accurately performed 16 to 24 hours after tracer injection.[17] Because of the short half-life of technetium (6 hours), delaying procedures for this amount of time may reduce the radioactivity at the injection site and lower the background interference, but because TSC is retained in the SLN dendritic cells, the SLNs can still be easily identified.

Step 2: Intraoperative Lymphatic Mapping and Identification of SLN

It is our practice to review the lymphoscintigram when the patient arrives in the OR, then evaluate him or her with the gamma probe before deciding on positioning; access to nodal basins may be difficult in certain positions. Probe evaluation begins by defining the diffusion zone around the primary tumor site, where SLN identification is not possible. The area between this diffusion zone and the possible nodal drainage sites is then mapped for possible in-transit nodes by means of a systematic but expeditious evaluation for radioactive "hot spots." The gamma probe is moved in a linear fashion between the diffusion zone and the nodal basin. It is then shifted medial or lateral to the previous line, and the process is repeated until the entire area is evaluated. The location of a radioactive hot spot is confirmed by identifying a discrete location where the radioactive counts are higher than the counts found in the tissue 1 to 2 cm more proximal to the injection site (the background skin count). The counts from the hot spot and the background are recorded. The hot-spot site is marked on the skin to allow more direct dissection to the SLN.

Concomitant use of a vital blue dye [see Sidebar Choice of Radiocolloid and Vital Blue Dye for Lymphatic Mapping] is favored by many surgeons. The blue dye is complementary to the radiolabeled tracer; the combination of the two marking agents improves the chances of identifying the SLN and facilitates node retrieval. The blue dye is injected into the dermis immediately adjacent to the melanoma. For lesions on an extremity, the dye may be injected along the proximal margin of the lesion or biopsy site; for lesions on other areas, it should be injected circumferentially. The general recommendation is to wait 5 to 10 minutes after injecting the dye before initiating SLN retrieval.

To minimize the dissection required for node resection, the incision for the SLN biopsy should be made through the hot spot identified by the gamma probe. The incision should also be situated so that it can be incorporated into a longer incision should the finding of a positive SLN necessitate performance of a completion lymph node dissection (CLND). The gamma probe is placed in a sterile sheath and used again after the incision is made to guide further dissection. If blue dye was used, the surgeon can visually follow the blue lymphatic channels to the blue-stained SLN.

An SLN is defined as either (1) the most radioactive node in the basin or (2) a node that either is stained blue or clearly has a blue-stained lymphatic vessel entering it. When an SLN is removed, the ex vivo radioactivity count in the node is recorded. This count is then used as a reference for determining which, if any, of the remaining nodes in that basin (some of which may be potential SLNs) should be removed. In our view, if the radioactivity count in the hottest remaining node in the basin is less than 10% of the ex vivo count in the hottest SLN, none of the remaining nodes should be considered SLNs, and none should be removed.[18] Any nodes whose radioactivity counts exceed this 10% threshold, however, should be removed.

A final count of the SLN biopsy bed is then taken to document that all significantly radiolabeled SLNs have been accounted for and removed. In addition, the tissues are examined for blue-stained lymphatic channels or lymph nodes regardless of radioactivity; as noted, blue staining confers SLN status even if the node is not radioactive. Finally, when it appears that all relevant SLNs have been removed, as confirmed by the final bed count, the tissues are palpated for grossly suspicious nodes. Firm tumor-involved nodes with obstructed afferent lymphatics may divert lymph flow to non-SLNs, and such diversion is a significant cause of false negative SLN biopsy results.

Once an SLN is identified, it should be dissected out with as little trauma to the surrounding tissues as possible. Lymphatic channels to the node should be identified and either tied or clipped to reduce the risk of postoperative seroma formation. Because the gamma probe can localize SLNs with great accuracy, routine dissection of motor nerves is not required; however, knowledge of the likely location of the motor nerves is critical for preventing inadvertent injury to these structures during dissection.

Step 3: Pathologic Evaluation of SLN

The optimal extent of pathologic evaluation of SLNs in patients with melanoma has been the subject of some debate. SLN biopsy allows pathologists to focus their efforts on one node or a small number of nodes, and this focus has led to a process of ultrastaging. Currently employed methods include serial sectioning, immunohistochemical (IHC) staining for melanoma-associated antigens (e.g., S-100 and HMB-45), and reverse transcriptase polymerase chain reaction (RT-PCR) for identification of messenger RNA (mRNA) transcripts of the enzyme tyrosinase. It is clear that these techniques can improve identification of node-positive patients, but it is not yet clear what their prognostic value may be with respect to determining patient outcome and guiding further therapy. Additional study in this area is required to resolve this issue.

COMPLICATIONS

Complications of SLN biopsy are quite uncommon. Allergic reactions to the blue dyes occur in fewer than 1% of patients but can range in severity from mild urticaria to anaphylaxis; thus, the surgical team and the anesthesia team should always be prepared for this uncommon but potentially serious problem.[19] Motor nerve injury is rare. In a series of 30 patients who had head and neck melanomas with SLN drainage to the parotid region, there were no injuries to the facial nerve when the SLN was removed without nerve dissection.[20] Similar results have been reported for nodes in the posterior triangle of the neck and the spinal accessory nerve, as well as for axillary nodes and the long thoracic and thoracodorsal nerves. The incidence of wound complications is quite low (1.7% wound complication rate; 3.0% seroma rate), as is the incidence of postbiopsy lymphedema (0.7%). In the Sunbelt Melanoma Trial, the complication rate in 2,120 patients undergoing SLN biopsy was 4.6%, compared with 23.2% in 444 patients undergoing CLND.[21]

OUTCOME EVALUATION

Studies of SLN biopsy in melanoma patients have demonstrated consistently good technical success and high pathologic accuracy with a variety of different techniques. There have been three studies in which SLN biopsy was done with confirmatory CLND of all lymph node basins in which SLNs were identified.[11,22,23] When the results of these studies are considered together, the pathologic false negative rate for SLN biopsy in clinically node-negative melanoma patients is about 6%. The pathologic accuracy rate (i.e., the rate at which the pathologic status of the SLN is the same as that of the entire nodal basin) is 98%.

Several trials have prospectively followed patients treated with SLN biopsy and subsequent observation if the SLN was negative.[24-27] These trials reported similar rates of technical success (94%–98%) and of node positivity (12% to 16%). The rates of first relapse in the regional nodes in these patients were similar as well (range, 3.8%–8%; mean, 4.4%), a finding that is consistent with the rates of false negative SLNs in the series in which CLND was performed. These studies also found that the pathologic status of the SLNs was the most important predictor of disease-free survival and overall survival, a result that further underscores the accuracy of the procedure and the importance of nodal staging in predicting melanoma outcomes.

The available data suggest that lymphatic mapping is applicable to all primary body sites, including the head and the neck (the most technically demanding sites).[17,28] The best results are achieved with a combination mapping approach that employs both a vital blue dye and a radiocolloid. The procedure is associated with slightly higher false negative rates in patients with head and neck melanoma than in those with melanoma of the trunk or extremities (10% versus 1% to 2%). Nevertheless, the false negative rates with head and neck melanoma are still low enough to justify offering lymphatic mapping to patients—especially given that the only alternative method of obtaining the nodal staging information is CLND, a procedure that carries a much higher morbidity.

Lymphatic Mapping and SLN Biopsy in Breast Cancer

RATIONALE

Assessment of Nodal Status

In early breast cancer, as in melanoma, the pathologic status of the regional lymph nodes is the most important predictor of outcome. The presence of regional lymph node metastases in breast cancer reduces 5-year survival by 28% to 40%.[29,30] Prognostic factors related to primary tumor characteristics have consistently been shown to be inferior to nodal status as predictors of disease outcome. In addition, regional lymph node dissection in the setting of breast cancer is superior to observation and at least equivalent to irradiation for regional disease control in clinically node-negative patients.[31] There is some evidence that adequate regional disease control may confer a small survival benefit.[32]

Invasive breast cancer has a relatively high rate of nodal metastasis in clinically node-negative patients. The risk of metastasis is clearly related to the size of the primary tumor, but it is significant (15% or higher) even in patients with early (T1a) lesions.[33,34] The primary nodal drainage basin for the breast is the ipsilateral axilla; however, drainage to extra-axillary sites (e.g., the internal mammary lymph node chain, the supraclavicular nodes, and the intramammary nodes) is also reported. Other potential sites of lymphatic drainage notwithstanding, the recommended surgical procedure for evaluating the regional lymph nodes in clinically node-negative breast cancer patients has been level I and II axillary lymph node dissection (ALND). Such dissections are, however, associated with a significant risk of long-term morbidity, primarily related to the risk of lymphedema in the affected arm. For this reason, SLN biopsy was developed and investigated as a possible substitute for standard ALND in the treatment of breast cancer.

PREOPERATIVE EVALUATION

Selection of Patients

All clinically node-negative patients with a diagnosis of invasive breast cancer are potential candidates for SLN biopsy. Ideal candidates are those patients with unifocal lesions who have no history of previous axillary surgery or prior cancer treatment. Performing an SLN biopsy after a previous excisional biopsy is technically feasible; however, SLN biopsy may be easier if the lesion is still in place. Patients who have undergone extensive breast procedures (e.g., breast reduction, placement of breast implants, or multiple open biopsies) may have significant alterations in the lymphatic pathways, which may compromise the accuracy of SLN biopsy. Patients with multifocal tumors or inflammatory cancer also are generally poor candidates for SLN biopsy, though there is some evidence suggesting that using periareolar injection sites may allow the procedure to be performed accurately in patients with multifocal disease.[35] The use of SLN biopsy in patients who have received preoperative chemotherapy has been reported in only a very modest number of cases.[36-38]

OPERATIVE PLANNING

Positioning and Anesthesia

Patients should be placed in the supine position, with all potential nodal sites within the operative field. Preoperative lym-

phoscintigraphy may help the surgeon identify SLNs located in extra-axillary sites (e.g., the internal mammary chain). Although SLN biopsy may be performed with the patient under local anesthesia, we favor general anesthesia for this procedure, particularly when it is done in conjunction with the breast excision.

OPERATIVE TECHNIQUE

Step 1: Injection of Radiolabeled Tracer and Lymphoscintigraphy

In the United States, the radiocolloid most commonly employed for SLN biopsy in breast cancer patients is TSC, which may be used either unfiltered or filtered (< 220 nm) [see Sidebar Choice of Radiocolloid and Vital Blue Dye for Lymphatic Mapping]. The ^{99m}Tc dose generally ranges from 0.45 to 1.0 mCi, and the injectate volume ranges from 4 to 8 ml. TSC is injected directly into the breast parenchyma in four to eight locations around the primary tumor site or the biopsy cavity. Because there are fewer lymphatic vessels in the breast parenchyma than in the dermis, it takes longer for the tracer to be transported in sufficient quantity to the SLNs than it does in the setting of melanoma. A minimum of 30 minutes is generally necessary before lymphoscintigraphy is performed or the patient is brought to the OR [see Figure 2].

When the lesion is palpable, injection is guided by the size, shape, and location of the mass. When the lesion is not palpable, injection is guided by ultrasonography or needle-wire localization. If an excisional biopsy was previously performed, the tracer should be injected into the breast parenchyma rather than into the biopsy cavity; it will not diffuse out of the cavity. This is best done under ultrasonographic guidance. In addition, injections should not be made into the retromammary fat or the pectoral fascia, because doing so would lead to wide diffusion of tracer throughout the chest area, which would make nodal identification very difficult.

As in melanoma, the timing of SLN biopsy after tracer injection is not of critical importance. Good results have been obtained with injection-to-biopsy intervals ranging from 30 minutes to 24 hours. The usual recommendation is to wait 1 to 2 hours.

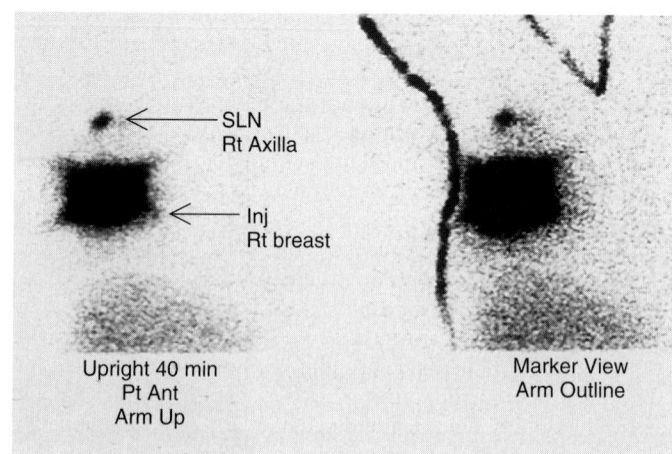

Figure 2 Lymphatic mapping and SLN biopsy for breast cancer. Whereas flow of the radiocolloid to the SLN takes 5 to 10 minutes for melanoma mapping, it takes 30 to 40 minutes for breast cancer mapping. In addition, the primary site is usually closer to the regional basin in breast cancer than it is in melanoma, and shine-through from the primary site may be a problem. Invariably, the lumpectomy or mastectomy is performed first, followed by axillary SLN harvesting.

Comment Several alternative routes of tracer injection have been investigated for SLN biopsy in breast cancer patients, primarily in response to the difficulties sometimes associated with peritumoral injection (e.g., delayed tracer uptake and wide diffusion zones that can overlap the nodal basins). These routes include intradermal or subdermal injection in the area overlying the tumor, subareolar injection, and periareolar injection. The rationale for the development of these alternatives is that there is significant overlap between the lymphatic vessels of the breast skin and those of the breast parenchyma. Multiple studies have confirmed that the use of these injection routes yields high localization rates and results in accurate removal of SLNs that reflect the pathologic nodal status of individual patients. A notable deficiency of these techniques, however, has been the low reported rate of tracer migration to nodes outside the axilla, particularly to the internal mammary lymph node chain. This result is thought to be attributable to a unique set of lymphatic channels deep in the breast parenchyma, separate from the overlying skin, that drain to the internal mammary chain.

Another injection route that has been described is intratumoral injection. This technique employs a very small volume of injectate, thereby avoiding much of the injection-site diffusion issues associated with peritumoral injection. Intratumoral injection gives the radiolabeled tracer access to the deeper lymphatic vessels and identifies SLN drainage to the extra-axillary nodal sites significantly more frequently than even peritumoral injection does.

The various tracer-injection methods have not been directly compared; thus, at present, the optimal route of injection can only be inferred by comparing studies from different institutions. The potential importance of the extra-axillary sites is not entirely clear, but it appears that these sites may be the sole locations of metastatic disease in as many as 20% of the node-positive patients from whom they are removed.[39,40] Most patients in whom SLNs are found outside the axilla have additional SLNs in the axillary basin.

Step 2: Intraoperative Lymphatic Mapping and Removal of SLN

Intraoperative mapping of SLNs is done in essentially the same fashion for breast cancer as for melanoma. Our approach begins by performing a primary survey of the potential nodal sites with the handheld gamma detector. First, the radiotracer injection-site diffusion zone is defined [*see Figure 3*]. The points at which the probe's audio output peaks are marked circumferentially on the skin surrounding the injection site. Within this zone, the probe is unable to identify an SLN.

Next, as in a melanoma survey, the probe is placed close to the skin and moved away from the diffusion zone in a linear manner. As the probe moves further from the injection site, the radioactivity counts decrease. If there is an SLN beneath the area being evaluated, a discrete radioactive hot spot will be identified. The location of the hot spot is marked on the skin, and the remainder of the primary survey is completed, focusing on detecting any additional SLNs. All potential nodal sites (including the supraclavicular and infraclavicular nodes, the internal mammary chain, intramammary sites, and the upper abdomen) are carefully assessed, and finally, the axilla is evaluated. By routinely assessing the other potential sites before the axilla, the surgeon can ensure that they are not overlooked and can confirm that each patient has been optimally evaluated.

Once the hot spots have been identified and marked, the radioactivity counts over each hot spot are recorded, as well as a background count from an area between the hot spot and the injection site, about 2 to 3 cm from the hot spot. If there is indeed a

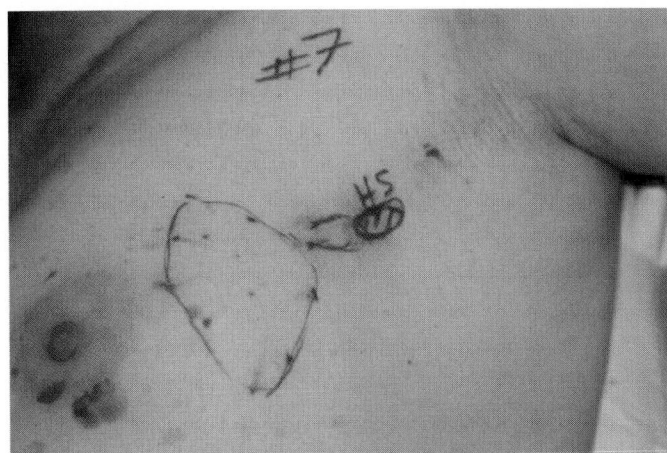

Figure 3 **Lymphatic mapping and SLN biopsy for breast cancer. The diffusion zone of radioactivity around the injection site is circled on the breast. The hot spot in the axilla is marked (HS) as well.**

radioactive SLN below the marked hot spot, the background count should be significantly lower than the hot-spot count.

Next, after the primary survey and counts have been recorded, 5 ml of vital blue dye is injected into the breast parenchyma around the tumor or the biopsy cavity. The breast is gently massaged for 5 to 10 minutes to enhance transport of the dye to the SLNs. A small incision is made at the hot-spot location marked on the skin. The gamma probe is placed in a sterile sheath and inserted into the wound, and the "line of sight" to the point of maximal radioactivity, along which dissection proceeds to the hot node or nodes, is identified. During the dissection, the surgeon looks for blue-stained lymphatic channels and nodes [*see Figure 4*]. Most of the time, the radiocolloid and the vital blue dye identify the same SLNs. The SLNs are then carefully removed, and the lymphatic vessels entering them are tied off whenever possible.

Once the SLNs have been excised, the ex vivo radioactivity count for each one is recorded, as is the presence or absence of blue dye in either the node itself or the lymphatic vessels entering it. The ex vivo count of the excised node is then used as a guide for

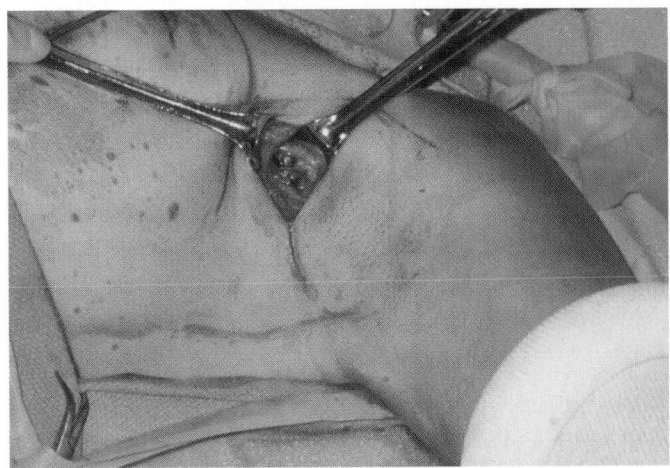

Figure 4 **Lymphatic mapping and SLN biopsy for breast cancer. A small incision is made in the axilla on the basis of the hot-spot location. The SLNs identified are both radioactive and stained blue.**

a   *b*

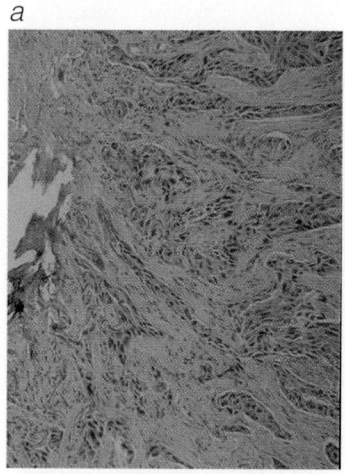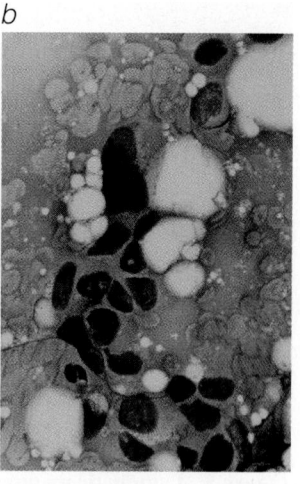

Figure 5 **Lymphatic mapping and SLN biopsy for breast cancer. In touch-imprint cytology, slides are touched to tissue from a "hot" specimen, and cells on the section or the margin are exfoliated onto the slide for cytologic preparation. Shown are (*a*) permanent histology of an infiltrating ductal carcinoma extending down to an inked margin and (*b*) a touch preparation demonstrating bizarre malignant cells from the sampling of the margin. The advantages of this technique are that the entire margin can be sampled and that tissue is not lost in the cryostat.**

determining the completeness of radioactive SLN removal. As in melanoma, if the remaining radioactivity in the nodal basin is more than 10% of that in the hottest node removed, there may be SLNs still in place that should be sought out and, if found, removed. If the residual radioactivity in the nodal basin is less than 10% of that in the hottest node, the remaining nodes should not be removed. These guidelines apply equally to SLN biopsy in extra-axillary locations. The remaining nodes in the nodal basin should also be evaluated for blue staining of the nodes themselves or of the lymphatic channels entering them; any nodes meeting these criteria should be removed and labeled as SLNs.

Finally, before the SLN procedure is completed, the remaining nodes in the basin should be palpated. If a firm, hard tumor-replaced node is identified, it should be removed and categorized as an SLN. As in melanoma, the presence of a tumor-replaced node can increase the risk of a false negative SLN biopsy.

Step 3: Pathologic Evaluation of SLN

Pathologic SLN evaluation in breast cancer patients has two main aspects. The first is intraoperative evaluation of the SLN when the pathologic status of the node is being used to determine the need for axillary dissection; the second is permanent evaluation of the nodes to determine whether micrometastatic disease is present.

Two techniques are commonly employed for intraoperative evaluation of SLNs: frozen-section analysis and touch-imprint cytology. Frozen-section histopathology is available in most hospitals, and all surgical pathologists have some experience with it. This technique has a drawback, however, in that it sometimes uses up a large portion of the SLN, leaving a remnant that is insufficient for permanent paraffin-embedded sections. In addition, the sectioning of radioactive nodes on a cryostat raises radiation-safety issues for the pathologists.

Studies of frozen-section techniques of evaluating SLNs for metastatic breast cancer report false negative rates of 27% and 32%.[41,42] When 60 frozen sections are made from each SLN, the

false negative rate can be reduced to about 5%,[41,43] but at the cost of 45 to 60 minutes of operating time and loss of tissues for permanent histopathologic evaluation. In comparison, touch-imprint cytology consumes much less time and tissue, is far more accurate (false negative rate, 0.8%),[44] and does not contaminate the cryostat. It has also been applied to the evaluation of lumpectomy margins [*see Figure 5*]. The chief limitation of the touch-imprint method is that for optimal results, it requires a pathologist who is highly skilled in the cytologic evaluation of lymph nodes. Some centers use rapid immunohistochemical (IHC) analysis for cytokeratin staining to detect tumor cells in touch-imprint or frozen-section specimens, anticipating that detection of such cells can thereby be improved, particularly in patients with invasive lobular or well-differentiated ductal carcinomas.

Techniques used to date for permanent pathologic evaluation of SLNs in the setting of breast cancer include (1) serial sectioning of the nodes with routine hematoxylin-eosin (H&E) staining, (2) cytokeratin IHC staining [*see Figure 6*], and (3) RT-PCR detection of mRNA transcripts specific for epithelial cells. Each of these techniques is more sensitive in detecting tumor cells in the SLNs than routine H&E analysis of bivalved nodes. There is, however, some controversy surrounding their use, centering on the clinical relevance of a positive result. Some of these techniques (i.e., IHC and RT-PCR) are sensitive enough to identify single tumor cells in SLNs, but it is not clear whether such individual cells are actually capable of forming metastases. In the current staging system for breast cancer, metastases large enough to be seen on H&E sections are the benchmark for nodal staging. Metastases 2 mm in size or larger are known to have a negative impact on survival[45]; however, it is not certain that the same can be said of smaller metastatic lesions. In 1999, the College of American Pathologists issued a consensus statement recommending that the staging of SLNs be based on routine histologic evaluation of the nodes cut at approximately 2 mm intervals.[46] Routine use of cytokeratin IHC staining should not be adopted as standard until its significance is demonstrated in clinical trials.

COMPLICATIONS

The complications of SLN biopsy in breast cancer patients are similar to those seen in melanoma patients. There is a minor

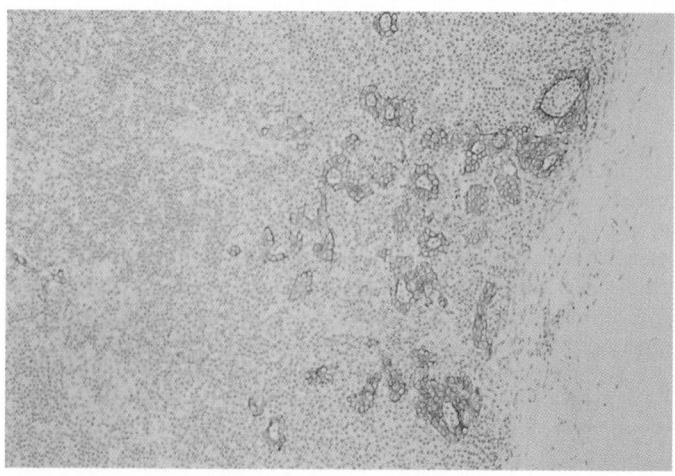

Figure 6 **Lymphatic mapping and SLN biopsy for breast cancer. Cytokeratin immunohistochemical staining finds metastatic cells in 9.4% of breast cancer patients whose SLNs are histologically negative on routine examination.**

Table 1 SLN Identification by Nodal Basin at Different Injection Sites[39,41,50-52,54-95]

Nodal Basin	Injection Location			
	Peritumoral*	Intradermal/Subdermal†	Periareolar/Subareolar‡	Intratumoral§
Axilla	92.0% (range, 86%–100%)	96.4% (range, 93%–100%)	98.4% (range, 94.2%–100%)	92.0% (range, 88%–96%)
Internal mammary chain	4.9% (range, 0%–25.3%)	0.6% (range, 0%–4%)	0%	18.4% (range, 13%–43%)
Other	0.6% (range, 0%–8.4%)	0%	0%	4.3% (range, 0%–33.1%)

*28 trials; 5,924 patients. †11 trials; 1,872 patients. ‡5 trials; 486 patients. §5 trials; 669 patients.

(< 1%) risk of allergic reactions to the blue dye. There is a small risk of sensory or motor nerve injury or lymphedema whenever an axillary node procedure is performed; this risk is substantially reduced, though not entirely eliminated, with SLN biopsy.[47] With an internal mammary SLN biopsy, there is a risk of pneumothorax from unintended opening of the parietal pleura. This risk is very small with careful technique, however, and the problem can almost always be corrected by closing the wound around a rubber catheter inserted through a small stab incision and removing it at the end of a positive pressure breath given by the anesthesiologist. Surgical site infections occur in fewer than 1% of cases, and small seromas occur in about 10%.

OUTCOME EVALUATION

The first report of SLN biopsy in breast cancer, published in 1993, described the use of the gamma-probe localization technique for SLN identification.[48] A second report, published the following year, described the use of the vital blue dye technique for this purpose.[49] Since these initial reports, many single-center and multicenter studies have been published that achieved remarkably similar results using either or both of these techniques.

The early studies of SLN biopsy tended to use either a radiolabeled tracer or a vital blue dye alone. The first trial in which the two agents were used together was published in 1996.[50] This study documented an improvement in SLN localization and a 0% false negative rate, albeit in a small series of patients. Subsequent multicenter trials incorporating larger study groups yielded more reliable indications of the applicability of these techniques to the overall surgical community. In one such study, surgeons from 11 centers performed SLN biopsies and confirmatory axillary dissection in clinically node-negative patients with invasive breast cancer.[51] The overall success rate for identifying and removing an SLN was 93%, the pathologic accuracy rate for predicting the presence

of nodal metastases from the SLNs removed was 97%, and the pathologic false negative rate was 11.4%. A subsequent multicenter trial, using a combination of blue-dye staining and the gamma-probe technique in most patients, reported an SLN retrieval rate of 88% and a pathologic false negative rate of 7.2%.[52] A third trial, using the gamma-probe technique, reported an SLN retrieval rate of 87% and a pathologic false negative rate of 13%.[53] A fourth, using both blue-dye staining and the gamma-probe technique, reported an SLN retrieval rate of 86% and a pathologic false negative rate of 4%.[54]

The numerous single-institution reports on SLN biopsy have made use of a variety of techniques. The technical variable of greatest interest has been the route by which the radiolabeled tracer is injected into the breast. The routes evaluated include peritumoral injection (as in the early studies), superficial injection into the dermis of the skin overlying the tumor site, periareolar or subareolar injection, and, most recently, intratumoral injection.

We have reviewed the literature on the use of different routes of injection and the associated rates of SLN localization by nodal basin, node positivity rates, and false negative rates. This review included those studies in which a radiolabeled tracer was used for SLN identification (either by lymphoscintigraphy or by intraoperative gamma probe localization) and in which the location of the SLN basins and the pathologic status of the SLNs could be ascertained [*see Tables 1, 2, and 3*]. Data on 8,951 patients were reviewed.[39,41,50-52,54-95] The results of our review indicated that all of the approaches have acceptable SLN retrieval rates but that the rates are slightly higher with the more superficial ones (i.e., the dermal, subareolar, and periareolar techniques). There are, however, significant differences in the locations of the SLN basins identified with the different methods: with the superficial injection techniques, drainage is essentially confined to the axillary basin, whereas with the deeper injection techniques, as many as 22% of patients

Table 2 SLN Pathologic Positive Rates by Nodal Basin at Different Injection Sites[39,41,50-52,54-95]

Nodal Basin	Injection Location			
	Peritumoral*	Intradermal/Subdermal†	Periareolar/Subareolar‡	Intratumoral§
Axilla	34.0% (range, 21%–50%)	35.2% (range, 18.2%–51.3%)	26.2% (range, 23.1%–42.1%)	37.8% (range, 12.7%–43.7%)
Internal mammary chain	21.2% (range, 0%–29.2%)	0%	0%	13% (range, 4.2%–25.9%)
Other	NA	0%	0%	3.4%

*28 trials; 5,924 patients. †11 trials; 1,872 patients. ‡5 trials; 486 patients. §5 trials; 669 patients.

Table 3 False Negative SLN Identification Rates at Different Injection Sites[39,41,50-52,54-95]

Injection Location	Evaluable Patients (No.)	False Negative Rate
Peritumoral*	3,909	6.0%
Intradermal/subdermal†	1,734	6.5%
Periareolar/subareolar‡	19	0%
Intratumoral§	126	5.2%

*28 trials; 5,924 patients. †11 trials; 1,872 patients. ‡5 trials; 486 patients. §5 trials; 669 patients.

are found to have nodal basins outside the axilla. Approximately 16% to 21% of the extra-axillary SLNs will be found to have metastatic disease if removed. The clinical ramifications of these findings are that some patients may be understaged if the extra-axillary sites are not evaluated, and such understaging may affect the recommendations for systemic adjuvant therapy. What impact this possibility might have on tumor recurrence rates and patient survival is unknown at present; to resolve the uncertainty would require a large prospective, randomized trial.

To date, the only prospective, randomized trial of SLN biopsy in breast cancer is that of Veronesi and coworkers.[96] In this trial, a total of 516 evaluable patients were randomly assigned to undergo either SLN biopsy with confirmatory axillary dissection (257 patients) or SLN biopsy with axillary dissection done only if the biopsy yielded positive results (259 patients). At a median follow-up point of 46 months, no significant survival differences were reported, and there were no regional nodal recurrences in either arm. Admittedly, the study size was quite small. Other, larger trials that will have greater statistical power to evaluate the safety of SLN biopsy when completed are the National Surgical Adjuvant Breast and Bowel Project (NSABP) B32 trial and the American College of Surgeons Oncology Group (ACOSOG) Z0010 trial. Another ongoing study is the ACOSOG Z0011 trial, the aim of which is to evaluate the effectiveness of SLN biopsy as the sole surgical procedure in patients with pathologically positive SLNs.

Training and Credentialing

Credentialing criteria for new operative procedures have traditionally been under the jurisdiction of local hospital credentialing committees. When new technology becomes available, adequate training is essential, both to ensure that surgeons can perform the new procedures competently and to address medicolegal liability concerns. The American College of Surgeons (ACS) has a committee (the Committee on Emerging Surgical Technology and Education) that monitors this activity. With some new techniques (e.g., laparoscopic cholecystectomy and image-guided breast biopsy), hospitals have required surgeons to attend formal training courses and to have their first cases proctored by surgeons with experience in the new technique before they are allowed to perform the procedure on their own.

National organizations continue to struggle with the problem of educating and credentialing surgeons to perform new procedures. This problem takes on increasing urgency as medicolegal issues proliferate, as other specialists begin to move into areas once generally considered to be the domain of surgeons (e.g., radiologists performing breast biopsies), and as new technical developments promise to revolutionize surgical care. In an effort to address this problem as it bears on lymphatic mapping, the ACS, in association with the Moffitt Cancer Center, initiated a program designed to investigate how best to train teams (comprising surgeons, nuclear medicine physicians, radiologists, and pathologists) in the new technology. This formal training course is a 2-day session composed of didactic lectures, live surgery (including extensive surgeon-audience interaction during the procedure), and a hands-on laboratory. The program offers mentoring of initial cases as registrants go back to their institutions, maintains national registries on the Internet so that different experiences can be compared, and, finally, facilitates the participation of other university and community physicians in national protocols. Further information may be obtained from the Center for Minimally Invasive Surgical Techniques (888-456-2840; www.slnmapping.org). Participation in programs such as this one provides a certain degree of protection against medicolegal risk as new technology and procedures are introduced.

Another avenue of training that has been available to surgeons is participation in clinical trials such as the NSABP B32 trial. Previous experience with SLN biopsy is not a requirement for participation in this trial, and all participating surgeons are required to undergo a training process to gain experience with the procedure and familiarity with the specifics of the protocol. The techniques used in this trial represented a combination of common methods designed to maximize the efficacy of the procedure. The training phase included distribution of a detailed training manual, the opportunity to view a video of the procedure, and a site visit by a protocol-designated core trainer to explain the specifics of the procedure.

Radiation Exposure Guidelines and Policies

The amount and type of radioactivity injected in the course of lymphatic mapping and SLN biopsy are relatively limited. Typically, from 0.4 to 1.2 mCi of ^{99m}Tc is injected. This agent is a pure gamma emitter with a short half-life (6 hours); thus, the risks of potentially harmful beta radiation are avoided. The total radiation dose used is quite small—only about 5% of that used in common nuclear scanning techniques (e.g., bone scans). It has been estimated that a maximum of 0.45 Gy could be absorbed at the injection site. Of hospital workers, the surgeon is exposed to the highest levels of radiation. A study from Walter Reed Army Medical Center found that the hands of surgeons performing lymphatic mapping and SLN biopsy were exposed to an average of 9.4 ± 3.6 mrem per operation.[97] Therefore, on the basis of skin dosage recommendations set by the Nuclear Regulatory Commission, a surgeon would have to perform more than 5,000 SLN procedures a year to incur more than the minimal level of risk.

The low risk notwithstanding, proper handling of radioactive specimens is recommended. All such specimens should be handled as little as possible for at least 24 to 48 hours and should be appropriately labeled. Each institution performing these procedures should develop guidelines for handling and processing specimens in accordance with their own institution's radiation safety policies.

References

1. Jemal A, Murray T, Samuels A, et al: Cancer Statistics, 2003. CA Cancer J Clin 53:5, 2003

2. Kirkwood JM, Strawderman MH, Ernstoff MS, et al: Adjuvant therapy of high-risk resected cutaneous melanoma: the Eastern Oncology Group Trial EST 1684. J Clin Oncol 14:7, 1996

3. Group EBCTC: Polychemotherapy for early breast cancer: an overview of the randomized trials. Lancet 352:930, 1998

4. Group EBCTC: Tamoxifen for early breast cancer: an overview of the randomized trials. Lancet 351:1451, 1998

5. Veronesi U, Adamus J, Bandiera DC, et al: Inefficacy of immediate node dissection in stage I melanoma of the limbs. N Engl J Med 297:627, 1977

6. Sim FH, Taylor WF, Pritchard DJ, et al: Lymphadenectomy in the management of stage I malignant melanoma: a prospective randomized study. Mayo Clin Proc 61:697, 1986

7. Balch C, Soong S, Ross M, et al: Long-term results of a multi-institutional trial comparing prognostic factors and surgical results for intermediate thickness melanomas (1.0 to 4.0 mm). Intergroup Melanoma Surgical Trial. Ann Surg Oncol 7:87, 2000

8. Balch CM, Soong SJ, Bartolucci A, et al: Efficacy of an elective regional lymph node dissection of 1 to 4 mm thick melanomas for patients 60 years of age and younger. Ann Surg 224:255, 1996

9. Kirkwood JM, Ibrahim JG, Sosman JA, et al: High-dose interferon alfa-2b significantly prolongs relapse-free and overall survival compared with the GM2-KLH/QS-21 vaccine in patients with resected stage IIB-III melanoma: results of intergroup trial E1694/S9512/C509801. J Clin Oncol 19:2370, 2001

10. Kirkwood JM, Ibrahim J, Sondak VK, et al: High and low dose interferon alfa 2-b in high-risk melanoma: first analysis of intergroup trial E1690/S9111/C9190. J Clin Oncol 18:2444, 2000

11. Morton D, Wen DR, Wong J, et al: Technical details of intraoperative lymphatic mapping for early stage melanoma. Arch Surg 127:392, 1992

12. Slingluff C, Vollmer R, Reintgen D, et al: Lethal thin malignant melanoma. Ann Surg 208:150, 1988

13. Heaton K, Sussman J, Gershenwald J, et al: Surgical margins and prognostic factors in patients with thick (> 4 mm) primary melanoma. Ann Surg Oncol 208:322, 1998

14. Evans H, Krag D, Teates C, et al: Lymphoscintigraphy and sentinel node biopsy accurately stage melanoma in patients presenting after wide local excision. Ann Surg Oncol 10:416, 2003

15. Kelemen P, Essner R, Foshag L, et al: Lymphatic mapping and sentinel lymphadenectomy after wide local excision of primary melanoma. J Am Coll Surg 189:247, 1999

16. Leong S, Thelmo M, Kim R, et al: Delayed harvesting of sentinel lymph nodes after previous wide local excision of extremity melanoma. Ann Surg Oncol 10:196, 2003

17. Byrd D, Nason K, Eary J, et al: Utility of sentinel lymph node dissection in patients with head and neck melanoma (abstr). Presented at the 54th Annual Cancer Symposium, Society of Surgical Oncology, Washington, DC, March 15–18, 2001

18. Krag D, Meijer S, Weaver D, et al: Minimal access surgery for staging regional nodes in malignant melanoma (abstr). Presented at the 48th Cancer Symposium, Society of Surgical Oncology, Boston, 1995

19. Leong S, Donegan E, Heffernon W, et al: Adverse reactions to isosulfan blue during selective lymph node dissection in melanoma. Ann Surg Oncol 7:361, 2000

20. Wells K, Reintgen D, Cruse C, et al: Parotid gland sentinel lymphadenectomy in malignant melanoma (abstr). Presented at the International Congress on Melanoma, Sydney, Australia, 1997

21. Wrightson W, Wong S, Edwards M, et al: Complications associated with sentinel lymph node biopsy for melanoma. Ann Surg Oncol 10:676, 2003

22. Reintgen D, Cruse C, Berman C: An orderly progression of melanoma nodal metastases. Ann Surg 220:759, 1994

23. Thompson J, McCarthy W, Bosch C, et al: Sentinel lymph node status as an indicator of the presence of metastatic melanoma in regional lymph nodes. Melanoma Res 5:255, 1995

24. Leong S, Steinnetz I, Habib F, et al: Optimal selective sentinel lymph node dissection in primary malignant melanoma. Arch Surg 132:666, 1997

25. Gadd M, Cosimi A, Yu J, et al: Outcome of patients with melanoma and histologically negative sentinel lymph nodes. Arch Surg 134:381, 1999

26. Gershenwald JE, Colome M, Lee J, et al: Patterns of recurrence following a negative sentinel lymph node biopsy in 243 patients with stage I or II melanoma. J Clin Oncol 16:2253, 1998

27. Harlow SP, Krag DN, Ashikaga T, et al: Gamma probe guided biopsy of the sentinel node in malignant melanoma: a multicentre study. Melanoma Res 11:45, 2001

28. Medina-Franco H, Beenken S, Heslin M, et al: Sentinel lymph node biopsy for cutaneous melanoma of the head and neck (abstr). Presented at the 54th Annual Cancer Symposium, Society of Surgical Oncology, Washington, DC, March 15–18, 2001

29. Hagensen C: Treatment of curable carcinoma of the breast. Int J Radiat Oncol Biol Phys 2:975, 1977

30. Bonnadona G: Conceptual and practical advances in the management of breast cancer: Karnofsky Memorial Lecture. J Clin Oncol 7:1380, 1989

31. Fisher B, Gedmond C, Fisher E, et al: Ten year results of a randomized clinical trial comparing radical mastectomy and total mastectomy with and without irradiation. N Engl J Med 312:674, 1985

32. Orr R: The impact of prophylactic axillary node dissection on breast cancer survival: a Bayesian meta-analysis. Ann Surg Oncol 6:109, 1999

33. Baker L: Breast cancer detection demonstration project: five year summary report. CA Cancer J Clin 32:194, 1982

34. Dewar J, Sarazin D, Benhamou E, et al: Management of the axilla in conservatively treated breast cancer: 592 patients treated at the Institut Gustave-Roussy. Int J Radiat Oncol Biol Phys 13:475, 1987

35. Mertz L, Mathelin C, Marin C, et al: [Subareolar injection of 99m-Tc sulfur colloid for sentinel nodes identification in multifocal invasive breast cancer]. Bull Cancer 86:939, 1999

36. Julian TB, Patel N, Dusi D, et al: Sentinel lymph node biopsy after neoadjuvant chemotherapy for breast cancer. Am J Surg 182:407, 2001

37. Tafra L, Verbanac KM, Lannin DR: Preoperative chemotherapy and sentinel lymphadenectomy for breast cancer. Am J Surg 182:312, 2001

38. Miller AR, Thomason VE, Yeh IT, et al: Analysis of sentinel lymph node mapping with immediate pathologic review in patients receiving preoperative chemotherapy for breast carcinoma. Ann Surg Oncol 9:243, 2002

39. Tanis PJ, Deurloo EE, Valdes Olmos RA, et al: Single intralesional tracer dose for radio-guided excision of clinically occult breast cancer and sentinel node. Ann Surg Oncol 8:850, 2001

40. Tanis PJ, Nieweg OE, Valdes Olmos RA, et al: Impact of non-axillary sentinel node biopsy on staging and treatment of breast cancer patients. Br J Cancer 87:705, 2002

41. Veronesi U, Paganelli G, Viale G, et al: Sentinel lymph node biopsy and axillary dissection in breast cancer: results in a large series. J Natl Cancer Inst 91:368, 1999

42. Dixon J, Mamman U, Thomas J: Accuracy of intraoperative frozen section analysis of axillary nodes. Edinburgh Breast Unit team. Br J Surg 86:392, 1999

43. Zurrida S, Mazzarol G, Galimberti V, et al: The problem of the accuracy of intraoperative examination of axillary sentinel nodes in breast cancer. Ann Surg Oncol 8:817, 2001

44. Rubio IT, Korourian S, Cowan C, et al: Use of touch preps for intraoperative diagnosis of sentinel lymph node metastases in breast cancer. Ann Surg Oncol 5:689, 1998

45. Group ILBCS: Prognostic importance of occult axillary lymph node micrometastases from breast cancer. Lancet 335:1565, 1990

46. Fitzgibbons PL, Page DL, Weaver D, et al: Prognostic factors in breast cancer. College of American Pathologists Consensus Statement 1999. Arch Pathol Lab Med 124:966, 2000

47. Temple LK, Baron R, Cody HS 3rd, et al: Sensory morbidity after sentinel lymph node biopsy and axillary dissection: a prospective study of 233 women. Ann Surg Oncol 9:654, 2002

48. Krag DN, Weaver DL, Alex JC, et al: Surgical resection and radiolocalization of the sentinel lymph node in breast cancer using a gamma probe. Surg Oncol 2:335, 1993

49. Giuliano AE, Kirgan DM, Guenther JM, et al: Lymphatic mapping and sentinel lymphadenectomy for breast cancer. Ann Surg 220:391, 1994

50. Albertini JJ, Lyman GH, Cox C, et al: Lymphatic mapping and sentinel node biopsy in the patient with breast cancer. JAMA 276:1818, 1996

51. Krag D, Weaver D, Ashikaga T, et al: The sentinel node in breast cancer—a multicenter validation study. N Engl J Med 339:941, 1998

52. McMasters KM, Tuttle TM, Carlson DJ, et al: Sentinel lymph node biopsy for breast cancer: a suitable alternative to routine axillary dissection in multi-institutional practice when optimal technique is used. J Clin Oncol 18:2560, 2000

53. Tafra L, Lannin DR, Swanson MS, et al: Multicenter trial of sentinel node biopsy for breast cancer using both technetium sulfur colloid and isosulfan blue dye. Ann Surg 233:51, 2001

54. Shivers S, Cox C, Leight G, et al: Final results of the Department of Defense multicenter breast lymphatic mapping trial. Ann Surg Oncol 9:248, 2002

55. van der Ent FW, Kengen RA, van der Pol HA, et al: Halsted revisited: internal mammary sentinel lymph node biopsy in breast cancer. Ann Surg 234:79, 2001

56. Watanabe T, Kimijima I, Ohtake T, et al: Sentinel node biopsy with technetium-99m colloidal rhenium sulphide in patients with breast cancer. Br J Surg 88:704, 2001

57. Allen B, Campbell I, Desai S, et al: Pilot study comparing the accuracy of lymphoscintigraphy sentinel lymph node localisation with axillary node dissection in women with operable breast cancer. N Z Med J 114:233, 2001

58. Birdwell RL, Smith KL, Betts BJ, et al: Breast cancer: variables affecting sentinel lymph node visualization at preoperative lymphoscintigraphy. Radiology 220:47, 2001

59. Sato K, Uematsu M, Saito T, et al: Sentinel lymph node identification for patients with breast cancer using large-size radiotracer particles: technetium-99m-labeled tin colloids produced excellent results. Breast J 7:388, 2001

60. Hodgson N, Zabel P, Mattar AG, et al: A new radiocolloid for sentinel node detection in breast cancer. Ann Surg Oncol 8:133, 2001

61. Byrd DR, Dunnwald LK, Mankoff DA, et al: Internal mammary lymph node drainage patterns in patients with breast cancer documented by breast lymphoscintigraphy. Ann Surg Oncol 8:234, 2001

62. Solorzano CC, Ross MI, Delpassand E, et al: Utility

of breast sentinel lymph node biopsy using day-be-fore-surgery injection of high-dose 99mTc-labeled sulfur colloid. Ann Surg Oncol 8:821, 2001

63. Jinno H, Ikeda T, Matsui A, et al: Sentinel lymph node biopsy in breast cancer using technetium-99m tin colloids of different sizes. Biomed Pharmacother 56(suppl 1):213S, 2002

64. Crossin JA, Johnson AC, Stewart PB, et al: Gamma-probe-guided resection of the sentinel lymph node in breast cancer. Am Surg 64:666, 1998

65. Roumen RM, Valkenburg JG, Geuskens LM: Lymphoscintigraphy and feasibility of sentinel node biopsy in 83 patients with primary breast cancer. Eur J Surg Oncol 23:495, 1997

66. Snider H, Dowlatshahi K, Fan M, et al: Sentinel node biopsy in the staging of breast cancer. Am J Surg 176:305, 1998

67. Pijpers R, Meijer S, Hoekstra OS, et al: Impact of lymphoscintigraphy on sentinel node identification with technetium-99m-colloidal albumin in breast cancer. J Nucl Med 38:366, 1997

68. Cox CE, Pendas S, Cox JM, et al: Guidelines for sentinel node biopsy and lymphatic mapping of patients with breast cancer. Ann Surg 227:645, 1998

69. Borgstein PJ, Meijer S, Pijpers R: Intradermal blue dye to identify sentinel lymph-node in breast cancer. Lancet 349:1668, 1997

70. De Cicco C, Chinol M, Paganelli G: Intraoperative localization of the sentinel node in breast cancer: technical aspects of lymphoscintigraphic methods. Semin Surg Oncol 15:268, 1998

71. Bass SS, Cox CE, Ku NN, et al: The role of sentinel lymph node biopsy in breast cancer. J Am Coll Surg 189:183, 1999

72. Winchester DJ, Sener SF, Winchester DP, et al: Sentinel lymphadenectomy for breast cancer: experience with 180 consecutive patients: efficacy of filtered technetium 99m sulphur colloid with overnight migration time. J Am Coll Surg 188:597, 1999

73. Haigh PI, Hansen NM, Giuliano AE, et al: Factors affecting sentinel node localization during preoperative breast lymphoscintigraphy. J Nucl Med 41:1682, 2000

74. Sato K, Uematsu M, Saito T, et al: Indications and technique of sentinel lymph node biopsy in breast cancer using 99m-technetium labeled tin colloids. Breast Cancer 7:95, 2000

75. Krause A, Dunkelmann S, Makovitzky J, et al: [Detection of atypical site of "sentinel lymph nodes" by lymph drainage scintigraphy in patients with breast carcinoma]. Zentralbl Gynakol 122:514, 2000

76. Sardi A, Spiegler E, Colandrea J, et al: The benefit of using two techniques for sentinel lymph node mapping in breast cancer. Am Surg 68:24, 2002

77. Mateos JJ, Vidal-Sicart S, Zanon G, et al: Sentinel lymph node biopsy in breast cancer patients: subdermal versus peritumoural radiocolloid injection. Nucl Med Commun 22:17, 2001

78. Martin RC, Derossis AM, Fey J, et al: Intradermal isotope injection is superior to intramammary in sentinel node biopsy for breast cancer. Surgery 130:432, 2001

79. Veronesi U, Paganelli G, Galimberti V, et al: Sentinel-node biopsy to avoid axillary dissection in breast cancer with clinically negative lymph-nodes. Lancet 349:1864, 1997

80. Boolbol SK, Fey JV, Borgen PI, et al: Intradermal isotope injection: a highly accurate method of lymphatic mapping in breast carcinoma. Ann Surg Oncol 8:20, 2001

81. Motomura K, Inaji H, Komoike Y, et al: Combination technique is superior to dye alone in identification of the sentinel node in breast cancer patients. J Surg Oncol 76:95, 2001

82. Rink T, Heuser T, Fitz H, et al: Results of a standardized protocol for sentinel node imaging in breast cancer with Tc-99m labeled nanocolloidal albumin. Nuklearmedizin 40:80, 2001

83. Rink T, Heuser T, Fitz H, et al: Lymphoscintigraphic sentinel node imaging and gamma probe detection in breast cancer with Tc-99m nanocolloidal albumin: results of an optimized protocol. Clin Nucl Med 26:293, 2001

84. Xavier NL, Amaral BB, Cerski CT, et al: Sentinel lymph node identification and sampling in women with early breast cancer using 99m Tc labelled dextran 500 and patent blue V dye. Nucl Med Commun 22:1109, 2001

85. Tavares MG, Sapienza MT, Galeb NA Jr, et al: The use of 99mTc-phytate for sentinel node mapping in melanoma, breast cancer and vulvar cancer: a study of 100 cases. Eur J Nucl Med 28:1597, 2001

86. Vargas HI, Tolmos J, Agbunag RV, et al: A validation trial of subdermal injection compared with intraparenchymal injection for sentinel lymph node biopsy in breast cancer. Am Surg 68:87, 2002

87. Doting MH, Jansen L, Nieweg OE, et al: Lymphatic mapping with intralesional tracer administration in breast carcinoma patients. Cancer 88:2546, 2000

88. Valdes-Olmos RA, Jansen L, Hoefnagel CA, et al: Evaluation of mammary lymphoscintigraphy by a single intratumoral injection for sentinel node identification. J Nucl Med 41:1500, 2000

89. Valdes Olmos RA, Tanis PJ, Hoefnagel CA, et al: Improved sentinel node visualization in breast cancer by optimizing the colloid particle concentration and tracer dosage. Nucl Med Commun 22:579, 2001

90. Ronka R, Krogerus L, Leppanen E, et al: Sentinel nodes outside level I-II of the axilla and staging in breast cancer. Anticancer Res 22:3109, 2002

91. Shimazu K, Tamaki Y, Taguchi T, et al: Comparison between periareolar and peritumoral injection of radiotracer for sentinel lymph node biopsy in patients with breast cancer. Surgery 131:277, 2002

92. Klimberg VS, Rubio IT, Henry R, et al: Subareolar versus peritumoral injection for location of the sentinel lymph node. Ann Surg 229:860, 1999

93. Smith LF, Cross MJ, Klimberg VS: Subareolar injection is a better technique for sentinel lymph node biopsy. Am J Surg 180:434, 2000

94. Kern KA: Concordance and validation study of sentinel lymph node biopsy for breast cancer using subareolar injection of blue dye and technetium 99m sulfur colloid. J Am Coll Surg 195:467, 2002

95. Tuttle TM, Colbert M, Christensen R, et al: Subareolar injection of 99mTc facilitates sentinel lymph node identification. Ann Surg Oncol 9:77, 2002

96. Veronesi U, Paganelli G, Viale G, et al: A randomized comparison of sentinel-node biopsy with routine axillary node dissection in breast cancer. N Engl J Med 349:546, 2003

97. Miner TJ, Shriver CD, Flicek PR, et al: Guidelines for the safe use of radioactive materials during localization and resection of the sentinel lymph node. Ann Surg Oncol 6:75, 1999

98. Tanabe K: Lymphatic mapping and epitrochlear node dissection for melanoma. Surgery 121:102, 1997

99. Hung JC, Wiseman GA, Wahner HW, et al: Filtered technetium-99m-sulfur colloid evaluated for lymphoscintigraphy. J Nucl Med 36:1895, 1995

100. Nathanson SD, Anaya P, Karvelis KC, et al: Sentinel lymph node uptake of two different technetium-labeled radiocolloids. Ann Surg Oncol 4:104, 1997

101. Wong J, Cagle L, Morton DL, et al: Lymphatic drainage of skin to a sentinel node in a feline model. Ann Surg 214:637, 1991

27 SURFACE RECONSTRUCTION PROCEDURES

Joseph J. Disa, M.D., F.A.C.S., Eric G. Halvorson, M.D., and Himansu R. Shah, M.D.

General Technical Issues in Plastic Surgical Wound Repair

The key to achieving optimal results in wound closure is correct approximation of the wound edges.[1] Because remodeling scars contract downward, it is essential that the edges be maximally everted to prevent the development of a depression at the closure site.[2] Such eversion can easily be accomplished either with carefully placed simple sutures or with vertical or horizontal mattress sutures. It is also important that closure be performed in layers so as to eliminate dead space. Accurate realignment of wound edges is especially critical with facial injuries. In the case of a defect involving the vermilion border of the lip, it is very helpful to mark the exact position of the lip margin with a marking pen. For a full-thickness laceration of the lip, the mucous membrane should be repaired first with absorbable suture material. The muscle layer should then be repaired with absorbable suture material. Skin closure is performed last. Placement of the initial suture at the vermilion border facilitates accurate alignment; a mismatch of more than 1 mm will be visible from a conversational distance.

Fundamental to any plastic surgical wound repair is good suturing technique. Careful handling of tissues and placement of sutures facilitates optimal wound healing and minimizes scar formation. A curved cutting needle is typically used to repair skin. With the surgeon's forearm fully pronated, the point of the needle is passed through the skin and the dermis at right angles to the skin surface. As the forearm is supinated, the curve of the needle causes the point to penetrate the dermis on the opposite side of the wound. At every step, it is vital to cause as little tissue trauma as possible. Gentle pressure on the skin with a closed Adson forceps or a skin hook will achieve eversion of the wound margins and allow proper suture placement without crushing the skin edge. Excessive pressure on the forceps can lead to ischemia of the wound edge and diminish the quality of wound healing.

Plastic surgical repair of an open wound may involve any of the following types of sutures: (1) simple interrupted sutures, (2) vertical mattress sutures, (3) horizontal mattress sutures, (4) subcuticular continuous sutures, (5) half-buried horizontal mattress sutures, or (6) continuous over-and-over sutures [see Figure 1]. No single suturing technique is ideal for all contexts; clearly, individual surgeons have differing preferences depending on the clinical situation or on personal choice. In general, however, simple, subcuticular, and continuous sutures are preferred because they tend to produce less wound edge ischemia and ultimately result in better scars. Whichever technique is employed, the mechanism of trauma will have some influence on the cosmetic outcome: crush or shear injuries, such as those that occur in falls or motor vehicle accidents, result in less favorable scars than those caused by sharp lacerations, such as glass or knife cuts.

Simple interrupted sutures are useful for closing simple wounds without excess tension. Subcuticular continuous sutures are useful for approximating wound edges without tension after the dermis has been approximated with buried deep dermal sutures.

Continuous over-and-over sutures are used for much the same purposes as simple sutures. They can be placed more quickly than interrupted sutures because knots are needed only at the beginning and the end; however, it is harder to distribute tension evenly over a nonlinear wound with a continuous over-and-over suture. When it is not possible to achieve a tension-free environment in which the dermis is properly apposed with buried sutures, mattress sutures may be preferred. These sutures generally provide better eversion of wound edges in areas where significant tension is present (e.g., on the lower extremities or over bony prominences); however, they tend to induce more wound edge ischemia and thus must be placed carefully. Half-buried mattress sutures are commonly employed for anchoring flaps and skin grafts, particularly at the corners.

The type of suture material used depends on personal preference to some extent; however, for the face, permanent suture material (e.g., 5-0 or 6-0 nylon) is generally preferred. Needle marks can be prevented by removing sutures earlier rather than later [see Table 1].

After a suture is placed, care should be taken to tie the knot properly. The knot should be brought to one side of the wound, and the tension should be adjusted so that the skin edges are apposed without compromising the blood supply. The optimal distance between sutures varies depending on the anatomic site undergoing repair; however, on the face, sutures should be approximately 3 to 4 mm apart and be placed 2 mm from the wound edge. Besides sutures, both staples and adhesive strips are currently used for wound closure. Whereas the former are commonly employed for lacerations of the scalp, where cosmetic outcome is of less importance, the latter are commonly employed when the wound is superficial and the edges can be easily approximated with little tension. Adhesive glues can also be used for superficial wounds; they are especially useful in children and in patients whose wounds are located in areas where a durable protective barrier is desired (e.g., the axilla or the groin).

Skin Grafts

Skin grafts are generally used to cover large open wounds that are not infected [see 23 Open Wound Requiring Reconstruction]. Healing requires a well-vascularized bed. Use of a skin graft is contraindicated in the presence of any of the following: (1) gross infection, (2) cortical bone denuded of periosteum, (3) a tendon denuded of paratenon, (4) cartilage denuded of perichondrium, and (5) heavily contaminated or irradiated areas (a relative rather than absolute contraindication).

CLASSIFICATION

Skin grafts are divided into two categories on the basis of thickness: (1) split-thickness (or partial-thickness) grafts and (2) full-thickness grafts. A full-thickness graft contains the entire epidermis and dermis, whereas a split-thickness graft contains the epidermis

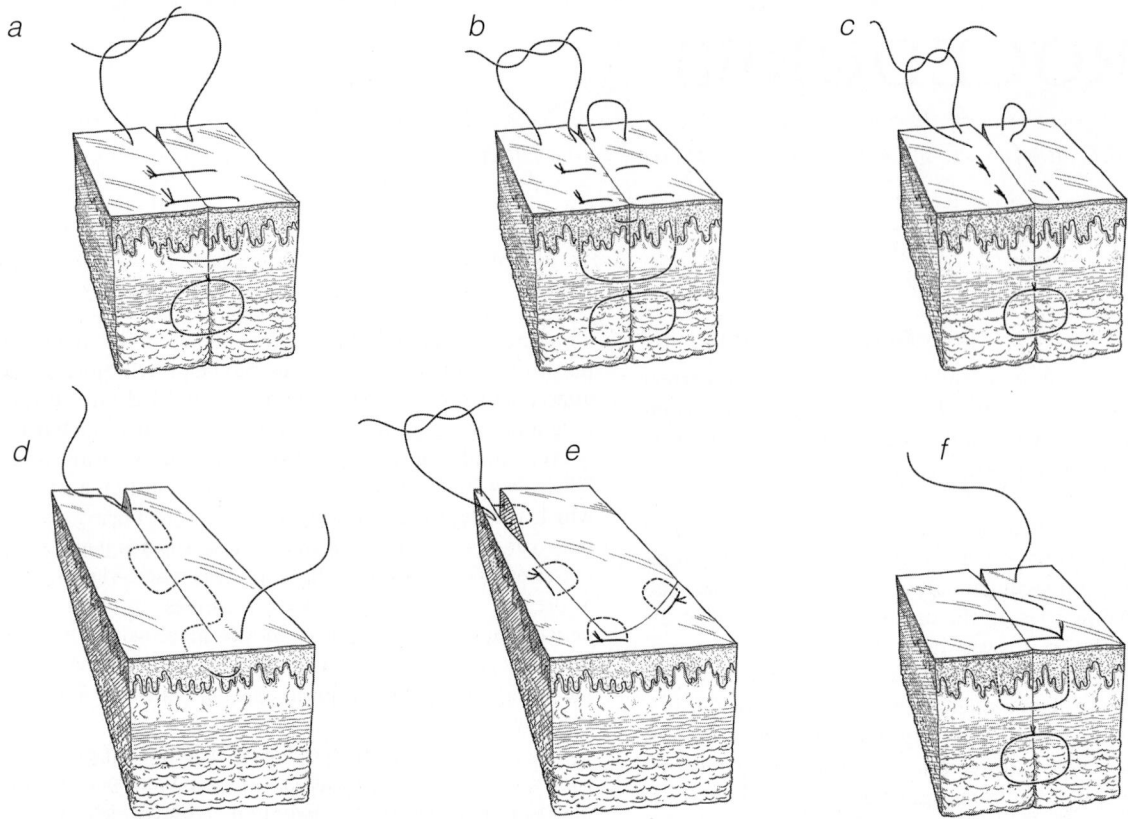

Figure 1 Shown are types of sutures used in plastic surgical wound repair. (*a*) Simple interrupted sutures. An equal bite of tissue is taken on each side of the wound; to ensure eversion of skin edges, a significant amount of deeper tissue is incorporated. (*b*) Vertical mattress sutures. Bites are taken either (1) first close to the wound and then distant from it or (2) vice versa. Bites on either side of the wound must be equally spaced from the skin edges. (*c*) Horizontal mattress sutures. As with vertical mattress sutures, all bites are equally spaced from the skin edges. (*d*) Subcuticular continuous suture. All bites, except for entrance and exit bites, are within the dermis at the same level; the suture should enter and exit the dermis at right angles. (*e*) Half-buried horizontal mattress sutures. These are similar to standard horizontal mattress sutures except that tissue opposite the side where the stitch enters the skin is grasped in the subcuticular level; thus, the needle passes into and out of the epidermis at only two locations. (*f*) Continuous over-and-over suture. This resembles a simple suture except that it is continuously passed through the wound until the desired terminus is reached.

but only part of the dermis [*see Figure 2*]. Split-thickness grafts are further subdivided into thin and thick split-thickness grafts.

Full-thickness skin grafts can be harvested from anywhere on the body, but they are most frequently taken from the upper eyelid, the buttocks, the arms, the groin, and the postauricular and supraclavicular areas. Because of their higher elastin content, such grafts are associated with more primary contraction than split-thickness grafts are; however, they are less often associated with secondary contraction. Full-thickness skin grafts are less likely to become hyperpigmented than split-thickness skin grafts are. Because primary closure of the donor site is required, the size of a full-thickness graft is limited by the dimensions of the site from which it comes.

Split-thickness skin grafts can be harvested from any of a number of broad, flat areas of the body, including the thigh, the buttocks, the back, the abdomen, the chest, and the posterior neck. In general, split-thickness grafts are more readily available than full-thickness grafts; in addition, they have better survival rates because plasmic imbibition (the process by which a skin graft is nourished by the underlying tissue) is more effective with thinner grafts. The main disadvantages of split-thickness grafts vis-à-vis full-thickness grafts are the increased secondary contraction and the higher incidence of hyperpigmentation.

OPERATIVE TECHNIQUE

Full-Thickness Grafts

The recipient site is adequately debrided, and the defect is measured. An outline of the defect is made on the graft site. If the graft is circular, it may have to be converted to an ellipse for smooth clo-

Table 1 Optimal Timing of Suture Removal after Wound Closure

Closure Site	Optimal Suture Removal Time (days after closure)
Eyelid	3–5
Face	5–7
Lip	5–7
Hands/feet	10–14
Trunk	7–10
Breast	7–10

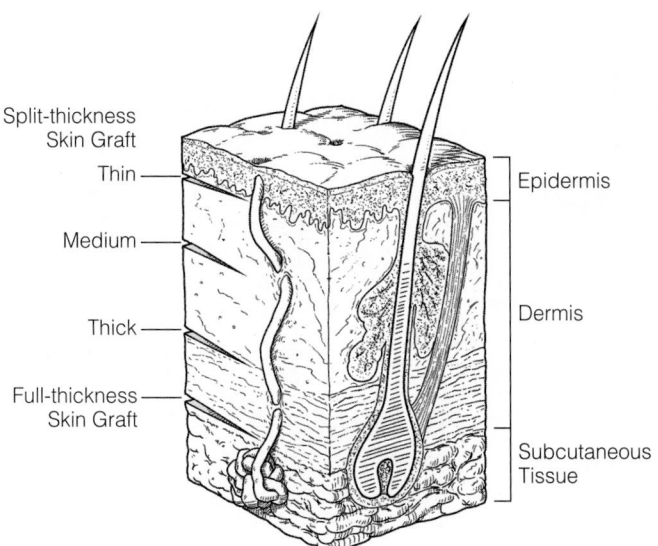

Figure 2 Skin grafts. Shown are the layers of the skin in cross section. The levels at which split-thickness and full-thickness skin grafts are harvested are noted.

sure [*see Figure 3a*]. An incision is made around the outline with a No. 10 or 15 blade. The edges of the graft are elevated with skin hooks. Meticulous dissection is performed in such a way that as little subcutaneous tissue as possible is included with the graft [*see Figure 3b*]. Once the graft is harvested, any subcutaneous tissue is sharply removed (a step known as defatting the graft). The graft is then wrapped in a saline-soaked sponge until ready for use.

The graft is properly positioned and secured with absorbable sutures [*see Figure 3c*]. A tie-over bolster dressing is applied—typ-

ically, Xeroform (Kendall Healthcare, Mansfield, Massachusetts) wrapped around cotton soaked with mineral oil or saline [*see Figure 3d*]. The donor site is then closed, either in two layers (for thicker donor sites, such as the groin) or in a single layer (for thinner donor sites, such as the eyelid).

Split-Thickness Grafts

A split-thickness graft may be harvested with a Humby knife, a Weck blade, or a power-driven dermatome. Currently, a power-driven dermatome is the most popular choice.

Harvesting and placement of a split-thickness skin graft is a relatively simple technique; however, attention to detail is necessary to optimize graft take. The key to how well a skin graft takes is the quality of the recipient bed; the relevant contraindications should be kept in mind (see above).

The recipient wound is debrided until a uniform bleeding surface is encountered. Extra care should be taken to debride areas of nonviable tissue because the graft will not take in such areas. Meticulous hemostasis is crucial because hematoma is the most common cause of graft loss. The defect is then measured [*see Figure 4a*], and the donor site is marked to indicate an appropriately sized graft. If the donor site is hairy, it is shaved before the graft is harvested. Any preparation solution remaining on the donor site is cleaned off, and mineral oil (or, as some surgeons prefer, water) is applied to lubricate the skin.

Next, the dermatome is prepared by inserting the blade and securing it by tightening the screws [*see Figure 4b*]. The graft thickness is determined by the calibration gauge, which, for most split-thickness grafts, is typically set at 14 (a setting equivalent to 0.014 in., or approximately 0.356 mm). As another method of setting the desired thickness, the edge of most No. 15 scalpels should just fit into the space created between the dermatome device and the

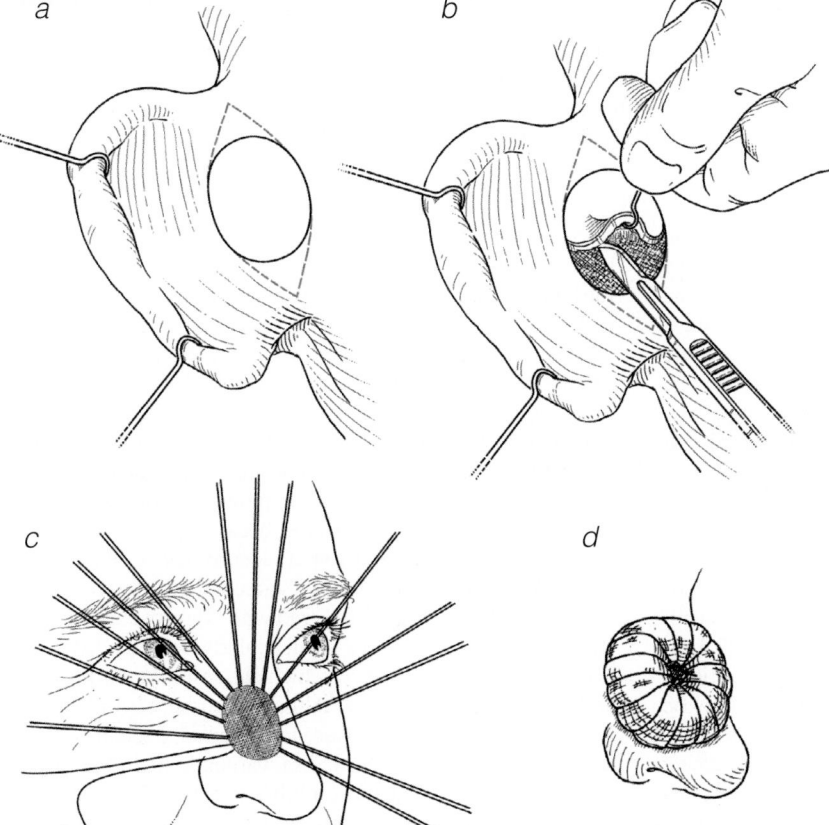

Figure 3 Skin grafts: full thickness. (*a*) A retroauricular full-thickness skin graft is outlined; conversion to an elliptical shape may facilitate closure. (*b*) The graft is elevated with skin hooks, with care taken to include as little subcutaneous tissue as possible. (*c*) The graft is sutured in place. (*d*) A tie-over bolster dressing is applied to maintain pressure on the graft and ensure good contact between it and the recipient bed.

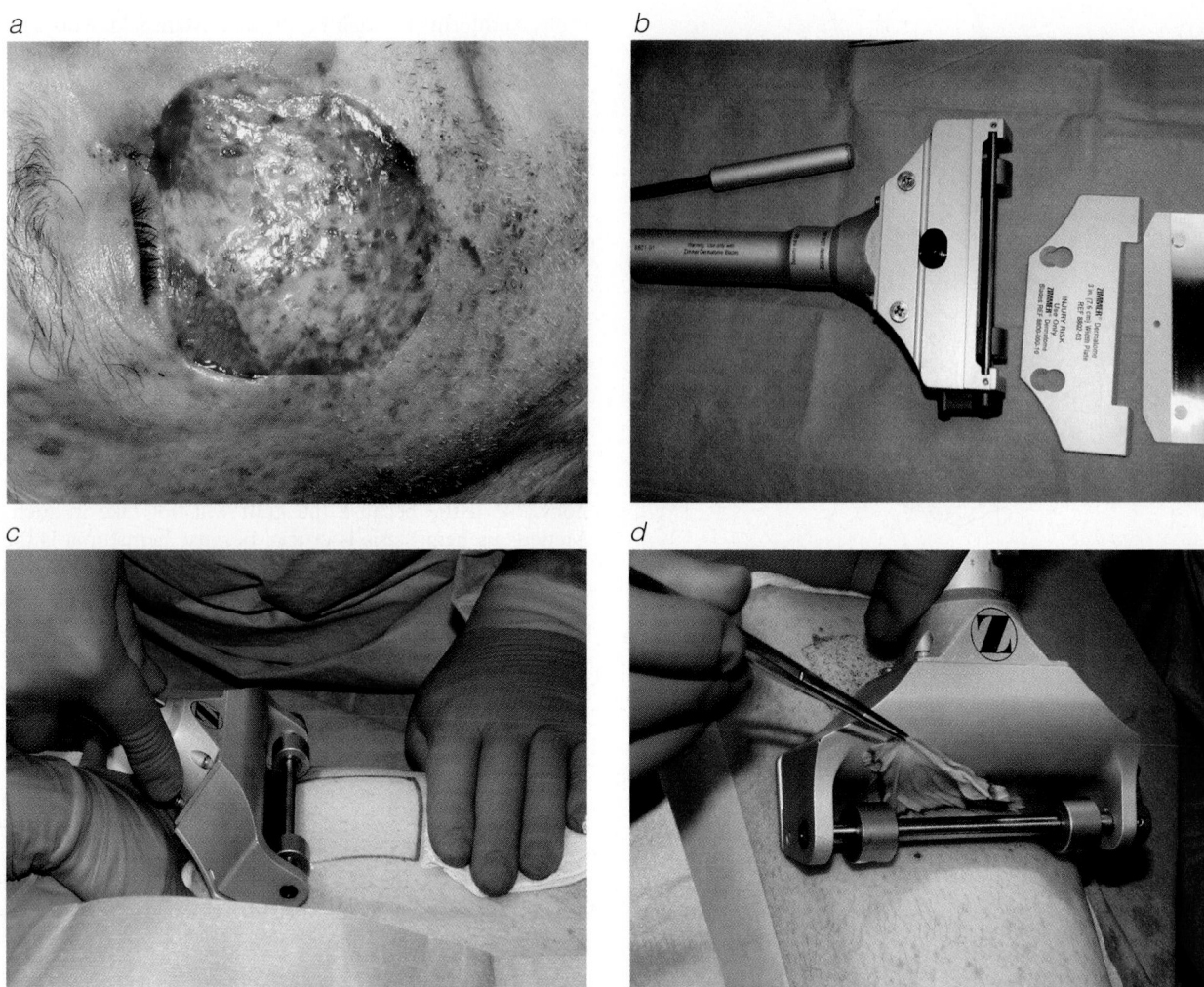

Figure 4 **Skin grafts: split thickness. (*a*) Shown is a cheek defect after excision of a melanoma in situ. (*b*) A dermatome is used to harvest the graft. It is set to obtain a specific thickness of skin; 0.014 in. (0.356 mm) is a common setting. (*c*) The graft is harvested by applying steady pressure to the skin with the dermatome while advancing it forward. The assistant retracts the skin to optimize contact between blade and skin. (*d*) The skin is gently removed from the dermatome. If necessary, it can be meshed to increase its size.**

blade. The skin surface is smoothed with gentle but steady traction to facilitate the harvest. Using an assistant to apply traction on the skin in all directions is very helpful [*see Figure 4c*]. The dermatome is turned on and placed so that it engages the skin at a slight angle [*see Figure 4d*]. It is then slowly advanced until an adequate amount of skin is harvested. Once harvested, the graft can be applied to the recipient area either with or without meshing.

Meshing a skin graft can be advantageous, first, because it allows a smaller graft to cover a larger area, and second, because it provides interstices through which fluid can drain in exudative environments. Meshed grafts generally take longer to heal than nonmeshed grafts do because the interstices must contract and fill with scar tissue; in addition, meshed grafts often heal with a cobblestone appearance. There are two basic types of graft meshers, those that contain grooved meshing boards and those that do not. Expansion ratios range from 1.5:1 to 3:1. The desired ratio is selected by choosing either the appropriate meshing board or the appropriate cutting blade, depending on the type of mesher used. In most circumstances, an expansion ratio of 1.5:1, which increases surface area by 50%, is sufficient. On rare occasions, an expansion ratio of 3:1 is needed, depending on the availability of donor sites in relation to the requirements of the recipient area. The graft

to be meshed is placed with the dermis side up on the grooved side of the meshing board. The meshing board is rolled through the mesher, and the meshed graft is ready for final placement over the recipient site.

The skin graft is secured to the recipient bed either with absorbable suture material or with staples [*see Figure 5a*]. A bolster dressing, made of Xeroform and of cotton soaked in saline or mineral oil, is applied over the graft. The bolster is fixed in place either by tying sutures over it (for broad, flat areas such as the trunk or the face) [*see Figure 5b*] or by wrapping gauze or an elastic bandage (or both) around it (for curved areas such as the extremities). Alternatively, a vacuum-assisted closure device (e.g., VAC Abdominal Dressing System; Kinetic Concepts, Inc., San Antonio, Texas) can be placed over a graft covered with Xeroform or a similar nonstick gauze.[3] Such a device is particularly helpful when the wound bed has an irregular surface, which can result in tenting of the graft and consequent graft loss. Although some clinical studies have found vacuum-assisted closure to be superior to conventional bolsters, this method does have disadvantages, including higher cost, greater complexity, and immobility resulting from attachment to the device. With a graft on an extremity, splinting may be necessary for immobilization. The donor site is then dressed with an

a

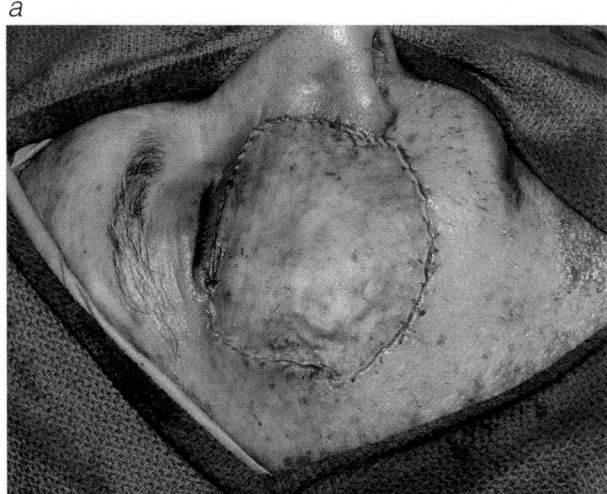

b

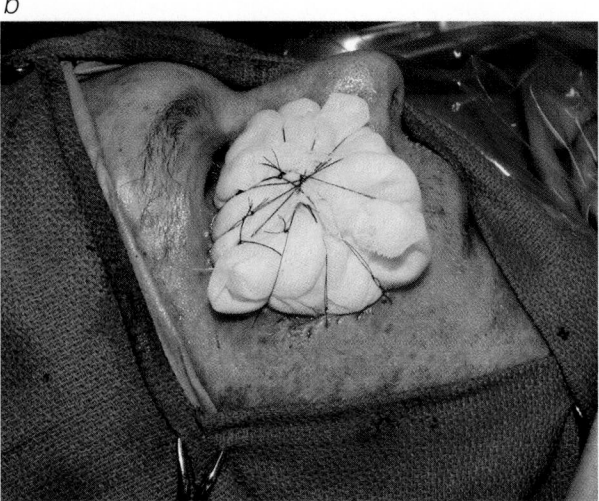

c

Figure 5 **Skin grafts: split thickness. (*a*) The skin graft is sutured in place. Care is taken to trim all excess skin and to ensure that the graft is in complete contact with the bed. (*b*) A tie-over bolster dressing is applied. (*c*) The donor site is dressed. In this case, calcium sodium alginate is applied to the bed, followed by a bio-occlusive dressing. The dressing is left intact until reepithelialization occurs (typically, 7 to 10 days).**

occlusive dressing (e.g., OpSite; Smith & Nephew, Hull, United Kingdom) or a semiocclusive dressing (e.g., Xeroform) until reepithelialization occurs [*see Figure 5c*].

POSTOPERATIVE CARE

The postoperative fate of a skin graft is largely determined by the circumstances of the wound (especially the presence or absence of infection) and the technical execution of the grafting procedure.[4] Successful healing of skin grafts requires immobilization of the recipient site for 5 to 7 days. Immobilization can be accomplished with tie-over bolsters; on extremities, skin grafts can be further immobilized with plaster casts. Proper immobilization is critical for graft survival because it prevents shearing in the plane between the graft and the wound bed. After 5 to 7 days of immobilization, the graft is inspected, and either a gauze dressing (e.g., Xeroform) or a lubricating antibiotic ointment is applied for another 5 to 7 days. Because grafted skin lacks oil glands, a nonirritating moisturizer should then be applied to the graft for several months thereafter, until the graft is capable of maintaining a more normal level of skin moisture without the moisturizer.

Grafts that are treated by closed methods (i.e., tie-over bolsters) are carefully observed for evidence of infection. Developing erythema or suppuration is an indication for immediate removal of the bolster dressing and inspection of the graft. On infrequent occasions, a graft may be threatened by infection; in such cases, the graft may be saved by switching to an open method of graft care with wet dressings changed three or four times a day.

Nonmeshed grafts may form a hematoma or seroma that will prevent the graft from taking. Accumulated fluid should be evacuated by puncturing the graft or by rolling cotton-tipped swabs over it until the fluid escapes from under its edges. Survival of the entire graft is possible if fluid is meticulously evacuated within the first few days after graft placement; plasmic imbibition will keep the graft viable over this period.

Meshed grafts are not subject to the problem of fluid accumulation, nor are they as vulnerable as nonmeshed grafts to the shear forces that can prevent graft survival. For meshed grafts, the postoperative goal is to prevent desiccation, because they are more exposed to the environment. After the initial dressing change, gauze dressings (e.g., Xeroform) should be placed over the graft and changed once a day. After 2 weeks, the dressings can be discontinued, but the graft should be kept well lubricated with either a skin cream or cocoa butter.

Meshed grafts that are placed over wounds at high risk for infection may be managed postoperatively with wet dressings changed three times a day. The dressing changes will not interfere with graft take and will maximize graft survival in the face of heavy bacterial contamination.

Extremities that are recipient sites for skin grafts should always be maintained above heart level for a minimum of 1 week postoperatively. Lower extremities with skin grafts should remain elevated for a minimum of 10 days to 2 weeks, particularly when the graft is below the knee. Patients should also be mobilized in a progressive manner, beginning with brief periods of limb dangling. Premature ambulation of patients with lower-extremity skin grafts can result in loss of the skin graft despite an early appearance of complete graft take.

Donor sites of split-thickness grafts heal by epithelialization. They are best managed by coverage with a gas-permeable polyurethane film dressing (e.g., OpSite). This dressing retains moisture underneath, which favors rapid reepithelialization. It is also impermeable to bacteria. The addition of calcium sodium alginate under

RANDOM PATTERN   AXIAL PATTERN   MYOCUTANEOUS

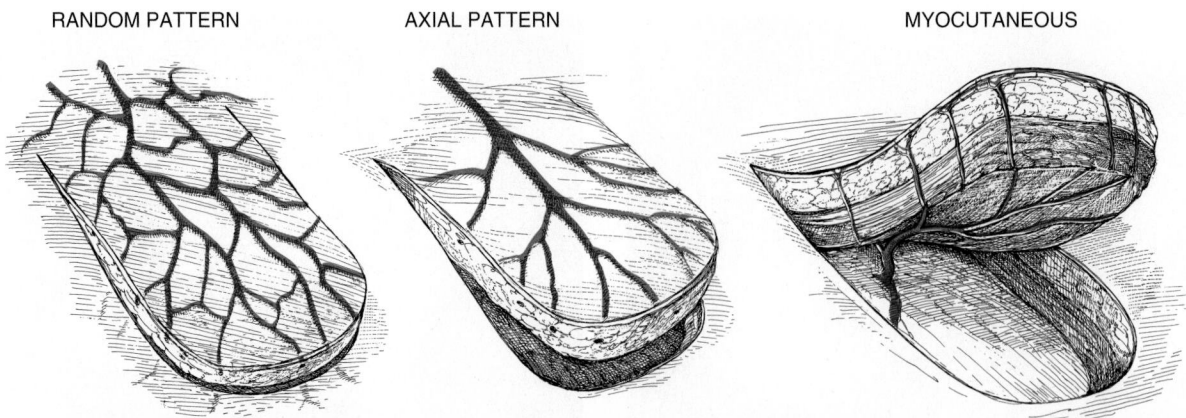

Figure 6 Local flaps. A random-pattern skin flap (left) is supplied by a subdermal plexus of small vessels that do not have an axial orientation. An axial-pattern skin flap (center) is designed parallel to the axis of a known major subcutaneous artery. It can have a greater length:width ratio because its blood supply is more reliable. A myocutaneous flap (right) derives the blood supply of its skin component from vertical perforators from the underlying muscle. The skin can be completely isolated over the muscle as an island.

the OpSite facilitates the absorption of the fluid that tends to collect there, thus further simplifying donor site management.[5]

Local Flaps

CLASSIFICATION

Flaps are classified according to the types of tissue that they contain, their blood supply [*see Figure 6*], and the method by which they are moved from the donor to the recipient site.

Tissue Contents

Flaps commonly consist of skin and subcutaneous tissue alone. However, they may also consist of skin combined with muscle, fascia, or bone; in these cases, the flaps are called myocutaneous, fasciocutaneous, or osteocutaneous, respectively. If a flap composed of skin and subcutaneous tissue that contains a known major artery (an axial-pattern, or arterialized, skin flap [*see* Blood Supply, *below*]) is raised at the donor site and remains attached only by the vascular pedicle, it is termed an island flap. The same flap is termed a free flap if the vascular pedicle is severed, the flap is transferred to a distant recipient site, and its circulation is restored by microvascular anastomoses.

Blood Supply

The earliest flaps in common use were skin flaps that had what is known as a random-pattern type of circulation [*see Figure 7a*], in which blood is supplied by the subdermal capillary plexus rather than by a named vessel.[6] The precarious nature of the blood supply of such flaps severely limited flap design and resulted in a preoccupation with suitable length:width ratios. Greater length:width ratios became possible after the empirical discovery that a more vigorous circulation develops in flaps raised in stages (the delay phenomenon).[7]

The next flaps to come into common use had an axial-pattern type of circulation, in which a sizable artery coursed directly to a specific cutaneous territory [*see Figure 7b*]. The groin was the first region where this arrangement was carefully described, and it remains a useful source of flaps for selected applications. Because longer flaps can be made in areas where the blood supply has an axial pattern, the length:width ratio and the delay phenomenon became less important issues.[8] Identification of an axial-pattern

blood supply to a given graft allows so-called islanding of the graft from the donor site except for the vascular connection, which is preserved. Such island flaps have greater mobility than flaps with a less attenuated attachment to the donor site.

A third type of flap was based on the myocutaneous blood supply, a network of vessels that perforate muscles vertically and supply the overlying skin [*see Figures 7c, d*]. These vessels are not necessarily the exclusive supply to the skin in a specific region, but they are able to support the skin entirely when other sources of blood supply are eliminated. Investigation of the body musculature showed that there were at least five basic patterns of blood supply to muscle, distinguished by the existence of and balance between primary pedicles and secondary sources of blood supply [*see Figure 8*]. Some muscles can be rotated or transposed as myocutaneous flaps on the basis of either their dominant or their secondary blood supply (e.g., the pectoralis major and the latissimus dorsi). Some muscles have two dominant supplies and can be transposed on either one (e.g., the rectus abdominis). Other muscles do not reliably support skin territories supplied by minor pedicles (e.g., the gracilis).

Other patterns of cutaneous blood supply are now well recognized. Fasciocutaneous flaps with high length:width ratios can be reliably raised on the trunk, arms, and legs. The blood supply of deep fascia appears to consist of both a deep and a superficial fascial plexus. These vessels connect both to perforating vessels from the underlying muscles and to the subcutaneous tissue vessels above them.[9] At least three types of fasciocutaneous flaps may be distinguished on the basis of the fascial blood supply to the skin [*see Figure 9*].[10]

In some areas, fascia supplies overlying subcutaneous tissue and skin more directly. Such a blood supply is most evident in the extremities, where direct branches from major vessels course through intermuscular septa to reach the deep fascia and supply the overlying skin and subcutaneous tissue. The forearm is a clinically important donor site because thin septocutaneous flaps fed by the radial artery can be raised as either pedicled or free flaps. Other examples of fasciocutaneous flaps include the lateral arm septocutaneous flap, fed by the profunda brachii artery; the scapular flap, fed by the circumflex scapular artery [*see Figure 7d*]; the fibular osteofasciocutaneous flap, fed by the peroneal artery; and the anterolateral thigh flap, fed by the descending branch of the lateral circumflex femoral artery.

Method of Movement to Recipient Site

Local flaps may be called either rotation, advancement, or transposition flaps, depending on how they are moved to reach their recipient sites.

A more complete characterization of flaps is achieved by combining all of the descriptive categories mentioned. For example, a muscle and skin flap that is rotated to cover an adjacent soft tissue defect is termed a myocutaneous rotation flap, and a skin and bone flap used to reconstruct a distant composite defect is termed an osteocutaneous free flap.

OPERATIVE TECHNIQUE

In all forms of plastic surgery, it is essential to cause as little tissue trauma as possible when raising a flap. Using skin hooks rather than forceps is helpful in this regard. The flap is marked and incised, and elevation is begun, first with a scalpel and then, at the base of the flap, with a blunt scissors to prevent injury to the blood supply. The electrocautery should be used judiciously in the elevation of skin flaps: although cauterization causes less bleeding, skin flaps often rely on the subdermal plexus for perfusion, and this plexus can be damaged by electrocautery dissection. Close attention to atraumatic technique throughout the procedure will result in less edema in the flap and, therefore, less circulatory compromise. Hemostasis is essential; in small flap procedures, bipolar coagulation controls bleeding with minimal damage to the flap's blood supply. Two-layer closure is recommended, with absorbable suture material in the deeper layer to decrease the tension and fine nylon for skin closure.

The recommendations just mentioned apply to local flap procedures in general. In what follows, we describe several different types of local flaps that are useful for the purposes of the general surgeon, and we summarize key technical points specific to each.

Transposition Flaps

A flap that is moved laterally into the primary defect is called a transposition flap. The essential concept in the design of such a flap is to ensure that the flap is long enough to cover the entire defect, so that the transfer can be done without tension [*see Figure 10*].

The skin is marked and incised with a scalpel, and dissection is carried through the subcutaneous fat. The flap is retracted with a skin hook, and dissection is performed with a blunt scissors until the flap is elevated sufficiently to allow it to be transposed into the defect without tension. The secondary defect is closed primarily; alternatively, depending on the location of the donor area and the

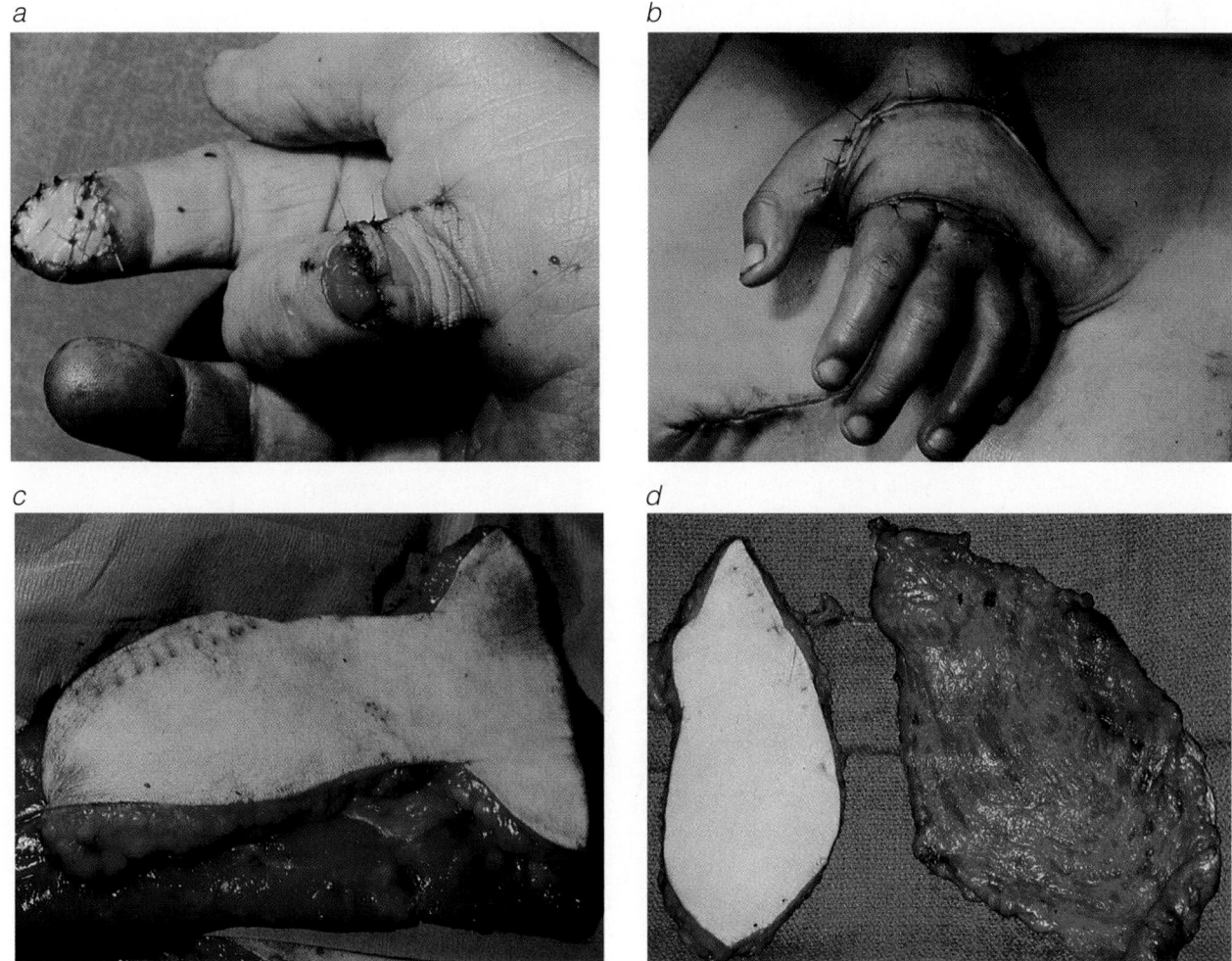

Figure 7 **Local flaps.** (*a*) **The blood supply of random-pattern skin flaps is limited; only small flaps (e.g., thenar flaps, shown here), are consistently reliable.** (*b*) **Shown is an axial-pattern skin flap.** (*c*) **The skin and subcutaneous tissue of a myocutaneous flap can exist as a complete island because the blood supply is derived from vertical muscular perforators.** (*d*) **Shown are a large free flap of scapular area skin and the entire latissimus dorsi. The subscapular vessels that connect the two will supply both components of the flap after microvascular anastomoses.**

TYPE I	TYPE II	TYPE III	TYPE IV	TYPE V

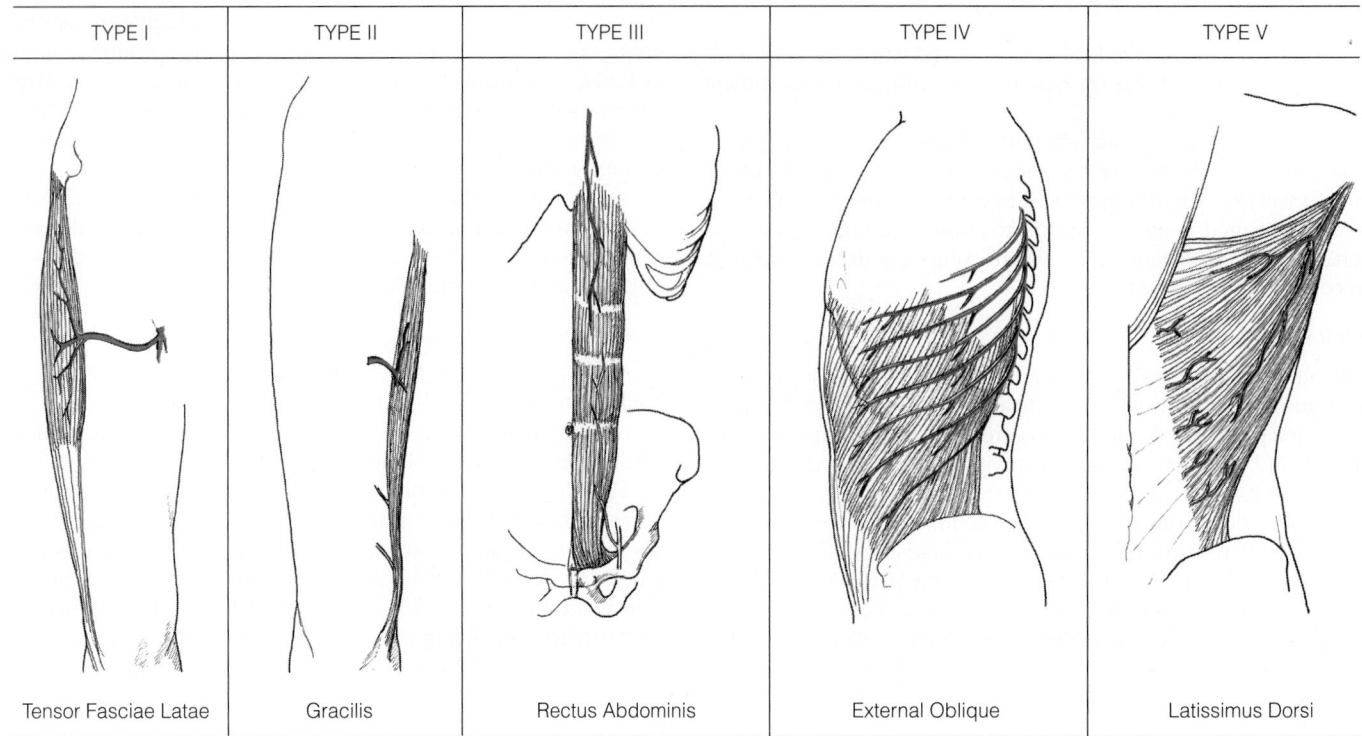

| Tensor Fasciae Latae | Gracilis | Rectus Abdominis | External Oblique | Latissimus Dorsi |

Figure 8 **Local flaps. Schematized are the five basic patterns of blood supply to muscle. Individual muscles are classified on the basis of the dominance, number, and size of the vessels that supply them. Type I is supplied by a single dominant pedicle. Type II is supplied by one dominant vessel and several much smaller vessels. Type III is supplied by two dominant pedicles. Type IV is supplied by multiple vessels of similar size. Type V is supplied by one dominant pedicle and several smaller segmental vascular pedicles.**

degree of skin tension present there, a skin graft may be indicated. As with any local flap, wide undermining of the surrounding tissues may be necessary for closure of the defect and the donor site. Closure is then performed in two layers.

Bilobed flap   A bilobed flap is a transposition flap consisting of two lobes of skin and subcutaneous tissue based on a common

pedicle [*see Figure 11*]. It is often used to correct nasal defects involving the lateral aspect, the ala, or the tip. The keys to a successful bilobed flap are (1) accurate design and (2) wide undermining of the surrounding tissue in the submuscular plane to allow a smooth transposition. The primary lobe is usually at an angle of 45° or less to the defect; the secondary lobe is designed to achieve closure of the donor defect and is substantially smaller

TYPE A	TYPE B	TYPE C

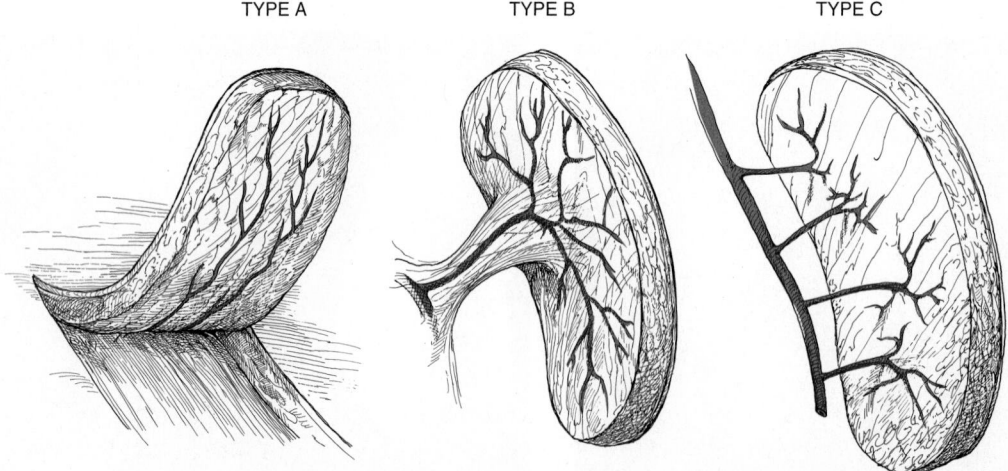

Figure 9 **Local flaps. At least three types of fasciocutaneous flaps exist, categorized by blood supply configuration. Type A is supplied by multiple small, longitudinal vessels coursing with the deep fascia. These flaps must retain a base of a certain width and cannot be raised as islands (e.g., longitudinally oriented flaps of skin and fascia on the lower leg). Type B is supplied by a single major vessel within the fascia (e.g., scapular flap). Type C is supplied by multiple perforating segments from a major vessel coursing through intermuscular septa (e.g., forearm flaps).**

Figure 10 **Local flaps: transposition flap. After excision of the defect, a transposition flap of adequate length is designed and elevated in the subcutaneous plane. The flap is moved laterally into the defect and inset. It may be necessary to excise a dog-ear of excess skin at the tip of the flap harvest site.**

than the primary lobe. The angle between the two is 90° to 100°. Both flaps are raised simultaneously in the submuscular plane. Wide undermining of the area (also in the submuscular plane) minimizes tension. The primary lobe of the bilobed flap is transposed into the initial defect, the secondary lobe is transposed into the donor defect left by the primary lobe, and the defect left by the secondary lobe is closed primarily. Closure is accomplished with 5-0 or 6-0 nylon.

Rhomboid flap (Limberg flap) A rhomboid flap is a transposition flap that is designed in a specific geometric fashion [*see Figure 12*]. The initial defect is converted to a rhomboid, with care taken to plan the flap in an area with minimal skin tension. The rhomboid must be an equilateral parallelogram with angles of 60° and 120°; this design allows the surgeon to excise less tissue than would be needed for an elliptical flap. One face of the rhomboid constitutes the first side of the flap (YZ). The short diagonal of the rhomboid is then extended outward for a distance equal to its own length. This extension should be oriented along relaxed skin tension lines, perpendicular to the line of maximum extensibility; it constitutes the second side of the flap (XY). Next, a line parallel and equal in length to YZ is drawn from X to outline the third side of the flap. Correct orientation of the rhomboid is vital for achieving flap repair with minimal tension, particularly with respect to the line of maximum extensibility: it is along this base line that maximum tension results when the donor defect is closed. Once the flap has been correctly designed and

elevated, it is transposed into the defect. Closure is done in two layers.

Rhomboid flaps work best on flat surfaces (e.g., the upper cheek, the temporal region, and the trunk). Extra attention to flap design is necessary when an attempt is made to close a defect over a convex surface with a rhomboid flap; improper flap design leads to excessive tension and potential flap necrosis.

Rotation Flaps

A flap that is rotated into the defect is called a rotation flap.[11,12] This type of flap is commonly used to repair a defect on the scalp, where large flaps must be designed to overcome the inelasticity of scalp tissue. A rotation flap takes the form of a semicircle of which the defect occupies a wedge-shaped segment [*see Figure 13*]. The original defect is converted to a triangular shape (ABC). One side of the triangular defect (AC) is extended to a point (D) that will serve as the pivot point for the flap. The distance between A and D should be at least 50% greater than that between A and C. A semicircular line extending from C to D is then defined.

The flap is incised with a scalpel, elevated, and rotated. As with all local skin flaps, wide undermining of the surrounding tissue may be necessary to allow tension-free rotation and wound closure. The flap is secured with a two-layer closure; the secondary defect may be closed primarily. Sometimes, a so-called back cut is required to gain adequate rotation. The most common technical error with rotation flaps is improper design: a flap that is too small will not cover the defect adequately.

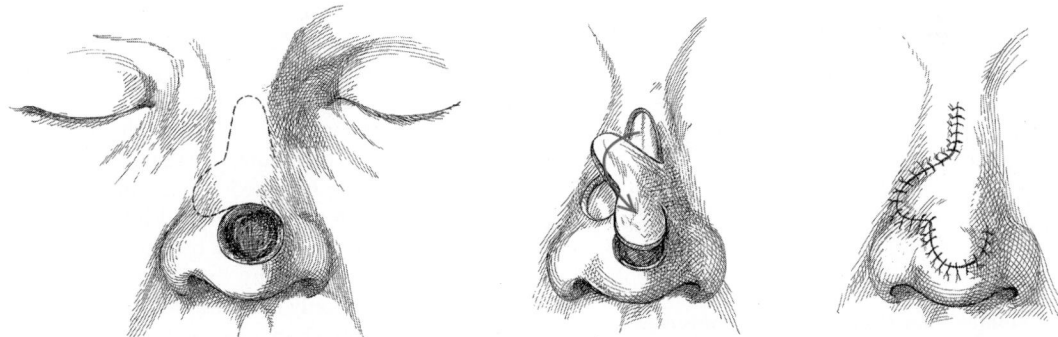

Figure 11 **Local flaps: bilobed flap. A flap with two lobes is created, with the first lobe the same size as the defect and the second lobe substantially (~50%) smaller than the first. The flap is elevated in the submuscular plane. Wide undermining at this level is necessary for tension-free transposition. The first lobe covers the initial defect, and the second covers the defect from the first. The second lobe is placed in an area of loose skin, and its area of origin is closed primarily.**

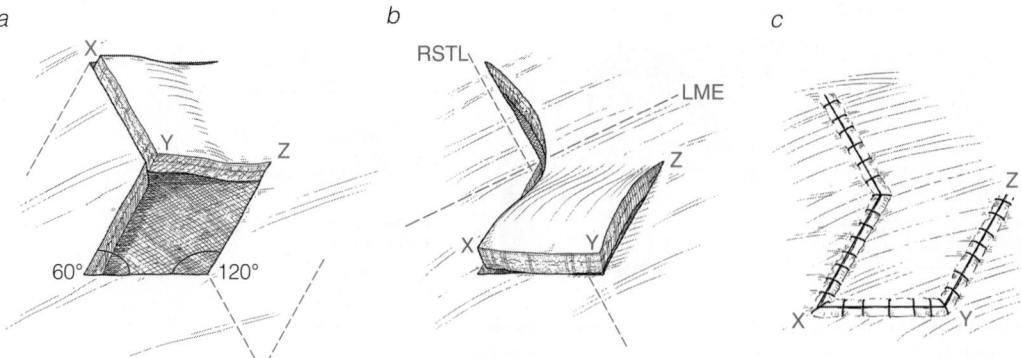

Figure 12 **Local flaps: rhomboid (Limberg) flap. (*a*) The defect is converted to a rhomboid, with all four sides of equal length and angles of 60° and 120°. An extension XY is made that is the same length as the short diagonal of the rhomboid, and a line of equal length is drawn from X paralleling YZ. (*b*) The flap is oriented so that XY follows the relaxed skin tension lines (RSTL) and YZ the line of maximum extensibility (LME). (*c*) The flap is inset.**

Advancement Flaps

Advancement flaps are moved directly forward into a defect without either rotation or lateral movement. The single-pedicle advancement flap is a rectangular or square flap of skin and subcutaneous tissue that is stretched forward. The flap is oriented with respect to the local skin tension, with care taken to plan the advancement in an area where the skin is extensible. A rectangular defect is created, and the flap is elevated in an area of loose skin and advanced to cover the defect [*see Figure 14*]. When closure is

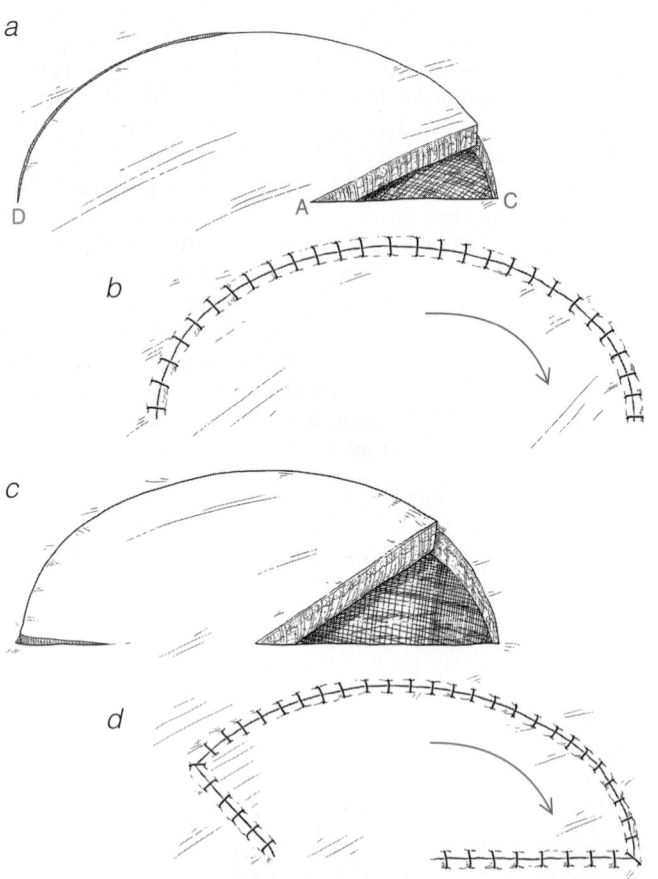

Figure 13 **Local flaps: rotation flap. (*a*) The defect is converted into a wedge. One side (AC) is extended to a pivot point D, so that AD is at least 50% longer than AC. A semicircle from C to D is defined. (*b*) The flap is elevated, rotated, and inset. (*c, d*) If there is too much tension, a back cut may be necessary to release the flap and allow rotation. Care is taken not to make the back cut excessively long; to do so could devascularize the flap.**

performed, some excess skin (dog-ears) at the base of the flap (Burow's triangles) may have to be excised.

V-Y advancement flap The V-Y advancement flap is a modification of a basic advancement flap [*see Figure 15*]. The use of a V-Y advancement flap eliminates the need to revise the dog-ears that sometimes result with rotation flaps. When possible, the flap should be oriented in accordance with the line of maximum extensibility. Its length should be 1.5 to 2 times that of the defect in the direction of the closure.

Incisions are made completely through skin. As with other flaps, skin hooks are used to retract the skin flap, and blunt scissors dissection is then performed. The point of the V on the flap is the area where tightness is most frequently encountered; this area may have to be released to facilitate advancement. Care must be taken not to undermine the advancing flap excessively: doing so may impair or interrupt the blood supply to the flap and result in necrosis. Once adequately advanced, the flap is sutured at the advancing edge and at the base of the Y.

Z-Plasty

When reconstruction is indicated for small, localized scars, soft tissue coverage is generally sufficient. With such coverage, there is no threat of breakdown leading to exposure of important structures; instead, the reconstructive problem is generally functional. An example is a flexion crease contracture, which is commonly seen after a burn injury. A local procedure that rearranges the existing tissue can relieve the tension by making more tissue available in one direction, even though the amount of tissue in the area is not actually increased.

The Z-plasty [*see Figure 16*] is an example of such tissue rearrangement.[13] Two triangular flaps are designed so that they have in common a central limb aligned in the direction along which additional length is desired. For example, the limb may be placed along the line of a contracture. Two lines, approximately equal in length to the central limb, are drawn from either end of the limb, diverging from it at equal angles varying from 30° to 90°. The degree of lengthening obtained is determined by the size of this angle [*see Table 2*]. In theory, maximal length gain is achieved by using the largest angle possible, but in practice, the maximum usable angle is determined by the limits of skin elasticity. A 60° angle, which is commonly used, will result in a 75% gain in length along the central limb. Triangular flaps are elevated, and the fibrous tissue band responsible for the contracture is divided. The triangular flaps are transposed and inset, yielding increased length in the desired direction, with the original Z rotated 90° and reversed.

Although Z-plasty is conceptually simple, it is not necessarily easy: experience is necessary for the surgeon to realize the limitations of technique and appreciate the subtleties of proper design. Important considerations in the use of Z-plasty include appropriate determination of the length of the central limb and correct orientation of the limbs so that the new central limb formed after transposition is parallel to skin tension lines. Multiple Z-plasties may be useful for some localized scars.

POSTOPERATIVE CARE

Local Flaps

The postoperative care of local flaps is not complex. Flap healing is supported by adequate nutrition and maintenance of a normal hemodynamic state, including normal blood volume. Tension must not be placed on the flap. Tension can develop in flaps on the trunk as a result of changes in patient position or in flaps on the limbs as a result of loss of immobilization. Generally, the tip of any local flap is not only its most valuable portion but also its most vulnerable area. At the tip, the blood supply is the most precarious, and the detrimental effects of tension are magnified. Unfortunately, no pharmacologic agents are of proven benefit in preventing necrosis of a flap with failing circulation. Any flap necrosis that might develop should be minimized by preventing infection of the necrotic tissue. Necrotic tissue must therefore be debrided after the extent of tissue loss becomes clear. Portions of the flap that are undergoing demarcation but do not appear actively infected can be protected by the application of a topical antibiotic (e.g., silver sulfadiazine cream).

Extremities that are recipient sites for flaps, like those that are recipient sites for skin grafts, should be immobilized and elevated after the operation until satisfactory wound healing has occurred.

Free Flaps

Survival of free flaps, unlike that of local flaps, tends to be an all-or-none phenomenon. Careful postoperative monitoring of flap circulation is essential because flap failure is likely to be the result of a problem at the vascular anastomoses. Flaps are usually monitored for 7 days. However, the most critical time for free-flap monitoring is the first 6 to 8 hours because the majority of vascular crises usually occur within this period. Early detection and aggressive investigation of such crises generally allow a flap to be salvaged. Maintenance of normal blood volume, treatment of hypothermia, and avoidance of pressors are particularly important in the early

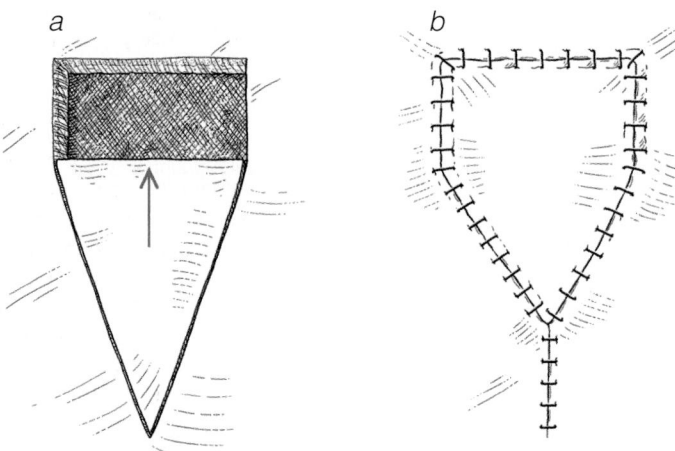

Figure 15 **Local flaps: V-Y advancement flap. (*a*) A V-shaped flap is created whose length is 1.5 to 2 times that of the defect. With subcutaneous connections to the skin preserved (because these constitute the blood supply to the flap), the flap is advanced into the defect. (*b*) The V incision is converted to a Y as the base is closed primarily.**

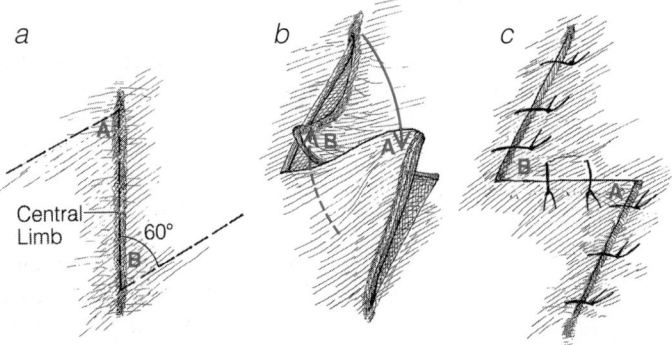

Figure 16 **Local flaps: Z-plasty. (*a*) The central limb of the Z is placed along the line of contracture. Incisions diverging from the scar at a 60° angle will yield an increase of approximately 75% in the direction of the central limb. (*b*) The flaps are transposed. (*c*) The length has been increased in the desired direction, and the original Z design has been rotated 90° and reversed.**

postoperative period to prevent vascular spasm. Spasm causes flaps to appear pale and to exhibit a significant temperature drop.

Free flaps exhibit venous engorgement when placed in a dependent position up to several weeks postoperatively. Such engorgement is generally not dangerous, though patients with free flaps below the knee should be gradually mobilized in the same fashion as patients with skin grafts in this location. These patients should also keep the lower extremity elevated for at least 10 to 14 days.

Free flaps in the head and neck area require that the patient's head motion be restricted somewhat for the first few days. It is important that electrocardiographic leads and tracheostomy tube ties not compress the external jugular vein if it was used as a recipient vessel for anastomosis. If central lines are used after operation, they should be placed on the contralateral side of the neck.

Free flaps should be monitored on an hourly basis during the early postoperative period. Most free flaps include an exposed skin island, which facilitates evaluation of the flap circulation. The flap is observed for color and for capillary refill—the most important indicators of flap viability. A pale flap generally indicates arterial insufficiency; however, this is not always the case, because certain

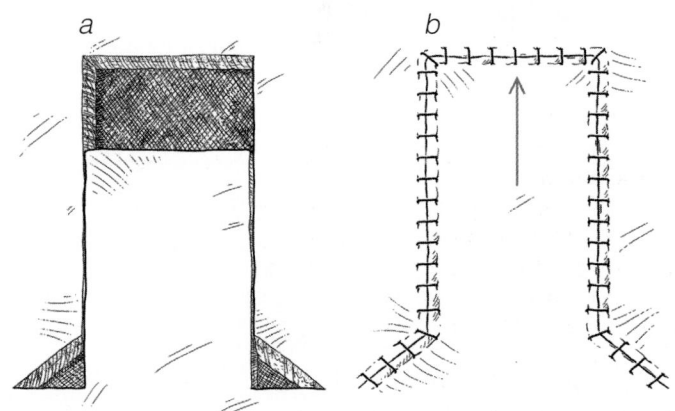

Figure 14 **Local flaps: direct advancement flap. (*a*) A flap whose shape corresponds to that of the defect is elevated in the subcutaneous plane and advanced into the defect. (*b*) Excision of Burow's triangles (excess skin at the flap base) may be necessary to permit advancement.**

Table 2   Z-Plasty: Incision Angle and Degree of Lengthening Theoretically Possible

Incision Angle (degrees)	Theoretical Amount of Lengthening (%)
30	25
45	50
60	75
75	100
90	120

donor sites, such as the abdomen, are relatively light in color under normal circumstances, which means that a flap from one of these sites may appear pale while still having an adequate arterial supply. Flaps with venous insufficiency are characteristically blue in color and exhibit rapid capillary refill. In such flaps, brisk capillary refill often precedes the blue discoloration, and it is cause for concern when observed. Bleeding from the edges of a flap is common in the presence of venous hypertension.

If a skin island is exposed, Doppler ultrasonography should reveal the presence of a triphasic arterial pulse. The site of this pulse should be marked with a suture or with permanent ink to facilitate monitoring by nursing staff. A trained ear can distinguish between triphasic, biphasic, and monophasic pulses, which (in that order) indicate increasing degrees of arterial compromise from arterial thrombosis or increasing venous hypertension.

Surface temperature probes can be used to monitor free flaps that have a skin island. The advantages of this method are simplicity and reliability. One probe is placed on the flap and another on a nearby area to serve as a control. The flap surface temperature is generally about 1.0° to 2.5° C lower than the control temperature. A progressive widening of this temperature difference is ominous and calls for critical assessment of the flap circulation. The absolute temperature of the flap probe is also significant: a flap temperature higher than 32° C indicates healthy circulation, whereas a temperature between 30° and 32° C indicates marginal circulation and a temperature lower than 30° C often indicates a vascular problem. In a healthy flap, temperature fluctuations may be caused by a dislodged probe, an exogenous heat source (e.g., a lamp), cooling of one of the probes from an oxygen mist mask, or cleaning of the flap skin with alcohol (which results in a precipitous drop in skin temperature).

To confirm the presence of an anastomotic problem, flap circulation is assessed directly by a full-thickness puncture of the flap skin with a 20-, 22-, or 25-gauge needle. If flap circulation is healthy, a drop of bright-red blood should appear at the puncture site within a few seconds, and another drop should appear each time the previous drop is wiped away by an alcohol swab. The failure of blood to appear or the delayed appearance of a clear, serous ooze instead of blood is an indication of arterial insufficiency. Vigorous, dark bleeding confirms a venous problem. Flaps that are pale as a result of vascular spasm are difficult to assess because their bleeding response to needle puncture is poor despite intact anastomoses. As a rule, clinical judgment of flap viability on the basis of all these methods of flap monitoring will be highly predictive. If, however, some uncertainty exists, surgical exploration should be undertaken because the entire flap may be in jeopardy.

Free flaps without skin islands are more difficult to monitor accurately. Muscle flaps can be followed in much the same way as skin free flaps by inserting needle temperature probes directly into the muscle belly. A healthy muscle free flap is red in color and typically has a serous ooze between the interstices of the overlying meshed skin graft. A flap with an arterial problem quickly becomes dry and dark in appearance. A muscle flap with a venous problem becomes dark and engorged with blood and exhibits bleeding from its surface and perimeter. A muscle free flap can be punctured with a needle to assess the quality of the bleeding if its circulatory status is unclear.

Fascial free flaps covered with skin grafts are more difficult to assess. They tend to transmit body core temperature readily because they are quite thin; therefore, needle temperature probes are generally unreliable. It is often possible in these cases either to observe the arterial pulsations in the flap directly or to monitor them with a conventional Doppler device.

Some free flaps are completely buried beneath the skin. Others, such as intraoral skin free flaps, are equally difficult to monitor postoperatively. Specialized transplants (e.g., jejunal transplants) are particularly vulnerable to short periods of anoxia and are not likely to be salvageable by the time a problem is recognized. Alternative methods of monitoring buried free flaps are being developed and are being used with increasing frequency. One example is the implantable Doppler monitor. This device is placed in direct contact with the artery or vein distal to the anastomosis to obtain a continuous Doppler signal.[14]

References

1. Weinzweig N, Weinzweig J: Basic principles and techniques in plastic surgery. Mastery of Plastic and Reconstructive Surgery, Vol 1. Choen M, Ed. Little, Brown, and Co, Boston, 1994
2. Borges AF: Elective Incisions and Scar Revision. Little, Brown, and Co, Boston, 1973
3. Schneider AM, Morkwas MJ, Argenta LC: A new and reliable method of securing skin grafts to the difficult recipient bed. Plast Reconstr Surg 102:1195, 1998
4. Smahel J: The healing of skin grafts. Clin Plast Surg 4:409, 1977
5. Disa JJ, Alizadeh K, Smith JW, et al: Evaluation of a combined sodium alginate and bioocclusive membrane dressing in the management of split thickness skin graft donor sites. Ann Plast Surg 46:405, 2001
6. Daniel RK, Kerrigan CL: Skin flaps: an anatomical and hemodynamic approach. Clin Plast Surg 6:181, 1979
7. Cederna PS, Chang P, Pittet-Cuenod BM, et al: The effect of the delay phenomenon on the vascularity of rabbit abdominal cutaneous island flaps. Plast Reconstr Surg 99:183, 1997
8. Milton SH: Pedicled skin-flaps: the fallacy of the length:width ratio. Br J Surg 57:502, 1970
9. Lamberty BG, Cormack GC: Fasciocutaneous flaps. Clin Plast Surg 17:713, 1990
10. Cormack GC, Lamberty BG: Arterial Anatomy of Skin Flaps. Churchill Livingstone, Edinburgh, 1987
11. Jackson IT: Local rotational flaps. Operative Plastic Surgery. Evans GRD, Ed. McGraw-Hill, New York, 2000
12. Worthen EF: Scalp flaps and the rotation forehead flap. Grabb's Encyclopedia of Flaps, Vol 1. Strauch B, Vasconez LO, Hall-Findlay EJ, Eds. Lippincott-Raven Publishers, Philadelphia, 1998
13. McGregor IA, McGregor AD: The z-plasty. Fundamental Techniques of Plastic Surgery. Churchill Livingstone, Edinburgh, 1995
14. Kind GM, Buntic RF, Buncke GM, et al: The effect of an implantable Doppler probe on the salvage of microvascular tissue transplants. Plast Reconstr Surg 101:1268, 1998

Acknowledgments

Figures 1 through 3, 10, 12 through 15   Tom Moore.
Figures 6, 8, 9, 11, 16   Carol Donner.

28 DYSPHAGIA

Ahmad S. Ashrafi, M.D., F.R.C.S.C., and R. Sudhir Sundaresan, M.D., F.A.C.S., F.R.C.S.C.

Evaluation of Dysphagia

Dysphagia may be defined as difficulty in transferring a food bolus from the mouth to the stomach. It may be associated with abnormalities in the oral, the pharyngeal, or the esophageal phase of swallowing. Unlike the term globus, which describes a painless sensation of fullness in the neck or throat, the term dysphagia implies actual interference with the swallowing mechanism [*see Sidebar The Swallowing Mechanism*]. Dysphagia may be classified as oropharyngeal or esophageal. Whereas oropharyngeal dysphagia (i.e., dysphagia resulting from abnormalities in the oral or the pharyngeal phase of swallowing) usually implies a functional disturbance in the swallowing mechanism, esophageal dysphagia may result from a discrete mechanical obstruction or from an esophageal motility disorder.

The exact prevalence of dysphagia is difficult to determine, but it is estimated that 35% of persons older than 50 years complain of dysphagia at least once a week. It is important to keep in mind, however, that the changes in swallowing physiology associated with aging rarely lead to true dysphagia. Esophageal dysphagia arises primarily from intrinsic diseases of the esophagus; oropharyngeal dysphagia frequently occurs as part of a neurologic, metabolic, myopathic, or infectious syndrome.[1]

In what follows, we review the diagnostic and therapeutic decision-making approaches employed in assessing patients with dysphagia. Although it is important that surgeons have a working knowledge of all causes of dysphagia, our focus here is on evaluation of conditions that give rise to esophageal dysphagia. We mention surgical management options but do not address them in detail; the operative procedures performed to treat the various clinical entities that cause dysphagia are described more fully elsewhere [*see 34 Open Esophageal Procedures, 35 Minimally Invasive Esophageal Procedures, and 37 Video-Assisted Thoracic Surgery*].

Clinical Evaluation

Evaluation of a patient with dysphagia must be performed in a systematic manner. Assessment begins with obtaining a detailed history, followed by physical examination. Ex-

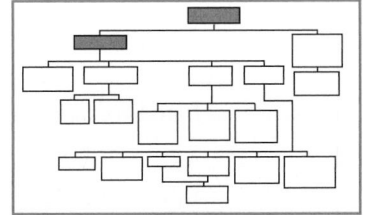

cept in the case of acute caustic ingestion, for which direct flexible esophagoscopy is the first line of assessment, the barium swallow, a readily available and noninvasive test, should be the first investigative tool. The barium swallow is a cost-effective, rapid, and easily available test that provides a "road map" of the esophagus and the lesion and yields a tremendous amount of information before endoscopic assessment. Additional diagnostic information can be obtained by means of fiberoptic esophagoscopy, manometry, 24-hour pH study, and, occasionally, bronchoscopy and endoscopic ultrasonography (EUS). Further diagnostic imaging, in the form of computed tomography and positron emission tomography

(PET), is particularly valuable in assessing patients with esophageal cancer.

OROPHARYNGEAL DYSPHAGIA

Oropharyngeal dysphagia is usually associated with symptoms that originate in the oropharynx, including inability to chew food, drooling, coughing during a meal, and nasal regurgitation of solids or liquids. In general, if a patient experiences dysphagia within 1 second of swallowing, an oropharyngeal origin is likely. A variety of different conditions are capable of causing oropharyngeal dysphagia. The common causes can be grouped into three broad categories: (1) generalized (systemic) conditions, (2) intrinsic functional disturbances, and (3) conditions that give rise to fixed mechanical obstruction [*see Table 1*]. Overall, the most common cause of oropharyngeal dysphagia is a cerebrovascular accident (CVA).

ESOPHAGEAL DYSPHAGIA

Esophageal dysphagia causes symptoms that are referable to the chest or the abdomen. In approximately 75% of cases, the patient's perception of the location of the obstructive site corresponds to the actual anatomic site of the lesion.[2] In addition to dysphagia, patients may experience associated symptoms, such as chest pain (with a character and a radiation pattern resembling those of coronary artery disease [CAD]), retrosternal burning, and regurgitation of undigested food.[3]

As a general rule, if the swallowing difficulty gradually progresses from solids to liquids, the dysphagia probably has a mechanical cause. Patients who have mechanical obstruction usually complain of dysphagia without pain and can relieve their symptoms only by regurgitating or by altering their diet. If significant weight loss and

---

The Swallowing Mechanism

Swallowing consists of both a voluntary phase (comprising the oral phase and the first part of the pharyngeal phase) and an involuntary phase (comprising the latter part of the pharyngeal phase and the esophageal phase). The voluntary phase starts with mastication and ends with the positioning of an appropriately sized food bolus in the back of the oropharynx via tongue retraction. The involuntary phase starts with the opening of the glossopalatal gate and the propulsion of the bolus into the pharynx, beyond the upper esophageal sphincter. Once in the esophagus, the food bolus is propelled into the stomach by primary and secondary esophageal peristaltic waves. The lower esophageal sphincter relaxes, allowing the food to be delivered into the stomach. The brain-stem swallowing center, located in the medulla and the pons, provides involuntary control of swallowing. Although swallowing begins in the oropharynx and is initially voluntary, the subsequent reflex mechanisms are based on peripheral input from the oropharyngeal innervation and are involuntary.

Evaluation of Dysphagia

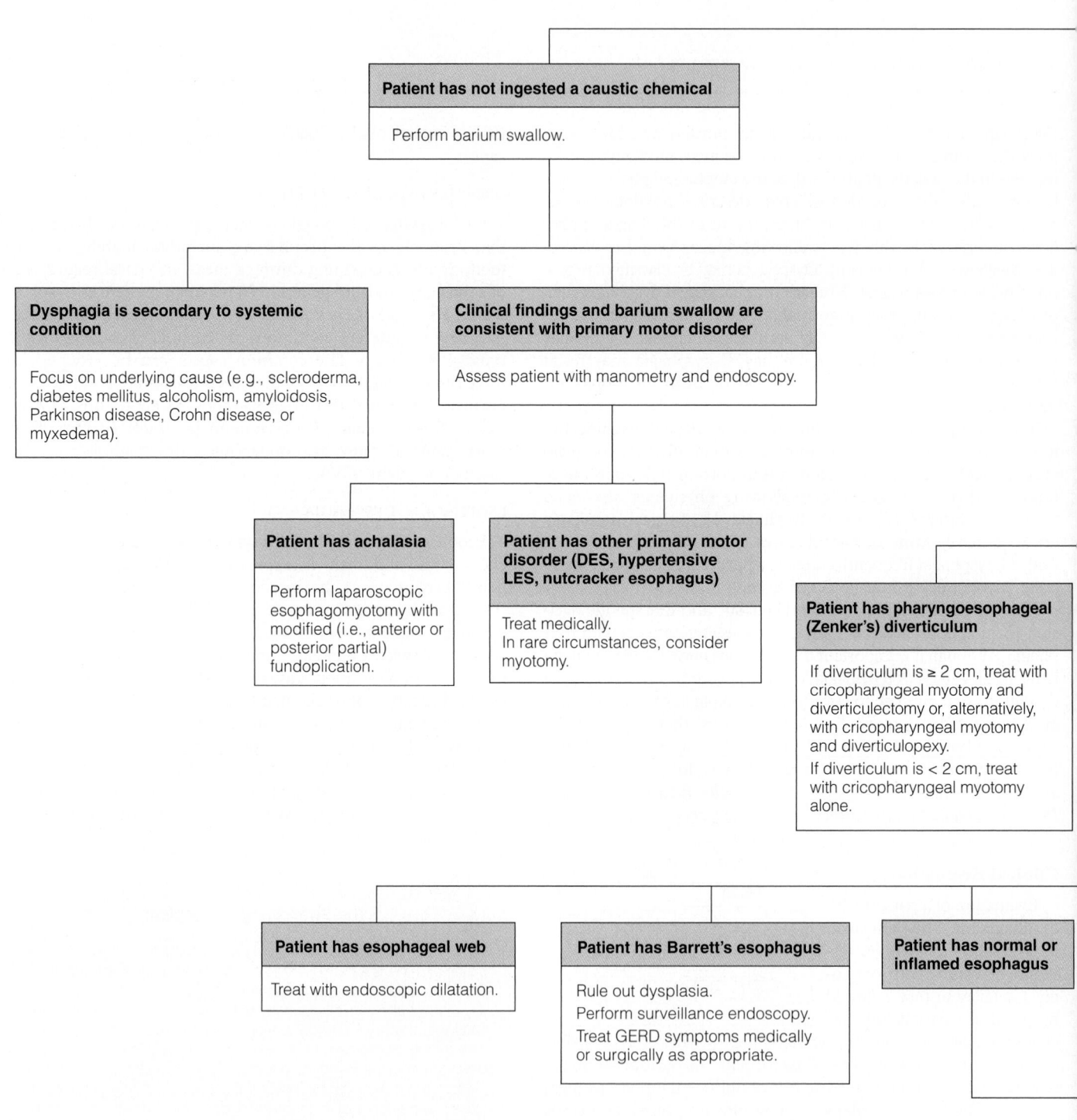

Patient has not ingested a caustic chemical

Perform barium swallow.

Dysphagia is secondary to systemic condition

Focus on underlying cause (e.g., scleroderma, diabetes mellitus, alcoholism, amyloidosis, Parkinson disease, Crohn disease, or myxedema).

Clinical findings and barium swallow are consistent with primary motor disorder

Assess patient with manometry and endoscopy.

Patient has achalasia

Perform laparoscopic esophagomyotomy with modified (i.e., anterior or posterior partial) fundoplication.

Patient has other primary motor disorder (DES, hypertensive LES, nutcracker esophagus)

Treat medically.
In rare circumstances, consider myotomy.

Patient has pharyngoesophageal (Zenker's) diverticulum

If diverticulum is ≥ 2 cm, treat with cricopharyngeal myotomy and diverticulectomy or, alternatively, with cricopharyngeal myotomy and diverticulopexy.
If diverticulum is < 2 cm, treat with cricopharyngeal myotomy alone.

Patient has esophageal web

Treat with endoscopic dilatation.

Patient has Barrett's esophagus

Rule out dysplasia.
Perform surveillance endoscopy.
Treat GERD symptoms medically or surgically as appropriate.

Patient has normal or inflamed esophagus

Patient presents with difficulty in swallowing

Obtain complete history.
Perform thorough examination.

Patient has ingested a caustic chemical

Perform direct flexible esophagoscopy.
Ensure adequate airway, breathing, and circulation.
Place patient on NPO regimen.
Give I.V. antibiotics.
Initiate total parenteral nutrition.
Perform barium swallow in 2–3 wk.

Follow up for stricture. Steroids are not helpful for stricture prophylaxis.
If stricture develops, treat with endoscopic dilatation. If stricture is tight and cannot be dilated, perform esophageal resection.

Barium swallow reveals esophageal diverticular disease

Treat according to anatomic level of diverticulum.

Barium swallow suggests fixed mechanical obstruction

Assess patient with endoscopy.

Patient has midesophageal diverticulum

Lesions result from periesophageal inflammation and are frequently asymptomatic; dysphagia is rare.
If there are no significant symptoms, they need not be treated, and therapy focuses on underlying inflammatory condition.

Patient has epiphrenic diverticulum

Assess patient with manometry and endoscopy.
If symptoms are absent or mild, manage conservatively.
If significant symptoms are present, manage surgically with myotomy, diverticulectomy, and partial fundoplication.

Patient has peptic stricture

Treat with endoscopic dilatation, and perform brush biopsy to rule out malignancy.

Give PPIs.
Consider manometry and 24-hr pH study.
Consider antireflux surgery.

Patient has Schatzki's ring

If lesion is asymptomatic, no treatment is required.
If lesion is symptomatic, treat with endoscopic dilatation and medical (or, if necessary, surgical) therapy for GERD.

Patient has esophageal cancer

Perform esophagoscopy for pathologic diagnosis.
Rule out distant metastatic disease with CT or PET. EUS may aid in locoregional staging.
Treat surgically according to stage of disease.
If cancer is localized and patient is medically fit, perform esophagectomy.

Table 1 Common Causes of Oropharyngeal Dysphagia

Generalized conditions	CVA Myasthenia gravis
Intrinsic functional disturbances	Cricopharyngeal achalasia Zenker's diverticulum
Conditions producing fixed mechanical obstruction	Neoplasm Webs Previous surgical treatment Previous radiation therapy

anorexia develop and symptoms are progressing rapidly, esophageal cancer is the likely cause of the dysphagia.

If, however, the patient has dysphagia for both liquids and solids, an underlying esophageal motor disorder is probably responsible. Patients who have motor disorders that cause dysphagia often develop certain unusual maneuvers to relieve their difficulty, including repeated swallowing, raising the arms over the head or assuming different positions during swallowing, and the Valsalva maneuver. Such patients also frequently complain of other associated symptoms (e.g., chest pain).

Physical examination is not as helpful as a detailed history. Clues that may help identify malignant conditions include the development of head and neck lymphadenopathy, the presence of an oropharyngeal mass, the appearance of subcutaneous lumps (suggestive of cutaneous metastasis), and the occurrence of clinical features associated with abdominal organ metastasis (jaundice, ascites, hepatomegaly). Muscle weakness, fatigability, and other neurologic deficits detected on physical examination may suggest a CVA or myasthenia gravis as the cause of dysphagia. Like oropharyngeal dysphagia, esophageal dysphagia may be caused by a number of different generalized conditions, intrinsic functional disturbances, or conditions that give rise to fixed mechanical obstruction [see Table 2].[4]

Workup and Management of Specific Causes of Dysphagia

SECONDARY MOTOR DISORDERS RESULTING FROM SYSTEMIC CONDITIONS

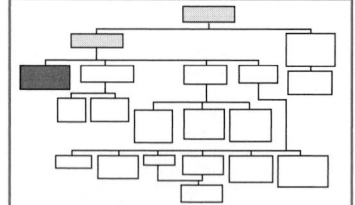

In patients with secondary motility disorders, the esophageal motor disturbance is a manifestation of a systemic condition; thus, organs other than the esophagus are also involved. The classic examples of systemic conditions that give rise to esophageal motility disorders are scleroderma, diabetes mellitus, and alcoholism. Patients who have one or more of these conditions may present with varying degrees of dysphagia, and their evaluation usually entails functional and structural evaluation of the esophagus.

Treatment is aimed at the underlying cause. Patients with scleroderma exhibit atrophy and sclerosis of distal esophageal smooth muscle with fragmentation of connective tissue. Consequently, primary peristalsis is absent, and the lower esophageal sphincter (LES) is hypotensive or virtually absent. Patients usually present with gastroesophageal reflux and heartburn. Because they also lack secondary peristalsis, there is no mechanism for clearing the refluxed acid back to the stomach, and as a result, patients are pre-

disposed to ulcerative esophagitis and peptic stricture [see Disorders Producing Fixed Mechanical Obstruction, Peptic Stricture, below].

Other causes of secondary esophageal motility disturbance resulting in dysphagia are amyloidosis, Parkinson disease, Crohn disease, and myxedema.

INTRINSIC FUNCTIONAL DISTURBANCES

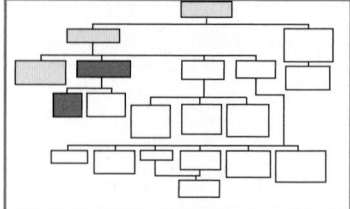

Primary Motor Disorders

Achalasia The majority of patients with achalasia present with dysphagia for liquids and solids. Most describe a long-standing history of swallowing difficulty, with or without associated weight loss. Other presenting symptoms include regurgitation, chest pain, heartburn, and coughing or choking spells. Typically, patients will have developed coping mechanisms to deal with the problem (e.g., changing position during eating, drinking liquids to "wash down" the food, and practicing repetitive swallowing and chewing).

A barium x-ray with fluoroscopy will show absent peristalsis and a dilated esophagus. Other findings include a tapered narrowing in the distal esophagus (a so-called bird's beak [see Figure 1]) and, occasionally, an epiphrenic diverticulum [see Esophageal Diverticula, below]. Because the study is dynamic, failure of LES relaxation must be watched for as it is performed. Over time, the esophagus can dilate significantly, to the point where it takes on a sigmoid shape.

Although some radiologists will declare a diagnosis of achalasia solely on the basis of barium x-rays and fluoroscopy, upper GI endoscopy is essential to rule out fixed mechanical obstruction (long-standing achalasia is a risk factor for squamous cell cancer of the esophagus because of chronic stasis and retention esophagitis) or so-called pseudoachalasia (a motility disorder resulting from a carcinoma on the underside of the cardia that extends proximally within the wall of the esophagus). The key diagnostic test in the setting of suspected achalasia is esophageal manometry. Characteristic manometric features of achalasia include aperistalsis and incomplete relaxation of the LES; the LES pressure may be either high or normal.

A detailed discussion of the management of achalasia is beyond the scope of this chapter. Briefly, medical management offers virtually no benefit. Pneumatic dilatation offers subjective improve-

Table 2 Common Causes of Esophageal Dysphagia

Generalized conditions	Scleroderma Diabetes mellitus Alcoholism
Intrinsic functional disturbances	GERD with decreased motility Motor disorders
Conditions producing fixed mechanical obstruction	Webs Peptic strictures Schatzki's ring Caustic injury Neoplasms Extrinsic compression Previous surgical treatment Previous radiation therapy

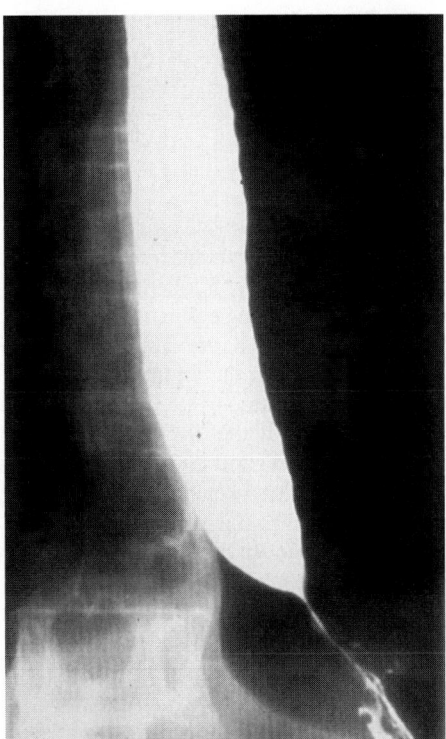

Figure 1 **Shown are proximal dilatation and classic bird's-beak narrowing consistent with achalasia in a 22-year-old woman being evaluated for dysphagia.**

ment in more than two thirds of patients; however, the result is durable in only a minority of cases, and the procedure carries a 4% to 5% risk of rupture. Laparoscopic esophagomyotomy with anterior (Dor) fundoplication (or, as some surgeons prefer, posterior partial fundoplication) [*see 35 Minimally Invasive Esophageal Procedures*] probably represents the current standard of care.

Diffuse esophageal spasm
Diffuse esophageal spasm (DES) is a motility disorder of unknown etiology that gives rise to dysphagia and chest pain. The dysphagia is non-progressive and is encountered with both liquids and solids.

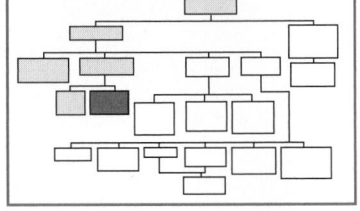

The chest pain is nonexertional but may respond to nitroglycerin.

A barium x-ray may show the classic corkscrew appearance [*see Figure 2*], but this finding is nondiagnostic. The diagnosis is established by manometry; the key finding is the periodic occurrence of simultaneous high-amplitude contractions with intervening periods of normal peristalsis. The presence of these intervals of normal peristalsis is important for distinguishing DES from nutcracker esophagus [*see Nutcracker Esophagus, below*]. An elaborate workup is often necessary to clarify the basis of the chest pain and rule out the possibility of CAD.

Once CAD has been ruled out, management is primarily medical and consists of reassurance, nitrates, and calcium channel blockers. Botulinum toxin injection and extended esophagomyotomy have been used to treat DES, with some success, but in general, surgery does not have an established role in this setting.

Hypertensive lower esophageal sphincter Hypertensive LES is a rare motility disorder of unknown etiology. Although it

can occur in isolation, it is usually seen in association with achalasia, nutcracker esophagus, or DES. Patients present with dysphagia for liquids and solids. Manometric evaluation shows a mean LES resting pressure higher than 45 mm Hg in midrespiration. Treatment is primarily medical, but balloon dilatation has been employed to relieve persistent dysphagia.

Nutcracker esophagus Nutcracker esophagus is an esophageal motility disorder of unknown etiology that affects women more often than men. Patients usually present with chest pain but may have associated dysphagia as well. Manometry typically shows peristaltic waves with significantly elevated amplitude (> 180 mm Hg). Barium x-rays are usually normal. Treatment is similar to that of DES and is primarily medical.

Esophageal Diverticula

Esophageal diverticula account for fewer than 5% of all cases of dysphagia. They may be classified into two broad categories: true and false. True diverticula include all layers of the esophageal

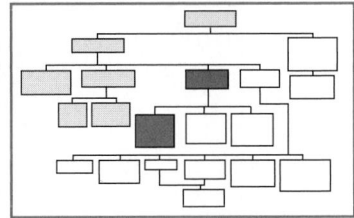

wall, whereas false diverticula include only the mucosal layer. True diverticula develop as a result of a periesophageal inflammatory process that places traction on the esophageal wall (and thus are also referred to as traction diverticula), whereas false diverticula are manifestations of an underlying motor dysfunction (and thus are also referred to as pulsion diverticula). Esophageal diverticula may also be classified into three categories on the basis of the anatomic level at which they occur: pharyngoesophageal (Zenker's), midesophageal, and epiphrenic. A few patients will exhibit

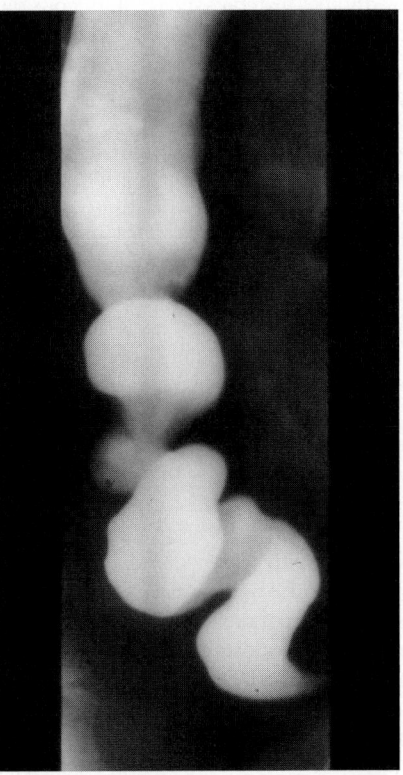

Figure 2 **Shown is classic corkscrew appearance of esophagus in a middle-aged man presenting with dysphagia and intermittent chest pain.**

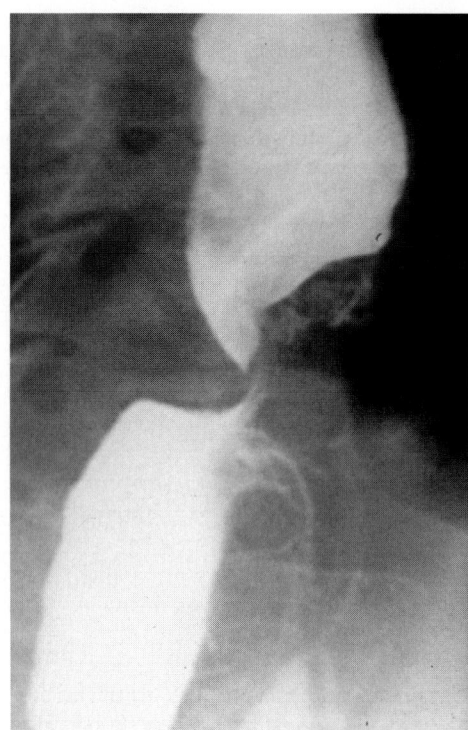

Figure 3 **Shown is a large pharyngoesophageal pouch (Zenker's diverticulum) in an elderly patient with dysphagia, regurgitation of old retained food, and recurrent pneumonia.**

diffuse intramural diverticulosis, a rare condition characterized by the development of multiple 1 to 5 mm outpouchings in association with esophageal inflammation and fibrosis. These outpouchings are believed to be dilated esophageal mucous glands resulting from chronic inflammation. Dysphagia is the most common presenting complaint for this condition, though one third of patients complain of gastroesophageal reflux.

Pharyngoesophageal diverticula Zenker's diverticula are the most common esophageal diverticula. These pulsion diverticula result from pharyngocricopharyngeal incoordination that leads to herniation of the mucosa in Killian's triangle (the posterior midline of the lower pharynx, between the oblique muscle fibers of the inferior pharyngeal constrictor and the transverse fibers of the cricopharyngeus). Dysphagia is the most common symptom, but patients may also complain of halitosis, regurgitation of undigested food, throat discomfort, a palpable neck mass, a gurgling noise during swallowing, and recurrent aspiration pneumonia.

The best initial diagnostic tool is a barium swallow [*see Figure 3*], which will establish the diagnosis and also may help diagnose any associated problems (e.g., gastroesophageal reflux disease [GERD] and hiatal hernia). Performing upper GI endoscopy without first obtaining a barium study is a potentially disastrous maneuver: because the endoscope will preferentially enter the pouch rather than the true esophageal lumen, there is a significant risk of inadvertent esophageal perforation. Endoscopy does play a role in assessing the esophageal mucosa, but it is best performed at the time of operation.

The fundamental component of surgical treatment is relief of the functional obstruction at the cricopharyngeus (via cricopharyngeal myotomy) [*see 34 Open Esophageal Procedures*]. Once this is done, diverticula larger than 2 cm should be excised; smaller diverticula can generally be managed with myotomy alone. Diverticulopexy is another option for dealing with the pouch.

Midesophageal diverticula Midesophageal diverticula are true (i.e., traction) diverticula that are caused by periesophageal inflammation. The usual cause is granulomatous inflammation of the subcarinal lymph nodes 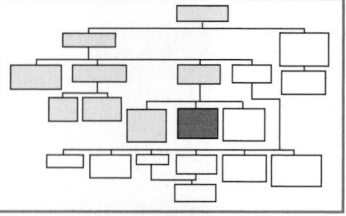 resulting from tuberculosis or fungal infection (typically, histoplasmosis). These diverticula are frequently asymptomatic and are often found incidentally during evaluation for some other disorder. Dysphagia does occur but is a rare symptom; the clinical manifestations are usually related to the underlying inflammatory disease or to associated complications (e.g., infection, bleeding, or fistulization to the airway). If the diverticula are not symptomatic, they need not be treated, and the therapeutic focus is on the underlying problem that prompted the evaluation.

Epiphrenic diverticula Epiphrenic diverticula are acquired pulsion diverticula that arise in the distal 10 cm of the esophagus [*see Figure 4*]. Although these diverticula are usually associated with other esophageal motor disorders 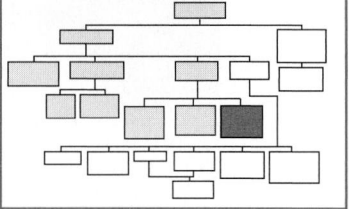 (e.g., achalasia, DES, and hypertensive LES), they occasionally occur in the absence of any underlying esophageal dysfunction. If symptoms are absent or mild, conservative management is appropriate. If significant symptoms (e.g., dysphagia) are present, however, surgical management—usually entailing myotomy, diverticulectomy, and modified fundoplication—is indicated. Before operation, patients should undergo a thorough functional assessment with manometry.

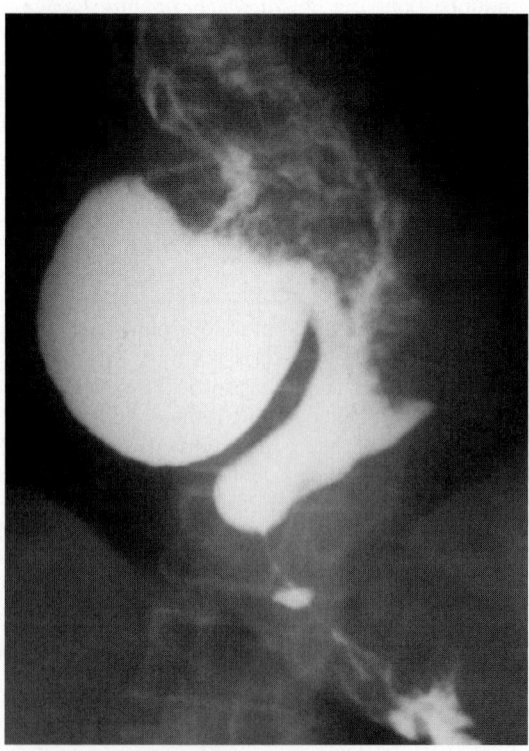

Figure 4 **Shown is a giant epiphrenic diverticulum in an elderly woman with progressive dysphagia and weight loss, in whom cancer was initially suspected.**

DISORDERS PRODUCING
FIXED MECHANICAL
OBSTRUCTION

Esophageal Webs

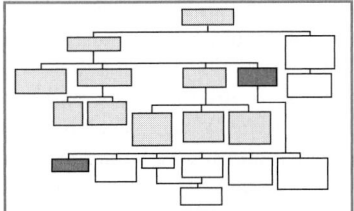

A web is a localized narrowing of the esophagus caused by intraluminal extension of the mucosa and part of the submucosa of the esophageal wall. Webs may be either congenital or, more commonly, acquired, usually secondary to conditions such as iron deficiency anemia, pemphigoid, and ulcerative colitis (among others). The main presenting symptom is dysphagia, the severity of which is proportional to the degree of obstruction. Treatment usually consists of simple endoscopic dilatation [*see 60 Gastrointestinal Endoscopy*] after careful verification of the nature of the lesion.

Peptic Stricture

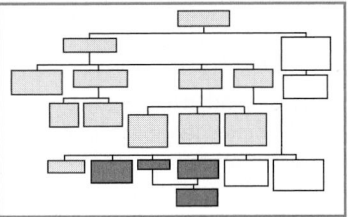

GERD is a very common problem. The majority of patients will present with heartburn and regurgitation. Although the associated hypomotility observed in some GERD patients can account for some of the dysphagia, it is important to consider (and, if possible, rule out) more significant complications, such as peptic stricture, Barrett's esophagus, and carcinoma.

Peptic stricture represents the end stage of ulcerative esophagitis, in which the healing of circumferential ulceration results in

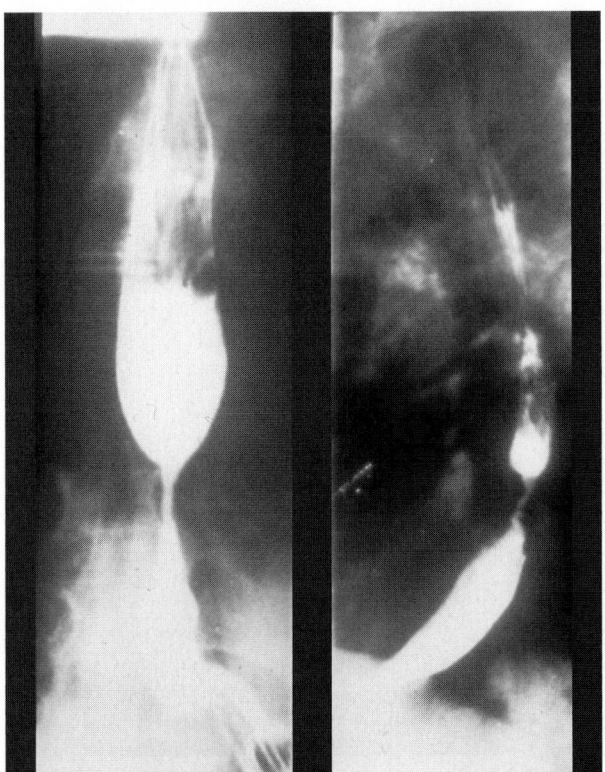

Figure 5 **Barium swallow shows severe ulcerative esophagitis, annular fibrosis (stricture), and evidence of acquired esophageal shortening. Shortness of narrowed segment suggests benign underlying cause.**

annular fibrosis. Proton pump inhibitors (PPIs) have proved highly effective in controlling GERD symptoms and enhancing the healing of esophageal ulcers; as a result of their widespread use, peptic stricture is now an infrequent complication.

Peptic strictures may occur at any age, and there is usually an antecedent history of GERD. The symptoms are progressive but unlike those of a malignant process, in that the dysphagia usually dates back several years and weight loss is usually absent. Typically, a patient with a peptic stricture describes gradually worsening dysphagia, initially for solids and eventually for liquids as well. If the patient has dysphagia for liquids before solids or has dysphagia for both liquids and solids, an associated motility disorder must be suspected. Strictures induced by reflux are located in the distal esophagus at the squamocolumnar junction [*see Figure 5*]; the presence of strictures in other parts of the esophagus raises the possibility of causes other than acid-peptic injury. The best initial diagnostic testing approach consists of a barium swallow [*see Figure 5*] followed by upper GI endoscopy, which shows ulcers and a concentric stenosis (which is usually short).

Management of GERD patients with peptic strictures is controversial. One approach consists of dilatation of the stricture [*see 60 Gastrointestinal Endoscopy*] in conjunction with high-dose PPI therapy. An important component of this approach is the performance of a brush biopsy at the time of dilatation to rule out a malignancy. If the stricture recurs, then dilatation with an antireflux procedure [*see 34 Open Esophageal Procedures and 35 Minimally Invasive Esophageal Procedures*] is indicated. In the rare cases in which the stricture cannot be dilated, esophageal resection [*see 34 Open Esophageal Procedures and 37 Video-Assisted Thoracic Surgery*] must be considered.

Schatzki's Ring

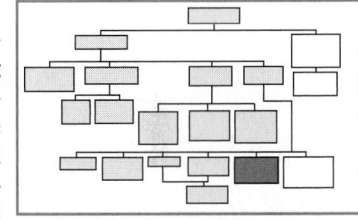

Schatzki's ring is a concentric, symmetrical narrowing at the squamocolumnar junction that arises from the development of submucosal annular fibrosis and is usually accompanied by a small hiatal hernia.[5] The exact cause is unknown, though there is a strong correlation with GERD. Dysphagia is usually for solids and is proportional to the diameter of the ring. Barium swallow establishes the diagnosis [*see Figure 6*], and esophagoscopy is recommended to confirm it.

For asymptomatic patients, no specific treatment is needed. For patients who present with food impaction, emergency treatment, involving rigid esophagoscopy and removal of the food bolus, is indicated. Definitive treatment entails dilatation of the ring in conjunction with medical therapy for GERD. If the ring proves refractory to this approach, dilatation plus antireflux surgery (fundoplication) [*see 34 Open Esophageal Procedures and 35 Minimally Invasive Esophageal Procedures*] may be indicated.

Chemical Ingestion

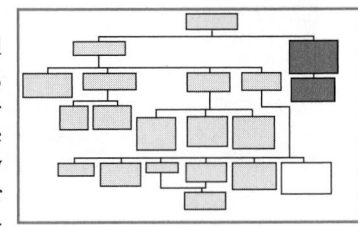

Alkali are commonly found in household cleaning agents, mostly in the form of sodium or potassium hydroxide (NaOH, KOH). The majority of alkali-related injuries occur accidentally in children; however, such injuries also occasionally occur in adults as part of a suicide attempt. The magnitude and site of the injury are directly relat-

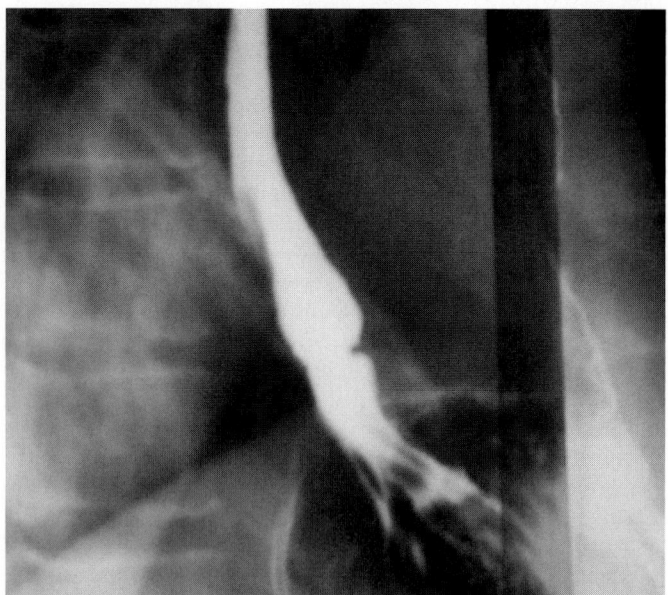

Figure 6 **Shown is Schatzki's ring in a middle-aged man with severe reflux symptoms and recent-onset dysphagia.**

ed to the length of the contact time between the offending substance and the esophageal mucosa. Injury can occur at any level, but the most common site is the distal esophagus; the proximal esophagus, where the transit time is very short, is frequently spared. The inflammation and injury eventually lead to submucosal scar formation, which in turn leads to stricture formation and dysphagia.

A careful endoscopic examination is an essential initial step. The scope should be advanced under direct vision to the proximal injury site; if severe injury is observed, the scope should not be advanced any further. A barium swallow should be done in the first month after injury to detect any stricture that may have formed and to determine its location, severity, and length. Serial barium swallows are helpful in following patients to monitor healing after caustic injury [*see Figure 7*].

At one time, it was common to administer steroids prophylactically to patients with caustic injuries to the esophagus as a strategy for preventing stricture formation. A 1990 study, however, found that this practice had no beneficial effect on healing and stricture formation rates in children,[6] and thus, steroids currently are not widely used in this setting. Strictures are treated by endoscopic dilatation as necessary [*see 60 Gastrointestinal Endoscopy*]. The ultimate solution for a tight, nondilatable stricture [*see Figure 7*] is esophageal resection [*see 34 Open Esophageal Procedures and 37 Video-Assisted Thoracic Surgery*].

Esophageal Cancer

The incidence of esophageal adenocarcinoma is rising at an alarming rate. Dysphagia is the presenting symptom in more than 90% of esophageal cancer patients. Dysphagia caused by cancer 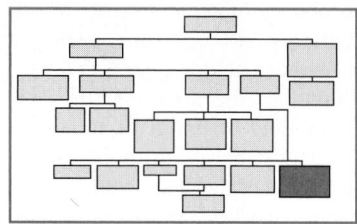 is usually gradual in onset and starts with solids, then progresses to include liquids. Other nonspecific presenting symptoms of esophageal cancer are odynophagia, regurgitation, and pain in the

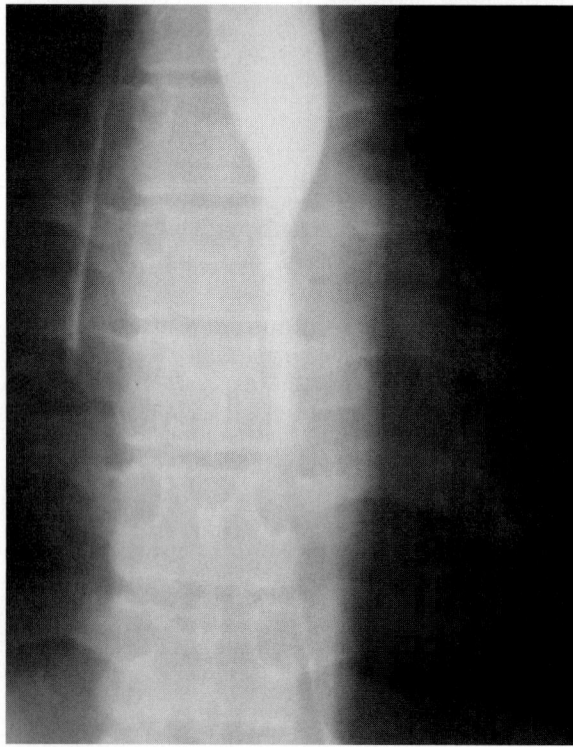

Figure 7 **Barium swallow from a 22-year-old patient who ingested toilet cleaner shows long, stringlike lumen from midesophagus to stomach. Dilatation was impossible in this case, and thus, management included esophageal resection with colonic interposition.**

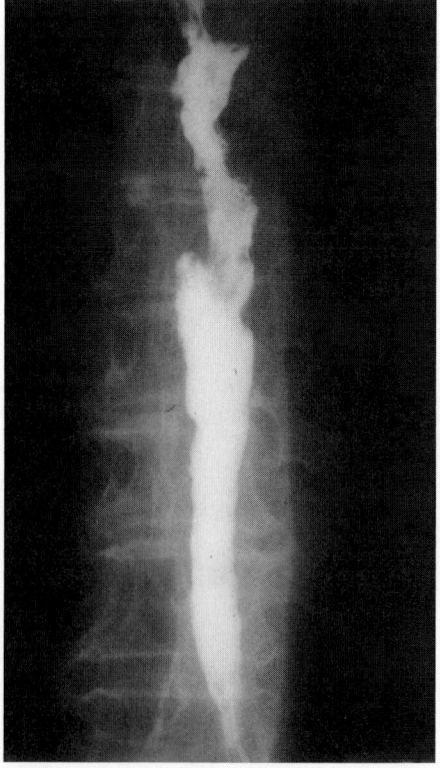

Figure 8 **Shown is classic appearance of midesophageal squamous cell carcinoma. Mucosal irregularity is apparent within lesion, along with proximal dilatation and shouldering at upper and lower borders. Bronchoscopy confirmed penetration of tumor into airway mucosa.**

neck, abdomen, or back. Fistulization of an esophageal tumor into the airway will result in ongoing aspiration (the so-called swallow-cough sequence) and pulmonary sepsis. Weight loss occurring in association with dysphagia is strongly suggestive of esophageal cancer and should prompt appropriate investigation.

A complete history and physical examination should be carried out, followed by a barium swallow. Characteristic features of esophageal cancer on barium x-ray include narrowing, mucosal irregularity, the presence of a mass, and, occasionally, a so-called shouldered stricture [see Figure 8]. Esophagoscopy is essential for establishing a pathologic diagnosis by means of biopsy, brushings, and washings.

Treatment is determined by the stage of the disease. In a medically fit patient with localized esophageal cancer, esophagectomy is indicated [see 34 Open Esophageal Procedures and 37 Video-Assisted Thoracic Surgery]. Traditionally, CT scanning of the neck, the chest, the abdomen, and the pelvis has been performed to rule out distant metastatic disease. More recently, PET scanning has also been used for this purpose. EUS, if available, may also aid in locoregional staging. For lesions in the upper third or the middle third of the esophagus, bronchoscopy is necessary to rule out direct tumor invasion of the airway.

References

1. Cook IA, Kahrilas PJ: AGA technical review on management of oropharyngeal dysphagia. Gastroenterology 116:455, 1999

2. Wilcox SM, Alexander LN, Clark WS: Localization of an obstructing esophageal lesion: is the patient accurate? Dig Dis Sci 40:2192, 1995

3. Richter JE: Heartburn, dysphagia, odynophagia, and other esophageal symptoms. Gastrointestinal Disease: Pathophysiology, Diagnosis and Management, 5th ed. Sleisinger MH, Fordtran JS, Eds. WB Saunders Co, Philadelphia, 1993, p 331

4. Dysphagia: Diagnosis and Management, 3rd ed. Groher ME, Ed. Butterworth-Heinemann, Boston, 1997

5. Schatzki R, Gary JE: Dysphagia due to a diaphragm-like localized narrowing in the lower esophagus (lower esophageal ring). Am J Roentgenol Radium Ther Nucl Med 70:911, 1953

6. Anderson KD, Rouse TM, Randolph JG: A controlled trial of corticosteroids in children with corrosive injury of the esophagus. N Engl J Med 323:637, 1990

Subroto Paul, M.D., and Raphael Bueno, M.D., F.A.C.S.

An acute or chronic cough is one of the most common chief presenting complaints. In the United States, it accounts for approximately 30 to 50 million physician visits each year, and more than $1 billion is spent annually on its workup and treatment.[1] A cough can result from a wide variety of conditions, ranging from fairly non–life-threatening causes (e.g., bronchitis) to life-threatening ones (e.g., lung cancer). Hemoptysis is also a common presenting complaint, with a similarly broad spectrum of possible causes. It may range in severity from mild blood streaking in sputum to massive hemorrhage that, if left untreated, can lead to shock and rapid death from blood loss and asphyxiation. Even mild hemoptysis is distressing to many patients and physicians and calls for prompt attention and diagnosis. In cases of massive hemoptysis, expedient evaluation and management are essential, often involving airway control with intubation and hemodynamic resuscitation.

Because both cough and hemoptysis may be signs of urgent or life-threatening disease, patients who present with either or both of these symptoms should undergo a thorough, methodical workup consisting of a detailed history, a careful physical examination, and appropriate diagnostic studies (usually computed tomography of the chest and bronchoscopy).

Cough

A cough is a forceful expiration that is mediated through the activation of a complex reflex arc. The cough reflex is triggered by the stimulation of various cough receptors, which are found not only in the epithelium of the respiratory tract but also in the lower esophagus, the stomach, and the diaphragm.[2,3] These receptors can be activated by mechanical, chemical, or thermal stimuli; once activated, they send signals to the medulla via the vagus nerve, the glossopharygneal nerve, the trigeminal nerve, or the phrenic nerve. A center in the medulla then activates the muscles of expiration by means of efferent signals transmitted via the vagus and phrenic nerves.[2,3]

Mechanical stimuli that can trigger the cough reflex include inhaled particulate matter and intrinsic and extrinsic tracheobronchial compression. Intrinsic compression may be caused by airway tumors, foreign bodies, granulomatous airway disease, or bronchial smooth muscle that is constricted as a result of disease or exposure to noxious materials. Extrinsic compression may be caused by aortic aneurysmal disease, a pulmonary parenchymal neoplasm (e.g., lung cancer or a tumor that has metastasized to the lung), edema from pulmonary parenchymal infection (e.g., pneumonia or abscess), or pulmonary parenchymal fibrosis resulting from any of a variety of interstitial lung diseases (e.g., idiopathic pulmonary fibrosis or sarcoidosis). Chemical stimuli that can trigger coughing include inhaled irritant gases and aspirated gastric acid or bile. A common thermal stimulus is hot or cold inhaled air (or other gas).[4-7]

CLINICAL EVALUATION

An acute or self-limited cough is defined as one that resolves within 3 weeks. Usually, an acute cough is the result of minor infection or inhalation of irritant gases or particulate matter; sometimes, however, it is associated with a more serious condition. Generally, a cough requires diagnostic attention when it persists for 3 weeks or longer, at which time it is deemed chronic. Numerous conditions are capable of causing a chronic cough [see Table 1], and the differential diagnosis of this complaint is broad.

Careful diagnostic evaluation is required to identify potentially life-threatening causes of chronic coughing [see Figure 1]. Such evaluation relies heavily on the history. Medications, tobacco use, and occupational exposure must all be considered in the effort to narrow the differential diagnosis. Associated symptoms offer important clues; for example, in a patient with water brash and a chronic cough, reflux is more likely to be the cause of the cough than it would be in a patient with copious nasal secretions.[5,7,8] The quality of the sputum is a particularly significant variable: purulent sputum may lead one to suspect infection, whereas bloody sputum may lead one to suspect malignancy, especially in a smoker. Substantial experience and acute clinical judgment are required to distinguish the relatively few patients with serious diseases from the millions of patients who present with a benign cough each year.

MANAGEMENT OF SPECIFIC CAUSES

Common causes of a chronic cough include acute and chronic bronchitis, bronchiectasis, asthma, postnasal drip, and gastroesophageal reflux.[4,5,9-15] Other, less common causes include drugs (e.g., angiotensin-converting enzyme [ACE] inhibitors), interstitial lung disease, congestive heart failure (CHF), bronchogenic carcinoma, tracheobronchial foreign bodies, and endobronchial tumors (benign or malignant).[7,16-18]

Table 1 Differential Diagnosis of Cough

Most common causes	Acute and chronic bronchitis Bronchiectasis Asthma Postnasal drip Gastroesophageal reflux
Less common causes	Drugs Angiotensin-converting enzyme inhibitors Interstitial lung disease Eosinophilic bronchitis Congestive heart failure Bronchogenic carcinoma Tracheobronchial foreign body Psychogenic

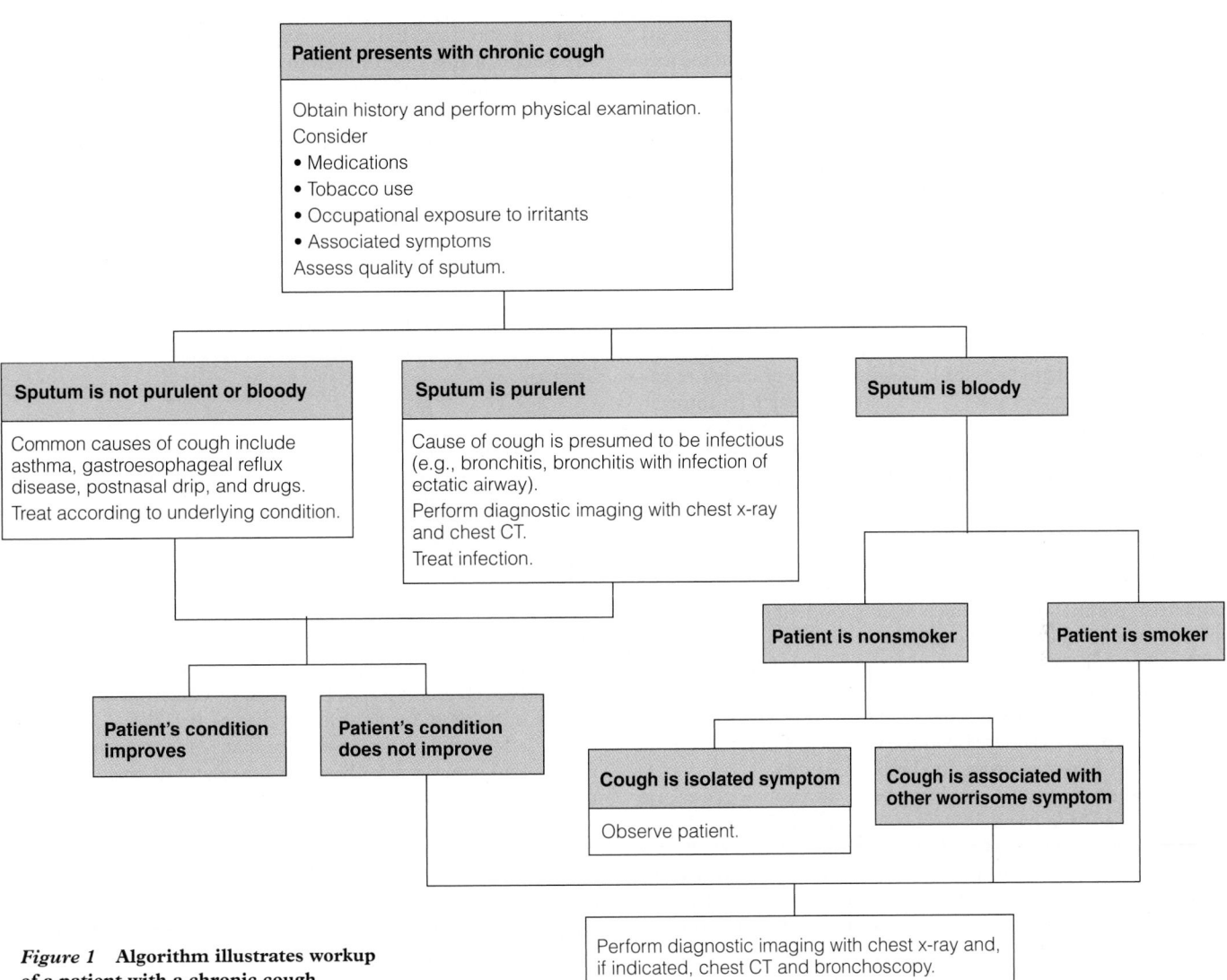

Figure 1 Algorithm illustrates workup of a patient with a chronic cough.

Tracheobronchial irritation can trigger the cough reflex. Acute irritation from inhaled substances (e.g., toxic fumes or cigarette smoke) can lead to bronchospasm and thence to coughing. In addition, patients with asthma or reactive airway disease may present with a cough. Asthma, in fact, is one of the most common causes of cough. Although asthma is typically associated with shortness of breath and expiratory wheezing, some variants of asthma have cough as the sole presenting symptom (so-called cough-variant or cough-type asthma).[5,15,19] Most persons with cough resulting from tracheobronchial irritation have a family history of atopy or asthma. Diagnosis rests on a history of symptom exacerbation with irritants or upper respiratory infections on the associated findings of end-expiratory wheeze; it is confirmed by spirometry.

Tracheobronchial infection can also lead to a chronic cough. Acute bronchitis from viral or bacterial infection (either primary infection or superinfection) is typically signaled by thick, purulent secretions. It is usually self-limited, though in some cases, it may have to be treated with a short course of antibiotics.[20] Chronic bronchitis is defined by the presence of a cough with sputum production that persists for at least 3 months and sometimes for years. The sputum is clear or white, and there is no evidence of systemic infection. Chronic bronchitis almost always occurs in current smokers (or recent quitters), who almost invariably have chronically inflamed airways.[5,6] In a smoker, a chronic cough is not a particularly worrisome symptom; however, if the character of the cough or the quality of the sputum changes, further workup is indicated to look for a possible superimposed infection or neoplasm.[21] With both acute and chronic bronchitis, the diagnosis can usually be made on the basis of the history and the physical findings (especially the sputum quality).

Persistent airway inflammation from any cause (e.g., chronic bronchitis, asthma, granulomatous airway disease, or cystic fibrosis) can lead to bronchiectasis, a state characterized by chronic airway dilatation with cystic changes in the lower bronchial tree. The anatomic abnormalities in the dilated, cystic bronchi cause pooling of mucus and secretions and impair clearance of secretions.[7,10,17] Cough, either dry or productive, is the major presenting symptom of bronchiectasis. This condition is often accompanied by infection of the ectatic airway, which leads to purulent secretion and systemic signs of illness that necessitate prompt antibiotic therapy. In patients with cystic fibrosis, for example, daily postural drainage of the bronchiectatic airways is required, and frequent hospitalization for intensive antibiotic therapy and chest physiotherapy is necessary. The diagnosis of bronchiectasis is made on the basis of the history and diagnostic imaging (including chest x-ray and, currently, chest CT).

Postnasal drip is one of the most common causes of cough. It usually results from allergic rhinitis, sinusitis, or nasopharyngitis. Nasal secretions irritate the larynx and trachea, leading to the activation of the cough reflex arc.[7,12,14] Generally, the diagnosis is made on the basis of the history and the symptom complex. Often, however, the symptoms are vague, and the diagnosis is confirmed only when the patient responds to empirical therapy directed at the presumed underlying cause. Steroid nasal sprays and antihistamines are useful for ameliorating symptoms. In recalcitrant cases, an otolaryngologic examination may be required to exclude sinus disorders.

Gastroesophageal reflux is increasingly being recognized as a cause of cough and asthma. Several mechanisms have been postulated for reflux-induced cough, including (1) mechanical aspiration of gastric contents that leads to stimulation of cough receptors in the distal airways and (2) stimulation of cough receptors in the distal esophagus and the proximal stomach from refluxed acid or bile. The data currently available tend to support the second mechanism for reflux-induced cough and bronchospasm.[9,11,13] Regardless of the mechanism responsible, the diagnosis is difficult to make if the typical symptoms of reflux and heartburn are absent. As awareness of reflux-induced asthma and cough grows, more patients are being evaluated with barium studies and esophageal pH monitoring, which often provide the correct diagnosis when clinical evaluation cannot.[9]

Specific medications may also give rise to a cough. In particular, cough is a well-recognized complication of ACE inhibitor therapy.[3,4,7,8] Cough may also result from nonselective beta-blocker therapy or may develop as a consequence of idiosyncratic reactions to a variety of drugs and herbal remedies.

The presence of bronchogenic cancer is always a concern in a smoker with a chronic cough.[3,5,8,21,22] Any irritation of the airway, whether intrinsic (by airway tumors) or extrinsic (by parenchymal tumors), with or without associated inflammation, can lead to coughing through mechanical or chemical stimulation of cough receptors. In the general population as a whole, a chronic cough is rarely the sole presenting symptom of developing lung cancer. In smokers, the presence of a chronic cough, in and of itself, is not particularly worrisome, but any change in the character of the cough, especially a change in sputum quality, is grounds for concern. Any degree of hemoptysis in a former smoker should be taken seriously, especially if it is not associated with an infection; prompt evaluation with a chest x-ray and, if indicated, chest CT and bronchoscopy is indicated.[23-25]

A chronic cough may also be a consequence of CHF (from any cause), though this is not a common occurrence. Mild CHF with symptoms of orthopnea at night may be associated with coughing. The diagnosis is made on the basis of a history of orthopnea and associated cardiac risk factors or valvular disease, followed by cardiac echocardiography.

Occasionally, the presence of a small unrecognized tracheobronchial foreign body can lead to chronic irritation of the bronchial epithelium and thence to a persistent cough; this presentation is more common in children than in adults.[16] The diagnosis is usually made by performing bronchoscopy in a patient who is believed to be harboring a foreign body on the basis of chest imaging.

Eosinophilic bronchitis is a rare cause of chronic cough that may be suspected in patients with no other clearly explainable diagnosis.[26,27] Patients typically have a history of atopy, and the diagnosis is made on the basis of clinical suspicion and the results of bronchial epithelial biopsy. Steroids are the mainstay of treatment.

In rare instances, a chronic cough may be the consequence of a fistula that connects some part of the airway or the lung to an adjacent structure (e.g., the esophagus, the mediastinum, or the pleura). Such a fistula can result from cancer, surgery, trauma, aspiration or swallowing of foreign objects (e.g., fish bones), radiation therapy, chemotherapy, or infection. In this setting, the cough is caused by secretions that enter the airway via the fistula.

In the occasional patient, a chronic cough may be of psychogenic origin.

Finally, a chronic cough can be caused by an endobronchial tumor (benign, malignant, or low-grade malignant). This is a quite rare circumstance that occasionally develops in patients who have no risk factors for lung cancer. Not uncommonly, a patient with a carcinoid tumor of the airway will have been treated with inhalers and steroids for years because of the presumptive diagnosis of asthma.

Hemoptysis

As noted (see above), hemoptysis may be a harbinger of life-threatening illness and should therefore be taken seriously in all circumstances. As a rule, the blood seen in the sputum derives from either the pulmonary arteries or the bronchial arteries[23,25,28]; only rarely does it come from the pulmonary veins. Although the bronchial arteries provide less blood flow than the pulmonary arteries do, they supply the bulk of the blood received by the airways and, accordingly, are the source of the blood in most cases of hemoptysis. Hemoptysis can be caused by either tracheobronchial disease or pulmonary parenchymal disease [see Table 2].[23,25,28] One should also consider the possibility that hemoptysis may be the result of an aneurysm of the aorta (or one of its main branches) that has ruptured into the lung.

CLINICAL EVALUATION

The differential diagnosis of hemoptysis, like that of cough, is quite broad. The history and the physical examination play important diagnostic roles. The presence of associated signs of other diseases (e.g., interstitial lung diseases) often helps narrow the differential diagnosis.[23,25,28]

INVESTIGATIVE STUDIES

Any patient with significant hemoptysis should be admitted to a hospital and evaluated promptly. Routine chest x-rays are insensitive. Chest CT with contrast can often identify the cause of hemoptysis for both tracheobronchial or parenchymal lesions[29,30]; CT scanners capable of three-dimensional helical reconstruction are especially useful in this regard. MRI has also been employed to evaluate hemoptysis, but it has no clear advantages over chest CT in this setting. Given that infection is commonly associated with hemoptysis, one should probably consider administering antibiotics to most patients. Antitussives may be helpful in patients whose hemoptysis is exacerbated by excessive coughing. Coagulopathy should be considered and, if present, corrected aggressively. Bronchoscopy is the key to the diagnosis, in that it is frequently able to define the pathology of the preceding hemoptysis (especially if the underlying condition is of tracheobronchial origin). It is particularly effective if performed within 48 hours of presentation.[23,25,28,31] Although either flexible bronchoscopy or rigid bronchoscopy may be used, flexible bronchoscopy is preferred because it is less traumatic to the airways and generally does not require general anesthesia.

Patients with massive hemoptysis should be promptly transported to the operating room (if there is time) and selectively intubated with a rigid bronchoscope or special endotracheal tubes. Balloon catheters may be placed for selective occlusion of the air-

Table 2 Differential Diagnosis of Hemoptysis

Tracheobronchial disease	Acute or chronic bronchitis Bronchiectasis Neoplasms Foreign bodies Trauma Tracheoinnominate fistula
Parenchymal disease	Infection Interstitial lung disease Pulmonary embolism Pulmonary arteriovenous malformations
Miscellaneous conditions	Mitral valve disease Coagulopathy

way or airways from which the hemoptysis originates, permitting ventilation to continue through the unaffected airways. A rapid evaluation must then be carried out to identify and manage the source of the bleeding. To this end, it may be necessary to perform urgent angiographic embolization of a bronchial artery, to place a stent in a pulmonary artery, or to resect a portion of the lung. Unfortunately, the majority of patients with massive hemoptysis do not survive, dying of hemorrhagic shock and suffocation. Thus, the goal of the treating physician should be to identify and treat these patients before they experience their final hemoptysis.

MANAGEMENT OF SPECIFIC CAUSES

Tracheobronchial disease is the most common cause of hemoptysis. Acute or chronic bronchitis leads to airway inflammation and sputum production, often associated with hemoptysis from the bronchial artery branches found within the mucosa; the bleeding is usually minor.[23,25,28] Bronchiectasis leads to bronchial artery dilatation, along with cystic dilatation of the bronchial tree[10,23,25,28]; the bleeding is often massive in this setting.

Numerous types of tracheobronchial neoplasms, including various benign and malignant primary epithelial and soft tissue tumors, have been associated with hemoptysis.[32-39] The majority of primary airway tumors are malignant, with squamous cell carcinoma and adenoid cystic carcinoma being the primary malignancies most frequently seen in the trachea.[32-38] The majority of malignant airway tumors, however, are metastases rather than primary malignancies. Invasion of the tracheobronchial tree by adjacent lung, thyroid, esophageal, or laryngeal tumors is not common, but it has been described.[33,34,39,40] Colon cancers, breast cancers, melanomas, and renal cancers have been reported to metastasize to the trachea, albeit very rarely.[39,41] There are also low-grade tumors

(e.g., carcinoid and mucoepidermal carcinoma) that present in the bronchial tree and may be associated with hemoptysis.

Tracheobronchial trauma, whether acquired or iatrogenic, is another cause of bloody sputum. Penetrating trauma to the bronchial tree or the pulmonary parenchyma, for example, can lead to significant hemoptysis, especially if a major branch of the bronchial artery is involved.[23,25,28,42] Particularly massive hemoptysis may occur if a tracheoinnominate fistula develops after tracheostomy.[43-45] There are two types of tracheoinnominate fistula: one develops at the tracheal stoma site as a consequence of erosion of the artery by the tracheostomy tube, and the other develops as a consequence of a more distal tracheal injury by a high-pressure cuff, which in turn injures the artery. Major bleeding can occur with either type. Prompt diagnosis with bronchoscopy is required in any patient with a tracheostomy who presents with hemoptysis; an initial "sentinel" bleed can be followed by life-threatening hemorrhage.[24,25,46,47] Treatment usually involves stabilization with rigid bronchoscopy and immediate sternotomy to control the artery and resect the fistula.

Other forms of iatrogenic injury may occur in patients with tracheobronchial stents, which often irritate the mucosa and cause bleeding. In most cases, such bleeding is mild, but on occasion, the stents (particularly the metallic expandable ones) erode through the bronchial wall and penetrate into a major blood vessel (usually the pulmonary artery or the aorta). Hemoptysis may also occur in patients who have undergone bronchial biopsies and those in whom pulmonary arterial catheters have been placed.[48,49] The same effect may be observed in patients who have harbored foreign bodies in the tracheobronchial tree for extended periods.[24]

Pulmonary parenchymal disease can lead to hemoptysis as well, though less often than tracheobronchial disease does. Parenchymal infection, especially from tuberculosis and aspergillosis, is a common cause of hemoptysis.[23,25,28,50] Aspergillosis, in particular, has a propensity for vascular invasion and thus can result in massive hemoptysis.[50] The various interstitial lung diseases (e.g., collagen vascular disorders, Goodpasture syndrome, and Wegener granulomatosis) often have hemoptysis as their primary presenting symptom.[51-53] Pulmonary embolism can lead to hemoptysis if it involves a significant portion of pulmonary parenchyma.[23,25,28,54] Mitral valve disease with resulting left atrial hypertension can also result in hemoptysis. Any form of coagulopathy resulting from a low platelet count or a deficiency in clotting factors, therapeutic or not, can lead to hemoptysis; such conditions must be corrected in patients who experience massive or persistent episodes. Another rare cause of bloody sputum is congenital pulmonary arteriovenous malformation, which typically is diagnosed only after chest imaging.[55,56]

References

1. Irwin RS, Boulet LP, Cloutier MM, et al: Managing cough as a defense mechanism and as a symptom: a consensus panel report of the American College of Chest Physicians. Chest 114:133S, 1998
2. Shannon R, Baekey DM, Morris KF, et al: Production of reflex cough by brainstem respiratory networks. Pulm Pharmacol Ther 17:369, 2004
3. Reynolds SM, Mackenzie AJ, Spina D, et al: The pharmacology of cough. Trends Pharmacol Sci 25:569, 2004
4. Page C, Reynolds SM, Mackenzie AJ, et al: Mechanisms of acute cough. Pulm Pharmacol Ther 17:389, 2004
5. McGarvey LP, Nishino T: Acute and chronic cough. Pulm Pharmacol Ther 17:351, 2004
6. McGarvey LP, Ing AJ: Idiopathic cough, prevalence and underlying mechanisms. Pulm Pharmacol Ther 17:435, 2004
7. Patrick H, Patrick F: Chronic cough. Med Clin North Am 79:361, 1995
8. Pratter MR, Bartter T, Akers S, et al: An algorithmic approach to chronic cough. Ann Intern Med 119:977, 1993
9. Ahmed T, Vaezi MF: The role of pH monitoring in extraesophageal gastroesophageal reflux disease. Gastrointest Endosc Clin N Am 15:319, 2005
10. Barker AF: Bronchiectasis. N Engl J Med 346:1383, 2002
11. Bocskei C, Viczian M, Bocskei R, et al: The influence of gastroesophageal reflux disease and its treatment on asthmatic cough. Lung 183:53, 2005
12. Ciprandi G, Buscaglia S, Catrullo A, et al: Loratadine in the treatment of cough associated with aller-

gic rhinoconjunctivitis. Ann Allergy Asthma Immunol 75:115, 1995

13. Leggett JJ, Johnston BT, Mills M, et al: Prevalence of gastroesophageal reflux in difficult asthma: relationship to asthma outcome. Chest 127:1227, 2005

14. Morice AH: Post-nasal drip syndrome—a symptom to be sniffed at? Pulm Pharmacol Ther 17:343, 2004

15. O'Connell EJ, Rojas AR, Sachs MI: Cough-type asthma: a review. Ann Allergy 66:278, 1991

16. Saquib Mallick M, Rauf Khan A, Al-Bassam A: Late presentation of tracheobronchial foreign body aspiration in children. J Trop Pediatr 51:145, 2005

17. Morrissey BM, Evans SJ: Severe bronchiectasis. Clin Rev Allergy Immunol 25:233, 2003

18. Perez RL: Interstitial lung disease: causes, treatment, and prevention. Ethn Dis 15:S45, 2005

19. Martinez FJ, Standiford C, Gay SE: Is it asthma or COPD? The answer determines proper therapy for chronic airflow obstruction. Postgrad Med 117:19, 2005

20. Brunton S, Carmichael BP, Colgan R, et al: Acute exacerbation of chronic bronchitis: a primary care consensus guideline. Am J Manag Care 10:689, 2004

21. Ebihara S, Ebihara T, Okazaki T, et al: Cigarette smoking, cough reflex, and respiratory tract infection. Arch Intern Med 165:814, 2005

22. Hamilton W, Sharp D: Diagnosis of lung cancer in primary care: a structured review. Fam Pract 21:605, 2004

23. Corder R: Hemoptysis. Emerg Med Clin North Am 21:421, 2003

24. Johnson JL: Manifestations of hemoptysis: how to manage minor, moderate, and massive bleeding. Postgrad Med 112:101, 2002

25. Hirshberg B, Biran I, Glazer M, et al: Hemoptysis: etiology, evaluation, and outcome in a tertiary referral hospital. Chest 112:440, 1997

26. Gibson PG, Fujimura M, Niimi A: Eosinophilic bronchitis: clinical manifestations and implications for treatment. Thorax 57:178, 2002

27. Birring SS, Berry M, Brightling CE, et al: Eosinophilic bronchitis: clinical features, management

and pathogenesis. Am J Respir Med 2:169, 2003

28. Thompson AB, Teschler H, Rennard SI: Pathogenesis, evaluation, and therapy for massive hemoptysis. Clin Chest Med 13:69, 1992

29. Fetita CI, Preteux F, Beigelman-Aubry C, et al: Pulmonary airways: 3-D reconstruction from multislice CT and clinical investigation. IEEE Trans Med Imaging 23:1353, 2004

30. Grenier PA, Beigelman-Aubry C, Fetita C, et al: New frontiers in CT imaging of airway disease. Eur Radiol 12:1022, 2002

31. Karmy-Jones R, Cuschieri J, Vallieres E: Role of bronchoscopy in massive hemoptysis. Chest Surg Clin N Am 11:873, 2001

32. D'Cunha J, Maddaus MA: Surgical treatment of tracheal and carinal tumors. Chest Surg Clin N Am 13:95, 2003

33. Gaissert HA: Primary tracheal tumors. Chest Surg Clin N Am 13:247, 2003

34. Meyers BF, Mathisen DJ: Management of tracheal neoplasms. Oncologist 2:245, 1997

35. Compeau CG, Keshavjee S: Management of tracheal neoplasms. Oncologist 1:347, 1996

36. Ampil FL: Primary malignant tracheal neoplasms: case reports and literature radiotherapy review. J Surg Oncol 33:20, 1986

37. Gaissert HA, Mathisen DJ, Moncure AC, et al: Survival and function after sleeve lobectomy for lung cancer. J Thorac Cardiovasc Surg 111:948, 1996

38. Pearson FG, Todd TR, Cooper JD: Experience with primary neoplasms of the trachea and carina. J Thorac Cardiovasc Surg 88:511, 1984

39. Litzky L: Epithelial and soft tissue tumors of the tracheobronchial tree. Chest Surg Clin N Am 13:1, 2003

40. Chan KP, Eng P, Hsu AA, et al: Rigid bronchoscopy and stenting for esophageal cancer causing airway obstruction. Chest 122:1069, 2002

41. Heitmiller RF, Marasco WJ, Hruban RH, et al: Endobronchial metastasis. J Thorac Cardiovasc Surg 106:537, 1993

42. Chu CP, Chen PP: Tracheobronchial injury secondary to blunt chest trauma: diagnosis and man-

agement. Anaesth Intensive Care 30:145, 2002

43. Cahill BC, Ingbar DH: Massive hemoptysis: assessment and management. Clin Chest Med 15:147, 1994

44. Epstein SK: Late complications of tracheostomy. Respir Care 50:542, 2005

45. Walts PA, Murthy SC, DeCamp MM: Techniques of surgical tracheostomy. Clin Chest Med 24:413, 2003

46. MacIntosh EL, Parrott JC, Unruh HW: Fistulas between the aorta and tracheobronchial tree. Ann Thorac Surg 51:515, 1991

47. Barben JU, Ditchfield M, Carlin JB, et al: Major haemoptysis in children with cystic fibrosis: a 20-year retrospective study. J Cyst Fibros 2:105, 2003

48. Zakaluzny SA, Lane JD, Mair EA: Complications of tracheobronchial airway stents. Otolaryngol Head Neck Surg 128:478, 2003

49. Abreu AR, Campos MA, Krieger BP: Pulmonary artery rupture induced by a pulmonary artery catheter: a case report and review of the literature. J Intensive Care Med 19:291, 2004

50. Soubani AO, Chandrasekar PH: The clinical spectrum of pulmonary aspergillosis. Chest 121:1988, 2002

51. Fox HL, Swann D: Goodpasture syndrome: pathophysiology, diagnosis, and management. Nephrol Nurs J 28:305, 2001

52. Semple D, Keogh J, Forni L, et al: Clinical review: vasculitis on the intensive care unit—part 1: diagnosis. Crit Care 9:92, 2005

53. Semple D, Keogh J, Forni L, et al: Clinical review: vasculitis on the intensive care unit—part 2: treatment and prognosis. Crit Care 9:193, 2005

54. Laack TA, Goyal DG: Pulmonary embolism: an unsuspected killer. Emerg Med Clin North Am 22:961, 2004

55. Thung KH, Sihoe AD, Wan IY, et al: Hemoptysis from an unusual pulmonary arteriovenous malformation. Ann Thorac Surg 76:1730, 2003

56. Kjeldsen AD, Oxhoj H, Andersen PE, et al: Pulmonary arteriovenous malformations: screening procedures and pulmonary angiography in patients with hereditary hemorrhagic telangiectasia. Chest 116:432, 1999

30 CHEST WALL MASS

John C. Kucharczuk, M.D., F.A.C.S.

Evaluation of Chest Wall Mass

Chest wall masses arise from a variety of different causes. The chest wall contains a number of distinct tissues, including skin, fat, muscle, bone, cartilage, lymphatic vessels, and fascia. Each of these component tissues can give rise to either a benign or a malignant primary chest wall mass. In addition, the chest wall is also in intimate proximity to a number of organs (e.g., the breast, the lung, the mediastinum, and the pleura) that may give rise to a chest wall mass through extension of a malignancy or infection. Finally, because of its large surface area, the chest wall can be the site of a secondary mass caused by metastasis from a distant malignancy (e.g., carcinoma or sarcoma) [*see Table 1*].

Chest wall masses, whether primary or secondary, are relatively uncommon in clinical practice. Accordingly, many surgeons lack a solid working knowledge of the causes, evaluation, treatment, and natural history of these lesions. Often, this unfamiliarity leads to inappropriate selection of diagnostic studies, unnecessary delays in treatment, and considerable frustration for patient and surgeon alike. In what follows, I outline a focused clinical approach aimed at streamlining the evaluation and treatment of patients with chest wall masses. Appropriate diagnostic studies and operative planning are discussed, and specific causes of chest wall masses are reviewed.

Clinical Evaluation

HISTORY AND PHYSICAL EXAMINATION

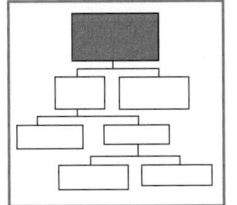

Initial evaluation of a patient with a chest wall mass begins with a careful history that notes the symptoms associated with the mass and records the history of its growth. Previously obtained radiographs, if available, are reviewed to determine how rapidly the mass has been growing. A complete physical examination is performed to rule out other sites of disease and to identify any comorbid medical conditions that may affect the patient's candidacy for resection. If the mass is palpable, its size and its salient characteristics (i.e., hard versus soft and fixed versus mobile) are noted. By itself, physical examination will not establish whether the lesion is benign or malignant.

Investigative Studies

DIAGNOSTIC IMAGING

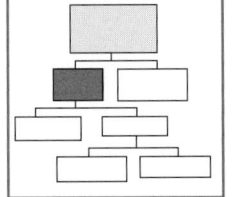

At presentation, most patients with chest wall masses have already undergone chest radiography and computed tomography. In the case of a primary chest wall mass, magnetic resonance imaging is useful for further characterization of the lesion. MRI allows precise delineation of tissue planes and major adjacent neurovascular structures[1]; however, as a stand-alone test, it cannot differentiate between benign and malignant chest wall lesions.

In general, given that neither physical examination nor diagnostic imaging can reliably distinguish benign from malignant chest wall masses, it is important to move quickly to tissue diagnosis. With very unusual tumors, it is often necessary to consult a highly specialized pathologist to make the diagnosis and an oncologist to assist in treatment planning.

BIOPSY

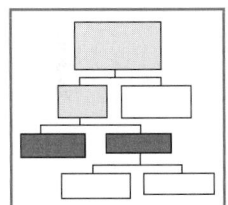

Whether a tissue diagnosis is needed before initiation of definitive therapy depends on the size and characteristics of the lesion. If the lesion is small (< 3 cm), regardless of whether it is believed to be benign or malignant, excisional biopsy is performed as both diagnosis and treatment. If the lesion is larger (≥ 3 cm) and its resection will lead to significant morbidity and necessitate extensive reconstruction, a preoperative tissue diagnosis is obtained.

Whether fine-needle aspiration (FNA) is useful for tissue diagnosis in this setting remains a subject of debate. FNA is a simple procedure that can be performed in the office during the initial patient evaluation, and several studies suggest that it is an effective technique for assessing chest wall masses.[2] Nevertheless, in routine clinical practice, cytologic analysis of a fine-needle aspirate from a primary chest wall mass frequently yields nondiagnostic results, and additional tissue is often requested. In such cases, a core-needle biopsy or an incisional biopsy is performed. Both techniques provide tissue for histologic evaluation, and both must be performed in such a way that the biopsy tract will be completely excised at the time of definitive surgical treatment. As a rule, in patients with a known primary malignancy and a secondary chest wall mass, I perform FNA. In patients with a primary chest wall mass larger than 3 cm and no underlying diagnosis, I proceed directly to incisional biopsy for diagnosis.

Table 1 Classification of Primary and Secondary Chest Wall Masses

Primary masses of chest wall	Benign
	  Infectious masses
	  Soft tissue neoplasms
	  Bone and cartilage neoplasms
	Malignant
	  Soft tissue neoplasms
	  Bone and cartilage neoplasms

Secondary masses of chest wall	Tumor invasion from contiguous organs Metastasis from distant organs

Evaluation of Chest Wall Mass

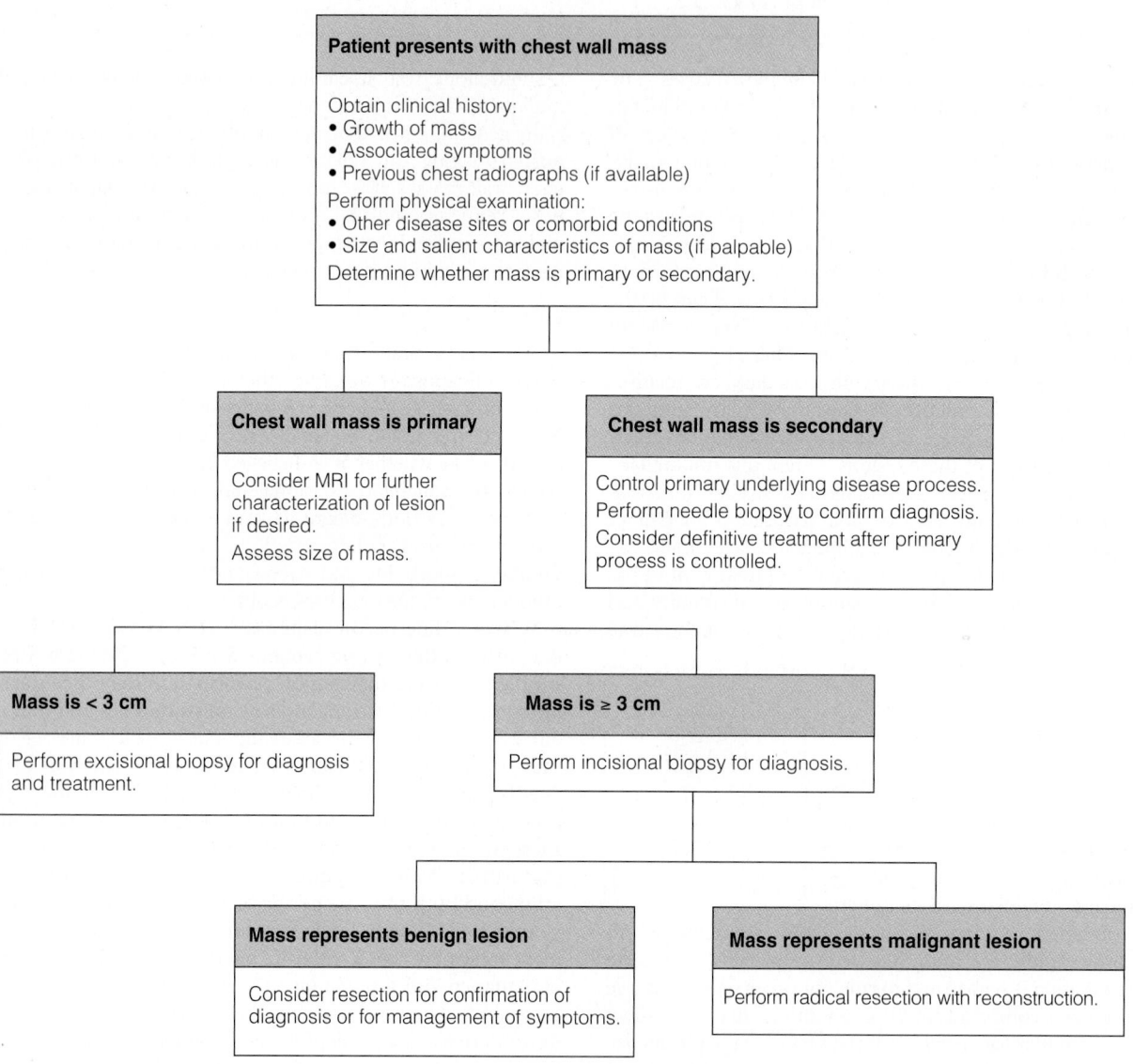

Patient presents with chest wall mass

Obtain clinical history:
- Growth of mass
- Associated symptoms
- Previous chest radiographs (if available)

Perform physical examination:
- Other disease sites or comorbid conditions
- Size and salient characteristics of mass (if palpable)

Determine whether mass is primary or secondary.

Chest wall mass is primary

Consider MRI for further characterization of lesion if desired.
Assess size of mass.

Chest wall mass is secondary

Control primary underlying disease process.
Perform needle biopsy to confirm diagnosis.
Consider definitive treatment after primary process is controlled.

Mass is < 3 cm

Perform excisional biopsy for diagnosis and treatment.

Mass is ≥ 3 cm

Perform incisional biopsy for diagnosis.

Mass represents benign lesion

Consider resection for confirmation of diagnosis or for management of symptoms.

Mass represents malignant lesion

Perform radical resection with reconstruction.

Management

PRIMARY BENIGN MASSES OF CHEST WALL

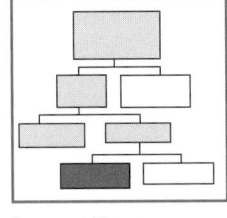

Infectious Masses

Sternal infection Primary sternal osteomyelitis may be seen in intravenous drug abusers but is otherwise rare. Much more common is osteomyelitis occurring after median sternotomy. Approximately 1% to 3% of median sternotomies for cardiac procedures are complicated by sternal wound infection.[3] Risk factors include diabetes, the use of bilateral internal mammary arteries, and reoperation.[4] Patients with poststernotomy osteomyelitis present with pain, drainage, and, often, a palpable mass overlying the incision. In most cases, the infection is not confined to the sternum but extends deeply into the mediastinum as well. The diagnostic study of choice is CT scanning of the chest, which will determine the extent of mediastinal soilage.

After CT, the patient is taken to the operating room for wide drainage and sternal debridement. A number of different techniques have been employed to treat these infections; of these, aggressive surgical debridement of the infected area with flap closure yields the best overall clinical outcomes [see 36 Chest Wall Procedures].[5]

The patient who presents with a pulsating sternal mass after sternotomy represents a special case. Such patients have a pseudoaneursym of the underlying aorta and are at risk for exsanguination. They should undergo an emergency CT angiogram or aortogram to confirm the diagnosis and then be taken directly to the OR, where they are placed on cardiopulmonary bypass through femoral cannulation and cooled to a hypothermic state before the sternum is opened.

Sternoclavicular joint infection Sternoclavicular joint (SCJ) infections present as painful palpable masses overlying the joint [see Figure 1]. These infections are often associated with I.V. drug abuse, infected indwelling subclavian catheters, or trauma. Most patients also have an underlying risk factor (e.g., diabetes or hepatic or renal insufficiency) or a history of sepsis. The diagnosis

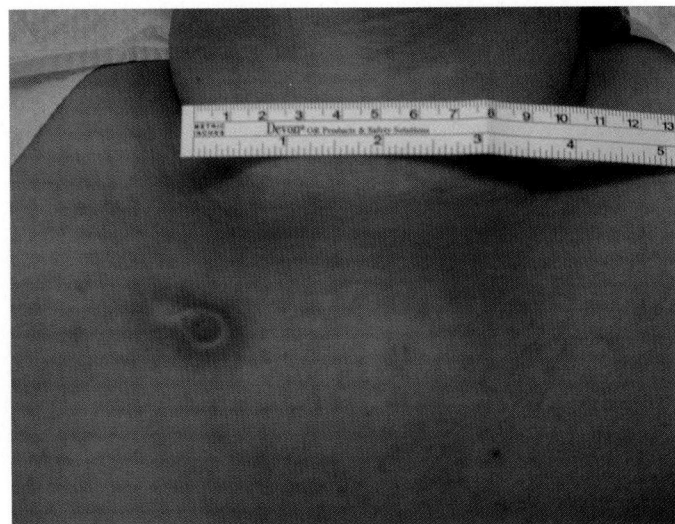

Figure 1 Sternoclavicular joint infections present as painful palpable masses overlying the joint.

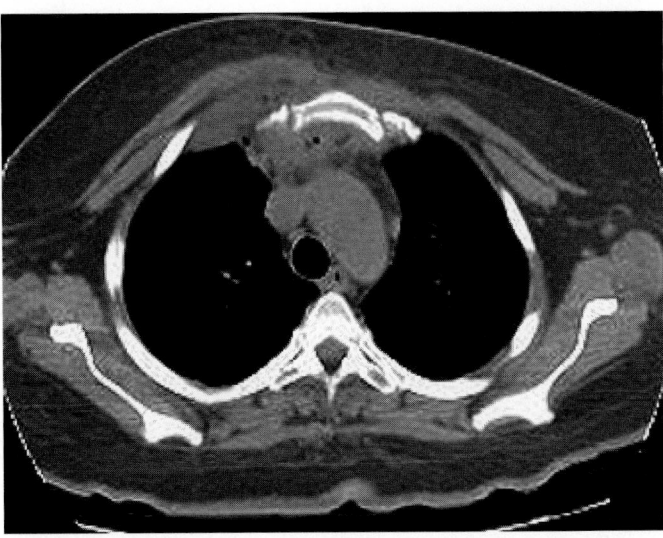

Figure 2 CT scan shows typical appearance of SCJ infection, including fluid collection around the joint and tissue stranding.

is made on the basis of the history, the physical examination, and CT scanning of the chest (with particular attention paid to the SCJ). Typical CT findings include tissue stranding and a collection around the joint [see Figure 2].

Treatment consists of wide resection of the SCJ and the proximal third of the clavicle, as well as debridement of the manubrium [see 36 Chest Wall Procedures].[6] Often, the proximal portion of the first rib is involved and also must be resected. Immediate reconstruction is performed by rotating a pectoralis muscle flap into the resection cavity. After operation, I.V. antibiotics are administered for 6 weeks. Most patients require intensive postoperative physical therapy to restore strength, function, and mobility in the upper extremity.

Osteomyelitis of rib Osteomyelitis of a rib presents as a painful, swollen mass overlying an infected segment of rib. Often, a draining sinus tract is present. The diagnosis is made on clinical grounds. A CT scan of the chest is obtained to rule out an underlying intrathoracic condition (e.g., empyema).

Treatment consists of resection of the infected bone and soft tissue coverage of the defect [see 36 Chest Wall Procedures]. Care must be taken to avoid contamination of the underlying pleural cavity during rib resection.

In children, the diagnosis is made on clinical grounds and may be facilitated by the use of ultrasonography, which demonstrates obliteration of the intermuscular planes adjacent to the infected rib and pericostal edema.[7] Again, a CT scan is usually obtained to rule out other underlying pleura-based abnormalities. As with adults, the range of pathologic organisms that may be recovered is quite wide.

Benign Neoplasms

Benign neoplasms of the chest wall may be divided into those arising from soft tissue and those arising from bone and cartilage [see Table 2].

Soft tissue neoplasms Benign soft tissue neoplasms of the chest wall usually present as slowly growing, painless masses. On examination, the lesions usually are soft and freely movable. Plain radiographs and a CT scan of the chest are obtained. The CT

Table 2 Primary Benign Chest Wall
Neoplasms by Tissue of Origin

Benign soft tissue neoplasms	Lipoma Fibroma Hemangioma Granuloma Neurofibroma Elastoma Desmoid
Benign bone and cartilage neoplasms	Osteochondroma Chondroma Fibrous dysplasia Eosinophilic granuloma

scan shows a homogeneous mass, with no necrosis and no infiltration of associated soft tissue or destruction of associated bone. Small soft tissue lesions (< 3 cm) are completely removed by means of excisional biopsy, which provides definitive diagnosis and treatment. Larger lesions (≥ 3 cm) undergo incisional biopsy first to rule out a malignant soft tissue neoplasm. If the lesion is confirmed as benign, it is resected with close negative margins to minimize the size of the surgical defect. If it is determined to be malignant, an aggressive wide excision is performed with immediate reconstruction [*see 36 Chest Wall Procedures*].

Desmoid tumors deserve special mention, in that they are borderline neoplasms.[8] These tumors generally arise in the muscle and fascia around the shoulder. Although they are histologically benign, they can infiltrate adjacent structures and exhibit a high tendency for local recurrence. Desmoid tumors are best treated by means of radical surgical excision. In patients with positive surgical margins, the recurrence rate is 89%, whereas in those with negative margins, the recurrence rate is less than 20%.[9]

Bone and cartilage neoplasms Osteochondromas are the most common bone tumors overall. These lesions are benign cartilaginous neoplasms that may occur in any bone that undergoes enchondral bone formation; essentially, they are hamartomas of the growth plate. The knee is the most common site of occurrence. In the chest, osteochondromas arise in the metaphyseal regions of the anterior ribs. Most are asymptomatic and are found when screening chest radiographs reveal an eccentric growth pattern at the costochondral junction. The diagnosis is made on the basis of a characteristic pattern on plain x-rays. In children, osteochondromas are followed; in postpubescent and adult patients, they are resected to confirm the diagnosis and rule out malignancy.

Chondromas are the next most common benign neoplasms of the chest wall. They occur along the costochondral junctions between the anterior ribs and the sternum. Unfortunately, it is not possible to distinguish between benign and malignant cartilage neoplasms on the basis of clinical or radiographic findings; therefore, excision is required for diagnosis. Excision results in a significant surgical defect that usually necessitates complex reconstruction, including the use of prosthetic material to provide rigid structure and soft tissue coverage [*see 36 Chest Wall Procedures*].

Fibrous dysplasia usually presents as a painless cystic bone lesion that is found incidentally on a screening chest x-ray. Replacement of the medulla by fibrous tissue creates a characteristic radiolucent appearance. These lesions are treated conservatively and are simply followed. Local resection is indicated if pain develops or if the lesion is seen to be enlarging on serial x-rays.

PRIMARY MALIGNANT MASSES OF
CHEST WALL

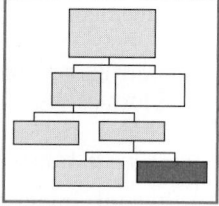

Like benign chest wall neoplasms, malignant chest wall neoplasms may be divided into those arising from soft tissue and those arising from bone and cartilage [*see Table 3*].

Soft Tissue Neoplasms

Sarcomas are the primary malignant soft tissue neoplasms of the chest wall. Most of the published series addressing soft tissue sarcoma of the chest wall have included small numbers of patients and have also addressed lesions arising in bone and cartilage. The largest surgical series of patients with soft tissue sarcomas of the chest wall was published in 1991.[10] This study included 149 patients who had undergone resection at the Memorial Sloan-Kettering Cancer Center in New York. The overall 5-year survival rate was 66%. Unfortunately, the study also included 32 patients with desmoid tumors, which are not histologically classified either as sarcomas or as malignant neoplasms. In 2005, a large retrospective study from a single institution in Brazil reported on 55 patients who underwent surgical treatment of soft tissue sarcomas of the chest wall.[11] Nearly 53% of the lesions were fibrosarcomas. With wide surgical resection, the disease-free survival rate was 75% at 5 years and 64% at 10 years. The histologic grade of the tumor and the type of surgical resection performed were found to be independent prognostic factors for disease-free survival. These findings are consistent with those of other studies that suggest that age, gender, symptoms, and lesion size do not have a significant impact on survival.[12]

Sarcomas of the chest wall can be quite sizable [*see Figure 3*]. They are painless in about 50% of patients. The typical clinical finding is a hard, fixed mass. No calcifications are visible on CT chest scans, but bone invasion is common. The standard treatment is wide surgical excision. Currently, the data are not sufficient to warrant recommendation of neoadjuvant therapy, which has become routine in managing soft tissue sarcomas of the extremities. In 2001, the University of Texas M. D. Anderson Cancer Center reported its multidisciplinary experience with primary chest wall sarcomas.[13] The retrospective review included patients with sarcomas of soft tissue, cartilage, and bone, as well as desmoid tumors. Nevertheless, the cumulative 5-year survival rate was 64%, which is about the rate to be expected from surgery alone.

Bone and Cartilage Neoplasms

A solitary plasmacytoma is a unique chest wall mass that is caused by a localized collection of monoclonal plasma cells. His-

Table 3 Primary Malignant Chest Wall
Neoplasms by Tissue of Origin

Malignant soft tissue neoplasms	Liposarcoma Leiomyosarcoma Rhabdomyosarcoma Malignant fibrous histiocytoma Angiosarcoma
Malignant bone and cartilage neoplasms	Solitary plasmacytoma Chondrosarcoma Osteosarcoma Ewing sarcoma Synovial cell sarcoma

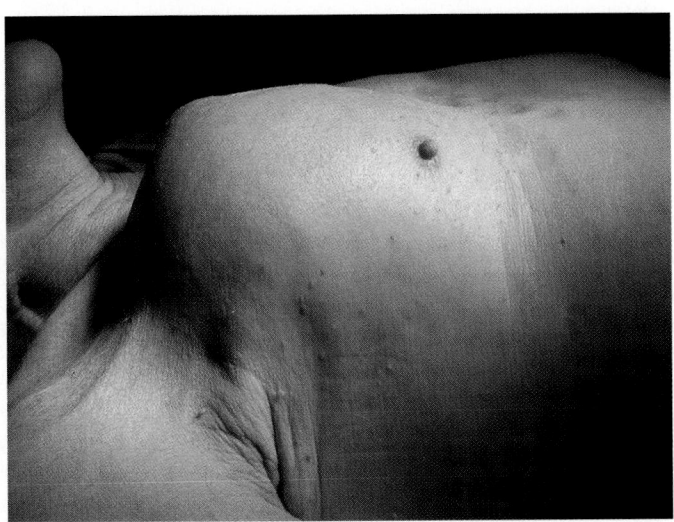

Figure 3 **Shown is the appearance of a chest wall sarcoma on physical examination. Such lesions can be quite large.**

tologically, the plasma cells are identical to those seen in patients with multiple myeloma; however, in a plasmacytoma, unlike multiple myeloma, these cells are confined to a single site. Patients generally present with pain and often have pathologic rib fractures. When soft tissue becomes involved, a palpable mass becomes evident. The role of surgery is limited to obtaining tissue for diagnosis via FNA, core-needle biopsy, or a small incisional biopsy. Tissue is sent for analysis by flow cytometry, which confirms the clonal nature of the cells.[14] Definitive local radiotherapy is the treatment of choice for solitary bone plasmacytoma.[15] Although local control is achieved in more than 90% of patients with radiation therapy alone, about 50% of patients progress to multiple myeloma within 2 years and require systemic treatment.[16]

Chondrosarcomas are the most common primary malignant tumors of the chest wall. They are found along the anterior sternal boarder or the costochondral arches and are substantially more common in males than in females. Pain is typically a presenting complaint. CT scanning is the primary imaging study; however, there are no distinguishing radiographic characteristics that establish a definitive diagnosis.[17] Complete surgical resection with adequate surgical margins and immediate reconstruction is the treatment of choice [*see 36 Chest Wall Procedures*]. A 2004 study from the Mayo Clinic reported a 5-year survival rate of 100% and a recurrence rate of less than 10% in patients with adequate surgical margins.[18] In contrast, patients with inadequate surgical margins had a 50% 5-year survival rate and a 75% local recurrence rate.

Ewing sarcoma is an aggressive primary malignant bone tumor that occurs in children and adolescents. It is more common in boys than in girls and usually develops between the ages of 10 and 20 years. Ewing sarcoma was initially distinguished from osteosarcoma on the basis of its sensitivity to radiation. The origin of Ewing sarcoma remains unclear, but there appear to be several tumors that share the same genetic translocation; these lesions are referred to as the Ewing family of tumors.[19]

The initial role of surgery in managing primary Ewing sarcoma of the chest wall consists of obtaining tissue for diagnosis. With smaller rib lesions, this may be done by means of an excisional biopsy. Generally, Ewing sarcoma is best managed with a multimodality approach that includes preoperative chemotherapy followed by complete resection of residual disease.[20] A 2003 review of three multi-institutional trials from the Pediatric Oncology Group suggests that in patients with Ewing sarcoma and closely related primitive neuroectodermal tumors of the chest wall, the likelihood of achieving a complete resection is improved by employing neoadjuvant chemotherapy followed by delayed resection.[21] The definitive resection is undertaken after four cycles of chemotherapy. If the resection is complete and the pathologic margins are negative, no radiation therapy is administered. Avoidance of radiation therapy may be particularly important in pediatric and adolescent patients, who are at significant (10% to 30%) risk for a radiation-induced malignancy over their lifetime.[22]

Askin tumors are members of the Ewing family of tumors. They are small round cell tumors of the thoracopulmonary region that arise from the same primordial stem cell. They are best managed by means of diagnostic biopsy, preoperative chemotherapy, and complete surgical resection.[23]

Synovial sarcomas are very uncommon, but they occasionally arise on the trunk, where they present as palpable chest wall masses. Although these tumors are referred to as synovial cell sarcomas, this term is a misnomer, in that the lesions do not arise from synovial cells or joint cavities. The name originally derived from the tumors' resemblance to developing synovial tissue under light microscopy; however, synovial sarcomas are now known to arise from primitive mesenchymal cells.[24] The most important prognostic factor is tumor size.[25] The limited data available at present suggest that although neoadjuvant chemotherapy may elicit an objective response, it apparently has no detectable beneficial effect on survival.[26] The current therapeutic recommendation is aggressive surgical resection. If the tumor is very large or margins are positive, postoperative adjuvant treatment is indicated.

SECONDARY MASSES OF CHEST WALL

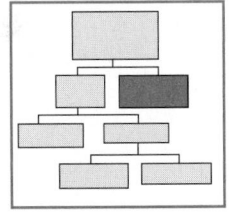

The secondary chest wall masses of surgical interest arise as direct extensions of a malignancy in a contiguous organ. The breast and the lung are the most common primary sites. The initial evaluation centers on the underlying disease, not the chest wall mass. For example, a patient with a chest wall mass resulting from direct invasion by a primary lung cancer should undergo a staging workup to determine the extent of the disease. If the patient is a stage-appropriate candidate for resection and is medically fit for surgery, he or she should undergo pulmonary resection with en bloc chest wall resection.[27] After resection, the patient should be referred for four cycles of postoperative chemotherapy. The interventional intent is cure, and the outcomes are stage specific.

Unfortunately, most women who present with a chest wall mass arising from a breast neoplasm have a local recurrence. From a technical standpoint, resection with reconstruction is feasible in this setting; however, it is unclear whether it offers any real benefit. In a study from the Memorial Sloan-Kettering Cancer Center, 38 women underwent extensive chest wall resection for recurrent breast cancer.[28] The operative mortality was 0%, but the 5-year survival rate was only 18%, and by 5 years, 87% of the patients had local recurrences. Currently, chest wall resection for locally recurrent breast cancer must be considered on a case-by-case basis.

References

1. Fortier M, Mayo JR, Swensen SJ, et al: MR imaging of chest wall lesions. Radiographics 14:597, 1994

2. Gattuso P, Castelli MJ, Reyes CV, et al: Cutaneous and subcutaneous masses of the chest wall: a fine-needle aspiration study. Diagn Cytopathol 15:374, 1996

3. Toumpoulis IK, Anagnostopoulos CE, DeRose JJ, et al: The impact of deep sternal wound infection on long-term survival after coronary artery bypass grafting. Chest 127:464, 2005

4. Ridderstolpe L, Gill H, Granfeldt H, et al: Superficial and deep sternal wound complications: incidence, risk factors and mortality. Eur J Cardiothorac Surg 20:1168, 2001

5. DeFeo M, Gregorio R, Della Corte A, et al: Deep sternal wound infection: the role of early debridement surgery. Eur J Cardiothorac Surg 19:811, 2001

6. Song HK, Guy TS, Kaiser LR, et al: Current presentation and optimal surgical management of sternoclavicular joint infections. Ann Thorac Surg 73:427, 2002

7. Bar-Ziv J, Barki Y, Maroko A, et al: Rib osteomyelitis in children: early radiologic and ultrasonic findings. Pediatr Radiol 15:315, 1985

8. Hayry P, Reitamo JJ, Totterman S, et al: The desmoid tumor: II. Analysis of factors possibly contributing to the etiology and growth behavior. Am J Clin Pathol 77:674, 1982

9. Abbas AE, Deschamps C, Cassivi SD, et al: Chest wall desmoid tumors: results of surgical intervention. Ann Thorac Surg 78:1219, 2004

10. Gordon MS, Hadju SI, Bains MS, et al: Soft tissue sarcomas of the chest wall. J Thorac Cardiovasc Surg 101:843, 1991

11. Gross JL, Younes RN, Haddad FJ, et al: Soft-tissue sarcomas of the chest wall: prognostic factors. Chest 127:902, 2005

12. King RM, Pairolero PC, Trastek VF, et al: Primary chest wall tumors: factors affecting survival. Ann Thorac Surg 41:597, 1986

13. Walsh GL, Davis BM, Swisher SG, et al: A single-institutional, multidisciplinary approach to primary sarcomas involving the chest wall requiring full-thickness resections. J Thorac Cardiovasc Surg 121:48, 2001

14. Jennings CD, Foon KA: Recent advances in flow cytometry: application to the diagnosis of hematologic malignancy. Blood 90:2863, 1997

15. Dimopoulos MA, Moulopoulos LA, Maniatis A, et al: Solitary plasmacytoma of bone and asymptomatic multiple myeloma. Blood 96:2037, 2000

16. Liebross RH, Ha CS, Cox JD, et al: Solitary bone plasmacytoma: outcome and prognostic factors following radiotherapy. Int J Radiat Oncol Biol Phys 41:1063, 1998

17. Murphey MD, Flemming DJ, Boyea SR, et al: Enchondroma versus chondrosarcoma in the appendicular skeleton: differentiating features. Radiographics 5:1213, 1998

18. Fong YC, Pairolero PC, Sim FH, et al: Chondrosarcoma of the chest wall. Clin Orthop Relat Res 427:184, 2004

19. Delattre O, Zucman J, Melot T, et al: The Ewing family of tumors—a subgroup of small-round-cell tumors defined by specific chimeric transcripts. N Engl J Med 331:294, 1994

20. Saenz NC, Hass DJ, Meyer P, et al: Pediatric chest wall Ewing's sarcoma. J Pediatr Surg 35:550, 2000

21. Shamberger RC, LaQuaglia MP, Gebhardt MC, et al: Ewing sarcoma/primitive neuroectodermal tumor of the chest wall: impact of initial versus delayed resection on tumor margins, survival and use of radiation therapy. Ann Surg 238:563, 2003

22. Paulussen M, Ahrens S, Lehnert M, et al: Second malignancies after Ewing tumor treatment in 690 patients from a cooperative German/Austrian/Dutch study. Ann Oncol 12:1619, 2001

23. Veronesi G, Spaggiari L, De Pas T, et al: Preoperative chemotherapy is essential for conservative surgery of Askin tumors. J Thorac Cardiovasc Surg 125:429, 2003

24. Miettinen M, Virtanen I: Synovial sarcoma: a misnomer. Am J Pathol 117:18, 1984

25. Deshmukh R, Mankin H, Singer S: Synovial sarcoma: the importance of size and location for survival. Clin Orthop Relat Res 419:155, 2004

26. Singer S, Baldini EH, Demetri GD, et al: Synovial sarcoma: prognostic significance of tumor size, margin of resection and mitotic activity for survival. J Clin Oncol 14:1201, 1996

27. Burkhart HM, Allen MS, Nichols FC, et al: Results of en bloc resection for bronchogenic carcinoma with chest wall invasions. J Thorac Cardiovasc Surg 123:670, 2002

28. Downey RJ, Rusch V, Hsu FI, et al: Chest wall resection for locally recurrent breast cancer: is it worthwhile? J Thorac Cardiovasc Surg 119:420, 2000

31 PLEURAL EFFUSION

Rafael S. Andrade, M.D., and Michael Maddaus, M.D., F.A.C.S.

Approach to the Patient with a Pleural Effusion

Pleural effusion is a common problem in surgical practice. It results from perturbations of normal pleural fluid transport, which are produced by three main mechanisms—abnormalities in Starling's equilibrium, increased capillary and mesothelial permeability, and interference with lymphatic drainage. These mechanisms are associated with a variety of different causes [see Table 1].[1,2] Often, more than one mechanism is involved. An inflammatory effusion, for instance, is marked by increases in capillary and mesothelial permeability, which lead to elevated intrapleural oncotic pressure.

Pleural effusion is classified as either transudative or exudative, depending on the chemical composition of the fluid. A transudate is an ultrafiltrate of serum and has a low total protein content (≤3 g/dl); an exudate is the result of increased permeability and has a high total protein content. Increased pleural permeability results from complex inflammatory mediator interactions between the mesothelium (whose cells play an active role in inflammation, phagocytosis, leukocyte migration, tissue repair, antigen presentation, coagulation, and fibrinolysis[3,4]) and the capillary endothelium. The distinction between transudative and exudative pleural effusion is clinically significant in that the two types of effusion have different causes [see Table 2].[1,4]

Clinical Evaluation

A complete history, physical examination, and clinical acuity are the initial tools used for diagnosing pleural effusion. Important facts from a patient's history (e.g., respiratory symptoms, pain, extrathoracic symptoms, duration of symptoms, previous medical conditions, and risk factors for cardiopulmonary diseases or can-

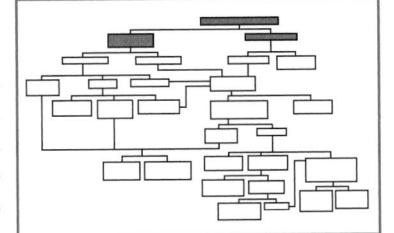

cer) can raise the index of suspicion for an effusion and provide guidance regarding possible causes. Careful physical examination of the chest can detect an effusion, and many physical signs may provide clues to the cause. Physical signs that are particularly useful for diagnostic purposes include jugular venous distention and tachycardia (suggestive of congestive heart failure); lymphadenopathy, digital clubbing, and localized bone tenderness (suggestive of lung cancer); and ascites (suggestive of ovarian tumors or cirrhosis).

Pleural effusion can occur in a wide variety of clinical situations, however, and it often evades clinical detection by history and physical examination. Consequently, imaging tests are indispensable in the workup of a patient with a possible pleural effusion. Pleural fluid analysis, pleural biopsy, and thoracoscopy may also be required for evaluation.

Investigative Studies

IMAGING

Chest Radiography

To be detectable on a standard upright posteroanterior chest radiograph, an effusion must have a volume greater than 150 ml. If the volume is 150 to 500 ml, the lateral costophrenic angle will be blunted; if the volume is greater than 500 ml, a meniscus will be created.[5,6] A lateral decubitus chest radiograph can detect an effusion as small as 5 ml. As a general rule, a layering effusion that is at least 1 cm thick is accessible to thoracentesis.[6,7] A loculated effusion may appear as a so-called pseudotumor on a chest radiograph and typically will not layer freely on a lateral decubitus radiograph. Subtle changes on an upright chest radiograph (e.g., accentuation of a fissure, elevation of a hemidiaphragm [see 33 Paralyzed Diaphragm], or increased separation between the lung and subdiaphragmatic gas [see Figure 1]) may also signal an effu-

Table 1 Pathophysiologic Mechanisms of Pleural Effusion

Mechanism	Specific Alteration	Cause
Abnormality in Starling's equilibrium	Increased capillary and lymphatic hydrostatic pressure	Increased venous pressure (e.g., biventricular heart failure, renal failure)
	Decreased capillary oncotic pressure	Hypoproteinemia (e.g., nephrotic syndrome)
	Decreased intrapleural hydrostatic pressure	Ex vacuo effusion (e.g., atelectasis)
	Increased intrapleural oncotic pressure	Inflammation (e.g., infection, cancer, autoimmune disease)
Increase in capillary and mesothelial permeability	Increased filtration	Inflammation (e.g., infection, cancer, autoimmune disease)
Interference with lymphatic drainage	Obstruction	Cancer, structural abnormalities

Approach to the Patient with a Pleural Effusion

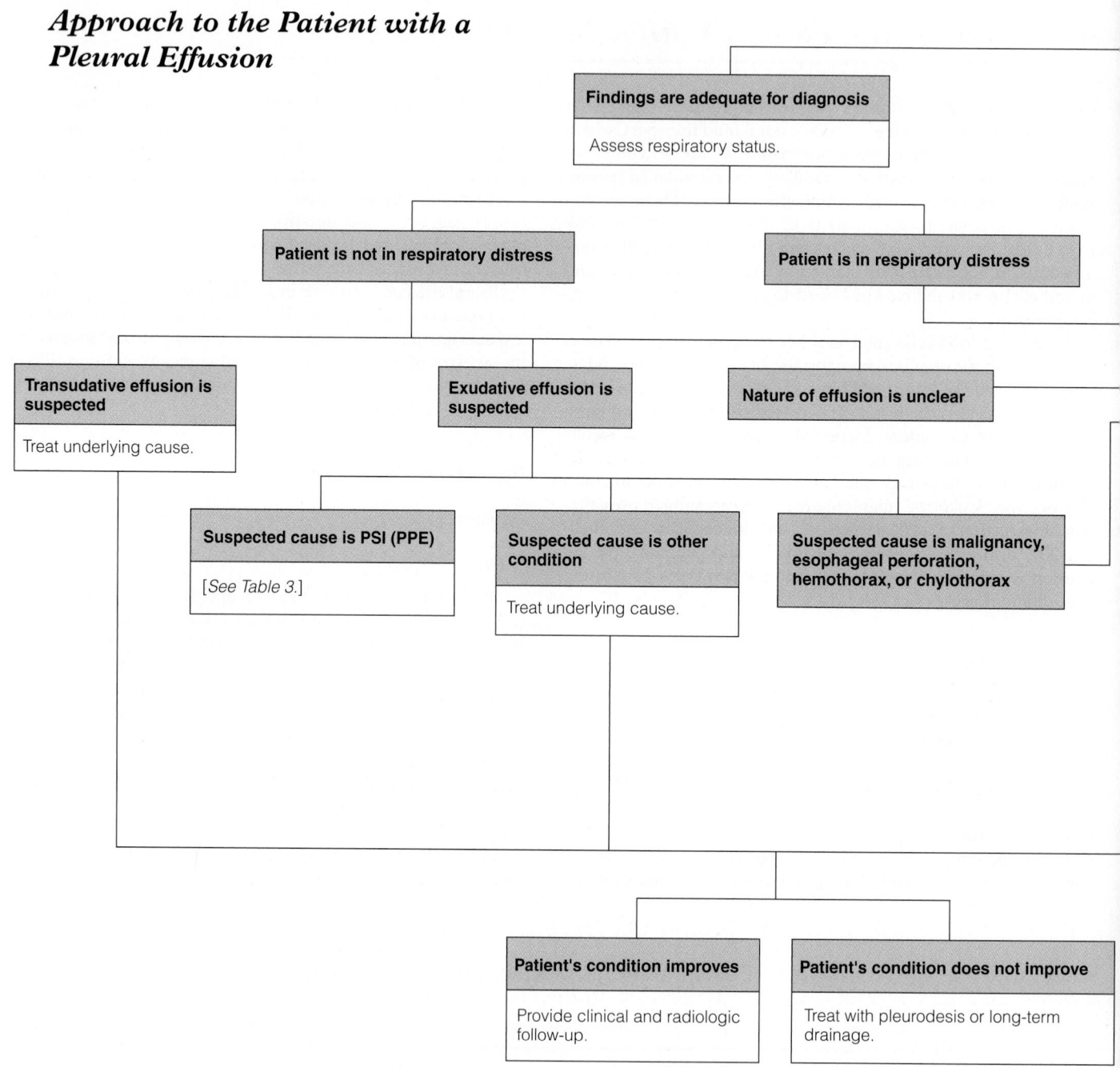

Findings are adequate for diagnosis

Assess respiratory status.

Patient is not in respiratory distress

Patient is in respiratory distress

Transudative effusion is suspected

Treat underlying cause.

Exudative effusion is suspected

Nature of effusion is unclear

Suspected cause is PSI (PPE)

[*See Table 3.*]

Suspected cause is other condition

Treat underlying cause.

Suspected cause is malignancy, esophageal perforation, hemothorax, or chylothorax

Patient's condition improves

Provide clinical and radiologic follow-up.

Patient's condition does not improve

Treat with pleurodesis or long-term drainage.

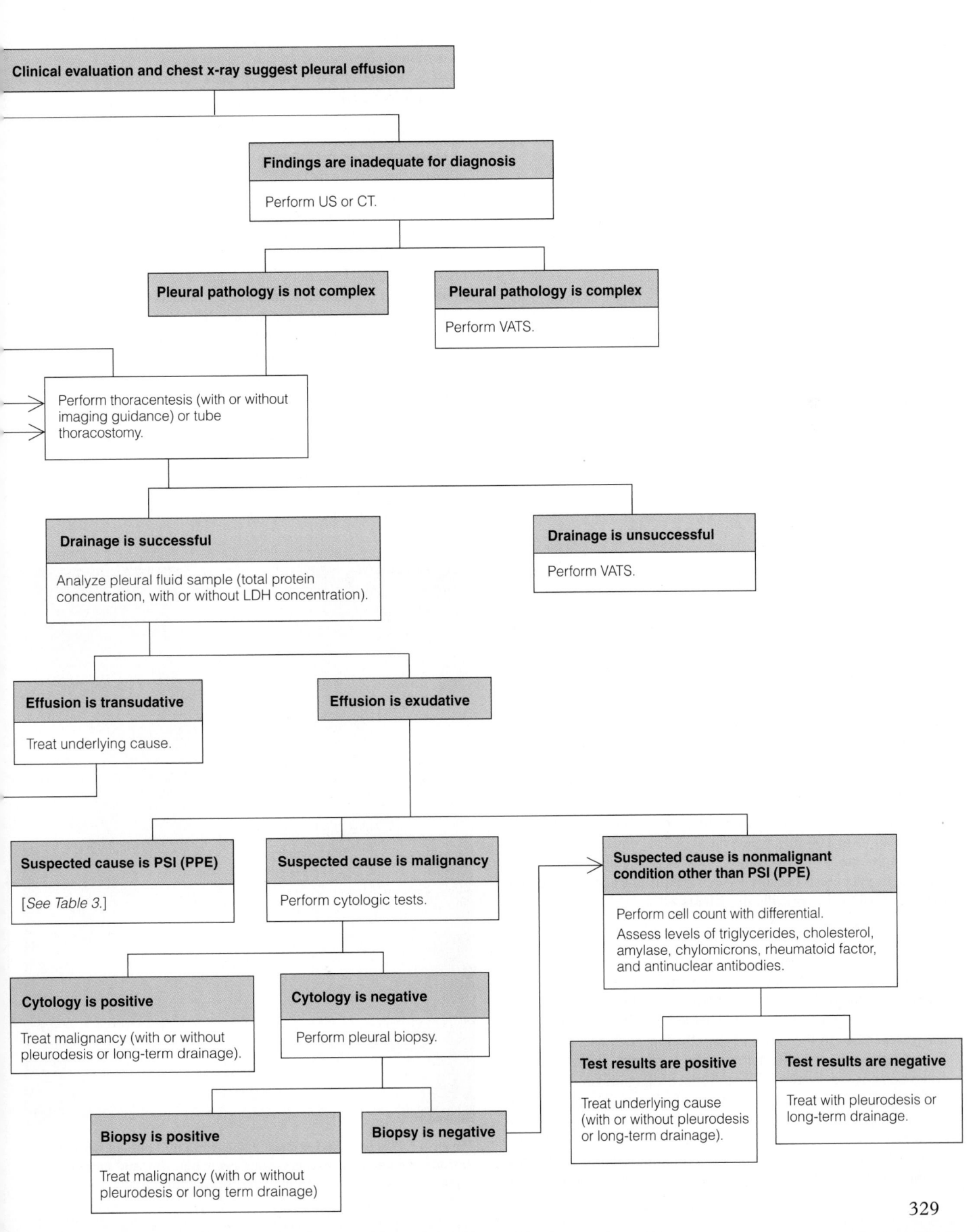

Clinical evaluation and chest x-ray suggest pleural effusion

Findings are inadequate for diagnosis

Perform US or CT.

Pleural pathology is not complex

Pleural pathology is complex

Perform VATS.

Perform thoracentesis (with or without imaging guidance) or tube thoracostomy.

Drainage is successful

Analyze pleural fluid sample (total protein concentration, with or without LDH concentration).

Drainage is unsuccessful

Perform VATS.

Effusion is transudative

Treat underlying cause.

Effusion is exudative

Suspected cause is PSI (PPE)

[*See Table 3.*]

Suspected cause is malignancy

Perform cytologic tests.

Suspected cause is nonmalignant condition other than PSI (PPE)

Perform cell count with differential.
Assess levels of triglycerides, cholesterol, amylase, chylomicrons, rheumatoid factor, and antinuclear antibodies.

Cytology is positive

Treat malignancy (with or without pleurodesis or long-term drainage).

Cytology is negative

Perform pleural biopsy.

Test results are positive

Treat underlying cause (with or without pleurodesis or long-term drainage).

Test results are negative

Treat with pleurodesis or long-term drainage.

Biopsy is positive

Treat malignancy (with or without pleurodesis or long term drainage)

Biopsy is negative

Table 2 Causes of Transudative and Exudative Pleural Effusion

Type of Effusion	Cause
Transudative	Congestive heart failure Cirrhosis Nephrotic syndrome Acute atelectasis Renal failure Peritoneal dialysis Postoperative state Myxedema Postpartum state
Exudative	Pneumonia Malignancy Infection Esophageal perforation Hemothorax Chylothorax Pseudochylothorax Connective tissue diseases Drug-induced pleuritis Pancreatitis Uremia Postmyocardial infarction (Dressler syndrome) Chronic atelectasis Radiation therapy Asbestos exposure Meigs syndrome Ovarian hyperstimulation
Transudative or exudative	Pulmonary embolus

sion. Additional findings on a standard chest radiograph (e.g., laterality, the size of the cardiac silhouette, the position of the mediastinum, pulmonary parenchymal changes, pleural calcifications, and osseous abnormalities) may point to a specific cause.

Supine chest radiographs are less sensitive than other chest radiographs. With these images, suspicion of an effusion is triggered by increased homogeneous density of the lower hemithorax, loss of normal diaphragmatic silhouette, blunting of the lateral costophrenic angle, or apical capping [see Figure 2].[8]

Ultrasonography

Chest ultrasonograms are more reliable for detecting and localizing small (5 to 100 ml) or loculated pleural effusions than chest radiographs are.[5,9,10] Ultrasonography is particularly helpful for guiding thoracentesis for small-volume effusions and for assessing pleural effusions in critically ill patients.[6,11]

Computed Tomography of the Chest

Computed tomography of the chest is a very sensitive tool for evaluating pleural effusion. Free-flowing fluid causes a sickle-shaped opacity in the most dependent portion of the thorax, and even small effusions are readily detected [see Figure 3]. CT may also reveal clues to the cause of the effusion, such as a fluid-fluid level (suggestive of acute hemorrhage), pleural thickening and enhancement (suggestive of pleural space infection [see Figure 4]), calcified pleural plaques (suggestive of asbestosis), and diffuse irregular nodularity and pleural thickening (suggestive of pleural metastases or mesothelioma). CT is especially useful for characterizing loculated effusions, for differentiating pleural thickening or pleural masses from pleural effusion, for distinguishing be-

tween effusion and lung abscess, and for guiding and monitoring closed drainage of effusions.[6,10,12,13]

Magnetic Resonance Imaging

Magnetic resonance imaging of the chest provides no useful information beyond what can be obtained with CT scanning. MRI is neither efficient nor cost-effective in standard evaluation of pleural effusion.[12,14]

THORACENTESIS

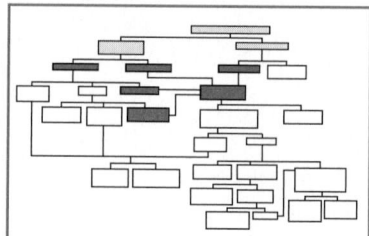

If the cause of a pleural effusion cannot be explained by the clinical circumstances (e.g., congestive heart failure or a recent surgical procedure), diagnostic thoracentesis [see Sidebar Techniques of Bedside Thoracentesis and Tube Thoracostomy] is indicated. Thoracentesis may also have therapeutic value, in that drainage of fluid may relieve dyspnea. Absolute contraindications to thoracentesis include lack of cooperation on the patient's part, clinical instability with hemodynamic or respiratory compromise, severe coagulopathy, and high-pressure ventilation. Relative contraindications to thoracentesis include a nonlayering effusion, loculations, and previous thoracic trauma, chest tube placement, or surgery.

A large effusion can be drained without any special imaging guidance other than an upright lateral chest radiograph. Thoracentesis for a small or loculated effusion is best done with ultrasound guidance; success rates are as high as 97%.[15]

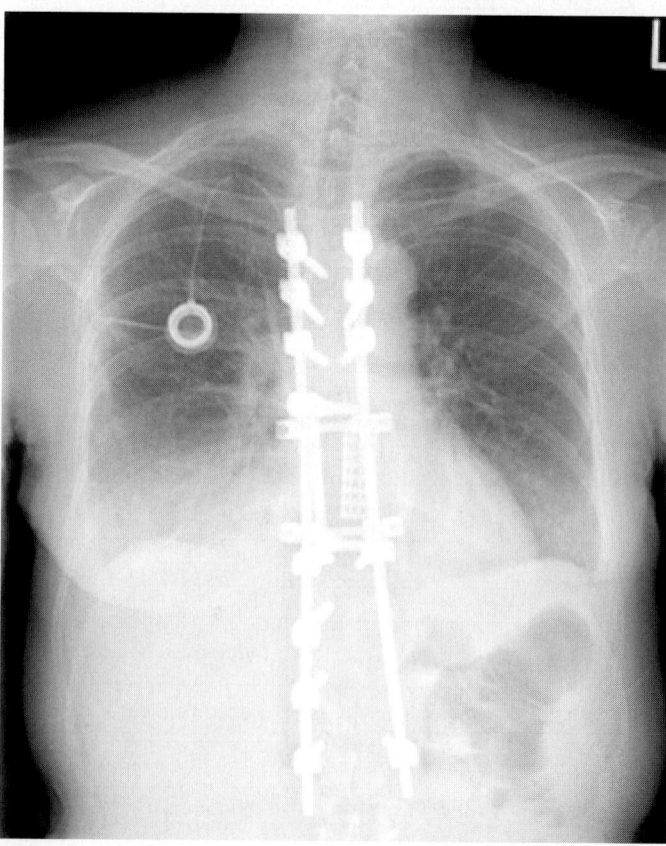

Figure 1 **Posteroanterior chest radiograph of a patient with bilateral pleural effusion reveals costophrenic blunting and increased separation between the left lung and subdiaphragmatic gas.**

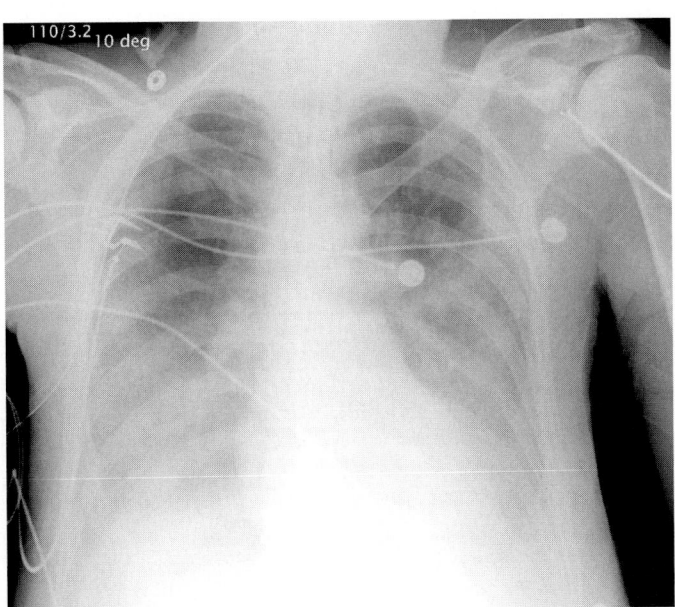

Figure 2 **Supine chest radiograph of a patient with bilateral pleural effusion shows increased homogeneous density of the lower hemithoraces.**

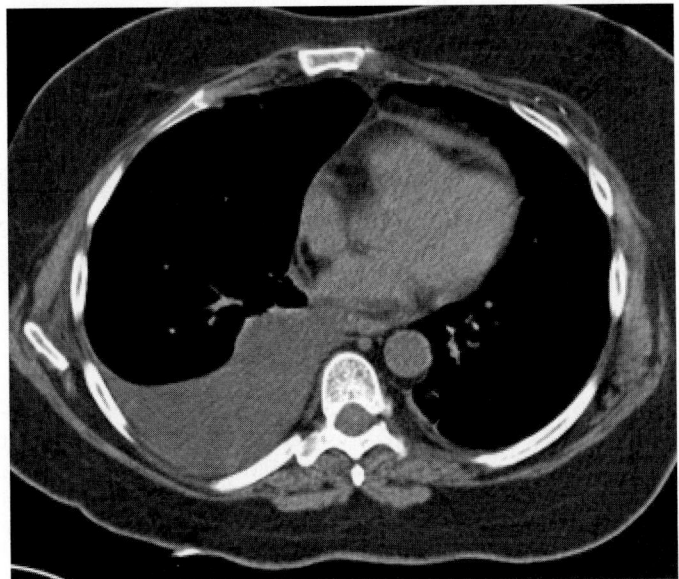

Figure 3 **Chest CT shows a free-flowing, sickle-shaped right-side effusion.**

The incidence of complications associated with thoracentesis varies, depending on the experience of the operator and on the use of imaging guidance. Pneumothorax occurs in 3% to 20% of patients, of whom approximately 20% require tube thoracostomy [*see Sidebar* Techniques of Bedside Thoracentesis and Tube Thoracostomy]. Patients commonly experience pain and cough with lung reexpansion during drainage. Reexpansion pulmonary edema is an uncommon complication that can occur with rapid drainage of a large-volume effusion. It is common practice to drain no more than 1 to 1.5 L at a time, even though no evidence supports this practice. Experimental data suggest that active aspiration of fluid can cause high negative intrapleural pressures, potentially precipitating edema formation; gravity drainage may be

preferable to minimize the chance of edema. Additional potential complications include so-called dry tap, vasovagal reaction, hemorrhage hypovolemia, and pleural space infection (PSI).[10,16-18]

PLEURAL FLUID ANALYSIS

Assessment of a pleural fluid sample is guided, to some extent, by the clinical context in which the pleural effusion occurs. When the cause of the effusion is unknown, evaluation of a pleural fluid sample typically in- 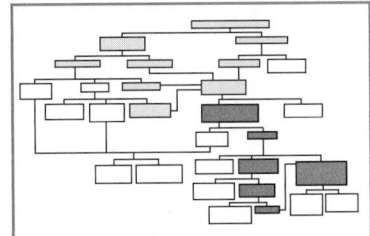 cludes measurement of total protein and lactic dehydrogenase (LDH) concentrations, a cell count with differential, cause-specific testing, and microbiologic and cytologic analysis.

Biochemical Analysis of Pleural Fluid

A total protein concentration higher than 3 g/dl is generally used as the main criterion for distinguishing a transudate from an exudate; however, the use of this criterion may result in misclassification of as many as 15% of effusions. According to Light's criteria,[19] which have a sensitivity of 99% and a specificity of 98% for identifying exudates, an effusion is an exudate if any of the following three findings is present:

1. A pleural fluid–to–serum protein ratio higher than 0.5
2. A pleural fluid–to–serum LDH ratio higher than 0.6
3. A pleural fluid LDH concentration higher than two thirds of the upper limit of the serum reference range

A 1997 meta-analysis of the diagnostic value of tests used to distinguish transudates from exudates did not find any test or combination of tests to be clearly superior.[20] The choice of a test for this purpose is therefore a matter of individual preference. If only one test is to be performed, measurement of the total protein concentration is the most practical choice, in view of its accuracy and availability.

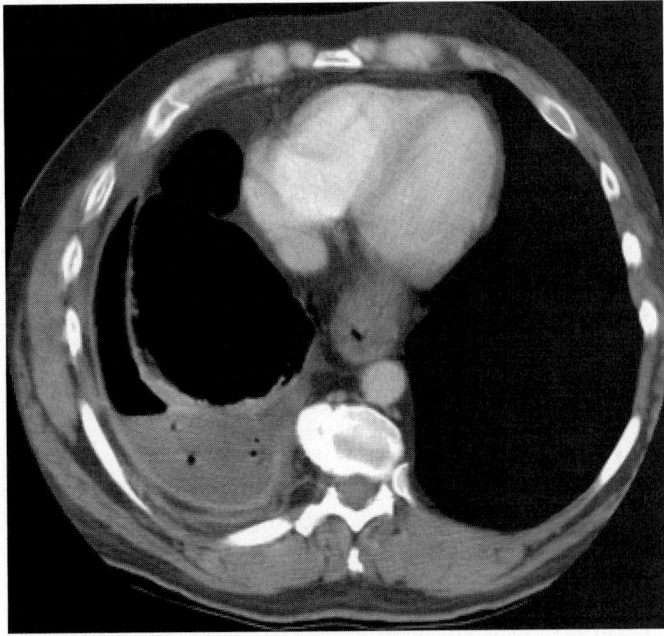

Figure 4 **Chest CT of a patient with right-side empyema shows a loculated effusion. The pleura is enhanced with I.V. contrast.**

Techniques of Bedside Thoracentesis and Tube Thoracostomy

Bedside Thoracentesis

Bedside thoracentesis should be performed on a bed or an examination table (as a safeguard if hypotension develops). The patient should be upright and seated (provided that he or she is awake and cooperative), with the arms leaning comfortably on a bedside table and the back facing the surgeon.

The proper intercostal space for catheter insertion is determined through physical examination and radiologic evaluation of the effusion; generally, the ninth or 10th intercostal space in the midscapular line is a good choice. The area is prepared and anesthetized with 1% lidocaine, 3 to 5 mg/kg, with care taken not to injure the intercostal bundle. To confirm that the catheter is in the correct location, we recommend drawing a small amount of pleural fluid at the time of local anesthetic infiltration. Several thoracentesis kits with one-way valves are available. To minimize the risk of reexpansion pulmonary edema, fluid should be allowed to drain by gravity, and drainage should not exceed 1.5 L. Frequently, a dry cough and pleuritic pain develop as drainage approaches its end. To minimize anxiety, the patient should be warned about this possibility in advance. After the completion of thoracentesis, a chest radiograph should be obtained.

Bedside Tube Thoracostomy

Bedside tube thoracostomy should be performed with the patient supine. The side on which the thoracostomy will be created should be elevated, and the patient's ipsilateral arm should be abducted. Supplemental oxygen should be supplied. Monitoring must include, at the least, continuous oxygen saturation plethysmography and intermittent measurement of blood pressure and heart rate. Tube thoracostomy is potentially very painful; accordingly, in a nonemergency situation, every effort should be made to minimize pain and anxiety. We usually administer intravenous ketorolac about 30 to 60 minutes before the procedure.

During preparation for chest tube placement, narcotics and sedatives should be administered intravenously; additional doses should then be administered at the beginning of and during the procedure.

The ideal location for chest tube placement is determined by clinical and radiographic examination. The area is prepared and draped widely, and a local anesthetic is used at a near-maximum dosage, with care taken to anesthetize skin, subcutaneous tissue, muscle, and periosteum. A 1.5 cm skin incision is made, a soft tissue tunnel is created with blunt instrument and finger dissection, the upper edge of the rib is identified clearly, and additional local anesthetic is applied to the periosteum and the intercostal muscles. The subcutaneous tunnel should generally be directed posteriorly so that the chest tube will sit along the posterior chest wall and will not be trapped in a fissure. The intercostal muscle is pierced bluntly, and digital examination of the pleural space is performed to confirm that an intrapleural location has been reached and to search for abnormalities such as adhesions or tumor implants. The chest tube is then directed to the desired location with the aid of a clamp. As with thoracentesis, fluid should be allowed to drain by gravity, but drainage should not exceed 1.5 L. If the effusion exceeds 1.5 L, the chest tube should be clamped and the remaining fluid allowed to drain intermittently in 200 ml aliquots every 2 hours. Immediately after completion of the procedure, a chest radiograph should be obtained to verify lung expansion and confirm the position of the chest tube. When chest tube output falls below 200 ml/day and reexpansion of the lung is verified, pleurodesis should be performed. We recommend that patient-controlled analgesia be employed while the chest tube remains in place.

The size of the chest tube is determined by the suspected cause and by the radiologic characteristics of the effusion. For a free-flowing transudative effusion, a small (20 to 24 French) chest tube or even a pigtail catheter usually suffices; for a thick exudative effusion or a hemothorax, a tube as large as 40 French may be required.

Assessment of pleural fluid pH and glucose levels may be used adjunctively for risk stratification in patients with PSI, but the clinical utility of these measurements is not well established (see below).[21]

There are numerous pleural fluid components whose concentrations can be measured to help determine the specific cause of a pleural effusion, such as triglycerides, chylomicrons, and cholesterol (to help diagnose chylothorax); amylase (to help diagnose esophageal perforation or pancreatitis); rheumatoid factor (to help diagnose rheumatoid effusion); antinuclear antibodies (to help diagnose lupus pleuritis); carcinoembryonic antigen (to help diagnose malignancy); and adenosine deaminase (to help diagnose tuberculous pleurisy).[3,22-25]

Cell Counts

Analysis of the number and type of white blood cells (WBCs) present in pleural fluid is often diagnostically useful. Pleural effusions can be categorized according to the type of WBC that is predominant. Generally, pleural fluid neutrophilia points to acute inflammation (e.g., from PSI or pulmonary infarction) as the underlying cause; however, the presence of a neutrophilic effusion does not exclude malignancy. Pleural fluid lymphocytosis, in which lymphocytes account for more than 50% of WBCs, most frequently is indicative of malignancy (occurring in 50% of malignant effusions), tuberculosis (occurring in 15% to 20% of tuberculous effusions), or chylothorax.[26] Pleural fluid eosinophilia, in which eosinophils account for more than 10% of WBCs, can be caused by a wide variety of benign and malignant conditions—even, in some cases, by the mere presence of air or blood in the pleural space. Approximately one third of eosinophilic effusions

are idiopathic. As a rule, the presence of mesothelial cells is of little diagnostic value; the exception to this rule is that if such cells account for more than 5% of WBCs, a tuberculous effusion is unlikely.[23,27]

Microbiologic Tests

If a PSI is suspected, Gram staining and standard bacterial cultures are indicated. If tuberculous pleurisy is a possibility, acid-fast stains and mycobacterial cultures should be performed. Fungal, viral, and parasitic PSIs are uncommon; accordingly, special stains and cultures for these conditions are indicated only if dictated by a specific clinical setting.[28]

Cytologic Tests

Cytologic testing of pleural fluid is routinely performed whenever the cause of an effusion is unclear. The diagnostic yield for malignancy varies depending on the stage of the disease, but it generally is in the range of 50% to 60% (higher in patients with bulky pleural tumors). Repeat cytologic testing may increase the yield to more than 70%,[10,29] and testing of three or more samples may increase the yield to 90%.[30]

PLEURAL BIOPSY

In approximately 25% of patients with exudative effusion, the cause remains unknown after clinical evaluation, imaging, and pleural fluid analysis. The next step in the evaluation of such patients is pleural biopsy.

Percutaneous pleural biopsy is an infrequently used tool that has a diagnostic yield of 57% for carcinoma. Its low yield for malignant effusion can be explained by the uneven distribution of pleural metastases. For tuberculous pleurisy, however, the diagnostic yield of percutaneous pleural biopsy is 75%, and the yield rises to 90% when this procedure is combined with pleural fluid culture. In about 10% to 20% of patients with exudative pleural effusion, laboratory analysis of pleural fluid and percutaneous biopsy fail to produce a specific diagnosis.[18] The contraindications and complications associated with percutaneous pleural biopsy are similar to those associated with thoracentesis.[31]

Video-assisted thoracoscopic surgery (VATS) is also employed for pleural biopsy; its diagnostic yield in this setting is 92% for malignancy and nearly 100% for tuberculous pleurisy. VATS is a therapeutic procedure as well, allowing the surgeon to perform pleurodesis, decortication, or pleurectomy if necessary. VATS pleural biopsy is typically performed with the patient under general anesthesia, but if the patient is highly debilitated, it can be done with regional and local anesthesia.[32] Procedure-specific complications include hypoxemia, hemorrhage, prolonged air leakage, subcutaneous emphysema, and empyema, each of which occurs at a rate of about 2%. The mortality associated with diagnostic thoracoscopy ranges from 0.01% to 0.09%.[29,31] When VATS is performed to remove a suspected malignant lesion, a protective plastic device is required to minimize the possibility of tumor seeding. Incisional tumor seeding after a VATS biopsy is rare but can occur at any time after the procedure (reported range, 2 weeks to 29 months).[33]

If mesothelioma is suspected, open lung biopsy (through a 5 to 7 cm incision) is the preferred diagnostic procedure. Ideally, the biopsy incision should be placed at the location of a potential thoracotomy incision so that future excision of the biopsy scar can be accomplished in a manner that minimizes the risk of local tumor recurrence.[34]

Management

PLEURAL EFFUSION IN THE INTENSIVE CARE UNIT

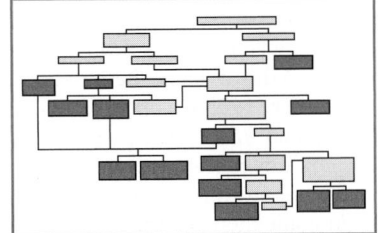

Pleural effusion develops in as many as 60% of intensive care unit patients who are evaluated with ultrasonography.[11] When pleural effusion occurs in the ICU, drainage should be liberally employed to optimize the patient's hemodynamic and respiratory status and to detect PSI early. Thoracentesis can be done in critically ill ventilator-dependent patients with the help of bedside ultrasonography. Chest tube thoracostomy does not require ultrasonographic guidance and may be a safer choice for patients on high-pressure ventilation.

MALIGNANT PLEURAL EFFUSION

Pleural effusion is associated with malignancy in 30% to 65% of patients, and approximately 75% of patients with malignant effusion have lung or breast cancer.[35] The principal aim of therapy is to relieve dyspnea and to limit the number of procedures and hospital days that patients with a limited life expectancy must endure.

Drainage can be achieved by means of thoracentesis, chest tube placement, or VATS. Thoracentesis is a valuable option for initial patient evaluation, particularly in the office setting. Because malignant pleural effusion recurs rapidly unless patients undergo effective systemic or local treatment, repeat thoracentesis is generally not recommended for anything other than urgent relief of symptoms. Chest tubes are placed primarily with the intention of performing bedside pleurodesis.

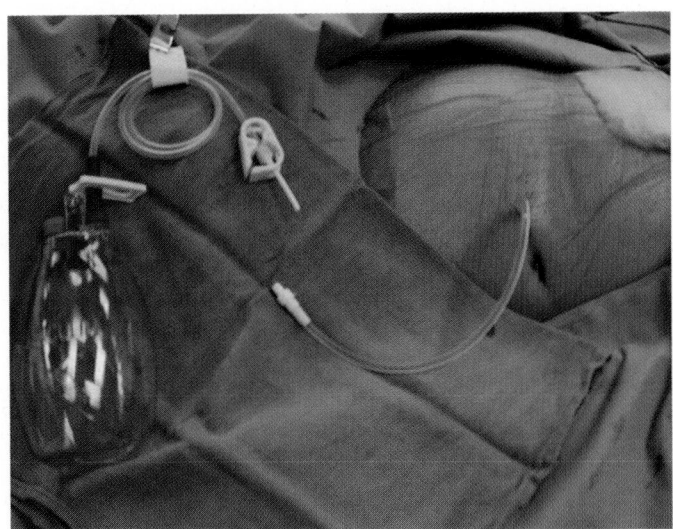

Figure 5 Shown is a Pleurx catheter after placement and subcutaneous tunneling. The vacuum container is not connected.

Small-bore subcutaneously tunneled catheters may be employed for long-term management of malignant pleural effusions. Two options are available: the Pleurx catheter (Denver Biomedical, Golden, Colorado) [*see Figure 5*] and the Tenckhoff peritoneal dialysis catheter. Regardless of which option is chosen, the procedure is essentially the same: the catheter is inserted with the patient under local or general anesthesia, the patient is discharged on the same day or on the day after insertion, and the pleural fluid is drained either according to a schedule or on an as-needed basis. Small-bore tunneled catheters are comfortable, but patients may object to having a permanent catheter or to undergoing home-based procedures. In 20% to 58% of patients with a permanent catheter, pleurodesis develops within 4 to 6 weeks. Catheter removal, if desired, is easily done in the office setting. Technical failures and infection may occur in as many as 20% of patients with permanent catheters, but such problems are easily managed.[36-39]

Pleuroperitoneal shunting has been advocated as an alternative for long-term management of malignant pleural effusions. Experience with this mode of drainage is limited, however, and the potential for technical complications is high.[40,41]

Recurrence of malignant pleural effusion is best prevented by using sclerosants to induce pleurodesis. The sclerosant may be instilled either via a bedside tube thoracostomy or thoracoscopically; a median hospitalization of 6.5 days is required.[36] Of the various sclerosants available, talc is the most efficacious, with an overall success rate of 80% to 96%.[42,43] The ideal talc dose has not been determined; the usual dose is 4 or 5 g. Talc pleurodesis with a 5 g dose has generally proved efficient and safe. For obvious reasons, simultaneous bilateral talc instillation should be avoided.[42] A phase III intergroup study (CALGB 9334) that compared bedside talc slurry pleurodesis with thoracoscopic talc insufflation pleurodesis found no difference in outcome at 30 days; however, subgroup analysis revealed that thoracoscopic talc insufflation pleurodesis was superior in patients with primary lung cancer or breast cancer.[44] Thoracoscopically guided talc pleurodesis can be performed with an operative mortality of less than 1%.[45,46]

Pain and fever are frequent side effects of talc pleurodesis, but the main concern is the possible development of acute lung injury (ALI) and respiratory failure. Respiratory failure occurs in approximately 1% to 4% of patients. The cause of respiratory failure sec-

Table 3 Categorization of PPE by Risk of Poor Outcome

Pleural Space Anatomy	Pleural Fluid Bacteriology	Category	Risk of Poor Outcome	Drainage
Minimal free-flowing effusion (< 10 mm on lateral decubitus x-ray)	Culture and Gram stain results unknown	1	Very low	No
Small to moderate free-flowing effusion (> 10 mm but < 50% hemithorax)	Negative culture and Gram stain	2	Low	No
Large free-flowing effusion (> 50% hemithorax), loculated effusion, or effusion with thickened parietal pleura (as seen on contrast-enhanced CT)	Positive culture or Gram stain	3	Moderate	Yes
	Pus	4	High	Yes

ondary to talc pleurodesis is not clear and is probably related to multiple factors (e.g., talc dose, talc absorption, underlying lung disease, reexpansion pulmonary edema, systemic inflammatory response, tumor burden, and lymphatic obstruction). There is no definitive evidence that the talc dose is correlated with the incidence of ALI; respiratory failure has been reported even with a 2 g talc dose.[42,47-51]

Treatment of malignant pleural effusion must be individualized. The key factors governing the choice of treatment approach are (1) the patient's performance status, (2) the prognosis, (3) the pleural tumor bulk, and (4) the ability of the lung to reexpand. Patients who have poor performance status (e.g., those with advanced tumors or significant comorbid conditions) or a very poor short-term prognosis should undergo the least invasive treatment—namely, drainage only. Patients who have better functional status and are expected to survive longer should undergo thoracoscopically guided talc pleurodesis. Intrathoracic tumor bulk is important in that a bulky pleural lesion will interfere with pleurodesis. The lung's ability to reexpand after drainage of a malignant effusion is significant because if the lung is atelectatic as a result of airway obstruction or trapped as a result of pleural seeding, no agent will be able to induce pleurodesis, and the best treatment will be long-term drainage.

PLEURAL SPACE INFECTION

PSI can be caused by a variety of factors, including pneumonia, trauma, and intrathoracic procedures. It has a wide clinical spectrum, ranging from a small parapneumonic effusion (PPE) to a pus-filled pleural space (empyema) with respiratory compromise and sepsis. (The terms PSI and PPE are often used interchangeably.) PSI can be classified either according to its pathophysiologic stage (exudative, fibrinopurulent, or organizing) or according to its anatomic appearance (nonloculated versus loculated or noncomplicated versus complicated). The term empyema is commonly reserved for the most advanced stage of PSI.[52]

The pathophysiology of PSI or PPE can be divided into three stages. The exudative stage is characterized by the development of an exudative effusion secondary to increased pleural permeability; the pleural space is often sterile initially, but if it is left untreated, bacterial infection is likely to ensue. The fibrinopurulent stage is marked by the progressive deposition of fibrin and the increasing presence of WBCs; gradual angioblastic and fibroblastic proliferation leads to extensive fibrin deposits, and the effusion becomes loculated (complicated). The organizing stage starts as early as 1 week after infection, with increasing collagen deposition and lung entrapment. After 3 or 4 weeks, the organized collagen has formed a peel, and the pleural fluid is grossly purulent. Eventually, dense fibrosis, contraction, and lung entrapment develop.[53,54]

In most patients, PSI is caused by bacteria. The most common pathogens are *Staphylococcus aureus*, *Streptococcus pneumoniae*, enteric gram-negative bacilli, and anaerobes. Approximately 30% to 40% of cultures are polymicrobial. In a subgroup of patients, there is sterile pus in the pleural space, as a consequence either of previous antimicrobial therapy or of bacterial autolysis. The pathogens identified vary according to the cause of PSI. For instance, *S. aureus* and *S. pneumoniae* predominate in PPE; *S. aureus*, in postthoracotomy PSI; mixed oropharyngeal organisms, in PSI resulting from esophageal perforation[28]; and acid-fast bacteria, in tuberculous empyema.[55]

Parapneumonic Effusion

PPE occurs in as many as 57% of patients hospitalized with pneumonia, and pneumonia accounts for 42% to 73% of cases of PSI. In most cases, early PPE is effectively treated by timely antibiotic therapy aimed at the underlying pneumonia.[21,28]

In 2000, a panel convened by the Health and Science Policy Committee of the American College of Chest Physicians (ACCP) reviewed the available literature with the aim of developing an evidence-based clinical practice guideline for the treatment of PPE.[21] The panel formulated a clear and relatively simple classification system that used pleural anatomy and bacteriology to stratify patients according to the risk of a poor outcome [*see Table 3*]. It then made therapeutic recommendations on the basis of this classification. Some authors have used pleural fluid chemistry test results (e.g., pH and glucose concentration) as additional criteria for categorizing PPE; for example, a pleural fluid pH lower than 7.20 or a glucose level lower than 60 mg/dl has been considered suggestive of moderate risk. To date, however, the clinical utility and decision thresholds of pH and glucose values have not been well defined. Accordingly, we prefer to omit pleural fluid chemistry from these guidelines.

The ACCP Health and Science Policy Committee evaluated six primary management approaches: no drainage, therapeutic thoracentesis, tube thoracostomy, fibrinolytic therapy, VATS, and open surgery. Overall, pooled outcomes favored patients treated with fibrinolytics, VATS, and open surgery. However, the success of an approach is related to the patient's risk category. The recommendations for drainage in relation to risk category are general guidelines, based on level C and D evidence (with level C referring to historically controlled series and case series and level D to expert opinion). With these recommendations (and their limitations) in mind, treatment should be tailored to the specific situation of each patient.

Category 1 and 2 PPE PPE in categories 1 (very low risk) and 2 (low risk) can be treated with antibiotic therapy directed at the underlying pneumonia. Some patients with category 2 PPE may require drainage for relief of dyspnea through either thoracentesis or tube thoracostomy.

Category 3 and 4 PPE Drainage options for categories 3 (moderate risk) and 4 (high risk) PPE include tube thoracostomy alone, tube thoracostomy with intrapleural fibrinolytic therapy, VATS drainage, and open surgical drainage. These various approaches are not mutually exclusive: in some cases, patient outcomes may be optimized by combining them.[56]

Tube thoracostomy alone may be appropriate for category 3 patients with free-flowing effusion. With loculated effusion, however, the key to successful therapy is breaking down the fibrin septations. Evidence from three small randomized, controlled trials suggested that intrapleural fibrinolytic therapy has an advantage over tube thoracostomy alone for patients with category 3 or 4 PPE; a large trial is being conducted to address this specific issue.[53] To date, only one randomized study, including 20 patients with category 3 or 4 PPE, has compared VATS with fibrinolytic therapy. The primary treatment success rate was significantly higher in the VATS treatment group, the duration of chest tube drainage was less, and the total hospital stay was shorter.[57] VATS allows not only adequate drainage and visualization of the pleural space but also decortication of the lung if required; however, if decortication cannot be thoroughly accomplished by means of VATS and satisfactory lung expansion cannot be achieved, a thoracotomy should be performed.[58]

The principles of PPE treatment can be applied to PSI from any cause, but in view of the paucity of reliable data, caution should be exercised.

Posttraumatic PSI

PSI occurs in about 1% to 5% of patients who have sustained blunt or penetrating thoracic injury. The incidence of PSI in the setting of trauma increases with the number of chest tubes placed and with the duration of chest tube drainage. The effect of an undrained hemothorax on the risk of PSI has not been completely defined, and prophylactic antibiotics have not been shown to reduce the incidence of PSI.[52]

As noted (see above), the general guidelines for the treatment of PPE apply to the treatment of posttraumatic PSI.

Iatrogenic PSI

Iatrogenic PSI develops when a preexisting pleural effusion is inoculated with bacteria during an invasive procedure (e.g., thoracentesis or tube thoracostomy). The presence of fluid in the pleural space appears to be a prerequisite for infection.[52]

A bronchopleural fistula (BPF) is by definition a PSI and therefore has a similarly broad spectrum of clinical presentation. The overall incidence of BPF after lobar resection is approximately 1%; it is somewhat higher after resections for inflammatory diseases than after resections for cancer. The incidence of BPF after pneumonectomy varies, depending on the side on which the pneumonectomy was done, the indications for surgery, the extent of preoperative irradiation, and the comorbid conditions present. In a report encompassing 464 pneumonectomies for cancer, the incidence of BPF was 8.6% after right pneumonectomy and 2.3% after left pneumonectomy. The overall incidence of postpneumonectomy empyema (generally but not always secondary to a BPF) is 1% to 3%.[59,60]

PSI that is not associated with a BPF is treated in accordance with the treatment guidelines for PPE, but if a BPF is present, operative management is required.

Tuberculous PSI

Pleural effusion is common in patients with clinically evident pulmonary tuberculosis. Most cases of tuberculous effusion are secondary to hypersensitivity and resolve spontaneously. Tuberculous empyema is relatively rare; it is typically the result of active pleural infection by acid-fast bacteria.[55]

Tuberculous PSI is also treated in accordance with the general treatment guidelines for bacterial PSI. Chronic tuberculous PSI may present specific problems, such as drug resistance and impaired ability (or even inability) to reexpand the lung. Surgical procedures performed to manage chronic tuberculous empyema include VATS, standard open decortication, thoracoplasty, parietal wall collapse, open drainage, myoplasty, and omentopexy.[55]

CHYLOTHORAX AND PSEUDOCHYLOTHORAX

Chylothorax is the presence of chyle in the pleural space as a consequence of blockage of or damage to the thoracic duct or one of its tributaries. The rate at which chyle flows through the thoracic duct can be higher than 100 ml/hr, and thus, large amounts of chyle can leak into the pleural space.[61] The principal causes of chylothorax are surgical trauma and malignancy (70% to 80% are caused by non-Hodgkin lymphoma).[46,61,62] Congenital chylothorax is more often due to malformation of the thoracic duct than to birth trauma.[24]

The diagnosis of chylothorax is made by measuring triglyceride levels in pleural fluid. Levels higher than 110 mg/dl are highly suggestive of chylothorax; levels between 50 and 100 mg/dl are equivocal; and levels lower than 50 mg/dl rule out chylothorax.[24] A pleura-to-serum triglyceride ratio higher than 1 can be a useful indicator[63]; the presence of chylomicrons is synonymous with chylothorax.[25]

Treatment of chylothorax depends on its cause and severity. Postoperative chylothorax may be treated initially with conservative measures (e.g., with a nihil per os [NPO] regimen, total parenteral nutrition, and administration of octreotide). However, drainage totaling more than 500 ml/day is considered to predict failure of conservative management. Thoracic duct ligation is the surgical treatment of choice and can often be performed thoracoscopically. To help identify the leak intraoperatively, it may be helpful to administer 100 to 200 ml of heavy cream or olive oil orally 2 to 3 hours before the operation.[64,65] Early surgical intervention is important because the ongoing loss of lymph has significant effects on fluid homeostasis, nutrition, and immunocompetence (secondary to lymphocyte loss). In the early postligation period, medical management should be continued to allow any small leaks to seal. An alternative to surgical ligation that has evoked some interest is transabdominal percutaneous embolization of the thoracic duct. This technique requires significant expertise.[66]

Lymphoma-related chylothorax is caused principally by obstruction and usually develops on the left side [*see Figure 6*]. In a stiff and infiltrated duct, minor triggers (e.g., a Valsalva maneuver) can lead to duct rupture. Although patients with chylothorax often have extensive disease, supradiaphragmatic disease is not always present. Lymphoma-related chylothorax is best managed with thoracentesis and with therapy directed at the underlying cause. If first-line therapy fails, thoracoscopic talc pleurodesis is recommended; a small series reported 100% resolution of lymphoma-related chylothorax with thoracoscopic talc pleurodesis. If the chylothorax does not respond to any of these approaches, it may respond to thoracic duct ligation or pleuroperitoneal shunting. Chylothorax in the presence of lymphoma-related chylous ascites is a difficult problem that is

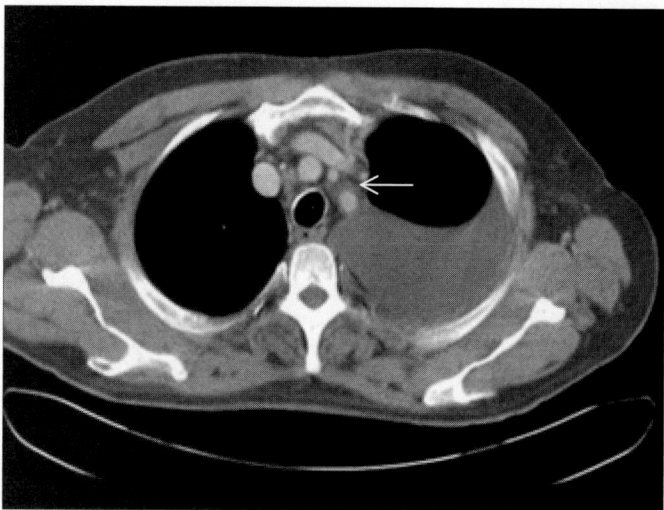

Figure 6   **Chest CT shows left-side chylothorax secondary to lymphoma. Subtle mediastinal lymphadenopathy obstructing the thoracic duct (arrow) is apparent.**

generally refractory to most forms of therapy (though pleurodesis is occasionally successful).[46,61,62,67,68]

Pseudochylothorax is a rare disorder associated with the formation of persistent exudates that last for months or years. The most common cause is tuberculosis; the second most common cause is rheumatoid arthritis. Biochemical analysis of pleural fluid from patients with pseudochylothorax reveals very high cholesterol levels (> 200 mg/dl) and the presence of cholesterol crystals. Treatment is generally conservative.[24,25]

IDIOPATHIC PERSISTENT PLEURAL EFFUSION

In a small percentage of patients, the cause of pleural effusion remains unknown despite extensive diagnostic evaluation. Tuberculosis and other granulomatous diseases, malignancy, and pulmonary embolism account for most cases of idiopathic effusion; those causes are identified later in the course of the disease or at autopsy. Other causes include constrictive pericarditis, subphrenic abscess, connective tissue diseases, drug-induced pleuritis, peritoneal dialysis, and cirrhosis.[23] In the management of persistent benign or idiopathic effusion, talc pleurodesis has a high success rate and minimal long-term implications.[69,70]

Discussion

Pleural Anatomy

The pleura is a continuous membrane that covers the parietal and visceral surfaces of the thorax. In adults, it has an estimated surface area of 2,000 cm².[71] Light microscopy shows the pleura to have five layers: (1) a mesothelial cell layer; (2) a mesothelial connective tissue layer with basal lamina; (3) a superficial elastic layer; (4) a loose connective tissue layer with adipose tissue, blood vessels, nerves, and lymphatic vessels; and (5) a deep fibroelastic layer. The parietal pleura establishes a pleurolymphatic communication on the diaphragm to allow clearance of large (> 1,000 nm) particles and cells from the normal pleural space. The structure of this pleurolymphatic communication consists of stomata 2 to 12 μm in diameter, which overlie bulblike lymphatic channels (lacunae) separated by a layer of loose connective tissue (the membrana cribriformis).

Electron microscopy reveals microvilli on the mesothelial cell surface of the pleura. The main function of these microvilli is to enmesh glycoproteins rich in hyaluronic acid for purposes of lubrication. The structure of the intercellular junction in the mesothelial cells of the pleura is similar to that in the endothelial cells of the venules, which suggests that the pleural mesothelial cell layer may be as leaky as the venular endothelium.[3,4,72]

Pleural Fluid Physiology

The amount of pleural fluid in an adult is 1 to 10 ml and forms a 10 μm–thick layer.[1,3,71,72] Fluid exchange across the pleural surface depends on three mechanisms: (1) passive filtration following Starling's equilibrium, (2) active solute transport, and (3) lymphatic clearance. In the normal pleura, Starling's equilibrium favors the flow of fluid in a parietal-to-visceral direction.[71] The rate at which fluid traverses the pleura ranges from 20 to 160 ml/day in adults; maximal lymphatic clearance is believed to be approximately 700 ml/day.[2,71,73-76]

The chemical composition of normal pleural fluid is similar to that of interstitial fluid. The protein concentration is typically 1 to 2 g/dl. The concentration of high-molecular-weight proteins (e.g., LDH) is approximately half that seen in serum. Cell counts in normal pleural fluid range from 1,400 to 4,500 cells/mm³; macrophages account for the majority of the cells.[3,72]

References

1. Tran AC, Lapworth RL: Biochemical analysis of pleural fluid: what should we measure? Clin Biochem 38:311, 2001
2. Jaker SA: Pleural anatomy, physiology and diagnostic procedures. Textbook of Pulmonary Diseases, 6th ed, Vol 1. Baum GL, Crapo JD, Celli BR, et al, Eds. Lippincott-Raven, New York, 1998, p 255
3. Antony VB, Mohammed KA: Pathophysiology of pleural space infections. Semin Respir Infect 14:9, 1999
4. Mutsaers S: Mesothelial cells: their structure, function and role in serosal repair. Respirology 7:171, 2002
5. Rubins JB, Colice GL: Evaluating pleural effu-

sions: how should you go about finding the cause? Postgrad Med 105:39, 1999
6. Levin DL, Klein JS: Imaging techniques for pleural space infections. Semin Respir Infect 14:31, 1999
7. Moskowitz H, Platt RT, Schachar R, et al: Roentgen visualization of minute pleural effusion—an experimental study to determine the minimum amount of pleural fluid visible on a radiograph. Radiology 109:33, 1973
8. Woodring JH: Recognition of pleural effusion on supine radiographs: how much fluid is required? AJR Am J Roentgenol 142:59, 1984
9. Eibenberger KL, Dock WI, Ammann ME, et al: Quantification of pleural effusions: sonography ver-

sus radiography. Radiology 191:681, 1994
10. Bartter T, Santarelli R, Akers SM, et al: The evaluation of pleural effusion. Chest 106:1209, 1994
11. Azoulay E: Pleural effusions in the intensive care unit. Curr Opin Pulm Med 9:291, 2003
12. McLoud TC: CT and MR in pleural disease. Clin Chest Med 19:261, 1998
13. Stark DD, Federle MP, Goodman PC, et al: Differentiating lung abscess and empyema: radiography and computed tomography. AJR Am J Roentgenol 141:163, 1983
14. Rusch VW: Mesothelioma and less common pleural tumors. Thoracic Surgery. Pearson FG, Cooper JD, Deslauriers J, et al, Eds. Churchill Livingstone, New York, 2002, p 1241

15. Tsai TH, Yang PC: Ultrasound in the diagnosis and management of pleural disease. Curr Opin Pulm Med 9:282, 2003

16. Light RW, Jenkinson SG, Minh VD, et al: Observations on pleural fluid pressures as fluid is withdrawn during thoracentesis. Am Rev Respir Dis 121:799, 1980

17. Grogan DR, Irwin RS, Channick R, et al: Complications associated with thoracentesis: a prospective, randomized study comparing three different methods. Arch Intern Med 150:873, 1990

18. American Thoracic Society. Guidelines for thoracentesis and needle biopsy of the pleura. Am Rev Respir Dis 140:257, 1989

19. Light R, Macgregor MI, Luchsinger PC, et al: Pleural effusions: the diagnostic separation of transudates and exudates. Ann Intern Med 77:507, 1972

20. Heffern JE, Brown LK, Barbier CA: Diagnostic value of tests that discriminate between exudative and transudative pleural effusion. Chest 111:970, 1997

21. Colice GL, Curtis A, Deslauriers J, et al: Medical and surgical treatment of parapneumonic effusions: an evidence-based guideline. Chest 18:1158, 2000

22. Banales JL, Pineda PR, Fitzgerald JM, et al: Adenoside deaminase in the diagnosis of tuberculous pleural effusions: a report of 218 patients and review of the literature. Chest 99:355, 1991

23. Ansari T, Idyll S: Management of undiagnosed persistent pleural effusion. Clin Chest Med 19:407, 1998

24. Hillerdal G: Chylothorax and pseudochylothorax. Eur Respir J 10:1157, 1997

25. Garcia-Zamalloa A, Ruiz-Irastorza G, Aguayo FJ, et al: Pseudochylothorax: report of 2 cases and review of the literature. Medicine 78:200, 1999

26. O'Callaghan AM, Meade GM: Chylothorax in lymphoma: mechanisms and management. Ann Oncol 6:603, 1995

27. Kalomenidis I, Light RW: Eosinophilic pleural effusions. Curr Opin Pulm Med 9:254, 2003

28. Everts RJ, Relle B: Pleural space infections: microbiology and antimicrobial therapy. Semin Respir Infect 1:18, 1999

29. Boutin C, Astoul P: Diagnostic thoracoscopy. Clin Chest Med 19:295, 1998

30. Light RW, Erozan YS, Ball WC Jr, et al: Cells in pleural fluid: their value in differential diagnosis. Arch Intern Med 13:854, 1973

31. Sahn SA: The pleura. Am Rev Respir Dis 13:184, 1988

32. Rusch VW, Mountain C: Thoracoscopy under regional anesthesia for the diagnosis and management of pleural disease. Am J Surg 154:274, 1987

33. Downey RJ, McCormack P, LoCicero J 3rd, et al: Dissemination of malignant tumors after video-assisted thoracic surgery: a report of twenty-one cases. J Thorac Cardiovasc Surg 111:954, 1996

34. Fleishman SB, et al: Quality of life (QOL) advantage of sclerosis for malignant pleural effusion (MPE) via talc thoracoscopy over chest tube infusion of talc slurry: a Cancer and Leukemia Group B study. Abstract 1418

35. Moghissi K: The malignant pleural effusion tissue diagnosis and treatment. Thoracic Surgery: Surgical Management of Pleural Diseases, Vol 6. Deslauriers J, Lacquet LK, Eds. Mosby, St Louis, 1990, p 397

36. Pollak J: Malignant pleural effusions: treatment with tunneled long-term drainage catheters. Curr Opin Pulm Med 8:302, 2002

37. Robinson R., Fullerton DA, Albert JD, et al: Use of pleural Tenckhoff catheter to palliate malignant pleural effusion. Ann Thorac Surg 57:286, 1994

38. Musani A, Haas AR, Seijo L, et al: Outpatient management of malignant pleural effusions with small-bore, tunneled pleural catheter. Respiration 71:559, 2004

39. Pollak JS, Burdge CM, Rosenblatt M, et al: Treatment of malignant pleural effusions with tunneled long-term drainage catheters. J Vasc Interv Radiol 2:201, 2001

40. Little A, Kadowaki MH, Ferguson MK, et al: Pleuro-peritoneal shunting: alternative therapy for pleural effusions. Ann Surg 208:443, 1988

41. Genc O, Petrou M, Ladas G, et al: The long-term morbidity of pleuroperitoneal shunts in the management of recurrent malignant effusions. Eur J Cardiothorac Surg 18:143, 2000

42. Sahn SA: Talc should be used for pleurodesis. Am J Respir Crit Care Med 162:2023, 2000

43. Shaw P, Agarwal R: Pleurodesis for malignant pleural effusions. Cochrane Database Syst Rev (1): CD002916, 2004

44. Dresler C, Olak J, Herndon JE 2nd, et al: Phase III intergroup study of talc poudrage vs talc slurry sclerosis for malignant pleural effusion. Chest 127:909, 2005

45. Cardillo G, Facciolo F, Carbone L, et al: Long-term follow-up of video-assisted talc pleurodesis in malignant recurrent pleural effusions. Eur J Cardiothorac Surg 21:302, 2002

46. Mares DC, Mathu PN: Medical thoracoscopic talc pleurodesis for chylothorax due to lymphoma: a case series. Chest 114:731, 1998

47. de Campos M, Ribas J: Thoracoscopy talc poudrage. Chest 119:801, 2001

48. Prevost A, Costa B, Elamarti R, et al: Long-term effect and tolerance of talc slurry for control of malignant pleural effusions. Oncol Reports 5:1327, 2001

49. Webb WR: Iodized talc pleurodesis for the treatment of pleural effusions. J Thorac Cardiovasc Surg 103:881, 1992

50. Kennedy L, Rusch VW, Strange C, et al: Pleurodesis using talc slurry. Chest 106:342, 1994

51. Montes JF, Ferrer J, Villarino MA, et al: Influence of talc dose on extrapleural talc dissemination after talc pleurodesis. Am J Respir Crit Care Med 168:348, 2003

52. Strange C, Sahn S: The definitions and epidemiology of pleural space infection. Semin Respir Infect 14:3, 1999

53. Cameron R, Davies HR: Intra-pleural fibrinolytic therapy versus conservative management in the treatment of parapneumonic effusions and empyema. Cochrane Database Syst Rev (2):CD002312, 2004

54. McLaughlin JS, Krasna MJ: Parapneumonic empyema. General Thoracic Surgery, 5th ed. LoCicero J III, Ponn RB, Shields TW, Eds. Lippincott Williams & Wilkins, New York, 2000, p 699

55. Sahn SA, Iseman M: Tuberculous empyema. Semin Respir Infect 14:82, 1999

56. Lim TK, Chin NK: Empirical treatment with fibrinolysis and early surgery reduces the duration of hospitalization in pleural sepsis. Eur Respir J 13:514, 1999

57. Wait MA: A Randomized trial of empyema therapy. Chest 111:1548, 1997

58. Landreneau R: Thoracoscopy for empyema and hemothorax. Chest 109:18, 1995

59. Shields TW, Ponn RB: Complications of pulmonary resection. General Thoracic Surgery, 5th ed. LoCicero J III, Ponn RB, Shields TW, Eds. Lippincott Williams & Wilkins, New York, 2000, p 481

60. Asamura H, Naruke T, Tsuchiya R, et al: Bronchopleural fistulas associated with lung cancer operations: univariate and multivariate analysis of risk factors, management and outcome. J Thorac Cardiovasc Surg 104:1456, 1992

61. Johnstone DW: Postoperative chylothorax. Chest Surg Clin N Am 12:597, 2002

62. Simpson L: Chylothorax in adults: pathophysiology and management. Thoracic Surgery: Surgical Management of Pleural Diseases, Vol 6. Deslauriers J, Lacquet LK, Eds. Mosby, St. Louis, 1990, p 366

63. Romero S: Nontraumatic chylothorax. Curr Opin Pulm Med 6:287, 2000

64. Peillon C, D'Hont C, Melki J, et al: Usefulness of video thoracoscopy in the management of spontaneous and post operation chylothorax. Surg Endosc 13:1106, 1999

65. Haniuda M, Nishimura H, Kobayashi O, et al: Management of chylothorax after pulmonary resection. J Am Coll Surg 180:537, 1995

66. Cope C: Management of chylothorax via percutaneous embolization. Curr Opin Pulm Med 10:311, 2004

67. Pratap U, Slavik Z, Ofoe VD, et al: Octreotide to treat postoperative chylothorax after cardiac operations in children. Ann Thorac Surg 72:1740, 2001

68. Gabbieri D, Bavutti L, Zaca F, et al: Conservative treatment of postoperative chylothorax with octreotide. Ital Heart J 5:479, 2004

69. Lange P, Mortensen J, Groth S: Lung function 22–35 years after treatment of idiopathic spontaneous pneumothorax with talc poudrage or simple drainage. Thorax 43:559, 1988

70. Glazer M, Berkman N, Lafair JS, et al: Successful talc slurry pleurodesis in patients with nonmalignant pleural effusion: report of 16 cases and review of the literature. Chest 117:1404, 2000

71. Jones JSP: The pleura in health and disease. Lung 179:397, 2002

72. Wang NS: Anatomy of the pleura. Clin Chest Med 19:229, 1998

73. Agostoni E, Zocchi L: Mechanical coupling and liquid exchanges in the pleural space. Clin Chest Med 19:241, 1988

74. Kinasewitz GT, Fishman AP: Influence of alterations in Starling forces on visceral pleural fluid movement. J Appl Phys 51:671, 1981

75. Miserocchi G: Physiology and pathophysiology of pleural fluid turnover. Eur Respir J 10:219, 1997

76. Pistolesi M, Miniati M, Giunti C: Pleural liquid and solute exchange. Am Rev Respir Dis 140: 825, 1989

32 SOLITARY PULMONARY NODULE

Shamus R. Carr, M.D., and Taine T. V. Pechet, M.D., F.A.C.S.

Assessment of a Solitary Pulmonary Nodule

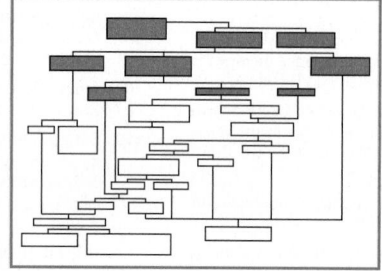

The solitary pulmonary nodule (SPN) is a common finding that is observed in more than 150,000 persons each year in the United States.[1] An SPN is defined as a single radiographically visible pulmonary lesion that is less than 3 cm in diameter, is completely surrounded by pulmonary parenchyma, and is not associated with atelectasis or adenopathy.[2] Any pulmonary lesion larger than 3 cm is considered a mass and as such has a greater likelihood of being malignant.[3,4] SPNs are detected on routine chest radiography at a rate of 1 in 500 x-rays, but with the growing use of computed tomographic scanning, they are now being diagnosed with increasing frequency.

The differential diagnosis of an SPN is broad and includes vascular diseases, infections, inflammatory conditions, congenital abnormalities, benign tumors, and malignancies [see Table 1]. Although most SPNs are benign, as many as one third represent primary malignancies, and nearly one quarter may be solitary metastases.[1,5,6] Various approaches have been developed to aid in the characterization and identification of SPNs. Certain clinical characteristics—such as greater age, history of tobacco use, and previous history of cancer—have been shown to increase the likelihood that the SPN is malignant.[7] Some authors have attempted to use Bayes's theorem, logistic regression models, or neural network analysis to predict the likelihood of malignancy.[7-9] Such methods are highly sensitive and specific, but they are cumbersome and of limited practical use in actual clinical evaluation of a patient with an SPN.

Clinical Evaluation

Once an SPN has been discovered, the essential task is to determine whether the lesion is benign or malignant. Evaluation and workup should be governed by the dictum "malignant until proven otherwise." The basis for this initial assumption of malignancy is the observation that the average overall 5-year survival rate is quite poor—10% to 15%—once a diagnosis of lung cancer is made.[10] Appropriate evaluation involves careful assessment of the patient's history and risk factors for malignancy in conjunction with the results of radiographic studies [see Investigative Studies, below] to develop an individualized care plan.

FACTORS INFLUENCING PROBABILITY OF MALIGNANCY

Of the various factors that influence the probability that cancer will be found in an SPN before radiographic evaluation, those most strongly associated with lung cancer are age, smoking history, and occupational history. Pulmonary function test results indicative of severe obstructive ventilatory impairment are also associated with an increased likelihood of malignancy.[11] In addition, the presence of endemic granulomatous disease has been shown to increase the probability that an SPN is harboring cancer.[7]

Other factors that influence the probability of malignancy in an SPN are based on the findings from CT scanning [see Investigative Studies, Imaging, Computed Tomography, below]. The size, contour, internal characteristics, and growth rate of the nodule are all potentially significant indicators of malignant disease [see Table 2].

Age

Lung cancer is rare before the age of 40 years, but its incidence steadily increases from that point until the age of 80.[5] Above the age of 70, the likelihood that an SPN is malignant increases.[8] After the age of 80, the incidence of malignancy in an SPN seems to level off or even decrease.

Tobacco Exposure

The link between cigarette smoking and lung cancer has been well established since the 1950s, and the incidence of lung cancer in smokers is directly correlated with the number of pack-years of smoking.[12] The Surgeon General's Report from 2004 states that "the evidence is sufficient to infer a causal relationship between smoking and lung cancer."[13]

Occupational History

Patients with a history of workplace exposure to a radioactive substance (e.g., uranium or plutonium) are at increased risk for lung cancer, but this association is not as well documented as the association of lung cancer with tobacco use. Miners of heavy metals (e.g., nickel, cadmium, and silica) are also at increased risk. There is some evidence to suggest that patients with idiopathic pulmonary fibrosis and pneumoconiosis are at increased risk for bronchoalveolar cell carcinoma.[14] Radon exposure is the second leading cause of lung cancer, and cigarette smoking further increases the risks associated with radon exposure.[15] Asbestos exposure in combination with cigarette smoking also places patients at significantly increased risk for lung cancer.

Investigative Studies

IMAGING

Chest Radiography

Whereas the prevalence of lung cancer is low in comparison to that of breast or prostate cancer,

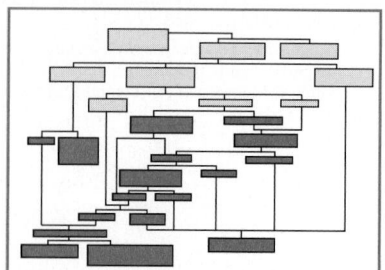

the mortality for lung cancer exceeds that for breast, prostate, and colon cancer combined. As noted [see Clinical Evaluation, above],

Table 1 Differential Diagnosis of Solitary Pulmonary Nodule

Benign	Vascular disease	Arteriovenous malformations Pulmonary artery aneurysm
	Infection	Tuberculosis *Mycobacterium avium* complex infection Aspergilloma Histoplasmosis Echinococcosis Blastomycosis Cryptococcosis Coccidioidomycosis Ascariasis Dirofilariasis
	Inflammatory condition	Rheumatoid nodule Sarcoidosis Wegener granulomatosis
	Congenital abnormality	Foregut duplication cyst
	Other	Rounded atelectasis Pulmonary amyloidosis
	Benign tumor	Hamartoma Lipoma Fibroma

Malignant	Primary lung cancer	Non–small cell lung cancer
		  Squamous cell carcinoma
		  Adenocarcinoma
		  Large cell cancer
		  Bronchoalveolar carcinoma
		Small cell lung cancer
		Carcinoid
		Lymphoma

	Metastatic cancer	Colon cancer Testicular cancer Melanoma Sarcoma Breast cancer

the overall 5-year survival rate for lung cancer patients is dismal, in part because lung cancer is typically identified at a more advanced stage than other cancers are. Several trials performed before the advent of CT scanning attempted to employ chest radiography for early screening of lung cancer, but they were unable to demonstrate that such screening yielded any better survival than no screening at all.[16-18] One explanation for these disappointing results may be that fewer than 10% of lung cancers are stage I at presentation.[16]

Although chest radiography is ineffective as a screening tool for early-stage lung cancer, it remains a valuable investigative tool in the evaluation of SPNs. If an SPN's appearance on chest x-rays has not changed for more than 2 years, the SPN will be benign in more than 90% of cases. In such cases, only yearly follow-up is typically required; additional diagnostic tests are usually unnecessary.[19,20] Therefore, an effort should always be made to obtain old chest radiographs if they are known to exist.

Computed Tomography

The advent of CT scanning has led to an increase in the number of SPNs detected[21]—but of course, it has also led to an increase in the number of SPNs found that prove to be benign.

Advocates of CT scanning for assessment of SPNs base their argument on two central points. First, as many as 83% of CT-detected stage I malignancies are not visible on chest x-ray.[22] Second, non–small cell lung cancer (NSCLC) is the malignancy most commonly identified, and the survival rate for stage I NSCLC is relatively high. In patients whose SPN proves to be NSCLC, the 5-year survival rate is 67% for stage IA disease. This figure falls rapidly as the disease stage rises: the 5-year survival rate is 55% for stage IIA NSCLC and only 10% for stage IIIA NSCLC with mediastinal nodal metastasis.[23]

Numerous studies have evaluated the use of screening CT both in the general population and in at-risk groups consisting of older patients with a smoking history.[22,24,25] The greatest drawback to screening CT is the high false positive rate: nodules are identified on 23% to 66% of all CT scans, depending on the thickness of the slices,[22,26] and nearly 98% of these nodules are eventually determined to be benign. Sequential CT scanning is often required to determine whether an SPN is benign or malignant. In 10% to 15% of patients, however, this determination cannot be made even when two CT scans are compared. Such patients may be assessed with other imaging modalities (e.g., positron emission tomography [PET]) or may be referred for transthoracic needle biopsy (TTNB) or other invasive diagnostic tests.

There is currently some controversy regarding the optimal timing of follow-up CT scanning after initial identification of an SPN. In the literature, the recommended interval between initial CT scanning and repeat CT scanning has ranged from 1 month to 1 year.[22,25,26] These varying recommendations are based on what is considered the doubling time for an SPN. In a study from 2000 that included 13 patients with a known diagnosis and lesions less than 10 mm in diameter at initial evaluation, volumetric growth rates were measured to establish the doubling times of the nodules.[10] The doubling times ranged from 51 days to more than 1 year. For malignant lesions, the average doubling time was less than 177 days, whereas for benign lesions, it was more than 396 days.

In addition to delineating the size and contours of an SPN, CT scans provide information on its internal characteristics. Certain lesion characteristics noted on CT, though not absolutely definitive, point more toward a benign condition, whereas others point more toward malignancy. For example, although cavitation may occur in either benign or malignant lesions, SPNs with walls thicker than 16 mm are much more likely to be malignant, whereas those with walls thinner than 4 mm are much more likely to be benign.[27] As another example, the presence of intranodular fat is a reliable indicator of a hamartoma (a benign lesion) and is seen in as many as 50% of hamartomas.[28] In addition, calcification is most commonly associated with hamartomas and other benign nodules. Unfortunately, between one third and two thirds of benign lesions visualized are not calcified, and as many as 6% of malignant lesions are calcified.[29-31] Finally, increased enhancement (measured in Hounsfield units [HU]) after injection with intravenous contrast is strongly suggestive of malignancy. Lesions that enhance by less than 15 HU are most likely benign (positive predictive value, 99%), whereas lesions that enhance by more than 20 HU are typically malignant (sensitivity, 98%; specificity, 73%).[32] Lesions that enhance by 15 to 20 HU should be considered indeterminate.

Because most SPNs are benign and because the risk of misdiagnosing a malignant lesion is so great, it is important to make use of all of the data obtained from CT scanning in the effort to make cost-effective, logical decisions regarding further evaluation or treatment. Careful evaluation of the size, contours, and internal

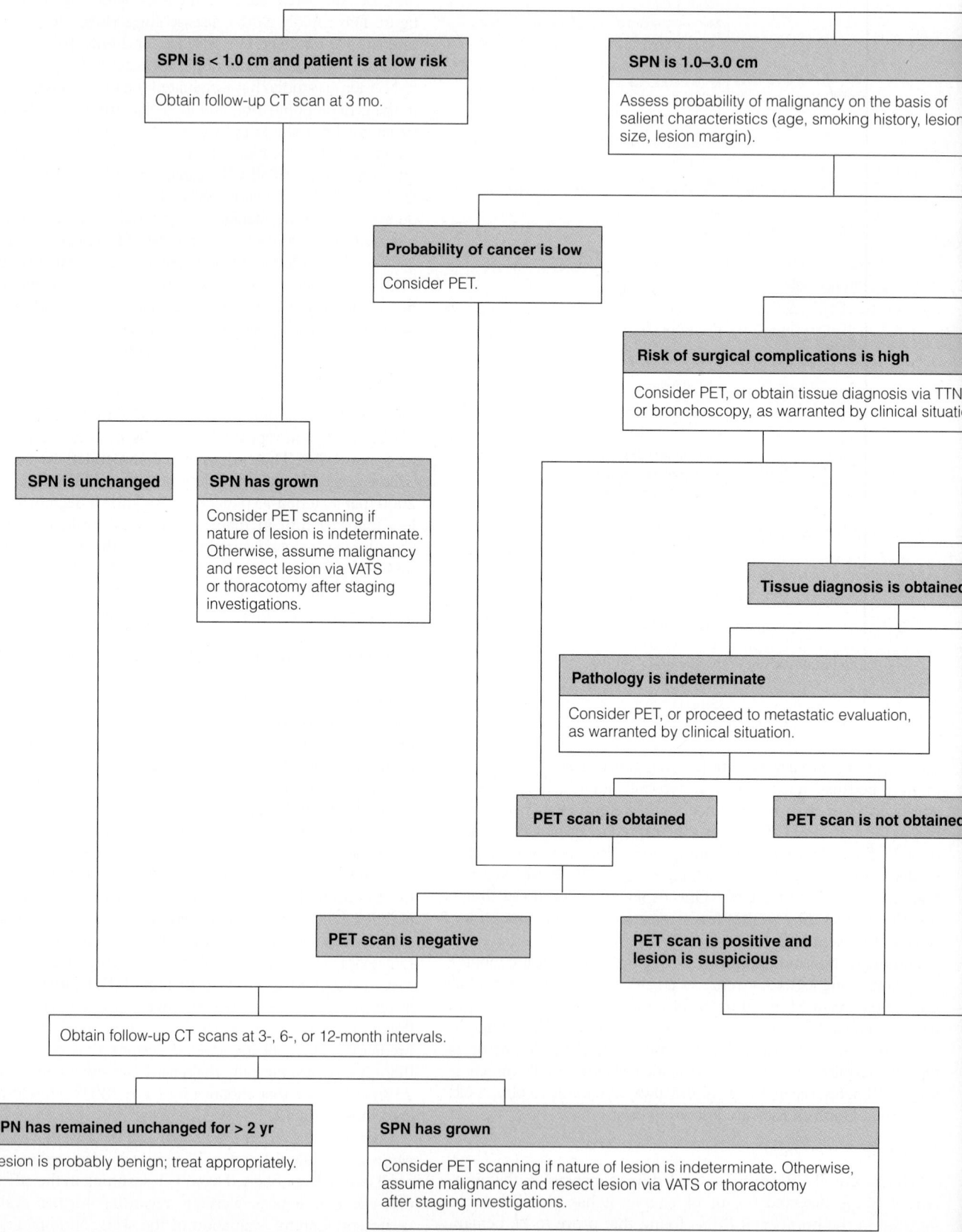

Assessment of a Solitary Pulmonary Nodule

SPN is seen on chest x-ray or CT scan

Obtain history and perform thorough physical examination.
Review previous diagnostic images (if available).

SPN is < 1.0 cm and patient is at low risk

Obtain follow-up CT scan at 3 mo.

SPN is 1.0–3.0 cm

Assess probability of malignancy on the basis of salient characteristics (age, smoking history, lesion size, lesion margin).

Probability of cancer is low

Consider PET.

Risk of surgical complications is high

Consider PET, or obtain tissue diagnosis via TTN or bronchoscopy, as warranted by clinical situatio

SPN is unchanged

SPN has grown

Consider PET scanning if nature of lesion is indeterminate. Otherwise, assume malignancy and resect lesion via VATS or thoracotomy after staging investigations.

Tissue diagnosis is obtained

Pathology is indeterminate

Consider PET, or proceed to metastatic evaluation, as warranted by clinical situation.

PET scan is obtained

PET scan is not obtained

PET scan is negative

PET scan is positive and lesion is suspicious

Obtain follow-up CT scans at 3-, 6-, or 12-month intervals.

SPN has remained unchanged for > 2 yr

Lesion is probably benign; treat appropriately.

SPN has grown

Consider PET scanning if nature of lesion is indeterminate. Otherwise, assume malignancy and resect lesion via VATS or thoracotomy after staging investigations.

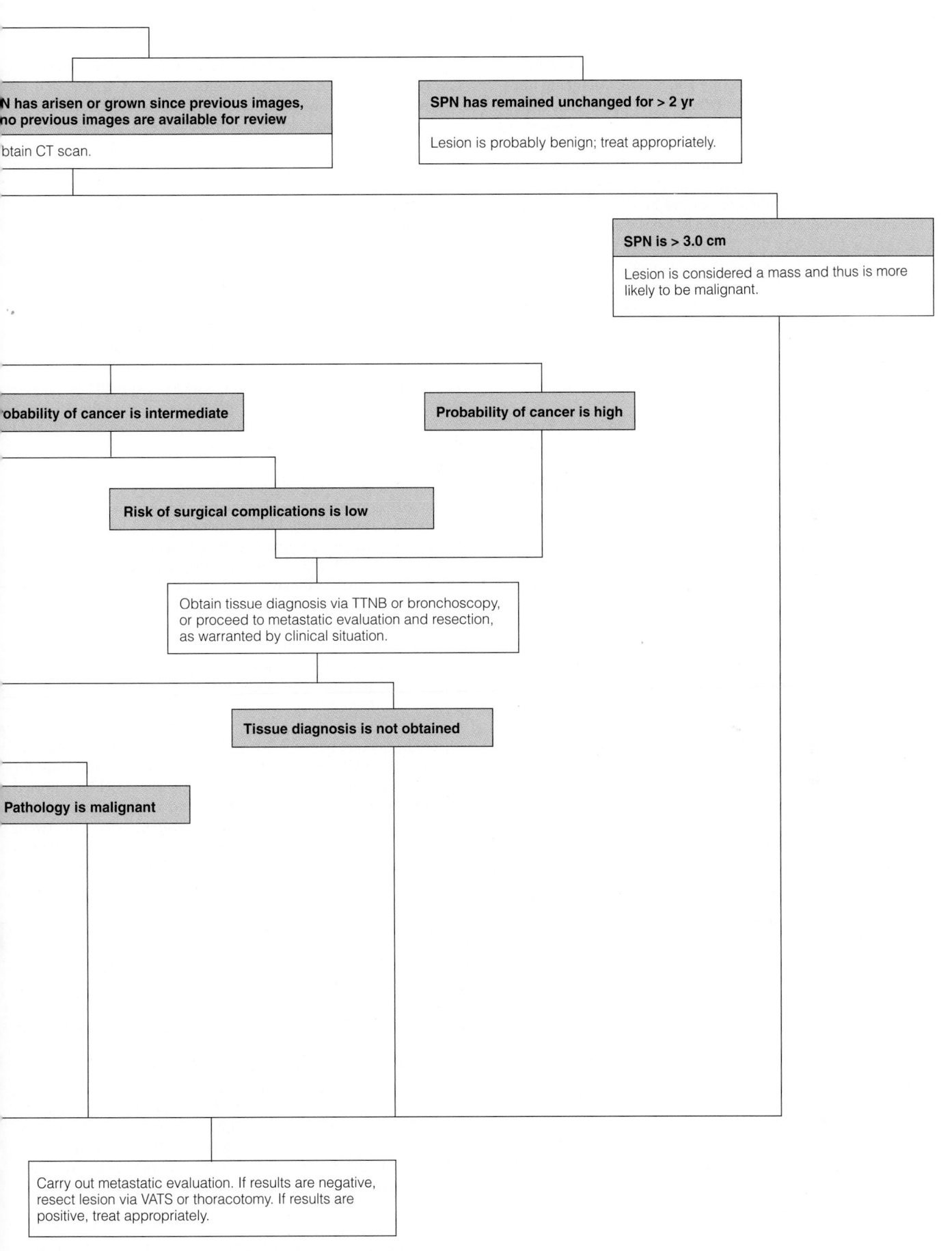

SPN has arisen or grown since previous images,
no previous images are available for review

Obtain CT scan.

SPN has remained unchanged for > 2 yr

Lesion is probably benign; treat appropriately.

SPN is > 3.0 cm

Lesion is considered a mass and thus is more
likely to be malignant.

Probability of cancer is intermediate

Probability of cancer is high

Risk of surgical complications is low

Obtain tissue diagnosis via TTNB or bronchoscopy,
or proceed to metastatic evaluation and resection,
as warranted by clinical situation.

Tissue diagnosis is not obtained

Pathology is malignant

Carry out metastatic evaluation. If results are negative,
resect lesion via VATS or thoracotomy. If results are
positive, treat appropriately.

characteristics of an SPN on successive CT scans—in conjunction with thoughtful consideration of the patient's age, smoking history, and occupational exposure—provides the framework for appropriate treatment. Because the doubling time is considerably shorter for malignant lesions than for benign lesions, a repeat CT scan should be performed 3 months after the initial study. If the lesion is visibly larger on the repeat scan, it is probably malignant, and further diagnostic evaluation should be carried out with an eye toward resection. If, however, the lesion is still present and has not grown, a follow-up CT scan between 3 months and 12 months is warranted; the precise timing remains controversial and should be determined on the basis of individual patient and SPN characteristics. New volumetric modeling methods have been developed that may be capable of detecting conformational changes over much shorter intervals, but at present, they are not frequently used.[33]

Positron Emission Tomography

PET is an imaging modality that employs radiolabeled isotopes of fluorine, carbon, or oxygen; the most commonly used isotope is ^{18}F-fluorodeoxyglucose (FDG). The rationale for FDG-PET scanning in the evaluation of SPNs is based on the higher metabolic rate of most malignancies and the preferential trapping of FDG in malignant cells.[34] However, increased FDG activity can also occur in benign SPNs,[35,36] especially those arising from active granulomatous diseases[37,38] or inflammatory processes.[39] These benign diseases can produce false positive PET scans and thereby reduce the sensitivity of the test. Conversely, some malignancies—bronchoalveolar carcinoma and carcinoid tumors, in particular—have low metabolic activity and commonly produce false negative PET scans.[40-44] Thus, a negative PET scan is not a particularly helpful result, and it is necessary to follow the lesion with serial CT scans.

Efforts have been made to increase the sensitivity and specificity of PET scanning in the diagnosis of SPNs. One such effort involves the use of the standardized uptake value (SUV), which is a numerical indication of the activity concentration in a lesion, normalized for the injected dose.[45] In many studies, an SPN is considered malignant when its SUV is higher than 2.5. Because of the method used to calculate the SUV, however, small tumors (<

1.0 cm) may have an SUV lower than 2.5 and still be malignant. The reason is that their small volume causes their true activity concentration to be underestimated, with the result that their SUV drops below the threshold value for malignancy. In one prospective study of patients with SPNs, the overall sensitivity of FDG-PET scanning was 79%, and the overall specificity was 65%.[46] When the SPN was smaller than 1.0 cm, however, all of the scans were negative, even though 40% of the nodules were malignant.

In cases where the SPN is larger than 1.0 cm and no previous radiographs or CT scans are available for comparison, PET scanning can provide information that may facilitate the decision whether to follow the lesion closely or to proceed with biopsy. PET scanning has a definite place in the evaluation of SPNs, but it is not appropriate for every patient. A study that examined the cost-effectiveness of PET in the evaluation of SPNs concluded that it was cost-effective for patients who had an intermediate pretest probability of a malignant SPN and who were at high risk for surgical complications.[47] In all other groups, PET was not cost-effective, and CT led to similar outcomes (in terms of quality-adjusted life years) and to lower costs.

BIOPSY

If an SPN demonstrates characteristics suggestive of malignancy, a tissue diagnosis should be obtained. There are several alternative biopsy techniques that may be performed in place of resection, including TTNB and bronchoscopy. Traditionally, open lung biopsy was performed for an SPN, but this approach has the drawback of the morbidity associated with a thoracotomy. For peripheral lesions, video-assisted thoracoscopic surgery (VATS) has now supplanted thoracotomy as the procedure of choice. For central lesions that cannot be diagnosed by means of less invasive techniques, more invasive approaches will still be required.

Transthoracic Needle Biopsy

Lesions that are between 1.0 and 3.0 cm in diameter should be considered for TTNB. The diagnostic yield of this procedure for SPNs is excellent, reaching 95% in some studies. The reported sensitivity ranges from 80% to 95%, and the specificity ranges from 50% to 88%.[48-50] A study of 222 patients who underwent TTNB for an SPN reported a positive predictive value of 98.6% and a negative predictive value of 96.6%[51]; however, several other studies reported false negative rates ranging from 3% to 29%.[48,52] The complication rate associated with TTNB is relatively high—potentially as high as 30% and rarely lower than 10%, in even the most experienced hands.[49,53] Most commonly, a pneumothorax results; however, chest tube placement is required only if the patient becomes symptomatic, a situation that occurs in approximately 50% of cases. In the absence of symptoms, observation with serial chest x-rays is generally appropriate. If no increase in the size of the SPN is observed, the patient can be discharged with the expectation that the pneumothorax will resolve.

For lesions smaller than 1.0 cm, the risk-to-benefit ratio of TTNB rises to the point where other techniques are typically preferred. The utility of TTNB depends primarily on the characteristics of the SPN—in particular, its location. Nodules that are central or close to the diaphragm or the pericardium are less well suited to this technique than those at other sites are.

Bronchoscopy

Bronchoscopy has a well-established role in the evaluation of central SPNs, which are amenable to direct visualization and biopsy. Most SPNs, however, are not central. Various adjunctive measures, including transbronchial needle biopsy and cytology brush-

---

Table 2 **Factors Affecting Malignant Probability of Solitary Pulmonary Nodule[8]**

Factor	Likelihood Ratio for Malignancy
Spiculated margins on CT scan	5.54
Age > 70 yr	4.16
Lesion size 2.1–3.0 cm	3.67
Doubling time < 465 days	3.40
History of smoking	2.27
Age 50–69 yr	1.90
Lesion size 1.1–2.0 cm	0.74
Lesion size < 1 cm	0.52
Smooth margins on CT scan	0.30
No history of smoking	0.19
Doubling time > 465 days	0.01

ings, are employed to improve the yield of bronchoscopy. Newer techniques, including the use of endobronchial ultrasonography, are currently under active investigation.

For SPNs between 2.0 and 3.0 cm in diameter, the diagnostic yield of bronchoscopy ranges from 20% to 80%, depending on the size of the lesion, the incidence of malignancy in the study population, and the proximity of the lesion to the bronchial tree.[54,55] For SPNs smaller than 1.5 cm, the yield drops to 10%.[56] Even though bronchoscopy has a low complication rate (about 5%), its low diagnostic yield for malignancy limits its utility in the evaluation of SPNs.

Excisional Biopsy

The decision whether to proceed to excisional lung biopsy (open or thoracoscopic) must be carefully considered. The risk-to-benefit ratio of excisional biopsy is determined by clinical characteristics affecting perioperative morbidity and mortality, as well as by the risk of malignancy.

Resection is the definitive diagnostic technique. The morbidity associated with VATS is less than that associated with thoracotomy; accordingly, when VATS lung biopsy is technically feasible, it is preferable to open lung biopsy. The overall morbidity is lower than 1% for VATS wedge resection, compared with 3% to 7% for the equivalent open procedure.[57] Patients who have undergone VATS lung biopsy experience less pain, have shorter hospital stays, and recover sooner than those who have undergone open biopsy.[57,58]

A technical consideration that must be taken into account when VATS is planned is possible conversion to a thoracotomy. The conversion rate for VATS to thoracotomy has been reported to be as high as 33%, but there is evidence to suggest that this rate can be significantly reduced with careful patient selection and increasing experience in minimally invasive techniques.[59,60]

Peripheral SPNs more than 1.0 cm in diameter are the lesions best suited to VATS excision. As SPNs become smaller and more central, they become harder to identify, and the rate of conversion to thoracotomy rises. A wide variety of techniques have been employed to improve the identification of SPNs for VATS, ranging from radioisotope use through guide-wire localization. None of these techniques have achieved wide acceptance, and most surgeons rely on simple finger palpation through one of the port sites.

Differential Diagnosis

MALIGNANT LESIONS

Non–Small Cell Lung Cancer

As noted, NSCLC is the malignancy most frequently identified in an SPN. Most lung cancer patients are asymptomatic, and those who are symptomatic usually have advanced disease, including mediastinal lymph node involvement. Arterial invasion has also been shown to have an adverse effect on survival in patients with early-stage NSCLC.[61] The most common sites of metastases are the lungs, the brain, the bones, and the adrenal glands. Accordingly, it is essential to perform a metastatic workup that focuses on these areas to identify metastatic disease before proceeding with resection.

Bronchoalveolar carcinoma is a subtype of NSCLC that is well differentiated and has a prolonged doubling time. Because of its slow growth rate, it may be missed by PET scanning.[42] Bronchoalveolar carcinoma may present as an SPN, as airspace disease, or as multiple nodules.

Small Cell Lung Cancer

Small cell carcinoma accounts for approximately 20% of lung cancers. Typically, it presents as a central mass in association with significant nodal disease, often accompanied by distant metastases.[62] Small cell carcinoma typically has a very short doubling time. Paraneoplastic syndromes are more common with small cell lung cancer than with NSCLC.

Pulmonary Carcinoid

Pulmonary carcinoid tumors are uncommon neuroendocrine neoplasms that account for 1% to 2% of lung cancers.[63] They are classified as either typical or atypical, depending on their histology.[64] Either type of carcinoid may present as an SPN, usually in the fifth or sixth decade of life. Typical carcinoid tumors have a very long doubling time—up to 80 months—and thus may be mistaken for benign lesions.[65] Atypical carcinoid tumors have a much shorter doubling time and are more likely to show an increase in size on serial CT scans. Typical carcinoid tumors have an extremely low incidence of recurrence and are not usually associated with nodal metastasis.

Metastatic Malignancies

Metastases to the lung frequently appear as smooth, round, well-demarcated lesions. They often are multiple and rarely are associated with mediastinal adenopathy. Most pulmonary metastases derive from the lungs, the colon, the testicles, the breasts, melanomas, or sarcomas. Treatment tends to be palliative, based on the diagnosis of the primary tumor, but it may be curative in cases of metastatic sarcoma or testicular carcinoma. In patients with these cancers, limited wedge resection of a metastasis to the lung has been shown to confer a survival advantage; this measure may also be beneficial for patients with metastatic colon or head and neck cancer and, occasionally, for those with metastatic melanoma.[66]

BENIGN LESIONS

Pulmonary Hamartoma

Pulmonary hamartomas are the most common benign pulmonary tumors and the third most common cause of SPNs overall. Most (90%) arise in the periphery of the lung, but endobronchial hamartomas are seen as well. Because they are most common in the periphery, hamartomas are usually asymptomatic. When a potential hamartoma appears as an SPN on a chest x-ray, CT scanning is warranted for further evaluation.

Certain typical CT findings suggest that the SPN is likely to be a hamartoma. One such finding is a particular pattern of calcification. Calcification is more common in benign lesions than in malignant tumors. There are four patterns of calcification that are considered benign: central, diffuse, laminated, and "popcornlike." The first three patterns are most commonly associated with an infectious condition (e.g., histoplasmosis or tuberculosis). The popcornlike pattern, however, indicates that the lesion is probably a hamartoma. Unfortunately, calcification is present in only about 50% of benign lesions, and only about 50% of hamartomas are calcified.[29] It is important to remember that pulmonary carcinoid tumors and metastases to the lung (especially those from osteosarcomas, chondrosarcomas, or synovial cell sarcomas) may also have calcifications.

Another reliable marker of a hamartoma is the finding of fat within the lesion on a CT scan; however, fewer than 50% of hamartomas demonstrate this characteristic.

Inflammatory Nodules

Sarcoidosis is known as the great mimicker, but it rarely presents as an SPN.[67] Most commonly, it presents as hilar and mediastinal lymphadenopathy and diffuse parenchymal involvement. When it does present as an SPN, it is almost invariably a solid lesion, hardly ever a cavitary one. The incidence of sarcoidosis is highest in African-American women between 20 and 40 years of age. If sarcoidosis is suspected during the evaluation of an SPN, an elevated angiotensin-converting enzyme level supports the diagnosis, but a normal level does not exclude it. If a biopsy is performed, the presence of noncaseating granulomas on pathologic evaluation establishes the diagnosis.

Pulmonary rheumatoid nodules are present in fewer then 1% of patients with rheumatoid arthritis.[68] They are usually associated with rheumatoid nodules in other parts of the body but may precede any systemic manifestations of the disease. Pulmonary rheumatoid nodules, though generally asymptomatic in themselves, arise from underlying rheumatoid activity. When the underlying disease is active, the nodules may grow, simulating malignancy. An elevated serum rheumatoid factor level is typical and helps confirm the diagnosis.

Wegener granulomatosis is a necrotizing vasculitis that affects both the upper and the lower respiratory tract, as well as the kidneys. It presents with an SPN in approximately 20% of patients.[69] If vasculitis is suspected during evaluation of an SPN, laboratory studies should include testing for cytoplasmic antineutrophil cytoplasmic antibodies (c-ANCA); a positive result on this test is highly suggestive of Wegener granulomatosis. Treatment includes the cytotoxic drug cyclophosphamide, either alone or in combination with corticosteroids.

Infectious Nodules

An SPN can also represent an infectious granuloma caused by tuberculosis, atypical mycobacterial diseases, histoplasmosis, coccidioidomycosis, or aspergillosis. Such granulomas normally have a cavitary appearance on CT scans. Occasionally, an upright chest x-ray taken with the patient in the lateral decubitus position shows shifting of the position of the cavity's contents or a crescent of air around the mass (the Monod sign).[70] This radiographic finding is characteristic of a mycetoma, usually aspergilloma. Depending on the circumstances—in particular, on whether there has been significant hemoptysis and whether pulmonary function is reasonably well preserved—many of these lesions are best treated by means of resection. Others are best diagnosed by noninvasive techniques and treated with antibiotics.

Pulmonary dirofilariasis is a rare but well-attested cause of SPNs that is the consequence of infestation of human lungs by the canine heartworm *Dirofilaria immitis*. This organism is transmitted to humans in larval form by mosquitoes that have ingested blood from affected dogs.[71] Because humans are not suitable hosts for this organism, the larvae die and embolize to the lungs, where they initiate a granulomatous response. Typically, these lesions are pleura based, and the diagnosis is made at the time of resection.[72] Once the diagnosis is made, no further therapy is required.

Echinococcosis is a hydatid disease caused by the tapeworm *Echinococcus granulosus*. It is endemic to certain areas of the world where sheep and cattle are raised. Normally, it is ingested incidentally; the parasite penetrates the bowel wall and travels to the lungs in 10% to 30% of cases.[73,74] A complete blood count usually demonstrates peripheral eosinophilia. If echinococcosis is suspected, a hemagglutination test, which has a sensitivity of 66% to 100% and a specificity of 98% to 99% for *Echinococcus*, should be performed. TTNB should not be performed, because there is a risk that cyst

rupture could result in an anaphylactic reaction to the highly antigenic contents. Patients may be treated with anthelmintic agents, but the incidence of persistent or recurrent disease is high. Accordingly, surgical resection should be considered.

OTHER CONSIDERATIONS

Pulmonary amyloidosis may present in either a diffuse or a nodular form. The prognosis is most favorable when it presents as an asymptomatic SPN. Typically, the nodule is well defined and between 2 and 4 cm in diameter. Unless the patient exhibits systemic manifestations of amyloidosis, the diagnosis can be confirmed only by biopsy of the nodule.[35]

Rounded atelectasis usually presents as a pleura-based nodular density that occurs secondary to pleural scarring and thickening. An effort should be made to look for associated pleural plaques resulting from asbestos exposure. The CT scan usually demonstrates an SPN with a "comet tail." Biopsy is not required unless mesothelioma is strongly suspected or the SPN is seen to have grown on successive CT scans.[75]

Management

Currently, there are no evidence-based guidelines that fully delineate a recommended approach to the workup and management of SPNs.[76] The following is a summary of our preferred approach.

The ultimate aim in the evaluation of an SPN is to classify the lesion as either benign or malignant. The first step toward that end is to compare current chest x-rays or CT scans with any previous images that are available. An SPN whose size has been stable for 2 years on diagnostic images will be benign 90% to 95% of the time. If no previous images are available for comparison, the patient should undergo a complete evaluation as if the nodule were an early-stage NSCLC. This evaluation must be individualized according to the characteristics of the patient and the lesion. On the basis of the patient's age and smoking history, the size of the SPN, and the characteristics of the lesion's borders, an SPN for which no previous diagnostic images are available can be initially classified as having a low, intermediate, or high probability of cancer [*see Table 3*].[7,77,78] This classification governs the subsequent workup. Whereas a patient with a high-probability SPN needs a complete workup, with the goal being resection, the same workup would not be cost-effective for a patient with a low-probability SPN. It is important not to subject a patient with a high-probability SPN to studies that will not change clinical management or outcome: doing so will delay diagnosis and treatment unnecessarily.

At this point in the evaluation, if the nature of the SPN is still

Table 3 Initial Assessment of Probability of Cancer in Solitary Pulmonary Nodule

Characteristics of Patient or Lesion	Probability of Cancer		
	Low	Intermediate	High
Patient age	< 40 yr	40–60 yr	> 60 yr
Patient smoking history	Never smoked	< 20 pack-years	20 pack-ye
Lesion size	< 1.0 cm	1.1–2.2 cm	2.3 cm
Lesion margin	Smooth	Scalloped	Spiculated

indeterminate and the lesion is larger than 1.0 cm, there may be a role for PET scanning. If PET scanning yields negative results, the SPN is probably benign, and follow-up with CT scanning is appropriate. If PET scanning yields positive results and the patient is a high surgical risk, TTNB may be performed to establish a diagnosis. If, however, the patient is a reasonable surgical risk, proceeding directly to VATS resection (and, potentially, to lobectomy) offers the best chance of a cure.

For patients with SPNs smaller than 1.0 cm, the optimal approach may be to perform serial CT scanning at 3-month intervals for a minimum of 2 years. The rationale for this approach is based on the difficulty of identifying these lesions with VATS, the low likelihood of establishing a diagnosis with TTNB, and the possibility that the lesion may be benign. If the lesion has grown visibly between scans, it is probably malignant, and proceeding with resection for diagnosis and treatment is appropriate. The likelihood that nodal metastases will develop in a closely followed SPN smaller than 1.0 cm is low.[60] If the SPN proves to be malignant, scanning at 3-month intervals is unlikely to alter the eventual outcome.

References

1. Leef JL 3rd, Klein JS: The solitary pulmonary nodule. Radiol Clin North Am 40:123, 2002

2. Tuddenham WJ: Glossary of terms for thoracic radiology: recommendations of the Nomenclature Committee of the Fleischner Society. AJR Am J Roentgenol 143:509, 1984

3. Lillington GA: Management of the solitary pulmonary nodule. Hosp Pract (Off Ed) 28(5):41, 1993

4. Midthun DE, Swensen SJ, Jett JR: Approach to the solitary pulmonary nodule. Mayo Clin Proc 68:378, 1993

5. Jemal A, Murray T, Ward E, et al: Cancer statistics, 2005. CA Cancer J Clin 55:10, 2005

6. Swanson SJ, Jaklitsch MT, Mentzer SJ, et al: Management of the solitary pulmonary nodule: role of thoracoscopy in diagnosis and therapy. Chest 116(6 suppl):523S, 1999

7. Swensen SJ, Silverstein MD, Ilstrup DM, et al: The probability of malignancy in solitary pulmonary nodules: application to small radiologically indeterminate nodules. Arch Intern Med 157:849, 1997

8. Gurney JW: Determining the likelihood of malignancy in solitary pulmonary nodules with Bayesian analysis: Part I. Theory. Radiology 186:405, 1993

9. Henschke CI, Yankelevitz DF, Mateescu I, et al: Neural networks for the analysis of small pulmonary nodules. Clin Imaging 21:390, 1997

10. Yankelevitz DF, Henschke CI: Small solitary pulmonary nodules. Radiol Clin North Am 38:471, 2000

11. Kishi K, Gurney JW, Schroeder DR, et al: The correlation of emphysema or airway obstruction with the risk of lung cancer: a matched case-controlled study. Eur Respir J 19:1093, 2002

12. Wynder EL, Graham EA: Tobacco smoking as a possible etiologic factor in bronchiogenic carcinoma. JAMA 143:329, 1950

13. The 2004 United States Surgeon General's Report: The Health Consequences of Smoking. N S W Public Health Bull 15(5-6):107, 2004

14. Pairon JC, Brochard P, Jaurand MC, et al: Silica and lung cancer: a controversial issue. Eur Respir J 4:730, 1991

15. Pawel DJ, Puskin JS: The U.S. Environmental Protection Agency's assessment of risks from indoor radon. Health Phys 87(1):68, 2004

16. Melamed MR, Flehinger BJ, Zaman MB, et al: Screening for early lung cancer: results of the Memorial Sloan-Kettering study in New York. Chest 86:44, 1984

17. Kubik A, Haerting J: Survival and mortality in a randomized study of lung cancer detection. Neoplasma 37:467, 1990

18. Kubik A, Parkin DM, Khlat M, et al: Lack of benefit from semi-annual screening for cancer of the lung: follow-up report of a randomized controlled trial on a population of high-risk males in Czechoslovakia. Int J Cancer 45:26, 1990

19. Lillington GA: Management of solitary pulmonary nodules. Dis Mon 37:271, 1991

20. Yankelevitz DF, Henschke CI: Does 2-year stability imply that pulmonary nodules are benign? AJR Am J Roentgenol 168:325, 1997

21. Diederich S, Lenzen H, Windmann R, et al: Pulmonary nodules: experimental and clinical studies at low-dose CT. Radiology 213:289, 1999

22. Henschke CI, Naidich DP, Yankelevitz DF, et al: Early lung cancer action project: initial findings on repeat screenings. Cancer 92:153, 2001

23. Mountain CF: Revisions in the International System for Staging Lung Cancer. Chest 111:1710, 1997

24. Sone S, Li F, Yang ZG, et al: Results of three-year mass screening programme for lung cancer using mobile low-dose spiral computed tomography scanner. Br J Cancer 84:25, 2001

25. Swensen SJ, Jett JR, Sloan JA, et al: Screening for lung cancer with low-dose spiral computed tomography. Am J Respir Crit Care Med 165:508, 2002

26. Libby DM, Smith JP, Altorki NK, et al: Managing the small pulmonary nodule discovered by CT. Chest 125:1522, 2004

27. Woodring JH, Fried AM: Significance of wall thickness in solitary cavities of the lung: a follow-up study. AJR Am J Roentgenol 140:473, 1983

28. Weisbrod GL, Towers MJ, Chamberlain DW, et al: Thin-walled cystic lesions in bronchioalveolar carcinoma. Radiology 185:401, 1992

29. Siegelman SS, Khouri NF, Leo FP, et al: Solitary pulmonary nodules: CT assessment. Radiology 160:307, 1986

30. Ledor K, Fish B, Chaise L, et al: CT diagnosis of pulmonary hamartomas. J Comput Tomogr 5:343, 1981

31. Mahoney MC, Shipley RT, Corcoran HL, et al: CT demonstration of calcification in carcinoma of the lung. AJR Am J Roentgenol 154:255, 1990

32. Swensen SJ, Viggiano RW, Midthun DE, et al: Lung nodule enhancement at CT: multicenter study. Radiology 214:73, 2000

33. Winer-Muram HT, Jennings SG, Tarver RD, et al: Volumetric growth rate of stage I lung cancer prior to treatment: serial CT scanning. Radiology 223:798, 2002

34. Wahl RL, Hutchins GD, Buchsbaum DJ, et al: ^{18}F-2-deoxy-2-fluoro-D-glucose uptake into human tumor xenografts: feasibility studies for cancer imaging with positron-emission tomography. Cancer 67:1544. 1991

35. Ollenberger GP, Knight S, Tauro AJ: False-positive FDG positron emission tomography in pulmonary amyloidosis. Clin Nucl Med 29:657, 2004

36. Alavi A, Gupta N, Alberini JL, et al: Positron emission tomography imaging in nonmalignant thoracic disorders. Semin Nucl Med 32:293, 2002

37. El-Haddad G, Zhuang H, Gupta N, et al: Evolving role of positron emission tomography in the management of patients with inflammatory and other benign disorders. Semin Nucl Med 34:313, 2004

38. Zhuang H, Yu JQ, Alavi A: Applications of fluorodeoxyglucose-PET imaging in the detection of infection and inflammation and other benign disorders. Radiol Clin North Am 43:121, 2005

39. Croft DR, Trapp J, Kernstine K, et al: FDG-PET imaging and the diagnosis of non–small cell lung cancer in a region of high histoplasmosis prevalence. Lung Cancer 36:297, 2002

40. Yap CS, Schiepers C, Fishbein MC, et al: FDG-PET imaging in lung cancer: how sensitive is it for bronchioloalveolar carcinoma? Eur J Nucl Med Mol Imaging 29:1166, 2002

41. Higashi K, Ueda Y, Seki H, et al: Fluorine-18-FDG PET imaging is negative in bronchioloalveolar lung carcinoma. J Nucl Med 39:1016, 1998

42. Heyneman LE, Patz EF: PET imaging in patients with bronchioloalveolar cell carcinoma. Lung Cancer 38:261, 2002

43. Erasmus JJ, McAdams HP, Patz EF Jr, et al: Evaluation of primary pulmonary carcinoid tumors using FDG PET. AJR Am J Roentgenol 170:1369, 1998

44. Marom EM, Sarvis S, Herndon JE 2nd, et al: T1 lung cancers: sensitivity of diagnosis with fluorodeoxyglucose PET. Radiology 223:453, 2002

45. Vansteenkiste J, Fischer BM, Dooms C, et al: Positron-emission tomography in prognostic and therapeutic assessment of lung cancer: systematic review. Lancet Oncol 5:531, 2004

46. Nomori H, Watanabe K, Ohtsuka T, et al: Evaluation of F-18 fluorodeoxyglucose (FDG) PET scanning for pulmonary nodules less than 3 cm in diameter, with special reference to the CT images. Lung Cancer 45:19, 2004

47. Gould MK, Sanders GD, Barnett PG, et al: Cost-effectiveness of alternative management strategies for patients with solitary pulmonary nodules. Ann Intern Med 138:724, 2003

48. Levine MS, Weiss JM, Harrell JH, et al: Transthoracic needle aspiration biopsy following negative fiberoptic bronchoscopy in solitary pulmonary nodules. Chest 93:1152, 1988

49. Lacasse Y, Wong E, Guyatt GH, et al: Transthoracic needle aspiration biopsy for the diagnosis of localised pulmonary lesions: a meta-analysis. Thorax 54:884, 1999

50. Larscheid RC, Thorpe PE, Scott WJ: Percutaneous transthoracic needle aspiration biopsy: a comprehensive review of its current role in the diagnosis and treatment of lung tumors. Chest 114:704, 1998

51. Conces DJ Jr, Schwenk GR Jr, Doering PR, et al: Thoracic needle biopsy: improved results utilizing a team approach. Chest 91:813, 1987

52. Yung RC: Tissue diagnosis of suspected lung cancer: selecting between bronchoscopy, transthoracic needle aspiration, and resectional biopsy. Respir Care Clin N Am 9:51, 2003

53. Geraghty PR, Kee ST, McFarlane G, et al: CT-guided transthoracic needle aspiration biopsy of pulmonary nodules: needle size and pneumothorax rate. Radiology 229:475, 2003

54. Wallace JM, Deutsch AL: Flexible fiberoptic bronchoscopy and percutaneous needle lung aspiration for evaluating the solitary pulmonary nodule. Chest 81:665, 1982

55. Cortese DA, McDougall JC: Bronchoscopic biopsy and brushing with fluoroscopic guidance in nodular metastatic lung cancer. Chest 79:610,1981

56. Swensen SJ, Jett JR, Payne WS, et al: An integrated approach to evaluation of the solitary pulmonary nodule. Mayo Clin Proc 65:173, 1990

57. Davies AL: The current role of video-assisted thoracic surgery (VATS) in the overall practice of thoracic surgery: a review of 207 cases. Int Surg 82:229, 1997

58. Asamura H: Thoracoscopic procedures for intrathoracic diseases: the present status. Respirology 4:9, 1999

59. Allen MS, Deschamps C, Jones DM, et al: Video-assisted thoracic surgical procedures: the Mayo experience. Mayo Clin Proc 71:351, 1996

60. Hazelrigg SR, Magee MJ, Cetindag IB: Video-assisted thoracic surgery for diagnosis of the solitary lung nodule. Chest Surg Clin N Am 8:763, 1998

61. Pechet TT, Carr SR, Collins JE, et al: Arterial invasion predicts early mortality in stage I non-small cell lung cancer. Ann Thorac Surg 78:1748, 2004

62. Chute CG, Greenberg ER, Baron J, et al: Presenting conditions of 1539 population-based lung cancer patients by cell type and stage in New Hampshire and Vermont. Cancer 56:2107, 1985

63. Harpole DH Jr, Feldman JM, Buchanan S, et al: Bronchial carcinoid tumors: a retrospective analysis of 126 patients. Ann Thorac Surg 54:50, 1992

64. McMullan DM, Wood DE: Pulmonary carcinoid tumors. Semin Thorac Cardiovasc Surg 15:289, 2003

65. DeCaro LF, Paladugu R, Benfield JR, et al: Typical and atypical carcinoids within the pulmonary APUD tumor spectrum. J Thorac Cardiovasc Surg 86:528, 1983

66. Greelish JP, Friedberg JS: Secondary pulmonary malignancy. Surg Clin North Am 80:633, 2000

67. Gotway MB, Tchao NK, Leung JW, et al: Sarcoidosis presenting as an enlarging solitary pulmonary nodule. J Thorac Imaging 16:117, 2001

68. Voulgari PV, Tsifetaki N, Metafratzi ZM, et al: A single pulmonary rheumatoid nodule masquerading as malignancy. Clin Rheumatol 24:556, 2005

69. Elrifai AM, Bailes JE, Shih SR, et al: Rewarming, ultraprofound hypothermia and cardiopulmonary bypass. J Extra Corpor Technol 24:107, 1993

70. Suen HC, Mathisen DJ, Grillo HC, et al: Surgical management and radiological characteristics of bronchogenic cysts. Ann Thorac Surg 55:476, 1993

71. Echeverri A, Long RF, Check W, et al: Pulmonary dirofilariasis. Ann Thorac Surg 67:201, 1999

72. Asimacopoulos PJ, Katras A, Christie B: Pulmonary dirofilariasis: the largest single-hospital experience. Chest 102:851, 1992

73. Morar R, Feldman C: Pulmonary echinococcosis. Eur Respir J 21:1069, 2003

74. Gottstein B, Reichen J: Hydatid lung disease (echinococcosis/hydatidosis). Clin Chest Med 23:397, 2002

75. Dial EM, Kane GC: Why the abnormal findings in this man without symptoms? J Respir Dis 24:537, 2003

76. Ost D, Fein AM, Feinsilver SH: Clinical practice: the solitary pulmonary nodule. N Engl J Med 348:2535, 2003

77. Cummings SR, Lillington GA, Richard RJ: Estimating the probability of malignancy in solitary pulmonary nodules: a Bayesian approach. Am Rev Respir Dis 134:449, 1986

78. Henschke CI, Yankelevitz D, Westcott J, et al: Work-up of the solitary pulmonary nodule. American College of Radiology. ACR Appropriateness Criteria. Radiology 215(suppl):607, 2000

33 PARALYZED DIAPHRAGM

Bryan F. Meyers, M.D., F.A.C.S., and Benjamin D. Kozower, M.D.

Evaluation of Elevated Hemidiaphragm

Paralysis of the diaphragm is an unusual and challenging clinical problem that may occur either in isolation or as part of a systemic disease. It can be caused by a number of disorders and should be considered in the differential diagnosis whenever a chest radiograph shows an elevated hemidiaphragm. At one time, diaphragmatic paralysis was generally considered to be a benign condition, but it is now clear that many patients experience various pulmonary, cardiac, and gastrointestinal symptoms. The symptoms reported are typically nonspecific, and the correct diagnosis is often difficult to make.

It is helpful to remember that the clinical manifestations of diaphragmatic paralysis are usually explained by the pathophysiology. Interruption of the phrenic nerve anywhere between the neck and the diaphragm results in paralysis of the ipsilateral hemidiaphragm [*see* Discussion, Diaphragmatic Anatomy, *below*]. Because the diaphragm is a continuous muscular sheet, one might suppose that paralysis of one side would adversely affect the other. Actually, the two sides of the diaphragm function independently: tension from one side is not distributed to the other across the central tendon.[1] Bilateral diaphragmatic paralysis is rarely encountered by the thoracic surgeon. When it does occur, it is usually a manifestation of neuromuscular or systemic disease.

The functional effects of hemidiaphragmatic paralysis are similar to but less striking than those of bilateral paralysis [*see* Discussion, Normal Diaphragmatic Function, *below*].[2] An elevated hemidiaphragm compresses the hemithorax and results in a restrictive pattern of lung disease. In the seated position, the patient's vital capacity and total lung capacity decrease by approximately 20%; in the supine position, vital capacity decreases by nearly 40%.[3] Ventilation and perfusion of the lower lobe are also reduced on the affected side. Mismatching may widen the alveolar-arterial oxygen difference and produce mild hypoxemia.[4] Generally, adults with healthy lungs tolerate these changes well; however, patients who are obese or have underlying lung disease are more likely to be symptomatic.

Diaphragmatic paralysis is frequently described in the literature in conjunction with eventration of the diaphragm. Eventration is a condition in which all or a portion of one hemidiaphragm is permanently elevated while retaining its continuity and its normal attachments to the costal margins. Although eventration and unilateral paralysis are technically different, they often give rise to the same physiologic disturbances and radiographic findings.

Clinical Evaluation

HISTORY

In adults, the clinical presentation of unilateral paralysis of the diaphragm is highly variable. Right and left hemidiaphragmatic paralysis seem to occur with equal frequency and usually cause little or no respiratory

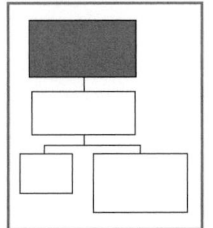

compromise. Patients may sleep in a semirecumbent position or in the lateral decubitus position with the affected hemidiaphragm down. Most patients have few respiratory symptoms at rest, but some complain of dyspnea, cough, or chest pain with exertion [*see Figure 1*]. Patients with left-side paralysis may experience GI complaints resulting from compression of the stomach [*see Figure 2*]. In addition, patients may suffer from recurrent pneumonia, bronchitis, or cardiac arrhythmias.

Bilateral diaphragmatic paralysis, on the other hand, is poorly tolerated. Patients with this condition depend more on their accessory muscles of respiration, avoid the supine position, and are more prone to chronic respiratory failure.[5]

In children, diaphragmatic paralysis may cause severe respiratory distress. Compared with adults, children have weaker intercostal muscles, a more compliant chest wall, and a more mobile mediastinum. Accordingly, children must depend on their diaphragms to achieve adequate tidal volumes. Unilateral diaphragmatic paralysis in a child usually necessitates mechanical ventilation; bilateral paralysis is often fatal without prompt ventilatory support.

Common Causes of Diaphragmatic Paralysis

As noted (see above), bilateral diaphragmatic paralysis is usually a manifestation of a systemic disease, such as a neuromuscular junction disorder, an immunologic phenomenon, or a myopathy. Because thoracic surgeons rarely treat these conditions, the ensu-

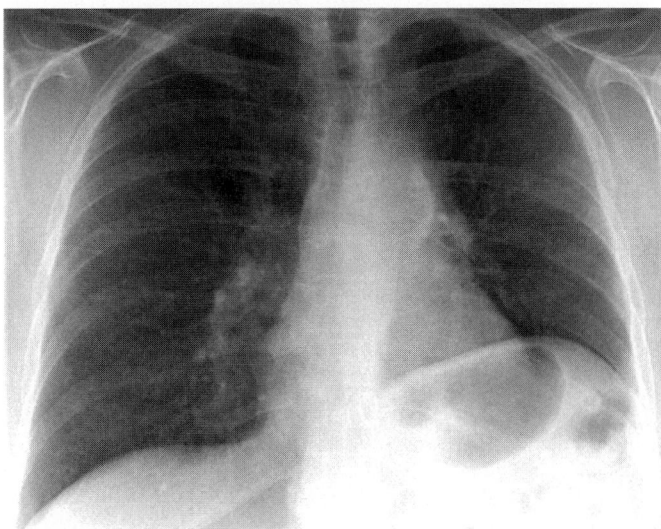

Figure 1 **Shown is a postoperative radiograph from a 55-year-old woman who underwent left upper lobectomy. Because the tumor was directly adherent to the phrenic nerve, a 2 cm portion of the left phrenic nerve was resected along with the tumor. Recovery was uneventful, and the only late symptom was mild dyspnea with exertion.**

Evaluation of Elevated Hemidiaphragm

Patient presents with elevated hemidiaphragm on chest x-ray

Obtain clinical history:
- Previous operations (iatrogenic phrenic nerve injury)
- Malignancy involving phrenic nerve
- Respiratory symptoms (exertional dyspnea, cough, difficulty in sleeping)
- GI symptoms (dysphagia, dyspepsia)
- Cardiac symptoms (dysrhythmia)

Perform physical examination:
- Auscultation for decreased breath sounds
- Percussion to assess diaphragmatic excursion

Order investigative studies:
- Inspiratory and expiratory chest x-ray (to confirm elevated hemidiaphragm)
- Fluoroscopy and sniff test (to distinguish diaphragmatic paralysis from weakness)
- Cervical phrenic nerve stimulation (to clarify diagnosis in patients on mechanical ventilation when sniff test is inconclusive—rarely necessary)

Patient is asymptomatic or has only mild symptoms

Treat conservatively:
- Physical therapy
- Pulmonary rehabilitation
- Weight loss

Patient has significant symptoms (e.g., dyspnea, recurrent pneumonia, chronic bronchitis, chest pain, poor exercise tolerance, cardiac dysrhythmia, or functional gastric disorder)

Order further tests as required:
- Pulmonary (pulmonary function tests)
- Cardiac (ECG, echocardiography)
- GI (gastric motility study)

Treat surgically with diaphragmatic plication (open or thoracoscopic).

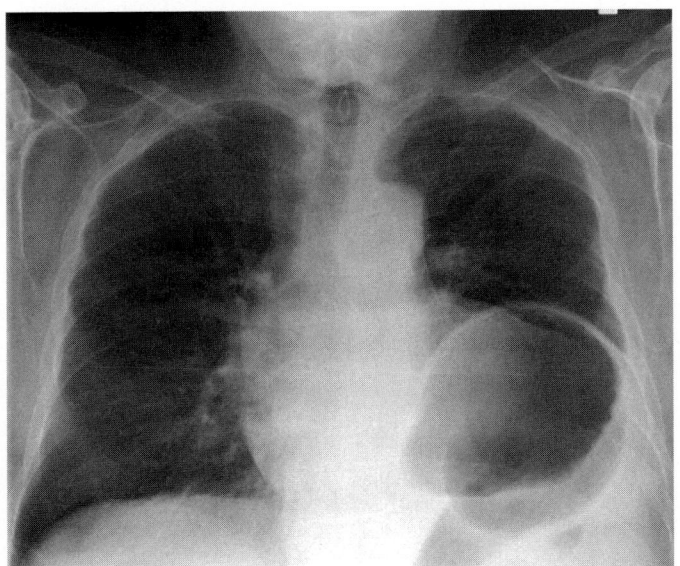

Figure 2 Shown is a postoperative radiograph of a 70-year-old man who underwent left upper lobectomy for removal of a peripheral 3 cm lesion. The phrenic nerve was injured with the electrocautery during mediastinal lymph node dissection. The radiograph shows permanent elevation of the left hemidiaphragm with gastric bloating 3 years after operation. The patient is neither dyspneic nor dyspeptic and does not require surgical intervention.

ing discussion focuses on conditions associated with isolated diaphragmatic paralysis [*see Table 1*]. The two most common causes of unilateral diaphragmatic paralysis are (1) iatrogenic injury after a cardiothoracic or cervical procedure and (2) malignancy.

Injury to phrenic nerve   Common mechanisms of phrenic nerve injury during cardiac procedures include stretching, crushing, transection, and hypothermia. During the mid-1980s, topical ice slush was frequently employed in cardiopulmonary bypass procedures, and this practice dramatically increased the incidence of phrenic nerve injury. After cooling jackets replaced topical ice slush in this setting, the incidence of elevated hemidiaphragms fell from 23% to 2%.[6,7] It has been suggested that harvesting the internal mammary artery may contribute to phrenic nerve injury, but a def-

---

Table 1   Causes of Isolated Diaphragmatic Paralysis

Idiopathic paralysis
Phrenic neuropathy
  Phrenic nerve injury
    Iatrogenic
    Malignancy (invasion or compression)
    Trauma
    Therapeutic (tuberculosis)
  Mononeuritis
    Viral infection (Guillain-Barré syndrome)
    Vasculitis
    Diabetes
    Connective tissue disease
Anterior horn cell lesions
  Herpes zoster
  Poliomyelitis
  Amyotrophic lateral sclerosis

---

inite connection between the two has not been established.

The outcome of phrenic nerve injury incurred during cardiac surgery has been well studied. In many cases, the injured phrenic nerves recover; typical recovery times for diaphragmatic function range from 6 months to 2 years.[6,8] In 20% of cases, however, the injury is permanent [*see Figure 3*]. Although morbidity is usually minimal, bilateral diaphragmatic paralysis after cardiac surgery has occasionally resulted in death. It should be kept in mind that diaphragmatic paralysis after cardiac surgery is a more serious problem in children than in adults. In pediatric patients, phrenic nerve injury usually results in respiratory distress, which may prevent weaning from mechanical ventilation.[9]

In current usage, the term iatrogenic phrenic nerve injury refers to either (1) unintentional injury to the nerve during an operation or (2) intentional resection of the nerve to permit complete excision of a chest neoplasm. In the past, however, phrenic nerve injury was sometimes deliberately induced to elevate or disable a hemidiaphragm for therapeutic purposes, either permanently or temporarily. Therapeutic phrenic nerve paralysis was originally achieved by crushing the nerve at the level of the diaphragm with a surgical clamp; subsequently, temporary paralysis was achieved by exposing the phrenic nerve in the neck and infiltrating the area around it with local anesthetics. This technique was employed in the treatment of pulmonary tuberculosis and was occasionally performed to elevate a hemidiaphragm and help obliterate a difficult pleural space problem. It must be emphasized that in current practice, therapeutic phrenic nerve paralysis is of historic interest only. It is never necessary, and it is no longer considered appropriate or beneficial.

Malignancy involving phrenic nerve   Neoplastic involvement of the phrenic nerve accounts for one third of cases of diaphragmatic paralysis.[10] Bronchogenic carcinomas are the lesions that most commonly affect the phrenic nerve, and paralysis is usually secondary to mediastinal lymph node involvement or direct mediastinal invasion by central tumors. Other mediastinal tumors that may affect the phrenic nerve include thymomas, lymphomas, and germ cell tumors. It is reassuring to note that in patients with unilateral diaphragmatic paralysis of no clear origin, malignancy turns out to be the cause in fewer than 5% of cases. Although patients with unexplained diaphragmatic paralysis are unlikely to have an occult malignancy, they are also unlikely to recover their diaphragmatic function.[10]

PHYSICAL EXAMINATION

Patients with diaphragmatic paralysis may be asymptomatic or may present with some of the nonspecific clinical findings mentioned (see above). Physical examination usually reveals decreased breath sounds on the affected side, a mediastinal shift during inspiration, or a scaphoid abdomen. Percussion may demonstrate an elevated hemidiaphragm with decreased excursion on inspiration.

Investigative Studies

In the majority of cases, an asymptomatic person is referred to the surgeon because a chest radiograph demonstrates an elevated hemidiaphragm. It is important to remember that there is a broad differential diagnosis for an elevated hemidiaphragm and that diaphragmatic paralysis is relatively rare [*see Table 2*].

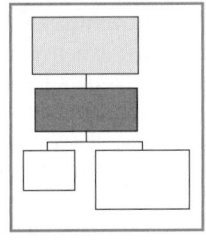

Workup usually begins with inspiratory and expiratory chest

a

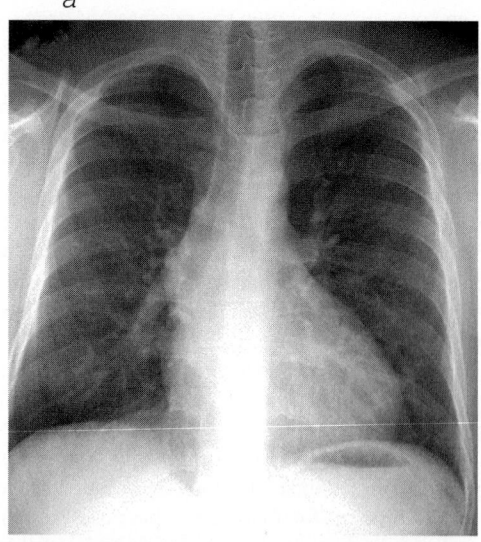

b

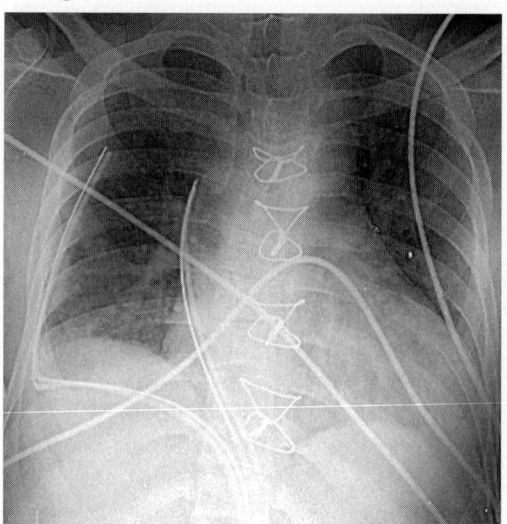

c

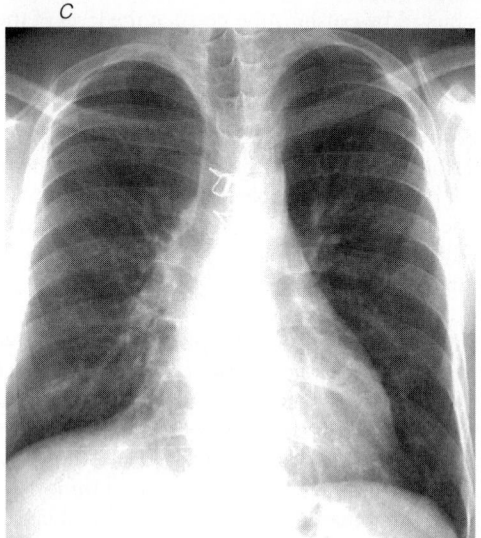

Figure 3 **Shown are three chest radiographs of a 25-year-old man with residual anterior mediastinal mass after treatment for germ cell tumor. (*a*) Preoperative view shows normal diaphragmatic positioning bilaterally. (*b*) Immediate postoperative view demonstrates an elevated right hemidiaphragm, attributed to stretch injury and electrothermal injury caused by dissection of mass from the vicinity of the phrenic nerve at the right hilum. (*c*) Late view, 3 months after operation, reveals gradual restoration of normal diaphragm positioning. Patient is asymptomatic.**

radiographs. However, fluoroscopic examination is the most practical method of assessing the movement of the diaphragm. The excursion of the domes of the diaphragm averages 3 to 5 cm and may range from 2 to 10 cm.[11] The examination is typically performed with the patient standing, but it is more sensitive when the patient is supine because the effect of gravity is removed. In a patient with unilateral paralysis, the paralyzed hemidiaphragm moves upward with rapid inspiration and downward with expiration. This paradoxical motion passively follows changes in intrapleural and intra-abdominal pressure.

The so-called sniff test is then performed to confirm that the abnormal diaphragm excursion is the result of paralysis rather than of weakness. During this test, the patient inhales forcefully and rapidly through the nose with the mouth closed. A sharp and brief downward motion in both hemidiaphragms is the normal response when paralysis is absent. If an entire hemidiaphragm exhibits a paradoxical upward motion greater than 2 cm, however, diaphragmatic paralysis is likely.[12] The diagnosis of diaphragmatic paralysis may be difficult to make in patients with severe chronic obstructive pulmonary disease, in whom normal hemidiaphragms move very little. The sniff test may also be inconclusive in weak, debilitated patients, who often are incapable of producing a forceful sniff. In patients who are undergoing mechanical ventilation and in whom the diagnosis remains in doubt after a

sniff test, a definitive diagnosis can be made by employing cervical phrenic nerve stimulation in conjunction with electromyographic measurement of phrenic nerve latency.[13] This final test is rarely necessary.

Management

CONSERVATIVE VERSUS SURGICAL
TREATMENT

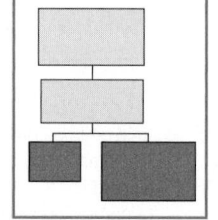

Treatment is individualized and depends on the degree to which the patient is incapacitated. Most healthy adults with isolated diaphragmatic paralysis are asymptomatic or suffer only from mild exertional dyspnea. The vast majority of these patients do not require surgical treatment and are best treated conservatively (e.g., with physical therapy, pulmonary rehabilitation, and counseling on weight loss, if necessary). Just as many patients with normal lung function can tolerate major pulmonary resections, most patients who are otherwise fit can tolerate unilateral diaphragmatic paralysis without the need for surgical intervention.

Operative management may, however, be indicated for children and for adults who have significant symptoms (e.g., dyspnea, recurrent pneumonia, chronic bronchitis, chest pain, poor exercise tolerance, cardiac arrhythmias, or functional disorders of the stomach).[14] The classic treatment is diaphragmatic plication, which may be performed either via a thoracotomy or thoracoscopically. Plication of the diaphragm was first performed in 1947 to treat congenital eventration of the diaphragm, and the basic principles of the procedure have changed little since then.[15]

PLICATION OF DIAPHRAGM

Open

A standard diaphragmatic plication is performed through a posterolateral thoracotomy in the eighth intercostal space. The lung and the mediastinum are examined to exclude any unsuspected pathologic conditions. The uncut diaphragm is plicated with four to six parallel rows of heavy nonabsorbable sutures. The stitches are placed in an anterolateral-to-posterolateral direction, and each row takes several bites of the diaphragm to form pleats. The sutures are tied only after all the rows have been placed. When all of the sutures are placed and tied, the diaphragm should be tight, and much of the plicated tissue should lie within the central tendon.

Open diaphragmatic plication is an effective procedure for treating diaphragmatic paralysis. In a study of 17 patients who underwent plication for exertional dyspnea,[16] no major complications were reported during a mean hospital stay of 11 days. At 6 months' follow-up, patients exhibited significant improvements with respect to dyspnea score, forced vital capacity (FVC), total lung capacity (TLC), functional residual capacity (FRC), and arterial oxygenation. Furthermore, the subjective and objective improvements were maintained for at least 5 years. In a subsequent series from the United Kingdom, similar results were observed at a mean follow-up of 10 years: 14 of 15 patients were satisfied with their plication and had returned to work.[17] In addition, FVC, forced expiratory volume in 1 second (FEV$_1$), FRC, and TLC improved by 12%, 15%, 26%, and 13%, respectively.

Research has also been performed on changes in respiratory mechanics after diaphragmatic plication. In 1980, one group noted that plication was more successful for hemiparalysis than for bilateral diaphragmatic paralysis.[18] These clinical results subsequently led another group to hypothesize that normal functioning of the contralateral hemidiaphragm might be required to derive significant benefit from diaphragmatic plication.[19] These investigators demonstrated that plication for unilateral paralysis improved the strength of the normal contralateral hemidiaphragm, so that the contralateral hemidiaphragm functioned as a better pressure generator and thus made a greater contribution to breathing. However, they found that bilateral plication for bilateral paralysis did not yield significant improvements with respect to diaphragmatic function, lung compliance, or work of breathing.

There was a small improvement in tidal volume after bilateral plication, but this was probably attributable to improved rib cage efficiency secondary to diaphragmatic fixation.

These findings may explain why bilateral plication has been more beneficial for adults than it has been for children,[20] who depend more on the diaphragmatic contribution to respiration. In infants, the small improvement in rib cage efficiency may not be large enough to allow them to be weaned from mechanical ventilation. In children with hemidiaphragmatic paralysis, however, plication is essential for improving diaphragmatic efficiency and preventing complications associated with long-term mechanical ventilation.[20]

Thoracoscopic

In 1996, a thoracoscopy-assisted approach to diaphragmatic plication was first described. The goal was to achieve an equivalent degree of plication by less invasive means.[21] Three patients were treated in this fashion. The procedure made use of a double-lumen endotracheal tube, two thoracoscopic ports, and a 5 cm minithoracotomy. The diaphragm was invaginated and stitched with two rows of continuous sutures. The results were excellent, and the average hospital stay was 8 days. All three patients showed significant improvements in FVC and FEV$_1$: FVC improved by 9% to 22%, and FEV$_1$ improved by 11% to 14%. These improvements were maintained for a minimum of 17 months.

Since this first description, several reports of successful diaphragmatic plication with a purely thoracoscopic approach (using three or four ports) have been published.[14,22] These case reports documented symptomatic improvement and reduced length of stay (4 days); however, they did not document significant improvements in FVC or FEV$_1$. Thoracoscopic diaphragmatic plication appears to be the surgical method of the future, but larger series with longer follow-up periods are needed. The main contraindication to thoracoscopic plication is extensive pleural adhesions from inflammatory reactions or previous operations.

SURGICAL PROPHYLAXIS AFTER PHRENIC NERVE INJURY

Phrenic Nerve Repair versus Prophylactic Plication

An area of investigation that, to date, has not been sufficiently explored is the potential role of prophylactic procedures in cases where one is confident that a phrenic nerve has been injured during an operation and wishes to reverse or at least mitigate the effect of the injury.

If the injury resulted from sharp dissection, so that the entire nerve is present but divided, one may elect to repair the nerve. On occasion, we have invited colleagues from plastic surgery to perform microsurgical anastomoses between the cut ends of the severed nerves, but we have never attempted a formal analysis of this practice. Such a repair would not, of course, be feasible in a case where the phrenic nerve was resected in the course of excision of an attached invasive tumor.

If the nerve was resected or was injured beyond hope of recovery, one may reasonably consider plicating the diaphragm during the same operation so as to minimize the impact of the diaphragmatic paralysis without having to perform another operation later. This strategy has not yet been studied in the surgical literature, but it should be kept in mind for the rare instances of phrenic nerve resection or injury during pulmonary or mediastinal resection.

PACING OF DIAPHRAGM

Although pacing of the diaphragm requires an intact phrenic nerve and thus is not useful in cases of classic diaphragmatic

---

> ### Table 2 Differential Diagnosis of Elevated Hemidiaphragm on Chest Radiograph
>
> Volume loss (atelectasis, lobar collapse, hypoplasia)
> Splinting
> Pleural disease (subpulmonic effusion, mass)
> Diaphragmatic hernia
> Eventration
> Phrenic nerve paralysis
> Abdominal disease (dilated viscera, abscess)
> Single-lung transplantation for pulmonary fibrosis

paralysis, it is an established mode of ventilatory support with which the thoracic surgeon should be familiar. The two main indications for diaphragmatic pacing are central alveolar hypoventilation and high cervical spinal cord injury; less common indications are intractable hiccups and end-stage chronic obstructive pulmonary disease. Central alveolar hypoventilation is a form of sleep apnea resulting from failure of the respiratory drive itself rather than from an anatomic obstruction. It is also known as Ondine's curse (from the German myth about the water nymph Ondine, who, finding that her mortal husband had been unfaithful, placed a fatal curse on him so that he would only breathe while awake).[23] The underlying cause is impaired sensitivity of the brain's respiratory control center to alterations in oxygenation. The clinical result is persistent hypoventilation with sleep apnea and the development of pulmonary hypertension.

The use of electricity to induce diaphragmatic contraction was first suggested by Hufeland in 1783.[24] Besides an intact phrenic nerve and a functioning diaphragm, diaphragmatic pacing also requires normal lungs with the ability to oxygenate and ventilate in response to diaphragmatic movement; severe restrictive lung disease and major chest wall deformities are contraindications to pacing. In addition, it is crucial that the patient be cooperative and motivated and have adequate support from nursing staff and family.

Phrenic nerve pacing involves the use of an extracorporeal generator with an antenna that transmits radiofrequency signals to a subcutaneous radio receiver; the receiver then translates the radiofrequency signal into direct current, which is delivered through electrodes to the phrenic nerves. The electrodes are placed on the phrenic nerves via bilateral anterior thoracotomies or neck incisions. Several different commercial pacing systems are available, but they all work according to the same basic concept.

Phrenic nerve pacing remains a relatively rare procedure. The largest series published to date included 165 patients, of whom 27% were paced on a full-time basis and 63% on a part-time basis.[25] Phrenic nerve pacing met the ventilatory requirements of 47% of the patients and was partially successful in 36%.

Discussion

Diaphragmatic Anatomy

For the purposes of discussion, the diaphragm may usefully be divided into left and right hemidiaphragms. In anatomic terms, the diaphragm is a dome-shaped muscle that can be described as having both muscular and tendinous components. The muscular portion of the diaphragm is divided into three parts, each of which originates from one of the three structural elements forming the lower thoracic aperture: the pars lumbalis diaphragmatis (originating from the lumbar spine), the pars costalis diaphragmatis (from the ribs), and the pars sternalis diaphragmatis (from the sternum). The pars lumbalis is the most powerful region of the diaphragm.[26] All three parts insert into a central aponeurosis known as the central tendon. This tendon has a cloverleaf shape, with one leaf directed anteriorly and two leaves directed laterally (one into each hemithorax).

The diaphragm possesses three major apertures, which allow passage of the inferior vena cava, the esophagus, and the aorta. The caval orifice is located in the right portion of the central tendon, typically at the level of T8. Diaphragmatic contraction stretches this orifice and may facilitate the return of blood to the heart during inspiration. The right phrenic nerve and some lymphatic vessels also pass through this orifice. The esophageal hiatus is located behind the central tendon at the level of T10. This aperture, unlike the other two, is ventrally framed by muscle. The aortic opening is anterior to T12, between the crura and behind the median arcuate ligament. The aortic opening also allows passage of the azygos vein, the thoracic duct, and lymphatic channels as they descend from the thorax into the abdomen.

The arterial supply to the cranial surface of the diaphragm consists of the pericardiophrenic, musculophrenic, and superior phrenic arteries. The posterior aspect of the diaphragm is supplied by small direct branches from the aorta. The caudal surface of the diaphragm is supplied by the inferior phrenic arteries, which arise from the aorta or the celiac trunk; these arteries are much larger than the superior phrenic arteries. Occasionally, the right inferior phrenic artery originates from the right renal artery.[27] The venous drainage from the diaphragm mirrors the arterial supply.

The left and right phrenic nerves arise from the C3–C5 nerve roots and travel a distance of 30 to 40 cm between their cervical origin and their termination on the surface of the diaphragm. A firm understanding of the anatomy of the phrenic nerves is crucial for the thoracic surgeon because iatrogenic injury during operation is a leading cause of diaphragmatic paralysis. Both nerves originate on the middle scalene muscle and cross to the anterior scalene muscle, where they descend within an investment of fascia. At the base of the neck, the left phrenic nerve crosses the thoracic duct, descending into the thorax on the anterior surface of the left subclavian artery. It then travels between the left common carotid and subclavian arteries, crosses in front of the vagus nerve, and passes lateral to the aortic arch, where it descends along the pericardium to a point just above the diaphragm. At the thoracic inlet, the right phrenic nerve is located behind the innominate vein and usually crosses in front of the internal mammary artery. It descends to the right of the innominate vein and the superior vena cava before reaching the pericardium, anterior to the lung. Finally, the right phrenic nerve descends along the inferior vena cava toward the diaphragm. Both phrenic nerves branch just proximal to the diaphragm, and small terminal branches innervate the muscle.

Normal Diaphragmatic Function

The diaphragm is the most important respiratory muscle. During inspiration, the diaphragm contracts and moves caudally in a pistonlike fashion. This motion forces the abdominal contents down and forward, increasing the vertical dimension of the chest cavity. In addition, the ribs lift the lateral aspect of the diaphragm during inspiration, causing the transverse diameter of the thorax to increase. As the diaphragm contracts, pleural pressure decreases, facilitating lung inflation. Normal diaphragmatic function accounts for 75% of air movement during normal respiration and is responsible for 60% of minute volume in the supine position. Diaphragmatic excursion averages about 1 cm during normal tidal breathing, but it can increase to 10 cm during forced inspiration and expiration.[28]

References

1. Whitelaw WA: Shape and size of the human diaphragm in-vivo. J Appl Physiol 62:180, 1987

2. Gibson GJ: Diaphragmatic paresis: pathophysiology, clinical features, and investigation. Thorax 44:960, 1989

3. Clague HW, Hall DR: Effect of posture on lung volume airway closure and gas exchange in hemidiaphragmatic paralysis. Thorax 34:523, 1979

4. Easton PA, Fleetham JA, de la Rocha A, et al: Respiratory function after paralysis of the right hemidiaphragm. Am Rev Respir Dis 127:125, 1983

5. Rochester DF: The diaphragm: contractile properties and fatigue. J Clin Invest 75:1397, 1985

6. Curtis JJ, Weerachai N, Walls J, et al: Elevated hemidiaphragm after cardiac operations: incidence, prognosis and relationship to the use of topical ice slush. Ann Thorac Surg 48:764, 1989

7. Wheeler WE, Rubis LJ, Jones CW, et al: Etiology and prevention of topical cardiac hypothermia-induced phrenic nerve injury and left lower lobe atelectasis during cardiac surgery. Chest 88:680, 1985

8. Markand ON, Moorthy SS, Mahomed Y, et al: Postoperative phrenic nerve palsy in patients with open-heart surgery. Ann Thorac Surg 39:68, 1985

9. De Leeuw M, Williams JM, Freedom RM, et al: Impact of diaphragmatic paralysis after cardiothoracic surgery in children. J Thorac Cardiovasc Surg 118:510, 1999

10. Piehler JM, Pairolero PC, Gracey DR, et al: Unexplained diaphragmatic paralysis: a harbinger of malignant disease? J Thorac Cardiovasc Surg 84:861, 1982

11. Gierada DS, Slone RM, Fleishman MJ: Imaging evaluation of the diaphragm. Chest Surg Clin N Am 8:237, 1998

12. Alexander C: Diaphragm movements and the diagnosis of diaphragmatic paralysis. Clin Radiol 17:79, 1966

13. Stochina M, Ferber I, Wolf E: Evaluation of the phrenic nerve in patients with neuromuscular disorders. Int J Rehabil Res 6:455, 1983

14. Suzumura Y, Terada Y, Sonobe M, et al: A case of unilateral diaphragmatic eventration treated by plication with thoracoscopic surgery. Chest 112:530, 1997

15. Bisgard JD: Congenital eventration of the diaphragm. J Thorac Surg 16:489, 1947

16. Graham FT, Kaplan D, Evans CC, et al: Diaphragmatic plication for unilateral diaphragmatic paralysis: a 10-year experience. Ann Thorac Surg 49:248, 1990

17. Higgs SM, Hussain A, Jackson M, et al: Long term results of diaphragmatic plication for unilateral diaphragm paralysis. Eur J Cardiothorac Surg 21:294, 2002

18. Schonfeld T, O'Neal MH, Platzker ACG, et al: Function of the diaphragm before and after plication. Thorax 35:631, 1980

19. Takeda S, Nakahara K, Fujii Y, et al: Effects of diaphragmatic plication on respiratory mechanics in dogs with unilateral and bilateral phrenic nerve paralyses. Chest 107:798, 1995

20. Simansky DA, Paley M, Refaely Y, et al: Diaphragm plication following phrenic nerve injury: a comparison of paediatric and adult patients. Thorax 57:613, 2002

21. Mouroux J, Padovani B, Poirier NC, et al: Technique for the repair of diaphragmatic eventration. Ann Thorac Surg 62:905, 1996

22. Sloane GT, Montany PF: Thoracoscopic diaphragmatic plication. Surg Laparosc Endosc 8:319, 1998

23. Goldblatt D: Historical note: Ondine's curse. Semin Neurol 15:218, 1995

24. Hufeland CW: Usum uis electriciae in asphyxia experimentis illustratum. Dissertatio Inauguralis Medica, Göttingen, Germany, 1783

25. Glenn WWL, Bouillette RT, Dentz B, et al: Fundamental consideration in pacing of the diaphragm for chronic ventilatory insufficiency: a multi-institutional study: part II. Pacing Clin Electrophysiol 11:2121, 1988

26. Fell SC: Surgical anatomy of the diaphragm and the phrenic nerve. Chest Surg Clin N Am 8:281, 1998

27. Schumpelick V, Steinau G, Schluper I, et al: Surgical embryology and anatomy of the diaphragm with surgical applications. Surg Clin North Am 80:213, 2000

28. West JB: Respiratory Physiology: The Essentials, 6th ed. Williams and Wilkins, Baltimore, 2000

John Yee, M.D., F.R.C.S.C., and Richard J. Finley, M.D., F.A.C.S., F.R.C.S.C.

The remarkable developments in diagnosis, imaging, and surgical treatment of esophageal diseases over the past 15 years have resulted in markedly better patient outcomes: the morbidity and mortality associated with surgery of the esophagus have been substantially reduced. In particular, the operative techniques employed to treat esophageal disease have advanced considerably, as a result of an improved understanding of esophageal anatomy and physiology and the successful introduction of minimally invasive approaches to the esophagus [*see 35 Minimally Invasive Esophageal Procedures*]. For a number of diseases (e.g., achalasia), minimally invasive procedures have proved to be as effective as their open counterparts while causing less postoperative morbidity. The growing stature of minimally invasive approaches does not, however, diminish the importance of the equivalent open approaches. In this chapter, we describe common open operations performed to excise Zenker's diverticulum, to manage complex gastroesophageal reflux disease (GERD), and to resect esophageal and proximal gastric tumors.

General Preoperative Considerations

METHODS OF PATIENT ASSESSMENT

The functional results achieved with esophageal procedures become more predictable when the approach to preoperative patient evaluation is precise and reproducible. The ciné barium swallow remains the most cost-effective method for initial evaluation of esophageal anatomy and function. It should be employed before endoscopy because the results may direct the endoscopist's attention to particular areas of concern. For example, a finding of abnormal angulation or strictures indicates that the endoscopist should either use a pediatric-caliber endoscope or exercise more caution in passing a standard adult endoscope. In addition, endoscopic examination alone is often insufficient for assessing esophageal motility disorders or defining the complex anatomy of a paraesophageal hiatal hernia.

Endoscopic ultrasonography (EUS) is an extension of the visual mucosal examination. The information it can provide about the extension of mass lesions beyond the confines of the esophageal wall is helpful in planning surgical resection. In addition, EUS can differentiate benign stromal tumors from cystic or malignant neoplasms on the basis of characteristic echogenicity patterns. The combination of EUS and computed tomography permits highly precise anatomic assessment of esophageal neoplasms, definition of the extent of local invasion, and identification of regional metastases.

Functional imaging with photodynamic or vital staining allows accurate diagnosis of dysplastic or malignant mucosal lesions in their earliest stages. Positron emission tomography (PET) yields similar results by localizing metabolically active tissue regionally or at distant sites. The combination of morphologic data from high-resolution CT and functional data from PET is particularly effective for identifying occult metastases that would preclude curative resection for esophageal cancer.

Esophageal manometry, 24-hour esophageal pH testing, and nuclear studies for assessment of esophageal and gastric transit provide functional data that can facilitate the diagnosis and treatment of GERD, achalasia, and other disorders of the esophagus. They are useful complements to standard investigations (e.g., ciné barium swallow and endoscopy).

Complete preoperative investigation of all patients, even those with classic histories and physical findings, is mandatory. The data from anatomic and functional testing allow the surgeon to plan the operation more appropriately and effectively (e.g., deciding on the need for esophageal lengthening in patients with paraesophageal hernias or choosing between a complete and a partial fundoplication in patients with hernias associated with varying degrees of esophageal dysmotility).

OPTIMIZATION OF PATIENT HEALTH STATUS

Patients with obstructing esophageal diseases are often elderly, debilitated, and malnourished. Although months of insufficient nutrition cannot be corrected in the space of a few hours, anemia, dehydration, and electrolyte abnormalities can be mitigated by means of intravenous support and appropriate laboratory monitoring. If esophageal obstruction prevents oral intake, endoscopic dilation of the stricture, accompanied by either nasogastric intubation or percutaneous endoscopic gastrostomy (PEG) [*see 60 Gastrointestinal Endoscopy*], is indicated; the patient should then be able to resume at least a liquid diet. If weight loss has exceeded 10%, enteral nutrition, comprising at least 2,000 kcal/day of a high-protein liquid diet, should be administered for at least 10 days before the operation. Cardiovascular, renal, hepatic, and respiratory function should be documented and optimized. If the patient is aspirating, the esophagus should be evacuated and the patient should be given nothing by mouth until after the operation. Aspiration pneumonia should always be corrected preoperatively.

Cricopharyngeal Myotomy and Excision of Zenker's Diverticulum

PREOPERATIVE EVALUATION

Patients who are candidates for cricopharyngeal myotomy usually present with difficulty initiating swallowing, cervical dysphagia or odynophagia [*see 28 Dysphagia*], and a history of pulmonary aspiration. These symptoms of cricopharyngeal dysfunction may or may not be associated with a Zenker's diverticulum. Ciné contrast studies may reveal poor pharyngeal contractility, pulmonary or nasal aspiration, abnormalities of the upper esophageal sphincter, pharyngeal pouches, or other structural abnormalities in the distal esophagus. Barium is the usual contrast agent, but if aspiration is suspected, a nonionic contrast agent can be used instead to prevent pneumonitis.

Zenker's diverticulum is a pulsion diverticulum that arises adjacent to the inferior pharyngeal constrictor, between the oblique fibers of the posterior pharyngeal constrictors and the cricopharyngeus muscle. This mucosal outpouching results from a transient incomplete opening of the upper esophageal sphinc-

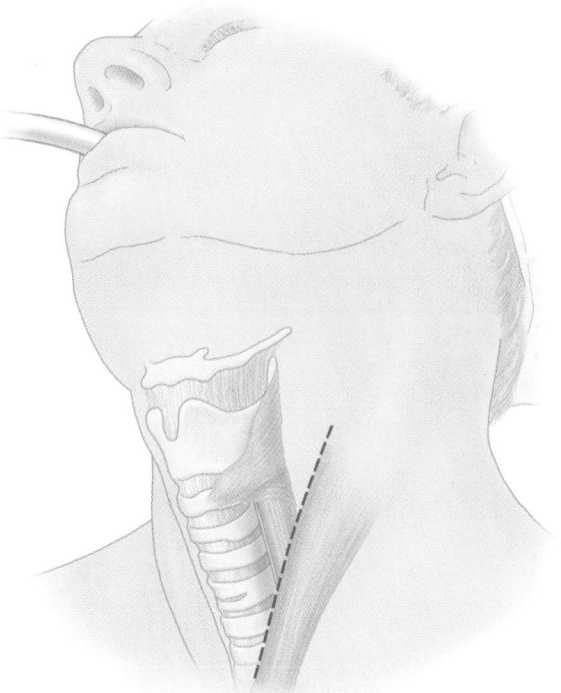

Figure 1 **Cricopharyngeal myotomy and excision of Zenker's diverticulum. A soft roll is placed behind the shoulders to extend the neck. The head is turned to the side opposite the incision. The cricoid cartilage is palpated and marked. The skin is incised obliquely along the sternocleidomastoid muscle, as shown, or transversely in a skin crease at the level of the cricoid.**

ter. The diverticulum ultimately enlarges, drapes over the cricopharyngeus, and dissects behind the esophagus into the prevertebral space. The pouch usually deviates to one side or the other; accordingly, the side on which the deviation occurs must be determined by means of a barium swallow so that the appropriate operative approach can be selected. Esophageal motility studies may show either incomplete upper esophageal relaxation on swallowing or poor coordination of the upper esophageal relaxation phase with pharyngeal contractions. Upper GI endoscopy is performed preoperatively to exclude the presence of a pharyngeal or esophageal carcinoma and to assess the upper GI anatomy. If there is evidence of GERD, proton pump inhibitors (PPIs) are given.

In symptomatic patients (e.g., those with dysphagia, nocturnal cough, or recurrent pneumonia from aspiration), surgical therapy is indicated regardless of whether a pouch is present or how large it may be. Such treatment involves correcting the underlying cricopharyngeal muscle dysfunction with a cricopharyngeal myotomy. If there is a diverticulum larger than 2 cm, it should be excised in addition to the cricopharyngeal myotomy. Alternatively, the diverticulum may be managed via endoscopic obliteration of the common wall between the pharyngeal pouch and the esophagus with either a stapler or a laser. Cricopharyngeal incoordination may be temporarily relieved by injecting botulinum toxin into the cricopharyngeus.

OPERATIVE PLANNING

The patient is placed on a clear fluid diet for 2 days before the operation. With the patient under general anesthesia, the trachea is intubated with a single-lumen endotracheal tube. Cricoid pressure is applied to prevent aspiration of diverticular contents. A soft

roll is placed behind the shoulders to extend the neck. The patient is placed in a 20° reverse Trendelenburg position, and the legs are wrapped with pneumatic calf compressors to prevent deep vein thrombosis (DVT). With the endotracheal tube placed to the left side of the mouth, a preliminary flexible esophagogastroscopy is performed to empty the diverticulum of all food and to examine the esophagus and the stomach. The scope is then brought back up into the oropharynx and moved into the pouch. The location of the diverticulum (on the left or the right side) is confirmed by turning off the room lights and noting which side is transilluminated by the gastroscope.

OPERATIVE TECHNIQUE

Step 1: Incision and Dissection of Pharyngeal Pouch

The patient lies with the head turned away from the side on which the incision is made. The cricoid cartilage is palpated and marked. A 4 cm skin incision is made, either obliquely along the sternocleidomastoid muscle [*see Figure 1*] or transversely in a skin crease at the level of the cricoid. The platysma is divided in the same line. Self-retaining retractors are inserted. The anterior border of the sternocleidomastoid muscle is incised throughout its length. The omohyoid muscle and the sternohyoid and sternothyroid muscles are retracted [*see Figure 2*]. The sternocleidomastoid muscle is retracted laterally to expose the carotid sheath and the internal jugular vein. The middle thyroid vein is ligated and divided, and the thyroid gland and the trachea are retracted medially by the assistant's finger to minimize the risk of injury to the underlying recurrent laryngeal nerve. There is no need to encircle the esophagus or to dissect in the tracheoesophageal groove. The deep cervical fascia is divided. The inferior thyroid artery is divided as laterally as possible. The carotid sheath is retracted laterally, and

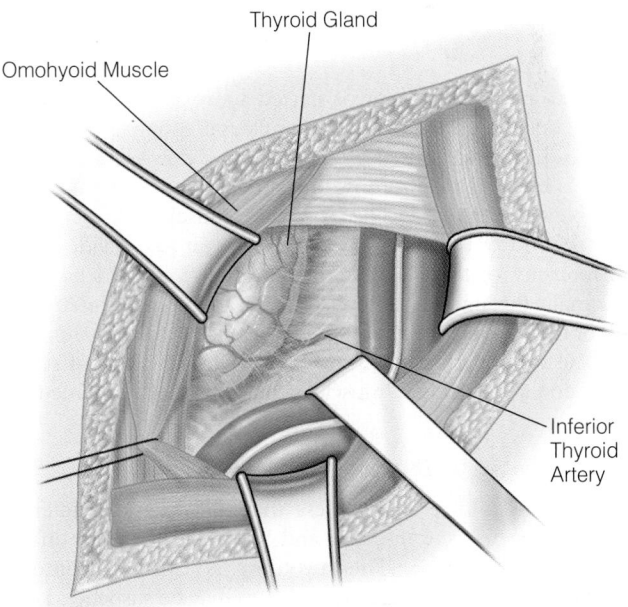

Figure 2 **Cricopharyngeal myotomy and excision of Zenker's diverticulum. The sternocleidomastoid is incised along the anterior border so as to expose the omohyoid muscle and the sternohyoid and sternothyroid muscles, which are retracted. The thyroid gland and the trachea are retracted medially by the assistant's finger, and the inferior thyroid artery is ligated and divided laterally to avoid injury to the recurrent laryngeal nerve.**

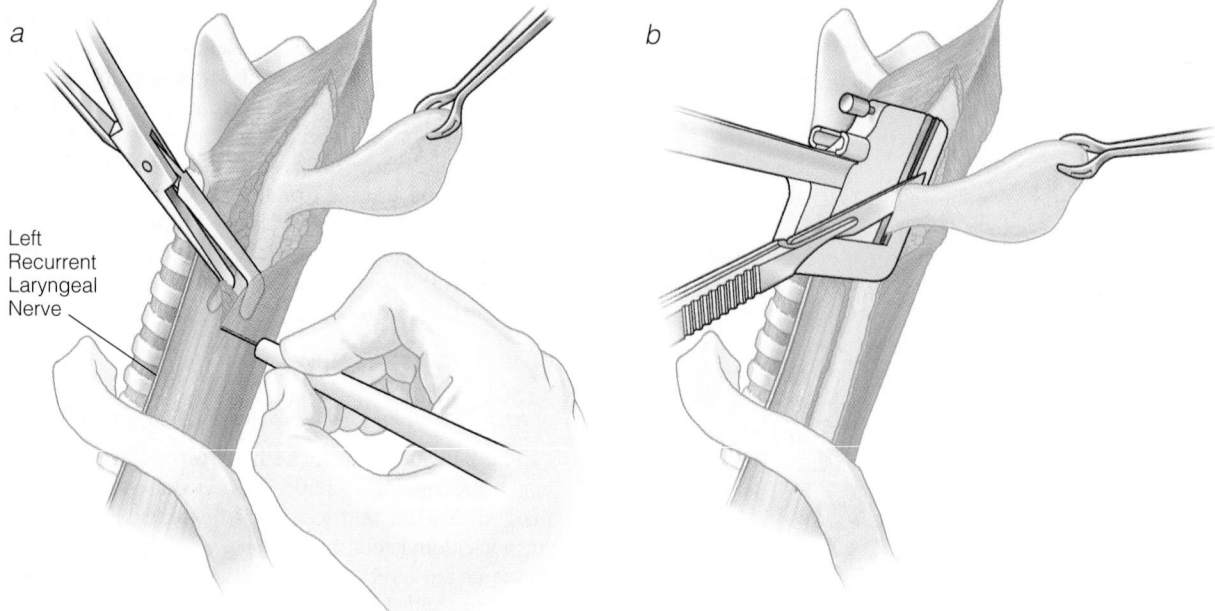

Figure 3 Cricopharyngeal myotomy and excision of Zenker's diverticulum. (*a*) The diverticulum is dissected away from the esophagus, and an esophageal myotomy is started approximately 3 cm below the cricopharyngeus. The myotomy is continued proximally through the cricopharyngeus, and the muscle around the diverticulum is freed. (*b*) A linear stapler is placed at the base of the sac and pressed firmly against the esophagoscope. The stapler is fired, and the diverticulum is excised.

dissection is carried down to the prevertebral fascia [*see Figure 2*]. The endoscope placed in the diverticulum is palpated, and the pouch is dissected away from the cervical esophagus up as far as the pharyngoesophageal junction. The flexible endoscope is then removed from the pouch and advanced into the thoracic esophagus so that it can be used as a stent for the cricopharyngeal myotomy. Dissection of the pharyngeal pouch is then completed.

Step 2: Myotomy

The esophageal myotomy is started approximately 3 cm below the cricopharyngeus on the posterolateral esophageal wall [*see Figure 3a*]. The esophageal muscle is divided down to the mucosa, which is recognizable from its bluish coloration with the submucosal plexus overlying it. The esophageal muscle is dissected away from the mucosa with a right-angle dissector and divided with a low-intensity diathermy unit. The myotomy is then continued proximally through the cricopharyngeus and up into the muscular wall of the hypopharynx for 2 cm if there is no diverticulum present. The hypopharynx is distinguished by a pronounced submucosal venous plexus. The muscle is then swept off the mucosa for 120°.

Step 3: Freeing or Excision of Diverticulum

If there is a diverticulum less than 2 cm in diameter, the cricopharyngeus is transected and the muscularis around the diverticulum is freed. The myotomy is extended onto the hypopharynx for 2 cm. The diverticulum may be suspended to the back wall of the pharynx. It should not be sutured to the prevertebral fascia, because the passage of sutures through the diverticulum can contaminate the fascia, leading to an increased risk of fascial infection.

If the diverticulum is more than 2 cm in diameter, it is excised with a linear stapler loaded with 2.5 mm staples, which is placed at the base of the sac and pressed firmly against the esophagoscope [*see Figure 3b*]. Particular care must be taken at this point so as not

to injure the recurrent laryngeal nerve. The stapler is fired, and the diverticulum is excised. The staple line is cleaned with an antiseptic solution, and the incision is filled with saline. The esophagus is insufflated with air to determine whether mucosal leakage has occurred, and the esophagoscope is removed; any mucosal leaks found are closed with fine absorbable sutures. In the absence of a stapler, the best way of excising the sac is to make a series of short incisions through the neck of the sac with scissors, suturing the edges after each cut with absorbable monofilament sutures (the so-called cut-and-sew technique). The esophagoscope ensures that the esophageal lumen is not narrowed.

Step 4: Drainage and Closure

Once hemostasis has been achieved, a short vacuum drain is placed through the skin into the retroesophageal space. The platysma is repaired with absorbable sutures, and the skin is closed with a subcuticular absorbable suture. Nasogastric intubation is unnecessary. Prokinetic agents and PPIs are administered to prevent gastroesophageal reflux. A water-soluble contrast study is done on the day of the operation. If the results are normal, the patient is started on a liquid diet, and the drain is removed on postoperative day 1, when the patient is discharged.

COMPLICATIONS

The main complications associated with cricopharyngeal myotomy are recurrent laryngeal nerve trauma (occurring in 0.5% of cases), fistulas (1%), hematoma formation, infection (2%), aspiration, and recurrence (4%). Hematomas and infections must be drained promptly. Fistulas usually close once the prevertebral space is drained and the associated infection controlled. Aspiration is the most serious complication after cricopharyngeal myotomy. Gastroesophageal reflux may contribute to oropharynygeal dysphagia. Division of the upper esophageal sphincter in a patient with an incompetent esophagogastric junction may lead to massive tracheobronchial aspiration. Therefore, documented gastroesophageal reflux, gastroesophageal regurgitation, and severe distal esophagitis may be relative contraindications to cricopharyngeal myotomy until the lower esophageal sphincter defect has been remedied with an antireflux operation.

OUTCOME EVALUATION

Of patients with a Zenker's diverticulum, at least 90% experience excellent results from surgical treatment. Of patients without a Zenker's diverticulum, one third experience excellent results, another third show moderate improvement, and the remaining third show no improvement.[1] Patients with poor pharyngeal contractility in conjunction with normal upper esophageal sphincter function show little improvement with cricopharyngeal myotomy. Patients with oropharyngeal dysphagia secondary to neurologic involvement who have intact voluntary deglutination, adequate pulsion of the tongue, and normal phonation may show improvement with cricopharyngeal myotomy. Appropriate selection of patients for cricopharyngeal myotomy leads to better surgical outcomes.

Transthoracic Hiatal Hernia Repair

Unlike most operations on the esophagus, which are extirpative procedures, hiatal hernia repair with fundoplication is a reconstructive procedure, the aim of which is to restore a high-pressure zone at the esophagogastric junction that prevents reflux but also permits comfortable swallowing. Currently, this repair is often accomplished via minimally invasive approaches; however, such approaches may be hampered by significant perceptual and motor limitations, such as loss of stereopsis, reduced tactile feedback, and decreased range of motion for the instruments. The degree of tension on the hiatal repair sutures, the quality of the crural tissue itself, and the caliber of the esophageal hiatus after repair all must be assessed. In certain patients, laparoscopic reconstruction of a competent gastroesophageal high-pressure zone may be very difficult and may demand a degree of tactile sensitivity that is not yet achievable via video laparoscopy.

The long-term success of antireflux surgery, whether done via the transthoracic approach or by means of laparoscopy, depends on three factors: (1) a tension-free repair that maintains a 4 cm long segment of esophagus in the intra-abdominal position, (2) durable approximation of the diaphragmatic crura, and (3) correct matching of the fundoplication technique chosen to the peristaltic function of the esophagus. The transthoracic approach should be considered whenever the standard abdominal approaches to hiatal hernia repair carry an increased risk of failure or complication—for example, in patients who have a foreshortened esophagus associated with a massive hernia and an incarcerated intrathoracic stomach, patients with severe peptic strictures of the esophagus, patients in whom the hiatal hernia coexists with an esophageal motility disorder or morbid obesity, and patients who have undergone multiple previous abdominal operations. The transthoracic repair is particularly useful when a previous open abdominal procedure has failed. In this situation, the reasons for such failure, whether technical or tissue-related, should be assessed so that a compensatory strategy can be devised.

PREOPERATIVE EVALUATION

Symptomatic Evaluation

All patients being considered for fundoplication to treat GERD must undergo a comprehensive evaluation to determine whether there is indeed an anatomic substrate for their symptoms and what the most appropriate form of repair is. Specifically, a history of heartburn and effortless regurgitation should be sought. Dysphagia and odynophagia are not typically associated with hiatal hernia unless there is a significant paraesophageal component. Persistent dysphagia may reflect the presence of a stricture or a neoplasm [see 28 Dysphagia]. Reflux-induced esophageal spasm may present with occasional episodes of cervical dysphagia, but the transient nature of the symptoms easily differentiates this condition from dysphagia caused by a fixed obstruction. Chest pain that radiates toward the back after meals and is relieved by nonbilious vomiting may indicate the presence of an incarcerated intrathoracic stomach that is hindering the emptying of the paraesophageal component. Atypical chest pain from cholelithiasis, peptic ulcer, or coronary artery disease may confound the diagnosis.

Imaging

Radiographic investigation should begin with a ciné barium swallow, which will yield valuable information regarding the length of the esophagus, its peristaltic function, and the integrity of the mucosal surface. The gastric views can be used for qualitative assessment of distal emptying. Any paraesophageal component will be clearly demonstrated, along with any associated organoaxial volvulus. A simple barium swallow often yields the most useful information for managing the complex problem of recurrent hiatal hernia and a slipped Nissen fundoplication.

Next, esophagogastroscopy should be performed to examine the mucosa for the presence of esophagitis, Barrett's mucosa, stricture, or malignancy. The locations of any lesions observed, along with the position of the squamocolumnar junction, should be carefully documented in terms of their distance from the incisors. All strictures must undergo cup or brush biopsy to rule out an occult malignancy. The presence of severe esophagitis raises the possibility of acquired shortening of the esophagus secondary to transmural inflammation and contraction scarring. Every effort should be made to measure the length of the esophagus accurately.

Dilation

If a stricture is found during esophagoscopy, a decision must be made about whether to attempt esophageal dilation. This procedure carries the risk of perforation and should be performed only after careful consideration. If the stricture is diagnosed at the time of the initial endoscopic examination, it is advisable to perform only the brush biopsy at this point, deferring dilation to a subsequent visit. Delaying dilation gives the surgeon time to reassess the anatomy depicted on the barium swallow, to decide whether wire-guided dilation is necessitated by angulation of the esophagus, to obtain informed consent, to assemble the requisite equipment, and to plan sedation for what is often an uncomfortable procedure. If a malignancy is suspected at the time of the initial endoscopic examination, dilation should be avoided. In this situation, repair is impossible; thus, if iatrogenic perforation of a malignant stricture occurs, the surgeon will have to attempt emergency resection in an inadequately prepared patient in whom proper staging is unlikely to have been completed.

The standard flexible adult esophagoscope is approximately 32 French in caliber. In advancing the scope into the stricture, only very gentle pressure should be necessary. As a rule, a mild stricture that is not associated with steep angulation of the esophagus will readily accept passage of the endoscope and will be amenable to subsequent blind dilation with Hurst-Maloney bougies.

After successful passage, the scope is removed, and sequential insertion of progressively larger dilators (starting at 32 French) into the stricture is attempted. The weight of the dilator alone should be sufficient to effect its passage, with little or no forward force applied. Although the patient will be able to swallow comfortably only after satisfactory passage of a dilator at least 48 French in caliber, it is essential never to try to force passage. To this end, the surgeon must take careful note of the subtle signs of increasing resistance transmitted through the dilator. Sequential dilation should be stopped whenever significant resistance is encountered or blood streaks appear on the dilator. Sudden pain during dilation is an ominous sign and calls for immediate investigation with a swallow study using a water-soluble contrast agent (e.g., Gastrografin; Schering AG, Berlin, Germany). Subcutaneous emphysema in the neck or mediastinal air on a plain chest radiograph may also indicate an injury to the esophagus. Perforation must be definitively ruled out before the patient can be discharged.

Highly stenotic strictures that do not allow the passage of a standard adult endoscope may be associated with a distorted and a steeply angulated esophagus. In such cases, the use of a pediatric endoscope may permit directed placement of a guide wire through the stricture; fluoroscopy is a useful adjunct for this purpose. A series of progressively larger Savary-Gillard dilators may then be passed over the guide wire to enlarge the lumen and allow subsequent endoscopic biopsy. As a rule, much less tactile feedback is available during wire-guided dilation than during passage of standard Maloney-Hurst bougies. Increased pressure is required to pass the Savary-Gillard dilators because of the resistance caused by the wire passing through the dilator itself. It is essential that the wire be well lubricated and not be allowed to dislodge proximally between the sequential insertions of progressively larger dilators. The caveats that apply to blind dilation also apply to wire-guided dilation.

Patients whose esophagus can be dilated to 48 French and who are candidates for antireflux surgery may undergo subsequent intraoperative dilation to 54 to 60 French. Patients who cannot be dilated to 48 French and fail to achieve comfortable swallowing should be classified as having a non-dilatable stricture and should be considered for transhiatal esophagectomy [see Resection of Esophagus and Proximal Stomach, below].

Functional Evaluation

Esophageal manometry permits quantitative assessment of peristalsis, a capability that is critically important for determining which type of fundoplication is most suitable for reconstructing a nonoccluding high-pressure zone at the esophagogastric junction. Stationary pH tests measure the capacity of the esophagus to clear acid, its sensitivity to instilled acid, the relationship of reflux episodes to body position, and the correlation between changes in esophageal pH and the subjective symptoms of heartburn. Ambulatory 24-hour pH testing allows further quantification of reflux episodes with respect to duration, frequency, and association with patient symptoms.

OPERATIVE PLANNING

The transthoracic hiatus hernia repair may be completed with either a partial fundoplication (as in the 240° Belsey Mark IV procedure) or a complete fundoplication (as in the 360° Nissen procedure). Acquired shortening of the esophagus may necessitate lengthening of the esophagus by means of a Collis gastroplasty, in which the portion of the gastric cardia along the lesser curvature and directly contiguous to the distal esophagus is fashioned into a tube [see Operative Technique, Step 6a, below].

A thoracic epidural catheter is placed for regional analgesia. General anesthesia is administered, and flexible esophagoscopy is performed by the operating team. Insufflation should be done with as little air as is practical, particularly in the case of large paraesophageal hernias. The extent of the pathologic condition is documented and the absence of malignancy verified. The stomach is decompressed with suction, and the endoscope is removed. An orogastric tube is placed while the patient is supine.

Tracheal intubation is performed with either a standard single-lumen endotracheal tube or a double-lumen tube. The former requires that the ventilated left lung be retracted cephalad with moist packs during the procedure; the latter allows lung isolation and is preferred by some surgeons. A Foley catheter is placed; central venous access generally is not required. Subcutaneous heparin is administered for DVT prophylaxis, and pneumatic calf compression devices are applied. Antibiotic prophylaxis is provided [see 5 Prevention of Postoperative Infection].

The patient is positioned for a left thoracotomy. The table is flexed to distract the ribs. An axillary roll is placed to protect the right brachial plexus. The right leg is bent at hip and knee while the left leg is kept straight. Pillows are placed between the legs, and all pressure points are padded. The arms are positioned so that the humeri are at right angles to the chest and the elbows are bent 90°.

OPERATIVE TECHNIQUE

Step 1: Incision and Entry into Chest

A standard left posterolateral thoracotomy is performed. The latissimus dorsi is divided. The serratus fascia is incised, but the muscle itself can generally be preserved. For most patients, the sixth interspace is the most appropriate incision site for exposing the hiatus. The seventh interspace can also be used, particularly if the patient is tall or has a hyperextended chest as a result of chronic pulmonary disease. The paraspinal muscles are elevated away from the posterior aspect of the adjacent ribs, and a 1 cm segment of the rib below the selected interspace is resected to facilitate exposure. The chest is then entered, and the lung and the pleural space are thoroughly inspected. The leaves of the retractor are spread slowly over the course of the next several minutes so as not to cause iatrogenic rib fractures.

Step 2: Mobilization of Esophagus and Excision of Hernia Sac

The inferior pulmonary ligament is divided with the electrocautery to the level of the inferior pulmonary vein [see Figure 4]. The mediastinal pleura overlying the esophagus is longitudinally incised to expose the esophagus from the level of the carina to the diaphragm. Particular care is taken to avoid injury to the vagi. Vessels supplying the esophagus and arising from the adjacent aorta are cauterized and divided. A few larger vessels may have to be ligated with 2-0 silk. The esophagus is encircled just below the inferior pulmonary vein with a wide Penrose drain [see Figure 4]. The two vagi are mobilized and carried with the esophagus. (The right vagus is located along the right anterior border of the descending aorta and can easily be missed.)

The esophagus is then elevated, and mobilization is circumferentially completed in the direction of the diaphragm, starting from the level of the carina. In cases of giant paraesophageal hernia or reoperation for a failed repair, the stomach will have a large intrathoracic component. Dissection continues inferiorly to separate the sac from the pericardium anteriorly and the aorta posteriorly. The right pleura is closely approximated to the esophagus for 2 to 5 cm above the diaphragm; in the presence of a substantial hiatal hernia and its sac, it may be difficult to identify. The right pleura should be gently dissected away from the sac without entry into

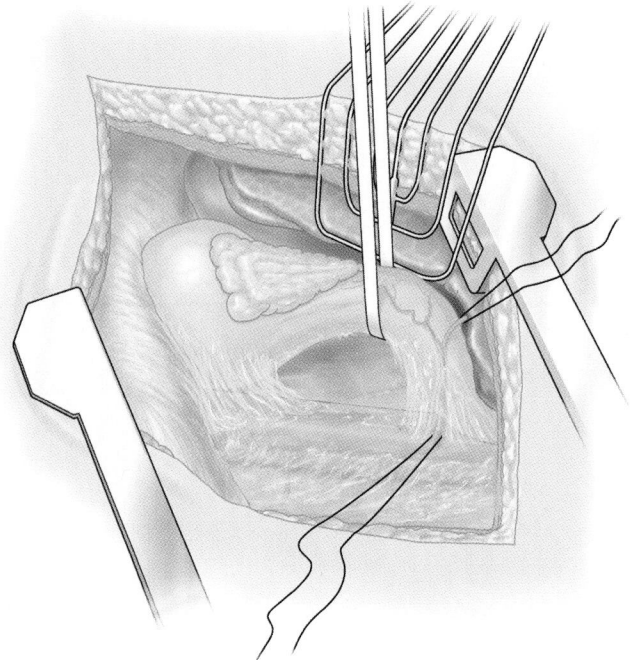

Figure 4 Transthoracic hiatal hernia repair. The lung is retracted, and the inferior pulmonary ligament is divided to the level of the inferior pulmonary vein. The mediastinal pleura overlying the esophagus is incised to expose the esophagus from the level of the carina to the diaphragm. The esophagus and both vagi are encircled just below the inferior pulmonary vein with a Penrose drain. Vessels supplying the esophagus and arising from the adjacent aorta are ligated and divided.

the right chest. This can generally be done with a small sponge on a stick. If a tear occurs, it should be closed with absorbable suture material to prevent accumulation of blood and fluid on the right side during the operation.

Dissection is continued inferiorly to expose the right and left crura. The left crus is generally more robust and is certain to be easily seen with this exposure. Its medial fibers may be attenuated and may blend into the hernia sac superiorly. The sac should be incised 1 cm above the muscle fibers because the muscle alone will not hold sutures well for the subsequent repair. Skeletonization of the crural muscle must be avoided; it is the fibroconnective tissue that provides the most tensile strength. The hernia sac is dissected away from the left crus in an anterior-to-posterior direction. The right crus is generally less robust than the left. In the case of a previous failed repair, the right crus may be very difficult to see, being obscured from the operator's view by the intrathoracic stomach. Dissection of the right crus is best accomplished in a posterior-to-anterior direction.

Once the sac is circumferentially freed from the crura, dissection proceeds cephalad along the esophagus. To minimize the risk of vagal injury, the sac should be incised parallel to the esophagus.

Step 3: Division of Phrenoesophageal Membrane and Gastrohepatic Ligament

The esophagus is retracted anteriorly to expose the posteriorly located phrenoesophageal membrane, which is then divided to yield entry into the lesser sac. The remainder of the phrenoesophageal membrane is elevated with a right-angle clamp as it courses anteriorly, yielding a view of the spleen below. The esophagus and the stomach are thus completely mobilized from the left crus. The esophageal branch of the left phrenic artery, visible near the left vagus, is divided near the crus.

The uppermost portion of the gastrohepatic ligament is found along the undersurface of the right crus. It is divided with the electrocautery. Belsey's artery, a communicating branch between the left gastric artery and the inferior phrenic artery, lies in this area and may have to be ligated directly. It is vital to divide the gastrohepatic ligament down to the level of the left gastric artery. The caudate lobe of the liver must be clearly visible beneath the right crus. This opening is essential for subsequent passage of the fundoplication wrap behind the esophagus.

Step 4: Mobilization of the Stomach

The highest short gastric arteries are ligated between ties to permit mobilization of the fundus. Excessive traction must be avoided to prevent splenic injury. Three or four vessels are usually divided. The esophagogastric junction is elevated well into the chest, and any organoaxial rotation of the stomach is released as the short gastric vessels are divided. It is crucial that ligation be limited to the vessels along the greater curvature. Inadvertent ligation of the vessels along the lesser curvature can easily occur, especially if there was a previous operation. Loss of blood supply from the branches of the left gastric artery along the lesser curvature will lead to ischemia of the Collis gastroplasty tube and will predispose to either leakage at the staple line or subsequent stricture formation.

In the case of a redo repair, the previous fundoplication often will have slipped down onto the cardia or even onto the body of the stomach. Generally, the inner aspect of the previous fundoplication can be freed from the esophagus without any difficulty; rarely will any major dissection have been done in this area during the original operation. The vagi will be found within the wrap and should be specifically visualized. Because of scarring, it may be difficult to see the point at which the previous fundoplication attaches to itself. Not uncommonly, a serosal tear develops on the fundus as the wrap is undone. Any areas of concern can be reinforced

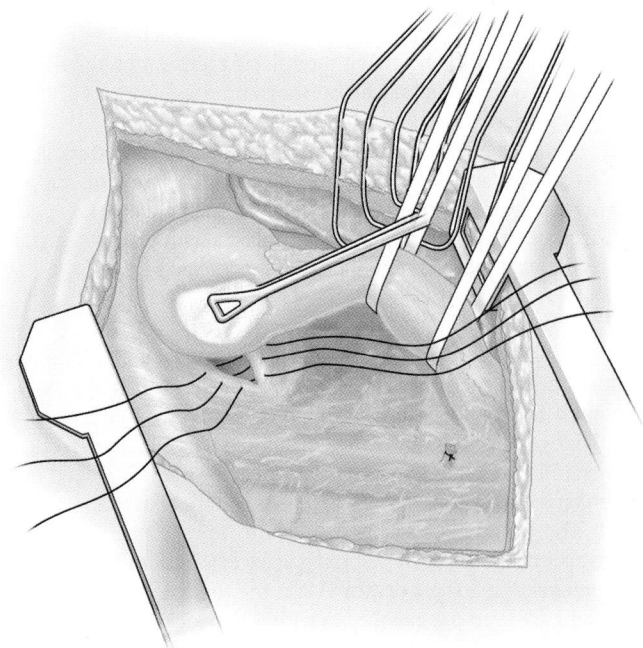

Figure 5 Transthoracic hiatal hernia repair. The esophagogastric junction is mobilized by dividing the phrenoesophageal ligament and some short gastric vessels. No. 1 silk sutures are passed through the exterior aspect of the right crus (with care taken to avoid the adjacent inferior vena cava) and through the left crus (with care taken to avoid the spleen).

with a simple stitch of 4-0 silk. Mobilization is complete when the fundus is restored to its original anatomic position and the greater curvature can be followed down to the left gastroepiploic artery.

Step 5: Closure of Crura

Because the right crus is often quite attenuated, it is crucial to incorporate an adequate amount of tissue into the repair. An Allis or Babcock clamp is placed at the apex of the hiatus and into the central tendon so that both crura can be placed under tension. The esophagus is retracted anteriorly, and a No. 1 silk suture is passed through the most posterior aspect of the left crus, with care taken to avoid the adjacent spleen [see Figure 5]. A notched spoon retractor is placed through the hiatus and into the abdomen behind the left crus. The spleen is thus protected while the suture is brought through the left crus.

Next, the suture is brought out through the right crus, with care taken to prevent injury to the aorta or entry through the right pleura. Three to five crural repair stitches are then placed at 1 cm intervals, from posterior to anterior. The sutures should be staggered slightly so that the needle entry points are not all in a straight line; this measure helps prevent longitudinal shredding of the muscle fibers when the sutures are placed under tension. The sutures are held together with hemostats but left untied at this point in the operation.

Placement of traction on the last suture should close the defect while still allowing easy passage of one finger along the esophagus. The final decision on whether to tie this last suture or to cut it out is made later, after construction of the fundoplication. It is better to err on the side of an overly narrow opening: removing a suture is easier than having to place an extra one at a time when exposure is less than optimal.

Step 6: Assessment of Esophageal Length and Removal of Anterior Fat Pad

After placement of the crural stitches, an assessment of the esophageal length is made. Ideally, the stomach can easily be reduced into the abdomen without placing tension on the thoracic esophagus. When esophageal foreshortening is found, a Collis gastroplasty is performed [see Step 6a, below].

If an esophageal stricture is present, the assistant performs dilation by passing a tapered bougie orally while the surgeon supports the esophagus. The anteriorly located esophageal fat pad is removed in anticipation of the gastroplasty, with care taken not to injure the vagi located on either side [see Figure 6].

Step 6a: Collis Gastroplasty

In a Collis gastroplasty for a short esophagus, a stapler is used to form a 4 to 5 cm neoesophagus out of the proximal stomach, thereby effectively lengthening the esophagus and transposing the esophagogastric junction more distally. A large-caliber Maloney bougie (54 French for women, 56 French for men) is placed in the esophagus to prevent narrowing of the lumen as the stapler is fired. The bougie is advanced well into the stomach so that its widest portion rests at the esophagogastric junction. The bougie is held against the lesser curvature, and the fundus is retracted away at a right angle to the esophagus with a Babcock clamp. A 60 mm gastrointestinal anastomosis (GIA) stapler loaded with 3.5 mm staples is applied immediately alongside the bougie on the greater curvature side [see Figure 7a] and fired, simultaneously cutting and stapling the cardia. The staple line is oversewn with nonabsorbable 4-0 monofilament suture material on both sides [see Figure 7b]. Two metal clips are placed to mark the distal extent of the gastroplasty tube, denoting the new esophagogastric junction.

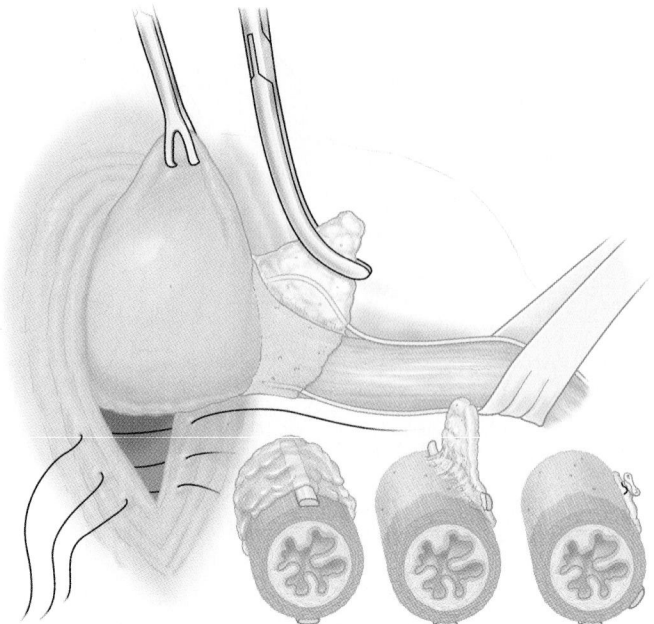

Figure 6 Transthoracic hiatal hernia repair. The anterior fat pad is removed from the esophagus with sharp dissection, with care taken to avoid injury to the vagi.

Step 7: Fundoplication and Reduction of Wrap into Abdomen

The fundus is passed posteriorly behind the esophagus and brought up against the anterior stomach, with care taken to avoid torsion of the fundal wrap. The fundus is then wrapped either over the lower 2 cm of the esophagus, if no gastroplasty was done, or over a 2 cm length of the gastroplasty tube while the bougie is in place. The seromuscular layer of the fundus is approximated to that of the esophagus or the gastroplasty tube and that of the adjacent anterior stomach with two interrupted 2-0 silk sutures [see Figure 8]. When tied, the wrap should still be loose enough to accommodate a finger alongside the esophagus. The fundoplication sutures are again oversewn with a continuous seromuscular nonabsorbable monofilament suture. Two clips are placed at the superior aspect of the wrap. These, along with the previously placed clips, help confirm both the length and the location of the wrap on chest x-ray.

Once the fundoplication is complete, the dilator is removed and the wrap is reduced into the abdomen. Two mattress sutures of 2-0 polypropylene are placed to secure the top of the fundoplication to the underside of the diaphragm. The crural sutures are then sequentially tied, from the most posterior one to the most anterior. When the final suture is tied, one finger should still be able to pass through the hiatus alongside the esophagus.

Step 8: Drainage and Closure

A nasogastric tube is passed into the stomach and secured. Hemostasis is verified, and a single thoracostomy tube is placed. The wound is closed in layers. A chest x-ray is performed to verify the position of the tubes and the location of the clips marking the wrap. The patient is then extubated in the OR and transported to the recovery area.

POSTOPERATIVE CARE

Patients typically remain in the hospital for 5 days. The nasogastric tube is left on low suction and removed on postoperative day 3. Patients then begin liquid oral intake, advancing to a full fluid

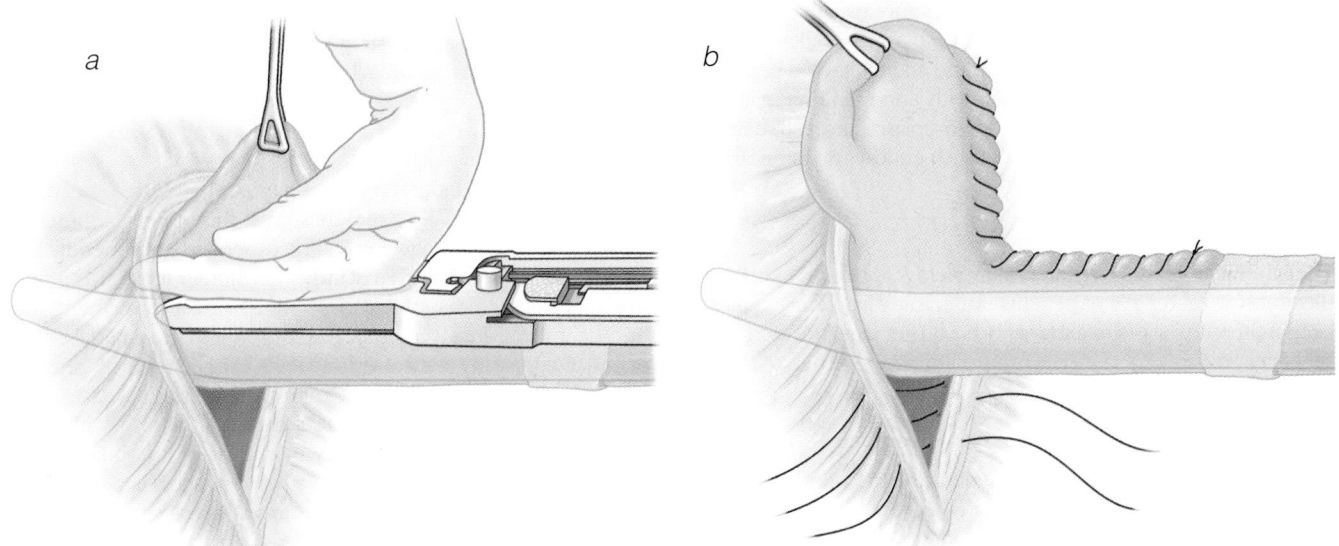

Figure 7 **Transthoracic hiatal hernia repair. (*a*) If esophageal foreshortening is present, a Collis gastro-plasty is performed. A 54 French Maloney bougie is inserted through the esophagogastric junction. A 4 to 5 cm neoesophagus is formed with a 60 mm GIA stapler loaded with 3.5 mm staples. (*b*) Both the fundal staple line and the lesser curvature staple line are oversewn with nonabsorbable monofilament suture.**

diet as tolerated. Early ambulation is encouraged to prevent respiratory complications. Judicious use of analgesics and antiemetics minimizes nausea and vomiting. The thoracostomy tube is removed as drainage subsides. The epidural and Foley catheters are generally removed later the same day. A barium swallow is performed on postoperative day 5 to verify the position of the wrap, to ensure that there is no significant esophageal obstruction, and to provide a qualitative impression of gastric emptying. Gastroparesis secondary to vagal nerve dysfunction may be apparent.

Once patients can tolerate a soft solid diet, they are discharged home with instructions about the gradual resumption of a normal diet at home. Large meals and carbonated beverages should be avoided in the early postoperative period.

COMPLICATIONS

The root causes of the complications arising after transthoracic hiatal hernia repair are often technical; thus, the best prevention, in most cases, is meticulous surgical technique. Mobilization of the stomach with ligation of short gastric vessels may result in injury to the spleen. Injury to the vagi predisposes to gastric dysfunction, early satiety, and so-called gas-bloat syndrome. Poor crural approximation increases the chances that the repair will fail. Dehiscence allows upward migration of the wrap into the chest or the development of a paraesophageal hernia. The gastroplasty may leak at the staple line. Overzealous dissection along the lesser curvature can devascularize the cardia and cause ischemic stenosis of the gastroplasty tube. Torsion of the fundus results in perforation and sepsis. Excessive distraction of the ribs can lead to pain and splinting with subsequent atelectasis or pneumonia. Inadequate mobilization of the fundus may place excessive tension on the wrap and promote later disruption and recurrent reflux. A slipped Nissen can result when the wrap is inadequately fixed to the esophagus or the gastroplasty tube and the stomach telescopes through the intact fundoplication to assume an hourglass configuration. This event leads to varying degrees of heartburn, regurgitation, and dysphagia because the proximal pouch tends to empty slowly and remain distended after meals. A wrap that is too tight or too long results in persistent dysphagia.

Recurrent heartburn and regurgitation call for evaluation with contrast studies and esophagoscopy. The barium swallow is the most useful test for assessing whether the repair has failed. If there is an anatomic condition that is responsible for recurrent symptoms (e.g., slipping of the fundoplication or disruption of the crural repair), reoperation is usually necessary; continued medical treatment of symptoms related to a structural failure invariably proves to be of little use. A barium swallow may also identify gastroparesis secondary to vagal nerve injury. Nuclear transit studies for gastric emptying will help confirm this diagnosis. Dysphagia that is not

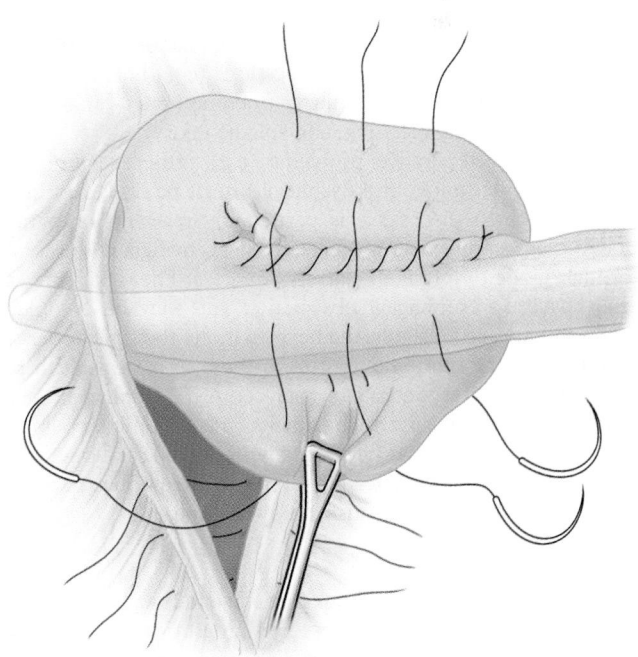

Figure 8 **Transthoracic hiatal hernia repair. The fundus is passed behind the esophagus and sewn to the neoesophagus and the anterior stomach over a 2 cm length with interrupted 2.0 silk sutures.**

related to recurrent reflux, ulceration, or stricture usually responds to dilation; reoperation is not required if the barium swallow shows contrast flowing through the esophagus and an intact wrap beneath the diaphragm. Given that patients with longstanding gastroesophageal reflux are at higher risk for dysplasia and esophageal adenocarcinoma, it is important to perform endoscopy in order to rule out malignancy.

OUTCOME EVALUATION

Transthoracic hiatal hernia repair yields good to excellent results in more than 85% of patients undergoing a primary repair. Approximately 75% of patients who have previously undergone hiatal hernia repair experience symptomatic improvement.[2]

Resection of Esophagus and Proximal Stomach

In the remainder of the chapter, we describe the standard open techniques for resection of the esophagus and the esophagogastric junction. Transhiatal esophagectomy is commonly performed to treat end-stage benign esophageal disease and carcinomas of the cardia and the lower esophagus. Esophageal resection through a combined laparotomy–right thoracotomy approach is ideal for cancers of the middle and upper esophagus. The gastric conduit may be anastomosed to the cervical esophagus either high in the right chest (as in an Ivor-Lewis esophagectomy) or in the neck (as in a transhiatal esophagectomy). The left thoracoabdominal approach is rarely used but may be indicated for resection of the distal esophagus and the proximal stomach in the case of a bulky tumor that is locally aggressive.

PREOPERATIVE EVALUATION

Thorough preoperative preparation is essential for good postoperative outcome. Smoking cessation and a graded regimen of home exercise will help minimize postoperative complications and encourage early mobilization. Schematic diagrams have proved useful for educating patients and shaping their expectations about quality of life and ability to swallow after esophagectomy. Illustrations, by emphasizing the anatomic relations, greatly facilitate discussion of potential complications (e.g., hoarseness from recurrent laryngeal nerve injury, pneumothorax, anastomotic leakage, mediastinal bleeding, and splenic injury).

Potential postoperative problems (e.g., reflux, regurgitation, early satiety, dumping, and dysphagia) must be discussed before operation. Such discussion is particularly relevant for patients undergoing esophagectomy for early-stage malignant tumors or for high-grade dysplasia in Barrett's mucosa. These patients generally have no esophageal obstruction and may be completely asymptomatic; accordingly, their expectations about postoperative function may be quite different from those of patients with profound dysphagia secondary to near-complete esophageal occlusion. Support groups in which patients with upcoming operations can contact patients that have already undergone treatment have proved to be highly beneficial to all parties. Realistic expectations improve the chances of a satisfactory outcome.

Evaluation of Operative Risk

Preoperative assessment should include a thorough review of the patient's cardiopulmonary reserve and an estimate of the level of operative risk. Spirometry, arterial blood gas analysis, and exercise stress testing should be considered. Even when a transhiatal esophagectomy without thoracotomy is planned, patients should be assessed with an eye to whether they can tolerate a laparotomy and a thoracotomy, in case the latter is made necessary by findings that

become apparent only at the time of operation. Thoracic epidural analgesia should be administered for pain control. If an Ivor-Lewis or thoracoabdominal approach is taken, a double-lumen endotracheal tube should be placed for separate lung ventilation.

Imaging

Contrast esophagography, esophagoscopy with biopsy, and contrast-enhanced CT of the chest and the upper abdomen are required before esophagectomy. The esophagogram identifies the location of the tumor and may indicate whether it extends into the proximal stomach. Esophagoscopy allows direct assessment of the mucosa, precise localization of the tumor, and collection of tissue for histologic study. Retroflexion views of the stomach, after distention with air, are particularly important if proximal gastric invasion is suspected, in which case esophagogastrectomy with reconstruction of alimentary continuity by means of intestinal interposition may be required. In cases of midesophageal cancer, a bronchoscopy is mandatory to rule out airway involvement. The carina and the proximal left mainstem bronchus are the sites that are most at risk for local invasion.

Contrast-enhanced CT scans of the chest and abdomen are standard. Thoracic and abdominal CT scans yield information on the extent of any celiac or mediastinal adenopathy, the degree of esophageal thickening, and the possibility of invasion of the adjacent aorta or tracheobronchial tree. The lung parenchyma is assessed for metastatic nodules, as are the liver and the adrenal glands. When the distal extent of tumor cannot be defined as a result of near-complete obstruction on endoscopy, a prone abdominal CT can help differentiate a tumor at the gastric cardia from a collapsed but normal stomach. If the obstruction is not complete, the stomach can be distended with air (through either the ingestion of effervescent granules or the passage of a small-bore nasogastric tube) to improve visualization. A prone CT also yields improved imaging of the gastrohepatic and celiac lymph nodes by allowing the stomach to fall away from these adjacent structures. Metastatic cancer in the celiac lymph nodes portends a very poor prognosis and is a contraindication to resection.

PET scanning is useful for the detection of occult distant metastases that preclude curative resection. Suspicious areas should undergo needle biopsy or laparoscopic or thoracoscopic assessment. Similarly, pleural effusions [*see 31 Pleural Effusion*] must be tapped for cytologic evaluation. Invasion of mediastinal structures and the presence of distant metastases are contraindications to transhiatal esophagectomy.

At present, EUS, though quite sensitive for detection of paraesophageal adenopathy, is incapable of differentiating reactive lymph nodes from nodes invaded by malignancy. CT and PET have limitations, and thus, locoregional involvement may not be recognized before resection is attempted. In patients who are marginal candidates for surgical treatment and in whom metastatic disease is suspected, thoracoscopy and laparoscopy have been advocated for histologic evaluation of mediastinal lymph nodes, pleural or peritoneal abnormalities, and celiac nodes. Although this approach adds to the cost of investigation, it can save the patient from having to undergo a major operation for what would later prove to be an incurable condition.

Neoadjuvant Therapy

Patients with esophageal cancer who are candidates for resection may benefit from neoadjuvant chemotherapy and concurrent radiation therapy. In particular, patients with good performance status and bulky disease should be considered for such therapy. To date, no randomized trials have conclusively demonstrated a survival benefit with this approach, but several series have documented a 20% to 30% rate of complete response with no viable tumor found at the time of resection. After chemoradiation, patients are restaged with a barium swallow and CT. PET scanning after treatment may yield spurious results, in that inflammatory conditions can mimic the increased tracer uptake seen in malignant tissue. Microscopic disease cannot be assessed, and scarring from radiation may further confound the situation by preventing tracer uptake in areas that actually harbor malignancy.

If there are no contraindications to surgical treatment, resection is scheduled 2 to 3 weeks after the completion of neoadjuvant therapy. This interval allows time for patients to return to their baseline activity level and for any induced hematologic abnormalities to be corrected. Previous chemoradiation therapy does not make transhiatal esophagectomy significantly more difficult or complicated. Many tumors are downstaged and less bulky at the time of resection. In centers with experience in this approach, the rates of bleeding and anastomotic leakage remain low.

OPERATIVE PLANNING

Transhiatal Esophagectomy

In transhiatal esophagectomy, the stomach is mobilized through a short upper midline laparotomy, the esophagus is mobilized from adjacent mediastinal structures via dissection through the hiatus without the use of a thoracotomy, and the stomach is transposed through the posterior mediastinum and anastomosed to the cervical esophagus at the level of the clavicles. The main advantages of this approach are (1) a proximal surgical margin that is well away from the tumor site, (2) an extrathoracic esophagogastric anastomosis that is easily accessible in the event of complications, and (3) reduced overall operative trauma. Single-center studies throughout the world have shown transhiatal esophagectomy to be safe and well tolerated, even in patients who may have significantly reduced cardiopulmonary reserve. Long-term survival is equivalent to that reported after transthoracic esophagectomy.

Although transhiatal esophagectomy has been used for resection of tumors at any location in the esophagus, it is best suited for resection of tumors in the lower esophagus and at the esophagogastric junction. It should also be considered the operation of choice for certain advanced nonmalignant conditions of the esophagus. Nondilatable strictures of the esophagus may occur as an end-stage complication of gastroesophageal reflux. Intractable reflux after failed hiatal hernia repair may not be amenable to further attempts at reconstruction of the esophagogastric junction and thus may call for esophagectomy. Because of the high cervical anastomosis, a transhiatal esophagectomy is less likely to predispose to postoperative reflux and recurrent stricture formation than a transthoracic esophagectomy would be. Achalasia may result in a sigmoid megaesophagus and dysphagia that cannot be managed without removal of the esophagus. Transhiatal esophagectomy permits complete removal of the thoracic esophagus and, in the majority of patients, restoration of comfortable swallowing without the need for a thoracotomy.

Generally, patients are admitted to the hospital on the day of the operation. Thoracic epidural analgesia is administered, both intraoperatively and postoperatively, and appropriate antibiotic prophylaxis is provided [*see 5 Prevention of Postoperative Infection*]. Heparin, 5,000 U subcutaneously, is given before induction, and pneumatic calf compression devices are applied. A radial artery catheter is placed to permit continuous monitoring of blood pressure. Central venous access is rarely required. General anesthesia is administered via an uncut single-lumen endotracheal tube.

Flexible esophagoscopy is performed (if it was not previously performed by the surgical team). A nasogastric tube is placed before final positioning and draping.

The patient is placed in the supine position with a small rolled sheet between the shoulders. The arms are secured to the sides, and the head is rotated to the right with the neck extended. The neck, the chest, and the abdomen are prepared as a single sterile field. The drapes are placed so as to expose the patient from the left ear to the pubis. The operative field is extended laterally to the anterior axillary lines to permit placement of thoracostomy tubes as needed. A self-retaining table-mounted retractor is used to facilitate upward and lateral traction along the costal margin.

Ivor-Lewis Esophagectomy

At many institutions, Ivor-Lewis esophagectomy is preferred because it provides excellent direct exposure for dissection of the intrathoracic esophagus, in that it combines a right thoracotomy with a laparotomy. This procedure should be considered when there is concern regarding the extent of esophageal fixation within the mediastinum. One advantage of Ivor-Lewis esophagectomy is that an extensive local lymphadenectomy can easily be performed through the right thoracotomy. Any attachments to mediastinal structures can be freed under direct vision. Whether any regional lymph node dissection is necessary is highly controversial; no significant survival advantage has yet been demonstrated. Long-term survival after Ivor-Lewis resection is equivalent to that after transhiatal esophagectomy.[3]

The main disadvantages of the Ivor-Lewis procedure are (1) the physiologic impact of the two major access incisions employed (a right thoracotomy and a midline laparotomy) and (2) the location of the anastomosis (in the chest, at the level of the azygos vein). Incision-related pain may hinder deep breathing and the clearing of bronchial secretions, resulting in atelectasis and pneumonia. Complications of the intrathoracic anastomosis may be hard to manage. Although the anastomotic leakage rate associated with Ivor-Lewis esophagectomy has typically been 5% or lower—and thus substantially lower than the rate cited for the cervical anastomosis after transhiatal esophagectomy—intrathoracic leaks are much more dangerous and difficult to handle than intracervial leaks. In many cases, drainage of the leak will be incomplete and empyema will result. Reoperation may prove necessary to manage mediastinitis.

Left Thoracoabdominal Esophagogastrectomy

The left thoracoabdominal approach is indicated for resection of the distal esophagus and the proximal stomach when removal of the stomach necessitates the use of an intestinal substitute to restore swallowing. If the proximal stomach must be resected for adequate resection margins to be obtained, then the distal stomach may be anastomosed to the esophagus in the chest. This operation is frequently associated with significant esophagitis from bile reflux, and dysphagia is common. Consequently, many surgeons prefer to resect the entire stomach and the distal esophagus and then to restore swallowing with a Roux-en-Y jejunal interposition anastomosed to the residual thoracic esophagus.

OPERATIVE TECHNIQUE

Transhiatal Esophagectomy

Transhiatal esophagectomy is best understood as consisting of three components: abdominal, mediastinal, and cervical. The abdominal portion involves mobilization of the stomach, pyloromyotomy, and placement of a temporary feeding jejunostomy.

Step 1: incision and entry into peritoneum A midline laparotomy is performed from the tip of the xiphoid to the umbilicus. The peritoneum is opened to the left of the midline so that the falciform and the preperitoneal fat may be retracted en bloc to the right. Body wall retractors are placed at 45° angles from the midline to elevate and distract both costal margins. The retractors are placed so as to lift up the costal margin gently and open the wound. The abdomen is then inspected for metastases.

Step 2: division of gastrohepatic ligament and mobilization of distal esophagus The left lobe of the liver is mobilized by dividing the triangular ligament, then folded to the right and held in this position with a moist laparotomy pad and a deep-bladed self-retaining retractor. Next, the gastrohepatic ligament is divided. Occasionally, there is an aberrant left hepatic artery arising from the left gastric artery [see Figure 9]. The peritoneum over the right crus is incised, and the hiatus is palpated; the extent and mobility of any tumor may then be assessed. The peritoneum over the left crus is similarly divided, and the esophagus is encircled with a 2.5 cm Penrose drain. Traction is applied to draw the esophagogastric junction upward and to the right; this measure facilitates exposure of the short gastric arteries coursing to the fundus and the cardia.

Step 3: mobilization of stomach The greater curvature of the stomach is inspected and the right gastroepiploic artery palpated. The lesser sac is generally entered near the midpoint of the greater curvature. The transition zone between the right gastroepiploic arcade and the short gastric arteries is usually devoid of blood vessels. A moist sponge is placed behind the spleen to elevate it and facilitate subsequent control of the short gastric vessels.

Dissection then proceeds along the greater curvature toward the pylorus. The omentum is mobilized from the right gastroepiploic artery. Vessels are ligated between 2-0 silk ties, and great care is exercised to avoid placing excessive traction on the arterial arcade. A 1 cm margin is always maintained between the line of dissection and the right gastroepiploic artery. Venous injuries, in particular, can occur with injudicious handling of tissue. The ultrasonic scalpel is particularly efficient and effective for mobilization of the stomach; again, this instrument must be applied well away from the gastroepiploic arcade. Dissection is continued rightward to the level of the pylorus. It should be noted that the location of the gastroepiploic artery in this area may vary; often, it is at some unexpected distance from the stomach wall. Posterior adhesions between the stomach and the pancreas are lysed so that the lesser sac can be completely opened.

The assistant's left hand is then placed into the lesser sac to retract the stomach gently to the right and place the short gastric vessels on tension. The Penrose drain previously placed around the esophagus facilitates exposure by retracting the cardia to the right. Dissection along the greater curvature proceeds cephalad. The vessels are divided well away from the wall of the stomach to prevent injury to the fundus. Clamps should never be placed on the stomach. A high short gastric artery is typically encountered just adjacent to the left crus. Precise technique is required to prevent injury to the spleen. The Penrose drain [see Step 2, above] is exposed as the peritoneum is opened over the left crus. Mobilization of the proximal stomach and liberation of the distal esophagus are thereby completed.

Once the stomach has been completely mobilized along the greater curvature, it is elevated and rotated to the right [see Figure

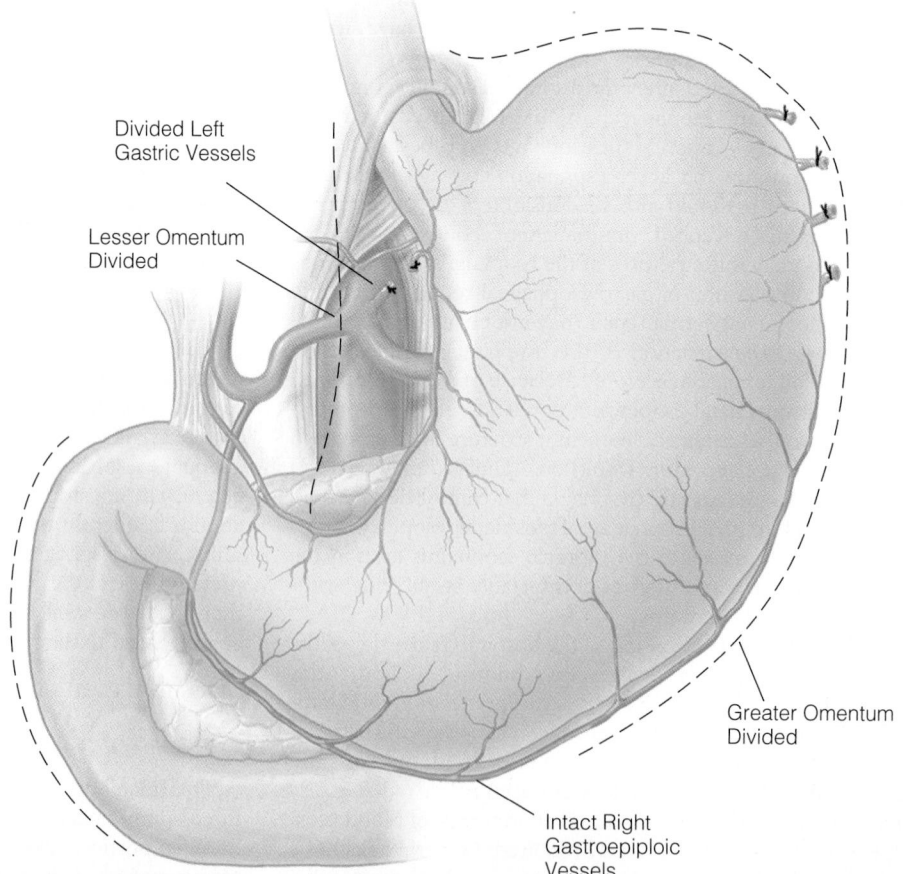

Divided Left Gastric Vessels

Lesser Omentum Divided

Greater Omentum Divided

Intact Right Gastroepiploic Vessels

Figure 9 **Transhiatal esophagectomy. The duodenum is mobilized, and the gastrohepatic and gastrocolic omenta are divided.**

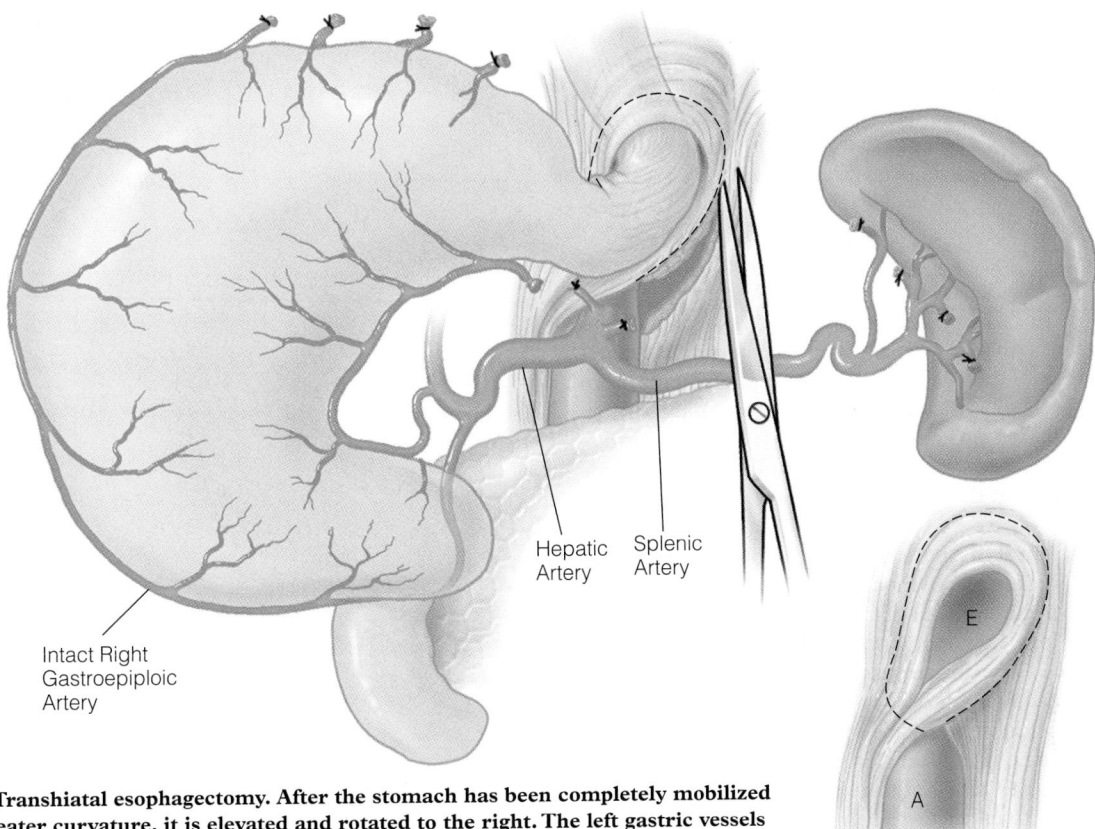

Hepatic Artery

Splenic Artery

Intact Right Gastroepiploic Artery

E

A

Figure 10   **Transhiatal esophagectomy. After the stomach has been completely mobilized along the greater curvature, it is elevated and rotated to the right. The left gastric vessels are suture-ligated and divided. A 1 cm margin of the diaphragmatic crura is taken in continuity with the esophagogastric junction, providing ample clearance of the tumor and improved exposure of the lower mediastinum.**

10]; the left gastric artery and associated nodal tissues can then be visualized via the lesser sac. The superior edge of the pancreas is visible, and the remaining posterior attachments of the stomach are divided along the hiatus and the left crus. These may be quite extensive if there has been a history of pancreatitis or preoperative radiation therapy.

If the operation is being done for malignant disease, a final determination of resectability can be made at this point. Tumor fixation to the aorta or the retroperitoneum can be assessed. Celiac and paraortic lymph nodes can be palpated and, if necessary, sent for biopsy. The left gastric artery and vein are then ligated proximally, either through the lesser sac or directly through the divided gastrohepatic ligament. All nodal tissue is dissected free in anticipation of subsequent removal en bloc with the specimen.

Step 4: mobilization of duodenum and pyloromyotomy
The duodenum is mobilized with a Kocher maneuver. Careful attention to the superior extent of this dissection is critical. Adhesions to either the porta hepatis or the gallbladder must be divided to ensure that the pylorus is sufficiently freed for later migration to the diaphragmatic hiatus.

Gastric drainage is provided by a pyloromyotomy. Two figure-eight traction sutures of 2-0 cardiovascular silk are placed deeply through both the superior and the inferior border of the pylorus; traction is then placed on these sutures to provide both exposure and some degree of hemostasis. The pyloromyotomy is begun 2 to 3 cm on the gastric side of the pylorus. The serosa and the muscle are divided with a needle-tipped electrocautery to expose the submucosa; generally, these layers of the stomach are robust, making the proper plane easy to find.

Dissection is extended toward the duodenum with the aid of a fine-tipped right-angle clamp. The duodenal submucosa, recognizable by its fatty deposits and yellow coloration, is exposed for approximately 0.5 cm. The duodenal submucosa is usually much more superficial than expected, and accidental entry into the duodenum often occurs just past the left edge of the circular muscle of the pylorus. Releasing the tension on the traction sutures helps the surgeon visualize the proper depth of dissection. Should entry into the lumen occur, a simple repair using interrupted fine monofilament (4-0 or 5-0 polypropylene) sutures to close the mucosa is performed. Small metal clips are applied to the knots of the traction sutures before removal of the ends; these clips serve to indicate the level of the pyloromyotomy on subsequent radiographic studies.

Step 5: feeding jejunostomy   Placement of a standard Weitzel jejunal feeding tube approximately 30 cm from the ligament of Treitz completes the abdominal portion of the transhiatal esophagectomy.

Step 6: exposure and encirclement of cervical esophagus
The cervical esophagus is exposed through a 6 cm incision along the anterior edge of the left sternocleidomastoid muscle [*see Figure 1*] that is centered over the level of the cricoid cartilage. The platysma is divided to expose the omohyoid, which is divided at its tendon. The strap muscles are divided low in the neck. The esophagus and its indwelling nasogastric tube can be palpated.

The carotid sheath is retracted laterally, and blunt dissection is employed to reach the prevertebral fascia. The inferior thyroid artery is ligated laterally; the recurrent laryngeal nerve is visible just deep and medial to this vessel. No retractor other than the surgeon's finger should be applied medially: traction injury to the recurrent laryngeal nerve will result in both vocal cord palsy and uncoordinated swallowing with aspiration. In particular, metal retractors must not be used in this area. The tracheoesophageal groove is incised close to the esophageal wall while gentle finger traction is applied cephalad to elevate the thyroid cartilage toward the right. This measure usually suffices to define the location of the nerve.

The esophagus is then encircled by passing a right-angle clamp posteriorly from left to right while the surgeon's finger remains in the tracheoesophageal groove. The tip of the clamp is brought into the pulp of the fingertip. The medially located recurrent laryngeal nerve and the membranous trachea are thereby protected from injury. The clamp is brought around, and a narrow Penrose drain is passed around the esophagus [see Figure 11]. Blunt finger dissection is employed to develop the anterior and posterior planes around the esophagus at the level of the thoracic inlet.

Step 7: mediastinal dissection   Some authors describe this portion of the procedure as a blunt dissection, but in fact, the vast majority of the mediastinal mobilization is done under direct vision. Narrow, long-handled, handheld, curved Harrington retractors are placed into the hiatus and lifted up to expose the distal esophagus. Caudal traction is placed on the esophagus, allowing excellent visualization of the hiatus and the distal esophagus. Long right-angle clamps are used to expose these attachments. Vascularity in this area is often minimal, and hemostasis can easily be achieved with either the electrocautery or the ultrasonic

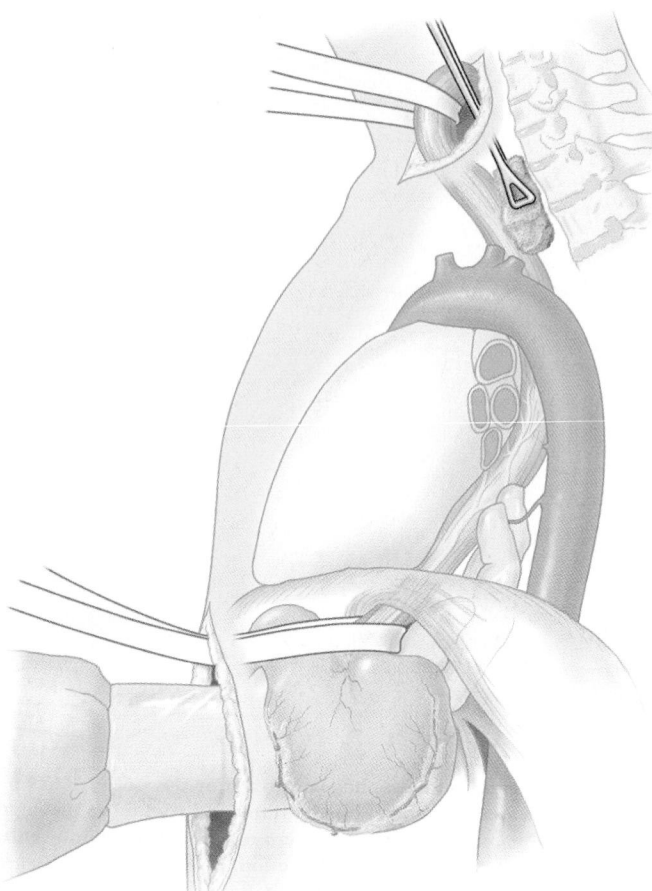

Figure 12   **Transhiatal esophagectomy. The plane posterior to the esophagus is developed by placing the surgeon's right hand into the hiatus along the prevertebral fascia. A moist sponge stick is placed through the cervical incision posterior to the esophagus, and the posterior plane is completed.**

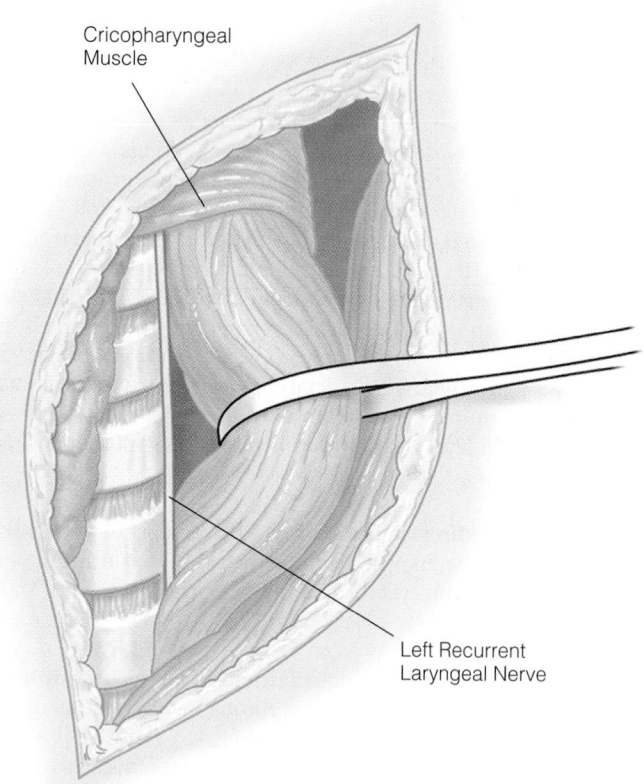

Cricopharyngeal Muscle

Left Recurrent Laryngeal Nerve

Figure 11   **Transhiatal esophagectomy. Once the cervical esophagus is exposed through an incision along the left sternocleidomastoid muscle, strap muscles are divided and retracted, and the cervical esophagus is dissected away from the left and right recurrent laryngeal nerves.**

scalpel. The left crus can be divided to facilitate exposure. Paraesophageal lymph nodes are removed either en bloc or as separate specimens. Dissection is continued cephalad with the electrocautery and a long-handled right-angle clamp. The two vagi are divided, and the periesophageal adhesions are lysed. Mobilization of the distal esophagus under direct vision is thus completed up to the level of the carina.

Three specific maneuvers are now carried out. First, the plane posterior to the esophagus is developed [see Figure 12]. The surgeon's right hand is advanced palm upward into the hiatus, with the fingers closely applied to the esophagus. The volar aspects of the fingers run along the prevertebral fascia, elevating the esophagus off the spine. A moist sponge stick is placed through the cervical incision, also posterior to the esophagus. The sponge is advanced toward the right hand, which is positioned within the mediastinum. As the sponge is advanced into the right palm, the posterior plane is completed. A 28 French mediastinal sump is then passed from the cervical incision into the abdomen along the posterior esophageal wall and attached to suction. Any blood loss from the mediastinum is collected and monitored.

Second, the anterior plane is developed [see Figure 13]. This is often much more difficult than developing the posterior plane because the left mainstem bronchus may be quite close to the esophagus. Again, the surgeon's right hand is placed through the hiatus, but it is now palm down and anterior to the esophagus. The fingertips enter the space between the esophagus and the left mainstem bronchus. The hand is gently advanced, and the airway is displaced anteriorly. A blunt curved suction handle is employed from above as a substitute finger. It is advanced along the anterior aspect of the esophagus through the cervical incision. The right hand guides the tip of the suction handle beneath the bronchus. Lateral displacement of the handle allows further mobilization of the bronchus away from the esophagus. Completion of the anterior and posterior planes usually results in a highly mobile esophagus.

Third, the lateral attachments of the upper and middle esophagus are divided. Upward traction is applied with the Penrose drain previously placed around the cervical esophagus, allowing further dissection at the level of the thoracic inlet. Lateral attachments are pushed caudally into the mediastinum, and traction applied to the esophagus from below allows these attachments to be visualized inferiorly through the hiatus, then isolated with long right-angle clamps and divided with the electrocautery. Caution must be exercised so as not to injure the azygos vein. Dissection on the right side must therefore be kept close to the esophagus. Once the last lateral attachment is divided, the esophagus is completely free and can be advanced into the cervical wound.

Close monitoring of arterial blood pressure is maintained throughout. Transient hypotension may occur as a result of mediastinal compression and temporary impairment of cardiac venous return as the surgeon's hand or retractors are passed through the hiatus. Vasopressors are never required for management: simple

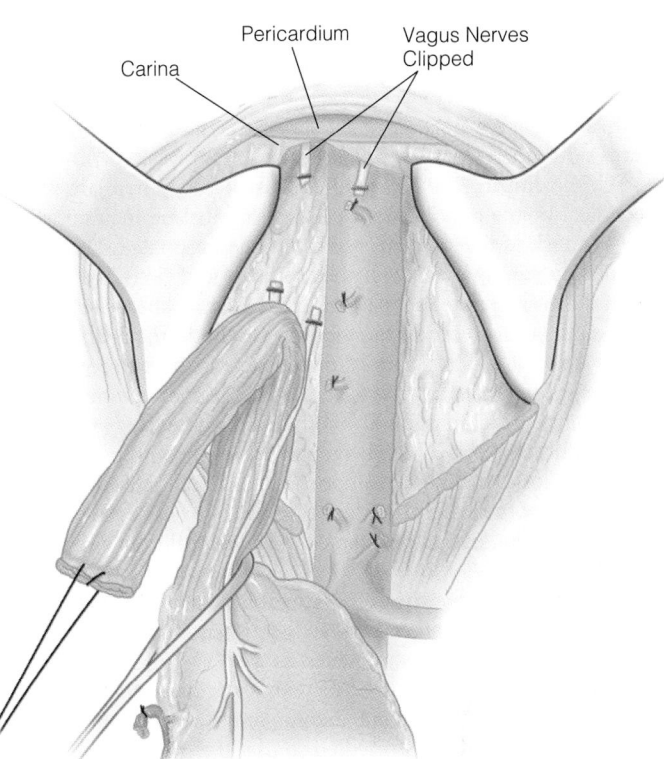

Figure 14 **Transhiatal esophagectomy. The esophagus is divided in the neck and delivered into the abdomen. Retractors are placed in the hiatus, and any vessels entering into the esophagus are clipped and divided. The vagi are also clipped and divided.**

repositioning of the retractors or removal of the dissecting hand usually results in prompt restoration of normal BP. Placement of the patient in a slight Trendelenburg position is often helpful.

Step 8: proximal transection of esophagus and delivery into abdomen The nasogastric tube is retracted to the level of the cricopharyngeus, and the esophagus is divided with a cutting stapler 5 to 6 cm distal to the muscle. The esophagus is then removed via the abdomen [*see Figure 14*]. Retractors are placed in the hiatus, and the mediastinum is inspected for hemostasis. The sump is removed. Both pleurae are inspected. The lungs are inflated so that it can be determined which pleural space requires thoracostomy drainage. The mediastinum is packed with dry laparotomy pads from below. A narrow pack is placed into the thoracic inlet from above. Chest tubes are then placed as required along the inframammary crease in the anterior axillary line. The drainage from these tubes should be closely monitored throughout the rest of the operation to ensure that any bleeding from the mediastinal dissection does not go unnoticed.

Step 9: excision of specimen and formation of gastric tube The gastric fundus is grasped, and gentle tension is applied along the length of the stomach. The esophagus is held at right angles to the body of the stomach, and the fat in the gastrohepatic ligament is elevated off the lesser curvature; all lymph nodes are thus mobilized. A point approximately midway along the lesser curvature is selected. The blood vessels traversing this area from the right gastric artery are ligated to expose the lesser curvature. The distal resection margin is then marked; it should be 4 to 6 cm from the esophagogastric junction, extending from the selected point on the lesser curvature to a point medial to the fundus. A 60

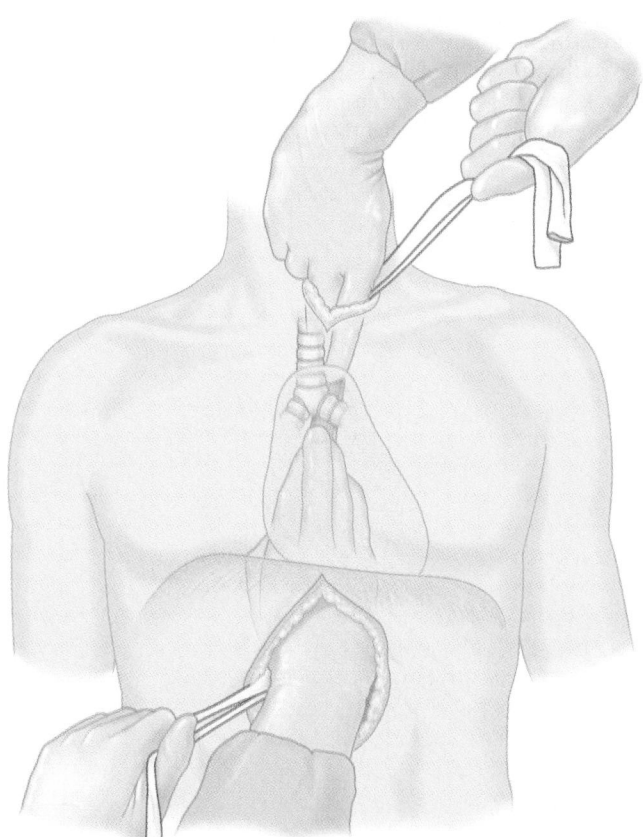

Figure 13 **Transhiatal esophagectomy. The anterior plane is developed by placing the surgeon's right hand through the hiatus anterior to the esophagus. The fingertips enter the space between the esophagus and the left mainstem bronchus, to be met by a blunt suction handle passed downward through the cervical incision. The lateral attachments of the esophagus are divided from above downward as far as the aortic arch.**

mm GIA stapler loaded with 3.5 mm staples is then used to transect the proximal stomach, proceeding from the lesser curvature toward the fundus [see Figure 15]. Resection of the cardia along with the adjacent portion of the lesser curvature effectively converts a J-shaped stomach into a straight tube.

For maximizing the length of the gastric tube, there are several technical points that are critical. Tension must be maintained on the stomach as the stapler is serially applied cephalad. The stapler should be simply placed on the stomach and fired: no attempt should be made to telescope tissue into the jaws, because to do so would effectively reconstitute the curve of the stomach and diminish its upward reach. Typically, three staple loads are required.

The specimen is removed, and frozen section examination is done on the distal margin. The completed staple line is then oversewn with a continuous Lembert suture of 4-0 polypropylene. Once again, tension is maintained along the stomach to prevent any foreshortening of the lesser curvature. The use of two separate sutures, each reinforcing half of the staple line, is helpful in this regard.

Step 10: advancement of stomach into chest or neck

The mediastinal packs are removed, and hemostasis is verified in the chest. The stomach is inspected as well. The ends of any short gastric vessels that were divided with the ultrasonic scalpel are now tied so that subsequent manipulation does not precipitate bleeding. The stomach is oriented so that the greater curvature is to the patient's left. There must be no torsion. The anterior surface of the fundal tip should be marked with ink so that proper orientation of the stomach can be confirmed after its passage into the neck. The stomach can usually be advanced through the posterior mediastinum without any traction sutures or clamps. The surgeon's hand is placed palm down on the anterior surface of the stomach, with the fingertips about 5 cm proximal to the tip of the fundus. The hand is then gently advanced through the chest, pushing the stomach ahead of itself. The tip of the fundus is gently grasped with a Babcock clamp as it appears in the neck. To prevent trauma at this most distant aspect of the gastric tube, the clamp should not be ratcheted closed.

No attempt should be made to pull the stomach up into the neck: the position of the fundus is simply maintained as the surgeon's hand is removed from the mediastinum. Further length in the neck can usually be gained by gently readvancing the hand along the anterior aspect of the stomach. This measure uniformly distributes tension along the tube and ensures proper torsion-free orientation in the chest. The stomach is pushed up into the neck rather than drawn up by the clamp.

A useful alternative approach for positioning the gastric tube involves passing a large-bore Foley catheter through the mediastinum from the neck incision. The balloon is inflated, and a 50 cm section of a narrow plastic laparoscopic camera bag is tied onto the catheter just above the balloon. The gastric tube is positioned within the bag, and suction is applied through the catheter, creating an atraumatic seal between the stomach and the surrounding plastic bag. As the bag is drawn upward through the neck with gentle traction on the Foley catheter, the stomach advances through the mediastinum. A small dry pack is placed in the neck behind the fundus to prevent retraction into the chest. The stomach is not secured to the prevertebral fascia in any way.

The feeding jejunal tube is brought out the left midabdomen through a separate stab incision. The hiatus is inspected for hemostasis, as is the splenic hilum. It may be necessary to reconstitute the hiatus with one or two simple sutures of 1-0 silk placed through the crura. These sutures must be placed with care to

ensure that injury to the gastroepiploic arcade does not occur at this late point in the procedure. The hiatus is narrowed, but not so much that three fingers cannot be easily passed alongside the gastric conduit. This reconstitution will help prevent herniation of other abdominal contents alongside the gastric conduit. The liver is returned to its anatomic position, thus also preventing any subsequent herniation of bowel into the chest. The pyloromyotomy is generally found at the level of the diaphragm. The laparotomy is then closed in the usual fashion. The viability of the fundus in the neck incision is checked periodically as the abdominal portion of the procedure is completed.

Step 11: cervical esophagogastric anastomosis

The construction of the esophagogastric anastomosis is the most important part of the entire operation: any anastomotic complication will greatly compromise the patient's ability to swallow comfortably. Accordingly, meticulous technique is essential.

A seromuscular traction suture of 4-0 polyglactin is placed through the anterior stomach at the level of the clavicle and drawn upward, thus elevating the fundus into the neck wound and greatly facilitating the anastomosis. The pack behind the fundus is then removed.

The site of the anterior gastrotomy is then carefully selected: it should be midway between the oversewn lesser curvature staple line and the greater curvature of the fundus (marked by the ligated ends of the short gastric vessels). The staple line on the cervical esophagus is removed, and the anterior aspect of the esophagus is grasped with a fine-toothed forceps at the level of the planned gastrotomy. A straight DeBakey forceps is then applied across the full width of the esophagus to act as a guide for division. The esophagus is cut with a new scalpel blade at a 45° angle so that the anterior wall is slightly longer than the posterior wall; the

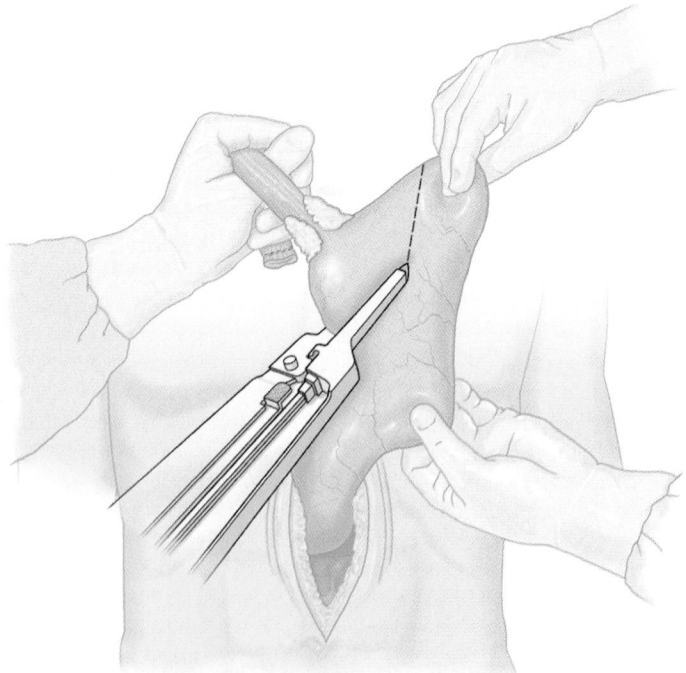

Figure 15 **Transhiatal esophagectomy. A gastric tube is formed by stapling along the lesser curvature of the stomach from the junction of the right and left gastric vessels to the top of the fundus. This staple line is oversewn with a continuous 3-0 suture, with care taken not to foreshorten the gastric tube.**

anterior wall then forms the hood of the anastomosis. The fine-toothed forceps is used to maintain orientation of the esophagus throughout. Two full-thickness stay sutures of 4-0 Vicryl are placed, one at the midpoint of the anterior cut edge of the esophagus and one at the corresponding location posteriorly. The posterior stitch is placed from inside the lumen, and the needle is left on the suture for later use.

A 2 cm gastrotomy is then performed with a needle-tipped electrocautery using cutting current. The incision is obliquely oriented, with the cephalad extent proceeding slightly medially. The needle from the stay suture previously placed on the posterior wall of the esophagus is then passed the full thickness of the cephalad aspect of the gastrotomy [see Figure 16a]. Traction on this untied suture brings the esophagus toward the stomach. A 45 mm endoscopic stapler loaded with 3.5 mm staples is used to form the back wall of the anastomosis. The thicker portion of the device (the cartridge) is advanced cephalad into the esophagus, with the narrower portion (the anvil) in the gastric lumen [see Figure 16b]. The tip of the stapler should be aimed toward the patient's right ear. Tension is applied to the stay suture holding the esophagus and stomach together so as to bring tissue into the jaws of the device. The portion of the fundus extending beyond the stapler is then rotated medially to ensure that the new staple line is well away from the one previously placed along the lesser curvature. This is a crucial point: crossing of the two staple lines may create an ischemic area that can give rise to a large leak in the postoperative period.

The stapler is then closed, holding the esophagus and stomach together, but not yet fired. The position of the nasogastric tube should be maintained just at the level of the cricopharyngeus during the construction of the anastomosis. This positioning keeps the tube out of the operative field and protects it from being entrapped by the jaws of the stapler; it also facilitates subsequent passage of the tube into the gastric conduit once the posterior wall of the anastomosis is complete. Two suspension sutures are placed on either side of the closed stapler, one toward the tip and the other near the heel of the jaws. These four sutures alleviate any potential tension on the staple line by approximating the muscular layer of the esophagus to the seromuscular layer of the stomach. The suspension sutures are tied, and the stapler is fired, thereby completing the posterior portion of the anastomosis [see Figure 16c].

The anterior portion of the anastomosis is closed in two layers. The inner layer consists of a continuous 4-0 polydioxanone suture placed as full-thickness inverting stitches, and the second layer consists of interrupted seromuscular Lembert sutures [see Figure 17]. The lateral and medial corners of the anastomosis, where the staple line meets the handsewn portion, merit extra attention. These corners are quite fragile, and excessive traction may result in dehiscence progressing cephalad along the staple line in a zipperlike fashion. The inner layer should therefore be started at each corner, incorporating the last 5 mm of the staple line. Once several stitches have been placed from the two corners, the nasogastric tube can be passed through the anastomosis. The nasogastric tube is properly positioned when the most distal black marker is at the nares. The inner layer is then completed as the two sutures are tied at the midpoint.

Step 12: drainage, closure, and completion x-ray A small Penrose drain is placed in the thoracic inlet below the anastomosis and brought out through the inferior end of the neck incision. The drain is secured, and the incision is irrigated. The strap muscles are not reapproximated but are merely attached loosely to the underside of the sternocleidomastoid muscle with two interrupted 4-0 polyglactin sutures. The platys-

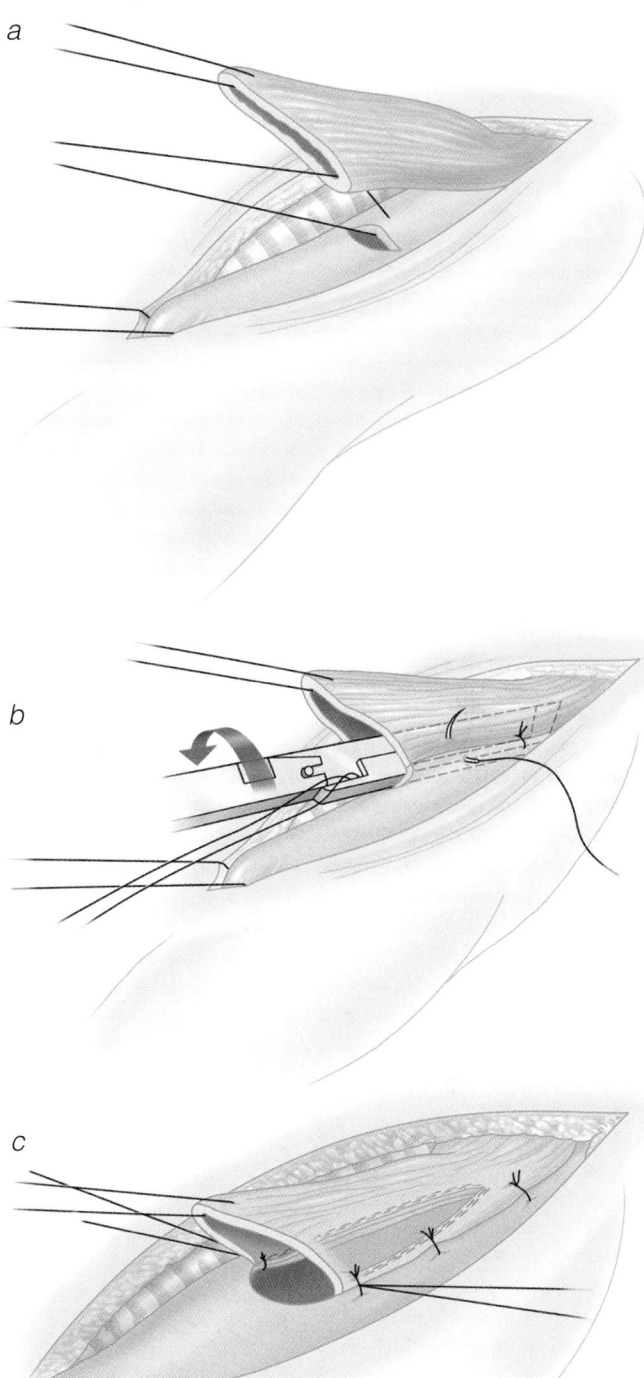

Figure 16 Transhiatal esophagectomy. (*a*) After the proximal end of the stomach tube is delivered into the neck, the esophagus is cut at a 45° angle so that the anterior wall is longer than the posterior wall. A gastrotomy is placed between the oversewn lesser curvature staple line and the greater curvature of the fundus. A full-thickness suture is placed through all layers of the esophagus and all layers of the gastrotomy. (*b*) An endoscopic GIA stapler is used to form the back wall of the anastomosis. The thicker portion of the device (the cartridge) is advanced cephalad into the esophagus, with the narrower portion (the anvil) in the gastric lumen. The tip of the stapler should be aimed toward the patient's right ear. The staple line must be well away from the lesser curvature staple line. Two suspension sutures are placed on either side of the closed stapler, one toward the tip and the other near the heel of the jaws. (*c*) The stapler is fired to complete the posterior portion of the anastomosis.

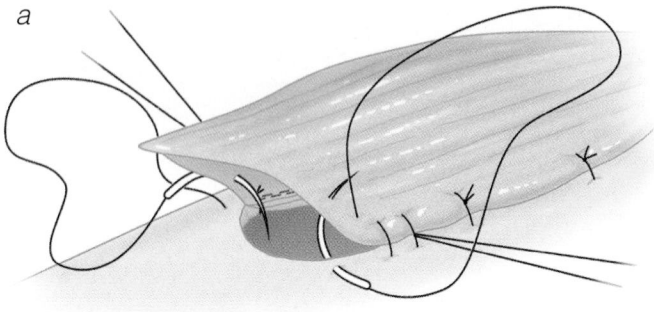

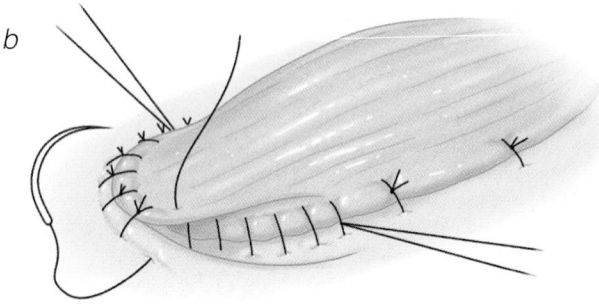

Figure 17 **Transhiatal esophagectomy. The anterior portion of the anastomosis is completed with (*a*) an inner layer consisting of a continuous 4-0 polydioxanone suture and (*b*) an outer layer consisting of interrupted sutures.**

ma is reconstituted with interrupted 4-0 polyglactin sutures. The nasogastric tube is secured.

A chest x-ray is obtained in the OR to verify the position of the drains and the absence of any abnormal collections in the chest. Patients are extubated in the OR and transported to the anesthetic recovery area. Extubation should be carried out only when the health care team is confident that subsequent reintubation is unlikely to be necessary. Emergency reintubation after a cervical anastomosis is hazardous, in that vigorous neck extension may threaten the suture line. Once patients are awake and alert, which is usually 3 to 4 hours after the operation, they are taken to the general ward. As a rule, admission to an intensive care unit is not required unless there are substantial comorbidities or intraoperative concerns. To prevent excessive traction on the anastomosis, the neck should be maintained in a flexed position with two pillows placed behind the head.

In certain patients, a stapled anastomosis may be impractical. In patients with a bull-neck habitus, for example, a partial sternal split may be required for adequate exposure of the cervical esophagus, and a handsewn true end-to-end anastomosis may be necessary. In addition, patients who have previously undergone antireflux surgery may have a relatively short gastric tube that will necessitate an end-to-end reconstruction.

Patients should, if possible, begin walking the morning after the operation. An incentive spirometer should be constantly within arm's length of the patient, and hourly use of this device should be encouraged. The nasogastric tube is removed on postoperative day 3, and the patient is allowed ice chips in the mouth. The thoracic epidural catheter is removed the afternoon after the chest tube is removed. The diet is gradually advanced so that a soft diet is begun on postoperative day 5 or 6. A barium swallow is performed on postoperative day 6 in preparation for hospital discharge on day 7 or 8.

Ivor-Lewis Esophagectomy

Steps 1 through 5 Esophagoscopy is performed to confirm the location of the tumor. Steps 1, 2, 3, 4, and 5 of an Ivor-Lewis esophagectomy are virtually identical to the first five steps (i.e., the abdominal portion) of a transhiatal esophagectomy. Once complete mobilization of the stomach is verified, the pylorus is manually advanced to the level of the diaphragm to ensure that it is not being tethered by the duodenum or the greater omentum. The stomach is then placed back into the anatomic position, and the laparotomy is closed.

Step 6: exposure and mobilization of esophagus The patient is shifted to the left lateral decubitus position and redraped. Single-lung ventilation is instituted, and the chest is entered through a right fifth or sixth interspace thoracotomy. The inferior pulmonary ligament is divided, and the lung is retracted cephalad. The esophagus is mobilized from the level of the diaphragm to a point above the azygos vein [*see Figure 18*], which is typically divided with a vascular stapler. The pleura overlying the esophagus is divided to the level of the thoracic inlet, superior to the azygos vein. The esophagus is encircled with a Penrose drain in the retrotracheal region. The pleura is then divided to the level of the diaphragm, with care taken to stay close to the right bronchus and the pericardium and avoid injury to the thoracic duct. The soft tissue between the esophagus and the aorta posteriorly and between the esophagus and the trachea or the pericardium anteriorly is dissected free and maintained en bloc with the esophagus. Periesophageal and subcarinal nodes are thereby mobilized [*see Figure 18b*].

Step 7: excision and removal of specimen The hiatus is incised and the abdomen entered. The stomach is drawn up into the chest, with care taken not to place excessive traction on the gastroepiploic pedicle. The esophagus is divided with a stapler proximally at least 5 cm away from any grossly evident tumor. A margin is sent for frozen section examination. The distal resection margin is completed in a similar manner, and the esophageal specimen is removed from the operative field [*see Figure 19*]. The gastric staple line is oversewn, and the stomach is positioned in the posterior mediastinum.

Step 8: intrathoracic esophagogastric anastomosis The site of the esophagogastric anastomosis should be about 2 cm above the divided azygos vein. Several interrupted sutures are used to secure the transposed stomach to the adjacent pleura. The staple line on the esophagus is removed, and a gastrotomy is performed in preparation for a side-to-side functional end-to-end anastomosis [*see Figure 20*]. With the aid of full-thickness traction sutures, the esophagus is positioned along the surface of the stomach and well away from the oversewn staple line defining the gastric resection margin. The posterior aspect of the anastomosis is completed with an endoscopic GIA stapler as described earlier [*see* Transhiatal Esophagectomy, Step 11, *above, and Figures 16 and 17*]. A nasogastric tube is passed, and the anterior wall is completed in two layers. The first layer consists of a full-thickness continuous 3-0 polydioxanone suture; the second consists of interrupted absorbable sutures approximating the seromuscular layer of the stomach to the muscular layer of the esophagus.

Two alternative methods of anastomosis are sometimes used: (1) a totally handsewn end-to-side anastomosis and (2) a totally stapled end-to-end anastomosis. The latter technique involves opening the previously placed gastric staple line and advancing the handle of an end-to-end anastomosis (EEA) stapler through

a

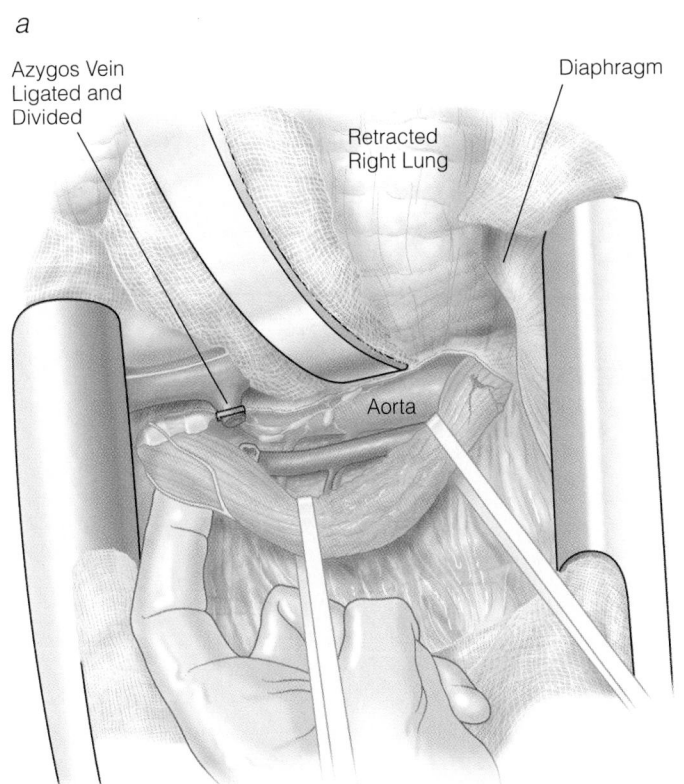

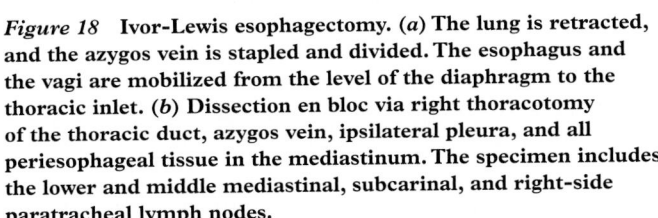

b

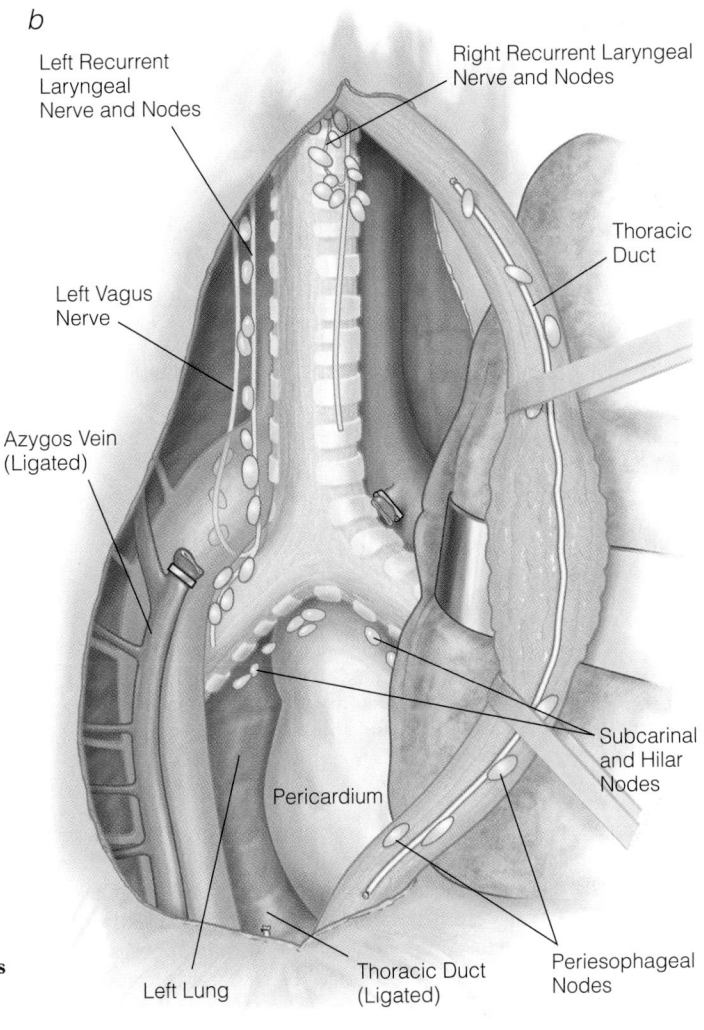

Figure 18 **Ivor-Lewis esophagectomy. (*a*) The lung is retracted, and the azygos vein is stapled and divided. The esophagus and the vagi are mobilized from the level of the diaphragm to the thoracic inlet. (*b*) Dissection en bloc via right thoracotomy of the thoracic duct, azygos vein, ipsilateral pleura, and all periesophageal tissue in the mediastinum. The specimen includes the lower and middle mediastinal, subcarinal, and right-side paratracheal lymph nodes.**

the stomach. The proximal esophagus is dilated sufficiently to accommodate at least a 25 mm head. The anvil is placed into the distal esophagus and secured with a purse-string suture. The tip of the stapler is brought out through the apical wall of the stomach and attached to the anvil. The stapler is then fired to create the end-to-end anastomosis, and the gastrotomy is closed. The advantages of this technique are its relative simplicity and the theoretical security of a completely stapled anastomosis; the main potential disadvantage is the risk of postoperative dysphagia resulting from an overly narrow anastomotic ring.

After completion of the anastomosis, the stomach is inspected for any potential redundancy or torsion in the chest. To prevent torsion, the stomach is anchored to the pericardium with nonabsorbable sutures. The diaphragmatic hiatus is then inspected: it should allow easy passage of two fingers into the abdomen alongside the transposed stomach. Interrupted sutures may be used to approximate the edge of the crura to the adjacent stomach wall, thereby preventing any later herniation of abdominal contents into the pleural space.

Step 9: drainage and closure Two chest tubes are placed through separate stab incisions. The tip of the posterior drain is positioned alongside the stomach at the level of the anastomosis. Fine gut sutures secured to the adjacent parietal pleura will help maintain the position of the tube. The thoracotomy is then closed in the standard fashion.

Patients should begin walking on postoperative day 1. The naso-

gastric tube is generally removed on postoperative day 3. Oral intake is not begun at this point; feeding is accomplished via the temporary jejunostomy. A barium contrast study is performed approximately 5 to 7 days after the operation. If there is no anastomotic leakage, oral intake is initiated and advanced as tolerated. The chest tubes are removed only after the reinstitution of oral intake. Patients are generally discharged from the hospital by postoperative day 8 to 10.

Left Thoracoabdominal Esophagogastrectomy

Step 1: incision and entry into peritoneum The patient is placed in the right lateral position, with the hips rotated backward about 30°. An exploratory laparotomy is performed through an oblique incision extending from the tip of the sixth costal cartilage to a point about halfway between the sternum and the umbilicus. The peritoneal cavity is carefully examined to rule out peritoneal and hepatic metastases. The region of the cardia is palpated and the mobility of the tumor assessed. If there is minor involvement of the crura or the tail of the pancreas, resection may still be possible; however, if the tumor is firmly fixed or there are peritoneal or hepatic metastases, resection should be abandoned. A feeding jejunostomy, an esophageal stent, or both may be inserted to improve swallowing and allow nutrition.

Step 2: assessment of gastric involvement and incision of diaphragm The extent to which the tumor involves the stom-

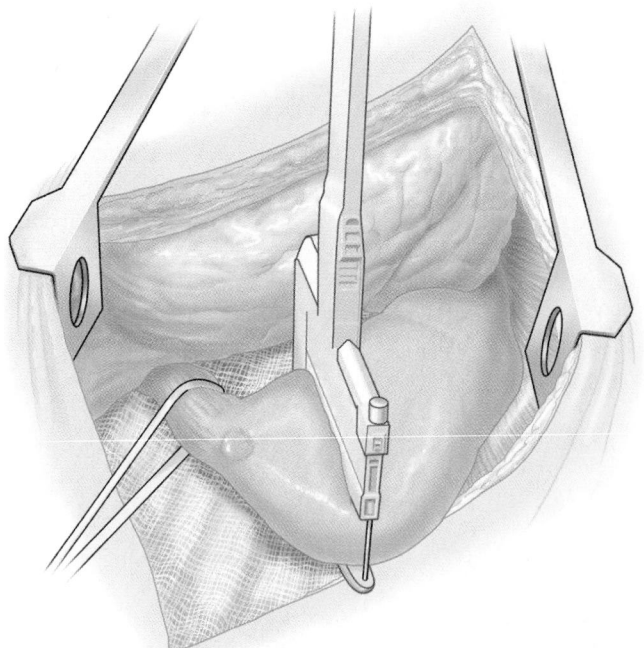

Figure 19 Ivor-Lewis esophagectomy. The esophagus and the proximal stomach are divided and stapled at least 5 cm away from the gross tumor.

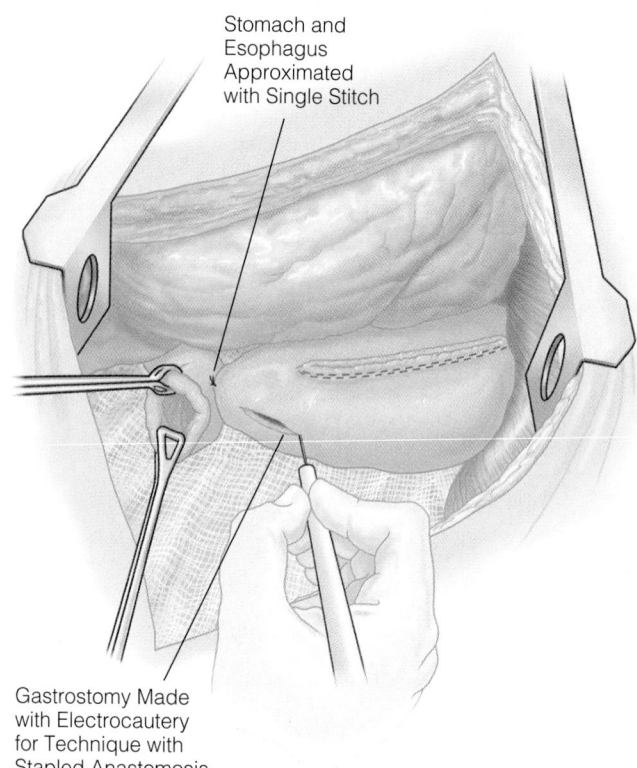

Stomach and Esophagus Approximated with Single Stitch

Gastrostomy Made with Electrocautery for Technique with Stapled Anastomosis

Figure 20 Ivor-Lewis esophagectomy. The transposed stomach is sutured to the adjacent pericardium, and a gastrotomy is carried out halfway between the lesser curvature staple line and the greater curvature. The anastomosis is completed as in a transhiatal esophagectomy [*see Figures 16 and 17*].

ach determines whether a total gastrectomy or a proximal gastrectomy is indicated along with the distal esophagectomy. If no metastases are found, the incision is extended and the chest is opened with a left posterolateral incision through the sixth interspace. If the thoracic component of the tumor appears to be resectable, the costal margin is divided. It is advisable to remove a 1 to 2 cm segment of the costal margin to facilitate repair of the diaphragm at the end of the operation and reduce postoperative costal margin pain. The diaphragm is incised radially [*see Figure 21*]. Branches of the pericardiophrenic artery are suture-ligated, and the sutures are left long so that they can be used as diaphragmatic retractors. Alternatively, a circumferential incision may be made about 2 cm from the costal margin to reduce the risk of postoperative diaphragmatic paralysis.

Step 3: division of pulmonary ligament and mobilization of esophagus and stomach   The pulmonary ligament is divided, and the mediastinal pleura is incised over the esophagus as far as the aortic arch. The esophagus is mobilized above the tumor and is retracted by a Penrose drain [*see Figure 21*]. The esophageal vessels are carefully dissected, ligated, and divided. The tumor is mobilized; the plane of the dissection is kept close to the aorta on the left, and if necessary, the right parietal pleura is taken in continuity with the lesion. About 1 cm of the crura is taken in continuity with the tumor to provide good local clearance. The stomach is then mobilized in much the same way as in a transhiatal esophagectomy [*see Figure 9*].

Step 4: assessment of pancreatic involvement and hepatic viability   The lesser sac is opened through the greater omentum so that it can be determined whether the primary tumor involves the distal pancreas. If so, it is reasonable to resect the distal pancreas, the spleen, or both in continuity with the stomach; if not, the short gastric vessels are ligated and divided, with the spleen preserved. The lesser omentum is detached from the right side of

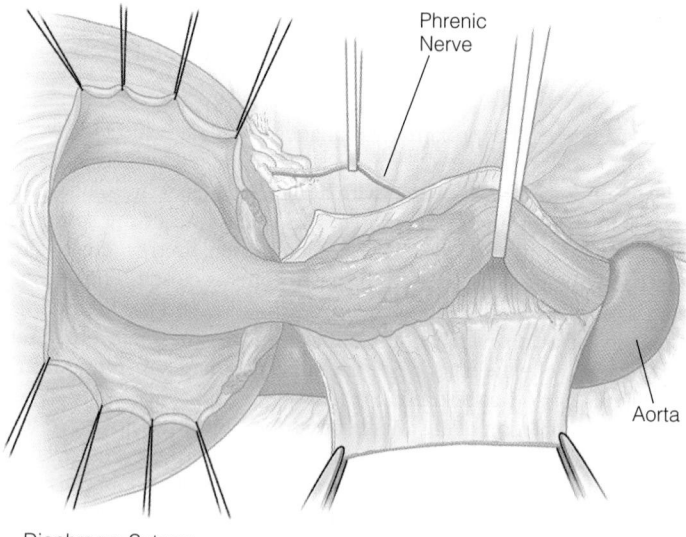

Phrenic Nerve

Aorta

Diaphragm Sutures

Figure 21 Left thoracoabdominal esophagogastrectomy. The diaphragm is incised radially. The branches of the pericardial phrenic artery are suture-ligated, and the sutures are left long to be used as diaphragmatic retractors. The pulmonary ligament is divided, and the esophagus is mobilized above the tumor and retracted with a Penrose drain. The esophageal vessels are ligated and divided. The tumor and the esophagus are mobilized off the aorta down to the hiatus; 1 cm of the diaphragmatic crura is taken in continuity with the tumor to provide local clearance. The stomach is then mobilized in much the same way as in a transhiatal esophagectomy [*see Figure 9*].

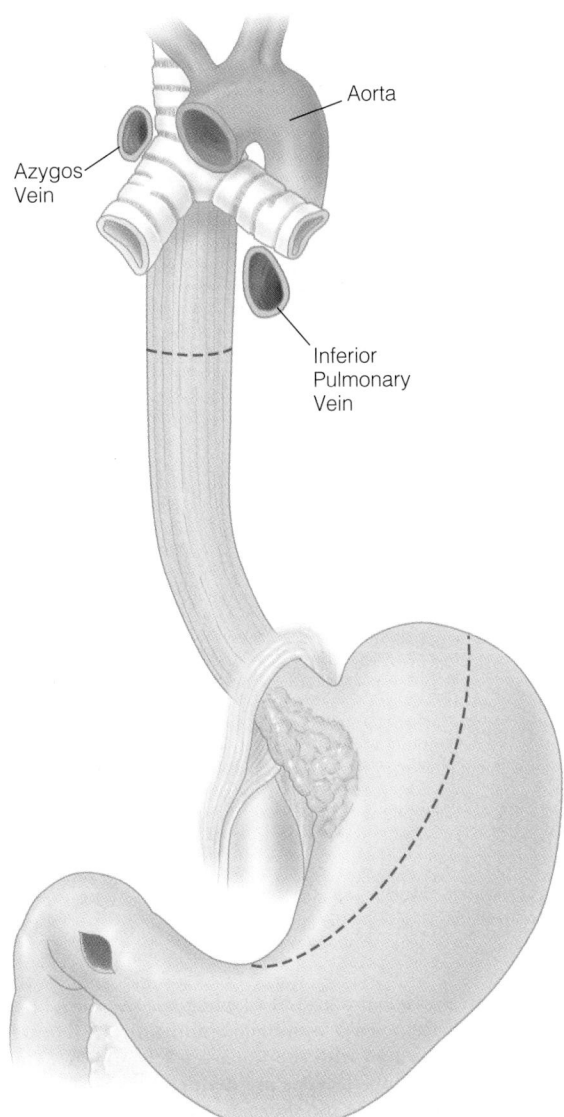

Figure 22 **Left thoracoabdominal esophagogastrectomy: proximal esophagogastrectomy with esophagogastrostomy. If the tumor can be completely resected by removing the proximal stomach, a proximal esophagogastrectomy is carried out.**

Step 6: choice of partial or total gastrectomy At this time, the surgeon determines whether the whole stomach must be resected to remove the gastric part of the cancer or whether a partial (i.e., proximal) gastrectomy will suffice.

Proximal esophagogastrectomy with esophagogastrostomy. If the surgeon decides that resection of the proximal stomach will remove all of the tumor while leaving at least 5 cm of tumor-free stomach, a proximal esophagogastrectomy is performed [*see Figure 22*]. A gastric tube is fashioned with a linear stapler [*see* Transhiatal Esophagectomy, Step 9, *above, and Figure 15*]. The staple line is oversewn with inverting 3-0 sutures. Because the vagus nerves are divided and gastric stasis may result, a pyloromyotomy is performed, much as in a transhiatal esophagectomy.

The proximal gastric resection margin is covered with a sponge and turned upward over the costal margin. The stomach tube is then brought up through the hiatus and into the thorax behind the proximal esophageal resection margin. The margin should be at least 10 cm from the proximal end of the esophagogastric cancer. If the esophageal resection margin is not adequate, the stomach tube is mobilized and brought to the left neck, then anastomosed to the cervical esophagus through a left neck incision; alternatively, the left colon is interposed between the gastric stump and the cervical esophagus. If the resection margin is adequate, the tip of the stomach tube is sewn to the posterior wall of the esophagus [*see Figure 23*].

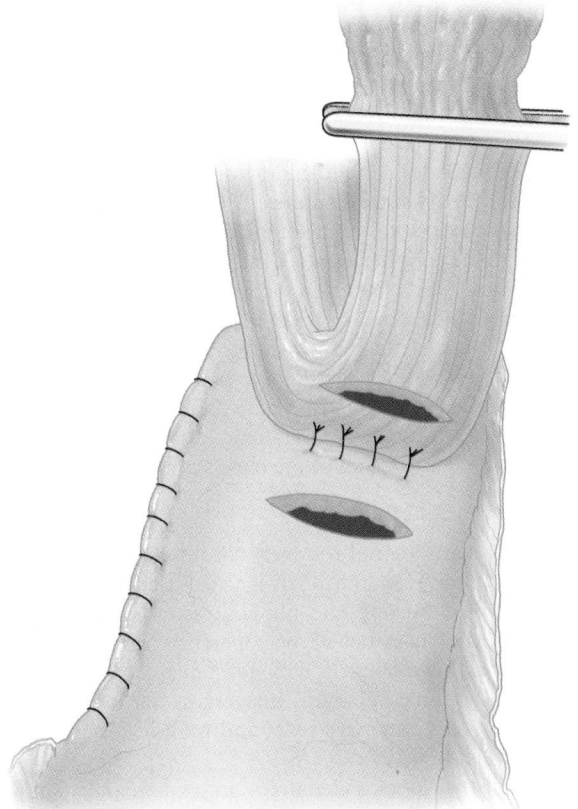

Figure 23 **Left thoracoabdominal esophagogastrectomy: proximal esophagogastrectomy with esophagogastrostomy. The esophagus is sewn to the tip of the stomach tube, halfway between the lesser curvature suture line and the greater curvature. An anastomosis is then fashioned with the stapling technique used in transhiatal esophagectomy [*see Figures 16 and 17*].**

the esophagus and the hilum of the liver, then divided down to the area of the pylorus, with the right gastric artery and vein preserved. There is often a hepatic branch from the left gastric artery running through the gastrohepatic omentum. If this hepatic branch is of significant size, a soft vascular clamp should be placed on the artery for 20 minutes so that the viability of the liver can be assessed. If the liver is viable, the artery is suture-ligated and divided.

Step 5: division of greater omentum and short gastric vessels The greater omentum is divided, with care taken to preserve the right gastroepiploic artery and vein. These two vessels are suture-ligated and divided well away from the stomach. Ligation and division of the short gastric vessels allow complete mobilization of the greater curvature of the stomach. Dissection is extended downward as far as the pylorus. The stomach is turned upward, and the left gastric vessels are exposed through the lesser sac [*see Figure 10*]. The lymph nodes along the celiac axis and the left gastric artery are swept up into the specimen, and the gastric vessels are either suture-ligated or stapled and divided.

The anastomosis is then performed with the stapling technique previously described for transhiatal esophagectomy [*see Figures 16 and 17*]. A nasogastric tube is passed down into the gastric remnant. The tube is sewn to the pericardium and the endothoracic fascia to prevent anastomotic dehiscence.

Total gastrectomy with Roux-en-Y esophagojejunostomy. If the surgeon decides that a total gastrectomy is necessary, the right gastroepiploic and right gastric vessels are suture-ligated and divided distal to the pylorus. The duodenum is divided just distal to the pylorus with a linear stapler. The staple line is inverted with interrupted 3-0 nonabsorbable sutures and covered with omentum to prevent duodenal stump blowout.

The esophagus is then mobilized up to the level of the inferior pulmonary vein. Two retaining sutures are placed in the esophageal wall. A monofilament nylon purse-string suture is placed around the circumference of the proximal esophagus in preparation for stapling. A No. 24 Foley catheter with a 20 ml balloon is advanced into the esophagus and gently inflated to distend the esophageal lumen. The resected specimen is sent to the pathologist for examination of the margins.

A jejunal interposition is then fashioned by using the Roux-en-Y technique. One or two jejunal arteriovenous arcades are divided to mobilize enough jejunum to allow anastomosis to the thoracic esophagus [*see Figure 24*]. After removal of the Foley catheter, a 25 or 28 mm EEA stapler is passed through the jejunum into the esophagus, fired, and removed. The jejunum is anchored to the pericardium and the proximal esophagus. The duodenal loop is anastomosed to the jejunum at least 45 to 50 cm distal to the esophagojejunal anastomosis to minimize bile reflux [*see Figure 24*]. The blind end of the jejunal loop is then stapled closed.

After careful irrigation of the chest, the first step in the closure is to repair the diaphragm around the hiatus. The gastric or jejunal interposition is sewn to the crura with interrupted nonabsorbable sutures. The remainder of the diaphragm is closed with interrupted nonabsorbable 0 mattress sutures. A chest tube is placed into the pleural space close to but not touching the anastomosis. The final sutures in the peripheral part of the diaphragm are placed but are not tied until the ribs are brought together with pericostal sutures. The left lung is reexpanded. The costal cartilages are not approximated but are left to float free. If the ends of the costal margin are abutting, another 2 cm of costal cartilage should be removed to reduce postoperative pain. Thoracic and abdominal skin layers are closed with a continuous absorbable suture. The skin and the subcutaneous tissue are closed in the usual fashion.

POSTOPERATIVE CARE

As a rule, patients are not routinely admitted to the ICU after esophagectomy; however, individual practices depend on the distribution of skilled nursing and physiotherapy personnel. Early ambulation is the mainstay of postoperative care. As a rule, patients are able to walk slowly, with assistance, on postoperative day 1. Patient-controlled epidural analgesia is particularly useful in facilitating good pulmonary toilet and minimizing the risk of atelectasis or pneumonia.

The nasogastric tube is removed on postoperative day 3; jejunostomy tube feedings are gradually started at the same time. Once bowel function normalizes, patients are allowed small sips of liquids. Chest tubes are removed as pleural drainage subsides. By postoperative day 6, most patients have progressed to a soft solid diet. Dietary education is provided, focusing primarily on eating smaller and more frequent meals, avoiding bulky foods (e.g., meat and bread) in the early postoperative period, and taking measures

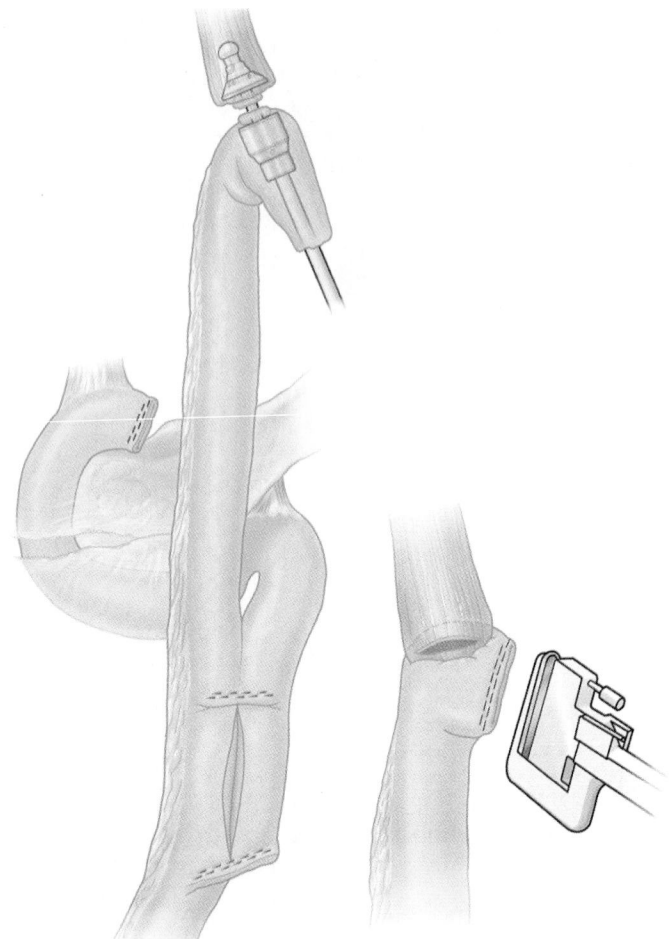

Figure 24 **Left thoracoabdominal esophagogastrectomy: total gastrectomy with Roux-en-Y esophagojejunostomy. A jejunal interposition is fashioned with the Roux-en-Y technique. One or two jejunal arteriovenous arcades are divided to mobilize enough jejunum for anastomosis to the thoracic esophagus. A 25 or 28 mm EEA stapler is passed through the jejunum into the esophagus. The jejunum is anchored to the pericardium and the proximal esophagus. The duodenal loop is anastomosed to the jejunum at least 45 to 50 cm distal to the esophagojejunal anastomosis. The blind end of the jejunal loop is then stapled closed.**

to minimize postprandial dumping. Patients are also taught how to care for their temporary feeding jejunostomy. Consumption of caffeine and carbonated beverages is usually limited during the first few weeks after discharge.

A barium swallow is performed on postoperative day 7 to verify the integrity of the anastomosis and the patency of the pyloromyotomy. Patients are usually discharged on postoperative day 7 or 8. The feeding jejunostomy is left in place until the first postoperative evaluation, which usually takes place 2 to 3 weeks after the operation. The feeding tube is removed during that visit if oral intake and weight are stable.

COMPLICATIONS OF ESOPHAGECTOMY

Pulmonary Impairment

Atelectasis and pneumonia should be considered preventable complications of esophagectomy. Patients with recognized preoperative impairment of pulmonary reserve should be considered for transhiatal esophagectomy. Existing pulmonary function can be optimized through incentive spirometry, use of bronchodilators, and physical rehabilitation. Chronic nocturnal aspiration from esophageal obstruction should be watched for in the preoperative patient; the head of the bed should be elevated 30° to 45° as a preventive measure. Effective pain control is essential to prevent postoperative atelectasis. Routine use of patient-controlled thoracic epidural analgesia should be considered. Deep breathing, early ambulation, and chest physiotherapy encourage the clearing of bronchial secretions. Certain patients will require nasotracheal aspiration or bronchoscopy for pulmonary toilet.

Tracheobronchial Injury

On rare occasions, lacerations of the membranous trachea or the left mainstem bronchus occur during esophagectomy. When such injuries occur during transthoracic resection, management is relatively simple, thanks to the already excellent operative exposure. Direct suture repair and tissue reinforcement with adjacent pleura or a pedicle of intercostal muscle provide safe closure in almost all cases. When tracheobronchial injuries occur during transhiatal esophagectomy, they are less obvious but no less urgent. This rare complication arises during mediastinal dissection. Typically, the anesthetic team notes a loss of ventilatory volume, and the surgeon may detect the smell of inhalational agents in the operative field. Bronchoscopy should be promptly performed to identify the site of the injury. The uncut endotracheal tube is then advanced over the bronchoscope and past the site of the laceration to restore proper ventilation. High tracheal injuries can usually be repaired by extending the cervical incision and adding a partial sternotomy. Injury to the carina or the left mainstem bronchus must be repaired via a right thoracotomy.

Bleeding

Hemorrhage should be rare during esophagectomy. In routine situations, blood loss should amount to less than 500 ml. The blood supply to the esophagus consists of small branches coming from the aorta, which are easily controlled and generally constrict even if left untied. Splenic injuries sometimes occur during mobilization of the stomach. The resultant hemorrhage can be immediate or delayed; blood loss may be significant, and splenectomy is usually required. Precise dissection around the left gastric artery is vital: the bleeding vessels may retract, and attempts at control may result in injury to the celiac artery or its hepatic branches. Similarly, peripancreatic vessels may be difficult to control if inadvertently injured during the Kocher maneuver.

Bleeding that arises during the mediastinal stage of the transhiatal esophagectomy generally subsides with packing if it derives from periesophageal arterial branches. Brisk loss of dark blood usually signifies injury to the azygos vein. The first step in addressing such injuries is to pack the mediastinum quickly so as to allow the anesthetic team to stabilize the patient and restore volume. Chest tubes are immediately placed to allow detection of any free hemorrhage into the pleural space. Precise localization of the bleeding site may then follow. Injury to the azygos vein may be addressed via an upper sternal split; however, when the exposure is poor, the surgeon should not hesitate to proceed to a full sternotomy. Bleeding from the subcarinal area is usually bright red and may involve bronchial arteries or small periesophageal vessels arising from the aorta, both of which can usually be controlled through the hiatus with a long-handled pistol-grip clip applier or electrocautery.

Laryngeal Nerve Injury

Injury to the recurrent laryngeal nerve is a major potential complication of transhiatal esophagectomy. Traction neuropraxia may be temporary and require no specific treatment. Permanent injury will lead to hoarseness and impaired protection of the airway during deglutition. Pneumonia from chronic aspiration is a major problem. Meticulous protection of the nerve during the cervical stage should minimize the incidence of this complication. If laryngeal nerve injury becomes apparent in the postoperative period, early medialization of the affected cord should be performed by an otolaryngologist.

Of particular concern is the risk of bilateral nerve injury after a transthoracic esophagectomy with a cervical esophagogastric anastomosis (i.e., a so-called three-hole esophagectomy). Any dissection of the upper esophagus performed through the right chest should be done as close to the esophagus as possible to avoid placing traction on the right recurrent laryngeal nerve; the subsequent left cervical dissection may put the left recurrent laryngeal nerve at risk for damage. Bilateral paralysis of the vocal cords is very poorly tolerated and has a devastating impact on quality of life.

Chylothorax

Thoracic duct injuries typically present by postoperative day 3 or 4. Dyspnea and pleural effusion may be noted if thoracostomy tubes are not in place. Thoracentesis yields an opaque, milky fluid. In patients who already have a chest drain in place, there is typically a high volume of serous drainage in the first 2 postoperative days. As enteral nutrition is established and dietary fat reintroduced, the fluid assumes a characteristic milky appearance. In most cases, the gross appearance is diagnostic, and there is rarely a need to confirm the diagnosis by measuring the triglyceride level. A thoracostomy drain is placed to monitor the volume of the chyle leak. Chest x-rays should be obtained to verify complete drainage of the pleural space and full expansion of the lung.

Patients with chylothorax should be converted to fat-free enteral nutrition. Persistent drainage exceeding 500 ml/8 hr is an indication for early operation and ligation of the thoracic duct; high-volume chyle leaks are unlikely to close spontaneously. Prolonged loss of chyle causes significant electrolyte, nutritional, and immunologic derangements that may prove fatal if allowed to progress. Accordingly, patients with persistent chyle leakage should undergo operation within 1 week of diagnosis. A feeding tube is placed in the duodenum before operation if a jejunostomy tube is not already in place. Jejunal feeding with 35% cream at a rate of 60 to 80 ml/hr is maintained for at least 4 hours before operation. Feeding is continued even during the procedure: the enteral fat stimulates a brisk flow of chyle and greatly facilitates visualization of any thoracic duct injury.

Right-side chyle leaks are approached via either a thoracotomy or video-assisted thoracoscopy. The magnification and excellent illumination associated with thoracoscopy are partially counterbalanced by the constraints imposed by port placement and limited tissue retraction. The inferior pulmonary ligament is divided, and the posterior mediastinum is inspected for extravasation of milky fluid. Any visible sources of chyle leakage can be controlled with clips or suture ligatures. In some cases, mass ligation of the thoracic duct at the level of the diaphragm, incorporating all the soft tissue between the aorta and the azygos vein, may be required.

Left-side leaks can be difficult to manage. The subcarinal area is typically involved; this is the level at which the thoracic duct crosses over from the right. Exploration should begin on the left side. If the leak cannot be visualized, a right-side approach may be necessary to control the thoracic duct as it first enters the chest.

Anastomotic Leakage

The consequences of anastomotic complications after esophagectomy vary considerably in severity, depending on their location and cause. The cervical anastomotic leaks that may develop after transhiatal esophagectomy are generally simple to treat. Leaks in the early postoperative period are usually related to technical factors (e.g., excessive tension across the anastomosis). A nonviable stomach may not give rise to obvious signs, and thus, any possibility of ischemia in the transposed stomach must be addressed promptly. Tachycardia, confusion, leukocytosis, cervical wound drainage, and neck tenderness may or may not be present.

The morbidity of an open cervical wound is not high—certainly lower than that of an untreated leak. Accordingly, any clinical suspicion of a leak should prompt a diagnostic contrast swallow study using dilute barium. Large leaks are manifested as persistent collections of contrast material outside the esophagus. Although such leaks rarely extend into the pleural space, any fluid in the chest must be drained so that its nature can be determined. The neck wound is opened by removing the sutures and performing gentle digital exploration of the prevertebral space behind the esophagus as the finger is advanced into the mediastinum; this is usually done at the bedside and requires little, if any, patient sedation.

Saline-moistened gauze packing is changed three or four times a day. Prolonged or copious cervical drainage may call for supplemental deep wound aspiration with a Yankauer suction handle. Administering water orally during aspiration facilitates removal of any necrotic debris. A fetid, malodorous breath associated with sanguineous discharge from the nasogastric tube and purulent fluid in the opened neck incision are ominous signs that should prompt early esophagoscopy. Diffuse mucosal ischemia may indicate the presence of a nonviable stomach; reoperation with completion gastrectomy and proximal esophagostomy is required to treat this rare catastrophic complication.

Generally, leaks that occur more than 7 days after operation are small and are related to some degree of late ischemic disruption along the anastomosis. They can usually be managed by opening the cervical wound at the bedside and packing the site with gauze. Oral diet is advanced as tolerated. It may be noted that the volume of the leak is markedly greater or less depending on the position of the head during swallowing. Accordingly, before discharge, patients are taught how to temporarily adjust their swallowing as well as how to manage their dressing changes. Applying gentle pressure to the neck wound and turning the head to the left may help the patient ingest liquids with minimal soiling of the open neck incision. Dysphagia, even with an opened neck incision, should be treated by passing tapered esophageal dilators orally between 2 and 4 weeks after surgery. When a bougie at least 48 French in caliber can be passed through the anastomosis, the patient can usually swallow comfortably. The size of the leak often decreases after dilation as food is allowed to proceed preferentially into the stomach. To maximize the diameter of the anastomosis and reduce the likelihood of a symptomatic stricture, subsequent dilations should be scheduled at 2-week intervals for the next few months.

When a routine predischarge barium swallow after transhiatal esophagectomy raises the possibility of an anastomotic leak in an asymptomatic patient, the question arises of whether the wound should be opened at all. For small, contained leaks associated with preferential flow of contrast material into the stomach, observation alone may suffice in selected cases. Patients must be closely watched for fever or other signs of major infection. Given the quite low morbidity of cervical wound exploration, the surgeon should not hesitate to drain the neck if the patient's condition changes.

The incidence of anastomotic leakage is low after Ivor-Lewis resection, but the consequences are significant. Leaks presenting early in the postoperative period are usually related to technical problems and are difficult to manage; those presenting later are generally related to some degree of ischemic tissue loss. Patients who have received radiation therapy or are nutritionally depleted may be especially vulnerable to problems with anastomotic healing. A contrast swallow with dilute barium is the best method of evaluating the anastomosis. Leaks may be manifested either as a free flow of contrast into the pleural space or as a contained fluid collection.

Small leaks that drain immediately into properly placed thoracostomy tubes can usually be managed by giving antibiotics and withholding oral intake. Local control of infection generally results in spontaneous healing. Anastomotic disruptions that are large or are associated with a major pleural collection typically necessitate open drainage with decortication; percutaneous drainage may be considered as a preliminary approach in selected patients. Persistent soiling of the mediastinum and the pleural space is fatal if untreated.

Early esophagoscopy is strongly advised to evaluate the viability of the gastric remnant. Ischemic necrosis of the stomach necessitates reexploration, decortication, takedown of the anastomosis, gastric debridement, return of any viable stomach into the abdomen, closure of the hiatus, and proximal diversion with a cervical esophagostomy. Repair or revision of the anastomosis in an infected field is certain to fail and should never be considered. In certain cases, diversion via a cervical esophagostomy and a completion gastrectomy may be required.

Late Complications

At every postoperative visit, symptoms of reflux, regurgitation, dumping, poor gastric emptying, and dysphagia must be specifically sought: these are the major quality-of-life issues for post-esophagectomy patients.[4] Reflux and regurgitation may complicate any form of alimentary reconstruction after esophagectomy, though cervical anastomoses are less likely to be associated with symptomatic reflux than intrathoracic anastomoses are. Reflux symptoms generally respond to dietary modifications, such as smaller and more frequent meals. Regurgitation is usually related to the supine position and thus tends to be worse at night; elevating the bed and avoiding late meals may suffice for symptom control. Dumping is exacerbated by foods with high fat or sugar content. Dysphagia may be related to narrowing at the anastomosis or, in rare instances, to poor emptying of the transposed stomach. Anastomotic strictures are most commonly encountered as a sequel to a postoperative leak. There may be excessive scarring at the anastomosis, associated with local distortion or angulation. Specific tests for gastric atony include nuclear medicine gastric emptying studies using radiolabeled food. A simple barium swallow may indicate an incomplete pyloromyotomy as a cause of poor gastric emptying; balloon dilation often corrects this problem.

Any form of anastomotic leak will increase the incidence of late stricture. Dysphagia may be treated by means of progressive dilation with Maloney bougies. This procedure is performed in the outpatient clinic and often does not require sedation or any other special patient preparation. Complications are rare if due care is exercised during the procedure. As noted [see Transthoracic Hiatal Hernia Repair, Preoperative Evaluation, Dilation, above], it is essential that the caliber of the dilators be increased gradually and that little or no force be applied in advancing them. The appearance of blood on a withdrawn dilator signals a breach of the mucosa; further dilation should be done cautiously lest a transmural injury result. Comfortable swallowing, of liquids at least, is usually achieved after the successful passage of a 48 French bougie. It is preferable, however, to advance dilation until at least a 54 French bougie can be passed with ease. For late strictures that are particularly difficult to dilate, endoscopic examination and histologic evaluation may be required to rule out a recurrent tumor. CT of the chest should also be performed whenever there is unexplained weight loss or fatigue late after esophagectomy.

The Savary system of wire-guided dilators has been particularly helpful in the management of tight or eccentric strictures. Patients are generally treated in the endoscopy suite. Temporary sedation with I.V. fentanyl and midazolam is required. Fluoroscopy is used to confirm proper placement of a flexible-tip wire across the stricture. Serial wire-guided dilation can then be performed with confidence and increased patient safety.

OUTCOME EVALUATION

Transhiatal Esophagectomy

A 1999 study from the University of Michigan presented data on 1,085 patients who underwent transhiatal esophagectomy without thoracotomy, of whom 74% had carcinoma and 26% had nonmalignant disease.[5] Transhiatal esophagectomy was completed in 98.6% of the patients; the remaining 1.4% were converted to a transthoracic esophagectomy as a result of either thoracic esophageal fixation or bleeding. Previous chemotherapy or radiation therapy did not preclude performance of a transhiatal esophagectomy. Nine patients experienced inordinate intraoperative blood loss; three died as a result. The overall hospital mortality was 4%. The overall 5-year survival rate for patients undergoing transhiatal esophagectomy is approximately 20% for adenocarcinoma of the cardia and the esophagus and 30% for squamous cell carcinoma of the esophagus.

The stapled anastomosis described earlier [*see* Operative Technique, Transhiatal Esophagectomy, Step 8, *above*] reflects numerous refinements introduced at the University of Michigan. The endoscopic GIA stapler has a low-profile head that is ideally suited to the tight confines of the neck, enabling the surgeon to fashion a widely patent side-to-side functional end-to-end anastomosis with three rows of staples along the back wall. The rate of anastomotic stricture is markedly lower with this anastomosis than with a totally handsewn anastomosis. As regards postoperative function, stomach interposition through the posterior mediastinum after transhiatal esophagectomy is associated with low rates of aspiration and regurgitation. Esophageal reflux and esophagitis—commonly seen with intrathoracic esophagogastric anastomoses—are usually not clinically significant problems with this approach. Patients are advised to elevate the head of their bed and to continue taking PPIs for about 3 months after the operation. Approximately one third will require esophageal dilation for dysphagia after the operation. Some 7% to 10% experience postvagotomy dumping symptoms, which in most cases can be controlled by simply avoiding high-carbohydrate foods and dairy products.

Ivor-Lewis Esophagectomy

Ivor-Lewis esophagectomy is associated with anastomotic leakage rates and operative mortalities of less than 3%.[3,6] Approximately 5% of patients will require anastomotic dilation. Again, patients are advised to elevate the head of the bed and to continue taking PPIs. In some patients, the gastric interposition rotates into the right posterolateral thoracic gutter, resulting in postprandial gastric tension and rendering them more susceptible to aspiration. Compared with transhiatal esophagectomy, extended transthoracic esophagectomy is associated with higher pulmonary morbidity and operative mortality but also with a superior 3-year survival rate.[7]

Left Thoracoabdominal Esophagogastrectomy

Left thoracoabdominal esophagogastrectomy is also associated with anastomotic leakage rates and operative mortalities of less than 3%.[8] Approximately 5% of patients will require esophageal dilation. Reconstructions involving anastomosis of the distal stomach to the esophagus are associated with a high incidence of delayed gastric emptying and bile gastritis and esophagitis. Of all the operations we have described, this one results in the lowest postoperative quality of life. Accordingly, most surgeons prefer to carry out a total gastrectomy. Swallowing is restored with a Roux-en-Y jejunal interposition.

References

1. Lahey FH, Warren K: Esophageal diverticula. Surg Gynecol Obstet 98:1, 1954

2. Stirling MC, Orringer MB: Continued assessment of the combined Collis-Nissen operation. Ann Thorac Surg 47:224, 1989

3. Mathiesen DJ, Grillo HC, Wilkens EW Jr: Transthoracic esophagectomy: a safe approach to carcinoma of the esophagus. Ann Thorac Surg 45:137, 1988

4. Finley RJ, Lamy A, Clifton J, et al: Gastro-intestinal function following esophagectomy for malignancy. Am J Surg 169:471, 1995

5. Orringer MB, Marshall B, Iannettoni MD: Transhiatal esophagectomy: clinical experience and refinements. Ann Surg 230:392, 1999

6. King RM, Pairolero PC, Trastek VF, et al: Ivor Lewis esophagogastrectomy for carcinoma of the esophagus: early and long-term results. Ann Thorac Surg 44:119, 1987

7. Hulscher JBF, van Sandick JW et al: Extended transthoracic resection compared with limited transhiatal resection for adenocarcinoma of the esophagus. N Engl J Med 347:1662, 2002

8. Akiyama H, Miyazono H, Tsurumaru M, et al: Thoracoabdominal approach for carcinoma of the cardia of the stomach. Am J Surg 137:345, 1979

Acknowledgment

Figures 1 through 24   Tom Moore.

Marco G. Patti, M.D., F.A.C.S.

During the 1970s and the 1980s, operations for benign esophageal disorders were often withheld or delayed in favor of less effective forms of treatment in an effort to prevent the postoperative discomfort, the long hospital stay, and the recovery time associated with open surgical procedures. For instance, pneumatic dilatation became first-line therapy for achalasia, even though surgical management had been shown to be clearly superior.[1]

In the first part of the 1990s, it became clear that treatment of benign esophageal disorders with minimally invasive procedures yielded results comparable to those of treatment with traditional operations while causing minimal postoperative discomfort, reducing the duration of hospitalization, shortening recovery time, and permitting earlier return to work.[2,3] Consequently, minimally invasive surgery was increasingly considered as first-line treatment for achalasia, and laparoscopic fundoplication was considered more readily and at an earlier stage in the management of gastroesophageal reflux disease (GERD).

Since then, minimally invasive esophageal procedures have continued to evolve, thanks to better instrumentation and improved surgical expertise. In addition, with greater experience and longer follow-up periods, it has become possible to analyze techniques and their results more rigorously. For instance, whereas a few years ago a left thoracoscopic Heller myotomy was considered the procedure of choice for achalasia, the current procedure of choice is a laparoscopic Heller myotomy with partial fundoplication, which has proved to be better at relieving dysphagia and controlling postoperative reflux.[4-7] Similarly, whereas total fundoplication and partial fundoplication were initially considered equally effective in treating GERD,[8] total fundoplication is now viewed as clearly superior for this purpose and should be used whenever feasible.[9]

In this chapter, I focus on minimally invasive approaches to the treatment of abnormal gastroesophageal reflux and esophageal motility disorders. The standard open counterparts of these operations are described elsewhere [*see 34 Open Esophageal Procedures*].

Laparoscopic Nissen Fundoplication

PREOPERATIVE EVALUATION

All patients who are candidates for a laparoscopic fundoplication should undergo a preoperative evaluation that includes the following: (1) symptomatic evaluation, (2) an upper GI series, (3) endoscopy, (4) esophageal manometry, and (5) ambulatory pH monitoring.

Symptomatic Evaluation

The presence of both typical symptoms (heartburn, regurgitation, and dysphagia) and atypical symptoms of GERD (cough, wheezing, chest pain, and hoarseness) should be investigated, and symptoms should be graded with respect to their intensity both before and after operation. Nonetheless, a diagnosis of GERD should never be based solely on symptomatic evaluation. Many authorities assert that the diagnosis can be made reliably from the clinical history,[10] so that a complaint of heartburn should lead to the presumption that acid reflux is present; however, testing of this diagnostic strategy demonstrates that symptoms are far less sensitive and specific than is usually believed.[11] For instance, a study from the University of California, San Francisco (UCSF), found that of 822 consecutive patients referred for esophageal function tests with a clinical diagnosis of GERD (based on symptoms and endoscopic findings), only 70% had abnormal reflux on pH monitoring.[12] Heartburn and regurgitation were no more frequent in patients who had genuine reflux than in those who did not; thus, symptomatic evaluation, by itself, could not distinguish between the two groups.

The response to proton pump inhibitors (PPIs) is a better predictor of abnormal reflux. For example, in the UCSF study just cited, 75% of patients with GERD reported a good or excellent response to PPIs, compared with only 26% of patients without GERD.[12] Similarly, a study involving multivariate analysis of factors predicting outcome after laparoscopic fundoplication concluded that a clinical response to acid suppression therapy was one of three factors predictive of a successful outcome, the other two being an abnormal 24-hour pH score and the presence of a typical primary symptom (e.g., heartburn).[13]

Upper Gastrointestinal Series

An upper GI series is useful for diagnosing and characterizing an existing hiatal hernia. The size of the hiatal hernia helps predict how difficult it will be to reduce the esophagogastric junction below the diaphragm. In addition, large hiatal hernias are associated with more severe disturbances of esophageal peristalsis and esophageal acid clearance.[14] Esophagograms are also useful for determining the location, shape, and size of a stricture and detecting a short esophagus.

Endoscopy

Endoscopy is typically the first test performed to confirm a symptom-based diagnosis of GERD. This approach has two pitfalls, however. First, even though the goal of endoscopy is to assess the mucosal damage caused by reflux, mucosal changes are absent in about 50% of GERD patients.[12] Second, major interobserver variations have been reported with esophageal endoscopy, particularly for low-grade esophagitis.[15] In one study, for instance, 60 (24%) of 247 patients with negative results on pH monitoring had been diagnosed as having grade I or II esophagitis.[12] Accordingly, I believe that endoscopy is most valuable for excluding gastric and duodenal pathologic conditions and detecting the presence of Barrett's esophagus.

Table 1   Instrumentation for Laparoscopic Nissen Fundoplication

Five 10 mm trocars

30° scope

Graspers

Babcock clamp

L-shaped hook cautery with suction-irrigation capacity

Scissors

Laparoscopic clip applier

Ultrasonic coagulating shears

Fan retractor

Needle holder

Penrose drain

2-0 silk sutures

56 French esophageal bougie

Esophageal Manometry

Esophageal manometry provides useful information about the motor function of the esophagus by determining the length and resting pressure of the lower esophageal sphincter (LES) and assessing the quality (i.e., the amplitude and propagation) of esophageal peristalsis. In addition, it allows proper placement of the pH probe for ambulatory pH monitoring (5 cm above the upper border of the LES).

Ambulatory pH Monitoring

Ambulatory pH monitoring is the most reliable test for the diagnosis of GERD, with a sensitivity and specificity of about 92%.[16] It is of key importance in the workup for the following four reasons.

1. It determines whether abnormal reflux is present. In the UCSF study mentioned earlier,[12] pH monitoring yielded normal results in 30% of patients with a clinical diagnosis of GERD, thereby obviating the continuation of inappropriate and expensive drugs (e.g., PPIs) or the performance of a fundoplication. In addition, pH monitoring prompted further investigation that in a number of cases pointed to other diseases (e.g., cholelithiasis and irritable bowel syndrome).
2. It establishes a temporal correlation between symptoms and episodes of reflux. Such a correlation is particularly important when atypical GERD symptoms are present because 50% of these patients experience no heartburn and 50% do not have esophagitis on endoscopy.[17]
3. It allows staging on the basis of disease severity. Specifically, pH monitoring identifies a subgroup of patients characterized by worse esophageal motor function (manifested by a defective LES or by abnormal esophageal peristalsis), more acid reflux in the distal and proximal esophagus, and slower acid clearance. These patients more frequently experience stricture formation and Barrett metaplasia and thus might benefit from early antireflux surgery.[18]
4. It provides baseline data that may prove useful postoperatively if symptoms do not respond to the procedure.

OPERATIVE PLANNING

The patient is placed under general anesthesia and intubated with a single-lumen endotracheal tube. Abdominal wall relaxation is ensured by the administration of a nondepolarizing muscle relaxant, the action of which is rapidly reversed at the end of the operation. Adequate muscle relaxation is essential because increased abdominal wall compliance allows increased pneumoperitoneum, which yields better exposure. An orogastric tube is inserted at the beginning of the operation to keep the stomach decompressed; it is removed at the end of the procedure.

The patient is placed in a steep reverse Trendelenburg position, with the legs extended on stirrups. The surgeon stands between the patient's legs. To keep the patient from sliding as a result of the steep position used during the operation, a bean bag is inflated under the patient, and the knees are flexed only 20° to 30°. A Foley catheter is inserted at the beginning of the procedure and usually is removed in the postoperative period. Because increased abdominal pressure from pneumoperitoneum and the steep reverse Trendelenburg position decrease venous return, pneumatic compression stockings are always used as prophylaxis against deep vein thrombosis.

The equipment required for a laparoscopic Nissen fundoplication includes five 10 mm trocars, a 30° laparoscope, a hook cautery, and various other instruments [see Table 1]. In addition, we use a three-chip camera system that is separate from the laparoscope.

OPERATIVE TECHNIQUE

In all patients except those with very poor esophageal motility—for whom partial fundoplication [see Laparoscopic Partial (Guarner) Fundoplication, below] is preferable—we advocate performing a 360° wrap of the gastric fundus around the lower esophagus as described by Nissen, but we always take down the short gastric vessels to achieve what is called a floppy fundoplication. This type of wrap is very effective in controlling gastroesophageal reflux.[19,20] The operation can be divided into nine key steps as follows.

Step 1: Placement of Trocars

Five 10 mm trocars are used for the operation [see Figure 1]. Port A is placed about 14 cm below the xiphoid process; it can also be placed slightly (2 to 3 cm) to the left of the midline to be in line with the hiatus. This port is used for insertion of the scope. Port B is placed at the same level as port A but in the left midclavicular line. It is used for insertion of the Babcock clamp; insertion of a grasper to hold the Penrose drain once it is in place surrounding the esophagus; or insertion of the clip applier, the ultrasonic coagulating shears, or both to take down the short gastric vessels. Port C is placed at the same level as the previous two ports but in the right midclavicular line. It is used for insertion of the fan retractor, the purpose of which is to lift the lateral segment of the left lobe of the liver and expose the esophagogastric junction. I do not divide the left triangular ligament. The fan retractor can be held in place by a self-retaining system fixed to the operating table. Ports D and E are placed as high as possible under the costal margin and about 5 to 6 cm to the right and the left of the midline so that they are about 15 cm from the esophageal hiatus; in addition, they should be placed so that their axes form an angle of 60° to 120°. These ports are used for insertion of the graspers, the electrocautery, and the suturing instruments.

Troubleshooting   If the ports are placed too low in the abdomen, the operation is made more difficult. If port C is too low, the fan retractor will not retract the lateral segment of the left lobe of the liver well, and the esophagogastric junction will not be exposed. If port B is too low, the Babcock clamp will not reach the esophagogastric junction, and when the ultrasonic coagulating shears or the clip applier is placed through the same port, it will not reach the upper short gastric vessels. If ports D and E are too low, the dissection at the beginning of the case and the suturing at the end are problematic.

Other mistakes of positioning must be avoided as well. Port C must not be placed too medially, because the fan retractor may clash with the left-hand instrument; the gallbladder fossa is a good landmark for positioning this port. Port A must be placed with extreme caution in the supraumbilical area: its insertion site is just above the aorta, before its bifurcation. Accordingly, I recommend initially inflating the abdomen to a pressure of 18 mm Hg just for placement of port A; increasing the distance between the abdominal wall and the aorta reduces the risk of aortic injury. I also recommend directing the port toward the coccyx. Once port A is in place, the intraperitoneal pressure is reduced to 15 mm Hg. A Hasson cannula can be used in this location, particularly if the patient has already had one or more midline incisions. Maintaining the proper angle (60° to 120°) between the axes of the two suturing instruments inserted through ports D and E is also important: if the angle is smaller, the instruments will cover part of the operating field, whereas if it is larger, depth perception may be impaired. Finally, if a trocar is not in the ideal position, it is better to insert another one than to operate through an inconveniently placed port.

If the surgeon spears the epigastric vessels with a trocar, bleeding will occur, in which case there are two options. The first option is to pull the port out, insert a 24 French Foley catheter with a 30 ml balloon through the site, inflate the balloon, and apply traction with a clamp. The advantage of this maneuver is that the vessel need not be sutured; the disadvantage is that the surgeon must then choose another insertion site. At the end of the case, the balloon is deflated. If some bleeding is still present, it must be controlled with sutures placed from outside under direct vision. The second option is to use a long needle with a suture, with which one can rapidly place two U-shaped stitches, one above the clamp and one below. The suture is tied outside over a sponge and left in place for 2 or 3 days.

Step 2: Division of Gastrohepatic Ligament; Identification of Right Crus of Diaphragm and Posterior Vagus Nerve

Once the ports are in place, the gastrohepatic ligament is divided. Dissection begins above the caudate lobe of the liver, where this ligament usually is very thin, and continues toward the diaphragm until the right crus is identified. The crus is then separated from the right side of the esophagus by blunt dissection, and the posterior vagus nerve is identified. The right crus is dissected inferiorly toward the junction with the left crus.

Troubleshooting An accessory left hepatic artery originating from the left gastric artery is frequently encountered in the gastrohepatic ligament. If this vessel creates problems of exposure, it may be divided; in my experience, doing so has not caused problems. When dissecting the right crus from the esophagus, the electrocautery should be used with particular caution. Because the monopolar current tends to spread laterally, the posterior vagus nerve may sustain damage simply from being in proximity to the device, even when there is no direct contact. The risk of neuropraxia can be reduced by using the cut mode rather than the coagulation mode when the electrocautery is close to the nerve. The cut mode has problems of its own, however, and is not recommended in most laparoscopic procedures. A better alternative is to use the ultrasonic coagulating shears.

Step 3: Division of Peritoneum and Phrenoesophageal Membrane above Esophagus; Identification of Left Crus of Diaphragm and Anterior Vagus Nerve

The peritoneum and the phrenoesophageal membrane above the esophagus are divided with the electrocautery, and the anterior vagus nerve is identified. The left crus of the diaphragm is dissected downward toward the junction with the right crus.

Troubleshooting Care must be taken not to damage the anterior vagus nerve or the esophageal wall. To this end, the nerve should be left attached to the esophageal wall, and the peritoneum and the phrenoesophageal membrane should be lifted from the wall by blunt dissection before they are divided.

Step 4: Creation of Window between Gastric Fundus, Esophagus, and Diaphragmatic Crura; Placement of Penrose Drain around Esophagus

The esophagus is retracted upward with a Babcock clamp applied at the level of the esophagogastric junction. Via blunt and sharp dissection, a window is created under the esophagus between the gastric fundus, the esophagus, and the diaphragmatic crura. The window is enlarged with the ultrasonic coagulating shears, and a Penrose drain is passed around the esophagus. This drain is then used for traction instead of the Babcock clamp to reduce the risk of damage to the gastric wall.

Troubleshooting The two main problems to watch for during this part of the procedure are (1) creation of a left pneumothorax and (2) perforation of the gastric fundus.

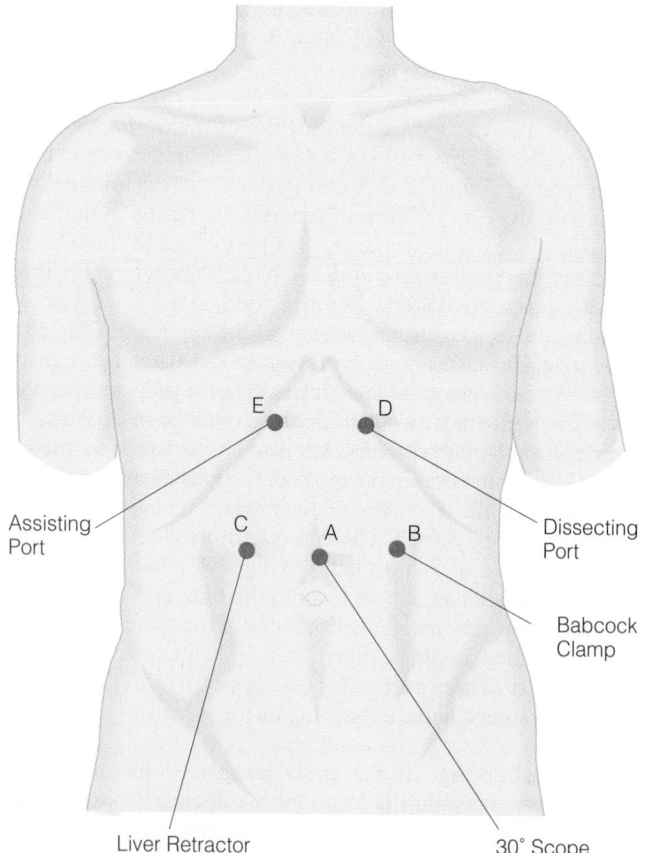

Figure 1 **Laparoscopic Nissen fundoplication. Illustrated is the recommended placement of the trocars.**

A left pneumothorax is usually caused by dissection done above the left crus in the mediastinum rather than between the crus and the gastric fundus. This problem can be avoided by properly dissecting and identifying the left crus.

Perforation of the gastric fundus is usually caused by pushing a blunt instrument under the esophagus and below the left crus without having done enough dissection. Care must be exercised in taking down small vessels from the fundus when the area behind the esophagus is approached from the right: the anatomy is not as clear from this viewpoint, and perforation can easily occur. Sometimes, perforation is caused by the use of a monopolar electrocautery for dissection. An electrocautery burn can go unrecognized during dissection and manifest itself in the form of a leak during the first 48 hours after operation.

Step 5: Division of Short Gastric Vessels

The ultrasonic coagulating shears or the clip applier is introduced through port B. A grasper is introduced by the surgeon through port D, and an assistant applies traction on the greater curvature of the stomach through port E. Dissection begins at the level of the middle portion of the gastric body and continues upward until the most proximal short gastric vessel is divided and the Penrose drain is reached.

Troubleshooting Again, there are two main problems to watch for during this part of the procedure: (1) bleeding, either from the gastric vessels or from the spleen, and (2) damage to the gastric wall.

Bleeding from the gastric vessels is usually caused by excessive traction or by division of a vessel that is not completely occluding with clips on both sides. Vessels up to 5 mm in diameter can be taken down with the ultrasonic coagulating shears; this process requires about half of the amount of time needed when only clips are used. The lower blade has a sharp, oscillating inferior edge that must always be kept in view to prevent damage to other structures (e.g., the pancreas, the splenic artery and vein, and the spleen). Damage to the gastric wall can be caused by a burn from the electrocautery used to dissect between vessels or by traction applied via the graspers or the Babcock clamp.

Step 6: Closure of Crura

The diaphragmatic crura are closed with interrupted 2-0 silk sutures on a curved needle; the sutures are tied intracorporeally. Exposure is provided by retracting the esophagus upward and toward the patient's left with the Penrose drain. The lens of the 30° laparoscope is angled slightly to the left by moving the light cable of the scope to the patient's right. The first stitch should be placed just above the junction of the two crura. Additional stitches are placed 1 cm apart, and a space of about 1 cm is left between the uppermost stitch and the esophagus.

Troubleshooting Care must be taken not to spear the posterior wall of the esophagus with either the tip or the back of the needle. So as not to limit the space available for suturing, the bougie is not placed inside the esophagus during this part of the procedure.

Step 7: Insertion of Bougie into Esophagus and through Esophagogastric Junction

The esophageal stethoscope and the orogastric tube are removed, and a 56 French bougie is inserted by the anesthesiologist and passed through the esophagogastric junction under laparoscopic vision. The crura must be snug around the esopha-gus but not too tight: a closed grasper should slide easily between the esophagus and the crura.

Troubleshooting The most worrisome complication during this step is perforation of the esophagus. This can be prevented by lubricating the bougie and instructing the anesthesiologist to advance the bougie slowly and to stop if any resistance is encountered. In addition, it is essential to remove any instruments from the esophagogastric junction and to open the Penrose drain; these measures prevent the creation of an angle between the stomach and the esophagus, which can increase the likelihood of perforation. The position of the bougie can be confirmed by pressing with a grasper over the esophagus, which will feel full when the bougie is in place.

Step 8: Wrapping of Gastric Fundus around Lower Esophagus

The gastric fundus is gently pulled under the esophagus with the graspers. The left and right sides of the fundus are wrapped above the fat pad (which lies above the esophagogastric junction) and held together in place with a Babcock clamp introduced through port B. (The Penrose drain should be removed at this point because it is in the way.) Usually, three 2-0 silk sutures are used to secure the two ends of the wrap to each other. The first stitch does not include the esophagus and is used for traction; the second and the third include a bite of the esophageal muscle. The bougie is passed into the stomach after the first stitch to assess the size of the wrap. If the wrap seems at all tight, the stitch is removed and repositioned more laterally. Two coronal stitches are then placed between the top of the wrap and the esophagus, one on the right and one on the left. Finally, one additional suture is placed between the right side of the wrap and the closed crura.

To avoid the risk of injuring the inferior vena cava at the beginning of the dissection, some surgeons use a different method—the so-called left crus approach.[19] In this approach, the operation begins with identification of the left crus of the diaphragm and division of the peritoneum and the phrenoesophageal membrane overlying it. The next step is division of the short gastric vessels, starting midway along the greater curvature of the stomach and continuing upward to join the area of the previous dissection. When the fundus has been thoroughly mobilized, the peritoneum is divided from the left to the right crus, and the right crus is dissected downward to expose the junction of the right and left crura. With this technique, the vena cava is never at risk. In addition, the branches of the anterior vagus nerve and the left gastric artery are less exposed to danger. This technique can be very useful, particularly for management of very large paraesophageal hernias and for second antireflux operations [see Reoperation for GERD, below].

Troubleshooting To determine whether the wrap is going to be floppy, the surgeon must deliver the fundus under the esophagus, making sure that the origins of the short gastric vessels that have been transected are visible. Essentially, the posterior wall of the fundus is being used for the wrap. If the wrap remains to the right of the esophagus without retracting back to the left, then it is floppy, and suturing can proceed. If not, the surgeon must make sure that the upper short gastric vessels have been transected. If tension is still present after these maneuvers, it is probably best to perform a partial wrap [see Laparoscopic Partial (Guarner) Fundoplication, below].

Damage to the gastric wall may occur during the delivery of the fundus. Atraumatic graspers must be used, and the gastric fundus must be pulled gently and passed from one grasper to the other.

Sometimes, it is helpful to push the gastric fundus under the esophagus from the left. The wrap should measure no more than 2 to 2.5 cm in length and, as noted, should be done with no more than three sutures. The first stitch is usually the lowest one; it must be placed just above the fat pad where the esophagogastric junction is thought to be.

If the anesthesiologist observes that peak airway pressure has increased (because of a pneumothorax) or that neck emphysema is present (because of pneumomediastinum), the pneumoperitoneum should be reduced from 15 mm Hg to 8 or 10 mm Hg until the end of the procedure. Pneumomediastinum tends to resolve without intervention within a few hours of the end of the procedure. Small pneumothoraces (usually on the left side) tend to resolve spontaneously, rendering insertion of a chest tube unnecessary. Larger pneumothoraces (> 20%), however, call for the insertion of a small (18 to 20 French) chest tube.

Step 9: Final Inspection and Removal of Instruments and Ports from Abdomen

After hemostasis is obtained, the instruments and the ports are removed from the abdomen under direct vision.

Troubleshooting If any areas of oozing were observed, they should be irrigated and dried with sponges rolled into a cigarette-like shape before the ports are removed. In addition, if some grounds for concern remain, the oozing areas should be examined after the pneumoperitoneum is decreased to 7 to 8 mm Hg to abolish the tamponading effect exerted by the high intra-abdominal pressure.

All the ports should be removed from the abdomen under direct vision so that any bleeding from the abdominal wall can be readily detected. Such bleeding is easily controlled, either from inside or from outside.

COMPLICATIONS

A feared complication of laparoscopic Nissen fundoplication is esophageal or gastric perforation, which may result either from traction applied with the Babcock clamp or a grasper to the esophagus or the stomach (particularly when the stomach is pulled under the esophagus) or from inadvertent electrocautery burns during any part of the dissection. A leak will manifest itself during the first 48 hours. Peritoneal signs will be noted if the spillage is limited to the abdomen; shortness of breath and a pleural effusion will be noted if spillage also occurs in the chest. The site of the leak should always be confirmed by a contrast study with barium or a water-soluble contrast agent. Optimal management consists of laparotomy and direct repair. If a perforation is detected intra-operatively, it may be closed laparoscopically.

About 50% of patients experience mild dysphagia postoperatively. This problem usually resolves after 4 to 6 weeks, during which period patients receive pain medications in an elixir form and are advised to avoid eating meat and bread. If, however, dysphagia persists beyond this period, one or more of the following causes is responsible.

1. A wrap that is too tight or too long (i.e., > 2.5 cm).[21]
2. Lateral torsion with corkscrew effect. If the wrap rotates to the right (because of tension from intact short gastric vessels or because the fundus is small), a corkscrew effect is created.
3. A wrap made with the body of the stomach rather than the fundus. The relaxation of the LES and the gastric fundus is controlled by vasoactive intestinal polypeptide and nitric oxide[22,23]; after fundoplication, the two structures relax simultaneously

with swallowing. If part of the body of the stomach rather than the fundus is used for the wrap, it will not relax as the LES does on arrival of the food bolus.
4. Choice of the wrong procedure. In patients who have severely abnormal esophageal peristalsis (as in end-stage connective tissue disorders), a partial wrap is preferable. A 360° wrap may cause postoperative dysphagia and gas bloat syndrome.

If the wrap slips into the chest, the patient becomes unable to eat and prone to vomiting. A chest radiograph shows a gastric bubble above the diaphragm, and the diagnosis is confirmed by means of a barium swallow. This problem can be prevented by using coronal sutures and by ensuring that the crura are closed securely.

Paraesophageal hernia may occur if the crura have not been closed or if the closure is too loose. In my opinion, closure of the crura not only is essential for preventing paraesophageal hernia but also is important from a physiologic point of view, in that it acts synergistically with the LES against stress reflux. Sometimes, it is possible to reduce the stomach and close the crura laparoscopically. More often, however, because the crural opening is very tight and the gastric wall is edematous, laparoscopic repair is impossible and laparotomy is preferable.

POSTOPERATIVE CARE AND OUTCOME EVALUATION

Postoperative care and outcome evaluation of laparoscopic Nissen fundoplication are considered elsewhere in conjunction with the discussion of partial fundoplication [see Laparoscopic Partial (Guarner) Fundoplication, Postoperative Care *and* Outcome Evaluation, *below*].

Laparoscopic Partial (Guarner) Fundoplication

PREOPERATIVE EVALUATION AND OPERATIVE PLANNING

Preoperative evaluation and operative planning are essentially the same for partial (Guarner) fundoplication as for Nissen fundoplication. This operation should be performed only in patients with the most severe abnormalities of esophageal peristalsis: it is less effective than a 360° wrap for long-term control of reflux.[9] In addition, laparoscopic partial fundoplication may be performed after laparoscopic Heller myotomy for achalasia [see Laparoscopic Heller Myotomy with Partial Fundoplication, *below*].[24]

OPERATIVE TECHNIQUE

The first seven steps in a Guarner fundoplication are identical to the first seven in a Nissen fundoplication. The wrap, however, differs in that it extends around only 240° to 280° of the esophageal circumference. Once the gastric fundus is delivered under the esophagus, the two sides are not approximated over the esophagus. Instead, 80° to 120° of the anterior esophagus is left uncovered, and each of the two sides of the wrap (right and left) is separately affixed to the esophagus with three 2-0 silk sutures, with each stitch including the muscle layer of the esophageal wall. The remaining stitches (i.e., the coronal stitches and the stitch between the right side of the wrap and the closed crura) are identical to those placed in a Nissen fundoplication.

POSTOPERATIVE CARE

Currently, my average operating time for a laparoscopic fundoplication is approximately 2 hours. I start patients on a soft mechanical diet on the morning of postoperative day 1 and usually discharge them after 23 to 48 hours. The recovery time usually ranges from 10 to 14 days.

OUTCOME EVALUATION

The initial results of laparoscopic fundoplication obtained in the early 1990s indicated that the operation was effective in controlling reflux but that postoperative dysphagia occurred more often than had been anticipated.[8] Many experts thought that this problem could be avoided by tailoring the fundoplication to the strength of esophageal peristalsis as measured by esophageal manometry.[8] Accordingly, partial fundoplication (240°) was recommended for patients with impaired peristalsis, and total fundoplication (360°) was recommended for those with normal peristalsis. The short-term results of this tailored approach were promising.[8] Gradually, however, it became evident that partial fundoplication was not as durable as total fundoplication[9] and that total fundoplication did not pose a special problem for patients with weak peristalsis.[25]

Long-term follow-up of patients operated on in accordance with the tailored approach at UCSF between October 1992 and December 1999 indicated that the promising short-term results reported earlier[8] were not maintained over time.[20] After a mean follow-up period of 70 months, 56% of the patients who underwent partial fundoplication had recurrent reflux as documented by pH monitoring, compared with only 28% of those who underwent total fundoplication. (These figures probably overestimate the real incidence of postoperative reflux, in that most of the patients studied had heartburn and very few were asymptomatic.) In addition, more of the patients in the partial fundoplication group needed acid-suppressing medication (25% versus 8%) or a second operation (9% versus 3%). The incidence of postoperative dysphagia, however, was the same in the two groups, which indicated that the completeness of the wrap played no role in causing this largely transient complication. These findings suggest that the initial problems with postoperative dysphagia were primarily attributable to unknown technical factors that were largely eliminated from the procedure as surgeons garnered more experience with it. As a result, total fundoplication is currently considered the procedure of choice for patients with GERD, regardless of the strength of their esophageal peristalsis.

Laparoscopic Heller Myotomy with Partial Fundoplication

Minimally invasive surgical procedures for primary esophageal motility disorders (achalasia, diffuse esophageal spasm, and nutcracker esophagus) yield results that are comparable to those of open procedures but are associated with less postoperative pain and with a shorter recovery time.[26] Today, laparoscopic Heller myotomy with partial fundoplication has supplanted left thoracoscopic myotomy as the procedure of choice for esophageal achalasia.[4-7] Long-term studies demonstrated that even though left thoracoscopic myotomy led to resolution of dysphagia in about 85% to 90% of patients, it had the following four drawbacks.

1. Gastroesophageal reflux developed postoperatively in about 60% of patients because no fundoplication was performed in conjunction with the myotomy.[4] With the laparoscopic approach, in contrast, a partial fundoplication can easily be performed, which prevents reflux in the majority of patients[4,5] and corrects many instances of preexisting reflux arising from pneumatic dilatation.[4] A prospective, randomized, double-blind clinical trial that compared Heller myotomy alone with Heller myotomy and Dor fundoplication clearly demonstrated that the addition of a fundoplication is essential: the incidence of postoperative reflux (as measured by pH monitoring) was 47.6% in patients who underwent myotomy alone but only 9.1% in those

who underwent myotomy and Dor fundoplication.[27]
2. The extension of the myotomy onto the gastric wall (clearly the most critical and challenging part of the operation) proved difficult because of poor exposure, with the consequent risk of a short myotomy and persistent dysphagia. With the laparoscopic approach, in contrast, excellent exposure of the esophagogastric junction is easily achieved, and the myotomy can be extended onto the gastric wall for about 2 to 2.5 cm.[4]
3. Double-lumen endotracheal intubation and single-lung ventilation were required, with the patient in the right lateral decubitus position. In contrast, the setting for a laparoscopic myotomy (the same as that for a laparoscopic fundoplication) is much easier for the patient, the anesthesiologist, and the OR personnel. In addition, most surgeons have by now acquired substantial experience with laparoscopic antireflux procedures and thus are more familiar and comfortable with laparoscopic exposure of the distal esophagus and the esophagogastric junction.
4. The average postoperative hospital stay was about 3 days because of the chest tube left in place at the time of the operation and the discomfort arising from the thoracic incisions. After a laparoscopic Heller myotomy, the hospital stay is only 1 or 2 days; there is no need for a chest tube, and patients are more comfortable.

Because of these drawbacks, left thoracoscopic myotomy is now largely reserved for patients with achalasia who have undergone multiple abdominal operations (which may rule out a laparoscopic approach). A laparoscopic Heller myotomy and Dor fundoplication is considered the procedure of choice for achalasia.

PREOPERATIVE EVALUATION

All candidates for a laparoscopic Heller myotomy should undergo a thorough and careful evaluation to establish the diagnosis and characterize the disease.[28]

An upper GI series is useful. A characteristic so-called bird's beak is usually seen in patients with achalasia. A dilated, sigmoid esophagus may be present in patients with long-standing achalasia. A corkscrew esophagus is often seen in patients with diffuse esophageal spasm. Endoscopy is performed to rule out a tumor of the esophagogastric junction and gastroduodenal pathologic conditions.

Esophageal manometry is the key test for establishing the diagnosis of esophageal achalasia. The classic manometric findings are (1) absence of esophageal peristalsis and (2) a hypertensive LES that fails to relax appropriately in response to swallowing.

Ambulatory pH monitoring should always be done in patients who have undergone pneumatic dilatation to rule out abnormal gastroesophageal reflux. In addition, pH monitoring should be performed postoperatively to detect abnormal reflux, which, if present, should be treated with acid-reducing medications.[28]

In patients older than 60 years who have experienced the recent onset of dysphagia and excessive weight loss, secondary achalasia or pseudoachalasia from cancer of the esophagogastric junction should be ruled out. Endoscopic ultrasonography or computed tomography can help establish the diagnosis.[29]

OPERATIVE PLANNING

Patient preparation (i.e., anesthesia, positioning, and instrumentation) is identical to that for laparoscopic fundoplication.

OPERATIVE TECHNIQUE

Many of the steps in a laparoscopic Heller myotomy are the same as the corresponding steps in a laparoscopic fundoplication. The

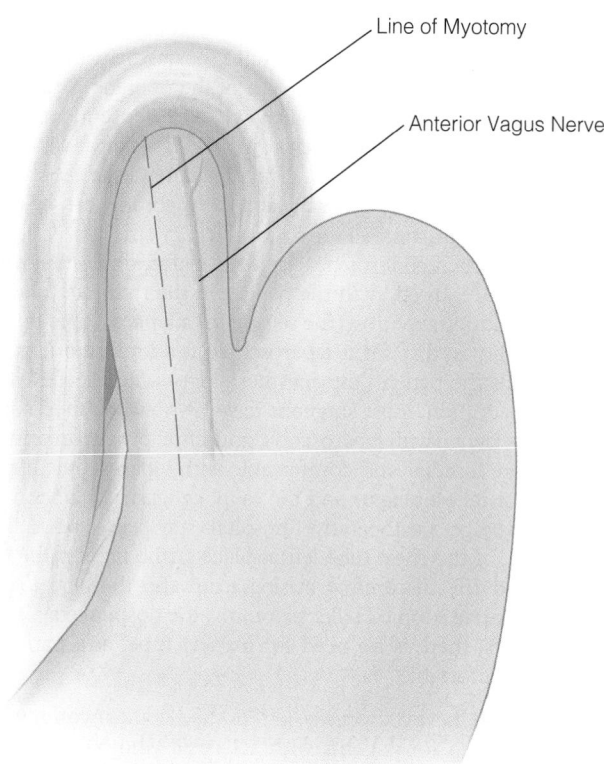

Line of Myotomy

Anterior Vagus Nerve

Figure 2 **Laparoscopic Heller myotomy with partial fundoplication. The proposed myotomy line is marked on the surface of the esophagus.**

ensuing description focuses on those steps that differ significantly.

Either a Dor or a Guarner fundoplication [*see* Laparoscopic Partial (Guarner) Fundoplication, *above*] may be performed in conjunction with a Heller myotomy. The Dor fundoplication is an anterior 180° wrap. Its advantages are that (1) it does not require posterior dissection and the creation of a window between the esophagus, the stomach, and the left pillar of the crus; (2) it covers the exposed esophageal mucosa after completion of the myotomy; and (3) it is effective even in patients with GERD.[30] Its main disadvantage is that achieving the proper geometry can be difficult, and a wrong configuration can lead to dysphagia even after a properly performed myotomy.[31] The advantages of the Guarner fundoplication are that (1) it is easier to perform; (2) it keeps the edges of the myotomy well separated; and (3) it might be more effective than a Dor procedure in preventing reflux. Its main disadvantages are that (1) it requires more dissection for the creation of a posterior window and (2) it leaves the esophageal mucosa exposed.

Steps 1 through 6

Steps 1, 2, 3, 4, 5, and 6 of a laparoscopic Heller myotomy are essentially identical to the first six steps of a laparoscopic fundoplication. Steps 4 and 6, however, are necessary only if a posterior partial fundoplication is to be performed. Care must be taken not to narrow the esophageal hiatus too much and push the esophagus anteriorly.

Step 7: Intraoperative Endoscopy

The esophageal stethoscope and the orogastric tube are removed, and an endoscope is inserted. The endoscopic view allows easy identification of the squamocolumnar junction, so that the myotomy can be extended downward onto the gastric wall for about 2 cm distal to this point. In addition, if possible mucosal

perforation is a concern, the esophagus can be covered with water from outside while air is insufflated from inside; bubbling will be observed over the site of any perforation present.

At the beginning of a surgeon's experience with laparoscopic Heller myotomy, intraoperative endoscopy is a very important and helpful step; however, once the surgeon has gained adequate experience with this procedure and has become familiar with the relevant anatomy from a laparoscopic perspective, it may be omitted.

Troubleshooting The most worrisome complication during intraoperative endoscopy is perforation of the esophagus. This complication can be prevented by having the procedure done by an experienced endoscopist who is familiar with achalasia.

Step 8: Initiation of Myotomy and Entry into Submucosal Plane at Single Point

The fat pad is removed with the ultrasonic coagulating shears to provide clear exposure of the esophagogastric junction. A Babcock clamp is then applied over the junction, and the esophagus is pulled downward and to the left to expose the right side of the esophagus. The myotomy is performed at the 11 o'clock position. It is helpful to mark the surface of the esophagus along the line through which the myotomy will be carried out [*see Figure 2*]. The myotomy is started about 3 cm above the esophagogastric junction. Before it is extended upward and downward, the proper submucosal plane should be reached at a single point; in this way, the likelihood of subsequent mucosal perforation can be reduced.

Troubleshooting The myotomy should not be started close to the esophagogastric junction, because at this level the layers often are poorly defined, particularly if multiple dilatations or injections of botulinum toxin have been performed. At the preferred starting point, about 3 cm above the esophagogastric junction, the esophageal wall is usually normal. As a rule, I do not open the entire longitudinal layer first and then the circular layer; I find it easier and safer to try to reach the submucosal plane at one point and then move upward and downward from there. In the course of the myotomy, there is always some bleeding from the cut muscle fibers, particularly if the esophagus is dilated and the wall is very thick. After the source of the bleeding is identified, the electrocautery must be used with caution. The most troublesome bleeding comes from the submucosal veins encountered at the esophagogastric junction (which are usually large). In most instances, gentle compression is preferable to electrocautery. A sponge introduced through one of the ports facilitates the application of direct pressure.

Step 9: Proximal and Distal Extension of Myotomy

Once the mucosa has been exposed, the myotomy can safely be extended [*see Figure 3*]. Distally, it is extended for about 2 to 2.5 cm onto the gastric wall; proximally, it is extended for about 6 cm above the esophagogastric junction. Thus, the total length of the myotomy is typically about 8 cm [*see Figure 4*].

Troubleshooting The course of the anterior vagus nerve must be identified before the myotomy is started. If this nerve crosses the line of the myotomy, it must be lifted away from the esophageal wall, and the muscle layers must then be cut under it. In addition, care must be taken not to injure the anterior vagus nerve while removing the fat pad. Treatment with botulinum toxin occasionally results in fibrosis with scarring and loss of the normal

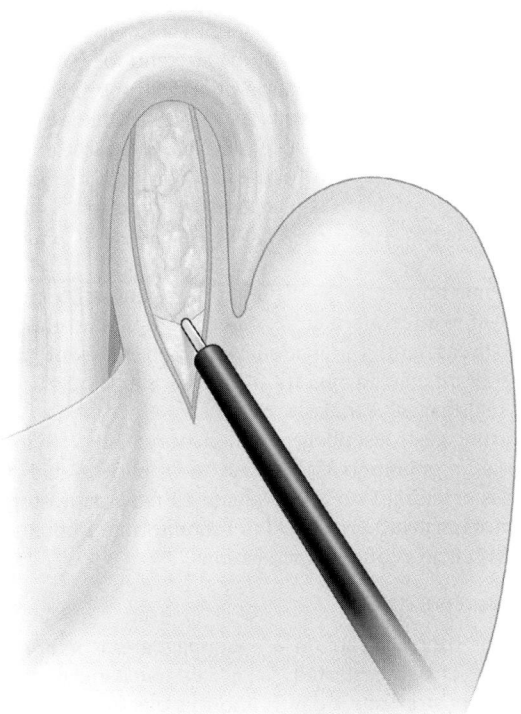

Figure 3   **Laparoscopic Heller myotomy with partial fundoplication. The myotomy is extended proximally and distally.**

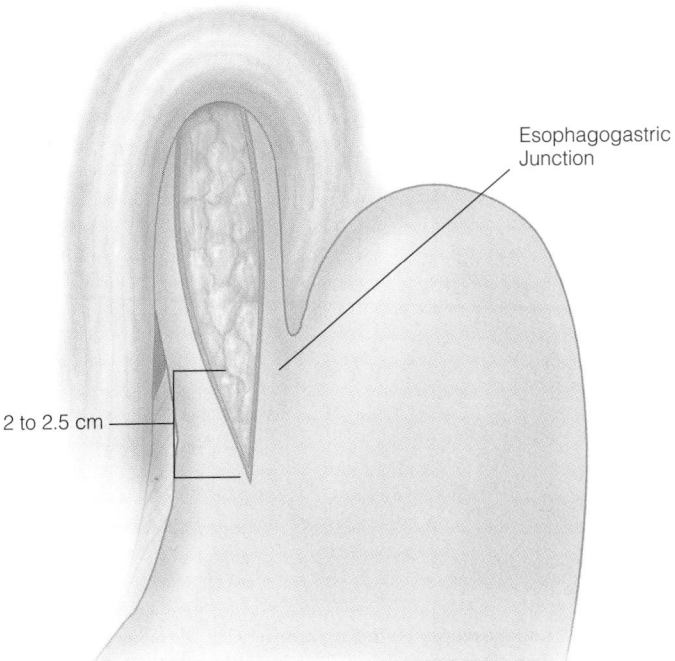

Figure 4   **Laparoscopic Heller myotomy with partial fundoplication. The myotomy is approximately 8 cm long, extending distally for about 2 to 2.5 cm onto the gastric wall and proximally for about 6 cm above the esophagogastric junction.**

anatomic planes; this occurs more frequently at the level of the esophagogastric junction.

If a perforation seems possible or likely, it should be sought as described earlier [*see* Step 7, *above*]. Any perforation found should be repaired with 5-0 absorbable suture material, with interrupted sutures employed for a small perforation and a continuous suture for a larger one. When a perforation has occurred, an anterior fundoplication is usually chosen in preference to a posterior one because the stomach will offer further protection against a leak.

Step 10 (Dor Procedure): Anterior Partial Fundoplication

Two rows of sutures are placed. The first row (on the left side) comprises three stitches: the uppermost stitch incorporates the gastric fundus, the esophageal wall, and the left pillar of the crus [*see Figure 5*], and the other two incorporate only the gastric fundus and the left side of the esophageal wall [*see Figure 6*]. The gastric fundus is then folded over the myotomy, and the second row (also comprising three stitches) is placed on the right side between the fundus and the right side of the esophageal wall, with only the uppermost stitch incorporating the right crus [*see Figures 7 and 8*]. Finally, two additional stitches are placed between the anterior rim of the hiatus and the superior aspect of the fundoplication [*see Figure 9*]. These stitches remove any tension from the second row of sutures.

Troubleshooting   Efforts must be made to ensure that the fundoplication does not become a cause of postoperative dysphagia. Accordingly, I always take down the short gastric vessels, even though some authorities suggest that this step can be omitted.[5,29] In addition, the gastric fundus rather than the body of the stomach should be used for the wrap, and only the uppermost stitch of the right row of sutures should incorporate the right pillar of the crus.[30]

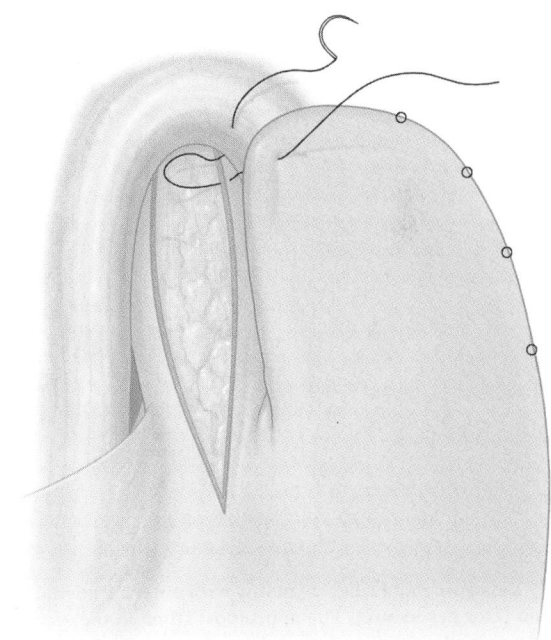

Figure 5   **Laparoscopic Heller myotomy with anterior partial fundoplication (Dor procedure). The uppermost stitch in the first row incorporates the fundus, the esophageal wall, and the left pillar of the crus.**

Step 10 (Guarner Procedure): Posterior Partial Fundoplication

Alternatively, a posterior 220° fundoplication may be performed. The gastric fundus is delivered under the esophagus, and each side of the wrap (right and left) is attached to the esophageal wall, lateral to the myotomy, with three sutures [*see Figure 10*].

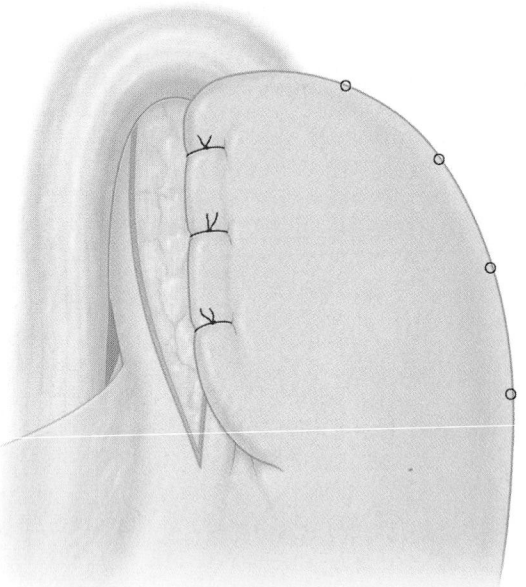

Figure 6 **Laparoscopic Heller myotomy with anterior partial fundoplication (Dor procedure). The second and third stitches in the first row incorporate only the fundus and the left side of the esophageal wall.**

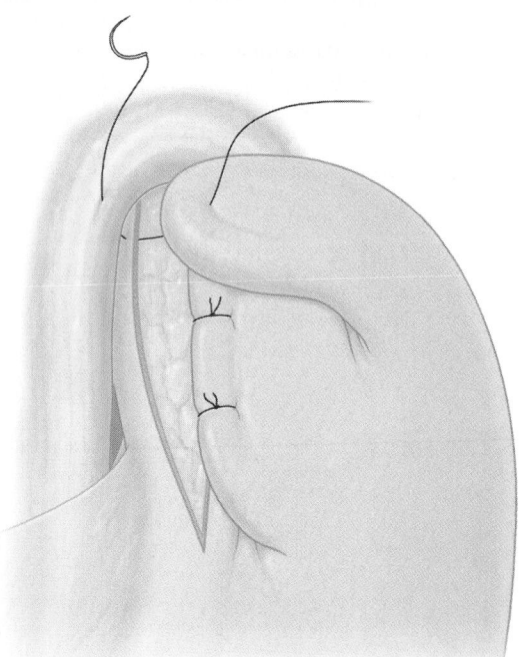

Figure 7 **Laparoscopic Heller myotomy with anterior partial fundoplication (Dor procedure). The uppermost stitch in the second row incorporates the fundus, the esophageal wall, and the right crus.**

Step 11: Final Inspection and Removal of Instruments and Ports from Abdomen

Step 11 of a laparoscopic Heller myotomy is identical to step 9 of a laparoscopic Nissen fundoplication.

COMPLICATIONS

Delayed esophageal leakage, usually resulting from an electrocautery burn to the esophageal mucosa, may occur during the first 24 to 36 hours after operation. The characteristic signals are chest pain, fever, and a pleural effusion on the chest x-ray. The diagno-

sis is confirmed by an esophagogram. Treatment options depend on the time of diagnosis and on the size and location of the leak. Early, small leaks can be repaired directly. If the site of the leak is high in the chest, a thoracotomy is recommended; if the site is at the level of the esophagogastric junction, a laparotomy is preferable, and the stomach can be used to reinforce the repair. If the damage to the esophagus is too extensive to permit repair, a transhiatal esophagectomy [*see 34 Open Esophageal Procedures*] is indicated.

Dysphagia may either persist after the operation or recur after a symptom-free interval. In either case, a complete workup is necessary, and treatment is individualized on the basis of the specific cause of dysphagia. Reoperation may be indicated [*see Reoperation for Esophageal Achalasia, below*].

Abnormal gastroesophageal reflux occurs in 7% to 20% of patients after operation.[4,5] Because most patients are asymptomatic, it is essential to try to evaluate all patients postoperatively with manometry and prolonged pH monitoring. Reflux should be treated with acid-reducing medications.

POSTOPERATIVE CARE

I do not routinely obtain an esophagogram before initiating feeding. Patients are started on a soft mechanical diet on the morning of postoperative day 1, and this diet is continued for the rest of the first week. Patients are discharged after 24 to 48 hours and are able to resume regular activities in 7 to 14 days.

OUTCOME EVALUATION

The results obtained to date with laparoscopic Heller myotomy and partial fundoplication are excellent and are generally comparable to those obtained with the corresponding open surgical procedures: dysphagia is reduced or eliminated in more than 90% of patients.[4-7] Laparoscopic treatment clearly outperforms balloon dilatation and botulinum toxin injection in the treatment of achalasia. Its high success rate has caused a shift in practice, to the

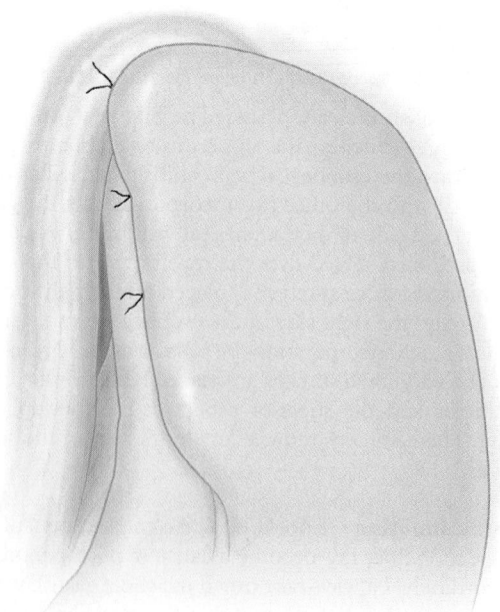

Figure 8 **Laparoscopic Heller myotomy with anterior partial fundoplication (Dor procedure). The second and third stitches in the second row incorporate only the fundus and the right side of the esophageal wall.**

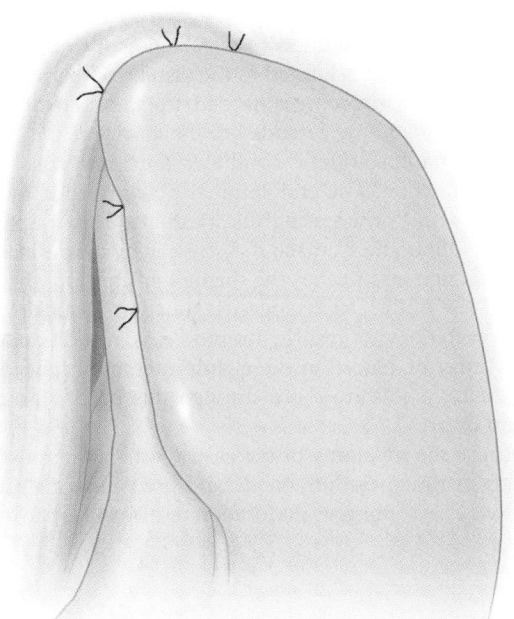

Figure 9   **Laparoscopic Heller myotomy with anterior partial fundoplication (Dor procedure). Two final stitches are placed between the superior portion of the wrap and the anterior rim of the hiatus.**

point where most referring physicians currently regard surgery as the preferred treatment.[32]

Left Thoracoscopic Myotomy

PREOPERATIVE EVALUATION

Preoperative evaluation is essentially the same as that for laparoscopic Heller myotomy.

OPERATIVE PLANNING

The patient is placed under general anesthesia and intubated with a double-lumen endotracheal tube so that the left lung can be deflated during the procedure. As for a left thoracotomy, the patient is placed in the right lateral decubitus position over an inflated bean bag. The instrumentation is similar to that for a laparoscopic Nissen or Guarner fundoplication. Instead of conventional trocars, four or five thoracoports with blunt obturators are employed, because insufflation of the thoracic cavity is not required. The myotomy can be performed with a monopolar hook cautery, bipolar scissors, or an ultrasonic scalpel. A 30° scope and a 45° scope are essential for thoracoscopic procedures. In addition, an endoscope is used for intraoperative endoscopy.

OPERATIVE TECHNIQUE

Step 1: Placement of Thoracoports

Five ports are usually placed [*see Figure 11*]. Port A, used for the 30° scope, is inserted in the sixth intercostal space about 3.5 to 5 cm behind the posterior axillary line. Port B, used for the lung retractor, is placed in the third intercostal space about 1.25 to 2.5 cm anterior to the posterior axillary line. Port C, used for insertion of a grasper, is placed in the sixth intercostal space in the anterior axillary line. Port D, used for insertion of the instrument employed for the myotomy, is placed in the seventh intercostal space in the midaxillary line. Port E is placed in the eighth intercostal space between the anterior axillary line and the midaxillary line. This

port is optional: it is needed in about 30% of cases to allow the surgeon to obtain further exposure of the esophagogastric junction through retraction of the diaphragm.

Troubleshooting   A common mistake is to insert port A too anteriorly. This port must be placed well beyond the posterior axillary line to provide the best angle for the 30° scope. Often, the other ports are placed one or two intercostal spaces too high. This mistake hampers the performance of the most delicate portion of the operation, the myotomy of the distal portion of the esophagus and the stomach.

Sometimes, chest wall bleeding occurs as a consequence of port insertion. This bleeding will obscure the operating field and therefore must be stopped before the intrathoracic portion of the procedure is begun. This is accomplished either by using the cautery from the inside or by applying a stitch from the outside if an intercostal vessel has been damaged.

Step 2: Retraction of Left Lung and Division of Inferior Pulmonary Ligament

Once the ports are in place, the deflated left lung is retracted cephalad with a fan retractor introduced through port B. This maneuver places tension on the inferior pulmonary ligament, which is then divided. After the ligament is divided, the fan retractor can be held in place by a self-retaining system fixed to the operating table.

Troubleshooting   Before the inferior pulmonary ligament is divided, the inferior pulmonary vein must be identified to prevent a life-threatening injury to this vessel. If oxygen saturation decreases, particularly in patients with lung disease, the retractor should be removed and the lung inflated intermittently.

Step 3: Division of Mediastinal Pleura and Dissection of Periesophageal Tissues

The mediastinal pleura is divided, and the tissues overlying the esophageal wall are dissected until the wall of the esophagus is vis-

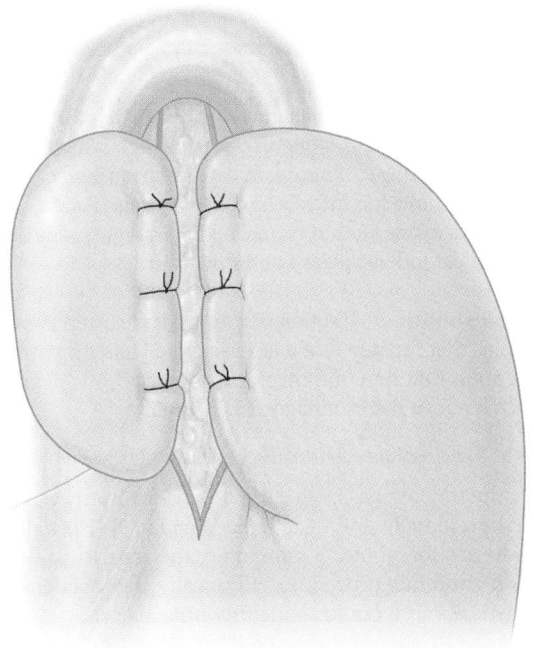

Figure 10   **Laparoscopic Heller myotomy with posterior partial fundoplication (Guarner procedure). Each side of the posterior 220° wrap is attached to the esophageal wall with three sutures.**

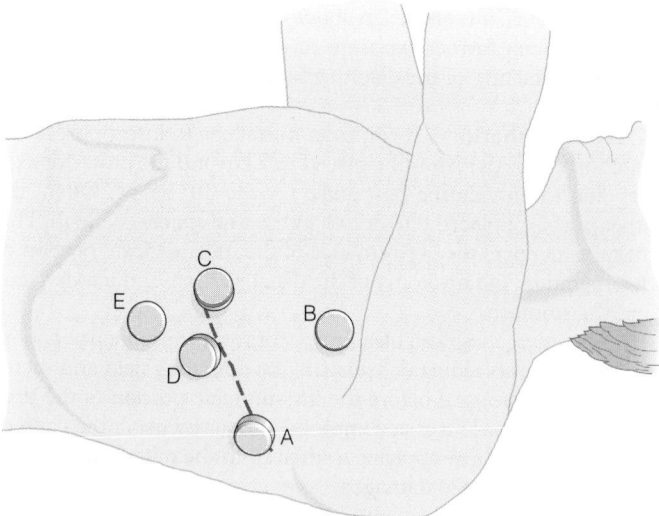

Figure 11 **Left thoracoscopic myotomy. Illustrated is the recommended placement of the thoracoports.**

ible. This maneuver varies in difficulty depending on the width of the space between the aorta and the pericardium (which sometimes is very small) and on the size and shape of the esophagus. Large (sigmoid) esophagi tend to curve to the right, which makes identification of the wall difficult. If the esophagus is not immediately apparent, it can be easily identified in the groove between the heart and the aorta by means of transillumination provided by an endoscope [*see Figure 12*].

Troubleshooting The endoscope placed inside the esophagus at the beginning of the procedure plays an important role. In the early stages of the procedure, it allows identification of the esophagus via transillumination. When the light intensity of the 30° scope is turned down, the esophagus appears as a bright structure. In addition, tilting the tip of the endoscope brings the esophagus into view as it is lifted from the groove between the aorta and the heart.

Step 4: Initiation of Myotomy and Entry into Submucosal Plane at Single Point

As in a laparoscopic Heller myotomy, it is helpful to mark the surface of the esophagus along the line through which the myotomy will be carried out. The myotomy is started halfway between the diaphragm and the inferior pulmonary vein. Again, the proper submucosal plane should be reached at a single point before the myotomy is extended upward and downward.

Troubleshooting Troubleshooting for this step is essentially the same as that for step 8 of a laparoscopic Heller myotomy, with the exception that here the myotomy is started 4 to 5 cm (rather than 3 cm) above the esophagogastric junction.

Step 5: Proximal and Distal Extension of Myotomy

Once the mucosa has been exposed, the myotomy can safely be extended proximally and distally [*see Figure 13*]. I usually extend the myotomy for about 5 mm onto the gastric wall, without adding an antireflux procedure.[3,4] Typically, the total length of the myotomy is about 6 cm for patients with achalasia.

Troubleshooting Proximally, the myotomy is extended all the way to the inferior pulmonary vein only in cases of vigorous achalasia (high-amplitude simultaneous contractions associated

with chest pain in addition to dysphagia) or diffuse esophageal spasm; otherwise, it is limited to the distal 5 to 6 cm of the esophagus. If a longer myotomy is needed, the lung is displaced anteriorly and the myotomy extended to the aortic arch.

Distally, the myotomy is continued for 5 mm past the esophagogastric junction. The endoluminal view provided by the endoscope is useful for assessing the location of the esophagogastric junction. Often, the stomach is distended by the air insufflated by the endoscope and pushes the diaphragm upward, thereby limiting the view of the esophagogastric junction. If sucking air out of the stomach does not resolve this problem, an additional port (i.e., port E) may be placed in the eighth intercostal space, and a fan retractor may be introduced through this port to push the diaphragm down.

Because the myotomy of the gastric wall is the most challenging part of the operation, good exposure is essential. It is at this level that an esophageal perforation is most likely to occur. The

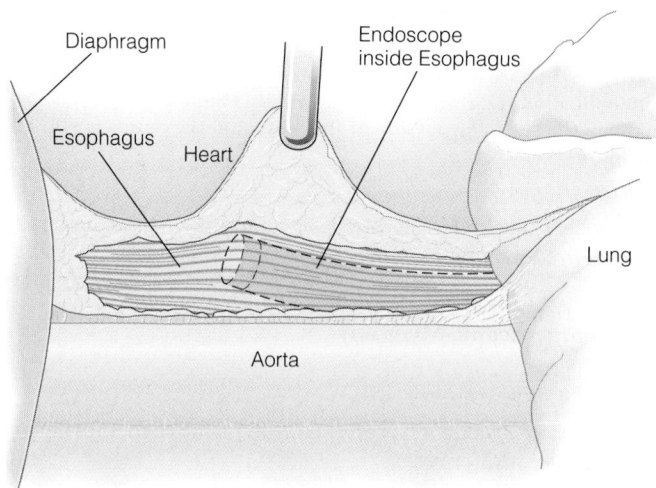

Figure 12 **Left thoracoscopic myotomy. The esophagus may be identified by means of transillumination from the endoscope.**

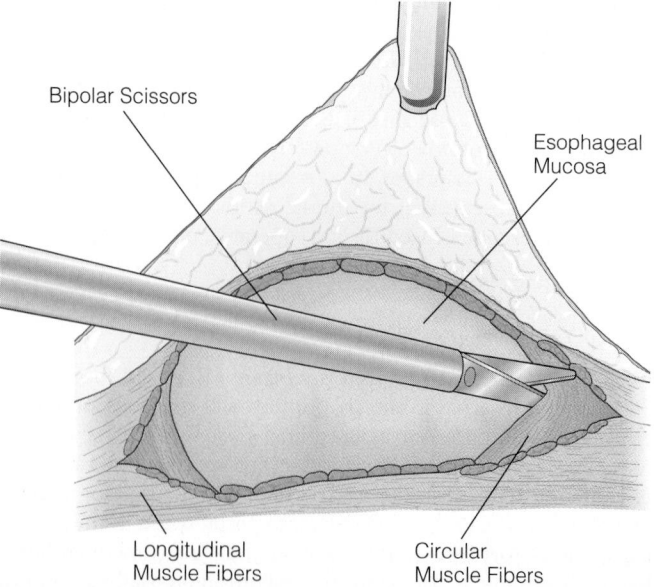

Figure 13 **Left thoracoscopic myotomy. Shown are the distal and proximal extensions of the myotomy.**

risk is particularly high in patients who have undergone pneumatic dilatation or injection of botulinum toxin, both of which may lead to the replacement of muscle layers by scar tissue and the consequent loss of the regular planes. Perforations recognized in the OR can be repaired by thoracoscopic intracorporeal suturing or, if this fails, by thoracotomy and open repair. The gastric fundus can be used to buttress the repair. If it is unclear whether a perforation has occurred, the esophagus should be covered with water and air insufflated through the endoscope as described earlier [see Laparoscopic Heller Myotomy with Partial Fundoplication, Operative Technique, Step 7, above].

Step 6: Insertion of Chest Tube and Removal of Thoracoports

A 24 French angled chest tube is inserted under direct vision through port D or port E. The ports are removed under direct vision, and the thoracic wall is inspected for bleeding.

COMPLICATIONS

As with laparoscopic Heller myotomy, delayed esophageal leakage is a common postoperative complication, and treatment options are similar.

If the myotomy is not extended far enough onto the gastric wall, residual dysphagia occurs. To prevent this problem, the distal extent of the myotomy should be assessed by means of endoscopy with the goal of including 5 mm of the gastric wall. Patients with residual dysphagia must be evaluated by means of esophageal manometry, which will document the extent of the residual high-pressure zone and the pressure within it. The myotomy can be easily extended by a laparoscopic approach, and a Dor fundoplication can be added.

If, on the other hand, the myotomy is extended too far onto the gastric wall, abnormal gastroesophageal reflux occurs. Some patients present with heartburn; others are asymptomatic. It is essential to evaluate patients postoperatively with manometry and prolonged pH monitoring. Mild reflux can be treated with acid-reducing medications, particularly in elderly patients. In younger patients, abnormal reflux should be corrected with a laparoscopic partial fundoplication (e.g., Dor fundoplication).

POSTOPERATIVE CARE

Patients are started on a liquid diet the morning of postoperative day 1; on postoperative day 2, they are started on a soft mechanical diet, which is continued for the rest of the first week. I do not routinely obtain an esophagogram before starting feedings. The chest tube is removed after 24 hours if the lung is fully expanded and there is no air leak. Patients are discharged after 48 to 72 hours and are able to resume regular activities in 7 to 10 days.

OUTCOME EVALUATION

The results obtained with thoracoscopic myotomy are generally comparable to those obtained with open surgical procedures. In a 1999 study from UCSF,[4] 26 (87%) of the first 30 patients with achalasia who were treated in this fashion experienced good or excellent results [see Table 2]. Currently, however, this procedure is rarely used to treat esophageal achalasia: laparoscopic Heller myotomy and Dor fundoplication is now the treatment of choice.[32]

Right Thoracoscopic Myotomy

A right thoracoscopic myotomy extending from the diaphragm to the thoracic inlet is the preferred procedure for patients who have nutcracker esophagus or diffuse esophageal spasm involving the entire length of the esophagus but whose LES function is nor-

Table 2 Results of Thoracoscopic Myotomy in 30 Patients with Achalasia[4]

Results	Patients (% of Total)
Excellent (no dysphagia)	21 (70)
Good (dysphagia < once/wk)	5 (17)
Fair (dysphagia > once/wk)	3 (10)
Poor (persistent dysphagia)	1 (3)

mal. On the whole, this procedure is technically simpler than a left thoracoscopic myotomy: because there is no need to go through the esophagogastric junction, perforation, postoperative dysphagia, and abnormal gastroesophageal reflux are largely prevented.

PREOPERATIVE EVALUATION

Preoperative evaluation of patients being considered for right thoracoscopic myotomy is essentially the same as that of patients being considered for left thoracoscopic myotomy.

OPERATIVE PLANNING

Operative planning is similar to that for a left thoracoscopic myotomy. The double-lumen tube is used to deflate the right lung rather than the left, and the patient is placed in the left lateral decubitus position over an inflated bean bag, as for a right thoracotomy. The instrumentation is identical except for the endovascular 30 mm stapler used to transect the azygos vein. A thoracotomy tray should be kept ready in case an emergency thoracotomy is necessary to control bleeding.

OPERATIVE TECHNIQUE

Step 1: Insertion of Thoracoports

Only port B is inserted where it would be for a left thoracoscopic myotomy. All the other ports are inserted one intercostal space higher because the myotomy need not be extended all the way to the stomach but must be extended to the thoracic inlet. Usually, only four ports are placed; however, an additional port may be placed in the fourth intercostal space in the anterior axillary line to facilitate the proximal extension of the myotomy.

Step 2: Dissection of Periesophageal Tissues and Division of Azygos Vein

The periesophageal tissues above and below the azygos vein are dissected away from the esophagus. A tunnel is created between the azygos and the esophagus with a dissector or a right-angle clamp. The vein is then transected with an endovascular 30 mm stapler. (Alternatively, the azygos is spared and simply lifted off the esophagus with umbilical tape.)

Troubleshooting Dissection of the azygos vein is the most critical part of this procedure. I find it easier to transect the azygos vein than to keep the vein lifted away from the esophagus and perform the myotomy under it.

Steps 3, 4, and 5

Steps 3, 4, and 5 of a right thoracoscopic myotomy are virtually identical to steps 4, 5, and 6 of a left thoracoscopic myotomy, with a few minor exceptions. Once the submucosal plane is reached, the myotomy is extended distally to the diaphragm and proximally to the thoracic inlet. The endoscope plays a less critical role than in a left thoracoscopic myotomy because the esophagus is easily identified and because the myotomy is not extended through the esophagogastric junction. Instead, a 52 to 56 French bougie is placed inside the esophagus; this facilitates division of the circular fibers and separates the edges of the myotomy nicely.

COMPLICATIONS

A delayed esophageal leak is the most common postoperative complication. It should be handled as described earlier [*see* Laparoscopic Heller Myotomy with Partial Fundoplication, Complications, *above*].

POSTOPERATIVE CARE

The postoperative course of patients who have undergone this procedure is usually identical to that of patients operated on for achalasia.

OUTCOME EVALUATION

Long-term follow-up has confirmed the excellent results initially obtained for diffuse esophageal spasm with either a thoracoscopic or a laparoscopic approach.[26,33] The results for nutcracker esophagus, however, have been disappointing: a number of patients have experienced postoperative dysphagia and recurrent chest pain. In my view, the optimal treatment of nutcracker esophagus remains uncertain. The results of operative management are less predictable with nutcracker esophagus than with other esophageal disorders, and chest pain often is not alleviated.[33]

Reoperation for GERD

At the UCSF Swallowing Center, an increasing number of patients are being seen for evaluation and treatment of foregut symptoms after laparoscopic antireflux surgery. These patients are treated as follows.

PREOPERATIVE EVALUATION

Some degree of dysphagia, bloating, and abdominal discomfort is common during the first 6 to 8 weeks after a fundoplication. If these symptoms persist or heartburn and regurgitation occur, a thorough evaluation (with barium swallow, endoscopy, esophageal manometry, and pH monitoring) is carried out with the aim of answering the following three questions:

1. Are the symptoms attributable to persistent gastroesophageal reflux?
2. Are the symptoms attributable to the fundoplication itself?
3. Can the cause of the failure of the first operation be identified and corrected by a second operation?

Many patients report heartburn after a fundoplication. It is often assumed that this symptom must be the result of a failed operation and that acid-reducing medications should be restarted. In most cases, however, this assumption is mistaken: postoperative pH monitoring yields abnormal results in only about 20% of patients.[34] The value of manometry lies in its ability to document the changes caused by the operation at the level of the LES and the esophageal body. The pH monitoring assesses the reflux status and determines whether there is a correlation between symptoms and actual episodes of reflux. If abnormal reflux is in fact present, the therapeutic choice is between medical therapy and a second operation. Other patients complain of dysphagia arising de novo after the operation. This symptom is usually attributable to the operation itself and may occur in the absence of abnormal reflux. In addition

to manometry and pH monitoring, a barium swallow is essential to define the anatomy of the esophagogastric junction. A study from the University of Washington[35] found that the anatomic configurations observed could be divided into three main types: (1) type I hernia, in which the esophagogastric junction was above the diaphragm (subdivided into type IA, with both the esophagogastric junction and the wrap above the diaphragm, and type IB, with only the esophagogastric junction above the diaphragm); (2) type II hernia, a paraesophageal configuration; and (3) type III hernia, in which the esophagogastric junction was below the diaphragm and there was no evidence of hernia but in which the body of the stomach rather than the fundus was used for the wrap. In 10% of patients, however, the cause of the failure could not be identified preoperatively.[33]

Some patients present with a mix of postprandial bloating, nausea, and diarrhea. These symptoms may be the result of damage to the vagus nerves. Radionuclide evaluation of gastric emptying often helps quantify the problem.

OPERATIVE PLANNING

Patient preparation (i.e., anesthesia, positioning, and instrumentation) for a reoperation for reflux is identical to that for the initial laparoscopic fundoplication.

OPERATIVE TECHNIQUE

I routinely attempt a second antireflux operation laparoscopically, but if the dissection does not proceed smoothly, I convert to a laparotomy. To provide a stepwise technical description that would be suitable for all reoperations for reflux is impossible because the optimal procedure depends on the original approach (open versus laparoscopic), the severity of the adhesions, and the specific technique used for the first operation (total or partial fundoplication). The key goals of reoperation for reflux are as follows.

1. To dissect the wrap and the esophagus away from the crura. This is the most difficult part of the operation. The major complications seen during this part of the procedure are damage to the vagus nerves and perforation of the esophagus and the gastric fundus.
2. To take down the previous repair. The earlier repair must be completely undone and the gastric fundus returned to its natural position. If the short gastric vessels were not taken down during the first procedure, they must be taken down during the second.
3. To dissect the esophagus in the posterior mediastinum so as to have enough esophageal length below the diaphragm and avoid placing tension on the repair.
4. To reconstruct the cardia. The same steps are followed as for a first-time repair. If, after extensive esophageal mobilization, the esophagogastric junction remains above the diaphragm (short esophagus), esophageal lengthening can be accomplished by adding a thoracoscopic Collis gastroplasty to the fundoplication. To date, however, I have never found this step to be necessary.

COMPLICATIONS

Because the risk of gastric or esophageal perforation or damage to the vagus nerves is much higher during a second antireflux operation, the surgeon must be ready to convert to a laparotomy if the dissection is too cumbersome or the structures are not properly identified. Most perforations are recognized and repaired intraoperatively. Leaks manifest themselves during the first 48 hours. Peritoneal signs are noted if the spillage is limited to the abdomen; shortness of breath and a pleural effusion are noted if spillage also occurs in the chest. The site of the leak should always be confirmed by means of a contrast study with barium or a water-soluble agent. Perforation is best handled with laparotomy and direct repair of the leak.

OUTCOME EVALUATION

Whereas the success rate is around 80% to 90% for a first antireflux operation, it falls to 70% to 80% for a second such operation. In my view, a second operation should be attempted by an expert team only if medical management fails to control heartburn or pneumatic dilatation has not relieved dysphagia.

Reoperation for Esophageal Achalasia

Laparoscopic Heller myotomy improves swallowing in more than 90% of patients. What causes the relatively few failures reported is still incompletely understood. Typically, a failed Heller myotomy is signaled either by persistent dysphagia or by recurrent dysphagia that develops after a variable symptom-free interval following the original operation.

A complete workup (routinely including barium swallow, endoscopy, manometry, and pH monitoring) is required before treatment is planned. In addition, it is my practice to review the video of the first operation to search for technical errors that might have been responsible for the poor outcome. Such errors typically fall into one of the following three categories.

1. A myotomy that is too short either distally or proximally. If the myotomy is too short distally, a barium swallow shows persistent distal esophageal narrowing and manometry shows a residual high-pressure zone. If the myotomy is too short proximally, it will be apparent from the barium swallow.
2. A constricting Dor fundoplication. Often, manometry and pH monitoring yield normal results, but a barium swallow shows slow passage of contrast media from the esophagus into the stomach. In one study from UCSF,[31] problems with Dor fundoplications occurred in four (4%) of 102 patients. Analysis of the video records of the first operations showed that in three of the four patients, all the stitches in the right suture row had incorporated the esophagus, the right pillar of the crus, and the

stomach, thereby constricting the myotomy. In one patient, the short gastric vessels had not been taken down, and the body of the stomach rather than the fundus had been used for the fundoplication.
3. Transmural scarring caused by previous treatment. In patients treated with intrasphincteric injection of botulinum toxin, transmural fibrosis can sometimes be found at the level of the esophagogastric junction. This unwelcome finding makes the myotomy more difficult and the results less reliable.

There are two treatment options for persistent or recurrent dysphagia after Heller myotomy: (1) pneumatic dilatation and (2) a second operation tailored to the results of preoperative evaluation. In a 2002 study,[36] pneumatic dilatation was successfully used to treat seven of 10 patients who experienced dysphagia postoperatively; of the remaining three patients, two required a second operation and one refused any treatment.

In the UCSF study just cited,[31] however, pneumatic dilatation was effective in only one of the eight patients in whom it was tried. That patient was the one with a short distal myotomy; none of the four patients with dysphagia resulting from a poorly constructed Dor fundoplication derived any benefit. In two patients who had a short proximal myotomy, the myotomy was successfully extended to the inferior pulmonary vein through a left thoracoscopic approach. Of the four patients with a constricting Dor fundoplication, two underwent a second operation during which the Dor was taken down, and one of these two had a second myotomy. Currently, both patients are free of dysphagia; however, they experience abnormal reflux and are being treated with acid-reducing medications.

Reoperation for achalasia is a technically challenging procedure. It is of paramount importance to avoid perforating the exposed esophageal mucosa during the dissection. A small hole can be repaired, but a larger laceration might necessitate an esophagectomy. This option should always be discussed with the patient before the operation.

Overall, about 10% of patients have some degree of dysphagia after a Heller myotomy. Pneumatic dilatation, a second operation, or both should always be tried before a radical procedure such as esophagectomy is decided on.

References

1. Csendes A, Braghetto I, Henriquez A, et al: Late results of a prospective randomized study comparing forceful dilatation and oesophagomyotomy in patients with achalasia. Gut 30:299, 1989

2. Hinder RA, Filipi CJ, Wetscher G, et al: Laparoscopic Nissen fundoplication is an effective treatment for gastroesophageal reflux disease. Ann Surg 220:472, 1994

3. Pellegrini CA, Wetter LA, Patti MG, et al: Thoracoscopic esophagomyotomy: initial experience with a new approach for the treatment of achalasia. Ann Surg 216:291, 1992

4. Patti MG, Pellegrini CA, Horgan S, et al: Minimally invasive surgery for achalasia: an 8 year experience with 168 patients. Ann Surg 230:587, 1999

5. Zaninotto G, Costantini M, Molena D, et al: Treatment of esophageal achalasia with laparoscopic Heller myotomy and Dor partial anterior fundoplication: prospective evaluation of 100 consecutive patients. J Gastrointest Surg 4:282, 2000

6. Ackroyd R, Watson DI, Devitt PG, et al: Laparo-

scopic cardiomyotomy and anterior partial fundoplication for achalasia. Surg Endosc 15:683, 2001

7. Finley RJ, Clifton JC, Stewart KC, et al: Laparoscopic Heller myotomy improves esophageal emptying and the symptoms of achalasia. Arch Surg 136:892, 2001

8. Patti MG, Arcerito M, Feo CV, et al: An analysis of operations for gastroesophageal reflux disease: identifying the important technical elements. Arch Surg 133:600, 1998

9. Horvath KD, Jobe BA, Herron DM, et al: Laparoscopic Toupet fundoplication is an inadequate procedure for patients with severe reflux disease. J Gastrointest Surg 3:583, 1999

10. Sonnenberg A, Delco F, El-Serag HB: Empirical therapy versus diagnostic tests in gastroesophageal reflux disease: a medical decision analysis. Dig Dis Sci 43:1001, 1998

11. Johnsson F, Joelsson B, Gudmundsson K, et al: Symptoms and endoscopic findings in the diagnosis of gastroesophageal reflux disease. Scand J Gastroenterol 22:714, 1987

12. Patti MG, Diener U, Tamburini A, et al: Role of

esophageal function tests in the diagnosis of gastroesophageal reflux disease. Dig Dis Sci 46:597, 2001

13. Campos GM, Peters JH, DeMeester TR, et al: Multivariate analysis of factors predicting outcome after laparoscopic Nissen fundoplication. J Gastrointest Surg 3:292, 1999

14. Patti MG, Goldberg HI, Arcerito M, et al: Hiatal hernia size affects the lower esophageal sphincter function, esophageal acid exposure, and the degree of mucosal injury. Am J Surg 171:182, 1996

15. Bytzer P, Havelund T, Moller Hansen J: Interobserver variation in the endoscopic diagnosis of reflux esophagitis. Scand J Gastroenterol 28:119, 1993

16. Fuchs KH, DeMeester TR, Albertucci M: Specificity and sensitivity of objective diagnosis of gastroesophageal reflux disease. Surgery 102:575, 1987

17. Patti MG, Arcerito M, Tamburini A, et al: Effect of laparoscopic fundoplication on gastroesophageal reflux disease–induced respiratory symptoms. J Gastrointest Surg 4:143, 2000

18. Diener U, Patti MG, Molena D, et al: Esophageal dysmotility and gastroesophageal reflux disease. J Gastrointest Surg 5:260, 2001

19. Horgan S, Pellegrini CA: Surgical treatment of gastroesophageal reflux disease. Surg Clin North Am 77:1063, 1997

20. Patti MG, Robinson T, Galvani C, et al: Total fundoplication is superior to partial fundoplication even when esophageal peristalsis is weak. J Am Coll Surg 198:863, 2004

21. Patterson EJ, Herron DM, Hansen PD, et al: Effect of an esophageal bougie on the incidence of dysphagia following Nissen fundoplication: a prospective, blinded, randomized clinical trial. Arch Surg 135:1055, 2000

22. Guelrud M, Rossiter A, Souney PF, et al: The effect of vasoactive intestinal polypeptide on the lower esophageal sphincter in achalasia. Gastroenterology 103:377, 1992

23. Tottrup A, Svane D, Forman A: Nitric oxide mediating NANC inhibition in opossum lower esophageal sphincter. Am J Physiol 260:G385, 1991

24. Champion JK, Delisle N, Hunt T: Laparoscopic esophagomyotomy with posterior partial fundoplication for primary esophageal motility disorders. Surg Endosc 14:746, 2000

25. Oleynikov D, Eubanks TR, Oelschlager BK, et al: Total fundoplication is the operation of choice for patients with gastroesophageal reflux and defective peristalsis. Surg Endosc 16:909, 2002

26. Patti MG, Pellegrini CA, Arcerito M, et al: Comparison of medical and minimally invasive surgical therapy for primary esophageal motility disorders. Arch Surg 130:609, 1995

27. Richards WO, Torquati A, Holzman MD, et al: Heller myotomy versus Heller myotomy and Dor fundoplication for achalasia: a prospective randomized, double-blind clinical trial. Ann Surg 240:405, 2004

28. Patti MG, Diener U, Molena D: Esophageal achalasia: preoperative assessment and postoperative follow-up. J Gastrointest Surg 5:11, 2001

29. Moonka R, Patti MG, Feo CV, et al: Clinical presentation and evaluation of malignant pseudoachalasia. J Gastrointest Surg 3:456, 1999

30. Watson DI, Liu JF, Devitt PG, et al: Outcome of laparoscopic anterior 180-degree partial fundoplication for gastroesophageal reflux disease. J Gastrointest Surg 4:486, 2000

31. Patti MG, Molena D, Fisichella PM, et al: Laparoscopic Heller myotomy and Dor fundoplication for achalasia: analysis of successes and failures. Arch Surg 136:870, 2001

32. Patti MG, Fisichella PM, Perretta S, et al: Impact of minimally invasive surgery on the treatment of esophageal achalasia: a decade of change. J Am Coll Surg 196:698, 2003

33. Patti MG, Gorodner MV, Galvani C, et al: The spectrum of esophageal motility disorders: implications for diagnosis and treatment. Arch Surg (in press)

34. Lord RVN, Kaminski A, Oberg S, et al: Absence of gastroesophageal reflux disease in a majority of patients taking acid suppression medications after Nissen fundoplication. J Gastrointest Surg 6:3, 2002

35. Horgan S, Pohl D, Bogetti D, et al: Failed antireflux surgery: what have we learned from reoperations? Arch Surg 134:809, 1999

36. Zaninotto G, Costantini M, Portale G, et al: Etiology, diagnosis and treatment of failures after laparoscopic Heller myotomy for achalasia. Ann Surg 235:186, 2002

Acknowledgment

Figures 1 through 13   Tom Moore.

36 CHEST WALL PROCEDURES

Seth D. Force, M.D.

Chest wall procedures are an important component of any thoracic surgeon's practice. The approach to these procedures is somewhat different from the approach to esophageal or pulmonary resections and requires specific knowledge of thoracic musculoskeletal anatomy, as well as of the different types of autologous and artificial grafts available for chest wall reconstruction. Broadly, chest wall procedures may be divided into those performed to treat congenital chest wall disease and those done to treat acquired disease. In what follows, I describe the major surgical techniques in both categories and review the pitfalls that may accompany them.

Procedures for Congenital Chest Wall Disease

Congenital chest wall defects arise from abnormal development of the sternum, the costal cartilages, and the ribs. Such defects include pectus excavatum (funnel chest), pectus carinatum (pigeon chest), cleft sternum, and Poland syndrome (absence of the breast and the underlying pectoralis muscle and ribs). Of these, pectus excavatum is by far the most common, accounting for more than 90% of all congenital chest wall procedures; accordingly, the ensuing discussion focuses on the surgical aspects of pectus excavatum repair.

REPAIR OF PECTUS EXCAVATUM

Preoperative Evaluation

Because pectus excavatum occurs in varying degrees of severity, patients may seek surgical treatment for any of a number of different reasons, such as shortness of breath, early fatigue with exercise, or simple dissatisfaction with their appearance. Thus, one of the most important tasks for surgeons treating pectus excavatum is determining which patients are candidates for operative management. In an attempt to facilitate this determination, the Congenital Heart Surgery Nomenclature and Database Project has developed a classification system for pectus excavatum, in which a deformity less than 2 cm in depth is classified as mild, a deformity 2 to 3 cm in depth is classified as moderate, and a deformity greater than 3 cm in depth is classified as severe.[1] A computed tomography–based index has also been devised, in which the transverse chest diameter is divided by the anteroposterior diameter; an index greater than 3.2 is considered indicative of severe disease.[2]

These classification attempts notwithstanding, the precise indications for surgery remain unclear. Many studies have attempted to show that the depressed sternum leads to pulmonary compromise, but for the most part, these studies have had small sample sizes and have employed differing measures of lung function, both of which have made accurate comparisons difficult. In one study that included 25 United States Air Force personnel with symptomatic pectus excavatum, lung volumes were comparable to those in normal persons, but there was a significant difference in maximum voluntary ventilation.[3] In a study that compared 37 patients who had undergone surgical repair of pectus excavatum both with normal persons and with persons who had uncorrected deformities, no differences in physical working capacity among the three groups were noted.[4] Other studies have reported improvements in exercise tolerance and regional ventilation and perfusion after surgical repair of pectus excavatum.[5,6] On the other hand, some investigators have reported decreases in pulmonary function in symptomatic patients after corrective surgery. One group attributed this result to overly aggressive resection in very young patients that led to growth restriction of the chest wall; accordingly, they recommended delaying surgical repair until 6 to 8 years of age.[7]

Severe pectus excavatum has also been reported to cause cardiac dysfunction secondary to sternal compression of the right ventricle. Several early studies found stroke volume and cardiac output to be lower in exercising upright patients than in supine patients.[8,9] However, improvement in cardiac function after pectus excavatum repair has not been universally documented. In one study, first-pass radionuclide angiocardiography failed to show any improvements in left ventricular function after repair of pectus excavatum.[10] At present, there is no consensus on the cardiopulmonary benefits of pectus excavatum repair, and the major reasons for surgical treatment are still patient discomfort and dissatisfaction with appearance.

Operative Technique

A number of different procedures have been employed to treat pectus excavatum, but for present purposes, I focus on (1) the Ravitch procedure (and variations thereof) and (2) the Nuss procedure. For historical reasons, the turnover technique, originally described by Judet and Judet[11] and later employed by Wada,[12] warrants a brief mention. Wada's series included 199 patients whose deformities were corrected with a version of this technique; good results were achieved in 63% of patients, and there were only three instances of partial sternal necrosis. Today, however, the turnover technique is rarely used because of the good results that can be achieved with techniques that do not carry a risk of sternal necrosis. It is usually reserved for extreme cases of pectus excavatum, which often include deformities of the sternum in addition to abnormalities of the costal cartilages.

Ravitch procedure   Repair of pectus excavatum is based on the principle that the deformity is secondary to abnormal growth of the costal cartilages. Accordingly, correction involves (1) resection of the abnormal cartilages, (2) a transverse anterior sternal osteotomy to allow anterior displacement of the sternum, and (3) sternal fixation to prevent posterior displacement after the repair. Most of the variations in the Ravitch procedure have to do with the use of different sternal fixation techniques.

Step 1: initial incision and exposure.   Either a midline incision or a

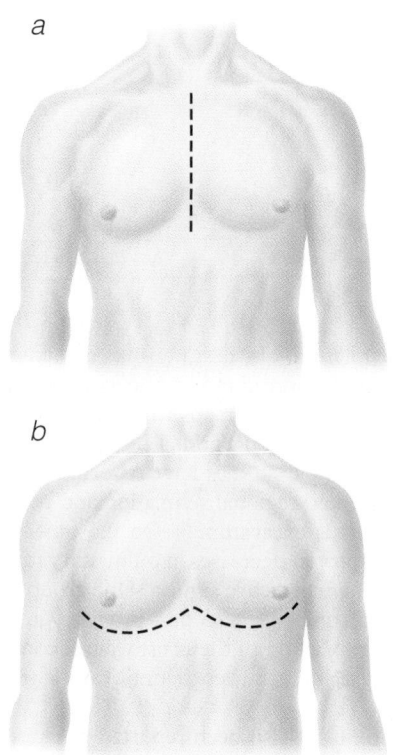

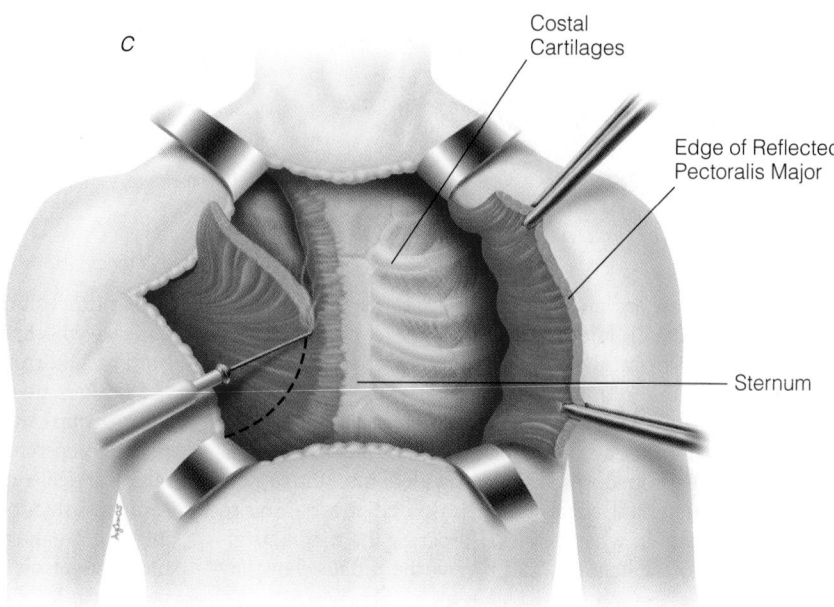

Costal
Cartilages

Edge of Reflected
Pectoralis Major

Sternum

Figure 1 **Repair of pectus excavatum: Ravitch procedure. The procedure begins with a midline incision (*a*) or a bilateral inframammary incision (*b*). The pectoralis muscles are then dissected off the chest wall (*c*).**

bilateral inframammary incision is made [*see Figure 1a, b*]; the latter incision yields superior cosmetic results, especially in female patients, but necessitates the elevation of large subcutaneous skin flaps to the level of the angle of Louis or the sternal notch superiorly and to the xiphoid process inferiorly. The pectoralis muscles are then mobilized from the chest wall, beginning medially and proceeding laterally until the costal cartilages are exposed [*see Figure 1c*].

Step 2: resection of abnormal cartilages. For each abnormal costal cartilage, the anterior perichondrium is scored with the electrocautery along the length of the cartilage, and the cartilage is dissected from the perichondrium with a periosteal elevator [*see Figure 2a*].

The posterior plane between the cartilage and the perichondrium is then developed in one area, and the cartilage is divided with a scalpel between the jaws of a right-angle clamp [*see Figure 2b*]. The cut end of the cartilage is grasped with a clamp, and the rest of the cartilage is dissected from the perichondrium. Once the correct plane is established, the dissection can be facilitated by gently pushing the perichondrium off the cartilage with a finger. The entire cartilage should be removed from the sternum to the rib, with every attempt made to maintain the integrity of the perichondrium. During this part of the procedure, the xiphoid process is also detached from the sternum. The extent of cartilage removal depends on the individual defect present but usually includes the third rib.

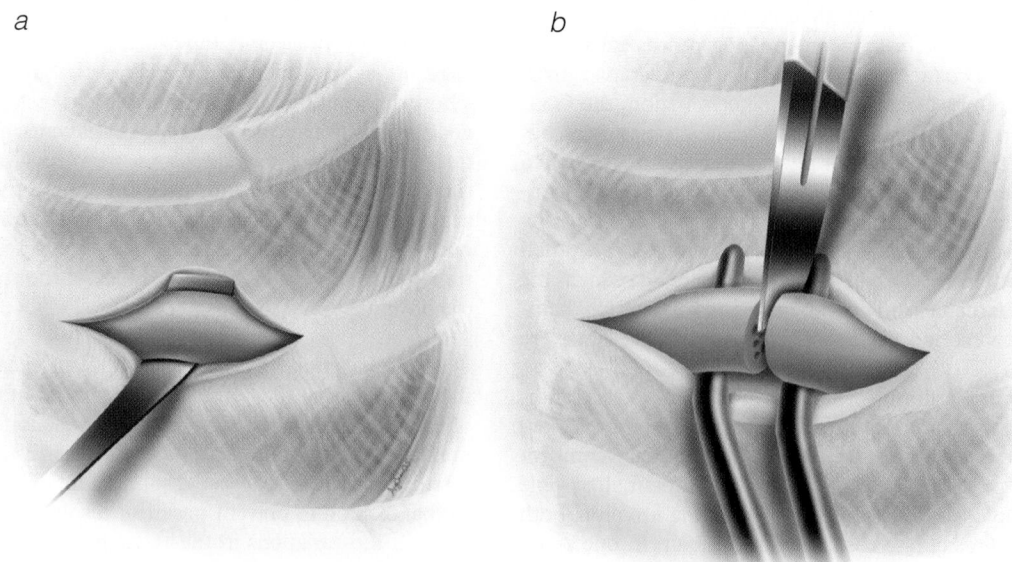

Figure 2 **Repair of pectus excavatum: Ravitch procedure. (*a*) The anterior perichondrium is opened, and the abnormal cartilage is dissected free with a periosteal elevator. (*b*) The cartilage is divided.**

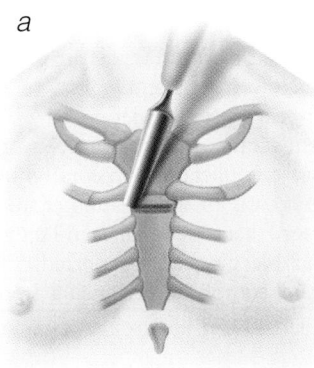

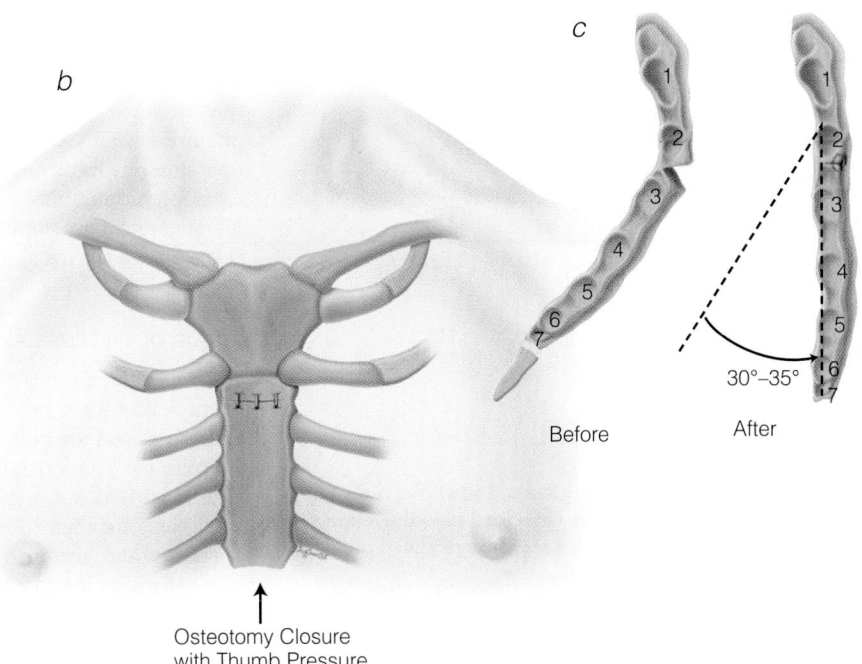

Figure 3 **Repair of pectus excavatum: Ravitch procedure. (*a*) An osteotomy is made in the upper sternum. (*b*) The sternum is angled anteriorly; when the desired angle is reached, the osteotomy is closed. (*c*) Shown is a lateral view of the sternal angle before and after correction.**

Osteotomy Closure
with Thumb Pressure

Before   After

30°–35°

Step 3: sternal osteotomy. An osteotomy is made in the upper anterior table of the sternum with either a periosteal elevator or a small reticulating bone saw [*see Figure 3a*], and the posterior table of the sternum is fractured. The sternum can then be angled anteriorly. When the desired angle is reached, the osteotomy is closed with three interrupted nonabsorbable sutures or with microplates and screws [*see Figure 3b, c*]. At this point, rotational sternal defects can be corrected by making anterior and posterior lateral osteotomies on either side of the sternum and then closing the osteotomies with sutures or microplates.

Step 4: sternal fixation. Sternal fixation can be accomplished by any of several means. Posterior sternal support can be achieved by placing a Kirschner wire or retrosternal bar that is secured to the periosteum of the rib and left in place for approximately 3 months after operation [*see Figure 4*]. Alternatively, the sternum can be supported with a piece of polypropylene mesh or with two polypropylene sutures sutured to the xiphoid process and then brought around the right and left second ribs.[13]

Step 5: closure and drainage. The pectoralis muscles are reapproximated in the midline, closed suction drains are placed in the subcutaneous flaps, and the subcutaneous layer and the skin are closed. To prevent seroma formation, one closed suction drain may be placed posterior to the pectoralis muscles and another between the pectoralis muscles and the subcutaneous layer; the right pleural space may then be opened anteriorly and a right pleural tube placed through a separate incision.[14]

Nuss procedure   Minimally invasive repair of pectus excavatum, also referred to as the Nuss procedure, has gained popularity over the past decade.

Step 1: configuration of bar. The patient is placed in the supine position with the arms abducted, and marks are made on either side of the chest at spots that correspond to the deepest point of

the defect. The bar that will be used for the repair is shortened to a length equivalent to the measured distance between the two midaxillary lines minus 1 cm. A complex series of bends are then placed in the bar to match its contours to those of the patient's deformity.

Step 2: initial incisions and creation of intrathoracic tunnel. Incisions are made in the right and left midaxillary lines at the level of the marks, and a subcutaneous flap is raised from each incision and extended to the defect. A Crawford vascular clamp or a

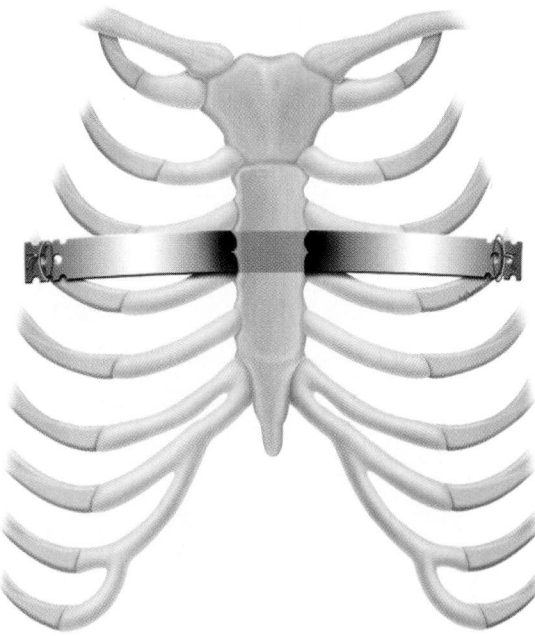

Figure 4 **Repair of pectus excavatum: Ravitch procedure. Sternal fixation is accomplished through placement of a retrosternal bar.**

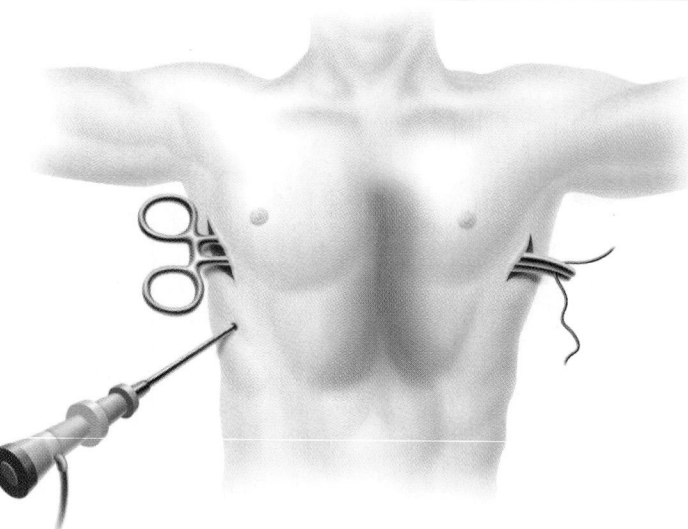

Figure 5 **Repair of pectus excavatum: Nuss procedure. Incisions are made on either side of the chest. A Crawford vascular clamp is inserted through the right intercostal space and advanced along the sternum and out the left intercostal space.**

Lorenz pectus introducer is then placed through the right intercostal space under thoracoscopic visualization and advanced along the posterior sternum and out the corresponding left intercostal space [*see Figure 5*].

Step 3: placement and fixation of bar. An umbilical tape is pulled through the anterior mediastinum and attached to the bar, which is then gently pulled, with the concave side up, through the intercostal space. A Lorenz pectus bar rotator is employed to flip the bar over, and the ends of the bar are positioned in the subcutaneous space [*see Figure 6*]. Occasionally, for proper alignment, the bar may have to be removed and rebent, or stabilizers may have to be placed alongside it. When the bar is correctly positioned, it is sutured to the chest wall musculature with an absorbable suture on one end and a permanent suture on the other.

The bar is usually left in place for 2 years. Excellent results have been reported.[15] Significant complications include bar displacement necessitating reoperation (9.2% of procedures), pneumothorax (4.8%), infection (2%), and pleural effusion (2%). Rare complications include cardiac injury, thoracic outlet syndrome (TOS), pericarditis, and sternal erosion caused by the bar.

Outcome Evaluation

In general, the results of pectus excavatum repair are good, and the overall complication rate is low. In one study, 90% of 76 patients operated on over a 30-year period experienced excellent outcomes, and only one patient required reoperation for a recurrent defect.[14] The incidence of complications (pleural effusions, pneumonia, and wound seromas) was 14%.[14] In another study, no operative deaths occurred in more than 800 repairs, and only a few cases of serious infections and bleeding were reported.[16] Other investigators have reported rare complications arising from the migration of sternal support bars and wires.[17]

REPAIR OF PECTUS CARINATUM

Surgical repair of pectus carinatum resembles surgical repair of pectus excavatum in several respects. The same skin incision is employed, and the pectoralis major muscles are elevated in a similar manner. Subperichondrial resection of the abnormal cartilages is then carried out, usually extending to the second costal cartilage. Next, a generous V-shaped osteotomy is made in the upper portion of the sternum at the point of maximal protrusion, which is usually near the insertion of the second cartilage. Occasionally, a second osteotomy is required near the caudal end of the sternum to facilitate elevation of the manubrium and depression of the sternum. Finally, the osteotomy is closed with nonabsorbable monofilament sutures, drains are placed, and soft tissue is closed as in a pectus excavatum repair.

The results of pectus carinatum repair are generally comparable to those of pectus excavatum repair. Most patients experience good outcomes, and operative morbidity is low.

Procedures for Acquired Chest Wall Disease

TRANSAXILLARY FIRST RIB RESECTION FOR THORACIC OUTLET SYNDROME

Preoperative Evaluation

TOS results from compression of the subclavian blood vessels or the brachial plexus as these structures exit the bony thorax. Symptoms may be primarily vascular (e.g., arm swelling or loss of pulse) or neurogenic (e.g., pain and paresthesias). The workup for TOS includes a detailed physical examination, as well as imaging and nerve conduction studies.

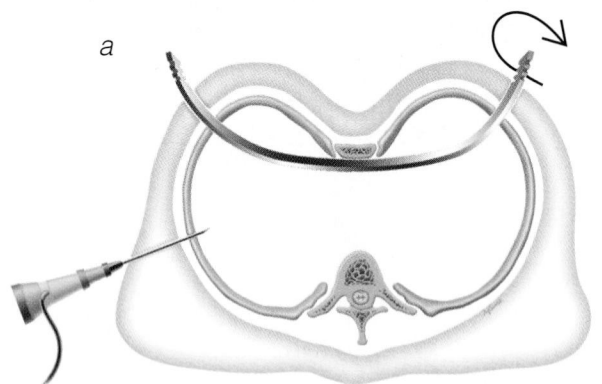
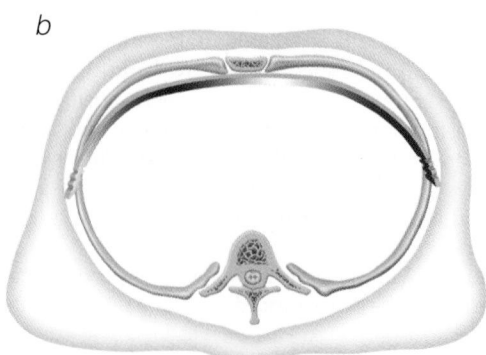

Figure 6 **Repair of pectus excavatum: Nuss procedure. (*a*) The pectus bar is pulled into the tunnel opened by the vascular retractor, then flipped to provide the desired chest contour. (*b*) The ends of the bar are then sutured to the chest wall musculature.**

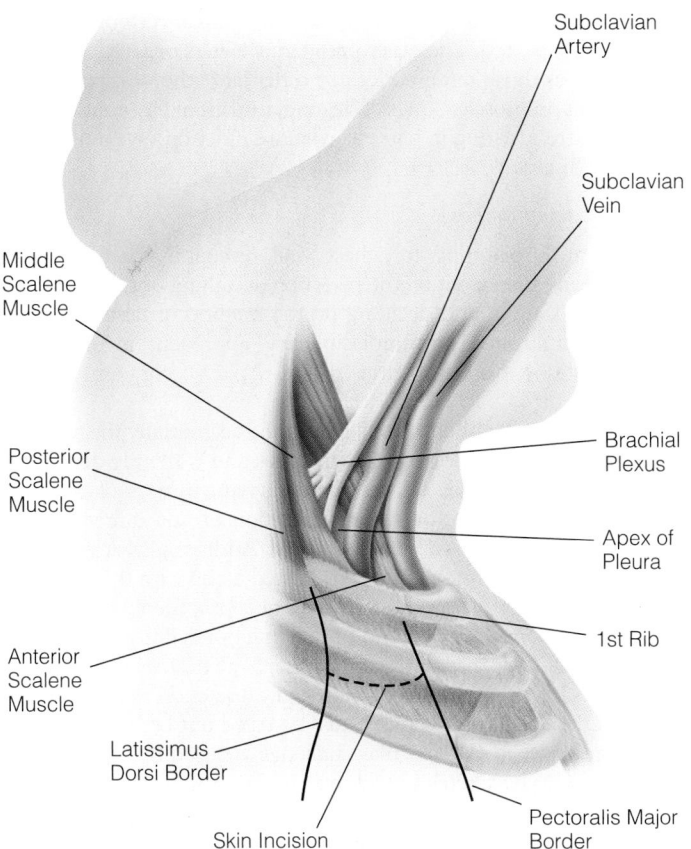

Figure 7 **Transaxillary first rib resection. Shown are the transaxillary incision and the thoracic outlet anatomy.**

Operative Planning

Surgical treatment of TOS typically involves resection of the first rib, which widens the thoracic outlet and relieves the neurovascular impingement. First rib resection can be accomplished via several different approaches, including posterior, supraclavicular, infraclavicular, transthoracic, and transaxillary. I focus here on the transaxillary approach, which provides good exposure of the first rib and allows the surgeon to avoid the subclavian blood vessels and the brachial plexus. Regardless of the specific surgical approach followed, any surgeon embarking on a first rib resection must have a detailed knowledge of the thoracic outlet to keep from injuring the neurovascular structures in the area.

Operative Technique

The patient is placed in the lateral decubitus position, and the affected arm is kept at a 90° angle either by an arm holder or, alternatively, by an assistant. Care must be taken not to hyperabduct or hyperextend the shoulder. The arm, the axilla, and the chest are prepared and draped into the sterile field.

Step 1: initial incision and exposure An incision is made just below the axillary hair line and extended from the pectoralis major to the latissimus dorsi [*see Figure 7*]. The subcutaneous tissue is incised down to the chest wall with the electrocautery, with care taken to stay perpendicular to the axis of the chest. Dissection is then begun along the chest wall and carried toward the first rib. The intercostal brachial nerve is identified where it exits between the first and second ribs. This nerve should be spared: dividing it leads to numbness of the upper inner biceps region.

Step 2: dissection and division of anterior portion of first rib When the first rib is encountered, it is dissected from the periosteum with a periosteal elevator. Dissection is continued anteriorly along the rib until just past the subclavian vein, at which point a right-angle clamp can be passed around the rib in the subperiosteal plane. A Gigli saw or a first rib cutter is then used to divide the anterior portion of the rib [*see Figure 8a*].

Next, the first rib is retracted inferiorly to permit visualization of the anterior scalene muscle, which is then divided at its attachment to the rib. To prevent thermal injury to the phrenic nerve, a scalpel rather than an electrocautery is used to divide the muscle [*see Figure 8b*]. Care should also be taken not to injure the subcla-

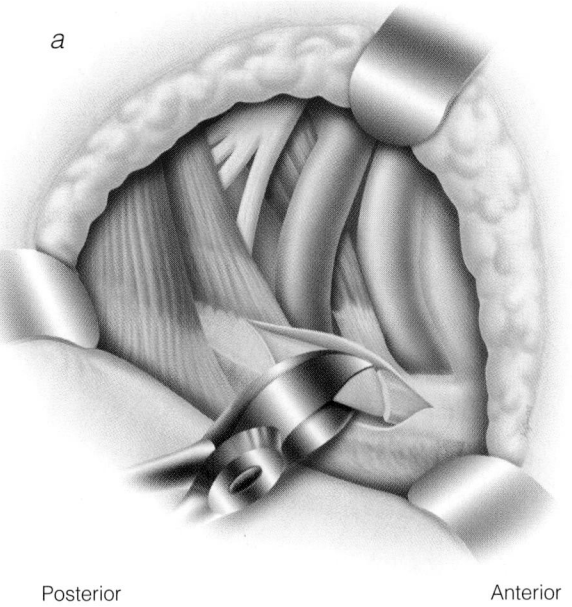

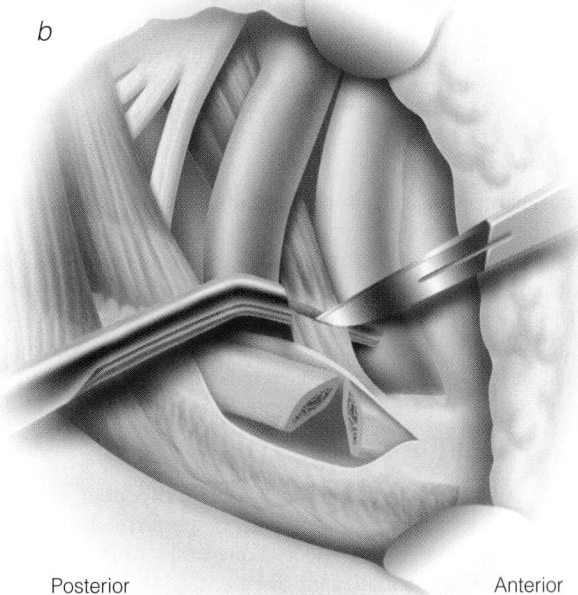

Figure 8 **Transaxillary first rib resection. (*a*) The anterior portion of the first rib is cut. (*b*) The anterior scalene muscle is then divided.**

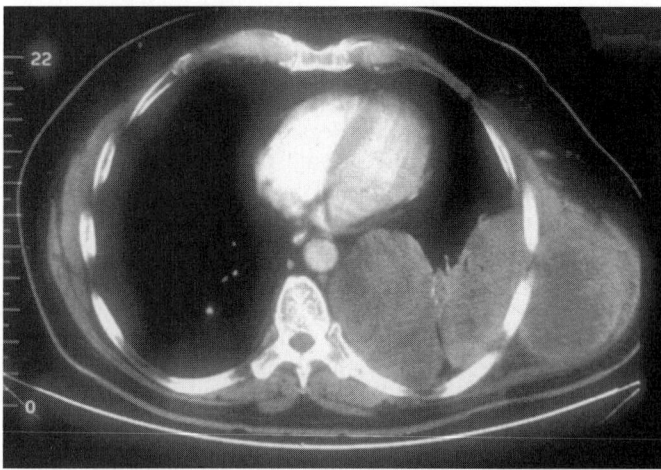

Figure 9 Chest CT reveals a large pulmonary and chest wall mass.

vian vein and artery, which lie anterior and posterior to the anterior scalene muscle, respectively. As an alternative, the anterior scalene muscle may be divided before the anterior portion of the rib is cut.

Step 3: dissection and division of posterior portion of first rib The subperiosteal dissection is continued posteriorly, freeing the first rib from the pleura, the subclavian vessels, and the brachial plexus. The posterior portion of the rib is then divided with a first rib cutter as close as possible to the articulation of the rib with the transverse process. Every effort should be made to keep from injuring the C8 and T1 nerve roots.

Step 4: closure The incision is closed without drainage. If the pleura was inadvertently entered, air may be aspirated from the chest with a red rubber tube, which is removed before the subcutaneous tissue is closed. One authority recommends further neurolysis of the C7 to T1 nerve roots and the middle and lower trunks of the brachial plexus, as well as resection of the anterior and middle scalene muscles up into the neck.[18]

Complications

Surgical complications include injuries to the subclavian vein and artery (leading to massive blood loss), the brachial plexus, the phrenic nerve, the long thoracic nerve, and the thoracic duct.

Outcome Evaluation

The long-term results of first rib resection appear to be independent of the exposure technique employed. Good results, defined as relief of major symptoms, have been reported in as many of 90% of patients in the first year and in as many as 70% of patients 5 to 10 years after operation. There continues to be considerable debate over the preferred surgical approach, but to date, no studies have shown any one approach to have significant advantages over any of the others.

CHEST WALL RESECTION

Chest wall resection has become a critical component of the thoracic surgeon's armamentarium. It may be performed to treat either benign conditions (e.g., osteoradionecrosis, osteomyelitis, and benign neoplasms) or malignant disease.

Preoperative Evaluation

Preoperative imaging studies may include chest x-ray, chest CT

[*see Figure 9*], and magnetic resonance imaging if vertebral involvement is suspected. The other preoperative tests ordered are much the same as those required for any other large thoracic procedure, including pulmonary function testing, nutritional assessment, and cardiac stress testing in patients who are older or have a history of cardiac disease.

Operative Planning

Operative planning for chest wall resection should include establishing the extent of the resection, weighing options for chest wall stabilization, and deciding on the method of tissue coverage to be employed. A multidisciplinary approach, involving the participation of a neurosurgeon and a plastic surgeon, may be required.

The technique of chest wall resection is essentially the same for benign conditions as for malignant ones and is mainly dependent on the location of the lesion. For malignant tumors of the chest wall, a 5 cm margin, or at least resection of one uninvolved rib above and below the tumor, is required. Additionally, any involved skin and any biopsy site must be resected along with the chest wall specimen. For infection or osteoradionecrosis, the resection must include all nonviable skin and underlying bone; if it does not, skin and muscle flaps may not heal properly. Any destroyed lung tissue may also have to be resected along with the chest wall specimen. In addition, recurrent cancer must be ruled out before the operation can proceed. A particular challenge is posed by breast cancer patients who have already had muscle flaps for breast reconstruction; in these patients, tissues other than muscle (e.g., omentum) may be required for tissue coverage after chest wall resection.

Standard Chest Wall Resection

In cases in which a concomitant lung resection is required, the

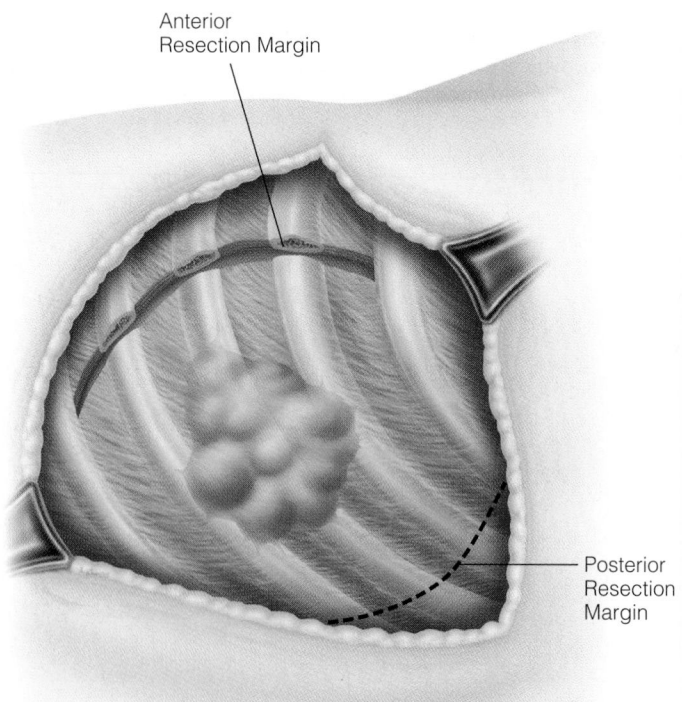

Figure 10 Chest wall resection. The anterior and posterior margins of the required resection are determined. The anterior margin is completed first.

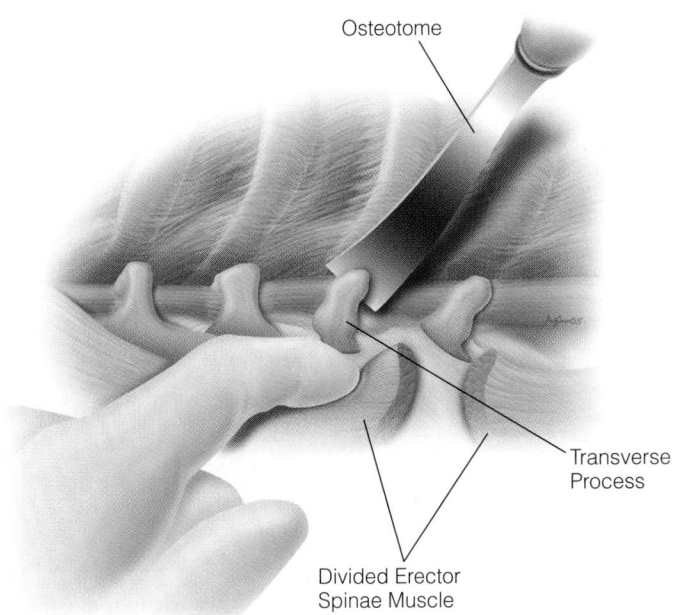

Osteotome

Transverse
Process

Divided Erector
Spinae Muscle

Figure 11 **Chest wall resection. Depicted is disarticulation of the rib from the transverse process.**

chest wall resection is usually performed first; this measure renders the lung more mobile and facilitates the pulmonary resection. The lateral decubitus position is the best choice for most combined lung–chest wall procedures, whereas the supine position is preferable for isolated anterior chest wall procedures. If a larger chest wall resection is expected, every attempt should be made to spare major muscle groups so that these muscles can be used later to cover any prosthetic material used in reconstruction.

Operative technique *Step 1: initial incision and exposure.* The usual incision is a standard posterolateral thoracotomy incision through the fifth interspace.

Step 2: determination of extent of required chest wall resection. As soon as the pleura is opened, the surgeon should palpate the tumor to evaluate the extent of chest wall involvement, which determines the extent of the resection. Removal of uninvolved ribs may make reconstruction of the chest wall more complicated. For example, posterior resections that do not require removal of the fifth rib are protected by the scapula, so that reconstruction is unnecessary. If the fifth rib is removed, however, the tip of the scapula will tend to become stuck under the sixth rib with shoulder movement; this is very uncomfortable for the patient, and chest wall reconstruction will therefore be required at the time of resection.

At this point, the surgeon should also rule out diffuse pleural disease before proceeding with resection. In some cases, the tumor can be removed by means of extrapleural dissection, without any need for chest wall resection. If there is any suspicion of chest wall involvement, however, chest wall resection is mandatory because leaving any tumor behind guarantees a recurrence.

The extent of the chest wall resection is marked with the electrocautery on the outside of the thoracic cavity. At least one grossly uninvolved rib should be included both above and below the tumor.

Step 3: completion of anterior boundary of resection. Initially, the periosteum over the lowest rib to be resected is scored, and a periosteal elevator is used to separate the intercostal bundle from

the rib. Alternatively, the intercostal bundle can be doubly ligated and divided at the anterior resection margin. Once the intercostal vessels are cleared from the lowest rib, the electrocautery is used to divide the pleura below the rib toward the anterior boundary of the resection. The rib is then divided with a rib cutter, with care taken to ensure a margin of at least 5 cm from the tumor [*see Figure 10*]. Next, the intercostal bundle of the next higher rib is ligated and divided, the intercostal muscle is divided with the electrocautery, and the rib is cut with a rib cutter in the same manner as the previous rib. This process is repeated until the anterior boundary of resection is completed. A subperiosteal plane is then developed over the highest rib to be resected, the adjacent intercostal bundle is separated from the rib, and the parietal pleura is divided with the electrocautery.

Step 4: completion of posterior boundary of resection. If the tumor margin does not involve the vertebrae, the posterior portion of the chest wall resection is identical to the anterior portion [*see* Step 3, *above*]. If, however, the tumor appears to encroach on the head of the rib or the transverse process, it will be necessary to disarticulate the rib from the transverse process or, in the latter situation, remove the transverse process entirely.

Disarticulation of the rib from the transverse process is performed by dissecting the paraspinal ligament and erector spinae muscles away from the spine with the electrocautery, thereby exposing the joint between the head of the rib and the transverse process. The ligaments attaching the rib to the transverse process are then incised with the electrocautery, and an osteotome is inserted into the joint, which is then levered anteriorly and posteriorly to disarticulate the rib from the transverse process [*see Figure 11*]. The intercostal neurovascular bundle must be ligated and divided at this point: failure to do so will result in bleeding and possibly in leakage of cerebrospinal fluid. If bleeding occurs, it can be controlled with bipolar electrocauterization and temporary packing with a hemostatic agent. The hemostatic agent must not be left in place permanently, because it may expand or result in a neural foramen hematoma, and either of these events can lead to spinal cord compression and significant neurologic injury. If at any time the surgeon feels uncomfortable about ongoing intercostal bleeding or a possible CSF leak, intraoperative neurosurgical consultation should be obtained. In cases in which the tumor involves the transverse process, this structure must be removed from the vertebral body with an osteotome and a mallet or with a first rib cutter. If the tumor has invaded the vertebral body and resection is still being considered, neurosurgical consultation should be obtained. Generally, if the tumor involves more than one quarter of the vertebral body or extends into multiple vertebral levels, it is considered unresectable.

Step 5: lung resection (if required). Once the posterior chest wall margin has been completed, the lung resection (if required) is performed. The entire lung–chest wall specimen is then be submitted for pathologic examination, and histopathologic margins are obtained both on the lung and on the chest wall. If the chest wall margins are positive, the involved area must be trimmed back and a new margin submitted.

Step 6: chest wall reconstruction. Chest wall reconstruction is required for all anterior defects and for posterior defects that involve any rib lower than the fourth rib. Reconstruction can be performed either with polypropylene or Gore-Tex (W. L. Gore and Associates, Flagstaff, Arizona) mesh or with a polypropylene-methylmethacrylate sandwich. The latter is employed when rigid recon-

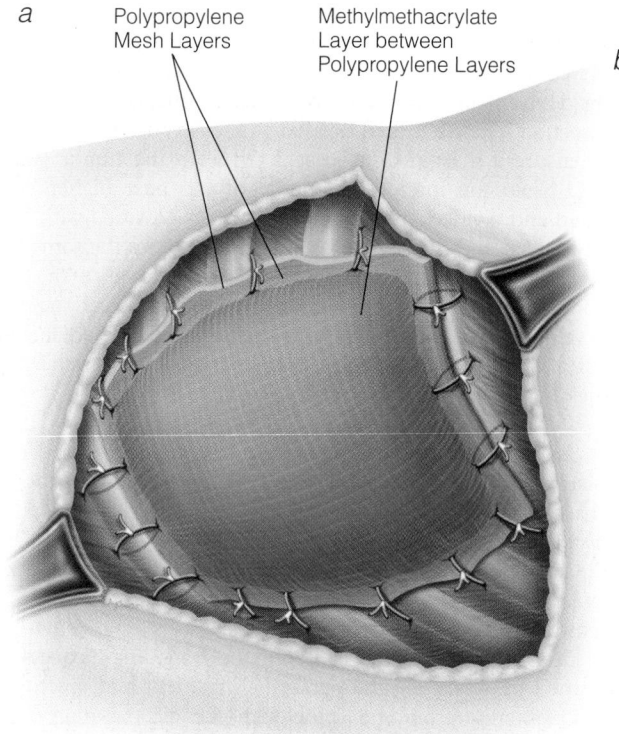

a Polypropylene Mesh Layers   Methylmethacrylate Layer between Polypropylene Layers

b

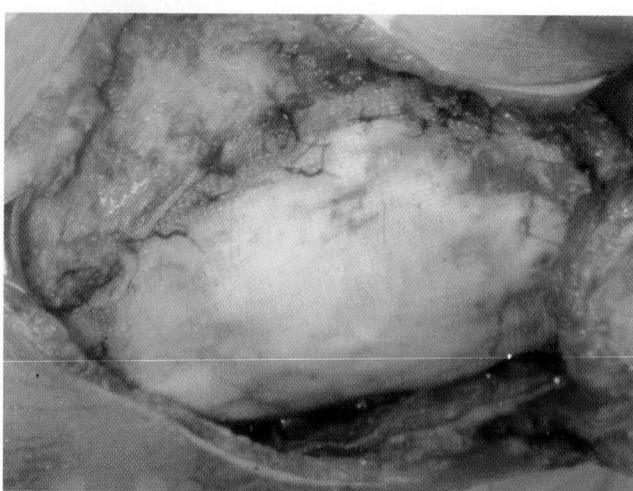

Figure 12 **Chest wall resection. (a) A polypropylene-methylmethacrylate sandwich is created by spreading a layer of methylmethacrylate cement between two pieces of polypropylene mesh. When sufficiently hardened, the sandwich is sutured to the ribs. (b) Photograph shows a polypropylene-methylmethacrylate sandwich sutured in place.**

struction is warranted (as in anterior reconstruction); it not only provides added protection of pleural and mediastinal structures but also creates a better cosmetic effect by recreating the shape of the chest wall.

To create the polypropylene-methylmethacrylate sandwich, two pieces of polypropylene mesh are cut to the size of the defect. A thin layer of methylmethacrylate cement is spread on one of the mesh pieces, and the other piece is then applied over the methylmethacrylate layer. As this sandwich begins to harden, it is molded to the contours of the chest wall, with care taken to protect the patient's skin against injury from the heat given off by the hardening cement. When the sandwich is sufficiently hardened, it is sewn to the ribs with 0 polypropylene sutures [see Figure 12a]. The sutures may be passed around the uppermost and lowermost ribs and may be placed directly through the anterior and posterior margins [see Figure 12b]. If rib disarticulation was required to complete the posterior margin, holes may be drilled in the transverse processes and the sutures passed through these holes; alternatively, the sandwich may be sutured to the paraspinal ligament.

If polypropylene or Gore-Tex mesh is used without cement, it should be cut to a size smaller than that of the defect. Thus, the mesh will effectively be stretched when it is sutured to the chest wall, and any laxity in the reconstruction will thereby be alleviated.

Step 7: closure and drainage. The serratus anterior and the latissimus dorsi are closed in the standard fashion, as are the subcutaneous and skin layers. With the exception of pleural tubes, drains are not routinely used. Special attention should be paid to postoperative analgesia: patients who have undergone extensive resections often experience considerable pain and are therefore prone to atelectasis and pneumonia. Epidural analgesia should be employed routinely in such cases.

Troubleshooting If chest wall infection is a possibility (as with osteoradionecrosis or osteomyelitis), alternative reconstructive techniques are required to obviate concerns about superinfec-

tion resulting from the use of synthetic material. In particular, radiation injury may involve all layers of the chest wall, necessitating very large resections [see Figure 13a]. Muscle or omental flaps with split-thickness skin grafts may be required for coverage; thus, preoperative consultation with an experienced plastic surgeon is advisable. A particular concern is what to use to reconstruct the chest wall. Various tissues (e.g., fascia lata and ribs) have been employed, but an easier substitute that works quite well is an absorbable synthetic mesh (e.g., Vicryl). The mesh is sewn to the ribs as previously described [see Step 6, above], and the tissue flap is placed on top of the mesh, followed by a skin graft [see Figure 13b, c]. Alternatively, some authors recommend the use of muscle or myocutaneous flaps without rigid chest wall reconstruction after resection, particularly in infected fields.[19]

Outcome evaluation The results achieved after major chest wall resection have generally been excellent. One study reviewed 200 patients who underwent resection and reconstruction over a 25-year period.[20] The reconstructions ranged from relatively straightforward two-rib resections to more complex forequarter amputations. The indications for resection were lung cancer (38%), osteoradionecrosis (29%), chest wall tumor (27%), and osteomyelitis (16%). Immediate reconstruction was performed in 98% of patients. The major muscle flaps utilized were latissimus dorsi (20%), rectus abdominis (17%), pectoralis major (16%), and serratus anterior (9%). Free flaps were utilized in only 9% of cases, and split-thickness skin grafts were required in 12% of patients. Reconstruction was performed with Prolene mesh (25%), Marlex mesh (11%), Vicryl mesh (6%), or a polypropylene-methylmethacrylate sandwich (6%). Operative mortality was 7%, and major morbidity occurred in 24% of patients. Most of the morbidity was accounted for by pneumonia (14%) and acute respiratory distress syndrome (6%).

Manubrial and Clavicular Resection

Resection of the manubrium or the clavicle may be necessary if

a

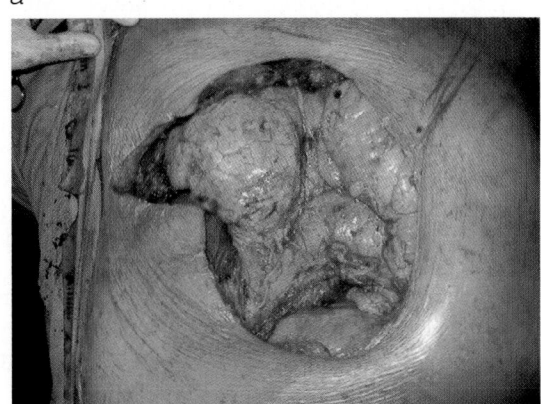

b

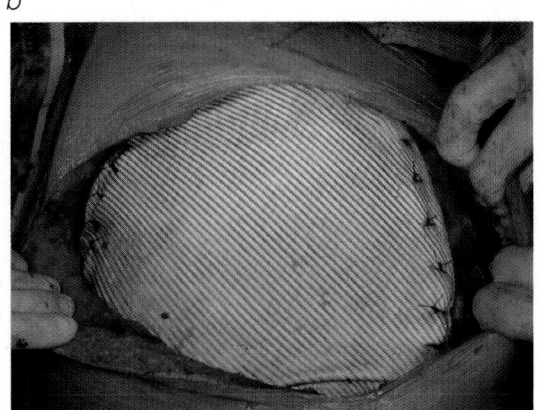

c

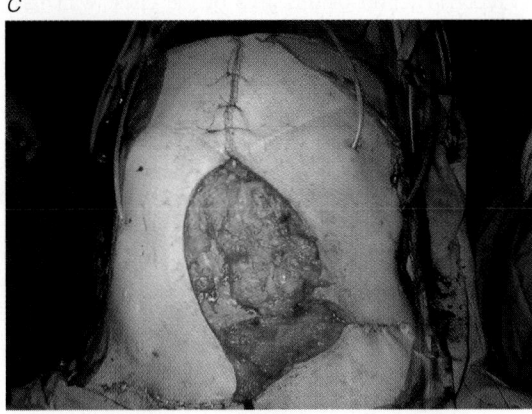

Figure 13   Chest wall resection. The presence of osteoradionecrosis may necessitate very large resections and resulting defects (*a*). Such defects may be covered with absorbable mesh (*b*), followed by an omental flap (*c*) or a muscle flap.

Resection of sternoclavicular joint for infection   Clavicular resections are rarely performed but may be required to treat tumors, vascular compression from healed fractures, or infection. Occasionally, infections involve the sternoclavicular joint (SCJ). Patients with osteomyelitis of this joint are often immunosuppressed and may have had an indwelling subclavian vein catheter that became infected. In a study of seven patients who underwent SCJ resection for infection, five of six patients initially treated with antibiotics and simple drainage experienced recurrences, whereas six of six patients treated with resection of the joint and pectoralis muscle advancement flaps were cured. None of the patients experienced problems with arm mobility in the course of long-term follow-up.[21]

these structures become infected or involved with tumors. Clavicular and manubrial resections follow the same operative approach as other chest wall resections. Specifically, attention must be paid to how much bone to resect, how to reconstruct the defect, and how to provide tissue coverage.

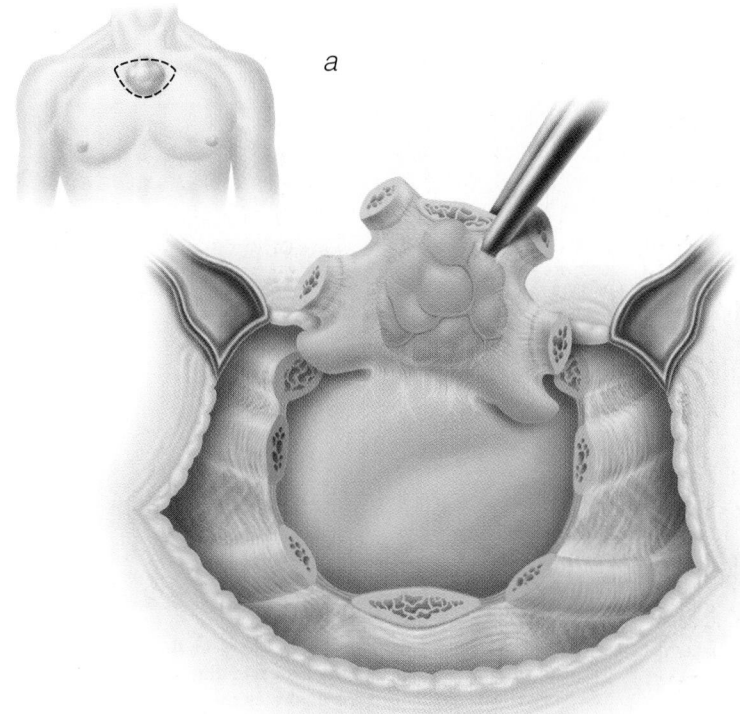

a

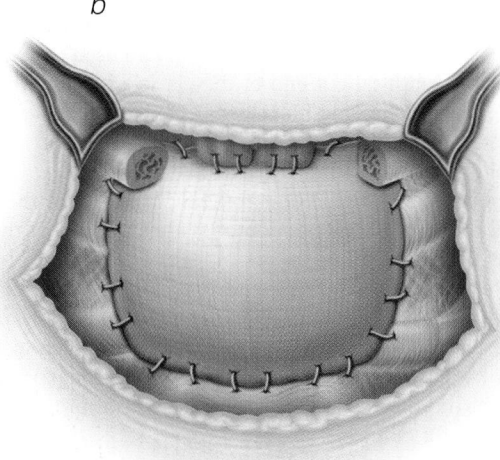

b

Figure 14   Manubrial resection and reconstruction. (*a*) The clavicles and ribs are divided as in clavicular and other chest wall resections. (*b*) A polypropylene-methylmethacrylate sandwich may be used to reconstruct the chest wall.

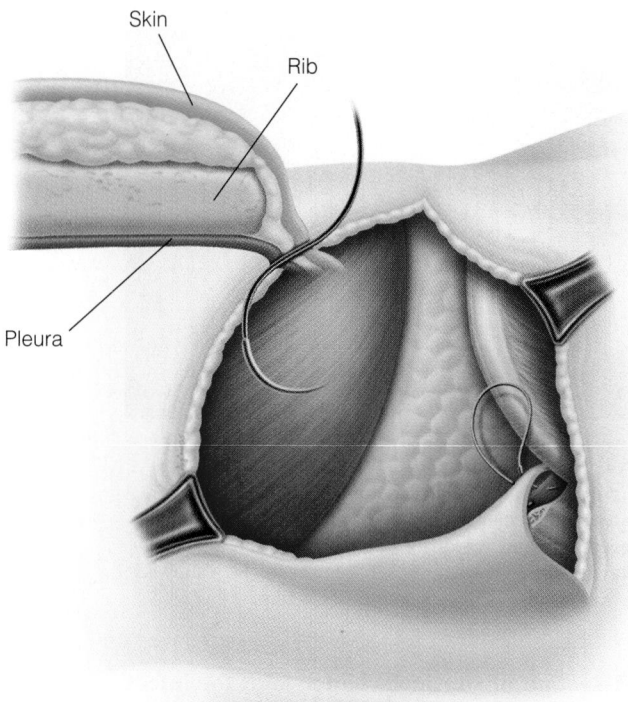

Skin

Rib

Pleura

Figure 15 **Open chest drainage (Eloesser flap). Once the ribs have been resected, the skin overlying the thoracostomy is marsupialized to the parietal pleura to permit packing and open pleural drainage.**

Operative technique. An incision is made that extends along the distal clavicle and curves down onto the manubrium. The soft tissue is divided with the electrocautery down to the clavicle and the manubrium. The muscular attachments of the pectoralis major and the sternocleidomastoid muscle are dissected off the clavicle and the manubrium with a periosteal elevator. Dissection in the subperiosteal plane is then continued circumferentially around the distal clavicle, with special care taken to keep from injuring the subclavian vessels that lie deep to the clavicle. A Gigli saw is passed around the clavicle with a right-angle clamp and used to divide the distal clavicle. The distal cut end of the clavicle is grasped with a penetrating towel clamp and bluntly dissected away from the deep tissue toward the manubrium. Any pockets of infection encountered should be cultured, drained, and debrided.

At this point, a large separation in the SCJ, caused by the infection, should be apparent. Resection of a small portion of the manubrium is usually required to remove all of the infected bone. Once the tissue deep to the manubrium has been dissected, a small band retractor is placed beneath the manubrium, and an oscillating sternal saw is used to resect the lateral portion of the manubrium, adjacent to the SCJ. Alternatively, a rongeur may be used to debride infected bone from the manubrium. All tissue should be sent for culture.

Severe infections may necessitate more extensive resection of bone or soft tissue, but if the infection is caught early, simple resection of the SCJ is generally curative. In more extensive resections, muscle flap coverage may be required, but in simple SCJ resections, good results can be obtained by using only deep closed suction drainage, followed by multilayer closure of the wound. To prevent any recurrent osteomyelitis, antibiotics should be continued for several weeks after resection.

Resection of manubrium for cancer Manubrial resections may be required for rare cases of primary or metastatic cancers.

Operative technique. Because of the relative paucity of tissue overlying the manubrium, cancers in this area may involve the dermis. In such cases, it may be necessary to resect skin along with the specimen. Alternatively, if the skin is not involved, an upper midline incision may be employed. The incision is carried down circumferentially to the chest wall, with care taken to maintain a 2 to 3 cm margin from the tumor. The clavicles and ribs are divided in the same fashion as for chest wall and clavicular resections [*see Figure 14a*]. Associated structures (e.g., the thymus) can be resected along with the manubrium; these tumors rarely involve the innominate vein.

A polypropylene-methylmethacrylate sandwich is useful for reconstruction of this area of the chest wall [*see Figure 14b*]. The patch is secured to the remaining ribs and clavicles with 0 polypropylene sutures. Coverage is then provided with a pectoralis major

a

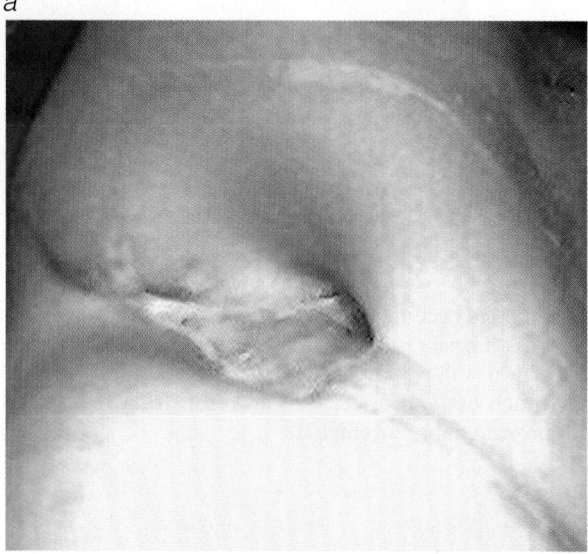

b

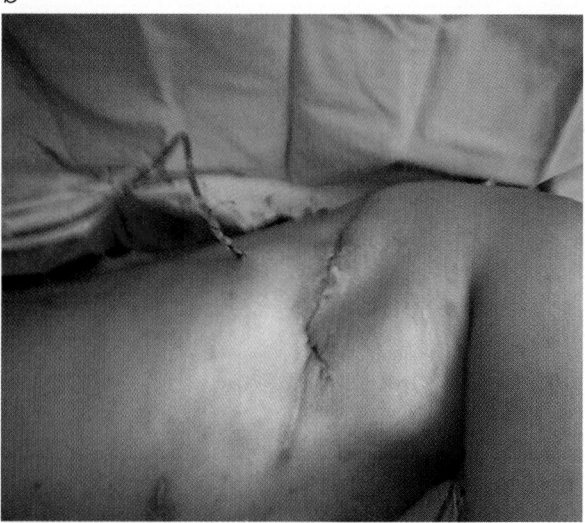

Figure 16 **Open chest drainage (Eloesser flap). (*a*) Photograph shows a right Eloesser flap 8 months after creation. (*b*) Photograph shows an Eloesser flap that was closed with a muscle flap.**

advancement flap or, if skin was excised, a pedicled pectoralis myocutaneous flap. A pleural drain may be placed if either pleural space was entered, but this measure is not routinely employed.

Open Chest Drainage (Eloesser Flap)

Open drainage procedures are usually included in discussions of treatment of empyema, but they really represent a type of chest wall resection. Open drainage techniques for empyema were first described in the late 1800s by Poulet and subsequently by Schede. Graham, who headed the Army Empyema Commission during World War I, is credited with the observation that ensuring pleural-pleural symphysis was the key to preventing the often fatal complication of pneumothorax.[22] Indications for open chest drainage include postpneumonectomy empyema or bronchopleural fistula, long-standing empyema in a patient who cannot undergo decortication, and chronic bronchopleural fistula in a high-risk patient.

Operative technique The technique currently employed by most thoracic surgeons follows Symbas's modification of Eloesser's open drainage technique.[23] This procedure has come to be known as the Eloesser flap. Preoperative chest CT is essential for identifying the exact location of the empyema, which determines the placement of the incision.

Step 1: initial incision and exposure. The patient is placed in the decubitus position, and a 6 to 8 cm incision is made over the area corresponding to the most dependent area of the infected cavity. Symbas employed a U-shaped incision; however, a simple linear incision can also be used with good results. The subcutaneous tissue and muscle are then divided down to the chest wall with the electrocautery.

Step 2: resection of ribs and creation of thoracostomy. The pleural space is opened with the electrocautery, any pus present is drained, and the chest cavity is manually and visually explored. Next, 6 to 8 cm segments of two or three adjacent ribs are resected according to the same principles employed for other chest wall resections. The resulting thoracostomy is large enough to permit drainage and packing. The skin overlying this thoracostomy is then marsupialized to the thickened parietal pleura with absorbable sutures [*see Figure 15*]. If the pleura does not possess sufficient integrity to hold the sutures, they can be placed through the periosteum of the ribs.

Step 3: packing and drainage. The wound is irrigated with normal saline and packed with saline-moistened gauze. Postoperatively, a chest x-ray should be obtained to rule out pneumothorax, and twice- to thrice-daily packing is initiated. Packing is continued on an outpatient basis, and the wound is monitored. The wound will begin to close over the next several weeks. If the empyema or bronchopleural fistula has not healed by the time the wound starts closing, the thoracostomy will have to be revised. In some cases, this can be accomplished merely by manually dilating the opening in the operating room; in others, the entire thoracostomy must be revised. In either case, the goal is to maintain a large enough opening to allow adequate packing.

Step 4: closure of thoracostomy. Once the lung and the pleural space have healed, the thoracostomy is closed. The procedure for closing the thoracostomy depends on the size and nature of the remaining defect [*see Figure 16a*]. For small defects, simple closure of the skin will suffice. For larger defects or residual spaces in the pleura, however, muscle flap closure will be required [*see Figure 16b*]. Improvements in radiographic techniques and greater emphasis on early intervention for empyemas have significantly reduced the need for open chest drainage; however, this technique can still be valuable in the appropriate clinical situation.

References

1. Backer CL, Mavroudis C: Congenital heart surgery nomenclature and database project: vascular rings, tracheal stenosis, pectus excavatum. Ann Thorac Surg 69(4 suppl):S308, 2000

2. Haller JA, Kramer Ss, Lietman SA: Use of CT scans in selection of patients for pectus excavatum surgery: a preliminary report. J Pediatr Surg 22:904, 1987

3. Weg JG, Krumholz RA, Harkleroad LE: Pulmonary dysfunction in pectus excavatum. Am Rev Respir Dis 96:936, 1967

4. Gyllensward A, Irnell L, Michaelsson M, et al: Pectus excavatum: a clinical study with long term postoperative follow-up. Acta Paediatr 255(suppl): 2, 1975

5. Cahill JL, Lees GM, Robertson HT: A summary of preoperative and postoperative cardiorespiratory performance in patients undergoing pectus excavatum and carinatum repair. J Pediatr Surg 19:430, 1984.

6. Blickman JG, Rosen PR, Welch KJ, et al: Pectus excavatum in children: pulmonary scintigraphy before and after corrective surgery. Radiology 156:781, 1985

7. Haller JA, Colombani PM, Humphries CT, et al: Chest wall constriction after too extensive and too early operations for pectus excavatum. Ann Thorac Surg 61:1618, 1996

8. Bevegard S: Postural circulatory changes at rest and during exercise in patients with funnel chest, with special reference to the influence on the stroke volume. Acta Physiol Scand 49:279, 1960

9. Gattiker H, Buhlmann A: Cardiopulmonary function and exercise tolerance in supine and sitting position in patients with pectus excavatum. Helv Med Acta 33:122, 1967

10. Peterson RJ, Young WG Jr, Godwin JD, et al: Noninvasive assessment of exercise cardiac function before and after pectus excavatum repair. J Thorac Cardiovasc Surg 90:251, 1985

11. Judet J, Judet R: Sternum en entonnoir par resection et retournement. Mem Acad Chir 82:250, 1956

12. Wada J, Ikeda K, Ishida T, et al: Results of 271 funnel chest operations. Ann Thorac Surg 10:526, 1970

13. Robicsek F, Cook JW, Daugherty HK, et al: Pectus carinatum. J Thorac Cardiovasc Surg 78:52, 1979

14. Mansour KA, Thourani VH, Odessey EA, et al: Thirty-year experience with repair of pectus deformities in adults. Ann Thorac Surg 76:391, 2003

15. Hebra A: Minimally invasive pectus surgery. Chest Surg Clin N Am 10:329, 2000

16. Robicsek F: Surgical treatment of pectus excavatum. Chest Surg Clin N Am 10:277, 2000

17. Stefani A, Morandi U, Lodi R: Migration of pectus excavatum correction metal support into the abdomen. Eur J Cardiothorac Surg 14:434, 1998

18. Urschel HC: The transaxillary approach for treatment of thoracic outlet syndrome. Chest Surg Clin N Am 9:771, 1999

19. Arnold PG, Pairolero PC: Use of pectoralis major muscle flaps to repair defects of anterior chest wall. Plast Reconstruct Surg 63:105, 1979

20. Mansour KA, Thourani VH, Losken A, et al: Chest wall resections and reconstruction: a 25-year experience. Ann Thorac Surg 73:1720, 2002

21. Song HK, Guy TS, Kaiser LR, et al: Current presentation and optimal surgical management of sternoclavicular joint infections. Ann Thorac Surg 73:427, 2002

22. Somers J, Faber LP: Historical developments in the management of empyema. Chest Surg Clin N Am 6:404, 1996

23. Symbas PN, Nugent JT, Abbott OA, et al: Nontuberculous pleural empyema in adults. Ann Thorac Surg 12:69, 1971

Acknowledgment

Figures 1 through 8, 10 through 12, 14, and 15   Alice Y. Chen.

37 VIDEO-ASSISTED THORACIC SURGERY

Raja M. Flores, M.D., Bernard Park, M.D., and Valerie W. Rusch, M.D., F.A.C.S.

The technique of thoracoscopy was first described in 1910 by Jacobeus, a Swedish physician who used a cystoscope to examine the pleural space.[1] Although thoracoscopy was initially performed for diagnostic purposes, it later evolved into a therapeutic procedure. During the 1930s and 1940s, it was used to lyse intrapleural adhesions after collapse therapy for tuberculosis. During the 1950s, when effective antituberculous chemotherapy became available, thoracoscopy fell into disuse in the United States[2]; however, it remained popular in Europe, where it was employed in diagnosing and treating problems such as pleural effusion, empyema, traumatic hemothorax, persistent air leak after pulmonary resection, and spontaneous pneumothorax.[3-5] During the 1970s and 1980s, a few North American surgeons revived the practice of thoracoscopy, both to manage pleural disease and to perform small peripheral lung biopsies in patients with diffuse pneumonitis.

In the first stages of its revival, thoracoscopy was often performed with open endoscopes that were originally designed for other procedures (e.g., mediastinoscopes).[6,7] As optics and lighting systems improved, smaller-caliber endoscopes were created specifically for thoracoscopic applications[8]; however, these instruments were limited, in that only one person could visualize the operative field at a given time. In 1991, the application of video technology to thoracoscopy revolutionized the procedure because it allowed several persons to see the operative field simultaneously and to operate together as they would during an open procedure. In addition, the development of endoscopic instruments, particularly endoscopic staplers, enabled surgeons to perform major operations using minimally invasive techniques. The impact of this new technology was so profound that within a 2-year period, traditional thoracoscopic techniques were abandoned in favor of video-assisted thoracic surgery (VATS).[9,10]

In what follows, therefore, we focus on current VATS procedures rather than on traditional thoracoscopic techniques. There are numerous accepted diagnostic and therapeutic indications for VATS [see Table 1]. Accordingly, there are numerous operations that can be performed by VATS; we describe the most important of these, with the exception of esophageal myotomy and fundoplication, which are covered elsewhere [see 35 Minimally Invasive Esophageal Procedures]. In addition, we describe the application of telerobotics to VATS lobectomy.

A major force that drives surgeons to perform VATS procedures has been patient demand. Unfortunately, the application of VATS has not always been accompanied by careful evaluation of outcomes. Feasibility has sometimes been confused with success. Although VATS appears to have beneficial effects in terms of cosmesis and postoperative pain in the short term, it has not yet been proved to have beneficial effects on pulmonary function and a return to normal activity in the long term.[11,12] It is therefore the responsibility of thoracic surgeons to perform these procedures selectively rather than indiscriminately, either in settings where the effectiveness of VATS is clearly proved or, where the role of VATS

has not been fully established, within the context of well-designed clinical trials.

In particular, questions remain about the oncologic soundness of some VATS procedures. It appears that levels of cytokines and other acute-phase reactants are lower with minimally invasive procedures than with the corresponding open procedures.[13,14] However, it remains to be determined whether this decrease will ultimately result in decreased tumor growth or reduced recurrence rates. Rigorous evaluation is needed to determine how VATS may be most appropriately and safely employed in cancer patients.

Operative Planning

POSITIONING AND PORT PLACEMENT

Patient preparation and positioning are much the same for most VATS procedures. As a rule, the lateral decubitus position offers the best exposure, and it permits easy conversion to a thoracotomy if necessary. There are occasional exceptions to this rule, however, and in such cases the choice of position is dictated by the procedure planned. For instance, if a cervical mediastinoscopy or a Chamberlain procedure is being performed for lung cancer staging and the pleura must be examined to rule out the presence of metastases, the patient can be left in the supine position and the videothoracoscope introduced through the parasternal incision or a separate inferior incision.[15]

Port placement, the use of so-called access incisions (utility thoracotomies), and instrumentation may vary from one procedure to the next. In approximately 20% of patients undergoing VATS, intraoperative conversion to a standard thoracotomy will be necessary for any of several reasons, including extensive pleural adhesions and pulmonary lesions that cannot be located thoracoscopically or that necessitate a more extensive resection than can be accomplished endosurgically. With experience, one can learn to predict the likelihood of such conversion in a given case. It is important to discuss this possibility with the patient before operation and to obtain informed consent to conversion. Any patient who is likely to require conversion to a thoracotomy or who may be undergoing lobectomy or pneumonectomy should receive the cardiopulmonary evaluation that is usual for such procedures before VATS is performed.

ANESTHESIA AND MONITORING

VATS procedures are performed with the patient under general anesthesia. Very limited operations (e.g., pleural biopsies) can be done with a single-lumen endotracheal tube in place, but most procedures should be performed with single-lung ventilation using a double-lumen endotracheal tube or a bronchial blocker. The degree of intraoperative monitoring needed depends on the extent of the planned procedure and on the patient's general medical condition. Standard monitoring techniques (including pulse oximetry) are always used, but arterial lines are placed selectively. A central venous catheter or a Swan-Ganz catheter is inserted only when the patient's baseline cardiac status demands precise hemodynamic monitoring. A Foley catheter is inserted at the beginning of all VATS procedures to monitor urine output because it is not always possible to predict how long the operation will take or whether conversion to thoracotomy will prove necessary.

INSTRUMENTATION

Instrumentation for VATS comprises (1) video equipment, (2) endoscopes and thoracoports, (3) staplers, (4) thoracic instruments (e.g., lung clamps and retractors) modified for endoscopic use, and (5) various devices for tissue cauterization, including lasers. Because immediate conversion to thoracotomy is occasionally necessary, a basic set of thoracotomy instruments should be an integral part of a VATS instrument tray.[16]

Video Equipment

Minor variations in lighting and optics aside, the basic components of all video systems used for thoracoscopy are similar: a large-screen (21 in.) video monitor, a xenon light source, a video recorder, and a printer for still photography, mounted together on a cart. A second video monitor, also mounted on a cart, is connected by cable to the main monitor and is placed across from it at the head of the operating table. Thus, both the surgeon and the first assistant are able to look directly at a video display without having to turn away from the surgical field. Alternatively, a single monitor can be placed at the head of the operating table. The only additional item of equipment necessary for laparoscopy is an insufflator. Therefore, to maximize cost-efficiency, hospitals acquiring video monitors and endoscopes should coordinate the choice of this expensive equipment among the specialties using it, including thoracic surgery, general surgery, gynecology, and urology. Hospitals performing many endoscopic procedures may find it advisable to dedicate one or more rooms to video endoscopic surgery and to mount video equipment on the ceilings or walls.

Endoscopes and Thoracoports

Some procedures are performed with a forward-viewing (0°) rigid scope; however, 30° angled scopes are useful for visualizing the sulci and the superior and posterior mediastinum and provide better overall visualization of the pleural space. In addition to the standard 10 mm thoracoscopes, there are 5 mm thoracoscopes whose resolution is nearly as good. The scope is attached to the light source by a light cable and is coupled to the video-monitor system by a camera cable [*see Figure 1*]. Although camera cables can be sterilized, it is best to cover the camera head and cable with a clear plastic bag so that the cable can remain in the OR at all times. Videoscopes are now available in which the camera chip is located at the tip of the scope rather than in the connecting camera cable; these are replacing the endoscopes previously used because they provide a sharper image. For complex procedures (e.g., VATS lobectomy), we currently use a 30° rotating scope, which allows better orientation and visualization around structures such as the pulmonary artery and bronchus. Flexible thoracoscopes, which look like a short, heavy version of a flexible bronchoscope but have a more rigid distal end, are also available. Some surgeons feel that flexible thoracoscopes enhance their ability to visualize the entire pleural space, but these devices are very expensive and continue to be premium purchases for most hospitals.

Originally, thoracoscopy made use of trocar cannulas designed for laparoscopy to access the pleural space. However, these devices are too long and have sharp ends that can injure the lung. Because

---

Table 1   Indications and Contraindications for VATS Procedures

Diagnostic indications
   Undiagnosed pleural effusion
   Indeterminate pulmonary nodule
   Undiagnosed interstitial lung disease
   Pulmonary infection in the immunosuppressed patient
   To define cell type in known thoracic malignancy
   To define extent of a primary thoracic tumor
   Nodal staging of a primary thoracic tumor
   Diagnosis of intrathoracic pathology to stage a primary extrathoracic tumor
   Evaluation of intrapleural infection
Therapeutic indications
   Lung
      Spontaneous pneumothorax
      Bullous disease
      Lung volume reduction
      Persistent parenchymal air leak
      Benign pulmonary nodule
      Resection of pulmonary metastases (in highly selected cases)
      Resection of primary lung tumor (in highly selected cases)
   Mediastinum
      Drainage of pericardial effusion
      Excision of bronchogenic or pericardial cyst
      Resection of selected primary mediastinal tumors
      Esophageal myotomy
      Facilitation of transhiatal esophagectomy
      ? Resection of primary esophageal tumors
      ? Thymic resection
      Ligation of thoracic duct
   Pleura
      Drainage of a multiloculated effusion
      Drainage of an early empyema
      Pleurodesis
Contraindications
   Extensive intrapleural adhesions
   Inability to sustain single-lung ventilation
   Extensive involvement of hilar structures
   Preoperative induction chemotherapy or chemoradiotherapy
   Severe coagulopathy

---

patients undergoing thoracoscopy are under general anesthesia and have a double-lumen endotracheal tube in place, the cannulas need not maintain an airtight seal, as they do in laparoscopy. Accordingly, thoracoports, which are shorter than laparoscopy cannulas and have a corkscrew configuration on the outside that stabilizes them within the chest wall, are routinely used. The trocar is simply a blunt-tip obturator that facilitates passage of the cannula through the chest wall [*see Figure 2a*]. Thoracoports are available in several sizes (5, 10.5, 12, and 15 mm in diameter) to accommodate various instruments.

Staplers

Endoscopic staplers that cut between two simultaneously applied triple rows of staples (gastrointestinal anastomosis [GIA] staplers) are available in lengths of 30 and 60 mm and in staple depths of 2.0, 2.5, 3.5, and 4.8 mm [*see Figure 2b*]. Like their counterparts designed for open procedures, they are disposable multicartridge instruments. The endoscopic GIA stapler with 2.0 and 2.5 mm staples is designed for division of pulmonary vessels. Some surgeons are reluctant to use it on hilar vessels because if the

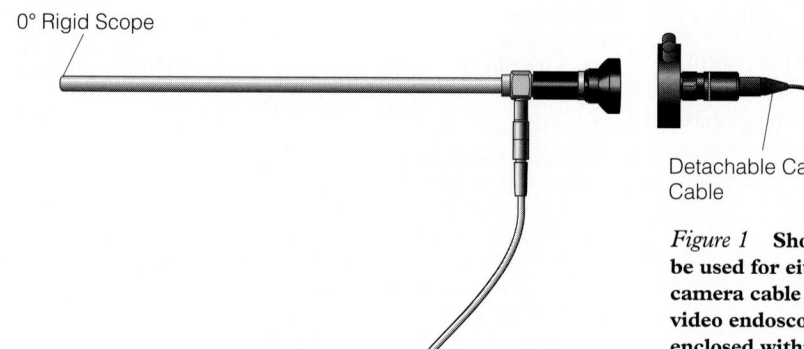

0° Rigid Scope

Detachable Camera
Cable

Figure 1 **Shown is a forward-viewing (0°) rigid scope that can be used for either laparoscopy or thoracoscopy. A detachable camera cable is clipped onto the eyepiece of the scope for video endoscopy. The camera cable can be sterilized or enclosed within a plastic sheath if it is used frequently.**

stapler fails mechanically (e.g., cuts without applying both staple lines properly), life-threatening hemorrhage can ensue. Endoscopic staplers that do not cut (transverse anastomosis [TA] staplers) are also available.

Some advocate using two applications of the endovascular stapling device to minimize the risk of transecting the vessel as a consequence of a stapling misfire. In this approach, the stapler is first fired proximally with the knife removed, leaving six rows of staples in place. Next, the stapler is fired again more distally with the cutting mechanism intact to transect the vessel, leaving a total of nine rows of staples on the patient side and three rows of staples on the specimen side.

Endoscopic GIA staplers have revolutionized surgeons' ability to perform minimally invasive pulmonary resections. These devices are highly reliable and provide excellent hemostasis and closure of air leaks. There are also stapler cartridges that buttress

the staple line with prosthetic materials (e.g., Gore-Tex; W. L. Gore, Boulder, Colorado) to reduce postoperative air leakage in patients with emphysematous lung tissue.

Although they have been largely supplanted by endoscopic GIA staplers, standard stapling instruments can also be used during some VATS procedures. They are unnecessary for most pulmonary wedge resections but may be helpful for more complex procedures (e.g., lobectomies). Standard GIA staplers and articulated rotating TA staplers (Roticulator; AutoSuture, Norwalk, Connecticut) are the most practical devices for VATS because they can be inserted and positioned through an access incision.

Instruments

Various types of Pennington and Duval clamps are available [*see Figure 2c*]. Sponge sticks modified by the introduction of various curves and a line of DeBakey-type teeth on the end can also be

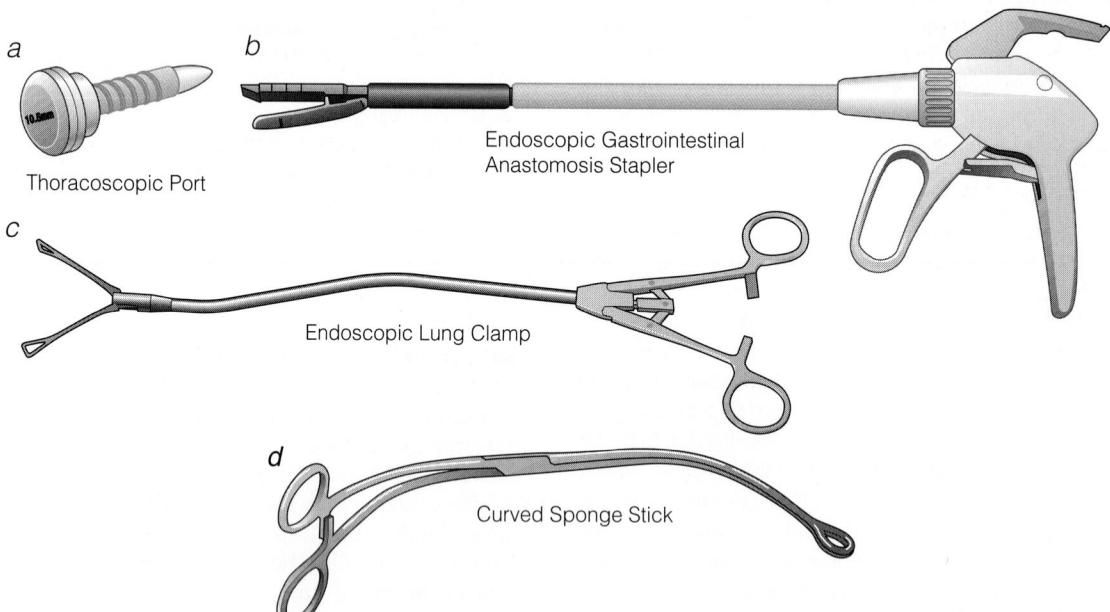

a Thoracoscopic Port

b Endoscopic Gastrointestinal Anastomosis Stapler

c Endoscopic Lung Clamp

d Curved Sponge Stick

Figure 2 **Shown are instruments commonly used during VATS. Modified trocar cannulas, called thoracoports (*a*), facilitate access to the pleural space. They are shorter than the cannulas used in laparoscopy and have a corkscrew configuration on the outside that maintains their position on the chest wall. The trocar is a blunt-tipped plastic obturator that facilitates passage of the cannula through the chest wall. A thin plastic diaphragm stabilizes the position of the instruments or can be removed to facilitate access to the pleural space. Endoscopic GIA staplers that make incisions between two triple rows of staples (*b*) can be inserted through these ports. Like staplers designed for open procedures, endoscopic GIA staplers are disposable multifire instruments that hold three replacements of the staple cartridge. Another instrument that can be inserted through these ports is the nondisposable endoscopic lung clamp (*c*), which is available in various shapes with serrations at the end or along the full length of the clamp. Finally, the port allows insertion of curved sponge sticks (*d*), which have been modified for endoscopic use as lung clamps or lymph node holders.**

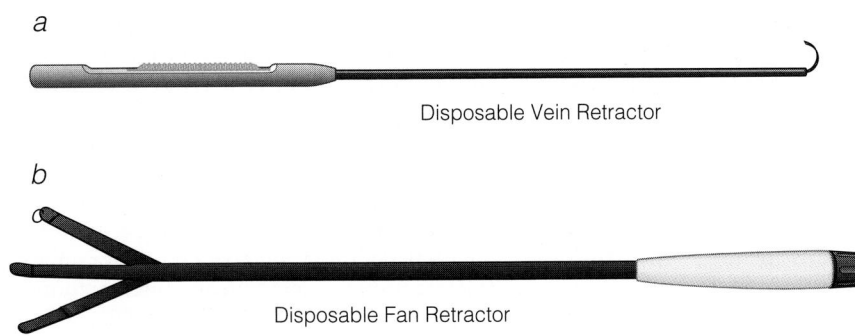

a

Disposable Vein Retractor

b

Disposable Fan Retractor

Figure 3 **Shown are retractors used for VATS. Vein retractors are best suited for gentle retraction of hilar or mediastinal structures, such as the vessels, bronchi, esophagus, and lymph nodes. The tip of the disposable vein retractor (*a*) can be extended from or withdrawn into the shaft to allow insertion of the retractor through a 12 mm port. The most useful retractor for general purposes is the fan retractor (*b*). A knob on the end of the handle opens and closes the fan, allowing the retractor to be inserted through a port and opened for retraction in the pleural space.**

used as lung clamps or lymph node holders [*see Figure 2d*].

Several retractors have been developed for endoscopic surgery. One such device is a modified Finochietto retractor with long, narrow blades, which is particularly helpful for retracting the chest wall soft tissues in an access incision. Others are the disposable vein retractor [*see Figure 3a*], the tip of which can be withdrawn into the straight instrument shaft, and the fan retractor, which can be opened and closed like a fan by turning a knob on the end of the retractor [*see Figure 3b*]. Of these, the fan retractor is the most useful general retractor for thoracoscopic procedures. Vein retractors are best suited for gentle retraction of hilar or mediastinal structures (e.g., vessels, bronchi, esophagus, or lymph nodes).

In major VATS procedures (e.g., VATS lobectomy), the soft tissues of the access incision may be retracted by means of a cerebellar (or Weitlaner) retractor. This measure allows the surgeon to encircle the hilar vascular structures by using two instruments simultaneously through the same incision. A Harken clamp is useful, in that it is long enough to reach behind a vascular structure

and pass a monofilament suture to the tip of the instrument. A polyp forceps is an excellent instrument for holding and retracting lymph nodes during a mediastinal lymph node dissection (MLND). Because polyp forceps have a slightly curved configuration and a blunt tip, they can also be used to dissect around hilar vessels.

Although biopsy forceps have been specifically created for laparoscopy and thoracoscopy, those used for mediastinoscopy are, in fact, well suited for thoracoscopy. Because laparoscopy instruments were developed before thoracoscopy instruments, many types of grasping forceps are available; however, most are too traumatizing for thoracic surgery. DeBakey forceps, modified for endoscopic use, are the gentlest type available. Various curved and right-angle dissecting clamps, needle holders, and scissors have been developed [*see Figure 4*]. In addition, standard thoracotomy instruments can be inserted through a minithoracotomy incision and used just as they would be in an open procedure.

Devices for Tissue Cauterization

Most scissors have an electrocautery attachment that permits simultaneous cutting and cauterizing. The neodymium:yttrium-aluminum-garnet (Nd:YAG) laser is sometimes applied to VATS resection of pulmonary lesions. This is done by inserting the YAG laser-fiber through angled or straight handpieces [*see Figure 5*]. Laser-assisted pulmonary resection is helpful in removing lesions on the flat surface of the lung, where a stapler cannot be easily applied.[17]

The argon beam electrocoagulator (ABC) (ConMed Corporation, Utica, New York) is a noncontact form of electrocautery that provides superb hemostasis on raw surfaces (e.g., denuded pulmonary parenchyma or the chest wall after pleurectomy) and helps seal air leaks from the surface of the lung.[18] The standard disposable ABC handpiece used for open procedures is narrow enough to pass through a thoracoport and thus may be used for VATS. The optional Bend-a-Beam handpiece is extremely useful in VATS lobectomy because it allows the surgeon to shape the shaft of the instrument for easier coagulation of hard-to-reach areas.

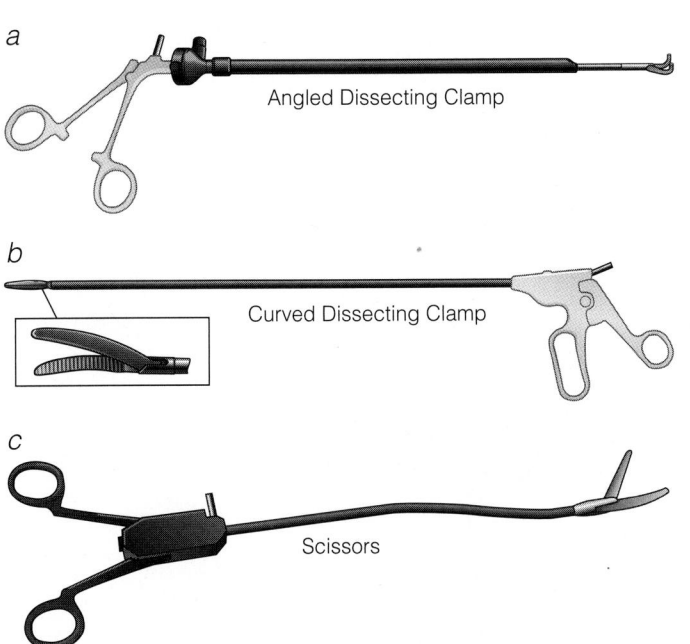

a

Angled Dissecting Clamp

b

Curved Dissecting Clamp

c

Scissors

Figure 4 **Various right-angle (*a*) and curved (*b*) dissecting clamps are available. On the angled model shown (*a*), the knob close to the handle rotates the shaft of the clamp 360°. Many types of endoscopic scissors (*c*) are also available. Some scissors incorporate an attachment for an electrocautery so that the surgeon can cut and cauterize simultaneously.**

YAG Laser Fiber

Angled Hand Piece

Figure 5 **Shown is an angled handpiece through which an yttrium-aluminum-garnet (YAG) laser can be placed during VATS. The handpiece is narrow enough to be used during thoracoscopy as well as during open procedures.**

Instrumentation for videothoracoscopy continues to evolve, especially as minimally invasive cardiac surgical procedures become commonplace. Nevertheless, to put together the best set of instruments, it still is necessary to combine disposable and nondisposable instruments from different manufacturers and to borrow instruments originally designed for other procedures. Rather than create separate instrument trays for different VATS procedures, it is best to maintain a single standard tray that includes the basic instruments required for most operations and to add instruments as needed. Again, this tray should also include the instruments needed for conversion to thoracotomy.

Basic Operative Technique

VATS procedures include both true videothoracoscopies and video-assisted procedures that are really a cross between videothoracoscopies and standard thoracotomies. Because VATS procedures are still evolving, there is no firm consensus among surgeons with respect to the number, size, and location of incisions.

The basic videothoracoscopy techniques have been well described.[19] The primary strategy is to place the instruments and the thoracoscope so that all are oriented in the same direction, facing the target disease within a 180° arc [see Figure 6]; this positioning prevents mirror imaging. The incisions should also be placed widely distant from each other so that the instruments do not crowd one another.

For most procedures, the videothoracoscope is inserted through a thoracoport placed between the midaxillary and the posterior axillary line at the seventh or eighth intercostal space. Instruments are introduced through two thoracoports: one is placed at approximately the fifth intercostal space in the anterior axillary line, and the other is placed at the fifth space, parallel to and about 2 to 3 cm away from the posterior border of the scapula [see Figure 6a]. If the procedure is converted to a thoracotomy, the two upper incisions can be incorporated into the thoracotomy incision and the lower incision can be used as a chest tube site. When a patient is being operated on for an apical lesion (e.g., bullae causing a spontaneous pneumothorax) [see Figure 6b], the camera port can be placed at the fifth or sixth intercostal space, and the two instrument ports may also be moved higher, with one in the axilla and the other higher on the posterior chest wall at approximately the third intercostal space. Depending on the location of the lesion being removed, a fourth port incision may be helpful to permit the introduction of additional instruments.

When the lung must be palpated so that a small or deep-seated lesion can be located or when complex video-assisted procedures are being performed, a small (4 cm) intercostal incision is added to the three port incisions. This utility thoracotomy, or access incision, is usually placed in the midaxillary line or in the auscultatory triangle. An infant Finochietto retractor or a Weitlaner retractor is used to retract the soft tissues without actually spreading the ribs [see Figure 7].

These basic concepts regarding incision placement are modified as necessary to accommodate the procedure being performed and the location of the lesion being removed (see below).

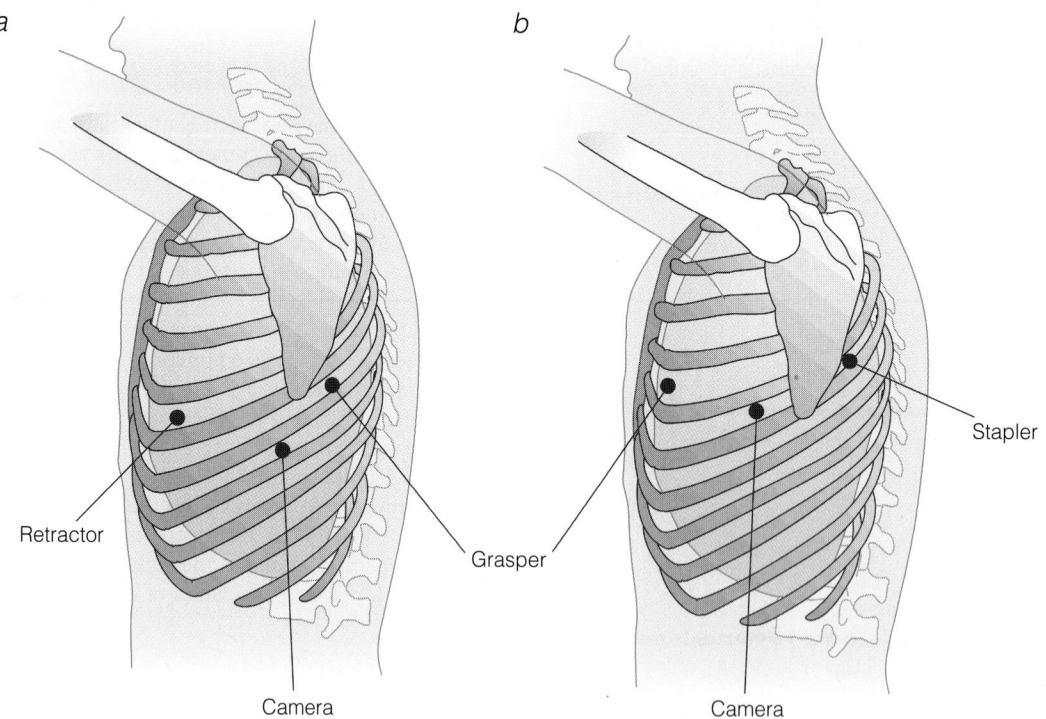

a

b

Retractor

Grasper

Camera

Stapler

Camera

Figure 6 **Basic operative technique. Shown is the typical positioning of instruments and the video camera for patients undergoing VATS for a lesion in the superior segment of the left lower lobe of the lung. Instruments are introduced through two port incisions made anteriorly at approximately the fifth intercostal space in the anterior axillary line and posteriorly parallel to and 2 to 3 cm away from the border of the scapula (*a*). For patients undergoing thoracoscopy for apical bullous disease in the left upper lobe of the lung, the camera port can be placed at the fifth or sixth intercostal space; one instrument port can be inserted in the axilla and the other port inserted higher on the posterior chest wall at approximately the third intercostal space (*b*).**

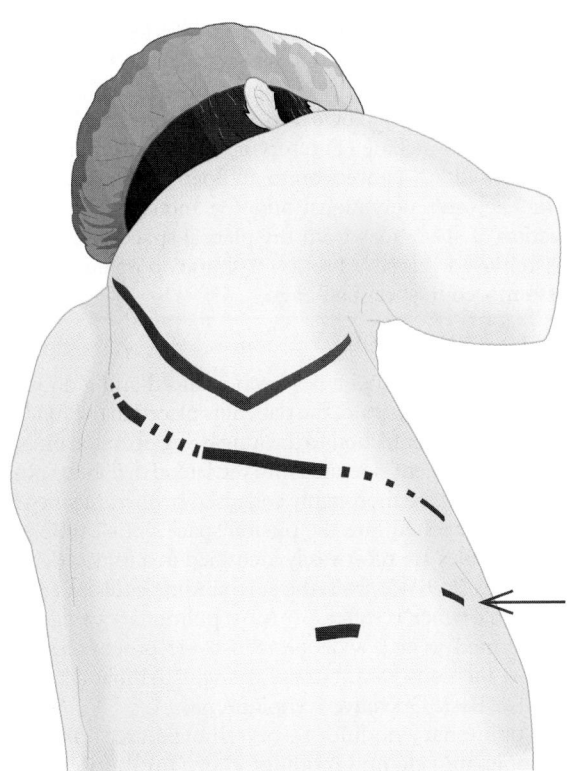

Figure 7   **Basic operative technique. Shown are the incisions used for common VATS procedures. The thoracoscope is inserted through the bottom incision. Anterior and posterior incisions are used for the introduction of instruments. Only one additional low anterior incision (arrow) is needed for thoracoscopic pleural procedures. If necessary, a so-called utility thoracotomy (dotted line) can be added at the fifth intercostal space. The tip of the scapula is outlined. These incisions can be incorporated into a standard thoracotomy incision if the VATS procedure is converted to an open procedure.**

VATS Procedures for Pleural Disease

OPERATIVE TECHNIQUE

A double-lumen endotracheal tube is inserted and the patient is placed in the lateral decubitus position. Two 1.5 cm incisions are made, one for the videothoracoscope and one for the instruments. The videothoracoscope is inserted through a 10.5 mm thoracoport at the seventh or eighth intercostal space in the midaxillary line; the instruments are inserted through a port placed a couple of interspaces higher in the anterior axillary line. If a talc poudrage is performed, both incisions are reused for placement of chest tubes, with a right-angle tube inserted on the diaphragm through the lower incision and a straight tube advanced up to the apex of the pleural space through the upper incision. The addition of a diaphragmatic chest tube helps prevent loculated basilar fluid collections after a talc pleurodesis. If a thoracotomy is subsequently performed, the upper port site is incorporated into the anterior aspect of the incision and the lower site can be reused as a chest tube site. Proper placement of port incisions is especially important in patients with suspected malignant mesothelioma because of the propensity of this tumor to implant in incisions and needle tracks.[8,20,21]

Once the videothoracoscope has been inserted, pleural biopsies are obtained under direct vision by introducing a biopsy forceps through a port placed in the upper incision. (The mediastinoscopy biopsy forceps are well suited to this task.) Pleural fluid is evacu-

ated with a Yankauer or pool-tip suction device. Fibrinous debris can be removed by irrigating the pleural space with a pulsating water jet lavage device designed for debridement of orthopedic wounds. This technique is particularly useful for the debridement and drainage of loculated fibrinopurulent empyemas.[22] At the end of the procedure, intercostal blocks are performed by using a mediastinoscopy aspiration needle, and talc can be insufflated for pleurodesis, if indicated. All of these instruments are introduced sequentially through the upper incision.[23]

An alternative approach is to make a single incision in the midaxillary line at the sixth or seventh intercostal space and to use an operating thoracoscope that incorporates a biopsy forceps. This approach has the advantage of requiring only one incision; however, it does not allow as much latitude in draining or debriding the pleural space. Moreover, the biopsy forceps in an operating thoracoscope is of a smaller caliber than a mediastinoscopy biopsy forceps and thus cannot obtain as large a biopsy specimen.

TROUBLESHOOTING

In patients with loculated effusion, thoracoport placement must sometimes be modified. The preoperative chest computed tomographic scan and chest x-ray should help ensure that the ports are placed in areas where the lung is not adherent to the chest wall.

In some cases, the pleural space is obliterated by adhesions or tumor. This event occurs most frequently in patients who have had severe inflammatory disease (e.g., pneumonia, empyema, or tuberculosis) or extensive pleural malignancy (e.g., locally advanced malignant mesothelioma). In these circumstances, the anterior thoracoport incision can be extended to a length of 5 to 6 cm, the underlying rib section can be resected, and the parietal pleura can undergo biopsy directly; a full thoracotomy is not required. If thoracotomy is subsequently warranted for therapeutic reasons (e.g., for pleurectomy, decortication, or extrapleural pneumonectomy for mesothelioma), this small incision can be incorporated into the thoracotomy incision.

VATS Pulmonary Wedge Resection

VATS pulmonary wedge resection has become a standard approach to diagnosing small indeterminate pulmonary nodules, especially those not technically amenable to transthoracic needle biopsy.[24,25] It is also an accepted method of diagnosing pulmonary infiltrates of uncertain origin, particularly in immunocompromised patients in whom transbronchial biopsy is either unsafe or inappropriate.[26,27]

The role of VATS wedge resection is less well defined in the management of primary lung cancers. It is an appropriate compromise operation for primary lung cancers in patients with cardiac or pulmonary function status that rules out lobectomy. However, it remains a highly controversial approach to the treatment of pulmonary metastases.[28] In an often-quoted 1993 study,[29] patients with CT-documented pulmonary metastases underwent first thoracoscopic resection and then thoracotomy in the same setting. Many additional lesions, both benign and malignant, were found at thoracotomy that had been missed by VATS. The study was terminated early because of the failure of thoracoscopy to identify these lesions. One criticism of the study is that the preoperative CT scans were not comparable to the spiral (helical) CT scans currently available and therefore probably missed many pulmonary nodules that modern scanning methods would have identified.

A 2000 nonrandomized multicenter study of patients undergoing VATS metastasectomy for colon cancer suggested that minimal residual disease not identified by helical CT and not resected by VATS may not affect survival significantly.[30] This conclusion, however, is completely at odds with all of the previously published surgical literature on pulmonary metastasectomy performed via thoracotomy. Improved survival in patients with pulmonary metastases appears to be directly linked to the ability to remove all gross tumor, and VATS does not allow the careful bimanual palpation that is critical to detecting pulmonary metastases that are too small or too deep to be visible endoscopically.[30-32] Accordingly, most centers reserve VATS for diagnosis rather than treatment of pulmonary metastases. Until a well-designed prospective, randomized trial is conducted with survival as an end point, the standard of care remains thoracotomy and metastasectomy.

Anecdotal reports of port-site recurrence have also raised concerns about VATS as a treatment method in patients with malignancies. However, a 2001 study of 410 patients from a prospective

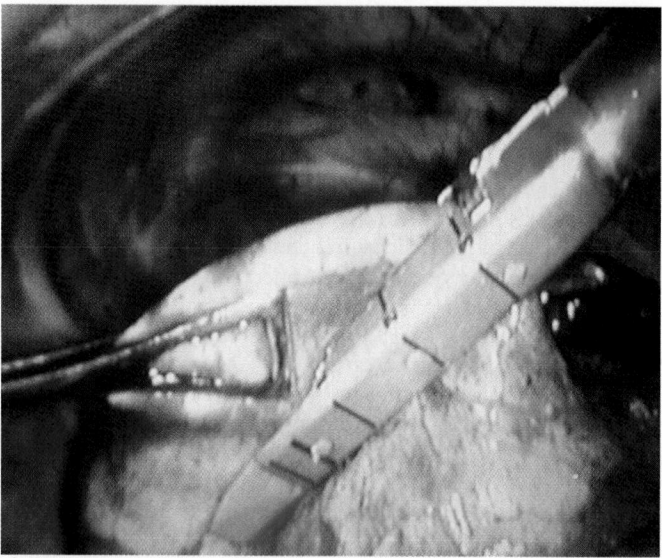

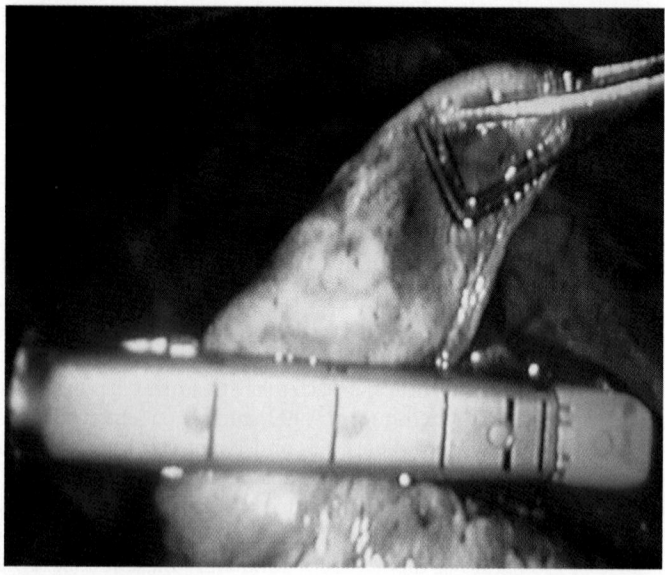

Figure 8 **VATS pulmonary wedge resection. A double-lumen endotracheal tube is used to render the lung partially atelectatic. The pulmonary nodule is lifted upward with a lung clamp, and an endoscopic GIA stapler is applied to the lung underneath (top). During the wedge resection, the lung clamp and the stapler are alternately inserted through opposite ports to obtain the correct angle for performance of the wedge resection (bottom).**

VATS database at the Memorial Sloan-Kettering Cancer Center (MSKCC) found only one case of port-site recurrence.[33] The authors concluded that the incidence of such recurrences can be kept low if surgical oncologic principles are respected. At MSKCC, these principles include (1) reserving VATS for lesions that can be widely excised; (2) conversion to an open thoracotomy for definitive or extensive operations; and (3) meticulous technique for extraction of specimens from the pleural space, with small specimens removed directly through a thoracoport and larger specimens removed in specimen bags.

OPERATIVE TECHNIQUE

Once general anesthesia has been induced and a double-lumen endotracheal tube inserted, the patient is placed in the full lateral decubitus position. Ventilation to the lung being operated on is stopped as soon as the patient is rotated into the lateral decubitus position, so that the lung will be thoroughly collapsed by the time the videothoracoscope is inserted into the pleural space. Small subpleural pulmonary nodules are most easily identified in a fully atelectatic lung because they protrude from the surrounding collapsed pulmonary parenchyma, which is softer.[19,20] Most pulmonary wedge resections are performed as true videothoracoscopic procedures using just three port incisions placed in the triangulated manner already described [*see* Basic Operative Technique, *above*].

The pulmonary nodules to be removed are grasped with an endoscopic lung clamp (Pennington or Duval) inserted through one instrument port, and wedge resection is done with repeated applications of an endoscopic stapler inserted through the opposite port.[24,34] As the resection is performed, it is often helpful to introduce the stapler through each of two instrument ports to obtain the correct angle for application to the lung [*see Figure 8*]. To prevent tumor implantation in the chest wall, small specimens (usually those resected with three or fewer stapler applications) are removed via the thoracoport. Larger specimens are placed in a disposable plastic specimen retrieval bag, which is then brought out through a very slightly enlarged anterior thoracoport incision.

When the wedge resections have been completed, intercostal blocks are performed under direct vision with a mediastinoscopy aspiration needle, and a single chest tube is inserted through the inferior port after the videothoracoscope is withdrawn.[35] The videothoracoscope can be placed through the anterior incision to check the position of the chest tube and to confirm reinflation of the lung after the double-lumen endotracheal tube is unclamped. The remaining incisions are then closed with sutures.

TROUBLESHOOTING

Four techniques may be used to locate pulmonary nodules that are either too deep or too small to be easily visible on simple inspection of the lung. All of these should be used in conjunction with a high-quality preoperative chest CT scan to identify the lung segment in which the nodule is located.

First, an endoscopic lung clamp may be gently run across the surface of the lung as an extension of digital palpation.[20,36] With some patience and experience, one can achieve considerable success with this technique. Second, ultrasonographic examination of the collapsed lung may be used to locate deep pulmonary nodules; at present, however, this approach appears to have lost favor.[37] Third, CT-guided needle localization may be used preoperatively if a nodule is likely to be difficult to locate. Localization is accomplished by injecting methylene blue or by inserting a barbed mammography localization needle, which is then cut off at the skin exit site and later retrieved thoracoscopically.[38] Needle localization techniques are effective, but they are also costly and time-consuming and hence are not used by most surgeons. Finally, if careful endoscopic examination of the lung does not reveal the location of a nodule, an access incision is added to the videothoracoscopy.[24,39] Each lobe of the lung is sequentially rotated up to this non–rib-spreading utility thoracotomy for direct digital palpation. This technique almost always allows identification of a nodule when other techniques fail. As the endoscopist gains experience with these techniques, conversion to thoracotomy solely for the purpose of locating a pulmonary nodule is rarely necessary.[40]

Pulmonary nodules located on the broad surface of the lung may not be amenable to a wedge resection with an endoscopic stapler. Such nodules can be removed by means of electrocauterization, just as in an open thoracotomy. An extension is placed on the handle of the electrocautery, which is then introduced into the pleural space through either a port or an access incision. Another approach is to resect the pulmonary nodule with a laser in either a contact or a noncontact mode. The potassium-titanyl-phosphate (KTP)/YAG laser is particularly suited to this task because it is capable of both cutting and coagulation. To minimize bleeding and air leakage, raw pulmonary surfaces can be cauterized with either the Nd:YAG laser or the ABC.[17] Numerous types of absorbable sealant patches or materials are also available to control air leaks from areas of raw pulmonary parenchyma.

Occasionally, after a wedge resection, it is necessary to suture together the pleural edges over an area of raw pulmonary parenchyma. The suturing can be done directly through a non–rib-spreading access incision or through port sites. In the latter case, the ports are removed and a 3-0 polypropylene suture is passed through the anterior port site with a standard needle holder. A second needle holder is introduced via the posterior port site and used in place of a forceps to pick up and reposition the needle as it is passed through the lung. The surgeon and the first assistant work together to oversew the lung, in contrast with the normal practice for an open procedure, in which the surgeon uses a needle holder and a forceps to place the sutures.

VATS Procedures for Spontaneous Pneumothorax and Bullous Disease

OPERATIVE TECHNIQUE

VATS is now frequently performed for the management of recurrent spontaneous pneumothorax and for bullous disease.[41,42] The approach is similar to that followed in a wedge resection, with three or four port sites being utilized. The videothoracoscope is inserted at the fifth intercostal space in the midaxillary line, and two other port sites are added at the fourth intercostal space in the anterior and posterior axillary lines.

In patients with spontaneous pneumothorax, the responsible bulla (which is usually apical in location) is identified, and wedge resection is done with an endoscopic stapler.[43,44] Bullae can be excised by applying the stapler across the base of the area of bullous disease. They can also be ablated with the ABC or the Nd:YAG laser, then suture-plicated if necessary; however, this approach may not be as successful over the long term.[45,46]

Taking note of the lower rate of recurrence, the shorter hospital stay, and the relative cost-effectiveness, some surgeons advocate performing VATS for the first episode of spontaneous pneumothorax.[47,48] To justify this approach in patients with primary spontaneous pneumothorax, however, well-designed clinical trials rather than retrospective reviews will be required.

TROUBLESHOOTING

The placement of port incisions should be determined by the location of the bullae. Because bullous disease is generally apical, port sites are correspondingly higher than for the average wedge resection (i.e., at the fourth and sixth intercostal spaces rather than at the fifth or sixth and eighth spaces). The precise placement should, however, be determined by pinpointing the disease site or sites on the preoperative chest x-ray and CT scans.

The main problem after resection for bullous disease is prolonged leakage of air from the staple line. This problem can be minimized by applying commercially available sleeves made of bovine pericardium or Gore-Tex over the arms of the stapler to reinforce the staple line and by performing some form of pleu-

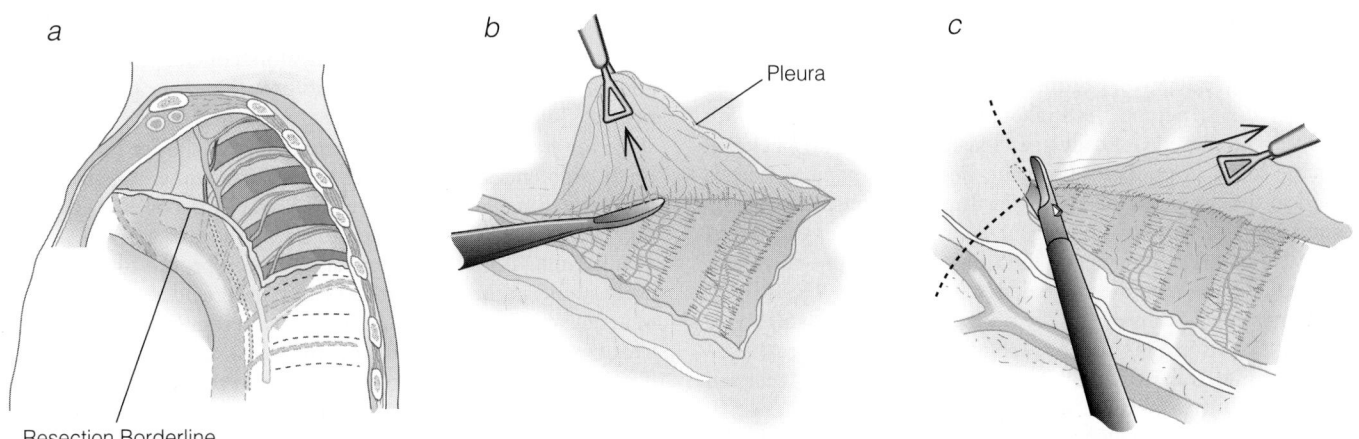

Figure 9   **VATS procedures for spontaneous pneumothorax and bullous disease. Limited apical pleurectomy is a useful alternative to chemical pleurodesis in young patients with spontaneous pneumothorax because these patients may need to undergo thoracotomy later in life. Shown is an outline of the pleural resection (*a*) performed in this procedure. The pleura is grasped at the inferior border with forceps and lifted in the avascular layer in a cranial or ventral direction (*b*). A T-shaped incision is made in the pleura at the level of the subclavian artery or the truncus brachiocephalicus. The dissection of the pleural flap thus created is extended in either the ventral or the parasternal direction and in either the apical or the mediastinal direction (*c*).**

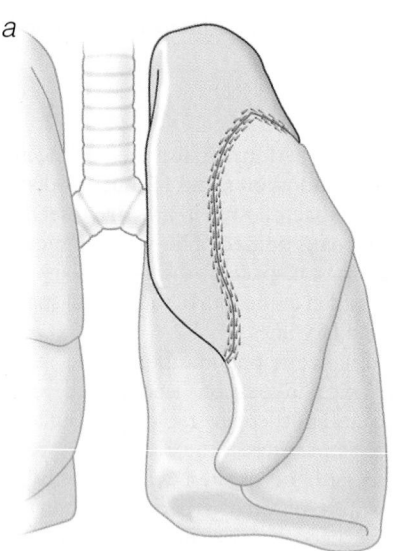

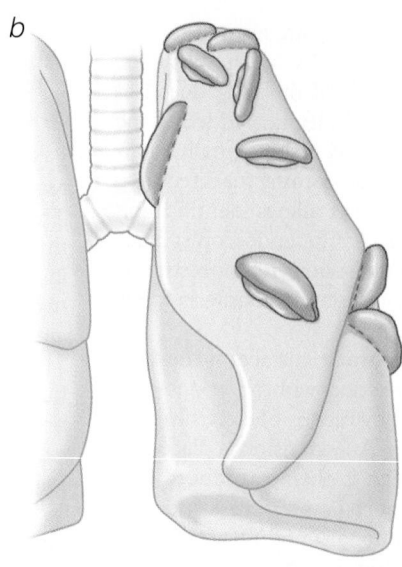

Figure 10 **VATS lung volume reduction surgery. Thoracoscopic lung volume reduction can be accomplished through either (*a*) resection or (*b*) plication without cutting.**

rodesis. Mechanical pleurodesis is done with a small gauze sponge passed through a port site. Some surgeons scarify the pleura by cauterizing it with the ABC or the Nd:YAG laser, but this is not as successful as mechanical pleurodesis. Chemical pleurodesis by talc poudrage is an appropriate option for older patients with emphysema and bullous disease but is unwise in young patients with spontaneous pneumothorax, who might require a thoracotomy later in life.[49] Another option in younger patients is a limited apical pleurectomy [*see Figure 9*]. Special angulated instruments and blunt dissectors have been designed for this procedure; however, a parietal pleurectomy is also easily performed with combinations of standard blunt and sharp instruments.[50]

VATS Lung Volume Reduction Surgery

OPERATIVE TECHNIQUE

VATS may also be applied to the performance of lung volume reduction surgery (LVRS). If unilateral LVRS is planned, the patient is placed in the lateral decubitus position and port placement is similar to that for a patient undergoing a wedge resection of the upper lobe. Most patients undergoing LVRS, however, benefit from bilateral LVRS. For this procedure, the patient is placed in the standard supine bilateral lung transplant position, with shoulder rolls placed vertically in an I fashion behind the back and with the arms positioned above the head. The camera port is placed in the anterior axillary line at the sixth interspace. A lung compression clamp is placed on the area that will be resected. A Gore-Tex–reinforced stapler is then inserted into the chest and fired sequentially until the desired area is excised [*see Figure 10a*].

Another approach used to help buttress the tenuous staple line in emphysematous lung tissue is lung plication [*see Figure 10b*].[51] In this method, the defunctionalized, bullous lung tissue is stapled to itself to form a plicated autologous buttress [*see Figure 11*]. Because the diseased bullous lung is not cut, the risk of postoperative air leakage is minimized.

TROUBLESHOOTING

A major cause of morbidity and mortality with this procedure is the occurrence of air leaks, which sometimes are large enough to compromise ventilation significantly. Thus, once LVRS has been done on one side, the lung is reexpanded and any air leaks

carefully assessed. If the leak is small, the other side is operated on in the same setting; if the leak is large, the contralateral procedure is put off to a later date. The use of fibrin glue or another commercially available pneumostatic sealant along the staple line should be considered to minimize postoperative air leakage.

VATS Lobectomy and Pneumonectomy

Although VATS lobectomy is much less frequently performed than VATS pulmonary wedge resection, standard techniques have been developed for it.[52] VATS pneumonectomy, on the other hand, is less well accepted. Both operations are done as video-assisted procedures using a utility thoracotomy, which facilitates insertion of standard thoracotomy instruments, extraction of the resected specimen from the pleural space, and performance of the technically complex aspects of the procedure, including dissection of the hilar vessels and the mediastinal lymph nodes.

A 1998 retrospective study addressing the adequacy of VATS lobectomy as an oncologic procedure reported on 298 patients who underwent VATS lobectomy with MLND for primary non–small cell lung cancer.[53] On the basis of a 70% 4-year survival rate for stage I tumors, the investigators concluded that outcome after VATS lobectomy is comparable to that after open thoracotomy. At 5 years, however, survival rates after VATS are inferior, stage for stage, to the rates generally reported after thoracotomy. Such differences could reflect either inaccurate staging or true oncologic differences between VATS and thoracotomy; additional prospective studies are needed to clarify these issues.

Although VATS lobectomy has not been proved to be oncologically sound in the long term, there is good evidence that it is safe in acute settings.[54] Therefore, it should certainly be performed to treat benign diseases (e.g., bronchiectasis).[55] As with all minimally invasive procedures, conversion to open thoracotomy is indicated if technical issues require it. Some authors advocate VATS lobectomy for low-grade malignancies (e.g., carcinoids) as well.[56] It must be recognized, however, that although carcinoids have a lower malignant potential than non–small cell lung cancer, they are still malignancies and must be treated appropriately for optimal long-term outcome.

Two approaches to lobectomy have been developed. One involves sequential anatomic ligation of the hilar structures, much as in a standard lobectomy,[57,58] and the other involves mass ligation of the

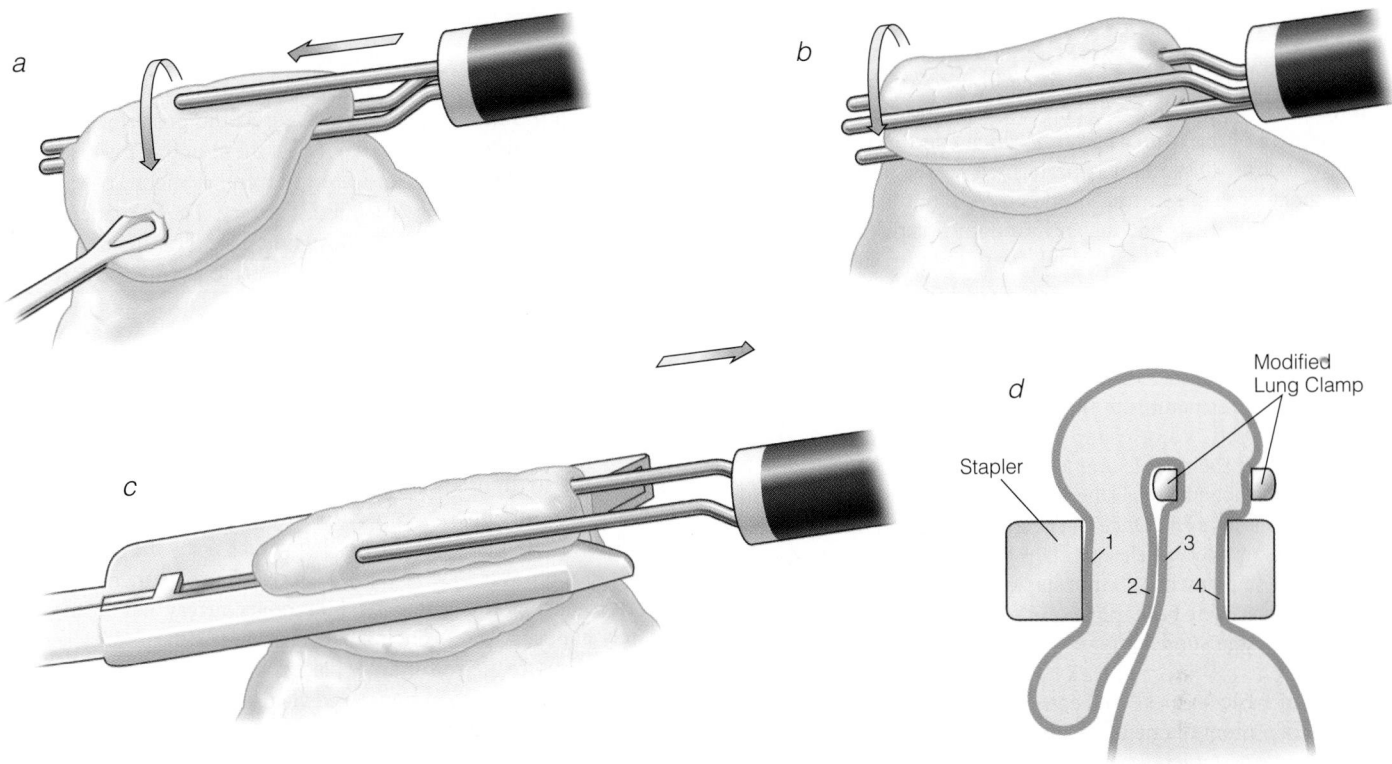

Figure 11 **VATS lung volume reduction surgery. Shown are the key steps in the plication method of LVRS. (a) The apex of the lung area selected for plication is drawn to one side over a lung plication clamp, and the retractable guidebar of the clamp is extended into position. (b) The clamp is rotated 180° to fold the lung over itself. (c) The guidebar is retracted, a stapler is positioned with its jaws around the folded lung (but not yet closed), and the plication clamp is removed. (d) Shown is a cross-section of the folded lung after the stapler has been positioned but before the clamp has been removed. The stapler is then fired to complete the plication.**

pulmonary vessels and the bronchus. Both approaches require at least two port incisions in addition to the utility thoracotomy incision. The sequential anatomic ligation approach has been well described and follows sound surgical oncologic principles.[57] Accordingly, it is our preferred method of performing VATS lobectomy. It must be remembered, however, that VATS lobectomy is a procedure for which there is no accepted uniform definition. In a survey aimed at defining the criteria used by minimally invasive thoracic surgeons for VATS lobectomy,[14] the length of the utility incision ranged from 4 to 10 cm, the number of incisions ranged from three to five, and the use of rib spreading was variable. In an effort to standardize the approach at our own institution (MSKCC), we define a VATS lobectomy as an anatomic dissection that is performed entirely under thoracoscopic visualization, proceeds in an anterior-to-posterior fashion, employs a 4 cm utility incision, involves absolutely no rib spreading, and uses two thoracoscopy ports (one for the camera and one for retraction). Our definition also includes nodal evaluation (either sampling or dissection) of levels 4, 7, and 9 on the right and levels 5, 6, 7, and 9 on the left.

OPERATIVE TECHNIQUE

Lobectomy (Sequential Anatomic Ligation)

Positioning and port placement Correct positioning and port placement are essential for a successful VATS lobectomy. The patient is placed in the maximally flexed lateral decubitus position to prevent the hip from impeding downward movement of the thoracoscope. Tilting the hip posteriorly, especially in obese patients, greatly increases the range of movement of the thoracoscope. After the initi-

ation of single-lung ventilation, the camera port is placed at the eighth interspace in the anterior axillary line (for right-side lesions) or in the posterior axillary line (for left-side lesions). The posterior port is then placed where the lower lobe edge touches the diaphragm (at the ninth or 10th interspace) along the anterior border of the paraspinous muscle. A retractor is placed through the posterior port, and the upper lobe is retracted laterally to allow visualization of the superior pulmonary vein. The utility incision (no longer than 4 cm) is placed directly over the superior pulmonary vein for upper lobectomies (at approximately the third or fourth interspace) and one interspace lower for middle and lower lobectomies. A Weitlaner (or cerebellar) retractor is used to retract the soft tissues, and there is no need for rib spreading. A rotating 30° videothoracoscope is always used for these procedures.

Right-side resections *Right upper lobe.* The superior pulmonary vein is dissected from the overlying pleura via the access incision with long Metzenbaum scissors and DeBakey forceps, much as in an open lobectomy. A Harken clamp is passed behind the superior pulmonary vein after clear identification of the middle lobe vein. The superior pulmonary vein is encircled with a monofilament tie and retracted upward via the utility incision. An empty sponge stick is then placed through the utility incision, and the upper lobe is retracted posteriorly. An endovascular stapler is placed through the posterior port and, with the suture as a guide, passed behind the superior pulmonary vein.

Once the pulmonary vein has been divided, the anterior and apical segmental branches of the pulmonary artery are visualized. The level 10 lymph nodes are removed. A Harken clamp is passed around the anterior and apical pulmonary arterial branches, and a monofilament suture is passed around them and brought out through the utility incision. The endovascular stapler is passed though the posterior port and used to transect the vessels. Transection of the truncus artery branch exposes the right upper lobe bronchus. Dissection is performed to separate the ongoing pulmonary artery from the bronchus. A monofilament suture is passed around the bronchus and brought out through the utility incision. An endoscopic GIA stapler with 4.8 mm staples is placed through the posterior port, and the right upper lobe bronchus is transected. This step exposes the branch of the pulmonary artery to the posterior segment of the right upper lobe, which is transected in the same manner through the posterior port.

Once all the structures to the upper lobe have been divided, the fissure is assessed. A lung clamp placed through the posterior port is used to retract the middle and lower lobes inferiorly, and a second lung clamp placed through the utility incision is used to retract the upper lobe superiorly. Once the fissure is exposed, a long curved sponge stick is used to elevate the right upper lobe, and an endoscopic GIA stapler with 4.8 mm staples is passed through the utility incision to complete both minor and major fissures. The lobe is then placed in a large surgical tissue pouch and removed via the utility incision.

Certain basic surgical concepts—dissection of hilar structures, passage of a monofilament suture around the structure, and transection with a stapler—are similar for all lobectomies. However, the order in which structures are transected and the ports through which staplers are passed differ.

Right lower lobe. The lower lobe is retracted superiorly, the inferior pulmonary ligament is transected, and the level 9 lymph nodes are removed. Once the entire inferior pulmonary vein has been dissected, a stapler is placed via the utility incision to transect the vessel. The lower lobe bronchus is exposed from its inferior aspect to its bifurcation with the middle lobe bronchus. The bronchus is left intact until the pulmonary artery to the right lower lobe is exposed medially and superiorly from the overlying fissure. Once the pulmonary artery has been adequately exposed, the bronchus is transected with a 4.8 mm universal stapler placed through the utility incision. The pulmonary artery is then transected via the utility incision, followed by the fissure.

Right middle lobe. With the middle lobe retracted laterally, the pleura overlying the middle lobe vein is incised. Once dissection of the vein is complete, the vessel is transected with an endovascular stapler placed via the posterior port, and the middle lobe bronchus is exposed. The bronchus is encircled with a monofilament suture, and an endoscopic GIA stapler with 3.5 mm staples is placed via the posterior port to transect the bronchus. An empty sponge stick is then used to place traction on the middle lobe bronchus, exposing the one or two branches of the middle lobe artery, which are then transected via the posterior port. On occasion, the angle is such that the middle lobe artery must be transected via the utility incision. The minor fissure is then completed by passing staplers via the utility incision.

Left-side resections *Left upper lobe.* The left upper lobe is retracted laterally, and the superior pulmonary vein is dissected free and transected via the posterior port. The first apical branch of the pulmonary artery is dissected free and transected with an endoscopic GIA vascular stapler introduced via the posterior port. The anterior aspect of the fissure is opened with one or two applications of an

endoscopic GIA stapler introduced via the access incision. The bifurcation of the left upper and left lower lobe bronchi is identified, and the left upper lobe bronchus is transected with an endoscopic GIA stapler with 4.8 mm staples introduced via the posterior port. An empty sponge stick is then used to retract the stump of the bronchus laterally, which facilitates exposure of several branches of the pulmonary artery, including the lingular artery. These branches are transected individually via the posterior port. The fissure is then completed by passing an endoscopic GIA stapler with 4.8 mm staples via the posterior port.

Left lower lobe. The lower lobe is retracted superiorly, the inferior pulmonary ligament is transected, and level 9 lymph nodes are removed. Once the inferior pulmonary vein has been dissected free, an endoscopic GIA vascular stapler is placed via the utility incision to transect the vessel. The lower lobe bronchus is exposed from its inferior aspect to its bifurcation with the upper lobe bronchus. The bronchus is left intact until the pulmonary artery to the lower lobe is exposed medially and superiorly from the overlying fissure. After the pulmonary artery has been adequately exposed, the bronchus is transected with an endoscopic GIA stapler with 4.8 mm staples placed via the utility incision. The pulmonary artery is then transected via the utility incision, and the fissure is completed via the posterior port. In cases with a very thick incomplete fissure, the fissure between the lingula and lower lobe should be opened before dissection of the pulmonary artery to facilitate subsequent arterial exposure.

Lobectomy (Mass Ligation)

The mass ligation method, or so-called SIS (simultaneous individual stapling) lobectomy, has also been used for VATS lobectomy.[59] Four incisions are made: an incision for the camera port at the seventh intercostal space, a 2 cm incision in the midaxillary line at the sixth intercostal space for the insertion of staplers, and two 3 cm incisions at the fourth intercostal space in the anterior and posterior axillary lines for the insertion of additional instruments. In the initial report of this technique, the bronchus and the pulmonary vessels were ligated separately, but the vessels were stapled en masse.[60] Subsequently, the technique was refined so that the bronchus and the vessels were stapled simultaneously by applying the stapler twice, the first time loosely to obtain closure of the bronchus and the second time more tightly to obtain hemostatic closure of the vessels.

Although the early results of SIS lobectomy were satisfactory,[61] concerns arose about the long-term risks of bronchovascular or arteriovenous fistula formation resulting from mass ligation of the hilar structures. Consequently, this approach has not gained wide acceptance and is rarely used at present.

Pneumonectomy

The approach to VATS pneumonectomy is similar to the sequential anatomic ligation approach to VATS lobectomy. The thoracoscope is inserted at the seventh intercostal space in the midaxillary line, and a utility thoracotomy is performed at the fourth intercostal space in the same line. Two port sites are then created at the sixth intercostal space in the anterior and posterior axillary lines. The hilar vessels are sequentially isolated, ligated, and divided with endoscopic or standard staplers. The inferior pulmonary vein is done first, followed by the superior pulmonary vein and the pulmonary artery. The bronchus is stapled and divided last.[62,63]

TROUBLESHOOTING

If ambiguous anatomy or excessive bleeding is encountered at any point during the procedure or if oncologic principles are violated, conversion to a thoracotomy is mandatory to ensure patient safety. A sponge on a stick, an open thoracotomy tray, and a polypropylene suture should always be readily available for emergency control of hemorrhage.

To prevent too-distal or too-proximal dissection (which can lead to bleeding and violation of oncologic principles), the surgeon should alternate frequently between panoramic and close-up views. In addition, to ensure that the mainstem bronchus has not been inadvertently dissected, the remaining lobes may be reinflated before bronchial transection.

Robot-Assisted VATS Lobectomy

Current minimally invasive surgical technology has several notable weaknesses. First, the camera platform is unstable, which means that the operating surgeon must rely on an assistant with a variable amount of experience and knowledge of the technical aspects of the procedure to provide the needed visualization. Second, the straight instruments used are limited with respect to range of movement and degrees of freedom when placed through small incisions—a limitation that can be particularly significant with thoracic procedures in which incision size is further limited by the size of the intercostal space. Third, the cameras provide only two-dimensional imaging. Finally, as a result of all of the preceding factors, the ergonomics of these minimally invasive procedures for the operating surgeon and the assistants are often very poor.[64] These weaknesses provided the impetus for the application of robotic techniques to minimally invasive surgery.

The first generation of surgical robots focused primarily on the issue of the unstable camera platform. In 1994, the Automated Endoscopic System for Optimal Positioning (AESOP) (Computer Motion, Santa Barbara, California), a voice-activated robotic camera holder, was approved by the Food and Drug Administration for clinical use in abdominal surgery. Subsequently, the EndoAssist (Armstrong Healthcare Limited, High Wycombe, United Kingdom), which allows the operating surgeon to control camera movement through natural head movement, was also approved by the FDA.

The newest generation of surgical robots was designed to address issues beyond the camera platform by employing telerobotic technology to enable the operating surgeon to control the surgical robot and its instruments by using a remote computer console. At present, two FDA-approved systems are commercially available: the da Vinci Surgical System (Intuitive Surgical, Sunnyvale, California) and the ZEUS Surgical System (Computer Motion, Santa Barbara, California). Both were originally designed for closed-chest cardiac surgery,[65,66] and most of the published literature to date has been concerned with this application. Nevertheless, the published experience with surgical telerobotics in minimally invasive surgery continues to expand, ranging from laparoscopic cholecystectomy to laparoscopic Nissen fundoplication to laparoscopic radical prostatectomy.[67-69]

At MSKCC, we employ the da Vinci Surgical System, which consists of three main parts. The first part is the basic robot. The robot has three arms—two instrument arms with a camera arm between them—all attached to a central column. Each instrument arm attaches to an 8 mm trocar, and the whole unit is placed into the patient; surgical instruments are then introduced through the trocar for intracorporeal use. The camera arm attaches to a 12 mm trocar that is already positioned inside the patient. The second part of the system is the surgeon's console, an ergonomically comfortable worksta-

tion that contains the computer, the three-dimensional imaging center, and the master controls that govern the robot's function. The third part is the equipment tower, which holds the light source, the camera, and additional necessary components (e.g., the electrocautery, the ultrasonic scalpel, and the insufflator).

For our purposes, the da Vinci robot has three signal advantages. First, it offers a true three-dimensional imaging system with binocular vision. The scope is 12 mm in diameter, with a separate 5 mm scope for each eye. The left and right images remain separated from the telescopes to the surgeon's eyes, so that the right eye sees the right image and the left eye sees the left image. Second, the instrument and camera arms are all controlled by the surgeon through the master controls and their interface with the computer; no voice or visual activation is necessary. Third, all of the surgical instruments, with the exception of the SonoSurg (Olympus America, Melville, New York), have seven degrees of freedom and two degrees of axial rotation, which means that they can be articulated in a manner that replicates the action of a human wrist.

OPERATIVE TECHNIQUE

To date, there have been only two published reports of the use of robotic technology during VATS lobectomy. One is a case report of a VATS left lower lobectomy done with robotic assistance,[70] and the other is a series of five patients, two of whom were converted to thoracotomy for technical reasons.[71] It is clear from the lack of a substantial literature that a standardized approach has not yet been established. At MSKCC, however, we have developed a technique of robot-assisted VATS lobectomy that employs the da Vinci Surgical System as an adjunct to our standard VATS lobectomy technique. This robot-assisted approach has proved to be safe and feasible in more than 30 consecutive patients.

Step 1: Initial Exploration of Chest and Positioning of Robot

The patient is placed in a maximally flexed lateral decubitus position after single-lung ventilation is established. Initial thoracic exploration is conducted by means of conventional thoracoscopy to verify resectability and to establish the three standard VATS lobectomy access incisions. As noted [see VATS Lobectomy and Pneumonectomy, Operative Technique, above], the location of the main utility incision varies slightly, depending on the lobe of interest. Employing standard VATS lobectomy incisions has the benefit of allowing conversion to a conventional VATS procedure if the need arises (e.g., as a result of minor bleeding, inadequate exposure, or mechanical or technical problems with the robot). Once the incisions have been made, the conventional VATS instruments are removed, and the robot is brought into position from the posterior aspect of the patient, with the center column at an angle of approximately 45° with respect to the patient's longitudinal axis. This positioning allows the field of dissection to include the hilar structures and most of the chest.

A 12 mm trocar is placed through the anterior inferior access incision, and the camera arm is attached to the trocar. The three-dimensional 30° scope is introduced through the trocar and secured to the camera arm. The remainder of the positioning is accomplished under direct vision, both from outside the patient and from within the thorax. The trocars attached to the two instrument arms are introduced into the two remaining access incisions. Care must be taken to ensure that the instrument arms have full range of motion and do not collide with each other or with any portion of the patient.

Once the camera and the instrument arms are in place, surgical instruments are inserted through the attached trocars under direct thoracoscopic vision. Our practice is to start the procedure with a Cadiere forceps in the left instrument arm (placed in the main utility incision) and a blunt permanent spatula hooked to an electrocautery in the right instrument arm. When all instruments have been positioned optimally, the operating surgeon scrubs out and moves to the control console.

Step 2: Robot-Assisted VATS Dissection

Two assistants are required: the first stands at the anterior aspect of the patient and assists through the main utility incision by providing additional retraction of the lung and suction when necessary, and the second is positioned at the posterior inferior access incision.

At MSKCC, we typically begin the procedure with MLND. All major nodal stations are explored with a combination of electrocauterization and blunt dissection, and all nodal tissue is removed and sent for frozen-section analysis to rule out occult stage III disease in patients with non–small cell lung cancer. Currently, we use the SonoSurg in an effort to prevent postoperative chyle leakage, though we have not yet encountered this complication.

If there are no contraindications to lobectomy, individual isolation of the hilar structures proceeds with dissection around the hilar vessels and bronchi performed with a combination of cauterization and sharp and blunt dissection, much as would be done through a thoracotomy. The tissues overlying each structure, particularly the regional lymph nodes, are precisely dissected away. When either a vessel or the bronchus is sufficiently mobilized, two blunt-tipped Cadiere forceps are used to reach around the structure, place a tie, and create sufficient space for placement of an endovascular stapler.

Step 3: Lobectomy

Right upper lobe   The main utility incision is created in the midaxillary line at the level of the superior pulmonary vein. The right upper lobe is retracted inferiorly and posteriorly for MLND from the right paratracheal space, then anteriorly for the subcarinal space. Next, the right upper lobe is retracted laterally, and the mediastinal pleura overlying the superior pulmonary vein is incised with the Cadiere forceps in the left instrument arm and the permanent spatula attached to the cautery in the right instrument arm. The full extent of the vein is defined by identifying the takeoff of the middle lobe vein inferiorly and the junction between the superior vein and the truncus arteriosus superiorly. Any regional nodes present are resected. The spatula is replaced with a second Cadiere forceps, and the vein is encircled with a tie to allow gentle retraction. The left instrument arm is removed from the posterior inferior access incision just far enough to permit introduction of a 2.5 mm endoscopic GIA vascular stapler that is passed behind the vessel. The tie is removed, the stapler is closed, and the vessel is stapled and divided. The left instrument arm is replaced, and dissection continues by dividing the mediastinal pleura superiorly and posteriorly over the truncus arteriosus toward the bronchus with a combination of cauterization and blunt dissection. Any additional regional nodes encountered are resected.

The truncus branches are isolated with the Cadiere forceps and divided in the same manner as the vein. Attention is turned to the right upper lobe bronchus, and the peribronchial tissue is bluntly swept distally. The bronchus is mobilized with the Cadiere forceps, and an endoscopic GIA stapler with 4.8 mm staples is introduced again via the posterior access incision and closed around the bronchus. The remaining lung is minimally ventilated to ensure that the middle and the lower lobe are uncompromised; if this is the case,

the upper lobe bronchus is stapled and divided. The upper lobe is then retracted laterally and inferiorly. Additional hilar nodal tissue is resected, and the origins of the posterior ascending (or recurrent) artery, middle lobe artery, and superior segment pulmonary artery branches are defined. The recurrent artery branch is divided with an endoscopic GIA vascular stapler with 2.5 mm staples.

Once each of the hilar structures of the upper lobe has been divided, only the fissure remains. At this point, the robotic portion of the procedure is terminated. The instruments and the instrument arms are removed under direct vision, followed by the camera, the camera arm, and, finally, the robot. Conventional thoracoscopy is reestablished, and the fissure between the upper lobe and the remaining middle and lower lobes is completed with multiple firings of the 4.8 mm endoscopic GIA stapler. The specimen is placed in a large laparotomy sac and brought out through the anterior superior access incision. Hemostasis is confirmed, intercostal nerve blocks are created with 0.5% bupivacaine, and a single chest tube is placed under direct vision. The remaining lung is inflated, and the wounds are closed in the standard fashion.

Right middle lobe   The main access incision is created in the midaxillary line one interspace below the level of the superior pulmonary vein, and MLND of the right paratracheal and subcarinal spaces is performed. With the middle lobe retracted laterally, the mediastinal pleura overlying the middle lobe pulmonary vein is incised with the Cadiere forceps in the left instrument arm and the permanent spatula attached to the cautery in the right arm. The mediastinal pleura is further incised down to the level of the inferior pulmonary vein. The spatula is replaced with a second Cadiere forceps; the vein is encircled with a tie and divided with the 2.5 mm endoscopic GIA vascular stapler inserted via the posterior access incision.

Next, the anterior portion of the major fissure is completed with the spatula and the cautery, and all regional lymph nodes encountered are excised. The middle lobe bronchus is identified and mobilized, with the peribronchial tissue swept distally. Division of the bronchus with a 3.5 mm endoscopic GIA stapler placed via the posterior incision facilitates subsequent dissection and ligation of the middle lobe branches of the pulmonary artery. This is best accomplished by resecting the tissue overlying the ongoing pulmonary artery proximally up to the takeoff of the middle lobe arterial supply. The middle lobe pulmonary artery is encircled and divided with the 2.5 mm endoscopic GIA vascular stapler through the posterior incision. The minor fissure is completed with multiple firings of the 4.8 mm endoscopic GIA stapler through the anterior superior utility incision. The lobe is placed in a large tissue pouch and brought out through the anterior utility incision. The robot is removed, and the procedure is completed in the same manner as a right upper lobectomy.

Right lower lobe   As in a right middle lobectomy, the anterior utility incision is placed in the midaxillary line one interspace inferior to the level of the superior pulmonary vein, and MLND of the subcarinal space is performed. The lower lobe is retracted toward the apex of the chest, the inferior pulmonary ligament is divided with the electrocautery, and additional mediastinal lymph nodes from levels 8 and 9 are resected. The pleura overlying the inferior pulmonary vein is incised superiorly both anterior and posterior to the vessel. The Cadiere forceps are used to isolate this vein, and a 2.5 mm endoscopic GIA vascular stapler placed through the utility incision is used to divide the vessel. Retraction of the lung is maintained superiorly and posteriorly while the major fissure is completed anteriorly with the spatula and the attached cautery.

The plane between the lower lobe bronchus and the basilar segmental pulmonary artery is developed bluntly. This step facilitates dissection of the pulmonary artery branches, especially if the major fissure is incomplete. In this instance, the bronchus may be divided before the artery with the 4.8 mm endoscopic GIA stapler inserted via the utility incision. The remainder of the pulmonary artery may be approached either inferiorly or via the fissure and may be similarly ligated with the 2.5 mm endoscopic GIA vascular stapler. The basilar and superior segmental branches may be divided separately if doing so is technically more feasible. The posterior aspect of the major fissure is completed with the stapler, and the lobe is removed. The robot is extracted, and the procedure is completed in the same manner as a right upper lobectomy.

Left upper lobe   The main utility incision is created in the midaxillary line at the level of the superior pulmonary vein. The left upper lobe is retracted inferiorly and posteriorly to allow MLND from the aortopulmonary window. The lung is then retracted laterally, and the mediastinal pleura overlying the superior pulmonary vein is incised. As on the right side, the Cadiere forceps is in the left instrument arm and the permanent spatula attached to the cautery in the right. The mediastinal pleura is further incised down to the level of the inferior pulmonary vein. The full extent of the vein is defined by identifying the upper lobe bronchus inferiorly and the junction between the superior vein and the anterior pulmonary artery branches superiorly. Any regional nodes present are resected. The spatula is replaced with a second Cadiere forceps, and the vein is encircled with a tie. The left instrument arm is removed from the posterior inferior access incision to permit introduction of a 2.5 mm endoscopic GIA vascular stapler, which is passed behind the vessel. The tie is removed, the stapler is closed, and the vessel is stapled and divided.

The left instrument arm is replaced, and dissection is continued to mobilize the anterior pulmonary artery branches, which are encircled and divided with a 2.5 mm endoscopic GIA vascular stapler introduced through the posterior access incision. Ligating these arterial branches greatly facilitates division of the upper lobe bronchus. The upper lobe bronchus is then mobilized by means of blunt dissection and cauterization, with care taken not to include the entire left mainstem bronchus. A 4.8 mm endoscopic GIA stapler is used to staple and divide the bronchus. Once this is accomplished, the upper lobe is retracted laterally, which allows quick and easy identification, mobilization, and division of the apicoposterior and lingular pulmonary artery branches with multiple firings of the 2.5 mm endoscopic GIA vascular stapler. Conventional thoracoscopy is then reestablished, and the fissure between the upper and lower lobes is completed with multiple firings of the 4.8 mm endoscopic GIA stapler. The lobe is placed in a large laparotomy sac and brought out through the anterior utility incision, and the procedure is completed in the same manner as a right upper lobectomy.

Left lower lobe   The anterior utility incision is placed in the midaxillary line one interspace below the level of the superior pulmonary vein. The left upper lobe is retracted inferiorly and posteriorly to allow MLND from the aortopulmonary window. Once this is done, the lower lobe is retracted toward the apex of the chest, the inferior pulmonary ligament is divided with the electrocautery, and additional mediastinal lymph nodes from levels 8 and 9 are resected. The pleura overlying the inferior pulmonary vein is incised superiorly both anterior and posterior to the vessel. The Cadiere forceps are used to isolate the inferior vein, and a 2.5 mm

endoscopic GIA vascular stapler is placed through the utility incision to divide the vessel. Retraction of the lung is maintained superiorly and posteriorly while the major fissure is completed anteriorly with the spatula and the attached cautery.

The plane between the lower lobe bronchus and the basilar segmental pulmonary artery is developed bluntly. This step facilitates dissection of the pulmonary artery branches, especially if the major fissure is incomplete. In this instance, the bronchus may be divided before the artery with the 4.8 mm endoscopic GIA stapler placed via the utility incision. The remainder of the pulmonary artery may be approached either inferiorly or via the fissure and may be similarly ligated with the 2.5 mm endoscopic GIA vascular stapler. The basilar and superior segmental branches may be divided separately if doing so is technically more feasible. The posterior aspect of the major fissure is completed with the stapler, and the lobe is removed. A subcarinal lymph node dissection is performed using blunt and cautery dissection with the Cadiere forceps and the spatula. The robot is removed, and the procedure is completed in the same manner as a right upper lobectomy.

TROUBLESHOOTING

If concerns arise at any time during robot-assisted VATS lobectomy about exposure, accurate identification of anatomic structures, the oncologic adequacy of the procedure, or safety, the surgeon must carefully consider whether it would be best to convert to a standard VATS lobectomy or even to a thoracotomy. If such conversion is indicated at any point in the procedure, the robot can be quickly and easily moved away from the patient. The instruments are removed under direct vision, followed by the camera. The instrument arms and the camera arm are backed away from the patient, and the robot can then be taken away.

There are several unique caveats that apply to robot-assisted VATS procedures. First, before even attempting such a procedure, the operating surgeon, the assistants, and all other operating personnel must be fully trained on the particular robotic surgical system being used. In the early stages of a center's experience with a system, it is advisable to have a company representative present to help manage any complex technical issues that may arise. Second, care must be taken both during initial positioning and throughout the procedure to ensure that the arms of the robot do not collide with one another or, more important, with the patient. Third, there must be constant communication between all team members and constant vigilance during the procedure. Untimely or unintended manipulation of any component of the robotic system during dissection around delicate hilar structures can be potentially disastrous and should be completely avoidable.

VATS Mediastinal Lymph Node Dissection

OPERATIVE TECHNIQUE

For biopsy of the aortopulmonary window nodes or anterior mediastinal masses, VATS MLND is often performed as an alternative to a Chamberlain procedure and is thought by some surgeons to provide better exposure and a superior cosmetic result.[72] The thoracoscope is inserted at the fifth or sixth intercostal space in the posterior axillary line. Instruments for retracting the lung inferiorly are introduced via a port at the seventh intercostal space in the midaxillary line. Instruments for dissecting nodes are introduced through ports placed at the fourth intercostal space in the anterior axillary line and in the auscultatory triangle. The lymph nodes are dissected free with graspers (e.g., curved sponge sticks or polyp forceps), scissors, the electrocautery, and endoscopic hemostatic clips. A similar approach can be used for biopsy of other mediastinal nodes, including the paratracheal and periesophageal nodes. Dissection of level 4 and level 2 nodes on the right is facilitated by transection of the azygos vein. This method has become an accepted approach to the surgical staging of esophageal cancer.[73,74] It is more difficult to do a complete en bloc subcarinal lymph node dissection on the left than on the right with this method, though nodal sampling of this region by means of VATS is certainly feasible, especially when an access incision is used.

TROUBLESHOOTING

Care should be taken not to injure the phrenic nerve as it courses along the superior vena cava on the right and across the anterior aspect of the aortopulmonary window on the left. The vagus nerve should be visualized, and the origin of the recurrent laryngeal nerve avoided during dissection. The recurrent laryngeal nerve is easily injured on the left side, where it passes around the ligamentum arteriosum before traveling under the aortic arch; however, it can also be injured on the right side if MLND is carried too high superiorly along the origin of the innominate artery.

It is unwise to perform a VATS MLND after induction chemotherapy or chemoradiotherapy because the lymph nodes will often be densely adherent to surrounding structures. This is especially true on the right side, where the superior mediastinal lymph nodes are usually densely adherent to the superior vena cava, the azygos vein, and the right main pulmonary artery. A thoracotomy, with extensive exposure and sharp dissection, is usually required for a safe and complete MLND.

All lymphatic branches should be ligated during node biopsy or dissection to prevent leakage of chyle. There are often large lymphatic branches in the distal right paratracheal area. In addition, the thoracic duct can be injured if periesophageal or posterior mediastinal lymph nodes are being removed.

VATS Esophagectomy

OPERATIVE TECHNIQUE

To date, surgeons' experience with thoracoscopic esophageal resection has been limited. VATS esophagectomy can take either a transhiatal or a transthoracic approach.

Transhiatal Approach

The technique originally described for VATS transhiatal esophagectomy[75] is a modification of the open technique advocated by Orringer[76] [see 34 Open Esophageal Procedures] and allows the esophagectomy to be performed entirely under direct vision with the help of a specially designed operating mediastinoscope. This instrument has a partially concave olive tip that distracts the mediastinal tissues away from the mediastinoscope and cradles the esophagus in a stable position during the dissection. The mediastinoscope incorporates an optical system, an irrigation canal, and an operating channel for insertion of scissors, suction devices, and monopolar and bipolar cautery forceps.

The mediastinoscope is introduced through the neck incision used to expose the cervical esophagus, after the stomach and the distal esophagus have been mobilized via laparotomy. The thoracic esophagus is circumferentially freed from the surrounding mediastinal structures, beginning at the thoracic inlet and moving inferiorly to the hiatus, primarily by means of blunt dissection with the suction device. Vessels are cauterized or clipped. Dissection is performed first along the posterior wall of the esophagus, then along both lateral walls, and finally on the anterior surface of the esoph-

agus. At the level of the primary tumor, periesophageal soft tissues are resected en bloc to ensure complete removal of the cancer.

When the esophagus has been fully mobilized down to the diaphragmatic hiatus, a plastic tube is passed into the hiatus, where it is grasped by the mediastinoscope. Both the mediastinoscope and the plastic tube are then withdrawn to the cervical incision. The cervical esophagus is transected at the sternal notch with the GIA stapler, and the plastic tube is sutured to the distal end of the divided esophagus. The tube is then gently pulled back down to the diaphragmatic hiatus; in the process, the thoracic esophagus is folded onto itself. The mediastinoscope is reintroduced and used to follow the esophagus as it is removed from the mediastinum. Any undivided vessels or lymphatics are easily visualized and are either ligated or cauterized. After the esophagus is extracted, the stomach is passed up to the neck via the posterior mediastinum, and the esophagogastric anastomosis is performed in the standard manner for a transhiatal esophagectomy [see Figure 12].

Transthoracic Approach

Transthoracic thoracoscopic techniques for esophagectomy have been described by several authors.[77-79] One group has refined a clinical VATS technique that is based on results from animal studies.[80] The most widely accepted method of performing a thoracoscopic and laparoscopic esophagectomy, however, is the one developed by Luketich and associates, who have performed more than 200 cases to date and have published a report of 77 patients that demonstrated the feasibility of their approach.[81]

A double-lumen endotracheal tube is inserted, the patient is placed in the left lateral decubitus position, and four thoracoports are placed. A 0 suture is placed in the central tendon of the diaphragm and brought out through an inferior anterior 1 mm skin nick to provide downward traction on the diaphragm and adequate exposure of the esophagus. The mediastinal pleura is opened widely, and the anterior edge is retracted with two stay sutures. The azygos vein is divided with an endoscopic stapler, and the inferior half of the thoracic esophagus is mobilized away from the aorta and the pericardium. The subcarinal lymph nodes are removed en bloc. The upper third of the thoracic esophagus is mobilized away from the trachea, and the right paratracheal lymph nodes are removed, with care taken not to injure the recurrent laryngeal nerve. A Penrose drain is placed around the esophagus and placed through the thoracic inlet for later retrieval via the neck incision. Once the esophagus has been fully mobilized, the pleural traction sutures are removed, a chest tube is inserted through the camera port site, and the other port incisions are closed.

The patient is then moved to the supine position. The stomach is mobilized laparoscopically. Port placement is similar to that for laparoscopic Nissen fundoplication. The patient is placed in a steep reverse Trendelenburg position. The gastrohepatic ligament is divided to expose the right crus of the diaphragm. The short gastric vessels are divided with ultrasonic shears; the right gastroepiploic artery is preserved. The stomach is retracted superiorly to facilitate nodal dissection of the celiac and gastric vessels. The left gastric artery and the left gastric (coronary) vein are then divided with an endovascular stapler. A pyloroplasty is performed, with ultrasonic shears used for the incision and an endoscopic suturing device for the repair. The gastric tube is then created with a universal 4.8 stapler, with care taken to preserve the right gastric vessels. Once the gastric tube is complete, it is attached to the specimen with several applications of the suturing device in preparation for transport to the neck. A laparoscopic jejunostomy is then performed. The right and left crural areas are opened last to facilitate passage on the conduit without loss of pneumoperitoneum.

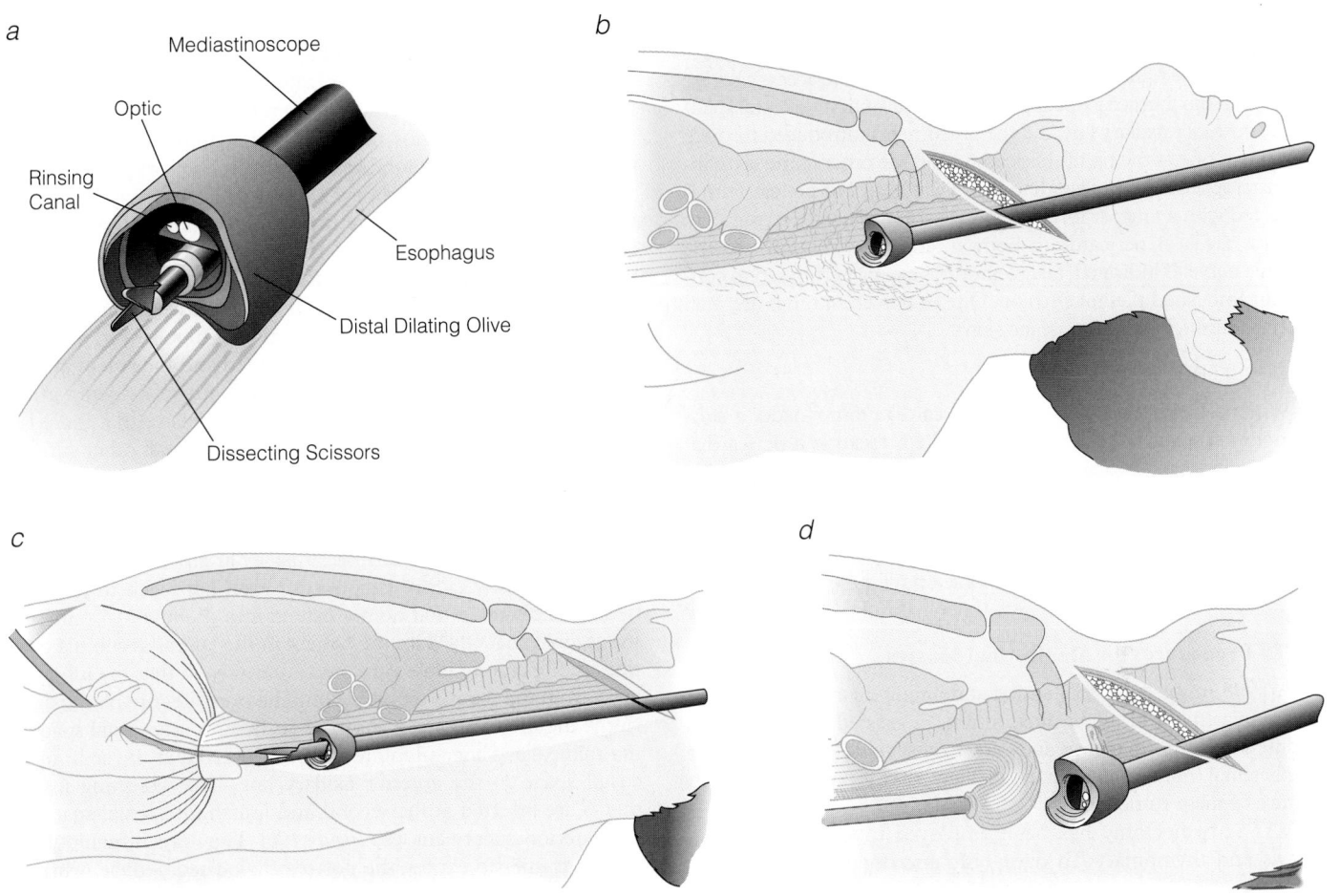

Figure 12 **VATS esophagectomy. In the transhiatal approach, a specially designed operating mediastinoscope with an olive-shaped tip (*a*) is used. This tip mechanically distracts the mediastinal tissues away from the mediastinoscope and keeps the esophagus in a stable position during dissection. The scope is shown cradling the esophagus with the dissecting scissors inserted. During periesophageal dissection, the distal dilating olive of the mediastinoscope is placed behind the esophagus (*b*). The olive creates and maintains space by careful probing of the periesophageal areolar tissue. When the esophagus has been fully mobilized down to the diaphragmatic hiatus, a plastic tube is passed into the hiatus, where it is grasped by the mediastinoscope. Both the mediastinoscope and the plastic tube are pulled up from the hiatus (*c*). After esophageal resection with an endoscopic GIA stapler, the esophagus is folded over by using endoscopic control (*d*). Structures still attached to the esophagus are placed in traction, coagulated, and divided.**

A 5 cm collar incision is made to the left of the midline, and the cervical esophagus is exposed. The Penrose drain that was left in the thoracic inlet is then delivered into the wound to facilitate mobilization of the desired portion of the esophagus. The esophagus is divided in the neck, and the specimen and the conduit are delivered through the posterior mediastinum under laparoscopic visualization to ensure proper alignment of the conduit. The cervical anastomosis may be either handsewn or stapled.[82]

TROUBLESHOOTING

The technical problems associated with VATS esophagectomy are similar to those associated with open thoracic esophagectomy, including thoracic duct injury, recurrent nerve palsy, bleeding from the intercostal vessels, and anastomotic leakage [*see 34 Open Esophageal Procedures*]. These problems are best prevented by obtaining good visualization of the superior and posterior mediastinum, which can be achieved by using a 30° angled thoracoscope. The most common reason for conversion to thoracotomy is the presence of a locally advanced tumor that necessitates exten-

sive dissection for safe mobilization away from adjacent mediastinal structures.

To date, comparison of the results of VATS esophagectomy with those of open esophagectomy has not shown VATS to yield a significant decrease in major complications, especially postoperative respiratory insufficiency and cardiac arrhythmias.[83,84] As a result, most centers still prefer the standard open transhiatal or transthoracic approaches to esophagectomy.

VATS may also be used in the management of postoperative chylothorax.[85] The thoracic duct can be ligated thoracoscopically, though it is sometimes difficult to identify and ligate the primary site of a postoperative lymphatic leak without reopening the thoracotomy.

VATS Pericardial Window

OPERATIVE TECHNIQUE

Some surgeons create a pericardial window by means of VATS as an alternative to taking the subxiphoid approach or the left anterior thoracotomy approach.[86,87] A double-lumen endotracheal tube is inserted with the patient under general anesthesia, and the patient is rotated into the right lateral decubitus position. Three access sites are used, with the thoracoscope inserted at the seventh intercostal space in the posterior axillary line and the instruments introduced through two ports, one at the tip of the scapula and the other at the sixth intercostal space in the axillary line [see Figure 13a]. The pericardium is retracted with a grasper forceps, and scissors are used to resect 8 to 10 cm² areas of pericardium both anterior and posterior to the phrenic nerve. If indicated, talc pleurodesis can be performed to control an associated pleural effusion. One or two chest tubes are then inserted through the port-site incisions.

TROUBLESHOOTING

When a pericardial effusion causes cardiac tamponade, a subxiphoid approach is preferable to VATS for creating a pericardial window because it is safer to perform in a hemodynamically unstable patient. A VATS pericardial window is also inadvisable in patients with constrictive physiology or with intrapericardial adhesions discovered at the time of operation. Conversion to an open procedure with formal pericardiectomy is advisable under these circumstances.

VATS Procedures for Mediastinal Masses

A 1998 multicenter trial aimed at defining the role of VATS in the management of mediastinal tumors suggested that VATS can be used safely to diagnose and resect most middle and posterior mediastinal masses, especially in view of the typically benign nature of these tumors.[88]

VATS thymectomy has been employed to treat myasthenia gravis and thymoma.[89] To date, only anecdotal experience has been reported, and no studies examining long-term outcome have been published. Although a VATS approach to myasthenia gravis may appear attractive at first, it is not the least invasive approach to the thymus. Transcervical thymectomy is a minimally invasive approach to the thymus that does not require a chest incision, does not violate the pleural space, and allows most patients to be discharged home the next day.[90] There is still a degree of controversy as to whether complete thymic resection, including all ectopic thymic tissue, is necessary to obtain clinical remission in patients with myasthenia gravis.[91] For patients with a thymic mass, we prefer a transsternal approach. It is imperative to maintain oncologic surgical principles; accordingly, en bloc resection is emphasized, so that pleural seeding is avoided and the risk of incomplete resection minimized. For patients with myasthenia gravis who do not have a thymoma, however, we believe that there is a need for prospective studies comparing VATS with other surgical approaches to thymectomy.

OPERATIVE TECHNIQUE

VATS has been used to resect masses in all of the mediastinal compartments. VATS resection is an ideal approach to posterior neurogenic tumors that do not extend into the neural foramen or the spinal canal.[92,93] With the patient in the lateral decubitus position, the operating table is rotated anteriorly so that the lung falls away from the paravertebral region. The port sites are placed anteriorly: the thoracoscope is inserted at the fifth intercostal space in the midaxillary line, a lung retractor is inserted at the sixth intercostal space in the anterior axillary line, and dissecting instruments are inserted at the second and fourth intercostal spaces in the anterior axillary line [see Figure 13b]. The mass is manipulated with a grasper to expose the posteriorly located pedicle, which is

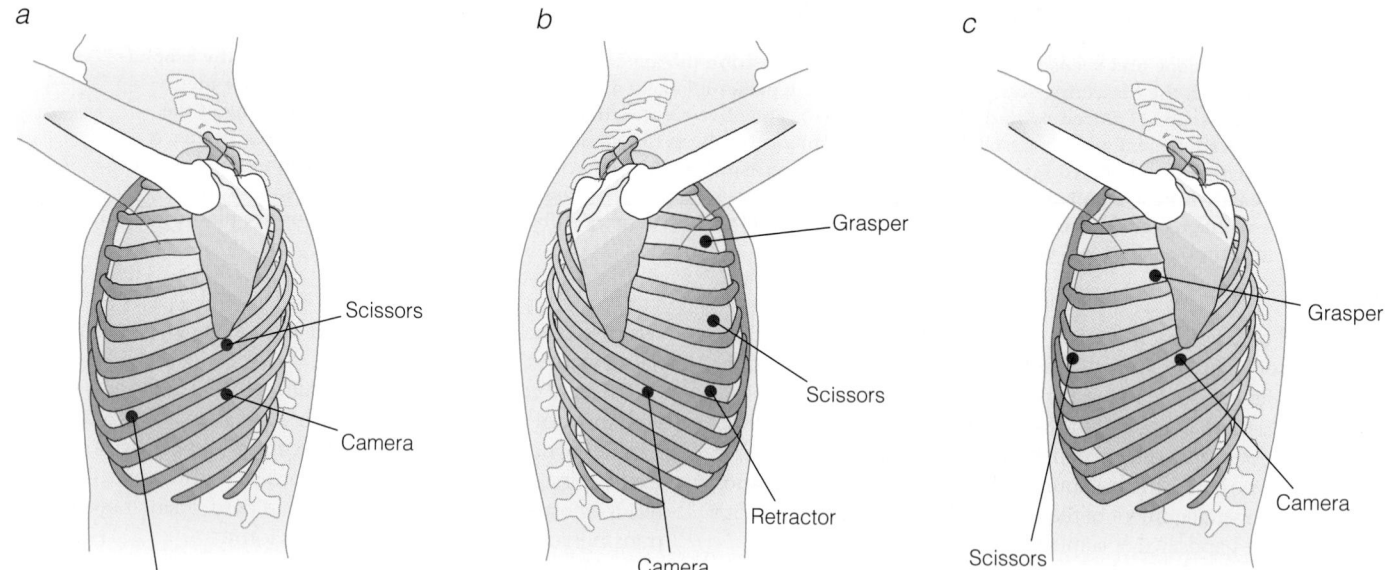

Figure 13 (*a*) **VATS pericardial window. Three access sites are used. The thoracoscope is inserted in the posterior axillary line at the seventh intercostal space, the endoscopic scissors are inserted through one port at the tip of the scapula, and the grasper forceps is inserted through another port in the anterior axillary line at the sixth intercostal space. (*b, c*) VATS procedures for mediastinal masses. For posterior masses, the port sites are placed anteriorly (*b*), and the thoracoscope is inserted at the fifth intercostal space in the midaxillary line. A lung retractor is inserted at the sixth intercostal space in the anterior axillary line, and dissecting instruments are inserted at the second and fourth intercostal spaces in the anterior axillary line. For anterior mediastinal masses and thymectomy, the port sites are placed in more posterior locations (*c*). The thoracoscope is introduced at the fifth intercostal space in the midaxillary or the posterior axillary line, and instruments are inserted through one port at the second intercostal space in the midaxillary line and another at the fifth or sixth intercostal space in the anterior axillary line.**

then dissected, ligated, and divided with the scissors, clip appliers, and the electrocautery.[94,95]

For removal of anterior mediastinal masses, the port sites are placed in more posterior locations. The thoracoscope is introduced at the fifth intercostal space in the midaxillary or posterior axillary line, and instruments are inserted through two ports, one at the second intercostal space at the midaxillary line and the other at the fifth or sixth intercostal space in the anterior axillary line [see Figure 13c]. The mass is retracted with a grasper and dissected free with a combination of sharp and blunt dissection, clip appliers, and the electrocautery.[96,97]

A similar technique is used to resect middle mediastinal masses, most of which are pericardial or bronchogenic cysts.[98,99] The access sites should be chosen according to the location of the mass on the preoperative CT scan. Generally, however, the triangulated site placement used for pulmonary wedge resections provides more suitable exposure than the site placement used for anterior or posterior mediastinal masses.

TROUBLESHOOTING

The placement of the thoracoports and the positioning of the operating team for the resection of posterior mediastinal tumors or for thoracic diskectomy differ significantly from the usual practice in most other VATS procedures. In place of the standard arrangement of trocars in an inverted triangle, the viewing port is placed in the posterior axillary line and the operating ports in the anterior axillary line. The thoracic surgeon and the neurosurgeon both stand on the anterior side of the patient, each viewing a monitor on the opposite side. In addition, a 30° scope is essential for visualizing the intervertebral disk space.[93,95]

Removal of dumbbell neurogenic tumors can be accomplished thoracoscopically if immediately preceded by posterior surgical removal of the spinal component of the tumor via laminectomy and intervertebral foraminotomy. Preoperative MRI scanning is crucial for defining the extent of the tumor within the spinal canal.[94] Resection of posterior mediastinal tumors is sometimes associated with significant bleeding from intercostal or spinal arteries. If such bleeding occurs, there should be no hesitation in converting to a thoracotomy.

Ideally, anterior mediastinal cysts should be resected in toto to prevent recurrence. However, if the cysts are firmly adherent to vital mediastinal structures, partial excision with cauterization of the endothelial lining may be safer.

VATS Management of Thoracic Trauma

The major contraindication to thoracoscopy in thoracic trauma is hemodynamic instability. For major life-threatening injuries involving the great vessels and the mediastinum, thoracotomy is required to obtain expeditious control of injured structures [see 104 Injuries to the Chest]. However, hemodynamically stable patients with certain thoracic problems (e.g., diaphragmatic injury, slow continued intrathoracic bleeding, persistent air leakage, and empyema) may be diagnosed and often treated by means of VATS.[100,101]

In the assessment of a trauma patient with a potential diaphragmatic injury, it is important not to ignore the high incidence of associated intra-abdominal injury. If intra-abdominal injury has been ruled out and there is concern about the presence of a diaphragmatic tear, thoracoscopic assessment of the diaphragm is justified. Such assessment allows a more thorough evaluation of the entire diaphragm than the laparoscopic approach, which is limited by the liver on the right side. In the largest series published to date, 60 of 171 patients who underwent thoracoscopy for pen-

etrating chest injuries had diaphragmatic injuries that necessitated repair.[102] For hemodynamically stable patients with suspected diaphragmatic injuries, the VATS approach appears reasonable.

When a patient has an ongoing intrathoracic problem (e.g., persistent bleeding or a large air leak 24 to 48 hours after a traumatic injury), VATS should be considered before a thoracotomy is done because most problems encountered at this time (e.g., chest wall bleeding and laceration of the lung parenchyma) can be managed endoscopically, without the need for a thoracotomy.

TROUBLESHOOTING

The main pitfall in thoracoscopic evaluation of the diaphragm is failure to assess the abdomen appropriately and consequent failure to recognize an occult intra-abdominal injury. When laparoscopy is performed in a patient with a diaphragmatic injury, insufflation of CO_2 may cause a tension pneumothorax to develop on the side of the diaphragmatic injury. Accordingly, whenever diaphragmatic injury is a possibility, the chest should be included in the operative field to allow chest tube insertion if required. Because thoracoscopy does not require CO_2 insufflation, it is safer in such situations.

VATS Sympathectomy and Splanchnicectomy

Thoracic sympathectomy is known to be the most effective treatment for upper limb hyperhidrosis, and VATS is now an accepted approach to this operation.

The main indication for splanchnicectomy is intractable abdominal pain from unresectable malignancies (e.g., pancreatic or gastric carcinoma) and chronic pancreatitis. The effects of celiac ganglion blocks are transient, and surgical manipulation of this area is usually very difficult because of the primary disease process, previous operations, or both. In the past, thoracotomy was generally considered too invasive an approach to splanchnic denervation in these patients. Currently, however, because of the less invasive nature of thoracoscopy and the quicker recovery time associated with it, thoracoscopic splanchnicectomy is an attractive therapeutic option.[103]

OPERATIVE TECHNIQUE

Sympathectomy

VATS sympathectomy is performed with the patient under general anesthesia and a double-lumen tube in place. Several techniques have been described. Initially, the common practice was to use three port sites: one for the thoracoscope at the third intercostal space in the midaxillary line, one at the third intercostal space in the anterior axillary line, and one at the tip of the scapula. Currently, the procedure is most often performed with two incisions: one at the fifth interspace at the border of the pectoralis and one at the fourth interspace in the anterior axillary line. The pleura is incised and divided from T2 to T5, and the sympathetic chain is dissected free with scissors and excised. For complete control of upper limb hyperhidrosis, VATS must be done bilaterally.[104,105]

A 1998 study reviewed the long-term results in 630 patients who had undergone thoracoscopic sympathectomy for hyperhidrosis (median follow-up, 15 years).[106] Of these patients, 68% were fully satisfied, and 26% were only partially satisfied but nevertheless would agree again to the operation. Hyperhidrosis was cured permanently in 93%. Compensatory sweating and gustatory sweating occurred in 67% and 47% of cases, respectively. Overall, patients were well satisfied with the results and considered the compensatory sweating less of a problem than the original hyperhidrosis.

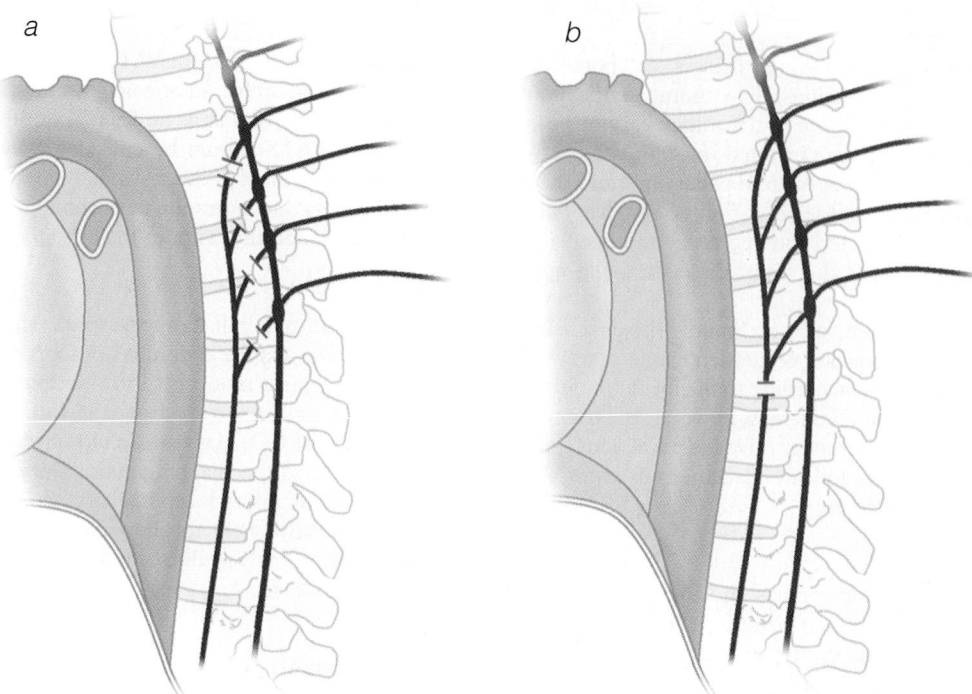

Figure 14 **VATS splanchnicectomy. Splanchnicectomy may be accomplished by either (*a*) dividing the roots of the splanchnic nerves or (*b*) dividing the splanchnic nerve itself.**

Splanchnicectomy

The technical aspects of VATS splanchnicectomy are quite simple: a sound knowledge of the splanchnic anatomy and a basic set of thoracoscopic instruments are all that is needed. Single-lung ventilation is required. Three thoracoports are placed. A silk stitch is placed in the central tendon of the diaphragm and pulled through the most anterior and inferior port to allow better visualization of the splanchnic nerves. The camera is also placed through this port. An endoscopic grasper and an endoscopic scissors with an electrocautery attachment are used to remove the nerve segment from T5 to T9. The greater and lesser splanchnic nerves are resected [*see Figure 14*]. The least splanchnic nerve is rarely visualized.

TROUBLESHOOTING

Care should be taken to identify the first and second ribs. Division of the sympathetic trunk at the level of the first rib causes Horner syndrome and does not reduce palmar hyperhidrosis.

Division of the rami communicantes rather than the main sympathetic trunk reduces the incidence of undesirable side effects, especially compensatory hyperhidrosis of the trunk, but its overall success rate in controlling upper limb hyperhidrosis is lower. Abolition of only the T2 and T3 ganglia may control palmar hyperhidrosis without being as likely to result in unacceptable compensatory truncal sweating. Some have advocated limited T3 sympathectomy for primary hyperhidrosis to prevent compensatory sweating.[107] Target areas for axillary sweating also include T4 and T5. In addition, an accessory sympathetic nerve fiber that runs lateral to the sympathetic chain (known as the nerve of Kuntz) should be sought and, if identified, divided. Compensatory hyperhidrosis of the inner thighs is a not uncommon complication.

Neuralgia is frequent after VATS sympathectomy. Some authors advocate a 2-day postoperative course of dexamethasone to reduce the incidence of this problem.[108]

Miscellaneous VATS Procedures

Several other procedures have been performed by VATS, including ligation of the thoracic duct[109] and resection of the adrenal gland.[110] For adrenal resection, three incisions are placed at the ninth or 10th intercostal space, extending from the anterior axillary line to the posterior axillary line. A fan retractor is inserted through a radial incision in the diaphragm and used to retract the perirenal fat. The adrenal gland is dissected free and removed, and the associated vessels are clipped or cauterized.[110]

Cost Considerations

It is hard to estimate the cost-effectiveness of VATS procedures because the instrumentation, the types of procedures performed, and the surgical expertise with these operations are all still evolving. Initially, VATS procedures proved expensive for several reasons (e.g., the cost of purchasing video and endoscopic equipment, the cost of disposable instrumentation, and the need for long operating times as surgeons and nursing staff gained experience with the procedures). Soon after VATS was introduced, a study from the Mayo Clinic compared the cost of performing VATS pulmonary wedge resections with that of the same operation done by thoracotomy.[111] The VATS approach was associated with substantially shorter hospital stays but also with increased OR costs; hence, the use of VATS did not result in any significant overall savings. Since that study, however, as some VATS procedures (e.g., pulmonary wedge resection) have become standard operations and more reusable instrumentation has become available, the cost of VATS has undoubtedly decreased. Whether other, more complex VATS procedures (e.g., thoracoscopic esophagectomy) are cost-effective remains to be determined.

Training and Certification in VATS and Robotic Surgery

Thoracoscopy is most frequently performed by thoracic surgeons.[2] In some centers, however (particularly in Europe), pulmonologists became highly experienced in the application of traditional thoracoscopic techniques to the diagnosis of pleural disease. The experience of Boutin epitomizes the involvement of physicians who do not have specific surgical training.[4,8] The development of small-caliber endoscopes that could be used with local anesthesia outside the OR made it easy for nonsurgeons to perform thoracoscopy.

After the 1950s, thoracoscopy was largely forgotten by surgeons and pulmonologists in the United States until the advent of VATS. The dramatic initial popularity of this technique generated considerable debate about whether nonsurgeons should perform VATS in the same way as they perform other invasive endoscopic procedures.[112-114] During this period, laparoscopic cholecystectomy became widely practiced, often by persons who lacked adequate training, and reports of serious complications emerged.

Within this context, the Society of Thoracic Surgeons (STS) and the American Association for Thoracic Surgery (AATS) formed a joint committee to establish standards and guidelines for training and certification in VATS [*see Sidebar* Statement of AATS/STS Joint Committee on Thoracoscopy and Video Assisted Thoracic Surgery].[115] As a result of the educational efforts of this committee, many surgeons were trained within a short time, and VATS was quickly incorporated into thoracic surgical practice and residency training.

The important considerations with respect to the training and practice of VATS have been well articulated.[114,115] VATS is not minor surgery: it is a minimally invasive, complex intrathoracic procedure that should be performed only by persons who are familiar with intrathoracic anatomy and pathology and are fully competent to manage complications and make intraoperative decisions in such a way as to ensure safe outcomes for thoracic surgical patients. The complications encountered during thoracoscopic operations are potentially immediately life-threatening, whereas those encountered during other endoscopic procedures usually are not. For that reason, VATS procedures should not be performed by anyone—surgeon or nonsurgeon—who lacks the training and experience to perform immediate thoracotomy and repair of intrathoracic injuries.

VATS is now an integral part of the practice of thoracic surgery.[116] The direct involvement of the major thoracic societies in the dispersion of this technology has discouraged the casual and unsafe application of VATS and has promoted an ongoing critical appraisal of VATS procedures.

The use of robotic assistance in a particular VATS procedure imposes two special requirements on the individual practitioner. First, the robot must be FDA approved for use in that procedure. The list of approved procedures continues to grow and currently includes the majority of general thoracic operations. Second, the practitioner must complete system training for the specific surgical robotic system being used. For the da Vinci Surgical System, Intuitive Surgical runs a 2-day certification course that includes thorough system training, as well as practical instruction with animal and cadaver models. At present, however, although each institution has its own individual requirements for robotic use, there is no standardized method for demonstrating competence.

References

1. Jacobeus HC: The practical importance of thoracoscopy in surgery of the chest. Surg Gynecol Obstet 34:289, 1922

2. Bloomberg AE: Thoracoscopy in perspective. Surg Gynecol Obstet 147:433, 1978

3. Weissberg D, Kaufman M: Diagnostic and therapeutic pleuroscopy: experience with 127 patients. Chest 78:732, 1980

4. Boutin C, Viallat JR, Cargnino P, et al: Thoracoscopy in malignant pleural effusions. Am Rev Respir Dis 124:588, 1981

5. Wihlm JM, Roeslin N, Morand G, et al: Résultats comparés de la ponction, de la biopsie à l'aiguille, de la pleuroscopie et de la thoracotomie dans le diagnostic des pleurésies chroniques. Poumon Coeur 37:57, 1981

6. Rodgers BM, Ryckman FC, Moazam F, et al: Thoracoscopy for intrathoracic tumors. Ann Thorac Surg 31:414, 1981

7. Rusch VW, Mountain C: Thoracoscopy under regional anesthesia for the diagnosis and management of pleural disease. Am J Surg 154:274, 1987

8. Boutin C, Viallat JR, Aelony Y: Practical Thoracoscopy. Berlin, Springer-Verlag, 1991

9. Hazelrigg SR, Nunchuck SK, LoCicero JI: Video Assisted Thoracic Surgery Study Group data. Ann Thorac Surg 56:1039, 1993

10. Krasna MJ, Deshmukh S, McLaughlin JS: Complications of thoracoscopy. Ann Thorac Surg 61:1066, 1996

11. Nakata M, Saeki H, Yokoyama N, et al: Pulmonary function after lobectomy: video-assisted thoracic surgery versus thoracotomy. Ann Thorac Surg 70:938, 2000

12. Kaseda S, Aoki T, Hangai N, et al: Better pulmonary function and prognosis with video-assisted thoracic surgery than with thoracotomy. Ann Thorac Surg 70:1644, 2000

13. Craig SR, Leaver HA, Yap PL, et al: Acute phase re-

sponses following minimal access and conventional thoracic surgery. Eur J Cardiothorac Surg 20:455, 2001

14. Yim AP, Wan S, Lee TW, et al: VATS lobectomy reduces cytokine responses compared with conventional surgery. Ann Thorac Surg 70:243, 2000

15. Deslauriers J, Beaulieu M, Dufour C, et al: Mediastinopleuroscopy: a new approach to the diagnosis of intrathoracic diseases. Ann Thorac Surg 22:265, 1976

16. Rusch VW: Instrumentation for video-assisted thoracic surgery. Chest Surg Clin North Am 3:215, 1993

17. Landreneau RJ, Herlan DB, Johnson JA, et al: Thoracoscopic neodymium:yttrium-aluminum garnet laser-assisted pulmonary resection. Ann Thorac Surg 52:1176, 1991

18. Rusch VW, Schmidt R, Shoji Y, et al: Use of the argon beam electrocoagulator for performing pulmonary wedge resections. Ann Thorac Surg 49:287, 1990

19. Landreneau RJ, Mack MJ, Hazelrigg SR, et al: Video-assisted thoracic surgery: basic technical concepts and intercostal approach strategies. Ann Thorac Surg 54:800, 1992

20. Rusch VW, Bains MS, Burt ME, et al: Contribution of videothoracoscopy to the management of the cancer patient. Ann Surg Oncol 1:94, 1994

21. Ohri SK, Oswal SK, Townsend ER, et al: Early and late outcome after diagnostic thoracoscopy and talc pleurodesis. Ann Thorac Surg 53:1038, 1992

22. Angelillo Mackinlay TA, Lyons GA, Chimondeguy DJ, et al: VATS debridement versus thoracotomy in the treatment of loculated postpneumonia empyema. Ann Thorac Surg 61:1626, 1996

23. Hartman DL, Gaither JM, Kesler KA, et al: Comparison of insufflated talc under thoracoscopic guidance with standard tetracycline and bleomycin pleurodesis for control of malignant pleural effusions. J Thorac Cardiovasc Surg 105:743, 1993

24. Landreneau RJ, Hazelrigg SR, Ferson PF, et al: Thoracoscopic resection of 85 pulmonary lesions. Ann Thorac Surg 54:415, 1992

25. Jimenez MF, Spanish Video-Assisted Thoracic Surgery Group: Prospective study on video-assisted thoracoscopic surgery in the resection of pulmonary nodules: 209 cases from the Spanish Video-Assisted Thoracic Surgery Group. Eur J Cardiothorac Surg 19:562, 2001

26. Ferson PF, Landreneau RJ, Dowling RD, et al: Comparison of open versus thoracoscopic lung biopsy for diffuse infiltrative pulmonary disease. J Thorac Cardiovasc Surg 106:194, 1993

27. Miller JD, Urschel JD, Cox G, et al: A randomized, controlled trial comparing thoracoscopy and limited thoracotomy for lung biopsy in interstitial lung disease. Ann Thorac Surg 70:1647, 2000

28. Dowling RD, Keenan RJ, Ferson PF, et al: Video-assisted thoracoscopic resection of pulmonary metastases. Ann Thorac Surg 56:772, 1993

29. McCormack PM, Ginsberg KB, Bains MS, et al: Accuracy of lung imaging in metastases with implications for the role of thoracoscopy. Ann Thorac Surg 56:863, 1993

30. Landreneau RJ, De Giacomo T, Mack MJ, et al: Therapeutic video-assisted thoracoscopic surgical resection of colorectal pulmonary metastases. Eur J Cardiothorac Surg 18:671, 2000

31. Dowling RD, Ferson PF, Landreneau RJ: Thoracoscopic resection of pulmonary metastases. Chest 102:1450, 1992

32. McCormack PM, Bains MS, Begg CB, et al: Role of video-assisted thoracic surgery in the treatment of pulmonary metastases: results of a prospective trial. Ann Thorac Surg 62:213, 1996

33. Parekh K, Rusch V, Bains M, et al: VATS port site recurrence: a technique dependent problem. Ann Surg Oncol 8:175, 2001

34. Miller DL, Allen MS, Trastek VF, et al: Videothoracoscopic wedge excision of the lung. Ann Thorac Surg 54:410, 1992

35. Bolotin G, Lazarovici H, Uretzky G, et al: The efficacy of intraoperative internal intercostal nerve block during video-assisted thoracic surgery on postoperative pain. Ann Thorac Surg 70:1872, 2000

36. Normori H, Horio H: Endofinger for tactile localization of pulmonary nodules during thoracoscopic resection. Thorac Cardiovasc Surg 44:50, 1996

37. Shennib H, Bret P: Intraoperative transthoracic ultrasonographic localization of occult lung lesions. Ann Thorac Surg 55:767, 1993

38. Plunkett MB, Peterson MS, Landreneau RJ, et al: Peripheral pulmonary nodules: preoperative percutaneous needle localization with CT guidance. Radiology 185:274, 1992

39. Lewis RJ, Caccavale RJ, Sisler GE, et al: One hundred consecutive patients undergoing video-assisted thoracic operations. Ann Thorac Surg 54:421, 1992

40. Demmy TL, Nielson D, Curtis JJ: Improved method for deep thoracoscopic lung nodule excision. Missouri Med 93:86, 1996

41. Mouroux J, Elkaïm D, Padovani B, et al: Video-assisted thoracoscopic treatment of spontaneous pneumothorax: technique and results of one hundred cases. J Thorac Cardiovasc Surg 112:385, 1996

42. Schramel FMNH, Sutedja TG, Braber JCE, et al: Cost-effectiveness of video-assisted thoracoscopic surgery versus conservative treatment for first time or recurrent spontaneous pneumothorax. Eur Respir J 9:1821, 1996

43. Hazelrigg SR, Landreneau RJ, Mack M, et al: Thoracoscopic stapled resection for spontaneous pneumothorax. J Thorac Cardiovasc Surg 105:389, 1993

44. Cole FH Jr, Cole FH, Khandekar A, et al: Video-assisted thoracic surgery: primary therapy for spontaneous pneumothorax? Ann Thorac Surg 60:931, 1995

45. Wakabayashi A: Expanded applications of diagnostic and therapeutic thoracoscopy. J Thorac Cardiovasc Surg 102:721, 1991

46. Wakabayashi A: Thoracoscopic laser pneumoplasty in the treatment of diffuse bullous emphysema. Ann Thorac Surg 60:936, 1995

47. Torresini G, Vaccarili M, Divisi D, et al: Is video-assisted thoracic surgery justified at first spontaneous pneumothorax? Eur J Cardiothorac Surg 20:42, 2001

48. Yim AP: Video-assisted thoracoscopic management of primary spontaneous pneumothorax. Ann Acad Med Singapore 25:668, 1996

49. Colt HG, Russack V, Chiu Y, et al: A comparison of thoracoscopic talc insufflation, slurry, and mechanical abrasion pleurodesis. Chest 111:442, 1997

50. Inderbitzi RGC, Furrer M, Striffeler H, et al: Thoracoscopic pleurectomy for treatment of complicated spontaneous pneumothorax. J Thorac Cardiovasc Surg 105:84, 1993

51. Swanson SJ, Mentzer SJ, DeCamp MM, et al: No-cut thoracoscopic lung plication: a new technique for lung volume reduction surgery. J Am Coll Surg 185:25, 1997

52. Yim APC, Ko K-M, Ma C-C, et al: Thoracoscopic lobectomy for benign diseases. Chest 109:554, 1996

53. McKenna RJ Jr, Wolf RK, Brenner M, et al: Is lobectomy by video-assisted thoracic surgery an adequate cancer operation? Ann Thorac Surg 66:1903, 1998

54. Demmy TL, Curtis JJ: Minimally invasive lobectomy directed toward frail and high-risk patients: a case-control study. Ann Thorac Surg 68:194, 1999

55. Weber A, Stammberger U, Inci I, et al: Thoracoscopic lobectomy for benign disease—a single centre study on 64 cases. Eur J Cardiothorac Surg 20:443, 2001

56. Solaini L, Prusciano F, Bagioni P, et al: Video-assisted thoracic surgery major pulmonary resections:

present experience. Eur J Cardiothorac Surg 20:437, 2001

57. Kirby TJ, Mack MJ, Landreneau RJ, et al: Initial experience with video-assisted thoracoscopic lobectomy. Ann Thorac Surg 56:1248, 1993

58. Kohno T, Murakami T, Wakabayashi A: Anatomic lobectomy of the lung by means of thoracoscopy: an experimental study. J Thorac Cardiovasc Surg 105:729, 1993

59. Lewis RJ: Simultaneously stapled lobectomy: a safe technique for video-assisted thoracic surgery. J Thorac Cardiovasc Surg 109:619, 1995

60. Lewis RJ, Sisler GE, Caccavale RJ: Imaged thoracic lobectomy: should it be done? Ann Thorac Surg 54:80, 1992

61. Lewis RJ: Personal communication, 1993

62. Roviaro GC, Rebuffat C, Varoli F, et al: Videoendoscopic thoracic surgery. Int Surg 78:4, 1993

63. Roviaro GC, Varoli F, Rebuffat C, et al: Videothoracoscopic staging and treatment of lung cancer. Ann Thorac Surg 59:971, 1995

64. Ballantyne GH: Robotic surgery, telerobotic surgery, telepresence and telemonitoring: review of early clinical results. Surg Endosc 16:1389, 2002

65. Falk V, Diegler A, Walther T, et al: Developments in robotic cardiac surgery. Curr Opin Cardiol 15:378, 2000

66. Reichenspurner H, Damiano RJ, Mack M, et al: Use of the voice-controlled and computer-assisted surgical system ZEUS for endoscopic coronary artery bypass grafting. J Thorac Cardiovasc Surg 118:11, 1999

67. Himpens J, Leman G, Cadiere GB: Telesurgical laparoscopic cholecystectomy (letter). Surg Endosc 12:1091, 1998

68. Cadiere GB, Himpens J, Vertruyen M, et al: Nissen fundoplication done by remotely controlled robotic technician. Ann Chir 53:137, 1999

69. Pasticier G, Rietbergen JB, Guillonneau B, et al: Robotically-assisted laparoscopic radical prostatectomy: feasibility study in men. Eur Urol 40:70, 2001

70. Morgan JA, Ginsburg ME, Sonett JR, et al: Thoracoscopic lobectomy using robotic technology. Heart Surg Forum 6:E167, 2003

71. Melfi FM, Menconi GF, Mariani AM, et al: Early experience with robotic technology for thoracoscopic surgery. Eur J Cardiothorac Surg 21:864, 2002

72. Landreneau RJ, Hazelrigg SR, Mack MJ, et al: Thoracoscopic mediastinal lymph node sampling: useful for mediastinal lymph node stations inaccessible by cervical mediastinoscopy. J Thorac Cardiovasc Surg 106:554, 1993

73. Krasna MJ: Minimally invasive staging for esophageal cancer. Chest 112:191S, 1997

74. Krasna MJ, Flowers JL, Attar S, et al: Combined thoracoscopic/laparoscopic staging of esophageal cancer. J Thorac Cardiovasc Surg 111:800, 1996

75. Buess G, Becker HD, Lenz G: Perivisceral endoscopic oesophagectomy. Operative Manual of Endoscopic Surgery. Cuschieri A, Ed. Springer-Verlag, Berlin, 1992, p 149

76. Orringer MB: Transhiatal esophagectomy without thoracotomy for carcinoma of the thoracic esophagus. Ann Surg 200:282, 1984

77. Law S, Fok M, Chu KM, et al: Thoracoscopic esophagectomy for esophageal cancer. Surgery 122:8, 1997

78. Collard J-M, Lengele B, Otte J-B, et al: En bloc and standard esophagectomies by thoracoscopy. Ann Thorac Surg 56:675, 1993

79. Gossot D, Fourquier P, Celerier M: Thoracoscopic oesophagectomy. Ann Chir Gyn Fenniae 83:162, 1994

80. Akaishi T, Kaneda I, Higuchi N, et al: Thoracoscopic en bloc total esophagectomy with radical mediastinal

lymphadenectomy. J Thorac Cardiovasc Surg 112:1533, 1996

81. Luketich JD, Schauer PR, Christie NA, et al: Minimally invasive esophagectomy. Ann Thorac Surg 70:906, 2000

82. Litle VR, Luketich JD: Minimally invasive esophagectomy. CTSNET Experts' Techniques, General Thoracic Experts' Techniques. Ferguson MK, Ed. Accessed October 2004 http://www.ctsnet.org/doc/6762

83. Collard J-M: En bloc and standard esophagectomies by thoracoscopy: update. Ann Thorac Surg 61:769, 1996

84. Peracchia A, Rosati R, Fumagalli U, et al: Thoracoscopic esophagectomy: are there benefits? Sem Surg Onc 13:259, 1997

85. Fahimi H, Casselman FP, Mariani MA, et al: Current management of postoperative chylothorax. Ann Thorac Surg 71:448, 2001

86. Mack MJ, Landreneau RJ, Hazelrigg SR, et al: Video thoracoscopic management of benign and malignant pericardial effusions. Chest 103:390S, 1993

87. Flores RM, Jaklitsch MT, DeCamp MM Jr, et al: Video-assisted thoracic surgery pericardial resection for effusive disease. Chest Surg Clin North Am 8:835, 1998

88. Demmy TL, Krasna MJ, Detterbeck FC, et al: Multicenter VATS experience with mediastinal tumors. Ann Thorac Surg 66:187, 1998

89. Mack MJ, Landreneau RJ, Yim AP, et al: Results of video-assisted thymectomy in patients with myasthenia gravis. J Thorac Cardiovasc Surg 112:1352, 1996

90. Cooper JD, Al-Jilaihawi AN, Pearson FG, et al: An improved technique to facilitate transcervical thymectomy for myasthenia gravis. Ann Thorac Surg 45:242, 1988

91. Jaretzki A III, Wolff M: 'Maximal' thymectomy for myasthenia gravis: surgical anatomy and operative technique. J Thorac Cardiovasc Surg 96:711, 1988

92. Riquet M, Mouroux J, Pons F, et al: Videothoracoscopic excision of thoracic neurogenic tumors. Ann Thorac Surg 60:943, 1995

93. Bousamra M II, Haasler GB, Patterson GA, et al: A comparative study of thoracoscopic vs open removal of benign neurogenic mediastinal tumors. Chest 109:1461, 1996

94. Vallières E, Findlay JM, Fraser RE: Combined microneurosurgical and thoracoscopic removal of neurogenic dumbbell tumors. Ann Thorac Surg 59:469, 1995

95. Mack MJ, Regan JJ, McAfee PC, et al: Video-assisted thoracic surgery for the anterior approach to the thoracic spine. Ann Thorac Surg 59:1100, 1995

96. Yim APC, Kay RLC, Ho JKS: Video-assisted thoracoscopic thymectomy for myasthenia gravis. Chest 108:1440, 1995

97. Knight R, Ratzer ER, Fenoglio ME, et al: Thoracoscopic excision of mediastinal parathyroid adenomas: a report of two cases and review of the literature. J Am Coll Surg 185:481, 1997

98. Hazelrigg SR, Landreneau RJ, Mack MJ, et al: Thoracoscopic resection of mediastinal cysts. Ann Thorac Surg 56:659, 1993

99. Lewis RJ, Caccavale RJ, Sisler GE: Imaged thoracoscopic surgery: a new thoracic technique for resection of mediastinal cysts. Ann Thorac Surg 53:318, 1992

100. Lang-Lazdunski L, Mouroux J, Pons F, et al: Role of videothoracoscopy in chest trauma. Ann Thorac Surg 63:327, 1997

101. Spann JC, Nwariaku FE, Wait M: Evaluation of video-assisted thoracoscopic surgery in the diagnosis of diaphragmatic injuries. Am J Surg 170:628, 1995

102. Freeman RK, Al-Dossari G, Hutcheson KA, et al: Indications for using video-assisted thoracoscopic surgery to diagnose diaphragmatic injuries after penetrating chest trauma. Ann Thorac Surg 72:342, 2001

103. Le Pimpec-Barthes F, Chapuis O, Riquet M, et al: Thoracoscopic splanchnicectomy for control of intractable pain in pancreatic cancer. Ann Thorac Surg 65:810, 1998

104. Dumont P, Denoyer A, Robin P: Long-term results of thoracoscopic sympathectomy for hyperhidrosis. Ann Thorac Surg 78:1801, 2004

105. Krasna MJ, Demmy TL, McKenna RJ, et al: Thoracoscopic sympathectomy: the U.S. experience. Eur J Surg Suppl 580:19, 1998

106. Zacherl J, Huber ER, Imhof M, et al: Long-term results of 630 thoracoscopic sympathicotomies for primary hyperhidrosis: the Vienna experience. Eur J Surg Suppl 580:43, 1998

107. Yoon do H, Ha Y, Park YG, et al: Thoracoscopic limited T-3 sympathicotomy for primary hyperhidrosis: prevention for compensatory hyperhidrosis. J Neurosurg Spine 99:39, 2003

108. Wong C-W: Transthoracic video endoscopic electrocautery of sympathetic ganglia for hyperhidrosis palmaris: special reference to localization of the first and second ribs. Surg Neurol 47:224, 1997

109. Shirai T, Amano J, Takabe K: Thoracoscopic diagnosis and treatment of chylothorax after pneumonectomy. Ann Thorac Surg 52:306, 1991

110. Mack MJ, Aronoff RJ, Acuff TE, et al: Thoracoscopic transdiaphragmatic approach for adrenal biopsy. Ann Thorac Surg 55:772, 1993

111. Allen MS, Deschamps C, Lee RE, et al: Video-assisted thoracoscopic stapled wedge excision for indeterminate pulmonary nodules. J Thorac Cardiovasc Surg 106:1048, 1993

112. Mathur P, Martin WJ Jr: Clinical utility of thoracoscopy. Chest 102:2, 1992

113. Forum: Who should perform thoracoscopy? Chest 102:1553, 1992

114. Thoracoscopy forum, continuing dialogue. Chest 102:1915, 1992

115. McKneally MF, Lewis RJ, Anderson RP, et al: Statement of the AATS/STS Joint Committee on Thoracoscopy and Video Assisted Thoracic Surgery. J Thorac Cardiovasc Surg 104:1, 1992

116. Mack MJ, Scruggs GR, Kelly KM, et al: Video-assisted thoracic surgery: has technology found its place? Ann Thorac Surg 64:211, 1997

Acknowledgment

Figures 1 through 7 and 9 through 14   Tom Moore.

Joseph B. Shrager, M.D., F.A.C.S., and Vivek Patel, M.B.B.S.

Procedures for Lesions of the Anterior Mediastinum

More than half of all mediastinal masses arise from the anterior compartment. Most primary malignancies of the mediastinum also develop in the anterior mediastinum. Because of the narrowness of the space that makes up the thoracic inlet, as well as the presence of the trachea and esophagus traversing this region, anterior mediastinal masses become symptomatic earlier than their counterparts in other anatomic spaces of the mediastinum. Whereas adults with masses of the middle or posterior mediastinum usually report no significant symptoms, more than 50% of patients with anterior mediastinal masses present with chest pain, fever, cough, dyspnea, dysphagia, or vascular obstruction. Thymic neoplasms and lymphoma, the two most common masses in the anterior mediastinum, may have systemic manifestations (e.g., weakness associated with myasthenia gravis [MG] or symptoms associated with International Working Formulation [IWF] group B lymphoma).

In what follows, we focus on surgical approaches to diagnosis and treatment of the more common neoplasms of the anterior mediastinum, including thymic tumors, lymphomas, and germ cell tumors. Embryologic anomalies and neoplasms arising from normal structures in this region broaden the differential diagnosis [see Table 1]. Finally, we address thymectomy for MG, a procedure that is frequently performed even in the absence of neoplastic disease.

PREOPERATIVE EVALUATION

In a patient with an anterior mediastinal mass, it is frequently possible to make a strong provisional diagnosis of the tumor type on the basis of clinical evaluation and diagnostic imaging.[1] As noted (see above), the presence of systemic manifestations may be helpful. Physical examination must include examination of peripheral lymph node groups and testes. Computed tomography yields valuable information about the anatomic location of the tumor, its characteristics (i.e., fatty, solid, or cystic), and its degree of invasiveness (if any) [see Figure 1]. Occasionally, magnetic resonance imaging provides useful additional information about the obliteration of normal tissue planes.

Lymphoma is the most likely diagnosis in persons younger than 40 years, and the presence of IWF group B symptoms further raises the level of suspicion. The presence of palpable remote adenopathy or an elevated serum lactic dehydrogenase (LDH) level is also suggestive.[2] When peripheral nodes are palpable, the diagnosis may be most easily obtained by excising one of them. Patients with suspected lymphoma who have an isolated anterior mediastinal mass should undergo core-needle biopsy or a Chamberlain procedure (anterior mediastinotomy), depending on the pathologists' level of comfort with classifying lymphoma on the basis of small specimens at one's institution. Resection of lymphoma is not indicated; it may be avoided by performing a diagnostic biopsy whenever lymphoma is suspected.

Unlike lymphomas, thymic neoplasms are uncommon before the fourth decade of life. Thymoma [see Figure 1a] may be associated with any of several paraneoplastic syndromes. MG occurs in conjunction with a pathologic condition of the thymus—either thymoma or thymic hyperplasia—in 80% to 90% of cases. Thymoma may also be associated with pure red cell aplasia, agammaglobulinemia, systemic lupus erythematosus, and various autoimmune disorders. The presence of any of these associated syndromes essentially clinches the diagnosis of thymoma. Autoantibodies to the acetylcholine receptor (anti-AChR antibodies) should be measured: their presence is diagnostic of MG, and they are found in nearly 60% of patients who have thymoma without neurologic symptoms.[3] Once the diagnosis of thymoma has been made, the goal is to proceed to direct resection without preliminary biopsy; these tumors have a predilection for local recurrence once the capsule has been violated.

The majority of germ cell tumors, whether malignant or be-

Table 1 Differential Diagnosis of Anterior Mediastinal Mass

Neoplastic conditions	Thyroid
	  Substernal goiter
	  Ectopic thyroid tissue
	Thymus
	  Thymic hyperplasia
	  Thymoma
	  Thymic carcinoma
	  Thymic carcinoid
	  Thymic small cell carcinoma
	  Thymic cyst
	  Thymolipoma
	Teratoma
	  Mature teratoma
	  Immature teratoma
	  Teratoma with malignant component
	Lymphoma
	Ectopic parathyroid with adenoma
	Germ cell tumors
	  Seminoma
	  Nonseminoma
	    Yolk sac tumor
	    Embryonal carcinoma
	    Choriocarcinoma
	Hemangioma
	Lipoma
	Liposarcoma
	Fibroma
	Fibrosarcoma
	Cervicomediastinal hygroma

Infectious conditions	Acute descending necrotizing mediastinitis Subacute mediastinitis
Vascular conditions	Aneurysm of aortic arch with projection in anterior mediastinum Innominate vein aneurysm Superior vena cava aneurysm Dilation of superior vena cava (with anomalous pulmonary venous return) Persistent left superior vena cava

a

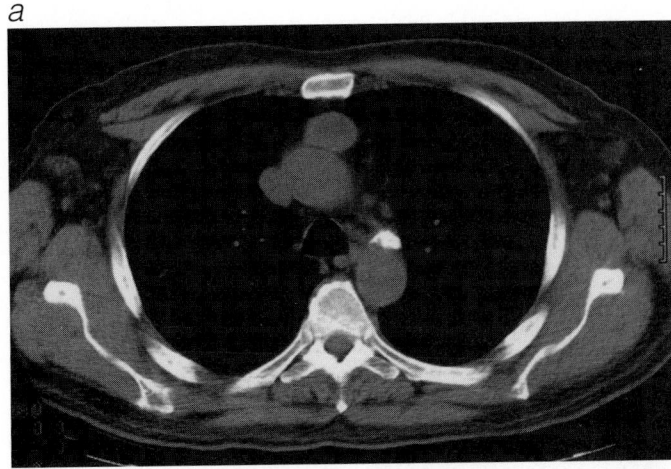

b

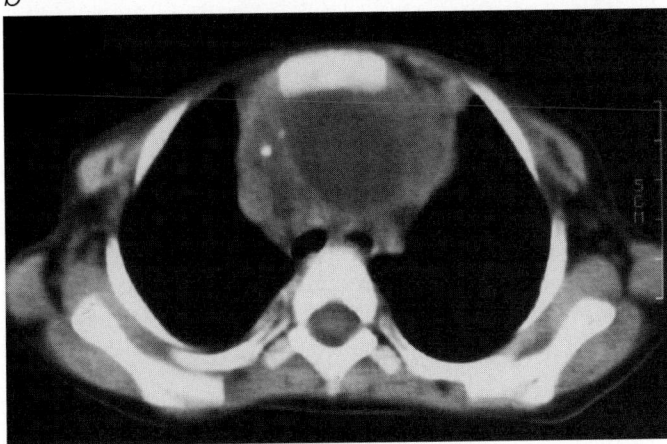

Figure 1 (*a*) **CT scan shows a well-encapsulated anterior mediastinal mass—a thymoma.** (*b*) **CT scan shows a benign teratoma of the anterior mediastinum; calcification and varying tissue densities may be seen.**

nign, are diagnosed in the second or third decade of life. Benign teratomas are usually well encapsulated, with frequent recapitulation of one or more tissue elements seen on radiography.[4] The appearance of the lesions on CT is often diagnostic [*see Figure 1b*]. Surgical extirpation is the mainstay of treatment for these mature germ cell tumors, and biopsy is not indicated. Malignant germ cell tumors, on the other hand, are treated with primary chemotherapy, radiotherapy, or both; when suspected, they should undergo biopsy rather than proceed directly to resection. Characteristic serum tumor markers, including β–human chorionic gonadotropin (β-hCG) and alpha-fetoprotein (AFP), are elaborated by most malignant germ cell neoplasms but are not found in benign germ cell tumors.[5] Elevation of the AFP level beyond 500 ng/ml is considered diagnostic of a nonseminomatous component in a malignant germ cell tumor and is usually associated with a concomitant increase in serum β-hCG levels.[6] In the absence of any marked elevation in the AFP or β-hCG level, percutaneous needle biopsy usually suffices to establish the diagnosis.

OPERATIVE PLANNING

Biopsy versus Resection

Clearly, the decision whether to perform a biopsy of an anteri-

or mediastinal mass is not a simple one. Routine biopsy should be avoided, not only because of the cost and the unnecessary morbidity but also because of the risk that biopsy may spread thymoma. The choice to proceed with biopsy should be made according to which tumor type is believed to be most likely on the basis of the diagnostic workup.

Well-encapsulated lesions that are believed not to represent lymphoma are resected, without a preceding biopsy, for both diagnosis and treatment. Neoplasms that commonly fall into this category include noninvasive thymomas, mature teratomas, mesenchymal tumors, and, occasionally, benign cysts. Patients with MG should be offered thymectomy, whether they have a thymic mass or not.

When lymphoma is suspected, biopsy is required. The technique employed should be minimally invasive while still permitting the acquisition of a sufficient tissue sample. CT-guided core needle biopsy may be attempted, but frequently, this technique does not provide enough tissue for the analyses required to classify the tumor.[7,8]

For anterior mediastinal masses that appear to be locally invasive or frankly unresectable, biopsy is also preferable to immediate resection. Such lesions may represent aggressive thymomas that may benefit from neoadjuvant treatment, malignant germ cell tumors, or other rare disease processes. Once the decision has been made to proceed with biopsy rather than resection, selection of a biopsy approach is based on anatomic considerations and patient factors.

BIOPSY OF ANTERIOR MEDIASTINAL MASS

Chamberlain Approach

Anterior parasternal mediastinotomy (the Chamberlain procedure) is favored by most surgeons for biopsy of lesions in the anterior mediastinum and the aortopulmonary window. It is usually done under general anesthesia, though local anesthesia may be used instead, and it does not require single-lung ventilation. This operation affords good exposure and allows generous biopsy specimens to be taken, and it can be performed as an outpatient procedure.

Operative technique *Step 1: initial incision.* A 5 cm transverse incision is made over the second costal cartilage on the side to be operated on (the second cartilage is identified by its continuity with the sternal angle). The pectoralis major is separated in a direction parallel to the direction of its fibers, and the cartilage is resected in a subperichondrial plane [*see Figure 2*]. Leaving perichondrium behind facilitates postoperative regrowth of the cartilage.

Step 2: dissection and exposure. The posterior perichondrium is incised, and the parietal pleura is bluntly dissected laterally with a peanut sponge; this affords entry into the mediastinal fat and direct access to the tumor mass. Almost invariably, the internal mammary vessels can be mobilized medially and preserved, but if necessary, they may be ligated to improve exposure.

Step 3: biopsy. A generous wedge-shaped portion of the mass is excised with a scalpel. Frozen-section examination is then performed to confirm that diagnostic tissue has been obtained. It is important to remember to request that flow cytometry be performed on the specimen.

Step 4: closure. The posterior perichondrium is reapproximated, followed by the pectoralis major, the subcutaneous fat, and the skin.

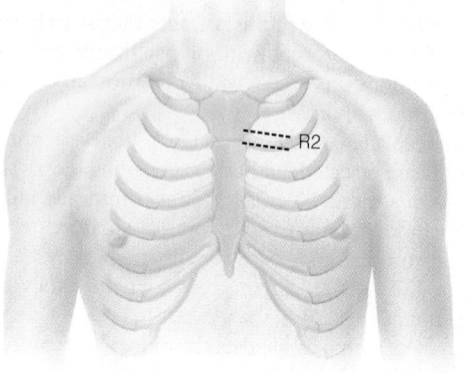

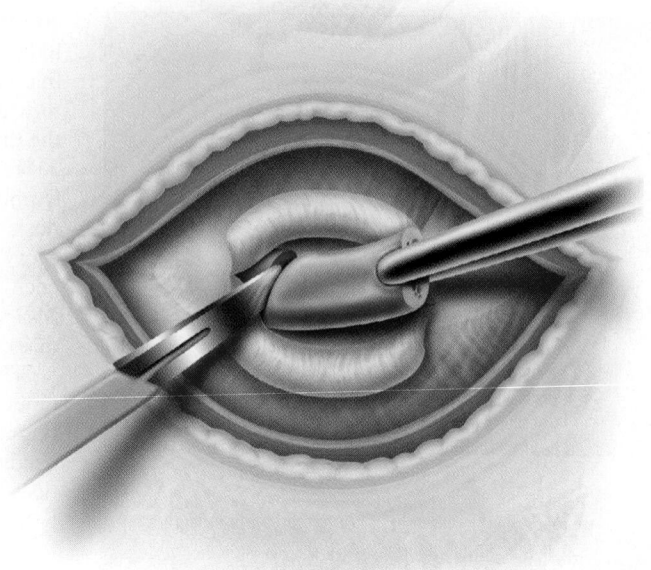

Figure 2 **Biopsy of anterior mediastinal mass: Chamberlain approach. Depicted are incision and subperichondrial resection of the second costal cartilage.**

Troubleshooting If the pleura was entered, a red rubber catheter is used to evacuate the pleural space as the lung is inflated with a large positive pressure breath, and the catheter is withdrawn through the layers of closure. A small postoperative pneumothorax is almost always attributable to residual air rather than to an ongoing air leak.

Sometimes, the tumors are fairly vascular and bleed moderately after biopsy is performed. This bleeding can always be controlled with electrocauterization. We often leave an absorbable hemostatic agent in place as well.

Transcervical Approach

As an alternative to the Chamberlain procedure, a mass of the anterior mediastinum may be approached for biopsy through a cervical incision, exactly as in a transcervical thymectomy [*see* Resection of Anterior Mediastinal Mass, Transcervical Approach, *below*]. The use of a Cooper thymectomy retractor (Pilling Company, Fort Washington, Pennsylvania), which elevates the sternum, affords excellent exposure of the anterior mediastinum and sometimes allows direct examination to ascertain the invasiveness of an otherwise uncertain mass. In most cases, general anesthesia is required, but transcervical biopsy can be performed as an outpatient procedure. We have used this technique at our institution and have achieved results comparable to those of anterior mediastinotomy.[9] Proper performance of this procedure does, however, require a level of experience with the technique that is not widely available.

Video-Assisted Thoracic Surgery

Video-assisted thoracic surgery (VATS) has been applied to diagnostic biopsy [*see 37 Video-Assisted Thoracic Surgery*], but VATS biopsy procedures are not widely employed in the anterior mediastinum. The necessity of single-lung ventilation adds a level of complexity to the procedure beyond what is required for the Chamberlain procedure or the transcervical approach. Furthermore, intercostal incisions are frequently more painful than transcervical incisions or anterior mediastinotomies. VATS does have certain advantages that may be of value in individual cases, such as the capacity to provide simultaneous access to other compartments of the mediastinum and the ability to evaluate the pleural

space for evidence of tumor dissemination. Robot-assisted thoracoscopic procedures for anterior mediastinal masses have also been described,[10] but their availability does not eliminate the major objection to transpleural approaches to mediastinal masses—namely, the possibility of spreading a disease that had been contained within the mediastinum into the pleural space.

RESECTION OF ANTERIOR MEDIASTINAL MASS

Operative Planning

The most frequent indications for resection (as opposed to biopsy) of an anterior mediastinal mass are (1) thymoma and (2) thymectomy for MG. The principles underlying thymoma resection can be applied to resection of other, rarer anterior mediastinal masses. The first successful resection of a thymic mass for MG was described in 1939.[11] Since the introduction of transcervical thymectomy (TCT), there has been ongoing debate regarding the optimal method for thymectomy in patients with nonthymomatous MG. There is little debate, however, regarding the optimal approach to resection of anterior mediastinal malignancies.

For all primary invasive masses of the anterior mediastinum—including invasive thymomas, malignant germ cell tumors (after systemic treatment), thymic carcinomas, and other, less common malignancies—the most important prognostic factor is complete resection. Accordingly, the operative approach must be selected with an eye to providing optimal exposure. There is little doubt that a full median sternotomy is ideal in this regard. However, a less than full sternotomy is a reasonable choice for small (< 3 cm) noninvasive thymomas or other noninvasive mediastinal tumors (e.g., mature teratomas), particularly when the diagnosis of thymoma is in doubt before operation. In such situations, we usually begin with TCT,[12] but we do not hesitate to convert to a sternotomy if unexpected invasion is identified. Some surgeons have employed a partial upper sternotomy in these settings; however, this approach limits exposure, and we do not believe that it actually reduces morbidity in comparison with a full sternotomy.

En bloc resection of malignancies is mandatory, and resection of adjacent serosal membranes (including pleura or pericardium) is required if there is any suggestion of attachment during the operation. Resection of adjacent lung parenchyma is not uncom-

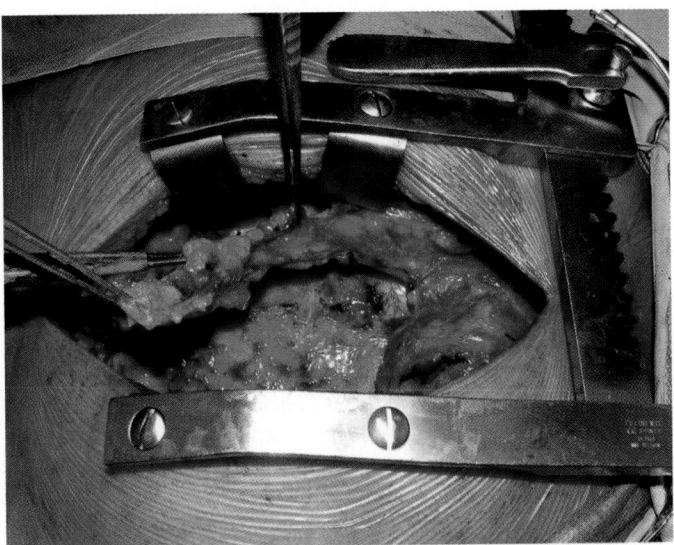

Figure 3 **Resection of anterior mediastinal mass: median sternotomy approach. Intraoperative photo shows dissection of the right inferior thymic pole and associated mediastinal fat.**

mon, and resection of the great vessels has been performed with both technical success and good long-term survival. All great vessels resected must be reconstructed, with the exception of the innominate vein, which may be ligated with little deleterious effect. Every effort should be made to preserve the phrenic nerves: damage to even one of these nerves can be disastrous in an already weakened myasthenia patient. In a patient with a malignancy, however, one phrenic nerve may be sacrificed if tumor invasion necessitates this step, provided that the patient's preoperative respiratory status is acceptable and curative resection is likely.

In cases of thymectomy for advanced MG, every effort must be made to optimize the patient's condition preoperatively. To this end, a multidisciplinary approach that includes a neurologist and, possibly, a pulmonologist is necessary. If the disease does not stabilize with medication (e.g., pyridostigmine, steroids, or intravenous γ-globulin), preoperative plasmapheresis may be required. The question of which MG patients should be offered thymectomy is, at best, difficult to answer. Most studies have found the impact of thymectomy to be greater if it is performed early. Accordingly, our practice is to offer TCT sooner in the course of the disease rather than later; however, we will perform the procedure at any stage, from ocular-only disease to severe, generalized weakness. Because TCT is associated with minimal morbidity, requires only a small incision, and can generally be done as an outpatient procedure, it is a very attractive option for patients with milder disease. At the same time, it is also more easily tolerated by patients with severe disease than a median sternotomy is.

An approach to thymectomy for MG that is favored by a few surgeons is so-called maximal transsternal-transcervical thymic resection, which combines a median sternotomy with an additional neck incision to provide wide access to all areas where thymic tissue has been identified. The rationale for such extensive exposure is the observation that thymic tissue may reside in several extrathymic locations. Proponents of the maximal approach argue that if thymectomy for MG is to provide optimal benefit, it should include removal of all of this extraglandular thymic tissue. This approach has never been compared with TCT in a randomized trial, but in our view, most of the available data suggest that remission rates after maximal transsternal-transcervical thymic resection

are not remarkably different from those after TCT, which is much less invasive. Because we do not personally perform the maximally invasive procedure, we do not describe it in this chapter.

Median Sternotomy Approach

As noted (see above), the standard approach to masses of the anterior mediastinum is via a median sternotomy. Resection of a thymoma of the anterior mediastinum is performed as follows.

Operative technique *Step 1: initial incision and exposure.* The patient is placed in the supine position and intubated with a single-lumen tube. If direct extension to the lung is considered a possibility, a double-lumen tube is placed. The skin incision typically extends from 2 cm below the jugular notch to the xiphisternal junction; however, depending on the extent of the expected pathologic condition, the incision may be shortened further and the full sternum divided by reaching beneath skin flaps. Finger dissection is performed beneath the sternum to rule out tumor invasion into the posterior sternal table. If the posterior sternal table is clear, the sternum is divided, hemostasis is achieved, and the edges are separated with a sternal retractor.

Step 2: determination of resectability. The anterior mediastinum is inspected, the mass is visually identified, and an initial assessment of resectability is undertaken.

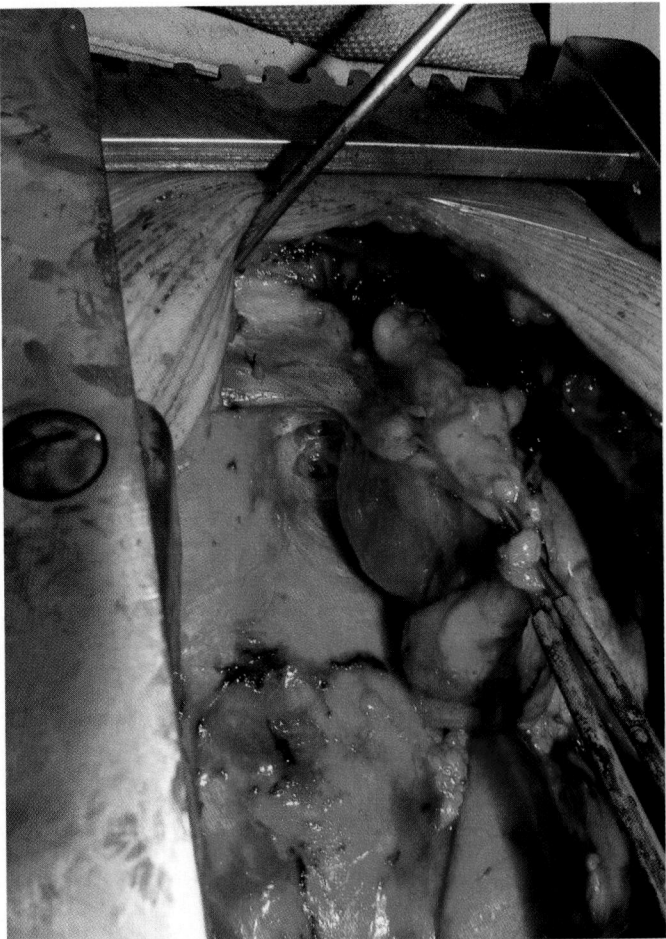

Figure 4 **Resection of anterior mediastinal mass: median sternotomy approach. View from feet shows the thymus and tumor mobilized off the innominate vein. The entire right thymus (both the upper and the lower pole) has been fully mobilized.**

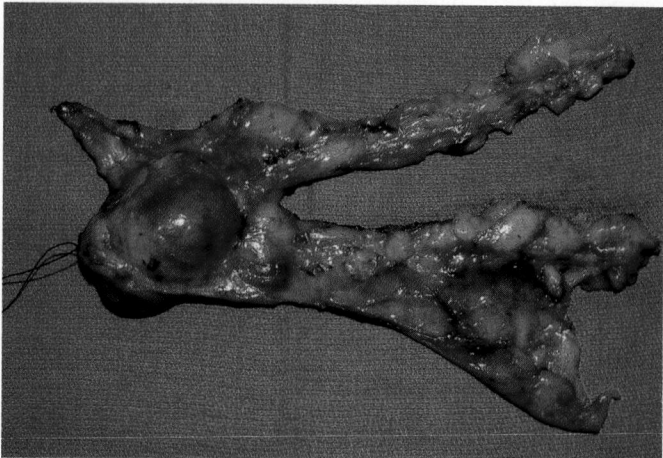

Figure 5 Resection of anterior mediastinal mass: median sternotomy approach. Shown is the resected thymoma specimen.

Step 3: mobilization of inferior poles of thymus. Dissection of the thymus begins at the caudad aspect, with the inferior poles mobilized first from the underlying pericardium through electrocautery dissection. It is difficult to determine by visual means precisely where thymic tissue merges into simple mediastinal fat; accordingly, to ensure complete resection of the thymus, all fatty tissue between the phrenic nerves and down to the level of the diaphragm is removed with the specimen. The mediastinal pleura, to which this fatty and thymic tissue tends to be adherent, is also taken with the specimen [see Figure 3].

Step 4: continuation of dissection cephalad. As dissection proceeds cephalad, the phrenic nerves are identified and followed along their entire path up to the point where they course beneath the innominate vein. Sharp dissection often must be carried very close to the nerves to secure an adequate tumor margin. It is advisable to clip small vessels near the nerve before dividing them, so as to prevent irritating bleeding, which can be difficult to control without compromising the nerve.

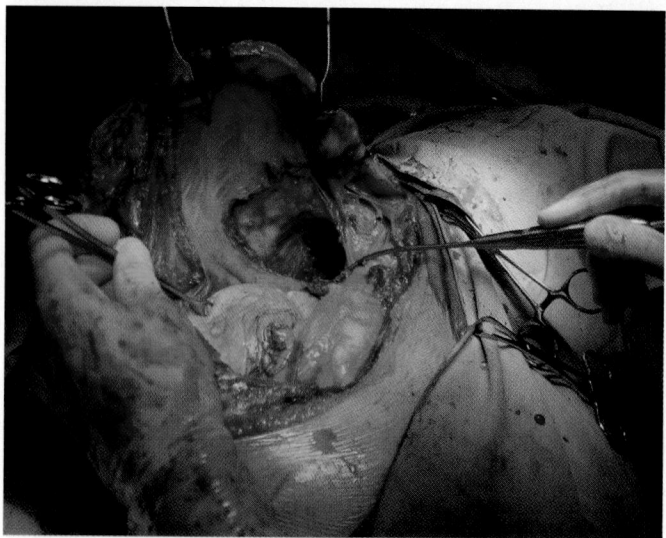

Figure 6 Resection of anterior mediastinal mass: median sternotomy approach. Hemiclamshell incision provides exposure to masses located at the thoracic apex.

The arteries supplying the thymus, arising laterally via branches from the internal mammary vessels, are ligated and divided as they are encountered. Care must be taken to stay away from the phrenic nerves while controlling the arterial blood supply.

Step 5: mobilization of superior poles of thymus. Dissection is then continued in the neck, where the two cervical extensions are isolated by means of gentle traction and blunt dissection and followed until they trail off into the thyrothymic ligament. This ligament is clamped, divided, and ligated superiorly at a point where only a small blood vessel is present and no visible glandular tissue remains.

Step 6: dissection of thymus from innominate vein. The cervical poles are followed down over the innominate vein. Sharp dissection is continued onto the surface of the vein, and the two to five veins draining the gland into the innominate vein are ligated and divided [see Figure 4].

Step 7: removal of specimen. Once the body of the thymus has been freed from the innominate vein, the H-shaped gland and the associated mass are removed [see Figure 5]. If the clean plane between the mass and the underlying pericardium—a plane normally composed of fine, filmy adhesions—is at all compromised, one should not hesitate to resect a portion of the pericardium en bloc with the specimen, with care taken to maintain a gross margin of at least 2 cm at all times.

Step 8: closure. Two pleural drains that traverse the mediastinum and reach the apex of each hemithorax are placed, and the sternum and the soft tissues are reapproximated in layers.

Troubleshooting If invasion of great vessels is considered a possibility before the start of the operation, the groin should be prepared and draped into the field to provide access for cardiopulmonary bypass if needed. Giant anterior mediastinal masses may necessitate extension of a partial median sternotomy incision into an ipsilateral intercostal space (usually the fourth space). Such extension may be achieved by making an ipsilateral incision in the neck along the anterior border of the sternocleidomastoid muscle and making a submammary skin incision continuous with the incision over the sternum (a hemiclamshell incision) [see Figure 6].

Transcervical Approach

Although the transcervical approach to thymic resection was the first one used in the early 1900s, it fell into disuse during the middle of the 20th century, when the median sternotomy approach became feasible. During the past 20 years, however, there has been a resurgence of interest in TCT. Today, TCT is used primarily for thymectomy in the setting of MG, though, as noted (see above), a transcervical approach can be useful for biopsy or resection of other anterior mediastinal processes as well. Proponents of TCT have published data establishing that complete remission rates from MG after so-called extended TCT using the sternum-lifting Cooper retractor[13] are virtually equivalent to remission rates after the more invasive approaches.[14,15] Because TCT is an outpatient procedure, hospital stay and operative recovery are certainly dramatically shorter than after thymectomy by sternotomy.

TCT should be employed very cautiously in cases in which a neoplasm is suspected or proved on the basis of preoperative studies or is identified during the course of intraoperative exploration. Because thymoma is often an indolent tumor, with recurrence developing many years after resection, long-term follow-up studies are required before TCT can be firmly recommended for treatment of even small thymomas. On the other hand, it is likely that surgeons who have extensive experience with TCT can safely resect small (< 3 cm) thymomas via this approach without risking tumor spillage or incomplete resection.

Operative technique *Step 1: initial incision and exposure.* The patient is placed on the operating table in the supine position, with the head supported by a foam doughnut and an inflatable bag placed horizontally beneath the scapulae. The bag is inflated until the cervical spine is maximally extended. It is important that the top of the patient's head be all the way up to the edge of the table, so that the surgeon can easily reach all areas of the mediastinum from a seated position at the head.

A 5 to 6 cm curvilinear incision is made about 2 cm superior to the jugular notch and extending about 1 cm above each clavicular head [*see Figure 7*]. Electrocautery dissection is continued through the platysma, and subplatysmal flaps are elevated. The strap muscles are separated in the midline, and the interclavicular ligament is divided. Separating a small portion of the attachment of each sternocleidomastoid muscle from the corresponding clavicular head allows the sternum to be elevated somewhat higher, thereby improving exposure.

Step 2: mobilization of superior poles of thymus. The superior poles of the thymus are located (usually on the left side first) by means of gentle blunt dissection beneath the strap muscles. After one pole is identified, it is divided between ties at its superior extent. Its medial edge is then followed down to where it meets the medial edge of the opposite superior pole, and this opposite pole can then be similarly traced upward into the neck, ligated, and divided. A very important part of the procedure is the placement of 0 silk ligatures around an area containing strong tissue within each superior pole. These ligatures are left long and clamped. The surgeon or an assistant places traction on them during the remaining course of the dissection to manipulate and progressively mobilize the gland [*see Figure 8*].

Step 3: continuation of dissection downward into superior mediastinum. As traction is being placed on the upper poles, sharp and blunt dissection, staying outside the well-defined capsule of the gland, is extended downward into the superior mediastinum to the level of the innominate vein. The procedure becomes much more difficult if the capsule is violated.

Step 4: elevation of sternum. Finger dissection is performed in the substernal plane, and the arm of a Cooper thymectomy retractor is placed into the retromanubrial space to elevate the sternum. The retracting arm is placed under upward tension as the inflatable bag beneath the shoulders is deflated. This step leaves most patients actually hanging from the retractor, thereby opening up a sizable space that allows good visualization and ready passage of dissecting instruments into the anterior mediastinum. Army-Navy retractors are placed in each of the two upper corners of the incision, and their distal ends are tied to the siderails of the table with Penrose drains to provide countertraction and to hold the skin incision open.

Step 5: dissection of venous tributaries to innominate vein. With the superior poles gently pulled upward by an assistant (and at times looped over the Cooper retractor), the inferior surface of the gland is dissected until the innominate vein is encountered. The venous tributaries draining the thymus into the innominate vein are isolated sharply, ligated with fine silk sutures, and divided.

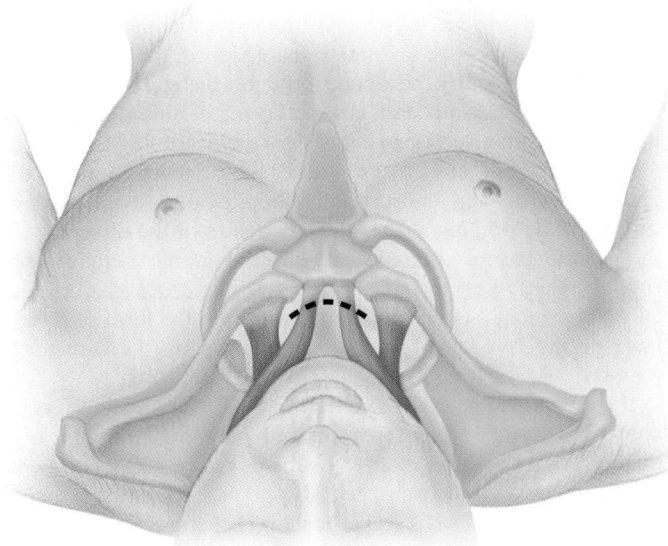

Figure 7 **Resection of anterior mediastinal mass: transcervical approach. Shown is the location of the skin incision for TCT in relation to the sternal notch and the heads of the clavicles.**

Step 6: dissection of posterior aspect of thymus. Once the thymus is freed from the innominate vein, dissection of the posterior aspect of the gland must be continued directly on the surface of the pericardium. This posterior dissection is carried as far down as possible, primarily in a blunt fashion. Most of the time, the surgeon holds one ring clamp containing a sponge dissector in each hand, while an assistant holds the upper poles. Occasionally, the surgeon holds the sutures attached to the upper poles in one hand while employing the sponge dissector in the other hand.

Step 7: removal of specimen. When the posterior dissection has been extended as far as possible toward the diaphragm, further mobilization of the thymus is typically accomplished by working the glandular tissue laterally, first off the pleura on one side, then off the sternum anteriorly, and finally off pleura on the opposite side. In this way, the entire gland is ultimately removed between the phrenic nerves and down to the diaphragm. During this final mobilization, the surgeon periodically asks to have ventilation held temporarily so that the pleura can fall back and thus permit improved visualization. Small feeding vessels from the mammary are doubly clipped and divided as they are encountered.

Often, the final stages of blunt dissection may be facilitated by placing a ring clamp on the body of the gland to allow slightly more vigorous retraction than can be achieved by using the upper poles alone. If any suspicious residual tissue is seen in the mediastinum at this point, it can be removed piecemeal; however, this is an unusual occurrence.

Step 8: closure. After inspection of the surgical field for hemostasis, the strap muscles and the platysma are closed over a red rubber catheter, to which suction may be applied. The catheter is subsequently removed, and the skin is closed.

Troubleshooting In the course of preoperative evaluation before TCT, it is important to be sure that the patient is able to extend the neck to a reasonable degree. TCT is simplest in young persons who are capable of good extension; it can be difficult or impossible in persons with cervical spine disease that hinders extension.

During the procedure itself, it is important that the branches of the innominate vein be tied rather than clipped; the space anterior to the vein becomes the avenue through which dissecting instruments are passed into and out of the mediastinum, and these instruments often rub against the vein fairly vigorously.

When working laterally, one must take care not to injure the phrenic nerves, and one certainly should not use the electrocautery while working at the lateral extremes of the dissection. If the pleural space is entered while one is working laterally, a red rubber catheter [see Operative Technique, Step 8, above] is advanced well into that pleural space, and suction in the form of several large positive pressure breaths is applied before the catheter is removed.

If a thymoma is encountered during TCT, continuation via this approach may be considered. In our view, most noninvasive thymic lesions less than 3 cm in diameter can be safely and completely resected via the transcervical approach. In addition, it generally is not difficult to resect a portion of the anterior pericardium as well if a tumor or the thymus is adherent to it. However, because the evidence currently available does not conclusively establish that TCT is equivalent to resection via sternotomy for thymoma, some surgeons prefer to convert to a sternotomy if a suspicious mass is discovered during transcervical exploration. Certainly, if any difficulty is encountered that might lead to an incomplete thymectomy or incomplete removal of a thymoma, the incision should be extended.

Approximately 90% of patients are able to go home on the same day as their procedure. The most common cause for hospital admission is a pneumothorax that must be monitored or drained.

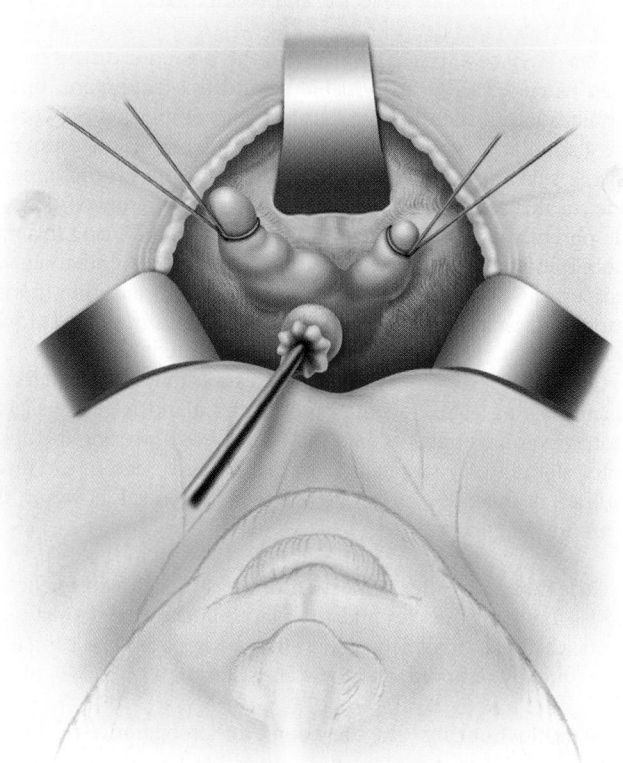

Figure 8 **Resection of anterior mediastinal mass: transcervical approach. A Cooper thymectomy retractor is placed beneath the sternum, and retraction on the upper poles of the thymus is maintained with silk sutures.**

Occasionally, a seroma develops at the site of the incision, but it almost always resolves either spontaneously or after a single percutaneous drainage procedure in the office.

Procedures for Lesions of the Middle Mediastinum

The majority of masses found in the middle mediastinum in adults are malignant, representing either lymphoma or lymph node metastases from primary lung carcinoma. Accordingly, the procedures performed in this anatomic area primarily involve biopsy for staging or diagnosis rather than curative or palliative resection. On infrequent occasions, however, benign or primary malignant lesions of the middle mediastinum occur for which resection is appropriate. In what follows, we briefly discuss resection of such lesions; for the most part, the principles are the same as those underlying resection of masses in the posterior mediastinum [see Procedures for Lesions of the Posterior Mediastinum, below].

Of particular surgical interest in the middle mediastinum are benign cysts, which may arise from the pleura, the pericardium, the airways, or the esophagus. Bronchogenic cysts, which typically develop in proximity to the carina, are probably the middle mediastinal cysts most commonly encountered in clinical practice, with pericardial cysts running a close second. On rare occasions, ectopic remnants from cervical structures (e.g., the parathyroid and thyroid glands) are encountered in this compartment.[16]

PREOPERATIVE EVALUATION

CT generally provides an accurate preoperative diagnosis of a benign middle mediastinal cyst, as well as information regarding abutment of adjacent structures, the consistency of the mass, and potential invasiveness. MRI may be helpful if there is concern that a cyst might actually represent an aberrant vascular structure or an aneurysm, if the simple nature of the cyst is in doubt, or if clearer delineation of suspected invasion of surrounding structures is required. Radionuclide scans (e.g., with technetium-99m or radioactive iodine) may be useful if the differential diagnosis includes a parathyroid or thyroid mass. Cystic structures adjacent to the airways and the esophagus are evaluated by means of bronchoscopy, esophagoscopy, barium esophagography, or some combination of these imaging modalities to rule out communication with the lumina.

OPERATIVE PLANNING

Middle mediastinal cysts that are symptomatic should be treated surgically. However, simple cysts of the middle mediastinum that are asymptomatic and meet all radiographic criteria for benignity may be followed. This conservative approach is often more appropriate for asymptomatic middle mediastinal cysts than for asymptomatic posterior mediastinal cysts, in that complete cyst resection (at least, for bronchogenic cysts) tends to be more complex in the middle mediastinum than in the posterior mediastinum, given the closer proximity to vital structures and the deeper placement within soft tissue. Complete resection of pericardial cysts, on the other hand, typically is easily accomplished by means of VATS; therefore, such cysts are probably best resected when discovered, even if they are asymptomatic. Although VATS resection of subcarinal bronchogenic cysts is feasible and has been described in published reports,[17] it is our experience that in many instances, this approach leaves behind more than a small portion of the cyst wall.

Thus, for a symptomatic subcarinal bronchogenic cyst (a not uncommon occurrence), one is left to choose between (1) thoracotomy for complete resection and (2) some other approach for incomplete resection. Because this area is easily accessible by means of mediastinoscopy, and because we believe that mediastinoscopy both is simpler and causes less morbidity than VATS, we prefer partial resection via mediastinoscopy as the initial approach to these lesions.[18] If cysts treated in this manner recur with associated symptoms, one can always perform thoracotomy for complete resection at that time, and little will have been lost in the meantime.

MEDIASTINOSCOPIC PARTIAL RESECTION OF SUBCARINAL BRONCHOGENIC CYST

Operative Technique

Step 1: mediastinoscopy and pretracheal dissection A standard cervical mediastinoscopy is performed, with dissection in the pretracheal plane down to the level of the carina.

Step 2: freeing of cyst from surrounding tissues With the cyst wall kept intact, as much of the wall as can safely be exposed is visualized by bluntly dissecting it away from the undersurface of the carina and the mainstem bronchi. Next, the mass is dissected away from the soft tissues anterior and posterior to it; obviously, this must be done with caution, given that the right main pulmonary artery and the esophagus are located nearby (anteriorly and posteriorly, respectively).

Step 3: aspiration of cyst contents and excision of exposed cyst wall The contents of the cyst are aspirated for cytologic and microbiologic examination, and the exposed portion of cyst wall is excised. Typically, approximately 50% of the cyst wall can be removed in this fashion. Some of the remaining cyst wall may be cauterized; this too must be done with caution, given the proximity of the adjacent vital structures.

Procedures for Lesions of the Posterior Mediastinum

The majority of posterior mediastinal masses occurring in adults are benign. These lesions may be usefully classified according to their radiologic appearance—that is, as either cystic or solid. Cystic masses in this region typically are bronchogenic cysts or esophageal duplication cysts, whereas solid masses most frequently are benign neurogenic tumors (e.g., schwannomas, neurofibromas, or ganglioneuromas). Esophageal leiomyomas (benign intramuscular tumors within the esophageal wall) are often grouped with these posterior mediastinal lesions and are managed in a similar fashion. In many cases, posterior mediastinal masses come to light as asymptomatic radiographic abnormalities; however, they may also be associated with signs of infection (in the case of infected cysts), dysphagia, chest pain, or respiratory complaints. At present, because of the growing availability of less morbid, minimally invasive approaches to posterior mediastinal masses, most authors recommend resection even when the lesion is asymptomatic. Although this recommendation remains somewhat controversial, we agree with it.

OPERATIVE PLANNING

VATS versus Thoracotomy

Resection of posterior mediastinal masses may be accomplished by means of either VATS or thoracotomy. The procedure is essentially the same with either approach, and the goal is complete resection. With some exceptions, VATS [see 37 Video-Assisted Thoracic Surgery] is considered preferable to thoracotomy in this setting;

Table 2 **Indications for Planned Thoracotomy Approach to Middle or Posterior Mediastinal Mass**

Suggestion of malignancy on preoperative radiography
Presence of inflammation or infection, blurring tissue planes
Large mass (> 5–6 cm)
Esophageal duplication cyst believed to communicate with esophageal lumen on the basis of preoperative CT, barium esophagography, or esophagoscopy
Esophageal lesions without evidence of overlying normal esophageal mucosa on preoperative esophagoscopy or endoscopic ultrasonography
Previous ipsilateral thoracotomy with adhesions
Tumor located at apex of the chest, which may necessitate thoracosternotomy

generally, VATS results in less postoperative pain and quicker functional recovery.[19,20] Some surgeons argue that a VATS approach may be more likely to leave a patient with microscopic residual disease. In our experience and that of others, however, recurrences of these lesions are very rare after VATS excision.[21,22] Given the low recurrence rate and the fact that these masses are almost always benign, we believe that the risk-benefit ratio is better with VATS in most cases.

There are, however, several circumstances in which thoracotomy is indicated from the outset [see Table 2]. A suggestion of malignancy (in particular, invasion of surrounding structures) on preoperative radiography mandates exploration and resection by thoracotomy; in this situation, the potential consequences of positive margins justify the more aggressive approach. The presence of active infection within a cyst is a relative indication for thoracotomy, in that it can cause disruption of normal tissue planes and thereby render VATS dissection more hazardous. Masses larger than approximately 6 cm also call for an open approach: such lesions are typically more difficult to mobilize safely from underlying structures than smaller lesions are, they are more likely to be malignant, and their removal between the ribs is likely to necessitate rib spreading, which may negate some of the benefit of true VATS.

When a cyst is arising from or abutting the esophagus, the possibility of a communication between the cyst and the esophageal

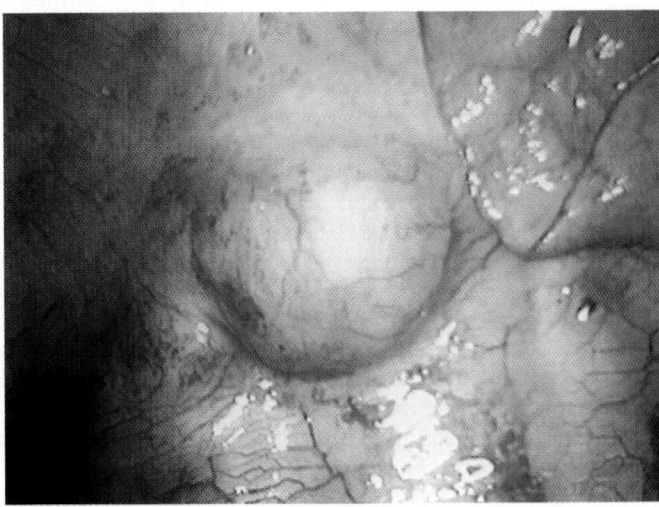

Figure 9 **Resection of neurogenic tumor of posterior mediastinum. Intraoperative photo shows a solid neurogenic tumor of the costovertebral sulcus.**

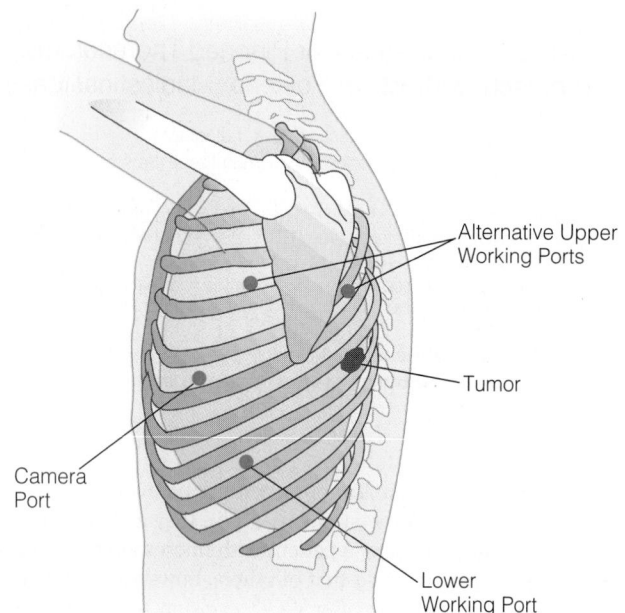

Figure 10 Resection of neurogenic tumor of posterior mediastinum. Shown is typical port placement for VATS resection of a posterior mediastinal mass.

lumen should be investigated preoperatively. Such a communication may be suggested on CT scans by the presence of an air-fluid level. To rule out this phenomenon, we perform barium esophagography during the preoperative workup, followed by intraoperative esophagoscopy at the commencement of the operation. If a communication is identified or cannot be ruled out, thoracotomy is performed. After excision of an esophageal duplication cyst with a communication, reapproximation of the esophageal mucosa is a paramount consideration; in our view, this is best done through an open approach.

In cases of suspected leiomyoma of the esophagus, preoperative investigation should be done to confirm the presence of intact overlying mucosa, which is virtually pathognomonic of this disease. Esophagoscopy is done to assess the mucosa; if the mucosa is intact, the possibility of malignancy is essentially ruled out. Simultaneously, endoscopic ultrasonography may be performed to establish the depth to which the esophageal wall is involved. With a preoperative diagnosis of probable leiomyoma, VATS is the approach of choice in our practice.

So-called dumbbell neurogenic tumors (tumors that invade the neural foramen) are special cases. Any solid mass in the costovertebral sulcus should be evaluated by means of MRI to determine whether it is invading the neural foramen if the absence of invasion was not clearly established by CT. Although invasion of the neural foramen by tumor is not in itself an indication for thoracotomy, it does necessitate a combined anterior-posterior approach with neurosurgical involvement for the intraspinal portion of the procedure. Several versions of such an approach have been described.[23-25] We prefer to perform the posterior neurosurgical resection of the intraspinal component (laminectomy and intervertebral foraminotomy) first, then to reposition the patient and carry out the remainder of the procedure (via VATS or thoracotomy).[26]

Although VATS is often an excellent approach to posterior mediastinal lesions, it must be emphasized that one should never hesitate to convert a VATS procedure to a thoracotomy if required. Accordingly, informed consent to undergo thoracotomy should be

sought before operation from all patients being treated for posterior mediastinal lesions, even when VATS is the intended approach.

VATS RESECTION OF NEUROGENIC TUMOR OF POSTERIOR MEDIASTINUM

Operative Technique

Resection of a solid neurogenic tumor of the posterior mediastinum that does not invade the neural foramen [*see Figure 9*] proceeds as follows.

Step 1: intubation and endoscopy The patient is intubated with a double-lumen endotracheal tube to allow single-lung ventilation. Preoperative bronchoscopy (for cystic lesions) or esophagoscopy (for lesions abutting the esophagus) is performed as indicated (see above).

Step 2: patient positioning and placement of ports The patient is placed in the lateral thoracotomy position and stabilized with bean bags so that the operating table can safely be tilted as much as 45° to either side. With this degree of tilt, the lung tends to fall away from the field of vision; thus, there usually is no need to place an additional port for a lung retractor.

The port for the scope is placed through an incision in the midaxillary line at the level of the mass; if it is placed much more anteriorly than the midaxillary line, the surgeon's view of posterior lesions may be obscured by the lung. The two working ports are placed through separate incisions in the posterior axillary line, made as far cephalad and caudad as possible. Sometimes, placement of an alternative upper working port posterior to the scapula is advantageous [*see Figure 10*]. The main working instruments are an endoscopic scissors-cautery, a ring clamp, an endoscopic peanut dissector, a Maryland dissector, a long right-angle clamp, and an endoscopic clip applier.

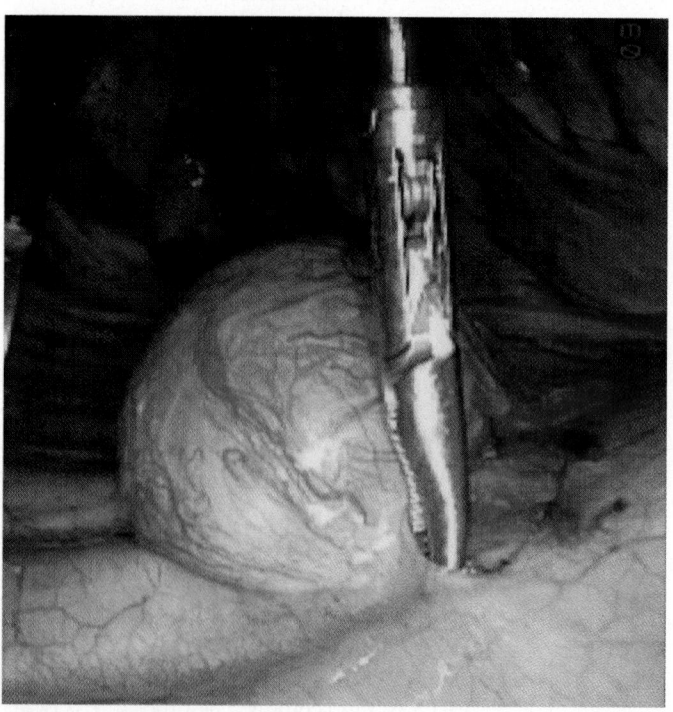

Figure 11 Resection of neurogenic tumor of posterior mediastinum. Shown is circumferential incision of the pleura around a neurogenic mass.

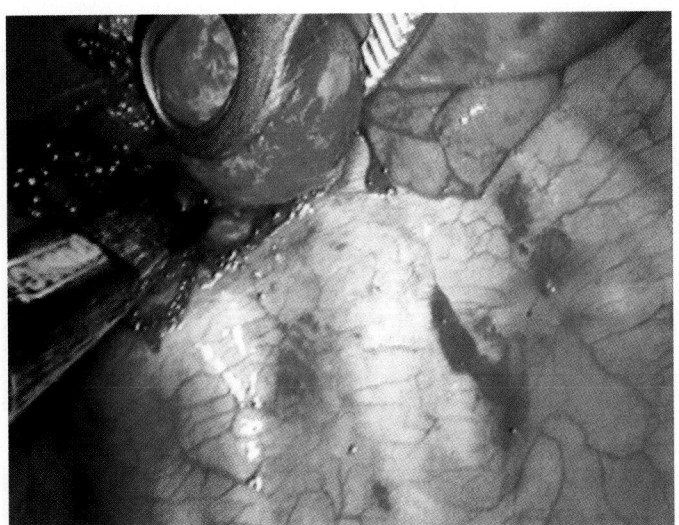

Figure 12 **Resection of neurogenic tumor of posterior mediastinum. The final remaining intercostal stalk is divided.**

Step 3: incision of pleura The parietal pleura is incised around the mass, with a margin of approximately 2 cm circumferentially. The pleura is tented up with the aid of the right-angle clamp or the Maryland dissector to separate it from the underlying structures [*see Figure 11*]. This separation allows the use of the electrocautery, which provides hemostasis while protecting the underlying esophagus, vagus and intercostal nerves, and azygos vein. This dissection and all subsequent work are facilitated by placing gentle traction on the mass with a sponge stick or, for smaller masses, by grasping the entire mass within a ring clamp.

Step 4: dissection of soft tissue attachments Once the pleura has been incised circumferentially, the soft tissue attachments are further dissected bluntly with the endoscopic peanut dissector. Attachments that are relatively thick or vascular are best controlled by double-clipping and division. If the tumor originates from an intercostal nerve, gentle dissection is done beneath the tumor to identify the intercostal bundle that is the source of the lesion.

Step 5: division of source intercostal bundle The source intercostal bundle lateral to the tumor is mobilized, doubly clipped, and divided. Once this has been accomplished, blunt dissection is performed until the nerve root emerging from the neural foramen and the associated intercostal vessels are the last remaining attachments. If the tumor originates from the sympathetic chain, the chain is clipped above and below the tumor, and the intercostal bundle is spared if possible.

Step 6: removal of specimen The remaining stalk is doubly clipped and divided [*see Figure 12*], and the mass is removed in an endoscopic bagging device.

Step 7: drainage A 24 French chest tube is positioned posteriorly at the apex.

Troubleshooting

Care must be taken to ensure that only very gentle traction is exerted on a mass adjacent to the neural foramen. Overzealous traction can cause tearing of the nerve root proximal to the extraspinal extent of the dura, and this tearing can lead to a cere-

brospinal fluid leak, which most often becomes evident only postoperatively (in the form of persistent clear chest tube output). The diagnosis of CSF leakage can be confirmed by measuring the β_2-transferrin level in the fluid. If CSF leakage is confirmed, reoperation with a neurosurgeon is mandatory; the leak is repaired and buttressed with vascularized tissue.

After resection of a tumor at the costovertebral sulcus, regular neurologic examinations of the lower extremities are indicated. Tamponade with hemostatic agents should never be employed for bleeding at the neural foramen: doing so can result in an intraspinal hematoma with subsequent cord compression. Careful use of the electrocautery at the bony margins of the foramen or watchful waiting is preferable. If hemostasis cannot be achieved with these measures, a neurosurgical consultation should be obtained. In the event of oozing from the vicinity of a foramen that is not easily controlled, there should be no hesitation in converting a VATS procedure to an open procedure.

In a minority of patients, clipping and division of an intercostal nerve results in intercostal neuralgia after the procedure; the possibility that this may occur must be discussed with the patient preoperatively. Many patients who undergo division of a lower thoracic intercostal nerve that supplies an upper abdominal dermatome notice postoperative bulging of the ipsilateral abdomen in the area supplied by that nerve.

RESECTION OF BENIGN CYST OF POSTERIOR MEDIASTINUM

Resection of a benign cystic mass of the posterior mediastinum closely resembles resection of a neurogenic tumor [*see* Resection of Neurogenic Tumor of Posterior Mediastinum, *above*]; the differences are relatively minor [*see* Troubleshooting, *below*].

Troubleshooting

In the initial stages of dissection of a benign cyst of the posterior mediastinum, care should be taken not to rupture the cyst; initial mobilization from surrounding structures is easier when the cyst wall is under tension [*see Figure 13*]. If the area of the cyst wall that directly abuts the mediastinum is found to be too adherent to underlying structures to be removed safely, we intentionally rupture the cyst, then remove as much of the cyst wall as possible. As much as 35% of the cyst wall may be left in place. In such cases,

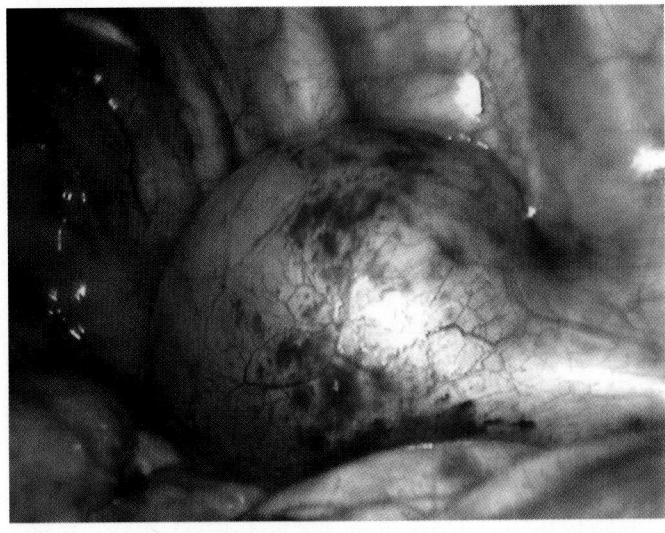

Figure 13 **Resection of benign cyst of posterior mediastinum. Intraoperative photo shows a fluid-filled posterior mediastinal cyst. The tenseness of the cyst wall facilitates initial dissection.**

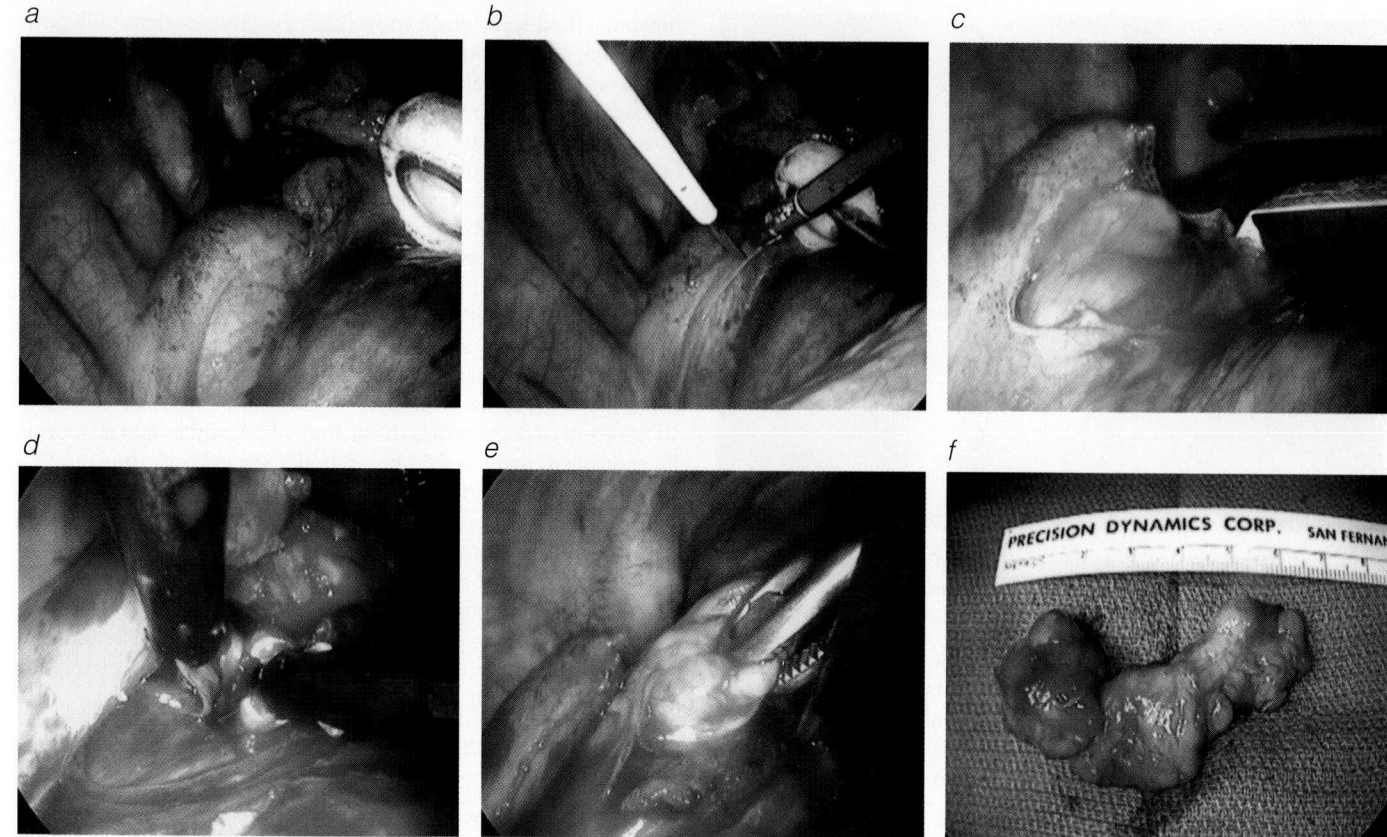

Figure 14 Resection of esophageal leiomyoma. (*a*) Shown is an esophageal leiomyoma beneath the azygos vein. (*b*) The mediastinal pleura overlying the leiomyoma is incised. (*c*) The azygos vein is divided with an endoscopic stapler. (*d*) The muscle fibers overlying the mass are divided. (*e*) Gentle traction is applied to facilitate blunt dissection. (*f*) Shown is a completely resected horseshoe-shaped esophageal leiomyoma.

we ablate the residual intact cyst wall with the electrocautery to destroy any potential secretory tissue. If more than approximately 35% of the cyst must be left in place, conversion to thoracotomy should be considered.

RESECTION OF ESOPHAGEAL LEIOMYOMA

Operative Technique

In addition to the steps described for resection of a neurogenic mass, there are several special maneuvers that facilitate resection of esophageal intramural masses, such as leiomyomata [*see Figure 14a*] and duplication cysts.

1. The pleura is incised longitudinally with the electrocautery after it is tented up away from the esophagus, the vagus nerve, and the azygos vein with a right-angle clamp or a Maryland dissector [*see Figure 14b*].
2. In some cases, exposure is facilitated by dividing the azygos vein with an endoscopic stapler [*see Figure 14c*].
3. The longitudinal esophageal muscle fibers that overlie the mass are separated bluntly or with the electrocautery. These fibers are often markedly attenuated as a result of the expansion of the mass [*see Figure 14d*].
4. Blunt dissection with an endoscopic peanut dissector allows careful, progressive mobilization of the mass, first from the muscle layer and then from the underlying mucosa. Gentle traction on the mass facilitates exposure at this point in the pro-

cedure [*see Figure 14e*]. Having an assistant place the endoscope within the esophageal lumen to distend and illuminate the mucosa also may be helpful at this stage. Once the mass has been completely resected, it is sent for pathologic examination [*see Figure 14f*].
5. The esophagus is distended by insufflating air from above while the distal esophagus is occluded with a sponge stick. The air-filled esophagus is then submerged in saline, and the area of the resection is examined for air leakage.

Troubleshooting

Some surgeons routinely close the muscular defect in the esophagus after resection so as to reduce the risk that an esophageal diverticulum will develop. Such closure may be accomplished by means of thoracoscopic suturing. Often, though, the muscle layer is attenuated to the point where useful reapproximation is nearly impossible. For this reason, as well as because we believe that a diverticulum is unlikely to develop in the absence of a distal functional obstruction, we do not routinely close the muscular defect.

Frequently, duplication cysts are more adherent to the underlying esophageal mucosa than leiomyomata are, and transillumination of the esophageal wall helps define the plane at which blunt dissection should be performed. Where the cyst wall becomes difficult to separate from the mucosa, a small amount of the wall may be left in place if, in the surgeon's judgment, attempting to remove all of it might lead to a breach in the mucosa.

References

1. Hoerbelt R, Keunecke L, Grimm H: The value of a noninvasive diagnostic approach to mediastinal masses. Ann Thorac Surg 75:1086, 2003

2. Koduri P: The diagnostic approach to mediastinal masses. Ann Thorac Surg 78:1888, 2004

3. Vernino S, Lennon VA: Autoantibody profiles and neurological correlations of thymoma. Clin Cancer Res 10:7270, 2004

4. Drevelegas A, Palladas P, Scordalaki A: Mediastinal germ cell tumors: a radio-pathological review. Eur Radiol 11:1925, 2001

5. Schneider DT, Calaminus G, Reinhard H, et al: Primary germ cell tumors in children and adolescents: results of the German cooperative protocols MEKEI 83/86, 89 and 96. J Clin Oncol 18:832, 2000

6. Wood DE: Mediastinal germ cell tumors. Semin Thorac Cardiovasc Surg 12:278, 2000

7. Watanabe M, Takagi K, Aoki T: A comparison of biopsy through a parasternal anterior mediastinotomy under local anesthesia and percutaneous needle biopsy for malignant anterior mediastinal tumors. Surg Today 28:1022, 1998

8. Powers CN, Silverman JF, Geisinger KR, et al: Fine-needle aspiration biopsy of the anterior mediastinum: a multi-institutional analysis. Am J Clin Pathol 105:168, 1996

9. Deeb ME, Brinster CJ, Kucharzuk J, et al: Expanded indication for transcervical thymectomy in the management of anterior mediastinal masses. Ann Thorac Surg 72:208, 2001

10. Savitt MA, Gao G, Furnary AP, et al: Application of robotic-assisted techniques to the surgical evaluation and treatment of the anterior mediastinum.

11. Ann Thorac Surg 79:450, 2005

11. Blalock A, Masoj MF, Riven SS: Myasthenia gravis and tumors of the thymic region. Ann Surg 110:544, 1939

12. Shrager JB, Deeb ME, Mick R, et al: Transcervical thymectomy for myasthenia gravis achieves results comparable to thymectomy by sternotomy. Ann Thorac Surg 74:320, 2002

13. Cooper JD, Al-Jilaihawa AN, Pearson FG, et al: An improved technique to facilitate transcervical thymectomy for myasthenia gravis. Ann Thorac Surg 45:242, 1988

14. Bril V, Kojic J, Ilse WK, et al: Long-term clinical outcome after transcervical thymectomy for myasthenia gravis. Ann Thorac Surg 65:1520, 1998

15. Calhoun RF, Ritter JH, Guthrie TJ, et al: Results of transcervical thymectomy for myasthenia gravis in 100 consecutive patients. Ann Surg 230:555, 1999

16. Nwariaku F, Snyder WH, Burkey SH, et al: Inframanubrial parathyroid glands in patients with primary hyperparathyroidism: alternatives to sternotomy. World J Surg, March 22, 2005 [Epub ahead of print]

17. Demmy TL, Krasna MJ, Detterbeck FC, et al: Multicenter VATS experience with mediastinal tumors. Ann Thorac Surg 66:187, 1998

18. Smythe WR, Bavaria JE, Kaiser LR: Mediastinoscopic subtotal removal of mediastinal cysts. Chest 114:1794, 1998

19. Santambrogio L, Nosotti M, Bellaviti N, et al: Videothoracoscopy versus thoracotomy for the diagnosis of the intermediate solitary pulmonary nodule. Ann Thorac Surg 59:868, 1995

20. Nagahiro I, Andou A, Aoe M, et al: Pulmonary function, postoperative pain, and serum cytokine level after lobectomy: a comparison of VATS and conventional procedure. Ann Thorac Surg 72:362, 2001

21. Martinod E, Pons F, Azorin J, et al: Thoracoscopic excision of mediastinal bronchogenic cysts: results in 20 cases. Ann Thorac Surg 69:1525, 2000

22. Zambudio AR, Lanzas JT, Calvo MJ, et al: Nonneoplastic mediastinal cysts. Eur J Cardiothorac Surg 22:712, 2002

23. Shadmehr MB, Gaissert HA, Wain JC, et al: The surgical approach to "dumbbell tumors" of the mediastinum. Ann Thorac Surg 76:1650, 2003

24. Osada H, Aoki H, Yokote K, et al: Dumbbell neurogenic tumor of the mediastinum: a report of three cases undergoing single-staged complete removal without thoracotomy. Jpn J Surg 21:224, 1991

25. Rzyman W, Skokowski J, Wilimski R, et al: One step removal of dumb-bell tumors by postero-lateral thoracotomy and extended foraminectomy. Eur J Cardiothorac Surg 25:509, 2004

26. Vallieres E, Findlay JM, Fraser RE: Combined microneurosurgical and thorascopic removal of neurogenic dumbbell tumors. Ann Thorac Surg 59:469, 1995

Acknowledgments

Figure 1b   Photo courtesy of Wallace T. Miller, Sr., M.D., University of Pennsylvania School of Medicine.

Figures 2, 7, and 8   Alice Y. Chen.

Figure 10   Tom Moore.

39 PERICARDIAL PROCEDURES

Shari L Meyerson, M.D., and Thomas A. D'Amico, M.D., F.A.C.S.

Surgical procedures are performed on the pericardium either for diagnostic purposes or for relief of the hemodynamic consequences of pericardial disease. The pericardial processes for which intervention is required can be divided into two broad categories: pericardial effusion and constrictive pericarditis. The decisions that must be made regarding the selection of patients, the timing of surgery, and the choice of technique or approach often pose substantial challenges to the surgeon. Accordingly, a thorough knowledge of the anatomy, physiology, and pathophysiology of the pericardium is essential for successful management of pericardial disease processes.

Anatomic and Physiologic Considerations

ANATOMY

Like the pleura, the pericardium consists of two layers. The inner layer, the visceral pericardium (or epicardium), is a monolayer of mesothelial cells that is adherent to the heart. The outer layer, the parietal pericardium, is a tough fibrous structure composed of dense bundles of collagen fibers with occasional elastic fibers. The fibrous structure of this layer renders the pericardial sac relatively noncompliant, and this noncompliance plays a significant role in pericardial function and pathophysiology.

The pericardium surrounds the heart and the great vessels [*see Figure 1*]. Its parietal and visceral surfaces meet superiorly at the ascending aorta and the superior vena cava. From that point, it continues down the right border of the heart and over the anterior surface of the pulmonary veins to the inferior vena cava. After crossing the inferior vena cava, the inferior pericardium is densely adherent to the diaphragm. Just past the apex of the heart, it turns superiorly again and runs over the pulmonary veins back to the aorta.

Anteriorly, there are normally no connections between the visceral and parietal layers of the pericardium. Posteriorly, the pattern of pericardial reflections around the pulmonary veins and the venae cavae creates two sinuses. The oblique pericardial sinus is the space in the center of the pulmonary veins, directly behind the left atrium. The transverse pericardial sinus is bordered anteriorly by the aorta and the main pulmonary artery and posteriorly by the dome of the left atrium and the superior vena cava.

PHYSIOLOGY

The pericardium is normally filled with 15 to 50 ml of serous fluid, which serves as lubrication to facilitate the motion of the heart within this structure. By virtue of its relative noncompliance, the pericardium exerts an influence on cardiac hemodynamics. This influence can easily be seen in the normal inspiratory varia-

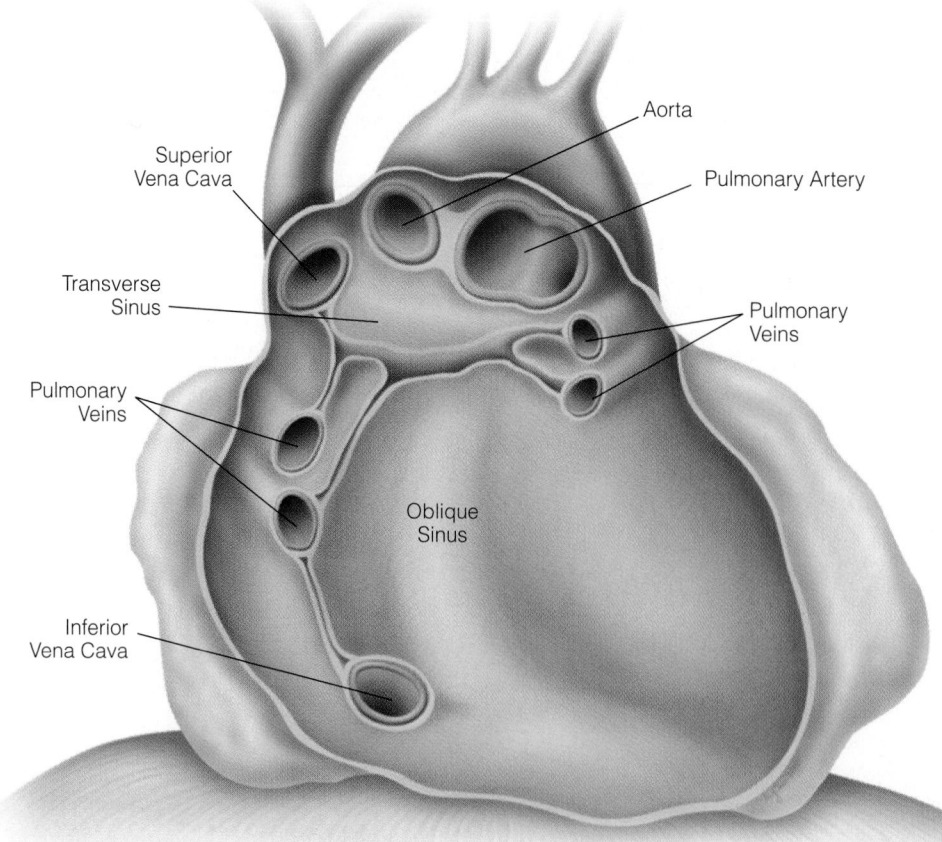

Aorta

Superior
Vena Cava

Pulmonary Artery

Transverse
Sinus

Pulmonary
Veins

Pulmonary
Veins

Oblique
Sinus

Inferior
Vena Cava

Figure 1 **Shown is a view of the pericardium with the heart removed.**

Table 1   Causes of Constrictive Pericarditis

Common causes	Unknown
	Infection
	  Tuberculosis
	  Viral infection (coxsackievirus B)
	  Bacterial infection
	  Fungal infection (histoplasmosis, coccidioidomycosis)
	  Parasitic infection (amebiasis, echinococcosis)
	Cardiac surgery or pacemaker insertion
	Penetrating, nonpenetrating, or iatrogenic trauma
	Radiation therapy
	Connective tissue disorders (rheumatoid arthritis, systemic lupus erythematosus, scleroderma)
	Renal failure
	Neoplasm
	  Metastatic disease (breast, lung, lymphatic system, skin)
	  Primary mesothelioma
	Drugs (procainamide, methysergide, hydralazine)

Uncommon causes	Myocardial infarction Asbestosis Amyloidosis Sarcoidosis Dermatomyositis Actinomycosis Lassa fever Whipple disease Mulibrey nanism

tion in systemic arterial pressure. Under normal circumstances, intrapericardial pressure is slightly less than 0 mm Hg, becoming more negative during inspiration and less negative during expiration. Negative intrathoracic pressure during inspiration augments right ventricular filling. Because the pericardium does not allow significant acute right ventricular dilation, the ventricular cavity enlarges by shifting the septum toward the left ventricle. In addition, the noncompliance of the pericardium prevents the free wall of the left ventricle from distending to recapture its normal cavitary volume. Thus, the volume ejected from the left ventricle is slightly decreased, resulting in lower systemic arterial pressure. Normally, this effect is exceedingly small. However, it becomes more pronounced when the pericardium is filled with fluid: ventricular distention is restricted even further, and paradoxical pulse becomes clinically apparent.

Although the pericardium is resistant to rapid distention, it is capable of distending over time. If filled slowly, it can expand to contain significant amounts of fluid (sometimes more than 1 L) before hemodynamic consequences develop. In the setting of an acute pericardial effusion (e.g., from trauma), however, devastating hemodynamic consequences may occur with only 100 to 200 ml of blood in the pericardium. When the elastic capacity of the pericardium is exceeded, even small increases in volume cause large increases in intrapericardial pressure.

Constrictive pericarditis is defined as a chronic fibrous thickening of the pericardium that causes cardiac compression sufficient to prevent normal diastolic filling. It can best be thought of as the chronic sequela of acute pericarditis or of any situation resulting in pericardial irritation and adhesion formation. Almost any cause of acute pericarditis can result in pericardial constriction [see Table 1]. In many patients, there is no clear antecedent event, and the cause of the constrictive pericarditis cannot be determined with certainty. Pathologic examination typically demonstrates end-stage fibrosis, and these cases are presumed to be viral in origin. Historically, mycobacterial tuberculosis has been the most common infectious

cause of constrictive pericarditis, and it is still the dominant infectious cause in many developing countries today.[1,2] In the United States, tuberculosis is the cause of constrictive pericarditis in approximately 6% of patients who undergo pericardiectomy.[3] Constrictive pericarditis also occurs after instrumentation of the pericardium and is seen occasionally (in 0.2% to 0.3% of cases) after cardiac surgery.[4,5] It also may develop after iatrogenic cardiac perforation in the course of catheterization or pacemaker placement and after blunt or penetrating trauma—essentially, after any process resulting in an incompletely drained hemopericardium.[6,7]

The pericardium may harbor metastatic disease or locally advanced disease (e.g., mesothelioma), which may lead to pericardial constriction.[8,9] Connective tissue disorders (e.g., rheumatoid arthritis and lupus) can cause recurrent acute pericarditis and pericardial effusions, eventually resulting in constrictive pericarditis. A similar situation may arise in patients receiving radiation therapy and patients with renal failure.

The stiffening and thickening of the pericardium have three major physiologic effects. First, the thicker pericardium isolates the heart from changes in intrathoracic pressure. Normally, the pulmonary veins (which are intrathoracic structures) and the cardiac chambers experience the same changes in intrathoracic pressure. In the presence of pericardial constriction, however, the negative intrathoracic pressure generated during inspiration cannot be transmitted to the heart. This isolation of the heart results in decreased flow through the pulmonary veins during inspiration and reduced left-side filling.

Second, the ventricles become interdependent. Because total pericardial volume does not change, the inspiratory decrease in left ventricular filling seen with constriction must be accompanied by an increase in right ventricular filling, with a resultant septal shift toward the left ventricle. During expiration, the opposite occurs: left ventricular filling increases and right ventricular filling decreases, and there is a septal shift toward the right ventricle.

Third, the encasement of the heart impairs the diastolic filling of all cardiac chambers. Elevated atrial pressure causes rapid initial filling of the ventricle (with as much as 75% of the ventricle filled during the first 25% of diastole), but by the middle of diastole, filling abruptly decreases as a result of the rigid pericardium. Because of this limit to diastolic filling, increasing the heart rate becomes the most effective method of increasing cardiac output.[10]

Pericardial Drainage Procedures for Pericardial Effusion

A number of different processes can result in the accumulation of fluid in the pericardial space [see Table 2]. Regardless of the origin of the fluid accumulation, once the pericardium has reached the limits of its elasticity, the only way in which it can increase its volume is by reducing the volume occupied by the heart within it. Increases in pericardial pressure result in progressive cardiac compression and reductions in intracardiac volumes and myocardial

Table 2   Common Causes of Pericardial Effusion

Malignancy	Myocardial infarction
Trauma	Iatrogenesis (intracardiac procedures)
Uremia	
Infection (viral, bacterial, fungal, tubercular)	Aortic dissection
	Radiation
Autoimmune processes	Idiopathic origin
Cardiac surgery (postoperative complication)	

diastolic compliance. This effect is most pronounced in the chambers with the lowest normal intracavitary pressures—namely, the right atrium and the right ventricle.[11] Changes in systemic cardiac output occur as a result of right heart compression, which leads to diminished right ventricular stroke volume, reduced pulmonary blood flow, and decreased left ventricular filling. In the early stages of pericardial effusion, various compensatory changes act to preserve cardiac output. Such changes include an increased ejection fraction, tachycardia, increased intravascular volume via renal conservation of salt and water, increased peripheral vascular resistance, and time-dependent pericardial stretch.[12,13]

PREOPERATIVE EVALUATION

The presenting symptoms of pericardial effusion may be nonspecific and related to the underlying disorder (e.g., fever, chest pressure, and fatigue). Fluid accumulation that is substantial enough to have hemodynamic consequences is defined as cardiac tamponade. Patients with early tamponade may have dyspnea, tachycardia, mild hypotension, decreased urine output, and paradoxical pulse. As tamponade progresses, patients may manifest signs of end-organ hypoperfusion (e.g., mental status changes, renal insufficiency, and shock). The classic physical findings known as Beck's triad (i.e., jugular venous distention, systemic hypotension, and distant heart sounds) are more common with acute tamponade (such as results from trauma) than with slow-developing tamponade (such as results from medical processes). In patients with slow-developing tamponade, systemic fluid retention is observed, often manifested by peripheral edema or ascites.

Most commonly, pericardial effusion is diagnosed when a patient exhibits new symptoms in the context of an underlying disorder associated with pericardial effusion (e.g., renal failure or malignancy). Chest x-rays may reveal a globular heart or an increasing cardiac silhouette on serial films. Currently, echocardiography is the most commonly employed and most useful modality for the diagnosis of pericardial effusion: it reliably determines the presence, location, and relative volume of fluid accumulations. In many cases, echocardiography can identify early tamponade, often before symptoms develop. A variety of echocardiographic findings have been associated with pericardial effusion, of which the most useful are right atrial collapse and right ventricular collapse. Right atrial collapse during late diastole tends to occur early in the development of tamponade because of the normally low right atrial filling pressures. Right ventricular free wall collapse during early diastole suggests progression of tamponade. Other useful signs are loss of the normal inspiratory collapse of the inferior vena cava and an increase in right ventricular diameter with a reciprocal decrease in left ventricular diameter during inspiration.

In patients who are undergoing invasive hemodynamic monitoring (e.g., those who have just undergone cardiac surgery), hemodynamic findings suggestive of tamponade include elevation of right atrial pressure and equalization of right atrial pressure and pulmonary capillary wedge pressure. It is important to remember, however, that localized tamponade can occur (especially in the postoperative period) without these changes. A common cause is localized clot in the oblique pericardial sinus behind the left atrium, which causes reduced left atrial compliance.

OPERATIVE PLANNING

Choice of Procedure

There are three procedures that are commonly performed for surgical diagnosis and treatment of pericardial effusion: peri-

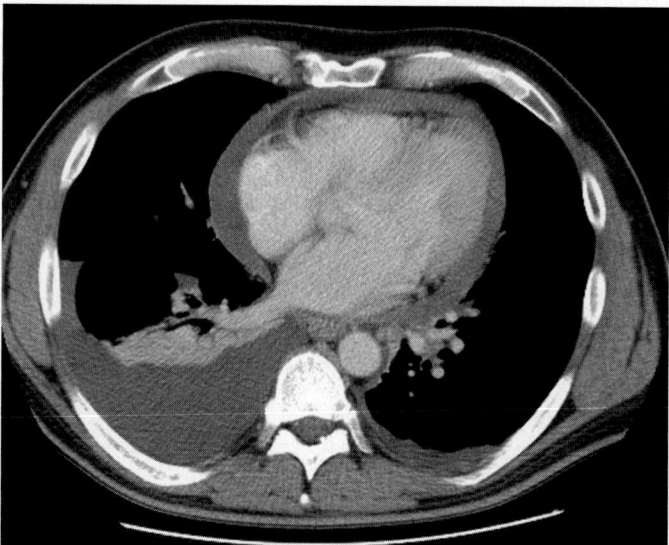

Figure 2 **Computed tomography demonstrates right pleural and pericardial effusions, for which a right thoracoscopic approach is ideal.**

cardiocentesis, subxiphoid pericardiostomy (pericardial window), and thoracoscopic pericardiostomy (via either the right or the left pleural space). The choice of a surgical approach to the pericardial space depends on the clinical condition of the patient, as well as on the underlying diagnosis (if known). Patients with tamponade may decompensate rapidly during the vasodilatation and positive pressure ventilation associated with general anesthesia. Accordingly, careful consideration must be given to the type of anesthesia employed for pericardial drainage procedures.

Pericardiocentesis is routinely done with local anesthesia only, and it may be the best choice in an acutely unstable patient with tamponade. If this option is chosen, however, the choice must be made with the understanding that pericardiocentesis, because of its high recurrence rate and its limited diagnostic capacity, is unlikely to constitute definitive therapy. Subxiphoid pericardiostomy is generally done with initial local anesthesia followed by induction of general anesthesia, and most patients with tamponade can undergo this procedure. The subxiphoid approach provides the hemodynamic benefits of pericardiocentesis, offers the enhanced diagnostic capability of pericardial biopsy, and has a low recurrence rate. Consequently, it is the procedure of choice for patients with tamponade who are stable enough to be transported to the operating suite. Thoracoscopic pericardiostomy has the advantage of enabling simultaneous treatment of pleural processes, which are commonly present in these patients [*see Figure 2*]. Ipsilateral pleural and pericardial spaces can be fully explored, pleural effusions can be drained, loculations can be divided, and biopsy specimens can be obtained as needed. The thoracoscopic approach can be especially useful in the case of a known loculated effusion that is limited to one area of the pericardium, in that a pericardial window can be created via either pleural space. This approach also allows resection of a larger segment of pericardium, which may improve the diagnostic yield and reduce the likelihood of recurrent effusion. The major limitation of thoracoscopic pericardiostomy is the need for lung isolation and lateral positioning, which should not be attempted in patients with evidence of tamponade. By weighing the relative risks and benefits of these three procedures, the surgeon can choose the optimal approach for each patient.

PERICARDIOCENTESIS

Operative Technique

Pericardiocentesis is performed either at the bedside in an urgent situation or, preferably, under echocardiographic guidance in a catheterization laboratory. The basic technique is simple.

Step 1: placement of needle A local anesthetic is infiltrated along the left side of the xiphoid. An 18-gauge spinal needle attached to a three-way stopcock and syringe is then advanced into the pericardial space and directed cephalad toward the left shoulder at a 45° angle until fluid is aspirated [*see Figure 3*]; if air is aspirated, the needle is withdrawn and redirected more medially. Once fluid is aspirated freely, it is inspected. If the fluid is bloody, 5 ml is withdrawn and placed on a sponge. If the fluid on the sponge clots, it is fresh blood, probably from a cardiac injury occurring during the procedure or from intracardiac positioning of the needle; blood that has been in the pericardium for even a short time becomes defibrinated and will not clot.[14]

Troubleshooting. The inherent danger of cardiac injury during pericardiocentesis should be obvious. The risk is highest with small or loculated effusions and patients with coagulation abnormalities. The possibility of cardiac aspiration or injury can be minimized, though not eliminated, by means of various safety measures. The simplest of these measures is to attach an ECG lead to the needle and employ continuous ECG monitoring. If the needle contacts the epicardium, ST segment elevation will be observed, in which case the needle is withdrawn until the ST elevation disappears. Another useful safety measure is to employ echocardiographic guidance to help direct aspiration of a loculated area. Simultaneous cardiac catheterization has also been used to locate the right coronary artery and the atrioventricular groove.

Step 2: placement of drainage catheter and aspiration of fluid Once the needle is within the pericardial space, a guide wire is placed through it, and a small-bore drainage catheter is advanced into the effusion by means of a modified Seldinger technique. Fluid is aspirated and sent for laboratory evaluation (including cell count, chemistry, culture, and cytology). The catheter is then connected to a closed drainage system for 24 to 72 hours; this may help reduce recurrence.

Complications

The most common complications of pericardiocentesis are pneumothorax, cardiac injury, misdiagnosis, and recurrence of pericardial effusion. In every patient undergoing pericardiocentesis, pneumothorax must be ruled out by means of chest x-ray at the completion of the procedure or, if respiratory or hemodynamic changes develop intraoperatively, during the procedure. Cardiac injuries range from minor needle lacerations to the epicardium, which are self-limited in patients with normal coagulation parameters, to potentially fatal injuries that lead to acute cardiac tamponade. Incorrect diagnoses based on pericardiocentesis are not uncommon. Although a diagnosis can be confirmed by positive results from fluid culture or cytology, negative results from cytology do not rule out malignant effusion. Cytologic analysis of pericardial fluid is diagnostic in only 55% to 85% of patients.[15] Further diagnostic maneuvers often must be undertaken, usually involving subxiphoid or thoracoscopic approaches with pericardial biopsy. Recurrence of pericardial effusion after pericardiocentesis is extremely common. In a review that included 139 patients with malignant pericardial effusions who were treated with pericardio-

centesis, successful fluid removal with symptomatic relief was achieved in 97.1% of cases.[16] Of the 139 patients, 2.9% experienced complications (e.g., pneumothorax and ventricular laceration), and one (0.7%) died. In all, 45 of the patients received no further therapy, and in 25 (55%) of the 45, recurrent effusions developed that necessitated reintervention.

Several techniques for preventing recurrent pericardial effusion have been tried. Instillation of a sclerosing agent (e.g., tetracycline, thiotepa, or bleomycin) into the pericardium to promote fusion of the two layers of the pericardium has been shown to increase the success rate of pericardiocentesis by as much as 85%.[17-19] Placement of an indwelling catheter (see above) also has been shown to improve the success rate.[16,20] Several authors have described creating a pericardial window percutaneously by means of balloon dilation of the tract created by pericardiocentesis, which theoretically allows fluid to drain into the pleural space or the subcutaneous tissues, where it can be absorbed.[21,22] However, it is unclear how long a window created in this fashion will remain patent. Although pericardiocentesis provides initial symptomatic relief in most patients, the observation that 15% to 45% of patients require a further procedure for diagnosis and as many as 55% require reintervention for recurrence has led some authorities to question its benefit.

SUBXIPHOID PERICARDIOSTOMY (PERICARDIAL WINDOW)

Operative Technique

Subxiphoid pericardiostomy may be performed either to diagnose pericardial effusion or to manage tamponade. For diagnosis, the procedure is usually done with general anesthesia. In an unstable patient with significant tamponade, who would be at risk for hemodynamic collapse with general anesthesia, the procedure may be performed with the patient under local anesthesia and mild sedation and breathing spontaneously. If there is any question of tamponade, the patient is prepared and draped while awake, and anesthesia is induced only when the surgeon is ready to begin. In all patients, the entire chest should be prepared, in case a full sternotomy is required. Ideally, the patient is sedated and the airway

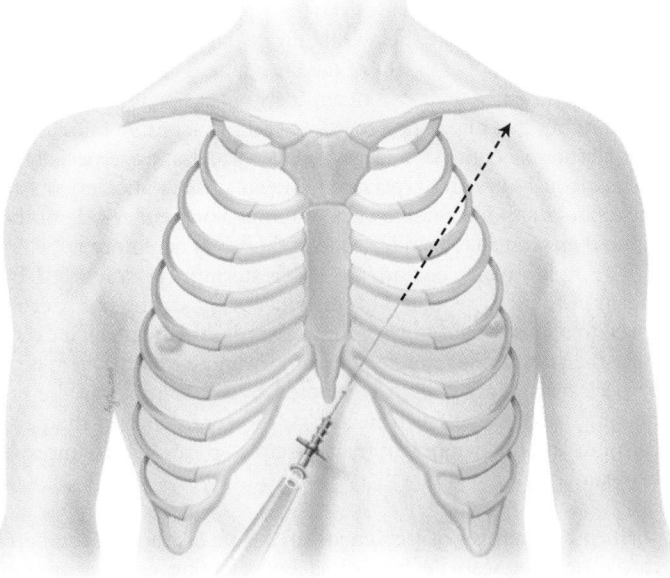

Figure 3 **Pericardiocentesis. The needle is angled toward the left shoulder at an angle of 45°.**

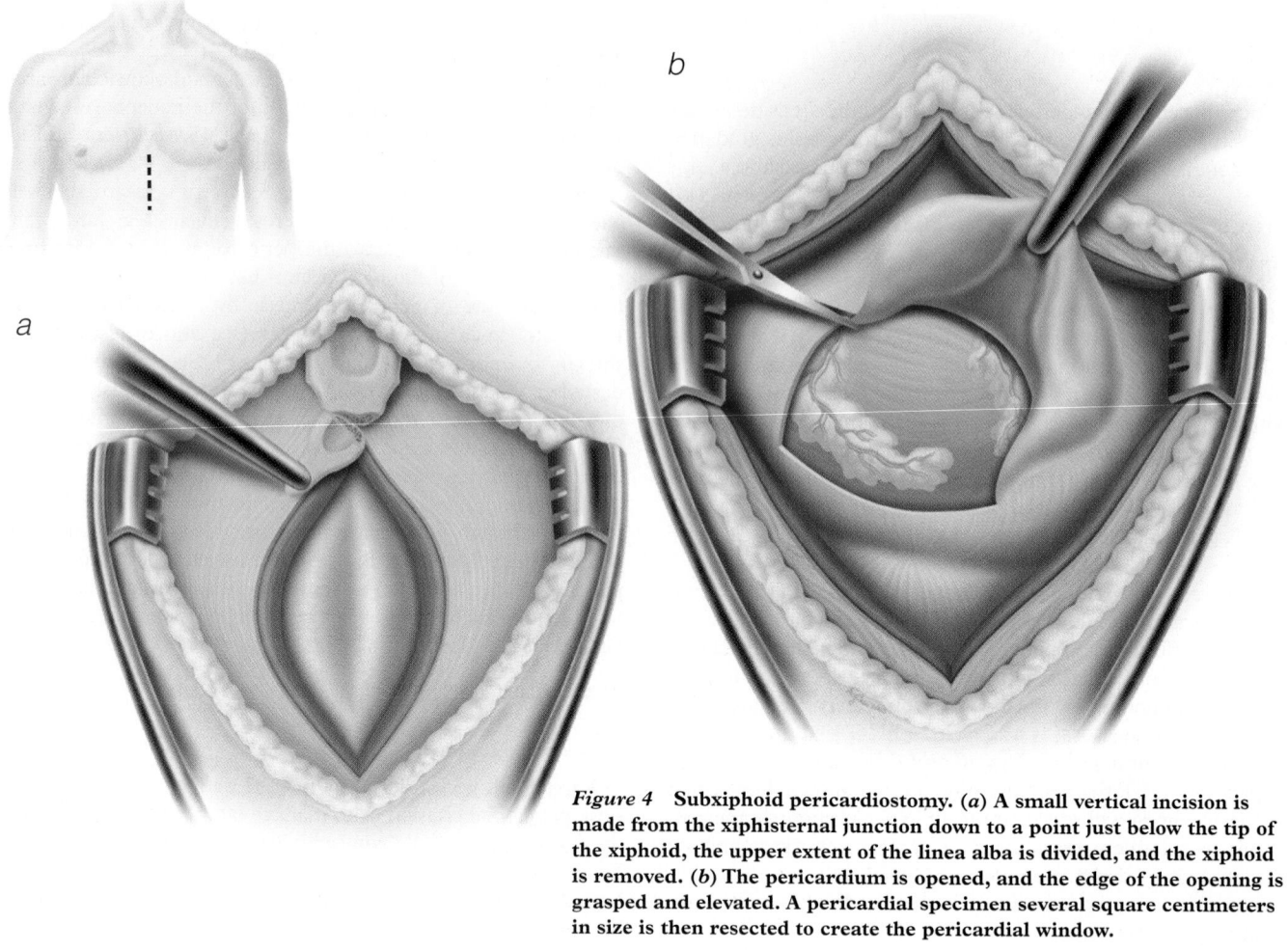

Figure 4 Subxiphoid pericardiostomy. (*a*) A small vertical incision is made from the xiphisternal junction down to a point just below the tip of the xiphoid, the upper extent of the linea alba is divided, and the xiphoid is removed. (*b*) The pericardium is opened, and the edge of the opening is grasped and elevated. A pericardial specimen several square centimeters in size is then resected to create the pericardial window.

controlled while spontaneous respiration is maintained to minimize hemodynamic effects. If necessary, a local anesthetic may be infiltrated and the incision made before induction of anesthesia.

Step 1: initial incision and exposure of pericardium   A small vertical incision is made from the xiphisternal junction downward to a point slightly below the tip of the xiphoid process [*see Figure 4a*]. The upper extent of the linea alba is divided, with care taken not to enter the peritoneum. Peritoneal openings are easily repaired but can make the procedure technically more difficult, in that abdominal contents tend to impede visualization, especially in spontaneously breathing patients. The soft tissue attachments to the xiphoid are divided, the veins running along either side of the xiphoid are controlled, and the xiphoid process is removed.

The tissue plane behind the lower sternum is developed by means of blunt dissection. This maneuver exposes the retrosternal space to allow visualization of the pericardium. To enhance exposure, the sternum is retracted upward by an assistant. The anterior pericardial surface is then exposed by sweeping away the remaining mediastinal fat. If necessary, the confluence of the pericardium and the diaphragm may be retracted caudally to improve exposure.

Step 2: opening of pericardium   The location of the pericardial incision can be confirmed by palpating cardiac motion through the exposed pericardium. The pericardium is then opened with a scalpel; shallow strokes should be employed to reduce the chances of injuring underlying myocardium that may be adherent

to the pericardium. Upon entry into the pericardium, there is an initial outrush of fluid. A sanguineous effusion can be difficult to differentiate from cardiac injury; therefore, the patient's hemodynamics should be carefully monitored during this time. When the pressure placed on the heart by an effusion is released, blood pressure will usually rise and heart rate fall; however, if the heart has been accidentally injured, the opposite will occur. Once hemodynamic stability is achieved, administration of a diuretic (e.g., furosemide) should be considered to reduce the risk of pulmonary edema developing as a result of systemic fluid retention.

Step 3: creation of pericardial window   Pericardial fluid is collected for microbiologic and cytologic analysis and for any additional testing suggested by the clinical scenario. The pericardial space is gently explored with the fingers, and all remaining fluid is evacuated. The edge of the pericardial opening is grasped with a clamp and elevated [*see Figure 4b*]. A pericardial specimen several square centimeters in size—or as large as can safely be managed—is resected and sent for pathologic and microbiologic analysis.

Step 4: drainage and closure   A separate stab incision for drain placement is made below and to one side of the lowermost aspect of the skin incision. Bringing the drainage tube out through a separate incision helps prevent incisional complications (e.g., infection and hernia). A 24 to 28 French chest tube (either straight or right-angle) is tunneled through the fascia at the entry site so that it lies beneath the divided linea alba in the preperitoneal space. The tube is then directed through the pericardial window and into the pericardial space and secured at skin level. The fascia at the linea alba is closed with interrupted sutures to provide secure closure and prevent late hernia; the skin and subcutaneous tissue are closed in the standard fashion. The chest tube is connected to a drainage system with a water seal. Pericardial drainage is maintained for several days postoperatively until the output falls below 100 ml/day. This period allows time for apposition and adhesion formation between the visceral pericardium and the parietal pericardium.

Although some fluid may initially drain into the subcutaneous tissues and be absorbed, the name pericardial window is something of a misnomer. The surgically created window in the pericardium is unlikely to remain patent over the long term, and in fact, obliteration of the pericardial space has been shown to be the mechanism responsible for the success of this procedure.[23,24]

Complications

Complications from subxiphoid pericardiostomy are rare; bleeding, infection, incisional hernia, anesthetic complications, and cardiac injury have been reported. In a study that included 155 patients who underwent subxiphoid pericardiostomy over a 5-year period, not a single death was attributable to the operative procedure itself.[23] The 30-day mortality was high but was related to the underlying disease process: 33% in patients with malignant effusions and 5% in those with benign effusions. Recurrent pericardial effusion necessitating additional procedures occurred in four patients (2.5%). In a study that compared 94 patients who underwent subxiphoid pericardiostomy with 23 patients who underwent pericardiocentesis, the rate of recurrent effusion that necessitated reintervention was 1.1% after subxiphoid window but 30.4% after pericardiocentesis.[25] In this series, the rate of major complications after the pericardial window procedure was 1.1% (one patient with bleeding that necessitated reexploration), compared with a major complication rate of 17% after pericardiocentesis (including a mortality of 4%).

Several studies have shown that the most important predictor of long-term outcome is the underlying disease process. In one, the median survival time was 800 days for patients with benign disease, 105 days for patients with known cancer but negative results from pericardial cytology and pathology, and only 56 days for patients with malignant effusions.[23] It appears, however, that cancer patients with hematologic malignancies and pericardial effusion survive significantly longer than patients with other malignancies. In another study, the mean survival time after drainage of pericardial effusion was 20 months for patients with hematologic malignancies, compared with 5 months for patients with any other malignancies.[26] The investigators suggested that this finding may be related to the relative responsiveness of hematologic cancers to systemic chemotherapy. Patients with HIV disease have been shown to have universally dismal outcomes after they present with pericardial effusion. In this population, surgical pericardial drainage generally is not diagnostically revealing and is of little therapeutic value. Several authors have questioned whether pericardial drainage should even be offered to these patients.[27]

THORACOSCOPIC PERICARDIOSTOMY

Operative Technique

Thoracoscopic pericardiostomy is a safe and effective approach to the diagnosis and management of pericardial effusion, especially in patients with a unilateral pleural disease process that can be simultaneously addressed in the course of the procedure. Tho-racoscopic pericardial drainage necessitates single-lung ventilation and thus is unsuitable for unstable patients, especially those with tamponade. Such ventilation can be accomplished by means of either a dual-lumen endotracheal tube or a bronchial blocker placed through a standard endotracheal tube.

Once the tube is in place, the patient is turned to the appropriate lateral decubitus position. The side of approach is chosen on the basis of the location of a loculated effusion or the site of any coexisting pathologic condition (e.g., a pleural effusion or pulmonary nodule). If the disease process or processes present do not dictate a particular side of approach, the right side is frequently preferred. It is often easier to operate on the right side because there is more working room within the pleural space; however, operating on the left side usually allows the surgeon to create a larger pericardial window. If tamponade is present in a patient for whom the thoracoscopic approach is desired, pericardiocentesis may be performed before induction of general anesthesia.[28]

Step 1: placement of ports and entry into pleural space
An initial camera port is placed in the posterior axillary line at the eighth intercostal space [see Figure 5]. The pleural space is entered and explored, and any effusion present is drained. Pleural fluid is sent separately for culture and cytologic analysis. To prevent inadvertent entry into the pericardium, which is often distended, a second incision is created anteriorly at the fifth intercostal space under camera visualization.

Step 2: opening of pericardium On the left side, the phrenic nerve, which runs midway between the hilum and the anterior chest wall, is carefully identified, and an initial pericardial incision is made approximately 1 cm anterior to this nerve. Care must be taken to place this first incision in an area that is free of cardiac adhesions. When grasped, the pericardium should tent outward slightly. Often, cardiac motion is visible through the pericardium.

Step 3: creation of pericardial window A pericardial window several square centimeters in area is removed. A similar window may be created posterior to the phrenic nerve—again, with care taken to stay at least 1 cm away from the nerve. The pericardial space is inspected, and any loculations are opened. The procedure is similar when performed on the right side, except that the phrenic nerve on the right runs much closer to the hilum; accordingly, instead of two pericardial windows (anterior and posterior to the nerve), only a single, larger pericardial window is created (anterior to the nerve).

In patients who can tolerate general anesthesia, a pericardial window can be created thoracoscopically with excellent diagnostic yield and relief of symptoms.[29] The thoracoscopic approach allows directed access and can be useful in treating effusions that recur after subxiphoid pericardiostomy.[30]

Pericardiectomy for Constrictive Pericarditis

PREOPERATIVE EVALUATION

Constrictive pericarditis appears to be about three times as common in males as in females, and it may occur at any point in life from childhood to the ninth decade.[31] The symptoms of constrictive pericarditis usually develop progressively over a period of years but may develop within weeks to months after a defined inciting event (e.g., mediastinal irradiation or cardiac surgery). Signs and symptoms are related to pulmonary venous congestion

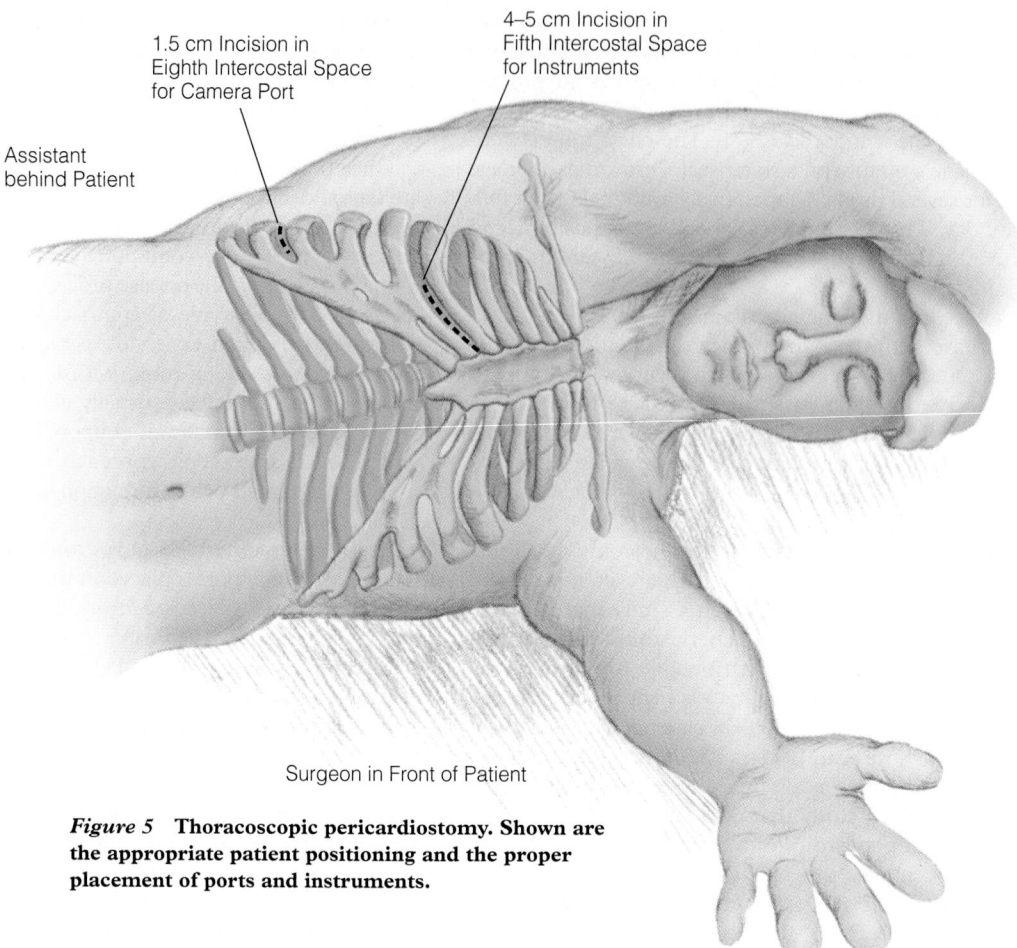

1.5 cm Incision in
Eighth Intercostal Space
for Camera Port

4–5 cm Incision in
Fifth Intercostal Space
for Instruments

Assistant
behind Patient

Surgeon in Front of Patient

Figure 5 **Thoracoscopic pericardiostomy. Shown are the appropriate patient positioning and the proper placement of ports and instruments.**

(e.g., exertional dyspnea) and systemic venous congestion (e.g., elevated jugular venous pressure, hepatomegaly, ascites, and peripheral edema).

The physiologic effects of the thickened pericardium form the basis for the diagnosis of constrictive pericarditis and, more important, for the differentiation of constrictive pericarditis from restrictive cardiomyopathy, which often presents a similar picture. Echocardiography can be employed to rule out other causes of right-side failure. Specific findings that suggest pericardial constriction include septal bounce (a respiratory phase–related septal shift) and decreased transmitral flow velocity during inspiration. Computed tomography and magnetic resonance imaging may demonstrate thickened, often calcified, pericardium; however, the degree of pericardial thickening does not necessarily correlate with the presence of hemodynamic effects.

Cardiac catheterization may demonstrate increases in and equalization of end-diastolic pressure in all four cardiac chambers, a dip-and-plateau pattern (the square-root sign) in the ventricular pressure curves as a result of rapid early filling and limited late filling, and rapid x and y descents in the atrial pressure curves. The most useful information obtainable through cardiac catheterization has to do with the respiratory variation of ventricular pressure. In a patient with a normal heart or a patient with restrictive cardiomyopathy, inspiration causes a decrease in both right ventricular pressure and left ventricular pressure as a consequence of decreased intrathoracic pressure. In a patient with constrictive pericarditis, because of the interdependence of the ventricles, inspiration causes a decrease in left ventricular pressure but an increase in right ventricular pressure.[32]

OPERATIVE PLANNING

Choice of Approach

Pericardiectomy may be performed via either a median sternotomy or a left anterolateral thoracotomy, with equivalent results. Median sternotomy provides better access to the right atrium and the great vessels, as well as easier access for cannulation if cardiopulmonary bypass is required; left anterolateral thoracotomy allows more complete release of the left ventricle. With either approach, the patient should undergo full monitoring, including radial artery catheterization and central venous catheterization, with consideration given to placement of a pulmonary arterial catheter if there is significant hemodynamic compromise. Because significant blood loss can occur when densely adherent pericardium is resected, large-bore intravenous access should be available as well.

OPERATIVE TECHNIQUE

Median Sternotomy

Step 1: initial incision and exposure The patient is placed in the supine position, and the skin incision is carried down to the level of the sternum. If there is no history of previous pericardial procedures and it is possible to develop the plane behind the sternum bluntly at the superior and inferior aspects, a standard sternotomy saw can be used for the median sternotomy. If, however, there are likely to be adhesions between the sternum and the pericardium or the heart (as in the case of constrictive pericarditis after coronary artery bypass grafting), a careful reoperative sternotomy should be performed with an oscillating saw. Access to the femoral vessels should be available within the sterile field; placement of a femoral arterial line will facilitate percutaneous cannulation in the event that the heart is injured during sternal reentry.

After the sternum is opened, all adhesions are dissected away from the sternum, with care taken to stay as close to the posterior surface of the sternum as possible. Both pleural spaces are opened, and the left and right phrenic nerves are identified.

Step 2: dissection and resection of pericardium The phrenic nerves define the limits of pericardial resection bilaterally. Small loculated spaces are often present within the pericardium, especially near the great vessels and the diaphragm, and provide good starting places for pericardiectomy. Once an initial flap is raised, it is used to provide retraction to facilitate further dissection. Careful attention must be paid to the coronary artery anatomy: coronary arteries and bypass grafts are vulnerable to injury. If the pericardium is densely adherent in the region of a coronary artery, small islands of pericardium may be left on the heart. Areas of calcification can be addressed with the use of bone-cutting instruments; however, if an island of calcification appears to extend into the myocardium, it should not be removed.

Epicardium can also be involved in the disease process and should be resected or scored until no further restriction to ventricular filling remains. The heart should be dissected free of the left

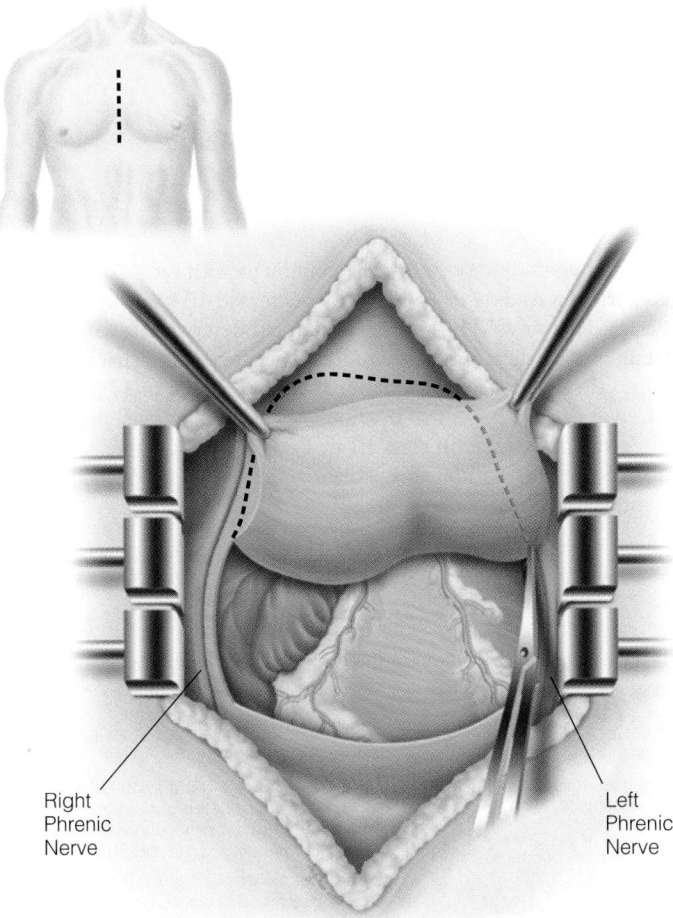

Figure 6 **Pericardiectomy: median sternotomy approach. The pericardium is resected from the left phrenic nerve to the right phrenic nerve.**

Right Phrenic Nerve

Left Phrenic Nerve

pulmonary veins all the way over to the right pulmonary veins (including the origins of the venae cavae). The pericardium is resected from the left phrenic nerve to the right phrenic nerve [*see Figure 6*].

Cardiopulmonary bypass can make dissection easier, but in view of the greater risk of bleeding and the increased transfusion requirements, it is best avoided if possible. Cardiopulmonary bypass does facilitate repair of cardiac injuries during sternal reentry or dissection, and it should be used if cardiac procedures are to be performed concomitantly.

Step 3: drainage and closure After completion of the pericardiectomy, mediastinal and pleural drains are placed, and the sternum is closed in the usual fashion.

Left Anterolateral Thoracotomy

Step 1: initial incision and exposure The patient is placed in the supine position, with a roll under the left side of the torso to elevate the left side 45°. It is often difficult to establish cardiopulmonary bypass through the chest via this approach; therefore, the femoral vessels should be available within the sterile field so that femorofemoral bypass can be instituted if necessary. A curvilinear submammary incision is created, and the chest is entered at the fifth interspace. For improved exposure, the internal thoracic vessels may be divided and the intercostal muscles divided posteriorly. The left phrenic nerve is carefully identified.

Step 2: dissection and resection of pericardium As with the median sternotomy approach, loculated spaces are often present near the great vessels and the diaphragm, and these vessels provide good starting places for dissection. The entire pericardium is dissected free over the left ventricle, and an island of pericardium is left attached to the phrenic nerve along its length [*see Figure 7*]. The pericardium is resected from the pulmonary veins to a point just posterior to the phrenic nerve. Resection resumes anterior to the nerve and continues across the anterior aspect of the heart as far as possible, ideally to the right atrioventricular groove. The same precautions should be taken around the coronary vessels as are taken with the median sternotomy approach.

Step 3: drainage and closure After completion of the pericardiectomy, mediastinal and pleural drains are placed, and the thoracotomy is closed in the usual fashion.

OUTCOME EVALUATION

There is no proven difference between the two approaches to pericardiectomy with respect to outcome. Accordingly, the choice between them is based on whether one option affords better access to the areas believed to be most involved (e.g., a median sternotomy is more effective for releasing the right side of the heart) and whether the surgeon is more comfortable with one approach or the other.

The underlying cause of constrictive pericarditis is a significant predictor of long-term survival. In a study of 163 patients who underwent pericardiectomy, 7-year survival rates were highest in patients with idiopathic constrictive pericarditis (88%), somewhat lower in patients with postoperative constriction (66%), and lowest in patients with radiation-induced constriction (27%).[33] Predictors of decreased survival included previous radiation therapy, renal dysfunction, pulmonary hypertension, and abnormal left ventricular systolic function. Perioperative mortality was 6% overall but 21% in patients who had received radiation therapy and 8% in postsurgical patients. The slightly higher mortality recorded in

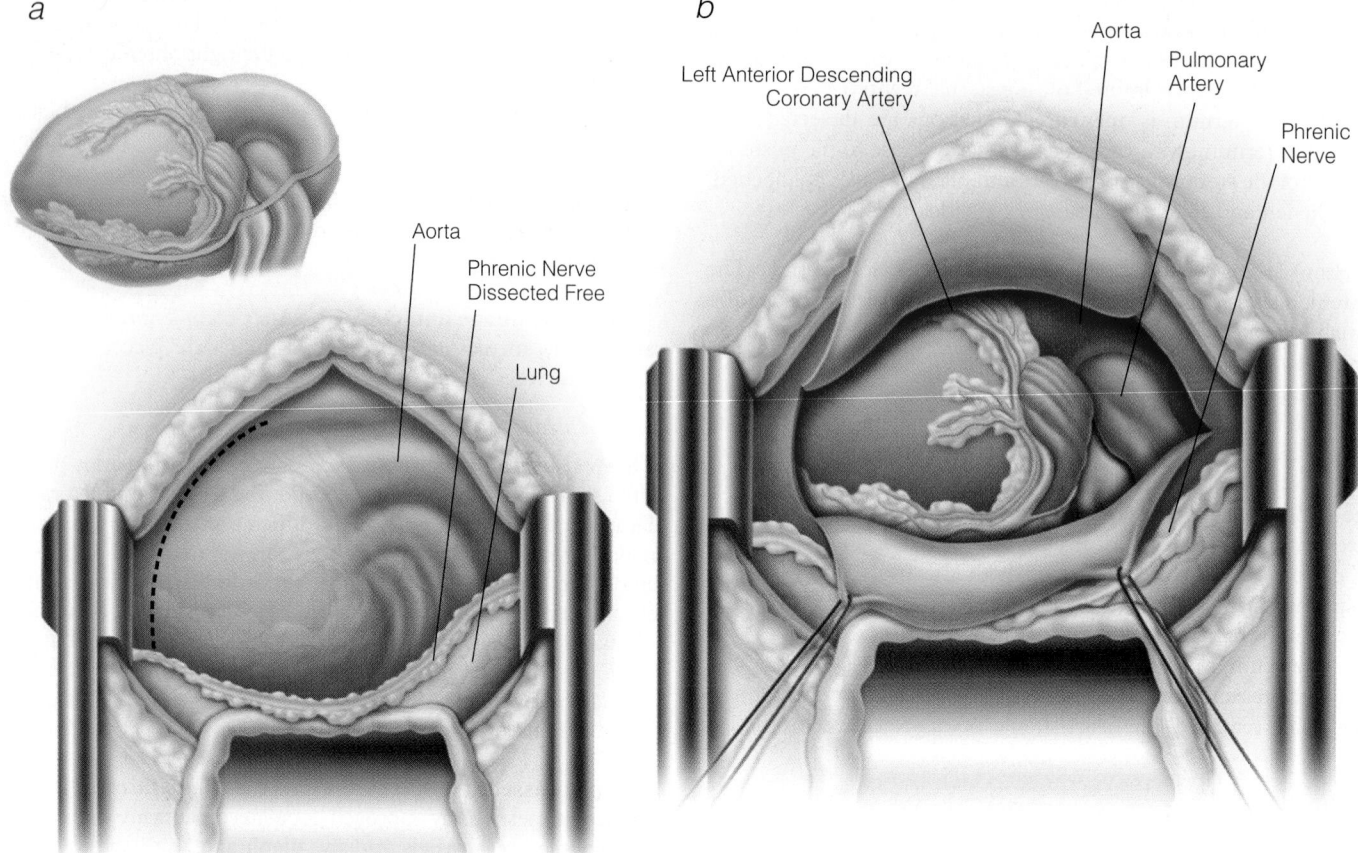

a

b

Figure 7 **Pericardiectomy: left anterolateral thoracotomy approach. (*a*) The left phrenic nerve is identified. (*b*) The entire pericardium is dissected free over the left ventricle, with an island of pericardium left attached to the phrenic nerve along its length. Care must be taken to avoid injuring coronary vessels.**

postoperative patients may reflect underlying cardiac dysfunction, as well as the vulnerability of previous bypass grafts to injury. The poor outcomes after pericardiectomy for radiation-induced constriction indicate that constriction is not the sole factor responsible for cardiac failure in this situation. Although cardiac failure has been attributed to myocardial atrophy caused by prolonged constriction, the excellent outcomes reported after pericardiectomy for idiopathic constrictive pericarditis suggest that constriction is rarely the only cause of cardiac failure.

Another study reported similar findings, with radiation-induced constriction leading to significantly decreased 10-year survival after pericardiectomy.[31] The authors also noted that patients who underwent pericardiectomy for radiation-induced constriction had demonstrably worse late functional status. Fifteen of 17 long-term survivors with a history of previous radiation therapy showed New York Heart Association class III or IV symptoms, whereas only 31 of 112 patients without a history of radiation therapy had major symptoms of heart failure.

References

1. Fowler NO: Tuberculous pericarditis. JAMA 266:95, 1991
2. Butany J, El Demellawy D, Collins MJ, et al: Constrictive pericarditis: case presentation and a review of the literature. Can J Cardiol 20:1137, 2004
3. Tuna IC, Danielson GK: Surgical management of pericardial diseases. Cardiol Clin 84:683, 1990
4. Cimino JJ, Kogan AD: Constrictive pericarditis after cardiac surgery: report of three cases and review of the literature. Am Heart J 118:1292, 1989
5. Matsuyama K, Matsumoto M, Sugita T, et al: Clinical characteristics of patients with constrictive pericarditis after coronary bypass surgery. Jap Circ J 65:480, 2001
6. Swallow RA, Thomas RD: Pericardial constriction after a stab wound to the chest. Heart 90:276, 2004
7. Isaacs D, Stark P, Nichols C, et al: Post traumatic pericardial calcification. J Thorac Imaging 18:250, 2003
8. Eren NT, Akar AR: Primary pericardial mesothelioma. Curr Treat Options Oncol 3:369, 2002
9. Quinn DW, Qureshi F, Mitchell IM: Pericardial mesothelioma: the diagnostic dilemma of misleading images. Ann Thorac Surg 69:1926, 2000
10. Myers RBH, Spodick DH: Constrictive pericarditis: clinical and pathophysiologic characteristics. Am Heart J 138:219, 1999
11. Fowler NO, Gabel M: The hemodynamic effects of cardiac tamponade: mainly the result of atrial, not ventricular, compression. Circulation 71:154, 1985
12. Ameli S, Shah PK: Cardiac tamponade: pathophysiology, diagnosis and management. Cardiol Clin 9:665, 1991
13. Spodick DH: Pathophysiology of cardiac tamponade. Chest 113:1372, 1998
14. Nkere UU, Whawell SA, Thompson EM, et al: Changes in pericardial morphology and fibrinolytic activity during cardiopulmonary bypass. J Thorac Cardiovasc Surg 106:339, 1993
15. Posner MR, Cohen GI, Skarin AT: Pericardial disease in patients with cancer. Am J Med 71:407, 1981
16. Vaitkus PT, Herrmann HC, LeWinter MM: Treatment of malignant pericardial effusion. JAMA 272:59, 1994
17. Shepherd FA, Morgan C, Evans WK, et al:

Medical management of malignant pericardial effusion by tetracycline sclerosis. Am J Cardiol 60:1161, 1987

18. Davis S, Rambotti P, Grignani F: Intrapericardial tetracycline sclerosis in the treatment of malignant pericardial effusion. J Clin Oncol 2:631, 1984

19. Girardi LN, Ginsberg RJ, Burt ME: Pericardiocentesis and intrapericardial sclerosis: effective therapy for malignant pericardial effusions. Ann Thorac Surg 64:1422, 1997

20. Kopecky SL, Callahan JA, Tajik AJ, et al: Percutaneous pericardial catheter drainage: report of 42 consecutive cases. Am J Cardiol 58:633, 1986

21. del Barrio LG, Morales JH, Delgado C, et al: Percutaneous balloon pericardial window for patients with symptomatic pericardial window. Cardiovasc Intervent Radiol 25:360, 2002

22. DiSegni E, Lavee J, Kaplinsky E, et al: Percutaneous balloon pericardiostomy for treatment of cardiac tamponade. Eur Heart J 16:184, 1995

23. Moores DWO, Allen KB, Faber LP, et al: Subxiphoid pericardial drainage for pericardial tamponade. J Thorac Cardiovasc Surg 109:546, 1995

24. Sugimoto JT, Little AG, Ferguson MF, et al: Pericardial window: mechanism of efficacy. Ann Thorac Surg 50:442, 1990

25. Allen KB, Faber LP, Warren WH, et al: Pericardial effusion: subxiphoid pericardiostomy versus percutaneous catheter drainage. Ann Thorac Surg 67:437, 1999

26. Dosios T, Theaskos N, Angouras D, et al: Risk factors affecting the survival of patients with pericardial effusion submitted to subxiphoid pericardiostomy. Chest 124:242, 2003

27. Flum DR, McGinn JT, Tyras DH: The role of the 'pericardial window' in AIDS. Chest 107:1522, 1995

28. Burfeind WR, D'Amico TA: VATS for mediastinal and pericardial diseases. Mastery of Endoscopic and Laparoscopic Surgery, 2nd ed. Soper NL, Swanstrom LL, Eubanks WS, Eds. Lippincott Williams & Wilkins, Philadelphia, 2005

29. Nataf P, Cocoub P, Regan M, et al: Video-thoracoscopic pericardial window in the diagnosis and treatment of pericardial effusions. Am J Cardiol 82:124, 1998

30. Campione A, Cacchiarelli M, Ghiribelli, et al: Which treatment in pericardial effusion? J Cardiovasc Surg 43:735, 2002

31. Ling LH, Oh JK, Schaff HV, et al: Constrictive pericarditis in the modern era: evolving clinical spectrum and impact on outcome after pericardiectomy. Circulation 100:1380, 1999

32. Nishimura RA: Constrictive pericarditis in the modern era: a diagnostic dilemma. Heart 86:619, 2001

33. Bertog SC, Thambidorai SK, Parakh K, et al: Constrictive pericarditis: etiology and cause-specific survival after pericardiectomy. J Am Coll Cardiol 43:1445, 2004

Acknowledgment

Figures 1 and 3 through 7   Alice Y. Chen.

Eric S. Lambright, M.D.

In normal circumstances, the pleural space is a potential cavity between the lung and the chest wall—more specifically, between the visceral pleura and the parietal pleura. In the average healthy patient, this space is less than 1 mm thick. There are a number of pathologic processes that can alter the transport of cells and fluid within this space and thus give rise to clinically significant sequelae. One such process is fibrothorax, which is defined as the presence of abnormal fibrous tissue within the pleural space, resulting in entrapment of the underlying pulmonary parenchyma (a state variously referred to as trapped lung, restrictive pleurisy, or encased lung). Decortication is the surgical procedure by which this restrictive fibrous layer is peeled away from the lung; the literal meaning of the term is the stripping away of a rind (from the Latin word *cortex* "bark, rind, shell"). The technical goals of the operation are to reexpand the lung and resolve the pathologic process affecting the pleural space so that pulmonary function and chest wall mechanics will improve and the patient's symptoms will be relieved.

Successful management of a patient with fibrothorax depends on close adherence to basic surgical tenets: appropriate selection of patients for surgical treatment, preoperative optimization of the patient's physiologic status, exacting attention to the technical aspects of the procedure, and timely intervention to address perioperative complications. If insufficient attention is paid to any of these important tenets, decortication may fail to achieve any significant improvement in the patient's symptoms or physiologic status, potentially leaving him or her in an even more debilitated state.

Preoperative Evaluation

PATHOPHYSIOLOGY OF FIBROTHORAX

Although any insult to the pleura can result in an inflammatory response with fibrin deposition,[1] hemothorax and infection (bacterial and mycobacterial) remain the most common causes of fibrothorax [see Table 1]. Typically, empyemas evolve over a 4- to 6-week period as the infection progresses throughout the pleural space. The first (exudative) phase is characterized by a thin, fibrin-containing fluid exudate. The second (fibropurulent) phase is characterized by a heavy fibrin deposit over the pleural surface with the development of loculations and fibrous debris in the thoracic cavity. The third (organizational) phase, which begins at about 3 to 5 weeks, is characterized by the formation of a thick fibrous peel that imprisons the lung and prevents expansion. When fully developed, this peel has three distinct layers: (1) an outer layer consisting of loosely organized vascular tissue, (2) a middle layer consisting of fibrous connective tissue that is relatively avascular and acellular, and (3) an inner layer consisting of necrotic tissue and fibrinoid masses.[2] Generally, if a hemothorax is small, it will be reabsorbed, provided that the lymphatic system is intact. However, if the hemothorax is relatively large, if there is continued bleeding, or if bacteria are present, there is a high likelihood that a fibrous peel will eventually form.[3]

HISTORY AND PHYSICAL EXAMINATION

The physiologic consequences of a fibrothorax culminate in pulmonary restriction, manifested by decreased lung volumes, reduced diffusion capacity, and lower expiratory flow rates. Movement of the chest is impaired.[4] The initial clinicial presentation of a fibrothorax depends on its cause and severity, as well as on the presence or absence of underlying parenchymal disease. Typically, dyspnea on exertion is the most common presenting symptom, though cough, fever, pleuritic chest discomfort, malaise, night sweats, weight loss, or chest pressure may also be present. In obtaining the clinical history, it is important to determine whether the condition is chronic and whether there are any other underlying disease processes that may be complicating the pulmonary disease process. Physical examination yields relatively nonspecific findings; typically, decreased breath sounds and decreased chest wall excursion are noted.

DIAGNOSTIC IMAGING AND PHYSIOLOGIC TESTING

Radiographic evaluation is the mainstay of diagnosis [see Figures 1, 2, and 3]. Computed tomography (CT) of the chest is the imaging modality of choice for delineating abnormalities of the pleural space and defining the character of the pleural disease process. CT scanning can assess the extent and thickness of pleural involvement and characterize associated parenchymal disease. It readily identifies parenchymal abnormalities such as fibrosis, bronchiectasis, and malignancy. Such factors play a role in surgical decision making. In particular, malignancy must be included in the differential diagnosis of fibrothorax and ruled out; the management options for malignant disease are quite different from those for benign disease.

Physiologic testing with spirometry and evaluation of diffusing capacity helps define the degree of pulmonary dysfunction and facilitates risk stratification. The results of pulmonary function testing may be quite abnormal preoperatively and are often worse than would have been expected from the radiographic evaluation. Marked abnormalities in physiologic testing should not be considered absolute contraindications to surgical intervention, because some degree of improvement may be anticipated. The improvement in dyspnea, pulmonary reexpansion, and parenchymal function that can realistically be expected after decortication may be

---

Table 1 Common Causes of Fibrothorax

Chronic empyema
Retained hemothorax (traumatic or iatrogenic)
Pleural effusive disease
   Transudative
   Chylous
   Pancreatic
Sequelae of *Mycobacterium tuberculosis* infection
Chronic pneumothorax

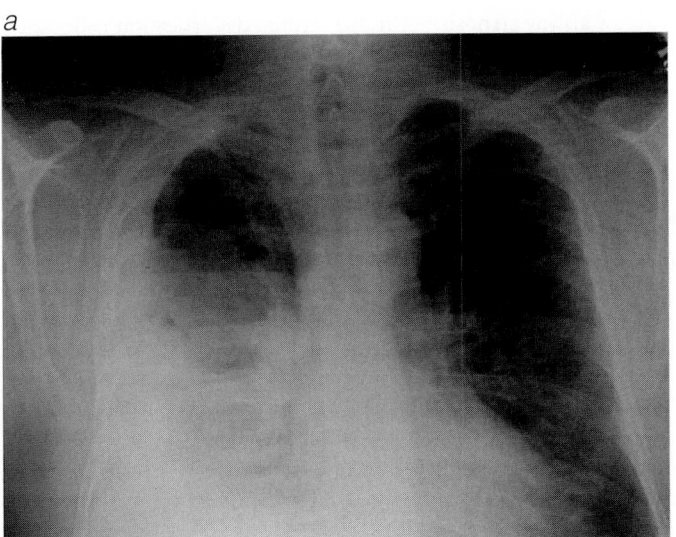

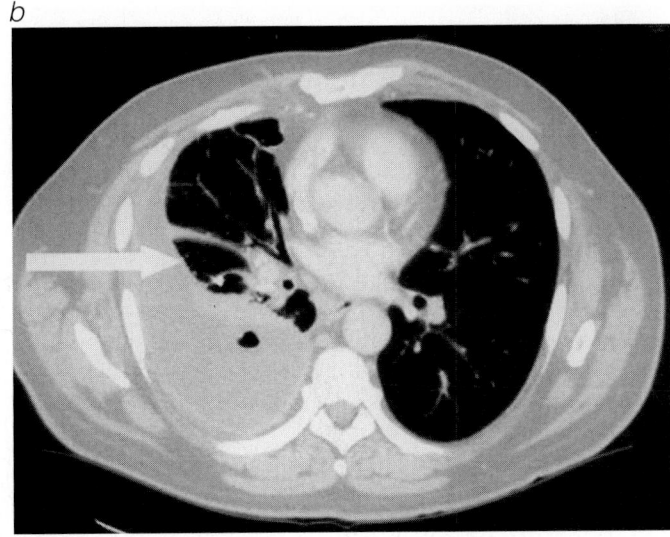

Figure 1 (*a*) Shown is a chest x-ray from a patient with a 2-month history of dyspnea and cough associated with intermittent fever and night sweats. Treatments included three courses of antibiotics and bronchodilator therapy. (*b*) A chest CT scan from the same patient shows a large pleural collection containing air and demonstrates pleural thickening (arrow). The findings are consistent with empyema. Thoracentesis was performed, demonstrating white, creamy purulence but failing to achieve reexpansion of the lung. Decortication was performed.

estimated on the basis of the preoperative diagnostic imaging and physiologic testing. Ultimately, the surgeon's judgment plays the key role in deciding for or against surgical intervention.

EXCLUSION OF MALIGNANCY

In the evaluation of a patient with a fibrothorax, it is essential to keep in mind the possibility of a malignant pleural process. If malignancy is a concern, this possibility should be excluded before a decision is made to proceed with decortication. Decortication of a malignant fibrous peel is difficult, and the outcome is not particularly satisfying from the standpoint of lung expansion; accordingly, for a pleural malignancy, a lesser, palliative intervention is generally more appropriate than decortication. Metastatic involve-

ment of the pleura (usually by adenocarcinoma) is far more common than malignant pleural mesothelioma, which is a primary malignancy of the pleural space. Cytologic evaluation of the pleural fluid will establish the diagnosis of metastatic pleural involvement in most cases; however, it tends to be less effective in establishing the diagnosis of malignant mesothelioma. If the presentation of a chronic pleural process is atypical and the etiology is poorly defined, a degree of suspicion for malignancy must be maintained. Appropriate initial pleural biopsies can be useful for ruling out underlying malignancy before decortication. Currently, pleural biopsy is usually performed by means of video thoracoscopy, but closed pleural biopsy is still done occasionally (though it is fast becoming a lost art). If a malignancy is identified, therapeutic alter-

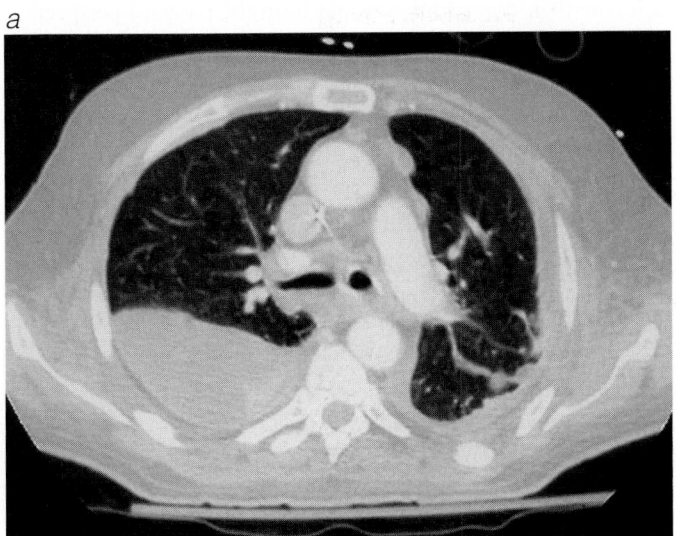

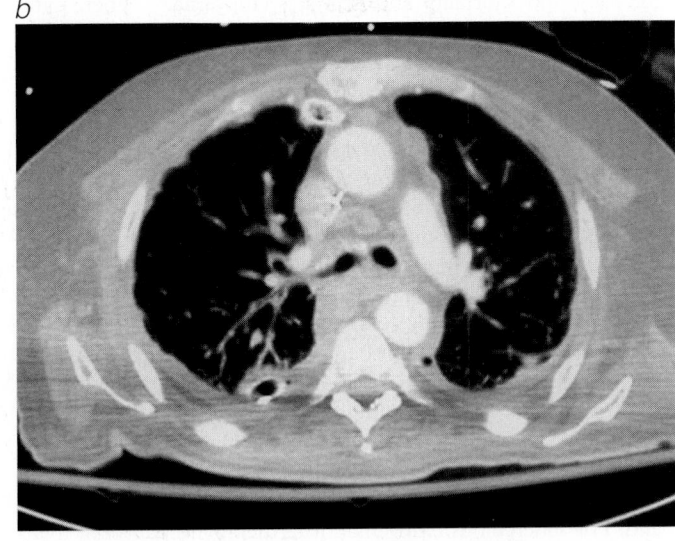

Figure 2 (*a*) Shown is a preoperative chest CT scan from a patient with a 6-week history of malaise and weight loss who ultimately presented with hypotension and respiratory insufficiency necessitating mechanical ventilatory support. (*b*) A chest CT scan obtained from the same patient after decortication shows complete reexpansion of the lung.

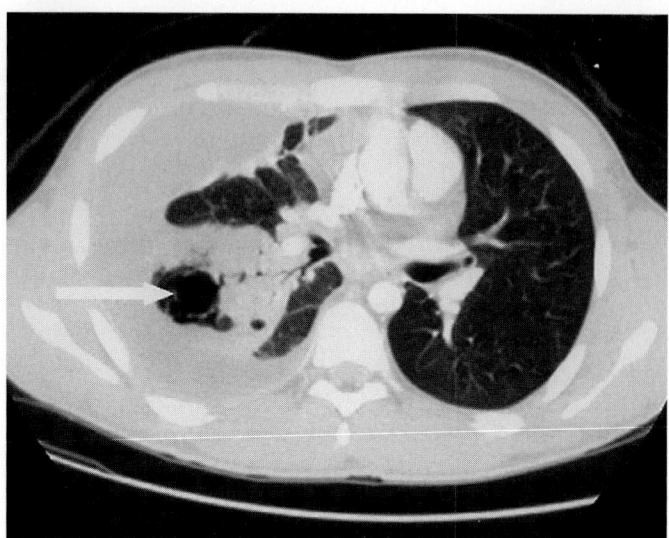

Figure 3 **Shown is a chest CT scan from a patient with a pulmonary abscess (arrow) complicated by pleural space infection. The pleural space was drained via a chest tube thoracostomy. The lung did not completely reexpand. Sepsis was controlled with antibiotics. Decortication was not considered, because of the extensiveness of the underlying pulmonary parenchymal process.**

natives such as pleurodesis or use of the Pleurx pleural catheter (Denver Biomedical, Golden, Colorado) may be indicated.

Operative Planning

INDICATIONS FOR SURGICAL INTERVENTION

Fibrothorax is a potentially preventable complication. As noted (see above), it is a manifestation of a chronic disease process; thus, the earlier a therapeutic intervention is initiated, the better the chances that fibrothorax can be prevented. In patients with a traumatic hemothorax, early and complete drainage often serves to prevent fibrothorax.[5] Observational studies have consistently demonstrated that early evacuation of a clotted hemothorax reduces morbidity and mortality and prevents empyema.[6,7] When parapneumonic effusions are thin, simple aspiration or chest tube drainage may suffice. Often, the fibropurulent stage characterized by loculated empyema or clotted hemothorax can be successfully managed by means of thoracoscopic intervention with debridement of the intrathoracic debris and irrigation; this approach allows the parenchyma to reexpand before a restrictive peel can be formed.[8]

The primary indication for decortication in a patient with fibrothorax is symptomatic pulmonary restriction resulting from the development of a fibrinous peel. The timing of the operation is an important consideration. In many cases, pleuropulmonary processes are self-limiting, and the symptoms resolve over time. As a rule, decortication should be considered (1) if pleural thickening has been present for a substantial period (> 4 to 6 weeks), (2) if respiratory symptoms remain disabling, and (3) if there is radiographic evidence of reversible entrapment of the lung. Decortication is often necessary when lesser interventions have not achieved control of a pleural space infection or have not enabled the lung to reexpand. For tuberculous empyema, drug therapy remains the treatment of choice. Decortication may also be performed to treat pleural effusions that persist despite long-term medical therapy.

A condition that poses a major challenge to the thoracic surgeon is pleural space infection with underlying parenchymal disease or airway stenosis.[9,10] In this setting, decortication is destined to fail: the lung parenchyma will not reexpand to fill the pleural space completely, and any surgical intervention carried out on the diseased lung will only aggravate the underlying disease process. Pleuropneumonectomy may be the only option, though it should be considered a last resort, to be used only if there is significant parenchymal destruction. Decortication may be precluded by invasive uncontrolled pulmonary infection, contralateral pulmonary disease, or a chronically debilitated state that results in a significant or even prohibitive level of operative risk. Medical optimization may be required as an initial step. Often, however, the underlying pleural infection process remains unresolved despite optimal medical management, and surgical intervention becomes necessary in a patient who remains medically fragile. Optimally, the patient's nutritional status should be normalized (with forced feedings, if necessary), and sepsis, if present, should be controlled with appropriate antibiotic therapy.

TECHNICAL CONSIDERATIONS

Essentially, pleural cavity infection and fibrosis are problems of residual intrapleural space. The lung cannot expand sufficiently to fill the hemithorax, and as a consequence, the residual space becomes or remains infected. These problems often prove difficult for the thoracic surgeon to address; good surgical judgment is crucial for ensuring optimal outcomes. In planning for decortication, there are a number of technical issues that must be considered, including the timing of intervention (taking into account whether the disease process is chronic or subacute), the quality of the underlying pulmonary parenchyma, the expected ability of the lung to reexpand, the possible need to address residual space issues, and the physiologic status of the patient. The goal of the procedure is to remove the peel from the visceral pleura so as to allow the lung to reexpand and, equally important, to ensure that any potential residual space is obliterated.[11]

There are few absolute contraindications to pulmonary decortication, other than a patient who is unfit to undergo surgery or the presence of underlying parenchymal or bronchial disease that would prevent lung reexpansion. There are, however, some situations in which a lesser intervention (e.g., chest tube thoracostomy, rib resection, or open window thoracostomy) might yield a better outcome than decortication would from the patient's perspective. In general, decortication is not required for a small, well-defined residual cavity; it is usually reserved for a diffuse pleural process. Whether the disease process is chronic or subacute will also influence the surgeon's choice of approach. For example, in the earlier stages of pleural space infection, when the peel is less organized, a thoracoscopic approach that includes cleansing of the pleural space, removal of the pleural debris, and breaking up of loculations may prove adequate. With a chronic process, however, an attempt at thoracoscopic decortication may do more harm than good.

Operative Technique

The first step in open decortication (which at times includes parietal pleurectomy in addition to decortication) is bronchoscopic evaluation aimed at identifying any endobronchial obstructions that might prevent satisfactory lung expansion. Such evaluation sometimes yields unexpected findings, such as malignancy, bronchial stenosis, or a broncholith.

The chest is entered at the appropriate predetermined interspace (usually the fifth or sixth) via a standard posterolateral thoracotomy [see Figure 4]; alternatively, a vertical axillary thoracotomy may be employed. With either approach, the latissimus dorsi

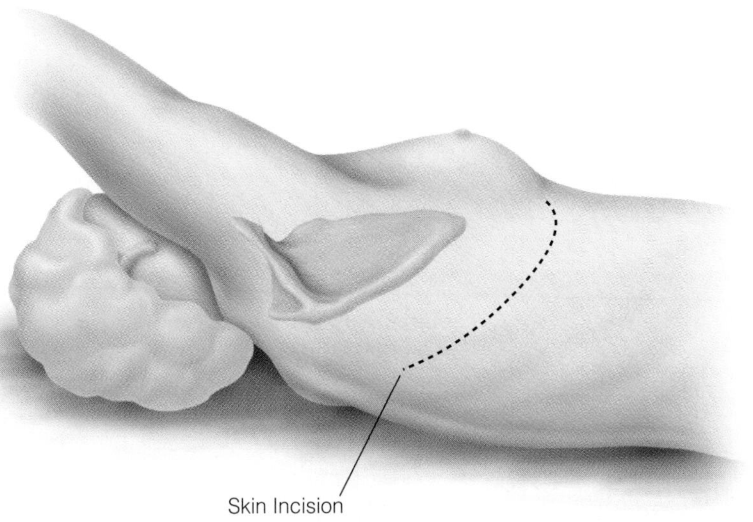

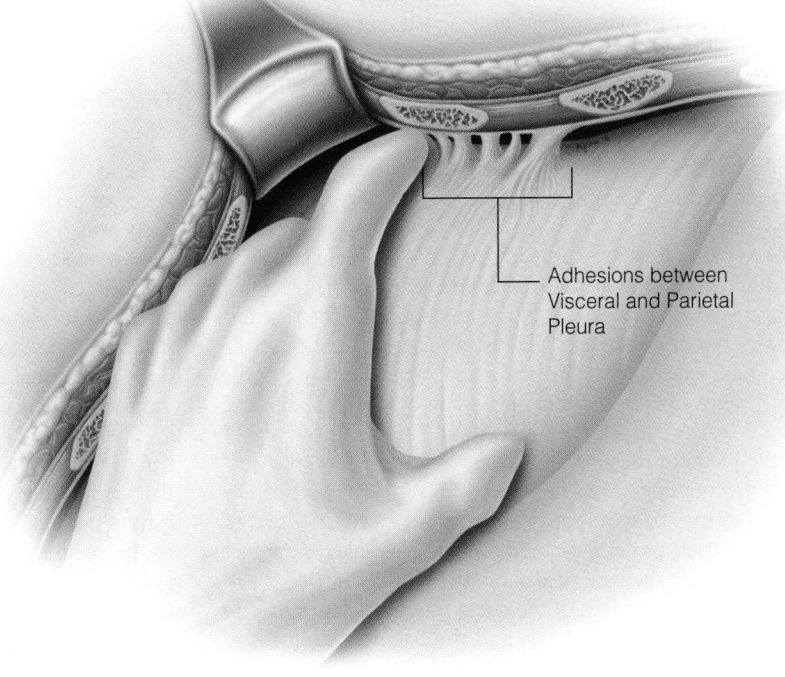

Figure 4 **Decortication. The chest is entered through a posterolateral thoracotomy at the fifth or sixth interspace.**

Skin Incision

and the serratus anterior should be spared because either or both might subsequently be required for a transposition muscle flap. Because the chest is often rigid and contracted as a result of the underlying inflammatory process, it may be helpful to resect a rib in a subperiosteal fashion. This measure facilitates exposure and helps define the extrapleural plane for the initiation of parietal pleurectomy.

When the disease process is chronic (i.e., has lasted longer than 6 weeks), the parietal pleura and the visceral pleura are often fused. In this situation, one would proceed with pleurectomy. When adhesions are present between the pleural layers but the visceral pleura has not fused with the parietal pleura [*see Figure 5*], the adhesions may be lysed with a combination of sharp dissection and electrocauterization.

The key to a technically successful decortication is to define the correct plane between the pleural peel and the visceral pleura. If the pleural resection is inadequate, lung expansion will be compromised. If the pleurectomy is too deep, parenchymal injury will result, bleeding and air leakage will occur, and postoperative recovery will be prolonged. Gentle manual ventilation of the lung

operated on, coupled with continuous positive airway pressure (CPAP), should provide appropriate countertraction from the underlying lung parenchyma.

An incision is made in the pleural peel, and the appropriate decortication plane is identified [*see Figure 6a*]. The pleural peel is then grasped with hemostats, and blunt and sharp dissection is carried out over a broad area to separate the peel from the visceral pleura [*see Figure 6b*]; a sponge-ball or peanut dissector may be useful for this purpose. Care must be taken to keep from injuring the underlying pulmonary parenchyma, which is fragile; inadvertent injury may result in prolonged and unnecessary air leaks. Some degree of patience is required, in that this operation often becomes tedious. For an optimal surgical outcome, all portions of the lung encased by the peel should be addressed. To this end, it is often necessary to follow the peel into the fissure, down onto the diaphragm, and into the posterior and anterior sulci. At times, a second entry point into the chest through another interspace may be required to achieve an optimal technical result. Should better exposure be deemed necessary, one should not hesitate to proceed with this counterincision.

Figure 5 **Decortication. Any adhesions between the visceral pleura and the parietal pleura are lysed with a combination of sharp dissection and electrocauterization.**

Adhesions between Visceral and Parietal Pleura

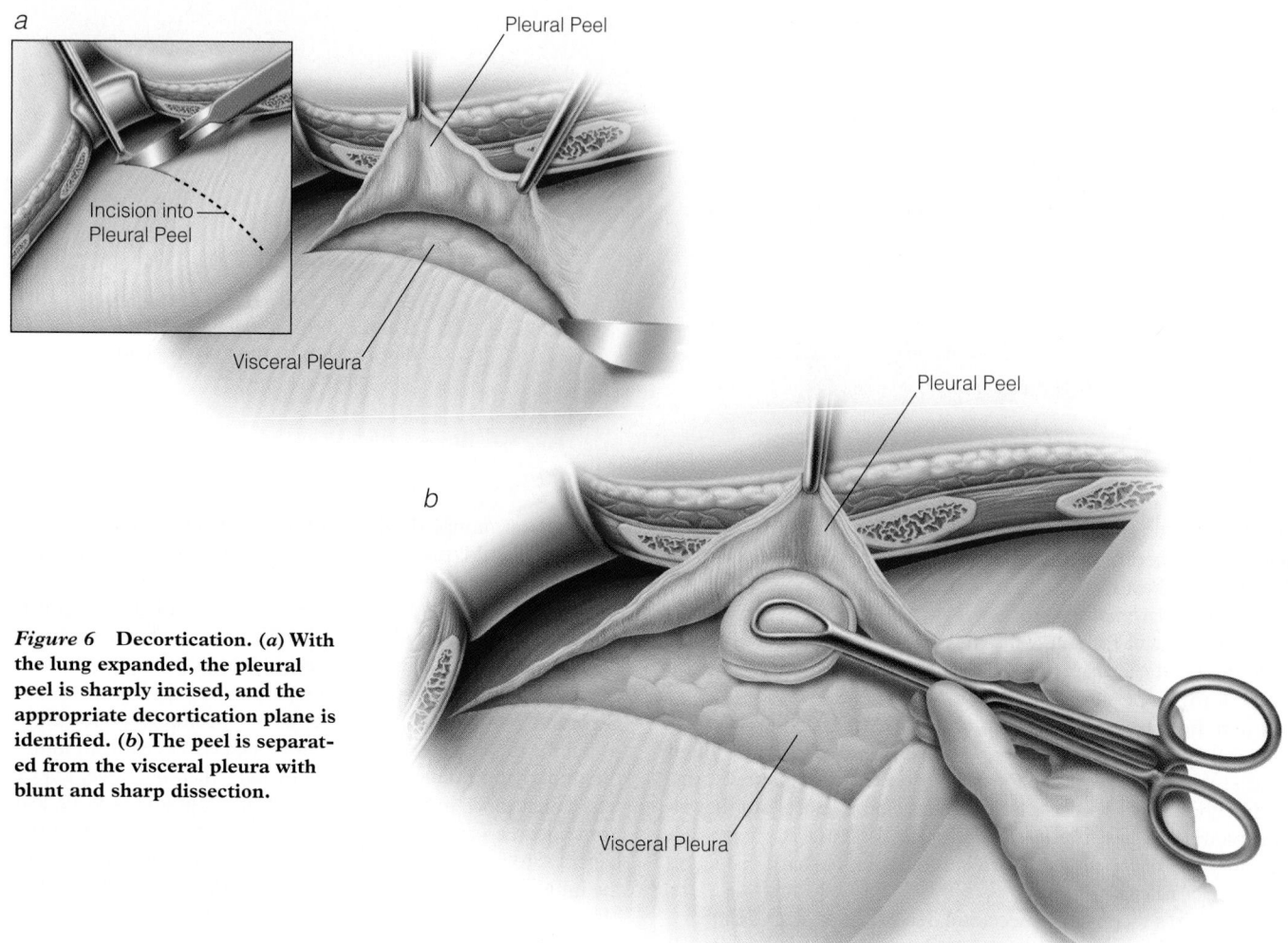

a

Pleural Peel

Incision into
Pleural Peel

Visceral Pleura

b

Pleural Peel

Visceral Pleura

Figure 6 **Decortication. (*a*) With the lung expanded, the pleural peel is sharply incised, and the appropriate decortication plane is identified. (*b*) The peel is separated from the visceral pleura with blunt and sharp dissection.**

Once resected, the peel is sent for pathologic and microbiologic evaluation. The lung is tested to confirm that it is capable of complete reexpansion. Any large parenchymal air leaks that are noted may be oversewn, but this step often is not necessary. The various pulmonary parenchymal sealants now commercially available may reasonably be considered for control of parenchymal air-leaks.[12] Chest tubes are placed—typically, one along the diaphragm, a second anteriorly, and a third posteriorly, toward the apex. Provided that the lung is satisfactorily reexpanded, air leaks will seal promptly. Hemostasis must be ensured: a residual hemothorax in a patient with a pleural space infection will serve as a nidus for ongoing infection.

The role of parietal pleurectomy in this setting remains unclear. Opinions differ, but objective data are sparse. Parietal pleurectomy does result in some improvement of the mechanics of the thoracic cage[12]; however, it also increases the risk of bleeding, prolongs the procedure, and places vital intrathoracic structures (e.g., the phrenic and vagus nerves, the esophagus, the brachial plexus, and certain blood vessels) at risk for injury. In addition, it is often possible that the pleural process will resolve without parietal pleurectomy once the underlying issues are addressed. The technically optimal strategy may be to adopt a compromise approach—that is, to perform a partial parietal pleurectomy and to take extra care when dissecting near the vital mediastinal structures.

Postoperative management of the chest tube is dictated by culture results, intraoperative findings, and the patient's clinical sta-

tus. Concerns related to residual space may be managed by means of open tube thoracostomy, open window thoracostomy, or placement of a muscle flap. On rare occasions, thoracoplasty with multiple rib resection may be considered to obliterate any infection in the residual space by bringing the chest wall down to fill the space.

Outcome Evaluation

The morbidity and mortality to be expected after decortication depend on the severity of the underlying illness and on the occurrence of perioperative complications. In a review from 1985, mortality was less than 8%.[13] Complications tend to be either infection related (e.g., perioperative sepsis syndrome) or technique related (e.g., bronchopleural fistula, hemorrhage, and persistent air leakage); some of them may necessitate additional surgical intervention. As with all operations in the chest, close attention to detail and meticulous surgical technique are critical for minimizing the incidence of postoperative complications.

The degree of functional improvement attained after decortication depends primarily on the presence and extent of disease in the underlying lung parenchyma.[14-16] If the parenchyma of the lung is normal, complete reexpansion of the lung and obliteration of the pleural space should be achievable. Lung volumes usually improve measurably after decortication, but they generally do not return to normal.[14,17] Changes within the chest (i.e., mediastinal shift and elevation of the diaphragm, with a resultant decrease in

Table 2 Causes of Failed Decortication

Underlying parenchymal disease	Active tuberculosis or invasive pulmonary infection Bronchial stenosis Chronic lung collapse
Technical considerations	Residual space Inadequate lung expansion Air leakage Postoperative hemothorax

the size of the thorax) may account for this finding. It is unclear to what extent the expected functional improvement is influenced by whether the pleural process is acute or chronic. Some authors have observed an association between shorter durations of pleural disease before treatment and improved outcomes[18,19]; others have not observed such an association.[14] Failure to achieve improvement after decortication appears to be most strongly related to errors of surgical judgment (in particular, poor patient selection) and to insufficiently meticulous surgical technique (leading to perioperative complications).

Although to date, no studies have dealt specifically with failure after decortication, it is likely that technical difficulties are the most common cause of such failure, with the main problem being inadequate obliteration of the pleural space [*see Table 2*].

Inability to define the plane of dissection between the peel and the visceral pleura is an especially troublesome technical challenge that can adversely affect results. If visceral pleurectomy is performed, air leakage and postoperative hemorrhage may compromise pulmonary function. Care must be taken throughout the operation to protect the phrenic nerve from injury; fortunately, this usually is not an issue, because the mediastinal pleura is rarely involved in the inflammatory process. Incomplete parietal pleurectomy or inability to free the diaphragm may also compromise results.

If patients are appropriately selected, complete reexpansion of the lung after decortication can usually be achieved. Occasionally, however, an issue related to residual pleural space may arise after an otherwise technically satisfactory decortication. If this space is not obliterated, failure is inevitable. Options for addressing the residual space problem include thoracoplasty and tissue transposition. Either the latissimus dorsi or the abdominal omentum will provide sufficient bulk for obliteration of the residual space.[20,21] The omentum is preferable when the space is in the inferior hemithorax, whereas the latissimus dorsi is preferable when the space is in the superior hemithorax. At the time of the initial incision, the surgeon should keep in mind the possibility that tissue transposition may eventually prove necessary and should therefore opt for a muscle-sparing thoracotomy if possible.

At present, the use of thoracoscopy to address fibrothorax definitively cannot be recommended.

References

1. Samson PC, Merrill DL, Dugan DJ, et al: Technical considerations in decortication for the pleural complications of pulmonary tuberculosis. J Thorac Surg Cardiovasc 36:431, 1958

2. Wachsmuth W, Schautz R: Untersuchungen uber die Lungen-Pleura-Grenzschicht beider extrapleuralen Dekortikation. Chirurg 22:237, 1961

3. Drummond DS, Craig RH: Traumatic hemothorax: complications and management. Am Surg 33:404, 1967

4. Bollinger CT, de Kock MA: Influence of a fibrothorax on the flow volume curve. Respiration 54:197, 1988

5. Wilson JM, et al: Traumatic hemothorax: is decortication necessary? J Thorac Cardiovasc Surg 77:494, 1979

6. Milfield DJ, Mattox KL, Beall AC: Early evacuation of clotted hemothorax. Am J Surg 136:686, 1978

7. Beall AC, Crawford HW, DeBakey ME: Considerations in the management of acute traumatic hemothorax. J Thorac Cardiovasc Surg 52:353, 1966

8. Deslauriers J, Mehran RJ: Role of thoracoscopy in the diagnosis and management of pleural disease. Semin Thorac Cardiovasc Surg 5:284, 1993

9. Savage T, Flemin JA: Decortication of the lung in tuberculous disease. Thorax 10:293, 1955

10. Magdeleinat P, Icard P, Pouzet B, et al: Indications actuelles et resultats des decortications pulmonaires pour pleurisies purulentes non tuberculeuses. Ann Chir 53:41, 1999

11. Kaiser LR: Pleurectomy and decortication. Atlas of General Thoracic Surgery. Philadelphia, Mosby-Year Book, 1997

12. Waterman DH, Domm SE, Roger WK: A clinical evaluation of decortication. J Thorac Cardiovasc Surg 33:1, 1957

13. Mayo P: Early thoracotomy and decortication for nontuberculous empyema in adults with and without underlying disease: a twenty-five year review. Am Surg 51:230, 1985

14. Patton WE, Watson TR, Gaensler EA: Pulmonary function before and at intervals after surgical decortication of the lung. Surg Gynecol Obstet 95:477, 1952

15. Siebens AA, Storey CF, Newman MM, et al: The physiological effects of fibrothorax and the functional results of surgical treatment. J Thorac Surg 32:53, 1956

16. Barker WL, Neuhaus H, Langston HT: Ventilatory improvement following decortication in pulmonary tuberculosis. Ann Thor Surg 1:532, 1965

17. LeMense GF, Strange CH, Sahn S: Empyema thoracis: therapeutic management and outcome. Chest 107:1532, 1994

18. Carroll D, McClement J, Himmelstein A, et al: Pulmonary function following decortication of the lung. Am Rev Tuberc 63:231, 1951

19. Morton JR, Boushy SF, Guinn GA: Physiological evaluation of results of pulmonary decortication. Ann Thorac Surg 4:321, 1970

20. Marshall MD, Kaiser LR, Kucharczuk JC: Simple technique for maximal thoracic muscle harvest. Ann Thorac Surg 4:1465, 2004

21. Shrager JB, Wain JC, Wright CD, et al: Omentum is highly effective in the management of complex cardiothoracic surgical problems. J Thorac Cardiovasc Surg 125:526, 2003

Acknowledgment

Figures 4 through 6   Alice Y. Chen.

41 PULMONARY RESECTION

Ara Vaporciyan, M.D., F.A.C.S.

Anatomic resections of the lung (including pneumonectomy and lobectomy) are the standard operative techniques employed to treat both neoplastic and nonneoplastic diseases of the lung. Any surgeon who intends to operate on the pulmonary system must be keenly aware of the anatomy of the pulmonary vasculature, the bronchi, and the relation between the two. There is no substitute for this degree of familiarity. Detailed discussions are available in existing anatomy textbooks. In what follows, I describe several of the more common techniques employed for anatomic resections of the lung.

Preoperative Evaluation

Detailed discussion of the physiologic evaluation of the patient and of the indications for lobectomy or pneumonectomy is beyond the scope of this chapter. In general, the patient must have sufficient pulmonary reserve to tolerate the planned resection. In addition, it is essential to carry out a thorough evaluation of all other systems, especially the cardiac system. In patients who have received preoperative chemotherapy, the hematologic and renal systems should receive particular attention.

Operative Planning

ANESTHESIA

Although pulmonary resections can be performed with bilateral lung ventilation, careful hilar dissection is greatly facilitated by using unilateral lung ventilation. The advent of double-lumen endotracheal tubes and bronchial blockers has made it possible to isolate the ipsilateral lung and has made it easier for surgeons to carry out complex hilar dissections with the required precision. In patients with centrally located tumors, care must be taken with tube placement: inadvertent trauma to an endobronchial tumor during placement of a double-lumen tube can lead to significant bleeding and compromise of the airway. Bronchoscopic confirmation of tube position is recommended after the patient has been positioned.

Requirements for monitoring and intravenous access are determined by the patient's preoperative status and by the complexity of the resection. In most cases, the standard practice is to place a radial arterial catheter, two large-bore peripheral intravenous catheters, and a Foley catheter, with more invasive monitoring employed if mandated by the patient's clinical condition. Thoracic epidural catheters are also commonly employed for postoperative pain control. If carefully placed by an experienced anesthesiologist, these catheters can remain in place for as long as 7 days or until the chest tubes are removed.

PATIENT POSITIONING

Patients are routinely placed in the lateral decubitus position, with the table flexed just cephalad to the superior iliac crest. This positioning allows sufficient access for most incisions. If an anterior thoracotomy or a sternotomy is planned, the patient may be placed in the supine position, with a pillow placed in such a way as to elevate the area of the thorax that will be operated on.

When the patient is in the lateral decubitus position, several measures should be adopted to guard against injury. Adequate padding should be employed to prevent the development of pressure points on the contralateral lower extremity. A low axillary roll should be used to prevent injury to the contralateral brachial plexus and shoulder girdle. Finally, adequate padding should be placed beneath the head to keep the cervical spine in a neutral position.

GENERAL TECHNICAL CONSIDERATIONS

Incisions

Posterior lateral thoracotomy remains the standard incision for anatomic pulmonary resections; however, safe and complete resections can also be performed through a variety of smaller incisions, including posterior muscle-sparing, anterior muscle-sparing, and axillary thoracotomies. In most cases, the thorax is entered at the fifth intercostal space, an approach that affords excellent exposure of the hilar structures. The anterior muscle-sparing thoracotomy is generally placed at the fourth intercostal space because of the more caudal positioning of the anterior aspects of the ribs. Although a sternotomy may be employed to gain access to the upper lobes, it does not provide good exposure of the lower lobes and the bronchi.

Thoracoscopic lobectomy [*see 37 Video-Assisted Thoracic Surgery*] is being performed with increasing frequency, especially for early-stage lesions. This procedure employs two or three 1 cm ports and a utility thoracotomy (frequently in the axillary position) for instrumentation and removal of the specimen. Rib spreading is not necessary, because visualization is achieved via the thoracoscope. The various thoracoscopic lobar resections are generally similar with regard to isolation and division of the hilar vessels and bronchi. Complete nodal dissections are also performed thoracoscopically. The main advantages of this approach seem to be reduced postoperative pain and earlier return to normal activity, but to date, no randomized trials have shown these advantages to be significant. Because of the technical challenges posed by thoracoscopic pulmonary resections, surgeons should have a complete mastery of the hilar anatomy before attempting these procedures.

Special Intraoperative Issues

Upon entry into the thoracic cavity, all benign-appearing filmy adhesions should be mobilized. Any malignant-appearing, broad-based, or dense adhesions should be noted, and a decision whether to perform an extrapleural dissection or a chest wall resection should be made on the basis of the depth of involvement and the preoperative imaging studies. If there is reason to believe that the chest wall or the parietal pleura may be involved, a more aggressive approach may be required to achieve a complete resection. These techniques are beyond the scope of this chapter.

Once the lung is freed of all adhesions, the inferior pulmonary ligament is divided and the lung rendered completely atelectatic. The entire lung and the parietal pleura are inspected and palpated. In patients with malignant disease, biopsies of any suspicious nodules are performed. The presence or absence of pleural fluid should be noted; if fluid is present, it should be aspirated and sent for immediate cytologic analysis.

Frequently, the fissures are incomplete as a consequence of congenital absence, inflammatory disease, or a neoplasm. If the adhesions within the fissure are filmy, they may be divided sharply or with the electrocautery while the lung is being ventilated. If the adhesions are more densely adherent, the fissures may have to be completed with staplers. During resection for malignancy, any evidence of tumor extension across a fissure or of hilar nodal involvement should be noted. A decision is then made regarding the extent of the required resection. If there is only minor extension, wedge resection of a portion of the additional lobe is indicated. If, however, the involvement is significant, segmentectomy, bilobectomy, or pneumonectomy may be indicated. Often, I develop the fissures during ventilation until a dense or incomplete region is encountered, at which point I complete the remainder of the fissure with staples. For this approach to work, the vascular and bronchial anatomy must already have been completely delineated. If the vascular structures cannot be identified in the fissure because the fissure is fused, the pulmonary artery branches will have to be approached from the anterior and posterior hilum.

Traditionally, during a lobectomy, the arterial branches are divided first, followed by the venous branches. However, if conditions exist that limit exposure (e.g., a centrally placed tumor or significant inflammation and scarring), the surgeon should start with the structures that provide the most accessible targets. Veins may be ligated first. Proponents of this approach believe that it may limit the escape of circulating tumor cells (an event that rarely, if ever, occurs); opponents claim that initial vein ligation may lead to venous congestion and retention of blood that is subsequently lost with the specimen, though peribronchial venous channels will frequently prevent this result. The bronchus may also be ligated first. However, there are two points that should be kept in mind if this is done. First, the distal limb of the bronchus (the specimen side) should be oversewn to prevent drainage of mucus into the chest. Second, after division of the bronchus, the lobe is much more mobile; therefore, to prevent avulsion of the pulmonary artery branches, care should be taken not to employ excessive torsion or traction.

The techniques used for dissection, ligation, and division of pulmonary arteries and their branches differ from those used for other vessels. Pulmonary vessels are low-pressure, high-flow, thin-walled, fragile structures. Accordingly, for rapid and safe dissection, a perivascular plane, known as the plane of Leriche, should be sought. This plane may be absent in the presence of long-standing granulomatous or tuberculous disease, after major chemotherapy, after thoracic radiotherapy, and in cases of reoperation. In these situations, proximal control of the main pulmonary artery and the two pulmonary veins may be necessary before the more peripheral arterial dissection can be started. Before any pulmonary vessel is divided, it should be controlled either with two separate suture ligatures proximal to the line of division or with vascular staples; stapling devices are especially useful for larger vessels.

Exposure of the bronchus should not involve stripping the bronchial surface of its adventitia. Aggressive dissection may compromise the vascular supply and lead to impaired healing and bronchial dehiscence. Overlying nodal tissues should be cleared, and major bronchial arteries should be clipped just proximal to the point of division. Bronchial closure has been greatly facilitated by the use of automatic staplers. Because the bronchus is frequently the last structure to be divided before removal of the specimen, I often apply staples only to the proximal side of the bronchus and divide the bronchus distal to the staple line. Once the stapler is applied, every effort should be made to minimize its movement during firing, so as to prevent injury to the remaining proximal bronchial segment. With the stapler applied but not yet fired, the remaining lung should be ventilated to determine whether there is any impairment of ventilation secondary to placement of the stapler too close to a proximal lobar bronchus. Only when the absence of ventilatory impairment has been confirmed should the stapler be fired. When bronchial length is limited, one may perform suture closure of the bronchial stump rather than attempt to force a stapler around the bonchus. Whenever there is a high risk of bronchial stump dehiscence (e.g., after chemotherapy, radiotherapy, or chemoradiotherapy; in patients for whom adjuvant therapy is planned; or after right pneumonectomy), a vascularized rotational tissue flap (e.g., from the pericardium, the pericardial fat pad, or intercostal muscle) should be used to reinforce the bronchial closure.

Closure and Drainage

Once the bronchial closure is complete, the next step is to test its adequacy. The bronchial stump is submerged under normal saline, and the lung is inflated to a tracheal pressure of 45 cm H_2O. Any area of hilar dissection and divided fissures should be evaluated in a similar fashion. Significant parenchymal air leaks should be repaired with interrupted fine sutures (e.g., 4-0 polypropylene). If the air leak is from a diffuse raw surface, especially after upper lobectomy, construction of a pleural tent should be considered. Any air leak from the bronchial stump should be assessed very carefully. A simple repair with fine absorbable sutures may suffice, or the entire closure may have to be redone. Strong consideration should be given to reinforcing the stump with vascularized tissue (see above).

The chest is usually drained with two chest tubes that are positioned anteriorly and posteriorly and exit through separate stab incisions in the chest wall. If an epidural or a paravertebral catheter is being employed for postoperative pain management, the chest tubes should exit through an intercostal space that is no more than two spaces below the intercostal space used for entry into the chest. Failure to follow this recommendation is likely to result in pain originating from the chest tube site that will not be adequately addressed postoperatively and will lead to a significant increase in discomfort.

After a pneumonectomy, the chest tubes can be omitted. If this option is chosen, a needle should be used to aspirate 1,000 to 1,200 ml of air from the hemithorax operated on after closure of the skin. If a chest tube is used, a balanced drainage system is employed without suction. At most institutions, suction is employed postoperatively for all other resections (i.e., lobectomy, segmentectomy, and wedge resection); however, careful use of water seal in selected patients (i.e., those with small air leaks whose lungs do not collapse while on water seal) may allow earlier withdrawal of the tube.

Operative Technique

RIGHT LUNG

Right Upper Lobectomy

Dissection begins within the interlobar fissure, and the pulmonary artery is exposed at the junction of the major and minor fissures [see Figure 1]. In many cases, the artery is partially obscured by a level 11 interlobar lymph node, which should be removed. Also present is the posterior segmental branch of the superior pulmonary vein, which traverses the fissure in a posterior-to-anterior direction. The pulmonary artery lies medial and inferior to this venous branch.

Once the pulmonary artery is identified, the branches within the fissure are exposed, including the posterior ascending artery to the right upper lobe, the right middle-lobe artery, the superior segmental artery to the right lower lobe, and the basilar branches to the right lower lobe. If the exposure is adequate, the posterior ascending branch can be ligated and divided. If additional length is required, the fissure between the superior segment of the lower lobe and the posterior segment of the upper lobe can be completed. This is accomplished by opening the pleura in the posterior hilum along the lateral edge of the bronchus intermedius. A level 11 lymph node will be encountered between the right upper-lobe bronchus and the bronchus intermedius. Removal of this interlobar node (sometimes referred to as the sump node) will expose the posterior ascending branch. Either the branch can be directly ligated and divided via this exposure, or the fissure can be completed with gastrointestinal anastomosis (GIA) staplers, with the vessel ligated and divided after completion of the fissure.

The lung is then rotated posteriorly, and the pleura is incised posterior to the course of the phrenic nerve, which usually passes close to the base of the superior pulmonary vein. The phrenic nerve is carefully and gently mobilized anteriorly. The superior pulmonary vein is dissected, and the apical, anterior, and posterior branches are encircled [see Figure 2]. Care is taken to preserve the middle-lobe branches. The branches draining the upper lobe are then ligated and divided or controlled with a vascular stapler. Division of the veins before division of the arterial supply will not cause the lobe to become engorged. Instead, through collateral venous drainage to the middle lobe or via bronchial venous channels, blood will be shunted away from the upper lobe.

The interlobar (or truncus posterior) branch of the right pulmonary artery will be visible as it courses posterior to the superior pulmonary vein branches. Dissection continues along the lateral surface of the interlobar artery. Once the branches to the middle-lobe artery are identified, the dissection should reach the region previously dissected within the fissure. The fissure between the middle lobe and the upper lobe can now be completed through serial application of GIA staplers.

The right upper lobe is then rotated more inferiorly to provide a better view of the superior aspect of the hilum. This step allows complete exposure of the truncus anterior branch. Frequently, the truncus anterior branch originates from the main right pulmonary artery medial to the course of the superior vena cava; some elements of the pericardium may also encircle the artery at this location. Once the vessel is exposed, it is either suture-ligated and divided or transected with an endovascular stapler.

The upper lobe is retracted superiorly and posteriorly, and the interlobar artery is gently retracted anteriorly. The bronchus to the right upper lobe is circumferentially exposed, and all nodal tissue surrounding the right upper-lobe bronchus is swept distally so that it can be included with the specimen. Every effort is made to avoid devascularizing the bronchus. Once an adequate length of the right upper-lobe bronchus is exposed, the lung is rotated anteriorly to allow visualization of the course of the bronchus intermedius [see Figure 3]. The bronchus is ligated with a transverse anastomosis (TA)-30 stapler loaded with 4.8 mm staples. Care is taken to achieve close apposition of the anterior wall to the posterior membranous wall of the bronchus. With the stapler applied but not

fired, the right lung is ventilated to confirm that the bronchus intermedius has not been compromised. The stapler is fired, the bronchus is divided, and the specimen is removed.

To prevent middle-lobe syndrome resulting from torsion of the narrow hilum of the middle lobe after an upper lobectomy, the middle lobe should be secured to the lower lobe. Once the lungs are reexpanded, a small portion of the lower lobe and a comparable portion of the middle lobe are grasped along the major fissure. A single application (or, at most, two applications) of a TA stapler should suffice to secure the lobes to each other at this site and thus prevent middle-lobe torsion.

Right Middle Lobectomy

The initial steps in a right middle lobectomy are similar to those in a right upper lobectomy. The pulmonary artery and its branches are identified within the fissure. The middle-lobe artery is identified [see Figure 1]. Not infrequently, there are two middle-lobe arteries. When this is the case, the most proximal branch is commonly located across from the posterior ascending branch to the right upper lobe. Once the anatomy has been confirmed, the arterial branches to the middle lobe can be individually ligated and divided. If additional exposure is needed before ligation, the fis-

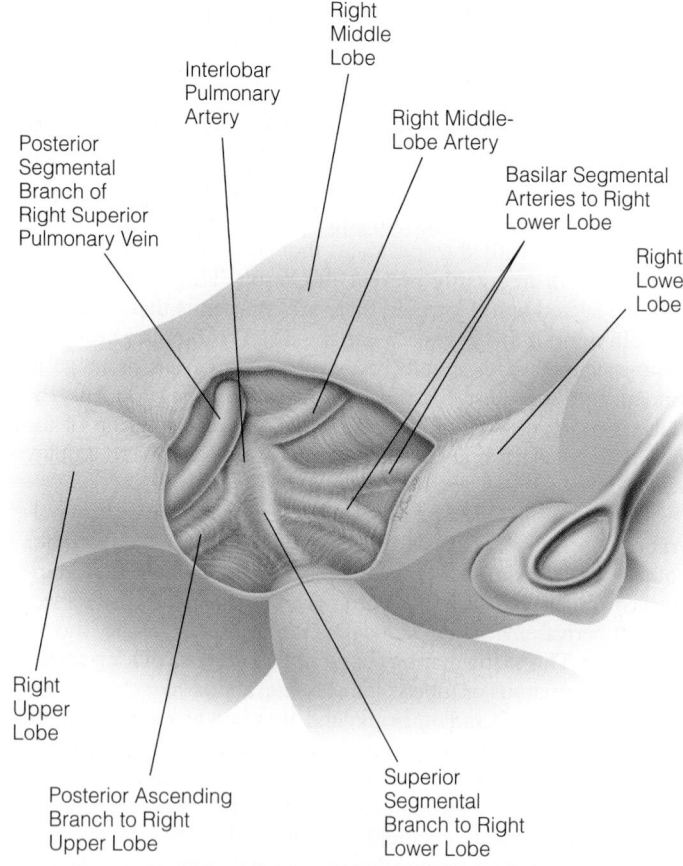

Figure 1 **Right upper lobectomy. Shown is the surgeon's view of the right interlobar fissure. The fissures have been completed, and the segmental arteries to the upper, middle, and lower lobes have been identified. The posterior ascending branch to the upper lobe most commonly varies with respect to size and origin. This vessel may be absent or diminutive and may arise from the superior segmental branch to the lower lobe. The posterior segmental vein draining into the superior pulmonary vein (not seen) is clearly visualized in the right upper lobe, lateral to the pulmonary artery branches.**

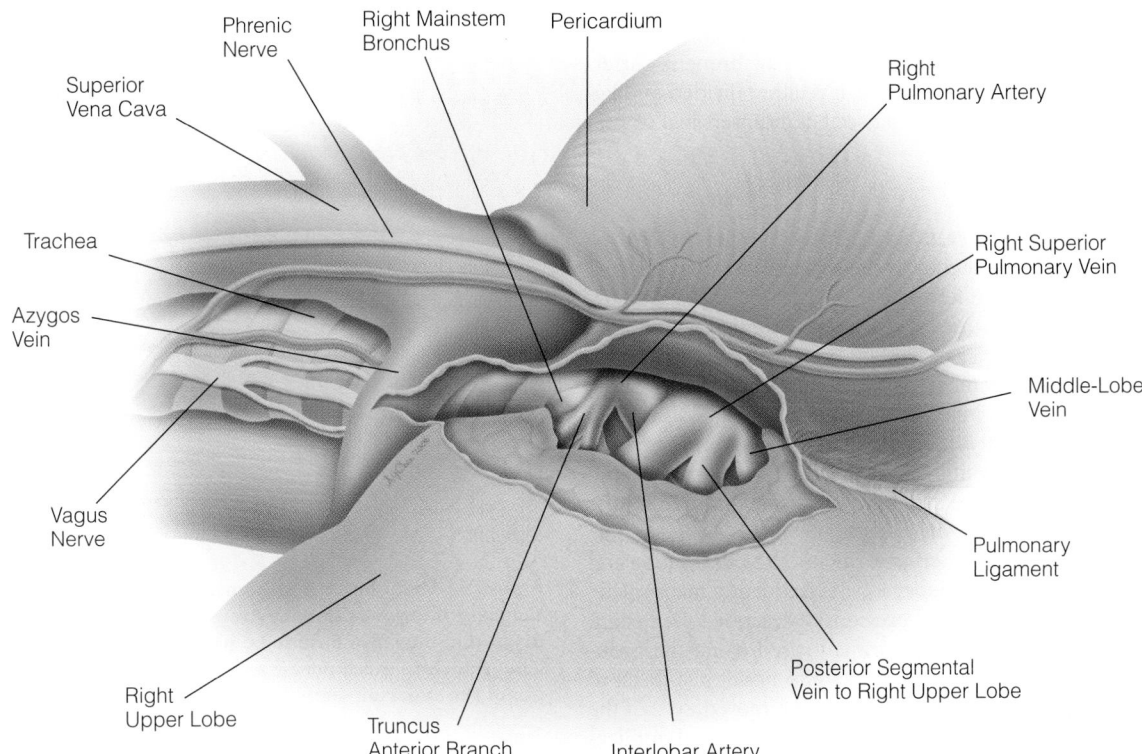

Figure 2 **Right upper lobectomy. Shown is the surgeon's view of the anterior right hilum. The apical venous branches of the superior pulmonary vein obscure the interlobar pulmonary artery and, to a lesser degree, the truncus anterior branch. Division of these venous branches during upper lobectomy improves exposure of the truncus anterior. The splitting of the main pulmonary artery into its two main branches may occur more proximally, and care should be taken to identify both branches before either one is divided. Another significant possible variation is a branch of the middle-lobe vein that arises from the intrapericardial portion of the superior pulmonary vein.**

sures can be completed to yield added exposure of a proximal middle-lobe artery.

Once the arteries are divided (or if additional exposure is required), the lung is rotated posteriorly to expose the superior pulmonary vein [see Figure 2]. The branches to the middle lobe are carefully identified, doubly ligated, and divided. The posterior segmental branch of the superior pulmonary vein should now be easily identifiable, originating just cephalad to the middle-lobe vein and coursing posteriorly (lateral to the interlobar artery) to drain the posterior segment of the right upper lobe. As noted (see above), this venous branch is easily identified during dissection of the interlobar artery within the fissure. To complete the fissure between the upper and middle lobes, dissection continues along the caudal and lateral surface of the posterior segmental venous branch until the previously performed dissection of the interlobar artery within the fissure is reached. The fissure is then completed through serial application of GIA staplers. When the fissure is complete, the surgeon has a clear view of the posterior segmental branch of the superior pulmonary vein and the interlobar branch of the pulmonary artery coursing posterior and medial to the veins. If the proximal arterial branch to the middle lobe could not be safely ligated from the fissure before, it should be easily accessible now.

The middle lobe is then rotated superiorly and posteriorly to expose the right middle-lobe bronchus [see Figure 4], which usually arises anterior and inferior to the right middle-lobe branches of the pulmonary artery. The basilar artery branches to the right lower lobe are gently mobilized posteriorly to expose the bronchus intermedius and the origin of the right middle-lobe bronchus.

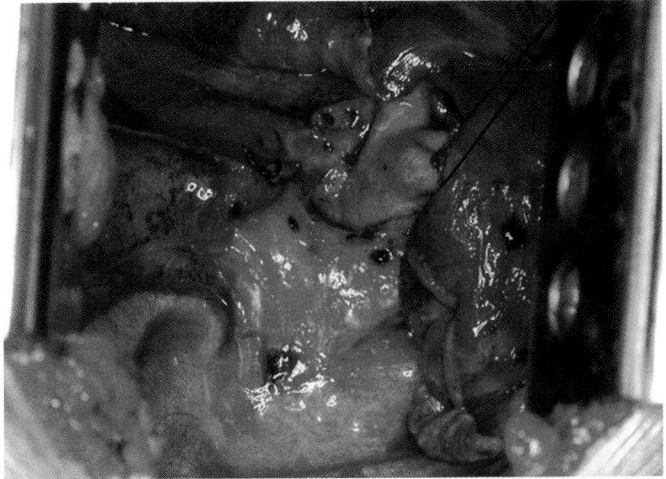

Figure 3 **Right upper lobectomy. Shown is the surgeon's view of the posterior right hilum. The carina, the right mainstem bronchus, the right upper lobe, and the bronchus intermedius are easily seen. The interlobar sump node has been removed and the fissure completed, and the posterior ascending branch of the pulmonary artery is visible. Care should be taken not to injure this vessel during division of the fissure. It can be ligated via this approach if it cannot be adequately exposed from the fissure. Both the truncus anterior and the posterior ascending branch of the pulmonary artery lie directly anterior to the right upper-lobe bronchus, and care should be taken not to injure these vessels during bronchial encirclement. The bronchial arteries course along the medial and lateral edges of the bronchus intermedius.**

Peribronchial lymph nodes located in this region should be dissected and removed, with care taken not to injure the bronchial arterial branches. Once the bronchus is free, it is either divided and ligated with an automatic stapler or transected and oversewn as previously described (see above).

Right Lower Lobectomy

Once again, the pulmonary artery is exposed within the oblique fissure. The pulmonary branches to the superior segment and the basilar segments of the right lower lobe are identified [*see Figure 1*]. All branches within the fissure are identified, including the middle-lobe artery and the posterior ascending branch to the right upper lobe. The superior segmental artery is encircled and doubly ligated, with care taken not to injure the posterior ascending branch if it arises from or close to the origin of the superior segmental branch. The basilar segmental branches are then encircled and doubly ligated, with the same care taken not to injure the middle-lobe branch. Both vessels are then divided.

The fissure between the superior segment of the lower lobe and the posterior segment of the upper lobe is frequently incomplete. If necessary, it is completed as previously described [*see* Right Upper Lobectomy, *above*]. The pleura is incised along the bronchus intermedius, and the lymph node (sump node) just distal to the takeoff of the right upper-lobe bronchus is removed, so that the previously dissected pulmonary artery is exposed. Serial application of GIA staplers is employed to complete the fissure.

The fissure between the middle and lower lobes may also have to be completed (though in many cases, it is congenitally com-

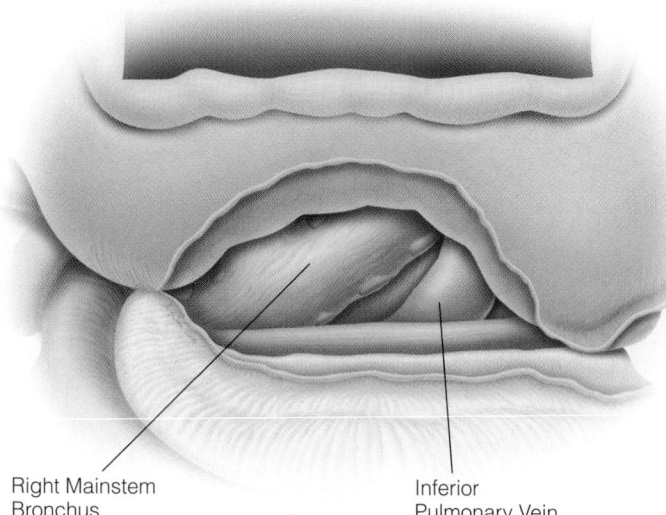

Right Mainstem Bronchus   Inferior Pulmonary Vein

Figure 5 **Right lower lobectomy. Shown is the surgeon's view of the right inferior pulmonary vein. For encirclement of this vein, dissection may also have to be performed on its anterior surface. The branch to the superior segment can be seen overlying the origin of the superior segmental bronchus.**

plete). The pleura is incised within the anterior hilum to allow identification of the superior and inferior pulmonary veins. The basilar segmental bronchi and the middle-lobe bronchus should be exposed. Removal of lymphoid tissue allows easy application of a GIA stapler to complete the fissure.

The inferior pulmonary vein is then encircled as it exits the pericardium [*see Figure 5*]. This step is facilitated by dissecting the superior edge of the inferior pulmonary vein with the lung rotated first anteriorly and then posteriorly. Once encircled, the pulmonary vein can easily be ligated and divided with a vascular stapler.

Division of the lower-lobe bronchus is best accomplished through the fissure; this approach facilitates identification of the middle-lobe bronchus and helps prevent inadvertent damage to or compromise of the origin of this structure. Level 11 and 12 lymph nodes are cleared distally along the bronchi to expose the origin of the superior segmental bronchus [*see Figure 6*]. In some patients, there is adequate length to permit oblique placement of a stapler for control of all the lower-lobe segmental bronchi without compromise of the middle-lobe bronchus. If this step is not possible, separate ligation and division of the superior segmental bronchus and of all the basilar bronchi as a unit should be performed.

The lung is rotated anteriorly, and the bronchus intermedius is dissected distally until the origin of the superior segmental bronchus is identified from this side. The branch of the inferior pulmonary vein draining the superior segment will be encountered and should be mobilized distally to allow adequate exposure of the superior segmental bronchus origin. This bronchus can now be encircled, ligated, and divided with a stapler or divided and oversewn.

Next, the basilar segmental bronchi are encircled at a point where closure will not affect airflow to the middle-lobe bronchus. Appropriate placement is confirmed by asking the anesthesiologist to ventilate the right lung while the stapler or clamp is applied to the base of the basilar bronchi. If placement is adequate, the basilar segmental bronchi are ligated and divided.

Right Pneumonectomy

With the pleura incised circumferentially around the hilum, the lung is rotated inferiorly and posteriorly [*see Figure 2*]. The main

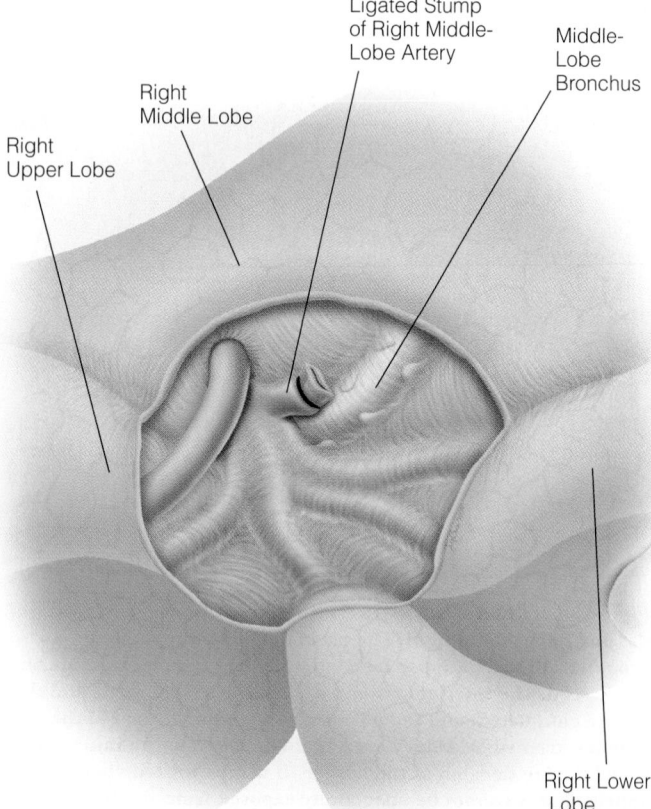

Right Upper Lobe

Right Middle Lobe

Ligated Stump of Right Middle-Lobe Artery

Middle-Lobe Bronchus

Right Lower Lobe

Figure 4 **Right middle lobectomy. Shown is the surgeon's view of the right middle-lobe bronchus. Gentle retraction of the basilar segmental artery to the lower lobe posteriorly allows clear visualization of the origin of the middle-lobe bronchus.**

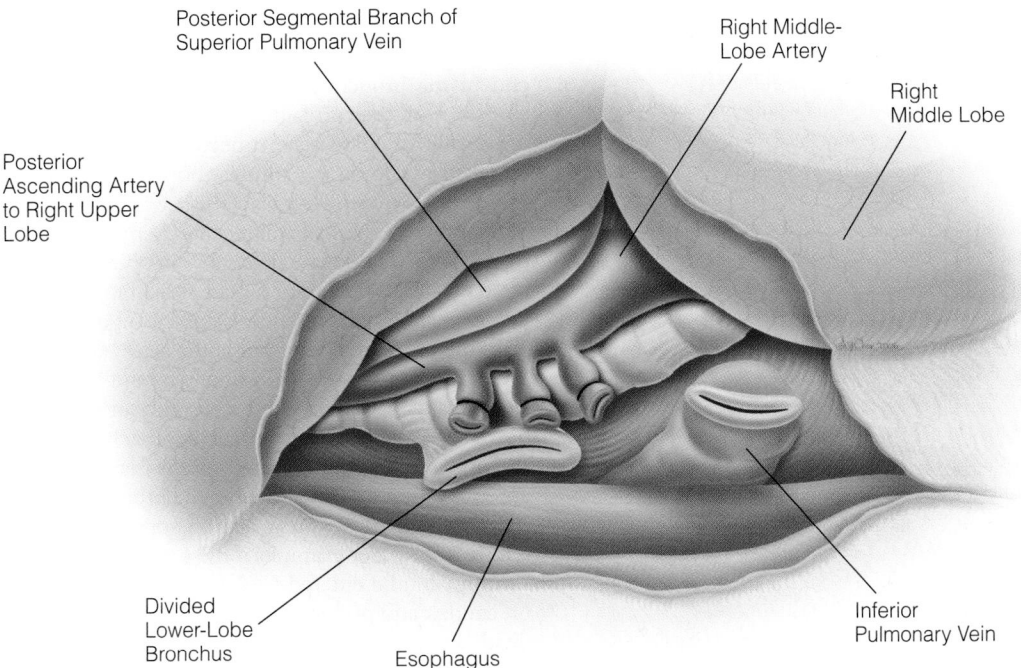

Posterior Segmental Branch of Superior Pulmonary Vein

Right Middle-Lobe Artery

Right Middle Lobe

Posterior Ascending Artery to Right Upper Lobe

Divided Lower-Lobe Bronchus

Esophagus

Inferior Pulmonary Vein

Figure 6 **Right lower lobectomy. Shown is the surgeon's view of the right fissure after division of the lower-lobe vessels. The decision whether to divide the bronchi separately or to transect them with a single oblique application of the stapler depends on the proximity of the middle-lobe bronchus to the superior segmental and basilar bronchi.**

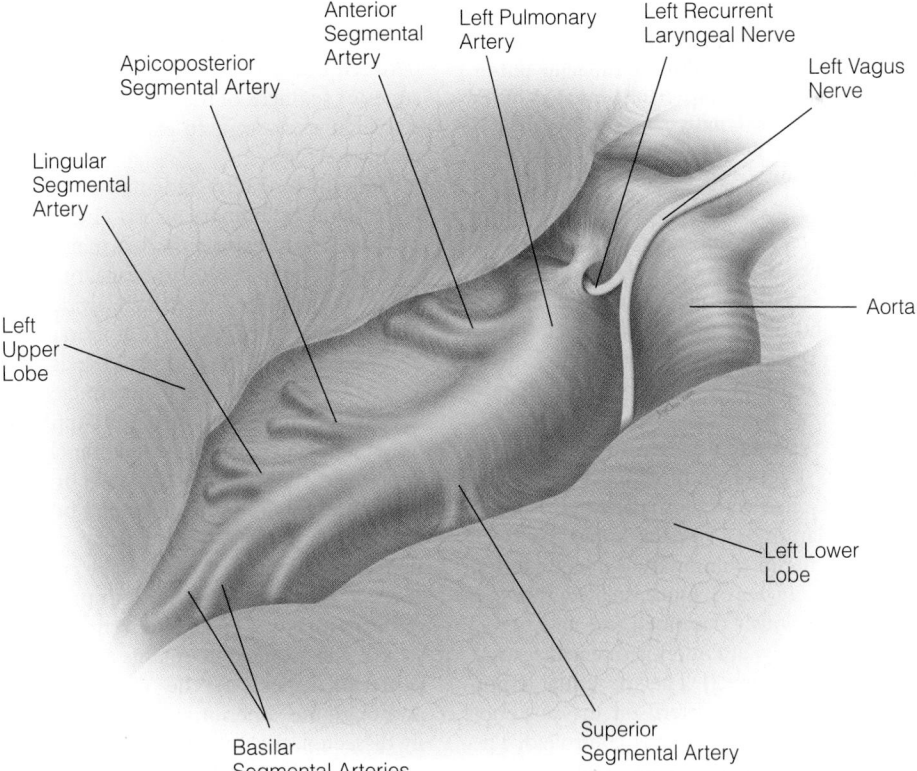

Apicoposterior Segmental Artery

Anterior Segmental Artery

Left Pulmonary Artery

Left Recurrent Laryngeal Nerve

Left Vagus Nerve

Lingular Segmental Artery

Left Upper Lobe

Aorta

Left Lower Lobe

Basilar Segmental Arteries

Superior Segmental Artery

Figure 7 **Left upper lobectomy. Shown is the surgeon's view of the left interlobar fissure. The recurrent laryngeal nerve can be seen coursing lateral to the ligamentum arteriosum. The arterial branches supplying the left upper lobe between the apicoposterior segmental branch and the lingular branch can vary substantially in number and size. Another frequently encountered variation is a distal lingular branch that arises from a basilar segmental branch.**

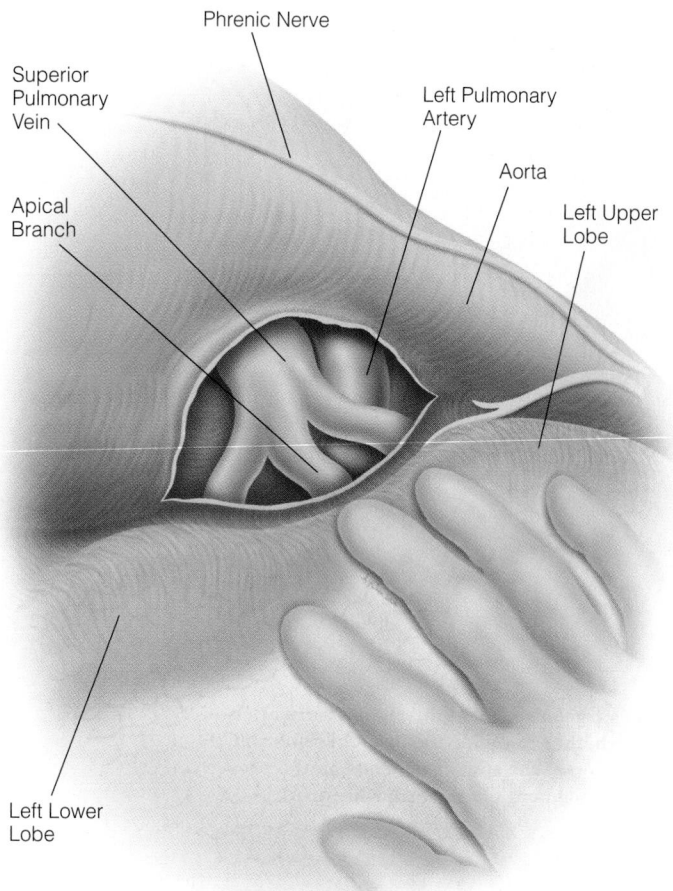

Apical
Branch

Superior
Pulmonary
Vein

Phrenic Nerve

Left Pulmonary
Artery

Aorta

Left Upper
Lobe

Left Lower
Lobe

Figure 8 **Left upper lobectomy. Shown is the surgeon's view of the anterior left hilum. The apical branches of the superior pulmonary vein course anterior to the apicoposterior branches of the pulmonary artery. If additional vessel length is needed because of the presence of a central tumor, the pericardium may be entered and the vein divided at that location.**

trunk of the right pulmonary artery is exposed as it exits the pericardium posterior to the vena cava. Care is taken not to dissect distally on the vessel and not to encircle only the truncus anterior branch by mistake. Ligation and division of the right pulmonary artery can be accomplished in several different ways; either dividing the vessel between clamps and oversewing it with 3-0 nonabsorbable suture material or using vascular staplers is acceptable.

Next, attention is directed toward the superior pulmonary vein. The vessel is mobilized on its superior and inferior aspects with blunt and sharp dissection, encircled with blunt dissection, and ligated and divided with either clamps or a vascular stapler. With the lung retracted superiorly, the inferior pulmonary vein is dissected as in a right lower lobectomy [*see Figure 5*]. Once isolated, this vein is also ligated and divided as previously described (see above).

With the lung retracted anteriorly, attention is directed toward the right mainstem bronchus [*see Figure 3*]. The subcarinal lymph nodes are mobilized, and the bronchial artery on the posterior medial aspect of the right mainstem bronchus is controlled. The remaining peribronchial tissues are then mobilized distally with blunt and sharp dissection. To avoid leaving a long bronchial stump, exposure of the bronchus to within 1 cm of the carina is advisable.

The bronchus can be closed with a TA stapler loaded with 4.8 mm staples. The staples should be oriented so as to allow good approximation of the anterior and posterior membranous walls. If

suture closure is selected instead, the bronchus is divided with the clamp placed on the distal bronchus to prevent spillage. The open end of the bronchus is then closed with nonabsorbable simple sutures, with the cartilaginous wall approximated to the membranous wall. To guard against necrosis of the bronchus, care should be taken not to tie the sutures too tightly. Coverage of the pneumonectomy stump with viable tissue is preferred, especially if the patient has received or will receive chemotherapy, radiation therapy, or both. The ideal choice for this purpose is either a rotated intercostal muscle flap or a pericardial fat pad rotational flap. The flap is secured with carefully placed 4-0 polypropylene sutures.

In the preceding description, the artery is divided first, followed by the individual veins and finally by the bronchus; however, the steps of this operation can be carried out in any order. The position of the tumor may make the approach I describe difficult. For example, an anteriorly placed tumor may hinder exposure of the anterior hilum. In this situation, the bronchus can be divided first, and the pulmonary artery can be approached from the posterior hilum. As another example, if the tumor is very proximal, the pericardium can be entered via a U-shaped incision along the anterior, caudal, and posterior hilum. The pulmonary veins can then be divided en masse as they originate from the left atrium, and the pulmonary artery can be divided as it courses posterior to the ascending aorta.

LEFT LUNG

Left Upper Lobectomy

After the thorax is entered, the lung is rendered atelectatic and the thorax is explored. The inferior pulmonary ligament is divided. The interlobar fissure is developed with a combination of sharp and electrocautery dissection. The posterior aspect of the fissure, between the apicoposterior segment of the left upper lobe and the superior segment of the left lower lobe, is completed (with a linear stapler if necessary) to expose the proximal portion of the pulmonary artery.

With the lung retracted inferiorly, dissection continues proximally along the pulmonary artery. The pleura is incised under the arch of the aorta to expose the left main pulmonary artery. A variable number of small vessels and vagal branches to the lung are encountered that must be ligated and divided. Care is taken not to injure the recurrent laryngeal nerve as it branches from the vagus and travels under the arch just distal to the ligamentum arteriosum.

The left upper lobe is then retracted anteriorly and superiorly to expose the pulmonary arteries supplying the lobe [*see Figure 7*]. There is an anterior segmental branch that frequently arises directly opposite the superior segmental branch to the lower lobe, as well as a more distally situated lingular branch. These vessels should be identified, individually ligated, and divided. Not infrequently, multiple posterior apical branches are encountered; in fact, as many as seven vessels supplying the left upper lobe may be identified.

Next, the whole lung is retracted caudally and inferiorly to expose the aortic arch. A large arterial branch supplying the apicoposterior aspect of the upper lobe is usually encountered. Although the superior and posterior aspects of this artery are easily dissected, the anterior aspect is frequently obscured by an apical branch of the superior pulmonary vein; division of this venous branch may improve exposure and facilitate control of the artery. Once the artery is encircled, it is ligated and divided. To prevent avulsion of this vessel from the main pulmonary artery, care must be taken not to exert excessive traction on the lung.

With the lung now retracted posteriorly, the mediastinal pleura is opened parallel to and posterior to the course of the phrenic

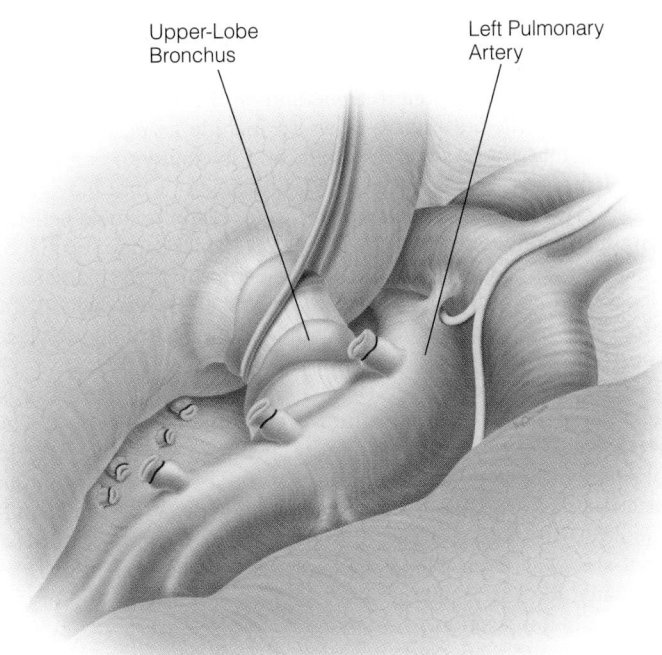

Figure 9 Left upper lobectomy. Shown is the surgeon's view of the left fissure after division of the upper-lobe arteries. Care should be taken not to injure the pulmonary artery inadvertently when applying a stapler.

the lingula and the lower lobe is completed with serial application of GIA staplers [see *Figure 9*]. The left upper lobe bronchus is encircled and either clamped or controlled with a TA stapler. To prevent inadvertent injury, the pulmonary artery branches to the lower lobe should be gently retracted posteriorly during stapler placement. With the stapler applied (or the clamp in place), the anesthesiologist ventilates the left lung to verify that air is flowing freely to the entire left lower lobe. Once unobstructed airflow is confirmed, the stapler is fired and the bronchus divided.

Left Lower Lobectomy

As in a left upper lobectomy, dissection begins within the interlobar fissure. The pulmonary artery is identified, and the branches to the upper and lower lobes are dissected [see *Figure 7*]. The superior segmental artery is encircled first and is ligated and divided; not uncommonly, there are actually two separate superior segmental arteries. The basilar segmental arteries are then encircled distal to the origin of the lingular artery. These vessels are also ligated and divided, with care taken not to encroach on the blood flow to the lingula.

The lung is rotated superiorly to expose the inferior pulmonary vein. As in a right lower lobectomy, the vein is encircled by dissecting first on its anterior surface with the lung rotated posteriorly, then on its posterior surface with the lung rotated anteriorly [see *Figure 10*]. Once the vein is encircled, it is ligated and divided.

Attention is then redirected toward the interlobar fissure, and the left lower lobe bronchus is identified [see *Figure 11*]. The origin of the bronchus is cleared by sweeping nodal tissue distally with blunt and sharp dissection. The upper-lobe branches of the pulmonary artery are gently retracted superiorly to allow placement of a TA stapler on the bronchus. With the stapler applied, the anesthesiologist ventilates the left lung to confirm the adequacy of airflow to the upper lobe. The stapler is fired, and the bronchus is divided distal to the staple line.

Left Pneumonectomy

The initial steps of a left pneumonectomy are similar to those of a left upper lobectomy. The lung is retracted caudally, and the pleu-

nerve [see *Figure 8*]. The superior pulmonary vein can then be identified easily. If the apical branch was not previously ligated, the surgeon should make every effort not to damage the pulmonary artery branches that lie posterior to this portion of the vein. The majority of the superior pulmonary vein lies anterior to the left upper lobe bronchus. Once this vein is encircled, it is ligated and divided.

Attention is then redirected toward the fissure, and the peribronchial nodal tissue surrounding the left upper lobe bronchus is swept distally with blunt and sharp dissection. The fissure between

Figure 10 Left lower lobectomy. Shown is the surgeon's view of the left inferior pulmonary vein. The left side, unlike the right side, affords only limited access to the subcarinal space. However, the length of the inferior pulmonary vein outside the pericardium is greater on the left side than on the right.

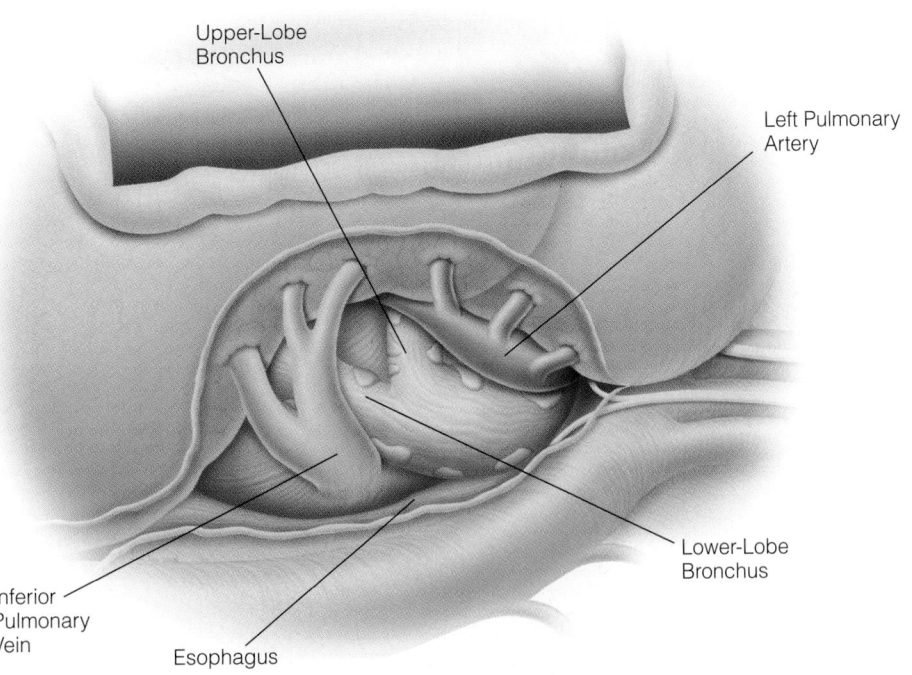

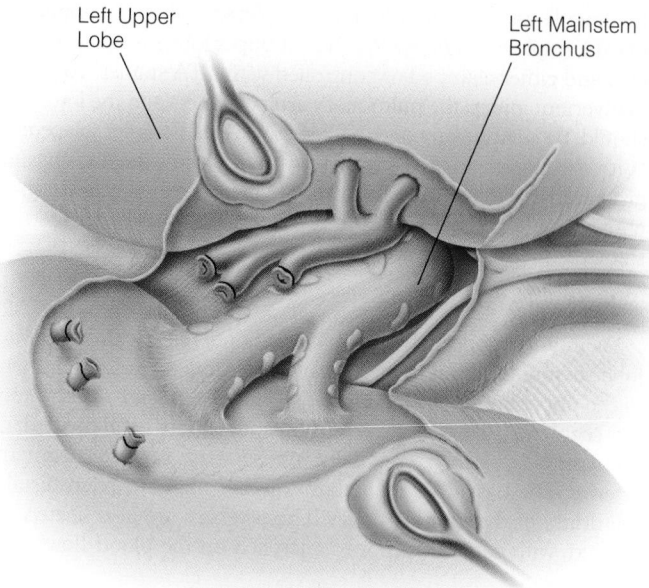

Figure 11 Left lower lobectomy. Shown is the surgeon's view of the left fissure after division of the lower-lobe vessels. In this procedure, a single oblique transection of the entire left lower-lobe bronchus can be employed without any concern that a proximal bronchus will be compromised; this step would not be feasible in a right lower lobectomy, in that the right middle-lobe bronchus arises from the bronchus intermedius.

ra is incised along the course of the aortic arch [*see Figure 7*]. The superior and posterior surfaces of the pulmonary artery are dissected as it enters the thorax under the aortic arch. Once the perivascular space is entered, the entire vessel can usually be encircled with blunt dissection. If the superior pulmonary vein's apical branch limits access to the anterior surface of the pulmonary artery, the branch may be ligated and divided first to improve exposure of the artery; alternatively, the superior pulmonary vein itself may be ligated and

divided first to facilitate arterial exposure (see below).

Once the pulmonary artery is encircled, the vessel can be ligated and divided. My preferred method is to use an endovascular GIA stapler, the advantages of which include its rapidity of use, its consistently reproducible results, and its ability to control the vessel along a broad surface. Mass ligation is not advisable, because the risk of dislocation of the tie is too great. When the length of exposed artery is too short or a stapler cannot be placed safely, the surgeon may apply vascular clamps to the proximal and distal portions of the vessel instead. Once the vessel is divided, the proximal end may be oversewn with a continuous polypropylene suture.

If additional vessel length is required because of the presence of a proximal tumor, the ligamentum arteriosum may be divided. The recurrent laryngeal nerve should be identified and preserved. In dividing the left pulmonary artery proximal to the ligamentum arteriosum, care should be taken not to narrow the main pulmonary artery and thereby reduce right-side blood flow. For maximal safety, systemic blood pressures and oxygenation should be evaluated for 1 to 2 minutes after application of the clamp or stapler but before ligation.

With the lung retracted posteriorly, the pleura is incised posterior to the course of the phrenic nerve, and the superior pulmonary vein is identified [*see Figure 8*]. The vein is encircled with blunt dissection, then ligated and divided. As noted (see above), the apical branch usually travels across the apical branch of the pulmonary artery, and care should be taken not to injure this vessel during dissection.

The lung is then retracted superiorly to expose the inferior pulmonary vein. Dissection is performed on the anterior and posterior aspects of the inferior pulmonary vein, and blunt dissection is used to achieve complete encirclement of the vein [*see Figure 10*], which is ligated and divided.

Next, the lung is retracted anteriorly and superiorly. Complete dissection of the subcarinal lymph nodes is performed, facilitated by division of one or two pulmonary branches of the left vagus nerve and both bronchial arteries. Gentle traction is applied in

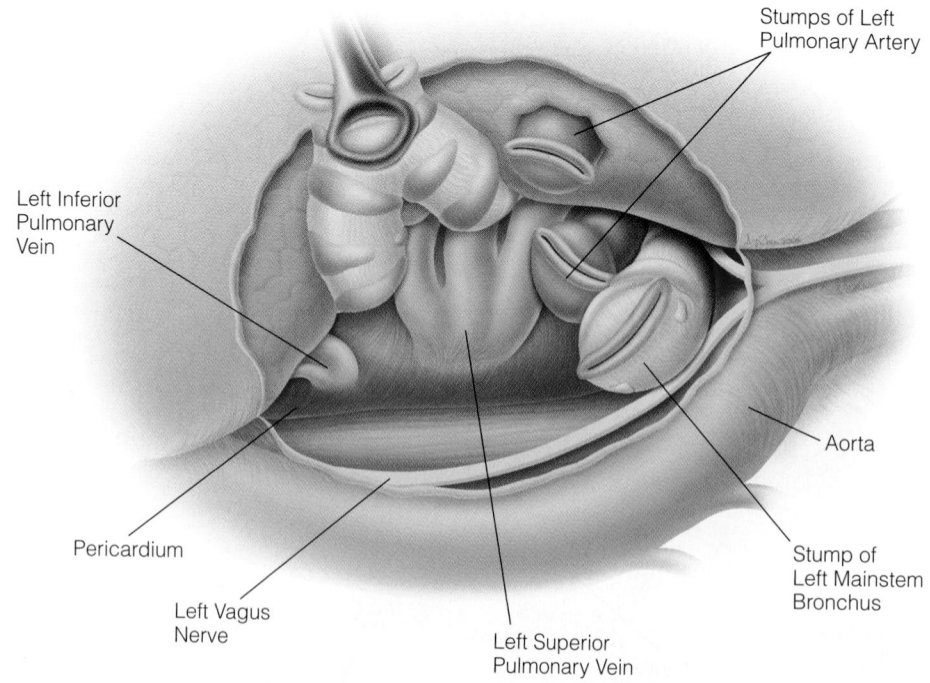

Figure 12 Left pneumonectomy. Shown is the surgeon's view of the posterior left hilum. The carina is located deep under the aortic arch. A left-side double-lumen tube or bronchial blocker may have to be withdrawn to afford better exposure of the proximal left mainstem bronchus. The orientation of the superior pulmonary vein and the pulmonary artery (anterior and superior to the bronchus, respectively) should be noted.

conjunction with blunt dissection to allow encirclement of the proximal left mainstem bronchus [*see Figure 12*]. An effort should be made to encircle the bronchus within 1 cm of the carina. A TA stapler is then passed around the left mainstem bronchus and applied at this point. If excessive traction is required to achieve this placement, the bronchial stump can be left slightly longer: 1 to 1.5 cm, as measured from the carina. The stapler is fired, and the bronchus is divided distal to the staple line.

Frequently, the position of the bronchial stump under the aortic arch and deep within the mediastinum renders coverage of the stump unnecessary. If the surgeon is concerned about possible stump dehiscence (e.g., in a patient who has undergone high-dose preoperative radiotherapy), coverage with a flap from the pericardial fat pad or intercostal muscle is appropriate.

Selected Reading

Fell SC, Kirby TJ: Technical aspects of lobectomy. General Thoracic Surgery, 6th ed. Shields TW, LoCicero J, Ponn RB, et al, Eds. Lippincott Williams & Wilkins, Philadelphia, 2005, p 433

Hood RM: Techniques in General Thoracic Surgery, 2nd ed. Lea & Febiger, Philadelphia, 1993

Kirby TJ, Fell SC: Pneumonectomy and its modifica-

tions. General Thoracic Surgery, 6th ed. Shields TW, LoCicero J, Ponn RB, et al, Eds. Lippincott Williams & Wilkins, Philadelphia, 2005, p 470

Martini N, Ginsberg RJ: Lobectomy. Thoracic Surgery, 2nd ed. Pearson FG, Cooper JD, Deslauriers J, et al, Eds. Churchill Livingstone, Philadelphia, 2002, p 981

Waters PF: Pneumonectomy. Thoracic Surgery, 2nd ed.

Pearson FG, Cooper JD, Deslauriers J, et al, Eds. Churchill Livingstone, Philadelphia, 2002, p 974

Acknowledgment

Figures 1, 2, and 4 through 12 Alice Y. Chen.

42 DIAPHRAGMATIC PROCEDURES

Ayesha S. Bryant, M.S.P.H., and Robert James Cerfolio, M.D., F.A.C.S., F.C.C.P.

Although the diaphragm is sometimes thought of as little more than a partition between the thoracic organs and the abdominal organs, it is in fact a dynamic anatomic structure that plays a pivotal role in the physiology of respiratory mechanics. For example, paralysis of just one hemidiaphragm can lead to the loss of 50% of a patient's vital capacity.[1] Like any other anatomic structure, the diaphragm may be affected by either benign or malignant conditions. Overall, benign diseases of the diaphragm (e.g., paralysis) are far more common than malignant ones. With either type of condition, however, the development of a safe surgical treatment strategy depends on a solid knowledge of diaphragmatic anatomy and physiology. Accordingly, we begin with a brief review of the embryology and anatomy of the diaphragm. We then describe the main procedures performed to treat the more common congenital diseases (e.g., congenital diaphragmatic hernia [CDH]) and acquired pathologic conditions (e.g., paralysis and tumor) that affect this structure.

Anatomic Considerations

DEVELOPMENTAL ANATOMY

The diaphragm is a modified half-dome of musculofibrous tissue that lies between the chest and the abdomen and serves to separate these two compartments. It is formed from four embryologic components: (1) the septum transversum, (2) two pleuroperitoneal folds, (3) cervical myotomes, and (4) the dorsal mesentery. Development of the diaphragm begins during week 3 of gestation and is complete by week 8. Failure of the pleuroperitoneal folds to develop, with subsequent muscle migration, results in congenital defects.

CLASSICAL ANATOMY

The diaphragmatic musculature originates from the lower six ribs on each side, from the posterior xiphoid process, and from the external and internal arcuate ligaments. A number of different structures traverse the diaphragm, including three distinct apertures (foramina) that allow the passage of the vena cava, the esophagus, and the aorta [*see Figure 1*]. The aortic aperture is the lowest and most posterior of the diaphragmatic foramina, lying at the level of the 12th thoracic vertebra. Besides the aorta, the thoracic duct and, sometimes, the azygos and hemiazygos veins also pass through this aperture. The esophageal aperture is the middle foramen; it is surrounded by diaphragmatic muscle and lies at the level of the 10th thoracic vertebra. The vena caval aperture is the highest of the three foramina, lying level with the disk space between T8 and T9.

VASCULAR SUPPLY

The diaphragm is supplied by the right and left phrenic arteries, the intercostal arteries, and the musculophrenic branches of the internal thoracic arteries. Some blood is supplied by small branches of the pericardiophrenic arteries that run with the phrenic nerve, mainly where the nerves penetrate the diaphragm. Venous drainage occurs via the inferior vena cava and the azygos vein on the right and via the suprarenal and renal veins and the hemiazygos vein on the left.

INNERVATION

The diaphragm receives its muscular neurologic impulse from the phrenic nerve, which arises primarily from the fourth cervical ramus but also has contributions from the third and fifth rami. The phrenic nerve originates around the level of the scalenus anterior and runs inferiorly through the neck and thorax before reaching its terminal point, the diaphragm. Because the phrenic nerve follows such a long course before reaching its final destination, a number of processes can disrupt the transmission of neurologic impulses through the nerve at various points and thereby cause diaphragmatic paralysis [*see 33 Paralyzed Diaphragm*].

Procedures for Congenital Diaphragmatic Hernia

REPAIR OF BOCHDALEK HERNIA

Bochdalek hernia, named after the Czech anatomist Vincent Alexander Bochdalek, is the most common form of CDH and is also the most common surgical emergency in neonates.[1] The usual presenting symptoms are severe respiratory distress and a scaphoid

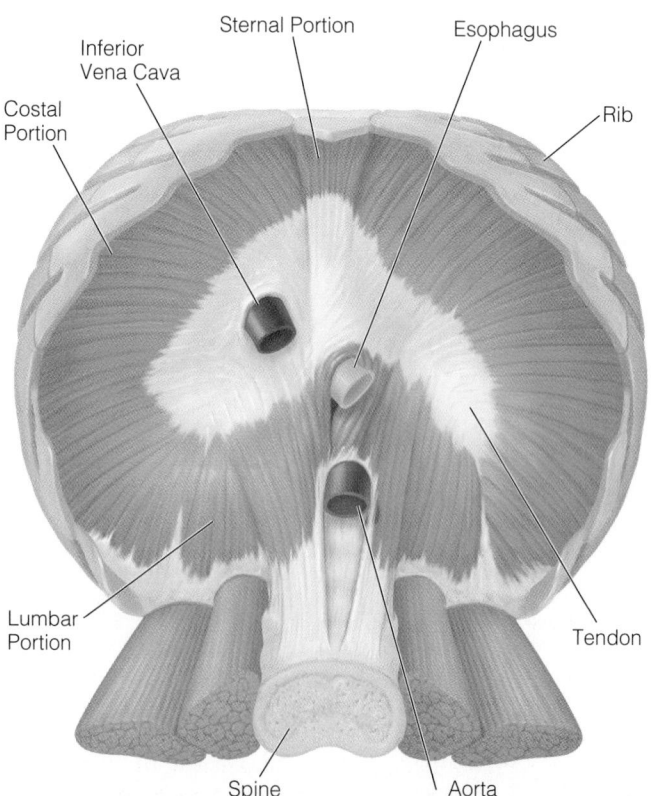

Figure 1 **Shown is an inferior view of the diaphragm.**

abdomen. The primary pathologic condition is the presence of posterolateral defects of the diaphragm, which result either in maldevelopment of the pleuroperitoneal folds or in improper or absent migration of the diaphragmatic musculature.

Bochdalek hernias occur in approximately one of every 2,500 live births and are twice as common in male neonates as in female neonates. Mortality ranges from 45% to 50%. The bulk of the morbidity and mortality of CDH is attributable to the resultant hypoplasia of the lung on the affected side and to various associated abnormalities (e.g., malrotation of the gut, neural tube defects, and cardiovascular anomalies).

Preoperative Evaluation

Prenatal ultrasound examination accurately diagnoses CDH in 40% to 90% of cases.[2] In most instances, the examination is performed to rule out polyhydramnios. It is noteworthy that polyhydramnios is present in as many as 80% of pregnant women whose fetuses have CDH.[3] In neonates with CDH, besides the upper gastrointestinal tract, parts of the colon, the spleen, the kidneys, and the pancreas may herniate, and the abnormal position of these organs can be identified by means of ultrasonography. Malrotation and malfixation of the small bowel should be ruled out. Once the diagnosis is confirmed, additional radiographic, echocardiographic, and ultrasonographic studies should be performed to rule out associated anomalies.

Operative Technique

As a rule, neonates with Bochdalek hernias are taken to the operating room immediately after birth. Some studies, however, have shown that delayed surgical repair yields improved survival rates.[4]

For left-side hernias, a transabdominal subcostal approach is generally preferred, whereas for right-side hernias, a transthoracic approach may be more useful. The herniated organs are returned to the peritoneal cavity. The lung is inspected, but no attempt to expand the hypoplastic lung should be made. If any extralobar pulmonary sequestration is present (as is occasionally the case), it should be excised. Most of the defects may be closed primarily with interrupted nonabsorbable sutures; particularly large defects may be closed with a prosthetic patch. The left pleural space is drained with a chest tube, which should be placed on water seal.

Alternative technique Some surgeons have attempted surgical correction of severe Bochdalek hernias in the prenatal period. The safety and feasibility of this therapeutic approach continue to be debated. Prenatal correction of these hernias poses a risk to both the mother and the fetus, with possibly fatal results for both.[5]

REPAIR OF MORGAGNI HERNIA

Morgagni hernias, named after the Italian anatomist and pathologist Giovanni Battista Morgagni, are related to maldevelopment of the embryologic septum transversum and to failed fusion of the sternal and costal fibrotendinous elements of the diaphragm.[6] These hernias are generally asymptomatic[7] and are usually detected as incidental findings on radiographs. Accordingly, the average age at diagnosis is typically greater for Morgagni hernia than for Bochdalek hernia: in one report, the mean age at which the former was diagnosed was 45 years.[8] Morgagni hernias are most commonly seen on the right side. The hernia sac usually contains omentum, but it may also contain part of the transverse colon or, less commonly, parts of the stomach, the liver, or the small bowel; almost any upper abdominal structure may herniate in this setting.

Preoperative Evaluation

On chest radiography, a Morgagni hernia appears as a mass at the right cardiophrenic angle [see Figure 2]. Computed tomography of the chest and abdomen, liver scintigraphy, and multiplanar magnetic resonance imaging are occasionally helpful in the diagnostic process.

Operative Technique

Morgagni hernias can be repaired via a subcostal, a paramedian, or a midline incision. We prefer to use an upper midline abdominal incision. Once the peritoneal cavity is entered, the hernia sac is identified just posterior to the xiphoid and the posterior sternal border, then opened. The herniated abdominal viscera are restored to their normal abdominal anatomic positions, and the sac is ligated. The entire hernia sac is defined, resected, and closed. The diaphragmatic defect may be repaired in several different ways, depending on its size and position. Because there is weak tissue in the area of the defect, we generally use a prosthetic patch for the repair. Either polypropylene mesh (e.g., Marlex; C. R. Bard, Inc., Murray Hill, New Jersey) or polytetrafluoroethylene (PTFE) mesh (e.g., Gore-Tex; W. L. Gore and Associates, Newark, Delaware) may be used for this purpose. We prefer PTFE because it may cause fewer adhesions to the underlying abdominal structure, which may be an important consideration if further abdominal surgery subsequently proves necessary. The prosthetic patch is sewn to the midline abdominal fascia, with wide bites taken to prevent an abdominal incisional hernia. The rest of the patch is sewn to the thickened investing fascia that made up the edges of the hernia sac. As noted, the frequently marginal quality of this tissue is the reason why a patch repair is almost always required.

Repair of a Morgagni hernia via a thoracic incision follows the same basic principles. The hernia sac is entered, the visceral contents are mobilized and reduced into the abdomen, the sac is resected, and the diaphragm is repaired. Again, the closure should be completed without tension. If the defect cannot be closed with horizontal mattress sutures, a prosthetic patch should be used.

Complications

The potential complications of surgical treatment of Morgagni hernia depend to an extent on the type of procedure undertaken to repair the defect. Laparoscopy may result in failure to reduce the contents of the hernia sac, which necessitates conversion to an open procedure. Laparotomy has been associated with postoperative pleural effusion,[9] wound infection,[10] deep vein thrombosis,[11] and pulmonary embolism.[12] Thoracotomy has been associated with pneumonia, sepsis, and bowel obstruction in the postoperative period.[13]

Outcome Evaluation

Most patients do not have any significant postoperative limitations after repair of a Morgagni hernia, nor are such hernias likely to recur. In one study, 16 patients who underwent transthoracic repair of a Morgagni hernia were followed for 5.7 years; no recurrences or symptoms related to the operation were reported.[14]

Procedures for Diaphragmatic Paralysis

The diaphragm is the most important of the respiratory muscles: diaphragmatic contraction decreases intrapleural pressure during inspiration, expands the rib cage, and thereby facilitates the movement of gases into the lungs. Accordingly, paralysis of the diaphragm can have a major adverse effect on respiratory function [see 33 Paralyzed Diaphragm]. Diaphragmatic paralysis may involve

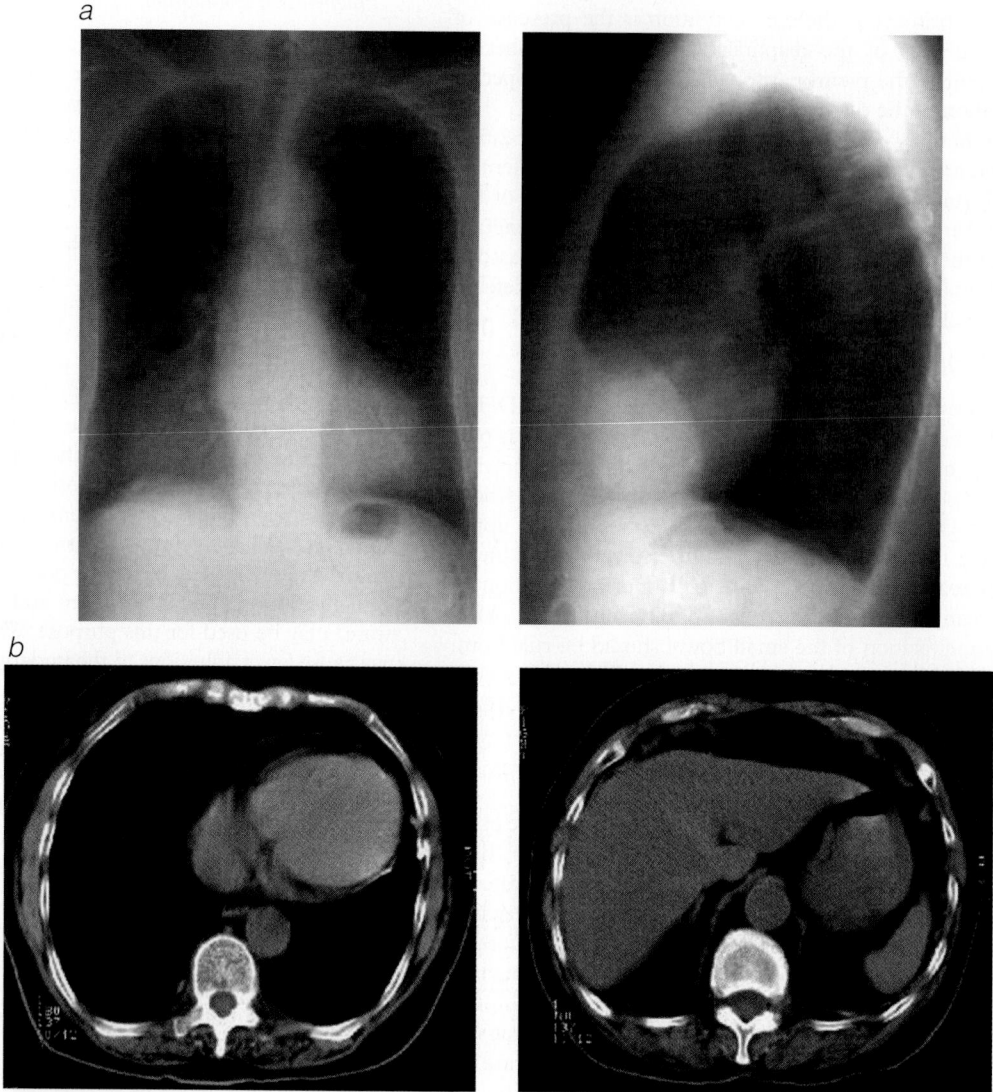

Figure 2 Repair of Morgagni hernia. The differential diagnosis of a cardiophrenic-angle mass includes pericardial fat, a lipoma, a pericardial cyst, a Morgagni hernia, and a thymoma. Shown are (*a*) chest x-rays and (*b*) chest CT scans from a 33-year-old man with an incidental finding of a Morgagni hernia.

either the whole diaphragm (bilateral paralysis) or only one leaflet or hemidiaphragm (unilateral paralysis). The possible causes of diaphragmatic paralysis are numerous [*see Table 1*]; the most common causes are phrenic nerve trauma related to a surgical procedure (e.g., stretching, crushing, or transection) and invasion by a malignant neoplasm.

DIAPHRAGMATIC PLICATION FOR UNILATERAL PARALYSIS

Preoperative Evaluation

With unilateral diaphragmatic paralysis, the paralyzed hemidiaphragm paradoxically moves upward on inspiration and downward on expiration, passively following changes in intrapleural and intra-abdominal pressure. Patients with a paralyzed hemidiaphragm who are otherwise healthy usually have no symptoms at rest but experience dyspnea during exertion and show a decrease in exercise performance. Physical examination may reveal dullness to percussion and an absence of breath sounds over the lower chest on the involved side.

In most cases, the diagnosis of hemidiaphragmatic paralysis is suspected on the basis of incidental findings on a chest x-ray. Typically, the roentgenogram reveals an elevated hemidiaphragm, diminished lung volume, and basilar atelectasis. Fluoroscopy may also be performed. The diagnosis is confirmed by performing a fluoroscopic sniff test, in which paradoxical elevation of the paralyzed diaphragm is observed with sniffing.[15] The sniff test is the gold standard for the diagnosis of this condition. In certain patients, a chest CT scan may be indicated for evaluating the potential cause of the paralysis. If an obvious cause is not apparent from the history or a previous evaluation, CT scanning of the chest should be performed to ensure there is no pathologic process that is compressing or invading the phrenic nerve. Similarly, MRI of the neck or the spine may be indicated in certain patients to look for conditions that might be causing the diaphragmatic paralysis.

Two other tests that are also (albeit less commonly) used for the diagnosis of unilateral diaphragmatic paralysis are electromyography and transdiaphragmatic pressure assessment. In the first, the phrenic nerve is electrically stimulated in the neck in an effort to

Table 1 Common Causes of Diaphragmatic Paralysis

Neurologic conditions	Spinal cord transection
	Multiple sclerosis
	Amyotrophic lateral sclerosis
	Cervical spondylosis
	Poliomyelitis
	Guillain-Barré syndrome
	Phrenic nerve dysfunction
	Compression by tumor
	Cardiac surgery cold injury
	Blunt trauma
	Idiopathic phrenic neuropathy
	Diabetes mellitus
	Postviral phrenic neuropathy (herpes zoster)
	Radiation therapy
	Cervical chiropractic manipulation
Myopathic conditions	Limb-girdle dystrophy
	Hyperthyroidism/hypothyroidism
	Malnutrition
	Acid maltase deficiency
	Connective tissue disease
	Systemic lupus erythematosus
	Dermatomyositis
	Mixed connective tissue disease
	Amyloidosis
	Idiopathic myopathy
	Muscular dystrophy
	Multiple sclerosis

distinguish between neuropathic and myopathic causes of paralysis. In the second, transdiaphragmatic pressures are measured by placing a thin-walled balloon transnasally at the lower end of the esophagus in such a way as to reflect changes in pleural pressure; a second balloon manometer is then placed in the stomach in such a way as to reflect changes in intra-abdominal pressure. The difference between the two pressures is the transdiaphragmatic pressure. Measurement of transdiaphragmatic pressure can help differentiate diaphragmatic paralysis from other causes of respiratory failure.

Yet another test involves measurement of maximal inspiratory pressures. Patients with diaphragmatic dysfunction and paralysis show a decrease in their maximal inspiratory pressures. These patients cannot generate high negative inspiratory pressures, and thus, their maximal inspiratory pressures will be less negative than -60 cm H_2O.

Operative Planning

Surgical treatment of hemidiaphragmatic paralysis is reserved for symptomatic patients who, after a follow-up period of at least 6 months, have persistent shortness of breath with exertion that is sufficiently pronounced to interfere with lifestyle. For a patient to be considered for operation, the sniff test should show significant paradoxical motion.

The basic principle of the surgical procedure is to "reef" (i.e., reduce the surface area of) the redundant floppy diaphragm by plicating it. This measure lowers the resting position of the hemidiaphragm and thus affords the lung the opportunity to expand fully. The effective result is an increase in the functional vital capacity of the ipsilateral lung. A 2002 study found that plication of the diaphragm led to long-term improvements in pulmonary function test results, as well as reduced dyspnea.[16]

Operative Technique

Diaphragmatic plication may be performed with either sutures or staples; we prefer sutures for this procedure. The chest is entered through a thoracotomy in the seventh or eighth intercostal space. Horizontal mattress sutures buttressed with Teflon pledgets are then placed in a lateral-to-medial direction [see Figure 3]. We typically use monofilament nonabsorbable sutures that pass easily through the muscle and can be tightened without dragging through tissue. To distribute the tension, multiple sutures must be placed; this is especially important on the right side, where the diaphragm must be pulled down against the upward force exerted by the presence of the right hemiliver. When the sutures are tied, the hemidiaphragm should be almost back to its normal anatomic location. Care must be taken to ensure that the repair is not under undue tension: excessive tension is likely to result in early dehiscence. Occasionally, a prosthetic patch may be used to buttress the repair further, but in the majority of cases, this measure should be unnecessary. If the choice is made to use staples rather than sutures, care must be taken to ensure that the underlying abdominal contents are not caught in the staple line.

DIAPHRAGMATIC PACING FOR BILATERAL PARALYSIS

Preoperative Evaluation

In patients with bilateral diaphragmatic paralysis, the respiratory accessory muscles assume all the work of breathing by contracting more intensely. Both hemidiaphragms move upward on inspiration, concomitant with inward (rather than the normal outward) movement of the abdominal wall.[17] Patients typically present with severe respiratory failure or with dyspnea (sometimes misinterpreted as a sign of heart failure) that worsens in the supine position, and they generally exhibit tachypnea and rapid, shallow

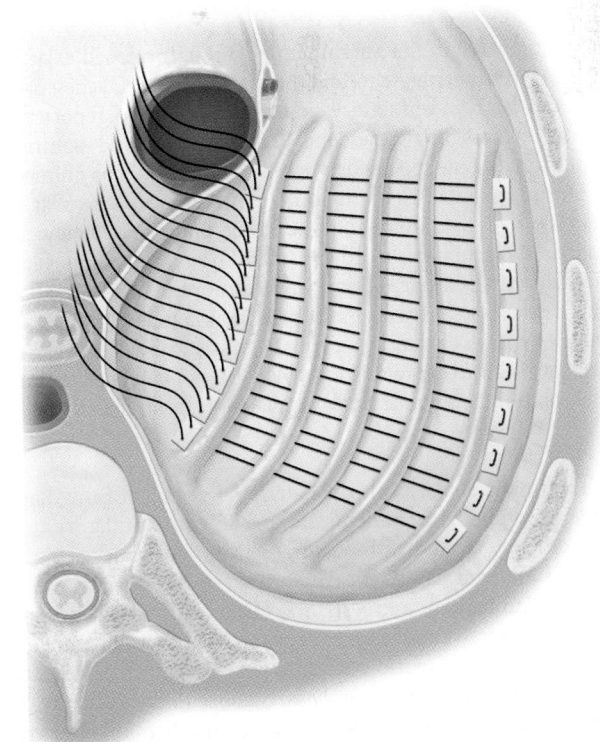

Figure 3 Diaphragmatic plication. Shown is suture plication of the right hemidiaphragm. Placement of sutures buttressed with pledgets extends anteriorly to the level of the vena cava.

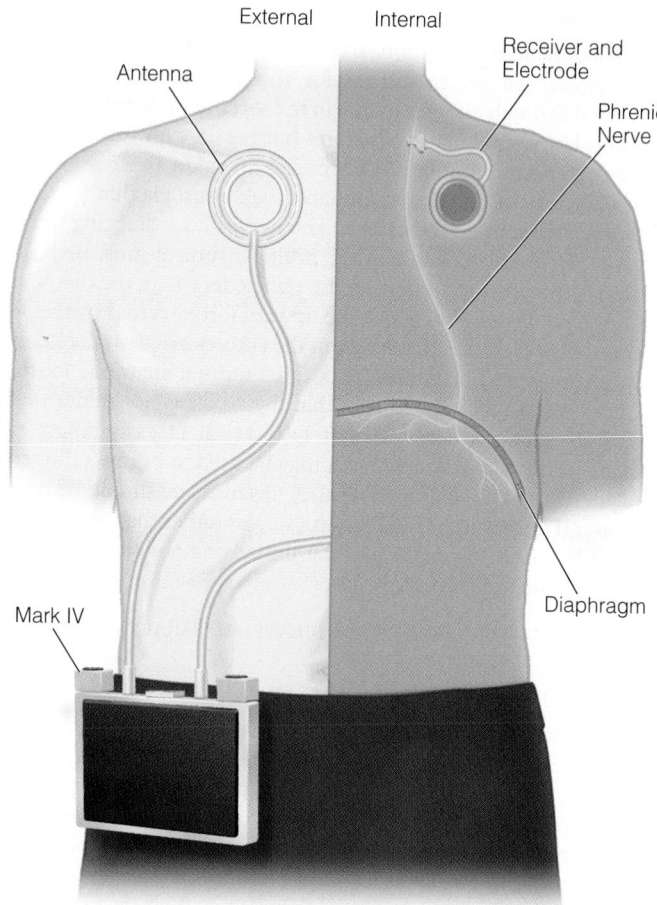

External   Internal

Antenna

Receiver and
Electrode

Phrenic
Nerve

Mark IV

Diaphragm

Figure 4 **Diaphragmatic pacing. Shown are internal and external pacer connections.**

breathing when in the recumbent position. Increased expenditure of effort in the struggle to breathe may fatigue the accessory muscles and lead to ventilatory failure. Patients also report anxiety, insomnia, morning headache, excessive daytime somnolence, confusion, fatigue, poor sleep habits, and signs of cor pulmonale.[18]

During physical examination, auscultation of the chest reveals limitation of diaphragmatic excursion and bilateral lower-chest dullness with absent breath sounds. The finding that establishes the diagnosis is a paradoxical inward movement of the abdomen with inspiration. As with unilateral diaphragmatic paralysis, however, it is more common for the diagnosis to be suspected on the basis of a chest roentgenogram that shows bilateral diaphragmatic elevation, then confirmed by means of the sniff test.

Operative Planning

Treatment depends on the cause and severity of the diaphragmatic paralysis. Most patients are treated with ventilatory support, but some are treated with bilateral plication or with pacing. Plication for bilateral paralysis is performed in the same way as plication for unilateral paralysis [*see* Diaphragmatic Plication for Unilateral Paralysis, *above*], except that both hemidiaphragms are lowered. Diaphragmatic pacing is not useful in the treatment of unilateral diaphragmatic paralysis, because of the difficulty of synchronizing the contractions of the normal hemidiaphragm with those of the paralyzed hemidiaphragm. However, it is sometimes an appropriate choice for the treatment of bilateral paralysis, especially in patients who have a central condition that is causing their apnea. Because the phrenic nerve stimulates the C3, C4, and C5

anterior horn cells in the nerve roots, diaphragmatic pacing is feasible only when the lesion is above the C2-C3 level. Accordingly, it is sometimes employed in patients with high spinal cord injuries.

To date, only one pacing device has been approved by the Food and Drug Administration: the Mark IV Breathing Pacemaker System (Avery Biomedical Devices, Commack, New York). This device possesses an internal component and an external component [*see Figure 4*]. The internal component is surgically placed adjacent to the skeletonized phrenic nerve and is connected to a small, wafer-shaped receiving unit placed under the skin. A battery-powered external transmitting box connected to an antenna is taped over the surface of the skin, just above the subcutaneous receiver. This transmitting box permits adjustment of pulse duration, pulse train duration, respiratory rate, pulse frequency, and current amplitude. In most patients, the only parameters that the clinician adjusts are current amplitude and respiratory rate.

Implantation of a diaphragmatic pacer requires significant experience on the part of the surgeon—not so much because of any particular technical demands imposed by the implantation itself but because of the procedures for diaphragm training that must be carried out in the postoperative period.

Choice of surgical approach Surgical implantation of a diaphragmatic pacer can be done via either a cervical approach or a thoracic approach. The primary advantage of the cervical approach is that it avoids the morbidity associated with bilateral thoracotomies, which may not be well tolerated in patients who have marginal pulmonary function or a history of severe pulmonary contusions. However, there are other ways of avoiding this morbidity, such as using video-assisted thoracoscopic surgery (VATS) or performing small muscle-sparing, rib-sparing, nerve-sparing thoracotomies.[19] One disadvantage of the cervical approach is that in a small percentage of patients, the current amplitude necessary to stimulate the phrenic nerve results in transmission of the current through the soft tissues. The transmitted current stimulates the functioning portions of the brachial plexus, causing rhythmic jerking motions of the upper extremities. Another disadvantage is that there are a number of accessory nerve branches arising distal to the neck.

One advantage of the thoracic approach is that inadvertent stimulation of portions of the brachial plexus (as sometimes occurs with the cervical approach) may be avoided. Another advantage is that there is some neuroanatomic evidence that a small branch of the phrenic nerve joins the main nerve trunk only after it enters the chest cavity; thus, the thoracic approach may stimulate a larger portion of the phrenic nerve than the cervical approach would. The disadvantage of the thoracic approach is the preconceived notion that entry into the chest is associated with a higher morbidity than entry into the neck.

Operative Technique

Cervical placement In the neck, the phrenic nerve runs between the scalenus anterior and the scalenus medius. A transverse skin incision is made in the midportion of the neck, just lateral to the sternocleidomastoid muscle, and the borders of the two scalene muscles are dissected. The scalene muscles are then divided, and the phrenic nerve is identified lying in a layer of fascia just anterior to the anterior surface of the scalenus medius. Identification of this nerve is often facilitated by the use of a hand-held nerve stimulator. Intraoperative fluoroscopy allows observation of diaphragmatic contraction in response to phrenic nerve stimulation, which confirms that pacing is successful.

Once the phrenic nerve is identified, it is carefully dissected free of its investing fascia, and the Y-shaped electrode is placed under

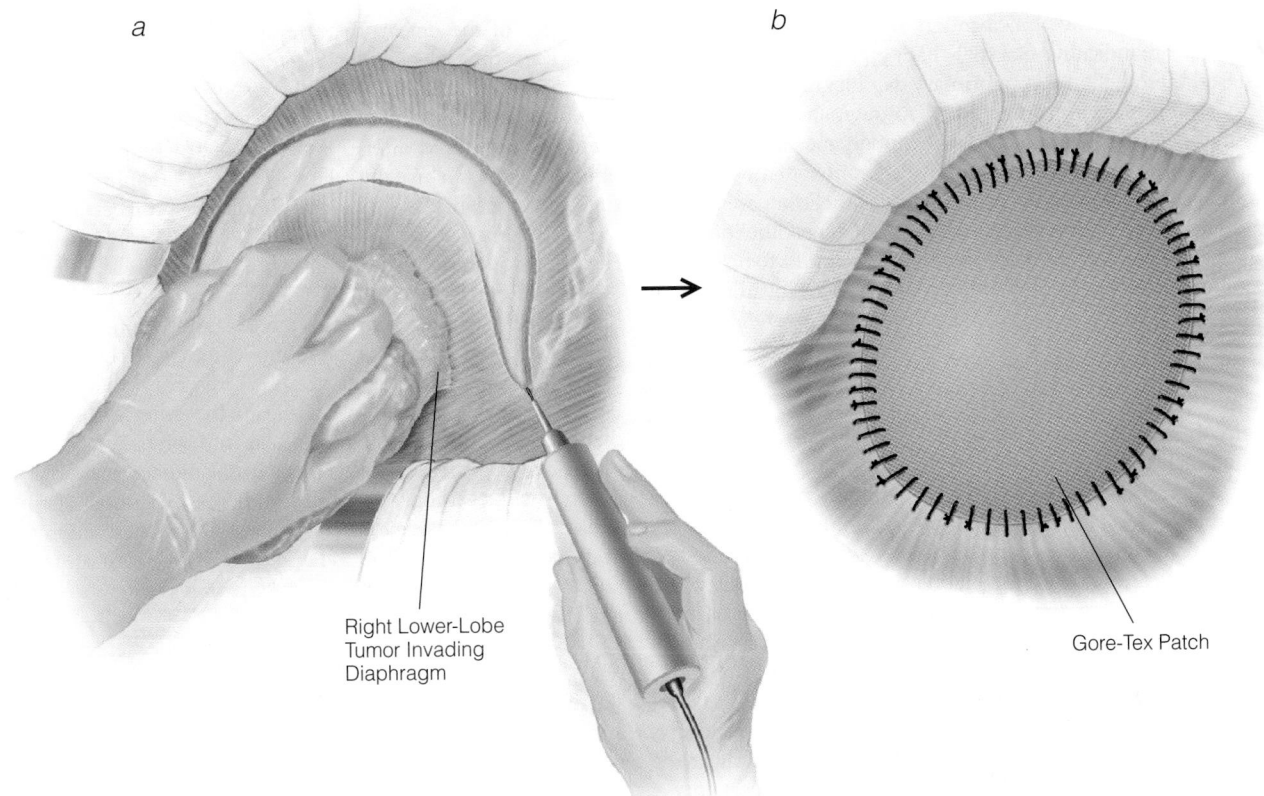

a

b

Right Lower-Lobe
Tumor Invading
Diaphragm

Gore-Tex Patch

Figure 5 **Resection of diaphragmatic tumor. The patient has a right lower-lobe bronchogenic malignancy with erosion into the right hemidiaphragm. (*a*) The tumor is resected en bloc with the diaphragmatic fibers; the electrocautery is used to achieve clear surgical margins and hemostasis. (*b*) The defect in the right hemidiaphragm is closed with a mesh patch.**

it and secured with sutures. Care must be taken to ensure that the nerve is not injured during this step. The connecting wire from the electrode is then tunneled subcutaneously to a subcutaneous pocket that is created just below the ipsilateral clavicle. The connections are made and sealed, and the small incisions are closed.

Thoracic placement In the thoracic approach, the chest is entered through a high thoracotomy (usually over the fourth interspace), and the proximal phrenic nerve is identified. On the right side, the nerve lies along the mediastinum, situated just anterior to the vena cava and coursing along the pericardial surface. On the left side, it lies on the pericardium for most of its length. The proximal nerve is freed of its fibrous investments, and the electrode is placed under it and secured with sutures. The electrode is connected to the receiver, which is placed in a subcutaneous pocket.

As noted (see above), there are alternative approaches to pacer implantation that avoid the cervical approach but also do not involve standard thoracotomies. For example, there is limited (but growing) experience with thoracoscopic placement of phrenic nerve pacing leads.[20] In addition, laparoscopic implantation of intramuscular pacing electrodes onto the inferior aspect of the diaphragm has been reported.[21]

Taking into account all the advantages and disadvantages of each approach to pacer implantation, we generally prefer the thoracic approach, either via VATS or via a thoracotomy.[20,22] The evolution of less invasive surgical techniques may allow the thoracic approach to be employed in patients who are unable to tolerate thoracotomy.

Complications

Besides the usual complications associated with any thoracic procedure (i.e., infection, bleeding, atrial fibrillation, and pneumonia),

there are several specific complications associated with diaphragmatic pacing. The most common of these are dislodgment of the pacer electrode, transmission of pacer impulses to the brachial plexus with resultant rhythmic jerking of the upper extremity (seen with cervical placement of the electrode), and hardware malfunction.

Outcome Evaluation

Retrospective analysis of the collective experience at a single center between 1981 and 1987 suggested that long-term pacing did not lead to progressive diaphragmatic dysfunction.[23] Six of the 12 patients in this cohort continued to undergo diaphragmatic pacing on a full-time basis for a median period of more than 14 years. Pacing was well tolerated in this group; the reasons for discontinuance included intercurrent medical illness and lack of social support. Concerns have been raised that prolonged diaphragmatic pacing might damage the phrenic nerve. In the series cited, however, the ability to pace the phrenic nerve was not lost in any of the patients, and the mean threshold currents for pacing did not change significantly over time.

Resection of Diaphragmatic Tumors

Primary tumors of the diaphragm are extremely rare. Benign tumors (e.g., lipomas and cystic masses) are more common than malignant tumors, which mostly are sarcomas of fibrous or muscular origin. Thoracic and abdominal tumors (e.g., bronchogenic carcinomas, pleural malignancies, and chest wall malignancies [*see 30 Chest Wall Mass*]) may involve the diaphragm secondarily through direct extension. Malignant pleural mesothelioma represents a different scenario and is not discussed here. Schwannomas, chondromas, pheochromocytomas, and endometriomas have all been reported. Bilateral occurrence, calcification, sharp margins, and flattened contours are indicative of a malignant process, such as pleural metastases, mesothelioma, or a primary diaphragmatic tumor.

The most common indication for diaphragmatic resection is mesothelioma. This remains true even though mesothelioma is relatively uncommon in comparison with bronchogenic malignancy and even though few patients with mesothelioma are actually candidates for resection. Again, resection of a mesothelioma is not addressed here. The ensuing operative description focuses on diaphragmatic resection to treat either a lung cancer invading the diaphragm or a primary diaphragmatic tumor [see Figure 5].

OPERATIVE TECHNIQUE

Once the decision is made to resect a tumor involving the diaphragm, the key considerations are (1) the surgical approach to be taken and (2) the placement of the incision in the diaphragm. We prefer a skin incision that is lower and slightly more anterior than a normal posterolateral thoracotomy; such an incision allows easy entry over the top of the seventh rib. After entry into the chest, the lung, the pericardium, and the pleural surface are carefully visualized and palpated to search for any signs of metastatic disease.

Next, the incision in the diaphragm is planned. Ideally, the incision should be made anterior or lateral to the tumor so that a hand can be placed easily into the peritoneal cavity [see Figure 5a]. Intra-abdominal palpation confirms that the tumor has not extended into underlying structures. This information is almost always gleaned from the preoperative CT scan, but if any uncertainty remains after the scan, diagnostic laparoscopy may be performed before the thoracotomy to look for possible tumor extension.

The tumor is then resected with 2 to 4 cm margins. The large arteries that course through the diaphragmatic fibers are ligated. It is our practice also to place a few silk sutures (stay stitches) in the edges of the defect; this prevents the edges from retracting, helps keep the defect as small as possible, and keeps abdominal contents from interfering with the resection. In addition, we place clips on the edges for guidance purposes, in case adjuvant radiotherapy is delivered after the operation. If adequate margins are obtained, which is usually relatively easy in a diaphragmatic resection, postoperative radiotherapy should be unnecessary. If, however, the tumor abuts vital structures (e.g., the suprahepatic vena cava), postoperative radiotherapy may have a useful role to play.

Once the entire tumor has been resected and clear margins have been confirmed by frozen-section examination, the diaphragm is reconstructed. Primary repair is rarely indicated, because in most cases, the defect is too large and the tension on the repair would be too great. Moreover, the tissue in the anterior aspect of the diaphragm is thin and is likely to tear under tension. Accordingly, repair with a prosthetic patch is the usual choice. Infection of such a patch is exceedingly rare, and with the exception of the cost, there is little downside to the use of prosthetic material in this setting. As in the repair of a CDH, we prefer PTFE mesh [see Figure 5b] to polypropylene mesh because it is less likely to adhere to underlying abdominal structures.

The mesh patch is sewn to the edges of the defect (preferably with nonabsorbable suture material, such as 0 polypropylene), starting at the most anterior and inferior portion of the opening and continuing toward the surgeon [see Figure 5]. The inferior half of the repair is done with a continuous suture. The repair is completed with two or three sutures, which are tied circumferentially. To prevent paradoxical motion, the diaphragm must not be too redundant or floppy. It should remain in the normal anatomic position so that the remaining lung can expand completely. In general, however, it is best to keep the repair taut so as to optimize pulmonary mechanics after the procedure.

References

1. Kirks DR, Caron KH: Gastrointestinal tract. Practical Pediatric Imaging, 2nd ed. Kirs DR, Ed. Little, Brown & Co, Boston, 1991

2. Lewin D, Bowerman R: Hirschel R: Prenatal ultrasonogram frequently fails to diagnose congenital diaphragmatic hernia. J Pediatr Surg (in press)

3. Adzick NS, Harrison MR, Glick PL, et al: Diaphragmatic hernia in the fetus: prenatal diagnosis and outcome in 94 cases. J Pediatr Surg 20:357, 1985

4. Breaux CW Jr, Rouse TM, Cain WS, et al: Improvement in survival of patients with congenital diaphragmatic hernia utilizing a strategy of delayed repair after medical and/or extracorporeal membrane oxygenation stabilization. J Pediatr Surg 26:333, 1991

5. Wenstrom KD, Weiner CP, Hanson JW: A five year statewide experience with congenital diaphragmatic hernia. Am J Obstet Gynecol 165:838, 1991

6. Panicek DM, Benson CB, Gottlieb RH, et al: The diaphragm: anatomic, pathologic, and radiologic considerations. Radiographics 8:385, 1988

7. Fraser RS, Pare JAP, Fraser RG, et al: Synopsis of Diseases of the Chest, 2nd ed. WB Saunders Co, Philadelphia, 1984

8. Minneci PC, Deans KJ, Kim P, et al: Foramen of Morgagni hernia: changes in diagnosis and treatment. Ann Thorac Surg 77:1956, 2004

9. Jani PG: Morgagni hernia: case report. East Afr Med J 78:559, 2001

10. Ngaage DL, Young RA, Cowen ME: An unusual combination of diaphragmatic hernias in a patient presenting with the clinical features of restrictive pulmonary disease: report of a case. Surgery Today 31:1079, 2001

11. Missen AJB: Foramen of Morgagni hernia. Proc R Soc Med 66:654, 1973

12. Dawson RE, Jansing CW: Case report: foramen of Morgagni hernias. J Kentucky Med Assoc 75:325, 1997

13. Lev-Chelouche D, Ravid A, Michowitz M, et al: Morgagni hernia: unique presentations in elderly patients. J Clin Gastroenterol 28:81, 1999

14. Kiliç D, Nadir A, Döner E, et al: Transthoracic approach in surgical management of Morgagni hernia. Eur J Cardiothorac Surg 20:1016, 2001

15. Miller JM, Moxham J, Green M: The maximal sniff in the assessment of diaphragm function in man. Clin Sci (Colch) 69:91, 1985

16. Higgs SM, Hussain A, Jackson M, et al: Long term results of diaphragmatic plication for unilateral diaphragm paralysis. Eur J Cardiothorac Surg 21:294, 2002

17. Higgenbottam T, Allen D, Loh L, et al: Abdominal wall movement in normals and patients with hemi-diaphragmatic and bilateral diaphragmatic palsy. Thorax 32:589, 1977

18. Piehler JM, Pairolero PC, Gracey DR, et al: Unexplained diaphragmatic paralysis: a harbinger of malignant disease? J Thorac Cardiovasc Surg 84:861, 1982

19. Cerfolio RJ, Bryant AS, Patel B, et al: Intercostal muscle flap decreases the pain of thoracotomy: a prospective randomized trial. J Thorac Cardiovasc Surg 130:987, 2005

20. Morgan JA, Morales DL, John R, et al: Endoscopic, robotically assisted implantation of phrenic pacemakers. J Thorac Cardiovasc Surg 126:582, 2003

21. DiMarco AF, Onders RP, Kowalski KE, et al: Phrenic nerve pacing in a tetraplegic patient via intramuscular diaphragm electrodes. Am J Respir Crit Care Med 166:1604, 2002

22. Cerfolio RJ, Price TN, Bryant AS, et al: Intracostal sutures decrease the pain of thoracotomy. Ann Thorac Surg 76:407, 2003

23. Elefteriades JA, Quin JA, Hogan JF, et al: Long-term follow-up of pacing of the conditioned diaphragm in quadriplegia. Pacing Clin Electrophysiol 25:897, 2002

Acknowledgment

Figures 1 and 3 through 5   Tom Moore.

43 ACUTE ABDOMINAL PAIN

David I. Soybel, M.D., F.A.C.S., and Romano Delcore, M.D., F.A.C.S.

The term acute abdominal pain generally refers to previously undiagnosed pain that arises suddenly and is of less than 7 days' (usually less than 48 hours') duration.[1] It may be caused by a great variety of intraperitoneal disorders, many of which call for surgical treatment, as well as by a range of extraperitoneal disorders,[2] which typically do not call for surgical treatment [see Clinical Evaluation, Tentative Differential Diagnosis, *below*]. Abdominal pain that persists for 6 hours or longer is usually caused by disorders of surgical significance.[3] The primary goals in the management of patients with acute abdominal pain are (1) to establish a differential diagnosis and a plan for confirming the diagnosis through appropriate imaging studies, (2) to determine whether operative intervention is necessary, and (3) to prepare the patient for operation in a manner that minimizes perioperative morbidity and mortality.

In many cases, these goals are easily accomplished. On occasion, however, the evaluation of patients with acute abdominal pain can be one of the most difficult challenges in clinical surgery. It is essential to keep in mind that most (at least two thirds) of the patients who present with acute abdominal pain have disorders for which surgical intervention is not required.[2,4,5] In addition, most clinicians depend on recognition of specific patterns and sequences of symptoms and signs to determine the need for further testing and to make decisions regarding the timing of operation; however, at least one third of patients with acute abdominal pain exhibit atypical features that render pattern recognition unreliable.[2,5] Finally, it is not clear that individual clinicians always or even usually agree on presenting symptoms and physical signs. In one study of abdominal pain in children, agreement between individual observers was reached 50% of the time for the physical sign of rebound tenderness; however, for five other signs (abdominal distention, abdominal tenderness to percussion, abdominal tenderness to palpation, abdominal guarding, and bowel sounds), interobserver agreement was not reached in more than one third of patients. These findings highlight the difficulties inherent in evaluation and management of acute abdominal pain. In addition, they emphasize the importance of integrating care among different providers to minimize loss of information and maximize continuity of care.

Clinical Evaluation

HISTORY

A careful and methodical clinical history should be obtained. Key features of the history include the di-

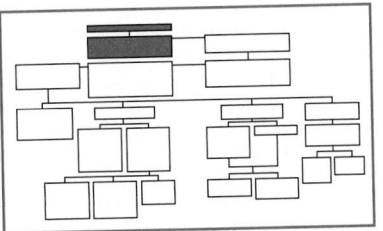

mensions of pain (i.e., mode of onset, duration, frequency, character, location, chronology, radiation, and intensity), as well as the presence or absence of any aggravating or alleviating factors and associated symptoms. Often, such a history is more valuable than any single laboratory or x-ray finding and determines the course of subsequent evaluation and management.

Unfortunately, when the ability of clinicians to take an organized and accurate history has been studied, the results have been disappointing.[6] For this reason, the use of standardized history and physical forms, with or without the aid of diagnostic computer programs, has been recommended.[7-10] A large-scale study that included 16,737 patients with acute abdominal pain demonstrated that integration of computer-aided diagnosis into management yielded a 20% improvement in diagnostic accuracy.[7] The study also documented statistically significant reductions in inappropriate admissions, negative laparotomies, serious management errors (e.g., failure to operate on patients who require surgery), and length of hospital stay, as well as statistically significant increases in the number of patients who were immediately discharged home without adverse effects and the promptness with which those requiring surgery underwent operation. Although many factors may have contributed to the observed benefits of computer-aided decision-making, it is clear that the use of structured and standardized means of collecting clinical and laboratory data was crucial. An example of such a structured data sheet is the pain chart developed by the World Organization of Gastroenterology (OMGE) [see Figure 1]. Because this pain chart is not exhaustive and does not cover all potential situations, individual surgeons may want to add to it; however, they would be well advised not to omit any of the symptoms and signs on the OMGE data sheet from their routine examination of patients with acute abdominal pain.[11]

The patient's own words often provide important clues to the correct diagnosis. The examiner should refrain from suggesting specific symptoms, except as a last resort. Any questions that must be asked should be open-ended—for example, "What happens when you eat?" rather than "Does eating make the pain worse?" Leading questions should be avoided. When a leading question must be asked, it should be posed first as a negative question (i.e., one that calls for an answer in the negative) because a negative answer to a question is more likely to be honest and accurate. For example, if peritoneal inflammation is suspected, the question asked should be "Does coughing make the pain better?" rather than "Does coughing make the pain worse?"

The mode of onset of abdominal pain may help the examiner determine the severity of the underlying disease. Pain that has a sudden onset suggests an intra-abdominal catastrophe, such as a ruptured abdominal aortic aneurysm (AAA), a perforated viscus, or a ruptured ectopic pregnancy; a near loss of consciousness or stamina associated with sudden-onset pain should heighten the level of concern for such a catastrophe. Rapidly progressive pain that becomes intensely focused in a well-defined area within a period of a few minutes to an hour or two suggests a condition such as acute cholecystitis or pancreatitis. Pain that has a gradual onset over several hours, usually beginning as slight or vague discomfort and slowly progressing to steady and more localized pain, suggests a subacute process and is characteristic of processes that lead to peritoneal inflammation. Numerous disorders may be associated with this mode of onset, including acute appendicitis, diverticulitis, pelvic inflammatory disease (PID), and intestinal obstruction.

Pain can be either intermittent or continuous. Intermittent or cramping pain (colic) is pain that occurs for a short period (a few minutes), followed by longer periods (a few minutes to one-half

Assessment of Acute Abdominal Pain

Patient presents with acute abdominal pain

Obtain clinical history

Assess mode of onset, duration, frequency, character, location, chronology, radiation, and intensity of pain.
Look for aggravating or alleviating factors and associated symptoms.
Use structured data sheets if possible.

Generate working diagnosis

Proceed with subsequent management on the basis of the working diagnosis.
Reevaluate patient repeatedly. If patient does not respond to treatment as expected, reassess working diagnosis and return to differential diagnosis.

Perform basic investigative studies

Laboratory: complete blood count, hematocrit, electrolytes, creatinine, blood urea nitrogen, glucose, liver function tests, amylase, lipase, urinalysis, pregnancy test, ECG (if patient is elderly or has atherosclerosis).
Imaging: Perform US or CT as indicated by results of examination and basic laboratory studies.

Patient has acute surgical abdomen

Operate immediately.
Conditions necessitating immediate laparotomy include ruptured abdominal aortic or visceral aneurysm, ruptured ectopic pregnancy, spontaneous hepatic or splenic rupture, major blunt or penetrating abdominal trauma, and hemoperitoneum from various causes.
Severe hemodynamic instability is the essential indication.

Patient has subacute surgical abdomen

Treat surgically when diagnosis is confirmed.

Patient requires urgent laparotomy or laparoscopy

Conditions necessitating urgent laparotomy include perforated hollow viscus, appendicitis, Meckel diverticulitis, strangulated hernia, mesenteric ischemia, and ectopic pregnancy (unruptured).
Laparoscopy is recommended for acute appendicitis and perforated ulcers (provided that surgeon has sufficient experience and competence with the technique).

Patient should be hospitalized and observed

Observe patient carefully, and reevaluate condition periodically.
Consider additional investigative studies (e.g., CT, US, diagnostic peritoneal lavage, radionuclide imaging, angiography, MRI, and GI endoscopy).
Diagnostic laparoscopy is recommended if pain persists after a period of observation.

Patient requires early laparotomy or laparoscopy

Early laparotomy or laparoscopy is reserved for patients whose conditions are unlikely to become life threatening if operation is delayed for 24–48 hr (e.g., those with uncomplicated intestinal obstruction, uncomplicated acute cholecystitis, uncomplicated acute diverticulitis, or nonstrangulated incarcerated hernia).

Patient is candidate for elective laparotomy or laparoscopy

Elective laparotomy or laparoscopy is reserved for patients who are highly likely to respond to conservative medical management or whose conditions are highly unlikely to become life threatening during prolonged evaluation (e.g., those with IBD, peptic ulcer disease, pancreatitis, or endometriosis).

Diagnosis is uncertain, or patient has suspected nonsurgical abdomen

Reevaluate patient as appropriate
(see facing page).

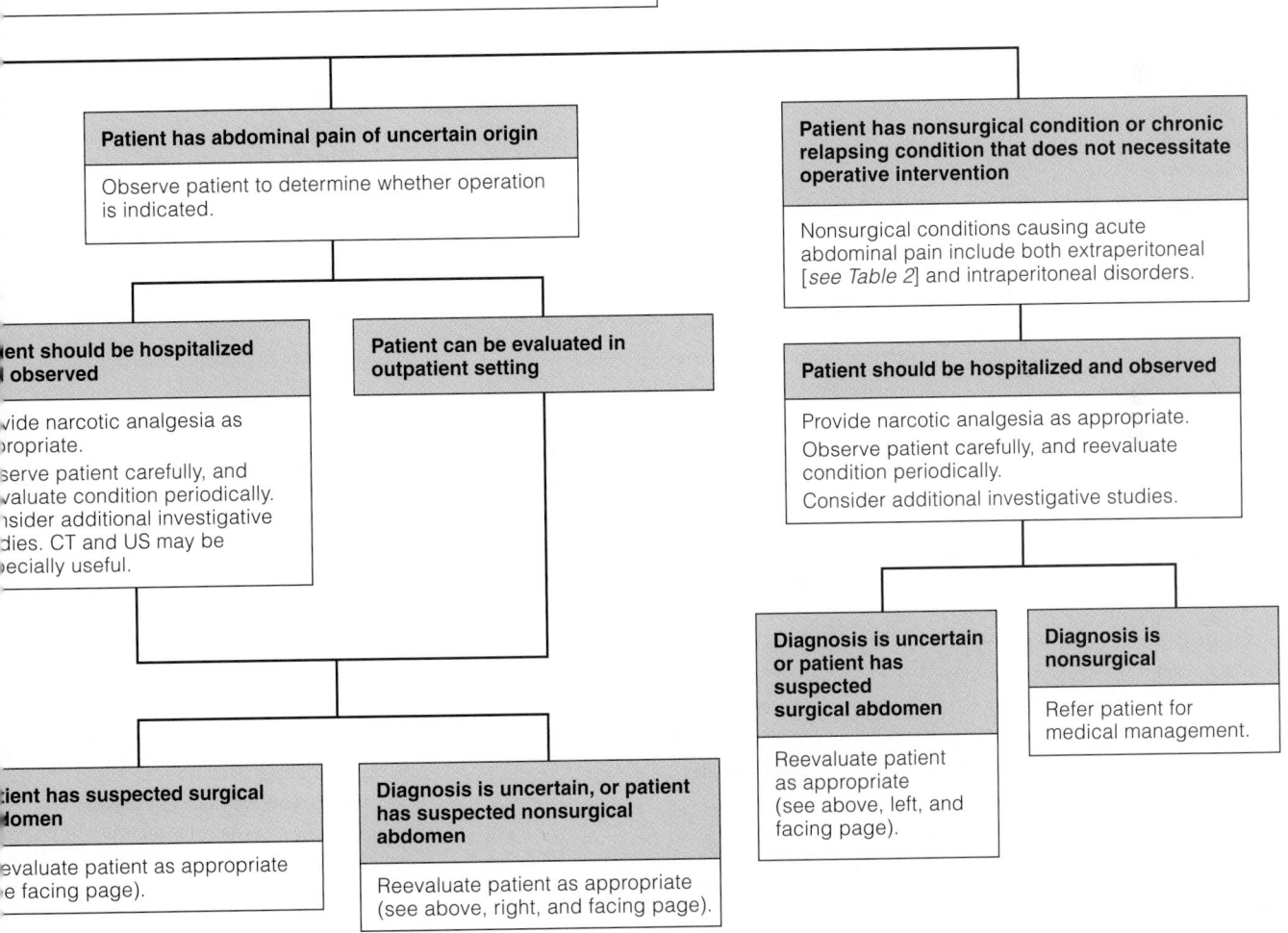

erate tentative differential diagnosis

ember that the majority of patients will turn out to have nonsurgical
noses.
into account effects of age and gender on diagnostic possibilities.

orm physical examination

uate general appearance and ability to answer questions; estimate
ree of obvious pain; note position in bed; identify area of maximal
; look for extra-abdominal causes of pain and signs of systemic illness.
orm systematic abdominal examination: (1) inspection,
uscultation, (3) percussion, (4) palpation.
orm rectal, genital, and pelvic examinations.

Patient has abdominal pain of uncertain origin

Observe patient to determine whether operation
is indicated.

Patient has nonsurgical condition or chronic
relapsing condition that does not necessitate
operative intervention

Nonsurgical conditions causing acute
abdominal pain include both extraperitoneal
[see Table 2] and intraperitoneal disorders.

ient should be hospitalized
observed

vide narcotic analgesia as
ropriate.
serve patient carefully, and
valuate condition periodically.
nsider additional investigative
dies. CT and US may be
ecially useful.

Patient can be evaluated in
outpatient setting

Patient should be hospitalized and observed

Provide narcotic analgesia as appropriate.
Observe patient carefully, and reevaluate
condition periodically.
Consider additional investigative studies.

Diagnosis is uncertain
or patient has
suspected
surgical abdomen

Reevaluate patient
as appropriate
(see above, left, and
facing page).

Diagnosis is
nonsurgical

Refer patient for
medical management.

ient has suspected surgical
domen

evaluate patient as appropriate
e facing page).

Diagnosis is uncertain, or patient
has suspected nonsurgical
abdomen

Reevaluate patient as appropriate
(see above, right, and facing page).

ABDOMINAL PAIN CHART

NAME _____   REG. NUMBER _____

MALE _____ FEMALE _____ AGE _____   FORM FILLED BY _____

MODE OF ARRIVAL _____   DATE _____   TIME _____

PAIN

Site of Pain

At Onset

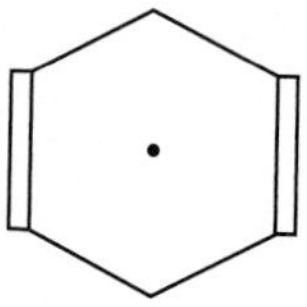

At Present

Radiation

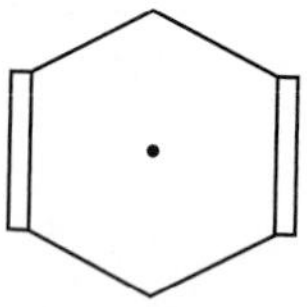

Aggravating Factors
- movement
- coughing
- respiration
- food
- other
- none

Relieving Factors
- lying still
- vomiting
- antacids
- food
- other
- none

Progression of Pain
- better
- same
- worse

Duration

Type
- intermittent
- steady
- colicky

Severity
- moderate
- severe

HISTORY

Nausea
  yes   no

Vomiting
  yes   no

Anorexia
  yes   no

Indigestion
  yes   no

Jaundice
  yes   no

Bowels
- normal
- constipation
- diarrhea
- blood
- mucus

Micturition
- normal
- frequency
- dysuria
- dark
- hematuria

Previous Similar Pain
  yes   no

Previous Abdominal Surgery
  yes   no

Drugs for Abdominal Pain
  yes   no

Female-LMP
- pregnant
- vaginal discharge
- dizzy/faint

EXAMINATION

Temp.   Pulse
BP

Mood
- normal
- upset
- anxious

Color
- normal
- pale
- flushed
- jaundiced
- cyanotic

Intestinal Movement
- normal
- poor/nil
- peristalsis

Scars
  yes   no

Distention
  yes   no

Location of Tenderness

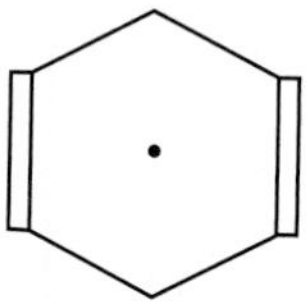

Rebound
  yes   no

Guarding
  yes   no

Rigidity
  yes   no

Mass
  yes   no

Murphy's Sign Present
  yes   no

Bowel Sounds
- normal
- absent
- increased

Rectal-Vaginal Tenderness
- left
- right
- general
- mass
- none

Initial Diagnosis & Plan

Results
- amylase
- blood count (WBC)
- urine
- x-ray

other

Diagnosis & Plan after Investigation

(time   )

Discharge Diagnosis

History and examination of other systems on separate case notes.

Figure 1   **Shown above is a data sheet modified from the abdominal pain chart developed by the OMGE.**[10]

hour) of complete remission during which there is no pain at all. Intermittent pain is characteristic of obstruction of a hollow viscus and results from vigorous peristalsis in the wall of the viscus proximal to the site of obstruction. This pain is perceived as deep in the abdomen and is poorly localized. The patient is restless, may writhe about incessantly in an effort to find a comfortable position, and often presses on the abdominal wall in an attempt to alleviate the pain. Whereas the intermittent pain associated with intestinal obstruction (typically described as gripping and mounting) is usually severe but bearable, the pain associated with obstruction of small conduits (e.g., the biliary tract, the ureters, and the uterine tubes) often becomes unbearable. Obstruction of the gallbladder or the bile ducts gives rise to a type of pain often referred to as biliary colic; however, this term is a misnomer, in that biliary pain is usually constant because of the lack of a strong muscular coat in the biliary tree and the absence of regular peristalsis.

Continuous or constant pain is pain that is present for hours or days without any period of complete relief; it is more common than intermittent pain. Continuous pain is usually indicative of a process that will lead, or has already led, to peritoneal inflammation or ischemia. It may be of steady intensity throughout, or it may be associated with intermittent pain. For example, the typical colicky pain associated with simple intestinal obstruction changes when strangulation occurs, becoming continuous pain that persists between episodes or waves of cramping pain.

Certain types of pain are generally held to be typical of certain pathologic states. For example, the pain of a perforated ulcer is often described as burning, that of a dissecting aneurysm as tearing, and that of bowel obstruction as gripping. One may imagine that the first type of pain is explained by the efflux of acid, the second by the sudden expansion of the retroperitoneum, and the third by the churning of hyperperistalsis. Colorful as these images may be, in most cases, the pain begins in a nondescript way. It is only by carefully following the patient's description of the evolution and time course of the pain that such images may be formed with confidence.

For several reasons—atypical pain patterns, dual innervation by visceral and somatic afferents, normal variations in organ position, and widely diverse underlying pathologic states—the location of abdominal pain is only a rough guide to diagnosis. It is nevertheless true that in most disorders, the pain tends to occur in characteristic locations, such as the right upper quadrant (cholecystitis), the right lower quadrant (appendicitis), the epigastrium (pancreatitis), or the left lower quadrant (sigmoid diverticulitis) [see Figure 2]. It is important to determine the location of the pain at onset because this may differ from the location at the time of presentation (so-called shifting pain). In fact, the chronological sequence of events in the patient's history is often more important for diagnosis than the location of the pain alone. For example, the classic pain of appendicitis begins in the periumbilical region and settles in the right lower quadrant. A similar shift in location can occur when escaping gastroduodenal contents from a perforated ulcer pool in the right lower quadrant.

It is also important to take into account radiation or referral of the pain, which tends to occur in characteristic patterns [see Figure 3]. For example, biliary pain is referred to the right subscapular area, and the boring pain of pancreatitis typically radiates straight through to the back. Obstruction of the small intestine and the proximal colon is referred to the umbilicus, and obstruction distal to the splenic flexure is often referred to the suprapubic area. Spasm in the ureter often radiates to the suprapubic area and into the groin. The more severe the pain is, the more likely it is to be associated with referral to other areas.

The intensity or severity of the pain is related to the magnitude of the underlying insult. It is important to distinguish between the intensity of the pain and the patient's reaction to it because there appear to be significant individual differences with respect to tolerance of and reaction to pain. Pain that is intense enough to awaken the patient from sleep usually indicates a significant underlying organic cause. Past episodes of pain and factors that aggravate or relieve the pain often provide useful diagnostic clues. For example, pain caused by peritonitis tends to be exacerbated by motion, deep breathing, coughing, or sneezing, and patients with peritonitis tend to lie quietly in bed and avoid any movement. The typical pain of acute pancreatitis is exacerbated by lying down and relieved by sitting up. Pain that is relieved by eating or taking antacids suggests duodenal ulcer disease, whereas diffuse abdominal pain that appears 30 minutes to 1 hour after meals suggests intestinal angina.

Associated gastrointestinal symptoms (e.g., nausea, vomiting, anorexia, diarrhea, and constipation) often accompany abdominal pain; however, these symptoms are nonspecific and therefore may not be of great value in the differential diagnosis. Vomiting in particular is common: when sufficiently stimulated by pain impulses traveling via secondary visceral afferent fibers, the medullary vomiting centers activate efferent fibers and cause reflex vomiting. Once again, the chronology of events is important, in that pain often precedes vomiting in patients with conditions necessitating operation, whereas the opposite is usually the case in patients with medical (i.e., nonsurgical) conditions.[5,12] This is particularly true for adult patients with acute appendicitis, in whom pain almost always precedes vomiting by several hours. In children, vomiting is commonly observed closer to the onset of the pain, though it is rarely the initial symptom.

Similarly, constipation may result from a reflex paralytic ileus when sufficiently stimulated visceral afferent fibers activate efferent sympathetic fibers (splanchnic nerves) to reduce intestinal peristalsis. Diarrhea is characteristic of gastroenteritis but may also accompany incomplete intestinal or colonic obstruction. More significant is a history of obstipation, because if it can be definitely established that a patient with acute abdominal pain has not passed gas or stool for 24 to 48 hours, it is certain that some degree of intestinal obstruction is present. Other associated symptoms that should be noted include jaundice, melena, hematochezia, hematemesis, and hematuria. These symptoms are much more specific than the ones just discussed and can be extremely valuable in the differential diagnosis. Most conditions that cause acute abdominal pain of surgical significance are associated with some degree of fever if they are allowed to continue long enough. Fever suggests an inflammatory process; however, it is usually low grade and often absent altogether, particularly in elderly and immunocompromised patients. The combination of a high fever with chills and rigors indicates bacteremia, and concomitant changes in mental status (e.g., agitation, disorientation, and lethargy) suggest impending septic shock.

A history of trauma (even if the patient considers the traumatic event trivial) should be actively sought in all cases of unexplained acute abdominal pain; such a history may not be readily volunteered (as is often the case with trauma resulting from domestic violence). The history may be particularly relevant in a patient taking anticoagulants and presenting with acute onset of abdominal pain accompanied by tenderness but no clear signs of inflammation. Hematoma within the rectus muscle sheath can easily be mistaken for appendicitis or other lower abdominal illnesses; hematoma elsewhere can produce symptoms of obstruction or acute bleeding into the peritoneum and the retroperitoneum. In female patients, it is essential to obtain a detailed gynecologic history that includes the timing of symptoms within the menstrual cycle, the date of the last menses, previous and current use of contraception, any abnormal vaginal bleeding or discharge, an obstetric history, and any risk fac-

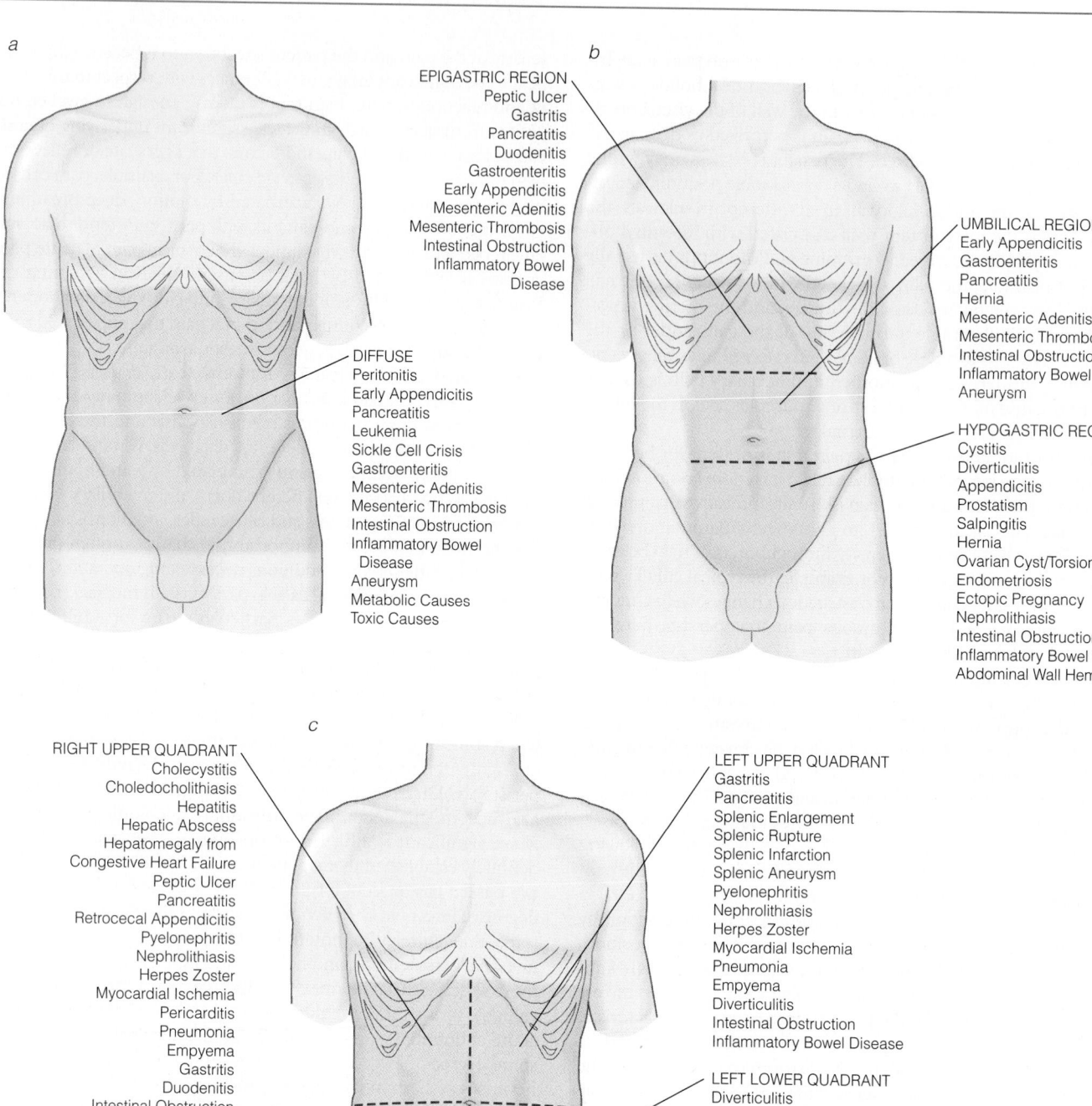

a

b

EPIGASTRIC REGION
Peptic Ulcer
Gastritis
Pancreatitis
Duodenitis
Gastroenteritis
Early Appendicitis
Mesenteric Adenitis
Mesenteric Thrombosis
Intestinal Obstruction
Inflammatory Bowel
Disease

DIFFUSE
Peritonitis
Early Appendicitis
Pancreatitis
Leukemia
Sickle Cell Crisis
Gastroenteritis
Mesenteric Adenitis
Mesenteric Thrombosis
Intestinal Obstruction
Inflammatory Bowel
Disease
Aneurysm
Metabolic Causes
Toxic Causes

UMBILICAL REGION
Early Appendicitis
Gastroenteritis
Pancreatitis
Hernia
Mesenteric Adenitis
Mesenteric Thrombosis
Intestinal Obstruction
Inflammatory Bowel Disease
Aneurysm

HYPOGASTRIC REGION
Cystitis
Diverticulitis
Appendicitis
Prostatism
Salpingitis
Hernia
Ovarian Cyst/Torsion
Endometriosis
Ectopic Pregnancy
Nephrolithiasis
Intestinal Obstruction
Inflammatory Bowel Disease
Abdominal Wall Hematoma

c

RIGHT UPPER QUADRANT
Cholecystitis
Choledocholithiasis
Hepatitis
Hepatic Abscess
Hepatomegaly from
Congestive Heart Failure
Peptic Ulcer
Pancreatitis
Retrocecal Appendicitis
Pyelonephritis
Nephrolithiasis
Herpes Zoster
Myocardial Ischemia
Pericarditis
Pneumonia
Empyema
Gastritis
Duodenitis
Intestinal Obstruction
Inflammatory Bowel Disease

RIGHT LOWER QUADRANT
Appendicitis
Intestinal Obstruction
Inflammatory Bowel Disease
Mesenteric Adenitis
Diverticulitis
Cholecystitis
Perforated Ulcer
Leaking Aneurysm
Abdominal Wall Hematoma
Ectopic Pregnancy
Ovarian Cyst/Torsion
Salpingitis
Mittelschmerz
Endometriosis
Ureteral Calculi
Pyelonephritis
Nephrolithiasis
Seminal Vesiculitis
Psoas Abscess
Hernia

LEFT UPPER QUADRANT
Gastritis
Pancreatitis
Splenic Enlargement
Splenic Rupture
Splenic Infarction
Splenic Aneurysm
Pyelonephritis
Nephrolithiasis
Herpes Zoster
Myocardial Ischemia
Pneumonia
Empyema
Diverticulitis
Intestinal Obstruction
Inflammatory Bowel Disease

LEFT LOWER QUADRANT
Diverticulitis
Intestinal Obstruction
Inflammatory Bowel Disease
Appendicitis
Leaking Aneurysm
Abdominal Wall Hematoma
Ectopic Pregnancy
Mittelschmerz
Ovarian Cyst/Torsion
Salpingitis
Endometriosis
Ureteral Calculi
Pyelonephritis
Nephrolithiasis
Seminal Vesiculitis
Psoas Abscess
Hernia

Figure 2 In most disorders that give rise to acute abdominal pain, the pain tends to occur in specific locations. (*a*) Diffuse pain suggests a certain set of diagnostic possibilities. (*b*) Differing groups of disorders give rise to abdominal pain in the epigastric, umbilical, and hypogastric regions. (*c*) Disorders that give rise to acute abdominal pain may be grouped according to the quadrant of the abdomen in which pain tends to occur.

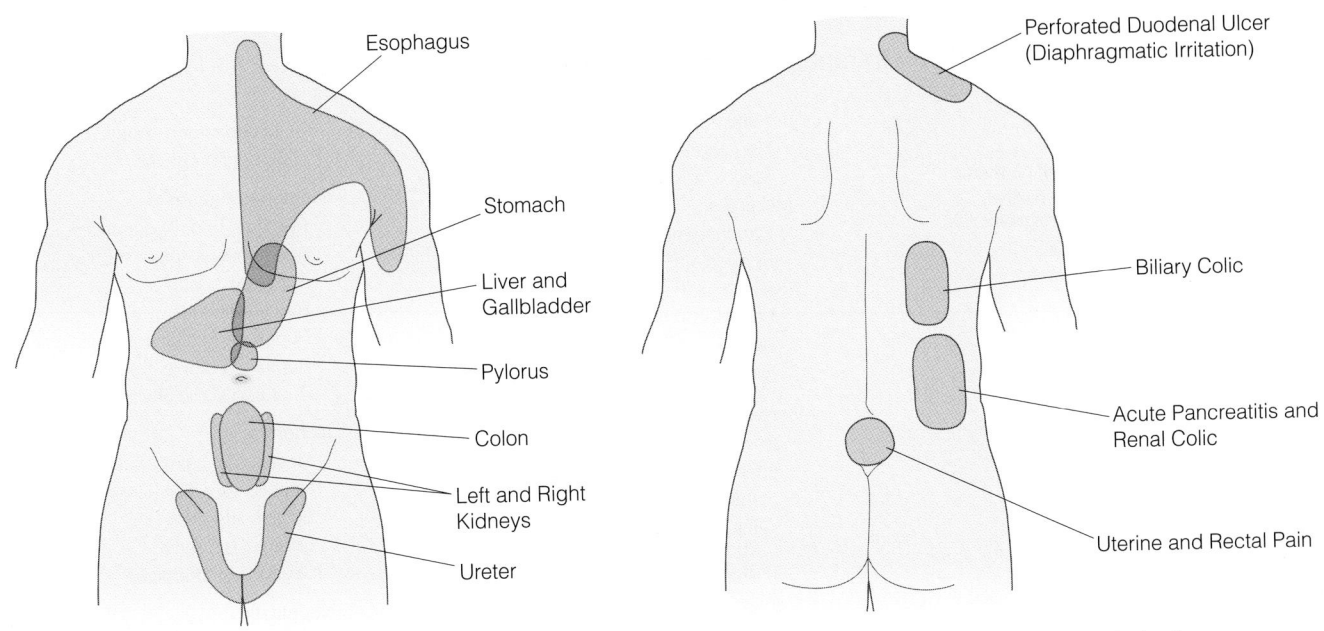

Figure 3 **Pain of abdominal origin tends to be referred in characteristic patterns.[80] The more severe the pain is, the more likely it is to be referred. Shown are anterior (left) and posterior (right) areas of referred pain.**

tors for ectopic pregnancy (e.g., PID, use of an intrauterine device, or previous ectopic or tubal surgery).

A complete history of previous medical conditions must be obtained because associated diseases of the cardiac, pulmonary, and renal systems may give rise to acute abdominal symptoms and may also significantly affect the morbidity and mortality associated with surgical intervention. Weight changes, past illnesses, recent travel, environmental exposure to toxins or infectious agents, and medications used should also be investigated. A history of previous abdominal operations should be obtained but should not be relied on too heavily in the absence of operative reports. A careful family history is important for detection of hereditary disorders that may cause acute abdominal pain. A detailed social history should also be obtained that includes any history of tobacco, alcohol, or illicit drug use, as well as a sexual history.

TENTATIVE DIFFERENTIAL
DIAGNOSIS

Once the history has been obtained, the examiner should generate a tentative differential diagnosis and carry out the physical examination in search of

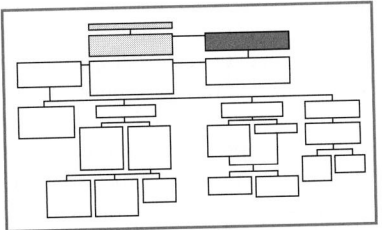

specific signs or findings that either rule out or confirm the diagnostic possibilities. Given the diversity of conditions that can cause acute abdominal pain [*see Tables 1 and 2*], there is no substitute for general awareness of the most common causes of acute abdominal pain and the influence of age, gender, and geography on the likelihood of any of these potential causes. Although acute abdominal pain is the most common surgical emergency and most non–trauma-related surgical admissions (and 1% of all hospital admissions) are accounted for by patients complaining of abdominal pain, little information is available regarding the clinical spectrum of disease in these patients.[13] Nevertheless, detailed epidemiologic information can be an invaluable asset in the diagnosis and treatment of acute abdominal pain. Now that patients from different parts of the world are increasingly being seen in

North American emergency rooms, it is important to consider endemic diseases, including tuberculosis,[14,15] parasitic diseases,[16-18] bezoars from unusual dietary habits,[19,20] and unusual malignancies.[21,22]

The value of detailed epidemiologic knowledge notwithstanding, it is worthwhile to keep in mind the truism that common things are common. Regarding which things are common, the most extensive information currently available comes from the ongoing survey begun in 1977 by the Research Committee of the OMGE. As of the last progress report on this survey, which was published in 1988,[23] more than 200 physicians at 26 centers in 17 countries had accumulated data on 10,320 patients with acute abdominal pain [*see Table 3*]. The most common diagnosis in these patients was nonspecific abdominal pain (NSAP)—that is, the retrospective diagnosis of exclusion in which no cause for the pain can be identified.[24,25] Nonspecific abdominal pain accounted for 34% of all patients seen; the four most common diagnoses accounted for more than 75%. The most common surgical diagnosis in the OMGE survey was acute appendicitis, followed by acute cholecystitis, small bowel obstruction, and gynecologic disorders. Relatively few patients had perforated peptic ulcer, a finding that confirms the current downward trend in the incidence of this condition. Cancer was found to be a significant cause of acute abdominal pain. There was little variation in the geographic distribution of surgical causes of acute abdominal pain (i.e., conditions necessitating operation) among developed countries. In patients who required operation, the most common causes were acute appendicitis (42.6%), acute cholecystitis (14.7%), small bowel obstruction (6.2%), perforated peptic ulcer (3.7%), and acute pancreatitis (4.5%).[23] The OMGE survey's finding that NSAP was the most common diagnosis in patients with acute abdominal pain has been confirmed by several studies[12,13,25]; the finding that acute appendicitis, cholecystitis, and intestinal obstruction were the three most common diagnoses in patients with acute abdominal pain who require operation has also been amply confirmed [*see Table 3*].[1,12,13]

The data described so far provide a comprehensive picture of the most likely diagnoses for patients with acute abdominal pain in many centers around the world; however, this picture does not take

Table 1 Intraperitoneal Causes of Acute Abdominal Pain[81]

Inflammatory
  Peritoneal
    Chemical and nonbacterial peritonitis
      Perforated peptic ulcer/biliary tree,
        pancreatitis, ruptured ovarian cyst,
        mittelschmerz
    Bacterial peritonitis
      Primary peritonitis
        Pneumococcal, streptococcal,
          tuberculous
        Spontaneous bacterial peritonitis
      Perforated hollow viscus
        Esophagus, stomach, duodenum, small
          intestine, bile duct, gallbladder, colon,
          urinary bladder
  Hollow visceral
    Appendicitis
    Cholecystitis
    Peptic ulcer
    Gastroenteritis
    Gastritis
    Duodenitis
    Inflammatory bowel disease
    Meckel diverticulitis
    Colitis (bacterial, amebic)
    Diverticulitis
  Solid visceral
    Pancreatitis
    Hepatitis

Pancreatic abscess
Hepatic abscess
Splenic abscess
  Mesenteric
    Lymphadenitis (bacterial, viral)
    Epiploic appendagitis
  Pelvic
    Pelvic inflammatory disease (salpingitis)
    Tubo-ovarian abscess
    Endometritis

Mechanical (obstruction, acute distention)
  Hollow visceral
    Intestinal obstruction
      Adhesions, hernias, neoplasms, volvulus
      Intussusception, gallstone ileus, foreign
        bodies
      Bezoars, parasites
    Biliary obstruction
      Calculi, neoplasms, choledochal cyst,
        hemobilia
  Solid visceral
    Acute splenomegaly
    Acute hepatomegaly (congestive heart
      failure, Budd-Chiari syndrome)
  Mesenteric
    Omental torsion
  Pelvic
    Ovarian cyst

Torsion or degeneration of fibroid
Ectopic pregnancy

Hemoperitoneum
  Ruptured hepatic neoplasm
  Spontaneous splenic rupture
  Ruptured mesentery
  Ruptured uterus
  Ruptured graafian follicle
  Ruptured ectopic pregnancy
  Ruptured aortic or visceral aneurysm

Ischemic
  Mesenteric thrombosis
  Hepatic infarction (toxemia, purpura)
  Splenic infarction
  Omental ischemia
  Strangulated hernia

Neoplastic
  Primary or metastatic intraperitoneal
    neoplasms

Traumatic
  Blunt trauma
  Penetrating trauma
  Iatrogenic trauma
  Domestic violence

Miscellaneous
  Endometriosis

into account the effect of age on the relative likelihood of the various potential diagnoses. It is well known that the disease spectrum of acute abdominal pain is different in different age groups, especially in the very old[4,26,27] and the very young.[28-30] In the OMGE survey, well over 90% of cases of acute abdominal pain in children were diagnosed as acute appendicitis (32%) or NSAP (62%).[28] Similar age-related differences in the spectrum of disease have been confirmed by other studies,[16] as have various gender-related differences.

This variation in the disease spectrum is readily apparent when the 10,320 patients from the OMGE survey are segregated by age [*see Table 4*]. In patients 50 years of age or older,[27] cholecystitis was more common than either NSAP or acute appendicitis; small bowel obstruction, diverticular disease, and pancreatitis were all approximately five times more common than in patients younger than 50 years. Hernias were also a much more common problem in older patients. In the entire group of patients, only one of every 10 instances of intestinal obstruction was attributable to a hernia, whereas in patients 50 years of age or older, one of every three instances was caused by an undiagnosed hernia. Cancer was 40 times more likely to be the cause of acute abdominal pain in patients 50 years of age or older; vascular diseases (including myocardial infarction, mesenteric ischemia, and ruptured AAA) were 25 times more common in patients 50 years of age or older and 100 times more common in patients older than 70 years. What is more, outcome was clearly related to age: mortality was significantly higher in patients older than 70 years (5%) than in those younger than 50 years (< 1%). Whereas the peak incidence of acute abdominal pain occurred in patients in their teens and 20s,[28] the great majority of deaths occurred in patients older than 70 years.[27]

PHYSICAL EXAMINATION

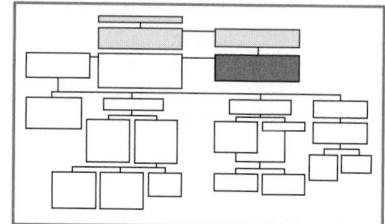

In the physical examination of a patient, as in the taking of the history, there is no substitute for organization and patience; the amount of information that can be obtained is directly proportional to the gentleness and thoroughness of the examiner. The physical examination begins with a brief but thorough evaluation of the patient's general appearance and ability to answer questions. The degree of obvious pain should be estimated. The patient's position in bed should be noted. A patient who lies motionless with flexed hips and knees is more likely to have generalized peritonitis. A restless patient who writhes about in bed is more likely to have colicky pain.

The area of maximal pain should be identified before the physical examination is begun. The examiner can easily do this by simply asking the patient to cough and then to point with two fingers to the area where pain seems to be focused. This allows the examiner to avoid the area in the early stages of the examination and to confirm it at a later stage without causing the patient unnecessary discomfort in the meantime.

The physical examination should be directed, in the sense that it should address critical findings that would confirm or exclude the likeliest disorders in the differential diagnosis. In this context, however, it should be complete. Some processes that can cause abdominal pain occur within the chest (e.g., pneumonia, ischemic heart disease or arrhythmia, esophageal muscular disorders); thus, auscultation of the lungs and the heart is integral to the examination. Pelvic examination should be performed in women, and examination of the rectum and the groin should be performed in all patients. It should not be assumed that advanced imaging technology (e.g., CT, MRI, or ultrasonography [US]) will provide the diagnosis most quickly or with the highest level of confidence. The sensitivity and specificity (not to mention the cost-effectiveness) of any laboratory or imaging study are grounded in the intelligent gathering and categorization of signs and symptoms.[31,32]

Before attention is directed to the patient's abdomen, signs of systemic illness should be sought. Systemic signs of shock (e.g., diaphoresis, pallor, hypothermia, tachypnea, tachycardia with orthostasis, and frank hypotension) usually accompany a rapidly progressive or advanced intra-abdominal condition and, in the absence of extra-abdominal causes, are indications for immediate laparotomy. The absence of any alteration in vital signs, however, does not necessarily exclude a serious intra-abdominal process.

Examination of the abdomen begins with the patient resting in a comfortable supine position. A right-handed examiner should stand on the patient's right side, and the patient's abdomen should be level with the elbow at rest. In some cases, to make sure that the examination is unhurried and the patient's anxiety is allayed, the examiner may find it useful to sit at the bedside. The examination should include inspection, auscultation, percussion, and palpation of all areas of the abdomen, the flanks, and the groin (including all hernia orifices) in addition to rectal and genital examinations (and, in female patients, a full gynecologic examination). A systematic approach is crucial: an examiner who methodically follows a set pattern of abdominal examination every time will be rewarded more frequently than one who improvises haphazardly with each patient.

The first step in the abdominal examination is careful inspection of the anterior and posterior abdominal walls, the flanks, the perineum, and the genitalia for previous surgical scars (possible adhesions), hernias (incarceration or strangulation), distention (intestinal obstruction), obvious masses (distended gallbladder, abscesses, or tumors), ecchymosis or abrasions (trauma), striae (pregnancy or ascites), an everted umbilicus (increased intra-abdominal pressure), visible pulsations (aneurysm), visible peristalsis (obstruction), limitation of movement of the abdominal wall with ventilatory movements (peritonitis), or engorged veins (portal hypertension).

The next recommended step in the abdominal examination is auscultation. Although it is important to note the presence (or absence) of bowel sounds and their quality, auscultation is probably the least rewarding aspect of the physical examination. Severe intra-abdominal conditions, even intra-abdominal catastrophes, may occur in patients with normal bowel sounds, and patients with silent abdomens may have no significant intra-abdominal pathology at all. In general, however, the absence of bowel sounds indicates a paralytic ileus; hyperactive or hypoactive bowel sounds often are variations of normal activity; and high-pitched bowel sounds with splashes, tinkles (echoing as in a large cavern), or rushes (prolonged, loud gurgles) indicate mechanical bowel obstruction.

Table 2 **Extraperitoneal Causes of Acute Abdominal Pain**

Genitourinary
Pyelonephritis
Perinephric abscess
Renal infarct
Nephrolithiasis
Ureteral obstruction (lithiasis, tumor)
Acute cystitis
Prostatitis
Seminal vesiculitis
Epididymitis
Orchitis
Testicular torsion
Dysmenorrhea
Threatened abortion

Pulmonary
Pneumonia
Empyema
Pulmonary embolus
Pulmonary infarction
Pneumothorax

Cardiac
Myocardial ischemia
Myocardial infarction
Acute rheumatic fever
Acute pericarditis

Metabolic
Acute intermittent porphyria
Familial Mediterranean fever
Hypolipoproteinemia
Hemochromatosis
Hereditary angioneurotic edema

Endocrine
Diabetic ketoacidosis
Hyperparathyroidism (hypercalcemia)
Acute adrenal insufficiency (Addisonian crisis)
Hyperthyroidism or hypothyroidism

Musculoskeletal
Rectus sheath hematoma
Arthritis/diskitis of thoracolumbar spine

Neurogenic
Herpes zoster
Tabes dorsalis
Nerve root compression
Spinal cord tumors
Osteomyelitis of the spine
Abdominal epilepsy
Abdominal migraine
Multiple sclerosis

Inflammatory
Schönlein-Henoch purpura
Systemic lupus erythematosus
Polyarteritis nodosa
Dermatomyositis
Scleroderma

Infectious
Bacterial
Parasitic (malaria)
Viral (measles, mumps, infectious mononucleosis)
Rickettsial (Rocky Mountain spotted fever)

Hematologic
Sickle cell crisis
Acute leukemia
Acute hemolytic states
Coagulopathies
Pernicious anemia
Other dyscrasias

Vascular
Vasculitis
Periarteritis

Toxins
Bacterial toxins (tetanus, staphylococcus)
Insect venom (black widow spider)
Animal venom
Heavy metals (lead, arsenic, mercury)
Poisonous mushrooms
Drugs
Withdrawal from narcotics

Retroperitoneal
Retroperitoneal hemorrhage (spontaneous adrenal hemorrhage)
Psoas abscess

Psychogenic
Hypochondriasis
Somatization disorders

Factitious
Munchausen syndrome
Malingering

Table 3 Frequency of Specific Diagnoses in Patients with Acute Abdominal Pain

Diagnosis	Frequency in Individual Studies (% of Patients)					
	OMGE[23] (N = 10,320)	Wilson[82] (N = 1,196)	Irvin[13] (N = 1,190)	Brewer[12] (N = 1,000)	de Dombal[1] (N = 552)	Hawthorn[83] (N = 496)
Nonspecific abdominal pain	34.0	45.6	34.9	41.3	50.5	36.0
Acute appendicitis	28.1	15.6	16.8	4.3	26.3	14.9
Acute cholecystitis	9.7	5.8	5.1	2.5	7.6	5.9
Small bowel obstruction	4.1	2.6	14.8	2.5	3.6	8.6
Acute gynecologic disease	4.0	4.0	1.1	8.5	—	—
Acute pancreatitis	2.9	1.3	2.4	—	2.9	2.1
Urologic disorders	2.9	4.7	5.9	11.4	—	12.8
Perforated peptic ulcer	2.5	2.3	2.5	2.0	3.1	—
Cancer	1.5	—	3.0	—	—	—
Diverticular disease	1.5	1.1	3.9	—	2.0	3.0
Dyspepsia	1.4	7.6	1.4	1.4	—	—
Gastroenteritis	—	—	0.3	6.9	—	5.1
Inflammatory bowel disease	—	—	0.8	—	—	2.1
Mesenteric adenitis	—	3.6	—	—	—	1.5
Gastritis	—	2.1	—	1.4	—	—
Constipation	—	2.4	—	2.3	—	—
Amebic hepatic abscess	1.2	—	1.9	—	—	—
Miscellaneous	6.3	1.3	5.2	15.5	4.0	8.0

The third step is percussion to search for any areas of dullness, fluid collections, sections of gas-filled bowel, or pockets of free air under the abdominal wall. Tympany may be present in patients with bowel obstruction or hollow viscus perforation. Percussion can be useful as a way of estimating organ size and of determining the presence of ascites (signaled by a fluid wave or shifting dullness). Gentle percussion over the four quadrants of the abdomen can also be used to elicit a sign of peritoneal irritation, and patients tolerate this maneuver reasonably well. Pain associated with mild levels of percussion is a good indicator of peritonitis if the maneuver is performed in the same way each time. In general, however, maneuvers associated with palpation are best for determining whether peritonitis is present.

The last step, palpation, is the most informative aspect of the physical examination. Palpation of the abdomen must be done very gently to avoid causing additional pain early in the examination. It should begin as far as possible from the area of maximal pain and then should gradually advance toward this area, which should be the last to be palpated. The examiner should place the entire hand on the patient's abdomen with the fingers together and extended, applying pressure with the pulps (not the tips) of the fingers by flexing the wrists and the metacarpophalangeal joints. It is essential to determine whether true involuntary muscle guarding (muscle spasm) is present. This determination is made by means of gentle palpation over the abdominal wall while the patient takes a long, deep breath. If guarding is voluntary, the underlying muscle immediately relaxes under the gentle pressure of the palpating hand. If, however, the patient has true involuntary guarding, the muscle remains in spasm

(i.e., taut and rigid) throughout the respiratory cycle (so-called boardlike abdomen). True involuntary guarding is indicative of localized or generalized peritonitis. It must be remembered that mus-

Table 4 Frequency of Specific Diagnoses in Younger and Older Patients with Acute Abdominal Pain in the OMGE Study[23,27]

Diagnosis	Frequency (% of Patients)	
	Age < 50 Yr (N = 6,317)	Age ≥ 50 Yr (N = 2,406)
Nonspecific abdominal pain	39.5	15.7
Appendicitis	32.0	15.2
Cholecystitis	6.3	20.9
Obstruction	2.5	12.3
Pancreatitis	1.6	7.3
Diverticular disease	< 0.1	5.5
Cancer	< 0.1	4.1
Hernia	< 0.1	3.1
Vascular disease	< 0.1	2.3

Table 5   Common Abdominal Signs and Findings Noted on Physical Examination[6]

Sign or Finding	Description	Associated Clinical Condition(s)
Aaron sign	Referred pain or feeling of distress in epigastrium or precordial region on continued firm pressure over the McBurney point	Acute appendicitis
Ballance sign	Presence of dull percussion note in both flanks, constant on left side but shifting with change of position on right side	Ruptured spleen
Bassler sign	Sharp pain elicited by pinching appendix between thumb of examiner and iliacus muscle	Chronic appendicitis
Beevor sign	Upward movement of umbilicus	Paralysis of lower portions of rectus abdominis muscles
Blumberg sign	Transient abdominal wall rebound tenderness	Peritoneal inflammation
Carnett sign	Disappearance of abdominal tenderness when anterior abdominal muscles are contracted	Abdominal pain of intra-abdominal origin
Chandelier sign	Intense lower abdominal and pelvic pain on manipulation of cervix	Pelvic inflammatory disease
Charcot sign	Intermittent right upper quadrant abdominal pain, jaundice, and fever	Choledocholithiasis
Chaussier sign	Severe epigastric pain in gravid female	Prodrome of eclampsia
Claybrook sign	Transmission of breath and heart sounds through abdominal wall	Ruptured abdominal viscus
Courvoisier sign	Palpable, nontender gallbladder in presence of clinical jaundice	Periampullary neoplasm
Cruveilhier sign	Varicose veins radiating from umbilicus (*caput medusae*)	Portal hypertension
Cullen sign	Periumbilical darkening of skin from blood	Hemoperitoneum (especially in ruptured ectopic pregnancy)
Cutaneous hyperesthesia	Increased abdominal wall sensation to light touch	Parietal peritoneal inflammation secondary to inflammatory intra-abdominal pathology
Dance sign	Slight retraction in area of right iliac fossa	Intussusception
Danforth sign	Shoulder pain on inspiration	Hemoperitoneum (especially in ruptured ectopic pregnancy)
Direct abdominal wall tenderness	—	Localized inflammation of abdominal wall, peritoneum, or an intra-abdominal viscus
Fothergill sign	Abdominal wall mass that does not cross midline and remains palpable when rectus muscle is tense	Rectus muscle hematoma

(continued)

cle rigidity is relative: for example, muscle guarding may be less pronounced or absent in debilitated and elderly patients who have poor abdominal musculature. In addition, the evaluation of muscle guarding is dependent on the patient's cooperation.

Palpation is also useful for determining the extent and severity of the patient's tenderness. Diffuse tenderness indicates generalized peritoneal inflammation. Mild diffuse tenderness without guarding usually indicates gastroenteritis or some other inflammatory intestinal process without peritoneal inflammation. Localized tenderness suggests an early stage of disease with limited peritoneal inflammation. Rebound tenderness is elicited by applying gentle but deep pressure to the region of interest and then letting go abruptly. As a means of distraction, the examiner may use the stethoscope to apply the pressure. The main difficulties associated with palpation are that the deep pressure may increase anxiety and that the surprise of the sudden withdrawal may elicit pain where peritoneal irritation is not the cause.

Careful palpation can elicit several specific signs [*see Table 5*], such as the Rovsing sign (pain in the right lower quadrant when the left lower quadrant is palpated deeply), which is associated with acute appendicitis, and the Murphy sign (arrest of inspiration when the right upper quadrant is deeply palpated), which is associated with acute cholecystitis. These signs are indicative of localized peritoneal inflammation. Similarly, specific maneuvers can elicit signs of localized peritoneal irritation. The psoas sign is elicited by placing

the patient in the left lateral decubitus position and extending the right leg. In settings where appendicitis is suspected, pain on extension of the right leg indicates that the psoas is irritated and thus that the inflamed appendix is in a retrocecal position. The obturator sign is elicited by raising the flexed right leg and rotating the thigh internally. In settings where appendicitis is suspected, pain on rotation of the right thigh indicates that the obturator is irritated and thus that the inflamed appendix is in a pelvic position. The Kehr sign is elicited when the patient is placed in the Trendelenburg position. Pain in the shoulder indicates irritation of the diaphragm by a noxious fluid (e.g., gastric contents from a perforated ulcer, pus from a ruptured appendix, or free blood from a fallopian tube pregnancy). Another useful maneuver is the Carnett test, in which the patient elevates his or her head off the bed, thus tensing the abdominal muscles. When the pain is caused by abdominal wall conditions (e.g., rectal sheath hematoma), tenderness to palpation persists, but when the pain is caused by intraperitoneal conditions, tenderness to palpation decreases or disappears (the Carnett sign).

Rectal, genital, and (in women) pelvic examinations are essential to the evaluation of all patients with acute abdominal pain. The rectal examination should include evaluation of sphincter tone, tenderness (localized versus diffuse), and prostate size and tenderness, as well as a search for the presence of hemorrhoids, masses, fecal impaction, foreign bodies, and gross or occult blood. The genital examination should search for adenopathy, masses, discoloration,

Table 5   (continued)

Sign or Finding	Description	Associated Clinical Condition(s)
Grey Turner sign	Local areas of discoloration around umbilicus and flanks	Acute hemorrhagic pancreatitis
Iliopsoas sign	Elevation and extension of leg against pressure of examiner's hand causes pain	Appendicitis (retrocecal) or an inflammatory mass in contact with psoas
Kehr sign	Left shoulder pain when patient is supine or in the Trendelenburg position (pain may occur spontaneously or after application of pressure to left subcostal region)	Hemoperitoneum (especially ruptured spleen)
Kustner sign	Palpable mass anterior to uterus	Dermoid cyst of ovary
Mannkopf sign	Acceleration of pulse when a painful point is pressed on by examiner	Absent in factitious abdominal pain
McClintock sign	Heart rate > 100 beats/min 1 hr post partum	Postpartum hemorrhage
Murphy sign	Palpation of right upper abdominal quadrant during deep inspiration results in right upper quadrant abdominal pain	Acute cholecystitis
Obturator sign	Flexion of right thigh at right angles to trunk and external rotation of same leg in supine position result in hypogastric pain	Appendicitis (pelvic appendix); pelvic abscess; an inflammatory mass in contact with muscle
Puddle sign	Alteration in intensity of transmitted sound in intra-abdominal cavity secondary to percussion when patient is positioned on all fours and stethoscope is gradually moved toward flank opposite percussion	Free peritoneal fluid
Ransohoff sign	Yellow pigmentation in umbilical region	Ruptured common bile duct
Rovsing sign	Pain referred to the McBurney point on application of pressure to descending colon	Acute appendicitis
Subcutaneous crepitance	Palpable crepitus in abdominal wall	Subcutaneous emphysema or gas gangrene
Summer sign	Increased abdominal muscle tone on exceedingly gentle palpation of right or left iliac fossa	Early appendicitis; nephrolithiasis; ureterolithiasis; ovarian torsion
Ten Horn sign	Pain caused by gentle traction on right spermatic cord	Acute appendicitis
Toma sign	Right-sided tympany and left-sided dullness in supine position as a result of peritoneal inflammation and subsequent mesenteric contraction of intestine to right side of abdominal cavity	Inflammatory ascites

edema, and crepitus. The pelvic examination in women should check for vaginal discharge or bleeding, cervical discharge or bleeding, cervical mobility and tenderness, uterine tenderness, uterine size, and adnexal tenderness or masses. Although a carefully performed pelvic examination can be invaluable in differentiating nonsurgical conditions (e.g., pelvic inflammatory disease and tubo-ovarian abscess) from conditions necessitating prompt operation (e.g., acute appendicitis), the possibility that a surgical condition is present should not be prematurely dismissed solely on the basis of a finding of tenderness on pelvic or rectal examination.

Investigative Studies

Laboratory tests and imaging studies rarely, if ever, establish a definitive diagnosis by themselves; however, if used in the correct clinical setting, they can confirm or exclude specific diagnoses suggested by the history and the physical examination.

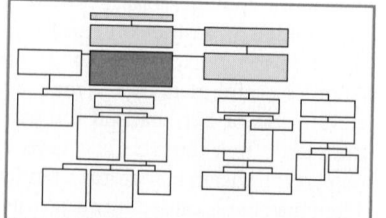

LABORATORY TESTS

In all patients except those in extremis, a complete blood count, blood chemistries, and a urinalysis are routinely obtained before a decision to operate. The hematocrit is important in that it allows the surgeon to detect significant changes in plasma volume (e.g., dehydration caused by vomiting, diarrhea, or fluid loss into the peri-

toneum or the intestinal lumen), preexisting anemia, or bleeding. An elevated white blood cell (WBC) count is indicative of an inflammatory process and is a particularly helpful finding if associated with a marked left shift; however, the presence or absence of leukocytosis should never be the single deciding factor as to whether the patient should undergo an operation. A low WBC count may be a feature of viral infections, gastroenteritis, or NSAP. Other tests, such as C-reactive protein assay, may be useful for increasing confidence in the diagnosis of an acute inflammatory condition. An important consideration in the use of any such test is that derangements develop over time, becoming more likely as the illness progresses; thus, serial examinations might be more useful than a single test result obtained at an arbitrary point. Indeed, for the diagnosis of acute appendicitis, serial observations of the leukocyte count and the C-reactive protein level have been shown to possess greater predictive value than single observations.[33]

Serum electrolyte, blood urea nitrogen (BUN), and creatinine concentrations are useful in determining the nature and extent of fluid losses. Blood glucose and other blood chemistries may also be helpful. Liver function tests (serum bilirubin, alkaline phosphatase, and transaminase levels) are mandatory when abdominal pain is suspected of being hepatobiliary in origin. Similarly, amylase and lipase determinations are mandatory when pancreatitis is suspected, though it must be remembered that amylase levels may be low or normal in patients with pancreatitis and may be markedly elevated in patients with other conditions (e.g., intestinal obstruction, mesenteric thrombosis, and perforated ulcer).

Urinalysis may reveal red blood cells (RBCs) (suggestive of renal or ureteral calculi), WBCs (suggestive of urinary tract infection or inflammatory processes adjacent to the ureters, such as retrocecal appendicitis), increased specific gravity (suggestive of dehydration), glucose, ketones (suggestive of diabetes), or bilirubin (suggestive of hepatitis). A pregnancy test should be considered in any woman of childbearing age who is experiencing acute abdominal pain.

Electrocardiography is mandatory in elderly patients and in patients with a history of cardiomyopathy, dysrhythmia, or ischemic heart disease. Abdominal pain may be a manifestation of myocardial disease, and the physiologic stress of acute abdominal pain can increase myocardial oxygen demands and induce ischemia in patients with coronary artery disease.

IMAGING

Until relatively recently, initial radiologic evaluation of the patient with acute abdominal pain included plain films of the abdomen in the supine and standing positions and chest radiographs.[34] Currently, CT scanning (when available) is generally considered more likely to be helpful in most situations.[35,36] Still, there remain some situations in which plain films may be a more useful and safe form of investigation—as, for example, when a strangulating obstruction is thought to be the most likely diagnosis and plain films are used for rapid confirmation. If the diagnosis of strangulating obstruction is in doubt, however, CT scanning—particularly with the newer generations of scanning instruments—is useful for making a definitive diagnosis and for identifying clinically unsuspected strangulation.[37-39]

When performed in the correct clinical setting, imaging studies may confirm diagnoses such as pneumonia (signaled by pulmonary infiltrates); intestinal obstruction (air-fluid levels and dilated loops of bowel); intestinal perforation (pneumoperitoneum); biliary, renal, or ureteral calculi (abnormal calcifications); appendicitis (fecalith); incarcerated hernia (bowel protruding beyond the confines of the peritoneal cavity); mesenteric infarction (air in the portal vein); chronic pancreatitis (pancreatic calcifications); acute pancreatitis (the so-called colon cutoff sign); visceral aneurysms (calcified rim); retroperitoneal hematoma or abscess (obliteration of the psoas shadow); and ischemic colitis (so-called thumbprinting on the colonic wall).

Although in most settings, CT is the preferred modality for primary evaluation of acute abdominal pain, there are certain settings in which US should be considered. When gallstones are considered a likely diagnosis, US is more apt to be diagnostic than CT is, given that about 85% of gallstones are not detectable by x-rays. In disorders of the female genitourinary tract, US is also quite sensitive and specific for diagnoses such as ovarian cyst, fallopian tube pregnancy, and intrauterine pregnancy. Although there are reassuring reports that the risks of radiation from CT scanning can be managed in children and pregnant women with abdominal pain,[40,41] there remain theoretical concerns regarding the teratogenicity of the radiation dose.[42] Accordingly, it would seems prudent to consider US the preferred initial imaging test for such patients. In these circumstances, CT is employed only if the diagnosis remains unresolved and if the potential delay in diagnosis (from not obtaining a CT scan) is likely to cause harm.

Working or Presumed Diagnosis

The tentative differential diagnosis developed on the basis of the clinical history is refined on the basis of the physical examination and the investigative studies per-

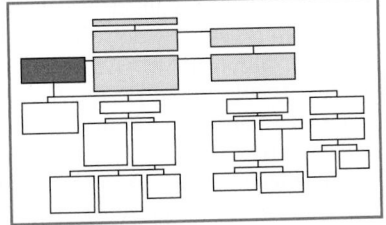

formed, and a working or presumed diagnosis is generated. Once a working diagnosis has been established, subsequent management depends on the accepted treatment for the particular condition believed to be present. In general, the course of management follows four basic pathways [see Management: Surgical versus Nonsurgical Treatment, below], depending on whether the patient (1) has an acute surgical condition that necessitates immediate laparotomy, (2) is believed to have an underlying surgical condition that does not necessitate immediate laparotomy but does call for urgent or early operation, (3) has an uncertain diagnosis that does not necessitate immediate or urgent laparotomy and that may prove to be nonsurgical, or (4) is believed to have an underlying nonsurgical condition.

It must be emphasized that the patient must be constantly reevaluated (preferably by the same examiner) even after the working diagnosis has been established. If the patient does not respond to treatment as expected, the working diagnosis must be reconsidered, and the possibility that another condition exists must be immediately entertained and investigated by returning to the differential diagnosis.

Management: Surgical versus Nonsurgical Treatment

ACUTE SURGICAL ABDOMEN

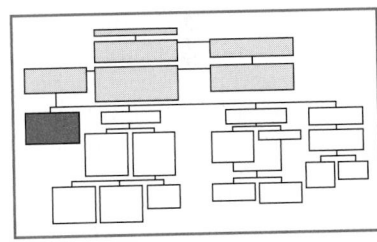

A thorough but expeditious approach to patients with acute abdominal pain is essential because in some patients, action must be taken immediately and there is not enough time for an exhaustive evaluation. As outlined (see above), such an approach should include a brief initial assessment, a complete clinical history, a thorough physical examination, and targeted laboratory and imaging studies. These steps can usually be completed in less than 1 hour and should be insisted on in the evaluation of most patients. In most cases, it is wise to resist the temptation to rush to the operating room with an incompletely evaluated, unprepared, and unstable patient. Sometimes, the anxiety of the patient or the impatience of the health care providers requesting the surgeon's consultation creates an unwarranted feeling of urgency. Often, however, the anxiety or impatience is on the part of the surgeon and, if indulged, may be a cause of subsequent regret.

There are very few abdominal crises that mandate immediate operation, and even with these conditions, it is still necessary to spend a few minutes on assessing the seriousness of the problem and establishing a probable diagnosis. Among the most common of the abdominal catastrophes that necessitate immediate operation are ruptured AAAs or visceral aneurysms, ruptured ectopic pregnancies, and spontaneous hepatic or splenic ruptures. The relative rarity of such conditions notwithstanding, it must always be remembered that patients with acute abdominal pain may have a progressive underlying intra-abdominal disorder causing the acute pain and that unnecessary delays in diagnosis and treatment can adversely affect outcome, often with catastrophic consequences.

SUBACUTE SURGICAL ABDOMEN

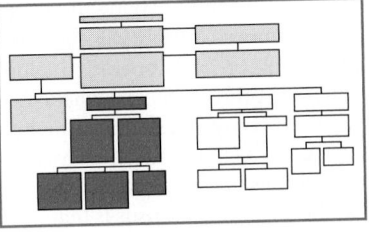

When immediate operation is not called for, the physician must decide whether urgent laparotomy or nonurgent but early operation is necessary. Urgent laparotomy implies operation within 4 hours of the patient's arrival; thus, there is usually sufficient time for adequate resuscitation, with proper rehydration and restoration of vital organ function, before the procedure. Indications for urgent laparotomy may be encountered during the physical examination, may be revealed by the basic laboratory and radiologic studies, or may not become apparent until other investigative studies are performed. Involuntary guarding or rigidity during the physical examination, particularly if spreading, is a strong indication for urgent laparotomy. Other indications include increasing severe localized tenderness, progressive tense distention, physical signs of sepsis (e.g., high fever, tachycardia, hypotension, and mental-status changes), and physical signs of ischemia (e.g., fever and tachycardia). Basic laboratory and radiologic indications for urgent laparotomy include pneumoperitoneum, massive or progressive intestinal distention, signs of sepsis (e.g., marked or rising leukocytosis, increasing glucose intolerance, and acidosis), and signs of continued hemorrhage (e.g., a falling hematocrit). Additional findings that constitute indications for urgent laparotomy include free extravasation of radiologic contrast material, mesenteric occlusion on angiography, endoscopically uncontrollable bleeding, and positive results from peritoneal lavage (i.e., the presence of blood, pus, bile, urine, or GI contents). Acute appendicitis, perforated hollow viscera, and strangulated hernias are examples of common conditions that necessitate urgent laparotomy.

If early operation is contemplated, it may still be prudent to obtain additional studies to obtain information related to the site of the lesion or to associated anatomic pitfalls. In deciding whether to order such studies, it is important to consider not only whether the additional information obtained will increase confidence in the diagnosis but also whether the extra time, expense, and discomfort involved will be justified by the quality and usefulness of the information.[43] During a short, defined period of resuscitation, it may be possible to employ CT scanning to identify the location of the inflamed appendix in difficult (i.e., retrocecal or pelvic) locations. Knowing the location of the appendix and its morphology can be helpful in directing the incision in an open operation or determining the most expeditious exposure in a laparoscopic procedure. CT scanning may also be used to identify an atypical site of a visceral perforation (e.g., the proximal stomach, the distal or posterior wall of the duodenum, or the transverse colon), thereby guiding placement of the incision and obviating needless dissection of tissue planes. In the setting of distal bowel obstruction, an expeditious Gastrografin (Bracco Diagnostics, Princeton, New Jersey) enema or CT scan may alert the surgeon to the possibility of an otherwise undetectable malignancy (e.g., cecal carcinoma causing distal bowel obstruction). In cases where ischemic bowel is suspected, the site of vascular blockage can be localized by using a CT-angiogram imaging protocol. In each of these examples, the information gained may permit the surgeon to plan the operation, to optimize time spent under anesthesia, and to minimize postoperative discomfort after laparotomy.

The use of preoperative imaging has become increasingly important as an operative planning tool, particularly when laparoscopic approaches are contemplated for management of acute abdominal emergencies. In the 1990s and the first few years of the 21st century, a number of trials were performed to determine whether laparoscopy or open operation should be the approach of choice when the primary clinical diagnosis is acute appendicitis. This topic has been reviewed extensively in the literature[44-46] and in a 2004 update of a Cochrane meta-analysis.[47] In some environments, the answer to this question remains unclear.[48,49] In many settings, however, the current consensus is that uncomplicated appendicitis can be treated laparoscopically, with a clear expectation of less postoperative pain, a shorter hospital stay, and an earlier return to work and regular activities. These advantages, though significant, do not indicate that a laparoscopic approach is to be preferred in all or most clinical settings or that it is necessarily more cost-effective than an open approach.[47] Laparoscopic appendectomy requires a high level of organization with respect to operating room resources, and this level of organization may be difficult to achieve in institutions where the procedure is not performed regularly (particularly in the middle of the night). In addition, it is not clear whether patients with appendicitis that is complicated by a well-established abscess or bowel obstruction benefit from laparoscopic approaches.

Anatomic considerations also enter into the decision whether to perform the procedure laparoscopically. For instance, it can be very difficult to separate a perforated retrocecal appendix from adherent colon in a safe manner. In many cases, it is prudent not to persist in attempting to extract the appendix without a standard open incision, excellent exposure, and controlled technique. The importance of anatomic considerations underscores the usefulness of preoperative CT in identifying pathologic anatomy, associated abnormalities, and potential pitfalls for either open or laparoscopic approaches.

The advantages of laparoscopy in the management of other abdominal emergencies are less clear-cut. It is important that the surgeon determine not only whether the particular clinical scenario is amenable to a laparoscopic approach but also whether the experience of the entire team and that of the institution as a whole are sufficient for what may be an advanced procedure performed in an acute situation. With this caveat in mind, various investigators have demonstrated that laparoscopy can be employed safely and with good clinical results in selected patients with perforated peptic ulcers.[50-54] Two prospective, randomized, controlled trials comparing open repair of perforated peptic ulcers with laparoscopic repair found that the latter was safe and reliable and was associated with shorter operating times, less postoperative pain, fewer chest complications, shorter postoperative hospital stays, and earlier return to normal daily activities than the former.[52,54]

ACUTE ABDOMINAL PAIN REQUIRING OBSERVATION

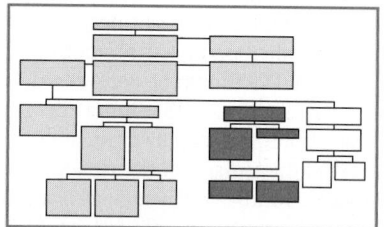

It is widely recognized that of all patients admitted for acute abdominal pain, only a minority require immediate or urgent operation.[2,12] It is therefore both cost-effective and prudent to adopt a system of evaluation that allows for thought and investigation before definitive treatment in all patients with acute abdominal pain except those identified early on as needing immediate or urgent laparotomy. The traditional wisdom has been that spending time on observation opens the door for complications (e.g., perforating appendicitis, intestinal perforation associated with bowel obstruction, or strangulation of an incarcerated hernia). However, clinical trials evaluating active in-hospital observation of patients with acute abdominal pain of uncertain origin have demonstrated that such observation is safe, is not accompanied by an increased incidence of complications, and results in fewer negative laparotomies.[55] Many institutions now employ CT scanning liberally in patients with uncertain diagnoses; this practice should greatly minimize the incidence of diagnostic failures or delays in patients with acute conditions necessitating surgical intervention.[32]

The initial resuscitation and assessment are followed by appropriate imaging studies and serial observation. Specific monitoring measures are chosen (e.g., examination of the abdomen, measurement of urine output, a WBC count, and repeat CT scans), and end points of therapy should be identified. Active observation allows the surgeon to identify most of the patients whose acute abdominal pain is caused by NSAP or by various specific nonsurgical conditions. It must be emphasized that active observation involves more than simply admitting the patient to the hospital and passively watching for obvious problems: it implies an active process of thoughtful, discriminating, and meticulous reevaluation (preferably by the same examiner) at intervals ranging from minutes to a few hours, complemented by appropriately timed additional investigative studies.

A major point of contention in the management of patients with acute abdominal pain is the use of narcotic analgesics during the observation period. The main argument for withholding pain medication is that it may obscure the evolution of specific findings that would lead to the decision to operate. The main argument for giving narcotic analgesics is that in a controlled setting where patients are being observed by experienced clinicians, outcomes are not compromised and patients are more comfortable.[56] It has also been suggested that providing early pain relief may allow the more critical clinical signs to be more clearly identified[57] and that severe pain persisting despite adequate doses of narcotics suggests a serious condition for which operative intervention is likely to be necessary.

In my view, the decision whether to provide or withhold narcotic analgesia must be individualized.[58] The current consensus is that for most patients undergoing evaluation and observation for acute abdominal pain, it is safe to provide medication in doses that would "take the edge off" the pain without rendering the patient unable to cooperate during the observation period. It may be especially desirable to provide medication in a manner that allows the patient to be comfortable while lying in the CT scanner. In these cases, the goal of pain relief is to make it easier to obtain accurate information that will facilitate and expedite the diagnosis and the development of a treatment plan. Given the high diagnostic yield and accuracy of the new generation of CT scanners, it is generally safe to provide pain medication while obtaining the diagnosis.

On occasion, however, reflex administration of pain medication solely with the aim of relieving pain may be undesirable or even harmful. For example, in situations where advanced imaging is unavailable, physical examination may be so crucial to decision making that any risk of obscuring important physical findings is deemed unacceptable, and therefore, pain medication should be withheld. In addition, narcotic analgesia should be used cautiously in patients with acute intestinal obstruction when strangulation is a concern.[59] These patients present with abdominal pain that is out of proportion to the physical findings, a syndrome whose differential diagnosis includes acute intestinal ischemia, pancreatitis, ruptured aortic aneurysm, ureteral colic, and various medical causes (e.g., sickle cell crisis and porphyria). A period of resuscitation and evaluation, in conjunction with advanced imaging studies (e.g., CT) may then yield a tentative diagnosis of intestinal obstruction caused by adhesions (e.g., if the patient has a history of abdominal surgery and no evidence of herniation or obturation) without evidence of bowel ischemia. In this setting, the decision whether to admit the patient for observation rather than immediate operation depends on the extent to which the surgeon is confident that the obstruction is not a "closed loop."[59] However, within a relatively short period (perhaps 4 to 24 hours), the surgeon must determine whether any indications for operation will arise, and the main parameters for observation include the WBC count, the urine output, and the development of peritoneal findings. In such cases, it may well be prudent to withhold pain medication until there is a high level of confidence that the timing of surgery will not be delayed.

A final point is that over the course of a 24- to 48-hour observation period, the patient's condition may neither deteriorate nor improve, and supplemental investigation may be considered. Diagnostic laparoscopy has been recommended in cases where surgical disease is suspected but its probability is not high enough to warrant open laparotomy.[60,61] It is particularly valuable in young women of childbearing age, in whom gynecologic disorders frequently mimic acute appendicitis.[62-64] A 1998 report showed that diagnostic laparoscopy had the same diagnostic yield as open laparotomy in 55 patients with acute abdomen; 34 (62%) of these patients were safely managed with laparoscopy alone, with no increase in morbidity and with a shorter average hospital stay.[63] Diagnostic laparoscopy has also been shown to be useful for assessing acute abdominal pain in acutely ill patients in the intensive care unit.[60,65]

In patients with AIDS,[66,67] there are a number of unusual diagnoses that may be related to or coincident with an episode of abdominal pain. The differential diagnosis includes lymphoma, Kaposi sarcoma, tuberculosis and variants thereof, and opportunistic bacterial, fungal, and viral (especially cytomegaloviral) infections. Laparoscopy has been used for the purposes of diagnosis, biopsy, and treatment in patients with an established AIDS diagnosis who manifest acute abdominal pain syndrome.[66,67] The complication rate and mortality associated with surgery are related to the underlying illness, and outcomes have improved steadily over the years.[68] It is important to note that patients who are infected with HIV but have no clinical manifestations of AIDS are evaluated and managed in the same fashion as patients without HIV infection when they present with acute abdominal pain. The differential diagnosis and the outcomes are essentially no different, unless there are reasons to think that the new onset of pain in an HIV-infected patient is a manifestation of AIDS.[58,68]

Subacute or Chronic Relapsing Abdominal Pain: Role of Outpatient Evaluation and Management

For every patient who requires hospitalization for acute abdominal pain, there are at least two or three others who have self-limiting conditions for which neither operation nor hospitalization is necessary. Much or all of the evaluation of such patients, as well as any treatment that may be needed, can now be completed in the outpatient department. To treat acute abdominal pain cost-effectively and efficiently, the surgeon must be able not only to identify patients who need immediate or urgent laparotomy or laparoscopy but also to reliably identify those whose condition does not present a serious risk and who therefore can be managed without hospitalization. The reliability and intelligence of the patient, the proximity and availability of medical facilities, and the availability of responsible adults to observe and assist the patient at home are factors that should be carefully considered before the decision is made to evaluate or treat individuals with acute abdominal pain as outpatients.

SUSPECTED NONSURGICAL ABDOMEN

There are numerous disorders that cause acute abdominal pain but do not call for surgical intervention. These nonsurgical conditions are often extremely

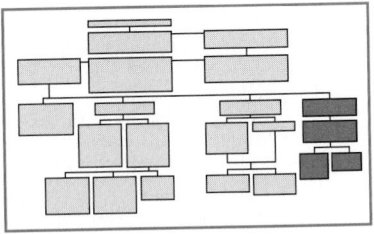

difficult to differentiate from surgical conditions that present with almost indistinguishable characteristics.[2] For example, the acute abdominal pain of lead poisoning or acute porphyria is difficult to differentiate from the intermittent pain of intestinal obstruction, in that marked hyperperistalsis is the hallmark of both. As another example, the pain of acute hypolipoproteinemia may be accompanied by pancreatitis, which, if not recognized, can lead to unnecessary laparotomy. Similarly, acute and prostrating abdominal pain accompanied by rigidity of the abdominal wall and a low hematocrit may lead to unnecessary urgent laparotomy in patients with sickle cell anemia crises. To further complicate the clinical picture, cholelithiasis is also often found in patients with sickle cell anemia.

In addition to numerous extraperitoneal disorders [see Table 2], nonsurgical causes of acute abdominal pain include a wide variety of intraperitoneal disorders, such as acute gastroenteritis (from enteric bacterial, viral, parasitic, or fungal infection), acute gastritis, acute duodenitis, hepatitis, mesenteric adenitis, salpingitis, Fitz-Hugh–Curtis syndrome, mittelschmerz, ovarian cyst, endometritis, endometriosis, threatened abortion, spontaneous bacterial peritonitis, and tuberculous peritonitis. As noted (see above), acute abdominal pain in immunosuppressed patients or patients with AIDS is now encountered with increasing frequency and can be caused by a number of unusual conditions (e.g., cytomegalovirus enterocolitis, opportunistic infections, lymphoma, and Kaposi sarcoma), as well as by the more usual ones.

Although such disorders typically are not treated by operative means, operation is sometimes required when the diagnosis is uncertain or when a surgical illness cannot be excluded with confidence. In such cases, laparoscopy can be very helpful, permitting relatively complete and systematic exploration without involving the potential morbidity or the longer postoperative recovery and rehabilitation period associated with open exploration.[69-72] From the surgeon's point of view, an optimal outcome for laparoscopic exploration in these settings is one in which a diagnosis is established by means of visualization, with or without biopsy, and in which symptoms improve as a consequence of a therapy directed by the laparoscopic findings. Overall, candidate lesions—including appendiceal pathology (e.g., chronic appendicitis or carcinoid tumor), adhesions, hernias, endometriosis, mesenteric lymphadenopathy—are identified in about 50% of cases, with pelvic adhesions the most common finding. From the patient's point of view, however, establishing a precise diagnosis may not be particularly critical, and symptomatic improvement, by itself, may suffice to render the outcome successful. Indeed, a number of reports have emphasized that laparoscopy often leads to improvement in symptoms even if no lesion is identified or treated.[69,70] This point may be illustrated by considering pelvic adhesions.

Given the frequency with which laparoscopic exploration identifies pelvic adhesions, adhesiolysis might be expected to alleviate abdominal pain in many cases. However, it is unclear whether adhesiolysis is therapeutically beneficial when there is no firm evidence that the adhesions are contributing to the pain syndrome. In one prospective, randomized trial,[73] 100 patients with laparoscopically identified adhesions were randomly allocated to either a group that underwent adhesiolysis or one that did not. Both groups reported substantial pain relief and a significantly improved quality of life, but there were no differences in outcome between them, which suggested that the benefit of laparoscopy could not be attributed to adhesiolysis. Longer-term studies also failed to support the hypothesis that pelvic adhesions are responsible for chronic pelvic pain.[74] However, in a study conducted concurrently with the aforementioned randomized trial, 224 consecutive patients underwent laparoscopically assisted adhesiolysis, and 74% of the 224 obtained short-term relief.[75] Factors that contributed to a successful outcome were gender, age, and adhesions severe enough to have led to inadvertent enterotomy and a consequent need for open exploration. It may, therefore, be possible to identify specific subgroups that would benefit from the addition of adhesiolysis to exploratory laparoscopy.

A similar issue arises with respect to pathologic conditions of the appendix—namely, whether appendectomy should be performed when no other source of the abdominal pain can be identified. Early enthusiasm for appendectomy in patients with chronic right lower quadrant pain was sparked by observations of acute or chronic inflammation in specimens that seemed visibly normal.[76,77] In subsequent reports, however, this enthusiasm was tempered by the recognition that these pathologic findings were not very prevalent and that appendectomy did not always reduce the pain.[78,79] No randomized trial of appendectomy for chronic abdominal pain has been performed in a clearly defined patient group, as has been done for adhesiolysis.[73]

At present, the surgeon can only use his or her best judgment as to the likelihood that a given episode of abdominal pain may originate from a set of visible adhesions or a visually normal appendix. It should be remembered that unnecessary or potentially meddlesome interventions are always best avoided; however, it should also be remembered that failure to alleviate chronic relapsing abdominal pain will lead to a program of chronic pain management, including long-term management with potentially addictive and enervating agents. Thus, if adhesiolysis or appendectomy can be performed with the expectation of low morbidity and without conversion to laparotomy, it seems reasonable to perform these procedures during laparoscopy if no other source of pain can be identified.

References

1. de Dombal FT: Diagnosis of Acute Abdominal Pain, 2nd ed. Churchill Livingstone, London, 1991

2. Purcell TB: Nonsurgical and extraperitoneal causes of abdominal pain. Emerg Med Clin North Am 7:721, 1989

3. Silen W: Cope's Early Diagnosis of the Acute Abdomen, 20th ed. Oxford University Press, New York, 2000

4. Marco CA, et al: Abdominal pain in geriatric emergency patients: variables associated with adverse outcomes. Acad Emerg Med 5:1163, 1998

5. Flasar MH, Goldberg E: Acute abdominal pain. Med Clin North Am 90:481, 2006

6. Hickey MS, Kiernan GJ, Weaver KE: Evaluation of abdominal pain. Emerg Med Clin North Am 7:437, 1989

7. Adams ID, Chan M, Clifford PC, et al: Computer aided diagnosis of acute abdominal pain: a multi-centre study. Br Med J 293:800, 1986

8. de Dombal FT, Dallos V, McAdam WA: Can computer aided teaching packages improve clinical care in patients with acute abdominal pain? BMJ 302:1495, 1991

9. Korner H, Sondenaa K, Soreide JA, et al: Structured data collection improves the diagnosis of acute appendicitis. Br J Surg 85:341, 1998

10. American College of Emergency Physicians: Clinical policy for the initial approach to patients presenting with a chief complaint of nontraumatic acute abdominal pain. Ann Emerg Med 23:906, 1994

11. de Dombal FT: Surgical Decision Making in Practice: Acute Abdominal Pain. Butterworth-Heinemann Ltd, Oxford, 1993, p 65

12. Brewer RJ, Golden GT, Hitch DC, et al: Abdominal pain: an analysis of 1,000 consecutive cases in a university hospital emergency room. Am J Surg 131:219, 1976

13. Irvin TT: Abdominal pain: a surgical audit of 1190 emergency admissions. Br J Surg 76:1121, 1989

14. Di Placido R, Pietroletti R, Leardi S, et al: Primary gastroduodenal tuberculous infection presenting as pyloric outlet obstruction. Am J Gastroenterol 91:807, 1996

15. Padussis, J, Loffredo B, McAneny D: Minimally invasive management of obstructive gastroduodenal tuberculosis. Am Surg 71:698, 2005.

16. Petro M, Iavu K, Minocha A: Unusual endoscopic and microscopic view of Enterobius vermicularis: a case report with a review of the literature. South Med J 98:927, 2005

17. Ross AG, Bartley PB, Sleigh AC, et al: Schistosomiasis. N Engl J Med 346:1212, 2002

18. Akgun Y: Intestinal obstruction caused by Ascaris

lumbricoides. Dis Colon Rectum 39:1159, 1996

19. Krausz MM, Moriel EZ, Ayalon A, et al: Surgical aspects of gastrointestinal persimmon phytobezoar treatment. Am J Surg 152:526, 1986

20. Lee JF, Leow CK, Lai PB, et al: Food bolus intestinal obstruction in a Chinese population. Aust NZ J Surg 67:866, 1997

21. Parente F, Anderloni A, Greco S, et al: Ileocecal Burkitt's lymphoma. Gastroenterology 127:368, 2004

22. Qiu DC, Hubbard AE, Zhong B, et al: A matched, case-control study of the association between *Schistosoma japonicum* and liver and colon cancers, in rural China. Ann Trop Med Parasitol 99:47, 2005

23. de Dombal FT: The OMGE acute abdominal pain survey. Progress Report, 1986. Scand J Gastroenterol 144(suppl):35, 1988

24. Jess P, Bjerregaard B, Brynitz S, et al: Prognosis of acute nonspecific abdominal pain: a prospective study. Am J Surg 144:338, 1982

25. Lukens TW, Emerman C, Effron D: The natural history and clinical findings in undifferentiated abdominal pain. Ann Emerg Med 22:690, 1993

26. Martinez JP, Mattu A: Abdominal pain in the elderly. Emerg Med Clin North Am 24:371, 2006

27. Telfer S, Fenyo G, Holt PR, et al: Acute abdominal pain in patients over 50 years of age. Scand J Gastroenterol 144(suppl):47, 1988

28. Dickson JAS, Jones A, Telfer S, et al: Acute abdominal pain in children. Progress Report, 1986. Scand J Gastroenterol 144(suppl):43, 1988

29. Scholer SJ, Pituch K, Orr DP, et al: Clinical outcomes of children with acute abdominal pain. Pediatrics 98:680, 1996

30. Malaty HM, Abudayyeh S, O'Malley KJ, et al: Development of a multidimensional measure for recurrent abdominal pain in children: population-based studies in three settings. Pediatrics 115:e210, 2005

31. Gill BD, Jenkins JR: Cost-effective evaluation and management of the acute abdomen. Surg Clin North Am 76:71, 1996

32. Rao PM, Rhea JT, Novelline RA, et al: Effect of computed tomography of the appendix on treatment of patients and use of hospital resources. N Engl J Med 338:141, 1998

33. Thompson MM, Underwood MJ, Dookeran KA, et al: Role of sequential leucocyte counts and C-reactive protein measurements in acute appendicitis. Br J Surg 79:822, 1992

34. Plewa MC: Emergency abdominal radiography. Emerg Med Clin North Am 9:827, 1991

35. Ahn SH, Mayo-Smith WW, Murphy BL, et al: Acute nontraumatic abdominal pain in adult patients: abdominal radiography compared with CT evaluation. Radiology 225:159, 2002

36. MacKersie AB, Lane MJ, Gerhardt RT, et al: Nontraumatic acute abdominal pain: unenhanced helical CT compared with three-view acute abdominal series. Radiology 237:114, 2005

37. Balthazar EJ, Liebeskind ME, Macari M: Intestinal ischemia in patients in whom small bowel obstruction is suspected: evaluation of accuracy, limitations, and clinical implications of CT in diagnosis. Radiology 205:519, 1997

38. Zalcman M, Sy M, Donckier V, et al: Helical CT signs in the diagnosis of intestinal ischemia in small-bowel obstruction. AJR Am J Roentgenol 175:1601, 2000

39. Mallo RD, Salem L, Lalani T, et al: Computed tomography diagnosis of ischemia and complete obstruction in small bowel obstruction: a systematic review. J Gastrointest Surg 9:690, 2005

40. Wagner LK, Huda W: When a pregnant woman with suspected appendicitis is referred for a CT scan, what should a radiologist do to minimize potential radiation risks? Pediatr Radiol 34:589, 2004

41. Fefferman NR, Bomsztyk E, Yim AM, et al: Appen-

dicitis in children: low-dose CT with a phantom-based simulation technique—initial observations. Radiology 237:641, 2005

42. Hurwitz LM, Yoshizumi T, Reiman RE, et al: Radiation dose to the fetus from body MDCT during early gestation. AJR Am J Roentgenol 186:871, 2006

43. Ng CS, Watson CJ, Palmer CR, et al: Evaluation of early abdominopelvic computed tomography in patients with acute abdominal pain of unknown cause: prospective randomised study. BMJ 325:1387, 2002

44. Garbutt JM, Soper NJ, Shannon WD, et al: Meta-analysis of randomized controlled trials comparing laparoscopic and open appendectomy. Surg Laparosc Endosc 9:17, 1999

45. Sauerland S, Lefering R, Holthausen U, et al: Laparoscopic vs conventional appendectomy—a meta-analysis of randomised controlled trials. Langenbecks Arch Surg 383:289, 1998

46. Guller U, Hervey S, Purves H, et al: Laparoscopic versus open appendectomy: outcomes comparison based on a large administrative database. Ann Surg 239:43, 2004

47. Sauerland S, Lefering R, Neugebauer EA: Laparoscopic versus open surgery for suspected appendicitis. Cochrane Database Syst Rev (4):CD001546, 2004

48. Katkhouda N, Mason RJ, Towfigh S, et al: Laparoscopic versus open appendectomy: a prospective randomized double-blind study. Ann Surg 242:439, 2005

49. Moberg AC, Berndsen F, Palmquist I, et al: Randomized clinical trial of laparoscopic versus open appendicectomy for confirmed appendicitis. Br J Surg 92:298, 2005

50. Fritts LL, Orlando R: Laparoscopic appendectomy: a safety and cost analysis. Arch Surg 128:521, 1993

51. Hansen JB, Smithers BM, Schache D, et al: Laparoscopic versus open appendectomy: prospective randomized trial. World J Surg 20:17, 1996

52. Lau WY, Leung KL, Kwong KH, et al: A randomized study comparing laparoscopic versus open repair of perforated peptic ulcer using suture or sutureless technique. Ann Surg 224:131, 1996

53. Matsuda M, Nishiyama M, Hanai T, et al: Laparoscopic omental patch repair for the perforated peptic ulcer. Ann Surg 221:236, 1995

54. Siu WT, Leong HT, Law BK, et al: Laparoscopic repair for perforated peptic ulcer: a randomized controlled trial. Ann Surg 235:313, 2002

55. Thomson HJ, Jones PF: Active observation in acute abdominal pain. Am J Surg 152:522, 1986

56. McHale PM, LoVecchio F: Narcotic analgesia in the acute abdomen—a review of prospective trials. Eur J Emerg Med 8:131, 2001

57. Attard AR, Corlett MJ, Kidner NJ, et al: Safety of early pain relief for acute abdominal pain. BMJ 305:554, 1992

58. Soybel DI: Appendix. Surgery: Basic Science and Clinical Evidence. Norton JA, Barie PS, Bollinger RR, Eds. Springer, New York, 2000, p 647

59. Saund M, Soybel DI: Ileus and bowel obstruction. Greenfield's Surgery: Scientific Principles and Practice, 4th ed. Mulholland MW, Lillemoe KD, Doherty GM, Eds. Lippincott Williams & Wilkins, Philadelphia, 2006, p 767

60. Majewski W: Diagnostic laparoscopy for the acute abdomen and trauma. Surg Endosc 14:930, 2000

61. Golash V, Willson PD: Early laparoscopy as a routine procedure in the management of acute abdominal pain: a review of 1,320 patients. Surg Endosc 19:882, 2005

62. Taylor EW, Kennedy CA, Dunham RH, et al: Diagnostic laparoscopy in women with acute abdominal pain. Surg Laparosc Endosc 5:125, 1995

63. Chung RS, Diaz JJ, Chari V: Efficacy of routine laparoscopy for the acute abdomen. Surg Endosc 12:219, 1998

64. Ou CS, Rowbotham R: Laparoscopic diagnosis and treatment of nontraumatic acute abdominal pain in women. J Laparoendosc Adv Surg Tech A 10:41, 2000

65. Orlando R, Crowell KL: Laparoscopy in the critically ill. Surg Endosc 11:1072, 1997

66. Box JC, Duncan T, Ramshaw B, et al: Laparoscopy in the evaluation and treatment of patients with AIDS and acute abdominal complaints. Surg Endosc 11:1026, 1997

67. Endres JC, Salky BA: Laparoscopy in AIDS. Gastrointest Endosc Clin N Am 8:975, 1998

68. Saltzman DJ, Williams RA, Gelfand DV, et al: The surgeon and AIDS: twenty years later. Arch Surg 140:961, 2005

69. Klingensmith ME, Soybel DI, Brooks DC: Laparoscopy for chronic abdominal pain. Surg Endosc 10:1085, 1996

70. Onders RP, Mittendorf EA: Utility of laparoscopy in chronic abdominal pain. Surgery 134:549, 2003

71. Paajanen H, Julkunen K, Waris H: Laparoscopy in chronic abdominal pain: a prospective nonrandomized long-term follow-up study. J Clin Gastroenterol 39:110, 2005

72. Salky BA, Edye MB: The role of laparoscopy in the diagnosis and treatment of abdominal pain syndromes. Surg Endosc 12:911, 1998

73. Swank DJ, Swank-Bordewijk SC, Hop WC, et al: Laparoscopic adhesiolysis in patients with chronic abdominal pain: a blinded randomised controlled multi-centre trial. Lancet 361:1247, 2003

74. Dunker MS, Bemelman WA, Vijn A, et al: Long-term outcomes and quality of life after laparoscopic adhesiolysis for chronic abdominal pain. J Am Assoc Gynecol Laparosc 11:36, 2004

75. Swank DJ, Van Erp WF, Repelaer Van Driel OJ, et al: A prospective analysis of predictive factors on the results of laparoscopic adhesiolysis in patients with chronic abdominal pain. Surg Laparosc Endosc Percutan Tech 13:88, 2003

76. Chao K, Farrell S, Kerdemelidis P, et al: Diagnostic laparoscopy for chronic right iliac fossa pain: a pilot study. Aust NZ J Surg 67:789, 1997

77. Greason KL, Rappold JF, Liberman MA: Incidental laparoscopic appendectomy for acute right lower quadrant abdominal pain. Its time has come. Surg Endosc 12:223, 1998

78. Teh SH, O'Ceallaigh S, Mckeon JG, et al: Should an appendix that looks 'normal' be removed at diagnostic laparoscopy for acute right iliac fossa pain? Eur J Surg 166:388, 2000

79. van den Broek WT, Bijnen AB, de Ruiter P, et al: A normal appendix found during diagnostic laparoscopy should not be removed. Br J Surg 88:251, 2001

80. Cheung LY, Ballinger WF: Manifestations and diagnosis of gastrointestinal diseases. Hardy's Textbook of Surgery. Hardy JD, Ed. JB Lippincott Co, Philadelphia, 1983, p 445

81. McFadden DW, Zinner MJ: Manifestations of gastrointestinal disease. Principles of Surgery, 6th ed. Schwartz SI, Shires GT, Spencer FC, Eds. McGraw-Hill, New York, 1994, p 1015

82. Wilson DH, Wilson PD, Walmsley RG, et al: Diagnosis of acute abdominal pain in the accident and emergency department. Br J Surg 64:249, 1977

83. Hawthorn IE: Abdominal pain as a cause of acute admission to hospital. J R Coll Surg Edinb 37:389, 1992

Acknowledgments

Figures 2 and 3 Tom Moore.

The authors would like to thank Laurence Y. Cheung, M.D., F.A.C.S., for his contributions to a previous iteration of this chapter on which the current version is partially based.

44 ABDOMINAL MASS

Wilbur B. Bowne, M.D., and Michael E. Zenilman, M.D., F.A.C.S.

Evaluation of an Abdominal Mass

Abdominal masses are commonly addressed by surgeons, as well as by members of many clinical subspecialties. In terms of clinical importance, abdominal masses cover a broad spectrum: some have few or no apparent consequences, others significantly impair quality of life, and still others represent severe conditions that are associated with poor outcomes and high mortalities. For each patient, therefore, it is essential to formulate a management approach that is tailored to the particular clinical situation. Effective decision-making in this regard involves establishing the correct diagnosis, introducing an effective treatment plan, eliminating risks and complicating factors, initiating preventive measures, and determining the prognosis.

The history of the abdominal mass in the medical literature is ancient, dating back to the Egyptians. The varied differential diagnosis of such masses was discussed in the Papyrus Ebers (ca. 1500 B.C.).[1] Egyptian medical scholars kept detailed notes chronicling conditions encountered and describing methods of abdominal examination that were based on studies of basic anatomy and embalming practices. Centuries later, in his *Book of Prognostics*, the Greek physician Hippocrates (ca. 400 B.C.) discussed the prognostic significance of various types of abdominal masses:

> The state of the hypochondrium is best when it is free from pain, soft, and of equal size on the right side and the left. But if inflamed, or painful, or distended; or when the right and left sides are of disproportionate sizes; all of these appearances are to be dreaded. A swelling in the hypochondrium, that is hard and painful, is very bad…. Such swellings at the commencement of disease prognosticate speedy death. Such swellings as are soft, free from pain, and yield to the finger, occasion more protracted crises, and are less dangerous than others.[2]

Along with the basic methods of clinical evaluation known since antiquity, the modern surgeon has an armamentarium of sophisticated diagnostic studies that aid in the detection, diagnosis, and appropriate treatment of abdominal masses.

In this chapter, we begin with essential definitions and anatomic considerations and then outline our fundamental approach to evaluating patients with an abdominal mass, which integrates the clinical history, the physical examination, and various investigative studies. In particular, we address current developments in investigative techniques, including radiographic and molecular imaging studies that facilitate anatomic evaluation, diagnosis, and determination of the biologic significance of the abdominal mass; we also address minimally invasive diagnostic interventions. Throughout, we emphasize an algorithmic, evidence-based approach to detection and evaluation of abdominal masses. Specific perioperative and operative strategies for addressing particular diagnoses are outlined in other chapters.

Clinical Evaluation

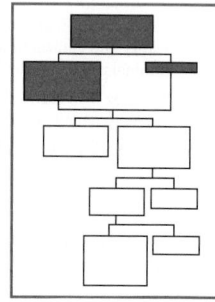

In general, the term abdominal mass refers to a palpable mass that lies anterior to the paraspinous muscles in a region bordered by the costal margins, the iliac crests, and the pubic symphysis. One method of description divides the abdomen into nine areas: epigastric, umbilical, suprapubic, right hypochondriac, left hypochondriac, right lumbar, left lumbar, right inguinal, and left inguinal.[3] Our preferred method divides the abdominal cavity into four quadrants—right upper, right lower, left upper, and left lower—and makes specific reference to the epigastrium and the hypogastrium as necessary. This method of description also includes masses discovered within the retroperitoneum and the abdominal wall. For practical purposes, the abdominal wall begins from the diaphragm superiorly and continues inferiorly to the pelvic cavity through the pelvic inlet. The anterior, posterior, and lateral boundaries of the abdominal wall should be familiar to surgeons. Further anatomic detail is available in other sources.[4,5]

A sound understanding of the normal anatomy in each abdominal quadrant is essential for the evaluation of the abdominal mass. Particular abnormalities tend to be associated with particular regions or quadrants of the abdomen, and these associations should be considered first in the differential diagnosis. Commonly, an abnormal enlargement or mass in the abdomen comes to the clinician's attention in one of three ways: it is detected and reported by the patient, it is discovered by the clinician on physical examination, or it is noticed as an unrelated incidental finding on a radiographic study. Subsequent clinical decision making is then influenced by whether the lesion is intraabdominal, pelvic, retroperitoneal, or situated within the abdominal wall. In certain cases, a prompt diagnosis can be made after the physical examination, with no further investigation required; obesity, ascites, pregnancy, hernias, infection or abscess, cysts, and lipomas are examples of conditions that can generally be diagnosed at this point.

Of the various factors that go into making the diagnosis and implementing therapy, clinical experience is undoubtedly paramount. Nevertheless, even the most experienced physicians are subject to some degree of clinical inaccuracy. A randomized study from 1981 found that even when experienced clinicians were certain about the presence of a mass, there was still an appreciable (22%) chance that further investigation would not reveal any abnormality.[6] The evaluation of abdominal masses continues to pose many clinical challenges for the surgeon. There is no magical

Evaluation of an Abdominal Mass

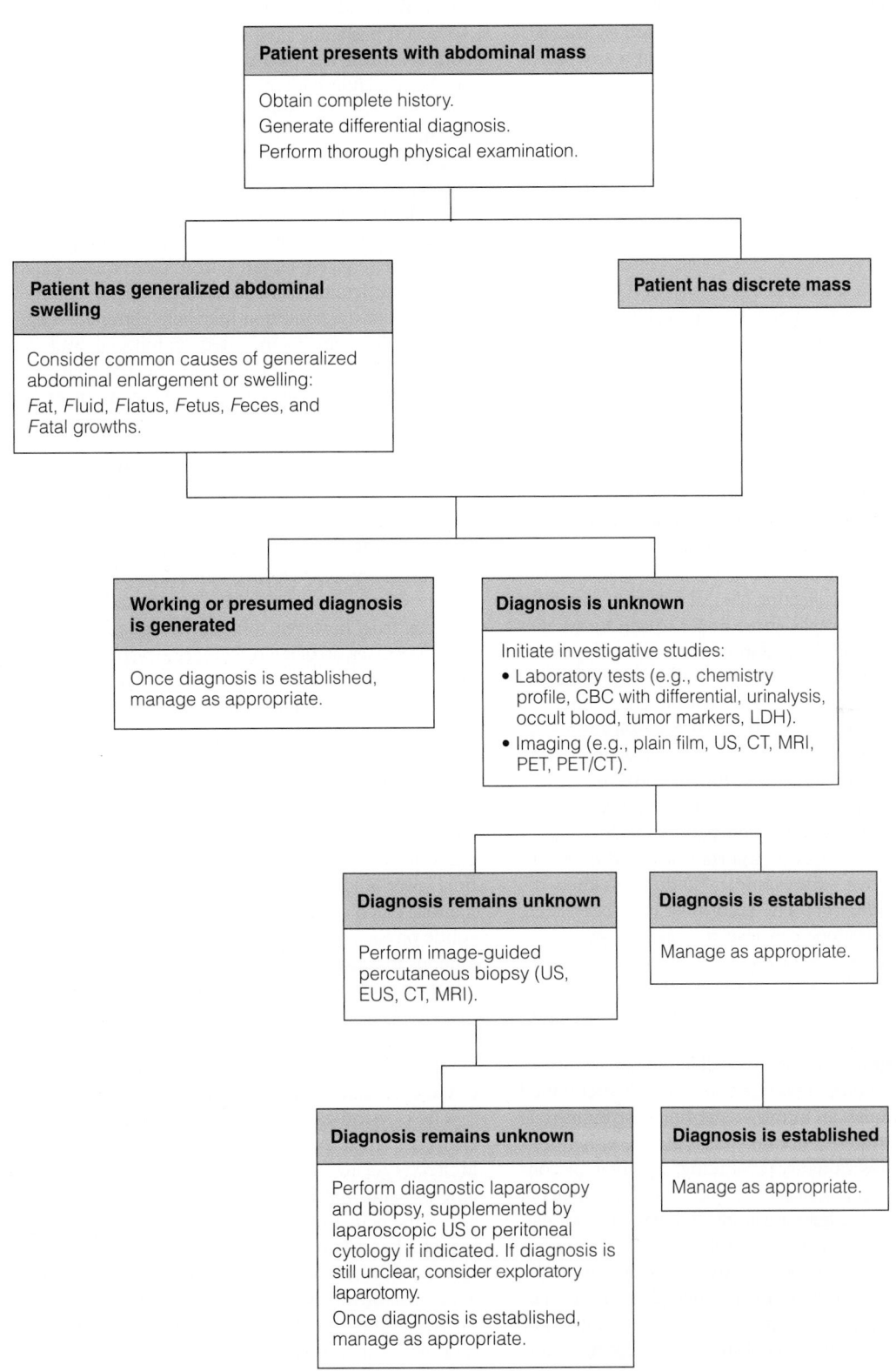

Patient presents with abdominal mass

Obtain complete history.
Generate differential diagnosis.
Perform thorough physical examination.

Patient has generalized abdominal swelling

Consider common causes of generalized abdominal enlargement or swelling:
Fat, *Fluid*, *Flatus*, *Fetus*, *Feces*, and *Fatal growths*.

Patient has discrete mass

Working or presumed diagnosis is generated

Once diagnosis is established, manage as appropriate.

Diagnosis is unknown

Initiate investigative studies:
- Laboratory tests (e.g., chemistry profile, CBC with differential, urinalysis, occult blood, tumor markers, LDH).
- Imaging (e.g., plain film, US, CT, MRI, PET, PET/CT).

Diagnosis remains unknown

Perform image-guided percutaneous biopsy (US, EUS, CT, MRI).

Diagnosis is established

Manage as appropriate.

Diagnosis remains unknown

Perform diagnostic laparoscopy and biopsy, supplemented by laparoscopic US or peritoneal cytology if indicated. If diagnosis is still unclear, consider exploratory laparotomy.
Once diagnosis is established, manage as appropriate.

Diagnosis is established

Manage as appropriate.

formula for mastering the necessary diagnostic skills; the closest thing to such a formula is an approach that combines knowledge and application of fundamental anatomic principles with continuous development and appropriate utilization of new diagnostic modalities. For accurate assessment of the origin and character of the abdominal mass, it is essential to possess a thorough understanding of the normal anatomy, the anatomic variations that may be observed, and the distortions that may be caused by the various potential disease processes. As has been said of many professions besides surgery, "You must know the territory." Ultimately, whether a correct diagnosis calls for further intervention or for referral to colleagues with complementary technical expertise depends on the experience of the practitioner.

Fundamental to the successful diagnosis of any abdominal mass are a detailed medical and surgical history and a meticulous physical examination (see below).

HISTORY

Establishing a solid surgeon-patient relationship is vital for building patient trust and confidence, particularly during a period of great uncertainty and vulnerability in the patient's life. Accordingly, our philosophy in dealing with an abdominal mass is to evaluate the patient first and then consider radiographic and laboratory studies if the initial assessment does not yield a diagnosis. A careful and methodical clinical history should be taken that includes all factors pertaining to the lesion. Information about the lesion's mode of onset, duration, character, chronology, and location should be obtained, as well as confirmation of the presence or absence of associated symptoms.

Interviewing strategies for collecting clinical data may vary from surgeon to surgeon.[7] For example, some prefer to conduct a clinical history while sitting rather than standing because this posture tends to suggest the absence of undue haste and the presence of appropriate concern and empathy. A focused, comprehensive interview usually provides all the information necessary for making the correct diagnosis. Our practice is to start by asking nondirective questions—for example, "When did you first notice the mass on your left side?" or "How long did you experience this pain in your abdomen?" It is important to allow patients to describe the history in their own words. It is also important to avoid questions with a built-in degree of bias—for example, "Didn't you know the mass was on your left side?" or "The pain must have been there for some time?" Such questions can lead to biased answers that may misrepresent the chronology or the true natural history of the disease. In most cases, we then proceed to ask questions designed to elicit more specific information (e.g., previous operations, previous medical conditions or therapies, family medical history, or recent travel). It is sometimes necessary to fill in the details by asking direct questions about particular points not already mentioned by the patient. For example, an inquiry regarding gastrointestinal symptoms associated with the abdominal mass may be either nonspecific (e.g., concerned with nausea, vomiting, diarrhea, or constipation) or specific (e.g., concerned with jaundice, melena, hematochezia, hematemesis, hematuria, or changes in stool caliber). Non-GI symptoms (including urologic, gynecologic or obstetric, vascular, and endocrinologic symptoms) should not be overlooked. A history of surgery, trauma, or neoadjuvant or adjuvant cancer therapy may be diagnostically important.[8] For instance, the presence of an abdominal mass representing recurrent cancer raises important clinical questions concerning the advisability of additional therapy or palliative measures, which may carry significant morbidity and mortality.[9-12]

DIFFERENTIAL DIAGNOSIS

For practical purposes, the differential diagnosis for an abdominal mass is divided into categories corresponding to the anatomic divisions of the abdomen (i.e., the four quadrants, the epigastrium, and the hypogastrium) [see Figure 1]. The challenge for the modern surgeon is how to narrow down the diagnostic possibilities while avoiding needlessly extensive and expensive evaluations. To accomplish this goal with efficiency, the surgeon must draw both on his or her own reservoir of fundamental knowledge and on the available patient data (e.g., age, gender, associated symptoms, and comorbidities).

After obtaining a thorough clinical history, the surgeon should be able to generate a differential diagnosis. The physical examination may then help confirm or rule out diagnostic possibilities. For example, the presence or absence of pain or tenderness may distinguish an inflammatory or nonneoplastic process from a neoplastic one (e.g., cholecystitis from Courvoisier gallbladder or, perhaps, diverticulitis from carcinoma of the colon). Likewise, the acuteness of the condition may help eliminate diagnostic possibilities, as when an incarcerated abdominal wall hernia is distinguished from a lipomatous mass. So too may the nature of the process, as when a pulsatile mass such as an aneurysm is distinguished from a nonpulsatile one such as a hematoma or a cyst.

Masses of the abdominal wall commonly are subcutaneous lipomas, and care should be taken to differentiate them from neoplastic lesions such as desmoid tumors,[13] dermatofibrosarcoma protuberans (DFSP),[14] and other related[15] or nonrelated tumors.[16,17] When an abdominal mass is associated with uncommon or unexpected findings, the surgeon must be alert to the possibility of an uncommon or unexpected disease process.[18,19] It remains true, however, that knowledge of the most common disease processes associated with region-specific abdominal masses, combined with familiarity with the characteristic signs and symptoms, is the foundation of the clinical assessment of such masses.

PHYSICAL EXAMINATION

The physical examination plays an essential role in the evaluation and workup of an abdominal mass. Current investigative studies are also important in this setting, but all too often, clinicians become overly reliant on various imaging modalities, sometimes overlooking the importance of a careful and thorough examination. Such overreliance can increase the chances of missing subtle physical findings—such as an enlarged lymph node, subcutaneous irregularity, or referred pain—that could have a significant effect on the management of the abdominal mass. Our practice in examining patients with an abdominal mass is to follow an organized, systematic approach consisting of inspection, auscultation, percussion, and palpation, in that order. More detailed discussions of these specific maneuvers are available elsewhere.[20]

The physical examination has three main objectives. First, the examiner must evaluate the patient's condition as it directly or indirectly relates to the mass (e.g., by noting associated systemic illness, pain, malaise, or cachexia). Second, the examiner must assess the acuteness of the patient's condition (e.g., by determining whether a left upper quadrant mass is likely to be a ruptured spleen or simply a long-standing mass in the abdominal wall), which will dictate whether the next step is immediate treatment or further evaluation. Third, the examiner must carefully examine each abdominal quadrant, assessing both normal and abnormal anatomic relations as possible sources of the presumed mass.

How to distinguish a normal abdominal mass or swelling from an abnormal one remains a common challenge for the surgeon.

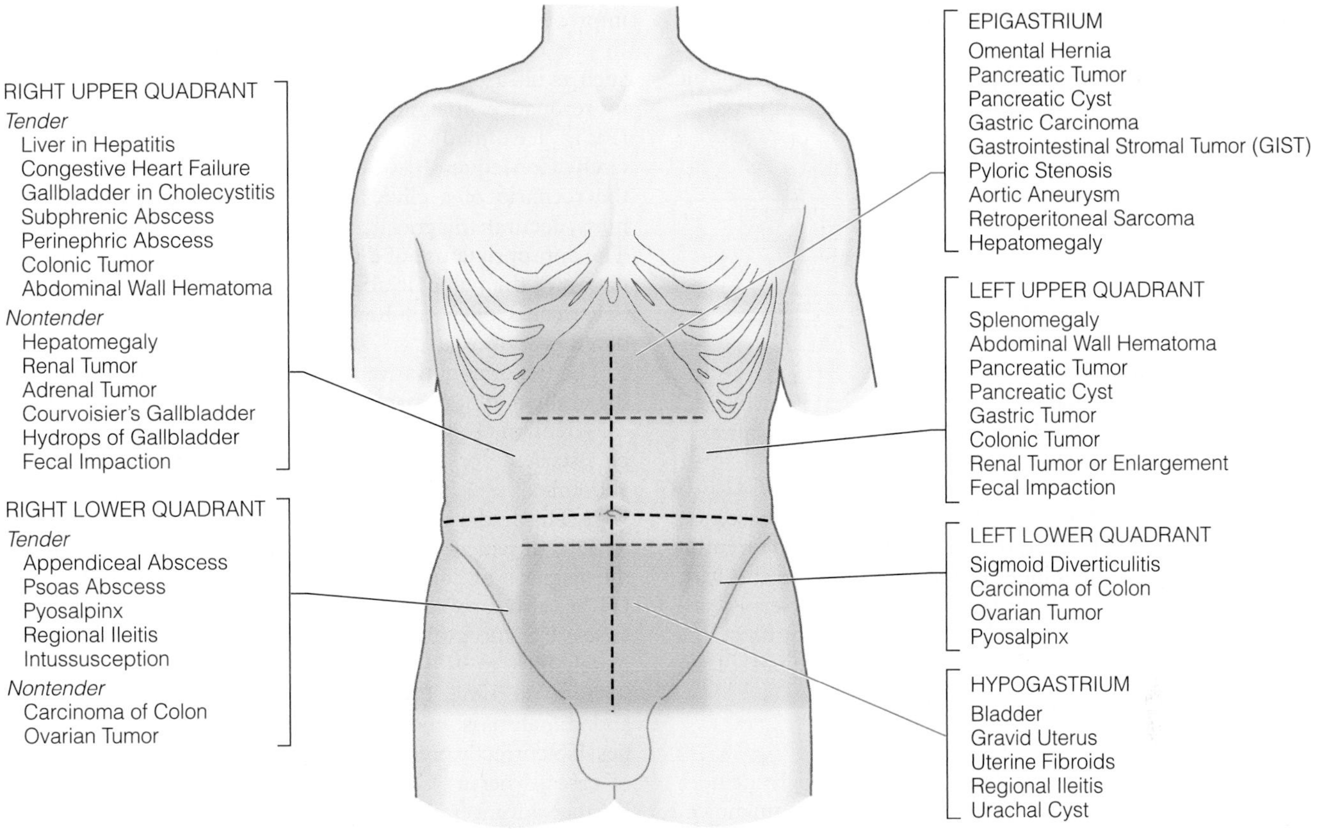

RIGHT UPPER QUADRANT
Tender
Liver in Hepatitis
Congestive Heart Failure
Gallbladder in Cholecystitis
Subphrenic Abscess
Perinephric Abscess
Colonic Tumor
Abdominal Wall Hematoma
Nontender
Hepatomegaly
Renal Tumor
Adrenal Tumor
Courvoisier's Gallbladder
Hydrops of Gallbladder
Fecal Impaction

RIGHT LOWER QUADRANT
Tender
Appendiceal Abscess
Psoas Abscess
Pyosalpinx
Regional Ileitis
Intussusception
Nontender
Carcinoma of Colon
Ovarian Tumor

EPIGASTRIUM
Omental Hernia
Pancreatic Tumor
Pancreatic Cyst
Gastric Carcinoma
Gastrointestinal Stromal Tumor (GIST)
Pyloric Stenosis
Aortic Aneurysm
Retroperitoneal Sarcoma
Hepatomegaly

LEFT UPPER QUADRANT
Splenomegaly
Abdominal Wall Hematoma
Pancreatic Tumor
Pancreatic Cyst
Gastric Tumor
Colonic Tumor
Renal Tumor or Enlargement
Fecal Impaction

LEFT LOWER QUADRANT
Sigmoid Diverticulitis
Carcinoma of Colon
Ovarian Tumor
Pyosalpinx

HYPOGASTRIUM
Bladder
Gravid Uterus
Uterine Fibroids
Regional Ileitis
Urachal Cyst

Figure 1 **Schema represents differential diagnosis of an abdominal mass by quadrant or region. Fundamental knowledge of normal anatomy and clinical presentations is the basis for distinguishing the various disease processes. Abdominal wall hernia is considered a possibility in every region or quadrant.**

Physical findings on examination are sometimes variable and can be affected by factors such as obesity, body habitus, associated medical conditions, and the patient's ability to cooperate. For example, the normal aorta is often palpable within the epigastrium and may be slightly tender; in elderly, asthenic patients, the normal aorta may be mistaken for an aneurysm. Likewise, the cecum and the descending colon, both of which are usually palpable in thin patients (especially when they contain feces), sometimes masquerade as a cancerous mass; subsequent disimpaction causes such "masses" to resolve. Obesity may preclude evaluation of a potential abdominal mass: it can be difficult to identify discrete palpable masses amid the often remarkable adiposity present within the abdominal wall and the surrounding structures. Ascites may also obscure abdominal masses, making examination more problematic. Transient gaseous distention or intestinal bloating occasionally presents a similar problem, but it usually resolves spontaneously, except in cases of intestinal obstruction. Either gastric dilatation or intestinal obstruction may lead to abdominal distention that is severe enough to necessitate nasogastric decompression. Not uncommonly, in women of childbearing age, a lower abdominal mass may represent a gravid uterus. In such cases, a gynecologic examination must be conducted and a pregnancy test performed before further studies are ordered. The multiplicity of potential benign causes notwithstanding, the possibility of a neoplasm (single or multiple) clearly remains a matter of considerable concern in the evaluation of any patient with abdominal distention. A convenient method of recalling the main causes of generalized enlargement or distention of the abdomen is to use the so-called "six Fs" mnemonic device: *F*at, *F*luid, *F*latus, *F*etus, *F*eces, and *F*atal growths.[21-23]

Palpable or discrete masses should always be localized with respect to the previously described landmarks (see above), and they should, if possible, be described in terms of size, shape, consistency, contour, presence or absence of tenderness, pulsatility, and fixation. Knowledge of the location of the mass in the abdomen shortens the list of structures or organs to be considered and may give insight into the nature and extent of the pathologic process. Frequently, however, the mass's location can only be vaguely outlined, particularly when fluid is present, when the abdomen is tender or tense, or when the patient is obese. Gastric neoplasms, pancreatic neoplasms, colonic neoplasms, sarcomas, pancreatic cysts, and distended gallbladders may be palpable, typically at advanced stages of disease. Recognition of such masses can be facilitated by repeating the abdominal examination after analgesics have been administered or after the patient has been anesthetized in preparation for a procedure.

Working or Presumed Diagnosis

Once a thorough clinical history has been obtained and a careful physical examination conducted, it is usually possible to generate a working diagnosis. Once the working diagnosis has been established, subsequent management is considered in light of its appropriateness for the presumed condition. Sometimes, however, the diagnosis remains unknown even after a comprehensive clinical history and physical examination; in such cases, further studies are required. A wide range of laboratory and imag-

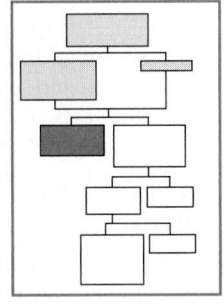

ing studies are now available for establishing the diagnosis. If these studies do not resolve the diagnostic uncertainty, additional procedures, including image-guided percutaneous biopsy, diagnostic laparoscopy, and exploratory laparotomy, may be employed as necessary.

Investigative Studies

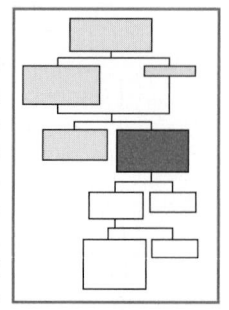

Surgeons are in a unique position to care for patients presenting with an abdominal mass and should guide the collaborative management effort and the choice of appropriate investigative studies. It is therefore essential that surgeons be familiar with every available method for efficient and cost-effective diagnosis of an abdominal mass. For any given situation, the selection of investigative studies should be based on the preferences of the patient, the knowledge and judgment of the surgeon, and the capabilities of the institution. In this way, surgeons who practice outside large, specialized referral centers will still be able to provide integral leadership for most disease management efforts arising from the diagnosis of an abdominal mass.

LABORATORY STUDIES

The diagnostic workup of an abdominal mass usually includes laboratory evaluation. If the cause of the mass remains unknown, preliminary laboratory analysis should include a chemistry profile (electrolyte, blood urea nitrogen [BUN], and creatinine concentrations, as well as liver function tests), a complete blood count (CBC) with differential, and urinalysis. An abnormal laboratory value sometimes plays an important role in establishing the identity or pathogenesis of an abdominal mass. For example, an elevated alkaline phosphatase or liver transaminase level may suggest metastasis to the liver. Likewise, an elevated serum amylase concentration may be suggestive of a pancreatic pseudocyst rather than a cystic neoplasm or an adenocarcinoma; however, an elevated total serum bilirubin level (i.e., > 10 mg/dl) may be more suggestive of a malignant process secondary to adenocarcinoma of the pancreatic head or cholangiocarcinoma. Routine testing for occult blood in the stool should not be overlooked. Tumor markers (e.g., carcinoembryonic antigen [CEA], the cancer antigens CA 19-9 and CA 125, and α-fetoprotein [AFP]) may also help differentiate between benign disease processes and malignant ones, distinguish high-level disease from low-level disease, and, in some cases, establish a disease diagnosis (e.g., elevated AFP levels in patients with hepatocellular carcinoma). Similarly, an elevated serum lactate dehydrogenase (LDH) level may prove invaluable in the staging and prognosis of certain diseases (e.g., melanoma) connected with an abdominal mass.[24] Furthermore, the ability to distinguish between functional abdominal masses and nonfunctional ones (e.g., adrenal tumors) also has important implications for evaluation and management.

In some cases, when the type of mass remains unknown, needless and expensive laboratory analysis can and should be avoided if it appears that other studies may prove more beneficial.

IMAGING

Diagnostic radiology is a dynamic specialty that has undergone rapid change in conjunction with the ongoing evolution of imaging technology. Not only has the number of imaging modalities increased, but each modality continues to be improved and refined for use in evaluating abdominal masses. In particular, advances in cross-sectional imaging techniques, such as ultrasonography (US), computed tomography, magnetic resonance imaging, and positron emission tomography (PET), have made it possible to assess these lesions more precisely. Consequently, whenever the surgeon is confronted with the scenario of a clinically suspected or palpable abdominal mass, accurate diagnostic imaging is of paramount importance. The appropriate use of different imaging modalities in the evaluation of the palpable abdominal mass is well described by the American College of Radiology guidelines,[25,26] which are updated every 6 years.

The use of noninvasive US and CT as first-line procedures for the evaluation of palpable masses has received considerable clinical attention.[6,27-30] Investigators have found both US and CT to be excellent for affirming or excluding a clinically suspected abdominal mass, with sensitivity and specificity values exceeding 95%. This finding is particularly noteworthy because in only 16% to 38% of patients referred for a suspected abdominal mass will the diagnosis be corroborated by an imaging study.[31] Both US and CT are also capable of visualizing the organ from which the mass arises: US successfully determines the organ of origin approximately 88% to 91% of the time, and CT does so approximately 93% of the time. Prediction of the pathologic diagnosis of an abdominal mass, however, remains a challenge for both modalities. US correctly predicts the pathologic diagnosis in 77% to 81% of cases, whereas CT suggests the diagnosis in 88% of cases. Further advancements in cross-sectional imaging (e.g., multidetector CT [MDCT] with three-dimensional reconstruction and magnetic resonance angiography [MRA]) and the addition of molecular and functional imaging modalities (e.g., PET) will undoubtedly improve the predictive abilities of CT and US. At any rate, the current state of imaging technology affords clinicians the ability to distinguish benign from malignant processes, to assess tumor biology, and to detect lesions that impose a minimal disease burden. As a consequence, clinicians are more likely to detect clinically occult disease or discover it incidentally.

Employing an integrative assessment approach (which includes clinical history, physical examination, and investigative studies) should lead to more targeted, efficient, and cost-effective strategies for evaluating abdominal masses. For example, the surgeon can correlate the clinical location of the abdominal mass with pertinent findings from the history and laboratory studies to determine which imaging modality is the most expeditious and cost-effective for a given circumstance. Each imaging modality has unique strengths and weaknesses.

Plain Abdominal Radiographs

By definition, a plain film is a radiograph made without the use of an artificially introduced contrast substance.[32] Commonly employed for initial surveillance of the abdomen, the plain film still has an important place within the investigative armamentarium. Otherwise known as a KUB (kidney-ureter-bladder) study, this low-cost technique may reveal nonspecific or indirect evidence of an abdominal mass, such as variations in the size and density of an organ or displacement of normal structures or fat planes. Furthermore, the radiolucency of air within the bowel may also prove helpful for recognizing worrisome displacement of viscera as a result of a large abdominal mass. Occasionally, a simple plain radiograph can assist the surgeon in making a specific diagnosis, such as calcified aortic aneurysm, acute gastric distention, fecal impaction, porcelain gallbladder, and certain malignancies [see Figure 2].

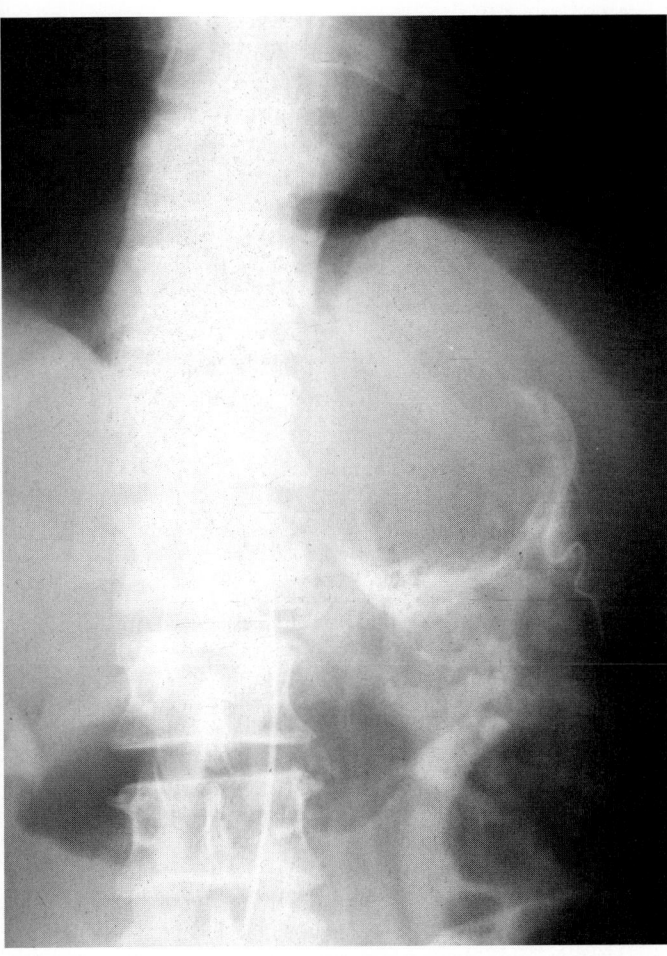

Figure 2 **Plain abdominal radiograph shows a 10 cm functional left adrenocortical carcinoma. Calcifications creating a rim enhancement are easily identified. The diagnosis was confirmed by means of laboratory analysis and abdominal CT.**

Conventional Gastrointestinal Imaging

As a consequence of the technical advances in cross-sectional imaging and endoscopy, conventional GI contrast studies are now largely relegated to more adjunctive roles in the evaluation of abdominal masses. In the upper and middle portions of the abdomen, we occasionally use upper GI studies, small bowel follow-through (SBFT), or enteroclysis to evaluate inflammatory masses (e.g., lesions arising from Crohn disease), masses that are inaccessible to endoscopy, or unusual masses with uncertain diagnoses. For such lesions, we employ single- or double-contrast barium protocols to ensure that significant pathology is not missed; however, these studies are notoriously insensitive and do not provide an opportunity for tissue diagnosis. In the lower portion of the abdomen, barium studies still play a significant role in the evaluation of masses whose history includes GI symptoms (e.g., anemia and weight loss) suggestive of a colonic neoplasm, as well as for evaluating inflammatory masses arising from diverticular disease. In certain cases, we employ a single-contrast barium enema for masses that are causing near-complete obstruction; this study is also helpful for assessing the remaining large bowel for synchronous disease. For small lesions (masses < 1 cm), we typically favor a double-contrast barium enema.

Currently, in the evaluation of an abdominal mass, barium studies are used mainly to complement colonoscopy and CT.

Novel approaches (e.g., CT virtual colonoscopy), in conjunction with advances in cross-sectional imaging, may eventually render conventional GI imaging unnecessary.

Ultrasonography

Compared with other modalities, US has several advantages in the evaluation of suspected abdominal masses, including widespread availability, speed of use, the absence of ionizing radiation, low cost, and the ability to document the size, consistency (solid or cystic), and origin of a mass with real-time images.[27,33] When directed at solving a specific clinical problem, US generally provides more diagnostic information. Moreover, the necessary equipment can easily be transported to the patient's bedside or another clinical setting; thus, no patient preparation is required, and only minimal patient cooperation is needed.

We consider US indispensable in the assessment of abdominal masses. At the same time, we acknowledge that one disadvantage of US is the extent to which the quality of the results depends on the technical proficiency and diligence of the operator or technician (though this disadvantage can actually become an advantage when personnel are well trained and experienced). In the hands of an inexperienced operator, US may yield inconclusive or untrustworthy results that contribute to delayed diagnosis or even misdiagnosis. In an effort to help minimize this problem, we encourage the surgeons at our institution (who are trained in US) to perform their own studies in the clinic and the operating room. This approach further expedites recognition of disease [*see Figure 3*], positively influences management, and facilitates operative decision making regarding abdominal masses [*see Figure 4*].

Another disadvantage of US is its inability to visualize the entire abdominal cavity as a consequence of the acoustic barriers presented by gas-containing structures (e.g., the bowel) and the absorptive interfaces (acoustic shadowing) provided by soft tissue and bone. For optimal visualization of abdominal masses, US should be performed through "acoustic windows" that allow adequate transmission of sound. Accordingly, US is most effective as a tool for evaluating masses in those regions of the abdomen where an acoustic window exists (e.g., the right and left upper quadrants and the

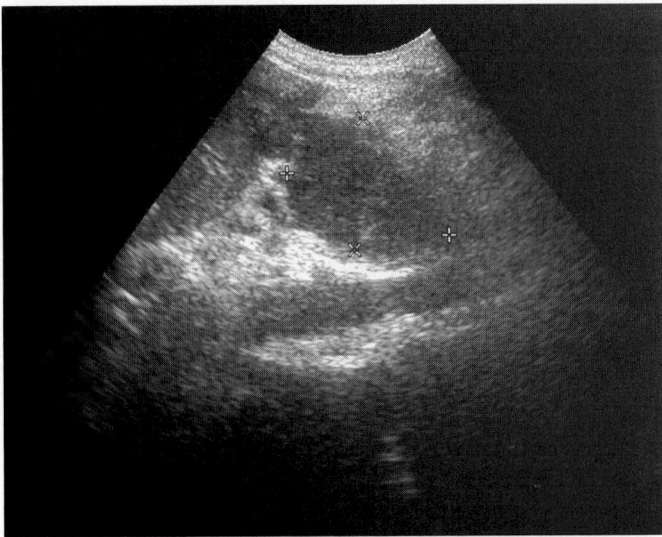

Figure 3 **Sagittal ultrasonogram of the pancreas demonstrates a large mass in the pancreatic head of a 71-year-old patient referred for "gallstones" after experiencing a 10 lb weight loss. The mass lies anterior to the inferior vena cava.**

a

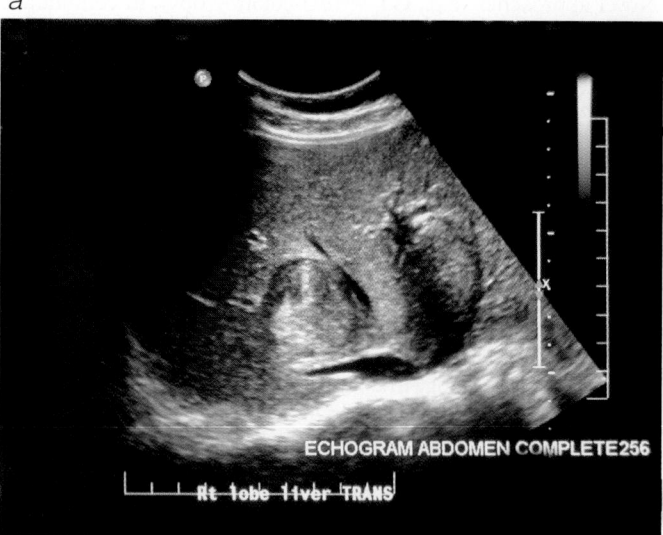

b

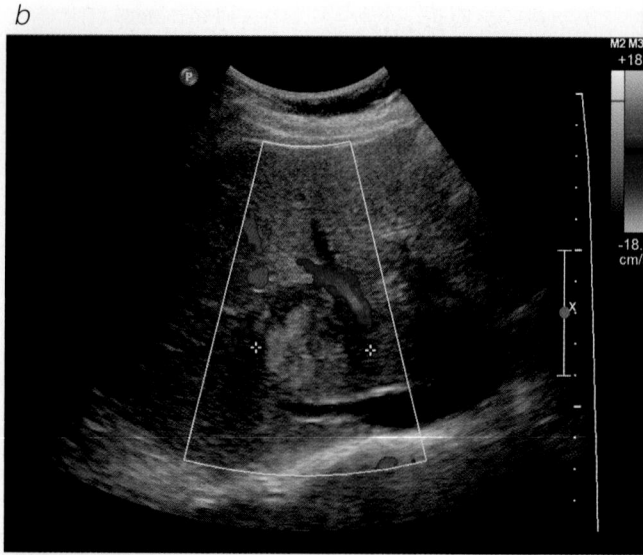

Figure 4 (*a*) **Transverse ultrasonogram of the liver of a 72-year-old cirrhotic patient with a hepatitis C infection shows a 4.0 × 3.5 cm hepatoma, nestled between the right and middle hepatic veins and closely apposed to the inferior vena cava. (*b*) Color Doppler ultrasonogram from the same patient displays blood flow in the middle hepatic vein and the surrounding liver parenchyma. Blood flow toward the transducer is usually displayed in shades of red, whereas blood flow away from the transducer is displayed in shades of blue. Color Doppler ultrasonography allows evaluation of the patency and flow characteristics of the hepatic circulation as it relates to the mass.**

pelvis). Fortunately, the shortcomings of US can be compensated for by employing other cross-sectional imaging modalities.

Computed Tomography

At present, helical (spiral) CT is the most efficient and cost-effective imaging modality for the evaluation of abdominal masses.[6,27,34,35] Unlike US, CT provides cross-sectional images with excellent spatial resolution and exquisite density discrimination that are unaffected by bowel gas, bone, or excessive abdominal fat. CT routinely visualizes the abdominal wall, the viscera, the mesentery, and the retroperitoneum, clearly defining important tissue planes

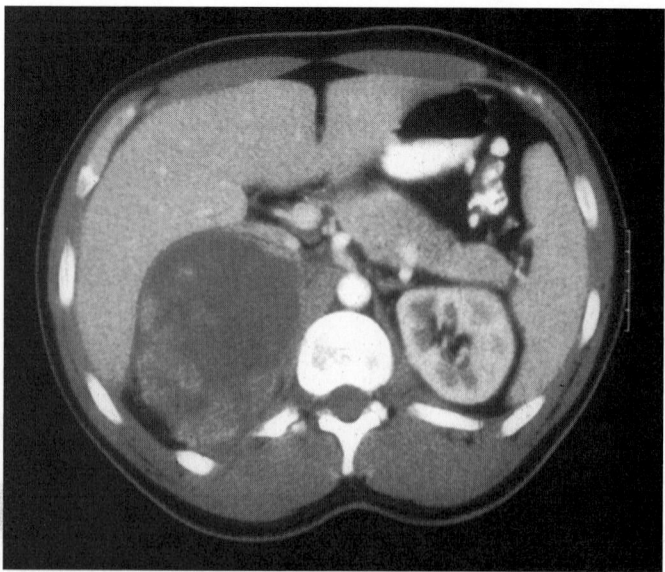

Figure 5 **CT scan of a 65-year-old man with a large retroperitoneal leiyomyosarcoma clearly demonstrates close association of this mass with the right hemiliver, as well as displacement of the inferior vena cava.**

and delineating the relations between the abdominal mass and adjacent structures [*see Figure 5*]. Such data are essential for guiding diagnostic procedures, determining whether operative management is indicated, and selecting the optimal operative approach. Although modalities such as MRI, PET, and endoscopic ultrasonography (EUS) have advantages over CT in one area or another, CT continues to be superior overall for assessing abdominal masses and remains our preferred imaging method for this purpose.

The use of contrast during the acquisition of CT scans is vital. Opacification of the bowel enables the examiner to distinguish the abdominal mass from surrounding viscera or other adjacent structures. Contrast-enhanced scans also allow delineation of the relevant vascular anatomy; in fact, CT angiography has now relegated conventional angiography to a minimal role in the evaluation of certain abdominal masses.[36,37] Triple-phase or multiphase scanning that includes noncontrast images is now recommended. Such scans achieve optimal definition and characterization of liver and pancreatic masses. This achievement is of significant clinical value: state-of-the-art CT imaging of malignant pancreatic masses, as well as of other malignancies, has the potential to improve outcome not only by correctly detecting the mass but also by accurately assessing the extent of disease, thereby helping determine which patients may benefit from surgical management or neoadjuvant therapy [*see Figure 6*].

The advent of MDCT technology offers the possibility of even better imaging of abdominal masses than standard contrast CT provides. MDCT scanners can image specific organs or masses with 1 mm slices in less than 20 seconds, and the resultant data can be displayed not only as an axial image but also in a three-dimensional representation that includes detailed vascular mapping.[35] Studies suggest that MDCT may be the most useful modality for preoperative assessment of the resectability of pancreatic and other abdominal masses.[36] MDCT has a sensitivity of 90% and a specificity of 99%, respectively, and it is not observer dependent.

Currently, although MRI (see below) offers unique tissue contrast and inherent multiplanar capabilities for imaging abdominal

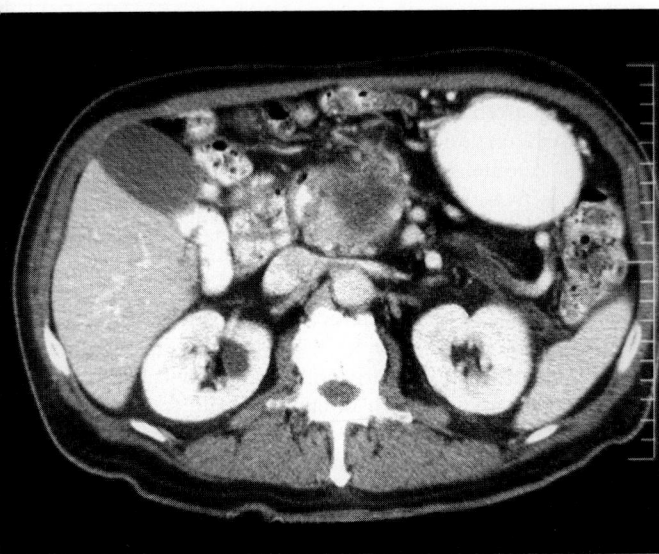

Figure 6 **CT angiography performed to evaluate vascular invasion in a 58-year-old patient with a pancreatic mass demonstrates nearly complete encasement of the superior mesenteric vein. The superior mesenteric artery is not involved with the mass.**

masses, CT has several advantages—high resolution, short scan times, and fast patient throughput—that make it a more widely preferred imaging modality for this purpose.

Magnetic Resonance Imaging

Since its introduction in the mid-1980s, MRI has become one of radiology's great success stories (though, because it still is not as widely available as US or CT, its cost-effectiveness has yet to be determined). Few would dispute the enormous impact MRI has had on our ability to diagnose pathologic conditions of the brain, the spine, and the musculoskeletal system. Whereas MRI has clear advantages over CT in these areas of the body, this is not the case in the abdomen. Nevertheless, there are situations in which MRI

is a better choice than CT for evaluating an abdominal mass. An example is a case in which the use of iodinated contrast material is contraindicated. The extracellular gadolinium chelates used in MRI are very safe and can be given to patients with mild to moderate azotemia without causing renal impairment. MRI has unique characteristics that can be effectively employed to distinguish normal from pathologic tissue in a patient with an abdominal mass.[38]

Detailed information about the principles and practices of abdominal MRI is beyond the scope of this chapter and is readily available elsewhere.[39] A brief technical summary may, however, be worthwhile. The abdomen and its contents are subjected to a momentary radiofrequency pulse, then allowed to return to a state of equilibrium. During the return to equilibrium, the nuclei within each specific tissue will emit specific radiofrequency signals. The strength and type of the emitted signal determine the image intensity. The way in which the different tissues are visually rendered depends on (1) the longitudinal relaxation time (T_1) and the transverse relaxation time (T_2) of the nuclei in the tissues and (2) the method of image weighting employed. By convention, tissues with short T_1 values (such as solid structures) appear bright on T_1-weighted images, whereas structures with long T_2 values (e.g., fluid-containing tissues) appear bright on T_2-weighted images. The tissue contrast and multiplanar capabilities of MRI allow surgeons and radiologists to distinguish not only obvious but also subtle differences between abdominal masses and normal anatomy. For example, T_1-weighted images may be valuable for detecting abdominal masses that contain fluid (e.g., cystic masses or masses containing necrotic tissue), whereas T_2-weighted images may be useful for characterizing these masses as either benign or malignant [*see Figure 7*]. Similarly, magnetic resonance cholangiopancreatography (MRCP) uses T_2-weighted images to distinguish masses with different signal intensities in the pancreas, the liver, and the biliary tract.[40]

Positron Emission Tomography

In 1930, Warburg reported that cancer cells show higher rates of glycolysis than normal cells do.[41] This discovery has stood the

a

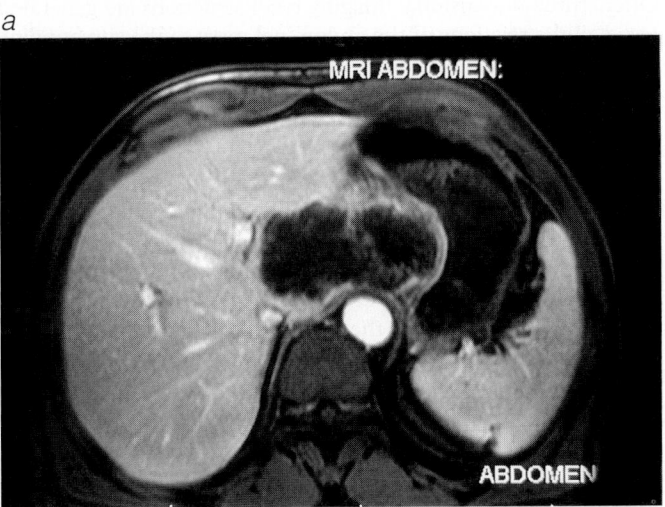

b

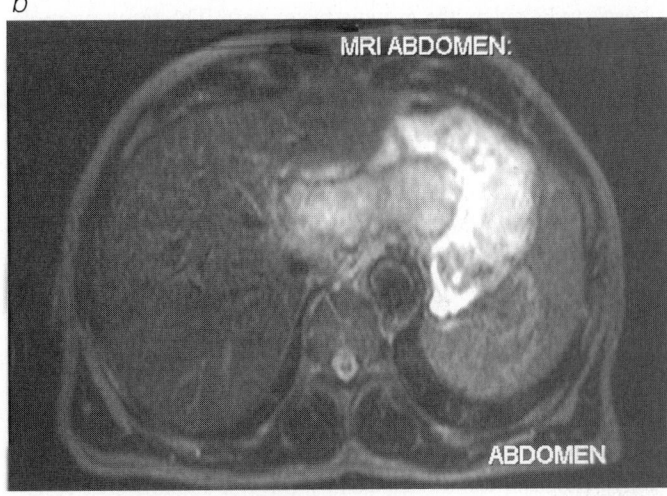

Figure 7 **(a) Gadolinium-enhanced, T_1-weighted MRI shows a large mass that appears dark and well-circumscribed in comparison with the normal-appearing enhanced liver and spleen. This abnormal mass clearly contains some fluid. The fluid-filled stomach also appears dark. (b) T_2-weighted MRI of the same patient details subtle inhomogeneities characteristic of a malignant mass (less organized appearance with an enhanced necrotic component). Subsequent biopsy showed this mass to be a poorly differentiated adenocarcinoma from recurrent colon cancer.**

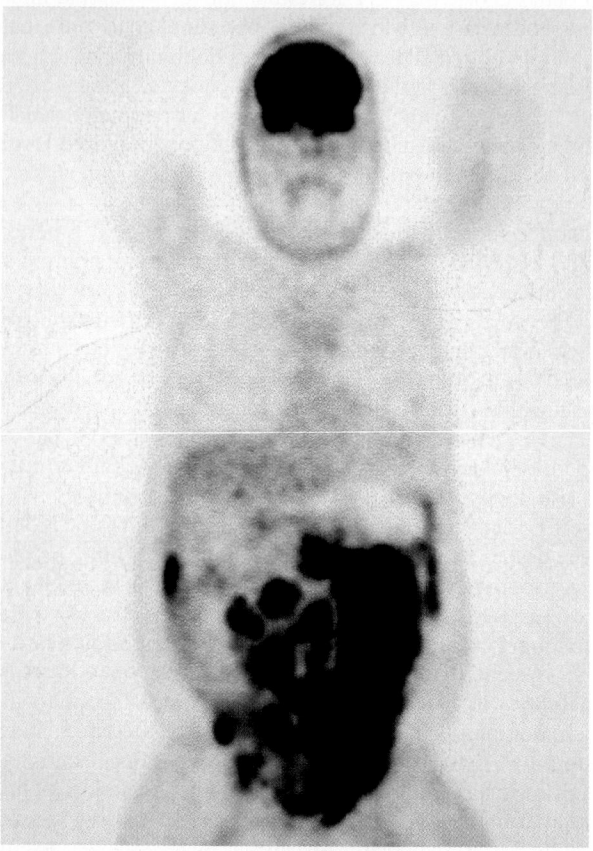

Figure 8 18FDG PET scan demonstrates a large metabolically active non-Hodgkin lymphoma giving rise to an abdominal mass.

test of time and now serves as the theoretical rationale for the use of 18F-fluorodeoxyglucose (18FDG) PET imaging to assess abdominal masses caused by cancer. Briefly, 18FDG is a glucose analogue that crosses the cell membrane by sharing the glucose transporter molecules used by glucose. Like glucose, it undergoes phosphorylation by the enzyme hexokinase. The resulting molecule, 18FDG-6-phosphate, is polar and is unable to cross cell membranes or serve as a substrate for metabolism. The net effect is that 18FDG both accumulates in and is retained by cancer cells.

The molecular information obtained from PET, as measured by standard uptake values (SUV), allows identification of hypermetabolic (18FDG-avid) abdominal masses (typically arising from lymphomas, melanomas, or certain GI malignancies [*see Figure 8*]).[42] PET may also prove to be an important surrogate modality for distinguishing malignant abdominal masses from benign ones.[43] When PET is used alone, it has the disadvantage of being unable to provide sufficient anatomic information to guide biopsy or further therapy. When PET is used with CT in PET/CT fusion imaging, however, the functional advantages of PET and the structural advantages of CT combine to enhance the detection rate for abdominal masses.[42] If a mass is anatomically evident but metabolically inactive, it will be detected by CT. If it shows increased glycolysis but few or no CT abnormalities, it will be detected by PET. The apparent advantages of PET/CT notwithstanding, prospective, randomized validation is necessary before the widespread application of this approach to the evaluation of abdominal masses can be justified. At present, the use of PET/CT is mostly restricted to large tertiary referral centers.

BIOPSY

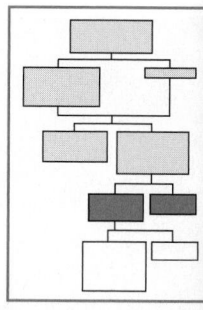

In many cases, the pathologist is the surgeon's greatest teacher. Despite the surgeon's most strenuous efforts, the biology of the disease or lesion will inevitably dictate the outcome. Nowhere is this statement more true than in the evaluation of the abdominal mass, and its truth becomes increasingly evident as ongoing refinements in molecular diagnosis permit ever more sophisticated discrimination among different tumor types and their respective behaviors.[44] Aside from the treatment of lymphoma, in which the surgeon is frequently called on to provide technical assistance in obtaining tissue for diagnosis, the decision whether to perform a biopsy (as well as when and how to do so) rests on the surgeon's understanding of the probable disease. For example, surgeons who treat pancreatic cancer usually proceed to surgery without biopsy if the evidence for malignancy is strong. In other cases, biopsy is performed to confirm what is already suspected on the basis of clinical and radiographic findings. Moreover, establishing the type of tumor or mass present has important implications for the use of neoadjuvant or adjuvant therapy, as well as for the planning of the surgical approach. We view the biopsy of an abdominal mass as the first stage of surgery. This procedure, though seemingly innocuous, has the potential to contaminate tissue planes and must therefore be performed carefully. Accordingly, in order to make the appropriate choice when confronted with an abdominal mass, the surgeon must possess a thorough understanding of the various methods of obtaining an accurate and safe biopsy. Factors related to the size and location of the abdominal mass, as well as factors related to institutional preference and experience, may influence the choice of biopsy technique.

Image-Guided Percutaneous Biopsy

The value of image-guided percutaneous biopsy in the evaluation of the abdominal mass is well established.[45,46] In practice, the procedure begins with identification of the mass by means of a cross-sectional imaging modality such as US, CT, or MRI. Often, three-dimensional imaging reconstructions are generated to detail the relations of the abdominal mass to the surrounding anatomy. Once the mass is identified, decisions are made regarding the safest approach and the most appropriate technique. The biopsy needle is then inserted percutaneously under the guidance of US, CT, or MRI. The choice among the different modalities depends on several factors, including the size and location of the mass, the surgeon's judgment regarding which method is best in the circumstances, and the availability of the various modalities at a particular institution. The most important consideration, however, is the personal preference and experience of the radiologist performing the biopsy. We favor either US or CT, both of which yield good results.

In general, we prefer US-guided biopsy for large, superficial, and cystic masses. This technique is also appropriate for lesions lying at moderate depths in thin to average-size persons. In some cases, US can be employed to guide biopsy of small, deep, and solid abdominal masses; however, US-guided biopsy of these deep-seated masses (as well as of masses in obese patients) often proves difficult because of inadequate visualization resulting from sound attenuation in the soft tissues. Similarly, lesions located within or behind bone or gas-filled bowel cannot be easily visualized (a consequence of the nearly complete reflection of sound from bone or air interfaces).

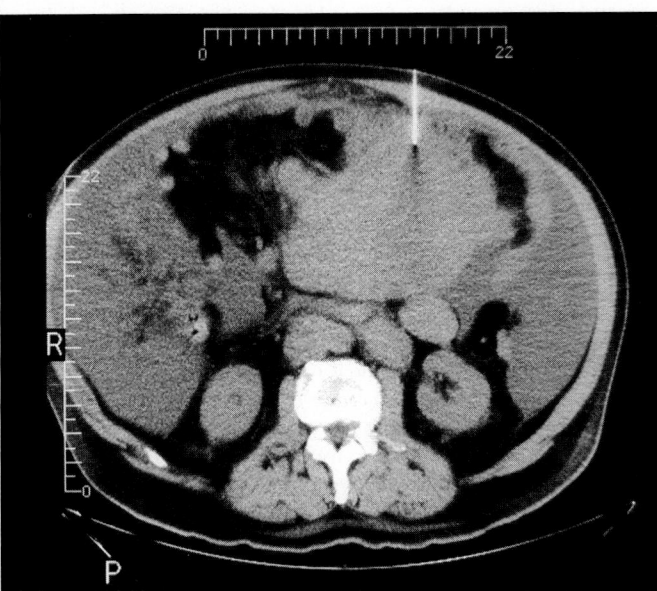

Figure 9 **In a percutaneous biopsy of a large abdominal mass, CT guidance is a reliable means of determining the direction and depth of the needle.**

US possesses several strengths as a guidance modality for percutaneous biopsy. It is readily available, inexpensive, and portable, and it provides guidance in multiple transverse, longitudinal, or oblique planes. Moreover, it offers real-time visualization of the needle tip as it passes through tissue planes into the target area,[47] thereby allowing the surgeon to place the needle precisely and to avoid important intervening structures. In addition, color flow Doppler imaging can help prevent complications of needle placement by identifying the blood vessels involved with the mass, as well as any vessels lying within the needle path. Because of its real-time capabilities, US guidance has the potential to allow quicker, more accurate, and less expensive biopsies than CT guidance does.[48] In theory, any mass that is well visualized with US should be amenable to US-guided biopsy. In practice, however, this modality remains best suited for superficial to moderately deep abdominal masses and for patients with a thin to average body habitus.

The utility of US notwithstanding, CT remains indispensable at our institution as a guidance method for percutaneous biopsy of most regions in the body. It is particularly useful when an abdominal mass is in a location that is inaccessible to US as a result of bowel gas or body habitus. In the abdomen, CT provides excellent spatial resolution of all structures between the skin and the mass, regardless of body habitus or lesion depth, and it provides an accurate image of the needle tip. We favor CT guidance for abdominal masses that are located deep in the abdomen or in the retroperitoneum. The only limitation of CT in this setting is that it does not offer continuous visualization of the needle during insertion and biopsy. In most cases, however, CT guidance can reliably establish the direction and depth of the needle [*see Figure 9*].

Numerous different needles, covering a broad spectrum of calibers, lengths, and tip designs, are commercially available for use in percutaneous image-guided fine-needle aspiration (FNA) biopsy. For convenience, these needles can be grouped into two main size categories: small caliber (20 to 25 gauge) and large caliber (14 to 19 gauge). Small-caliber needles are used primarily for cytologic analysis but may also be employed to obtain small pieces of tissue for histologic analysis. The flexible shaft of small-caliber needles allows them to be passed with minimal risk of tissue or organ

laceration or of damage from tearing. Such needles are often used to confirm tumor recurrence or metastasis in patients with a pathologically confirmed primary malignancy. Large-caliber needles are typically used to obtain greater amounts of material for histologic or cytologic analysis.[49] In practice, the choice of a biopsy needle is often influenced by whether the suspected pathology is benign or malignant. For example, large-caliber needles may be necessary to obtain a sufficiently large histologic specimen when certain types of malignancies (e.g., lymphoma) are suspected. When an inflammatory mass is suspected and material is needed for culture, however, a small-caliber needle may be preferred.

Additional considerations for image-guided biopsy include the accuracy, safety, and potential complications of the proposed technique. These considerations are essential for an evidence-based approach to diagnosis of an abdominal mass.

The reported accuracy of US-guided biopsy ranges from 66% to 97%. The location, size, and histologic origin of the abdominal mass appear to influence the diagnostic accuracy of the procedure.[47] In a series that included 126 consecutive small (< 3 cm) solid masses distributed among various anatomic locations and histologic types, US-guided biopsies showed an overall accuracy of 91%.[47] Biopsy results improved as the size of the mass increased: accuracy rose from 79% in masses 1 cm or less in diameter to 98% in masses 2 to 3 cm in diameter. The accuracy of US-guided biopsy in the liver, where most of the biopsies were performed, exceeded 96%. Another study found US-guided biopsy to be 91% accurate for abdominal masses less than 2.5 cm in diameter.[50] Two organ-specific reviews concluded that US-guided biopsy of hepatic masses had an accuracy of 94%[51] and that US-guided biopsy of pancreatic masses had an accuracy of 95%.[52]

The reported accuracy of CT-guided biopsy ranges from 80% to 100%. As with US-guided biopsy, the size, location, and histologic origin of the mass influence the results.[53-55] In a study of 200 consecutive CT-guided needle biopsies, the overall accuracy for all sites biopsied was 95%. The reported organ-specific accuracy was as follows: kidneys, 100%; liver, 99%; retroperitoneum, 87.5%; and pancreas, 82%.[56] In a prospective study of 1,000 consecutive CT-guided biopsies, the reported sensitivity was 91.8% and the specificity 98.9%.[55] At our institution, as well as others, CT-guided biopsy is now considered a reliable tool for the diagnosis and classification of malignant abdominal lymphomas.[57]

The safety of image-guided percutaneous biopsy is well documented. Several large multi-institutional reviews reported major complication rates ranging from 0.05% to 0.18% and mortalities ranging from 0.008% to 0.031%.[58-60] A large prospective study of 3,393 biopsies (1,825 US-guided; 1,568 CT-guided) documented an overall mortality of 0.06%, a major complication rate of 0.34% (0.3% with US; 0.5% with CT), and a minor complication rate of 2.9% (2.4% with US; 3.3% with CT).[47] Procedure-related morbidity and mortality appear to be largely unaffected by whether a small-caliber or a large-caliber biopsy needle is used. A review of 11,700 patients who underwent percutaneous abdominal biopsy with 20- to 23-gauge needles found an overall complication rate of only 0.05% and an overall mortality of only 0.008%.[58] A single-institution review of 8,000 US-guided needle biopsies performed with both small- and large-caliber needles reported equivalent results: a major complication rate of 0.187% and a mortality of 0.038%.[61] Of the rare major complications that occur, hemorrhage is the most frequently reported; pneumothorax, pancreatitis, bile leakage, peritonitis, and needle track seeding may also develop.

Needle-track seeding remains an important theoretical consideration when an abdominal mass appears likely to be malignant. According to some investigators, percutaneous needle biopsy has the potential to seed between 10^3 to 10^4 tumor cells into the needle track.[62,63] Nevertheless, tumor dissemination after percutaneous biopsy remains exceedingly rare: with fewer than 100 cases reported in the world literature, it has an estimated frequency of 0.005%,[64-66] mostly occurring after biopsy of pancreatic, hepatic, or retroperitoneal masses. Poorly planned biopsies of malignant abdominal masses have the potential to exert adverse effects on subsequent surgery and to compromise local tumor control; fortunately, such negative consequences remain rare.

EUS-Guided Imaging and Biopsy

EUS provides unique imaging information because it involves the close apposition of a high-frequency ultrasound transducer, called an echoendoscope (whereby image resolution is directly related to frequency), to the structures being studied. As a result, it can delineate abdominal masses and associated structures with greater anatomic detail than standard transcutaneous ultrasonography can. In general, EUS-guided biopsy is well suited for abdominal masses that are too small for visualization by means of other cross-sectional imaging modalities or that are inaccessible to percutaneous biopsy.[67] The most frequently used EUS device is the radial echoendoscope, which creates a 360° tomographic image perpendicular to the scope. The circumferential view obtained with this instrument facilitates orientation and therefore is more efficient for diagnostic imaging. Alternatively, the linear-array echoendoscope, which generates an image parallel to the shaft of the scope, may be used. This instrument produces high-quality gray-scale images, as well as color and duplex images. EUS-guided biopsy with a linear scanning system offers clear and consistent visualization of the biopsy needle along its entire path in real time, with excellent delineation of intervening tissues and without any interference from intestinal gas.

EUS has proved to be superior to other cross-sectional imaging modalities for detection and staging of pancreatic, gastric, and esophageal masses.[68-71] For instance, in a patient with a pancreatic mass, EUS not only identifies the size of the mass and the peripancreatic lymph nodes but also delineates the relations of these structures to major blood vessels. EUS has also proved to be helpful in selecting patients for various neoadjuvant protocols. Furthermore, the availability of high-frequency catheter-based intraductal ultrasonography (IDUS) now enables surgeons to visualize masses within the biliary tree and obtain biopsy specimens from them.[72]

Advantages notwithstanding, EUS technology has several important limitations. As with all forms of ultrasonography, a substantial period is required before the operator achieves proficiency. EUS is highly operator dependent; when it is done by an inexperienced operator, the potential exists for serious misinterpretations. For example, if an operator obtains only one view of a mass in the head of the pancreas, the mass may appear to be invading vascular structures when it is not actually doing so. In the evaluation of pancreatic masses around vessels, the operator should always obtain multiple views. It cannot be overemphasized that EUS and EUS-guided biopsy require personnel with sufficient experience and skill in both ultrasonography and endoscopy.

EUS is frequently employed for diagnosis and staging of upper GI malignancies. In a large single-institution study of 267 pancreatic masses that were sampled by means of EUS-guided biopsy and subsequently resected, the overall diagnostic accuracy was 95.6%, the sensitivity was 94.6%, and the specificity was 100%.[73] In studies of gastric and esophageal masses, diagnostic accuracy was related to the location of the biopsy,[74] the histology of the dis-

ease,[75] and the number of samples obtained. In one series that included more than 200 patients with esophageal or gastric masses, a diagnosis was made in 70% of patients after the first biopsy, 95% of patients after the fourth biopsy, and 98.9% of patients after the seventh biopsy.[76] Several other studies have confirmed the high sensitivity and specificity of EUS-guided biopsy (especially for the diagnosis of extraluminal abdominal masses) and verified the safety of the procedure (reported complication rates range from 0.3% to 2%).[68-71,77] It is worth noting that in the resection of a potentially curable abdominal mass, concern about needle-track contamination is obviated when the path of the needle is removed as part of the surgical specimen (as in pancreaticoduodenectomy for a pancreatic head mass or gastrectomy for a stomach mass).

We consider EUS-guided biopsy for the diagnosis of masses that are not readily accessible to percutaneous biopsy, on the grounds that it can obviate more invasive procedures (e.g., laparoscopy and laparotomy). In a 10-year study of the impact of EUS on patient management, 86% of patients required no further imaging, and 25% were able to avoid unnecessary laparotomy.[77] Overall, EUS changed clinical management significantly in as many as one third of the 537 patients studied.[77] Nevertheless, despite the high diagnostic yield achieved with EUS-guided biopsy, results that are negative for tumor should not always be interpreted as proving that no tumor is present; laparoscopic or open biopsy may still be indicated.

DIAGNOSTIC LAPAROSCOPY

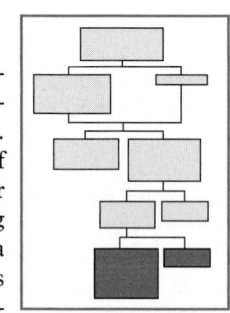

The available evidence now clearly supports the role of laparoscopy in the diagnosis and management of abdominal masses. We and others advocate the liberal use of laparoscopy as a primary staging tool for upper and lower GI malignancies, believing it to be a safe, cost-effective tool that offers a clear benefit in more than 20% of patients with these diseases.[78,79] Preventing unnecessary laparotomy in selected patients by performing diagnostic laparoscopy is associated with shorter hospital stays and earlier initiation of locoregional or systemic therapy. Moreover, laparoscopic ultrasonography[80] and peritoneal cytology[81] are known to provide added value in the staging of disease. Furthermore, diagnostic laparoscopy can safely provide tissue samples from suspected lymphomatous masses for full diagnostic analysis.[82] With the growth of dedicated minimally invasive fellowships and the improved quality and availability of laparoscopic training for general surgery residents and related subspecialties, the skill sets required for diagnostic laparoscopy are coming to be more widely mastered, and the concerns once commonly expressed regarding intra-abdominal adhesions and effective biopsy techniques for abdominal masses now appear to be less problematic.

Indications for Exploratory Laparotomy

Advances in diagnostic imaging, endoscopy, and minimally invasive surgery have nearly eliminated the need for open exploration for the sole purpose of establishing a diagnosis in patients with an abdominal mass. In selected cases, however, exploratory laparotomy may still help in the assessment of abdominal masses that were initially misinterpreted on preoperative evaluation. In general, exploratory laparotomy should be reserved for those rare instances in which other modalities have failed to yield crucial information needed for evaluation and diagnosis of an abdominal mass.

References

1. Ancient Egyptian Medicine–Smith Papyrus–Ebers Papyrus http://crystalinks.com/egyptmedicine.html

2. Hippocrates: The Book of Prognostics. Francis Adams, Transl. http://etext.library.adelaide.edu.au/h/hippocrates/h7w/prognost.html

3. Swartz MH: Textbook of Physical Diagnosis: History and Examination, 5th ed. Saunders Elsevier, Philadelphia, 2006, p 479

4. Wood WC, Skandalakis JE: Anatomic Basis of Tumor Surgery. Quality Medical Publishing, St. Louis, 1999, p 307

5. Hart FD: French's Index of Differential Diagnosis, 11th ed. Year Book Medical, Chicago, 1979, p 9

6. Dixon AK, Kingham JGC, Fry IK, et al: Computed tomography in patients with an abdominal mass: effective and efficient? A controlled trial. Lancet 1:1199, 1981

7. Walker HK, Hall WD, Hurst JW: Clinical Methods: The History, Physical, and Laboratory Examinations, 3rd ed. Butterworth, Stoneham, Massachusetts, 1990, p 415

8. Brady MS, Gaynor JJ, Brennan MF: Radiation-associated sarcoma of bone and soft tissue. Arch Surg 127:1379, 1992

9. Bowne WB, Lee B, Wong WD, et al: Operative salvage for locoregional recurrent colon cancer: an analysis of 100 cases. Dis Colon Rectum 5:897, 2003

10. Miner TJ, Jaques DP, Karpeh MS, et al: Defining palliative surgery in patients receiving non-curative resections for gastric cancer. J Am Coll Surg 198:1013, 2004

11. Miner TJ, Jaques DP, Shriver C: A prospective evaluation of patients undergoing surgery for palliation of an advanced malignancy. Ann Surg Oncol 9:696, 2002

12. Miner TJ, Brennan MF, Jaques DP: A prospective, symptom related outcomes analysis of 1022 palliative procedures for advanced cancer. Ann Surg 240:719, 2004

13. Stojadinovic A, Hoos A, Karpoff HM, et al: Soft tissue tumors of the abdominal wall: analysis of disease patterns and treatment. Arch Surg 136:70, 2001

14. Bowne WB, Antonescu CR, Leung DH, et al: Dermatofibrosarcoma protuberans: a clinicopathologic analysis of patients treated and followed at a single institution. Cancer 88:2711, 2000

15. Lewis JJ, Brennan MF: Soft tissue sarcomas. Curr Probl Surg 33:817, 1996

16. Reeves WM, Coit DG: Melanoma: a multidisciplinary approach for the general surgeon. Surg Clin North Am 80:581, 2000

17. Allen PJ, Bowne WB, Jaques DP: Merkel cell carcinoma: prognosis and treatment of patients from a single institution. J Clin Oncol 23:2300, 2005

18. Brooks AD, Bowne WB, Delgado R, et al: Soft tissue sarcomas of the groin: diagnosis, management, and prognosis. 193:130, 2001

19. Bowne WB, Lewis JJ, Filippa DA, et al: The management of unicentric and multicentric Castleman's disease: a report of 16 cases and a review of the literature. Cancer 85:706, 1999

20. Judge RD, Zuidema GD, Fitzgerald FT: Clinical Diagnosis, 5th ed. Little, Brown and Co, Boston and Toronto, 1989, p 339

21. Schaffner F: Abdominal enlargement and masses. Gastroenterology. Haubrich WS, Schaffner F, Berk JE, Eds. WB Saunders, Philadelphia, 1998, p 138

22. Morales TG, Fennerty MB: Abdominal distention. Clinical Medicine, 2nd Ed. Greene HL, Fincher RME, Johnson WP, et al, Eds. Mosby, St Louis, 1996, p 290

23. DeGowin EL, DeGowin RL: Bedside diagnostic examination. Macmillan, New York, 1976, p 471

24. Balch CM, Soong SJ, Atkins MB, et al: An evidence-based staging system for cutaneous melanoma. CA Cancer J Clin 54:131, 2004

25. DiSantis DJ, Ralls PW, Balfe DM, et al: Imaging evaluation of the palpable abdominal mass. American College of Radiology. ACR Appropriateness Criteria. Radiology 215(suppl):201, 2000

26. Grollman J, Bettman MA, Boxt LM, et al: Pulsatile abdominal mass. American College of Radiology. ACR Appropriateness Criteria. Radiology 215(suppl):55, 2000

27. Williams MP, Scott IHK, Dixon AK: Computed tomography in 101 patients with a palpable abdominal mass. Clin Radiol 35:293, 1984

28. Holm HH, Gammelgaard J, Jensen F, et al: Ultrasound in the diagnosis of a palpable abdominal mass: a prospective study of 107 patients. Gastrointest Radiol 7:149, 1982

29. Barker CS, Lindsell DR: Ultrasound of the palpable abdominal mass. Clin Radiol 41:98, 1990

30. Aspelin P, Hildell J, Karlsson S, et al: Ultrasonic evaluation of palpable abdominal masses. Acta Chir Scand 156:501, 1980

31. Colquhoun IR, Saywell WR, Dewbury KC: An analysis of referrals for primary diagnostic abdominal ultrasound to a general X-ray department. Br J Radiol 61:297

32. Squire LF, Novelline RA: Fundamentals of Radiology, 4th ed. Harvard University Press, 1988, p 156

33. Barker CS, Lindsell DRM: Ultrasound of the palpable abdominal mass. Clin Radiol 41:98, 1990

34. Gore RM: Palpable abdominal masses. Diagnostic Imaging: An Algorithmic Approach. Eisenberg RL, Ed. JB Lippincott, Philadelphia, 1988, p 214

35. Lawler LP, Fishman EK: Three-dimensional CT angiography with multidetector CT data: study optimization, protocol design, and clinical applications in the abdomen. Crit Rev Comput Tomogr 43:77, 2002

36. Fishman EK, Horton KM: Imaging pancreatic cancer: the role of multidetector CT with three-dimensional CT angiography. Pancreatology 1:610, 2001

37. Murugiah M, Windsor JA, Redhead DN, et al: The role of selective visceral angiography in the management of pancreatic and periampullary cancer. World J Surg 17:796, 1993

38. Brown JJ: Body MR: no longer optional. European Society of Gastrointestinal and Abdominal Radiology 2006 http://www.diagnosticimaging.com/bodymri/body.jhtml

39. Weisskoff RM, Edelman RR: Basic principles of MRI. Clinical Magnetic Resonance Imaging, 2nd ed. Edelman RR, Hesselink JR, Zlatkin MB, Eds. WB Saunders, Philadelphia, 1990, p 3

40. Schwartz LH, DeCorato DR: Magnetic resonance imaging of the liver and biliary tract. Surgery of the Liver and Biliary Tract, 3rd ed. Blumgart LH, Fong Y, Eds. WB Saunders, Edinburgh, 2003, p 341

41. Warburg O: The metabolism of tumors. Richard R Smith, New York, 1931, p 129

42. Schröder H, Larson SM, Yeung HWD: PET/CT in oncology: integration into clinical management of lymphoma, melanoma, and gastrointestinal malignancies. J Nucl Med 45(suppl):1, 2004

43. Sperti C, Pasquali C, Chierichetti F, et al: Value of 18-fluorodeoxyglucose positron emission tomography in the management of patients with cystic tumors of the pancreas. Ann Surg 234:675, 2001

44. Brennan MF: Pre-emptive surgery and increasing demands for technical perfection. Br J Surg 90:3, 2002

45. Gazelle GS, Haaga JR: Guided percutaneous biopsy of intraabdominal lesions. AJR Am J Radiol 153:929, 1989

46. Welch TJ, Reading CC: Imaging-guided biopsy. Mayo Clin Proc 64:1295, 1989

47. Caspers JM, Reading CC, McGahan JP, et al: Ultrasound-guided biopsy and drainage of the abdomen and pelvis. Diagnostic Ultrasound, 2nd ed. Rumack CM, Wilson SR, Charboneau JW, Eds. Mosby, St Louis, 1998, p 600

48. Sheafor DH, Paulson EK, Simmons CM, et al: Abdominal percutaneous interventional procedures: comparison of CT and US guidance. Radiology 207:705, 1998

49. Silverman JF, Geisinger KR: Interventional radiology of deep organs. Fine Needle Aspiration Cytology of the Thorax and Abdomen. Churchhill Livingstone, New York, 1996, p 263

50. Downey DB, Wilson SR: Ultrasonographically guided biopsy of small intra-abdominal masses. Can Assoc Radiol J 44:350, 1993

51. Buscarini L, Fornari F, Bolondi L, et al: Ultrasound-guided fine-needle biopsy of focal liver lesions: technique, diagnostic accuracy and complications: a retrospective study on 2091 biopsies. J Hepatology 11:344, 1990

52. Brandt KR, Charboneau JW, Stephens DH, et al: CT- and US-guided biopsy of the pancreas. Radiology 187:99, 1993

53. Sundaram M, Wolverson MK, Heiberg E, et al: Utility of CT-guided abdominal aspiration procedures. AJR Am J Radiol 139:1111, 1982

54. Smith C, Butler JA: Efficacy of directed percutaneous fine-needle aspiration cytology in the diagnosis of intra-abdominal masses. Arch Surg 123:820, 1988

55. Welch TJ, Sheedy PF, Johnson CD, et al: CT-guided biopsy: prospective analysis of 1,000 procedures. Radiology 171:493, 1989

56. Staab EV, Jaques PF, Partain CL: Percutaneous biopsy in the management of solid intra-abdominal masses of unknown etiology. Radiol Clin North Am 17:435, 1979

57. Balestreri L, Morassut S, Bernardi D, et al: Efficacy of CT-guided percutaneous needle biopsy in the diagnosis of malignant lymphoma at first presentation. Clin Imaging 29:123, 2005

58. Livraghi T, Damascelli B, Lombardi C, et al: Risk in fine-needle abdominal biopsy. J Clin Ultrasound 11:77, 1983

59. Fornari F, Civardi G, Cavanna L, et al: Complications of ultrasonically guided fine-needle abdominal biopsy: results of a multi-centre Italian study and a review of the literature (The Cooperative Italian Study Group). Scand J Gastroenterol 24:949, 1989

60. Smith EH: Complications of percutaneous abdominal fine needle biopsy. Radiology 178:253, 1991

61. Nolsoe C, Nielsen L, Torp-Pedersen S, et al: Major complications and deaths due to interventional ultrasonography: a review of 8000 cases. J Clin Ultrasound 18:179, 1990

62. Ryd W, Hagmar B, Eriksson O: Local tumor cell seeding by fine-needle aspiration biopsy: a semi-quantitative study. Acta Pathol Microbiol Immunol Scand [A] 91:17, 1983

63. Eriksson O, Hagmar B, Ryd W: Effects of fine-needle aspiration and other biopsy procedures on tumor dissemination in mice. Cancer 54:73, 1984

64. Smith EH: The hazards of fine-needle aspiration biopsy. Ultrasound Med Biol 10:629, 1984

65. Engzell U, Esposti PL, Rubio C, et al: Investigation on tumor spread in connection with aspiration biopsy. Acta Radiol Ther Phys Biol 10:385, 1971

66. Smith FP, Macdonald JS, Schein PS, et al: Cu-

taneous seeding of pancreatic cancer by skinny-needle aspiration biopsy. Arch Intern Med 140:855, 1980

67. Ingram M, Arregui ME: Endoscopic ultrasonography. Surg Clin North Am 84:1035, 2004

68. Pfau PR, Chak A: Endoscopic ultrasonography. Endoscopy 34:21, 2002

69. Harewood GC, Wiersema MJ: Endosonography-guided fine needle aspiration biopsy in the evaluation of pancreatic masses. Am J Gastroenterol 97:1386, 2002

70. Catalano MF, Sial S, Chak A, et al: EUS-guided fine needle aspiration of idiopathic abdominal masses. Gastrointest Endosc 55:854, 2002

71. Williams DB, Sahai AV, Aabakken L, et al: Endoscopic ultrasound guided fine needle aspiration biopsy: a large single centre experience. Gut 44:720, 1999

72. Tamada K, Ido K, Ueno N, et al: Preoperative staging of extrahepatic bile duct cancer with intraductal ultrasonography (IDUS). Am J Gastroenterol 89:239, 1994

73. Mitsuhashi T, Ghafari S, Chang CY, et al: Endoscopic ultrasound-guided fine-needle aspiration of the pancreas: cytomorphological evaluation with emphasis on adequacy assessment, diagnostic criteria and contamination from the gastrointestinal tract. Cytopathology 17:34, 2006

74. Hatfield AR, Slavin G, Segal AW, et al: Importance of the site of endoscopic gastric biopsy in ulcerating lesions of the stomach. Gut 16:884, 1975

75. Winawer SJ, Posner G, Lightdale CJ, et al: Endoscopic diagnosis of advanced gastric cancer: factors influencing yield. Gastroenterology 69:1183, 1975

76. Graham DY, Schwartz JT, Cain GD, et al: Prospective evaluation of biopsy number in the diagnosis of esophageal and gastric carcinoma. Gastroenterology 82:228, 1982

77. Kaffes AJ, Mishra A, Simpson SB, et al: Upper gastrointestinal endoscopic ultrasound and impact on patient management: 1990–2000. Intern Med J 32:372, 2002

78. Conlon KC, Brennan MF: Laparoscopy for staging abdominal malignancies. Adv Surg 34:331, 2000

79. Grobmyer SR, Fong Y, D'Angelica M, et al: Diagnostic laparoscopy prior to planned hepatic resection for colorectal metastases. Arch Surg 139:1326, 2004

80. Minnard EA, Conlon KC, Hoos A, et al: Laparoscopic ultrasound enhances standard laparoscopy in the staging of pancreatic cancer. Ann Surg 228:182, 1998

81. Bentrem D, Wilton A, Mazumdar M, et al: The value of peritoneal cytology as a preoperative predictor in patients with gastric carcinoma undergoing a curative resection. Ann Surg Oncol 12:347, 2005

82. Mann GB, Conlon KC, LaQuaglia M, et al: Emerging role of laparoscopy in the diagnosis of lymphoma. J Clin Oncol 16:1909, 1998

Acknowledgments

Figure 1   Tom Moore.

Figure 2   Courtesy of Bimal C. Ghosh, M.D., F.A.C.S.

45 JAUNDICE

Jeffrey S. Barkun, M.D., F.A.C.S., Prosanto Chaudhury, M.D., and Alan N. Barkun, M.D.

Approach to the Jaundiced Patient

The term jaundice refers to the yellowish discoloration of skin, sclerae, and mucous membranes that results from excessive deposition of bilirubin in tissues. It usually is unmistakable but on occasion may manifest itself subtly. It is generally held that jaundice develops when serum bilirubin levels rise above 34.2 µmol/L (2 mg/dl)[1]; however, the appearance of jaundice also depends on whether it is conjugated or unconjugated bilirubin that is elevated and on how long the episode of jaundice lasts.

In what follows, we outline a problem-based approach to the jaundiced patient that involves assessing the incremental information provided by successive clinical and laboratory investigations, as well as the information obtained by means of modern imaging modalities. We also propose a classification of jaundice that stresses the therapeutic options most pertinent to surgeons. We have not attempted a detailed review of bilirubin metabolism and the various pediatric disorders that cause jaundice; such issues are beyond the scope of this chapter. Finally, we emphasize that modern decision making in the approach to the jaundiced patient includes not only careful evaluation of anatomic issues but also close attention to patient morbidity and quality-of-life concerns, as well as a focus on working up the patient in a cost-effective fashion. For optimal treatment, in our view, an integrated approach that involves the surgeon, the gastroenterologist, and the radiologist is essential.

Clinical Evaluation and Investigative Studies

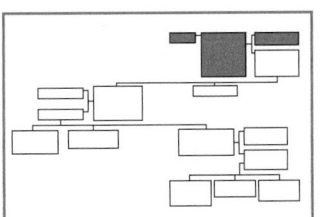

HISTORY AND PHYSICAL EXAMINATION

When a patient presents with a skin discoloration suggestive of jaundice, the first step is to confirm that icterus is indeed present. To this end, the mucous membranes of the mouth, the palms, the soles, and the sclerae should be examined in natural light. Because such areas are protected from the sun, photodegradation of bile is minimized; thus, the yellowish discoloration of elastic tissues may be more easily detected. Occasionally, deposition of a yellowish pigment on skin may mimic jaundice but may in fact be related to the consumption of large quantities of food containing lycopene or carotene or drugs such as rifampin or quinacrine. In these cases, the skin is usually the only site of coloration, and careful inspection of sclerae and mucous membranes generally reveals no icteric pigmentation. In certain cultures, long-term application of tea bags to the eyes may lead to a brownish discoloration of the sclerae that can mimic jaundice.[2]

DIRECT VERSUS INDIRECT HYPERBILIRUBINEMIA

Once the presence of jaundice has been confirmed, further clinical assessment determines whether the hyperbilirubinemia is predominantly direct or indirect. This distinction is based on the division of bilirubin into conjugated and unconjugated fractions, which are also known, respectively, as direct and indirect fractions on the basis of their behavior in the van den Bergh (diazo) reaction.[3] If the patient has normal-colored urine and stools, unconjugated bilirubin [see Sidebar Unconjugated (Indirect) Bilirubin] is predominant [see Table 1]. If the patient has dark urine, pale stools, or any other signs or symptoms of a cholestatic syndrome (see below), the serum bilirubin fractionation usually indicates that conjugated bilirubin is predominant. Rarely, the clinical picture may be secondary to a massive increase in both direct and indirect bilirubin production after the latter has overcome the ability of the hepatocytes to secrete conjugated bilirubin.

It is nearly always possible to distinguish between direct and indirect hyperbilirubinemia on clinical grounds alone.[4] Our emphasis here is on direct hyperbilirubinemia, which is the type that is more relevant to general surgeons.

Cholestatic Syndrome

The term cholestasis refers to decreased delivery of bilirubin into the intestine (and subsequent accumulation in the hepato-

Approach to the Jaundiced Patient

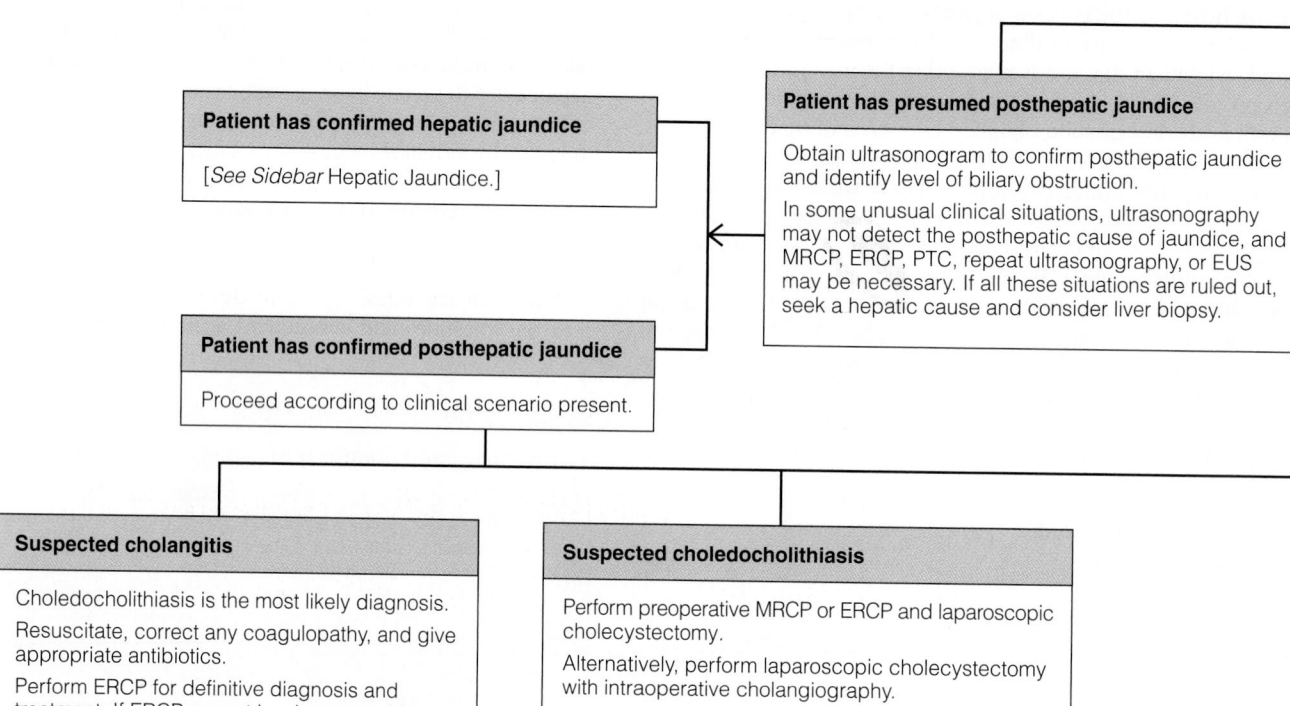

Patient has confirmed hepatic jaundice

[*See Sidebar* Hepatic Jaundice.]

Patient has presumed posthepatic jaundice

Obtain ultrasonogram to confirm posthepatic jaundice and identify level of biliary obstruction.

In some unusual clinical situations, ultrasonography may not detect the posthepatic cause of jaundice, and MRCP, ERCP, PTC, repeat ultrasonography, or EUS may be necessary. If all these situations are ruled out, seek a hepatic cause and consider liver biopsy.

Patient has confirmed posthepatic jaundice

Proceed according to clinical scenario present.

Suspected cholangitis

Choledocholithiasis is the most likely diagnosis.

Resuscitate, correct any coagulopathy, and give appropriate antibiotics.

Perform ERCP for definitive diagnosis and treatment. If ERCP cannot be done, consider transhepatic drainage or surgery.

Suspected choledocholithiasis

Perform preoperative MRCP or ERCP and laparoscopic cholecystectomy.

Alternatively, perform laparoscopic cholecystectomy with intraoperative cholangiography.

Patient presents with skin discoloration suggestive of jaundice

Perform clinical assessment

Perform physical exam and obtain history.

Confirm icterus by examining oral mucous membranes, palms, soles, and sclerae in natural light.

Distinguish indirect (unconjugated) from direct (conjugated) hyperbilirubinemia:

- Normal-colored urine and stools suggest indirect hyperbilirubinemia
- Dark urine, pale stools, and signs or symptoms of a cholestatic syndrome suggest direct hyperbilirubinemia

Measure total serum bilirubin and percentage of conjugated bilirubin.

Patient has indirect hyperbilirubinemia

[*See Sidebar* Unconjugated (Indirect) Bilirubin.]

Patient has direct hyperbilirubinemia

Distinguish hepatic ("medical") jaundice from posthepatic ("surgical") jaundice.

- Acute hepatitis, alcohol abuse, and physical evidence of cirrhosis or portal hypertension suggest hepatic jaundice
- Abdominal pain, rigors, itching, and a palpable liver > 2 cm below costal margin suggest posthepatic jaundice

Patient has presumed hepatic jaundice

[*See Sidebar* Hepatic Jaundice.]

Suspected lesion other than choledocholithiasis

The most common single cause is pancreatic cancer; many of the other possible causes also involve malignancy.

Perform spiral CT or MRI with MRCP to diagnose lesion and assess resectability.

Consider EUS with biopsy for distal-third obstruction.

Perform Doppler ultrasonography to stage lesion further; CT angiography or MRA may be considered if ultrasonogram is abnormal.

Perform MRCP to assess intrahepatic biliary system in patients with middle-third or upper-third obstruction.

Lesion appears unresectable, and surgical palliation is not indicated

Treat with ERCP or PTC and drainage. For advanced malignant disease, supportive care alone may be indicated.

Lesion appears resectable, or surgical palliation is indicated

Treat with surgical bypass or resection as appropriate for level of obstruction.

Perform laparoscopy to confirm resectability before laparotomy.

Upper-third obstruction

Palliation: bypass with left (segment III) hepaticojejunostomy.

Resection for cure: resection of tumor, possibly with hepatectomy or segmentectomy, and reconstruction with hepaticojejunostomy or cholangiojejunostomy.

Middle-third obstruction

Palliation: bypass with hepaticojejunostomy.

Resection for cure: resection of tumor and reconstruction with hepaticojejunostomy.

Lower-third obstruction

Palliation: bypass with Roux-en-Y choledochojejunostomy.

Resection for cure: resection of tumor with pancreaticoduodenectomy or local ampullary excision.

Table 1 Causes of Unconjugated Hyperbilirubinemia

Increased RBC breakdown
  Acute hemolysis
  Chronic hemolytic disorders
  Large hematoma resorption, multiple blood transfusions
  Gilbert syndrome

Decreased hepatic bilirubin conjugation
  Gilbert syndrome
  Crigler-Najjar syndrome types I and II
  Familial unconjugated hyperbilirubinemia

cytes and in blood), irrespective of the underlying cause. When cholestasis is mild, it may not be associated with clinical jaundice. As it worsens, a conjugated hyperbilirubinemia develops that presents as jaundice. The conjugated hyperbilirubinemia may derive either from a defect in hepatocellular function (hepatic jaundice, also referred to as nonobstructive or medical jaundice) or from a blockage somewhere in the biliary tree (posthepatic jaundice, also referred to as obstructive or surgical jaundice). In this chapter, we refer to hepatic and posthepatic causes of jaundice, reserving the term cholestasis for the specific clinical syndrome that is attributable to a chronic lack of delivery of bile into the intestine. This syndrome is characterized by signs and symptoms that are related either to the conjugated hyperbilirubinemia or to chronic malabsorption of fat-soluble vitamins (i.e., vitamins A, D, E, and K): jaundice, dark urine, pale stools, pruritus, bruising, steatorrhea, night blindness, osteomalacia, and neuromuscular weakness.[5]

HEPATIC VERSUS POSTHEPATIC JAUNDICE

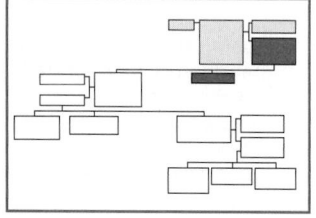

Once the presence of direct hyperbilirubinemia is confirmed, the next step is to determine whether the jaundice is hepatic or posthepatic. A number of authors have studied the reliability of clinical assessment for making this determination.[6-17] The sensitivities of history, physical examination, and blood tests alone range from 70% to 95%,[6-11] whereas the specificities are approximately 75%.[10,11] The overall accuracy of clinical assessment of hepatic and posthepatic causes of jaundice ranges from 87% to 97%.[8,12] Clinically, hepatic jaundice is most often signaled by acute hepatitis, a history of alcohol abuse, or physical findings reflecting cirrhosis or portal hypertension[13]; posthepatic jaundice is most often signaled by abdominal pain, rigors, itching, or a palpable liver more than 2 cm below the costal margin.[14]

By using discriminant analysis in a pediatric patient population, two investigators were able to isolate three biochemical tests that differentiated between biliary atresia and intrahepatic cholestasis with an accuracy of 95%: total serum bilirubin concentration, alkaline phosphatase level, and γ-glutamyltranspeptidase level.[15] Serum transaminase levels added no independent information of significance to the model. Another multivariate analysis model demonstrated that patients with posthepatic jaundice were younger, had a longer history of jaundice, were more likely to present with fever, and had greater elevations of serum protein concentrations and shorter coagulation times than patients with hepatic jaundice.[16]

This model, however, despite its 96% sensitivity (greater than that of any single radiologic diagnostic modality), could not accurately predict the level of a biliary obstruction. Other investigators have reported similar findings,[8,12,13] and most agree that strategies that omit ultrasonography are clearly inferior.[17]

In summary, a clinical approach supported by simple biochemical evaluation displays good predictive ability to distinguish hepatic from posthepatic jaundice; however, a clinical approach alone does not accurately identify the level of biliary obstruction in a patient with posthepatic jaundice.

The remainder of this chapter focuses primarily on management of posthepatic jaundice; hepatic jaundice is less often seen and dealt with by general surgeons [see Table 2 and Sidebar Hepatic Jaundice].

IMAGING

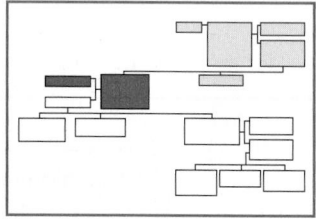

Once the history has been obtained and bedside and laboratory assessments have been completed, the next step is imaging, the goals of which are (1) to confirm the presence of an extrahepatic obstruction (i.e., to verify that the jaundice is indeed posthepatic rather than hepatic), (2) to determine the level of the obstruction, (3) to identify the specific cause of the obstruction, and (4) to provide complementary information relating to the underlying diagnosis (e.g., staging information in cases of malignancy).

Of the many imaging methods available today, the gold standard for defining the level of a biliary obstruction before operation in a jaundiced patient remains direct cholangiography, which can be performed either via endoscopic retrograde cholangiopancreatography (ERCP) [see 60 Gastrointestinal Endoscopy] or via percutaneous transhepatic cholangiography (PTC). Unlike other imaging modalities, direct cholangiography poses significant risks to the patient: there is a 4% to 7% incidence of pancreatitis or cholangitis after ERCP,[18,19] and there is a 4% incidence of bile leakage, cholangitis, or bleeding after PTC.[20] There are also several risks that are particular to the manipulation of an obstructed biliary system (see below). For these reasons, the role of ERCP and PTC is increasingly a therapeutic one; therefore, it is important to

Table 2 Causes of Hepatic Jaundice[133]

Hepatitis
  Viral
  Autoimmune
  Alcoholic
Drugs and hormones
Diseases of intrahepatic bile ducts
Liver infiltration and storage disorders
Systemic infections
Total parenteral nutrition
Postoperative intrahepatic cholestasis
Cholestasis of pregnancy
Benign recurrent intrahepatic cholestasis
Infantile cholestatic syndromes
Inherited metabolic defects
No identifiable cause (idiopathic hepatic jaundice)

Hepatic Jaundice

Hepatic jaundice may be either acute or chronic and may be caused by a variety of conditions [see Table 2].

Acute hepatic jaundice may arise de novo or in the setting of ongoing liver disease. Historical clues may suggest a particular cause, such as medications or viral hepatitis. Physical examination usually reveals little. In the presence of preexisting chronic liver disease, bedside stigmata (e.g., ascites, spider nevi, caput medusae, palmar erythema, gynecomastia, or Dupuytren contracture) may be present. Although specific therapies exist for certain clinical problems (e.g., acetylcysteine for acetaminophen ingestion and penicillin plus silibinin for *Amanita phalloides* poisoning), treatment in most cases remains supportive. Patients in whom encephalopathy develops within 2 to 8 weeks of the onset of jaundice are usually classified as having fulminant hepatic failure [see 124 Hepatic Failure]. Evidence of encephalopathy, renal failure, or a severe coagulopathy is predictive of poor outcome in this setting.[128] The most common causes of fulminant hepatic failure are viral hepatitis and drug toxicity. The mortality from fulminant hepatic failure remains high even though liver transplantation has favorably affected the prognosis.[129]

In cases of chronic hepatic jaundice, the patient may have chronic hepatitis or cholestasis, with or without cirrhosis. The cause usually is determined on the basis of the history in conjunction with the results of serology, biochemistry, viral DNA analysis, and, occasionally, histology. Causes include viral infection, drug-induced chronic hepatitis, autoimmune liver disease, genetic disorders (e.g., Wilson disease and α_1-antitrypsin deficiency), chronic cholestatic disorders, alcoholic liver disease, and steatohepatitis.[130] Physical examination reveals the stigmata of chronic liver disease and occasionally suggests a specific cause (e.g., Kayser-Fleischer rings on slit-lamp examination in Wilson disease). Treatment, once again, is usually supportive, depending on the clinical presentation; whether more specific therapy is needed and what form it takes depend on the cause of liver disease. Although physiologic tests have been developed to quantify hepatic reserve, the most widely used and best-validated prognostic index remains the Child-Pugh classification (see below), which correlates with individual survival and has been shown to predict operative risk.[131] Liver transplantation is the treatment of choice in most cases of end-stage liver disease.

The Child-Pugh Classification[131]
Numerical Score (*points*)

Variable	1	2	3
Encephalopathy	Nil (0)	Slight to moderate (1, 2)	Moderate to severe (3–5)
Ascites	Nil	Slight	Moderate to severe
Bilirubin, mg/dl (μmol/L*)	< 2 (< 34)	2–3 (34–51)	> 3 (> 51)
Albumin, g/dl (g/L*)	> 3.5 (> 35)	2.8–3.5 (28–35)	< 2.8 (< 28)
Prothrombin index	> 70%	40%–70%	< 40%

Modified Child's risk grade (depending on total score): 5 or 6 points, grade A; 7 to 9 points, grade B; 10 to 15 points, grade C.
*Système International d'Unités, or SI units.

The Model for End-Stage Liver Disease (MELD) score is now used to prioritize the allocation of organs for liver transplantation by the United Network for Organ Sharing.[132] This score is based on the serum bilirubin and creatinine concentrations, the international normalized ratio (INR), and the presence of hepatocellular carcinoma; it does not make use of some of the more subjective components of the Child-Pugh score (e.g., ascites and encephalopathy).

gather as much imaging information as possible on the likely cause of the jaundice before performing either investigation.[21] We have found the following approach to be an efficacious, cost-effective,[22] and safe way of obtaining such information in a patient with presumed posthepatic jaundice.

The presence of ductal dilatation of the intrahepatic or extrahepatic biliary system confirms that a posthepatic cause is responsible for the jaundice. Ultrasonography detects ductal dilatation with an accuracy of 95%, though results are to some extent operator-dependent.[23] If ultrasonography does not reveal bile duct dilatation, it is unlikely that an obstructing lesion is present. In some cases, even though ductal dilatation is absent, other ultrasonographic findings may still point to a specific hepatic cause of jaundice (e.g., cirrhosis or infiltration of the liver by tumor).

There are a few specific instances in which ultrasonography may fail to detect a posthepatic cause of jaundice. For instance, very early in the course of an obstructive process, not enough time may have elapsed for biliary dilatation to occur. In this setting, a hepato-iminodiacetic acid (HIDA) scan has often helped identify bile duct blockage.[24] The yield from this test is highest when the serum bilirubin level is lower than 100 μmol/L.[1] Occasionally, the intrahepatic biliary tree is unable to dilate; possible causes of such inability include extensive hepatic fibrosis, cirrhosis, sclerosing cholangitis, and liver transplantation. If one of these diagnoses is suspected, ERCP, magnetic resonance cholangiopancreatography (MRCP), or PTC will eventually be required to confirm the diagnosis of biliary obstruction. Occasionally, the biliary tree dilatation may be intermittent; possible causes of this condition include choledocholithiasis and some biliary tumors. In a patient with gallstones, transient liver test abnormalities by themselves may suggest an intermediate to high likelihood of common bile duct (CBD) stones, even if there is no biliary ductal dilatation.[25,26] If one of these diagnoses is suspected, ultrasonography may be repeated after a short period of observation (when clinically applicable); biliary ductal dilatation then generally becomes apparent. If all of these unusual clinical situations have been ruled out, a hepatic cause for the jaundice should be sought [see Table 2] and a liver biopsy considered.[27,28]

Besides being able to identify the presence of extrahepatic ductal obstruction with a high degree of reliability, ultrasonography can accurately determine the level of the obstruction in 90% of cases.[29] For example, a dilated gallbladder suggests that the obstruction is probably located in the middle third or the distal third of the CBD.

Some centers prefer CT to ultrasonography as the initial imaging modality,[30] but we, like a number of other authors,[31] find ultrasonography to be the most expedient, least invasive, and most economical imaging method for differentiating between hepatic and posthepatic causes of jaundice, as well as for suggesting the level of obstruction.[32] Traditional imaging techniques, such as oral or intravenous cholangiography, have a negligible role to play in this setting because of their very poor accuracy and safety, especially in jaundiced patients.

MRCP [see Figure 1] and endoscopic ultrasonography (EUS) have been used to visualize the biliary and pancreatic trees in various populations of patients with obstructive jaundice.[33-37]

Compared with direct cholangiography, both appear to be excellent at diagnosing biliary obstruction and establishing its location and nature.[38,39] MRCP exhibits more modest detection rates when diagnosing small CBD stones.[40,41] Spiral (helical) CT scanning is also useful in diagnosing biliary obstruction and determining its cause, though concomitant oral or I.V. cholangiography is required to detect choledocholithiasis.[42-44]

In addition to their ability to detect choledocholithiasis, spiral CT, EUS, and MRCP in combination with abdominal magnetic resonance imaging (e.g., of the pancreas) are very useful in diagnosing and staging biliopancreatic tumors.[45-47] Cytology specimens are readily obtained via fine-needle aspiration (FNA) during CT or EUS.[46]

It is our current practice to employ these modalities as second-line tests after the initial abdominal ultrasonographic examination. To obtain a diagnosis, we favor EUS for periampullary pathologic conditions and MRI with MRCP for more proximal diseases of the biliary tree.

In making the choice among the various available second-line tests, local expertise and cost-effectiveness become important considerations. Unfortunately, the reports on cost-effectiveness published to date have suffered either from limited assumptions (when the methodology involved decision modeling) or from the lack of an effectiveness-type design (when the methodology involved allocation of patients).

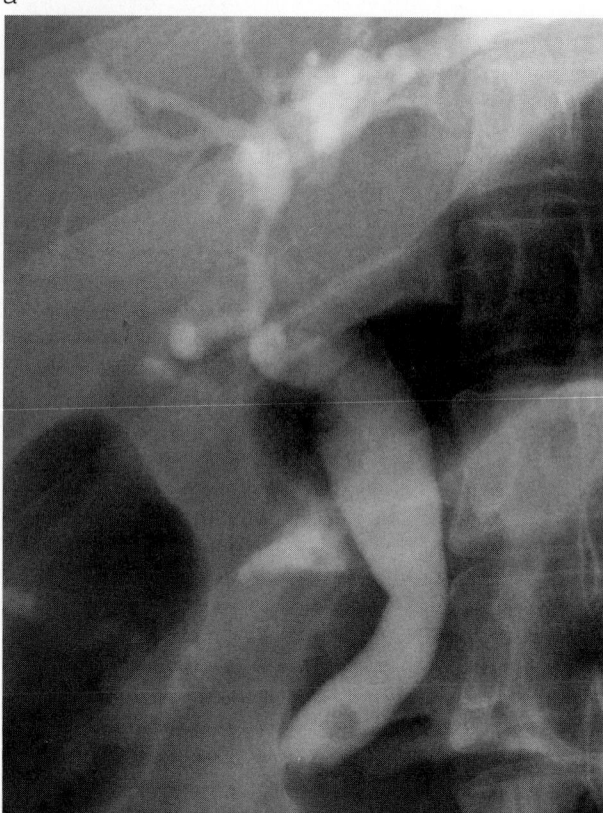

a

Workup and Management of Posthepatic Jaundice

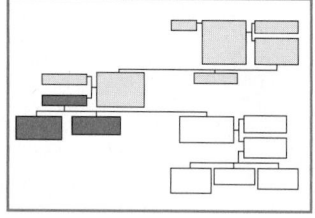

Once ultrasonography has confirmed that ductal obstruction is present, there are three possible clinical scenarios: suspected cholangitis, suspected choledocholithiasis without cholangitis, and a suspected lesion other than choledocholithiasis. The direction of the subsequent workup depends on which of the three appears most likely.

SUSPECTED CHOLANGITIS

If a jaundiced patient exhibits a clinical picture compatible with acute suppurative cholangitis (Charcot's triad or Raynaud's pentad), the most likely diagnosis is choledocholithiasis. After appropriate resuscitation, correction of any coagulopathies present, and administration of antibiotics, ERCP is indicated for diagnosis and treatment.[48] If ERCP is unavailable or is not feasible (e.g., because of previous Roux-en-Y reconstruction), transhepatic drainage or surgery may be necessary. It is important to emphasize here that the mainstay of treatment of severe cholangitis is not just the administration of appropriate antibiotics but rather the establishment of adequate biliary drainage.

SUSPECTED CHOLEDOCHOLITHIASIS WITHOUT CHOLANGITIS

Choledocholithiasis is the most common cause of biliary obstruction.[13,14] It should be strongly suspected if the jaundice is episodic or painful or if ultrasonography has demonstrated the presence of gallstones or bile duct stones. Patients with suspected choledocholithiasis should be referred for laparoscopic cholecystectomy with either preoperative ERCP, intraoperative cholangiography, or intraoperative ultrasonography [*see 63 Cholecystotomy and Common Bile Duct Exploration*].[49] We favor preoperative ERCP in this setting of jaundice because its diagnostic yield is high,[50] it allows confirmation of the diagnosis preoperatively (thus obviating intraoperative surprises), and it is capable of clearing the

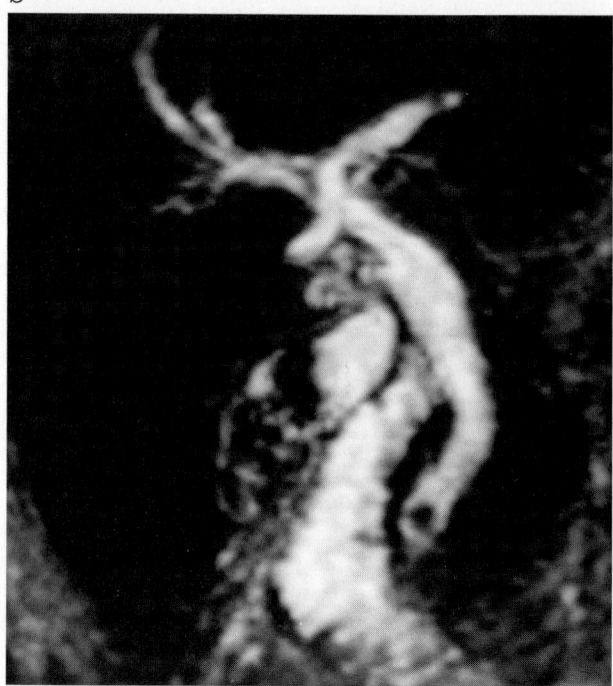

b

Figure 1 **ERCP (*a*) and corresponding MRCP (*b*) demonstrate presence of a stone in the distal CBD.**

CBD of stones in 95% of cases. Decision analyses appear to confirm the utility of this strategy when laparoscopic CBD exploration is not an option.[51-55] Many authors, however, favor a fully laparoscopic approach, in which choledocholithiasis is detected in the

OR by means of intraoperative cholangiography[56,57] or ultrasonography[58-60] and laparoscopic biliary clearance is performed when choledocholithiasis is confirmed. Given that both the ERCP approach and the fully laparoscopic approach have advantages and limitations, the optimal approach in a particular setting should be dictated by local expertise.

SUSPECTED LESION OTHER THAN CHOLEDOCHOLITHIASIS

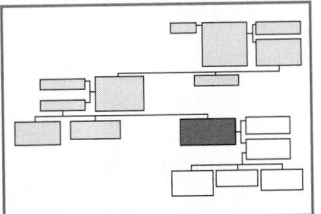

If no gallstones are identified, if the clinical presentation is less acute (e.g., constant abdominal or back pain), or if there are associated constitutional symptoms (e.g., weight loss, fatigue, and longstanding anorexia), the presence of a lesion other than choledocholithiasis should be suspected. In such cases, another imaging modality besides the ultrasonography already performed must be considered before the decision is made to proceed to cholangiography or operation.

Possible causes of posthepatic obstruction (other than choledocholithiasis) may be classified into three categories, depending on the location of the obstructing lesion (as suggested by the pattern of gallbladder and biliary tree dilatation on the ultrasonogram): the upper third of the biliary tree, the middle third, or the lower (distal) third [see Table 3]. Once it has been determined that choledocholithiasis is unlikely, the most common cause of such obstruction is pancreatic cancer [see 51 Tumors of the Pancreas, Biliary Tract, and Liver].[13,14] In adults, many of the other possible causes also involve malignant processes. Consequently, the next step in the workup of the patient is typically the assessment of resectability and operability [see 64 Procedures for Benign and Malignant Biliary Tract Disease].

Diagnosis and Assessment of Resectability

Assessment of the resectability of a tumor usually hinges on whether the superior mesenteric vein, the portal vein, the superior mesenteric artery, and the porta hepatis are free of tumor and on whether there is evidence of significant local adenopathy or extrapancreatic extension of tumor. Unfortunately, the majority of lesions will be clearly unresectable, either because of tumor extension or because of the presence of hepatic or peritoneal metastases.

Many imaging modalities are currently used to determine resectability, and several of these have been established as effective alternatives to direct cholangiography because they involve little if any morbidity. Their accuracy varies according to the underlying pathology and the expertise of the user. They have been studied mostly with respect to the staging and diagnosis of pancreatic, periampullary, and biliary hilar cancers.

For determining resectability and staging lesions before operation, we rely mainly on spiral CT. The advent and widespread availability of multidetector CT have made this modality the dominant second-line imaging method in cases of suspected pancreatic masses. For optimal evaluation of the pancreas, a fine-cut dualphase (arterial phase and portal venous phase) scan should be obtained. Oral administration of water allows better evaluation of the duodenum and the ampulla.[61,62] At present, spiral CT is considered to be superior for the diagnosis and staging of lesions such as pancreatic cancer.[45,63,64] It exhibits a high negative predictive value and has a false positive rate of less than 10%; its sensitivity is optimal for pancreatic lesions larger than 1.5 cm in diameter. Ascites, liver metastases, lymph nodes larger than 2 cm in diameter, and invasion into adjacent organs are all signs of advanced disease.[65] On the basis of these criteria, spiral CT can predict that a lesion will not be resectable with an accuracy approaching 95%; however, as many as 33% of tumors that appear to be resectable on CT are found to be unresectable at operation.[64]

MRI-based staging, along with MRCP, can further dictate the subsequent choice of therapy.[65-68] MRI may be particularly useful for following up patients in whom clip artifacts interfere with a CT image.[65] It also appears to be successful in detecting cholangiocarcinoma spreading along the proximal biliary tree.[69] Given the renewed interest in biliary contrast media and the availability of software optimized for multidetector scanners, CT cholangiography may soon rival MRCP for evaluation of the biliary tree in cases of suspected malignancy.[70]

Only in a few very rare instances is traditional angiography used to assess resectability or stage a hepatobiliary or pancreatic neoplasm. Increasingly, it is being replaced by CT angiography or duplex Doppler ultrasonography, which can confirm the presence of flow in the hepatic arterial or portal venous systems and occasionally can demonstrate invasion of these vessels by tumor.[71] Magnetic resonance angiography (MRA) has also been used with excellent results. As yet, none of these noninvasive modalities has been shown to be clearly superior to any of the others.[72]

Table 3 Causes of Posthepatic Jaundice

Upper-third obstruction
Polycystic liver disease
Caroli disease
Hepatocellular carcinoma
Oriental cholangiohepatitis
Hepatic arterial thrombosis (e.g., after liver transplantation or chemotherapy)
Hemobilia (e.g., after biliary manipulation)
Iatrogenic bile duct injury (e.g., after laparoscopic cholecystectomy)
Cholangiocarcinoma (Klatskin tumor)
Sclerosing cholangitis
Papillomas of the bile duct

Middle-third obstruction
Cholangiocarcinoma
Sclerosing cholangitis
Papillomas of the bile duct
Gallbladder cancer
Choledochal cyst
Intrabiliary parasites
Mirizzi syndrome
Extrinsic nodal compression (e.g., from breast cancer or lymphoma)
Iatrogenic bile duct injury (e.g., after open cholecystectomy)
Cystic fibrosis
Benign idiopathic bile duct stricture

Lower-third obstruction
Cholangiocarcinoma
Sclerosing cholangitis
Papillomas of the bile duct
Pancreatic tumors
Ampullary tumors
Chronic pancreatitis
Sphincter of Oddi dysfunction
Papillary stenosis
Duodenal diverticula
Penetrating duodenal ulcer
Retroduodenal adenopathy (e.g., lymphoma, carcinoid)

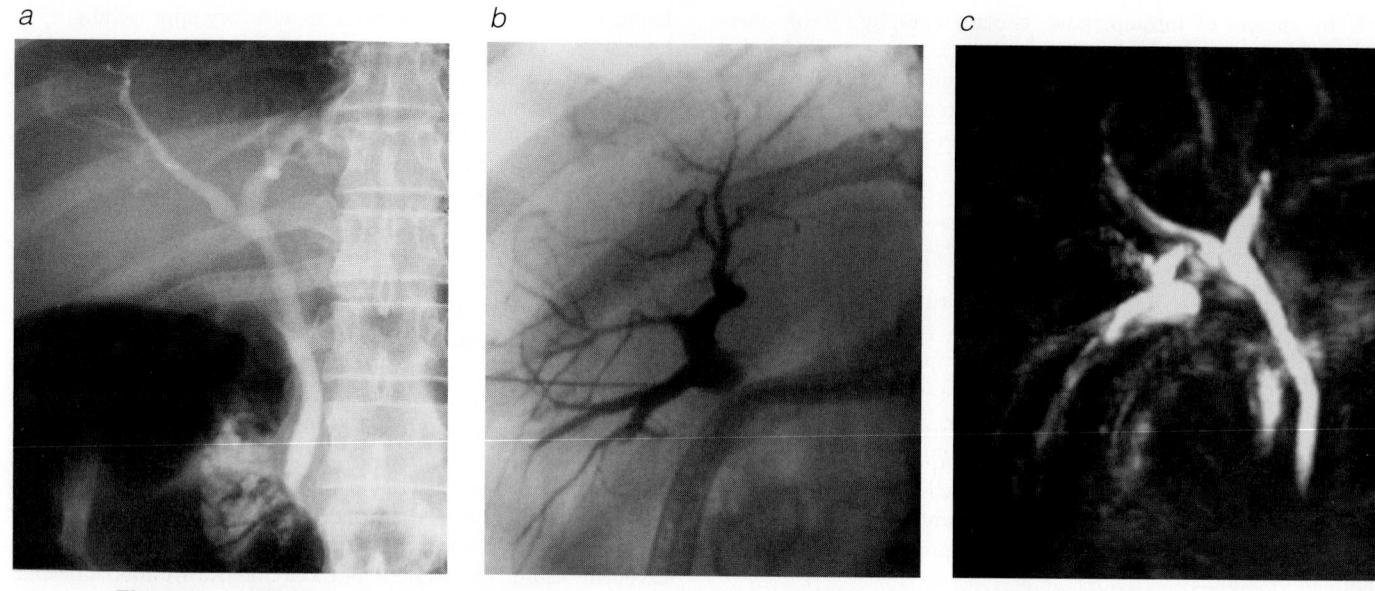

a   *b*   *c*

Figure 2 (*a*) **ERCP demonstrates missing liver segments.** (*b*) **Transhepatic cholangiography of segment 6 reveals the excluded liver ductal system.** (*c*) **MRCP shows the excluded liver segments, as well as the biliary system, which still communicates with the common hepatic duct.**

EUS is a highly sensitive method of imaging the pancreas and the duodenum.[46,73,74] In two large studies, it was found to be superior to CT and standard ultrasonography in staging pancreatic and ampullary cancers.[75,76] Subsequent studies indicated that whereas EUS is superior to CT for detection and staging, it provides similar information regarding nodal status and overall assessment of resectability.[61,77] From a cost-minimization point of view, the optimal strategy is to begin with a dual-phase CT scan and to follow up with EUS only in cases in which further information or a tissue diagnosis is required.[78,79] In another large series, EUS was reported to be more accurate than CT in the comparative staging of pancreatic and ampullary cancers. It has also been found useful for identifying small (< 2 cm) pancreatic tumors, which may be suspected in a patient who has an obstruction of the distal third of the bile duct and whose CT scan is normal.[74] Furthermore, EUS is currently the dominant technique for staging ampullary tumors.[80]

In patients with a suspected pancreatic tumor, direct FNA of the lesion at the time of EUS has become the gold-standard method for obtaining a tissue diagnosis. In the case of potentially resectable lesions, however, this measure adds very little to the decision-making process. The limited data currently available suggest that assays of tumor markers in serum and pancreatic fluid are useful, particularly for cystic lesions of the pancreas.[81]

At this point in the evaluation, patients can be referred either for cholangiography (ERCP or MRCP) to clarify a still-unclear diagnosis or for biliary decompression (see below). MRI of the pancreas with MRCP continues to improve rapidly. It is a noninvasive modality that evaluates the pancreas, vasculature, and the pancreatobiliary ductal system in a single examination, with the additional benefit of avoiding ionizing radiation and iodinated contrast agents.[82] MRCP remains our test of choice for evaluation of middle- and upper-third lesions in cases in which decompression is not required.

In the event that none of these modalities point to a diagnosis, the use of ^{18}F-fluorodeoxyglucose (FDG) positron emission tomography (PET) may be considered to help differentiate benign pancreatic conditions from malignant ones.[83,84] Besides facilitating diagnosis, FDG-PET provides information regarding occult metastases and can be useful in detecting recurrent disease. Experience with FDG-PET is growing rapidly as this imaging modality becomes more readily accessible.

When a biliary stricture is detected at cholangiography, brush cytology or biopsy is mandatory. Biliary cytology, however, has been disappointing, particularly at ERCP: diagnostic accuracy ranges from 40% to 85%,[85,86] mostly because the negative predictive value is poor. Accuracy improves with multiple sampling and when a biliary rather than a pancreatic malignancy is detected. In addition, biopsy tends to be more accurate than brush cytology.[85]

Nonoperative Management: Drainage and Cholangiography

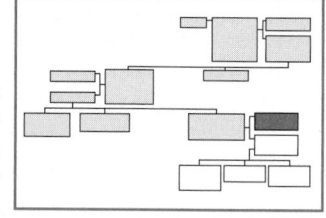

In the majority of patients with malignant obstructions, treatment is palliative rather than curative. It is therefore especially important to recognize and minimize the iatrogenic risks related to the manipulation of an obstructed biliary system; this is why staging and cholangiography are currently being performed with EUS and MRCP.

Cholangiography and decompression of obstructed biliary system As a rule, we favor ERCP, though PTC may be preferable for obstructions near the hepatic duct bifurcation. Whichever imaging modality is used, the following four principles apply.

1. In the absence of preexisting or concomitant hepatocellular dysfunction, drainage of one half of the liver is generally sufficient for resolution of jaundice.[87]
2. Because of its external diameter, a transhepatic drain, once inserted, does not necessarily permit equal drainage of all segments of the liver, particularly if there are a number of intrahepatic ductal stenoses. Accordingly, some patients with conditions such as sclerosing cholangitis or a growing tumor may experience persistent sepsis from an infected excluded liver segment even when the prosthesis is patent [*see Figure 2*]. An excluded segment may even be responsible for severe persistent pruritus.

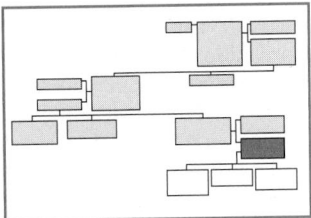

3. Any attempt at opacifying an obstructed biliary tree introduces a significant risk of subsequent cholangitis, even when appropriate antibiotic prophylaxis is provided. Accordingly, when one elects to perform direct cholangiography, there should be a plan for biliary drainage either at the time of ERCP or PTC or soon thereafter.

4. Even though jaundice is believed to be associated with multiple adverse systemic effects (e.g., renal failure, sepsis, and impaired wound healing),[88,89] routine preoperative drainage of an obstructed biliary system does not benefit patients who will soon undergo resection.[90,91] There is a growing body of evidence suggesting that in patients with either pancreatic[92,93] or hepatic[94] malignancies, routine preoperative direct cholangiography with decompression is associated with a higher incidence of postoperative complications when tumor resection is ultimately carried out.

When direct cholangiography is ordered, it should be thought of as more than just a diagnostic test: it is the ideal setting for cytology, biopsy, or even drainage of the obstructed bile duct via a sphincterotomy, a nasobiliary tube, or a catheter or stent. Accordingly, it is essential that the surgeon, the gastroenterologist, and the radiologist discuss the possible need for drainage well before it is required. Early, open communication among all the members of the treating team is a hallmark of the modern management of biliary obstruction.

Palliation in patients with advanced malignant disease

When a patient has advanced malignant disease, drainage of the biliary system for palliation is not routinely indicated, because the risk of complications related to the procedure may outweigh the potential benefit. Indeed, the best treatment for a patient with asymptomatic obstructive jaundice and liver metastases may be supportive care alone.[95] Biliary decompression is indicated if cholangitis or severe pruritus interferes with quality of life.

We, like others,[22] consider a stent placed with ERCP to be the palliative modality of choice for advanced disease, though upper-third lesions may be managed most easily through the initial placement of an internal/external catheter at the time of PTC. Metal expandable stents remain patent longer than large conventional plastic stents,[96,97] but the high price of the metal stents has kept them from being widely used, and their overall cost-effectiveness has yet to be clearly demonstrated. Whether plastic biliary stents should be replaced prophylactically or only after obstruction has occurred remains controversial; however, results from a randomized, controlled trial (RCT) favor the former approach.[98] In another RCT, the use of prophylactic ciprofloxacin did not prolong stent patency but did reduce the incidence of cholangitis and improve quality of life scores.[99]

RCTs suggest that surgical biliary bypass should be reserved for patients who are expected to survive for 6 months or longer because bypass is associated with more prolonged palliation at the cost of greater initial morbidity.[100]

The role of prophylactic gastric drainage at the time of operative biliary drainage remains controversial,[101,102] though two RCTs demonstrated a reduced incidence of subsequent clinical gastric outlet obstruction when this measure was employed. Jaundiced patients with unresectable lesions who also present with duodenal or jejunal obstruction should be referred for gastrojejunostomy at the time of biliary bypass surgery. There is evidence to suggest that when a pancreatic malignancy is present, intraoperative celiac ganglion injection should be performed for either prophylactic or therapeutic pain control.[103]

Operative Management at Specific Sites: Bypass and Resection

Surgical treatment of tumors causing biliary obstruction is determined primarily by the level of the biliary obstruction. Current evidence indicates that modern surgical approaches are resulting in lower postoperative morbidity and, possibly, improved 5-year survival[104]; however, the prognosis is still uniformly poor, except for patients with ampullary tumors. In fact, the surgical procedure rarely proves curative, even after meticulous preoperative patient selection.

At one time, there was considerable enthusiasm for routine use of staging laparoscopy; at present, however, selective use is recommended.[105] The benefits of staging laparoscopy include more accurate assessment of resectability and prevention of the prolonged hospital stay and convalescence associated with an unnecessary laparotomy. Laparoscopy is used mostly to detect peritoneal carcinomatosis, liver metastases, malignant ascites, and gross hilar adenopathy.[106,107] The main limitation of laparoscopy in this setting appears to be that it does not accurately detect the spread of tumors to lymph nodes or the vascular system.[108] In several studies, a combined approach that included both laparoscopy and laparoscopic ultrasonography was associated with shorter hospital stays and lower costs.[105,107-109]

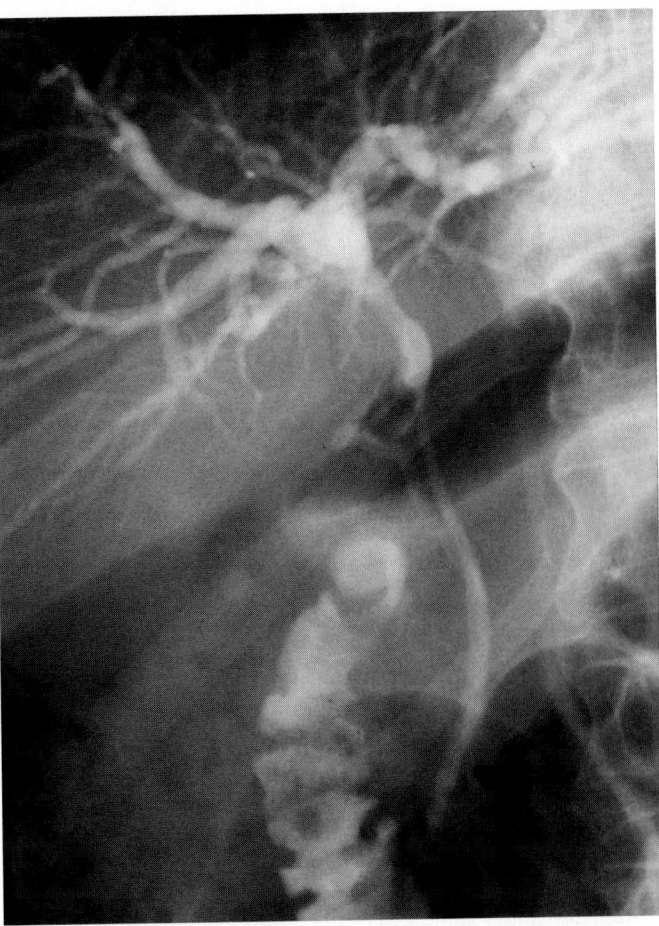

Figure 3 ERCP demonstrates extrinsic compression of the common hepatic duct by a stone in Hartmann's pouch. A biliary stent has been inserted for drainage.

In what follows, only the general principles of resection or bypass at each level of obstruction are discussed; operative technical details are addressed elsewhere [*see 64 Procedures for Benign and Malignant Biliary Tract Disease*]. Our preferred method of biliary anastomosis, for either reconstruction or bypass, involves the fashioning of a Roux-en-Y loop, followed by a mucosa-to-mucosa anastomosis. In all cases, a cholecystectomy is performed to facilitate access to the biliary tree.

Upper-third obstruction

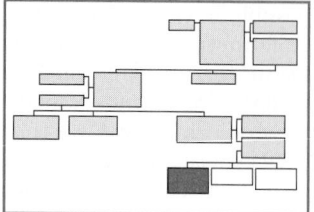

Palliation. Because the left hepatic duct has a long extrahepatic segment that makes it more accessible, the preferred bypass technique for an obstructing upper-third lesion is a left (or segment 3) hepaticojejunostomy. This operation has superseded the Longmire procedure because it does not involve formal resection of liver parenchyma. Laparoscopic bypass techniques that make use of segment 3 have been developed, but their performance has yet to be formally assessed, and they cannot yet be incorporated into a management algorithm.[110,111]

Resection for cure. The hilar plate is taken down to lengthen the hepatic duct segment available for subsequent anastomosis. Often, a formal hepatectomy or segmentectomy is required to ensure an adequate proximal margin of resection. If the resection must be carried out proximal to the hepatic duct bifurcation, several cholangiojejunostomies will have to be done to anastomose individual hepatic biliary branches. Frozen-section examination of the proximal and distal resection margins is important because of the propensity of tumors such as cholangiocarcinoma to spread in a submucosal or perineural plane.

The results of aggressive hilar tumor resections that included as much liver tissue as was necessary to obtain a negative margin appear to justify this approach.[112] In cases of left hepatic involvement, resection of the caudate lobe (segments 1 and 9) is indicated as well.[113,114]

Middle-third obstruction

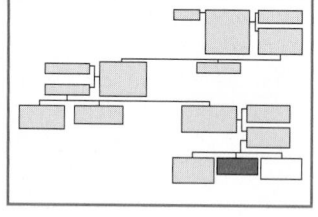

Palliation. Surgical bypass of middle-third lesions is technically simpler because a hepaticojejunostomy can often be performed distal to the hepatic duct bifurcation, which means that exposure of the hilar plate or the intrahepatic ducts is unnecessary.

Resection for cure. Discrete tumors in this part of the bile duct, though uncommon, are usually quite amenable to resection along with the lymphatic chains in the porta hepatis. Resection of an early gallbladder cancer may, on occasion, necessitate the concomitant resection of segment 5, though the value of resecting this segment prophylactically has not been conclusively demonstrated.[115] Sometimes, jaundice from a suspected middle-third lesion is in fact caused by a case of Mirizzi syndrome [*see Figure 3*]. In such cases, a gallstone is responsible for extrinsic obstruction of the CBD, either by causing inflammation of the gallbladder wall or via direct impingement. Proper treatment of this syndrome may involve hepaticojejunostomy in addition to cholecystectomy if a cholecystocholedochal fistula is present.[116]

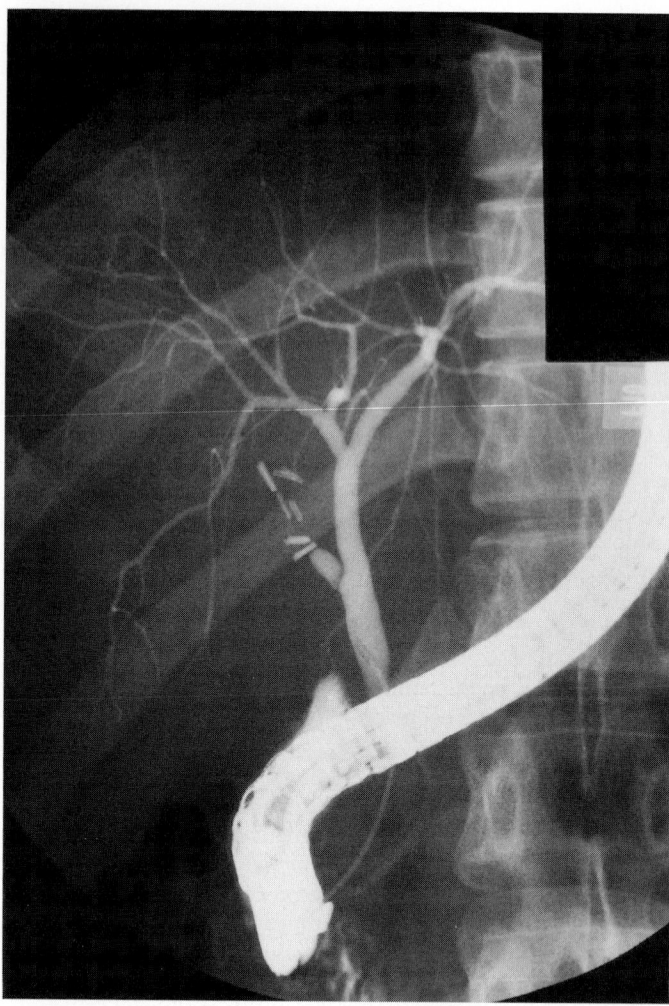

Figure 4 **Jaundice has occurred after laparoscopic cholecystectomy as a result of bile leakage from a distal biliary tributary. A stent has been inserted to decrease bile duct luminal pressure and foster spontaneous resolution.**

Lower-third obstruction

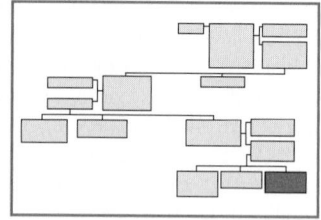

Palliation. The preferred bypass technique for lower-third lesions is a Roux-en-Y choledochojejunostomy. Cholecystojejunostomy carries a higher risk of complications and subsequent development of jaundice[117]; this remains true even when it is performed laparoscopically. Occasionally, it may be done as a temporizing measure before a more definitive procedure in the context of an upcoming transfer to a specialized center.

Resection for cure. Occasionally, an impacted CBD stone at the duodenal ampulla mimics a tumor and is not clearly identified preoperatively. Because of the growing use of EUS and MRCP, such a situation is increasingly uncommon. Resection of a lower-third lesion usually involves a pancreaticoduodenectomy [*see 66 Procedures for Benign and Malignant Pancreatic Disease*], though transduodenal ampullary resection may be an acceptable alternative for a small adenoma of the ampulla [*see 62 Procedures for Benign and Malignant Gastric and Duodenal Disease*]; local duodenal resection without removal of the head of the pancreas has also been described.[118] For optimal results, pancreaticoduodenectomy is best performed in specialized centers.[119]

It has been suggested that postoperative adjuvant therapy may improve the prognosis after resection of a pancreatic adenocarcinoma,[104] but this debate falls outside the scope of our discussion.

Postoperative Jaundice

A clinical scenario of particular pertinence to surgeons that we have not yet addressed is the development of jaundice in the postoperative setting.

Jaundice develops in approximately 1% of all surgical patients after operation.[120] When jaundice occurs after a hepatobiliary procedure, it may be attributable to specific biliary causes, such as retained CBD stones, postoperative biliary leakage (through reabsorption of bile leaking into the peritoneum) [see Figure 4], injury to the CBD, and the subsequent development of biliary strictures. In most instances, however, the jaundice derives from a combination of disease processes, and only rarely is invasive testing or active treatment required.[121]

A diagnostic approach similar to the one outlined earlier (see above) is applicable to postoperative jaundice; however, another useful approach is to consider the possible causes in the light of the time interval between the operation and the subsequent development of jaundice.

- Jaundice may develop within 48 hours of the operation; this is most often the result of the breakdown of red blood cells, occurring in the context of multiple blood transfusions (particularly with stored blood), the resorption of a large hematoma, or a transfusion reaction. Hemolysis may also develop in a patient with a known underlying hemolytic anemia and may be precipitated by the administration of specific drugs (e.g., sulfa drugs in a patient who has glucose-6-phosphate dehydrogenase deficiency).[122] Cardiopulmonary bypass or the insertion of a prosthetic valve may be associated with the development of early postoperative jaundice as well. Gilbert syndrome [see Sidebar Hepatic Jaundice] may first manifest itself early in the postoperative period. Occasionally, a mild conjugated hyperbilirubinemia may be related to Dubin-Johnson syndrome, which is an inherited disorder of bilirubin metabolism. This condition is usually self-limited and is characterized by the presence of a melaninlike pigment in the liver.
- Intraoperative hypotension or hypoxemia or the early development of heart failure can lead to conjugated hyperbilirubinemia within 5 to 10 days after operation. The hyperbilirubinemia may be associated with other end-organ damage (e.g., acute tubular necrosis). In fact, any impairment of renal function causes a decrease in bilirubin excretion and can be responsible for a mild hyperbilirubinemia.
- Jaundice may develop 7 to 10 days after operation in association with a medication-induced hepatitis attributable to an anesthetic agent. This syndrome has an estimated incidence of 1/10,000 after an initial exposure.[122] More commonly, the jaundice is related to the administration of antibiotics or other medications used in the perioperative setting.[122]
- After the first week, jaundice associated with intrahepatic cholestasis is often a manifestation of a septic response and usually presents in the setting of overt infection, particularly in patients with multiple organ dysfunction syndrome. Gram-negative sepsis from an intra-abdominal source is typical; if it persists, the outcome is likely to be poor. Jaundice may occur in as many as 30% of patients receiving total parenteral nutrition (TPN). It may be attributable to steatosis, particularly with formulas containing large amounts of carbohydrates. In addition, decreased export of bilirubin from the hepatocytes may lead to cholestasis, the severity of which appears to be related to the duration of TPN administration. Acalculous cholecystitis or even ductal obstruction may develop as a result of sludge in the gallbladder and the CBD. An elevated postoperative bilirubin level at any time may also result from unsuspected hepatic or post-hepatic causes (e.g., occult cirrhosis, choledocholithiasis, or cholecystitis). A rare cause of postoperative jaundice is the development of thyrotoxicosis. Another entity to consider (as a diagnosis of exclusion) is so-called benign postoperative cholestasis, a primarily cholestatic, self-limited process with no clearly demonstrable cause that typically arises within 2 to 10 days after operation. Benign postoperative cholestasis may be attributable to a combination of mechanisms, including an increased pigment load, impaired liver function resulting from hypoxemia and hypotension, and decreased renal bilirubin excretion caused by varying degrees of tubular necrosis.[123] The predominantly conjugated hyperbilirubinemia may reach 40 mg/dl and remain elevated for as long as 3 weeks.[122]
- In the late postoperative period, the development of non-A, non-B, non-C viral hepatitis after transfusion of blood products will usually occur within 5 to 12 weeks of operation.

References

1. Schiff L: Jaundice: a clinical approach. Diseases of the Liver, 7th ed. Schiff L, Schiff ER, Eds. JB Lippincott Co, Philadelphia, 1993, p 334
2. Jabbari M: Personal communication
3. Scharschmidt BF, Gollan JL: Current concepts of bilirubin metabolism and hereditary hyperbilirubinemia. Progress in Liver Diseases. Popper H, Schaffner F, Eds. Grune & Stratton, New York, 1979, p 187
4. Frank BB: Clinical evaluation of jaundice: a guideline of the Patient Care Committee of the American Gastroenterological Association. JAMA 262:3031, 1989
5. Schiff's Diseases of the Liver, 8th ed. Schiff ER, Sorrell MF, Maddrey WC, Eds. Lippincott-Raven, Philadelphia, 1999, p 119
6. Lindberg G, Björkman A, Helmers C: A description of diagnostic strategies in jaundice. Scand J Gastroenterol 18:257, 1983
7. Lumeng L, Snodgrass PJ, Swonder JW: Final report of a blinded prospective study comparing current non-invasive approaches in the differential diagnosis of medical and surgical jaundice. Gastroenterology 78:1312, 1980
8. Martin W, Apostolakos PC, Roazen H: Clinical versus actuarial prediction in the differential diagnosis of jaundice. Am J Med Sci 240:571, 1960
9. Matzen P, Malchow-Möller A, Hilden J, et al: Differential diagnosis of jaundice: a pocket diagnostic chart. Liver 4:360, 1984
10. O'Connor K, Snodgrass PJ, Swonder JE, et al: A blinded prospective study comparing four current non-invasive approaches in the differential diagnosis of medical versus surgical jaundice. Gastroenterology 84:1498, 1983
11. Schenker S, Balint J, Schiff L: Differential diagnosis of jaundice: report of a prospective study of 61 proved cases. Am J Dig Dis 7:449, 1962
12. Theodossi A, Spiegelhalter D, Portmann B, et al: The value of clinical, biochemical, ultrasound and liver biopsy data in assessing patients with liver disease. Liver 3:315, 1983
13. Pasanen PA, Pikkarainen P, Alhava E, et al: The value of clinical assessment in the diagnosis of icterus and cholestasis. Ital J Gastroenterol Hepatol 24:313, 1992
14. Theodossi A: The value of symptoms and signs in the assessment of jaundiced patients. Clin Gastroenterol 14:545, 1985
15. Fung KP, Lau SP: Differentiation between extrahepatic and intrahepatic cholestasis by discriminant analysis. J Paediatr Child Health 26:132, 1990
16. Pasanen PA, Pikkarainen P, Alhava E, et al: Evaluation of a computer-based diagnostic score system in the diagnosis of jaundice and cholesta-

sis. Scand J Gastroenterol 28:732, 1993

17. Malchow-Möller A, Gronvall S, Hilden J, et al: Ultrasound examination in jaundiced patients: is computer-assisted preclassification helpful? J Hepatol 12:321, 1991

18. Loperfido S, Angelini G, Benedetti G, et al: Major early complications from diagnostic and therapeutic ERCP: a prospective multicenter study. Gastrointest Endosc 48:1, 1998

19. Freeman ML, DiSario JA, Nelson DB, et al: Risk factors for post-ERCP pancreatitis: a prospective, multicenter study. Gastrointest Endosc 54:425, 2001

20. Lillemoe KD: Surgical treatment of biliary tract infections. Am Surg 66:138, 2000

21. NIH state-of-the-science statement on endoscopic retrograde cholangiopancreatography (ERCP) for diagnosis and therapy. NIH Consens State Sci Statements 19:1, 2002

22. Rossi LR, Traverso W, Pimentel F: Malignant obstructive jaundice: evaluation and management. Surg Clin North Am 76:63, 1996

23. Taylor KJW, Rosenfield A: Grey-scale ultrasonography in the differential diagnosis of jaundice. Arch Surg 112:820, 1977

24. Kaplun L, Weissman HS, Rosenblatt RR, et al: The early diagnosis of common bile duct obstruction using cholescintigraphy. JAMA 254:2431, 1985

25. Abboud PA, Malet PF, Berlin JA, et al: Predictors of common bile duct stones prior to cholecystectomy: a meta-analysis. Gastrointest Endosc 44:450, 1996

26. Roston AD, Jacobson IM: Evaluation of the pattern of liver tests and yield of cholangiography in symptomatic choledocholithiasis: a prospective study. Gastrointest Endosc 45:394, 1997

27. Richter JM, Silverstein MD, Schapiro R: Suspected obstructive jaundice: a decision analysis of diagnostic strategies. Ann Intern Med 99:46, 1983

28. Bravo AA, Sheth SG, Chopra S: Liver biopsy. N Engl J Med 344:495, 2001

29. Blackbourne LH, Earnhardt RC, Sistrom CL, et al: The sensitivity and role of ultrasound in the evaluation of biliary obstruction. Am Surg 60:683, 1994

30. Sherlock S: Ultrasound (US), computerized axial tomography (CT) and magnetic resonance imaging (MRI). Diseases of the Liver and Biliary System 5:70, 1989

31. Cosgrove DO: Ultrasound in surgery of the liver and biliary tract. Surgery of the Liver and Biliary Tract, 2nd ed, Vol 1. Blumgart LH, Ed. New York, Churchill Livingstone, 1994, p 189

32. Lindsell DRM: Ultrasound imaging of pancreas and biliary tract. Lancet 335:390, 1990

33. Gillams A, Gardener J, Richards R, et al: Three-dimensional computed tomography cholangiography: a new technique for biliary tract imaging. Br J Radiol 67:445, 1994

34. Low RN, Sigeti JS, Francis IR, et al: Evaluation of malignant biliary obstruction: efficacy of fast multiplanar spoiled gradient-recalled MR imaging vs spin-echo MR imaging, CT, and cholangiography. AJR Am J Roentgenol 162:315, 1994

35. Amouyal P, Amouyal G, Levy P, et al: Diagnosis of choledocholithiasis by endoscopic ultrasonography. Gastroenterology 106:1062, 1994

36. Guibaud L, Bret PM, Reinhold C, et al: Bile duct obstruction and choledocholithiasis: diagnosis with MR cholangiography. Radiology 197:109, 1995

37. Ishizaki Y, Wakayama T, Okada Y, et al: MR cholangiography for evaluation of obstructed jaundice. Am J Gastroenterol 88:2072, 1993

38. Bardou M, Romagnuolo J, Barkun AN, et al: Magnetic resonance cholangiopancreatography:

a meta-analysis of test performance in suspected biliary disease. Ann Intern Med 139:547, 2002

39. Mallery S, Van Dam J: Current status of diagnostic and therapeutic endoscopic ultrasonography. Radiol Clin North Am 39:449, 2001

40. Sugiyama M, Atomi Y, Hachiya J: Magnetic resonance cholangiography using half-Fourier acquisition for diagnosing choledocholithiasis. Am J Gastroenterol 93:1886, 1998

41. Jendresen MB, Thorboll JE, Adamsen S, et al: Preoperative routine magnetic resonance cholangiopancreatography before laparoscopic cholecystectomy: a prospective study. Eur J Surg 168:690, 2002

42. Soto JA, Alvarez O, Munera F, et al: Diagnosing bile duct stones: comparison of unenhanced helical CT, oral contrast-enhanced CT cholangiography, and MR cholangiography. AJR Am J Roentgenol 175:1127, 2000

43. Soto JA, Velez SM, Guzman J: Choledocholithiasis: diagnosis with oral-contrast-enhanced CT cholangiography. AJR Am J Roentgenol 172:943, 1999

44. Stabile Ianora AA, Memeo M, Scardapane A, et al. Oral contrast enhanced three-dimensional helical-CT cholangiography: clinical applications. Eur Radiol 13(4):867, 2003

45. Freeny PC: Computed tomography in the diagnosis and staging of cholangiocarcinoma and pancreatic carcinoma. Ann Oncol 10(suppl 4):12, 1999

46. Hawes RH, Xiong Q, Waxman I, et al: A multispecialty approach to the diagnosis and management of pancreatic cancer. Am J Gastroenterol 95:17, 2000

47. Megibow AJ, Lavelle MT, Rofsky NM: MR imaging of the pancreas. Surg Clin North Am 81:307, 2001

48. Lai EC, Mok FP, Tan ES, et al: Endoscopic biliary drainage for severe acute cholangitis. N Engl J Med 326:1582, 1992

49. Siperstein AE, Pearl J, Macho J, et al: Comparison of laparoscopic ultrasonography and fluorocholangiography in 300 patients undergoing laparoscopic cholecystectomy. Surg Endosc 13:967, 1999

50. Barkun JS, Fried GM, Barkun AN, et al: Cholecystectomy without operative cholangiography: implications for bile duct injury and common bile duct stones. Ann Surg 218:371, 1993

51. Sahai AV, Mauldin PD, Marsi V, et al: Bile duct stones and laparoscopic cholecystectomy: a decision analysis to assess the roles of intraoperative cholangiography, EUS, and ERCP. Gastrointest Endosc 49(3 pt 1):334, 1999

52. Abraham N, Barkun AN, Barkun JS, et al: What is the optimal management of patients with suspected choledocholithiasis in the era of laparoscopic cholecystectomy? a decision analysis. Gastroenterology 116:G0012, 1999

53. Tse F, Barkun JS, Barkun AN. The elective evaluation of patients with suspected choledocholithiasis undergoing laparoscopic cholecystectomy. Gastrointest Endosc 60:437, 2004

54. Erickson RA, Carlson B: The role of endoscopic retrograde cholangiopancreatography in patients with laparoscopic cholecystectomies. Gastroenterology 109:252, 1995

55. Urbach DR, Khajanchee YS, Jobe BA, et al: Cost-effective management of common bile duct stones: a decision analysis of the use of endoscopic retrograde cholangiopancreatography (ERCP), intraoperative cholangiography, and laparoscopic bile duct exploration. Surg Endosc 15:4, 2001

56. Memon MA, Hassaballa H, Memon MI: Laparoscopic common bile duct exploration: the past, the present, and the future. Am J Surg 179:309, 2000

57. Crawford DL, Phillips EH: Laparoscopic common bile duct exploration. World J Surg 23:343, 1999

58. Falcone RA Jr, Fegelman EJ, Nussbaum MS, et al: A prospective comparison of laparoscopic ultrasound vs intraoperative cholangiogram during laparoscopic cholecystectomy. Surg Endosc 13:784, 1999

59. Thompson DM, Arregui ME, Tetik C, et al: A comparison of laparoscopic ultrasound with digital fluorocholangiography for detecting choledocholithiasis during laparoscopic cholecystectomy. Surg Endosc 12:929, 1998

60. Wu JS, Dunnegan DL, Soper NJ: The utility of intracorporeal ultrasonography for screening of the bile duct during laparoscopic cholecystectomy. J Gastrointest Surg 2:50, 1998

61. Stroszczynski C, Hunerbein M: Malignant biliary obstruction: value of imaging findings. Abdom Imaging 30:314, 2005

62. Legmann P, Vignaux O, Dousset B, et al: Pancreatic tumors: comparison of dual-phase helical CT and endoscpic sonography. AJR Am J Roentgenol 170:1315, 1998

63. Freeny PC, Traverso LW, Ryan JA: Diagnosis and staging of pancreatic adenocarcinoma with dynamic computed tomography. Am J Surg 165:600, 1993

64. Moosa AR, Gamagami RA: Diagnosis and staging of pancreatic neoplasms. Surg Clin North Am 75:871, 1995

65. Megibow AJ, Zhou XH, Rotterdam H, et al: Pancreatic carcinoma: CT vs MR imaging in the evaluation of resectability. Radiology 195:327, 1995

66. Hann LE, Winston CB, Brown KT, et al: Diagnostic imaging approaches and relationship to hepatobiliary cancer staging and therapy. Semin Surg Oncol 19:94, 2000

67. Zidi SH, Prat F, Le Guen O, et al: Performance characteristics of magnetic resonance cholangiography in the staging of malignant hilar strictures. Gut 46:103, 2000

68. Kim MJ, Mitchell DG, Ito K, et al: Biliary dilatation: differentiation of benign from malignant causes—value of adding conventional MR imaging to MR cholangiopancreatography. Radiology 214:173, 2000

69. Georgopoulos SK, Schwartz LH, Jarnagin WR, et al: Comparison of magnetic resonance and endoscopic retrograde cholangiopancreatography in malignant pancreaticobiliary obstruction. Arch Surg 134:1002, 1999

70. McNulty N, Francis I, Platt J, et al: Multi-detector row helical CT of the pancreas: effect of contrast-enhanced multiphasic imaging on enhancement of the pancreas, peripancreatic vasculature, and pancreatic adenocarcinoma. Radiology 220:97, 2001

71. Smits NJ, Reeders JW: Current applicability of duplex Doppler ultrasonography in pancreatic head and biliary malignancies. Baillieres Clin Gastroenterol 9:153, 1995

72. Arslan A, Buanes T, Geitung JT: Pancreatic carcinoma: MR, MR angiography and dynamic helical CT in the evaluation of vascular invasion. Eur J Radiol 38:151, 2001

73. Giovannini M, Seitz JF: Endoscopic ultrasonography with a linear-type echoendoscope in the evaluation of 94 patients with pancreatobiliary disease. Endoscopy 26:579, 1994

74. Snady H, Cooperman A, Siegel J: Endoscopic ultrasonography compared with computed tomography and E.R.C.P. in patients with obstructive jaundice or small peri-pancreatic mass. Gastrointest Endoscopy 38:27, 1992

75. Nakaizumi A, Uehara H, Iishi H, et al: Endoscopic ultrasonography in diagnosis and staging of pancreatic cancer. Dig Dis Sci 40:696, 1995

76. Bakkevold KE, Arnesjo B, Kambestad B: Carcinoma of the pancreas and papilla of Vater—assessment of resectability and factors influencing resectability in stage I carcinomas: a prospective multicentre trial in 472 patients. Eur J Surg Oncol 18:494, 1992

77. DeWitt J, Devereaux B, Chiswell M, et al: Comparison of endoscopic ultrasonagraphy and multidetector computed tomography for detecting and staging pancreatic cancer. Ann Intern Med 141:753, 2004

78. Soriano A, Castells A, Ayuso C, et al: Preoperative staging and tumor resectability assessment of pancreatic cancer: prospective study comparing endoscopic ultrasonography, helical computed tomography, magnetic resonance imaging and angiography. Am J Gastroenterol 99:492, 2004.

79. Agarwal B, Abu-Hamda E, Molke KL, et al: Endoscopic Ultrasound-guided fine needle aspiration and multidetector spiral CT in the diagnosis of pancreatic cancer. Am J Gastroenterol 99:844, 2004

80. Cannon ME, Carpenter SL, Elta GH, et al: EUS compared with CT, magnetic resonance imaging, and angiography and the influence of biliary stenting on staging accuracy of ampullary neoplasms. Gastrointest Endosc 50:27, 1999

81. Brugge WR, Lauwers GY, Sahani D, et al: Current concepts: cystic neoplasms of the pancreas. N Engl J Med 351:1218, 2004

82. Keppke AL, Miller FH: Magnetic resonance imaging of the pancreas: the future is now. Semin Ultrasound CT MR 26:132, 2005

83. Delbeke D, Pinson CW: Pancreatic tumors: role of imaging in the diagnosis, staging and treatment. J Hepatobiliary Pancreat Surg 11:4, 2004

84. Heinrich S, Goerres G, Schafer M, et al: Positron emission tomography/computed tomography influences in the management of resectable pancreatic cancer and its cost-effectiveness. Ann Surg 242:235, 2005

85. Davidson BR: Progress in determining the nature of biliary strictures. Gut 34:725, 1993

86. Hawes RH: Endoscopy and non-calculus biliary obstruction. Annuals of Gastrointestinal Endoscopy, 8th ed. Cotton PB, Tytgat GNJ, Williams CB, Eds. Current Science, England, 1995, p 101

87. Baer HU, Rhyner M, Stain SC, et al: The effect of communication between the right and left liver on the outcome of surgical drainage from jaundice due to malignant obstruction at the hilus of the liver. HPB Surg 8:27, 1994

88. Rege RV: Adverse effects of biliary obstruction: implications for treatment of patients with obstructive jaundice. AJR Am J Roentgenol 164:287, 1995

89. Grande L, Garcia-Valdecasas JC, Fuster J, et al: Obstructive jaundice and wound healing. Br J Surg 77:440, 1990

90. Pitt HA, Gomes AS, Lois JF: Does preoperative percutaneous biliary drainage reduce operative risk or increase hospital cost? Ann Surg 201:545, 1985

91. McPherson GA, Benjamin IS, Hodgson HJ, et al: Preoperative percutaneous transhepatic biliary drainage: results of a controlled trial. Br J Surg 71:371, 1984

92. Povoski SP, Karpeh MS Jr, Conlon KC, et al: Preoperative biliary drainage: impact on intraoperative bile cultures and infectious morbidity and mortality after pancreaticoduodenectomy. J Gastrointest Surg 3:496, 1999

93. Sohn TA, Yeo CJ, Cameron JL, et al: Do preoperative biliary stents increase postpancreaticoduodenectomy complications? J Gastrointest Surg 4:258, 2000

94. Jarnagin WR, Bodniewicz J, Dougherty E, et al: A prospective analysis of staging laparoscopy in patients with primary and secondary hepatobiliary malignancies. J Gastrointest Surg 4:34, 2000

95. Abraham N, Barkun J, Barkun AN, et al: Clinical risk factors of plastic biliary stent obstruction: a prospective trial. Am J Gastroenterol 95:2471, 2000

96. Knyrim K, Wagner HJ, Pausch J, et al: A prospective, randomized controlled trial of metal stents for malignant obstruction of the common bile duct. Endoscopy 25:207, 1993

97. Davids P, Groen A, Rauws E, et al: Randomized trial of self-expanding metal stents versus polyethylene stents for distal malignant biliary obstruction. Lancet 340:1488, 1992

98. Prat F, Chapat O, Ducot B, et al: A randomized trial of endoscopic drainage methods for inoperable malignant strictures of the common bile duct. Gastrointest Endosc 47:1, 1998

99. Chan G, Barkun J, Barkun AN, et al: The role of ciprofloxacin in prolonging polyethylene biliary stent patency: a multicenter, double-blinded effectiveness study. J Gastrointest Surg 9:481, 2005

100. Smith AC, Dowsett JF, Russell RC, et al: Randomized trial of endoscopic stenting vs surgical bypass in malignant low bile duct obstruction. Lancet 344:1655, 1994

101. Lillemoe KD, Sauter P, Pitt HA, et al: Current status of surgical palliation of periampullary carcinoma. Surg Gynecol Obstet 176:1, 1993

102. Van Heek NT, De Castro SM, Van Eijck CH, et al: Need for a prophylactic gastrojejunostomy for unresectable periampullary cancer: a propsective randomized multicenter trial with special focus on assessment of quality of life. Ann Surg 238:894, 2003

103. Lillemoe KD, Cameron JL, Kaufman HS, et al: Chemical splanchnicectomy in patients with unresectable pancreatic cancer: a prospective randomized trial. Ann Surg 217:447, 1993

104. Lillemoe KD, Cameron JL, Yeo CJ, et al: Pancreaticoduodenectomy: does it have a role in the palliation of pancreatic cancer? Ann Surg 223:718, 1996

105. D'Angelica M, Fong Y, Weber S, et al: The role of staging laparoscopy in hepatobiliary malignancy: prospective analysis of 401 cases. Ann Surg Oncol 10:183, 2003

106. Conlon KC, Dougherty E, Klimstra DS, et al: The value of minimal access surgery in the staging of patients with potentially resectable pancreatic malignancy. Ann Surg 223:134, 1996

107. John TG, Greig JD, Carter DC, et al: Carcinoma of the pancreatic head and periampullary region: tumor staging with laparoscopy and laparoscopic ultrasonography. Ann Surg 221:156, 1995

108. Jarnagin WR, Bodniewicz J, Dougherty E, et al: A prospective analysis of staging laparoscopy in patients with primary and secondary hepatobiliary malignancies. J Gastrointest Surg 4:34, 2000

109. Hunerbein M, Rau B, Schlag PM: Laparoscopic ultrasound for staging of upper gastrointestinal tumours. Eur J Surg Oncol 21:50, 1995

110. Scott-Conner CE: Laparoscopic biliary bypass for inoperable pancreatic cancer. Semin Laparosc Surg 5:185, 1998

111. Date RS, Siriwardena AK: Current status of laparoscopic biliary bypass in the management of non-resectable peri-ampullary cancer. Pancreatology 5:325, 2005.

112. Chamberlain RS, Blumgart LH: Hilar cholangiocarcinoma: a review and commentary. Ann Surg Oncol 7:55, 2000

113. Ogura Y, Kawarada Y: Surgical strategies for carcinoma of the hepatic duct confluence. Br J Surg 85:20, 1998

114. Jarnagin W, Shoup M. Surgical management of cholangiocarcinoma. Seminars in liver disease 24:189, 2004

115. Bartlett D: Gallbladder cancer. Semin Surg Oncol 19:145, 2000

116. Baer HU, Matthews JB, Schweizer WP, et al: Management of the Mirizzi syndrome and the surgical implications of cholecystocholedochal fistula. Br J Surg 77:743, 1990

117. Sarfeh MG, Rypins EB, Jakowatz JG, et al: A prospective, randomized clinical investigation of cholecystoenterostomy and choledochoenterostomy. Am J Surg 155:411, 1988

118. Kalady MF, Clary BM, Tyler DS, Pappas TN. Pancreas-preserving duodenectomy in the management of duodenal familial adenomatous polyposis. J Gastrointest Surg 6:82, 2002

119. Lieberman MD, Kilburn H, Lindsey M, et al: Relation of perioperative deaths to hospital volume among patients undergoing pancreatic resection for malignancy. Ann Surg 222:638, 1995

120. Lamont JT, Isselbacher KJ: Current concepts of postoperative hepatic dysfunction. Conn Med 39:461, 1975

121. Matlof DS, Kaplan MM: Postoperative jaundice. Orthop Clin North Am 9:799, 1978

122. Moody FG, Potts JR III: Postoperative jaundice. Diseases of the Liver, 7th ed. Schiff L, Schiff ER, Eds. JB Lippincott Co, Philadelphia, 1993, p 370

123. Isselbacher KJ: Bilirubin metabolism and hyperbilirubinemia. Harrison's Principles of Internal Medicine, 12th ed. Wilson JD, Braunwald E, Isselbacher KJ, et al, Eds. McGraw-Hill, New York, 1991, p 1320

124. Watson CJ: Prognosis and treatment of hepatic insufficiency. Ann Intern Med 31:405, 1959

125. Sherlock S: Jaundice. Diseases of the Liver and Biliary System, 8th ed. Sherlock S, Ed. Blackwell Scientific Publications, Oxford, 1989, p 230

126. Gollan JL, Keefe EB, Scharschmidt BF: Cholestasis and hyperbilirubinemia. Current Hepatology, Vol I. Gitnick G, Ed. Houghton Mifflin, Boston, 1980, p 277

127. Bosma PJ, Chowdhury JR, Bakker C, et al: The genetic basis of the reduced expression of bilirubin UCP-glucuronosyltransferase 1 in Gilbert's syndrome. N Engl J Med 333:1171, 1995

128. O'Grady JG, Portmann B, Williams R: Fulminant hepatic failure. Diseases of the Liver, 7th ed. Schiff L, Schiff ER, Eds. JB Lippincott Co, Philadelphia, 1993, p 1077

129. Bismuth H, Samuel D, Castaing D, et al: Orthotopic liver transplantation in fulminant and subfulminant hepatitis. Ann Surg 222:109, 1995

130. Boyer JL, Reuben A: Chronic hepatitis. Diseases of the Liver, 7th ed. Schiff L, Schiff ER, Eds. JB Lippincott Co, Philadelphia, 1993, p 586

131. Pugh RN, Murray-Lyon IM, Dawson JL, et al: Transection of the esophagus for bleeding esophageal varices. Br J Surg 60:646, 1973

132. Kamath PS, Wiesner RH, Malinchoc M, et al: A model to predict survival in patients with end-stage liver disease. Hepatology 33:464, 2001

133. Fallon MB, Anderson JM, Boyer JL: Intrahepatic cholestasis. Diseases of the Liver, 7th ed. Schiff L, Schiff ER, Eds. JB Lippincott Co, Philadelphia, 1993, p 343

Acknowledgment

Figure 2c From *MRI of the Abdomen and Pelvis: A Text-Atlas*, by R. C. Semelka, S. M. Asher, and C. Reinhold. John Wiley and Sons, New York, 1997. Used with permission.

46 INTESTINAL OBSTRUCTION

W. Scott Helton, M.D., F.A.C.S., and Piero M. Fisichella, M.D.

Assessment of Intestinal Obstruction

Intestinal obstruction is a common medical problem and accounts for a large percentage of surgical admissions for acute abdominal pain [*see 43 Acute Abdominal Pain*].[1] It develops when air and secretions are prevented from passing aborally as a result of either intrinsic or extrinsic compression (i.e., mechanical obstruction) or gastrointestinal paralysis (i.e., nonmechanical obstruction in the form of ileus or pseudo-obstruction). Small intestinal ileus is the most common form of intestinal obstruction; it occurs after most abdominal operations and is a common response to acute extra-abdominal medical conditions and intra-abdominal inflammatory conditions [*see Table 1*].[2] Mechanical small bowel obstruction is somewhat less common; such obstruction is secondary to intra-abdominal adhesions, hernias, or cancer in about 90% of cases [*see Table 2*]. Mechanical colonic obstruction accounts for only 10% to 15% of all cases of mechanical obstruction and most often develops in response to obstructing carcinoma, diverticulitis, or volvulus [*see Table 3*]. Acute colonic pseudo-obstruction occurs most frequently in the postoperative period or in response to another acute medical illness.

There are several different methods of classifying mechanical obstruction: acute versus chronic, partial versus complete, simple versus closed-loop, and gangrenous versus nongangrenous. The importance of these classifications is that the natural history of the condition, its response to treatment, and the associated morbidity and mortality all vary according to which type of obstruction is present.

When chyme and gas can traverse the point of obstruction, obstruction is partial; when this is not the case, obstruction is complete. When the bowel is occluded at a single point along the intestinal tract, leading to intestinal dilatation, hypersecretion, and bacterial overgrowth proximal to the obstruction and decompression distal to the obstruction, simple obstruction is present. When a segment of bowel is occluded at two points along its course by a single constrictive lesion that occludes both the proximal and the distal end of the intestinal loop as well as traps the bowel's mesentery, closed-loop obstruction is present. When the blood supply to a closed-loop segment of bowel becomes compromised, leading to ischemia and eventually to bowel wall necrosis and perforation, strangulation is present. The most common causes of simple obstruction are intra-abdominal adhesions, tumors, and strictures; the most common causes of closed-loop obstruction are hernias, adhesions, and volvulus.

One of the most difficult tasks in general surgery is deciding when to operate on a patient with intestinal obstruction. The purpose of the following discussion is to outline a safe, efficient, and cost-effective stepwise approach to making this often difficult decision and to optimizing the management of patients with this problem. Absolutes are few and far between: treatment must always be highly individualized. Consequently, the following recommendations are intended only as guidelines, not as surgical dicta.

Clinical Evaluation

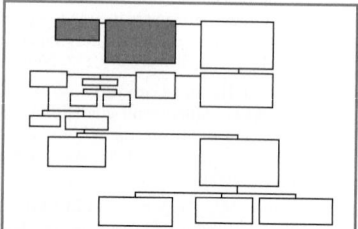

HISTORY AND CLINICAL SETTING

When a patient complains of acute obstipation, abdominal pain and distention, nausea, and vomiting, the probability that either mechanical bowel obstruction or ileus is present is very high.[3] Mechanical obstruction can often be distinguished from ileus or pseudo-obstruction on the basis of the location, character, and severity of abdominal pain. Pain from mechanical obstruction is usually located in the middle of the abdomen, whereas pain from ileus and pseudo-obstruction is diffuse. Pain from ileus is usually mild, and pain from obstruction is typically more severe. In general, pain increases in severity and depth over time as obstruction progresses; however, in mechanical obstruction, pain severity may decrease over time as a result of bowel fatigue and atony. The periodicity of pain can help localize the level of obstruction: pain from proximal intestinal obstruction has a short periodicity (3 to 4 minutes), and distal small bowel or colonic pain has longer intervals (15 to 20 minutes) between episodes of nausea, cramping, and vomiting.

Abdominal distention, nausea, and vomiting usually develop after pain has already been felt for some time. The patient should be asked what degree of abdominal distention is present and whether there has been a sudden or rapid change. Distention developing over many weeks suggests a chronic process or progressive partial obstruction. Massive abdominal distention coupled with minimal crampy pain, nausea, and vomiting suggests long-standing intermittent mechanical obstruction or some form of chronic intestinal pseudo-obstruction. The combination of a gradual change in bowel habits, progressive abdominal distention, early satiety, mild crampy pain after meals, and weight loss also suggests chronic partial mechanical bowel obstruction. If the patient has undergone evaluation for similar symptoms before, any previous abdominal radiographs or contrast studies should be reviewed. The patient should be asked when flatus was last passed: failure to pass flatus may signal a transition from partial to complete bowel obstruction. Patients with an intestinal stoma (ileostomy or colostomy) who present with signs and symptoms of obstruction often report abdominal distention and pain after a sudden change in stomal output of stool, liquid, or air.

The patient should also be asked about (1) previous episodes of bowel obstruction, (2) previous abdominal or pelvic operations, (3) a history of abdominal cancer, and (4) a history of intra-abdominal inflammation (e.g., inflammatory bowel disease, cholecystitis, pancreatitis, pelvic inflammatory disease, or abdominal trauma). Any of these factors increases the chance that the obstruction is secondary to an adhesion or recurrent cancer. Obstructive symptoms that come and go suddenly over several days in a patient older than 65 years should increase the index of suspicion for gallstone ileus.[4]

Table 1 Causes of Ileus

Intra-abdominal causes
  Intraperitoneal problems
    Peritonitis or abscess
    Inflammatory condition
      Mechanical: operation, foreign body
      Chemical: gastric juice, bile, blood
      Autoimmune: serositis, vasculitis
    Intestinal ischemia: arterial or venous, sickle-cell disease
  Retroperitoneal problems
    Pancreatitis
    Retroperitoneal hematoma
    Spine fracture
    Aortic operation
    Renal colic
    Pyelonephritis
    Metastasis

Extra-abdominal causes
  Thoracic problems
    Myocardial infarction
    Pneumonia
    Congestive heart failure
    Rib fractures
  Metabolic abnormalities
    Electrolyte imbalance (e.g., hypokalemia)
    Sepsis
    Lead poisoning
    Porphyria
    Hypothyroidism
    Hypoparathyroidism
    Uremia
  Medicines
    Opiates
    Anticholinergics
    Alpha agonists
    Antihistamines
    Catecholamines
  Spinal cord injury or operations
  Head, thoracic, or retroperitoneal trauma
  Chemotherapy, radiation therapy

gic side effects. Patients who are receiving chemotherapy or have undergone abdominal radiation therapy are prone to ileus. Severe infection, fluid and electrolyte imbalances, narcotic and anticholinergic medications, and intra-abdominal inflammation of any origin may be implicated. Acute massive abdominal distention in a hospitalized patient usually results from acute gastric distention, small bowel ileus, or acute colonic pseudo-obstruction. Excessive anticoagulation can lead to retroperitoneal, intra-abdominal, or intramural hematoma that can cause mechanical obstruction or ileus. Finally, there are specific problems that tend to arise in the postoperative period; these are discussed more fully elsewhere [*see* Urgent Operation, Early Postoperative Technical Complications, *and* No Operation, Early Postoperative Obstruction, *below*].

PHYSICAL EXAMINATION
AND RESUSCITATION

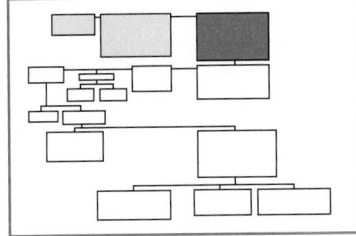

The initial steps in the physical examination are (1) developing a gestalt of the patient's illness and (2) assessing the patient's vital signs, hydration status, and cardiopulmonary system. A nasogastric tube, a Foley catheter, and an I.V. line are placed immediately while the physical examination is in progress. The volume and character of the gastric aspirate and urine are noted. A clear, gastric effluent is suggestive of gastric outlet obstruction. A bilious, nonfeculent aspirate is a typical sign of medial to proximal small bowel obstruction or colonic obstruction

Table 2 Causes of Small Bowel Obstruction in Adults

Extrinsic causes
  Adhesions*
  Hernias (external, internal [paraduodenal], incisional)*
  Metastatic cancer*
  Volvulus
  Intra-abdominal abscess
  Intra-abdominal hematoma
  Pancreatic pseudocyst
  Intra-abdominal drains
  Tight fascial opening at stoma

Intraluminal causes
  Tumors*
  Gallstones
  Foreign body
  Worms
  Bezoars

Intramural abnormalities
  Tumors
  Strictures
  Hematoma
  Intussusception
  Regional enteritis
  Radiation enteritis

*Approximately 85% of all small bowel obstructions are secondary to adhesions, hernias, or tumors.

If the patient has experienced episodes of obstruction before, one should ask about the etiology and the response to treatment. If the patient has ever undergone an abdominal operation, one should try to obtain and read the operative report, which can provide a great deal of helpful information (e.g., description of adhesions, assessment of their severity, and evaluation of intra-abdominal pathology and anatomy). If abdominal cancer was present, one should find out what operation was performed and attempt to determine the likelihood of intra-abdominal recurrence.

The clinical setting often provides clues to the cause and type of bowel obstruction. In hospitalized patients, there is likely to be an associated medical condition or metabolic derangement that led to obstruction. A thorough review of the patient's medical history and hospital course should be undertaken to identify precipitating events that could have led to intestinal obstipation. One should ask the patient about any previous abdominal irradiation and should note and take into account all medications the patient is taking, especially anticoagulants and agents with anticholiner-

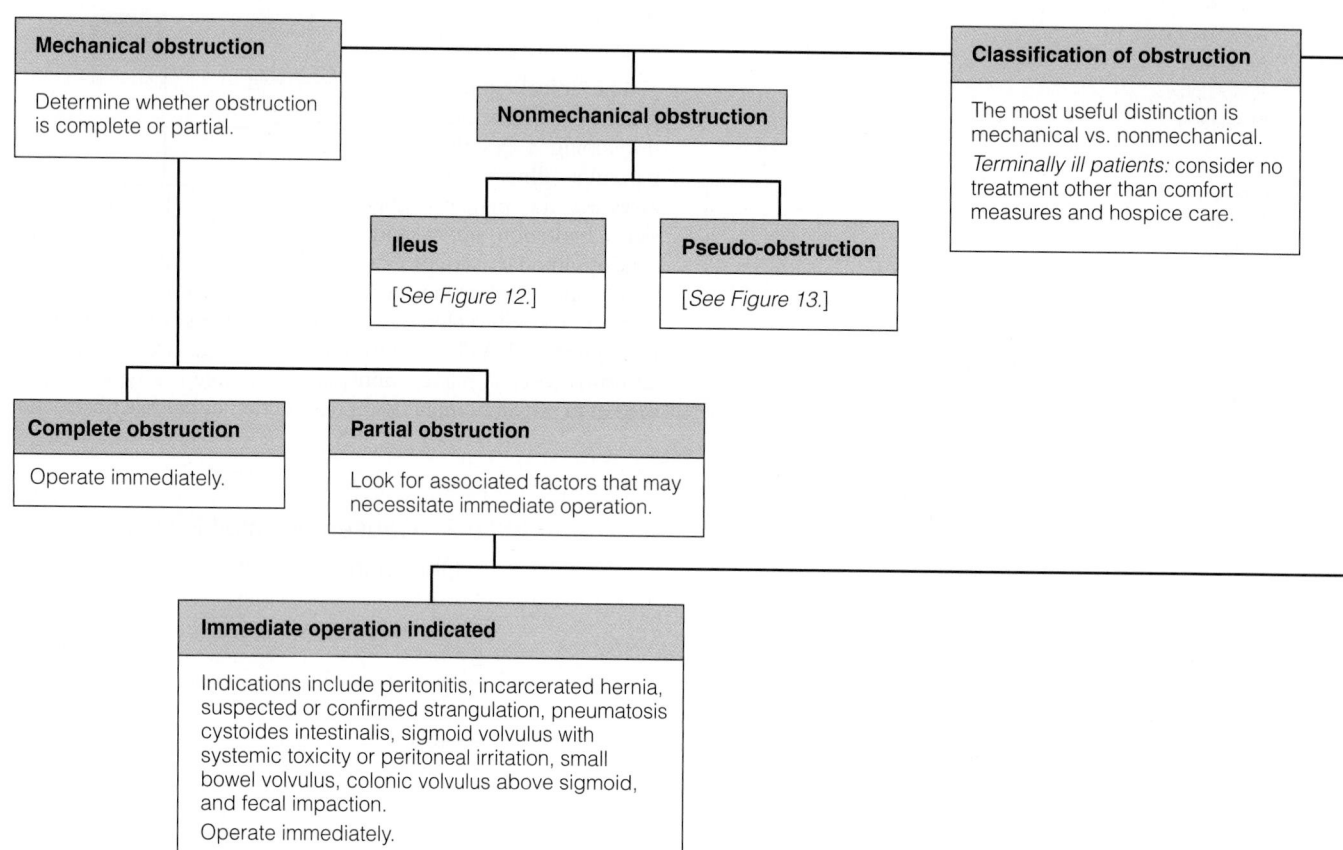

Signs and symptoms of intestinal obstruction

Signs and symptoms include abdominal pain or distention, nausea, vomiting, and obstipation.

Clinical history

Assess character, severity, location, and periodicity of pain.

Assess degree of abdominal distention, and ask about any sudden or rapid changes.

Ask about changes in bowel habits, weight loss, and last passage of flatus.

Ask about (1) previous obstruction, (2) previous abdominal or pelvic procedures, (3) abdominal cancer, (4) intra-abdominal inflammation.

Consider clinical setting: ask about medical conditions or metabolic derangements, exposure to radiation, all medications. Immediate postoperative state is special situation.

Mechanical obstruction

Determine whether obstruction is complete or partial.

Nonmechanical obstruction

Classification of obstruction

The most useful distinction is mechanical vs. nonmechanical.

Terminally ill patients: consider no treatment other than comfort measures and hospice care.

Ileus

[*See Figure 12.*]

Pseudo-obstruction

[*See Figure 13.*]

Complete obstruction

Operate immediately.

Partial obstruction

Look for associated factors that may necessitate immediate operation.

Immediate operation indicated

Indications include peritonitis, incarcerated hernia, suspected or confirmed strangulation, pneumatosis cystoides intestinalis, sigmoid volvulus with systemic toxicity or peritoneal irritation, small bowel volvulus, colonic volvulus above sigmoid, and fecal impaction.

Operate immediately.

Assessment of Intestinal Obstruction

Urgent operation

Indications include
- Lack of response to 24–48 hr of nonoperative therapy (increasing abdominal pain, distention, or tenderness; NG aspirate changing from nonfeculent to feculent; ↑ proximal small bowel distention with ↓ distal gas).
- Early technical complications of operation (abscess, phlegmon, hematoma, hernia, intussusception, anastomotic obstruction).

Physical exam and resuscitate as necessary

Develop gestalt of patient's illness, and assess patient's vital signs, hydration, and cardiopulmonary system.

Place NG tube, Foley catheter, and I.V. line immediately. Assess volume and character of NG aspirate, and measure urine output.

Replace lost fluid with isotonic saline or lactated Ringer solution. Look for signs of abscess, pneumonia, or myocardial infarction, and be alert for dyspnea, labored breathing, or jaundice.

Perform systematic abdominal examination: observation → auscultation → palpation and percussion. Look for abdominal masses, tenderness, incisions, and hernias; assess bowel sounds; examine rectum for masses, fecal impaction, and occult blood.

Investigative studies

Obtain chest x-rays and abdominal films.

If uncertainty about presence or nature of colonic obstruction remains, perform sigmoidoscopy and barium enema examination.

Measure serum electrolytes and creatinine, determine hematocrit, and order coagulation profile. If ileus is suspected, measure serum magnesium and calcium and order urinalysis.

Perform CT (with oral or I.V. contrast agents), fast MRI, or abdominal ultrasonography.

Immediate operation not indicated

Manage initially with nonoperative measures.

Reassess patient every 4 hr.

For partial obstruction, administer oral diatrizoate meglumine.

Look for changes in pain, abdominal findings, and volume and character of NG aspirate.

Repeat abdominal x-rays, and look for changes in gas distribution, pneumatosis cystoides intestinalis, and free intraperitoneal air.

Classify patient's condition as improved, unchanged, or worse.

Decide whether operative treatment is necessary and, if so, whether it should be done on urgent or elective basis.

Arrival of contrast agent in right colon within 24 hr is highly predictive of successful resolution of adhesive obstruction without operation.

No operation

Conditions that typically resolve with nonoperative therapy include adhesive obstruction (unless it does not improve in 12 hr), early postoperative obstruction (unless it does not improve in 2 wk), and various inflammatory conditions (IBD, radiation enteritis, diverticulitis, acute Crohn disease).

Elective operation

Indications include nontoxic, nontender sigmoid volvulus with sigmoidoscopically managed obstruction; recurrent adhesive or stricture-related small bowel obstruction; partial colonic obstruction unresponsive to 24 hr of nonoperative therapy; development and resolution of small bowel obstruction in patient who has never undergone abdominal operation.

Table 3 Causes of Colonic Obstruction

Common causes
   Cancer (primary, anastomotic, metastatic)
   Volvulus
   Diverticulitis
   Pseudo-obstruction
   Hernia
   Anastomotic stricture

Unusual causes
   Intussusception
   Fecal impaction
   Strictures (from one of the following)
     Inflammatory bowel disease
     Endometriosis
     Radiation therapy
     Ischemia
   Foreign body
   Extrinsic compression by a mass
     Pancreatic pseudocyst
     Hematoma
     Metastasis
     Primary tumors

with a competent ileocecal valve. A feculent aspirate is a typical sign of distal small bowel obstruction. Volume replacement, if necessary, is initiated with isotonic saline solution or lactated Ringer solution. Urine output must be adequate (at least 0.5 ml/kg/hr) before the patient can be taken to the OR; supplemental potassium chloride (40 mEq/L) is administered once this is achieved.

Fever may be present, suggesting that the obstruction may be a manifestation of an intra-abdominal abscess. Signs of pneumonia or myocardial infarction should be sought: these conditions, like intestinal obstruction, can have upper abdominal pain, distention, nausea, and vomiting as presenting symptoms. Dyspnea and labored breathing may occur secondary to severe abdominal distention or pain, in which case immediate relief should be provided by placing the patient in the lateral decubitus position and offering narcotics as soon as the initial physical examination is performed. Jaundice raises the possibility of gallstone ileus or metastatic cancer.

Examination of the abdomen proceeds in an orderly manner from observation to auscultation to palpation and percussion. The patient is placed in the supine position with the legs flexed at the hip to decrease tension on the rectus muscles. The degree of abdominal distention observed varies, depending on the level of obstruction: proximal obstructions may cause little or no distention. Abdominal scars should be noted. Abdominal asymmetry or a protruding mass suggests an underlying malignancy, an abscess, or closed-loop obstruction. The abdominal wall should be observed for evidence of peristaltic waves, which are indicative of acute small bowel obstruction.

Auscultation should be performed for at least 3 to 4 minutes to determine the presence and quality of bowel sounds. High-pitched bowel tones, tingles, and rushes are suggestive of an obstructive process, especially when temporally associated with waves of crampy pain, nausea, or vomiting. The absence of bowel tones is typical of intestinal paralysis but may also indicate intestinal fatigue from long-standing obstruction, closed-loop obstruction, or pseudo-obstruction.

Approximately 70% of patients with bowel obstruction have symmetrical tenderness, whereas fewer than 50% have rebound tenderness, guarding, or rigidity.[3] The traditional teaching is that localized tenderness and guarding indicate underlying strangulated bowel; however, prospective studies have demonstrated that these physical findings are neither specific nor sensitive for detecting underlying strangulation[5] or even obstruction.[3] Nevertheless, most surgeons still believe that guarding, rebound tenderness, and localized tenderness reflect underlying strangulation and therefore are indications for operation. Patients with ileus tend to have generalized abdominal tenderness that cannot be distinguished from the tenderness of mechanical obstruction. Gentle percussion is performed over all quadrants of the abdomen to search for areas of dullness (suggestive of an underlying mass), tympany (suggestive of underlying distended bowel), and peritoneal irritation.

A thorough search is made for inguinal, femoral, umbilical, and incisional hernias. The rectum is examined for masses, fecal impaction, and occult blood. If the patient has an ileostomy or a colostomy, the stoma is examined digitally to make sure that there is no obstruction at the level of the fascia.

Investigative Studies

IMAGING

One should obtain a chest x-ray in all patients with bowel obstruction to exclude a pneumonic process and to look for subdiaphragmatic

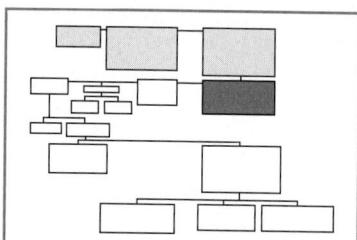

air. In most cases, supine, upright, or lateral decubitus films of the abdomen can distinguish the type of obstruction present (mechanical or nonmechanical, partial or complete) and establish the location of the obstruction (stomach, small bowel, or colon). A useful technique for evaluating abdominal radiographs is to look systematically for intestinal gas along the normal route of the GI tract, beginning at the stomach, continuing through the small bowel, and, finally, following the course of the colon to the rectum. The following questions should be kept in mind as this is done.

- Are there abnormally dilated loops of bowel, signs of small bowel dilatation, or air-fluid levels?
- Are air-fluid levels and bowel loops in the same place on supine and upright films?
- Is there gas throughout the entire length of the colon (suggestive of ileus or partial mechanical obstruction)?
- Is there a paucity of distal colonic gas or an abrupt cutoff of colonic gas with proximal colonic distention and air-fluid levels (suggestive of complete or near-complete colonic obstruction)?
- Is there evidence of strangulation (e.g., thickened small bowel loops, mucosal thumb printing, pneumatosis cystoides intestinalis, or free peritoneal air)?
- Is there massive distention of the colon, especially of the cecum or sigmoid (suggestive of either volvulus or pseudo-obstruction)?
- Are there any biliary or renal calculi, and is there any air in the biliary tree (suggestive of gallstone ileus[6] or a renal stone that could be causing ileus)?

It is important to be able to distinguish between small and large bowel gas. Gas in a distended small bowel outlines the valvulae conniventes, which traverse the entire diameter of the bowel lumen [see Figure 1]. Gas in a distended colon, on the other hand, outlines the colonic haustral markings, which cross only part of the bowel lumen and typically interdigitate [see Figures 2 and 3]. Distended

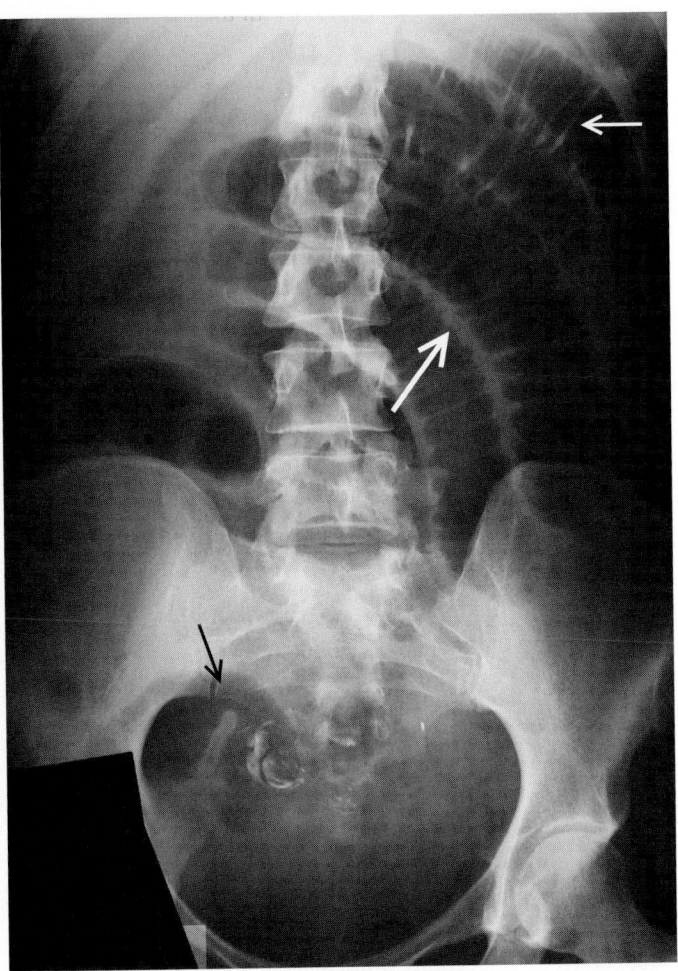

Figure 1 Supine radiograph from a patient with complete small bowel obstruction shows distended small bowel loops in the central abdomen with prominent valvulae conniventes (small white arrow). Bowel wall between the loops is thickened and edematous (large white arrow). No air is seen in the colon or the rectum. Note the presence of an isolated small bowel loop in the right lower quadrant (black arrow), which is seen fixed in the same location on upright films, as shown in Figure 4.

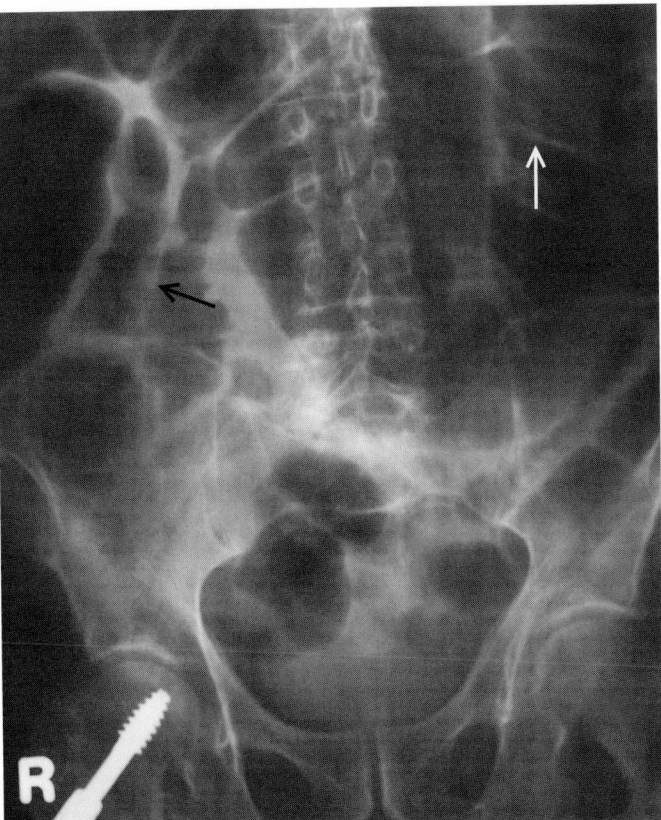

Figure 2 Radiograph from a patient with acute colonic pseudo-obstruction shows a dilated colon with haustral markings (white arrow) and edematous small bowel loops (black arrow). Air extends down to the distal sigmoid. This picture is also consistent with rectal obstruction, which could have been excluded by rigid sigmoidoscopy.

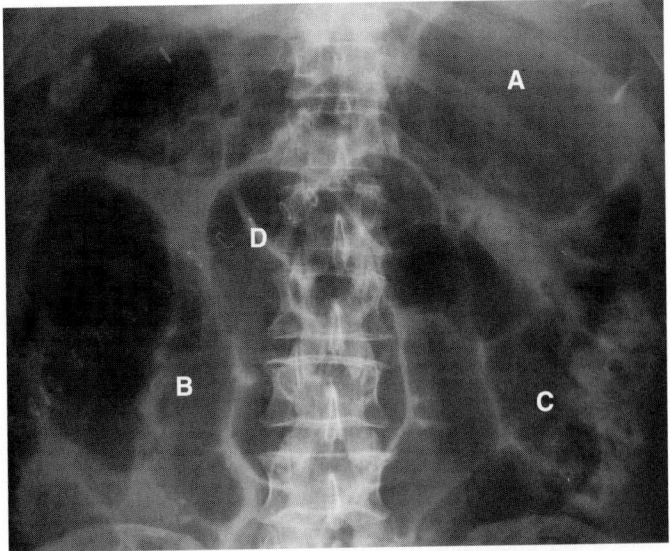

Figure 3 Radiograph from a patient with postoperative ileus shows massive gastric distention (A), distended small bowel loops (B), air throughout the colon, mild dilatation of the sigmoid colon (C) with air mixed with stool, and a haustral fold in the apex of the sigmoid colon (D).

small bowel loops usually occupy the central abdomen [*see Figure 1*], whereas distended large bowel loops are typically seen around the periphery [*see Figure 2*]. In patients with ileus, distention usually extends uniformly throughout the stomach, the small bowel, and the colon [*see Figure 3*], and air-fluid levels may be found in the colon and the small intestine.

Patients with gastric outlet obstruction or gastric atony typically have a giant gastric bubble if no nasogastric tube has been placed, with little or no air in the small bowel or the colon. Patients with mechanical small bowel obstruction usually have multiple air-fluid levels, with distended bowel loops of varying sizes arranged in an inverted U configuration [*see Figure 4*]. A dilated loop of small bowel appearing in the same location on supine and upright films suggests obstruction of a fixed segment of bowel by an adhesion or an internal hernia [*see Figures 1 and 4*]. Small bowel obstruction is often accompanied by a paucity of gas in the colon. The complete absence of colonic gas is strongly suggestive of complete small bowel obstruction; however, the presence of colonic gas does not exclude complete small bowel obstruction, in that there may have been unevacuated gas distal

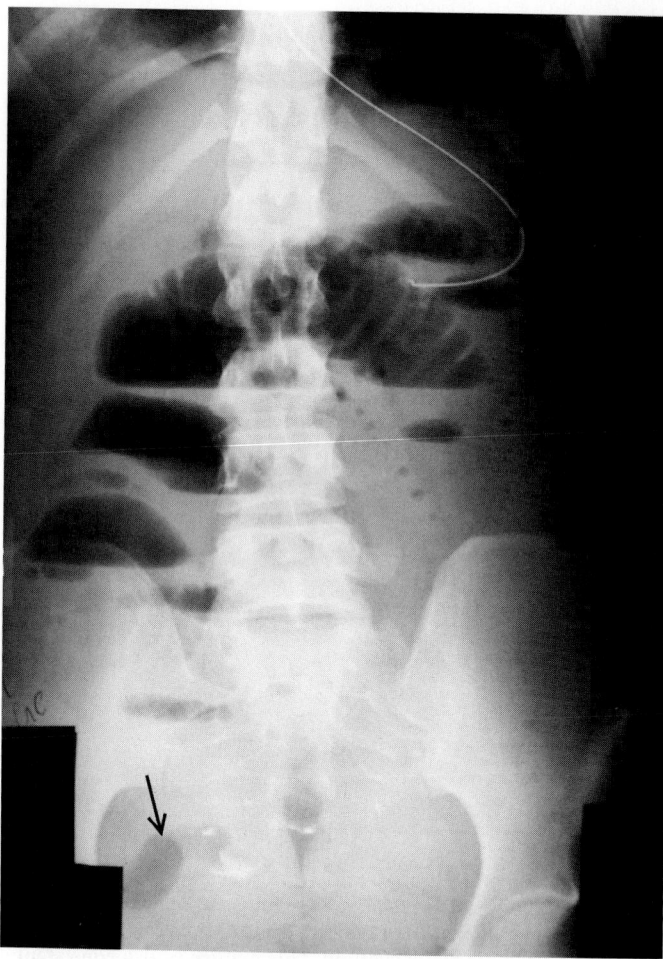

Figure 4 **Upright radiograph from the same patient as the supine radiograph in Figure 1 shows multiple air-fluid levels of varying size arranged in inverted Us. In the right lower pelvis, a loop of small bowel is seen in exactly the same location as on the supine abdominal film (black arrow), a finding suggestive of adhesive obstruction.**

to a point of complete obstruction before the radiograph was taken. On the other hand, if repeat radiographs demonstrate decreased or absent colonic or rectal gas in a patient with small bowel obstruction who previously had more colonic or rectal gas, it is probable that partial obstruction has become complete, and immediate operation is almost always indicated. High-grade obstruction of the colon with an incompetent ileocecal valve may manifest itself as distended small bowel loops with air-fluid levels, thereby mimicking small bowel obstruction. Hence, it is sometimes necessary to perform a barium enema to exclude colonic obstruction.

Massive gaseous distention of the colon is usually secondary to distal colonic or rectal obstruction, volvulus, or pseudo-obstruction [see Figures 2, 5, 6, and 7]. There are well-defined radiographic criteria that are highly sensitive and specific for sigmoid volvulus.[6] If there is any uncertainty regarding the presence, type, or level of colonic obstruction, immediate sigmoidoscopy followed by barium enema is diagnostic.

LABORATORY TESTS

Serum electrolyte concentrations, the hematocrit, the serum

creatinine concentration, and the coagulation profile (prothrombin time [or international normalized ratio—INR] and platelet count) are helpful in determining the severity of volume depletion and guiding resuscitative efforts. If ileus is suspected, serum magnesium and calcium levels should be measured, and urinalysis should be done to check for hematuria.

Determination of Need for Operation and Classification of Obstruction

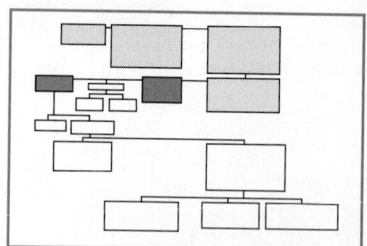

The combination of a thorough history, a carefully performed physical examination, and correctly interpreted abdominal radiographs usually allows one to identify the type of bowel obstruction present and to decide whether a patient requires immediate, urgent, or delayed operation [see Table 4] or can safely be treated initially with nonoperative measures. To this end, it is particularly important and useful to stratify patients into those with mechanical obstruction and those with nonmechanical obstruction. In patients with mechanical bowel obstruction, an effort should be made to determine whether the obstruction is complete or partial. Except for a few clinical situations, patients with complete bowel obstruction require immediate operation; conversely, patients with partial bowel obstruction rarely do. Finally, an effort should be made to establish the level and cause of obstruction because these factors often help guide therapy and affect the probability of success in response to specific therapeutic intervention. Patients with nonmechanical obstruction, which derives from ileus or pseudo-obstruction [see Ileus and Pseudo-obstruction, below], do not require immediate operation.

ADJUNCTIVE TESTS FOR EQUIVOCAL SITUATIONS

Sigmoidoscopy

When one is uncertain whether the obstruction is mechanical or not on the basis of the information in hand, additional diagnostic measures are immediately indicated. When large amounts of colonic air extend down to the rectum, flexible or rigid sigmoidoscopy will readily exclude a rectal or distal sigmoid obstruction. Care must be exercised to avoid insufflating large amounts of air during endoscopy: excessive insufflation can cause overdistention of the colon above the level of the possible obstruction, which can be counterproductive and harmful. If sigmoidoscopy yields normal findings but partial colonic obstruction seems to be the correct diagnosis, a water-soluble contrast enema should be administered.[7] Barium studies may be harmful in patients with acute obstruction when they are performed before the nature of the obstruction (complete or partial) is determined. Abdominal ultrasonography, though not as definitive as a contrast examination, is also able to diagnose suspected colonic obstruction in 85% of patients.[8]

Ultrasonography, Computed Tomography, and Fast Magnetic Resonance Imaging

Abdominal radiographs can be entirely normal in patients with complete, closed-loop, or strangulation obstruction.[9] Therefore, if the patient's clinical profile and the results of physical examination are consistent with intestinal obstruction despite normal abdominal radiographs, abdominal ultrasonography, CT scanning, or fast MRI should be performed immediately.[9-18] All three modalities are

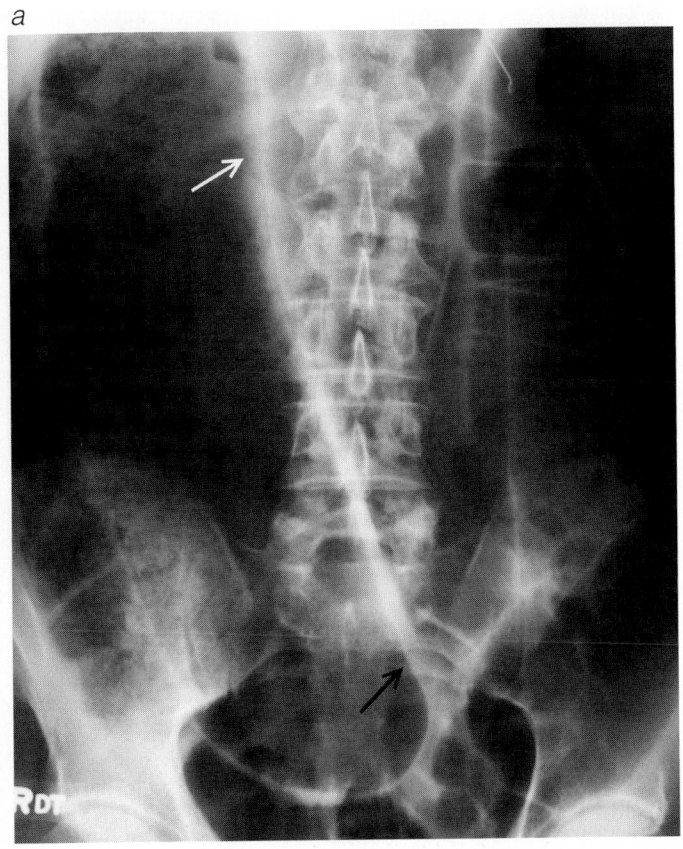

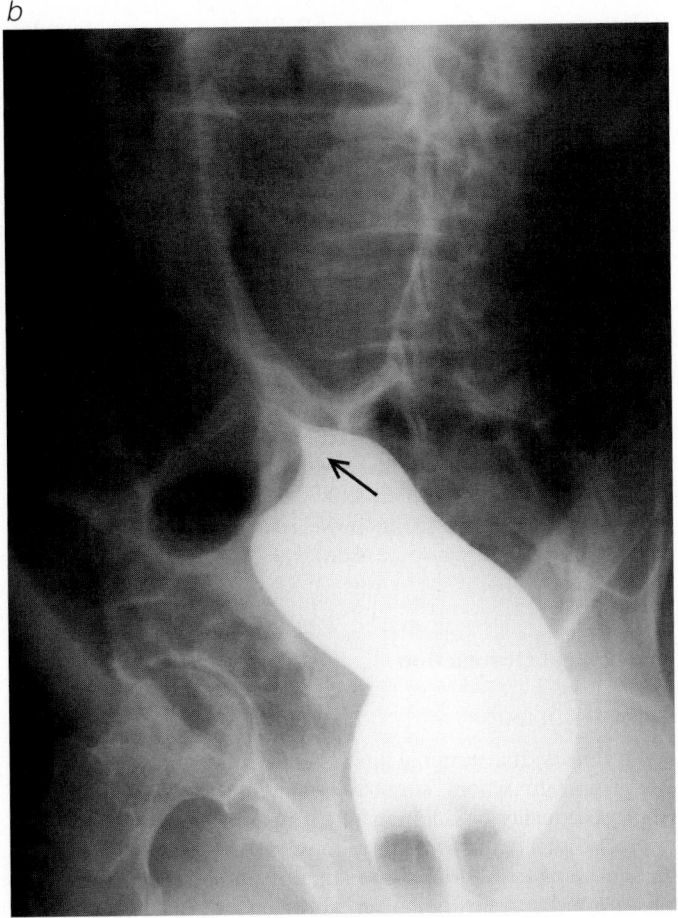

highly sensitive and specific for intestinal obstruction when performed properly and interpreted by experienced clinicians. Two prospective clinical trials found ultrasonography to be as sensitive as and more specific than abdominal radiography in diagnosing intestinal obstruction.[19,20] Ultrasonography, CT, and fast MRI are all capable of detecting the cause of the obstruction, as well as the presence of closed-loop or strangulation obstruction.[8,10,15-18,21-24]

Sonographic criteria have been established for small bowel and colonic obstruction[8,21,22]: (1) simultaneous observation of distended and collapsed bowel segments, (2) free peritoneal fluid, (3) inspissated intestinal contents, (4) paradoxical pendulating peristalsis, (5) highly reflective fluid within the bowel lumen, (6) bowel wall edema between serosa and mucosa, and (7) a fixed mass of aperistaltic, fluid-filled, dilated intestinal loops. One group of authors has recommended that when abdominal radiographs are inconclusive or normal in patients with suspected colonic obstruction, ultrasonography, rather than CT or barium enema, should be the next diagnostic step.[8] Ultrasonography is well suited to critically ill patients: because it can be performed at the bedside, the risk associated with transport to the radiology suite is avoided. Given that ultrasonography is relatively inexpensive, is easy and quick to perform, and often can provide a great deal of information about the location, nature, and severity of the obstruction, it should be employed early on in the evaluation of all patients with intestinal obstruction.[19]

Several authors have recommended that patients with suspected small bowel obstruction and equivocal plain abdominal films undergo CT scanning before a small bowel contrast series is ordered.[11-14] CT scanning has several advantages over a small bowel contrast examination in this setting: (1) it can ascertain the level of obstruction, (2) it can assess the severity of the obstruction and determine its cause, and (3) it can detect closed-loop obstruction and early strangulation [*see Figures 8, 9, 10, and 11*]. CT can also detect inflammatory or neoplastic processes both outside and inside the peritoneal cavity and can visualize small amounts of intraperitoneal air or pneumatosis cystoides intestinalis not seen on conventional films [*see Figure 10*]. Prospective studies have demonstrated that the accuracy of CT in diagnosing bowel obstruction is higher than 95% and that its sensitivity and specificity are each higher than 94%.[23,24] CT scanning distinguishes colonic mechanical obstruction from pseudo-obstruction more accurately than conventional films do and thus is the preferred modality in many cases.[25]

There is evidence to indicate that fast MRI with T_2-weighted images is more sensitive, specific, and accurate than contrast-enhanced helical CT scanning in establishing the location and cause of bowel obstruction.[17] The advantages of fast MRI over helical CT scanning are (1) that the image acquisition time is short (1 to 2 seconds per slice), which means that the image can be acquired in the space of a single held breath, and (2) that no contrast agents are required. In addition, because of its multiplanar capability, MRI is also more effective at demonstrating the transition point of the obstruction. When helical CT scanning is nondiagnostic in a patient with suspected bowel obstruction and fast MRI is not available, a small bowel follow-through examination with dilute barium is often useful.[14]

Figure 5 (*a*) **Radiograph from a patient with massive sigmoid volvulus shows a distended ahaustral sigmoid loop (white arrow), inferior convergence of the walls of the sigmoid loop to the left of the midline, and approximation of the medial walls of the sigmoid loop as a summation line (black arrow). (*b*) Barium enema of the colon shows a tapered obstruction at the rectosigmoid junction with a typical bird's-beak deformity (black arrow).**

a

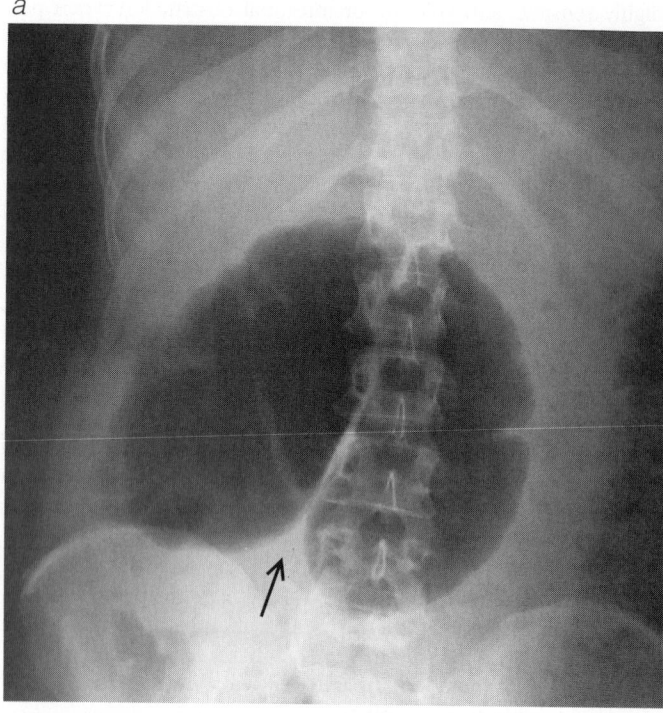

b

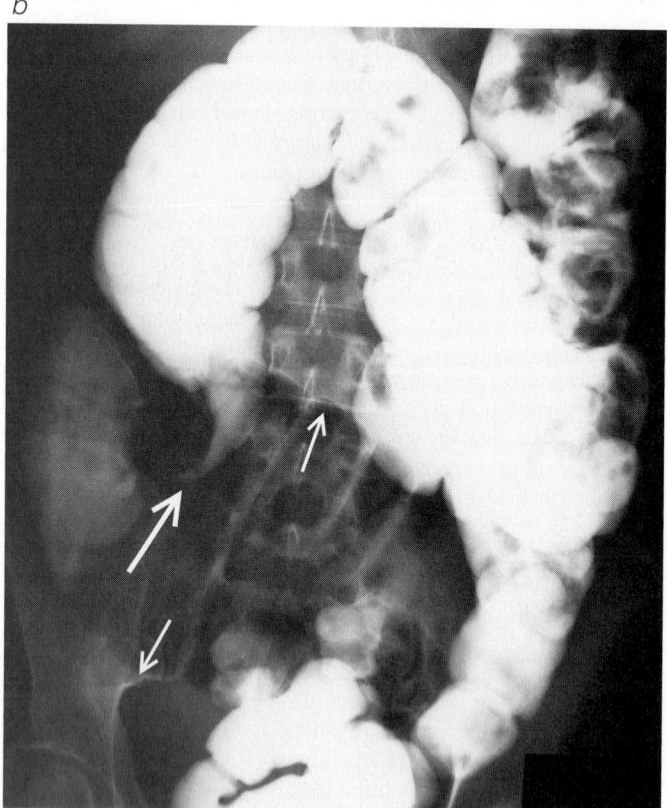

Figure 6 (*a*) Radiograph from a patient with cecal volvulus shows a dilated cecum with no air distally in the colorectum. Convergence of the medial walls of the loop (black arrow) points to the right, a typical finding in cecal volvulus. (*b*) Barium examination demonstrates a bird's-beak deformity tapering at the point of volvulus (large white arrow). Note walls of dilated cecum (small white arrows).

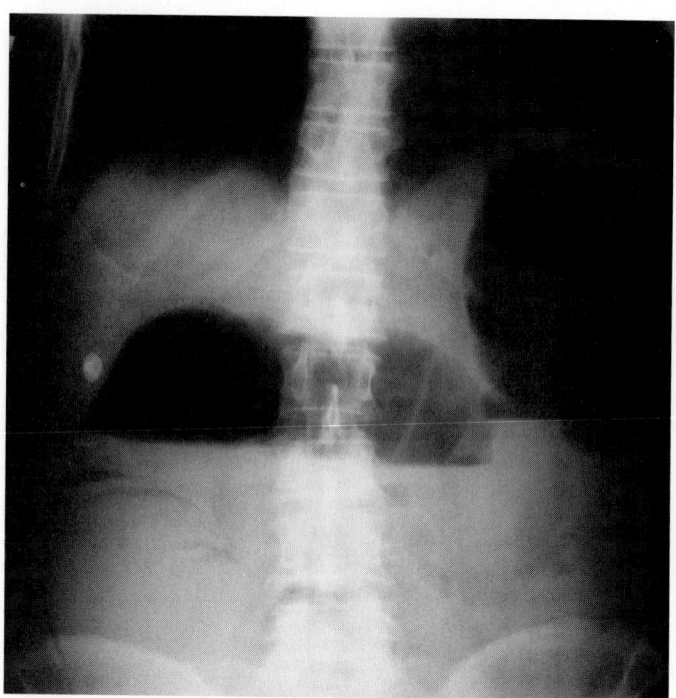

Figure 7 Shown is a radiograph from a patient with complete colonic obstruction from an obstructing carcinoma in the descending left colon with proximal air-fluid levels. The absence of air distally in the rectum or the sigmoid is suggestive of complete obstruction. The ileocecal valve is competent, and thus, there is no small bowel air.

Contrast Studies

Enteroclysis (direct injection of $BaSO_4$ into the small bowel) is generally considered the most sensitive method of distinguishing between ileus and partial mechanical small bowel obstruction: it has a diagnostic sensitivity of 87% for adhesive obstruction.[26,27] Many surgeons are concerned that injection of barium might cause partial obstruction to progress to complete obstruction; however, there is no evidence that this ever occurs, and one therefore should not refrain from using barium to diagnose partial small bowel obstruction.[28-31] If complete obstruction is identified, the patient should undergo immediate operation. If partial obstruction is identified in either the small or the large bowel, the patient is treated accordingly. If (1) mechanical obstruction is not identified and (2) a point of obstruction, as evidenced by the finding of both dilated and decompressed intestinal loops, cannot be identified through abdominal ultrasonography, CT scanning, or fast MRI, then the diagnosis is almost certainly ileus, in which case one's attention is directed toward identifying and correcting the underlying precipitating cause [*see Table 1 and* Mechanical Obstruction, No Operation, Adhesive Partial Small Bowel Obstruction, *below*].

Mechanical Obstruction

TERMINAL ILLNESS

Patients with a terminal illness (e.g., AIDS or advanced carcinomatosis) to whom surgical treatment offers little hope of improved quality or duration of life may choose not to undergo operative intervention for acute bowel obstruction. These patients should be offered comfort measures, including continuous morphine infusion, rehydration, and administration of antisecretory

Table 4   Guidelines for Operative and Nonoperative Therapy

Situations necessitating emergent operation

Incarcerated, strangulated hernias

Peritonitis

Pneumatosis cystoides intestinalis

Pneumoperitoneum

Suspected or proven intestinal strangulation

Closed-loop obstruction

Nonsigmoid colonic volvulus

Sigmoid volvulus associated with toxicity or peritoneal signs

Complete bowel obstruction

Situations necessitating urgent operation

Progressive bowel obstruction at any time after nonoperative measures are started

Failure to improve with conservative therapy within 24–48 hr

Early postoperative technical complications

Situations in which delayed operation is usually safe

Immediate postoperative obstruction

Sigmoid volvulus successfully decompressed by sigmoidoscopy

Acute exacerbation of Crohn disease, diverticulitis, or radiation enteritis

Chronic, recurrent partial obstruction

Paraduodenal hernia

Gastric outlet obstruction

Postoperative adhesions

Resolved partial colonic obstruction

agents.[32-34] In some of these patients, endoscopic deployment of plastic stents may relieve high-grade partial obstruction, thus rendering laparotomy unnecessary.[35,36] Patients who do not wish to

die of malignant bowel obstruction in a hospital should be offered hospice care or home visiting nurse services with continuous octreotide infusion, I.V. rehydration, and gastrostomy decompression.[37,38] Three prospective, randomized clinical trials demonstrated that octreotide significantly attenuated the severity of nausea and vomiting and the degree of subjective discomfort in patients with inoperable obstruction and permitted the discontinuance of nasogastric tube decompression.[33,34,39] One of these studies also demonstrated that octreotide significantly reduced the degree of fatigue and anorexia experienced.[39] When long-term gastric decompression is required for palliation in a terminally ill patient, percutaneous endoscopic gastrostomy or jejunostomy should be considered [see 60 Gastrointestinal Endoscopy].[40] Attention must always be paid to quality-of-life issues and to the patient's potential interest in pursuing nonoperative forms of palliation. For many terminally ill or incurable patients with bowel obstruction, the most humane and sensible treatment comprises nothing more than instituting palliative measures such as those described.

IMMEDIATE OPERATION

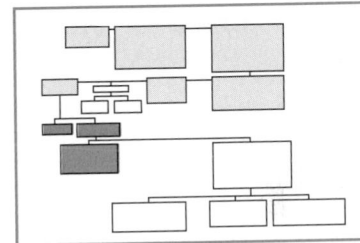

All patients with complete bowel obstruction, whether of the small intestine or the large, should undergo immediate operation unless extraordinary circumstances (e.g., diffuse carcinomatosis, terminal illness, or sigmoid volvulus that responds to sigmoidoscopic decompression) are present. If one attempts to manage complete intestinal obstruction nonoperatively, one risks delaying definitive treatment of patients with intestinal ischemia and subjecting them to significantly increased morbidity and mortality should perforation or severe infection develop.[5,41]

Immediate operation is also indicated when bowel obstruction is associated with peritonitis; incarcerated strangulated hernias;

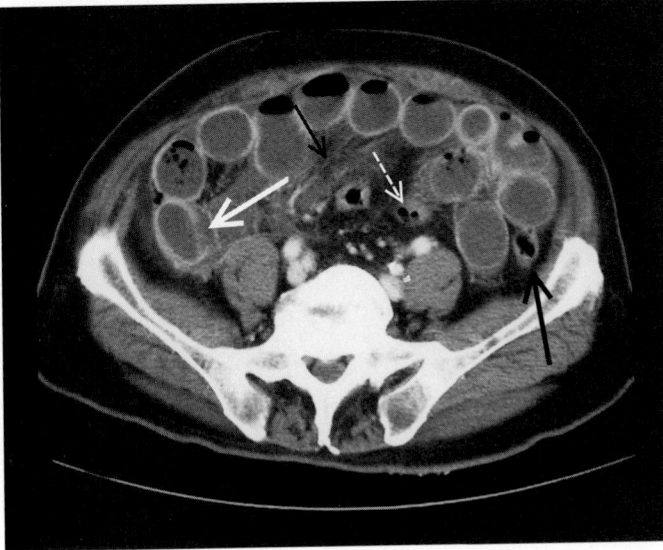

Figure 8   CT scan from a patient with partial small bowel obstruction shows distended, fluid-filled loops of small bowel with air-fluid levels, hyperemia, and bowel wall thickening (large white arrow). Note the discrepancy in caliber between dilated small bowel and decompressed small bowel (dashed white arrow) and the stranding (small black arrow) in the small bowel mesentery. Air in a decompressed descending colon (large black arrow) is indicative of partial obstruction.

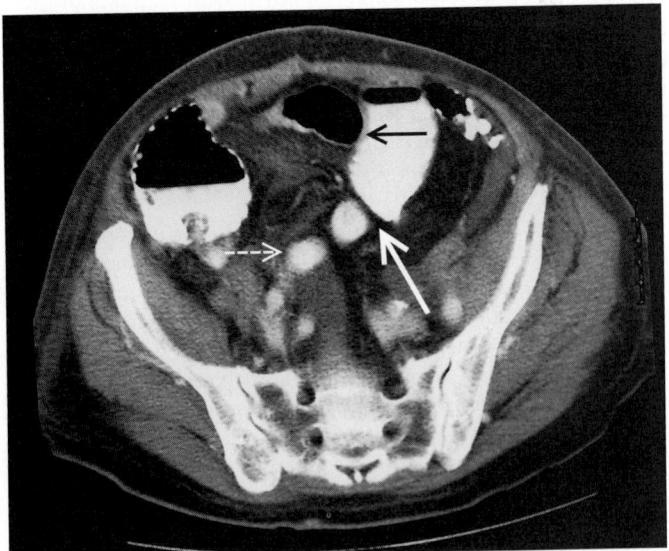

Figure 9   CT scan from a patient with adhesive partial small bowel obstruction shows massively dilated small intestine (black arrow) proximal to a thick adhesive band (large white arrow) and decompressed small bowel distal to the adhesion (dashed white arrow). The patient was operated on because of the low probability that this obstruction would resolve with conservative management.

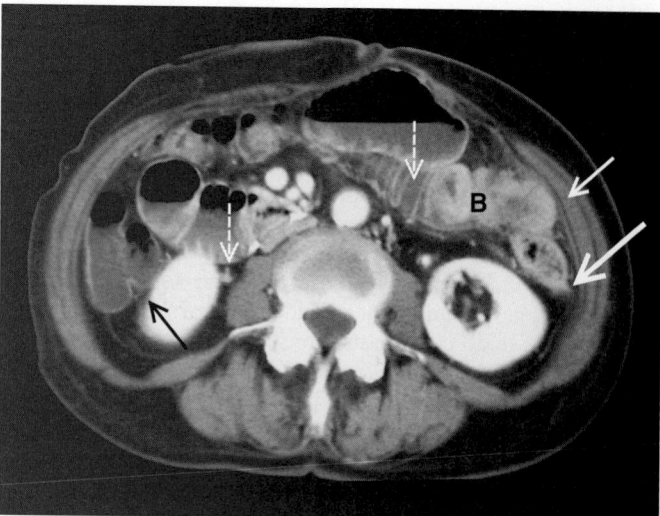

Figure 10 CT scan from a patient with partial small bowel obstruction from cancer shows distended small bowel (dashed white arrows) proximal to a mass (small white arrow). There is air in the cecum (black arrow), the transverse colon, and the descending colon (large white arrow). The small bowel is maximally dilated, with hyperemic, edematous bowel wall (B) just proximal to an obstructing recurrent colon carcinoma. Even though plain radiographs showed partial small bowel obstruction, this CT scan led to early operation because continued nonoperative management would not resolve the problem.

suspected or confirmed strangulation; pneumatosis cystoides intestinalis; sigmoid volvulus accompanied by systemic toxicity or peritoneal irritation; colonic volvulus above the sigmoid colon; or fecal impaction. These conditions will not resolve without operation and are associated with increased morbidity, mortality, and cost if diagnosis and treatment are delayed. The only time one would not operate immediately on any patient with one of these diagnoses is when the patient requires cardiopulmonary stabilization, additional resuscitation, or both. Whenever there is any doubt as to the presence of any of these conditions, additional diagnostic tests (e.g., ultrasonography, CT, fast MRI, or contrast studies) are indicated to confirm or exclude them.

Strangulation and Closed-Loop Obstruction

Morbidity and mortality from intestinal obstruction vary significantly and depend primarily on the presence of strangulation and subsequent infection. Strangulation obstruction occurs in approximately 10% of all patients with small intestinal obstruction. It carries a mortality of 10% to 37%, whereas simple obstruction carries a mortality of less than 5%.[5,28,42,43] Early recognition and immediate operative treatment of strangulation obstruction are the only current means of decreasing this mortality. Strangulation obstruction occurs most frequently in patients with incarcerated hernias, closed-loop obstruction, volvulus, or complete bowel obstruction; hence, identification of any of these specific causes of obstruction is an important and clear indication for immediate operation. Radiographic evidence of pneumatosis cystoides intestinalis or free intraperitoneal air in a patient with a clinical picture of bowel obstruction is indicative of strangulation, perforation, or both and constitutes an indication for operation. High-quality abdominal CT with I.V. contrast can detect advanced strangulation and identify early, reversible strangulation [see Figure 11].[13,15,16]

Abdominal ultrasonography can also identify edematous, hemorrhagic loops of intestine. Accordingly, whenever one is concerned about possible strangulation or closed-loop obstruction but is not yet committed to taking the patient immediately to the OR, an ultrasonogram or a CT scan should be obtained. In fact, given that ultrasonography, CT, and fast MRI are the only well-established means of diagnosing strangulation obstruction short of exploratory laparotomy or laparoscopy, an argument can be made that one of these modalities should be performed in all patients who have been admitted to the hospital with bowel obstruction and are initially being treated nonoperatively.

Many surgeons base the decision whether to operate on patients with bowel obstruction on the presence or absence of the so-called classic signs of strangulation obstruction—continuous abdominal pain, fever, tachycardia, peritoneal signs, and leukocytosis—and on their clinical experience. Unfortunately, these classically taught signs, even in conjunction with abdominal x-rays and clinical judgment, are incapable of reliably detecting closed-loop or gangrenous bowel obstruction.[5,28,41,44] In fact, one prospective clinical trial concluded that the five classic signs of strangulation obstruction and experienced clinical judgment were not sensitive for, specific for, or predictive of strangulation[5]: in more than 50% of the patients who had intestinal strangulation, the condition was not recognized preoperatively. Such findings suggest that early nonoperative recognition of intestinal strangulation is not feasible without ultrasonography, CT, or fast MRI.

Incarcerated or Strangulated Hernias

A hernia that is incarcerated, tender, erythematous, warm, or edematous is an indication for immediate operation. Primary or incisional hernias may not be palpable in obese patients, in which case ultrasonography, CT scanning, or fast MRI should be performed.

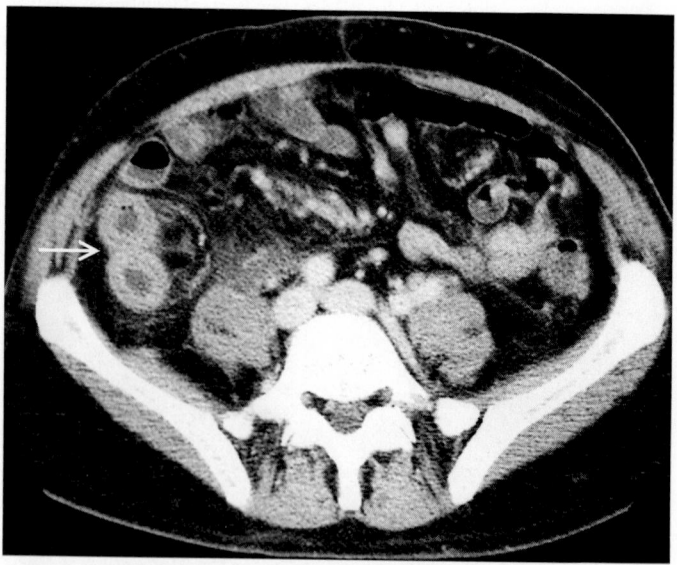

Figure 11 Early closed-loop small bowel obstruction CT scan from a patient with early closed-loop obstruction of the small intestine shows markedly edematous, hyperemic small bowel, a finding indicative of early strangulation (white arrow). The patient had minimal symptoms, and there was air in the transverse colon and the descending colon (a finding indicative of partial small bowel obstruction); however, the finding of gangrenous, nonperforated small bowel on this CT scan led to early operation.

Nonsigmoid Volvulus and Sigmoid Volvulus with Systemic Toxicity or Peritoneal Signs

All intestinal volvuli are closed-loop obstructions and thus carry a high risk of intestinal strangulation, infarction, and perforation. Patients typically present with acute, colicky abdominal pain, massive distention, nausea, and vomiting. Sigmoid volvulus is the most common form of colonic volvulus, followed by cecal volvulus. Abdominal radiographs are fairly diagnostic for colonic volvulus [*see Figures 5 and 6*]. In contrast, small bowel volvulus may not be visualized on plain radiographs, because the closed loop fills completely with fluid and no air-fluid level can be seen. Small bowel volvulus is readily detected by ultrasonography or CT scanning; one or both of these procedures should be performed in patients presenting with signs and symptoms of bowel obstruction and normal abdominal radiographs. Small bowel volvulus is an indication for immediate operation.

If one observes signs of systemic toxicity, a bloody rectal discharge, fever, leukocytosis, or peritoneal irritation in a patient with sigmoid volvulus, the patient should undergo immediate operation; if all of these signs are absent, the patient should undergo sigmoidoscopy. When there are no signs of peritonitis or generalized toxicity, sigmoidoscopic decompression is safe and effective in more than 95% of patients with sigmoid volvulus.[45] If mucosal gangrene or a bloody effluent is noted at the time of sigmoidoscopy, immediate operative intervention is necessary even in the absence of any clinical signs or symptoms of strangulation. After sigmoidoscopy, the patient can undergo elective bowel preparation and a single-stage sigmoid resection before being discharged from the hospital. If, however, clinical toxicity, a bloody rectal discharge, fever, or peritoneal irritation arises at any time after sigmoidoscopic decompression while the patient is being prepared for an elective procedure, immediate operation is indicated.

Patients with volvulus proximal to the sigmoid colon should undergo immediate operation regardless of whether peritoneal irritation is present. The incidence of strangulation infarction is high in such patients, and nonoperative therapy often fails. If the diagnosis of nonsigmoid colonic volvulus is in doubt, a barium enema is indicated to exclude colonic pseudo-obstruction.

Fecal Impaction

Complete colonic obstruction secondary to fecal impaction in the rectum can sometimes be successfully relieved through disimpaction at the bedside; however, this can be difficult and extremely uncomfortable for the patient. The most expeditious and successful method of relieving the obstruction is to disimpact the patient while he or she is under general or spinal anesthesia. In one study, the pulsed-irrigated enhanced-evacuation (PIEE) procedure, which can be performed at the bedside, successfully resolved fecal impaction in approximately 75% of geriatric patients.[46] In another study, administration of a polyethylene glycol 3350 solution over 3 days successfully resolved intestinal obstruction from fecal impaction in 75% of pediatric patients.[47]

URGENT OPERATION

Lack of Response to Nonoperative Therapy within 24 to 48 Hours

It is usually safe to manage partial bowel obstruction initially by nonoperative means: a nihil per os (NPO) regimen, nasogas-

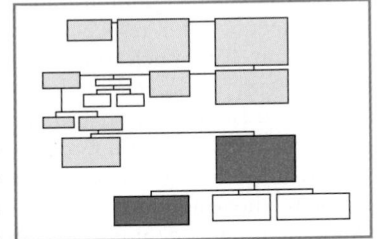

tric decompression, analgesics, and octreotide. Such therapy is successful in most cases, especially if the cause of obstruction is postoperative adhesions, but there is always the risk that complete bowel obstruction or strangulation already exists but is undetected. Furthermore, there is the risk that while the patient is being observed, partial obstruction will progress to complete obstruction or strangulation and perforation will develop. It is therefore crucial to be alert to changes in the patient's condition.

Repeated examination of the abdomen by the same clinician is the most sensitive way of detecting progressive obstruction. Examinations should be performed no less frequently than every 3 hours. If abdominal pain, tenderness, or distention increases or the gastric aspirate changes from nonfeculent to feculent, abdominal exploration is usually indicated. Abdominal radiographs should be repeated every 6 hours after nasogastric decompression and reviewed by the surgeon who is following the patient. If proximal small bowel distention increases or distal intestinal gas decreases, nonoperative therapy is less likely to be successful; in these circumstances, early operative intervention should be seriously considered. Conversely, if the patient's condition appears stable or improved and x-rays indicate that the obstruction either has resolved somewhat or at least is no worse, it is generally safe to continue nonoperative care for another 12 to 24 hours. If the clinical picture is stable after 24 hours of observation, one must decide whether to operate or to continue nonoperative therapy. Clinical judgment and experience, coupled with thorough and accurate assessment of the patient's underlying diagnosis and clinical condition, have traditionally been the most reliable guides for making this decision. Currently, however, it appears that the decision whether to operate can be made more cost-effectively and reliably on the basis of abdominal imaging studies [*see No Operation, Adhesive Partial Small Bowel Obstruction, below*].

Early Postoperative Technical Complications

When normal bowel function initially returns after an abdominal operation but then is replaced by a clinical picture suggestive of early postoperative mechanical obstruction, the explanation may be a technical complication of the operation (e.g., phlegmon, abscess, intussusception, a narrow anastomosis, an internal hernia, or obstruction at the level of a stoma). An early, aggressive diagnostic workup should be performed to identify or exclude these problems because they are unlikely to respond to nasogastric decompression or other forms of conservative management. It is critical to know exactly what was done within the abdomen in the course of the operation. To this end, one should try to speak directly with the operating surgeon rather than attempt to deduce the needed information from the operative report.

If the patient had peritonitis or a colonic anastomosis at the initial operation, one should order a CT scan to look for an intraabdominal abscess. An abscess or a phlegmon at the site of an anastomosis is usually secondary to anastomotic leakage and is an indication for reoperation. CT scanning can also identify intraabdominal hematomas, which should be evacuated through early reoperation. In patients recovering from a proctectomy, herniation of the small bowel through a defect in the pelvic floor is a common cause of intestinal obstruction. Oral contrast studies can help identify patients with an internal hernia, intussusception, or anastomotic obstruction and should be performed after the CT scan. A retrograde barium examination should be performed in patients thought to have a problem related to a stoma or an intestinal anastomosis. When none of the above factors appears to be the cause of the postoperative obstruction, it is reasonable for the surgeon to assume that the obstruction is secondary to postoperative adhesions, which are best treated conservatively (see below).

NO OPERATION

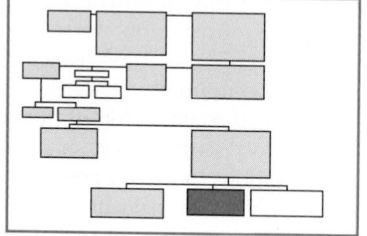

In selected patients, nonoperative management of partial small bowel obstruction is highly successful and carries an acceptably low mortality. Such patients include those whose partial obstruction is secondary to intra-abdominal adhesions, occurs in the immediate postoperative period, or derives from an inflammatory condition (e.g., inflammatory bowel disease, radiation enteritis, or diverticulitis).

Adhesive Partial Small Bowel Obstruction

Adhesions are the major cause of bowel obstruction. Obstruction resulting from adhesions can occur as early as 1 month or as late as 20 years after operation.[48] Adhesive partial small bowel obstruction is treated initially with nasogastric decompression, I.V. rehydration, and analgesia. Parenteral nutrition should be begun if one believes that oral or enteral nutrition will not be adequate within 5 days. Nonoperative therapy leads to resolution of adhesive partial obstruction in as many as 90% of patients[49,50]; however, such resolution is followed by recurrence of obstruction in approximately 50% of cases.[51,52] When operative adhesiolysis is performed, the mortality is less than 5% for patients with simple obstruction but may be as high as 30% for patients with strangulation or necrotic bowel necessitating intestinal resection.[48] In view of this substantial difference in mortality, it is extremely important to be able to confidently distinguish obstruction that is likely to resolve with nonoperative treatment from obstruction that is not. Patients with adhesive partial obstruction that can be accurately predicted to resolve with medical therapy can and should be treated nonoperatively.

Some studies suggest that the nature of the previous abdominal operation or the type of adhesions present may influence the probability that the obstruction will not respond to medical therapy.[53-57] Operations associated with a lower likelihood of response to medical therapy include those performed through a midline incision; those involving the aorta, the colon, the rectum, the appendix, or the pelvic adnexa; and those done to relieve previous carcinomatous obstruction. Matted adhesions, which are more common in patients who have undergone midline incisions or colorectal procedures, are less amenable to conservative management than a simple obstructive band is.[53] In the context of this kind of operative history, strong consideration should be given to surgical intervention if the obstruction does not resolve within 24 hours—unless comorbid medical conditions tip the risk-benefit balance in the direction of nonoperative therapy.

There is an ongoing debate regarding how long patients with partial adhesive obstruction should be treated conservatively. After 48 hours of nonoperative management, the risk of complications increases substantially, and the probability that the obstruction will resolve diminishes.[43] Generally, if the obstruction is going to resolve with nonoperative therapy, there will be a fairly prompt response within the first 8 to 12 hours. Therefore, if a patient's condition has deteriorated or has not significantly improved by 12 hours after nasogastric decompression and resuscitation, exploratory laparotomy is advisable. During this obser-

vation period, the patient must be constantly reevaluated, ideally by the same examiner. Analgesics can be safely administered, and repeat abdominal examinations should be performed at 3-hour intervals when the influence of narcotics has waned. Repeat abdominal x-rays should be obtained no later than 6 hours after nasogastric decompression, and the pattern of gas distribution should be compared with that seen on the admission films. A decrease in intestinal gas distal to a point of obstruction coupled with an increase in proximal dilatation suggests that the obstruction is worsening; conversely, a decrease in intestinal distention coupled with the appearance of more gas distally in the colon suggests that the obstruction is being reduced. The degree of abdominal distention, the passage of flatus, and the nature of the nasogastric aspirate should be evaluated periodically. If abdominal distention does not decrease or the gastric aspirate changes from bilious to feculent, the patient should be operated on.

Experimental and clinical studies suggest that patients undergoing nonoperative treatment of bowel obstruction may benefit from the administration of somatostatin analogues as a result of the potent effects these substances exert on intestinal sodium, chloride, and water absorption.[57] In one study, animals with either complete or closed-loop partial small bowel obstruction were given either long-acting somatostatin or saline; the treatment group had significantly less intestinal distention, less infarction, and longer survival than the control group.[57,58] In a prospective, randomized clinical trial evaluating the use of somatostatin in patients who had complete small bowel obstruction without clinical or radiologic evidence of strangulation, the treatment group was less likely to need operation, had less proximal intestinal distention, and exhibited decreased mucosal necrosis proximal to the point of obstruction.[59] In other trials, long-acting somatostatin analogues and other nonsecretagogues significantly decreased the amount of gastric contents aspirated and alleviated the symptoms of intestinal obstruction in terminally ill patients with nonoperable malignant disease.[32,33,37-40]

It should be possible to determine with a high degree of accuracy and safety which patients will require operation for adhesive small bowel obstruction within 24 to 48 hours of admission to the hospital. As a rule, patients with closed-loop or complete bowel obstruction, who require immediate or urgent operation, can be readily identified by means of abdominal CT or MRI.[12-14,17,18] For the remaining patients, who have some degree of partial obstruction, the success or failure of conservative management can be predicted with high accuracy by recording the arrival of contrast material (either a water-soluble agent or a mixed barium preparation) in the right colon within a defined time.[14,30,60-63] One prospective study documented the arrival of diatrizoate meglumine–diatrizoate sodium in the colon within 24 hours and found this measure to have a sensitivity of 98%, a specificity of 100%, an accuracy of 99%, a positive predictive value of 100%, and a negative predictive value of 96% as a predictor of successful nonoperative treatment.[64] Other studies achieved comparable results with shorter arrival times (e.g., 4 or 8 hours).[14,61,65]

Several prospective, randomized clinical trials have addressed the issue of whether administration of contrast material can itself be therapeutic with respect to resolving adhesive small bowel obstruction. Two such studies examined small bowel followthrough with barium, either alone or mixed with diatrizoate meglumine.[30,31] Both found that the intervals between admission and operation were shorter for patients randomized to the contrast arm than for those in the control group but that contrast examination did not lead to more expeditious resolution of obstruction. Both studies also demonstrated that barium could be administered to patients with small bowel obstruction safely and without complications.

Four prospective, randomized trials have investigated the effects of administering water-soluble hyperosmolar contrast agents to patients with small bowel obstruction.[60,62,63,66] In one study, administration of 100 ml of diatrizoate meglumine (1,900 mOsm/L) through the nasogastric tube promoted resolution of adhesive partial obstruction and shortened hospital stay but had no effect on whether laparotomy was required.[60] No contrast-related complications were observed. In the second study, administration of a different water-soluble hyperosmolar contrast agent, ioxitalamate meglumine (1,500 mOsm/L), had no therapeutic effect on patients with partial small bowel obstruction.[66] Again, no contrast-related complications were observed. In the third study, administration of 100 ml of diatrizoate meglumine through the nasogastric tube significantly accelerated the resolution of adhesive partial small bowel obstruction and shortened hospital stay.[62] Patients in whom contrast reached the colon within 24 hours were able to tolerate immediate oral feeding. In addition, the time needed to decide on operative adhesiolysis was shorter in patients receiving the contrast agent. In the fourth study, patients whose partial adhesive small bowel obstruction did not resolve after 48 hours either received 100 ml of diatrizoate meglumine or underwent operative adhesiolysis.[63] If administration of the contrast agent revealed complete bowel obstruction, operative treatment was immediately initiated. If it revealed partial obstruction, conservative treatment was continued; in 100% of these patients, the obstruction then resolved without operation. No contrast-mediated complications, no bowel strangulation, and no deaths were reported. The significant treatment effect reported in three of the four randomized clinical trials, along with the absence of any deleterious contrast-related complications in all four, constitutes sufficient evidence to support the administration of 100 ml of diatrizoate meglumine to patients with adhesive partial small bowel obstruction.

By accelerating the resolution of partial small bowel obstruction and ileus, administration of water-soluble contrast agents can shorten the expected hospital stay and thereby reduce the cost of care. Thus, it is reasonable that the first step in managing suspected partial small bowel obstruction from adhesions or postoperative ileus should be to administer water-soluble contrast material intragastrically. When bowel function does not return within 24 hours and the obstruction is demonstrated to be partial, continued observation is safe and resolution without operation is still highly probable. Eventually, however, there will be a point beyond which continued observation is no longer cost-effective in comparison with operative adhesiolysis (especially laparoscopic adhesiolysis). Additional prospective trials are necessary to determine precisely how long the waiting period before operative treatment should be.

Laparoscopic adhesiolysis Several clinical reports have demonstrated that laparoscopic adhesiolysis for acute small bowel obstruction is both feasible and safe.[67-72] Laparoscopic or laparoscopic-assisted lysis of adhesions relieves bowel obstruction in more than 50% of patients and is associated with lower morbidity, earlier return of bowel function, quicker resumption of normal diet, and a shorter hospital stay than open operative lysis.[67-71,73] To minimize the risk for bowel injury at the beginning of the operation, the first trocar is inserted under direct vision by means of an open technique, and the incision is placed well away from any previous scars.[74,75]

At present, there are no prospective, randomized, controlled clinical trials comparing laparoscopic with open adhesiolysis. Perhaps

the best study published to date on this issue is a retrospective, matched-pair analysis that used an intention-to-treat analysis.[71] In this study, 52% of the patients in the laparoscopic group underwent conversion to open lysis of adhesions either for completion of adhesiolysis or for management of complications. No perforations or recurrent obstructions were missed. Perforations were more common overall in the laparoscopic group than in the open group, though this difference was largely eliminated when patients from the laparoscopic group who underwent conversion to open lysis were not considered. Patients with two or more previous laparotomies had a higher incidence of intraoperative complications than those with fewer laparotomies. Accordingly, the authors recommended against laparoscopic adhesiolysis in patients with two or more previous laparotomies. The high conversion rate in this study notwithstanding, the laparoscopic group as a whole (including conversions) experienced an overall reduction in postoperative complications.

Another potential advantage of laparoscopic adhesiolysis is that it results in fewer intra-abdominal adhesions than open laparotomy[76,77] and thus may reduce the risk of recurrent bowel obstruction. However, one study found that despite a reduction in median length of stay, patients treated laparoscopically were at increased risk for early unplanned reoperation as a consequence of either incomplete relief of obstruction or complications.[70] In fact, bowel perforation in the course of laparoscopic adhesiolysis often is not detected during the procedure and presents in a delayed fashion.[75] Many such injuries are attributable either to insertion of the initial trocar or to delayed perforation of a thermal injury. When laparoscopic adhesiolysis fails to identify and relieve an obvious point of obstruction or when adhesiolysis is inadequate or unsafe, conversion to an open approach is indicated.

Early Postoperative Obstruction

Early postoperative mechanical small bowel obstruction is not uncommon: it occurs in approximately 10% of patients undergoing abdominal procedures.[78] Postoperative bowel obstruction is often difficult to diagnose because it gives rise to many of the same signs and symptoms as postoperative ileus: obstipation, distention, nausea, vomiting, abdominal pain, and altered bowel sounds. In most cases, there are roentgenographic signs indicative of small bowel obstruction rather than ileus; however, in some cases, abdominal x-rays fail to diagnose the obstruction.[79] Traditionally, when plain radiographs are equivocal, an upper GI barium study with follow-through views is the next test performed to distinguish ileus from partial or complete small bowel obstruction[80]; however, such studies may yield the wrong diagnosis in as many as 30% of cases.[26,79,81] A number of authorities believe that abdominal ultrasonography is excellent at distinguishing postoperative ileus from mechanical obstruction and recommend that it be done before any contrast study.[22]

Early postoperative obstruction is caused by adhesions in about 90% of patients.[79,82] When there are no signs of toxicity and no acute abdominal signs, such obstruction can usually be managed safely with nasogastric decompression.[78,79,81,82] As many as 87% of patients respond to nasogastric suction within 2 weeks. About 70% of the patients who respond to nonoperative treatment do so within 1 week, and an additional 25% respond during the following 7 days. If postoperative obstruction does not resolve in the first 2 weeks, it is unlikely to do so with continued nonoperative therapy, and reoperation is probably indicated[79,82]; about 25% of patients whose postoperative obstruction was initially treated nonoperatively eventually require reoperation. An exception to this guideline arises in patients known to have severe dense adhesions (sometimes referred to as obliterative peritonitis) in response to multiple sequential laparotomies. These patients may have a combination of mechanical obstruction and diffuse small bowel and colonic ileus. The risk of closed-loop obstruction, volvulus, or strangulation in this group of patients is low. Repeat laparotomies and attempts to lyse adhesions may lead to complications, the development of enterocutaneous fistulae, or exacerbation of the adhesions. Often, the best approach to managing these patients is observation for prolonged periods (i.e., months). Total parenteral nutrition (TPN) is indicated. The addition of octreotide to the TPN solution may be helpful and may make patients more comfortable.

Because the risk of intestinal strangulation in patients with postoperative adhesive obstruction is extremely low (< 1%),[79,83] one can generally treat these patients nonoperatively for longer periods. In fact, the conservative approach is often the wise one: reoperation may do more harm than good (e.g., by causing enterotomies and inducing denser adhesions). The traditional indications for operation in patients with early postoperative obstruction include (1) deteriorating clinical status, (2) worsening obstructive symptoms, and (3) failure to respond to nonoperative management within 2 weeks. With the rising cost of hospitalization, it might in fact be more cost-effective to reoperate on patients who have persistent obstruction after 7 days. This speculation would have to be tested by a well-organized cost-benefit study conducted in a prospective fashion.

Some physicians have maintained that long intestinal tubes are beneficial in the management of postoperative bowel obstruction.[50] However, there is no convincing evidence that long intestinal tubes are any better for resolving bowel obstruction than conventional nasogastric tubes are. In fact, some authorities have reported that the use of such tubes increases morbidity.[28,43,44] One prospective, randomized clinical trial that addressed this issue found no differences between the two types of tube with respect to the percentage of patients who were able to avoid operation, the incidence of complications, the time between admission and operation, or the duration of postoperative ileus.[84]

Inflammatory Conditions

Partial bowel obstruction secondary to inflammatory bowel disease, radiation enteritis, or diverticulitis usually resolves with nonoperative therapy. Bowel obstruction accompanying an acute exacerbation of Crohn disease usually resolves with nasogastric suction, I.V. antibiotics, and anti-inflammatory agents. If, however, CT scanning detects intra-abdominal abscess, there is evidence of a chronic stricture, or the patient exhibits persistent obstructive symptoms, operation may be necessary. Similarly, bowel obstruction arising from acute enteritis caused by radiation exposure or chemotherapy usually resolves with supportive care. Chronic radiation-induced strictures are problematic; astute clinical judgment must be exercised to determine when operative treatment is the best option.

Patients with acute diverticulitis typically present with a history of altered bowel movements, fever, leukocytosis, localized pain, tenderness, and guarding in the left lower quadrant of the abdomen. Approximately 20% of patients with colonic diverticulitis also present with signs and symptoms of partial colonic obstruction. A CT scan should be obtained early in all patients with diverticulitis to ascertain whether there is a pericolic abscess that could be drained percutaneously.[85] Partial colonic obstruction in these patients usually resolves with antibiotic therapy, an NPO regimen, and nasogastric decompression. If obstructive symptoms persist for more than 7 days or if obstructive symptoms from a documented stricture recur, operation is indicated.

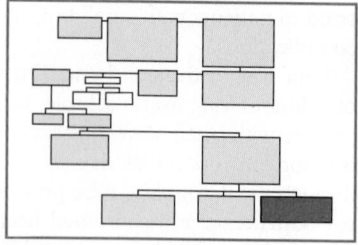

ELECTIVE OPERATION

Nontoxic, Nontender Sigmoid Volvulus

Patients with nontoxic, nontender sigmoid volvulus whose bowel obstruction is initially treated successfully with sigmoidoscopic decompression are at risk for recurrent colonic obstruction. Accordingly, these patients should undergo elective sigmoid resection after complete bowel preparation.

Recurrent Adhesive or Stricture-Related Partial Small Bowel Obstruction

Many patients whose adhesive bowel obstruction resolves experience no further obstructive episodes. If a patient does present with recurrent obstruction from presumed adhesions, either a contrast examination of the bowel or CT scanning is indicated to determine whether there is a surgically correctable point of stenosis. A strong argument can be made that non–high-risk patients should undergo elective operation after presenting with their second episode of mechanical obstruction. Similarly, patients with recurrent obstruction from strictures of any sort should undergo elective operation, given that these lesions are unlikely to resolve.

Partial Colonic Obstruction

The most common causes of partial colonic obstruction are colon cancer, strictures, and diverticulitis. Cancer and strictures usually must be managed surgically because they generally go on to cause obstruction later. Strictures from ischemia or endometriosis usually call for elective colonic resection. Inflammatory strictures from diverticulitis may resolve; however, if obstructive symptoms persist or if barium enema examination continues to yield evidence of colonic narrowing, elective resection is warranted.

When abdominal x-rays suggest distal colonic obstruction, digital examination and rigid sigmoidoscopy are performed to exclude fecal impaction, tumors, strictures, and sigmoid volvulus. If obstruction is proximal to the sigmoidoscope, barium contrast examination is indicated. If barium examination does not demonstrate mechanical obstruction, a presumptive diagnosis of colonic pseudo-obstruction is made.

The morbidity and mortality associated with elective colorectal procedures are significantly lower than those associated with emergency colonic surgery. Furthermore, immediate operation for left-side colonic obstruction almost always necessitates the creation of a diverting colostomy. If a colostomy takedown subsequently proves necessary, the overall cost of caring for the patient will be significantly higher than it would have been had a single-stage procedure been performed. For these reasons, one should initially treat partial colonic obstruction with nasogastric suction, enemas, and I.V. rehydration in the hope that the obstruction will resolve and that the patient thus can undergo mechanical and antibiotic bowel preparation and a single-stage procedure comprising resection and primary anastomosis. Patients who do not respond to nonoperative measures within 24 hours should undergo operation within 12 hours with the aim of preventing perforation.

In patients with partially obstructing rectal or distal sigmoid tumors or strictures that can be traversed with a radiologic guide wire, balloon dilatation can be performed and a self-expanding stent deployed.[36,86-89] Clinical improvement and resolution of obstruction occur in more than 90% of patients within 96

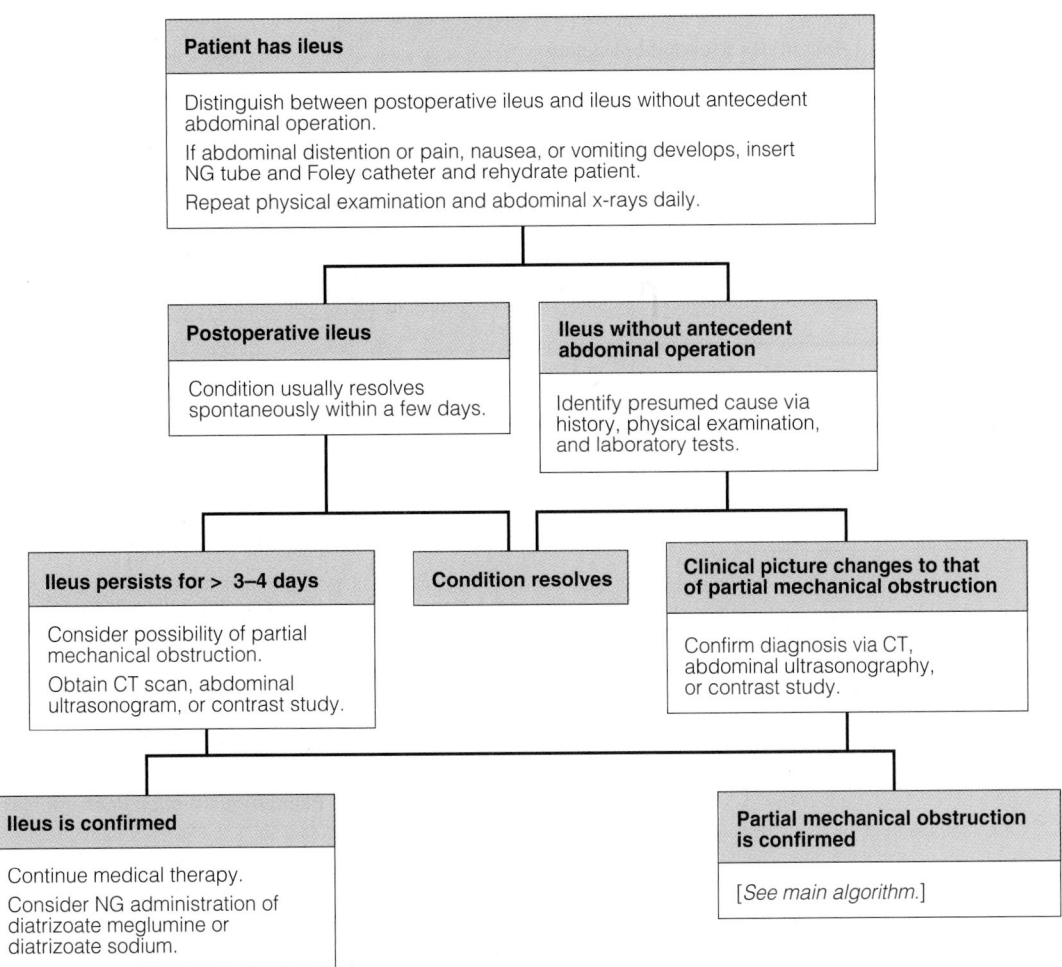

Figure 12 **Shown is an algorithm outlining an approach to management of ileus.**

hours.[36,88] With restoration of the bowel lumen, patients can be prepared for elective surgery, can be spared the creation of a diverting colostomy, and can avoid the extra expense and morbidity associated with the performance of two operations.[88,89] This approach is also highly successful as primary therapy for bowel obstruction in patients who are not surgical candidates.[36] In patients with large, fixed rectal masses, one should obtain CT scans of the pelvis to assess the extent of the tumor. Transrectal laser fulguration and endoluminal stenting are palliative options for restoring bowel lumen patency that may be considered for patients with nonresectable recurrent rectal cancer or radiation strictures in whom operative risk is prohibitively high.

Bowel Obstruction without Previous Abdominal Operation

When partial small bowel obstruction develops and resolves in a patient who has not previously undergone an abdominal operation, a diagnostic workup should be performed to identify the cause of the obstruction; there may be an underlying condition that is likely to cause recurrent obstruction (e.g., an internal hernia, a tumor, malrotation, or metastatic cancer). The first diagnostic test to be ordered should be a CT scan, followed by an upper GI barium study with follow-through views and a barium enema.[90] If a pathologic lesion is identified, elective operation is indicated. An argument can be made that no additional diagnostic tests should be performed in these patients and that diagnostic laparoscopy should be performed instead to enable laparoscopic surgery in case a cause of obstruction is identified that can be treated with

a minimally invasive procedure. If no cause of obstruction is found at laparoscopy, open laparotomy is performed.

Paraduodenal hernia Paraduodenal hernia, a congenital defect resulting from intestinal malrotation, is probably more common than was once thought. It accounts for approximately 50% of internal hernias. Patients with paraduodenal hernia may present with a catastrophic closed-loop obstruction; more often, however, they exhibit mild, nonspecific GI symptoms such as nausea, vomiting, esophageal reflux, and abdominal pain. Duodenogastric reflux and prominent bile gastritis in the absence of a previous operation or diabetic gastroparesis are indirect signs of a paraduodenal hernia. The diagnosis is established by means of either an upper GI contrast study with small bowel follow-through or CT scanning. When a paraduodenal hernia is identified, operative treatment is indicated. Such treatment is usually successful in alleviating symptoms and preventing strangulation obstruction.[91]

Nonmechanical Obstruction

ILEUS

Ileus, or intestinal paralysis, is most common after abdominal operations but can also occur in response

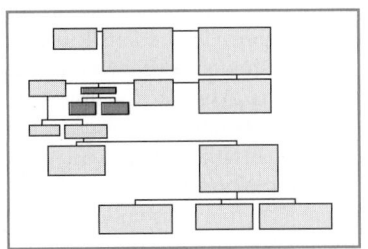

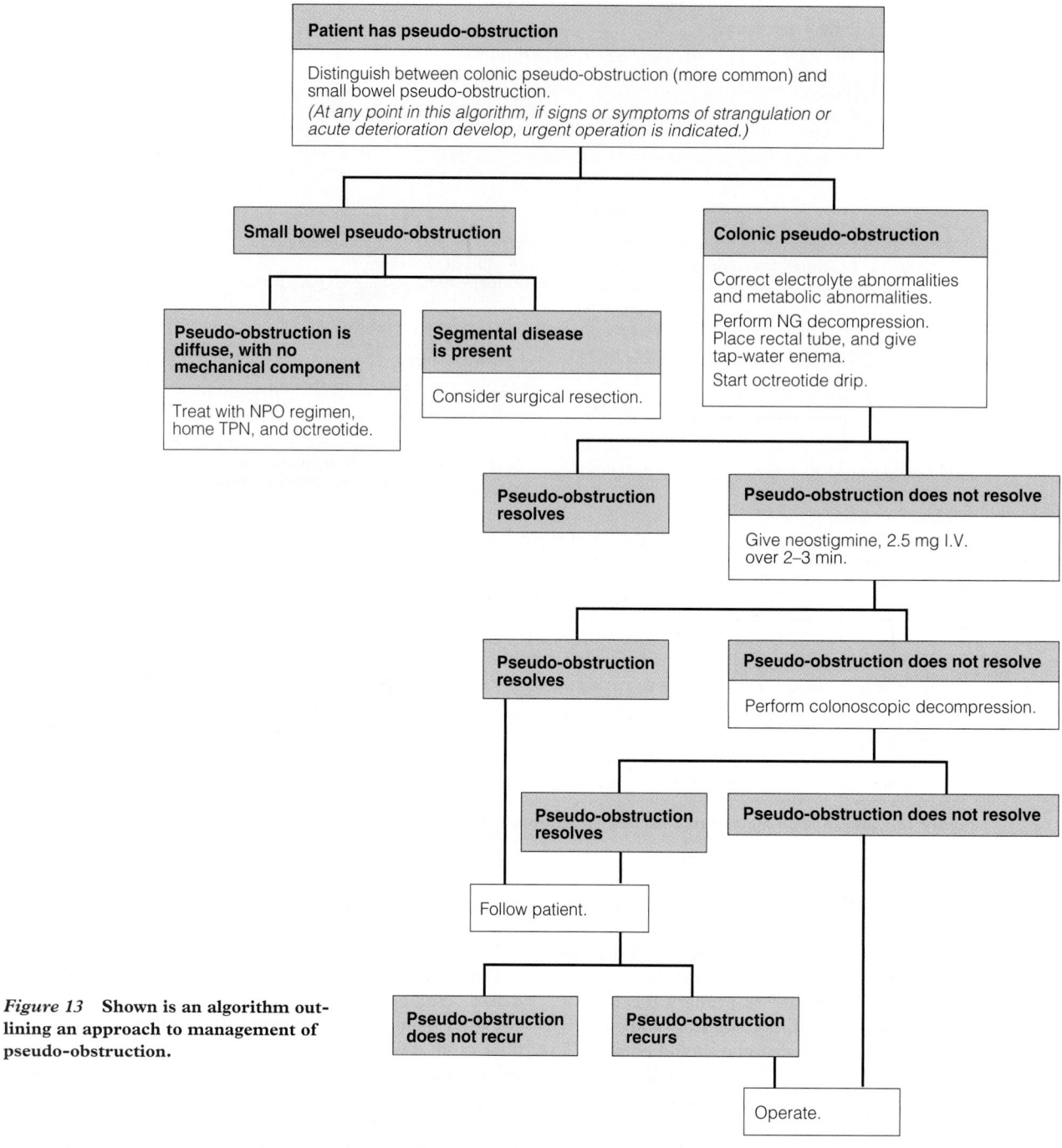

Figure 13 **Shown is an algorithm outlining an approach to management of pseudo-obstruction.**

to any acute medical condition or metabolic derangement [*see Table 1*]. The pathophysiologic mechanisms that cause ileus are incompletely understood but appear to involve disruption of normal neurohumoral responses.[92] Ileus may be classified into two broad categories: postoperative ileus and ileus without antecedent abdominal operation. Postoperative ileus is manifested by atony of the stomach, the small intestine, and the colon and usually resolves spontaneously within a few days as normal bowel motility returns. Typically, the small bowel regains its motility within 24 hours of operation, followed 3 to 4 days later by the stomach and the colon. Initial therapy of ileus is directed at identifying and correcting the presumed cause [*see Figure 12*]. If the patient experiences abdominal distention, abdominal pain, nausea, or vomiting, then nasogastric decompression, placement of a Foley catheter,

and I.V. rehydration are indicated. In postoperative patients, it is best not to use strong narcotics for analgesia and instead to rely on epidural anesthesia and nonsteroidal anti-inflammatory drugs. When ileus develops in patients who have not recently undergone an operation, a thorough history, a careful physical examination, and well-chosen laboratory tests are necessary to identify the possible causes.

When ileus persists for what is, in one's best clinical judgment, an inordinate length of time for the operation performed (typically, longer than 3 to 4 days), the possibility of partial mechanical obstruction, possibly associated with an intra-abdominal abscess or another source of infection, must be considered. If an abscess is suspected, an abdominal CT scan should be obtained. Abdominal ultrasonography has been reported to distinguish postoperative ileus from mechanical obstruction reliably.[22] A small bowel contrast examination with barium identifies partial mechanical small bowel obstruction in about 75% of patients.[26,28] CT scanning distinguishes ileus from obstruction in about 80% of patients.

Intragastric administration of a water-soluble contrast agent has shown great potential in the treatment of ileus.[93,94] In one study, administration of 120 ml of diatrizoate meglumine or diatrizoate sodium via nasogastric tube to 40 adults with postoperative small bowel ileus led to restored intestinal motility within 6 hours in all 40, allowing them to resume oral alimentation within 24 hours.[93] Given these results, a prospective, randomized trial that addresses cost-management end points is warranted.

PSEUDO-OBSTRUCTION

Pseudo-obstruction [see Figure 13] can exist in the small bowel or the colon and can be either acute or chronic. Acute colonic pseudo-obstruction, also known as Ogilvie syndrome, is the most common form. Colonic pseudo-obstruction occurs most commonly in hospitalized patients in the postoperative period or in response to a nonsurgical acute illness (e.g., pneumonia, myocardial infarction, hypoxia, shock, intestinal ischemia, or electrolyte imbalance). The pathophysiologic mechanisms underlying idiopathic pseudo-obstruction appear to be related to an imbalance in the parasympathetic and sympathetic influences on colonic motility.

The presenting symptoms of acute colonic pseudo-obstruction are massive dilatation of the colon (with the cecum more dilated than the distal colon), crampy pain, nausea, and vomiting.[95] If peritoneal irritation or systemic toxicity is present, immediate laparotomy is indicated; if not, treatment involves nasogastric decompression, placement of a rectal tube, tap-water enemas, correction of any underlying metabolic disturbances, and avoidance of narcotic and anticholinergic medications. With conservative management, acute colonic pseudo-obstruction resolves within 4 days in more than 80% of cases.[96] Colonoscopy was previously the method of choice for decompression in this setting.[97] It has been shown, however, that I.V. administration of neostigmine, 2.5 mg over 2 to 3 minutes, leads to prompt resolution of acute colonic pseudo-obstruction within minutes in nearly all cases.[98,99] Now that this previously difficult and potentially lethal problem can readily be treated pharmacologically, colonoscopic decompression and surgical intervention should be reserved for cases in which pharmacologic measures fail.

Chronic intestinal pseudo-obstruction is a rare acquired disorder that is caused by various diseases involving GI smooth muscle, the enteric nervous system, or the extrinsic autonomic nerve supply to the gut.[100] These disorders are treated with an NPO regimen, home TPN, and octreotide. Patients with chronic intestinal pseudo-obstruction should be followed closely for long periods and should undergo repeat contrast studies: a condition occasionally develops that can cause mechanical obstruction and that may be surgically correctable.[101,102]

Cost Considerations

Cost considerations are exerting an ever-growing influence on surgical care in general and on the decision whether to operate in particular. A large percentage of the high total cost of caring for patients with ileus or mechanical intestinal obstruction is accounted for by the cost associated with hospitalization or the need for laparotomy.

Strategies for reducing the overall cost of managing patients with bowel obstruction may take several forms: the development of diagnostic and therapeutic methods that lead to more rapid diagnosis and resolution of ileus and partial small bowel obstruction; the development of techniques for rapid identification of patients with complete or closed-loop obstruction and early reversible strangulation, which would permit earlier operative intervention and thereby reduce the incidence of complications; the development of therapeutic approaches that prevent postoperative ileus; and the development of methods for preventing intra-abdominal adhesions, which would significantly reduce the overall incidence of bowel obstruction. Two prospective, randomized clinical trials demonstrated that placement of a bioresorbable membrane composed of sodium hyaluronate and carboxymethylcellulose underneath abdominal fascial closures significantly reduced the severity and density of postoperative adhesions.[103,104] In theory, use of such a product should reduce the incidence of adhesion-related bowel obstruction; however, longer-term studies are required to determine whether this will actually be the case.

From a management viewpoint, if a specific diagnostic test, medication, or approach (e.g., laparoscopy) costs less than a day of hospitalization does, it immediately becomes cost-effective if it reduces complications and shortens length of stay by 1 day. Intragastric administration of a water-soluble contrast agent to relieve small bowel ileus or partial adhesive obstruction is an example of an innovative, cost-effective therapeutic strategy. Diagnostic laparoscopy, abdominal ultrasonography, CT scanning, and fast MRI have all been successfully used to make earlier definitive management decisions and to prevent gangrenous obstruction. Laparoscopic adhesiolysis also leads to earlier hospital discharge. On the basis of the collective experience reported in a substantial number of studies (see above), a logical proposal for cost-effective management of patients with bowel obstruction would be to perform ultrasonography or abdominal CT scanning immediately after initial resuscitation, then to perform laparoscopic surgery on those patients in whom the contrast agent does not arrive in the right colon within 24 hours. However, prospective, randomized clinical trials are needed to evaluate the cost-effectiveness of this and other newer management strategies.

References

1. Irvin T: Abdominal pain: a surgical audit of 1190 emergency admissions. Br J Surg 76:1121, 1989

2. Lucky A, Livingston E, Tache Y: Mechanisms and treatment of postoperative ileus. Arch Surg 138:206, 2003

3. Eskelinen M, Ikonen J, Lipponen P: Contributions of history-taking, physical examination, and computer assistance to diagnosis of acute small-bowel obstruction: a prospective study of 1333 patients with acute abdominal pain. Scand J Gastroenterol 29:715, 1994

4. Reisner R, Cohen J: Gallstone ileus: a review of 1001 reported cases. Am Surg 60:441, 1994

5. Sarr M, Bulkley G, Zuidema G: Preoperative recognition of intestinal strangulation obstruction: prospective evaluation of diagnostic capability. Am J Surg 145:176, 1983

6. Burrell H, Baker D, Wardrop P, et al: Significant plain film findings in sigmoid volvulus. Clin Radiol 49:317, 1994

7. Fatarr S, Schulman A: Small bowel obstruction masking synchronous large bowel obstruction: a need for emergency barium enema. AJR Am J Roentgenol 140:1159, 1983

8. Lim J, Ko Y, Lee D, et al: Determining the site and causes of colonic obstruction with sonogra-

phy. AJR Am J Roentgenol 163:113, 1994

9. Gough I: Strangulating adhesive small bowel obstruction with normal radiographs. Br J Surg 65:431, 1978

10. Ko Y, Lim J, Le D, et al: Small bowel obstruction: sonographic evaluation. Radiology 188:649, 1993

11. Balthazar E: For suspected small-bowel obstruction and an equivocal plain film, should we perform CT or a small-bowel series? AJR Am J Roentgenol 163:1260, 1994

12. Daneshmand S, Hedley C, Stain S: The utility and reliability of computed tomography scan in the diagnosis of small bowel obstruction. Am Surg 65:922, 1999

13. Donckier V, Closset J, Van Gansbeke D, et al: Contribution of computed tomography to decision making in the management of adhesive small bowel obstruction. Br J Surg 85:1071, 1998

14. Peck J, Milleson T, Phelan J: The role of computed tomography with contrast and small bowel follow-through in management of small bowel obstruction. Am J Surg 177:375, 1999

15. Zalcman M, Sy M, Donckier V, et al: Helical CT signs in the diagnosis of intestinal ischemia in small-bowel obstruction. AJR Am J Roentgenol 175:1601, 2000

16. Ha H: CT in the early detection of strangulation in intestinal obstruction. Semin Ultrasound CT MRI 16:141, 1995

17. Beall DP, Fortman BJ, Lawler BC, et al: Imaging bowel obstruction: a comparison between fast magnetic resonance imaging and helical computed tomography. Clin Radiol 57:719, 2002

18. Matsuoka H, Takahara T, Masaki T, et al: Preoperative evaluation by magnetic resonance imaging in patients with bowel obstruction. Am J Surg 183:614, 2002

19. Ogata M, Mateer J, Condon R: Prospective evaluation of abdominal sonography for the diagnosis of bowel obstruction. Ann Surg 223:237, 1996

20. Grunshaw N, Renwick IG, Scarisbrick G, et al: Prospective evaluation of ultrasound in distal ileal and colonic obstruction. Clin Radiol 55:356, 2000

21. Meiser G, Meissner K: Intermittent incomplete intestinal obstruction: a frequently mistaken identity. Ultrasonographic diagnosis and management. Surg Endosc 3:46, 1989

22. Meiser G, Meissner K: Ileus and intestinal obstruction—ultrasonographic findings as a guideline to therapy. Hepatogastroenterology 34:194, 1987

23. Megibow A: Bowel obstruction: evaluation with CT. Radiol Clin North Am 32:861, 1994

24. Balthazar E: CT of small-bowel obstruction. AJR Am J Roentgenol 162:255, 1994

25. Frager D, Rovno HD, Baer JW, et al: Prospective evaluation of colonic obstruction with computed tomography. Abdom Imaging 23:141, 1998

26. Dunn JT, Halls JM, Berne TV: Roentgenographic contrast studies in acute small-bowel obstruction. Arch Surg 119:1305, 1984

27. Caroline DF, Herlinger H, Laufer I, et al: Small bowel enema in the diagnosis of adhesive obstructions. AJR Am J Roentgenol 142:1133, 1984

28. Brolin R: Partial small bowel obstruction. Surgery 95:145, 1984

29. Maglinte D, Peterson D, Vahey T, et al: Enteroclysis in partial small bowel obstruction. Am J Surg 147:325, 1984

30. Anderson C, Humphry W: Contrast radiography in small bowel obstruction: a prospective randomized trial. Mil Med 162:749, 1997

31. Fevang BT, Jensen D, Fevang J, et al: Upper gas-

trointestinal contrast study in the management of small bowel obstruction—a prospective randomised study. Eur J Surg 166:39, 2000

32. Muir J, von Gunten C: Antisecretory agents in gastrointestinal obstruction. Clin Geriatr Med 16:327, 2000

33. Mercadante S, Ripamonti C, Casuccio A, et al: Comparison of octreotide and hyoscine butylbromide in controlling gastrointestinal symptoms due to malignant inoperable bowel obstruction. Support Care Cancer 8:188, 2000

34. Ripamonti C, Mercadante S, Groff L, et al: Role of octreotide, scopolamine butylbromide, and hydration in symptom control of patients with inoperable bowel obstruction and nasogastric tubes: a prospective randomized trial. J Pain Symptom Manage 19:23, 2000

35. Matsushita M, Hajiro K, Takakawa H, et al: Plastic prosthesis in the palliation of small bowel stenosis secondary to recurrent gastric cancer: initial cost savings. Gastrointest Endosc 52:571, 2000

36. de Gregorio MA, Mainar A, Tejero E, et al: Acute colorectal obstruction: stent placement for palliative treatment—results of a multicenter study. Radiology 209:117, 1998

37. Khoo D, Hall E, Motson R, et al: Palliation of malignant intestinal obstruction using octreotide. Eur J Cancer 30A:28, 1994

38. Stiefel F, Morant R: Vapreotide, a new somatostatin analogue in the palliative management of obstructive ileus in advanced cancer. Support Care Cancer 1:57, 1993

39. Mystakidou K, Tsilika E, Kalaidopoulou O, et al: Comparison of octreotide administration vs. conservative treatment in the management of inoperable bowel obstruction in patients with far advanced cancer: a randomized, double-blind, controlled clinical trial. Anticancer Res 22:1187, 2002

40. Scheidbach H, Horbach T, Groitl H, et al: Percutaneous endoscopic gastrostomy/jejunostomy (PEG/PEJ) for decompression in the upper gastrointestinal tract. Initial experience with palliative treatment of gastrointestinal obstruction in terminally ill patients with advanced carcinomas. Surg Endosc 13:1103, 1999

41. Silen W, Hein MF, Goldman L: Strangulation obstruction of the small intestine. Arch Surg 85:137, 1962

42. Laws H, Aldrete J: Small bowel obstruction: a review of 465 cases. South Med J 69:733, 1976

43. Sosa J, Gardner B: Management of patients diagnosed as acute intestinal obstruction secondary to adhesions. Am Surg 59:125, 1993

44. Snyder EN, McCranie D: Closed loop obstruction of the small bowel. Am J Surg 111:398, 1966

45. Mangiante E, Croce M, Fabian T, et al: Sigmoid volvulus: a four-decade experience. Am Surg 55:41, 1989

46. Gilger MA, Wagner ML, Barrish JO, et al: New treatment for rectal impaction in children: an efficacy, comfort, and safety trial of the pulsed-irrigation enhanced-evacuation procedure. J Pediatr Gastroenterol Nutr 18:92, 1994

47. Youssef NN, Peters JM, Henderson W, et al: Dose response of PEG 3350 for the treatment of childhood fecal impaction. J Pediatr 141:410, 2002

48. Ellis H: The clinical significance of adhesions: focus on intestinal obstruction. Eur J Surg Suppl 577:5, 1997

49. Bizer L, Liebling R, Delany H, et al: Small bowel obstruction: the role of non-operative treatment in simple intestinal obstruction and predictive criteria for strangulation obstruction. Surgery 89:407, 1981

50. Gowen GF: Long tube decompression is successful in 90% of patients with adhesive small

bowel obstruction. Am J Surg 185:512, 2003

51. Barkan H, Webster S, Ozeran S: Factors predicting the recurrence of adhesive small-bowel obstruction. Am J Surg 170:361, 1995

52. Landercasper J, Cogbill TH, Merry WH, et al: Long-term outcome after hospitalization for small-bowel obstruction. Arch Surg 128:765, 1993

53. Miller G, Boman J, Shrier I, et al: Natural history of patients with adhesive small bowel obstruction. Br J Surg 87:1240, 2000

54. Ellis H, Moran BJ, Thompson JN, et al: Adhesion-related hospital readmissions after abdominal and pelvic surgery: a retrospective cohort study. Lancet 353:1476, 1999

55. Parker MC, Ellis H, Moran BJ, et al: Postoperative adhesions: ten-year follow-up of 12,584 patients undergoing lower abdominal surgery. Dis Colon Rectum 44:822, 2001

56. Meagher AP, Moller C, Hoffmann DC: Non-operative treatment of small bowel obstruction following appendicectomy or operation on the ovary or tube. Br J Surg 80:1310, 1993

57. Mulvihill S, Pappas T, Fonkalsrud Z, et al: The effect of somatostatin on experimental intestinal obstruction. Ann Surg 207:169, 1988

58. Gittes G, Nelson M, Debas H, et al: Improvement in survival of mice with proximal small bowel obstruction treated with octreotide. Am J Surg 163:231, 1992

59. Bastounis E, Hadjinikolaou L, Ioannou N, et al: Somatostatin as adjuvant therapy in the management of obstructive ileus. Hepatogastroenterology 36:538, 1989

60. Assalia A, Schein M, Kopelman D, et al: Therapeutic effect of oral Gastrografin in adhesive, partial small-bowel obstruction: a prospective randomized trial. Surgery 115:433, 1994

61. Blackmon S, Lucius C, Wilson JP, et al: The use of water-soluble contrast in evaluating clinically equivocal small bowel obstruction. Am Surg 66:238, 2000

62. Biondo S, Pares D, Mora L, et al: Randomized clinical study of Gastrografin administration in patients with adhesive small bowel obstruction. Br J Surg 90:542, 2003

63. Choi H, Chu K, Law W: Therapeutic value of Gastrografin in adhesive small bowel obstruction after unsuccessful conservative treatment, a prospective randomized trial. Ann Surg 223:1, 2002

64. Chen SC, Chang KJ, Lee PH, et al: Oral urografin in postoperative small bowel obstruction. World J Surg 23:1051, 1999

65. Chen SC, Lin FY, Lee PH, et al: Water-soluble contrast study predicts the need for early surgery in adhesive small bowel obstruction. Br J Surg 85:1692, 1998

66. Feigin E, Seror D, Szold A, et al: Water-soluble contrast material has no therapeutic effect on postoperative small-bowel obstruction: results of a prospective, randomized clinical trial. Am J Surg 171:227, 1996

67. Leon EL, Metzger A, Tsiotos GG, et al: Laparoscopic management of small bowel obstruction: indications and outcome. J Gastrointest Surg 2:132, 1998

68. Strickland P, Lourie DJ, Suddleson EA, et al: Is laparoscopy safe and effective for treatment of acute small-bowel obstruction? Surg Endosc 13:695, 1999

69. Suter M, Zermatten P, Halkic N, et al: Laparoscopic management of mechanical small bowel obstruction: are there predictors of success or failure? Surg Endosc 14:478, 2000

70. Bailey IS, Rhodes M, O'Rourke N, et al: Laparoscopic management of acute small bowel obstruction. Br J Surg 85:84, 1998

71. Wullstein C, Gross E: Laparoscopic compared with conventional treatment of acute adhesive small bowel obstruction. Br J Surg 90:1147, 2003

72. Fischer CP, Doherty D: Laparoscopic approach to small bowel obstruction. Semin Laparosc Surg 9:40, 2002

73. Bohm B, Milsom JW, Fazio VW: Postoperative intestinal motility following conventional and laparoscopic intestinal surgery. Arch Surg 130:415, 1995

74. Vrijland WW, Jeekel J, van Geldorp HJ, et al: Abdominal adhesions, intestinal obstruction, pain, and infertility. Surg Endosc 117:1017, 2003

75. Chapron C, Pierre F, Harchaoui Y, et al: Gastrointestinal injuries during gynaecological laparoscopy. Hum Reprod 14:333, 1999

76. Garrard CL, Clements RH, Nanney L, et al: Adhesion formation is reduced after laparoscopic surgery. Surg Endosc 13:10, 1999

77. Tittel A, Treutner KH, Titkova S, et al: Comparison of adhesion reformation after laparoscopic and conventional adhesiolysis in an animal model. Langenbecks Arch Surg 386:141, 2001

78. Ellozy SH, Harris MT, Bauer JJ, et al: Early postoperative small-bowel obstruction: a prospective evaluation in 242 consecutive abdominal operations. Dis Colon Rectum 45:1214, 2002

79. Pickleman J, Lee R: The management of patients with suspected early postoperative small bowel obstruction. Ann Surg 212:216, 1989

80. Brolin R: The role of gastrointestinal tube decompression in the treatment of mechanical intestinal obstruction. Am Surg 49:131, 1983

81. Quatromoni J, Rosoff L, Halls J, et al: Early postoperative small bowel obstruction. Ann Surg 191:72, 1980

82. Stewart R, Page C, Brender J, et al: The incidence and risk of early postoperative small bowel obstruction. Am J Surg 154:643, 1987

83. Spears H, Petrelli N, Herrera L, et al: Treatment of small bowel obstruction after colorectal carcinoma. Am J Surg 155:383, 1988

84. Fleshner PR, Siegman MG, Slater GI, et al: A prospective, randomized trial of short versus long tubes in adhesive small-bowel obstruction. Am J Surg 170:366, 1995

85. Hulnick D, Megibow A, Balthazar E, et al: Computed tomography in the evaluation of diverticulitis. Radiology 152:491, 1984

86. Tejero E, Mainar A, Fernández L, et al: New procedure for the treatment of colorectal neoplastic obstructions. Dis Colon Rectum 37:1158, 1994

87. Itabashi M, Hamano K, Kameoka S, et al: Self-expanding stainless steel stent application in rectosigmoid stricture. Dis Colon Rectum 36:508, 1993

88. Binkert C, Ledermann H, Jost R, et al: Acute colonic obstruction: clinical aspects and cost-effectiveness of preoperative and palliative treatment with self-expanding metallic stents—a preliminary report. Radiology 206:199, 1998

89. Mainar A, DeGregorio Ariza MA, Tejero E, et al: Acute colorectal obstruction: treatment with self-expandable metallic stents before scheduled surgery—results of a multicenter study. Radiology 210:65, 1999

90. Stelmach W, Cass A: Small bowel obstructions: the case for investigation for occult large bowel carcinoma. Aust NZ J Surg 59:181, 1989

91. Yoo HY, Mergelas J, Seibert DG: Paraduodenal hernia: a treatable cause of upper gastrointestinal tract symptoms. Clin Res 31:226, 2000

92. Fromm D: Ileus and obstruction. Surgery: Scientific Principles and Practice. Greenfield LJ, Mulholland MW, Oldham KT, et al, Eds. JB Lippincott Co, Philadelphia, 1993, p 731

93. Watkins D, Robertson C: Water-soluble radiocontrast material in the treatment of the postoperative ileus. Am J Obstet Gynecol 152:450, 1985

94. Zer M, Kanzenelson D, Feigenberg Z, et al: The value of Gastrografin in the differential diagnosis of paralytic ileus and mechanical obstruction. Dis Colon Rectum 20:573, 1977

95. Vanek V, Al-Salti M: Acute pseudo-obstruction of the colon (Ogilvie's syndrome): an analysis of 400 cases. Dis Colon Rectum 29:203, 1986

96. Sloyer A, Panella V, Demas B: Ogilvie's syndrome: successful management with colonoscopy. Dig Dis Sci 33:1391, 1988

97. Nakhgevany KB: Colonoscopic decompression of the colon in patients with Ogilvie's syndrome. Am J Surg 148:317, 1984

98. Hutchinson R, Griffiths C: Acute colonic pseudo-obstruction: a pharmacological approach. Ann R Coll Surg Engl 74:364, 1992

99. Ponec RJ, Saunders MD, Kimmey MB: Neostigmine for the treatment of acute colonic pseudo-obstruction. N Engl J Med 341:137, 1999

100. Faulk D, Anuras S, Christensen J: Chronic intestinal pseudo-obstruction. Gastroenterology 74:922, 1978

101. Schuffler M, Deitch E: Chronic idiopathic intestinal pseudo-obstruction: a surgical approach. Ann Surg 192:752, 1980

102. Knoll RF Jr, Schuffler MD, Helton WS: Small bowel resection for relief of chronic intestinal pseudo-obstruction. Am J Gastroenterol 90:1142, 1995

103. Vrijland WW, Tseng L, Eijkman H, et al: Fewer intraperitoneal adhesions with use of hyaluronic acid-carboxymethylcellulose membrane, a randomized clinical trial. Ann Surg 235:193, 2002

104. Becker JM, Dayton MT, Fazio VW, et al: Prevention of postoperative abdominal adhesions by a sodium hyaluronate-based bioresorbable membrane: a prospective, randomized, double-blind multicenter study. J Am Coll Surg 183:297, 1996

Acknowledgment

Figures 12 and 13 Marcia Kammerer.

47 UPPER GASTROINTESTINAL BLEEDING

Kristi L. Harold, M.D., F.A.C.S., and Richard T. Schlinkert, M.D., F.A.C.S.

Assessment and Management of Upper Gastrointestinal Bleeding

The most common causes of upper gastrointestinal bleeding are chronic duodenal ulcers, chronic gastric ulcers, esophageal varices, gastric varices, Mallory-Weiss tears, acute hemorrhagic gastritis, and gastric neoplasms [*see* Management of Specific Sources of Upper GI Bleeding, *below*]. Less common causes include various other gastrointestinal conditions and certain hepatobiliary and pancreatic disorders.

Presentation and Initial Management

INITIAL ASSESSMENT AND MANAGEMENT

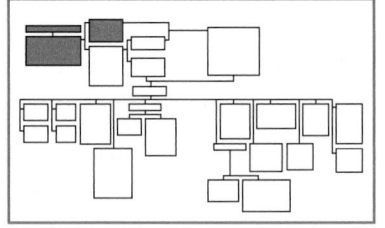

Upper gastrointestinal hemorrhage may present as severe bleeding with hematemesis, hematochezia, and hypotension; as gradual bleeding with melena; or as occult bleeding detected by positive tests for blood in the stool. The initial steps in the evaluation of patients with upper GI bleeding are based on the perceived rate of bleeding and the degree of hemodynamic stability. Hemodynamically stable patients who show no evidence of active bleeding or comorbidities and in whom endoscopic findings are favorable may be treated on an outpatient basis, whereas patients who show evidence of serious bleeding should be managed aggressively and hospitalized.

The airway, breathing, and circulation should be rapidly assessed, and the examiner should note whether the patient has a history of or currently exhibits hematemesis, melena, or hematochezia. Blood should be drawn for a complete blood count, blood chemistries (including tests of liver function and renal function), and measurement of the prothrombin time (PT) and the partial thromboplastin time (PTT). Blood should be sent to the blood bank for typing and crossmatching.

If the patient is stable and shows no evidence of recent or active hemorrhage, the surgeon may proceed with the workup.

If, however, the patient is stable but shows evidence of recent or active bleeding, a large-bore intravenous line should be placed before workup is begun; the presence of the line ensures immediate I.V. access should the patient subsequently become unstable.

If the patient is unstable, resuscitation should be begun immediately.

RESUSCITATION

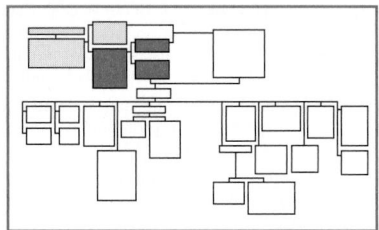

Resuscitation of an unstable patient is begun by establishing a secure airway and ensuring adequate ventilation. Oxygen should be given as necessary, either by mask or by endotracheal tube and ventilator. A large-bore I.V. line should then be placed, through which lactated Ringer solution should be infused at a rate high enough to maintain tissue perfusion. A urinary catheter should be inserted and urine output monitored. Blood should be given as necessary, and any coagulopathies should be corrected if possible. It is all too easy to forget these basic steps in a desire to evaluate and manage massive GI hemorrhage.

If the patient remains unstable and continues to bleed despite supportive measures, he or she should be taken to the operating room for intraoperative diagnosis. The abdomen should be opened through an upper midline incision, and an anterior gastrotomy should be performed. If inspection does not reveal the source of the bleeding or if bleeding is observed beyond the pylorus, a duodenotomy is made, with care taken to preserve the pylorus if possible. Bleeding from the proximal stomach may be difficult to verify, but it should be actively sought if no other bleeding site is identified.

Clinical Evaluation

HISTORY

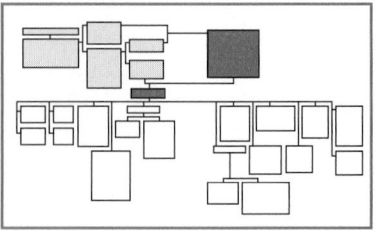

Only after the initial measures to protect the airway and stabilize the patient have been completed should an attempt be made to establish the cause of the bleeding. The history should focus on known causes of upper GI bleeding (e.g., ulcers, recent trauma or stress, liver disease, varices, alcoholism, and vomiting) and on the possible use of medications that interfere with coagulation (e.g., aspirin, nonsteroidal anti-inflammatory drugs [NSAIDs], and dipyridamole) or alter hemodynamics (e.g., beta blockers and antihypertensive agents). The cardiac history is particularly important for assessing the patient's ability to withstand varying degrees of anemia.

PHYSICAL EXAMINATION

The physical examination is seldom of much help in determining the exact site of bleeding, but it may reveal jaundice, ascites, or other signs of hepatic disease; a tumor mass; or a bruit from an abdominal vascular lesion.

NASOGASTRIC ASPIRATION

The next step is nasogastric aspiration. A bloody aspirate is an indication for esophagogastroduodenoscopy (EGD), as is a clear, nonbilious aspirate if a bleeding site distal to the pylorus has not been excluded. If the aspirate is clear and bile-stained, the source of the bleeding is unlikely to be the stomach, the duodenum, the liver, the biliary tree, or the pancreas. Nonetheless, if subsequent evaluation of the lower GI tract for the source of the bleeding is unrewarding, an upper GI site that had stopped bleeding when the nasogastric tube was passed or that was distal to the ligament of Treitz should still be considered.

Investigative Tests

UPPER GI ENDOSCOPY (ESOPHAGOGASTRODUODENOSCOPY)

EGD [see 60 Gastrointestinal Endoscopy] almost always reveals the source of upper GI bleeding; its utility and accuracy have been well documented in the literature. This procedure requires considerable skill: identification of bleeding sites in a blood-filled stomach is far from easy. Hematemesis is an indication for emergency EGD, usually within 1 hour of presentation. If the rate of bleeding is high, saline lavage may be performed to clear the stomach of blood and clots. If the rate of bleeding is moderate or low, as is often the case in patients with melena, urgent EGD is indicated.

EGD is not only an excellent diagnostic tool but also a valuable therapeutic modality. Indeed, most upper GI hemorrhages may be controlled endoscopically, though the degree of success to be expected in individual cases varies according to the expertise of the endoscopist and the specific cause of the bleeding. Therapeutic endoscopic maneuvers include injection, thermal coagulation, and mechanical occlusion of bleeding sites (by means of clip application or variceal banding). The choice of therapy depends on the cause, the site, and the rate of bleeding.

OTHER TESTS

If endoscopic examination reveals no lesions in the stomach or the duodenum and bleeding has ceased, enteroclysis (direct introduction of $BaSO_4$ into the small bowel) and roentgenography of the duodenum and the jejunum should be done next. This is probably a more sensitive radiologic test than a standard small bowel roentgenogram. Nonetheless, the absence of a lesion on this test does not rule out the small bowel as the source of the hemorrhage; not uncommonly, the x-ray is negative when a bleeding small bowel lesion is present.

Tagged red cell scans may confirm the presence of an active bleeding site; however, scans are fairly nonspecific with respect to determining the anatomic location of the bleeding. Arteriography may demonstrate that a lesion is present, but it cannot reliably identify a bleeding site unless the bleeding is brisk (> 1 ml/min). Occasionally, arteriography reveals the cause of the bleeding even if the bleeding has stopped. Recurrent bleeding or bleeding that is suspected to be secondary to small bowel pathology may be evaluated by means of video capsule endoscopy, which is capable of localizing a variety of lesions (including arteriovenous malformations, ulcers, strictures, and malignancies) so as to direct surgical

intervention. Video capsule endoscopy should be used with caution in patients exhibiting obstructive symptoms: if the capsule becomes trapped, complete obstruction may result.

Intraoperative endoscopic exploration may also prove useful in this situation. Before the small bowel is manipulated, a pediatric colonoscope is introduced either orally or through a distal jejunal enterotomy; the latter method allows easier viewing of the entire small bowel. The mucosal detail is examined as the surgeon guides the scope through the small bowel. The bowel must be handled gently to avoid a mucosal injury, which could mimic a significant lesion.

These tests, in conjunction with EGD, should allow the surgeon to establish the cause of upper GI bleeding at least 90% of the time.

Management of Specific Sources of Upper GI Bleeding

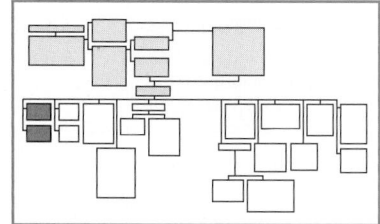

CHRONIC DUODENAL ULCER

The development of effective medical regimens for controlling uncomplicated duodenal ulcers has led to a drastic reduction in the number of elective surgical procedures performed for this purpose. Nevertheless, the incidence of bleeding from duodenal ulcers that is severe enough to necessitate emergency endoscopic or operative intervention has not decreased over the past decade.

Once EGD has demonstrated that a duodenal ulcer is the source of the bleeding, the first question that must be addressed is whether active bleeding is present. If it is, an attempt should be made to control the hemorrhage endoscopically [see Figure 1]. Because ongoing blood loss eventually leads to coagulopathies, the surgeon must exercise good judgment in deciding how long to pursue endoscopic treatment before concluding that such treatment has failed and that surgical treatment is necessary. In general, substantial bleeding (four to six units or more) that is not easily controlled endoscopically is an indication for immediate surgical intervention. Likewise, ongoing hemorrhage in a hemodynamically unstable patient (especially an elderly one) calls for immediate surgical therapy.

If bleeding is controlled endoscopically, then a proton pump inhibitor (PPI)—such as pantoprazole, 40 mg/day—should be given intravenously. In addition, antibiotic therapy directed against *Helicobacter pylori* (e.g., a 14-day course of metronidazole, 500 mg p.o., t.i.d.; omeprazole, 20 mg p.o., b.i.d.; and clarithromycin, 500 mg p.o., b.i.d.) should be considered if the organism is present; such therapy has been shown to decrease rebleeding rates after antacid medication has been stopped. Food need not be withheld unless the likelihood of rebleeding is high, in which case operation or repeat endoscopy would be necessary. Resumption of oral feeding does not appear to affect rebleeding rates.

If bleeding continues despite medical and endoscopic therapy, it should be managed surgically. In addition, certain patients whose bleeding was controlled endoscopically—such as those with a visible gastroduodenal artery and a clot in the base of the ulcer, those who experience rebleeding despite medical and endoscopic therapy, and those with giant ulcers—should be strongly considered for surgical therapy.

Surgical management may be accomplished either laparoscopically or via an open approach. The latter [see 62 Procedures for Benign and Malignant Gastric and Duodenal Disease] begins with an upper midline incision. The duodenum is mobilized and an anterior lon-

Assessment and Management of Upper Gastrointestinal Bleeding

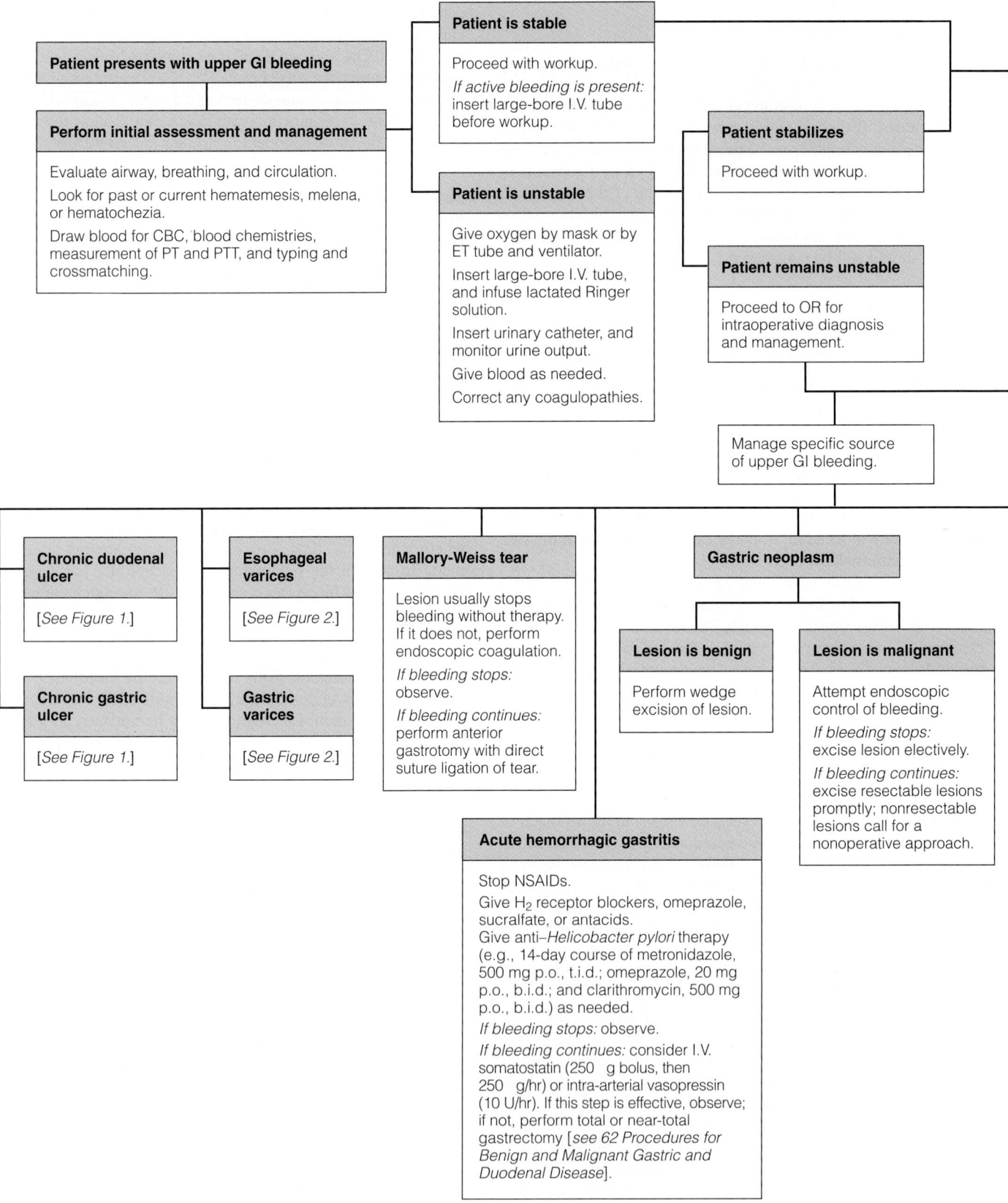

Patient presents with upper GI bleeding

Perform initial assessment and management

Evaluate airway, breathing, and circulation.
Look for past or current hematemesis, melena, or hematochezia.
Draw blood for CBC, blood chemistries, measurement of PT and PTT, and typing and crossmatching.

Patient is stable

Proceed with workup.
If active bleeding is present: insert large-bore I.V. tube before workup.

Patient is unstable

Give oxygen by mask or by ET tube and ventilator.
Insert large-bore I.V. tube, and infuse lactated Ringer solution.
Insert urinary catheter, and monitor urine output.
Give blood as needed.
Correct any coagulopathies.

Patient stabilizes

Proceed with workup.

Patient remains unstable

Proceed to OR for intraoperative diagnosis and management.

Manage specific source of upper GI bleeding.

Chronic duodenal ulcer

[See Figure 1.]

Chronic gastric ulcer

[See Figure 1.]

Esophageal varices

[See Figure 2.]

Gastric varices

[See Figure 2.]

Mallory-Weiss tear

Lesion usually stops bleeding without therapy. If it does not, perform endoscopic coagulation.
If bleeding stops: observe.
If bleeding continues: perform anterior gastrotomy with direct suture ligation of tear.

Gastric neoplasm

Lesion is benign

Perform wedge excision of lesion.

Lesion is malignant

Attempt endoscopic control of bleeding.
If bleeding stops: excise lesion electively.
If bleeding continues: excise resectable lesions promptly; nonresectable lesions call for a nonoperative approach.

Acute hemorrhagic gastritis

Stop NSAIDs.
Give H_2 receptor blockers, omeprazole, sucralfate, or antacids.
Give anti–*Helicobacter pylori* therapy (e.g., 14-day course of metronidazole, 500 mg p.o., t.i.d.; omeprazole, 20 mg p.o., b.i.d.; and clarithromycin, 500 mg p.o., b.i.d.) as needed.
If bleeding stops: observe.
If bleeding continues: consider I.V. somatostatin (250 g bolus, then 250 g/hr) or intra-arterial vasopressin (10 U/hr). If this step is effective, observe; if not, perform total or near-total gastrectomy [*see 62 Procedures for Benign and Malignant Gastric and Duodenal Disease*].

Work up patient

Obtain history, focusing on known causes of upper GI bleeding and suspect medications.

Perform physical examination.

Perform NG aspiration.

Perform esophagogastroduodenoscopy [*see 60 Gastrointestinal Endoscopy*].

Use other tests as appropriate:
- tagged red cell scans
- arteriography
- roentgenography with BaSO$_4$
- video capsule endoscopy
- intraoperative endoscopic exploration

Dieulafoy lesion

Attempt endoscopic control of bleeding.

If bleeding stops: observe.

If bleeding continues: ligate or excise vessel.

Hemosuccus pancreaticus

Perform distal pancreatectomy [*see 66 Procedures for Benign and Malignant Pancreatic Disease*], including excision of pseudocyst and ligation of bleeding vessel.

Vascular ectases

Attempt endoscopic control of bleeding.

Consider I.V. somatostatin (250 g bolus, then 250 g/hr).

If bleeding stops: observe.

If bleeding continues: resect lesion.

Jejunal ulcer

Manage underlying causes if known (e.g., medications, infections, or gastrinomas).

If bleeding stops: observe.

If bleeding continues: excise bleeding segment of jejunum.

Esophageal hiatal hernia

Hemobilia

Perform arteriographic embolization of affected portion of liver.

Other options are hepatic artery ligation and hepatic resection.

Aortoenteric fistula

Resect aortic graft.

Close enteric site of fistula.

Place extra-anatomic or in situ arterial graft.

Duodenal or jejunal diverticula

Excise lesion, with or without the aid of intraoperative endoscopy.

Paraesophageal hernia

Repair surgically (either via open laparotomy or via minimally invasive approach) [*see 34 Open Esophageal Procedures and 35 Minimally Invasive Esophageal Procedures*].

Sliding hernia

Give PPI and, if applicable, anti–*H. pylori* therapy (e.g., 14-day course of metronidazole, 500 mg p.o., t.i.d.; omeprazole, 20 mg p.o., b.i.d.; and clarithromycin, 500 mg p.o., b.i.d.).

If bleeding stops: continue medical therapy.

If bleeding continues: perform Nissen fundoplication [*see 34 Open Esophageal Procedures and 35 Minimally Invasive Esophageal Procedures*].

537

Patient has bleeding from chronic duodenal or gastric ulcer

Attempt to control hemorrhage endoscopically.
If bleeding stops: manage patient medically.
If bleeding continues: perform suture ligation of bleeding vessel.

Duodenal ulcer

Administer aggressive acid-suppressive therapy (proton pump inhibitor or H₂ receptor antagonist) and, if indicated, anti–*H. pylori* therapy (e.g., a 14-day course of metronidazole, 500 mg p.o., t.i.d.; omeprazole, 20 mg p.o., b.i.d.; and clarithromycin, 500 mg p.o., b.i.d) postoperatively.

Gastric ulcer

Perform wedge excision.
Administer aggressive acid-suppressive therapy (proton pump inhibitor or H₂ receptor antagonist) and, if indicated, anti–*H. pylori* therapy (e.g., a 14-day course of metronidazole, 500 mg p.o., t.i.d.; omeprazole, 20 mg p.o., b.i.d.; and clarithromycin, 500 mg p.o., b.i.d) postoperatively.

Figure 1 **Shown is an algorithm for management of bleeding from chronic duodenal or gastric ulcers.**

gitudinal duodenotomy performed over the site of the ulcer. The bleeding vessel, which is usually on the posterior wall of the first portion of the duodenum, is ligated with nonabsorbable sutures at sites proximal and distal to the bleeding point. A third stitch is placed posterior to the bleeding vessel. Pains must be taken to avoid injury to the common bile duct during the placement of these sutures. The duodenotomy is then closed.

The role of vagotomy in the management of bleeding duodenal ulcers has been called into question. Previously, proximal gastric vagotomy was recommended for stable patients. It was considered preferable to truncal vagotomy because it is less likely to result in gastric atony, alkaline reflux gastritis, dumping, and diarrhea. In unstable patients, truncal vagotomy was typically performed in conjunction with pyloroplasty [*see 62 Procedures for Benign and Malignant Gastric and Duodenal Disease*]. Frozen section to confirm the presence of nerve tissue is helpful for ensuring that the vagotomy is complete.

The recommendation for truncal vagotomy was based on data from studies done before PPI and anti–*H. pylori* therapy came into use. Subsequent studies that evaluated rebleeding rates with current medical regimens, however, demonstrated much lower rebleeding rates. Furthermore, it seems probable that long-term PPI therapy (e.g., omeprazole, 20 mg p.o., q.d.)—the medical equivalent of vagotomy—in conjunction with eradication of *H. pylori* and avoidance of NSAIDs, should decrease rebleeding rates significantly. Therefore, one may consider an alternative treatment approach in patients who had not been receiving ulcer therapy before the bleeding began—namely, ligation of the bleeding vessel, postoperative administration of PPIs, and anti–*H. pylori* therapy. This approach avoids the complications associated with truncal vagotomy.

CHRONIC GASTRIC ULCER

Initially, bleeding from a chronic gastric ulcer is managed in much the same way as that from a chronic duodenal ulcer (i.e., endoscopically) [*see Figure 1*]. To prevent aggravation of the bleeding, early biopsy generally is not recommended; repeat endoscopy

and biopsy are done at a later date. Emergency surgical indications for gastric ulcers are the same as those for duodenal ulcers. In addition, if a gastric ulcer does not resolve after 6 weeks of medical therapy, surgical excision is often indicated.

In stable patients, surgical management of a nonhealing chronic gastric ulcer generally consists of a hemigastrectomy that includes the ulcer site; if the ulcer is located more proximally, it may be removed by means of wedge excision [*see 62 Procedures for Benign and Malignant Gastric and Duodenal Disease*]. Excision of the ulcer should be immediately followed by frozen section to rule out cancer. There is no need for a vagotomy in these instances. In unstable patients, hemigastrectomy should probably be avoided because of the increased morbidity and mortality that can follow it. Wedge excision should be combined with aggressive acid-suppressive therapy (PPIs or H₂ receptor antagonists), followed by anti–*H. pylori* treatment. Truncal vagot-omy with pyloroplasty is rarely indicated; however, it may be considered in a patient with previous complications from ulcer disease.

ESOPHAGEAL VARICES

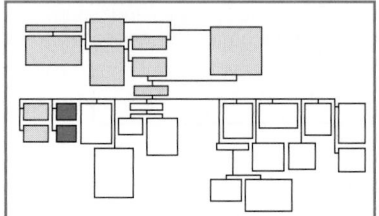

The value of endoscopy in the diagnosis and management of variceal bleeding cannot be overemphasized. Even in patients with known varices, the site of bleeding is frequently non-variceal; endoscopy is therefore essential. If bleeding varices are identified, rubber banding or intravariceal sclerotherapy with a sclerosing agent (1.5% sodium tetradecyl sulfate, ethanolamine, sodium morrhuate, or absolute alcohol) is performed [*see Figure 2*]. If these measures do not control the hemorrhage, balloon tamponade is indicated. Patients who are to undergo this procedure should have an endotracheal tube in place. The tube we prefer to use for balloon tamponade is the four-port Minnesota tube, although the Sengstaken-Blakemore tube is also acceptable. The Minnesota tube has a gastric balloon, an esophageal balloon, and aspiration ports for the esophagus and the stomach. The gastric balloon is inflated first and placed on traction. If the bleeding is not controlled, the esophageal balloon is then inflated. The pressure in the balloons should be released in 24 to 48 hours to prevent necrosis of the esophageal or the gastric wall. Successful balloon tamponade is followed by endoscopic variceal injection or variceal banding.

I.V. somatostatin (250 μg bolus, followed by infusion of 250 μg/hr) should be administered in conjunction with the abovementioned steps. Vasopressin (10 U/hr) may also be given; however, it causes diffuse vasoconstriction, and nitroglycerin is required to alleviate cardiac side effects. Somatostatin has proved superior to placebo in controlling variceal hemorrhage when used in conjunction with endoscopic sclerotherapy. It is as effective as vasopressin while giving rise to fewer side effects. Octreotide, a synthetic analogue of somatostatin, shares many of the properties of somatostatin but perhaps not all. Both agents decrease secretion of gastric acid and pepsin; to date, however, the decreased gastric blood flow observed with somatostatin administration has not been reported with octreotide administration. Nevertheless, some clinicians in the United States elect to use octreotide (25 to 50 μg/hr) in place of I.V. somatostatin because the former tends to be more widely available in the United States. Multiple prospective, randomized trials showed that propranolol (40 mg b.i.d., p.o.) decreased the incidence of first-time variceal bleeding as well as the incidence of recurrent variceal bleeding. Propranolol should

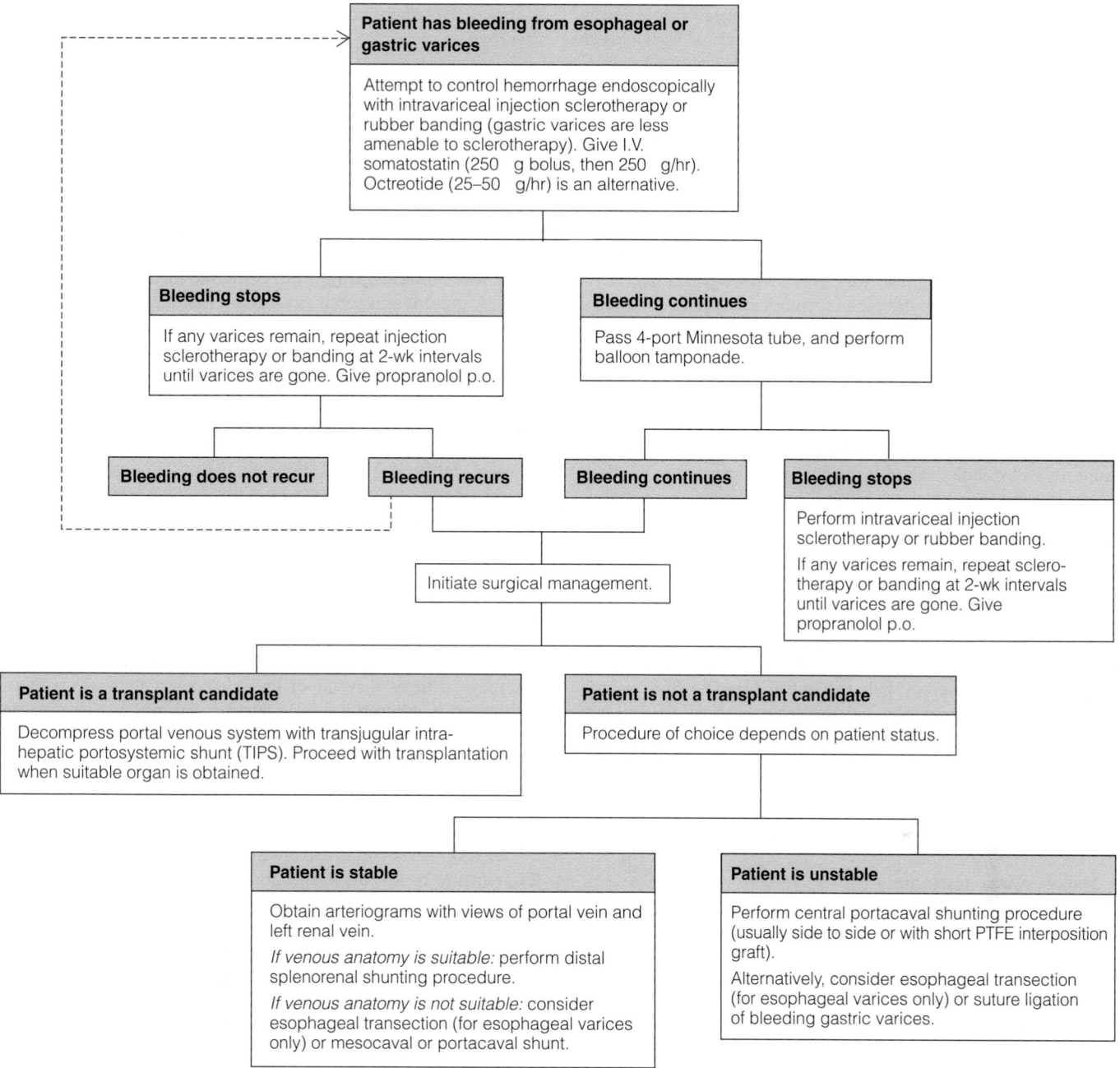

Patient has bleeding from esophageal or gastric varices

Attempt to control hemorrhage endoscopically with intravariceal injection sclerotherapy or rubber banding (gastric varices are less amenable to sclerotherapy). Give I.V. somatostatin (250 g bolus, then 250 g/hr). Octreotide (25–50 g/hr) is an alternative.

Bleeding stops

If any varices remain, repeat injection sclerotherapy or banding at 2-wk intervals until varices are gone. Give propranolol p.o.

Bleeding continues

Pass 4-port Minnesota tube, and perform balloon tamponade.

Bleeding does not recur

Bleeding recurs

Bleeding continues

Bleeding stops

Perform intravariceal injection sclerotherapy or rubber banding.

If any varices remain, repeat sclerotherapy or banding at 2-wk intervals until varices are gone. Give propranolol p.o.

Initiate surgical management.

Patient is a transplant candidate

Decompress portal venous system with transjugular intrahepatic portosystemic shunt (TIPS). Proceed with transplantation when suitable organ is obtained.

Patient is not a transplant candidate

Procedure of choice depends on patient status.

Patient is stable

Obtain arteriograms with views of portal vein and left renal vein.

If venous anatomy is suitable: perform distal splenorenal shunting procedure.

If venous anatomy is not suitable: consider esophageal transection (for esophageal varices only) or mesocaval or portacaval shunt.

Patient is unstable

Perform central portacaval shunting procedure (usually side to side or with short PTFE interposition graft).

Alternatively, consider esophageal transection (for esophageal varices only) or suture ligation of bleeding gastric varices.

Figure 2 Shown is an algorithm for management of bleeding from esophageal or gastric varices.

not be used during active bleeding but should be started once bleeding stops.

After the acute variceal bleeding has been controlled, any remaining varices should be subjected to injection sclerotherapy or banding at 2-week intervals until they too are obliterated.

The main indications for surgical intervention in patients with bleeding esophageal varices are uncontrolled hemorrhage and persistent rebleeding despite endoscopic and medical therapy. When such intervention is planned, it is essential to determine whether the patient is a transplant candidate. If so, operation should be avoided and bleeding managed by decompressing the portal venous system with a transjugular intrahepatic portosystemic shunt (TIPS) [*see 52 Portal Hypertension*]. TIPS yields excellent short-term results with respect to stopping bleeding and providing time to locate a liver suitable for transplantation; however, it has not been shown to control hemorrhage by itself over the

long term. Its use in patients who are not transplant candidates is questionable.

If the patient is not a transplant candidate and is not actively bleeding, a distal splenorenal shunt is preferable. Arteriograms with views of the portal vein and the left renal vein are obtained. Alternatively, computed tomographic angiography with three-dimensional reconstruction may be performed. If the venous anatomy is suitable—that is, if the diameter of the splenic vein is greater than 0.75 cm (preferably greater than 1.0 cm) and the vein is within one vertebral body of the renal vein on venography—a distal splenorenal shunting procedure should be feasible. If the venous anatomy is not suitable, then esophageal transection, a mesocaval venous graft, or a portacaval shunt is required.

In the emergency setting, we prefer a central portacaval shunt, usually in a side-to-side orientation or with a short polytetrafluoroethylene (PTFE) interposition graft. Esophageal transection is also a reasonable choice. This procedure is associated with a lower incidence of encephalopathy than a portacaval shunting procedure; however, it is associated with higher rates of rebleeding (particularly late rebleeding), and it can be difficult to perform when active bleeding is present. Suture ligation of the bleeding varices with devascularization (the Segura procedure) should also be considered.

In general, prognosis is related to the underlying liver disease. For example, patients with varices that are secondary to chronic extrahepatic portal venous or splenic venous occlusion generally have a much better prognosis than those whose portal hypertension is secondary to hepatic parenchymal causes. The severity of the cirrhosis also determines short-term and long-term survival and may influence the decision whether to perform a shunting procedure.

Varices in children are generally secondary to portal vein thrombosis. A conservative, nonoperative approach is preferred. If operation is required, either a portacaval shunt, a distal splenorenal shunt, or a devascularization procedure is performed. In children or adults with varices that are secondary to splenic vein thrombosis (sinistral portal hypertension), a splenectomy is usually curative; the procedure may be performed laparoscopically [*see 67 Splenectomy*].

GASTRIC VARICES

Gastric varices are managed in much the same way as esophageal varices [*see Figure 2*], though they are less amenable to sclerotherapy. If sclerotherapy fails to control bleeding from gastric varices, surgical intervention—in the form of distal splenorenal shunting, portosystemic shunting, or suture ligation with gastric devascularization—is indicated. If the patient is a suitable candidate, liver transplantation may be performed as an alternative to shunting.

MALLORY-WEISS TEARS

Mallory-Weiss tears are linear tears at the esophagogastric junction that are usually caused by vomiting. Any patient who presents with vomiting that initially is not bloody but later turns

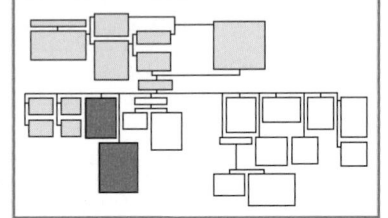

so should be suspected of having a Mallory-Weiss tear. As a rule, these lesions stop bleeding without therapy. If bleeding is substantial or persistent, however, endoscopic coagulation may be necessary. In rare instances, the tear will have to be oversewn at operation. This is accomplished via an anterior gastrotomy and direct suture ligation of the tear.

ACUTE HEMORRHAGIC GASTRITIS

Bleeding from gastritis is virtually always managed medically with H$_2$ receptor blockers, PPIs, sucralfate, or antacids (either alone or in combination), along with antibiotics if *H. pylori* is present. Somatostatin may be beneficial. Sometimes, administration of vasopressin via the left gastric artery is needed to control bleeding. In rare cases, total or near-total gastrectomy [*see 62 Procedures for Benign and Malignant Gastric and Duodenal Disease*] is required; however, the mortality associated with this operation in this setting is high. Stress ulcer prophylaxis in severely ill or traumatized patients is essential to prevent this problem. The gastric pH should be kept as close to neutral as possible. If the gastritis is relatively mild, a biopsy specimen should be obtained and tested for

H. pylori. Treatment consists of acid reduction and anti–*H. pylori* therapy.

NEOPLASMS

Benign tumors of the upper GI tract (e.g., leiomyomas, hamartomas, and hemangiomas) bleed at times. Wedge excision of the offending lesion is the procedure of choice. Gastrointestinal stro-

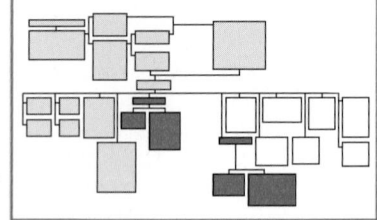

mal tumors run the gamut from benign to highly aggressive. They typically present as a submucosal mass that may cause bleeding as a result of mucosal ulceration. The bleeding may be treated with wedge excision of the tumor. Such excision can often be accomplished laparoscopically [*see 62 Procedures for Benign and Malignant Gastric and Duodenal Disease*].

Bleeding from malignant neoplasms, whether early stage or late stage, generally can be controlled initially by endoscopic means; however, rebleeding rates are high. If the lesion is resectable, it should be excised promptly once the patient is stable and any coagulopathies have been corrected. If disease is advanced, however, surgical options are limited, and a nonoperative approach, though necessarily imperfect, is preferable.

ESOPHAGEAL HIATAL HERNIA

Not infrequently, the source of chronic enteric blood loss is an esophageal hiatal hernia. Major bleeding is rare in this condition but may occur as a result of linear erosions at the level of the diaphragm (Cameron lesions), gastritis within the hernia, or torsion of a paraesophageal hernia. Endoscopy is generally diagnostic, though the sources of chronic blood loss are not always obvious. Recognition that the bleeding derives from a Cameron lesion should incline the surgeon toward operative intervention [*see 34 Open Esophageal Procedures and 35 Minimally Invasive Esophageal Procedures*]: this lesion is usually mechanically induced and therefore tends to be less responsive to antacid therapy.

Chronic bleeding from a sliding esophageal hiatal hernia should be treated initially with a PPI; anti–*H. pylori* therapy should be added if biopsy shows this organism to be present. Operation (i.e., laparoscopic Nissen fundoplication [*see 35 Minimally Invasive Esophageal Procedures*]) should be considered for fit patients who have complications associated with their hiatal hernia. A paraesophageal hernia should be repaired surgically; we prefer the laparoscopic approach when feasible.

DIEULAFOY LESION

A Dieulafoy lesion (also termed exulceratio simplex) is the rupturing of a 1 to 3 mm bleeding vessel through the gastric mucosa (usually in the proximal stomach) without surounding ulcera-

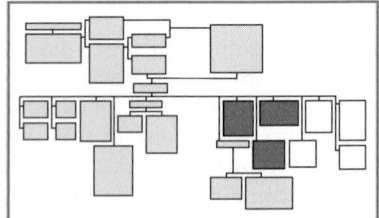

tion. It tends to be found high on the lesser curvature but can also occur in other locations. Histologic studies have not shown any intrinsic abnormalities of the mucosa or the vessel.

Initial treatment consists of either coagulation of the bleeding vessel with a heater probe or mechanical control with clips or rubber bands; local injection of epinephrine may help control acute hemorrhage while this is being done. In skilled hands, endoscopic therapy has a 95% success rate, and long-term control is excellent. If endoscopic therapy fails, surgical options, including ligation or excision of the vessel involved, come into play. Arteriographic embolization may be employed in patients who are too ill to tolerate surgical intervention.

HEMOBILIA

Hemobilia should be suspected in all patients who present with the classic triad of epigastric and right upper quadrant pain, GI bleeding, and jaundice; however, only about 40% of patients with hemobilia present with the entire triad. Endoscopy demonstrating blood coming from the ampulla of Vater points to a source in the biliary tree or the pancreas (hemosuccus pancreaticus).

Arteriography may provide the definitive diagnosis: a bleeding tumor, a ruptured artery from trauma, or another cause. Arteriographic embolization of the affected portion of the liver is the preferred treatment option; hepatic artery ligation (selective if possible) or hepatic resection [see 65 Hepatic Resection] may be required.

HEMOSUCCUS PANCREATICUS

Bleeding into the pancreatic duct, generally from erosion of a pancreatic pseudocyst into the splenic artery, is signaled by upper abdominal pain followed by hematochezia. If endoscopy is performed when hematochezia is present, the bleeding site may not be seen; however, if endoscopy is performed when pain is first noted, blood may be seen coming from the ampulla of Vater. The combination of significant GI bleeding, abdominal pain, a history of alcohol abuse or pancreatitis, and hyperamylasemia should suggest the diagnosis. Angiography can be diagnostic and, at times, therapeutic. Distal pancreatectomy [see 66 Procedures for Benign and Malignant Pancreatic Disease], including excision of the pseudocyst and ligation of the splenic artery, is the preferred treatment and generally leads to cure.

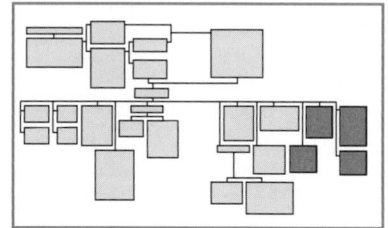

AORTOENTERIC FISTULA

Aortoenteric fistulas may occur spontaneously as a result of rupture of an aortic aneurysm or perforation of a duodenal lesion; more often, they arise after aortic surgery. A common initial manifestation of an aortoenteric fistula is a small herald bleed that is followed a few days later by a massive hemorrhage. Patients often present with the triad of GI hemorrhage, a pulsatile mass, and infection; however, not all of these symptoms are invariably present. A high index of suspicion facilitates diagnosis. Endoscopy may show an aortic graft eroding into the enteric lumen, but this is an uncommon finding. CT scanning is the procedure of choice for diagnosis. The finding of air around the aorta or the aortic graft is diagnostic and is an indication for emergency exploration. The preferred surgical treatment is resection of the graft with extra-abdominal bypass. Some authorities, however, advocate resection of the graft with in situ graft replacement.

VASCULAR ECTASES

Vascular ectases (also referred to as vascular dysplasia, angiodysplasia, angiomata, telangiectasia, and arteriovenous malformations) may bleed briskly. As a rule, gastric lesions are readily identified and the bleeding controlled by endoscopic means. Lesions that continue to bleed, either acutely or chronically, despite endoscopic measures should be excised. Some patients have multiple and extensive lesions that necessitate resection of large portions of the stomach or the small intestine. Pharmacotherapy and hormone therapy have been tried; the results have been mixed.

DUODENAL AND JEJUNAL DIVERTICULA

Duodenal and jejunal diverticula are rare causes of upper GI bleeding. Accurate identification of a bleeding site within a given diverticulum is difficult, but an attempt should be made to accomplish this by means of peroral enteroscopy or video capsule endoscopy. Excision is the preferred treatment and is accomplished by means of segmental resection. Great care must be taken in the treatment of duodenal diverticula in the region of the ampulla of Vater to ensure that the pancreatic duct and the bile ducts are not injured during excision.

JEJUNAL ULCER

Ulcerations of the jejunum are also rare. They may be secondary to medications (e.g., NSAIDs), infection, a gastrinoma, or idiopathic causes. Offending medications should be stopped, infections should be treated, and gastrinomas should be excised. If these measures do not control the hemorrhage, the bleeding segment of the jejunum should be excised.

Recommended Reading

PROSPECTIVE, RANDOMIZED, CONTROLLED TRIALS

Avgerinos A, Nevens F, Raptis S, et al: Early administration of somatostatin and efficacy of sclerotherapy in acute oesophageal variceal bleeds: the European Acute Bleeding Oesophageal Variceal Episodes (ABOVE) randomised trial. Lancet 350:1495, 1997

Cello JP, Grendell JH, Crass RA, et al: Endoscopic sclerotherapy versus portacaval shunt in patients with severe cirrhosis and variceal hemorrhage. N Engl J Med 311:1589, 1984

Clark AW, Westaby D, Silk DBA, et al: Prospective controlled trial of injection sclerotherapy in patients with cirrhosis and recent variceal hemorrhage. Lancet 2:552, 1980

Conn HO, Grace ND, Bosch J, et al: Propranolol in the prevention of the first hemorrhage from esophagogastric varices: a multicenter, randomized clinical trial. Hepatology 13:902, 1991

Garcia-Pagan JC, Feu F, Bosch J, et al: Propranolol compared with propranolol plus isosorbide-5-mono-nitrate for portal hypertension in cirrhosis: a randomized controlled study. Ann Intern Med 114:869, 1991

Graham DY, Hepps KS, Ramirez FC, et al: Treatment of Helicobacter pylori reduces the rate of rebleeding in peptic ulcer disease. Scand J Gastroenterol 28:939, 1993

Gregory PB: Prophylactic sclerotherapy for esophageal varices in men with alcoholic liver disease: a randomized, single-blind, multicenter trial. N Engl J Med 324:1779, 1991

Groszmann RJ, Bosch J, Grace ND, et al: Hemodynamic events in a prospective randomized trial of propranolol versus placebo in the prevention of a first variceal hemorrhage. Gastroenterology 99:1401, 1990

Hartigan PM, Gebhard RL, Gregory PB: Sclerotherapy for actively bleeding esophageal varices in male alcoholics with cirrhosis. Gastrointest Endosc 46:1, 1997

Krejs GJ, Little KH, Westergaard H, et al: Laser photocoagulation for the treatment of acute peptic-ulcer bleeding: a randomized controlled clinical trial. N Engl J Med 316:1618, 1987

Laine L: Multipolar electrocoagulation versus injec-tion therapy in the treatment of bleeding peptic ulcers: a prospective, randomized trial. Gastroenterology 99:1303, 1990

Laine L, Cohen H, Brodhead J, et al: Prospective evaluation of immediate versus delayed refeeding and prognostic value of endoscopy in patients with upper gastrointestinal hemorrhage. Gastroenterology 102:314, 1992

Metz CA, Livingston DH, Smith JS, et al: Impact of multiple risk factors and ranitidine prophylaxis on the development of stress-related upper gastrointestinal bleeding: a prospective, multicenter, double-blind, randomized trial. Crit Care Med 21:1844, 1993

Pascal JP, Cales P: Propranolol in the prevention of first upper gastrointestinal tract hemorrhage in patients with cirrhosis of the liver and esophageal varices. N Engl J Med 317:856, 1987

Saeed ZA, Winchester CB, Michaletz PA, et al: A scoring system to predict rebleeding after endoscopic therapy of nonvariceal upper gastrointestinal hemorrhage, with a comparison of heat probe and ethanol injection. Am J Gastroenterol 88:1842, 1993

Vinel JP, Lamouliatte H, Cales P, et al: Propranolol reduces the rebleeding rate during endoscopic sclerotherapy before variceal obliteration. Gastroenterology 102:1760, 1992

Warren WD, Henderson JM, Millikan WJ, et al: Distal splenorenal shunt versus endoscopic sclerotherapy for long-term management of variceal bleeding: preliminary report of a prospective, randomized trial. Ann Surg 203:454, 1986

META-ANALYSES

Cook DJ, Guyatt GH, Salena BJ, et al: Endoscopic therapy for acute nonvariceal upper gastrointestinal hemorrhage: a meta-analysis. Gastroenterology 102:139, 1992

Poynard T, Cales P, Pasta L, et al: Beta-adrenergic-antagonist drugs in the prevention of gastrointestinal bleeding in patients with cirrhosis and esophageal varices. N Engl J Med 324:1532, 1991

Tryba M: Prophylaxis of stress ulcer bleeding: a meta-analysis. J Clin Gastroenterol 13(suppl 2):S44, 1991

PROSPECTIVE STUDIES

Barkun AN, Cockeram AW, Plourde V, et al: Review article: acid suppression in non-variceal acute upper gastrointestinal bleeding. Aliment Pharmacol Ther 13:1565, 1999

Branicki FJ, Coleman SY, Pritchett CJ, et al: Emergency surgical treatment for nonvariceal bleeding of the upper part of the gastrointestinal tract. Surg Gynecol Obstet 172:113, 1991

Cebollero-Santamaria F, Smith J, Gioe S, et al: Selective outpatient management of upper gastrointestinal bleeding in the elderly. Am J Gastroenteral 94:1242, 1999

Costamagna G, Shah SK, Riccioni ME, et al: A prospective trial comparing small bowel radiographs and video capsule endoscopy for suspected small bowel disease. Gastroenterology 4:123, 2002

Gostout CJ, Wang KK, Ahlquist DA, et al: Acute gastrointestinal bleeding: experience of a specialized management team. J Clin Gastroenterol 14:260, 1992

Hunt PS, Fracs MS, Korman MG, et al: An 8-year prospective experience with balloon tamponade in emergency control of bleeding esophageal varices. Dig Dis Sci 27:413, 1982

Loftus EV, Alexander GL, Ahlquist DA, et al: Endoscopic treatment of major bleeding from advanced gastroduodenal malignant lesions. Mayo Clin Proc 69:736, 1994

Rockey DC, Cello JP: Evaluation of the gastrointestinal tract in patients with iron-deficiency anemia. N Engl J Med 329:1691, 1993

Terblanche J, Northoever JMA, Bornman P, et al: A prospective evaluation of injection sclerotherapy in the treatment of acute bleeding from esophageal varices. Surgery 85:239, 1979

Wilcox CM, Alexander LN, Straub RF, et al: A prospective endoscopic evaluation of the causes of upper GI hemorrhage in alcoholics: a focus on alcoholic gastropathy. Am J Gastroenteral 91:1343, 1996

Zuckerman G, Benitez J: A prospective study of bidirectional endoscopy (colonoscopy and upper endoscopy) in the evaluation of patients with occult gastrointestinal bleeding. Am J Gastroenterol 87:62, 1992

RETROSPECTIVE STUDIES

Corley DA, Stefan AM, Wolf M, et al: Early indicators of prognosis in upper gastrointestinal hemorrhage. Am J Gastroenterol 93:336, 1998

Cotton PB, Rosenberg MT, Waldram RPL, et al: Early endoscopy of oesophagus, stomach, and duodenal bulb in patients with haematemesis and melaena. Br Med J 2:505, 1973

Dempsey DT, Burke DR, Reilly RS, et al: Angiography in poor-risk patients with massive nonvariceal upper gastrointestinal bleeding. Am J Surg 159:282, 1990

Fox JG, Hunt PS: Management of acute bleeding gastric malignancy. Aust NZ J Surg 63:462, 1993

Gaisford WD: Endoscopic electrohemostasis of active upper gastrointestinal bleeding. Am J Surg 137:47, 1979

Henriksson AE, Svensson J-O: Upper gastrointestinal bleeding (with special reference to blood transfusion). Eur J Surg 157:193, 1991

Himal HS, Perrault C, Mzabi R: Upper gastrointestinal hemorrhage: aggressive management decreases mortality. Surgery 84:448, 1978

Jacobson AR, Cerqueira MD: Prognostic significance of late imaging results in technetium-99m-labeled red blood cell gastrointestinal bleeding studies with early negative images. J Nucl Med 33:202, 1992

Jim G, Rikkers LF: Cause and management of upper gastrointestinal bleeding after distal splenorenal shunt. Surgery 112:719, 1992

Kaye GL, McCormick A, Siringo S, et al: Bleeding from staple line erosion after esophageal transection: effect of omeprazole. Hepatology 15:1031, 1992

Kollef MH, O'Brien JD, Zuckerman GR, et al: Bleed: a classification tool to predict outcomes in patients with acute upper and lower gastrointestinal hemorrhage. Crit Care Med 25:1125, 1997

Liebler JM, Benner K, Putnam T, et al: Respiratory complications in critically ill medical patients with acute upper gastrointestinal bleeding. Crit Care Med 19:1152, 1991

Lipper B, Simon D, Cerrone F: Pulmonary aspiration during emergency endoscopy in patients with upper gastrointestinal hemorrhage. Crit Care Med 19:330, 1991

Miller AR, Farnell MB, Kelly KA, et al: The impact of therapeutic endoscopy on the treatment of bleeding duodenal ulcers, 1980–90. World J Surg 19:89, 1995

Norton ID, Petersen BT, Sorbi D, et al: Management and long-term prognosis of Dieulafoy lesion. Gastrointest Endosc 50:762, 1999

Sakorafas GH, Sarr MG, Farley DR: Hemosuccus pancreaticus complicating chronic pancreatitis: an obscure cause of upper gastrointestinal bleeding. Langenbeck Arch Surg 385:124, 2000

Sugawa C, Benishek D, Walt AJ: Mallory-Weiss syndrome: a study of 224 patients. Am J Surg 145:30, 1983

Sugawa C, Steffes CP, Nakamura R, et al: Upper gastrointestinal bleeding in an urban hospital: etiology, recurrence, and prognosis. Ann Surg 212:521, 1990

Wilairatana S, Sriussadaporn S, Tanphaiphat C: A review of 1338 patients with acute upper gastrointestinal bleeding at Chulalongkorn University Hospital, Bangkok. Gastroenterologia Japonica 26:58, 1991

Reviews

Cuschieri A: Laparoscopic gastric resection. Surg Clin North Am 80:1269, 2000

De Franchis R: Emerging strategies in the management of upper gastrointestinal bleeding. Digestion 60(suppl 3):17, 1999

Groszmann RJ, Grace ND: Complications of portal hypertension: esophagogastric varices and ascites. Gastroenterol Clin North Am 21:103, 1992

Jenkins SA: Drug therapy for non-variceal upper gastrointestinal bleeding. Digestion 60(suppl 3):39, 1999

Kankaria AG, Fleischer DE: The critical care management of nonvariceal upper gastrointestinal bleeding. Crit Care Clin 11:347, 1995

Katz PO, Salas L: Less frequent causes of upper gastrointestinal bleeding. Gastroenterol Clin North Am 22:875, 1993

Montgomery RS, Wilson SE: Surgical management of gastrointestinal fistulas. Surg Clin North Am 76:1148, 1996

Savides TJ, Jensen DM: Therapeutic endoscopy for nonvariceal upper gastrointestinal bleeding. Gastroenterol Clin North Am 29:465, 2000

Stabile BE: Hemorrhagic complications of pancreatitis and pancreatic pseudocysts. The Pancreas: A Clinical Textbook. Beger HG, Warshaw AL, Buchler MW, et al, Eds. Blackwell Scientific Publications, Oxford, 1997

Weiner FR, Simon DM: Gastric vascular ectases. Gastrointest Endosc Clin North Am 6:681, 1996

Zoller WG, Gross M: Beta-blockers for prophylaxis of bleeding from esophageal varices in cirrhotic portal hypertension: review of the literature. Eur J Med Res 1:407, 1995/96

48 LOWER GASTROINTESTINAL BLEEDING

Michael J. Rosen, M.D., and Jeffrey L. Ponsky, M.D., F.A.C.S.

Approach to Lower GI Bleeding

Lower gastrointestinal bleeding is defined as abnormal hemorrhage into the lumen of the bowel from a source distal to the ligament of Treitz. In the majority of cases, lower GI bleeding derives from the colon; however, the small bowel is identified as the source of bleeding in as many as one third of cases,[1,2] and the upper GI tract is identified as the source in as many as 11% of patients presenting with bright-red blood per rectum.[3]

Lower GI bleeding is more common in men than in women. The incidence rises steeply with advancing age, exhibiting a greater than 200-fold increase from the third decade of life to the ninth. This increase is largely attributable to the various colonic disorders commonly associated with aging (e.g., diverticulosis and angiodysplasia).[4-6] The exact incidence of lower GI bleeding is not known, because there is no standardized technique for localizing it. Several investigators, however, estimate the incidence to be in the range of 20 to 27 cases per 100,000 adults.[4,7] A 1997 survey of GI bleeding from the American College of Gastroenterology found that lower GI hemorrhage accounted for 24% of all GI bleeding events.[8] Another study published the same year found that 0.7% of 17,941 discharges from a Veterans Affairs hospital were for patients who had had lower GI bleeding.[9]

The basic components of management are (1) initial hemodynamic stabilization, (2) localization of the bleeding site, and (3) site-specific therapeutic intervention. There are many conditions that can cause lower GI hemorrhage [*see* Discussion, Etiology of Lower GI Bleeding, *below*]; accordingly, successful localization depends on timely and appropriate use of a variety of diagnostic tests. Despite the abundance of diagnostic modalities available, attempts to localize the source of the hemorrhage fail in as many as 8% to 12% of patients.[10,11] Once the bleeding site is localized, the appropriate therapeutic intervention must be carried out as expeditiously as possible.

Lower GI bleeding can be acute and life-threatening, chronic, or even occult. In what follows, we focus on severe, life-threatening hematochezia, reviewing the wide array of possible causes of lower GI bleeding and outlining the diagnostic and therapeutic modalities available for treating this difficult clinical problem.

Initial Evaluation and Resuscitation

Initial evaluation of a patient with lower GI bleeding should include a focused history and physical examination, to be carried out simultaneously with resuscitation. Of particular importance in taking the history is to ascertain

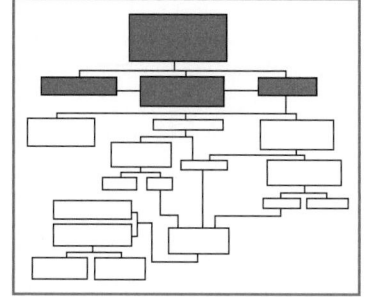

the nature and duration of the bleeding, including stool color and frequency. The patient should also be asked about any associated symptoms of potential significance (e.g., abdominal pain, changes in bowel habits, fever, urgency, tenesmus, or weight loss), as well as about relevant past medical events (e.g., previous GI bleeding episodes, injuries, surgical procedures, peptic ulcer disease, inflammatory bowel disease [IBD], and abdominal or pelvic irradiation). Any complicating comorbid conditions (e.g., heart or liver disease and clotting disorders) should be investigated. A comprehensive review of medications—in particular, nonsteroidal anti-inflammatory drugs (NSAIDs) and anticoagulants—is mandatory.[12]

The physical examination should include determination of postural vital signs so that intravascular volume status can be accurately estimated. A drop in the orthostatic blood pressure greater than 10 mm Hg or an increase in the pulse rate greater than 10 beats/min indicates that more than 800 ml of blood (> 15% of the total circulating blood volume) has been lost. Marked tachycardia and tachypnea in association with hypotension and depressed mental status indicates that more than 1,500 ml of blood (> 30% of the total circulating blood volume) has been lost. A complete abdominal examination, including digital rectal examination and anoscopy, should be performed.

Laboratory evaluation should include a complete blood count, measurement of serum electrolyte concentrations, a coagulation profile (prothrombin time and partial thromboplastin time) [*see 8 Bleeding and Transfusion*], and typing and crossmatching.

A nasogastric tube should be placed for gastric lavage. If lavage yields positive results (i.e., the aspirate contains gross blood or so-called coffee grounds), esophagogastroduodenoscopy (EGD) is indicated [*see 60 Gastrointestinal Endoscopy*]. An aspirate that contains copious amounts of bile is strongly suggestive of a lower GI source of bleeding, and the workup proceeds accordingly [*see Investigative Studies, below*]. The choice is less clear-cut with a clear aspirate. In the absence of bile, such an aspirate cannot rule out a duodenal source for the bleeding. Accordingly, there is some degree of latitude for clinical judgment: depending on the overall clinical picture, the surgeon may choose either to perform EGD to rule out a duodenal bleeding source or to proceed with colonoscopy on the assumption that the source of the bleeding is in the lower GI tract.

Resuscitative efforts should begin immediately, with the aim of maintaining the patient in a euvolemic state. Two large-bore peripheral intravenous catheters should be inserted and isotonic I.V. fluid administered. A Foley catheter should be placed to facilitate monitoring of intravascular volume status. Whether and in what form to administer blood products is determined on an individual basis, with appropriate weight given to the presence or absence of comorbid conditions, the rate of blood loss, and the

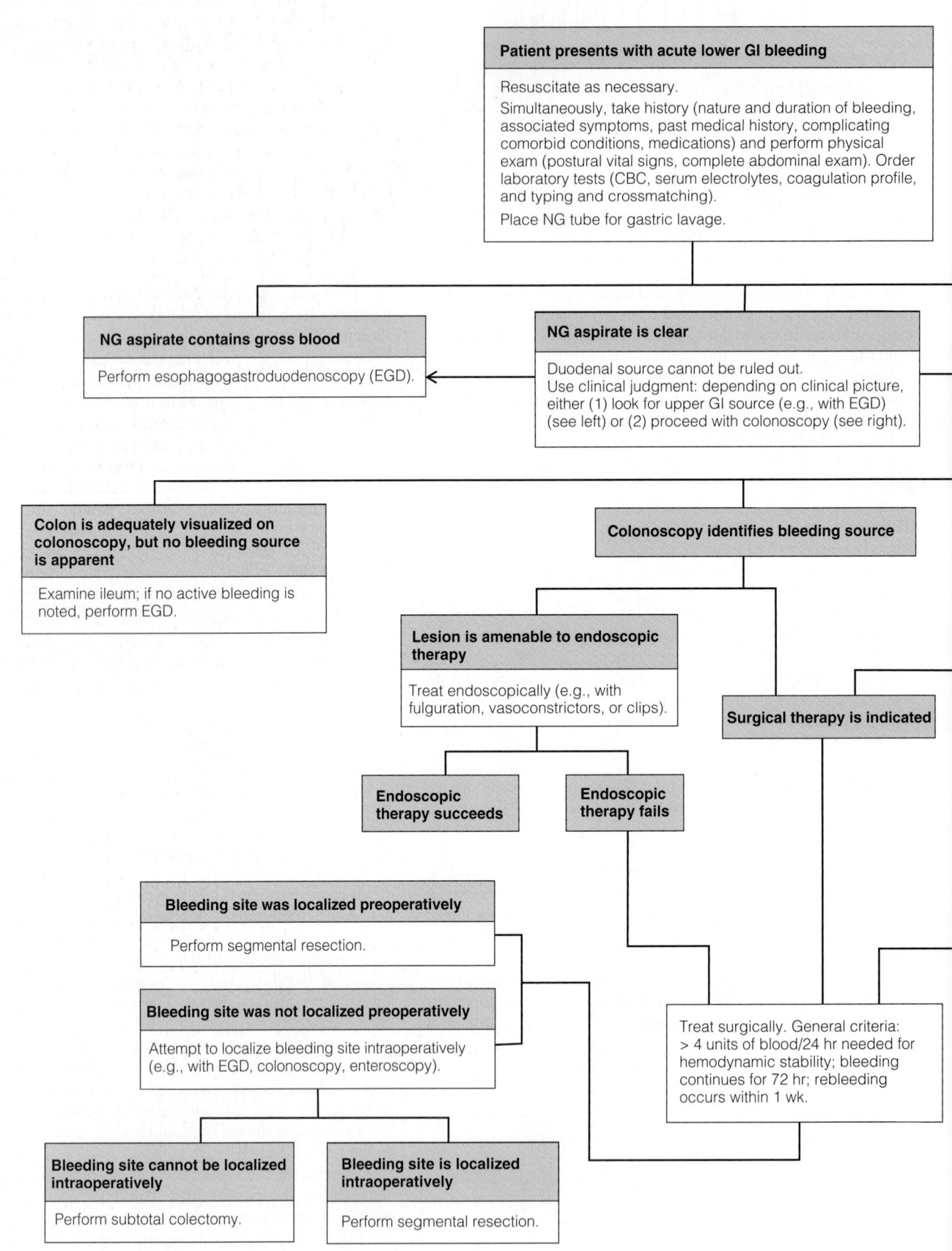

Patient presents with acute lower GI bleeding

Resuscitate as necessary.

Simultaneously, take history (nature and duration of bleeding, associated symptoms, past medical history, complicating comorbid conditions, medications) and perform physical exam (postural vital signs, complete abdominal exam). Order laboratory tests (CBC, serum electrolytes, coagulation profile, and typing and crossmatching).

Place NG tube for gastric lavage.

NG aspirate contains gross blood

Perform esophagogastroduodenoscopy (EGD).

NG aspirate is clear

Duodenal source cannot be ruled out.
Use clinical judgment: depending on clinical picture, either (1) look for upper GI source (e.g., with EGD) (see left) or (2) proceed with colonoscopy (see right).

Colon is adequately visualized on colonoscopy, but no bleeding source is apparent

Examine ileum; if no active bleeding is noted, perform EGD.

Colonoscopy identifies bleeding source

Lesion is amenable to endoscopic therapy

Treat endoscopically (e.g., with fulguration, vasoconstrictors, or clips).

Surgical therapy is indicated

Endoscopic therapy succeeds

Endoscopic therapy fails

Bleeding site was localized preoperatively

Perform segmental resection.

Bleeding site was not localized preoperatively

Attempt to localize bleeding site intraoperatively (e.g., with EGD, colonoscopy, enteroscopy).

Treat surgically. General criteria: > 4 units of blood/24 hr needed for hemodynamic stability; bleeding continues for 72 hr; rebleeding occurs within 1 wk.

Bleeding site cannot be localized intraoperatively

Perform subtotal colectomy.

Bleeding site is localized intraoperatively

Perform segmental resection.

Approach to Lower GI Bleeding

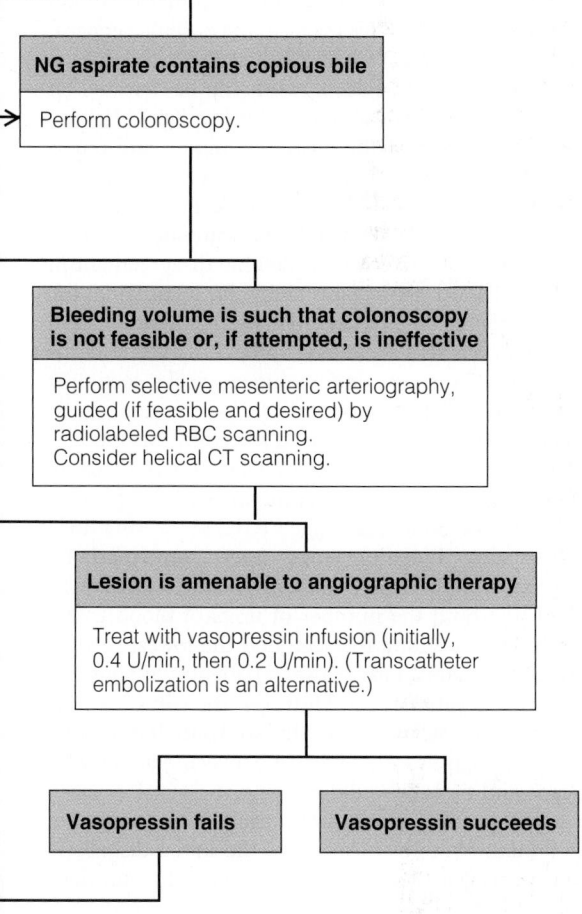

NG aspirate contains copious bile

Perform colonoscopy.

Bleeding volume is such that colonoscopy is not feasible or, if attempted, is ineffective

Perform selective mesenteric arteriography, guided (if feasible and desired) by radiolabeled RBC scanning.
Consider helical CT scanning.

Lesion is amenable to angiographic therapy

Treat with vasopressin infusion (initially, 0.4 U/min, then 0.2 U/min). (Transcatheter embolization is an alternative.)

Vasopressin fails

Vasopressin succeeds

degree of hemodynamic stability. Severe hemodynamic instability may necessitate monitoring in the intensive care unit.

Investigative Studies

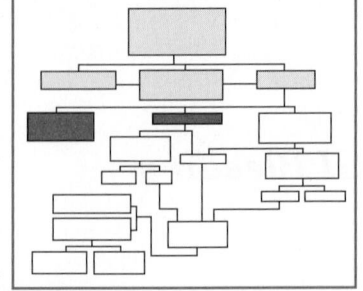

A number of diagnostic techniques are available for determining the source of lower GI hemorrhage, the most useful of which are colonoscopy [see 60 Gastrointestinal Endoscopy], radionuclide scanning, computed tomography, and angiography (in the form of selective mesenteric arteriography). The goal of these tests is to locate the site of bleeding accurately so that definitive therapy can be properly directed. Which diagnostic test is chosen for a specific patient depends on several factors, including the hemodynamic stability of the patient, the bleeding rate, the comorbid conditions present, and the local expertise available at the physician's hospital.

COLONOSCOPY

Several large series that evaluated the diagnostic utility of colonoscopy in patients with lower GI bleeding found this modality to be moderately to highly accurate, with overall diagnostic yields ranging from 53% to 97% [see Table 1].[3,13-17] Those studies that reported morbidity found colonoscopy to be safe as well, with an average complication rate of 0.5%. Colonoscopy has both a higher diagnostic yield and a lower complication rate than arteriography in this setting and thus would appear to be a more attractive initial test in most circumstances.[3,18] An argument has been made—one with which we agree—that colonoscopy should be considered the procedure of choice for structural evaluation of lower GI bleeding and that arteriography should be reserved for patients with massive, ongoing bleeding in whom endoscopy is not feasible or colonoscopy fails to reveal the source of the hemorrhage.[12]

The merits of colonic purging have been extensively debated in the literature.[3,11,14] Although no firm conclusion has been reached, we feel that adequate colonic purging can improve both the diagnostic yield and the safety of colonoscopy. Given the absence of any definitive data suggesting that colonic purging either reactivates or increases bleeding,[12] it is our practice to administer an oral purge after the patient has been adequately resuscitated.

If the entire colon has been adequately visualized and no source for the bleeding has been identified, the ileum should be intubated; fresh blood in this region suggests a possible small bowel source. If no active bleeding is observed in the ileum, upper GI endoscopy should be performed to rule out an upper GI bleeding site.

When colonoscopy and routine upper GI endoscopy fail to locate a bleeding source, push enteroscopy may be helpful. This procedure can be carried out in several ways. It can be performed purely endoscopically with a pediatric colonoscope. This approach generally requires a high level of skill on the part of the endoscopist, in that the lack of retroperitoneal attachments of the small intestine makes endoscopic navigation extremely challenging. In most cases, only the proximal 150 cm of the small intestine can be evaluated in this way. Alternatively, push enteroscopy can be performed in the operating room at the time of exploratory laparotomy. The surgeon can manually "milk" the small bowel over the scope to evaluate its distal portion. In addition, an enterotomy can be made, and the scope can be passed in both a retrograde and an antegrade fashion so that the entire small intestine can be evaluat-

ed. Depending on the indication and on the technique employed, the diagnostic yield from push enteroscopy has ranged from 13% to 78%.[19] Typically, yields are highest (40% to 60%) in patients with significant GI hemorrhage.

RADIOLABELED RED BLOOD CELL SCANNING

Radionuclide scanning is highly sensitive for lower GI hemorrhage: it is capable of detecting bleeding at rates as slow as 0.1 to 0.4 ml/min.[20] Two imaging tracers, both labeled with technetium-99m (^{99m}Tc), are currently available for radionuclide scanning in this setting: ^{99m}Tc-labeled sulfur colloid (^{99m}Tc-SC) and ^{99m}Tc-labeled red blood cells (RBCs). ^{99m}Tc-SC requires no preparation time and can be injected immediately into the patient; however, its rapid absorption into the liver and the spleen can often hinder accurate localization of overlying bleeding sites.[9] At our institution, we prefer to use ^{99m}Tc-labeled RBCs. This agent requires some preparation time, but it has a much longer half-life than ^{99m}Tc-SC does, it is not taken up by the liver and spleen, and it can be detected on images as long as 24 to 48 hours after injection [see Figure 1].[21,22]

One study directly compared these two techniques and found ^{99m}Tc-labeled RBC scanning to have an accuracy of 93%, compared with an accuracy of only 12% for ^{99m}Tc-SC scanning.[23] The high sensitivity of ^{99m}Tc-labeled RBC scanning—80% to 98%—is well attested, but there is considerable disagreement in the literature with regard to its specificity in identifying the anatomic site of bleeding.[24-27] For example, on one hand, a 1996 study found radiolabeled RBC scanning to be 97% accurate for localizing bleeding in 37 patients undergoing surgical resection[27]; on the other hand, a 1990 study reported a 42% rate of incorrect resection when surgical therapy was based solely on this modality.[26] In 2005, one group retrospectively reviewed 127 bleeding scans in an effort to identify factors that might predict a positive scan.[28] The investigators found that tagged RBC scans were 48% accurate in localizing bleeding sites later confirmed by endoscopy, surgery, or pathologic evaluation. Multivariate analysis demonstrated that both the number of units of blood transfused in the 24 hours preceding the scan and the lowest recorded hematocrit differed significantly between patients with positive scans and those with negative scans. However, the clinical significance of a positive scan was unclear in this study, in that the rate of endoscopy was not significantly different between patients who had positive scans and those who did not.

To date, no prospective, randomized trials have compared radionuclide scanning with colonoscopy as the initial diagnostic procedure for patients with lower GI hemorrhage. In our view,

Table 1 Diagnostic Accuracy of Colonoscopy in Localizing Source of Lower GI Hemorrhage

Study	No. of Patients	Diagnostic Yield (%)
Richter[13]	78	70 (90%)
Jensen[3]	80	68 (85%)
Rossini[14]	409	311 (76%)
Goenka[15]	166	141 (85%)
Ohyama[16]	345	307 (89%)
Chaudhry[17]	85	82 (97%)
Total	1,163	979 (84%)

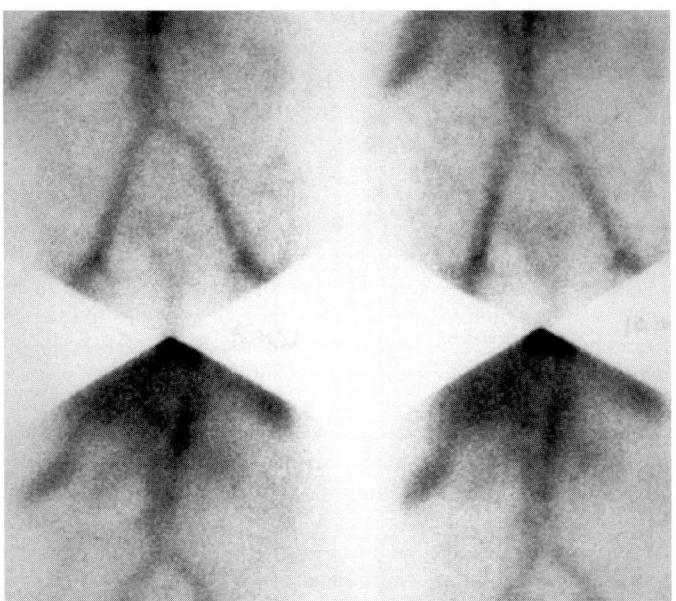

Figure 1 ⁹⁹ᵐTc-labeled RBC scan demonstrates collection of tracer at hepatic flexure.

however, given that radionuclide scanning (unlike colonoscopy and angiography) has no therapeutic intervention capabilities, its best use is in patients with non–life-threatening lower GI bleeding as a prelude and a guide to mesenteric angiography after active hemorrhage has been confirmed.

COMPUTED TOMOGRAPHY

With the ongoing improvements in high-speed abdominal CT scanning, there has been growing interest in the evaluation of GI bleeding with CT.[29] Helical CT scanners can provide direct or indirect evidence of the source of GI bleeding. Typical findings that can facilitate localization of bleeding sites include spontaneous hyperdensity of the peribowel fat, contrast enhancement of the bowel wall, vascular extravasation of the contrast medium, thickening of the bowel wall, polyps, tumors, and vascular dilatation.

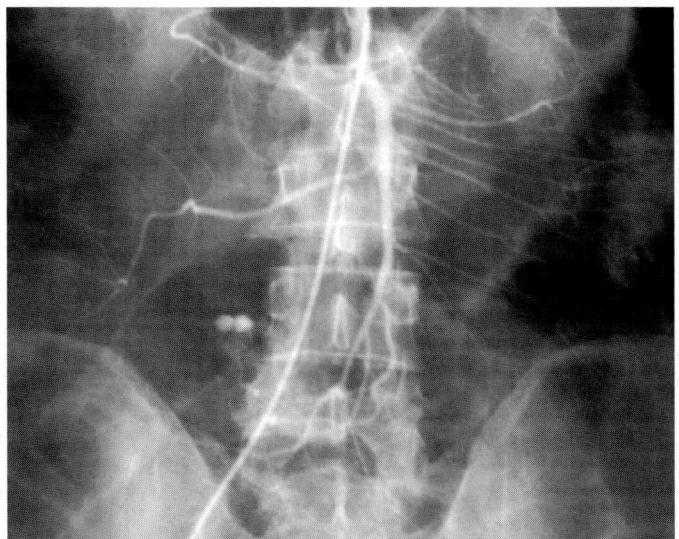

Figure 2 Angiographic study documents extravasation of contrast into small bowel.

CT evaluation of GI bleeding has several noteworthy advantages: the scanners typically are readily available, mobilization of special teams or units is not required, the scans can be completed rapidly in the emergency department, and bowel preparation is unnecessary. In one experimental study, CT scanners were able to detect arterial bleeding at rates as low as 0.07 ml/min, which suggests that CT scanning is more sensitive than angiography for this purpose.[30] In addition, CT scans are noninvasive and carry little morbidity. Unfortunately, like radionuclide scanning, CT has no therapeutic capability.

A 2003 study of 19 patients with GI hemorrhage compared triphasic helical CT evaluation with colonoscopy and surgery for localization of bleeding sites.[30] In this series, five patients had small bowel bleeding sites, and 14 had colonic sites. Helical CT scanning correctly identified four of the five small bowel lesions and 11 of the 14 colonic lesions. These findings, though preliminary, suggest that CT is a potentially valuable evaluation method in certain cases of GI bleeding. Perhaps CT scanning can eventually replace radionuclide scanning, which is often inaccurate. One potential drawback to the use of CT in this setting is the excessive dye load if angiography is employed as well.

ANGIOGRAPHY

Selective Mesenteric Arteriography

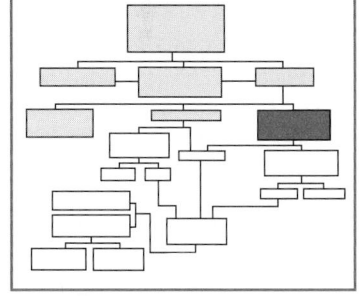

Selective mesenteric arteriography is somewhat less sensitive than radionuclide scanning for lower GI hemorrhage: bleeding must be occurring at a rate of at least 1.0 to 1.5 ml/min to be detectable with this test.[31] The procedure involves percutaneous placement of a transfemoral arterial catheter for evaluation of the superior mesenteric, inferior mesenteric, and celiac arteries. A positive test result is defined as extravasation of contrast into the lumen of the bowel [*see Figure 2*]. Once the bleeding vessel has been localized angiographically, the area must be marked so that it can be successfully identified intraoperatively; this is commonly accomplished by infusing methylene blue into the bleeding artery [*see Figure 3*].[32,33]

In several large series [*see Table 2*], the overall diagnostic yield of arteriography ranged from 27% to 67%.[27,34-38] The complication rate for arteriography performed for lower GI bleeding ranges from 2% to 4%.[2,38] Reported complications include contrast allergy, renal failure, bleeding from arterial puncture, and embolism from a dislodged thrombus.[12]

Unlike radionuclide scanning, arteriography provides several therapeutic options, including vasopressin infusion and embolization of bleeding vessels. Nonetheless, given that arteriography has a lower diagnostic yield and a higher complication rate than colonoscopy does, it is reasonable to attempt colonoscopy first in patients with lower GI hemorrhage and to reserve angiography for patients in whom the volume of bleeding is such that colonoscopy would be neither safe nor accurate.

Provocative Angiography for Continued Obscure Bleeding

In a minority of patients, obscure bleeding persists despite negative findings from endoscopy, mesenteric arteriography, and radiolabeled RBC scanning. This obscure bleeding presents a considerable diagnostic challenge, which some investigators have proposed addressing by means of so-called provocative angiography.[39,40]

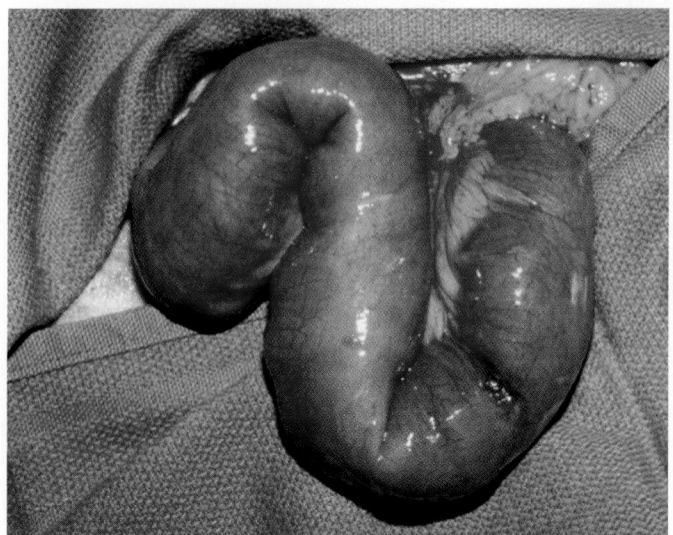

Figure 3 **Intraoperative examination of the bowel is aided by injection of methylene blue dye, which facilitates localization of the bleeding site and thereby helps direct surgical resection.**

Provocative angiography involves the use of short-acting anticoagulant agents (unfractionated heparin, vasodilators, thrombolytics, or combinations thereof) in association with angiography. Once the bleeding point has been localized, methylene blue is injected and the patient is immediately brought to the OR for surgical treatment. To date, unfortunately, little has been published on this technique, but it does appear to be a promising approach to this difficult problem.

Management

Although, in the majority of cases, lower GI bleeding stops spontaneously, in a significant number of cases, hemorrhage continues and necessitates therapeutic intervention. Treatment options include endoscopic therapy, angiographic therapy, and surgical resection.

ENDOSCOPIC THERAPY

When colonoscopy identifies a bleeding source, endoscopic treatment may be an option [*see 60 Gastrointestinal Endoscopy*]. Endoscopic modalities used to treat lower GI bleeding include use of thermal contact probes,[41,42] laser photocoagulation,[43] electrocauterization,[44] injection of vaso-

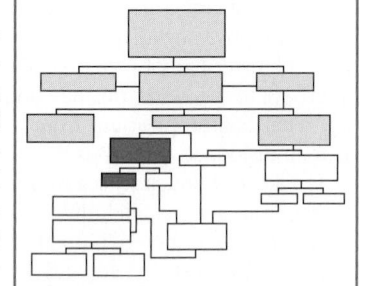

constrictors, application of metallic clips,[45] and injection sclerotherapy.[46] The choice of a specific modality often depends on the nature of the offending lesion and on the expertise and resources available locally. A 1995 survey of members of the American College of Gastroenterology found that endoscopic therapy was used in 27% of patients presenting with lower GI bleeding.[8]

Diverticular hemorrhage can be difficult to treat endoscopically because of the high bleeding rate and the location of the bleeding point within the diverticulum. In 2000, one group of investigators reported their experience with endoscopic therapy for severe

hematochezia and diverticulosis in a prospective series of 121 patients.[47] In this series, none of the patients treated endoscopically with epinephrine injections, bipolar coagulation, or both required surgery and none experienced recurrent bleeding episodes. A 2001 study from another group, however, reported high rates of recurrent bleeding episodes in both the early and the late post-treatment periods.[48] In the absence of prospective, randomized trials, it is difficult to draw definitive conclusions about the utility of endoscopic therapy in treating diverticular hemorrhage.

Angiodysplasias resulting in GI hemorrhage typically are amenable to endoscopic treatment. That these lesions are frequently found in the right colon makes perforation a concern; this complication is reported in approximately 2% of patients.[49] Good success rates have been reported with both injection and thermal methods.[50] In one series, endoscopic fulguration was successful in 87% of patients, and no rebleeding episodes occurred over a 1- to 7-year follow-up period.[50] Bleeding from multiple telangiectatic lesions in the distal colon resulting from radiation injury can be treated with thermal contact probes, lasers, or noncontact devices such as the argon plasma coagulator.[51]

Postpolypectomy hemorrhage can often be successfully treated by endoscopic means. Methods used include simple resnaring of the stalk while pressure is maintained[52]; electrocauterization, with or without epinephrine injection; endoscopic band ligation; and placement of metallic clips. For patients whose bleeding is attributable to benign anorectal causes, endoscopic therapy may include epinephrine injection, sclerosant injection, or band ligation of internal hemorrhoids.[53]

ANGIOGRAPHIC THERAPY

Diagnostic use of angiography in patients with lower GI bleeding can often be followed by angiographic therapy. The two main angiographic treatment options are intra-arterial injection of vasopressin and transcatheter embolization.

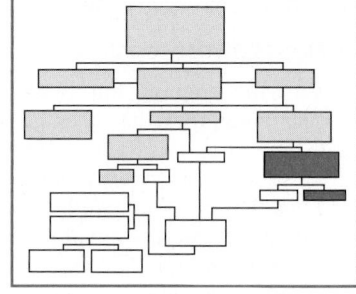

Vasopressin acts to control bleeding by causing arteriolar vasoconstriction and bowel wall contraction.[9] Once the bleeding site has been localized angiographically, the catheter is positioned in

Table 2 Diagnostic Accuracy of Mesenteric Angiography in Localizing Source of Lower GI Hemorrhage

Study	No. of Patients	No. of Positive Angiograms (%)
Pennoyer[34]	131	37 (28%)
Ng[27]	49	22 (45%)
Rantis[35]	30	8 (27%)
Leitman[36]	68	27 (40%)
Casarella[37]	69	46 (67%)
Colacchio[38]	98	40 (41%)
Total	445	180 (40%)

the main trunk of the vessel. Infusion of vasopressin is initiated at a rate of 0.2 U/min and can be increased to a rate of 0.4 U/min. Within 20 to 30 minutes, another angiogram is performed to determine whether the bleeding has ceased. If the bleeding is under control, the catheter is left in place and vasopressin is continuously infused for 6 to 12 hours. If the bleeding continues to be controlled, infusion is continued for an additional 6 to 12 hours at 50% of the previous rate. Finally, vasopressin infusion is replaced by continuous saline infusion, and if bleeding does not recur, the catheter is removed.[54,55]

The vasoconstrictive action of vasopressin can have deleterious systemic side effects, including myocardial ischemia, peripheral ischemia, hypertension, dysrhythmias, mesenteric thrombosis, intestinal infarction, and death.[9,36] Occasionally, simultaneous I.V. administration of nitroglycerin is necessary to counteract these systemic effects. The reported success rate of vasopressin in controlling lower GI bleeding ranges from 60% to 100%, and the incidence of major complications ranges from 10% to 20%.[56-58] Rebleeding rates as high as 50% have been reported.[57,58]

An alternative for patients with coronary vascular disease, severe peripheral vascular disease, or other comorbidities that prevent safe administration of vasopressin is transcatheter embolization. In this technique, a catheter is superselectively placed into the identified bleeding vessel and an embolizing agent (e.g., a gelatin sponge, a microcoil, polyvinyl alcohol particles, or a balloon) is injected. Several small series found this technique to be 90% to 100% successful at stopping bleeding.[59-63] Equally impressive was the finding that the rebleeding rates in these series were 0%. The complication rates of this procedure are generally reasonable as well; however, intestinal infarction has been reported.[36,64]

The use of small microcatheters and the ability to superselectively embolize individual vessels have reduced the potential for ischemic perforation. It is possible that as more experience is gained with these techniques, superselective embolization may replace catheter-directed vasoconstrictive therapy, thus obviating the potential deleterious systemic effects of vasopressin administration. Some researchers have suggested that with the exception of cases of diffuse bleeding lesions or cases whose demands exceed the technical limitations of superselective catheterization, embolization therapy should be the first choice for angiographic treatment of lower GI bleeding.[65,66]

SURGICAL THERAPY

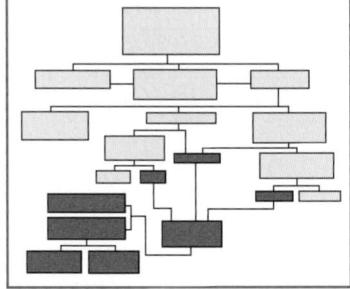

Although there are no absolute criteria for surgical treatment of lower GI bleeding, there are several factors— including hemodynamic status, associated comorbidities, transfusion requirements, and persistent bleeding—that are instrumental in making an appropriate and timely decision whether to operate. In general, patients who require more than 4 units of blood in a 24-hour period to remain hemodynamically stable, whose bleeding has not stopped after 72 hours, or who experience rebleeding within 1 week after an initial episode should undergo surgery.[9]

If the patient's hemodynamic status permits, surgical treatment should be undertaken after accurate localization of the bleeding site. When possible, directed segmental resection is the procedure of choice: it is associated with rebleeding rates ranging from 0% to 14% and mortality rates ranging from 0% to 13%.[10,36,67] Blind segmental colectomy should never be performed: it is associated with rebleeding rates as high as 75% and mortality rates as high as 50%.[68] If hemodynamic compromise and ongoing hemorrhage make it necessary to perform surgical exploration before the bleeding site can be localized, every effort should be made to identify the source of bleeding intraoperatively before embarking on resection. Intraoperative options for bleeding-site localization include colonoscopy (to allow for this option, patients should always be placed in the lithotomy position), EGD, and transoral passage of a pediatric colonoscope for enteroscopy with simultaneous intraperitoneal assistance for small bowel manipulation.[9] If the bleeding site still cannot be accurately localized, subtotal colectomy is the procedure of choice. This procedure is associated with mortality rates ranging from 5% to 33%,[69,70] which underscores the importance of accurate preoperative localization of bleeding before surgical intervention.

Discussion

Etiology of Lower GI Bleeding

As noted, lower GI bleeding has a wide array of possible causes [*see Table 3*].[9,71] Of these, diverticular disease is the most common, accounting for 30% to 40% of all cases.[72] Arteriovenous malformations (AVMs), though extensively described in the literature, are considerably less common causes, accounting for 1% to 4% of cases.[73,74] Other significant causative conditions are IBD, benign and malignant neoplasms, ischemia, infectious colitis, anorectal disease, coagulopathy, use of NSAIDs, radiation proctitis, AIDS, and small bowel disorders.

DIVERTICULAR DISEASE

The reported prevalence of colonic diverticulosis in Western societies is 37% to 45%.[75] The vast majority of colonic diverticula are actually false diverticula (pseudodiverticula) that contain only serosa and mucosa [*see 54 Diverticulitis*]. They occur at weak points in the colonic wall where the vasa recta penetrate the muscularis to supply the mucosa[9]; as the diverticulum expands, these vessels are displaced. A 1976 anatomic study of colonic specimens from patients with diverticular bleeding used angiography to demonstrate that in all cases, the vasa recta overlying the diverticulum ruptured into the lumen of the diverticulum, not into the peritoneum [*see Figure 4*].[76]

It has been estimated that approximately 17% of patients with colonic diverticulosis experience bleeding, which may range from minor to severe and life-threatening.[77] As many as 80% to 85% of diverticular hemorrhages stop spontaneously.[78] In one series, surgery was unlikely to be necessary if fewer than 4 units of packed RBCs were transfused in a 24-hour period, whereas 60% of patients receiving more than 4 units of packed RBCs in a 24-hour period required surgical intervention.[5] The risk of a second bleeding episode is approximately 25%.[3] Semielective surgical therapy is usually offered after a second diverticular bleeding episode because once a second such episode has occurred, the risk that a

Table 3 Common Causes of Lower GI Hemorrhage

Cause of Bleeding	Frequency
Diverticulosis	17%–40%
Arteriovenous malformation	2%–30%
Colitis	9%–21%
Neoplasia (including postpolypectomy bleeding)	7%–33%
Benign anorectal disease	4%–10%
Upper GI source	0%–11%
Small bowel source	2%–9%

third will follow exceeds 50%.[79] In a series of 83 conservatively managed cases of diverticular disease, the predicted yearly recurrence rates were 9% at 1 year, 10% at 2 years, 19% at 3 years, and 25% at 4 years.[4]

COLITIS

The broad term colitis includes IBD, infectious colitis, radiation colitis, and idiopathic ulcers. IBD, in turn, includes Crohn disease [see 53 Crohn Disease] and ulcerative colitis [see 55 Fulminant Ulcerative Colitis]. Patients with IBD usually present with bloody diarrhea that is not life-threatening; however, 6% to 10% of patients with ulcerative colitis have lower GI bleeding severe enough to necessitate emergency surgical resection,[80,81] and 0.6% to 1.3% of patients with Crohn disease have acute life-threatening lower GI bleeding.[80,82] In one review, 50% of patients with intestinal hemorrhage from IBD experienced spontaneous cessation of bleeding.[80] Approximately 35% of patients whose bleeding stops without intervention will have another bleeding episode. Because of this high recurrence rate, semielective surgery is recommended after the first episode of severe GI bleeding secondary to IBD.

Colitis caused by various infectious agents (e.g., *Salmonella typhi*,[83,84] *Escherichia coli* O157:H7,[85] *Clostridium difficile*,[86] and

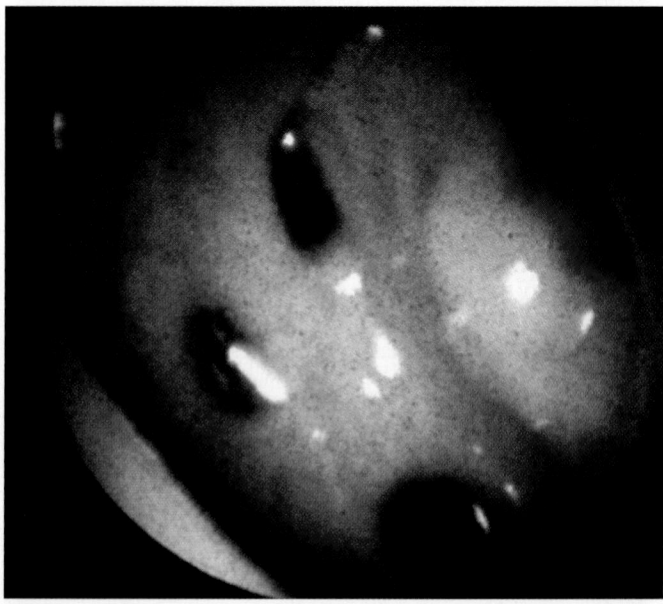

Figure 4 **Shown is the appearance of a bleeding diverticulum on colonoscopy.**

cytomegalovirus) can result in severe lower GI bleeding, but this is a relatively rare occurrence.

Increasing use of radiation therapy to treat pelvic malignancies has led to a corresponding increase in the incidence of chronic radiation proctitis.[87] Radiation therapy damages bowel mucosa, resulting in the formation of vascular telangiectases that are prone to bleeding.[88] From 1% to 5% of cases of acute lower GI bleeding from radiation-induced proctocolitis are severe enough to necessitate hospitalization.[4,14] In a survey of patients with prostate cancer who underwent pelvic irradiation, 5% of the patients reported hematochezia daily.[89] Initial therapy for clinically significant hematochezia related to radiation proctitis should include some form of endoscopic treatment (e.g., argon-beam coagulation). Surgery should be reserved for unstoppable hemorrhage or other major complications, such as fistulas and strictures.[87]

NEOPLASIA

Significant GI bleeding from colorectal neoplasia [see 57 Adenocarcinoma of the Colon and Rectum] accounts for 7% to 33% of cases of severe lower GI hemorrhage.[3,11,14,36,90] Such bleeding is believed to result from erosions on the luminal surface.[91] One report identified ulcerated cancers as the cause in 21% of cases of hematochezia.[14] Adenomatous polyps are implicated in 5% to 11% of cases of acute lower GI bleeding.[7,8,14,92,93] Lower GI hemorrhage, either immediate or delayed, is the most common reported complication after endoscopic polypectomy, occurring in 0.2% to 6% of cases.[3,4,94,95] Immediate postpolypectomy bleeding is believed to result from incomplete coagulation of the stalk before transection.[52] Delayed bleeding has been reported as long as 15 days after polypectomy and is thought to be secondary to sloughing of the coagulum; it is less common than immediate bleeding, occurring in only 0.3% of cases.[14,52]

COAGULOPATHY

Lower GI bleeding can be a presenting symptom both for patients with iatrogenic coagulopathy from heparin or warfarin therapy and for patients with a hematologic coagulopathy from thrombocytopenia [see 8 Bleeding and Transfusion]. It is unclear, however, whether severe coagulopathy leads to spontaneous hemorrhage or whether it predisposes to bleeding from an existing lesion.[96,97] In an early series of leukemic patients with thrombocytopenia and severe GI hemorrhage, 50% of bleeding patients had platelet counts lower than 20,000/mm³ without any identifiable mucosal lesions; furthermore, when the platelet count rose above 20,000/mm³, the incidence of bleeding decreased to 0.8%.[96] The investigator concluded that severe thrombocytopenia led to spontaneous GI hemorrhage. Other investigators subsequently challenged this conclusion, arguing that spontaneous bleeding from coagulopathy is in fact rare.[98] In one report, the distribution of pathologic lesions in patients with GI bleeding who were taking heparin or warfarin was essentially equivalent to that in the general population.[98] Regardless of what the precise relation between coagulopathy and GI hemorrhage may be, a thorough investigation for an anatomic lesion is imperative in the workup of patients with lower GI bleeding even in the face of coagulopathy or thrombocytopenia.

BENIGN ANORECTAL DISEASE

Hemorrhoids, ulcer/fissure disease, and fistula in ano [see 59 Benign Rectal, Anal, and Perineal Problems] must not be overlooked as causes of GI hemorrhage: in one review comprising almost 18,000 cases of lower GI bleeding, 11% were attributable to anorectal pathology. It is crucial to remember that identification of

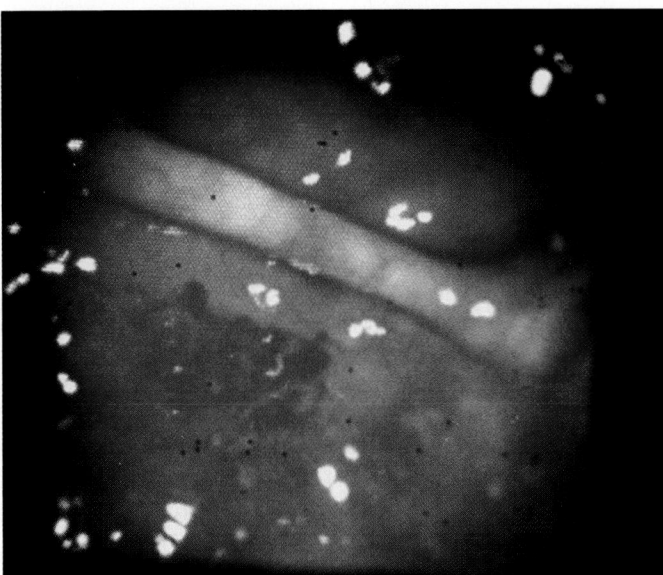

Figure 5 Shown is the appearance of an arteriovenous malformation on colonoscopy.

a benign anorectal lesion does not eliminate the possibility of a more proximal cause of hemorrhage. In general, patients with hemorrhoids identified on physical examination should still undergo thorough endoscopic evaluation of the colon to rule out other pathologic conditions.

Portal hypertension [*see 52 Portal Hypertension*], congestive heart failure, and splenic vein thrombosis can cause colonic or anorectal varices, which can result in massive lower GI hemorrhage.[99] The reported incidence of anorectal varices in patients with portal hypertension ranges from 78% to 89%.[100,101] If local measures fail to control hemorrhage, some form of portosystemic shunting is indicated.

COLONIC ARTERIOVENOUS MALFORMATIONS

The term arteriovenous malformation includes vascular ectasias, angiomas, and angiodysplasias. AVMs are ectatic blood vessels seen in the mucosa and submucosa of the GI tract. They are degenerative lesions of the GI tract, occurring more frequently with advancing age.[9] In autopsy series, the reported incidence of colonic AVMs is 1% to 2%.[102] In patients older than 50 years, the incidence of colonic AVMs is estimated to range from 2% to 30%.[103-106] In healthy asymptomatic adults, the prevalence is estimated to be approximately 0.8%.[107]

Colonic AVMs are believed to derive from chronic colonic wall muscle contraction, which leads to chronic partial obstruction of the submucosal veins, causing the vessels to become dilated and tortuous. This process eventually renders the precapillary sphincters incompetent, resulting in direct arterial-venous communication.[108,109] Colonic AVMs are most commonly found in the cecum.[10] They have been associated with several systemic diseases, including atherosclerotic cardiovascular disease, aortic stenosis, chronic renal disease, collagen vascular disease, von Willebrand disease, chronic obstructive pulmonary disease, and cirrhosis of the liver; to date, however, no definite causal relationship to any of these conditions has been established.[6,21,44,110]

The diagnosis of a colonic AVM is made at the time of angiography or colonoscopy. During angiography, visualization of ectatic, slow-emptying veins, vascular tufts, or early-filling veins estab-

lishes the diagnosis.[111] During endoscopy, angiodysplasias appear as red, flat lesions about 2 to 10 mm in diameter, sometimes accompanied by a feeding vessel [*see Figure 5*].[6,41,44,72]

Typically, the bleeding caused by colonic AVMs is chronic, slow, and intermittent.[9] Although these lesions can cause severe lower GI hemorrhage, they are a relatively uncommon cause: in most large series, they account for only about 2% of cases of acute bleeding.[74,104] The bleeding stops spontaneously in 85% to 90% of cases,[10] but it recurs in 25% to 85%.[112] Accordingly, definitive surgical or colonoscopic treatment should be rendered once the lesion has been identified.

COLONIC ISCHEMIA

Acute lower GI bleeding can also be a presenting symptom of colonic ischemia. In several large series, colonic ischemia accounted for 3% to 9% of cases of acute lower GI hemorrhage.[4,7,8,14,92] Other vascular diseases reported as potential causes are polyarteritis nodosa, Wegener granulomatosis, and rheumatoid vasculitis.[113,114] The resultant vasculitis can cause ulceration, necrosis, and ultimately hemorrhage.[115]

SMALL INTESTINAL SOURCES

Small intestinal sources account for 0.7% to 9% of cases of acute lower GI bleeding.[3,4,116-118] About 70% to 80% of cases of small bowel hemorrhage are attributable to AVMs; other, less common causes are jejunoileal diverticula, Meckel's diverticulum,[119] neoplasia, regional enteritis, and aortoenteric fistulas [*see Figure 6*].[90,120,121]

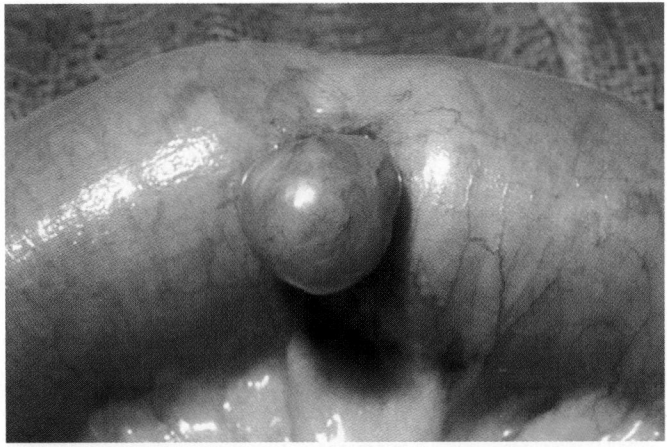

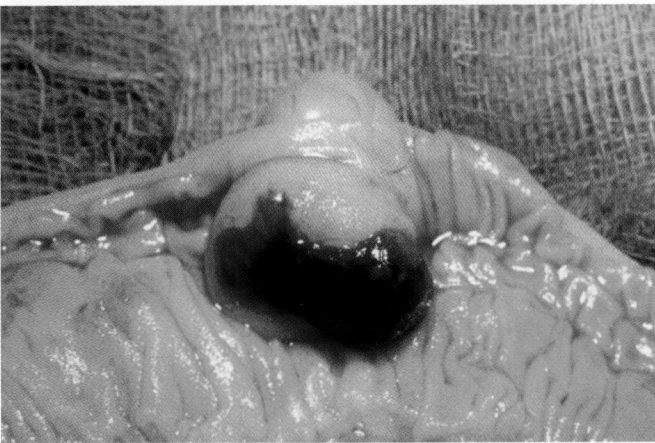

Figure 6 Shown are intraoperative specimens of small bowel tumors causing lower GI hemorrhage.

Accurate localization of a bleeding site in the small intestine can be highly challenging: the length and the free intraperitoneal position of the small bowel make endoscopic examination difficult, and the nature of the overlying loops makes angiographic localization imprecise. For these reasons, the small intestine is usually left for last in the attempt to localize the source of lower GI bleeding and is examined only after sources in the colon, the upper GI tract, and the anorectum have been ruled out.[9]

AIDS

The etiology of lower GI bleeding in patients with AIDS differs from that in the general population.[91] In AIDS patients, lower GI bleeding is caused predominantly by conditions related to the underlying HIV infection. Cytomegalovirus colitis is the most common cause of such bleeding in this population, occurring in 39% of cases.[122] AIDS patients with hemorrhoids or anal fissures often experience significant bleeding as a result of HIV-induced thrombocytopenia.[122] A 1998 study reported that in 23% of AIDS patients hospitalized for lower GI bleeding, benign anorectal disease was the cause.[123] Other significant causes of lower GI hemorrhage in this population are colonic histoplasmosis, Kaposi sarcoma of the colon, and bacterial colitis.[123,124]

NSAID USE

The association between NSAID use and upper GI hemorrhage is well known.[125] Current data suggest that NSAIDs have a toxic effect on colonic mucosa as well.[126] An epidemiologic study estimated the incidence of NSAID-associated large bowel bleeding to be 7/100,000.[127] A retrospective review found that patients who had experienced lower GI bleeding were twice as likely to have taken NSAIDs as those who had not.[128] NSAIDs have also been linked to diverticular hemorrhage: in one study, 92% of patients with diverticular bleeding were taking NSAIDs.[107] The exact mechanism of NSAID-induced colonic injury is unknown; nevertheless, heightened clinical awareness of this potential cause of lower GI bleeding is warranted.[91]

References

1. Briley CA Jr, Jackson DC, Johnsrude IS, et al: Acute gastrointestinal hemorrhage of small-bowel origin. Radiology 136:317, 1980

2. Koval G, Benner KG, Rosch J, et al: Aggressive angiographic diagnosis in acute lower gastrointestinal hemorrhage. Dig Dis Sci 32:248, 1987

3. Jensen DM, Machicado GA: Diagnosis and treatment of severe hematochezia: the role of urgent colonoscopy after purge. Gastroenterology 95:1569, 1988

4. Longstreth GF: Epidemiology and outcome of patients hospitalized with acute lower gastrointestinal hemorrhage: a population-based study. Am J Gastroenterol 92:419, 1997

5. McGuire HH Jr: Bleeding colonic diverticula: a reappraisal of natural history and management. Ann Surg 220:653, 1994

6. Foutch PG: Angiodysplasia of the gastrointestinal tract. Am J Gastroenterol 88:807, 1993

7. Bramley PN, Masson JW, McKnight G, et al: The role of an open-access bleeding unit in the management of colonic haemorrhage: a 2-year prospective study. Scand J Gastroenterol 31:764, 1996

8. Peura DA, Lanza FL, Gostout CJ, et al: The American College of Gastroenterology. Bleeding Registry: preliminary findings. Am J Gastroenterol 92:924, 1997

9. Vernava AM 3rd, Moore BA, Longo WE, et al: Lower gastrointestinal bleeding. Dis Colon Rectum 40:846, 1997

10. Boley SJ, DiBiase A, Brandt LJ, et al: Lower intestinal bleeding in the elderly. Am J Surg 137:57, 1979

11. Caos A, Benner KG, Manier J, et al: Colonoscopy after Golytely preparation in acute rectal bleeding. J Clin Gastroenterol 8:46, 1986

12. Zuccaro G Jr: Management of the adult patient with acute lower gastrointestinal bleeding. American College of Gastroenterology Practice Parameters Committee. Am J Gastroenterol 93:1202, 1998

13. Richter JM, Christensen MR, Kaplan LM, et al: Effectiveness of current technology in the diagnosis and management of lower gastrointestinal hemorrhage. Gastrointest Endosc 41:93, 1995

14. Rossini FP, Ferrari A, Spandre M, et al: Emergency colonoscopy. World J Surg 13:190, 1989

15. Goenka MK, Kochhar R, Mehta SK: Spectrum of lower gastrointestinal hemorrhage: an endoscopic study of 166 patients. Indian J Gastroenterol 12:129, 1993

16. Ohyama T, Sakurai Y, Ito M, et al: Analysis of urgent colonoscopy for lower gastrointestinal tract bleeding. Digestion 61:189, 2000

17. Chaudhry V, Hyser MJ, Gracias VH, et al: Colonoscopy: the initial test for acute lower gastrointestinal bleeding. Am Surg 64:723, 1998

18. Cohn SM, Moller BA, Zieg PM, et al: Angiography for preoperative evaluation in patients with lower gastrointestinal bleeding: are the benefits worth the risks? Arch Surg 133:50, 1998

19. Lin S, Branch MS, Shetzline M: The importance of indication in the diagnostic value of push enteroscopy. Endoscopy 35:315, 2003

20. Alavi A, Dann RW, Baum S, et al: Scintigraphic detection of acute gastrointestinal bleeding. Radiology 124:753, 1977

21. Gupta N, Longo WE, Vernava AM 3rd: Angiodysplasia of the lower gastrointestinal tract: an entity readily diagnosed by colonoscopy and primarily managed nonoperatively. Dis Colon Rectum 38:979, 1995

22. McKusick KA, Froelich J, Callahan RJ, et al: 99mTc red blood cells for detection of gastrointestinal bleeding: experience with 80 patients. AJR Am J Roentgenol 137:1113, 1981

23. Bunker SR, Lull RJ, Hattner RS, et al: The ideal radiotracer in gastrointestinal bleeding detection. AJR Am J Roentgenol 138:982, 1982

24. Kester RR, Welch JP, Sziklas JP: The 99mTc-labeled RBC scan: a diagnostic method for lower gastrointestinal bleeding. Dis Colon Rectum 27:47, 1984

25. Suzman MS, Talmor M, Jennis R, et al: Accurate localization and surgical management of active lower gastrointestinal hemorrhage with technetium-labeled erythrocyte scintigraphy. Ann Surg 224:29, 1996

26. Hunter JM, Pezim ME: Limited value of technetium 99m-labeled red cell scintigraphy in localization of lower gastrointestinal bleeding. Am J Surg 159:504, 1990

27. Ng DA, Opelka FG, Beck DE, et al: Predictive value of technetium Tc 99m-labeled red blood cell scintigraphy for positive angiogram in massive lower gastrointestinal hemorrhage. Dis Colon Rectum 40:471, 1997

28. Olds GD, Cooper GS, Chak A, et al: The yield of bleeding scans in acute lower gastrointestinal hemorrhage. J Clin Gastroenterol 39:273, 2005

29. Yamaguchi T, Yoshikawa K: Enhanced CT for initial localization of active lower gastrointestinal bleeding. Abdom Imaging 28:634, 2003

30. Ernst O, Bulois P, Saint-Drenant S, et al: Helical CT in acute lower gastrointestinal bleeding. Eur Radiol 13:114, 2003

31. Baum S, Athanasoulis CA, Waltman AC: Angiographic diagnosis and control of large-bowel bleeding. Dis Colon Rectum 17:447, 1974

32. Athanasoulis CA, Moncure AC, Greenfield AJ, et al: Intraoperative localization of small bowel bleeding sites with combined use of angiographic methods and methylene blue injection. Surgery 87:77, 1980

33. Schrodt JF, Bradford WR: Presurgical angiographic localization of small bowel bleeding site with methylene blue injection. J Ky Med Assoc 94:192, 1996

34. Pennoyer WP, Vignati PV, Cohen JL: Management of angiogram positive lower gastrointestinal hemorrhage: long term follow-up of non-operative treatments. Int J Colorectal Dis 11:279, 1996

35. Rantis PC Jr, Harford FJ, Wagner RH, et al: Technetium-labelled red blood cell scintigraphy: is it useful in acute lower gastrointestinal bleeding? Int J Colorectal Dis 10:210, 1995

36. Leitman IM, Paull DE, Shires GT 3rd: Evaluation and management of massive lower gastrointestinal hemorrhage. Ann Surg 209:175, 1989

37. Casarella WJ, Galloway SJ, Taxin RN, et al: "Lower" gastrointestinal tract hemorrhage: new concepts based on arteriography. Am J Roentgenol Radium Ther Nucl Med 121:357, 1974

38. Colacchio TA, Forde KA, Patsos TJ, et al: Impact of modern diagnostic methods on the management of active rectal bleeding: ten year experience. Am J Surg 143:607, 1982

39. Bloomfeld RS, Smith TP, Schneider AM, et al: Provocative angiography in patients with gastrointestinal hemorrhage of obscure origin. Am J Gastroenterol 95:2807, 2000

40. Shetzline MA, Suhocki P, Dash R, et al: Provocative

angiography in obscure gastrointestinal bleeding. South Med J 93:1205, 2000

41. Krevsky B: Detection and treatment of angiodysplasia. Gastrointest Endosc Clin N Am 7:509, 1997

42. Foutch PG: Colonic angiodysplasia. Gastroenterologist 5:148, 1997

43. Rutgeerts P, Van Gompel F, Geboes K, et al: Long term results of treatment of vascular malformations of the gastrointestinal tract by neodymium Yag laser photocoagulation. Gut 26:586, 1985

44. Rogers BH: Endoscopic diagnosis and therapy of mucosal vascular abnormalities of the gastrointestinal tract occurring in elderly patients and associated with cardiac, vascular, and pulmonary disease. Gastrointest Endosc 26:134, 1980

45. Binmoeller KF, Thonke F, Soehendra N: Endoscopic hemoclip treatment for gastrointestinal bleeding. Endoscopy 25:167, 1993

46. Jaspersen D, Korner T, Schorr W, et al: Diagnosis and treatment control of bleeding intestinal angiodysplasias with an endoscopic Doppler device. Bildgebung 62:14, 1995

47. Jensen DM, Machicado GA, Jutabha R, et al: Urgent colonoscopy for the diagnosis and treatment of severe diverticular hemorrhage. N Engl J Med 342:78, 2000

48. Bloomfeld RS, Rockey DC, Shetzline MA: Endoscopic therapy of acute diverticular hemorrhage. Am J Gastroenterol 96:2367, 2001

49. Naveau S, Aubert A, Poynard T, et al: Long-term results of treatment of vascular malformations of the gastrointestinal tract by neodymium YAG laser photocoagulation. Dig Dis Sci 35:821, 1990

50. Santos JC Jr, Aprilli F, Guimaraes AS, et al: Angiodysplasia of the colon: endoscopic diagnosis and treatment. Br J Surg 75:256, 1998

51. Eisen GM, Dominitz JA, Faigel DO, et al: An annotated algorithmic approach to upper gastrointestinal bleeding. Gastrointest Endosc 53:853, 2001

52. Habr-Gama A, Waye JD: Complications and hazards of gastrointestinal endoscopy. World J Surg 13:193, 1989

53. Trowers EA, Ganga U, Rizk R, et al: Endoscopic hemorrhoidal ligation: preliminary clinical experience. Gastrointest Endosc 48:49, 1998

54. Athanasoulis CA, Baum S, Rosch J, et al: Mesenteric arterial infusions of vasopressin for hemorrhage from colonic diverticulosis. Am J Surg 129:212, 1975

55. Rahn NH 3rd, Tishler JM, Han SY, et al: Diagnostic and interventional angiography in acute gastrointestinal hemorrhage. Radiology 143:361, 1982

56. Levinson SL, Powell DW, Callahan WT, et al: A current approach to rectal bleeding. J Clin Gastroenterol 3:9, 1981

57. Clark RA, Colley DP, Eggers FM: Acute arterial hemorrhage: efficacy of transcatheter control. AJR Am J Roentgenol 136:1185, 1981

58. Browder W, Cerise EJ, Litwin MS: Impact of emergency angiography in massive lower gastrointestinal bleeding. Ann Surg 204:530, 1986

59. Matolo NM, Link DP: Selective embolization for control of gastrointestinal hemorrhage. Am J Surg 138:840, 1979

60. Encarnacion CE, Kadir S, Beam SA, et al: Gastrointestinal bleeding: treatment with gastrointestinal arterial embolization. Radiology 183:505, 1992

61. Bookstein JJ, Chlosta EM, Foley D, et al: Transcatheter hemostasis of gastrointestinal bleeding using modified autogenous clot. Radiology 113:277, 1974

62. Peck DJ, McLoughlin RF, Hughson MN, et al: Percutaneous embolotherapy of lower gastrointestinal hemorrhage. J Vasc Interv Radiol 9:747, 1998

63. Gady JS, Reynolds H, Blum A: Selective arterial embolization for control of lower gastrointestinal bleeding: recommendations for a clinical manage-

ment pathway. Curr Surg 60:344, 2003

64. Gomes AS, Lois JF, McCoy RD: Angiographic treatment of gastrointestinal hemorrhage: comparison of vasopressin infusion and embolization. AJR Am J Roentgenol 146:1031, 1986

65. Funaki B: Microcatheter embolization of lower gastrointestinal hemorrhage: an old idea whose time has come. Cardiovasc Intervent Radiol 27:591, 2004

66. Darcy M: Treatment of lower gastrointestinal bleeding: vasopressin infusion versus embolization. J Vasc Interv Radiol 14:535, 2003

67. Wright HK, Pelliccia O, Higgins EF Jr, et al: Controlled, semielective, segmental resection for massive colonic hemorrhage. Am J Surg 139:535, 1980

68. Eaton AC: Emergency surgery for acute colonic haemorrhage—a retrospective study. Br J Surg 68:109, 1981

69. McGuire HH Jr, Haynes BW Jr: Massive hemorrhage for diverticulosis of the colon: guidelines for therapy based on bleeding patterns observed in fifty cases. Ann Surg 75:847, 1972

70. Setya V, Singer JA, Minken SL: Subtotal colectomy as a last resort for unrelenting, unlocalized, lower gastrointestinal hemorrhage: experience with 12 cases. Am Surg 58:295, 1992

71. Jensen DM, Machicado GA: Colonoscopy for diagnosis and treatment of severe lower gastrointestinal bleeding: routine outcomes and cost analysis. Gastrointest Endosc Clin N Am 7:477, 1997

72. Foutch PG, Rex DX, Lieberman DA: Prevalence and natural history of colonic angiodysplasia among healthy asymptomatic people. Am J Gastroenterol 90:564, 1995

73. Heer M, Ammann R, Buhler H: Clinical significance of colonic angiodysplasias. Schweiz Med Wochenschr 114:1416, 1984

74. Sebastian JJ, Lucia F, Botella MT, et al: Diffuse gastrointestinal angiodysplasia associated with cryptogenic hepatic cirrhosis and coagulopathy simulating von Willebrand disease. Rev Esp Enferm Dig 88:631, 1996

75. Hughes LE: Postmortem survey of diverticular disease of the colon: I. Diverticulosis and diverticulitis. Gut 10:336, 1969

76. Meyers MA, Alonso DR, Gray GF, et al: Pathogenesis of bleeding colonic diverticulosis. Gastroenterology 71:577, 1976

77. Rushford AJ: The significance of bleeding as a symptom in diverticulitis. Proc R Soc Med 49:577, 1956

78. Bokhari M, Vernava AM, Ure T, et al: Diverticular hemorrhage in the elderly—is it well tolerated? Dis Colon Rectum 39:191, 1996

79. Luk GD, Bynum TE, Hendrix TR: Gastric aspiration in localization of gastrointestinal hemorrhage. JAMA 241:576, 1979

80. Robert JR, Sachar DB, Greenstein AJ: Severe gastrointestinal hemorrhage in Crohn's disease. Ann Surg 213:207, 1991

81. Binder SC, Miller HH, Deterling RA Jr: Emergency and urgent operations for ulcerative colitis: the procedure of choice. Arch Surg 110:284, 1975

82. Cirocco WC, Reilly JC, Rusin LC: Life-threatening hemorrhage and exsanguination from Crohn's disease: report of four cases. Dis Colon Rectum 38:85, 1995

83. Reyes E, Hernandez J, Gonzalez A: Typhoid colitis with massive lower gastrointestinal bleeding: an unexpected behavior of *Salmonella typhi*. Dis Colon Rectum 29:511, 1986

84. Maguire TM, Wensel RH, Malcolm N, et al: Massive gastrointestinal hemorrhage cecal ulcers and *Salmonella* colitis. J Clin Gastroenterol 7:249, 1985

85. Cohen MB, Giannella RA: Hemorrhagic colitis associated with *Escherichia coli* O157:H7. Adv Intern Med 37:173, 1992

86. Gould PC, Khawaja FI, Rosenthal WS: Antibiotic-associated hemorrhagic colitis. Am J Gastroenterol 77:491, 1982

87. Tagkalidis PP, Tjandra JJ: Chronic radiation proctitis. ANZ J Surg 71:230, 2001

88. den Hartog Jager FC, van Haastert M, Batterman JJ, et al: The endoscopic spectrum of late radiation damage of the rectosigmoid colon. Endoscopy 17:214, 1985

89. Crook J, Esche B, Futter N: Effect of pelvic radiotherapy for prostate cancer on bowel, bladder, and sexual function: the patient's perspective. Urology 47:387, 1996

90. Ellis DJ, Reinus JF: Lower intestinal hemorrhage. Crit Care Clin 11:369, 1995

91. Zuckerman GR, Prakash C: Acute lower intestinal bleeding. Part II: etiology, therapy, and outcomes. Gastrointest Endosc 49:228, 1999

92. Wagner HE, Stain SC, Gilg M, et al: Systematic assessment of massive bleeding of the lower part of the gastrointestinal tract. Surg Gynecol Obstet 175:445, 1992

93. Makela JT, Kiviniemi H, Laitinen S, et al: Diagnosis and treatment of acute lower gastrointestinal bleeding. Scand J Gastroenterol 28:1062, 1993

94. Geenen JE, Schmitt MG Jr, Wu WC, et al: Major complications of coloscopy: bleeding and perforation. Am J Dig Dis 20:231, 1975

95. Macrae FA, Tan KG, Williams CB: Towards safer colonoscopy: a report on the complications of 5000 diagnostic or therapeutic colonoscopies. Gut 24:376, 1983

96. Gaydos LA, Freireich EJ, Mantel N: The quantitative relation between platelet count and hemorrhage in patients with acute leukemia. N Engl J Med 266:905, 1962

97. Wilkinson JF, Nour-Eldin F, Israels MC, et al: Haemophilia syndromes: a survey of 267 patients. Lancet 2:947, 1961

98. Mittal R, Spero JA, Lewis JH, et al: Patterns of gastrointestinal hemorrhage in hemophilia. Gastroenterology 88:515, 1985

99. Cappell MS, Price JB: Characterization of the syndrome of small and large intestinal variceal bleeding. Dig Dis Sci 32:422, 1987

100. Chawla Y, Dilawari JB: Anorectal varices—their frequency in cirrhotic and non-cirrhotic portal hypertension. Gut 32:309, 1991

101. Goenka MK, Kochhar R, Nagi B, et al: Rectosigmoid varices and other mucosal changes in patients with portal hypertension. Am J Gastroenterol 86:1185, 1991

102. Baer JW, Ryan S: Analysis of cecal vasculature in the search for vascular malformations. AJR Am J Roentgenol 126:394, 1976

103. Danesh BJ, Spiliadis C, Williams CB, et al: Angiodysplasia—an uncommon cause of colonic bleeding: colonoscopic evaluation of 1,050 patients with rectal bleeding and anaemia. Int J Colorectal Dis 2:218, 1987

104. Heer M, Sulser H, Hany A: Angiodysplasia of the colon: an expression of occlusive vascular disease. Hepatogastroenterology 34:127, 1987

105. Richter JM, Hedberg SE, Athanasoulis CA, et al: Angiodysplasia: clinical presentation and colonoscopic diagnosis. Dig Dis Sci 29:481, 1984

106. Zuckerman G, Benitez J: A prospective study of bidirectional endoscopy (colonoscopy and upper endoscopy) in the evaluation of patients with occult gastrointestinal bleeding. Am J Gastroenterol 87:62, 1992

107. Foutch PG: Diverticular bleeding: are nonsteroidal anti-inflammatory drugs risk factors for hemorrhage and can colonoscopy predict out-

come for patients? Am J Gastroenterol 90:1779, 1995

108. Boley SJ, Sammartano R, Adams A, et al: On the nature and etiology of vascular ectasias of the colon: degenerative lesions of aging. Gastroenterology 72:650, 1977

109. Mitsudo SM, Boley SJ, Brandt LJ, et al: Vascular ectasias of the right colon in the elderly: a distinct pathologic entity. Hum Pathol 10:585, 1979

110. Imperiale TF, Ransohoff DF: Aortic stenosis, idiopathic gastrointestinal bleeding, and angiodysplasia: is there an association? A methodologic critique of the literature. Gastroenterology 95:1670, 1988

111. Boley SJ, Sprayregen S, Sammartano RJ, et al: The pathophysiologic basis for the angiographic signs of vascular ectasias of the colon. Radiology 125:615, 1977

112. Helmrich GA, Stallworth JR, Brown JJ: Angiodysplasia: characterization, diagnosis, and advances in treatment. South Med J 83:1450, 1990

113. Burt RW, Berenson MM, Samuelson CO, et al: Rheumatoid vasculitis of the colon presenting as pancolitis. Dig Dis Sci 28:183, 1983

114. Moses FM: Gastrointestinal bleeding and the athlete. Am J Gastroenterol 88:1157, 1993

115. Sokol RJ, Farrell MK, McAdams AJ: An unusual presentation of Wegener's granulomatosis mimicking inflammatory bowel disease. Gastroenterology 87:426, 1984

116. Klinvimol T, Ho YH, Parry BR, et al: Small bowel causes of per rectum haemorrhage. Ann Acad Med Singapore 23:866, 1994

117. Gilmore PR: Angiodysplasia of the upper gastrointestinal tract. J Clin Gastroenterol 10:386, 1988

118. Netterville RE, Hardy JD, Martin RS Jr: Small bowel hemorrhage. Ann Surg 167:949, 1968

119. Lu CL, Chen CY, Chiu ST, et al: Adult intussuscepted Meckel's diverticulum presenting mainly lower gastrointestinal bleeding. J Gastroenterol Hepatol 16:478, 2001

120. Longo WE, Vernava AM 3rd: Clinical implications of jejunoileal diverticular disease. Dis Colon Rectum 35:381, 1992

121. Buchman TG, Bulkley GB: Current management of patients with lower gastrointestinal bleeding. Surg Clin North Am 67:651, 1987

122. Chalasani N, Wilcox CM: Gastrointestinal hemorrhage in patients with AIDS. AIDS Patient Care STDS 13:343, 1999

123. Chalasani N, Wilcox CM: Etiology and outcome of lower gastrointestinal bleeding in patients with AIDS. Am J Gastroenterol 93:175, 1998

124. Becherer PR, Sokol-Anderson M, Joist JH, et al: Gastrointestinal histoplasmosis presenting as hematochezia in human immunodeficiency virus–infected hemophilic patients. Am J Hematol 47:229, 1994

125. Allison MC, Howatson AG, Torrance CJ, et al: Gastrointestinal damage associated with the use of nonsteroidal antiinflammatory drugs. N Engl J Med 327:749, 1992

126. Davies NM: Toxicity of nonsteroidal anti-inflammatory drugs in the large intestine. Dis Colon Rectum 38:1311, 1995

127. Langman MJ, Morgan L, Worrall A: Use of anti-inflammatory drugs by patients admitted with small or large bowel perforations and haemorrhage. Br Med J (Clin Res Ed) 290:347, 1985

128. Holt S, Rigoglioso V, Sidhu M, et al: Nonsteroidal antiinflammatory drugs and lower gastrointestinal bleeding. Dig Dis Sci 38:1619, 1993

49 MORBID OBESITY

Harvey J. Sugerman, M.D., F.A.C.S.

Approach to the Morbidly Obese Patient

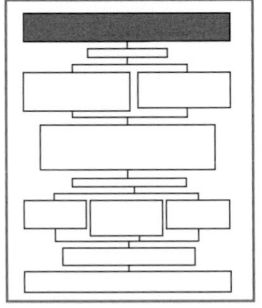

Many surgeons are afraid to operate on the morbidly obese patient (i.e., a patient whose weight is 100 lb greater than ideal body weight or who has a body mass index [BMI] greater than 35 kg/mg²) because they presuppose a marked increase in perioperative morbidity and mortality. Although the morbidly obese patient is certainly at greater risk, this risk can be markedly reduced by paying careful attention to detail in preoperative and postoperative care. The increased risks encountered in these patients include wound infection, dehiscence, thrombophlebitis, pulmonary embolism, anesthetic calamities, acute postoperative asphyxia in patients with obstructive sleep apnea syndrome (SAS), acute respiratory failure, right ventricular or biventricular cardiac failure, and missed acute catastrophes of the abdomen, such as an anastomotic leak. In a series of about 3,000 gastric procedures for morbid obesity itself, we have observed the following incidence of complications: wound infection that delayed hospital discharge, 5%, as well as minor infections or seromas in an additional 10%; clinically apparent phlebitis, 0.4%; clinically diagnosed fatal pulmonary embolism, 0.2%; and pneumonia, 0.5%. We have observed a 1% operative mortality. Although many of these patients had severe preoperative morbidity (respiratory insufficiency, pseudotumor cerebri, or insulin-dependent diabetes), the risks of complications approach the risks associated with major abdominal operation in nonobese patients. In what follows, the focus is on issues that the surgeon should carefully consider when operating on an extremely overweight patient.

Cardiac Dysfunction

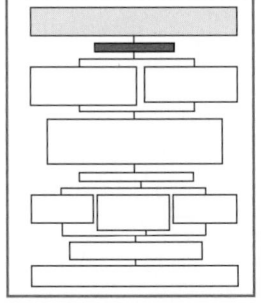

Morbidly obese patients are at significant risk of coronary artery disease as a result of an increased incidence of systemic hypertension, hypercholesterolemia, and diabetes. Because of this increased risk for cardiac dysfunction, preoperative electrocardiography probably should be performed on all obese patients 30 years of age or older.

Most morbidly obese patients have minimal evidence of cardiac dysfunction as detected by Swan-Ganz catheterization. Markedly elevated pulmonary arterial pressure (PAP) and pulmonary arterial wedge pressure (PAWP) values will frequently be noted in patients with the respiratory insufficiency of obesity, especially those with obesity hypoventilation syndrome (OHS) [see Respiratory Insufficiency, Obesity Hypoventilation Syndrome, below].[1] Intubation and ventilation in these patients will often be followed by a vigorous diuresis, and it is not unusual for a patient to lose 50 lb or more of retained fluid. In a few obese patients, acute respiratory insufficiency will be caused by a greatly expanded central blood volume and heart failure. Abnormal blood gas values in these individuals will be corrected by vigorous diuresis alone. As with most other abnormalities related to morbid obesity, weight loss will also correct cardiac dysfunction.

Respiratory Insufficiency

Morbidly obese patients may suffer from obstructive SAS or OHS. The simultaneous presence of SAS and OHS is known as the pickwickian syndrome [see Discussion, Respiratory Insufficiency of Obesity, below].[2-4]

SLEEP APNEA SYNDROME

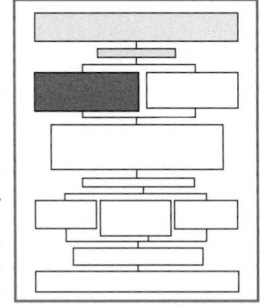

SAS is a potentially fatal complication of morbid obesity. A diagnosis of SAS should be suspected when there is a history of loud snoring, frequent nocturnal awakening with shortness of breath, and daytime somnolence. It is estimated that 2% of middle-aged women and 4% of middle-aged men in the United States workforce have SAS, and the incidence is markedly higher in the severely obese.[5] Patients will often admit to falling asleep while driving and waking up with their car on the road's median strip or bumping its guardrail. It is extremely important that trauma surgeons be aware of the relation between obesity and somnolence should a morbidly obese patient be seen in the emergency room after an automobile accident in which he or she fell asleep at the wheel. Elective patients with suspected sleep apnea syndrome should undergo preoperative polysomnography at a sleep center to confirm the diagnosis. Medications are usually ineffective. Stimulants, such as methylphenidate hydrochloride (Ritalin), should not be used. If a patient has a respiratory disturbance index (RDI) greater than 25—indicating more than 25 apneic or hypopneic episodes per hour of sleep—or has cardiac arrhythmias in association with apnea, treatment by nocturnal nasal continuous positive airway pres-

Approach to the Morbidly Obese Patient

Patient is morbidly obese (current weight at least 100 lb > ideal body weight, body mass index ≥ 35 kg/m², or both)

Increased risks include
- Missed abdominal catastrophe
- Respiratory failure
- Cardiac failure

- Anesthetic calamities
- Pulmonary embolism
- Internal hernia
- Acute gastric distention

- Wound infection
- Postoperative asphyxia
- Dehiscence
- Thrombophlebitis

Evaluate cardiopulmonary status preoperatively

Patient reports loud snoring, frequent nocturnal awakening, and daytime somnolence, or trauma victim has fallen asleep at the wheel

Suspect sleep apnea syndrome (SAS).

Confirm SAS by polysomnography in elective patients. Provide nocturnal nasal CPAP if apneic episodes are ≥ 25/hr of sleep or are associated with arrhythmias. If patient does not respond to — or does not tolerate — CPAP, perform tracheostomy with extra-long tube.

Patient has heart failure or extreme shortness of breath

Suspect obesity hypoventilation syndrome (OHS).
OHS is confirmed by $P_aO_2 ≤ 55$ mm Hg or $P_aO_2 ≥ 47$ mm Hg
- If PAWP ≥ 18 mm Hg, try I.V. furosemide.
- If PAP ≥ 40 mm Hg, consider insertion of Greenfield vena caval filter.
- If Hb ≥ 16 g/dl, phlebotomize to Hb of 15 g/dl.

Give prophylaxis against thromboembolism, induce anesthesia, and intubate

Administer regular or low-molecular-weight heparin 30 min preoperatively and at appropriate intervals thereafter until the patient is ambulatory.

Use intermittent sequential venous compression boots during anesthesia induction and throughout operation.

Two anesthesia personnel are required for induction and intubation of patients with SAS or OHS (one to hold the mask and one to squeeze the ventilation bag).

Insert oral airway after administration of succinylcholine and sodium pentobarbital. Ventilate with 100% O_2 for several minutes before intubation. If intubation is unsuccessful, reinsert oral airway and ventilate with a mask. Patient should be in reverse Trendelenburg position.

In the recovery room, keep patient in reverse Trendelenburg position

---

Patient does not have respiratory insufficiency of obesity

Extubate in recovery room when patient is fully alert and ventilatory effort is adequate; return patient to room.

Patient has SAS

In the absence of OHS, wean and extubate the day after operation. If patient was on nasal CPAP before operation, reinstitute on second night after operation. Monitor for prolonged apnea or arrhythmia; if either occurs, awaken patient.

Patient has OHS

Continue mechanical ventilation after operation until pain of breathing resolves. Wean to preoperative arterial blood gas levels; several days may be required.

Encourage early postoperative ambulation

Use intermittent sequential venous compression boots until patient is fully ambulatory.

Maintain high index of suspicion for recognition of abdominal catastrophes

Guarding, tenderness, and rigidity may be absent. Signs of infection (fever, tachypnea, tachycardia) may be absent. Acute respiratory failure may be secondary to peritonitis. Radiographic contrast studies and laparotomy may be indicated even when clinical signs are few.

sure (nasal CPAP) should be provided. If the patient has severe SAS with an RDI greater than 40 and does not respond with elimination of the apneic episodes or cannot tolerate nasal CPAP, a tracheostomy should be considered. An extra-long tracheostomy tube is usually necessary because of the depth of the trachea in the morbidly obese patient.

OBESITY HYPOVENTILATION SYNDROME

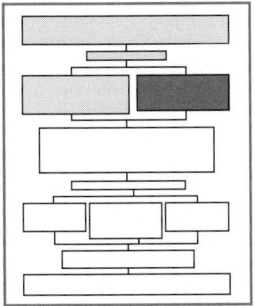

OHS should be suspected in patients who present with heart failure or extreme shortness of breath. Patients who have a BMI of 50 kg/m² or greater or who have a history of pulmonary problems (e.g., smoking, chronic obstructive pulmonary disease, sarcoidosis, pulmonary fibrosis, or asthma) should undergo a baseline arterial blood gas (ABG) determination before operation. Diagnosis of OHS is confirmed when the patient's arterial oxygen tension (P_aO_2) is 55 mm Hg or less or the arterial carbon dioxide tension (P_aCO_2) is 47 mm Hg or greater. These patients often have marked elevations in mean PAP, mean PAWP, or both, as well as severe polycythemia. In patients with obesity hypoventilation syndrome, a Swan-Ganz catheter should be inserted as part of the preoperative evaluation. If PAWP is 18 mm Hg or greater, diuresis with intravenous furosemide is indicated. In many of these patients, however, an elevated PAWP reflects an increased intrathoracic pressure and is necessary to maintain adequate cardiac output; such patients do not have congestive heart failure, despite a markedly elevated filling pressure [see Discussion, below]. Little can be done for the pulmonary hypertension that is seen in many of these patients; raising the P_aO_2 above 60 mm Hg usually will not lower PAP acutely.

Polycythemia can significantly increase the incidence of phlebothrombosis. If the hemoglobin (Hb) concentration is 16 g/dl or greater, phlebotomy to a concentration of 15 g/dl should be performed to reduce the postoperative risk of venous thrombosis. If PAP is 40 mm Hg or greater, consideration should be given to prophylactic insertion of a Greenfield vena caval filter because of the high risk of a fatal pulmonary embolism in these patients.[6] Placement of this filter can be a challenge because the appropriate landmarks cannot be identified in the operating room with fluoroscopy. It is necessary before operation to tape a quarter to the patient's back over the second lumbar vertebra with the aid of fixed radiographs and then during operation to aim for the quarter with the insertion catheter, using fluoroscopy. Because these patients are usually too heavy for angiography tables, the Greenfield filter usually cannot be inserted percutaneously in the radiology department.

Embolism

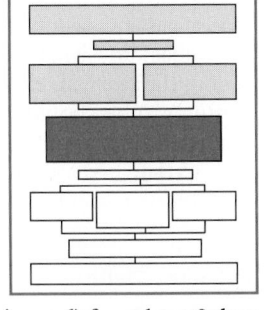

The risk of deep vein thrombosis [see 85 Venous Thromboembolism] increases with a prolonged operation or a postoperative period of immobilization, and it increases even further in the morbidly obese patient. Standard or low-molecular-weight heparin should be administered subcutaneously 30 minutes before operation and at appropriate intervals thereafter (depending on the type of heparin used) for at least 2 days or until the patient is ambulatory. Because respiratory function in the morbidly obese patient is greatly enhanced with the reverse Trendelenburg position, intermittent sequential venous compression boots should be used to counteract the increased venous stasis and the propensity for clotting. It is important that the intermittent venous compression boots be used before induction of anesthesia and throughout the operative procedure. Compression boots are usually part of a standard preoperative protocol in gastric procedures for weight control; their use should not be unintentionally neglected in preparation for other elective or emergency procedures on morbidly obese patients. Patients with severe venous stasis disease (e.g., pretibial stasis ulcers or bronze edema) are at significantly increased risk for fatal pulmonary embolism (PE).[7] Prophylactic insertion of a Greenfield vena cava filter should be considered in both patients with severe venous stasis disease and patients with OHS and a high PAP. Bariatric surgery–induced weight loss will correct the venous stasis disease in most cases.[7]

Anesthesia in Patients with Respiratory Insufficiency

Morbidly obese patients can be intimidating to the anesthesiologist because they are at significant risk for complications from anesthesia, especially during induction. The risk is particularly great for obese patients with respiratory insufficiency. An obese patient often has a short, fat neck and a heavy chest wall, which make intubation and ventilation a challenge. If endotracheal intubation proves difficult, however, these patients can usually be well ventilated with a mask. Awake intubation can be performed, with or without fiberoptic aids, but is quite unpleasant and rarely necessary.

It is extremely important that at least two anesthesia personnel be present during induction and intubation for patients with respiratory insufficiency of obesity. An oral airway is inserted after muscle paralysis with succinylcholine and sodium pentobarbital induction. One person elevates the jaw, hyperextends the neck, and ensures a tight fit of the mask, using both hands. To ensure adequate oxygen delivery, a second person compresses the ventilation reservoir bag, using two hands because of the resistance to air flow from the poorly compliant, heavy chest wall. After ventilation with 100% oxygen for several minutes, intubation is attempted. If difficulties are encountered within 30 seconds, the steps above should be repeated until the patient has been successfully intubated. A volume ventilator is required during operation. Placing the patient in the reverse Trendelenburg position expands total lung volume and facilitates ventilation[8]; however, the reverse Trendelenburg position increases lower extremity venous pressure and therefore mandates the use of intermittent sequential venous compression boots [see Embolism, above]. It is helpful to monitor blood gases through a radial arterial line or digital pulse oximeter.

Postoperative Management

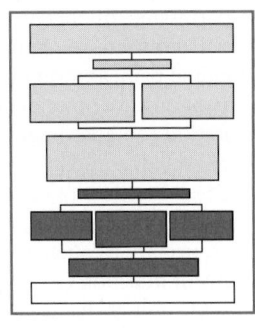

After operation, the obese patient should be kept in the reverse Trendelenburg position and should not be extubated until he or she is fully alert and showing evidence of adequate ventilatory effort [see 121 Mechanical Ventilation]. In the absence of respiratory insufficiency, most obese patients can be extubated in the OR or the recovery room and returned to a standard hospital room.

Patients with SAS, however, should be managed with overnight mechanical ventilation in the ICU. In the absence of concomitant OHS, they can usually be weaned and extubated the day after operation. Patients who were receiving ventilatory support with nasal CPAP before operation should have this treatment reinstituted the second night after operation; monitoring for prolonged apnea should be continued in the ICU or in a stepdown unit with digital oximetry. If apnea occurs, simply waking the patient should correct the problem. Patients who required tracheostomy can also usually be weaned from the ventilator the morning after operation.

Patients with OHS require prolonged mechanical volume ventilation until the pain of breathing resolves. One cannot expect such patients to manifest normal ABG levels, and they should be weaned to their preoperative values. This is why baseline ABG values are obtained preoperatively. The weaning process may require several days. It is important that these patients remain in the reverse Trendelenburg position to maximize diaphragmatic excursion. Positive end-expiratory pressure (PEEP) ventilation may be detrimental in patients with OHS because it can overdistend alveoli, thereby leading to capillary compression, decreased cardiac output, and increased dead space, all of which can exacerbate retention of carbon dioxide.

Swan-Ganz catheters, inserted preoperatively in patients with severe OHS, are useful in monitoring postoperative intravascular volume and oxygen delivery status. Excessive diuresis or restriction of fluids should be avoided [see Discussion, below].

It is extremely important to encourage early postoperative ambulation for the morbidly obese patient. These patients have surprisingly little pain, and it is not unusual to see them walking in the afternoon or early evening after a major abdominal procedure. If the patients have been advised preoperatively of the merits of early postoperative ambulation and know it is for their own welfare, they are usually willing to cooperate.

Complications of Gastric Surgery for Obesity

Current gastric procedures for obesity include open and laparoscopic gastric bypass (GBP), gastroplasty, and laparoscopic adjustable gastric banding. The procedures themselves are described in more detail elsewhere [see 61 Bariatric Procedures]; the following are some of the main complications associated with any abdominal operation in a severely obese patient.

ABDOMINAL CATASTROPHE

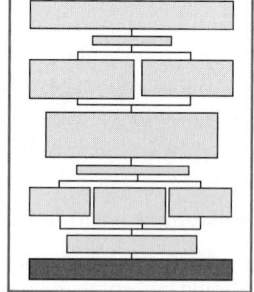

It may be very difficult to recognize an abdominal catastrophe in patients who are very young, very old, or morbidly obese or who are receiving high doses of steroids. The obese patient, for example, may present in the emergency room with a perforated duodenal ulcer or a ruptured diverticulum, complaining of abdominal pain, and yet on abdominal examination have no evidence of peritoneal irritation (no guarding, tenderness, or rigidity). This situation has been well documented in patients in whom an anastomotic or gastric leak has developed after operation for morbid obesity.[9] Symptoms include shoulder pain, pelvic or scrotal pain, back pain, tenesmus, urinary frequency, and, of great importance, marked anxiety. Signs of infection (e.g., fever, tachypnea, and tachycardia) may be absent, though tachycardia is often the first sign of a significant problem. Patients with peritonitis often have clinical symptoms and signs suggesting a massive pulmonary embolus: severe tachypnea, tachycardia, and sudden hypotension. Such acute pulmonary failure is probably secondary to sepsis-induced acute respiratory dis-

tress syndrome (ARDS). Thus, peritonitis must be suspected in any morbidly obese patient with acute respiratory failure. Patients who have undergone a laparoscopic bariatric procedure may be reexplored without much difficulty if there is concern about a possible leak.

Because a high index of suspicion of peritonitis is required to detect the condition in morbidly obese patients, radiographic contrast studies with water-soluble agents such as diatrizoate meglumine (Gastrografin) may be indicated even when there are few clinical signs. If a perforated viscus is suspected, an exploratory laparotomy may be necessary despite normal findings on radiographic contrast study.

INTERNAL HERNIA

GBP places patients at risk for internal hernia with a closed-loop obstruction, leading to bowel strangulation. There are three potential locations for these internal hernias: the Roux-en-Y anastomosis; the opening in the transverse mesocolon through which the retrocolic Roux limb is brought; and the Petersen hernia, which is located behind the retrocolic Roux limb. The primary symptom of an internal hernia is periumbilical pain, usually in the form of cramping consistent with visceral colic. These internal hernias may be very difficult to diagnose. Upper gastrointestinal radiographic series and abdominal CT scans are often normal, providing a false sense of security. The resulting assumption that no problem exists may be devastating for the patient should bowel infarction occur as a consequence of closed-loop obstruction. One should always carefully inspect the plain abdominal radiograph for the abnormal placement or spreading of the Roux-en-Y anastomotic staples. The safest course of action in patients with recurrent attacks of cramping periumbilical pain is abdominal surgical exploration. The frequency of this complication seems to have increased with the advent of laparoscopic GBP, presumably because of the difficulty of closing the potential hernia spaces completely. Some attribute the problem to the decreased tendency toward adhesion formation after laparoscopic surgery.

ACUTE GASTRIC DISTENTION

After GBP, massive gaseous distention occasionally develops in the distal bypassed stomach; this can lead to a gastric perforation or disruption of the gastrojejunostomy. The primary symptoms of this complication are hiccups and a bloated feeling. Massive gastric dilatation can lead to severe left shoulder pain and shock. The problem is usually secondary to edema at the Roux-en-Y anastomosis but can also be secondary to a mechanical problem. The diagnosis is made by means of an urgent upright abdominal radiograph, which reveals the markedly dilated and air-filled bypassed stomach. Occasionally, the stomach is filled with fluid, and the diagnosis may be more difficult. In those few cases in which the dilatation is primarily caused by air, the problem can be relieved by percutaneous transabdominal skinny-needle decompression with subsequent passage of gas and gastric and biliopancreatic juices through the Roux-en-Y anastomosis. Should the dilatation recur or the patient be in serious difficulty, an emergency laparotomy with insertion of a gastrostomy tube should be performed and the jejunojejunostomy evaluated. If a patient has extensive adhesions from previous abdominal surgery, a gastrostomy tube should be inserted at the time of GBP to prevent gastric dilatation.

Diabetes Mellitus

Type 2 (non–insulin-dependent) diabetes mellitus, a nonketotic form of diabetes that is usually noted after age 40, is markedly exacerbated by obesity. Patients with this type of diabetes often require large amounts of insulin for blood glucose control because of a significant reduction in insulin receptors. It is not unusual, however, to note a complete absence of the requirement for insulin in the immediate postoperative period in morbidly obese patients. Therefore, insulin should be withheld on the morning of operation. There is often a marked reduction in the requirement for insulin throughout the postoperative period and even at discharge in morbidly obese patients who have undergone GBP, probably because of increased release of gastric inhibitory peptide (GIP) from the proximal small bowel. Therefore, regular subcutaneous insulin should be administered to GBP patients according to a sliding scale after operation until insulin requirements can be determined. Before discharge, the patient should be taking an appropriate dose of neutral protamine Hagedorn (NPH) or Lente insulin but must perform frequent finger-stick blood glucose determinations afterward, given that the need for insulin will decrease progressively with weight loss.

In one study of 23 patients with diabetes mellitus who underwent gastric bariatric operation, the average requirement for insulin decreased from 74 units/day before operation to 8 units/day after operation.[10] Fourteen of the 23 patients were able to discontinue insulin completely, 11 by the time of discharge from the hospital 1 week after operation. These benefits were maintained during long-term follow-up to 39 months and were a result of a major decrease in insulin resistance that was associated with decreased food intake as well as weight loss.

Wound Care

Morbidly obese patients have been reported to have an increased risk of wound infection and dehiscence. However, the incidence of these complications in this group of patients can be very low. In a randomized, prospective trial comparing a running, continuous absorbable No. 2 polyglycolic acid suture with a No. 28 stainless-steel wire in morbidly obese patients who weighed an average of 320 lb, there was no significant difference in complications, including the incidence of incisional hernia, between the types of closure.[11] However, the running absorbable suture closure required significantly less time. Similar results comparing continuous with interrupted sutures have been noted by others.[12] Subcutaneous sutures should not be used, because the subcutaneous fat becomes reapproximated during skin closure, and subcutaneous sutures have been found to increase the risk of wound infection.[13] Obese patients undergoing clean-contaminated intestinal procedures should be given a parenteral antibiotic immediately before the operation and for only 24 hours after the operation[14]; it is important to note that morbidly obese patients should receive a double dose of prophylactic antibiotics because of the increased volume of distribution. If a gastric or gallbladder operation is planned, only aerobic bacterial coverage is necessary; a colon operation will necessitate anaerobic coverage as well.

It has been our experience that the incidence of incisional hernia is much higher in morbidly obese patients than in thin patients with ulcerative colitis who are taking large doses of corticosteroids and who undergo the same fascial wound closure with running No. 2 polyglycolic acid sutures.[15] This increased risk in morbidly obese patients is probably secondary to the increased intra-abdominal pressures (IAP) present in patients with central, or android, obesity.[16]

Obese diabetic patients are at risk for rapidly spreading panniculitis secondary to mixed aerobic and anaerobic organisms.[17] Subcutaneous gas and extensive necrosis, which usually does not involve the underlying muscle, are often present. It is uncommon to culture clostridia from these wounds. Even after extensive and repeated debridement, mortality remains high [see 22 Soft Tissue Infection].

Other Obesity-Related Diseases

GALLSTONES

Approximately one third of morbidly obese patients either have had a cholecystectomy or may have had gallstones noted at the time of another intra-abdominal operative procedure, such as gastric operation for morbid obesity. Preoperative evaluation of the gallbladder may be technically quite difficult in morbidly obese patients because gallstones may be missed with either ultrasonography or oral cholecystography. Intraoperative sonography is probably much more accurate. Should stones be present in a patient undergoing gastric operation for obesity, the gallbladder should be removed. In the past, obese patients with intermittent attacks of biliary colic were told to lose weight before an elective cholecystectomy for fear of significant morbidity and mortality from an elective operation. This attitude is no longer valid, because among the large numbers of obese patients who now undergo major elective abdominal procedures, morbidity is similar to that seen in thin patients if appropriate precautions are taken. Furthermore, obese patients have great difficulty losing large amounts of weight by diet alone and should be allowed to undergo definitive corrective operative procedures before weight reduction.

Rapid weight loss may lead to the development of gallstones in 25% to 40% of patients who undergo GBP. The risk of cholelithiasis in this setting can be reduced to 2% by administering ursodeoxycholic acid, 300 mg orally twice daily.[18]

PSEUDOTUMOR CEREBRI

Pseudotumor cerebri is an unusual complication of morbid obesity that is associated with benign intracranial hypertension, papilledema, blurred vision, headache, and elevated cerebrospinal fluid pressures.[19] It has been our experience that patients with pseudotumor cerebri are not at any additional perioperative risk and that cerebrospinal fluid does not have to be removed before anesthesia and major abdominal operation. Weight reduction will cure pseudotumor cerebri.[20,21]

DEGENERATIVE OSTEOARTHRITIS

Degenerative osteoarthritis of the knees, hips, and back is a common complication of morbid obesity. Weight reduction alone may greatly reduce the pain and immobility that afflict these patients, although the damage may be so extensive that a total joint replacement may be desirable. However, joint replacement in patients who weigh more than 250 lb is associated with an unacceptable incidence of loosening.[22] Weight reduction by means of a gastric bariatric operation may be the most sensible initial approach, to be followed by joint replacement after weight loss if pain and dysfunction persist.

Discussion

Morbidity Associated with Central Fat Deposition

Much has been written about the increased health risks inherent in central, or android, fat deposition as compared with peripheral, or gynoid, fat deposition. It is thought that in the former, the increased metabolic activity of mesenteric fat is associated with increased metabolism of amino acids to sugar, which leads to hyperglycemia and hyperinsulinism. Hyperinsulinism gives rise to increased sodium absorption and hypertension. Furthermore, central obesity has been linked to hypercholesterolemia. Hence, these patients have a significantly higher incidence of diabetes, hypertension, hypercholesterolemia, and gallstones[23]—which explains the higher mortality of the apple distribution of body fat as compared with the pear distribution. In the past, fat distribution was measured on the basis of the waist-to-hip ratio; however, computed tomography scans have shown that abdominal circumference is a more accurate measurement of central fat distribution.[24] We have found that morbidly obese women have significantly increased IAP and that this is associated with stress and urge overflow urinary incontinence.[25] With weight loss comes a significant decrease in bladder pressure and correction of incontinence. We have found IAP, as reflected in bladder pressure, to be closely correlated with sagittal abdominal diameter and waist circumference but not with waist-to-hip ratio (many morbidly obese patients have both central and peripheral obesity). We have also found that the increased IAP associated with central obesity may cause additional comorbid factors, including venous stasis ulcers, OHS, gastroesophageal reflux, and inguinal and incisional hernias.

Respiratory Insufficiency of Obesity

Obese patients are at risk for respiratory difficulties, which may be present before operation or may be exacerbated by an operation. The term pickwickian syndrome (which derives from *The Posthumous Papers of the Pickwick Club*, by Charles Dickens) was resurrected from the late 1800s to describe a morbidly obese man 52 years of age who fell asleep in a poker game while holding a hand containing a full house.[2] He was taken to the hospital by friends who presumed he was ill. The pickwickian syndrome is now known to comprise two pulmonary syndromes associated with morbid obesity: obstructive SAS and OHS.[3]

Patients with SAS suffer from repeated attacks of upper airway obstruction during sleep. The cause is probably related to a large, fat tongue as well as to excessive fat deposition in the uvula, pharynx, and hypopharynx. The normal genioglossus reflex is depressed, but this depression may be secondary to the excessive weight of the tongue. These patients are notorious snorers. As a result of inadequate stage IV and rapid eye movement (REM) sleep, they are markedly somnolent during the day.

Patients with SAS are at great risk for acute upper airway obstruction and respiratory arrest after operation and general anesthesia. A high index of suspicion is necessary before operation. Patients with severe SAS often have ventricular arrhythmias and sinus arrest during their apneic episodes, thereby placing them at even greater risk. A history of heavy snoring, early morning headaches, frequent awakening at night with shortness of breath, severe daytime somnolence (including falling asleep at the wheel), and frequent headaches should prompt further study. The syndrome is confirmed by sleep polysomnography, which is available at sleep centers in most major cities.

In most instances, severe SAS can be treated with nocturnal nasal CPAP. With this technique, air flowing through a nasal mask against a constant airway resistance enters the nasal pharynx and pushes the tongue forward to prevent recurrent obstruction.[26] The pressure can be adjusted for each patient. Unfortunately, many patients cannot tolerate the device, because it is cumbersome and noisy and tends to dry out the upper airway, although dryness can be prevented with an inexpensive room humidifier. If nasal CPAP cannot be tolerated by the patient, or if it is ineffective and the problem is severe (i.e., causing cardiac arrhythmias or severe hypoxia), tracheostomy is indicated. This procedure can be very difficult and dangerous and therefore should not be relegated to the youngest house officer in a surgical residency program. Because of the extremely deep neck in obese patients, a standard tracheostomy tube is usually inadequate, and a special tube with a deep bend should be used.

OHS is a condition associated with morbid obesity in which an individual suffers from hypoxemia and hypercapnia when breathing room air while awake but resting.[27] Spirometry reveals decreases in forced vital capacity, residual lung volume, expiratory reserve volume, functional residual capacity, and maximum minute volume ventilation, usually without obstruction to airflow [*see Figure 1*]. The most profound decrease is that in expiratory reserve volume; it is probably secondary to increased intra-abdominal pressure and a high-riding diaphragm. Thus, these patients have a restrictive rather than an obstructive pulmonary disease. The decreased expiratory reserve volume implies that many alveolar units are collapsed at end-expiration, which leads to perfusion of unventilated alveoli, or shunting. Patients with OHS often are heavy smokers or have additional pulmonary problems, such as asthma, sarcoidosis, idiopathic pulmonary fibrosis, or recurrent pulmonary emboli. One study of patients who underwent operation for morbid obesity showed no statistically significant difference in weight between those who had OHS and those who did not.[3]

As a result of chronic and severe hypoxemia, patients with OHS are often markedly polycythemic. The polycythemia further increases their already significant risk for venous thrombosis and pulmonary embolism. Because we have had several patients who later had a subclavian venous thrombosis and one patient who probably had a transient sagittal sinus thrombosis, patients with OHS should probably undergo phlebotomy to a hemoglobin concentration of 15 g/dl before elective operation.

Chronic hypoxemia also leads to pulmonary arterial vasoconstriction and severe pulmonary hypertension[1,28] and eventually to

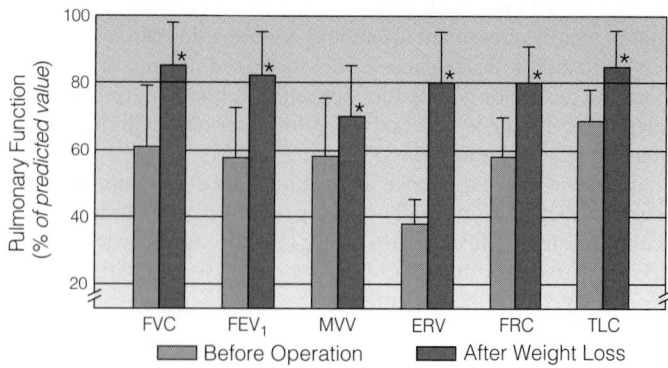

Figure 1 Impaired pulmonary function in the morbidly obese improved significantly after weight loss induced by gastric operation.[3]

right-sided heart failure or cor pulmonale with neck vein distention, tricuspid valvular insufficiency, right upper quadrant tenderness secondary to acute hepatic engorgement, and massive peripheral edema. Such patients may also have significantly elevated PAWP, which suggests left ventricular dysfunction.[1] Morbidly obese patients with a history of pulmonary disease or a BMI higher than 50 kg/m[2] should have preoperative determinations of blood gas values. If ABG measurement reveals severe hypoxemia (i.e., $P_aO_2 \leq 55$ mm Hg), severe hypercapnia ($P_aCO_2 \geq 47$ mm Hg), or both, the patient should undergo Swan-Ganz catheterization. If PAWP is 18 mm Hg or greater, intravenous furosemide should be administered for diuresis before elective operation. However, some patients may require a high ventricular filling pressure. A low cardiac output and hypotension may follow diuresis, necessitating volume reexpansion. If mean PAP is 40 mm Hg or greater, consideration should be given to the prophylactic insertion of a Greenfield inferior vena caval filter [see Thrombophlebitis, Venous Stasis Ulcers, and Pulmonary Embolism in the Morbidly Obese Patient, below].

It is highly probable that some of the elevated PAP and PAWP measurements are caused by the increased IAP in the morbidly obese [see Figure 2].[16,29] This leads to an elevated diaphragm, which in turn increases intrapleural pressure and thereby PAP and PAWP; if the pleural pressure is measured with an esophageal transducer, the transmyocardial pressure can be estimated. For this reason, these patients may require a markedly elevated PAWP to maintain an adequate cardiac output, and excessive diuresis may lead to hypotension. The same reasoning may be applied to a patient with a distended abdomen resulting from peritonitis and pancreatitis in whom what seem to be unusually high cardiac filling pressures are necessary. Therefore, one must rely on relative changes in cardiac output in response to either volume challenge or diuresis to determine the optimal PAWP in morbidly obese patients.

Patients with OHS respond rapidly to supplemental oxygen. However, oxygen administration is occasionally associated with significant CO_2 retention, which necessitates intubation and mechanical ventilation. Because their pulmonary disease is restrictive rather than obstructive, these patients are usually easy to ventilate without high peak airway pressures. Arterial blood gases need not return to normal before extubation; it is only necessary that they return to their preoperative values. These values are achieved, on average, 4 days after major upper abdominal operation, when the patients no longer have abdominal pain.[3]

It is important to emphasize that morbidly obese patients, especially those with respiratory insufficiency, should be placed in the reverse Trendelenburg position to maximize diaphragmatic excursion and to increase residual lung volume.[8] These patients will often complain of air hunger and respiratory distress when they lie supine. So-called breaking of the bed at the waist may exacerbate the problem by pushing the abdominal contents into the chest, thereby raising the diaphragm and further reducing lung volumes. Placing these patients in the leg-down position may predispose them to venous stasis, phlebitis, and pulmonary embolism, which should be offset with intermittent venous compression boots [see Thrombophlebitis, Venous Stasis Ulcers, and Pulmonary Embolism in the Morbidly Obese Patient, below].[30]

Both SAS and OHS can be completely corrected with weight reduction after gastric operation for morbid obesity: the nocturnal apneas resolve, the P_aO_2 rises, and the P_aCO_2 falls to normal as lung volumes improve.[3]

Cardiac Dysfunction in the Morbidly Obese Patient

Cardiac dysfunction in the morbidly obese patient is usually as-

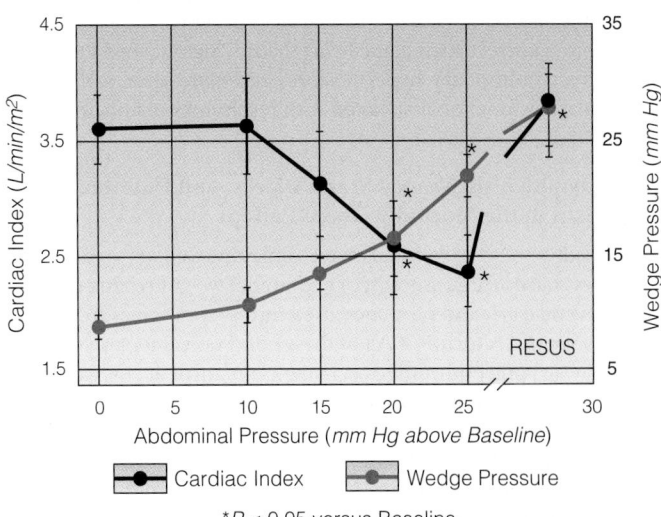

Figure 2 In a porcine model,[29] raising IAP caused cardiac index to fall and PAWP to rise. At an IAP of 25 mm Hg, saline was given to restore intravascular volume; cardiac index returned to baseline levels, but PAWP remained elevated. (IAP—intra-abdominal pressure; PAWP—pulmonary arterial wedge pressure)

sociated with respiratory insufficiency of obesity, especially OHS.[2] Elevated PAP in these patients may be secondary to hypoxemia-induced pulmonary arterial vasoconstriction, to elevated left atrial pressures secondary to left ventricular dysfunction, or to a combination of these; they may also be secondary to the increased pleural pressures arising from an elevated diaphragm secondary to increased IAP.[1,29,30] It is unusual for morbidly obese patients without respiratory insufficiency to experience significant cardiac dysfunction in the absence of severe coronary artery disease. Morbidly obese patients often have systemic hypertension, which can aggravate left ventricular dysfunction; however, mild left ventricular dysfunction can be documented in many morbidly obese patients in the absence of systemic hypertension.[31,32] Circulating blood volume, plasma volume, and cardiac output increase in proportion to body weight.[32] Massively obese patients may occasionally present with acute heart failure: it is reasonable to assume that the enormous metabolic requirements of such patients can present a greater

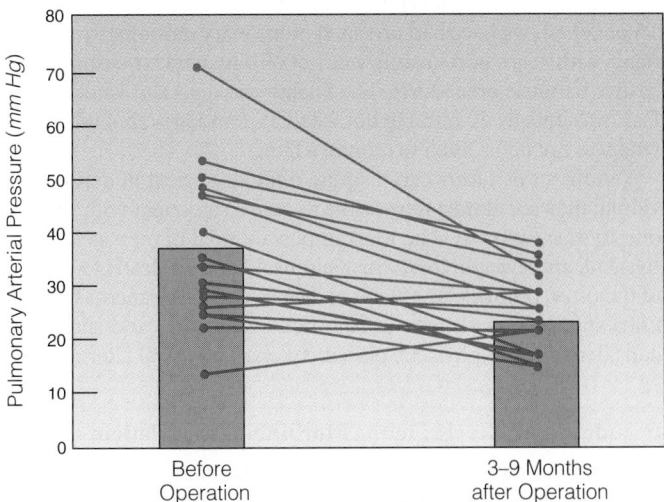

Figure 3 Mean pulmonary arterial pressure was significantly improved in 18 patients 3 to 9 months after gastric surgery–induced weight loss of 42% ± 19% of excess weight.[1]

demand for blood flow than the heart can provide. Vigorous diuresis will often correct such acute heart failure. Significant weight loss will correct pulmonary hypertension [see Figure 3] as well as left ventricular dysfunction associated with respiratory insufficiency.[1,33]

Thrombophlebitis, Venous Stasis Ulcers, and Pulmonary Embolism in the Morbidly Obese Patient

Morbidly obese individuals have difficulty walking; tend to be sedentary; have a large amount of abdominal weight resting on their inferior vena cava; and have increased intrapleural pressure, which impedes venous return.[28,29] All of these conditions increase the tendency toward phlebothrombosis. Patients are most at risk when immobilized in the supine position for long periods in the OR. These patients have also been shown to have low levels of antithrombin, which may increase their tendency toward venous thrombosis.[34] It has also been suggested that starvation, particularly in the postoperative period, may be associated with high levels of free fatty acids, which may predispose to perioperative thrombotic complications.[35]

Intermittent venous compression boots have been shown in randomized trials to reduce the incidence of deep vein thrombosis.[30] Administration of low-dose subcutaneous heparin must be started immediately before operation. However, because morbidly obese patients show a significant improvement in pulmonary function when placed in the reverse Trendelenburg position,[8] and because this position further increases venous pressure in the legs and the tendency toward stasis, it is preferable to use this position and intermittent venous compression boots. All patients, but especially the morbidly obese, should make every attempt to walk during the evening after operation.

Because pulmonary embolism is quite unusual when the appropriate precautions have been taken, acute air hunger, tachypnea, and hypoxemia should suggest the equal likelihood that sepsis-induced ARDS is present secondary to an intra-abdominal anastomotic leak.

Patients with severe OHS often have noticeably elevated PAP, which can lead to right-sided heart failure and can increase the risk of venous stasis and thrombosis. Investigators have noted that patients with primary idiopathic pulmonary hypertension are at significant risk for fatal PE.[5] For this reason, it has been our policy to place a prophylactic Greenfield vena caval filter in patients with respiratory insufficiency of obesity and a mean PAP of 40 mm Hg or greater. With this approach (in which a vena caval filter was used in 15 patients), we have had one fatal pulmonary embolus in 156 patients with respiratory insufficiency of obesity who have undergone gastric bariatric procedures. The fatality was a patient whose mean PAP was initially 40 mm Hg but fell to 35 mm Hg with diuresis and who was not considered to require a filter.

Venous stasis ulcers can be quite difficult to treat in a thin individual; they are almost impossible to cure in a patient with morbid obesity [see Figure 4]. The most important goal in management of these ulcers is weight loss, which almost invariably leads to healing of the ulcer, probably as a result of decreased IAP.[7] Patients with venous stasis ulcers also are at high risk for fatal PE and should be considered for prophylactic placement of a vena caval filter.

Pseudotumor Cerebri in the Morbidly Obese Patient

Pseudotumor cerebri (also known as idiopathic intracranial hypertension) associated with obesity is almost certainly secondary to increased IAP. The rise in IAP causes a rise in intrathoracic pressure, which in turn raises central venous pressure and PAWP [see Figure 2], thus decreasing venous drainage from the brain.[29] This se-

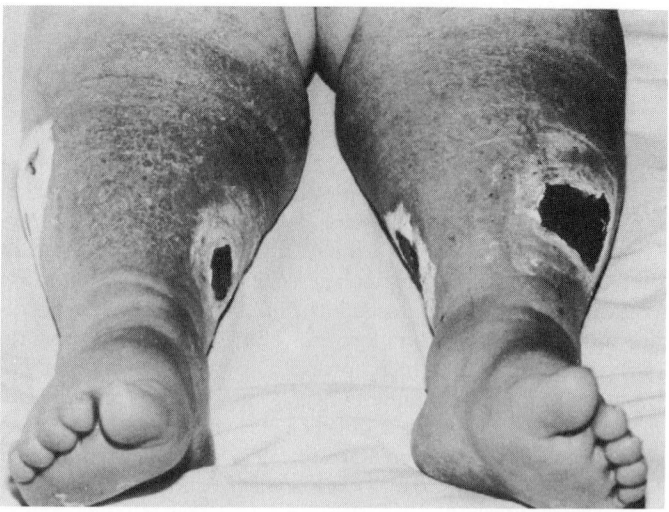

Figure 4 This chronic venous stasis ulcer was present for several years in a morbidly obese patient. Healing promptly followed weight loss induced by a gastric operation.

quence of events has been reproduced in a porcine model.[36] The elevated intracranial pressure (ICP) can be prevented by means of median sternotomy and pleuropericardiotomy [see Figure 5].[37] In humans studied 3 years after weight-reduction surgery, surgically induced weight loss was associated with a significant decrease in ICP (from 353 ± 35 mm H_2O to 168 ± 12 mm H_2O; $P < 0.001$) and with relief of headache and pulsatile tinnitus.[20,21]

Conclusion

Although the morbidly obese patient is potentially at risk for significant perioperative morbidity and mortality, attention to detail in preoperative preparation as well as in postoperative management

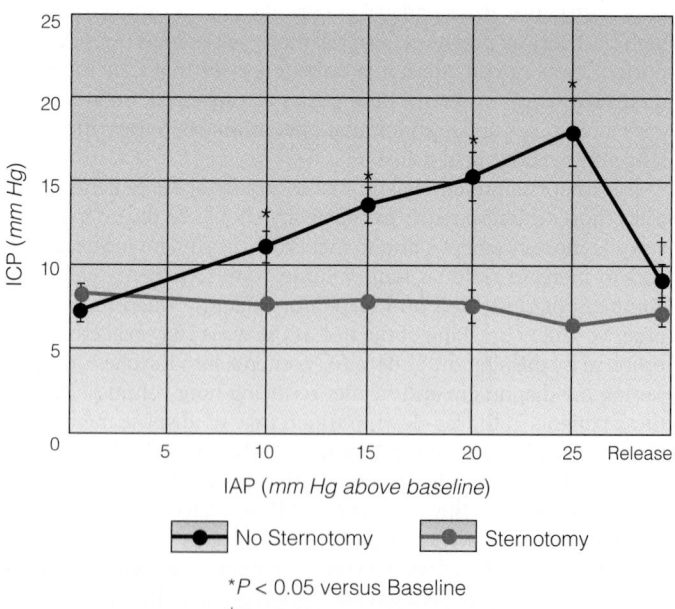

*P < 0.05 versus Baseline
†P < 0.05 versus Maximum IAP

Figure 5 In a porcine model,[37] IAP was increased to 25 mm Hg in 12 animals, of which three underwent median sternotomy and pleuropericardiotomy (red line) and nine did not (black line). Sternotomy and pleuropericardiotomy prevented the expected increase in ICP. (ICP—intracranial pressure)

should reduce this risk almost to that of the general population. A high index of suspicion for peritonitis must be maintained after an intra-abdominal procedure or when the patient complains of abdominal pain in the emergency room. Awareness of the problems associated with respiratory insufficiency in obese patients should enable the surgeon to avoid pitfalls when managing the patient with obstructive SAS or OHS. These patients may require preoperative pulmonary arterial catheterization for optimal fluid management before and after operation. The risks of venous thrombosis and PE are high, but the use of intermittent compression boots and early ambulation can minimize the dangers. The obese patient with non–insulin-dependent diabetes has been surprisingly easy to manage after major operation.

Weight reduction by diet is associated with a 95% incidence of recidivism. The average morbidly obese patient can be expected to lose two thirds of the excess weight within 1 year after a standard GBP or, if superobese, after a long-limb gastric bypass. Furthermore, recent reports note that this weight loss is long-lasting and averages 60% of excess weight at 5 years and more than 50% of excess weight up to 10 years after operation. This weight loss is associated with the correction of insulin-dependent diabetes, obstructive SAS, OHS, pseudotumor cerebri, hypertension, chronic venous stasis ulcers, stress incontinence, gastroesophageal reflux, and female sex hormone abnormalities, which may be related to dysmenorrhea, infertility, hirsutism, and an increased risk of endometrial carcinoma. Weight loss can markedly improve the patient's self-image and employability. Because techniques for operation for morbid obesity continue to change as understanding of pathophysiology improves, it is important for surgeons to keep abreast of the latest developments.

References

1. Sugerman HJ, Baron PL, Fairman RP, et al: Hemodynamic dysfunction in obesity hypoventilation syndrome and the effects of treatment with surgically induced weight loss. Ann Surg 207:604, 1988
2. Burwell CS, Robin ED, Whaley RD, et al: Extreme obesity associated with alveolar hypoventilation—a pickwickian syndrome. Am J Med 21:811, 1956
3. Sugerman HJ, Fairman RP, Baron PL, et al: Gastric surgery for respiratory insufficiency of obesity. Chest 89:81, 1986
4. Sugerman HJ, Fairman RP, Sood RK, et al: Long-term effects of gastric surgery for treating respiratory insufficiency of obesity. Am J Clin Nutr 55(2 suppl): 597S, 1992
5. Young T, Palta M, Dempsey J, et al: The occurrence of sleep-disordered breathing among middle-aged adults. N Engl J Med 328:1230, 1993
6. Greenfield LJ, Scher LA, Elkins RC: KMA-Greenfield® filter placement for chronic pulmonary hypertension. Ann Surg 189:560, 1979
7. Sugerman HJ, Sugerman EL, Wolfe L, et al: Risks/ benefits of gastric bypass in morbidly obese patients with severe venous stasis disease. Ann Surg 234:41, 2001
8. Vaughan RW, Bauer S, Wise L: Effect of position (semirecumbent versus supine) on postoperative oxygenation in markedly obese subjects. Anesth Analg 55:37, 1976
9. Mason EE, Printen KJ, Barron P, et al: Risk reduction in gastric operations for obesity. Ann Surg 190:158, 1979
10. Herbst CA, Hughes TA, Gwynne JT, et al: Gastric bariatric operation in insulin-treated adults. Surgery 95:209, 1984
11. McNeill PM, Sugerman HJ: Continuous absorbable vs interrupted nonabsorbable fascial closure: a prospective, randomized comparison. Arch Surg 121:821, 1986
12. Richards PC, Balch CM, Aldrete JS: Abdominal wound closure: a randomized prospective study of 571 patients comparing continuous vs. interrupted suture techniques. Ann Surg 197:238, 1983
13. De Holl D, Rodeheaver G, Edgerton MT, et al: Potentiation of infection by suture closure of dead space. Am J Surg 127:716, 1974
14. Stone HH, Hooper CA, Kolb LD, et al: Antibiotic prophylaxis in gastric, biliary, and colonic surgery. Ann Surg 184:443, 1976
15. Sugerman HJ, Kellum JM, Reines HD, et al: Incisional hernia: greater risk with morbidly obese than steroid dependent patients; low recurrence rate with prefascial polypropylene mesh repair. Am J Surg 171:80, 1996
16. Sugerman H, Windsor A, Bessos M, et al: Intra-abdominal pressure, sagittal abdominal diameter, and obesity co-morbidity. J Intern Med 241:71, 1997
17. Rouse TM, Malangoni MA, Schulte WJ: Necrotizing fasciitis: a preventable disaster. Surgery 92:765, 1982
18. Sugerman HJ, Brewer WH, Shiffman ML, et al: A multicenter, placebo-controlled, randomized, double-blind, prospective trial of prophylactic ursodiol for the prevention of gallstone formation following gastric-bypass-induced rapid weight loss. Am J Surg 169:91, 1995
19. Corbett JJ, Mehta MP: Cerebrospinal fluid pressure in normal obese subjects and patients with pseudotumor cerebri. Neurology 33:1386, 1983
20. Sugerman HJ, Felton WL, Salvant JB, et al: Effects of surgically induced weight loss on pseudotumor cerebri in morbid obesity. Neurology 45:1655, 1995
21. Sugerman HJ, Felton WL III, Sismanis A, et al: Gastric surgery for pseudotumor cerebri associated with severe obesity. Ann Surg 229:634, 1999
22. Goldin RH, McAdam L, Louie JS, et al: Clinical and radiologic survey of the incidence of osteoarthritis among obese patients. Ann Rheum Dis 35:349, 1976
23. Kissebah AH, Vydelingum N, Murray R, et al: Relation of body fat distribution to metabolic complications of obesity. J Clin Endocrinol Metab 54:254, 1982
24. Kvist H, Chowdhury B, Grangard U, et al: Total and visceral adipose-tissue volumes derived from measurements with computed tomography in adult men and women: predictive equations. Am J Clin Nutr 48:1351, 1988
25. Bump RC, Sugerman HJ, Fantl JA, et al: Obesity and lower urinary tract function in women: effect of surgically induced weight loss. Am J Obstet Gynecol 167: 392, 1992
26. Sullivan CE, Issa FG, Berthon-Jones M, et al: Reversal of obstructive sleep apnoea by continuous positive airway pressure applied through the nares. Lancet 1:862, 1981
27. Rochester DR, Enson Y: Current concepts in the pathogenesis of the obesity hypoventilation syndrome: mechanical and circulatory factors. Am J Med 57: 402, 1974
28. Alexander JK, Amad KH, Cole VW: Observations on some clinical features of extreme obesity, with particular reference to cardiorespiratory effects. Am J Med 32:512, 1962
29. Ridings PC, Bloomfield GL, Blocher CR, et al: Cardiopulmonary effects of raised intra-abdominal pressure before and after volume expansion. J Trauma 39:1168, 1995
30. Coe NP, Collins RE, Klein LA, et al: Prevention of deep vein thrombosis in urological patients: a controlled, randomized trial of low-dose heparin and external pneumatic compression boots. Surgery 83:230, 1978
31. Kaltman AJ, Goldring RM: Role of circulatory congestion in the cardiorespiratory failure of obesity. Am J Med 60:645, 1976
32. De Divitiis O, Fazio S, Petitto M, et al: Obesity and cardiac function. Circulation 64:477, 1981
33. Alpert MA, Terry BE, Kelly DL: Effect of weight loss on cardiac chamber size, wall thickness and left ventricular function in morbid obesity. Am J Cardiol 55: 783, 1985
34. Batist G, Bothe A, Bern M, et al: Low antithrombin III in morbid obesity: return to normal with weight reduction. JPEN 7:447, 1983
35. Printen HJ, Miller EV, Mason EE, et al: Venous thromboembolism in the morbidly obese. Surg Gynecol Obstet 147:63, 1978
36. Bloomfield GL, Ridings PC, Blocher CR, et al: Effects of increased intra-abdominal pressure upon intracranial and cerebral perfusion before and after volume expansion. J Trauma 40:936, 1996
37. Bloomfield GL, Ridings PC, Blocher CR, et al: A proposed relationship between increased intra-abdominal, intrathoracic, and intracranial pressure. Crit Care Med 25:496, 1997

Acknowledgments

Figures 1 and 3   Albert Miller.
Figures 2 and 5   Marcia Kammerer.

50 TUMORS OF THE STOMACH, DUODENUM, AND SMALL BOWEL

Jeffrey D. Wayne, M.D., F.A.C.S., and Mark S. Talamonti, M.D., F.A.C.S.

Gastric Adenocarcinoma

The incidence of gastric carcinoma exhibits significant geographic variability. The disease is most common in Japan and China, and high rates of occurrence have also been reported in Central and South America, Eastern Europe, and parts of the Middle East.[1] In most of the more developed nations, however, gastric carcinoma is relatively uncommon. The overall incidence of this condition has decreased in the past few decades, but gastric carcinoma remains the second leading cause of cancer death worldwide. The reported reductions in gastric cancer mortality may be linked to better refrigeration and a concomitant decrease in the intake of salted, pickled, smoked, and chemically preserved foods; however, this link remains controversial. An inverse association with the consumption of fresh fruits and vegetables has also been noted.[2]

Gastric cancer occurs 1.5 to 2.5 times more frequently in males than in females. It is rarely diagnosed before the age of 40, and its incidence peaks in the seventh decade of life. African Americans, Hispanic Americans, and Native Americans are two times more likely to have gastric cancer than white Americans are.[3]

In the United States in particular, the incidence of stomach cancer has fallen substantially over the past 70 years.[4] Whereas this disease was once a leading cause of cancer-related death in the United States, it now ranks 13th among major causes. Unfortunately, the decline in incidence has not translated into an improvement in the 5-year survival rate.[5] Across all races, the 5-year relative survival was 23% for the period extending from 1992 to 1999.[3] This result is probably related to the advanced stage at which most patients present. A 1995 study from the Commission on Cancer of the American College of Surgeons (ACS) found that 66% of patients with gastric cancer presented with locally advanced or metastatic disease.[6] Resection rates ranged from 30% to 50%, and 5-year survival rates after resection with curative intent were directly related to stage at presentation. For stage I disease, the survival rate was 43%; for stage II, 37%; for stage III, 18%; and for stage IV, 20%.

Another relevant change in the epidemiology of gastric cancer is a shift in the distribution of primary lesion sites within the stomach. In the first quarter of the 20th century, two thirds of gastric cancers were located in the antrum and the prepyloric area, and only 10% arose in the cardia or the esophagogastric junction. Since the 1970s, however, adenocarcinoma of the proximal stomach has become increasingly common. In one study, the incidence of adenocarcinoma of the gastric cardia rose from 29.1% to 52.2% in the period between 1984 and 1993.[7] In another, which included 18,365 gastric cancer patients from ACS-approved hospitals, a full 31% of tumors were found to be in the proximal stomach, compared with only 26% in the distal third.[8] In the United States, carcinoma of the cardia occurs primarily in whites, with a male-to-female ratio of approximately 2:1. Cancer of the cardia appears to be distinct from adenocarcinoma of the distal esophagus, which frequently arises in the setting of Barrett's esophagus.[9] Associations have also been

reported between cancer of the gastric cardia and infection with *Helicobacter pylori* or Epstein-Barr virus.[10,11]

CLASSIFICATION

Adenocarcinoma of the stomach may be divided into two histologic subtypes, intestinal and diffuse.[12] Each subtype has unique pathologic, epidemiologic, etiologic, and prognostic features. The intestinal (or glandular) subtype usually arises in the distal stomach (often after a long precancerous phase), is more common in elderly patients, and has been closely associated with atrophic gastritis and diets high in nitrates and nitrose compounds.[13] The characteristic histologic finding is cohesive neoplastic cells that form glandlike tubular structures. The diffuse subtype occurs more frequently in younger patients and has no identifiable precursor lesion. It may develop in any part of the stomach but shows a predilection for the cardia. Cell cohesion is absent; thus, individual cancer cells infiltrate and thicken the stomach wall without forming a discrete ulcer or mass.

In general, the prognosis for the diffuse subtype is worse than that for the intestinal subtype. Whereas intestinal lesions are seen more frequently in regions with a high incidence of gastric cancer, the incidence of diffuse lesions is constant among various populations throughout the world.[14] Accordingly, the overall decline in gastric cancer over the past century has been attributed to a decline in intestinal lesions and to a decline in the incidence of *H. pylori* infection (see below).

RISK FACTORS

Historical studies of specimens obtained during operation or at autopsy suggest that gastric carcinoma, especially of the intestinal subtype, frequently develops in the presence of chronic atrophic gastritis and associated intestinal metaplasia. It has generally been assumed that adenocarcinoma of the distal stomach progresses from chronic gastritis to metaplasia through the teratogenic influence of environmental factors. The most commonly studied environmental factors are the nitrates and nitrose compounds present in high levels in salted, smoked, or pickled foods consumed in areas where gastric cancer is endemic.[15] To date, however, no prospective studies have conclusively demonstrated that modern refrigeration practices and the subsequent decline in the salting, smoking, and pickling of food have been responsible for the relative decline in intestinal gastric cancer. Furthermore, the intestinal subtype may arise in the absence of metaplasia. Finally, the emergence of chronic infection with *H. pylori* as the dominant risk factor for gastric adenocarcinoma has challenged the paradigm of the atrophic gastritis–intestinal metaplasia–gastric cancer sequence.

Epidemiologic studies across various populations worldwide have consistently demonstrated a strong association between *H. pylori* infection and gastric cancer.[16] Prospective serologic studies have confirmed that persons with evidence of such infection are three to six times more likely to have gastric cancer than persons

Table 1 American Joint Committee of Cancer TNM Clinical Classification of Gastric Carcinoma

Primary tumor (T)	TX	Primary tumor cannot be assessed
	T0	No evidence of primary tumor
	Tis	Carcinoma in situ: intraepithelial tumor without invasion of lamina propria
	T1	Tumor invades lamina propria or submucosa
	T2	Tumor invades muscularis propria or subserosa
		T2a: tumor invades muscularis propria
		T2b: tumor invades subserosa
	T3	Tumor penetrates serosa (visceral peritoneum) without invasion of adjacent structures
	T4	Tumor invades adjacent structures
Regional lymph nodes (N)	NX	Regional lymph node(s) cannot be assessed
	N0	No regional lymph node metastasis
	N1	Metastasis in 1–6 regional lymph nodes
	N2	Metastasis in 7–15 regional lymph nodes
	N3	Metastasis in > 15 regional lymph nodes
Distant metastasis (M)	MX	Distant metastasis cannot be assessed
	M0	No distant metastasis
	M1	Distant metastasis

who are seronegative.[17] Still, only a very small fraction of infected persons have gastric cancer. It has been estimated that more than half of the world's inhabitants may be infected with *H. pylori*—a number that dwarfs the actual incidence of gastric cancer. What is clear is that *H. pylori* infection of the gastric mucosa leads to a state of chronic active inflammation that lasts for decades. This inflammatory process appears to be modulated by multiple forces, including genetic and environmental factors.[18] Inherited traits may confer susceptibility or resistance to carcinogenesis. Indeed, first-degree relatives of gastric cancer patients have a two to three times higher relative risk of contracting the disease.[19] Gastric irritants may act as promoters, and antioxidants may have a protective effect (which may be part of the reason for the reduced risk of gastric cancer associated with diets rich in fruits and vegetables).[20]

Unlike intestinal cancers, diffuse cancers appear not to be associated with *H. pylori* infection. Diffuse adenocarcinoma of the stomach is more common in young patients and has no known precursor lesion.[9] The incidence of genetically associated diffuse cancers is estimated to be in the range of 5% to 10%.[19] Familial cases of diffuse gastric cancer occur at an average age of 38 years and are inherited in an autosomal dominant fashion with 70% penetrance.[21] Patients with blood group A have a 16% to 20% increased risk of gastric cancer.[22]

CLINICAL EVALUATION

In high-risk areas (e.g., Japan), mass screening programs have been successful in identifying early gastric cancer, which is generally amenable to surgical cure.[23] In fact, in some Japanese studies, as many as 40% of newly diagnosed patients had early gastric cancer. Unfortunately, in Western countries, the disease is almost always diagnosed relatively late, when it is locally advanced or metastatic. When it is superficial, gastric cancer typically produces no symptoms. As it progresses, however, a constellation of vague, nonspecific symptoms may develop, including anorexia, fatigue, weight loss, and epigastric discomfort. Dysphagia, early satiety, vomiting, and hematemesis also are seen, albeit rarely; when present, they often indicate advanced disease. Indeed, early gastric cancer has no characteristic physical findings, and many patients are not diagnosed until they present with jaundice, ascites, or a palpable mass, all of which signal incurable disease.

INVESTIGATIVE STUDIES

Until comparatively recently, an upper gastrointestinal series was often the first diagnostic test ordered to evaluate symptoms related to the upper GI tract. However, even with double-contrast techniques, which allow improved visualization of mucosal detail, false negative rates as high as 25% were reported, especially with small lesions (i.e., 5 to10 mm).[24] Accordingly, in most large series, fiberoptic endoscopy with biopsy has replaced contrast radiography as the primary diagnostic technique.[25] Upper GI endoscopy with biopsy has been reported to have a diagnostic accuracy of 95%.[20] However, false negatives have been reported, especially in the context of inadequate biopsies. Thus, it is recommended that at least four biopsy specimens taken from the region of any atypical findings.[26]

STAGING

Two major classification systems are available for staging gastric cancer. The first is the one used in Japan, where gastric cancer is staged according to the general rules for gastric study in surgery and pathology published by the Japanese Research Society for Gastric Cancer (JRSGC).[27] This elaborate system focuses on the anatomic involvement of specifically numbered lymph node stations. The second system is the one generally used in Western countries—namely, the familiar tumor-node-metastasis (TNM) system developed by the American Joint Committee on Cancer (AJCC) and the International Union Against Cancer (UICC) [*see Tables 1 and 2*].[28] The AJCC/UICC staging system is based on a gastric cancer database and classifies lesions according to the depth to which the primary tumor penetrates the gastric wall, the extent of lymph node involvement, and the presence or absence of distant metastases.

The primary goal in the evaluation of gastric cancer patients is to stratify them into two clinical stage groups: those with locoregional disease (AJCC stages I to III) and those with systemic disease (AJCC stage IV).[29] The National Comprehensive Cancer Network (NCCN) has developed consensus guidelines for the clinical evaluation and staging of patients with possible gastric cancer. These guidelines are accessible to any practitioner via

Table 2 American Joint Committee on Cancer Staging System for Gastric Carcinoma

Stage	T	N	M
Stage 0	Tis	N0	M0
Stage IA	T1	N0	M0
Stage IB	T1	N1	M0
	T2a, T2b	N0	M0
Stage II	T1	N2	M0
	T2a, T2b	N1	M0
	T3	N0	M0
Stage IIIA	T2a, T2b	N2	M0
	T3	N1	M0
	T4	N0	M0
Stage IIIB	T3	N2	M0
Stage IV	T4	N1, N2, N3	M0
	T1, T2, T3	N3	M0
	Any T	Any N	M1

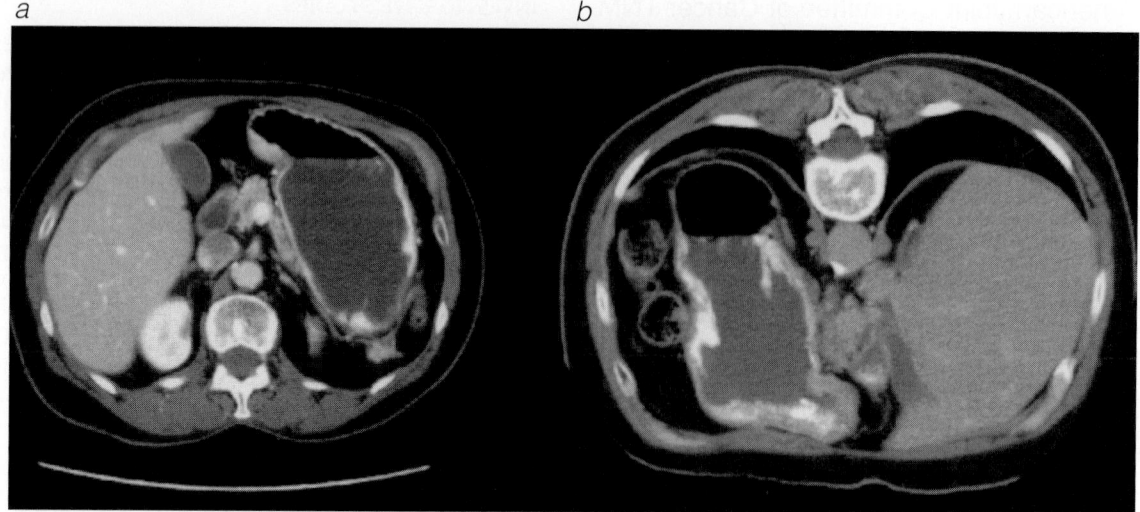

Figure 1 **Shown are CT scans of a patient with a T3 carcinoma involving the posterior wall of the gastric antrum, taken with the patient supine (*a*) and prone (*b*). By placing the patient in the prone position and distending the stomach with water, better definition of the extent of the tumor and clearer delineation of the interface between the stomach and the pancreas is achieved.**

the Internet (http://www.nccn.org/professionals/physician_gls/PDF/gastric.pdf) and are updated annually. Multidisciplinary evaluation is recommended for all patients. A careful history is obtained and a thorough physical examination performed, with special attention paid to comorbid conditions that might preclude operative intervention. Initial laboratory studies include a complete blood cell count with a platelet count; determination of serum electrolyte, blood urea nitrogen, creatinine, and glucose concentrations; and a liver function panel. Chest radiography is performed, along with computed tomography of the abdomen and pelvis.

Whereas CT is invaluable for detecting ascites, bulky adenopathy, and significant visceral metastases, its overall accuracy in staging tumors is modest: only 70% for advanced lesions and 44% for early lesions.[30] CT assesses lymph node involvement primarily on the basis of node size. Thus, its sensitivity for N1 and N2 disease is low, ranging from 24% to 43%; however, its specificity is high, approaching 100%. Technical advances, such as spiral (helical)

CT with intravenous contrast plus appropriate gastric distention with 600 to 800 ml of water (a negative contrast agent), have allowed modest improvements in overall staging with CT [*see Figure 1*]. Nevertheless, CT is still limited in its ability to evaluate peritoneal disease and liver metastases smaller than 5 mm.[31]

Given the limitations of CT, we believe that in the absence of obvious metastatic disease, locoregional staging with endoscopic ultrasonography (EUS) is vital for accurately assessing tumor penetration through the gastric wall (T stage) and ascertaining whether regional nodes (N stage) or even mediastinal or para-aortic lymph nodes may be involved (which would be considered M1 disease) [*see Figure 2*]. EUS is unique among imaging modalities in its ability to image the gastric wall as a five-layer structure, with each layer correlating with an actual histologic layer.[32] The overall accuracy of EUS in determining the extent of infiltration ranges from 67% to 92%.[33] EUS features that suggest lymph node metastasis include a rounded shape, hypoechoic patterns, and a

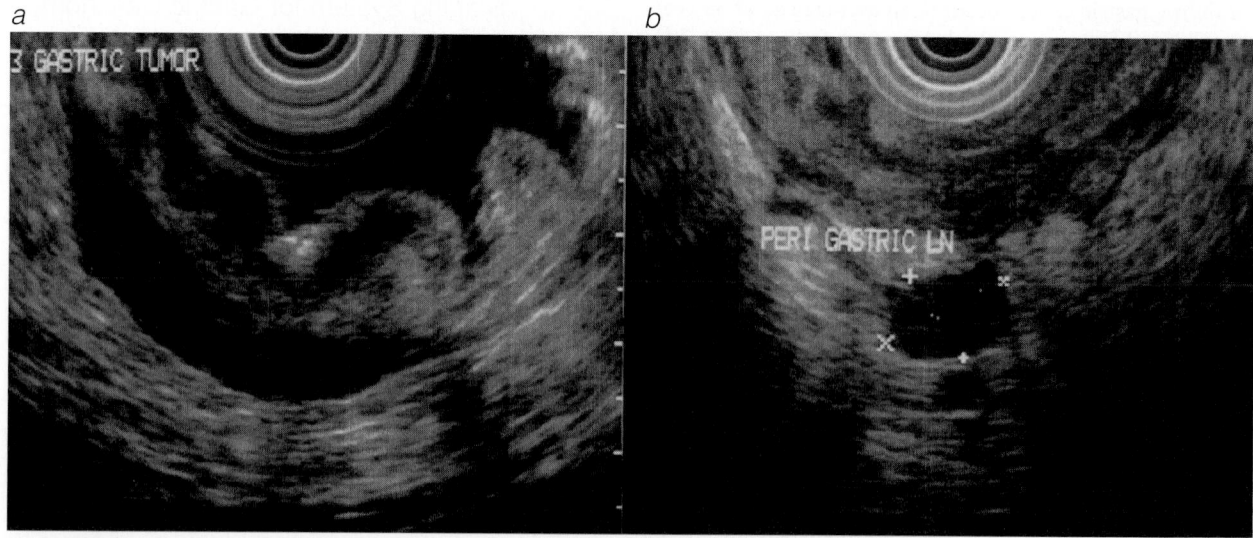

Figure 2 (*a*) **Shown is an EUS image of a T3 gastric neoplasm.** (*b*) **EUS reveals the presence of suspicious perigastric (N1) nodes, later confirmed as malignant at operation.**

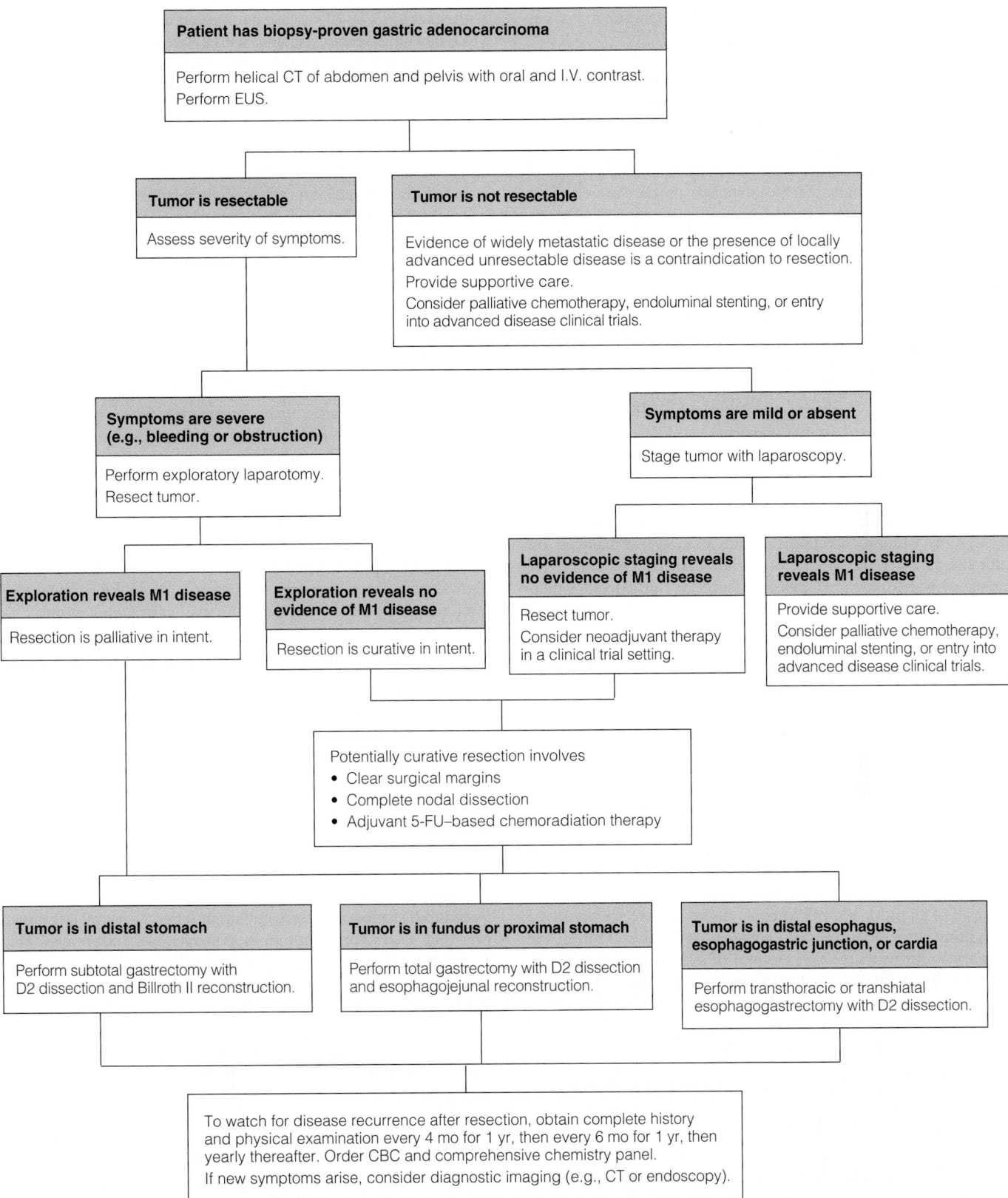

Figure 3 **Algorithm illustrates workup and treatment of patient with gastric carcinoma.**

size larger than 1 cm. In one study comparing preoperative findings from EUS with pathologic findings at operation, EUS was 100% sensitive for N0 disease and 66.7% sensitive for N1 disease.[34] EUS also allows identification and aspiration of small-volume ascites. If cytologic study of the ascitic fluid so obtained confirms the presence of malignant cells, the patient is considered to have metastatic disease and therefore is not eligible for curative-intent surgery. For all of these reasons, EUS is now widely accepted as superior to conventional CT in the regional staging of gastric cancer.[9]

Role of Laparoscopy

The ultimate goal of any staging evaluation is to ensure that patients with metastatic disease are not treated with nontherapeutic laparotomy or other local therapies (e.g., radiation therapy), which are generally ineffective against advanced disease. Even small-volume metastatic disease identified on the surface of the liver or the peritoneum at laparotomy is associated with poor survival: in one study, patients with such disease had a life expectancy of only 6 to 9 months.[35] In these situations, there is little to be gained from attempts at palliative resection.

Staging laparoscopy [see 62 Procedures for Benign and Malignant Gastric and Duodenal Disease] has proved to be highly relevant to the evaluation of patients with gastric cancer. In a study from the Memorial Sloan-Kettering Cancer Center (MSKCC), the investigators performed laparoscopic exploration on 110 of 111 patients with newly diagnosed gastric cancer.[36] Of these 110 patients, 94% were accurately staged, with a sensitivity of 84% and a specificity of 100%, and 37% were found to have subclinical metastatic disease. Hospital stay was substantially shorter in the 24 patients who underwent diagnostic laparoscopy with biopsy only (average, 1.4 days) than in comparable patients who underwent exploratory laparotomy without resection (average, 6.5 days). Finally, at the time the data were reported, none of the patients who underwent laparoscopy had required palliative surgery. Subsequent single-institution series confirmed the utility of staging laparoscopy, reporting accuracy rates ranging from 95% to 97% and occult M1 disease rates approaching 30%.[37,38] Taken as a whole, the data, though derived from relatively small single-institution experiences, are compelling, and they have led the NCCN to encourage laparoscopic staging strongly, either before or at the time of the planned resection.[39]

MANAGEMENT

Surgical Therapy

Surgical resection [see 62 Procedures for Benign and Malignant Gastric and Duodenal Disease] remains the only potentially curative therapy for localized gastric cancer [see Figure 3]. Cure requires removal of all gross and microscopic disease. More specifically, a margin-negative (R0) resection entails wide local excision of the primary tumor with en bloc removal of all associated lymphatic vessels and any local or regional extension of disease. The downside of surgical resection as a sole modality of therapy is that it is associated with a high rate of relapse. Consequently, several areas of surgical treatment of stomach cancer remain subject to controversy. In particular, the extent of gastric resection, the extent of lymph node dissection, the optimal approach to proximal stomach lesions, and the role of splenectomy and adjacent organ resection continue to generate significant debate.

Extent of gastric resection R0 resection (i.e., resection of all gross disease with microscopically negative margins) has been shown to have a clear impact on overall survival after potentially curative surgery. In the German Gastric Cancer Study, a prospective multicenter observational trial, the calculated 10-year survival rate in the entire population was 26.3%, compared with 36.1% in patients who underwent an R0 resection.[40] In a large multi-institutional adjuvant therapy trial, 19% of patients underwent an R1 resection (i.e., had resection-line involvement); only 9% of patients

with stage I, II, or III disease and resection-line involvement survived beyond 5 years, compared with 27% of those who underwent an R0 resection.[41] Given the propensity of tumor for submucosal spreading, many authors consider proximal margins of 5 to 6 cm, with routine frozen-section analysis, to be optimal.[42,43]

In an effort to lower the positive margin rate, some surgeons have proposed that total gastrectomy be considered the operation of choice for all operable gastric cancers. This approach, originally based on historical data from single institutions, has been tested in three clinical trials. In the first trial, elective total gastrectomy was compared with subtotal gastrectomy as curative-intent therapy for adenocarcinoma of the antrum.[44] Elective total gastrectomy did not increase mortality, but it also did not improve 5-year survival (which was 48% in both treatment arms). In the second trial, patients with antral cancer were randomly assigned to undergo either subtotal gastrectomy or total gastrectomy with extended lymph node dissection (ELND) and en bloc distal pancreatectomy and splenectomy.[45] Total gastrectomy was associated with increased operative time, greater transfusion requirements, and longer hospital stay; however, median survival was significantly better in the subtotal gastrectomy group (1,511 days versus 922 days). In the third trial, the investigators concluded that subtotal gastrectomy should be the procedure of choice for cancer of the distal half of the stomach, provided that an adequate negative proximal margin could be achieved.[46] This conclusion was based on their finding that 5-year survival probabilities were essentially equivalent in the two groups studied (65.3% in the subtotal gastrectomy group versus 62.4% in the total gastrectomy group).

Options for proximal gastric cancer As noted (see above), adenocarcinoma of the gastric cardia and the esophagogastric junction appears to be clinically distinct from adenocarcinoma of the distal stomach,[47] and its incidence is currently escalating across all races and age groups. Accordingly, it is imperative that surgeons understand the surgical options for treatment of proximal gastric cancer.[48]

For tumors originating from the distal esophagus, esophagectomy—either transhiatal esophagectomy with a cervical anastomosis or transthoracic (Ivor-Lewis) esophagectomy with a thoracic anastomosis—is clearly the procedure of choice [see 34 Open Esophageal Procedures]. For tumors of the cardia, it has been suggested that esophagogastrectomy might offer a survival advantage over total gastrectomy with an esophagojejunal anastomosis. This suggestion was evaluated in a study of 1,002 patients with adenocarcinoma of the esophagogastric junction.[49] The investigators divided tumors into three types on the basis of the location of the tumor center—cancers of the distal esophagus (type I), cancers of the cardia (type II), and cancers of the subcardial fundus (type III)—and analyzed the demographic and long-term survival data. Operative mortality proved to be higher with esophagogastrectomy than with extended total gastrectomy. Furthermore, R0 resection and lymph node status were found to be the dominant prognostic factors influencing survival. Finally, in patients with type II lesions, the pattern of lymphatic spread was primarily to paracardial, lesser curvature, and left gastric node groups. These data, taken together, led the authors to conclude that total gastrectomy is preferable to esophagogastrectomy in this setting if a margin-negative resection can be achieved.

An alternative approach to treating proximal gastric cancer is to perform a proximal subtotal gastrectomy. To date, no prospective studies have compared this method with total gastrectomy or transhiatal esophagogastrectomy for esophagogastric junction tumors, but surgeons from MSKCC have published their retrospective experience with 98 patients who underwent either total gastrectomy or proximal subtotal gastrectomy for proximal gastric cancer over a 10-year period.[50] There were no significant differences between the groups with respect to morbidity, mortality, or 5-year survival. It remains to be seen whether such excellent results can be achieved at other centers.

Thus, the evidence at present does not support routine performance of total gastrectomy for lesions of the distal fundus or antrum, provided that histologically negative margins are achievable without compromise of the gastric inlet. Our current practice is to perform a subtotal gastrectomy with Billroth II reconstruction for tumors of the distal stomach, a total gastrectomy with Roux-en-Y esophagojejunostomy for most cancers of the fundus and the proximal stomach [*see 62 Procedures for Benign and Malignant Gastric and Duodenal Disease*], and either a transthoracic esophagogastrectomy or a transhiatal esophagogastrectomy with gastric interposition for tumors of the esophagogastric junction and the cardia [*see 34 Open Esophageal Procedures*].

Extent of lymph node dissection   Over the past decade, few topics in the surgical literature have generated more debate than the optimal extent of regional lymphadenectomy for gastric cancer. In Japan, where radical surgery for gastric cancer is now universally accepted, the JRSGC has codified the extent of lymphatic dissection according to the level of nodes dissected.[51] A D1 lymph node dissection involves resection of the perigastric lymph nodes along the greater and lesser curvature of the stomach. A D0 dissection is anything less than a D1 dissection. A D2 dissection entails resection of the D1 nodes along with nodes along the common hepatic artery, the left gastric artery, the celiac axis, and the splenic artery. A D3 lymph node dissection adds resection of nodes in the hepatoduodenal ligament and the root of the mesentery. Finally, a D4 resection calls for a D3 dissection plus resection of the retroperitoneal para-aortic and paracolic lymph nodes.[52] The JRSGC defines a curative operation as a gastric resection that includes lymph nodes one level beyond the level of pathologic nodal involvement. Thus, in Japan, a D2 lymph node dissection is considered the standard resection for even relatively early cancers, and numerous studies have cited the benefits of D3 and even D4 lymphadenectomy for advanced carcinoma.[53-55]

Western surgeons have been reluctant to embrace radical lymphadenectomy, arguing that it has yet to demonstrate an unequivocal survival advantage in any prospective, randomized trial from a Western institution or cooperative group. Detractors further argue that the survival advantage associated with more radical procedures simply reflects stage migration, a higher incidence of early gastric cancers, and differences in tumor biology and body habitus between Japanese and Western populations, and they point to the increases in operating time and morbidity that often accompany extended gastric resections. One retrospective review of the tumor registries of over 2,000 hospitals in the United States found that D2 lymph node dissection had no survival advantage over D1 lymph node dissection in terms of either the median survival time or the 5-year survival rate.[56]

Two prospective trials from Western Europe examined this issue further in an effort to evaluate the safety and efficacy of ELND. In the Dutch Gastric Cancer Group trial, 711 patients were randomly assigned to undergo either D1 or D2 lymphadenectomy as part of a potentially curative gastrectomy for biopsy-proven adenocarcinoma.[57] This trial was unique in its use of extensive quality control measures, which included instruction and operative supervision by an expert gastric cancer surgeon from Japan (who

also assisted with the processing and pathologic examination of the surgical specimens). Patients without evidence of disseminated metastases underwent either total gastrectomy or, if 5 cm proximal margins could be obtained, distal gastrectomy. In this study, a D2 lymph node dissection entailed distal pancreatectomy and splenectomy. Both morbidity and mortality were significantly higher in the D2 group than in the D1 group, and D2 dissection conferred no demonstrable survival advantage at a median follow-up of 72 months.

In a trial from the Medical Research Council in the United Kingdom, 400 patients with stage I to IIB disease were randomly assigned to undergo either a D1 or a D2 lymph node dissection.[58] There was no significant difference in overall 5-year survival between the two arms, but multivariate analysis demonstrated that clinical stages II and III, advanced age, male sex, and removal of the pancreas and the spleen were independently associated with poor outcome. The authors concluded that the classic Japanese D2 dissection offered no survival advantage over D1 dissection. However, they hypothesized that D2 dissection with preservation of the distal pancreas and the spleen might lead to decreased morbidity and mortality within the extended resection group and thus potentially to superior outcomes.

Further support for this hypothesis was provided by two nonrandomized trials from specialized centers. The Italian Gastric Cancer Study Group (IGCSG) completed a phase II multicenter trial designed to evaluate the safety and efficacy of pancreas-preserving D2 lymph node dissection.[59] Quality control measures included supervision by a surgeon who had studied the technique of D2 lymph node dissection at the National Cancer Center Hospital in Tokyo. At a median follow-up time of 4.38 years, the overall morbidity rate for D2 dissection in the 191 patients enrolled was 20.9%, and the in-hospital mortality was 3.1%. The 5-year survival rate for eligible patients was 55%. In a prospective series of 125 patients undergoing standardized D2 lymph node dissection at a single Western center, the investigators reported a mortality of 1.37% and an overall morbidity of 33.5%.[60] As in the IGCSG study, distal pancreatectomy was avoided in all cases, except when direct extension was suspected on the basis of macroscopic findings (5.5% of cases). Overall 5- and 10-year survival rates for this highly selected cohort were 52.3% and 40%, respectively. These studies suggest D2 lymph node dissection may be safely performed in Western centers, when accompanied by careful selection of patients, strict standardization of technique, and a strategy of pancreatic preservation.

Current AJCC guidelines state that pathologic examination of at least 15 lymph nodes is required for adequate staging.[28] In an effort to confirm the benefit of this staging system, investigators from MSKCC reviewed their experience with 1,038 patients who underwent R0 resection for gastric cancer.[61] The location of positive lymph nodes (within 3 cm of the primary tumor versus more than 3 cm away) did not significantly affect median survival; however, the number of positive lymph nodes had a profound effect on survival. Furthermore, in cases in which at least 15 nodes were examined (27% of the total), the median survival for patients with N1 (metastasis in one to six regional lymph nodes), N2 (metastasis in seven to 15 regional lymph nodes), and N3 disease (metastasis in more than 15 regional lymph nodes) was significantly longer than the median survival reported in cases in which 14 or fewer nodes were resected with the specimens. These findings are consistent with published data from our own institution (Northwestern University Feinberg School of Medicine), which indicate that the number of positive lymph nodes is a highly significant predictor of survival.[62] In our series of 110 patients, those with N2 or

Table 3 Survival after Curative Resection of Gastric Cancer
According to AJCC Lymph Node Status

Lymph Node Status	Roder et al[1]		Kodera et al[105]		Karpeh et al[61]	
	Cases (% of Total)	5-Year Survival (%)	Cases (% of Total)	5-Year Survival (%)	Cases (% of Total)	5-Year Survival (%)
N1 (1–6 positive nodes)	258 (54)	45	306 (62)	70	392 (62)	38
N2 (7–15 positive nodes)	137 (29)	30	94 (19)	39	178 (28)	12
N3 (> 15 positive nodes)	82 (17)	10	93 (19)	24	65 (10)	5

N3 disease (seven or more positive lymph nodes) had a median disease-free survival (DFS) of 17.6 months, whereas those with N0 or N1 disease (six or fewer positive nodes) had a median DFS of 44 months. Data from other centers support this view as well [*see Table 3*].

It is our current practice to perform a D2 lymph node dissection, with resection of all perigastric lymph nodes along the greater and lesser curvatures of the stomach, as well as those along the common hepatic artery, the left gastric artery, the celiac axis, and the splenic artery [*see 62 Procedures for Benign and Malignant Gastric and Duodenal Disease*]. We make every attempt to preserve the tail of the pancreas and spleen, with multivisceral resection reserved for cases of overt direct extension of malignant disease in the absence of disseminated metastasis. This strategy should provide adequate staging in terms of the AJCC guidelines, minimize morbidity, and possibly confer a survival advantage on certain patient subgroups, as suggested by the results of the trials mentioned.

Role of splenectomy Routine splenectomy has been proposed as a means of facilitating clearance of metastatic nodes along the splenic artery and in the splenic hilum, but there is little evidence to support this practice in the treatment of proximal gastric cancers. Indeed, numerous studies have documented the deleterious effect of splenectomy when it is performed as part of an extended gastric resection.

In a retrospective study of 392 patients who underwent curative gastrectomy at a high-volume cancer center, the impact of splenectomy on survival and postoperative morbidity was evaluated.[63] Splenectomy was not predictive of death on multivariate analysis, but complications were far more frequent in patients who underwent splenectomy as part of surgical treatment than in those who did not (45% versus 21%). Specifically, the incidence of infectious complications was far higher in the splenectomy group than in the nonsplenectomy group (75% versus 47%).

In a review of data from an American College of Surgeons Pattern of Care Study, the investigators reported that the operative mortality was 9.8% in patients who underwent splenectomy during gastric resection, compared with 8.6% for those who did not.[64] More significantly, the 5-year observed survival rate was 20.9% in the splenectomy group, compared with 31% in the nonsplenectomy group.

In a randomized, prospective trial, early and late results of total gastrectomy alone were compared with those of total gastrectomy plus splenectomy in patients being treated for cancers of the upper third of the stomach.[65] All patients underwent a D2 lymph node dissection. The operative mortalities and the 5-year survival rates were similar in the two groups, but the splenectomy group had more infectious complications. Specifically, the splenectomy group had higher incidences of pulmonary complications, postoperative

fever higher than 38° C (100° F), and subphrenic abscess formation. We agree with the conclusions of the authors of this study: routine splenectomy does not increase survival, and it should be reserved for situations in which the gastric tumor directly invades the splenic hilum or there is evidence of gross nodal metastases along the splenic artery.

Nonsurgical Therapy

Adjuvant therapy As noted (see above), the majority of patients who present with gastric carcinoma and undergo potentially curative surgical treatment will experience locoregional failure, distant metastasis, or both and will succumb to their disease. Accordingly, numerous adjuvant approaches—including chemotherapy, radiotherapy, chemoradiation, immunochemotherapy, and intraperitoneal chemotherapy—have been tried in gastric cancer patients with the aim of improving overall survival and DFS. The results, for the most part, have been disappointing.

Results from prospective, randomized, controlled trials of adjuvant radiation therapy in this setting have failed to establish a survival benefit. In a multi-institutional trial from 1994, patients were randomly assigned to undergo surgery alone, surgery plus adjuvant radiation, or surgery plus adjuvant multiagent chemotherapy.[66] There was no significant benefit to either adjuvant regimen: overall 5-year survival was 20% for surgery alone, compared with 12% for surgery plus radiation therapy and 19% for surgery plus chemotherapy.

Results from trials of chemotherapy alone have been equally unsatisfactory. Because of the established inefficacy of single-agent 5-fluorouracil (5-FU) therapy, combination chemotherapy regimens have been employed. Such regimens have included nitrosourea compounds, mitomycin-C, anthracyclines, and members of the cisplatin family.[23] In a meta-analysis of 13 trials comparing adjuvant chemotherapy with observation in non-Asian countries, the odds ratio for death in the treated group was 0.8, corresponding to a relative risk of 0.94.[67] This result did not, however, reflect a statistically significant improvement. Most oncologists have now abandoned the use of chemotherapy by itself in the adjuvant setting.

In an effort to derive greater therapeutic benefit than can be achieved with either radiation therapy or chemotherapy alone, combinations of the two have been used in the adjuvant setting. In Intergroup Trial 0116, 556 patients who had undergone R0 resection of adenocarcinoma of the stomach or the esophagogastric junction were randomly assigned to treatment with either surgery alone or surgery plus postoperative chemoradiotherapy.[68] Patients with tumors ranging from stage IB to stage IVM0 were included; the majority had T3 tumors and node-positive disease. The therapeutic regimen consisted of 5-FU and leucovorin administered concomitantly with 45 Gy of external-beam irradiation over a period of 5 weeks. Median overall survival in the surgery-only group was

27 months, compared with 36 months in the surgery-chemoradiation group. In addition, the 3-year survival rate was 41% in the surgery-only group, compared with 50% in the surgery-chemoradiation group. The hazard ratio for death in the surgery-only group as compared with the surgery-chemoradiation group was 1.35.

In the United States, the results of Intergroup Trial 0116 have led to the acceptance of chemoradiotherapy as standard adjuvant therapy for patients who have undergone curative-intent resection of gastric cancer. Nonetheless, numerous criticisms of this trial have been expressed. Specifically, a review of the operative and pathology reports of 453 of the patients revealed a lack of surgical standardization.[69] When the extent of lymphadenectomy was categorized, the majority (54.2%) of the patients were found to have undergone a D0 dissection; 38.1% underwent a D1 dissection, and only 7.5% underwent a D2 or D3 dissection. These findings suggest that the main effect of the chemoradiation therapy may have been simply to compensate for inadequate surgery. This suggestion is supported by the observation that the number of patients with local and regional recurrences was higher in the surgery-only group (178 versus 101), whereas the number of patients with distant failure was slightly higher in the adjuvant-therapy arm (40 versus 32). Furthermore, when the Maruyama Index of Unresected Disease (a computer model developed for accurate prediction of nodal station involvement in gastric cancer) was applied to the 556 patients eligible for the Intergroup Trial, the median Maruyama Index was 70.[70] This value was far above the level considered to represent optimal surgical therapy (i.e., Maruyama Index < 5) and led the authors to conclude that the vast majority of patients in the trial had been surgically undertreated.

Currently, physicians, especially in Europe, generally eschew adjuvant therapy after R0 resection of gastric cancer, except under the auspices of a clinical trial.[9] The Radiation Therapy Oncology Group has initiated a phase II trial of adjuvant chemoradiotherapy using 45 Gy of external beam radiation with cisplatin and paxitaxel, with or without 5-FU. If promising results are found, a phase III trial will follow. It is to be hoped that ongoing trials will shed further light on this complex management issue.

Neoadjuvant therapy As a response to the disappointing results of adjuvant therapy and the inability of many patients to regain adequate performance status after radical gastric surgery, neoadjuvant therapy protocols have been proposed.[71] The theoretical benefits of a neoadjuvant treatment strategy include treatment-induced tumor downstaging, which may enhance resectability, and early administration of systemic therapy, which allows almost all patients to receive and complete the prescribed treatment. Furthermore, because treatment is administered when measurable disease is present, response to therapy may be assessed and continued only in patients who are likely to benefit. Finally, patients who are found to have rapidly progressive disease during preoperative chemotherapy may be spared having to undergo a nontherapeutic gastrectomy.[72]

In a report of three phase II trials from the M. D. Anderson Cancer Center, encompassing 83 patients who received neoadjuvant chemotherapy before planned surgical resection, clinical response rates ranged from 24% to 38%, with three patients (4%) exhibiting a complete pathologic response.[72] Sixty-one patients (73%) were able to undergo a curative-intent resection, and the response to chemotherapy was the only significant predictor of survival on multivariate analysis.

Preoperative chemoradiation therapy has also been shown to be feasible in phase II trials. In a 2001 trial that included 23 patients, 96% of the study population received combined-modality therapy.[71] Nineteen patients (83%) were able to undergo surgical resection with D2 lymphadenectomy; four patients (17%) had progressive disease and did not undergo resection. Morbidity and death rates were acceptable (32% and 5%, respectively), and 11% of patients exhibited complete pathologic responses. Overall, 63% of patients showed pathologic evidence of a significant treatment effect.

Newer neoadjuvant treatment strategies employ multiagent induction chemotherapy followed by chemoradiotherapy and planned gastric resection in patients with locally advanced but potentially resectable gastric cancer.[73]

FOLLOW-UP AND MANAGEMENT OF RECURRENT DISEASE

Even after gross resection of all disease with microscopically negative margins (R0 resection), recurrence of gastric carcinoma is common. Adenocarcinoma of the stomach may spread through direct extension, via lymphatic channels to regional and distant lymph nodes, or via the bloodstream to distant sites. Furthermore, once tumors have penetrated the serosa (T3), peritoneal metastasis becomes a possibility. Through autopsy series and clinical studies, certain definite patterns of locoregional failure and distant metastasis have been established. Locoregional recurrences are common in the gastric bed and the adjacent lymph nodes. Clinical and reoperative evaluation have documented recurrent disease at the anastomosis, in the retroperitoneum, or in the regional lymph nodes in 3% to 69% of patients; the incidence of recurrence may vary, depending on whether the patients had received adjuvant therapy.[23] One autopsy series documented a locoregional recurrence rate of 94% in patients treated with surgery alone. The peritoneum is ultimately involved in 17% to 50% of all patients. The most common sites of visceral metastases are the liver and the lungs.

In view of the high recurrence rates, all patients who have undergone resection should be seen for routine surveillance examinations. Currently, the NCCN recommends that a complete history and physical examination be conducted every 4 months for 1 year, then every 6 months for 1 year, and then yearly thereafter.[39] A complete blood count, serum electrolyte concentrations, and liver function studies should also be considered. Imaging studies (e.g., CT and endoscopy) are ordered as indicated, usually in response to new symptoms. In addition, long-term vitamin B_{12} supplementation should be initiated for patients who have undergone a proximal or subtotal gastrectomy.

Other Gastric Malignancies

GASTRIC LYMPHOMA

Gastric lymphoma is the second most common malignancy of the stomach, accounting for 2% to 9% of gastric tumors in the United States. Lymphomas of the stomach are of the non-Hodgkin type. The stomach is the most common site of extranodal involvement of non-Hodgkin lymphoma (NHL) and accounts for nearly 50% of all such cases.[74]

Clinical Evaluation

The presenting symptoms of gastric lymphoma, like those of gastric adenocarcinoma, are nonspecific and include loss of appetite, weight loss, vomiting, and bleeding. Overt clinical symptoms (e.g., fever and night sweats) are relatively rare: in one multicenter trial concerned with primary gastric lymphoma, they occurred in fewer than 12% of patients enrolled.[75] Risk factors for gastric lymphoma include *H. pylori* infection, immunosuppression after solid-organ transplantation, celiac disease, inflammatory bowel disease, and HIV infection.[76]

Investigative Studies

The diagnosis of gastric lymphoma is most frequently established by means of endoscopy with biopsy. Staging studies include a comprehensive blood count, a lactate dehydrogenase (LDH) level, and a comprehensive chemistry panel; CT of the chest, the abdomen, and the pelvis; and, often, a bone marrow biopsy. All pathology slides should be reviewed by an experienced hematopathologist.[77]

Staging and Prognosis

Numerous staging systems have been employed to stage NHL of the GI tract. Of these, the one most commonly applied is a modification of the Ann Arbor staging system for lymphoma.[76] For surgeons, the most important determination is often whether the NHL (1) is confined to the stomach and the perigastric nodes (stage I and II disease), (2) involves other intra-abdominal nodes and organs (stage III), or (3) extends outside the abdomen (stage IV).[78]

Management

Over the past decade, the management of patients with gastric lymphoma has undergone significant changes. Generally, there has been a shift away from surgical management, even in relatively localized cases (stages I and II).[79] This shift is the result not only of the documented success of chemotherapy alone for more advanced cases (stages III and IV) but also of a better understanding of the etiology of gastric lymphoma.[80] Approximately 45% of all gastric lymphomas are low-grade mucosa-associated lymphoid tissue (MALT) lymphomas.[75] The gastric mucosa is normally devoid of lymphoid tissue. It is hypothesized that MALT develops in the stomach in response to chronic *H. pylori* infection.[81]

Nonsurgical therapy Low-grade MALT lymphoma usually presents as stage I or II disease and has an indolent course. Since 1993, when regression of low-grade MALT lymphoma after eradication of *H. pylori* was first reported, numerous trials have documented the efficacy of anti–*H. pylori* therapy, with complete remission rates ranging from 50% to 100%.[79] In the German MALT Lymphoma Study, the complete remission rate was 81%; 9% of patients exhibited partial responses, and 10% showed no response.[82] Low-grade lymphomas that are more advanced or do not regress with antibiotic therapy may be treated with *H. pylori* eradication and radiation (with or without chemotherapy).[83] For localized persistent disease, modest doses of radiation, on the order of 30 Gy, may be employed. When chemotherapy is required, multiagent regimens, such as cyclophosphamide-vincristine-prednisolone (COP), are often used.

Approximately 55% of gastric lymphomas are high-grade lesions, which can occur with or without a low-grade MALT component.[75] These lymphomas are treated with chemotherapy and radiation therapy according to the extent of the disease. The cyclophosphamide-doxorubicin-vincristine-prednisolone (CHOP) regimen is the one most frequently employed. In some studies, the anti-CD20 monoclonal antibody rituximab has been either added to standard therapy or used alone, with encouraging results.[84]

Surgical therapy Surgical resection, once thought to be essential for the diagnosis, staging, and treatment of early-stage gastric lymphoma, now is used mainly in patients who experience bleeding or perforation. In the German Multicenter Study Group trial, 185 patients with stage I or II gastric lymphoma were treated either with gastrectomy followed by radiation or (in the case of high-grade lesions) chemotherapy plus radiation or with chemotherapy and radiotherapy alone.[75] There was no significant difference in survival between the group receiving surgical treatment and the group receiving nonoperative therapy: overall 5-year survival rates were 82.5% and 84%, respectively. There were no perforations, and there was only one hemorrhage (in a patient treated with chemotherapy alone). Similarly, in a single-institution, prospective, randomized trial comparing chemotherapy alone with chemotherapy plus surgery for stage I and II lymphoma, there were no instances of perforation and only three instances of GI bleeding in the chemotherapy group, compared with two bleeding episodes in the surgery plus chemotherapy group.[79]

Currently, patients with early-stage high-grade gastric lymphomas are treated primarily with chemotherapy or radiation therapy; only rarely do they require surgical intervention for complications encountered during therapy. Patients with locally advanced (stage III) or disseminated (stage IV) gastric lymphoma are clearly best treated with chemotherapy, with or without radiation. Occasionally, surgery is indicated in such patients to treat residual disease confined to the stomach or to palliate bleeding or obstruction that does not resolve with nonoperative therapy. Primary surgical therapy is to be avoided in these patients because of the significant risk of complications and the delay in initiating systemic therapy.

GASTROINTESTINAL STROMAL TUMOR

Gastrointestinal stromal tumor (GIST), though relatively rare in absolute terms, is the most common sarcoma of the GI tract,[85] with approximately 6,000 cases reported each year in the United States alone. The stomach is the most common site of involvement, accounting for 60% to 70% of cases[86]; the small intestine (25%), the rectum (5%), the esophagus (2%), and a variety of other locations account for the remainder. On the basis of their appearance on light microscopy, GISTs were once thought to be of smooth muscle origin, and most were classified as leiomyosarcomas.[87] Thus, extended gastric resection, often including contiguous organs, was advised. Recurrence developed after R0 resection in approximately 50% of cases.[88] With the advent of immunohistochemistry and electron microscopy, it became clear that GIST has both smooth muscle and neural elements, and the cell of origin is now believed to be the interstitial cell of Cajal, an intestinal pacemaker cell.[89] The diagnosis of GIST is secured by immunohistochemical staining for the tyrosine kinase receptor KIT (CD117), which highlights the presence of interstitial cells of Cajal. More than 95% of GISTs exhibit unequivocal staining for KIT.[86] Approximately two thirds of GISTs also express CD34. Histologically, these tumors may exhibit a spindle cell pattern, an epithelioid pattern, or a mixed subtype.

Clinical Evaluation

The median age of incidence is 63 years, and tumors are generally between 0.5 and 44 cm in diameter at the time of diagnosis (median diameter, 6 cm).[86] Mass-related symptoms (e.g., abdominal pain, bloating, and early satiety) may be present. Melena or anemia from overlying mucosal ulceration may be present as well. A small subset of patients have peritonitis as a consequence of tumor rupture and subsequent hemorrhage. Finally, many GISTs are discovered incidentally during operation, abdominal imaging, or endoscopy.

Investigative Studies

When a GIST is suspected, abdominal and pelvic imaging with either CT or MRI is indicated. Chest imaging is performed as well. Endoscopy, with or without EUS, may occasionally help with surgical planning, but because of the infrequency of mucosal involvement, it is rarely diagnostic.[90] Surgical consultation should be obtained to determine whether the lesion can be resected. If the tumor is resectable, biopsy should not be performed, because of the risk of tumor rupture and intra-abdominal dissemination. Biopsy may be required, however, if the patient has widespread disease or may be enrolling in a trial of neoadjuvant therapy. In such cases, biopsy may be performed percutaneously or at the time of EUS.

Staging and Prognosis

Although the majority of gastric GISTs have a benign course, a wide spectrum of biologic behavior has been observed. Of the prognostic factors examined to date, tumor size and mitotic rate appear to be the most valuable. If the tumor is less than 2 cm in diameter and the mitotic count is lower than five per high-power field (HPF), the risk of an aggressive disease course is considered to be very low. Conversely, if the tumor is larger than 10 cm, if the mitotic count is higher than 10/HPF, or if the tumor is larger than 5 cm with a mitotic count higher than 5/HPF, the risk of aggressive clinical behavior is considered to be high. For all other tumors, the risk of aggressive disease is considered to be intermediate.[86]

Management

Surgical therapy The role of surgery in the treatment of a GIST is to resect the tumor with grossly negative margins and an intact pseudocapsule. Lymph node involvement is rare with GISTs, and thus, no effort is made to perform ELND. The tumor must be handled with care to prevent intra-abdominal rupture. Formal gastric resection is rarely required: as a rule, it is indicated only for lesions in close proximity to the pylorus or the esophagogastric junction.

Nonsurgical therapy If the tumor has metastasized or has advanced locally to the point where surgical therapy would result in excessive morbidity, the patient is treated with the tyrosine kinase inhibitor imatinib mesylate. Imatinib is a selective inhibitor of a family of protein kinases that includes the KIT-receptor tyrosine kinase, which is expressed in the majority of GISTs. Originally indicated for the treatment of chronic myelocytic leukemia, imatinib was approved for the treatment of KIT-positive GIST in 2002, when phase II clinical trials documented sustained objective responses in a majority of patients with advanced unresectable or metastatic GIST.[91] Patients with borderline resectable lesions should be treated with imatinib until they exhibit a maximal response as documented by CT and positron emission tomography (PET); surgery may then be undertaken to resect any residual foci of disease. Similarly, whereas patients with metastatic disease are unlikely to manifest a complete response to imatinib therapy, they should be periodically reevaluated and considered for resection should surgical treatment become technically feasible.[90]

After an R0 resection of a GIST, no adjuvant therapy is indicated unless the patient is participating in a clinical trial. The American College of Surgeons Oncology Group is currently conducting two trials of imatinib in the postoperative setting. A phase II trial (Z9000) of imatinib, 400 mg/day, for patients with high-risk GIST, has reached accrual, and a phase III trial (Z9001) comparing 1 year of imatinib, 400 mg/day, with placebo in patients with intermediate-risk GIST is currently under way.

GASTRIC CARCINOID

Gastric carcinoid tumors are rare, accounting for fewer than 11% to 30% of all GI carcinoids and fewer than 1% of all gastric tumors.[92] The median age at diagnosis is 62, and tumors are equally distributed between men and women.

Clinical Evaluation and Investigative Studies

Gastric carcinoid tumors are often discovered during endoscopic examination of patients experiencing chronic abdominal pain; patients may also complain of vomiting and diarrhea. These tumors are rarely associated with symptoms of the carcinoid syndrome. Diagnosis is usually confirmed by endoscopic biopsy, and EUS is helpful in determining the extent of gastric wall penetration and the degree of regional lymph node involvement.

Gastric carcinoid tumors have been divided into three types, primarily on the basis of their association (or lack thereof) with hypergastrinemia. Type I tumors are associated with chronic atrophic gastritis, are generally small (< 1 cm), and are often multiple and polypoid. They grow slowly and only rarely metastasize to regional nodes or distant sites. Type II tumors are associated with the Zollinger-Ellison syndrome and multiple endocrine neoplasia type I (MEN I) and, like type I tumors, are usually small and multiple. They also grow slowly, but they are more likely to metastasize than type I gastric carcinoids are. Type III (sporadic) gastric carcinoid tumors are the most biologically aggressive type. They are often large (> 1 cm) at the time of diagnosis and are not associated with hypergastrinemia. Type III lesions frequently metastasize to regional nodes (54%) or the liver (24%).[92]

Management

For patients with small, solitary type I tumors, endoscopic polypectomy [see 60 Gastrointestinal Endoscopy] or open resection via gastrotomy (local excision) [see 62 Procedures for Benign and Malignant Gastric and Duodenal Disease] is the procedure of choice. For patients with multiple or recurrent tumors, antrectomy [see 62 Procedures for Benign and Malignant Gastric and Duodenal Disease] is indicated to remove the source of the hypergastrinemia. For patients with type II lesions, treatment is similar to that for patients with type I lesions, with the extent of gastric resection determined

Table 4 American Joint Committee of Cancer TNM Clinical Classification of Small Bowel Carcinoma

Primary tumor (T)	TX	Primary tumor cannot be assessed
	T0	No evidence of primary tumor
	Tis	Carcinoma in situ
	T1	Tumor invades lamina propria or submucosa
	T2	Tumor invades muscularis propria
	T3	Tumor penetrates < 2 cm into subserosa or into nonperitonealized perimuscular tissue (mesentery for jejunum or ileum, retroperitoneum for duodenum)
	T4	Tumor penetrates visceral peritoneum or directly invades > 2 cm into adjacent structures
Regional lymph nodes (N)	NX	Regional lymph node(s) cannot be assessed
	N0	No regional lymph node metastasis
	N1	Regional lymph node metastasis
Distant metastasis (M)	MX	Distant metastasis cannot be assessed
	M0	No distant metastasis
	M1	Distant metastasis

Table 5 American Joint Committee on Cancer Staging System for Small Bowel Carcinoma

Stage	T	N	M
Stage 0	Tis	N0	M0
Stage I	T1, T2	N0	M0
Stage II	T3, T4	N0	M0
Stage III	Any T	N1	M0
Stage IV	Any T	Any N	M1

by the size and number of lesions. For patients with type III lesions, however, either distal or total gastrectomy with ELND is required.[93] All patients undergoing a less than total gastrectomy should be followed with serial endoscopy at regular intervals.[94]

Small Bowel Malignancies

Malignant tumors of the small intestine are rare, accounting for fewer than 5% of all GI tract malignancies. In the United States, only a few thousand new cases of small bowel cancer are reported each year.[95] The majority of small bowel malignancies are adenocarcinomas, lymphomas, or carcinoid tumors,[96] though GISTs are being noted with increasing frequency in the small intestine. Treatment of lymphomas, carcinoid tumors, and GISTs in the small bowel is nearly identical to treatment of the same lesions in the stomach [*see Other Gastric Malignancies, above*] and thus will not be covered further in this chapter. Our focus here is on the presentation, diagnosis, and treatment of adenocarcinoma of the small bowel. Like gastric adenocarcinoma, small bowel adenocarcinoma is usually staged according to the AJCC/UICC TNM classification system [*see Tables 4 and 5*].

CLINICAL EVALUATION

Between 46% and 55% of small bowel adenocarcinomas occur in the duodenum.[96,97] Patients frequently present with nausea, vomiting, abdominal pain, weight loss, and GI bleeding[98]; occasionally, they present with iron deficiency anemia or a positive fecal occult blood test result. In rare cases, small bowel obstruction, often with the tumor serving as a lead point for intussusception, is the first manifestation of the disease.[97]

INVESTIGATIVE STUDIES

When an adenocarcinoma is located in the duodenum, the diagnosis is often made by means of esophagogastroduodenoscopy (EGD). Lesions within the first 100 cm of the small bowel may be evaluated with push enteroscopy. When the adenocarcinoma is situated elsewhere in the small bowel, it is localized with small bowel radiographs. Some authors consider enteroclysis to be superior to the more commonly used small bowel follow-through in this setting, in that enteroclysis is better able to demonstrate fine mucosal detail.[99] In experienced hands, enteroclysis may therefore be more sensitive.[100] Some lesions are identified when CT or MRI is performed to evaluate complaints of abdominal pain. Furthermore, abdominal imaging may yield complementary staging information (e.g., the presence of regional adenopathy or metastatic disease). One promising new method for the identification of small bowel tumors is wireless capsule endoscopy.[101] This minimally invasive technique may be particularly useful in identifying small lesions in the distal jejunum and ileum that cannot be identified radiographically.

MANAGEMENT

Aggressive surgical resection remains the cornerstone of therapy for adenocarcinoma of the small intestine.[102] For periampullary lesions, pancreaticoduodenectomy is typically required to achieve a margin-negative resection. For lesions in the distal duodenum, a segmental sleeve resection with a duodenojejunostomy is appropriate. For lesions in the jejunum or the ileum, segmental resection may be performed with a wide mesenteric resection to encompass potentially involved regional lymph nodes. Contiguous organs are resected en bloc as necessary.[98]

Because the presenting signs and symptoms are often vague and nonspecific, diagnosis is often delayed. In one series, only 6 (11%) of the 53 patients were suspected of having a small bowel tumor at admission.[102] In a retrospective review of patients with small bowel tumors treated at our institution, the mean duration of symptoms before surgical management was 110 months, and more than 50% of the patients were found to have stage III or IV disease.[98]

The 5-year survival rate continues to be low (24% to 37%).[98,103,104] Significant predictors of good overall survival include complete (R0) resection and low AJCC tumor stage.[98,103,104] The available evidence indicates that all patients with small bowel neoplasms should be offered an oncologically sound surgical resection. In one series, curative (R0) resection was accomplished in 51% of cases.[103]

References

1. Roder DM: The epidemiology of gastric cancer. Gastric Cancer 5(1):5, 2002

2. Neugut AI, Hayek M, Howe G: Epidemiology of gastric cancer. Semin Oncol 23:281, 1996

3. Jemal A, Tiwari RC, Murray T, et al: Cancer Statistics. CA Cancer J Clin 54:8, 2004

4. Alberts SR, Cervantes A, van de Velde CJ: Gastric cancer: epidemiology, pathology and treatment. Ann Oncol 14(2):ii, 2003

5. Cancer Statistics Working Group. United States Cancer Statistics: 1999–2001 Incidence and Mortality Web-based Report Version. Department of Health and Human Services, Centers for Disease Control and Prevention, and National Cancer Institute, Atlanta, 2004 http://www.cdc.gov/cancer/npcr/uscs

6. Lawrence W Jr, Menck HR, Steele GD Jr, et al: The National Cancer Data Base report on gastric cancer. Cancer 75:1734, 1995

7. Wayman J, Forman D, Griffin SM: Monitoring the changing pattern of esophago-gastric cancer: data from a UK regional cancer registry. Cancer Causes Control 12:943, 2001

8. Wanebo HJ, Kennedy BJ, Chmiel J, et al: Cancer of the stomach: a patient care study by the American College of Surgeons. Ann Surg 218:579, 1993

9. Hohenberger P, Gretschel S: Gastric cancer. Lancet 362:305, 2003

10. Corvalan A, Koriyama C, Akiba S, et al: Epstein-Barr virus in gastric carcinoma is associated with location in the cardia and with a diffuse histology: a study in one area of Chile. Int J Cancer 94:527, 2001

11. Fukayama M, Chong JM, Uozaki H: Pathology and molecular pathology of Epstein-Barr virus-associated gastric carcinoma. Curr Top Microbiol Immunol 258:91, 2001

12. Lauren P: The two histological main types of gastric carcinoma: diffuse and so-called intestinal-type carcinoma: an attempt at a histological classification. Acta Pathol Micrbiol Scand 64:31, 1965

13. Ogimoto I, Shibata A, Fukuda K: World Cancer Research Fund/American Institute of Cancer Research 1997 recommendations: applicability to digestive tract cancer in Japan. Cancer Causes Control 11(1):9, 2000

14. Plummer M, Franceschi S, Munoz N: Epidemiology of gastric cancer. IARC Sci Publ 157:311, 2004

15. Hansson LE, Nyren O, Bergstrom R, et al: Nutrients and gastric cancer risk: a population-based cases-control study in Sweden. Int J Cancer 57:638, 1994

16. Gastric cancer and *Helicobacter pylori*: a combined analysis of 12 case control studies nested within prospective cohorts. Helicobacter and Cancer Collaborative Group. Gut 49:347, 2001

17. Correa P: Bacterial infections as a cause of cancer. JNCI 95(7):E3, 2003

18. Peek RM Jr, Blaser MJ: *Helicobacter pylori* and gastrointestinal tract adenocarcinomas. Nat Rev Cancer 2:28, 2002

19. La Vecchia C, Negri E, Franceschi S, et al: Family history and the risk of stomach and colorectal cancer. Cancer 70:50, 1992

20. Fuchs CS, Mayer RJ: Gastric carcinoma. N Engl J Med 333:32, 1995

21. Lin J, Beer DG: Molecular biology of upper gastrointestinal malignancies. Sem Oncol 31:476, 2004

22. Ebert MP, Malfertheiner P: Review article: pathogenesis of sporadic and familial gastric cancer—implications for clinical management and cancer prevention. Aliment Pharmacol Ther 16:1059, 2002

23. Karpeh MS, Kelsen DP, Tepper JE: Cancer of the stomach. Cancer Principles and Practice of Oncology, 6th ed. DeVita VT Jr, Hellman S, Rosenberg S, Eds. Lippincott Williams & Wilkins, Philadelphia, 2001, p 1092

24. Oohara T, Aono G, Ukawa S, et al: Clinical diagnosis of minute gastric cancer less than 5 mm in diameter. Cancer 53:162, 1984

25. Grise K, McFadden D: Gastric cancer: three decades of surgical management. Am J Surg 64: 930, 1998

26. Yalmarthi S, Witherspoon P, McCole D, et al: Missed diagnosis in patients with upper gastrointestinal cancers. Endoscopy 36:874, 2004

27. Nio Y, Tsubono M, Kawabata K, et al: Comparison of survival curves of gastric cancer patients after surgery according to the UICC stage classification and the general rules for gastric cancer study by the Japanese Research Society for gastric cancer. Ann Surg 218:47, 1993

28. American Joint Committee on Cancer: Stomach. AJCC Cancer Staging Manual, 6th ed. Greene F, Page DL, Fleming ID, et al, Eds. Springer-Verlag, New York, 2002, p 99

29. Abdalla EK, Pisters PWT: Staging and preoperative evaluation of upper gastrointestinal malignancies. Semin Oncol 31:513, 2004

30. Takao M, Fukuda T, Iwanaga S, et al: Gastric cancer: evaluation of triphasic spiral CT and radiologic-pathologic correlation. J Comput Assist Tomogr 22:288, 1998

31. Davies J, Chalmers AG, Sue-Ling HM, et al: Spiral computed tomography and operative staging of gastric carcinoma: a comparison with histopathological staging. Gut 41:314, 1997

32. Pollack BJ, Chak A, Sivak MV Jr: Endoscopic ultrasonography. Semin Oncol 23:336, 1996

33. Messmann H, Schlottmann K: Role of endoscopy in the staging of esophageal and gastric cancer. Semin Surg Oncol 20:70, 2001

34. De Manzoni G, Di Leo M, Bonfiglio P, et al: Experience of endoscopic ultrasound in staging adenocarcinoma of the cardia. Eur J Surg Oncol 25:595, 1999

35. Macdonald JS, Gohmann JJ: Chemotherapy of advanced gastric cancer: present status, future prospects. Semin Oncol 15:42, 1988

36. Burke EC, Karpeh MS Jr, Conlon KC, et al: Laparoscopy in the management of gastric adenocarcinoma. Ann Surg 225:262, 1997

37. Feussner H, Omote K, Fink U, et al: Pretherapeutic laparoscopic staging in advanced gastric carcinoma. Endoscopy 31:342, 1999

38. Charukhchyan SA, Lucas GW: Laparoscopy and lesser sac endoscopy in gastric carcinoma operability assessment. Am Surg 64:160, 1998

39. Gastric Cancer, Practice Guidelines in Oncology, v.1.2005. National Comprehensive Cancer Center Network http://www.nccn.org

40. Siewert JR, Bottcher K, Stein HJ, et al: Relevant prognostic factors in gastric cancer: ten-year results of the German Gastric Cancer Study. Ann Surg 228:449, 1998

41. Hallissey MT, Jewkes AJ, Dunn JA, et al: Resection-line involvement in gastric cancer: a continuing problem. Br J Surg 80:1418, 1993

42. Jakl RJ, Miholic J, Koller R, et al: Prognostic factors in adenocarcinoma of the cardia. Am J Surg 169:316, 1995

43. Kooby DA, Coit DG: Controversies in the surgical management of gastric cancer. J National Comprehensive Cancer Network 1(1):115, 2003

44. Gouzi JL, Huguier M, Fagniez PL, et al: Total versus subtotal gastrectomy for adenocarcinoma of the gastric antrum: a French prospective controlled study. Ann Surg 209:162, 1989

45. Robertson CS, Chung SC, Woods SD, et al: A prospective randomized trial comparing R1 subtotal gastrectomy with R3 total gastrectomy for antral cancer. Ann Surg 220:176, 1994

46. Bozzetti F, Marubini E, Bonfanti G, et al: Subtotal versus total gastrectomy for gastric cancer: five-year survival rates in a multicenter randomized Italian trial. Italian Gastrointestinal Tumor Study Group. Ann Surg 230:170, 1999

47. Spechler SJ: The role of gastric carditis in metaplasia and neoplasia at the gastroesophageal junction. Gastroenterology 117:218, 1999

48. Devesa SS, Blot WJ, Fraumeni JF Jr: Changing patterns in the incidence of esophageal and gastric carcinoma in the United States. Cancer 83: 2049, 1998

49. Rudiger Siewert J, Feith M, Werner M, et al: Adenocarcinoma of the esophagogastric junction: results of surgical therapy based on anatomical/topographic classification in 1,002 consecutive patients. Ann Surg 232:353, 2000

50. Harrison LE, Karpeh MS, Brennan MF: Total gastrectomy is not necessary for proximal gastric cancer. Surgery 123:127, 1998

51. Kajitani T: The general rules for the gastric cancer study in surgery and pathology. Japan J Surg 2:127, 1981

52. Japanese Gastric Cancer Association: Japanese Classification of Gastric Adenocarcinoma—2nd English edition. Gastric Cancer 1:10, 1998

53. Maeta M, Yamashiro H, Saito H, et al: A prospective pilot study of extended (D3) and super-extended para-aortic lymphadenectomty (D4) in patients with T3 or T4 gastric cancer managed by total gastrectomy. Surgery 125:325, 1999

54. Baba M, Hokita S, Natsugoe S, et al: Paraaortic lymphadenectomy in patients with advanced carcinoma of the upper-third of the stomach. Hepatogastroenterology 47:893, 2000

55. Isozaki H, Okajima K, Fujii K, et al: Effectiveness of paraaortic lymph node dissection for advanced gastric cancer. Hepatogastroenterology 46:549, 2000

56. Wanebo HJ, Kennedy BJ, Winchester DP, et al: Gastric carcinoma: does lymph node dissection alter survival? J Am Coll Surg 183:616, 1996

57. Bonenkamp JJ, Hermans J, Sasako M, et al: Extended lymph node dissection for gastric cancer. N Engl J Med 340:908, 1999

58. Cuscheri A, Weeden S, Fielding J, et al: Patient survival after D1 and D2 resections for gastric cancer: long term results of the MMC randomized surgical trial. Br J Cancer 70:1522, 1999

59. Degiuli M, Sasako M, Ponyi A, et al: Survival results of a multicentre phase II study to evaluate D2 gastrectomy for gastric cancer. Br J Cancer 90:1727, 2004

60. Roukos DH, Lorenz M, Encke A: Evidence of survival benefit of extended (D2) lymphadenectomy in Western patients with gastric cancer based on a new concept: a prospective long-term follow-up study. Surgery 123:573, 1998

61. Karpeh MS, Leon L, Klimstra D, et al: Lymph node staging in gastric cancer: is location more important than number? An analysis of 1,038 patients. Ann Surg 232:362, 2000

62. Talamonti MS, Kim SP, Yao KA, et al: Surgical outcomes of patients with gastric carcinoma: the importance of primary tumor location and microvessel invasion. Surgery 134:720, 2003

63. Brady MS, Rogatko A, Dent LL, et al: Effect of splenectomy on morbidity and survival following curative gastrectomy for carcinoma. Arch Surg 126:359, 1991

64. Wanebo HJ, Kennedy BJ, Winchester DP, et al: Role of splenectomy in gastric cancer surgery: adverse effect of elective splenectomy on long-term survival. J Am Coll Surg 185:177, 1997

65. Csendes A, Burdiles P, Rojas J, et al: A prospective randomized study comparing D2 total gastrectomy versus D2 total gastrectomy plus splenectomy in 187 patients with gastric carcinoma. Surgery 131:401, 2002

66. Hallissey MT, Dunn JA, Ward LC, et al: The second British stomach cancer group trial of adjuvant radiotherapy or chemotherapy in respectable gastric cancer: five-year follow-up. Lancet 343: 1309, 1994

67. Earle CC, Maroun JA: Adjuvant chemotherapy after curative resection for gastric cancer in non-Asian patients: revisiting a meta-analysis of randomized trials. Eur J Cancer 35:1059, 1999

68. MacDonald JS, Smalley SR, Benedetti J, et al: Chemoradiotherapy after surgery compared with surgery alone for adenocarcinoma of the stomach or gastroesophageal junction. N Engl J Med 345:725, 2001

69. Estes NC, MacDonald JS, Touijer K, et al: Inadequate documentation and resection for gastric cancer in the United States: a preliminary report. Am Surg 64:680, 1998

70. Hundahl SA, MacDonald JS, Bendetti J, et al: Surgical treatment variation in a prospective, randomized trial of chemoradiotherapy in gastric cancer: the effect of undertreatment. Ann Surg Oncol 9:278, 2002

71. Lowy AM, Feig BW, Janjan N, et al: A pilot study of preoperative chemoradiotherapy for respectable gastric cancer. Ann Surg Oncol 8:519, 2001

72. Lowy AM, Mansfield PF, Leach SD, et al: Response to neoadjuvant chemotherapy best predicts survival after curative resection of gastric cancer. Ann Surg 229:303, 1999

73. Yao JC, Mansfield PF, Pisters PWT, et al: Combined-modality therapy for gastric cancer. Sem Surg Oncol 21:223, 2003

74. Gurney KA, Cartwright RA, Gilman EA: Descriptive epidemiology of gastrointestinal non-Hodgkin's lymphoma in a population-based registry. Br J Cancer 79:1929, 1999

75. Koch P, del Valle F, Berdel WE, et al: Primary gastrointestinal non-Hodgkin's lymphoma: II. Combined surgical and conservative or conservative management only in localized gastric lymphoma—results of the prospective German Multicenter Study GIT NHL 01/92. J Clin Oncol 19:3874, 2001

76. Crump M, Gospodarowicz M, Shepherd FA: Lymphoma of the gastrointestinal tract. Semin Oncol 26:324, 1999

77. Non-Hodgkin's Lymphoma, Practice Guidelines

in Oncology, v.1.2005. National Comprehensive Cancer Center Network http://www.nccn.org

78. Talamonti MS: Gastric cancer. Cancer Surgery for the General Surgeon. Winchester D, Jones RS, Murphy GP, Eds. Lippincott Williams & Wilkins, Philadelphia, 1998

79. Yoon SS, Coit DG, Portlock CS, et al: The diminishing role of surgery in the treatment of gastric lymphoma. Ann Surg 240:28, 2004

80. Parsonnet J, Hansen S, Rodriguez L, et al: *Helicobacter pylori* infection and gastric lymphoma. N Engl J Med 330:1267, 1994

81. Isaacson PG: Recent developments in our understanding of gastric lymphomas. Am J Surg Pathol 20:S1, 1996

82. Stolte M, Bayerdorffer E, Morgner A, et al: *Helicobacter* and gastric MALT lymphoma. Gut 50:III19, 2002

83. Schechter NR, Yahalom J: Low-grade MALT lymphoma of the stomach: a review of treatment options. Int J Radiat Oncol Biol Phys 46:1093, 2000

84. Martinelli G, Laszlo D, Ferreri AJ, et al: Clinical activity of rituximab in gastric marginal zone non-Hodgkin's lymphoma resistant to or not eligible for anti–*Helicobacter pylori* therapy. J Clin Oncol 23:1979, 2005

85. Nilsson B, Bumming P, Meis-Kindblom JM, et al: Gastrointestinal stromal tumors: the incidence, prevalence, clinical course, and prognostication in the preimatinib mesylate era—a population-based study in western Sweden. Cancer 103:821, 2005

86. Miettinen M, Sobin LH, Lasota J: Gastrointestinal stromal tumors of the stomach: a clinicopathologic, immunohistochemical, and molecular genetic study of 1765 cases with long-term follow-up. Am J Surg Pathol 29:52, 2005

87. Ng EH, Pollock RE, Munsell MF, et al: Prognostic factors influencing survival in gastrointestinal leiomyosarcomas: implications for surgical management and staging. Ann Surg 215: 68, 1992

88. Conlon KC, Casper ES, Brennan MF: Primary gastrointestinal sarcomas: analysis of prognostic variables. Ann Surg Oncol 2:26, 1995

89. Corless CL, Fletcher JA, Heinrich MC: Biology of gastrointestinal stromal tumors. J Clin Oncol 22:3813, 2004

90. Soft Tissue Sarcoma, Practice Guidelines in Oncology, v.1.2005. National Comprehensive Cancer Center Network http://www.nccn.org

91. Demetri GD, von Mehren M, Blanke CD, et al: Efficacy and safety of imatinib mesylate in advanced gastrointestinal stromal tumors. N Engl J Med 347:472, 2002

92. Gilligan CJ, Lawton GP, Tang LH, et al: Gastric carcinoid tumors: the biology and therapy of an enigmatic and controversial lesion. Am J Gastroenterol 90:338, 1995

93. Schindl M, Kaserer K, Niederle B: Treatment of gastric neuroendocrine tumors: the necessity of a type-adapted treatment. Arch Surg 136:49, 2001

94. Modlin IM, Cornelius E, Lawton GP: Use of an isotopic somatostatin receptor probe to image gut endocrine tumors. Arch Surg 130:367, 1995

95. Jemal A, Murray T, Ward E, et al: Cancer Statistics, 2005. CA Cancer J Clin 55:10, 2005

96. Frost DB, Mercado PD, Tyrell JS: Small bowel cancer: a 30-year review. Ann Surg Oncol 1:290, 1994

97. Torres M, Matta E, Chinea B, et al: Malignant tumors of the small intestine. J Clin Gastroenterol 37:372, 2003

98. Talamonti MS, Goetz LH, Rao S, et al: Primary cancers of the small bowel. Arch Surg 137:564, 2002

99. Zuckerman GR, Prakash C, Askin MP, et al: AGA technical review on the evaluation and management of occult and obscure gastrointestinal bleeding. Gastroenterology 118:201, 2000

100. Lewis BS: Small intestinal bleeding. Gastroenterol Clin North Am 29:67, 2000

101. de Mascarenhas-Saravina MN, de Silva Araujo Lopes LM: Small bowel tumors diagnosed by wireless capsule endoscopy: report of five cases. Endoscopy 35:865, 2003

102. Lambert P, Minghini A, Pincus W, et al: Treatment and prognosis of primary malignant small bowel tumors. Am Surg 62:709, 1996

103. Ito H, Perez A, Brooks DC, et al: Surgical treatment of small bowel cancer: a 20-year single institution experience. J Gastrointest Surg 7:925, 2003

104. Dabaja BS, Suki D, Pro B, et al: Adenocarcinoma of the small bowel: presentation, prognostic factors, and outcome of 217 patients. Cancer 101:518, 2004

105. Kodera Y, Yamamura Y, Shimizu Y, et al: Lymph node status assessment for gastric carcinoma: is the number of metastatic lymph nodes really practical as a parameter for N category in the TNM Classification? Tumor Node Metastasis. J Surg Oncol 69:15, 1998

51 TUMORS OF THE PANCREAS, BILIARY TRACT, AND LIVER

Steven M. Strasberg, M.D., F.A.C.S., and David C. Linehan, M.D., F.A.C.S.

Numerous types of tumors affect the pancreas, the biliary tree, and the liver. Each year, hundreds of papers are published on the topics of pancreatic, biliary, and hepatic cancer. Accordingly, in this chapter, we concentrate on essential principles rather than details. In particular, we focus on common malignant tumors, addressing benign tumors and uncommon tumors only insofar as they are important in differential diagnosis.

When a patient presents with an apparent cancer of the pancreas, the biliary tree, or the liver, the surgeon must attempt to answer the following three important questions:

1. What is the diagnosis?
2. What is the surgical stage of the disease—that is, is the tumor resectable?
3. What is the operative rationale that will encompass the disease and produce a margin-free resection (and, for pancreatobiliary cancers, an N1 resection)?

These questions form the underpinning for the process of investigation and management. In what follows, we describe our approach to each of the cancers in these terms.

Pancreatic Cancer

DUCTAL ADENOCARCINOMA

Adenocarcinoma of Head of Pancreas

Adenocarcinoma of the pancreatic head is common (with 30,000 new cases occurring annually in the United States) but remains one of the hardest GI cancers to cure. In the past 25 years, the efficacy of surgical treatment has improved dramatically, but 5-year actual survival rates in patients who have undergone resection are still low (about 15%).[1] Cancer of the head of the pancreas is the prototypical tumor that causes painless jaundice; however, other cancers that obstruct bile ducts also cause jaundice, including extrahepatic bile duct cancers, gallbladder cancers, ampullary malignancies, and some duodenal cancers. Some of the following discussion is generalized with an eye to determining the diagnosis in patients presenting with obstructive jaundice [see 45 Jaundice].

Clinical evaluation *History.* The classic presentation of cancer of the head of the pancreas is unremitting jaundice, usually accompanied by dark urine, light stool, and pruritus. Darkening of the urine or pruritus is often the first symptom, and scleral icterus frequently is first noted by family members or coworkers. The pruritus is often severe. The jaundice sometimes is painless but more frequently is associated with epigastric pain. This pain usually is not severe; severe, acute pain is more often associated with other conditions that may cause jaundice (e.g., choledocholithiasis and pancreatitis). Back pain suggests that the tumor has invaded tissues outside the pancreas and is unresectable.

Significant weight loss (≥ 10% of body weight) is common even when the pancreatic cancer is resectable.

In some patients, steatorrhea or diarrhea from obstruction of the pancreatic duct, weight loss, pain, or a combination of these is the presenting symptom, rather than jaundice. A presentation with steatorrhea or diarrhea is usually the result of a tumor in the uncinate process that obstructs the pancreatic duct but not the bile duct. Often, these symptoms are overlooked until the tumor extends and causes jaundice. About 5% of patients have a history of diabetes of recent onset. Migratory thrombophlebitis (the Trousseau sign) is uncommon and usually signifies metastatic disease. Pancreatobiliary malignancies cause biliary obstruction, but such obstruction is not commonly associated with biliary tract infection before instruments have been employed in the biliary tree. Therefore, in patients presenting with cholangitis who have not undergone biliary tract instrumentation, other diagnoses should be suspected. Patients with pancreatic cancer may also present with acute pancreatitis as the first manifestation. Vomiting and GI bleeding are uncommon presenting symptoms and suggest the presence of advanced tumors that are obstructing or eroding the duodenum.

Physical examination. Examination reveals scleral icterus. In some cases, the distended gallbladder may be palpable. In advanced cases, signs of metastatic disease (e.g., hepatomegaly and ascites) may be detected.

Investigative studies *Laboratory tests.* Liver function tests (LFTs) are of limited value in diagnosis. The serum bilirubin level is elevated in jaundiced patients, with the direct fraction exceeding 50%. The serum alkaline phosphatase level is almost always elevated when the bile duct is obstructed, and levels three to five times normal are common. Aminotransferase levels usually are moderately elevated as well. Very high aminotransferase levels suggest a hepatocellular cause of jaundice, usually viral, though impaction of a stone in the bile duct can cause transient rises in serum aspartate aminotransferase (AST) to levels higher than 1,000 IU/ml. By themselves, LFTs cannot effectively distinguish among jaundice arising from a hepatocellular cause (e.g., viral hepatitis or drug-induced cholestasis), jaundice resulting from a disease of microscopic bile ducts (e.g., primary biliary cirrhosis), and jaundice caused by any of the malignancies that obstruct the major bile ducts. To make this distinction, radiologic imaging tests are required [see Imaging, *below*].

Serum concentrations of the tumor marker CA 19-9 are often elevated in patients with pancreatic or biliary adenocarcinomas.[2] The upper limit of the normal range is 37 U/ml. Concentrations higher than 100 U/ml are highly suggestive of malignancy, but elevations between 37 and 100 U/ml are less specific. Serum levels generally reflect the extent of the tumor: small tumors (< 1 cm in diameter) are rarely associated with levels higher than 100 U/ml,

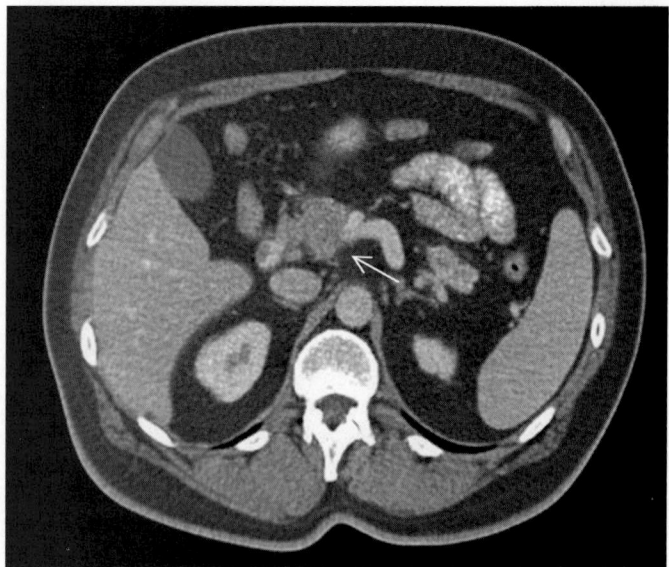

Figure 1 Shown is a typical hypoattenuating cancer of the pancreatic head. The tumor is invading the right side of the portosplenic confluence, as evidenced by the "beaking" of the vein at that point.

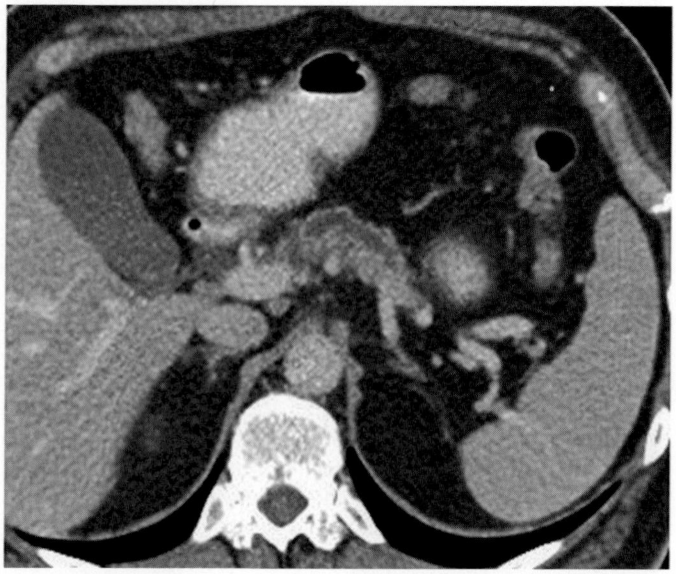

Figure 2 In the same patient as in Figure 1, pancreatic duct dilation is apparent in the body of the pancreas, with atrophy of the parenchyma.

whereas very high levels (> 1,000 U/ml) suggest metastatic disease. High levels may also accompany cholangitis. Measurement of CA 19-9 concentrations may be employed to detect recurrences in patients who have elevated CA 19-9 levels that return to normal after tumor resection; a second rise in the CA 19-9 level in the follow-up period is indicative of recurrence in most cases.

Imaging. Several different imaging tests may be used for diagnostic purposes in jaundiced patients, including computed tomography, magnetic resonance imaging, endoscopic retrograde cholangiopancreatography (ERCP), endoscopic ultrasonography (EUS), and transabdominal ultrasonography. The technical advances in imaging achieved over the past few years are remarkable. CT and MRI, which only a few years ago were limited to axial images, on one hand, and fuzzy MRI cholangiopancreatography (MRCP), on the other, can now provide high-quality images of blood vessels and ducts and their anatomic relation to tumors. These images can even be projected in three dimensions if desired.

Selection of appropriate imaging tests in a jaundiced patient is influenced by patient characteristics and by the symptoms observed. For instance, the type and order of investigations appropriate for an older patient presenting with obstructive jaundice, who is likely to have a malignancy, differ from those appropriate for a young woman with severe pain, who is more likely to have choledocholithiasis. The best initial imaging test in a patient in whom malignancy is suspected is either a fine-cut (3 mm between slices) three-phase (no-contrast phase, arterial phase, and venous phase) helical (spiral) CT scan or a high-quality MRI scan. Although MRI has the advantage of being able to provide a cholangiogram (i.e., with MRCP), small and medium-sized radiologic facilities currently tend to be more skilled at CT than at MRI; this difference should be taken into account when the first test is ordered. High-quality MRI scanners and the very latest generation of CT scanners are capable of providing cholangiograms and angiograms, as well as axial images.

The typical pancreatic cancer appears as a lucent zone in the pancreatic head [*see Figure 1*], associated with upstream dilatation of the bile ducts and the gallbladder. Often, the pancreatic duct is

also obstructed. As a result, the pancreatic duct may be dilated in the tail, body, and neck of the pancreas, with dilatation terminating sharply at the edge of the tumor. Pancreatic duct dilatation is often accompanied by atrophy of the body and the tail of the pancreas [*see Figure 2*].

When a jaundiced patient is discovered to have a typical-appearing localized cancer of the pancreatic head on CT scanning, no further diagnostic tests are needed, and operative management should be the next step. Tissue diagnosis is unnecessary. Negative biopsy results rarely change the therapeutic approach, and in that they are sometimes falsely negative, they are potentially misleading. Furthermore, omitting biopsy eliminates the small risk of tumor implantation in the needle tract. Selection of axial imaging as the first test often renders diagnostic ERCP, which is a more invasive test, unnecessary as well. Cholangiography also is not required for staging pancreatic head tumors [*see Surgical Staging, below*]. The advantages of starting with axial imaging in jaundiced patients with suspected cancer are discussed in greater detail elsewhere [*see Biliary Tract Cancer, Extrahepatic Cholangiocarcinoma, Upper-Duct Cholangiocarcinoma, Investigative Studies, below*].

Additional diagnostic imaging for atypical CT or MRI findings. In many patients with adenocarcinoma of the pancreatic head, the typical CT findings are absent and additional diagnostic imaging is required. Such patients may be categorized into two groups: those with an atypical mass and those with no mass on axial imaging. In either case, before ordering additional tests, it is appropriate to determine whether the CT scan is of adequate quality. For example, the scan may have been performed without contrast, the arterial and venous phases may not have been captured appropriately, or the slice thickness may have been too great for precise visualization of the head of the pancreas. Small adenocarcinomas may be missed when the venous phase is timed poorly, especially if slice thickness is 5 mm or greater, and masses that appear atypical initially may exhibit a typical appearance when the CT scan is optimized. Neuroendocrine cancers commonly display arterial-phase enhancement, which will be missed if the scan is mistimed. In our experience, about 40% of referred patients who underwent

CT scanning before arrival require a so-called pancreas protocol CT scan (i.e., a fine-cut three-phase helical scan) when they are first seen; in many of these cases, the second CT scan yields important diagnostic findings.

When no mass is present in a jaundiced patient with a peri-ampullary tumor or another focal obstructing process (e.g., pancreatitis), the CT scan usually shows bile duct dilatation extending down to the intrapancreatic portion of the duct. The dilatation may terminate anywhere from the upper border of the pancreas to the duodenum, depending on the site of the tumor and the nature of the process obstructing the bile duct. In these conditions, ERCP is a good choice as the second test.

ERCP provides an endoscopic view of the duodenum that allows identification and biopsy of ampullary and duodenal tumors that may be blocking the bile duct and producing jaundice. It confirms the presence of a bile duct stricture and displays its form, which is helpful in diagnosis. Focal strictures, especially those with shoulders, suggest malignancy. Long, tapering strictures limited to the intra-pancreatic portion of the bile duct suggest chronic pancreatitis. Concomitant narrowing of the pancreatic duct in the head of the pancreas (the double-duct sign) suggests the presence of a small pancreatic cancer that is not visible on the CT scan. Longer or multiple pancreatic strictures suggest chronic pancreatitis. A single focal bile duct stricture in the absence of pancreatic duct abnormalities is the hallmark of cancer of the lower bile duct. Infiltrating cancers of the bile duct may cause more than one stricture along the bile duct, but when more than one stricture is present, other diagnoses (e.g., primary sclerosing cholangitis) should be considered. Both pancreatic and bile ducts may be assessed with brush cytology. This test has a 45% to 50% sensitivity for cancer[3]; therefore, only a positive test result is significant.

ERCP findings in a patient with no mass must be evaluated in the light of findings from other investigations. Patients with the classic double-duct sign or single focal shouldered bile duct strictures are likely to have small pancreatic or bile duct tumors. Further diagnostic support is usually not needed before laparotomy, though such support may be reassuring when the CA 19-9 concentration is higher than 100 U/ml. When doubt persists, EUS often helps resolve it. EUS may identify a small mass that was not seen on the CT scan, and biopsies may then be done. Occasionally, EUS reveals enlarged lymph nodes, which may also undergo biopsy. However, negative EUS-guided biopsy results in patients who present with painless jaundice do not exclude malignancy. When such patients have an identifiable mass on EUS, pancreaticoduodenectomy is recommended, even if EUS-guided biopsy yields negative results. If a non-operative approach is taken, short-term follow-up at 4 to 6 weeks with repeat imaging and biopsy is mandatory. If the findings persist, laparotomy is advisable.

Occasionally, preoperative testing reveals no mass, but a mass is subsequently discovered by intraoperative palpation or intraoperative ultrasonography (IOUS). A mass palpated in the head of a pancreas that is otherwise normal or near normal in texture is highly suggestive of malignancy and constitutes sufficient justification for resection. The same is true of a mass detected by IOUS if the mass has characteristics of malignancy (i.e., is hypoechoic). If the IOUS findings are inconclusive, biopsy with frozen-section examination is a reasonable approach. In many such cases, the whole pancreas is diffusely firm or hard, and IOUS demonstrates a diffuse change in the normal texture of the gland. When the pancreas is diffusely firm and no localized process is seen on IOUS, biopsies should be directed toward the stent in the bile duct at the point where the bile duct narrows (as seen on ultrasonography).

The ultimate diagnostic test is pancreaticoduodenectomy. If there is a strong suspicion of cancer before laparotomy or the findings at laparotomy are strongly suggestive, this procedure should be performed without preliminary biopsy. When this approach is followed, a small number of patients with suspected malignant disease will ultimately turn out to have benign disease when operated on; this possibility should be explained to patients who do not undergo confirmatory tissue diagnosis before operation. Because of the limited negative predictive value of currently available tests, pancreaticoduodenectomy is sometimes still required to make a definitive diagnosis.

The finding of an atypical pancreatic head mass on a CT scan poses an additional challenge. Atypical masses may take different forms. In some cases, they exhibit attenuation that differs only slightly from that of the surrounding pancreas; in others, they have a ground-glass appearance. They may extend into the body and tail of the pancreas, or they may be localized to the head. With atypical masses, the most common problem is how to differentiate focal pancreatitis from adenocarcinoma. This differentiation can be very difficult to achieve. Pancreatitis may be present without antecedent acute attacks; without a history of alcoholism, gallstones, or hyperlipidemia; without diabetes or steatorrhea; and without calcifications in the gland. Cancer appears to be more common in patients who have had chronic pancreatitis, and the diseases may coexist. Therefore, one cannot feel confident that cancer is absent simply because chronic pancreatitis is present. Cancer should be suspected in patients with an established diagnosis of chronic pancreatitis who undergo a rapid change in status (e.g., weight loss). Diabetes is common in patients with chronic pancreatitis, but it may also be the first sign of pancreatic cancer in patients without chronic pancreatitis. Chronic pancreatitis can cause painless jaundice. A rare immune form of chronic pancreatitis, known as lymphoplasmacytic sclerosing pancreatitis, has been recognized that is particularly hard to differentiate from cancer.[4]

EUS is becoming increasingly important in the management of patients with atypical pancreatic head masses.[5] When jaundice is present, ERCP followed by EUS is our usual approach; when it is absent, EUS without ERCP is preferred. EUS-guided biopsy is superior to CT-guided transabdominal biopsy, in that access to the head of the pancreas is easier and the chance of needle tracking is reduced (because the biopsy is taken through the duodenal wall, which is resected if a Whipple procedure is done).

At the conclusion of all of the preceding investigations, it still may not be clear whether a malignancy is present. Clinical judgment must be exercised in deciding whether to operate or to repeat investigative studies after an interval of 2 to 3 months. Operation is favored in patients who are jaundiced, who have less pain, who have elevated CA 19-9 levels, and whose mass is suspicious for cancer. Elevation of the CA 19-9 concentration beyond 100 U/ml should be regarded as a very important finding. When EUS is inconclusive, ultrasound-guided diagnostic laparoscopy may be performed to obtain core tissue biopsies from several areas of the mass. This technique is especially useful when chronic pancreatitis is strongly suspected,[6] in that the multiple long core biopsies obtainable with this procedure provide a greater degree of assurance against false-negative findings for cancer. Even this test, however, is not 100% accurate in this regard. The penultimate diagnostic test is laparotomy with mobilization of the pancreatic head and IOUS-guided transduodenal core biopsies of the mass. The ideal outcome with this approach is to perform pancreaticoduodenectomy in all patients who actually have cancer while reducing to a reasonable minimum resection in patients with benign disease, who in most cases are better served by biliary bypass.

Surgical staging   The term staging is currently used to denote the process by which the surgeon determines whether a tumor is resectable. We prefer to use the term surgical staging for this process so as to distinguish it from those staging classifications that define the life history and prognosis of tumors and provide the basis for comparison of results—namely, the TNM classifications developed by the American Joint Committee on Cancer (AJCC). These latter systems are also of great importance to the surgeon dealing with pancreatic tumors.

Surgical staging is started preoperatively and completed intraoperatively. Preoperative staging tests determine operability—that is, whether the tumor appears resectable after preoperative testing. However, the final decision regarding resectability is made only during the operation, on the basis of intraoperative staging. A tumor of the head of the pancreas is deemed unresectable when it is determined to have extended beyond the boundaries of a pancreaticoduodenectomy. Common reasons for unresectability include (1) vascular invasion (i.e., invasion of the superior mesenteric vein, the portal vein, the superior mesenteric artery, or, less commonly, the hepatic artery); (2) lymph node metastases that fall outside the scope of a pancreaticoduodenectomy (e.g., metastases to para-aortic and celiac lymph nodes); (3) hepatic metastases; (4) peritoneal metastases; and (5) extra-abdominal metastases (usually pulmonary). Limited vascular invasion of the superior mesenteric vein and the portal vein may be overcome by resection and reconstruction and thus is only a relative contraindication to resection. This is especially true when the tumor is small and has arisen in the vicinity of the veins. In a series from our institution (Washington University in St. Louis), about 20% of resections done for pancreatic cancer involved resection of these veins.[7]

The tests used to establish the diagnosis and those used to accomplish surgical staging go hand in hand. Abdominal CT scans, abdominal MRI, thoracic CT scans, and chest radiographs are obtained to detect hepatic metastases, vascular invasion, and pulmonary metastases. To assess vascular invasion, fine-cut three-phase helical CT scans or MRI scans are required. These tests may detect enlarged lymph nodes, but it should be remembered that nodes may be enlarged for reasons other than cancer. Sometimes, ascitic fluid collections or peritoneal or omental nodules are iden-

Table 1   American Joint Committee on Cancer TNM Clinical Classification of Pancreatic Cancer

Primary tumor (T)	TX	Primary tumor cannot be assessed
	T0	No evidence of primary tumor
	Tis	Carcinoma in situ
	T1	Tumor limited to pancreas, ≤ 2 cm in greatest dimension
	T2	Tumor limited to pancreas, > 2 cm in greatest dimension
	T3	Tumor extends beyond pancreas but without involvement of celiac axis or SMA
	T4	Tumor involves celiac axis or SMA
Regional lymph nodes (N)	NX	Regional lymph nodes cannot be assessed
	N0	No regional lymph node metastasis
	N1	Regional lymph node metastasis
Distant metastasis (M)	MX	Distant metastasis cannot be assessed
	M0	No distant metastasis
	M1	Distant metastasis

SMA—superior mesenteric artery

Table 2   American Joint Committee on Cancer Staging System for Pancreatic Cancer

Stage	T	N	M
Stage 0	Tis	N0	M0
Stage IA	T1	B0	M0
Stage IB	T2	N0	M0
Stage IIA	T3	N0	M0
Stage IIB	T1, T2, T3	N1	M0
Stage III	T4	Any N	M0
Stage IV	Any T	Any N	M1

tified; ascitic fluid may be sent for cytologic analysis, and omental nodules may undergo ultrasound-guided biopsy. Invasion of the mesentery, the mesocolon, or retroperitoneal tissues may also be detected by CT scanning. In the view of some surgeons, such invasion may render the tumor unresectable, but in our experience, this is rarely the case in the absence of concomitant vascular invasion: the resection may still be accomplished with clear margins by resecting the portion of the mesocolon or the mesentery that was locally invaded.

EUS may be used to guide biopsy of suspicious lymph nodes when these lie outside the planned resection zone. It has also been employed to assess vascular invasion, but in our experience, it has no advantage over CT scanning in this regard; what is more, it is highly operator dependent. Staging laparoscopy is particularly effective at finding small hepatic and peritoneal nodules. About 20% of patients thought to have resectable pancreatic adenocarcinoma of the head of the pancreas before staging laparoscopy are found to have liver or peritoneal metastases upon laparoscopy.[8] Staging is completed intraoperatively by carefully inspecting the intra-abdominal contents, opening the lesser sac, mobilizing the head of the pancreas, performing biopsies of suspicious nodules or nodes outside the planned resection zone, and attempting dissection of the superior mesenteric vein or the portal vein. Formal clinicopathologic staging according to the AJCC's TNM system is useful for establishing the prognosis and planning additional treatment [*see Tables 1 and 2*].

All authorities agree that axial imaging of the abdomen and chest (or roentgenography of the chest) is standard practice for staging pancreatic cancer; however, not all agree on the value of other staging tests. Many authorities advocate omission of staging laparoscopy or EUS-guided biopsy of nodes, on the grounds that patients are better served by palliative surgery than by endoscopic stenting of the bile duct. There is no advantage in knowing whether small liver metastases or celiac node metastases are present if laparotomy is to be undertaken anyway. The literature on this issue is unclear regarding what constitutes best practice. The two randomized trials published to date reported differing outcomes, with one favoring surgical bypass[9] and the other endoscopic stenting. We continue to recommend staging laparoscopy in patients with adenocarcinoma of the pancreas. In those considered likely to have a short life expectancy because of peritoneal or hepatic metastases discovered upon laparoscopy, the procedure is discontinued, and endoscopic stenting with metal stents is performed. We no longer advocate using staging laparoscopy with ultrasonography to determine if the tumor is unresectable solely because of local vascular invasion; these patients are likely to have a longer life expectancy and are treated with a double-bypass procedure. Finally, ^{18}F-fluorodeoxyglucose positron emission tomography (FDG-PET) may be useful in staging pancreatic cancer, but at present, its role is unclear. Given that inflammation is frequently confused with cancer, the major role of this modality will probably be in the detection of distant metastases.

Management   *Preoperative preparation.* All jaundiced patients should receive vitamin K, a fat-soluble vitamin whose absorption is reduced by biliary or pancreatic duct obstruction. Routine preoperative bile duct decompression is unnecessary, except when jaundice has been prolonged or operative treatment will be delayed (e.g., for correction of cardiac or other comorbid conditions). Several studies have shown that surgical outcome is not improved by routine preoperative decompression in jaundiced patients. In fact, stent placement may increase the incidence of postoperative infection.[10]

Rationale for pancreaticoduodenectomy. The technical details of pancreaticoduodenectomy are discussed more fully elsewhere [*see 66 Procedures for Benign and Malignant Pancreatic Disease*]. Therapeutic decision-making necessarily includes consideration of the extent of the procedure. The operative goal is to remove the tumor with clear margins, as well as the N1 regional lymph nodes. Numerous attempts have been made to improve results by extending the operation, either through more extensive lymph node dissections[11] or through resection of the superior mesenteric artery.[12] None of these attempts have been successful in improving overall survival. The lesson is that invasion of additional lymph node regions or the superior mesenteric artery signals an aggressive tumor biology that is unlikely to be overcome by wider resections. Except for resection of the portal vein or the superior mesenteric vein to address invasion of these structures by otherwise favorable tumors, extended resections are no longer recommended. Even these recommended venous resections are probably best restricted to tumors that have arisen close to the veins and involved them while still small; resections of large adenocarcinomas that have grown over time to involve long stretches of the veins are best avoided.

There is also continuing controversy regarding the respective merits of the standard version of the operation and its pylorus-preserving variant. There is no evidence that the two procedures differ with respect to overall survival. Pylorus preservation is associated with gastric-emptying problems in the postoperative period, but overall, it seems to be associated with less postoperative GI dysfunction.[13] We employ pylorus preservation selectively in older, thinner patients, with the aim of minimizing disruption of GI function.

Adenocarcinoma of Body and Tail of Pancreas

Adenocarcinoma of the body and tail of the pancreas is less common than adenocarcinoma of the head. Because it does not produce jaundice, it tends to be recognized relatively late. Accordingly, patients are often in an advanced stage of disease at presentation. Tumors of the midbody tend to invade posteriorly to involve the superior mesenteric artery or the celiac axis, even when these lesions are only 2 to 3 cm in diameter. As a result, tumors of the tail are more likely to be resectable than tumors of the midbody when they are discovered. Many resectable tumors are discovered incidentally; by the time the tumors give rise to symptoms, they are frequently unresectable.

Clinical evaluation   Symptoms are nonspecific, consisting of abdominal and back pain (which is usually relieved by sitting up and leaning forward), weight loss, and diabetes of recent onset.

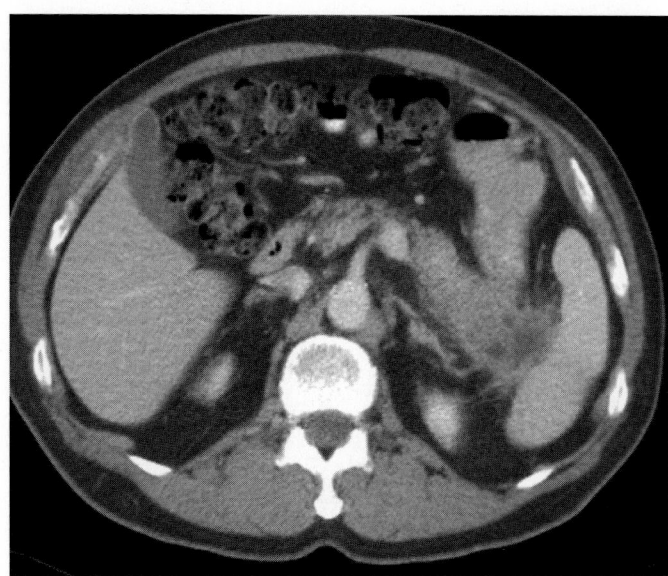

Figure 3   **Shown is a typical hypoattenuating cancer of the tail of the pancreas with invasion of the hilum of the spleen and the splenic flexure of the colon. Peritumoral stranding suggests inflammation or invasion of peripancreatic fat.**

Investigative studies   The CA 19-9 concentration may be elevated. CT usually shows a lucent mass [*see Figure 3*], often with extension outside the pancreas and dilatation of the distal pancreatic duct, when the tumor is proximal to the tail of the gland. EUS is very useful for assessing indeterminate lesions.

Surgical staging   Surgical staging of cancers of the body and the tail is similar to that of cancers of the pancreatic head and is based primarily on CT scanning of the abdomen and the thorax. Unresectability by reason of local invasion is usually attributable to the involvement of the superior mesenteric artery or the celiac artery and less commonly to the involvement of the portal vein, the superior mesenteric vein, or the aorta. Another indicator of unresectability is enlarged para-aortic nodes, which sometimes appear along the aorta below the pancreas. Invasion of the spleen, the stomach, the left adrenal gland, the mesocolon, the colon, the retroperitoneum, or even the left kidney is not a contraindication to resection, provided that clear margins may be expected.[14] Staging laparoscopy is of great value in this context: between 20% and 50% of patients are found to have unresectable tumors with this modality.[15] Cancer of the body and the tail differs from cancer of the head in that there is no effective palliation and therefore no rationale for laparotomy if the lesion is unresectable. Celiac nerve block, which is very helpful in reducing the use of narcotics for pain control, may also be performed laparoscopically or endoscopically.

Management   *Rationale for radical antegrade modular pancreatosplenectomy.* Logically, the goal of resection of tumors of the body and tail should be the same as that of resection of tumors of the head—namely, excision of the tumor with clear margins, along with the N1 lymph nodes. In practice, this goal generally is not achieved by the traditional retrograde distal pancreatectomy, in which the spleen is taken first and which is not based on the lymph node drainage of the pancreas. Lymph node counts have been low with the traditional procedure, and positive posterior margin rates have been high. As an alternative, we have developed a technique referred to as radical antegrade modular pancreatosplenectomy

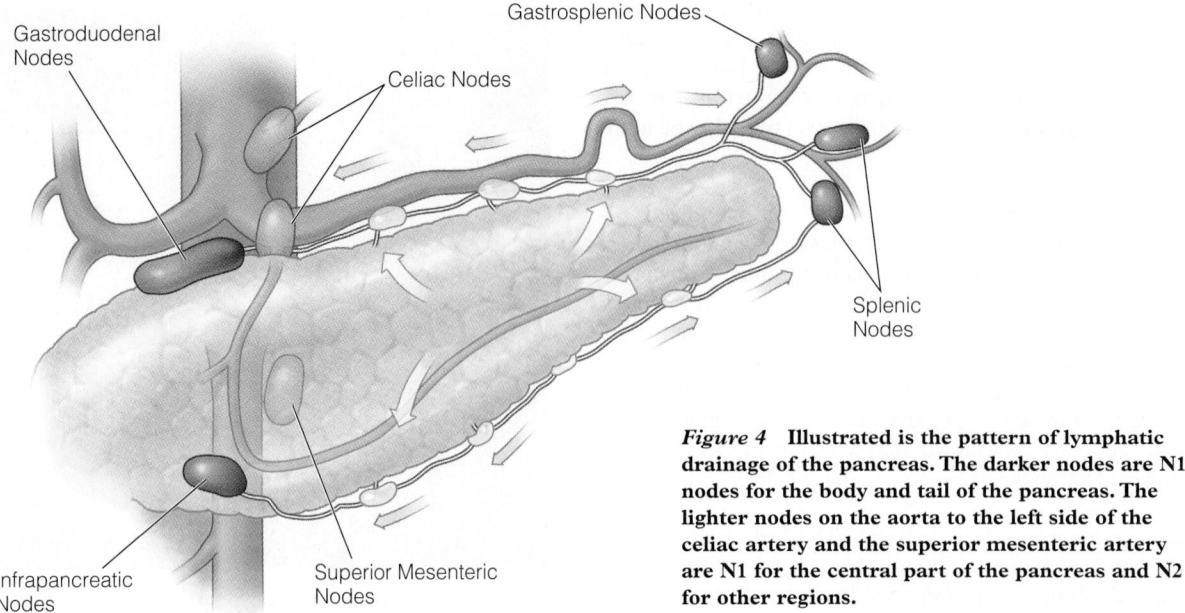

Figure 4 **Illustrated is the pattern of lymphatic drainage of the pancreas. The darker nodes are N1 nodes for the body and tail of the pancreas. The lighter nodes on the aorta to the left side of the celiac artery and the superior mesenteric artery are N1 for the central part of the pancreas and N2 for other regions.**

(RAMPS), which accomplishes the desired goals by performing the resection in an antegrade manner from right to left and which is based on the established lymph node drainage of the gland [*see Figure 4*].[16] RAMPS also allows early control of the vasculature.

Mucinous Adenocarcinoma

Mucin-producing cancers are special variants of adenocarcinoma of the pancreas that often arise in preexisting lesions. The two main types are mucinous cystic neoplasm (MCN) and intraductal papillary mucinous neoplasm (IPMN) (also referred to as intraductal papillary mucinous tumor [IPMT]).[17] A complete discussion of pancreatic cyst disease is beyond the scope of this chapter. Accordingly, we briefly address such disease as it relates to cancer of the pancreas, omitting discussion of less common cystic malignancies of the pancreas.

MCN MCN occurs most often in middle-aged women, typically in the body and tail of the pancreas. MCNs are unilocular or septated cysts whose diameter ranges from subcentimeter size to 15 cm or larger. Occasionally, calcium is present in the wall. Excrescences may be present on the inner wall; if so, malignancy is likely. Most symptomatic MCNs are between 4 and 7 cm in diameter.

Clinical evaluation and investigative studies. Patients with MCNs typically present with left-side pain, often in the flank and the back, though these lesions also are frequently discovered incidentally. Pancreatitis is rare and jaundice is uncommon, even when the lesions are situated in the head of the pancreas. MCNs must be differentiated from pseudocysts and from serous cystadenomas (SCAs), which are benign cysts. Differentiation between MCNs and pseudocysts is based on the history, imaging studies, and cyst fluid analysis. The diagnosis of pseudocyst is supported by a history of pancreatitits; a thick-walled, uncalcified cyst with associated radiologic signs of pancreatitis; and cyst fluid with high levels of amylase and lipase and a relatively low level of carcinoembryonic antigen (CEA) (< 500 ng/ml).

SCAs have the same clinical presentation as MCNs. SCAs are more frequently polycystic than MCNs are, but this difference is not a certain means of discriminating between the two. In a minority (25%) of cases, SCAs have a pathognomonic central calcification

with radiating arms ringed by multiple grape-sized cysts. When the cysts are tiny (honeycomb pattern), SCAs may also appear to be solid tumors. Unlike pseudocysts and IPMNs, neither MCNs nor SCAs communicate with the pancreatic duct, though they may compress it. Measurement of the CEA level in cyst fluid is a good means of distinguishing MCN from SCA. SCAs have very low levels of CEA, with the cutoff being 5 ng/ml.[18] In MCNs, the cyst fluid is often mucinous, and cytologic assessment may show mucin-producing cells; typically, the fluid is high in CEA. The CA 19-9 concentration may also be used to distinguish MCNs from SCAs, but it is not as reliable as the CEA concentration for this purpose.[18]

Surgical staging. Surgical staging is required when MCNs are malignant, and essentially the same methods are used as for any pancreatic adenocarcinoma (see above). Malignancy is suggested by a solid intracystic or extramural component. Sometimes, a mucinous tumor is frankly malignant with a large or dominant solid component. Such a tumor is better termed a mucinous adenocarcinoma, and it should be evaluated and treated from the outset in the same manner as any other adenocarcinoma of the pancreas.

Management. In symptomatic patients, preoperative differentiation between MCNs and SCAs is unnecessary, because resection is the treatment for both. In asymptomatic patients, MCNs more than 2 cm in diameter should be excised because of the possibility of malignant degeneration. The standard procedure has been open distal pancreatectomy with splenectomy, though lesser procedures, such as spleen-sparing distal pancreatectomy,[19] laparoscopic distal pancreatectomy,[20] central pancreatectomy, and enucleation,[21] have all been used as well. These procedures appear to be reasonable choices, provided that there is no suggestion of invasive malignancy on imaging (i.e., that there are no excrescences on the inner lining and that the surrounding pancreas appears normal). Enucleation may be associated with a higher incidence of postoperative fistula. If invasive cancer is not detected in the resected specimen, the chances that the malignancy will recur are small; in fact, we have never seen such a recurrence.

The 2 cm cutoff for treatment of MCNs in asymptomatic patients is arbitrary. It is still possible that malignant degeneration could occur in a cyst smaller than 2 cm, but many cysts of this size are found in the course of axial imaging performed for other reasons. Such cysts are difficult to diagnose because of the small volume of cyst fluid present, and the benefit to be gained from performing a large number of pancreatectomies for these small cysts is questionable, even when they are diagnosable as MCNs. Some authorities feel that large SCAs should also be excised because of rare instances of malignant degeneration. Occasionally, MCNs or symptomatic SCAs are located in the head of the pancreas and must be treated with pancreaticoduodenectomy.

IPMN IPMN begins as the cells lining the pancreatic ducts undergo a metaplastic alteration from a low cuboidal serous type of cell to a mucin-producing type. These cells are prone to dysplasia and eventual malignant transformation. Overall, IPMNs appear to undergo malignant transformation much more regularly than MCNs do. There are two recognized types of IPMN, which may occur either separately or together. The more common type affects the main pancreatic duct [*see Figure 5*], which becomes dilated and filled with mucin. As the disease progresses toward malignancy, papillary processes may project into the lumen. The less common type, so-called side-branch IPMN, affects the smaller ducts and presents as multiple (usually small) pancreatic cysts. In either type of IPMN, the disease may be either diffuse or focal; when it is focal, the head of the pancreas is the site of disease in the majority (60%) of cases. About 20% of IPMN patients have a malignancy at the time of diagnosis, though the cancer may not be evident until the specimen is examined pathologically.

Clinical evaluation and investigative studies. IPMN occurs predominantly in males and usually affects patients in their 60s. Pain (usually attributable to pancreatitis arising from mucous obstruction of the pancreatic duct) is a common presenting symptom. Another common presentation is pancreatic insufficiency with diabetes or steatorrhea. Accordingly, it is not surprising that formerly, many IPMN patients were diagnosed as having chronic pancreatitis. IPMN may also be discovered incidentally or may present as a cancer with signs and symptoms similar to those of other pancreatic cancers, depending on the part of the gland in which they arise. On rare occasions, cholangitis from obstruction of the common channel by mucus is the presenting problem.

The diagnosis is made on the basis of the presentation and the findings from axial imaging and ERCP. ERCP sometimes shows mucus bulging from the mouth of the pancreatic duct when the duodenum is inspected. In main duct disease, the pancreatic duct is dilated, but sometimes, the mucus prevents complete filling. In this situation, CT scans or MRI with MRCP may be quite useful for detecting ductal dilatation and atrophy of the pancreas. MRCP is best at detecting excrescences emanating from the surface of the duct, which signal progression of the disease toward neoplasia. In side-branch IPMN, ERCP typically demonstrates communication between the cysts and the main duct, which is often normal in size; this finding is not present in MCN or SCA and is very useful for distinguishing side-branch IPMN from these other types of cysts.

Management. IPMN is treated by resecting the involved portion of the gland. In about 50% of patients, the resection margin is involved with atypia or cancer, and the planned resection may have to be extended.[22] In some cases (about 20%), total pancreatectomy is required; in others, partial pancreatectomy and close follow-up of the pancreatic remnant with MRCP and serum CA 19-9 measurement are indicated. Most patients who require total pancreatectomy tolerate the procedure well when they are enrolled in a program keyed to this operation. The mucinous cancers associated with IPMN have a better prognosis than ductal adenocarcinomas do.[23] Frank mucinous cancers may appear in patients with IPMN as well; they should be managed in much the same fashion as other adenocarcinomas, with the additional requirement that the resection should encompass the entire IPMN-bearing portion of the pancreas.

NEUROENDOCRINE CANCERS

In most large centers, neuroendocrine cancers account for fewer than 5% of surgically treated pancreatic malignancies. Some of these cancers are functional tumors, which produce hormones leading to paraneoplastic syndromes. Examples include gastrinoma, insulinoma, glucagonoma and vasoactive intestinal polypeptide–secreting tumor (VIPoma), all of which are associated with characteristic clinical syndromes. These syndromes are often produced while the tumors are still small. A detailed discussion of functional neuroendocrine tumors is beyond the scope of this chapter.

a

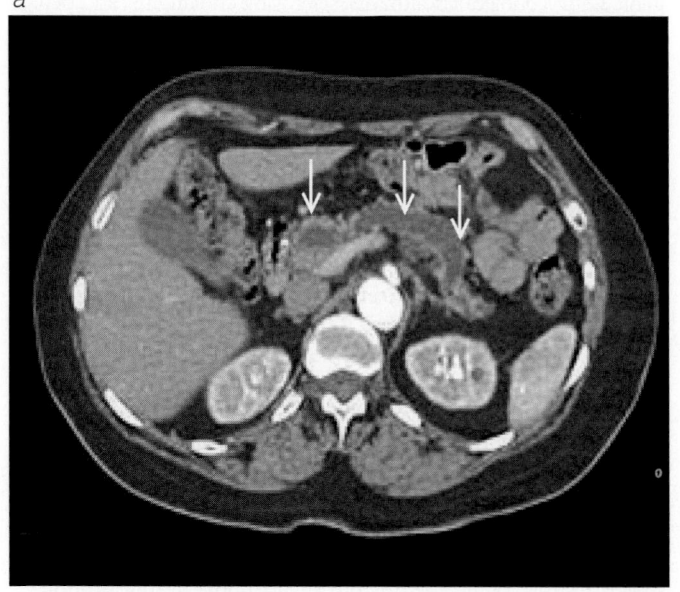

b

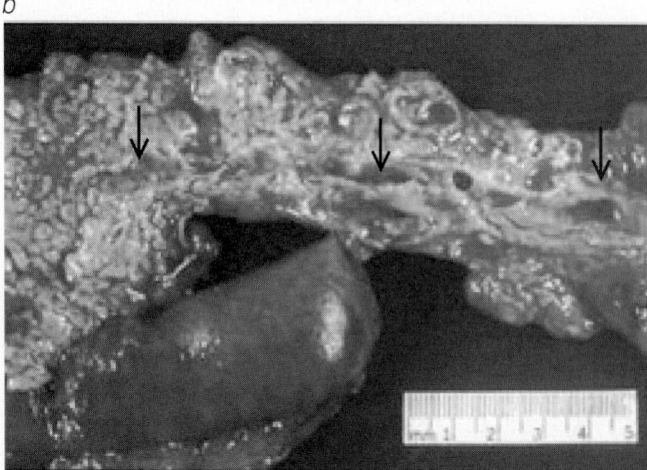

Figure 5 (*a*) **CT scan of a patient with main duct IPMN involving the entire length of the pancreatic duct reveals substantial distention of the duct.** (*b*) **Shown is a cross-section through the resected specimen.**

Other neuroendocrine tumors are nonfunctional and, as a result, reach a larger size before giving rise to symptoms. These lesions present with symptoms caused by the mass effect and must be differentiated from ductal adenocarcinomas. Nonfunctional neuroendocrine cancers are slow-growing tumors that tend to push rather than invade structures but are capable of metastasizing to lymph nodes, as well as to the liver and other organs. Pain is the most common presenting symptom. Jaundice, pancreatitis, and systemic symptoms (e.g., weight loss) are less common with these tumors than with adenocarcinoma of the pancreas. Because of the propensity of neuroendocrine tumors to deflect rather than invade the bile duct, jaundice may be absent even when tumors are located in the head of the gland.

Diagnosis, surgical staging, and treatment rationale are essentially the same for neuroendocrine cancers as for ductal adenocarcinomas. On CT scans, these lesions characteristically show enhancement in the arterial phase and are seen to push on bile ducts and vascular structures rather than encase them. Complete resection by means of pancreatoduodenectomy or distal pancreatectomy [*see 66 Procedures for Benign and Malignant Pancreatic Disease*] is indicated. Given the slow growth rate of neuroendocrine cancers and their relatively favorable prognosis (50% to 60% 5-year survival rate), removal of the primary lesion and any hepatic secondary lesions is justified if all tumor tissue can be removed with clear margins.

Biliary Tract Cancer

EXTRAHEPATIC CHOLANGIOCARCINOMA

Extrahepatic cholangiocarcinoma (CCA) may be subdivided into lower-duct CCA and upper-duct CCA, with the former arising in the intrapancreatic or retroduodenal portion of the bile duct and the latter arising above it. In practice, most upper-duct CCAs (also referred to as hilar CCAs or Klatskin tumors) arise just below the union of the right and left hepatic ducts, at the union of the ducts, or in the main right or left hepatic ducts. Cancer of the midportion of the bile duct at the cystic duct's usual insertion point is more likely to be an extension of a gallbladder cancer than a primary CCA. AJCC staging criteria for these tumors are useful

Table 3 American Joint Committee on Cancer TNM Clinical Classification of Extrahepatic Bile Duct Cancer

Primary tumor (T)	TX	Primary tumor cannot be assessed
	T0	No evidence of primary tumor
	Tis	Carcinoma in situ
	T1	Tumor confined to bile duct histologically
	T2	Tumor invades beyond wall of bile duct
	T3	Tumor invades liver, gallbladder, pancreas, or unilateral branches of portal vein or hepatic artery
	T4	Tumor invades any of the following: main portal vein or branches bilaterally, coronary artery, or other adjacent structures (e.g., colon, stomach, duodenum, or abdominal wall)
Regional lymph nodes (N)	NX	Regional lymph nodes cannot be assessed
	N0	No regional lymph node metastasis
	N1	Regional lymph node metastasis
Distant metastasis (M)	MX	Distant metastasis cannot be assessed
	M0	No distant metastasis
	M1	Distant metastasis

Table 4 American Joint Committee on Cancer Staging System for Extrahepatic Bile Duct Cancer

Stage	T	N	M
Stage 0	Tis	N0	M0
Stage IA	T1	N0	M0
Stage IB	T2	N0	M0
Stage IIA	T3	N0	M0
Stage IIB	T1, T2, T3	N1	M0
Stage III	T4	Any N	M0
Stage IV	Any T	Any N	M1

for establishing the prognosis and planning further treatment [*see Tables 3 and 4*].

Lower-Duct Cholangiocarcinoma

Clinical evaluation and investigative studies   Much of what the surgeon needs to know about lower-duct CCA has already been addressed elsewhere [*see* Pancreatic Cancer, Adenocarcinoma of Head of Pancreas, *above*]. By far the most common presentation is painless jaundice with its constellation of associated symptoms (especially pruritus). Laboratory tests reveal the characteristic pattern of obstructive jaundice. A serum CA 19-9 concentration higher than 100 U/ml facilitates the diagnosis. Axial imaging reveals dilation of the intrahepatic bile ducts, the gallbladder (in most cases), and the extrahepatic bile ducts down to the level of the pancreatic head, where the dilatation terminates abruptly. Usually, no mass is visible. ERCP or MRCP shows a focal stricture, and ERCP brushings are positive in about 50% of cases. EUS may be helpful, in that it is more sensitive for small tumors than CT scanning is. Needle biopsy is directed toward the mass or, if no mass is visible, toward the narrowest segment of the bile duct. A negative biopsy result does not rule out a small bile duct cancer.

The differential diagnosis includes other potential causes of focal strictures of the bile duct.[24] The most common cause of a benign stricture of the intrapancreatic bile duct is pancreatitis, which may be diffuse or focal. Other causes of benign stricture include iatrogenic injury, choledocholithiasis, sclerosing cholangitis, and benign inflammatory pseudotumors [*see* Upper-Duct Cholangiocarcinoma, Investigative Studies, Imaging, *below*]. Iatrogenic injuries rarely involve the intrapancreatic portion of the bile duct, though such injuries can occur in this area as a consequence of forceful instrumentation. Sclerosing cholangitis may affect this section of the bile duct but usually affects other areas of the biliary tree as well. The diagnostic steps for differentiating benign neoplasms from malignant tumors are essentially the same for lower-duct CCA as for pancreatic cancer. As noted, resection may be required to make the diagnosis. In any patient presenting with jaundice and a focal stricture of the bile duct, lower-duct CCA should be strongly suspected.

Surgical staging   Surgical staging of lower-duct CCAs is usually straightforward. These tumors are usually remote from major vascular structures and thus are not subject to the same local staging considerations as adenocarcinomas of the pancreatic head are. The exception is a tumor that extends to the top of the retroduodenal portion of the bile duct. At this point, the bile duct is apposed to the portal vein and the hepatic artery, and these structures may be invaded by bile duct tumors in this location.

Management   The treatment for resectable lesions is pancreaticoduodenectomy.

Upper-Duct Cholangiocarcinoma

Upper-duct (or hilar) CCA is a sporadically occurring tumor that may also be seen in patients with primary sclerosing cholangitis, ulcerative colitis, or parasitic infestation. It is characteristically slow growing and locally invasive, and it metastasizes more readily to lymph nodes than systemically, though intrahepatic and peritoneal metastases are not uncommon. Most hilar CCAs are cicatrizing diffusely infiltrating cancers, but some are nodular, and others present as papillary ingrowths. These tumors are divided into four types according to the Bismuth classification, which is based on the upper extent of the tumor [*see Figure 6*].[25]

When the CCA originates in one of the hepatic ducts, that duct may be obstructed for a considerable period before the tumor causes jaundice by growing into the other hepatic duct or the common bile duct. Such prolonged unilateral obstruction before the onset of the presenting symptom of jaundice may result in atrophy of the obstructed side of the liver, which may affect subsequent management. For example, because the disease is more advanced on the obstructed side, it is the atrophied half of the liver that will be removed in almost all cases where resection is indicated. In addition, when one side of the liver undergoes atrophy, the other side undergoes hypertrophy. These changes lead to rotation of the liver, which in turn may cause the structures in the hepatoduodenal ligament to be rotated out of their normal anatomic location. For instance, if hypertrophy of the left hemiliver develops, the hepatic artery may come to lie directly in front of the bile duct.

Clinical evaluation   The usual presentation of hilar CCA consists of painless jaundice with its accompanying symptoms (especially pruritus), though some pain may be present. Cholangitis before instrumentation of the bile duct is uncommon. In patients who present in the late stages of the disease, general manifestations of cancer (e.g., malaise, weight loss, or ascites) may be noted.

Investigative studies   *Laboratory tests.*   Laboratory testing follows the pattern previously described for obstructive jaundice [*see Pancreatic Cancer, above*]. Again, the most helpful diagnostic laboratory test is the serum CA 19-9 concentration: levels higher than 100 U/ml are strongly suggestive of cancer. In patients with primary sclerosing cholangitis, the presence of CCA is often suggested by a rapid deterioration in condition. It is not unusual for patients with hilar CCA to have undergone a cholecystectomy in the recent past; the symptoms of pain and jaundice may be mistaken for symptoms of gallbladder disease in patients who happen also to have gallstones.

Imaging.   Earlier [*see Pancreatic Cancer, Ductal Adenocarcinoma, Adenocarcinoma of Head of Pancreas, above*], the point was made that it is preferable to employ axial imaging rather than ERCP as the first imaging test in the jaundiced patient because doing so will often render ERCP, an invasive test, unnecessary. This point carries even more force in the setting of hilar CCA. Injection of dye

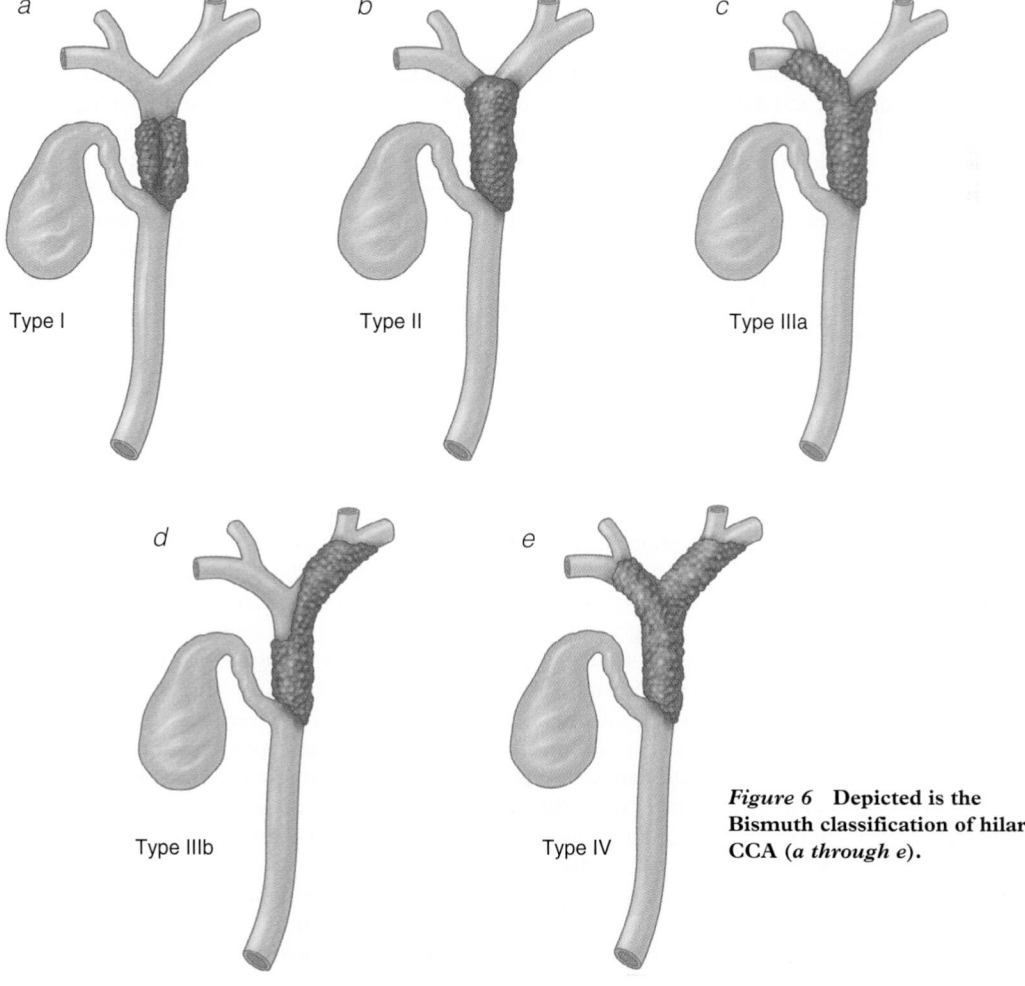

Figure 6   **Depicted is the Bismuth classification of hilar CCA (*a through e*).**

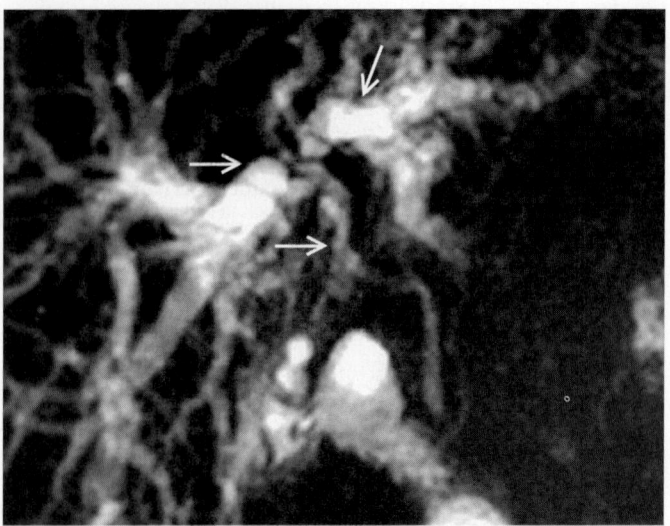

Figure 7 **Shown is Bismuth type II CCA. The right and left hepatic ducts are dilated (upper arrows), whereas the common hepatic duct is normal sized.**

above the malignant stricture is an integral part of ERCP. Once the dye has been injected, stents must be placed to prevent post-ERCP cholangitis. This process may involve insertion of bilateral stents, including a stent in the atrophic hemiliver. Bilateral stenting is disadvantageous, because the aim is to encourage atrophy of the hemiliver to be resected and hypertrophy of the hemiliver to be retained, and insertion of a stent in the atrophic side contravenes that aim. Starting with CT or MRI rather than with ERCP allows detection of any hilar CCA present simultaneously with detection of atrophy. At this point, the patient can be evaluated by a multidisciplinary team with expertise in this disease, and a decision can be made regarding which side of the biliary tree to decompress (if either). Whether stents should be employed in treating hilar CCA is debatable, but if a stent is inserted, only the side to be retained should be intubated. MRCP now provides resolution that is close to that obtained with direct cholangiography [*see Figure 7*].

ERCP does have one significant advantage, in that it allows brushings to be obtained; however, brushings at this high level in the biliary tree are even less sensitive than those at lower levels. Bile cytology has been tried, without much success. EUS has been employed to obtain diagnostic tissue, with some degree of success; however, because the biopsy needle passes through the peritoneal cavity, concerns have been expressed regarding possible tumor seeding. Such seeding has not been an issue with lower-duct cancers, because the biopsy tract is entirely within the future resection specimen. In many cases, a tissue diagnosis cannot be obtained preoperatively, and the diagnosis is based on the presence of a focal hilar stricture that causes jaundice.

Focal strictures of the upper bile ducts are strongly suggestive of cancer, but CCAs must also be differentiated from benign inflammatory tumors (also referred to as hepatic inflammatory pseudotumors and benign fibrosing disease).[26] These inflammatory masses mimic upper-duct CCAs but consist of chronic inflammatory cells and fibrous material. Even today, they are very difficult to distinguish from cancers before pathologic examination of a resected specimen.[27] Benign inflammatory tumors appear to occur most frequently in extrahepatic upper ducts, but they also occur intrahepatically and, less commonly, in lower ducts.

Gallbladder cancer may invade the porta hepatis and appear as a CCA, especially on ERCP. Gallstones are usually present.

Axial imaging usually shows thickening of the gallbladder wall or the presence of a mass involving the infundibulum. Mirizzi syndrome is another cause of a focal stricture of the middle or upper bile duct. This syndrome results from compression of the bile duct by a large gallstone in the infundibulum and is usually associated with severe inflammation of the gallbladder and the characteristic signs and symptoms of acute cholecystitis. The duct is typically bowed to the left rather than focally narrowed, as in cancer. Iatrogenic causes should be considered if the patient has had a cholecystectomy. On occasion, a stricture appears years after the operation. In these cases, the probable cause of the stricture is ischemic injury to the bile duct. The presence of clips close to or indenting the duct is a clue that such injury is a possibility. Choledocholithiasis may also cause strictures, especially if cholangitis has occurred. Strictures are also frequent with recurrent pyogenic (oriental) cholangitis. Other rare tumors of the bile duct (e.g., neuroendocrine tumors) may mimic cholangiocarcinoma.

Surgical staging Often, the first axial imaging test reveals only the presence of intrahepatic bile duct dilatation, which stops abruptly as the ducts merge in the hepatic hilum. This finding, however, leads to MRI or CT aimed at providing high-quality cholangiograms and angiograms of the hepatic arteries and the portal veins. Surgical staging of hilar CCA, unlike that of lower-duct CCA, requires exact knowledge of the macroscopic upper extent of the tumor in the bile duct. Furthermore, invasion of hepatic arteries and portal veins is common and frequently affects resectability. Thus, surgical staging also requires accurate determination of the extent of hepatic arterial or portal venous invasion and assessment of the degree of atrophy.

Bismuth type IV tumors are not resectable, except by liver transplantation. Type I through III tumors are resectable, provided that the main portal vein and the proper hepatic artery, as well as the portal vein and the hepatic artery to the side of the liver to be retained, are not invaded by tumor and that the side to be retained is not atrophic. Involvement of the main portal vein or the hepatic artery is a relative rather than an absolute contraindication; lesser degrees of involvement can be handled by means of vascular resection and reconstruction in specialized centers. Unusual combinations of events may prelude resection (e.g., atrophy on one side of the liver and invasion of the hepatic artery supplying the other side, or invasion of the portal vein to one side and the bile duct on the other side to the level of the secondary biliary branches).

MRI (with MRCP and magnetic resonance angiography [MRA]) or CT with the latest generation of scanners can provide complete information regarding the extent of bile duct involvement and the degree of vascular invasion. Doppler ultrasonography is also excellent for evaluating vascular invasion. ERCP may be used for additional assessment of the extent of the tumor on the side to be retained if a stent on that side is deemed necessary. The use of percutaneous cholangiography is controversial, the main concern being the risk of tumor seeding along the tube, into the peritoneal cavity, and onto the surface of the liver or the abdominal wall. Nevertheless, this procedure is used extensively in Japan, where surgeons have considerable experience with selective decompression of parts of the liver as a preoperative strategy.[28]

Assessment of distant metastases is achieved by means of axial imaging of the chest and the abdomen. Staging laparoscopy identifies 10% to 15% of cancers that are unresectable because of peritoneal or liver metastases. FDG-PET identifies about 15% of patients with distant metastases. At present, neither of these tests is routinely employed in this setting.

Table 5 American Joint Committee on Cancer TNM Clinical Classification of Gallbladder Cancer

Primary tumor (T)	TX	Primary tumor cannot be assessed
	T0	No evidence of primary tumor
	Tis	Carcinoma in situ
	T1	Tumor invades lamina propria or muscle layer
		T1a: Tumor invades lamina propria
		T1b: Tumor invades muscle layer
	T2	Tumor invades perimuscular connective tissue
	T3	Tumor perforates serosa (visceral peritoneum) or directly invades one adjacent organ (≤ 2 cm into liver)
	T4	Tumor extends > 2 cm into liver or invades two or more adjacent organs (e.g., duodenum, colon, pancreas, omentum, or extrahepatic bile ducts)
Regional lymph nodes (N)	NX	Regional lymph nodes cannot be assessed
	N0	No regional lymph node metastasis
	N1	Metastasis in cystic duct, pericholedochal, or hilar lymph nodes (i.e., in hepatoduodenal ligament)
	N2	Metastasis in peripancreatic (head only), periduodenal, periportal, celiac, or mesenteric lymph nodes
Distant metastasis (M)	MX	Distant metastasis cannot be assessed
	M0	No distant metastasis
	M1	Distant metastasis

Management *Preoperative preparation.* Unlike cancers of the lower bile duct, cancers of the upper bile duct usually necessitate major liver resection [*see 64 Procedures for Benign and Malignant Biliary Tract Disease*]. Consequently, it has been argued that the risk of postoperative hepatic failure may be lowered by preoperative decompression, especially decompression of the side to be retained, which has the dual purpose of allowing that side to recover function and of actually encouraging hypertrophy. On the other hand, stents may introduce bacteria and cause cholangitis. As noted (see above), selective percutaneous decompression is an accepted strategy in Japan; often, multiple stents are inserted.[28]

A reasonable strategy is to proceed to operation if (1) the patient is relatively young (< 70 years), (2) there are no serious comorbid conditions, (3) the jaundice has been present for less than 4 weeks, (4) the serum bilirubin concentration is lower than 10 mg/dl, (5) the future remnant liver will include more than 30% of the total liver mass, and (6) the patient has not undergone biliary instrumentation (which always contaminates the obstructed biliary tract). In all other cases, we routinely decompress the side of the liver to be retained and wait until the serum bilirubin concentration falls to 3 mg/dl. When the future remnant liver will include less than 30% to 35% of the total liver mass, portal vein embolization (PVE) of the side to be resected may be performed to induce hypertrophy of the remnant. Because resection for hilar CCA is a major procedure in a somewhat compromised liver, it is contraindicated in patients who are in poor general condition or who have major organ dysfunction.

Rationale for surgery. Patients with upper-duct CCA are candidates for resection if they have no distant metastases (including intrahepatic metastases) and if the tumor can be removed in its entirety by means of bile duct resection [*see 64 Procedures for Benign and Malignant Biliary Tract Disease*] combined with liver resection [*see 65 Hepatic Resection*]. The goal of resection is to achieve clear margins by removing the tumor, the portal and celiac lymph nodes, the side of the liver in which the ductal involvement is greater (via hemihepatectomy or trisectionectomy), and the caudate lobe. (The caudate lobe is resected because

cholangiocarcinomas tend to invade along the short caudate bile ducts, which enter the posterior surfaces of the main right and left bile ducts at the bifurcation of the common hepatic duct.)

Liver transplantation has been used successfully to manage Bismuth type IV tumors and is usually performed after neoadjuvant chemoradiation therapy and staging laparotomy in highly selected patients.[29]

GALLBLADDER CANCER

The incidence of gallbladder cancer in the United States is about 9,000 cases a year. This cancer almost always arises in patients with preexisting gallstones and is most often seen in elderly patients. Like ductal adenocarcinoma of the pancreas, it is highly malignant, and it tends to spread at an early stage to lymph nodes, to peritoneal surfaces, and through the bloodstream. AJCC staging criteria are helpful for planning management of this cancer [*see Tables 5 and 6*].

Clinical Evaluation

Gallbladder cancer is discovered incidentally either during performance of cholecystectomy for symptomatic cholelithiasis or when the tumor causes symptoms related to invasion of the bile duct or metastatic disease. In stage I and II disease, which is confined to the wall of the gallbladder, the symptoms are usually those of the associated stones—that is, the patient has biliary colic, and the cancer is silent. In later stages of disease, jaundice, weight loss, a palpable right upper quadrant mass, hepatomegaly, or ascites may develop. Jaundice occurs in about 50% of patients. It is a poor prognostic sign because it signifies extension of the tumor beyond the gallbladder and obstruction of the extrahepatic bile ducts. Consequently, most gallbladder cancer patients with jaundice have unresectable tumors. Because the signs and symptoms of gallbladder cancer are nonspecific, delays in diagnosis are common. As a result, most gallbladder cancers are not diagnosed until they have reached stage III or IV; thus, most of these aggressive tumors are unresectable at presentation, even when the patient is not jaundiced.

Investigative Studies

Laboratory tests In stages I and II, LFTs usually yield normal results. In later stages, laboratory test abnormalities may be noted that are not diagnostic but are consistent with bile duct obstruction. Elevated alkaline phosphatase and bilirubin levels are common. An elevation in the serum CA 19-9 concentration is the most helpful diagnostic indicator.

Table 6 American Joint Committee on Cancer Staging System for Gallbladder Cancer

Stage	T	N	M
Stage 0	Tis	N0	M0
Stage I	T1	N0	M0
Stage II	T2	N0	M0
Stage III	T1, T2	N1	M0
	T3	N0, N1	M0
Stage IVA	T4	N0, N1	M0
Stage IVB	Any T	N2	M0
	Any T	Any N	M1

Imaging Because gallbladder cancer is most curable in its early stages and because the symptoms in those stages are those of cholelithiasis, it is helpful to be aware of subtle signs of gallbladder cancer that are occasionally present on sonograms. These signs include thickening of the gallbladder wall, a mass projecting into the lumen, multiple masses or a fixed mass in the gallbladder, calcification of the gallbladder wall (so-called porcelain gallbladder), and an extracholecystic mass. Displacement of a stone to one side of the gallbladder should also be viewed with suspicion.

In later stages of disease, CT scans usually show a gallbladder mass with or without invasion of the liver or other adjacent organs. Obstruction of the bile duct produces the usual features associated with obstructive jaundice. Percutaneous CT-guided biopsy is a useful technique for confirming the diagnosis in patients with unresectable tumors. Porcelain gallbladder is a premalignant condition, though there is some evidence that the incidence of cancer depends on the pattern of calcification: selective mucosal calcification apparently carries a significant risk of cancer, whereas diffuse intramural calcification does not.[30] It seems reasonable to resect only tumors with the former pattern, but whenever there is a question about the pattern of calcification, one should err on the side of resection.

Surgical Staging

Staging of gallbladder cancer requires knowledge of the extent of direct invasion into the liver and other adjacent organs and tissues (especially the bile duct, the portal veins, and the hepatic arteries). As in hilar CCA, this information may be obtained by means of MRCP and MRA or CT with the latest-generation scanners. Staging laparoscopy is very helpful in managing gallbladder cancer. As many as 50% of patients with this disease are found to have peritoneal or liver metastases upon staging laparoscopy,[8] and as with carcinoma of the body of the pancreas, there are no useful palliative measures that can be undertaken at laparotomy.

Management

Rationale for surgery When early-stage gallbladder cancer is suspected on the basis of diagnostic imaging, open (rather than laparoscopic) cholecystectomy is probably the procedure of choice [see 63 Cholecystectomy and Common Bile Duct Exploration and 64 Procedures for Benign and Malignant Biliary Tract Disease]. Intraoperatively, if there is no evidence of spread outside the gallbladder, we recommend performing an extraserosal cholecystectomy, in which the fibrous liver plate is excised along with the gallbladder so that bare liver is exposed. It is possible to perform an extraserosal resection laparoscopically; however, in our opinion, this should not be attempted, because gallbladder perforation and bile spillage are more common with the laparoscopic version of the procedure. The negative consequences of tumor implantation or incomplete excision far outweigh any benefit that a minimally invasive approach might confer.

The excised specimen should be inked and a frozen section obtained. If there is gallbladder cancer in the specimen but the resection margins are clear and the tumor is a T1 lesion (i.e., has not penetrated the muscularis), the procedure is considered complete, in that lymph node metastases are uncommon with T1 tumors (incidence < 10%). However, lymph node metastases are present in 50% of patients with T2 lesions (i.e., tumors that have invaded the muscularis). Therefore, if margins are positive or the tumor is a T2 lesion, resection of segments 4b and 5 of the liver and dissection of portal and celiac lymph nodes, along with resection of the extrahepatic bile duct and hepaticojejunostomy, are recommended. If it is already clear at the commencement of the operation that the tumor is T2, one should proceed directly to liver, lymph node, and bile duct resection.

In more advanced stages of disease (T3 and T4), the aim is still excision with clear margins and resection of portal and celiac lymph nodes. To obtain clear local margins with these tumors, in addition to what is required for T2 tumors, more extensive hepatic resections—up to a trisectionectomy (resection of segments 4 through 8) [see Liver Cancer, Anatomic Considerations, below][31]—may be necessary, as well as resection of adjacent organs.

Incidentally discovered gallbladder cancer Gallbladder cancer may be an incidental finding at laparoscopic cholecystectomy, as it has been at open cholecystectomy. The incidence of this finding ranges from 0.3% to 1.0%. A concern that has arisen in the current era, in which the laparoscopic approach to cholecystectomy is dominant, is the risk of port-site implantation of tumor. Port-site implantation may simply be the result of contact between the malignancy and the tissues surrounding the port site at the time of gallbladder extraction; however, positive pressure pneumoperitoneum may also play a causative role. When evidence of gallbladder wall thickening is noted intraoperatively, the gallbladder should be extracted in a sac. The gallbladder should be inspected at the time of extraction, and any questionable areas should undergo biopsy.

If a gallbladder cancer is discovered at the time of operation, it should be treated without delay according to the principles stated earlier (i.e., depending on whether the margins on the excised gallbladder are clear and on the T stage of the tumor). From an oncologic viewpoint, it would seem ideal to resect the tissue around all trocar port sites. From a technical viewpoint, however, it would be very difficult and impractical to excise the full thickness of the abdominal wall circumferentially around four port sites, especially because the tract of the port site often is not at a 90° angle to the abdominal wall. If the gallbladder was extracted through a port site without having been placed into a bag, it is reasonable to attempt excision of that one port site.

Sometimes, cancer is suspected, but frozen-section examination is inconclusive and the definitive diagnosis of cancer is not made until the early postoperative period. More often, cancer is not suspected intraoperatively, and the diagnosis is made only when permanent sections of the gallbladder are examined. In these situations, patients with completely excised T1 lesions require no further therapy, and patients with higher-stage lesions should undergo reoperation in accordance with the principles outlined earlier (see above). Other appropriate reasons for not performing the additional surgery at the time of the cholecystectomy are (1) the desire to discuss the management scheme with the patient and (2) lack of experience with the procedure for T2 tumors. Not infrequently, patients are referred to hepatic-pancreatic-biliary (HPB) centers 10 to 14 days after surgery, which is an inopportune time for reoperation, especially if the first procedure was difficult. Surgery may then be delayed for 3 to 4 weeks. We restage patients with abdominal CT scans when they are referred with this diagnosis, and it is not unusual to find hepatic metastases when this is done. The survival rate is much higher after radical resection than after cholecystectomy, even when cholecystectomy was the first procedure.[32]

Gallbladder polyps Gallbladder polyps are discovered incidentally on ultrasonograms or CT scans or are diagnosed when they cause biliary colic. They may be malignant but are rarely so when less than 1 cm in diameter, especially when they are multiple. Most gallbladder polyps are less than 0.5 cm in diameter; these are almost always benign cholesterol polyps and may be followed if they are not giving rise to symptoms. Single polyps between 0.5 and 1 cm in diameter should probably be removed by means of cholecystectomy; multiple polyps in this size range should be followed. About one quarter of all single gallbladder polyps more than 1 cm in diameter are malignant, and such polyps should be treated as malignant as a matter of policy. Almost all polyps more than 1.8 cm in diameter are malignant.[33]

Liver Cancer

ANATOMIC CONSIDERATIONS

A long-standing problem in discussing any surgical liver disease, especially liver cancer, has been the confusing terminology applied to liver anatomy and the various hepatic resections. Fortunately, a lucid and cogent terminology has emerged that is sanctioned by both the International Hepato-Pancreato-Biliary Association (IHPBA) and the American Hepato-Pancreato-Biliary Association (AHPBA).[31] This terminology has been widely adopted around the world and translated into many languages. It may be briefly summarized as follows.

The fundamental principle is that the anatomic divisions of the liver are based on vascular and biliary anatomy rather than on surface markings [see Figure 8]. This is an important point because surgical resection is a process of isolating specific liver volumes serviced by specific vascular and biliary structures. The anatomic ramifications of the hepatic artery and the bile duct are regular and virtually identical. Liver anatomy is best understood by first following these structures through a series of orderly divisions. The branching of the portal vein on the right side is similar to that of the bile duct and the hepatic artery, but its branching on the left side, because of the fetus's need to use the umbilical portion of the portal vein as a conduit, is unusual.

The first-order division of the proper hepatic artery and the common hepatic duct into the right and left hepatic arteries and the right and left hepatic ducts, respectively, results in division of the liver into two parts (or volumes), referred to as the right and left hemilivers (or the right and left livers) [see Figure 8 and Table 7]. In this system of terminology, the term lobe is never used to denote a hemiliver, because it bears no relation to the internal vascular anatomy. The right hepatic artery supplies the right hemiliver, and the left hepatic artery supplies the left hemiliver. The right and left hepatic ducts drain the corresponding hemilivers. The plane between these two zones of vascular supply is called a watershed. The border or watershed of the first-order division is a plane that intersects the gallbladder fossa and the fossa for the inferior vena cava and is called the midplane of the liver.

The second-order division divides each of the hemilivers into two parts [see Figure 8 and Table 7], referred to as sections. The right hemiliver comprises the right anterior section and the right

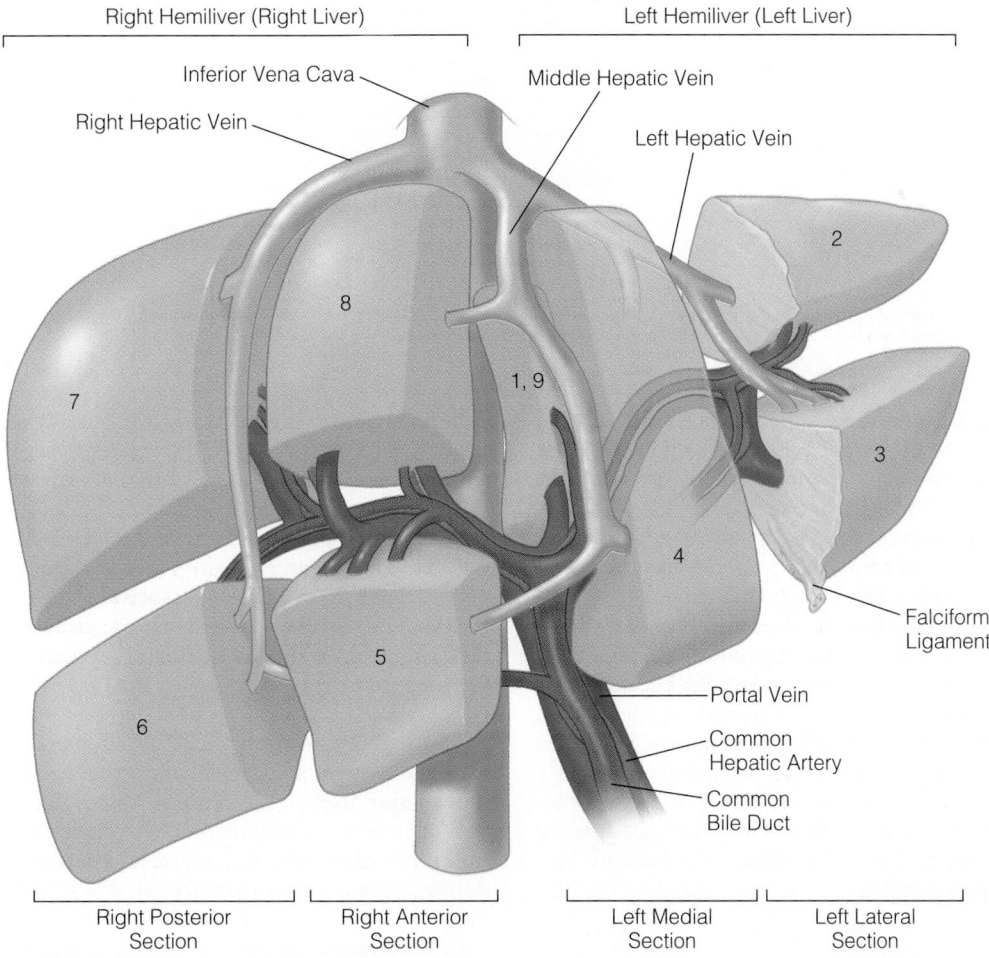

Figure 8 **Illustrated are the anatomic divisions of the liver according to IHPBA/AHPBA-sanctioned terminology, including first-order divisions (hemilivers), second-order divisions (sections) and third-order divisions (segments).**

Table 7 Brisbane 2000 Terminology for Hepatic Anatomy and Resections from IHPBA

Level of Division	Preferred Anatomic Term	Corresponding Couinaud Segments (Sg)	Preferred Term for Surgical Resection*	Comments
First order (hemiliver)	Right hemiliver *or* Right liver	Sg 5–8 (± caudate lobe†)	Right hepatectomy *or* Right hemihepatectomy (stipulate ± caudate lobe)	The border or watershed separating the two hemilivers is a plane that intersects the gallbladder fossa and the inferior vena cava fossa; this plane is referred to as the midplane of the liver
	Left hemiliver *or* Left liver	Sg 2–4 (± caudate lobe)	Left hepatectomy *or* Left hemihepatectomy (stipulate ± caudate lobe)	
Second order (section)	Right anterior section	Sg 5, 8	Right anterior sectionectomy	The borders or watersheds separating the sections within the hemilivers are planes referred to as the right intersectional plane (for which there is no surface marking) and the left intersectional plane (which passes through the umbilical fissure and the attachment of the falciform ligament)
	Right posterior section	Sg 6, 7	Right posterior sectionectomy	
	Left medial section	Sg 4	Left medial sectionectomy	
	Left lateral section	Sg 2, 3	Left lateral sectionectomy	
	—	Sg 4–8 (± caudate lobe)	Right trisectionectomy (preferred) *or* Extended right hepatectomy *or* Extended right hemihepatectomy (stipulate ± caudate lobe)	
	—	Sg 2, 3, 4, 5, 8 (± caudate lobe)	Left trisectionectomy (preferred) *or* Extended left hepatectomy *or* Extended left hemihepatectomy (stipulate ± caudate lobe)	
Third order (segment)	Segments 1–9	Any Sg	Segmentectomy (stipulate Sg— e.g., segmentectomy 7)	The borders or watersheds of the segments are planes referred to as the intersegmental planes
	Two contiguous segments	Any two Sg in continuity	Bisegmentectomy (stipulate Sg— e.g., bisegmentectomy 7, 8)	

*It is also permissible to refer to any resection in terms of its third-order components. Thus, a left hemihepatectomy may be referred to as a resection Sg 2–4 (or 1–4).
†The caudate lobe comprises segments 1 and 9. IHPBA—International Hepato-Pancreato-Biliary Association

posterior section. These sections are supplied by a right anterior sectional hepatic artery and a right posterior sectional hepatic artery and are drained by a right anterior sectional hepatic duct and a right posterior sectional hepatic duct. The left hemiliver comprises the left medial section and the left lateral section. These sections are supplied by a left medial sectional hepatic artery and a left lateral sectional hepatic artery and are drained by a left medial sectional hepatic duct and a left lateral sectional hepatic duct.

The third-order division divides the liver into nine segments, each of which has its own segmental artery and bile duct [*see Figure 8 and Table 7*]. The caudate lobe, a unique portion of the liver that is separate from the right and left hemilivers, comprises segments 1 and 9. The left lateral section comprises segments 2 and 3; the left medial section comprises segment 4 (which is sometimes further divided into segments 4a and 4b); the right anterior section comprises segments 5 and 8; and the right posterior section comprises segments 6 and 7.

PRIMARY CANCERS

Hepatocellular Cancer

Hepatocellular cancer (HCC), or hepatoma, is the fifth most common cancer in the world. About 90% of cases arise in patients with chronic liver disease, especially when the disease has progressed to cirrhosis. Although any condition that produces cirrhosis may lead to HCC, the most common cause is viral hepatitis. In the United States, some 3 million people are infected with hepatitis C virus (HCV), and more than 1 million people have liver disease associated with hepatitis B virus (HBV). HCV infection is much more likely to lead to HCC than HBV infection is. AJCC staging criteria are useful for planning the management of liver cancer [*see Tables 8 and 9*].

Clinical evaluation The usual presentation of sporadic HCC consists of pain, mass, and systemic symptoms of cancer, though the disease may also be discovered incidentally. HCC occurring as a complication of liver disease may present similarly, but it is often manifested first as a deterioration of liver function with the onset of jaundice, ascites, or encephalopathy.

Investigative studies Screening programs are employed in high-risk populations. These programs, which use α-fetoprotein (AFP) levels and ultrasonographic examination of the liver to detect early HCC, may detect asymptomatic tumors.

Table 8 American Joint Committee on Cancer TNM Clinical Classification of Adult Primary Liver Cancer

Primary tumor (T)	TX	Primary tumor cannot be assessed
	T0	No evidence of primary tumor
	T1	Solitary tumor without vascular invasion
	T2	Solitary tumor with vascular invasion; multiple tumors, none > 5 cm in greatest dimension
	T3	Multiple tumors > 5 cm in greatest dimension or tumor involving major branch of portal or hepatic vein
	T4	Tumor or tumors with direct invasion of adjacent organs (other than gallbladder) or visceral peritoneum
Regional lymph nodes (N)	NX	Regional lymph nodes cannot be assessed
	N0	No regional lymph node metastasis
	N1	Regional lymph node metastasis
Distant metastasis (M)	MX	Distant metastasis cannot be assessed
	M0	No distant metastasis
	M1	Distant metastasis

The diagnosis of sporadic HCC is based on elevation of AFP levels (an indicator with 50% to 60% sensitivity) and the presence of a hepatic mass on axial images. HCCs typically demonstrate hypervascularity, which is best seen on arterial-phase images [*see Figure 9*]. A pseudocapsule is often visualized, which is best seen on portal venous–phase images. Multifocality is also common in HCC, and this finding often serves to differentiate it from other hepatic neoplasms. Routine biopsy is not indicated in patients with a characteristic mass, those who have a mass and an elevated AFP level, or those who are symptomatic and require treatment for pain. HCC may be very well differentiated and difficult to distinguish from hepatic adenoma and focal nodular hyperplasia on biopsy. It may also be hard to distinguish from cirrhotic nodules. Biopsy is associated with a small risk of bleeding or tumor seeding.

Surgical staging Staging of sporadic HCC requires axial imaging of the abdomen and imaging of the chest. FDG-PET scanning is only marginally useful: HCCs are typically well differentiated, and as a result, only 50% of the tumors are visualized. Staging laparoscopy is helpful: additional tumors are found in about 15% of patients.[34]

Staging also requires evaluation of the extent of liver disease. The Child-Pugh classification is used to determine operability. With few exceptions, resection is limited to Child class A patients with near-normal bilirubin levels (< 1.5 mg/dl), a normal or marginally raised prothrombin time (PT), and no or minimal portal hypertension. The extent of resection must be tailored to the severity of the liver

disease. For instance, resection of more than two segments is limited to patients with normal liver function. Too-extensive resection puts the patients at risk for liver failure in the postoperative period. In Japan and China, indocyanine green (ICG) clearance is used in Child class A patients to determine the possible extent of resection.

Management *Rationale for surgery.* The rationale for surgery is clear in patients without liver disease or in Child class B or C patients with chronic liver disease. The rationale for surgery in Child class A patients, however, remains controversial.

Partial liver resection [*see 65 Hepatic Resection*] is the procedure of choice for sporadic HCC in patients with normal livers. In Child class B or C patients with chronic liver disease, liver resection can be hazardous, and orthotopic liver transplantation (OLT) is the procedure of choice. To justify the use of donor organs, however, it is necessary to select patients with HCC so that the long-term outcome of OLT for HCC is similar to that of OLT for benign conditions. To achieve this goal, OLT is restricted to patients with a single tumor less than 5 cm in diameter or to patients with as many as three tumors, none of which are more than 3 cm in diameter (the Milan criteria). These criteria have been shown to be associated with OLT outcomes comparable to those for benign conditions.[35]

In Child class A patients with liver disease, hepatic resection and OLT are options if the Milan criteria are met. The optimal therapeutic approach in this situation has been the subject of considerable debate, with proponents arguing for one of two strategies—namely, (1) primary OLT or (2) resection followed by OLT if HCC recurs, provided that the patients still meet criteria for OLT (so-called salvage OLT). A complete discussion of this controversy is beyond the scope of this chapter. Currently, it would seem that the best strategy in patients who meet the criteria for OLT is to perform primary OLT for HCV-associated disease[36] and to perform resection and salvage OLT for HBV-associated disease[37] and other HCCs of non-HCV origin. In patients who do not meet the OLT criteria, resection would be performed even if the tumor is of HCV origin. At present, there is a trend toward liberalizing the OLT criteria to include single tumors 6 or 7 cm in diameter, especially if the source of the organ is a living donor.

When OLT is to be performed, it is important that the waiting time be short; these tumors progress over a timescale of a few months, and when viewed on an intention-to-treat basis, the results of OLT deteriorate significantly if the waiting time is long.[38] In the United States, this concern has been dealt with by

Table 9 American Joint Committee on Cancer Staging System for Adult Primary Liver Cancer

Stage	T	N	M
Stage I	T1	N0	M0
Stage II	T2	N0	M0
Stage IIIA	T3	N0	M0
Stage IIIB	T4	N0	M0
Stage IIIC	Any T	N1	M0
Stage IV	Any T	Any N	M0

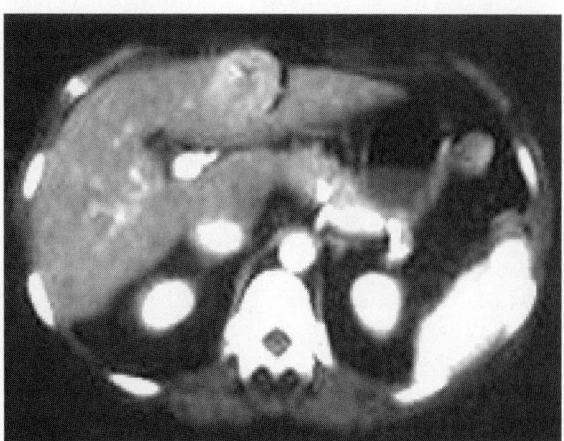

Figure 9 **CT scan shows a hypervascular HCC of the left liver.**

the introduction of the Model for End-stage Liver Disease (MELD) scoring system, which gives priority to recipients with HCC. It is common in the United States—and usual in countries with longer waiting times—to inhibit the growth of the HCC with various bridging-to-transplantation strategies during the waiting period for OLT. Such strategies include systemic chemotherapy, local treatments (e.g., radiofrequency [RF] ablation and alcohol injection), transarterial chemoembolization (TACE), and even resection of the HCC (so-called bridge resection).

In patients with nondiseased livers, the extent of the resection depends on the size and position of the tumor. As much as 70% of the liver may be safely excised when normal liver function is present. The size of the future hepatic remnant may be determined by means of imaging. PVE of the side of the liver to be resected may be performed preoperatively to increase the size of the future remnant. It may also be used for this purpose in patients with liver disease. In these patients, PVE functions as a test of the liver's ability to regenerate. Failure to respond to PVE is itself a contraindication to surgery in patients with chronic liver disease.

As a rule, liver resections for HCC should be anatomic [see 65 Hepatic Resection]. Recurrence rates are higher with nonanatomic resections because HCCs grow along portal veins and metastasize locally within segments, sections, or hemilivers, depending on how far they reach back along the portal veins. When HCC reaches the main portal vein, resection is generally contraindicated; the results are very poor in this situation.

Intrahepatic Cholangiocarcinoma

Clinical evaluation   Intrahepatic CCAs arise from intrahepatic bile ducts. There are three types: a mass-forming type (MF), a periductal infiltrating type (PI), and a type that grows as an intraductal papillary tumor (IG). The MF type is by far the most common. Intrahepatic CCA tumor usually occurs in normal livers. The presentation is similar to that of sporadic HCC.

Investigative studies   On diagnostic imaging, the appearance of intrahepatic CCA is suggestive of a secondary tumor [see Figure 10]. Unlike diagnosis of HCC, diagnosis of intrahepatic CCA usually requires a biopsy, which reveals an adenocarcinoma

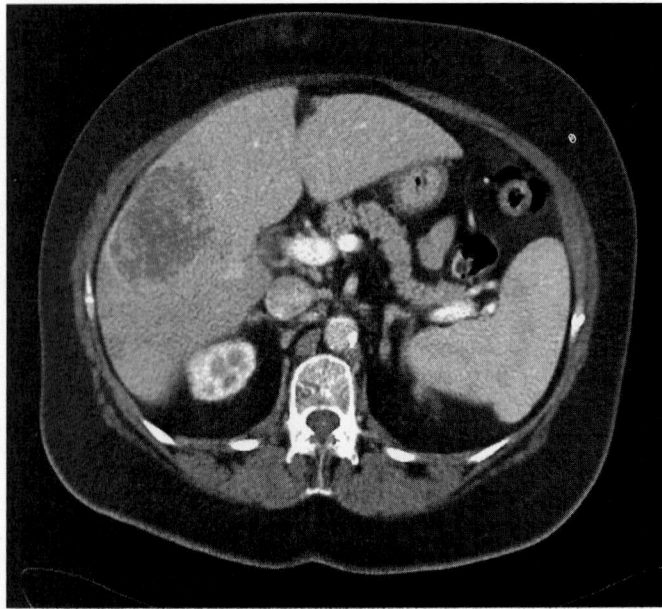

Figure 10   **CT scan shows a mass-forming intrahepatic CCA.**

that is indistinguishable from a hepatic metastasis arising from a primary adenocarcinoma in one of several intra-abdominal or extra-abdominal sites. Special stains may be helpful in differentiating this tumor from a true secondary malignancy, but the differentiation is rarely certain. An elevated CA 19-9 concentration is strongly suggestive of this diagnosis if it is higher than 100 U/ml. To make the diagnosis of intrahepatic CCA, primary tumors in other sites must be excluded by means of axial imaging of the chest, the abdomen, and the pelvis; upper and lower GI endoscopy; and mammography. FDG-PET scanning is another means by which an extrahepatic primary may be identified, but it has not been fully evaluated in this setting.

Surgical staging   FDG-PET scanning appears to be a promising staging tool for identifying portal lymph node and distant metastases when the primary is actually an intrahepatic CCA. Portal lymph node metastases are a contraindication to resection in patients with MF tumors; the results of resection in this situation are very poor. Left-side tumors may metastasize to lymph nodes at the cardia of the stomach and along the lesser curvature.

Management   The considerations related to resection for intrahepatic CCA are similar to those for sporadic HCC (see above). Liver transplantation generally is not performed for this tumor, because of the typically poor results.

SECONDARY CANCERS

Colorectal Metastases

Clinical evaluation and investigative studies   About 50% of the 150,000 patients who are diagnosed with colorectal cancer annually in the United States either have or will have liver metastases. About 10% of patients with these colorectal metastases (CRMs) are eligible for liver resection. CRMs may be diagnosed either at the time of treatment of the primary colorectal cancer (synchronous tumors) or at a later stage (metachronous tumors).

Synchronous tumors are diagnosed by means of either preoperative CT scanning [see Figure 11] or intraoperative palpation. LFTs may show elevations (especially of the serum alkaline phosphatase level), but these results are not specific. CEA levels are not helpful as long as the primary tumor is in place. Metachronous tumors are most often diagnosed in the course of a postcolectomy surveillance program, either by imaging the liver with CT scans or FDG-PET scans or by detecting a rise in the CEA level. When synchronous metastases are discovered preoperatively, a FDG-PET scan should be done to complete the staging.

Surgical staging   In about 25% of patients, FDG-PET scanning changes management by detecting unsuspected extrahepatic or intrahepatic disease. Sometimes, it demonstrates that apparent metastases are actually benign lesions. Second primaries are not uncommon in patients with metachronous lesions; accordingly, such patients should also be staged by means of colonoscopy, if this procedure was not done in the preceding 6 months, as well as FDG-PET scanning. Staging laparoscopy adds little to staging if an FDG-PET scan has been done.

Intraoperative staging consists of careful palpation of intra-abdominal structures, including hepatic and portal venous lymph nodes. In patients with metachronous lesions, however, palpation of the entire abdomen may be limited by adhesions from previous operations. IOUS of the liver may also detect unsuspected lesions, though this is less likely if the patient has already been staged by means of FDG-PET.

a *b*

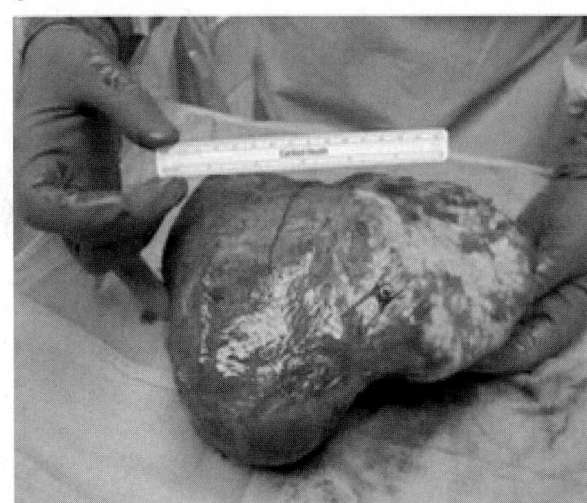

Figure 11   (*a*) **CT scan shows a single large CRM.** (*b*) **Shown is the specimen after resection.**

The main value of FDG-PET in this setting is its ability to discover unsuspected extrahepatic disease. In so doing, it helps eliminate futile hepatic resections. If a patient with extrahepatic disease is treated with hepatic resection, a "recurrence" is inevitable. Elimination of pointless resections has a positive effect on survival: a 2004 study from our institution found that the overall 5-year survival rate after FDG-PET was about 60%, compared with 40% after conventional imaging.[39] Furthermore, the study showed that after FDG-PET scanning, the classic prognostic factors of the secondary tumor (e.g., tumor number and tumor size) were no longer significant; rather, the most important prognostic factor was the grade of the primary tumor. FDG-PET–scanned patients with poorly differentiated primary tumors did very poorly in terms of overall survival after hepatic resection.[39] Currently, standard PET scanners are rapidly being replaced with CT-PET scanners, which fuse the images and provide superior diagnosis and staging. For planning surgical extirpation, however, the level of detail provided by high-quality contrast-enhanced CT or MRI is also required.

Management   *Rationale for surgery.*   The criteria that determine eligibility for resection are (1) that the primary tumor has been or can be completely resected, (2) that (with uncommon exceptions) there is no extrahepatic tumor (other than the primary), and (3) that it is possible to resect all tumors in the liver while leaving enough of a hepatic remnant to ensure that hepatic failure does not develop postoperatively. The considerations governing the extent of the resection and the use of PVE are similar to those for sporadic HCC.

Treatment of multiple tumors is much more common with CRMs than with HCC. However, nonanatomic resections are as effective as anatomic resections as long as the resection margin is microscopically clear. The traditional view has been that resection margins of 1 cm are mandatory. Whereas 1 cm margins may still be a reasonable goal, margins as narrow as 1 mm are satisfactory and are probably as effective as traditional margins, provided that they are free of microscopic and gross cancer. When close margins are expected, transection of the liver with a saline-linked RF ablation device may be useful, in that this device leaves a margin of devitalized tissue in the patient, as well as in the specimen.[40] When the margin is very close, it may be extended by painting the cut surface of the hepatic remnant with the RF device.

Synchronous resection of the primary tumor and the liver metastases has proved to be safe[41] and is desired by many patients. The decision to proceed with hepatic resection should not be made until resection of the primary tumor has been completed and it has been determined that the margins are clear and the patient is stable. Some patients with a small number of lung lesions in addition to liver lesions have been cured by resection.

Ablation of colorectal metastases.   In situ destruction of tumors with cryotherapy or RF ablation may expand the surgeon's ability to eradicate CRMs localized to the liver.[42] RF ablation has largely supplanted cryotherapy in this context as a result of its lower incidence of complications and greater ease of use. Ablation may be used either as an adjunct to operative management or as the sole treatment when there are many metastases (but usually < 10). The efficacy of RF ablation as an adjunct to surgery remains to be determined. It is doubtful, however, that using this modality alone to eradicate multiple lesions will improve overall survival significantly, because the tumor biology in such cases is likely to be that of an aggressive tumor. FDG-PET scans should be performed in all such patients; the likelihood of discovering extrahepatic tumors increases as the number of hepatic tumors increases.[39]

RF ablation is not recommended for treatment of resectable metastases: it is not approved for this purpose, and using it in this way would mean substituting an unproven therapy of unknown efficacy for a proven therapy of known value. If a consenting patient with resectable metastases nevertheless insists on this less invasive therapy, the surgeon should document that the preceding considerations have been explained to him or her. RF ablation may be applied by means of open, laparoscopic, or percutaneous methods. There is good reason to believe that targeting ability is degraded as one moves to less invasive methods. This consideration should also be explained to patients, though undoubtedly there are some patients who, because of comorbid conditions, are candidates only for percutaneous or laparoscopic approaches.

Neuroendocrine Metastases

Neuroendocrine metastases are characteristically slow growing. Some are functional, especially if they arise from the ileum; metastatic liver disease from this source may produce carcinoid syndrome.

[111]In-pentetreotide imaging (OctreoScan; Mallinckrodt Inc., Hazelwood, Missouri) provides staging information comparable to that provided by FDG-PET in patients with CRMs.

The aims of surgical treatment are (1) to eradicate the cancer and (2) to reduce hormonal symptoms. The considerations regarding tumor eradication for neuroendocrine metastases are similar to those for CRMs—that is, resection should be performed if all cancer can be removed and no extrahepatic cancer is detectable. In highly symptomatic patients in whom conservative therapy with octreotide has failed, debulking the tumor by means of either chemoembolization or surgery may provide relief. The former is more suitable for patients with multiple small, diffuse metastases, whereas the latter is preferred for patients with large localized tumors. RF ablation may also be employed, either combined with surgical treatment or alone; this is an excellent use of this procedure, in that the aim is cytoreduction rather than eradication. Debulking tumors in asymptomatic patients with the intention of extending survival is controversial.

Noncolorectal, Nonneuroendocrine Metastases

Occasionally, liver metastases from other primary sites behave like CRMs, in that they are localized to part of the liver in the absence of extrahepatic disease. Such patients can be managed according to the same approach employed for CRMs, though the outcome is somewhat less satisfactory. Tumors that have been treated in this way with acceptable results include breast cancers, renal cell cancers, gastric cancers, acinar cell cancers of the pancreas, and ovarian cancers. Liver resection for more aggressive malignancies (e.g., metastases from gallbladder cancer and pancreatic ductal adenocarcinomas) can be expected to yield very poor results.

INCIDENTALLY DISCOVERED ASYMPTOMATIC HEPATIC MASS

Now that transaxial imaging of the abdomen is commonly performed for a variety of complaints, the problem of the incidentally discovered asymptomatic hepatic mass is being encountered with increased frequency. Generally, cysts are easily distinguished from solid tumors; the main diagnostic issue is differentiation of the various solid lesions.

The differential diagnosis of the benign solid hepatic mass includes hepatic adenoma, focal nodular hyperplasia (FNH), focal fatty infiltration, cavernous hemangioma, and other rare neoplasms (e.g., mesenchymal hamartoma and teratoma)—all of which must be distinguished not only from one another but also from malignant tumors. In the past, several diagnostic tests (e.g., ultrasonography, CT, sulfur colloid scanning, and angiography) were used to differentiate these neoplasms. Currently, our usual practice is to perform MRI with gadolinium contrast enhancement, which generally allows accurate differentiation among benign tumors with a single test. Cavernous hemangiomas are usually easy to distinguish because they have a characteristic appearance on MRI (hypointense on T_1-weighted images, very intense on T_2-weighted images, and filling in from the periphery with gadolinium injection); if they are asymptomatic, they need not be resected. It is important to distinguish asymptomatic FNHs from hepatic adenomas: whereas resection is recommended for adenomas, because of their potential for hemorrhage or malignant degeneration, asymptomatic FNHs can safely be observed. An FNH is nearly isointense on T_1- and T_2- weighted images; it shows slightly more enhancement than normal liver parenchyma in the early phase after contrast injection, then becomes isointense. A central scar is often, but not always, seen. Conversely, a hepatic adenoma exhibits strong early-phase enhancement with contrast administration, and it tends to be hyperintense on T_1-weighted images.

Given that a symptomatic hepatic mass is usually treated with resection, preoperative biopsy for tissue diagnosis is rarely necessary or desirable. Modern noninvasive radiologic tests, in conjunction with a careful patient history, are often quite accurate in predicting histologic diagnosis. Biopsy of hepatic lesions should not be performed indiscriminately, because there is a small risk of complications or tumor tracking and because biopsy results often do not change management. As a rule, biopsies should be performed when definitive surgical intervention is not planned and when pathologic confirmation is necessary for institution of nonsurgical therapy.

References

1. Cleary SP, Gryfe R, Guindi M, et al: Prognostic factors in resected pancreatic adenocarcinoma: analysis of actual 5-year survivors. J Am Coll Surg 198:722, 2004

2. Patel AH, Harnois DM, Klee GG, et al: The utility of CA 19-9 in the diagnoses of cholangiocarcinoma in patients without primary sclerosing cholangitis. Am J Gastroenterol 95:204, 2000

3. Logrono R, Wong JY: Reporting the presence of significant epithelial atypia in pancreaticobiliary brush cytology specimens lacking evidence of obvious carcinoma: impact on performance measures. Acta Cytologica 48:613, 2004

4. Hardacre JM, Iacobuzio-Donahue CA, Sohn TA, et al: Results of pancreaticoduodenectomy for lymphoplasmacytic sclerosing pancreatitis. Ann Surg 237:853, 2003

5. Kahl S, Malfertheiner P: Role of endoscopic ultrasound in the diagnosis of patients with solid pancreatic masses. Dig Dis 22:26, 2004

6. Strasberg SM, Middleton WD, Teefey SA, et al: Management of diagnostic dilemmas of the pancreas by ultrasonographically guided laparoscopic biopsy. Surgery 126:736, 1999

7. Strasberg SM, Drebin JA, Mokadam NA, et al: Prospective trial of a blood supply–based technique of pancreaticojejunostomy: effect on anastomotic failure in the Whipple procedure. J Am Coll Surg 194:746, 2002

8. Vollmer CM, Drebin JA, Middleton WD, et al: Utility of staging laparoscopy in subsets of peripancreatic and biliary malignancies. Ann Surg 235:1, 2002

9. Nieveen van Dijkum EJ, Romijn MG, Terwee CB, et al: Laparoscopic staging and subsequent palliation in patients with peripancreatic carcinoma. Ann Surg 237:66, 2003

10. Povoski SP, Karpeh MS Jr, Conlon KC, et al: Preoperative biliary drainage: impact on intraoperative bile cultures and infectious morbidity and mortality after pancreaticoduodenectomy. J Gastrointest Surg 3:496, 1999

11. Pedrazzoli S, DiCarlo V, Dionigi R, et al: Standard versus extended lymphadenectomy associated with pancreatoduodenectomy in the surgical treatment of adenocarcinoma of the head of the pancreas: a multicenter, prospective, randomized study. Lymphadenectomy Study Group. Ann Surg 228:508, 1998

12. Sindelar WF: Clinical experience with regional pancreatectomy for adenocarcinoma of the pancreas. Arch Surg 124:127, 1989

13. Wenger FA, Jacobi CA, Haubold K, et al: [Gastrointestinal quality of life after duodenopancreatectomy in pancreatic carcinoma. Preliminary results of a prospective randomized study: pancreatoduodenectomy or pylorus-preserving pancreatoduodenectomy]. Chirurg 70:1454, 1999

14. Shoup M, Conlon KC, Klimstra D, et al: Is extended resection for adenocarcinoma of the body or tail of the pancreas justified? J Gastrointest Surg 7:946, 2003

15. Fernandez-del Castillo C, Rattner DW, Warshaw AL: Further experience with laparoscopy and peritoneal cytology in the staging of pancreatic cancer. Br J Surg 82:1127, 1995

16. Strasberg SM, Drebin JA, Linehan D: Radical antegrade modular pancreatosplenectomy. Surgery 133:521, 2003

17. Sarr MG, Murr M, Smyrk TC, et al: Primary cystic neoplasms of the pancreas. Neoplastic disorders of emerging importance: current state-of-the-art and unanswered questions. J Gastrointest Surg 7:417, 2003

18. Hammel P, Levy P, Voitot H, et al: Preoperative cyst fluid analysis is useful for the differential diagnosis of

cystic lesions of the pancreas. Gastroenterology 108:1230, 1995

19. Shoup M, Brennan MF, McWhite K, et al: The value of splenic preservation with distal pancreatectomy. Arch Surg 137:164, 2002

20. Tagaya N, Kasama K, Suzuki N, et al: Laparoscopic resection of the pancreas and review of the literature. Surg Endosc 17:201, 2003

21. Kiely JM, Nakeeb A, Komorowski RA, et al: Cystic pancreatic neoplasms: enucleate or resect? J Gastrointest Surg 7:890, 2003

22. D'Angelica M, Brennan MF, Suriawinata AA, et al: Intraductal papillary mucinous neoplasms of the pancreas: an analysis of clinicopathologic features and outcome. Ann Surg 239:400, 2004

23. Sohn TA, Yeo CJ, Cameron JL, et al: Intraductal papillary mucinous neoplasms of the pancreas: an updated experience. Ann Surg 239:788, 2004

24. Kim HJ, Lee KT, Kim SH, et al: Differential diagnosis of intrahepatic bile duct dilatation without demonstrable mass on ultrasonography or CT: benign versus malignancy. J Gastroenterol Hepatol 18:1287, 2003

25. Bismuth H, Nakache R, Diamond T: Management strategies in resection for hilar cholangiocarcinoma. Ann Surg 215:31, 1992

26. Stamatakis JD, Howard ER, Williams R: Benign inflammatory tumour of the common bile duct. Br J Surg 66:257, 1979

27. Knoefel WT, Prenzel KL, Peiper M, et al: Klatskin tumors and Klatskin mimicking lesions of the biliary tree. Eur J Surg Oncol 29:658, 2003

28. Kamiya S, Nagino M, Kanazawa H, et al: The value of bile replacement during external biliary drainage: an analysis of intestinal permeability, integrity, and microflora. Ann Surg 239:510, 2004

29. Heimbach JK, Gores GJ, Haddock MG, et al: Liver transplantation for unresectable perihilar cholangiocarcinoma. Semin Liver Dis 24:201, 2004

30. Stephen AE, Berger DL: Carcinoma in the porcelain gallbladder: a relationship revisited. Surgery 129:699, 2001

31. Terminology Committee of the International Hepato-Pancreato-Biliary Association: Brisbane 2000 terminology of liver anatomy and resections. HPB 2:333, 2000

32. Fong Y, Jarnagin W, Blumgart LH: Gallbladder cancer: comparison of patients presenting initially for definitive operation with those presenting after prior noncurative intervention. Ann Surg 232:557, 2000

33. Kubota K, Bandai Y, Noie T, et al: How should polypoid lesions of the gallbladder be treated in the era of laparoscopic cholecystectomy? Surgery 117:481, 1995

34. Lo CM, Lai EC, Liu CL, et al: Laparoscopy and laparoscopic ultrasonography avoid exploratory laparotomy in patients with hepatocellular carcinoma. Ann Surg 227:527, 1998

35. Mazzaferro V, Regalia E, Doci R, et al: Liver transplantation for the treatment of small hepatocellular carcinomas in patients with cirrhosis. N Engl J Med 334:693, 1996

36. Adam R, Azoulay D, Castaing D, et al: Liver resection as a bridge to transplantation for hepatocellular carcinoma on cirrhosis: a reasonable strategy? Ann Surg 238:508, 2003

37. Poon RT, Fan ST, Lo CM, et al: Long-term survival and pattern of recurrence after resection of small hepatocellular carcinoma in patients with preserved liver function: implications for a strategy of salvage transplantation. Ann Surg 235:373, 2002

38. Llovet JM, Fuster J, Bruix J: Intention-to-treat analysis of surgical treatment for early hepatocellular carcinoma: resection versus transplantation. Hepatology 30:1434, 1999

39. Fernandez FG, Drebin JA, Linehan DC, et al: Five-year survival after resection of hepatic metastases from colorectal cancer in patients screened by positron emission tomography with F-18 fluorodeoxyglucose (FDG-PET). Ann Surg 240:438, 2004

40. Topp SA, McClurken M, Lipson D, et al: Saline-linked surface radiofrequency ablation: factors affecting steam popping and depth of injury in the pig liver. Ann Surg 239:518, 2004

41. de Santibanes E, Lassalle FB, McCormack L, et al: Simultaneous colorectal and hepatic resections for colorectal cancer: postoperative and longterm outcomes. J Am Coll Surg 195:196, 2002

42. Strasberg SM, Linehan D: Radiofrequency ablation of liver tumors. Curr Probl Surg 40:459, 2003

Acknowledgment

Figures 4, 6, and 8   Tom Moore.

Clifford S. Cho, M.D., and Layton F. Rikkers, M.D., F.A.C.S.

Clinical strategies for managing portal hypertension have undergone significant refinements over the past half-century. This evolution has been driven by advances in our understanding of the physiology of both the disease and the therapies employed against it. Today, clinical management of the portal hypertensive patient is a truly multidisciplinary endeavor, requiring the coordinated efforts of skilled intensivists, gastroenterologists, hepatologists, interventional radiologists, and surgeons. Nevertheless, portal hypertension and its manifold complications remain some of the most vexing problems encountered in modern medicine and surgery.

In this chapter, we briefly review portal venous anatomy and the pathophysiology of portal hypertension [*see Sidebar* Portal Hypertension: Anatomic and Physiologic Considerations]; however, our main focus is on current practical approaches to managing portal hypertension and its associated sequelae (variceal bleeding, ascites, and hepatic encephalopathy). Of particular relevance to surgeons is that the role of surgical therapy has shifted significantly. Operative treatment now occupies only the final steps in modern treatment protocols for portal hypertension—that is, it serves as a form of salvage for intractable cases that are refractory to other forms of therapy.

Clinical Evaluation

The ultimate aims of diagnostic evaluation in a patient with portal hypertension are (1) to determine the cause of portal hypertension [*see Table 1*], (2) to estimate hepatic functional reserve, (3) to define the portal venous anatomy and assess hemodynamic status, and (4) to identify the site of GI hemorrhage (if present). Any history of chronic alcohol abuse, hepatitis, or exposure to hepatotoxins raises the suspicion of cirrhotic liver disease. Confirmatory evidence of chronic liver disease on physical examination may be found in the form of jaundice, chest wall spider angiomata, palmar erythema, Dupuytren contractures, testicular atrophy, or gynecomastia. Ascites, splenomegaly, caput medusae, encephalopathic alterations in mental status, and asterixis are all suggestive of portal hypertension.

Investigative Studies

Laboratory studies can also provide indicators of hepatic dysfunction. The hypersplenism that often accompanies cirrhosis can produce mild to moderate pancytopenia. Anemia may also reflect variceal hemorrhage, hemolysis, or simply the chronic malnutrition or bone-marrow suppression associated with chronic alcoholism. Associated hyperaldosteronism, emesis, or diarrhea may give rise to electrolyte derangements, including hyponatremia, hypokalemia, metabolic alkalosis, and prerenal azotemia. Coagulopathy is usually attributable to chronic deficiencies in clotting factors that are normally synthesized by the liver; thus, elevation of the prothrombin time (PT) or the international normalized ratio (INR) often reflects the degree of chronic hepatic impairment. Similarly, the degree of hyperbilirubinemia can be a measure of both acute and chronic hepatic dysfunction. Hepato-

cellular necrosis results in marked elevations in serum aminotransferases that are readily observed in patients with chronic active viral or alcoholic hepatitis. An alanine aminotransferase (ALT)–aspartate aminotransferase (AST) ratio of 2 or higher is often seen in patients with alcoholic liver disease.

The Child-Pugh scoring system is a useful tool for quantifying hepatic functional reserve [*see Table 2*].[1] Based on total bilirubin and albumin levels, PT (INR), and the clinical severity of ascites and hepatic encephalopathy, the Child-Pugh score predicts both the likelihood of variceal hemorrhage and its anticipated mortality. A newer assessment tool, the Model for End-Stage Liver Disease (MELD) scoring system, which takes the degree of renal impairment and the cause of hepatic dysfunction into account, has also been used to predict outcomes in cirrhotic patients.[2]

Management of Variceal Bleeding

The prognosis of variceal hemorrhage depends on the presence or absence of underlying cirrhosis. In noncirrhotic patients, the mortality associated with a first episode of variceal hemorrhage ranges from 5% to 10%; in cirrhotic patients, the range is from 40% to 70%. Esophagogastric varices ultimately develop in approximately one half of cirrhotic patients, and bleeding episodes occur in approximately one third of cirrhotic patients with varices. If the initial hemorrhagic episode resolves spontaneously, 30% of patients experience rebleeding within 6 weeks, and 70% experience rebleeding within 1 year. It is noteworthy that overall mortality in patients who survive 6 weeks after an episode of variceal bleeding is statistically indistinguishable from that in persons who have never experienced such an episode.

Table 1 Causes of Portal Hypertension

Presinusoidal obstruction	Extrahepatic
	  Portal vein thrombosis
	  Splenic vein thrombosis
	Intrahepatic
	  Congenital hepatic fibrosis
	  Primary biliary cirrhosis
	  Sarcoidosis
	  Schistosomiasis

Sinusoidal obstruction	Steatohepatitis Wilson disease

Postsinusoidal obstruction	Extrahepatic
	  Budd-Chiari syndrome
	  Right heart failure
	Intrahepatic
	  Hemochromatosis
	  Laennec (alcoholic) cirrhosis
	  Secondary biliary cirrhosis
	  Posthepatitic cirrhosis

High-flow states	Arteriovenous fistula Massive splenomegaly

Portal Hypertension: Anatomic and Physiologic Considerations

Anatomy of Portal Venous System

The 6 to 8 cm portal vein is formed by the confluence of the splenic vein and the superior mesenteric vein behind the pancreatic neck and is the most posterior component of the portal triad in the hepatoduodenal ligament. The inferior mesenteric vein, though prone to anatomic variation, typically enters the splenic vein at or near its confluence with the superior mesenteric vein. The left gastric vein drains the lesser curvature of the stomach and typically enters the portal vein near its origin.

The unique dual blood supply of the liver, consisting of the portal vein and the hepatic artery, is coordinated by a compensatory regulatory system. Total hepatic blood flow, which averages 1.5 L/min, accounts for about one quarter of cardiac output. The portal circulation typically accounts for two thirds of this hepatic blood flow but provides only one third of hepatic oxygen content. Portal blood flow is an indirect function of splanchnic arterial vasoconstriction and vasodilatation; in contrast, hepatic arterial flow is directly regulated by sympathetic innervation and circulatory catecholamines. As a result, changes in portal blood flow resulting from splanchnic circulatory changes can be compensated for by hepatic arteriolar dilatation or constriction. In this manner, hepatic arterial autoregulatory vasodilatation can preserve normal hepatic blood flow even in the setting of significant decreases in portal flow resulting from shock, hypovolemia, splanchnic vasoconstriction, or portosystemic shunting. Although hepatic oxygenation may be preserved in this fashion, augmented hepatic arterial flow does not replace the essential regulators of hepatic metabolism and growth (e.g., insulin) that are found in portal venous blood. As a consequence, prolonged restriction of portal perfusion, as is seen with portal hypertension–induced portosystemic collateralization or surgically created portosystemic shunts, results in deprivation of these hepatotrophic factors, which can ultimately contribute to hepatic atrophy and failure.

Pathophysiology of Portal Hypertension

Traditionally, the various causes of portal hypertension have been categorized according to the anatomic locus of increased resistance to portal flow. In reality, this categorization is an oversimplification, in that individual causes have been shown to exert their inciting effects at multiple levels. For example, portal hypertension arising from alcoholic cirrhosis has classically been considered an intrahepatic postsinusoidal obstructive process resulting from regenerative hepatic nodules and fibrosis causing hepatic venule compression; however, the demonstration of collagen deposition within Disse's space in cirrhotic livers suggests the presence of a concurrent sinusoidal locus as well. Similarly, the extrahepatic postsinusoidal Budd-Chiari syndrome often produces cirrhotic changes that create a secondary intrahepatic sinusoidal cause of portal hypertension.

Normal portal vein pressures range from 3 to 6 mm Hg, with daily circadian variation. Transient pressure elevations are commonly detected after eating, exercise, and Valsalva maneuvers. Sustained elevations in portal vein pressure to levels higher than 10 mm Hg can result in gradual shunting of blood from the portal circulation into the adjacent low-pressure systemic circulation via certain collateral vessels. Formation and expansion of these collaterals are thought to progress by means of active angiogenesis. The most clinically significant of these vessels are the left gastric vein and the short gastric veins, which decompress hypertensive portal flow into the azygous vein via esophageal and gastric submucosal veins, respectively. Collateral filling from the left portal vein to the epigastric veins through recanalization of the obliterated umbilical vein can result in the caput medusae pattern of dilated abdominal wall veins that is readily appreciated on physical examination. Portosystemic shunting also takes place via retroperitoneal and anorectal collateral vessels.

Long-term shunting of high-pressure portal venous blood through systemic venous vessels evolved for low-pressure capacitance can eventually result in variceal dilatation of the latter. Sustained portal pressures of 12 mm Hg or higher are necessary to produce sufficient distention of these thin-walled vessels to induce rupture. Variceal rupture presents as GI hemorrhage. Although varices can form throughout the entire length of the alimentary canal, the majority of portal hypertensive bleeding is from esophagogastric varices. Unfortunately, prediction of variceal hemorrhage can be difficult; only one third to one half of patients with portal pressures exceeding 12 mm Hg will experience bleeding episodes. On the basis of Laplace's law, one can expect variceal size, intraluminal variceal pressure, and overlying epithelial wall thickness to be predictive of the likelihood of variceal rupture. Clinically, variceal size and the presence and severity of red-wale markings on upper GI endoscopy (a marker of epithelial thickness) can be used in conjunction with the Child-Pugh score to predict the likelihood of variceal hemorrhage.[54]

Further risk stratification is based on the extent of hepatic decompensation. The mortality associated with variceal hemorrhage is 5% for patients with Child class A cirrhosis, 25% for those with Child class B cirrhosis, and over 50% for those with Child class C cirrhosis. The likelihood of recurrent hemorrhage is 28% for patients with Child class A cirrhosis, 48% for those with Child class B cirrhosis, and 68% for those with Child class C cirrhosis.[3]

TREATMENT OF ACUTE VARICEAL HEMORRHAGE

Management of acute variceal hemorrhage [see Figure 1] begins with the establishment of adequate airway protection. The risk of aspiration and consequent respiratory deterioration is particularly high among patients with hepatic encephalopathy and those undergoing endoscopic therapy. Accordingly, the threshold for early endotracheal intubation should be low, particularly if endosopic therapy is considered. As with all cases of brisk hemorrhage, adequate venous access is mandatory; placement of a central venous catheter for accurate volume assessment is particularly useful in cases of major bleeding. The presence of chronic liver disease often necessitates vigorous replacement of circulatory volume and coagulation factors, often involving infusion of colloids and transfusion of fresh frozen plasma and packed red blood cells. Antibiotic prophylaxis therapy is recommended because of the propensity of bacterial infections to develop in patients with chronic liver disease after bleeding episodes.

Pharmacologic Therapy

First-line pharmacotherapy for acute variceal bleeding relies on the long-acting somatostatin analogue octreotide, which has been shown to decrease splanchnic blood flow and portal venous pressure. Octreotide is administered in a 250 μg I.V. bolus, followed by infusion of 25 to 50 μg/hr for 2 to 4 days.[4] In addition, vasopressin, a strong splanchnic vasoconstrictor, has been shown to control approximately 50% of acute variceal bleeding episodes.[4,5] Vasopressin is typically administered in a 20 U I.V. bolus over 20 minutes, followed by infusion of 0.2 to 0.4 U/min. The therapeutic benefits of octreotide and vasopressin appear to be similar, though the side-effect profile of octreotide appears to be much lower than that of vasopressin monotherapy.[4] Adjunctive use of nitroglycerin at an initial rate of 50 µg/min (titrated according to blood pressure tolerance) effectively reduces the cardiac complications of vasopressin and thereby facilitates its administration.[6] The long-acting vasopressin analogue terlipressin has been shown to be approximately as effective as octreotide.[7]

Endoscopic Therapy

Endoscopic treatment, in the form of sclerosant injection or band ligation, has become a standard form of therapy for acute variceal hemorrhage. Experienced endoscopists achieve initial control of hemorrhage in 74% to 95% of cases; however, rebleeding rates ranging from 20% to 50% are typically observed.

In endoscopic sclerotherapy, a sclerosant—typically either 5% sodium morrhuate (more common in the United States) or 5% ethanolamine oleate (more common in Europe and Japan)—is injected either intravariceally to obliterate the varix or paravariceally to induce submucosal fibrosis and thereby prevent variceal rupture. Three prospective, randomized, controlled trials demonstrated that endoscopic sclerotherapy, compared with traditional balloon tamponade, achieved better initial hemorrhage control, resulted in fewer episodes of rebleeding, and, in selected cohorts of patients, led to improved long-term survival.[8-10] Furthermore, routine use of balloon tamponade after sclerotherapy appeared not to confer any additional therapeutic benefit.[8] There are, however, significant risks associated with the use of endoscopic sclerotherapy, including pulmonary complications, transient chest pain, esophageal stricture formation with recurrent sclerotherapy, iatrogenic portal vein thrombosis, hemorrhagic esophageal ulceration, bacteremia, and esophageal perforation.[11]

Partially in response to the potential complications of endoscopic sclerotherapy, endoscopic variceal band ligation has been advocated as a sclerosant-free therapeutic alternative. The limited data comparing the two approaches suggest a trend toward fewer rebleeding episodes, fewer endoscopic interventions, and significantly lower procedure-related morbidity and overall mortality after variceal ligation.[12]

Pharmacologic versus Endoscopic Therapy

Two meta-analyses compared medical pharmacotherapy with emergency sclerotherapy as first-line treatment of acute variceal hemorrhage.[13,14] No significant differences between the two approaches were demonstrated with respect to initial hemorrhage

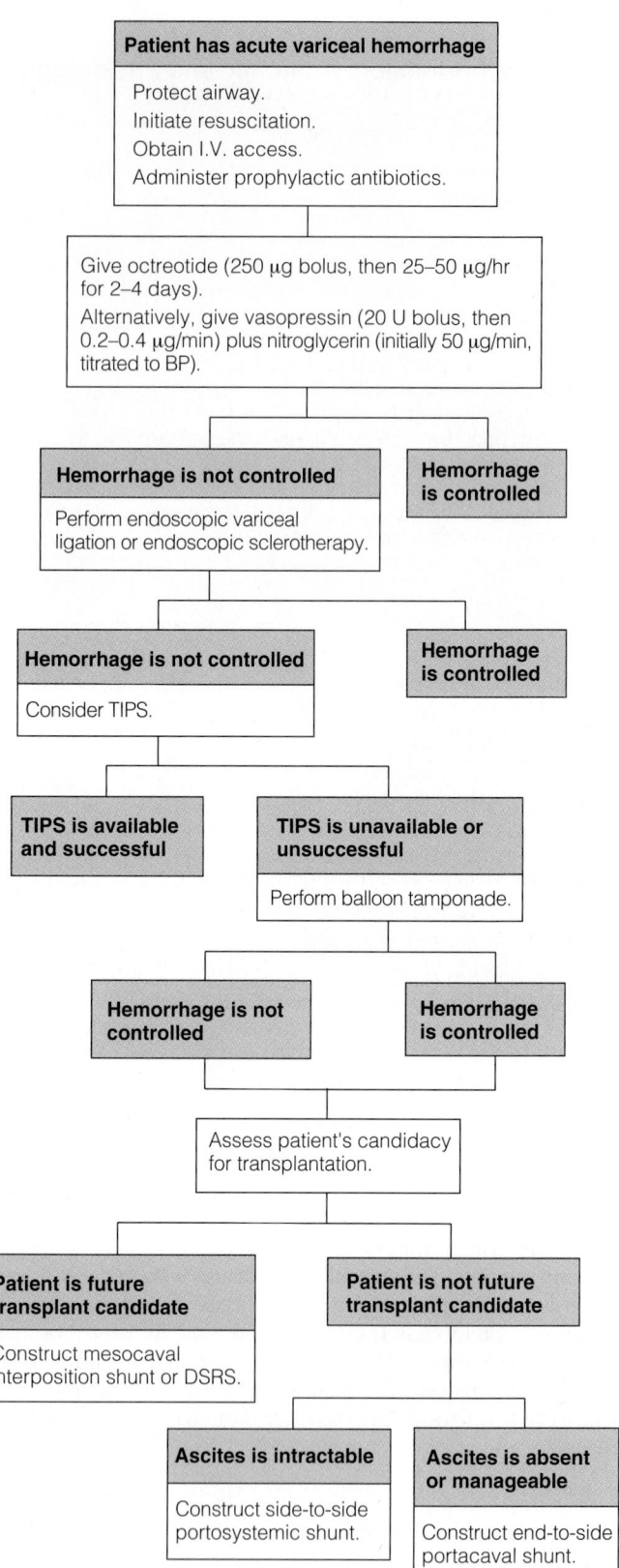

Figure 1 **Algorithm outlines treatment of acute variceal bleeding.**

control or mortality, though treatment-related complications appeared to be significantly more common after sclerotherapy. On the basis of these studies, it has been suggested that endoscopic treatment should be reserved for cases of pharmacotherapeutic failure or that pharmacologic therapy should be initiated in situa-

Table 2 Child-Pugh System for Classifying Cirrhosis

Parameter	Score*		
	1	2	3
Total bilirubin (mg/dl)	1–2	2.1–3	3.1
Albumin (g/dl)	3.5	2.8–3.5	2.7
INR	< 1.7	1.8–2.3	2.4
or			
PT (sec)	1–4	4.1–6	6.1
Ascites	None	Mild	Moderate
Hepatic encephalopathy	None	Mild	Advanced

*Class of cirrhosis is determined on the basis of total points scored: 5 to 6 points, class A; 7 to 9 points, class B; 10 to 15 points, class C.

tions where endoscopy is not immediately available. At present, however, it is more common for the two forms of treatment to be employed concurrently. Pharmacotherapy is often initiated in preparation for endoscopy; early mitigation or control of variceal hemorrhage can make endoscopic visualization and intervention easier, safer, and more effective. Indeed, administration of somatostatin before and after endoscopic sclerotherapy has been shown to improve treatment efficacy and decrease transfusion requirements in comparison with endoscopic sclerotherapy alone.[15,16]

Balloon Tamponade

Although the devices used for balloon tamponade have evolved through numerous different forms over the years, all of them rely on the same basic principle—application of direct upward pressure against varices at the esophagogastric junction. Patients for whom balloon tamponade is considered should be intubated endotracheally to prevent airway occlusion and aspiration. The tube is inserted into the stomach, and the gastric balloon is partially inflated with 40 to 50 ml of air [see Figure 2]. An abdominal radiograph is obtained to ensure that the gastric balloon is correctly positioned within the stomach and below the diaphragm. This balloon is then further inflated until it holds 300 ml of air, and the tube is pulled upward with external traction. If hemorrhage is not controlled at this point, the esophageal balloon is inflated to a pressure of 35 to 40 mm Hg. Suction drainage is applied to both the esophageal port and the gastric port to minimize aspiration risk and monitor for recurrent hemorrhage.

When properly applied, direct tamponade therapy is 90% effective in controlling acute hemorrhage. The primary limitation of such therapy is that bleeding resumes in as many as 50% of patients after takedown and removal of the balloon. Furthermore, serious potential complications (e.g., gastric or esophageal perforation, aspiration, and airway obstruction) result in treatment-related mortalities as high as 20%.[17,18] Nevertheless, in cases of brisk variceal hemorrhage refractory to pharmacologic and endoscopic therapy, balloon tamponade may have a role to play as a bridge therapy to more definitive forms of treatment, such as transjugular intrahepatic portosystemic shunting (TIPS) (see below) or operative intervention.

Transjugular Intrahepatic Portosystemic Shunting

A nonoperative technique for creating an intrahepatic portosystemic fistula for decompression of portal hypertension was proposed in 1969[19] and first performed in 1982.[20] As currently practiced, TIPS is performed by (1) cannulating a hepatic vein (usually the right hepatic vein) via the internal jugular vein, (2) passing a needle from the hepatic vein through the liver parenchyma and into a portal vein branch, (3) passing a guide wire through the needle, (4) dilating the needle tract with a balloon passed over the guide wire, and (5) stenting the tract to a desired diameter, thus effectively constructing a nonselective side-to-side portosystemic shunt [see Figure 3].

Experience with TIPS in the setting of acute variceal hemorrhage is limited. However, one meta-analysis of studies comparing the efficacy of conventional endoscopic therapy (with or without pharmacotherapy) with that of TIPS in treating acute hemorrhagic episodes demonstrated a significant improvement in hemorrhage control with TIPS.[21] Unfortunately, this improvement came at the cost of increased rates of hepatic encephalopathy as a consequence of the nonselective shunting of portal venous flow into the systemic venous circulation. Furthermore, the meta-analysis failed to demonstrate a significant improvement in overall mortality with TIPS.[21]

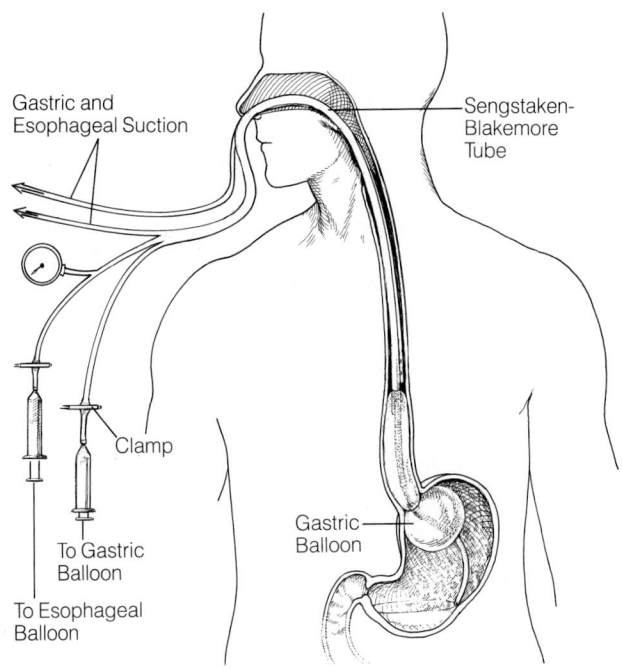

Figure 2 The Sengstaken-Blakemore tube permits tamponade of both the distal esophagus and the gastric fundus. An accessory nasogastric tube permits aspiration of secretions from above the esophageal balloon.

Given the relative paucity of data on the use of TIPS as first-line therapy for acute variceal hemorrhage, it is logical to recommend that TIPS be employed in cases of pharmacotherapeutic and endoscopic failure; the efficacy of TIPS as salvage therapy in this setting is well documented.[22] Contraindications to TIPS include right heart failure and polycystic liver disease. Portal vein thrombosis is a relative contraindication.

Surgical Therapy

The role of surgical management in the treatment of acute variceal bleeding has changed considerably over the past 50 years. At present, operative intervention is reserved for cases that have proved refractory to pharmacotherapy, endoscopy, balloon tamponade, and TIPS. Numerous operations have been developed, each with its own merits and flaws.

Esophageal transection with an end-to-end anastomosis (EEA) stapler has been employed as a means of interrupting blood flow into bleeding esophageal varices. In this technique, the esophagus is mobilized, and the EEA stapler is passed into the distal esophagus through a gastrotomy. With care taken not to injure the vagus nerves and the external periesophageal veins that may be providing collateral venous drainage, a full-thickness segment of the esophagus is transected. When this technique is used on an emergency basis in a patient with acutely bleeding varices, operative mortality is as high as 76%, and the rate of operative complications (e.g., esophageal perforation, stricture, esophagitis, and infection) is approximately 26%.[23] Accordingly, esophageal transection is not commonly advocated as a useful form of surgical therapy for acutely bleeding esophageal varices.

In contrast, portosystemic shunting operations have been widely used to treat acute variceal hemorrhage. The largest single body of data on this practice comes from Orloff and associates,[24] who reported remarkable outcomes—71% survival at 10 years—in 400 consecutive patients undergoing emergency portacaval shunt operations (mostly side-to-side) over a 28-year period. Unfortunately, these investigators' experience stands in stark contrast to that of most other groups, who uniformly reported operative mortalities of about 40% and 5-year survival rates of about 30%.

Another potential drawback to urgent operative shunting is the manipulation and dissection that are often necessary in the region of the porta hepatis: these measures can result in adhesions and scarring, which can complicate future orthotopic liver transplantation. For this reason, some surgeons have advocated using the mesocaval interposition shunt [see Prevention of Recurrent Variceal Hemorrhage, Surgical Therapy, Portosystemic Shunts, Nonselective Shunts, below] in the emergency setting because of its ability to lower portal pressure without complicating the hilar dissection that will be necessary if transplantation is carried out later.[25] In addition, surgeons familiar with the distal splenorenal shunt (DSRS) can employ this selective shunt in some cases of acute variceal hemorrhage unaccompanied by refractory ascites.

PREVENTION OF RECURRENT VARICEAL HEMORRHAGE

Pharmacotherapy

Without further treatment, the likelihood that hemorrhage will recur within 1 year after control of an acute episode of variceal bleeding is approximately 70%.[26] The pharmacologic maneuver that has been used most extensively to prevent recurrent variceal bleeding [see Figure 4] is nonselective beta-adrenergic blockade, most commonly with propranolol. Although beta blockade has been shown to lower portal pressure and hepatic vein wedge pressure, its ability to induce this effect is variable and unpredictable.[27] Nevertheless, a meta-analysis of multiple trials studying the effectiveness of nonselective beta blockade demonstrated a significant decline in recurrent bleeding and a trend toward improved overall survival.[4] Patients with decompensated hepatic function appear to derive less benefit from beta blockade, possibly because of the downregulation of beta-adrenergic receptors

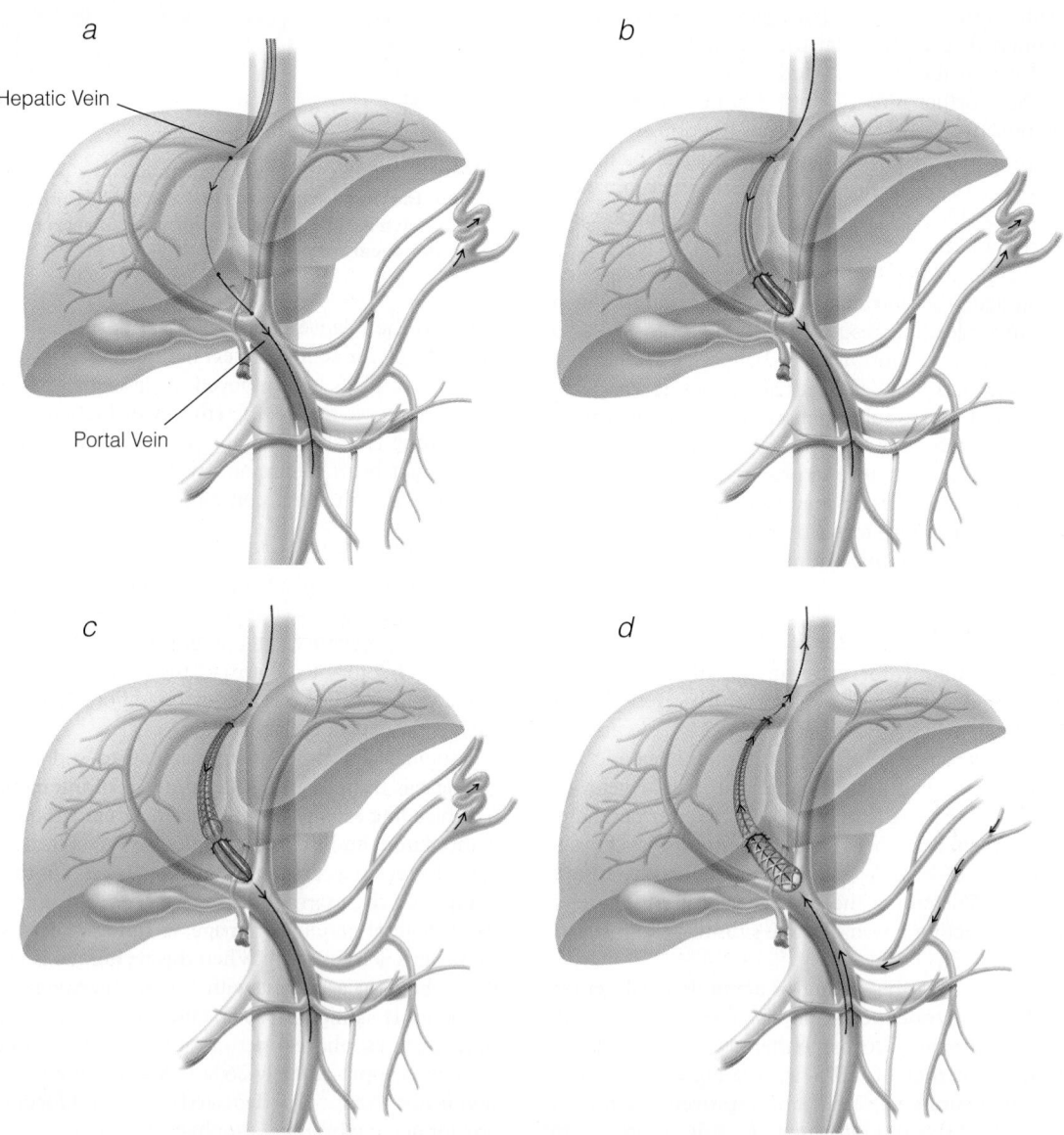

Figure 3 Depicted is the procedure for performing TIPS. (*a*) A needle is passed under radiologic guidance from a hepatic vein into a major portal venous branch, and a guide wire is advanced through this needle. (*b*) A balloon is passed over the guide wire, creating a tract in the hepatic parenchyma. (*c*) An expandable stent is placed though this tract. (*d*) The effective result is a nonselective portosystemic shunt.

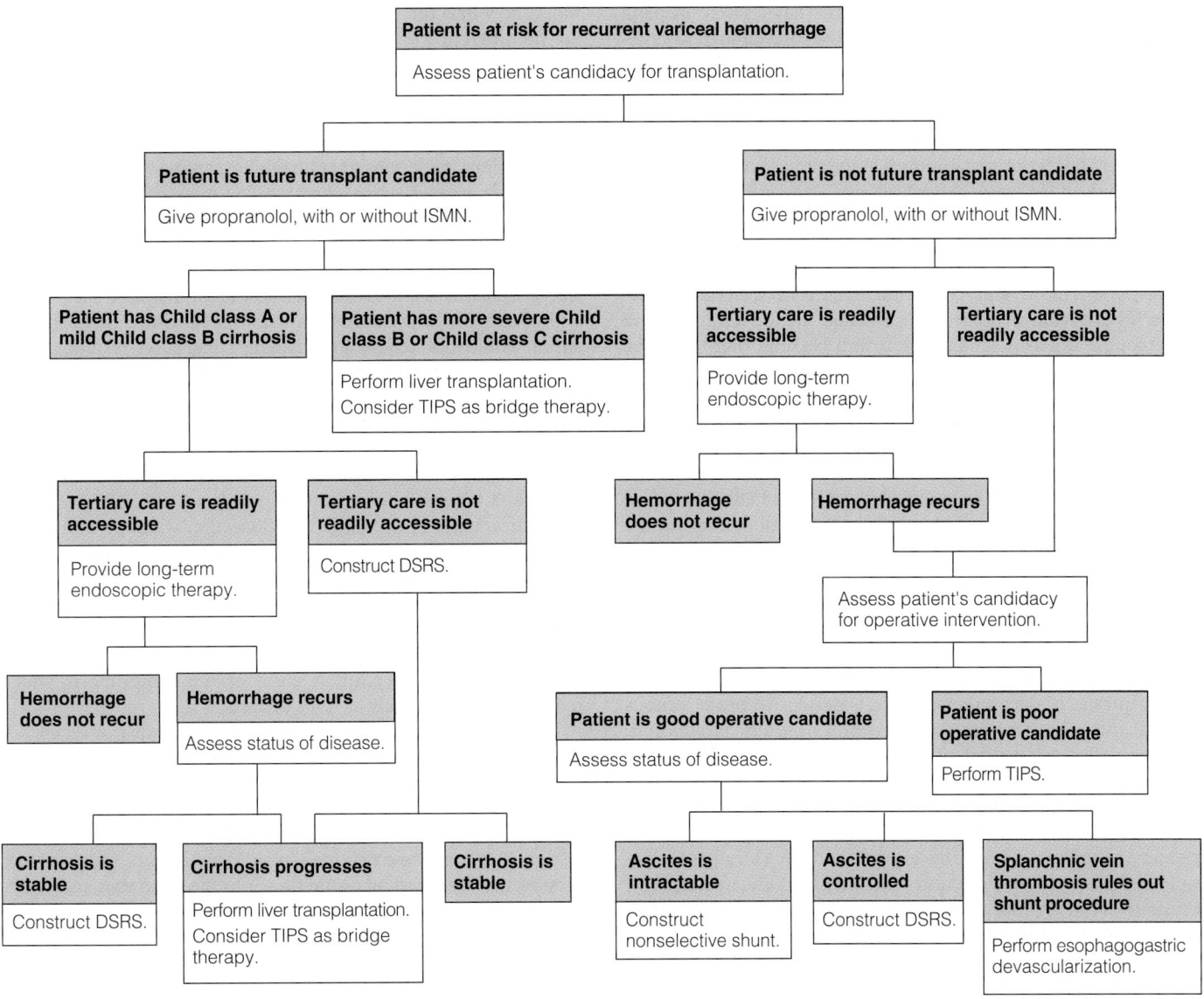

Figure 4 **Algorithm outlines prevention of recurrent variceal bleeding.**

associated with cirrhosis.[28] Adjunctive use of the long-acting vasodilator isosorbide 5-mononitrate (ISMN) appears to potentiate the efficacy of propranolol therapy.[29]

Endoscopic Therapy

Repeated endoscopic therapy with sclerosant injection or band ligation has been advocated as a means of completely eradicating esophageal varices. Once the varices are eliminated, routine endoscopy is performed at 6- to 12-month intervals to prevent recurrent hemorrhage. Compared with medical treatment, long-term endoscopic therapy results in fewer rebleeding episodes.[4] Nevertheless, approximately one half of endoscopically treated patients eventually experience recurrent hemorrhage, usually within the first year. Approximately one third of patients treated with repeated endoscopy ultimately must be converted to another form of therapy because of unrelenting major bleeding.[30,31] For this reason, such extended endoscopic surveillance and treatment should be reserved for compliant patients who live in proximity to tertiary medical care and should be administered with the understanding that conversion to a more definitive form of therapy may be necessary if endoscopy fails.

Transjugular Intrahepatic Portosystemic Shunting

TIPS [*see Figure 3*] has been employed to prevent recurrent episodes of variceal hemorrhage, particularly as a form of bridge therapy for patients awaiting orthotopic liver transplantation. The potential advantage TIPS has over surgical portosystemic shunting is the ability to decompress the portal system without the risks associated with general anesthesia and without postoperative complications. The major limitation of TIPS is the shunt stenosis (caused by neointimal hyperplasia or thrombosis) that occurs in as many as 50% of patients in the first year after the procedure. Fortunately, most such episodes of stenosis are amenable to balloon dilatation or secondary shunt insertion; however, 10% to 15% of TIPS recipients experience total shunt occlusion that cannot be reversed. Furthermore, TIPS functions as a nonselective shunt, leading to hepatic encephalopathy in approximately one third of patients.[32]

Meta-analytic comparison of TIPS with endoscopic therapy indicates that rebleeding episodes are markedly reduced in patients treated with TIPS, but at the cost of a higher incidence of encephalopathy and a shunt malfunction rate of at least 50%. That the efficacy of TIPS is relatively short-lived makes this modality an ideal form of bridge therapy for patients who are awaiting orthotopic liver transplantation or those who have severe hepatic decompensation and thus are unlikely to live long enough to experience failure of TIPS. TIPS can reduce the number of bleeding episodes for patients on the transplant waiting list. In addition, the significant reduction in portal pressure produced by TIPS technically facilitates future liver transplantation. Finally, unlike surgical shunts, TIPS is completely removed at the time of recipient native hepatectomy.

Surgical Therapy

Surgical therapy is the most effective method of controlling portal hypertension and preventing recurrent variceal hemorrhage. The operative procedures available to the surgeon have undergone numerous modifications and become more effective over the years. Review of the surgical experience reveals that with the onset of alternative modalities (e.g., TIPS and transplantation), the risk status of patients undergoing surgical therapy (as predicted by Child's classification) and the frequency of emergency operations have steadily declined. As a result, the incidence of postoperative hepatic encephalopathy has gradually fallen and overall survival has gradually improved.[33] Surgical options for the prevention of recurrent variceal hemorrhage in patients with portal hypertension may be divided into three categories: (1) portosystemic shunt procedures, (2) esophagogastric devascularization, and (3) orthotopic liver transplantation.

Portosystemic shunts Surgical portosystemic shunting provides a means of decompressing the hypertensive portal venous system into the low-pressure systemic venous circulation. Diversion of portal blood flow from the liver also deprives the liver of important hepatotrophic hormones that are present in portal venous blood while routing cerebral toxins normally metabolized by the liver directly into the systemic circulation. As a result, the primary complications of surgical portosystemic shunting are accelerated hepatic dysfunction and hepatic encephalopathy. Primarily in an attempt to minimize these adverse sequelae, various forms of portosystemic shunting operations have evolved, which may be classified as nonselective shunts, selective shunts, or partial shunts.

Nonselective shunts. The classic nonselective portosystemic shunt is the end-to-side portacaval shunt (the so-called Eck fistula) [see Figure 5a]. This is the only nonselective shunt that has been rigorously compared with conventional nonoperative therapy. Several randomized, controlled trials demonstrated superior control of bleeding after operative shunting: 9% to 25% of patients experienced rebleeding after portacaval shunting (mostly related to nonvariceal hemorrhage or shunt thrombosis), whereas 65% to 98% of patients experienced rebleeding after medical therapy.[34-37] Markedly higher rates of spontaneous posttreatment encephalopathy were reported in the operative shunt groups; however, the overall rates of encephalopathy did not differ between the operative groups and the medical groups, because the encephalopathy seen in the medically treated patients (mainly attributable to hemorrhage and infection) eventually became equivalent to that seen in the surgically treated patients. There were trends toward improved overall survival in the surgical groups, but these trends did not attain statistical significance.

The side-to-side portacaval shunt [see Figure 5b] maintains the anatomic continuity of the portal vein as it passes into the liver. However, the high sinusoidal resistance typically present in the setting of cirrhosis effectively renders this shunt a nonselective one, with no measurable antegrade (i.e., hepatopetal) portal blood flow into the liver. Consequently, the encephalopathy rates are no different from those observed after end-to-side portacaval shunting. Side-to-side portacaval shunting does offer the benefit of decompressing the hepatic sinusoidal pressure via reversed (i.e., hepatofugal) flow of blood from the liver into the portal vein. Because transudation of interstitial fluid from both the liver and the intestines is thought to contribute to ascites formation, better control of ascites is achieved with a side-to-side portacaval shunt, which effectively decompresses both the splanchnic veins and the intrahepatic sinusoids, than with an end-to-side portosystemic shunt, which decompresses only the splanchnic veins. The side-to-side portacaval shunt is therefore also recommended for patients with Budd-Chiari syndrome, in whom an end-to-side portacaval shunt would not relieve intrahepatic congestion resulting from hepatic venous outflow occlusion. Otherwise, no significant outcome differences between end-to-side and side-to-side portacaval shunts have been documented. The end-to-side variant is, however, technically easier to construct.

Placement of an interposition mesocaval shunt [see Figure 5c] composed of prosthetic or autogenous vein grafts offers the technical advantages of avoiding hilar dissection (thereby making future liver transplantation less complicated) and permitting intentional shunt ligation in the event of refractory postoperative encephalopathy. Like the side-to-side portacaval shunt, the interposition shunt functions physiologically as a nonselective shunt because of the hepatofugal portal venous blood flow. The major drawback to the interposition shunt is shunt thrombosis, which may develop in as many as 35% of cases.

The conventional (proximal) splenorenal shunt [see Figure 5d] was initially advocated as a means of decompressing portal venous flow while retaining hepatopedal hepatic portal perfusion. This shunt is constructed by performing a splenectomy and anastomosing the proximal splenic vein to the left renal vein. Physiologic testing of patent conventional splenorenal shunts suggests that they eventually divert all portal flow into the renal vein and therefore effectively function as nonselective shunts. Indeed, long-term rates of hepatic encephalopathy appear to be no lower after conventional splenorenal shunting than after portacaval shunting.[38] Shunt occlusion develops in about 18% of cases.[39]

In short, nonselective portosystemic shunts are an effective means of controlling variceal hemorrhage in cases that are refractory to other therapeutic approaches. Given the absence of any major differences in the rate of encephalopathic complications after the various nonselective shunts, the choice of a nonselective shunting procedure should be based on the surgeon's technical familiarity with the operations and on the patient's candidacy for future transplantation. The end-to-side portacaval shunt can be constructed relatively quickly but should be avoided in patients who have intractable ascites or Budd-Chiari syndrome and those who may subsequently undergo liver transplantation. The side-to-side portacaval shunt may provide better control of ascites but is technically more challenging to construct and should also be avoided if future transplantation is an option. The interposition mesocaval shunt is relatively easy to construct and avoids hepatic hilar dissection but is associated with a relatively high rate of shunt occlusion when a nonautogenous conduit is used. The conventional splenorenal shunt also avoids hilar dissection but is associated with a high shunt occlusion rate and is technically challenging to construct.

Selective shunts. In response to the postoperative complications seen after nonselective portosystemic shunting (hepatic encephalopathy and hepatic failure), Warren and colleagues intro-

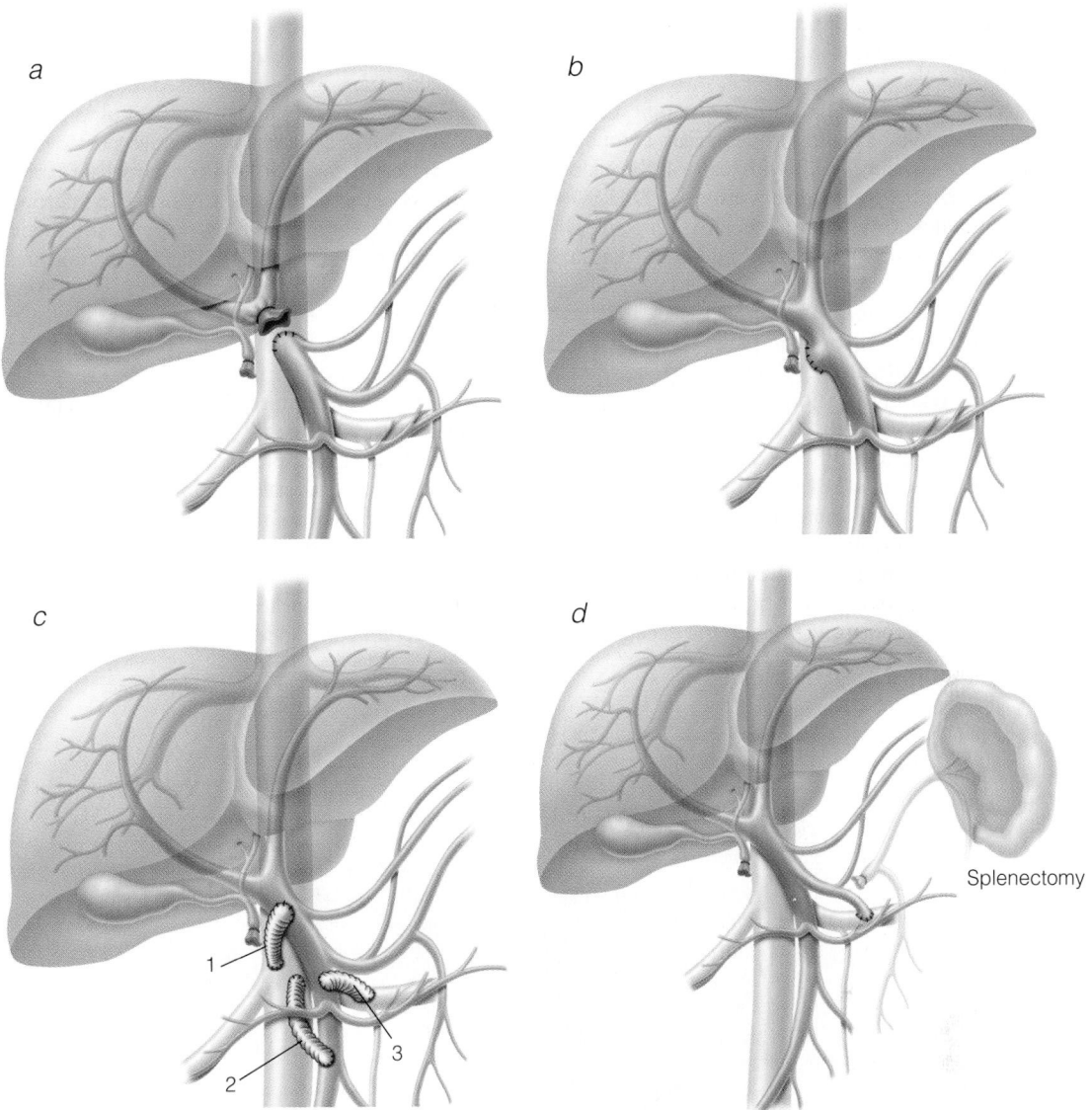

Figure 5 **Nonselective portosystemic shunts either immediately or eventually divert all portal blood flow from the liver into the systemic venous circulation. Shown are the four main variants: (*a*) end-to-side portacaval shunt, (*b*) side-to-side portacaval shunt, (*c*) interposition shunt (portacaval [1], mesocaval [2], and mesorenal [3]), and (*d*) conventional (proximal) splenorenal shunt.**

duced the distal splenorenal shunt in 1967.[40] The DSRS has become the prototypical selective shunt, in that it selectively decompresses the esophagogastric veins while maintaining hepatopetal flow from the mesenteric veins. It is performed by anastomosing the distal splenic vein to the left renal vein and interrupting venous collaterals (e.g., the left gastric and right gastroepiploic veins) [*see Figure 6*]. As a result, the DSRS effectively separates the portal system into two components: (1) a decompressed esophagogastric venous circuit and (2) a persistently hypertensive mesenteric venous circuit that continues to provide hepatopetal portal flow. Thus, the DSRS does not address the mesenteric and sinusoidal hypertension that is responsible for ascites formation. Indeed, it is believed that the extensive retroperitoneal dissection required to construct this shunt may actually contribute to ascites formation through inadvertent disruption of retroperitoneal lymphatic vessels. The DSRS is contraindicated in patients who have refractory ascites or splenic vein thrombosis, those who have previously undergone splenectomy, and those with an excessively small (< 7 mm) splenic vein diameter.

Unfortunately, perfusion studies indicate that approximately one half of patients lose hepatopetal flow within 1 year after a DSRS procedure. This is a particular problem in patients with alcoholic cirrhosis. The loss of shunt selectivity is believed to result from progressive collateral diversion of portal flow into the splenic vein via a network of pancreatic and peripancreatic veins (the so-called pancreatic siphon effect). Extensive skeletonization of the splenic vein off the pancreas (so-called splenopancreatic disconnection) has been proposed as a means of minimizing this unwanted collateralization,[41] but at present, the evidence is insufficient to support routine employment of this measure.

The complications of DSRS procedures are well described. Depending on patient selection, postoperative ascites formation is seen in 7% to 98% of cases; however, in only 0% to 14% of cases is ascites clinically significant and refractory to dietary sodium restriction and diuresis.[23] Hepatic encephalopathy is reported in 0% to 32% of cases; several clinical trials comparing DSRS with nonselective shunting demonstrated significantly lower rates of encephalopathy after DSRS, whereas other trials found no statistically significant difference. With respect to overall survival and hemorrhage control, DSRS and nonselective shunts appear to be equivalent.[42]

Comparison of DSRS construction with endoscopic therapy has yielded interesting results. Two controlled trials comparing endoscopic therapy and salvage DSRS with early DSRS alone demonstrated superior hemorrhage control with early DSRS.[30,31] Rates of hepatic encephalopathy did not differ between the two groups. One of the trials, conducted in an urban-suburban area where 85% of sclerotherapy failures could be rescued with salvage DSRS, found survival to be improved in patients treated with endoscopic therapy and salvage DSRS, compared with survival in patients treated with early DSRS alone.[30] The other, performed in a less densely populated region where only 31% of sclerotherapy failures could be rescued with salvage DSRS, found survival to be improved in the early DSRS group.[31] These data suggest that early definitive surgical intervention may be preferable for patients who are too far from a tertiary medical center to be able to reach one expeditiously in the event of uncontrollable hemorrhage.

Attention is now being turned toward comparisons between the DSRS and TIPS. One uncontrolled comparative study found that with DSRS, hemorrhage control was better, the encephalopa-thy rate was lower, and shunt occlusion was reduced, but the incidence of postoperative ascites was higher.[43] A National Institutes of Health–sponsored randomized comparison between DSRS and TIPS is currently under way at multiple centers.

The other main form of selective portosystemic shunt is the coronary-caval shunt, initially described in Japan in 1984.[44] This shunt is constructed by anastomosing an interposition graft to the left gastric (coronary) vein on one end and the inferior vena cava on the other. To date, the applicability of this procedure has been limited, and most surgeons have relatively little experience with it.

Partial shunts.   Various small-diameter interposition portosystemic shunts have been proposed as partial shunts, designed to achieve partial decompression of the entire portal venous system while maintaining a degree of hepatopetal portal flow to the liver. The most successful of these partial shunts has been the small-diameter portacaval interposition shunt. The use of a 10 mm or smaller interposition shunt, combined with extensive disruption of portosystemic collateral venous circuits, serves to maintain some degree of hepatic portal perfusion. Early experience with the 8 mm ringed polytetrafluoroethylene graft suggests that hepatic encephalopathy rates are lower with this shunt than with nonse-

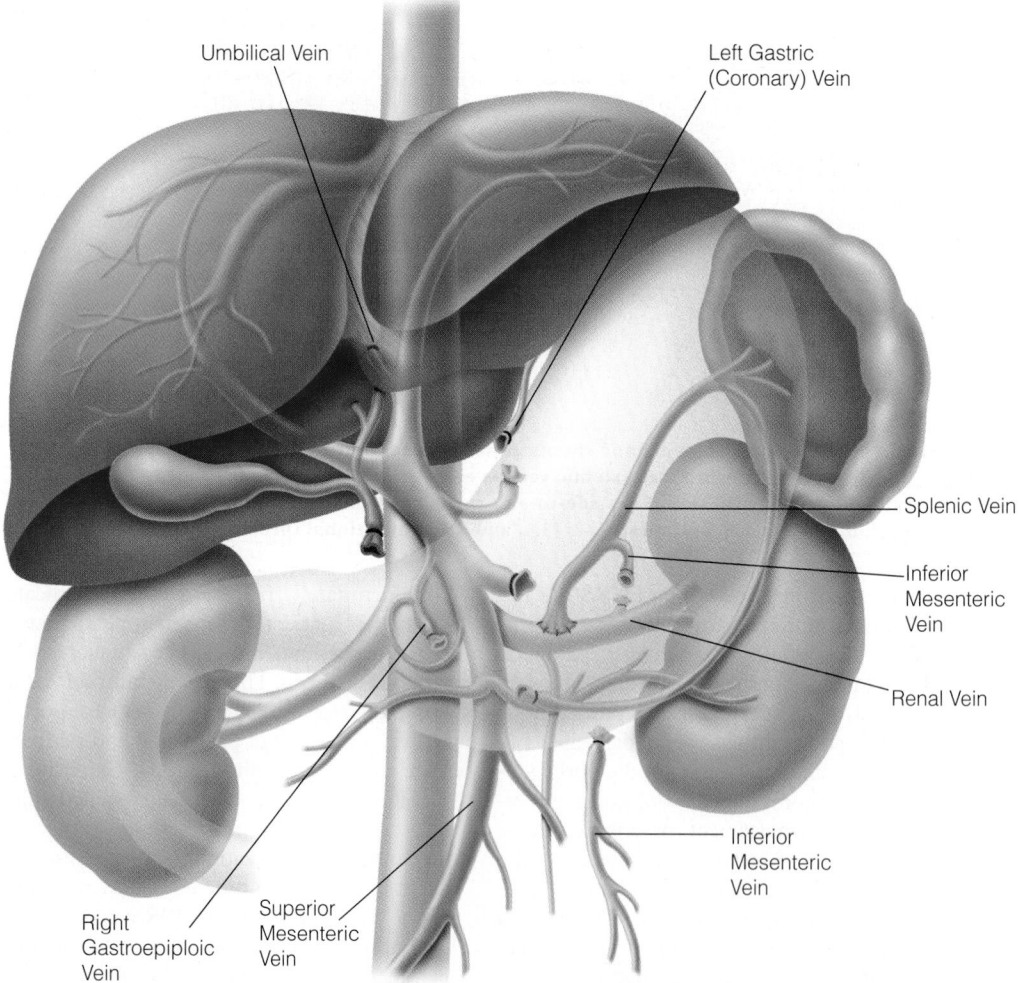

Figure 6   **The distal splenorenal shunt diverts portal flow from the spleen and short gastric veins into the left renal vein. The DSRS provides selective shunting by preserving portal flow from the mesenteric circulation. Potential sites of collateralization (e.g., the left gastric vein, the gastroepiploic vein, and the umbilical vein) are routinely interrupted to preserve hepatopedal portal flow.**

lective 16 mm grafts and that use of the smaller shunt yields comparable long-term survival.[45] An early comparison of the small-diameter portacaval shunt with TIPS demonstrated lower rates of shunt occlusion and treatment failure in the operative therapy group.[46]

Esophagogastric devascularization The most effective nonshunt operation for preventing recurrent variceal hemorrhage is esophagogastric devascularization with esophageal transection and splenectomy, as advocated by Sugiura and associates.[47] Unlike simple esophageal transection, which has been used with limited success in the setting of acute hemorrhage, the Sugiura procedure and its subsequent modifications [see Figure 7] involve ligation of venous branches entering the distal esophagus and the proximal stomach from the level of the inferior pulmonary vein, combined with selective vagotomy and pyloroplasty [see 62 Procedures for Benign and Malignant Gastric and Duodenal Disease]. A key point is that the left gastric (coronary) vein and the paraesophageal collateral veins are preserved to permit portoazygous collateralization, which inhibits future varix formation. Initial reports from Japan cited a 5.2% operative mortality and a 6.3% rate of recurrent hemorrhage (most often from nonvariceal causes).[47,48] Unfortunately, these successes have not been easily replicated in the United States, where operative mortality with this procedure has exceeded 20%, with bleeding recurring in 35% to 55% of patients.[49,50] Nevertheless, modifications of the Sugiura procedure continue to be performed in patients who are unable to undergo shunting procedures because of extensive splanchnic vein thrombosis.

Orthotopic liver transplantation Orthotopic liver transplantation is the most definitive form of therapy for complications of portal hypertension. The cost of cadaveric and living-donor liver transplantation and its attendant immunosuppression, as well as the paucity of available allografts, make liver replacement an option for only a select minority of patients presenting with portal hypertensive sequelae. Accordingly, careful analysis of the outcomes of transplantation procedures in comparison with those of nontransplantation procedures is necessary for optimal allocation of this limited resource.

For patients whose portal hypertension has become refractory to nonoperative management strategies, the decision whether to employ transplantation or nontransplantation operative therapy can be based on the level of hepatic functional reserve. Patients with Child class A or mild class B cirrhosis appear to do well with nontransplantation therapy as first-line operative treatment, with the understanding that liver transplantation may remain an option for salvage therapy in the event of future hepatic functional deterioration. In contrast, patients with more advanced Child class B or Child class C cirrhosis appear to benefit from early transplantation, with nonoperative strategies employed strictly as bridge therapy for maintenance during the time spent on the allograft waiting list.[51,52]

PROPHYLAXIS OF INITIAL VARICEAL HEMORRHAGE

The significant mortality associated with variceal hemorrhage has prompted efforts to devise effective means of preventing the onset of initial variceal bleeding. The difficulty of identifying those 20% to 33% of cirrhotic patients who will experience bleeding episodes remains the primary challenge in the application of prophylaxis for variceal hemorrhage. Patient characteristics that predict an increased likelihood of variceal bleeding include alcoholic cirrhosis, active alcohol consumption, and severe hepatic dysfunction.[53] Certain anatomic features of varices seen at the time of endoscopic examination have been shown to predict the likelihood of rupture: evidence of variceal wall thinning (cherry-red spots, red wales), variceal tortuosity, superimposition of varices on other varices, and the presence of gastric varices all appear to be correlated with a higher likelihood of hemorrhage.[54]

At present, pharmacologic therapy is the only measure that provides effective prophylaxis against variceal hemorrhage. Nonselective beta-adrenergic blockade, either with propranolol or the long-acting agent nadolol, reduces portal venous pressure by decreasing cardiac output and favoring splanchnic vasoconstriction. Clinical trials examining the efficacy of propranolol therapy demonstrated lowered rates of initial variceal bleeding, though the ultimate influence of beta blockade on patient survival was mixed.[55-57]

Endoscopic sclerotherapy has not been consistently effective in preventing initial variceal bleeding. In fact, several trials found survival to be poorer in patients treated with prophylactic sclerotherapy than in those managed with prophylactic pharmacotherapy.[4,58] This difference is probably attributable to the well-documented complications associated with endoscopic sclerotherapy.

The flaws of prophylactic endoscopic sclerotherapy have led some authorities to advocate endoscopic variceal band ligation as a more effective form of prophylaxis. One trial demonstrated that variceal band ligation achieved better prophylaxis of initial variceal bleeding than propranolol therapy did.[59] Clearly, this observation warrants further investigation.

Early trials comparing prophylactic portosystemic shunting with medical prophylaxis definitively showed that early operative intervention conferred no significant benefit. In fact, the significant morbidity associated with surgical shunting and the substantial risk of accelerated hepatic dysfunction and encephalopathy led to lower survival rates in patients treated with prophylactic surgical procedures.[6,60] At present, the data are insufficient to recommend the use of prophylactic TIPS to prevent acute variceal hemorrhage.

Management of Ascites

The presence of ascites in a patient with portal hypertension is typically an ominous finding that is of significant prognostic importance: 1-year mortalities as high as 50% have been reported in cirrhotic patients with new-onset ascites, whereas baseline 1-year mortalities in cirrhotic patients without ascites are in the range of 10%.[61] The pathogenesis of ascites formation appears to be related to the relative hypovolemia and the primary avidity of renal sodium retention that develop in patients with cirrhosis. Hypovolemia induces renin-angiotensin activation and salt and water reabsorption, which, in the setting of chronic liver dysfunction, results in excessive transudation of fluid out of the liver and the intestines and into the peritoneal cavity. The major complications of this process are spontaneous bacterial peritonitis (SBP) and hepatorenal syndrome (HRS) [see Complications, below], which account for the bulk of the morbidity and mortality associated with ascites in patients with portal hypertension.

NONSURGICAL THERAPY

By addressing the hyperavidity of sodium retention that drives much of ascites formation, restriction of dietary salt intake (to levels as low as 2 g of sodium a day) can resolve ascites in approximately 25% of cases. The hyperaldosteronemic state that exists can be countered by initiating diuresis with spironolactone, which, at dosages ranging from 100 to 400 mg/day, can relieve ascites in an additional 60% to 70% of patients. Although automatic addi-

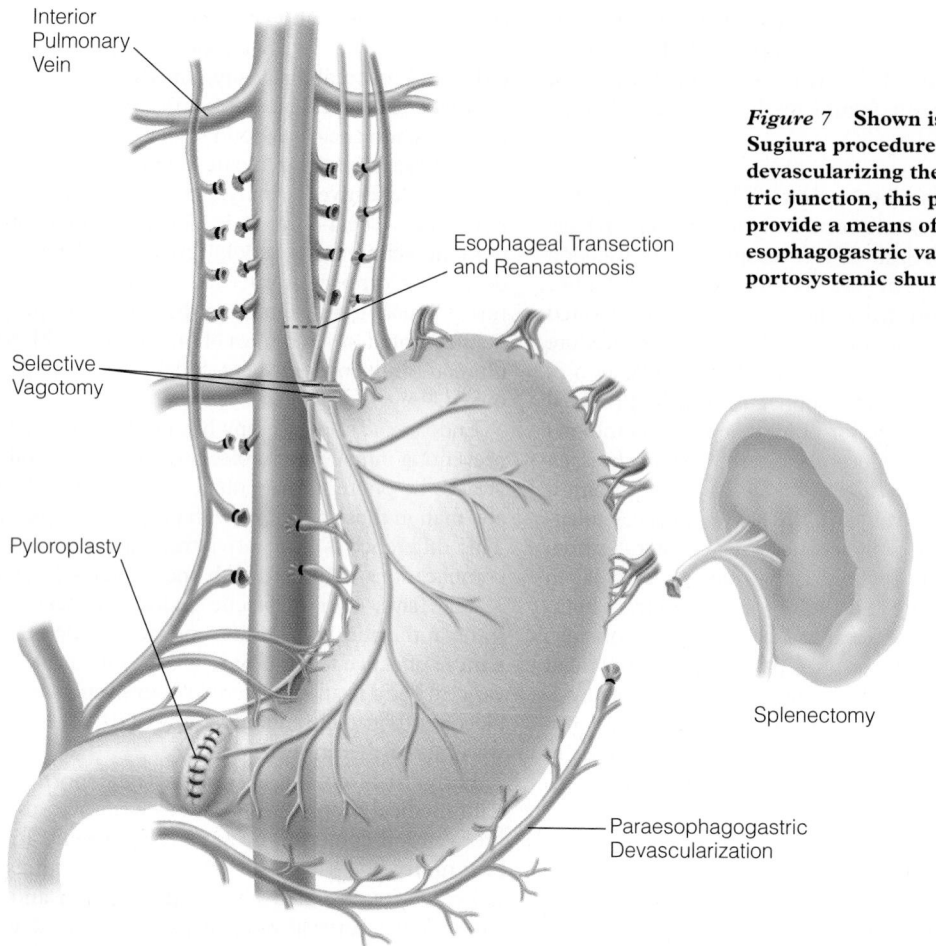

Interior Pulmonary Vein

Esophageal Transection and Reanastomosis

Selective Vagotomy

Pyloroplasty

Splenectomy

Paraesophagogastric Devascularization

Figure 7 **Shown is the modified Sugiura procedure. By extensively devascularizing the esophagogastric junction, this procedure may provide a means of interrupting esophagogastric varices without portosystemic shunting.**

tion of loop diuretics has not been proved to enhance the clinical efficacy of spironolactone, augmentation of spironolactone therapy with furosemide can be helpful for patients whose ascites is refractory to spironolactone monotherapy or who have hyperkalemia as a result of spironolactone treatment. Gradual diuresis is necessary to prevent potential complications (e.g., prerenal azotemia and HRS).[62]

In cases of ascites that is refractory to medical dietary restriction and diuretic therapy, large-volume paracentesis has been employed with some success. Albumin is typically infused at a dose of 6 to 8 g per liter of ascitic fluid to prevent the hypotension that results from acute volume shifts. Patients in whom ascites recurs after multiple rounds of large-volume paracentesis should be considered for TIPS. TIPS is particularly useful in patients with ascites and a history of bleeding esophageal varices; it corrects as many as 80% of medically refractory cases of ascites.[63] However, the efficacy of TIPS is counterbalanced by its attendant risks (i.e., hepatic encephalopathy, shunt occlusion, and accelerated hepatic failure), especially in patients with poor hepatic functional reserve.

SURGICAL THERAPY

Operative intervention plays only a limited role in the management of ascites. Surgically inserted peritoneovenous shunts have been compared with large-volume paracentesis in patients with ascites refractory to medical therapy. No significant differences in early control of ascites have been detected, but patients treated with peritoneovenous shunting appear to benefit from faster ascites resolution, longer palliation, and fewer hospital readmis-

sions.[64] Long-term follow-up, however, indicates that shunt occlusion occurs in 47% of patients so treated and disseminated intravascular coagulation in as many as 35%.

The morbidity and mortality associated with operative therapy make routine use of side-to-side portacaval shunts a poor option for managing ascites. The exceptions to this general statement are cases in which ascites proves refractory to medical and TIPS therapy or in which concomitant refractory variceal hemorrhage is present.

COMPLICATIONS

SBP is the most common form of ascitic infection. It typically is signaled by fever and abdominal tenderness and often is also accompanied by acute hepatic and renal deterioration. The diagnosis is generally made by analyzing ascitic fluid collected through paracentesis and is defined by the presence of a positive bacterial culture and a neutrophil count higher than 250/mm³ in the absence of an obvious intra-abdominal source of infection. Unlike secondary peritonitis, SBP is typically monomicrobial, and the frequency with which enteric gram-negative rods are found with SBP suggests intestinal bacterial translocation as a potential cause. SBP carries a mortality of 25% and should therefore be treated aggressively with I.V. antibiotic therapy. Given the 70% recurrence rate after an initial episode of SBP, continuation of suppressive antimicrobial therapy until ascites resolves is warranted.[65]

HRS, a poorly understood state characterized by progressive and refractory renal impairment, typically occurs in the setting of tense ascites and hepatic disease. Management of HRS is strictly supportive, in that the syndrome often responds only to correction of the underlying liver dysfunction. Accordingly, the only proven therapy for HRS is liver transplantation.

Management of Hepatic Encephalopathy

Hepatic encephalopathy is a complex of symptoms characterized by mental status changes ranging from impaired mentation to frank stupor. The classic neurologic finding associated with this symptom complex is asterixis. Typically, hepatic encephalopathy develops in the setting of significant portosystemic shunting or significant hepatic functional impairment. It is most commonly observed after the creation of a therapeutic nonselective portosystemic shunt. Its onset is usually precipitated by dehydration, GI hemorrhage, sepsis, or excessive protein intake; in fact, the spontaneous development of hepatic encephalopathy mandates workup for these physiologic triggers. It has been speculated that the shunting of intestinally absorbed cerebral toxins (e.g., ammonia,

mercaptans, and γ-aminobutyric acid) away from hepatic metabolism is what causes hepatic encephalopathy; however, the absolute level of circulating ammonia correlates poorly with the magnitude of encephalopathic symptoms.

Correction of the triggers that cause hepatic encephalopathy often reverses the psychoneurologic disturbances. In severe cases, patients should also receive neomycin (1.5 g every 6 hours), which covers enteric urease-positive bacteria, and lactulose (20 to 30 g two to four times daily), a disaccharide GI cathartic. Both agents are believed to reduce intestinal levels of ammonia and inhibit its enteric absorption. Whereas neomycin has long-term side effects (i.e., nephrotoxicity and ototoxicity), long-term lactulose therapy is generally well tolerated. Dietary protein restriction should also be employed for long-term suppression of hepatic encephalopathy. On occasion, refractory cases of shunt-induced hepatic encephalopathy may be treated by means of intentional ligation or occlusion of the portosystemic shunt.

References

1. Pugh RN, Murray-Lyon IM, Dawson JL, et al: Transection of the oesophagus for bleeding oesophageal varices. Br J Surg 60:646, 1973

2. Kamath PS, Wiesner RH, Malinchoc M, et al: A model to predict survival in patients with end-stage liver disease. Hepatology 33:464, 2001

3. Sherlock S: Esophageal varices. Am J Surg 160:9, 1990

4. D'Amico G, Pagliaro L, Bosch J: The treatment of portal hypertension: a meta-analytic review. Hepatology 22:332, 1995

5. Vlavianos P, Westaby D: Management of acute variceal hemorrhage. Eur J Gastroenterol Hepatol 13:335, 2001

6. Gimson AE, Westaby D, Hegarty J, et al: A randomized trial of vasopressin and vasopressin plus nitroglycerin in the control of acute variceal hemorrhage. Hepatology 6:410, 1986

7. Silvain C, Carpentier S, Sautereau D, et al: Terlipressin plus transdermal nitroglycerin vs. octreotide in the control of acute bleeding from esophageal varices: a multicenter randomized trial. Hepatology 18:61, 1993

8. Barsoum MS, Bolous FI, El-Rooby AA, et al: Tamponade and injection sclerotherapy in the management of bleeding oesophageal varices. Br J Surg 69:76, 1982

9. Paquet KJ, Feussner H: Endoscopic sclerosis and esophageal balloon tamponade in acute hemorrhage from esophagogastric varices: a prospective controlled randomized trial. Hepatology 5:580, 1985

10. Larson AW, Cohen H, Zweiban B, et al: Acute esophageal variceal sclerotherapy: results of a prospective randomized controlled trial. JAMA 255:497, 1986

11. Eckhauser FE, Sarosi G: Endoscopic treatment of esophageal varices and transjugular intrahepatic portal-systemic shunts. Shackleford's Surgery of the Alimentary Tract. Zuidema GD, Yeo CJ, Eds. WB Saunders Co, Philadelphia, 2001

12. Stiegmann GV, Goff JS, Michaletz-Onody PA, et al: Endoscopic sclerotherapy as compared with endoscopic ligation for bleeding esophageal varices. N Engl J Med 326:1527, 1992

13. Escorsell A, Ruiz del Arbol L, Planas R, et al: Multicenter randomized controlled trial of terlipressin versus sclerotherapy in the treatment of acute variceal bleeding: the TEST study. Hepatology 32:471, 2000

14. D'Amico G, Pietrosi G, Tarantino I, et al: Emergency sclerotherapy versus vasoactive drugs for variceal bleeding in cirrhosis: a Cochrane meta-analysis. Gastroenterology 124:1277, 2003

15. Avgerinos A, Nevens F, Raptis S, et al: Early administration of somatostatin and efficacy of sclerotherapy in acute oesophageal variceal bleeds: the ABOVE randomized trial. Lancet 350:1495, 1997

16. Banares R, Albillos A, Rincon D, et al: Endoscopic treatment versus endoscopic plus pharmacologic treatment for acute variceal bleeding: a meta-analysis. Hepatology 35:609, 2002

17. Panes J, Teres J, Bosch J, et al: Efficacy of balloon tamponade in treatment of bleeding gastric and esophageal varices: results in 151 consecutive episodes. Dig Dis Sci 33:454, 1988

18. Avgerinos A, Klonis C, Rekoumis G, et al: A prospective randomized trial comparing somatostatin, balloon tamponade and the combination of both methods in the management of acute variceal haemorrhage. J Hepatol 13:78, 1991

19. Rosch J, Hanafee WN, Snow H: Transjugular portal venography and radiologic portacaval shunt: an experimental study. Radiology 92:1112, 1969

20. Colapinto RF, Stronell RD, Birch SJ, et al: Creation of an intrahepatic portosystemic shunt with a Gruntzig balloon catheter. Can Med Assoc J 126:267, 1982

21. Luca A, D'Amico G, La Galla R, et al: TIPS for the prevention of recurrent bleeding in patients with cirrhosis: meta-analysis of randomized clinical trials. Radiology 212:411, 1999

22. Sanyal AJ, Freedman AM, Luketic VA, et al: Transjugular intrahepatic portosystemic shunts compared with endoscopic sclerotherapy for the prevention of recurrent variceal hemorrhage: a randomized, controlled trial. Ann Intern Med 126:849, 1997

23. Maley WR, Klein AS: Portal hypertension. Shackleford's Surgery of the Alimentary Tract. Zuidema GD, Yeo CJ, Eds. WB Saunders Co, Philadelphia, 2001

24. Orloff MJ, Orloff MS, Orloff SL, et al: Three decades of experience with emergency portacaval shunt for acutely bleeding esophageal varices in 400 unselected patients with cirrhosis of the liver. J Am Coll Surg 180:257, 1995

25. Brems JJ, Hiatt JR, Klein AS, et al: Effect of prior portosystemic shunt on subsequent liver transplantation. Ann Surg 209:51, 1989

26. Grace ND: A hepatologist's view of variceal bleeding. Am J Surg 160:26, 1990

27. Garcia-Tsao G, Grace ND, Groszmann RJ, et al: Short-term effect of propranolol on portal venous pressure. Hepatology 6:101, 1986

28. Gerbes A, Remien J, Jungst D, et al: Evidence for down regulation of beta 2 adrenoceptors in cirrhotic patients with severe ascites. Lancet 21:1409, 1986

29. Garcia-Pagan JC, Fe F, Bosch J, et al: Propranolol compared with propranolol plus isosorbide-mononitrate for portal hypertension in cirrhosis: a randomized controlled study. Ann Intern Med 114:869, 1991

30. Henderson JM, Kutner MH, Millikan WJ Jr, et al: Endoscopic variceal sclerosis compared with distal splenorenal shunt to prevent recurrent variceal bleeding in cirrhosis: a prospective, randomized trial. Ann Intern Med 112:22, 1990

31. Rikkers LF, Jin G, Burnett DA, et al: Shunt surgery versus endoscopic sclerotherapy for variceal hemorrhage: late results of a randomized trial. Am J Surg 165:27, 1993

32. Riggio O, Merlli M, Pedretti G, et al: Hepatic encephalopathy after transjugular intrahepatic portosystemic shunt: incidence and risk factors. Dig Dis Sci 41:578, 1996

33. Rikkers LF: The changing spectrum of treatment for variceal bleeding. Ann Surg 228:536, 1998

34. Jackson FC, Perrin EB, Felix W, et al: A clinical investigation of the portacaval shunt: V. Survival analysis of the therapeutic operation. Ann Surg 174:672, 1971

35. Resnick RH, Iber FL, Ishihara AM, et al: A controlled study of the therapeutic portacaval shunt. Gastroenterology 67:843, 1974

36. Rueff B, Prandi D, Degos F, et al: A controlled study of therapeutic portacaval shunt in alcoholic cirrhosis. Lancet 27:655, 1976

37. Reynolds TB, Donovan AJ, Mikkelsen WP, et al: Results of a 12-year randomized trial of portacaval shunt in patients with alcoholic liver disease and bleeding varices. Gastroenterology 80:1005, 1981

38. Malt RA, Nabseth DC, Orloff MJ, et al: Occasional notes: portal hypertension, 1979. N Engl J Med 301:617, 1979

39. Mehigan, DG, Zuidema GD, Cameron JL: The incidence of shunt occlusion and portosystemic decompression. Surg Gynecol Obstet 10:661, 1980

40. Warren WD, Zeppa R, Fomon JJ: Selective transplenic decompression of gastroesophageal varices by distal splenorenal shunt. Ann Surg 166:437, 1967

41. Inokuchi K, Beppu K, Koyanagi N, et al: Exclusion of nonisolated splenic vein in distal splenorenal shunt for prevention of portal malcirculation. Ann Surg 200:711, 1984

42. Jin GL, Rikkers LF: Selective variceal decompression: current status. HPB Surg 5:1, 1991

43. Khaitiyar JS, Luthra SK, Prasad N, et al: Transjugular intrahepatic portosystemic shunt versus distal splenorenal shunt—a comparative study. Hepatogastroenterology 47:492, 2000

44. Inokuchi K, Beppu K, Koyanagi N, et al: Fifteen years' experience with left gastric venous caval shunt for esophageal varices. World J Surg 8:716, 1984

45. Sarfeh IJ, Rypins EB: Partial versus total portacaval shunt in alcoholic cirrhosis: results of a prospective, randomized clinical trial. Ann Surg 219:353, 1994

46. Rosemurgy AS, Serafini FM, Zweibel BR, et al: Transjugular intrahepatic portosystemic shunt versus small-diameter prosthetic H-graft portacaval shunt: extended follow-up of an expanded randomized prospective trial. J Gastrointest Surg 4:589, 2000

47. Sugiura M, Futagawa S: Results of six hundred thirty-six esophageal transactions with paraesophagogastric devascularization in the treatment of esophageal varices. J Vasc Surg 1:254, 1984

48. Idezuki Y, Kokudo N, Sanjo K, et al: Sugiura procedure for management of variceal bleeding in Japan. World J Surg 18:216, 1994

49. Gouge TH, Ranson JHC: Esophageal resection and paraesophagogastric devascularization for bleeding esophageal varices. Am J Surg 151:47, 1986

50. Jin G, Rikkers LF: Transabdominal esophagogastric devascularization as treatment for variceal hemorrhage. Surgery 120:641, 1996

51. Henderson JM: The role of portosystemic shunts for variceal bleeding in the liver transplantation era. Arch Surg 129:886, 1994

52. Rikkers LF, Jin G, Langnas AN, et al: Shunt surgery during the era of liver transplantation. Ann Surg 228:536, 1997

53. DeFrancis R, Primignani M: Why do varices bleed? Gastroenterol Clin North Am 21:85, 1992

54. Prediction of the first variceal hemorrhage in patients with cirrhosis of the liver and esophageal varices: the North Italian endoscopic club for the study and treatment of esophageal varices. N Engl J Med 319:983, 1988

55. Feu F, Bordas JM, Garcia-Pagan JC, et al: Double-blind investigation of the effects of propranolol and placebo in the pressure of esophageal varices in patients with portal hypertension. Hepatology 13:917, 1991

56. LeBrec D: Current status and future goals of the pharmacologic reduction of portal hypertension. Am J Surg 160:19, 1990

57. Conn HO, Grace ND, Bosch J, et al: Propranolol in the prevention of the first hemorrhage from esophagogastric varices: a multicenter, randomized clinical trial. Hepatology 13:902, 1991

58. Prophylactic sclerotherapy for esophageal varices in alcoholic liver disease: a randomized, single-blind, multicenter clinical trial. N Engl J Med 324:1779, 1991

59. Sarin SK, Lamba GS, Kumar M, et al: Comparison of endoscopic ligation and propranolol for the primary prevention of variceal bleeding. N Engl J Med 340:988, 1999

60. Jackson FC, Perrin EB, Smith AG, et al: A clinical investigation of the portacaval shunt: II. Surgical analysis of the prophylactic operation. Am J Surg 115:22, 1968

61. Gines P, Quintero E, Arroyo V: Compensated cirrhosis: natural history and prognosis. Hepatology 7:122, 1987

62. Fogel MR, Sawhney VK, Neal EA, et al: Diuresis in the ascitic patient: a randomized controlled trial of three regimens. J Clin Gastroenterol 93:234, 1987

63. Ochs A, Rossle M, Haag K, et al: The transjugular intrahepatic portosystemic stent-shunt procedure for refractory ascites. N Engl J Med 32:1192, 1995

64. Gines P, Arroyo V, Vargas V, et al: Paracentesis with intravenous infusion of albumin as compared with peritoneovenous shunting in cirrhosis with refractory ascites. N Engl J Med 325:829, 1991

65. Gines P, Rimola A, Planas R, et al: Norfloxacin prevents spontaneous bacterial peritonitis recurrence in cirrhosis: results of a double-blind, placebo-controlled trial. Hepatology 12:716, 1990

Acknowledgments

Figure 2   Carol Donner.
Figures 3 and 5 through 7   Alice Y. Chen.

53 CROHN DISEASE

Susan Galandiuk, M.D., F.A.C.S., F.A.S.C.R.S.

The role of surgery in the management of Crohn disease has undergone a dramatic evolution over the past 50 years. Currently, surgical treatment of Crohn disease is seldom performed in the emergency setting; it is nearly always performed after failed medical therapy. The decision to proceed with operative management is based on careful patient evaluation, with full awareness of the potential complications and ramifications of treatment. In particular, attention must be paid to the risk of recurrent disease, the possible surgical sequelae, and the side effects of medical therapy.

Classification

There are many systems for classifying Crohn disease. One of the simplest is the classification developed by Farmer and associates,[1] which categorizes the disease on the basis of disease location alone (ileocolic, purely colonic, small bowel, and perianal). A more elaborate system is the Vienna classification, which categorizes the disease on the basis not only of location but also of age of onset and disease behavior.[2] In this system, there are four categories for disease location: terminal ileum (L1), colon (L2), terminal ileum and colon (L3), and any location proximal to the terminal ileum (L4). There are two categories for age of onset: less than 40 years of age (A1) and 40 years of age or older (A2). Finally, there are three categories for disease behavior: nonstricturing and nonpenetrating (B1), stricturing (B2), and penetrating (B3).

Given that there are as many types and combinations of Crohn disease as there are patients with this condition, the most sensible approach is probably to use some combination of these two classification schemes. Careful evaluation of the specifics of each case will yield the best treatment results; however, general classification of the disease can help guide therapy. Broadly speaking, Crohn disease of the small bowel has the highest recurrence rate. Because of the important function of the small bowel in digestion, surgeons tend to emphasize conserving small bowel length during operative treatment of Crohn disease. Currently, however, there is an increasing focus on colon conservation with the aims of maintaining water absorption in patients and delaying (or perhaps eliminating) the need for a stoma.

Roles of Medical Therapy and Surgical Therapy

In planning treatment of Crohn disease, it is important not to make the use of medical therapy or surgical therapy an either-or issue. Just as one tool cannot be expected to fill every household need, operative management cannot be expected to solve every problem related to Crohn disease. Overall, careful use of medical therapy, appropriately combined with surgical therapy, provides the best treatment of Crohn disease. Single-minded reliance on either therapy to the exclusion of the other often leads to inadequate patient care.

Generally speaking, except in the case of a free perforation, cancer, or dysplasia, one should not operate on a patient with Crohn disease without first attempting medical therapy. With the dramatically improved medical treatment options currently available, surgery can be avoided in many cases. This is often a desirable result, given

the known risk of disease recurrence after surgical treatment of Crohn disease and the significant associated operative morbidity. In one single-center study, the reoperation rate for Crohn disease was 34% at 10 years.[3] The agents used to treat Crohn disease can be divided into several broad groups: probiotics, antibiotics, anti-inflammatory drugs, immunosuppressive drugs, and biologic agents. These can be used alone or in combination to treat disease, as well as to maintain remission [see Table 1].

Few good studies have been done on the cost-effectiveness of medical or surgical therapy[4,5] versus that of timely surgery followed by maintenance medical therapy. There is clearly a need for such studies. The use of potent and expensive immunomodulator therapy (e.g., maintenance infliximab) for simple ileocolic disease is questionable, especially in the light of studies indicating that such treatment is not at all innocuous.[6,7]

CHANGING CONCEPTS IN SURGERY FOR CROHN DISEASE

Although first described in the beginning of the 19th century, Crohn disease was not recognized as a discrete clinical entity until the first part of the 20th century.[8] At one point, it was treated surgically in much the same way as cancer, with frozen-section margins obtained at the time of resection. This approach did not yield any substantial reduction in the recurrence rate.[9] In fact, overzealous resections often resulted in Crohn patients' requiring lifelong parenteral nutritional support.[10] Accordingly, conservative surgery is now the rule: only gross macroscopic disease is resected into palpably normal margins (in particular, a palpably normal mesenteric border of the bowel).

General Indications for Surgical Treatment

SIDE EFFECTS OF MEDICAL THERAPY

Significant side effects of medical therapy include those associated with failure to wean from prednisone (e.g., cataract forma-

Table 1 Medical Treatment of Crohn Disease

Category	Example	Application Form	Expense
Probiotics	*Lactobacillus*	Food, capsules, pills, powders	$–$$
Antibiotics	Metronidazole, ciprofloxacin	p.o., I.V.	$–$$
Anti-inflammatories	Sulfasalazine 5-ASA products	p.o. p.o., suppositories, enemas	$ $$
Immunosuppressives	Conventional steroids Budesonide Antimetabolites Methotrexate Cyclosporine	p.o., I.V. p.o. p.o. p.o. or I.M. p.o. or I.V.	$ $$ $$ $ $$
Biologics	Infliximab Investigational agents	—	$$$$ NA

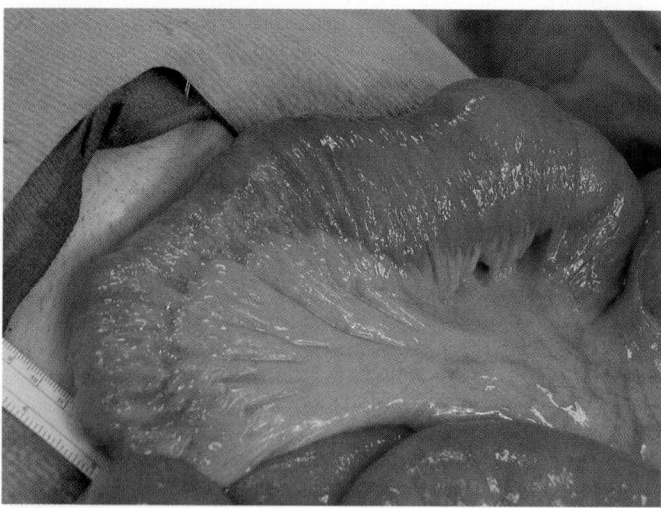

Figure 1 Shown is an example of stenotic ileocolic Crohn disease resulting in obstructive symptoms that were not relieved by medical therapy.

tion, aseptic necrosis of the femoral head, and weight gain). Side effects of antimetabolite therapy include pancreatitis, neutropenia, and opportunistic infections.

COMPLICATIONS OF DISEASE

Lack of Response to Medical Therapy

Many patients with so-called toxic colitis do not respond satisfactorily to medical treatment. In severe cases of refractory disease, if surgery is not performed, colonic perforation, peritonitis, and multiple organ failure may ensue. Such cases are much less frequent now than they once were.

Obstruction

In many patients with Crohn disease, the behavior of the disease changes over time, from a more inflammatory and edematous process to one characterized more by fibrosis and scarring. Whereas anti-inflammatory drugs are ideal for treating the former, surgery is frequently necessary for the latter. Failure to refer for surgical treatment of obstruction is, unfortunately, a common error among gastroenterologists. Severe abdominal pain is always a warning sign of obstruction and should be taken seriously [*see 43 Acute Abdominal Pain and 46 Intestinal Obstruction*]. The importance of this point is illustrated by a case from my experience, involving a patient who had obstructing ileocolic Crohn disease with gross proximal distention of the terminal ileum [*see Figure 1*]. This patient lost 20 lb, was experiencing severe abdominal pain, and was treated for more than a year with 6-mercaptopurine before being referred for operative management. Ileocolic resection led to rapid resolution of the symptoms.

Symptomatic Fistulas

Enteroenteric fistulas, by themselves, are no longer considered an absolute indication for operation in the absence of other complicating factors. Symptomatic fistulas, such as those associated with obstruction or those associated with disabling symptoms (e.g., rectovaginal fistulas or enterocutaneous fistulas [*see Figure 2*]), may have to be treated surgically. Ileosigmoid fistulas, which effectively bypass the entire colon, may be associated with profound and refractory diarrhea (i.e., ≥ 20 bowel movements/day) and may also have to be treated operatively.

Abscess Formation

Abscesses are particularly common with ileocolic Crohn disease. If they cannot be controlled by means of computed tomography–guided drainage, surgical therapy may be indicated.

Cancer or Dysplasia

The risk of colorectal cancer is approximately three times higher in patients with Crohn disease than in the general population.[11-13]

Failure to Grow

In children, failure to grow and develop normally is one of the main indications that medical therapy for Crohn disease has been unsuccessful. Timely surgical therapy will permit normal development. On occasion, when bone age lags significantly behind chronological age, treatment with recombinant human growth hormone is required.

Special Considerations

PREGNANCY

Persons who have Crohn disease may be less fertile than healthy age-matched persons. One possible explanation for this difference is that feeling ill may result in reduced sexual desire or decreased sexual activity. Another is that pelvic inflammation caused by Crohn disease or by scarring and adhesion formation resulting from surgery may impair fertility. To reduce the chances of the latter, hyaluronic acid sheets may be placed around the tubes and ovaries; alternatively, the ovaries may be tacked to the undersurface of the anterior abdominal wall with absorbable sutures and thereby prevented from entering the pelvis.

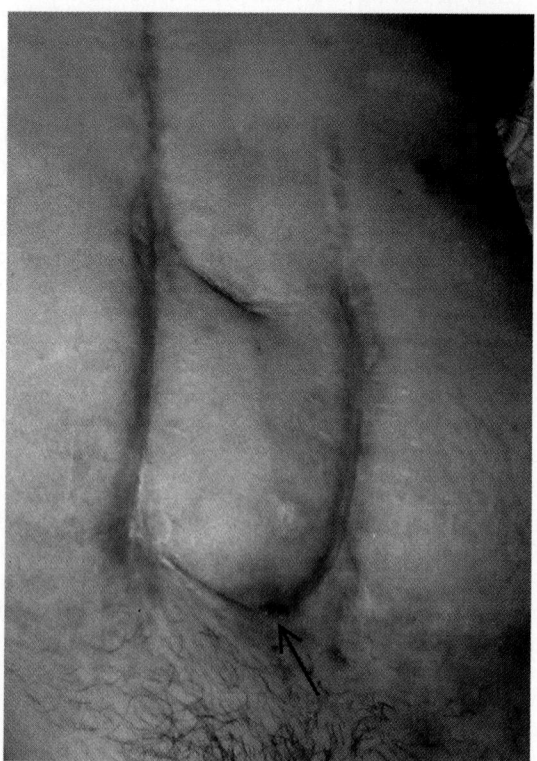

Figure 2 Shown is an enterocutaneous fistula that persisted for more than 1 year after an ileocolic resection (arrow). The choice of parallel incisions by the previous surgeon made selection of a temporary stoma site much more difficult.

There is no evidence that pregnancy exacerbates Crohn disease; however, there are some specific concerns that apply to pregnant patients with this condition. Because patients with Crohn disease often have more-liquid bowel movements, they have a particular need for a well-functioning anal sphincter. If there is any chance of an obstetrics-related injury (e.g., from a large baby in a prima-gravida or from a breech presentation), a cesarean section is advisable to minimize the risk of sphincter trauma. The same is true in the presence of severe perianal Crohn disease. During pregnancy, prednisone and 5-aminosalicylic acid (5-ASA) medications are safe, whereas drugs such as metronidazole are not. If imaging studies are needed, magnetic resonance imaging and ultrasonography are the modalities of choice.

MARKING OF STOMA SITES AND CHOICE OF INCISION

When a patient with Crohn disease is expected to need an ileostomy [see 72 Intestinal Stomas], it is extremely important to mark the site preoperatively. What looks flat when the patient is on the operating table may not be flat when he or she is upright. The patient must be asked to sit and lean over to confirm that the marked stoma site is in an area without folds, creases, or previous incisions. Stoma appliances do not adhere well to areas of previous scarring, and these should be avoided whenever possible.

Patients with Crohn disease do not react to intra-abdominal infection in a typical fashion. It is not unusual to find unsuspected abscesses that were not revealed by preoperative CT scans and other imaging studies. If there is even a remote chance of an unsuspected abscess (particularly in cases of obstructing ileocolic Crohn disease), the possibility of a temporary stoma should be raised with the patient and the proposed stoma site marked preoperatively.

A key point is the necessity of planning for the future. Many patients with Crohn disease will eventually require a stoma. Operating through a midline abdominal incision preserves all four quadrants for possible future stoma sites (if needed).

LAPAROSCOPY

Laparoscopic surgical techniques have gained acceptance in the treatment of Crohn disease. In performing a laparoscopic operation for Crohn disease, it is essential to adhere to the same technical standards that apply to corresponding open procedures. Careful intraoperative exploration of the abdomen is important, in that many patients have multifocal disease. Without such exploration, patients may experience persistent postoperative symptoms as a consequence of persistent proximal pathologic states that were not addressed. As with other treatment modalities, there are some circumstances in which laparoscopy is particularly useful and others in which it should not be used. For example, a laparoscopic approach is ideal for fecal diversion in patients with perianal Crohn disease.

Ileocolic resection for Crohn disease also lends itself well to a laparoscopic-assisted approach; compared with open resection, laparoscopic resection has been reported to result in shorter hospital stays and reduced costs.[14,15] The ileocolic vessels originate centrally, and they only lie over the retroperitoneum. Once the lateral peritoneal attachments are divided, the colon and the small bowel mesentery can be exteriorized, and the mesentery can be divided and the anastomosis performed extracorporeally.

Many studies have shown that even fistulizing Crohn disease can be safely addressed laparoscopically, depending on the skill of the surgeon. A hand-assisted approach is often useful with cases of dense fixation, in which fistulas are common and finger dissection may facilitate definition of the anatomy. If in doubt, one should not hesitate to convert to an open procedure. Typically, most areas that feel fibrotic or contain fibrotic adhesions are actually areas of fistulizing disease and should be treated as such until proved otherwise. In one study, patients with recurrent disease, those older than 40 years, and those with an abdominal mass were more likely to require conversion to an open procedure.[16]

Surgical Management of Crohn Disease at Specific Sites

ESOPHAGEAL, GASTRIC, AND DUODENAL DISEASE

Crohn disease of the upper alimentary tract can be difficult to diagnose, largely because it is relatively uncommon. Obstructing strictures due to Crohn disease in this area are unusual; the unsuspected finding of noncaseating granulomas in biopsies of erythematous areas in a patient with Crohn disease in other locations is diagnostic.

Occasionally, a patient with Crohn disease of the distal esophagus requires dilatations, but this is uncommon. Surgical treatment for Crohn disease of the upper alimentary tract is almost exclusively reserved for disease affecting the duodenum. Diagnosis of duodenal Crohn disease can be difficult and requires a certain amount of suspicion. Frequently, the diagnosis is not made until relatively late, because diagnostic imaging tends to focus on endoscopy and because the degree of duodenal obstruction is often not evident except on barium studies. The rigidity and luminal narrowing of the second portion of the duodenum is typically much more readily apparent on contrast studies than on endoscopy. Duodenal Crohn disease can lead to gastric outlet obstruction. In children, it can be mistaken for annular pancreas.

When duodenal Crohn disease does not respond to medical therapy, gastrojejunostomy with vagotomy is the preferred surgical treatment.[17,18] Failure to perform a vagotomy may result in marginal ulcer formation and obstruction. Some surgeons have performed duodenal strictureplasty to treat duodenal Crohn disease. The results have been conflicting[19,20]; the feasibility of this operative approach is limited by the pliability of the duodenum. Many patients experience prompt and full recovery of normal gastric emptying after operation, but some patients with long-standing gastric outlet obstruction continue to experience impaired emptying. The latter may benefit from administration of a prokinetic agent (e.g., metoclopramide or erythromycin).

JEJUNOILEAL DISEASE

Short Bowel Syndrome

Although Crohn disease of the small bowel is not common and accounts for a relatively small proportion of all cases, disease in this area is associated with one of the highest overall recurrence rates. Resection of large portions of the small bowel can result in short bowel syndrome. For this reason, before proceeding with any type of small bowel or ileocolic resection, one should measure the length of the existing small bowel to determine the patient's "bowel resource." One naturally would more readily perform a resection in a patient who has 400 cm of normal small bowel than in one who has only 200 cm.

Resection versus Strictureplasty

The major advance in the surgical treatment of Crohn disease over the past quarter-century has been the technique of small bowel strictureplasty, first proposed by Lee and subsequently popularized by Williams, Fazio, and others.[17,18] Currently, the two most prevalent strictureplasty techniques are Heineke-Mikulicz strictureplasty [*see Figure 3*] and Finney strictureplasty [*see Figure 4*]. The former is best suited for strictures up to 5 to 7 cm long [*see Figure 5*], the latter for strictures up to 10 to 15 cm long. The side-to-side strictureplasty described by Michelassi[21] is suitable for longer areas of stricture; however, this technique involves longer suture lines and is mainly considered for patients who already have, or are at high risk for, short bowel syndrome.

The short, isolated strictures characteristic of diffuse jejunoileal Crohn disease are more frequently described in patients with long-standing Crohn disease. It has been postulated that over time, Crohn disease progresses from an edematous condition to a more fibrotic, stricturing condition.[22] It is the fibrotic strictures characteristic of the later stage of the disease that are amenable to treatment with strictureplasty. Patients with these short fibrotic strictures typically have obstructive symptoms and often are unable to tolerate solid food, experiencing dramatic weight loss as a result. Although strictureplasty leaves active disease in situ, it usually leads to prompt resolution of obstructive symptoms, regaining of lost body weight, and restoration of normal nutritional status.

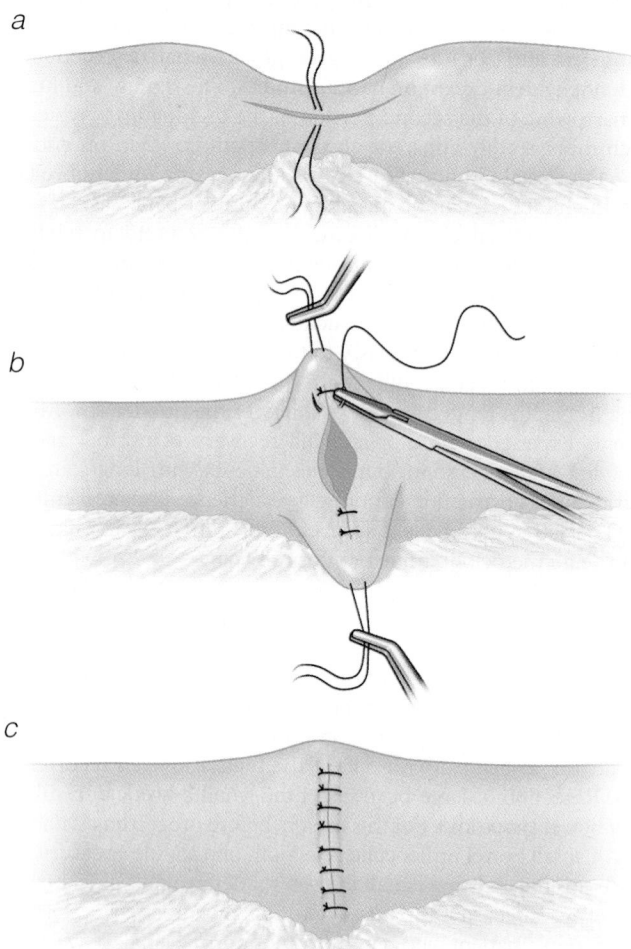

Figure 3 **Heineke-Mikulicz strictureplasty. Stay sutures are placed parallel to each other on the antimesenteric border of the bowel over the area of the stricture. (*a*) The antimesenteric border of the bowel is then opened with the electrocautery over the area of the stricture, and the opening is extended for approximately 1 to 2 cm on either side of the stricture. (*b, c*) Traction is placed on the stay sutures, and the original longitudinal enterotomy is closed in a horizontal fashion in one or two layers.**

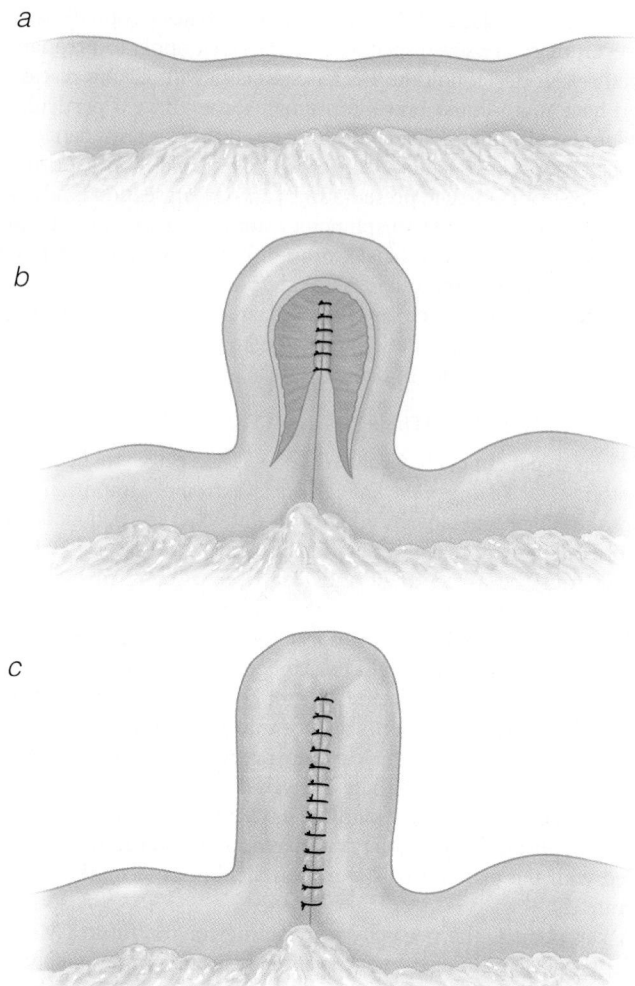

Figure 4 **Finney strictureplasty. (*a*) This procedure is suitable for longer areas of stricture (up to 10 to 15 cm). (*b*) The strictured bowel is bent into the shape of an inverted U. Stay sutures are placed at the apex of the U, which is at the midpoint of the stricture, and at the far ends, which lie 1 to 2 cm proximal and distal to the stricture. A longitudinal enterotomy is made on the antimesenteric border of the bowel with the electrocautery. A side-to-side anastomosis is then performed, with the posterior wall done first. (*c*) Shown is the completed anastomosis.**

A significant concern with strictureplasty is the possibility that small bowel adenocarcinoma may develop; several cases have been reported.[23,24] I have treated a patient in whom a poorly differentiated jejunal adenocarcinoma developed at the site of a strictureplasty that had been performed 10 years earlier. Accordingly, many surgeons advocate routine biopsy of the active ulcer on the mesenteric side of the bowel at the time of strictureplasty [*see Figure 6*]. Another concern has to do with the number of strictureplasties that can safely be performed in a single patient in the course of a single operation. As many as 19 strictureplasties have been performed during one procedure without increased morbidity.[25]

Strictureplasty can be performed with either a single-layer or a double-layer anastomosis. It should not be performed in the presence of an abscess, a phlegmon, or a fistula; and like any other anastomosis, it should not be performed proximal to an existing obstruction that is not treated at the time of operation.

Areas of small bowel Crohn disease that are too long to be treated with strictureplasty can be treated with segmental resection.

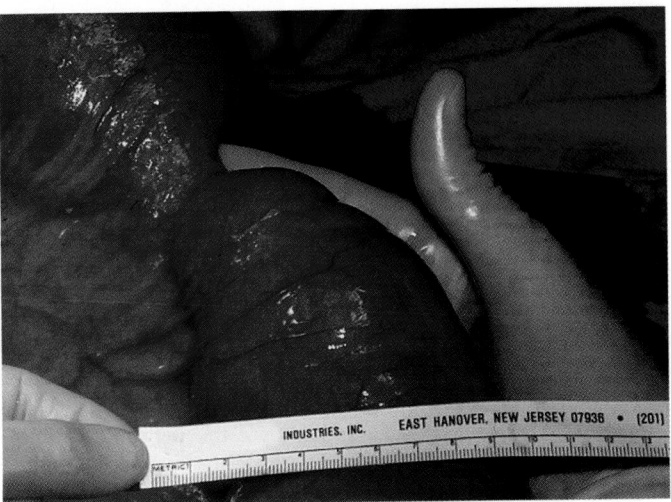

Figure 5 **Shown is a short fibrotic stricture that is ideally suited to treatment with Heineke-Mikulicz strictureplasty.**

The area to be resected should be as short as possible. There is no need to obtain frozen-section margins to determine the extent of resection; doing so leads to unnecessary loss of small bowel length.[26] The resection should extend into palpably normal areas of small bowel. The easiest way of determining the area to be resected is to feel the mesenteric margin of the bowel until palpably normal tissue is reached. Because Crohn disease is generally more severe on the mesenteric side of the bowel, palpation in this area gives the most accurate impression of the intraluminal character of the bowel. Because it is not uncommon for patients to have multifocal Crohn disease, the entire small bowel should always be inspected at the time of operation. Operating on one area of disease while failing to treat a more proximal lesion is clearly not in the patient's interest.

Because of the high rate of recurrence in patients with isolated small bowel disease, postoperative chemoprophylaxis should be strongly considered. In these patients, I prefer to use a more potent agent, such as an antimetabolite, rather than a 5-ASA agent.

ILEOCOLIC DISEASE

Approximately half of those diagnosed with Crohn disease have ileocolic disease. Ileocolic resection is, in fact, the operation most frequently performed to treat Crohn disease. Currently, there is a trend toward more aggressive medical management of Crohn disease; at the same time, surgeons are seeing more complicated disease at the time of operation. These developments have implications for management. An easy ileocolic resection is an experience that a patient generally tolerates well and recovers from very quickly; however, delaying operative management with years of aggressive medical therapy can lead to more complicated disease associated with enteroenteric fistulas, which can be difficult to treat. Ileosigmoid fistulas are among the most common fistulas associated with ileocolic Crohn disease, along with fistulas between the terminal ileum and the ascending colon and fistulas between the terminal ileum and adjacent loops of small bowel.

Disease recurrence is common after ileocolic resection. Colonoscopy is the most accurate modality for postoperative surveillance and the easiest to use; it is more sensitive than either small bowel follow-through or air-contrast barium enema. For this reason, I favor an end-to-end anastomosis after ileocolic resection. In the event of recurrent disease, an end-to-side, side-to-end, or side-to-side anastomosis may be difficult to intubate. There is some evidence in the literature to suggest that the postoperative recurrence rate may be lower with a wider anastomosis.[27] The anastomosis can be performed in either one or two layers. If the bowel is thicker, a handsewn anastomosis is preferred to a stapled one.

The incidence of reoperation for recurrent disease after ileocolic resection is high and increases with the number of resections.[28] Postoperative chemoprophylaxis with mesalamine can significantly reduce the recurrence rate.[29] Patients who smoke should be strongly encouraged to stop: the rate and severity of recurrence are increased in smokers.[20]

Special Circumstances

Ileocolic Crohn disease is often associated with intra-abdominal abscesses or fistulas. If an associated abscess is known to be present, CT-guided drainage should be done preoperatively so that a single-stage procedure can then be performed. If an unsuspected abscess is identified at the time of operation, the safest approach is to proceed with bowel resection, perform the posterior wall of the anastomosis, and exteriorize the anastomosis as a loop ileostomy. This loop ileostomy can then be safely closed, often without a formal laparotomy, 8 weeks after operation if there are no signs of ongoing sepsis. If the abscess or the terminal ileal loop is adherent to the sigmoid colon, an ileosigmoid fistula may be present. The decision whether to resect the sigmoid colon is dictated by the appearance and feel of the sigmoid in the involved areas. If only a portion of the anterior colon wall is involved, that portion can be excised in a wedgelike fashion and the excision site closed primarily. If the entire circumference of the sigmoid colon at that point is indurated and woody feeling, a short segmental resection with anastomosis is the best option.

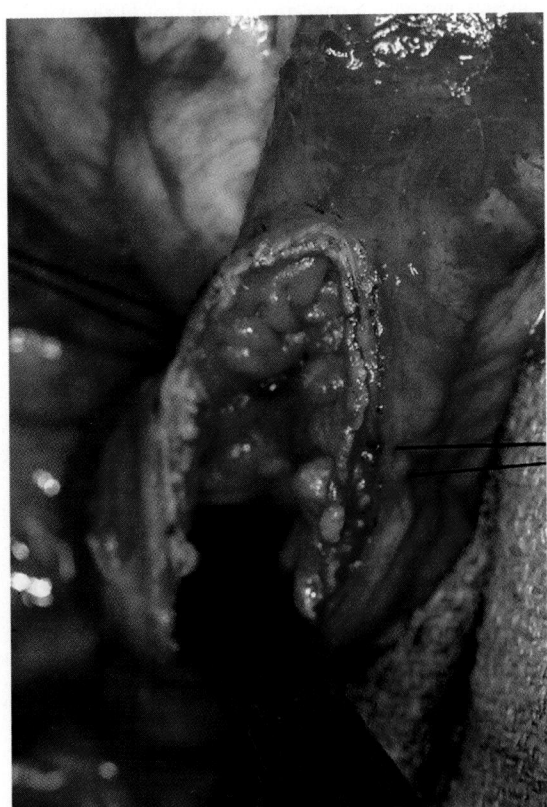

Figure 6 **A large ulcer is nearly always present on the mesenteric luminal border of small bowel strictures.**

COLONIC DISEASE

Colonic involvement is present in 29% to 44% of patients with Crohn disease.[30] One of the challenges in treating colonic Crohn disease is obtaining the correct diagnosis. Whereas Crohn disease of the small bowel is fairly easy to diagnose, colonic disease often is not. Because granulomas are not present in most cases of colonic Crohn disease and because this condition can look very similar to ulcerative colitis both endoscopically and macroscopically, differentiation between Crohn colitis and ulcerative colitis can be difficult in the absence of small bowel or anal disease. Colonic Crohn disease appears to be more frequently associated with cutaneous manifestations (e.g., pyoderma gangrenosum) [see Figure 7].

Indications for Surgical Treatment

The main indications for operative management of colonic Crohn disease are stricture [see Figure 8], malignancy, side effects of medical therapy, and failure of medical therapy. In children, failure to recognize and treat this condition promptly may result in growth retardation. It is important to monitor both bone age and insulinlike growth factor–1 levels. If these are abnormal, timely institution of human growth hormone therapy, operative management of inflammatory bowel disease, or both may still permit normal growth and development.

Side effects of medical therapy can be substantial. They may include such varied complications as aseptic necrosis of the femoral head and cataract formation (both related to steroid use), as well as an increased incidence of opportunistic infections (from immunosuppression secondary to antimetabolite therapy).

Failure of medical therapy can refer to continuing severe disease activity or, at worst, to so-called toxic megacolon. The term toxic megacolon is actually a misnomer, in that not all patients with this condition actually have a true megacolon [see Figure 9a]. In common usage, the term toxic megacolon refers to any condition associated with colitis that is severe enough to result in sloughing of the colonic mucosa; such sloughing permits endotoxins to enter the circulatory system and evoke a septic response. The signs and symptoms of toxic megacolon include those characteristic of sepsis—leukocytosis, fever, tachycardia, and hypoalbuminemia. These patients are very ill and often manifest ileus, which is an ominous development that frequently signals impending perforation. Emergency surgical intervention is required. At operation, the colon is often distended, and when the specimen is opened, the colon may appear almost autolytic [see Figure 9b]. In this state, the bowel frequently does not hold staples well; accordingly, it is often helpful to sew the distal Hartmann stump between the left and right halves of the anterior inferior rectus fascia at the lower abdominal incision and then to close the skin over it.[31] Thus, if the staple line is disrupted, the result is essentially a surgical site infection that can be opened and drained, rather than the pelvic abscess [see Figure 9c] that could develop if the rectal stump were located deep within the pelvis.

Types of Disease

Segmental disease In a 2003 review of 92 consecutive cases of patients with Crohn colitis, the number of patients with segmental colonic Crohn disease and the number of those with pancolonic disease were nearly equal.[30] Approximately 63% of those with segmental colitis had other disease involvement as well (e.g., jejunoileal, ileocolic, or perianal), compared with only 12% of those with pancolitis. The recurrence rate, however, was higher in patients with segmental colitis than in those with pancolitis. In addition, the risk of recurrence was higher in patients who had granulomatous disease than in those who did not.

Pancolonic disease In cases of pancolonic Crohn disease with associated perianal, jejunoileal, or ileocolic involvement, diagnosis is not difficult. However, most patients with Crohn pancolitis do not have other sites of disease involvement, nor do they have granulomas.[30] Consequently, differentiation of Crohn pancolitis

a

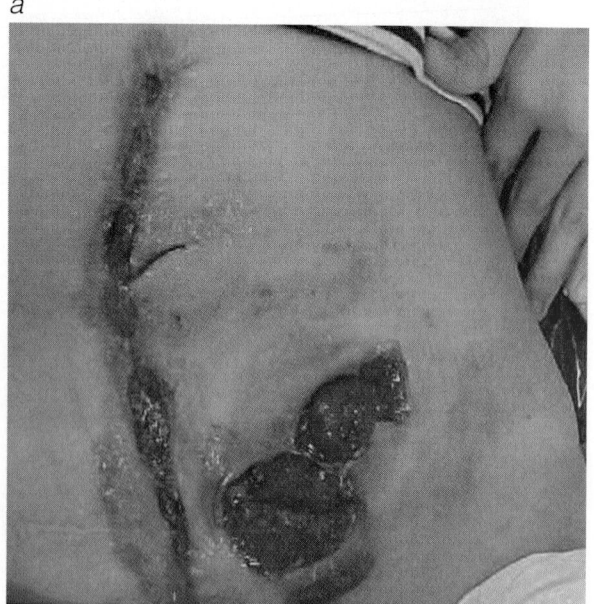

b

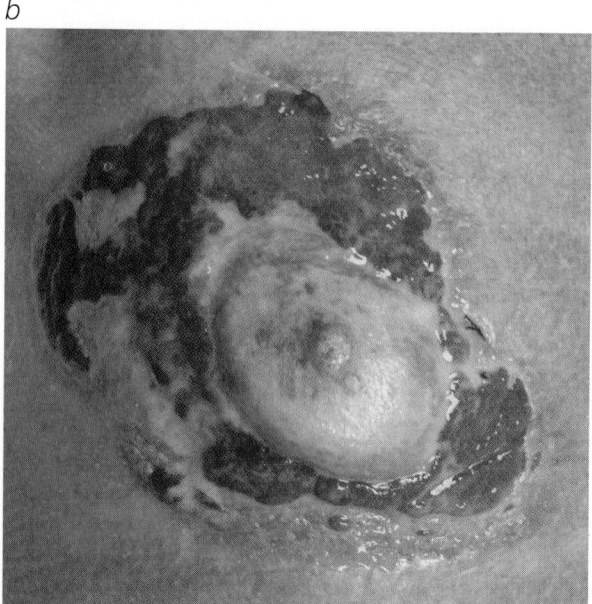

Figure 7 (*a*) Shown is pyoderma gangrenosum affecting the peristomal and incisional area 6 months after creation of a loop ileostomy in a 16-year-old girl who had undergone colectomy with IPAA for a presumed initial diagnosis of ulcerative colitis. (*b*) Shown is peristomal gangrenosum of the breast in an otherwise asymptomatic patient with Crohn colitis and perianal Crohn disease who had a diverting loop ileostomy.

Figure 8 Shown is a sigmoid colon stricture secondary to Crohn disease that caused obstructing symptoms refractory to medical therapy.

from ulcerative colitis can be very difficult. Many patients with Crohn disease have been inappropriately subjected to colectomy with ileal pouch–anal anastomosis (IPAA) because they were initially presumed to have ulcerative colitis.

Operative Procedures

Total proctocolectomy with end ileostomy The traditional procedure for colonic Crohn disease is total proctocolectomy with end ileostomy, which is associated with an 8% to 15% rate of recurrence in the bowel proximal to the stoma.[32-34] This operation remains the best choice in patients with severe rectal and anal Crohn disease (e.g., those with so-called watering-can perineum [*see Figure 10*]) and carries the lowest risk of disease recurrence. In contrast to the approach taken in patients with rectal cancer, which involves excising the external anal sphincter and a large portion of the levator muscles, the approach taken in those with colonic Crohn disease is intersphincteric, with dissection performed in the plane between the internal and external anal sphincters to reduce the size of the perineal wound and facilitate healing. Even with the intersphincteric approach, delayed healing of the perineal wound is common, occurring in as many as 30% of patients.

Subtotal colectomy with ileorectal or ileosigmoid anastomosis Because many patients with Crohn disease are young, surgeons have long been interested in operations that do not involve an ileostomy. In the absence of significant rectal and anal disease, subtotal colectomy with ileorectal or ileosigmoid anastomosis is an option. Unfortunately, this operation is associated with high recurrence rates (up to 70%)[35]; however, with the advent of more effective immunosuppressive and biologic therapy, it is hoped that these rates can be reduced. As much palpably normal distal rectum and colon as possible should be spared. The anastomosis can be stapled, though if the bowel wall is thickened, many surgeons would feel more secure with a handsewn anastomosis in either one or two layers.

Segmental resection Currently, more surgeons are advocating colon-sparing procedures [*see 76 Segmental Colon Resection*] for Crohn disease. Although this is a relatively new approach,

a
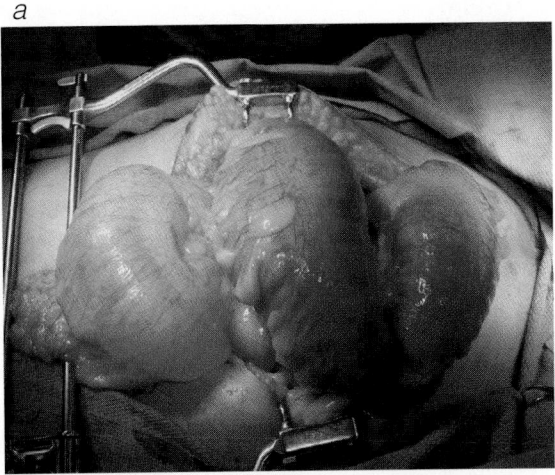

b

c
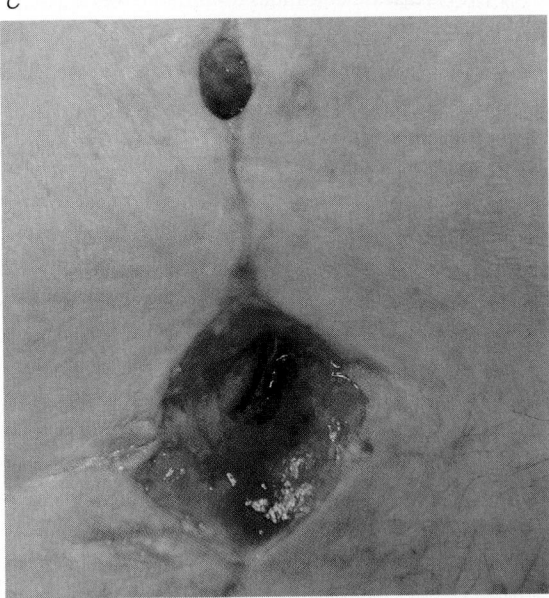

Figure 9 (*a*) Shown is toxic megacolon in a 17-year-old girl with Crohn colitis. The colon is massively distended and near perforation at the time of operation. (*b*) When the specimen is opened, it is apparent that large segments of the mucosa have sloughed off, leaving denuded muscle wall. (*c*) The distal rectosigmoid is incorporated between the left and right halves of the anterior inferior rectus fascia at the lower abdominal incision and placed underneath the skin, which is then closed over it. Thus, in the event of disruption of the distal stump, the contents drain harmlessly through the wound.

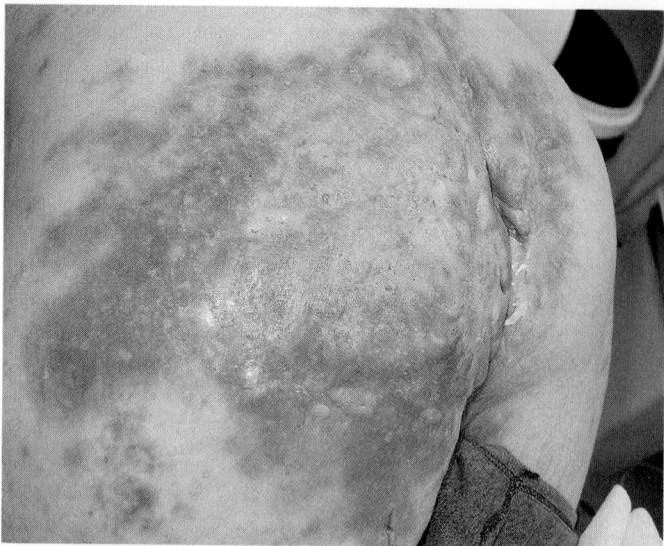

Figure 10 **Shown is so-called watering-can perineum secondary to severe perianal Crohn disease.**

there have already been some reports documenting the safety of segmental resection in cases of limited disease.[36] In patients with colonic strictures resulting in obstruction, segmental resection into palpably normal areas of the bowel yields prompt resolution of symptoms. Because the colon performs an important water-absorbing function, many patients with a limited amount of small bowel can still live without intravenous supplementation if a significant segment of the colon is left in situ. However, patients with segmental Crohn disease appear to have a higher recurrence rate than those with pancolitis, as do patients with granulomas.[30] Surgical treatment of Crohn disease continues to undergo reevaluation and reassessment of results on the basis of the availability of newer medical therapies.

Colectomy with IPAA Although colectomy with IPAA [*see 75 Procedures for Ulcerative Colitis*] is not an operation that one

would knowingly perform in a patient with Crohn disease, every year there are many such patients who undergo this procedure as treatment of colonic inflammatory bowel disease that initially is incorrectly presumed to be ulcerative colitis but later is diagnosed as Crohn disease (on the basis of either final pathologic analysis of the resected specimen or the disease's clinical behavior). Generally speaking, in the absence of fistulizing disease, most of these patients are able to maintain their pouch, but they require medical therapy for disease control.[30,37-40]

ANAL DISEASE

Types of Disease

With stenosis For patients with anal strictures that are not regularly dilated, the outlook is poor. Such strictures pose functional obstructions and typically lead to continuing problems with fistulas and suppurative disease. They frequently become more and more fibrotic over time and often extend proximally. Most of these patients eventually require fecal diversion. Management generally involves self-dilation, which can often be done with Hegar dilators. If the stenosis is not dealt with, all other treatment of the Crohn disease is doomed to failure; obstruction at the level of the anal canal inevitably results in the persistence of anorectal disease.

Without stenosis Anal Crohn disease without stenosis is much easier to treat medically. Long-term oral metronidazole therapy is often helpful; other medications (e.g., anti–tumor necrosis factor antibody) may be useful as well. Broad fissures are usually asymptomatic. Surgical treatment should be avoided unless the lesions are causing symptoms. Because they tend to have more liquid bowel movements, patients with Crohn disease need an optimally functioning anal sphincter; hence, fistulotomies, which divide portions of the sphincter, should be avoided if at all possible. Placement of setons through fistula tracts can often prevent abscess formation, provide drainage, and thereby prevent perianal pain while minimizing sphincter trauma. Silk sutures, vessel loops, or Penrose drains also can be used as setons [*see Figure 11*]. Rectovaginal fistulas pose a particular challenge. In the presence of active Crohn disease, advancement flap repair of such fistulas has a low success rate.[41] Laparoscopic-assisted loop ileostomy improves the success rate, but unfortunately, the fistulas may recur when intestinal continuity is reestablished.

Postoperative Management

CHEMOPROPHYLAXIS

In 1995, a prospective, randomized study showed that patients who underwent ileocolic resection and were given mesalamine postoperatively had a significant reduction in both the symptomatic and the endoscopic rate of recurrence.[29] Not all of the work done since then has confirmed these results, but several studies and a meta-analysis have indicated that mesalamine does reduce the postoperative recurrence rate of Crohn disease.[42] Many patients undergoing surgical treatment of Crohn disease are advised to take some type of postoperative preventive medical therapy—either a 5-ASA derivative (e.g., mesalamine) or a stronger immunosuppressive agent (e.g., 6-mercaptopurine or azathioprine). Better studies are required to document the efficacy of the latter agents in preventing recurrence. It is hoped that chemoprophylaxis will reduce the anticipated recurrence rates by 30% to 40%.

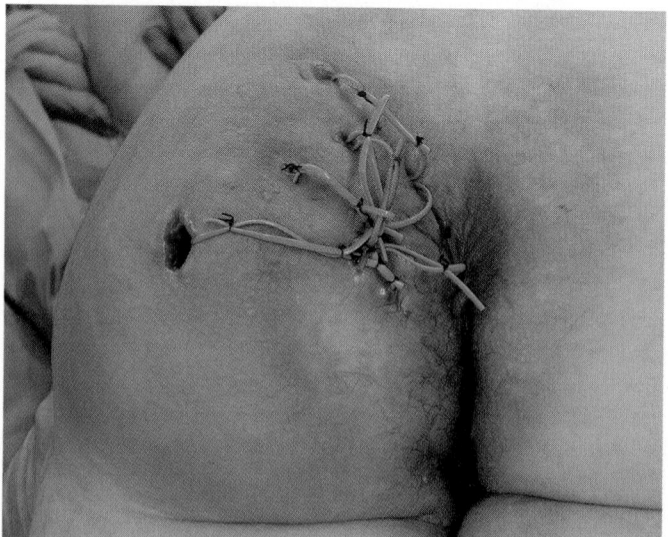

Figure 11 **Vessel loops can be used as setons for drainage of abscesses caused by perianal Crohn disease. They can be left in as long as necessary and help prevent recurrent abscess formation.**

SURVEILLANCE

At present, there are no clear guidelines for surveillance after operative treatment of Crohn disease. In my opinion, however, given the increased risk of colorectal cancer in this setting, patients with Crohn disease who retain some colon should undergo colonoscopy every 2 years, not only to detect any development of colonic neoplasia but also to identify any recurrence of disease in a timely manner. If recurrent Crohn disease is detected, appropriate medical therapy should be promptly instituted, with the aim of avoiding subsequent operation if possible.

BEHAVIORAL MODIFICATION

Exposure to cigarette smoke is known to exacerbate the symptoms of Crohn disease. Smoking has been reported to affect the overall severity of the disease, with smokers having a 34% higher recurrence rate and a higher rate of reoperation than nonsmokers.[43-45] A 1999 study of 141 Crohn disease patients who had undergone ileocolic resection, of whom 79 were nonsmokers and the remainder were smokers, found that the respective 5- and 10-year recurrence-free rates were 65% and 45% in smokers and 81% and 64% in nonsmokers. The recurrence rates were higher in heavy smokers ($\geq$ 15 cigarettes/day) than in moderate smokers.[46]

References

1. Farmer RG, Hawk WA, Turnbull RB Jr: Clinical patterns in Crohn's disease: a statistical study of 615 cases. Gastroenterology 68:627, 1975

2. Gasche C, Scholmerich J, Brynskov J, et al: A simple classification of Crohn's disease: report of the Working Party for the World Congresses of Gastroenterology, Vienna 1998. Inflamm Bowel Dis 6:8, 2000

3. Michelassi F, Balestracci T, Chappell R, et al: Primary and recurrent Crohn's disease: experience with 1379 patients. Ann Surg 214:230, 1991

4. Bodger K: Cost of illness of Crohn's disease. Pharmacoeconomics 20:639, 2002

5. Feagan BG, Vreeland MG, Larson LR, et al: Annual cost of care for Crohn's disease: a payor perspective. Am J Gastroenterol 95:1955, 2000

6. Colombel JF, Loftus EV Jr, Tremaine WJ, et al: The safety profile of infliximab in patients with Crohn's disease: the Mayo clinic experience in 500 patients. Gastroenterology 126:19, 2004

7. Ljung T, Karlen P, Schmidt D, et al: Infliximab in inflammatory bowel disease: clinical outcome in a population based cohort from Stockholm County. Gut 53:849, 2004

8. Crohn BB, Ginzburg L, Oppenheimer GD: Landmark article Oct 15, 1932. Regional ileitis: a pathological and clinical entity. By Burril B. Crohn, Leon Ginzburg, and Gordon D. Oppenheimer. JAMA 251:73, 1984

9. Fazio VW, Marchetti F, Church M, et al: Effect of resection margins on the recurrence of Crohn's disease in the small bowel: a randomized controlled trial. Ann Surg 224:563, 1996

10. Galandiuk S, O'Neill M, McDonald P, et al: A century of home parenteral nutrition for Crohn's disease. Am J Surg 159:540, 1990

11. Greenstein AJ: Cancer in inflammatory bowel disease. Mt Sinai J Med 67:227, 2000

12. Rhodes JM, Campbell BJ: Inflammation and colorectal cancer: IBD-associated and sporadic cancer compared. Trends Mol Med 8:10, 2002

13. Gillen CD, Walmsley RS, Prior P, et al: Ulcerative colitis and Crohn's disease: a comparison of the colorectal cancer risk in extensive colitis. Gut 35:1590, 1994

14. Milsom JW, Hammerhofer KA, Bohm B, et al: Prospective, randomized trial comparing laparoscopic vs. conventional surgery for refractory ileocolic Crohn's disease. Dis Colon Rectum 44:1, 2001

15. Young-Fadok TM, HallLong K, McConnell EJ, et al: Advantages of laparoscopic resection for ileocolic Crohn's disease: improved outcomes and reduced costs. Surg Endosc 15:450, 2001

16. Moorthy K, Shaul T, Foley RJ: Factors that predict conversion in patients undergoing laparoscopic surgery for Crohn's disease. Am J Surg 187:47, 2004

17. Murray JJ, Schoetz DJ Jr, Nugent FW, et al: Surgical management of Crohn's disease involving the duodenum. Am J Surg 147:58, 1984

18. Ross TM, Fazio VW, Farmer RG: Long-term results of surgical treatment for Crohn's disease of the duodenum. Ann Surg 197:399, 1983

19. Worsey MJ, Hull T, Ryland L, et al: Strictureplasty is an effective option in the operative management of duodenal Crohn's disease. Dis Colon Rectum 42:596, 1999

20. Yamamoto T, Bain IM, Connolly AB, et al: Outcome of strictureplasty for duodenal Crohn's disease. Br J Surg 86:259, 1999

21. Michelassi F, Hurst RD, Melis M, et al: Side-to-side isoperistaltic strictureplasty in extensive Crohn's disease: a prospective longitudinal study. Ann Surg 232:401, 2000

22. Marshak RH, Wolf BS: Chronic ulcerative granulomatous jejunitis and ileojejunitis. AJR 70:93, 1953

23. Jaskowiak NT, Michelassi F: Adenocarcinoma at a strictureplasty site in Crohn's disease: report of a case. Dis Colon Rectum 44:284, 2001

24. Marchetti F, Fazio VW, Ozuner G: Adenocarcinoma arising from a strictureplasty site in Crohn's disease: report of a case. Dis Colon Rectum 39:1315, 1996

25. Dietz DW, Laureti S, Strong SA, et al: Safety and long-term efficacy of strictureplasty in 314 patients with obstructing small bowel Crohn's disease. J Am Coll Surg 192:330, 2001

26. Hamilton SR, Reese J, Pennington L, et al: The role of resection margin frozen section in the surgical management of Crohn's disease. Surg Gynecol Obstet 160:57, 1985

27. Munoz-Juarez M, Yamamoto T, Wolff BG, et al: Wide-lumen stapled anastomosis vs. conventional end-to-end anastomosis in the treatment of Crohn's disease. Dis Colon Rectum 44:20, 2001

28. Greenstein AJ, Sachar DB, Pasternack BS, et al: Reoperation and recurrence in Crohn's colitis and ileocolitis: crude and cumulative rates. N Engl J Med 293:685, 1975

29. McLeod RS, Wolff BG, Steinhart AH, et al: Prophylactic mesalamine treatment decreases postoperative recurrence of Crohn's disease. Gastroenterology 109:404, 1995

30. Morpurgo E, Petras R, Kimberling J, et al: Characterization and clinical behavior of Crohn's disease initially presenting predominantly as colitis. Dis Colon Rectum 46:918, 2003

31. Hull T, Fazio VW: Surgery for toxic megacolon. Mastery of Surgery, 3rd ed. Nyhus LM, Baker RJ, Frischer JE, Eds. Little Brown & Co, Boston, 1996, p 1437

32. Goligher JC: The outcome of excisional operations for primary and recurrent Crohn's disease of the large intestine. Surg Gynecol Obstet 148:1, 1979

33. Ritchie JK, Lockhart-Mummery HE: Nonrestorative surgery in the treatment of Crohn's disease of the large bowel. Gut 14:263, 1973

34. Goligher JC: The long-term results of excisional surgery for primary and recurrent Crohn's disease of the large intestine. Dis Colon Rectum 28:51, 1985

35. Goligher JC: Surgical treatment of Crohn's disease affecting mainly or entirely the large bowel. World J Surg 12:186, 1988

36. Allan A, Andrews H, Hilton CJ, et al: Segmental colonic resection is an appropriate operation for short skip lesions due to Crohn's disease in the colon. World J Surg 13:611, 1989

37. Hyman NH, Fazio VW, Tuckson WB, et al: Consequences of ileal pouch-anal anastomosis for Crohn's colitis. Dis Colon Rectum 34:653, 1991

38. Galandiuk S, Scott NA, Dozois RR, et al: Ileal pouch-anal anastomosis. Reoperation for pouch-related complications. Ann Surg 212:446, 1990

39. Panis Y, Poupard B, Nemeth J, et al: Ileal pouch/anal anastomosis for Crohn's disease. Lancet 347:854, 1996

40. Ricart E, Panaccione R, Loftus EV, et al: Successful management of Crohn's disease of the ileoanal pouch with infliximab. Gastroenterology 117:429, 1999

41. Sonoda T, Hull T, Piedmonte MR, et al: Outcomes of primary repair of anorectal and rectovaginal fistulas using the endorectal advancement flap. Dis Colon Rectum 45:1622, 2002

42. Achkar JP, Hanauer SB: Medical therapy to reduce postoperative Crohn's disease recurrence. Am J Gastroenterol 95:1139, 2000

43. Duffy LC, Zielezny MA, Marshall JR, et al: Cigarette smoking and risk of clinical relapse in patients with Crohn's disease. Am J Prev Med 6:161, 1990

44. Sutherland LR, Ramcharan S, Bryant H, et al: Effect of cigarette smoking on recurrence of Crohn's disease. Gastroenterology 98:1123, 1990

45. Cottone M, Rosselli M, Orlando A, et al: Smoking habits and recurrence in Crohn's disease. Gastroenterology 106:643, 1994

46. Yamamoto T, Keighley MR: The association of cigarette smoking with a high risk of recurrence after ileocolonic resection for ileocecal Crohn's disease. Surg Today 29:579, 1999

Acknowledgment

Figures 3 and 4   Tom Moore.

John P. Welch, M.D., F.A.C.S., and Jeffrey L. Cohen, M.D., F.A.C.S., F.A.S.C.R.S.

Management of Diverticulitis

Diverticula are small (0.5 to 1.0 cm in diameter) outpouchings of the colon that occur in rows at sites of vascular penetration between the single mesenteric taenia and one of the antimesenteric taeniae. At the sites of most diverticula, the muscular layer is absent [*see Figure 1*]. Technically, such lesions are really pseudodiverticula; true diverticula (which are much less common than pseudodiverticula) involve all layers of the bowel wall. Nevertheless, both pseudodiverticula and true diverticula are generally referred to as diverticula.

The sigmoid colon is the most common site of diverticula: in 90% of patients with diverticulosis, the sigmoid colon is involved.[1] If a diverticulum becomes inflamed as a result of obstruction by feces or hardened mucus or of mucosal erosion, a localized perforation (microperforation) may occur—a process known as diverticulitis. The incidence of diverticulitis is about 10% to 25% in patients with colonic diverticula.[1] Both diverticulosis and variants of diverticulitis may be subsumed under the more encompassing term diverticular disease.

The incidence of diverticular disease increases with age. Diverticula are quite common in elderly patients, being present in more than 80% of patients older than 85 years.[2] Consequently, as the population of the United States continues to age, the overall risk of diverticular complications continues to increase.[3] Before the 20th century, diverticular disease was rare in the United States. By 1996, however, 131,000 patients were being admitted to hospitals with diverticulitis each year.[4]

A diet containing refined carbohydrates and low-fiber substances, such as is currently widespread in many developed countries (especially in the West), has been associated with the emergence of this disease entity.[5,6] A low-residue diet facilitates the development of constipation, which can lead to increased intraluminal pressure in the large bowel. In addition, elevated elastin levels are commonly noted at colon wall sites containing diverticula,[7] and this change causes shortening of the taeniae.[1] High-pressure zones or areas of segmentation may develop [*see Figure 2*], usually in the sigmoid colon, and diverticula begin to protrude at these locations. If microperforation of a thin-walled diverticulum takes place, local or, sometimes, widespread contamination with fecal organisms may ensue. The pericolic tissue (typically, the mesentery and the pericolic fat) thus becomes inflamed while the mucosa tends to remain otherwise normal.

Several factors appear to promote the development of diverticular disease and its complications, including decreased physical activity,[8] intake of nonsteroidal anti-inflammatory drugs (NSAIDs),[9,10] smoking,[11] and constipation from any cause (e.g., diet or medications). The well-known Western afflictions cholelithiasis, diverticulosis, and hiatal hernia frequently occur together (Saint's triad). Obesity has been associated with the intake of low-fiber diets,[12] and growing numbers of young, obese patients with diverticulitis are being seen by physicians.

Clinical Evaluation

HISTORY

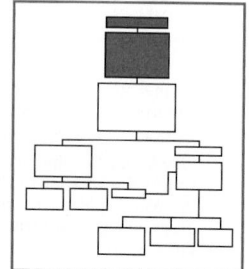

Uncomplicated (Simple) Diverticulitis

The classic symptoms of uncomplicated acute diverticulitis are left lower quadrant abdominal pain, a low-grade fever, irregular bowel habits, and, possibly, urinary symptoms if the affected colon is adjacent to the bladder. If the sigmoid colon is highly redundant, pain may be greatest in the right lower quadrant. Diarrhea or constipation may occur, together with rectal urgency.

The differential diagnosis includes gynecologic and urinary disorders, perforated colon carcinoma, Crohn disease, ischemic colitis, and, sometimes, appendicitis. Chronic diarrhea, multiple areas of colon involvement, perianal disease, perineal or cutaneous fistulas, or extraintestinal signs are suggestive of Crohn disease. Rectal bleeding should raise the possibility of inflammatory bowel disease, ischemia, or carcinoma; such bleeding is uncommon with diverticulitis alone. Given the prevalence of diverticula, it is not surprising that colon carcinoma may coexist with diverticular disease [*see Figure 3*].

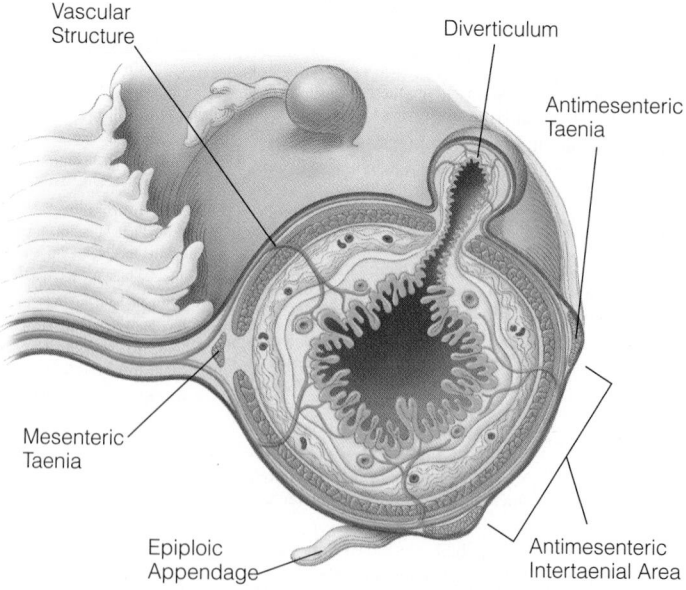

Figure 1 **Illustrated are anatomic findings in a segment of colon containing diverticula. Diverticula are located at sites where blood vessels enter the colonic wall.**[87]

Management of Diverticulitis

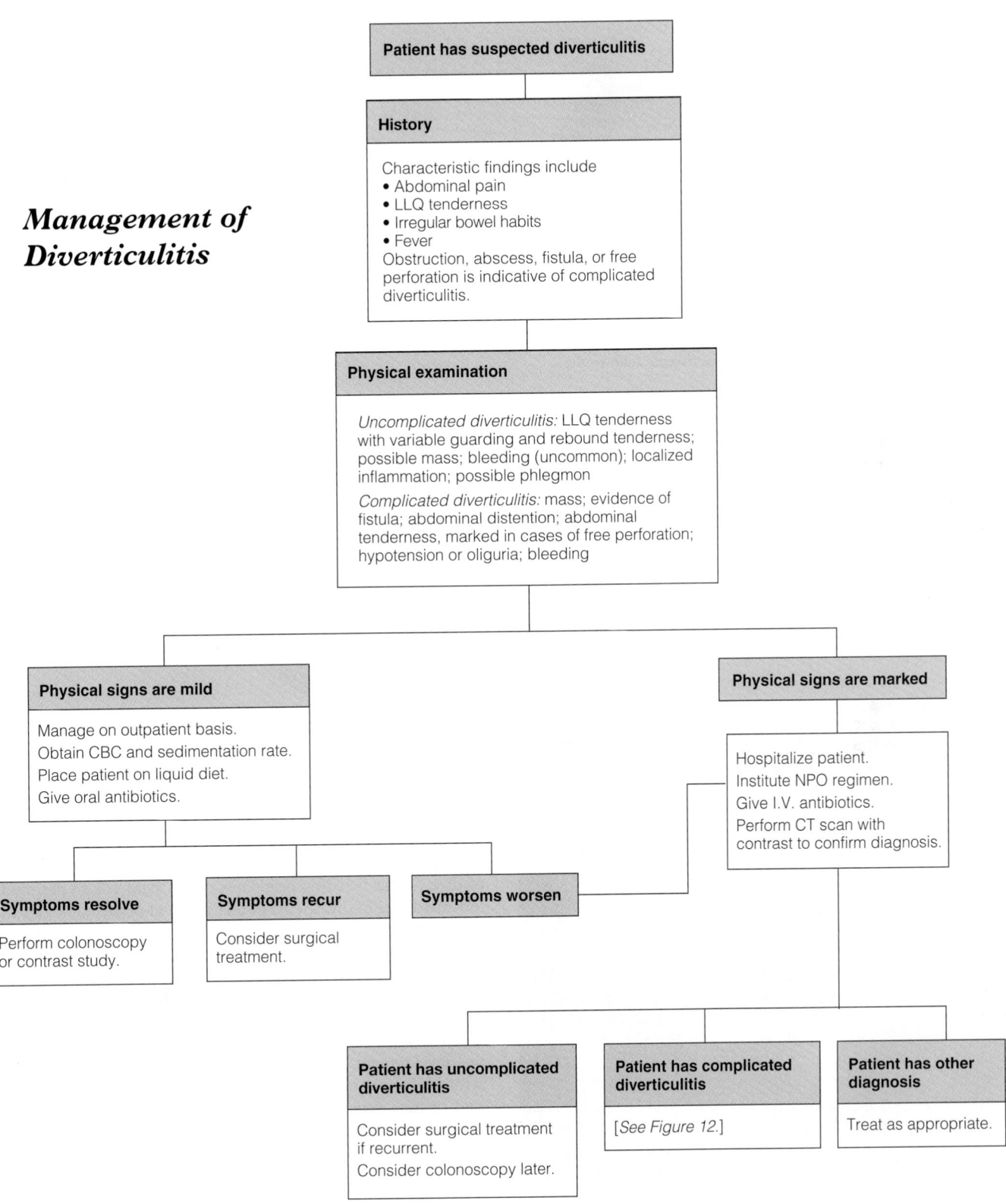

Patient has suspected diverticulitis

History

Characteristic findings include
- Abdominal pain
- LLQ tenderness
- Irregular bowel habits
- Fever

Obstruction, abscess, fistula, or free perforation is indicative of complicated diverticulitis.

Physical examination

Uncomplicated diverticulitis: LLQ tenderness with variable guarding and rebound tenderness; possible mass; bleeding (uncommon); localized inflammation; possible phlegmon

Complicated diverticulitis: mass; evidence of fistula; abdominal distention; abdominal tenderness, marked in cases of free perforation; hypotension or oliguria; bleeding

Physical signs are mild

Manage on outpatient basis.
Obtain CBC and sedimentation rate.
Place patient on liquid diet.
Give oral antibiotics.

Physical signs are marked

Hospitalize patient.
Institute NPO regimen.
Give I.V. antibiotics.
Perform CT scan with contrast to confirm diagnosis.

Symptoms resolve

Perform colonoscopy or contrast study.

Symptoms recur

Consider surgical treatment.

Symptoms worsen

Patient has uncomplicated diverticulitis

Consider surgical treatment if recurrent.
Consider colonoscopy later.

Patient has complicated diverticulitis

[*See Figure 12.*]

Patient has other diagnosis

Treat as appropriate.

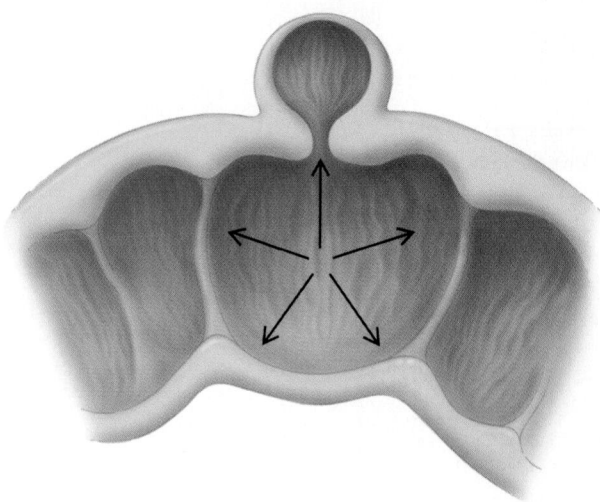

Figure 2 Depicted is a schematic representation of the process termed segmentation in the colon. It has been theorized that high-pressure compartments lead to the development of diverticula.[88]

Complicated Diverticulitis

Some cases of diverticulitis are classified as complicated, meaning that the disease process has progressed to obstruction, abscess or fistula formation, or free perforation [see Figure 4]. Complicated diverticulitis may be particularly challenging to manage,[13,14] especially because patients may have no known history of diverticular disease.[15] Lower gastrointestinal bleeding is also a complication of diverticular disease in 30% to 50% of cases[16]; in fact, diverticula are the most common colonic cause of lower GI bleeding.[16] When diverticular hemorrhage occurs [see

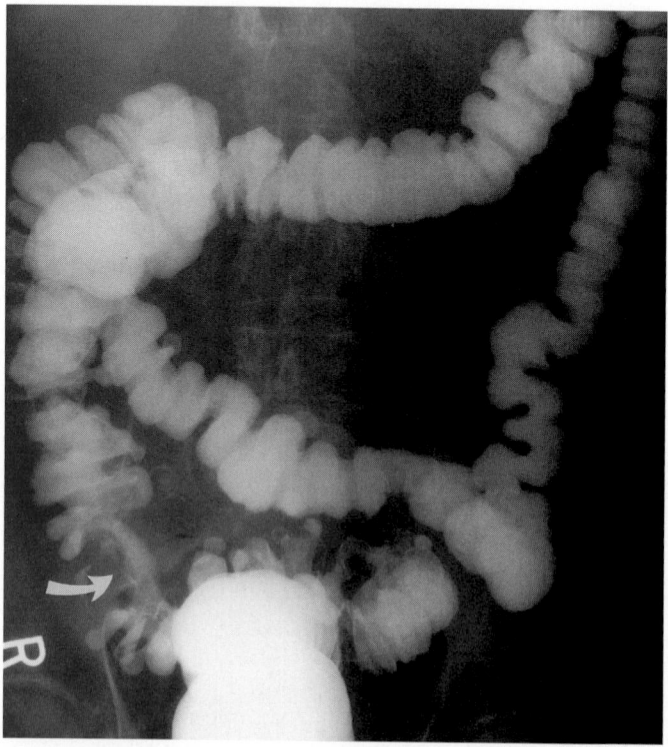

Figure 3 Barium enema shows a napkin-ring carcinoma (arrow) in the middle of multiple diverticula in a redundant sigmoid colon.

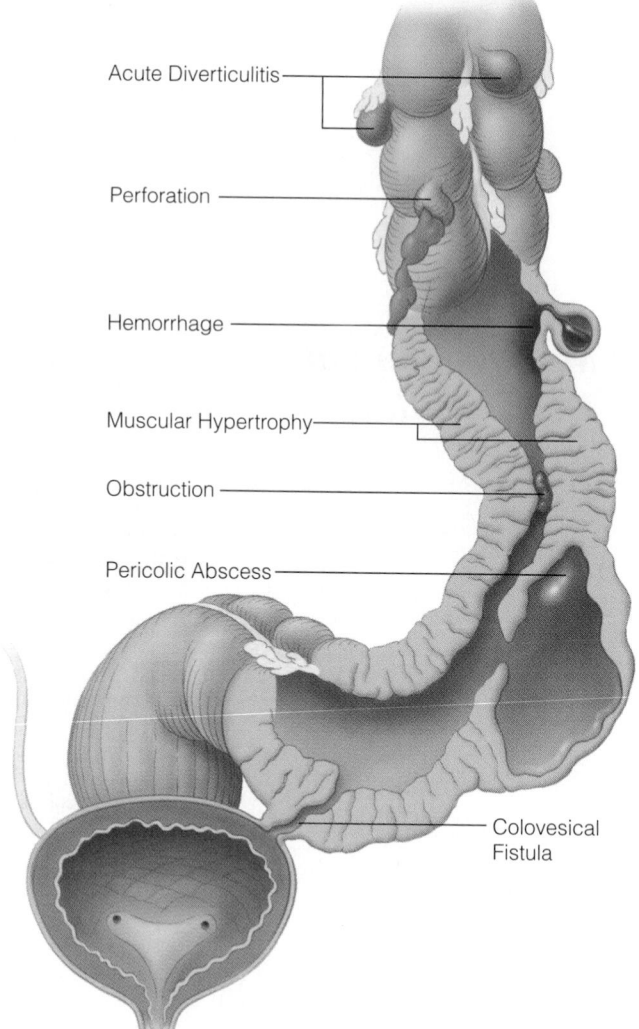

Acute Diverticulitis

Perforation

Hemorrhage

Muscular Hypertrophy

Obstruction

Pericolic Abscess

Colovesical Fistula

Figure 4 Shown are major complications of diverticular disease of the sigmoid colon.[89]

48 Lower Gastrointestinal Bleeding], it is usually associated with diverticulosis rather than with diverticulitis. Approximately 50% of diverticular bleeding originates in the right colon, despite the low incidence of diverticula in this segment of the colon. Patients tend to be elderly[13] and to have cardiovascular disease and hypertension. Regular intake of NSAIDs may increase the risk of this complication. Although patients may lose 1 to 2 units of blood, the bleeding usually ceases spontaneously,[17] and expeditious operative treatment generally is not necessary.

The most common form of complicated diverticulitis involves the development of a pericolic abscess, typically signaled by high fever, chills, and lassitude. Such abscesses may be small and localized or may extend to more distant sites (e.g., the pelvis). They may be categorized according to the Hinchey classification of diverticular perforations,[18] in which stage I refers to a localized pericolic abscess and stage II to a larger mesenteric abscess spreading toward the pelvis [see Figure 5]. On rare occasions, an abscess forms in the retroperitoneal tissues, subsequently extending to distant sites such as the thigh or the flank. The location of the abscess can be defined precisely by means of computed tomography with contrast.

Some abscesses rupture into adjacent tissues or viscera, resulting in the formation of fistulas. The fistulas most commonly seen in this

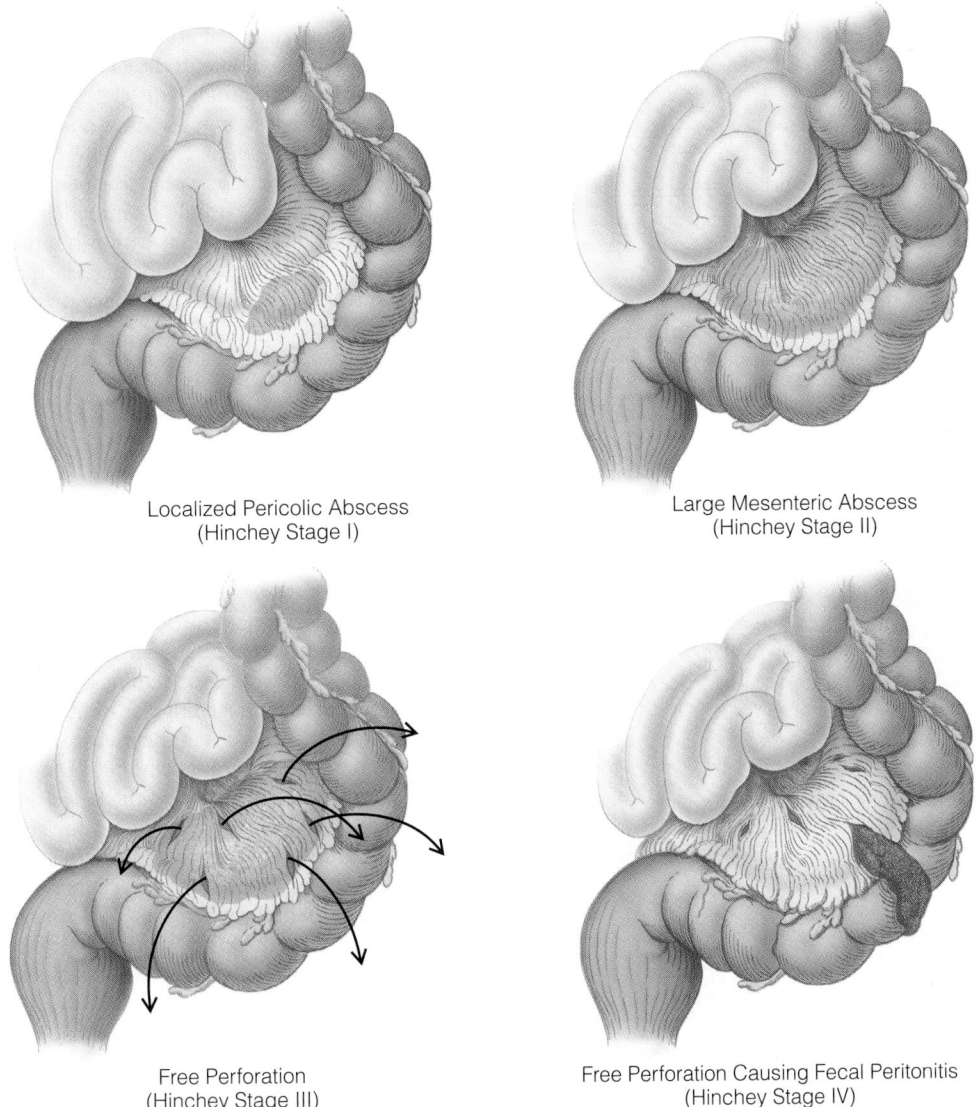

Localized Pericolic Abscess
(Hinchey Stage I)

Large Mesenteric Abscess
(Hinchey Stage II)

Free Perforation
(Hinchey Stage III)

Free Perforation Causing Fecal Peritonitis
(Hinchey Stage IV)

Figure 5 **The Hinchey classification divides diverticular perforations into four stages. Mortality increases significantly in stages III and IV.**[18]

setting (50% to 65% of cases) are colovesical fistulas. This complication is less common in women because of the protection afforded by the uterus. Symptoms of colovesical fistulas tend to involve the urinary tract (e.g., pneumaturia, hematuria, and urinary frequency). Fecaluria is diagnostic of colovesical or enterovesical fistulas. Colovaginal fistulas (which account for 25% of all diverticular fistulas) are usually seen in women who have undergone hysterectomies.[19] The diseased colon is adherent to the vaginal cuff. Most commonly, patients complain of a foul vaginal discharge; however, some patients present with stool emanating from the vagina.

About 10% of colon obstructions are attributable to diverticulitis. Acute diverticulitis can cause colonic edema and a functional obstruction that usually resolves with antibiotic infusion and bowel rest. Stricture formation is more common, usually occurring as a consequence of recurrent attacks of diverticulitis. Circumferential pericolic fibrosis is noted, and marked angulation of the pelvic colon with adherence to the pelvic sidewall may be seen. Patients complain of constipation and narrowed stools. Colonoscopy can be difficult and potentially dangerous in this setting. Differentiating a diverticular stricture from carcinoma may be impossible by any means short of resection.

The term malignant diverticulitis has been employed to describe an extreme form of sigmoid diverticulitis that is characterized by an extensive phlegmon and inflammatory reaction extending below the peritoneal reflection, with a tendency toward obstruction and fistula formation.[20] Malignant diverticulitis is seen in fewer than 5% of patients older than 50 years who are operated on for diverticulitis.[20] The process is reminiscent of Crohn disease, and CT scans demonstrate extensive inflammation. In this setting, a staged resection might be preferable to attempting a primary resection through the pelvic phlegmon. The degree of pelvic inflammation may subside significantly after diversion.[20]

A dangerous but rare complication of acute diverticulitis (occurring in 1% to 2% of cases) is free perforation,[21] a term that includes both perforation of a diverticular abscess throughout the abdomen leading to generalized peritonitis (purulent peritonitis; Hinchey stage III) and free spillage of stool thorough an open diverticulum into the peritoneal cavity (fecal peritonitis; Hinchey stage IV). The incidence of free perforations may be increasing, at least in the southwestern United States.[22] The overall mortality in this group is between 20% and 30%; that for purulent peritonitis is approximately 13%, and that for fecal peritonitis is about 43%.[21]

PHYSICAL EXAMINATION

Uncomplicated Diverticulitis

Physical examination reveals localized left lower quadrant abdominal tenderness with variable degrees of guarding and rebound tenderness. A mass is occasionally felt. The stool may contain traces of blood, but gross bleeding is unusual. Localized inflammation of the perforated diverticulum and the adjacent mesentery is present, and a phlegmon may be seen as well. Depending on the severity of the physical findings, patients may be managed either as inpatients or outpatients.

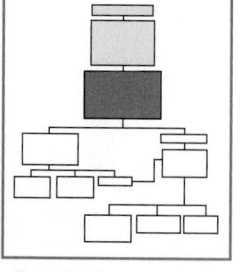

Complicated Diverticulitis

In a patient with a pericolic abscess, a mass may be detectable on abdominal, rectal, or pelvic examination. In a patient with a colovaginal fistula, a site of granulation tissue and drainage is seen at the apex of the vaginal cuff. In a patient with obstruction, there may be marked abdominal distention, usually of slow onset; abdominal tenderness may or may not be present, but if tears develop in the cecal taeniae, right lower quadrant tenderness is typically seen. In a patient with a free perforation, there is marked abdominal tenderness, usually commencing suddenly in the left lower quadrant and spreading within hours to the remainder of the abdomen. Hypotension and oliguria may develop later. Patients with rectal bleeding usually have no complaints of abdominal pain or tenderness, and they may be hypovolemic and hypotensive, depending on the rapidity of the bleeding.

Investigative Studies

IMAGING

The most useful diagnostic imaging study in the setting of suspected diverticulitis is a CT scan with oral and rectal contrast.[23] Localized thickening of the bowel wall or inflammation of the adjacent pericolic fat is suggestive of diverticulitis; extraluminal air or fluid collections are sometimes seen together with diverticula [see Figure 6]. The most frequent findings (seen in 70% to 100% of cases) are bowel wall thickening, fat stranding, and diverticula.[24] In some cases, small abscesses in the mesocolon or bowel wall are not detected. The diagnosis of carcinoma cannot be excluded definitively when there is thickening of the bowel wall [see Figure 7].[2]

Although CT scanning has tended to replace contrast studies in the evaluation of diverticulitis, the latter may be more useful in differentiating carcinoma from diverticulitis. A contrast study can also be complementary when the CT scan raises the suspicion of carcinoma.[23] When diverticulitis is suspected, water-soluble contrast material should be used instead of barium because of the complications that follow extravasation of barium [see Figures 8 and 9]. Furthermore, in the acute setting, only the left colon should be evaluated. Carcinoma is suggested by an abrupt transition to an abnormal mucosa over a relatively short segment; diver-

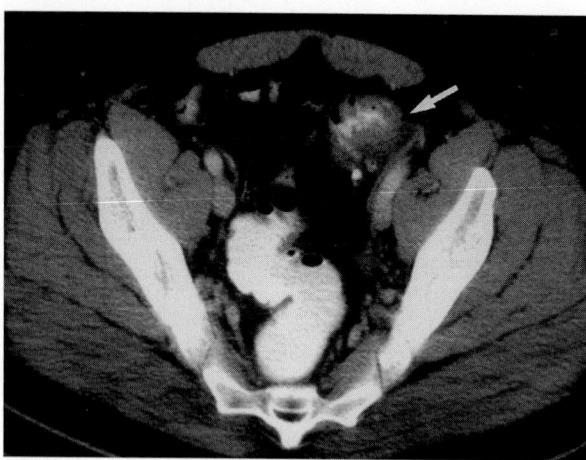

Figure 6 CT scan shows thickening of the sigmoid colon (arrow) caused by acute diverticulitis.

a   b

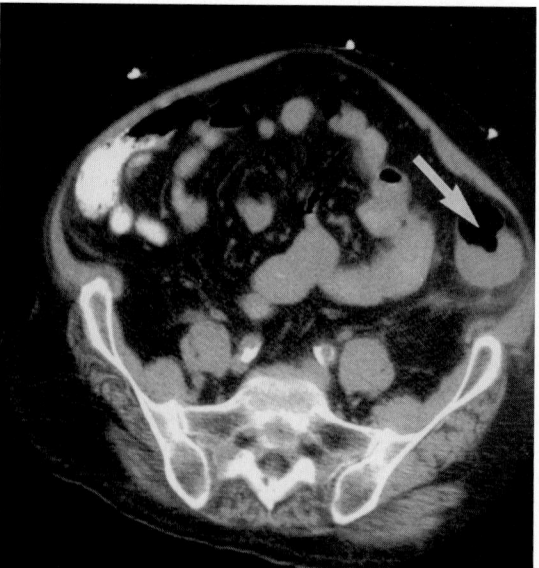

Figure 7 (a) CT scan shows a thickened left colonic wall and diverticulum (arrow). Diverticulitis was considered the most likely diagnosis. (b) CT scan through an adjacent plane shows deformity of the mucosa, suggesting a possible apple-core lesion (arrow). Subsequent endoscopy revealed a carcinoma that was obstructing the colon almost completely.

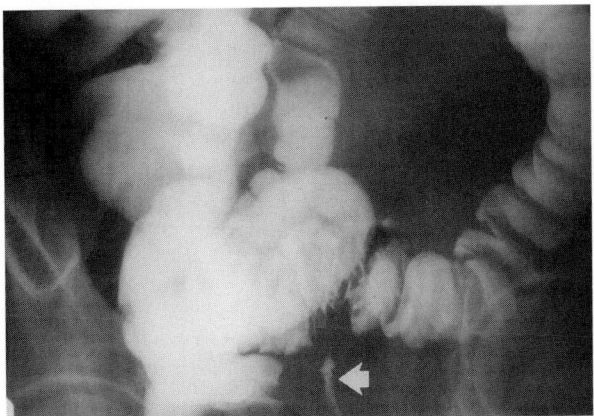

Figure 8 **Contrast study shows local extravasation from the sigmoid colon (arrow); a diverticulum is visible.**

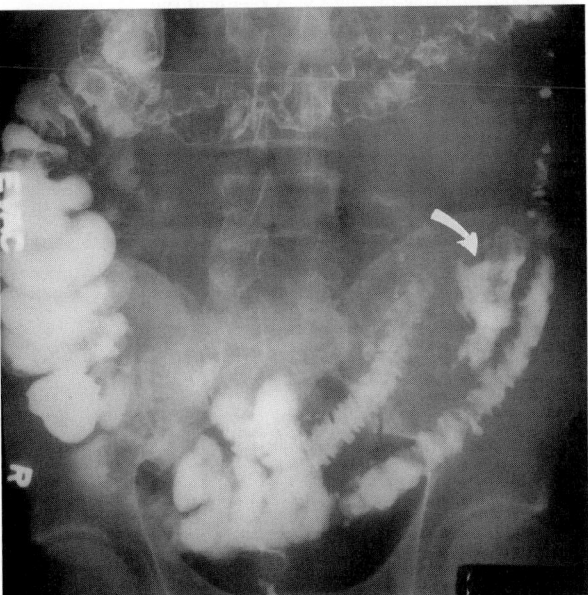

Figure 9 **Shown is extravasation into an abscess cavity (arrow) from diverticulitis at the sigmoid colon–descending colon junction in a postevacuation film.**

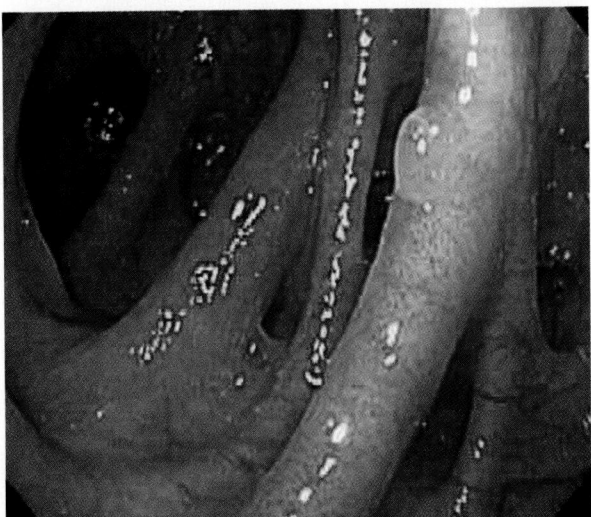

Figure 10 **Colonoscopic view of several sigmoid diverticula reveals no evidence of active diverticulitis (e.g., edema or narrowing).**

ticulitis is usually characterized by a gradual transition into diseased colon over a longer segment, with the mucosa remaining intact. If the contrast study reveals extravasation of contrast outlining an abscess cavity [*see Figure 9*], an intramural sinus tract, or a fistula, diverticulitis is likely.[1]

Colonoscopy is avoided when acute diverticulitis is suspected, because of the risk of perforation. It may, however, be done 6 to 8 weeks after the process subsides to rule out other disorders (e.g., colon cancer) [*see Figure 10*]. If diverticular disease is advanced, the endoscopic procedure may be difficult; the diverticular segment must be fully traversed for the examiner to be able to exclude a neoplasm with confidence. When major lower GI bleeding occurs, colonoscopy is done to search for polyps, carcinoma, or a site of diverticular bleeding. In the case of massive bleeding, selective arteriography is useful for localizing the source, and superselective embolization frequently quells the hemorrhage. The actual risk of bowel ischemia is low when superselective techniques are employed. Bleeding at the time of arteriography may be facilitated by the infusion of heparin or urokinase; however, this is a risky approach that should be taken only when other attempts at localization have failed and recurrent bouts of bleeding have occurred.

When a colovesical fistula occurs, contrast CT with narrow cuts in the pelvis can be very helpful. The classic findings are sigmoid diverticula, thickening of the bladder and the colon, air in the bladder, opacification of the fistula tract and the bladder, and, possibly, an abscess [*see Figure 11*]. Cystoscopy is less specific, showing possible edema or erythema at the site of the fistula. A contrast enema helps rule out malignant disease. The diagnostic tests that are most useful for detecting colovaginal fistulas are contrast CT and vaginography via a Foley catheter. Charcoal ingestion helps confirm the presence of colovesical or colovaginal fistulas. On rare occasions, colocutaneous fistulas may develop, causing erythema and breakdown of the skin. Colouterine fistulas may occur as well; these are also quite rare.[25]

Management

MEDICAL

Uncomplicated diverticulitis is usually managed on an outpatient basis by instituting a liquid or low-residue diet and administering an oral antibiotic combination that covers anaerobes and gram-negative organisms (e.g., ciprofloxacin

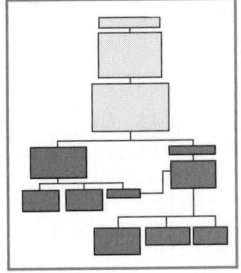

with metronidazole or clindamycin) over a period of 7 to 10 days. Provided that symptoms and signs have subsided, the colon may be evaluated more fully several weeks later with a contrast study or colonoscopy if the diagnosis of diverticular disease has not already been established. If symptoms worsen, hospitalization should be considered. Over the long term, patients should be maintained on a high-fiber diet, though it may take months for the diet to have an effect on symptoms.[26]

If more significant physical findings and symptoms of toxicity develop, hospitalization is warranted [*see Figure 12*]. Patients are placed on a nihil per os (NPO) regimen, and intravenous fluids and antibiotics are administered (e.g., a third-generation cephalosporin with metronidazole) until abdominal pain and tenderness have resolved and bowel function has returned. As a rule, resolution occurs within several days. If there is clinical evidence of intestinal obstruction or ileus, a nasogastric tube is placed. In most cases, ileus-related symptoms resolve with antibiotic treatment. CT scans are useful for establishing the correct diagnosis in

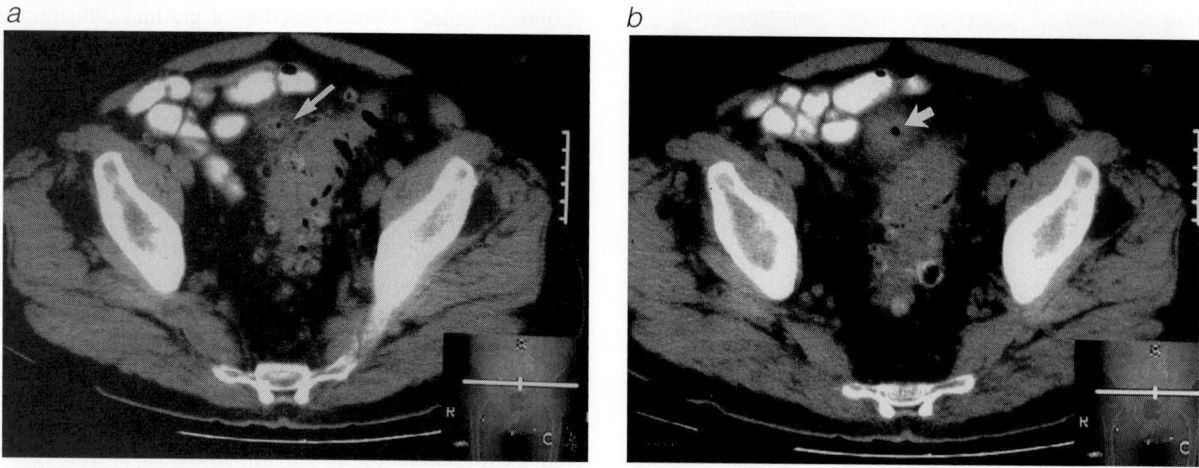

Figure 11 (*a*) CT scan in a patient with a colovesical fistula shows air in the thickened tract (arrow) adjacent to the sigmoid colon. (*b*) CT scan through an adjacent plane shows air in the bladder (arrow) as a result of the fistula. No contrast is present in the bladder.

the emergency department[27]; furthermore, the severity of diverticulitis on CT scans predicts the risk of subsequent medical failure.[28] Following the sedimentation rate may be helpful in assessing the effectiveness of treatment. It has been estimated that 15% to 30% of patients admitted with acute diverticulitis will require surgical treatment during the same admission.[1]

If fever and leukocytosis persist despite antibiotic therapy, the presence of an abscess should be suspected. Small (< 5 cm)

abscesses may respond to antibiotics and bowel rest. Larger abscesses that are localized and isolated may be accessible to percutaneous drainage [*see Figure 13*].[28] Generally, this technique is reserved for abscesses greater than 5 cm in diameter in low-risk patients who are not immunocompromised. It often leads to resolution of sepsis and the resulting symptoms and signs (e.g., abdominal pain and tenderness and leukocytosis), usually within 72 hours, thereby facilitating subsequent elective surgical resec-

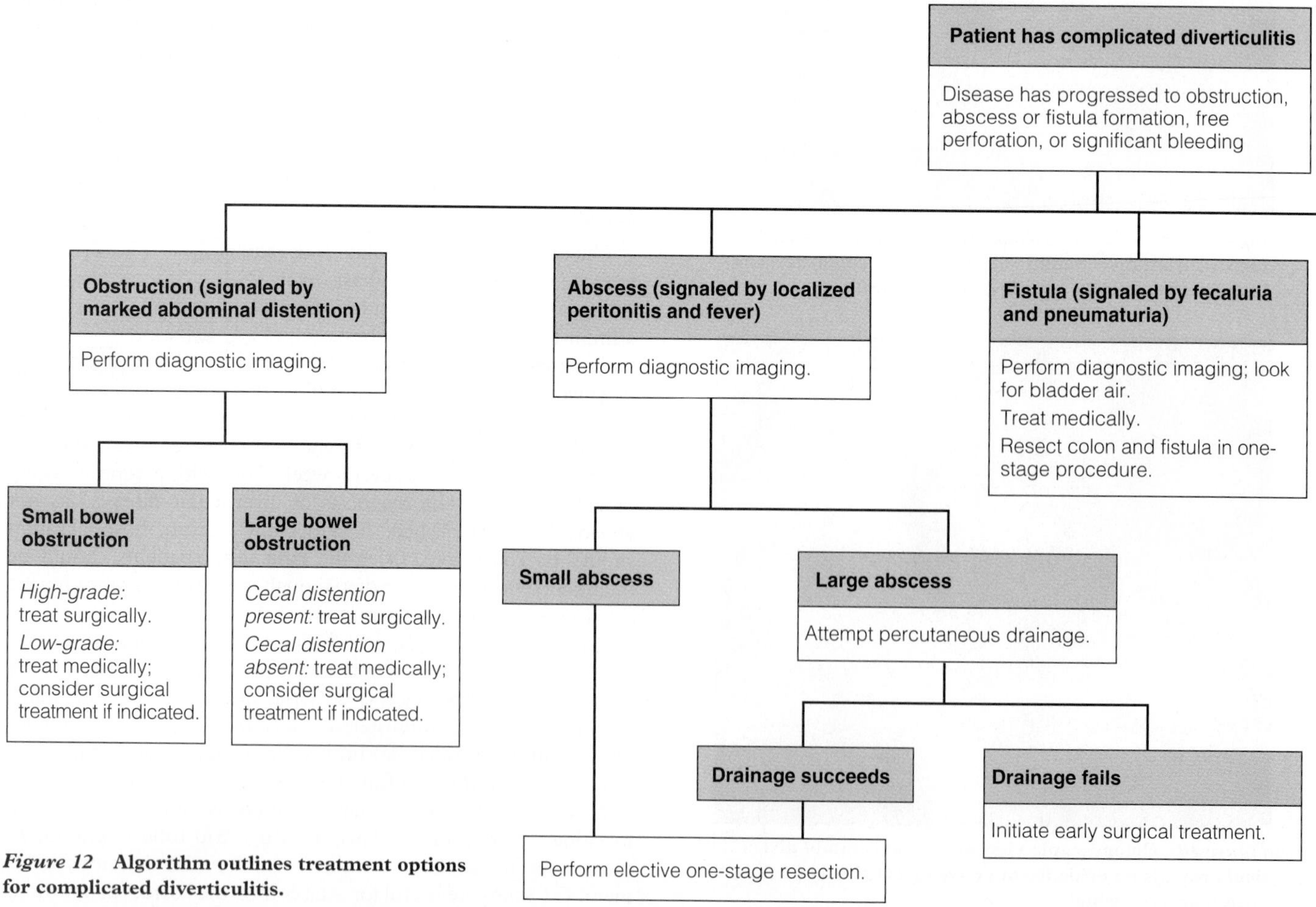

Patient has complicated diverticulitis

Disease has progressed to obstruction, abscess or fistula formation, free perforation, or significant bleeding

Obstruction (signaled by marked abdominal distention)

Perform diagnostic imaging.

Abscess (signaled by localized peritonitis and fever)

Perform diagnostic imaging.

Fistula (signaled by fecaluria and pneumaturia)

Perform diagnostic imaging; look for bladder air.
Treat medically.
Resect colon and fistula in one-stage procedure.

Small bowel obstruction

High-grade:
treat surgically.
Low-grade:
treat medically;
consider surgical treatment if indicated.

Large bowel obstruction

Cecal distention present: treat surgically.
Cecal distention absent: treat medically;
consider surgical treatment if indicated.

Small abscess

Large abscess

Attempt percutaneous drainage.

Drainage succeeds

Drainage fails

Initiate early surgical treatment.

Perform elective one-stage resection.

Figure 12 Algorithm outlines treatment options for complicated diverticulitis.

tion of the colon. In addition, percutaneous drainage offers cost advantages, in that it reduces the number of operative procedures required and shortens hospital stay.

Access to a pelvic collection may be difficult to obtain, and the drainage procedure typically must be done with the patient in a prone or lateral position. If the catheter drainage amounts to more than 500 ml/day after the first 24 hours, a fistula should be suspected. Before the catheter is removed, a CT scan is done with injection of contrast material through the tube to determine whether the cavity has collapsed. If this approach fails (as it usually does in patients with multiple or multiloculated abscesses), an expeditious operation may be necessary.[22] An initial surgical procedure is required in about 20% of cases.[29]

SURGICAL

Overall, approximately 20% of patients with diverticulitis require surgical treatment.[2,30] Most surgical procedures are reserved for patients who experience recurrent episodes of acute diverticulitis that necessitate treatment (inpatient or outpatient) or who have complicated diverticulitis. The most common indication for elective resection is recurrent attacks—that is, several episodes of acute diverticulitis documented by studies such as CT. Estimates of the risk of such attacks range from 30% to 45%. A task force of the American Society of Colon and Rectal Surgeons recommended sigmoid resection after two attacks of diverticulitis.[31] A cost analysis using a Markov model suggested that cost savings can be achieved if resection is done after three attacks.[32] Efforts are made to time surgical treatment so that it takes place during a quiescent period 8 to 10 weeks after the last attack. Barium enema or colonoscopy may be employed to evaluate the diverticular disease and rule out carcinoma. The bowel can then be prepared mechanically and with antibiotics (e.g., oral neomycin and metronidazole on the day before operation).

Elective resection is a common sequel to successful percutaneous drainage of a pericolic abscess in an otherwise healthy, well-nourished patient. The timing of surgery may be guided by the extent of the inflammatory changes (as documented by CT scanning) and the patient's clinical course. Most patients can be operated upon within 6 weeks. Elective resection is the preferred approach to diverticular fistulas as well. Colovesical fistulas are usually resected because of the risk of urinary sepsis and the concern that a malignancy might be overlooked. Preferably, the operation is done when the acute inflammation has subsided.

Elective resection is done via either the open route or, increasingly, the laparoscopic route[33]; a few telerobotic-assisted laparoscopic colectomies have also been attempted.[34] The learning curve for laparoscopic colectomy is 20 to 50 cases.[35] Obese patients with severe colonic inflammation are poorer candidates for laparoscopic resection.[33] In our institution, the development of hand-assisted procedures has widened the opportunities for utilizing minimally invasive surgery [see 74 Procedures for Diverticular Disease], allowing all types of diverticular resections to be performed more safely. Minimally invasive procedures have several advantages over conventional procedures: decreased intraoperative trauma, fewer postoperative adhesions, reduced postoperative pain, shorter duration of ileus, quicker discharge from the hospi-

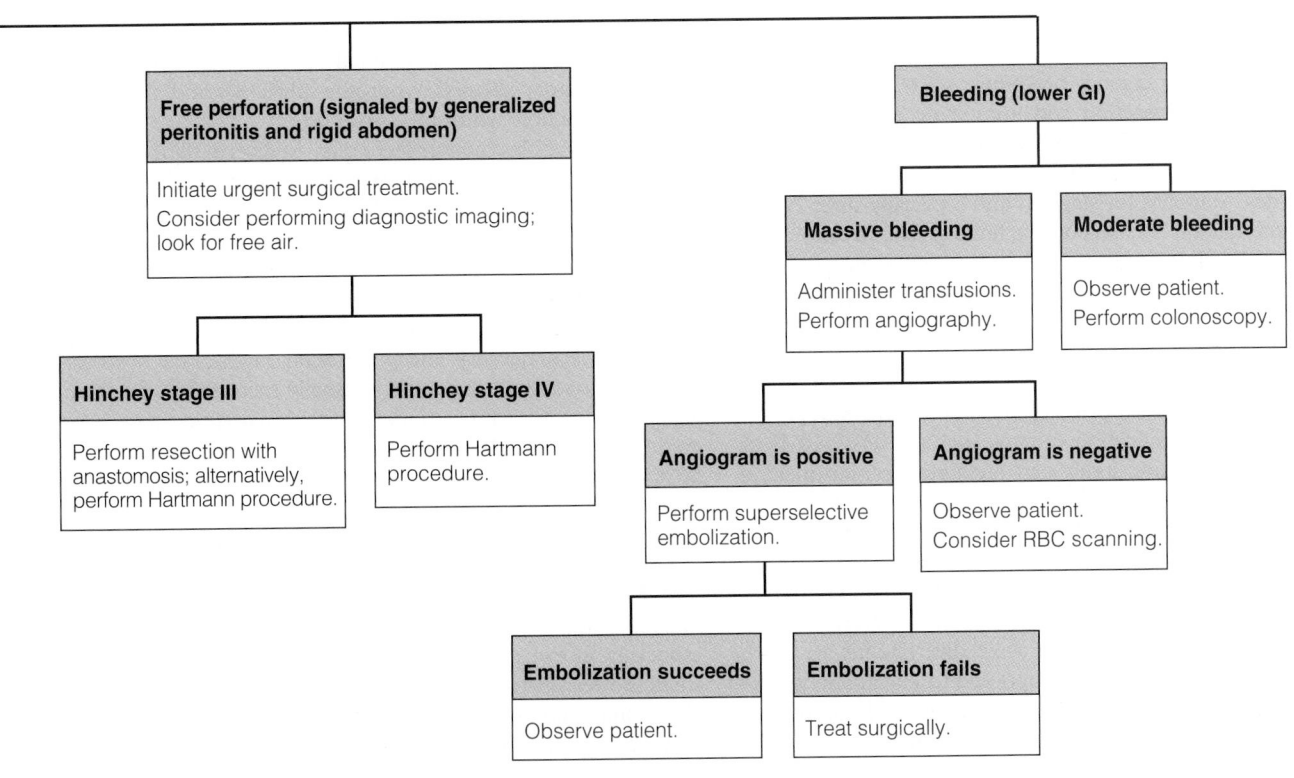

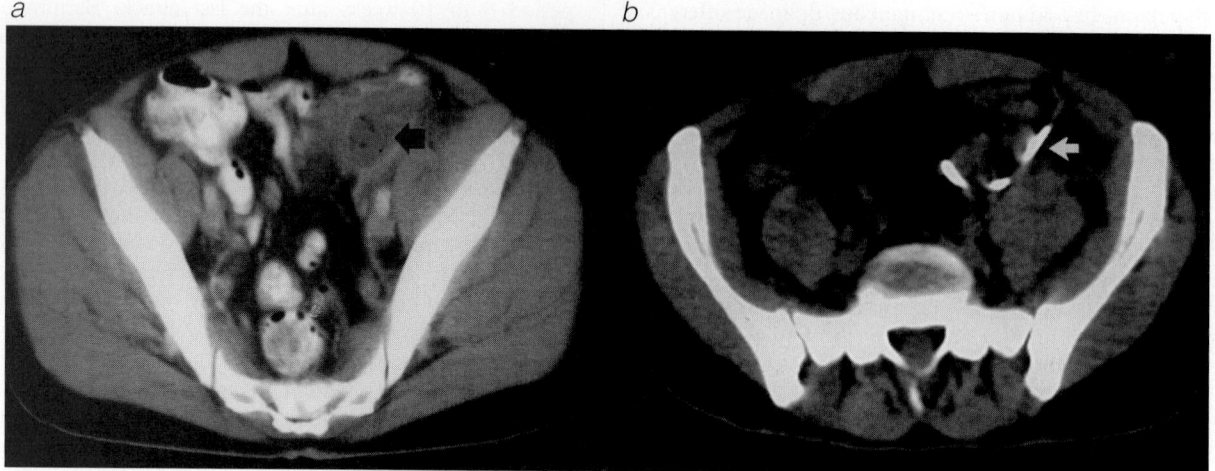

Figure 13 (*a*) CT scan shows a pericolic abscess (arrow) caused by a contained perforation arising from sigmoid diverticulitis. (*b*) A pigtail catheter (arrow) has been placed into the abscess cavity by the interventional radiologist.

tal, and earlier return to work.[36-38] Such procedures can be done safely in obese patients,[38] and the conversion rate is now low.[35,39] Technical details of the procedures are addressed elsewhere [*see 74 Procedures for Diverticular Disease*].[40,41]

Some patients with complicated diverticulitis require emergency resection because of free perforation and widespread peritonitis. In such patients, the American Society of Anesthesiologists (ASA) physical status score and the degree of preoperative organ failure may be significant predictors of outcome.[42,43] Unfavorable systemic factors (e.g., hypotension, renal failure, diabetes, malnutrition, immune compromise, and ascites) play a vital role in determining patient outcome,[43] as does the severity of the peritonitis (i.e., extent, contents, and speed of development).[44,45] One of the unfortunate limitations of the Hinchey classification is that it does not take comorbidities into account.[44] Because the bowel is not prepared before operation, the surgeon may feel uncomfortable doing an anastomosis. On-table lavage may be considered if contamination is minimal, but it adds to the time spent under anesthesia during an emergency procedure.

As a general rule, resection and immediate anastomosis are suitable for Hinchey stage I and perhaps stage II diverticular perforations, whereas resection with diversion (the Hartmann procedure) is the gold standard for stage III and especially stage IV.[46-48] This recommendation is based on the finding that an anastomosis involving the left colon is risky when performed under emergency conditions.[49] The once-popular three-stage procedures are now of historic interest only. There are some reports of successful outcomes for type III and type IV cases after extensive abdominal lavage and two-layer anastomoses[50] or after on-table lavage of the colonic contents to allow primary anastomosis.[51] Grading of comorbidities with classification systems such as APACHE II or the Mannheim peritonitis index can facilitate decision-making with respect to the question of anastomosis versus diversion.[52] The surgeon's decision must be individualized on the basis of each patient's condition and needs. The literature on this topic is confusing, in that most of the published reports are small and retrospective, with only limited classification of disease severity.

Currently, surgeons encountering acute diverticulitis are more likely to do one-stage resections, as opposed to Hartmann procedures, than they once were.[43,53] The advantage of the one-stage approach is that the colostomy takedown and the attendant 4%

mortality are avoided.[54] Furthermore, at least 30% of patients who undergo a Hartmann procedure never return for colostomy closure. A primary anastomosis can be protected with a proximal ileostomy as well.[46,55,56] Transverse colostomy and loop ileostomy appear to be equally safe, though skin changes may be more problematic after a colostomy[57] and an ileostomy closure tends to be less complex than a colostomy closure. On-table lavage may also be used as an adjunct to anastomosis.[58]

The risk of complications inherent in operations on the colon should always be kept in mind, especially in the relatively few patients undergoing emergency procedures. In this setting, the bowel is unprepared and systemic sepsis may be present. Potential complications include ureteral injuries; anastomotic leakage, anastomotic stricture, and postoperative intra-abdominal abscesses; perioperative bleeding involving the mesentery, adhesions, the splenic capsule, or the presacral venous plexus; postoperative small bowel obstruction; stomal complications; wound infection, wound dehiscence, and abdominal compartment syndrome; the acute respiratory distress syndrome (ARDS); and the multiple organ dysfunction syndrome (MODS).

Large bowel obstruction secondary to diverticulitis can lead to considerable morbidity and may necessitate surgical intervention.[55] The obstruction is usually partial [*see Figures 14 and 15*], allowing preparation of the bowel in many cases. High-grade obstruction represents a complex problem. If the cecum is dilated to a diameter of 10 cm or greater and there is tenderness in the right lower quadrant, expeditious surgery is necessary because of the risk of cecal necrosis and perforation. High-grade obstruction with fecal loading of the colon is usually managed by performing a Hartmann procedure, though on-table lavage may be considered.[22] A survey of GI surgeons in the United States indicated that 50% would opt for a one-stage procedure in low-risk patients with obstruction, whereas 94% would opt for a staged procedure in high-risk patients.[59]

Small bowel obstruction may also complicate the clinical picture. Mechanical small bowel obstruction may occur as a consequence of adherence of the small bowel to a focus of diverticulitis, especially in the presence of a large pericolic abscess. Whereas small bowel obstruction tends to cause periumbilical crampy abdominal pain and vomiting, these characteristic manifestations may be obscured in part by pain attributed to diverticulitis. The

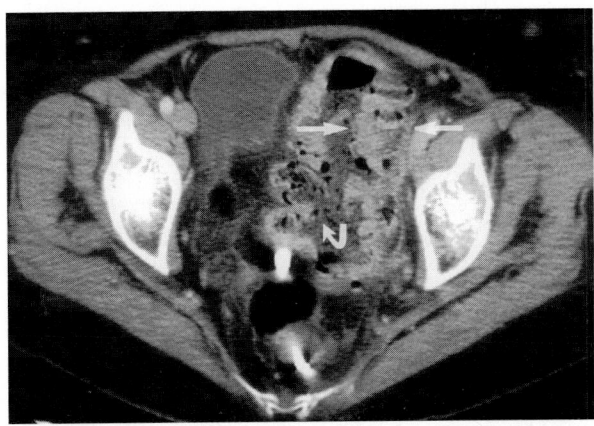

Figure 14 CT scan shows marked thickening of the sigmoid wall (arrows) in a patient with diverticular disease who presented with symptoms of intractable constipation. No contrast is present in the lumen (curved arrow).

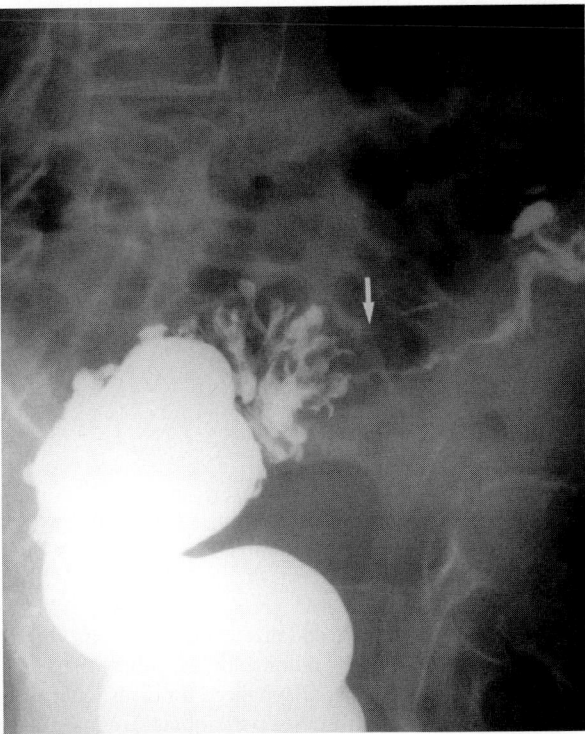

Figure 15 Contrast study shows high-grade retrograde obstruction, multiple diverticula, and a long proximal sigmoid stricture. A tiny extraluminal tract (possibly intramural) from a diverticulum (arrow) is seen.

concern in this situation is that ischemic small bowel may be ignored, with potentially disastrous consequences. Diarrhea should trigger the suspicion of colonic disease, and formation of a fistula into the small bowel should raise the possibility of Crohn disease. CT scanning often helps the surgeon differentiate between primary and secondary small bowel obstruction, but ultimately, exploratory surgery may be required both for diagnosis and for treatment.

Lower GI bleeding caused by diverticular disease rarely calls for emergency resection, because the bleeding is self-limited in most patients (80% to 90%). Furthermore, active diverticulitis is rare when active bleeding is the presenting symptom. Attempts are made to establish the active bleeding site by means of colonoscopy, tagged red blood cell nuclear scans, or angiography; barium contrast studies have no role to play in this situation. Emergency resection is indicated if the bleeding is life-threatening and if colonic angiography and attempted superselective embolization prove unsuccessful. In an unstable patient, total abdominal colectomy is necessary if the site of bleeding is unknown, though identification of the bleeding site with intraoperative colonoscopy has been reported. In a stable patient with ongoing bleeding, repeat angiography at a later time is appropriate, or so-called pharmacoangiography (infusion of heparin) can be employed in an attempt to induce bleeding.

Special Types of Diverticulitis

CECAL DIVERTICULITIS

In the United States, diverticulitis rarely involves the cecum or the right colon. Right-side diverticula occur in only 15% of patients in Western countries, compared with 75% in Singapore.[1] The incidence of cecal diverticulitis appears to be related to the number of diverticula present.[60] A classification system has been proposed that divides cecal diverticulitis into four grades [*see Figure 16*] to facilitate comparisons between different clinical series and to help surgeons formulate treatment plans in the OR.[60] Some cecal diverticula are true diverticula, containing all layers of the bowel wall, but the majority are pseudodiverticula. Diverticulitis of the hepatic flexure and the transverse colon is even less common and can present with symptoms suggesting appendicitis.[61,62]

Patients with right-side disease tend to be younger and to have less generalized peritonitis than patients with left-side diverticulitis.[60,61] Because they typically present with right lower quadrant pain, fever, and leukocytosis, acute appendicitis is usually suspected. CT scans are helpful for differentiating cecal diverticulitis from appendicitis or colon cancer [*see Figure 17*].[63,64] If cecal diverticulitis is suspected (as in a patient who has previously undergone appendectomy or in a patient with known right-side diverticulosis who has experienced similar attacks in the past), medical management with observation and antibiotics is generally the favored strategy, just as with simple sigmoid diverticulitis. In Japan, where right-side diverticulitis is more common, medical treatment has been successfully used for recurrent attacks of uncomplicated right-side diverticulitis.[65] After a few weeks, colonoscopy should be performed to rule out a colonic neoplasm.

If the patient has significant peritonitis or the diagnosis is unclear, laparoscopy or laparotomy is indicated. It is important that one or the other be done because the mortality associated with delayed treatment of perforated cecal diverticulitis is high. In our institution, laparoscopy is usually employed; if the diagnosis is unclear, laparotomy is recommended. When inflammation is localized and minimal, colectomy is unnecessary, and incidental appendectomy should be considered if the cecum is uninvolved at the base of the appendix.[66] If desired, the diverticulum may be removed as well.

Diverticulectomy should be done only if (1) carcinoma can be ruled out, (2) the resection margins are free of inflammation, (3) the ileocecal valve and the blood supply of the bowel are not compromised, and (4) perforation, gangrene, and abscess are absent.[60] Localized diverticulectomy, in general, should be reserved for grade I and grade II disease.[60] Sometimes, the ostium of the inflamed diverticulum is palpable if the cecum is mobilized surgically.[67] On-table cecoscopy thorough the appendiceal stump has also been helpful in establishing the diagnosis in the OR.[66] Grade III and IV cecal diverticulitis may be difficult to differentiate from

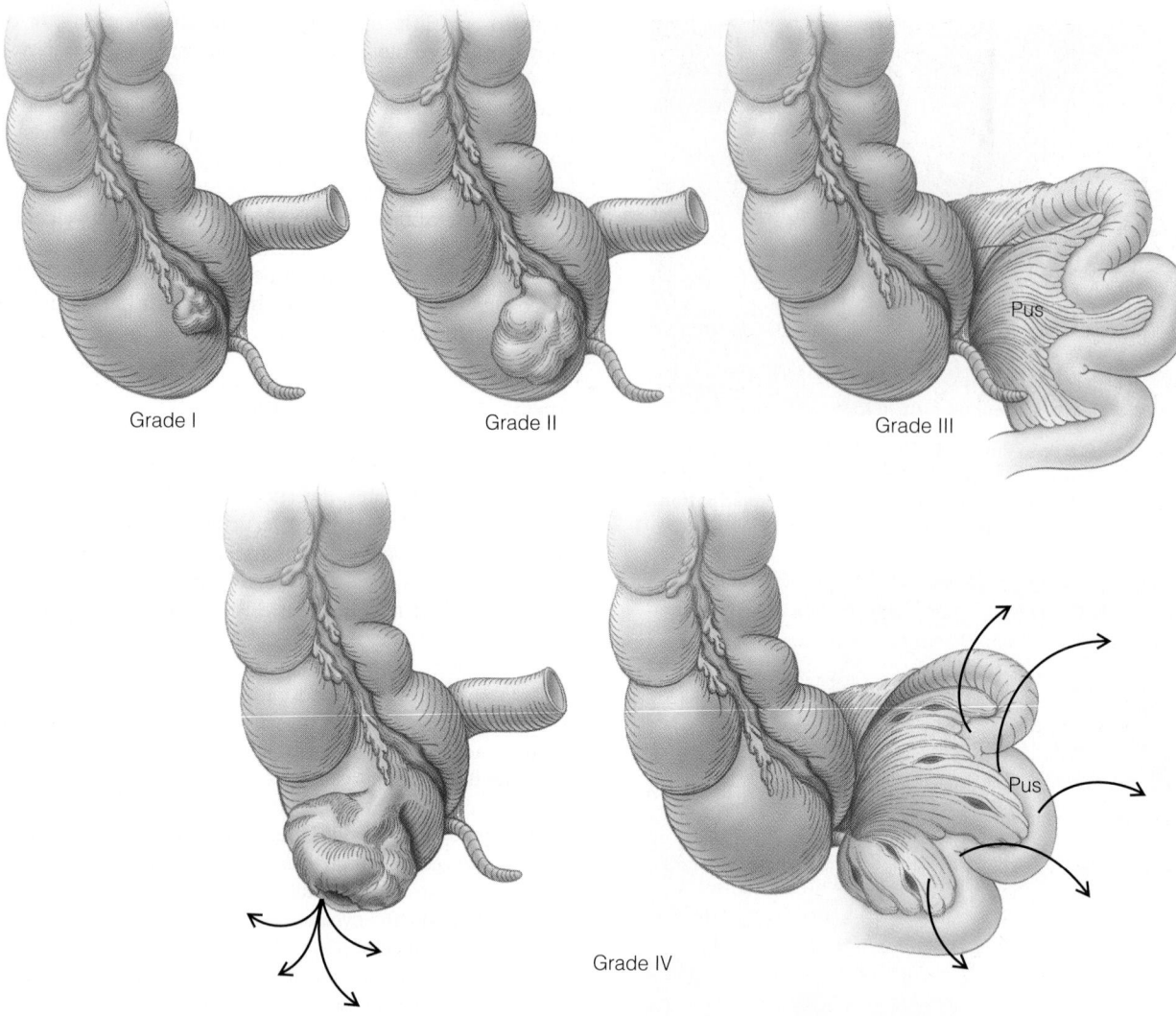

Figure 16 **Illustrated is a proposed classification of pathologic types of cecal diverticulitis. Grade I is a specific inflamed diverticulum; grade II is a cecal mass; grade III is characterized by a localized abscess or fistula; and grade IV represents a free perforation or a ruptured abscess with peritonitis.**[59]

carcinoma; resection is favored for these lesions.[67] An anastomosis may be created if contamination is limited, but generally, primary resection, ileostomy, and a mucous fistula are favored for treatment of grade IV disease.

DIVERTICULITIS IN YOUNG PATIENTS

Diverticulitis in patients younger than 40 years has been a focus of considerable attention in the literature, though this group only represents about 2% to 5% of the patients in large series.[31] The incidence of diverticulitis in young patients may be increasing, and obese Latino men appear to be at particular risk.[68] This predominance in males reflects a tendency to underdiagnose acute diverticulitis in young women.[69] Some authors have asserted that diverticulitis is particularly virulent in young patients; however, current data tend not to support this concept, suggesting that patients with mild diverticulitis are misdiagnosed when hospitalized or are treated as outpatients. The high rate of early operation in young patients probably reflects misdiagnosis of diverticulitis as acute appendicitis rather than the development of particularly severe forms of diverticulitis.[68] Patients found to have uncomplicated acute diverticulitis may, if desired, undergo incidental appendectomy in conjunction with medical treatment of diverticulitis.

Unlike elderly patients, hospitalized young patients with diverticulitis tend to have few comorbidities other than obesity. Furthermore, young patients hospitalized for diverticulitis tend to have relatively advanced disease, perhaps as a consequence of delayed diagnosis,[2] whereas elderly patients hospitalized with an admitting diagnosis of diverticulitis tend to exhibit a wider spectrum of disease severity. Young patients appear not to have a higher rate of recurrent diverticulitis than older patients do, and thus, aggressive resection is not necessary at the time of the first attack.[42,68] However, a finding of advanced diverticulitis on CT scans is a predictor of subsequent disease complications in this population.[70,71]

In general, diverticulitis should be approached in the same fashion in younger patients as in older patients.[71] The pathophysiology of the disease is probably identical. As in the elderly, elective resection is recommended after recurrent attacks, not after a single attack; with follow-up, the majority of patients hospitalized with acute diverticulitis do not require operation.[71,72]

DIVERTICULITIS IN IMMUNOCOMPROMISED PATIENTS

In view of their known predisposition to infection, immunocompromised patients (e.g., chronic alcoholics, transplant

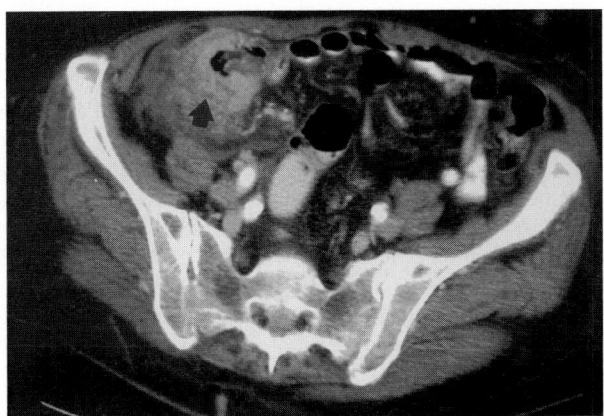

Figure 17 **CT scan shows inflammation in the pericecal area (arrow) and cecal edema, which could represent cecal diverticulitis. Because the appendix is not clearly visualized, appendicitis cannot be ruled out.**

patients, and persons with metastatic tumors who are receiving chemotherapy) with diverticulitis are at particular risk. There is no evidence that the incidence of diverticulitis is higher in this population than in the general population, but it is clear that immunocompromised patients have higher rates of operation once diverticulitis develops and that their postoperative mortality is higher.[73,74] Corticosteroid intake causes a number of significant problems, such as thinning of the colonic wall, lessening of the physical findings with diverticulitis, and an attenuated inflammatory response.

Any immunocompromised patient with abdominal pain should be evaluated aggressively. Contrast-enhanced CT is the imaging study of choice. The risk of perforation is increased in this setting, as is the risk of postoperative complications such as wound dehiscence. For an immunocompromised patient who has recovered from an episode of symptomatic diverticulitis, elective surgical treatment is recommended. A renal transplant patient with asymptomatic diverticulosis, however, need not undergo prophylactic colectomy. Pretransplantation colonic screening of patients older than 50 years does not reliably predict posttransplantation colonic complications.[75]

ATYPICAL PRESENTATIONS

Diverticulitis may give rise to various unusual manifestations involving multiple organ systems [*see Table 1*]. Not surprisingly, immunocompromised patients are at particular risk.

Retroperitoneal abscesses can track into anatomic planes (e.g., along the psoas muscle) or through the obturator foramen to areas such as the neck, the thigh,[76] the knee, the groin,[77] and the genitalia.[78,79] CT scanning is essential to outline the extent of such abscesses. Contrast enemas show the diverticula along with a sinus tract into the abscess cavity. Cultures of the abscess demonstrate the presence of colonic organisms such as *Bacteroides fragilis*. Definitive treatment consists of wide abscess drainage and colon resection. Without aggressive surgical management, mortality is high.

The protean manifestations of diverticulitis also include pylephlebitis (which causes liver abscesses), arthritis, and skin changes. Diverticulitis has in fact replaced appendicitis as the most common source of liver abscesses of portal origin. Simple abscesses may be drained percutaneously if they are not too large, and multiple loculated abscesses may be managed with open drainage. The main risk factors for mortality from liver abscesses are immunosuppression, underlying malignancy, the presence of

multiple organisms, and liver dysfunction. If the decision is made to perform a colectomy, the procedure may be done after drainage of the liver abscess or simultaneously with drainage during an open procedure.

GIANT DIVERTICULA

An anatomic curiosity sometimes encountered in patients with diverticular disease is a giant diverticulum, also termed a giant gas cyst or a pneumocyst of the colon.[80] These lesions, which may reach diameters of 40 cm, are believed to develop as a consequence of a ball-valve mechanism created by intermittent occlusion of the neck by fecal material that traps air in the diverticulum. Most giant diverticula are minimally symptomatic, causing only mild abdominal pain, and perforation is rare. A mobile mass may be palpable, and the gas-filled cyst can be seen on plain abdominal films. As many as two thirds of giant diverticula are opacified during a barium enema and can thereby be differentiated from other abnormalities (e.g., a mesenteric cyst, emphysematous cholecystitis, or a colon duplication). The cyst tends to adhere densely to adjacent structures (e.g., the bladder and the small bowel). The treatment of choice is resection of the colon and the cyst; performing diverticulectomy alone can lead to the development of a colocutaneous fistula.

RECURRENT DIVERTICULITIS AFTER RESECTION

Recurrent diverticulitis is rare after a colectomy for diverticulitis, occurring in 1% to 10% of patients.[81] As many as 3% of patients who have undergone resection for diverticulitis will require repeat resection.[3] The differential diagnosis includes Crohn disease, irritable bowel syndrome, carcinoma, and ischemic colitis. CT imaging and colonoscopy should be carried out. Particular care should be taken to review pathologic specimens for evidence of Crohn disease.

The only significant determinant of recurrent diverticulitis is the level of the anastomosis; the high pressure in the sigmoid colon distal to the anastomosis appears to be responsible. In one study, the risk of recurrence was four times greater in patients with

Table 1 Unusual Extra-abdominal Presentations of Diverticulitis[90]

Dermatologic	Pyoderma gangrenosum
Urinary	Ureteral obstruction Coloureteral fistula
Soft tissue	Thigh abscess Necrotizing fasciitis
Orthopedic	Osteomyelitis Arthritis
Gynecologic	Colouterine fistula Ovarian tumor/abscess
Genital	Epididymitis Pneumoscrotum
Neurologic	Coloepidural fistula
Vascular	Femoral vein thrombosis Mesenteric vein thrombosis Pylephlebitis Colovenous fistula
Perineal	Fournier gangrene Complex anal fistula

a colosigmoid anastomosis than in those with a colorectal anastomosis.[82] Reoperation requires a dissection that commences in noninflamed tissue. Dissection may be particularly difficult near the pelvic sidewall because of fibrosis; ureteral stenting may facilitate identification of the ureters.

SUBACUTE AND ATYPICAL DIVERTICULITIS

A small number of patients experience recurrent episodes of left lower quadrant abdominal pain that are not accompanied by the classic findings of acute diverticulitis (e.g., fever and leukocytosis). The inflammatory changes associated with diverticula in this subgroup have been referred to as atypical, subacute, or smoldering diverticulitis.[83,84] In this setting, there is not always a direct association between endoscopic and clinical findings; endoscopic evidence of diverticular inflammation has been seen in asymptomatic patients.[85] It has been suggested that there is a relation between diverticular disease and colitis.[86] Patients with chronic lower abdominal pain should undergo imaging studies and endoscopic evaluation, and other disorders (e.g., irritable bowel syndrome, inflammatory bowel disease, drug-induced symptoms, and bowel ischemia) should be excluded. In most cases of atypical diverticulitis, endoscopic findings are normal.[84] In carefully selected patients, colectomy often eliminates the abdominal pain, and many of these patients are eventually found to have histologic signs of acute and chronic mucosal inflammation.[84]

References

1. Stollman NH, Raskin JB: Diverticular disease of the colon. J Clin Gastroenterol 29:241, 1999

2. Ferzoco LB, Raptopoulos V, Silen W: Acute diverticulitis. N Engl J Med 338:1521, 1998

3. Kang JY, Hoare J, Tinto, et al: Diverticular disease of the colon. Aliment Pharm Therap 17:1189, 2003

4. Munson KD, Hensien MA, Jacob LN, et al: Diverticulitis: a comprehensive follow-up. Dis Colon Rectum 39:318, 1996

5. Makela J, Kiviniemi H, Laitinen S: Prevalence of perforated sigmoid diverticulitis is increasing. Dis Colon Rectum 45:955, 2002

6. Fisher N, Berry CS, Fearn T, et al: Cereal dietary fiber consumption and diverticular disease: a lifespan study in rats. Am J Clin Nutr 43:788, 1985

7. Whiteway J, Morson BC: Elastosis in diverticular disease of the sigmoid colon. Gut 26:258, 1985

8. Alsoori WH, Giovannucci EL, Rimm EB, et al: Prospective study of physical activity and the risk of symptomatic diverticular disease in men. Gut 36:276, 1995

9. Goh H, Bourne R: Non-steroidal anti-inflammatory drugs and perforated diverticular disease: a case-control study. Ann R Coll Surg Engl 84:93, 2002

10. Morris CR, Harvey IM, Stebbing WS, et al: Epidemiology of perforated colonic diverticular disease. Postgrad Med J 78:654, 2002

11. Papagrigoriadis S, Macey L, Bourantas N, et al: Smoking may be associated with complication in diverticular disease. Br J Surg 86:923, 1999

12. Pereira MA, Ludwig DS: Dietary fiber and body weight regulation: observations and mechanisms. Pediatr Clin North Am 48:969, 2001

13. McConnell EJ, Tessier DJ, Wolff BG: Population-based incidence of complicated diverticular disease of the sigmoid colon based on gender and age. Dis Colon Rectum 46:1110, 2003

14. Hughes LE: Complications of diverticular disease: inflammation, obstruction and bleeding. Clin Gastroenterol 4:147, 1975

15. Somasekar K, Foster ME, Haray PN: The natural history of diverticular disease: is there a role for elective colectomy. J R Coll Surg Edinb 47:481, 2002

16. Leitman IM, Paull DE, Shires DT III: Evaluation and management of massive lower gastrointestinal hemorrhage. Ann Surg 209:175, 1989

17. McGuire HH: Bleeding colonic diverticula: a reappraisal of natural history and management. Ann Surg 220:653, 1994

18. Hinchey GC, Schall GH, Richards MB: Treatment of perforated diverticulitis of the colon. Adv Surg 12:85, 1978

19. Woods RJ, Lavery IC, Fazio VW, et al: Internal fistulas in diverticular disease. Dis Colon Rectum 31:591, 1988

20. Morgenstern L: "Malignant" diverticulitis: a clinical entity. Arch Surg 114:1112, 1979

21. Sanford MB, Ryan JA Jr: The proper surgical treatment of perforated sigmoid diverticulitis with generalized peritonitis. Diverticular Disease: Management of the Difficult Surgical Case. Welch JP, Cohen JL, Sardella WV, et al, Eds. Williams & Wilkins, Baltimore, 1998, p 223

22. Schwesinger WH, Page CP, Gaskill HV III, et al: Operative management of diverticular emergencies: strategies and outcomes. Arch Surg 135:558, 2000

23. Ambrosetti P, Jenny A, Becker C, et al: Acute left colonic diverticulitis—compared performance of computed tomography and water-soluble contrast enema: prospective evaluation of 420 patients. Dis Colon Rectum 43:1363, 2000

24. Kircher MF, Rhea JT, Kihiczak D, et al: Frequency, sensitivity, and specificity of individual signs of diverticulitis on thin-section helical CT with colonic contrast material: experience with 312 cases. AJR Am J Roentgenol 178:1313, 2002

25. Huettner PC, Finkler NJ, Welch WR: Colouterine fistula complicating diverticulitis: charcoal challenge test aids in diagnosis. Obstet Gynecol 80:550, 1992

26. Brodribb AJ: Treatment of symptomatic diverticular disease with a high fiber diet. Lancet 1:664, 1977

27. Tsushima Y, Yamada S, Aoki J, et al: Effect of contrast-enhanced computed tomography on diagnosis and management of acute abdomen in adults. Clin Radiol 57:507, 2002

28. Harisinghani MG, Gervais DA, Maher MM, et al: Transgluteal approach for percutaneous drainage of deep pelvic abscesses: 154 cases. Radiology 228:701, 2003

29. Boulos PB: Complicated diverticulosis. Best Pract Res in Clin Gastroenterol 16:649, 2002

30. Chappius CW, Cohn I Jr: Acute colonic diverticulitis. Surg Clin North Am 68:301, 1988

31. Wong WD, Wexner SD, Lowry A, et al: Practice parameters for the treatment of sigmoid diverticulitis—supporting documentation. The Standards Task Force. Dis Colon Rectum 43:290, 2000

32. Richards RJ, Hammitt JK: Timing of prophylactic surgery in prevention of diverticulitis recurrence: a cost-effectiveness analysis. Dig Dis Sci 47:1903, 2002

33. Bouillot JL, Berthou JC, Champault G, et al: Elective laparoscopic colonic resection for diverticular disease: results of a multicenter study in 179 patients. Surg Endosc 16:1320, 2002

34. Weber PA, Merola S, Wasielewski A: Telerobotic-assisted laparoscopic right and sigmoid colectomies for benign disease. Dis Colon Rectum 45:1689, 2002

35. Senagore AJ, Duepree HJ, Delaney CP, et al: Results of a standardized technique and postoperative care plan for laparoscopic sigmoid colectomy: a 20-month experience. Dis Colon Rectum 46:503, 2003

36. Dwivedi A, Chahin F, Agrawal S, et al: Laparoscopic colectomy vs. open colectomy for sigmoid diverticular disease. Dis Colon Rectum 45:1309, 2002

37. Lawrence DM, Pasquale MD, Wasser TE: Laparoscopic versus open sigmoid colectomy for diverticulitis. Am Surg 69:499, 2003

38. Tuech J-J, Regenet N, Hennekinne S, et al: Laparoscopic colectomy for sigmoid diverticulitis in obese and nonobese patients: a prospective comparative study. Surg Endosc 15:1427, 2001

39. Trebuchet G, Lechaux D, Lecalve JL: Laparoscopic left colon resection for diverticular disease: results from 170 consecutive cases. Surg Endosc 16:18, 2002

40. Tocchi A, Mazzani G, Fornasari V, et al: Preservation of the inferior mesenteric artery in colorectal resection for complicated diverticular disease. Am J Surg 182:162, 2001

41. Senagore AJ: Laparoscopic techniques in intestinal surgery. Semin Laparosc Surg 8:183, 2001

42. Biondo S, Pares D, Marti Rague J, et al: Acute colonic diverticulitis in patients under 50 years of age. Br J Surg 89:1137, 2002

43. Zorcolo L, Covotta L, Carlomagno N, et al: Safety of primary anastomosis in emergency colorectal surgery. Colorect Dis 5:262, 2003

44. Nespoli A, Ravizzini C, Trivella M, et al: The choice of surgical procedure for peritonitis due to colonic perforation. Arch Surg 128:814, 1993

45. Krukowski ZH, Matheson NA: Emergency surgery for diverticular disease complicated by generalized fecal peritonitis: a review. Br J Surg 71:921, 1984

46. Illert B, Engemann R, Thiede A: Success in treatment of complicated diverticular disease is stage related. Int J Colorectal Dis 16:276, 2001

47. Maggard MA, Chandler CF, Schmit PJ, et al: Surgical diverticulitis: treatment options. Am Surg 67:1185, 2001

48. Farthmann EH, Ruckauer KD, Haring RU: Evidence-based surgery: diverticulitis—a surgical disease? Langenbeck Arch Surg 385:143, 2000

49. Scott-Conner CE, Scher KS: Implications of emergency operation on the colon. Am J Surg 153:535, 1987

50. Schilling MK, Maurer CA, Kollmar O, et al: Primary vs. secondary anastomosis after sigmoid colon resection for perforated diverticulitis (Hinchey Stage III and IV): a prospective outcome and cost analysis. Dis Colon Rectum 44:699, 2001

51. Regenet N, Teuch JJ, Pessaux P et al: Intraoperative colonic lavage with primary anastomosis vs. Hartmann's procedure for perforated diverticular disease of the colon: a consecutive study. Hepatogastroenterol 49:664, 2002

52. Blair NP, Germann E: Surgical management of acute sigmoid diverticulitis. Am J Surg 183:525, 2002

53. Zeitoun G, Laurent A, Rouffett F, et al: Multicenter randomized clinical trial of primary versus secondary sigmoid resection in generalized peritonitis complicating sigmoid diverticulitis. Br J Surg 87:1366, 2000

54. Belmonte C, Klas JV, Perez JJ, et al: The Hartmann procedure: first choice or last resort in diverticular disease? Arch Surg 131:612, 1996

55. Gooszen AW, Gooszen HG, Veerman W, et al: Operative treatment of acute complications of diverticular disease: primary or secondary anastomosis after sigmoid resection. Eur J Surg 167:35, 2001

56. Bahadursingh AM, Virgo KS, Kaminski DL, et al: Spectrum of disease and outcome of complicated diverticular disease. Am J Surg 186:696, 2003

57. Sakai Y, Nelson H, Larson D, et al: Temporary transverse colostomy vs loop ileostomy in diversion: a case-matched study. Arch Surg 136:338, 2001

58. Murray J, Schoetz D, Coller J: Intraoperative colonic lavage and primary anastomosis in nonelective colon resection. Dis Colon Rectum 34:527, 1991

59. Goyal A, Schein M: Current practices in left-sided colonic emergencies: a survey of US gastrointestinal surgeons. Dig Surg 18:399, 2001

60. Thorsen AG, Ternent CA: Cecal diverticulitis. Diverticular Disease: Management of the Difficult Surgical Case. Welch JP, Cohen JL, Sardella WV, et al, Eds. Williams & Wilkins, Baltimore, 1998, p 428

61. Law WL, Liu CL, Chan WF, et al: Perforated diverticulitis of the transverse colon. Eur J Surg 166:579, 2000

62. McClure ET, Welch JP: Acute diverticulitis of the transverse colon with perforation: report of three cases and review of the literature. Arch Surg 114:1068, 1979

63. Jang HJ, Lim HK, Lee SJ, et al: Acute diverticulitis of the cecum and ascending colon: the value of thin-section helical CT findings in excluding colonic carcinoma. AJR Am J Roentgenol 174:1397, 2000

64. Jhaveri KS, Harisinghani MG, Wittenberg J, et al: Right-sided colonic diverticulitis: CT findings. J Comput Assist Tomogr 26:84, 2002

65. Komuta K, Yamanaka S, Okada K, et al: Toward therapeutic guidelines for patients with acute right colonic diverticulitis. Am J Surg 187:233, 2004

66. Chiu PW, Lam CY, Chow TL, et al: Conservative approach is feasible in the management of acute diverticulitis of the right colon. Aust NZ J Surg 71:634, 2001

67. Fang JF, Chen RJ, Lin C, et al: Aggressive resection is indicated for cecal diverticulitis. Am J Surg 185:135, 2003

68. Schweizer J, Casillas RA, Collins JC: Acute diverticulitis in the young adult is not "virulent." Am Surg 68:1044, 2002

69. Edelstein PS, Goldberg SM: Diverticular disease and the younger patient. Diverticular Disease: Management of the Difficult Surgical Case. Welch JP, Cohen JL, Sardella WV, et al, Eds. Williams & Wilkins, Baltimore, 1998, p 319

70. Chautems RC, Ambrosetti P, Ludwig A, et al: Long-term follow-up after first acute episode of sigmoid diverticulitis: is surgery mandatory? a prospective study of 118 patients. Dis Colon Rectum 45:962, 2002

71. West SD, Robinson RK, Delu AN, et al: Diverticulitis in the younger patient. Am J Surg 186:743, 2003

72. Vignati PV, Welch JP, Cohen JC: Long-term management of diverticulitis in young patients. Dis Colon Rectum 38:627, 1995

73. Perdrizet G, Akbari C: Diverticular disease in the immunocompromised patient. Diverticular Disease: Management of the Difficult Surgical Case. Welch JP, Cohen JL, Sardella WV, et al, Eds. Williams & Wilkins, Baltimore, 1998, p 309

74. Tyau ES, Prystowsky JB, Joehl RJ, et al: Acute diverticulitis: a complicated problem in the immunocompromised patient. Arch Surg 126:855, 1991

75. Helderman JH, Goral S: Gastrointestinal complications of transplant immunosuppression. J Am Soc Nephrol 13:277, 2002

76. Chankowsky J, Dupuis P, Gordon PH: Sigmoid diverticulitis presenting as a lower extremity abscess: report of a case. Dis Colon Rectum 44:1711, 2001

77. Girotto JA, Shaikh AY, Freeswick PD et al: Diverticulitis presenting as a strangulated inguinal hernia. Dig Surg 19:67, 2002

78. Ravo B, Khan SA, Ger R et al: Unusual extraperitoneal presentations of diverticulitis. Am J Gastroenterol 80:346, 1985

79. Meyers MA, Goodman KJ: Pathways of extrapelvic spread of disease: anatomic-radiologic correlation. AJR Am J Roentgenol 125:900, 1975

80. Naber A, Sliutz A-M, Freitas H: Giant diverticulum of the sigmoid colon. Int J Colorectal Dis 10:168, 1995

81. Benn PL, Wolff BC, Ilstrup DM: Level of anastomosis and recurrent colonic diverticulitis. Am J Surg 151:269, 1986

82. Thaler K, Baig MK, Berho M, et al: Determinants of recurrence after sigmoid resection for uncomplicated diverticulitis. Dis Colon Rectum 46:385, 2003

83. Sardella WV, Pingpank J: Subacute diverticulitis. Diverticular Disease: Management of the Difficult Surgical Case. Welch JP, Cohen JL, Sardella WV, et al, Eds. Williams & Wilkins, Baltimore, 1998, p 242

84. Horgan AF, McConnell EJ, Wolff BG, et al: Atypical diverticular disease: surgical results. Dis Colon Rectum 44:1315, 2001

85. Ghorai S, Ulbright TM, Rex DK: Endoscopic findings of diverticular inflammation in colonoscopy patients without clinical acute diverticulitis: prevalence and endoscopic spectrum. Am J Gastroenterol 98:802, 2003

86. Makapugay LM, Dean PJ: Diverticular disease-associated chronic colitis. Am J Clin Pathol 20:94, 1996

87. Hackford AW, Veidenheimer MC: Diverticular disease of the colon: current concepts and management. Surg Clin North Am 65: 347, 1985

88. Pemberton JH, Armstrong DN, Dietzen CD: Diverticulitis. Textbook of Gastroenterology, 2nd ed. Yamada T, Ed. JB Lippincott Co, Philadelphia, 1995, p 1879

89. Zollinger RW, Zollinger RM: Diverticular disease of the colon. Adv Surg 5:255, 1971

90. Polk HC, Tuckson WB, Miller FB: The atypical presentations of diverticulitis. Diverticular Disease: Management of the Difficult Surgical Case. Welch JP, Cohen JL, Sardella WV, et al, Eds. Williams & Wilkins, Baltimore, 1998, p 384

Acknowledgment

Figures 1, 2, 4, 5, and 16   Alice Y. Chen.

Roger D. Hurst, M.D., F.A.C.S., F.R.C.S.Ed., and Fabrizio Michelassi, M.D., F.A.C.S.

Management of Fulminant Ulcerative Colitis

Fulminant ulcerative colitis is a potentially life-threatening disorder that must be expertly managed if optimal outcomes are to be achieved. This condition was once associated with a very high mortality,[1] but medical and surgical treatments have improved dramatically, to the point where the mortality associated with fulminant ulcerative colitis is now lower than 3%.[2,3] Optimal management depends on close coordination between medical and surgical therapy, and multidisciplinary strategies are essential.

Classification

The most commonly applied system of classifying the severity of ulcerative colitis has been the one devised by Truelove and Witts, who identified clinical parameters by which colitis could be categorized as mild, moderate, or severe.[4] The Truelove-Witts classification does not, however, specify a unique category for fulminant disease. Accordingly, Hanauer modified this classification scheme to include a category for fulminant colitis [*see Table 1*].[5] Unfortunately, there is no universally agreed upon distinction between severe ulcerative colitis and fulminant ulcerative colitis.[6] Some authors use the terms severe and fulminant interchangeably, whereas others, concerned about the lack of a clear distinction between the two, recommend that the term fulminant ulcerative colitis be avoided altogether.[7] This latter recommendation has not been widely followed: the term fulminant ulcerative colitis remains an established component of the medical vernacular, the absence of a clear definition notwithstanding.[8-10]

Fulminant ulcerative colitis is certainly a severe condition that is associated with systemic deterioration related to progressive ulcerative colitis. Most authorities would agree that a flare of ulcerative colitis can be considered fulminant if it is associated with one or more of the following: high fever, tachycardia, profound anemia necessitating blood transfusion, dehydration, low urine output, abdominal tenderness with distention, profound leukocytosis with a left shift, severe malaise, or prostration. Patients with these symptoms should be hospitalized for aggressive resuscitation while clinical assessment and treatment are being initiated.[11]

Clinical Evaluation

When a patient is admitted with severe or fulminant ulcerative colitis, a complete history and a thorough physical examination are required. The abdominal examination should focus on signs of peritoneal irritation that may suggest perforation or abscess formation. Any patient admitted with severe ulcerative colitis may have already received substantial doses of corticosteroids, which can mask the physical findings of peritonitis.

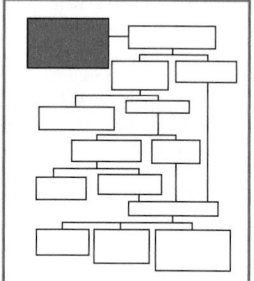

Investigative Studies

LABORATORY TESTS

Initial laboratory studies should include a complete blood count with differential, a coagulation profile, and a complete metabolic profile with assessment of nutritional parameters (e.g., serum albumin concentration). Multiple stool specimens should be sent to be tested for *Clostridium difficile*, cytomegalovirus, and *Escherichia coli* 0157:H7.[12,13] It is important to rule out the presence of opportunistic infections, particularly with *C. difficile*, even in patients with an established diagnosis of ulcerative colitis; superinfection with *C. difficile* is common in such patients.

IMAGING

Abdominal films and an upright chest x-ray should be obtained to look for colonic distention (indicative of toxic megacolon) and free intraperitoneal air (indicative of perforation).

Endoscopic evaluation of the colon and rectum in the presence

---

Table 1 Criteria for Evaluating Severity of Ulcerative Colitis

Variable	Mild Disease	Severe Disease	Fulminant Disease
Stools	< 4/day	> 6/day	> 10/day
Blood in stool	Intermittent	Frequent	Continuous
Temperature	Normal	> 37.5° C	> 37.5° C
Pulse	Normal	> 90 beats/min	> 90 beats/min
Hemoglobin	Normal	< 75% of normal	Transfusion required
Erythrocyte sedimentation rate	30 mm/hr	> 30 mm/hr	> 30 mm/hr
Colonic features on radiography	—	Air, edematous wall, thumbprinting	Dilatation
Clinical signs	—	Abdominal tenderness	Abdominal distention and tenderness

Management of Fulminant Ulcerative Colitis

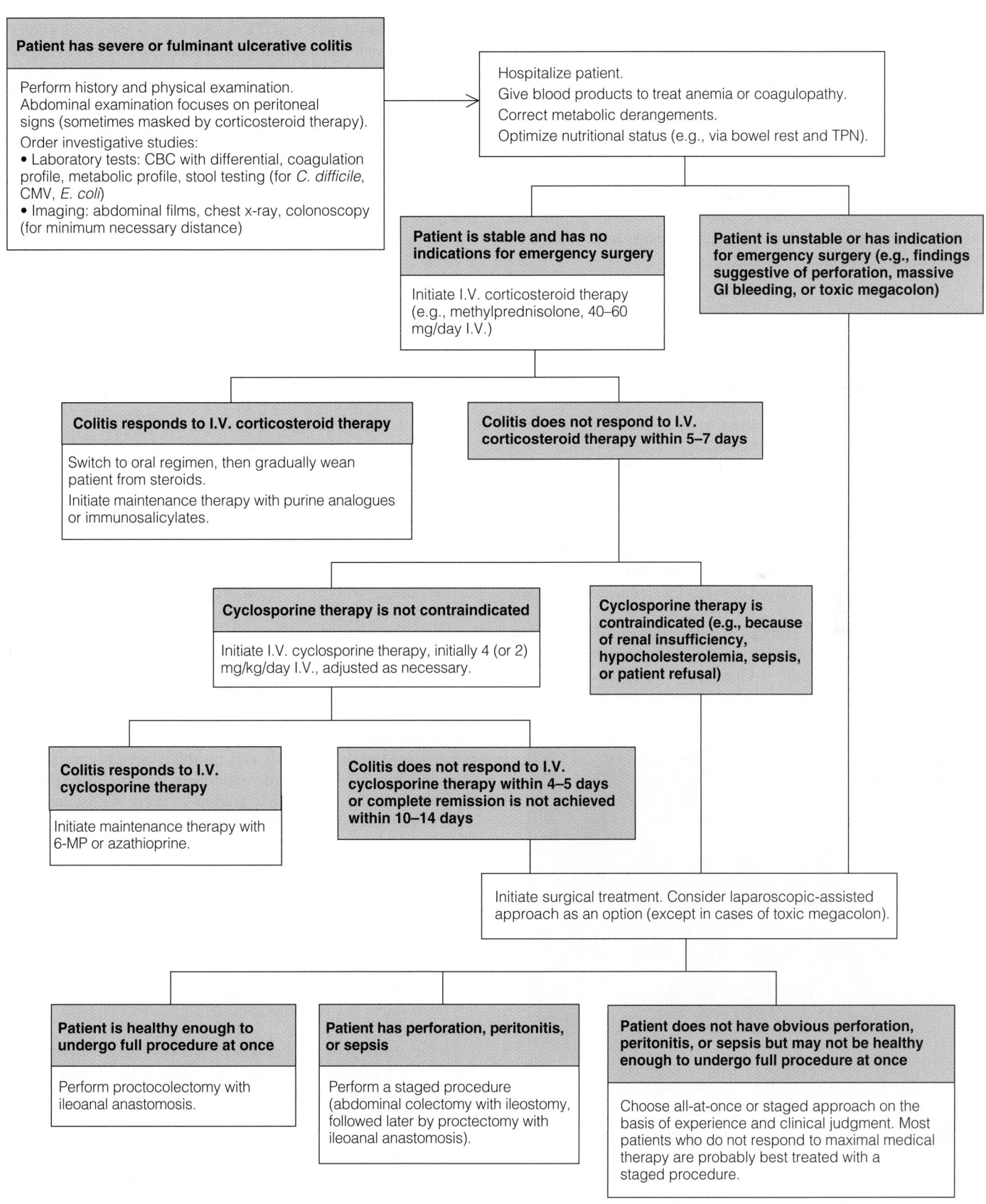

Patient has severe or fulminant ulcerative colitis

Perform history and physical examination.
Abdominal examination focuses on peritoneal signs (sometimes masked by corticosteroid therapy).
Order investigative studies:
• Laboratory tests: CBC with differential, coagulation profile, metabolic profile, stool testing (for *C. difficile*, CMV, *E. coli*)
• Imaging: abdominal films, chest x-ray, colonoscopy (for minimum necessary distance)

Hospitalize patient.
Give blood products to treat anemia or coagulopathy.
Correct metabolic derangements.
Optimize nutritional status (e.g., via bowel rest and TPN).

Patient is stable and has no indications for emergency surgery

Initiate I.V. corticosteroid therapy (e.g., methylprednisolone, 40–60 mg/day I.V.)

Patient is unstable or has indication for emergency surgery (e.g., findings suggestive of perforation, massive GI bleeding, or toxic megacolon)

Colitis responds to I.V. corticosteroid therapy

Switch to oral regimen, then gradually wean patient from steroids.
Initiate maintenance therapy with purine analogues or immunosalicylates.

Colitis does not respond to I.V. corticosteroid therapy within 5–7 days

Cyclosporine therapy is not contraindicated

Initiate I.V. cyclosporine therapy, initially 4 (or 2) mg/kg/day I.V., adjusted as necessary.

Cyclosporine therapy is contraindicated (e.g., because of renal insufficiency, hypocholesterolemia, sepsis, or patient refusal)

Colitis responds to I.V. cyclosporine therapy

Initiate maintenance therapy with 6-MP or azathioprine.

Colitis does not respond to I.V. cyclosporine therapy within 4–5 days or complete remission is not achieved within 10–14 days

Initiate surgical treatment. Consider laparoscopic-assisted approach as an option (except in cases of toxic megacolon).

Patient is healthy enough to undergo full procedure at once

Perform proctocolectomy with ileoanal anastomosis.

Patient has perforation, peritonitis, or sepsis

Perform a staged procedure (abdominal colectomy with ileostomy, followed later by proctectomy with ileoanal anastomosis).

Patient does not have obvious perforation, peritonitis, or sepsis but may not be healthy enough to undergo full procedure at once

Choose all-at-once or staged approach on the basis of experience and clinical judgment. Most patients who do not respond to maximal medical therapy are probably best treated with a staged procedure.

of fulminant ulcerative colitis is a controversial measure.[14-16] Undoubtedly, colonoscopy with biopsy can provide useful diagnostic information in this setting, and numerous reports indicate that in experienced hands, colonoscopy poses little risk to patients with severe colitis.[14,15] In general, however, it is recommended that endoscopic examination proceed no further than the minimum distance necessary to confirm severe colitis. If an endoscopic examination is to be performed, insufflation of air must be minimized; overdistention of the colon may lead to perforation or the development of megacolon. In addition to diagnostic information, endoscopy can provide useful prognostic information. In one study, the presence of deep, extensive colonic ulcerations indicated a low probability for successful medical treatment of fulminant ulcerative colitis: fewer than 10% of patients with such ulcerations responded to medical measures.[14] Thus, an endoscopic finding of deep ulcers [*see Figure 1*] may facilitate the decision to proceed with early operative treatment if medical therapy does not lead to rapid and significant improvement.

Management

GENERAL CARE

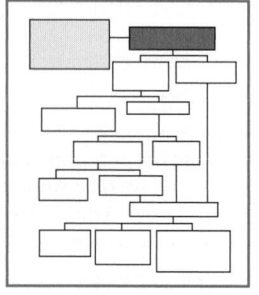

All patients with fulminant ulcerative colitis should be hospitalized. Blood products should be administered to treat significant anemia or coagulopathy. Metabolic derangements should be corrected.[17] Patients with a perforation or massive lower GI hemorrhage are taken to the operating room for emergency surgical treatment; more stable patients are initially managed with medical therapy. Narcotics, antidiarrheal agents, and other anticholinergic medications should be avoided because they can precipitate toxic dilation of the colon.

Bowel rest typically reduces the volume of diarrhea, but whether it affects the clinical course of the fulminant colitis remains to be established.[18,19] One study of patients with acute flares of ulcerative colitis reported no significant difference in outcome between those who were managed with total parenteral nutrition (TPN) and bowel rest and those who received enteral nutrition. This study, however, included patients with colitis of varying degrees of severity, and apparently, only a small number of them had fulminant ulcerative colitis.[19] A subsequent study found that bowel rest and TPN did have a potential clinical advantage in patients with fulminant ulcerative colitis.[18] The most common approach to nutritional management of these patients is first to place them on bowel rest with hyperalimentation, then to initiate oral feeding once the symptoms of the fulminant attack begin to be alleviated. Whether patients are being maintained on bowel rest or are receiving oral feedings, adequate nutritional support must always be ensured. Hence, TPN, if employed, should be maintained until the patient is receiving and tolerating full enteral feedings.

MEDICAL THERAPY

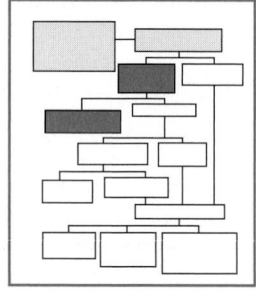

The standard medical approach to fulminant ulcerative colitis involves induction of remission by means of I.V. corticosteroid therapy, followed by long-term maintenance treatment (in the form of purine analogues) once remission has been achieved. If treatment with steroids fails to induce remission, I.V. cyclosporine therapy is considered.

Steroids

For decades, steroid treatment has been the frontline therapy for acute flares of ulcerative colitis. Response rates in cases of fulminant ulcerative colitis range from 50% to 60% when the steroids are given over a period of 5 to 10 days.[20,21] Methylprednisolone, 40 to 60 mg/day in a continuous I.V. infusion, is a common regimen.[5,22-24]

The length of time that should be allowed for patients to respond to I.V. steroid therapy has been a subject of debate. In 1974, Truelove and Jewell recommended urgent operative treatment after 5 days if there is no response to I.V. steroid therapy.[25] This 5-day rule has been widely adopted, but more recent experience suggests that steroids can be safely administered for as long as 7 to 10 days to allow patients more time to respond.[12] Patients who respond to I.V. steroid therapy are switched to an oral steroid regimen (typically prednisone). It is important, however, to stress that corticosteroids should never be employed as long-term maintenance therapy.[5,26] The toxic effects of corticosteroids are related to not only the dosage but also the duration of treatment. Severe complications are common with extended use of even modest doses of steroids. Accordingly, patients should be slowly but completely weaned from steroid therapy. Because symptomatic colitis recurs in 40% to 50% of patients who initially respond to I.V. therapy, maintenance therapy with either purine analogues or immunosalicylates should be instituted.[5,20]

Unfortunately, corticosteroid dependency is frequently encountered in patients with ulcerative colitis. Often, the steroid dosage cannot be tapered without an increase in disease activity and exacerbation of symptoms. In such cases, if the patient cannot be weaned from steroids and switched to purine analogues within 3 to 6 months, surgical consultation is indicated. In addition, if complications related to ulcerative colitis or to corticosteroid therapy develop, the colitis must be treated surgically.

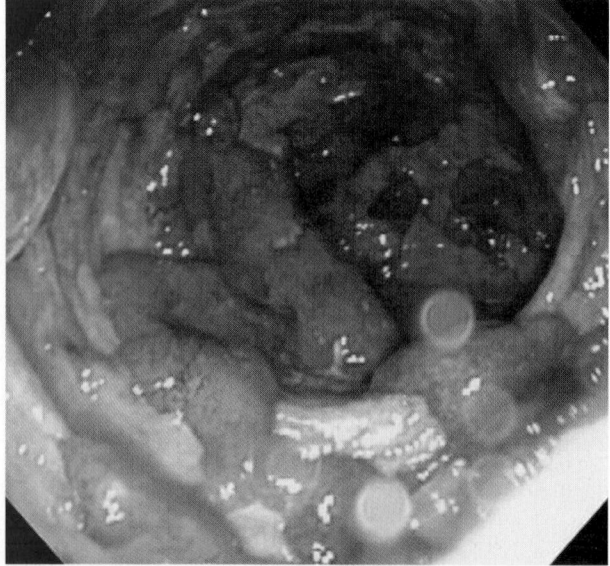

Figure 1 **Sigmoidoscopy demonstrates deep ulcerations in a patient with fulminant ulcerative colitis.**

Cyclosporine

At one time, patients who did not respond to I.V. steroid treatment were invariably referred for surgical treatment. Currently, such patients are most often treated with I.V. cyclosporine therapy. Cyclosporine is an immunosuppressant macrolide that suppresses the production of interleukin-2 by activated T cells through a calcineurin-dependent pathway.[27] Originally employed to prevent tissue rejection after transplantation, cyclosporine has become the standard treatment of steroid-refractory severe ulcerative colitis.

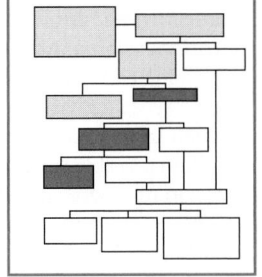

The first report of the use of cyclosporine to treat ulcerative colitis was published in 1984.[28] It was not until 10 years later, however, that a randomized, placebo-controlled trial of cyclosporine therapy for steroid-refractory ulcerative colitis convincingly demonstrated the effectiveness of cyclosporine in this setting.[29] In this trial, patients with steroid-refractory ulcerative colitis who received cyclosporine (4 mg/kg) had an 82% response rate, compared with a 0% response rate in those treated with continued I.V. steroid therapy alone. Since this initial report, response rates ranging from 56% to 91% have been reported in the medical literature, confirming cyclosporine as a major advance in the treatment of severe and fulminant ulcerative colitis.[30-32]

The beneficial effects of cyclosporine therapy are not always durable: as many as 60% of patients experience recurrence of disease after initial cyclosporine-induced remission.[33] Fortunately, recurrence rates can be substantially lowered by means of maintenance therapy with 6-mercaptopurine (6-MP) or azathioprine. With appropriate maintenance therapy, the rate of early recurrence of symptoms after successful I.V. cyclosporine treatment may be reduced to levels as low as 22%.[31,34] Even if the disease does recur, the initial success of cyclosporine therapy in aborting the acute phase of the ulcerative colitis allows patients to recover from the acute illness, so that they are in better condition to undergo elective surgical treatment at a later date if such treatment ultimately proves necessary. This is a major benefit, in that operative management of ulcerative colitis carries a much higher risk of complications when carried out on an urgent basis than when carried out in an elective setting.[18,35,36]

The major side effects of cyclosporine treatment are renal insufficiency, opportunistic infections, and seizures. The risk of seizures appears to be highest in patients with hypocholesterolemia. Consequently, cyclosporine should not be given to patients with significant hypocholesterolemia (serum cholesterol concentration < 100 mg/dl). Hypomagnesemia is commonly seen in patients with fulminant ulcerative colitis who undergo cyclosporine treatment; accordingly, serum magnesium levels should be closely followed.

Dosing regimens for cyclosporine vary. The typical starting dosage is 4 mg/kg/day I.V., which is then adjusted to achieve a whole-blood level between 150 and 400 ng/ml, as measured by high-power liquid chromatography or radioimmunoassay.[37,38] Whole-blood levels as high as 800 ng/ml are considered acceptable by some investigators.[29] If the patient shows no improvement within 4 to 5 days or if complete remission is not achieved by 10 to 14 days, surgical treatment is advised.[12] Most of the side effects of cyclosporine therapy are dose dependent. Several studies have shown that an initial dosage of 2 mg/kg/day I.V. can also be effective in achieving remission.[39-41] Some physicians prefer to begin at this lower dosage and then increase it as necessary on the basis of the measured cyclosporine levels.

Concerns have been raised about the possibility that prolonging medical therapy in patients with severe colitis who have already

Table 2 Indications for Operation in Patients with Fulminant Ulcerative Colitis

Inability to tolerate medical treatment
Failure to respond to medical treatment
Inability to be weaned from corticosteroids
Presence of complications of ulcerative colitis (e.g., perforation, peritonitis, progressive signs of sepsis, hemorrhage, and toxic megacolon)
Development of complications related to medical treatment

received large amounts of corticosteroids may increase the risk of perioperative morbidity and mortality in those who respond to neither steroids nor cyclosporine therapy and thus require operative management. At present, however, there is no evidence that patients who do not respond to cyclosporine therapy are at increased risk for perioperative complications; such therapy does not appear to compromise surgical results.[42]

SURGICAL THERAPY

Indications

Indications for surgical treatment of fulminant ulcerative colitis have been established [see Table 2]. One such indication, of course, is the exhaustion of options for appropriate medical treatment. Because most patients with fulminant ulcerative colitis respond to aggressive medical therapy, such treatment is

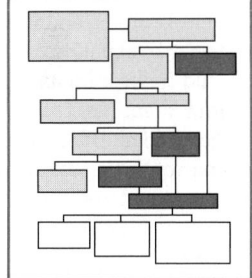

warranted in almost all cases. Care must be exercised, however, not to overtreat patients with fulminant ulcerative colitis who are otherwise stable. The immunosuppressive effects of high-dose corticosteroids and I.V. cyclosporine, along with the debilitation induced by prolonged severe disease, can place patients at high risk for perioperative complications. Patients who do not show significant improvement in response to I.V. steroid therapy within 5 to 7 days should be started on I.V. cyclosporine therapy or referred for operative treatment.[12] Those who do not respond to cyclosporine therapy within 4 days or in whom remission of major symptoms is not achieved within 2 weeks should be treated surgically. Patients whose symptoms progress during the course of I.V. therapy or who show no sign of improvement at all should be considered for early surgery. Patients known to have deep longitudinal ulcerations are less likely to respond to I.V. medical therapy and thus may also be referred for early surgery. The decision regarding when to abandon medical therapy for fulminant ulcerative colitis in favor of surgical therapy is difficult and requires considerable experience and special expertise. Accordingly, patients with fulminant ulcerative colitis are best managed in a center specializing in inflammatory bowel disease.

Patients with perforation or severe GI bleeding require urgent surgical treatment.[43] The debilitation resulting from the disease, coupled with the immunosuppression resulting from intensive medical therapy, can mask the signs and symptoms of sepsis and peritonitis associated with perforation. Perioperative mortality in cases of fulminant colitis is as much as 10 times higher when perforation occurs than when it does not.[44] For this reason, patients with high fever, marked leukocytosis, and persistent tachycardia should be referred for early surgery, regardless of whether other indications of perforation or peritonitis are noted.

Toxic megacolon, though an uncommon complication of severe ulcerative colitis, is important in that it is associated with impending colonic perforation and therefore must be watched for and aggressively managed if present. Two specific conditions must be satisfied to establish the diagnosis of toxic megacolon.[45] First, there must be colonic dilatation; second, the patient must be in a toxic state. Patients with mild symptoms of ulcerative colitis may experience a degree of colonic dilatation, perhaps in conjunction with colonic ileus. This condition is distinctly different from and considerably less worrisome than toxic megacolon. Patients admitted to the hospital with fulminant ulcerative colitis will, by definition, exhibit some degree of toxicity. Colonic dilatation in these patients is a very worrisome phenomenon, in that it completes the picture of toxic megacolon. Accordingly, in all patients with fulminant ulcerative colitis, an abdominal x-ray should be obtained to look for colonic dilatation. Those in whom abdominal distention develops or who experience a sudden decrease in the number of bowel movements without signs of significant clinical improvement should also be assessed for colonic dilatation and toxic megacolon.

In patients with toxic megacolon who are otherwise stable, conservative management, consisting of elimination of narcotics and anticholinergic agents, may be briefly tried. Changes in patient position may be tried as well: moving the patient from side to side, from supine to prone, and into the knee-elbow prone position is thought to facilitate expulsion of colonic gas.[46] Patients with toxic megacolon should be kept on a nihil per os (NPO) regimen, and broad-spectrum I.V. antibiotics should be given. Endoscopic decompression is to be avoided. Blind placement of rectal tubes is ineffective and may be harmful. Patients who do not rapidly respond to conservative management and those who show signs of peritonitis or are otherwise unstable require urgent surgical treatment.[47]

Preparation for Operation

With patients who are stable but are not responding to medical therapy, there may be time for preoperative preparation. Patients who are not on NPO status should be maintained on clear liquids, then kept on an NPO regimen for 6 to 8 hours before operation. On occasion, a patient may be able to tolerate mild bowel preparation with either polyethylene glycol or Fleet Phospho-soda (Fleet Pharmaceuticals, Lynchburg, Virginia). Any bowel preparations that are used need be employed only until bowel movements are free of residue. If time allows, the patient should be counseled by an experienced enterostomal therapist, and an optimal site for the ostomy should be marked on the abdomen. Prophylactic antibiotics should be given before the the surgical incision is made, and appropriate stress-dose steroids should be administered.

Surgical Strategies

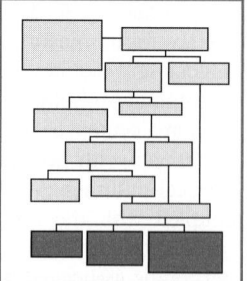

The operative strategies for treating fulminant ulcerative colitis are controversial. Ultimately, almost all patients end up undergoing a restorative proctocolectomy with ileoanal anastomosis [*see 75 Procedures for Ulcerative Colitis*]. In most cases, however, the final surgical goal is achieved in multiple steps. Performing an extensive resection in conjunction with a prolonged and delicate reconstruction in an acutely ill patient is a procedure of questionable safety. Accordingly, many surgeons elect first to perform a total abdominal colectomy with an ileostomy, leaving the rectal stump as either a Hartmann pouch or a mucous fistula,[43,44] then to perform a restorative proctectomy with ileoanal anastomosis at a later date. This staged approach allows the patient to recover from the acute illness, to be

weaned from immunosuppressive agents, and to achieve improved nutritional status. Although the remaining rectal stump continues to be affected by ulcerative colitis, the fecal diversion greatly diminishes disease activity, so that almost all patients can be completely weaned from steroids and other immunosuppressive medications. It is then possible to perform the proctectomy with ileoanal anastomosis in more controlled conditions.

The exact circumstances in which it is best to follow a staged approach have not been clearly defined. It is universally accepted that a staged procedure is mandatory in patients with perforation, peritonitis, or sepsis, but beyond this point, there is no clear consensus. The studies published to date have been inconclusive on this issue: either they included only a small number of patients, they did not clearly define what constituted fulminant colitis, or they did not directly compare the results of the two alternative strategies (i.e., staged colectomy and immediate ileoanal anastomosis). A 1995 study reported excellent long-term results and acceptable short-term morbidity in 12 patients undergoing immediate restorative proctocolectomy with ileal pouch–anal anastomosis (IPAA) for fulminant colitis.[48] These 12 patients, however, represented an extraordinarily small percentage of the total number of ileoanal procedures performed by the authors. In addition, this study used a somewhat liberal definition of fulminant colitis and thus might have included a number of cases that would not have qualified as fulminant colitis—or, possibly, even as severe colitis—according to the criteria cited earlier [*see Table 1*]. Finally, the study provided no data on the experience of patients undergoing a staged procedure for the management of severe or fulminant colitis.

A 1994 study also reported excellent long-term results and exceptionally low perioperative morbidity in 20 patients undergoing restorative proctocolectomy with IPAA for urgent treatment of ulcerative colitis.[49] Another study from the same year, however, reported a 41% anastomotic leakage rate in 12 patients also undergoing an urgent ileoanal procedure for ulcerative colitis, compared with an 11% leakage rate in patients undergoing ileoanal anastomosis under more controlled conditions.[50] On the basis of these results, the authors counseled against ileoanal anastomosis in the urgent setting. A later study also noted a higher incidence of anastomotic leakage (36%) in patients undergoing urgent ileoanal anastomosis.[51] These authors likewise advised against ileoanal anastomosis in the urgent setting.

The fact of the matter is that the distinction between severe and fulminant ulcerative colitis may be little more than an academic exercise. At one end of the disease spectrum, there is a small subset of patients who have symptoms severe enough to necessitate hospitalization yet are healthy enough to undergo a primary ileoanal anastomosis without undue risk. At the other end of the spectrum, there is a subset of severely ill patients with fulminant colitis for whom a staged procedure is mandatory. The middle of the spectrum remains something of a gray area. Because specific criteria for quantifying the risk have not been defined, the decision whether to follow a staged operative approach ultimately is made on the basis of the experienced surgeon's clinical judgment. It has been our experience, however, that the majority of patients who fit the criteria of fulminant colitis [*see Table 1*] and who do not respond to maximal medical therapy are best managed with a staged approach.

Technical Considerations

Surgical exploration is performed via either a midline or a transverse incision. The abdomen is carefully examined, with particular attention paid to the small intestine in an effort to detect any signs of Crohn disease. The colon often shows the changes typical of colitis: serosal hyperemia, corkscrew vessels, and edema [*see Figure 2*].

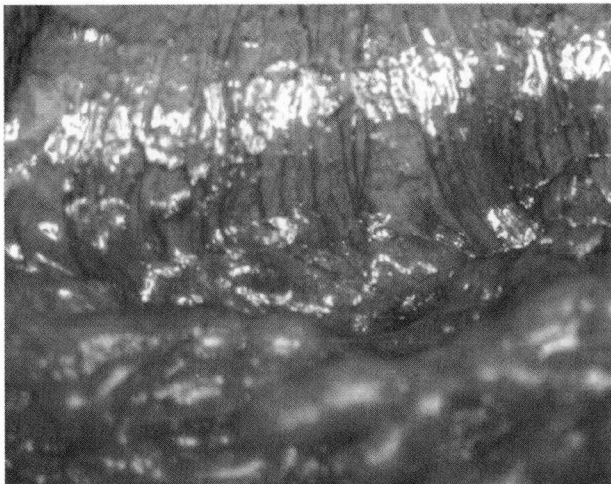

Figure 2 In a colon affected by fulminant ulcerative colitis, changes on the serosal aspect are typically subtle. Serosal hyperemia with small corkscrew vessels is present.

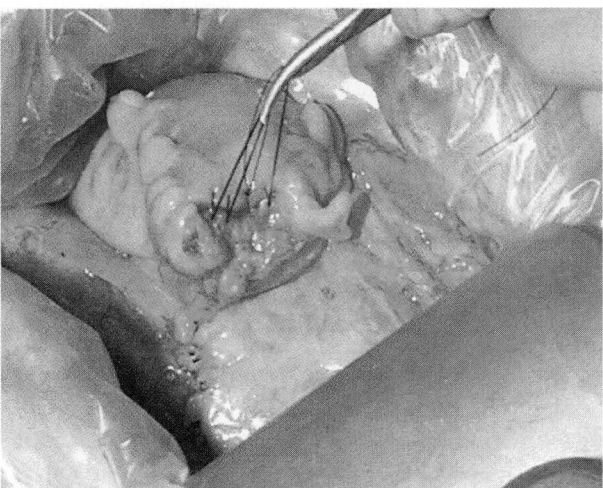

Figure 3 Shown is a Hartmann pouch constructed at the level of the sacral promontory. TA staple line is reinforced with interrupted silk Lembert sutures.

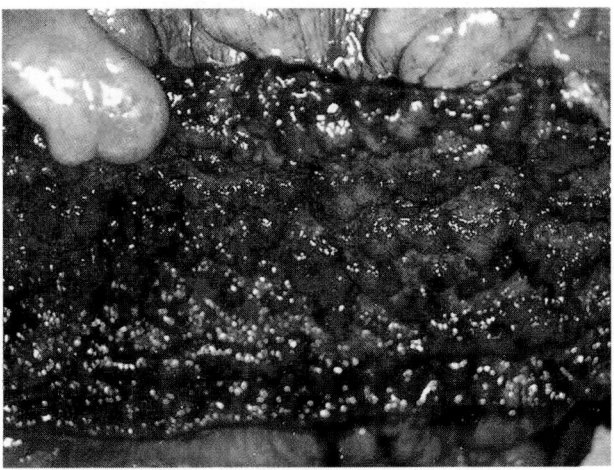

Figure 4 Surgical specimen from a patient with fulminant ulcerative colitis shows severe ulceration and inflammation.

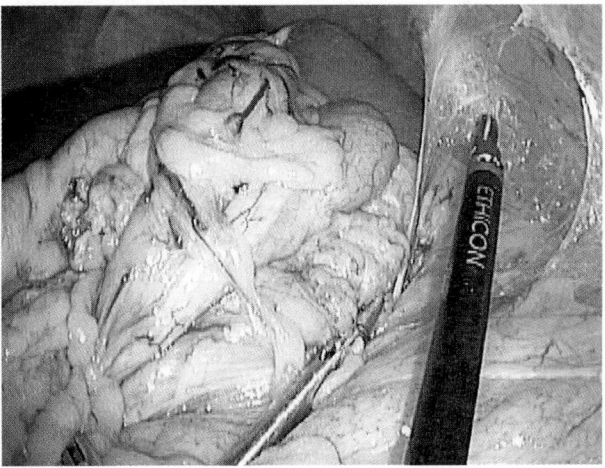

Figure 5 Shown is mobilization of splenic flexure during laparoscopic colectomy for fulminant ulcerative colitis.

Colectomy may be performed in the standard fashion, with mesenteric division occurring at a convenient distance from the bowel; wide mesenteric resection is not necessary. If a staged colectomy is to be performed, the colon is removed, and the rectum is left either as a Hartmann pouch or as a mucous fistula. In most cases, a Hartmann pouch can safely be created. In the construction of a Hartmann pouch, it is important that the stump be of the appropriate length. If the stump is too short, the proctectomy to be performed in the second stage may prove very difficult; if it is too long, there is an increased risk of complications related to persistent disease in the rectum (e.g., bleeding, discharge, and tenesmus). Ideally, the Hartmann pouch should be made at the level of the sacral promontory [*see Figure 3*]. During the colectomy, the sigmoid branches of the inferior mesenteric artery should be divided and the terminal branches of the inferior mesenteric artery preserved. This measure ensures a good blood supply to the remaining rectal stump and helps the Hartmann closure to heal. Preservation of the terminal branches of the inferior mesenteric artery and the superior rectal artery also simplifies the subsequent proctectomy by keeping the pelvic sympathetic nerves free of surrounding scar tissue and by providing a key anatomic landmark

that will assist the surgeon in locating the appropriate presacral dissection plane for any future planned proctectomy.

To create the Hartmann pouch, the mesenteric and pericolonic fat are removed from the bowel wall for a distance of approximately 2 cm. A transverse anastomosis (TA) stapler loaded with 4.8 mm staples is placed on the prepared bowel and fired to close the pouch. The bowel is then divided proximal to the staple line. The staple line should be closely examined to confirm that the staples are closed properly into two rows of well-formed Bs and that individual staples are not cutting into the muscularis propria of the bowel. To provide additional protection against dehiscence, the staple line may be oversewn with interrupted Lembert sutures [*see Figure 3*]. If sutures are employed, they should be carefully placed so that the anterior and posterior serosal surfaces are approximated without undue tension. With a well-constructed Hartmann pouch, pelvic drains are unnecessary and may even be harmful, in that they can promote dehiscence if situated close to the suture line.

In some cases, the colon at the level of the sacral promontory is affected by deep ulcerations and severe inflammation, to the point where closure of the Hartmann pouch at this level poses an unacceptably high risk of dehiscence [*see Figure 4*]. If the severity of disease precludes safe closure of the Hartmann pouch, creation of a mucous fistula should be considered. A mucous fistula requires a longer segment of bowel than a Hartmann pouch does and thus is associated with a higher risk of bleeding from the retained segment. In addition, a mucous fistula is unsightly and often generates a very foul odor. As a compromise approach, some surgeons advocate creating a Hartmann pouch of moderate length and placing the proximal end of the stump through the fascia at the lower edge of the midline incision; the end of the stump is then left buried in the subcutaneous tissue. The benefit of this approach is that if dehiscence of the staple line occurs, any ensuing infection is limited to the subcutaneous space and does not result in an intra-abdominal or pelvic abscess.

If attempts to fashion a secure Hartmann closure fail and the remaining rectal stump is too short to be brought out as a mucous fistula, the proximal rectum should be resected, and closure of the Hartmann pouch should be performed just below the peritoneal reflection. In this situation, closed suction drains should be placed deep in the pelvis, and the peritoneum should be closed over the rectal stump. Such a short Hartmann pouch, however, will be more difficult to locate during the subsequent restorative proctectomy and ileoanal anastomosis.

With a staged colectomy, an end ileostomy is created in the standard fashion [*see 72 Intestinal Stomas*], and the abdomen is closed. Placing a rectal tube to drain rectal secretions may be beneficial in reducing the risk of dehiscence of the Hartmann pouch.

Laparoscopic Approaches

Experience has demonstrated that laparoscopic-assisted approaches to abdominal colectomy can be safely employed in patients with ulcerative colitis.[52] Mobilization of the colon and division of the mesentery can be accomplished laparoscopically [*see Figure 5*], with the specimen being removed through a small Pfannenstiel incision. An end ileostomy can also be fashioned with the aid of inspection through the Pfannenstiel incision. Alternatively, the Pfannenstiel incision can be made early in the procedure and used for placement of a hand port, and the colon can be removed by means of a hand-assisted laparoscopic approach.

Whether a laparoscopic-assisted approach to the management of fulminate ulcerative colitis possesses any significant clinical advantages remains to be determined. However, a growing body of experience with this approach indicates that in experienced hands, laparoscopic-assisted colectomy is a safe and reasonable alternative that may well result in shorter hospital stays and decreased postoperative pain. The laparoscopic-assisted approach may therefore be considered as an option for patients with fulminant ulcerative colitis. Patients with toxic megacolon, however, should be managed by means of an open surgical approach; the instruments used to grasp the bowel in a laparoscopic-assisted colectomy are likely to cause perforation of the severely thinned walls of the dilated megacolon.

References

1. Banks B, Korelitz B, Zetzel I: The course of non-specific ulcerative colitis: review of twenty years experience and late results. Gastroenterology 32:983, 1952

2. Daperno M, Sostegni R, Rocca R, et al: Medical treatment of severe ulcerative colitis. Aliment Pharmacol Ther 16(suppl 4):7, 2002

3. Jarnerot G, Rolny P, Sandberg-Gertzen H: Intensive intravenous treatment of ulcerative colitis. Gastroenterology 89:1005, 1985

4. Truelove SC, Witts LJ: Cortisone in ulcerative colitis: final report on a therapeutic trial. BMJ 2:1041, 1955

5. Hanauer SB: Inflammatory bowel disease. N Engl J Med 334:841, 1996

6. Ludwig D, Stange EF: Treatment of ulcerative colitis. Hepatogastroenterology 47:83, 2000

7. Hyde GM, Jewell DP: The management of severe ulcerative colitis. Aliment Pharmacol Ther 11:419, 1997

8. Modigliani R: Medical management of fulminant colitis. Inflamm Bowel Dis 8:129, 2002

9. Swan NC, Geoghegan JG, O'Donoghue DP, et al: Fulminant colitis in inflammatory bowel disease: detailed pathologic and clinical analysis. Dis Colon Rectum 41:1511, 1998

10. Danovitch SH: Fulminant colitis and toxic megacolon. Gastroenterol Clin North Am 18:73, 1989

11. Han PD, Cohen RD: The medical approach to the patient with inflammatory bowel disease. The Clinician's Guide to Inflammatory Bowel Disease. Lichtenstein GR, Ed. Slack, Thorofare, New Jersey, 2003

12. Chang JC, Cohen RD: Medical management of severe ulcerative colitis. Gastroenterol Clin North Am 33:235, 2004

13. Kaufman HS, Kahn AC, Iacobuzio-Donahue C, et al: Cytomegaloviral enterocolitis: clinical associations and outcome. Dis Colon Rectum 42:24, 1999

14. Carbonnel F, Lavergne A, Lemann M, et al: Colonoscopy of acute colitis: a safe and reliable tool for assessment of severity. Dig Dis Sci 39:1550, 1994

15. Alemayehu G, Jarnerot G: Colonoscopy during an attack of severe ulcerative colitis is a safe procedure and of great value in clinical decision making. Am J Gastroenterol 86:187, 1991

16. Marion JF, Present DH: The modern medical management of acute, severe ulcerative colitis. Eur J Gastroenterol Hepatol 9:831, 1997

17. Travis SP, Farrant JM, Ricketts C, et al: Predicting outcome in severe ulcerative colitis. Gut 38:905, 1996

18. Mikkola KA, Jarvinen HJ: Management of fulminating ulcerative colitis. Ann Chir Gynaecol 81:37, 1992

19. McIntyre PB, Powell-Tuck J, Wood SR, et al: Controlled trial of bowel rest in the treatment of severe acute colitis. Gut 27:481, 1986

20. Kornbluth A, Marion JF, Salomon P, et al: How effective is current medical therapy for severe ulcerative and Crohn's colitis? An analytic review of selected trials. J Clin Gastroenterol 20:280, 1995

21. Faubion WA Jr, Loftus EV Jr, Harmsen WS, et al: The natural history of corticosteroid therapy for inflammatory bowel disease: a population-based study. Gastroenterology 121:255, 2001

22. Rosenberg W, Ireland A, Jewell DP: High-dose methylprednisolone in the treatment of active ulcerative colitis. J Clin Gastroenterol 12:40, 1990

23. Farthing MJ: Severe inflammatory bowel disease: medical management. Dig Dis 21:46, 2003

24. Wolf JM, Lashner BA: Inflammatory bowel disease: sorting out the treatment options. Cleve Clin J Med 69:621, 2002

25. Truelove SC, Jewell DP: Intensive intravenous regimen for severe attacks of ulcerative colitis. Lancet 1:1067, 1974

26. Sachar DB: Maintenance therapy in ulcerative colitis and Crohn's disease. J Clin Gastroenterol 20:117, 1995

27. Faulds D, Goa KL, Benfield P: Cyclosporin: a review of its pharmacodynamic and pharmacokinetic properties, and therapeutic use in immunoregulatory disorders. Drugs 45:953, 1993

28. Gupta S, Keshavarzian A, Hodgson HJ: Cyclosporin in ulcerative colitis. Lancet 2:1277, 1984

29. Lichtiger S, Present DH, Kornbluth A, et al: Cyclosporine in severe ulcerative colitis refractory to steroid therapy. N Engl J Med 330:1841, 1994

30. Stack WA, Long RG, Hawkey CJ: Short- and long-term outcome of patients treated with cyclosporin for severe acute ulcerative colitis. Aliment Pharmacol Ther 12:973, 1998

31. Loftus CG, Loftus EV Jr, Sandborn WJ: Cyclosporin for refractory ulcerative colitis. Gut 52:172, 2003

32. Santos J, Baudet S, Casellas F, et al: Efficacy of intravenous cyclosporine for steroid refractory attacks of ulcerative colitis. J Clin Gastroenterol 20:285, 1995

33. Cohen RD, Stein R, Hanauer SB: Intravenous cyclosporin in ulcerative colitis: a five-year experience. Am J Gastroenterol 94:1587, 1999

34. Kamm MA: Review article: maintenance of remission in ulcerative colitis. Aliment Pharmacol Ther 16(suppl 4):21, 2002

35. Hawley PR: Emergency surgery for ulcerative colitis. World J Surg 12:169, 1988

36. Hurst RD, Finco C, Rubin M, et al: Prospective analysis of perioperative morbidity in one hundred consecutive colectomies for ulcerative colitis. Surgery 118:748, 1995

37. Stein RB, Hanauer SB: Medical therapy for inflammatory bowel disease. Gastroenterol Clin North Am 28:297, 1999

38. Sandborn WJ: Cyclosporine in ulcerative colitis: state of the art. Acta Gastroenterol Belg 64:201, 2001

39. Actis GC, Ottobrelli A, Pera A, et al: Continuously infused cyclosporine at low dose is sufficient to avoid emergency colectomy in acute attacks of ulcerative colitis without the need for high-dose steroids. J Clin Gastroenterol 17:10, 1993

40. Van Assche G, D'Haens G, Noman M, et al: Randomized, double-blind comparison of 4 mg/kg versus 2 mg/kg intravenous cyclosporine in severe ulcerative colitis. Gastroenterology 125:1025, 2003

41. Rayner CK, McCormack G, Emmanuel AV, et al: Long-term results of low-dose intravenous ciclosporin for acute severe ulcerative colitis. Aliment Pharmacol Ther 18:303, 2003

42. Fleshner PR, Michelassi F, Rubin M, et al: Morbidity of subtotal colectomy in patients with severe ulcerative colitis unresponsive to cyclosporin. Dis Colon Rectum 38:1241, 1995

43. Berg DF, Bahadursingh AM, Kaminski DL, et al: Acute surgical emergencies in inflammatory bowel disease. Am J Surg 184:45, 2002

44. Binderow SR, Wexner SD: Current surgical therapy for mucosal ulcerative colitis. Dis Colon Rectum 37:610, 1994

45. Gan SI, Beck PL: A new look at toxic megacolon: an update and review of incidence, etiology, pathogenesis, and management. Am J Gastroenterol 98:2363, 2003

46. Panos MZ, Wood MJ, Asquith P: Toxic megacolon: the knee-elbow position relieves bowel distension. Gut 34:1726, 1993

47. Foley WJ, Coon WW, Bonfield RE: Toxic megacolon in acute fulminant ulcerative colitis. Am J Surg 120:769, 1970

48. Ziv Y, Fazio VW, Church JM, et al: Safety of urgent restorative proctocolectomy with ileal pouch–anal anastomosis for fulminant colitis. Dis Colon Rectum 38:345, 1995

49. Harms BA, Myers GA, Rosenfeld DJ, et al: Management of fulminant ulcerative colitis by primary restorative proctocolectomy. Dis Colon Rectum 37:971, 1994

50. Heyvaert G, Penninckx F, Filez L, et al: Restorative proctocolectomy in elective and emergency cases of ulcerative colitis. Int J Colorectal Dis 9:73, 1994

51. Fukushima T, Sugita A, Koganei K, et al: The incidence and outcome of pelvic sepsis following hand-sewn and stapled ileal pouch anal anastomoses. Surg Today 30:223, 2000

52. Bell RL, Seymour NE: Laparoscopic treatment of fulminant ulcerative colitis. Surg Endosc 16:1778, 2002

José G. Guillem, M.D., M.P.H., F.A.C.S., and Harvey G. Moore, M.D.

The majority of cases of inherited colorectal cancer (CRC) are accounted for by two syndromes: hereditary nonpolyposis colorectal cancer (HNPCC) and familial adenomatous polyposis (FAP). In both, the predisposition to disease is a germline mutation transmitted in an autosomal dominant fashion. Although the two syndromes are similar in some respects, differences in their phenotypic expression and in the certainty of disease development mandate distinctly different surgical approaches, including the timing and extent of prophylactic procedures in carefully selected patients. In the management of FAP, the role of prophylactic surgery is clearly defined, though the optimal procedure for an individual patient depends on a number of factors. In the management of HNPCC, the indications for prophylactic procedures are emerging, particularly for unaffected mutation-positive patients.

Two less common polyposis syndromes, Peutz-Jeghers syndrome (PJS) and juvenile polyposis syndrome (JPS), are also inherited in an autosomal dominant fashion and are associated with a significant risk of CRC. Carefully selected persons affected by these syndromes may also benefit from prophylactic surgical procedures. Current evidence supports a role for prophylactic colectomy in JPS but not in PJS.

Finally, there are a few other, less common, inherited hamartomatous polyposis syndromes, such as Cowden disease and Ruvalcaba-Myhre-Smith syndrome. At present, these syndromes appear to be associated with an exceedingly low risk of CRC; accordingly, prophylactic surgery is not indicated.[1]

Familial Adenomatous Polyposis

FAP is caused by mutations in the tumor suppressor gene *APC*, located at 5q21. Nearly 80% of FAP patients belong to known FAP kindreds; 10% to 30% have new mutations.[1] More than 300 distinct mutations have been identified within the *APC* gene locus in persons manifesting the FAP phenotype. More than half of the known germline mutations associated with the classic FAP phenotype are concentrated in the 5′ region of exon 15.[1] Genotype-phenotype correlative studies have revealed a wide range of phenotypic heterogeneity, ranging from the relatively mild presentation associated with attenuated FAP, which is caused by mutations in the 3′ and 5′ ends of the *APC* gene,[2] to the severe presentation associated with mutations downstream from codon 1250, particularly those in codon 1309. It has been reported that as many as 7.5% of patients with a classic FAP phenotype and no demonstrable *APC* mutation may have biallelic germline mutations in the base excision repair gene *MYH*.[3]

CLINICAL EVALUATION

FAP, which accounts for less than 1% of the annual CRC burden, is characterized by the presence of more than 100 adenomatous polyps of the colorectum, virtually 100% penetrance, and a nearly 100% risk of CRC by the age of 40 if prophylactic colectomy is not performed.[1,4] Extracolonic manifestations are common and include desmoid tumors, osteomas, odontomas, sebaceous and epidermoid cysts, congenital hypertrophy of the retinal pigment epithelium, and periampullary neoplasms.[1]

INVESTIGATIVE STUDIES

Pathologic Findings

The polyps, which develop by the age of 20 years in 75% of cases, are typically less than 1 cm in size. In severe FAP, they may carpet the entire surface of the colorectal epithelium or, alternatively, may spare portions of the epithelial lining (e.g., the rectum). Adenomas may be either pedunculated or sessile and may have tubular, villous, or tubulovillous histology. Microscopic evaluation may reveal innumerable microadenomas within grossly normal-appearing colorectal mucosa. Foci of carcinoma in situ and invasive carcinoma may be found within larger polyps, and the incidence of invasive cancer is proportional to the extent of polyposis. Unlike CRC in the setting of HNPCC, CRC in the setting of FAP is more commonly located on the left side.[1]

Screening and Surveillance

Screening (genetic testing or annual or biennial flexible sigmoidoscopy) for at-risk family members should begin around puberty (i.e., at 10 to 12 years of age) [see Table 1]. In families with a demonstrated *APC* mutation, informative genetic testing can be carried out with the protein truncation test [see Table 2]. This test, which detects foreshortened proteins resulting from truncating *APC* mutations, is approximately 80% sensitive[5]; however, the test results are commonly misinterpreted, even by physicians.[6] Patients with normal protein truncation test results and a previously identified mutation in the family may be discharged from further screening with a nearly 100% certainty that the mutation is absent, but they should still undergo CRC screening starting at the age of 50 years, as is recommended for average-risk persons. When an *APC* mutation has not previously been identified in the family of an affected person, the patient should be tested first to identify the causative mutation. In families in which the protein truncation test fails to provide conclusive information on carrier status, at-risk individuals should continue with the recommended endoscopic surveillance program. Other options for detecting *APC* mutations include linkage analysis, single-stranded confirmation polymorphism, and direct sequence analysis.[1]

Genetic counseling is an essential component of the evaluation of patients for FAP. Patients who have a positive genotype or who have adenomatous polyps on sigmoidoscopy should undergo full colonoscopy to establish the extent of polyposis.

MANAGEMENT

Medical Therapy

A number of nonsteroidal anti-inflammatory drugs, including sulindac, celecoxib, and the sulindac metabolite exisulind, have been shown to reduce the number and size of polyps in FAP

Table 1   Genetic Basis, Clinicopathologic Features, Diagnosis, Surveillance, and Surgical Management of Hereditary CRC and Polyposis Syndromes

Syndrome	Genetic Basis	Diagnosis	GI Manifestations	Extracolonic Manifestations	Pathologic Features	CRC Screening and Surveillance	Surgical Management
FAP	*APC*, 5q21 (> 90%); *MYH* (8%)	100 adenomatous polyps of colorectum *or* *APC* mutation demonstrated	Adenomatous polyps of colon and rectum 100% risk of colorectal cancer by age 40 without colectomy	Desmoids Osteomas Odontomas Sebaceous and epidermoid cysts CHRPE Periampullary neoplasms	Tubular, villous, or tubulovillous histology	Consider genetic counseling/testing Carry out early surveillance with sigmoidoscopy (at age 10–12 yr)[98,99] For at-risk untested individuals, perform FS every 1–2 yr	If polyposis is confirmed, colectomy is indicated Options include the following: TPC with ileostomy TAC with IRA TPC with IPAA
HNPCC	MMR genes: *MLH1* and *MSH2* (90%), *MSH6* (10%), *PMS1*, *PMS2*, *MLH3*, *MSH3*	MMR mutation demonstrated *or* Family meets Amsterdam I or II criteria[50,51]	Possibly few or no colorectal polyps Right-side tumor (60%–70%) MSI-high tumor (80%–90%) Synchronous/metachronous tumors 80% lifetime risk of CRC	Associated tumors of endometrium, small bowel, ureter, or renal pelvis	Adenocarcinoma, frequently mucinous or signet-ring cell histology Solid or cribriform growth pattern Tumor-infiltrating or peritumoral lymphocytes	Consider genetic counseling/testing If patient is mutation positive or is untested but meets criteria, perform colonoscopy at 20–25 yr (or 10 yr earlier than youngest affected individual), then every 1–2 yr, then annually after age 40[98,99]	*Affected patient with identified mutation or meeting Amsterdam criteria:* Colon cancer or advanced adenoma: perform TAC with IRA or segmental colectomy with annual colonoscopy Rectal cancer: perform TPC with IPAA or LAR and annual colonoscopy *Unaffected patient with identified mutation or meeting Amsterdam criteria:* Consider TAC with IRA or colonoscopy every 1–3 yr
PJS	*LKB1/STK11*, 19p13.3 (18%–63%)	Hamartomas of GI tract *and* At least two of the following: Small bowel disease Mucocutaneous melanin Family history of PJS	Hamartomatous polyps throughout entire GI tract (small intestine, 90%; colon, 50%) Relative risk of CRC = 84	Mucocutaneous pigmentation (perioral and buccal areas, 95%)	Hyperplasia of smooth muscle of muscularis mucosa Arborization Pseudoinvasion	Consider genetic counseling/testing Perform colonoscopy starting between puberty and age 25, then every 2–3 yr[88]	Perform operative or laparoscopy-assisted polypectomy or segmental colectomy for polyps > 1.5 cm that are not amenable to endoscopic resection Perform segmental bowel resection for invasive cancers In the setting of laparotomy, perform intraoperative endoscopy (peroral or via enterotomy) *Prophylactic colectomy has no role*[88]
JPS	*SMAD4/DPC4*, 18q21.1 (50%); *BMPR1A*, 10q22.3	3 juvenile polyps of colon and juvenile polyps throughout GI tract *or* Any number of polyps with family history of JPS	Multiple hamartomatous polyps throughout gastroduodenum 15% risk of CRC by age 35, 68% risk by age 65	Tumors of stomach, pancreas, duodenum	50–200 polyps Cystic, mucus-filled spaces with epithelial lining Attenuated smooth muscle layer Focal epithelial hyperplasia and dysplasia	Consider genetic counseling/testing Perform colonoscopy in middle to late teenage years, with EGD and SBS; if results are negative, repeat in 3 yr, then every 3 yr if results remain negative; if results are positive, perform biopsy of polyps and intestinal mucosa	*Disease is local, and no significant symptoms are present:* Manage endoscopically, with colonoscopic surveillance every 1–3 yr *Disease is diffuse or significant symptoms are present:* Perform TAC with IRA, and carry out rectal surveillance every 1–3 yr

CHRPE—congenital hypertrophy of retinal pigment epithelium   CRC—colorectal cancer   EGD—esophagogastroduodenoscopy   FAP—familial adenomatous polyposis   FS—flexible sigmoidoscopy   HNPCC—hereditary nonpolyposis colorectal cancer   IPAA—ileal pouch–anal anastomosis   IRA—ileorectal anastomosis   JPS—juvenile polyposis syndrome   LAR—low anterior resection   MMR—mismatch repair   MSI—microsatellite instability   PJS—Peutz-Jeghers syndrome   SBS—small bowel series   TAC—total abdominal colectomy   TPC—total proctocolectomy

patients.[7-10] However, long-term use of chemopreventive agents for primary treatment of FAP is not recommended.[11] In a randomized, placebo-controlled, double-blind study of genotype-positive, phenotype-negative patients, the use of sulindac had no effect on the subsequent development of colorectal polyposis.[12] Furthermore, the development of rectal cancer has been reported in patients whose rectal polyps were effectively controlled with sulindac.[10] Finally, these medications necessitate continued compliance[9] and may be associated with significant side effects. Chemopreventive agents may be useful for reducing polyp load and facilitating endoscopic management of polyps in patients who have an ileal pouch or in patients who have an iliorectal anastomosis, are at high risk for polyp development, and refuse proctectomy. In such cases, however, it is still necessary to perform careful surveillance of the residual rectum or the ileoanal pouch every 6 months.[11]

Surgical Therapy

The timing of surgical treatment depends to some degree on the extent of polyposis, in that the risk of CRC is partially dependent on the number of polyps present.[13] Patients with mild polyposis (and thus a lower cancer risk) can undergo surgery in their midteens.[11] Practically speaking, the best time is usually the summer between high school and college. Patients who have severe polyposis, dysplasia, adenomas larger than 5 mm, and significant symptoms should undergo surgery as soon after diagnosis as is practical.[11]

There are three basic surgical options for treating FAP: (1) total proctocolectomy (TPC) with permanent ileostomy, (2) total abdominal colectomy with ileorectal anastomosis (IRA), and (3) proctocolectomy with ileal pouch–anal anastomosis (IPAA) [*see 75 Procedures for Ulcerative Colitis*]. The optimal procedure for a given patient is determined on the basis of a number of factors, including disease characteristics, differences in postoperative functional outcome, preoperative anal sphincter status, and patient preference.

TPC TPC with permanent ileostomy is rarely chosen as a primary procedure. More commonly, it is considered as an option for patients in whom a proctectomy is required but an IPAA is contraindicated (e.g., those with rectal tumors involving the sphincters or the levator complex or those with poor baseline sphincter function) or for patients in whom an IPAA is not technically feasible (e.g., those with desmoid disease and foreshortening of the small bowel mesentery). Occasionally, however, TPC is chosen as a primary procedure in patients whose lifestyle would be compromised by frequent bowel movements.

IPAA versus IRA The choice between IPAA and IRA is generally more challenging. The main considerations to be taken into account are the risk of rectal cancer development if the rectum is left in situ and the differences in functional outcome (and associated quality of life) between procedures.

It has been estimated that the risk of rectal cancer after IRA may be as high as 4% to 8% at 10 years and 26% to 32% at 25 years.[14,15] The true risk, however, may be somewhat lower. Most of the studies from which these figures were derived were completed before IPAA became available; thus, patients and physicians might have been more likely to choose IRA even in the setting of more extensive rectal disease, given that TPC and permanent ileostomy was the only other option at the time. The magnitude of risk in an individual patient is related to the overall extent of colorectal polyposis. IRA may be an option for patients with fewer than 1,000 colorectal polyps (including those with attenuated FAP) and fewer than 20 rectal adenomas, because these patients appear to be at relatively low risk for rectal cancer.[11,13,16] Ideally, patients with severe rectal (> 20 adenomas) or colonic (> 1,000 adenomas) polyposis, an adenoma larger than 3 cm, or an adenoma with severe dysplasia should be treated with IPAA.[11,13]

The risk of secondary rectal excision as a consequence of uncontrollable rectal polyposis or rectal cancer may be estimated on the basis of the specific location of the causative *APC* mutation.[15-17] In a study of 87 FAP patients with an identified *APC* mutation who underwent IRA, those with a mutation located downstream from codon 1250 had an approximately threefold higher incidence of secondary rectal resection than those with a mutation located upstream of codon 1250.[14] Furthermore, patients with a mutation located between codons 1250 and 1464 had a 6.2-fold higher risk of rectal cancer than those with a mutation before codon 1250 or after codon 1464.[15]

The risk of polyp and cancer development after index surgery is not limited to patients undergoing IRA. In patients undergoing IPAA, the pouch-anal anastomosis may be either handsewn after

Table 2 Availability of Commercial Genetic Testing for Autosomal Dominant Inherited CRC Syndromes

Test	Approximate Time Frame	Approximate Cost	Clinical Availability (in United States)
Protein truncation test	4–6 wk	$1,100; if mutation known, $475	Mayo Clinic, Rochester, Minn.; (800) 533-1710 Washington University, St. Louis, Mo.; (314) 454-7601
DNA sequencing, germline *APC*	3 wk	$1,475	Baylor College of Medicine, Houston, Tex.; (800) 411-GENE Huntington Medical Research Institute, Pasadena, Calif.; (626) 795-4343 Myriad Inc., Salt Lake City, Utah; (800) 469-7423 University of Pennsylvania, Philadelphia, Pa.; (215) 573-9161
MSI analysis	2–4 wk	$350–850	ARUP Laboratories, Salt Lake City, Utah; (801) 583-2787 Baylor College of Medicine, Houston, Tex.; (800) 411-GENE Mayo Clinic, Rochester, Minn.; (800) 533-1710 Memorial Sloan-Kettering Cancer Center, New York, N.Y.; (212) 639-5170 Ohio State University, Columbus, Ohio; (614) 293-7774
MSI and IHC	2–3 wk	$750	Mayo Clinic, Rochester, Minn.; (800) 533-1710
DNA sequencing, germline MMR mutation (*MLH1, MSH2*)	3 wk	$1,950; if mutation known, $350	Baylor College of Medicine, Houston, Tex.; (800) 411-GENE Huntington Medical Research Institute, Pasadena, Calif.; (626) 795-4343 Myriad Inc., Salt Lake City, Utah; (800) 469-7423 Quest Diagnostics, Inc., San Juan Capistrano, Calif.; (949) 728-4279 University of Pennsylvania, Philadelphia, Pa.; (215) 573-9161
LKB1/STK11 testing	6–12 wk	$1,176–1,400; if mutation known, $200–350	Ohio State University, Columbus, Ohio; (614) 293-7774 GeneDx Inc., Gaithersburg, Md.; (301) 519-2100
SMAD4/BMPR1A testing	3 mo	$1,234–1,260; if mutation known, $200	Ohio State University, Columbus, Ohio; (614) 293-7774

IHC—immunohistochemistry   MMR—mismatch repair   MSI—microsatellite instability complete anal mucosectomy or stapled to a 1 to 2 cm anal transition zone. Neoplasia may occur at the site of the anastomosis, and the incidence appears to be higher after stapled anastomosis (28% to 31%) than after mucosectomy and handsewn anastomosis (10% to 14%).[18,19] Function, however, may be better after stapled anastomosis.[19] In the case of anal transition zone neoplasia after stapled anastomosis, transanal mucosectomy can often be performed, followed by advancement of the pouch to the dentate line. Of additional concern is the development of adenomatous polyps in the ileal pouch itself, which occurs in 35% to 42% of patients at 7 to 10 years.[20-22]

With respect to postoperative bowel function and associated quality of life, IPAA has been associated with a higher frequency of both daytime and nocturnal bowel movements, a higher incidence of passive incontinence and incidental soiling, and higher postoperative morbidity than IRA.[23] Accordingly, some authors recommend IRA for patients with mild rectal polyposis. Other authors, however, have found the two approaches to be equivalent in terms of functional results[24] and quality of life[25] and therefore recommend IPAA for most patients because of the risk of rectal cancer associated with IRA.

Regardless of which procedure is performed, however, lifetime surveillance of the rectal remnant (after IRA) or the ileal pouch (after IPAA) is required.[11] Endoscopic surveillance of the bowel at intervals of 6 months to 1 year after index surgery is recommended.[5,11] After IRA, small (< 5 mm) adenomas may be safely observed, with biopsy performed to rule out severe dysplasia. If adenomas increase in number, the frequency of surveillance should be increased, and polyps larger than 5 mm should be removed. When fulguration and polypectomy are repeated over a period of many years, subsequent polypectomy may become difficult, rectal compliance may be reduced, and flat cancers may be hard to identify against a background of scar tissue. The development of severe dysplasia or a villous adenoma larger than 1 cm is an indication for proctectomy.[11]

Extracolonic Disease

After total abdominal colectomy with IRA and regular surveillance, the risk of death appears to be three times higher for FAP patients than for an age- and sex-matched control population.[26] The main causes of death after IRA are desmoid disease and upper gastrointestinal malignancy.

Desmoid disease Desmoids are histologically benign tumors that arise from fibroaponeurotic tissue and occur in 12% to 17% of FAP patients.[11,27,28] Unlike those in the general population, desmoids in FAP patients tend to be intra-abdominal (up to 80% of cases) and mainly occur after abdominal surgical procedures.[27,28] Patients with *APC* mutations located between codons 1310 and 2011 are at increased risk for these tumors.[29] Desmoids often involve the small bowel mesentery (> 50% of cases),[28] making complete resection difficult or impossible, and they may also involve the ureters.[27] Not uncommonly, patients present with small bowel obstruction.[27,28] Morbidity after attempted resection, which often involves removal of a significant length of small bowel, is substantial. The recurrence rate after attempted resection is also high, and the recurrent disease is often more aggressive than the initial desmoid.[27,28]

Intra-abdominal desmoid formation may be more common after IRA than after IPAA, and the disease may be more severe after IRA as well.[28,30] When desmoid tumors involve the small bowel mesentery, the mesentery may become foreshortened and thereby render IPAA impracticable, especially in patients under-

going a subsequent completion proctectomy after an initial IRA.[11] This possibility should be considered in making the choice between IRA and IPAA as the initial procedure for FAP.

Medical therapy. When desmoid tumors are clinically inert, they may be treated with sulindac.[11] Tamoxifen or other antiestrogens may be added for slow-growing or mildly symptomatic tumors.[11,31,32] More aggressive desmoid tumors may be treated with chemotherapy. Vinblastin and methotrexate achieve some degree of response in 40% to 50% of patients.[33] For more rapidly growing desmoids, antisarcoma agents, such as doxorubicin and dacarbazine, may be administered.[34,35] Radiation therapy may also be effective, but it can result in substantial small bowel morbidity.

Surgical therapy. Surgical treatment of intra-abdominal desmoid tumors should be reserved for small, well-defined lesions with clear margins.[11] When intra-abdominal desmoids involve the small bowel mesentery, they should be treated according to their initial presentation and rate of growth. In patients with desmoid lesions that are refractory to all medical treatment and call for surgical treatment with extensive small bowel resection, small bowel transplantation may be feasible in selected cases.[36]

Periampullary neoplasms In approximately 80% to 90% of persons with FAP, duodenal adenomas, periampullary adenomas, or both will develop.[37] Of these patients, 14% to 50% will eventually exhibit advanced polyposis, and as many as 6% will eventually have invasive cancer.[1,38-42] Although the risk of periampullary or duodenal cancer in FAP patients is relatively low, it is still several hundred times higher than that in the general population. Among FAP patients, those with *APC* mutations between codons 976 and 1067 appear to have the highest incidence of duodenal adenoma.

Surveillance should begin with side-viewing esophagogastroduodenoscopy (EGD) and biopsy of suspicious polyps either at the age of 20 years or at the time of prophylactic colectomy, whichever is earlier.[11] The purpose of screening is not to remove all disease but to watch for the development of high-grade dysplasia. Small, tubular adenomas without high-grade dysplasia may be biopsied and observed; adenomas that are larger than 1 cm or that exhibit high-grade dysplasia, villous changes, or ulceration should be removed. Surgical options include endoscopic removal and transduodenal excision, but both approaches have drawbacks: endoscopic ablation generally requires multiple settings,[38] and recurrence is high after either procedure.[38,43] Endoscopic ablation is a reasonable initial approach for most patients without invasive cancer and is an attractive alternative for patients who are unfit for duodenal resection. For patients with persistent or recurrent high-grade dysplasia in the papilla or duodenal adenomas and for patients with Spigelman stage IV disease, pancreas-preserving duodenectomy or pancreaticoduodenectomy is recommended.[11] The results reported for duodenal resection in patients with premalignant lesions are encouraging, with good local control and low morbidity.[38,44,45] Duodenectomy also greatly reduces the need for upper GI surveillance.

Hereditary Nonpolyposis Colorectal Cancer

HNPCC, which accounts for 5% to 7% of CRCs, results from a mutation in one of the DNA mismatch repair (MMR) genes (*MLH1, MSH2, MSH6, PMS1, PMS2, MLH3,* and *MSH3*).[46,47] Two genes (*MLH1, MSH2*) may be responsible for as many as 90% of causative germline MMR mutations. However, only 50%

to 70% of patients meeting clinical criteria for HNPCC have an identifiable germline MMR mutation, which suggests that one or more unidentified genes may be involved. A significant percentage of cases may be attributable to large germline deletions that are difficult to detect by means of direct sequencing. It appears that genomic deletions may account for as many as 7% of HNPCC cases defined on the basis of clinical criteria.[48]

CLINICAL EVALUATION

HNPCC is characterized by early-onset CRC, a predominance of lesions proximal to the splenic flexure (60% to 70% of cases), benign and malignant extracolonic tumors, and a predilection for synchronous and metachronous colorectal tumors.[4] Microsatellite instability (MSI), reflecting a deficiency in DNA repair secondary to a mutation in the MMR genes, is noted in approximately 80% to 90% of HNPCC-related tumors.[4] The lifetime risk of CRC in HNPCC patients is approximately 80%.[11,49]

Establishing a clinical diagnosis of HNPCC is much more challenging than establishing a clinical diagnosis of FAP, in that it requires a careful and detailed family history. The Amsterdam II criteria [see Table 3] require that there be three relatives (of which one must be a first-degree relative of the other two) with an HNPCC-related cancer (of the colorectum, the endometrium, the small bowel, the ureter, or the renal pelvis), that two or more successive generations be involved, and that at least one relative have a CRC diagnosed before the age of 50.[50,51] Finally, FAP should be excluded. CRC occurs in 78% to 80% of MMR mutation–positive patients at a mean age of 46 years.[1,49,52] Endometrial cancer occurs in 43%, gastric cancer in 19%, urinary tract cancer in 18%, and ovarian cancer in 9%.[53]

INVESTIGATIVE STUDIES

Pathologic Findings

Adenomas in HNPCC patients show high-grade dysplasia and villous changes more frequently than adenomas in sporadic CRC patients.[1] Adenomas may also appear at an earlier age and are often larger than those found in the general population. Other pathologic features reported to be more common in HNPCC-related cancers include a mucinous or poorly differentiated histology, a solid or cribriform growth pattern, signet-ring cell tumors, and the presence of tumor-infiltrating and peritumoral lymphocytes. HNPCC-related CRCs have also been shown to have a lower rate of lymph node involvement.[54]

Screening and Surveillance

CRC patients who belong to known HNPCC kindreds, who have a pedigree suggestive of HNPCC, or who meet the Bethesda criteria [see Table 4][55] should be offered screening by MSI testing. MSI evaluation will yield positive results (i.e., an MSI-high tumor) in 80% to 90% of patients belonging to families that meet the Amsterdam criteria. Patients with MSI-high tumors should undergo testing for germline MMR mutations (tests for *MSH2* and *MLH1* are available commercially [see Table 2]). If tumor tissue is not available, initial germline testing may be considered. As in FAP, a mutation in an affected individual must first be established for testing in at-risk individuals to be informative.[5]

Recommended surveillance for HNPCC includes colonoscopy, initially every 1 to 2 years beginning at the age of 20 to 25, then annually after the age of 40.[56] Given the increasing evidence of an accelerated adenoma-carcinoma sequence in HNPCC, annual colonoscopy should be strongly considered.[4] Female patients should undergo annual transvaginal ultrasonography and mea-

Table 3 Clinical Criteria for Diagnosis of HNPCC

Amsterdam criteria I[50]	Three or more relatives with CRC One first-degree relative of the other two One CRC diagnosed at age < 50 yr Two or more successive generations FAP excluded
Amsterdam criteria II[51]	Three or more relatives with an HNPCC-associated cancer (in colorectum, endometrium, small bowel, ureter, or renal pelvis) One first-degree relative of the other two Two or more successive generations One CRC diagnosed at age < 50 yr FAP excluded

surement of CA125 levels starting at 25 to 35 years of age, as well as annual endometrial aspiration.[56] Annual EGD is recommended for patients belonging to kindreds with a history of gastric cancer. Finally, ultrasonography and urine cytology every 1 to 2 years may be considered to screen for urinary tract malignancy.

MANAGEMENT

Surgical Therapy

Although the development of CRC in persons with HNPCC is not a certainty, the 80% lifetime risk,[1] the 45% rate of metachronous tumors, and the possibility of an accelerated adenoma-carcinoma sequence[4] mandate consideration of prophylactic surgical options. Patients who have HNPCC as defined by their genotype or the Amsterdam criteria [see Table 3] and who have a colon cancer or more than one advanced adenoma should be offered either (1) prophylactic total abdominal colectomy with IRA or (2) segmental colectomy with yearly colonoscopy [see 76 Segmental Colon Resection].[11,57,58] (The first option, however, is open only to patients with normal rectal and anal sphincter function.) Although the risk of metachronous colon cancers may be higher after partial colectomy than after total colectomy with IRA, intensive colonoscopic surveillance and polypectomy may minimize the number of metachronous cancers in the remaining colon.[52,59] Careful surveillance is also necessary after total colectomy and IRA, given that the risk of metachronous rectal cancer after total colectomy is approximately 12% at 10 to 12 years.[60]

HNPCC patients with an index rectal cancer that is amenable to a sphincter-preserving resection should be offered either (1) total proctocolectomy with IPAA [see 75 Procedures for Ulcerative Colitis] or (2) low anterior resection (LAR) with primary reconstruction [see 77 Procedures for Rectal Cancer].[11,58] The rationale for

Table 4 Revised Bethesda Guidelines for Testing CRC Patients for MSI[55]

CRC diagnosed at age < 50 yr

Presence of synchronous or metachronous CRC or other HNPCC tumors (regardless of age)

CRC with HNPCC-like histology at age < 60 yr

CRC in one or more FDR with an HNPCC-related tumor (one diagnosed at age < 50 yr)

CRC in two or more first- or second-degree relatives with HNPCC-related tumors (regardless of age)

FDR—first-degree relative

total proctocolectomy is based on the 17% to 45% rate of metachronous cancer in the remaining colon associated with an index rectal cancer in HNPCC patients.[61] The decision between the two procedures depends in part on the patient's willingness to undergo intensive surveillance of the retained proximal colon, as well as on the level of bowel function.

Mutation-positive patients with a normal colorectum may also be offered prophylactic colectomy in selected cases.[56,62] This approach is supported by the similarity of lifetime cancer risk between patients with germline *APC* mutations and those with MMR mutations, as well as by the observation that total abdominal colectomy with IRA yields less functional disturbance than the prophylactic procedure recommended for FAP (total proctocolectomy with IPAA).[56,62] An alternative strategy in these patients is to carry out colonoscopic surveillance at 1- to 3-year intervals. This strategy has proved to be cost-effective[63] and to reduce both the rate of CRC development and overall mortality.[52,64,65] There is a risk that CRC may develop in the intervals between colonoscopies[64,66]; however, when the surveillance interval is shorter than 2 years, tumors tend to be found in their early stages and to be curable when found.[52,64]

A study using a decision-analysis model suggested that prophylactic total abdominal colectomy at the age of 25 might offer a survival benefit of 1.8 years when compared with colonoscopic surveillance. The benefit of prophylactic colectomy decreased when surgery was delayed until later in life and became negligible when it was performed at the time of cancer development.[65] However, surveillance provided a greater benefit with respect to quality of life (measured in quality-adjusted life years).[65] On the basis of this evidence, some surgeons recommend that prophylactic colectomy be performed only in highly selected situations (e.g., when colonoscopic surveillance is not technically possible or when a patient refuses to undergo regular surveillance). Thus, the decision between prophylactic surgery and surveillance for gene-positive unaffected patients is based on many factors, including the penetrance of disease in a family, the age of cancer onset in family members, functional and quality-of-life considerations, and the likelihood of patient compliance with surveillance.

Extracolonic Disease

Management of extracolonic cancers in HNPCC patients is not yet well defined. Female patients with a family history of uterine cancer should be offered prophylactic total abdominal hysterectomy (TAH) if their childbearing is complete or if they are undergoing abdominal surgery for other conditions.[11] This recommendation is based on the high (43%) rate of endometrial cancer in mutation-positive persons,[53] particularly those with *hMSH2* mutations, and on the inefficacy of screening in some studies.[67] Oophorectomy should be added to TAH because of the high (9%) incidence of ovarian cancer in HNPCC patients[53] and the frequent coexistence of endometrial cancer with ovarian cancer.[68] The optimal timing for prophylactic TAH is unclear; however, endometrial cancer has been reported in HNPCC patients before the age of 35. At present, it seems reasonable to begin surveillance at the age of 25 and delay prophylactic surgery until childbearing is complete.[11]

Peutz-Jeghers Syndrome

Like FAP and HNPCC, PJS follows an autosomal dominant pattern of inheritance with variable penetrance. It is caused in part by mutations in the gene *LKB1/STK11*, which maps to the telomeric region of chromosome 19p13.3. This gene, which codes for a multifunctional serine-threonine kinase, is thought to function as a tumor suppressor gene.[69-72] Germline mutations in *LKB1/STK11* can be demonstrated in 18% to 63% of PJS patients, which suggests the existence of additional PJS loci.[72-75] Genetic testing for PJS can be accomplished through direct sequencing of the *LKB1/STK11* gene [*see Table 2*]; however, such testing is not widely available. In families with an established mutation, genetic testing of at-risk individuals is informative, with a reported accuracy of 95%.[76]

CLINICAL EVALUATION

PJS is a hereditary polyposis syndrome characterized by hamartomas of the GI tract, as well as by mucocutaneous melanin pigmentation. Hamartomatous polyps may occur throughout the GI tract but are most frequently found in the small intestine (90%). Other common sites of hamartomas in PJS are the large intestine (50%) and the stomach; less common sites are the renal pelvis, the bile ducts, the urinary bladder, the lungs, and the nasopharynx.[1,77,78] Mucocutaneous pigmentation generally appears during infancy. The perioral and buccal areas are involved in 95% of cases; the periorbital and facial areas, the genital region, and the acral areas (including the hands and feet) may be involved as well.[1] The average age of diagnosis of PJS is 22 years in men and 26 years in women.

In as many as 86% of cases, the initial presentation of PJS is small bowel obstruction secondary to intussusception of hamartomas. Other presentations include acute or chronic GI bleeding, biliary and gastric outlet obstruction, and anal protrusion of polyps. The diagnosis of PJS is established by the presence of histologically confirmed hamartomas of the GI tract plus two of the following three criteria: (1) small bowel polyposis, (2) mucocutaneous melanotic pigmentation, and (3) a family history of PJS [*see Table 1*].[79]

Patients with PJS are at significantly increased risk for both intestinal and extraintestinal malignancies. A meta-analysis found that in comparison with the general population, PJS patients were at a relative risk of 15.2 for the development of any malignancy.[80] The relative risks for the development of specific cancers were as follows: small bowel, 520; gastric, 213; pancreatic, 132; colorectal, 84; esophageal, 57; ovarian, 27; lung, 17; endometrial, 16; and breast, 15. The cumulative risk for the development of any cancer between the ages of 15 and 64 was 93%.[80] Other cancers associated with PJS are cholangiocarcinomas, testicular neoplasms, and duodenal tumors.[1]

Although the relative risk for the development of CRC was high in this study,[80] the reported magnitude of risk in the individual studies included in the meta-analysis varied considerably. Previous studies also reported a wide range of CRC incidences in these patients.[1] Thus, the true incidence of CRC in PJS patients remains unclear.

INVESTIGATIVE STUDIES

Pathologic Findings

The polyps seen in PJS are hamartomas characterized by hypertrophy or hyperplasia of the smooth muscle of the muscularis mucosa. Smooth muscle extends into the superficial epithelial layer of the bowel wall in a treelike fashion (a process referred to as arborization). Epithelial cells may become entrapped within the muscle layer, and this "pseudoinvasion" can be mistaken for malignant transformation. Therefore, to diagnose a malignancy in a PJS polyp, cellular atypia or an elevated mitotic rate must be documented.[81] Sporadic PJS polyps do occur, generally secondary to somatic *LKB1/STK11* mutations in one or both alleles, and are histologically identical to their hereditary counterparts. These sporadic polyps appear not to be associated with an increased risk of GI cancer.[82]

Histologically, areas of cutaneous pigmentation reveal an increased number of melanocytes at the dermal-epidermal junction, with elevated melanin levels in the basal cells. These lesions do not appear to have any malignant potential.

Screening and Surveillance

Clinical screening of asymptomatic persons is facilitated by the appearance of perioral hyperpigmentation during early childhood. Once the diagnosis of PJS is made, patients generally enter a surveillance program. Recommended surveillance for GI disease includes annual serum hemoglobin measurement and EGD every 2 to 3 years, beginning between the ages of 10 and 25.[79,83-85] Contrast radiography is employed to examine the remainder of the small bowel, beginning at the age of 10 and repeated every 2 to 3 years.[79,85] The frequency of surveillance examinations may be modified in individual circumstances. Colonoscopic surveillance is also important, commencing between puberty and the age of 25 and repeated every 2 to 3 years.[83,85] Sigmoidoscopy should not be employed for surveillance, because the rectum may be spared in some patients with more proximal disease. Organ-specific surveillance for other associated malignancies should also be initiated in accordance with current high-risk recommendations.

MANAGEMENT

Medical Therapy

Cyclooxygenase-2 (COX-2) is known to be overexpressed in the hamartomatous tissue of PJS patients, and there is a correlation between expression of the COX-2 protein and expression of the LKB1/STK11 protein in PJS polyps and cancers.[86,87] These findings suggest that COX-2 may be a potential target for chemoprevention of PJS.

Surgical Therapy

Indications for surgical management of PJS include the presence of polyps larger than 1.5 cm that cannot be removed endoscopically, incomplete removal of polyps with adenomatous changes, the development of polyp-associated complications (e.g., obstruction, intussusception, and bleeding), and the management of malignant disease.[88]

Endoscopic polypectomy is generally employed as initial therapy when it is technically feasible. For some polyps, however, operative polypectomy performed through an enterotomy is required. Segmental resection should be avoided. In the context of a laparotomy, intraoperative endoscopy (either peroral or via an enterotomy) allows direct visualization of the remainder of the small bowel and endoscopic clearance of any synchronous polyps. This procedure significantly reduces the need for subsequent laparotomy. The St. Mark's Hospital group in London found that none of 25 patients who underwent enteroscopy during laparotomy required subsequent laparotomy within a 4-year period, whereas 17% of historical control patients who did not undergo intraoperative enteroscopy required repeat laparotomy within a 1-year period.[89]

Laparoscopy-assisted polypectomy and laparoscopic management of small bowel intussusception are additional surgical options.

Given the risk of CRC development in PJS patients, careful colonoscopic surveillance is clearly warranted. However, the role of prophylactic colectomy in patients who are at risk or are mutation

positive is unclear. Because the true risk of CRC in these patients is unknown and genetic testing for PJS is not widely available, no recommendations can be made at present regarding the role of prophylactic colectomy in the PJS population.[88]

Juvenile Polyposis Syndrome

Initial evidence suggested that mutations in the *PTEN* gene were responsible for JPS[90]; however, subsequent evidence implicated *SMAD4/DPC4* at 18q21.1 as a more common cause, accounting for as many as 50% of familial cases.[91-93] Mutations in *BMPR1A* at 10q22–q23 have also been reported to cause JPS but display variable penetrance [*see Table 2*].[94,95] Clonal genetic alterations are detected in stromal rather than epithelial cells, which suggests that the genetic changes in juvenile polyps originate in the nonepithelial component of the polyps.

CLINICAL EVALUATION

Like PJS, JPS is characterized by the development of multiple hamartomas throughout the GI tract. Isolated juvenile polyps are common in children and are found in approximately 1% of persons younger than 21 years. Juvenile polyposis, however, is much less common. A family history of juvenile polyposis is present in 20% to 50% of patients.[1] Although JPS is an autosomal dominant disorder, its variable penetrance results in a less obvious pattern of inheritance than is seen with FAP or HNPCC.

JPS affects the two sexes equally and generally manifests itself during the first or second decade of life (mean age at diagnosis, 18.5 years).[1] Common presenting symptoms include chronic anemia, acute GI bleeding, prolapse of rectal polyps, protein-losing enteropathy, and intussusception with or without obstruction.[1]

Extracolonic manifestations of JPS include gastroduodenal and small bowel polyps, malrotation of the midgut, and mesenteric lymphangiomas. Extraintestinal manifestations include clubbing, hypertrophic pulmonary osteoarthropathy, hydrocephalus and macrocephaly, alopecia, cleft lip and palate abnormalities, supernumerary teeth, porphyria, congenital cardiac and arteriovenous malformations, psoriasis, vitellointestinal duct abnormalities, renal structural abnormalities, and bifid uterus and vagina. JPS is also part of the phenotype for Ruvalcaba-Myhre-Smith syndrome and Gorlin syndrome. Cowden disease, which is characterized by hamartomatous polyposis and is associated with breast and thyroid cancer, may be a phenotypic variant of JPS.[1,95]

The diagnostic criteria for JPS are as follows: (1) the presence of three or more juvenile polyps of the colon; (2) the presence of juvenile polyps throughout the entire GI tract; or (3) the presence of any number of polyps in a patient with known family history of JPS [*see Table 1*].[85] The clinical presentation of JPS can be divided into three main clinical variants: (1) JPS of infancy, which is a non–sex-linked recessive condition characterized by failure to thrive, susceptibility to infections, protein-losing enteropathy, bleeding, diarrhea, rectal prolapse, intussusception, and death by the age of 2 years in severe cases; (2) generalized JPS, which occurs in the first decade of life and is characterized by juvenile polyps throughout the GI tract; and (3) JPS of the colon, the most common presentation, which is characterized by colonic polyposis only.[1]

Patients with JPS appear to be at increased risk for GI malignancies, especially CRC. One study estimated the risk of CRC to be 15% by age 35 and 68% by age 65.[96] In another study, GI malignancies (mostly CRC) were diagnosed in 36 (17%) of 218 JPS patients at a mean age of 33 years.[97] Associated gastric, pancreatic, and duodenal cancers have also been reported. CRCs are thought to arise from malignant transformation of dysplastic polyps.[1] Adenocarcinomas occur, on average, 15 years after diagnosis of JPS and generally are poorly differentiated or mucinous tumors with a poor prognosis.[1]

INVESTIGATIVE STUDIES

Pathologic Findings

The number of polyps seen in JPS patients varies but typically ranges from 50 to 200. The polyps are usually smaller than 1.5 cm but can be as large as 3 cm. Grossly, they appear as red-brown, smooth, pedunculated lesions with lobulated or spherical heads and superficial ulceration; the cut surface demonstrates cystic spaces corresponding to mucus-filled glands. Histologically, polyps are characterized by an inflammatory infiltration of the lamina propria, an attenuated smooth muscle layer, and cystically dilated mucus-filled glands lined by columnar epithelium. Focal epithelial hyperplasia and dysplasia may be present.

Screening and Surveillance

Initial evaluation of the proband and the first-degree relatives, which ideally would be done in the middle to late teenage years, should include colonoscopy, EGD, and a small bowel series. If the initial evaluation yields negative results, a repeat evaluation should be performed in 3 years, then every 3 years thereafter as long as the results remain negative. If disease is encountered, random biopsies of polyps and intervening mucosa should be performed to detect adenomatous and dysplastic changes. Management depends on the presence of symptoms and on the extent and severity of polyposis. When polyposis is mild, endoscopic management may be feasible. Continued annual surveillance after endoscopic management is required; the surveillance interval may be lengthened to 3 years if subsequent evaluations reveal no disease.[1,85]

MANAGEMENT

Surgical Therapy

When polyposis is severe or significant symptoms are apparent, prophylactic colectomy with IRA may be considered for suitable surgical candidates. Although rectal polyposis can generally be managed with rigid or flexible proctoscopy, IPAA may be considered if the polyposis is extensive. Continued annual surveillance of the rectal remnant (after IRA) or the ileal pouch (after IPAA) is required initially. Surveillance intervals may be increased to 3 years if subsequent evaluations find no evidence of disease.[1,85]

References

1. Guillem JG, Smith AJ, Puig-La Calle J, et al: Gastrointestinal polyposis syndromes. Curr Probl Surg 36:217, 1999

2. Hernegger GS, Moore HG, Guillem JG: Attenuated familial adenomatous polyposis: an evolving and poorly understood entity. Dis Colon Rectum 45:127, 2002

3. Sieber OM, Lipton L, Crabtree M, et al: Multiple colorectal adenomas, classic adenomatous polyposis, and germ-line mutations in MYH. N Engl J Med 348:791, 2003

4. Lynch HT, de la Chapelle A: Hereditary colorectal cancer. N Engl J Med 348:919, 2003

5. Giardiello FM, Brensinger JD, Petersen GM: AGA technical review on hereditary colorectal cancer and genetic testing. Gastroenterology 121:198, 2001

6. Giardiello FM, Brensinger JD, Petersen GM, et al: The use and interpretation of commercial APC gene testing for familial adenomatous polyposis. N Engl J Med 336:823, 1997

7. Giardiello FM, Hamilton SR, Krush AJ, et al: Treatment of colonic and rectal adenomas with sulindac in familial adenomatous polyposis. N Engl J Med 328:1313, 1993

8. Steinbach G, Lynch PM, Phillips RK, et al: The effect of celecoxib, a cyclooxygenase-2 inhibitor, in familial adenomatous polyposis. N Engl J Med 342:1946, 2000

9. Winde G, Schmid KW, Schlegel W, et al: Complete reversion and prevention of rectal adenomas in colectomized patients with familial adenomatous polyposis by rectal low-dose sulindac maintenance treatment: advantages of a low-dose nonsteroidal anti-inflammatory drug regimen in reversing adenomas exceeding 33 months. Dis Colon Rectum 38:813, 1995

10. Cruz-Correa M, Hylind LM, Romans KE, et al: Long-term treatment with sulindac in familial adenomatous polyposis: a prospective cohort study. Gastroenterology 122:641, 2002

11. Church J, Simmang C: Practice parameters for the treatment of patients with dominantly inherited colorectal cancer (familial adenomatous polyposis and hereditary nonpolyposis colorectal cancer). Dis Colon Rectum 46:1001, 2003

12. Giardiello FM, Yang VW, Hylind LM, et al: Primary chemoprevention of familial adenomatous polyposis with sulindac. N Engl J Med 346:1054, 2002

13. Debinski HS, Love S, Spigelman AD, et al: Colorectal polyp counts and cancer risk in familial adenomatous polyposis. Gastroenterology 110:1028, 1996

14. Vasen HF, van der Luijt RB, Slors JF, et al: Molecular genetic tests as a guide to surgical management of familial adenomatous polyposis. Lancet 348:433, 1996

15. Bertario L, Russo A, Radice P, et al: Genotype and phenotype factors as determinants for rectal stump cancer in patients with familial adenomatous polyposis. Hereditary Colorectal Tumors Registry. Ann Surg 231:538, 2000

16. Bulow C, Vasen H, Jarvinen H, et al: Ileorectal anastomosis is appropriate for a subset of patients with familial adenomatous polyposis. Gastroenterology 119:1454, 2000

17. Wu JS, Paul P, McGannon EA, et al: APC genotype, polyp number, and surgical options in familial adenomatous polyposis. Ann Surg 227:57, 1998

18. van Duijvendijk P, Vasen HF, Bertario L, et al: Cumulative risk of developing polyps or malignancy at the ileal pouch-anal anastomosis in patients with familial adenomatous polyposis. J Gastrointest Surg 3:325, 1999

19. Remzi FH, Church JM, Bast J, et al: Mucosectomy vs. stapled ileal pouch-anal anastomosis in patients with familial adenomatous polyposis: functional outcome and neoplasia control. Dis Colon Rectum 44:1590, 2001

20. Wu JS, McGannon EA, Church JM: Incidence of neoplastic polyps in the ileal pouch of patients with familial adenomatous polyposis after restorative proctocolectomy. Dis Colon Rectum 41:552, 1998

21. Parc YR, Olschwang S, Desaint B, et al: Familial adenomatous polyposis: prevalence of adenomas in the ileal pouch after restorative proctocolectomy. Ann Surg 233:360, 2001

22. Thompson-Fawcett MW, Marcus VA, Redston M, et al: Adenomatous polyps develop commonly in the ileal pouch of patients with familial adenomatous polyposis. Dis Colon Rectum 44:347, 2001

23. van Duijvendijk P, Slors JF, Taat CW, et al: Functional outcome after colectomy and ileorectal anastomosis compared with proctocolectomy and ileal pouch-anal anastomosis in familial adenomatous polyposis. Ann Surg 230:648, 1999

24. Kartheuser AH, Parc R, Penna CP, et al: Ileal pouch-anal anastomosis as the first choice operation in patients with familial adenomatous polyposis: a ten-year experience. Surgery 119:615, 1996

25. van Duijvendijk P, Slors JF, Taat CW, et al: Quality of life after total colectomy with ileorectal anastomosis or proctocolectomy and ileal pouch-anal anastomosis for familial adenomatous polyposis. Br J Surg 87:590, 2000

26. Nugent KP, Spigelman AD, Phillips RK: Life expectancy after colectomy and ileorectal anastomosis for familial adenomatous polyposis. Dis Colon Rectum 36:1059, 1993

27. Clark SK, Neale KF, Landgrebe JC, et al: Desmoid tumours complicating familial adenomatous polyposis. Br J Surg 86:1185, 1999

28. Soravia C, Berk T, McLeod RS, et al: Desmoid disease in patients with familial adenomatous polyposis. Dis Colon Rectum 43:363, 2000

29. Bertario L, Russo A, Sala P, et al: Multiple approach to the exploration of genotype-phenotype correlations in familial adenomatous polyposis. J Clin Oncol 21:1698, 2003

30. Heiskanen I, Jarvinen HJ: Occurrence of desmoid tumours in familial adenomatous polyposis and results of treatment. Int J Colorectal Dis 11:157, 1996

31. Tsukada K, Church JM, Jagelman DG, et al: Noncytotoxic drug therapy for intra-abdominal desmoid tumor in patients with familial adenoma-

tous polyposis. Dis Colon Rectum 35:29, 1992

32. Bus PJ, Verspaget HW, van Krieken JH, et al: Treatment of mesenteric desmoid tumours with the anti-oestrogenic agent toremifene: case histories and an overview of the literature. Eur J Gastroenterol Hepatol 11:1179, 1999

33. Skapek SX, Hawk BJ, Hoffer FA, et al: Combination chemotherapy using vinblastine and methotrexate for the treatment of progressive desmoid tumor in children. J Clin Oncol 16:3021, 1998

34. Lynch HT, Fitzgibbons R Jr, Chong S, et al: Use of doxorubicin and dacarbazine for the management of unresectable intra-abdominal desmoid tumors in Gardner's syndrome. Dis Colon Rectum 37:260, 1994

35. Poritz LS, Blackstein M, Berk T, et al: Extended follow-up of patients treated with cytotoxic chemotherapy for intra-abdominal desmoid tumors. Dis Colon Rectum 44:1268, 2001

36. Chatzipetrou MA, Tzakis AG, Pinna AD, et al: Intestinal transplantation for the treatment of desmoid tumors associated with familial adenomatous polyposis. Surgery 129:277, 2001

37. Wallace MH, Phillips RK: Upper gastrointestinal disease in patients with familial adenomatous polyposis. Br J Surg 85:742, 1998

38. Alarcon FJ, Burke CA, Church JM, et al: Familial adenomatous polyposis: efficacy of endoscopic and surgical treatment for advanced duodenal adenomas. Dis Colon Rectum 42:1533, 1999

39. Groves CJ, Saunders BP, Spigelman AD, et al: Duodenal cancer in patients with familial adenomatous polyposis (FAP): results of a 10 year prospective study. Gut 50:636, 2002

40. Vasen HF, Bulow S, Myrhoj T, et al: Decision analysis in the management of duodenal adenomatosis in familial adenomatous polyposis. Gut 40:716, 1997

41. Saurin JC, Gutknecht C, Napoleon B, et al: Surveillance of duodenal adenomas in familial adenomatous polyposis reveals high cumulative risk of advanced disease. J Clin Oncol 22:493, 2004

42. Bjork J, Akerbrant H, Iselius L, et al: Periampullary adenomas and adenocarcinomas in familial adenomatous polyposis: cumulative risks and APC gene mutations. Gastroenterology 121:1127, 2001

43. Soravia C, Berk T, Haber G, et al: Management of Advanced Duodenal Polyposis in Familial Adenomatous Polyposis. J Gastrointest Surg 1:474, 1997

44. Ruo L, Coit DG, Brennan MF, et al: Long-term follow-up of patients with familial adenomatous polyposis undergoing pancreaticoduodenal surgery. J Gastrointest Surg 6:671, 2002

45. Kalady MF, Clary BM, Tyler DS, et al: Pancreas-preserving duodenectomy in the management of duodenal familial adenomatous polyposis. J Gastrointest Surg 6:82, 2002

46. Muller A, Fishel R: Mismatch repair and the hereditary non-polyposis colorectal cancer syndrome (HNPCC). Cancer Invest 20:102, 2002

47. Wheeler JM, Bodmer WF, Mortensen NJ: DNA mismatch repair genes and colorectal cancer. Gut 47:148, 2000

48. Wijnen J, van der Klift H, Vasen H, et al: MSH2 genomic deletions are a frequent cause of HNPCC. Nat Genet 20:326, 1998

49. Vasen HF, Wijnen JT, Menko FH, et al: Cancer risk in families with hereditary nonpolyposis colorectal cancer diagnosed by mutation analysis. Gastroenterology 110:1020, 1996

50. Vasen HF, Mecklin JP, Khan PM, et al: The International Collaborative Group on Hereditary Non-Polyposis Colorectal Cancer (ICG-HNPCC). Dis Colon Rectum 34:424, 1991

51. Vasen HF, Watson P, Mecklin JP, et al: New clinical criteria for hereditary nonpolyposis colorectal cancer (HNPCC, Lynch syndrome) proposed by the International Collaborative group on HNPCC. Gastroenterology 116:1453, 1999

52. de Vos tot Nederveen Cappel WH, Nagengast FM, Griffioen G, et al: Surveillance for hereditary non-polyposis colorectal cancer: a long-term study on 114 families. Dis Colon Rectum 45:1588, 2002

53. Aarnio M, Mecklin JP, Aaltonen LA, et al: Lifetime risk of different cancers in hereditary non-polyposis colorectal cancer (HNPCC) syndrome. Int J Cancer 64:430, 1995

54. Jass JR, Walsh MD, Barker M, et al: Distinction between familial and sporadic forms of colorectal cancer showing DNA microsatellite instability. Eur J Cancer 38:858, 2002

55. Umar A, Boland CR, Terdiman JP, et al: Revised Bethesda Guidelines for hereditary nonpolyposis colorectal cancer (Lynch syndrome) and microsatellite instability. J Natl Cancer Inst 96:261, 2004

56. Lynch HT, Riley BD, Weissman SM, et al: Hereditary nonpolyposis colorectal carcinoma (HNPCC) and HNPCC-like families: problems in diagnosis, surveillance, and management. Cancer 100:53, 2004

57. Lynch HT: Is there a role for prophylactic subtotal colectomy among hereditary nonpolyposis colorectal cancer germline mutation carriers? Dis Colon Rectum 39:109, 1996

58. Burke W, Petersen G, Lynch P, et al: Recommendations for follow-up care of individuals with an inherited predisposition to cancer. I. Hereditary nonpolyposis colon cancer. Cancer Genetics Studies Consortium. JAMA 277:915, 1997

59. van Dalen R, Church J, McGannon E, et al: Patterns of surgery in patients belonging to Amsterdam-positive families. Dis Colon Rectum 46:617, 2003

60. Rodriguez-Bigas MA, Vasen HF, Pekka-Mecklin J, et al: Rectal cancer risk in hereditary nonpolyposis colorectal cancer after abdominal colectomy. International Collaborative Group on HNPCC. Ann Surg 225:202, 1997

61. Moslein G, Nelson H, Thibodeau S, et al: [Rectal carcinomas in HNPCC]. Langenbecks Arch Chir Suppl Kongressbd 115:1467, 1998

62. Lynch HT, Lynch JF, Fitzgibbons R Jr: Role of prophylactic colectomy in Lynch syndrome. Clin Colorectal Cancer 3:99, 2003

63. Vasen HF, van Ballegooijen M, Buskens E, et al: A cost-effectiveness analysis of colorectal screening of hereditary nonpolyposis colorectal carcinoma gene carriers. Cancer 82:1632, 1998

64. Jarvinen HJ, Aarnio M, Mustonen H, et al: Controlled 15-year trial on screening for colorectal cancer in families with hereditary nonpolyposis colorectal cancer. Gastroenterology 118:829, 2000

65. Syngal S, Weeks JC, Schrag D, et al: Benefits of colonoscopic surveillance and prophylactic colectomy in patients with hereditary nonpolyposis colorectal cancer mutations. Ann Intern Med 129:787, 1998

66. Vasen HF, Nagengast FM, Khan PM: Interval cancers in hereditary non-polyposis colorectal cancer (Lynch syndrome). Lancet 345:1183, 1995

67. Dove-Edwin I, Boks D, Goff S, et al: The outcome of endometrial carcinoma surveillance by ultrasound scan in women at risk of hereditary nonpolyposis colorectal carcinoma and familial colorectal carcinoma. Cancer 94:1708, 2002

68. Watson P, Butzow R, Lynch HT, et al: The clinical features of ovarian cancer in hereditary nonpolyposis colorectal cancer. Gynecol Oncol 82:223, 2001

69. Hemminki A, Markie D, Tomlinson I, et al: A serine/threonine kinase gene defective in Peutz-Jeghers syndrome. Nature 391:184, 1998

70. Jenne DE, Reimann H, Nezu J, et al: Peutz-Jeghers syndrome is caused by mutations in a novel serine threonine kinase. Nat Genet 18:38, 1998

71. Amos CI, Bali D, Thiel TJ, et al: Fine mapping of a genetic locus for Peutz-Jeghers syndrome on chromosome 19p. Cancer Res 57:3653, 1997

72. Lim W, Hearle N, Shah B, et al: Further observations on LKB1/STK11 status and cancer risk in Peutz-Jeghers syndrome. Br J Cancer 89:308, 2003

73. Jiang CY, Esufali S, Berk T, et al: STK11/LKB1 germline mutations are not identified in most Peutz-Jeghers syndrome patients. Clin Genet 56:136, 1999

74. Boardman LA, Couch FJ, Burgart LJ, et al: Genetic heterogeneity in Peutz-Jeghers syndrome. Hum Mutat 16:23, 2000

75. Westerman AM, Entius MM, Boor PP, et al: Novel mutations in the LKB1/STK11 gene in Dutch Peutz-Jeghers families. Hum Mutat 13:476, 1999

76. Burt RW: Colon cancer screening. Gastroenterology 119:837, 2000

77. Keller JJ, Westerman AM, de Rooij FW, et al: Molecular genetic evidence of an association between nasal polyposis and the Peutz-Jeghers syndrome. Ann Intern Med 136:855, 2002

78. Corredor J, Wambach J, Barnard J: Gastrointestinal polyps in children: advances in molecular genetics, diagnosis, and management. J Pediatr 138:621, 2001

79. Aaltonen LA: Hereditary intestinal cancer. Semin Cancer Biol 10:289, 2000

80. Giardiello FM, Brensinger JD, Tersmette AC, et al: Very high risk of cancer in familial Peutz-Jeghers syndrome. Gastroenterology 119:1447, 2000

81. Westerman AM, van Velthuysen ML, Bac DJ, et al: Malignancy in Peutz-Jeghers syndrome? The pitfall of pseudo-invasion. J Clin Gastroenterol 25:387, 1997

82. Oncel M, Remzi FH, Church JM, et al: Course and follow-up of solitary Peutz-Jeghers polyps: a case series. Int J Colorectal Dis 18:33, 2003

83. Spigelman AD, Arese P, Phillips RK: Polyposis: the Peutz-Jeghers syndrome. Br J Surg 82:1311, 1995

84. Dunlop MG: Guidance on gastrointestinal surveillance for hereditary non-polyposis colorectal cancer, familial adenomatous polyposis, juvenile polyposis, and Peutz-Jeghers syndrome. Gut 51(suppl 5):V21, 2002

85. Wirtzfeld DA, Petrelli NJ, Rodriguez-Bigas MA: Hamartomatous polyposis syndromes: molecular genetics, neoplastic risk, and surveillance recommendations. Ann Surg Oncol 8:319, 2001

86. McGarrity TJ, Peiffer LP, Amos CI, et al: Overexpression of cyclooxygenase 2 in hamartomatous polyps of Peutz-Jeghers syndrome. Am J Gastroenterol 98:671, 2003

87. Wei C, Amos CI, Rashid A, et al: Correlation of staining for LKB1 and COX-2 in hamartomatous polyps and carcinomas from patients with Peutz-Jeghers syndrome. J Histochem Cytochem 51:1665, 2003

88. Chessin DB, Markowitz AJ, Guillem JG: Peutz-Jeghers syndrome. Câncer de Cólon, Reto Ânus. Mauro Rossi B, Nakagawa WT, Ferreira FO, et al, Eds. Lemar and Tecmedd, São Paulo, Brazil, 2004

89. Edwards DP, Khosraviani K, Stafferton R, et al: Long-term results of polyp clearance by intraoperative enteroscopy in the Peutz-Jeghers syndrome. Dis Colon Rectum 46:48, 2003

90. Huang SC, Chen CR, Lavine JE, et al: Genetic heterogeneity in familial juvenile polyposis. Cancer Res 60:6882, 2000

91. Howe JR, Roth S, Ringold JC, et al: Mutations in the SMAD4/DPC4 gene in juvenile polyposis. Science 280:1086, 1998

92. Kim IJ, Ku JL, Yoon KA, et al: Germline mutations of the dpc4 gene in Korean juvenile polyposis patients. Int J Cancer 86:529, 2000

93. Woodford-Richens K, Williamson J, Bevan S, et al: Allelic loss at SMAD4 in polyps from juvenile polyposis patients and use of fluorescence in situ hybridization to demonstrate clonal origin of the epithelium. Cancer Res 60:2477, 2000

94. Sayed MG, Ahmed AF, Ringold JR, et al: Germline SMAD4 or BMPR1A mutations and phenotype of juvenile polyposis. Ann Surg Oncol 9:901, 2002

95. Zhou XP, Woodford-Richens K, Lehtonen R, et al: Germline mutations in BMPR1A/ALK3 cause a subset of cases of juvenile polyposis syndrome and of Cowden and Bannayan-Riley-Ruvalcaba syndromes. Am J Hum Genet 69:704, 2001

96. Desai DC, Neale KF, Talbot IC, et al: Juvenile polyposis. Br J Surg 82:14, 1995

97. Coburn MC, Pricolo VE, DeLuca FG, et al: Malignant potential in intestinal juvenile polyposis syndromes. Ann Surg Oncol 2:386, 1995

98. Smith RA, Cokkinides V, Eyre HJ: American Cancer Society guidelines for the early detection of cancer. CA Cancer J Clin 53:27, 2003

99. Winawer S, Fletcher R, Rex D, et al: Colorectal cancer screening and surveillance: clinical guidelines and rationale—update based on new evidence. Gastroenterology 124:544, 2003

Bruce M. Brenner, M.D., F.A.C.S., and David M. Ota, M.D., F.A.C.S.

Colorectal cancer (CRC) remains a major public health problem throughout the world. In the United States, CRC is the third most frequently diagnosed cancer in both men and women and the second most common fatal cancer (behind lung cancer).[1] During 2004, there were an estimated 106,000 cases of colon cancer and 41,000 cases of rectal cancer in the United States, resulting in 57,000 total deaths.[1] The cost of treating colorectal cancer in the United States is believed to be between 5.5 and 6.5 billion dollars a year.[2] Worldwide, the risk of death from CRC is highest in developed countries and especially low in Asia and Africa.[3]

Data from the Surveillance, Epidemiology, and End Results (SEER) program indicate that the overall incidence of and mortality from CRC have been decreasing in the United States among both men and women,[4] though they remain generally higher among men than among women. Overall, the incidence of and mortality from CRC are highest among African Americans, somewhat lower among European Americans, and lowest among Native, Asian, and Hispanic Americans [see Table 1].[5] Most CRCs still occur in the distal colon (beyond the splenic flexure), but the incidence of proximal adenocarcinomas relative to that of distal adenocarcinomas has been increasing over the past 25 years [see Figure 1].[6] The cause of this shift is not known.

Genetics

The development of CRC involves a progression from normal mucosa through adenoma to carcinoma.[7] A genetic model of colorectal carcinogenesis has been proposed that describes a sequence of key mutations driving the process of colorectal carcinogenesis [see Figure 2].[8] This process may involve the accumulation of mutations in both tumor suppressor genes and proto-oncogenes, as well as epigenetic phenomena such as DNA hypermethylation or hypomethylation.[9] The onset of genomic instability increases the mutation rate and accelerates this progression. Inactivation of the adenomatous polyposis coli (APC) gene on chromosome 5q is thought to be one of the earliest mutations in sporadic cancers and is seen as a germline mutation in patients with familial polyposis [see 56 Hereditary Colorectal Cancer and Polyposis Syndromes]. Mutations in other tumor suppressor genes play an important role

in this pathway as well, including mutations in DCC, SMAD2, and SMAD4 on chromosome 18q and p53 on chromosome 17p; these events are thought to occur at a later stage of tumor progression. Mutations in the K-ras oncogene occur at an intermediate stage. The accumulation of additional mutations (as yet poorly defined) allows metastases to develop.

Microsatellite instability (MSI) is an alternative pathway to genomic instability and subsequent colorectal carcinogenesis. This phenomenon arises from defects in mismatch repair genes, which cause significantly increased mutation rates in comparison with those in normal cells. MSI in hereditary nonpolyposis colorectal cancer (HNPCC) [see Risk Factors, below] is most commonly attributable to germline mutations in the hMLH1 and hMSH2 genes.[10] MSI in sporadic CRC is most frequently associated with hypermethylation of the promoter region of the hMLH1 gene,[11] which leads to inactivation of the gene and loss of expression of the hMLH1 protein.

Risk Factors

A number of risk factors for CRC have been described, including a family history of cancer or adenomatous polyps, familial CRC syndromes, inflammatory bowel disease (both ulcerative colitis and Crohn disease), and dietary and lifestyle factors.[12,13] The vast majority of CRCs worldwide are sporadic—that is, they are not associated with known genetic syndromes. In the United States, no more than 5% of CRCs are associated with known genetic syndromes.

In a meta-analysis of studies addressing CRC risk and family history, the relative risk of CRC in those with an affected first-degree relative was 2.25; this figure rose to 4.25 if more than one relative was involved and to 3.87 if CRC was diagnosed before the age of 45.[14] The National Polyp Study found that the relative risk of CRC was 1.78 in first-degree relatives of patients with adenomatous polyps.[15] In another study, the relative risk of CRC was 1.74 in first-degree relatives of patients with adenomatous polyps and was especially high (4.36) in those diagnosed with polyps at or before the age of 50.[16]

The most common of the genetic syndromes known to be asso-

Table 1 Incidence and Mortality of CRC by Race and Sex[5]

Race	Incidence (No./100,000)		Mortality (No./100,000)	
	Male	Female	Male	Female
White	64.1	46.2	25.3	17.5
African American	72.4	56.2	34.6	24.6
Asian/Pacific Islander	57.2	38.8	15.8	11.0
Native American	37.5	32.6	18.5	12.1
Hispanic	49.8	32.9	18.4	11.4

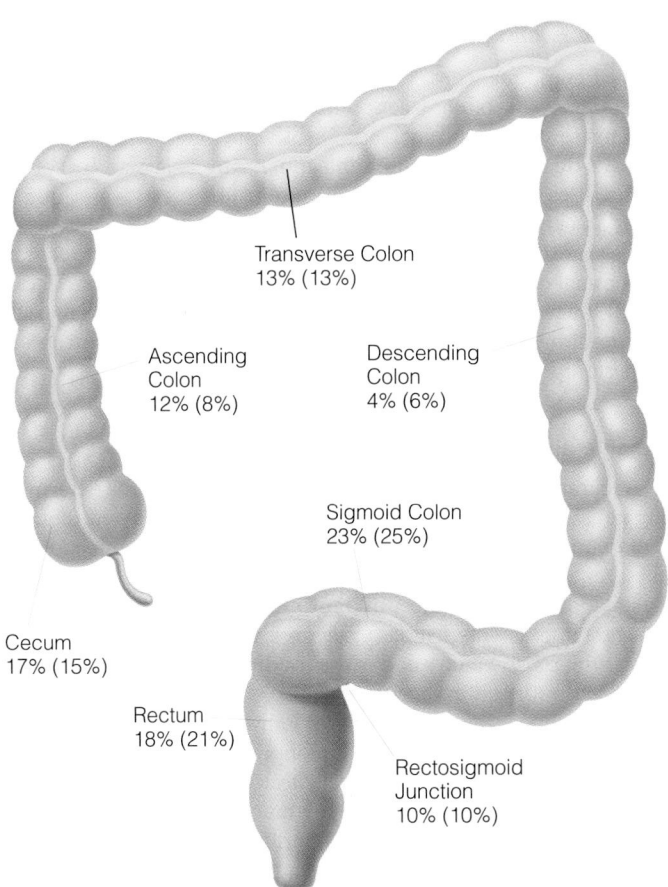

Cecum
17% (15%)

Ascending
Colon
12% (8%)

Transverse Colon
13% (13%)

Descending
Colon
4% (6%)

Sigmoid Colon
23% (25%)

Rectum
18% (21%)

Rectosigmoid
Junction
10% (10%)

Figure 1 **Shown are the relative frequencies of CRC for various anatomic subsites of the colon in 1996. For comparative purposes, figures for 1976 are provided in parentheses.**

ciated with CRC is HNPCC, which accounts for the majority of patients with familial CRC. MSI is the characteristic finding of HNPCC, though it is also present in approximately 15% of all sporadic CRCs. HNPCC can be diagnosed clinically on the basis of what are known as the Amsterdam Criteria.[17] Polyposis syndromes (e.g., familial polyposis and juvenile polyposis) account for the remainder of patients with familial CRC syndromes. HNPCC and polyposis syndromes are discussed further elsewhere [*see 56 Hereditary Colorectal Cancer and Polyposis Syndromes*].

As determined by a 2001 meta-analysis, the lifetime risk of CRC for patients with ulcerative colitis is 3.7%, which increases to

5.4% for patients with pancolitis and rises further with greater duration of disease.[18] Despite the common misconception, Crohn disease may be associated with a similarly increased risk of CRC.[19]

Numerous lifestyle and dietary factors have been put forward as potential causes of increased CRC risk. Lower levels of physical activity and increased body mass are associated with an increased risk of CRC in both men and women.[20] The Western-style diet, which is high in calories and fat and low in fiber, is associated with high rates of CRC. There is evidence that increased dietary intake of calcium may confer some protection against the development of CRC and adenomatous polyps. The Calcium Polyp Prevention Study, a large randomized trial done in the United States, reported a small but statistically significant reduction in the incidence of recurrent colorectal adenomas with dietary calcium supplementation.[21] To date, the evidence from randomized trials has not shown dietary fiber supplementation to have a similar effect. In Japan, where the incidence of CRC has traditionally been low, CRC has become considerably more common in the past few decades.[22] This increased incidence is believed to be the result of post–World War II lifestyle changes (e.g., increased consumption of animal fat and decreased expenditure of energy) that mirror Western habits.

Screening

Early diagnosis of colorectal neoplasms at a presymptomatic stage is important for improving survival. Polypectomy has consistently been shown to decrease the subsequent development of CRC: the National Polyp Study found that the incidence of CRC in patients who underwent colonoscopic polypectomy was as much as 90% less than would otherwise have been expected.[23] Identifying patients with early-stage disease that has not yet metastasized can prevent many CRC-related deaths. Early detection of and screening for CRC have become important components of routine care and public health programs both in the United States and abroad. The benefits of screening for CRC are especially substantial in patients who are at high risk for CRC (e.g., those with affected first-degree relatives), but even average-risk patients derive some benefit.

There is no ideal method of screening for CRC that is applicable to all patients. Physical examination is generally not helpful in making the diagnosis; various investigative tests are used instead. Modalities commonly employed for CRC screening and early detection include fecal occult blood testing (FOBT), double-contrast barium enema (DCBE), flexible sigmoidoscopy, and colonoscopy. Of these, only FOBT and sigmoidoscopy have been

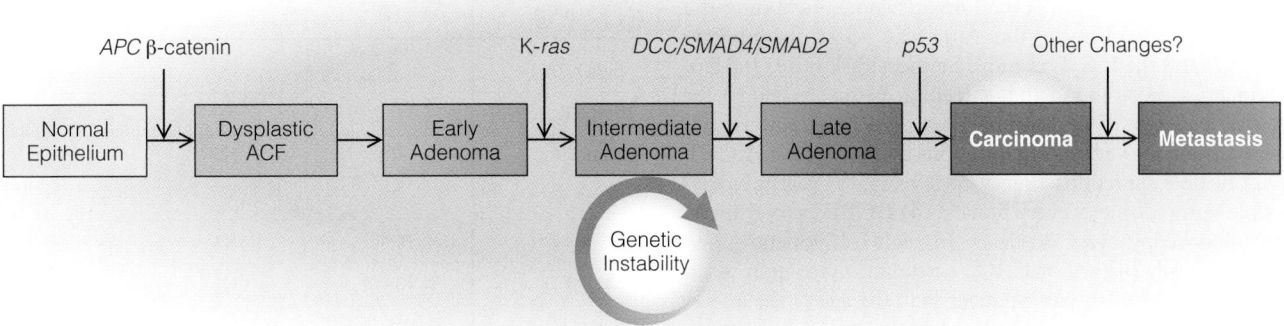

Figure 2 **Diagram illustrates genetic model of colorectal tumorigenesis.[8]**

Table 2 American Joint Committee on Cancer TNM Clinical Classification of Colorectal Cancer

Primary tumor (T)	T0	No evidence of primary tumor
	Tis	Carcinoma-in-situ, intraepithelial or invasion of lamina propria
	T1	Tumor invades submucosa
	T2	Tumor invades muscularis propria
	T3	Tumor invades through muscularis propria
	T4	Tumor invades other organs or perforates visceral peritoneum
Regional lymph nodes (N)	N0	No regional lymph node metastases
	N1	Metastases in 1 to 3 regional lymph nodes
	N2	Metastases in 4 or more regional lymph nodes
Distant metastasis (M)	M0	No distant metastasis
	M1	Distant metastasis

tested in randomized trials.[24] It is clear, however, that these tests are less sensitive and specific than colonoscopy. There is evidence that colonoscopy detects many CRCs in asymptomatic patients that would not be detected by sigmoidoscopy.[25,26] Colonoscopy has been shown to be a safe and effective method of CRC screening in asymptomatic, average-risk patients.[27]

Newer screening modalities, such as virtual colonoscopy and stool DNA assays, are currently being developed and tested. Virtual colonoscopy, which uses high-resolution computed tomographic scanning to image the colon, has been evaluated in at least two multicenter trials in the United States, with varying results.[28,29] One of the studies reported a sensitivity and a specificity of 89% and 80%, respectively, for polyps larger than 6 mm and up to 94% and 96%, respectively, for polyps larger than 10 mm.[28] The sensitivities were equivalent to those of optical colonoscopy in this group of asymptomatic average-risk patients. The second study, however, found that virtual colonoscopy had a sensitivity of only 39% for lesions larger than 6 mm and 55% for lesions larger than 10 mm.[29] Given these divergent findings, it appears that there are issues related to equipment, software, and training that remain to be addressed before virtual colonoscopy can be recommended as a routine screening modality. Another consideration is that patients with lesions detected by means of virtual colonoscopy must still undergo optical colonoscopy for treatment or tissue diagnosis. Fecal DNA assays have been developed to test for mutations in multiple genes known to be involved in colorectal neoplasia and are currently being evaluated in clinical trials.[30] These assays are not as sensitive as colonoscopy but may be useful in patients who are unable or unwilling to comply with endoscopic screening.[31]

Many groups have advocated CRC screening, and published guidelines are available from several organizations, including the American Cancer Society,[32] the American Gastroenterologic Association,[33] and the U.S. Preventive Services Task Force.[34] All of these guidelines recommend that screening begin at age 50 for average-risk patients. The recommended screening options are consistent among the various organizations and include (1) FOBT yearly, (2) flexible sigmoidoscopy every 5 years, (3) yearly FOBT and flexible sigmoidoscopy every 5 years, (4) DCBE every 5 years, and (5) colonoscopy every 10 years. In high-risk patients (e.g., those with a family history of CRC), screening may begin at an earlier age—generally, 10 years younger than the age of the affected first-degree relative. There are also specific intensive screening and follow-up regimens for patients with known or suspected familial cancer syndromes.

Clinical Evaluation

As a consequence of the use of screening modalities, patients with CRC are often asymptomatic at diagnosis. Some CRC patients present with occult GI bleeding and anemia. Many patients do not exhibit symptoms until relatively late in the course of the disease. The duration of symptoms, however, is not necessarily associated with the stage of the tumor.[35]

The most common symptoms of CRC are bleeding per rectum, abdominal or back pain, and changes in bowel habits or stool caliber. Other symptoms are fatigue, anorexia, weight loss, nausea, and vomiting. Some patients present with acute bowel obstruction or perforation.

Staging and Prognosis

Accurate staging of CRC is extremely important for determining patient prognosis and assessing the need for adjuvant therapy. Traditionally, staging of CRC has been based on modifications of the Dukes classification, which was initially developed as a prognostic tool for rectal cancer in the 1930s.[36] Since this classification was first implemented, it has undergone multiple modifications, of which the most widely used is the modified Astler-Coller system, initially introduced in the 1950s.[37] Currently, the TNM classification, developed by the American Joint Committee on Cancer (AJCC) and the International Union against Cancer (UICC), is the preferred staging system [*see Tables 2 and 3*].[38] This system takes into account the depth of penetration into the bowel wall (T) [*see Figure 3*], the presence and number of involved mesenteric nodes (N), and the presence of distant metastases (M).

CLINICAL STAGING

Clinical staging is based on the history and the physical examination, endoscopic findings, and biopsy results. If colonoscopy cannot be completed, an air-contrast barium enema study should be performed to evaluate the remainder of the colon. Additional staging information may be obtained by means of imaging studies (e.g., roentgenography, CT, magnetic resonance imaging, and positron emission tomography [PET]). A chest x-ray is routinely obtained to rule out metastases and prepare for operation.

There is some debate regarding the utility of preoperative CT scans in the management of primary colon cancer. The rationale for obtaining these scans includes evaluation of potential metastatic disease and assessment of the local extent of disease. In a 2002 study of preoperative CT in patients with intraperitoneal colon

Table 3 American Joint Committee on Cancer Staging of Colorectal Cancer

Stage	T	N	M
Stage 0	Tis	N0	M0
Stage I	T1, T2	N0	M0
Stage IIA	T3	N0	M0
Stage IIB	T4	N0	M0
Stage IIIA	T1, T2	N1	M0
Stage IIIB	T3, T4	N1	M0
Stage IIIC	Any T	N2	M0
Stage IV	Any T	Any N	M1

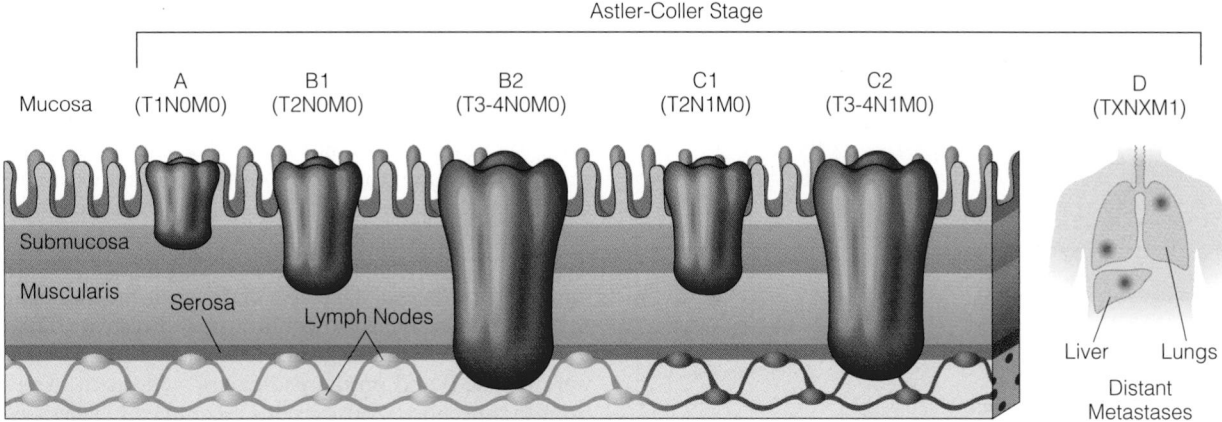

Figure 3   **Classification of CRC takes into account depth of tumor penetration and involvement of lymph nodes.**

cancer, however, the results of the imaging changed management in only 19% of patients, and CT had a sensitivity of only 78% for all metastatic disease.[39] Nonetheless, many surgeons routinely perform staging CT in patients with primary colon cancer. PET is a sensitive study, but its routine use for staging primary CRC is not generally recommended. PET may be considered for high-risk patients in whom the detection of metastases would change initial management.[40]

In cases of rectal cancer, locoregional staging may significantly affect therapeutic decision making. Such staging includes determination of the depth of invasion of the rectal wall and the degree of regional node involvement. Modalities commonly used include CT, MRI, and endoscopic ultrasonography (EUS). In a 2004 meta-analysis that examined the relative utility of each of these studies in rectal cancer staging,[41] EUS proved to be the most accurate technique for evaluating muscularis propria involvement and perirectal tissue invasion. The various techniques were equally accurate in assessing lymph node involvement, with none of them being highly sensitive.

PATHOLOGIC STAGING

Definitive pathologic staging is carried out after surgical exploration and examination of the resected specimen. The final stage of the cancer is then determined on the basis of the TNM system [*see Tables 2 and 3*]. Survival is correlated with the stage of the tumor [*see Figures 4 and 5*]. In the current (sixth) edition of the AJCC staging system,[38] stage II is subdivided into stages IIA and IIB, and stage III is subdivided into stages IIIA, IIIB, and IIIC on the basis of both the extent of wall penetration and the number of nodes involved. These changes were implemented as a result of studies demonstrating differences in survival among these subgroups [*see Figure 6*].[42]

Numerous other criteria have been evaluated as additional prognostic factors in CRC. The degree of lymphatic invasion and the extent of vascular invasion are important adjuncts to the TNM staging system and are incorporated in the current schema.[38] Certain histologic types, including signet-ring and mucinous carcinomas, are associated with poor outcomes. The preoperative serum carcinoembryonic antigen (CEA) level may be an independent prognostic factor that is predictive of resectability and the presence of distant metastases.[43]

MOLECULAR MARKERS

Various molecular markers have been investigated with respect to prognosis and response to therapy in CRC patients. Unfortunately, there are conflicting data on the prognostic impact and clin-

ical utility of most of these markers. As noted [*see Risk Factors, above*], MSI is seen in as many as 15% of patients with sporadic CRC. Patients with MSI typically have proximal, poorly differentiated tumors with mucinous or signet-ring components, but they usually exhibit improved overall survival.[44] These patients may be less sensitive to 5-fluorouracil (5-FU)–based chemotherapy.[45]

The long arm of chromosome 18 (18q) harbors at least three candidate tumor suppressor genes, including *DCC, SMAD2,* and *SMAD4*. Deletions of chromosome 18q in CRC patients are associated with decreased survival. One study found that patients with stage II cancers and 18q allelic loss had a prognosis similar to that of patients with stage III disease.[46] In addition, *p53* mutations and overexpression are associated with poor outcomes in CRC.[47] Thymidylate synthase is an enzyme active in DNA synthesis that is targeted by 5-FU and similar chemotherapeutic agents. Overexpression of this enzyme is associated with a poor prognosis but also with improved sensitivity to 5-FU–based chemotherapy.[48]

All of these molecular alterations, as well as others (e.g., K-*ras* mutations and 5q deletions), are commonly observed in CRC patients, but further study is required to establish their real prognostic significance.

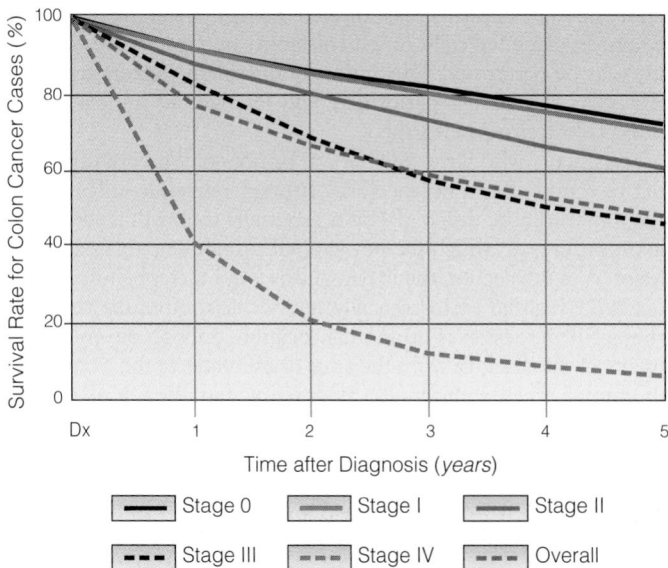

Figure 4   **Shown are 5-year survival rates for cases of colon cancer diagnosed in 1,735 U.S. hospitals in 1995 and 1996.**

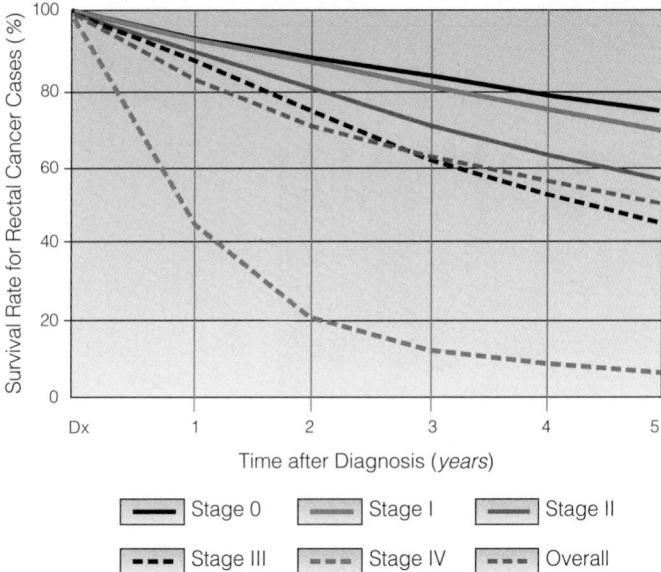

Figure 5 Shown are 5-year survival rates for cases of rectal cancer diagnosed in 1,683 U.S. hospitals in 1995 and 1996.

Management of Colon Cancer

SURGICAL THERAPY

Surgery with curative intent remains the mainstay of therapy for colon cancer [*see Figure 7*]. Complete R0 resection (leaving no gross or microscopic disease) with wide margins along the bowel wall, coupled with regional lymphadenectomy, is the standard of care. The major arterial vessels supplying the segment of the colon containing the tumor should be excised at their origins. A minimum margin of 5 cm of normal bowel on each side of the tumor is considered adequate.

Extent of Resection

The standard extent of resection for various colon cancers has been defined. For tumors of the cecum and the ascending colon, a right hemicolectomy that includes the right branch of the middle colic artery at its origin should be performed. For tumors of the hepatic flexure, an extended right colectomy that includes the entire middle colic artery is indicated. For tumors of the transverse colon, an extended right or left colectomy or a transverse colectomy may be performed. For tumors of the splenic flexure region, a left hemicolectomy is performed, and for sigmoid tumors, a sigmoid colectomy is performed.

In patients who have small or flat tumors or who are undergoing resection after a polypectomy, intraoperative identification of the tumor may be difficult. This is especially true with laparoscopic procedures, in which the bowel often cannot be palpated. If the lesion is in the cecum, the ileocecal valve and the appendiceal orifice are visualized endoscopically, and localization of the tumor is simple. If the lesion is at another location, endoscopic measurements of the distance from the anus or estimates of the location of the tumor may be inaccurate. Endoscopic tattooing, a process in which an agent is injected into the bowel wall submucosally at or near the site of the lesion, has been employed to facilitate intraoperative identification of the tumor site. India ink is the agent most commonly used for this purpose and generally yields excellent results.[49] As an alternative, many institutions use a commercially available sterile suspension of carbon particles, which is also very safe and effective.[50] Intraoperative endoscopy is another option for locating these lesions.

Surgical Staging

The selection of patients for adjuvant therapy relies heavily on accurate staging. A significant percentage of patients with early-stage node-negative disease present with recurrences or metastases; such a presentation implies that the patients had occult metastatic disease at the time of operation. Surgical resection of CRC should include division of the appropriate mesenteric vessels at their origins, along with resection of the regional nodes. Optimal staging of CRC patients, especially with regard to nodal status, remains controversial. One area of debate is the number of nodes that must be examined to confirm node-negativity. This number depends both on the surgeon's technique (i.e., how many nodes were resected) and on the pathologist's efforts to harvest nodes from the specimen. Most groups recommend analysis of at least 12 nodes to confirm node-negativity.[51]

Because of the importance of nodal status, ultrastaging of harvested nodes with techniques such as serial sectioning, immunohistochemistry (IHC), and reverse transcriptase polymerase chain reaction (RT-PCR) has been proposed as a means of detecting micrometastases. All of these techniques may result in upstaging of patients who are node negative on standard pathologic analysis, which involves only bivalving the nodes and examining a limited number of sections. The prognostic impact of micrometastases that are detected only by IHC or RT-PCR and are not verified by hematoxylin-eosin staining remains unclear. It is impractical to perform these assays on all nodes harvested; accordingly, the use of lymphatic mapping to identify sentinel lymph nodes (SLNs) has been proposed as a means of selecting a small number of nodes for further analysis.

SLN biopsy in the setting of CRC remains investigational. Lymphatic mapping may be done with either in vivo or ex vivo injection of tracer dye. The dye rapidly diffuses through the lymphatic vessels, and SLNs can be identified and marked in the mesocolon within minutes. This procedure has been shown to be feasible in a number of studies[52]; however, its sensitivity and false negative rates have been variable. In a 2004 multicenter trial, SLN biopsy with serial sectioning had a false negative rate of 54% in patients with node-positive colon cancer.[53] In a large single-insti-

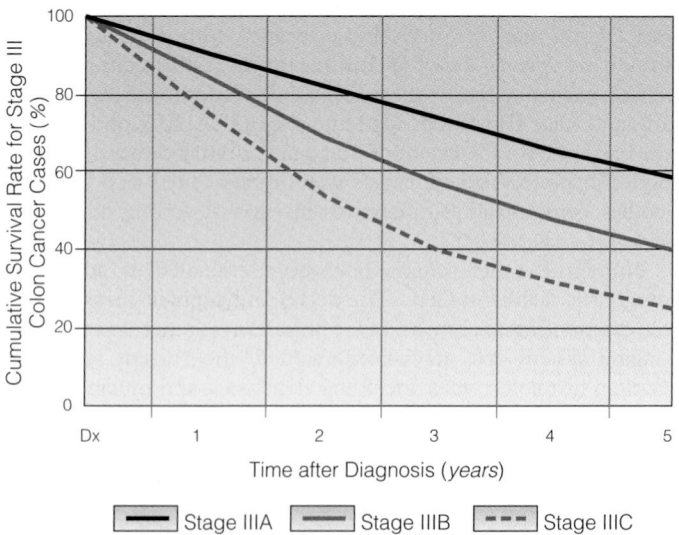

Figure 6 Shown are 5-year survival rates for cases of stage III colon cancer diagnosed between 1987 and 1993, stratified according to stage III subgroups established by 6th edition of AJCC Staging Manual.[38]

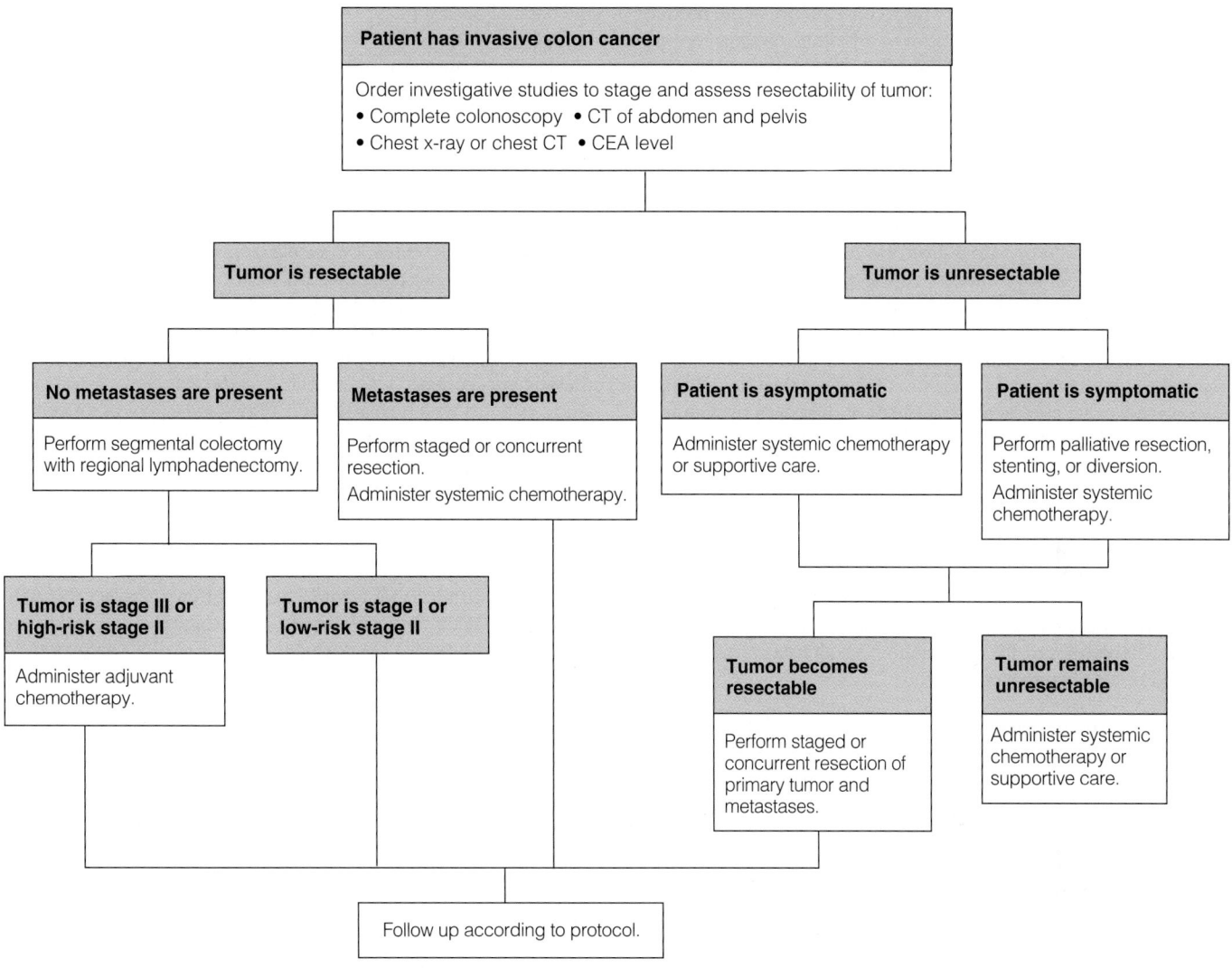

Figure 7 Algorithm outlines treatment of colon cancer.

tution trial, both SLNs and non-SLNs were studied with serial sectioning and IHC in patients who were node negative on routine pathologic analysis[54]; 19.5% of patients were upstaged by the combination of serial sectioning and IHC of SLNs. These results imply that the main role of this technique may be in upstaging patients who are node negative on routine pathologic analysis. Further study is required before the use of SLN techniques in the context of CRC becomes standard clinical practice.

Occult metastatic disease may also be present in the peritoneal cavity or systemically in the blood or bone marrow at the time of operation. The presence of tumor cells in the peritoneum may be detected by performing cytologic analysis of washings done at the time of operation. In one study, disseminated tumor cells were identified in peritoneal washings or blood in 25% of patients, and their presence was found to be an independent prognostic factor for survival.[55] In another study, patients with positive peritoneal washings had significantly higher rates of local recurrence and peritoneal carcinomatosis but manifested no differences in survival.[56] Again, further study is required before these assays can be routinely used for staging CRC.

Laparoscopic versus Open Colectomy

At present, open colectomy is the most widely accepted treatment of resectable colon cancer. Laparoscopic techniques have

been developed and are being tested in prospective, randomized multicenter trials [*see 75 Segmental Colon Resection*]. Initially, there were concerns about port-site recurrences,[57] but current data suggest that these concerns are unfounded.[58] With respect to comparative cost, data from a subset of patients in the European COlon cancer Laparoscopic or Open Resection (COLOR) trial demonstrated that although the total cost to society from laparoscopic colectomy is similar to that from open colectomy, the costs to the health care system are significantly higher with the former.[59] The Clinical Outcomes of Surgical Therapy (COST) study group, a large, randomized, multicenter trial conducted in the United States, found that laparoscopic-assisted colectomy conferred only minimal (though statistically significant) short-term quality-of-life benefits when compared with open colectomy.[60,61] Cancer-specific outcomes (e.g., recurrence rates, wound recurrences, and overall survival rates) were similar with the two approaches.[61] The COST investigators concluded that laparoscopic colectomy is an acceptable alternative to open colectomy. Recurrence and survival data from other large multicenter trials (e.g., the COLOR trial[62]) are not yet available.

Special Situations

Obstructing and perforated cancers Obstructing and perforated colon cancers are associated with a poor prognosis and with increased surgical morbidity (as a consequence of the need for emergency surgery). Perforation can occur either via direct erosion of the tumor through the wall of the colon or secondary to obstruction with resultant bowel distention proximal to the tumor. Patients with perforated colon cancer are managed with emergency laparotomy, washout, and resection of the primary lesion to prevent further soilage. A diverting stoma is usually indicated, with either a Hartmann pouch or a mucous fistula constructed distally. Select patients may be managed by means of primary anastomosis, with or without a proximal diverting colostomy or ileostomy.

Obstructing right-side cancers (up to the splenic flexure) can usually be treated with resection and primary anastomosis. The traditional emergency treatment of obstructing left-side colon cancers is a diverting colostomy, with or without resection of the lesion. In many such cases, the stoma is never taken down. Some surgeons advocate emergency treatment of these lesions with total abdominal colectomy and ileorectal anastomosis as a means of improving outcomes.[63] Another treatment option is primary resection and anastomosis, with or without on-table intestinal lavage. Yet another option for managing obstructing left-side colon and rectal cancers is the use of colorectal stents with the aim of avoiding emergency surgery. Stents can serve as a bridge to definitive resection by decompressing the colon and thereby allowing subsequent bowel preparation. In patients with advanced disease, stents may also be employed for palliation as an alternative to surgical resection or a diverting stoma.

Synchronous primary colorectal cancers The incidence of synchronous CRCs is reported to range from 3% to 5%[64,65] but may be as high as 11%.[66] Stage for stage, there appear to be no differences in survival between synchronous cancers and single primary cancers.[67,68] Synchronous adenomatous polyps are present in as many as 35% of patients undergoing surgical treatment of CRC.[65,68] In one study, the presence of synchronous lesions made the surgical procedure more extensive than was initially planned for resection of the primary tumor in 11% of patients.[65]

Most synchronous polyps are identified on preoperative colonoscopy, and the colon can often be cleared of these lesions before operation. Management of adenomas not amenable to endoscopic resection and management of synchronous cancers are more challenging. Each primary cancer must be managed surgically according to sound oncologic principles. One option is to perform multiple segmental resections with multiple anastomoses. Another is to perform an extended resection that encompasses all of the lesions or even total abdominal colectomy if needed. The presence of a rectal cancer and a second synchronous lesion makes surgical treatment even more challenging, especially if sphincter preservation and a low rectal or coloanal anastomosis are contemplated.

ADJUVANT THERAPY

Significant progress in systemic adjuvant therapy for patients undergoing resection of a colorectal adenocarcinoma has been made in the past 20 years, primarily through a series of phase III randomized trials and the development of new drugs. The evolution of adjuvant therapies is likely to continue for the foreseeable future, and surgeons will play a pivotal role as the primary entrance point for standard adjuvant therapy and new phase III randomized trials. Surgeons' awareness of past accomplishments, current study findings, and future phase III trials is crucial for improving the survival of potentially cured patients.

The 5-year survival rate after resection of colon cancer is inversely correlated with the pathologic stage [see Figure 4]. The diminishing 5-year survival rates for stage II and III colon cancer became

the basis of several phase III randomized trials designed to test the hypothesis that postoperative systemic adjuvant chemotherapy would significantly improve survival in patients with resected but high-risk cancers. Multi-institutional, cooperative cancer group trials were necessary to obtain populations large enough to test this hypothesis. The North Central Cancer Treatment Group (NCCTG) initiated a randomized trial of postoperative systemic adjuvant 5-FU plus levamisole for Dukes stage B and C (AJCC stage II and III) colon carcinomas.[69] Patients were randomly assigned to receive either levamisole alone or 5-FU plus levamisole. Overall survival was significantly improved in stage C patients treated with 5-FU plus levamisole. This was the first randomized trial to demonstrate the efficacy of systemic adjuvant therapy.

The NCCTG trial led to second-generation trials of adjuvant therapy for patients with resected colon cancers. In one such study, patients with high-risk stage II or stage III colon cancer were randomly assigned to receive either 5-FU plus leucovorin and levamisole or 5-FU plus levamisole.[70] Survival rates after 12 months of adjuvant chemotherapy were no better than those after 6 months of chemotherapy; however, 5-FU plus levamisole proved to be inferior to 5-FU plus leucovorin and levamisole with respect to survival.

National Surgical Adjuvant Breast and Bowel Project (NSABP) protocol C-04 randomly assigned Dukes stage B and C colon cancer patients to receive (1) postoperative 5-FU plus leucovorin, (2) 5-FU plus levamisole, or (3) 5-FU plus leucovorin and levamisole.[71] A slight improvement in 5-year disease-free survival was noted with 5-FU plus leucovorin, but overall 5-year survival did not differ significantly among the three treatment arms. Accordingly, 5-FU plus leucovorin became the standard adjuvant regimen.

Intergroup Trial 0089 randomly assigned patients with high-risk stage II and III disease to receive either 5-FU plus high-dose leucovorin or 5-FU plus low-dose leucovorin. The investigators concluded that (1) the high-dose and low-dose regimens were equivalent, (2) a regimen consisting of four cycles of 5-FU with high-dose weekly leucovorin was equivalent to the low-dose leucovorin Mayo Clinic regimen, and (3) the addition of levamisole to the 5-FU plus leucovorin regimen did not improve survival.

These clinical trials have established 5-FU plus leucovorin as standard therapy for patients with high-risk stage II and stage III colon cancer. The next generation of clinical investigations should provide data on the potential benefits of augmenting this regimen with irinotecan or oxaliplatin in an adjuvant setting.[72]

Routine use of systemic adjuvant therapy for stage II colon cancer remains controversial. Patients with stage II colon cancers, including those at high risk (e.g., those who present with large bowel obstruction or perforation), are typically included in adjuvant chemotherapy trials. A meta-analysis of stage II patients included in NSABP colon cancer trials demonstrated that adjuvant chemotherapy did confer a survival benefit at this disease stage.[73] This study was criticized, however, for having included patients from trials that lacked a surgery-only arm, as well as from trials that employed outmoded chemotherapeutic regimens.[74] Another meta-analysis, which included only trials that compared 5-FU plus leucovorin with observation after curative resection in stage II patients, found no statistically significant survival benefit with chemotherapy.[75] A 2004 meta-analysis formulated recommendations on this controversial topic and provided a Web-based tool for calculating risk.[76] This report included data from seven randomized trials that compared surgery alone with surgery plus chemotherapy. Patients with node-negative disease derived a much lower reduction in risk and no statistically significant improvement in overall survival. The authors concluded that the use of postoperative adjuvant chemotherapy for stage II colon cancer patients should be individualized on the basis of the estimated prognosis and the potential treatment benefit.

In summary, postoperative systemic adjuvant therapy is the standard of care in patients with stage III disease. In stage II colon cancer patients who have undergone complete surgical resection, the relative risk of recurrence is small enough that adjuvant chemotherapy yields relatively little benefit in terms of survival. There is, however, a subgroup of patients who have recognized prognostic factors that significantly reduce survival and in whom adjuvant therapy is therefore more likely to be beneficial. These risk factors include (1) bowel obstruction, (2) colonic perforation, (3) high-grade or lymphovascular invasion, and (4) the presence of fewer than 12 lymph nodes in the resected specimen.

Management of Rectal Cancer

Rectal cancer presents special management issues with respect to local recurrence after surgical resection. With cancer of the intraperitoneal colon, local recurrence is rare. With rectal cancer, however, surgical treatment alone results in recurrence rates of 16.2% after low anterior resection (LAR) and 19.3% after abdominoperineal resection (APR).[77] Higher stages are associated with higher recurrence rates: 8.5% for Dukes stage A, 16.3% for stage B, and 26% for stage C.[77] Multimodality management, including adjuvant radiation therapy or chemotherapy (or both) in combination with appropriate operative therapy, can reduce local recurrence rates significantly.

SURGICAL THERAPY

Extent of Resection

Sphincter preservation has become a major goal in the multimodality treatment of rectal cancer. Surgical procedures are chosen and performed with this goal firmly in mind.

Radical resection Traditionally, tumors of the rectum have been treated with either LAR or APR [see Figure 8]; in numerous series, APR rates of 60% or higher have been reported. Surgical techniques such as stapled or handsewn coloanal anastomoses [see 71 Intestinal Anastomosis], when combined with total mesorectal excision (TME), have led to excellent cancer-related outcomes without the need for permanent colostomy. The use of preoperative chemoradiation therapy for tumor downstaging may also reduce the need for APR.[78] Technical details of surgical procedures for rectal cancer are discussed elsewhere [see 77 Procedures for Rectal Cancer].

The morbidity associated with radical rectal resection can be substantial. Anastomotic leakage rates vary widely, ranging from less than 10% to more than 30% after resection with anastomosis. Leaks can lead to substantial morbidity and mortality and can necessitate reoperation. Such concerns have prompted the use of temporary diverting ileostomies or colostomies in patients with low rectal anastomoses. Defunctioning stomas may be overused, however, thereby increasing the cost of care in low-risk patients.[79] Preoperative chemoradiation therapy has not been shown to increase anastomotic leakage rates. Urinary and sexual dysfunction are also fairly common after radical resection of rectal cancer. Autonomic nerve preservation in conjunction with TME may improve the functional results of these procedures.[80] The use of local resection techniques (see below) is another means of reducing surgical morbidity and mortality in rectal cancer patients.

Local excision Local excision—including transanal, transsphincteric, and transcoccygeal techniques, as well as transanal endoscopic microsurgery (TEM) [see 77 Procedures for Rectal Cancer]—is another option for curative resection of low rectal cancers with preservation of sphincter function. These procedures were initially implemented for local control in patients who were medically unfit for or unwilling to undergo major resections. Transsphincteric and transcoccygeal resections have been associated with an increased incidence of complications, including fecal fistulas and incontinence, and have largely been abandoned now that other, better techniques are available.

Local excision with curative intent is generally reserved for the treatment of early-stage (T1–2N0) lesions. Selection of patients for these procedures is critical and is based on preoperative staging and on the probability of harboring nodal metastases, which increases with the T stage. EUS has become an important staging procedure in these patients, both for assessing the depth of tissue invasion and for detecting the presence of nodal disease. CT is generally performed to rule out distant metastases. Palliative procedures (e.g., fulguration and endocavitary irradiation) may also be considered in patients who are unfit for major surgery.

Several criteria have been established to identify patients who may be candidates for transanal excision (TAE).[81] Generally, the lesion must be no more than 4 cm in diameter, must encompass no more than one third of the circumference of the rectum, and must be less than 8 cm from the anal verge. With the advent of TEM, these criteria have been expanded to include patients with higher lesions. Poorly differentiated tumors and the presence of lymphovascular invasion may also be associated with increased nodal involvement and higher recurrence rates. At least two prospective trials have reported their results with TAE.[82,83] Local recurrence rates ranged from 5% to 7% for T1 lesions treated with surgery alone. Results were not as promising for T2 lesions: local recurrence rates ranged from 14% to 16%, even when adjuvant radiation or chemoradiation therapy was provided.

The use of local excision in patients with more locally advanced disease is even more controversial. Such patients are at considerably greater risk for nodal metastases and thus for local recurrence even after adequate resection of the primary lesion. Traditionally, local excision in patients with locally advanced disease has been associated with unacceptably high recurrence rates. Some authors advocate combining chemoradiation therapy with local excision to manage these patients. In a 2004 retrospective series, the results of local excision were comparable to those of radical resection in T3 patients who had a good response to preoperative chemoradiation therapy and who refused or were medically unfit for major surgery.[84] The role of local excision in these patients remains poorly defined.

Patients undergoing local resection must receive careful follow-up, including digital examination, measurement of CEA levels, proctoscopy, and, possibly, transanal ultrasonography. A subset of these patients with local-only recurrences who are medically fit for surgery may be candidates for resection. At present, few good data are available on the results of salvage surgery for local recurrence after local excision of rectal cancer, but it is unlikely that outcomes are equivalent to those of initial radical resection.[85]

Importance of Radial and Distal Resection Margins

There has been a great deal of debate about what constitutes an adequate margin of resection in surgical treatment of rectal cancer. With respect to distal margins, 2 to 5 cm has traditionally been considered to be the minimum necessary for curative resection. Growing interest in sphincter preservation has led investigators to consider smaller distal margins (i.e., < 2 cm).

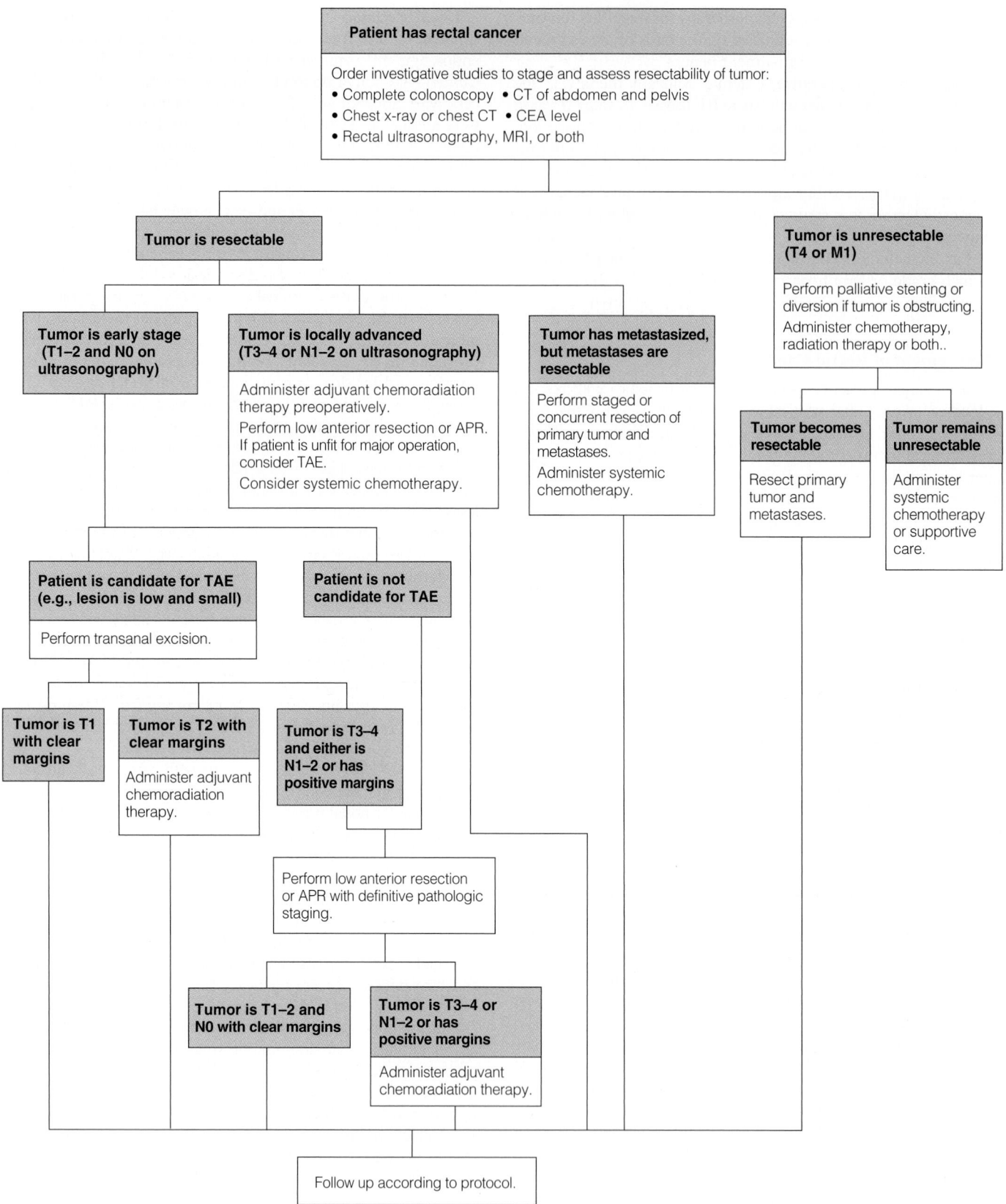

Figure 8 **Algorithm outlines treatment of rectal cancer.**

Studies have shown that clear margins smaller than 2 cm are not associated with higher local recurrence rates or reduced survival.[86] Subsequent reports have suggested that even smaller histologically negative margins (i.e., < 1 cm) may be adequate in patients receiving adjuvant chemoradiation therapy.[87,88]

The importance of radial margin involvement after rectal cancer resection was not recognized until comparatively recently.[89] Radial margins are assessed by means of serial slicing and evaluation of multiple coronal sections of the tumor and the mesorectum.[89] Involvement of radial margins is a predictor of both local recurrence and survival after potentially curative rectal cancer surgery[90] and may be associated with an increased risk of distant metastases.[91] Radial margins smaller than 2 mm are associated with increased local recurrence rates.[91] Adjuvant radiation therapy does not compensate for the adverse impact of positive margins on local recurrence rates.[92]

ADJUVANT THERAPY

Adjuvant therapy for rectal cancer has focused both on locoregional control of disease and on treatment of systemic disease. Several large studies have evaluated local recurrence of disease after surgical resection alone. Local failure rates of 30% to 40% for T2N0 disease and 50% to 70% for node-positive disease strongly suggested that postoperative adjuvant therapy was needed.[93-95] In distinct contrast to these data, however, other series in which TME was performed reported extremely low local recurrence rates with surgery alone.[96,97]

A series of randomized trials were conducted to assess adjuvant therapy for rectal cancer. Initial studies reported a decrease in local recurrence rates with postoperative radiation therapy.[98,99] In a multi-institutional trial conducted by the NCCTG, the combination of 5-FU with radiation therapy led to improvements in local control rates and in survival.[100] These results were confirmed in large intergroup trials, the results of which indicated that continuous infusion of 5-FU during radiation therapy resulted in significantly better disease-free survival and overall survival than bolus infusion of 5-FU.

Simultaneously with the ongoing development of postoperative locoregional adjuvant therapy for rectal cancer, interest in preoperative therapy has been growing. Preoperative radiation therapy has been associated with excellent local control of disease, sphincter preservation, and acceptable postoperative recovery. There is evidence that rectal adenocarcinoma is sensitive to preoperative radiation therapy, with or without 5-FU. Pathologic complete response rates of 10% to 20% have been noted in resected rectal specimens[101]; pathologic complete response is associated with improved outcomes.[102]

Perhaps the strongest reason to consider preoperative therapy for rectal cancer is its potential for inducing significant tumor regression before surgical resection. Such regression makes clear radial and distal margins easier to obtain. Moreover, tumor regression with preoperative therapy may result in higher sphincter preservation rates. In many published series, the APR rate in rectal cancer patients is between 40% and 60%; more aggressive preoperative efforts to induce regression may give surgeons a better chance to achieve sphincter preservation without compromising local control of disease.[101]

There remains significant controversy regarding the choice between preoperative and postoperative radiation therapy for rectal cancer. An advantage of the postoperative approach is that the disease is more accurately staged before adjuvant therapy begins, and thus, patients with early-stage disease are less likely to be overtreated. Two trials attempted to compare preoperative and postoperative radiation therapy for rectal cancer in an effort to determine their relative effects on local control, overall survival, and sphincter preservation. Both studies were unsuccessful, however—probably because of bias on the part of the treating physicians in favor of either preoperative or postoperative radiation therapy—and were closed because of slow accrual. At present, there is greater enthusiasm for preoperative therapy and pretreatment staging with transrectal ultrasonography, which is 90% accurate for determining the T stage. Patients with T3 or T4 rectal cancer on ultrasonography would be eligible for preoperative treatment.

Two Swedish studies studied the role of preoperative radiation therapy in treating rectal cancer. The first demonstrated that a short course of preoperative radiation therapy (2.5 Gy in 5 fractions) was comparable to high-dose postoperative radiation therapy (60 Gy over a period of 8 weeks). The local recurrence rate was significantly lower with the short-course preoperative regimen (12% versus 21%), and there was no overall survival difference between the two regimens.[103] In the second trial, patients received either a short course of preoperative radiation therapy or surgery alone.[104] The local recurrence rate for preoperative therapy plus surgery was 11%, compared with 27% for surgery alone. The combined regimen also resulted in significantly better 5-year survival (58% versus 48%).

The question of the relative merits of preoperative and postoperative radiation therapy may be resolved by the findings from a 2004 German trial that randomly assigned patients to receive either preoperative or postoperative 5-FU plus radiation, followed by systemic 5-FU therapy.[78] This study was limited to patients with locally advanced disease, including those who had T3 or T4 disease or were node positive on ultrasonography. TME was performed in all patients and was done 6 weeks after treatment in patients receiving preoperative chemoradiation therapy. The primary end point of this study was overall survival; secondary end points included disease-free survival, local and distant control of disease, sphincter preservation, toxicity of adjuvant therapy, surgical complications, and quality of life. There was no difference between the preoperative group and the postoperative group with respect to 5-year survival, but the local recurrence rate was significantly lower with the former (6% versus 13%), as were both the short-term and the long-term toxicity of adjuvant therapy. Although overall, the rates of complete (R0) resection and sphincter preservation were similar in the two groups, the APR rate was significantly lower in patients determined by the surgeon to require APR before randomization.

Special Considerations

SYNCHRONOUS METASTATIC (STAGE IV) DISEASE

As many as 20% of CRC patients have metastatic disease at the time of initial presentation. The need for surgical intervention in this group of patients is not well defined. Clearly, surgical resection or diversion is indicated in patients who present with significant bleeding, perforation, or obstruction. In asymptomatic patients with unresectable metastatic disease, the role of surgical resection of the primary lesion remains controversial. In patients with resectable metastatic disease (e.g., isolated liver or lung metastases), curative resection may be undertaken.

In a retrospective review of patients presenting with unresectable stage IV CRC, there was no difference in survival between those who were initially managed surgically and those who were initially managed nonoperatively.[105] In the surgical group, the morbidity rate was 30% and the mortality 5%. Only 9% of the nonoperative patients subsequently required surgical intervention for bowel obstruction. In another retrospective series, patients managed surgically had significantly better overall survival than those managed nonoperatively but had a lesser tumor burden[106]; 29% of the nonoperative patients eventually required surgery for bowel obstruction. When prognostic factors were evaluated in the surgical arm of this series, the only factor associated with improved outcomes was a less than 25% extent of liver involvement. On the basis of these and other studies, asymptomatic patients with unresectable metastatic CRC should be managed selectively: those with limited tumor burdens may benefit from surgical treatment, whereas those with more extensive disease (especially extensive liver involvement) may initially be managed nonoperatively.

Management of patients with synchronous resectable isolated liver metastases continues to evolve. Many studies have documented improved survival after liver resection in patients with metastatic disease that is confined to the liver. Patients presenting with synchronous lesions have a worse prognosis than those presenting with metachronous lesions.[107] Many of these patients have been managed with staged resections of the primary cancers and the liver metastases. Several groups have reported that such combined procedures do not substantially increase surgical morbidity and mortality or compromise cancer survival.[108,109] These combined procedures should be done only in carefully selected patients at specialized centers with significant experience in resection of both CRC and liver tumors.

PERITONEAL CARCINOMATOSIS

Peritoneal carcinomatosis develops in approximately 13% of all CRC patients.[110] The survival rate of patients who present with peritoneal carcinomatosis from CRC is dismal. In patients with stage IV CRC, the presence of carcinomatosis is associated with a significant reduction in survival (from 18.1 months to 6.7 months).[111] Treatment has traditionally included systemic chemotherapy, with surgery reserved for palliation of symptoms such as bowel obstruction. Newer chemotherapy regimens that include agents such as oxaliplatin may improve survival, but they certainly are not curative.

Peritoneal carcinomatosis is often associated with hematogenous metastases, but in some 25% of patients, the peritoneal cavity is the only site of disease. Several groups have advocated the use of cytoreductive surgery and hyperthermic intraperitoneal chemotherapy (HIPEC) as a means of improving survival in these patients.[112] This treatment, however, is associated with significant morbidity and mortality.[113] A randomized trial from the Netherlands that compared cytoreduction surgery plus HIPEC with systemic chemotherapy plus palliative surgery found that patients in the former group exhibited a statistically significant improvement in median survival (22.3 months versus 12.6 months).[114] Cytoreductive surgery plus HIPEC seems to be a viable option for the treatment of peritoneal carcinomatosis. Patient selection for these aggressive procedures remains a major issue, given the substantial morbidity and mortality associated with them.

Follow-up and Management of Recurrent Colorectal Cancer

The goal of any CRC follow-up regimen should be to detect any recurrences or metachronous lesions that are potentially curable. In a large, multicenter trial, the incidence of second primary CRCs in patients with resected stage II and III lesions was found to be 1.5% at 5 years.[115] Between 40% and 50% of patients experience relapses after potentially curative resection of CRC. Detection and treatment of recurrent disease before symptom development may improve survival. The time to recurrence is critical, in that as many as 80% of recurrences occur within the first 2 years and as many as 90% within the first 4 years. Patterns of recurrence should also be taken into account—for example, the markedly increased risk of local recurrence in rectal cancer patients compared with that in colon cancer patients. Even when recurrent CRC is detected, only a small percentage of patients are candidates for reoperation, and resection in these patients may not improve overall survival.

Systemic therapy may improve survival in some patients who have unresectable recurrent lesions.

Various modalities are available for follow-up after surgical treatment of CRC. The history and the physical examination continue to be useful, in that a significant percentage of patients present with symptomatic recurrences. Measurement of serum CEA levels has proved effective in detecting asymptomatic recurrences. Other studies, such as liver function tests (LFTs), complete blood count (CBC), chest x-ray, and imaging studies (e.g., CT and ultrasonography), have not been consistently shown to detect asymptomatic resectable recurrences. One study that evaluated routine CEA measurement and CT scanning of the chest, the abdomen, and the pelvis for follow-up of stage II and III CRC demonstrated that both modalities were able to identify asymptomatic patients with resectable disease.[116] Colonoscopy is valuable for detecting metachronous cancers and polyps.

Some authorities advocate so-called intensive follow-up. However, this term lacks a standard definition, and such follow-up has not been conclusively shown to be beneficial. In a meta-analysis that compared an intensive follow-up regimen (including history, physical examination, and CEA measurement) with no follow-up, the former detected more candidates for curative re-resection and led to improvements in both overall survival and survival of patients with recurrences.[117] Two other meta-analyses have been published that assessed the value of intensive follow-up of CRC patients.[118,119] Both of these meta-analyses included only randomized, controlled trials, and both documented a survival advantage with intensive follow-up. Some caution is required in interpreting these results, however, because the meta-analyses included trials with vastly different follow-up regimens in their baseline and intensive groups.

At present, the ideal follow-up regimen for CRC patients remains to be determined. Intensive follow-up regimens obviously are more costly. Patients with stage I disease are at very low risk for recurrence and therefore do not require intensive follow-up.[120] Patients with stage II and III disease are at significantly higher risk for recurrence and therefore need more specific cancer-related follow-up, but how intensive such a follow-up regimen should be is still a matter of debate.

Several organizations, including the American Society of Clinical Oncology,[121] the National Comprehensive Cancer Network (NCCN),[122,123] and the American Society of Colon and Rectal Surgeons,[124] have developed algorithms for postoperative surveillance of CRC patients. Their recommendations generally apply to patients with stage II or III disease (and sometimes patients with T2 lesions) who are candidates for resection of recurrent disease. The recommendations vary somewhat among groups, but the following are generally agreed on:

1. Measurement of CEA levels every 2 to 3 months for 2 years, then every 3 to 6 months for 3 years, then annually.
2. Clinical examination every 3 to 6 months for 3 years, then annually.
3. Colonoscopy perioperatively, then every 3 to 5 years if the patient remains free of polyps and cancer (the NCCN also recommends colonoscopy 1 year after primary therapy).

Imaging studies (e.g., CT and chest x-ray) are not routinely recommended, nor are other blood tests (e.g., CBC and LFTs).

A complete review of the treatment of recurrent CRC is beyond the scope of this chapter. The primary aim of postoperative surveillance is the detection of treatable recurrences or metastatic disease. The most common sites of metastasis in CRC patients are the liver and the peritoneal cavity. Surgery is the only potentially curative therapy for recurrent CRC. Only a select group of patients with isolated peritoneal, liver, or lung metastases are candidates for surgical resection. As noted [see Special Considerations, Peritoneal Carcinomatosis, above], cytoreductive surgery and HIPEC improve survival in patients with peritoneal carcinomatosis and may lead to long-term survival in a very select group of patients.

Numerous studies have addressed the treatment of patients with isolated liver metastases from CRC. Resection of isolated hepatic metastases has been reported to yield 5-year survival rates higher than 30%, with acceptable surgical morbidity and mortality. Investigators from the Memorial Sloan-Kettering Cancer Center developed a staging system known as the clinical score in an attempt to predict which patients are likely to benefit from aggressive surgical resection.[125] This system used five factors that were found to be independent predictors of poor outcome: (1) node-positive primary disease, (2) a disease-free interval shorter than 12 months, (3) the presence of more than one hepatic tumor, (4) a maximum hepatic tumor size exceeding 5 cm, and (5) a CEA level higher than 200 ng/ml. Patients who met no more than two of these criteria generally had good outcomes, whereas those who met three or more were recommended for inclusion in adjuvant therapy trials.

PET scanning has also been used to detect occult metastatic disease and thus to aid in the selection of patients for surgical resection. In one series, a 5-year overall survival of 58% was reported after resection of CRC liver metastases in patients screened with PET.[126] When combined with the clinical risk score, PET was found to be helpful only in patients with a score of 1 or higher.[127]

Modalities for treating unresectable disease confined to the liver include cryotherapy, radiofrequency (RF) ablation, hepatic artery infusion of chemotherapeutic agents, and hepatic perfusion. Of these, RF ablation is the one most commonly employed. It may be performed via an open approach, percutaneously, or laparoscopically; it may also be combined with resection and with local or systemic chemotherapy. The survival benefit (if any) associated with use of these modalities has not been well established.

Patients with isolated lung metastases from CRC may also benefit from surgical resection. Because there are relatively few of these patients, treatment of such metastases has not been studied as well as treatment of liver metastases. Some series have reported 5-year survival rates higher than 40% after complete resection. Patient selection remains a major issue. Several prognostic factors that may predict poor outcomes have been identified, including (1) a maximum tumor size greater than 3.75 cm, (2) a serum CEA level higher than 5 ng/ml, and (3) pulmonary or mediastinal lymph node involvement.[128,129] Patients with both pulmonary and hepatic metastases may also be considered for surgical resection.

Pelvic recurrences of rectal cancer present another difficult management issue. These tumors may cause significant pain and disability, and if they are not treated, survival is measured in months. Radiation and chemotherapy provide symptomatic relief and yield a modest increase in survival. Surgery may provide excellent palliation and is potentially curative in patients who do not have distant metastases.

Multimodality therapy has been advocated as a means of improving the chances of cure. In one study, a 37% 5-year survival rate was reported in patients who underwent multimodality therapy, including resection with negative margins.[130] A subgroup of patients in whom complete resection was impossible underwent intraoperative radiation therapy; the 5-year survival in this subgroup was 21%. Several predictors of poor outcomes were identified, including incomplete resection, multiple points of tumor fixation, and symptomatic pain. In another series, hydronephrosis was associated with the presence of unresectable disease.[131] Selection of appropriate patients for curative surgery remains a major issue in the management of locally recurrent rectal cancer.

Chemotherapy is the mainstay of palliative treatment for patients with CRC and unresectable recurrent or metastatic disease. Combinations of 5-FU and leucovorin with newer agents such as irinotecan and oxaliplatin define the current standard. Patients in whom these regimens fail may be considered for treatment with other newer agents, including cetuximab, a monoclonal antibody against epidermal growth factor receptor, and bevacizumab, a monoclonal antibody against the vascular endothelial growth factor receptor.

References

1. Jemal A, Tiwari RC, Murray T, et al: Cancer statistics, 2004. CA Cancer J Clin 54:8, 2004

2. Redaelli A, Cranor CW, Okano GJ, et al: Screening, prevention and socioeconomic costs associated with the treatment of colorectal cancer. Pharmacoeconomics 21:1213, 2003

3. Pisani P, Parkin DM, Bray F, et al: Estimates of the worldwide mortality from 25 cancers in 1990. Int J Cancer 83:18, 1999

4. Weir HK, Thun MJ, Hankey BF, et al: Annual report to the nation on the status of cancer, 1975-2000, featuring the uses of surveillance data for cancer prevention and control. J Natl Cancer Inst 95:1276, 2003

5. Ward E, Jemal A, Cokkinides V, et al: Cancer disparities by race/ethnicity and socioeconomic status. CA Cancer J Clin 54:78, 2004

6. Hawk ET, Limburg PJ, Viner JL: Epidemiology and prevention of colorectal cancer. Surg Clin North Am 82:905, 2002

7. Muto T, Bussey HJ, Morson BC: The evolution of cancer of the colon and rectum. Cancer 36:2251, 1975

8. Fearon ER, Vogelstein B: A genetic model for colorectal tumorigenesis. Cell 61:759, 1990

9. Rodriguez-Bigas MA, Stoler DL, Bertario L, et al: Colorectal cancer: how does it start? How does it metastasize? Surg Oncol Clin N Am 9:643, 2000

10. Chung DC, Rustgi AK: The hereditary nonpolyposis colorectal cancer syndrome: genetics and clinical implications. Ann Intern Med 138:560, 2003

11. Herman JG, Umar A, Polyak K, et al: Incidence and functional consequences of hMLH1 promoter hypermethylation in colorectal carcinoma. Proc Natl Acad Sci U S A 95:6870, 1998

12. Slattery ML, Levin TR, Ma K, et al: Family history and colorectal cancer: predictors of risk. Cancer Causes Control 14:879, 2003

13. Le Marchand L, Zhao LP, Quiaoit F, et al: Family history and risk of colorectal cancer in the multiethnic population of Hawaii. Am J Epidemiol 144:1122, 1996

14. Johns LE, Houlston RS: A systematic review and meta-analysis of familial colorectal cancer risk. Am J Gastroenterol 96:2992, 2001

15. Winawer SJ, Zauber AG, Gerdes H, et al: Risk of colorectal cancer in the families of patients with adenomatous polyps. National Polyp Study Workgroup. N Engl J Med: 334:82, 1996

16. Ahsan H, Neugut AI, Garbowski GC, et al: Family history of colorectal adenomatous polyps and increased risk for colorectal cancer. Ann Intern Med 28:900, 1998

17. Park JG, Vasen HF, Park YJ, et al: Suspected HNPCC and Amsterdam criteria II: evaluation of mutation detection rate, an international collaborative study. Int J Colorectal Dis 17:109, 2002

18. Eaden JA, Abrams KR, Mayberry JF: The risk of colorectal cancer in ulcerative colitis: a meta-analysis. Gut 48:526, 2001

19. Bernstein CN, Blanchard JF, Kliewer E, et al: Cancer risk in patients with inflammatory bowel disease: a population-based study. Cancer 91:854, 2001

20. Le Marchand L, Wilkens LR, Kolonel LN, et al: Associations of sedentary lifestyle, obesity, smoking, alcohol use, and diabetes with the risk of colorectal cancer. Cancer Res 57:4787, 1997

21. Baron JA, Beach M, Mandel JS, et al: Calcium supplements for the prevention of colorectal adenomas. Calcium Polyp Prevention Study Group. N Engl J Med 340:101, 1999

22. Yiu HY, Whittemore AS, Shibata A: Increasing colorectal cancer incidence rates in Japan. Int J Cancer 109:777, 2004

23. Winawer SJ, Zauber AG, Ho MN, et al: Prevention of colorectal cancer by colonoscopic polypectomy. The National Polyp Study Workgroup. N Engl J Med 329:1977, 1993

24. Walsh JM, Terdiman JP: Colorectal cancer screening: scientific review. JAMA 289:1288, 2003

25. Imperiale TF, Wagner DR, Lin CY, et al: Risk of advanced proximal neoplasms in asymptomatic adults according to the distal colorectal findings. N Engl J Med 343:169, 2000

26. Lieberman DA, Weiss DG, Bond JH, et al: Use of colonoscopy to screen asymptomatic adults for colorectal cancer. Veterans Affairs Cooperative Study Group 380. N Engl J Med 343:162, 2000

27. Nelson DB, McQuaid KR, Bond JH, et al: Procedural success and complications of large-scale screening colonoscopy. Gastrointest Endosc 55:307, 2002

28. Pickhardt PJ, Choi JR, Hwang I, et al: Computed tomographic virtual colonoscopy to screen for colorectal neoplasia in asymptomatic adults. N Engl J Med 349:2191, 2003

29. Cotton PB, Durkalski VL, Pineau BC, et al: Computed tomographic colonography (virtual colonoscopy): a multicenter comparison with standard colonoscopy for detection of colorectal neoplasia. JAMA 291:1713, 2004

30. Deenadayalu VP, Rex DK: Fecal-based DNA assays: a new, noninvasive approach to colorectal cancer screening. Cleve Clin J Med 71:497, 2004

31. Ladabaum U, Song K, Fendrick AM: Colorectal neoplasia screening with virtual colonoscopy: when, at what cost, and with what national impact? Clin Gastroenterol Hepatol 2:554, 2004

32. Smith RA, Cokkinides V, Eyre HJ: American Cancer Society guidelines for the early detection of cancer, 2004. CA Cancer J Clin 54:41, 2004

33. Winawer S, Fletcher R, Rex D, et al: Colorectal cancer screening and surveillance: clinical guidelines and rationale-Update based on new evidence. Gastroenterology 124:544, 2003

34. Screening for colorectal cancer: recommendation and rationale. U.S. Preventive Services Task Force. Ann Intern Med 137:129, 2002

35. Majumdar SR, Fletcher RH, Evans AT: How does colorectal cancer present? Symptoms, duration, and clues to location. Am J Gastroenterol 94:3039, 1999

36. Dukes C: The classification of cancer of the rectum. J Pathol Bacteriol 34:323, 1932

37. Astler VB, Coller FA: The prognostic significance of direct extension of carcinoma of the colon and rectum. Ann Surg 139:846, 1954

38. AJCC Cancer Staging Manual, 6th ed. Greene F, Page DL, Fleming ID, et al, Eds. Springer Verlag New York, Inc, New York, 2002

39. Barton JB, Langdale LA, Cummins JS, et al: The utility of routine preoperative computed tomography scanning in the management of veterans with colon cancer. Am J Surg 183:499, 2002

40. Delbeke D, Martin WH: PET and PET-CT for evaluation of colorectal carcinoma. Semin Nucl Med 34:209, 2004

41. Bipat S, Glas AS, Slors FJ, et al: Rectal cancer: local staging and assessment of lymph node involvement with endoluminal US, CT, and MR imaging—a meta-analysis. Radiology 232:773, 2004

42. Greene FL, Stewart AK, Norton HJ: A new TNM staging strategy for node-positive (stage III) colon cancer: an analysis of 50,042 patients. Ann Surg 236:416, 2002

43. Marchena J, Acosta MA, Garcia-Anguiano F, et al: Use of the preoperative levels of CEA in patients with colorectal cancer. Hepatogastroenterology 50:1017, 2003

44. Lawes DA, SenGupta S, Boulos PB: The clinical importance and prognostic implications of microsatellite instability in sporadic cancer. Eur J Surg Oncol 29:201, 2003

45. Carethers JM, Smith EJ, Behling CA, et al: Use of 5-fluorouracil and survival in patients with microsatellite-unstable colorectal cancer. Gastroenterology 126:394, 2004

46. Jen J, Kim H, Piantadosi S, et al: Allelic loss of chromosome 18q and prognosis in colorectal cancer. N Engl J Med 331:213, 1994

47. Petersen S, Thames HD, Nieder C, et al: The results of colorectal cancer treatment by p53 status: treatment-specific overview. Dis Colon Rectum 44:322, 2001

48. Edler D, Glimelius B, Hallstrom M, et al: Thymidylate synthase expression in colorectal cancer: a prognostic and predictive marker of benefit from adjuvant fluorouracil-based chemotherapy. J Clin Oncol 20:1721, 2002

49. Botoman VA, Pietro M, Thirlby RC: Localization of colonic lesions with endoscopic tattoo. Dis Colon Rectum 37:775, 1994

50. Askin MP, Waye JD, Fiedler L, Harpaz N: Tattoo of colonic neoplasms in 113 patients with a new sterile carbon compound. Gastrointest Endosc 56:339, 2002

51. Nelson H, Petrelli N, Carlin A, et al: Guidelines 2000 for colon and rectal cancer surgery. J Natl Cancer Inst 93:583, 2001

52. Saha S, Dan AG, Bilchik AJ, et al: Historical review of lymphatic mapping in gastrointestinal malignancies. Ann Surg Oncol 11(3 Suppl):245S, 2004

53. Bertagnolli M, Miedema B, Redston M, et al: Sentinel node staging of resectable colon cancer: results of a multicenter study. Ann Surg 240:624, 2004

54. Wong JH, Johnson DS, Namiki T, et al: Validation of ex vivo lymphatic mapping in hematoxylin-eosin node-negative carcinoma of the colon and rectum. Ann Surg Oncol 11:772, 2004

55. Bosch B, Guller U, Schnider A, et al: Perioperative detection of disseminated tumour cells is an independent prognostic factor in patients with colorectal cancer. Br J Surg 90:882, 2003

56. Kanellos I, Demetriades H, Zintzaras E, et al: Incidence and prognostic value of positive peritoneal cytology in colorectal cancer. Dis Colon Rectum 46:535, 2003

57. Wexner SD, Cohen SM: Port site metastases after laparoscopic colorectal surgery for cure of malignancy. Br J Surg 82:295, 1995

58. Zmora O, Weiss EG: Trocar site recurrence in laparoscopic surgery for colorectal cancer. Myth or real concern? Surg Oncol Clin N Am 10:625, 2001

59. Janson M, Bjorholt I, Carlsson P, et al: Randomized clinical trial of the costs of open and laparoscopic surgery for colonic cancer. Br J Surg 91:409, 2004

60. Weeks JC, Nelson H, Gelber S, et al: Short-term quality-of-life outcomes following laparoscopic-assisted colectomy vs open colectomy for colon cancer: a randomized trial. JAMA 287:321, 2002

61. A comparison of laparoscopically assisted and open colectomy for colon cancer. N Engl J Med 350:2050, 2004

62. Hazebroek EJ: COLOR: a randomized clinical trial comparing laparoscopic and open resection for colon cancer. Surg Endosc 16:949, 2002

63. Arnaud JP, Bergamaschi R: Emergency subtotal/total colectomy with anastomosis for acutely obstructed carcinoma of the left colon. Dis Colon Rectum 37:685, 1994

64. Fante R, Roncucci L, Di Gregorio C, et al: Frequency and clinical features of multiple tumors of the large bowel in the general population and in patients with hereditary colorectal carcinoma. Cancer 77:2013, 1996

65. Arenas RB, Fichera A, Mhoon D, et al: Incidence and therapeutic implications of synchronous colonic pathology in colorectal adenocarcinoma. Surgery 122:706, 1997

66. Cunliffe WJ, Hasleton PS, Tweedle DE, et al: Incidence of synchronous and metachronous colorectal carcinoma. Br J Surg 71:941, 1984

67. Passman MA, Pommier RF, Vetto JT: Synchronous colon primaries have the same prognosis as solitary colon cancers. Dis Colon Rectum 39:329, 1996

68. Chen HS, Sheen-Chen SM: Synchronous and "early" metachronous colorectal adenocarcinoma: analysis of prognosis and current trends. Dis Colon Rectum 43:1093, 2000

69. Moertel CG, Fleming TR, Macdonald JS, et al: Fluorouracil plus levamisole as effective adjuvant therapy after resection of stage III colon carcinoma: a final report. Ann Intern Med 122:321, 1995

70. O'Connell MJ, Laurie JA, Kahn M, et al: Prospectively randomized trial of postoperative adjuvant chemotherapy in patients with high-risk colon cancer. J Clin Oncol 16:295, 1998

71. Wolmark N, Rockette H, Mamounas E, et al: Clinical trial to assess the relative efficacy of fluorouracil and leucovorin, fluorouracil and levamisole, and fluorouracil, leucovorin, and levamisole in patients with Dukes' B and C carcinoma of the colon: results from National Surgical Adjuvant Breast and Bowel Project C-04. J Clin Oncol 17:3553, 1999

72. Andre T, Boni C, Mounedji-Boudiaf L, et al: Oxaliplatin, fluorouracil, and leucovorin as adjuvant treatment for colon cancer. N Engl J Med 350:2343, 2004

73. Mamounas E, Wieand S, Wolmark N, et al: Comparative efficacy of adjuvant chemotherapy in patients with Dukes' B versus Dukes' C colon cancer: results from four National Surgical Adjuvant Breast and Bowel Project adjuvant studies (C-01, C-02, C-03, and C-04). J Clin Oncol 17:1349, 1999

74. Pignon JP, Ducreux M, Rougier P: More patients needed in stage II colon cancer trials. J Clin Oncol 18:235, 2000

75. Efficacy of adjuvant fluorouracil and folinic acid in B2 colon cancer. International Multicentre Pooled Analysis of B2 Colon Cancer Trials (IMPACT B2) Investigators. J Clin Oncol 17:1356, 1999

76. Gill S, Loprinzi CL, Sargent DJ, et al: Pooled analysis of fluorouracil-based adjuvant therapy for stage II and III colon cancer: who benefits and by how much? J Clin Oncol 15:1797, 2004

77. McCall JL, Cox MR, Wattchow DA: Analysis of local recurrence rates after surgery alone for rectal cancer. Int J Colorectal Dis 10:126, 1995

78. Sauer R, Becker H, Hohenberger W, et al: Preoperative versus postoperative chemoradiotherapy for rectal cancer. N Engl J Med 351:1731, 2004

79. Koperna T: Cost-effectiveness of defunctioning stomas in low anterior resections for rectal cancer: a call for benchmarking. Arch Surg 138:1334, 2003

80. Havenga K, Enker WE: Autonomic nerve preserving total mesorectal excision. Surg Clin North Am 82:1009, 2002

81. Moore HG, Guillem JG: Local therapy for rectal cancer. Surg Clin North Am 82:967, 2002

82. Steele GD Jr, Herndon JE, Bleday R, et al: Sphincter-sparing treatment for distal rectal ade-

nocarcinoma. Ann Surg Oncol 6:433, 1999

83. Russell AH, Harris J, Rosenberg PJ, et al: Anal sphincter conservation for patients with adenocarcinoma of the distal rectum: long-term results of radiation therapy oncology group protocol 89-02. Int J Radiat Oncol Biol Phys 46:313, 2000

84. Bonnen M, Crane C, Vauthey JN, et al: Long-term results using local excision after preoperative chemoradiation among selected T3 rectal cancer patients. Int J Radiat Oncol Biol Phys 60:1098, 2004

85. Friel CM, Cromwell JW, Marra C, et al: Salvage radical surgery after failed local excision for early rectal cancer. Dis Colon Rectum 45:875, 2002

86. Pollett WG, Nicholls RJ: The relationship between the extent of distal clearance and survival and local recurrence rates after curative anterior resection for carcinoma of the rectum. Ann Surg 198:159, 1983

87. Kuvshinoff B, Maghfoor I, Miedema B, et al: Distal margin requirements after preoperative chemoradiotherapy for distal rectal carcinomas: are < or = 1 cm distal margins sufficient? Ann Surg Oncol 8:163, 2001

88. Andreola S, Leo E, Belli F, et al: Adenocarcinoma of the lower third of the rectum surgically treated with a <10-MM distal clearance: preliminary results in 35 N0 patients. Ann Surg Oncol 8:611, 2001

89. Quirke P, Durdey P, Dixon MF, et al: Local recurrence of rectal adenocarcinoma due to inadequate surgical resection. Histopathological study of lateral tumour spread and surgical excision. Lancet 2:996, 1986

90. Wibe A, Rendedal PR, Svensson E, et al: Prognostic significance of the circumferential resection margin following total mesorectal excision for rectal cancer. Br J Surg 89:327, 2002

91. Nagtegaal ID, Marijnen CA, Kranenbarg EK, et al: Circumferential margin involvement is still an important predictor of local recurrence in rectal carcinoma: not one millimeter but two millimeters is the limit. Am J Surg Pathol 26:350, 2002

92. Marijnen CA, Nagtegaal ID, Kapiteijn E, et al: Radiotherapy does not compensate for positive resection margins in rectal cancer patients: report of a multicenter randomized trial. Int J Radiat Oncol Biol Phys 55:1311, 2003

93. Rich T, Gunderson LL, Lew R, et al: Patterns of recurrence of rectal cancer after potentially curative surgery. Cancer 52:1317, 1983

94. Pilipshen SJ, Heilweil M, Quan SH, et al: Patterns of pelvic recurrence following definitive resections of rectal cancer. Cancer, 53:1354, 1984

95. Mendenhall WM, Million RR, Pfaff WW: Patterns of recurrence in adenocarcinoma of the rectum and rectosigmoid treated with surgery alone: implications in treatment planning with adjuvant radiation therapy. Int J Radiat Oncol Biol Phys 9:977, 1983

96. Zaheer S, Pemberton JH, Farouk R, et al: Surgical treatment of adenocarcinoma of the rectum. Ann Surg 227:800, 1998

97. Cecil TD, Sexton R, Moran BJ, et al: Total mesorectal excision results in low local recurrence rates in lymph node-positive rectal cancer. Dis Colon Rectum 47:1145, 2004

98. Prolongation of the disease-free interval in surgically treated rectal carcinoma. Gastrointestinal Tumor Study Group. N Engl J Med 312:1465, 1985

99. Wolmark N, Wieand HS, Hyams DM, et al: Randomized trial of postoperative adjuvant chemotherapy with or without radiotherapy for carcinoma of the rectum: National Surgical Adjuvant Breast and Bowel Project Protocol R-02. J Natl Cancer Inst 92:388, 2000

100. O'Connell MJ, Martenson JA, Wieand HS, et al: Improving adjuvant therapy for rectal cancer by combining protracted-infusion fluorouracil with radiation therapy after curative surgery. N Engl J Med 331:502, 1994

101. Ota DM, Jacobs L, Kuvshinoff B: Rectal cancer: the sphincter-sparing approach. Surg Clin North Am 82:983, 2002

102. Garcia-Aguilar J, Hernandez de Anda E, Sirivongs P, et al: A pathologic complete response to preoperative chemoradiation is associated with lower local recurrence and improved survival in rectal cancer patients treated by mesorectal excision. Dis Colon Rectum 46:298, 2003

103. Pahlman L, Glimelius B: Pre- or postoperative radiotherapy in rectal and rectosigmoid carcinoma. Report from a randomized multicenter trial. Ann Surg 211:187, 1990

104. Bekdash B, Harris S, Broughton CI, et al: Outcome after multiple colorectal tumours. Br J Surg 84:1442, 1997

105. Scoggins CR, Meszoely IM, Blanke CD, et al: Nonoperative management of primary colorectal cancer in patients with stage IV disease. Ann Surg Oncol, 6:651, 1999

106. Ruo L, Gougoutas C, Paty PB, et al: Elective bowel resection for incurable stage IV colorectal cancer: prognostic variables for asymptomatic patients. J Am Coll Surg 196:722, 2003

107. Scheele J, Stangl R, Altendorf-Hofmann A, et al: Indicators of prognosis after hepatic resection for colorectal secondaries. Surgery 110:13, 1991

108. Martin R, Paty P, Fong Y, et al: Simultaneous liver and colorectal resections are safe for synchronous colorectal liver metastasis. J Am Coll Surg 197:233, 2003

109. Chua HK, Sondenaa K, Tsiotos GG, et al: Concurrent vs. staged colectomy and hepatectomy for primary colorectal cancer with synchronous hepatic metastases. Dis Colon Rectum 47:1310, 2004

110. Jayne DG, Fook S, Loi C, et al: Peritoneal carcinomatosis from colorectal cancer. Br J Surg 89:1545, 2002

111. Rosen SA, Buell JF, Yoshida A, et al: Initial presentation with stage IV colorectal cancer: how aggressive should we be? Arch Surg 135:530, 2000

112. Elias DM, Pocard M: Treatment and prevention of peritoneal carcinomatosis from colorectal cancer. Surg Oncol Clin N Am 12:543, 2003

113. Stephens AD, Alderman R, Chang D, et al: Morbidity and mortality analysis of 200 treatments with cytoreductive surgery and hyperthermic intraoperative intraperitoneal chemotherapy using the coliseum technique. Ann Surg Oncol 6:790, 1999

114. Verwaal VJ, van Ruth S, de Bree E, et al: Randomized trial of cytoreduction and hyperthermic intraperitoneal chemotherapy versus systemic chemotherapy and palliative surgery in patients with peritoneal carcinomatosis of colorectal cancer. J Clin Oncol 21:3737, 2003

115. Green RJ, Metlay JP, Propert K, et al: Surveillance for second primary colorectal cancer after adjuvant chemotherapy: an analysis of Intergroup 0089. Ann Intern Med 136:261, 2002

116. Chau I, Allen MJ, Cunningham D, et al: The value of routine serum carcino-embryonic antigen measurement and computed tomography in the surveillance of patients after adjuvant chemotherapy for colorectal cancer. J Clin Oncol 22:1420, 2004

117. Rosen M, Chan L, Beart RW Jr, et al: Follow-up of colorectal cancer: a meta-analysis. Dis Colon Rectum 41:1116, 1998

118. Renehan AG, Egger M, Saunders MP, et al: Impact on survival of intensive follow up after curative resection for colorectal cancer: systematic review and meta-analysis of randomised trials. BMJ 324:813, 2002

119. Jeffery GM, Hickey BE, Hider P: Follow-up strategies for patients treated for non-metastatic colorectal cancer. Cochrane Database Syst Rev (1):CD002200, 2002

120. Wichmann MW, Muller C, Hornung HM, et al: Results of long-term follow-up after curative resection of Dukes A colorectal cancer. World J Surg 26:732, 2002

121. Benson AB 3rd, Desch CE, Flynn PJ, et al: 2000 update of American Society of Clinical Oncology colorectal cancer surveillance guidelines. J Clin Oncol 18:3586, 2000

122. NCCN colon cancer clinical practice guidelines in oncology. J Natl Compr Cancer Network 1:40, 2003

123. NCCN colon cancer clinical practice guidelines in oncology. J Natl Compr Cancer Network 1:54, 2003

124. Anthony T, Simmang C, Hyman N, et al: Practice parameters for the surveillance and follow-up of patients with colon and rectal cancer. Dis Colon Rectum 47:807, 2004

125. Fong Y, Fortner J, Sun RL, et al: Clinical score for predicting recurrence after hepatic resection for metastatic colorectal cancer: analysis of 1001 consecutive cases. Ann Surg 230:309, 1999

126. Fernandez FG, Drebin JA, Linehan DC, et al: Five-year survival after resection of hepatic metastases from colorectal cancer in patients screened by positron emission tomography with F-18 fluorodeoxyglucose (FDG-PET). Ann Surg 240:438, 2004

127. Schussler-Fiorenza CM, Mahvi DM, Niederhuber J, et al: Clinical risk score correlates with yield of PET scan in patients with colorectal hepatic metastases. J Gastrointest Surg 8:150, 2004

128. Pfannschmidt J, Muley T, Hoffmann H, et al: Prognostic factors and survival after complete resection of pulmonary metastases from colorectal carcinoma: experiences in 167 patients. J Thorac Cardiovasc Surg 126:732, 2003

129. Vogelsang H, Haas S, Hierholzer C, et al: Factors influencing survival after resection of pulmonary metastases from colorectal cancer. Br J Surg 91:1066, 2004

130. Hahnloser D, Nelson H, Gunderson LL, et al: Curative potential of multimodality therapy for locally recurrent rectal cancer. Ann Surg 237:502, 2003

131. Cheng C, Rodriguez-Bigas MA, Petrelli N: Is there a role for curative surgery for pelvic recurrence from rectal carcinoma in the presence of hydronephrosis? Am J Surg 182:274, 2001

Acknowledgment

Figure 1 Alice Y. Chen.

58 MOTILITY DISORDERS

Nancy N. Baxter, M.D., Ph.D., F.R.C.S.C., F.A.S.C.R.S., and Robert D. Madoff, M.D., F.A.C.S., F.A.S.C.R.S.

Surgeons commonly encounter patients with gastrointestinal motility disorders. The management of such patients is frequently challenging, in that the etiology of the disorder is often multifactorial. Furthermore, even when surgical therapy is appropriate, management of symptoms remains a key component of effective treatment.

In what follows, we discuss two of the most common motility disorders, constipation and fecal incontinence. Although constipation usually is not treated surgically, surgeons regularly see patients with this presenting symptom. It is therefore critical that surgeons have a practical method of diagnosing and managing the primary and secondary causes of constipation. Fecal incontinence is an understudied and undertreated condition that can have a dramatic impact on quality of life. Effective treatment of incontinence has a dramatic positive influence on patients' lives; thus, it is important for surgeons to have both an effective approach to diagnosis and an informed awareness of the various therapeutic options available (including experimental treatments).

Constipation

CLINICAL EVALUATION

History

Constipation is the most common digestive complaint, with as much as 20% of the population reporting this symptom.[1] The meaning of the term constipation, however, is variable: when patients describe themselves as constipated, they may be referring to decreased stool frequency, reduced stool volume, altered stool consistency, or difficulty with defecation.[2] Accordingly, when a patient presents with a complaint of constipation, a thorough history of the presenting illness is essential [see Figure 1].

The patient should be asked about the frequency of bowel movements, the volume of stool per movement, the caliber of the stool, and, in particular, any changes in bowel habits over time. Patients with idiopathic constipation tend to have long-standing problems, with no abrupt change in bowel habits. Thus, if the history reveals constipation of sudden onset, an underlying cause (e.g., cancer) is more likely and should be sought. Other important symptoms that should lead to a search for a secondary cause are weight loss, anorexia, nausea and vomiting, rectal bleeding, changes in stool caliber, and fever. The patient should always be asked about previous colon cancer screening or other GI investigations. Although chronic constipation is common, severe constipation that has been present since early childhood should alert the clinician to the possibility of undiagnosed short-segment Hirschsprung disease; this rare diagnosis is easily missed if it is not given appropriate consideration. Other symptoms may be indicative of an outlet problem (e.g., rectocele or nonrelaxing puborectalis syndrome); such symptoms include requiring a prolonged period to evacuate stool from the rectum, a feeling of incomplete rectal emptying, and the need to support the perineum (through digitation of the vagina or rectum) to achieve complete evacuation.

Diet can contribute significantly to constipation. Because high-fiber foods tend to increase stool bulk and frequency, detailed information on dietary fiber intake should be obtained. Because dehydration increases fluid resorption from stool and thereby results in the formation of hard stools, total daily fluid intake should be determined as well. A specific effort should be made to assess intake of fluids that contain caffeine, which exerts a diuretic effect. Most patients with long-standing constipation will already have tried some form of self-medication. Such attempts should be documented, both to help assess the severity of the symptom and to determine the likelihood of response to simple measures.

Various other diseases and certain common medications [see Table 1] also can cause or contribute to constipation. When such factors are present, treating the underlying condition or changing medications can result in substantial improvement. Therefore, a thorough past medical history and an accurate medication history are essential. A family history of colonic neoplasia or inflammatory bowel disease is potentially suggestive and may lead to a more intensive search for secondary causes. Victims of physical or sexual abuse may present with constipation; however, they are unlikely to mention the abuse if not directly questioned about the possibility.

Physical Examination

During physical examination, it is important to make a quick assessment of the patient's nutritional status. In general, patients with idiopathic constipation should not appear malnourished; the appearance of malnutrition should prompt a more extensive search for a secondary cause. An abdominal examination should be conducted to look for any significant abdominal distention, tenderness, or masses. Distention is a common and expected finding with idiopathic constipation, but significant tenderness or masses should prompt a full investigation.

All patients presenting with constipation should undergo a rectal examination. The anus should be examined for evidence of scarring or stricture. A digital rectal examination should be done to assess anal tone; high anal tone and inability to increase pressure when asked to squeeze are common findings in patients with obstructed defecation resulting from a nonrelaxing puborectalis. An effort should be made to look for any anterior defect in the rectovaginal septum, which would indicate the presence of a rectocele; such a defect, if present, may be made more prominent by having the patient strain. The finding of a rectal mass warrants further investigation.

INVESTIGATIVE STUDIES

In general, diagnostic studies are conducted to rule out an underlying cause of constipation (e.g., partially obstructing colon cancer) and to diagnose specific disorders associated with severe constipation (e.g., a nonrelaxing puborectalis and slow-transit constipation). Therefore, the choice of investigative studies should be individualized according to the clinical situation. In

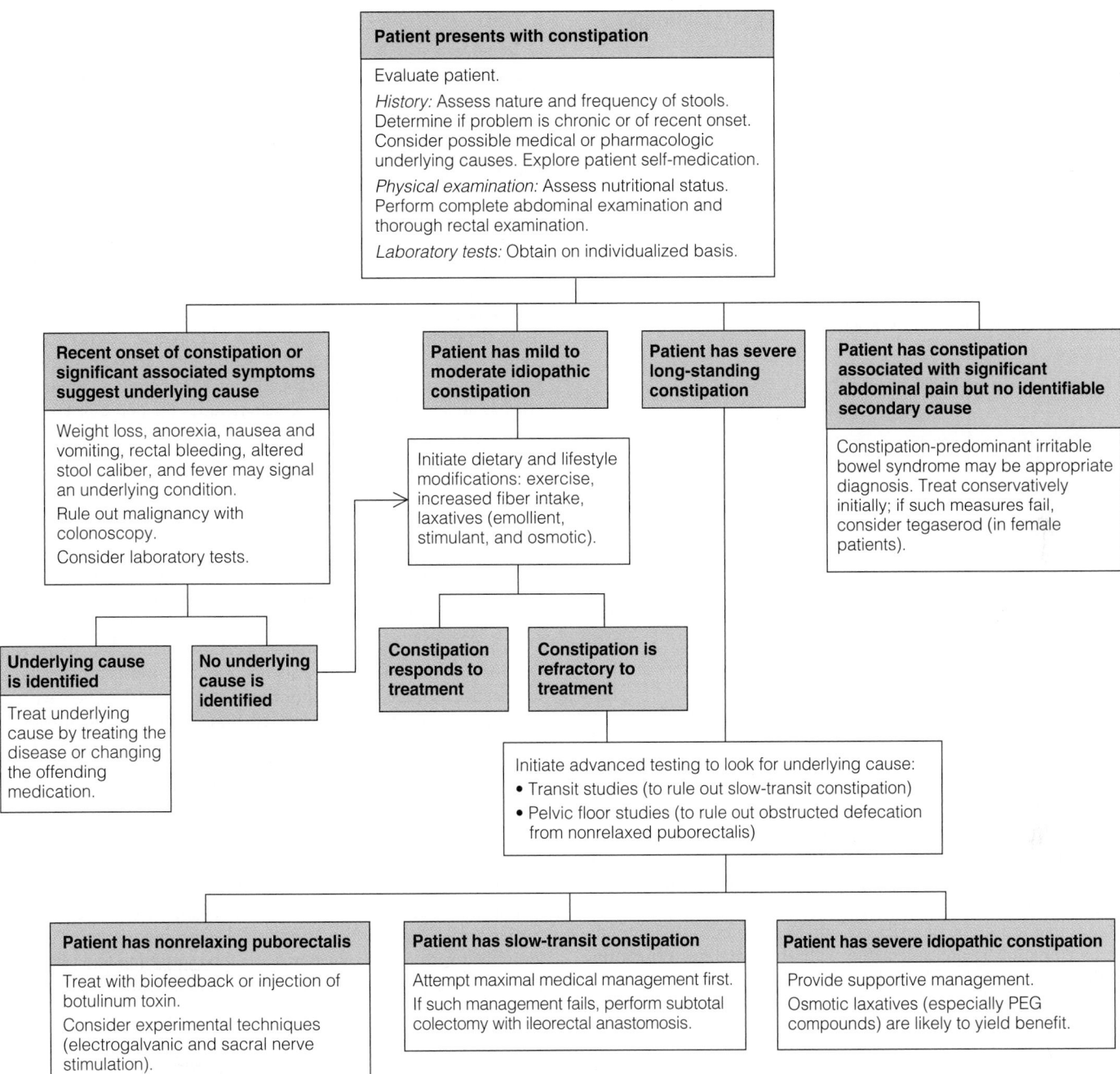

Figure 1 **Algorithm outlines workup and management of constipation.**

patients with mild symptoms and poor dietary habits who have no indications of any secondary causes of constipation, no investigations need be done on a routine basis. In patients with severe constipation, however, serum calcium concentrations, thyroid function tests, hemoglobin concentrations, glucose levels, serum electrolyte levels, and creatinine concentrations may be helpful.

Constipation with Suspected Underlying Cause

Whenever any of the findings from the history or the physical examination indicate a possible secondary cause of constipation, further investigation is mandatory. In particular, if a patient presents with any sign, symptom, or laboratory test result consistent with colorectal cancer (e.g., a sudden change in bowel habits, blood in the stool, weight loss, anorexia, a suggestive family history, abdom-

inal masses, or anemia), colonoscopy is necessary, irrespective of the patient's age or history of previous colonic investigations.

Patients with other secondary causes of constipation (e.g., hypothyroidism and hypercalcemia) often respond to treatment of the underlying disease or manipulation of medications. If such measures are ineffective, the constipation should be treated symptomatically, in much the same fashion as idiopathic constipation is. Patients requiring long-term opioid administration for pain control generally experience constipation as a side effect, and this effect does not dissipate with time. Thus, many of these patients will require laxative therapy for the duration of their opioid use.[3]

Mild to Moderate Idiopathic Constipation

In patients who have mild to moderate symptoms and no

Table 1 Causes of Secondary Constipation

Neuromuscular disorders	Spinal cord injury Parkinson disease Multiple sclerosis Stroke Autonomic neuropathy/diabetes Depression Hirschsprung disease
Metabolic abnormalities	Hypercalcemia Hyperparathyroidism Hypothyroidism Multiple endocrine neoplasia type IIB Chronic renal failure
Medications	Opioids Anticholinergics (tricyclic antidepressants, levodopa, antipsychotics) Supplements (iron, calcium) Antacids (calcium- or aluminum-containing) Anticonvulsants (phenytoin, valproic acid) Antihypertensives (calcium channel blockers, diuretics, clonidine) Cholestyramine
Others	Pregnancy Amyloidosis Scleroderma Chagas disease Anorexia nervosa

findings from the history or the physical examination that would indicate a secondary cause, extensive investigations are not necessary. Routine colonoscopy is not mandatory for patients younger than 50 years. For patients older than 50 years, the baseline risk of colorectal cancer is sufficiently high that screening colonoscopy is recommended even in the absence of symptoms. These older patients should therefore undergo routine colonoscopy, and many authors recommend that patients younger than 50 years undergo routine flexible sigmoidoscopy. Random endoscopic biopsies are unnecessary, because idiopathic constipation is not associated with abnormalities on routine processing of mucosal biopsies.

Severe, Long-standing Constipation or Refractory Constipation

In patients who have very severe constipation or in whom medical management fails, further investigative tests are warranted. These tests are conducted to classify patients into three categories, each of which calls for a different treatment approach: (1) slow-transit constipation, (2) nonrelaxing puborectalis, and (3) normal-transit constipation.[4] The initial investigations should include assessment of colonic transit time to determine if slow-transit constipation is present, as well as evaluation of pelvic floor function to determine if a nonrelaxing puborectalis is present.

There are two main methods for evaluating colonic transit: the radiopaque marker study and colonic scintigraphy. Both tests have advantages and disadvantages. In general, the choice between them depends on local expertise; the radiopaque marker study is more widely available. For the radiopaque marker study, 20 radiopaque markers (prepackaged in gelatin capsules) are ingested, and an abdominal x-ray (which includes the pelvis) is taken on day 5. The patient abstains from laxatives for the duration of the study. At 3 days, most patients with normal transit have excreted more than 80% of the markers; however, because there is substantial variation among asymptomatic persons, only patients who retain more than 20% of the markers for at least 5 days are considered to have abnormal transit. Abnormal transit may be demonstrated either throughout the colon or within a limited portion thereof (most commonly, the sigmoid and the rectum) [*see Figure 2*].

Colonic scintigraphy shares certain principles with the radiopaque marker study. Patients ingest a meal containing a radioactive isotope, and abdominal images are obtained with a gamma camera at 12, 24, and 48 hours. The results provide a quantitative assessment of colonic transit. In addition, unlimited numbers of images may be taken with the single isotope dose, and this feature of the test may be especially useful in children. For optimal accuracy, this technique requires standardization, and its availability is generally limited to centers with specific interest and expertise in it.

Pelvic floor studies are valuable for ruling out obstructed defecation as a cause of constipation. The balloon expulsion test can be performed in the office as an initial screening measure.[5] A balloon filled with 50 ml of water is attached to tubing and placed in the rectum; patients with a nonrelaxing puborectalis generally can-

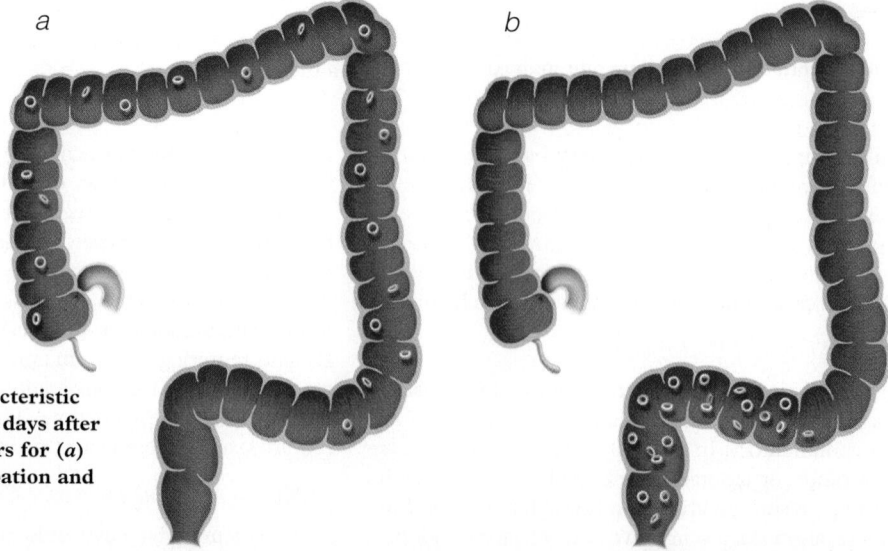

a   *b*

Figure 2 **Illustrated are characteristic colonic transit study findings 5 days after ingestion of radiopaque markers for (*a*) pancolonic slow-transit constipation and (*b*) outlet obstruction.**

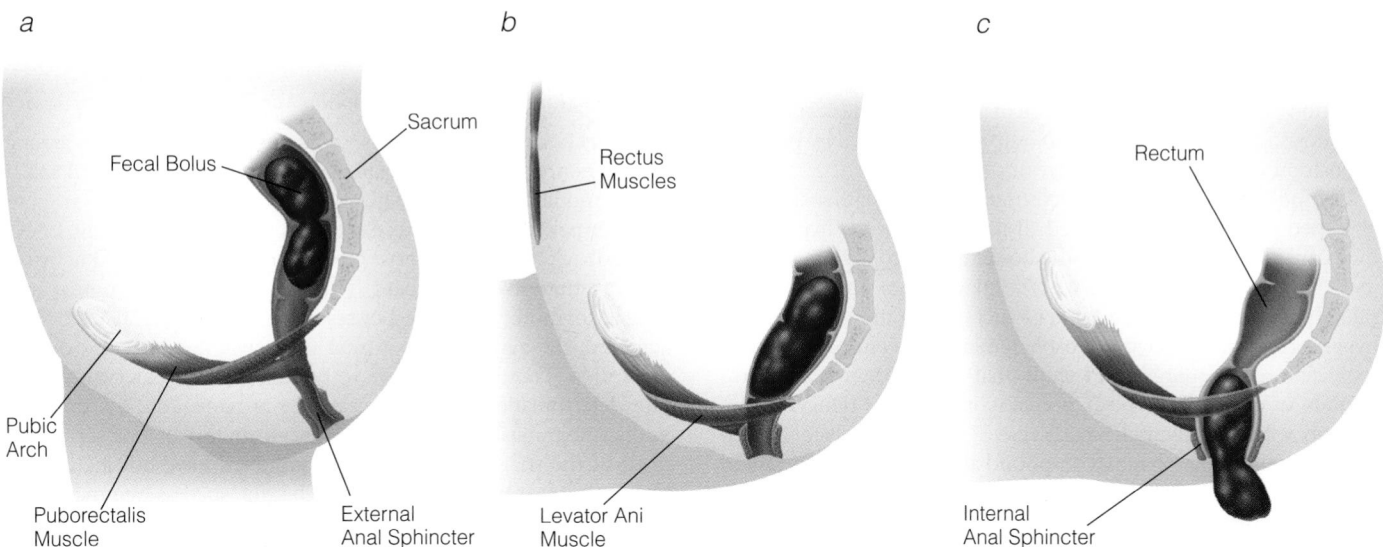

Figure 3 Schematic representation of normal defecation depicts (*a*) initial contraction of pelvic floor muscles with urge to defecate, (*b*) relaxation of puborectalis and external sphincter, and (*c*) relaxation of internal sphincter and evacuation of stool with rectal contraction.

not expel the balloon from the rectum in 1 minute while sitting on a commode. It should be kept in mind, however, that as many as 12% of patients with normal pelvic floor function will have difficulty with balloon expulsion in this setting.[6]

A thorough pelvic floor evaluation is best conducted in a pelvic floor laboratory with a specific interest in anorectal function. In addition to the balloon expulsion test, the evaluation generally involves manometry, including assessment of the reflexive relaxation of the internal sphincter after rectal distention. The presence of this reflexive relaxation rules out Hirschsprung disease as a cause of constipation. In patients with a nonrelaxing puborectalis, manometry during straining effort demonstrates abnormal function of the external sphincter—either failure to relax to enable expulsion or, on occasion, paradoxical contraction. Similar findings during straining can be documented by means of electromyography (EMG) with a sponge electrode in the anal canal.

Defecography is commonly performed as well. Barium paste is formulated so as to simulate a fecal bolus and placed in the rectum. The patient is asked to defecate on a radiolucent commode, and the event is recorded with fluoroscopy. During normal defecation, the puborectalis and the anal sphincter muscles relax, and the rectum assumes a more vertical position with respect to the anal canal, facilitating evacuation of stool [*see Figure 3*]. In a patient with a nonrelaxing puborectalis, defecography typically demonstrates failure to open the anorectal angle and persistence of the puborectalis impression during defecation, as well as failure to empty completely.[7] Other important findings that may be noted include rectocele, internal intussusception, and rectal prolapse. When appropriately selected, patients with obstructed defecation resulting from such abnormalities may benefit from surgical correction; however, even when these anatomic abnormalities are present, they may not be the underlying cause of constipation. Interpretation of defecography is subjective, and there is wide normal variation. Therefore, the diagnosis of a nonrelaxing puborectalis should be based not on a single test result but, rather, on the totality of the diagnostic findings.

The diagnosis of nonrelaxing puborectalis syndrome is made in persons with constipation in whom there is evidence of failure of the pelvic floor to relax appropriately (or paradoxical contraction of the pelvic floor) with defecation. The cause of this condition is not known; however, the syndrome is thought to be acquired over time. Patients with an underlying neurologic disorder (e.g., multiple sclerosis or Parkinson disease) are prone to spasticity of the puborectalis and may experience severe constipation as a result.

MANAGEMENT

Mild to Moderate Idiopathic Constipation

Many cases of constipation can be managed with dietary and lifestyle changes, such as modifying the diet to include foods high in fiber and drinking adequate amounts of water. Physical inactivity is associated with constipation, and encouraging moderate exercise may lead to significant symptomatic relief. Fiber supplementation is a key component of therapy for mild constipation.[8] Fiber products (e.g., psyllium, methylcellulose, and polycarbophil) increase stool bulk and stimulate colonic motility. Such products must be taken with sufficient amounts of fluid, or they may lead to stool hardening. Often, patients have already tried fiber products but did not achieve satisfactory results because the quantities were insufficient; daily doses as high as 20 g may be necessary for a therapeutic effect. Patients taking fiber products may experience an increase in flatulence, particularly with fermentable fiber products. To improve tolerance, the amount of fiber should be increased gradually, and patients should be informed that the effect of fiber may not be seen immediately.

Nonlaxative therapy should be stressed; however, if dietary changes and fiber supplementation fail, judicious use of laxatives can bring about significant symptomatic relief. It should be kept in mind that tachyphylaxis to laxatives is common and may lead to chronic dependence. Stool softeners, or emollient laxatives (e.g., ducosate sodium and mineral oil), enhance penetration of water and fat into the stool, thereby making it less hard. These agents may be of use on a relatively short-term basis. Ducosate sodium is less effective than fiber supplementation[9]; stool softeners should not be used as a substitute for fiber.

Stimulant laxatives, including cascara, anthraquinones (senna and rhubarb), castor oil, and bisacodyl, are common components of popular over-the-counter medications. These agents have direct neuromuscular or mucosal effects, resulting in enhanced GI motility and altered mucosal transport (and thus increased intestinal secretion).[8] Long-term use or abuse of anthraquinones can lead to melanosis (discoloration of the colonic mucosa caused by pigment deposition in colonic macrophages).

Osmotic laxatives contain compounds that either are not absorbed or are poorly absorbed. If the solutions are hypertonic, they cause water to move into the bowel lumen to maintain tonicity.[10] Common preparations include magnesium and phosphate salts. Ingestion of large amounts of such preparations can lead to hypermagnesemia or hyperphosphatemia, mainly in patients with renal failure. The large fluid shifts that result when these compounds are used for bowel preparation may be dangerous in patients with underlying heart disease. Polyethylene glycol (PEG) is a high-molecular-weight compound that is not absorbed and thus functions as an osmotic laxative. PEG preparations are commonly administered as isotonic solutions and therefore cause only minimal fluid or electrolyte shifts when consumed rapidly (as in bowel preparation). PEG compounds are available as laxatives that can be taken either intermittently or regularly.

Tegaserod, a 5-HT$_4$ partial agonist, has been shown to alleviate bloating and increase stool frequency by improving gut motility and decreasing visceral sensitivity.[11] It may be prescribed for women with constipation-predominant irritable bowel syndrome (IBS) (see below) and for either male or female patients younger than 65 years who have idiopathic constipation. Tegaserod has been associated with the development of diarrhea; typically, the diarrhea resolves when the drug is discontinued, but occasionally, it is severe. In addition, several cases of ischemic colitis have been reported in patients receiving tegaserod. Although no causal relation has been established, patients should be warned to cease taking tegaserod and immediately contact their physician if abdominal pain worsens.

Enemas and suppositories act via a number of mechanisms, including softening of the stool, stimulation of rectal contraction by rectal distention, and direct alteration of mucosal secretion. They may be useful for occasional administration.

Constipation-Predominant Irritable Bowel Syndrome

In patients with constipation, significant abdominal pain, and no identifiable secondary cause of constipation, the diagnosis of constipation-predominant IBS may be appropriate [*see Table 2*].[12,13] Often, patients with constipation-predominant IBS respond to reassurance and fiber supplementation. Tegaserod may be

employed in female patients who do not respond to conservative measures.

Severe, Long-standing Constipation or Refractory Constipation

Nonrelaxing puborectalis Patients with constipation arising from a nonrelaxing puborectalis often benefit from biofeedback.[14] In this modality, a device (e.g., an anorectal manometer) is used to monitor pelvic floor activity; electrodes may also be used for EMG biofeedback. Patients observe pressure changes (or EMG activity) during attempts to evacuate. Through trial and error, they are taught to modify their responses until appropriate relaxation is achieved, the aim being to retrain the pelvic floor to relax during defecation. Training may have to be reinforced at intervals. Accurate determination of the success rate of biofeedback is difficult, in that the published literature consists primarily of case series and most of the trials that have been conducted have not included a placebo arm. It has been estimated that the success rate may be as high as 70%; however, this estimate is probably overoptimistic.[15]

If biofeedback fails, injection of botulinum toxin into the puborectalis under ultrasonographic guidance may be attempted. To date, published reports have evaluated this approach only in relatively small study groups; the results, though not decisive, are promising, in that the use of botulinum toxin clearly brought about noticeable improvements in manometric and defecographic findings[16] and symptomatic improvements in the majority of patients.[17] Other experimental techniques available for treatment of nonrelaxing puborectalis syndrome are electrogalvanic stimulation[18] and sacral nerve stimulation (SNS).[19] Currently, surgical approaches do not play a role in the treatment of constipation secondary to a nonrelaxing puborectalis.

Slow-transit constipation Slow-transit constipation, also known as colonic inertia, is most common in young women and often starts at puberty. It is characterized by abnormally slow forward propulsion of colonic contents. The cause of slow-transit constipation is unknown, though abnormalities in a number of cellular and neuromuscular modulators of GI motility have been found in patients with this condition.[20,21] Although patients with idiopathic slow-transit constipation are frequently resistant to laxative therapy, many respond to osmotic PEG laxatives. Surgery should be considered as an option only in the most severely affected patients, in whom aggressive laxative therapy has repeatedly failed over a prolonged period. Even in specialized centers, only about 5% of patients presenting with constipation are considered appropriate candidates for surgical treatment.[22]

The operation most commonly performed to treat slow-transit constipation is subtotal colectomy with ileorectal anastomosis, performed via either an open or a laparoscopic approach. The colon is removed to the level of the sacral promontory in a standard fashion; the ileorectal anastomosis may be either stapled or handsewn. Constipation is less likely to recur with this anastomosis than with an ileosigmoid anastomosis.[23]

Surgical therapy is generally successful in improving bowel function: in most patients, stool frequency rises to one to three bowel movements a day. Unfortunately, surgery may not satisfactorily alleviate other symptoms (e.g., abdominal discomfort or bloating),[24] and patients should be made aware of this possibility before operation. The key to successful surgical treatment is patient selection. Overall, the majority of well-selected patients are satisfied with the results of surgical treatment[25,26]; however, long-term postoperative complications, particularly small bowel obstruction, are common. In addition, patients may manifest symptoms of a more global GI dysmotility disorder in the long term.

Table 2 **Rome II Criteria for Diagnosis of Constipation-Predominant Irritable Bowel Syndrome[8]**

At least 12 wk of abdominal pain or discomfort in the past year, with at least 2 of the following:
1. Relief with defecation
2. Onset associated with a change in frequency of stool
3. Onset associated with a change in form (appearance) of stool

Supportive symptoms of constipation-predominant IBS:
1. Abnormal stool frequency (< 3 bowel movements/wk)
2. Abnormal stool form (hard or lumpy stools)
3. Abnormal stool passage (straining during bowel movement, feeling of incomplete evacuation)

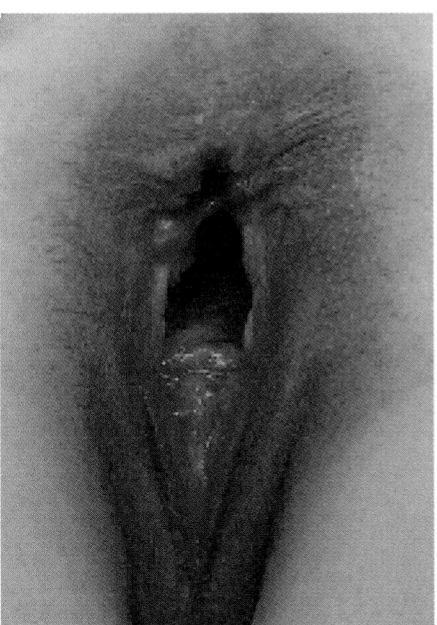

Figure 4 **Shown is an obstetric sphincter injury.**

Other surgical approaches sometimes employed in this setting are ileostomy [*see 72 Intestinal Stomas*], total proctocolectomy with ileal pouch–anal anastomosis (IPAA) [*see 75 Procedures for Ulcerative Colitis*], segmental colectomy [*see 76 Segmental Colon Resection*], and colectomy with cecorectal anastomosis; however, data on the long-term effectiveness of these approaches in large numbers of patients are lacking. Completion proctectomy with IPAA and ileostomy are options for patients who remain severely symptomatic after ileorectal anastomosis but who manifest no evidence of proximal dysmotility.

Not infrequently, patients have both slow-transit constipation and a nonrelaxing puborectalis. In such cases, it is essential that the obstructed defecation be addressed before any surgical treatment is carried out. Even after biofeedback, if surgical therapy is attempted in this setting, as many as 50% of patients will be dissatisfied with the results.[27]

Severe idiopathic constipation Patients who have severe constipation but show no signs of slow-transit constipation, pelvic floor dysfunction, or IBS should be treated with reassurance and symptomatic management. Osmotic laxatives—in particular, PEG products—may be very useful in this group. Operative treatment plays no role in management; however, experimental approaches (e.g., SNS) are being evaluated for possible use in this setting.

Fecal Incontinence

Fecal incontinence may be defined as the involuntary loss of rectal contents through the anal canal. It is a relatively common condition, occurring in an estimated 2.2% of persons in the United States.[28] Its exact prevalence is unknown, however, and appears to vary with the population being studied. For example, nearly 50% of nursing home patients are incontinent to stool.[28] Fecal incontinence is often treated inadequately, either because of underreporting of symptoms to the physician[29] or because of ignorance or disinterest on the physician's part.

Fecal incontinence makes a significant contribution to medical morbidity (e.g., urinary tract infections and decubitus ulcers),

but its main impact is on quality of life. Affected patients experience embarrassment and shame, and many dramatically alter their lifestyle in an effort to avoid accidents.

Normal continence depends on a chain of interdependent processes, and disruption of any of the links in the chain can lead to incontinence. Frequently, a combination of factors is responsible for the incontinence.

To care about continence, persons must have adequate mental function, and to maintain normal continence, they must have an intact neurologic arc from the brain to the anal sphincter. A wide array of neurologic disorders can lead to incontinence, including dementia, strokes, spinal cord injury, multiple sclerosis, and diabetic autonomic neuropathy. So-called idiopathic fecal incontinence is caused by pelvic floor denervation resulting from traction injury to the pudendal nerves.[30] The injury is usually caused by straining and consequent pelvic floor descent during obstetrical delivery or by chronic straining at stool.

Conditions characterized by abnormal GI function, especially diarrheal states, can cause or exacerbate incontinence. Common causative conditions include infectious diarrhea and inflammatory bowel disease. Diarrhea-predominant IBS can contribute to incontinence in patients with other associated disorders. Fecal impaction is an important cause of incontinence, particularly in older and institutionalized populations.[31]

Abnormalities of the pelvic floor are frequent causes of incontinence. Some such abnormalities are congenital malformations (e.g., imperforate anus, rectal agenesis, and cloacal defect). More often, abnormalities are attributable to acquired sphincter injuries. Common causes of sphincter injury include obstetric injury, pelvic fracture, and traumatic impalement [*see Figure 4*]. One of the most frequent causes is an anorectal procedure, such as fistulotomy,[32] sphincterotomy,[33] or anal dilatation.[34] Sphincter-sparing rectal resections can also lead to incontinence as a consequence of both the loss of the normal rectal reservoir and the sphincter injury caused by transanal introduction of intraluminal staplers.

CLINICAL EVALUATION

History

A careful patient history and a directed physical examination are the most important elements of clinical evaluation for a patient with fecal incontinence [*see Figure 5*]. The patient should be asked about the onset and nature of the incontinence (e.g., whether the stool is liquid or solid and whether flatus is present), any associated changes in stool consistency or bowel habits, and the frequency of incontinence. A pertinent but thorough medical, surgical, and obstetric history should be obtained, and any underlying contributory conditions (e.g., colitis) should be treated. The impact of the incontinence on the patient's quality of life should be assessed, at least qualitatively.

Physical Examination

Physical examination should focus primarily on the perineum. Seepage and secondary perineal skin breakdown should be noted, as should scars from previous surgical treatment or trauma. Perineal body deformity is an important sign of obstetric injury, and gaping of the anus with traction on the buttocks is suggestive of rectal prolapse. When prolapse is suspected but not evident, the patient should be asked to strain while seated on a commode. Digital rectal examination is useful for detecting low rectal tumors and fecal impaction; it also provides a qualitative assessment of both resting sphincter tone and voluntary squeeze pressure.

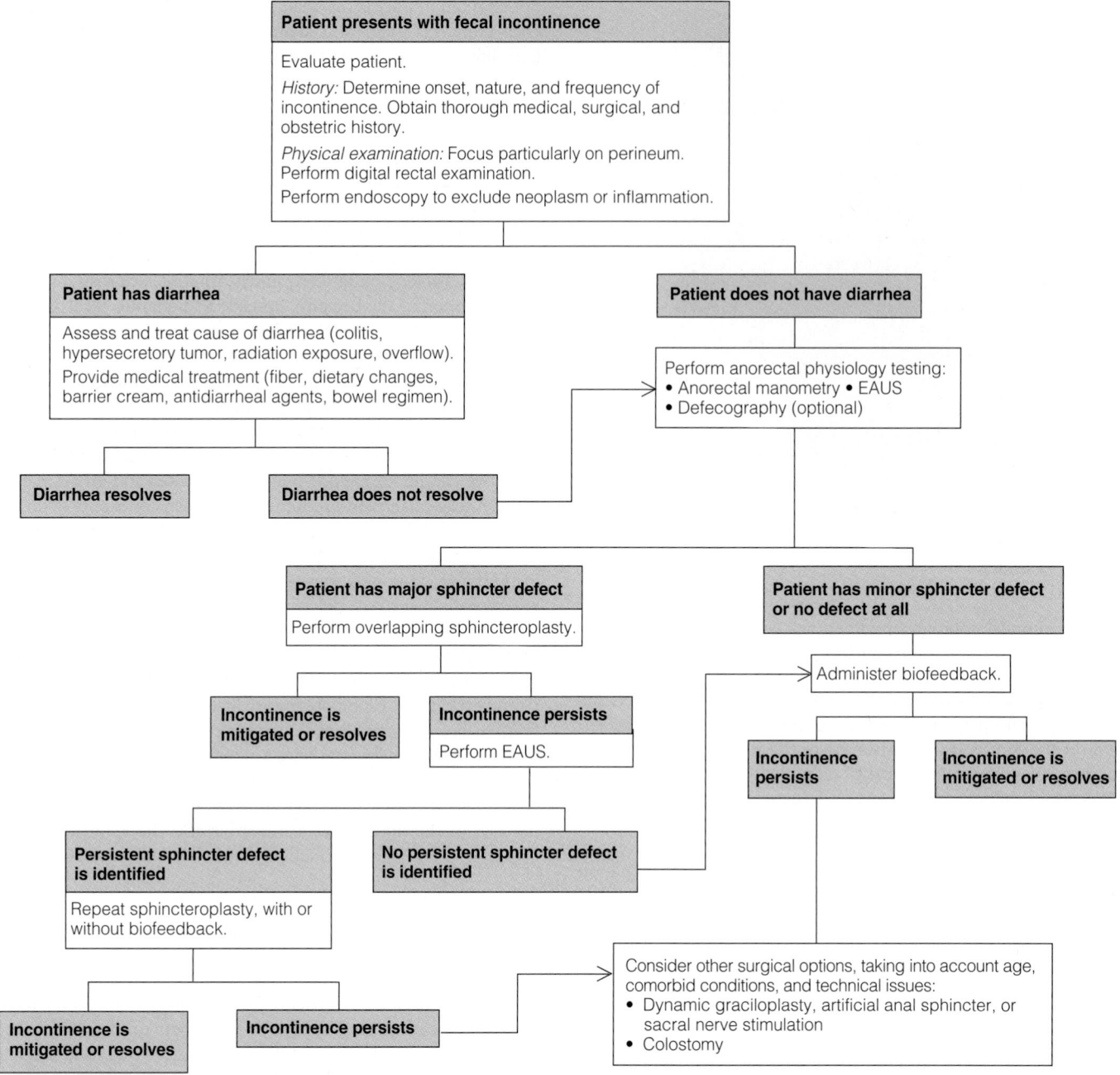

Patient presents with fecal incontinence

Evaluate patient.

History: Determine onset, nature, and frequency of incontinence. Obtain thorough medical, surgical, and obstetric history.

Physical examination: Focus particularly on perineum. Perform digital rectal examination.

Perform endoscopy to exclude neoplasm or inflammation.

Patient has diarrhea

Assess and treat cause of diarrhea (colitis, hypersecretory tumor, radiation exposure, overflow). Provide medical treatment (fiber, dietary changes, barrier cream, antidiarrheal agents, bowel regimen).

Patient does not have diarrhea

Perform anorectal physiology testing:
• Anorectal manometry • EAUS
• Defecography (optional)

Diarrhea resolves

Diarrhea does not resolve

Patient has major sphincter defect

Perform overlapping sphincteroplasty.

Patient has minor sphincter defect or no defect at all

Administer biofeedback.

Incontinence is mitigated or resolves

Incontinence persists

Perform EAUS.

Incontinence persists

Incontinence is mitigated or resolves

Persistent sphincter defect is identified

Repeat sphincteroplasty, with or without biofeedback.

No persistent sphincter defect is identified

Consider other surgical options, taking into account age, comorbid conditions, and technical issues:
• Dynamic graciloplasty, artificial anal sphincter, or sacral nerve stimulation
• Colostomy

Incontinence is mitigated or resolves

Incontinence persists

Figure 5 **Algorithm outlines workup and management of fecal incontinence.**

INVESTIGATIVE STUDIES

Endoscopy should be performed on all incontinent patients to exclude a neoplastic or inflammatory condition. In most cases, flexible sigmoidoscopy is adequate, but if the patient has unexplained diarrhea, bleeding, or changed bowel habits, complete colonoscopy should be performed.

Anorectal testing is indicated for most patients with significant incontinence, particularly if operative treatment is being considered. The most important test is endoanal ultrasonography (EAUS), which yields a highly accurate assessment of sphincter integrity [*see Figure 6*].[35] At some centers, magnetic resonance imaging has become the test of choice for evaluating the pelvic floor. Anal manometry provides a quantitative assessment of resting and squeeze anal pressures, which serve as indicators of internal anal sphincter function and external anal sphincter function,

respectively. EMG may be used to diagnose neuropathic injury of the pelvic floor. Although concentric-needle EMG is the most accurate technique, most centers employ a glove-mounted intra-anal electrode to measure pudendal nerve conduction time (i.e., pudendal nerve terminal motor latency [PNTML]). The practical utility of PNTML testing is debatable, however, and opinions vary regarding the test's ability to predict successful outcomes after anal sphincter repair.[36,37] When the cause of incontinence is uncertain, dynamic imaging of the pelvic floor with defecography or MRI may reveal an occult pathologic state (e.g., occult rectal prolapse).

MANAGEMENT

Conservative Management

Minor incontinence should be treated first with conservative measures. Dietary changes (e.g., avoidance of foods that cause diarrhea or urgency), fiber supplementation, and bowel habit training are helpful for most patients, as is regular use of loperamide. Perianal skin excoriation should be treated with a barrier cream, and seepage may be controlled either with placement of a small cotton wick at the anal orifice or, occasionally, with rectal washouts.

Biofeedback

Biofeedback appears to be an effective therapy for fecal incontinence in a high percentage of patients.[38,39] It is an inherently attractive approach because it is simple, painless, and risk-free. However, the biofeedback literature consists mostly of small, uncontrolled, retrospective studies; a randomized, controlled trial from 2003 found that biofeedback had no advantages over standardized medical and nursing care (i.e., advice) or advice plus sphincter exercises.[40]

Sphincteroplasty

Anal sphincter repair is the most widely accepted operation for fecal incontinence [see Figure 7]. In acute situations (e.g., when an obstetric sphincter injury is recognized), immediate direct repair is generally recommended. Unfortunately, as many as 75% of women have persistent external anal sphincter defects after primary repair, and about 60% have some degree of incontinence.[41] If immediate repair is not attempted, surgical treatment should be delayed at least 3 to 6 months to permit resolution of local tissue inflammation and edema.

For incontinent patients with established sphincter defects, overlapping sphincteroplasty is the procedure of choice. Complete bowel preparation is carried out before the procedure, and prophylactic antibiotics are administered.

Operative technique *Step 1: initial dissection.* The patient is placed in the prone jackknife position, with the buttocks taped apart and a large roll beneath the hips. A curvilinear incision is made over the perineal body, and the anoderm and the anal canal mucosa are raised as an endodermal flap [see Figure 7a]. The vaginal wall is mobilized anteriorly.

Step 2: mobilization of sphincter muscle. It is often easiest first to identify normal muscle laterally in the ischiorectal fossa and then to work medially toward the attenuated tissue in the midline. Lateral dissection is extended back on either side until enough healthy muscle is mobilized to allow overlapping without tension. Generally, however, lateral dissection should not extend beyond the midcoronal line, so as not to risk injury to the inferior rectal branches of the pudendal nerves, which cross the ischiorectal fossae posterolaterally. Dissection is then carried out cranially in the rectovaginal septum to the level of the puborectalis. The muscle is divided through its midline scar, but the scar is preserved to help prevent the sutures from tearing through.

Step 3: overlapping repair. The tapes on the buttocks are then released, and an overlapping sphincter repair is performed with absorbable mattress sutures [see Figures 7b, c]. A snug plication is universally advocated, but unfortunately, there are no generally accepted objective criteria to define exactly what "snug" means in this context. Many authorities advise plication of the puborectalis (so-called levatorplasty) at the cranial aspect of the repair to maximize the length of the anal canal.[42] Others favor individual dissection and repair of the internal and external sphincter muscles, but at present, there is no compelling evidence for the superiority of this approach.

Step 4: restoration of perineal body. The skin incision is closed in a V-Y configuration [see 27 Surface Reconstruction Procedures] to restore the perineal body and maximize the distance between the anus and the vaginal introitus. The wound is left partially open or closed loosely over small Penrose drains to minimize the risk of surgical site infection [see Figure 7d]. A diverting stoma is not generally indicated but may be considered in special situations (e.g., multiple previous failed repairs, Crohn disease, or various chronic diarrheal states).

Outcome evaluation Overlapping sphincteroplasty yields substantial clinical improvement in approximately 65% to 80% of patients.[43,44] Unfortunately, current data indicate that results deteriorate significantly over time.[45-47] When sphincteroplasty fails, repeat EAUS evaluation should be done to confirm that the muscle wrap is intact, and another repair should be performed after 6 to 12 months if a significant defect persists.[48] If the muscle wrap is intact, the functional outcome can often be improved by means of biofeedback.[49]

a

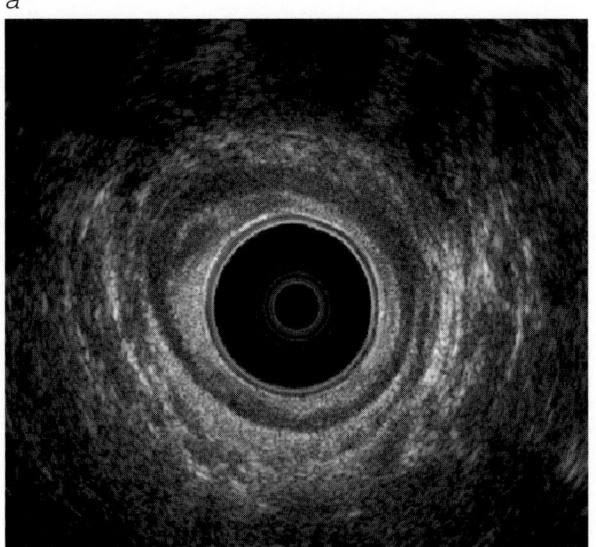

b

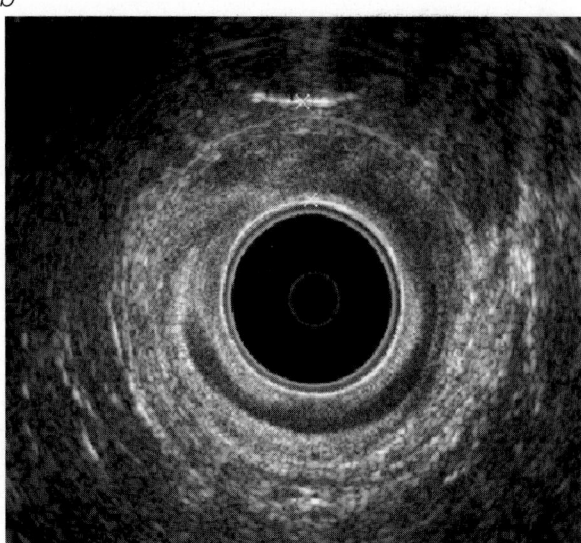

Figure 6 **Endoanal ultrasonograms show (a) a normal anal sphincter and (b) a sphincter defect.**

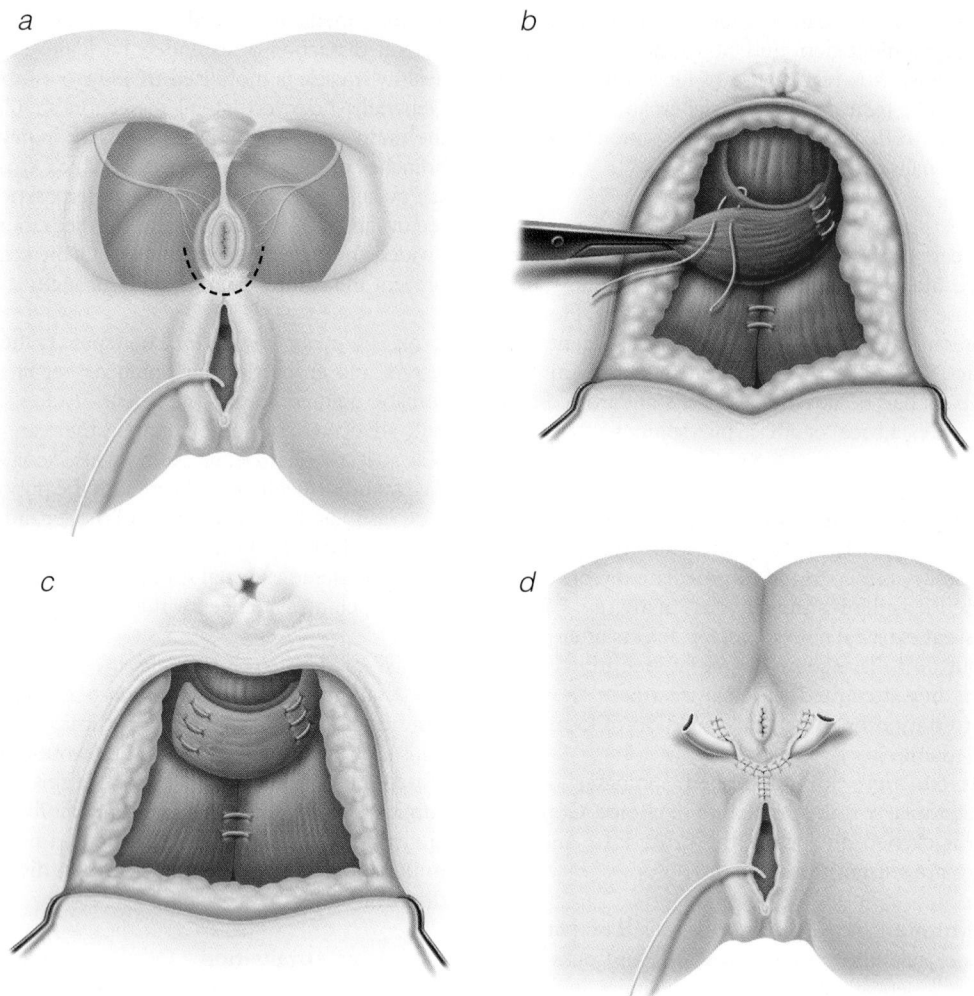

Figure 7 **Sphincteroplasty. (*a*) With the patient in the prone jackknife position, a curvilinear incision is made. Inferior rectal nerves cross the ischiorectal fossa posterolaterally. (*b*) Anterior levatorplasty is performed, and overlapping sphincter repair is then initiated. (*c*) Sphincter repair is completed. (*d*) The incision is closed, with drains in place (optional), and V-Y plasty is done to restore the perineal body.**

Various surgical options are available for patients in whom sphincteroplasty has failed or who are not candidates for the procedure (e.g., those with pudendal neuropathy and an anatomically intact sphincter). A number of these options are investigational, and further study is needed to determine their eventual role (if any) in incontinence therapy.

Postanal Repair

Sir Alan Parks devised the postanal repair in 1975 to treat patients with incontinence and intact sphincters. The initial results were encouraging but tended to deteriorate over time. Consequently, despite evidence of lasting improvement in some patients, this operation is rarely performed today.[50,51]

Injectable Biomaterials

A number of studies have explored the use of injectable biomaterials to provide bulk around the anal sphincter and thereby improve continence. The materials employed have included autologous fat, cross-linked collagen, silicone, and carbon-coated beads.[52,53] Several small, uncontrolled studies have reported promising results, but larger series with longer follow-up times are needed.

Nonstimulated Muscle Transposition

Attempts to restore continence by creating a neosphincter from transposed skeletal muscle date back to the early 20th century. Most such attempts have made use of either the gluteus maximus[54] or the gracilis.[55] Good results have frequently been reported, but many authorities believe that the quality of the resulting continence is poor. One of the main limitations of nonstimulated muscle transposition is that patients are typically unable to maintain voluntary contraction of the transposed muscle over the long term.

Stimulated (Dynamic) Graciloplasty

Successful electrical stimulation of a transposed gracilis by means of an implantable pulse generator was first reported in 1988.[56] Such stimulation has two main effects. First, it converts the fast-twitch, rapidly fatigable gracilis to a slow-twitch, fatigue-resistant muscle that is capable of tonic contraction for prolonged periods.[57] Second, electrical stimulation maintains tonic muscle contraction without the need for continuous voluntary control on the part of the patient. A small number of centers with particular expertise in dynamic graciloplasty and high patient volumes have reported good results with acceptable morbidities[58]; however, three large multicenter trials have reported less encouraging results with prohibitive morbidities.[59-61] In the United States, dynamic graciloplasty is not available, because it has not been approved by the Food and Drug Administration. Elsewhere in the world, the operation can be considered a salvage option at centers with the requisite expertise and experience.

Artificial Anal Sphincter

The artificial anal sphincter is an implantable system consisting of three parts: an inflatable perianal cuff, a pressure-regulating balloon, and a control pump that is implanted in the scrotum or the labia majora [see Figure 8]. Good results have been reported in individual case series,[62] but device infection has been a problem.[63,64] In a large multicenter trial, 46% of patients required surgical revision of the device, including 25% who required revision or explantation because of infection. Of the patients who underwent implantation, 53% had successful results; among those with a functioning device in place, the success rate was 85%.

Sacral Nerve Stimulation

In SNS, an electrode is inserted through a sacral foramen and used to stimulate the sacral nerves. To date, the procedure has been employed mainly in patients with intact anal sphincters (including those with intact repairs). It is available for treatment of fecal incontinence in Europe but has not yet received FDA approval for this indication in the United States.

SNS is generally carried out in two stages. The first stage, peripheral nerve evaluation (PNE), is performed to confirm a muscular response to stimulation of the sacral nerves, to identify the optimal site for stimulation (S2, S3, or S4) and to determine the clinical response to stimulation with an external pulse generator. In most cases, stimulation of the S3 nerves provides the optimal response.

PNE is performed with the patient prone and under local anesthesia, with or without sedation. The sacral foramina are located by means of bony landmarks; S3 is typically about 1.5 cm off the midline at the level of the sciatic notch.[65] Initial testing is performed with an insulated spinal needle and an external pulse generator. Stimulation of each foramen leads to a typical response: S3 causes a bellows-type contraction of the pelvic floor and dorsiflexion of the ipsilateral great toe. Usually, several levels are tested until the optimal site is identified. A temporary pacing wire or a permanent quadripolar lead is then inserted and connected to an external stimulator [see Figure 9].

Patients are asked to provide a baseline continence diary, and a second diary is recorded during the test stimulation period. If continence is significantly improved (e.g., by 50% or more), the second stage of SNS, implantation of a permanent lead (if not already in place) and a pulse generator, is carried out. This second stage is also performed with the patient prone, under local anesthesia, and sedated. The pulse generator is implanted in a subcutaneous pocket on the same side as the stimulating electrode.

Both stages of SNS are performed as outpatient procedures. The pulse generator is activated and its stimulation parameters set by means of a telemetric programmer. If problems (e.g., pain) develop or if the results of stimulation are inadequate, the system can be reprogrammed in a variety of ways: stimulation frequency can be altered, voltage can be increased or decreased, and the configuration of the stimulating electrodes can be modified.

SNS has been shown to be a highly effective treatment for fecal incontinence.[66-68] Unlike dynamic graciloplasty and the artificial anal sphincter, SNS is associated with only minimal morbidity. In a multicenter prospective trial, the frequency of incontinent events dropped from 16.4/wk at baseline to 3.1/wk at 12 months after SNS and 2.0/wk at 24 months. Fecal incontinence–related quality of life was significantly improved.

Because of its high success rate and excellent safety profile, many authorities now consider SNS the salvage procedure of choice for patients with refractory incontinence. If SNS fails, more aggressive treatments may still be tried at a later time.

a

b

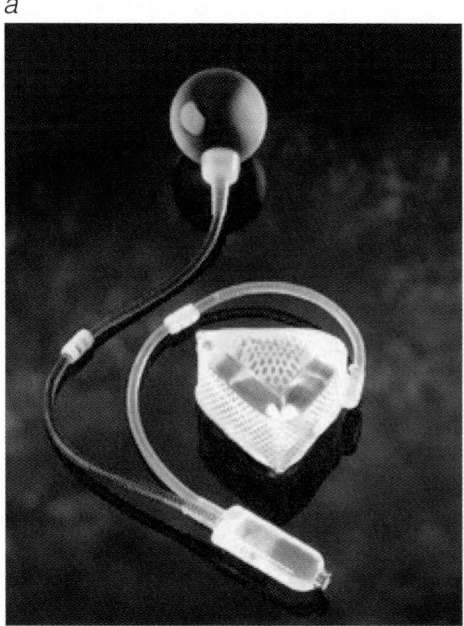
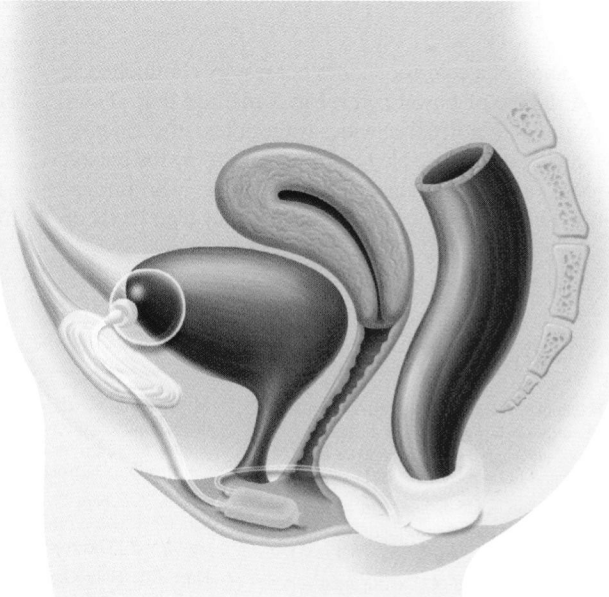

Figure 8 Artificial anal sphincter. (*a*) A three-part implantable system is used (shown is Acticon; American Medical Systems, Minneapolis, Minnesota). (*b*) Depicted is the recommended placement of the artificial sphincter device in the patient.

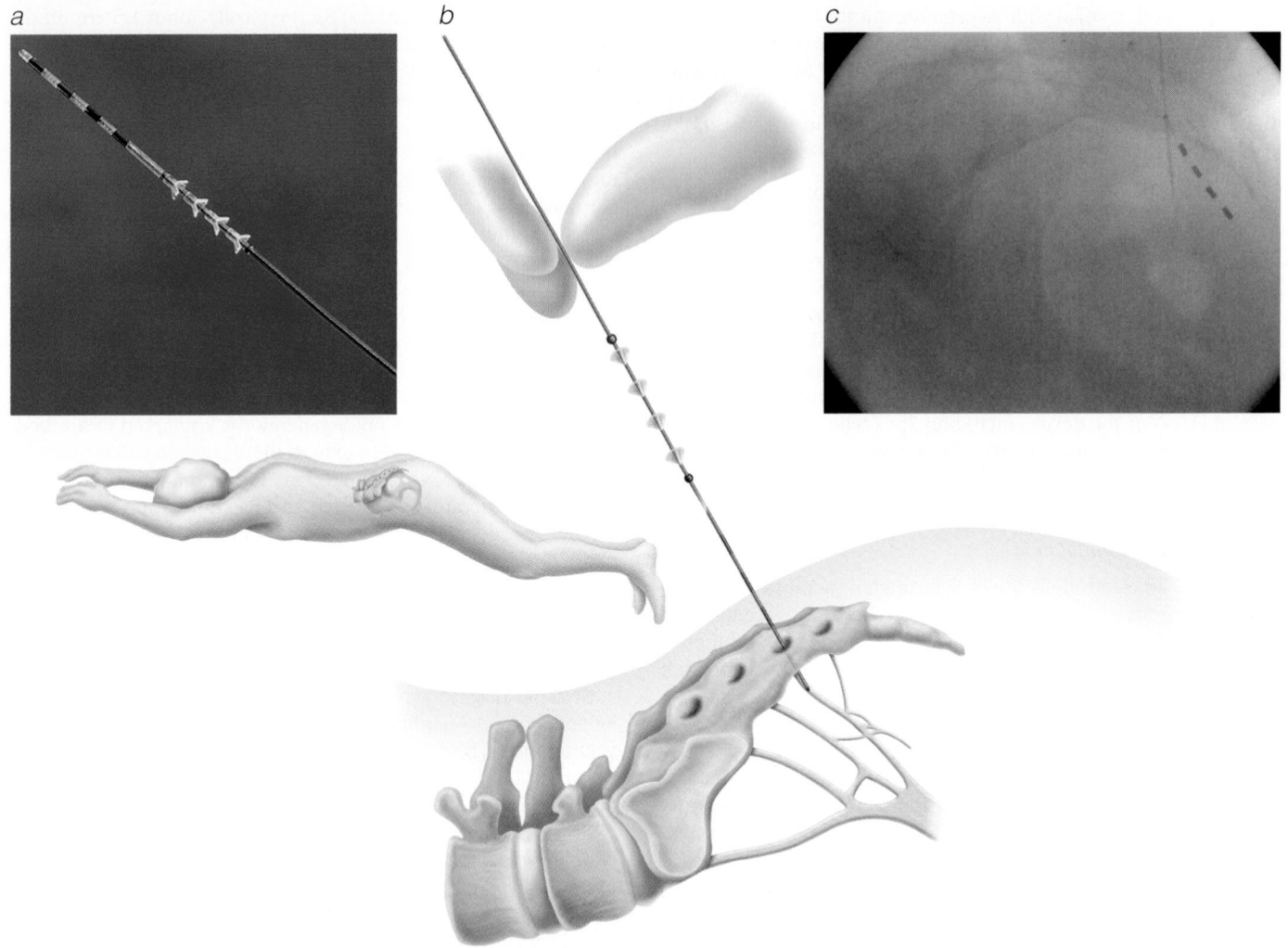

Figure 9   **Sacral nerve stimulation. (*a*) A lead containing four electrodes is used for SNS. (*b*) The sacral foramina are identified; in most cases, S3 is the optimal choice for stimulation. (*c*) Shown is the quadripolar lead in position.**

Colostomy

Although creation of a colostomy does not restore continence, it does provide a degree of bowel control in a manner that allows patients to resume their normal activities without fear of accidents. Surprisingly few data are available regarding colostomy for incontinence; however, one questionnaire study of patients who underwent colostomy for incontinence reported extremely high levels of

patient satisfaction and marked improvements in subjective quality of life.[69] In most cases, a simple end sigmoid colostomy with a Hartmann pouch is the appropriate procedure, and it can often be performed with relatively little operative trauma by using a laparoscopic or minilaparotomy technique. Patients should receive preoperative counseling from an enterostomal therapist, and the optimal stoma site should be marked before the procedure is initiated.

References

1. Walter S, Hallbook O, Gotthard R, et al: A population-based study on bowel habits in a Swedish community: prevalence of faecal incontinence and constipation. Scand J Gastroenterol 37:911, 2002

2. Talley NJ: Definitions, epidemiology, and impact of chronic constipation. Rev Gastroenterol Disord 4(suppl 2):S3, 2004

3. Klaschik E, Nauck F, Ostgathe C: Constipation—modern laxative therapy. Support Care Cancer 11:679, 2003

4. Prather CM: Subtypes of constipation: sorting out the confusion. Rev Gastroenterol Disord 4(suppl 2):S11, 2004

5. Minguez M, Herreros B, Sanchiz V, et al: Predictive value of the balloon expulsion test for excluding the diagnosis of pelvic floor dyssynergia in constipation. Gastroenterology 126:57, 2004

6. Glia A, Lindberg G, Nilsson LH, et al: Constipation assessed on the basis of colorectal physiology. Scand J Gastroenterol 33:1273, 1998

7. Jorge JM, Habr-Gama A, Wexner SD: Clinical applications and techniques of cinedefecography. Am J Surg 182:93, 2001

8. Schiller LR: The therapy of constipation. Aliment Pharmacol Ther 15:749, 2001

9. McRorie JW, Daggy BP, Morel JG, et al: Psyllium

is superior to docusate sodium for treatment of chronic constipation. Aliment Pharmacol Ther 12:491, 1998

10. DiPalma JA: Current treatment options for chronic constipation. Rev Gastroenterol Disord 4(suppl 2):S34, 2004

11. Muller-Lissner SA, Fumagalli I, Bardhan KD, et al: Tegaserod, a 5-HT(4) receptor partial agonist, relieves symptoms in irritable bowel syndrome patients with abdominal pain, bloating and constipation. Aliment Pharmacol Ther 15:1655, 2001

12. Lacy BE: Irritable bowel syndrome: a primer on management. Rev Gastroenterol Disord 3(suppl 3):S32, 2003

13. Rome II Diagnostic Criteria for the Functional Gastrointestinal Disorders. Appendix A, Diagnostic Criteria for Functional Gastrointestinal Disorders. http://www.romecriteria.org/documents/Rome_II_App_A.pdf, accessed October 21, 2004

14. Cheung O, Wald A: Review article: the management of pelvic floor disorders. Aliment Pharmacol Ther 19:481, 2004

15. Bassotti G, Chistolini F, Sietchiping-Nzepa F, et al: Biofeedback for pelvic floor dysfunction in constipation. BMJ 328:393, 2004

16. Maria G, Brisinda G, Bentivoglio AR, et al: Botulinum toxin in the treatment of outlet obstruction constipation caused by puborectalis syndrome. Dis Colon Rectum 43:376, 2000

17. Shafik A, El-Sibai O: Botulin toxin in the treatment of nonrelaxing puborectalis syndrome. Dig Surg 15:347, 1998

18. Chiarioni G, Chistolini F, Menegotti M, et al: One-year follow-up study on the effects of electrogalvanic stimulation in chronic idiopathic constipation with pelvic floor dyssynergia. Dis Colon Rectum 47:346, 2004

19. Kenefick NJ, Nicholls RJ, Cohen RG, et al: Permanent sacral nerve stimulation for treatment of idiopathic constipation. Br J Surg 89:882, 2002

20. Lembo A, Camilleri M: Chronic constipation. N Engl J Med 349:1360, 2003

21. Crowell MD: Pathogenesis of slow transit and pelvic floor dysfunction: from bench to bedside. Rev Gastroenterol Disord 4(suppl 2):S17, 2004

22. Locke GR 3rd, Pemberton JH, Phillips SF: AGA technical review on constipation. American Gastroenterological Association. Gastroenterology 119:1766, 2000

23. Vasilevsky CA, Nemer FD, Balcos EG, et al: Is subtotal colectomy a viable option in the management of chronic constipation? Dis Colon Rectum 31:679, 1988

24. Platell C, Scache D, Mumme G, et al: A long-term follow-up of patients undergoing colectomy for chronic idiopathic constipation. Aust N Z J Surg 66:525, 1996

25. FitzHarris GP, Garcia-Aguilar J, Parker SC, et al: Quality of life after subtotal colectomy for slow-transit constipation: both quality and quantity count. Dis Colon Rectum 46:433, 2003

26. Nyam DC, Pemberton JH, Ilstrup DM, et al: Long-term results of surgery for chronic constipation. Dis Colon Rectum 40:273, 1997

27. Bernini A, Madoff RD, Lowry AC, et al: Should patients with combined colonic inertia and nonrelaxing pelvic floor undergo subtotal colectomy? Dis Colon Rectum 41:1363, 1998

28. Nelson R, Furner S, Jesudason V: Fecal incontinence in Wisconsin nursing homes: prevalence and associations. Dis Colon Rectum 41:1226, 1998

29. Johanson JF, Lafferty J: Epidemiology of fecal incontinence: the silent affliction. Am J Gastroenterol 91:33, 1996

30. Snooks SJ, Swash M, Setchell M, et al: Injury to innervation of pelvic floor sphincter musculature. Lancet 2:546, 1984

31. Wrenn K: Fecal impaction. N Engl J Med 321:658, 1989

32. Garcia-Aguilar J, Belmonte C, Wong WD, et al: Open vs. closed sphincterotomy for chronic anal fissure: long-term results. Dis Colon Rectum 39:440, 1996

33. Garcia-Aguilar J, Belmonte C, Wong WD, et al: Anal fistula surgery: factors associated with recurrence and incontinence. Dis Colon Rectum 39:723, 1996

34. MacIntyre IM, Balfour TW: Results of the Lord non-operative treatment for haemorrhoids. Lancet 1:1094, 1972

35. Sultan AH, Kamm MA, Talbot IC, et al: Anal endosonography for identifying external sphincter defects confirmed histologically. Br J Surg 81:463, 1994

36. Gilliland R, Altomare DF, Moreira H Jr, et al: Pudendal neuropathy is predictive of failure following anterior overlapping sphincteroplasty. Dis Colon Rectum 41:1516, 1998

37. Buie WD, Lowry AC, Rothenberger DA, et al: Clinical rather than laboratory assessment predicts continence after anterior sphincteroplasty. Dis Colon Rectum 44:1255, 2001

38. Heymen S, Jones KR, Ringel Y, et al: Biofeedback treatment of fecal incontinence: a critical review. Dis Colon Rectum 44:728, 2001

39. Norton C, Kamm MA: Anal sphincter biofeedback and pelvic floor exercises for faecal incontinence in adults—a systematic review. Aliment Pharmacol Ther 15:1147, 2001

40. Norton C, Chelvanayagam S, Wilson-Barnett J, et al: Randomized controlled trial of biofeedback for fecal incontinence. Gastroenterology 125:1320, 2003

41. Pinta TM, Kylanpaa ML, Salmi TK, et al: Primary sphincter repair: are the results of the operation good enough? Dis Colon Rectum 47:18, 2004

42. Pemberton JH: Sphincter and pelvic floor reconstruction. Atlas of Colorectal Surgery. Keighley MR, Pemberton JH, Fazio VW, et al, Eds. Churchill Livingstone, New York, 1996, p 131

43. Engel AF, Kamm MA, Sultan AH, et al: Anterior anal sphincter repair in patients with obstetric trauma. Br J Surg 81:1231, 1994

44. Karoui S, Leroi AM, Koning E, et al: Results of sphincteroplasty in 86 patients with anal incontinence. Dis Colon Rectum 43:813, 2000

45. Halverson AL, Hull TL: Long-term outcome of overlapping anal sphincter repair. Dis Colon Rectum 45:345, 2002

46. Malouf AJ, Norton CS, Engel AF, et al: Long-term results of overlapping anterior anal-sphincter repair for obstetric trauma. Lancet 355:260, 2000

47. Bravo Gutierrez A, Madoff RD, Lowry AC, et al: Long-term results of anterior sphincteroplasty. Dis Colon Rectum 47:727, 2004

48. Pinedo G, Vaizey CJ, Nicholls RJ, et al: Results of repeat anal sphincter repair. Br J Surg 86:66, 1999

49. Jensen LL, Lowry AC: Biofeedback improves functional outcome after sphincteroplasty. Dis Colon Rectum 40:197, 1997

50. Setti Carraro P, Kamm MA, Nicholls RJ: Long-term results of postanal repair for neurogenic faecal incontinence. Br J Surg 81:140, 1994

51. van Tets WF, Kuijpers JH: Pelvic floor procedures produce no consistent changes in anatomy or physiology. Dis Colon Rectum 41:365, 1998

52. Kumar D, Benson MJ, Bland JE: Glutaraldehyde cross-linked collagen in the treatment of faecal incontinence. Br J Surg 85:978, 1998

53. Kenefick NJ, Vaizey CJ, Malouf AJ, et al: Injectable silicone biomaterial for faecal incontinence due to internal anal sphincter dysfunction. Gut 51:225, 2002

54. Devesa JM, Madrid JM, Gallego BR, et al: Bilateral gluteoplasty for fecal incontinence. Dis Colon Rectum 40:883, 1997

55. Faucheron JL, Hannoun L, Thome C, et al: Is fecal continence improved by nonstimulated gracilis muscle transposition? Dis Colon Rectum 37:979, 1994

56. Baeten C, Spaans F, Fluks A: An implanted neuromuscular stimulator for fecal continence following previously implanted gracilis muscle: report of a case. Dis Colon Rectum 31:134, 1988

57. Konsten J, Baeten CGMI, Havenith MG, et al: Morphology of dynamic graciloplasty compared with the anal sphincter. Dis Colon Rectum 36:559, 1993

58. Rongen MJ, Uludag O, El Naggar K, et al: Long-term follow-up of dynamic graciloplasty for fecal incontinence. Dis Colon Rectum 46:716, 2003

59. Mander BJ, Wexner SD, Williams NS, et al: Preliminary results of a multicentre trial of the electrically stimulated gracilis neoanal sphincter. Br J Surg 86:1543, 1999

60. Baeten CG, Bailey HR, Bakka A, et al: Safety and efficacy of dynamic graciloplasty for fecal incontinence: report of a prospective, multicenter trial. Dynamic Graciloplasty Therapy Study Group. Dis Colon Rectum 43:743, 2000

61. Madoff RD, Rosen HR, Baeten CG, et al: Safety and efficacy of dynamic muscle plasty for anal incontinence: lessons from a prospective, multicenter trial. Gastroenterology 116:549, 1999

62. Lehur PA, Roig JV, Duinslaeger M: Artificial anal sphincter: prospective clinical and manometric evaluation. Dis Colon Rectum 43:1100, 2000

63. Parker SC, Spencer MP, Madoff RD, et al: Artificial bowel sphincter: long-term experience at a single institution. Dis Colon Rectum 46:722, 2003

64. Malouf AJ, Vaizey CJ, Kamm MA, et al: Reassessing artificial bowel sphincters. Lancet 355:2219, 2000

65. Siegel SW: Management of voiding dysfunction with an implantable neuroprosthesis. Urol Clin North Am 19:163, 1992

66. Matzel KE, Stadelmaier U, Hohenfellner M, et al: Chronic sacral spinal nerve stimulation for fecal incontinence: long-term results with foramen and cuff electrodes. Dis Colon Rectum 44:59, 2001

67. Rosen HR, Urbarz C, Holzer B, et al: Sacral nerve stimulation as a treatment for fecal incontinence. Gastroenterology 121:536, 2001

68. Kenefick NJ, Vaizey CJ, Cohen RC, et al: Medium-term results of permanent sacral nerve stimulation for faecal incontinence. Br J Surg 89:896, 2002

69. Norton C: Patients' views of a colostomy for faecal incontinence. Neurourol Urodyn 22:403, 2003

Acknowledgment

Figures 2, 3, 7, 8, and 9   Alice Y. Chen.

59 BENIGN RECTAL, ANAL, AND PERINEAL PROBLEMS

David E. Beck, M.D., F.A.C.S., F.A.S.C.R.S.

Approach to Benign Rectal, Anal, and Perineal Problems

In this chapter, I briefly review the evaluation and management of common benign conditions affecting the rectum, the anus, and the perineum: hemorrhoidal disease, anal

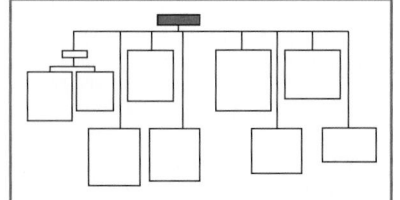

fissures, anorectal abscesses and fistulas, pilonidal disease, hidradenitis suppurativa, pruritus ani, and solitary rectal ulcer syndrome (SRUS). For proper diagnosis and treatment of these conditions, an understanding of the relevant anatomy is essential [*see Figure 1*].[1]

The dentate line divides the rectal mucosa, which is generally insensate and is lined with columnar mucosa, from the anoderm below it, which is highly sensitive (because of somatic innervation by the inferior hemorrhoidal nerve) and is lined with modified squamous mucosa. The anal canal is surrounded by two muscles. The internal anal sphincter, innervated by the autonomic nervous system, maintains resting anal tone and is under involuntary control. The external sphincter, innervated by somatic nerve fibers, generates the voluntary anal squeeze and plays the key role in maintaining anal continence. The area surrounding the anorectum is divided into four spaces—perianal, ischioanal, supralevator, and intersphincteric (intermuscular)—familiarity with which is particularly important in the evaluation of perirectal abscesses and fistulas.

Hemorrhoids

Hemorrhoids are fibromuscular cushions that line the anal canal. They are classically found in three locations: right anterior, right posterior,

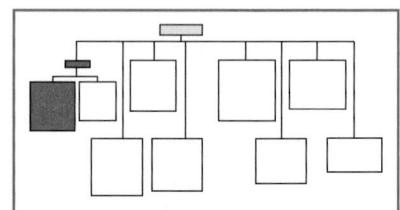

and left lateral.[2,3] On occasion, smaller secondary cushions may be found lying between these main cushions. Contrary to popular belief, hemorrhoids are not related to the superior hemorrhoidal artery and vein, to the portal vein, or to portal hypertension.[4] In fact, hemorrhoids are part of the normal anal anatomy. Their engorgement during straining or performance of the Valsalva maneuver is a component of the normal mechanism of fecal continence: it most likely completes the occlusion of the anal canal and prevents stool loss associated with nondefecatory straining. In the medical literature, however, the term hemorrhoid is used almost exclusively to refer to pathologic hemorrhoids, and I follow this usage throughout the chapter.

Hemorrhoids are broadly classified as either internal or external. Internal hemorrhoids are found proximal to the dentate line, whereas external hemorrhoids occur distally [*see Figure 2*]. External hemorrhoids are redundant folds of perianal skin that generally derive from previous anal swelling; they remain asymptomatic unless they are thrombosed and are treated entirely differently from internal hemorrhoids.

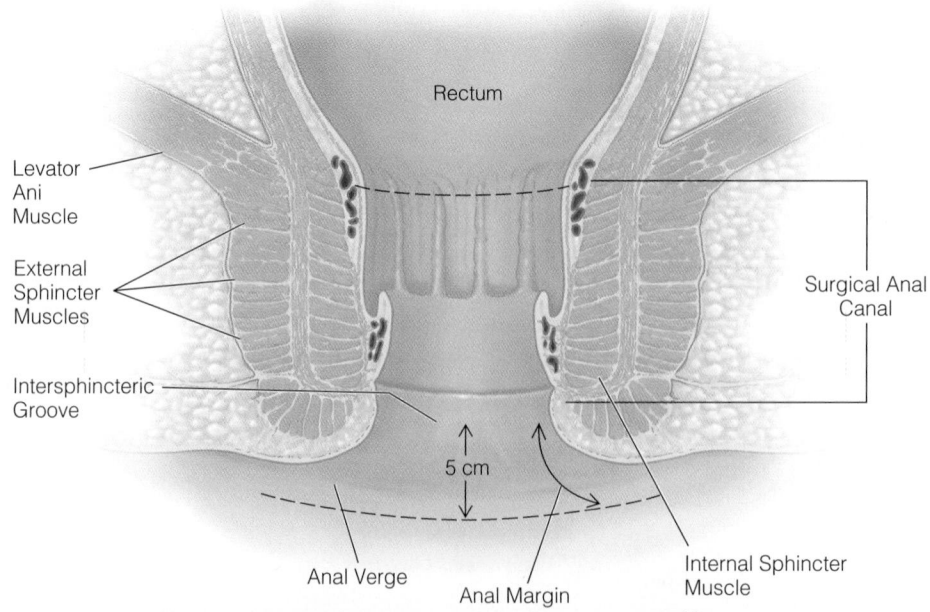

Figure 1 Depicted is the anatomy of the anal canal.[35]

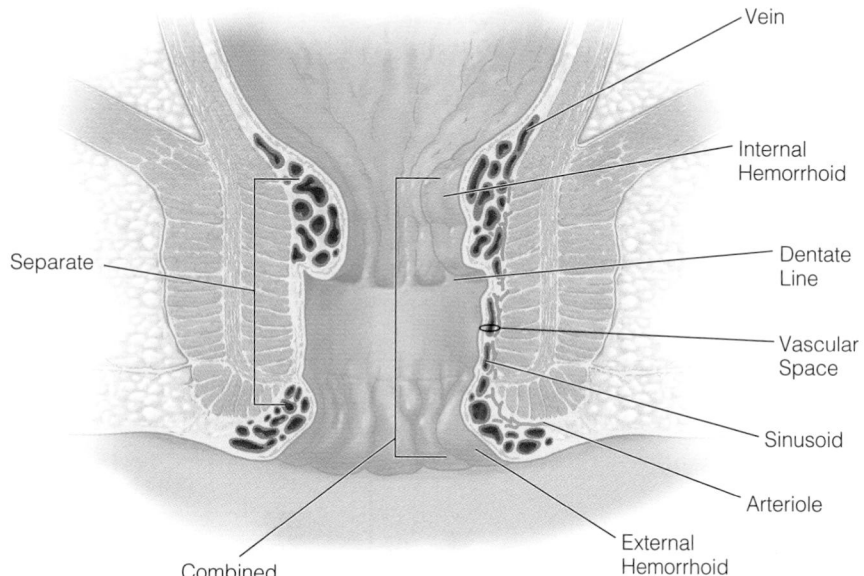

Figure 2 **External and internal hemorrhoids may occur either separately (left) or in combination (right).**

INTERNAL

Clinical Evaluation

Internal hemorrhoidal disease is manifested by two main symptoms: painless bleeding and protrusion.[4] Pain is rare because internal hemorrhoids originate above the dentate line in the insensate rectal mucosa. The most popular etiologic theory states that hemorrhoids result from chronic straining at defecation (with upright posture and heavy lifting possibly playing contributing roles as well). This straining not only causes hemorrhoidal engorgement but also generates forces that reduce the attachment between the hemorrhoids and the anal muscular wall. Continued straining causes further engorgement and bleeding, as well as hemorrhoidal prolapse. Internal hemorrhoids are classified into four grades on the basis of clinical findings and symptoms. Grade 1 represents bleeding without prolapse; grade 2, prolapse that spontaneously reduces; grade 3, prolapse necessitating manual reduction; and grade 4, irreducible prolapse.

Questioning often reveals a long history of constipation and straining at defecation. Many patients with internal hemorrhoids are extensive bathroom readers, spending many hours in the bathroom each week. Symptoms start with painless bleeding and may progress to anal protrusion. The physical examination begins with visual inspection and may reveal prolapsing hemorrhoidal tissue appearing as a rosette of three distinct pink-purple hemorrhoidal groups. Hemorrhoidal prolapse must be distinguished from true full-thickness rectal prolapse. When hemorrhoidal prolapse is not present, anoscopy typically reveals redundant anorectal mucosa just proximal to the dentate line in the classic locations.

Surgical treatment of hemorrhoids in a patient whose main disease process is Crohn disease, a pelvic floor abnormality, or fissure disease invariably yields imperfect results. It is especially important to recognize the anal pain and spasm associated with anal fissure because in patients with this problem, excision of the hemorrhoids without concomitant management of the fissure leads to increased postoperative pain and poor wound healing. Not uncommonly, patients are treated for hemorrhoids when the true primary condition is fissure disease.

Management

Treatment of symptomatic internal hemorrhoids ranges from simple reassurance to operative hemorrhoid excision, depending on hemorrhoid grade [*see Table 1*]. Therapies may be classified into three categories: (1) diet and lifestyle modifications, (2) nonoperative and office procedures, and (3) operative hemorrhoidectomies.

Diet and lifestyle modifications For all patients with grade 1 or 2 hemorrhoids and most patients with grade 3 hemorrhoids, treatment should begin with efforts to correct constipation. Recommendations should include a high-fiber diet, liberal water intake (six to eight 8 oz glasses of water daily), and fiber supplements (e.g., psyllium, methylcellulose, calcium polycarbophil, and gum). Sitz baths are recommended for their soothing effect and their ability to relax the anal sphincter muscles. Topical creams may reduce some of the associated symptoms, though they do not affect the hemorrhoids themselves. Suppositories are not helpful, because they deliver medication to the rectum, not the anus. Patients are instructed to avoid prolonged trips to the bathroom and to read in the bathroom only when sitting atop the toilet lid.

Table 1 Treatment Alternatives for Hemorrhoids

Treatment	Internal Hemorrhoids Grade				External Hemorrhoids
	1	2	3	4	
Diet modification	X				
Sclerotherapy	X	X			
Infrared coagulation	X	X	(X)		
Rubber band ligation	(X)	X	X		
Stapled hemorrhoidopexy (PPH)		X	X		
Excisional hemorrhoidectomy		(X)	X	X	X

(X)—selected patients   PPH—procedure for prolapsing hemorrhoids

Approach to Benign Rectal, Anal, and Perineal Problems

Patient has benign rectal, anal, or perineal lesion

Hemorrhoids

Internal

Clinical manifestations: painless bleeding, protrusion. Lesions are classified into four grades.

Management: depending on hemorrhoid grade, may include
- Diet and lifestyle modifications.
- Nonoperative and office procedures (rubber band ligation, infrared coagulation, sclerotherapy).
- Operative hemorrhoidectomy (open, closed, PPH).

External

Clinical manifestations: none unless thrombosed, in which case constant pain of acute onset is felt.

Management: none unless thrombosed. In first 24–72 hr, excision is warranted; after 72 hr, expectant treatment suffices.

Anorectal abscess

Lesions are classified as perianal, ischiorectal, supralevator, or intersphincteric.

Clinical manifestations: constant perianal pain, sometimes with fever, chills, or malaise; purulent discharge occasionally occurs, and systemic toxicity rarely develops. Visual inspection usually suffices for diagnosis.

Management: surgical drainage, usually in office but sometimes in OR.

Anal fissure

Clinical manifestations: pain, minor bright-red bleeding, split in anoderm (usually in midline). Chronic fissure is signaled by hypertrophic anal papilla, sentinel skin tag, and exposed internal sphincter muscle. Visual inspection suffices for diagnosis.

Management: for acute fissures, nonoperative measures (e.g., fiber, stool softeners); for chronic fissures, if such nonoperative measures fail, lateral internal sphincterotomy (alternatives: topical NTG, topical nifedipine, topical diltiazem, botulinum toxin injection).

Fistula in ano

Lesions are classified as intersphincteric, transsphincteric, suprasphincteric, or extrasphincteric.

Clinical manifestations: small opening in perianal skin, surrounding induration, ongoing drainage.

Management: surgical unroofing of entire fistula tract (fistulotomy), except in select cases (e.g., anterior fistulas in women) in which partial unroofing is recommended; closure of internal opening with advancement flap is an option.

Pilonidal disease

Clinical manifestations:
- Acute abscess (nearly all patients)
- Pilonidal sinus after resolution of abscess (many patients)
- Chronic or recurrent disease after treatment (few patients)

Management:
- Abscess: drainage
- Sinus: closed techniques; unroofing with healing by granulation, wide and deep excision of sinus alone, or excision and primary closure; nonoperative approach is an option
- Persistent, nonhealing disease: wide excision with split-thickness graft, cleft closure, or excision with flap closure

Pruritus ani

Clinical manifestations: uneasiness or itching around anus, reddened or thickened perianal skin (sometimes with excoriation or ulceration, occasionally with large weeping ulcer).

Management: identification and treatment of precipitating condition if possible; establishment and maintenance of healthy, clean, and dry perianal skin (washing, dietary changes, and topical hydrocortisone or antifungal if indicated). If standard measures fail, evaluation for fungal or neoplastic cause is indicated.

Hidradenitis suppurativa

Clinical manifestations: chronic inflammation of apocrine glands, pain, chronically draining wounds and sinus tracts.

Management: surgical. Wide excision with secondary granulation is most definitive therapy; local excision may be particularly suitable for perianal disease; incision and drainage or unroofing of sinus may be used for early acute disease.

Solitary rectal ulcer syndrome

Clinical manifestations: bleeding, pain, mucous discharge, difficult evacuation.

Management: conservative (high-fiber diet, lifestyle changes, biofeedback). Pharmacologic therapy may be considered. In select patients, localized resection may be considered if symptoms persist.

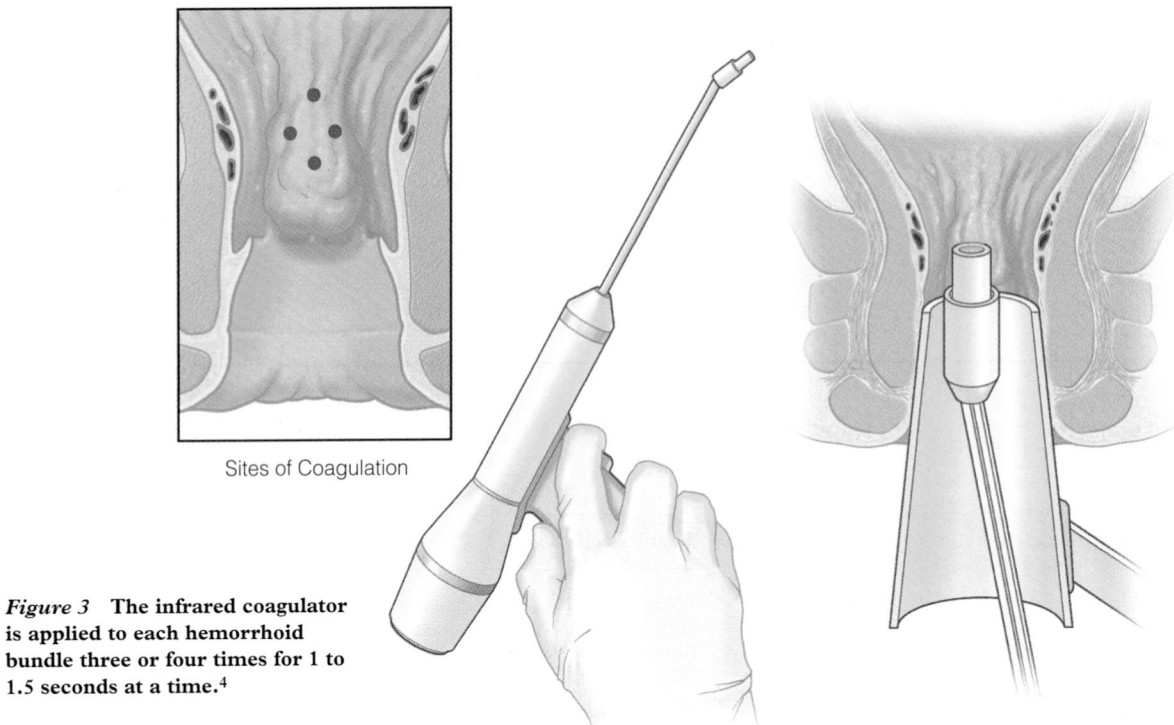

Sites of Coagulation

Figure 3 **The infrared coagulator is applied to each hemorrhoid bundle three or four times for 1 to 1.5 seconds at a time.**[4]

Nonoperative and office procedures If initial diet and lifestyle modifications are not effective, there are a number of nonoperative therapies that may be tried next. At present, the main recommended options are rubber band ligation, infrared photocoagulation, and sclerotherapy.

Rubber band ligation. Ligation of hemorrhoids with elastic bands is the method most commonly used in the outpatient setting [*see 79 Anal Procedures for Benign Disease*].[5] It is successful in two thirds to three quarters of all patients with grade 1 or 2 hemorrhoids.[2] Repeated banding may be necessary to resolve all symptoms. On rare occasions, patients do not respond to banding at all or cannot tolerate it. Some of these patients will respond to infrared coagulation; others may require formal hemorrhoidectomy.

Complications of rubber band ligation include bleeding, pain, thrombosis, and life-threatening perineal sepsis.[5,6] The cardinal signs of perineal sepsis are significant pain, fever, and difficult urination. Patients in whom any of these symptoms develop require urgent evaluation and treatment with broad-spectrum antibiotics, coupled with selective debridement of any necrotic anal tissue.

Infrared coagulation. The infrared coagulator generates infrared radiation, which coagulates tissue protein and evaporates water from cells.[7] The extent of the tissue destruction depends on the intensity and duration of the application. An anoscopic examination is performed, and the infrared coagulator is applied to the apex of each hemorrhoid at the top of the anal canal [*see Figure 3*]. Each hemorrhoid bundle receives three to four applications, each lasting 1 to 1.5 seconds.

The infrared coagulator was designed to decrease blood flow to the region. It is not particularly effective for treating large amounts of prolapsing tissue; it is most useful for treating grade 1 and small grade 2 hemorrhoids. Overall, it is slightly less painful than rubber banding. Infrared coagulation is especially beneficial for patients in whom rubber band ligation fails because of pain or who have symptomatic internal hemorrhoids that are too small to band.

Sclerotherapy. Sclerotherapy was once commonly employed to treat internal hemorrhoids, but with the advent of rubber band ligation, it has become less popular. The technique involves injection of a sclerosant into the anorectal submucosa to decrease vascularity and increase fibrosis. The agents used include phenol in oil, sodium morrhuate, and quinine urea.[2] Hemorrhoids are identified via anoscopy, and the sclerosant is infiltrated at the apex of the hemorrhoid (at the proximal anal rectal ring). After injection, patients occasionally experience a dull ache lasting 24 to 48 hours, but substantial bleeding and other significant complications are uncommon. Misplacement of the sclerosant, resulting in significant perianal infection and fibrosis, has been reported, albeit rarely.

Comparison of methods. A meta-analysis comparing a variety of modalities used to treat hemorrhoids found that rubber band ligation was superior to sclerotherapy for grade 1 through grade 3 hemorrhoids.[8] Patients who were treated with sclerotherapy or infrared coagulation were more likely to require further treatment than those treated with rubber band ligation. The authors concluded that hemorrhoidectomy should be reserved for patients in whom rubber band ligation or infrared coagulation fails or who have associated external hemorrhoidal disease.

Hemorrhoidectomies Various hemorrhoidectomies have been developed throughout the years. Although they differ with respect to detail, they incorporate similar basic principles—namely, reduction of blood flow to the anorectal ring, removal of redundant hemorrhoidal tissue, and fixation of redundant mucosa and anoderm.[9]

Open and closed hemorrhoidectomy. In the United Kingdom, open (Milligan and Morgan) hemorrhoidectomy, in which hemorrhoids are ligated and excised with the wound left open, is the most commonly performed operative excision procedure. In the United States, closed (Ferguson) hemorrhoidectomy is most commonly performed[10]; this procedure is described more fully elsewhere [*see 79 Anal Procedures for Benign Disease*]. With either type of hemorrhoidectomy, one, two, or three hemorrhoidal bundles may be excised. In performing a closed hemorrhoidectomy, it is essential to excise as little of the anoderm as possible: if large amounts are excised, closing the anal wounds or secondary healing can result in significant postoperative pain and perhaps even long-term anal stenosis.

Stapled hemorrhoidectomy. Stapled hemorrhoidectomy or anoplasty (commonly known as the procedure for prolapsing hemorrhoids [PPH]) is increasingly being performed as an alternative to standard open or closed hemorrhoidectomy with the aim of reducing the pain associated with traditional surgical techniques.[9] PPH involves transanal circular stapling of redundant anorectal mucosa with a modified circular stapling instrument (PPH-01, Ethicon Endo-Surgery Inc., Cincinnati, Ohio).[11] Because no incisions are made in the somatically innervated, highly sensitive anoderm, there should, theoretically, be significantly less postoperative pain.

Randomized, prospective trials comparing PPH with various operative hemorrhoidectomies and other therapies found it to be associated with significantly less pain then conventional treatments and to have similar complication rates.[9] PPH may, however, have a greater potential for disastrous complications (e.g., rectovaginal or rectourethral fistula from inclusion of too much tissue within the purse-string suture, perforation caused by placing the purse-string too high, and incontinence caused by placing the purse-string too low or too deep). Bleeding also remains a problem with PPH, and leaks have been reported. Finally, stapled hemorrhoidectomy has not yet been adequately compared with office procedures for grade 1 and 2 hemorrhoids and thus should not replace these techniques for treatment of minimally symptomatic hemorrhoidal disease.

EXTERNAL

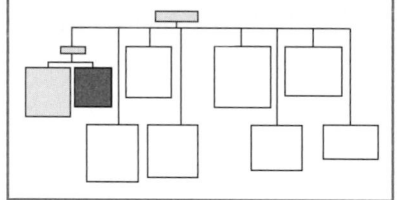

Clinical Evaluation

External hemorrhoids are asymptomatic except when secondary thrombosis occurs. Thrombosis may result from defecatory straining or extreme physical activity, or it may be a random event.[1] Patients present with constant anal pain of acute onset and often report feeling the sensation of sitting on a tender marble. Physical examination identifies the external thrombosis as a purple mass at the anal verge.

Management

Treatment depends on the patient's symptoms [*see Figure 4*].[4] In the first 24 to 72 hours after the onset of thrombosis, pain increases, and excision is warranted. After 72 hours, pain generally diminishes, and expectant treatment is all that is necessary. Patients should be advised that some drainage may occur. If operative treatment is chosen, the entire thrombosed hemorrhoid is excised with the patient under local anesthesia. Incision and drainage of the clot are avoided because they typically lead to rethrombosis and exacerbation of symptoms.

Anal Fissure

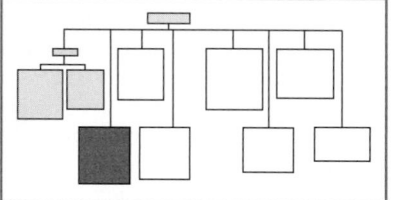

Anal fissures are tears or splits in the anoderm just distal to the dentate line.[12] They are characterized as acute or chronic. Generally, acute fis-

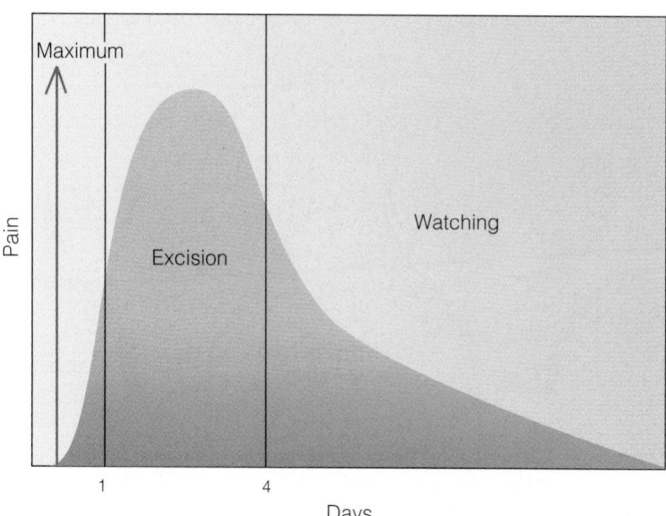

Figure 4 **Depicted is the timing of excision of thrombosed external hemorrhoids.**[36]

sures are caused by the mechanical force generated by the passage of a large, hard bowel movement through an anal canal that is too small to accommodate it safely and easily (though they can also be caused by diarrhea). These mechanical forces usually cause a split to occur in the posterior midline: 90% of the fissures in females and 99% of those in males are located posteriorly. Either decreased local blood flow or increased mechanical stress may account for the propensity of these fissures to occur in this location.[13] Repeated injury (e.g., from hard or watery bowel movements) may result in the development of a chronic fissure.

CLINICAL EVALUATION

Symptoms associated with anal fissures include anal pain and bright-red rectal bleeding after bowel movements. The pain is usually described as a knifelike or tearing sensation, and the associated anal sphincter spasm may persist for several hours after each bowel movement. The bleeding is usually minor and is seen mainly on the toilet paper.

Physical examination is difficult because the patient has an extremely tender anus and is fearful of further pain. Often, visual inspection with gentle eversion of the anoderm in the posterior midline is all that is required. Physical findings include a split in the anoderm approximately 1 cm long in the posterior midline just distal to the dentate line. In chronic fissures, the classic triad may be present: hypertrophy of the anal papilla, an anal fissure, and a sentinel skin tag [*see Figure 5*]. Once an anal fissure has been diagnosed, further examination is very painful, unrewarding, and unnecessary; more extensive investigations can be performed after the fissure has healed.

Multiple fissures are unusual, as are fissures that occur away from the anterior or posterior midline; either should raise suspicions that other problems may be present [*see Figure 6*].

MANAGEMENT

Acute fissures usually have been present for less than 4 to 6 weeks. As a rule, they are treated nonoperatively: fiber supplements, stool softeners, and generous intake of water, along with sitz baths and local anesthetic ointments, rapidly alleviate symptoms and usually bring about complete healing. Anal suppositories are avoided both because they are painful and because they rest in the rectum rather than the anal canal.

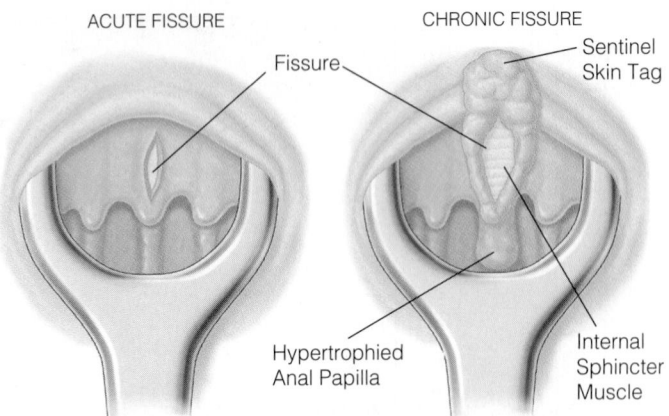

ACUTE FISSURE

CHRONIC FISSURE

Fissure

Sentinel
Skin Tag

Hypertrophied
Anal Papilla

Internal
Sphincter
Muscle

Figure 5 **Chronic anal fissures, as opposed to acute fissures, are characterized by hypertrophy of the anal papilla, a sentinel skin tag, rolled skin edges, and exposed internal anal sphincter muscle.**

Chronic fissures have been present for periods longer than 4 to 6 weeks. As noted (see above), they are typically characterized by an associated hypertrophied papilla, a skin tag, rolled skin edges, and exposed internal anal sphincter muscle at the base of the fissure. Chronic fissures respond less well to nonoperative measures than acute fissures do. The surgical procedure most frequently performed for anal fissure is lateral internal anal sphincterotomy [see 79 Anal Procedures for Benign Disease],[14] which results in cure in 95% to 98% of patients. Complications of this procedure include incontinence to flatus (0% to 18% of cases), soiling (0% to 7%), fecal incontinence (0% to 0.17%), and various other problems (0% to 7%).[14]

Several therapeutic alternatives for anal fissures have been proposed with the aim of avoiding the need for operation and the consequent risk of surgical complications.[15] On the basis of the theory that a fissure is actually an ischemic ulcer of the anoderm, topical nitroglycerin (NTG) ointment has been used to treat fissures, with success rates ranging from 48% to 78%. When metabolized, NTG releases nitric oxide, which is believed to be an inhibitory neurotransmitter for smooth muscle. The resulting neurogenic relaxation of the internal sphincter brings about a reduction in anal canal pressure, which diminishes pain and spasm. Typically, NTG is given in a concentration of 0.2% three to five times daily, but concentrations as high as 0.5% have been recommended. In practice, dosing is limited by NTG's side effects, which arise in as many as 88% of patients. Headaches are the predominant complaint, but dizziness, lightheadedness, and hypotension have also been reported. Caution must be exercised when NTG therapy is employed in patients receiving cardiac medications or those with sensitivities to nitrates. A meta-analysis comparing topical NTG therapy with sphincterotomy demonstrated that sphincterotomy results in better healing of chronic fissures.[16]

Another nonsurgical option is the use of nifedipine gel or ointment, which also has met with varying degrees of success. Nifedipine acts as a calcium antagonist, preventing calcium from flowing into the sarcoplasm of smooth muscle and thereby reducing local demand for oxygen and mechanical contraction of the muscle.[12] Like NTG ointment, nifedipine ointment is usually applied topically in a 0.2% concentration, but it seems to have fewer side effects than NTG does. Nifedipine should be used with caution in cardiac patients and patients who have demonstrated previous sensitivities. One multicenter study reported a 95% complete healing rate after 21 days of treatment.[12]

Topical 2% diltiazem has also been employed to treat chronic anal fissures, yielding a 67% healing rate.[12]

Botulinum toxin has been reported to facilitate healing in 78% to 90% of anal fissure patients, with an 8% recurrence rate at 6 months.[15,17] The toxin, produced by the bacterium *Clostridium botulinum*, acts by inhibiting the release of acetylcholine at the presynaptic membrane. The resulting blockage of neurotransmission diminishes or eliminates spasms and contractions of the sphincter mechanism. Typically, 2.5 to 10 units are injected at two to four sites in the internal sphincter at the level of the dentate line.[18] Pain relief is generally noted within 24 hours, though it still takes days for the fissure to heal. Postinjection incontinence is rare.[12] The major drawback is the cost of the toxin, which may be as high as $400 per 100 unit vial.

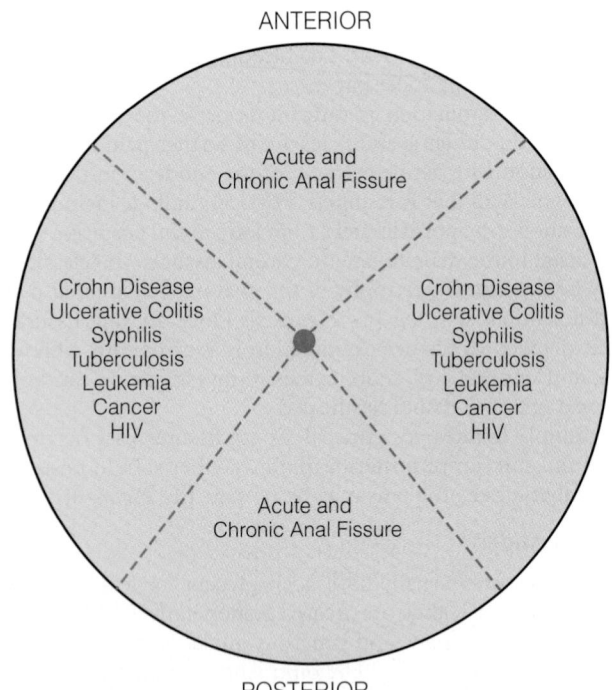

ANTERIOR

Acute and
Chronic Anal Fissure

Crohn Disease
Ulcerative Colitis
Syphilis
Tuberculosis
Leukemia
Cancer
HIV

Crohn Disease
Ulcerative Colitis
Syphilis
Tuberculosis
Leukemia
Cancer
HIV

Acute and
Chronic Anal Fissure

POSTERIOR

Figure 6 **Fissures occurring away from the anterior or posterior midline are likely to be associated with other conditions.**[4]

Anorectal Abscess

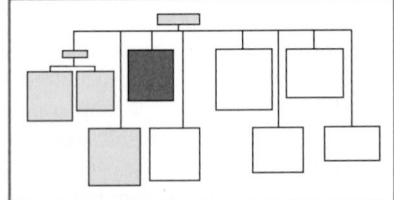

Anorectal abscesses, like abscesses elsewhere in the body, are the result of local, walled-off infections. Most perirectal abscesses are of cryptogenic origin—that is, they begin as infections in the anal glands that surround the anal canal and empty into the anal crypts at the dentate line.[18,19] It is thought that the ducts leading to and from these glands become obstructed by feces or traumatized tissue, and a secondary infection then develops that follows the path of least resistance, resulting in an anorectal abscess.

CLINICAL EVALUATION

Abscesses are categorized according to the space in which they occur: perianal, ischioanal, supralevator, or intersphincteric (intermuscular) [see Figure 7]. Perianal abscesses are the most

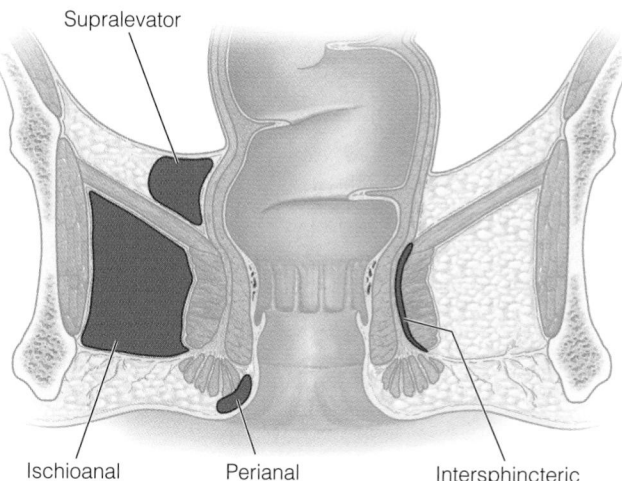

Figure 7 **Anorectal abscesses are classified according to the space in which they develop.**

common—together with ischioanal abscesses, they account for more than 90% of perianal infections. Perianal abscesses occur in the perianal space immediately adjacent to the anal verge. Ischioanal abscesses are larger and often more complex than their perianal counterparts, and they usually manifest themselves as a tender buttock mass. Supralevator abscesses occur above the levator ani muscles and are characterized by poorly localized pain; they are exceedingly rare. Intersphincteric abscesses occur in the plane between the internal and external sphincter muscles, high within the anal canal; these are also rare. The location of an abscess is important in that it dictates subsequent therapy.[20]

Regardless of location, all anorectal abscesses are associated with constant perianal pain. Accompanying symptoms may include fever, chills, and malaise. In rare cases, systemic toxicity may be evident. The history reveals rectal pain of gradual onset that progressively worsens until the time of presentation. Occasionally, spontaneous drainage decompresses the abscess, and the patient presents with a purulent discharge.

As with fissures, visual inspection of the perineum often clinches the diagnosis. A fluctuant, erythematous, tender area identifies the abscess. In the rare event of a supralevator or intersphincteric abscess, there may be no external manifestations. When this is the case, the presence of a tender mass on digital examination above the anal canal, either adjacent to the rectal ampulla (supralevator abscess) or within the anal canal (intersphincteric abscess), provides the clue to the diagnosis.

MANAGEMENT

Treatment of anorectal abscesses consists of adequate drainage performed in the office, in the emergency department, or in the operating room.[18] Most abscesses can be drained in the office, but recurrent or complex abscesses, abscesses in immunosupressed hosts (including some diabetic patients), intersphincteric abscesses, and supralevator abscesses are more appropriately drained in the OR.

Adequate drainage is essential and may be established in several ways. One method is to place a catheter (e.g., a 10 to 16 French Pezzar catheter) through a small stab incision [*see 79 Anal Procedures for Benign Disease*].[18] This measure allows the pus to drain through the catheter as the cavity closes down. A second option involves creating a larger elliptical incision.[20] Unroofing the abscess cavity allows it to heal without any need for packing. A

small incision should be avoided because it would require painful packing to keep the skin open until the abscess cavity heals.

The most difficult abscess to diagnose and manage is a deep postanal space abscess. Such abscesses are caused by fistulization from the posterior anal canal, usually in the bed of a chronic posterior fissure. The patient is highly uncomfortable and febrile, but there is no apparent sign of a problem perianally. A simple digital examination pushing posteriorly towards the coccyx and the deep postanal space will evoke severe pain, and this response should lead the examiner to suspect the diagnosis. The patient should be taken to the OR and anesthetized. On digital examination, the deep postanal space is often felt to be bulging. The diagnosis is confirmed by aspirating the space with an 18-gauge needle. Once the diagnosis is confirmed, an incision is made in the perianal skin posterior to the anal verge and deepened into the space, and the space is drained. In selected patients, a cutting seton is placed from the primary site in the posterior anal canal directly into the deep postanal space abscess. Horseshoe fistulas are dealt with as described elsewhere [*see 79 Anal Procedures for Benign Disease*].

Fistula in Ano

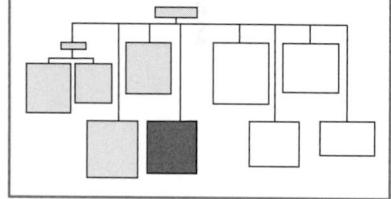

An anal fistula is a communication between the anal canal and the perianal skin. It usually begins in a crypt at the dentate line and follows a course either between the internal and external sphincters (the most common location), resulting in an ischioanal abscess, or above the sphincters, leading to a supralevator abscess.[18,20] After drainage of an abscess, one of three things typically occurs if a fistula is present: (1) the fistula heals spontaneously, and the patient

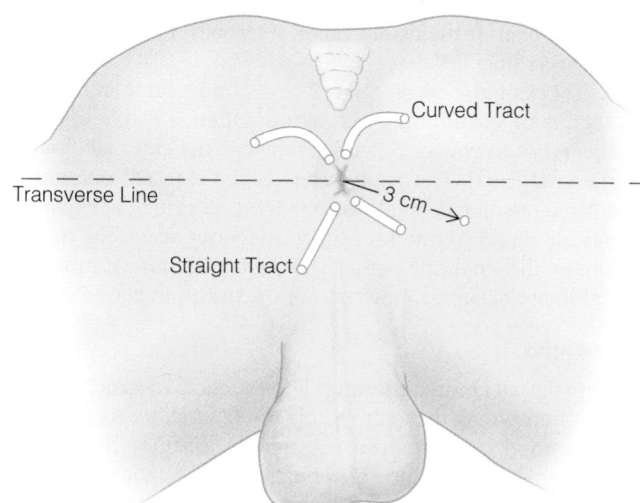

Figure 8 **The relation of the external opening of an anal fistula to the internal opening is suggested by Goodsall's rule. When the external opening is posterior to a line drawn transversely across the perineum, the fistula typically follows a curved course to an internal opening in the posterior midline. When the external opening is anterior to this line, the fistula typically follows a short, straight course to an internal opening in the nearest crypt (though this often does not hold true if the anterior exterior opening is more than 2 to 3 cm from the anus).[4]**

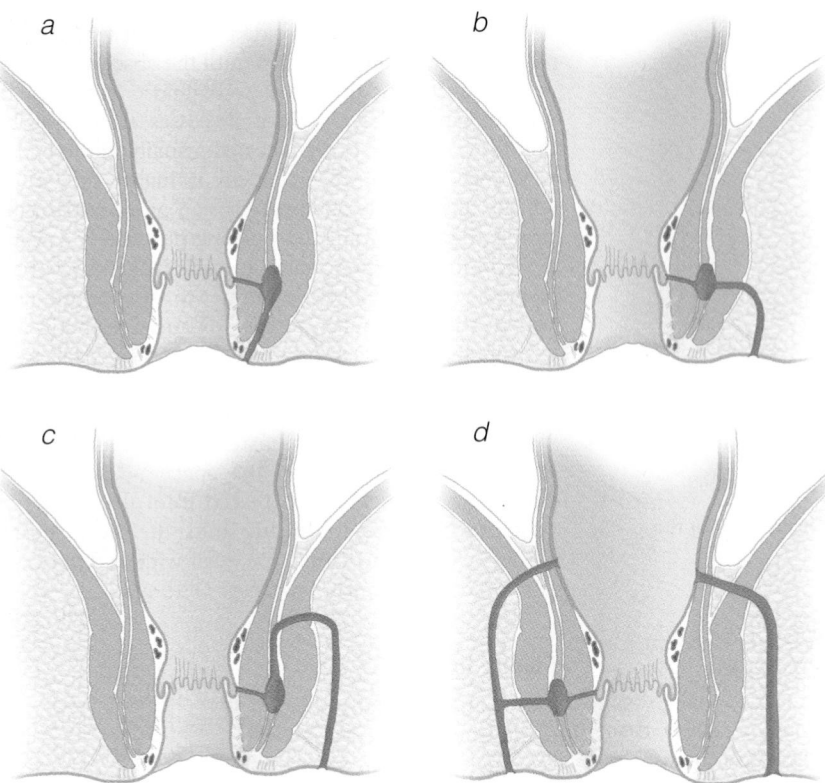

Figure 9 **Fistula in ano is classified on the basis of its relation to the anal sphincter muscles. Shown are (*a*) intersphincteric fistula, (*b*) transsphincteric fistula, (*c*) suprasphincteric fistula, and (*d*) extrasphincteric fistula.**

experiences no further symptoms; (2) the abscess heals, only to recur in the future; or (3) the abscess heals, but a chronic draining fistula remains. Only the third scenario is addressed here.

CLINICAL EVALUATION

After drainage of one or more abscesses, a fistula is usually associated with chronic serosanguineous to seropurulent drainage. As long as the fistula remains open and draining, patients report little pain. If the fistula closes externally, however, an anorectal abscess may develop.

Physical examination reveals a 2 to 3 mm opening in the perianal skin, with surrounding induration. Often, a fistula tract can be palpated as a firm cord running between the external opening and the anal canal. The relationship of the external opening to the internal opening is suggested by Goodsall's rule [*see Figure 8*]. Fistulas are classified into four main categories according to their relation to the anal sphincters [*see Figure 9*]: intersphincteric, transsphincteric, suprasphincteric, and extrasphincteric.[21]

MANAGEMENT

Essentially, all chronic fistulas call for surgical treatment, which consists of unroofing the entire fistula tract (fistulotomy) and leaving the wound open to heal secondarily. Fistulas that course through significant amounts of sphincter muscle, anterior fistulas in women, and fistulas associated with inflammatory bowel disease or weakened sphincter muscles, however, cannot be opened entirely, because incontinence will result. These fistulas may be partially opened, with the anal musculature left intact and encircled with a seton [*see 79 Anal Procedures for Benign Disease*].[20] Although some surgeons sequentially tighten the seton (making it a cutting seton), I prefer not to, because of the resultant patient discomfort. Another surgical option is to close the internal fistula opening with an advancement flap.[22] Advancement flap repairs result in high success rates with minimal effects on continence.

Pilonidal Disease

The term pilonidal disease is derived from the Latin words *pilus* ("hair") and *nidus* ("nest").[23] It denotes a chronic subcutaneous infection and foreign-body reaction to hairs embedded in the skin or to abnormalities of hair follicles in the natal cleft.[23] Pilonidal disease is most commonly seen in men between the onset of puberty and 40 years of age and in obese persons.[23]

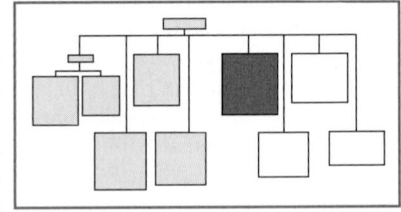

CLINICAL EVALUATION

Pilonidal disease has three common presentations. First, nearly all patients experience an episode of acute abscess formation. Second, after the abscess resolves, either spontaneously or with medical assistance, a pilonidal sinus tract develops in many cases. Third, although most of these sinus tracts resolve, chronic disease or recurrent disease after treatment develops in a small minority of cases.

Physical examination typically reveals one or more small (1 to 2 mm) dermal pits at the base of the intergluteal cleft [*see Figure 10*]. Tracking from the pits (usually proceeding in a cranial and lateral direction) appears as areas of induration. If there is an associated abscess, the diseased area may be tender and erythematous, and draining pus may be evident. The more extensive the disease, the more prominent the findings. Treatment varies according to the stage of the disease.

MANAGEMENT

Abscesses must be drained. In one study, incision and drainage in an office setting with local anesthesia led to healing in 60% of patients.[24] As many as 40% of acute pilonidal abscesses treated with incision and drainage develop into chronic sinus-

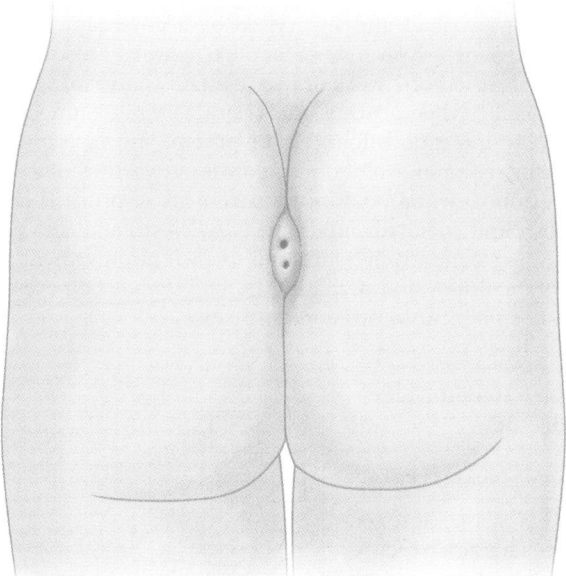

Figure 10 **Patients with pilonidal disease generally have one or two dermal pits in the intergluteal cleft, often associated with a sinus and an abscess.**

es for which additional treatment is necessary.

Several different approaches have been employed in the surgical treatment of pilonidal sinus tracts. A review of articles published over a period of 30 years on the treatment of pilonidal disease divided the procedures into the following four broad categories and reported the following findings.[25]

1. Closed techniques (coring out follicles and brushing the tracts). These techniques necessitated shaving of the area but could be performed on an outpatient basis. Mean healing time was about 40 days, and recurrence rates were slightly higher than those seen with other forms of treatment.
2. Laying open (unroofing) the tracts with healing by granulation. This approach resulted in average healing times of 48 days and necessitated frequent outpatient dressing changes. The incidence of recurrent sinus formation was lower than 13%.
3. Wide and deep excision of the sinus alone. This procedure resulted in an average healing time of 72 days. The recurrence rate was similar to that of simple unroofing of the sinus tract with healing by granulation.
4. Excision and primary closure. This technique resulted in wound healing within 2 weeks in successful cases (19 days overall). However, primary wound healing failed in as many as 30% of patients, and the average recurrence rate was 15%.

A nonoperative or conservative approach—involving meticulous hair control (through natal cleft shaving), improved perineal hygiene, and limited lateral incision and drainage for treatment of abscess—has been suggested as an alternative to conventional excision.[26] This approach has brought about a significant reduction in the number of excisional procedures and occupied-bed days.

Even with proper treatment of pilonidal abscesses and sinuses, a small number of patients are left with persistent, nonhealing wounds. A number of more aggressive approaches have been advocated for treatment of complex or recurrent disease, including wide excision with split-thickness skin grafting, cleft closure, and excision with flap closure.[24,27] Flap techniques, as a group, have been found to lead to primary healing within 15 days in

90% of cases.[24] These aggressive approaches nevertheless have certain disadvantages. For nearly all of them, hospitalization and general anesthesia are mandatory. In addition, as many as 50% of procedures involving the use of skin flaps for wound coverage or closure in this setting result in some loss of skin sensation or some degree of flap-tip necrosis.

My policy is to treat acute abscesses with drainage, followed by measures aimed at keeping the cleft free of hair. If a chronic sinus develops, it is managed with unroofing or, in selected patients, excision and closure. Flap procedures are reserved for cases of extensive, recurrent, and complex disease.[23]

Hidradenitis Suppurativa

CLINICAL EVALUATION

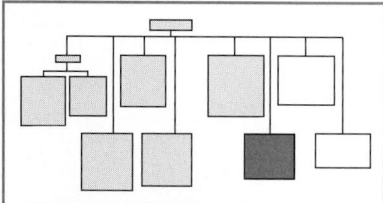

Hidradenitis suppurativa is a chronic, recurrent inflammatory process involving the apocrine glands of the axilla, the groin, the perineum, and the perianal region.[28] The disease can result in chronically draining wounds and sinus tracts and can become quite painful and debilitating.[29] Occlusion of follicles and abnormalities of apocrine ducts are believed to be causative factors.

MANAGEMENT

Medical management may afford temporary relief of symptoms; however, most patients eventually require surgical therapy.[30] In select patients, incision and drainage or unroofing of sinuses may provide relief, but these measures should be reserved for cases of early and acute disease. Local excision provides adequate control of symptoms; however, recurrence rates higher than 50% may be anticipated. Wide excision with secondary granulation of perineal wounds constitutes the most definitive therapy and generally can be accomplished safely.[29] Perianal disease is associated with considerably lower recurrence rates than perineal disease is and thus can more often be managed with local excision alone.

Pruritus Ani

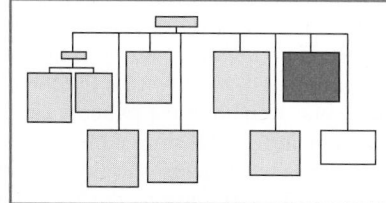

Pruritus ani is a dermatologic condition of the perianal skin characterized by uneasiness or itching in the area around the anus.[12,31] Multiple factors may predispose this area to irritation, including poor perianal hygiene (related to incontinence, diarrhea, or excessive hair), excessive moisture, irregularities of the perianal skin (from hemorrhoids, fistulas, or previous surgery), skin hypersensitivity, diet, decreased resistance to infection, and injury to the perianal skin.[31] The variety of possible causes is what often makes pruritus ani difficult to treat. Some patients improve only after the offending agents or conditions are identified and specific therapy instituted. Fortunately, many patients' symptoms can be alleviated by the application of nonspecific treatments.

CLINICAL EVALUATION

A thorough history and physical examination are necessary to suggest possible causes of pruritus. Initial inspection of the perianal skin should be conducted with gentle retraction of the buttocks under bright lighting. A characteristic finding is erythema-

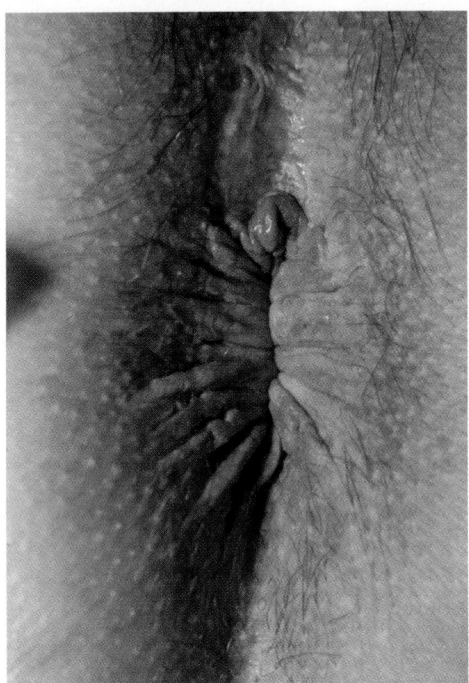

Figure 11 **A characteristic finding in idiopathic pruritus ani is erythematous or thickened perianal skin.**

tous or thickened perianal skin [*see Figure 11*]. This thickening results in a pale, whitish appearance, with accentuation of the radial anal skin creases. In addition, the skin may be excoriated or ulcerated; this process, when combined with thickening, is referred to as lichenification. Occasionally, the skin is so excoriated that a large, coalescing, weeping ulcer forms. Digital rectal examination should be performed to assess the competence of the anal sphincter both at rest and during maximal squeeze. Anoscopy and proctosigmoidoscopy may be performed after the administration of an enema.

MANAGEMENT

The basic principles of therapy for pruritus ani are uncomplicated. If an inciting cause can be identified, it should of course be eliminated or corrected. Frequently, the inciting cause is elusive, but even so, most patients can still be effectively managed by applying several simple measures.

Generally, patients should keep the perianal area dry and avoid further trauma to the area. The perianal area should be gently washed, never scrubbed. After showering, the area should be patted dry or dried with a hair dryer on a low heat setting. After bowel movements, the anus should be cleaned with moistened toilet paper. Excessive rubbing or wiping should be discouraged: scratching or rubbing the anal area damages the perianal skin, making it more susceptible to irritation. Patients should also be instructed to avoid irritating foods and drinks, such as tomatoes, peppers, citrus fruits and juices, coffee, colas, beer and other alcoholic beverages, milk, nuts, popcorn, and any other foodstuffs found to be associated with increased gas, indigestion, or diarrhea. After 2 weeks, food items eliminated from the diet can be reintroduced one at a time in an attempt to identify the offending agent more specifically.

A regular bowel habit should be maintained with the help of fiber supplementation or a high-fiber diet. Patients should be instructed to eschew all proprietary creams, lotions, and emol-lients. If prescribed and supervised by a physician, however, a hydrocortisone cream may be applied sparingly to the affected area for a period of 1 week or less to attain control of symptoms. Occasionally, when pruritus ani is refractory to treatment, a candidal yeast infection is found to be present, in which case a trial of antifungal lotion, solution, or powder is worthwhile.

The fundamental goal in the treatment of pruritus ani is to establish and maintain intact, healthy, clean, and dry perianal skin. When standard measures fail to elicit improvement, fungal and viral cultures and perhaps even biopsy may be necessary to exclude an infectious or neoplastic cause.

Solitary Rectal Ulcer Syndrome

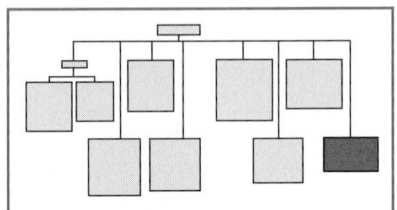

CLINICAL EVALUATION

SRUS is a clinical condition characterized by rectal bleeding, copious mucous discharge, anorectal pain, and difficult evacuation.[32] The name of the condition notwithstanding, SRUS patients can have a single rectal ulcer, multiple ulcers, or even no ulcers at all. When present, the ulcers usually occur on the anterior rectal wall, just above the anorectal ring; less commonly, they occur from just above the dentate line to 15 cm above it. The ulcers usually appear as shallow lesions with a punched-out gray-white base that is surrounded by hyperemia.[33]

Colitis cystica profunda (CCF) is a benign condition that is related to SRUS and is characterized by mucin-filled cysts located deep to the muscularis mucosae. CCF is a pathologic diagnosis, of which the most important aspect is differentiation of CCF from colorectal adenocarcinoma.

Precisely what causes SRUS and CCF remains unclear, but both conditions are known to be associated with chronic inflammation or trauma (e.g., internal intussception or prolapse of the rectum, direct digital trauma, or the forces associated with evacuating a hard stool). Endoscopic evaluation of the distal colon and rectum reveals the lesions described. For both CCF and SRUS, the differential diagnosis includes polyps, endometriosis, inflammatory granuloma, infection, drug-induced colitis, and mucus-producing adenocarcinoma. These entities can be confirmed or excluded by means of an adequate biopsy.

MANAGEMENT

Treatment is directed at alleviating symptoms or interfering with some of the proposed etiologic mechanisms. Conservative therapy (e.g., a high-fiber diet, lifestyle changes, and biofeedback) reduces symptoms in most patients and should be tried first. Patients without rectal intussusception are offered biofeedback for retraining their bowel function. Pharmacologic therapy (e.g., anti-inflammatory enemas and suppositories) has had only limited success but nonetheless may be worth trying before the decision is made to embark on surgery.

If symptoms persist, localized resection may be considered in selected patients. Patients with prolapse are considered for perineal procedures (i.e., mucosal or perineal proctectomy) and abdominal procedures (i.e., fixation or resection and rectopexy). Patients without prolapse may be offered excision, for which the options range from a transanal excision to a major resection with coloanal pull-through. Understandably, surgeons have been hesitant to offer surgical therapy for this benign condition; the results are often unsatisfactory.[34]

References

1. Beck DE: Hemorrhoids, anal fissure, and anorectal abscess and fistula. Conn's Current Therapy. Rakel RE, Ed. WB Saunders Co, Philadelphia, 1997, p 482

2. Beck DE: Hemorrhoidal disease. Fundamentals of Anorectal Surgery, 2nd ed. Beck DE, Wexner SD, Eds. WB Saunders Co, London, 1998, p 237

3. Thomsson WHE: The nature of haemorrhoids. Br J Surg 62:542, 1975

4. Beck DE: Hemorrhoids. Handbook of Colorectal Surgery, 2nd ed. Beck DE, Ed. Marcel Dekker, New York, 2003, p 325

5. Larach SW, Cataldo PA, Beck DE: Nonoperative treatment of hemorrhoidal disease. Complications of Colon and Rectal Surgery. Hicks TC, Beck DE, Opelka FG, et al, Eds. Williams & Wilkins, Baltimore, 1996, p 173

6. Scarpa FJ, Hillis W, Sabetta JR: Pelvic cellulitis: a life-threatening complication of hemorrhoidal banding. Surgery 103:383, 1988

7. Neiger S: Hemorrhoids in everyday practice. Proctology 2:22, 1979

8. MacRae HM, McLeod RS: Comparison of hemorrhoidal treatment modalities: a meta-analysis. Dis Colon Rectum 38:687, 1995

9. Cataldo PA: Hemorrhoids. Clin Colon Rectal Surg 14:203, 2001

10. Ferguson JA, Mazier WP, Ganchrow MI, et al: The closed technique of hemorrhoidectomy. Surgery 70:480, 1971

11. Sanger M, Abcarian H: Stapled hemorrhoidopexy. Clin Colon Rectal Surg (in press)

12. Beck DE, Timmcke AE: Pruritus ani and fissure-in-ano. Handbook of Colorectal Surgery, 2nd ed. Beck DE, Ed. Marcel Dekker, New York, 2003, p 367

13. Schouten WR, Briel JW, Auwerda JJ: Relationship between anal pressure and anodermal blood flow: the vascular pathogenesis of anal fissures. Dis Colon Rectum 37:664, 1994

14. Eisenhammer S: The evaluation of the internal anal sphincterotomy operation with special reference to anal fissure. Surg Gynecol Obstet 109:583, 1959

15. Wiley KS, Chinn BT: Anal fissures. Clin Colon Rectal Surg 14:193, 2001

16. Richard CS, Gregoire R, Plewes EA, et al: Internal sphincterotomy is superior to topical nitroglycerin in the treatment of chronic anal fissure. Dis Colon Rectum 43:1048, 2000

17. Minguez M, Melo F, Espi A, et al: Therapeutic effects of different doses of botulinum toxin in chronic anal fissure. Dis Colon Rectum 42:1016, 1999

18. Beck DE, Vasilevsky CA: Anorectal abscess and fistula-in-ano. Handbook of Colorectal Surgery, 2nd ed. Beck DE, Ed. Marcel Dekker, New York, 2003, p 345

19. Parks AG: Pathogenesis and treatment of fistula-in-ano. Br Med J 1:463, 1961

20. Luchtefeld MA: Anorectal abscess and fistula-in-ano. Clin Colon Rectal Surg 14:221, 2001

21. Parks AG, Gordon PH, Hardcastle JD: A classification of fistula-in-ano. Br J Surg 63:1, 1976

22. Lewis P, Bartolo DCC: Treatment of trans-sphincteric fistulae by full thickness anorectal advancement flap. Br J Surg 77:1187, 1990

23. Beck DE, Karulf RE: Pilonidal disease. Handbook of Colorectal Surgery, 2nd ed. Beck DE, Ed. Marcel Dekker, New York, 2003, p 391

24. Beck DE: Operative procedures for pilonidal disease. Oper Tech Gen Surg 3:124, 2001

25. Allen-Mersh TG: Pilonidal sinus: finding the right track for treatment. Br J Surg 77:123, 1990

26. Armstrong JH, Barcia PJ: Pilonidal sinus disease: the conservative approach. Arch Surg 129:914, 1994

27. Bascom JU: Repeat pilonidal operations. Am J Surg 154:118, 1987

28. Mitchel KM, Beck DE: Hidradenitis suppurativa. Surg Clin North Am 82:1187, 2002

29. Waters GS, Nelson H: Perianal hidradenitis suppurativa. Fundamentals of Anorectal Surgery, 2nd ed. Beck DE, Wexner SD, Eds. WB Saunders Co, London, 1998, p 233

30. Singer M, Cintron JR: Hidradenitis suppurativa. Clin Colon Rectal Surg 14:233, 2001

31. Hicks TC, Stamos MJ: Pruritus ani: diagnosis and treatment. Fundamentals of Anorectal Surgery, 2nd ed. Beck DE, Wexner SD, Eds. WB Saunders Co, London, 1998, p 198

32. Madoff RD: Rectal prolapse and intussusception. Fundamentals of Anorectal Surgery, 2nd ed. Beck DE, Wexner SD, Eds. WB Saunders Co, London, 1998, p 99

33. Beck DE: Surgical therapy for colitis cystica profunda and solitary rectal ulcer syndrome. Curr Treat Options Gastroenterol 5:231, 2002

34. Keighley MRB, Williams NS: Solitary rectal ulcer syndrome. Surgery of the Anus, Rectum, and Colon. WB Saunders Co, London, 1993, p 720

35. Beck DE, Wexner SD: Anal neoplasms. Fundamentals of Anorectal Surgery, 2nd ed. Beck DE, Wexner SD, Eds. WB Saunders Co, London, 1998, p 261

36. Nivatvongs S: Hemorrhoids. Principles and Practice of Surgery for the Colon, Rectum, and Anus, 2nd ed. Gordon PH, Nivatvongs S, Eds. Quality Medical Publishing, St Louis, 1999, p 193

Acknowledgment

Figures 1, 2, 3, 5, 7 through 10   Tom Moore.

Alicia Fanning, M.D., and Jeffrey L. Ponsky, M.D., F.A.C.S.

Since the beginning of the 1970s, flexible endoscopy of the gastrointestinal tract has been the dominant modality for the diagnosis of gastrointestinal disease. Over the same period, developments in technology and methodology have made possible the use of endoscopy to treat a host of conditions that once were considered to be manageable only by means of open surgical procedures. The integration of flexible endoscopic techniques into the armamentarium of the GI surgeon permits a more multidimensional approach to the treatment of digestive disease. The modern GI surgeon should be conversant in and adept at many of these procedures.

Diagnostic Esophagogastroduodenoscopy

Diagnostic esophagogastroduodenoscopy (EGD) is indicated when a patient has abnormal findings on traditional GI x-ray series, dysphagia, odynophagia, epigastric pain that does not respond to medical therapy, persistent heartburn, or upper GI bleeding; it is also indicated for surveillance of patients at high risk for malignancy and for sampling of GI tissue or fluid. One prepares for the examination by ensuring the patient's hemodynamic stability, having the patient fast for 6 to 8 hours beforehand, and performing conscious sedation, which generally involves applying a topical anesthetic to the posterior pharynx and administering a narcotic and a benzodiazepine intravenously. Monitoring of arterial blood pressure and oxygen saturation throughout the procedure is now standard practice.

TECHNIQUE

With the patient in the left lateral decubitus position, a topical anesthetic is applied to the posterior pharynx and an intravenous sedative administered. The forward-viewing panendoscope—a small-caliber instrument that is long enough to permit examination of the foregut from the mouth to the third portion of the duodenum—is employed.

The endoscope may be introduced either blindly, via finger-guided palpation of the pharynx, or under direct vision. The latter approach is preferable. In this approach, the instrument is advanced slowly until the epiglottis and vocal cords are visualized [*see Figure 1*]; it is then angled posteriorly to the esophageal introitus and gently advanced as the patient is asked to swallow. Insufflation of air is begun to distend the esophagus, which appears as a long, round tube. Frequent peristaltic waves are seen; these are normal. Mucosal surfaces must be closely inspected for signs of ulceration, stricture, tumor, or Barrett's (columnar) epithelium, which manifests itself as orange patches in otherwise pale salmon-pink esophageal (squamous) mucosa. When abnormalities are noted, biopsy, brushing for cytologic evaluation, or both should be performed. Staining of the esophagus with methylene blue may be useful in the search for Barrett's mucosa: the blue dye is avidly absorbed by

the intestinal absorptive cells of the columnar epithelium. Darkly stained areas may be biopsied for confirmation.

As the endoscope is advanced, insufflation is continued, and the curve of the lumen is followed to the left as the esophagus traverses the diaphragm to enter the stomach. There is a pinched area where the diaphragm compresses the esophagus; the pinching is exaggerated when the patient is asked to sniff. If gastric folds are seen above this pinched area, a hiatal hernia is present. When the stomach is entered, the tip of the endoscope is elevated so as to center it within the gastric lumen. It should be noted that with the patient lying in the left lateral decubitus position, the stomach is also on its side, with the greater curvature at 6 o'clock, the lesser curvature at 12 o'clock, the posterior wall at 3 o'clock, and the anterior wall at 9 o'clock. Air should be insufflated to distend the stomach fully and permit careful inspection of the mucosal surfaces.

As the instrument is advanced toward the gastric antrum, its tip should be slightly elevated because the stomach has a J shape and the prepyloric region curves upward. The pylorus is normally round and may be seen to open and close with gastric peristalsis. With the tip of the endoscope positioned at the proximal gastric antrum, just under the incisura angularis, a retroflex view of the cardia and the fundus is obtained by elevating the tip of the scope and rotating the shaft to the left. This maneuver provides visual and therapeutic access to the proximal stomach.

After the stomach has been viewed, the instrument is advanced under direct vision through the pylorus and into the duodenal bulb. Insufflation of air should continue as the scope is

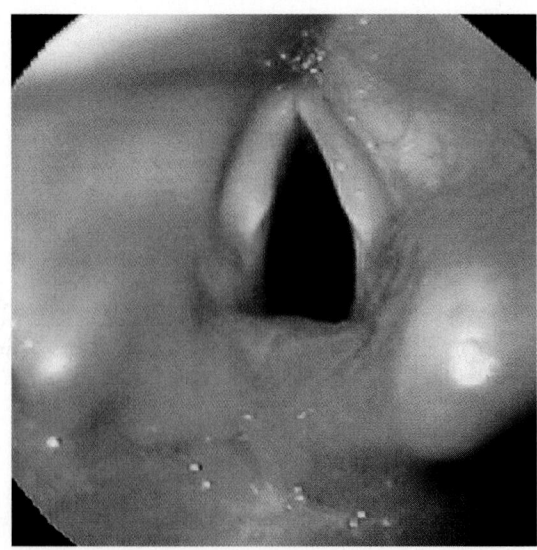

Figure 1 **Diagnostic esophagogastroduodenoscopy. As the endoscope is introduced under direct vision, the vocal cords are clearly noted. The esophageal opening is posterior to the cords.**

pressed against the pylorus to facilitate passage of the instrument. The scope tends to pop into the duodenal bulb rather than slide smoothly; it should be pulled back slightly to allow one to observe the mucosal surfaces of the bulb before moving ahead. Unlike the rest of the small bowel, the duodenal bulb has no semicircular folds. The tip of the scope must be rotated slightly to permit examination of the walls of the bulb. It is advisable to pull the instrument back into the stomach while observing the walls of the bulb and the pyloric channel for lesions; several such withdrawals may be required for full assessment of this area.

Once the duodenal bulb has been examined, the endoscope is advanced just past the bulb to the point where the first duodenal folds are observed. Here, the duodenum turns sharply to the rear and downward as it becomes retroperitoneal. Advancement of the scope into the second portion of the duodenum is one of the few endoscopic maneuvers that cannot be accomplished under direct vision. Because of the sharp angle of the turn, one will experience a moment of so-called red out as the tip of the endoscope touches the mucosa during the turn. To ensure that the turn is accomplished safely, the instrument is advanced as far through the bulb as is possible under direct vision. The control handle of the scope is then rotated approximately 90° to the right as the tip of the scope is turned to the right and angled first upward, then downward. As the second portion of the duodenum appears, the scope is rotated back to its neutral position. When done correctly, the turn is actually quite easy. It should never be forced: if the instrument does not proceed easily into the descending duodenum, the scope should be pulled back and the attempt repeated. Pushing against resistance may result in perforation.

Entering the descending duodenum causes the scope to form a large loop in the stomach. Therefore, once the second portion of the duodenum is successfully entered, the shaft of the instrument is pulled back. Paradoxically, as this movement straightens the gastric loop, it also advances the tip of the instrument deeper into the duodenum. Further advancement of the instrument under direct vision often permits entry into the third or even the fourth portion of the duodenum. Once the distal limit of intubation is reached, the scope is withdrawn and the luminal surfaces are carefully examined. Rotating the scope with small right-left movements of the controls and side-to-side movements of the control handle itself will help demonstrate the more subtle details of duodenal anatomy. Often, the upper GI tract is inspected more completely while the instrument is being withdrawn than while it is being advanced.

Mucosal abnormalities should be biopsied; liberal use of brush cytology in combination with biopsy enhances the yield.

COMPLICATIONS

EGD is an extremely safe procedure. Perhaps the most common problems associated with the technique arise from the preparatory sedation and analgesia. Respiratory depression and aspiration may occur during the procedure. Careful attention must be paid to the patient's state of consciousness and airway during the endoscopic procedure, appropriate drugs must be available to reverse sedative effects, and a suction apparatus must be ready for use at all times. Blind advancement of the endoscope by force may lead to perforation of the esophagus; this problem may be avoided by taking care never to advance the instrument against resistance.

Therapeutic Esophagogastroduodenoscopy

CONTROL OF VARICEAL HEMORRHAGE

In patients with massive upper GI hemorrhage, the first priori-

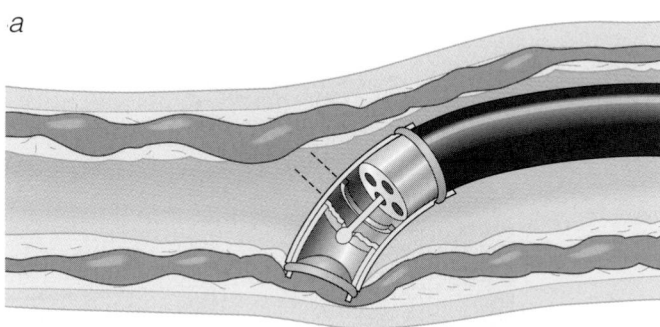

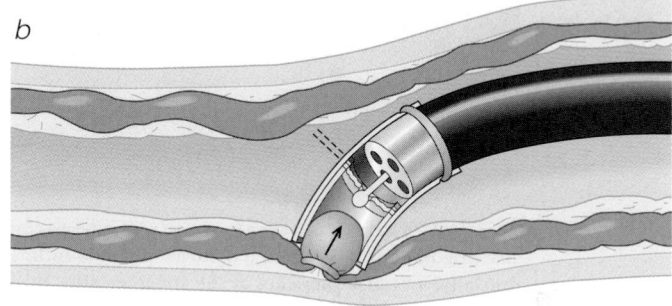

Figure 2 Therapeutic esophagogastroduodenoscopy: control of variceal hemorrhage. (*a*) A plastic tip on the endoscope is used to create a chamber. (*b*) An esophageal varix is suctioned into the chamber, and a rubber band is released around it.

ties are to establish a secure airway and to ensure hemodynamic stability. These priorities must be addressed before endoscopy is attempted. If the bleeding is thought to be coming from esophageal varices, it is frequently useful to perform endotracheal intubation for control of the airway before the endoscopic intervention.

Technique

A rapid but complete diagnostic upper GI endoscopic procedure is performed to determine whether varices are present and to identify the exact site of hemorrhage. Endoscopic therapy for variceal disease is then delivered by means of either sclerotherapy or rubber band ligation.

Sclerotherapy is commenced in the distal esophagus at the site of active or suspected bleeding: 2 to 3 ml of a sclerosant solution (e.g., sodium tetradecyl sulfate) is injected directly into the lumen of the varix. Additional varices can be treated in the same fashion. After the bleeding has stopped, further therapy is usually delivered at weekly intervals until total variceal obliteration is achieved.

Rubber band ligation of varices has become extremely popular and has been shown to possess some clear advantages over sclerotherapy [see Figure 2]. Originally, multiple passages of the endoscope were required to allow for reloading of the bands; however, newer ligating devices permit ligation of as many as 10 varices with a single passage of the endoscope. As with sclerotherapy, the site of active or suspected bleeding is attacked first; it is most often near the esophagogastric junction. The offending varix is centered in the field of view, and suction is applied to pull it into the ligator cup, which sits on the end of the endoscope. When the varix is deep within the cup, the trigger string on the ligator is pulled, and a rubber band is released around the varix. Suction is then released, and the ligated varix is visualized. Additional ligations may be performed at the initial session; follow-up sessions are usually held at weekly intervals until total variceal obliteration is achieved.

a

b

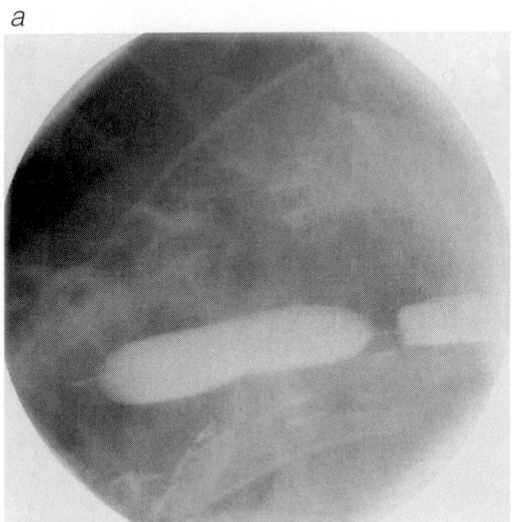
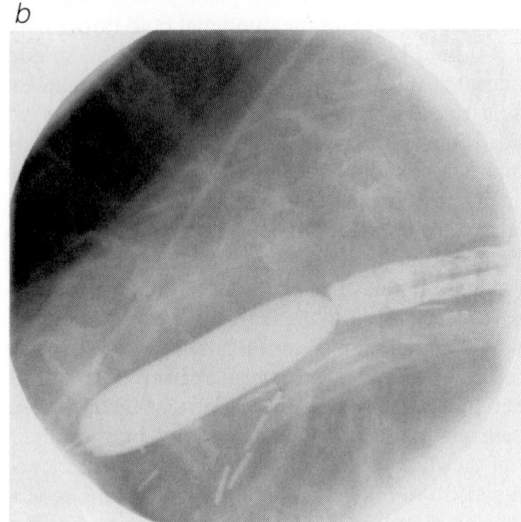

Figure 3 **Therapeutic esophagogastroduodenoscopy: dilation of esophageal strictures. (*a*) A hydrostatic dilating balloon filled with a contrast agent is inflated within the stricture under fluoroscopic guidance. Initially, a "waist" appears at the stricture site. (*b*) Inflation of the balloon is continued until the waist is ablated, which indicates complete dilation of the stricture.**

Complications

Because aspiration of blood and gastric contents may occur during endoscopic control of variceal hemorrhage, endotracheal intubation must be considered when bleeding is massive. In many cases, general anesthesia will permit adequate airway control and a quiet operating field. Violent patient motion when the injection needle is in a varix may result in perforation of the esophagus. This is a rare complication, however; tearing of the varix, with resultant hemorrhage, is more frequent. Injection of excessive amounts of sclerosant may lead to significant ulceration and necrosis of esophageal tissue. Fever, severe infection, pleural effusion, and subsequent esophageal stricture occasionally occur after sclerotherapy. Ulceration and necrosis of tissue, with subsequent stricture, occur after rubber band ligation as well, but severe infection is less common in this setting.

CONTROL OF NONVARICEAL HEMORRHAGE

Bleeding from peptic ulcer disease, gastritis, or vascular malformations is a common indication for EGD. Once the patient has been adequately resuscitated, endoscopy should be performed, and the entire esophagus, stomach, and duodenum should be examined thoroughly. Before the procedure is begun, the stomach should be vigorously irrigated through a large-bore tube so that as much clotted blood as possible can be evacuated. If a pool of blood is noted in the stomach, the position of the patient should be changed so as to move the pool and permit complete examination of the stomach.

The therapeutic modalities available for control of nonvariceal bleeding include (1) the injection of hypertonic saline, epinephrine (in a 1:10,000 solution), or 98% alcohol, (2) bipolar electrocoagulation, (3) the use of heater probes, (4) argon beam coagulation, (5) the application of acrylic glue, (6) the application of hemostatic clips, and (7) the use of the neodynium:yttrium-aluminum-garnet (Nd:YAG) laser.

Technique

The most popular therapeutic modalities are injection therapy, bipolar coagulation, and the use of the heater probe. Injection

therapy is performed around the bleeding lesion to create edema and vasospasm in the area. The bipolar coagulator or the heater probe is applied directly to the bleeding lesion in an attempt to coapt the bleeding vessel as heat is delivered. Frequently, injection therapy is employed in conjunction with coagulation; this combination is very effective.

If there is a clot covering the ulcer base, it must be removed with suction or a snare before coagulation is attempted. If a rapidly bleeding lesion is present, the best approach often is injection therapy in adjacent areas to slow or stop the bleeding, followed by coagulation by direct coaptation. Vascular lesions are often multiple or diffuse, as in so-called watermelon stomach. Such lesions are most effectively treated by means of modalities that can be applied in a spraying fashion, such as the Nd:YAG laser or the argon beam coagulator.

Complications

Nonvariceal hemorrhage is successfully controlled by endoscopic means in more than 90% of cases. At times, however, attempts at endoscopic control may exacerbate the bleeding. Several therapeutic modalities should always be available: one may succeed when another fails. Excessive injection therapy or persistent attempts at coagulation may lead to tissue necrosis and subsequent perforation. Although the argon beam coagulator can injure tissue only to a depth of several millimeters, excessive application may result in massive distention of the bowel if care is not taken to aspirate the constantly infused argon gas frequently. The Nd:YAG laser has the potential to cause full-thickness injury to the gastric wall.

DILATION OF ESOPHAGEAL STRICTURES

When patients complain of dysphagia or odynophagia, prompt endoscopic investigation is warranted. Strictures may be secondary to reflux disease, secondary to caustic burns, or of neoplastic origin.

Technique

Endoscopy is performed in the usual fashion. It is imperative that the endoscope be advanced only under direct vision. When a stricture is encountered, its location, morphology, and length should be determined. Biopsy and cytology specimens should be gathered from the circumference of the stricture. When a stricture is present at the esophagogastric junction and the scope can easily be passed by the stricture, it is helpful to view the area from below with the tip of the scope retroflexed.

Stricture dilation can be accomplished in several different ways and with several different kinds of dilators. One commonly employed method is to use the endoscope to guide the passage of a soft-tipped guide wire through the stricture; the scope is then removed, leaving the wire in place. Subsequently, dilators are passed over the guide wire, usually under fluoroscopic control. Another method for endoscopic dilation of strictures is the use of through-the-scope (TTS) hydrostatic dilating balloons. A balloon of the appropriate inflated diameter (usually no larger than 18 mm or 54 French) is selected, passed through the biopsy channel of the endoscope, and advanced under direct vision until its middle portion passes through the stricture. At the stricture site, the balloon is compressed, giving the appearance of a waist. The balloon is then inflated until the waist is fully expanded [see Figure 3]. Full expansion is verified by fluoroscopic surveillance and the use of contrast to inflate the balloon. This second method is extremely useful for initial dilation of tight strictures in preparation for the use of other, nonendoscopic dilators or the placement of an esophageal stent.

Complications

Dilation of esophageal strictures may result in bleeding (usually minor) or perforation of the esophagus. When a patient experiences severe pain after dilation, a chest x-ray is imperative. The finding of mediastinal or subcutaneous air should prompt the immediate performance of a contrast study with a water-soluble agent to determine whether a perforation is present. Some small perforations can be managed with intravenous antibiotics and observation, but most must be managed surgically. The incidence of perforation can be minimized by avoiding excessive or forceful dilation.

STENTING OF ESOPHAGEAL TUMORS

Under optimal circumstances, esophageal tumors should be treated by means of extirpative surgery. When surgical cure or palliation seems to have little to offer, placement of an esophageal prosthesis by endoscopic means is a reasonable approach.

Technique

Modern esophageal prostheses are placed under fluoroscopic guidance, frequently after endoscopic balloon dilation of the tumor. During the endoscopic examination, it is useful to inject a small amount of water-soluble contrast material into the muscular wall of the esophagus just above and below the tumor; this enables one to measure the length of the tumor and select the correct stent. Once the tumor has been dilated and marked endoscopically, the scope is removed, and the expandable stent is passed into the esophagus and positioned between the endoscopic injection markings seen on fluoroscopy. The stent is then deployed and allowed to expand [see Figure 4]. The endoscope may then be reintroduced to ensure that the prosthesis is patent and is correctly placed.

Complications

Incorrect positioning of the prosthesis is a frequent problem. Attention to the details of endoscopic marking is very important. Also crucial is correct selection of a stent: stents shorten from both ends as they are deployed, and this must be taken into account in selecting the correct stent length. On occasion, the stent may migrate as a result of tumor-related necrosis or incorrect placement. If it migrates into the stomach, it can usually be captured in a snare and retrieved.

RETRIEVAL OF FOREIGN BODIES

Many ingested foreign bodies pass through the GI tract uneventfully, but a good number must be removed by endoscopic means—in particular, foreign bodies in the esophagus, sharp objects that are likely to perforate the bowel, and objects that do not progress from the stomach.

If the ingested object is of an unfamiliar type, it is an extremely good idea to practice with a similar object outside the patient before attempting endoscopic retrieval. This preparatory step allows one to select the most appropriate accessory and technique for removing the object.

Technique

Objects with sharp edges should be removed with the sharp end trailing to prevent perforation. In some cases, this means that the object must be pushed into the stomach and turned

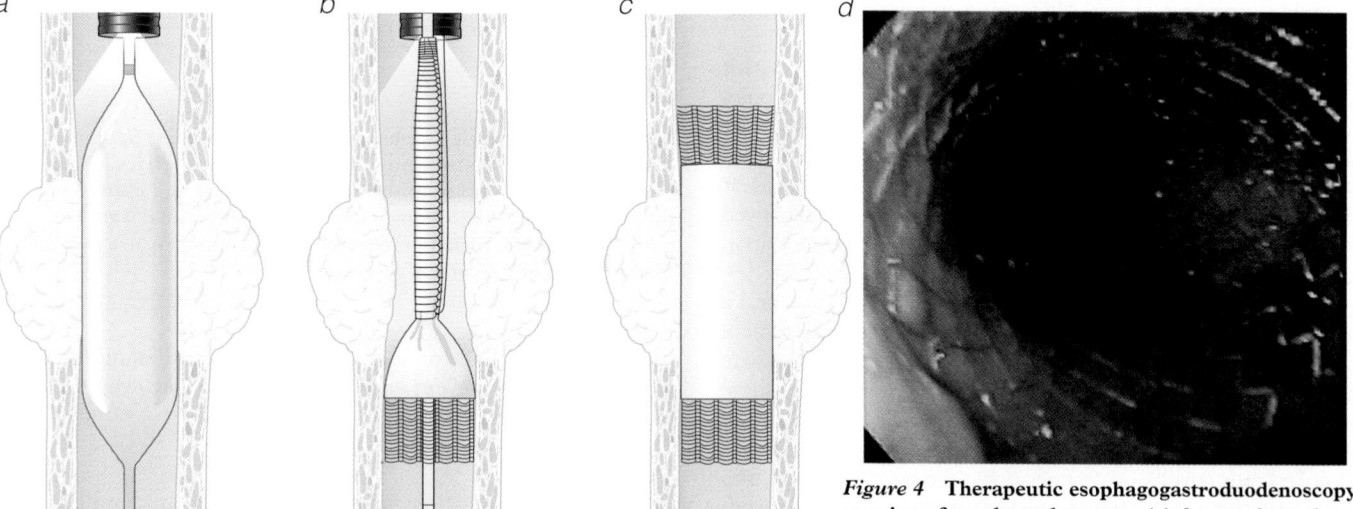

Figure 4 Therapeutic esophagogastroduodenoscopy: stenting of esophageal tumors. (*a*) An esophageal tumor is dilated. (*b, c*) A compressed expandable metal stent is positioned within the tumor and deployed. (*d*) The expanded stent yields a large enough lumen to permit the patient to continue oral alimentation.

around before being removed. If multiple foreign bodies are present or if it is highly likely that the foreign body will injure the esophagus if removed in the standard manner, an overtube should be placed over the scope before insertion. The overtube enables one to pass the instrument several times and retrieve any sharp objects without injuring the esophagus; it also helps ensure that the object is not aspirated into the airway. If the patient is a child, general anesthesia may be advisable.

Perhaps the best method of removing foreign bodies is to surround them with a simple polypectomy snare and secure them in the endoscope's grasp. Meat boluses that form in the esophagus or proximal to a gastric band may be extremely difficult to dislodge; the use of a variceal ligator cap to produce a suction chamber can be helpful in such situations.

Complications

Endoscopic removal of foreign bodies is extremely safe and effective. Care must be taken to ensure that the esophagus is not injured during removal of the object. If the object is deeply embedded or refractory to removal, a surgical approach is preferred.

PERCUTANEOUS ENDOSCOPIC GASTROSTOMY

Since 1980, endoscopically guided placement of a tube gastrostomy has been widely employed to provide access to the GI tract for feeding or decompression. Indications for percutaneous endoscopic gastrostomy (PEG) include various disease processes that interfere with swallowing, such as severe neurologic impairment, oropharyngeal tumors, and facial trauma. PEG has also been employed to establish a route for recycling bile in patients with malignant biliary obstruction, to provide supplemental feeding in selected patients with inflammatory bowel disease, and to accomplish gastric decompression in patients with conditions such as carcinomatosis, radiation enteritis, and diabetic gastropathy.

Technique

The patient fasts for 8 hours beforehand, and a single prophylactic dose of an antibiotic is administered just before the procedure is begun. The patient is placed in the supine position, a topical anesthetic is applied to the posterior pharynx, and intravenous sedation is begun. A forward-viewing endoscope is passed into the esophagus and advanced into the stomach. The abdomen is prepared in a sterile fashion and draped. The stomach and the duodenum are then inspected.

The room lights are dimmed, and the light of the endoscope is used to transilluminate the abdominal wall so as to indicate a point where the gastric wall and the abdominal wall are in close proximity. Finger pressure is applied to various areas of the abdomen until a spot is identified at which such pressure produces clear indentation of the gastric wall. An endoscopic snare is deployed through the biopsy channel of the endoscope to cover this spot, and a local anesthetic is infiltrated into the overlying skin [see Figure 5]. A 1 cm skin incision is made at the chosen spot, and a needle is passed through the incision and into the gastric lumen. The endoscopic snare is tightened around the needle, and a wire is passed through the needle and into the gastric lumen. The snare is moved so as to surround the wire, which is then pulled out of the patient's mouth. The gastrostomy tube is fastened to the wire and pulled in a retrograde manner down the esophagus and into the stomach. The gastroscope is subsequently reinserted to ensure that the head of the catheter is correctly positioned against the gastric mucosa [see Figure 6].

An outer crossbar is put in place to prevent inward migration of the tube and to hold the stomach in approximation to the

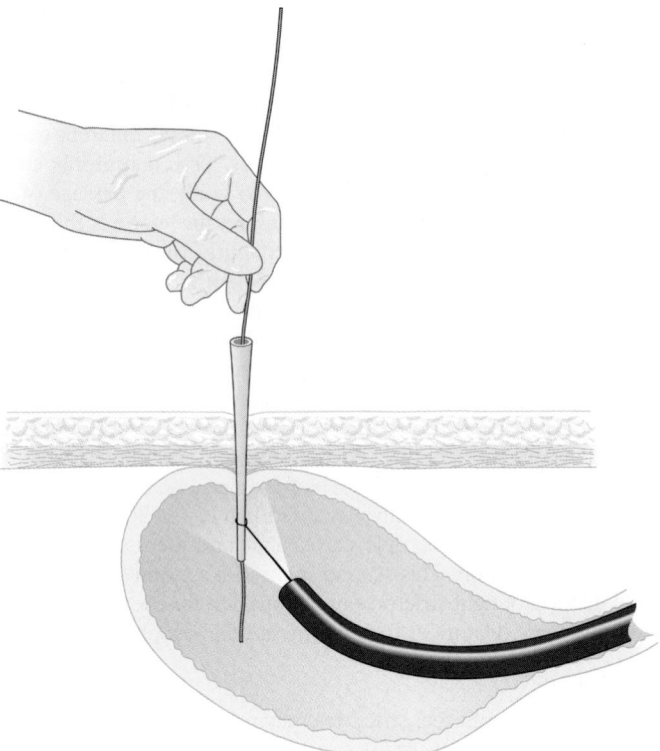

Figure 5 **Therapeutic esophagogastroduodenoscopy: percutaneous endoscopic gastrostomy. The first steps in the procedure involve selecting a proper site in the stomach and using a snare to surround a needle that has been passed through the abdominal and gastric walls.**

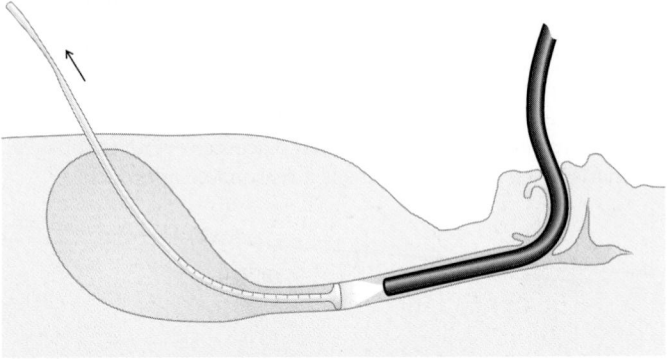

Figure 6 **Therapeutic esophagogastroduodenoscopy: percutaneous endoscopic gastrostomy. After the suture is retrieved from the stomach, it is affixed to the gastrostomy tube and used to pull the tube back into the stomach and out the abdominal wall. The gastroscope is reinserted to follow the process and ensure that the final position of the tube is correct.**

abdominal wall. The crossbar should remain several millimeters from the skin to prevent excessive tension, which would cause ischemic necrosis of the underlying tissue.

Complications

Local wound infections are the most common complications of PEG. They can be minimized by administering preoperative antibiotics and ensuring that excessive tension is not applied to the crossbar at the end of the procedure. When such infections do occur, they can usually be treated via simple drainage and local wound care; sacrifice of the gastrostomy is rarely necessary. Several other complications, such as early extrusion of the tube, progressive enlargement of the tract, and separation of the gastric and abdominal walls with leakage of feedings into the abdominal cavity, are also most often attributable to excessive crossbar tension and subsequent ischemia. Gastrocolic fistula can occur after PEG. This problem may not be obvious for months afterward, but severe diarrhea after feedings is grounds for suspicion. Once the PEG tract is mature, gastrocolic fistulas usually close quickly after simple removal of the gastrostomy tube.

Diagnostic Endoscopic Retrograde Cholangiopancreatography

Endoscopic retrograde cholangiopancreatography (ERCP) is an advanced procedure that is technically more challenging than standard upper GI endoscopy; however, it can be mastered by most endoscopists who are willing to dedicate sufficient time to learning the method. ERCP yields a radiologic image of the pancreatic and biliary trees, and in many cases, it provides access for therapy. Indications for ERCP include suspected benign or malignant maladies of the common bile duct (CBD), the ampulla of Vater, or the pancreas. Cholelithiasis per se is not an indication for ERCP unless choledocholithiasis is suspected.

TECHNIQUE

As with standard upper GI endoscopy, the patient fasts for 6 to 8 hours beforehand. Intravenous sedation is administered, and prophylactic antibiotics are given when biliary obstruction is suspected. The patient is initially placed in the left lateral decubitus position but is later rotated to the prone position after the scope is in place in the second portion of the duodenum. A side-viewing endoscope is employed because it allows the best visualization of the ampulla of Vater. The instrument is passed into the esophagus and maneuvered through the stomach, across the pylorus, and into the duodenum. Manipulation of a side-viewing instrument is a bit awkward for the novice but is easily learned.

Once the endoscope is in the second portion of the duodenum, it is pulled back so that the gastric loop is straightened and the tip of the scope occupies a better position with regard to the papilla. This so-called short scope position is generally best for work in the CBD [see Figure 7]. The papilla of Vater (also known as the major duodenal papilla) appears as a small longitudinal nubbin crossing the horizontal semicircular folds of the duodenum, generally in the 12 to 1 o'clock position. At its tip, a small, soft, reticulated area may be noted; this is the papillary orifice. Often, a small mucosal protuberance is seen just proximal and to the right of the papilla of Vater; this is the minor duodenal papilla.

A small plastic cannula is passed through the channel of the endoscope and introduced into the ampullary orifice, and contrast material is injected under fluoroscopic control to provide visualization of the CBD and the pancreatic duct. The two may share a single orifice within the ampulla or may have separate orifices. The CBD exits the papilla in a cephalad direction, tangential to the duodenal wall. The bulge of the ampulla within the duodenum represents the intramural segment of the duct. The orifice of the CBD is typically found at the 11 o'clock position in the ampulla. The pancreatic duct leaves the papilla in a perpendicular fashion. Its orifice is usually in the 1 o'clock area of the papilla [see Figure 8].

COMPLICATIONS

When contrast material is being injected into the pancreatic ductal system, care must be taken to avoid overfilling, which can

lead to acinarization, or rupture of the small ductules, with extravasation of contrast material into the pancreatic parenchyma; pancreatitis is a frequent consequence of acinarization. Cholangitis may result when contrast is injected proximal to an obstruction of the biliary tree. When obstruction is demonstrated, drainage of the system by means of stone extraction, stenting, or nasobiliary intubation is important to prevent cholangitis.

Therapeutic Endoscopic Retrograde Cholangiopancreatography

Therapeutic interventions that may be accomplished at the time of ERCP include sphincterotomy for ductal access or ampullary stenosis, removal of CBD stones, dilation of benign and malignant biliary strictures, and insertion of stents to maintain ductal patency. Pancreatic duct interventions include removal of stones, bridging of ductal disruptions, and drainage of pseudocysts.

TECHNIQUE

All therapeutic applications of ERCP must begin with selective cannulation of the duct being treated. Frequently, a guide wire is then introduced deep into the duct to provide a means of obtaining access to the duct on an ongoing basis and to ensure correct

a

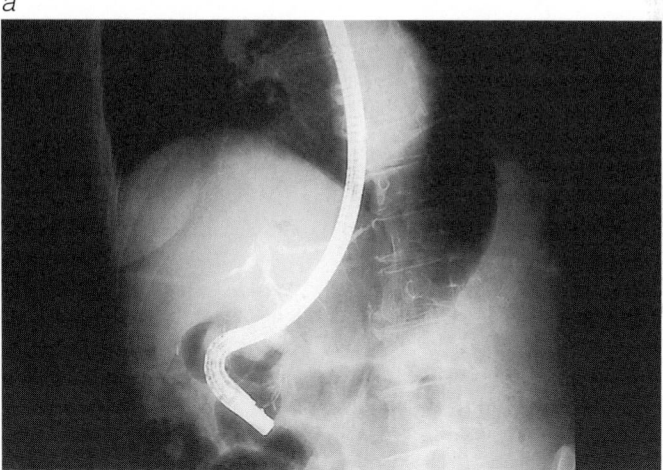

b

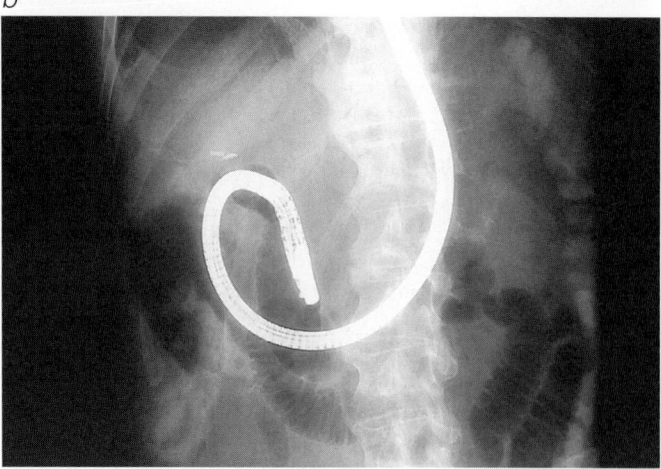

Figure 7 **Diagnostic endoscopic retrograde cholangiopancreatography. (*a*) The so-called short scope position, along the lesser curve of the stomach, is usually the most effective in biliary interventions. (*b*) The so-called long scope position may be necessary at times.**

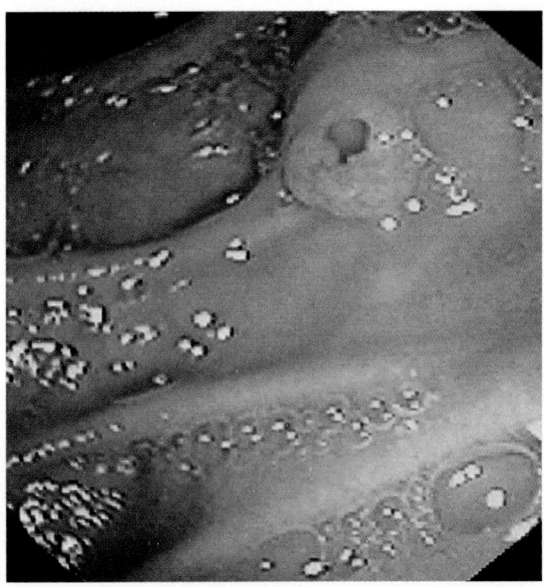

Figure 8 **Diagnostic endoscopic retrograde cholangiopancreatography. The so-called long scope position, along the greater curve of the stomach, may be useful in some pancreatic interventions; shown is the pancreatic duct orifice.**

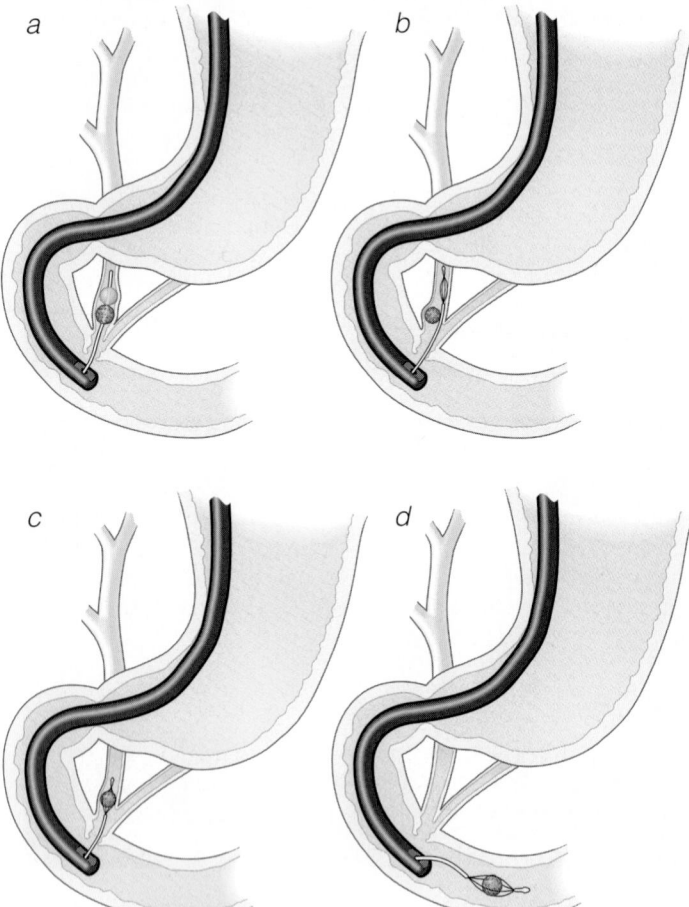

Figure 9 **Therapeutic endoscopic retrograde cholangiopancreatography. After endoscopic sphincterotomy, CBD stones may be retrieved with balloons (*a*) or baskets (*b, c, d*).**

positioning for intraductal manipulations. After electrosurgical division of the papilla, biliary stones are retrieved with balloon or baskets [*see Figure 9*]. Often, large stones can be captured within the duct in mechanical lithotripsy baskets and crushed before removal.

Strictures should be brushed for cytologic evaluation once they have been traversed by a wire. They may then be dilated with hydrostatic balloons under fluoroscopic guidance and stented [*see Figure 10*]. Plastic stents are used for most benign and many malignant strictures; however, self-expanding metal stents are now being used more frequently for malignant strictures because they remain patent longer [*see Figure 11*].

COMPLICATIONS

Perforation can occur during endoscopic sphincterotomy as a result of extension or tearing of the papilla beyond the junction of the CBD with the duodenal wall. Retroperitoneal or free intraperitoneal air may be seen. In many cases, intravenous antibiotics, hydration, and avoidance of oral intake are sufficient to manage such complications. If the patient's condition deteriorates, surgical exploration is indicated.

Bleeding may also occur with sphincterotomy. It is usually controllable with injection of epinephrine solution (1:10,000), electrocoagulation, or balloon tamponade. Arteriographic embolization of the gastroduodenal artery may be helpful in some cases. As with diagnostic ERCP, pancreatitis may occur; it usually responds to conservative measures.

Diagnostic Colonoscopy

Colonoscopy has become one of the most frequently performed endoscopic examinations. It has revolutionized the diagnosis and treatment of colonic disease and offers the promise of reducing the occurrence of colon cancer. Indications for colonoscopy include iron deficiency anemia, frank or occult rectal bleeding, a history of colonic cancer in the patient or in first-degree family members, a history or suspicion of colonic polyps, inflammatory bowel disease, and a persistent change in bowel habits. Preparation involves purging the bowel mechanically by placing the patient on a clear liquid diet for several days, then giving cathartics and enemas; alternatively, one may use osmotic lavage, in which 1 gal of lavage fluid is administered orally over a period of 4 hours. It is often helpful to administer 10 mg of metoclopramide to enhance gastric motility as preparation begins.

TECHNIQUE

Sedation is accomplished as for upper GI endoscopy, and the patient fasts for 6 to 8 hours before the procedure. With the patient in the left lateral decubitus position, a rectal examination is performed. This step helps relax the anal sphincter in preparation for insertion of the scope and ensures that low-lying rectal lesions are not overlooked.

The colonoscope is introduced into the rectal vault, and insufflation of air is commenced. The instrument is advanced only when the lumen is clearly apparent. At times, only a portion of the lumen may be visible, but this is usually enough to guide advancement of the scope. Frequently, when the lumen itself is not visible, light reflected onto the colonic folds can guide one to the lumen, with the concavity of the fold indicating the direction of the lumen. In contrast with upper GI endoscopy, in which torsion on the shaft of the endoscope is rarely necessary, such torsion is the rule in colonoscopy. The shaft of the instrument is rotated with the right hand to facilitate

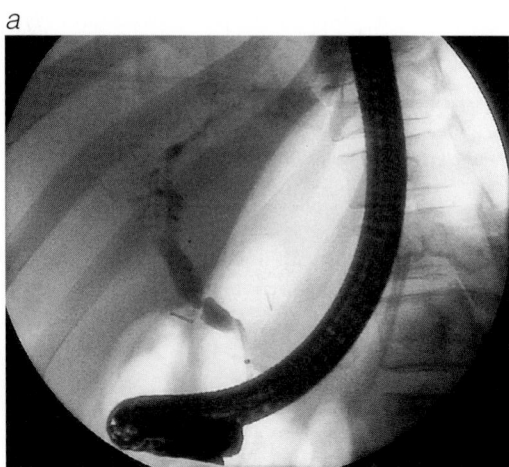
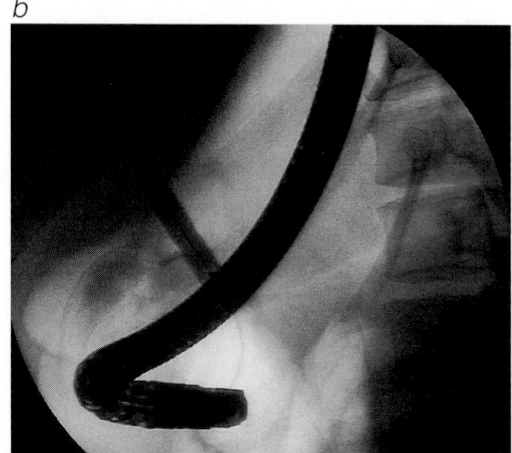

Figure 10   **Therapeutic endoscopic retrograde cholangiopancreatography. CBD strictures (*a*), whether benign or malignant, may be dilated effectively with hydrostatic balloons under fluoroscopic guidance (*b*).**

straightening and intubation of the colon. By applying torsion to the shaft frequently and pulling back the scope as necessary, one can pleat the colon on the instrument as it is advanced. Pulling back is one of the most useful techniques for advancing the colonoscope through the colon.

The colon exhibits a number of characteristic anatomic features that are readily observed during colonoscopy. The sigmoid colon, because of its frequent turns, yields elliptical views of the lumen. The descending colon appears as a long, round tunnel with little haustration. The transverse colon has well-defined triangular folds, and the hepatic flexure may exhibit a blue hue resulting from the proximity of the liver. The cecum is recognized on the basis of the appearance of the ileocecal valve on the lateral wall, the convergence of the colonic taenia to form the cecal strap (the so-called Mercedes sign), and the presence of the appendiceal orifice.

Insertion of the colonoscope as far as the hepatic flexure is rarely difficult. Occasionally, the sigmoid colon presents a challenge, in which case placement of the patient on the back or the abdomen to change the orientation may be helpful. Once again, pulling back and straightening the scope is a highly useful maneuver. Once the scope is in the hepatic flexure looking down the right colon, pulling back, counterclockwise torsion, and the application of suction may all assist in advancing the instrument into the cecum. Changing the patient's position or applying pressure to various points in the abdomen may also be helpful. Once the cecum is reached, the instrument is slowly withdrawn while the colonic parietes are carefully examined. Biopsy and cytologic brushing may be done as appropriate, and colonic contents may be aspirated into a suction trap for examination.

COMPLICATIONS

Perforation is the most common complication of diagnostic colonoscopy. It may result from direct tip pressure, bowing of the shaft of the scope while a large loop is being formed, blowout of a diverticulum secondary to air insufflation, or tearing of an adhesion of the colon to an adjacent structure. The risk of perforation can be minimized by observing the lumen directly as the scope is advanced, avoiding excessive insufflation, and minimizing loop formation. Close attention to patient discomfort is important. If the patient feels poorly after the procedure, an upright chest x-ray, an upright abdominal x-ray, or a lateral decubitus abdominal x-ray should be obtained to determine whether there is any free air, which would indicate a perforation. Such situations have been successfully managed by nonoperative means in some cases, but in most cases, prompt operative intervention with primary repair of the perforation is the best approach.

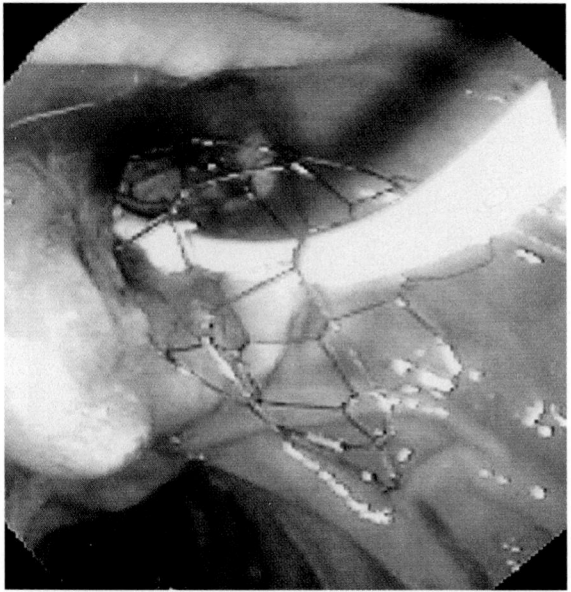

Figure 11   **Therapeutic endoscopic retrograde cholangiopancreatography. Self-expanding metal stents may provide effective long-term palliation of malignant biliary obstruction.**

Therapeutic Colonoscopy

By far the most common use of therapeutic colonoscopy is for the excision of polyps. Other applications include control of bleeding, dilation of strictures, and placement of enteral stents.

TECHNIQUE

The development of colonoscopic polypectomy—electrosurgical excision of the polyp with a wire snare—has rendered operative colotomy unnecessary in the management of colonic polyps. Pedunculated polyps are approached by placing the snare over the polyp's head and tightening the loop around the

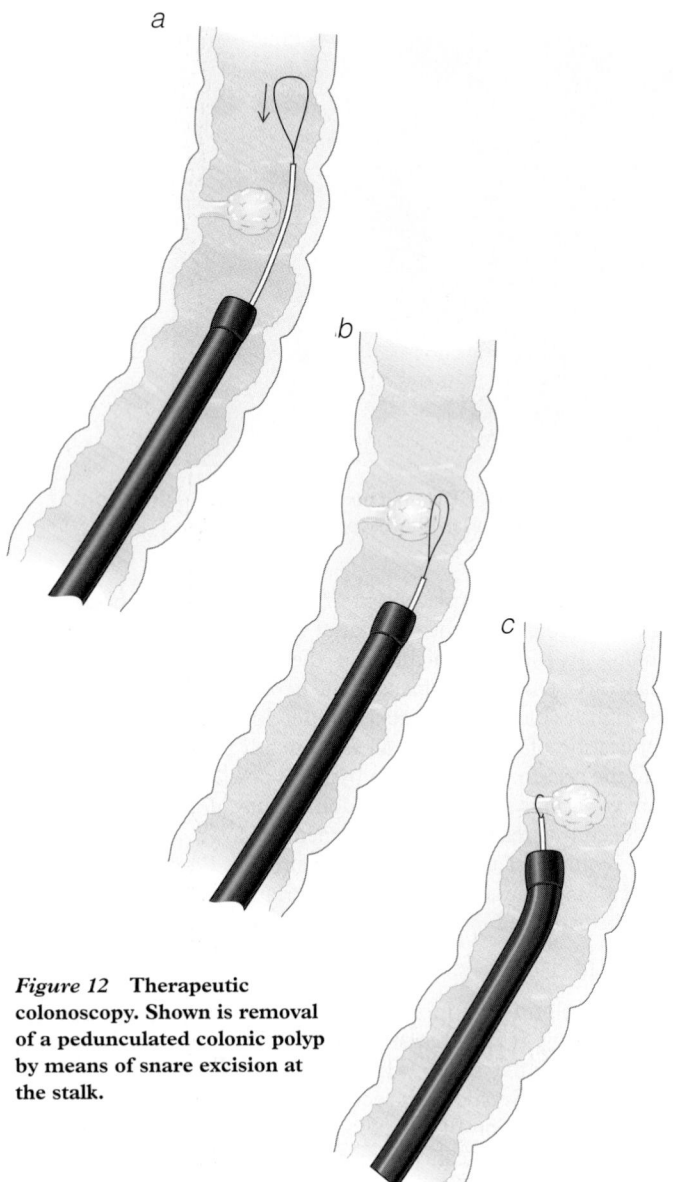

Figure 12 **Therapeutic colonoscopy. Shown is removal of a pedunculated colonic polyp by means of snare excision at the stalk.**

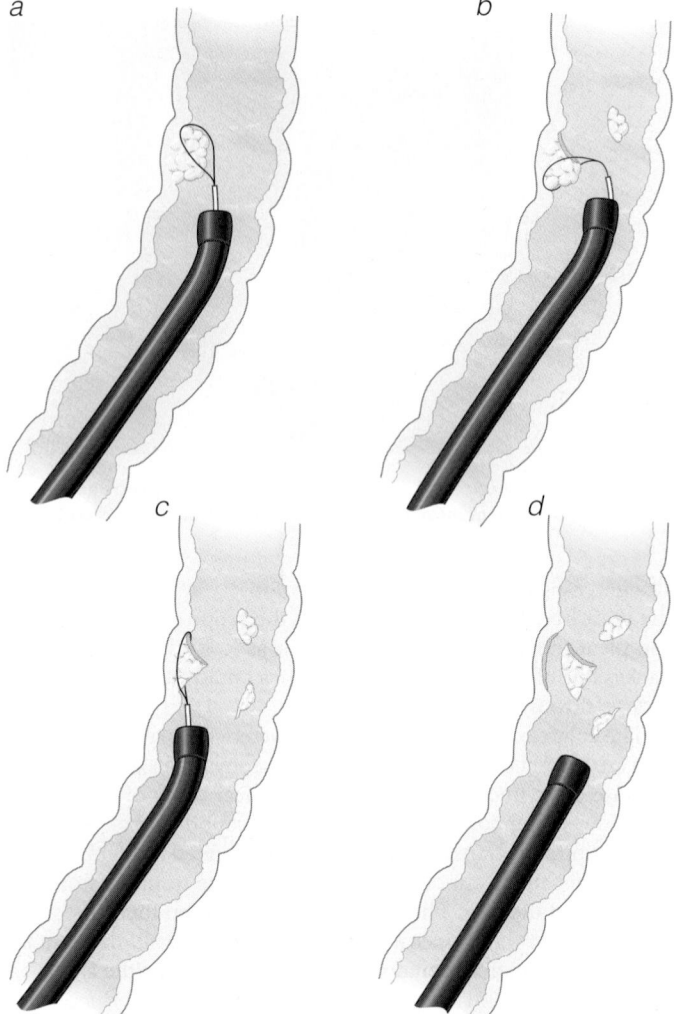

Figure 13 **Therapeutic colonoscopy. Illustrated is piecemeal excision of a sessile colonic polyp.**

stalk near the junction of the head and the stalk [*see Figure 12*]. Because the stalk is an extension of normal mucosa, it is unnecessary—and often unwise—to excise the stalk close to the colonic wall; excision near the head of the polyp is usually sufficient. Short bursts of coagulating current are applied to transect the stalk. During excision, the polyps must be moved around to prevent conduction burns to the opposing colonic wall. Once transection is complete, if the polyp is small, it may be suctioned into a trap; if it is large, it may be suctioned onto the tip of the scope and retrieved or captured in a snare or basket. Sessile polyps are more challenging and risky to excise. Accordingly, it is often preferable to excise such polyps in a piecemeal fashion [*see Figure 13*]. The snare is applied several times to successive portions of the polyp until it is excised down to the colonic wall. The excised fragments are then retrieved. Difficult or large sessile polyps may be elevated before excision by injecting epinephrine solution or saline submucosally into the polyp or the surrounding tissue. This maneuver makes transmural injury less likely (see below).

Although the use of colonoscopy to define the site of colonic bleeding is commonplace, its use to treat such bleeding is not.

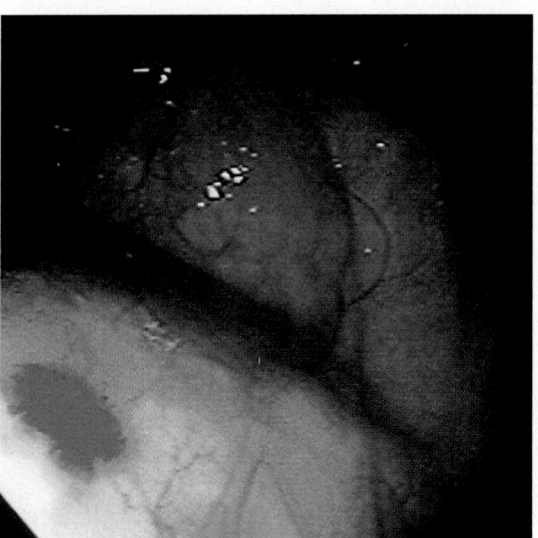

Figure 14 **Therapeutic colonoscopy. Shown is an angiodysplasia of the right colon, a frequent cause of lower GI hemorrhage.**

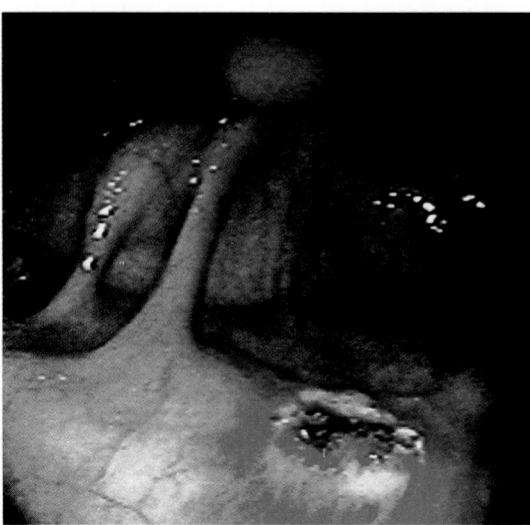

Figure 15 **Therapeutic colonoscopy. Shown is a right colonic angiodysplasia after treatment with bipolar electrocoagulation.**

Diverticular bleeding often stops when colonoscopy is done, and only in rare instances is the actual bleeding diverticulum seen. In such cases, injection of epinephrine solution around the mouth of the offending diverticulum is often effective. Angiodysplasias are frequently found in the right colon, though they are rarely identified while they are bleeding [*see Figure 14*]. They may be treated with a variety of modalities, including bipolar electrocoagulation, injection of a sclerosant solution, and laser therapy [*see Figure 15*]. Currently, the argon plasma coagulator is often employed for obliteration of these lesions. This device has the advantage of being able to obliterate angiodysplasias with minimal wall penetration, thereby increasing the safety of this intervention in the thin-walled right colon.

Strictures may occur in the colon, as in the rest of the GI tract. Colonic strictures usually develop at an anastomosis, though they may also be the result of ischemia. Hydrostatic balloon dilation is very effective in treating such strictures. The balloon is introduced through the lumen of the endoscope, and dilation is carried out under direct vision, often in conjunction with fluoroscopic observation to confirm that dilation is complete. In patients with fully or almost fully obstructing tumors of the colon, self-expanding metal stents may be placed to provide decompression and at least temporary relief of obstruction. This step may avert emergency surgery or, if the tumor is inoperable, provide palliation.

COMPLICATIONS

Perforation may occur as a result of transmural thermal injury during polypectomy. Some perforations are immediately apparent, but others may not be noticed for several days. When perforation is documented, surgical exploration is indicated. Occasionally, a patient may present with fever and abdominal tenderness several days after polypectomy but show no free air on abdominal films. Such a patient may have a thermal injury to the bowel wall or so-called postpolypectomy syndrome and can usually be treated with intravenous fluids, antibiotics, and observation. Bleeding from the stalk of a pedunculated polyp may occur after excision; it may present immediately or may be delayed until the coagulum on the stalk separates 3 to 5 days after polypectomy. Such bleeding is a rare occurrence. When it does occur, it can be treated by injecting epinephrine solution (1:10,000) into the stalk.

Chromoendoscopy

The development of extirpative endoscopy has allowed physicians to treat several conditions that previously required open or laparoscopic surgical procedures. However, it is not always possible to see the difference between diseased and healthy tissue on endoscopy, and this limitation has precluded one-stage procedures. Identification of tissue types required biopsy, and lesion margins were impossible to determine at the time of the procedure.

Chromoendoscopy can help to identify diseased tissue and define lesion borders. This process is essentially an in vivo staining technique in which a variety of specialized stains are applied to tissues to improve their characterization. It differs from carbon-dye injection (tattooing), a technique that is used for later surgical identification, in that the stains used for chromoendoscopy are specific to the anatomic area being examined. Several chromoendoscopic dyes are commercially available in the United States [*see Table 1*]. Selection of a particular agent is based on the type of tissue being studied, the disease state, and physician familiarity.

One of the first agents used for chromoendoscopy was methylene blue. It was initially used in Japan in the 1970s to detect intestinal metaplasia in the stomach. Subsequent studies in the United States, Japan, and Europe independently demonstrated that methylene blue will selectively stain metaplasia in Barrett's esophagus (see above). On routine screening endoscopy in patients with Barrett's esophagus, methylene blue chromoendoscopy offers improved detection of dysplasia and early malignancy compared with four-quadrant random biopsy studies. Other reported applications include esophageal carcinoma, gastric metaplasia, oropharyngeal cancer, mucosal lesions, and heterotopic gastric mucosa.

Endoscopic Mucosal Resection

Endoscopic polypectomy marked the beginning of extirpative procedures. Subsequently, endoscopic resection techniques have continued to advance, as a result of improvements in imaging and instrumentation, along with the development of chromoendoscopy and specific techniques designed as adjuncts to tissue removal. One such technique is endoscopic mucosal resection (EMR).

EMR has its basis in the anatomy of the GI tract. Histologically, the GI tract has three layers: a superficial mucosal, a middle submucosal, and an outer muscular layer. EMR is designed to help the endoscopist remove superficial mucosal tissue while leaving the deeper submucosal and muscular layers intact. These layers can be relatively easily separated from each other by injecting a liquid that spreads within the plane of injection. This step elevates the layers superficial to the injection, thus facilitating the resection of those layers. Advantages over other resection techniques include the preservation of histologic architecture (in contrast to electrocautery or laser ablation), which allows improved pathologic assessment; the ease with which EMR can be combined with endoscopic ultrasonography; and its safety and minimal invasiveness.

EMR was first described in 1955, when submucosal saline injections through a rigid sigmoidoscope were used in the resection of rectal and sigmoid polyps. In 1973, a submucosal saline injection was employed to assist with the removal of sessile polyps throughout the colon. Additional development was accomplished in Japan in 1983, when mucosal resection was used in the treatment of early gastric carcinoma in a technique termed strip-off biopsy. The technique has been refined and is now routinely used for lesions in the esophagus, stomach, duodenum, colon, and rectum. It is widely incorporated into aggressive screening programs designed to detect early GI cancers.

EMR can be used to treat dysplastic and other premalignant lesions, as well as superficial cancers of the GI tract. One must be careful to comply with all standard principles of cancer resection, including knowledge of the depth of the lesion, its radial extent, and staging. Consequently, several criteria must be fulfilled before EMR can be viewed as a curative intervention. Classification of lesions on the basis of their endoscopic appearance can be combined with information obtained through the use of chromoendoscopy and EUS to determine the potential for EMR.

Lesion location within the GI tract is important with respect to long-term outcomes. For example, EMR can be used to treat circumferential colonic lesions but is inappropriate for esophageal lesions that extend beyond one third of the circumference, because of the risk of a late stricture.

Although specific methods differ among practitioners, several generalizations about the technical aspects can be made. First, a liquid must be injected deep to the mucosal layer, allowing separation of the wall components. Although the ideal solution for injection has not been determined, the liquid chosen must be biodegradable, biocompatible, noninflammatory, and have viscoelastic properties allowing the development of an adequate bleb. Saline, hypertonic saline, epinephrine, hyaluronic acid, and glycerol solutions are all in current use. The elevated tissue is then held in place with a grasper or suction mechanism, and snares, needle knives, or lasers are used to cut the tissue at its base. Optimal results are obtained on nonulcerated lesions that are less than 2 cm after elevation; other lesions have a high probability of submucosal lymphatic and vascular invasion.

Although complications can occur, with proper patient selection and procedural refinement they are relatively rare. Perforation has been noted, particularly when submucosal bleb formation is suboptimal. Inadequate blebs may result from insufficient liquid being injected, improper needle depth, or severe scarring of the local tissues. Bleeding has been reported to occur in 1.6% of EMR cases. This complication is relatively easily handled with a combination of electrocautery and epinephrine injection. Infection in the absence of perforation is uncommon.

Overall, EMR provides a minimally invasive means to treat early cancers in favorable locations. Patients must understand that additional resection may be required if histopathologic assessment does not show curative margins. Future development of endoscopic instruments and injection liquids will likely broaden the applicability of the procedure.

Endoscopic Ultrasonography

The 1980s saw the introduction of EUS. Extracavitary ultrasonographic methods have been hampered by the presence of air within the GI tract, which precludes high-resolution imaging. Consequently, they had been relegated to gross estimates of disease and detection of displacement of other tissues or fluid accumulation proximal to stenoses, such as ductal dilation in patients with common bile duct stones.

Three advances have proved invaluable in allowing EUS to carve out a niche in the field of GI diagnosis. First is the improvement in endoscopes that allows transducer and receiver channels to traverse a tortuous path. Second is the development of multiple frequency options in conjunction with circumferential visualization. Higher frequencies provide higher resolutions, allowing useful differentiation of the various layers of the intestinal tract. Third is the evolution of treatment protocols keyed to the accu-

Table 1 Special Stains Used in Endoscopy

Stain	Site of Use	Comment
Lugol solution (2% iodine)	Esophagus	Normal mucosa stains green-brown (as a result of intracellular glycogen); dysplastic cells do not stain
Indigo carmine (0.4% solution)	Stomach, colon	Enhances contour of mucosa, giving tissue a three-dimensional appearance
Toluidine blue	Oropharynx, esophagus	Absorbed by the nucleic acid component of malignant epithelial cells
Congo red	Acid-secreting areas of gastric mucosa	Turns a blue-black color when pH < 3
Methylene blue (0.5% solution)	Intestinal metaplasia, Barrett's esophagus	Absorbed only by dysplastic tissue; however, absorption decreases as severe dysplasia develops

rate staging of tumors—information that is sometimes unobtainable from other imaging techniques.

This technology has now been firmly established as an accurate way to identify carcinoma. Subsequent developments are allowing EUS to expand from the field of diagnosis into the realm of intervention. Examples of EUS-guided procedures include fine-needle aspiration, lymph node sampling, and drainage of pancreatic pseudocysts.

EUS devices come in both linear and radial transducers. Radial transducers have the advantage of providing circumferential visualization that parallels the standard modes of perceiving the GI tract. Linear images allow EUS-directed biopsies and have the potential to provide color and pulsed Doppler imaging. Probes can be mounted on the top of an oblique viewing fiberoptic scope, or come in an over-the-wire format for use in the pancreaticobiliary tree. A series of frequencies is available, with the higher frequencies providing greater resolution but less tissue depth penetration. Lower-frequency probes allow deeper tissue assessment and a broader view, but at the price of reduced resolution. Nevertheless, any form of EUS will provide better resolution than transcutaneous ultrasonography, allowing markedly improved two-point discrimination and hence more accurate tissue diagnosis.

The benefits of accurate staging of GI tumors paved the way for EUS development. Tissue sampling techniques are further benefited by this technology. The sensitivity of EUS makes it one of the best modalities for the evaluation and detection of pancreatic tumors. Its sensitivity, which is in excess of 95%, contrasts favorably with those of other modalities, including ultrasonography (75%), computed tomography (80%), and angiography (89%). The accuracy of T staging by EUS in esophageal cancer (80% to 90%) is greater than that of staging determined by CT scanning (50% to 60%). This finding has led to the development of several staging schemes that are based solely on EUS findings. EUS has established a role in the identification of early pancreatitis; the detection of common bile duct stones and mediastinal masses; and the assessment of anastomotic strictures, thickened gastric folds, and the integrity of the anal sphincter. It has also proved a useful adjunct in the determination of whether a tumor is amenable to EMR techniques or is better served by adjuvant therapies or surgical interventions.

The sensitivity of EUS is rooted in its ability to delineate the various layers of the alimentary canal. Experienced endoscopists can easily evaluate the submucosa and differentiate intramural from extrinsic masses. Characteristic patterns are readily learned and rapidly recognized, obviating tissue diagnoses in straightforward cases. Criteria have also been established to aid in the differentiation of benign and malignant lesions. With the continued use of this technique, additional algorithms will be established in conjunction with more innovative interventional adjuncts. However, two limitations have caused many practitioners to remain skeptical: cost and training issues. Other imaging modalities, such as CT and magnetic resonance imaging, have also made tremendous strides in the recent past. Although these various modalities are often considered competitors—a view arising from the perceived need for a single imaging modality—the issue of which is superior to the others pales in comparison to the benefits that can be gained from combining imaging techniques in appropriate circumstances.

Endoscopic Suturing

The ability to suture through an endoscope would open up an entire arena of new possibilities, including antireflux procedures, morbid obesity surgery, and advances in the control of acute hemorrhage, as well as improved ability to manage complications of other endoscopic techniques. Despite the development and commercial availability of numerous devices, however, design problems have relegated most applications to investigational status. For such devices to enter clinical practice, they must encompass fundamental surgical techniques: the ability to cut, suture, tie knots, and staple. These are critical for maintaining hemostasis and constructing durable anastomoses. Although these techniques are plausible with modern devices, continued innovation and experience in conjunction with a new paradigm of disease management will direct the future of endoscopic interventions.

Natural Orifice Transvisceral Endoscopic Surgery

A new area of endoscopic exploration is emerging—namely, the performance of intraperitoneal surgical procedures by means of a flexible endoscope passed through the wall of a gastrointestinal viscus. This approach, referred to as natural orifice transvisceral endoscopic surgery (NOTES), is still investigational, but it has generated a great deal of excitement in the surgical and gastroenterologic communities. Transgastric gastrojejunostomy, liver biopsy, tubal ligation, and splenectomy in a porcine model have been reported. In addition, there have been anecdotal reports and presentations of natural orifice transvisceral appendectomy in human beings in India; however, to date, there have been no published cases. Extensive laboratory investigation and clinical trials will have to be carried out before the true utility and safety of NOTES can be established.

Recommended Reading

Abi-Hanna D, Williams SJ: Advances in gastrointestinal endoscopy. Med J Aust 170:131, 1999

Acosta MM, Boyce HW Jr: Chromoendoscopy—where is it useful? J Clin Gastroenterol 27:13, 1998

Brugge WR: Endoscopic ultrasonography: the current status. Gastroenterology 115:1577, 1998

Canto M: Methylene blue chromoendoscopy for Barrett's esophagus: coming soon to your GI unit? Gastrointest Endosc 54:403, 2001

Cotton PB, Williams CB: Practical Gastrointestinal Endoscopy, 3rd ed. Blackwell Scientific, Oxford, 1990

Hawes RH: Endoscopic ultrasound. Gastrointest Endosc Clin N Am 10:161, 2000

Hawes RH: Perspectives in endoscopic mucosal resection. Gastrointest Endosc Clin N Am 11:549, 2001

Inoue H: Endoscopic mucosal resection for the entire gastrointestinal mucosal lesions. Gastrointest Endosc Clin N Am 11:459, 2001

Kantsevoy SV, Jagannath SB, Niiyama H, et al: Endoscopic gastrojejunostomy with survival in a porcine model. Gastrointest Endosc 62:287, 2005

Matsuda K: Introduction to endoscopic mucosal resection. Gastrointest Endosc Clin N Am 11:439, 2001

Ponchon T: Endoscopic mucosal resection. J Clin Gastroenterol 32:6, 2001

Ponsky JL: Atlas of Surgical Endoscopy. Mosby–Year Book, St. Louis, 1992

Ponsky JL, King JF: Endoscopic marking of colonic lesions. Gastrointest Endosc 22:42, 1975

Rosch T, Lightdale CJ, Botel JF, et al: Localization of pancreatic endocrine tumors by endoscopic ultrasound. N Engl J Med 326:1721, 1992

Rosen M, Ponsky JL: Endoscopic therapy for gastroesophageal reflux disease. Semin Laparosc Surg 8:207, 2001

Schrock T: Colon and rectum: diagnostic techniques. Shackelford's Surgery of the Alimentary Tract. Vol 4: Colon and Anorectum, 3rd ed. Condon R, Ed. Philadelphia, WB Saunders Co, 1991, p 22

Schuman BM, Sugawa C: Diagnostic endoscopy of upper gastrointestinal bleeding. Gastrointestinal Bleeding. Sugawa C, Schuman BM, Lucas CE, Eds. Igaku Shoin, New York, 1992, p 222

Soetikno R, Inoue H, Chang KJ: Endoscopic mucosal resection: current concepts. Gastrointest Endosc Clin N Am 10:595, 2000

Swain CP: Endoscopic sewing and stapling machines. Endoscopy 29:205, 1997

Venu RP, Geenen JE: Overview of endoscopic sphincterotomy for common bile duct stone. Endoscopic Approach to Biliary Stones. Kozarek RA, Ed. Gastrointest Endosc Clin N Am 1:3, 1991

Acknowledgment

Figures 2, 4a, 4b, 4c, 5, 6, 9 12, 13 Tom Moore.

61 BARIATRIC PROCEDURES

Eric J. DeMaria, M.D., F.A.C.S.

It is clear that severe obesity is associated with a significant increase in morbidity[1] and a decreased life expectancy.[2] Morbid obesity has been shown to have a significant genetic basis.[3,4] To date, attempts to manage morbid obesity with medical weight reduction programs have met with an unacceptably high incidence of recidivism.[5] The approach that has had the greatest and longest-lasting success in achieving weight loss is bariatric surgery.

Operative Planning

CHOICE OF SURGICAL PROCEDURE

The gastric operations performed for morbid obesity include gastric bypass (GBP) procedures and gastric restrictive procedures (i.e., gastroplasty and gastric banding). Randomized, prospective trials have conclusively shown that GBP is as effective for weight control as the malabsorptive jejunoileal (JI) bypass is, while resulting in significantly fewer complications.[6,7] JI bypass is associated with a substantial incidence of both early complications (e.g., acute cirrhosis, electrolyte imbalance, and fulminant diarrhea)[8] and late complications (e.g., cirrhosis, interstitial nephritis, arthritis, enteritis, nephrocalcinosis, and recurrent oxalate renal stones).[9] If evidence of cirrhosis, renal failure secondary to interstitial nephritis, or other complications mandates reversal of a JI bypass, the patient, if not extremely ill, should be converted to a GBP; otherwise, all the lost weight is sure to be regained, and the obesity-related comorbidity will return. Admittedly, however, many patients have done well after JI bypass and do not need to have the operation reversed.

Several randomized, prospective trials have found that horizontal gastroplasty yields poorer results than GBP.[10-12] Failure of horizontal gastroplasty has generally been attributed to technical causes, such as enlargement of the proximal pouch or the stoma or disruption of the staple line. Vertical banded gastroplasty (VBG) was developed in the hope that it would solve these technical problems and yield weight loss comparable to that seen after GBP without incurring the significant risk of iron, calcium, and vitamin B$_{12}$ deficiencies associated with GBP. In the 1990s, a procedure known as adjustable silicone gastric banding was developed, which involved placement of a restrictive ring around the proximal stomach to create a small gastric pouch. In this restrictive procedure, which can be done laparoscopically in the vast majority of patients, weight loss can be enhanced and vomiting minimized by adjusting the ring diameter via transcutaneous access to the subcutaneous reservoir.

Although VBG and, presumably, other restrictive procedures appear to be excellent from a technical point of view,[13] multiple randomized, prospective trials have found such approaches to be significantly less effective than standard GBP. In one comparison trial, patients addicted to sweets lost much more weight after GBP than after VBG because they experienced symptoms of dumping syndrome when ingesting sweets.[14] The failure rate was high after VBG because these patients experienced no difficulties when eating candy or drinking nondietetic sodas. Subsequent randomized, prospective trials confirmed the superiority of GBP.[15,16] Furthermore, maintenance of successful weight loss after GBP appears to continue for as long as 14 years after operation: in the average patient, weight loss amounts to about two thirds of excess weight at 1 to 3 years after operation, three fifths at 5 years, and more than half in years 5 through 10.[17,18] It has been suggested that standard, or proximal, GBP will fail in 10% to 15% of patients because these patients will frequently nibble on high-fat snacks (e.g., corn chips, potato chips, and buttered popcorn). Such patients may have to be converted to a combined restrictive and malabsorptive procedure, such as partial biliopancreatic bypass (BPB).[19]

The original BPB involves hemigastrectomy and anastomosis of the distal 250 cm of intestine to the stomach; the bypassed small intestine is reanastomosed to the ileum 50 cm from the ileocecal valve. BPB with duodenal switch is a variant of the original procedure in which a linear gastric tube based on the lesser curvature is created (sleeve gastrectomy), with the pylorus left intact, and an ileal Roux limb is brought up for anastomosis to the proximal duodenum. BPB has been associated with a high incidence of deficiencies of fat-soluble vitamins, hypocalcemia-induced osteoporosis, and protein-calorie malnutrition.[20] These nutritional deficiencies may be more common in the United States, where fat intake is high, than in many other countries. In Italy, for example, starch intake (as in pasta) probably outstrips fat intake; still, a number of Italian patients have had to be readmitted for parenteral nutrition and extension of the common absorptive intestinal tract because of refractory malnutrition. In some patients, it might be possible to convert a failed proximal GBP into a modified BPB with a 150 cm absorptive ileal limb (a procedure often referred to as distal gastric bypass); however, these patients also must be monitored carefully for deficiencies of fat-soluble vitamins, for osteoporosis, and for malnutrition.

Superobese patients, defined as those whose weight is 225% of ideal body weight or greater or whose body mass index (BMI) is 50 kg/m^2 or higher, will lose, on average, only about half of their excess weight, rather than two thirds, after standard GBP. In these patients, a 150 cm proximal Roux-en-Y procedure (so-called long-limb GBP [*see* Proximal Gastric Bypass, Operative Technique, *below*]) may increase weight loss in the first few years after operation without causing an increase in nutritional complications.[21]

In choosing the appropriate surgical approach, it is important to take into account the tremendous surgical revolution that laparoscopy has brought about in the treatment of morbid obesity. Every operation performed to treat obesity can now be done laparoscopically, and laparoscopic bariatric surgery is now common in many centers. For this reason, as well as because laparoscopic obesity treatment requires advanced technical skills, minimally invasive bariatric procedures have become a cornerstone of training for surgeons now learning laparoscopic surgery.

PREPARATION FOR OPERATION

Many surgeons, exercising good clinical judgment and fearing increased perioperative morbidity and mortality, hesitate to operate on morbidly obese patients for routine elective problems. Complications do occur more often in this population than in the nonobese population, and even the simplest surgical treatment involves a measurable risk of morbidity and even mortality. Given that morbidly obese patients are at greater risk for complications and adverse results, it is all the more remarkable that they can undergo major abdominal surgery for weight loss with the low complication rates and mortalities reported in the literature. These results, however, can only be achieved if a comprehensive program for preoperative and postoperative surgical care is rigorously planned and followed. The key elements of preparation for operation in the morbidly obese patient are discussed in greater detail elsewhere [see 49 Morbid Obesity].

Vertical Banded Gastroplasty

OPERATIVE TECHNIQUE

The first step in VBG is to make a circular stapled opening in the stomach 5 cm from the esophagogastric junction. A 90 mm bariatric stapler with four parallel rows of staples is then applied once between this opening and the angle of His. (At this point, according to Mason, the originator of the procedure, the volume of the pouch should be measured by means of an Ewald tube placed by the anesthetist; ideally, pouch volume should be 15 ml.)

Next, a strip of polypropylene mesh is wrapped around the gastrogastric outlet on the lesser curvature and sutured to itself—but not to the stomach—in such a way as to create an outlet with a circumference of 5 cm for the small upper gastric pouch [see Figure 1a]. Some surgeons have used a stomal outlet 4.5 cm in circumference, but this smaller outlet has not led to better weight loss; in fact, many patients with the 4.5 cm outlet exhibit maladaptive eating behavior, drinking high-calorie liquids because meat tends to get caught in the small stoma.

Silastic ring gastroplasty [see Figure 1b] is a variant of VBG that uses a vertical staple line and a stoma reinforced with Silastic tubing.

COMPLICATIONS

Complications of VBG include erosion of the polypropylene mesh used to restrict the gastroplasty stoma into the gastric lumen, enlargement of the pouch, stomal stenosis, reflux esophagitis, and mild vitamin deficiencies.[22] To date, mesh erosion has been infrequently observed after VBG. Pouch enlargement is fairly common with horizontal gastroplasty but is much less likely to occur with VBG, in which the vertical staple line is placed in the thicker, more muscular part of the stomach. In addition, stomal diameter remains fixed with the mesh band. If mesh erosion, pouch enlargement, stomal stenosis, disabling GI reflux, or recurrent vomiting occurs, it is probably best to convert the patient to GBP. In particular, patients with a Silastic ring VBG may exhibit intractable vomiting of solid foods with no evidence of mechanical obstruction. In our experience, conversion of these patients to GBP yields good results and eliminates the vomiting problem. Finally, vitamin deficiencies can usually be prevented by having VBG patients take a standard multivitamin daily for life.

Laparoscopic Adjustable Gastric Banding

Gastric banding is another form of gastroplasty, in which a synthetic band is placed around the stomach just below the esophagogastric junction. In several series, gastric banding has yielded markedly variable results with respect to achievement of weight loss. Furthermore, it has been associated with slipping or kinking of the banded stoma, obstruction at the band, and intractable vomiting.

Laparoscopic adjustable gastric banding is potentially a significant advance over open gastric banding procedures, primarily because of the adjustability of the band. Open gastric banding procedures have used a variety of materials to constrict the gastric lumen and carry a recognized risk of postoperative nausea and vomiting that do not respond to any treatment short of reoperation. The adjustable gastric band (BioEnterics, Carpinteria, California) used in the laparoscopic procedure [see Figure 2] is a silicone device with an inflatable reservoir that can be inflated or deflated postoperatively through a subcutaneous port placed deep in the abdominal wall for percutaneous access. Saline is injected

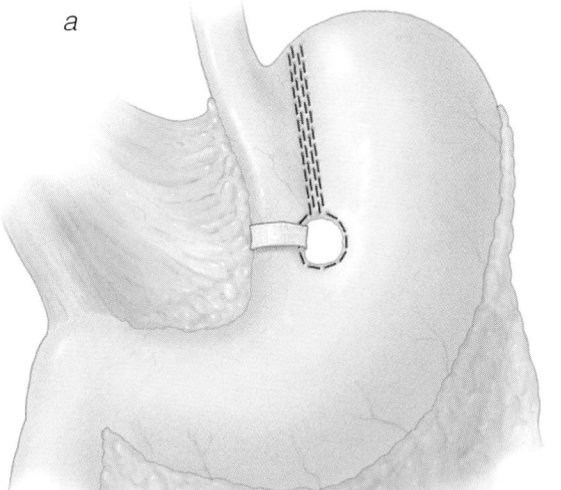
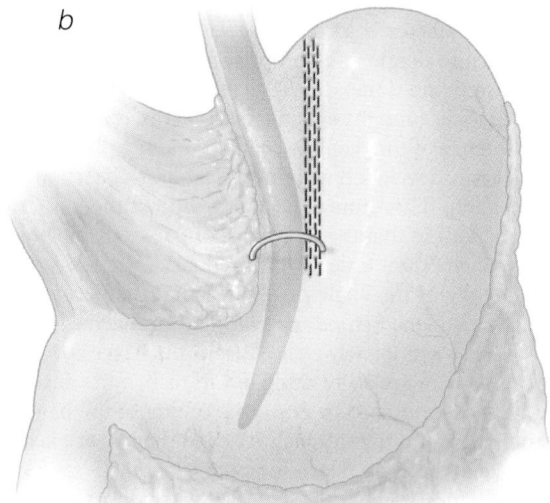

Figure 1 Vertical banded gastroplasty. Depicted are (*a*) standard VBG and (*b*) Silastic ring gastroplasty, a variant of VBG in which the stoma is reinforced with a Silastic tube.

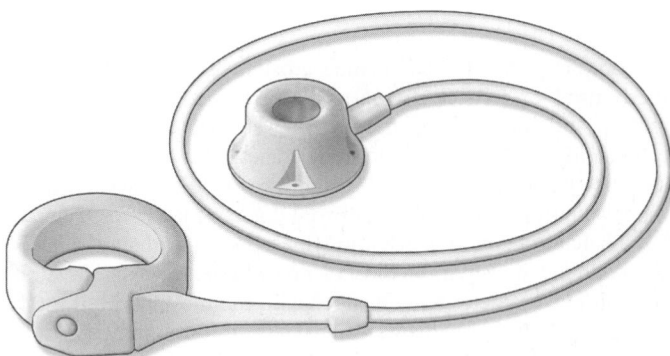

Figure 2 **Laparoscopic adjustable gastric banding. Shown is the adjustable gastric banding device used in the procedure.**

into or withdrawn from the reservoir to adjust gastric luminal diameter, as measured by barium contrast evaluations. Thus, if intractable vomiting develops, saline can be removed from the band to alleviate the problem; similarly, if the patient fails to lose weight after operation, additional saline may be injected into the band to narrow the gastric lumen further.

In June 2001, use of the laparoscopically placed adjustable gastric band was approved by the Food and Drug Administration. Key data on safety and effectiveness were provided by a prospective, single-arm trial involving 299 patients at eight centers in the United States. In this study, patients who completed 36 months of follow-up achieved a mean reduction in BMI of 39% and a mean overall loss of 18% of baseline body weight. However, 28% of patients lost less than 10% of their initial body weight (a clear definition of weight-loss failure). More than half (62%) of these patients lost more than 25% of their excess weight. Most patients (76%) experienced at least one adverse event, and 33% of patients required removal of the banding system.

OPERATIVE TECHNIQUE

Laparoscopic adjustable gastric banding is performed by using a six-port technique. Initial abdominal access is obtained via a supraumbilical trocar, and the remaining five ports are placed sequentially along the right and left costal margins. The liver is retracted via the right lateral port, and the proximal stomach is visualized via a laparoscope inserted through the umbilical port. A 20 ml balloon catheter is sometimes placed perorally into the proximal stomach to define an appropriately small pouch size.

Subsequent steps are done according to the pars flaccida technique. A retrogastric tunnel for band insertion is created at the posterior confluence of the diaphragmatic crura in a plane of dissection that is easily developed with minimal blunt dissection and electrocauterization. This tunnel is placed above the posterior peritoneal reflection, so that the free space of the lesser sac posterior to the stomach is not entered. Additional dissection is then carried out laterally at the angle of His to open the peritoneum and start clearing a plane behind the proximal stomach.

Once the plane is completely cleared from the lesser curvature to the angle of His, a specially designed implement is inserted behind the stomach and used to grasp the tubing of the banding device and pull it around the stomach. The banding device is then locked into place at the chosen location on the stomach [*see Figure 3*]. The band tubing is brought through the left midclavicular trocar port, which is placed via the left midclavicular line subcostal trocar incision and fixed to the abdominal wall fascia with sutures. The tubing is connected to the reservoir, which is filled with saline.

TROUBLESHOOTING

It is essential to place the band properly during the initial procedure. Early results suggest that the proximal pouch must be very small to optimize weight loss. In addition, proper placement minimizes—though it does not eliminate—the risk of band slippage and the complications thereof.

Several techniques have been suggested for posterior fixation of the band, but they are more difficult than anterior fixation techniques. With the pars flaccida technique, posterior fixation of the band is not usually necessary to prevent band slippage. Anterior fixation, however, is routinely performed, with interrupted sutures of nonabsorbable material placed between the distal and the proximal stomach to allow tissue to be apposed over the band and held in place.

Although laparoscopic adjustable gastric banding appears easier than many of the procedures done to treat obesity, there is a definite learning curve. A number of surgical misadventures have been reported, including gastric perforation, splenic injury, and malposition of the band.

COMPLICATIONS

Band slippage (usually posterior rather than anterior) may occur even after proper placement, resulting in intolerance of oral intake and vomiting. Such complaints are an indication for an upper GI series, which usually reveals dilatation of the proximal pouch and rotation of the band [*see Figure 4*]. Initial treatment consists of evacuating all saline from the band. Frequently, however, the proximal pouch does not return to its normal size, and symptoms recur or fail to resolve. Laparoscopic or open revision of the banding procedure is then required; if the patient also has not lost a sufficient amount of weight, conversion to GBP may be recommended. It is noteworthy that band erosion into the stom-

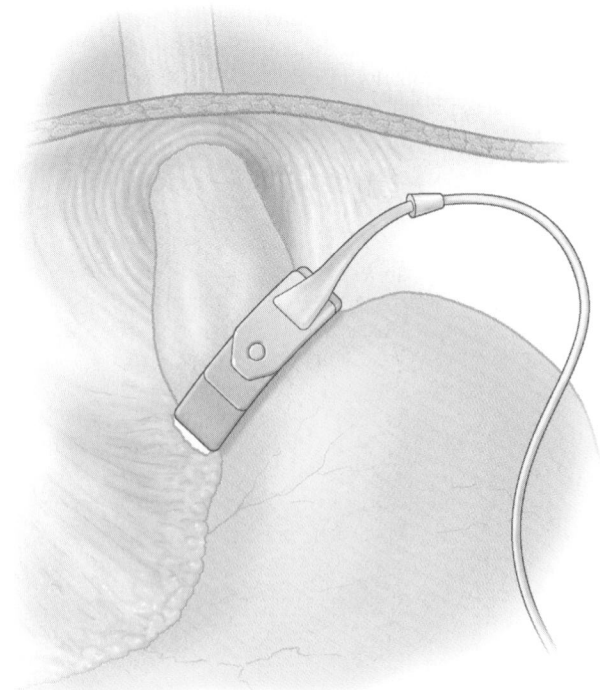

Figure 3 **Laparoscopic adjustable gastric banding. Once in the correct position on the proximal stomach, the adjustable band is locked into place.**

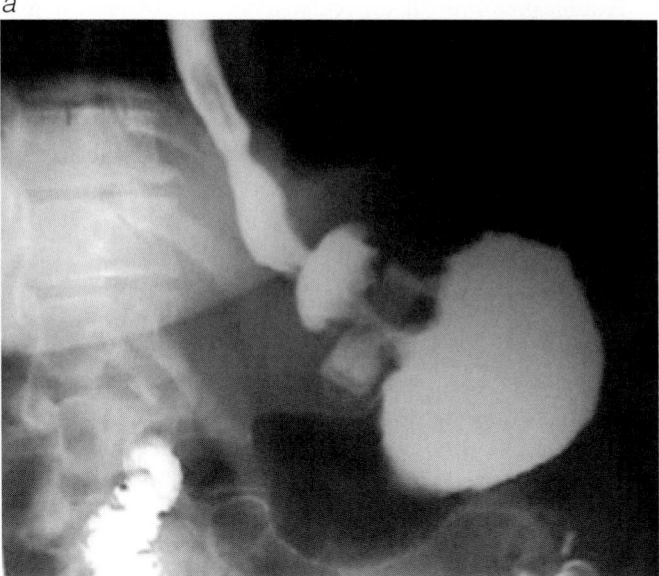
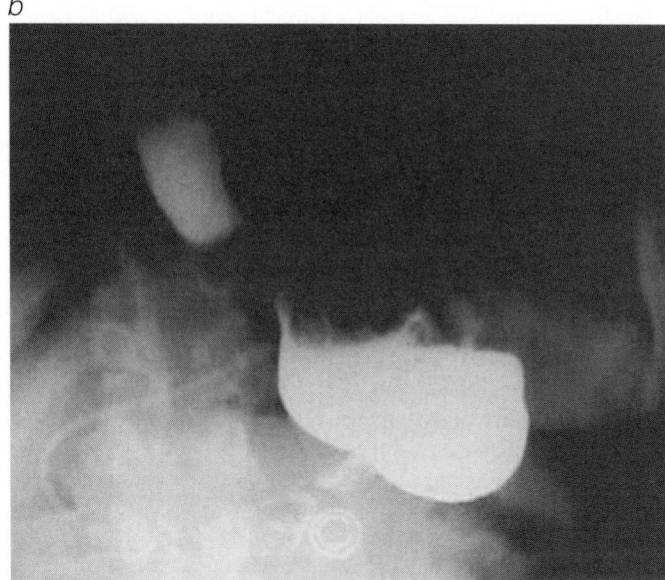

a

b

Figure 4 **Laparoscopic adjustable gastric banding. Contrast studies illustrate (*a*) a normally positioned laparoscopic adjustable gastric band and (*b*) a slipped band.**

ach, a not infrequent complication of the use of mesh in VBG or in the Angelchik prosthesis for gastroesophageal reflux treatment, has not been frequently reported. Longer follow-up will be necessary to evaluate the true extent of this risk.

As after any form of gastroplasty, the patient may fail to lose weight or may regain lost weight. Inappropriate eating behaviors (e.g., intake of high-calorie sweets) are the most likely cause. If obesity-related comorbid conditions persist, conversion to proximal GBP is appropriate.

OUTCOME EVALUATION

How successful laparoscopic adjustable gastric banding is at achieving weight loss over the long term remains unclear. The adjustability and reversibility of the operation, as well as the decreased disability that results, make it attractive to both patients and physicians. The procedure appears to avoid some of the major postoperative complications associated with open GBP (e.g., incisional hernia, marginal ulcer, and stomal stenosis). Band slippage remains a major postoperative concern, however, though the incidence of slippage does appear to decrease as one's experience with the procedure increases. More significant, there appears to be a high frequency of failed weight loss—as high as 15% to 20% of all patients undergoing the procedure and possibly even higher. European and Australian data confirm that there is a significant failure rate but also suggest that the remaining patients achieve a degree of weight loss approaching that seen with proximal GBP. Whether these reports will withstand the scrutiny of long-term follow-up remains to be seen.

Now that the laparoscopic adjustable gastric band has received the approval of the FDA, this procedure may come to play an important role in the management of more and more morbidly obese patients in the United States.

Proximal Gastric Bypass

Proximal GBP results in greater weight loss than the gastric restrictive procedures (see above) and carries a lower incidence of weight regain; consequently, it should be considered the superior procedure. At our institution, the focus since the beginning of the

1990s has been on developing techniques for minimizing complications after laparoscopic proximal GBP. Any surgeon currently performing this procedure ought to be able to achieve a gastrojejunal anastomotic leakage rate lower than 5%; many groups, in fact, report rates lower than 3%. In addition, other postoperative complications (e.g., acute dilatation of the excluded portion of the stomach) are usually preventable if strict attention is paid to mastering the technical aspects of the operation.

Compared with the version of GBP performed at our institu-

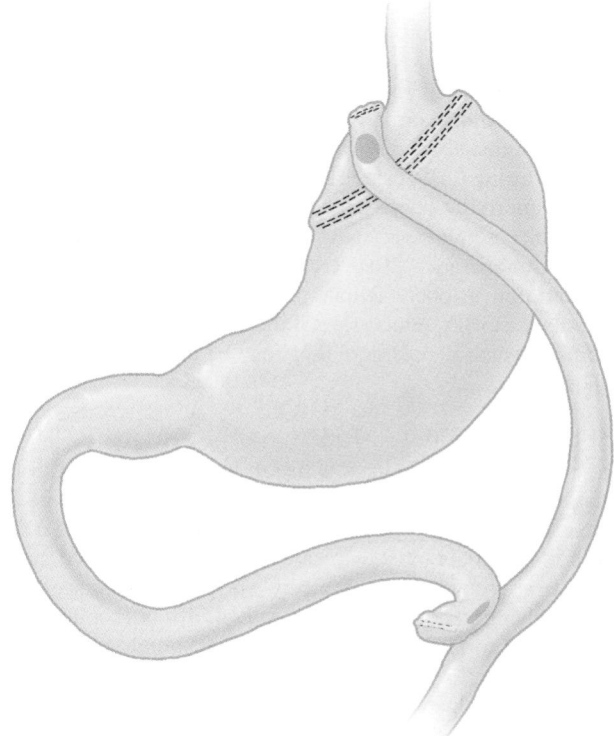

Figure 5 **Proximal gastric bypass. Depicted is the completed procedure.**

tion, the original GBP created a much larger proximal gastric pouch and a much wider anastomotic opening, and it was often associated with inadequate weight loss. In the later version, three superimposed 55 or 90 mm staple lines are placed across the proximal stomach in such a way as to create a gastric pouch no larger than 30 ml with a Roux limb at least 45 cm long and a stoma no larger than 1 cm [see Figure 5]. This anatomic situation is largely replicated when GBP is done laparoscopically, but an isolated gastric pouch is created with stapled transection of the stomach.

OPERATIVE TECHNIQUE

Step 1: Initial Incision and Abdominal Exploration

Once the patient is anesthetized, the abdomen receives a thorough, careful cleansing with povidone-iodine and is draped in a sterile fashion. An upper midline incision is made and extended through the fascia alongside the xiphoid process to facilitate cephalad exposure. The incision is routinely carried down to the supraumbilical area. The deep layer of subcutaneous fat can often be separated bluntly with aggressive lateral traction applied by the surgeon and the assistant, and the midline usually can then be identified for fascial incision. The electrocautery is used to enter the abdominal cavity, and a thick layer of subfascial preperitoneal fat is often encountered before entry into the peritoneal cavity. Abdominal exploration is undertaken in every patient, including examination of the liver for possible signs of liver disease. Other incidental findings may become apparent as well.

Troubleshooting Unexpected significant liver disease is occasionally discovered at the time of operation. If the patient has cirrhosis without portal hypertension, one should perhaps proceed with bypass if the patient's comorbid conditions make it mandatory; liver transplantation carries increased risk in morbidly obese patients. The gallbladder should be palpated for gallstones, which, if found, should be considered an indication for cholecystectomy at the time of the bypass procedure. If there are no visual or palpable gallbladder abnormalities, intraoperative ultrasonography may be used to examine the gallbladder, and cholecystectomy is performed if small stones, sludge, or polyps are identified.

It is not unusual to discover other previously unrecognized conditions during GBP, primarily because symptoms may not be obvious in morbidly obese patients and because their large size tends to make radiologic imaging difficult or even impossible. For example, intraoperative discovery of pelvic cysts and tumors is not uncommon in obese female patients. Such lesions may be excised during GBP; on occasion, if they appear benign and their location prevents safe excision, they may be managed with careful follow-up.

Step 2: Mobilization of Esophagus

The bypass procedure itself is begun by mobilizing the distal esophagus and encircling it with a soft rubber drain 0.5 in. in diameter. The gastrohepatic omentum is bluntly entered at a point overlying the caudate lobe, with care taken to look for and avoid injury to an aberrant left hepatic artery. The phrenoesophageal ligament overlying the anterior and lateral distal esophagus is sharply incised to facilitate subsequent blunt mobilization of the distal esophagus. To prevent esophageal injury, the nasogastric tube is carefully palpated within the lumen of the esophagus during mobilization, and blunt dissection proceeds widely around this important landmark. Laterally, dissection must be at the level of the esophagus or higher.

Troubleshooting If dissection is too low laterally, it may result in blunt injury to the short gastric vessels, bleeding, and the need for urgent splenectomy, which is no easy task in a morbidly obese patient. In addition, it may lead to creation of an inappropriately large pouch by keeping the surgeon from recognizing that some of the stomach is above the level at which the encircling rubber drain is placed.

Step 3: Division of Mesentery and Dissection around Stomach

Once the esophagus is mobilized, the assistant's left hand is placed through the gastrohepatic omental opening behind the stomach wall on the lesser curvature. The space between the first and second branches of the left gastric artery is then identified as a landmark for location of the gastric staple line, both to ensure that the pouch created is no larger than 30 ml and to prevent injury to the left gastric artery, which usually runs cephalad to this location. With the surgeon's posterior finger pressing anteriorly to place tension on the tissue, a fine-tip right-angle clamp and the electrocautery pencil are used to divide the mesentery carefully at this level immediately alongside the stomach wall so as to create a mesenteric opening that will admit a large right-angle clamp.

The avascular tissue on the posterior wall of the stomach is then bluntly dissected between the opening in the gastrohepatic omentum and the lateral angle of His, which is identified by the encircling rubber drain. The blunt tip of a large 28 French red rubber tube is placed behind the stomach in a medial-to-lateral direction along this dissected path to encircle the stomach [see Figure 6]. The open end of the red rubber tube is subsequently brought through the previously created mesenteric opening with a large right-angle clamp. The stomach is now ready for stapling, and the red rubber tube serves as a guide for introduction of the stapler. At this point, all intraluminal tubes and devices (e.g., the nasogastric tube and the esophageal stethoscope) are removed from the esophagus by the anesthetist.

Troubleshooting When a tube is inadvertently stapled within the stomach, excising it from the staple line can become a technical nightmare. To remove the stapled tube, it is usually necessary

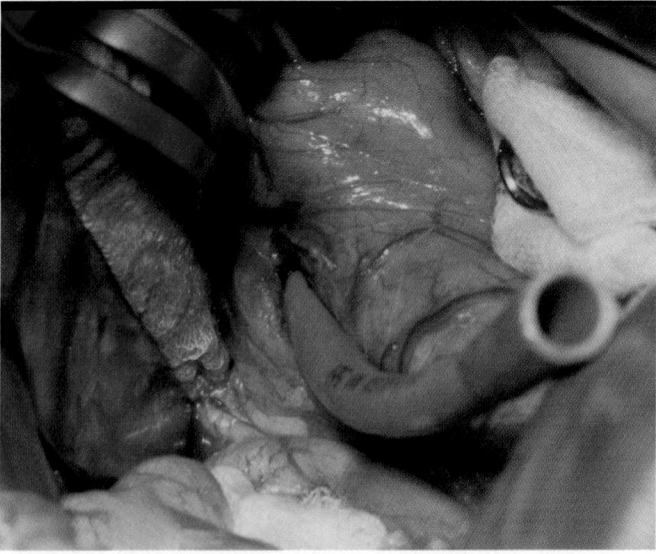

Figure 6 **Proximal gastric bypass. After dissection of the avascular tissue on the posterior gastric wall, a red rubber catheter is passed through the resulting space to encircle the stomach.**

to transect the stomach, thereby creating the potential for significant injury to the gastric tissue and possibly compromising the eventual anastomosis.

Step 4: Creation and Mobilization of Roux Limb and Jejunojejunostomy

The ligament of Treitz is identified, and the jejunum is measured to a point 45 cm beyond the ligament, where the jejunum is divided with a stapler. An 8 to 12 cm segment of jejunum is resected at this point to create a larger mesenteric defect, which should facilitate mobilization of the limb to the proximal stomach. Mesenteric dissection is carried posteriorly in fat with the sequential application of clamps until further dissection appears either unnecessary for mobilization or unwise (i.e., likely to cause mesenteric vascular injury).

A side-to-side jejunojejunostomy is then created with a 60 mm linear stapler either 45 cm beyond the initial point of jejunal division, for standard proximal GBP, or 150 cm downstream, for the long-limb modification of the procedure used in superobese patients [*see* Operative Planning, Choice of Surgical Procedure, *above*]. It is important not to narrow the efferent lumen at the jejunojejunostomy site, particularly with the long-limb modification, in which the lumen at the distal end of the Roux limb may be quite small. The enterotomies made to allow placement of the stapler can usually be closed with a 55 mm stapler loaded with 3.5 mm staples; however, if stapling would cause undue narrowing of the lumen, the closures should be handsewn instead.

Troubleshooting It may be preferable to mobilize the Roux limb before committing to stapling the stomach so that it can be determined whether the limb can be extended to reach the proximal stomach without tension being placed on it. In those rare cases in which the mesentery is too foreshortened to permit the limb to reach the proximal stomach, it is advisable to change the procedure to VBG rather than create a gastrojejunal anastomosis under tension and thereby incur the increased risk of leakage.

Step 5: Gastric Stapling and Gastrojejunostomy

The Roux limb is brought through the mesentery of the transverse colon with blunt dissection and then brought up to the proximal stomach. The 55 or 90 mm stapler, loaded with 4.8 mm staples, is guided behind the stomach by inserting its open-mouthed end into the lumen of the previously positioned red rubber tube. Once it is determined that the staple line will reach completely across the stomach and that the stomach is not folded on itself, the stomach is stapled three times in such a way that the three staple lines are superimposed [*see Figure 7*].

A 1 cm anastomosis is created between the proximal stomach pouch and the Roux limb, with an outer layer composed of interrupted 3-0 silk sutures and an inner layer composed of a continuous absorbable 2-0 polyglycolic acid (Dexon) suture. When the posterior aspect of the anastomosis is complete, a 30 French dilator is placed with the patient under anesthesia and is guided through the anastomosis by the surgeon to ensure that the stoma has the appropriate diameter [*see Figure 8*]. The anterior aspect of the anastomosis is then completed.

Troubleshooting A significant concern for many bariatric surgeons has been a high incidence of staple line disruption causing failed weight loss or weight regain; in one series, the incidence of such disruption was 35%. To minimize this risk, some surgeons

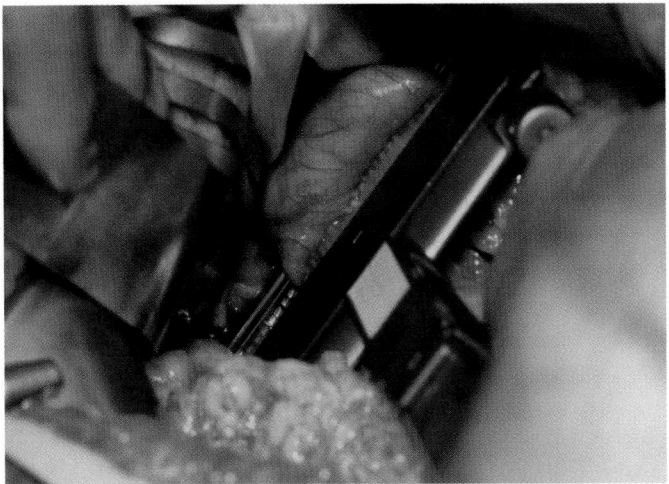

Figure 7 **Proximal gastric bypass. The stomach is stapled to create the small proximal pouch. The stapler is fired three times to create three superimposed staple lines, thereby decreasing the risk of staple line disruption.**

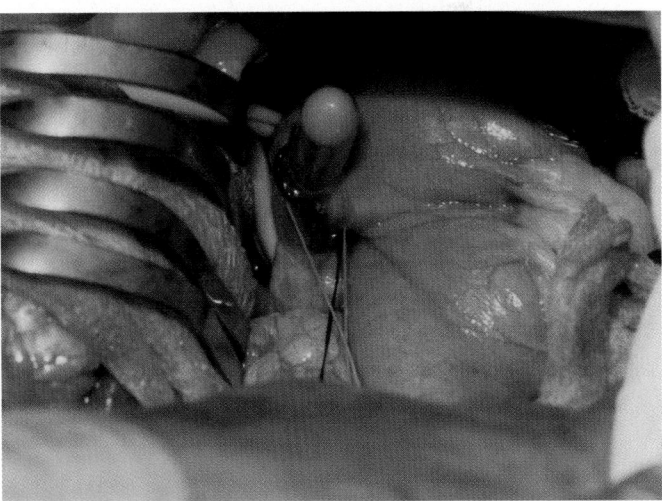

Figure 8 **Proximal gastric bypass. When the posterior aspect of the gastrojejunal anastomosis has been completed, a 30 French dilator is placed through the stoma to confirm that the opening is correctly sized.**

advocate transecting the stomach. This is done by inserting two parallel TA-90 staplers and cutting between them with a scalpel after the staplers are fired. Other surgeons, however, prefer to oversew the staple line. Using the technique of three superimposed staple lines has made it possible to reduce the incidence of staple line disruption to less than 2%; consequently, gastric transection is unnecessary on a routine basis (though occasionally useful in selected cases) and may increase the risk of the procedure.

Another advantage of gastric transection besides reduction of staple line disruption is that it allows the Roux limb to be brought up to the gastric pouch via a retrocolic and retrogastric tract, which is significantly shorter and places less tension on the limb. This approach is particularly helpful in severely obese patients with a fatty and foreshortened mesentery, in whom it is difficult to free the Roux limb sufficiently to reach the proximal stomach without tension. The possibility that gastric transection may prove helpful in a specific patient is another reason why it is advisable to delay stapling the stomach until the Roux limb is mobilized.

Step 6: Assessment of Anastomosis

When the entire anastomosis is complete, the dilator is removed and the tip of an 18 French nasogastric tube is advanced by the anesthetist and carefully guided through the anastomosis by the surgeon. The Roux limb is occluded with the assistant's left hand or with an atraumatic intestinal clamp, and the anesthetist injects a series of 10 ml aliquots of methylene blue dye through the nasogastric tube to determine whether the anastomosis is leaking. A total of 30 to 60 ml of methylene blue must usually be injected; lesser amounts will not stress the suture line enough to constitute an adequate test.

Troubleshooting When an intraoperative leak is identified, the area of leakage should be oversewn with silk sutures until injection of additional methylene blue dye via the nasogastric tube yields no further leakage. The most difficult area to repair is the posterior suture line, which is quite close to the gastric staple line. Posterior leaks are usually repaired by reinforcing the posterior suture line with additional sutures between the excluded stomach and the jejunal limb; often, the entire posterior suture line is oversewn. In addition, a viable pedicle of omentum may be mobilized and placed around the anastomosis for additional reinforcement. Closed suction drains may also be placed in this area, both to detect possible postoperative leakage and to control a postoperative fistula.

Finally, a gastrostomy tube may be placed in the excluded portion of the stomach. This measure provides postoperative decompression, which should prevent the development of undue tension on the Roux limb as a result of gastric distention, and establishes a route for enteral feeding if a fistula develops. Fortunately, such fistulas are rare. When they do occur, they often heal if (1) they are well drained, (2) there is no distal obstruction or local abscess, and (3) the patient is receiving nutritional support with no oral intake. A gastrostomy tube should also be placed in the distal gastric pouch when extensive adhesions from a previous procedure or a difficult gastric reoperation increases the risk of postoperative gastric distention.

Step 7: Closure

When the absence of leakage is confirmed or when any leaks identified have been controlled, the tip of the nasogastric tube may be positioned further down in the Roux limb and left to continuous suction overnight. All mesenteric defects—at the jejunojejunostomy, at the mesocolon, and behind the Roux limb (Peterson hernia)—are then closed to prevent an internal hernia. The abdominal fascia is reapproximated with a continuous No. 2 nonabsorbable suture, subcutaneous tissues are irrigated with a crystalloid solution containing 1% neomycin, and the skin is closed with skin staples. No subcutaneous sutures or drains are used in routine cases.

COMPLICATIONS

Proximal GBP is associated with a significant incidence of stomal stenosis and with marginal ulcer.[23] The former responds to endoscopic stomal dilatation, and the latter usually responds to H_2 receptor blocker or proton pump inhibitor therapy.

Iron, vitamin B_{12}, and folic acid deficiencies may occur but can usually be corrected with oral supplements[22]; accordingly, GBP patients, like VBG patients, should be advised to take a multivitamin daily for life. Compared with VBG, GBP results in significantly lower serum hemoglobin and iron concentrations. This is primarily a problem in menstruating women. All menstruating women who have undergone GBP should be treated prophylactically with supplemental oral ferrous sulfate, 325 mg/day. As many as six iron tablets a day may be required if menstrual bleeding is heavy. On occasion, intramuscular iron injections or, rarely, hysterectomy may be necessary. The risk of vitamin B_{12} deficiency is higher after GBP than after VBG, but this condition can be prevented with supplemental oral vitamin B_{12}, 500 mg/day. A few patients may require (or prefer) monthly B_{12} injections, which they can learn to administer themselves.

Concerns have been expressed that GBP can lead to other divalent cation deficiencies. Our group has not encountered zinc deficiencies 5 to 9 years after GBP, though we have observed calcium deficiencies leading to osteoporosis, which may take many years to become manifest and may not be biochemically evident because of normal serum calcium levels. It is therefore recommended that all GBP patients take oral calcium supplements. Magnesium deficiencies should be treated with $MgSO_4$ supplementation.

Although nutritional deficiencies do not appear to be a greater problem with long-limb GBP than with standard proximal GBP, monitoring patients for possible malabsorption of the fat-soluble vitamins A, D, and E after long-limb GBP is advisable.

BPB may be associated with all of the complications seen after GBP. In addition, patients who undergo BPB may experience diarrhea, severe protein malnutrition (manifested as hypoalbuminemia), and deficiencies of vitamins A (manifested as severe night blindness), D (manifested as severe osteoporosis), and E.[20] Hypoalbuminemia may respond to oral pancreatic enzymes but often must be treated with total parenteral nutrition. In some patients, it may prove necessary to lengthen the absorptive intestinal tract from 50 cm to 200 cm.

OUTCOME EVALUATION

A series of 672 open proximal GBP procedures reported a 1.2% incidence of anastomotic leak with peritonitis, a 4.4% incidence of severe wound infection (defined as infection serious enough to delay hospital discharge), an 11.4% incidence of minor wound infections and seromas (which were easily treated at home), a less than 1% incidence of gastric staple line disruption with the use of three superimposed applications of a 90 mm linear stapler, a 15% incidence of stomal stenosis, a 13% incidence of marginal ulcer, a 16.9% incidence of incisional hernia, and a 10% incidence of cholecystitis necessitating cholecystectomy.[17] Gallstones developed in 32% of the GBP patients who had a normal intraoperative gallbladder ultrasonogram within 6 months of surgery, and sludge was observed in another 10%. In a multicenter randomized, prospective trial,[24] the incidence of gallstones within 6 months of GBP was reduced from 32% to 2% by giving patients ursodeoxycholic acid, 300 mg twice daily. Gallstone formation beyond 6 months is very rare. The operative mortality in this series was less than 1%. Patients with respiratory insufficiency of obesity had a 2.2% operative mortality, whereas those without pulmonary dysfunction had a 0.4% mortality.

Neither the data from this randomized, prospective trial nor the data from selective studies support the contention that VBG is safer than GBP. Although GBP includes one more anastomosis than VBG, complications such as leaks and peritonitis occur with both operations. A common criticism of GBP is that it is difficult to evaluate the distal gastric pouch and duodenum after the operation. Such evaluation, however, can be done in 75% of patients by means of retrograde passage of an endoscope into the duodenum and the stomach and in others by means of percutaneous distal distention gastrography (DeMaria EJ, Sugerman HJ, unpublished data, 2000). Bleeding from either the distal gastric pouch or a duodenal ulcer is rare. In one patient, a perforation of the proximal gastric pouch developed after administration of high-dose nonsteroidal anti-inflammatory medication. Gastric mucosal metaplasia of the bypassed portion of the stomach was noted in 5% of patients after retrograde endoscopy, a finding that has raised concerns regarding the risk of carcinoma arising at that location. However, tens of thousands of these procedures have been performed since 1967, and only two cases of cancer in the bypassed stomach have been reported to date.

Laparoscopic Gastric Bypass

One would anticipate that laparoscopic GBP would yield much the same weight-loss results as open GBP but with less pain, reduced disability, and a shorter hospitalization period. In addition, one would anticipate a decrease in major wound infections as well as fewer incisional hernias. On the face of it, it seems likely that the laparoscopic procedure, though more expensive, would be cost-effective, but proving it is so will probably require an analysis of long-term follow-up that documents decreased subsequent hospitalizations for wound infections, hernia repairs, and complications of intra-abdominal adhesions (e.g., bowel obstruction), given that early results have not demonstrated a dramatic reduction in the length of hospitalization after the procedure. If the additional benefit of reduced disability-related absence from work is realized, this would help reduce overall costs as well.

TOTAL INTRACORPOREAL LAPAROSCOPIC GASTRIC BYPASS

Laparoscopic GBP poses significant technical challenges, even for surgeons with advanced laparoscopic skills. Most of the variations seen at different institutions are related to creation of the gastrojejunal anastomosis, with some groups using a circular stapler and others a linear stapler. The anvil of the circular stapler may be placed within the proximal gastric pouch either by means of flexible upper GI endoscopy, through an approach similar to the snare-and-wire technique used for placement of a percutaneous endoscopic gastrostomy (PEG) tube [see 60 Gastrointestinal Endoscopy], or by means of a gastrotomy of the pouch for intra-abdominal anvil placement followed by staple closure of the gastrotomy. Peroral placement of the stapler's anvil can be problematic: even the small 21 French anvil is hard to pass through the proximal esophagus in some patients. I routinely use the linear stapling method to create the gastrojejunal anastomosis; it is easier than circular stapling in this setting, and there is no risk of esophageal trauma from anvil passage.

Operative Technique

Step 1: initial access and trocar placement   Initial access to the abdomen is obtained through a left subcostal incision with either a Veress needle or a commercially available device that allows direct vision through the scope while a 12 mm trocar is inserted. Gas is then insufflated into the abdomen to a pressure of 15 mm Hg; on occasion, a pressure of 18 mm Hg may be necessary. Additional trocars are placed in specific locations [see Figure 9]. The liver is retracted with a metal Nathanson liver retraction device anchored to the bed, which is inserted after a 5 mm sharp trocar is used to enter the abdominal cavity in the subxiphoid position and removed. If the left lateral segment of the liver is very large (as in patients with steatosis), additional liver retractors may be necessary.

The enlarged fatty falciform ligament must occasionally be dis-

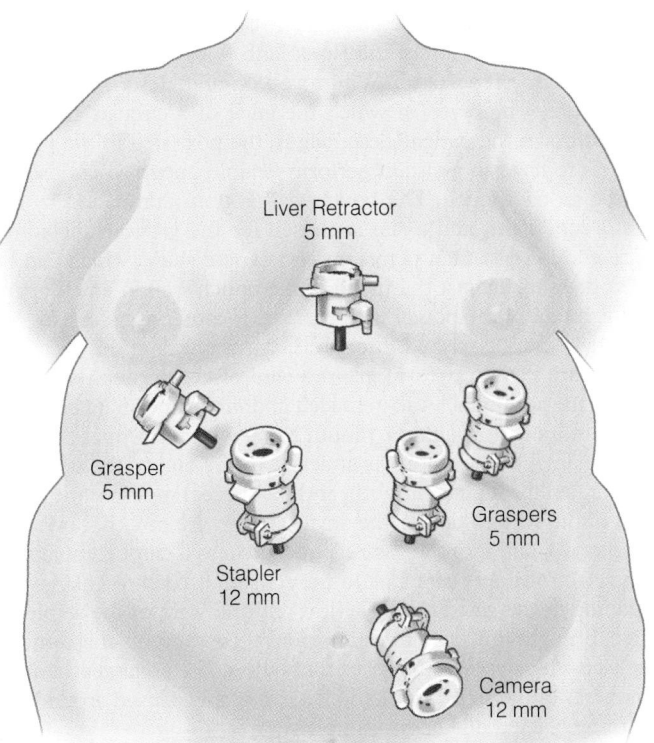

Figure 9   **Laparoscopic gastric bypass: total intracorporeal approach. Shown are the trocar incision sites for laparoscopic GBP.**

sected from the anterior abdominal wall with an ultrasonic scalpel. Trocar incisions near the costal margin and midline have been rendered unnecessary by the advent of long laparoscopic graspers, staplers, and ultrasonic dissectors, which facilitate operation on the proximal stomach. A 12 mm port placed in the right paramedian position serves as the surgeon's primary operative port; two lateral subcostal 5 mm ports allow both surgeon and assistant to employ two-handed techniques for the entire procedure.

Step 2: dissection around stomach and creation of gastric pouch   The mesentery of the lesser curvature is transected with a linear stapler loaded with 2.0 mm staples in a vascular cartridge to provide hemostasis. Despite the potential for problems with transection of the neurovascular bundle, no clear evidence of such problems has been found in hundreds of procedures performed with this access technique. Dissection posterior to the stomach is performed in the avascular free plane of the lesser sac. Additional dissection along the lesser curvature is not recommended, because it may increase the devascularization of the pouch. Further dissection is done with the ultrasonic scalpel at the angle of His to create a connection with the posterior gastric space. A linear endoscopic gastrointestinal anastomosis (GIA) stapler loaded with 3.5 mm staples in 60 mm cartridges is then used to transect the stomach and create the proximal gastric pouch; three firings are usually necessary [see Figure 10]. When reoperation is indicated or when buttressing materials are used to reinforce the staple line, 4.8 mm staples are usually required

Step 2a (circular stapling): placement of stapler in gastric pouch   As noted (see above), surgeons use several different techniques to complete the gastrojejunal anastomosis. With linear stapling, the surgeon proceeds directly from creation of the gastric pouch to mobilization of the Roux limb [*see* Step 3, *below*]. With the technique reported in Wittgrove's original description of the procedure,[25] however, in which the anvil of a circular stapler is passed down the patient's esophagus, the next step in the procedure is to have an assistant perform flexible upper GI endoscopy of the gastric pouch. The pouch wall is transilluminated by the endoscope light, and a site is chosen for the gastrojejunostomy. The endoscopist then places an endoscopic snare, which can be seen pressing against the tissue of the pouch wall. A small opening is made in the pouch with the electrocautery scissors so that the snare can be pushed through the gastric wall at this location. The snare is then used to grasp a wire placed through a needle across the abdominal wall in the left abdomen, and snare and wire are withdrawn through the mouth along with the scope.

The anvil of the stapler is attached to the end of the wire that was drawn through the mouth, and the surgeon pulls on the other end of the wire to deliver the anvil through the mouth, down the esophagus, and into the gastric pouch, where it can be visualized. The electrocautery attached to the scissors is used to enlarge the opening in the gastric wall slightly, and the stem of the stapler is then brought through the gastrotomy. To prevent anastomotic leakage after stapling, the gastrotomy should be no larger than the diameter of the stem; if it is too large, it can be closed around the stem by placing one or two simple sutures.

Troubleshooting. Difficulty in passing the anvil perorally may arise at the level where the trachea separates from the esophagus in the deep pharynx. This difficulty can usually be overcome either by having the endoscopist perform a jaw-thrust maneuver or by placing a large laryngoscope blade deep in the pharynx to make the anvil visible in the proximal esophagus and then nudging the anvil forward with either the tip of the blade or a McGill forceps. Deflating the endotracheal tube balloon may also help. Occasionally, a large, blunt esophageal dilator is used to place pressure on the top of the anvil. Given the potential for esophageal injury if the anvil will not advance, it is important not to apply excessive force. I have seen a case in which the anvil became

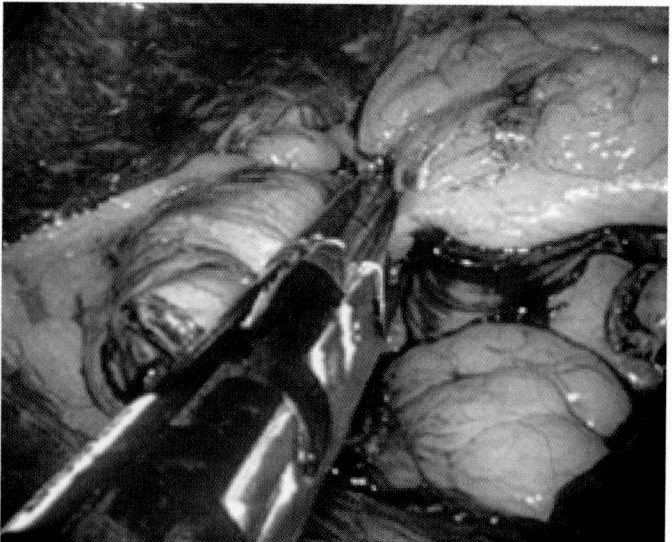

Figure 10 **Laparoscopic gastric bypass: total intracorporeal approach. Much as in open GBP, a linear endoscopic GIA stapler is fired three times to transect the stomach and create the gastric pouch.**

lodged in the proximal esophagus beyond the laryngoscopic view and the long suture holding it broke; retrograde passage of an esophageal dilator was required to dislodge the anvil. Other surgeons who use wire to draw the anvil down the esophagus have identified nontransmural esophageal injuries on postoperative contrast studies or have seen subcutaneous emphysema in the neck after operation.

Step 3: creation and mobilization of Roux limb and jejunojejunostomy In most reports of laparoscopic GBP, regardless of how the gastrojejunostomy is done, the approach to creating the Roux limb is essentially the same. The patient is placed in a supine position, and graspers are used to bring the omentum upward into the upper abdomen so that the transverse colon and the underlying mesocolon are exposed. Graspers are then placed on the transverse mesocolon and used to elevate it anteriorly so that the ligament of Treitz is exposed. The position of the ligament of Treitz is confirmed by careful manipulation and verification that the bowel is attached to the retroperitoneum at this location; this may be a more difficult task in patients who have previously undergone abdominal procedures.

With the help of a measuring instrument inserted into the abdomen, the small bowel is measured to a point 30 to 40 cm from the ligament of Treitz, where it is transected with the endoscopic GIA stapler, loaded with 2.5 mm staples. A 0.5 in. Penrose rubber drain is sutured to the cut end of the Roux limb so that it is not confused with the other cut end of the bowel. The Roux limb is then measured to a length of 45 to 60 cm. (As in open GBP, the Roux limb should be significantly longer—up to 150 cm—if the long-limb modification is being performed.) The afferent side of the previously transected small bowel is then attached with a simple absorbable suture to the proposed jejunojejunostomy site on the Roux limb. Intracorporeal suturing is facilitated by using an automatic suturing device. Positioning is important: the afferent limb should be kept toward the mesocolon, with the Roux limb brought toward the surgeon on the patient's right side.

A small (1 cm) enterotomy is then made in each of the two adjacent bowel limbs in preparation for passage of the linear stapler, loaded with 2.5 mm staples in a 60 mm cartridge, into the bowel. Two holding sutures are placed, one proximal to the enterotomy and the other distal, to help manipulate the bowel onto the stapler. The stapler is then fired, creating a 60 mm side-to-side anastomosis. A third suture is placed at the midpoint of the enterotomy, and all three sutures are grasped to facilitate closure of the enterotomy with another application of the linear stapler. Once completed, the anastomosis is inspected both for integrity and for possible narrowing. At this point, anterior traction is applied to the three sutures to facilitate placement of a continuous suture to close the mesenteric defect.

Next, the greater omentum is divided from its free edge to its junction with the transverse colon so as to facilitate passage of the Roux limb in an antecolic location. Alternatively, a retrocolic, retrogastric tunnel is created so that the Roux limb can be advanced to the proximal stomach for anastomosis. The retrocolic, retrogastric approach is superior if the antecolic approach appears to be placing undue tension on the limb as it is advanced to the proximal pouch. The ligament of Treitz is identified by lifting the transverse mesocolon anteriorly, and a spot 1 to 2 cm anterior and to the left of the ligament is chosen as the starting point for dissection with the ultrasonic scalpel. The middle colic artery should be visualized medial to this point of entry into the mesocolon. The goal of the dissection is to identify the posterior wall of the stomach, which may be difficult in patients who are extremely obese, have a fatty, foreshortened mesocolon, or have previously undergone abdominal surgery.

Once the stomach is visible, it is grasped and elevated through the mesocolic window, and the end of the Penrose drain is grasped and brought through the mesocolic defect into the lesser sac. When the Penrose is in place in the lesser sac, the omentum is pulled down from the epigastrium to allow visualization of the drain, now posterior to the divided distal stomach. The Penrose drain is grasped, and the patient is placed back into a steep reverse Trendelenburg position. Traction is applied to the Penrose drain to deliver the cut end of the Roux limb up into the lesser sac for anastomosis.

Troubleshooting. Some surgeons prefer to create a loop gastrojejunostomy, thus avoiding the technical challenges of creating a Roux limb laparoscopically. This approach was abandoned years ago in open GBP because of postoperative bile reflux and an increased severity of complications resulting from high output of digestive juices when a leak occurs at the gastrojejunal anastomosis; it should be abandoned in laparoscopic GBP as well. The practice of using such suboptimal methods for the purpose of performing this complex operation more expeditiously is poorly conceived and is to be condemned.

Step 4 (circular stapling): gastrojejunostomy In the circular stapling technique, the stapled end of the Roux limb is open to permit introduction of the stapler. The 12 mm trocar site in the left upper quadrant is dilated so that the circular stapler can be inserted through the abdominal wall without the need for a trocar; lubrication is helpful for this step. The stapler then cannulates the Roux limb. This step is facilitated by holding the open mouth of the limb in three locations, with one of the three holds involving traction on the Penrose drain previously sutured to the bowel. The stapler is advanced 3 to 4 cm down the limb, and the spike on the stapler is brought through the antimesenteric portion of the bowel by unscrewing the stapler under direct vision. Once the stapler has been opened completely, it is laparoscopically joined to the anvil in the gastric pouch, then closed and fired.

Once fired, the stapler is removed from the abdominal wall, and a balloon trocar device is used to close the dilated abdominal wall opening. A single firing of the endoscopic GIA stapler, loaded with 2.5 mm staples, is often all that is required to reclose the cut end of the small bowel. Interrupted or continuous absorbable sutures are then placed around the stapled anastomosis for added security.

Step 4 (linear stapling): gastrojejunostomy Initially, a continuous posterior row of nonabsorbable suture material is placed to secure the Roux limb to the posterior gastric pouch. An enterotomy and a gastrotomy are performed that are large enough to admit the jaws of the endoscopic GIA stapler, which is loaded with 3.5 mm staples in a 45 mm cartridge for a side-to-side anastomosis [*see Figure 11*] by means of the same techniques employed in creating the jejunojejunostomy. The cartridge is inserted to a distance of 2.5 to 3.0 cm and fired to create an inner stapled layer [*see Figure 12*]. A 30 French dilator or a flexible gastroscope is then passed into the pouch and guided through the anastomosis under direct vision to maintain the appropriate stomal diameter (10 to 12 mm) during closure of the open end. The subsequent defect is closed in two layers with continuous sutures (absorbable for the inner layer and nonabsorbable for the outer). The linear GIA stapler can generally be placed and retrieved without the need for dilatation of a trocar site, which appears to increase postoperative pain.

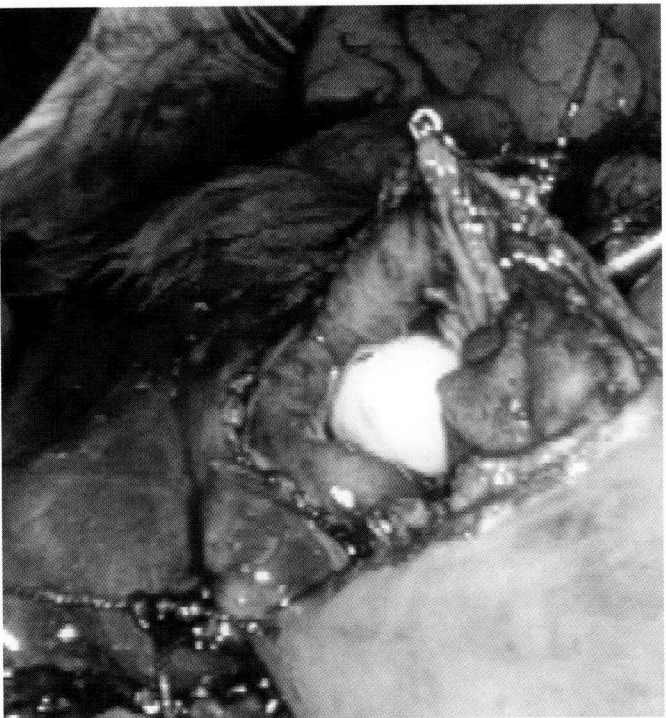

Figure 11 Laparoscopic gastric bypass: total intracorporeal approach. A 30 French dilator is placed into the proximal gastric pouch before closure of the gastrojejunal anastomosis with the endoscopic GIA stapler.

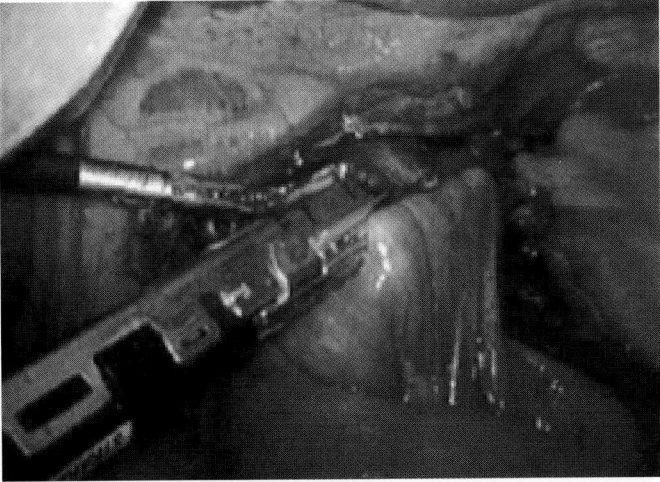

Figure 12 Laparoscopic gastric bypass: total intracorporeal approach. The gastrojejunal anastomosis is closed with the linear endoscopic GIA stapler.

In my experience, using the linear stapler for the gastrojejunostomy simplifies the procedure, reduces operating time, and eliminates the concerns about injury to the body of the esophagus that arise with passage of the circular stapler.

Step 5: assessment of anastomosis In every case, regardless of which stapling technique is employed, flexible upper GI endoscopy is performed to assess the anastomosis. The Roux limb is occluded with an intestinal clamp to prevent excessive bowel and distal gastric dilatation. The patient is placed in the supine position, and the area around the anastomosis is irrigated with saline; the presence of air bubbles, easily detectable in the irrigant, indicates that the anastomosis is leaking. In most cases, the pouch and the Roux limb can be distended tightly, and even tiny air leaks are reinforced with additional sutures. The anastomosis and the staple lines are visualized, and the endoscope is navigated through the anastomosis into the Roux limb whenever possible. After adequate visualization and testing, the gas is suctioned from the intestine, the Roux limb is unclamped, and the endoscope is removed.

Step 6: closure Finally, in selected cases, a 10 mm closed suction drainage tube is placed adjacent to the anastomosis to permit monitoring for postoperative leaks. This drain is removed after the patient begins oral intake if an upper GI series reveals no postoperative leakage [*see Figure 13*]. In antecolic Roux-en-Y procedures in which the greater omentum is divided, I routinely wrap the lateral tongue of greater omentum in a lateral-to-medial direction posteriorly around the gastrojejunostomy, then suture it to anterior gastrocolic fat so as to reinforce the anastomosis. The liver retractor is removed under direct vision to ensure that no bleeding occurs. Trocar sites 10 mm in diameter or larger are closed by using a needle suture passer to place 0 absorbable sutures under direct endoscopic visualization. Skin wounds are closed with skin staples or absorbable subcutaneous sutures.

HAND-ASSISTED LAPAROSCOPIC GASTRIC BYPASS

Because total intracorporeal laparoscopic GBP is such a challenging technical adventure, a hand-assisted version of the procedure was initially developed at our institution on the basis of previously published work.[26] This technique served as a bridge to the total intracorporeal approach, in that it made it possible to learn the technical aspects of a difficult, highly advanced laparoscopic procedure while enjoying the security provided by the presence of an intra-abdominal hand for palpation and manipulation during the procedure. This added security is the major advantage of the

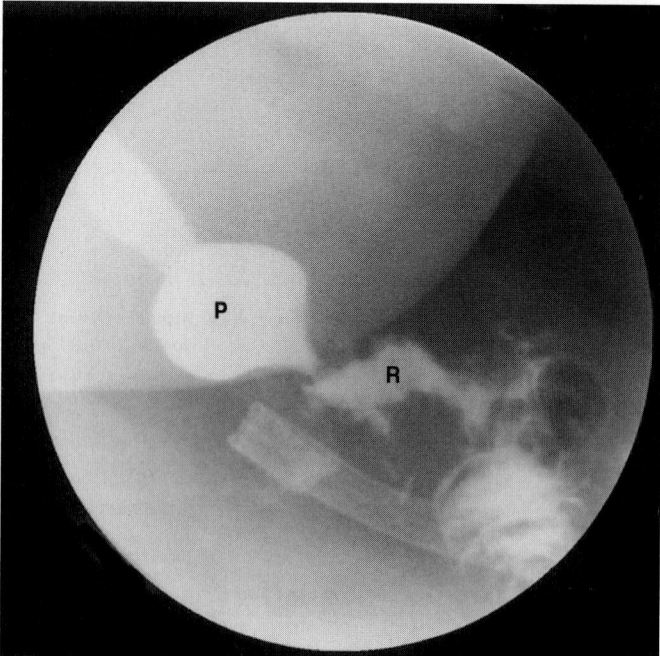

Figure 13 **Laparoscopic gastric bypass: total intracorporeal approach. Flexible upper GI endoscopy is performed to assess the completed anastomosis.**

hand-assisted approach. The major disadvantage is the potential for complications at the incision used for manual access. The complications seen at this site are reminiscent of those seen after open GBP, including major wound infection, dehiscence, and hernia formation.

In a series of hand-assisted laparoscopic GBP procedures from our institution, there was one major wound infection in the hand incision and one instance of postoperative fascial dehiscence. Subsequent study suggested that the hand-assisted procedure did not reduce the incidence of wound-related complications and incisional hernias and that it significantly increased the cost of surgical treatment when compared with open GBP. It appears, therefore, that the primary role of hand-assisted gastric bypass may be in helping surgeons to negotiate the steep learning curve associated with total laparoscopic GBP.

Operative Technique

Step 1: initial access and placement of hand-assisted device A left subcostal incision is made, a Veress needle is inserted, and gas is insufflated into the abdomen to a pressure of 15 mm Hg. A periumbilical location for a midline incision is then identified. This incision will allow insertion of the hand at a later point in the procedure; thus, its length in centimeters should roughly correspond to the surgeon's glove size. The assisting hand gains access to the abdomen via a device called the Pneumo Sleeve (Dexterity Surgical, Inc., Roswell, Georgia). This device includes a ring system at one end. Once pneumoperitoneum is obtained, the ring is glued to the skin of the abdominal wall in such a way that the proposed line of incision is in the middle of the ring.

Step 2: creation and mobilization of Roux limb, jejunojejunostomy, and creation of gastric pouch With the ring of the Pneumo Sleeve secured to the skin, the small midline incision is opened and extended directly through the midline fascia. The pneumoperitoneum is released as this incision is opened, and the ligament of Treitz is identified by palpation. Retractors are placed into the incision, and the Roux limb is constructed with an open surgical technique. The small bowel is mobilized into the wound to the extent possible and is transected 20 to 30 cm from the ligament of Treitz. A side-to-side stapled jejunojejunostomy is then constructed with an open technique. In my experience, using an endoscopic GIA stapler rather than a traditional surgical stapler for this step is both technically superior and more cost-efficient.

Once the anastomosis is created and the enterotomy is closed, the mesenteric defect is sutured in the usual fashion with an open technique. A Penrose drain is sutured to the cut end of the Roux limb. The surgeon, standing on the patient's left side, attaches the Pneumo Sleeve to the nondominant hand and places this into the abdominal cavity. Pneumoperitoneum is reestablished. The ligament of Treitz can then be manually identified, and a blunt mesocolic dissection into the retrogastric space can be performed. This manipulation can be visualized through a laparoscope with the placement of additional trocars, including two in the right subcostal area (as in total intracorporeal laparoscopic GBP); the laparoscope is usually placed through a left subcostal trocar site. The Penrose drain is then grasped with the surgeon's fingers and advanced through the mesocolic tunnel into the retrogastric space. The hand is then brought anterior to the stomach, and the patient is placed in a steep reverse Trendelenburg position.

The Nathanson liver retractor is inserted through a subxiphoid puncture as described earlier [*see* Total Intracorporeal Laparoscopic Gastric Bypass, *above*] and positioned to allow visualization of the esophagogastric junction and proximal stomach. The gastrohepatic ligament is bluntly opened, and the surgeon's hand is extended behind the stomach into the lesser sac to retrieve the Penrose drain. The hand is then used to facilitate the mesenteric dissection on the lesser curvature of the stomach 2 to 3 cm from the esophagogastric junction. An endoscopic GIA stapler loaded with 3.5 mm staples in 60 mm cartridges is fired three times to create the gastric pouch (as in total intracorporeal laparoscopic GBP).

Step 3: gastrojejunostomy Again, the gastrojejunal anastomosis can be created with either a circular stapler or a linear stapler [see Total Intracorporeal Laparoscopic Gastric Bypass, above]. The Roux limb is manipulated into view with the surgeon's hand. In the circular stapling technique, the stapler is placed into the Roux limb with the help of the intra-abdominal hand so that it can be opened, penetrating the antimesenteric portion of the bowel, and joined to the anvil in the gastric pouch. The hand also facilitates removal of the circular stapler, which is occasionally difficult.

Step 4: assessment of anastomosis The open end of the Roux limb is then stapled closed, and flexible upper GI endoscopy is performed as in total intracorporeal laparoscopic GBP, with the hand (rather than an intestinal clamp) occluding the limb to allow insufflation and testing of the anastomosis. Additional absorbable sutures can be placed around the anastomosis for added security; an automatic suturing device such as the Endostitch (United States Surgical, Norwalk, Connecticut) may be used for this purpose. If the sutures are left long, the surgeon can tie knots intra-abdominally, using the sleeved hand in a one-handed technique.

Step 5: closure Except for the hand incision, closure is accomplished in the same way as for total laparoscopic GBP. Although the hand incision is small, it may be difficult to close in severely obese patients who have a thick layer of subcutaneous fat. I typically use a continuous fascial closure with a heavy No. 1 or 2 nonabsorbable suture.

COMPLICATIONS

The complications observed to date after laparoscopic GBP include the usual problems that occur in some patients after open GBP, including marginal ulcer and stenosis at the gastrojejunal anastomosis necessitating dilatation. On rare occasions, a gastrogastric fistula may lead to a treatment-resistant marginal ulcer. The major advantage of laparoscopic GBP over open GBP is likely to be reduced wound complications (e.g., major wound infection and incisional hernia). I have seen several relatively minor trocar site infections but none carrying the long wound care disability characteristic of a major wound infection after open GBP. In my experience to date, weight loss with laparoscopic GBP is identical to that with open GBP.

Postoperative Management

For optimal results after bariatric surgery, postoperative management must be as well planned as preoperative preparation. The basic principles of postoperative care, including intubation, ambulation, feeding, and monitoring for complications (e.g., anastomotic leakage, abdominal catastrophe, acute gastric distention, and internal hernia), are discussed more fully elsewhere [see 49 Morbid Obesity].

These basic principles generally apply to laparoscopic cases as well, but with some differences. Unlike patients who have undergone open GBP, those who have undergone laparoscopic GBP do not have a nasogastric tube left in place. In addition, a contrast study of both the pouch and the anastomosis is ordered on postoperative day 1. A water-soluble contrast agent is initially used for this study, followed by barium if no leak or abnormality is identified. The patient may then begin to drink small amounts of liquids and may advance to a pureed diet with no sugar or concentrated sweets as soon as he or she can tolerate it. Discharge usually takes place 2 or 3 days after operation. Vitamin administration should be initiated early after operation; chewable tablets may be used if necessary. Thiamine deficiency may develop within weeks in patients who are kept on a liquid-only diet or who experience persistent vomiting.

FAILED WEIGHT LOSS AND WEIGHT REGAIN

A postoperative problem that deserves special mention is the risk of failed weight loss or weight regain. This is one of the greatest problems associated with bariatric surgery and may arise after any gastric procedure for morbid obesity. Approximately 20% of vertical banded gastroplasty patients have difficulty with solid foods and come to exhibit a maladaptive eating behavior involving frequent ingestion of high-calorie liquid carbohydrates; in about 10% of VBG patients, the procedure fails for this reason. In a study in which 53 VBG patients were converted to gastric bypass,[27] the average loss of excess weight after VBG was $31 \pm 5\%$; 2 years after conversion to GBP, it was $67 \pm 2\%$, a value virtually identical to that in the primary GBP group. Thirteen patients became sweets eaters and had lost only $15 \pm 5\%$ of their excess weight more than 1 year after VBG, though there were no radiographically demonstrated problems with the procedure; 1 year after conversion to GBP, they had lost an average of $78 \pm 11\%$ of their excess weight.

Inadequate weight loss is also seen in GBP patients. In some, stomal dilatation eventually develops after the procedure; however, no correlation between stomal size and weight loss has been demonstrated for GBP patients, and reoperation to make the pouch or the stoma smaller has not yielded any benefit when the initial procedure has failed. It appears that failure of GBP is generally due either to the loss or absence of dumping syndrome symptoms in a small percentage of patients, leading to resumption of high-calorie sweets ingestion or, more often, to frequent ingestion of high-fat junk foods (e.g., potato or corn chips, microwave popcorn, or peanut butter crackers) that crumble easily and empty quickly from the pouch, thereby keeping the patient from feeling full. Repeated dietary counseling over a period of years is required to educate patients to eat low-calorie, high-fiber foods (e.g., raw carrots, broccoli, cauliflower, apples, and oranges) that will stay in the small gastric pouch longer and provide a sensation of early satiety.

At our institution, the philosophy is to make clear to patients, well in advance of the operation, that bariatric surgery is designed to help them help themselves. Obesity can be beaten by surgical treatment, but to maintain the victory, patients must continue to make good food choices and exercise appropriately for the rest of their lives. Patients who begin to ingest more than 1,100 kcal/day often begin to gain weight; even if weight gain is only 0.5 lb/mo, this amounts to 6 lb/yr, or 60 lb in 10 years. Bariatric surgical patients need lifelong nutritional counseling to optimize the results of surgical management of morbid obesity.

References

1. Van Itallie TB: Obesity: adverse effects on health and longevity. Am J Clin Nutr 32:2723, 1979

2. Drenick EJ, Bale GS, Seltzer F, et al: Excessive mortality and causes of death in morbidly obese men. JAMA 243:443, 1980

3. Stunkard AJ, Foch TT, Hrubec Z: A twin study of human obesity. JAMA 256:51, 1986

4. Stunkard AJ, Sorensen TIA, Hanis C, et al: An adoption study of human obesity. N Engl J Med 314:193, 1986

5. Johnson D, Drenick EJ: Therapeutic fasting in morbid obesity: long-term follow-up. Arch Intern Med 137: 1381, 1977

6. Griffen WO, Young VL, Stevenson CC: A prospective comparison of gastric and jejunoileal bypass procedures for morbid obesity. Ann Surg 186:500, 1977

7. Buckwalter JA: A prospective comparison of the jejunoileal and gastric bypass operations for morbid obesity. World J Surg 1:757, 1977

8. Halverson JD, Wise L, Wazna MF, et al: Jejunoileal bypass for morbid obesity: a critical appraisal. Am J Med 64:461, 1978

9. Hocking MP, Duerson MC, O'Leary PJ, et al: Jejuno-ileal bypass for morbid obesity: late follow-up in 100 cases. N Engl J Med 308:995, 1983

10. Pories WJ, Flicinger EG, Meelheim D, et al: The effectiveness of gastric bypass over gastric partition in morbid obesity: consequences of distal gastric and duodenal exclusion. Ann Surg 196:389, 1982

11. Lechner GW, Elliott DW: Comparison of weight loss after gastric exclusion and partitioning. Arch Surg 118:685, 1983

12. Linner JH: Comparative effectiveness of gastric bypass and gastroplasty: a clinical study. Arch Surg 117: 695, 1982

13. Mason EE: Vertical banded gastroplasty for obesity. Arch Surg 117:701, 1982

14. Sugerman HJ, Starkey JV, Birkenhauer R: A randomized prospective trial of gastric bypass versus vertical banded gastroplasty for morbid obesity and their effects on sweets versus non-sweets eaters. Ann Surg 205:613, 1987

15. Hall JC, Watts JM, O'Brien PE, et al: Gastric surgery for morbid obesity: the Adelaide Study. Ann Surg 211:419, 1990

16. MacLean LD, Rhode BM, Sampalis J, et al: Results of the surgical treatment of obesity. Am J Surg 165:155, 1993

17. Sugerman HJ, Kellum JM, Engle KM, et al: Gastric bypass for treating severe obesity. Am J Clin Nutr 55(suppl 2):560S, 1992

18. Pories WJ, MacDonald KG Jr, Morgan EJ, et al: Surgical treatment of obesity and its effect on diabetes: 10-year follow-up. Am J Clin Nutr 55(suppl 2):582S, 1992

19. Scopinaro N, Bachi V: Evoluzione del bypass biliopancreatico parziale per l'obesita. Minerva Chir 39:1299, 1984

20. Liszka TG, Sugerman HJ, Kellum JM, et al: Risk/benefit considerations of distal gastric bypass. Int J Obes 12(suppl A):604, 1988

21. Brolin RE, Kenler HA, Gorman JH, et al: Long-limb gastric bypass in the superobese: a prospective randomized study. Ann Surg 215:387, 1992

22. MacLean LD, Rhode BM, Shizgal HM: Nutrition following gastric operations for morbid obesity. Ann Surg 198:347, 1983

23. Sanyal AJ, Sugerman HJ, Kellum JM, et al: Stomal complications of gastric bypass: incidence and outcome of therapy. Am J Gastroenterol 87:1165, 1992

24. Sugerman HJ, Brewer WH, Shiffman ML, et al: A multi-center, placebo-controlled, randomized, double-blind, prospective trial of prophylactic ursodiol for the prevention of gallstone formation following gastric bypass-induced rapid weight loss. Am J Surg 169:91, 1995

25. Wittgrove AC, Clark GW, Schubert KR: Laparoscopic gastric bypass: Roux-en-Y technique and results in 75 patients with 3–30 month follow-up. Obes Surg 6:500, 1996

26. Naihoth T, Gagner M: Laparoscopically assisted gastric bypass surgery using Dexterity Pneumo Sleeve. Surg Endosc 11:830, 1997

27. Sugerman HJ, Kellum JM, DeMaria EJ, et al: Conversion of failed or complicated vertical banded gastroplasty to gastric bypass in morbid obesity. Am J Surg 171:263, 1996

Acknowledgment

Figures 1, 2, 3, 5, and 9   Tom Moore.

62 PROCEDURES FOR BENIGN AND MALIGNANT GASTRIC AND DUODENAL DISEASE

Thomas E. Clancy, M.D., and Stanley W. Ashley, M.D., F.A.C.S.

Procedures for Benign Gastric and Duodenal Disease

Advances in the medical management of peptic ulcer disease, including the use of effective acid-suppressing medications (e.g., histamine receptor antagonists and proton pump inhibitors [PPIs]) and the treatment of *Helicobacter pylori*, have led to a dramatic decrease in the need for elective surgical management of uncomplicated duodenal and gastric ulcers. In the past, surgery was the only effective long-term option for peptic ulcer disease, but over the past two decades, it has become an increasingly rare choice.[1] Currently, operative therapy for peptic ulcer disease is largely reserved for the management of complications such as hemorrhage, perforation, and obstruction. The recognition that medical management successfully prevents ulcer recurrence in most patients has caused surgical management of complicated ulcer disease to evolve into a more minimalist strategy that favors damage-control surgery for complications and only infrequently resorts to acid-reducing operations.[2]

In this section of the chapter, we focus primarily on procedures performed to treat peptic ulcer disease, though we also briefly address diverticulectomy for duodenal diverticular disease. Other gastroduodenal procedures for nonmalignant disease are described in more detail elsewhere: gastric restrictive procedures and gastric bypass are discussed in the context of bariatric surgery [*see 61 Bariatric Procedures*]; choledochoduodenostomy and transduodenal sphincteroplasty are discussed in the context of biliary tract surgery [*see 64 Procedures for Benign and Malignant Biliary Tract Disease*]; cystogastrostomy for intractable pancreatic pseudocysts is discussed in the context of pancreatic surgery [*see 66 Procedures for Benign and Malignant Pancreatic Disease*]; and duodenal diverticularization is discussed in the context of pancreatic and duodenal trauma [*see 108 Injuries to the Pancreas and Duodenum*].

PREOPERATIVE EVALUATION

The appropriate extent of preoperative evaluation for a patient undergoing surgery for a benign gastroduodenal disorder is dictated primarily by the nature of the presenting problem. In the case of gastric outlet obstruction or a rare condition such as intractable peptic ulcer disease that is refractory to medical management, the preoperative workup may be extensive and include detailed endoscopy, contrast studies of the upper abdomen, cross-sectional imaging with computed tomography, and full laboratory panels. In most cases of complicated peptic ulcer disease, however, the emergency nature of the situation necessarily renders an extensive preoperative workup impractical. For instance, patients with perforated duodenal ulcers typically present in distress with an acute abdomen. A chest x-ray that demonstrates free intraperitoneal air is all that is needed before the patient is taken to the operating room; the decision to proceed to operation should not be delayed by waiting for further images (e.g., CT scans).

Patients who are experiencing upper GI hemorrhage secondary to peptic ulcer disease should undergo endoscopy to identify the source of bleeding [*see 47 Upper Gastrointestinal Bleeding*]. In many cases, endoscopic management of bleeding ulcers is possible, rendering surgical management unnecessary. Definitive surgical management is indicated, however, if bleeding leads to hemodynamic instability, an extensive transfusion requirement (i.e., more than 6 units), or rebleeding after initial endoscopic management. Objective criteria for surgery must be determined on a patient-by-patient basis. Precise preoperative localization of the bleeding source is essential; a bleeding posterior duodenal ulcer, for example, cannot be managed in the same way as hemorrhage from diffuse severe gastritis. Endoscopy should therefore be performed whenever possible. Alternatively, if brisk bleeding prevents clear intraluminal visualization of a bleeding site, angiographic localization may be attempted.

Occasionally, patients present for surgery with refractory gastric ulcers. If the ulcer has not healed after 12 weeks of optimal medical therapy, resection is indicated to rule out an occult gastric malignancy. In such cases, the preoperative workup should include endoscopic biopsies of the ulcer base and the surrounding gastric mucosa so that a preoperative diagnosis of malignancy can be made if possible. In view of the concern about a possible gastric malignancy, it is reasonable to obtain a preoperative chest x-ray and a CT scan of the abdomen so as to detect possible nodal or distant metastases.

OPERATIVE PLANNING

Patients undergoing gastroduodenal procedures should receive general anesthesia and have a nasogastric tube and Foley catheter in place. The supine position is preferred. The operation is usually done via an upper midline incision or, occasionally, via a bilateral subcostal incision, with fixed retractors used in either case.

The choice of procedure is primarily dictated by the indication for operation. Usually, several options are available. The first priority is to manage complications (e.g., bleeding and perforation); whether an accompanying acid-suppressing procedure is indicated and which one should be done depend on the clinical setting. Most commonly, duodenal perforation is treated with closure and omental patching, with or without an acid-reducing procedure. A bleeding ulcer is treated with oversewing of the the bleeding vessel, with or without an acid-reducing vagotomy and pyloroplasty. Gastric outlet obstruction may be managed with several different approaches, including vagotomy with antrectomy and vagotomy with drainage via pyloroplasty or gastroenterostomy. In the rare cases of intractability, highly selective vagotomy (HSV) is the procedure of choice.

An important component of preoperative evaluation is determination of the severity and duration of disease. If symptoms are longstanding or recurrent—particularly when the patient has already received acid-reducing or anti–*H. pylori* therapy—a definitive acid-reducing procedure should be considered. As has been demonstrated,[3] however, ulcer recurrence is significantly reduced even without an acid-reducing procedure when perforated ulcers are managed with anti–*H. pylori* agents in conjunction with a PPI. Therefore, a compliant patient who is presumed to be infected with *H. pylori* may not need to undergo an additional acid-reducing procedure. The evidence for this strategy is less clear with respect to bleeding or obstructing ulcers.

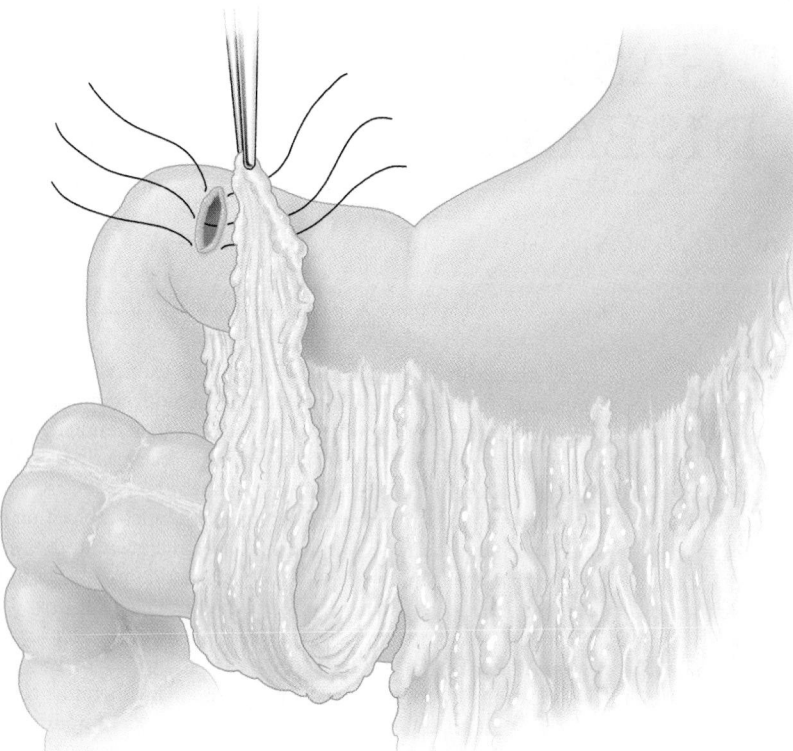

Figure 1 Omental (Graham) patch. Three or four interrupted sutures are placed along the ulcer edge. If possible, the ulcer is closed primarily and reinforced with omentum. Primary closure may be difficult; in a true Graham patch, primary closure is not attempted, and omentum is used to cover the tissue defect.

OMENTAL PATCH FOR DUODENAL PERFORATION (GRAHAM PATCH)

Operative Technique

Perforated duodenal ulcers are typically treated by oversewing the perforation, then placing a portion of the greater omentum over the suture line. The duodenal ulcer wall is carefully debrided and closed with three or four interrupted silk sutures; the tails of the sutures may be used to hold the omentum in place. Alternatively, if the ulcer edges are edematous and not expected to close easily, the perforation may be closed with a true Graham patch, which involves plugging the defect with a well-vascularized omental pedicle [see Figure 1]. Care should be taken to avoid tying sutures too tightly; this can lead to devascularization of the omental pedicle. Once the operation has been completed, the abdomen is generously irrigated to remove any contamination, and a search is made for occult collections in the subphrenic space and the pelvis.

Troubleshooting

To avoid placing excessive tension on the repair, primary closure should not be attempted if the duodenal wall is overly edematous and thickened. For large perforations that are expected to result in gastric outlet obstruction if closed, consideration should be given to incorporating the closure into a pyloroplasty.

There is some controversy regarding whether an acid-reducing operation should be added to the omental patch procedure. If the patient is stable and has a history of peptic ulcer disease, a definitive ulcer operation is included; HSV may be preferable to truncal vagotomy and pyloroplasty, in that it is less likely to give rise to dumping syndrome and postvagotomy diarrhea. If the patient has no history of peptic ulcer disease, has a severe medical illness, is hemodynamically unstable, has a long-standing perforation, or exhibits gross abdominal contamination, a definitive ulcer operation is omitted. In cases of gross contamination of the abdomen, it is probably inappropriate to divide the peritoneum over the esophagus during vagotomy and thereby expose the mediastinum to infection.

Complications

Persistent leakage should be uncommon after adequate closure. Duodenal scarring at the area of perforation and repair may lead to gastric outlet obstruction. Incomplete exploration and irrigation of the abdomen may result in late infection.

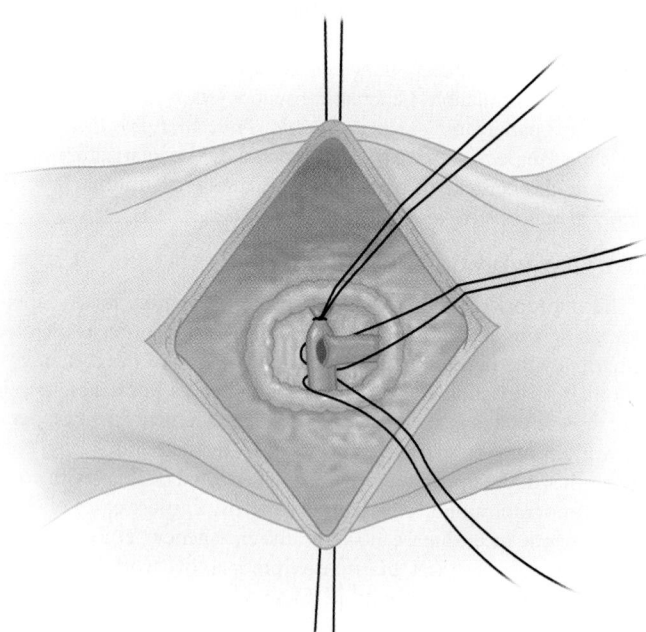

Figure 2 Vagotomy and pyloroplasty. To control a bleeding duodenal ulcer, traction sutures are placed along the cephalad and caudad borders of a longitudinal incision across the pylorus. Figure-eight sutures are placed at the cephalad and caudad portions of the ulcer to occlude the gastroduodenal artery. An additional U-stitch is placed to control small transverse pancreatic branches that may cause late bleeding. Care should be taken to avoid the underlying CBD.

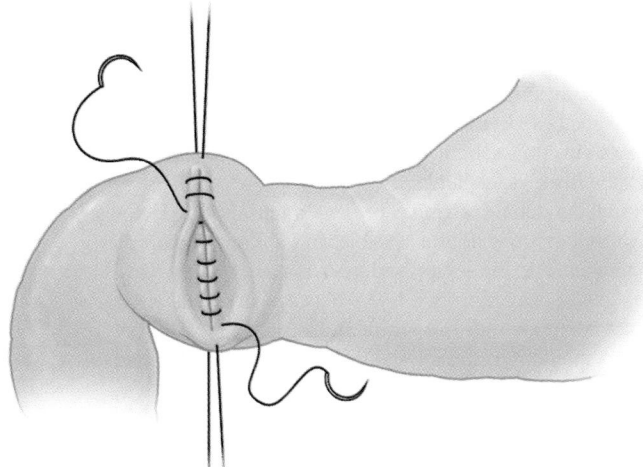

Figure 3 **Vagotomy and pyloroplasty. For a Heineke-Mikulicz pyloroplasty, a full-thickness longitudinal incision is made that extends from a point 1 cm proximal to the pylorus to a point 1 to 2 cm distal to the pylorus. The incision is closed transversely in two layers. Superior and inferior stay sutures help align the incision for closure.**

Outcome Evaluation

With adequate acid suppression and anti–*H. pylori* therapy, symptoms of duodenal ulcer are unlikely to recur. The 1-year recurrence rate after omental patching is substantially lower when both therapies are employed than when only a PPI is given (5% versus 38%).[3]

VAGOTOMY AND PYLOROPLASTY FOR BLEEDING DUODENAL ULCER

Truncal vagotomy with pyloric drainage via pyloroplasty is rarely employed as primary therapy for peptic ulcer disease, but it does play a role in emergency management of bleeding duodenal ulcers. This approach to acid suppression fits well with the proximal duodenotomy used to control the hemorrhage. Exposure of the first portion of the duodenum via a longitudinal incision in the pylorus is combined with truncal vagotomy; the pylorus is then closed in a transverse fashion to prevent the development of gastric outlet obstruction.

Operative Technique

Step 1: exposure and pyloric division A Kocher maneuver is performed. The pylorus is identified through palpation and through identification of the pyloric vein as it courses anteriorly. Two traction sutures are placed in the anterior aspect of the pylorus, one superiorly and one inferiorly. A longitudinal incision is made that extends approximately 2 to 3 cm on either side of the pylorus.

Step 2: ligation of bleeding vessel The bleeding ulcer bed is directly oversewn with at least three sutures. Figure-eight sutures are placed on the superior and inferior borders of the ulcer bed to ligate the gastroduodenal artery proximal and distal to the ulcer, and a third figure-eight suture is placed medially to control the transverse pancreatic branch [*see Figure 2*].

Step 3: pyloroplasty Tension is applied to the previously placed traction sutures to convert the longitudinal incision to a transverse one. The incision is then closed transversely in two layers with full-thickness bites of 3-0 or 2-0 nonabsorbable suture material (Heineke-Mikulicz pyloroplasty) [*see Figure 3*]. Tension-free closure is facilitated by adequate duodenal mobilization (by means of the Kocher maneuver) and lysis of surrounding adhesions.

Step 4: vagotomy To perform the vagotomy, further exposure may be needed, including mobilization of the left lateral section of the liver and division of the triangular ligament. Downward traction on the greater curvature of the stomach is essential to apply gentle tension to the esophagogastric junction and the proximal vagi. The peritoneum over the esophagus is divided transversely with the electro-cautery; exposure may be facilitated by surrounding the distal esophagus with a Penrose drain for downward traction. The left (anterior) vagus is best identified by applying traction to the right and posteriorly, so that the nerve can be traced into the posterior mediastinum. All fibers entering the distal esophagus are divided. The main nerve trunk is clipped proximally and distally, and a 2 cm long segment is excised. The right (posterior) vagus is exposed by applying traction to the left and anteriorly; the nerve can then be palpated as a taut cord and divided in much the same manner as the anterior vagus. For a complete vagotomy, the distal esophagus must be skeletonized for approximately 5 cm [*see Figure 4*].

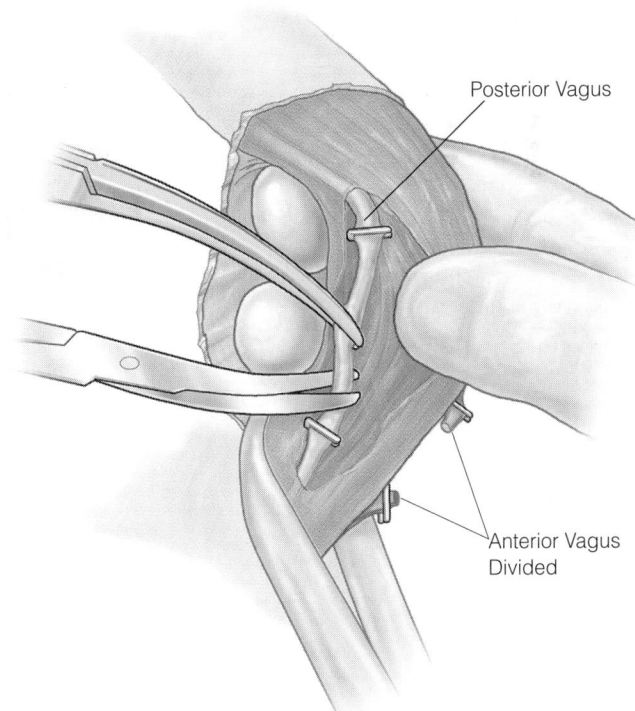

Posterior Vagus

Anterior Vagus Divided

Figure 4 **Vagotomy and pyloroplasty. For the truncal vagotomy, the peritoneum over the esophagogastric junction is opened widely to afford exposure. Gentle downward traction is applied to the stomach to facilitate identification of the two vagus nerves. Surgical clips are applied to each nerve in turn, and a 2 to 3 cm nerve segment is removed between the clips. These segments should be inspected to confirm removal of neural tissue.**

Troubleshooting

As this procedure becomes less frequent and surgeons' experience with it dwindles, location of the vagus nerves may prove an increasingly troublesome task. In most cases, complete skeletonization of the distal esophagus in conjunction with appropriate traction should allow palpation of the main vagal trunks.

If substantial duodenal scarring is present, a tension-free Heineke-Mikulicz pyloroplasty may not be possible, and a Finney pyloroplasty may be preferable. The Finney procedure is essentially a side-to-side anastomosis that is created in two layers between the distal stomach and the proximal duodenum [see Figure 5]. Complete mobilization of the duodenum, including adhesiolysis and a generous Kocher maneuver, is required.

Care should be taken to keep from injuring the common bile duct (CBD), particularly when the vascular inflow to a deeply penetrating duodenal ulcer is being sutured.

Complications

Leakage from a pyloroplasty is rare. Gastric outlet obstruction may occur secondary to either scarring or edema at the operative site; often, it is relieved by nasogastric decompression and conservative management. The incidence of ulcer recurrence and rebleeding is quite low with adequate anti–*H. pylori* treatment.

ANTRECTOMY

The primary indication for gastric resection in the setting of peptic ulcer disease is chronic obstruction caused by scarring, typically from a pyloric channel ulcer. Antrectomy removes the gastrin-secreting por-

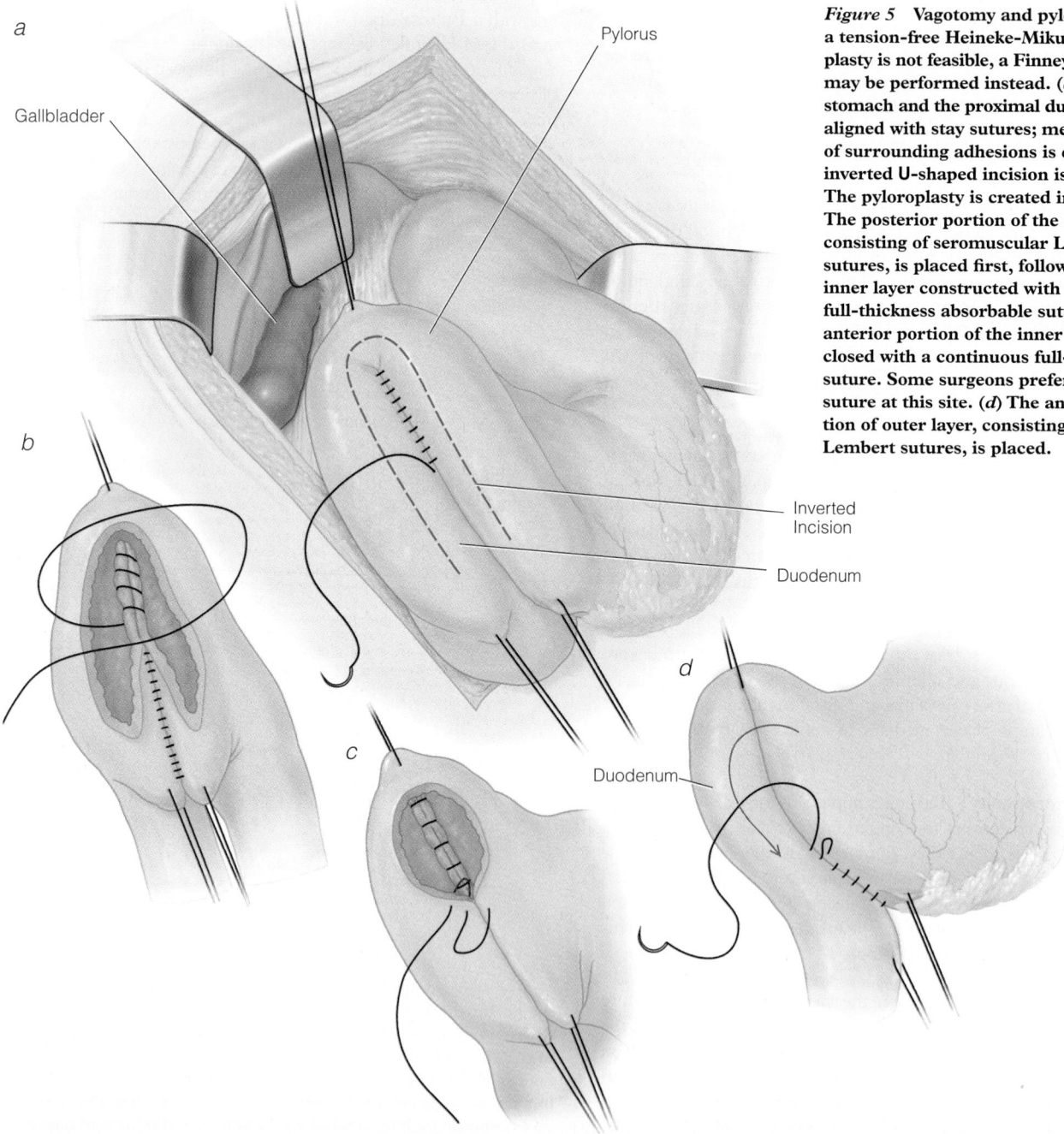

Figure 5 **Vagotomy and pyloroplasty. If a tension-free Heineke-Mikulicz pyloroplasty is not feasible, a Finney pyloroplasty may be performed instead. (*a*) The distal stomach and the proximal duodenum are aligned with stay sutures; meticulous lysis of surrounding adhesions is essential. An inverted U-shaped incision is made. (*b*) The pyloroplasty is created in two layers. The posterior portion of the outer layer, consisting of seromuscular Lembert sutures, is placed first, followed by an inner layer constructed with a continuous full-thickness absorbable suture. (*c*) The anterior portion of the inner layer is closed with a continuous full-thickness suture. Some surgeons prefer a Connell suture at this site. (*d*) The anterior portion of outer layer, consisting of silk Lembert sutures, is placed.**

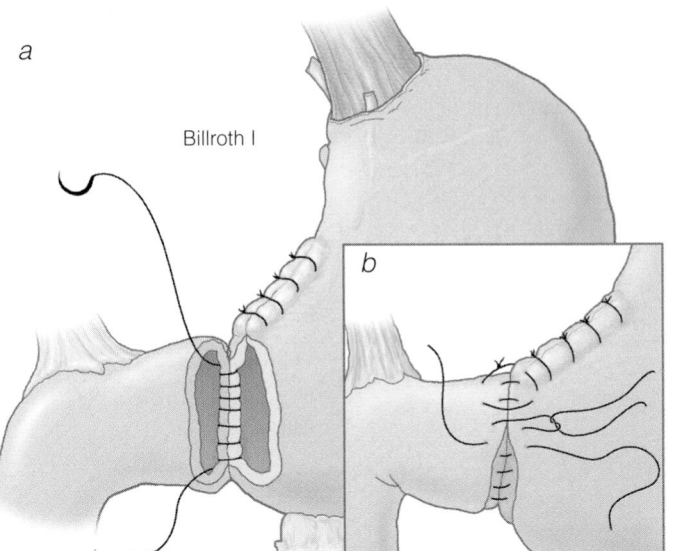

a

Billroth I

b

Figure 6 **Antrectomy: Billroth I reconstruction (gastroduodenostomy). (*a*) The anastomosis is done in two layers. The inner
layer is constructed by placing a continuous full-thickness suture.
(*b*) The outer layer is constructed with silk Lembert sutures. The
junction of the anastomosis and the gastric staple line has been
referred to as the angle of sorrow, a term that reflects the common complication of leakage at the intersection of suture or staple lines. This junction may be reinforced with additional
Lembert sutures.**

tion of the stomach. In addition, antrectomy may be required for
recurrent bleeding after an adequate vagotomy and pyloroplasty for a
bleeding duodenal ulcer. Alternatively, antrectomy may be the elective
operation of choice for intractable type I, II, and III gastric ulcers, as
well as a primary emergency surgical option for perforated or bleeding gastric ulcers. Historically, a primary Billroth I gastroduodenoto-
my has been the preferred procedure, but surrounding scar tissue may
limit the mobility of the duodenum, in which case a Billroth II gastrojejunostomy may be required for a tension-free anastomosis.
Antrectomy is typically combined with truncal vagotomy.

Operative Technique

Step 1: exposure The lesser sac is entered via the avascular
plane in the greater omentum, the plane between the stomach and the
pancreas is developed, and the lesser omentum is divided. The proximal border of the antrum must be identified before the stomach is
divided [*see* Step 2, *below*]. On the greater curvature, the antrum
extends to a point between the pylorus and the fundus; on the lesser
curvature, it extends to a point just above the incisura. Distally, the
dissection is carried past the pylorus. Along the lesser curvature, dissection necessitates division of the descending branch of the left gastric artery, as well as the right gastric artery. Dissection along the
pylorus must be meticulous to ensure that the pancreas is not damaged. If a Billroth I anastomosis is planned, dissection should continue 1 cm beyond the pylorus to expose a sufficient length of duodenum
for the anastomosis. If a Billroth II reconstruction is planned, dissection need extend only far enough to allow division of the duodenum
past the pylorus.

Step 2: division of stomach A gastrointestinal anastomosis
(GIA) stapler is used to divide the stomach at the estimated borders
of the antrum [*see* Step 1, *above*]. The antrum is gently retracted anteriorly and to the patient's left. The right gastroepiploic artery and vein

are divided just distal to the pylorus. The duodenum is then divided
distal to the pylorus with a tranverse anastomosis (TA) stapler.

Step 3: reconstruction When feasible, a Billroth I reconstruction (primary gastroduodenostomy) is preferred for maintenance of
physiologic antegrade flow (though there are no data establishing that
this maintenance of flow is beneficial). In addition, this reconstruction
avoids the complications associated with a Billroth II reconstruction
(e.g., afferent and efferent loop syndromes and duodenal stump
leaks). A generous Kocher maneuver, if not already performed, is necessary to minimize tension on the anastomosis. The lower portion of
the staple line is removed for the width of the duodenal stump, and
the anastomosis is performed in two layers or fashioned with a GIA
stapler through a gastrotomy [*see* Figure 6].

If a primary gastroduodenostomy is not possible, a Billroth II
reconstruction (gastrojejunostomy) is indicated. This procedure
involves a number of technical considerations: management of the
duodenal stump, the length of and placement of the afferent limb, and
the placement and method of the anastomosis. If the duodenum is not
scarred or inflamed, simple staple closure will suffice; if closure proves
difficult, a lateral duodenostomy tube may help decompress the
stump. The duodenal stump should be covered with an omental
patch.

The segment used for the anastomosis should be as short as possible while still being able to reach the stomach without tension;
approximately 20 cm of proximal jejunum should be sufficient to
serve as the afferent limb. Passing the jejunum through a retrocolic
window places less tension on the mesentery than an antecolic
approach does, though gastric emptying will occur with either
method. If a retrocolic approach is used, a window is created for the
jejunum; this must be closed and fixed to the small bowel.

The gastrojejunostomy may be constructed either to the posterior
wall of the stomach or to the inferior portion of the excised staple line.
If the anastomosis is placed at the gastric staple line, the inferior portion of the staple line is excised, often together with a wedge of stomach behind the staple line. A two-layer anastomosis is created with an
outer layer of Lembert sutures and an inner layer of absorbable full-
thickness sutures; the gastric staple line may be oversewn [*see* Figure
7]. Alternatively, the gastrojejunostomy may be created by means of
stapling. A GIA stapler is introduced via a gastrotomy and a small
enterotomy, and the defect is subsequently closed with a TA stapler.
Additional reinforcement is not necessary for this staple line.

Some authors recommend the use of a Braun enteroenterostomy
between the efferent and afferent limbs to reduce bile reflux and
decompress the duodenal stump [*see* Figure 8a]. Staple closure of the
afferent limb above the enteroenterostomy may also be performed to
limit bile reflux into the stomach; this measure creates a configuration
referred to as an uncut Roux-en-Y [*see* Figure 8b]. Enteroenterostomy
at this site may also be performed on an emergency basis to treat afferent limb syndrome. Staple closure of the afferent limb may discourage
bile reflux, but it may also lead to long-term bile reflux gastritis and
esophagitis.[4]

Troubleshooting

In most instances, a noninflamed duodenum can readily be closed
with a TA stapler. However, the thickened and inflamed tissue present
in the setting of inflammation with duodenal perforation is not
amenable to easy closure. Furthermore, poor afferent limb drainage
can lead to increased pressure in the afferent limb, thus contributing
to leakage. Lateral duodenostomy tubes may be used for decompression. The duodenum should be sutured to the abdominal wall in a
Stamm fashion at the exit site of the tube. Alternatively, if the duodenum cannot be closed without significant tension, closure may be

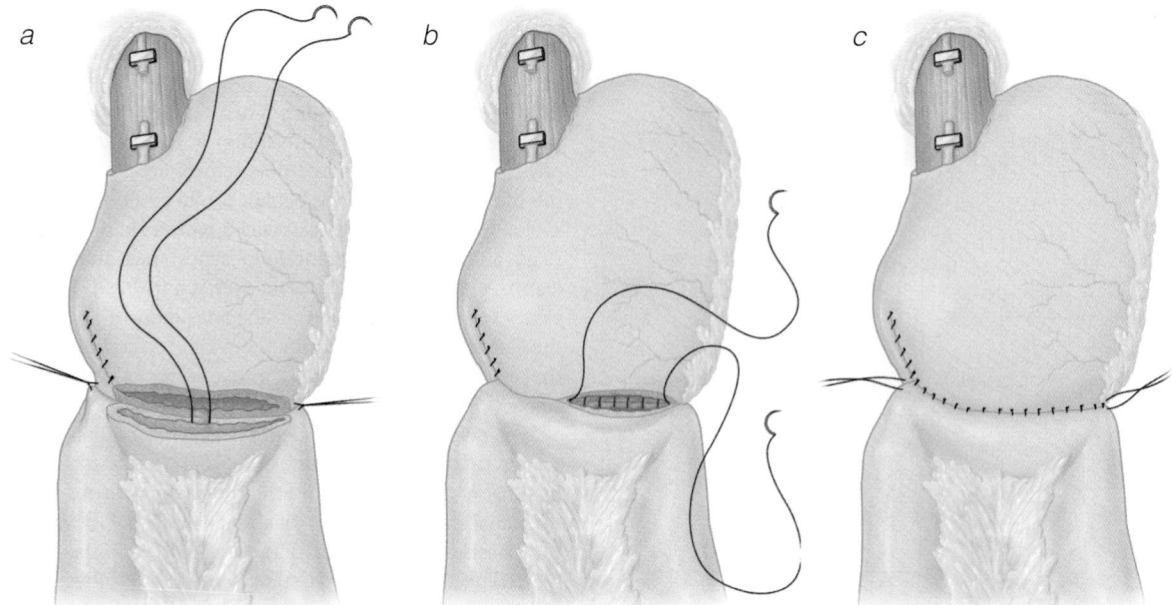

Figure 7 Antrectomy: Billroth II reconstruction (gastrojejunostomy). (*a*) The inferior portion of the gastric resection line is excised, along with a small wedge of the stomach. (*b, c*) A two-layer anastomosis is created, with an outer layer of Lembert sutures and an inner layer of full-thickness absorbable sutures. The upper gastric staple line may be oversewn with interrupted Lembert sutures.

accomplished around a red rubber or mushroom catheter. For especially thick tissue, primary suture closure is preferable to staple closure. Inversion of the duodenal suture line with Lembert sutures is not necessary. In addition, omental patch reinforcement of the duodenal stump may be desirable.

Complications

Leakage from the duodenal stump is a potentially devastating complication that necessitates prompt reoperation, washout, and drainage. The diagnosis of duodenal stump leakage is confirmed by aspirating bilious fluid from a right upper quadrant fluid collection or by per-

forming a technetium-99m (^{99m}Tc)-labeled hepato-iminodiacetic acid (HIDA) scan.

Duodenal leaks can rarely be closed primarily. Duodenostomy may be indicated to further decompress the afferent limb and prevent continuous leakage. The goals are to create a controlled fistula to the skin and to prevent the accumulation of biliary fluid in the abdomen.

Delayed gastric emptying after gastrojejunostomy may occur and is generally managed conservatively. On rare occasions, reoperation is required for delayed anastomotic function. In the case of a Billroth I reconstruction, takedown of the anastomosis is associated with devascularization and duodenal stump leakage. It is therefore preferable to

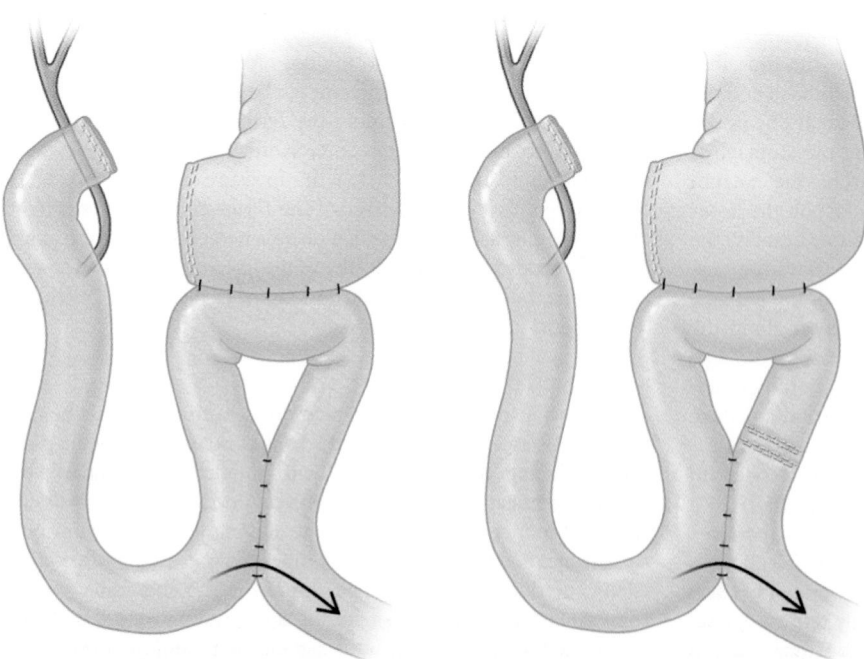

Figure 8 Antrectomy: Billroth II reconstruction (gastrojejunostomy). (*a*) A Braun enteroenterostomy facilitates decompression of the afferent limb in a Billroth II gastrojejunostomy. It may be done as either a sutured or a stapled anastomosis. (*b*) An option is to close the afferent limb above the enteroenterostomy with a TA stapler (so that the jejunal lumen is occluded but not divided). This configuration, often referred to as an uncut Roux-en-Y, temporarily discourages, but does not prevent, reflux of bile into the stomach.

leave the anastomosis in place and perform a gastrojejunostomy along the greater curvature of the stomach. In the case of a Billroth II reconstruction, revision may be required for better positioning of the anastomosis.

Afferent limb obstruction may occur as a consequence of adhesions, internal herniation, volvulus, or a kink at the angle formed with the gastric remnant. Obstruction to outflow of the afferent limb creates a closed-loop obstruction, with persistent secretion of bile and pancreatic fluids into the loop. Such obstruction often presents as recurrent pancreatitis. The diagnosis is facilitated by CT scanning; if it is confirmed, prompt exploration is mandated. Correction of the obstruction may necessitate conversion to a Roux-en-Y reconstruction, shortening of the afferent limb, or a side-to-side enteroenterostomy with the efferent limb (see above).

Bleeding, generally in the form of intraluminal blood loss, is a frequent occurrence after gastrectomy. A bloody aspirate from the nasogastric tube is a common presentation. If bleeding persists for more than 5 days after the initial operation, endoscopy with endoscopic coagulation or epinephrine injection may be considered. Endoscopic approaches should be undertaken with care to minimize the risk of distending the new anastomosis.

Alkaline reflux gastritis is one of the most common long-term complications of gastrectomy, developing in 5% and 15% of patients after gastric surgery.[5] This complication is most frequently associated with Billroth II reconstructions. Although reflux is common, symptoms (e.g., epigastric pain, nausea, and bilious emesis) are relatively rare. Medical management is generally ineffective. If surgery is required, conversion of the Billroth II reconstruction to a Roux-en-Y reconstruction is indicated. In those patients who have a Roux-en-Y rather than a Billroth II reconstruction, the preferred treatment is to divert alkaline contents to a location 45 to 60 cm beyond the gastric remnant.

HIGHLY SELECTIVE VAGOTOMY

Although both vagotomy with antrectomy and vagotomy with pyloroplasty drainage provide relief from duodenal ulcers, they are also associated with significant complications, including dumping syndrome, diarrhea, bile reflux, and poor gastric emptying. Highly selective vagotomy, also referred to as parietal cell vagotomy, was developed with these complications in mind; the idea was to avoid vagal denervation of viscera other than the parietal cell mass while keeping the pylorus mechanically and functionally intact.[6,7] HSV was found to reduce postvagotomy diarrhea and dumping dramatically; however, it was also found to be associated with a much higher rate of recurrent ulceration (greater than 10% at 5 years). Today, in an era characterized by greatly improved medical management of peptic ulcer disease, most GI surgeons perform HSV very rarely, if at all. One possible use for this procedure in the current context might be to treat intractable ulcer disease in young patients.

Operative Technique

Step 1: exposure and gastric mobilization Wide exposure is obtained with the help of upward retraction on the costal margin. The gastrocolic omentum is entered outside the gastroepiploic vessels to preserve the blood supply to the greater curvature. Adhesions to the peritoneum over the pancreas are divided sharply, and the stomach is rotated upward to allow visualization of the posterior leaf of the lesser omentum and the posterior nerve of Latarjet, which runs adjacent to the descending branch of the left gastric artery.

Step 2: dissection of anterior and posterior nerve branches to lesser curvature The distal branches of the nerve of Latarjet are defined, with care taken to preserve the so-called crow's foot, which is

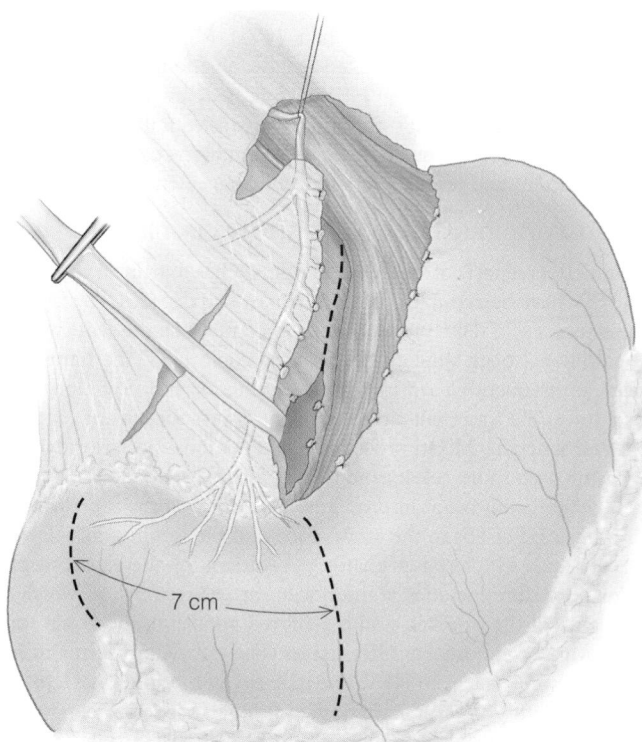

Figure 9 **Highly selective vagotomy. Anterior and posterior branches of the nerve of Latarjet to the lesser curvature are ligated and divided. The distal branches, comprising the so-called crow's foot, are left intact. The posterior branches may be approached via the lesser omentum.**

typically located near the incisura angularis, approximately 6 to 7 cm proximal to the pylorus. Gentle downward traction is applied to the stomach, the left gastric vascular arcade is identified, and all tissue between this arcade and the lesser curvature is divided and ligated. The dissection therefore includes individual branches of the vagus nerve to the stomach. It should proceed upward as far as the esophagogastric junction. The posterior branches are approached either by rotating the stomach or by proceeding directly through the lesser omentum [*see Figure 9*].

Step 3: dissection of esophagogastric junction The distal esophagus is cleared of all nerve fibers for a distance of approximately 5 cm above the esophagogastric junction. The dissection must stay close to the lesser curvature and the esophagus, avoiding the tissues to the right of the esophagus, where the main vagal trunks lie. The posterior esophagogastric junction is exposed by means of gentle traction and slight rotation of the distal esophagus. Exposure is facilitated by downward traction provided by a Penrose drain placed around the esophagogastric junction.

Troubleshooting

Incomplete denervation of the parietal cell mass is prevented by paying meticulous attention to dissection, particularly at the esophagogastric junction. The left side of the distal esophagus must be manually stripped so that the so-called criminal nerve of Grassi can be identified and ligated. About 4 to 5 cm of the distal esophagus should be stripped of vagal input.

Complications

The primary complication of HSV is recurrent ulceration. The reported rates vary, but the general view is that the 5-year ulceration recurrence rate may be higher than 10%.[8] Most recurrent ulcers occur in the setting of incomplete vagal denervation. Given the small number of patients for whom HSV is indicated, few GI surgeons are likely to have accumulated sufficient experience with this technique to be proficient at it. Fortunately, most recurrent ulcers can now be managed medically, and few call for surgical management.

LAPAROSCOPIC TREATMENT OF PEPTIC ULCER DISEASE

Numerous reports of laparoscopic approaches to truncal vagotomy and HSV have been published over the past two decades. The laparoscopic versions of these procedures proceed in much the same way as the traditional open versions. In a laparoscopic HSV, the ultrasonic shears are frequently used to divide the anterior and posterior vagal branches to the lesser curvature from the crow's foot to the esophagogastric junction. Mixed procedures that combine posterior truncal vagotomy with more selective anterior gastric denervation are common. In the Taylor procedure, an anterior seromyotomy is performed from the angle of His to the crow's foot, and the seromuscular layers are subsequently closed primarily.[9] A variant of the laparoscopic Taylor procedure includes a anterior linear gastrectomy, in which a linear strip of the stomach wall is removed parallel to the lesser curvature with an endoscopic GIA stapler. This procedure seems to be functionally equivalent to HSV. The majority of the studies of laparoscopic vagotomy, however, have been individual case series that do not compare the laparoscopic approach with a traditional open approach. Undoubtedly, the scarce comparative data reflect the declining indications for vagotomy for intractable peptic ulcer disease. Thus, whereas laparoscopic HSV has been well described, it is by no means clear that it should be recommended over open HSV for those rare patients in whom this procedure is indicated.

More data are available on laparoscopic treatment of perforated duodenal ulcers. A meta-analysis of 13 studies comparing laparoscopic and open approaches to perforated peptic ulcers found that laparoscopic repair yielded excellent results, albeit with a small but insignificant increase in the reoperation rate.[10] The laparoscopic approach is therefore considered as safe and effective as open Graham patch repair. The procedures generally involve either suture closure of the perforation followed by omentopexy or omentopexy alone, and they should be attempted only by surgeons with advanced laparoscopic skills. The threshold for conversion to an open procedure should be low if the ulcers are particularly large ulcers or prove difficult to localize.

DUODENAL DIVERTICULECTOMY

Incidental duodenal diverticula are common. Such diverticula consist of a sac that includes only mucosa and submucosa, and most occur within 2 cm of the ampulla of Vater. Complications include ulceration and bleeding, compression of the CBD with cholangitis or pancreatitis, and, in cases of perforation, abscess formation with peritonitis. CT scanning is useful for differentiating this condition from cholecystitis or pancreatitis. Surgery is rarely required; it is indicated primarily for complications such as bleeding, perforation, and biliary or duodenal obstruction.

Operative Technique

The main surgical options are simple diverticulectomy with drainage and transduodenal diverticulectomy (as described by Iida[11]). If the duodenum is free of inflammation, the transduodenal approach is preferred because it minimizes the need for dissection of the diverticulum from the surrounding pancreas. However, if the diverticulum does not involve the pancreas, simple excision flush with the duodenal wall, followed by closure in two layers, may be sufficient. The ensuing technical description focuses on transduodenal diverticulectomy.

Step 1: exposure and duodenotomy A generous Kocher maneuver is performed to elevate the head of the duodenum. The duodenum is then opened by making a 4 cm longitudinal incision along the antimesenteric border, and the ampulla is either visualized or palpated. To identify the ampulla, it may be necessary to place a catheter into the CBD via a separate choledochotomy.

Step 2: diverticulectomy The orifice of the diverticulum is identified, and the mucosa is inverted into the lumen of the duodenum. The neck of the diverticulum is transected 2 mm from the junction with the duodenal wall. The diverticular opening is then closed with interrupted seromuscular Lembert sutures of 3-0 silk and interrupted mucosal sutures of 4-0 polyglactin. The duodenum is closed in two layers, also with an inner layer of 4-0 polyglactin and an outer layer of seromuscular Lembert sutures of 3-0 silk. Closed suction drainage adjacent to the duodenum is indicated.

Special case: perforated duodenal diverticulum. In the setting of acute inflammation, duodenotomy is avoided. Instead, the abscess is evacuated, and the diverticulum is excised along with just enough of the adjacent duodenal wall to ensure that only healthy tissue is left. If the resulting duodenal defect is large, either sleeve resection of the duodenum or drainage of the open duodenal defect into a Roux-en-Y jejunal limb may be required.

Troubleshooting

Inadvertent closure of the CBD may be prevented by inserting a catheter into the duct. If the duodenum is markedly inflamed, suture line breakdown is likely, eventually leading to a duodenal fistula. The area can be isolated by means of pyloric exclusion or antrectomy with Billroth II reconstruction. In addition, bile flow can be diverted by performing a choledochojejunostomy to a Roux-en-Y intestinal limb to prevent combined leakage of pancreatic fluid and bile.

Diverticula arising from the third or the fourth portion of the duodenum may be approached via the transverse mesocolon and may be excised either primarily or via a transduodenal approach. Inverting the diverticulum without excising it is not recommended, because it may lead to duodenal obstruction.

Procedures for Gastric Cancer

Surgical resection remains the primary therapeutic modality for gastric cancer [*see 50 Tumors of the Stomach, Duodenum, and Small Bowel*]. The diagnosis of gastric cancer is primarily made by means of endoscopy with biopsy. There are numerous considerations that must be addressed before operation, including the stage of the cancer on diagnostic imaging, the use of staging laparoscopy, the extent of the planned gastrectomy, the extent of the planned lymphadenectomy, the placement of feeding enterostomies, and the patient's overall medical fitness for surgery.

PREOPERATIVE EVALUATION

Endoscopy, with or without endoscopic ultrasonography (EUS), is essential for diagnosis. Preoperative biopsy is helpful for confirming the suspected pathologic process, particularly because the extent of resection will be different if a less common lesion, such as a gastrointestinal stromal tumor (GIST), is identified. Endoscopic localization is critical because the extent of the gastrectomy will depend on the precise location of the tumor. It should be noted, however, that the true location of the tumor, as determined at laparotomy, may differ significantly from the preoperative estimate made on the basis of endoscopy. Abdominal CT scanning and chest radiography are indicated to rule out obvious metastatic disease, which would be an indication for a more conservative surgical approach or even for nonoperative therapy. The preoperative physical examination should also focus on the detection of occult metastatic disease, concentrating on such sites as the supraclavicular lymph nodes and the pouch of Douglas. A bone scan is indicated if metastasis to bone is suspected. Laparoscopic staging (see below) may be performed to identify occult metastatic disease (and, possibly, to prevent an unnecessary laparotomy in an otherwise ill patient).[12] If the tumor is not bleeding or causing an obstruction, palliative resection might be avoided. Generally, curative surgery should be attempted only when the tumor is believed to be limited to the stomach and the perigastric lymph nodes. On occasion, however, curative-intent surgery may be considered for tumors that involve nearby resectable structures (e.g., the transverse colon), provided that these structures can be removed en bloc with the primary lesion.

In Japan, where screening endoscopy is widespread, early gastric cancer is identified with some frequency. In Western countries, however, the situation is different, and patients tend to present with more advanced cancers. Accordingly, although procedures such as wedge resection for early gastric cancer have been described, most gastric cancer patients in the United States require formal gastrectomy and lymphadenectomy.

OPERATIVE PLANNING

Extent of Resection

The extent of the resection required for treatment of a gastric malignancy is determined primarily by the preoperative pathologic diagnosis and the site of the tumor. Considerably smaller surgical margins are required for rare mesenchymal tumors (e.g., GISTs) than are necessary for gastric adenocarcinomas, which tend to spread microscopically well beyond the gross extent of the tumor. Most mesenchymal tumors can be adequately treated with a wedge resection or partial gastrectomy that achieves a 1 cm gross margin. Laparoscopic approaches to such tumors have been described that employ either the endoscopic GIA stapler or excision with suture closure [see Laparoscopic Resection of Malignant Gastric Tumors, below]. Such approaches may be facilitated by endoscopic tattooing of an appropriate margin or by intraoperative endoscopic guidance. For adenocarcinomas, a margin of at least 5 cm is recommended.

A 5 cm margin may be particularly difficult to achieve when the tumor is located along the lesser curvature. In many such cases, although the tumor appears to be distal and possibly amenable to a subtotal gastrectomy, a 5 cm negative margin along the lesser curvature would place the proximal resection margin far above the incisura angularis and near the esophagogastric junction, thus necessitating total or near-total gastrectomy. For lesser-curvature tumors whose location allows adequate margins to be obtained, distal gastrectomy with Billroth II gastrojejunostomy is preferred; for more proximal tumors, total gastrectomy with esophagojejunostomy may be required.

Special consideration must be given to tumors of the esophagogastric junction. In the classification scheme described by Siewert and colleagues,[13] such tumors are defined as lying within 5 cm of the anatomic esophagogastric junction in either direction along the craniocaudal axis of the esophagus and the stomach. They are classified into three types as follows:

1. Type I: the center of the tumor lies 1 to 5 cm proximal to the esophagogastric junction.
2. Type II: the center of the tumor lies within 1 cm of the esophagogastric junction proximally or within 2 cm distally.
3. Type III: the center of the tumor lies 2 to 5 cm distal to the esophagogastric junction.

It is generally agreed that total esophagectomy is required for type I esophagogastric junction tumors [see 34 Open Esophageal Procedures]. The necessary extent of resection for type II and III esophagogastric junction tumors has been more controversial. A microscopically negative (R0) surgical margin is closely associated with survival after resection of esophagogastric junction adenocarcinomas, though R0 resection can be quite difficult to achieve, given the propensity of these tumors for intramural spreading. In our experience, positive margins have not been found in patients with T1 or T2 tumors, even when the margins are smaller than 4 cm. In patients with T3 or T4 tumors, however, proximal margins of at least 6 cm have proved necessary. For T1 and T2 tumors, total gastrectomy without thoracotomy may yield adequate margins. For T3 and T4 tumors, however, extended gastrectomy with thoracotomy or esophagectomy may be required.[14] It is well documented that the margin lengths measured on prefixed esophageal specimens are only about 50% of the corresponding lengths measured in situ before completion of resection.[15] Accordingly, intraoperative decisions about the extent of resection should be based on margin length requirements that may be considerably greater than those derived from resection specimens.

Extent of Lymphadenectomy

Considerable controversy has surrounded the question of how extensive lymphadenectomy should be for curative resection of gastric adenocarcinoma. One aspect of the controversy has to do with the minimum number of lymph nodes required for analysis. It has been suggested that a minimum of 15 lymph nodes must be removed during gastrectomy. In a study published in 2000, 5-year survival rates were significantly lower in patients with fewer than 15 lymph nodes sampled than in those with 15 or more lymph nodes examined.[16] This decreased survival has been attributed primarily to understaging as the result of inadequate lymphadenectomy (though, admittedly, there is some disagreement on this point).

The particular lymph node basins that should be sampled during gastrectomy has also been the subject of debate. Western surgeons have usually limited lymphadenectomy to the perigastric (D1) lymph nodes. Surgeons in other countries, particularly Japan, have tended to prefer a much more radical lymph node dissection that includes the second-order (D2) nodes [see Figure 10]. Whereas Japanese surgeons have reported better overall long-term stage-for-stage survival with D2 lymph node dissections, Western surgeons have not found this approach to be quite so beneficial. Consequently, it has not been clear whether more extensive lymph node dissection actually provides a survival benefit or simply improves surgical staging. To date, four randomized, controlled trials have failed to show any significant benefit from extended lymph node dissection. In the largest such study, performed by the Dutch Gastric Cancer Group, more than 700 patients were randomly assigned to undergo either D1 or D2 lymphadenectomy.[17] The 5-year survival rate was essentially the same in the two groups; perioperative morbidity and mortality were significantly higher after D2 lymphadenectomy.

A subsequent study from the same group found that at 10 years after operation, D2 lymphadenectomy provided a benefit (in terms of lower local recurrence) only in the subgroup with positive second-order nodes; however, these patients could not be identified preoperatively.[18] For the cohort as a whole, extended lymph node dissection generated no long-term survival benefit. Therefore, although some surgeons extend the lymphadenectomy to include lymph nodes along the left gastric, celiac, and common hepatic arteries (a so-called D1+ dissection), the standard of care for surgeons in the United States continues to be a D1 lymphadenectomy that includes all perigastric lymph nodes and the greater omentum.

TOTAL GASTRECTOMY

Operative Technique

Step 1: incision and exposure   The abdomen is entered via a midline or bilateral subcostal incision. If a subcostal incision is utilized, it may have to be extended past the xiphoid process in the midline for optimal exposure. Thorough exposure of the peritoneal cavity (including the liver, all peritoneal surfaces, and, in women, the ovaries) is undertaken to search for signs of metastatic disease. If the patient has a proximal lesion near the gastric cardia, there may be a need for a thoracotomy if the distal thoracic esophagus is to be included in the resection specimen. If an incision into the thoracic cavity is being considered, the left chest should be surgically prepared at the time of initial draping to allow extension of the incision across the lower left costal margin if desired. In this setting, if thoracotomy is possible, preoperative placement of a double-lumen endotracheal tube should be considered. The abdominal portion of a thoracoabdominal incision should be performed first to allow assessment of resectability.

Step 2: dissection of omentum from colon   The omentum is separated from the colon with an electrocautery or scissors through the relatively avascular plane. Gentle upward traction is placed on the omentum to facilitate entry into the correct surgical plane [*see Figure 11*]. If the procedure involves a formal D2 lymph node dissection, this is also a convenient time to enter the anterior leaf of the transverse mesocolon, which is resected with the anterior covering of the pancreas. (As noted, most U.S. surgeons perform a D1 resection or some modification thereof and thus do not dissect the anterior peritoneal surface of the mesocolon and pancreas.)

With the dissection starting on the right side, the right gastroepiploic artery is identified and ligated where it originates from the gastroduodenal artery. The short gastric vessels are divided as the dissection proceeds along the greater curvature. The lesser omentum is also divided near the liver and is included with the specimen; care should be taken to identify an aberrant left hepatic artery in the lesser omentum (if present). The dissection is continued onto the peritoneal surface of the distal esophagus.

Step 3: division of duodenum   The duodenum is divided just distal to the pyloric ring either with a GIA stapler or with a TA stapler applied twice [*see Figure 12*]. The right gastric artery is identified and ligated near its base. Division of the duodenum allows elevation and

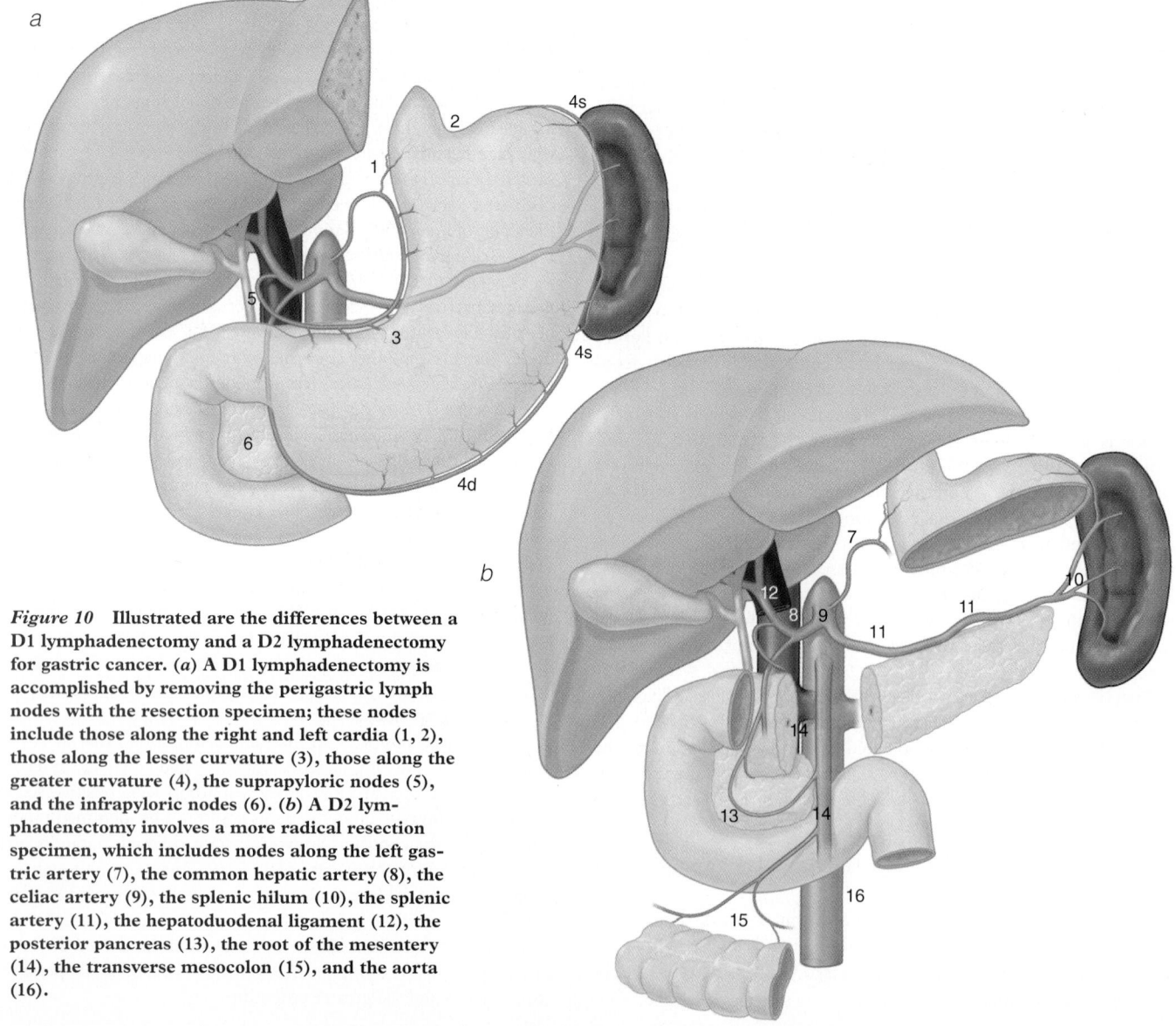

Figure 10   **Illustrated are the differences between a D1 lymphadenectomy and a D2 lymphadenectomy for gastric cancer. (*a*) A D1 lymphadenectomy is accomplished by removing the perigastric lymph nodes with the resection specimen; these nodes include those along the right and left cardia (1, 2), those along the lesser curvature (3), those along the greater curvature (4), the suprapyloric nodes (5), and the infrapyloric nodes (6). (*b*) A D2 lymphadenectomy involves a more radical resection specimen, which includes nodes along the left gastric artery (7), the common hepatic artery (8), the celiac artery (9), the splenic hilum (10), the splenic artery (11), the hepatoduodenal ligament (12), the posterior pancreas (13), the root of the mesentery (14), the transverse mesocolon (15), and the aorta (16).**

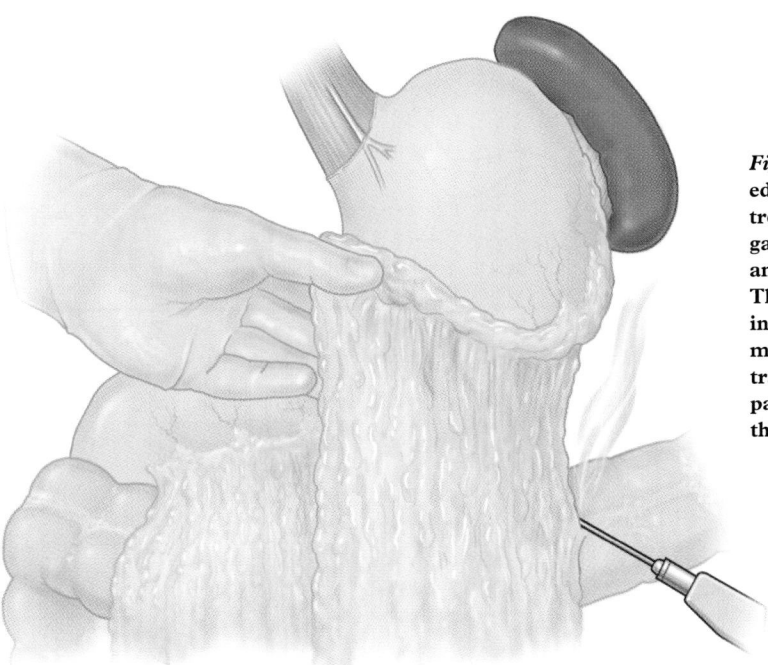

Figure 11 Total gastrectomy. The omentum is dissected from the transverse colon with scissors or the electrocautery. In the course of this dissection, the right gastroepiploic artery is encountered near the pylorus and divided near its base at the gastroduodenal artery. The dissection continues along the greater curvature, including ligation of the short gastric vessels. In a formal D2 lymphadenectomy, the anterior leaf of the transverse mesocolon and the anterior capsule of the pancreas are dissected. In a D1 lymphadenectomy, these structures are left alone.

rotation of the stomach, thereby facilitating access to the left gastric artery and the surrounding node-bearing tissue.

With the stomach gently retracted upward and anteriorly, dissection identifies the celiac axis and the left gastric artery [*see Figure 13a*]. The origin of the left gastric artery is ligated and divided, and a suture ligature is placed on the proximal end.

A standard D1 lymphadenectomy does not include splenectomy and distal pancreatectomy. The spleen and pancreas are left in situ and are separated from the resection specimen by dividing and ligating the short gastric vessels (see above).

Troubleshooting. Leakage from the duodenal stump is a potentially disastrous complication. If the stapled duodenum appears

ischemic, the staple line may be inverted with Lembert sutures of 3-0 silk.

Step 4: inclusion of necessary lymph nodes The degree of dissection to be performed in the porta hepatis depends on the extent of the planned lymphadenectomy. A D1 lymphadenectomy does not require any of the lymph nodes in this area, but a D1+ lymphadenectomy includes lymph nodes along the common hepatic artery. Gentle left lateral traction is placed on the stomach before division of the left gastric artery to apply some tension to the hepatic artery. The dissection proceeds along the celiac and hepatic arteries to the porta hepatis. The tissue surrounding the common hepatic artery and the left gastric artery is swept medially with the specimen.

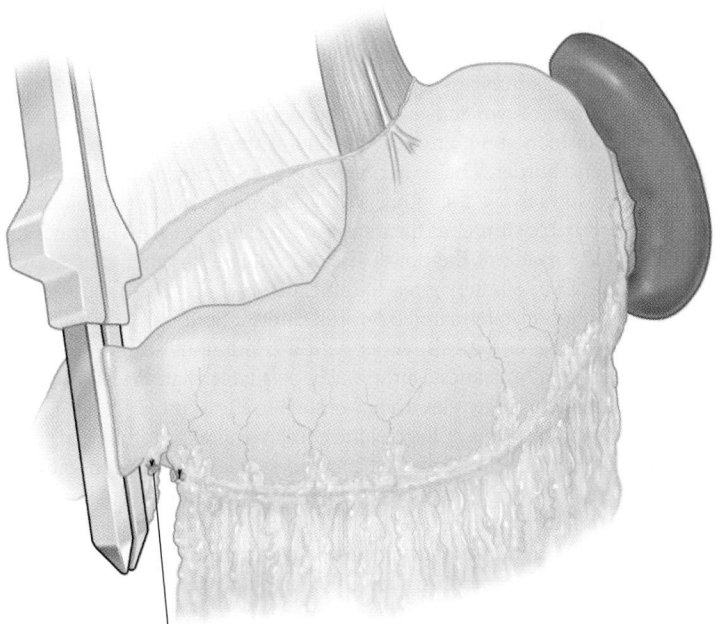

Right Gastroepiploic
Artery Divided

Figure 12 Total gastrectomy. The duodenum is divided just beyond the pylorus with a GIA or TA stapler. The duodenal staple line may be reinforced with interrupted Lembert sutures.

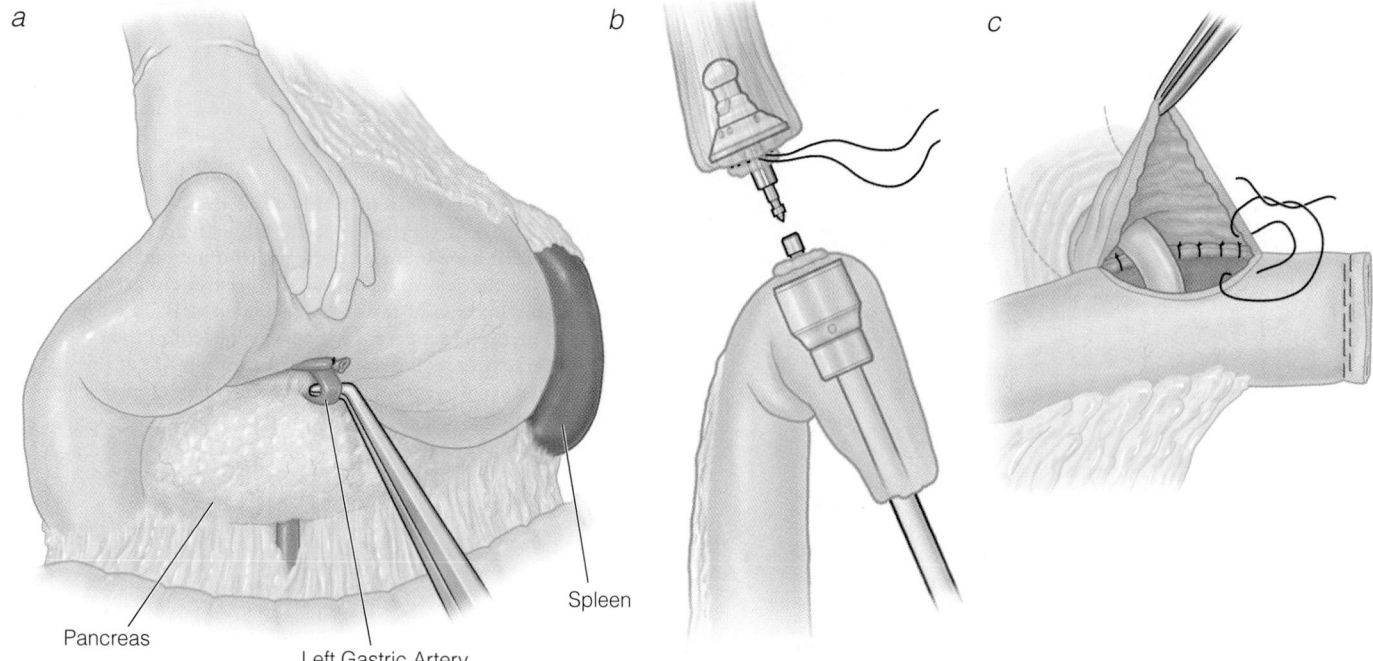

Pancreas

Left Gastric Artery

Spleen

Figure 13 **Total gastrectomy. (*a*) The stomach is retracted cephalad to expose the left gastric vessels, which may be divided and suture-ligated on the proximal side. Division of the distal esophagus should be preceded by placement of several stay sutures on the proximal esophagus to prevent it from retracting into the posterior mediastinum. Reconstruction is then carried out; options include stapled end-to-side esophagojejunostomy, hand-sewn end-to-side esophagojejunostomy, side-to-side esophagojejunostomy, and anastomosis to a jejunal pouch. (*b*) In a stapled esophagojejunostomy, the anvil is secured in the esophagus with a purse-string suture, an EEA stapler is inserted through the distal end of the Roux limb, and the anastomosis is created to the antimesenteric side of the bowel. Once the anastomosis is complete, the end of the Roux limb is amputated with a single firing of a GIA stapler. (*c*) A hand-sewn esophagojejunostomy may be fashioned with interrupted full-thickness sutures (as shown), with a continuous full-thickness suture, or as a two-layer anastomosis. After completion of the posterior row, a sump tube may be placed across the anastomosis into the proximal jejunum. After completion of the anterior row, several reinforcing seromuscular sutures may be placed to reduce tension on the anastomosis.**

Step 5: division of esophagus The peritoneum is divided over the anterior esophagus, and the esophagus is completely dissected free of surrounding tissue. The esophagus is then divided either with a TA stapler or with a scalpel after the placement of a noncrushing bowel clamp. To keep the stump from retracting too far proximally, stay sutures of 2-0 silk should be placed in the proximal esophagus before division. Alternatively, the specimen may be left attached and used as a handle to retract the proximal esophagus inferiorly. The esophagus may then be divided after placement of the posterior suture line. Evaluation of the proximal resection margin with frozen-section analysis is advisable.

Troubleshooting. The proximal margin may be found to harbor malignancy; if so, re-resection of the proximal margin should be performed. Placement of stay sutures in the proximal esophagus is important; if this is not done, the retracting esophagus may migrate into the posterior mediastinum.

Step 6: reconstruction via esophagojejunostomy The options for reconstruction after gastrectomy include stapled end-to-side esophagojejunostomy, hand-sewn end-to-side esophagojejunostomy, side-to-side esophagojejunostomy, and anastomosis to a jejunal pouch. A Roux-en-Y jejunal limb is fashioned; to prevent biliary reflux, it should be at least 40 to 50 cm long. The Roux limb is then brought up behind the colon to the esophagus. Some authors recommend antecolic placement of the Roux limb to prevent obstruction in the setting of recurrent disease; however, retrocolic placement may facilitate a more tension-free anastomosis.

For a stapled end-to-side esophagojejunostomy, a purse-string suture of 3-0 or 2-0 polypropylene is placed in the esophagus and used to secure the anvil of an end-to-end anastomosis (EEA) stapler. The body of the stapler is placed into the Roux limb, with the tip protruding through the end, and the esophagojejunostomy is created on the antimesenteric border of the jejunum [*see Figure 13b*]. The open end of the Roux limb is then closed with a TA stapler. To reduce tension on the anastomosis, the staple line may be reinforced with interrupted Lembert sutures of 3-0 silk.

A hand-sewn end-to-side esophagojejunostomy is created in a similar fashion at a point near the end of the Roux limb on the antimesenteric border. The posterior row is placed first, with interrupted 3-0 silk sutures as the outer layer and interrupted full-thickness 3-0 absorbable sutures as the inner layer [*see Figure 13c*]. The knots are tied on the inside of the bowel. The anterior row is then placed, with an inner layer of interrupted full-thickness 3-0 absorbable sutures and an outer layer of interrupted 3-0 silk sutures. Some surgeons prefer a single-layer anastomosis, either with a continuous suture or with interrupted full-thickness sutures. The available data do not favor either single-layer or two-layer anastomosis in this setting.

Side-to-side esophagojejunostomy requires a substantial length of intra-abdominal esophagus and necessitates extensive mobilization of the distal esophagus. The jejunum may be sutured to the underside of the diaphragm to relieve tension on the anastomosis.

Some authors report improved postoperative quality of life with a jejunal pouch reconstruction. For most patients with gastric cancer, however, pouch reconstruction offers no distinct advantage.

Drains are not routinely placed; drain placement may increase the rate of leakage from the esophagojejunostomy.

Troubleshooting. Without a sufficient length of intra-abdominal esophagus, primary reconstruction can be difficult. Full mobilization of the intra-abdominal esophagus is essential. Because the esophagus lacks a serosa, transversely oriented Cushing-type sutures may be preferable to Lembert sutures on the anterior and posterior outer layer of a hand-sewn anastomosis.

Step 7 (optional): feeding enterostomy Many patients with gastric adenocarcinoma become significantly malnourished after gastrectomy. The loss of the gastric pouch may adversely affect their ability to fulfill their caloric requirements in the early postoperative period. To prevent further malnutrition, some authors recommend creating a feeding jejunostomy at the time of total gastrectomy with esophagojejunostomy. The jejunostomy should be placed downstream from the jejunojejunostomy (i.e., more than 50 cm distal to the anastomosis). When a feeding enteroenterostomy is indicated, we prefer a Witzel jejunostomy.

Complications

D2 lymphadenectomy has been associated with numerous complications, including increased blood loss, longer operating time, colonic devascularization, pancreatitis, and pancreatic leakage. Although complication rates appear to be acceptably low when the procedure is done by an experienced surgeon, there is still the potential for the benefits of extensive lymphadenectomy to be outweighed by the additional complications.

Anastomotic leakage at an esophagojejunostomy may lead to postoperative infection. Intra-abdominal leaks may be managed by drainage via percutaneous drains or laparotomy, as well as by proximal nasogastric drainage. High anastomotic leaks may result in contamination of the posterior mediastinum or the pleural space, and thoracotomy or tube thoracostomy may be necessary to achieve external drainage.

Occasionally, bleeding may be substantial enough to necessitate reoperation. In this situation, the gastric remnant may be entered via a transverse incision just proximal to the anastomosis. As a rule, the bleeding can be successfully controlled by placing simple figure-eight sutures.

DISTAL OR SUBTOTAL GASTRECTOMY

Cancers of the distal stomach or antrum may be addressed by means of a distal gastrectomy. Particular attention should be paid to tumors on the lesser curvature, where obtaining an adequate proximal margin may be a problem [*see* Operative Planning, Extent of Resection, *above*]. The dissection proceeds as in a total gastrectomy,

but without division of the short gastric vessels. The omentum is separated from the transverse colon with the electrocautery, and the entire omentum is taken with the specimen. A 5 cm proximal margin is ideal. Commonly, the stomach is divided at a point inferior to the short gastric vessels and proximal to the incisura angularis.

Additional operative details and comments on postgastrectomy complications are available elsewhere [*see* Procedures for Benign Gastric and Duodenal Disease, Antrectomy, *above*].

LAPAROSCOPIC STAGING FOR GASTRIC CANCER

The goal of laparoscopic staging before attempted curative resection of gastric carcinoma is to detect occult metastatic disease, the presence of which may affect management. For example, if laparoscopy reveals peritoneal studding in a patient who does not have symptoms such as bleeding or obstruction, a decision may be made to forgo attempts at resection. In the setting of T2 or T4 tumors, laparoscopic staging has been shown to detect occult metastases in 20% to 30% of patients.[12]

The abdomen is explored with a 30° laparoscope inserted via an umbilical port. To facilitate exposure, additional 5 mm ports may be placed in the right upper and left upper quadrants. If laparoscopic ultrasonography is available, one of the port sites should be 10 mm to allow passage of the ultrasound probe. Any suspicious lesion encountered is sampled and sent for frozen-section analysis.

LAPAROSCOPIC RESECTION OF MALIGNANT GASTRIC TUMORS

Laparoscopic gastrectomy is being performed with increasing frequency. The principles of laparoscopic gastric resection are similar to those of the corresponding open procedure, though extensive lymph node dissections may be considerably more difficult with the minimally invasive approach. Currently, there are only a few centers where laparoscopic resection of advanced gastric carcinoma is being performed with any frequency. Accordingly, it seems appropriate, for the time being, to reserve laparoscopic gastrectomy for patients who have very early cancers and those who are candidates only for palliative resection.

Laparoscopic wedge resection may be appropriate for small lesions that are potentially benign or for malignant lesions for which extensive surgical margins are not required (e.g., GISTs [*see Figure 14*]). The lesion is visualized intraoperatively by means of endoscopy or marked preoperatively with India ink. Laparoscopic sutures are placed in the tissue surrounding the lesion, then retracted upward so that the portion of the gastric wall containing the lesion is elevated. A

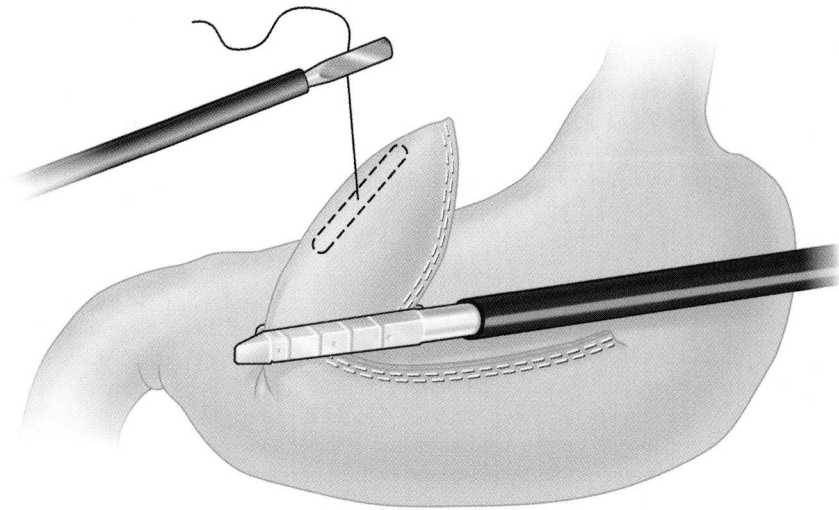

Figure 14 **Laparoscopic resection of GIST. The tumor is visualized preoperatively and marked with India ink; alternatively, the tumor may be identified intraoperatively by means of endoscopy and its location marked with a suture. Traction sutures may be employed to "tent up" the lesion, thereby isolating it from the remainder of the stomach. The tumor is then resected with several firings of an endoscopic linear stapler. For lesions higher along the greater curvature near the cardia, wedge resection should be performed with an esophageal bougie in place to prevent inadvertent narrowing of the esophagogastric junction.**

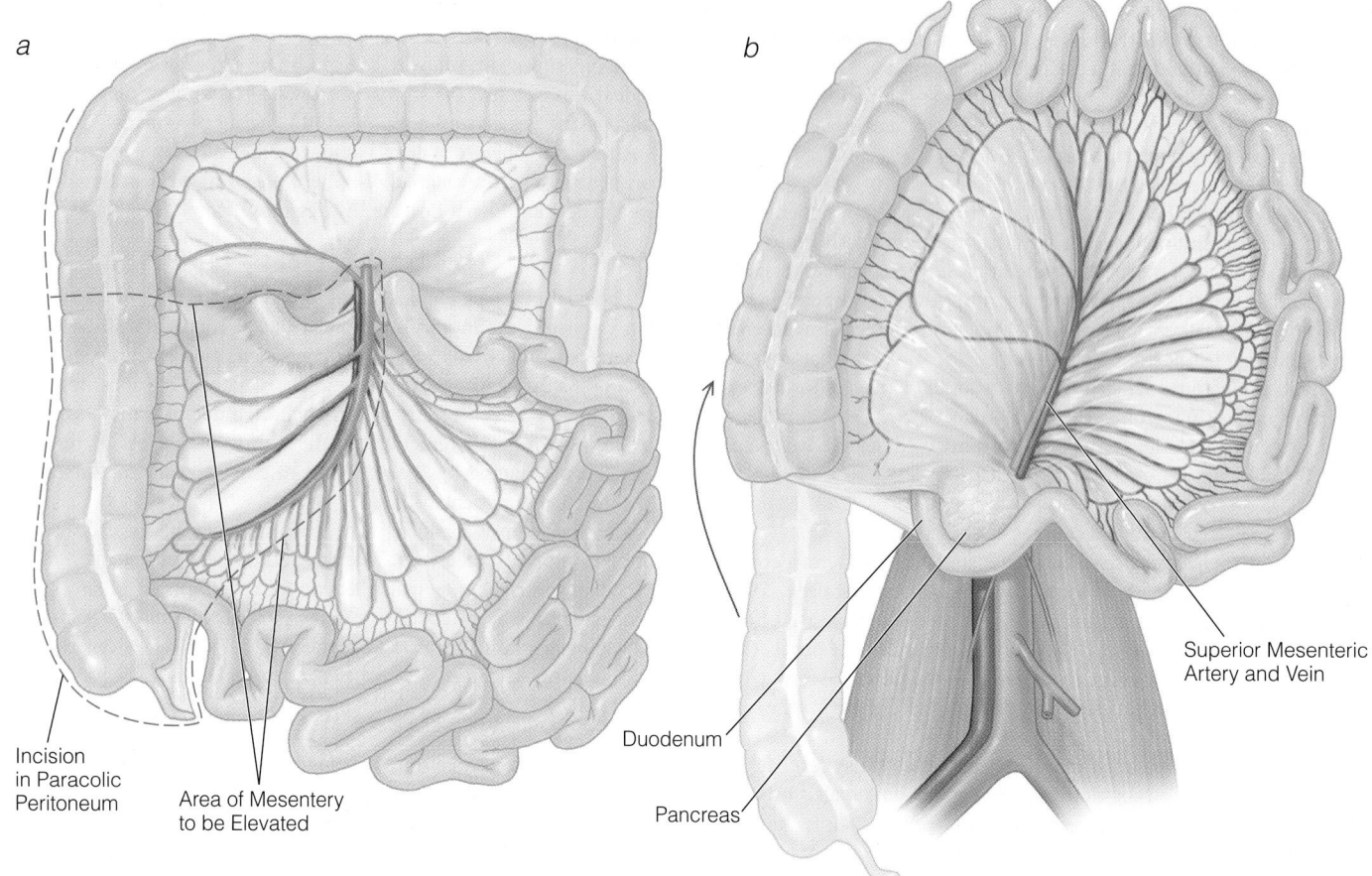

Figure 15 Local resection of duodenal tumors. Mobilization of the right colon and upward retraction of the small bowel mesentery allows direct access to the third and fourth portions of the duodenum. Sleeve resection of the duodenum with subsequent duodenojejunostomy can then be performed. (*a*) Avascular peritoneal attachments of the right colon are divided, as well as avascular attachments underneath the small bowel mesentery. Dotted lines enclose the area of mesentery to be elevated from posterior attachments. (*b*) Cephalad retraction of the right colon, the small bowel, and the mesenteric vessels allows exposure of the third and fourth portions of the duodenum.

wedge resection is then performed with an endoscopic stapler. Intraoperative assessment of the surgical margin by a pathologist is useful to ensure that the margin is negative.

Procedures for Duodenal Cancer

LOCAL RESECTION OF DUODENAL TUMORS

Small duodenal tumors (e.g., polyps, villous adenomas, small GISTs, and neuroendocrine tumors) are occasionally amenable to local surgical resection. The diagnosis must be confirmed by endoscopic biopsy before resection. Endoscopy is also useful for localization of the lesion with respect to the ampulla and pancreatic head. Lateral lesions are removed by local resection far more easily than lesions on the medial wall are.

Operative Planning

Endoscopic confirmation of the diagnosis and localization of the lesion are crucial for operative planning. In addition, appropriate patient selection is essential. Local resection may be inappropriate for lesions close to the ampulla of Vater, for large duodenal lesions, for carcinomas, or for lesions on the medial aspect of the duodenum abutting the pancreas. For lesions in the second or third portion of the duodenum that are not amenable to local excision, pancreaticoduo-

denectomy may be required. Exposure may be achieved through an upper midline or right upper quadrant incision.

Operative Technique

The duodenum is mobilized with an extensive Kocher maneuver. The tumor is palpated and approached via a longitudinal duodenotomy. The tumor is grasped and everted, and a full-thickness portion of the duodenal wall is resected with the mass. Stay sutures are placed at the ends of the duodenotomy, and the duodenotomy is closed transversely, either with a TA stapler or with sutures. If a transverse closure would place too much tension on the suture line, a longitudinal closure is undertaken. If possible, omentum is placed over the duodenal closure.

Troubleshooting

Intraoperative endoscopy may be required to locate small duodenal lesions that cannot be palpated. During dissection, the location of the ampulla can be determined by passing a Fogarty catheter into the cystic duct, down the CBD, and through the ampulla. This measure requires that a cholecystectomy be done.

RESECTION OF DISTAL DUODENAL TUMORS

Lesions of the distal duodenum (e.g., GISTs, carcinoids, and, rarely, adenocarcinomas) are occasionally amenable to sleeve resection. Preoperative CT and endoscopy are essential to the workup of such lesions. Endoscopic biopsy should be performed if it is technically feasible.

Operative Technique

Step 1: exposure of duodenum Operative access to the distal duodenum is limited by the presence of the superior mesenteric vessels and the transverse mesocolon. The third and fourth portions of the duodenum may be approached either by moving the duodenum under the mesenteric vessels or by temporarily mobilizing the mesenteric vessels. In the first approach, the distal duodenum and the proximal jejunum are mobilized upward by dissecting the ligament of Treitz away from its mesenteric attachments. The proximal jejunum is divided with a stapler. After extensive mobilization, the duodenum is passed under the superior mesenteric vein and artery and moved to the right side of the abdomen.

In the second approach, the superior mesenteric vessels are mobilized upward to expose the third portion of the duodenum. The right colon is mobilized cephalad by incising the peritoneum along the white line of Toldt from the hepatic flexure to the cecum [*see Figure 15a*]. Division of the peritoneum is then continued along the cecum and medially to liberate the terminal ileum. The avascular attachments between the small bowel mesentery and the retroperitoneum are divided by means of cauterization and gentle blunt dissection [*see Figure 15b*].

Step 2: resection and anastomosis The duodenum is divided with the stapler approximately 1 cm proximal to the tumor. If pancreatic invasion is identified, pancreaticoduodenectomy should be considered. The distal bowel is brought through the transverse mesocolon, and a side-to-side duodenojejunostomy is created with an outer layer of 3-0 silk and inner layer of 3-0 polyglactin. Alternatively, the anastomosis may be performed to the second portion of the duodenum.

Troubleshooting

The blood supply to the third portion of the duodenum arises from numerous branches of the inferior pancreaticoduodenal arcade, each of which must be meticulously dissected, divided, and ligated to prevent pancreatic trauma. The distal duodenum receives its blood supply from branches of the superior mesenteric artery.

The duodenum should not be simply closed distally and drained via a gastrojejunostomy; if this is done, the proximal duodenum will not be properly decompressed.

Complications

Delayed gastric emptying is common with duodenojejunostomy; it generally responds to prolonged conservative therapy. A delay in the return of bowel function should generally be treated with nasogastric suction; on occasion, a percutaneous gastrostomy

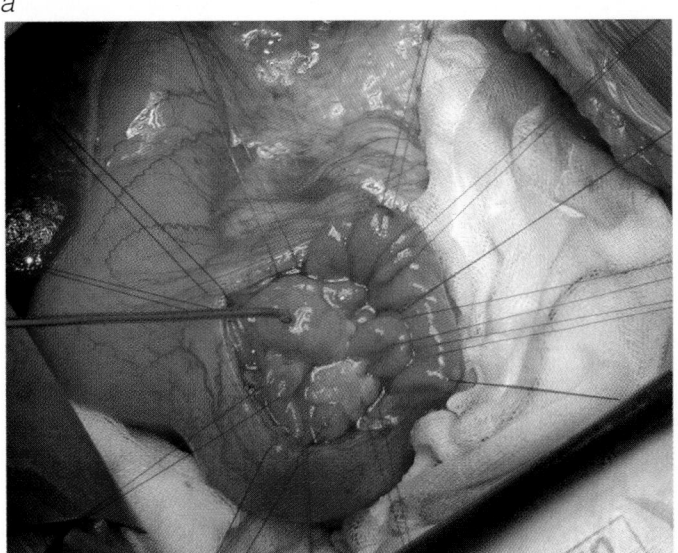
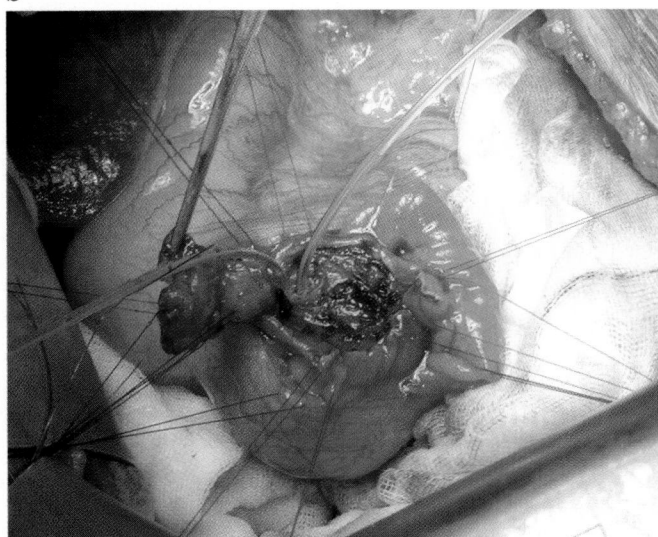
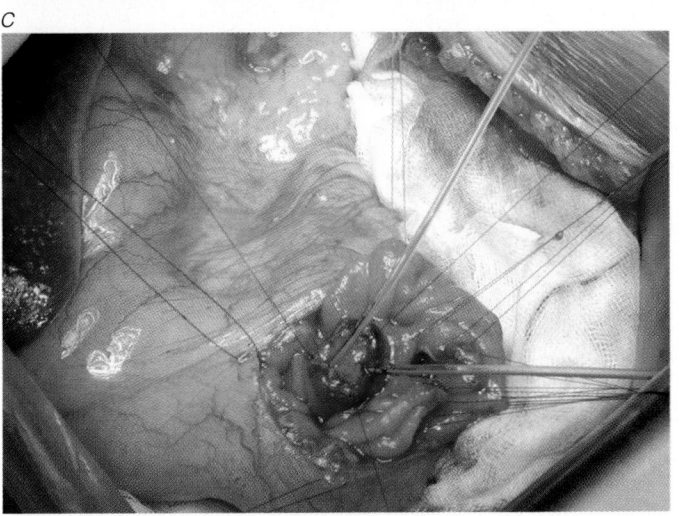

Figure 16 Ampullectomy. (*a*) After a longitudinal duodenotomy is made, the CBD is cannulated. Circumferential stay sutures of 4-0 polydioxanone are placed in the duodenal mucosa. A 2 cm periampullary tumor is visualized. (*b*) The ampullary tumor is removed from the underlying duodenum with the electrocautery. The CBD and the pancreatic duct are entered and separately cannulated. The CBD duct is typically seen at the 11 o'clock position, and the pancreatic duct is typically encountered at the 3 o'clock position. (*c*) The duodenal mucosa is sutured directly to the CBD and the pancreatic duct with 4-0 polydioxanone. In addition, the CBD and pancreatic duct are carefully connected with 4-0 polydioxanone sutures.

is required for proximal decompression. Postoperative pancreatitis may occur secondary to operative trauma; conservative management is usually sufficient.

AMPULLECTOMY

Local periampullary resection is indicated primarily for rare benign lesions, small neuroendocrine tumors of the pancreas, and small adenomatous or villous polyps. The likelihood of occult malignancy in an adenomatous periampullary tumor is significantly higher when the lesion is larger than 2 cm; caution is therefore indicated in attempting local resection of lesions of this size. The recurrence rate is high after local resection of any periampullary adenocarcinoma. The preoperative workup should include endoscopy with biopsy, EUS or transabdominal ultrasonography, CT scanning, and endoscopic retrograde cholangiopancreatography (ERCP).

Operative Technique

The ampulla of Vater is resected together with the distal CBD and the distal pancreatic duct [*see Figure 16*]. A Kocher maneuver is performed, and a longitudinal duodenotomy is made to expose the ampulla. Identification of the ampulla may be facilitated by placing a Fogarty catheter in the CBD via the cystic duct after a cholecystectomy. If the ampulla is identified during exploration, it may simply be cannulated. Circumferential stay sutures are placed in the mucosa. The CBD is entered at approximately the 11 o'clock position, and duodenal mucosa is reattached to the duct with 4-0 polydioxanone sutures. The pancreatic duct is encountered at approximately the 3 o'clock position; it may be cannulated separately to facilitate identification. The pancreatic duct is approximated to the CBD, and the inferior pancreatic duct is sewn to the duodenal wall. The duodenum is closed transversely in two layers.

Troubleshooting

Frozen-section analysis may identify invasive adenocarcinoma, which is an indication for pancreaticoduodenectomy. This possibility should be carefully considered before the operation.

References

1. Schwesinger WH, Page CP, Sirineck KR, et al: Operations for peptic ulcer disease: paradigm lost. J Gastrointest Surg 5:1038, 2001

2. Smith BR, Stablie BE: Emerging trends in peptic ulcer disease and damage control surgery in the *H. pylori* era. Am Surg 71:797, 2005

3. Ng EK, Lam YH, Sung JJ, et al: Eradication of *Helicobacter pylori* prevents recurrence of ulcer after simple closure of duodenal ulcer perforation: randomized controlled trial. Ann Surg 231:153, 2000

4. Tu BN, Sarr MG, Kelly KA: Early clinical results with the uncut Roux reconstruction after gastrectomy; limitations of the stapling technique. Am J Surg 170:262, 1995

5. Eagon JC, Miedema BW, Kelly KA: Postgastrectomy syndromes. Surg Clin North Am 72:445, 1992

6. Amdrup E, Jensen HE: Selective vagotomy of the parietal cell mass preserving innervation of the undrained antrum. Gastroenterology 59:522, 1970

7. Johnston D, Wilkinson AR: Highly selective vagotomy without a drainage procedure in the treatment of duodenal ulcer. Br J Surg 57:289, 1970

8. Adami HO, Enander L-K, et al: Recurrence 1 to 10 years after highly selective vagotomy in prepyloric and duodenal ulcer disease. Ann Surg 199:393, 1984

9. Taylor TV, Bunn AA, MacLeod DAD, et al: Anterior lesser curve seromyotomy and posterior truncal vagotomy in the treatment of chronic duodenal ulcer. Lancet 2:846, 1982

10. Lau H: Laparoscopic repair of perforated peptic ulcer. Surg Endosc 18:1013, 2004

11. Iida F: Transduodenal diverticulectomy for periampullary diverticula. World J Surg 3:103, 1979

12. Burke EC, Karpeh MS, Brennan MF: Laparoscopy in the management of gastric adenocarcinoma. Ann Surg 225:262, 1997

13. Siewert JR, Stein HJ: Classification of adenocarcinoma of the oesophagogastric junction. Br J Surg 85:1457, 1998

14. Ito H, Clancy TE, Osteen RT, et al: Adenocarcinoma of the gastric cardia: what is the optimal surgical approach? J Am Coll Surg 199:880, 2004

15. Siu KF, Cheung HC, Wong J: Shrinkage of the esophagus after resection for carcinoma. Ann Surg 203:173, 1986

16. Karpeh MS, Leon L, Klimstra D, et al: Lymph node staging in gastric cancer: is location more important than number? An analysis of 1,038 patients. Ann Surg 232:362, 2000

17. Bonekamp JJ, Hermans J, Sasako M, et al; for the Dutch Gastric Cancer Study Group: Extended lymph-node dissection for gastric cancer. N Engl J Med 340:908, 1999

18. Hartgrink HH, van der Velde CJH, Putter H, et al: Extended lymph node dissection for gastric cancer: who may benefit? Final results of the randomized Dutch Gastric Cancer Group trial. J Clin Oncol 22:1, 2004

Acknowledgments

Figures 1 through 15   Tom Moore.

Figure 16   Courtesy of Dr. John Windsor and Dr. Yatin Young, Auckland Hospital, Auckland, New Zealand.

63 CHOLECYSTECTOMY AND COMMON BILE DUCT EXPLORATION

Gerald M. Fried, M.D., F.A.C.S., Liane S. Feldman, M.D., F.A.C.S., and Dennis R. Klassen, M.D.

Cholecystectomy is the treatment of choice for symptomatic gallstones because it removes the organ that contributes to both the formation of gallstones and the complications ensuing from them.[1] The morbidity associated with cholecystectomy is attributable to injury to the abdominal wall in the process of gaining access to the gallbladder (i.e., the incision in the abdominal wall and its closure) or to inadvertent injury to surrounding structures during dissection of the gallbladder. Efforts to diminish the morbidity of open cholecystectomy have led to the development of laparoscopic cholecystectomy, made possible by modern optics and video technology.

Carl Langenbuch performed the first cholecystectomy in Berlin, Germany, in 1882. Erich Mühe performed the first laparoscopic cholecystectomy in Germany in 1985,[2] and by 1992, 90% of cholecystectomies in the United States were being performed laparoscopically. Compared with open cholecystectomy, the laparoscopic approach has dramatically reduced hospital stay, postoperative pain, and convalescent time. However, rapid adoption of laparoscopic cholecystectomy as the so-called gold standard for treatment of symptomatic gallstone disease was associated with complications, including an increased incidence of major bile duct injuries.

Since the early 1990s, considerable advances have been made in instrumentation and equipment, and a great deal of experience with laparoscopic cholecystectomy has been amassed worldwide. Of particular significance is the miniaturization and improvement of optics and instruments, which has reduced the morbidity of the procedure by making possible ever-smaller incisions. With proper patient selection and preparation, laparoscopic cholecystectomy is being safely performed on an outpatient basis in many centers.[3]

The primary goal of cholecystectomy is removal of the gallbladder with minimal risk of injury to the bile ducts and surrounding structures. Our approach is designed to maximize the safety of both routine and complicated cholecystectomies. In what follows, we describe our approach and discuss current indications and techniques for imaging and exploring the common bile duct (CBD).

Laparoscopic Cholecystectomy

PREOPERATIVE EVALUATION

To plan the surgical procedure, assess the likelihood of conversion to open cholecystectomy, and determine which patients are at high risk for CBD stones, the surgeon must obtain certain data preoperatively. Useful information can be obtained from the patient's history, from imaging studies, and from laboratory tests.

Preoperative Data

History and physical examination A good medical history provides information about associated medical problems that may affect the patient's tolerance of pneumoperitoneum. Patients with cardiorespiratory disease may have difficulty with the effects of CO_2 pneumoperitoneum on cardiac output, lung inflation pressure, acid-base balance, and the ability of the lungs to eliminate CO_2. Most bleeding disorders can also be identified through the history. A disease-specific history is important in identifying patients in whom previous episodes of acute cholecystitis may make laparoscopic cholecystectomy more difficult, as well as those at increased risk for choledocholithiasis (e.g., those who have had jaundice, pancreatitis, or cholangitis).[4-9]

Physical examination identifies patients whose body habitus is likely to make laparoscopic cholecystectomy difficult and is helpful for determining optimal trocar placement. Abdominal examination also reveals any scars, stomas, or hernias that are likely to necessitate the use of special techniques for trocar insertion.

Imaging studies Ultrasonography is highly operator dependent, but in capable hands, it can provide useful information. It is the best test for diagnosing cholelithiasis, and it can usually determine the size and number of stones.[4] Large stones indicate that a larger incision in the skin and the fascia will be necessary to retrieve the gallbladder. Multiple small stones suggest that the patient is more likely to require operative cholangiography (if a policy of selective cholangiography is practiced) [see Operative Technique, Step 5, *below*]. A shrunken gallbladder, a thickened gallbladder wall, and pericholecystic fluid on ultrasonographic examination are significant predictors of conversion to open cholecystectomy. The presence of a dilated CBD or CBD stones preoperatively is predictive of choledocholithiasis. Other intra-abdominal pathologic conditions, either related to or separate from the hepatic-biliary-pancreatic system, may influence operative planning.

Preoperative imaging studies of the CBD may allow the surgeon to identify patients with CBD stones before operation. Such imaging may involve endoscopic retrograde cholangiopancreatography (ERCP) [see 60 Gastrointestinal Endoscopy],[10] magnetic resonance cholangiopancreatography (MRCP) [see Figure 1],[11,12] or endoscopic ultrasonography (EUS). These imaging modalities also provide an anatomic map of the extrahepatic biliary tree, identifying unusual anatomy preoperatively and helping the surgeon plan a safe operation. Endoscopic sphincterotomy (ES) is performed during ERCP if stones are identified in the CBD. MRCP has an advantage over ERCP and EUS in that it is noninvasive and does not make use of injected iodinated contrast solutions.[11] Most surgeons would probably recommend that preoperative cholangiography be performed selectively in patients with clinical or biochemical features associated with a high risk of choledocholithiasis. The specific modality used in such a case varies with the technology and expertise available locally.

Laboratory tests Preoperative blood tests should include

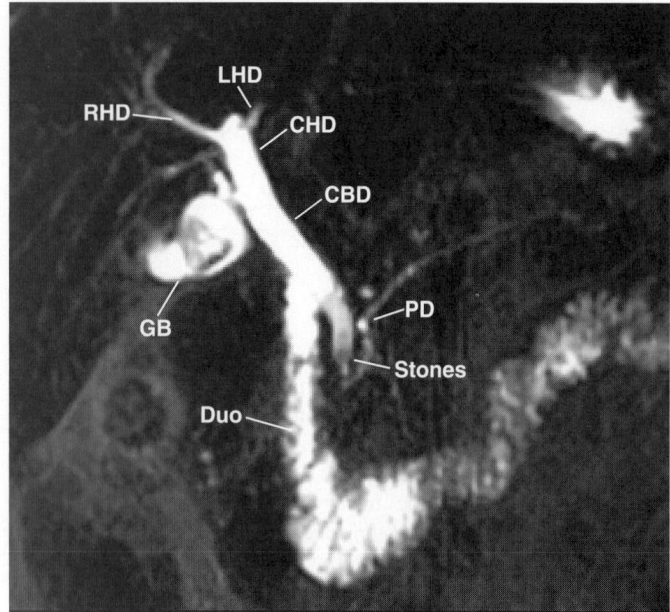 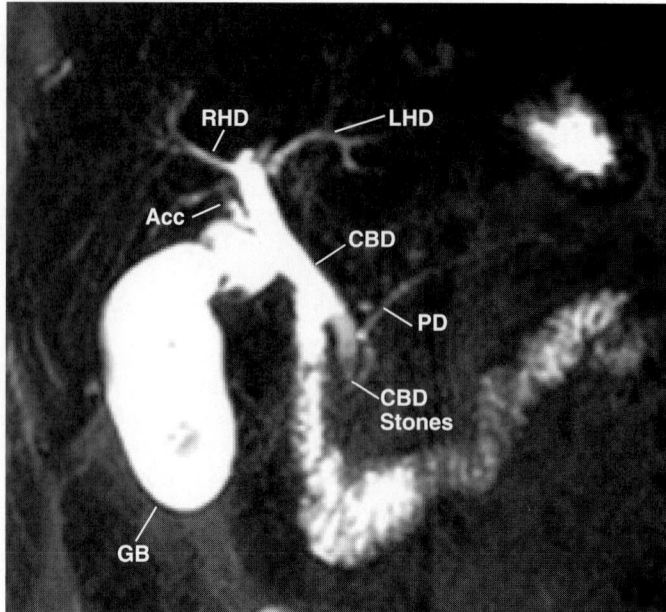

Figure 1 **Laparoscopic cholecystectomy. Preoperative MRCP alerts the surgeon to abnormal anatomy and the presence of stones in the distal CBD. (GB—gallbladder, containing stones; RHD—right hepatic duct; LHD—left hepatic duct; CHD—common hepatic duct; Acc—accessory duct entering common hepatic duct near neck of gallbladder; PD—pancreatic duct; Duo—duodenum)**

liver function, renal function, electrolyte, and coagulation studies. Abnormal liver function test results may reflect choledocholithiasis or primary hepatic dysfunction.

Selection of Patients

Patients eligible for outpatient cholecystectomy Patients in good general health who have a reasonable amount of support from family or friends and who do not live too far away from adequate medical facilities are eligible for outpatient cholecystectomy, especially if they are at low risk for conversion to laparotomy [*see* Special Problems, Conversion to Laparotomy, *below*].[3] These patients can generally be discharged home from the recovery room 6 to 12 hours after surgery, provided that the operation went smoothly, their vital signs are stable, they are able to void, they can manage at least a liquid diet without vomiting, and their pain can be controlled with oral analgesics.

Technically challenging patients Before performing laparoscopic cholecystectomy, the surgeon can predict which patients are likely to be technically challenging. These include patients who have a particularly unsuitable body habitus, those who are highly likely to have multiple and dense peritoneal adhesions, and those who are likely to have distorted anatomy in the region of the gallbladder.

Morbidly obese patients present specific difficulties [*see* Operative Technique, Step 1, Special Considerations in Obese Patients, *below*].[13] Small, muscular patients have a noncompliant abdominal wall, resulting in a small working space in the abdomen and necessitating high inflation pressures to obtain reasonable exposure.

Patients with a history of multiple abdominal operations, especially in the upper abdomen, and those who have a history of peritonitis are likely to pose difficulties because of peritoneal adhesions.[14] These adhesions make access to the abdomen more risky and exposure of the gallbladder more difficult. Patients who have undergone gastroduodenal surgery, those who have any history of acute cholecystitis, those who have a long history of recurrent gall-

bladder attacks, and those who have recently had severe pancreatitis are particularly difficult candidates for laparoscopic cholecystectomy. These patients may have dense adhesions in the region of the gallbladder, the anatomy may be distorted, the cystic duct may be foreshortened, and the CBD may be very closely and densely adherent to the gallbladder. Such patients are a challenge to the most experienced laparoscopic surgeon. When such problems are encountered, conversion to open cholecystectomy should be considered early in the operation.[14,15]

Predictors of choledocholithiasis CBD stones may be discovered preoperatively, intraoperatively, or postoperatively. The surgeon's goal is to clear the ducts but to use the smallest number of procedures with the lowest risk of morbidity. Thus, before elective laparoscopic cholecystectomy, it is desirable to classify patients into one of three groups: high risk (those who have clinical jaundice or cholangitis, visible choledocholithiasis, or a dilated CBD on ultrasonography), moderate risk (those who have hyperbilirubinemia, elevated alkaline phosphatase levels, pancreatitis, or multiple small gallstones), and low risk.

In our institution, where MRCP and EUS are available and reliable and where ERCP achieves stone clearance rates higher than 90%, we recommend the following approach: (1) preoperative ERCP and sphincterotomy (if required) for high-risk patients and (2) MRCP, EUS, or intraoperative fluoroscopic cholangiography for moderate-risk patients. Patients at low risk for CBD stones do not routinely undergo cholangiography [*see Figure 2*]. Laparoscopic CBD exploration and postoperative ERCP appear to be equally effective in clearing stones from the CBD.

Ultimately, surgeons and institutions must establish a reasonable approach to choledocholithiasis that takes into account the expertise and equipment locally available.

Contraindications There are few absolute contraindications to laparoscopic cholecystectomy. Certainly, no patient who poses an unacceptable risk for open cholecystectomy should be considered for laparoscopic cholecystectomy, because it is always possible that conversion will become necessary. Of the relative contraindications, surgical inexperience is the most important.

Neither ascites nor hernia is a contraindication to laparoscopic cholecystectomy. Ascites can be drained and the gallbladder visualized. Large hernias may present a problem, however, because with insufflation, the gas preferentially fills the hernia. Patients with large inguinal hernias may require an external support to minimize this problem and the discomfort related to pneumoscrotum. Patients with umbilical hernias can have their hernias repaired while they are undergoing laparoscopic cholecystectomy. For such patients, the initial trocar should be placed by open insertion according to the Hasson technique [see Operative Technique, Step 1, below], with care taken to avoid injury to the contents of the hernia. The sutures required to close the hernia defect can be placed before insertion of the initial trocar. A similar technique can be applied to patients with incisional hernias, although for large incisional hernias, laparoscopic cholecystectomy may have no advantages over open cholecystectomy if a large incision and dissection of adhesions are required. Patients with stomas may also undergo laparoscopic cholecystectomy, provided that the appropriate steps are taken to prevent injury to the bowel during placement of trocars and division of adhesions.

Patients with cirrhosis or portal hypertension are at high risk for morbidity and mortality with open cholecystectomy.[16,17] If absolutely necessary, laparoscopic cholecystectomy may be attempted by an experienced surgeon. The risk of bleeding can be minimized by rigorous preoperative preparation, meticulous dissection with the help of magnification available through the laparoscope, and use of the electrocautery.

Patients with bleeding diatheses, such as hemophilia, von Willebrand disease, and thrombocytopenia, may undergo laparoscopic cholecystectomy. They require appropriate preoperative and postoperative care and monitoring, and a hematologist should be consulted.

Questions have been raised about whether laparoscopic cholecystectomy should be performed in pregnant patients; it has been argued that the increased intra-abdominal pressure may pose a risk to the fetus. Because of the enlarged uterus, open insertion of the initial trocar is mandatory, and the positioning of other trocars may have to be modified according to the position of the uterus. Inflation pressures should be kept as low as possible, and prophylaxis of deep vein thrombosis (DVT) is recommended. Despite these potential problems, safe performance of laparoscopic cholecystectomy and other laparoscopic procedures in pregnant patients is increasingly being described in the literature. If cholecystectomy is necessary before delivery, the second trimester is the best time for it.[18-21]

Patients in whom preoperative imaging gives rise to a strong suspicion of gallbladder cancer should probably undergo open surgical management.

OPERATIVE PLANNING

Antibiotic Prophylaxis

Some surgeons recommend routine preoperative administration of antibiotics to all patients undergoing cholecystectomy, on the grounds that inadvertent entry into the gallbladder is not uncommon and can lead to spillage of bile or stones into the peritoneal cavity. Other surgeons do not recommend routine prophylaxis. Resolution of this controversy awaits appropriate prospective trials. We recommend selective use of antibiotic prophylaxis for patients at highest risk for bacteria in the bile (including those with acute cholecystitis or CBD stones, those who have previously undergone instrumentation of the biliary tree, and those older than 70 years) and for patients with prosthetic heart valves and joint prostheses.

Prophylaxis of DVT

The reverse Trendelenburg position used during laparoscopic cholecystectomy, coupled with the positive intra-abdominal pressure generated by CO_2 pneumoperitoneum and the vasodilatation induced by general anesthesia, leads to venous pooling in the lower extremities. This consequence may be minimized by using antiem-

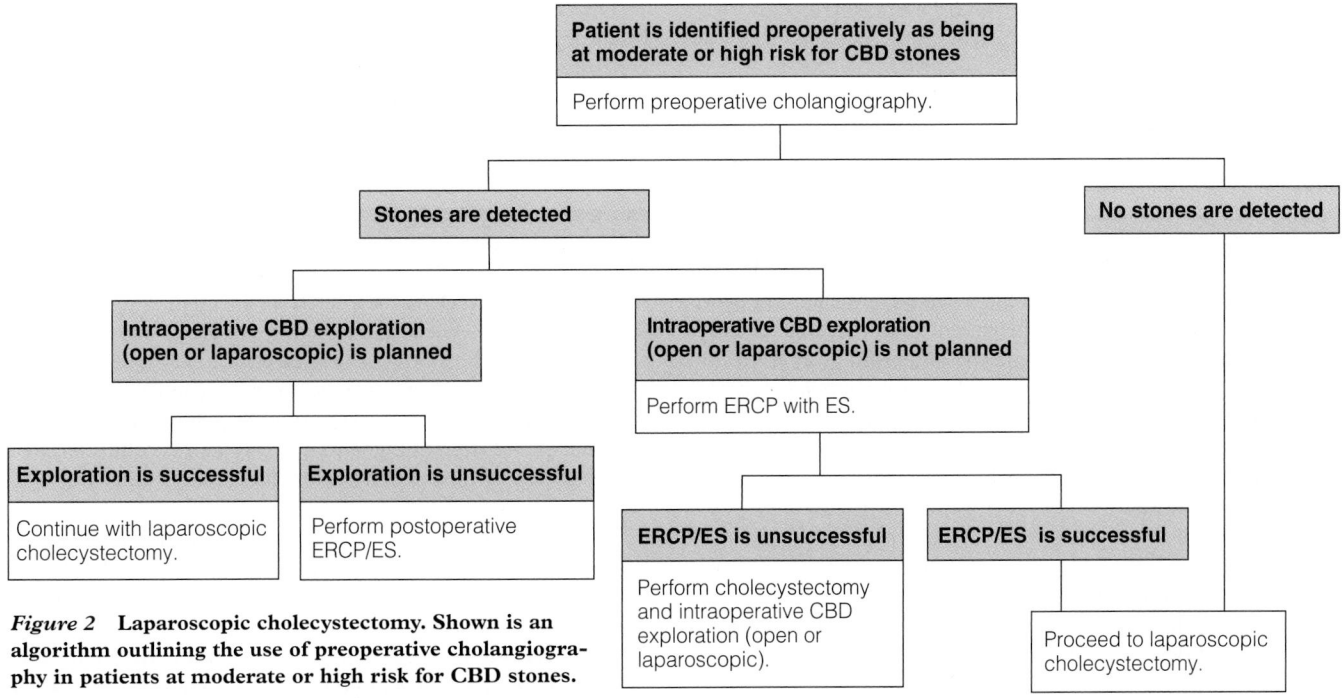

Figure 2 **Laparoscopic cholecystectomy. Shown is an algorithm outlining the use of preoperative cholangiography in patients at moderate or high risk for CBD stones.**

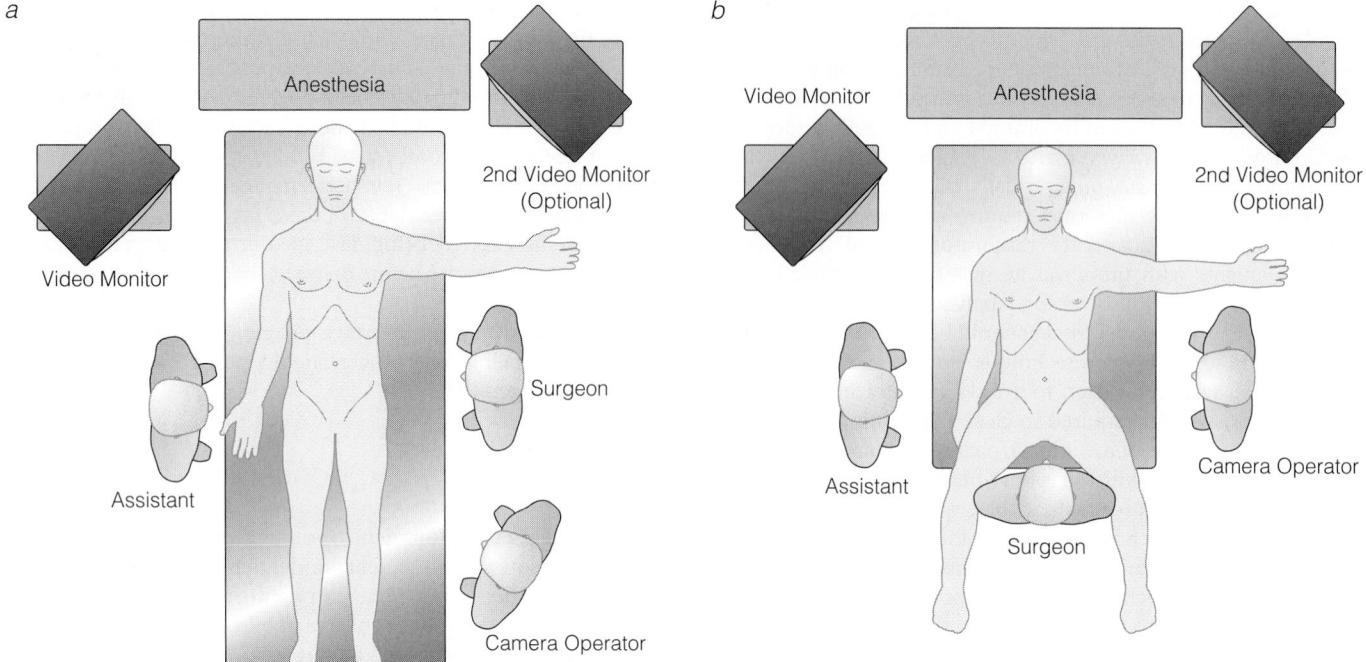

Figure 3 **Laparoscopic cholecystectomy. A patient undergoing laparoscopic cholecystectomy should be positioned so as to allow easy access to the gallbladder and a clear view of the monitors. Shown are the positions of the surgeon, the camera operator, and the assistant in the OR according to (*a*) North American positioning and (*b*) European positioning.**

bolic stockings or by wrapping the legs with elastic bandages. Subcutaneous heparin and pneumatic compression devices may be employed for patients at increased risk for DVT [*see 85 Venous Thromboembolism*]. As yet, however, there is no convincing evidence that the incidence of DVT is higher with laparoscopy than with open surgery.

Patient Positioning

In North American positioning, the patient is lying supine and the surgeon is positioned on the patient's left side [*see Figure 3a*]. In European positioning, the patient is in low stirrups and the surgeon is on the patient's left or between the patient's legs [*see Figure 3b*].

With North American positioning, the camera operator usually stands on the patient's left and to the left of the surgeon, while the assistant stands on the patient's right. The video monitor is positioned on the patient's right above the level of the costal margin. If a second monitor is available, it should be positioned on the patient's left to the right of the surgeon, where the assistant can have an unobstructed and comfortable view. Exposure can be improved by tilting the patient in the reverse Trendelenburg position and rotating the table with the patient's right side up. Gravity pulls the duodenum, the colon, and the omentum away from the gallbladder, thereby increasing the working space available in the upper abdomen.

The OR table should allow easy access for a fluoroscopic C arm, to facilitate intraoperative cholangiography. The table cover should be radiolucent.

Equipment

The equipment required for laparoscopic cholecystectomy includes an optical system, an electronic insufflator, trocars (cannulas), surgical instruments, and hemostatic devices [*see Table 1*].

Optical system The laparoscope can provide either a straight, end-on (0°) view or an angled (30° or 45°) view. Scopes that provide an end-on view are easier to learn to use, but angled scopes are more versatile. Scopes with a 30° angle cause less disorientation than those with a 45° angle and are ideal for laparoscopic cholecystectomy. Excellent 30° scopes are currently available in diameters of 10 mm, 5 mm, and 3.5 mm.

Fully digital flat-panel displays are now available that yield better resolution than analog video monitors, take up less space, are less subject to signal interference, and require less power.

The resolution and quality of the final image depend on (1) the brightness of the light source; (2) the integrity of the fiberoptic cord used to convey the light; (3) clean and secure connections between the light source and the scope; (4) the quality of the laparoscope, the camera, and the monitor; and (5) correct wiring of the components. The distal end of the scope must be kept clean and free of condensation: bile, blood, or fat will reduce brightness and distort the image. Lens fogging can be prevented by immersion in heated water or by antifogging solutions.

Insufflator CO_2 is the preferred insufflating gas for laparoscopic procedures because it is highly soluble in water and it does not support combustion when the electrocautery is used. The CO_2 should be insufflated with an electronic pump capable of a flow rate of at least 6 L/min; most current systems have a maximum flow rate of 20 L/min or higher. The insufflator is connected to one of the trocars by means of a flexible tube and a stopcock.

Trocars For cholecystectomy, at least one trocar site must be large enough to allow passage of the gallbladder and any stones removed. Most surgeons prefer to use a 10/12 mm trocar at the umbilicus for this purpose. The other trocars can range from 2 to 12 mm, depending on the size of the instruments to be placed through them. The conventional approach is to use a 10/12 mm

Table 1 Equipment for Laparoscopic Cholecystectomy

Instrument/Device	Number	Size	Comments

Laparoscopic cart
  High-intensity halogen light source
    (150–300 watts)
  High-flow electronic insufflator (minimum
    flow rate of 6 L/min)
  Laparoscopic camera box
  Videocassette recorder (optional)
  Digital still image capture system (optional)			

Laparoscope	1	3.5–10 mm	Available in 0° and angled views; we prefer to use a 30° 5 mm diameter laparoscope
Atraumatic grasping forceps	2–4	2–10 mm	Selection of graspers should allow surgeon choice appropriate to thickness and consistency of gallbladder wall; insulation is unnecessary
Large-tooth grasping forceps	1	10 mm	Used to extract gallbladder at end of procedure
Curved dissector	1	2–5 mm	Should have a rotatable shaft; insulation is required
Scissors	2–3	2–5 mm	One curved and one straight scissors with rotating shaft and insulation; additional microscissors may be helpful for incising cystic duct
Clip appliers	1–2	5–10 mm	Either disposable multiple clip applier or 2 manually loaded reusable single clip appliers for small and medium-to-large clips
Dissecting electrocautery hook or spatula	1	5 mm	Available in various shapes according to surgeon's preference; instrument should have channel for suction and irrigation controlled by trumpet valve(s); insulation required
High-frequency electrical cord	1		Cord should be designed with appropriate connectors for electrosurgical unit and instruments being used
Suction-irrigation probe	1	5–10 mm	Probe should have trumpet valve controls for suction and irrigation; may be used with pump for hydrodissection
10-to-5 mm reducers	2		Allow use of 5 mm instruments in 10 mm trocar without loss of pneumoperitoneum; these are often unnecessary with newer disposable trocars and may be built into some reusable trocars
5-to-3 mm reducer	1		Allows use of 2–3 mm instruments and ligating loops in 5 mm trocars
Ligating loops			
Endoscopic needle holders	1–2	5 mm	
Cholangiogram clamp with catheter	1	5 mm	Allows passage of catheter and clamping of catheter in cystic duct
Veress needle	1		Used if initial trocar is inserted by percutaneous technique
Allis or Babcock forceps	1–2	5 mm	Allow atraumatic grasping of bowel or gallbladder
Long spinal needle	1	14-gauge	Useful for aspirating gallbladder percutaneously in cases of acute cholecystitis or hydrops
Retrieval bag	1		Useful for preventing spillage of bile or stones in removal of inflamed or friable gallbladder; facilitates retrieval of spilled stones

trocar at the operating port site and 5 mm trocars for the other instruments; however, if a 5 mm laparoscope and a 5 mm clip applier are used, the operating port size can be reduced to 5 mm. Although 2 mm instrumentation is also available, it must be remembered that as a rule, the smaller the working port, the less versatile the instruments. In our experience, the combination of a 10 mm umbilical trocar, a 5 mm operating port, and 2 mm ports for grasping forceps is a good one: optical quality is maintained, little flexibility is lost with respect to selecting operating instruments, trocar size is minimized, and the cosmetic result is excellent.

Hemostatic devices Hemostasis can be achieved with monopolar or bipolar electrocauterization. A monopolar electrocautery can be connected to most available instruments; however, bipolar electrocauterization may eventually prove safer. With a monopolar electrocautery, depth of burn is less predictable, current can be conducted through noninsulated instruments and tro-

cars, and any area of the instrument that is stripped of insulation may conduct current and result in a burn. Caution is essential when the electrocautery is used near metallic hemostatic clips because delayed sloughing may occur.

Electrocauterization should be avoided near the CBD because delayed bile duct injuries and leaks may occur as a result of sloughing from a burned area and devascularization of the duct. Care must be exercised when a cautery is employed near the bowel and when intra-abdominal adhesions are being taken down. The electrocautery can be used with a forceps, scissors, hooks (L or J shaped), a spatula, and other instruments. Some cautery probes incorporate nonstick surfaces to prevent buildup of eschar. The use of hand-activated cautery probes and the presence of a channel that allows suction and irrigation through the cautery probes are especially convenient.

More advanced energy sources and instruments are also available. Bipolar devices designed to weld tissues have proved capable

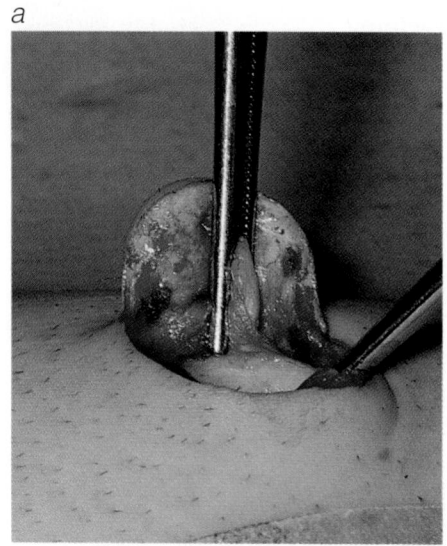 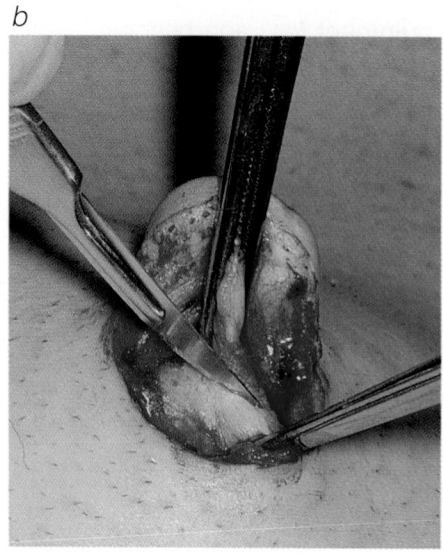 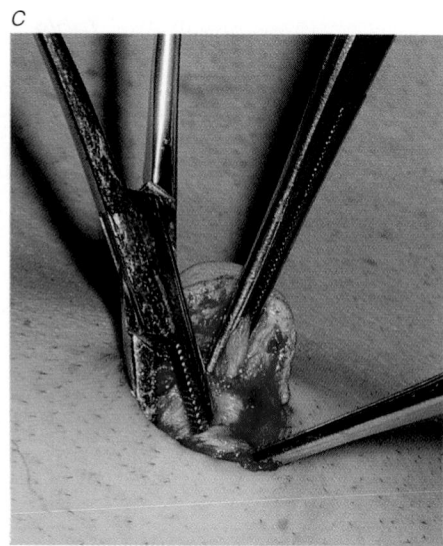

a *b* *c*

Figure 4 **Laparoscopic cholecystectomy. With the open insertion technique, the initial trocar is placed under direct vision. (*a*) The umbilical skin is elevated with a sharp towel clip. A curvilinear incision is made in the inferior umbilical fold. The skin flap is elevated, and the raphe leading from the dermis to the fascia is thereby exposed. (*b*) The fascia is grasped in the midline between forceps and elevated. The fascia and the underlying peritoneum are incised under direct vision. (*c*) A blunt instrument is placed into the peritoneum to ensure that the undersurface of the peritoneum is free of adhesions. The opening can be enlarged sufficiently to allow placement of a blunt 10/11 mm trocar.**

of achieving superb hemostasis. Ultrasonic dissecting shears can also be used to dissect and coagulate tissues effectively and precisely. For laparoscopic cholecystectomy, however, such advanced—and costly—devices are rarely needed.

OPERATIVE TECHNIQUE

Step 1: Placement of Trocars and Accessory Ports

Placement of initial trocar The first step in laparoscopic cholecystectomy is the creation of pneumoperitoneum and the insertion of an initial trocar through which the laparoscope can be passed. This step is critical because complications resulting from improper placement may cause serious morbidity and death. The surgeon may use either a percutaneous technique or an open technique. We prefer the open technique, which eliminates the risks inherent in the blind puncture [*see Figure 4*].[22,23]

Scars Patients who have previously undergone abdominal surgery may have adhesions, both to the undersurface of the abdominal wall and intra-abdominally. Adhesions to the undersurface of the abdominal wall make access to the abdominal cavity potentially hazardous, particularly when the percutaneous method is used for placement of the initial trocar. Scars from previous operations may affect insertion of the initial trocar, depending on its orientation and location. If a patient has a scar in the lower abdomen (e.g., from a Pfannenstiel incision or an incision in the right lower quadrant for an appendectomy), the position of the initial trocar need not be changed. If the scar is in the upper abdomen, the initial trocar may be inserted below the umbilicus in the midline. If there is a long midline scar that is impossible to avoid, careful dissection of the peritoneum through a vertical incision that is somewhat longer than usual affords safe access to the peritoneum in most cases.

An alternative is to insert the initial trocar high in the epigastrium or in the right anterior axillary line, where bowel adhesions are less common. The laparoscope is inserted through this trocar and

used to examine the undersurface of the old scar for a clear site near the umbilicus where a 10 mm trocar can be placed. Previous laparoscopy, which rarely creates significant intra-abdominal adhesions, rarely necessitates modification of trocar insertion.

The surgeon should also consider the reason for the previous surgery. For example, a patient who underwent an appendectomy for perforating appendicitis may have had diffuse peritonitis and may have adhesions well away from the old scar.

Placement of accessory ports In most cases, four ports are necessary. The first port is for the laparoscope; the remaining ports are for grasping forceps, dissectors, and clip appliers. The precise position of the accessory ports depends on the surgeon's preference, the patient's body habitus, and the presence or absence of previous scars or intra-abdominal adhesions. A rigid approach to port placement is inappropriate: trocar placement determines operative exposure, and improper placement will haunt the surgeon throughout the procedure. In some cases, a fifth trocar is required to elevate a floppy liver or to depress or retract the omentum or a bulky hepatic flexure of the colon. In trocar placement, as in patient positioning, European practice tends to differ from North American practice [*see Figure 5*].

Most surgeons elect to place one of the grasping forceps on the fundus of the gallbladder through an accessory port placed approximately in the anterior axillary line below the level of the gallbladder. Because the level of the gallbladder varies from patient to patient, the placement of this accessory port should not be decided on until the gallbladder is visualized. If the gallbladder is low lying and the trocar is placed too high, the surgeon will have difficulty achieving the appropriate angle of retraction. As a general rule, positioning the trocar in the anterior axillary line approximately halfway between the costal margin and the anterosuperior iliac spine provides the appropriate exposure. A 2 to 5 mm port usually suffices at this site because its only likely function is to allow retraction of the gallbladder. In some cases of acute cholecystitis, however, a larger port may be preferable, so that a larger grasper can be inserted and used to hold the gallbladder without tearing it.

A second accessory port (also 2 to 5 mm) allows the surgeon to grasp the gallbladder in the area of Hartmann's pouch for retraction. This port is usually positioned just beneath the right costal margin. Some surgeons prefer it to be approximately at the mid-clavicular line; others prefer it to be higher and more medial, just to the right of the falciform ligament.

The main operating port should be 5 or 10 mm in diameter, so that clip appliers can be readily placed through it and the laparoscope can be moved to this port at the end of the procedure. The positioning of this port is determined by the surgeon's preference and, in particular, by the patient's body habitus. The optimum placement is at about the same horizontal level as the gallbladder or slightly higher, so that during the operation, the laparoscope and the operating instrument form an angle of about 90°. Some surgeons prefer to place the operative port in the midline, to the right of the falciform ligament; others prefer to place it to the left of the falciform, passing the trocar underneath the ligament and elevating it with the trocar.

Surgeons should be encouraged to use both hands when performing laparoscopic cholecystectomy. One hand should control the grasping forceps holding Hartmann's pouch, so that the gallbladder can be moved to provide the best possible exposure. The other hand should control the dissecting instruments placed through the operating port.

Special considerations in obese patients Port placement in obese patients may be complicated by the thick abdominal wall, the large amount of intra-abdominal fat, or both. A thick abdominal wall makes it more difficult to rotate the trocar around the normal fulcrum point in the abdominal wall. Consequently, the trocar must be placed at the angle most likely to be used during the procedure. When a trocar is tunneled through the abdominal wall, more of the cannula is within the abdominal wall than if the trocar had been placed perpendicularly; accordingly, the trocar is less mobile. If the trocars are not easily rotated, the instruments placed through them will be difficult to manipulate smoothly. Thus, in the patient with a very thick pannus, a standard-length trocar may be too short. Displacement of trocars can lead to insufflation into the abdominal wall and consequently to subcutaneous emphysema, which further thickens the abdominal wall and hinders exposure.

To prevent such problems, special extra-length trocars designed for morbidly obese patients have been developed. It may also be necessary to place the trocars closer to the area of the gallbladder to ensure that the operating instruments can reach the gallbladder. For example, the initial port may have to be placed above the umbilicus.

In obese patients, the bulky falciform ligament and the large omentum may adversely affect exposure. A 30° laparoscope may help the surgeon see over the omentum and the high-lying hepatic flexure of the colon. In some cases, it is useful to place a fifth port so that the surgeon can retract the hepatic flexure downward. Fat may envelop the cystic duct and artery and the portal structures, obscuring normal anatomic landmarks. When the electrocautery is used, the heat melts the fat and causes it to sizzle and spray onto the lens of the laparoscope, resulting in a blurry image. To prevent this, the camera operator should pull the scope slightly away from the operative field during electrocauterization, then advance the scope during dissection. This should also be done when an ultrasonic dissector is being used.

Given that obese patients are more difficult candidates for open cholecystectomy and have a higher complication rate with laparotomy, the advantages of laparoscopic cholecystectomy in these individuals justify the effort needed to overcome the technical problems.

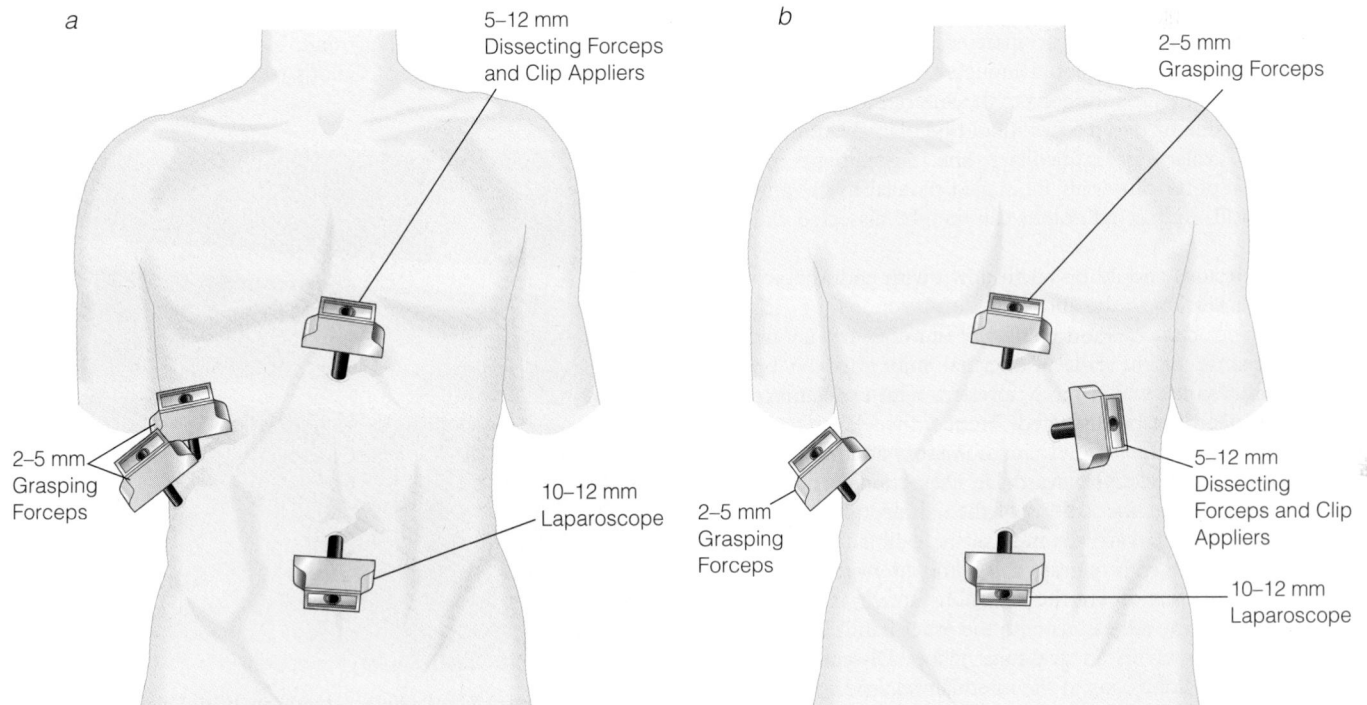

a

5–12 mm Dissecting Forceps and Clip Appliers

2–5 mm Grasping Forceps

10–12 mm Laparoscope

b

2–5 mm Grasping Forceps

2–5 mm Grasping Forceps

5–12 mm Dissecting Forceps and Clip Appliers

10–12 mm Laparoscope

Figure 5 **Laparoscopic cholecystectomy. Illustrated are the differences between typical North American practice (*a*) and typical European practice (*b*) with respect to the placement of the trocars and the instruments inserted through each port.**

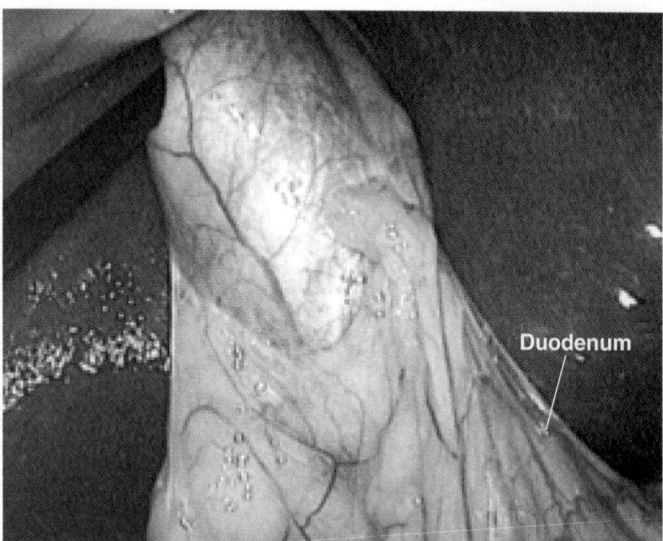

Figure 6 **Laparoscopic cholecystectomy. Adhesions of duodenum and omentum to gallbladder wall obscure view of structures of Calot's triangle.**

Step 2: Exposure of Gallbladder and Calot's Triangle

Dissection of adhesions Adhesions must be dissected to provide an unimpeded view of the gallbladder through the laparoscope. Not all intra-abdominal adhesions must be taken down, just enough to allow entry of accessory trocars under direct vision and thus permit access to the gallbladder. This process is facilitated by pneumoperitoneum, which provides traction on adhesions to the abdominal wall, and by the magnification provided by the optical system, which allows identification of the avascular plane of attachment.

The most difficult problem is positioning the dissecting instruments so that they can reach the undersurface of the anterior abdominal wall. A rigid trocar inserted through the anterior abdominal wall cannot be rotated enough to allow scissors passed through this port to cut adhesions to the anterior abdominal wall. In such cases, one or two trocars should be placed laterally, near the anterior axillary or midaxillary line. Instruments passed through these ports can easily be angled parallel to the anterior abdominal wall, and the adhesions can then be dissected without difficulty.

Bowel adhesions should be taken down with endoscopic scissors at their insertion to the abdominal wall, where they are least vascular. Electrocauterization, generally unnecessary, should be avoided because of the risk of thermal injury to the bowel. Interloop adhesions, which rarely interfere with exposure of the gallbladder, need not be dissected. Frequently, adhesions to the gallbladder occur as a reaction to inflammatory attacks [see Figure 6]. They are usually relatively avascular. Dissection of these adhesions should begin at the fundus of the gallbladder and should then proceed down toward the neck of the gallbladder. The best way to take them down is to grasp the gallbladder with one grasping forceps at the site where the adhesions attach and gradually place traction on the adhesions with the other hand. Usually, the adhesions peel down in an avascular plane. Dissection should continue until all adhesions to the inferolateral aspect of the gallbladder have been taken down. It is not necessary to divide adhesions between the superior surface of the liver and the undersurface of the diaphragm unless they impede superior retraction of the liver.

Exposing Calot's triangle Obtaining adequate exposure of Calot's triangle is a key step. First, the patient is placed in a reverse Trendelenburg position, with the table rotated toward the left side. Next, the fundus of the gallbladder and the right lobe of the liver are elevated toward the patient's right shoulder. One grasping forceps, inserted through the most lateral right-side port and held by an assistant, is placed on the fundus of the gallbladder [see Figure 7], and the gallbladder is retracted superiorly and laterally above the right hepatic lobe. This maneuver straightens out folds in the body of the gallbladder and permits initial visualization of the area of Calot's triangle. If Calot's triangle is still obscured, the patient can be placed in a steeper reverse Trendelenburg position, the stomach can be emptied of air via an orogastric tube inserted by the anesthetist, or, if necessary, a fifth trocar can be inserted on the patient's right side to push down the duodenum.

In some patients, such as those with acute cholecystitis and hydrops of the gallbladder, the gallbladder is tense and distended, making it difficult to grasp and easy to tear. In these patients, retraction of the fundus is difficult, and exposure of Calot's triangle is unsatisfactory. This problem is best managed by aspirating the contents of the gallbladder either percutaneously with a 14- or 16-gauge needle inserted into the fundus of the gallbladder under laparoscopic vision or by using the 5 mm trocar in the right upper abdomen to puncture the fundus and then aspirate with the suction irrigator. After the needle is withdrawn, a large atraumatic grasping forceps can be used to hold the gallbladder and occlude the hole; a 10 mm forceps may be preferred if the wall is markedly thickened. An alternative is to place a stitch or a ligating loop around the fundus of the collapsed gallbladder; the tail of the suture can then be grasped with a forceps to achieve a secure grip and also prevent further leakage of gallbladder contents from the needle hole.

Once the fundus of the gallbladder is retracted superiorly by the assistant, the surgeon places a grasping forceps in the area of Hartmann's pouch. Using both hands, the surgeon controls the grasper on Hartmann's pouch as well as the operating instrument. The surgeon maneuvers Hartmann's pouch to provide various angles for safe dissection of Calot's triangle. Initially, lateral and

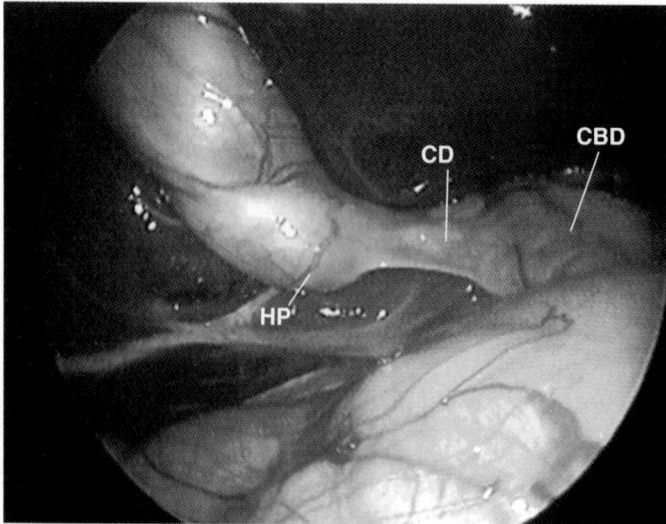

Figure 7 **Laparoscopic cholecystectomy. Initial view of gallbladder and related structures is facilitated by appropriate tilting of the operating table. Hartmann's pouch (HP), the cystic duct (CD), and the common bile duct (CBD) can be readily identified before any dissection.**

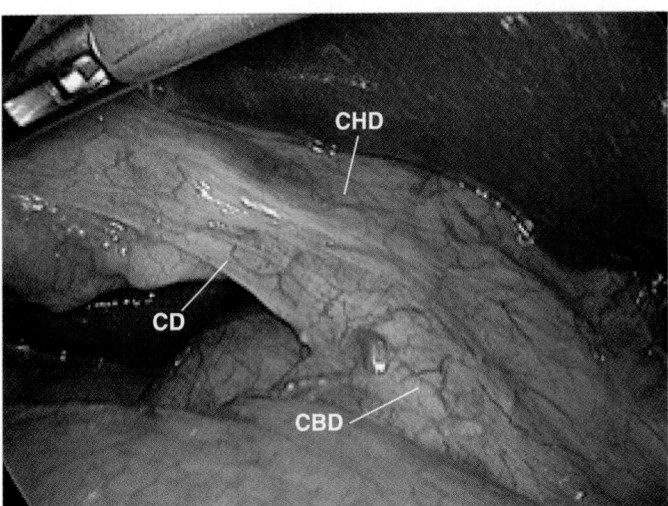

Figure 8 **Laparoscopic cholecystectomy. The area of Hartmann's pouch is retracted laterally. The cystic duct (CD) is seen at an angle to the common hepatic duct (CHD) and the common bile duct (CBD).**

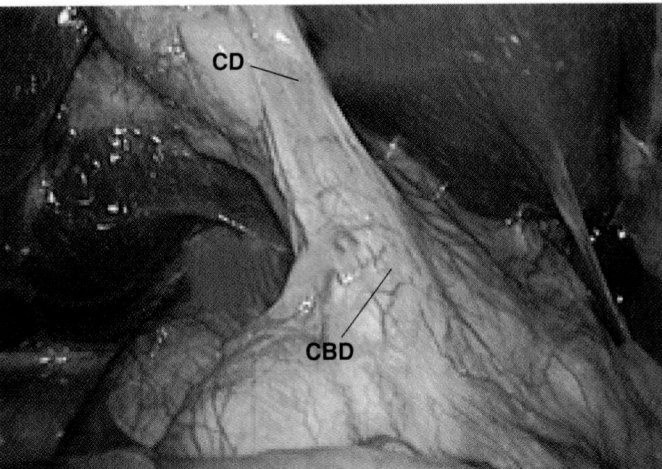

Figure 9 **Laparoscopic cholecystectomy. In this case, the gallbladder is retracted cephalad. The cystic duct (CD) can be seen running in the same direction as the common bile duct (CBD). The CBD may be misinterpreted as being the cystic duct and consequently is at risk for injury.**

inferior traction are placed on Hartmann's pouch, opening up the angle between the cystic duct and the common ducts [*see Figure 8*], avoiding their alignment [*see Figure 9*].

A large stone impacted in the gallbladder neck may impede the surgeon's ability to place the forceps on Hartmann's pouch. This problem can usually be managed by dislodging the stone early in the operation, as follows: the gallbladder is grasped as low as possible with one grasping forceps; a widely opening dissecting instrument, such as a right-angle dissector, a Babcock forceps, or a curved dissector, is used to dislodge the stone and milk it up toward the fundus; with the same forceps or another large grasper, the stone is held up and away from the neck of the gallbladder, and appropriate retraction is provided.

If the stone cannot be disimpacted, an instrument can be used to elevate the infundibulum of the gallbladder superiorly, allowing exposure of Calot's triangle. Alternatively, one can attempt to crush the stone, but small pieces of the stone may fall into the cys-

tic duct. A third option is to place a stitch in Hartmann's pouch and grasp the end of the stitch to provide exposure.

Step 3: Stripping of Peritoneum

The key to avoiding injury to the major ducts during laparoscopic cholecystectomy is accurate identification of the junction between the gallbladder and the cystic duct [*see Figure 10*]. Unless the gallbladder–cystic duct junction is immediately obvious upon examination of Calot's triangle anteriorly, our approach is to begin dissection of Calot's triangle posteriorly [*see Figure 11*]. From this approach, the insertion of the gallbladder neck into the cystic duct is usually more clearly identified, especially with the aid of a 30° laparoscope. Exposure is obtained by retracting Hartmann's

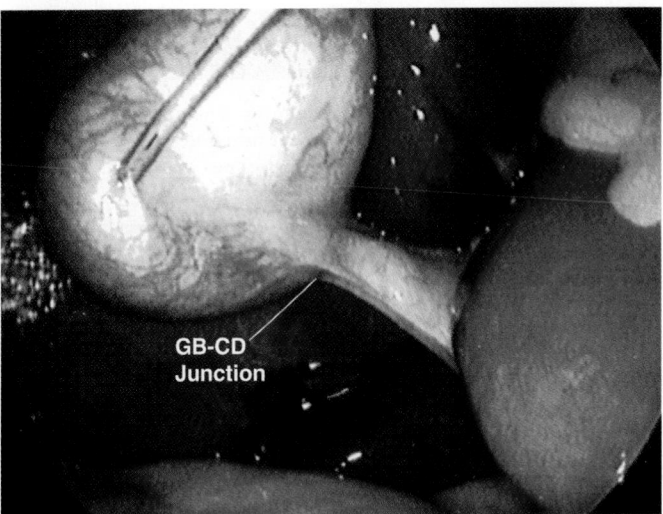

Figure 10 **Laparoscopic cholecystectomy. The gallbladder–cystic duct (GB-CD) junction can be identified as lateral traction is applied to the area of Hartmann's pouch.**

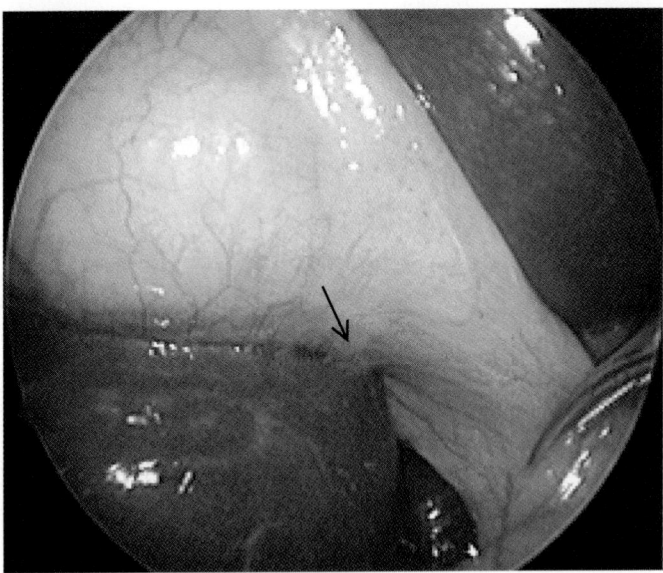

Figure 11 **Laparoscopic cholecystectomy. A view from below with a 30° laparoscope demonstrates the point for beginning dissection (arrow), where the gallbladder funnels down to its junction with the cystic duct. Just below this point can be seen a cleft in the liver known as Rouvier's sulcus. This cleft, present in 70% to 80% of livers, reliably indicates the plane of the CBD.**

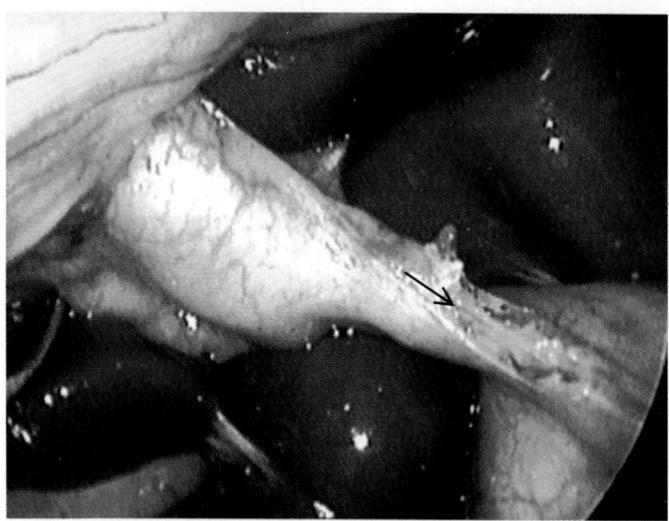

Figure 12 **Laparoscopic cholecystectomy. The peritoneum is dissected from the gallbladder–cystic duct junction (arrow), as seen from below through a 30° angled laparoscope.**

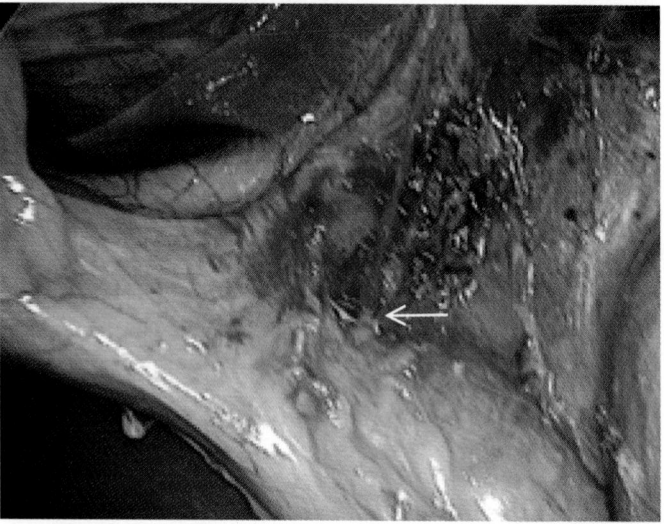

Figure 13 **Laparoscopic cholecystectomy. Arterial bleeding can be seen (arrow) from a branch of the cystic artery injured during dissection from the posterior approach.**

pouch superomedially and is facilitated by looking from below with a 30° scope.

Dissection should always start high on the gallbladder and hug the gallbladder closely until the anatomy is identified clearly. Using a curved dissector, the surgeon gently teases away peritoneum attaching the neck of gallbladder to the liver posterolaterally to visualize the funneling of the neck of the gallbladder into the cystic duct [*see Figure 12*]. Only the posterior layer of peritoneum is dissected; care must be taken not to dissect deeply in this area because of the risk of injury to the cystic artery [*see Figure 13*].

In some problem cases, edema, fibrosis, and adhesions make identification of the gallbladder–cystic duct junction very difficult. An anatomic landmark on the liver known as Rouvier's sulcus may be helpful in such circumstances [*see Figure 11*]. This sulcus, or the remnant of it, is present in 70% to 80% of livers and usually contains the right portal triad or its branches. Its location is consistently to the right of the hepatic hilum and anterior to the caudate process (Couinaud segment 1). This landmark reliably indicates

the plane of the CBD. Therefore, dissection dorsal to it should be done with caution. Once the funneling of the gallbladder into the cystic duct has been identified, the area of Hartmann's pouch should be again pulled laterally and inferiorly so that the anterior peritoneum can be dissected, while the 30° scope is angled to view the area. The two-handed technique facilitates the surgeon's movement between the posterior and anterior aspects of Calot's triangle, providing complete visualization. Dissection should always take place at the gallbladder–cystic duct junction, staying close to the gallbladder to avoid inadvertent injury to the CBD. A curved dissecting forceps is used to strip the fibroareolar tissue just superior to the cystic duct. The superior border of the cystic duct can then be identified and the cystic duct gently and gradually dissected [*see Figure 14*]. The cystic duct lymph node is a useful landmark at this location and may facilitate identification of the gallbladder–cystic duct junction.

When traction is placed as described, the cystic artery tends to run parallel and somewhat cephalad to the cystic duct. This artery can often be identified by noting its close relation to the cystic duct lymph node. Complete dissection of the area between the cystic duct and the artery develops a window through which the liver should be visible. The cystic duct is then encircled with a curved dissecting instrument or an L-shaped hook. Downward traction should be applied to the cystic duct to open this window and ensure that there is no ductal structure running through this space in Calot's triangle to join the cystic duct (i.e., the right hepatic duct).

Dissection of Calot's triangle should be completed before the cystic duct is clipped or divided. This is best accomplished by dissecting the neck of the gallbladder from the liver bed. Unequivocal identification of the gallbladder–cystic duct junction is imperative.[24,25] The cystic duct should be dissected for a length sufficient to permit secure placement of two clips; it is not necessary, and indeed may be hazardous, to attempt to dissect the cystic duct–CBD junction.

The cystic artery is exposed next [*see Figure 15*]. A small vein can usually be identified in the space between the cystic duct and the cystic artery; it can usually be pulled up anteriorly and cauterized. Because dissection is done near the gallbladder, it is not unusual to encounter more than one branch of the cystic artery. Each of these branches should be dissected free of the fibroareolar tissue. Care should also be taken to ensure that the right hepatic artery is not inadvertently injured as a result of being mistaken for the cystic artery.

Step 4: Control and Division of Cystic Duct and Cystic Artery

At this point, the cystic duct is clipped on the gallbladder side, and a cholangiogram is obtained if desired [*see Step 5, below*]. If a cholangiogram is not desired, three or four clips should be placed on the cystic duct and the cystic duct divided between them. Two or three hemostatic clips are placed on the cystic artery, and the vessel is divided. It is prudent to incise the artery partially before transecting it completely to ensure that the clips are secure and that there is no pulsatile bleeding. Once the artery is completely divided, the proximal end will retract medially, making it more difficult to expose and control the artery safely if bleeding occurs. Electrocauterization should be avoided near the cystic duct and all metallic clips. Electrical current will be conducted through metallic clips and may result in delayed sloughing of the duct or a clip. Delayed injuries to the CBD may be caused by a direct burn to the duct or by sparking from noninsulated instruments or clips during dissection. An alternative is to use locking polymer clips that fit through 5 mm ports, clip across a greater width of tissue, and do not conduct electricity.

Control of short or wide cystic duct Edema and acute inflammation may lead to thickening and foreshortening of the cystic duct, with subsequent difficulties in dissection and ligation. If the duct is edematous, clips may cut through it; if the duct is too wide, the clip may not occlude it completely. A modified clipping technique can be employed, with placement of an initial clip to occlude as much of the duct as possible. The occluded portion of the duct is then incised, and a second clip is placed flush with the first so as to occlude the rest of the duct. Alternatively, wider polymer clips may be used.

Because this technique is not always possible, the surgeon

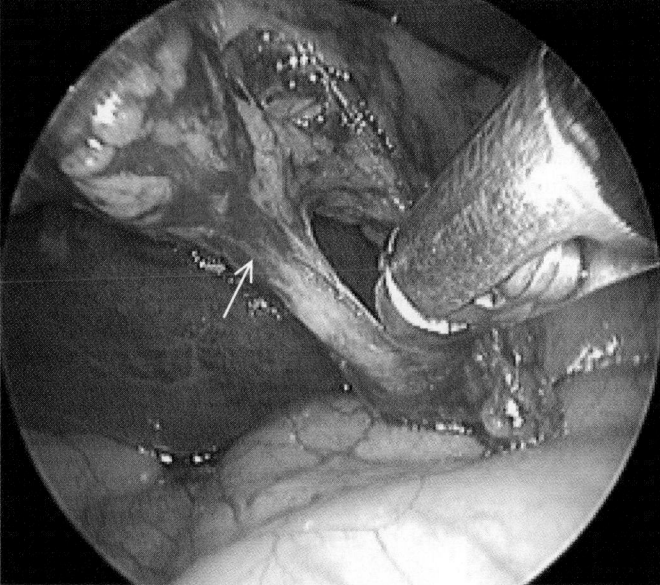

Figure 14 **Laparoscopic cholecystectomy. The superior border of the cystic duct has been dissected. Funneling of the gallbladder into the cystic duct is clearly seen (arrow).**

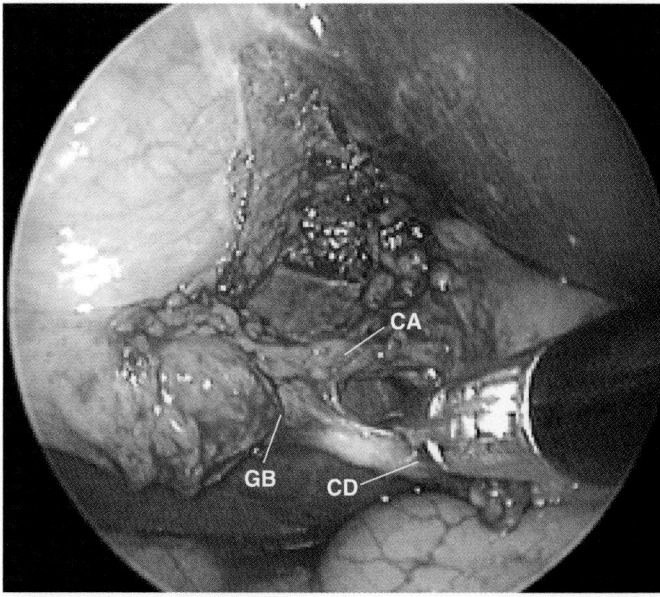

Figure 15 **Laparoscopic cholecystectomy. Dissection of Calot's triangle further exposes the cystic duct (CD) and the cystic artery (CA) near their entry into the gallbladder (GB) in preparation for clipping and division.**

should be familiar with techniques for ligating the duct with either intracorporeal or extracorporeal ties. It is extremely helpful to know how to tie extracorporeal ties so that the cystic duct can be ligated in continuity before it is divided. In some cases, the duct can be divided, held with a forceps, and controlled with a ligating loop. If there is concern about secure closure of the cystic duct, a closed suction drain may be placed. If inflammation, as in cholecystitis, has caused the duct to be shorter than usual, dissection must be kept close to the gallbladder to avoid inadvertent injury to the CBD. A short cystic duct is often associated with acute cholecystitis. Patient blunt dissection with the suction-irrigation device may be the safest technique.

Cystic duct stones Stones in the cystic duct may be visualized or felt during laparoscopic cholecystectomy. Every effort should be made to milk them into the gallbladder before applying clips. Placing a clip across a stone may push a fragment of the stone into the CBD and will increase the risk that the clip will become displaced, leading to a bile leak. If the stone cannot be milked into the gallbladder, a small incision can be made in the cystic duct (as is done for cholangiography), and the stone can usually be expressed and retrieved. Given that cystic duct stones are predictive of CBD stones, cholangiography or intraoperative ultrasonography is indicated.[26]

Step 5: Intraoperative Cholangiography

Whether intraoperative cholangiography should be performed routinely is still controversial. Advocates believe that this technique enhances understanding of the biliary anatomy, thus reducing the risk of bile duct injury[27,28]; at present, however, there are no objective data to confirm this impression. Cholangiography is not a substitute for meticulous dissection, and injuries to the CBD can occur before cystic duct dissection reaches the point at which cholangiography can be performed. Catheter-induced injuries and perforations of the biliary tree have been reported, and cholangiograms have been misinterpreted. On the other hand, one of the main advantages of cholangiography is that injuries can be recognized during the operation and promptly repaired. Another advantage of routine cholangiography is that it helps develop the skills required for more complex biliary tract procedures, such as transcystic CBD exploration.

The two methods of laparoscopic cholangiography differ in their technique for introducing the cholangiogram catheter into the cystic duct. In both approaches, a clip is placed at the gallbladder–cystic duct junction and a small incision made in the anterior wall of the cystic duct. In the first technique, a specially designed 5 mm cholangiogram clamp (the Olsen clamp) with a 5 French catheter is inserted via a subcostal trocar. For easy guidance of the catheter into the incision in the cystic duct, the catheter should be parallel, rather than perpendicular, to the cystic duct. This angle is facilitated by placing the subcostal port directly below the costal margin, near the anterior axillary line. A fifth trocar may occasionally be needed if exposure is lost when one of the grasping forceps is removed to allow passage of the cholangiogram clamp. The clamp and the catheter are then brought to the cystic duct under direct vision, and the catheter is steered into the duct [*see Figure 16*]. The clamp is then closed, holding the catheter in position and sealing the duct to avoid extravasation of dye.

In the second method, the cholangiogram catheter is introduced percutaneously through a 12- to 14-gauge catheter, inserted subcostally as described (see above). The surgeon then grasps the cholangiogram catheter and directs it into the cystic duct. A hemostatic clip is applied to secure the catheter in place. If passage

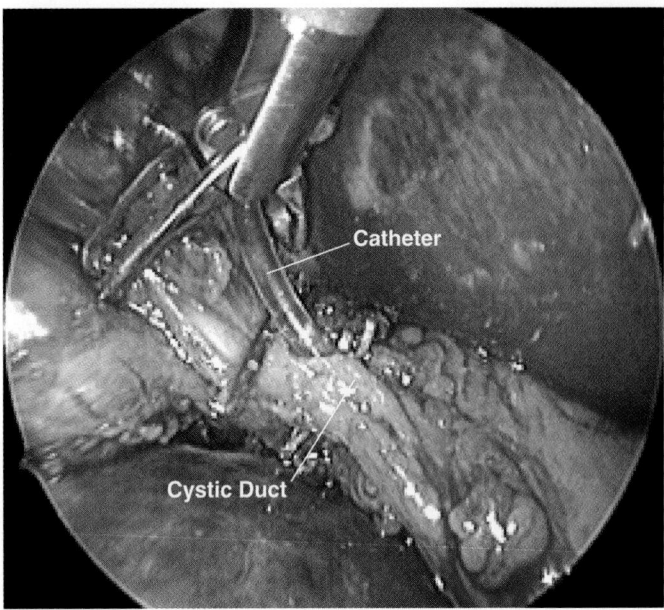

Figure 16 Laparoscopic cholecystectomy. The cystic duct has been clipped, a small incision has been made for placement of the cholangiogram catheter, and the catheter has been advanced through the specialized cholangiogram clamp into the cystic duct.

of the catheter into the cystic duct is prevented by Heister's valve, a guide wire can be passed initially.

If the cystic duct is tiny and cannulation is expected to be difficult or impossible, the gallbladder can be punctured, bile aspirated, and contrast material injected through the gallbladder until the biliary tree is filled.

The cannulas and operating instruments should be positioned so as not to obstruct the view of the biliary tree. If the cannulas cannot be positioned outside the x-ray window, radiolucent cannulas should be used, or the cannulas should be removed and replaced after the cholangiogram. A cholangiogram that does not visualize the biliary tree from the liver to the duodenum is inadequate.

Fluoroscopic cholangiography [*see Figure 17*] may be performed either with hard-copy film or with digital imaging and storage. After the C arm is positioned, with the operating staff protected behind a lead screen, full-strength contrast is slowly injected under fluoroscopic control. The goal is to visualize the biliary tree in its entirety, including the right and left hepatic ductal systems as well as the distal duct. Once the cholangiogram is obtained, the catheter is removed, and the cystic duct is double-clipped and transected.

Laparoscopic ultrasonography Evaluation of the biliary tree with intraoperative laparoscopic ultrasonography appears to be as accurate as intraoperative fluorocholangiography in identifying biliary stones.[28,29] This modality has several advantages over conventional cholangiography: it does not expose patients and staff to radiation; contrast agents are unnecessary; there is no need to cannulate the cystic duct; significantly less time is required; the capital cost of most ultrasound units is less than that of fluoroscopic equipment; and disposable cholangiogram catheters are not needed.

Most of the laparoscopic ultrasound devices in use at present are 7.5 MHz linear-array rigid probes 10 mm in diameter. Flexible probes capable of multiple frequencies are also available, and it is likely that future probes will be increasingly versatile. The probe is

inserted through a 10/12 mm port (usually a periumbilical or epigastric port) and placed directly on the porta hepatis, perpendicular to the structures of the hepatoduodenal ligament. The probe is then moved to the cystic duct–CBD junction. The transverse image obtained should show the three tubular structures of the hepatoduodenal ligament in the so-called Mickey Mouse head configuration: the CBD, the portal vein, and the hepatic artery [*see Figure 18*]. As the probe is moved distally, it is rotated clockwise to allow identification of the distal CBD and the pancreatic duct where they unite at the papilla. Instillation of saline into the right upper quadrant can enhance acoustic coupling and improve visualization.

Because of its many advantages, intraoperative laparoscopic ultrasonography may eventually replace fluorocholangiography in this setting, particularly for surgeons who practice routine intraoperative evaluation of the CBD.[30] Although the learning curve for effective performance of laparoscopic ultrasound examination is not long, surgeons should receive expert mentoring and formal instruction in ultrasonography before attempting it. During the first few attempts, it may be instructive to perform intraoperative laparoscopic ultrasonography in conjunction with fluorocholangiography. It should be emphasized that intraoperative laparoscopic ultrasonography is not a replacement for intraoperative cholangiography if the purpose of the examination is to define an anomalous anatomy or to evaluate a suspected injury or leak.

Step 6: Dissection of Gallbladder from Liver Bed

The gallbladder is grasped near the cystic duct insertion and

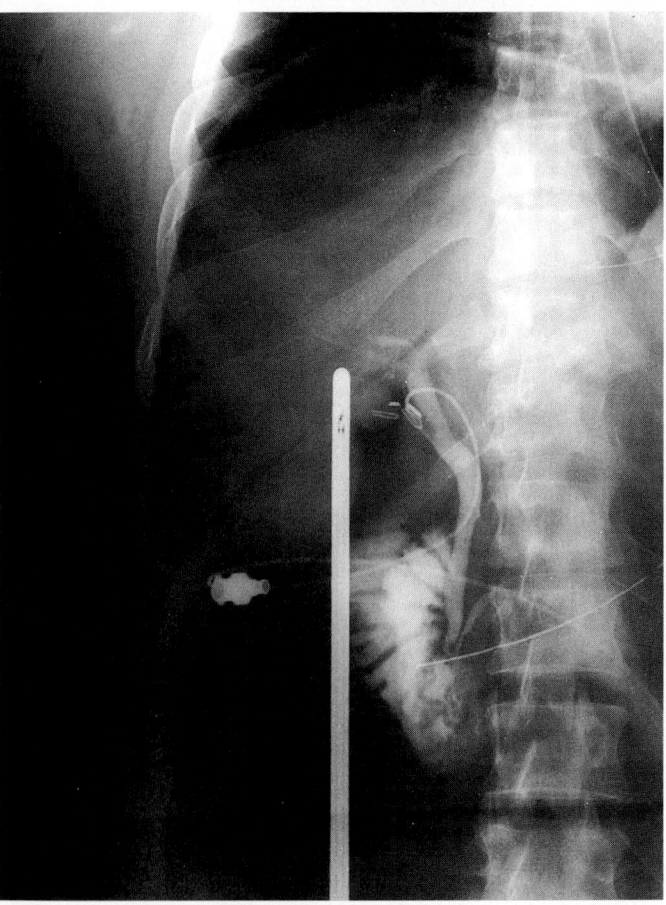

Figure 17 Laparoscopic cholecystectomy. Shown is a normal intraoperative cholangiogram.

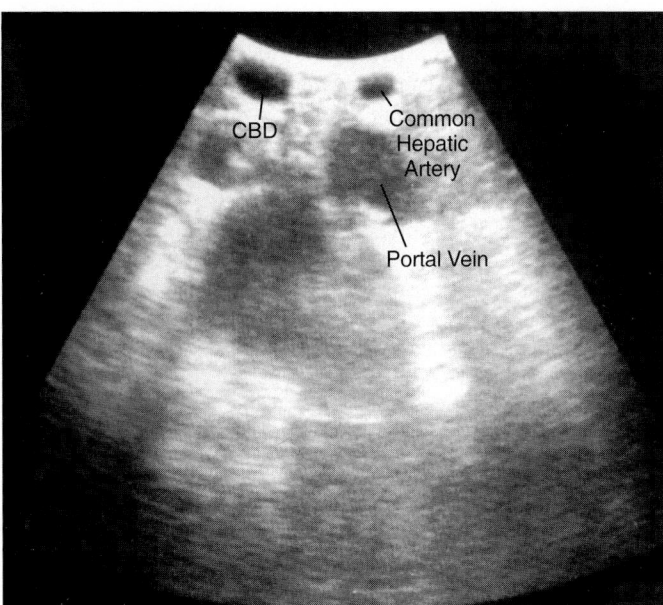

Figure 18 **Laparoscopic cholecystectomy. A transverse intraoperative ultrasound scan of the hepatoduodenal ligament reveals a typical "Mickey Mouse head" appearance. Visible are the CBD, the common hepatic artery, and the portal vein.**

pulled down toward the right anterosuperior iliac spine, placing the areolar tissue between the gallbladder and liver anteriorly under tension. The areolar tissue is cauterized with an L-shaped hook dissector or spatula, and dissection is carried upward as far as possible for as long as there is sufficient exposure. When exposure begins to diminish, the cystic duct end of the gallbladder should be pulled up toward or over the left lobe of the liver to expose the posteroinferior attachments of the gallbladder. A two-handed approach by the surgeon facilitates this dissection. It is sometimes helpful to apply downward and lateral traction on the forceps grasping the fundus. Bleeding during this stage generally indicates that the surgeon has entered the wrong plane and dissection has entered the liver. Bleeding can usually be readily controlled with the electrocautery. In some difficult cases (e.g., an intrahepatic gallbladder), it may be prudent to leave some of the posterior wall of the gallbladder in situ and cauterize it rather than persist with an excessively bloody dissection.[16]

Dissection continues until the gallbladder is attached only by a small piece of peritoneum at the fundus. Before the last attachment to the gallbladder is completely divided, the vital clips are reinspected to ensure that they have not slipped off, and the operative field is checked for hemostasis and the presence of any bile leakage. The final attachment to the gallbladder is then divided. The gallbladder is placed over the right lobe of the liver and laterally so that it can be found again to be retrieved. The grasping forceps on the gallbladder should not be removed.

Perforation of gallbladder The gallbladder may be accidentally breached at some point in the operation, with the result that bile and stones spill into the peritoneal cavity.[31,32] Efforts should be made to suction the spilled bile, which accumulates in the suprahepatic space, the right subhepatic space, and the lower abdomen because of the patient's position. Each of these areas should be irrigated and the effluent aspirated until it is clear. Stones should be located and removed whenever possible. An effective way of removing small stones is to irrigate the subhepat-

ic space copiously. Cholesterol stones usually float on the irrigation fluid and can then be suctioned through a 10 mm suction probe or through a 32 French chest tube passed through the 10 mm operating port. Unfortunately, small stones may be lost in the omentum or between bowel loops. In such cases, it is probably appropriate to leave the stones within the peritoneum rather than perform a laparotomy to attempt to retrieve them. However, there have been reports of serious morbidity, including intra-abdominal abscess, fistula, empyema, and bowel obstruction, resulting from lost stones.

If the gallbladder is perforated and it seems likely that multiple stones will be spilled, the surgeon should introduce a sterile bag into the peritoneal cavity, placing it close to the perforation. Spilled stones can then be transferred immediately into the bag. After the gallbladder is removed from the liver bed, it too is placed in the bag, affording some protection to the wound when it is removed from the abdominal cavity.

Step 7: Extraction of Gallbladder

The laparoscope is moved to the epigastric port, and a large-tooth grasping forceps is inserted through the umbilical port to grasp the gallbladder at the area of the cystic duct. Under direct vision, the gallbladder is then retrieved and pulled out as far as possible through the umbilical port. If the gallbladder is small enough, it can be drawn right into the trocar sleeve, and it and the trocar can then be removed together. It is sometimes necessary to stretch the fascial opening with a Kelly clamp or to aspirate bile from the gallbladder. It is far preferable to enlarge the incision than to have stones or bile spill into the abdominal cavity from a ripped gallbladder. Enlargement of this incision is easier if initial access was obtained via the Hasson technique. All of the other ports are then removed from the abdominal wall under direct vision to ensure that there is no bleeding. All residual CO_2 should be removed to prevent postoperative shoulder pain. The fascial opening at the umbilicus should be sutured closed to prevent subsequent herniation, and all skin incisions should be closed.

Need for drainage The decision to place a drain after laparoscopic cholecystectomy should be governed by the same principles applied to patients undergoing open cholecystectomy. There are two main indications for drainage: (1) the cystic duct was not closed securely, and (2) the CBD was explored by either a direct or a transcystic approach.

Drain placement is easily accomplished. A closed suction drain is inserted intra-abdominally through the 10 mm operative port. A grasping forceps placed through the right lateral port is used to pull one end of the drain out through the abdominal wall. The other end is then positioned according to the surgeon's preference, usually in the subhepatic space.

COMPLICATIONS

Intraoperative

Veress needle injury A syringe must always be attached to the Veress needle, and fluid must be aspirated before insufflation is initiated: failure to do so may lead to insufflation into a vessel and consequently to massive gas embolism. If the aspirate from the syringe attached to the Veress needle contains copious amounts of blood, a major vascular injury may have occurred, and immediate laparotomy is indicated. Because the problem at this point is a needle injury, it can usually be repaired easily and without serious sequelae.

Puncture of the bowel by a Veress needle is usually signaled by aspiration of bowel contents through the needle. If this occurs, the needle should be withdrawn and the approximate course and direction of the puncture remembered. The initial trocar should then be inserted by means of the open technique, under direct vision, to ensure that the undersurface of the abdominal wall is free of adherent bowel. Once pneumoperitoneum is created, careful examination of the abdomen through the laparoscope is undertaken. In most cases, either further leakage of bowel contents, staining of the serosal surface with bowel contents, or an ecchymosis on the serosal surface of the bowel helps the surgeon locate the site of the bowel injury. If ecchymosis is present without spillage of bowel contents, the bowel loop should be marked with a suture and reinspected at the end of the procedure. If ongoing leakage of bowel contents is noted, the injured loop of bowel can be either repaired by means of laparoscopic suturing or grasped with an atraumatic forceps and gently withdrawn through an enlarged umbilical incision for suture repair. The bowel is returned to the peritoneal cavity and the laparoscopic cholecystectomy completed.

Improper placement of the Veress needle into the omentum, the retroperitoneum, or the preperitoneal space may be signaled by high inflation pressures, uneven distribution of the gas on percussion, or marked subcutaneous emphysema. If such misplacement goes unrecognized, creation of a safe intraperitoneal space is impossible, and subsequent blind insertion of the trocar may result in injury to an intraperitoneal structure.

Trocar injury Trocar injury to blood vessels or bowel is much more dangerous than Veress needle injury to the same structures. Major vascular injuries virtually never occur when trocars are placed under direct vision; however, they remain a potentially lethal—though rare—complication of percutaneous trocar insertion. If active bleeding follows removal of the trocar from the cannula, prompt laparotomy is mandatory; if bleeding passes unnoticed and insufflation begins, massive air embolism will result. At the time of laparotomy, both the anterior and the posterior wall of the vessel must be examined after proximal and distal control of the vessel have been obtained.

Bowel injuries can result from either percutaneous or open insertion of the initial trocar. With open insertion, the bowel injury should be immediately obvious and can be repaired after the injured bowel is pulled through an enlarged umbilical incision; laparoscopic cholecystectomy can then proceed. Bowel injuries caused by percutaneous insertion may occur even in the absence of abdominal wall adhesions and can be managed in the same way as those caused by open insertion. The one caveat is that it is possible to spear the bowel in a through-and-through fashion so that when the laparoscope is inserted through the trocar, the view is normal and the injury is not recognized. This type of injury can be diagnosed only if the laparoscope is repositioned to the operating port at some time during the procedure and the undersurface of the umbilical site is carefully examined. This step is mandatory during the course of the operation, preferably early.

Bleeding *Abdominal wall.* Bleeding from the abdominal wall can usually be prevented by careful trocar placement. The abdominal wall should be transilluminated before percutaneous trocar insertion and the larger vessels avoided. If a vessel is speared, the cannula usually tamponades the bleeding reasonably effectively during the procedure.

Once the procedure is completed, each trocar is removed under direct vision. If bleeding follows the removal of a trocar, the puncture hole can be occluded with digital pressure to maintain pneumoperitoneum and the bleeding controlled by cauterization or suture repair. Alternatively, the surgeon may place a Foley catheter through the trocar site with a stylet, inflate the balloon, and place traction on the catheter for 4 to 6 hours; however, tissue ischemia can make this technique quite painful.

Omental or mesenteric adhesions. Generally, omental adhesions can be bluntly teased from their attachments to the gallbladder, with the plane of dissection kept close to the gallbladder, where the adhesions are less vascular. Adhesions to the liver should be taken down with the electrocautery to prevent capsular tears. Persistent bleeding from omental adhesions is unusual but can be managed by means of electrocauterization (with care taken to avoid damage to the duodenum or colon) or the application of hemostatic clips or a pretied ligating loop.

Cystic artery branch. Arterial bleeding encountered during dissection in Calot's triangle is usually from loss of control of the cystic artery or one of its branches. Biliary surgeons must be aware of the many anatomic variations in the vasculature of the gallbladder and the liver. Because the main cystic artery frequently branches, it is common to find more than one artery if dissection is maintained close to the gallbladder. If what seems to be the main cystic artery is small, a posterior cystic artery may be present and may have to be clipped during the dissection.

Prevention of arterial bleeding begins by dissecting the artery carefully and completely before clipping and by inspecting the clips to ensure that they are placed completely across the artery without incorporating additional tissue (e.g., a posterior cystic artery or right hepatic artery). When arterial bleeding is encountered, it is essential to maintain adequate exposure and to avoid blind application of hemostatic clips or cauterization. The laparoscope should be withdrawn slightly so that the lens is not spattered with blood. The surgeon should then pass an atraumatic grasping forceps through a port other than the operating port and attempt to grasp the bleeding vessel. An additional trocar may have to be inserted for simultaneous suction-irrigation. Once proximal control is obtained, the operative field should be suctioned and irrigated to improve exposure. Hemostatic clips are then applied under direct vision; in addition, a sponge may be introduced to apply pressure to the bleeding vessel. Conversion to open cholecystectomy is indicated whenever bleeding cannot be promptly controlled laparoscopically.

Liver bed. Bleeding from the liver bed may be encountered when the wrong plane is developed during dissection of the gallbladder. Patients who have portal hypertension, cirrhosis, or coagulation disorders are at particularly high risk. Control of bleeding requires good exposure, accomplished via lateral and superior retraction of the gallbladder; hence, all bleeding should be controlled before the gallbladder is detached from the liver bed. Most liver bed bleeding can be controlled with the electrocautery, and it should be controlled as it is encountered to allow exposure of the specific bleeding site. Either a hook-shaped or a spatula-shaped coagulation electrode is effective. If oozing continues, oxidized cellulose can be placed as a pack through the operative port and pressure applied on the raw surface of the liver. If needed, fibrin glue can be applied to the bleeding raw surface.

Postoperative

If a patient (1) complains of a great deal of abdominal pain necessitating systemic narcotics, (2) has a high or prolonged fever, (3) experiences ileus, or (4) becomes jaundiced, an intra-abdominal complication may have occurred. Blood should be drawn for

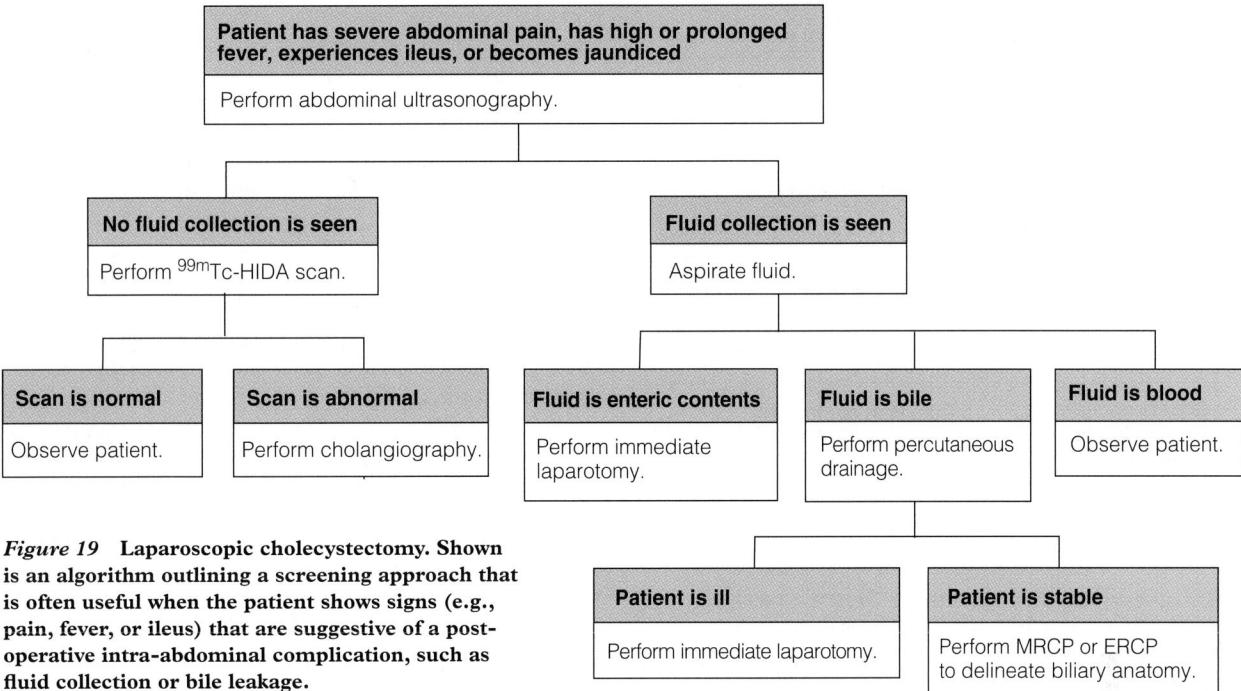

Figure 19 **Laparoscopic cholecystectomy. Shown is an algorithm outlining a screening approach that is often useful when the patient shows signs (e.g., pain, fever, or ileus) that are suggestive of a post-operative intra-abdominal complication, such as fluid collection or bile leakage.**

assessment of the white blood cell count, hemoglobin concentration, liver function, and serum amylase level. Abdominal ultrasonography may help diagnose dilated intrahepatic ducts and subhepatic fluid collections [*see Figure 19*].

Fluid collection or bile leakage When a significant fluid collection is seen, it should be aspirated percutaneously under ultrasonographic guidance. If the fluid is blood and the patient is hemodynamically stable and requires no transfusion, observation of the patient and culture of the fluid are usually sufficient. If the fluid is enteric contents, immediate laparotomy is indicated. If the fluid is bile and the patient is ill, immediate laparotomy should be considered; if the patient is stable and the appropriate facilities are available, MRCP or ERCP may be performed to identify the site of bile leakage, determine whether obstruction is also present, and assess the integrity of the extrahepatic biliary tree. If the bile ducts are in continuity and the bile is coming from the cystic duct stump or a small lateral tear in the bile duct, ES, with or without stenting, usually controls the leak. Percutaneous placement of a drain under ultrasonographic guidance allows control of the bile leakage and measurement of the quantity of fluid present.

Fever Postoperative fever is a common complication of laparoscopic cholecystectomy. As noted, it may be indicative of a complication such as a bile collection or bile leakage. Other common reasons for postoperative fever (e.g., atelectasis) should also be considered.

Abnormal liver function When postoperative blood tests indicate significantly abnormal liver function, possible causes include injury to the biliary tree and retained CBD stones [*see Figure 20*].[33] Cholangiography is required, even if it was performed intraoperatively. If MRCP or ERCP yields normal results, observation is sufficient; the abnormalities may be attributable to a passed stone or drug-related cholestasis. If stones are present, ES can usually solve the problem. If ERCP demonstrates extravasation of bile, it is important to establish whether the CBD is in continuity. If the duct is interrupted, early reoperation, ideally at a spe-

cialized center, is the best option. If the duct is in continuity, endoscopic and radiologic techniques may successfully resolve the problem without substantial morbidity.[34,35] Percutaneous drainage is instituted to control the fistula, and sphincterotomy or stenting is useful to overcome any resistance at the sphincter of Oddi. Any retained stones causing distal obstruction should also be removed. Major ductal injuries usually call for operative repair. When such an injury is identified at operation, the surgeon must decide whether to attempt repair immediately; this decision should be based on the surgeon's experience with reconstructive biliary surgery and on the local expertise available. At a minimum, adequate drainage must be established. Most major ductal injuries are not in fact identified intraoperatively. When such an injury is identified postoperatively, adequate drainage must be established and the anatomy of the injury clarified as well as possible before repair. MRCP or transhepatic cholangiography may be required to delineate the anatomy of the proximal biliary tree when ERCP does not opacify the biliary tract above the injury. If surgical repair is indicated, it should be performed by a surgeon experienced in complex biliary tract procedures. Often, referral to a specialized center is the most appropriate decision, especially in the case of more proximal biliary injuries.

SPECIAL CONSIDERATIONS

Conversion to Laparotomy

Conversion from laparoscopy to laparotomy may be required in any laparoscopic cholecystectomy, in accordance with the judgment of the surgeon. The most common reason for such conversion is the inability to identify important anatomic structures in the region of the gallbladder. Distorted anatomy may be the result of previous operations, inflammation, or anatomic variations. Conversion may also be required because of an intraoperative complication [*see Complications, Postoperative, above*]. Ideally, the surgeon would wish to convert before any complication occurs. It must be emphasized that conversion to open surgery should not be considered a failure or a complication. Rather, it should be considered a prudent maneuver for achieving the desired objective—

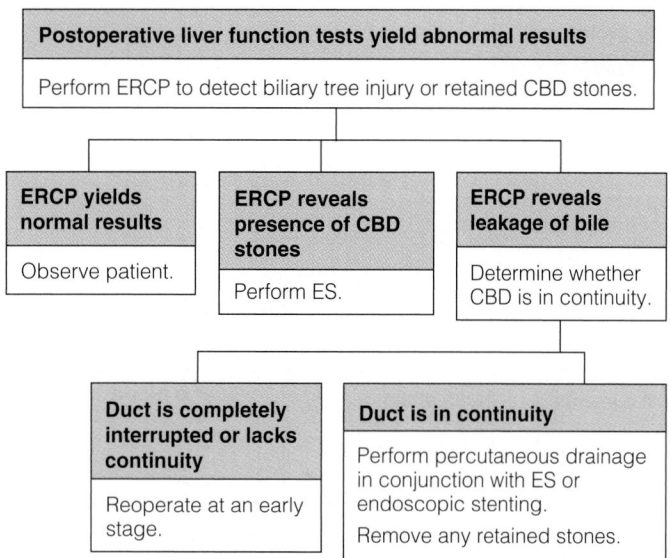

Figure 20 Laparoscopic cholecystectomy. Shown is an algorithm outlining an approach to abnormal liver function test results after laparoscopic cholecystectomy.

namely, safe removal of the gallbladder. Accordingly, every patient consent obtained for a laparoscopic cholecystectomy must explicitly allow for the possibility of conversion to an open procedure. Attempts have been made to predict the probability of conversion on the basis of preoperative information.[36,37] It is clearly useful to stratify patients according to likelihood of conversion. This information is helpful in selecting patients for laparoscopic cholecystectomy in an outpatient versus hospital setting, in determining the resources required in the OR, and in assisting patients in planning their work and family needs around the time of surgery.

Factors found to be predictive of an increased probability of conversion include acute cholecystitis, either at the time of surgery or at any point in the past; age greater than 65 years; male sex; and thickening of the gallbladder wall to more than 3 mm as measured by ultrasonography. Other factors more variably associated with an increased likelihood of conversion are obesity, previous upper abdominal operations (especially gastroduodenal), multiple gallbladder attacks over a long period, and severe pancreatitis. Factors not associated with an increased likelihood of conversion are jaundice, previous ES, previous lower abdominal procedures, stomas, mild pancreatitis, and diabetes.

On the basis of our data, a 45-year-old woman with no history of acute cholecystitis and no gallbladder wall thickening has a probability of conversion lower than 1%; such a patient is a good candidate for laparoscopic cholecystectomy in an outpatient setting. Conversely, a 70-year-old man with acute cholecystitis and ultrasonographic evidence of gallbladder wall thickening has a probability of conversion of about 30%; such a patient would be better managed in a traditional hospital environment.

Acute Cholecystitis

Laparoscopic cholecystectomy has been shown to be safe and effective for treating acute cholecystitis.[38,39] There are, however, several technical problems in this setting that must be addressed if the procedure is to be performed with minimal risk. It should also be recognized that the probability of conversion to laparotomy is greatly increased in these circumstances. There appears to be no advantage to delaying surgery in patients with acute cholecystitis, even if rapid improvement is noted with nonoperative manage-

ment.[40,41] Many patients return within a short time with recurrent attacks, and delaying surgery does not reduce the probability of conversion.

Technical difficulties associated with cholecystectomy for acute cholecystitis include dense adhesions, the increased vascularity of tissues, difficulty in grasping the gallbladder, an impacted stone in the gallbladder neck or the cystic duct, shortening and thickening of the cystic duct, and close approximation of the CBD to the gallbladder wall.

The surgeon should not hesitate to insert additional ports (e.g., for a suction-irrigation apparatus) if necessary. Because the tense, distended gallbladder is difficult to grasp reliably, it should be aspirated through the fundus early in the procedure, as previously described. If the graspers fail to grasp the wall or cause it to tear, exposure of Calot's triangle can be achieved by propping up or levering the neck of the gallbladder and the right liver with a blunt instrument. A sponge can be used for this purpose, thereby reducing the potential trauma of the retraction. This maneuver is also useful when an impacted stone in the neck of the gallbladder prevents the surgeon from grasping the gallbladder in the area of Hartmann's pouch. Dense adhesions that may be present between the gallbladder and the omentum, duodenum, or colon should be dissected bluntly (e.g., with a suction tip). Because the tissues are friable and vascular, oozing may be encountered. Electrocauterization should be only sparingly employed until the vital structures in Calot's triangle are identified. Instead, the surgeon should move to another area of dissection, allowing most of the oozing to coagulate on its own. Liberal use of suction and irrigation will keep the operative field free of blood.

In the identification of anatomic structures, it is important to keep dissection close to the gallbladder wall, working down from the gallbladder toward Calot's triangle. Dissection of the lower part of the gallbladder from the liver bed early in the operation may aid in identification of the gallbladder neck–cystic duct junction (analogous to an open, retrograde dissection). The surgeon should be aware that edema and acute inflammation may cause foreshortening of the cystic duct. If the anatomy cannot be identified, preliminary cholangiography through the emptied gallbladder may indicate the position of the cystic duct and the CBD.

Often, the obstructing stone responsible for the acute attack is in the neck of the gallbladder; thus, the cystic duct will be normal and easily secured with clips. If the stone is in the cystic duct, it must be removed before the duct is clipped or ligated. A thickened, edematous cystic duct is better controlled by ligation with an extracorporeal tie or a ligating loop than by clipping. If closure of the cystic duct is tenuous, closed suction drainage is advisable. Obviously, conversion to open cholecystectomy is indicated if the anatomy remains obscure. Conversion should also be considered if no progress is made after a predesignated period (e.g., 15 minutes) because at this point, the surgeon is unlikely to make any headway.

CBD Stones

Identification of patients at risk About 10% of all patients undergoing cholecystectomy for gallstones will also have choledocholithiasis. To select from the various diagnostic and therapeutic options for managing choledocholithiasis, it is helpful to know preoperatively whether the patient is at high, moderate, or low risk for stones. Patients with obvious clinical jaundice or cholangitis, a dilated CBD, or stones visualized in the CBD on preoperative ultrasonography are likely to have choledocholithiasis (risk > 50%). Patients who have a history of jaundice or pancreatitis, elevated preoperative levels of alkaline phosphatase or bilirubin, or ultrasonographic evidence of multiple small gallstones are some-

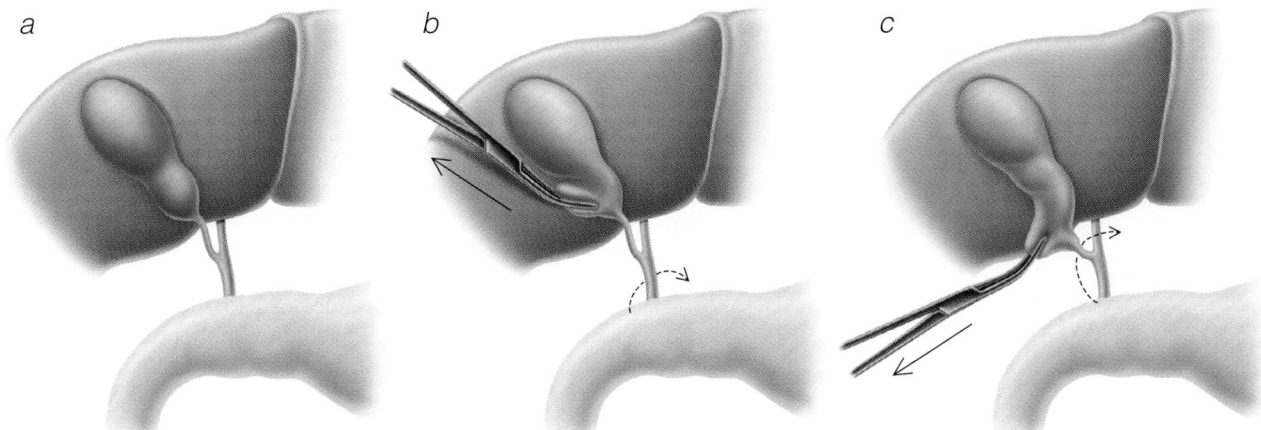

Figure 21 **Open cholecystectomy. (*a*) Shown are the resting positions of the cystic duct and the CBD (with Calot's triangle closed). (*b*) Improper upward retraction of Hartmann's pouch lines up the CBD and the cystic duct so that one can easily encircle the CBD or clamp the cystic duct and the CBD. (*c*) Correct downward and rightward retraction opens Calot's triangle; dissection proceeds lateral to the CBD.**

what less likely to have choledocholithiasis (risk, 10% to 50%). Patients with large gallstones, no history of jaundice or pancreatitis, and normal liver function are unlikely to have choledocholithiasis (risk < 5%).

Diagnostic and therapeutic options One argument for routine intraoperative cholangiography is that it is a good way of identifying unsuspected CBD stones. However, more selective approaches to diagnosing choledocholithiasis make use of preoperative cholangiography via MRCP, EUS, or, more invasively, ERCP [*see 60 Gastrointestinal Endoscopy*]. Preoperative identification of choledocholithiasis allows the surgeon to attempt preoperative clearance of the CBD by means of ES or intraoperative clearance during laparoscopy, depending on his or her expertise. Preoperative cholangiography is suggested when the patient's history and the results of laboratory and diagnostic tests suggest that there is a moderate or high risk of CBD stones. It is our practice to have patients at high risk for CBD stones undergo ERCP and ES if warranted. For patients at moderate risk, MRCP or EUS is done first, followed by therapeutic ERCP if CBD stones are identified. Intraoperative cholangiography can also be used to identify choledocholithiasis. ERCP with ES may result in pancreatitis, perforation, or bleeding and carries a mortality of approximately 0.2%.

When stones are detected during the operation, the options include laparoscopic transcystic duct exploration, laparoscopic choledochotomy and CBD exploration, open CBD exploration, and postoperative ERCP/ES.[10,42] If a single small (~ 2 mm) stone is visualized, it can probably be flushed into the duodenum by flushing the CBD via the cholangiogram catheter and administering glucagon, 1 to 2 mg I.V., to relax the sphincter of Oddi. Even if a stone of this size does not pass intraoperatively, it will usually pass on its own postoperatively.

Laparoscopic transcystic CBD exploration *Access to biliary tree.* The cholangiogram is reviewed; the size of the cystic duct, the site where the cystic duct inserts into the CBD, and the size and location of the CBD stones all contribute to the success or failure of transcystic CBD exploration.[43-45] For example, transcystic exploration is extremely challenging in a patient who has a long, spiraling cystic duct with a medial insertion. The size of the stones to be removed dictates the approach to the CBD: stones smaller than 4 mm can usually be retrieved in fluoroscopically

directed baskets and generally do not necessitate cystic duct dilatation; larger stones (4 to 8 mm) are retrieved under direct vision with the choledochoscope.

A hydrophilic guide wire is inserted through the cholangiogram catheter into the CBD under fluoroscopic guidance. The cholangiogram catheter is then removed. If the largest stone is larger than the cystic duct, dilatation of the duct is necessary, not only for passage of the stone but also to allow passage of the choledochoscope, which may be 3 to 5 mm in diameter.

Dilatation is accomplished with either a balloon dilator or sequential plastic dilators. Because plastic dilators may cause the cystic duct to split, balloon dilatation is recommended. A balloon 3 to 5 cm in length is passed over the guide wire and positioned with its distal end just inside the CBD and its proximal end just outside the incision in the cystic duct. The balloon is then inflated to the pressure recommended by the manufacturer and observed closely for evidence of shearing of the cystic duct. The cystic duct should not be dilated to a diameter greater than 8 mm. Larger stones in the CBD may be either fragmented with electrohydraulic or mechanical lithotripsy, if available, or removed via choledochotomy.

Once dilatation is complete, the guide wire may be removed or left in place to guide passage of a choledochoscope or baskets. When the choledochoscope is used, a second incision in the cystic duct, close to the CBD, avoids Heister's valves and allows removal of the guide wire. If baskets are used, a 6 French plastic introducer sheath may be inserted through the trocar used for cholangiography into the cystic duct. This sheath is especially useful if multiple stones must be removed.

Fluoroscopic wire basket transcystic CBD exploration. Stones smaller than 2 to 4 mm that do not pass with irrigation through the cholangiocatheter after injection of glucagon can usually be retrieved by using a 4 French or 5 French helical stone basket passed into the CBD over a guide wire under fluoroscopic guidance. The baskets can be passed alongside the cholangiocatheter or inserted via a plastic sheath replacing the cholangiocatheter. The basket is opened in the ampulla of Vater, pulled back into the CBD, and rotated clockwise until the stone is entrapped. The stone and basket are then removed together. A Fogarty catheter should not be used, because the stones are likely to be pulled up into the hepatic ducts, where they are much more difficult to remove.

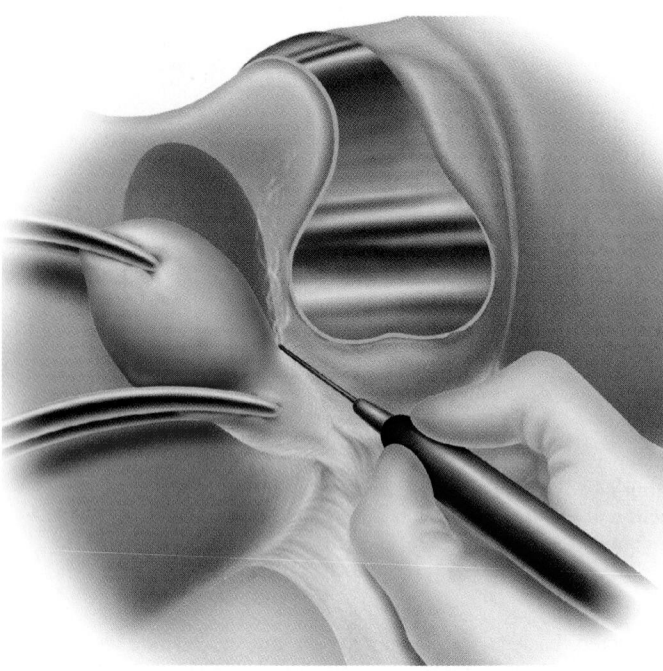

Figure 22 **Open cholecystectomy. In so-called fundus down dissection, the fundus and infundibulum are retracted up and away from the liver while dissection is performed with electrocautery. Sharp dissection with scissors or scalpel or blunt digital dissection all may be used, at the surgeon's discretion.**

Endoscopic transcystic CBD exploration. When stones are 4 to 8 mm in diameter, the helical stone basket wires are generally too close together to permit retrieval. Hence, choledochoscopic basketing is utilized. A 7 to 10 French choledochoscope with a working channel is either passed over the guide wire or inserted directly into the cystic duct. Because the usual grasping forceps may damage the choledochoscope, forceps with rubber-covered jaws should be used. A separate camera should be inserted onto the choledochoscope, and the image it produces can be displayed on the monitor by means of an audiovisual mixer (i.e., a picture within a picture) or displayed on a separate monitor.

Once the choledochoscope enters the cystic duct, warm saline irrigation is begun under low pressure to distend the CBD and provide a working space. The choledochoscope usually enters the CBD rather than the common hepatic duct. When a stone is seen, a 2.4 French straight four-wire basket is inserted through the operating port. The stones closest to the cystic duct are removed first, by advancing the closed basket beyond each stone, opening the basket, and pulling the basket back, thereby trapping the stone. The basket is then closed and pulled up against the choledochoscope so that they can be withdrawn as a unit. Multiple passes may be required until the duct is clear. A completion cholangiogram is done to ensure that the duct is clear and to rule out proximal stones. The dilated, traumatized cystic duct is ligated with a ligating loop rather than a hemostatic clip. If drainage is required, a red rubber catheter can be inserted into the CBD via the cystic duct.

Because of the angle created by the cephalad and superior retraction of the gallbladder, it may be difficult to pass the choledochoscope into the proximal ducts. If a common hepatic duct stone is seen on the cholangiogram, the patient is placed in a steep reverse Trendelenburg position. In this position, any nonimpacted stones may fall into the distal duct for retrieval. It may be possible to pass the choledochoscope into the proximal ducts by applying caudal traction to the cystic duct so as to align it with the common

hepatic duct. An additional access port in the right upper quadrant may be needed. If the cystic duct is long or spiraling or inserts medially, this measure may not be feasible, in which case access must be obtained by means of choledochotomy.

Laparoscopic CBD exploration   Large stones (> 1 cm), as well as most stones in the common hepatic ducts, are not retrievable with the techniques described above. Ductal clearance can be achieved via choledochotomy if the duct is dilated and the surgeon is sufficiently experienced.[46,47] The anterior wall of the CBD is bluntly dissected for a distance of 1 to 2 cm. When small vessels are encountered, it is preferable to apply pressure and wait for hemostasis rather than use the electrocautery in this area. Two stay sutures are placed in the CBD. An additional 5 mm trocar is placed in the right lower quadrant for insertion of an additional needle driver. A small longitudinal choledochotomy (a few millimeters longer than the circumference of the largest stone) is made with curved microscissors on the anterior aspect of the duct while the stay sutures are elevated. A choledochoscope is then inserted and warm saline irrigation initiated. In most cases, baskets should suffice for stone retrieval; however, lithotriptor probes and lasers are available for use through the working channel of the choledochoscope. The choice of approach depends on availability and individual surgical experience.

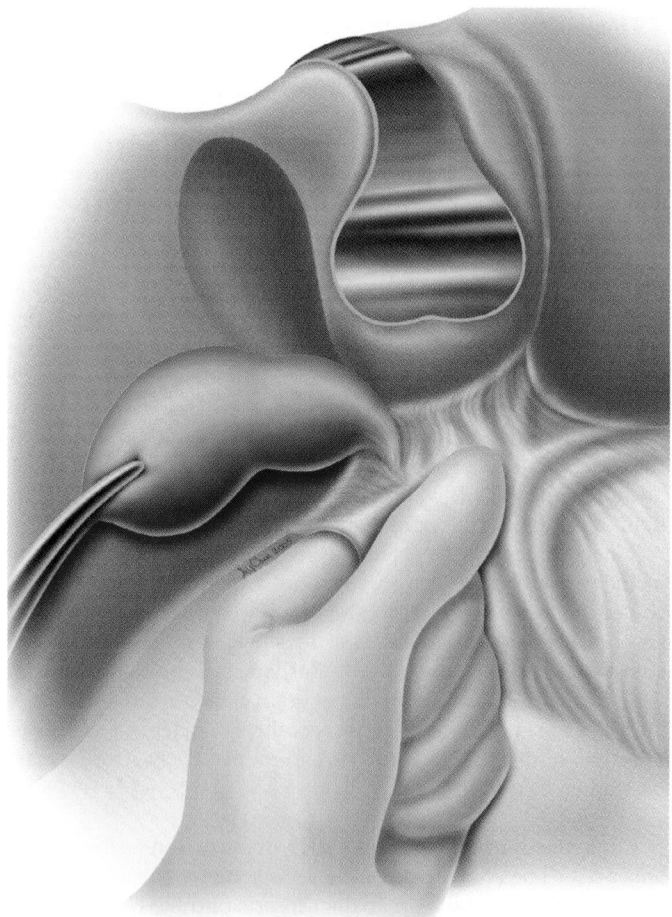

Figure 23 **Open cholecystectomy. In patients with severe inflammation and edema, the surgeon must be cautious when approaching Calot's triangle during fundus down dissection. In such circumstances, digital palpation can be very helpful in safely identifying the cystic duct and artery.**

a   *b*

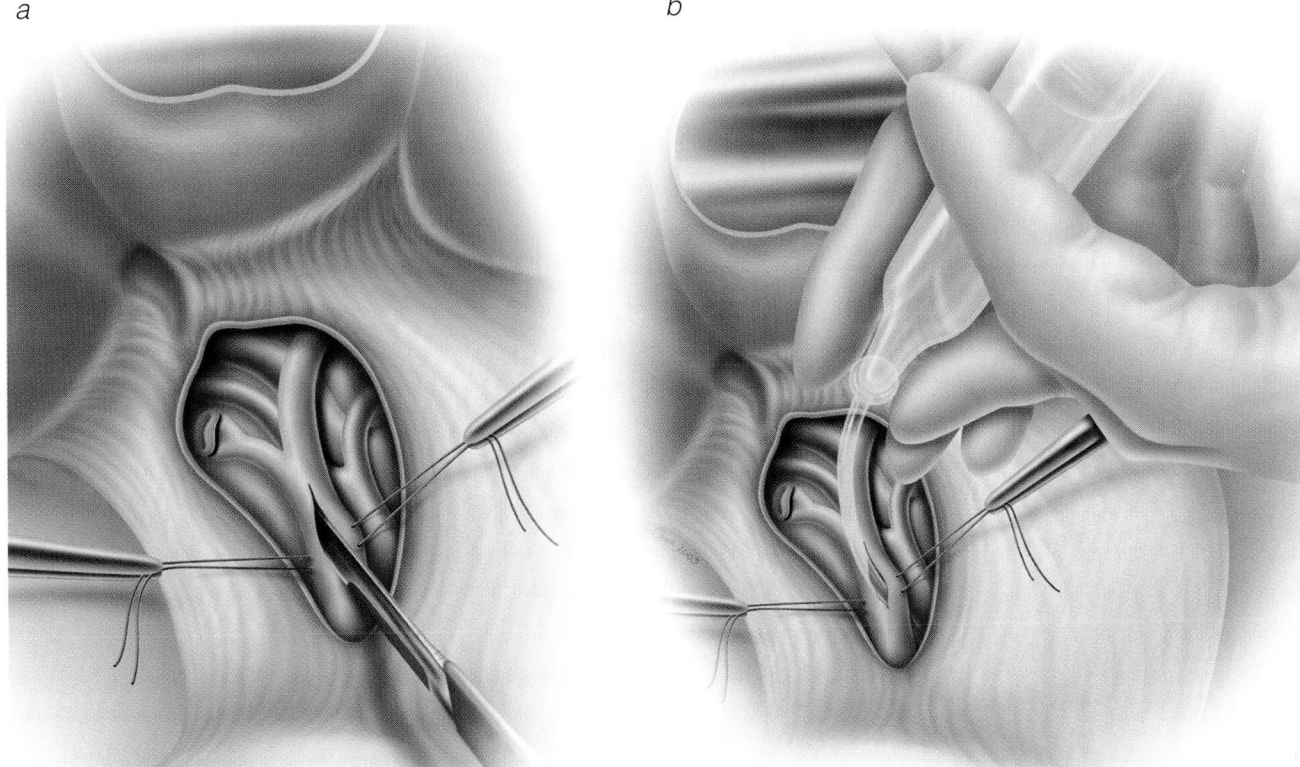

Figure 24 **Open common bile duct exploration. (*a*) The common bile duct is opened vertically between laterally positioned stay sutures. (*b*) A catheter is then used to irrigate and flush stones from the duct. If stones are
impacted within the duct, they can be retrieved with Fogarty catheters, wire stone retrieval baskets, or stone
retrieval forceps. The choledochoscope can be used if any of these methods fail or as the initial method of
exploration.**

Subsequently, a 12 or 14 French latex T tube is fashioned with
short limbs, placed entirely intraperitoneally to prevent CO_2 from
escaping, and positioned in the CBD. The choledochotomy is then
closed with fine interrupted absorbable sutures. The first suture is
placed right next to the T tube, securing it distally, and the second
is placed at the most proximal end of the choledochotomy; lifting
these two sutures facilitates placement of additional sutures.
Intracorporeal knots are preferred to avoid sawing of the delicate tissues. The end of the T tube is then pulled out through a trocar, and
cholangiography is performed after completion of the procedure.

Open Cholecystectomy

Open cholecystectomy is usually reserved for patients in whom
the laparoscopic approach is not feasible or is contraindicated. As
such, it is typically performed only in the most difficult situations
or when additional maneuvers such as CBD exploration are anticipated. Conversion from the laparoscopic to the open approach is
not considered a complication and does not represent failure.
Rather, conversion to this time-honored and effective procedure
represents the prudent judgment of a safe surgeon.

OPERATIVE TECHNIQUE

The choice of incision depends on the surgeon's experience and
preference, along with patient factors such as previous surgical
procedures and body habitus. Typically, open cholecystectomy is
performed through a right subcostal (Kocher) incision, but it can
also be approached through an upper midline incision or, less
commonly, through a right paramedian or transverse incision. A
mechanical retraction system should be used, if available, so that

the hands of the participating surgeons are free; there is no good
rationale for struggling to perform difficult biliary surgery with
handheld retractors.

The abdomen is opened and then explored; the abdominal viscera are inspected and palpated and a retraction system is put in
place. Long curved or angled clamps, such as Kelly or Mixter, are
placed on the gallbladder fundus and infundibulum for the application of gentle traction. The fundus is elevated and the
infundibulum is pulled laterally and away from the liver [*see Figure
21*]. If the gallbladder is not too inflamed and edematous, the procedure may be performed similarly to the typical laparoscopic
approach: the surgeon identifies and ligates the cystic duct and
artery, and then removes the gallbladder from the liver bed.

With more difficult open cases, the above technique may not be
possible. In such cases, a retrograde or so-called fundus down
approach is usually employed. Staying as close to the gallbladder
wall as is possible, the surgeon uses electrocautery or sharp and
digital blunt dissection to remove the gallbladder from the liver
bed, continuing downward to the cystic duct and artery [*see Figure
22*]. Anatomic variations of the duct and artery must always be
anticipated. These structures can be very difficult to identify and
safely dissect in cases of severe inflammation and markedly edematous tissues. In such cases, palpation and gentle digital blunt
dissection of the duct and artery between thumb and index finger
is useful [*see Figure 23*]. Opening the gallbladder to remove stones
or aspirate bile or pus may be necessary when it is tense and distended or necrotic and gangrenous. As with laparoscopic cholecystectomy, it is critical to identify the cystic duct and artery and
their anatomic relations to the gallbladder and common bile duct
before division and to avoid injury to the common bile duct or

a   b

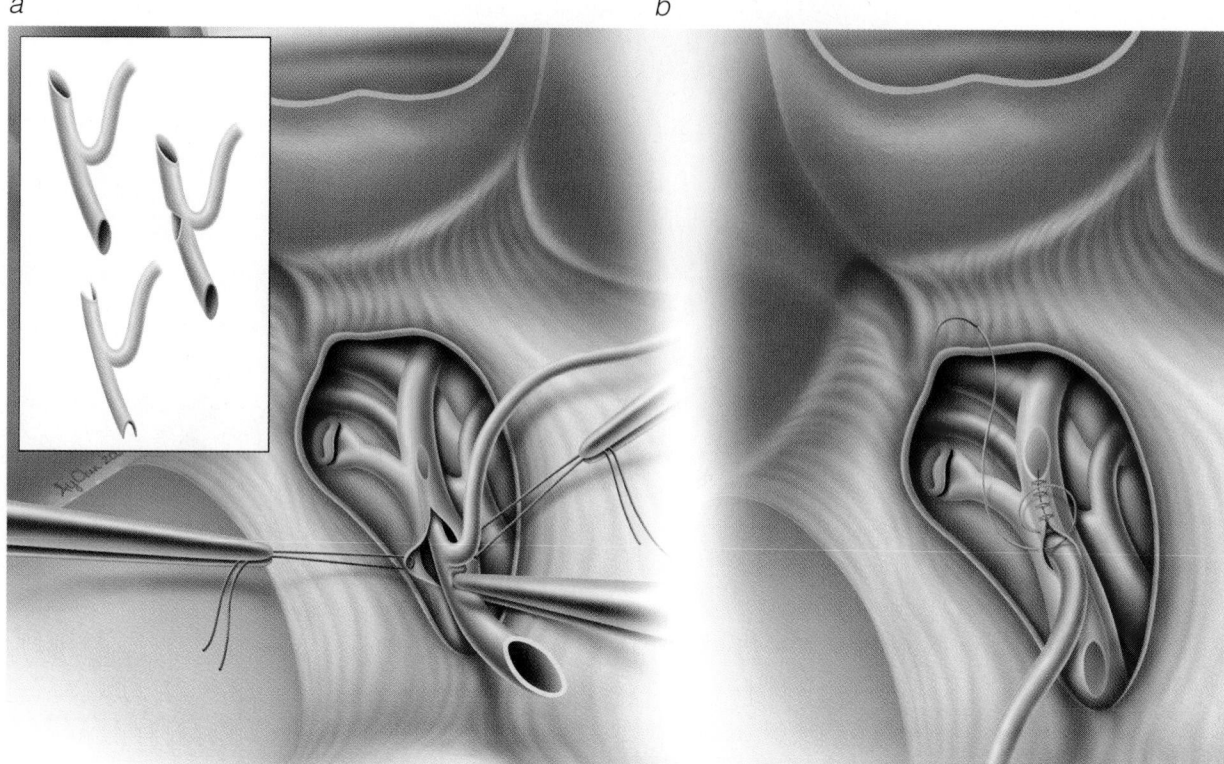

Figure 25 **Open common bile duct exploration.** (*a*) **After common bile duct exploration, a T tube is fashioned and is placed into the duct.** (*b*) **Interrupted 4-0 absorbable sutures are used to close the chole-dochotomy snug around the tube. A completion cholangiogram may then be performed. The tube is brought out through the right abdominal wall, through a separate stab incision, and secured to the skin.**

common hepatic duct. The cystic duct and artery may be suture ligated or divided between clips. Stones found in the cystic duct should be gently milked back into the gallbladder.

SPECIAL CONSIDERATIONS

Cholangiography

The indications for cholangiography are the same as for laparoscopic cholecystectomy. Several techniques for the performance of cholangiography can be utilized. Usually the same technique as for laparoscopic cholecystectomy is employed; the cystic duct is ligated or clipped high near the infundibulum and incised just below this point for insertion of a cholangiography catheter, which is secured against leakage by another clip or ligature. Alternatively, the cystic duct can be divided near the infundibulum and the gallbladder removed; then the cystic duct is cannulated. Needle puncture cholangiography can also be performed via the cystic duct or the common duct. Once cholangiography is complete, the gallbladder is removed and sent for pathologic examination. The operative field is inspected for hemostasis and irrigated. Any bile leak is identified. Drains are not routinely placed but can be used at the surgeon's discretion. If drains are used, a closed suction Jackson-Pratt or similar drain is recommended; the drain should be brought out through a separate stab incision.

Open CBD Exploration

Open common bile duct exploration has become a rare procedure, but it remains a skill that surgeons require. If ERCP has failed or is not possible, if the surgeon does not have the experience and necessary tools to perform laparoscopic duct explo-

ration, or if laparoscopic efforts have failed, then open exploration becomes necessary. Ductal stones are identified either preoperatively or intraoperatively by ultrasound, cholangiography, or palpation.

Appropriate retraction and exposure are crucial. The anterior aspect of the duct is exposed over a distance of 1 to 2 cm, avoiding electrocautery during dissection. Two stay sutures of a 3-0 monofilament are placed lateral to the midline of the duct. The common hepatic duct is sharply opened with a No. 11 or No. 15 scalpel and longitudinally incised further with a Potts' arteriotomy or similar scissors. When performing these maneuvers, the surgeon must respect the arterial blood supply of the duct, which courses laterally on either side of the duct in the 3 o'clock and 9 o'clock positions [*see Figure 24*]. In some cases, stones are immediately visible and can simply be plucked from the duct once it is opened. Flushing the duct with saline, proximally and then distally, through a 12 or 14 French Foley or red rubber catheter may also clear the duct of stones. The intravenous administration of 1 to 2 mg of glucagon will relax the sphincter of Oddi, which may help in the flushing of stones from the duct. In some cases, stones will be impacted within the duct and will require additional maneuvers. Kocher's maneuver (liberally mobilizing the lateral duodenum and head of the pancreas) will allow the surgeon to hold and palpate the duodenum, the head of the pancreas, and stones within the duct, facilitating instrumentation. Stone retrieval forceps, biliary Fogarty catheters, and wire baskets can all be employed to retrieve stones. A choledochoscope can also be used, either at the outset of exploration or for stone retrieval, if simpler maneuvers are not successful.

Either T tube cholangiography or choledochoscopy may be

employed to confirm clearance of ductal stones. If no stones are present, primary closure of the choledochotomy has been successfully employed, although most surgeons will leave in place a 12 or 14 French T tube, which is brought out through a separate stab incision in the right lateral abdominal wall [see Figure 25]. If stone clearance is not achieved, a T tube is mandatory for decompression of the biliary tract and to provide a route for future duct instrumentation. The T tube is connected to a bag for free drainage. Several days later, cholangiography is repeated. If it shows good flow into the duodenum without obstruction, the tube may be clamped and removed at the 2-week mark. If there are retained stones, a more mature tract must be allowed to develop over 4 to 6 weeks for future instrumentation and stone retrieval. Retained stones may require ERCP, percutaneous transhepatic instrumentation, T tube tract instrumentation, or combinations of these for removal.

References

1. McSherry CK: Cholecystectomy: the Gold Standard. Am J Surg 158:174, 1989

2. Mühe E: Die erste: cholecystecktomie durch das laparoskop. Langenbecks Arch Klin Chir 369:804, 1986

3. Lam D, Miranda R, Hom SJ: Laparoscopic cholecystectomy as an outpatient procedure. J Am Coll Surg 185:152, 1997

4. Abboud PC, Malet PF, Berlin JA, et al: Predictors of common bile duct stones prior to cholecystectomy: a meta-analysis. Gastrointest Endosc 44:450, 1996

5. Barkun AN, Barkun JS, Fried GM, et al: Useful predictors of bile duct stones in patients undergoing laparoscopic cholecystectomy. McGill Gallstone Treatment Group. Ann Surg 220:32, 1994

6. Jones DB, Soper NJ: Common duct stones. Current Surgical Therapy, 5th ed. Cameron JL, Ed. Mosby-Year Book, St. Louis, 1995

7. Paul A, Millat B, Holthhausen U, et al: Diagnosis and treatment of common bile duct stones (CBDS): results of a consensus development conference. Surg Endosc 12:856, 1998

8. Phillips EH: Controversies in the management of common duct calculi. Surg Clin North Am 74:931, 1994

9. Voyles CR, Sanders DL, Hogan R: Common bile duct evaluation in the era of laparoscopic cholecystectomy: 1050 cases later. Ann Surg 219:744, 1994

10. Cohen S, Bacon BR, Berlin JA, et al: National Institutes of Health state-of-the-science conference statement: ERCP for diagnosis and therapy, January 14–16, 2002. Gastrointest Endosc 56:803, 2002

11. Musella M, Barbalace G, Capparelli G, et al: Magnetic resonance imaging in evaluation of the common bile duct. Br J Surg 85:16, 1998

12. Guibaud L, Bret PM, Reinhold C, et al: Bile duct obstruction and choledocholithiasis: diagnosis with MR cholangiography. Radiology 197:109, 1995

13. Johnson AB, Fink AS: Alternative methods for management of the complicated gallbladder. Semin Laparosc Surg 5:115, 1998

14. Angrisani L, Lorenzo M, De Palma G, et al: Laparoscopic cholecystectomy in obese patients compared with nonobese patients. Surg Laparosc Endosc 5:197, 1995

15. Curet MJ: Special problems in laparoscopic surgery: previous abdominal surgery, obesity, and pregnancy. Surg Clin North Am 80:1093, 2000

16. Bornman PC, Terblanche J: Subtotal cholecystectomy: for the difficult gallbladder in portal hypertension and cholecystitis. Surgery 98:1, 1985

17. Lacy AM, Balaguer C, Andrade E, et al: Laparoscopic cholecystectomy in cirrhotic patients: indication or contraindication? Surg Endosc 9:407, 1995

18. Amos JD, Schorr SJ, Norman PF, et al: Laparoscopic surgery during pregnancy. Am J Surg 171:435, 1996

19. Curet MJ, Allen D, Josloff RK, et al: Laparoscopy during pregnancy. Arch Surg 131:546, 1996

20. SAGES Committee on Standards of Practice: SAGES Guidelines for Laparoscopic Surgery during Pregnancy. SAGES Publication #0023. Society of American Gastrointestinal Endoscopic Surgeons (SAGES), Santa Monica, California, 2000

21. Steinbrook RA, Brooks DC, Datta S: Laparoscopic cholecystectomy during pregnancy: review of anesthetic management, surgical considerations. Surg Endosc 10:511, 1996

22. Bhoyrul S, Vierra MA, Nezhat CR, et al: Trocar injuries in laparoscopic surgery. J Am Coll Surg 192:677, 2001

23. Sigman HH, Fried GM, Garzon J, et al: Risks of blind versus open approach to celiotomy for laparoscopic surgery. Surg Laparosc Endosc 3:296, 1993

24. Hunter JG: Avoidance of bile duct injury during laparoscopic cholecystectomy. Am J Surg 162:71, 1991

25. Martin RF, Rossi RL: Bile duct injuries: spectrum, mechanisms of injury, and their prevention. Surg Clin North Am 74:781, 1994

26. Mahmud S, Hamza Y, Nassar AHM: The significance of cystic duct stones encountered during laparoscopic cholecystectomy. Surg Endosc 15:460, 2001

27. Soper NJ, Brunt LM: The case for routine operative cholangiography during laparoscopic cholecystectomy. Surg Clin North Am 74:953, 1994

28. Fletcher DR, Hobbs MST, Tan P, et al: Complications of cholecystectomy: risks of the laparoscopic approach and protective effects of operative cholangiography. Ann Surg 229:449, 1999

29. Wu JS, Dunnegan DL, Soper NJ: The utility of intracorporeal ultrasonography for screening of the bile duct during laparoscopic cholecystectomy. J Gastrointest Surg 2:50, 1998

30. Ohtani T, Kawai C, Shirai Y, et al: Intraoperative ultrasonography versus cholangiography during laparoscopic cholecystectomy: a prospective comparative study. J Am Coll Surg 185:274, 1997

31. Sarli L, Pietra N, Costi R, et al: Gall-bladder perforation during laparoscopic cholecystectomy. World J Surg 23:1186, 1999

32. Schafer M, Suter L, Klaiber C, et al: Spilled gallstones after laparoscopic cholecystectomy. Surg Endosc 12:305, 1998

33. Halevy A, Gold-Deutch R, Negri M, et al: Are elevated liver enzymes and bilirubin levels significant after laparoscopic cholecystectomy in the absence of bile duct injury? Ann Surg 219:362, 1994

34. Ponsky JL: Endoscopic approaches to common bile duct injuries. Surg Clin North Am 76:505, 1996

35. Lillemoe KD, Martin SA, Cameron JL, et al: Major bile duct injuries during laparoscopic cholecystectomy: follow-up after combined surgical and radiologic management. Ann Surg 225:459, 1997

36. Fried GM, Barkun JS, Sigman HH, et al: Factors determining conversion to laparotomy in patients undergoing laparoscopic cholecystectomy. Am J Surg 167:35, 1994

37. Sanabria JR, Gallinger S, Croxford R, et al: Risk factors in elective laparoscopic cholecystectomy for conversion to open cholecystectomy. J Am Coll Surg 179:696, 1994

38. Zucker KA, Flowers JL, Bailey RW, et al: Laparoscopic management of acute cholecystitis. Am J Surg 165:508, 1993

39. Rattner DW, Ferguson C, Warshaw AL: Factors associated with successful laparoscopic cholecystectomy for acute cholecystitis. Ann Surg 217:233, 1993

40. Lo CM, Liu CL, Lai EC, et al: Early versus delayed laparoscopic cholecystectomy for treatment of acute cholecystitis. Ann Surg 223:37, 1996

41. Koo KP, Thirlby RC: Laparoscopic cholecystectomy in acute cholecystitis: what is the optimal timing for operation? Arch Surg 131:540, 1996

42. Park AE, Mastrangelo MJ: Endoscopic retrograde cholangiopancreatography in the management of choledocholithiasis. Surg Endosc 14:219, 2000

43. Petelin JB: Laparoscopic approach to common duct pathology. Am J Surg 165:487, 1993

44. Phillips EH: Laparoscopic transcystic duct common bile duct exploration-outcome and costs. Surg Endosc 9:1240, 1995

45. Rhodes M, Sussman L, Cohen L, et al: Randomized trial of laparoscopic exploration of common bile duct versus postoperative endoscopic retrograde cholangiography for common bile duct stones. Lancet 351:159, 1998

46. Hunter JG, Soper NJ: Laparoscopic management of bile duct stones. Surg Clin North Am 72:1077, 1992

47. Crawford DL, Phillips EH: Laparoscopic common duct exploration. World J Surg 23:343, 1999

Recommended Reading

Asbun HJ, Rossi RL: Techniques of laparoscopic cholecystectomy: the difficult operation. Surg Clin North Am 74:755, 1994

Barkun JS, Barkun AN, Sampalis JS, et al: Randomised controlled trial of laparoscopic versus mini cholecystectomy. The McGill Gallstone Treatment Group. Lancet 340:1116, 1992

Barkun JS, Fried GM, Barkun AN, et al: Cholecystectomy without operative cholangiography: implications for common bile duct injury and retained common bile duct stones. Ann Surg 218:371, 1993

Bass EB, Pitt HA, Lillemoe KD: Cost-effectiveness of laparoscopic cholecystectomy versus open cholecystectomy. Am J Surg 165:466, 1993

Bernard HR, Hartman TW: Complications after laparoscopic cholecystectomy. Am J Surg 165:533, 1993

Branum G, Schmitt C, Baillie J, et al: Management of major biliary complications after laparoscopic cholecystectomy. Ann Surg 217:532, 1993

Clair DG, Brooks DC: Laparoscopic cholangiography: the case for a selective approach. Surg Clin North Am 74:961, 1994

Cotton PB: Endoscopic retrograde cholangiopancreatography and laparoscopic cholecystectomy. Am J Surg 165:474, 1993

Crist DW, Gadacz TR: Laparoscopic anatomy of the biliary tree. Surg Clin North Am 73:785, 1993

Cuschieri A, Lezoche E, Morino M, et al: E.A.E.S. multicenter prospective randomised trial comparing two-stage vs single-stage management of patients with gallstone disease and ductal calculi. Surg Endosc 13:952, 1999

Deziel DJ: Complications of cholecystectomy: incidence, clinical manifestations, and diagnosis. Surg Clin North Am 74:809, 1994

Deziel DJ, Millikan KW, Economou SG, et al: Complications of laparoscopic cholecystectomy: a national survey of 4,292 hospitals and an analysis of 77,604 cases. Am J Surg 165:9, 1993

Freeman ML, Nelson DB, Sherman S, et al: Complications of endoscopic biliary sphincterotomy. N Engl J Med 335:909, 1996

Halpin VJ, Dunnegan D, Soper NJ: Laproscopic intracorporeal ultrasound vs fluoroscopic intraoperative cholangiography. Surg Endosc 16:336, 2002

Hunter JG, Trus T: Laparoscopic cholecystectomy, intraoperative cholangiography, and common bile duct exploration. Mastery of Surgery, 3rd ed. Nyhus LM, Baker RJ, Fischer JE, Eds. Little, Brown & Co, New York, 1997

Kane RL, Lurie N, Borbas C, et al: The outcomes of elective laparoscopic and open cholecystectomies. J Am Coll Surg 180:136, 1995

Korman J, Cosgrove J, Furman M, et al: The role of endoscopic retrograde cholangiopancreatography and cholangiography in the laparoscopic era. Ann Surg 223:212, 1996

Liberman MA, Phillips EH, Carroll BJ, et al: Cost-effective management of complicated choledocholithiasis: laparoscopic transcystic duct exploration or endoscopic sphincterotomy. J Am Coll Surg 182:488, 1996

MacFadyen BV, Vecchio R, Ricardo AE, et al: Bile duct injury after laparoscopic cholecystectomy: the United States experience. Surg Endosc 12:315, 1998

McGahan JP, Stein M: Complications of laparoscopic cholecystectomy: imaging and intervention. AJR Am J Roentgenol 165:1089, 1995

Menack MJ, Arregui ME: Laparoscopic sonography of the biliary tree and pancreas. Surg Clin North Am 80:1151, 2000

Millitz K, Moote DJ, Sparrow RK, et al: Pneumoperitoneum after laparoscopic cholecystectomy: frequency and duration as seen on upright chest radiographs. AJR Am J Roentgenol 163:837, 1994

National Institutes of Health Consensus Development Conference Statement on Gallstones and Laparoscopic Cholecystectomy. Am J Surg 165:390, 1993

Olsen D: Bile duct injuries during laparoscopic cholecystectomy. Surg Endosc 11:133, 1997

Phillips EH, Carroll BJ, Pearlstein AR, et al: Laparoscopic choledochoscopy and extraction of common bile duct stones. World J Surg 17:22, 1993

Ress AM, Sarr MG, Nagorney DM, et al: Spectrum and management of major complications of laparoscopic cholecystectomy. Am J Surg 165:655, 1993

Ros A, Gustafsson L, Krook H, et al: Laparoscopic cholecystectomy versus mini-laparotomy cholecystectomy: a prospective, randomized, single-blind study. Ann Surg 234:741, 2001

Schrenk P, Woisetschlager R, Wayand WU: Laparoscopic cholecystectomy: cause of conversions in 1300 patients and analysis of risk factors. Surg Endosc 9:25, 1995

Society of American Gastrointestinal Endoscopic Surgeons: Guidelines for the clinical application of laparoscopic biliary tract surgery. Surg Endosc 8:1457, 1994

Soper NJ, Flye MW, Brunt LM, et al: Diagnosis and management of biliary complications of laparoscopic cholecystectomy. Am J Surg 165:663, 1993

Strasberg SM, Hertl M, Soper NJ: An analysis of the problem of biliary injury during laparoscopic cholecystectomy. J Am Coll Surg 180:101, 1995

Traverso LW, Hargrave K: A prospective cost analysis of laparoscopic cholecystectomy. Am J Surg 169:503, 1995

Wherry DC, Rob CG, Marohn MR, et al: An external audit of laparoscopic cholecystectomy performed in medical treatment facilities of the Department of Defense. Ann Surg 220:626, 1994

Woods MS, Traverso LW, Kozarek RA, et al: Characteristics of biliary tract complications during laparoscopic cholecystectomy: a multi-institutional study. Am J Surg 167:27, 1994

Zucker KA, Josloff RK: Transcystic common bile duct exploration. Operative Laparoscopy and Thoracoscopy. MacFadyen BV, Ponsky JL, Eds. Lippincott-Raven Publishers, Philadelphia, 1996

Acknowledgments

Figures 2, 5   Tom Moore.

Figure 18   Courtesy of Nathaniel J. Soper, M.D., Northwestern University Feinberg School of Medicine, Chicago.

Figures 21 through 25   Alice Y. Chen.

64 PROCEDURES FOR BENIGN AND MALIGNANT BILIARY TRACT DISEASE

Bryce R. Taylor, M.D., F.A.C.S., F.R.C.S.C., and Bernard Langer, M.D., F.A.C.S., F.R.C.S.C.

Over the past few decades, remarkable advances in imaging technology have been made that allow more accurate diagnosis of biliary tract diseases and better planning of surgical procedures and other interventions aimed at managing these conditions. Operative techniques have also improved as a result of a better understanding of biliary and hepatic anatomy and physiology. Moreover, the continuing evolution of minimally invasive surgery has promoted the gradual adoption of laparoscopic approaches to these complex operations. Accordingly, biliary tract surgery, like many other areas of modern surgery, is constantly changing.

In what follows, we describe common operations performed to treat diseases of the biliary tract, emphasizing details of operative planning and intraoperative technique and suggesting specific strategies for preventing common problems. It should be remembered that complex biliary tract procedures, whether open or laparoscopic, are best done in specialized units where surgeons, anesthetists, intensivists, and nursing staff all are accustomed to handling the special problems and requirements of patients undergoing such procedures.

Preoperative Evaluation

IMAGING STUDIES

It is essential to define the pathologic anatomy accurately before embarking on any operation on the biliary tract. Extensive familiarity with the numerous variations of ductal and vascular anatomy in this region is crucial. High-quality ultrasonography and computed tomography are noninvasive and usually provide excellent information regarding mass lesions, the presence or absence of ductal dilatation, the extent and level of duct obstruction, and the extent of vessel involvement. Cholangiography—percutaneous transhepatic cholangiography (PTC), endoscopic retrograde cholangiopancreatography (ERCP), or magnetic resonance cholangiopancreatography (MRCP) [*see 45 Jaundice*]—can supply more detailed information about ductal anatomy and is used when CT and ultrasonography yield insufficient information. Angiography is rarely required to determine resectability. Magnetic resonance imaging and MRCP, which are noninvasive, are preferred where available. As newer MRCP technology becomes available, further improvements in definition of biliary anatomy appear to be obtainable. It may eventually prove possible to avoid the complications associated with ERCP (a more invasive alternative) entirely, at least for diagnostic indications.

MANAGEMENT OF BILIARY OBSTRUCTION

Although jaundice by itself does not increase operative risk, biliary obstruction has secondary effects that may increase operative mortality and the incidence of complications. There is little evidence to support the practice of routine preoperative biliary drainage in all jaundiced patients, but there are some elective situations in which preoperative drainage is required.

Infection

Patients with clinical cholangitis, whether spontaneous or in-duced by duct intubation (via PTC or ERCP), should be treated with biliary drainage and appropriate antibiotics until they are infection free; the recommended duration of treatment is at least 3 weeks. In addition, perioperative antibiotic prophylaxis with cefazolin or another agent with a comparable spectrum of activity should be employed routinely before any intervention or operation involving the biliary tract. For certain patients with biliary tract infection (e.g., associated with choledocholithiasis), urgent surgical decompression may be necessary, especially if antibiotics and endoscopic or transhepatic drainage are not immediately effective. If the patient was referred with a stent already in place (a frequent occurrence in our practice), broad-spectrum antibiotics should be given preoperatively to cover the anaerobes inevitably present.

Renal Dysfunction

The combination of a high bilirubin level and hypovolemia is a significant risk factor for acute renal failure, which can occur in the presence of a number of additional factors, such as acute infection, hypotension, and the infusion of contrast material. Patients with biliary obstruction should therefore be well hydrated before receiving I.V. contrast agents or undergoing operative procedures. In patients with acute renal dysfunction secondary to biliary obstruction, decompression of the bile duct until renal function returns to normal is advisable before any major elective procedure for malignant disease.

Impaired Immunologic Function or Malnutrition

Patients with long-standing biliary obstruction have impaired immune function and may become malnourished. Decompression of the bile duct until immune function and nutritional status are restored to normal is indicated before any major elective procedure is undertaken; this may take as long as 4 to 6 weeks.

Coagulation Dysfunction

Prolonged bile duct obstruction may lead to significant deficits in clotting factors. These deficits should be corrected with fresh frozen plasma and vitamin K before an operative procedure is begun. Even if there is no measurable coagulation dysfunction, vitamin K should be given to all patients with obstructive jaundice at least 24 hours before operation to replenish their depleted vitamin K stores.

Projected Major Liver Resection

If resection of an obstructing bile duct tumor is likely to necessitate major liver resection (e.g., a right trisectionectomy), it may be advisable to decompress the liver segments that are to be retained for approximately 4 to 6 weeks; a "normalized" area of the liver presumably regenerates more quickly than an obstructed one.

Operative Planning

PATIENT POSITIONING

The patient is placed in the supine position on an operating table that can be rotated and elevated. An x-ray cassette and machine should be available during major resections. Slight elevation of the right portion of the chest with an I.V. bag facilitates exposure of the liver and the biliary structures. A choledochoscope and equipment for intraoperative ultrasonography should also be available. Access to a pathology department that can perform cytologic or frozen-section examination of tissue is essential in operations intended as treatment of malignant disease.

GENERAL TECHNICAL CONSIDERATIONS

Exposure of Subhepatic Field in Open Procedures

A right subcostal incision provides excellent exposure for most open procedures on the gallbladder and biliary tract. For more extensive resections or reconstructions, the right subcostal incision can be extended laterally below the costal margin and across the midline to the left as a chevron incision. In patients with very narrow costal margins, a vertical midline incision may be more suitable for limited operations on the gallbladder and biliary tract, and a combination of a unilateral or bilateral subcostal incision and a midline vertical extension to the xiphoid may be required for more extensive operations. In any case, the incision must be long enough to allow sufficient visualization for safe performance of the procedure.

Adequate exposure and lighting are essential. The best retractors are those that can be fixed to the table while remaining flexible in terms of placement and angles of retraction. Modern high-intensity lights with focusing capabilities and headlamps are especially useful when the surgeon wears magnifying glasses.

Good access to the hepatoduodenal ligament and the structures in the porta hepatis is critical. In patients who have never undergone an abdominal procedure, identification of these structures is straightforward. In patients who have undergone previous operations or have a local inflammatory process, however, there may be considerable obliteration of planes. If this is the case, the following techniques may be useful in defining the anatomy.

1. *Using the falciform ligament as a landmark.* In reoperative surgery, the key to opening up the upper abdomen is the falciform ligament. This structure should be found immediately after the opening of the abdominal wall and retracted superiorly. The omentum, the colon, and the stomach are then dissected inferiorly, and a plane that leads to the hepatoduodenal ligament and the porta hepatis is thereby opened.
2. *Taking the right posterolateral approach.* When the colon and the duodenum are adherent to the undersurface of the right hemiliver, separation may be difficult. In most patients, an open space remains that can be approached by sliding the left hand posteriorly to the right of these adhesions and into the (usually open) subhepatic space in front of the kidney and behind the adhesions. Anterior retraction allows identification of the adherent structures by palpation and permits dissection of the adhesions in a lateral-to-medial direction. The undersurface of the liver is thus cleared, and the hepatoduodenal ligament can be approached.
3. *Taking the lesser sac approach.* Ordinarily, the foramen of Winslow is open, and the left index finger can be passed through it from the right subhepatic space. When the foramen of Winslow is obliterated, however, one should approach it from the left, dividing the lesser omentum and passing an index finger from the lesser sac behind the hepatoduodenal ligament to reopen the foramen of Winslow by blunt dissection.
4. *Using the round ligament to find the true porta hepatis.* Patients

who have already undergone one or more operations on the bile duct often have adhesions between the hepatoduodenal ligament and segment 4 of the liver. If one dissects this area via the anterior approach, one may think that the actual porta hepatis has been reached but notice that the hepatoduodenal ligament looks unusually short. In most cases, one can find the true porta more easily by tracing the round ligament to the point where it joins the left portal pedicle (including the ascending branch of the left portal vein) and then following that to the right along the true porta. The adhesions between the hepatoduodenal ligament and segment 4 can then be more easily divided from the left than from the front.

5. *Using aids to dissection.* Usually, structures in the hepatoduodenal ligament can be identified by inspection and palpation, especially if there is a biliary stent in place. In cases in which such identification is not easily accomplished, an intraoperative Doppler flow detector may be useful in identifying the hepatic artery and the portal vein, intraoperative ultrasonography may be helpful in identifying the bile duct (as well as vessels), and needle aspiration may also be used before the duct is incised if there is any doubt about its location. Either blunt or sharp dissection is effective in this area. Our preference is to use a long right-angle clamp (Mixter) to obtain exposure in a layer-by-layer fashion; we then electrocoagulate or ligate and divide the exposed tissue.

Guidelines for Biliary Anastomosis

As a rule, biliary anastomoses, whether of duct to bowel or of duct to duct, heal very well provided that the principles of preservation of adequate blood supply, avoidance of tension, and accurate placement of sutures are followed. In preparing the bile duct for anastomosis, it is essential to define adequate margins while avoiding excessive dissection that might compromise the blood supply to the duct. In repairs that follow acute injuries, it is important to resect crushed or devascularized tissue; however, in late repairs, it is not necessary to resect all scar tissue as long as an adequate opening can be made in the proximal obstructed duct through normal healthy tissue and as long as mucosa, rather than granulation tissue, is present at the duct margin. The length of the corresponding opening in the jejunal loop should be significantly smaller than the bile duct opening because the bowel opening tends to enlarge during the procedure.

Mucosa-to-mucosa apposition is essential for good healing and the prevention of late stricture. Sutures should be of a monofilament synthetic material (preferably absorbable) and should be as fine as is practical (e.g., 5-0 for a normal duct and 4-0 for a thickened duct). Because the bile duct wall has only one layer, biliary anastomoses should all be single layer. Sutures should pass through all layers of the bowel, taking sizable bites of the seromuscular layer and much smaller bites of the mucosa, and should take moderate-sized (1 to 3 mm, depending on duct diameter) bites in the bile duct. Interrupted sutures are used when access is difficult or the duct is small; continuous sutures, when access is easy and the duct is larger. Sutures should be securely placed but should not be so tight as to injure the tissues. It is sometimes wise to vary the spacing of the stitches: placing many stitches close together may cause ischemia of the suture line in a postage-stamp pattern. Magnification with loupes is particularly useful in anastomosing small ducts during open procedures. Stents are not routinely required for biliary anastomoses, and drainage of the operative field is seldom necessary.

There are several principles of suture placement that can be applied to most biliary anastomoses, whether end to side or side to

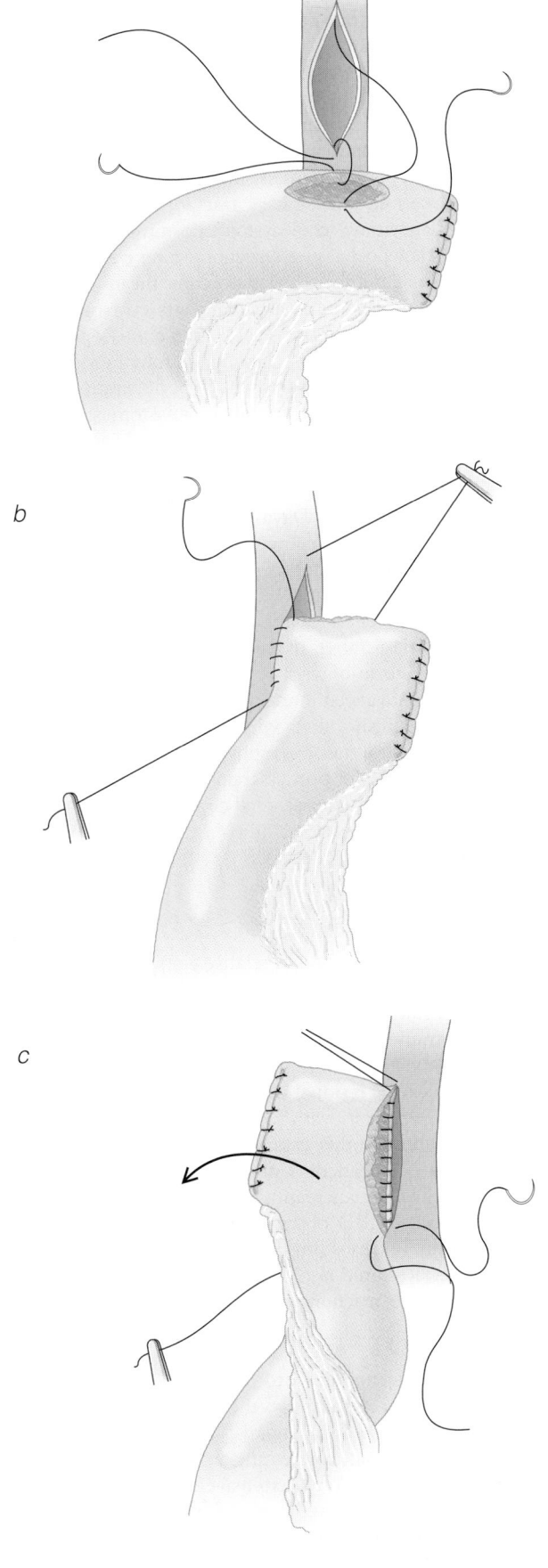

a

b

c

side. When the bile duct opening has a vertical configuration (as in side-to-side choledochoduodenostomy or choledochojejunostomy), stay sutures are placed inferiorly and superiorly in the duct and at corresponding points in the intestine. Traction is placed on these sutures to line up the adjacent walls. One side of the anastomosis is done first; the bowel is then rotated 180°, and the other side is completed [*see Figure 1*]. This maneuver may be facilitated by retracting the first interrupted posterior stitch to the opposite side to serve as a pivotal stitch. It is advisable to sew about two thirds of the first wall and two thirds of the second, leaving the anterior third of the circumference (the easiest part) to be closed last. This technique can also be used for end-to-side choledochojejunostomy and allows all the knots to be tied outside the lumen. When the bile duct opening lies transversely, as in bifurcation reconstruction, lateral stay sutures are placed first, and the posterior wall stitches are placed from inside the lumen. If interrupted sutures are used, they are all placed individually before any of them are tied, with the untied tails carefully arranged in order. When the posterior wall sutures have been tied, the anterior wall can then be sutured with either continuous or interrupted sutures [*see Figure 2*].

When the intended anastomosis is intrahepatic and access is particularly difficult because of some combination of an unfavorable position, a previous scar, or, perhaps, a stiff liver that is difficult to retract, another technique may be useful. All of the anterior wall stitches are placed into the duct, grouped together on a single retracting forceps with the needles left attached, and retracted superiorly to promote better exposure of the posterior duct wall [*see Figure 2c*]. The posterior stitches are placed into the duct and the bowel as described, tied in order, and cut; the anterior wall stitches are then completed by being placed into the bowel and tied.

When the duct is small, there are three techniques that may be useful for increasing the size of the lumen.

1. An anterior longitudinal incision can be made in a small common bile duct (CBD), and the sharp corners can be trimmed to enlarge the opening [*see Figure 3a*].
2. If the cystic duct is present alongside a divided CBD, an incision can be made in the shared wall to create a single larger lumen [*see Figure 3b*].
3. If the bifurcation has been resected, two small ducts can be brought together and sutures placed into their adjoining walls to form a single larger lumen [*see Figure 3c*].

Construction of Roux Loop

When the jejunum is used for long-term biliary drainage, a Roux loop is used to prevent reflux of small bowel content into the biliary system. In the creation of the loop, it is important to select a segment of jejunum with a well-defined vascular arcade that will be long enough to support a tension-free anastomosis. If access to the biliary system will be required in the future (e.g., in an operation for recurrent intrahepatic stones), the loop should be long enough to allow one to place a tube jejunostomy, fixing the loop to the abdominal wall with nonabsorbable sutures. The site of attachment should be marked with metallic clips to facilitate future percuta-

Figure 1 **Technical issues in biliary anastomosis. Shown is a side-to-side choledochojejunostomy using a vertical incision in the bile duct. The same technique can be used for choledochoduodenostomy or end-to-side choledochojejunostomy. (*a*) Inferior and superior corner continuous sutures are placed. (*b*) One side of the anastomosis is sewn first (here, the right side). (*c*) The bowel is rotated 180° so that the other side is exposed. The other side of the anastomosis is then sewn (here, the left side).**

neous puncture and cannulation and removal of recurrent or persistent stones. The tube can be removed after postoperative imaging studies confirm that the biliary tree is free of stones.

Principles of Laparoscopic Biliary Tract Procedures

The surgical principles that lead to successful outcomes are much the same for laparoscopic biliary tract procedures as for their open counterparts. An anastomosis that is done under excellent exposure

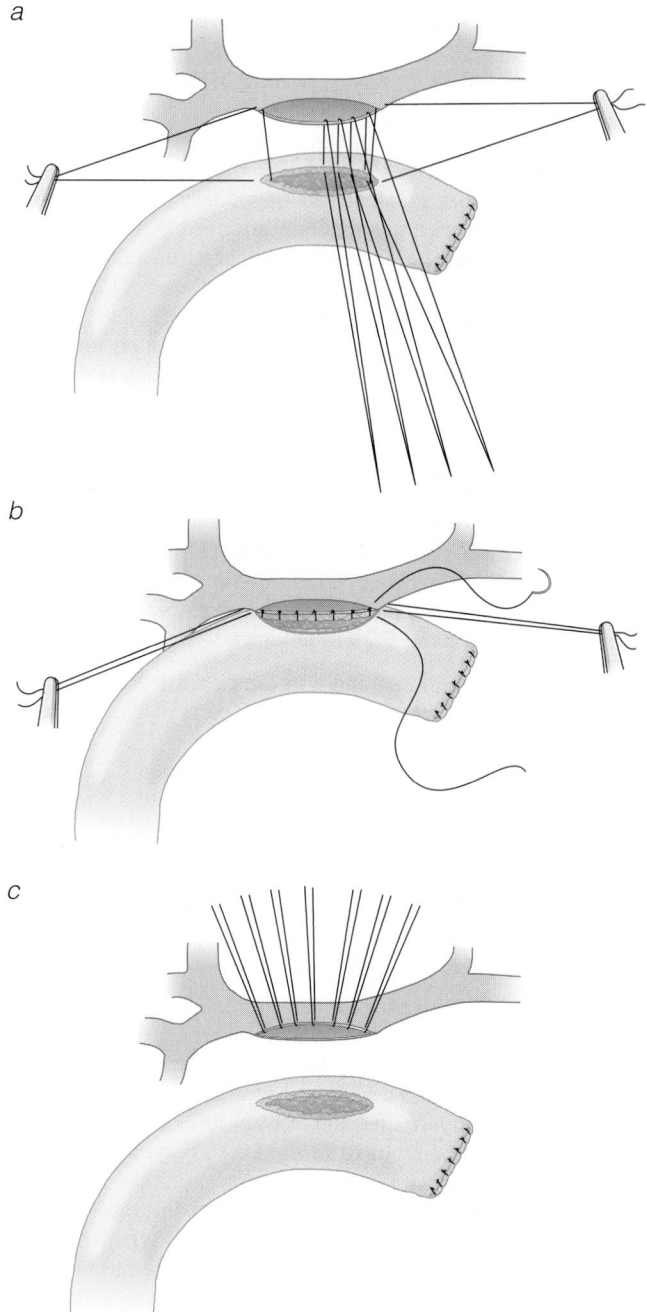

a

b

c

Figure 2 **Technical issues in biliary anastomosis. Shown is an end-to-side choledochojejunostomy using a transverse opening in the bile duct. This technique can be used at any level. (*a*) Corner sutures and posterior wall sutures are all placed before being tied. (*b*) The posterior wall is completed, and the anterior wall is sewn. (*c*) In difficult cases, the anterior wall sutures may be placed first, then retracted superiorly.**

and lighting, that is fashioned with meticulously placed sutures, and that is completed without tension usually heals without complications and remains patent, regardless of the approach followed. However, because stricturing can occur many years after operation, biliary tract anastomoses must be followed for relatively long periods before success can be claimed. Accordingly, the long-term results of biliary-enteric anastomoses remain to be established.

As a rule, laparoscopic biliary procedures should be performed by surgeons with substantial expertise and experience in both hepatobiliary surgery and minimally invasive surgery.

Most of the conventional biliary tract operations—including choledochoduodenostomy, cholecystojejunostomy, choledochojejunostomy, and choledochal cyst resection—have been successfully performed in small numbers by laparoscopic means. The laparoscopic approach may become a particularly attractive option in the palliative setting if it proves more reliable than endoscopic stenting or percutaneous transhepatic cholangiography and drainage (PTCD) with respect to safety and speed of postoperative recovery.

The laparoscopic approach to biliary anastomosis[1] involves placement of four or five ports in a fan pattern and usually is associated with a longer operating time than the open approach. Liver retraction is achieved with an articulated retractor (e.g., Endoflex; New Dynamics in Medicine, Dayton, Ohio), and dissection may be carried out with sharp instruments and an electrocautery, with or without an ultrasonic scalpel (e.g., Harmonic Scalpel; Ethicon Endo-Surgery, Inc., Cincinnati, Ohio).

Magnification may enhance the surgeon's ability to perform these demanding anastomoses in a meticulous fashion, and robotic assistance (in the form of wrist-type end-effectors) may further improve precision. Advanced intracorporeal knot-tying and suturing skills are a prerequisite, along with personal expertise in intraoperative laparoscopic ultrasonography, which is often helpful in assessing the liver and the porta hepatis. During intracorporeal creation of a biliary anastomosis, small clips may be used to organize multiple interrupted sutures, much as hemostats are used in the corresponding open procedures.

Choledochoduodenostomy

Choledochoduodenostomy is a relatively straightforward side-to-side biliary-enteric bypass procedure that is effective in certain restricted circumstances and has the advantage of being simpler and safer than transduodenal sphincteroplasty. It is most commonly used in patients with multiple bile duct stones when there is concern about leaving residual stones at the time of CBD exploration as well as in patients with recurrent bile duct stones when endoscopic papillotomy either cannot be done or has been unsuccessful. It is also used in patients with benign distal biliary obstruction (e.g., from chronic pancreatitis) and occasionally in patients with malignant distal CBD obstruction whose life expectancy is short. Choledochoduodenostomy works best if the CBD is at least 1 cm in diameter; it should not be used in patients with actual or potential duodenal obstruction.

OPERATIVE TECHNIQUE

The duodenum is mobilized to allow approximation to the CBD without tension. Ordinarily, the first part of the duodenum can easily be rolled up against the CBD; however, in patients who have chronic pancreatitis or have previously undergone an abdominal procedure, extensive kocherization may be required. If satisfactory approximation is not achieved with this maneuver, a choledochojejunostomy should be performed.

The CBD is exposed as described elsewhere [*see 63 Cholecys-*

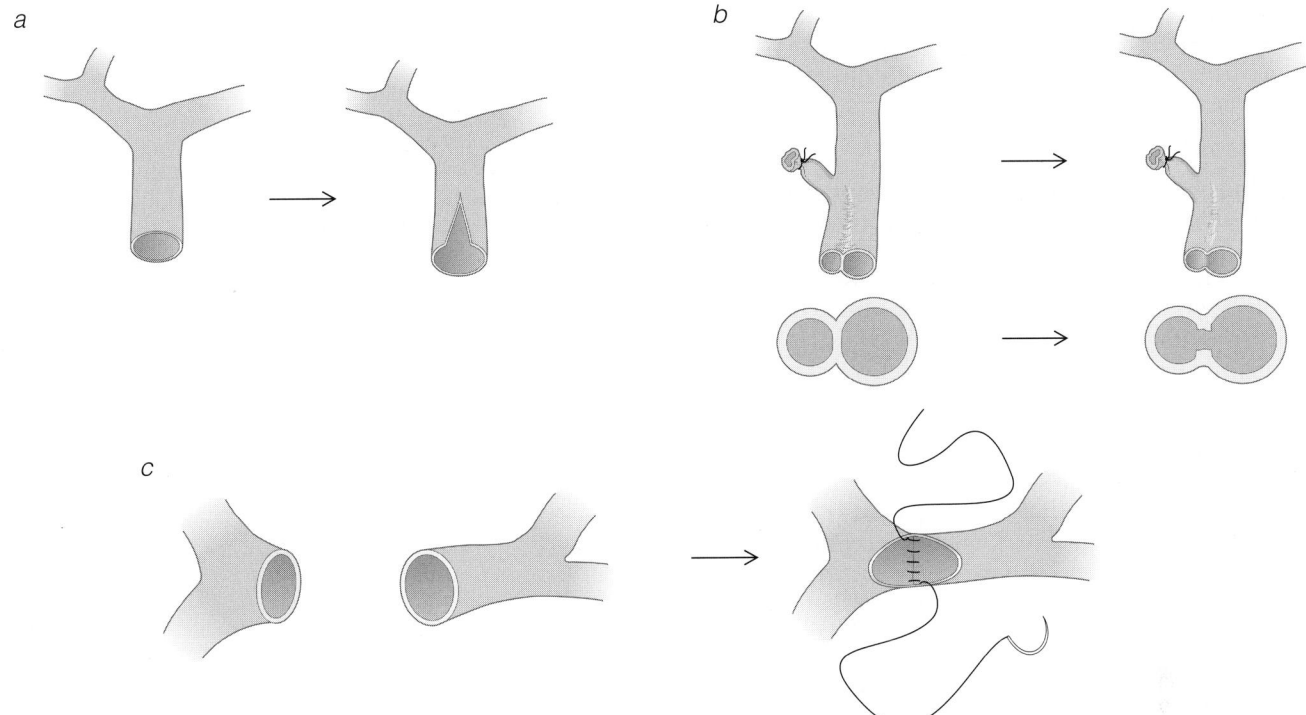

Figure 3 Technical issues in biliary anastomosis. Shown are three methods of enlarging a small duct. (*a*) An anterior longitudinal incision can be made in the duct wall. (*b*) A wall shared by the CBD and the cystic duct can be divided. (*c*) Adjoining walls of two small ducts can be sutured together to make a single opening for anastomosis.

tectomy and Common Bile Duct Exploration]. Longitudinal incisions are made in both the duodenum and the duct [*see Figure 1*], and the anastomosis is carried out as described previously [*see* Operative Planning, General Technical Considerations, Guidelines for Biliary Anastomosis, *above*].

Laparoscopic Considerations

Laparoscopic choledochoduodenostomy,[2] like all minimally invasive surgical procedures, follows the same principles proven in its open procedural counterpart—namely, adequate exposure, sufficient size of the CBD, and meticulous attention to creating a tension-free anastomosis with intracorporeally placed interrupted sutures. The diamond-shaped anastomosis fashioned should be indistinguishable from that fashioned in the corresponding open procedure.

COMPLICATIONS

Late closure or stricture of the anastomosis may occur if the CBD is small or malignant disease is present. Alternative methods of biliary decompression should be considered in these situations.

Cholangitis related to the presence of food in the CBD distal to the anastomosis (so-called sump syndrome) is an uncommon occurrence. The larger the anastomosis, the smaller the likelihood that this complication will occur.

Cholecystojejunostomy

Cholecystojejunostomy may be performed to treat malignant biliary obstruction in selected patients whose lesions are found to be unresectable at operation and whose life expectancy is expected to be short. Occasionally, it is indicated for patients in whom endoscopic or percutaneous stenting has been unsuccessful. This operation is not the preferred procedure for long-term decompression.

OPERATIVE TECHNIQUE

Step 1: Verification of Feasibility of Procedure

The cystic duct must be patent. Its junction with the CBD must be at least 1 cm above the tumor obstruction [*see Figure 4*]. The suitability of the anatomy for cholecystojejunostomy may have been verified by preoperative cholangiography; if not, intraoperative cholangiography via the gallbladder or the CBD is mandatory. If one still cannot be certain that the operation is feasible, the CBD should be opened and a choledochoenterostomy performed. The finding of a bile-filled gallbladder is not sufficient evidence that the patient is a suitable candidate for a cholecystojejunostomy. The gallbladder should be normal: there should be no evidence of cholecystitis or stones. Normal status is verified by inspection, palpation (in the open setting), and, if necessary, needle cholecystography. Finally, for the anastomosis to be feasible, one should be able to approximate the jejunum to the gallbladder easily.

Step 2: Preparation for Anastomosis

A site near the fundus is selected for the anastomosis, and an appropriate segment of proximal jejunum is anchored to the gallbladder with two fine stay sutures in anticipation of a transverse incision in the gallbladder and a longitudinal incision in the antimesenteric border of the bowel.

Step 3: Anastomosis

A 2 cm opening is made in the gallbladder and the adjacent segment of the jejunum, and a single-layer anastomosis is constructed with a continuous monofilament absorbable suture or a stapler.

Step 4: Optional Additional Procedures

A Roux loop, rather than a simple jejunal loop, may be used in the construction of the choledochojejunostomy, and a gastrojejunostomy [*see 62 Procedures for Benign and Malignant Gastric and Duodenal Disease*] may be added in patients with pancreatic head cancer in whom duodenal obstruction is either present or anticipated in the near future.

COMPLICATIONS

Bile leakage may occur if there is excessive tension on the anastomosis. In addition, jaundice may persist if there is unrecognized cystic duct obstruction resulting from inflammation or an unnoticed stone in the cystic duct or the gallbladder. Recurrent jaundice is usually the result of extension from an obstructing tumor that has involved the cystic duct–CBD junction.

Choledochojejunostomy

Choledochojejunostomy, one of the most commonly performed biliary tract procedures, is done to provide biliary drainage after CBD resection, repair of ductal injury, or relief of obstruction caused by a benign or malignant stricture. To reduce the likelihood of reflux of intestinal contents into the biliary tract, a Roux-en-Y jejunal loop is usually used for the anastomosis [*see* Operative Planning, General Technical Considerations, Construction of Roux Loop, *above*]. If long-term access to the biliary tract is required (e.g., in patients with recurrent intrahepatic strictures or stones), the Roux limb may be anchored to the abdominal wall rather than left free in the abdominal cavity.

When the operation is performed after CBD resection, an end-to-side choledochojejunostomy using the proximal transected duct is made. When the operation is performed for bile duct obstruction resulting from tumor or stricture and no resection has been performed, a side-to-side anastomosis is constructed. If a stent has already been placed endoscopically or percutaneously, the bile duct is often thickened.

OPERATIVE TECHNIQUE

Step 1: Preparation for Anastomosis

Preparation for an end-to-side anastomosis includes resection of any crushed or devitalized bile duct tissue. The CBD should be trimmed back to healthy, viable, bleeding duct wall. If the lumen of the duct is small, a short incision on the anterior wall will effectively increase its circumference to facilitate the anastomosis [*see Figure 3a*]. If the CBD has been transected at the level of the cystic duct, the lumina of the CBD and the cystic duct may be combined by incising and oversewing their common wall [*see Figure 3b*].

If a side-to-side anastomosis is being performed for stricture or tumor, the proximal duct is almost always dilated and has thicker walls, and thus a vertical incision is made on the anterior surface. When the procedure is being done for malignant disease, the incision should be made as high as possible above the malignancy to delay the eventual obstruction of the anastomosis by tumor growth.

Step 2: Anastomosis

When the duct is large, a secure, tension-free anastomosis can be constructed by means of the techniques previously illustrated [*see Figures 1 and 2*]. When the duct is small, extra effort must be made to place sutures carefully so as to prevent narrowing of the lumen. The laparoscopic variant of the procedure, like all laparoscopic biliary tract procedures, demands similar attention to detail.[1,3]

TROUBLESHOOTING

It is essential to preserve the blood supply to the CBD. Adequate debridement of injured ducts is mandatory, even if this

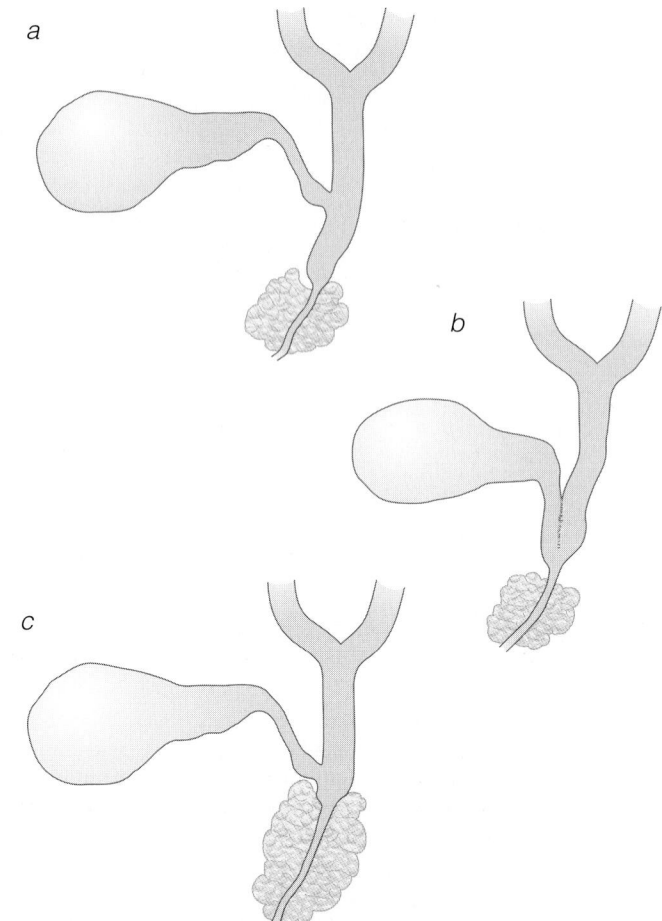

Figure 4 **Cholecystojejunostomy. Cholangiography is essential for determining whether the anatomy is suitable (*a*) or unsuitable (*b*, *c*) for the procedure.**

means extending the resection of the duct to the bifurcation. Longitudinal incisions should not be made in the medial or lateral portions of the CBD, where the major longitudinal blood supply is found. Finally, extensive mobilization of the duct from the surrounding tissues should be avoided so as to preserve the ductal blood supply.

Meticulous surgical technique is critical for ensuring good healing and preventing stricture. The finest suture material that will do the job should be employed, and magnifying devices should be used to facilitate the accurate placement of sutures. In very small ducts, the temporary placement of a small T tube at the anastomosis will allow most of the circumference to be completed without the risk of either picking up the opposite wall or placing sutures incorrectly. The T tube is then removed and the anastomosis completed. Routine postoperative stenting is unnecessary, but stents may be helpful in those rare cases in which mucosal apposition cannot be accomplished. In these situations, sutures may have to be placed in surrounding liver or scar tissue in much the same way as in a Kasai procedure. In difficult cases of proximal stricture, the surgeon may incise the liver plate and seek out viable duct above the bifurcation.

COMPLICATIONS

The main complications of choledochojejunostomy are bile leakage, late stricture, and recurrent jaundice as a result of tumor extension [see Cholecystojejunostomy *and* Choledochoduodenostomy, *above*].

Transduodenal Sphincteroplasty

Transduodenal sphincteroplasty is occasionally indicated when an impacted stone at the ampulla of Vater cannot be removed via a choledochotomy. It is also sometimes useful for clarifying the nature of an obstructive process at the ampulla, definitively treating ampullary stenosis, and gaining access to the main pancreatic duct if ERCP has been unsuccessful. Pancreatic sphincteroplasty may be added in selected cases.

Endoscopic techniques are usually successful for these purposes. A frequent use of the transduodenal approach is for local resection of a benign ampullary tumor (e.g., a villous adenoma) with reconstruction of the medial duodenal wall.

OPERATIVE TECHNIQUE

Step 1: Exposure of Ampulla

Mobilization of the duodenum and the pancreatic head is necessary for obtaining exposure of the lateral portion of the second part of the duodenum. The ampulla is located by palpation, which may be facilitated by passage of a sound down the CBD, out the ampulla, and into the duodenum. A longitudinal incision is made on the lateral surface of the duodenum; it should be at least 3 cm long to ensure good exposure. The duodenal edges are retracted gently. Crushing forceps should not be used; they may cause hematomas.

Step 2: Cannulation

If the bile duct has been opened, cannulation of the CBD is done from above. A metal sound may be used, but we generally prefer to insert a fine catheter and pass it through the ampulla, which can then be gently elevated into the field [see Figure 5]. This step facilitates accurate placement of an incision in the ampulla. If the duct has not been opened, cannulation is accomplished from below with a sound. Use of a grooved director may simplify the sphincterotomy.

Step 3: Sphincteroplasty

To prevent injury to the pancreatic duct, the incision in the ampulla is placed at the 11 o'clock position with either scissors or a scalpel rather than with the electrocautery. A so-called cut-and-sew approach, using interrupted 5-0 monofilament absorbable sutures placed 2 mm apart, is followed. The incision is started at the papillary orifice and extended above the ampullary sphincter along the line of the previously inserted catheter. The sutures should include both the bile duct and the duodenal wall. Once the sutures have been placed, lateral traction is applied to provide exposure of the bile duct lumen and to make each subsequent step in the cut-and-sew procedure easier. The pancreatic duct opening (usually found at the 4 o'clock position) must be identified and protected from being incorporated in the sutures.

Step 3 (Alternative): Ampullectomy

As noted, the transduodenal approach is often employed for local excision of a benign (or, sometimes, a malignant) ampullary tumor.[4] Ampullectomy is described in greater detail elsewhere [see 62 Procedures for Benign and Malignant Gastric and Duodenal Disease].

Step 4: Exploration of CBD

Exploration of the CBD should be completed from below with sounds and choledochoscopy to ensure that all stones are removed. If the presence of a tumor is suspected, biopsies of any suspicious areas should be performed.

Step 5: Closure and Postoperative Care

The duodenum is then closed in the direction in which the incision was made. This can be done in either one or two layers, provided that care is taken to prevent inversion and preserve the luminal diameter. Routine drainage is not necessary unless there is concern about the duodenotomy closure or the choledochotomy

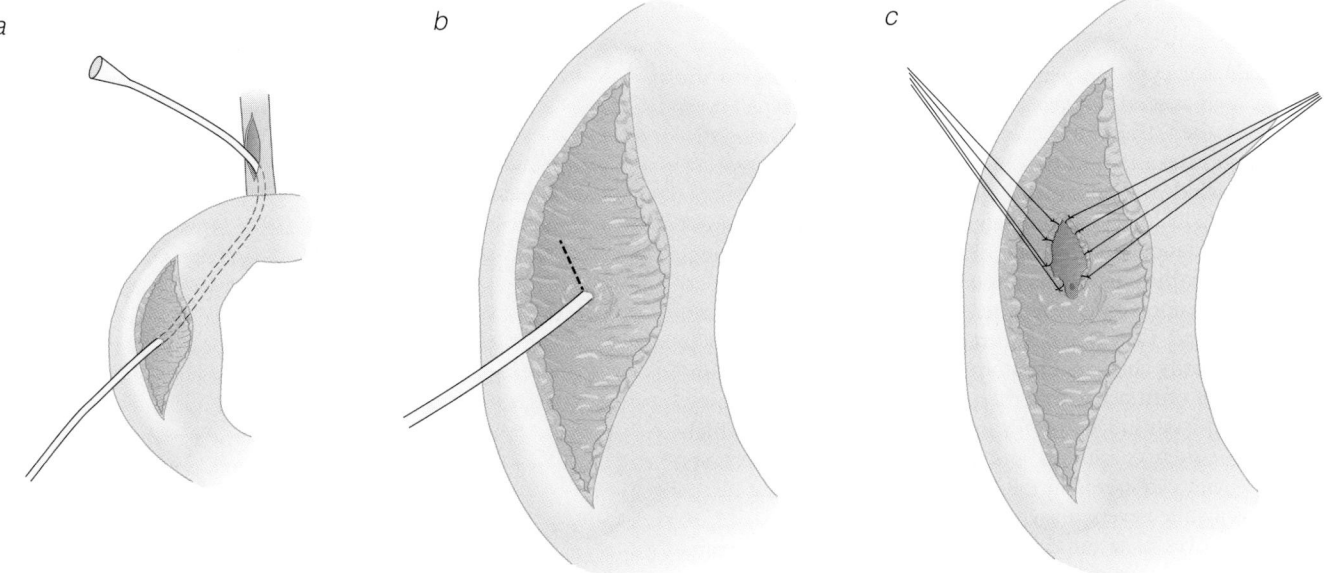

Figure 5 **Transduodenal sphincteroplasty. (*a*) A longitudinal incision is made in the duodenum, and a filiform catheter and a follower are used to find and elevate the ampulla. (*b*) An incision is made at the 11 o'clock position with scissors or a scalpel. (*c*) Interrupted sutures are placed through the bile duct wall and the duodenal wall. Lateral traction is applied.**

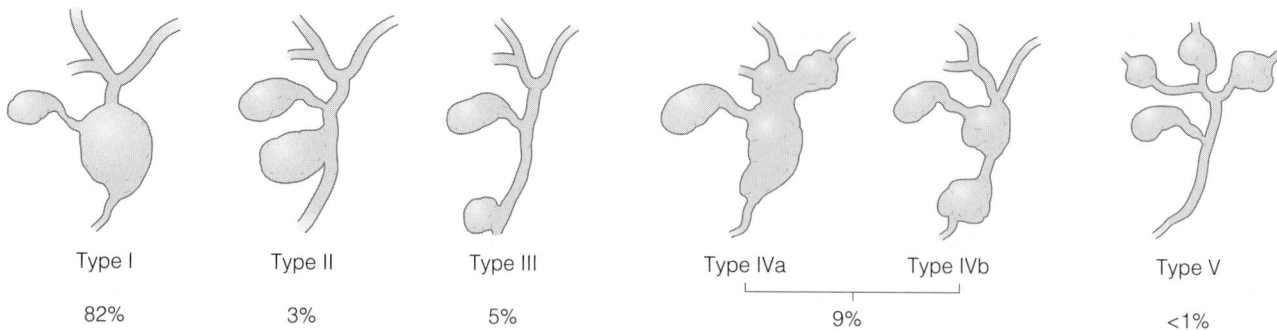

Type I   Type II   Type III   Type IVa   Type IVb   Type V

82%   3%   5%   9%   <1%

Figure 6   **Choledochal cyst resection. Illustrated is the Todani classification of choledochal cysts.**

closure. If a T tube has been left in place, a cholangiogram should be obtained before it is removed.

TROUBLESHOOTING

There may be an impacted stone at the distal end of the CBD that prevents cannulation from either above or below. Such a stone can usually be felt through the duodenal wall, in which case a vertical incision can be made in the medial duodenal wall directly onto the stone. Once the stone has been extracted, the incision can be extended down through the ampulla with a sound used as a guide.

Occasionally (e.g., in some patients with chronic pancreatitis), a long stricture of the CBD may extend above the ampulla. In such cases, the sphincteroplasty may have to be extended proximally to the point where it communicates with the retroperitoneal space. This will not be a problem as long as the duodenum-to-CBD repair is carefully executed. If the obstruction cannot be managed with an extended sphincteroplasty, a different decompressive procedure, such as choledochojejunostomy or choledochoduodenostomy, must be chosen.

Postoperative pancreatitis may develop if there was excessive manipulation of the ampulla, if the electrocautery was used at the ampulla, or if the pancreatic duct orifice is occluded by one of the sphincteroplasty sutures.

Choledochal Cyst Resection

Choledochal cysts are generally categorized according to the Todani classification [*see Figure 6*]. More than 80% are type I cysts that involve the CBD in its accessible portion. The following discussion addresses the resection of type I cysts and those type IV cysts that include the proximal right or left hepatic ducts.

Most choledochal cysts are related to an abnormal junction of the pancreatic duct and the distal CBD. Preoperative cholangiography to clarify the anatomy is important for preventing injury to the pancreatic duct, especially when an intrapancreatic resection may be required. Occasionally, intraoperative cholangiography is required to clarify abnormal anatomy. Patients may be symptomatic as a result of stones within the cyst, infection, or malignancy, any of which is an indication for operation. Because of the high incidence of such conditions and the extremely high mortality associated with carcinoma in this setting, prophylactic cyst resection seems justified even in asymptomatic patients.

The objectives of treatment are (1) to remove the cyst completely, along with the gallbladder and any stones that remain in the bile ducts proximal to the cyst, and (2) to achieve free biliary drainage. Resection of a choledochal cyst may be made more difficult by several factors, such as previous operations, recurrent bouts of infection and inflammation in the cyst, and portal hyper-

tension, which may develop as a result of long-standing cholangitis or portal vein thrombosis.

OPERATIVE TECHNIQUE

Resection of a choledochal cyst may be difficult and bloody, especially if inflammation is present. In addition, dissection of a choledochal cyst in its intrapancreatic portion may be hazardous because of the vascularity of this region and the difficulty of identifying anatomic structures.

Step 1: Clarification of Anatomy

The proximal and distal extent of the cyst and the presence or absence of stones or tumor may be determined preoperatively, as

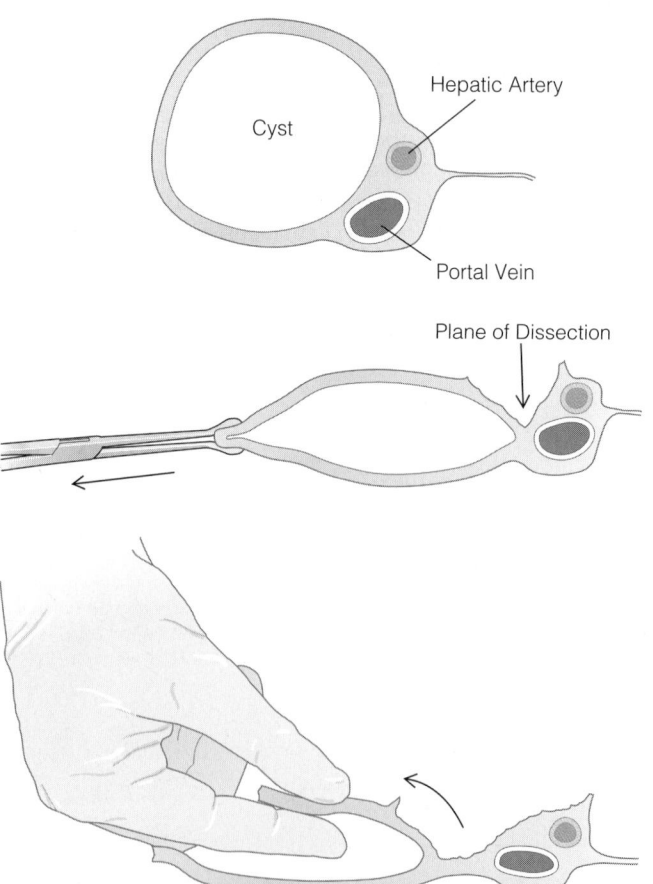

Figure 7   **Choledochal cyst resection. Illustrated is the proper plane of dissection in removal of a choledochal cyst. If necessary, dissection can be done with a finger inside the cyst.**

noted, but in many cases, intraoperative verification of the findings is necessary. Intraoperative cholangiography can be carried out by inserting a catheter through the gallbladder, by directly needling the cyst, or both. If cholangiography does not yield an accurate definition of the anatomy of the cyst, the cyst may then be opened and digital exploration and choledochoscopy used to clarify the anatomy.

Step 2: Initial Dissection

If the gallbladder is still in place, it is dissected free of the liver and left attached to the cyst via the cystic duct, then retracted to the right. If the patient has already undergone a cystoenteric anastomosis, this should be taken down at the beginning of the procedure, and the opening in the bowel should be carefully closed.

Step 3: Mobilization of Cyst

As noted, the vascularity of the region and the presence of inflammation may render dissection difficult. Rather than cleaning off the hepatic artery and the portal vein and dissecting them off the cyst, the surgeon should find a plane immediately adjacent to the wall of the cyst and remain close to it [see Figure 7]. This approach differs significantly from the corresponding approach in resection of a bile duct malignancy [see Resection of Middle-Third and Proximal Bile Duct Tumors, Operative Technique, below]. If necessary, the cyst may be opened and the dissection continued with a finger inside the cyst to yield a more accurate definition of its boundaries. The cyst should be cleared circumferentially in the middle third of the CBD so that a tape can be passed around it and traction applied to separate the cyst from the hepatic artery, the portal vein, and any remaining soft tissue in the hepatoduodenal ligament.

Step 4: Distal Dissection

Dissection then proceeds distally along the wall of the cyst until the junction of the cyst with the normal portion of the CBD is reached. If the intrapancreatic portion of the CBD is involved, the cyst must be separated from pancreatic tissue. There are a number of small vessels that must be individually identified and ligated to minimize the risk of early or delayed bleeding. If the cyst is close to the pancreatic duct junction, considerable care must be exercised not to injure the pancreatic duct.

Step 5: Proximal Dissection

If the proximal common hepatic duct is normal (as in a type I cyst), it is transected above the cyst. If the cystic dilatation includes the bifurcation (as in a type IVa cyst), a small button of proximal cyst is usually left attached to the intrahepatic ducts [see Figure 8].

Step 6: Reconstruction

Reconstruction is accomplished via an end-to-side anastomosis to a Roux jejunal loop to minimize the likelihood of reflux of enteric contents into the biliary tract.

Step 7: Closure

The abdomen is closed in the standard fashion. Stenting is not required, but the area should be drained with closed suction drains if an intrapancreatic resection has been done.

Laparoscopic Considerations

If the appropriate principles and techniques are used [see Operative Planning, General Technical Considerations, Principles of Laparoscopic Biliary Tract Surgery, above], choledochal cyst excision can be performed laparoscopically with excellent results.[5] A

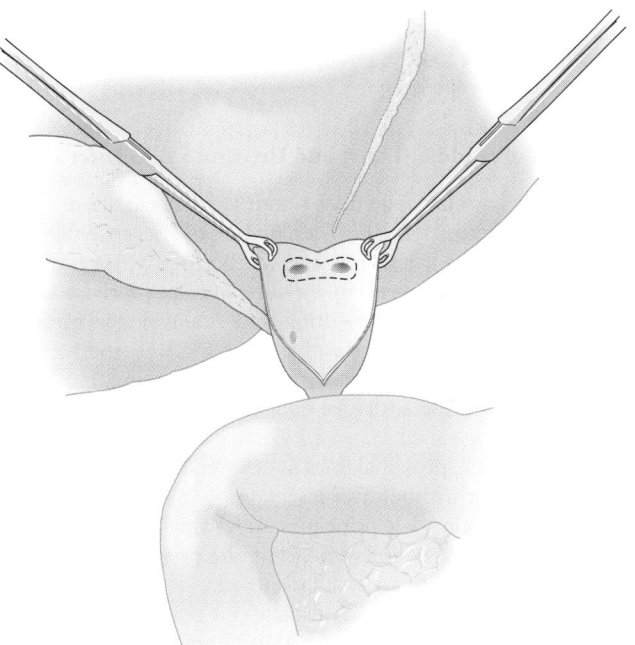

Figure 8 Choledochal cyst resection. If a cyst extends proximally past the bifurcation (e.g., a type IVa cyst), it may be necessary to open the cyst widely to identify the hepatic duct orifices. A small button of cyst wall is left attached to the hepatic ducts.

laparoscopic approach faces essentially the same challenges that an open approach does [see Complications, below].

TROUBLESHOOTING

If dissection of the cyst is carried distally into the pancreas, care must be taken to keep from injuring the pancreatic duct. The cyst should be transected as distally as possible, and the end should be carefully oversewn with absorbable sutures. Somatostatin, 100 µg subcutaneously during the operation and every 8 hours for 5 days afterward, should be given to reduce the likelihood of pancreatitis and pancreatic fistula. Occasionally, intraoperative cholangiography is useful to confirm the relationship of the cyst and the CBD to the pancreatic duct.

If the cystic process extends to include the bifurcation (type IVa), the hepatic ducts should be identified from within the cyst and their orifices preserved by leaving a small button of cyst wall in situ; this is preferable to performing an intrahepatic dissection to remove the entire cyst. The presence of this button simplifies and facilitates the anastomosis to the Roux loop.

COMPLICATIONS

Bleeding and pancreatitis are the main early complications of cystectomy. These can be largely prevented by meticulous dissection and ligation of all fine bleeding vessels as well as tissue adjacent to an intrapancreatic cyst. Late stricture of the anastomosis is an uncommon complication but may occur, especially if a small button of proximal cyst is left in place for the anastomosis; this particular complication is considered an acceptable hazard in a difficult situation.

OUTCOME EVALUATION

The immediate expected outcome is the relief of pain, jaundice, and cholangitis and the return of liver function to normal. The long-term expected outcome is the absence of any recurrence of symptoms of stone disease, cholangitis, or malignancy. Because of the rarity of this condition, no good data on the recurrence rate of problems are available.

Resection of Middle-Third and Proximal Bile Duct Tumors

The most common bile duct tumor is adenocarcinoma [*see 51 Tumors of the Pancreas, Biliary Tract, and Liver*]. Because this tumor responds poorly to irradiation and chemotherapy, surgical resection offers the best opportunity for cure. The appropriate operative approach depends on the location and extent of the tumor [*see Figure 9*]. Tumors in the distal third of the CBD (the pancreatic portion) are treated by means of a Whipple procedure that includes bile duct and periductal tissues right up to the bifurcation [*see 66 Procedures for Benign and Malignant Pancreatic Disease*]. Those in the middle third or the proximal third are treated by means of bile duct resection, with or without liver resection [*see 65 Hepatic Resection*].

There are certain basic principles underlying bile duct resection for tumor that must be followed. First, the proximal extent of the tumor must be identified so that the correct procedure can be planned. Preoperative PTC is usually not required for staging if high-quality ultrasonography and MRCP are available. Some authorities advocate bilateral percutaneous drainage to facilitate intraoperative dissection. We do not routinely use preoperative drainage

tubes, because of the risk of cholangitis.

Second, given that bile duct tumors spread by local extension to lymphatics, along perineural spaces, and along the bile radicles themselves directly into the liver, wide local excision beyond the visible edges of the tumor is required in the performance of curative resections. In proximal tumors, such excision necessitates resection of the adjacent segments of the liver. The principles of en bloc resection beyond tumor margins must be closely adhered to: dissection into or even close to the tumor must be avoided.

Third, intraoperative biopsy of the tumor should not be done, because of the difficulty of making a firm pathologic diagnosis on the basis of frozen-section examination and because of the risk of tumor dissemination.

Finally, given that liver resection is required in most cases, one must be careful to preserve enough healthy liver tissue to allow regeneration of the remnant. If there has been long-standing obstruction, biliary drainage on the side to be preserved is important for recovery of function in that portion of the liver. Some surgeons advocate preoperative portal vein embolization on the contralateral side to stimulate hepatic regeneration in the segments to be preserved, especially if the future remnant is marginal in size [*see 51 Tumors of the Pancreas, Biliary Tract, and Liver*].

On the whole, we are currently more aggressive in treating proximal tumors than we once were, for two main reasons: (1) the

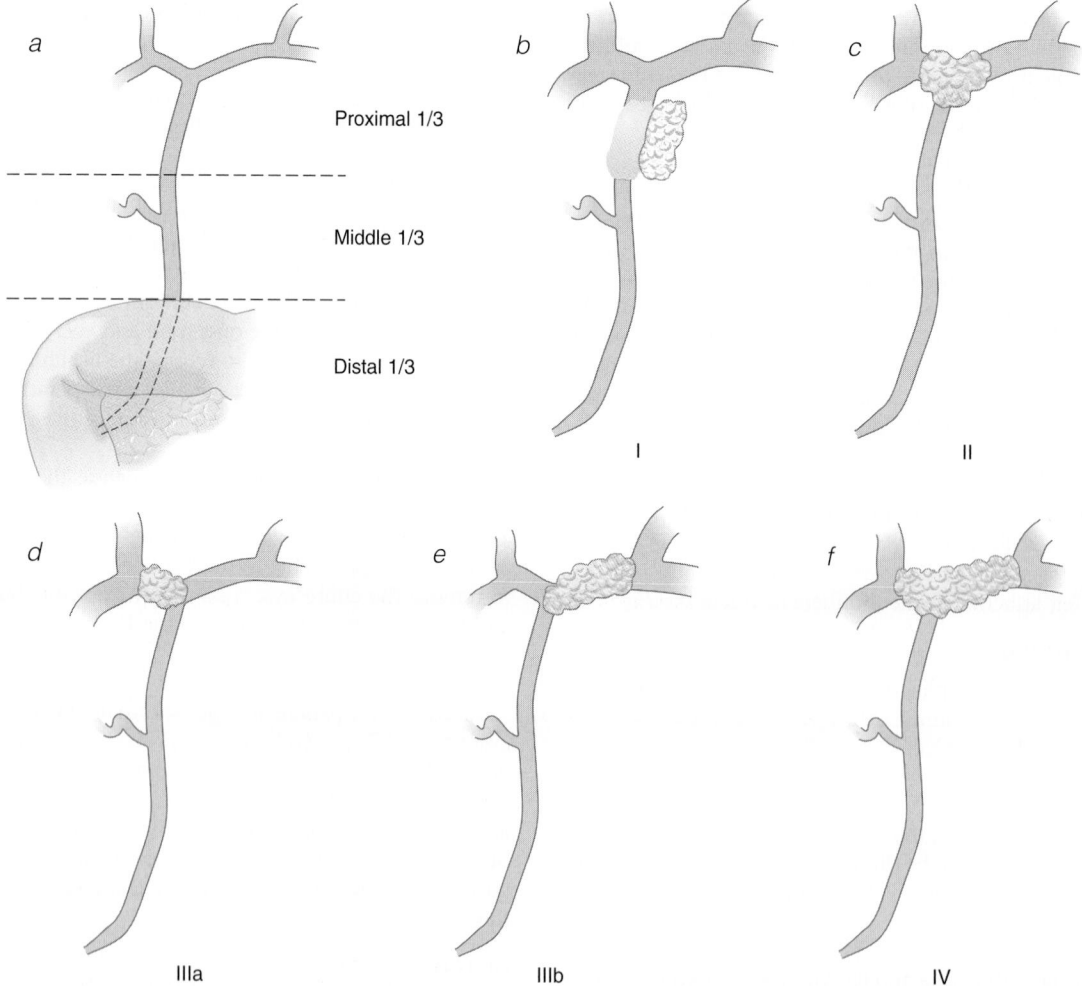

Figure 9 **Resection of middle-third and proximal bile duct tumors. The appropriate operation depends on the location and extent of the tumor. (*a*) Broadly, tumors may be localized to the proximal third, the middle third, or the distal third of the biliary tract. (*b through f*) Proximal tumors may be further categorized according to the Bismuth classification.**

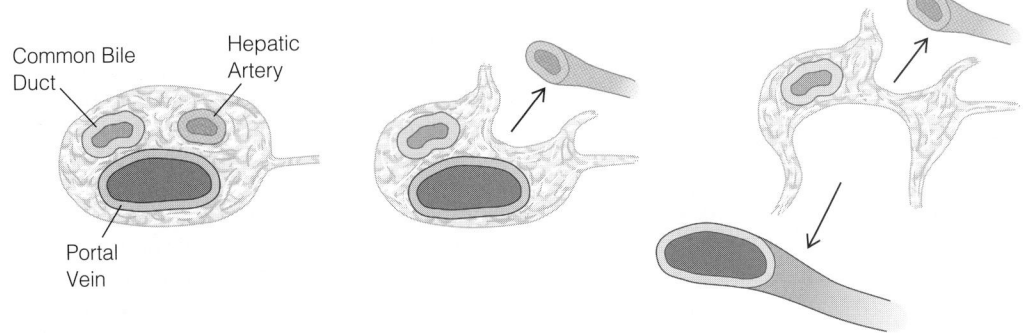

Figure 10 **Resection of middle-third and proximal bile duct tumors. Shown is the proper plane of dissection in the removal of a bile duct cancer. Except for the hepatic artery and the portal vein, all tissue stays with the CBD to be resected.**

accompanying liver resection can now be done with greater safety, and (2) this more radical approach has been shown to yield improved long-term results. For middle-third or type I proximal tumors, we favor resection of the bifurcation in conjunction with intrahepatic cholangiojejunostomy. For types II, III, and IV, we recommend additional liver resection: a right trisectionectomy (resection of segments 4, 5, 6, 7, and 8, along with the caudate lobe) for types II, IIIa, and IV and a formal left hepatectomy (resection of segments 1, 2, 3, and 4) for type IIIb [*see 65 Hepatic Resection*]. There is some controversy as to whether patients with these complex proximal biliary tumors have a better chance of long-term survival with liver transplantation than with a right tri-sectionectomy. This controversy has yet to be resolved, but given that organ availability remains a major issue, we continue to prefer radical resection in this setting.

OPERATIVE TECHNIQUE

Step 1: Assessment of Resectability

Before any dissection of the tumor or the CBD is done, a careful search for peritoneal metastases is undertaken. Spread within the liver is evaluated via palpation and intraoperative ultrasonography. Lymph nodes are assessed in the immediate and secondary drainage areas. Biopsies of any suspicious areas outside the planned resection margins are carried out. If tumor is found, stenting or a bypass procedure is indicated.

During dissection, determination of resectability is often difficult, especially with respect to assessment of tumor extension into the liver and the degree of vessel involvement. Therefore, any firm commitment to resection (e.g., dividing the blood supply) should be deferred until resectability is confirmed.

The gallbladder is mobilized from the liver bed by entering the usual plane superficial to the liver capsule without dissecting or dividing the cystic artery and the cystic duct. Exposure is improved by mobilizing the gallbladder and, if necessary, emptying the gallbladder of bile. The gallbladder can also be used as a retractor on the bile duct.

Dissection is then begun from below. The common hepatic artery and the portal vein are identified just above the neck of the pancreas and circumferentially cleared of all tissue. Dissection then proceeds proximally, with the hepatic artery retracted to the left and the portal vein to the right. Adjacent areolar tissue, nerve trunks, and lymph nodes are left in place around the CBD and the tumor [*see Figure 10*]. As noted, this approach differs from that used in resection of choledochal cysts [*see Choledochal Cyst Resection, Operative Technique, above*].

Step 2: Division of CBD

Once resectability is confirmed, the CBD is divided at the level of the pancreas. A clamp is placed on the upper end of the divided duct, which is then used as a retractor to facilitate the most proximal dissection of the CBD and the tumor away from the hepatic artery and the portal vein [*see Figure 11*].

Step 3: Proximal Dissection

With middle-third tumors or Bismuth type I proximal tumors, it is usually possible to palpate the proximal tumor margin and

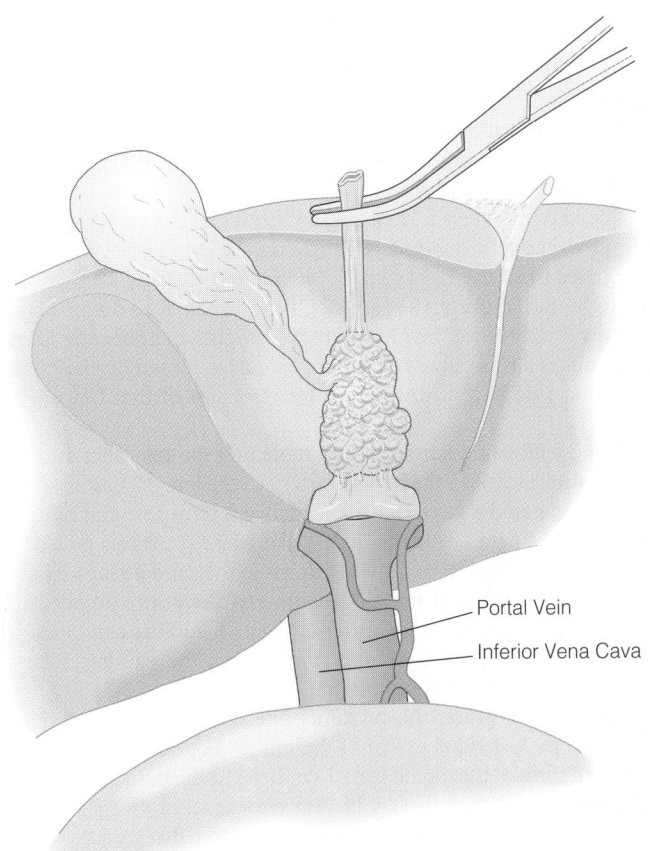

Figure 11 **Resection of middle-third and proximal bile duct tumors. When resectability is confirmed, the CBD is transected at the duodenum. The proximal portion of the divided duct is retracted anteriorly, and the CBD is cleaned off the portal vein up to a point above the bifurcation.**

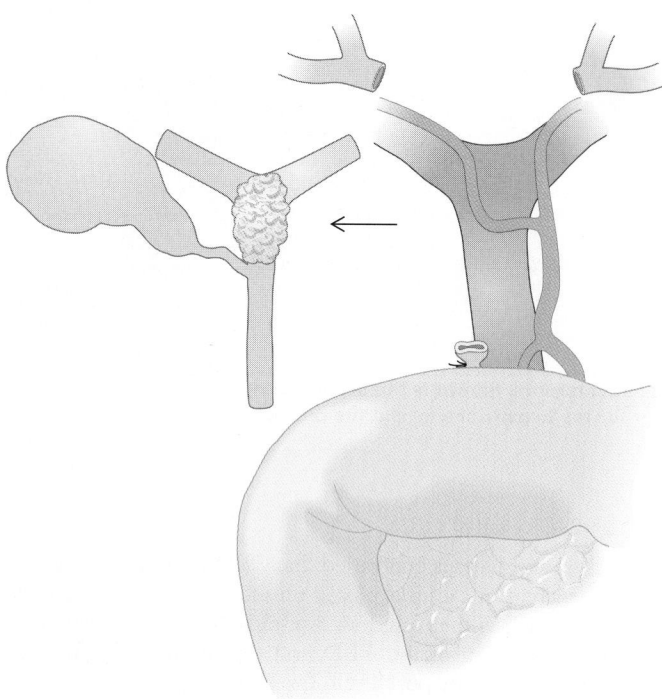

Figure 12   **Resection of middle-third and proximal bile duct tumors. Illustrated is the level of resection for middle-third and type I proximal tumors. The CBD is resected from the pancreas to a point above the bifurcation. Reconstruction is accomplished via Roux-en-Y hepaticojejunostomy (involving either one or two separate anastomoses).**

identify uninvolved right and left hepatic ducts. If this is not the case, the possibility of a type II or III tumor should be considered, and complete excision of the bifurcation, with or without part of the liver, should be planned.

The hepatic artery is dissected by retracting the vessel anteriorly and to the left, dividing and ligating the cystic artery where it originates from the right hepatic artery, and clearing all tissue off the right and left branches at least 1 cm proximal to the proximal margin of the tumor. Involvement of the right or left hepatic artery by tumor is almost always a sign of extensive spread on the corresponding side and an indication for resection of that half of the liver.

The portal vein is dissected by retracting the bile duct and the tumor anteriorly and the hepatic artery to the left. All tissue is then cleanly dissected away from the portal vein to expose the bifurcation and the region proximal to it [*see Figure 11*]. At this point, the duct may be found to be tethered down to the caudate lobe by several small branches. If these branches are clearly proximal to the tumor, they are divided and carefully ligated, and the caudate lobe is preserved. If there is tumor in this area, the caudate lobe is resected along with the bifurcation tumor.

The level at which the proximal bile ducts are transected depends on the proximal extent of the tumor. For all middle-third or proximal tumors that are at least 1 cm beyond the bifurcation, proximal resection should usually be above the level of the bifurcation. For type I or type II proximal tumors, proximal resection should always include all of the bifurcation along with the proximal right and left bile ducts out as far as the first major branch [*see Figure 12*]. With type III or IV proximal tumors, the proximal extent of the tumor cannot be determined in both right and left ducts unless the main pedicles are dissected out of the liver. Because these tumors tend to infiltrate locally, such dissection is not advisable. A decision

on whether liver resection is indicated should be made at an early stage so that the chances of a cure are not compromised. Intraoperative ultrasonography may help verify the extent of tumor at this point in the operation. Any major liver resection for type III or IV bile duct cancer should include the caudate lobe [*see Figure 13*].

Once the decision to resect part of the liver has been made, the operation consists of dissecting the hepatic artery and the portal vein branch to the part of the liver to be saved away from the tumor area. The hepatic artery and the portal vein branch to the side to be resected are then divided; this allows the tumor to be retracted further and provides better exposure of the duct to the side to be preserved [*see Figures 14 and 15*]. In selected cases, resection of an involved portal vein bifurcation may be carried out at this point [*see Figure 16*]; an end-to-end anastomosis is then fashioned.

The point at which the hepatic parenchyma will be divided is marked, and the parenchymal transection is performed. Division of the hepatic duct (or ducts) to the part of the liver being preserved is done as far from the tumor as possible.

Step 4: Reconstruction

After resection of the bifurcation or intrahepatic bile ducts, an intrahepatic cholangiojejunostomy is performed [*see Intrahepatic Cholangiojejunostomy, below*]. The duct tissue is usually healthy enough and the duct lumen large enough to allow mucosa-to-mucosa repair without stenting. Some surgeons place trans-

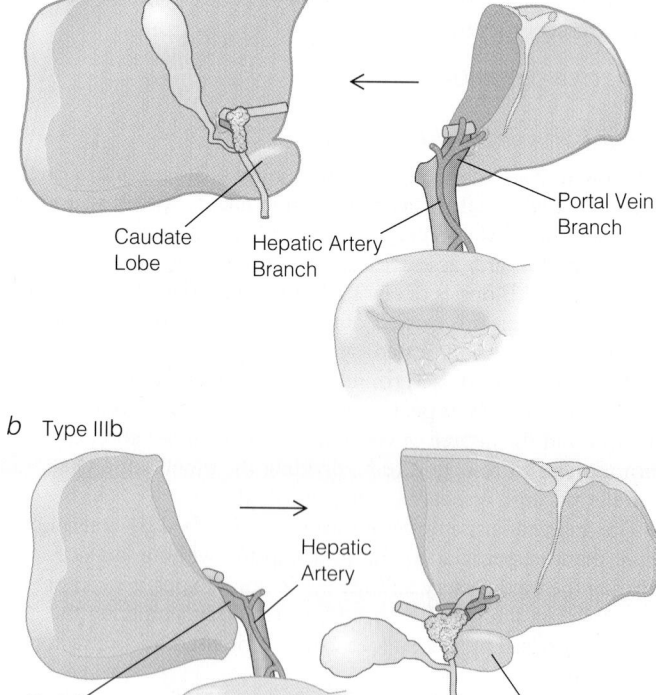

Figure 13   **Resection of middle-third and proximal bile duct tumors. Illustrated are (a) a right trisectionectomy (extended right hepatectomy) for type II, IIIa, and IV tumors and (b) a left hepatectomy (including the caudate lobe) for type IIIb tumors.**

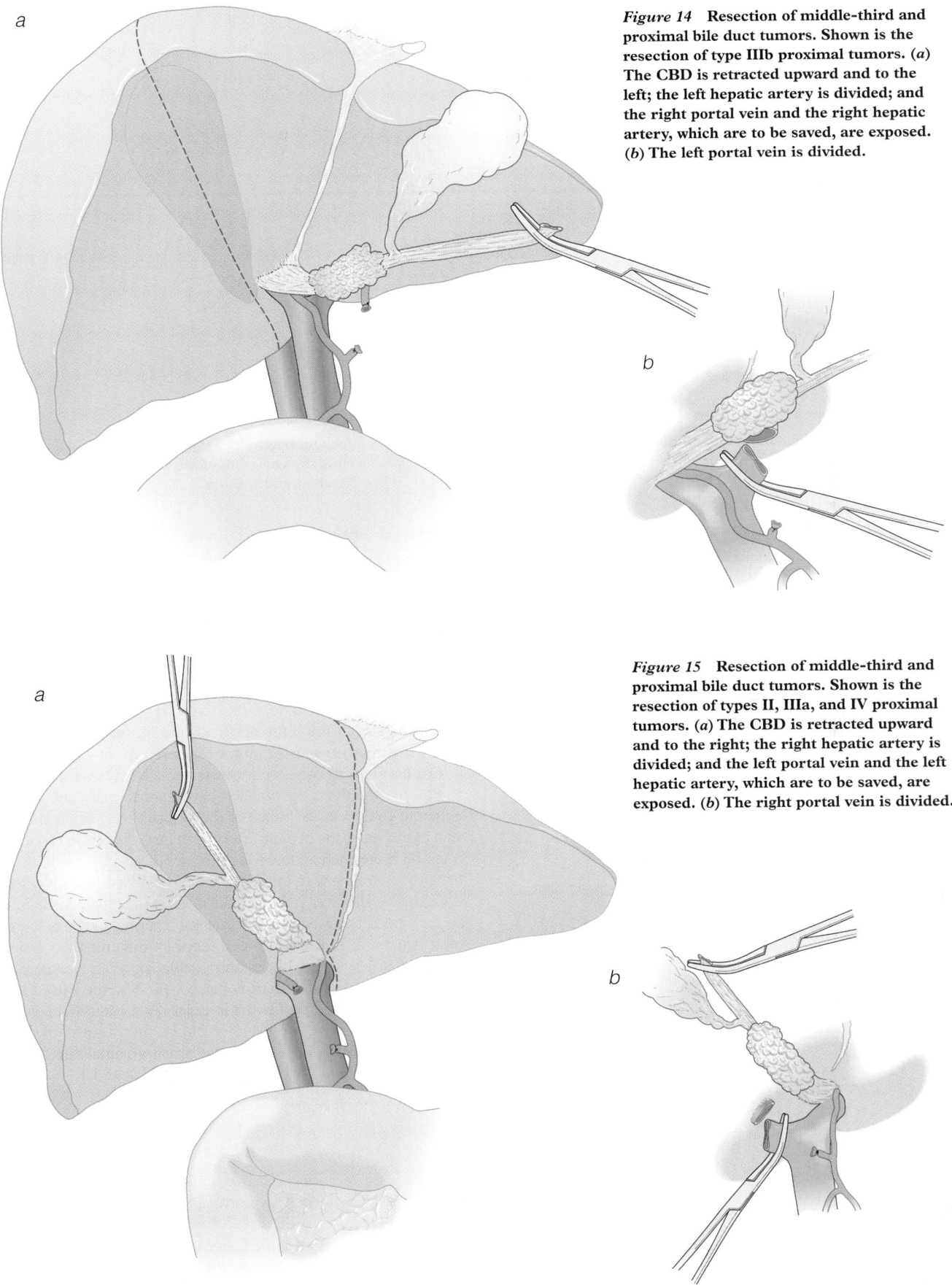

Figure 14 **Resection of middle-third and proximal bile duct tumors. Shown is the resection of type IIIb proximal tumors. (*a*) The CBD is retracted upward and to the left; the left hepatic artery is divided; and the right portal vein and the right hepatic artery, which are to be saved, are exposed. (*b*) The left portal vein is divided.**

Figure 15 **Resection of middle-third and proximal bile duct tumors. Shown is the resection of types II, IIIa, and IV proximal tumors. (*a*) The CBD is retracted upward and to the right; the right hepatic artery is divided; and the left portal vein and the left hepatic artery, which are to be saved, are exposed. (*b*) The right portal vein is divided.**

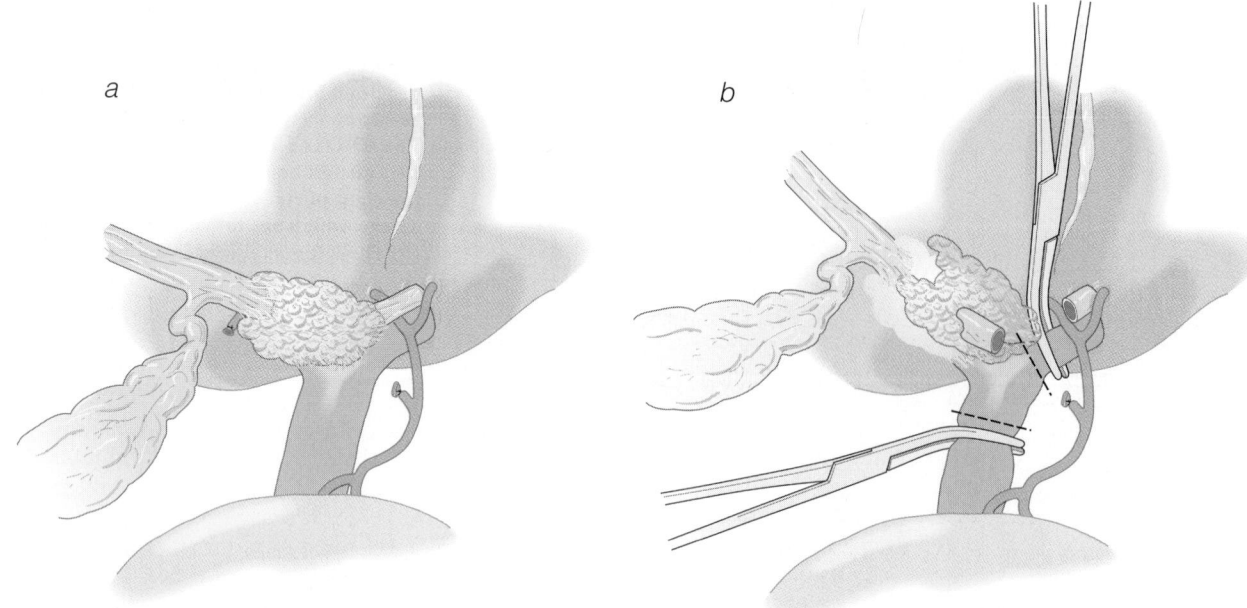

Figure 16 Resection of middle-third and proximal bile duct tumors. (*a*) Occasionally, a type III or IV proximal tumor will involve the portal vein bifurcation. (*b*) Shown is the resection of an involved portal vein bifurcation. Reconstruction is accomplished in an end-to-end fashion.

hepatic tubes through these anastomoses to facilitate postoperative treatment with internal radiation sources; however, there is no evidence that this practice reduces local recurrence or prolongs survival.

Step 5: Closure and Postoperative Care

The abdomen is closed in the standard fashion, and closed suction drains are placed. Liver function is monitored, particularly when a major liver resection has been done. Mild abnormalities in coagulation test results are common, and soluble coagulation factors are given only if there is evidence of bleeding.

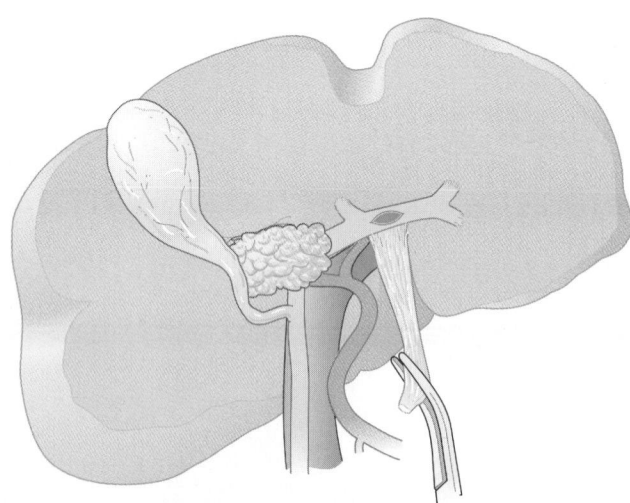

Figure 17 Intrahepatic cholangiojejunostomy. If a tumor involves the left main hepatic duct, the branch of the duct that supplies segment 3 of the liver may be used instead for anastomosis to the jejunum. This branch may be approached in the umbilical fissure, above the round ligament. Incision into the liver or wedge excision may be necessary to ensure adequate exposure.

COMPLICATIONS

Bile leakage, bleeding, and infection are the most important complications of bile duct resection for tumor. Parahepatic collections are treated with percutaneous drainage, and significant early bleeding is usually best managed by reexploration.

Intrahepatic Cholangiojejunostomy

Intrahepatic cholangiojejunostomy is commonly performed after resection of the bifurcation for a more proximal tumor; it is also performed to manage injury or stricture at the level of the bifurcation and to bypass an unresectable bifurcation tumor.

Because the ducts are smaller, have thinner walls, and are more adherent to the areolar tissue of the pedicles than either the portal vein branches or the hepatic artery branches, dissection of the ducts must be more meticulous. Magnification is an important aid, particularly in dealing with undilated ducts. Good exposure is essential; if necessary, the liver may be split to allow adequate visualization, access, and lighting. Anatomic mucosal suturing can be achieved in most situations. In rare instances, excessive inflammation, scarring, or tumor makes such suturing impossible, in which case periductal sutures are used and a stent is placed. As described [*see* General Considerations, Technical Issues in Biliary Anastomosis, *above*], separate ducts that are close together can be first sutured together at their adjacent walls to create a single larger proximal duct lumen so that a safer anastomosis can be created [*see* Figure 3*c*].

OPERATIVE TECHNIQUE

Step 1: Definition of Tissues for Anastomosis

In the case of injury, crushed, cauterized, or devitalized tissue must be debrided back to normal healthy tissue before reconstruction is begun. In the case of bile duct resection for tumor, there should be no attempt to clear a length of duct from surrounding areolar or liver tissue; the suturing should take place in situ, with the stitches passed through the duct wall and the areolar tissue of the portal pedicles. In the case of bypass for unresectable cancer, the duct being used should be opened as far from the tumor as possible. The left main hepatic duct can be approached between the bifurcation and the umbilical fissure. If the tumor involves the left main hepatic duct, the branch to segment 3 of the liver can be used instead; it can be approached in the umbilical fissure, above the round ligament. Occasionally, incision into the liver or excision of a wedge of liver tissue is necessary to provide adequate exposure [see Figure 17].

If an intrahepatic anastomosis is required for a bifurcation stricture, resection of the stricture is not necessary; however, it is important to identify a normal duct above the level of the bifurcation. If there is no communication from right to left, a horizontal incision can be made in the left duct and carried across into the right duct just above or through the bifurcation stricture, so that a single anastomosis can be made that incorporates both ducts. It is possible to enlarge duct openings by making a small longitudinal incision in the most accessible portion of the duct. This is easier to accomplish in the left hepatic duct (because of its extrahepatic transverse position) than in the right hepatic duct (which tends to run laterally and posteriorly directly in the liver substance).

Step 2: Anastomosis

A Roux-en-Y loop of sufficient length to make a tension-free anastomosis is constructed, and a biliary-enteric anastomosis is then performed. When adequate access is difficult to obtain, interrupted sutures are first placed in the anterior wall of the bile duct. This allows retraction of that wall, and it facilitates the accurate placement of interrupted sutures in the back wall.

Postoperative Care

In a patient who has impaired liver function or has undergone a major hepatic resection, the results of liver function tests, particularly coagulation studies, should be carefully monitored postoperatively. Transient worsening of these results is not unusual, especially if the procedure was long. Moderately elevated results from coagulation studies (e.g., international normalized ratio < 2.0) are not an indication for treatment with fresh frozen plasma or concentrated coagulation factors unless clinical bleeding is evident.

Postoperative infections may occur as a result of biliary tract contamination, especially if a bile duct stent was placed preoperatively. Antibiotic prophylaxis with broad-spectrum agents for periods longer than usual for perioperative treatment may be appropriate in such cases. If postoperative fever occurs, especially if it is accompanied by unusual pain and tenderness, imaging studies should be promptly obtained and fluid collections sought. In most cases, bile or pus can be drained satisfactorily through percutaneously placed tubes.

References

1. O'Rourke RW, Lee NN, Cheng J, et al: Laparoscopic biliary reconstruction. Am J Surg 187:621, 2004
2. Tang CN, Siu WT, Ha JPY, et al: Laparoscopic choledochoduodenostomy—an effective drainage procedure for recurrent pyogenic cholangitis. Surg Endosc 17:1590, 2003
3. Han HS, Yi NJ: Laparoscopic Roux-en-Y choledochojejunostomy for benign biliary disease. Surg Laparosc Endosc Percutan Tech 14:80, 2004
4. Li S, Zhuang GY, Pei YQ, et al: Extended local resection treatment of periampullary carcinoma of Vater. Hepatobiliary Pancreat Dis Int 3:303, 2004
5. Lipsett PA, Pitt HA: Surgical treatment of choledochal cysts. J Hepatobiliary Pancreat Surg 10:352, 2003

Recommended Reading

Bismuth H, Nakache R, Diamond T: Management strategies in resection for hilar cholangiocarcinoma. Ann Surg 215:31, 1992

Bornman PC, Terblanche J: Subtotal cholecystectomy: for the difficult gallbladder in portal hypertension and cholecystitis. Surgery 98:1, 1985

Braasch JW, Rossi RL: Reconstruction of the biliary tract. Surg Clin North Am 65:273, 1985

Fry DE: Surgical techniques in the management of distal biliary tract obstruction. American Surgeon 49:138, 1983

Gallinger S, Gluckman D, Langer B: Proximal bile duct cancer. Advances in Surgery, Vol 23. Cameron JL, Ed. Year Book Medical Publishers, St. Louis, 1990, p 89

Lillemoe KD, Pitt HA, Cameron JL: Current management of benign bile duct strictures. Advances in Surgery, Vol 25. Cameron JL, Ed. Year Book Medical Publishers, St. Louis, 1992, p 119

Russell E, Hutson DG, Guerra JJ Jr: Dilatation of biliary strictures through a stomatized jejunal limb. Acta Radiologica: Diagnosis 26:283, 1985

Smadja C, Blumgart LH: The biliary tract and the anatomy of biliary exposure. Surgery of the Liver and Biliary Tract. Blumgart LH, Ed. Churchill Livingstone, New York, 1988, p 11

Strom PR, Stone HH: A technique for transduodenal sphincteroplasty. Surgery 92:546, 1982

Acknowledgment

Figures 1 through 17 Tom Moore.

65 HEPATIC RESECTION

Yuman Fong, M.D., F.A.C.S., and Leslie H. Blumgart, M.D., F.A.C.S., F.R.C.S.

Liver resections were first described centuries ago, but until the latter half of the 20th century, the majority of such resections were performed for management of either injuries or infections. Today, these procedures are performed not only for treatment of acute emergencies (e.g., traumatic injuries or abscesses) but also as potentially curative therapy for a variety of benign and malignant hepatic lesions.

The first planned anatomic resection of a lobe of a liver is credited to Lortat-Jacob, who in 1952 performed a right lobectomy as treatment for metastatic colon cancer.[1] Major hepatectomies, however, did not become commonplace until the 1980s. Since then, the safety of these operations has improved dramatically, and as safety has improved, the indications for hepatic resection have become better refined as well. Currently, resection of as much as 85% of the functional liver parenchyma is being performed at numerous centers with an operative mortality of less than 2%. The duration of hospitalization is typically less than 2 weeks, and almost all individuals regain normal hepatic function.

In what follows, we focus on the technical aspects of hepatic resection, emphasizing efficiency and safety and taking into account recent developments, current controversies, and special operative considerations (e.g., the cirrhotic patient and repeat liver resection). Detailed discussions of the indications for hepatic resection are available elsewhere.[2-4]

Hepatic Anatomy

Familiarity with the surgical anatomy of the liver is essential for safe performance of a partial hepatectomy. The liver can be divided into two lobes (right and left) comprising eight segments [*see Figure 1*]. Each of these segments is a discrete anatomic unit that possesses its own nutrient blood supply and its own venous and biliary drainage. The right lobe consists of segments 5 through 8 and is nourished by the right hepatic artery and the right portal vein; the left lobe consists of segments 1 through 4 and is nourished by the left hepatic artery and the left portal vein. The anatomic division between the right lobe and the left is not at the falciform ligament (the most readily apparent visual landmark on the anterior liver) but follows a line projected through a plane (the principal plane, or Cantlie's line) that runs posterosuperiorly from the medial margin of the gallbladder to the left side of the vena cava.

The venous drainage of the liver consists of multiple small veins draining directly from the back of the right lobe and the caudate lobe to the vena cava, along with three major hepatic veins. These major hepatic veins occupy three planes, known as portal scissurae. The three scissurae divide the liver into four sectors, each of which is supplied by a portal pedicle; further branching of the pedicles subdivides the sectors into the eight segments [*see Figure 1*].[5-7] (Some surgeons refer to these sectors

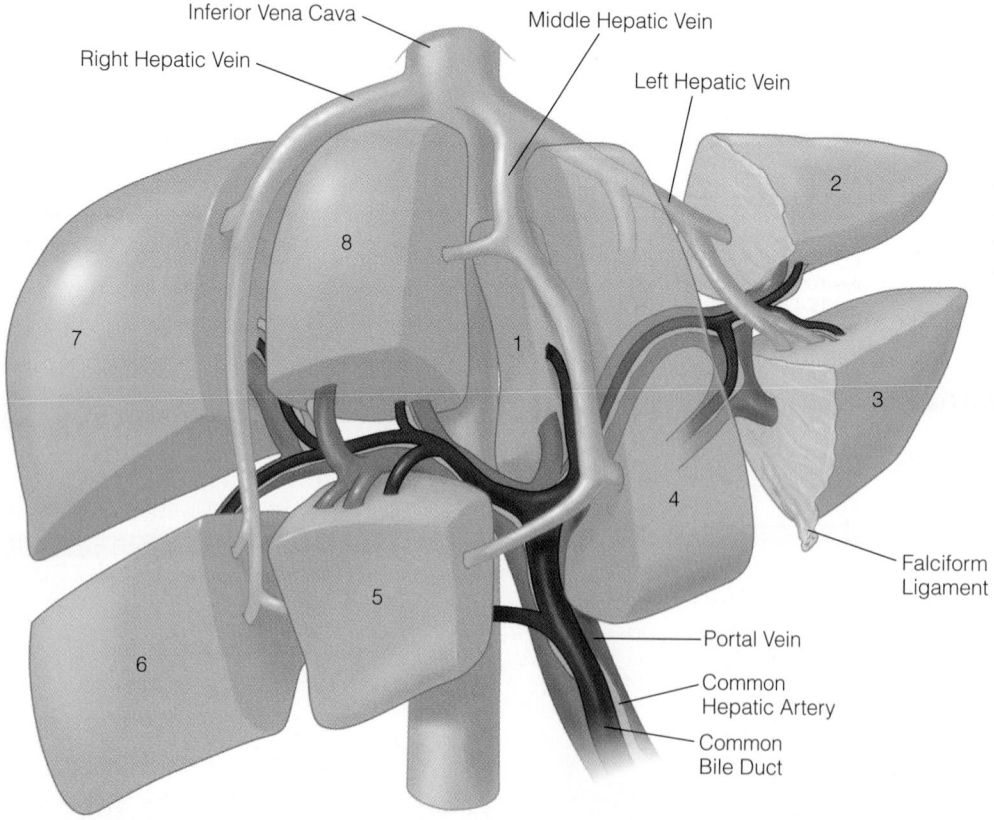

Figure 1 **The liver is separated into eight anatomic segments, each with an independent nutrient blood supply and venous and biliary drainage. Appreciation of this segmental anatomy is the basis of anatomic resection of the liver.**

a   *b*

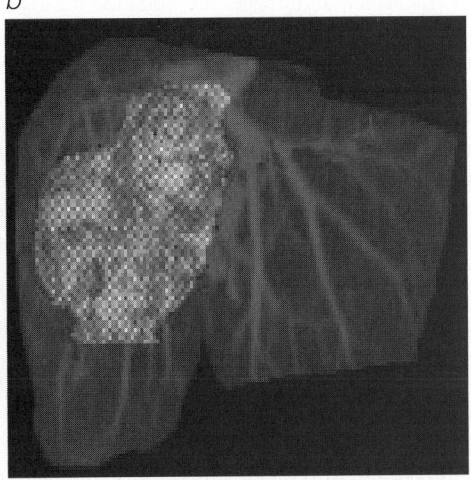

Figure 2 (*a*) **The arterial anatomy of the celiac axis is reconstructed from thin-slice CT images. (*b*) The hepatic venous anatomy is similarly reconstructed, with the tumor superimposed on the vascular reconstruction.**

as segments—hence the term trisegmentectomy.) The right hepatic vein passes between the right anterior sector (segments 5 and 8) and the right posterior sector (segments 6 and 7) in the right scissura. This vein empties directly into the vena cava near the atriocaval junction. The middle hepatic vein passes between the right anterior sector and the left medial sector (segment 4) in the central, or principal, scissura, which represents the division between the right lobe and the left. The left hepatic vein runs in the left scissura between segments 2 and 3. In most persons, the left and middle hepatic veins join to form a common trunk before entering the vena cava. Occasionally, a large inferior right hepatic vein is present that may provide adequate drainage of the right lobe after resection of the left even when all three major hepatic veins are ligated.[8]

The portal vein and the hepatic artery divide into left and right branches below the hilus of the liver. Unlike the hepatic veins, which run between segments, the portal venous and hepatic arterial branches, along with the hepatic ducts, typically run centrally within segments [*see Figure 1*]. On the right side, the hepatic artery and the portal vein enter the liver substance almost immediately after branching. The short course of the right-side extrahepatic vessels and the variable anatomy of the biliary tree make these vessels vulnerable to damage during dissection.[9] In contrast, the left branch of the portal vein and the left hepatic duct take a long extrahepatic course after branching beneath segment 4. When these vessels reach the base of the umbilical fissure, they are joined by the left hepatic artery to form a triad, which then enters the left liver substance at this point. It must be emphasized that proximal to the base of the umbilical fissure, the left-side structures are not a triad. A consequence of the long extrahepatic course of the left-side structures is that for tumors that involve the hilus (e.g., Klatskin tumors), when a choice exists between an extended right hepatectomy or an extended left hepatectomy, most surgeons choose the former because the greater ease of dissection on the left side facilitates preservation of the left-side structures. Knowledge of the relative anatomic courses of the portal veins, the hepatic arteries, and the hepatic ducts is the basis of the classical extrahepatic dissection for control of hepatic inflow [*see Operative Technique, Right Lobectomy, Step 6 (Extrahepatic Dissection and Ligation), below*].

The fibrous capsule surrounding the liver substance was described by Glisson in 1654.[10] It was Couinaud,[6] however, who demonstrated that this fibrous capsule extends to envelop the portal triads as they pass into the liver substance. Thus, within the liver, the portal vein, the hepatic artery, and the hepatic duct running to each segment of the liver lie within a substantial sheath. This dense sheath allows rapid control of inflow vessels to specific anatomic units within the liver and permits en masse ligation of these vascular structures in a maneuver known as pedicle ligation [*see Operative Technique, Right Lobectomy, Step 6—Alternative (Intrahepatic Pedicle Ligation), below*].[11]

Preoperative Evaluation

Cross-sectional imaging modalities such as computed tomography, magnetic resonance imaging, and ultrasonography play an important role in enhancing the safety and efficacy of hepatic resection. These modalities, along with biologic scanning techniques such as positron emission tomography (PET), are also invaluable for staging malignancies so as to improve patient selection and thereby optimize long-term surgical outcome.

At a minimum, all candidates for hepatic resection should undergo either CT or MRI. These imaging tests not only identify the number and size of any mass lesions within the liver but also delineate the relations of the lesions to the major vasculature—data that are crucial for deciding whether to operate and which operative approach to follow.

Use of contrast enhancement during CT scanning is vital for accurate definition of the vascular anatomy. In fact, data from thin-slice (1 to 2 mm) images captured by current spiral, or helical, CT scanners can be reconstructed to provide angiographic pictures whose level of detail rivals that of direct angiograms [*see Figure 2*]. Triple-phase scans (including a noncontrast phase, an arterial phase, and a venous phase) are recommended: these yield the best definition and characterization of intrahepatic lesions. For example, some vascular tumors become isodense with liver parenchyma after contrast injection. By first obtaining noncontrast scans and then obtaining contrast scans at two different times after contrast injection, the examiner stands a better chance of visualizing such tumors.

For small tumors, a CT variant known as CT portography is recommended. In this technique, contrast material is injected through the superior mesenteric artery, and images are obtained during the portal venous phase. The normal liver receives the majority of its nutrient blood from the portal vein and is therefore contrast-enhanced in this phase. Tumors, on the other hand, usually derive their nutrient blood from the hepatic artery and therefore appear as exaggerated perfusion defects. CT portography is the most sensitive test available for identifying small hepatic tumors.[12]

MRI may also be valuable for characterizing lesions and defining them vis-à-vis the vasculature. It is particularly helpful in diagnosing benign lesions such as hemangiomas, fibronodular hyperplasia, and adenomas. Whenever any of these benign lesions is suspected, MRI is usually indicated. With regard to surgical planning, MRI angiographic images are useful for identifying the major hepatic veins and clarifying their relations to any tumor masses.[13]

Imaging recommendations may be summed up as follows. A triple-phase CT should be obtained for most patients under consideration for hepatic resection. If diagnostic doubt remains after CT, particularly if the differential diagnosis includes an asymptomatic benign tumor, MRI should be performed. If questions remain after CT as to the extent of hepatic venous or major biliary involvement, MRI or duplex ultrasonography should be considered.[14] If small tumors are encountered, CT portography should be performed. Duplex ultrasonography, by demonstrating the vascular hilar structures, the hepatic veins, and the inferior vena cava, renders angiography unnecessary in many cases.[13,15] Currently, direct hepatic angiography is rarely required, and inferior vena cavography is almost never needed.

Operative Planning

PREPARATION

In general, preparation for hepatic resection is much the same as that for other major abdominal procedures. All patients who are older than 65 years or have a history of cardiopulmonary disease undergo a full cardiopulmonary assessment. It was once commonly believed that patients 70 years of age or older were poor candidates for major liver resection,[16,17] but this notion has been dispelled by more recent data.[18-20] Advanced chronologic age is not a complete contraindication to hepatectomy.

Anemia and coagulopathy, if present, are corrected. All patients are now encouraged to donate two units of autologous blood before a major hepatectomy. Appropriate single-dose antibiotic prophylaxis is administered [see 5 Prevention of Postoperative Infection].

ANESTHESIA

Decisions regarding anesthesia should take into account the possibility of baseline hepatic parenchymal dysfunction as well as the postoperative hepatic functional deficits resulting from resection of a major portion of the hepatic parenchyma.

The most important consideration, however, is the possibility of major intraoperative hemorrhage. Suitable monitoring and sufficient vascular access to permit rapid transfusion should be in place. At some centers, fluid resuscitation and blood transfusion are begun early in the course of resection to increase intravascular volume as a buffer against sudden blood loss. At the Memorial Sloan-Kettering Cancer Center (MSKCC), however, we favor the opposite approach, whereby a low central venous pressure is maintained during resection. The rationale for our preference is that generally, most of the blood lost during hepatic resection comes from the major hepatic veins or the vena cava.[21,22] If central venous pressure is kept below 5 mm Hg, there is less bleeding from the hepatic venous radicles during dissection.

Reduction of intrahepatic venous pressure can be facilitated by performing the dissection with the patient in a 15° Trendelenburg position, which increases venous return to the heart and enhances cardiac output. Central venous pressure is maintained at the desired level through a combination of anesthesia and early intraoperative fluid restriction. The minimal acceptable intraoperative urine output is 25 ml/hr.

The need for intraoperative blood transfusion can be minimized by accepting hematocrits lower than the common target figure of 30%: 24% in patients without antecedent cardiac disease and 29% in patients with cardiac disease. If blood loss is estimated to reach or exceed 20% of total volume or the patient becomes hemodynamically unstable, transfusion is indicated.[21]

PATIENT POSITIONING

The patient should be supine: to date, we have not found a lateral position to be necessary even for the largest of tumors. Electrocardiographic leads should be kept clear of the right chest wall and the presternal area in case a thoracoabdominal incision is necessitated by the position of a tumor or by intraoperative hemorrhage. Preparation and draping should therefore also allow for exposure of the lower chest and the entire upper abdomen down past the umbilicus. A crossbar or a similar device that holds self-retaining retractors should be used to elevate the costal margin. Some surgeons prefer ring-based self-retaining retractors. In our experience, although these retractors are adequate for most resections, the rings tend to restrict lateral access, thereby potentially hindering posterior dissection, particularly of the vena cava.

ANATOMIC VERSUS NONANATOMIC RESECTION

The key decision in planning a hepatectomy is whether the resection should be anatomic or nonanatomic. For treatment of malignant disease, anatomic resection is usually favored because the long-term outcome is better. Anatomic resections permit excision of parenchymal areas distal to the index tumors, where there is a high incidence of vascular micrometastases. In addition, they are significantly less likely to have positive margins than nonanatomic resections are. In a large series of hepatectomies for metastatic colorectal cancer, wedge or nonanatomic resections were associated with a 19% rate of positive margins.[23] In a recent examination of our increasing preference for anatomic resections over wedge resections, wedge resections were associated with a 16% rate of positive margins, compared with a 2% rate for anatomic resections.[24]

There are two oncologic settings where nonanatomic resections are favored. In patients with hepatocellular carcinoma, viral hepatitis and cirrhosis are often complicating factors. Cirrhotic patients tolerate resection of more than two segments of functional parenchyma poorly. Accordingly, for these patients, the smallest resection that will achieve complete tumor excision is favored, even if it is a wedge resection. For management of metastatic neuroendocrine tumors, in which resections are merely debulking procedures designed to alleviate symptoms, nonanatomic resections are accepted because cure is highly unlikely.

Hepatic resections for benign hepatic tumors are usually performed for one of three reasons: (1) to relieve symptoms (e.g., pain or early satiety), (2) because the diagnosis is uncertain, or (3) to prevent malignant transformation. A goal of such resections should be to spare as much normal parenchyma as possible. Consequently, lesions such as hemangiomas, adenomas, complex cysts, and fibronodular hyperplasia are often excised by means of enucleation or another nonanatomic resection with limited margins.

Operative Technique

Theoretically, any hepatic segment can be resected in isolation. For practical purposes, however, there are five types of major anatomic resections [see Figure 3]. We follow the most commonly used terminology, that of Goldsmith and Woodburne.[25] Some authors prefer other systems of nomenclature, based on the anatomic descriptions of Couinaud[6] or Bismuth.[7]

The essential principles of all anatomic hepatectomies are the same: (1) control of inflow vessels, (2) control of outflow vessels, and (3) parenchymal transection. To illustrate these principles, we begin by outlining the steps in a right lobectomy [see Figure 3a] in some detail, describing both extrahepatic vascular dissection and ligation and the alternative approach to inflow control, intrahepatic pedicle ligation. Left lobectomy [see Figure 3b] and other common anatomic resections share a number of steps with right lobectomy; accordingly, we discuss them in somewhat less detail. Further detail on these procedures is available in other sources.[26,27]

RIGHT LOBECTOMY

Step 1: Laparoscopic Inspection

Experience from MSKCC[28,29] and other centers[30,31] indicates that laparoscopy allows detection of unresectable disease and prevents the morbidity associated with a nontherapeutic laparotomy. We generally perform laparoscopy immediately before laparotomy during the same period of anesthesia. The laparoscopic port sites are placed in the upper abdomen along the line of the intended incision [see Step 2, below]. The first two ports are usually 10 mm ports placed in the right subcostal area along the midclavicular line and along the anterior axillary line. These

ports allow inspection of the abdomen and of the entire liver, including the dome and segment 7. The port along the right anterior axillary line is particularly suitable for laparoscopic ultrasound devices. If additional ports are necessary, a left subcostal midclavicular port is usually the best choice.

Step 2: Incision

For the majority of hepatic resections, most surgeons use a bilateral subcostal incision extended vertically to the xiphisternum [see Figure 4]. Our own preference, however, is to use an upper midline incision extending to a point approximately 2 cm above the umbilicus, with a rightward extension from that point to a point in the midaxillary line halfway between the lowest rib and the iliac crest [see Figure 4]. We find that this incision provides superb access for either right- or left-side resection, without the wound complications often encountered with trifurcated incisions (e.g., ascitic leakage and incisional hernia). On rare occasions (e.g., in the resection of large, rigid posterior tumors of the right lobe), a right thoracoabdominal incision may be required. In a recent series of nearly 2,000 resections at MSKCC, however, a thoracoabdominal incision proved necessary in only 3% of patients; the most common indication was repeat liver resection after previous right hepatic lobectomy [see Repeat Hepatic Resection, below].

Step 3: Abdominal Exploration and Intraoperative Ultrasonography

The liver is palpated bimanually. Intraoperative ultrasonography is systematically performed to identify all possible lesions and their relations to the major vascular structures. This modality is capable of identifying small lesions that preoperative imaging studies and palpation of the liver may miss.[32] The lesser omentum is incised to allow palpation of the caudate lobe and inspection of the celiac region for nodal metastases. A finger is passed from the lesser sac inferior to the caudate lobe through the foramen of Winslow to permit identification of the portal vein and palpation of the portocaval lymph nodes. The hilar lymph nodes are palpated, and any suspicious nodes are removed for frozen section examination. If the operation is being done for cancer, the entire abdomen is inspected for evidence of extrahepatic tumor.

Step 4: Mobilization of Liver

Once the decision is made to proceed with hepatic resection, the liver is fully mobilized by detaching all ligamentous attachments on the side to be resected. (Some surgeons defer completion of mobilization to a later stage in the procedure.) In particular, the suprahepatic inferior vena cava and the hepatic veins above the liver are dissected to facilitate the subsequent approach to the hepatic veins [see Step 7, below]. Once the liver is mobilized, further palpation is done to detect any small lesions that may have been obscured initially. This additional palpation is particularly important on the right side because before mobilization, the posterior parts of the liver cannot be effectively palpated, and intraoperative ultrasonography may fail to detect small lesions in this area.[32]

If, in the course of mobilization, tumor is found to be attached to the diaphragm, the affected area of the diaphragm may be excised and subsequently repaired.

Step 5: Identification of Arterial Anomalies

Any hepatic arterial anomalies present should be identified before resection is begun. With good preoperative imaging, the arterial anatomy is usually defined with sufficient exactitude before

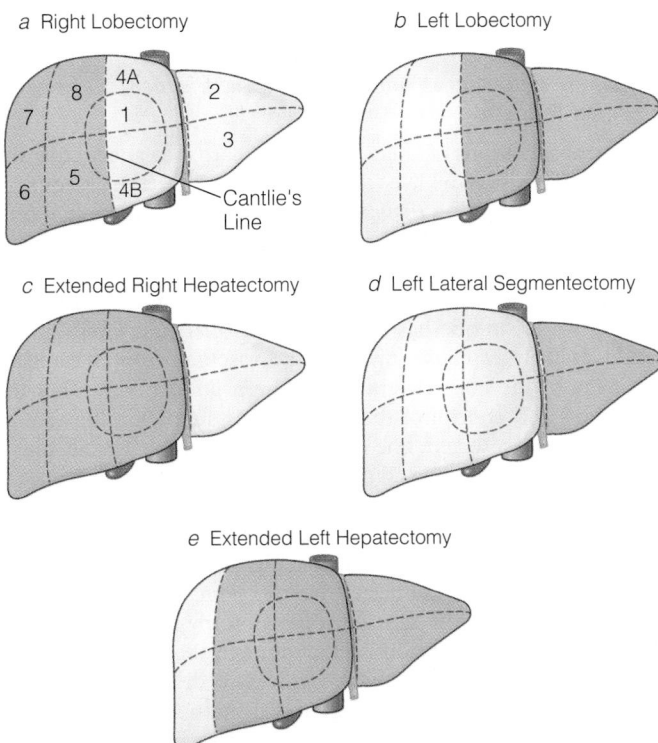

a Right Lobectomy   b Left Lobectomy

c Extended Right Hepatectomy   d Left Lateral Segmentectomy

e Extended Left Hepatectomy

Figure 3 **Shown are schematic illustrations of standard hepatic resections, with the shaded areas representing the resected portions: (*a*) right lobectomy, (*b*) left lobectomy, (*c*) extended right hepatectomy (or right trisegmentectomy), (*d*) left lateral segmentectomy, and (*e*) extended left hepatectomy (or left trisegmentectomy).**

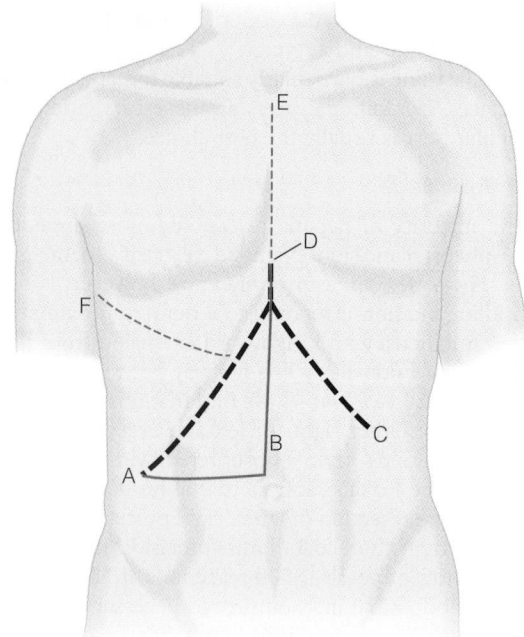

Figure 4 **Right lobectomy. A right subcostal incision (A) with a midline extension to the xiphoid (D) is the most common choice; an extension to the left subcostal area (C) is sometimes added to provide further operative exposure. We prefer a long midline incision from the xiphoid (D) to a point approximately 3 cm above the umbilicus (B) along with a rightward extension (A) because this incision provides superb exposure of both the right side and the left without the wound complications of a trifurcated incision. The chest can be entered through either a median sternotomy (E) or an anterolateral right thoracoabdominal incision (F).**

laparotomy. It is also possible to gain a clear picture of the arterial anatomy intraoperatively by means of simple maneuvers that do not involve major dissection.

The lesser omentum should be examined to determine whether there is a vessel coursing through its middle to the base of the umbilical fissure, and the hepatoduodenal ligament should be palpated with an index finger within the foramen of Winslow to see whether there is an artery in the gastropancreatic fold on its medial aspect. The usual bifurcation of the hepatic arteries occurs low and medially in the hepatoduodenal ligament, and the left hepatic artery normally travels on the medial aspect of the ligament to reach the base of the umbilical fissure. Thus, if an artery is palpable in the medial upper portion of the hepatoduodenal ligament, it is the main left hepatic artery. Any vessel seen in the lesser omentum must therefore be an accessory left artery. If, however, no pulse is found in the medial upper portion of the hepatoduodenal ligament, the vessel in the lesser omentum must be a replaced left hepatic artery. The right hepatic artery usually travels transversely behind the common bile duct (CBD) to reach the base of the cystic plate. A vertically traveling artery on the lateral hepatoduodenal ligament must therefore be either a replaced or an accessory right hepatic artery, probably arising from the superior mesenteric artery.

Step 6 (Extrahepatic Dissection and Ligation): Control of Inflow Vessels

The classic approach to extrahepatic control of the inflow vessels in a right lobectomy involves extrahepatic dissection and ligation [*see Figure 5*]. The cystic duct and the cystic artery are li-

gated and divided. The gallbladder may be either removed or left attached to the right liver, according to the surgeon's preference. The usual practice is first to ligate the right hepatic duct, then the right hepatic artery, and finally the right portal vein, working from anterior to posterior. Our preference, however, is to work from posterior to anterior, as follows.

The sheath of the porta hepatis is opened laterally. Dissection is then performed in the plane between the CBD and the portal vein. To facilitate this dissection, the CBD is elevated by applying forward traction to the ligated cystic duct. The portal vein is then followed cephalad until its bifurcation into the left and right portal veins is visible. In a small percentage of patients, the left portal vein arises from the right anterior branch of the portal vein. If the main right portal vein is ligated in a patient who exhibits this anatomic variant, the portion of the liver remaining after resection will lack any portal flow. There is usually a small portal branch that passes from the main right portal vein to the caudate process. Ligation of this branch untethers another 1 to 2 cm of the right portal vein, thereby allowing safer dissection and ligation. The right portal vein is usually clamped with vascular clamps, divided, and oversewn with nonabsorbable sutures. Once this is done, the right hepatic artery is visible behind the CBD and can easily be secured and ligated with nonabsorbable sutures. Because of the multitude of biliary anatomic variations, we usually leave the right hepatic duct intact until parenchymal dissection [*see Step 8, below*] is begun, when this structure can be secured higher within the hepatic parenchyma and divided with greater safety.

Staple ligation   Vascular staplers may be used for stapling the right or the left portal vein during extrahepatic vascular dissection[33,34]; however, suture ligation of the extrahepatic portal veins is such a straightforward technical exercise that staplers add little except cost.

Step 6—Alternative (Intrahepatic Pedicle Ligation): Control of Inflow Vessels

The observations of Glisson and Couinard (see above) that the nutrient vessels to the liver are contained within a thick connective tissue capsule [*see Figure 6*] were the basis for the initial proposal by Launois and Jamieson[11] that intrahepatic vascular pedicle ligation could serve as an alternative to extrahepatic dissection and ligation for controlling vascular inflow to the liver. This alternative technique has the advantages of being rapid and of being unlikely to cause injury to the vasculature or the biliary drainage of the contralateral liver. Given adequate intrahepatic definition and control of the portal triads supplying the area of the liver to be resected, one can readily isolate the various major pedicles by using simple combinations of hepatotomies at specific sites on the inferior surface of the liver [*see Figure 7*].

The right liver is completely mobilized from the retroperitoneum. The most inferior small hepatic veins are ligated, and the inferior right liver is mobilized off the vena cava. Incisions are then made in the liver capsule at hepatotomy sites A and B [*see Figure 7*]. The first incision is made though the caudate process. The full thickness of the caudate process is divided with a combination of diathermy, crushing, and ligation. The second incision is made almost vertically in the medial part of the gallbladder bed. Both incisions must be fairly substantial and reasonably deep. Care must be taken to avoid the terminal branches of the middle hepatic vein, which are the most common source of significant bleeding. By means of either finger dissection or the passage of a large curved clamp, a tape is then placed around the right main sheath [*see Figure 8*]. This tape can be pulled medial-

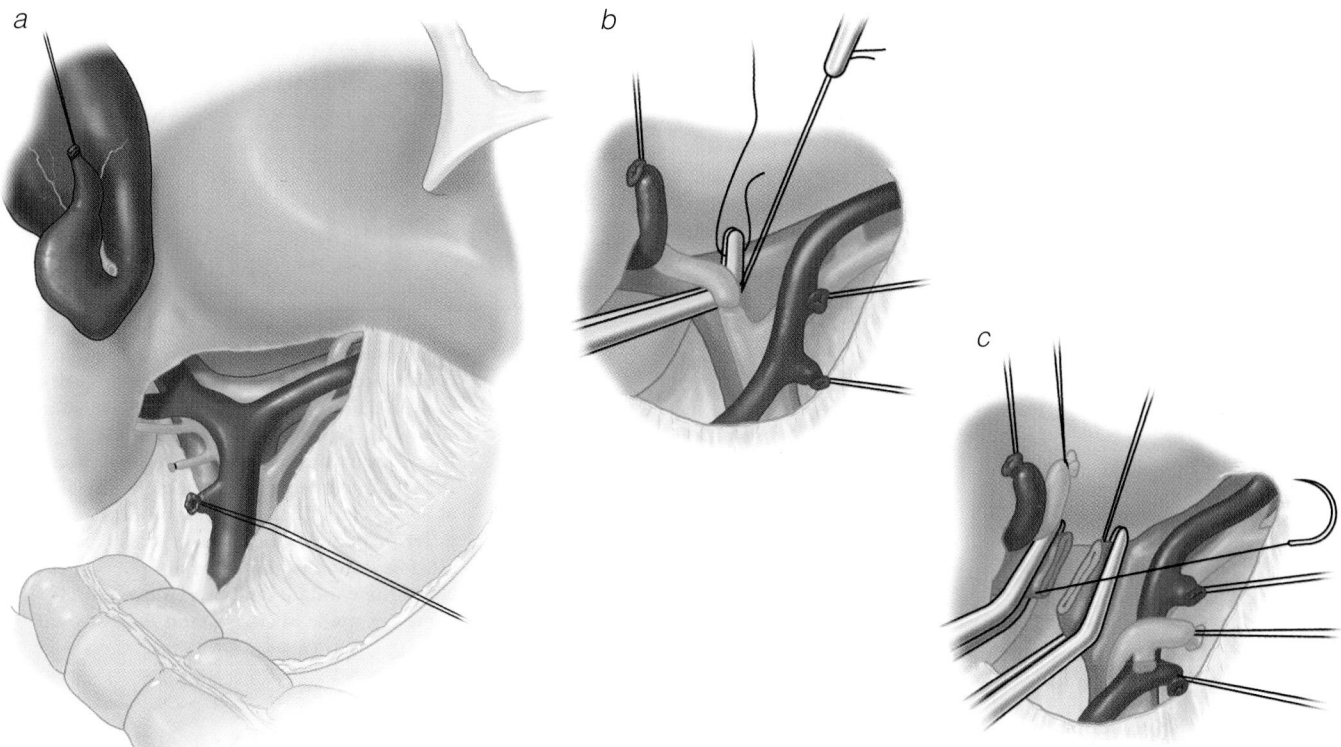

Figure 5 **Right lobectomy. For control of the inflow vessels of the right liver, the liver is retracted cephalad to allow exposure of the porta hepatis. (*a*) The gallbladder is resected to allow access to the bile duct and hepatic vessels. (*b*) The right hepatic duct is ligated to allow access to the hepatic artery and the portal vein. (*c*) After the right hepatic artery is divided, the right portal vein is controlled and divided. Alternatively, the vessels may be approached from a posterolateral direction and the portal vein and hepatic artery may be divided first, with the hepatic duct left intact until the parenchymal transection.**

ly to provide better exposure of the intrahepatic right pedicle and to retract the left biliary tree and portal vein away from the area to be clamped and divided. Clamps are then applied, the right pedicle is divided, and the stumps are suture-ligated.

In practice, for right lobectomies, we prefer to isolate the right anterior and posterior pedicles separately [*see Figure 8*] and ligate them individually. This measure ensures that the left-side structures cannot be injured. Any minor bleeding from a hepatotomy

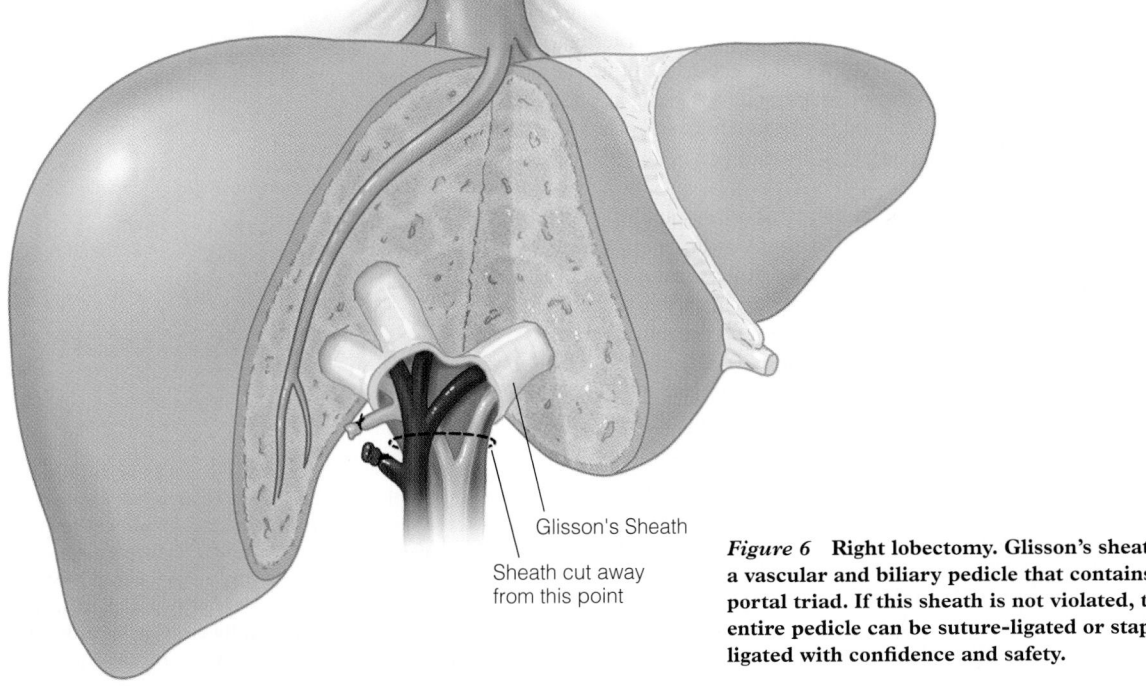

Glisson's Sheath

Sheath cut away
from this point

Figure 6 **Right lobectomy. Glisson's sheath is a vascular and biliary pedicle that contains the portal triad. If this sheath is not violated, the entire pedicle can be suture-ligated or staple-ligated with confidence and safety.**

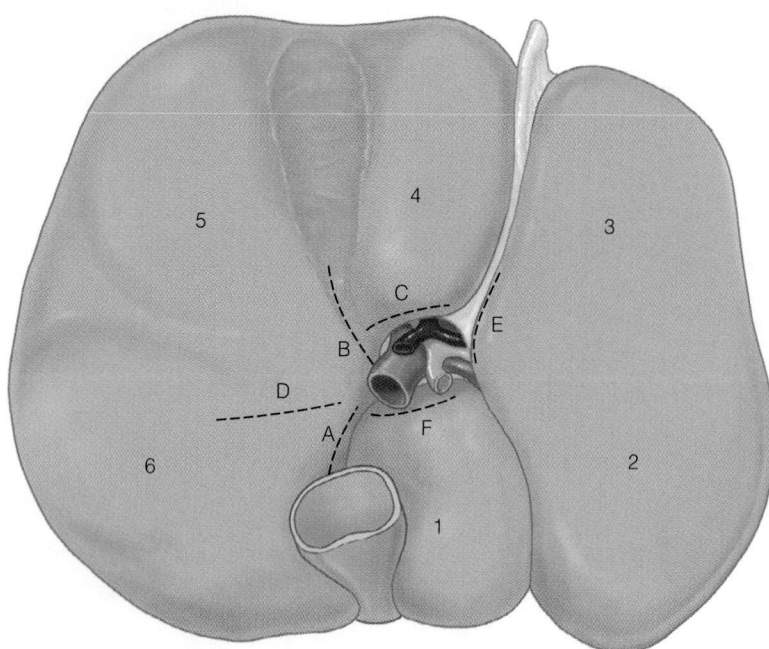

Figure 7 **Right lobectomy. Depicted are sites where hepatotomies can be made to permit isolation of various vascular pedicles. Incisions at sites A and B allow isolation of the right main portal pedicle. Incisions at sites A and D allow isolation of the right posterior portal pedicle. Incisions at sites B and D allow isolation of the right anterior pedicle. Incisions at sites C and E allow isolation of the left main portal pedicle; if the caudate is to be removed, incisions are made at sites C and F.**

usually ceases spontaneously or else stops when Surgicel is placed into the wound.

Staple ligation The use of staplers is now well established for liver resections,[33-38] and we find that staple ligation greatly increases the speed with which intrahepatic portal pedicle ligations can be performed. To control the intrahepatic portal pedicles for a right lobectomy, incisions are made at hepatotomy sites A and B [*see Figure 7*]. Ultrasonography directed from the inferior aspect of the liver helps determine the depth at which the right pedicle lies, which is usually 1 to 2 cm from the inferior surface. The right main pedicle is then secured either digitally or with a curved blunt clamp (e.g., a renal pedicle clamp), and an umbilical tape is placed around it [*see Figure 9a*]. The hilar plate in the back of segment 4 is lowered via an incision at hepatotomy site C [*see Figure 7*] to ensure that the left-side vascular and biliary structures are mobilized well away from the area of staple ligation. A transverse anastomosis (TA) vascular stapler is applied to the right main pedicle while firm countertraction is being applied to the umbilical tape to pull the hilus to the left [*see Figure 9a*]. The stapler is fired, and the pedicle is divided [*see Figure 9b*].

Troubleshooting There are several important guiding principles that should be followed in deciding on and performing intrahepatic pedicle ligation. The most important principle is that in patients undergoing operation for cancer, an intrahepatic pedicle approach should not be used when a tumor is within 2 cm of the hepatic hilus. In such cases, extrahepatic dissection should be performed to avoid violation of the tumor margin.

From a technical standpoint, removal of the gallbladder greatly facilitates isolation and control of right-side vascular pedicles in a right lobectomy. Application of the Pringle maneuver decreases bleeding during hepatotomy and isolation of the pedicle. Finally, the lowest hepatic veins behind the liver should be dissected before any attempt is made to isolate the right-side portal pedicles: incising the caudate process without dividing the small hepatic veins draining this portion of the liver to the vena cava can lead to significant hemorrhage.

Step 7: Control of Outflow Vessels

Control of the outflow vasculature begins with division of the hepatic veins passing from the posterior aspect of the right liver directly to the vena cava. After the right lobe is completely mobilized off the retroperitoneum by dividing the right triangular ligament, it is carefully dissected off the vena cava. Dissection proceeds upward from the inferior border of the liver until the right hepatic vein is exposed. Complete mobilization of the right liver

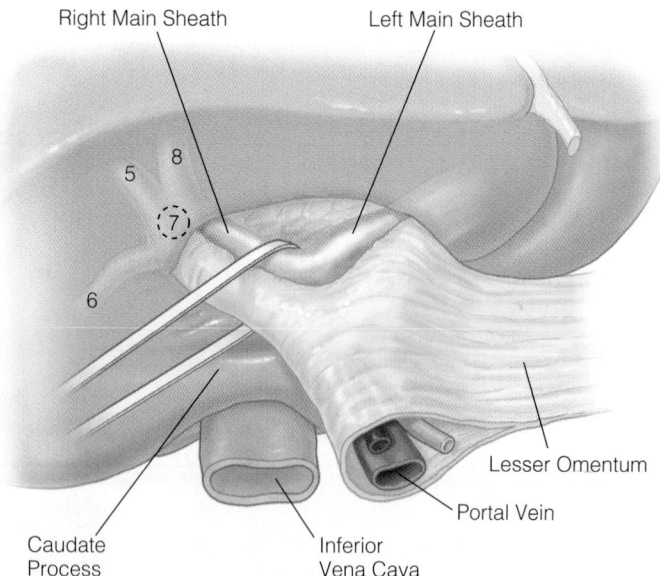

Figure 8 **Right lobectomy. Depicted is isolation of the main right portal pedicle. The pedicle is controlled with a vascular tape and retracted from within the liver substance. This tape can be used for countertraction when a vascular clamp or stapler is applied. The main right portal pedicle has anterior and posterior branches. The right anterior pedicle consists of pedicles to segments 5 and 8. The right posterior pedicle usually consists of only the segment 6 pedicle but may also give rise to the segment 7 pedicle.**

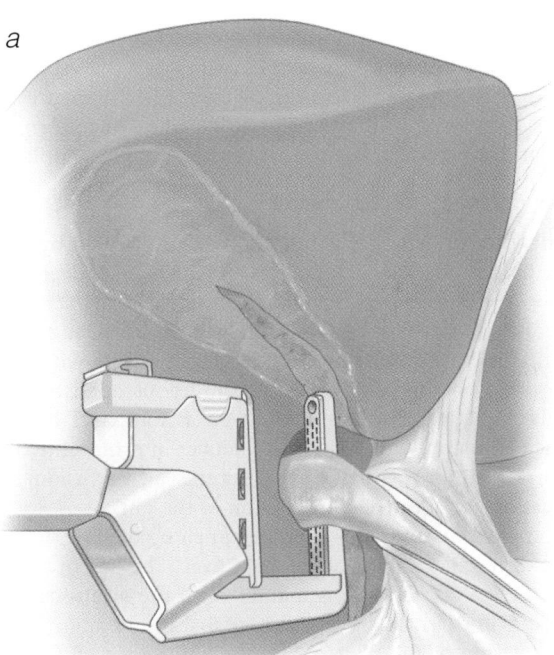

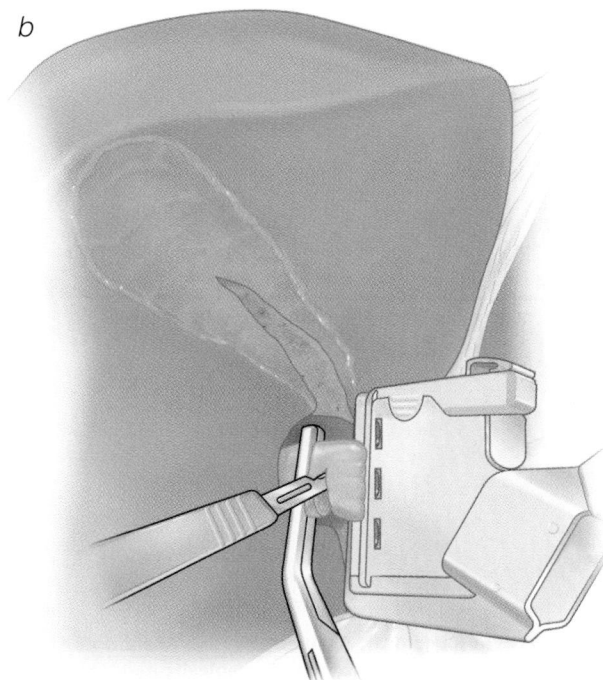

Figure 9 **Right lobectomy. Shown is staple ligation of the right portal pedicle. (*a*) After the liver is incised across the caudate process and along the gallbladder bed, the right main pedicle is isolated and held with an umbilical tape. Countertraction is placed on the umbilical tape while a TA vascular stapler is placed across the pedicle, allowing the left hepatic duct and the left vascular structures to be retracted away from the line of stapling. (*b*) After the stapler is fired, the pedicle is clamped and divided.**

is particularly critical for tumors close to the vena cava. The right hepatic vein is then isolated, cross-clamped, divided, and oversewn [*see Figure 10*]. Unless the tumor or lesion involves the middle hepatic vein close to its junction with the vena cava, the middle hepatic vein usually is not controlled extrahepatically for right-side resections and is easily secured during parenchymal transection.

If there is a large tumor residing at the dome of the liver, gaining control of the hepatic veins and the vena cava may prove very difficult. If so, one should not hesitate to extend the incision to the chest by means of a right thoracoabdominal extension. The morbidity of a thoracoabdominal incision is preferable to the potentially catastrophic hemorrhage that is sometimes encountered when the right hepatic vein is torn during mobilization of a rigid right hepatic lobe containing a large tumor.

Staple ligation Staple ligation has proved useful for outflow control during hepatectomy. When the tumor is in proximity to the hepatic vein–vena cava junction, extrahepatic control of the hepatic veins is essential for excision of the tumor with clear margins, and it limits blood loss during parenchymal transection.[39] Ligating the hepatic veins, particularly with a large and rigid tumor in the vicinity, can be a technically demanding and dangerous exercise. Tearing the hepatic vein or the vena cava during this maneuver is the most common cause of major intraoperative hemorrhage.[27] The endoscopic gastrointestinal anastomosis (GIA) stapler is well suited for ligation of the major hepatic veins in that it has a low profile and is capable of simultaneously sealing both the hepatic vein stump on the vena cava side and the one on the specimen side.

For staple ligation of the right hepatic vein, the right liver is mobilized off the vena cava. Any large accessory right hepatic

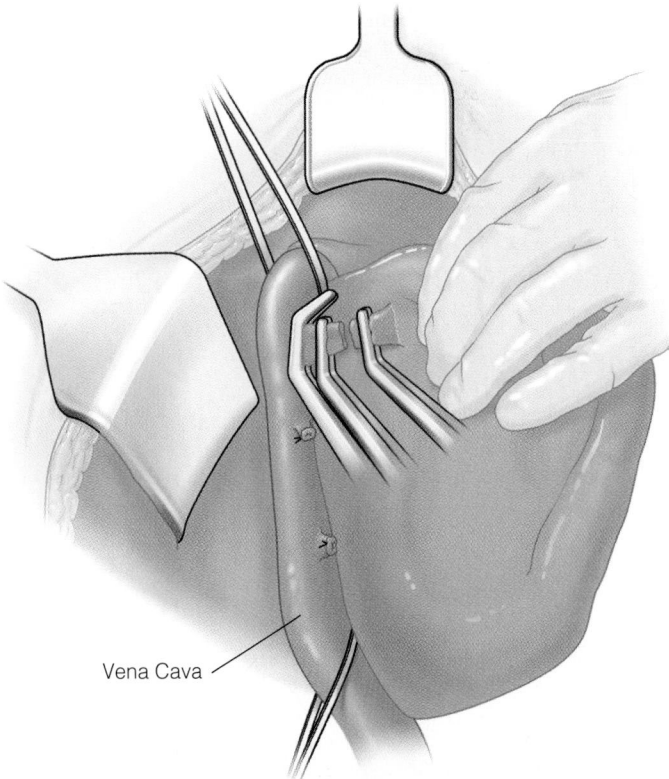

Vena Cava

Figure 10 **Right lobectomy. Once the small perforating vessels to the vena cava have been ligated, further dissection cephalad leads to the right hepatic vein. This vessel is controlled with vascular clamps and divided.**

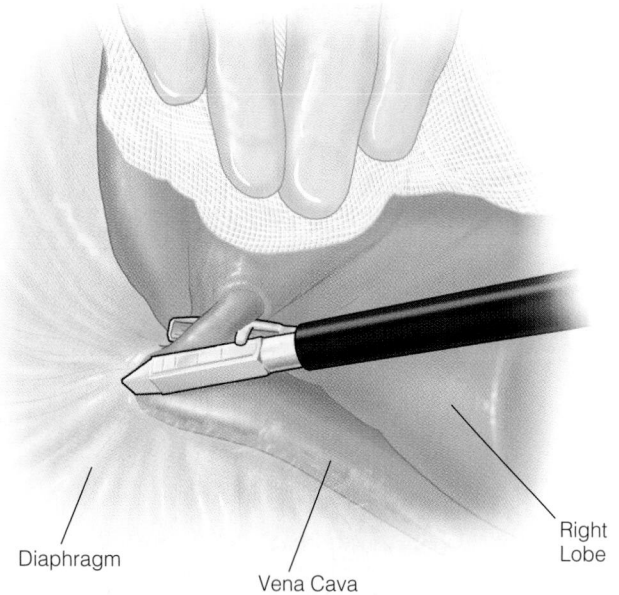

Figure 11 **Right lobectomy. As an alternative to clamping and division, the right hepatic vein may be staple-ligated. Once the small perforating tributaries from the right liver to the vena cava have been divided, the right hepatic vein is isolated and ligated with an endoscopic GIA vascular stapler. The safest method for introducing this stapler is to retract the liver cephalad and to the left while advancing the stapler cephalad in the direction of the vena cava.**

vein encountered can be staple-ligated, as can the tongue of liver tissue that often passes from the right lobe behind the vena cava to the caudate lobe. The right hepatic vein is then identified and isolated. It is the practice of some authors to introduce the stapler from the top of the liver downward,[34] but we find that in most patients, the liver is sufficiently high in the surgical wound

to render this angle of introduction technically impracticable. Accordingly, we introduce the stapler parallel to the vena cava and direct it from below upward [*see Figure 11*]. To ensure that the stapler does not misfire, care should be taken to confirm that no vascular clips are near the site where the stapler is applied.

Step 8: Parenchymal Transection

Inflow to the left liver is temporarily interrupted by clamping the hepatoduodenal ligament (the Pringle maneuver) [*see 106 Injuries to the Liver, Biliary Tract, Spleen, and Diaphragm*]. The safety of temporary occlusion of the vessels supplying the hepatic remnant is well documented. Even in patients with cirrhosis, the warm ischemia produced by continuous application of the Pringle maneuver is well tolerated for as long as 1 hour.[40] Our practice is to apply the Pringle maneuver intermittently for periods of 10 minutes, with 2 to 5 minutes of perfusion between applications to allow decompression of the gut.

Parenchymal division is then begun along the line demarcated by the devascularization of the right liver. The line of transection along the principal plane is marked with the electrocautery and then cut with scissors. Stay sutures of 0 chromic catgut are placed on either side of the plane of transection and used for traction, separation, and elevation as dissection proceeds.

Many special instruments have been proposed for use in parenchymal transection, including electrocauteries, ultrasonic dissectors, and water-jet dissectors. We find that for the majority of hepatic resections, blunt clamp dissection is the most rapid method and is quite safe. In essence, a large Kelly clamp is used to crush the liver parenchyma [*see Figure 12*]. The relatively soft liver substance dissects away, leaving behind the vascular and biliary structures, which are then ligated. With this technique, the principal plane of the liver can usually be transected in less than 30 minutes.

In cirrhotic patients, the clamp-crushing technique may not work as well because of the firmness of the liver substance: the vessels often tear before the parenchyma does. Accordingly, in

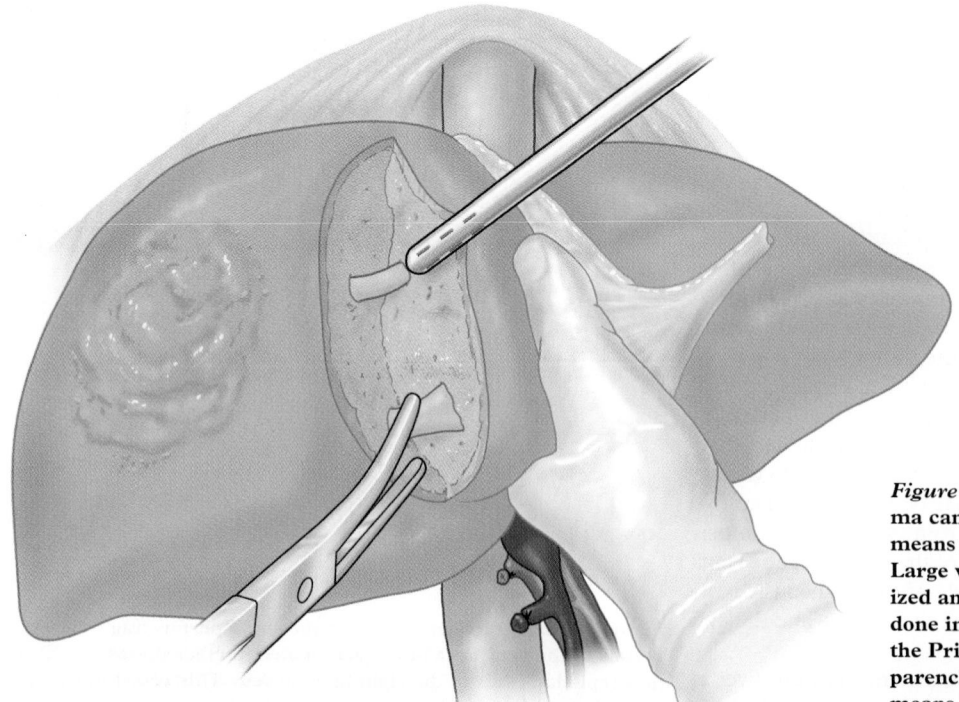

Figure 12 **Right lobectomy. The parenchyma can be quickly and safely transected by means of the clamp-crushing technique. Large vessels and biliary radicles are visualized and ligated or clipped. This is usually done in tandem with inflow occlusion (i.e., the Pringle maneuver). Alternatively, the parenchyma can be bluntly dissected away by means of the finger-fracture technique.**

cirrhotic patients, ultrasonic dissectors that coagulate while transecting the parenchyma may be a better choice. Water-jet dissectors may be useful in defining the major intrahepatic vascular pedicles or the junction of the hepatic vein and the vena cava, particularly if tumor is in close proximity.

After the specimen is removed, the raw surface of the hepatic remnant is carefully examined for hemostasis and bile leaks. Any oozing from the raw surface may be controlled with the argon beam coagulator. Biliary leaks should be controlled with clipping or suture ligation. The retroperitoneal surfaces should also be examined carefully for hemostasis, and the argon beam coagulator should be used where necessary.

Step 9: Closure and Drainage

The abdominal wall is closed in one or two layers with continuous absorbable monofilament sutures. The skin is closed with staples or with subcuticular sutures. Drains are unnecessary in most routine cases[41]; sometimes, in fact, they may exert harmful effects by leading to ascending infection or fluid management problems if ascites develops. There are four clinical situations in which we will routinely place a drain: (1) clear biliary leakage, (2) an infected operative field, (3) a thoracoabdominal incision, and (4) biliary reconstruction. In the case of the thoracoabdominal incision, a drain is placed to ensure that biliary leakage does not develop into a fistula into the chest.

LEFT LOBECTOMY

Steps 1 through 5

Left lobectomy involves removal of segments 2, 3, 4, and sometimes 1. The first five steps of the procedure are much the same as those of a right lobectomy.

Step 6 (Extrahepatic Dissection and Ligation): Control of Inflow Vessels

Extrahepatic control of vascular inflow vessels can be achieved in essentially the same fashion in a right-side resection. Our preference is to start the dissection at the base of the umbilical fissure. The left hepatic artery is divided first. The left branch of the portal vein is then easily identified at the base of the umbilical fissure. The point at which the left portal vein is to be divided depends on the extent of the planned parenchymal resection [see Figure 13]: if the caudate lobe is to be preserved, the left portal vein is ligated just distal to its caudate branch (line B); if the caudate lobe is to be removed, the left portal vein is ligated proximal to the origins of the portal venous branches to this lobe (line A).

Step 6—Alternative (Intrahepatic Pedicle Ligation): Control of Inflow Vessels

If the hepatectomy is being done to treat benign disease or to remove a malignancy that is remote from the base of the umbilical fissure, we highly recommend performing stapler-assisted pedicle ligation in preference to extrahepatic dissection and ligation.

The left portal pedicle is identified at the base of the umbilical fissure. The hilar plate is lowered through an incision at hepatotomy site C [see Figure 7], and a second incision is made in the back of segment 2 at hepatotomy site E [see Figure 7], thereby allowing isolation of the left portal pedicle with minimal risk of injury to the hilus. If the caudate lobe is to be removed as well, incisions should be made at hepatotomy sites C and F [see Figure 7] to allow isolation of the main left portal pedicle proximal to the vessels nourishing the caudate. The portal pedicle is isolated and secured with an umbilical tape. There is some risk that in the

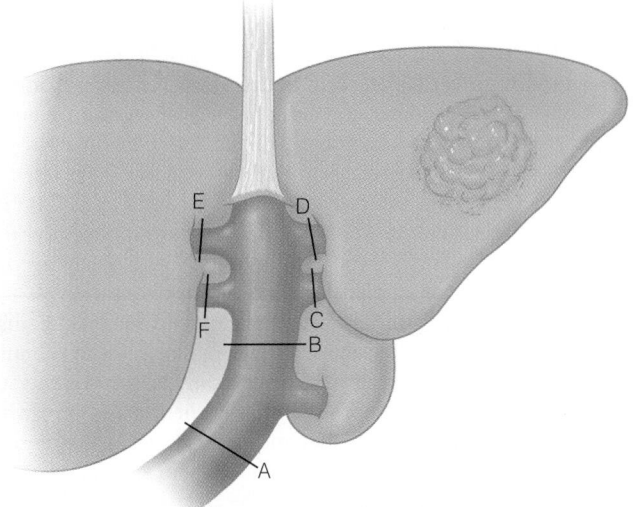

Figure 13 Left lobectomy. Ligation of vascular pedicles at specific sites in the left liver interrupts inflow to specific areas. Ligation at A interrupts inflow to the entire left liver, including the caudate lobe. Ligation at B interrupts blood flow to the left liver while sparing the caudate lobe. Ligation at C devascularizes segment 2, and ligation at D devascularizes segment 3. Ligation at E and F devascularizes segment 4.

course of securing the left portal pedicle, the middle hepatic vein, which lies immediately lateral to the left portal pedicle, may be injured. To minimize this risk, firm downward traction is applied to the umbilical tape, and a TA-30 vascular stapler is placed across the left portal pedicle [see Figure 14]. The pedicle is then stapled and divided.

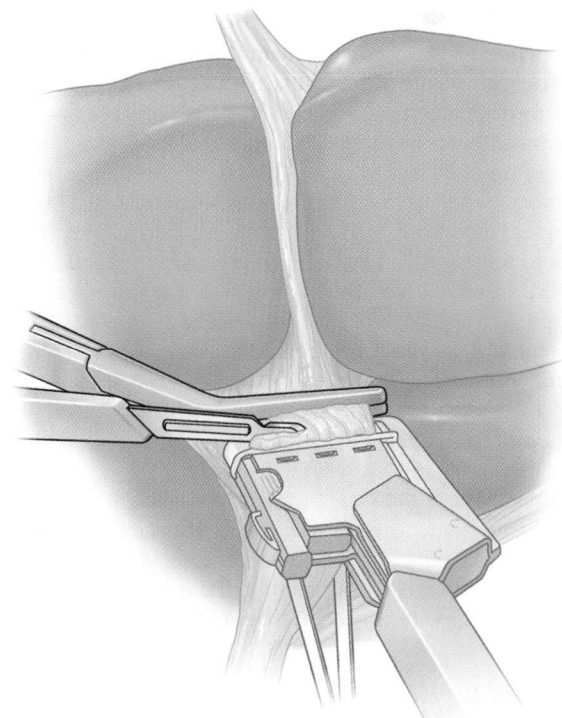

Figure 14 Left lobectomy. After hepatotomies in segment 4 and in the back of segment 2, the left portal pedicle is isolated, stapled, and divided.

Step 7: Control of Outflow Vessels

The left liver is retracted to the patient's right, and the entire lesser omentum is divided. The ligamentum venosum is identified between the caudate lobe and the back of segment 2 and is then divided near its attachment to the left hepatic vein; this measure facilitates identification and dissection of the left and middle hepatic veins anterior to the inferior vena cava. The left and middle hepatic veins are isolated in preparation for division.

Control of the left hepatic vein is quickly and safely accomplished by means of stapled ligation. In approximately 60% of patients, the left and middle hepatic veins join to form a single trunk before entering the vena cava. In a left lobectomy, the middle hepatic vein is often left intact; accordingly, if this is the surgeon's intent, it is vital to protect the middle hepatic vein while ligating the left. After the left hepatic vein is identified, an endoscopic GIA-30 vascular stapler is directed from above downward [see Figure 15] to ligate this vessel. The liver is retracted to the right to permit visualization of the junction of the left and middle hepatic veins. If ligation of the middle hepatic vein is desired as well, as is the case when there is tumor in proximity to the vessel, this can be accomplished with a stapler directed along the same path used for left hepatic vein ligation.

Steps 8 and 9

Parenchymal transection and closure are accomplished in much the same manner in a left lobectomy as in a right lobectomy (see above).

OTHER ANATOMIC RESECTIONS

In the ensuing discussion of the other major anatomic resections, we focus primarily on the major points in which they differ from right and left lobectomy. More detailed discussions of these operations are available in specialty texts on liver resection.[26,27]

Extended Right Hepatectomy (Right Trisegmentectomy)

An extended right hepatectomy involves removal of the right lobe along with segment 4—that is, all liver tissue to the right of the falciform ligament [see Figure 3c]. The initial steps of this operation are the same as those of a right lobectomy, up through division of the right inflow vessels and the right hepatic vein.

The next step is devascularization of segment 4. The umbilical fissure is dissected to permit identification of the vascular pedicles to segments 2, 3, and 4, which lie within this fissure [see Figure 13]. In most cases, the lower part of the umbilical fissure is concealed by a bridge of liver tissue fusing segments 2 and 3 to segment 4. After this tissue bridge is divided with diathermy, the ligamentum teres is retracted caudally to reveal the vascular pedicles from the umbilical fissure to segment 4 (lines E and F [see Figure 13]). We generally suture-ligate these pedicles before dividing them.

The liver tissue is then transected immediately to the right of the falciform ligament, from the anterior surface back toward the divided right hepatic vein. The middle hepatic vein is generally left intact until it is encountered in the upper part of the dissection, at which point it is controlled and either suture- or staple-ligated.

Left Lateral Segmentectomy

A left lateral segmentectomy involves removal of only segments 2 and 3—that is, all liver tissue to the left of the falciform ligament [see Figure 3d]. These segments are mobilized by dividing the left falciform and triangular ligaments. As this is done, care

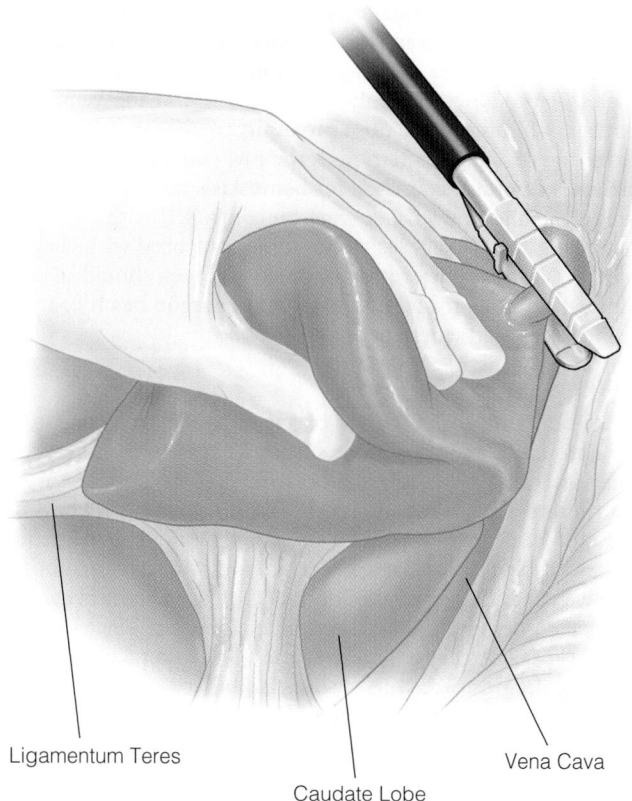

Ligamentum Teres

Caudate Lobe

Vena Cava

Figure 15 **Left lobectomy. Staple ligation of the left hepatic vein. After the left lobe is completely mobilized through division of the left triangular ligament and the lesser omentum, the left hepatic vein is isolated and ligated with an endoscopic GIA vascular stapler. The best angle for introducing the stapler is from the xiphoid posteriorly and caudad.**

must be taken not to injure the left hepatic and phrenic veins, which lie on the medial portion of the left triangular ligament.

The falciform ligament is retracted caudally, and the bridge of liver tissue between segment 4 and segments 2 and 3 is divided with diathermy. Dissection is then performed within the umbilical fissure to the left of the main triad. The vascular pedicles to segments 2 and 3 usually are then readily dissected and controlled (lines C and D [see Figure 13]). Control of these pedicles within the umbilical fissure is particularly important for tumor clearance if tumor is in proximity to the umbilical fissure: if the condition is benign or if tumor is remote from the umbilical fissure, the liver may be split anteroposteriorly just to the left of the ligamentum teres and the falciform ligament, and the vascular pedicles may be identified and ligated as they are encountered in the course of parenchymal transection.

Once the inflow vessels have been ligated, the left hepatic vein is identified and then divided either before parenchymal transection or as the vessel is encountered near the completion of parenchymal transection. If there is tumor near the dome, it is particularly important for tumor clearance that the left hepatic vein be controlled and ligated early and outside the liver.

Extended Left Hepatectomy (Left Trisegmentectomy)

An extended left hepatectomy involves resection of segments 2, 3, 4, 5, 8, and sometimes 1 [see Figure 3e]. In essence, it is a left lobectomy combined with a right anterior sectorectomy; it may or may not include excision of the caudate lobe. This complex resection is usually undertaken to excise large tumors that occupy the left lobe and cross the principal scissura into the right anterior sector.

In this procedure, it is essential to preserve the right hepatic vein, which constitutes the sole venous drainage of the hepatic remnant. Usually, however, parenchymal transection must be performed along the course of this vein; thus, the major potential danger in the operation is injury to the vessel, which could lead to hemorrhage or hepatic failure from venous congestion of the hepatic remnant. In addition, because the blood supply to segment 7 often arises from the right anterior portal pedicle or from the junction of the right anterior and posterior pedicles [see Figure 8], there is a risk that the operation may result in devascularization of a large portion of the hepatic remnant. Finally, because of the great variability of the biliary anatomy and the extensive intrahepatic dissection required in this procedure, there is a significant risk of biliary complications.[42] For all of these reasons, extended left hepatectomies are rarely performed outside major centers.[43]

In the planning of an extended left hepatectomy, particularly close attention must be paid to preoperative imaging investigations so that the right-side intrahepatic vessels and biliary structures can be accurately delineated. Thin-slice CT or MRI images in the form of arterial, portal venous, and hepatic venous reconstructions [see Figure 2] are quite helpful in this regard. For large tumors encroaching on the hepatic hilum or on the junction of the right anterior and posterior pedicles, direct angiography may still be necessary.

The liver is fully mobilized by dividing not only the left triangular ligament but also the ligaments on the right. This step is essential for identifying the correct plane of parenchymal dissection and for ensuring safe dissection along the right hepatic vein.

The initial dissection is the same as for a left lobectomy. The liver is turned to the right side and the portal triad approached. The inflow vessels to the left liver are ligated, and the left hepatic vein and the subdiaphragmatic inferior vena cava are dissected free. The left and middle hepatic veins are controlled and ligated in the extrahepatic portions of their courses.[43] The left liver is thereby freed, and dissection on the right liver is greatly facilitated.

Next, the plane of transection within the right liver is defined. This plane is horizontal and lies lateral to the gallbladder fossa and just anterior to the main right hepatic venous trunk in the right scissura, halfway between the right anterior pedicle and the right posterior pedicle. The plane can be approximated by drawing a line from just anterior to the right hepatic vein at its insertion into the vena cava to a point immediately behind the fissure of Gans. This line can be accurately defined by clamping the portal pedicle to the anterior right sector of the liver.[43] If the tumor is remote from the junction of the right anterior and posterior portal pedicles, the anterior pedicle is controlled as outlined earlier [see Right Lobectomy, Step 6—Alternative (Intrahepatic Pedicle Ligation), above]. A vascular clamp is placed on the pedicle and the line of demarcation on the liver surface inspected before the pedicle is divided. If segment 7 appears to be ischemic as well, further dissection must be done to identify and protect the origins of the vessels supplying segment 7.

Parenchymal dissection is then carried out from below upward, with bleeding controlled by means of low central venous pressure anesthesia and intermittent application of the Pringle maneuver. If the caudate lobe is to be removed as part of the total resection, the veins draining the caudate must be controlled before parenchymal transection.

Segment-Oriented Resection

Each segment of the liver can be resected independently. In addition, resections involving only the right posterior sector (segments 6 and 7) or the right anterior sector (segments 5 and 8) are not uncommon. Extensive and excellent descriptions of so-called segment-oriented hepatic resection are available elsewhere.[44,45]

Postoperative Care

I.V. fluids administered postoperatively should include phosphorus for support of liver regeneration. For large-volume hepatic resections, electrolyte levels, blood count, and prothrombin time (PT) are checked after the operation and then daily for 3 to 4 days. Packed red blood cells are administered if the hemoglobin level falls to 8 mg/dl or lower, and fresh frozen plasma is given if the PT is longer than 17 seconds. Postoperative pain control is best achieved with patient-controlled analgesia (PCA). Because of the decreased clearance of liver-metabolized drugs after a major hepatectomy, selection and dosing of pain medications should be adjusted accordingly. An oral diet can be resumed as early as postoperative day 3 unless a biliary-enteric anastomosis was performed.

Peripheral edema is common after major hepatic resections and may be treated with spironolactone. If an unexplained fever occurs or the bilirubin level rises when other hepatic function parameters are normal, an intra-abdominal bile collection may be present, and a CT scan should be obtained. Percutaneous drain placement usually brings about resolution of such collections after a few days; reoperation is rarely necessary.

Special Considerations

TOTAL VASCULAR ISOLATION FOR CONTROL OF BLEEDING

For control of bleeding during liver parenchymal transection, a technique known as total vascular isolation can be used as an alternative to the Pringle maneuver. In this technique, the liver is isolated by controlling the inferior vena cava (both above and below the liver), the portal vein, and the hepatic artery. This approach is based on techniques developed for liver transplantation and on the observation that the liver is capable of tolerating total normothermic ischemia for as long as 1 hour.[46] Its primary advantage is that while the liver is isolated, little or no bleeding occurs. It does, however, have disadvantages as well. In some patients, temporary occlusion of the inferior vena cava causes hemodynamic instability as a consequence of reduced cardiac output coupled with increased systemic vascular resistance.[47] Cardiac failure with marked hypotension, cardiac arrhythmia, and even cardiac arrest may ensue. In addition, when hepatic perfusion is restored, the sudden return of stagnant potassium-rich blood to the systemic circulation can aggravate the situation. For these reasons and because bleeding is generally well controlled with low central venous pressure anesthesia, we believe that total vascular isolation is useful only in rare cases. The clinical data published to date support this view. A prospective study from 1996 found that total vascular isolation had no major advantages over the approach described earlier [see Operative Technique, Right Lobectomy, Step 8, above] and was actually associated with greater blood loss.[39]

The one setting where we believe that total vascular isolation may have a significant role to play is in the surgical management of hepatic tumors, particularly very large tumors that compromise the vena cava or the hepatic veins. To extend the duration of vascular isolation in this setting, a venovenous bypass that vents the splanchnic blood into the systemic circulation may be used.[48] To further minimize parenchymal injury during vascular isolation, the liver may be perfused with cold organ preservation solutions. For extensive vascular invasion that necessitates major vena caval or hepatic venous reconstruction, some authors have suggested that the liver can be removed during venovenous bypass and resection and reconstruction performed extracorporeally.[49]

Although there are clinical situations that call for venovenous bypass and ex vivo resection, in practice, these techniques are very rarely necessary: short-length vena caval resection and reconstruction can be performed quite safely without resort to them. In fact, involvement of the retrohepatic vena cava at a level below the major hepatic veins can generally be treated with simple excision of the affected segment without replacement,[50] particularly if complete obstruction at this level has already led to established collateral circulation.

THE CIRRHOTIC PATIENT

Cirrhotic patients, by definition, have reduced hepatic functional capacity and reserve. Accordingly, these patients are at higher risk from hepatectomy and require careful assessment of liver function, appropriate selection for surgery and choice of operation, and greater attention to perioperative care.

Operative Planning

Selection of patients Hepatic failure is the major cause of hospital death and long-term morbidity after hepatic resection in cirrhotic patients.[51-55] Consequently, determination of a cirrhotic patient's candidacy for hepatectomy is based on preoperative assessment of baseline liver function.

A variety of tests have been proposed for assessment of hepatic reserve, including measurement of clearance of various dyes and metabolic substrates (e.g., indocyanine green[56,57] and aminopyrine[51]). Measurement of the urea-nitrogen synthesis rate has also been suggested as a way of predicting outcome after resection.[54] Another functional test involves administering lidocaine and measuring levels of monethylglycinexylidide (a metabolite of lidocaine that is generated mostly through the cytochrome P-450 enzyme system in the liver) as a gauge of liver function.[58] Measurement of the hepatic portal venous pressure gradient via invasive radiologic techniques has been found to predict postoperative hepatic failure.[59] Assessment of portal venous hemodynamics by means of noninvasive Doppler ultrasonography has also been found to predict outcome after hepatectomy.[60]

Currently, none of these functional tests are routinely done at most major liver resection centers. In practice, the Child-Pugh score [*see 45 Jaundice*] is the most commonly employed clinical tool for selection of surgical candidates. A Child-Pugh score higher than 8 is generally accepted as a contraindication to major hepatic resection.[53,55,61-64]

Choice of procedure The appropriate extent of resection for cirrhotic patients may be quite different from that for noncirrhotic patients. In cirrhotic patients, the majority of hepatectomies are performed to eradicate hepatocellular carcinoma. A prime consideration in such resections is the margin needed to ensure tumor clearance. Most clinicians aim for a tumor-free margin of 1 cm. A 1989 study, however, found that in cirrhotic patients with hepatocellular carcinoma, as long as the tumor margin was microscopically clear of cancer, the exact size of the margin was not correlated with the incidence of recurrence.[65] In fact, the acceptance

of limited margins, coupled with the acceptance of nonanatomic resections aimed at preserving as much functional parenchyma as possible, is the single change in technical practice that is most responsible for the great improvements in the safety of hepatic resection observed worldwide in cirrhotic patients.

The guiding principle for hepatectomy in cirrhotic patients is that limited resections should be favored, with as much functional parenchyma spared as possible. In general, even for patients with well-compensated Child's grade A cirrhosis, we try to limit resections to less than two segments of functional liver. Patients with large tumors are more likely to tolerate a major resection because little functional parenchyma must be removed along with the tumor. Major hepatic resections involving removal of at least one lobe are now reported to carry an operative mortality of less than 10% in cirrhotic patients.[66,67] Such procedures are usually performed in cirrhotic patients who have large tumors replacing most of one lobe, acceptable liver function, and no atrophy of the uninvolved lobe. Small tumors are often more difficult to manage. For patients with small, deeply placed tumors whose resection would necessitate removal of a large amount of functional parenchyma, an ablative alternative or even transplantation might be more suitable.

In an attempt to preserve as much functional liver as possible, many surgeons resort to more technically challenging operations. Most will perform multiple limited resections in order to avoid performing a full lobectomy.[68,69] Some go so far as to reconstruct the right hepatic vein for the purpose of preserving venous outflow in segments 5 and 6 after resection of segments 7 and 8.

Operative Technique

Hepatic resection in cirrhotic patients is associated with certain specific technical difficulties that substantially increase the complexity of the operation. The liver parenchyma is hard, which makes retraction of the liver difficult. In addition, anatomic landmarks are distorted and difficult to find as a consequence of fibrosis and atrophy-hypertrophy. Finally, portal hypertension and tissue friability contribute to increased blood loss during mobilization and parenchymal transection.

Exposure and mobilization Trifurcated incisions and thoracoabdominal incisions should be avoided in cirrhotic patients because of the potential for ascitic leakage externally or into the chest. The increased firmness of the cirrhotic liver and the consequent difficulty of retraction can lead to significant blood loss from retroperitoneal or phrenic collateral vessels during mobilization. To prevent such bleeding, it may be preferable to use an anterior approach in which the liver parenchyma is split within the principal interlobar plane down to the anterior surface of the vena cava before the right liver is mobilized off the retroperitoneum.[70] The right lobe is then mobilized in a medial-to-lateral direction, and the right hepatic vein is secured during mobilization of the right lobe off the vena cava.

Inflow control At one time, it was widely doubted whether the Pringle maneuver was safe in cirrhotic patients. Subsequently, however, many studies verified that this maneuver can be performed for extended periods in cirrhotic patients without increasing either morbidity or mortality.[71-76] Nevertheless, it is advisable to employ the Pringle maneuver sparingly in this population so as to minimize ischemic stress. Our practice is to clamp the portal triad with a vessel loop tourniquet for 10-minute periods with 5-minute breaks in between. We have not found additional protective maneuvers (e.g., topical cooling[77,78]) to be necessary.

a   *b*

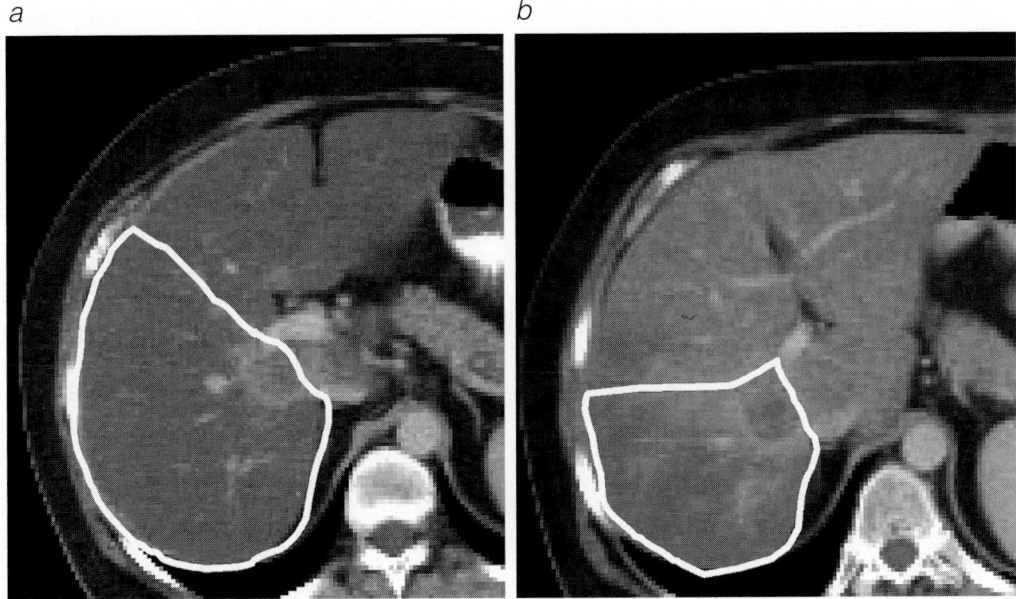

Figure 16   Liver atrophy and hypertrophy occur after right portal vein embolization. Shown are images of the liver (*a*) at baseline and (*b*) 6 weeks after PVE. The right liver is outlined in white.

Parenchymal transection   In patients with normal liver parenchyma, most experienced hepatic surgeons use blunt dissection, with either the clamp-crushing technique or the finger-fracture technique, to transect the liver tissue.[79] In patients with cirrhosis, however, the firmness of the parenchyma makes the clamp-crushing technique less than ideal: because the parenchyma is often harder than the underlying vasculature and biliary radicles, blunt dissection is likely to tear these vessels. Accordingly, ultrasonic dissectors that coagulate and seal vessels during dissection are more suitable for parenchymal transection in this population.

Closure and drainage   Because of the likelihood of postoperative ascites, the abdominal wall is closed with a heavy continuous absorbable monofilament suture to create a watertight closure. To prevent major fluid and protein losses and ascending infections, abdominal drains generally are not used.[41] Reports specifically examining the role of drainage in cirrhotic patients documented a much lower incidence of postoperative complications and a shorter hospital stay for patients in whom no drains were placed.[80,81]

Postoperative Care

The focus of postoperative care in cirrhotic patients is on management of cirrhosis and portal hypertension. In most such patients who undergo hepatic resection, transient hepatic insufficiency develops postoperatively, with hyperbilirubinemia, ascites formation, hypoalbuminemia, edema, and worsening of the baseline coagulopathy.

In the first 24 hours after the procedure, crystalloid must be administered at a level sufficient to maintain adequate portal perfusion.[82] If patients are stable after the first 24 hours, they are subjected to water and sodium restriction and receive liberal amounts of salt-poor albumin for volume expansion if needed. Spironolactone is started in all patients as soon as oral diet is resumed; furosemide is added as needed. On rare occasions, a peritoneovenous shunt may have to be employed to control postoperative ascites,[83] but this measure is usually unnecessary if patients were properly selected. The PT is checked twice daily

during the immediate postoperative period: a PT longer than 17 seconds is corrected by administering fresh frozen plasma.

Preoperative Portal Vein Embolization

Most liver surgeons would be reluctant to resect more than the equivalent of two segments of functional liver in a patient with documented cirrhosis.[84] Consequently, many cirrhotic patients with technically resectable tumors are relegated to noncurative ablative therapy out of concern over possible postoperative hepatic failure. The situation may be changing, however, with the growing use of preoperative portal vein embolization (PVE), a technique that may extend surgeons' ability to resect tumor in cirrhotic patients.

In PVE, access to the portal vein on the side of the liver to be resected is gained via a percutaneous transhepatic approach. The vein is embolized approximately 1 month before the planned resection so as to produce ipsilateral atrophy along with compensatory hypertrophy of the contralateral future hepatic remnant.[85] The degree of compensatory hypertrophy can be dramatic [*see Figure 16*] and may modulate postoperative hepatic dysfunction. PVE is also employed in patients with normal parenchyma in whom extensive resection may result in a very small hepatic remnant. In patients undergoing extended right hepatectomy, particularly those with congenitally small left lateral sectors, the entire area of the extended hepatectomy, including the main right portal vein and the segmental branches supplying segment 4, can be embolized.[86]

There is substantial evidence that preoperative PVE can be successfully used in patients with cirrhotic livers or impaired liver function and that such use is generally well tolerated.[87-90] This technique can also serve as a test of the regenerative capacity of the hepatic remnant. If no compensatory hypertrophy is seen 4 weeks after PVE, the decision to perform a major hepatectomy should be reconsidered.

Repeat Hepatic Resection

Since 1984, when one of the first reports of repeat hepatic resection was published,[91] a number of reports from around the world have demonstrated that repeat resection can be done safely and with good long-term results even for recurrent malignancies. The morbidity rates and mortalities reported after repeat hepatectomy for metastatic colorectal cancer[92-104] and hepatocellular carcinoma[105-112] are comparable to those reported after initial hepatectomy. Extended survival has been demonstrated, and in some cases, the survival rate is equivalent to or even better than that observed after initial resection.[93,100,107,113] In the following section, we concentrate on the key technical aspects of repeat hepatic resection. Discussions of indications, patient selection, and outcome are available in other sources.[93,100,107,113]

Repeat hepatic resection poses certain technical difficulties that are not commonly encountered during initial resection.[92,114,115] First, adhesions at the previous line of parenchymal transection can make reexposure of the liver difficult. Mobilizing the liver off the vena cava and reexposing the porta hepatis and the hepatic veins can be extremely hazardous if dissection was previously done in these areas. Second, liver regeneration and systemic chemotherapy can induce accumulation of fat within the liver, thereby rendering it more friable[93]; the increased friability further increases the difficulties of reexposure and predisposes to tearing of Glisson's capsule.[114] Third, regeneration alters the normal anatomic configuration of the portal structures [*see Figure 17*].[116] For example, after a right hepatectomy, the porta hepatis is rotated posteriorly and to the right. The normal relationship among the portal structures is altered, with the bile duct displaced posteriorly and the portal vein displaced anteriorly.

Preoperative imaging is even more important for repeat resections than for primary resections. This is because scarring limits access to the liver for intraoperative assessment via palpation or ultrasonography. Before embarking on a repeat resection, it is essential to know the exact number and locations of the lesions to be treated within the regenerated parenchyma. Preoperative imaging also facilitates operative planning by accurately delineating the vasculature within the regenerated liver.

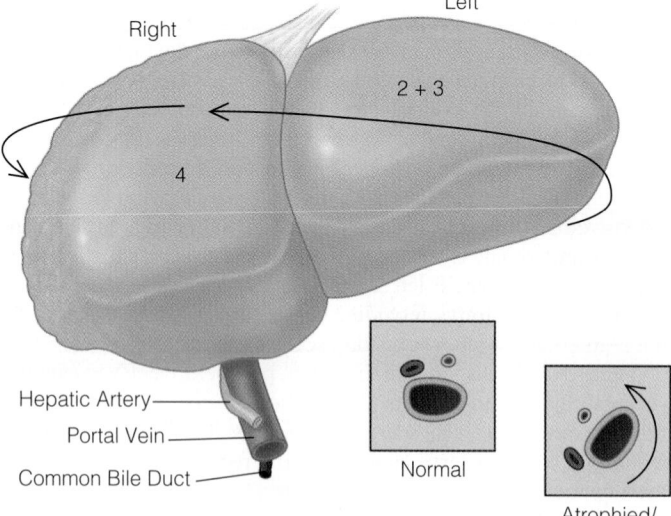

Figure 17 **Repeat hepatic resection. Depicted are the changes in the relations of the portal structures that occur as a result of right liver atrophy or resection and left-side hypertrophy. The structures in the porta hepatis rotate to the right, with the CBD coming to rest laterally rather than anteriorly.**

In a repeat resection after a previous major right hepatectomy, it is important to be prepared to convert the incision into a thoracoabdominal incision if necessary. Access through the right chest may be required for mobilization of the liver because of adherence of the previous resection margin to the diaphragm, or it may be required for access to the rotated CBD and portal vasculature at the porta hepatis.

In the dissection of the right upper quadrant after a previous right hepatectomy, three landmarks are particularly helpful in defining the anatomic structures within the regenerated left liver. The first landmark is remnants of the ligamentum teres, which defines the demarcation between the left lateral segment and segment 4; these should be found early on. The ligamentum teres may be followed to the base of the umbilical fissure to define the location of the left hepatic artery. Whether this artery arises from the common hepatic artery or from the left gastric artery, it passes into the liver parenchyma at the base of the umbilical fissure. The second landmark is the caudate lobe. The lesser omentum should be opened early on to reveal this lobe. An index finger should then be passed in front of the caudate toward the obliterated foramen of Winslow to define the porta hepatis and the location of the portal vein. The third landmark is the vena cava. Performing the Kocher maneuver to mobilize the duodenum off the vena cava allows this vessel to be dissected, thus further defining the portocaval plane. Definition of this plane leads to the correct plane for dissection and mobilization of the liver off the vena cava; it also allows isolation of the hepatoduodenal ligament for application of the Pringle maneuver and for extrahepatic dissection of the inflow vessels.

In a repeat resection after a previous left hepatectomy, the main concern with regard to mobilization of the liver is the anterior position of the portal vasculature after right-side hypertrophy. It is therefore prudent to mobilize the right liver, perform a Kocher maneuver, and follow the vena cava caudally to identify the portal vein from the right. The stomach and the colon usually are adherent to the edge of the previous resection and must be carefully dissected free to allow access to the liver. If the middle hepatic vein was preserved in the earlier left hepatectomy, it will lie immediately deep to the plane of the stomach or the colon and thus may be a source of hemorrhage during dissection.

Control of the inflow or outflow vasculature may be compromised by the scarring resulting from the previous operation. If extensive extrahepatic dissection was performed for control of inflow vasculature in the earlier procedure, control of these vessels in the repeat resection is more safely accomplished via intrahepatic pedicle ligation [*see* Operative Technique, Right Lobectomy, Step 6—Alternative (Intrahepatic Pedicle Ligation), *above*].

A major concern with repeat hepatectomy is that it is sometimes necessary to perform more limited resections than would otherwise be indicated. Normally, for removal of liver tumors, we avoid wedge excisions because these nonanatomic resections are more often associated with greater blood loss and positive margins than anatomic resections are.[99,117] In a repeat hepatectomy, however, anatomic considerations arising in the regenerated liver may make a wedge resection the best choice.

With appropriate patient selection and careful operative planning, very favorable perioperative and long-term results can be achieved after repeat hepatic resection. It is noteworthy that studies addressing repeat resection have not documented any substantial increases in blood loss, duration of operation, or rate of complications in comparison with the initial resection.[93-97,118]

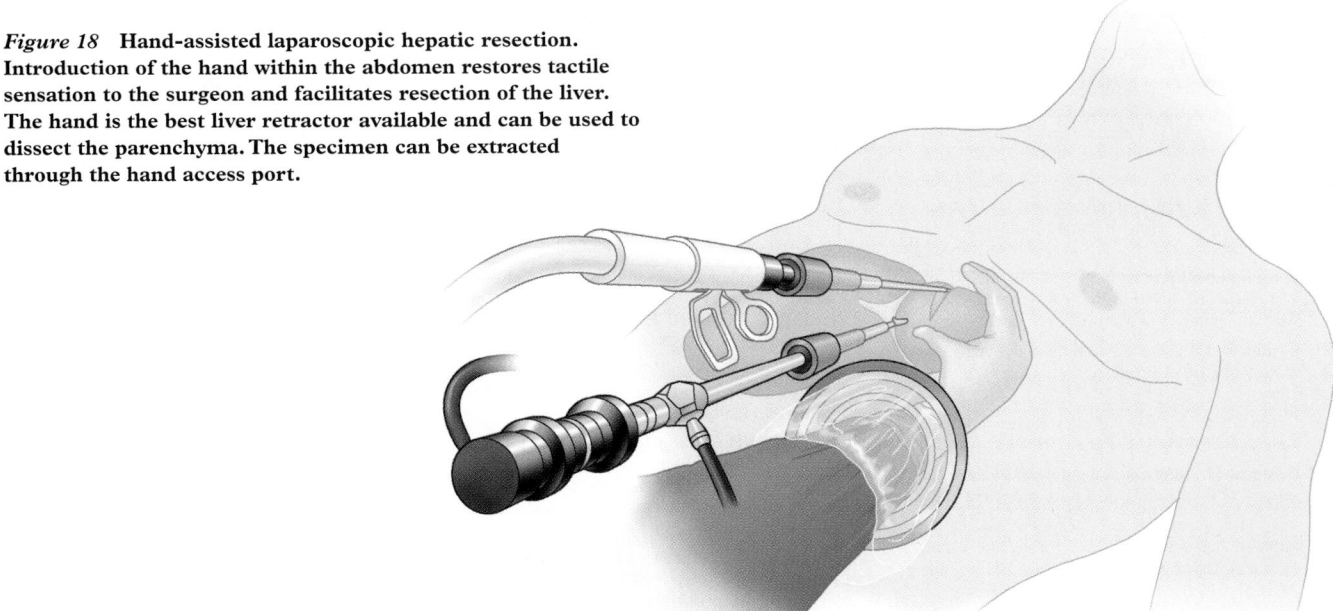

Figure 18 **Hand-assisted laparoscopic hepatic resection. Introduction of the hand within the abdomen restores tactile sensation to the surgeon and facilitates resection of the liver. The hand is the best liver retractor available and can be used to dissect the parenchyma. The specimen can be extracted through the hand access port.**

Hand-Assisted Laparoscopic Hepatic Resection

In addition to revolutionizing treatment of gallstone disease,[119] laparoscopic techniques are increasingly used for fenestration of benign cysts of the liver[120,121] and for staging of hepatobiliary malignancies to prevent unnecessary laparotomies.[29,122,123] Until recently, however, laparoscopic resection of liver tumors was described only in case reports or small series.[120,124-128] Perhaps the main reason for the strong resistance to laparoscopic hepatic resection has been fear of catastrophic bleeding. If inadvertent damage to a major hepatic vein or the vena cava occurs during an open operation, the bleeding can be controlled with direct manual compression until the vessel is repaired; however, if such damage occurs during a laparoscopic operation, control of the bleeding is considerably more difficult. In addition, damage to a hepatic vein or the vena cava during a laparoscopic procedure can theoretically result in CO_2 embolism. Another concern is that the loss of tactile sensation characteristic of laparoscopic surgery may lead to inadequate tumor clearance. Finally, whereas there are many liver retractors designed to hold the liver in one position, there is no good retractor for repeatedly moving the liver from side to side, as would be necessary during a laparoscopic hepatectomy. The human hand is still the best tool for this purpose.

Laparoscopic hepatic resection has been greatly facilitated by several recent technologic advances, including laparoscopic staplers[129] and ultrasonic dissectors,[130] which can be used for ligation of the hepatic vasculature and transection of liver parenchyma. The most important advance, however, is the hand access port, a small port through which one hand can be introduced into the abdomen for a hand-assisted laparoscopic resection [*see Figure 18*].[131-133] With this approach, the surgeon not only regains a measure of tactile sensation but also is able to employ the best liver retractor available. Moreover, direct manual compression of any bleeding vessels is once again possible, and the incision made for the hand access port is also used for extraction of the resected specimen.

Patient selection is essential for safe laparoscopic resection of liver tumors. Resection of any two segments along the lower edge of the liver is easily accomplished laparoscopically. At MSKCC, we have laparoscopically resected lesions from all segments.[38]

The procedure starts with the placement of a 10 mm port, usually in the right or left upper quadrant on the side opposite that on which the hand access port will be placed. After staging is performed to ensure that the lesion is resectable, a 5 to 6 cm incision is made for placement of the hand access port. The port site should be chosen so as to allow manual retraction of the part of the liver to be resected, with the falciform and triangular ligaments used to provide countertraction. Once the access port is in place, the abdomen is fully palpated under laparoscopic vision. A laparotomy sponge is placed into the abdomen to facilitate retraction and absorb blood, and a long bulldog clamp is inserted for use in the Pringle maneuver. A long umbilical tape is tied to the bulldog clamp beforehand so that the instrument can be easily located throughout the procedure. Additional ports are then placed as necessary for introduction of the stapler or the ultrasonic scalpel.

The area to be resected is outlined with the electrocautery. The liver is manually retracted, intermittent application of the Pringle maneuver is initiated, and the parenchyma is transected. Liver parenchyma remote from the major portal pedicles and hepatic veins may be transected either with the ultrasonic dissector or by means of finger fracture. Near the major portal pedicles and hepatic veins, an endoscopic GIA vascular stapler may be used. After removal of the specimen, the laparoscopic argon beam coagulator (Conmed Corporation, Utica, New York) and hemostatic agents may be used.

The laparoscopic approach is suitable for minor as well as major hepatic resections. At present, however, it is unclear whether this approach constitutes a significant advance in liver surgery. To clarify this issue, further study of laparoscopic hepatic resection with respect to perioperative outcome, quality of life, and long-term survival is required.

References

1. Lortat-Jacob JL, Robert HG: Hepatectomie droite reglee. Presse Med 60:549, 1952

2. Fong Y: Hepatic colorectal metastasis: current surgical therapy, selection criteria for hepatectomy, and role for adjuvant therapy. Adv Surg 34:351, 2000

3. Jarnagin WR, Fong Y, Blumgart LH: The current management of hilar cholangiocarcinoma. Adv Surg 33:345, 1999

4. Fong Y, Sun RL, Jarnagin W, et al: An analysis of 412 cases of hepatocellular carcinoma at a Western center. Ann Surg 229:790, 1999

5. Couinaud C: Bases anatomiques des hepatectomies gauche et droite reglées. J Chir 70:933, 1954

6. Couinaud C: Le Foie: Etudes Anatomiques et Chirurgicales. Masson, Paris, 1957

7. Bismuth H: Surgical anatomy and anatomic surgery of the liver. World J Surg 6:3, 1982

8. Baer HU, Dennison AR, Maddern GJ, et al: Subtotal hepatectomy: a new procedure based on the inferior right hepatic vein. Br J Surg 78:1221, 1991

9. Smadja C, Blumgart LH: The biliary tract and the anatomy of biliary exposure. Surgery of the Liver and Biliary Tract, 2nd ed. Blumgart LH, Ed. Churchill Livingstone, London, 1994

10. Glisson F: Anatomia Hepatis. O Pullein, London, 1654

11. Launois B, Jamieson GG: The importance of Glisson's capsule and its sheaths in the intrahepatic approach to resection of the liver. Surg Gynecol Obstet 174:7, 1992

12. Soyer P, Levesque M, Elias D, et al: Preoperative assessment of resectability of hepatic metastases from colonic carcinoma: CT portography vs sonography and dynamic CT. AJR Am J Roentgenol 159:741, 1992

13. Hann LE, Schwartz LH, Panicek DM, et al: Tumor involvement in hepatic veins: comparison of MR imaging and US for preoperative assessment. Radiology 206:651, 1998

14. Hann LE, Fong Y, Shriver CD, et al: Malignant hepatic hilar tumors: can ultrasonography be used as an alternative to angiography with CT arterial portography for determination of resectability? J Ultrasound Med 15:37, 1996

15. Gibson RN, Yeung E, Thompson JN, et al: Bile duct obstruction: radiologic evaluation of level, cause and tumor resectability. Radiology 160:43, 1986

16. Fortner JG, Lincer RM: Hepatic resection in the elderly. Ann Surg 211:141, 1990

17. Karl RC, Smith SK, Fabri PJ: Validity of major cancer operations in elderly patients. Ann Surg Oncol 2:107, 1995

18. Fong Y, Blumgart LH, Fortner JG, et al: Pancreatic or liver resection for malignancy is safe and effective for the elderly. Ann Surg 222:426, 1995

19. Hanazaki K, Kajikawa S, Shimozawa N, et al: Hepatic resection for hepatocellular carcinoma in the elderly. J Am Coll Surg 192:38, 2001

20. Fong Y, Brennan MF, Cohen AM, et al: Liver resection in the elderly. Br J Surg 84:1386, 1997

21. Cunningham JD, Fong Y, Shriver C, et al: One hundred consecutive hepatic resections: blood loss, transfusion and operative technique. Arch Surg 129:1050, 1994

22. Melendez J, Ferri E, Zwillman M, et al: Extended hepatic resection: a 6-year retrospective study of risk factors for perioperative mortality. J Am Coll Surg 192:47, 2001

23. Scheele J, Stangl R, Altendorf-Hofmann A, et al: Indicators of prognosis after hepatic resection for colorectal secondaries. Surgery 110:13, 1991

24. Weber SM, Jarnagin WR, DeMatteo RP, et al: Survival after resection of multiple hepatic colorectal metastases. Ann Surg Oncol 7:643, 2000

25. Goldsmith NA, Woodburne RT: The surgical anatomy pertaining to liver resection. Surg Gynecol Obstet 105:310, 1957

26. Blumgart LH, Jarnagin W, Fong Y: Liver resection for benign disease and for liver and biliary tumors. Surgery of the Liver and Biliary Tract, 3rd ed. Blumgart LH, Fong Y, Eds. WB Saunders, London, 2000, p 1639

27. Blumgart LH, Fong Y: Surgical management of colorectal metastases to the liver. Curr Probl Surg 5:333, 1995

28. Jarnagin WR, Conlon K, Bodniewicz J, et al: A clinical scoring system predicts the yield of diagnostic laparoscopy in patients with potentially resectable hepatic colorectal metastases. Cancer 91:1121, 2001

29. Jarnagin WR, Bodniewicz J, Dougherty E, et al: A prospective analysis of staging laparoscopy in patients with primary and secondary hepatobiliary malignancies. J Gastrointest Surg 4:34, 2000

30. Lo CM, Lai EC, Liu CL, et al: Laparoscopy and laparoscopic ultrasonography avoid exploratory laparotomy in patients with hepatocellular carcinoma. Ann Surg 227:527, 1998

31. Callery MP, Strasberg SM, Doherty GM, et al: Staging laparoscopy with laparoscopic ultrasonography: optimizing resectability in hepatobiliary and pancreatic malignancy. J Am Coll Surg 185:33, 1997

32. Castaing D, Kunstlinger F, Habib N: Intraoperative ultrasound study of the liver: methodology and anatomical results. Am J Surg 149:676, 1985

33. McEntee GP, Nagorney DM: Use of hepatic staplers in major hepatic resections. Br J Surg 78:40, 1991

34. Cohen AM: Use of laparoscopic vascular stapler at laparotomy for colorectal cancer. Dis Colon Rectum 35:910, 1992

35. Jurim O, Colonna II JO, Colquhoun SD, et al: A stapling technique for hepatic resection. J Am Coll Surg 178:510, 1994

36. Yanaga K, Nishizaki T, Yamamoto K, et al: Simplified inflow control using stapling devices for major hepatic resection. Arch Surg 131:104, 1996

37. Lefor AT, Flowers JL: Laparoscopic wedge biopsy of the liver. J Am Coll Surg 178:307, 1994

38. Fong Y, Jarnagin W, Conlon KC, et al: Hand-assisted laparoscopic liver resection: lessons from an initial experience. Arch Surg 135:854, 2000

39. Belghiti J, Noun R, Zante E, et al: Portal triad clamping or hepatic vascular exclusion for major liver resection. Ann Surg 224:155, 1996

40. Bothe AJ, Steele G Jr: Is there a role for perioperative nutritional support in liver resection? HPB Surgery 10:177, 1997

41. Fong Y, Brennan MF, Brown K, et al: Drainage is unnecessary after elective liver resection. Am J Surg 171:158, 1996

42. Starzl TE, Iwatsuki S, Shaw BW, et al: Left hepatic trisegmentectomy. Surg Gynecol Obstet 155:21, 1982

43. Blumgart LH, Baer HU, Czerniak A, et al: Extended left hepatectomy: technical aspects of an evolving procedure. Br J Surg 80:903, 1993

44. Scheele J: Segment oriented resection of the liver: rationale and technique in hepato-biliary and pancreatic malignancies. Lygidakis NJ, Tytgat GNJ, Eds. Thieme, Stuttgart, 1989

45. Scheele J, Stangl R: Segment oriented anatomical liver resections. Surgery of the Liver and Biliary Tract. Blumgart LH, Ed. Churchill Livingstone, London, 1994

46. Huguet C, Nordlinger B, Gallopin JJ, et al: Normothermic hepatic vascular occlusion for extensive hepatectomy. Surg Gynecol Obstet 147:689, 1978

47. Pappas G, Palmer WM, Martineau GL, et al: Hemodynamic alterations caused during orthotopic liver transplantation in humans. Surgery 70:872, 1971

48. Shaw BW, Martin DJ, Marquez JM, et al: Venous bypass in clinical liver transplantation. Ann Surg 200:524, 1984

49. Pichlmayr R, Grosse H, Hauss J, et al: Technique and preliminary results of extracorporeal liver surgery (bench procedure) and of surgery on the in situ perfused liver. Br J Surg 77:21, 1990

50. Cunci O, Coste T, Vacher B, et al: Resection de la veine cave inferieure retro-hepatique au cours d'une hepatectomie pour tumeur. Ann Chir 37:197, 1983

51. Lau H, Man K, Fan ST, et al: Evaluation of preoperative hepatic function in patients with hepatocellular carcinoma undergoing hepatectomy. Br J Surg 84:1255, 1997

52. Takenaka K, Kanematsu T, Fukuzawa K, et al: Can hepatic failure after surgery for hepatocellular carcinoma in cirrhotic patients be prevented? World J Surg 14:123, 1990

53. Nagasue N, Yukaya H, Kohno H, et al: Morbidity and mortality after major hepatic resection in cirrhotic patients with hepatocellular carcinoma. HPB Surg 1:45, 1988

54. Paquet KJ, Koussouris P, Mercado MA, et al: Limited hepatic resection for selected cirrhotic patients with hepatocellular or cholangiocellular carcinoma: a prospective study. Br J Surg 78:459, 1991

55. Fan ST, Lai EC, Lo CM, et al: Hospital mortality of major hepatectomy for hepatocellular carcinoma associated with cirrhosis. Arch Surg 130:198, 1995

56. Hasegawa H, Yamazaki S, Makuuchi M, et al: [Hepatectomy for hepatocarcinoma on a cirrhotic liver: decision plans and principles of perioperative resuscitation. Experience with 204 cases.] J Chir (Paris) 124:425, 1987

57. Makuuchi M, Kosuge T, Takayama T, et al: Surgery for small liver cancers. Semin Surg Oncol 9:298, 1993

58. Ercolani G, Grazi GL, Calliva R, et al: The lidocaine (MEGX) test as an index of hepatic function: its clinical usefulness in liver surgery. Surgery 127:464, 2000

59. Bruix J, Castells A, Bosch J, et al: Surgical resection of hepatocellular carcinoma in cirrhotic patients: prognostic value of preoperative portal pressure. Gastroenterology 111:1018, 1996

60. Yin XY, Lu MD, Huang JF, et al: Significance of portal hemodynamic investigation in prediction of hepatic functional reserve in patients with hepatocellular carcinoma undergoing operative treatment. Hepatogastroenterology 48:1701, 2001

61. Franco D, Capussotti L, Smadja C, et al: Resection of hepatocellular carcinomas: results in 72 European patients with cirrhosis. Gastroenterology 98:733, 1990

62. Wu CC, Ho WL, Yeh DC, et al: Hepatic resection of hepatocellular carcinoma in cirrhotic livers: is it unjustified in impaired liver function? Surgery 120:34, 1996

63. Noun R, Jagot P, Farges O, et al: High preoperative serum alanine transferase levels: effect on

the risk of liver resection in Child grade A cirrhotic patients. World J Surg 21:390, 1997

64. Capussotti L, Borgonovo G, Bouzari H, et al: Results of major hepatectomy for large primary liver cancer in patients with cirrhosis. Br J Surg 81:427, 1994

65. Yoshida Y, Kanematsu T, Matsumata T, et al: Surgical margin and recurrence after resection of hepatocellular carcinoma in patients with cirrhosis: further evaluation of limited hepatic resection. Ann Surg 209:297, 1989

66. Vauthey JN, Klimstra D, Franceschi D, et al: Factors affecting long-term outcome after hepatic resection for hepatocellular carcinoma. Am J Surg 169:28, 1995

67. Poon RT, Fan ST, Lo CM, et al: Intrahepatic recurrence after curative resection of hepatocellular carcinoma: long-term results of treatment and prognostic factors. Ann Surg 229:216, 1999

68. Makuuchi M, Hasegawa H, Yamazaki S, et al: Four new hepatectomy procedures for resection of the right hepatic vein and preservation of the inferior right hepatic vein. Surg Gynecol Obstet 164:68, 1987

69. Makuuchi M, Mori T, Gunven P, et al: Safety of hemihepatic vascular occlusion during resection of the liver. Surg Gynecol Obstet 164:155, 1987

70. Lai EC, Fan ST, Lo CM, et al: Anterior approach for difficult major right hepatectomy. World J Surg 20:314, 1996

71. Nagasue N, Uchida M, Kubota H, et al: Cirrhotic livers can tolerate 30 minutes ischaemia at normal environmental temperature. Eur J Surg 161:181, 1995

72. Wu CC, Hwang CR, Liu TJ, et al: Effects and limitations of prolonged intermittent ischaemia for hepatic resection of the cirrhotic liver. Br J Surg 83:121, 1996

73. Kim YI, Kobayashi M, Aramaki M, et al: "Early-stage" cirrhotic liver can withstand 75 minutes of inflow occlusion during resection. Hepatogastroenterology 41:355, 1994

74. Kim YI, Nakashima K, Tada I, et al: Prolonged normothermic ischaemia of human cirrhotic liver during hepatectomy: a preliminary report. Br J Surg 80:1566, 1993

75. Smadja C, Kahwaji F, Berthoux L, et al: [Value of total pedicle clamping in hepatic excision for hepatocellular carcinoma in cirrhotic patients.] Ann Chir 41:639, 1987

76. Elias D, Desruennes E, Lasser P: Prolonged intermittent clamping of the portal triad during hepatectomy. Br J Surg 78:42, 1991

77. Yamanaka N, Furukawa K, Tanaka T, et al: Topical cooling-assisted hepatic segmentectomy for cirrhotic liver with hepatocellular carcinoma. J Am Coll Surg 184:290, 1997

78. Kim YI, Kobayashi M, Nakashima K, et al: In situ and surface liver cooling with prolonged inflow occlusion during hepatectomy in patients with chronic liver disease. Arch Surg 129:620, 1994

79. Lin TY: A simplified technique for hepatic resection: the crush method. Ann Surg 180:285, 1974

80. Smadja C, Berthoux L, Meakins JL, et al: Patterns of improvement in resection of hepatocellular carcinoma in cirrhotic patients: results of a non drainage policy. HPB Surg 1:141, 1989

81. Franco D, Smadja C, Meakins JL, et al: Improved early results of elective hepatic resection for liver tumors: one hundred consecutive hepatectomies in cirrhotic and noncirrhotic patients. Arch Surg 124:1033, 1989

82. Tsuge H, Mimura H, Orita K, et al: Evaluation of preoperative and postoperative sodium and water loading in patients undergoing hepatectomy for liver cirrhosis complicated by hepatocellular carcinoma. Hepatogastroenterology 38(suppl 1):56, 1991

83. Maeda T, Shimada M, Shirabe K, et al: Strategies for intractable ascites after hepatic resection: analysis of two cases. Br J Clin Pract 49:149, 1995

84. Shirabe K, Shimada M, Gion T, et al: Postoperative liver failure after major hepatic resection for hepatocellular carcinoma in the modern era with special reference to remnant liver volume. J Am Coll Surg 188:304, 1999

85. Makuuchi M, Thai BL, Takayasu K, et al: Preoperative portal embolization to increase safety of major hepatectomy for hilar bile duct carcinoma: a preliminary report. Surgery 107:521, 1990

86. Nagino M, Nimura Y, Kamiya J, et al: Right or left trisegmental portal vein embolization before hepatic trisegmentectomy for hilar bile duct carcinoma. Surgery 117:677, 1995

87. Shimamura T, Nakajima Y, Une Y, et al: Efficacy and safety of preoperative percutaneous transhepatic portal embolization with absolute ethanol: a clinical study. Surgery 121:135, 1997

88. Lee KC, Kinoshita H, Hirohashi K, et al: Extension of surgical indications for hepatocellular carcinoma by portal vein embolization. World J Surg 17:109, 1993

89. Wakabayashi H, Okada S, Maeba T, et al: Effect of preoperative portal vein embolization on major hepatectomy for advanced-stage hepatocellular carcinomas in injured livers: a preliminary report. Surg Today 27:403, 1997

90. Azoulay D, Castaing D, Krissat J, et al: Percutaneous portal vein embolization increases the feasibility and safety of major liver resection for hepatocellular carcinoma in injured liver. Ann Surg 232:665, 2000

91. Tomas de la Vega JE, Donahue EJ, Doolas A, et al: A ten year experience with hepatic resection. Surg Gynecol Obstet 159:223, 1984

92. Bismuth H, Adam R, Navarro F: Re-resection for colorectal liver metastasis. Surg Oncol Clin North Am 5:353, 1996

93. Adam R, Bismuth H, Castaing D, et al: Repeat hepatectomy for colorectal liver metastases. Ann Surg 225:51, 1997

94. Fong Y, Blumgart LH, Cohen A, et al: Repeat hepatic resections for metastatic colorectal cancer. Ann Surg 220:657, 1994

95. Petrowsky H, Gonen M, Jarnagin W, et al: Second liver resections are safe and effective treatment for recurrent hepatic metastases from colorectal cancer: a bi-institutional analysis. Ann Surg 235:863, 2002

96. Pinson CW, Wright JK, Chapman WC, et al: Repeat hepatic surgery for colorectal cancer metastases to the liver. Ann Surg 223:765, 1996

97. Tuttle TM, Curley SA, Roh MS: Repeat hepatic resection as effective treatment for recurrent colorectal liver metastases. Ann Surg Oncol 4:125, 1997

98. Nordlinger B, Vaillant JC, Guiguet M, et al: Survival benefit of repeat liver resections for recurrent colorectal metastases: 143 cases. J Clin Oncol 12:1491, 1994

99. Fernandez-Trigo V, Sharmsa F, Sugarbaker PH, et al: Repeat liver resections from colorectal metastasis. Surgery 117:296, 1995

100. Yamamoto J, Kosuge T, Shimada K, et al: Repeat liver resection for recurrent colorectal liver metastases. Am J Surg 178:275, 1999

101. Muratore A, Polastri R, Bouzari H, et al: Repeat hepatectomy for colorectal liver metastases: a worthwhile operation? J Surg Oncol 76:127, 2001

102. Suzuki S, Sakaguchi T, Yokoi Y, et al: Impact of repeat hepatectomy on recurrent colorectal liver metastases. Surgery 129:421, 2001

103. Riesener K-P, Kasperk R, Winkeltau G, et al: Repeat resection of recurrent hepatic metastases: improvement in prognosis? Eur J Surg 162:709, 1996

104. Kin T, Nakajima Y, Kanehiro H, et al: Repeat hepatectomy for recurrent colorectal metastases. World J Surg 22:1087, 1998

105. Farges O, Regimbeau JM, Belghiti J: Aggressive management of recurrence following surgical resection of hepatocellular carcinoma. Hepatogastroenterology 45(suppl 3):1275, 1998

106. Nagasue N, Kohno H, Hayashi T, et al: Repeat hepatectomy for recurrent hepatocellular carcinoma. Br J Surg 83:127, 1996

107. Neeleman N, Andersson R: Repeated liver resection for recurrent liver cancer. Br J Surg 83:893, 1996

108. Lee PH, Lin WJ, Tsang YM, et al: Clinical management of recurrent hepatocellular carcinoma. Ann Surg 222:670, 1995

109. Hu RH, Lee PH, Yu SC, et al: Surgical resection for recurrent hepatocellular carcinoma: prognosis and analysis of risk factors. Surgery 120:23, 1996

110. Shimada M, Takenaka K, Gion T, et al: Prognosis of recurrent hepatocellular carcinoma: a 10-year surgical experience in Japan. Gastroenterology 111:720, 1996

111. Shuto T, Kinoshita H, Hirohashi K, et al: Indications for, and effectiveness of, a second hepatic resection for recurrent hepatocellular carcinoma. Hepatogastroenterology 43:932, 1996

112. Shimada M, Takenaka K, Taguchi K, et al: Prognostic factors after repeat hepatectomy for recurrent hepatocellular carcinoma. Ann Surg 227:80, 1998

113. Sugimachi K, Maehara S, Tanaka S, et al: Repeat hepatectomy is the most useful treatment for recurrent hepatocellular carcinoma. J Hepatobiliary Pancreat Surg 8:410, 2001

114. Elias D, Lasser P, Hoang JM, et al: Repeat hepatectomy for cancer. Br J Surg 80:1557, 1993

115. Hemming AW, Langer B: Repeat resection of recurrent hepatic colorectal metastases. Br J Surg 81:1553, 1994

116. Blumgart LH, Baer HU: Hilar and intrahepatic biliary-enteric anastomosis. Surgery of the Liver and Biliary Tract. Blumgart LH, Ed. Churchill Livingstone, London, 1994, p 1051

117. Polk W, Fong Y, Karpeh M, et al: A technique for the use of cryosurgery to assist hepatectomy. J Am Coll Surg 180:171, 1995

118. Chu QD, Vezeridis MP, Avradopoulos KA, et al: Repeat hepatic resection for recurrent colorectal cancer. World J Surg 21:292, 1997

119. The Southern Surgeons Club: A prospective analysis of 1518 laparoscopic cholecystectomies. N Engl J Med 324:1073, 1991

120. Katkhouda N, Hurwitz M, Gugenheim J, et al: Laparoscopic management of benign solid and cyctsic lesions of the liver. Ann Surg 229:460, 1999

121. Jeng KS, Yang FS, Kao CR, et al: Management of symptomatic polycystic liver disease: laparoscopy adjuvant with alcohol sclerotherapy. J Gastroenterol Hepatol 10:359, 1995

122. Cuesta MA, Meijer S, Borgstein PJ, et al: Laparoscopic ultrasonography for hepatobiliary and pancreatic malignancy. Br J Surg 80:1571, 1993

123. Ravikumar TS: Laparoscopic staging and intraoperative ultrasonography for liver tumor management. Surg Oncol Clin North Am 5:271, 1996

124. Asahara T, Dohi K, Nakahara H, et al: Laparoscopy-assisted hepatectomy for a large tumor of the liver. Hiroshima J Med Sci 47:163, 1998

125. Huscher CGS, Lirici MM, Chiodini S: Laparoscopic liver resections. Semin Laparosc Surg 5:204, 1998

126. Kaneko H, Takagi S, Shiba T: Laparoscopic partial hepatectomy and left lateral segmentectomy: technique and results of a clinical series. Surgery 120:468, 1996

127. Rau HG, Meyer G, Cohnert TU, et al: Laparoscopic liver resection with the water-jet dissector. Surg Endosc 9:1009, 1995

128. Yamanaka N, Tanaka T, Tanaka W, et al: Laparoscopic partial hepatectomy. Hepatogastroenterology 45:29, 1998

129. Fong Y, Blumgart LH: Useful stapling techniques in liver surgery. J Am Coll Surg 185:93, 1997

130. Jackman SV, Cadeddu JA, Chen RN, et al: Utility of the harmonic scalpel for laparoscopic partial nephrectomy. J Endourol 12:441, 1998

131. Wolf JSJ, Moon TD, Nakada SY: Hand assisted laparoscopic nephrectomy: comparison to standard laparoscopic nephrectomy. J Urol 160:22, 1998

132. Klingler PJ, Hinder RA, Menke DM, et al: Hand-assisted laparoscopic distal pancreatectomy for pancreatic cystadenoma. Surg Laparosc Endosc 8:180, 1998

133. Nakada SY, Moon TD, Gist M, et al: Use of the pneumo sleeve as an adjunct in laparoscopic nephrectomy. Urology 49:612, 1997

Acknowledgment

Figures 1, 3 through 15, 17, 18   Tom Moore.

66 PROCEDURES FOR BENIGN AND MALIGNANT PANCREATIC DISEASE

Attila Nakeeb, M.D., F.A.C.S., Keith D. Lillemoe, M.D., F.A.C.S., and John L. Cameron, M.D., F.A.C.S.

Over the past two decades, both the mortality and the morbidity associated with pancreatic surgery have been reduced substantially. In many high-volume centers, the perioperative mortality for pancreatic resection is now less than 3%.[1-3] This decline in mortality may be attributed to more careful patient selection, better understanding of surgical anatomy, advances in critical care medicine, and improvements in the management of perioperative complications.

In what follows, we describe the operative techniques we employ in the management of both benign and malignant pancreatic disease, including pancreaticoduodenectomy (the Whipple procedure), distal pancreatectomy (open and laparoscopic), longitudinal pancreaticojejunostomy (the Puestow procedure), enteric drainage of pancreatic pseudocysts (open and laparoscopic), and palliative bypass for unresectable periampullary cancer.

Preoperative Evaluation

A number of different imaging options are available to help determine the appropriate surgical approach to management of pancreatic disease [see 51 Tumors of the Pancreas, Biliary Tract, and Liver]. These options include both noninvasive modalities (e.g., transabdominal ultrasonography, computed tomography, and magnetic resonance imaging) and invasive modalities (e.g., endoscopic retrograde cholangiopancreatography [ERCP] and endoscopic ultrasonography [EUS]).

Transabdominal ultrasonography can identify changes associated with chronic pancreatitis, biliary and pancreatic duct dilation, and the presence of pseudocysts. In the setting of malignant disease, it may demonstrate dilated intrahepatic and extrahepatic bile ducts, liver metastases, pancreatic masses, ascites, and enlarged peripancreatic lymph nodes. A malignancy of the pancreas typically appears as a hypoechoic mass; ultrasonography reveals a pancreatic mass in 60% to 70% of pancreatic cancer patients.

Currently, helical (spiral) CT is the preferred noninvasive imaging test for pancreatic disease, having largely supplanted ultrasonography in this context. Helical CT can delineate the anatomy of the pancreas and the surrounding organs in considerable detail, and it can easily define pancreatic calcifications, inflammation, necrosis, and masses. Pancreatic cancer usually appears as an area of pancreatic enlargement with a localized hypodense lesion. A triple-phase intravenous contrast study is ideal for the assessment of pancreatic lesions. Thin cuts are obtained through the pancreas and the liver during both the arterial phase and the venous phase after the injection of I.V. contrast material. Besides being used to determine the primary tumor size, CT is used to look for and evaluate invasion into local structures or metastatic disease.

In general, MRI has no significant advantages over CT: its signal-to-noise ratio is low, it is prone to motion artifacts, it does not opacify the bowel, and it has low spatial resolution. Nevertheless, magnetic resonance cholangiopancreatography (MRCP) can be quite useful for defining the anatomy and pathology of the bile ducts and the pancreatic duct noninvasively. It can be especially useful in cases where the ampulla of Vater is not accessible (as in patients who have previously undergone Roux-en-Y or Billroth II reconstructions).

ERCP allows direct imaging of the pancreatic and bile ducts and is the gold standard for diagnosing chronic pancreatitis. It also allows therapeutic stenting of biliary and pancreatic duct strictures. The sensitivity of ERCP for the diagnosis of pancreatic cancer approaches 90%. The presence of a long, irregular stricture in an otherwise normal pancreatic duct is highly suggestive of a pancreatic malignancy. Often, the pancreatic duct is obstructed with no distal filling.

EUS, though newer than the aforementioned modalities, has begun to play an important role in the evaluation of pancreatic diseases. It is a semi-invasive test that can be performed with a very low rate of complications (< 0.1%). EUS can diagnose the most common causes of extrahepatic biliary obstruction (e.g., choledocholithiasis and pancreaticobiliary malignancies) with a degree of accuracy equaling or exceeding that of direct cholangiography or ERCP, and it is the most sensitive modality for the diagnosis of pancreatic carcinoma. The particular strengths of EUS in the diagnosis of pancreatic cancer are (1) that it can clarify small (< 2 cm) lesions when CT findings are questionable or negative, (2) that it can detect malignant lymphadenopathy, and (3) that it can guide fine-needle aspiration (FNA) for definitive diagnosis and staging. On average, EUS without FNA is 85% accurate for T stage disease and 70% accurate for N stage disease. The combination of EUS and FNA is 93% sensitive and 100% specific for T stage disease and 88% accurate for N stage disease.[4]

Pylorus-Preserving Pancreaticoduodenectomy (Whipple Procedure)

Surgical resection of a periampullary carcinoma can be accomplished by means of either a pylorus-preserving pancreaticoduodenectomy (PPPD) or the classic Whipple resection (including an antrectomy). Multiple randomized trials have failed to show any significant differences between the two in terms of either relative ease of performance or short- or long-term outcome (including survival). The choice between them is usually made on the basis of individual surgeons' preferences (unless there is obvious tumor encroachment on the first portion of the duodenum). In the ensuing technical description, we focus primarily on the pylorus-preserving modification but also refer to certain important components of the classic Whipple resection.

OPERATIVE PLANNING

Operative management of periampullary cancer is carried out in two phases. First, the resectability of the tumor is assessed; then, if the tumor is resectable, a pancreaticoduodenectomy is performed and gastrointestinal continuity restored. Selective use of staging laparoscopy should be considered for patients at high risk for occult metastatic disease, such as patients with large primary tumors; patients with lesions in the neck, body, or tail of the pancreas; patients with equivocal radiographic findings suggestive of occult distant metastatic disease (e.g., low-volume ascites, CT findings indicating possible carcinomatosis, and small hypodense regions in the hepatic parenchyma indicating possible hepatic metastases that are not amenable to percutaneous biopsy); and patients with clinical and laboratory findings

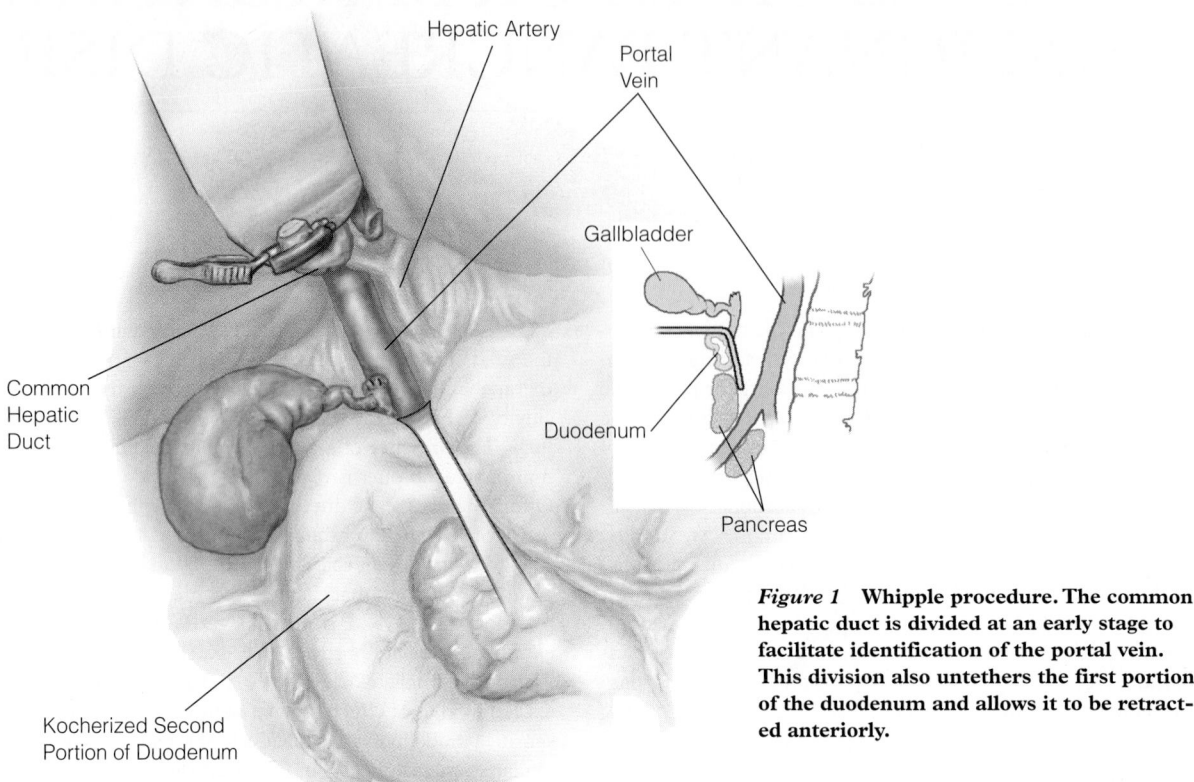

Figure 1 **Whipple procedure. The common hepatic duct is divided at an early stage to facilitate identification of the portal vein. This division also untethers the first portion of the duodenum and allows it to be retracted anteriorly.**

suggesting more advanced disease (e.g., marked hypoalbuminemia or weight loss, significant increases in the CA 19-9 level, and severe back or abdominal pain).

OPERATIVE TECHNIQUE

The peritoneal cavity is entered through an upper midline incision or a bilateral subcostal incision. The liver, the omentum, and the peritoneal surfaces are inspected and palpated. Biopsy is performed on suspicious lesions, and specimens are submitted for frozen-section analysis. Regional lymph nodes are examined for evidence of tumor involvement. The presence of tumor in the periaortic lymph nodes of the celiac axis indicates that the tumor has extended beyond the limits of normal resection; however, the presence of tumor in lymph nodes that normally would be incorporated within the resection specimen does not constitute a contraindication to resection.

Once distant metastases have been excluded, the resectability of the primary tumor is assessed. Various local factors may preclude pancreaticoduodenal resection, including retroperitoneal extension of the tumor to involve the inferior vena cava or the aorta and direct involvement or encasement of the superior mesenteric artery (SMA), the superior mesenteric vein (SMV), or the portal vein. Often, the determination of resectability is made on the basis of a careful review of the preoperative imaging (CT plus EUS) in conjunction with operative exploration.

Operative assessment of resectability begins with a Kocher maneuver and mobilization of the duodenum and the head of the pancreas from the underlying inferior vena cava and aorta. When the duodenum and head of the pancreas have been mobilized sufficiently, a hand is placed under the duodenum and the head of the pancreas to palpate the tumor mass and determine its relation to the SMA. Inability to identify a plane of normal tissue between the mass and the arterial pulsation indicates that the tumor directly involves the SMA, which means that complete tumor resection is not possible.

The final operative step for determining resectability involves dissection of the SMV and the portal vein to rule out tumor invasion. Identification of the portal vein is greatly simplified if the common hepatic duct is divided early in the dissection.[5] Once the hepatic duct has been divided, the anterior surface of the portal vein is easily and quickly identified [*see Figure 1*]. The lymph node tissue lateral to the hepatic duct and the portal vein should be dissected off the structures to be included in the surgical specimen. It must be remembered that important variations in the hepatic arterial anatomy, including a replaced right hepatic artery, may be encountered during this dissection. If the appropriate plane is found along the anterior surface of the portal vein, it should be easy to pass the index finger of the left hand on top of the vessel posterior to the first portion of the duodenum and the neck of the pancreas (because there usually are no veins joining the anterior surface of the portal vein). If this maneuver proves difficult, the gastroduodenal artery should be identified where it comes off the common hepatic artery. Once adequate dissection has been carried out, the artery should first be clamped with a nonoccluding vascular clamp, then, if the hepatic artery pulse is preserved, it should be divided and ligated with 2-0 silk ties. (The initial clamping of the gastroduodenal artery with a vascular clamp is done to confirm that the arterial supply to the liver will not be interrupted should either variations in hepatic arterial anatomy or important collateral circulation be present in the face of celiac artery stenosis.) After the artery has been divided and ligated, an additional ligature of 3-0 polypropylene should be placed on the proximal stump. Division of the gastroduodenal artery unroofs part of the tunnel through which the index finger is slipped, thereby greatly facilitating the separation of the portal vein from the posterior aspect of the first portion of the duodenum and the neck of the pancreas.

Once the anterior surface of the portal vein has been dissected posterior to the neck of the pancreas, the next step is to identify the SMV and dissect its anterior surface. This is most easily accomplished by

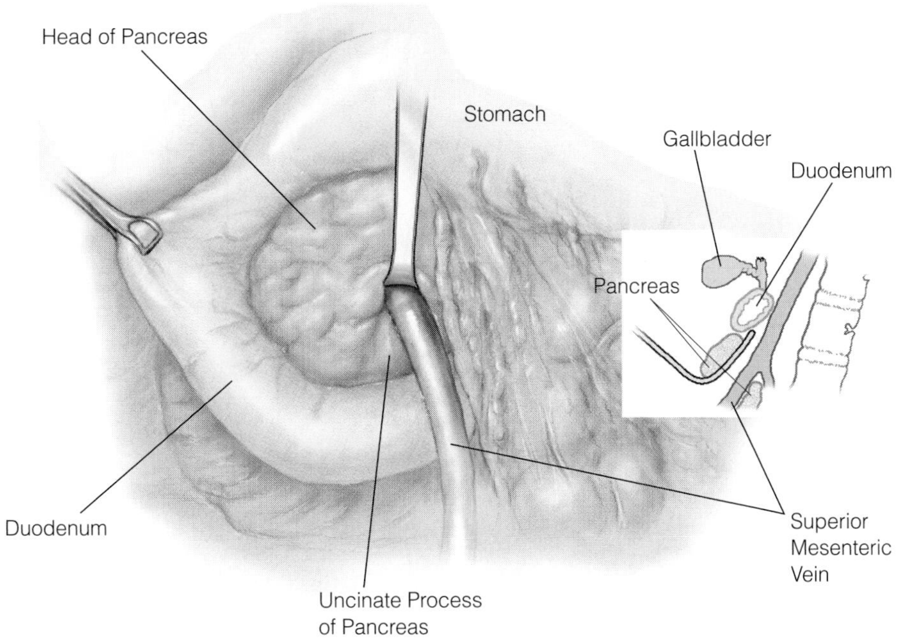

Figure 2 Whipple procedure. Kocherization of the duodenum is continued along the third portion until the superior mesenteric vein is reached. This vein can then be easily cleaned up to its connection with the portal vein.

extending the Kocher maneuver past the second portion of the duodenum to include the third and fourth portions. During this extensive kocherization, the first structure encountered anterior to the third portion of the duodenum is the SMV [see Figure 2]. The anterior surface of the vein can then be cleaned rapidly and dissected under direct vision by retracting the neck of the pancreas anteriorly. This dissection

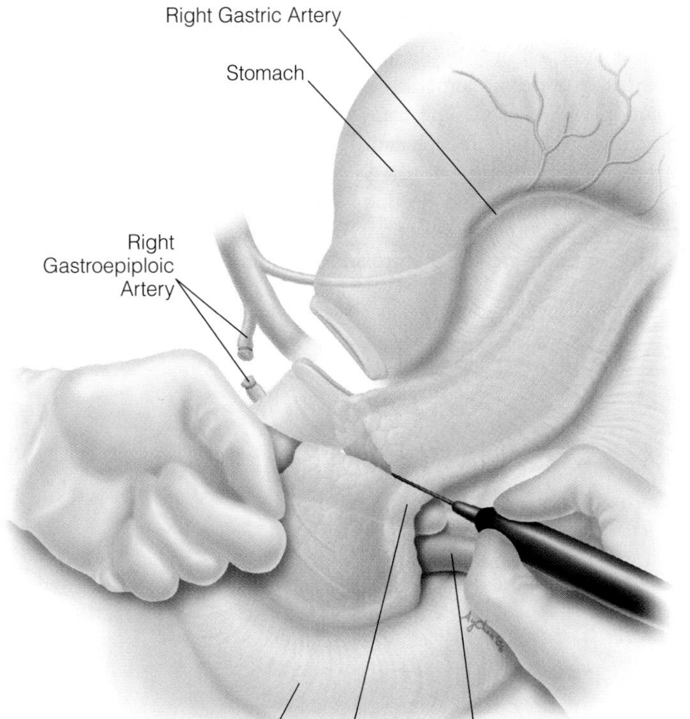

Figure 3 Whipple procedure. Transection of the neck of the pancreas with electrocautery.

is continued until it connects to the portal vein dissection from above. If this maneuver can be completed without evidence of SMV or portal vein involvement, the tumor can generally be considered resectable. It is still possible, however, for an uncinate tumor to involve the right lateral surface and the undersurface of the SMV, and this possibility should be carefully evaluated.

If the neck of the pancreas can be successfully dissected off of the anterior and lateral surfaces of the portal vein and the SMV, most experienced pancreatic surgeons will proceed with pancreaticoduodenectomy without obtaining a tissue diagnosis. In defining the diagnosis of malignancy, an intraoperative biopsy is less conclusive than the combination of the clinical presentation, the results of preoperative CT scanning and cholangiography, and the operative finding of a palpable mass in the head of the pancreas.

In a PPPD,[6] the duodenum is first mobilized and divided approximately 2 cm distal to the pylorus with a gastrointestinal anastomosis (GIA) stapler. The posterior surface of the proximal first portion of the duodenum is dissected until the lesser sac is entered. At this point, the soft tissue attachments from the inferior border of the duodenum to the inferior border of the pancreas are divided. The right gastroepiploic vessels, which can be sizable, are clamped, divided, and ligated. In a similar fashion, the soft tissue areolar attachments found superiorly are divided with the electrocautery. Care must be taken to identify and preserve the right gastric artery, which comes off the common hepatic artery and actually joins the foregut along the proximal part of the first portion of the duodenum.

In a classic Whipple procedure, an antrectomy is performed. The right gastroepiploic arcade and the right gastric vessels are divided to permit mobilization of the antrum. The stomach is then divided with a GIA stapler, usually at the level of the incisura. At this point, if the gastroduodenal artery was not divided earlier, it is identified, divided, and ligated as described (see above). During this step, particular care must be taken to ensure that the lumen of the common hepatic artery is not encroached on by one of the proximal ties.

The neck of the pancreas is then divided with the electrocautery [see Figure 3], with care taken not to injure the underlying SMV and portal vein. These veins are mobilized away from the uncinate process of the pancreas; the dissection should continue until the SMV, clearly palpable with the index finger of the left hand, is visualized. If a

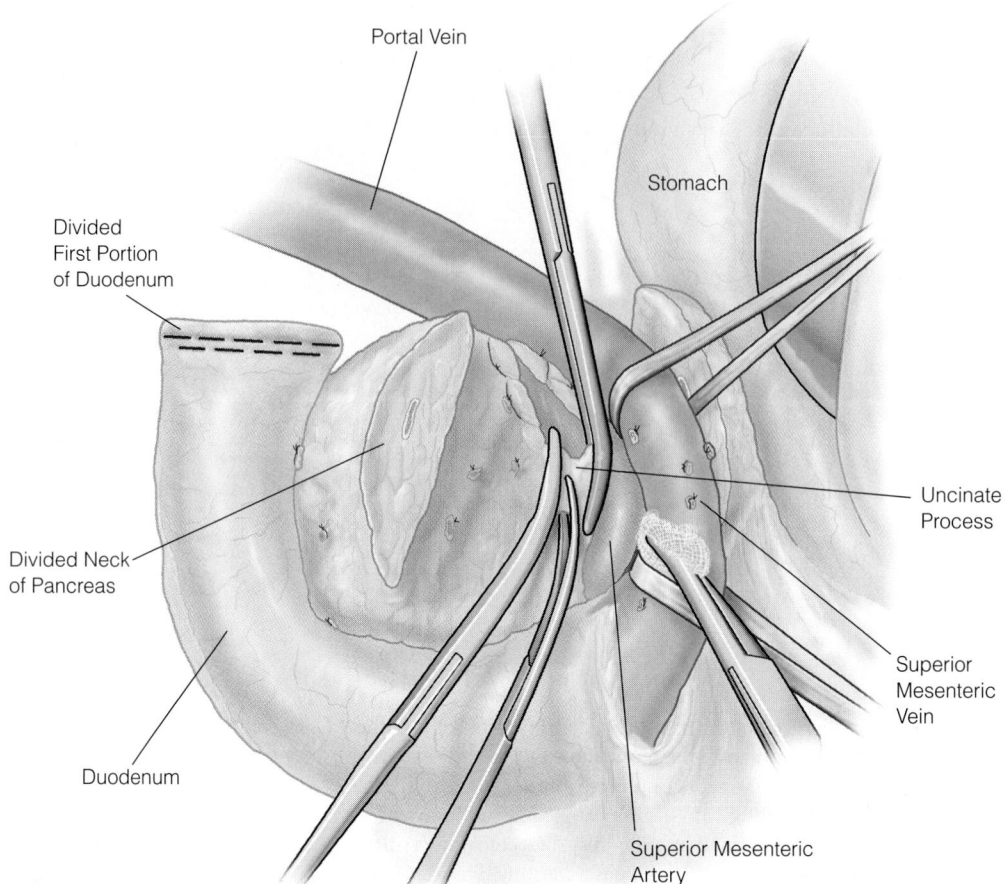

Figure 4 **Whipple procedure. The uncinate process is divided flush with the superior mesenteric artery.**

replaced right hepatic artery is present, its origin from the SMA will be encountered at this point and must be preserved. The uncinate process is divided between clamps flush with the SMA [*see Figure 4*], then ligated with 2-0 silk ties; alternatively, either a vessel-sealing system (e.g., LigaSure; Valleylab, Boulder, Colorado) or an ultrasonic shears may be used. The SMA is completely exposed during this dissection, which proceeds from cephalad to caudad. As a rule, there are two large veins joining the SMV inferiorly that must be dissected free, doubly ligated, and divided.

Once the uncinate process has been completely divided, the specimen is attached only by the third portion of the duodenum. At this point, the upper abdomen is copiously irrigated with an antibiotic solution and packed. The transverse colon, along with the greater omentum, is reflected cephalad. The proximal jejunum and the ligament of Treitz, along with the fourth portion of the duodenum, are dissected free, and the dissection is continued until it meets the right-side upper abdominal dissection. At a convenient point where there is a wide vascular arcade, the proximal jejunum is divided with a GIA

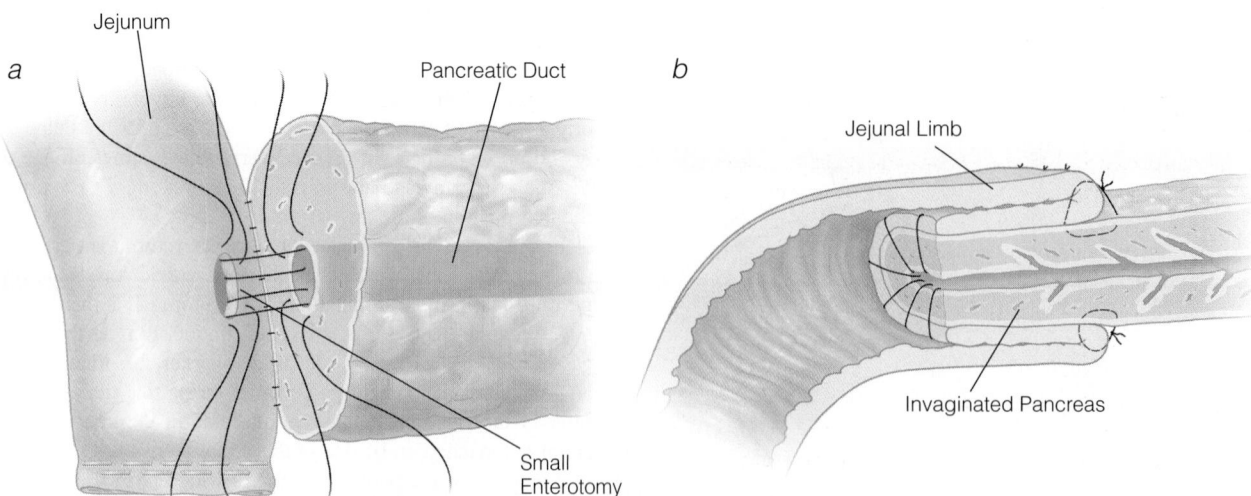

Figure 5 **Whipple procedure. (*a*) An end-to-side mucosa-to-mucosa pancreaticojejunostomy is done in two layers with an outer layer of interrupted 3-0 silk sutures and an inner layer of interrupted 5-0 absorbable synthetic sutures. (*b*) Alternatively, the end of the pancreas can be invaginated into the end of the jejunum for approximately 2 cm. The anastomosis is done with an outer interrupted layer of 3-0 silk and an inner continuous layer of 3-0 absorbable synthetic suture material.**

stapler approximately 10 to 12 cm from the ligament of Treitz. The proximal jejunum is then grasped with a Babcock clamp and retracted cephalad. The mesentery to the proximal jejunum is divided between clamps and ligated with 2-0 silk (or divided with a vessel-sealing device such as the LigaSure).

When division of the mesentery is complete, the specimen is free and can be removed from the operative field. The bile duct, the pancreatic neck, and the uncinate margins should be tagged with sutures and sent for frozen-section analysis. The bed of the tumor should be carefully inspected for hemostasis and its margins marked with ligating clips (e.g., LigaClip; Ethicon Endo-Surgery, Inc., Cincinnati, Ohio) to facilitate postoperative radiation therapy.

There are several technical options for restoring GI continuity after a pancreaticoduodenal resection. Our preferred technique is to bring the end of the divided jejunum through the transverse mesocolon to the right of the middle colic vessels in a retrocolic fashion and to perform an end-to-side pancreaticojejunostomy. A row of interrupted 3-0 silk Lembert sutures is placed between the side of the jejunum and the posterior capsule of the end of the pancreas. A small enterotomy, matching the size of the pancreatic duct, is made in the jejunum, and an inner layer of interrupted 5-0 absorbable monofilament sutures is placed to create a duct-to-mucosa anastomosis [see Figure 5a]. Meticulous stitch placement is crucial, and many surgeons use some degree of magnification to complete the anastomosis in small ducts. Often, a short segment of a pediatric feeding tube is placed across the anastomosis to be used as a temporary indwelling stent. The anastomosis is completed with an outer layer of 3-0 silk Lembert sutures placed between the anterior pancreatic capsule and the jejunum. A popular alternative to this duct-to-mucosa technique is to create an enterotomy approximately the same size as the pancreatic neck and to place an inner continuous layer of 3-0 absorbable synthetic suture material circumferentially around the entire gland. The neck is then invaginated 1 to 2 cm into the lumen of the bowel, and an outer interrupted layer of 3-0 silk is placed to complete the anastomosis [see Figure 5b].

The biliary-enteric anastomosis is performed 6 to 10 cm distal to the pancreaticojejunostomy. An end-to-side hepaticojejunostomy is fashioned with a single interrupted layer of 4-0 absorbable synthetic suture material [see Figure 6]. Generally, there is no need for a T tube or a stent.

Approximately 15 cm distal to the biliary-enteric anastomosis, an end-to-side duodenojejunostomy is performed with an inner continuous layer of 3-0 absorbable synthetic suture material and an outer interrupted layer of 3-0 silk [see Figure 7]. Some experienced pancreatic surgeons prefer to perform the duodenojejunostomy further distally in an antecolic position, in the belief that doing so reduces the incidence of early postoperative delayed gastric emptying. If an antrectomy was performed, the medial half of the gastric staple line is reinforced with interrupted 3-0 silk seromuscular Lembert sutures. The gastrojejunal anastomosis is completed to the lateral (greater curvature) aspect of the staple line as a two-layer Hofmeister-style anastomosis.

The abdomen is copiously irrigated with an antibiotic solution. The jejunal loop is tacked to the rent in the transverse mesocolon with interrupted 3-0 silk sutures. The defect in the retroperitoneum previously occupied by the fourth portion of the duodenum is closed with a continuous 2-0 silk suture. One or two closed suction Silastic drains are placed in the vicinity of the hepaticojejunostomy and the pancreaticojejunostomy and brought out through a stab wound in the right upper quadrant. The abdomen is closed in a standard fashion.

Distal Pancreatectomy with Splenectomy

Distal pancreatic resection is performed for a variety of conditions, including inflammatory processes, benign tumors and cysts, and pan-

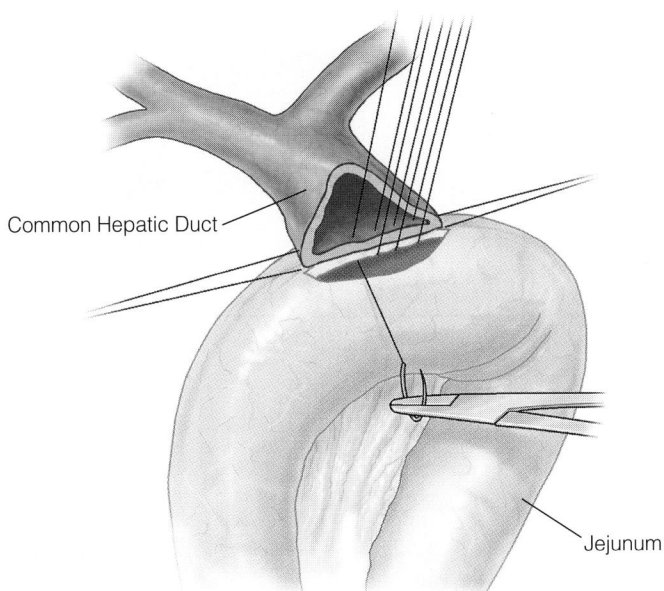

Common Hepatic Duct

Jejunum

Figure 6 **Whipple procedure. The common hepatic duct is anastomosed to the jejunum in an end-to-side fashion with a single layer of 4-0 interrupted absorbable synthetic sutures.**

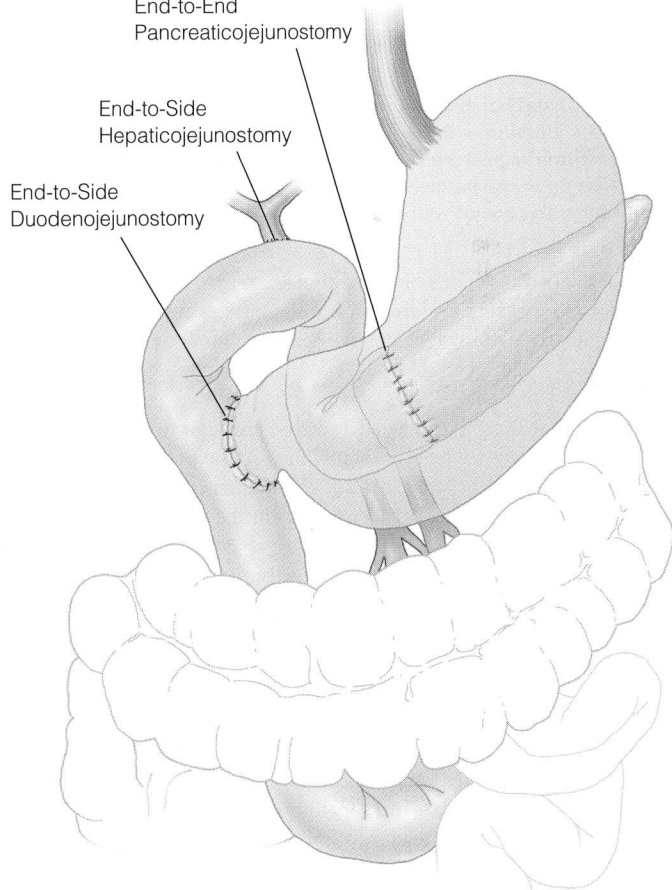

End-to-End Pancreaticojejunostomy

End-to-Side Hepaticojejunostomy

End-to-Side Duodenojejunostomy

Figure 7 **Whipple procedure. After the end-to-end pancreatico-jejunostomy and the end-to-side hepaticojejunostomy, the duodenum is anastomosed to the jejunum in an end-to-side fashion with an inner continuous layer of 3-0 absorbable suture material and an outer interrupted layer of 3-0 silk.**

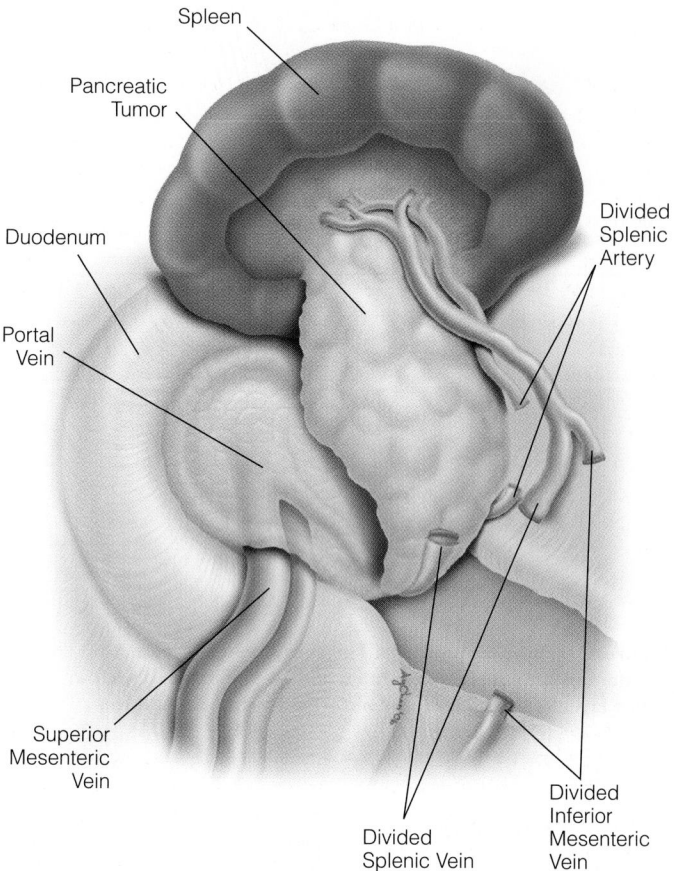

Figure 8 **Distal pancreatectomy. The splenic vein is divided just distal to its junction with the inferior mesenteric vein, then dissected away from the posterior surface of the pancreas from the point of division up to the point where it joins the superior mesenteric vein to form the portal vein.**

creatic malignancies. The following discussion focuses on distal pancreatectomy for malignant disease, but the basic technical principles of distal pancreatectomy for benign disease are much the same.

OPERATIVE TECHNIQUE

The peritoneal cavity is usually entered through a left subcostal incision that extends to the right of midline. In thin patients, an upper midline incision may be used instead. Upon entry into the abdomen, a careful exploration is performed to confirm the absence of disseminated disease.

The lesser sac is entered by dividing the gastrocolic omentum. Generally, this is best done by separating the greater omentum off the transverse colon and leaving it attached to the greater curvature of the stomach. Once the lesser sac has been entered, the posterior wall of the stomach is separated from the pancreas with sharp and blunt dissection to expose the body and tail of the pancreas. The duodenum is kocherized, and the head and the uncinate process of the pancreas are palpated and visualized; the entire gland can then be inspected and palpated. Intraoperative ultrasonography may be employed for further delineation of the tumor's relation to the surrounding vascular structures.

Once the pancreas has been exposed, the celiac axis and the superior mesenteric vessels are identified and assessed to determine whether the tumor is resectable. The splenic artery is identified where it comes off the celiac axis, and a vessel loop is placed around it; in this way, the vessel is controlled at an early stage of the procedure and can be promptly ligated if bleeding should occur. A patient with a

thrombosed splenic vein may have left-side portal hypertension and multiple collateral vessels leading from the spleen to the stomach via the short gastric vessels. With such a patient, it is usually preferable to ligate and divide the splenic artery early in the procedure.

The spleen is retracted toward the midline with the left hand; it should be compressed medially toward the spine rather than retracted anteriorly. It is then mobilized out of the retroperitoneum with the electrocautery. The retroperitoneum usually consists of loose areolar tissue that is easily mobilized. The omental attachments anterior to the hilum of the spleen are divided between Kelly clamps and ligated with 2-0 silk. The line of division is easily determined if the omentum has previously been completely taken off the transverse colon. As the division extends up toward and then along the greater curvature of the stomach, the vasa brevia are encountered and are doubly clamped, divided, and ligated. The splenic flexure of the colon is carefully dissected away from the inferior pole of the spleen, and the peritoneal attachments that make up the splenocolic ligament are divided.

The tail and the body of the pancreas are further mobilized out of the retroperitoneum by retracting the spleen and the pancreatic tail medially. In the course of this mobilization, care must be taken not to injure the left adrenal gland, which often occupies a fairly superficial position in the retroperitoneum, anterior and medial to the superior pole of the left kidney; care must also be taken not to carry the dissection too deep and thereby risk injuring the kidney or the renal vessels. The splenic vein is easily identified in the middle portion of the posterior aspect of the pancreas. The inferior mesenteric vein (IMV), which joins the splenic vein at the middle of the body of the pancreas, is identified in the retroperitoneum just lateral to the ligament of Treitz and can be divided at this point.

Further mobilization of the pancreas to the midline exposes the splenic artery where it takes off from the celiac axis. As noted (see

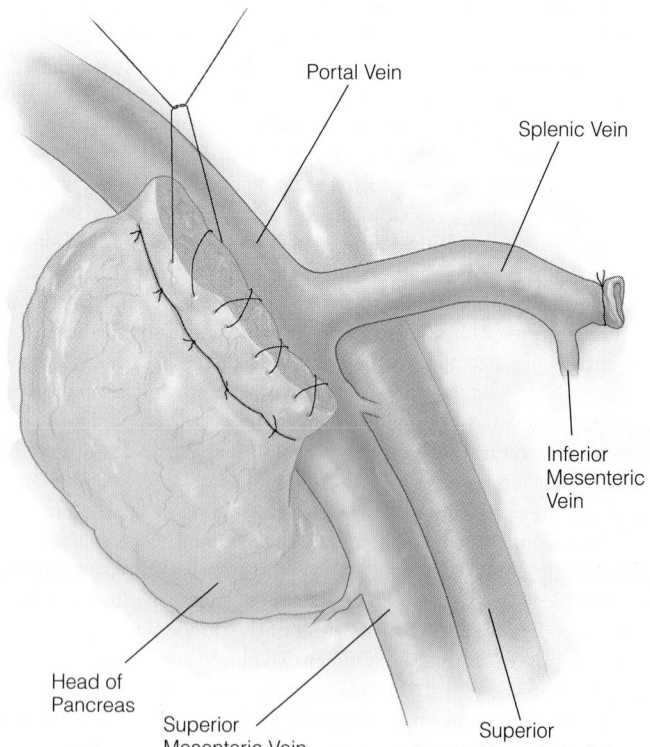

Figure 9 **Distal pancreatectomy. A row of overlapping horizontal mattress sutures is placed in the neck of the pancreas just proximal to where it is to be divided, the neck is divided with the electrocautery, and a row of figure-eight sutures of 3-0 absorbable synthetic suture material is placed over the end of the pancreas.**

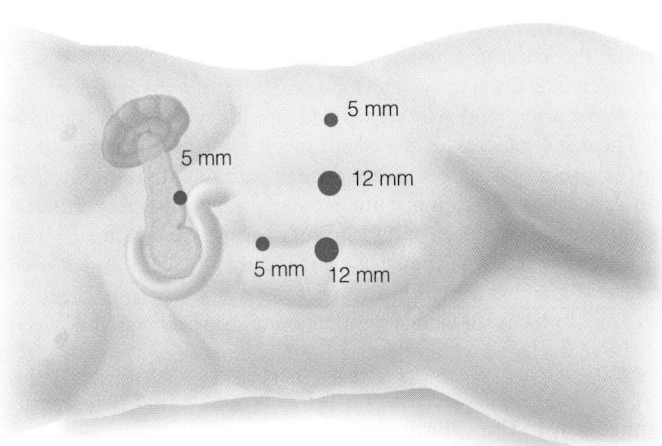

Figure 10 **Laparoscopic distal pancreatectomy. Shown is the placement of ports for distal pancreatectomy.**

above), this artery will already have been isolated with a vessel loop. The splenic artery is triply clamped, divided, and triply ligated with 2-0 silk and a 4-0 polypropylene suture near its point of origin.

The SMV can then be identified. A plane is developed by dissecting between the anterior surface of the SMV and the neck of the pancreas; a Penrose drain may be looped around the neck to facilitate exposure. With larger pancreatic cancers, tumor extension into the retroperitoneum may involve the splenic vein. Dividing the pancreatic neck with the electrocautery at this point may facilitate dissection of the splenic vein–portal vein confluence under direct vision. The splenic vein is clamped, divided (without compromising the portal vein–SMV complex), and ligated with 0 silk ties and a 4-0 polypropylene suture on the proximal stump [*see Figure 8*]. If there is a pancreatic tumor arising from the proximal body of the gland, the splenic vein may be ligated flush with the SMV. At this location, it is best to oversew the vein with a continuous 3-0 polypropylene suture so as not to compromise the portal vein–SMV complex.

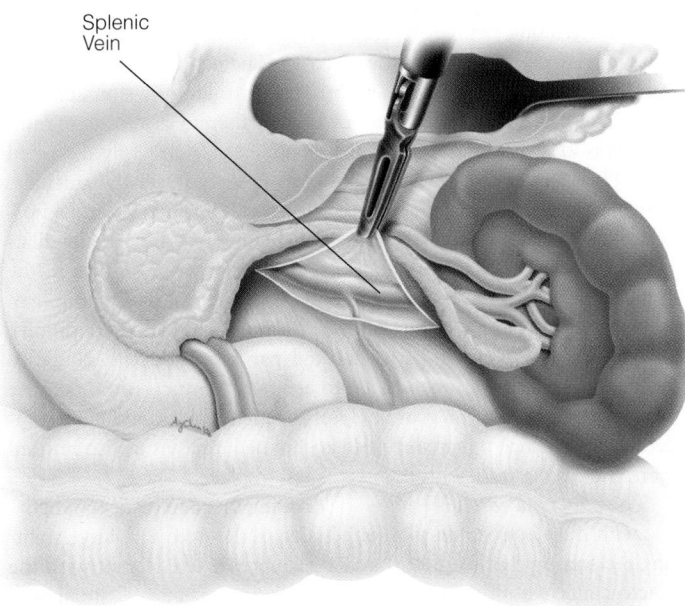

Figure 11 **Laparoscopic distal pancreatectomy. Once the pancreatic body has been mobilized from the retroperitoneum, the splenic vein can be identified.**

The portal vein and the SMV are carefully dissected away from the undersurface of the neck of the pancreas. Stay sutures of 2-0 silk are placed at the superior and inferior edges of the pancreas proximal to the site of transection, and the neck of the pancreas is divided with the electrocautery (or, alternatively, with a transverse anastomosis [TA] or GIA stapler). The operative specimen should be sent for frozen-section evaluation to ensure a negative microscopic margin.

A row of figure-eight sutures of 3-0 absorbable synthetic suture material is placed over the end of the pancreas [*see Figure 9*]. Using large needles that have been straightened makes this task simple even if the head-neck junction through which the needles are passed is thickened. If the pancreatic duct can be identified, it should be separately oversewn with a figure-eight or mattress suture of 5-0 absorbable synthetic suture material. The resection bed should be marked with titanium clips to guide postoperative radiation therapy if necessary.

The abdomen is copiously irrigated with an antibiotic solution. The pancreatic remnant is drained with a closed suction Silastic drain brought out through a stab wound in the left upper quadrant. There is no need to drain the splenic bed. The abdomen is then closed in a standard fashion.

Laparoscopic Distal Pancreatectomy with or without Splenectomy

Selected patients may benefit from a laparoscopic spleen-preserving distal pancreatectomy (SPDP) or a laparoscopic distal pancreatectomy with splenectomy. Conditions that are potentially amenable to treatment with a laparoscopic distal pancreatectomy include benign or premalignant cystic neoplasms, islet cell tumors of the pancreas, chronic pancreatitis with symptomatic ductal obstruction, and pancreatic pseudocysts confined to the distal body and tail of the pancreas.

OPERATIVE TECHNIQUE

The patient can be placed either supine in a low lithotomy position or in a semilateral position with the left side up. For lesions in the distal body or tail of the pancreas, we prefer the semilateral position; for lesions closer to the neck of the pancreas, we prefer the low lithotomy position. Five ports are placed [*see Figure 10*], and a 10 mm 30° laparoscope is used. As in all pancreatic procedures, the peritoneal surfaces, the omentum, the mesentery, and the viscera should all be carefully inspected to rule out metastatic disease. Intraoperative ultrasonography may be employed to evaluate the liver and locate the lesion in the pancreas.

The body and tail of the pancreas are exposed by opening the lesser sac. The gastrocolic omentum is divided and widely mobilized with an ultrasonic scalpel (e.g., Harmonic Scalpel; Ethicon Endo-Surgery, Inc., Cincinnati, Ohio), with care taken to stay outside the gastroepiploic vessels. A retractor is advanced into the lesser sac through the subxiphoid port and used to elevate the stomach anteromedially. The splenocolic ligament is divided, and the splenic flexure of the colon is reflected inferiorly.

After these maneuvers, the inferior pancreatic margin should be exposed. The peritoneum is then incised along the inferior pancreatic border, and the pancreatic body is separated from the retroperitoneum by means of sharp and blunt dissection along its inferior border. Laparoscopic ultrasonography and direct visual inspection, combined with the findings from preoperative imaging, may be employed to determine the extent of the dissection. Initially, the dissection should be directed so that it is medial to the pancreatic lesion. The pancreatic body is elevated by means of blunt and sharp dissection, after which the splenic vein should be easily identifiable [*see Figure 11*]. Care must be exercised to prevent inadvertent injury to this vessel. Once the splenic vein has been identified, a careful circumferential dissection around the splenic vein is performed with a right-angle

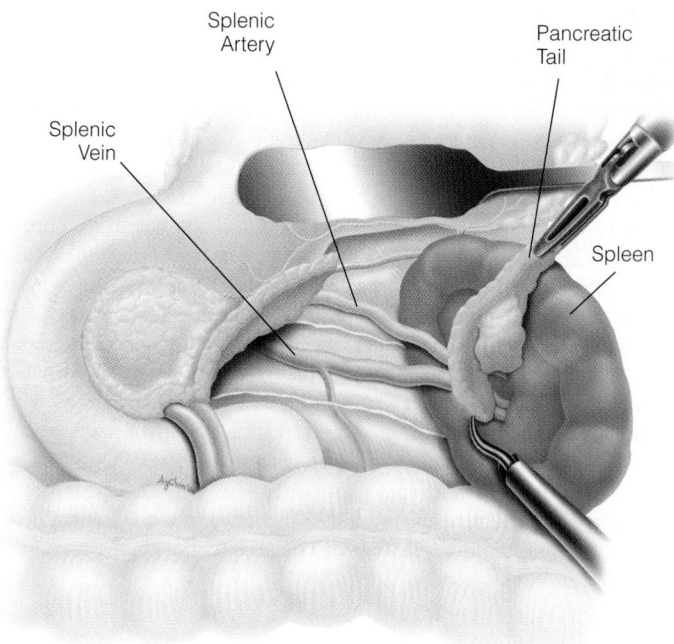

Splenic
Vein

Splenic
Artery

Pancreatic
Tail

Spleen

Figure 12 **Laparoscopic distal pancreatectomy. After having been transected, the distal portion of the pancreas is dissected away from the splenic vessels in a medial-to-lateral direction. The pancreatic branches of the splenic vessels are divided sequentially as they are encountered.**

clamp, and a vessel loop is placed around the vein. This dissection helps identify the splenic artery as well, which also is controlled with a vessel loop. These precautionary measures allow quick control of bleeding should a vascular tear occur later in the procedure.

Once the pancreatic body has been adequately mobilized from the splenic vessels, the pancreatic parenchyma is divided with the ultrasonic scalpel. Alternatively, an endoscopic stapler can be placed across the body of the pancreas, sparing the main splenic vessels. Once the proximal pancreatic tissue is divided, the specimen is grasped and gently retracted anteriorly to allow further dissection of the vessels. The dissection proceeds toward the splenic hilum in a medial-to-lateral direction. The pancreatic branches of the splenic vein are sequentially identified, dissected free with laparoscopic Metzenbaum scissors, and divided with the ultrasonic scalpel [*see Figure 12*]. The branches of the splenic artery, which runs just superior to the vein, are treated similarly. Special care must be taken as the dissection approaches the hilum of the spleen.

At the completion of an SPDP, the specimen is placed and removed in a standard endoscopic retrieval device (e.g., Endo Catch; United States Surgical, Norwalk, Connecticut). The pancreatic remnant is then oversewn with a series of interrupted absorbable horizontal mattress sutures. A single round Jackson Pratt drain is placed near the pancreatic transection line and brought out through one of the 5 mm lateral ports.

An alternative approach to SPDP involves dividing the splenic vessels proximally and distally while preserving the short gastric and left gastroepiploic vessels to maintain splenic perfusion [*see Figure 13*]. The initial steps of this technique are essentially the same as those already described (see above), up to the point where the pancreas is divided. In the alternative approach to SPDP, after pancreatic transection, the splenic artery and vein are divided with an endovascular stapler. The left portion of the pancreas is lifted up and mobilized posteriorly along with the splenic artery and vein, and the vessels are again divided as they emerge from the pancreatic tail to enter the hilum of

the spleen. The spleen is then supplied solely by the short gastric vessels and the left gastroepiploic vessels.

If an en bloc distal pancreatectomy with splenectomy is performed, the splenic artery and vein are divided after the pancreas is transected. The distal pancreas is dissected free in a medial-to-lateral direction. The short gastric vessels are divided with the ultrasonic scalpel, with care taken not to injure the stomach wall. The retroperitoneal attachments of the spleen and the tail of the pancreas are divided with the ultrasonic scalpel. The specimen is then placed in a specimen retrieval bag and extracted from a port site that has been enlarged to a size of 3 to 6 cm. To facilitate extraction of the specimen, the spleen may be morcellated within the bag [*see 67 Splenectomy*].

Laparoscopic Pancreatic Enucleation

Laparoscopic techniques have now been applied to the enucleation of benign neuroendocrine tumors of the pancreas. This approach is indicated for tumors in the body and tail of the pancreas that, on preoperative imaging, appear not to involve the pancreatic duct. Patients are positioned and trocars placed in much the same way as for laparoscopic distal pancreatectomy [*see* Laparoscopic Distal Pancreatectomy with and without Splenectomy, Operative Technique, *above*].

The body and the tail of the pancreas are widely exposed by entering the lesser sac through the gastrocolic omentum. Intraoperative ultrasonography is extremely useful for identifying the tumor and for further delineating its relation to the splenic vessels and the pancreatic duct. Once identified, the lesion is dissected out of the pancreatic parenchyma with the ultrasonic shears and the electrocautery. The specimen is placed in a specimen retrieval bag and removed. The enucleation bed is then inspected for hemostasis, and a closed suction drain is placed to control any pancreatic leakage that may develop.

Longitudinal Pancreaticojejunostomy (Puestow Procedure)

OPERATIVE TECHNIQUE

The abdomen is entered through an upper midline incision. The lesser sac is entered by removing the greater omentum from the transverse colon along virtually its entire length, thereby exposing the entire tail, body, neck, and head of the pancreas. The pancreas often appears markedly fibrotic and scarred. The posterior wall of the stomach may be adherent to a portion of the body of the pancreas as a result of multiple episodes of inflammation; if it is adherent, it is easily dissected free. The duodenum is kocherized, and the head and the uncinate process of the pancreas are palpated from both an anterior and a posterior direction. In many cases, the pancreatic duct is markedly dilated and can actually be palpated through the anterior surface in the middle portion of the body of the pancreas. The rest of the abdomen is explored to check for the presence of other pathologic conditions. To confirm the position of the dilated pancreatic duct, a 20-gauge needle on a 10 ml syringe is used to aspirate the duct. Intraoperative ultrasonography can be quite helpful for identifying the dilated pancreatic duct. Once pancreatic juice is obtained, the syringe is removed from the needle hub, with the needle left in place.

The pancreatic duct is entered by dividing the pancreatic parenchyma with the electrocautery on either side of the needle. A large right-angle clamp is then inserted, and the duct is filleted open with the electrocautery both proximally and distally [*see Figure 14*]. Small pancreatic ductal concretions are carefully removed. At least 6 cm of the duct must be opened to yield a good chance of long-term success. Ideally, if the duct is dilated all the way out to the tail, it can be filleted open virtually to the tip of the pancreas. In the proximal direction, the duct can easily be opened as far as the neck of the pancreas. Beyond this point, however, the duct passes posteriorly and inferiorly into the head of the pancreas; because the head can be very thick, opening up the duct any further can be difficult.

A Bakes dilator is carefully passed proximally through the open pancreatic duct, down through the pancreatic duct in the unopened head, through the ampulla of Vater, and into the duodenum. If a Bakes dilator cannot be passed into the duodenum, some surgeons elect to open the duodenum and perform a sphincteroplasty [*see 64 Procedures for Benign and Malignant Biliary Tract Disease*], so that by working both from within the duodenum and from within the open pancreatic duct, they can ensure the patency of the entire pancreatic duct.

A Roux-en-Y jejunal loop approximately 60 cm long is constructed. The most proximal loop of jejunum in which there is a good vascular arcade is selected. A 2 cm segment of this loop is cleaned and divided with a GIA stapler. The small bowel mesentery is divided between clamps down through the arcade vessel and is ligated with 3-0 silk. The end of the distal jejunum is oversewn with a layer of 3-0 silk Lembert sutures. A 60 cm length is then measured. Alimentary tract continuity is reestablished by means of an end-to-side jejunojejunostomy, in which the most proximal portion of the divided jejunum is anastomosed to the side of the Roux-en-Y jejunal loop 60 cm distally with an inner continuous layer of 3-0 absorbable synthetic suture material and an outer interrupted layer of 3-0 silk. The defect in the small bowel mesentery is closed with a continuous 4-0 silk suture.

The Roux-en-Y jejunal loop is brought up into the lesser sac in a retrocolic position through a small rent in the transverse mesocolon. A side-to-side pancreaticojejunostomy is performed in two layers. Before the Roux loop is opened, an outer interrupted layer of 3-0 silk is placed between the jejunal loop and the pancreatotomy, passing through the capsule of the pancreas and out through the opened pancreatic parenchyma along the inferior border of the pancreas. When this layer is complete, an enterotomy approximately 2 mm from the jejunal suture line is made along the entire length of this line. Starting at the distal pancreatic tail, an inner continuous layer of 3-0 absorb-

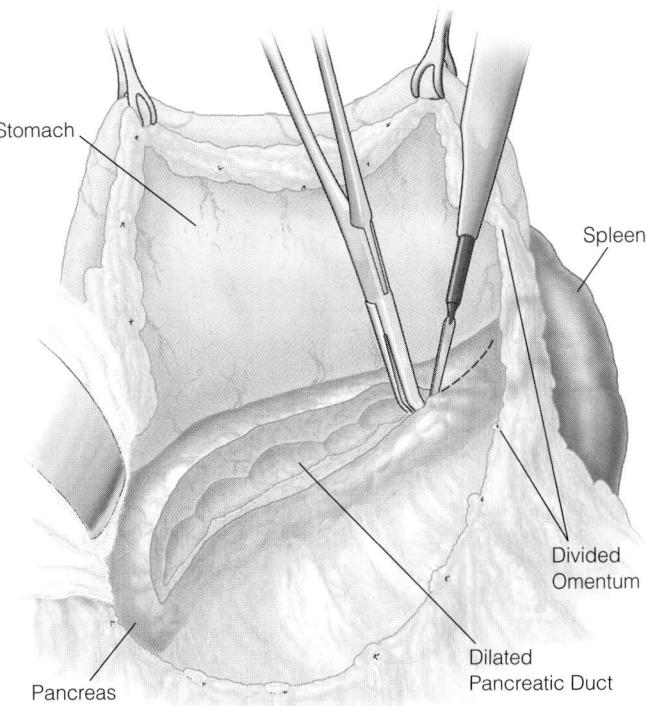

Figure 14 **Puestow procedure. The dilated pancreatic duct is filleted open with the electrocautery both proximally and distally. At least 6 cm of the duct should be opened.**

able synthetic suture material is placed in an over-and-over locking fashion through the entire wall of the jejunum and the entire divided surface of the pancreas and into the duct [*see Figure 15*]. The inner layer of the superior suture line is placed in an over-and-over fashion without locking, again with a continuous 3-0 absorbable synthetic suture. The outer layer of the superior suture line consists of interrupted 3-0 silk sutures placed in a Lembert fashion.

When the pancreatic duct is dilated to a diameter of 1 cm or greater, a two-layer anastomosis is possible and is in fact preferred. When the diameter of the duct is between 5 mm and 1 cm, however, a two-layer anastomosis is generally difficult, and a one-layer anastomosis is preferred. A single layer of interrupted 3-0 silk sutures is placed so that the knots are tied on the outside. This is easily accomplished with the superior suture line. With the inferior suture line, which is placed first, the suture passes from outside inward on the pancreas and then from inside outward on the jejunum. In a single-layer side-to-side pancreaticojejunostomy, the jejunotomy must be performed before any sutures are placed.

The procedure is completed by tacking the Roux-en-Y jejunal loop to the rent in the transverse mesocolon with interrupted 3-0 silk sutures. The pancreaticojejunostomy is drained with closed suction Silastic drains that are placed on either side of the anastomosis and brought out through separate stab wounds in the left upper quadrant. The abdomen is copiously irrigated with an antibiotic solution and closed in a standard fashion.

Drainage of Pancreatic Pseudocyst

OPERATIVE TECHNIQUE

Drainage into Roux-en-Y Jejunal Loop

The peritoneal cavity is entered through a midline incision, and the abdomen is explored. Typically, a substantial mass that is cystic and

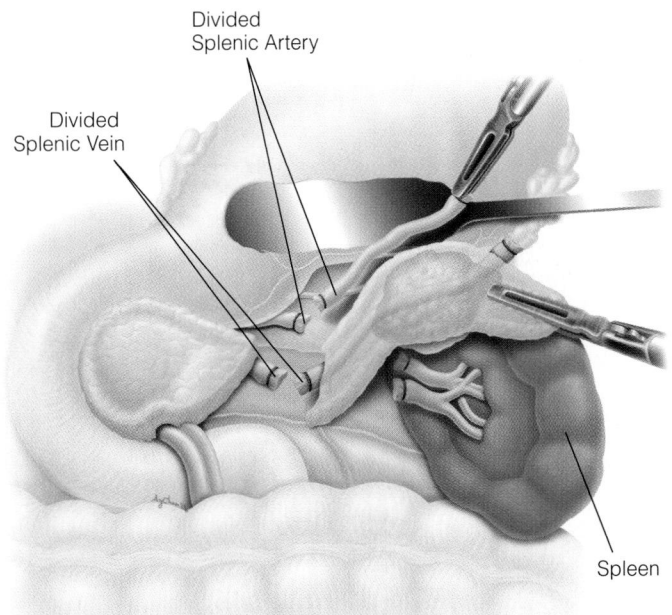

Figure 13 **Laparoscopic distal pancreatectomy. In an alternative approach to spleen-preserving distal pancreatectomy, the splenic artery and the splenic vein are divided, and the viability of the spleen is maintained by preserving the short gastric and left gastroepiploic vessels.**

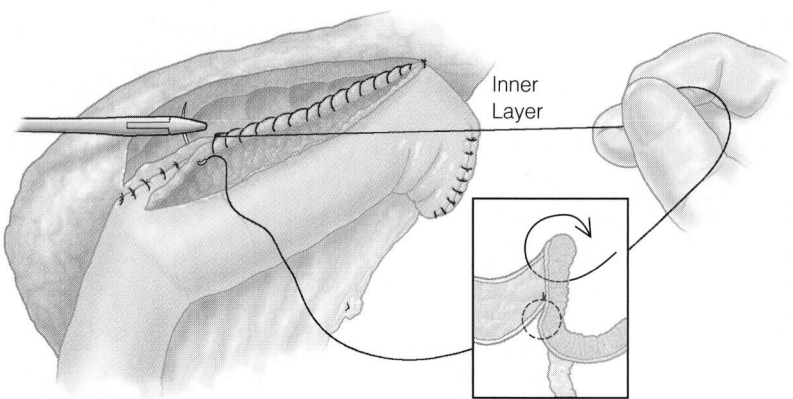

Figure 15 **Puestow procedure. When the diameter of the dilated pancreatic duct is 1 cm or wider, a side-to-side pancreaticojejunostomy should be done in two layers. Once an outer layer of interrupted 3-0 silk sutures is placed between the jejunal loop and the pancreatotomy, an enterotomy is made along the entire length of the jejunal suture line, and an inner layer consisting of a continuous 3-0 absorbable synthetic suture is placed.**

easily ballotable is palpable posterior to the stomach. The duodenum and the head of the pancreas are kocherized so that the head may be palpated both anteriorly and posteriorly. The physical characteristics of chronic pancreatitis are usually present. The body and the tail of the pancreas are palpated as well; the pancreas is usually fibrotic, firm, and somewhat enlarged. The rest of the abdomen is explored to check for the presence of other pathologic conditions.

At this point, the size and configuration of the cyst are compared with the size and configuration on the preoperative CT scan. If the CT scan shows a unilocular solitary cyst and if, at the time of laparotomy, there appears to be a mass that coincides exactly with what is seen on the CT scan, there is no need to enter the lesser sac. The lesion can be

drained into a Roux-en-Y jejunal loop through the transverse mesocolon, and the lesser sac need not be explored. Most pseudocysts are formed by anterior disruptions of the main pancreatic duct. When pancreatic secretions leak out into the lesser sac, the body walls off the leak through its inflammatory response. The transverse mesocolon becomes adherent to the posterior wall of the stomach, which in turn becomes adherent to other adjacent structures in and around the retroperitoneum, and the leak is sealed off. Thus, the transverse mesocolon is usually the inferior and most dependent portion of the pseudocyst, and this site is the ideal location for drainage [see Figure 16].

The transverse colon is retracted cephalad, and the cyst is easily visualized and palpated through the transverse mesocolon. The loca-

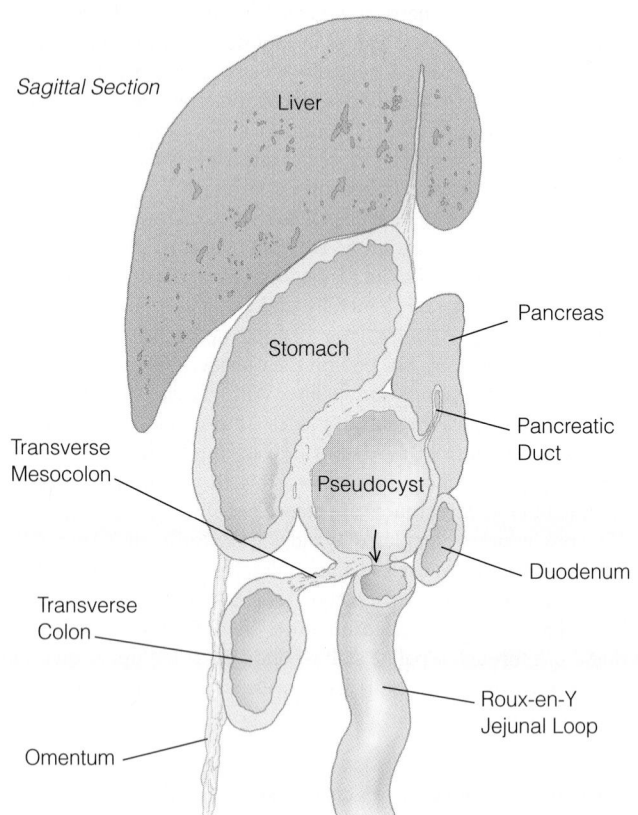

Figure 16 **Drainage of pancreatic pseudocyst into Roux-en-Y jejunal loop. The transverse mesocolon is usually the most inferior and dependent part of a pancreatic pseudocyst; thus, drainage through the transverse mesocolon into a Roux loop is usually the ideal approach.**

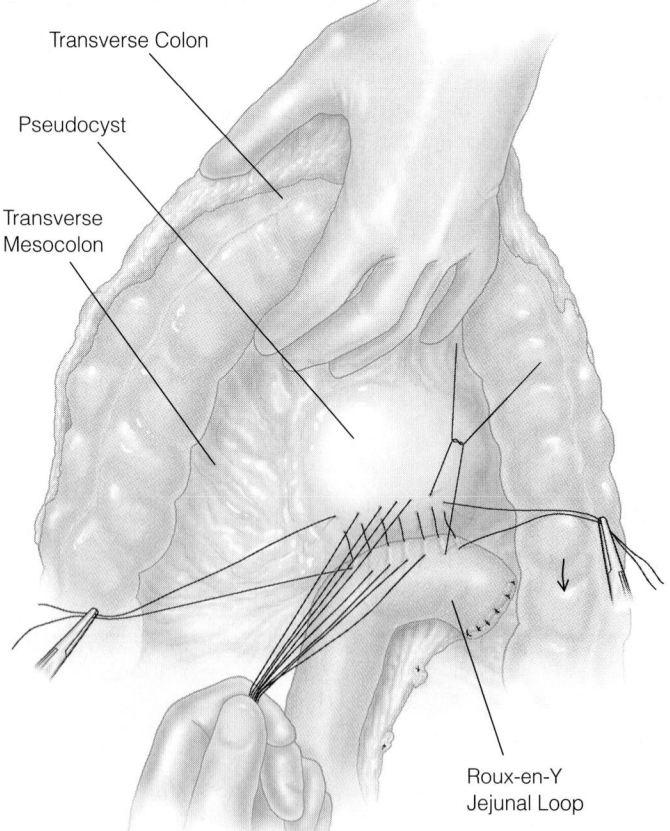

Figure 17 **Drainage of pancreatic pseudocyst into Roux-en-Y jejunal loop. The outer posterior layer of the side-to-side cystojejunostomy comprises a series of 3-0 silk sutures placed through and through the jejunal loop and the transverse mesocolon.**

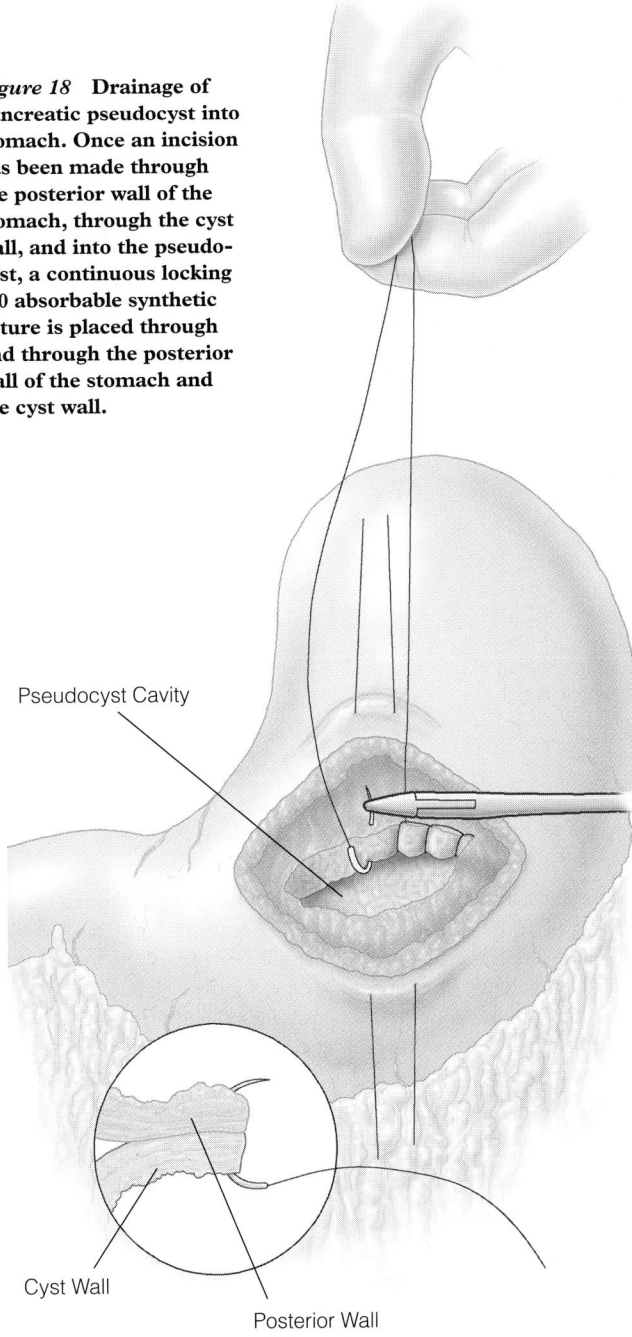

Figure 18 **Drainage of pancreatic pseudocyst into stomach. Once an incision has been made through the posterior wall of the stomach, through the cyst wall, and into the pseudocyst, a continuous locking 3-0 absorbable synthetic suture is placed through and through the posterior wall of the stomach and the cyst wall.**

Pseudocyst Cavity

Cyst Wall

Posterior Wall of Stomach

A side-to-side cystojejunostomy is performed with an outer interrupted layer of 3-0 silk and an inner continuous layer of 3-0 absorbable synthetic suture material. The posterior outer layer of the anastomosis consists of a series of 3-0 silk sutures passed through and through the jejunal loop and through and through the transverse mesocolon (which is the inferior wall of the pseudocyst) [*see Figure 17*]. The suture line should be approximately 2.5 to 5 cm long. After the posterior layer has been secured, a cystotomy is performed with the electrocautery. An ellipse of cyst wall is removed and sent for frozen-section examination. No matter how clear it seems to be that the lesion is a pseudocyst, a specimen from the cyst wall should always be sent for frozen-section examination. Some cystic lesions of the pancreas are cystic neoplasms, which must be resected rather than drained. If no epithelial lining is found on frozen-section examination, it is safe to assume that the lesion is not a cystic neoplasm but a pancreatic pseudocyst and to proceed accordingly.

A parallel enterotomy is made in the jejunum. An inner continuous layer of 3-0 absorbable synthetic suture material is placed inferiorly in a locking fashion, then brought around superiorly in a Connell stitch. An outer interrupted layer of 3-0 silk is placed superiorly. With the cyst decompressed, a sizable lumen should be easily palpable in the anastomosis between the cyst and the jejunal loop.

A closed suction Silastic drain is left near the anastomosis and brought out through a stab wound in the left upper quadrant. The

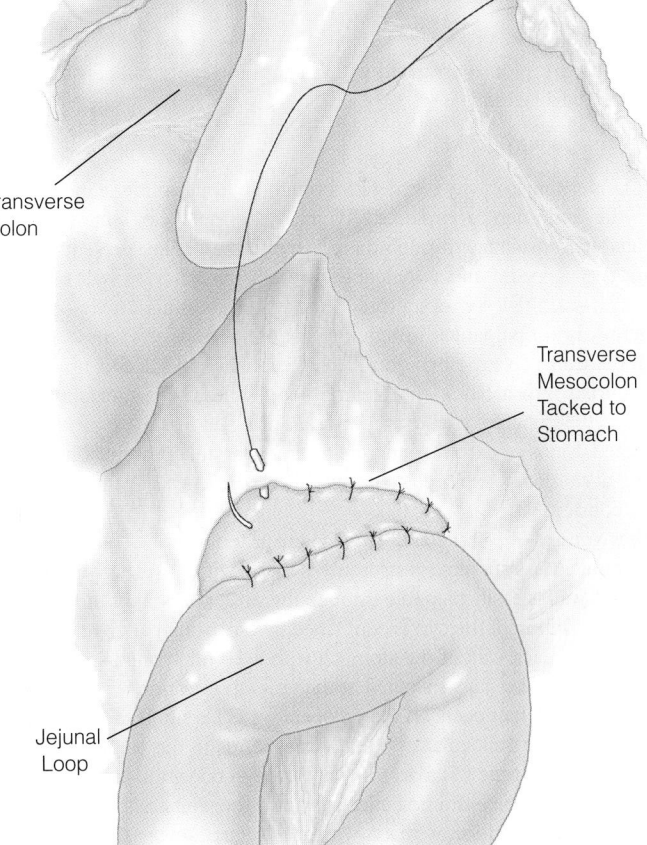

Transverse Colon

Transverse Mesocolon Tacked to Stomach

Jejunal Loop

Figure 19 **Palliative double bypass for unresectable pancreatic cancer. Once the retrocolic gastrojejunostomy is complete, the anastomosis is tacked to the rent in the transverse mesocolon on the gastric side with interrupted 3-0 silk sutures.**

tion of the cyst is confirmed by aspirating pancreatic juice through the transverse mesocolon with a 10 ml syringe and a 20-gauge needle. The middle colic vessels must be carefully identified and avoided. A 60 cm long Roux-en-Y jejunal loop is constructed. The proximal jejunum is divided with a GIA stapler at the first convenient arcade. The small bowel mesentery is divided down through the arcade. The distal end of the jejunum is inverted with an interrupted layer of 3-0 silk Lembert sutures.

Alimentary tract continuity is reestablished by means of an end-to-side jejunojejunostomy, in which the proximal jejunum is anastomosed to the side of the Roux-en-Y jejunal loop 60 cm from the inverted end. This anastomosis is performed with an inner continuous layer of 3-0 absorbable synthetic suture material and an outer interrupted layer of 3-0 silk. The rent in the small bowel mesentery is closed with a continuous 3-0 silk suture.

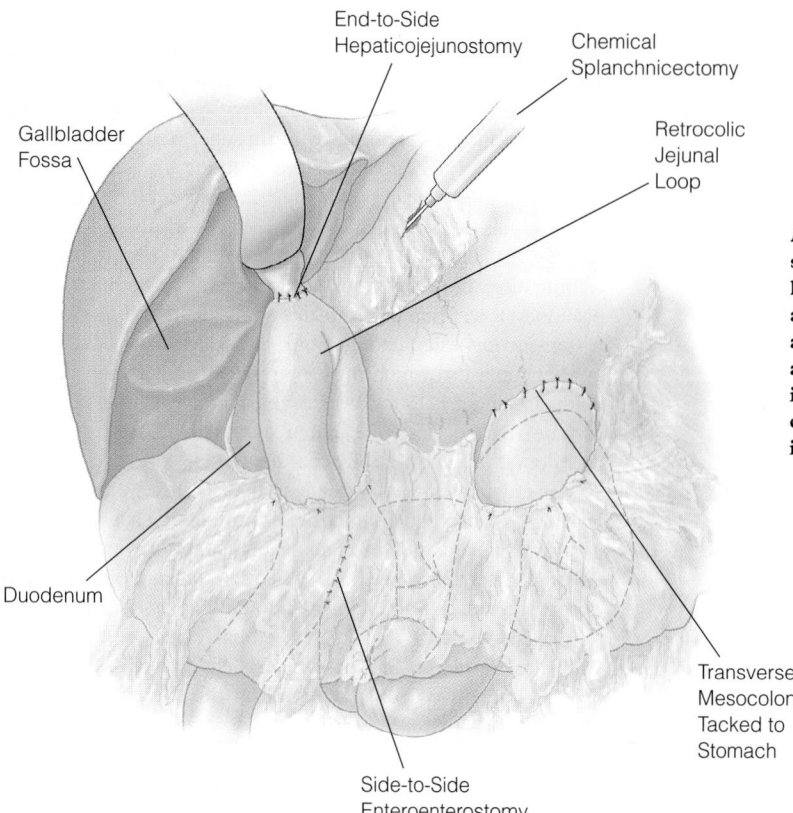

Figure 20   **Palliative double bypass for unresectable pancreatic cancer. An end-to-side hepaticojejunostomy is performed, followed by a side-to-side jejunojejunostomy between the afferent loop leading to the biliary anastomosis and the efferent loop leading from it. An opening is made in the lesser omentum, and a chemical splanchnicectomy is performed by injecting alcohol into the celiac plexus.**

abdomen is copiously irrigated with an antibiotic solution and closed in a standard fashion.

Drainage into Stomach

The peritoneal cavity is entered through an upper midline incision, and the abdomen is explored. Typically, a pseudocyst that is not amenable to drainage through the transverse mesocolon presents as a mass that is cystic and is palpable through the anterior wall of the stomach and the lesser omentum in the upper abdomen; such a mass generally is not palpable through the root of the transverse mesocolon with the transverse mesocolon reflected cephalad and thus is not easily drained into a Roux-en-Y jejunal loop. The duodenum and the head of the pancreas are kocherized, and the head of the pancreas is palpated. Signs of chronic pancreatitis are invariably present. The rest of the abdomen is explored to check for the presence of other pathologic conditions.

Stay sutures of 3-0 silk are placed in the anterior wall of the body of the stomach. A transverse gastrotomy is made with the electrocautery. The cyst wall is easily palpable through the posterior wall of the stomach. The location of the cyst is confirmed by aspirating pancreatic juice through the back wall of the stomach with a 10 ml syringe and a 20-gauge needle. The mass palpated at the time of operation is compared with the cyst as it appears on the preoperative CT scan. If the CT scan shows a solitary unilocular cyst that corresponds to the palpable mass identified at the time of laparotomy, it is safe to conclude that the cyst is solitary and can be drained effectively into the stomach.

A transverse incision is made with the electrocautery through the posterior wall of the stomach, through the cyst wall, and into the pseudocyst. It is often desirable to leave the 20-gauge needle in place and to perform the posterior wall gastrotomy on either side of the needle. An ellipse of cyst wall is sent for frozen-section examination. Again, this step is mandatory, no matter how obvious it seems that the lesion is an inflammatory cyst. A continuous locking suture of 3-0

absorbable synthetic material is placed through and through the posterior wall of the stomach and the anterior wall of the cyst [*see Figure 18*]. This step may or may not actually be important for achieving long-term patency of the opening between the cyst and the posterior wall of the stomach, but it does ensure good hemostasis. The anterior gastrotomy is closed with an inner continuous layer of 3-0 absorbable synthetic suture material in a Connell stitch and an outer interrupted layer of 3-0 silk. The abdomen is closed in a standard fashion.

Laparoscopic Drainage of Pancreatic Pseudocysts

Five distinct laparoscopic approaches have been employed for the drainage of pancreatic pseudocysts: (1) transgastric cystogastrostomy, (2) intragastric cystogastrostomy, (3) minilaparoscopic intragastric cystogastrostomy, (4) cystogastrostomy via the lesser sac approach, and (5) Roux-en-Y cystojejunostomy.

In a laparoscopic transgastric cystogastrostomy, an anterior gastrotomy is created, and the electrocautery is used to open the cyst wall through the posterior wall of the stomach. A cystogastrostomy is then created; it may be either stapled (with an endoscopic stapler) or handsewn (with intracorporeal sutures).

In an intragastric cystogastrostomy, trocars are inserted percutaneously through the abdominal wall and directly into the gastric lumen under simultaneous laparoscopic and gastroscopic guidance. A cystogastrostomy is then created by means of electrocauterization and sharp dissection. The technique for a minilaparoscopic intragastric cystogastrostomy is essentially the same, except that 2 mm intragastric ports are used to reduce the invasiveness of the procedure and minimize the trauma to the anterior gastric wall.

When the anatomy is favorable, laparoscopic cystogastrostomy via the lesser sac approach is the preferred technique for minimally invasive pseudocyst drainage. The advantages of this technique are (1) that it does not require an anterior gastrotomy and (2) that it ensures a large anastomosis that is not dependent on the adherence of the cyst to the posterior gastric wall. Because the entire anastomosis is either stapled or sutured, the risk of bleeding is minimized. In this procedure, a window is created in the gastrocolic omentum, through which the lesser sac is entered. The stomach is elevated, and a cystotomy is made adjacent to a posterior gastric wall gastrotomy. A cystogastrostomy is then created with an endoscopic stapler, and the opening is sutured closed.

For cysts that are large or are not in direct contact with the posterior wall of the stomach, a laparoscopic Roux-en-Y cystojejunostomy may be performed instead. The omentum and the transverse colon are retracted cephalad. Often, the pseudocyst is then visible through the transverse mesocolon. Laparoscopic ultrasonography may also be used to help identify the location of the cyst. The jejunum is divided approximately 30 cm distal to the ligament of Treitz to create a Roux limb. The pseudocyst is opened through the transverse mesocolon with the ultrasonic scalpel. A small enterotomy is made in the Roux limb, and a stapled cystojejunostomy is created. The cystoenterostomy is then closed with a continuous suture. The procedure is completed by performing a jejunojejunostomy at least 30 cm distal to the cystojejunostomy.

Palliative Bypass for Unresectable Periampullary Cancer

The peritoneal cavity is entered through an upper midline incision, and the abdomen is examined for evidence of liver metastases, serosal spread, carcinomatosis, involvement of regional lymph nodes, and invasion of major vascular structures. Once the tumor has been shown to be unresectable and histologic confirmation of malignancy has been received, a palliative double bypass procedure is begun, in which the duodenum is bypassed with a retrocolic gastrojejunostomy and the distally obstructed biliary tree is bypassed with a hepaticojejunostomy. A chemical splanchnicectomy is also performed to reduce pain.

Approximately 4 cm of the most dependent portion of the greater curvature of the stomach is cleaned by doubly clamping, dividing, and ligating attachments of the greater omentum. Once this is accomplished, a small rent is made in the transverse mesocolon, and a proximal loop of jejunum is brought up through this rent and anastomosed in an isoperistaltic fashion to the dependent wall of the stomach. The anastomosis is performed with an outer interrupted layer of 3-0 silk and an inner continuous layer of 3-0 absorbable synthetic suture material.

In the past, palliative duodenal bypasses for pancreatic cancer were frequently performed by carrying out an anterior antecolic gastrojejunostomy. Delayed gastric emptying proved to be a common occurrence with this approach. Fortunately, this complication can be virtually eliminated by performing a posterior gastroenterostomy. Once the posterior gastroenterostomy is complete, the anastomosis is tacked to the rent in the transverse mesocolon on the gastric side with interrupted 3-0 silk sutures to prevent the afferent and efferent jejunal limbs from herniating up through the transverse mesocolon [see Figure 19].

The gallbladder is mobilized out of the liver bed in a retrograde fashion and placed on traction to facilitate identification of the common hepatic duct. Once identified, the common hepatic duct is divided just proximal to the cystic duct. The gallbladder is removed, and the distal biliary segment is oversewn with a continuous 3-0 polypropylene suture. The jejunum is divided approximately 30 cm distal to the gastrojejunostomy, and a Roux-en-Y limb is brought up into the right upper quadrant through a second opening in the transverse mesocolon. An end-to-side hepaticojejunostomy is performed with a single layer of interrupted 4-0 absorbable synthetic sutures [see Figure 20]. An end-to-side jejunojejunostomy is then performed 60 cm downstream to restore enteric continuity and complete the Roux-en-Y. This anastomosis is performed with an inner continuous layer of 3-0 absorbable synthetic suture material and an outer interrupted layer of 3-0 silk. The Roux limb is tacked to the opening in the transverse mesocolon to prevent herniation.

The lesser omentum is divided, and a chemical splanchnicectomy is performed by injecting 20 ml of 50% alcohol into the celiac plexus on each side of the aorta at the level of the celiac axis. The level of the celiac axis is easily determined by palpating the thrill that is invariably present in the common hepatic artery as it comes off the celiac axis.

A closed suction Silastic drain may be left posterior to the area of the hepaticojejunostomy and brought out through a stab wound in the right upper quadrant. If tissue confirmation of the presence of adenocarcinoma of the head of the pancreas was not obtained preoperatively, it should be obtained during the operation. As a rule, this is most easily accomplished by performing a transduodenal needle biopsy (e.g., with a Tru-Cut needle; Cardinal Health, Dublin, Ohio). The abdomen is irrigated with an antibiotic solution and closed in a standard fashion.

References

1. Yeo CJ, Cameron JL, Sohn TA, et al: Six hundred fifty consecutive pancreaticoduodenectomies in the 1990s: pathology, complications, and outcomes. Ann Surg 226:248, 1997

2. Trede M, Schwall G, Saeger HD: Survival after pancreatoduodenectomy: 118 consecutive resections without an operative mortality. Ann Surg 211:447, 1990

3. Fernandez-del Castillo C, Rattner DW, Warshaw AL: Standards for pancreatic resection in the 1990s. Arch Surg 130:295, 1995

4. Dye CE, Waxman I: Endoscopic ultrasound. Gastroenterol Clin North Am 31:863, 2002

5. Cameron JL: Rapid exposure of the portal and superior mesenteric veins. Surg Gynecol Obstet 176:395, 1995

6. Traverso LW, Longmire WP Jr: Preservation of the pylorus in pancreaticoduodenectomy. Surg Gynecol Obstet 146:959, 1978

Recommended Reading

Cameron JL, Pitt HA, Yeo CJ, et al: One hundred and forty-five consecutive pancreaticoduodenectomies without mortality. Ann Surg 217:430, 1993

Fernandez-Cruz L, Martinez I, Gilabert R, et al. Laparoscopic distal pancreatectomy combined with preservation of the spleen for cystic neoplasms of the pancreas. J Gastrointest Surg 8:493, 2004

Fernandez-del Castillo C, Rattner DW, Warshaw AL: Standards for pancreatic resection in the 1990s. Arch Surg 130:295, 1995

Lillemoe KD, Cameron JL, Kaufman HS, et al: Chemical splanchnicectomy in patients with unresectable pancreatic cancer: a prospective randomized trial. Ann Surg 217:447, 1993

Lillemoe KD, Cameron JL, Hardacre JM, et al: Is prophylactic gastrojejunostomy indicated for unresectable periampullary cancer? a prospective randomized trial. Ann Surg 230:322, 1999

Lillemoe KD, Yeo CJ, Cameron JL: Pancreatic cancer: state-of-the-art care. CA Cancer J Clin 50:241, 2000

Sohn TA, Lillemoe KD, Cameron JL, et al: Surgical palliation of unresectable periampullary adenocarcinoma in the 1990s. J Am Coll Surg 188:658, 1999

Yeo CJ, Cameron JL, Lillemoe KD, et al: Does prophylactic octreotide decrease the rates of pancreatic fistula and other complications after pancreaticoduodenectomy? results of a prospective randomized placebo-controlled trial. Ann Surg 232:419, 2000

Yeo CJ, Cameron JL, Lillemoe KD, et al: Pancreaticoduodenectomy for cancer of the head of the pancreas: 201 patients. Ann Surg 221:721, 1995

Acknowledgments

Figures 1, 2, and 5 Tom Moore.
Figures 3, 8, and 10 through 13 Alice Y. Chen.
Figures 4, 6, 7, 9, and 14 through 20 Tom Moore.
Adapted from originals by Corinne Sandone.

Eric C. Poulin, M.D., M.Sc., F.A.C.S., F.R.C.S.C., Christopher M. Schlachta, M.D., F.A.C.S., and Joseph Mamazza, M.D., F.A.C.S., F.R.C.S.C.

Medicine is not an exact science, and nowhere is this observation more appropriate than in the operating room when a spleen is being removed.[1]

The first reported splenectomy in the Western world was performed by Zacarello in 1549, though the veracity of his operative description has been questioned. Between this initial report and the 1800s, very few cases were recorded. The first reported splenectomy in North America was performed by O'Brien in 1816. The patient was in the act of committing a rape when his victim plunged a large knife into his left side. As in this case, most early splenectomies were done in patients who had undergone penetrating trauma; often, the spleen was protruding from the wound and the surgeon proceeded with en masse ligation. The first elective splenectomy was performed by Quittenbaum in 1826 for sequelae of portal hypertension, and soon afterward, Wells performed one of the first splenectomies using general anesthesia; both patients died. In 1866, Bryant was the first to attempt splenectomy in a patient with leukemia. Over the following 15 years, 14 splenectomies were attempted as therapy for leukemia; none of the patients survived. In a 1908 review of 49 similar cases, Johnston reported a mortality of 87.7%.[2] These dismal results led to the abandonment of splenectomy for leukemia. In 1916, Kaznelson, of Prague, was the first to report good results from splenectomy in patients with thrombocytopenic purpura.

As the 20th century progressed, splenectomy became more common in direct proportion to the increase in the use of the automobile. The eventual recognition of the syndrome known as overwhelming postsplenectomy infection (OPSI) made splenic conservation an important consideration. Partial splenectomy had initially been described by the French surgeon Péan in the 19th century. This procedure received little further study until almost 100 years later, when the Brazilian surgeon Campos Cristo reevaluated Péan's technique in his report of eight trauma patients treated with partial splenectomy.[3] Simpson's report on 16 children admitted for splenic trauma to the Hospital for Sick Children in Toronto between 1948 and 1955 was instrumental in establishing the validity of nonoperative treatment of splenic trauma [see 106 Injuries to the Liver, Biliary Tract, Spleen, and Diaphragm].[4]

In late 1991 and early 1992, four groups working independently—Delaître in Paris, Carroll in Los Angeles, Cushieri in the United Kingdom, and our group in Canada—published the first reports of laparoscopic splenectomy in patients with hematologic disorders.[5-7] Since then, the development of operative techniques for partial laparoscopic splenectomy has tested the limits of minimally invasive surgery and encouraged clinical research into methods of simplifying the execution of the operation.[8,9] The adoption of laparoscopic splenectomy has led to a gradual decrease in the indications for open splenectomy; however, both procedures are still essential components of spleen surgery.

Anatomic Considerations

Most anatomy texts suggest that the splenic artery is constant in its course and branches; however, as the classic essay by Michels made clear, each spleen has its own peculiar pattern of terminal artery branches.[10]

SPLENIC ARTERY

The celiac axis is the largest but shortest branch of the abdominal aorta: it is only 15 to 20 mm long. The celiac axis arises above the body of the pancreas and, in 82% of specimens, divides into three primary branches: the left gastric artery, which is the first branch, and the hepatic and splenic arteries, which derive from a common stem. In rare instances, the splenic artery originates directly from the aorta; even less often, a second splenic artery arises from the celiac axis. There are numerous other possible variations, in which the splenic artery may originate from the aorta, the superior mesenteric artery, the middle colic artery, the left gastric artery, the left hepatic artery, or the accessory right hepatic artery. As a rule, however, the splenic artery arises from the celiac axis to the right of the midline, which means that the aorta must be crossed to reach the spleen and that selective angiography is likely to be difficult at times. The splenic artery can take a very tortuous course, particularly in patients who are elderly or who have a longer artery.

In his study of 100 cadaver spleens,[10] Michels divided splenic arterial geography into two types, distributed and magistral (or bundled) [see Figure 1]. In the distributed type, found in 70% of dissections, the splenic trunk is short, and six to 12 long branches enter the spleen over approximately 75% of its medial surface. The branches originate between 3 and 13 cm from the hilum [see Figure 1a]. In the bundled type, found in the remaining 30% of dissections, there is a long main splenic artery that divides near the hilum into three or four large, short terminal branches that enter the spleen over only 25% to 35% of its medial surface. These short splenic branches originate, on average, 3.5 cm from the spleen, and they reach the center of the organ as a compact bundle [see Figure 1b]. Early identification of the type of splenic blood supply present can help the surgeon estimate how difficult a particular splenectomy is likely to be. Operation on a spleen with a distributed vascular anatomy usually involves dissection of more blood vessels; however, the vessels, being spread over a wider area of the splenic hilum, are relatively easy to deal with. Operation on a spleen with a bundled-type blood supply typically involves dissection of fewer vessels; however, because the hilum is narrower and more compact, dissection and separation of the vessels are more difficult.

BRANCHES OF SPLENIC ARTERY

The splenic branches vary so markedly in length, size, and origin that no two spleens have the same anatomy. Outside the spleen, the arteries also frequently form transverse anastomoses with each other that, like most collaterals, arise at a 90° angle to the vessels involved [see Figure 1].[11] As a consequence, attempts to occlude a branch of the splenic artery by means of clips or embolization, if carried out proximal to such an anastomosis, may fail to devascularize the corresponding splenic segment. Before the splenic trunk divides, it usually gives off a few slender branch-

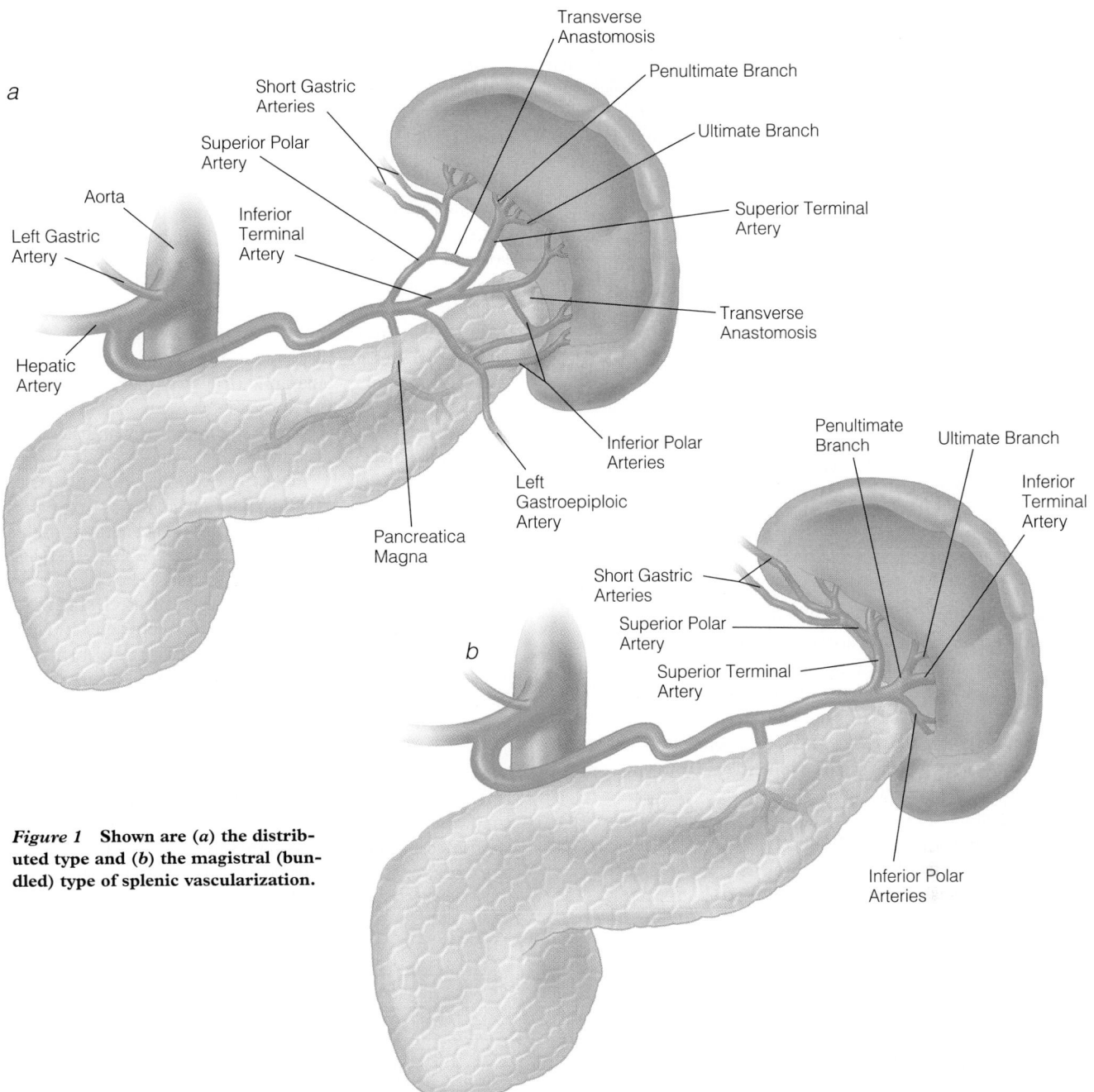

a

Short Gastric
Arteries

Superior Polar
Artery

Aorta

Left Gastric
Artery

Inferior
Terminal
Artery

Hepatic
Artery

Transverse
Anastomosis

Penultimate Branch

Ultimate Branch

Superior Terminal
Artery

Transverse
Anastomosis

Inferior Polar
Arteries

Left
Gastroepiploic
Artery

Pancreatica
Magna

b

Penultimate
Branch

Ultimate Branch

Inferior
Terminal
Artery

Short Gastric
Arteries

Superior Polar
Artery

Superior Terminal
Artery

Inferior Polar
Arteries

Figure 1 **Shown are (*a*) the distributed type and (*b*) the magistral (bundled) type of splenic vascularization.**

es to the tail of the pancreas. The most important of these is called
the pancreatica magna (a vessel familiar to vascular radiologists);
occlusion of this branch with embolic material has been reported
to result in pancreatitis. Next, the splenic artery divides into two
to six first and second terminal branches, and these branches
undergo two further levels of division into two to 12 penultimate
and ultimate branches. Segmental and subsegmental division can
occur either outside or inside the spleen. The number of arteries
entering the spleen ranges from six to 36. The size of the spleen
does not determine the number of arteries entering it; however,
the presence of notches and tubercles usually correlates well with
a higher number of entering arteries.

A reasonable general scheme of splenic artery branches might
include as many as seven principal branches at various division
levels and in various anatomic arrangements: (1) the superior

terminal artery, (2) the inferior terminal artery, (3) the medial
terminal artery, (4) the short gastric arteries, (5) the left gastroepiploic artery, (6) the inferior polar artery, and (7) the superior polar artery [*see Figure 2*]. Veins are usually located behind
the corresponding arteries, except at the ultimate level of division, where they may be either anterior or posterior.

First Terminal Division Branches

A classic study from 1917 found that 72% of specimens had
three terminal branches (superior polar, superior terminal, and
inferior terminal) and 28% had two[12]; the medial terminal artery
was observed in only 20% of cases. When the superior terminal
artery is excessively large, the inferior terminal is rudimentary,
with an added blood supply often coming from the left gastroepiploic and polar vessels.

Second Terminal Division Branches

Superior polar artery   The superior polar artery is present in 65% of patients. It usually arises from the main splenic trunk (75% of cases) or the superior terminal artery (20% of cases), but on occasion, it may originate from the inferior terminal artery or separately from the celiac axis (thus providing the spleen with a double splenic artery). In most instances, the superior polar artery gives rise to one or two short gastric branches; rarely, it gives rise to the left inferior phrenic and pancreatic rami. The presence and size of this artery appear to be correlated with tubercle formation, in that it is more prominent in spleens with large tubercles. The superior polar artery is frequently very long and slender and thus easily torn during splenectomy; accordingly, it was suggested in 1928 that ligation of splenic branches be started from the inferior pole of the spleen.[13]

Inferior polar artery   The inferior polar artery is present in 82% of cases. As many as five collateral branches may arise from the splenic trunk, the inferior terminal artery, or, as noted, the left gastroepiploic artery. Inferior polar branches may have multiple origins, and they tend to be of smaller caliber than the superior polar artery.

Left gastroepiploic artery   The left gastroepiploic artery, the most varied of the splenic branches, courses along the left side of the greater curvature in the anterior layer of the greater omentum. In 72% of cases, it arises from the splenic trunk several centimeters from its primary terminal division, and in 22% of cases, it originates from the inferior terminal artery or its branches; however, it may also originate from the middle of the splenic trunk or from the superior terminal artery. Characteristically, the left gastroepiploic artery gives off inferior polar arteries, which vary in number (ranging from one to five), size, and length. Typically, these branches are addressed first during laparoscopic splenectomy. When they are small, they can usually be controlled with the electrocautery.

Collaterals

Short gastric arteries   As many as six short gastric arteries may arise from the fundus of the stomach, but as a rule, only the one to three that open into the superior polar artery must be ligated during laparoscopic splenectomy [*see Figure 1*].

SUSPENSORY LIGAMENTS OF SPLEEN AND TAIL OF PANCREAS

Duplications of the peritoneum form the many suspensory ligaments of the spleen [*see Figure 3*]. Medially and posteriorly, the splenorenal ligament contains the tail of the pancreas and the splenic vessels. Anteriorly, the gastrosplenic ligament contains the short gastric and gastroepiploic arteries. In the lateral approach to laparoscopic splenectomy [*see* Operative Technique, *below*], the splenorenal and gastrosplenic ligaments are easily distinguished, and dissection of the anatomic structures they contain is relatively simple. In the anterior approach, these two ligaments lie on top of each other, and to separate them correctly and safely requires considerable experience with splenic anatomy.

The phrenicocolic ligament courses laterally from the diaphragm to the splenic flexure of the colon; its upper portion is called the phrenicosplenic ligament. The attachment of the lower pole on the internal side is called the splenocolic ligament. Between these two structures, a horizontal shelf of areolar tissue, known as the sustentaculum lienis, is formed on which the inferior pole of the spleen rests. The sustentaculum lienis is often molded into a sac that opens cephalad and acts as a support for the lower pole. This structure, often overlooked during open procedures, is readily visible through a laparoscope. The phrenicocolic ligament, the splenocolic ligament, and the sustentaculum lienis are usually avascular, except in patients who have portal hypertension or myeloid metaplasia.

A 1937 study found that the tail of the pancreas was in direct contact with the spleen in 30% of cadavers.[14] A subsequent report confirmed this finding and added that in 73% of patients, the distance between the two structures was no more than 1 cm.[15] Care must be exercised to avoid damage with the electrocautery during

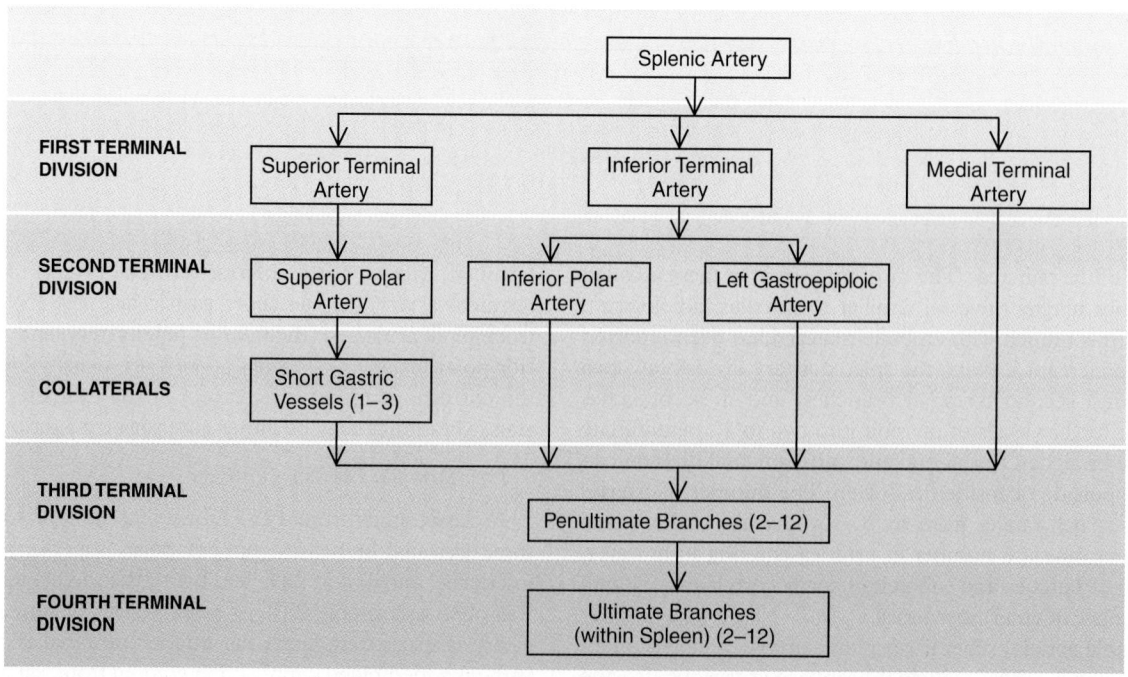

Figure 2   **Outlined is a general scheme of the levels of division of the splenic artery branches.**

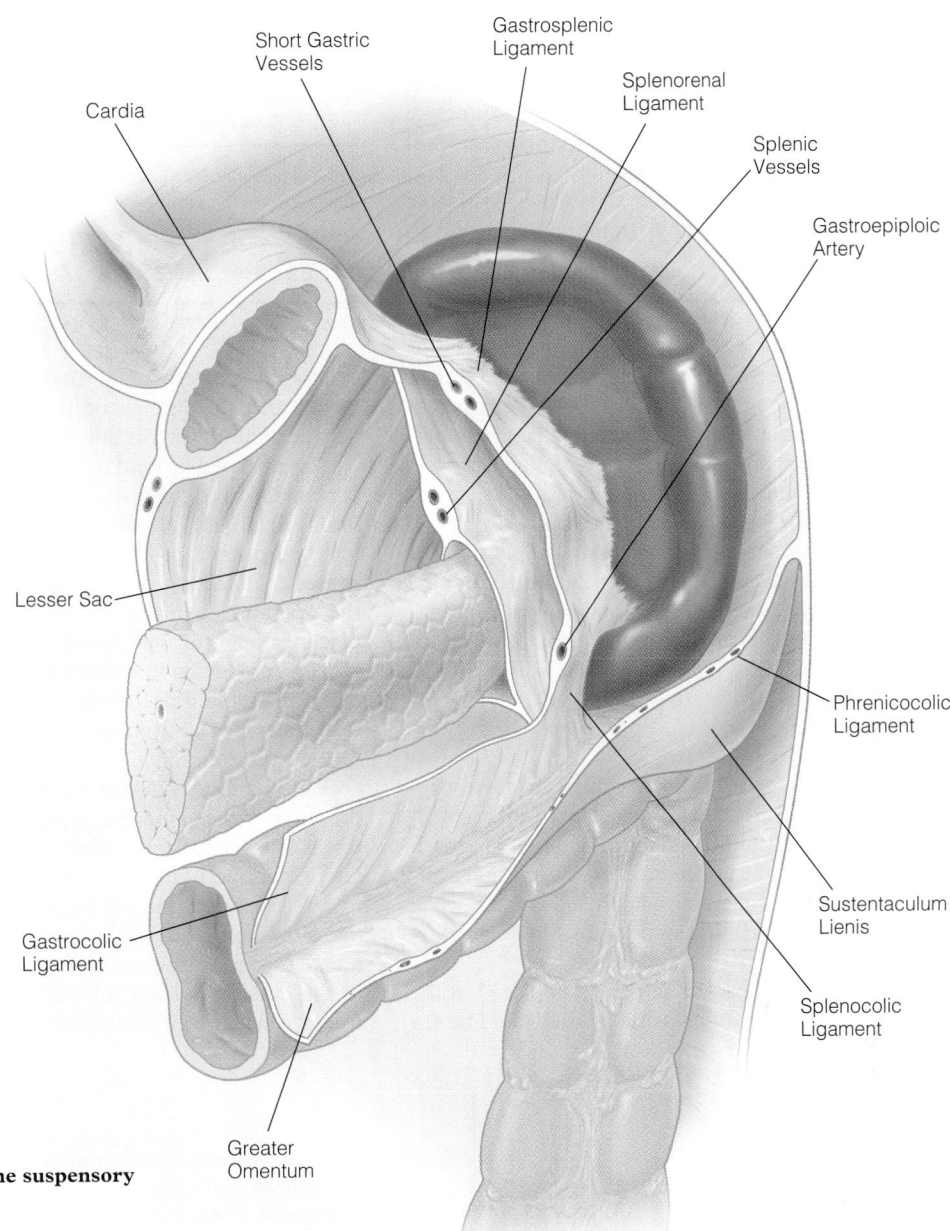

Cardia

Short Gastric
Vessels

Gastrosplenic
Ligament

Splenorenal
Ligament

Splenic
Vessels

Gastroepiploic
Artery

Lesser Sac

Phrenicocolic
Ligament

Gastrocolic
Ligament

Sustentaculum
Lienis

Splenocolic
Ligament

Greater
Omentum

Figure 3 **Depicted are the suspensory ligaments of the spleen.**

dissection as well as damage with the linear stapler in the course of en masse ligation of the splenic hilum (a maneuver more easily performed via the lateral approach to laparoscopic splenectomy).

Laparoscopic Splenectomy

PREOPERATIVE EVALUATION

Currently, we consider all patients evaluated for elective splenectomy to be potential candidates for laparoscopic splenectomy. Contraindications to a laparoscopic approach include severe portal hypertension, uncorrectable coagulopathy, severe ascites, and most traumatic injuries to the spleen. Extreme splenomegaly remains a relative contraindication as well. Because most patients scheduled for laparoscopic splenectomy have hematologic disorders, they undergo the same hematologic preparation that patients scheduled for open surgery do—namely, steroids and γ-globulins (when required). Ultrasonography is performed to determine the size of the spleen. Spleen size is expressed in terms of the maximum interpole length (i.e., the length of the line joining the two organ poles) and is generally classified into three categories: (1) normal spleen size (< 11 cm), (2) moderate splenomegaly (11 to 20 cm), and (3) severe splenomegaly (> 20 cm).[16] Because extremely large spleens present special technical problems that test the current limits of laparoscopic surgery, we make use of a fourth category for spleens longer than 30 cm or heavier than 3 kg, which we call megaspleens [*see Table 1*]. The ultrasonographer is also asked to try to identify any accessory spleens that may be present. Computed tomography is done when there is doubt about the exactness of the ultrasonographic measurement; such measurement is sometimes inaccurate at the upper pole and with spleens longer than 16 cm.

Patients receive thorough counseling about the consequences of the asplenic state. Polyvalent pneumococcal vaccine is administered at least 2 weeks before operation in all cases; preoperative vaccination against *Haemophilus influenzae* and meningococci is also advisable. Heparin prophylaxis for thrombophlebitis is administered according to standard guidelines, provided that there is no hematologic contraindication [*see 85 Venous Thromboembolism*]. Nonsteroidal anti-inflammatory drugs (NSAIDs) are often given orally before operation to minimize postoperative pain; however, on empirical grounds, NSAIDs are not used when heparin prophylaxis is employed. Platelets are rarely, if ever, required when laparoscopic splenectomy is performed for idiopathic (immune) thrombocytopenic purpura (ITP).

OPERATIVE PLANNING

Laparoscopic splenectomy presents special problems, such as the necessity of dealing with a fragile and richly vascularized organ that is situated close to the stomach, the colon, and the pancreas and the difficulty of devising an extraction strategy that is compatible with proper histologic confirmation of the pathologic process while maintaining the advantages of minimal access surgery. For successful performance of laparoscopic splenectomy, a detailed knowledge of both splenic anatomy and potential complications is essential. The operative strategy is largely determined by the anatomic features, which, as noted [*see Anatomic Considerations, above*], may vary considerably from patient to patient.[17]

OPERATIVE TECHNIQUE

Lateral Approach

This approach was first described in connection with laparoscopic adrenalectomy and is currently used for most laparoscopic splenectomies.[18] At present, the only indication for the anterior approach to laparoscopic splenectomy is the presence of massive splenomegaly or a megaspleen. Typically, this alternative approach is taken when a spleen reaches or exceeds 23 cm in length or 3 kg in weight.

Step 1: placement of trocars The patient is placed in the right lateral decubitus position, much as he or she would be for

Table 1 Classification of Spleens According to Spleen Length*

Spleen Class	Spleen Length
Normal-size spleen	7–11 cm
Moderate splenomegaly	12–20 cm
Massive splenomegaly	21–30 cm
Megaspleen	> 30 cm

*Spleen length is defined as interpole length, measured along a straight line connecting the two poles.

a left-side posterolateral thoracotomy. The operating table is flexed and the kidney bolster raised to increase the distance between the lower rib and the iliac crest. Usually, four 12 mm trocars are used around the costal margin so that the camera, the clip applier, and the linear stapler can be interchanged with maximum flexibility [*see Figure 4*]. The trocars must be far enough apart to permit good working angles. Some advantage may be gained from tilting the patient slightly backward; this step gives the operating team more freedom in moving the instruments placed along the left costal margins, especially during lifting movements, when it is easy for instrument handles to touch the operating table. For the same reason, it is also advisable to place the anterior or abdominal side of the patient closer to the edge of the operating table.

A local anesthetic is infiltrated into the skin at the midpoint of the anterior costal margin, and a 12 mm incision is made. The first trocar is inserted under direct vision, and a symmetrical 15 mm Hg pneumoperitoneum is created. The locations of the remaining trocars are determined by considering the anatomic configuration in relation to the size of the spleen to be excised. In most cases, the fourth posterior trocar cannot be inserted until the splenic flexure of the colon has been mobilized. Accordingly, the procedure is usually started with three trocars in place.

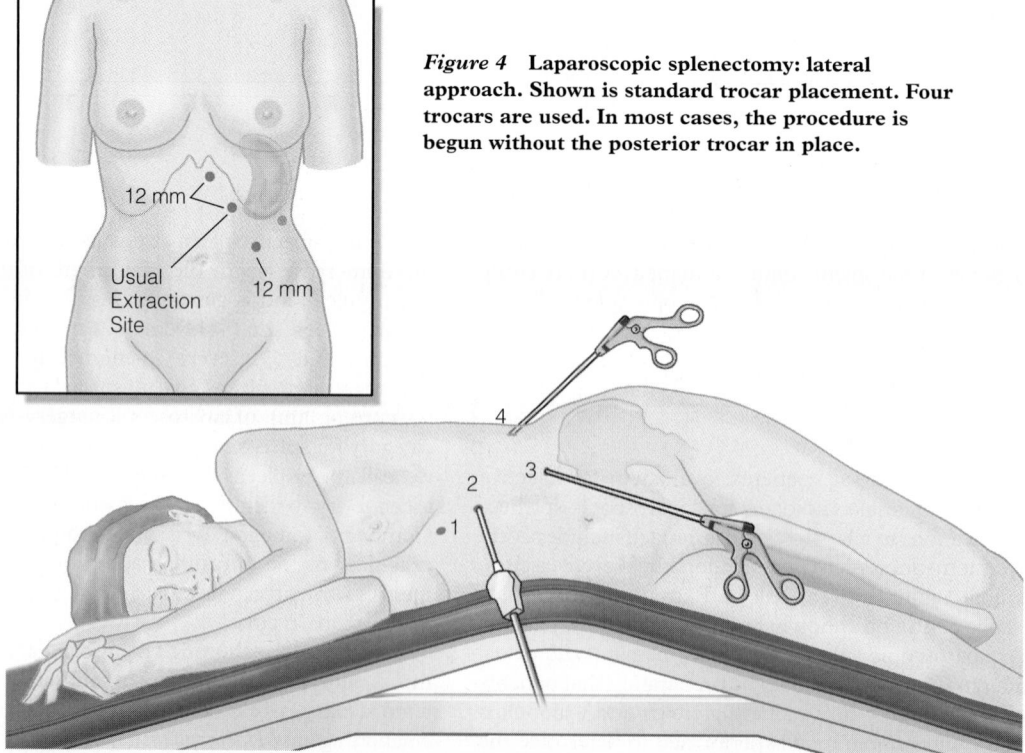

Figure 4 **Laparoscopic splenectomy: lateral approach. Shown is standard trocar placement. Four trocars are used. In most cases, the procedure is begun without the posterior trocar in place.**

Troubleshooting. After years of using the Veress needle, we now prefer the open method of inserting the first trocar. It is true that use of the Veress needle is for the most part safe; however, the small number of catastrophic complications that occur with blind methods of first trocar insertion are more and more difficult to justify. Admittedly, these complications are infrequent, and thus, it is unlikely that even a large randomized trial would be able to show any significant differences between various methods of first trocar insertion. Nevertheless, even though complications occur with the open method of first trocar insertion as well, they are very uncommon and tend to be limited to trauma to the intestine or the omental blood vessels; they do not have the same serious consequences as the major vessel injury that may arise from blind trocar insertion.

Trocar placements differing from the ones we describe may be considered. More experienced surgeons (or those simply wishing to make the procedure easier) may choose to replace one or two 12 mm trocars with 5 mm trocars [*see Figure 5a*]. The procedure can also be performed with only three trocars. In leaner patients, one of the trocars can be inserted into the umbilicus to gain a cosmetic advantage. The advent of needlescopic techniques has made it possible to replace some of the 5 and 12 mm trocars with 3 mm trocars. The ultimate (i.e., least invasive) technique, usually reserved for lean patients with ITP and normal-size spleens, involves one 12 mm trocar placed in the umbilicus and two 3 mm trocars placed subcostally [*see Figure 5b*]. This approach requires two different camera-laparoscope setups, so that a 3 mm laparoscope can be interchanged with a 10 mm laparoscope as necessary to permit application of clips or staplers through the umbilical incision once the dissection is completed. The specimen is then retrieved through the umbilicus. Because the use of 3 mm laparoscopes is accompanied by a decrease in available intra-abdominal light and focal width, a meticulously bloodless field and sophisticated surgical judgment are critical for successful performance of needlescopic splenectomy.

Step 2: search for and retrieval of accessory spleens The camera is inserted, and the stomach is retracted medially to expose the spleen. Then a fairly standard sequence is followed. A thorough search is then made for accessory spleens. To maximize retrieval, all known locations of accessory spleens should be carefully explored [*see Figure 6*]. Any accessory spleens found should be removed immediately; they are considerably harder to locate once the spleen is removed and the field is stained with blood.

Troubleshooting. It is especially important to retrieve accessory spleens from patients with ITP, in whom the presence of overlooked accessory spleens has been associated with recurrence of the disease. Remedial operation for excision of missed accessory spleens has been reported to bring remission of recurrent disease; such operation can be performed laparoscopically. The overall retrieval rate for accessory spleens should fall between 15% and 30%.

Splenic activity has been demonstrated after open and laparoscopic splenectomy for trauma and hematologic disorders[19,20]; accordingly, it is advisable to wash out and recover all splenic fragments resulting from intraoperative trauma at the end of the procedure. This step is particularly important for patients with ITP, in whom intraoperative trauma to the spleen is thought to contribute to postoperative scan-detectable splenic activity. As of this writing, we have recovered accessory spleens in 33% of ITP cases treated laparoscopically.

Step 3: control of vessels at lower pole, demonstration of "splenic tent," and incision of phrenicocolic ligament The splenic flexure is partially mobilized by incising the splenocolic ligament, the lower part of the phrenicocolic ligament, and the sustentaculum lienis. The incision is carried slightly into the left side of the gastrocolic ligament. This step affords access to the gastrosplenic ligament, which can then be readily separated from the splenorenal ligament to create what looks like a tent. This maneuver cannot be accomplished in all cases, but when it can be done, it simplifies the procedure considerably. The walls of this so-called splenic tent are made of the gastrosplenic ligament on the left and the splenorenal ligament on the right, and the floor is made up of the stomach. In fact, this maneuver opens the lesser sac in its lateral portion (a point that is better demonstrated with gentle upward retraction of the splenic tip) [*see Figure 7*].

The branches of the left gastroepiploic artery are controlled with the electrocautery or with clips, depending on the size of the branches. The avascular portion of the gastrosplenic ligament, situated between the gastroepiploic artery and the short gastric ves-

a 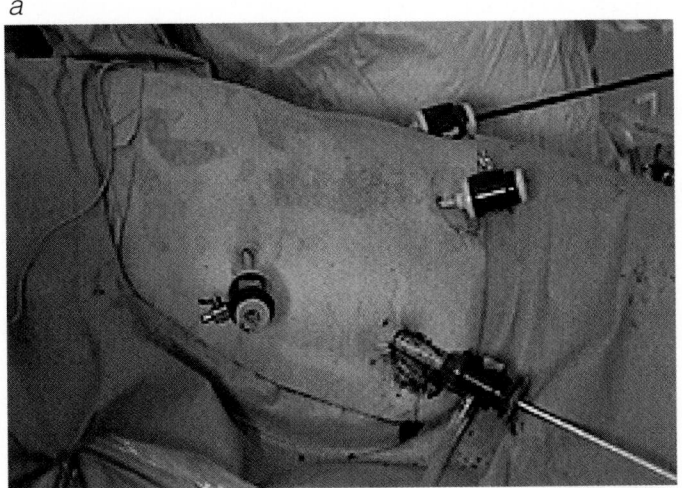 *b*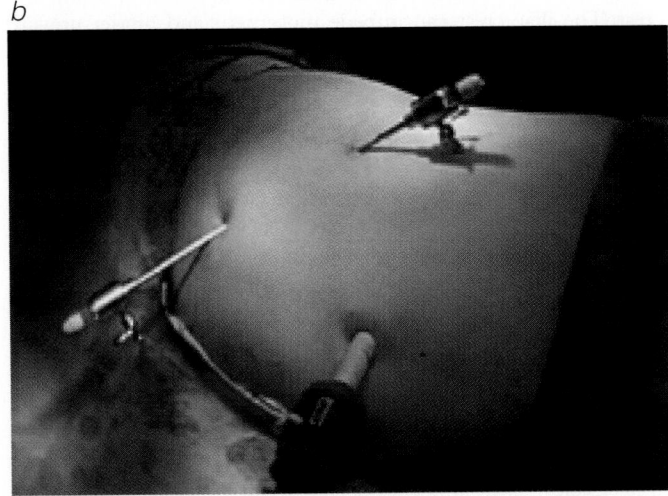

Figure 5 **Laparoscopic splenectomy: lateral approach. Shown are alternative trocar placements. (*a*) In some patients (e.g., thin patients with normal-size spleens), a 12 mm trocar may be placed in the umbilicus to gain a cosmetic advantage, and most of the other trocars may be downsized to 5 mm. (*b*) In the needlescopic approach, only three trocars are placed: a 12 mm trocar in the umbilicus and two 3 mm subcostal trocars. Two camera-laparoscope setups (3 and 10 mm) are required.**

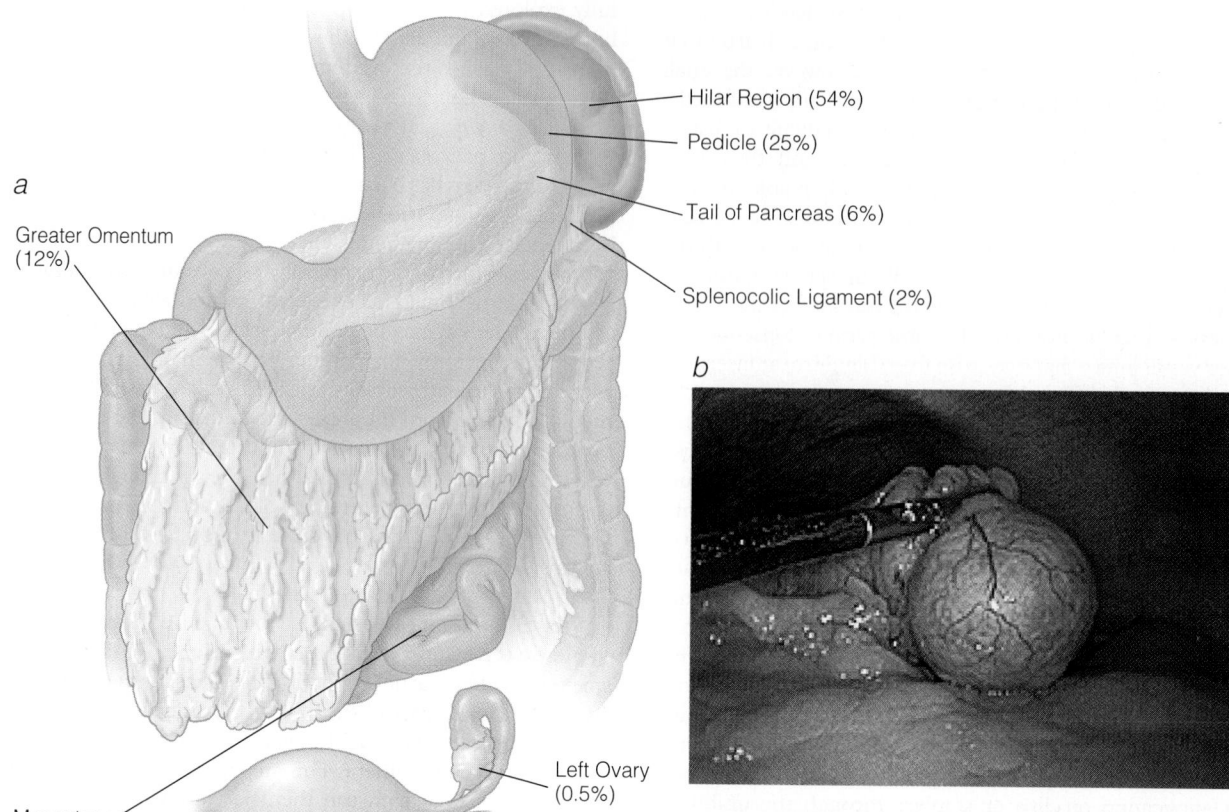

a

Greater Omentum
(12%)

Hilar Region (54%)

Pedicle (25%)

Tail of Pancreas (6%)

Splenocolic Ligament (2%)

Mesentery
(0.5%)

Left Ovary
(0.5%)

b

Figure 6 **Laparoscopic splenectomy: lateral approach.
(*a*) Accessory spleens are known to occur at specific
sites. (*b*) Shown is an accessory spleen.**

sels, is then incised sufficiently to expose the hilar structures in the splenorenal ligament. To accomplish this, the lower pole is gently elevated; in this position, the spleen almost retracts itself as it naturally falls toward the left lobe of the liver. At this point, the surgeon can usually assess the geography of the hilum and determine the degree of difficulty of the operation. The fourth trocar, if needed, is then placed posteriorly under direct vision, with care taken to avoid the left kidney. Caution must also be exercised in placing the trocars situated immediately anterior and posterior to the iliac crest. The iliac crest can impede movement and hinder upward mobilization of structures if the trocars are placed over it rather than in front of or behind it [*see Figure 8*].

Finally, the phrenicocolic ligament is incised all the way to the left crus of the diaphragm, either with a monopolar electrocautery with an L hook or with scissors. A small portion of the ligament is left to keep the spleen suspended and facilitate subsequent bagging. The phrenicocolic ligament is avascular except in patients with portal hypertension or myeloproliferative disorders (e.g., myeloid metaplasia). Leaving 1 to 2 cm of ligament all along the spleen side facilitates retraction and handling of the spleen with instruments.

Troubleshooting. Remarkably few instruments are needed for laparoscopic splenectomy: most of the operation is done with three reusable instruments. A dolphin-nose 5 mm atraumatic grasper is used to elevate and hold the spleen. It is also used to separate tissue planes and vessels with blunt dissection because its atraumatic tip is easily insinuated between tissue planes. A gently curved 5 mm fine-tip dissector (Crile or Maryland) and a 10 mm 90° right-angle dissector are the only other tools required for cost-efficient dissection.

When a powered instrument is called for, we use a monopolar electrocautery with an L hook or a gently curved scissors. Alternatively, an ultrasonic dissector or a tissue-welding device may be used, albeit at a much higher cost.

Step 4: dealing with splenic hilum and tailoring operative strategy to anatomy It is advisable to base one's operative strategy on the specific splenic anatomy. If a distributed anatomy

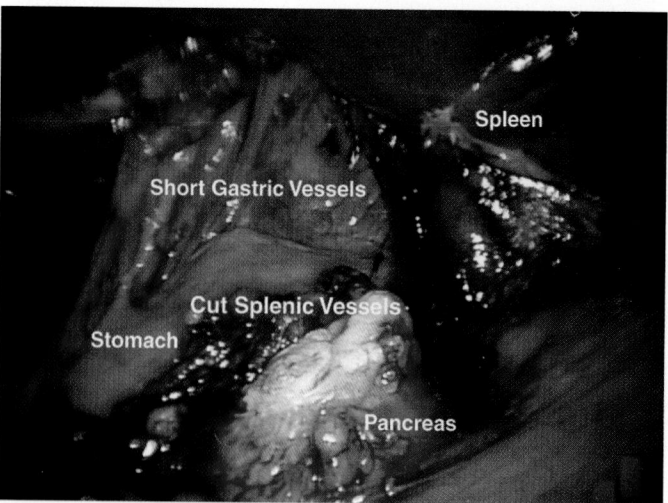

Spleen

Short Gastric Vessels

Cut Splenic Vessels

Stomach

Pancreas

Figure 7 **Laparoscopic splenectomy: lateral approach. The so-called splenic tent is formed by the gastrosplenic and splenorenal ligaments laterally and the stomach below.**

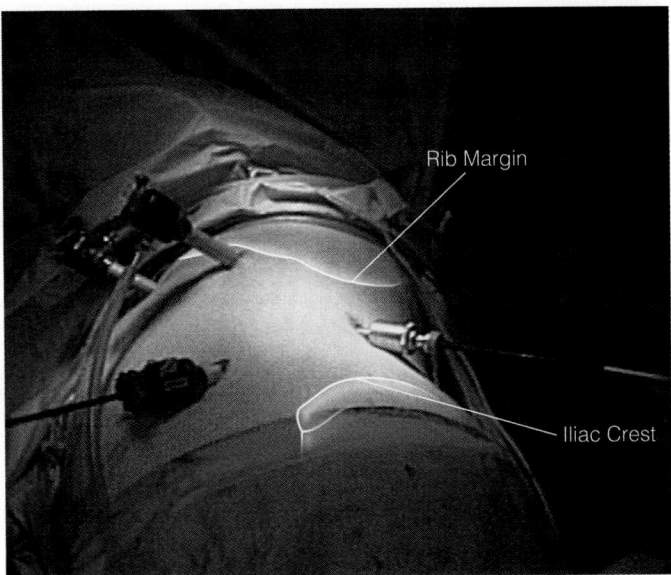

Figure 8 Laparoscopic splenectomy: lateral approach. Shown is the recommended trocar placement around the iliac crest.

is present, the splenic branches are usually dissected and clipped. This is not only the least costly approach but also the simplest, in that the vessels are spread over a wider area of the splenic hilum and are easier to dissect and separate [*see Figure 9*].

A bundled anatomy lends itself more to a single use of the linear stapler, provided that the tail of the pancreas is identified and dissected away when required. When possible, a window is created above the hilar pedicle in the splenorenal ligament so that all structures can be included within the markings of the linear stapler under direct vision [*see Figure 10*]. The angles provided by the various trocars make this maneuver much easier via the lateral approach than via the anterior approach. Dissection continues with individual dissection and clipping of the short gastric vessels; occasionally, these vessels can also be taken en masse with the linear stapler. So far, we have not used sutures in this setting, except once to control a short gastric vessel that was too short to be clipped safely. This portion of the operation is performed while the spleen is hanging from the upper portion of the phrenicocolic ligament, which has not yet been entirely cut.

Troubleshooting. It is at this point in the procedure that experience in designing the operative strategy pays off in reduced operating time. Because of the many variations in size, shape, vascular patterns, and relations to adjacent organs, spleens are almost as individual as fingerprints. Accordingly, an experienced spleen surgeon learns to keep an open mind with regard to operative strategy and must be able to call on a wide range of skills to facilitate the procedure.

The surgeon should start by looking at the internal surface of the spleen. If the splenic vessels cover more than 75% of the internal surface (as is the case in 70% of patients), a distributed anatomy is present. With a distributed vascular anatomy, the vessels tend to be easier to dissect and isolate and thus can be readily (and cost-effectively) controlled with clips. On the other hand, if the splenic vessels entering the spleen cover only 25% to 35% of the inner surface of the hilum (30% of patients), the pattern is bundled. With a bundled vascular anatomy, the vessels, being fewer and closer together, can usually be controlled with a single application of the vascular stapler across the hilum, provided that the tail of the pancreas can be protected.

Step 5: extraction of spleen A medium-size or large heavy-duty plastic freezer bag, of the sort commercially available in grocery stores, is used to bag the spleen. This bag is sterilized and folded, then introduced into the abdominal cavity through one of the 12 mm trocars [*see Figure 11*]. The bag is unfolded and the spleen slipped inside to prevent splenosis during the subsequent manipulations. Grasping forceps are used to hold the two rigid edges of the bag and to effect partial closure. Bagging is facilitated by preserving the upper portion of the phrenicocolic ligament. After final section of the phrenicocolic ligament and any diaphragmatic adhesions present, extraction is performed through one of the anterior port sites. Extraction through a posterior site is more difficult because of the thickness of the muscle mass; usually, the incision must be opened, and more muscle must be fulgurated than is desirable.

The subcostal or umbilical incision through which extraction is to take place is extended slightly. A grasping forceps is inserted through the extraction incision to hold the edges of the bag inside the abdomen. Gentle traction on the bag from outside brings the spleen close to the peritoneal surface of the umbilical incision and then out of the wound [*see Figure 12*]. Specimen retrieval bags

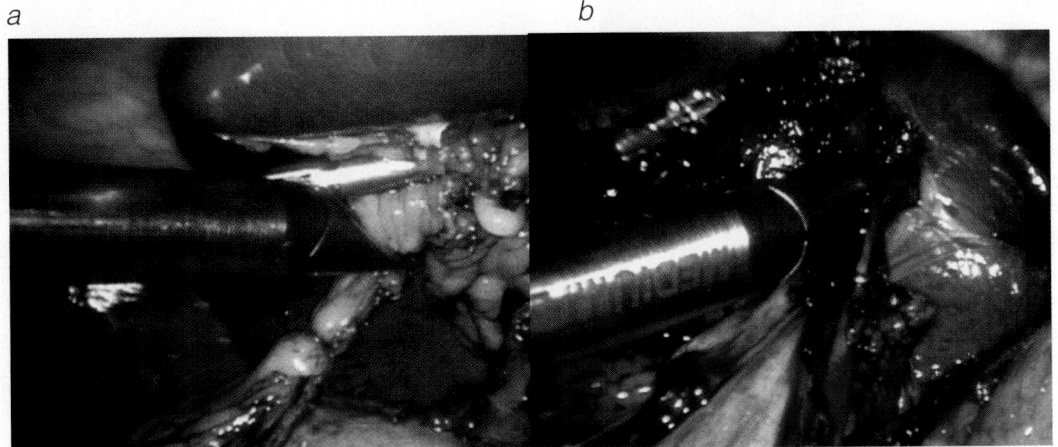

Figure 9 Laparoscopic splenectomy: lateral approach. (*a, b*) Clipping is well suited to controlling short gastric or gastroepiploic vessels. It is also appropriate for distributed-type splenic vasculatures, in which more splenic vessels are spread over a wider area of the hilum.

a

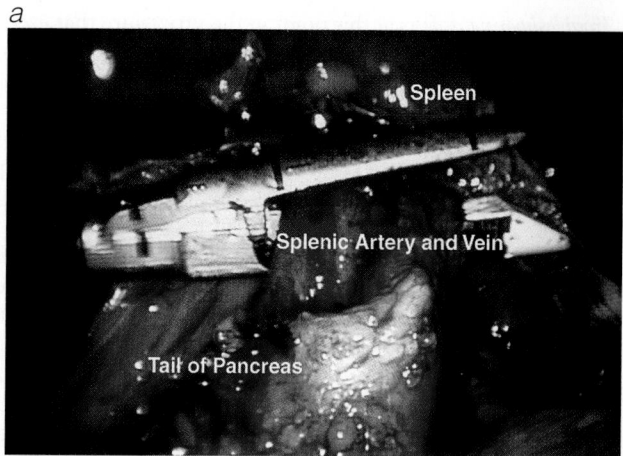

b

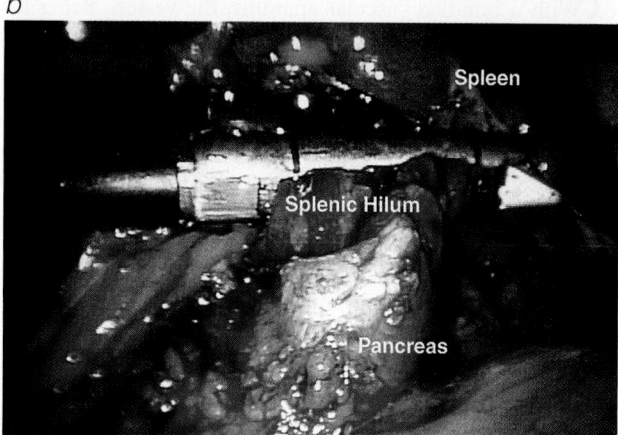

c

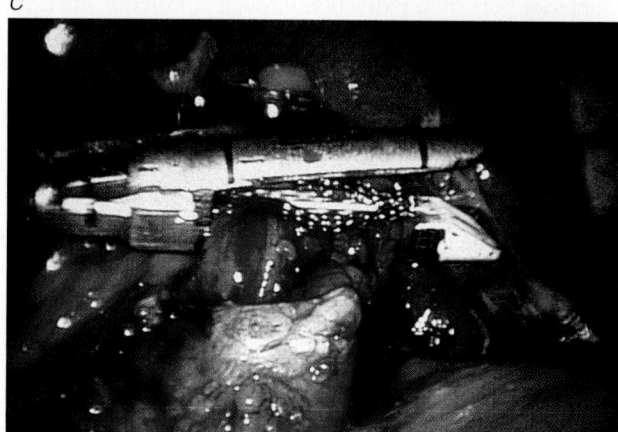

Figure 10 Laparoscopic splenectomy: lateral approach. (*a through c*) Stapling is particularly well suited to the compact hilum found in the magistral-type distribution of splenic vessels. As shown, all of the vascular structures are within the stapler markers, and the tail of the pancreas is well protected.

have been developed that can accommodate a normal-size spleen and thus make bagging much easier, but they are costly.

A biopsy specimen of a size suitable for pathologic identification is obtained by incising the splenic tip. The spleen is then fragmented with finger fracture, and the resulting blood is suctioned. The remaining stromal tissue of the spleen is then extracted through the small incision, hemostasis is again verified, and all trocars are removed. No drains are used. The incisions are closed with absorbable sutures and paper strips.

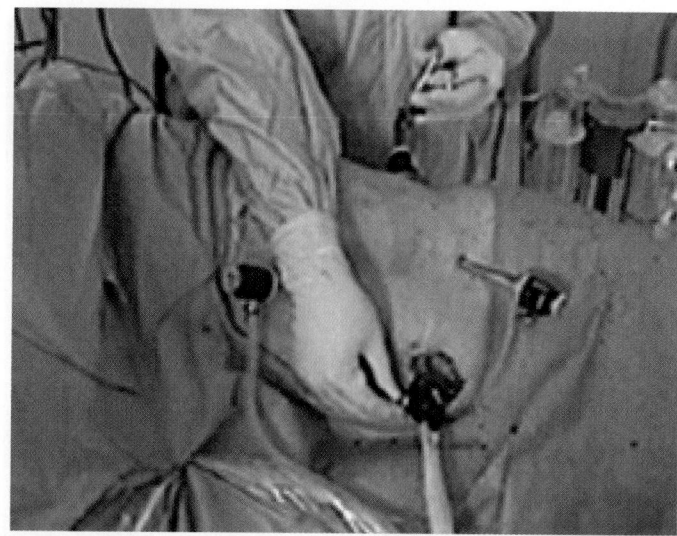

Figure 11 Laparoscopic splenectomy: lateral approach. Illustrated is the introduction of a sterile freezer bag for specimen extraction via the pull method. A toothed grasper is passed across the abdomen between two trocars and brought out through the 12 mm umbilical trocar site. This grasper is used to pull the extraction bag back into the abdomen.

Troubleshooting. The freezer bags can be more easily introduced into the abdomen if they are pulled in rather than pushed in [*see Figure 11*]. This may be accomplished by bringing out a 5 mm toothed grasper through the introduction trocar from another properly angled trocar, grasping the specimen bag, and pulling the bag back down through the trocar. A laparoscopic hernia mesh introducer may also be used.

Slipping the spleen into a freezer bag is also an acquired skill that takes some time to master. It is an important skill that is useful in many other instances where specimen retrieval is needed (e.g., in procedures involving the gallbladder, the appendix, the adrenal glands, or the colon). In addition, it is highly cost-effective, in that these commercially available bags cost only a few cents each. Admittedly, laparoscopic retrieval bags are easier to use, but their substantially higher cost can become a factor in a busy min-

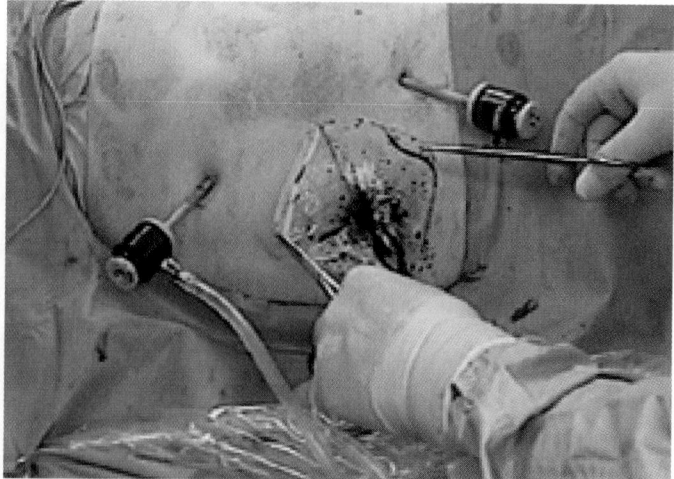

Figure 12 Laparoscopic splenectomy: lateral approach. Shown is the position of the specimen bag before finger fragmentation or pulp suction.

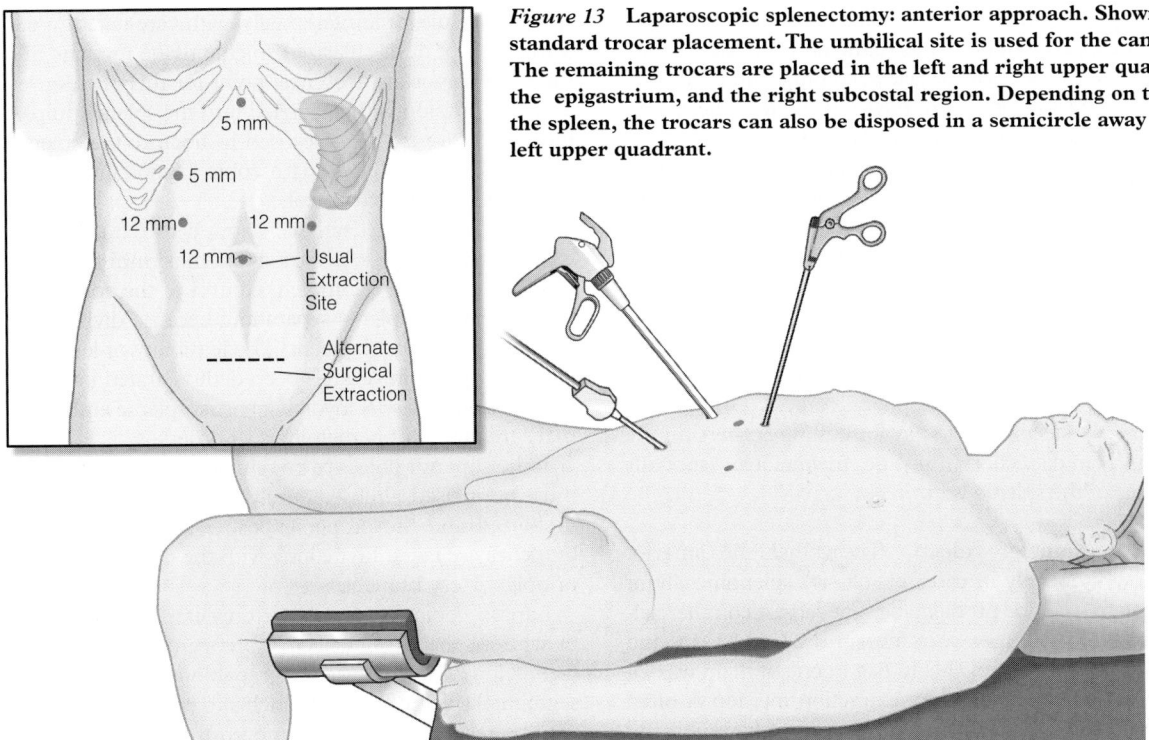

Figure 13 **Laparoscopic splenectomy: anterior approach. Shown is standard trocar placement. The umbilical site is used for the camera. The remaining trocars are placed in the left and right upper quadrants, the epigastrium, and the right subcostal region. Depending on the size of the spleen, the trocars can also be disposed in a semicircle away from the left upper quadrant.**

imally invasive surgery unit. We use a powerful suction machine (–70 mm Hg) and a custom-made sharp beveled 10 mm cannula to suction splenic tissue from the plastic retrieval bag.

Anterior Approach

The anterior approach is seldom used nowadays; however, it remains the preferable approach in some patients with massive splenomegaly (21 to 30 cm long) and all patients with megaspleens (> 30 cm or > 3 kg) with the aid of hand-assisted devices [*see* Special Considerations, Hand-Assisted Laparoscopic Splenectomy, *below*]. Very large spleens are extremely heavy and difficult to manipulate with laparoscopic instruments, and it is complicated to lift them so as to gain access to the phrenicocolic ligament posteriorly. The anterior approach can also be considered if another procedure (e.g., cholecystectomy) is being contemplated; alternatively, in this situation, the lateral approach can be used, and the patient can be repositioned for the secondary procedure.

Step 1: placement of trocars Under general anesthesia, the patient is placed in a modified lithotomy position to allow the surgeon to operate between the patient's legs and to allow the assistants to stand on each side of the patient. The procedure is performed through five trocars in the upper abdomen [*see Figure 13*], with the patient in a steep Fowler position with left-side elevation. A 12 mm trocar is introduced through an umbilical incision, and a 10 mm laparoscope (0° or 30°) is connected to a video system. A 12 mm trocar is placed in each upper quadrant, and two 5 mm trocars are inserted close to the rib margin on the left and right sides of the abdomen. Alternatively, trocars can be deployed in a semicircle away from the left upper quadrant. Trocar sites are carefully selected to optimize working angles. The 12 mm ports are used to allow introduction of clip appliers, staplers, or the laparoscope from a variety of angles as needed.

Troubleshooting. With increasing experience, we find that we prefer to do as many laparoscopic splenectomies as possible via

the lateral approach because it is so much easier, even with spleens that are longer than 20 cm and are readily palpable. The decision is arbitrarily made on the basis of estimated available working space. If the spleen comes too close to the iliac crest or the midline, the anterior approach should be taken instead.

Step 2: isolation of lower pole and control of blood supply The left hepatic lobe is retracted, and the stomach is retracted medially to expose the spleen. Accessory spleens are searched for, and the phrenicocolic ligament, the splenocolic ligament, and the sustentaculum lienis are incised near the lower pole with an electrocautery and a hook probe or with scissors. Vascular adhesions—frequently found on the medial side of the spleen—are cauterized. The gastrocolic ligament is carefully dissected close to the spleen, and the left gastroepiploic vessels are ligated one by one with metallic clips or, if small, simply cauterized. The upper and lower poles of the spleen are gently lifted with one or both palpators (placed through the 5 mm ports) to expose the splenic hilum and the tail of the pancreas within the splenorenal ligament, thereby facilitating individual dissection and clipping of all the branches of the splenic artery and vein close to the spleen. The short gastric vessels are then identified and ligated with clips or, occasionally, with staples. No sutures are used. Alternatively, the splenic artery itself can be isolated and clipped within the lesser sac before extensive dissection of the lower pole and suspensory ligaments.

Because of the segmental and terminal distribution of splenic arteries, it is easy to determine the devascularized portions of the spleen: these segments exhibit a characteristic grayish color, whereas the vascularized segments retain a pinkish hue. When the organ is completely isolated, it is left in its natural cavity, and hemostasis is verified.

Troubleshooting. If one elects first to clip the splenic artery within the lesser sac, there are a few precautions that must be taken. First, the clipping must be done distal to the pancreatica magna to prevent pancreatic injury. Second, one must make sure that the splenic artery proper is clipped, not one of its branches (e.g., the superior terminal branch). This is an easy mistake to commit with the distributed type of splenic vasculature [see Figure 1] because the splenic artery itself is short and the branches can take off very early. Third, one must always keep in mind the possibility of an anastomotic branch between the major splenic branches, as described by Testut.[11] Should a major terminal branch be clipped rather than the splenic artery proper, there will be no spleen ischemia if such an anastomosis is present [see Figure 1].

Yet another challenge posed by the anterior approach is that if bleeding occurs, the blood tends to pool in the area of the hilum and obscure vision even more, whereas in the lateral approach, the blood tends to flow away from the operative field. One quickly learns that there is a steep price to pay for cutting corners during the dissection. The dissection must be meticulous, especially behind branches of the splenic vein.

Step 3: extraction of spleen Given that the anterior approach is now used only in cases of massive splenomegaly or megaspleen, bagging can be problematic. The largest commercially available freezer bag we have seen measures 27 by 28 cm, and the largest spleen we have been able to bag in one of them was 24 cm long. Furthermore, an accessory extraction incision is often required; a Pfannenstiel incision gives better cosmetic results, but a left lower quadrant incision can also be used. Hand-assisted devices are used with increasing frequency in laparoscopic removal of large spleens [see Special Considerations, Hand-Assisted Laparoscopic Splenectomy, below].

If the spleen cannot be bagged, it may be fragmented in the pelvis before extraction, provided that the abdomen is copiously washed and cleaned of any residual spleen fragments before closure to prevent splenosis. Most patients with large spleens have hematologic malignancies; thus, residual splenic activity is not as crucial an issue in these patients as it would be in others.

Laparoscopic Partial Splenectomy

Concern regarding the risk of OPSI has encouraged the practice of preserving splenic tissue and function whenever possible. For this reason, partial splenectomy has occasionally been indicated for treatment of benign tumors of the spleen and for excision of cystic lesions.[21] Its use has been described in connection with the management of type I Gaucher disease, cholesteryl ester storage disease, chronic myelogenous leukemia, and thalassemia major, as well as with the staging of Hodgkin disease.[22,23] Partial splenectomy has also been an option in the management of splenic trauma when the patient's condition is stable enough to permit the meticulous dissection required for the operation.[24,25]

Like standard laparoscopic splenectomy, laparoscopic partial splenectomy is performed with the patient in the right lateral decubitus position. Trocar placement is similar as well. The splenocolic ligament and the lower part of the phrenicocolic ligament are incised to permit mobilization of the lower pole of the spleen. If the lower portion of the spleen is to be excised, branches of the gastroepiploic vessels supplying the lower pole are dissected and clipped close to the parenchyma. An appropriate number of penultimate branches of the inferior polar artery are then taken in such a way as to create a clear line of demarcation between normal spleen and devascularized spleen. This process is continued until the desired number of splenic segments are devascularized.

Next, a standard monopolar electrocautery is used to score the splenic capsule circumferentially, with care taken to ensure that a 5 mm rim of devascularized splenic tissue remains in situ; this is the most important technical point for this procedure [see Figure 14]. The incision is then carried into the splenic pulp. Atraumatic intestinal graspers are also used to fracture the splenic pulp in a bloodless fashion. The laparoscopic L hook and scissors provide excellent hemostatic control.

Once the spleen has been allowed to demarcate, resection is remarkably bloodless, provided that the 5 mm rim of ischemic tissue is left in place. Complete control of the splenic artery is not required before splenic separation, because division occurs in an ischemic segment of spleen.[9] The feasibility of leaving portions of ischemic spleen in situ has been demonstrated in a large prospective, randomized trial involving partial splenic embolization as primary treatment of hematologic disorders.[26]

If the superior pole is to be removed, the phrenicocolic ligament must be incised almost entirely so that the spleen can be easily mobilized and the proper exposure achieved. The short gastric branches are taken first, along with the desired number of superior polar artery branches.

Laparoscopic partial splenectomy can be performed either with or without the aid of selective preoperative arterial embolization (see below). Radiologists are capable of cannulating the desired segmental splenic arterial branch and embolizing the segment that is to be resected. We have removed the superior pole in a patient with a class IV isolated splenic injury sustained while skiing[8]; laparoscopic partial splenectomy was made possible largely by the accuracy of selective arterial embolization, which permitted control of the bleeding and allowed laparoscopy to be performed in unhurried conditions.[27]

Preoperative Splenic Artery Embolization

Preoperative splenic artery embolization is used as an adjuvant in a few patients to make laparoscopic splenectomy possible and to reduce blood loss. Although it is now infrequently used, it remains a useful tool in the armamentarium of spleen surgeons.

Generally speaking, the technique involves embolization of the spleen with coils placed proximally in the splenic artery and absorbable gelatin sponges and small coils placed distally in each splenic arterial branch (the double embolization technique), with care taken to spare vessels supplying the tail of the pancreas [see Figure 15].

The procedure is ended when it is estimated radiologically that 80% or more of the splenic tissue has been successfully embolized. In most cases, successful embolization is achieved with both proximal and distal emboli; in a minority of cases, it is achieved with proximal emboli alone or with distal emboli alone.[28]

Troubleshooting Preoperative splenic artery embolization is safe, provided that two main principles are adhered to. First, embolization must be done distal to the pancreatica magna to avoid damaging the pancreas. Second, neither microspheres nor absorbable gelatin powder should be used, because particles of this small size may migrate to unintended target organ capillaries and cause tissue necrosis; only coils and absorbable gelatin sponge fragments should be used.

POSTOPERATIVE CARE

Postoperative care for patients who have undergone laparoscopic splenectomy is usually simple. The nasogastric tube inserted after induction of general anesthesia is removed either in the recovery room, once stomach emptying has been verified, or the

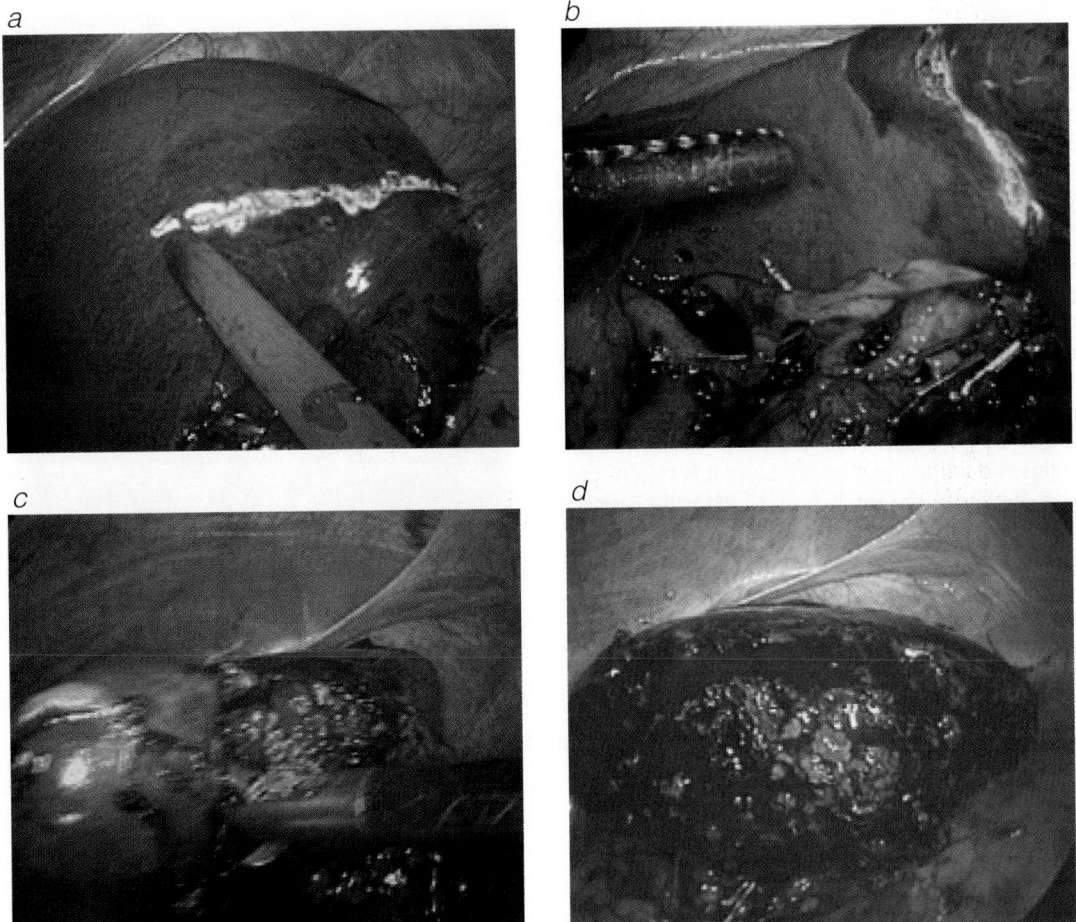

Figure 14 Laparoscopic splenectomy: partial splenectomy. (*a, b*) The splenic capsule is scored with the monopolar cautery, and a 5 mm margin of devitalized tissue is left. (*c*) The splenic pulp is fractured with an atraumatic grasper. The electrocautery with the L hook is also used to control parenchymal bleeding. (*d*) Shown is the cut surface of the spleen after transection. The operative field remains remarkably dry.

next morning, depending on the duration and the degree of technical difficulty of the procedure. The urinary catheter is usually removed before the patient leaves the recovery room. The patient is allowed to drink clear fluids on the morning after the operation; when clear fluids are well tolerated, the patient is allowed to proceed to a diet of his or her choice.

If the patient has no history of ulcer or dyspepsia, one naproxen sodium tablet (500 mg) is given with sips of water on the morning before operation. Meperidine injections (1 mg/kg) are administered during the first night, followed by oral acetaminophen (1 g every 6 hours). If pain is not well controlled, coanalgesia with an NSAID is added; this combination produces the best results. Because of its side effects (i.e., nausea, vomiting, abdominal fullness, and constipation), codeine is currently avoided if at all possible. When naproxen sodium is used, prophylactic doses of subcutaneous heparin are avoided on empirical grounds, especially if the platelet count is low or platelet function is abnormal.

Patients receiving I.V. cortisone are given oral steroids on postoperative day 1 after an overlap I.V. injection; thereafter, steroids are gradually tapered. Patients are allowed to shower 12 hours after surgery and are advised to keep the paper strips covering the trocar incisions in place for 7 to 10 days. No drains are used. No limitations are imposed on physical activity, and patients are allowed to tailor their activities to their degree of asthenia or discomfort.

COMPLICATIONS

Postoperative complications directly related to splenectomy include intraoperative and postoperative hemorrhage; left lower lobe atelectasis and pneumonia; left pleural effusion; subphrenic

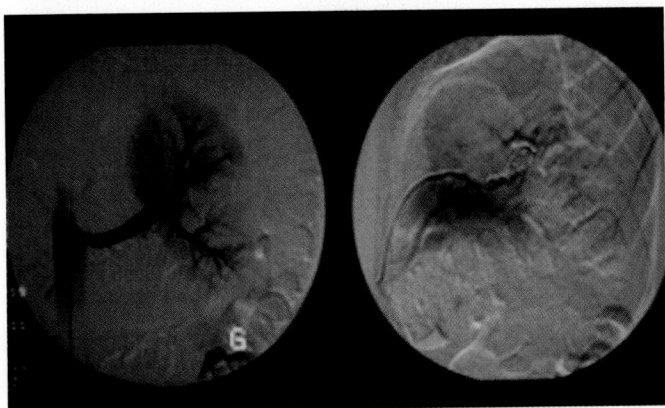

Figure 15 Laparoscopic splenectomy: splenic artery embolization. Shown are splenic angiograms of a patient with thrombotic thrombocytopenic purpura before (left) and after (right) splenic artery embolization with 3, 5, and 7 cm coils and absorbable gelatin sponge fragments.

collection; iatrogenic pancreatic, gastric, and colonic injury; and venous thrombosis.[24-31]

Successful laparoscopic splenectomy depends to a large extent on proper preparation. Recognition of anatomic elements and their arrangement is paramount. As with other laparoscopic procedures, the keys are avoiding complications and minimizing technical misadventures. Vascular structures should be cleanly isolated and dissected from surrounding fat; they then can usually be controlled with two clips proximally and distally. Staplers should be used with care and should not be applied blindly. The stapler tip should be clearly seen to be free of tissue before it is closed; otherwise, hemorrhage from partial section of a major splenic branch might occur after the instrument is released. Blind application of the stapler may also result in damage to the tail of the pancreas, which often lies in close proximity to the inner surface of the spleen. If both clips and a linear stapler are used, it is vital to prevent interposition of clips in the staple line, which will cause the stapler to misfire and possibly to jam.

Improper use of the electrocautery during the procedure can cause iatrogenic injury to the stomach, the colon, or the pancreas. In a smoke-filled environment, where controlling vessels is difficult and time consuming, blind fulguration of fat in the hilum can lead to bleeding. Structures close to the lower pole in the gastrocolic ligament can be approached more aggressively, but not those in the hilum. To prevent arcing and spot necrosis, which may result in delayed perforation and sepsis, the instrument should be activated only in proximity to the target organ.

The assistants also play an important role in preventing complications. All instruments, including those handled by assistants, should be moved under direct vision. Especially in the anterior approach, retraction of the liver and stomach and elevation of the spleen require constant concentration if lacerations and subsequent hemorrhage or perforation are to be avoided.

SPECIAL CONSIDERATIONS

Extraction of Specimens

Spleens removed via the anterior approach are extracted through the umbilical trocar site after finger fragmentation in a plastic bag. It is rarely necessary to enlarge the umbilical incision to more than 2 or 3 cm. When the lateral approach is used, extraction is more easily performed through one of the ports situated anteriorly. This extraction site also requires little or no enlargement. On occasion, for a spleen longer than 20 cm, a 7.5 to 10 cm Pfannenstiel incision is made, and the operator's forearm is introduced into the abdomen to deliver the spleen into the pelvis for extraction in large fragments under direct vision.[32] The abdomen is copiously irrigated before closure.

Special mention should be made of extraction of the splenic specimen from patients with malignant disease. If lymphoma or Hodgkin disease is suspected, neither preoperative splenic artery embolization nor finger fragmentation in a plastic bag should be performed, for fear of making the histologic diagnosis difficult. Extraction of intact spleens through a small left subcostal or median incision has also been employed when preservation of tissue architecture is required. Alternatively, a port site may be slightly enlarged, and a knife or a Mayo scissors may be used to furnish the pathologist with intact specimen pieces of various sizes. The various techniques of fragmentation and extraction of splenic tissue during laparoscopic splenectomy should be discussed and agreed on with the pathologist ahead of time to ensure that proper pathologic diagnoses are not compromised by either necrotic

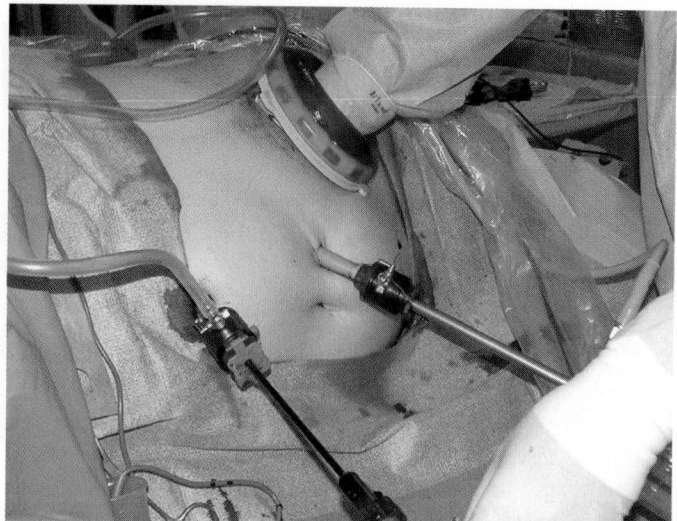

Figure 16 **Laparoscopic splenectomy: hand-assisted. Shown is the use of a hand port in the left lower quadrant to facilitate laparoscopic splenectomy in a patient with a large spleen.**

tissue (in the case of preoperative splenic artery embolization) or altered tissue architecture (in the case of finger fragmentation), especially if malignancy is suspected but not proved. In practice, however, we have found that the diagnosis is made preoperatively in more than 90% of patients with benign and malignant hematologic disease; hence, the issue rarely arises.

Hand-Assisted Laparoscopic Splenectomy

The term hand-assisted laparoscopic surgery refers to laparoscopic procedures performed with the aid of a plastic device inserted in a 7.5 to 10 cm wound. This plastic hand port consists of a sealed cuff that enables a hand to be inserted into and withdrawn from the abdomen without loss of pneumoperitoneum during the operation; in this way, the surgeon regains some of the tactile feedback lost in conventional laparoscopic surgery [*see Figure 16*]. A number of different models have been developed, some of them quite expensive. Most use either an inflatable sleeve clipped to an O-ring, a spiral inflatable valve, or a flap valve to maintain pneumoperitoneum.

The optimal placement of the incision for a hand-assisted laparoscopic splenectomy remains a subject of debate: recommended locations have included the upper midline, the right upper quadrant, the left iliac fossa, and, for very large spleens, the Pfannenstiel position. Whether the surgeon is left-handed or right-handed plays a role; most surgeons agree that the nondominant hand should be used in the device.

There are obvious advantages and drawbacks to hand-assisted laparoscopic splenectomy. The most apparent disadvantage is the cosmetic cost of a longer abdominal incision (except when a Pfannenstiel incision is employed). More generally, the use of a longer incision would seem to be at odds with the current trend toward developing surgical techniques that reduce surgical trauma as much as possible. Nevertheless, comparative studies of splenectomy in patients with large spleens (> 700 g) seem to indicate that for the most part, the hand-assisted approach yields outcomes similar to those of conventional laparoscopic splenectomy.[33]

Although the precise role of hand-assisted laparoscopic splenectomy remains to be defined, it is likely that this technique will find a place in the surgical management of patients with large spleens. In addition, the hand-assisted approach may be a valuable aid for

Table 2 Clinical Results of Laparoscopic Splenectomy

Authors	N	ITP/Non-ITP	Conversion Rate (%)	OR Time (min)	Morbidity (%)	Mortality (%)	Length of Stay (days)	Accessory Spleen Present (%)
All diagnoses								
Katkhouda et al (1998)[38]	103	67/36	3.9	161	6	0	2.5	16.5
Targarona et al (2000)[36]	122	54/68	7.4	153	18	0	4.0	12
Park et al (2000)[37]	203	129/74	3.0	145	9	0.5	2.7	12.3
Poulin et al (2001)[39]	100	50/50	8.0	180	15	4	3.0	25
ITP								
Trias et al (2000)[40]	48	—	4.2	142	12	N/A	4.0	11
Poulin et al (2001)[39]	51	—	3.9	160	5.9	0	2.0	32
Malignancy								
Schlachta et al (1999)[41]	14	—	21	239	18	9	3.0	—
Trias et al (2000)[40]	28	—	14*	171	28	N/A	5.5	—

*71% required accessory incision because of spleen size.

surgeons who have not yet completed the learning curve for conventional laparoscopic splenectomy. Finally, this technique may render preoperative splenic embolization unnecessary for most very large spleens.

OUTCOME EVALUATION

No randomized, prospective trials comparing open splenectomy with laparoscopic splenectomy have yet been conducted. At present, such trials are unlikely to be held, for a variety of reasons. For one thing, randomization is difficult with procedures that are still in evolution. At one end of the spectrum, laparoscopic splenectomy is done for patients with ITP, who usually are relatively healthy and have normal-size spleens. In many of these patients, needlescopic instruments (< 3 mm) can be used in conjunction with a single 12 mm port site in the umbilicus. This approach permits hospital discharge within 24 hours of operation in a significant number of cases. At the other end of the spectrum, laparoscopic splenectomy is done for patients with myeloid metaplasia and spleens longer than 30 cm. In this setting, a laparoscopic approach poses formidable challenges, and the optimal technique and its justification remain to be determined. The window of opportunity for randomized comparative trials may have been lost.

Large case series and nonrandomized comparative trials, however, have consistently reported better outcomes from laparoscopic splenectomy than from open splenectomy.[34-41] For example, in one set of 528 patients [see Table 2],[36-39] the rate of postoperative pneumonia was 1.1% (6/528), and no subphrenic abscesses occurred as postoperative complications. Many surgeons who have completed the learning curve associated with the procedure feel that there is still room for improvement regarding complication rates and length of stay for patients with ITP and other relatively benign conditions necessitating laparoscopic splenectomy. The more serious conditions and the mortality seen in conjunction with the procedure tend to occur in patients with advanced hematologic malignancies or megaspleens. In such cases, most of the adverse results are related to the disease state rather than to the operation, and it remains to be seen whether laparoscopic splenectomy will have a positive effect on outcome.

One of the great attractions of minimally invasive surgery has been the prospect of significant cost reductions. At this point in the development of laparoscopic splenectomy, however, we are reluctant to place too much trust in premature cost analyses that do not take into account the "work in progress" nature of minimally invasive surgery. Most surgeons can now perform most

laparoscopic splenectomies with simplified trays of reusable instruments. Our basic laparoscopic tray contains a few instruments and two sizes of reusable clip appliers with inexpensive clips. As noted [see Operative Technique, above], clips are used for distributed-type spleens, and single-use linear staplers are mostly used for magistral-type spleens. To reduce costs, ultrasonic dissectors are rarely used. In addition, the use of commercially available freezer bags instead of laparoscopic retrieval bags further reduces the cost of specimen extraction. Finally, even if intraoperative costs are higher with laparoscopic splenectomy, our experience is that the increase is offset by reductions in postoperative stay.

We, like most authorities, believe that as a surgeon gains experience with laparoscopic splenectomy, operating time tends to fall until it approaches that of open splenectomy. We also concur with the numerous authors who have suggested that once laparoscopic splenectomy is mastered, use of blood products tends to decrease substantially.

Open Splenectomy

PREOPERATIVE EVALUATION

With the growing acceptance of laparoscopic splenectomy, the indications for open splenectomy have essentially been reduced to (1) elective removal of megaspleens and (2) treatment of splenic trauma when conservative treatment either is not indicated or has failed. In rare cases, open splenectomy may be done for iatrogenic injuries incurred during left upper quadrant surgical procedures.

Preoperative evaluation for elective open splenectomy is similar to that for laparoscopic splenectomy [see Laparoscopic Splenectomy, Preoperative Evaluation, above]. Preoperative evaluation of trauma patients is covered in more detail elsewhere [see *100 Initial Management of Life-Threatening Trauma*]. Essentially, a coagulogram and blood typing and crossmatching are required. A preoperative CT scan will have established the size of the spleen, the grade of the splenic injury, the presence of other injuries (if any), and, in elective cases, the location and configuration of any masses or cysts.

OPERATIVE PLANNING

Most surgeons would agree that the lessons learned from successful performance of minimally invasive procedures have had a positive impact on the refinement of the corresponding open procedures. The principles of careful appreciation of fine anatomic details (as described for laparoscopic splenectomy) and maximal reduction of tissue trauma from retractors or excessive tissue handling should be incorporated into the planning of open splenectomy.

Total versus Partial Splenectomy

As a consequence of the recognition that splenectomy renders patients susceptible to a lifelong risk of OPSI, it is now routine practice to attempt splenic conservation. Accordingly, saving normally functioning splenic parenchyma has become the most important goal in the management of splenic injuries. In some 50% of adults (and over 80% of children), this goal can be achieved by means of nonoperative treatment. In approximately 20% of adults, splenorrhaphy and partial splenectomy are possible; splenectomy is indicated in the remainder. Partial splenectomy is also favored on occasion when excision of splenic tissue is required for the treatment of other elective conditions.

For the sake of brevity, we describe the surgical technique for total splenectomy and partial splenectomy concurrently, noting differences only where significant.

OPERATIVE TECHNIQUE

Step 1: Incision

The patient is supine, in a reverse Tredelenburg position with a 15° tilt to the right. For maximal exposure, a midline incision is made, starting on the left side of the xiphoid process [*see Figure 17*]. The incision is extended below the umbilicus for a variable distance, depending on circumstances such as the size of the patient, the surgical situation (traumatic versus nontraumatic), the possibility of associated injury, and the size of the spleen. Occasionally, a left subcostal incision may be used for nontraumatic indications in patients with normal-size spleens. This incision may be extended onto the right side to form a chevron incision if necessary; however, this may impede the search for accessory spleens. Some surgeons have per-

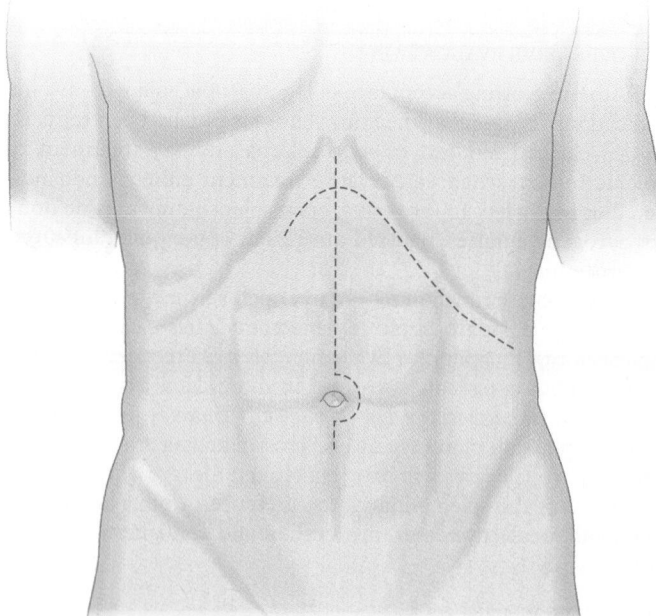

Figure 17 **Open splenectomy. Shown are midline and left subcostal incisions.**

formed splenectomy via a thoracoabdominal approach, but most have abandoned this approach. Appropriate retraction of the left lobe of the liver and the abdominal wall is achieved with the help of surgical assistants placed on each side of the table or the use of self-retaining retractors.

Troubleshooting In trauma cases, the anesthetist should always be informed when the peritoneum is opened; release of a tense hemoperitoneum can precipitate hypotension with the loss of tamponade.

Step 2: Evacuation of Blood and Packing of the Abdomen

In trauma cases, gross blood and clots are evacuated manually with large laparotomy sponges. All quadrants of the abdomen are then packed with laparotomy pads. Standard suction equipment is not very useful for evacuating large quantities of blood from the abdomen.

Step 3: Control of Splenic Artery

Once other major injuries are excluded, the first decision to be made is whether to control the splenic artery first or to mobilize the spleen to the midline. This decision is dictated by the urgency of the clinical situation, the spleen size, and the presence of underlying disease.

If the decision is made to control the splenic artery first, the main splenic trunk is identified above the pancreas via an approach that leads to the lesser sac either through the gastrocolic ligament or through the avascular plane of the greater omentum above the distal transverse colon. Once dissected, the artery is controlled with a vascular loop. The main artery can also be accessed and dissected posteriorly after the spleen is mobilized [*see Figure 18*].

Troubleshooting One advantage of dissecting the splenic artery in the lesser sac (as opposed to the hilum) is that the splenic vein is rarely damaged, being located under the pancreas and away from the artery. Good proximal control of the splenic blood supply facilitates the performance of the more complex variations of partial splenectomy or total splenectomy for megaspleens.

Step 4: Mobilization of Spleen

If the decision is made to mobilize the spleen first, as in most trauma cases, mobilization should be carried out in a carefully planned manner; it is all too easy to compound splenic injury with ill-advised maneuvers that obligate the surgeon to perform a total splenectomy.

Gastric decompression is ensured with a properly placed nasogastric tube. The spleen is then retracted anteromedially with the left hand, with care taken to confirm proper retraction of the left abdominal wall. The phrenicocolic ligament is thereby placed on stretch, and the ligament insertion on the lateral abdominal wall serves as countertraction. The phrenicocolic ligament is then incised from the bottom up with either long scissors or the 45°-angle tip of a monopolar cautery [*see Figure 19*]. Efforts should be made to leave 2 cm of ligament on the spleen side and to avoid capsular injury. If the surgeon cannot put a finger behind the ligament, an assistant should elevate the ligament between the jaws of a right-angle clamp. The incision of the phrenicocolic ligament is then extended to the left crus of the diaphragm. Except in patients with portal hypertension or myeloproliferative disorders, this ligament is avascular. The left lateral portion of the gastrocolic ligament (the greater omentum) is also dissected away from the splenic flexure of the colon to facilitate mobilization of the spleen.

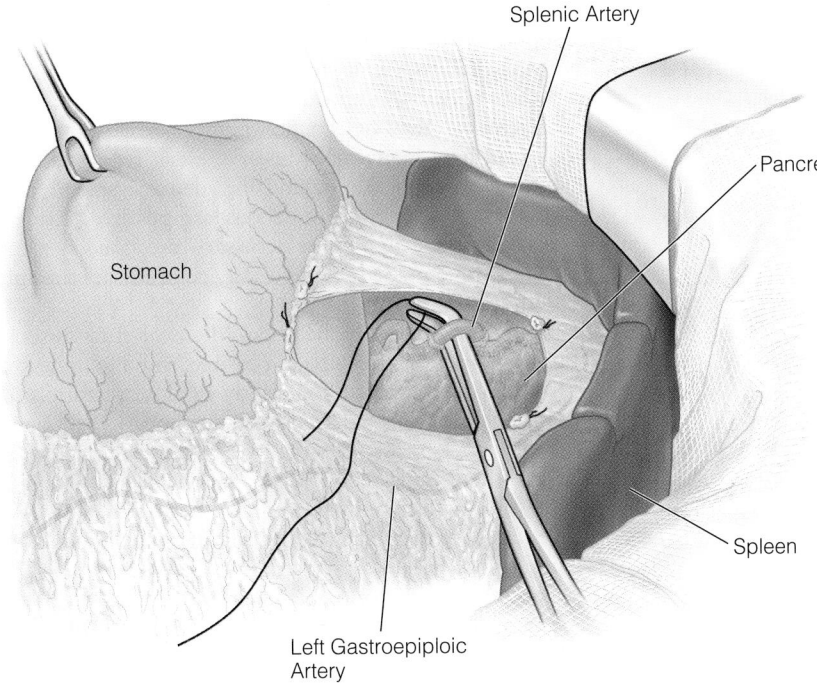

Figure 18 **Open splenectomy. The splenic artery is controlled above the pancreas in the lesser sac. The artery must be ligated distal to the pancreatica magna artery.**

At this point, the splenocolic ligament and the sustentaculum lienis are left alone.

After complete division of the phrenicocolic ligament, a plane is developed between the pancreas and the retroperitoneal structures with gentle blunt finger dissection. The spleen can then be delivered to the midline, where the splenectomy can be planned in an unhurried manner [see Figure 20]. Continuing splenic bleeding during this maneuver can be controlled with manual compression of the organ. The splenic pedicle may also be gently compressed between the thumb and the index finger at this stage. Laparotomy sponges are placed in the left subphrenic space.

Troubleshooting When performing elective resections of very large spleens, experienced spleen surgeons use a few tricks to simplify the procedure. In most patients with megaspleens, the suspensory ligaments have been stretched over time, allowing the surgeon much more leeway in mobilizing or turning the spleen. This greater leeway allows the surgeon to rotate the spleen from the lower pole so as to deliver it transversely into the incision. Thus, the presence of a large spleen does not always necessitate the creation of a long xiphopubic incision, because a transversely placed spleen can be extracted into the abdominal wall through a shorter incision.

Step 5a (Total Splenectomy): Planning of Resection

To devise the appropriate operative strategy, the surgeon performing open total splenectomy must address the same anatomic issues that he or she would if performing laparoscopic total splenectomy—for example, the nature of the splenic blood supply (distributed or bundled) and the distance between the tip of the pancreas and the splenic hilum. The anatomy must be appreciated before the operative strategy can be defined.

Once the spleen has been delivered into the abdominal wall, various techniques may be employed to control the blood supply. The classic approach is to serially clamp, ligate, or suture-ligate the vessels between curved clamps, starting from the lower pole. Alternatively, the vessels may be controlled with clips.

Troubleshooting We frequently use laparoscopic clip appliers to achieve vascular control in open splenectomy. The long, slender design of these devices is particularly useful in obese patients, in whom it is often difficult to achieve complete mobilization of the spleen without causing additional splenic trauma. With laparoscopic clip appliers, vessels can be safely controlled inside the abdomen. Locking plastic clips may also be used.

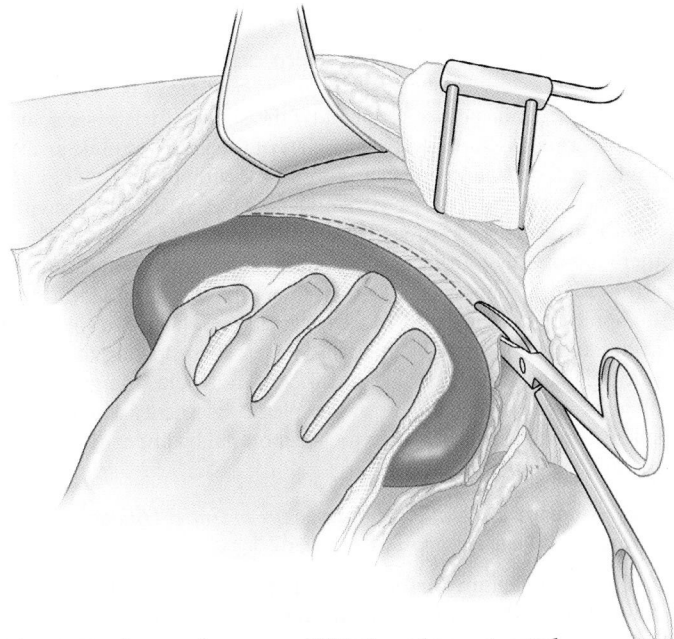

Figure 19 **Open splenectomy. With the spleen retracted medially, the phrenicocolic ligament is incised.**

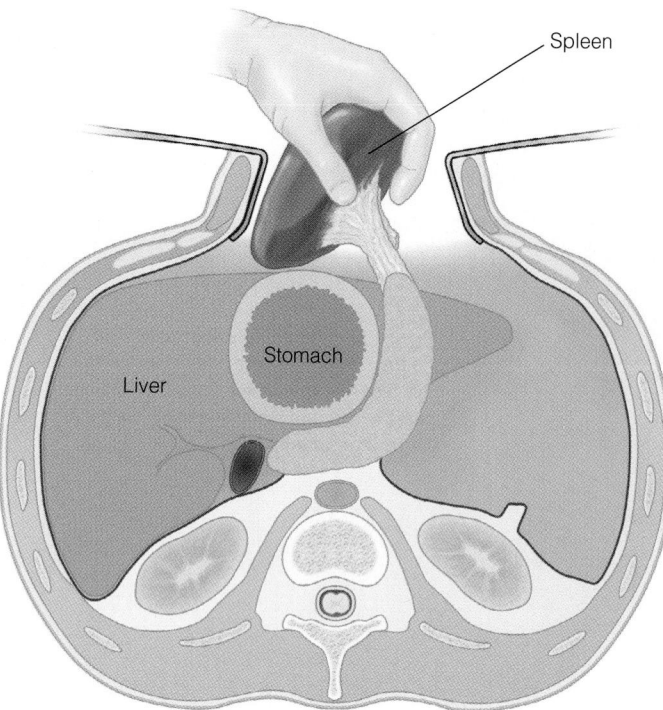

Spleen

Stomach

Liver

Figure 20 Open splenectomy. The spleen is delivered to the mid-line by means of blunt and sharp dissection of the areolar plane between the kidney and the pancreas.

Moreover, provided that the same precautions are taken as in laparoscopic splenectomy, a linear stapler with a vascular cartridge may be used to control the hilum in one step once the gastroepiploic branches have been controlled.

Step 5b (Partial Splenectomy): Planning of Resection

Once the spleen is appropriately placed for full evaluation and adequate hemostasis is ensured, planning for partial splenectomy can start. In trauma cases, such planning is guided by the extent of the injury, and in elective cases, it is guided by the nature of the underlying pathologic condition [*see Table 3*].

In most cases, as noted, the spleen can be divided into independent lobes or segments, each with its own terminal blood supply. The superior pole is supplied by the short gastric vessels, and the lower pole is supplied by branches of the gastroepiploic artery, which are known to form anastomoses with the inferior polar artery. In addition, most patients, possible variations notwithstanding, have two or three major vessels entering the hilum. Thus, there are usually four or five discrete regions or lobes that may be removed, individually or in combination, in a partial splenectomy. It should be kept in mind that the vessels supplying the spleen lie in different supportive ligaments. The vessels supplying the superior pole (the short gastrics) and the inferior pole (the gastroepiploic branches) rest in the gastrosplenic ligament, whereas the splenic branches proper lie in the splenorenal ligament along with the tail of the pancreas.

Step 6 (Partial Splenectomy): Exposure of Entire Hilum and Ligation of Appropriate Arteries

The entire hilum of the spleen is then exposed close to the parenchyma. The gastrosplenic ligament and the splenorenal ligament must be separated, with care taken to preserve the blood supply to both poles of the spleen. There is a fairly avascular area

of the gastrosplenic ligament, between the short gastric vessels supplying the superior pole and the gastroepiploic branches supplying the lower pole, that must be opened; once this is done, a complete view of the entire splenic blood supply is available. The surgeon can then determine whether partial splenectomy is feasible and how many lobes he or she can resect while still leaving enough spleen tissue behind for adequate splenic function. Any number of segmental resections are possible. If the surgeon is unsure of the extent of the necessary resection, an accurate assessment can be made by temporarily compressing the splenic arterial branches.

Selected arterial branches are then carefully dissected as close to the spleen parenchyma as possible, with the understanding that the veins are situated posteriorly in close proximity. The vessels may be doubly ligated, transfixed, or clipped. If clips are used, care is taken not to dislodge them with inappropriate manipulations. Once the arterial blood supply is controlled, the affected area of the spleen will rapidly become visibly demarcated. If the devitalized area of the spleen corresponds to the intended resection, a similar technique is applied to the venous side. Access to the venous side can also be achieved from the posterior aspect of the spleen. When this approach is followed, it is helpful to identify the tail of the pancreas if possible to avoid inadvertent damage: the tail of the pancreas touches the hilum of the spleen in 30% of cases and lies within 1 cm of the hilum in 70%.

Step 7 (Partial Splenectomy): Incision of Splenic Capsule and Partial Resection of Spleen

The capsule of the spleen is incised circumferentially with a scalpel or a monopolar cautery, and a 5 mm rim of devitalized tissue is left in situ. The splenic fragments may be transected with a scalpel, scissors, a monopolar cautery, or a combination thereof. Various techniques have been used to control residual bleeding, including use of a monopolar cautery on spray current; use of a cutaneous ultrasonic surgical aspirator; use of an argon beam

---

Table 3 Indications and Contraindications for Partial Splenectomy

Indications

Selected grade II–IV splenic injuries with the following:
   Hemodynamic stability
   No evidence of other intra-abdominal organ injury
   No associated head injury
   No coagulopathy
   CT confirmation of isolated splenic injury

Selective elective indications
   Resection of nonparasitic cysts
   Hamartomas and other benign splenic tumors
   Inflammatory pseudotumor of the spleen
   Type I Gaucher disease
   Cholesteryl ester storage disease
   Chronic myelogenous leukemia
   Thalassemia major
   Spherocytosis
   Staging of Hodgkin disease in children

Absolute/relative contraindications in trauma

Inadequate exposure
Inability to mobilize spleen and tail of pancreas to midline
Inability to leave > 25% of splenic mass for complete splenic function

coagulator; suture compression, with or without Teflon pledgets; and omental pedicle packing. One low-tech way of dealing with residual hemostatic requirements is to employ the hollow part of a Poole suction device to aspirate blood while employing a coagulating monopolar current on the suction tip. In some cases, wrapping the splenic remnant in an absorbable polyglycolic mesh is useful. Our experience suggests that when enough residual devitalized tissue (i.e., at least 5 mm) is left behind circumferentially, good hemostasis is easily achieved, typically requiring nothing more than simple measures and topical agents. No drains are used unless the tail of the pancreas has been damaged, in which case a closed-suction drain is placed.

POSTOPERATIVE CARE

The principles of postoperative care are essentially the same for open splenectomy as for laparoscopic splenectomy [see Laparoscopic Splenectomy, Postoperative Care, above], though most authors agree that the pace of aftercare is slower with the former.

It should be kept in mind that acute postoperative gastric distention occurs more frequently in children and may necessitate more prolonged gastric decompression.

COMPLICATIONS

The complications seen after open splenectomy are the same as those seen after its laparoscopic counterpart [see Laparoscopic Splenectomy, Complications, above]. Hemorrhagic complications may necessitate transfusion, reoperation, or both.

Although the rate of serious postoperative infection after splenic surgery is generally considered to be 8%, it is thought to be lower in patients undergoing splenorrhaphy or partial splenectomy. The lower rate is probably attributable to the presence of less severe underlying injuries, rather than to the preservation of splenic tissue. Infectious complications usually manifest themselves between postoperative days 5 and 10 and are typically diagnosed by means of physical examination, chest x-ray, ultrasonography, and CT.

References

1. Cole F: Is splenectomy harmless? Surg Gynecol Obstet 133:98, 1971
2. Johnston GB: Splenectomy. Ann Surg 48:50, 1908
3. Campos Cristo M: Segmental resections of the spleen: report on the first eight cases operated on. O Hosp (Rio) 62:205, 1962
4. Upadhyaya P, Simpson JS: Splenic trauma in children. Surg Gynecol Obstet 126:781, 1968
5. Delaitre B, Maignien B: Splénectomie par voie laparoscopique, 1 observation. Presse Médicale 20:2263, 1991
6. Carroll BJ, Phillips EH, Semel CJ, et al: Laparoscopic splenectomy. Surg Endosc 6:183, 1992
7. Thibault C, Mamazza J, Létourneau R, et al: Laparoscopic splenectomy: operative technique and preliminary report. Surg Laparosc Endosc 2:248, 1992
8. Poulin EC, Thibault C, DesCôteaux JG, et al: Partial laparoscopic splenectomy for trauma: technique and case report. Surg Laparosc Endosc 5:306, 1995
9. Seshadri PA, Poulin EC, Mamazza J, et al: Technique for laparoscopic partial splenectomy. Surg Laparosc Endosc 10:106, 2000
10. Michels NA: The variational anatomy of the spleen and splenic artery. Am J Anat 70:21, 1942
11. Testut L: Traité d'anatomie humaine, 7th ed. Librairie Octave Doin, Paris, 1923, p 942
12. Lipshutz B: A composite study of the coeliac axis artery. Ann Surg 65:159, 1917
13. Henschen C: Die chirurgische Anatomie der Milzgefiisse. Schweiz Med Wochenschr 58:164, 1928
14. Ssoson-Jaroschewitsch A: Zür chirurgischen Anatomie des Milzhilus. Zeitsch f. d. ges. Anat I Abt 84:218, 1937
15. Baronofsky ID, Walton W, Noble JF: Occult injury to the pancreas following splenectomy. Surgery 29:852, 1951
16. Goerg C, Schwerk WB, Goerg K, et al: Sonographic patterns of the affected spleen in malignant lymphoma. J Clin Ultrasound 18:569, 1990
17. Poulin EC, Thibault C: The anatomical basis for laparoscopic splenectomy. Can J Surg 36:485, 1993
18. Gagner M, Lacroix A, Bolte E, et al: Laparoscopic adrenalectomy: the importance of a flank approach in the lateral decubitus position. Surg Endosc 8:135, 1994
19. Gigot JF, Jamar F, Ferrant A, et al: Inadequate detection of accessory spleens and splenosis with laparoscopic splenectomy: a shortcoming of the laparoscopic approach in hematologic diseases. Surg Endosc 12:101, 1998
20. Nielsen JL, Ellegard J, Marqversen J, et al: Detection of splenosis and ectopic spleens with 99mTc-labeled heat damaged autologous erythrocytes in 90 splenectomized patients. Scand J Haematol 27:51, 1981
21. Pachter HL, Hofstetter SR, Elkowitz A, et al: Traumatic cysts of the spleen: the role of cystectomy and splenic preservation: experience with seven consecutive patients. J Trauma 35:430, 1993
22. Guzetta PC, Ruley EJ, Merrick HFW, et al: Elective subtotal splenectomy: indications and results in 33 patients. Ann Surg 211:34, 1990
23. Hoeckstra HJ, Tamminga RY, Timens W: Partial instead of complete splenectomy in children for the pathological staging of Hodgkin's disease. Ned Tijdschr Geneeskd 137:2491, 1993
24. Sheldon GF, Croom RD, Meyer AA: The spleen. Textbook of Surgery, 14th ed. Sabiston DC, Ed. WB Saunders Co, Philadelphia, 1991, p 1108
25. Jalovec LM, Boe BS, Wyffels PL: The advantages of early operation with splenorrhaphy versus nonoperative management for the blunt splenic trauma patient. Am Surg 59:698, 1993
26. Mozes MF, Spigos DG, Pollak R, et al: Partial splenic embolization, an alternative to splenectomy: results of a prospective randomized study. Surgery 96:694, 1984
27. Poulin E, Thibault C, Mamazza J, et al: Laparoscopic splenectomy: clinical experience and the role of preoperative splenic artery embolization. Surg Laparosc Endosc 3:445, 1993
28. Poulin EC, Mamazza J, Schlachta CM: Splenic artery embolization before laparoscopic splenectomy: an update. Surg Endosc 12:870, 1998
29. Hoeffer RA, Scullin DC, Silver LF, et al: Splenectomy for hematologic disorders: a 20 year experience. J Ky Med Assoc 89:446, 1991
30. Ly B, Albrechtson D: Therapeutic splenectomy in hematologic disorders. Effects and complications in 221 adult patients Acta Med Scand 209:21, 1981
31. Macrae HM, Yakimets WW, Reynolds T: Perioperative complications of splenectomy for hematologic disease. Can J Surg 35:432, 1992
32. Poulin EC, Thibault C: Laparoscopic splenectomy for massive splenomegaly: operative technique and case report. Can J Surg 38:69, 1995
33. Targarona EM, Balague C, Cerdan G, et al: Hand-assisted laparoscopic splenectomy (HALS) in cases of splenomegaly: a comparison analysis with conventional laparoscopic splenectomy. Surg Endosc 16:426, 2002
34. Poulin EC, Mamazza J: Laparoscopic splenectomy: lessons from the learning curve. Can J Surg 41:28, 1998
35. Cathode N, Hurwitz MB, Rivera RT, et al: Laparoscopic splenectomy: outcome and efficacy in 103 consecutive patients. Ann Surg 228:568, 1998
36. Targarona EM, Espert JJ, Bombuy E, et al: Complications of laparoscopic splenectomy. Arch Surg 135:1137, 2000
37. Park AE, Birgisson G, Mastrangelo MJ, et al: Laparoscopic splenectomy: outcomes and lessons learned from over 200 cases. Surgery 128:660, 2000
38. Katkhouda N, Hurwitz MB, Rivera RT, et al: Laparoscopic splenectomy: outcome and efficacy in 103 consecutive patients. Ann Surg 228:568, 1998
39. Poulin EC, Schlachta CM, Mamazza J: Unpublished data, February 2001
40. Trias M, Targarona EM, Espert JJ, et al: Impact of hematological diagnosis on early and late outcome after laparoscopic splenectomy: an analysis of 111 cases. Surg Endosc 14:556, 2000
41. Schlachta CM, Poulin EC, Mamazza J: Laparoscopic splenectomy for hematologic malignancies. Surg Endosc 13:865, 1999

Acknowledgment

Figures 1, 3, 4, 6a, 13, and 17 through 20   Tom Moore.

Abdelrahman A. Nimeri, M.D., and L. Michael Brunt, M.D., F.A.C.S.

The surgical approach to the adrenals has evolved substantially over the past decade with the development and refinement of techniques for performing laparoscopic adrenalectomy. At present, the majority of adrenal tumors are removed laparoscopically because minimally invasive approaches result in reduced pain, faster recovery, and fewer complications and because the rate of adrenal malignancy is low. Nevertheless, open adrenalectomy still has a role in the management of selected patients with large or malignant tumors. With both open adrenalectomy and laparoscopic adrenalectomy, several different surgical approaches to the adrenals are possible [*see* Operative Planning, Choice of Procedure, *below*]. Regardless of the particular approach followed, the keys to successful adrenalectomy are the same: proper patient selection for operation, a solid understanding of adrenal pathophysiology, and a thorough knowledge of adrenal anatomy.

Anatomic Considerations

The adrenal glands are retroperitoneal organs that lie along the superomedial aspects of the two kidneys [*see Figure 1*]. Each gland comprises two discrete anatomic and functional units: the adrenal cortex, which is the site for synthesis and secretion of cortisol, aldosterone, and adrenal androgens; and the medulla, which is derived from the neural crest and is the site for synthesis of the catecholamines epinephrine and norepinephrine. A normal adrenal gland typically weighs between 4 and 6 g and measures approximately 4 to 5 cm by 2 to 3 cm by 0.5 to 1 cm. The right adrenal is relatively pyramidal in shape, whereas the left is somewhat flattened and is more closely applied to the kidney. Grossly, the adrenals may be distinguished from the surrounding retroperitoneal fat by their golden-orange color, which is a result of the high intracellular lipid content. The glands have a fibrous capsule but are relatively fragile and can be easily cracked or fragmented with surgical manipulation.

RIGHT ADRENAL

Anteriorly, the right adrenal is partially covered by the liver and the right triangular ligament. The gland abuts the inferior vena cava (IVC) medially and may, in part, lie posterior to the lateral aspect of the vena cava. Inferiorly, the adrenal sits just above the

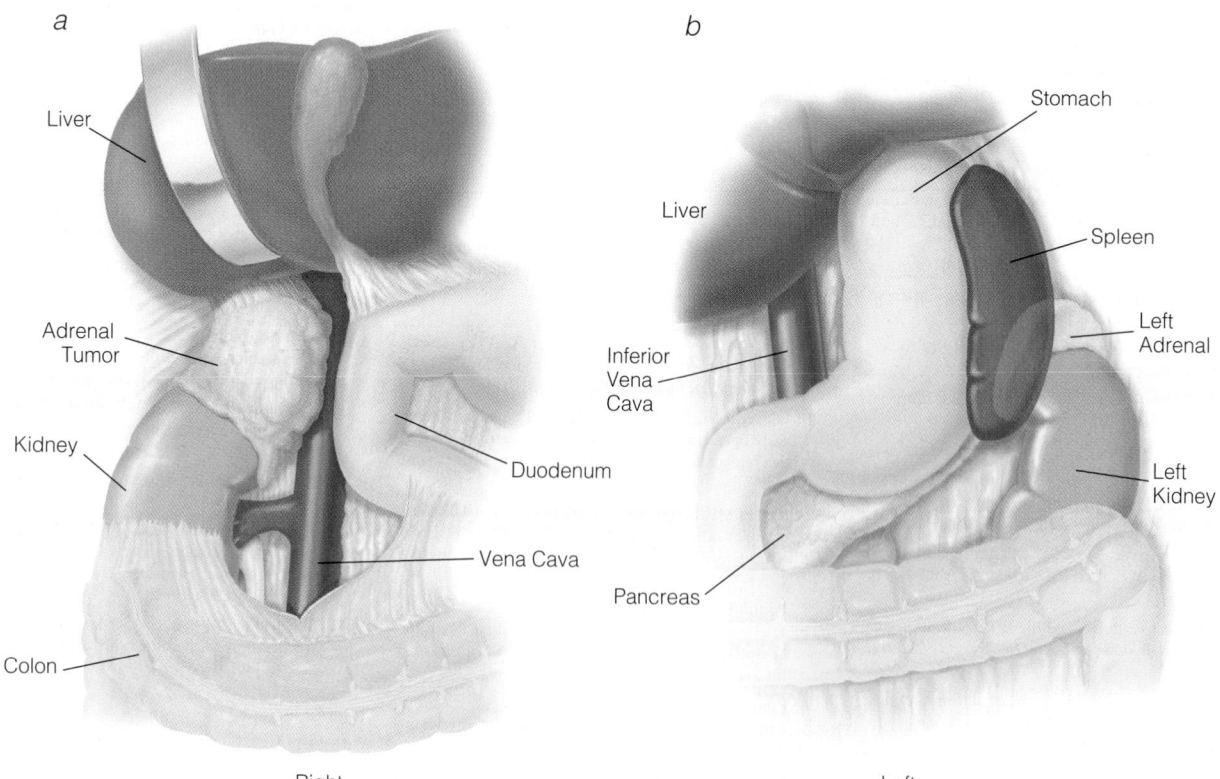

Figure 1 **Depicted is the relation of the adrenal glands to adjacent structures. (IVC—inferior vena cava)**

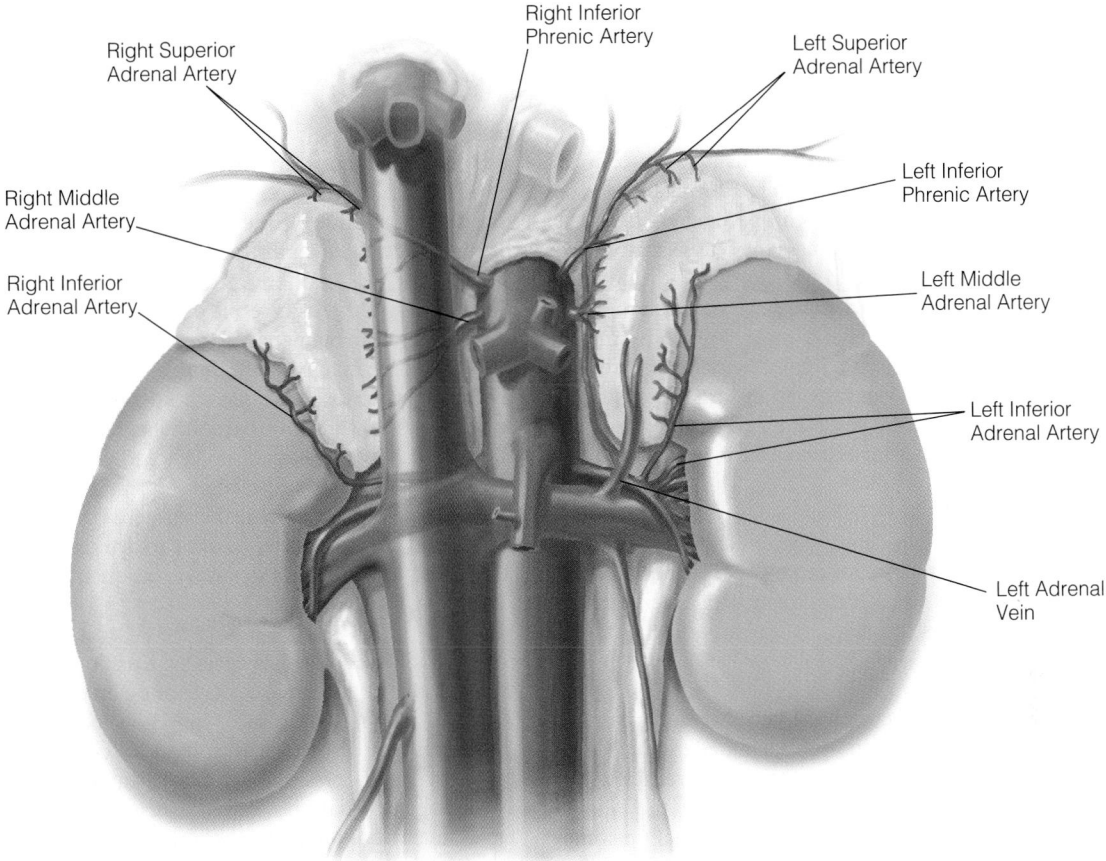

Figure 2 **Depicted is the adrenal blood supply. Multiple adrenal arteries are present; a single central adrenal vein drains into the IVC on the right side and the renal vein on the left side.**

upper pole of the kidney. The diaphragm forms the posterior and lateral boundaries of the gland.

The blood supply of the right adrenal is derived from branches of the inferior phrenic artery, the right renal artery, and the aorta [*see Figure 2*]. Typically, multiple small branches enter the gland along its superior, medial, and inferior aspects. Arterial branches from the aorta generally course posterior to the vena cava before entering the adrenal. Each adrenal is drained by a single central vein. On the right, this vein is short (1 to 1.5 cm long), runs transversely, and joins the lateral aspect of the inferior vena cava. In some cases, a more superiorly located accessory adrenal vein may enter either the IVC or one of the hepatic veins. Control of the adrenal vein is the most critical aspect of right adrenalectomy, in that the short course of this vessel makes it susceptible to tearing or avulsion from the IVC.

LEFT ADRENAL

The spleen and tail of the pancreas overlie the anterior and medial borders of the left adrenal. The inferolateral aspect of the gland lies over the superomedial aspect of the left kidney, to which it is more closely applied than the right adrenal is to the right kidney. The inferior aspect of the adrenal is in close proximity to the renal vessels, especially the renal vein. As on the right side, the posterior aspect of the adrenal rests on the diaphragm.

The arterial blood supply of the left adrenal is similar to that of the right adrenal [*see Figure 2*]. The left adrenal vein is longer than the right adrenal vein and runs somewhat obliquely from the inferomedial aspect of the gland to enter the left renal vein. The inferior phrenic vein courses in a superior-to-inferior direction just

medial to the adrenal and usually joins the left adrenal vein cephalad to its junction with the renal vein.

Preoperative Evaluation

INDICATIONS FOR OPERATION

The main indications for adrenalectomy are well established [*see Table 1*]. Any adrenal lesion that either is hypersecretory for one of

---

Table 1 Indications for Adrenalectomy

Aldosteronoma
Cushing syndrome
   Cortisol-producing adenoma
   Primary adrenal hyperplasia
   Failed treatment of ACTH-dependent Cushing syndrome
Pheochromocytoma
   Sporadic or familial
   Malignant pheochromocytoma
Nonfunctioning incidental lesion
   4–5 cm or atypical radiologic appearance
Adrenal metastasis
   Solitary, unilateral in the absence of extra-adrenal cancer
Adrenal cortical carcinoma
Adrenal sarcoma
Adrenal myelolipomas (only if symptomatic or enlarging)
Miscellaneous other lesions (atypical cysts, ganglioneuromas)

the adrenal hormones or appears to be malignant or possibly malignant should be removed. In selected cases, it may be appropriate to remove adrenal metastases if they are solitary and if there is no evidence of extra-adrenal metastatic disease. Nonfunctioning adrenal lesions that appear to be benign on the basis of their size (< 4 cm) and their appearance on computed tomography or magnetic resonance imaging need not be removed unless they enlarge during follow-up. Adrenal myelolipomas and cysts usually can be diagnosed radiographically and should not be removed unless they cause symptoms.

Most of the conditions for which adrenalectomy is indicated are amenable to a laparoscopic approach. However, the role of laparoscopy in patients with large adrenal tumors (> 6 to 8 cm) or potentially malignant primary adrenal lesions remains controversial. In the presence of a locally invasive tumor, a laparoscopic approach is contraindicated because of the need to perform en bloc resection of the tumor and any adjacent involved structures.

COMMON ADRENAL TUMORS

A brief review of the pertinent clinical and biochemical features of the various hypersecretory adrenal tumors [see Table 2] will facilitate evaluation of adrenal lesions (including adrenal incidentalomas) and planning for adrenal surgery.

Aldosteronoma

Primary hyperaldosteronism is the most common form of secondary hypertension, and aldosterone-producing adenoma is the most common hypersecretory adrenal tumor. The prevalence of this diagnosis is much higher than was previously thought,[1,2] reaching levels as high as 12% of hypertensive individuals in some series.[1] The classic finding in primary hyperaldosteronism is hypertension in conjunction with hypokalemia, but many patients have a normal or low-normal serum potassium level. Therefore, any patient who becomes hypertensive at an early age or who has malignant or difficult-to-control hypertension should be screened for this diagnosis. Screening consists of measuring plasma aldosterone concentration (PAC) and plasma renin activity (PRA). A PAC-to-PRA ratio higher than 20 to 30, in conjunction with a plasma aldosterone concentration higher than 15 ng/dl, is suggestive of the diagnosis and should be confirmed by measuring 24-hour urine aldosterone levels while the patient is on a high-sodium diet.[2] A 24-hour urine aldosterone level higher than 12 μg/24 hr in this setting is confirmatory.

Because 25% or more of cases of primary hyperaldosteronism may be idiopathic as a result of bilateral adrenal hyperplasia and should therefore be managed medically and not surgically, the next step should be imaging with thin-section (3 mm cuts) CT or MRI. The finding of a discrete unilateral adenoma larger than 1 cm on CT in conjunction with a normal contralateral adrenal is sufficient localization to allow the surgeon to proceed with adrenalectomy. If CT shows bilateral nodules, bilateral normal adrenals, or a unilateral nodule smaller than 1 cm, then adrenal vein sampling for aldosterone and cortisol should be done to determine whether a unilateral gradient of increased aldosterone production exists.[3]

Cortisol-Producing Adenoma

Approximately 20% of cases of Cushing syndrome are related to increased production of cortisol by an adrenal cortical tumor. Adrenal Cushing syndrome is most commonly attributable to adenoma but may also result from adrenal cortical carcinoma or primary adrenal hyperplasia. The classic features of full-blown Cushing syndrome are usually obvious and include centripetal obesity, moon facies, hypertension, purple skin striae, proximal muscle weakness, osteopenia, and amenorrhea. Not all patients present with advanced clinical signs, however, and the high prevalence of hypertension and obesity in the general population necessitates liberal use of diagnostic testing.

Table 2 Clinical and Diagnostic Features of Common Adrenal Tumors

Adrenal Tumor	Clinical Presentation	Biochemical Testing	Preferred Method of Imaging/Localization
Aldosteronoma	Hypertension ± hypokalemia	Elevated PAC with suppressed PRA (PAC:PRA > 20–30) Urine aldosterone > 12 μg/24 hr Urine potassium > 30 mEq/24 hr	Thin-section (3 mm) adrenal CT Adrenal vein sampling
Cortisol-producing adenoma (Cushing syndrome)	Centripetal obesity, moon facies, hypertension, purple skin striae, osteopenia, plethora, amenorrhea	Elevated 24-hr urinary free cortisol Nonsuppressed low-dose dexamethasone test Decreased plasma ACTH	Abdominal CT
Pheochromocytoma	Severe episodic hypertension or hypertension with spells of tachycardia, headache, anxiety, and diaphoresis	Elevated plasma fractionated metanephrines or urinary catecholamines and metabolites	MRI (T$_2$-weighted sequences showing bright-appearing adrenal lesion) ^{123}I-MIBG scan or Octreoscan if MRI is negative or if malignant or extra-adrenal tumor is suspected
Adrenal cortical carcinoma	Cushing syndrome, virilizing features, local pain or mass	24-hr urinary free cortisol and metabolites Plasma DHEA-sulfate	CT of chest/abdomen/pelvis
Adrenal metastasis	None (often seen on follow-up imaging) or local pain	Plasma fractionated metanephrines and low-dose DM test to exclude functioning lesion FNA biopsy only if unresectable	Abdominal CT, PET imaging to evaluate for extra-adrenal metastatic disease
Myelolipoma	None; occasionally local pain	None if radiographic appearance is unequivocal for myelolipoma	Presence of macroscopic fat on CT or MRI

ACTH—adrenocorticotropic hormone   DHEA—dehydroepiandrosterone   DM—dexamethasone   FNA—fine-needle aspiration   MIBG—meta-iodylbenzylguanidine   PAC—plasma aldosterone concentration   PET—positron emission tomography   PRA—plasma renin activity

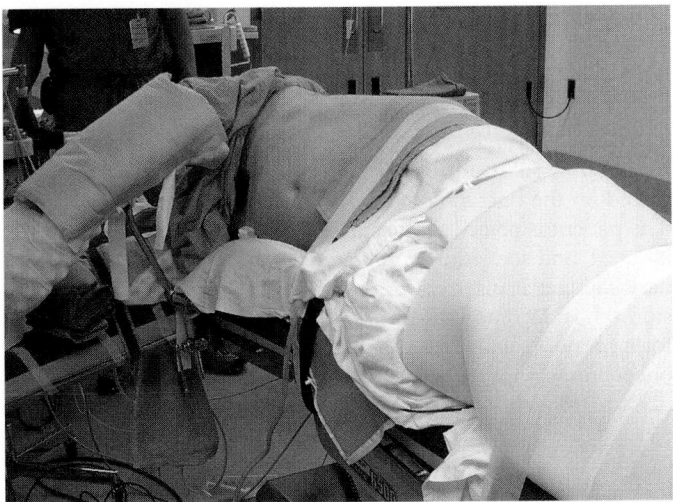

Figure 3 **Laparoscopic adrenalectomy: transabdominal approach. The patient is placed in a lateral decubitus position with the affected side up (here, right lateral decubitus for left adrenalectomy).**

Suspected Cushing syndrome should be evaluated initially by measuring 24-hour urinary free cortisol levels or by administering a single low-dose dexamethasone test. If plasma cortisol does not fall to a level below 3 to 5 µg/dl the morning after administration of 1 mg of dexamethasone at 11 P.M., Cushing syndrome is a strong possibility and further testing is required. Once the diagnosis of hypercortisolism is established, plasma levels of adrenocorticotropic hormone (ACTH) should be measured to differentiate ACTH-dependent (resulting from increased ACTH production by a pituitary tumor or an ectopic source) from ACTH-independent (primary adrenal) causative conditions. The plasma ACTH level should be in the low-normal or suppressed range in patients with primary adrenal tumors, whereas it is normal or elevated in patients with ACTH-dependent Cushing syndrome. Imaging should then be carried out with CT (or MRI) to localize the adrenal tumor.

Pheochromocytoma

Pheochromocytoma should be suspected in any patient who experiences either severe episodic hypertension or hypertension that is associated with spells of tachycardia, headache, anxiety, and diaphoresis. Biochemical evaluation consists of measuring urinary concentrations of catecholamines and metabolites (e.g., metanephrine and normetanephrine), plasma concentrations of fractionated metanephrines, or both. MRI is our preferred imaging modality for suspected pheochromocytomas because of the typical bright appearance these tumors exhibit on T_2-weighted imaging sequences. Occasionally, radionuclide imaging with iodine-123–metaiodylbenzylguanidine (^{123}I-MIBG) or octreotide scintigraphy is necessary to localize an extra-adrenal pheochromocytoma.

Adrenocortical Carcinoma

Adrenocortical carcinomas are rare, with an incidence of approximately one per 1.5 to 2.0 million in the general population. These tumors are typically large (> 6 to 8 cm) at diagnosis, and most patients have advanced (stage III or IV) disease at presentation. Consequently, patients often have a mass or complain of abdominal or back pain. A significant percentage of patients with adrenocortical carcinoma present with evidence of hormone overproduction in the form of Cushing syndrome or virilizing features. Complete surgical resection offers the only chance for cure; thus,

the role of laparoscopic adrenalectomy in the treatment of adrenocortical carcinoma remains controversial [*see* Troubleshooting, Large Tumors, *below*].

Adrenal Incidentaloma

Adrenal incidentalomas are the adrenal lesions most frequently referred to surgeons and are seen on 1% to 5% of all abdominal CT scans.[4] Practical, current recommendations for evaluation and management of patients with incidentally discovered adrenal lesions are available.[5] The most common adrenal incidentaloma is a nonfunctioning cortical adenoma for which adrenalectomy is not usually required. All patients with adrenal incidentalomas should be screened for hypercortisolism by administering an overnight low-dose dexamethasone test and for pheochromocytoma by measuring plasma concentrations of fractionated metanephrines or urine levels of catecholamines and metanephrines. Patients who are hypertensive or hypokalemic should also undergo testing for hyperaldosteronism with measurement of plasma aldosterone and renin levels. Some patients with adrenal incidentalomas are found to have subclinical Cushing syndrome with evidence of autonomous corticoid steroid production, as demonstrated by lack of suppressibility with a dexamethasone test and by low plasma ACTH levels.[6] These patients do not exhibit the classic features of Cushing syndrome but do have a high incidence of hypertension, diabetes, and osteoporosis. Adrenalectomy is generally indicated if the operative risk is suitably low. Supplemental corticosteroids should be given before, during, and after operation because contralateral adrenal function is often suppressed and adrenal insufficiency may ensue.

The nonfunctioning adrenal lesion should also be assessed for malignant potential on the basis of its size and appearance on diagnostic imaging. Cortical adenomas typically have low attenuation values (< 10 Hounsfield units) on unenhanced CT imaging and show loss of signal intensity on MRI chemical-shift imaging sequences. Needle biopsy is not useful in differentiating benign from malignant primary adrenal lesions and is rarely indicated. Adrenal biopsy should never be done unless a pheochromocytoma has first been excluded biochemically. Most experts recommend removing any nonfunctioning adrenal lesion larger than 4 to 5 cm unless the radiographic appearance of the lesion is diagnostic of a cyst or myelolipoma. Smaller tumors should be followed with imaging at 4 and 12 months after the initial presentation.

Operative Planning

PREPARATION FOR OPERATION

Preoperative preparation of the patient for adrenalectomy entails control of hypertension and correction of any electrolyte imbalances. Patients with a pheochromocytoma should receive 7 to 10 days of alpha-adrenergic blockade with phenoxybenzamine to minimize any exacerbation of hypertension during the operation. The usual starting dosage is 10 mg twice daily, which is increased by 10 to 20 mg/day until the hypertension and tachycardia are controlled and the patient is mildly orthostatic. Patients with Cushing syndrome or subclinical Cushing syndrome should receive perioperative dosages of stress steroids. Mechanical bowel preparation is not routinely employed.

CHOICE OF PROCEDURE

The retroperitoneal location of the adrenals renders them accessible via either transabdominal or retroperitoneal approaches. The choice of surgical approach in any given patient depends on a number of factors, including the nature of the underlying adrenal pathology, the size of the tumor, the patient's body habitus, and the experience of the operating surgeon. For the vast majority of adrenal lesions, laparoscopic adrenalectomy is preferred. Most centers favor the transabdominal lateral approach to laparoscopic adrenalectomy,[7] which has the advantages of a large working space, familiar anatomic landmarks, and widespread success. Some centers, however, prefer a retroperitoneal endoscopic approach.[8,9] The advantages of this technique are that the peritoneal cavity is not entered, there is no need to retract overlying organs, and the incidence of postoperative ileus may be lower. The disadvantages are that the retroperitoneal approach employs a smaller working space, is more difficult to learn with fewer anatomic landmarks for orientation, and is usually restricted to tumors smaller than 5 cm.

The only absolute contraindications to laparoscopic adrenalectomy are local tumor invasion and the presence of regional lymphadenopathy. A large tumor (> 8 to 10 cm), a suspected primary adrenal malignancy, and a history of previous nephrectomy, splenectomy, or liver resection on the side of the lesion to be removed are all indicators that a case is likely to be more difficult and should be considered relative contraindications to a laparoscopic approach in all but the most experienced hands. Portal hypertension is also a contraindication to a laparoscopic approach because of the dilated collateral vessels in the retroperitoneum.

Options for open adrenalectomy include transabdominal, flank, posterior retroperitoneal, and thoracoabdominal approaches. The lateral flank approach and the posterior retroperitoneal approach have been replaced by laparoscopic approaches and are now rarely used. A posterior retroperitoneal adrenalectomy is done through a hockey-stick incision in the back, with subperiosteal resection of the 12th rib. This approach has low morbidity and yields adequate exposure of the adrenal gland, but the visual field is often limited, and there is a high incidence of residual incisional complaints. The current consensus is that open posterior retroperitoneal adrenalectomy is indicated only in patients who require bilateral adrenalectomy but are not candidates for laparoscopic adrenalectomy. Most large or malignant adrenal tumors that necessitate an open approach can be removed via an anterior abdominal incision, usually a unilateral or bilateral subcostal incision (with subxiphoid extension if necessary); a thoracoabdominal incision is rarely needed.

Table 3 Instrumentation for Laparoscopic Adrenalectomy

Veress needle
Angled (30°) laparoscope
5 and 12 mm laparoscopic ports
5 mm liver retractor for right adrenalectomy
L-hook electrocautery
Atraumatic graspers, blunt dissector
Right-angle dissector
Medium-large clip applier
Ultrasonic coagulator for left adrenalectomy (optional)
Suction irrigation cannula
Specimen extraction bag
Laparoscopic ultrasonography device*
Endovascular stapler*

---

* Not routinely needed but should be available.

Operative Technique

LAPAROSCOPIC ADRENALECTOMY

Transabdominal Approach

Patient positioning A gel-padded bean-bag mattress is placed on the operating table before the patient enters the room. The patient is placed in the supine position, general anesthesia is induced, and sequential compression stockings are placed. A urinary catheter is inserted for monitoring of urine output, and the stomach is decompressed with an orogastric tube. Invasive monitoring is not usually necessary unless the patient has a vasoactive pheochromocytoma, in which case an arterial line is routinely placed.

Next, the patient is moved into a lateral decubitus position with the affected side up [see Figure 3]. A soft roll is placed underneath the chest wall to protect the axilla. The bean-bag mattress is molded around the patient and the legs are wrapped in a foam pad to minimize all pressure points. The patient is secured to the operating table with tape placed across the padded lower extremities and a safety strap across the pelvis. The operating table is then flexed at the waist. The combination of the lateral position, the flexed operating table, and the reverse Trendelenburg position facilitates placement of the laparoscopic ports and provides optimal access to the superior retroperitoneum.

Equipment Our preferred instrumentation for laparoscopic adrenalectomy is as follows [see Table 3]. An angled (30°) laparoscope, preferably 5 mm in diameter, is used to optimize viewing angles. One 10/12 mm port is employed to allow insertion of a clip applier and extraction of the specimen; the other ports can all be 5 mm if a 5 mm laparoscope is employed. The principal instruments needed for dissection and hemostasis are atraumatic graspers, an L-hook electrocautery, and a medium-large clip applier. An ultrasonic coagulator is not essential for a right adrenalectomy, but it may facilitate mobilization of the splenic ligaments and dissection of the adrenal from the retroperitoneal fat during a left adrenalectomy. An endovascular stapler should be available for a right adrenalectomy because it will occasionally be needed to divide the right adrenal vein. Other essential items are a suction-irrigation device and an impermeable specimen retrieval bag.

Initial access and placement of trocars Because the patient is in a lateral position, initial access to the peritoneal cavity is usually achieved in a closed fashion with a Veress needle. After insufflation to a pressure of 15 mm Hg, a 5 mm direct-view trocar is placed to afford direct visualization of the peritoneal cavity. An open insertion technique may be used instead, but this approach requires a larger incision and is hindered somewhat by the bulky overlapping muscle layers in the subcostal region. Open insertion at the umbilicus is an option in some patients.

The initial access site is generally at or somewhat medial to the anterior axillary line about two fingerbreadths below the costal margin [see Figure 4]. Subsequent ports should be placed at least 5 cm apart to allow freedom of movement externally. The most dorsal port should be approximately at the posterior axillary line. It is helpful to outline the anterior and posterior axillary lines with a marker before the patient is prepared to ensure that the ports are positioned properly. Whereas four ports are required for a right adrenalectomy, a left adrenalectomy can be done with either three or four ports, depending on the surgeon's preference and experience. On the left side, the splenic flexure of the colon usually must be mobilized before the fourth port (the most dorsal one) can be inserted.

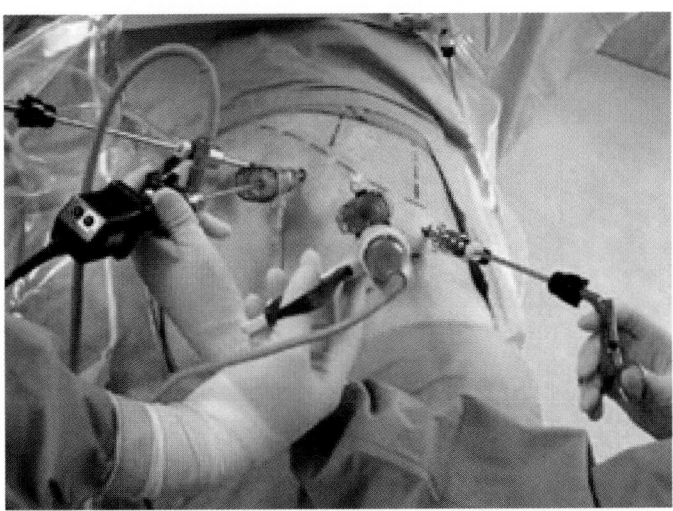

Figure 4 **Laparoscopic adrenalectomy: transabdominal approach. Shown is the recommended port site placement for laparoscopic adrenalectomy (here, left adrenalectomy). Dashed lines indicate the costal margin and the anterior and posterior axillary lines.**

Right adrenalectomy *Step 1: exposure of right adrenal gland and vein.* The key to exposure of the right adrenal gland is extensive division of the right triangular ligament of the liver. This maneuver should be continued until the liver can be easily elevated and retracted medially and both the right adrenal and the IVC are visible. A retractor is then inserted through the most medial port to hold the right lobe of the liver up and away from the operative site.

Next, the plane between the medial border of the adrenal and the lateral aspect of the IVC is developed. An L-hook cautery is used for gentle elevation and division of the peritoneum and the small arterial branches here [*see Figure 5*]. The adrenal is pushed laterally with an atraumatic grasper to apply traction to the dissection site; however, the gland itself should not be grasped, because it is fragile and the capsule and adrenal parenchyma are easily fractured. At all times, it is imperative to know where the lateral border of the IVC is, both to ensure that the dissection is extra-adrenal and to avoid injuring the IVC. The right adrenal vein should come into view as the medial border is dissected.

Step 2: isolation, clipping, and division of right adrenal vein. The right adrenal vein is first exposed by gentle blunt spreading, and a right-angle dissector is then used to isolate enough of the vein's length to permit clip placement [*see Figure 6*]. A medium-large clip is usually sufficient for securing the vein, though sometimes it is necessary to use larger clips or even an endovascular stapler. (We use an endovascular stapler primarily in cases in which the tumor is located in the medial area of the adrenal and the vein must be taken along with a portion of the IVC junction.) Usually, two clips are placed on the IVC side and one or two on the adrenal side, depending on the length of vein available. Meticulous hemostasis throughout the dissection is important: even minimal bleeding will stain the tissue planes and make the dissection more difficult and potentially treacherous.

Step 3: mobilization and detachment of specimen. Once the adrenal vein is divided, dissection is continued superiorly and inferiorly with the L-hook cautery. The numerous small arteries that enter the gland at its superior, medial, and inferior margins can be

safely cauterized, but larger branches may have to be clipped. Superiorly, as the adrenal is mobilized, the musculature of the posterior diaphragm is exposed and serves as a marker of the proper plane for the posterior dissection. Inferiorly, the dissection should stay close to the margin of the adrenal so as not to injure branches of the renal hilar vessels. The inferior dissection then proceeds in a medial-to-lateral direction as the gland is elevated off the superior pole of the right kidney. The remaining attachments to the back muscles and the retroperitoneal fat are relatively avascular and can be divided with the electrocautery.

Once the specimen has been detached, it is placed in an impermeable bag. The retroperitoneum is then irrigated and inspected for hemostasis and for secure placement of the clips on the IVC.

Step 4: extraction of specimen. The fascial opening at the 10/12 mm port site is enlarged somewhat, and the specimen bag is removed through this site. For larger tumors, a remote extraction site (e.g., the umbilicus or the suprapubic region) may be a preferable alternative. Large pheochromcytomas may be morcellated within the entrapment bag and removed piecemeal, but ideally, cortical tumors and metastatic lesions should be extracted intact to permit full pathologic examination.

Left adrenalectomy *Step 1: exposure of left adrenal gland and vein.* The splenic flexure of the colon is mobilized. The lateral attachments of the flexure are divided to allow placement of the fourth port (if needed), and the colon is then released from the

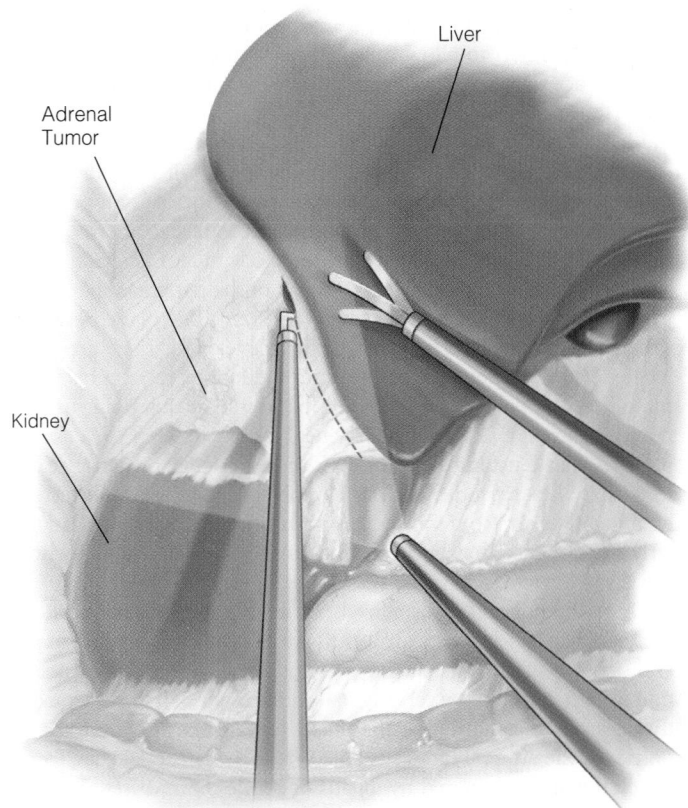

Figure 5 **Laparoscopic right adrenalectomy: transabdominal approach. Depicted is the anatomic exposure for right adrenalectomy. The liver is retracted medially, and the right triangular ligament of the liver is divided with an L-hook electrocautery.**

a

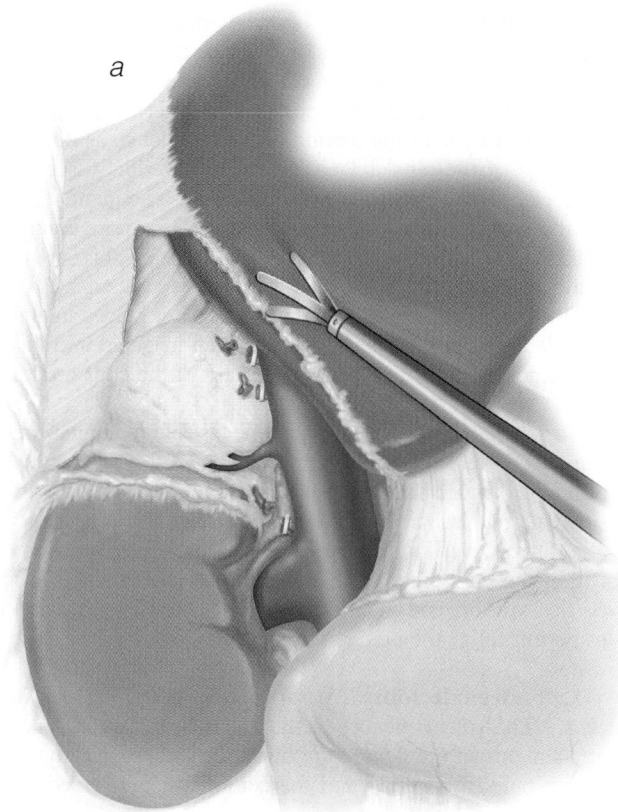

b

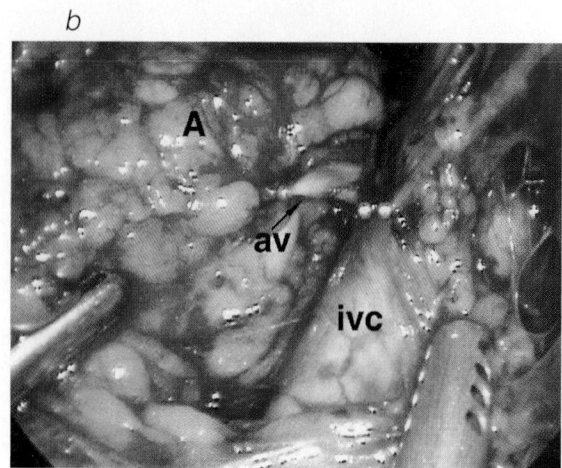

Figure 6 **Laparoscopic right adrenalectomy: transabdominal approach. Once the right adrenal and adrenal
vein are exposed, the vein is isolated and clipped.
Shown are (*a*) a schematic representation and (*b*) an
intraoperative view showing the right adrenal
gland/tumor (A), the right adrenal vein (AV), and the
inferior vena cava (IVC).**

inferior pole of the spleen and away from the left kidney. Next, the
splenorenal ligament is incised from the inferior pole of the spleen
to the diaphragm to allow full medial rotation of the spleen and
provide access to the left retroperitoneum [*see Figure 7*]. It is
important not to dissect lateral to the kidney; doing so will cause
the kidney to tilt forward and will interfere with exposure. Once
the spleen is completely mobilized, it should fall medially, with
minimal or no retraction needed to keep it out of the operative
field. Division of the ligaments can be accomplished more quickly and with less bleeding if an ultrasonic coagulator is used.

At this point in the dissection, the tail of the pancreas should be
visible, along with the splenic artery and vein. The plane between
the pancreas and the left kidney is then developed. The adrenal is
located on the superomedial aspect of the kidney just cephalad to
the tail of the pancreas and should be visible at this point unless
there is a great deal of retroperitoneal fat (as is often the case in
patients with Cushing syndrome). If the adrenal gland is not readily visible, laparoscopic ultrasonography should be employed to
help locate it and to delineate the surrounding anatomy, particularly the upper kidney and the renal hilar vessels. If the dissection
starts too low, the renal hilar vessels or the ureter could be injured.

Once the adrenal is visualized, the medial and lateral borders
are usually defined by means of dissection with the hook cautery
and division of areolar attachments and small vessels. The dissection is then continued inferiorly to locate the adrenal vein as it exits
the inferomedial border of the gland [*see Figure 8*]. The inferior
border of the adrenal often sits adjacent to the left renal vein, from
which it can be separated by means of gentle blunt dissection and
judicious use of the electrocautery.

Step 2: isolation, clipping, and division of left adrenal vein. Once
the adrenal vein has been visualized, it is isolated, doubly clipped,
and divided. Because the adrenal vein is usually joined by the inferior phrenic vein cephalad to its junction with the renal vein, it is

often necessary to clip the inferior phrenic vein again as the dissection proceeds more proximally.

Step 3: mobilization and detachment of specimen. Once the left
adrenal vein has been securely clipped and divided, the dissection
is continued cephalad along both the lateral and the medial borders of the gland. Because of the surrounding retroperitoneal fat,
it is advisable to use the ultrasonic coagulator for this part of the
left-side dissection. Because the left adrenal is more flattened out
on the superomedial aspect of the left kidney than the right adrenal is on the right kidney, more of the kidney will be exposed during dissection in a left adrenalectomy than in a right adrenalectomy. Finally, the posterior and superior attachments to the diaphragm and the retroperitoneal fat are divided.

Step 4: extraction of specimen. Once the gland is free, the
retroperitoneum is inspected and the specimen extracted as in a
right adrenalectomy. If there is any possibility that the pancreatic
parenchyma may have been violated, a closed suction drain is left
in place.

Retroperitoneal Approach

Retroperitoneal endoscopic adrenalectomy can be carried out
with the patient in either a lateral or a prone position. In general,
this technique is more challenging to learn than transabdominal
adrenalectomy, the working space is more cramped, and it is easier for surgeons to become disoriented unless they have experience
working in the retroperitoneum. On the other hand, the retroperitoneal approach allows surgeons to avoid having to reposition
patients for bilateral adrenalectomy (if the prone position is used),
and it may simplify access in patients who have previously undergone extensive upper abdominal procedures.

Initial access is usually achieved through open insertion of a 12
mm port into the retroperitoneum either (1) just lateral or inferi-

a

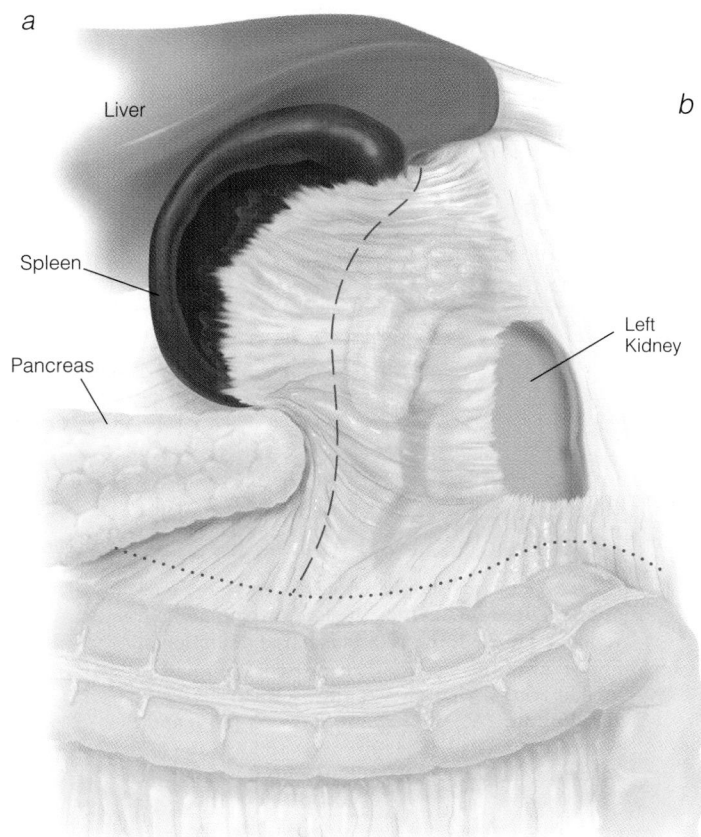

Liver

Spleen

Pancreas

Left Kidney

b

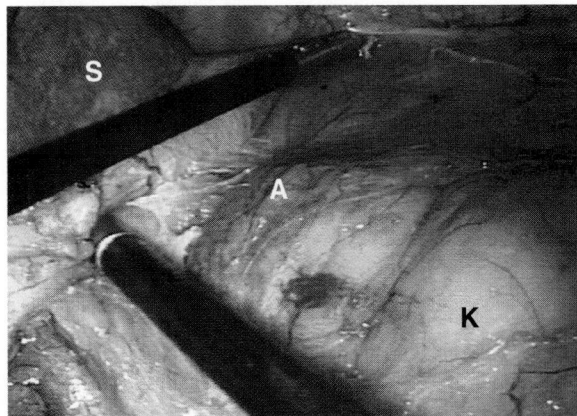

S

A

K

Figure 7 **Laparoscopic left adrenalectomy: transab-dominal approach. Depicted is the anatomic exposure for left adrenalectomy. (*a*) The splenic flexure of the colon is divided first (dotted line), and the splenorenal ligament is then divided (dashed line). (*b*) Shown is an intraoperative view. (S—spleen; A—adrenal; K—kidney)**

or to the tip of the 12th rib (for the prone position) or (2) in the midaxillary line about 3 cm above the iliac crest (for the lateral position). A potential advantage of the lateral approach is that it can be converted to a transperitoneal approach if difficulty is encountered.

Once the retroperitoneum is entered, a balloon device is deployed to create an initial working space, which is further developed by means of CO_2 insufflation and blunt dissection. The second and third ports are then placed [*see Figure 9*]. The principles of dissection are the same as in a transabdominal adrenalectomy [*see* Transabdominal Approach, *above*]. Laparoscopic ultrasonography may be useful for defining the upper portion of the kidney and the adrenal gland and tumor.

OPEN ADRENALECTOMY

Of the four approaches to open adrenalectomy [*see* Operative Planning, Choice of Procedure, *above*], the anterior transabdominal approach is the preferred method for any tumors that are too large to be removed laparoscopically and for all invasive adrenal malignancies. The incision most commonly used is an extended unilateral or bilateral subcostal incision, though a midline incision is also an option [*see Figure 10*]. The extended subcostal incision yields exposure of both adrenal glands, as well as the rest of the peritoneal cavity. If necessary, it may be extended superiorly in the midline to the xiphoid to provide better upper abdominal exposure for full mobilization of the liver and access to the hepatic veins and the vena cava. The exposure obtained with this incision is sufficient for all but the most extensive adrenal malignancies. If the tumor involves the vena cava, the incision may be extended into a median sternotomy to provide access to the superior vena cava and the heart. The classic thoracoabdominal incision, which extends from the abdomen up through the seventh or eighth inter-

costal space and through the diaphragm, provides excellent exposure but is associated with increased incision-related morbidity and is rarely used.

Much of the exposure and dissection is the same as in a laparoscopic adrenalectomy; however, because open adrenalectomy is often employed for removal of particularly large tumors, some additional maneuvers may be necessary to achieve adequate exposure and vascular control. For example, it may be helpful to elevate the flank with a roll or a bean-bag mattress and then flex the operating table to open up the space between the costal margin and the iliac crest. Once the abdomen is entered, exploration is carried out for the presence of metastatic disease.

Exposure of the adrenal on the right side is achieved by dividing the right triangular ligament of the liver, as in the laparoscopic approach. The hepatic flexure of the colon is also reflected inferiorly. With large tumors, a Kocher maneuver should be performed to afford better exposure of the vena cava and the renal vessels. The remainder of the dissection proceeds in much the same manner as in a laparoscopic right adrenalectomy. For suspected adrenal malignancies, a wide resection should be carried out, with removal of periadrenal fat and lymphatic tissue and any suspicious lymph nodes. For tumors that appear to involve the vena cava, vascular control of both the IVC proximal and distal to the tumor and the renal veins should be achieved before the lesion is removed.

Open left adrenalectomy entails mobilization of the splenic flexure of the colon and division of the splenorenal ligament. The spleen, the tail of pancreas, and the stomach are reflected medially en bloc to expose the left kidney and the left adrenal. The left adrenal vein is ligated with clips or silk ties near its junction with the renal vein. The remainder of the dissection proceeds as in a laparoscopic left adrenalectomy. For left-side primary adrenal

a

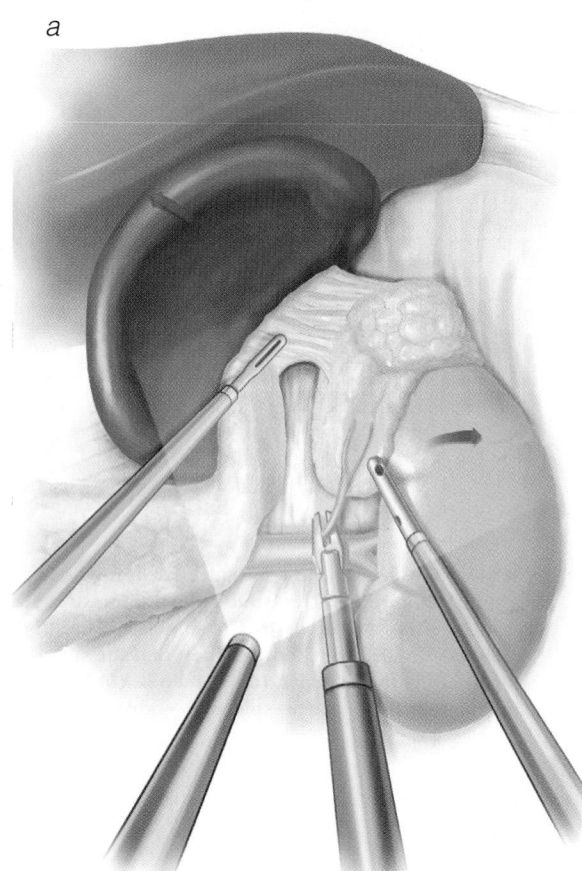

b

Figure 8 **Laparoscopic left adrenalectomy: transabdominal approach. Once the left adrenal and adrenal vein are exposed, the vein is isolated and clipped. Shown are (*a*) a schematic representation and (*b*) an intraoperative view showing the left adrenal gland/tumor (A), the left adrenal vein (AV), and the phrenic vein (PV). The phrenic vein joins the left adrenal vein above its junction with the renal vein.**

malignancies, periaortic lymphatic vessels and lymph nodes should be removed along with the specimen. If a large left-side tumor is invading adjacent structures, removal may require en bloc resection of the spleen, the distal pancreas, and the kidney.

Troubleshooting

INABILITY TO LOCATE ADRENAL

The adrenal is usually not difficult to find on the right side, where it should be visible once the right hemiliver has been mobilized. Important landmarks on that side are the IVC, which is medial to the adrenal, and the kidney, which is inferior to the adrenal. Once these structures have been identified, the location of the adrenal should be apparent. In contrast, the adrenal can be difficult to find on the left side, especially if the tumor is small or the patient is obese. To locate the left adrenal, the splenorenal ligament should be fully divided, and then the plane between the kidney and the tail of the pancreas should be developed, with the tail of the pancreas rotated medially. As dissection proceeds superiorly, the adrenal can be visually distinguished from the retroperitoneal fat by its golden-orange appearance. If the adrenal is not yet visualized at this point, laparoscopic ultrasonography should be used to verify the locations of the superior pole of the left kidney and the renal vessels. Ultrasonography should also be able to image the adrenal gland and tumor within the retroperitoneal fat [*see Figure 11*].

BLEEDING

The best means of managing bleeding problems during adrenalectomy is prevention. Important measures for minimizing bleed-

ing risk include obtaining good exposure of the operative field and employing meticulous dissection and gentle handling of the adrenal and surrounding structures. When bleeding does occur, it may be from the adrenal veins, the adrenal gland itself, the IVC, the renal veins, the liver, the pancreas, the spleen, or the kidney. For bleeding during laparoscopic adrenalectomy, the first maneuver should be to tamponade the bleeding site with an atraumatic instrument. If this maneuver is successful, dissection should be directed away from the bleeding site for a while, until better exposure of the area can be obtained. Major hemorrhage from the IVC or the renal veins that is not immediately controlled should be managed by prompt conversion to open adrenalectomy (see below). Lesser bleeding may also be an indication for conversion to open adrenalectomy if it obscures the tissue planes and thereby increases the risk of inadvertent entry into the adrenal gland or tumor.

CONVERSION TO OPEN ADRENALECTOMY

Conversion to open adrenalectomy may sometimes be necessary because of bleeding, failure to progress with the dissection, or a locally invasive tumor. If the patient is in the lateral decubitus position, conversion may be accomplished by means of a subcostal incision extended into the flank. With the patient on a bean-bag mattress, the operating table can be rotated out of the straight lateral plane so that the patient comes to occupy more of a hemilateral position. If the procedure is a bilateral adrenalectomy, then either a bilateral subcostal incision or a midline incision may be employed after the patient has first been returned to more of a supine position. For this reason, it is important to extend the initial preparation and draping past the midline of the abdomen. Alternatively, if the conversion is not being done on an urgent

For large invasive adrenal malignancies, an open approach, involving a generous bilateral subcostal incision, is indicated, and the chest should be prepared in case a thoracoabdominal or median sternotomy extension proves necessary. The important principles are to obtain wide exposure of the operative field and to control all major vessels that may be involved before removing the tumor.

OBESE PATIENTS

Obese patients present a particular challenge during adrenalectomy, for several reasons: initial access is more difficult; retraction and exposure are more challenging; and the copious amount of retroperitoneal fat makes it difficult to identify the adrenal and to clearly define the margins of the gland within the retroperitoneum. Our practice is to attempt to gain initial access to the peritoneal cavity by using a closed Veress needle technique. Because resting intra-abdominal pressure may be higher in obese patients, especially if they are in the lateral position, it may be necessary to increase the CO_2 pressure to 20 mm Hg temporarily until the first trocar is inserted. If it proves difficult to establish pneumoperitoneum with the Veress needle technique, the initial trocar should be placed at the umbilicus by means of an open insertion technique. The subcostal and flank ports are then inserted in the usual locations under direct vision.

On the right side, the presence of a bulky, fatty liver should be anticipated, and the locations of the port sites should be adjusted accordingly by placing them somewhat more caudad. Ample time should be taken to mobilize the liver fully so that the adrenal and the IVC can be safely accessed. On the left, the ports may be placed in the standard locations. The splenic flexure should be

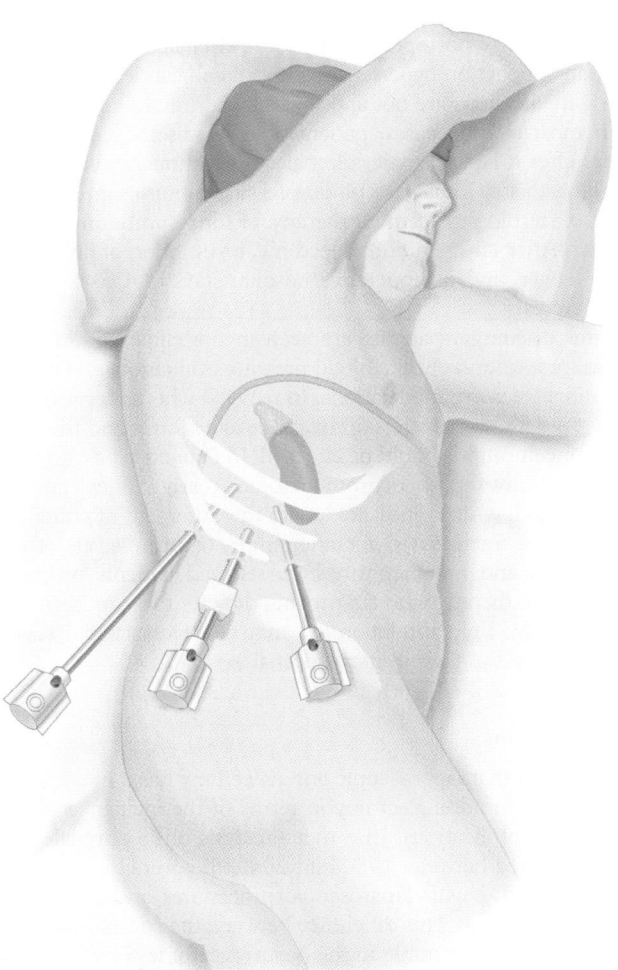

Figure 9 **Laparoscopic adrenalectomy: retroperitoneal endoscopic approach. Shown is the recommended port site placement.**

basis because of bleeding, the port sites may be closed, and the patient may then be moved into the supine position, reprepared, and redraped.

An option that may be considered before conversion to an open procedure is the use of a hand access port. A hand-assisted technique may be particularly useful for larger, noninvasive tumors that are harder to manipulate with laparoscopic instruments. The location of the incision for the hand port may vary according to the patient's body habitus; generally, however, an ipsilateral subcostal location medial to the working ports allows adequate hand access while preserving visualization through the more lateral ports.

LARGE TUMORS

Large adrenal tumors (> 6 to 8 cm) are more difficult to remove than smaller ones because they are bulkier and more vascular and because they are harder to manipulate and retract. Accordingly, the dissection should stay extra-adrenal, and care must be exercised during manipulation to avoid entering the tumor. Although surgeons have not yet had a great deal of experience with hand-assisted laparoscopic adrenalectomy, it appears that this approach may be useful for exposure and retraction of large tumors and may facilitate extraction of large specimens. Laparoscopic ultrasonography should also be employed to verify that the tumor is well circumscribed and noninvasive. Surgeons who attempt to remove large adrenal tumors laparoscopically should be highly experienced in laparoscopic adrenalectomy techniques.

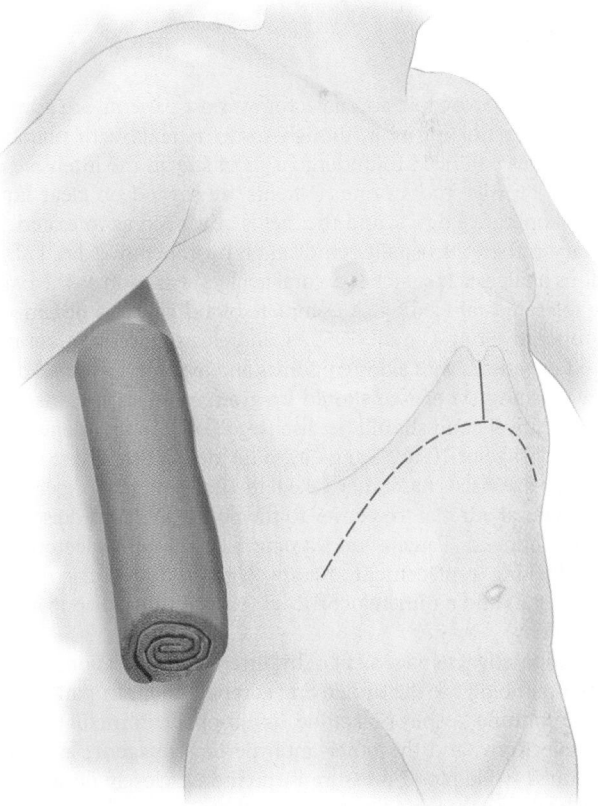

Figure 10 **Open adrenalectomy. The procedure is generally done through a unilateral or bilateral subcostal incision. For better exposure for large adrenal malignancies, the incision may be extended cephalad in the midline.**

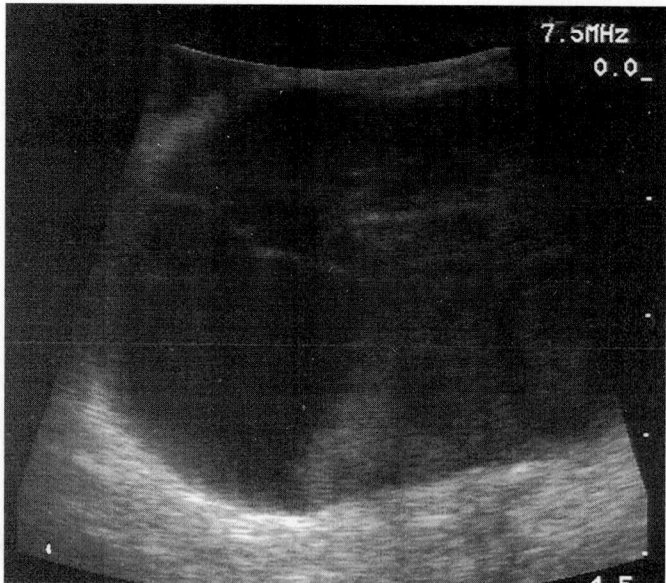

Figure 11 **If the left adrenal proves difficult to find, laparoscopic ultrasonography may be employed to locate the gland and the lesion within the retroperitoneal fat. This laparoscopic ultrasonogram shows an enlarged left adrenal gland secondary to metastatic squamous cell carcinoma of the lung.**

fully mobilized, as should the spleen and the tail of the pancreas. Laparoscopic ultrasonography is often needed to locate the gland in the retroperitoneal fat. In addition, use of an ultrasonic coagulator may facilitate division of the retroperitoneal fat.

Postoperative Care

After a laparoscopic adrenalectomy, most patients are admitted to a regular nursing unit, though some patients with pheochromocytomas will need to undergo a short stay in the intensive care unit for invasive monitoring. Patients are started on clear liquids on postoperative day 1, and the diet is advanced as tolerated. The urinary catheter is usually removed on postoperative day 1. Intravenous analgesia is switched to oral analgesia as soon as the patient can tolerate oral feeding. A complete blood count is obtained on postoperative day 1 in all patients, and electrolyte levels are monitored in patients with aldosteronomas and hypercortisolism. Patients with Cushing syndrome should be given stress doses of steroids perioperatively and should be discharged on a maintenance prednisone dosage of 10 to 15 mg/day in divided doses. These patients should be advised that it may take 6 to 12 months or longer for the contralateral adrenal to recover to the point where prednisone can be discontinued. Patients undergoing bilateral adrenalectomy will need lifelong replacement therapy with a glucocorticoid (e.g., prednisone) and a mineralocorticoid (e.g., fludrocortisone acetate, 0.1 mg/day).

Postoperative management of hypertensive medications depends on the pathology of the underlying adrenal lesion. In patients with aldosteronomas, spironolactone is stopped immediately after adrenalectomy, and the other antihypertensive agents are usually continued while blood pressure is monitored closely on an outpatient basis; further medication reductions are made as clinically warranted. In most patients with Cushing syndrome, antihypertensive medications are continued, whereas in most patients with pheochromocytomas, they are not. In both sets of patients, however, close outpatient monitoring of blood pressure should be carried out in the early postoperative period. Adrenalectomy can have a dramatic impact on hypertensive control and can lead to hypotension if medications are not appropriately adjusted.

In most routine cases, patients can be discharged within 24 hours after a laparoscopic adrenalectomy, though some patients will have to stay longer for blood pressure monitoring, for adjustment of steroid replacement therapy, or for resumption of a regular diet. After an open adrenalectomy, resumption of an oral diet takes longer, and postoperative hospital stays of 4 to 5 days are more typical.

After discharge, patients are seen in the clinic within 2 to 3 weeks for a wound check, blood pressure evaluation, and a review of antihypertensive medications. In patients who underwent adrenalectomy for an aldosteronoma, electrolyte levels and the creatinine concentration should be checked. In patients who underwent adrenalectomy for pheochromocytoma, yearly clinical and biochemical follow-up is indicated, with measurement of either plasma levels of fractionated metanephrines or urine levels of catecholamines and metanephrines. In selected patients on steroid replacement therapy who are proving difficult to wean from prednisone, an ACTH stimulation test may be necessary to assess the responsiveness of the pituitary-adrenal axis.

Complications

It appears that laparoscopic adrenalectomy has a major advantage over open adrenalectomy in terms of the incidence of postoperative complications. In a meta-analysis of 98 adrenalectomy series reported between 1980 and 2000, the overall complication rate was 10.9% with laparoscopic procedures and 25.2% with open procedures.[10] This difference between the complication rates was primarily attributable to the occurrence of fewer wound, pulmonary, and infectious complications in the laparoscopic series. The most common complication of laparoscopic adrenalectomy is bleeding, which was reported in 4.7% of patients from the series reviewed in the meta-analysis. Bleeding is also the most common reason for conversion to open adrenalectomy; however, major bleeding that leads to transfusion is relatively uncommon. The risk of bleeding can be minimized by obtaining meticulous hemostasis, taking care not to grasp the adrenal gland, and handling tissue gently. If bleeding does occur, the prudent course of action is to maintain pressure on the bleeding source while obtaining better exposure or even starting the dissection in another area, rather than to resort to indiscriminate use of clips or electrocautery. The surgeon must be prepared to convert rapidly to an open procedure should major hemorrhage occur.

Other potential complications of adrenalectomy (either laparoscopic or open) include injury to the tail of the pancreas (with resultant pancreatic leakage or pancreatitis), injury to the diaphragm, and pneumothorax. Wound infections are uncommon with laparoscopic adrenalectomy. Trocar site hernias are infrequent as well, provided that the fascia is closed at all port sites that are 10 mm or larger. Deep vein thrombosis occurs in 0.8% of cases, pulmonary embolism in 0.5%.[10] Pneumatic compression stockings should be used perioperatively to minimize the risk of venous thromboembolism. Renovascular hypertension from injury to the renal artery has also been reported.[11,12] The operative mortality associated with laparoscopic adrenalectomy is about 0.3%.

Several cases of local or regional tumor recurrence have been reported after laparoscopic adrenalectomy. In most of these cases, the tumors removed were either suspected or unsuspected adrenal malignancies, and the extensive nature of the recurrences was probably related to aggressive tumor biology rather than to the minimally invasive surgical technique. In some of the cases, however, the pattern of recurrence, characterized by the development of multiple intraperitoneal or port site metastases, suggested that laparoscopic dissection and pneumoperitoneum might have contributed to tumor spread.[13-16] One group treated three patients for recurrent pheochromocytomatosis that developed after laparoscopic adrenalectomy.[17] These patients were found to have multiple small tumor nodules in the adrenalectomy bed during open reoperation after removal of apparently benign pheochromocytomas. Fragmentation of the tumor and excessive tumor manipulation during the laparoscopic dissection were considered the probable mechanisms of tumor recurrence.

These reports highlight the need for caution in approaching large, malignant, or potentially malignant adrenal tumors. Surgeons who attempt a laparoscopic approach in this setting should be highly experienced in laparoscopic adrenalectomy techniques, and the tumor should be well circumscribed and not locally invasive. The use of a hand port may be a valuable adjunct to resection in these cases. Regardless of the specific surgical approach followed, wide excision of the lesion along with the surrounding periadrenal fat is crucial for minimizing recurrence rates in this population.

Outcome Evaluation

The safety and efficacy of laparoscopic adrenalectomy for the removal of small, benign adrenal tumors have been clearly estab-lished. Rates of conversion to open adrenalectomy in high-volume centers have ranged from 3% to 13%, and operating times have averaged 2 to 3 hours.[9,11,18-23] Most patients are now discharged from the hospital within 24 to 48 hours after operation. Although no prospective, randomized trial comparing laparoscopic with open adrenalectomy has been carried out, several retrospective studies have consistently shown that the laparoscopic approach is associated with decreased pain, a shorter hospital stay, and a faster recovery.[24-27] Complication rates have also been low, and overall, complications appear to be less common than with open adrenalectomy.[10]

The results of a laparoscopic approach in patients with large (> 6 cm) adrenal tumors or malignant primary or metastatic adrenal lesions have been reviewed[28]; generally, the conversion rates for large or malignant tumors have been higher than those reported in other laparoscopic adrenalectomy series. Overall, tumor recurrence rates after laparoscopic adrenalectomy have been low.[29-33] In one series, however, local or regional tumor recurrence developed in three of five patients with adrenocortical carcinomas that were treated laparoscopically.[34] Other groups have also published anecdotal reports of local tumor recurrences after resection of unsuspected adrenal carcinomas.[13-16] Whether these recurrences were related primarily to the surgical technique employed or to the underlying tumor biology is unclear. It would appear, therefore, that in most cases, primary adrenal malignancies are best approached in an open fashion unless the tumor is small and well circumscribed and the surgeon is highly experienced.

References

1. Mulatero P, Stowasser M, Loh K-C, et al: Increased diagnosis of primary aldosteronism, including surgically correctable forms, in centers from five continents. J Clin Endocrinol Metab 89:1045, 2004

2. Young WF Jr: Primary aldosteronism: a common and curable form of hypertension. Cardiol Rev 7:207, 1999

3. Young WF, Stanson AW, Thompson GB, et al: Role for adrenal venous sampling in primary aldosteronism. Surgery 136:1227, 2004

4. Brunt LM, Moley JF: Adrenal incidentaloma. World J Surg 25:905, 2001

5. Mansmann G, Lau J, Balk E, et al: The clinically inapparent adrenal mass: update in diagnosis and management. Endocr Rev 25:309, 2004

6. Reincke M: Subclinical Cushing's syndrome. Endocrinol Metab Clin N Am 29:43, 2000

7. Gagner M, Lacroix A, Bolte E, et al: Laparoscopic adrenalectomy: the importance of a flank approach in the lateral decubitus position. Surg Endosc 8:135, 1994

8. Mercan S, Seven R, Ozarmagan S, et al: Endoscopic retroperitoneal adrenalectomy. Surgery 118:1071, 1995

9. Bonjer HJ, Berends FJ, Kazemier G, et al: Endoscopic retroperitoneal adrenalectomy: lessons learned from 111 consecutive cases. Ann Surg 232:796, 2000

10. Brunt LM: The positive impact of laparoscopic adrenalectomy on complications of adrenal surgery. Surg Endosc 16:252, 2001

11. Gagner M, Pomp A, Heniford BT, et al: Laparoscopic adrenalectomy: lessons learned from 100 consecutive cases. Ann Surg 226:238, 1997

12. Wu T-H, Tsai S-H, Tsai C-Y, et al: Renovascular hypertension after laparoscopic adrenalectomy in a patient with adrenal adenoma. Nephron 74:464, 1996

13. Foxius A, Ramboux A, Lefebvre Y, et al: Hazards of laparoscopic adrenalectomy for Conn's adenoma. Surg Endosc 13:715, 1999

14. Deckers S, Derdelinckx L, Col V, et al: Peritoneal carcinomatosis following laparoscopic resection of an adrenocortical tumor causing primary hyperaldosteronism. Horm Res 52:97, 1999

15. Iino K, Oki Y, Sasano H: A case of adrenocortical carcinoma associated with recurrence after laparoscopic adrenalectomy. Clin Endocrinol 53:243, 2000

16. Iacconi P, Bendinelli C, Miccoli P, et al: Re: A case of Cushing's syndrome due to adrenocortical carcinoma 19 months after laparoscopic adrenalectomy (letter). J Urol 161:1580, 1999

17. Li ML, Fitzgerald PA, Price DC, et al: Iatrogenic pheochromocytomatosis: a previously unreported result of laparoscopic adrenalectomy. Surgery 130:1072, 2001

18. Terachi T, Matsuda T, Terai A, et al: Transperitoneal laparoscopic adrenalectomy: experience in 100 cases. J Endourol 11:361, 1997

19. Henry J-F, Defechereux T, Raffaelli M, et al: Complications of laparoscopic adrenalectomy: results of 169 consecutive cases. World J Surg 24:1342, 2000

20. Brunt LM, Moley JF, Doherty GM, et al: Outcomes analysis in patients undergoing laparoscopic adrenalectomy for hormonally active adrenal tumors. Surgery 130:629, 2001

21. Kebebew E, Siperstein AE, Duh Q-Y: Laparoscopic adrenalectomy: the optimal surgical approach. J Laparoendosc Adv Surg Tech 11:409, 2001

22. Lezoche E, Guerrieri M, Paganini AM, et al: Laparoscopic adrenalectomy by the transperitoneal approach. Surg Endosc 14:920, 2000

23. Zeh HJ, Udelsman R: One hundred laparoscopic adrenalectomies: a single surgeon's experience. Ann Surg Oncol 10:1012, 2003

24. Brunt LM, Doherty GM, Norton JA, et al: Laparoscopic compared to open adrenalectomy for benign adrenal neoplasms. J Am Coll Surg 183:1, 1996

25. Imai T, Kikumori T, Phiwa M, et al: A case-controlled study of laparoscopic compared with open lateral adrenalectomy. Am J Surg 178:50, 1999

26. Prinz RA: A comparison of laparoscopic and open adrenalectomies. Arch Surg 130:489, 1995

27. Thompson GB, Grant CS, van Heerden JA, et al: Laparoscopic versus open posterior adrenalectomy: a case-control study. Surgery 122:1132, 1997

28. Brunt L: Minimal access adrenal surgery. Surg Endosc (in press)

29. Heniford BT, Arca MJ, Walsh RM, et al: Laparoscopic adrenalectomy for cancer. Semin Surg Oncol 16:293, 1999

30. Henry J-F, Defechereux T, Gramatica L, et al: Should laparoscopic approach be proposed for large and/or potentially malignant adrenal tumors? Langenbecks Arch Surg 384:366, 1999

31. Hobart MG, Gill IS, Schweizer D, et al: Laparoscopic adrenalectomy for large-volume (> 5 cm) adrenal masses. J Endourol 14:149, 2000

32. Sarela A, Murphy I, Coit DG, et al: Metastasis to the adrenal gland: the emerging role of laparoscopic surgery. Ann Surg Oncol 10:1191, 2003

33. Miccoli P, Materazzi G, Mussi A, et al: A reappraisal of the indications for laparoscopic treatment of adrenal metastases. J Laparoendosc Adv Surg Tech 14:139, 2004

34. Kebebew E, Siperstein AE, Clark OH, et al: Results of laparoscopic adrenalectomy for suspected and unsuspected malignant adrenal neoplasms. Arch Surg 137:948, 2002

Acknowledgment

Figures 1, 2, 5, 6a, 7a, 8a, 9, 10   Tom Moore.

Robert J. Fitzgibbons, Jr., M.D., F.A.C.S., Alan T. Richards, M.D., F.A.C.S., and Thomas H. Quinn, Ph.D.

Herniorrhaphy is one of the most commonly performed operations in all of surgery. Worldwide, some 20 million groin hernia repairs are accomplished each year.[1] In the United States, over 1,000,000 herniorrhaphies are performed each year, of which 750,000 are for inguinal hernias, 166,000 for umbilical hernias, 97,000 for incisional hernias, 25,000 for femoral hernias, and 76,000 for miscellaneous hernias.[2] The significance of these large numbers is that small variations in practice patterns can have huge socioeconomic implications. Operations that might seem unimportant because they account for only a small percentage of herniorrhaphies actually are important in that they account for a large absolute number of procedures. Accordingly, though this chapter is necessarily selective, focusing on the most pertinent of the abdominal wall and groin herniorrhaphies being performed today, it addresses a wide variety of operative approaches to hernia repair.

Epidemiology of Hernia

Approximately 75% of all abdominal wall hernias occur in the groin. Inguinal hernias are more common on the right than on the left and are seven times more likely in males than in females. Indirect inguinal hernias are twice as common as direct hernias. Femoral hernias are much less common than either, accounting for fewer than 10% of all groin hernias; however, 40% of femoral hernias present as emergencies, with incarceration or strangulation, and mortality is higher for emergency repair than for elective repair. Femoral hernias are more common in older patients and in those who have previously undergone inguinal hernia repair. Females are at higher risk than males, by a factor of 4 to 1.[3]

The prevalence of abdominal wall hernias is difficult to determine, as illustrated by the wide range of published figures in the literature. The major reasons for this difficulty are (1) the lack of standardization in how inguinal and ventral hernias are defined, (2) the inconsistency of the data sources used (which include self-reporting by patients, audits of routine physical examinations, and insurance company databases, among others), and (3) the subjectivity of physical examination, even when done by trained surgeons. Prevalence was reported in a United States Health, Education and Welfare study conducted by interview in 1960 for hernia [*see Figure 1*].[4] Given that a number of persons must have had hernias without knowing it, it can be assumed that these figures underestimate the actual prevalence. Nevertheless, they provide a rough idea of the scope of the hernia problem.

Modern data concerning the risk of major complications from untreated abdominal wall hernias are scarce. Typically, surgeons are taught that all hernias, even if asymptomatic, should be repaired at diagnosis to prevent strangulation or bowel obstruction and that herniorrhaphy becomes more difficult the longer repair is delayed. As a result, it is hard to find a whole patient population in which at least some of the members do not undergo routine hernia repair regardless of symptoms. This state of affairs makes accurate estimates of the natural history of hernia impossible.

Examination of obscure data from the 1800s and some unique data from South America suggests that both the risk of complications from an untreated hernia and the operative mortality

from managing them have been overstated.[5] At the same time, it is becoming clear that abdominal wall herniorrhaphy is associated with a higher morbidity than was previously appreciated. Currently, numerous patients either choose or are counseled by their primary care physicians not to undergo herniorrhaphy if the hernia is not "bothering them too much." A better understanding of the natural history therefore becomes particularly important for identifying patient subgroups who might be at greater risk for complications.

Classification of Hernia Types

Numerous classification schemes for groin hernias have been devised, usually bearing the name of the responsible investigator or investigators (e.g., Casten, Lichtenstein, Gilbert, Robbins and Rutkow, Bendavid, Nyhus, and Schumpelick). The variety of classifications in current use indicates that the perfect system has yet to be developed.[6] The main problem in developing a single classification scheme suitable for wide application is that it is impossible to eliminate subjective measurements and thus impossible to ensure consistency from observer to observer. The advent of laparoscopic herniorrhaphy has further complicated the issue in that some of the measurements needed cannot be obtained via a laparoscopic approach. At present, the Nyhus system enjoys the greatest degree of acceptance [*see Table 1*].

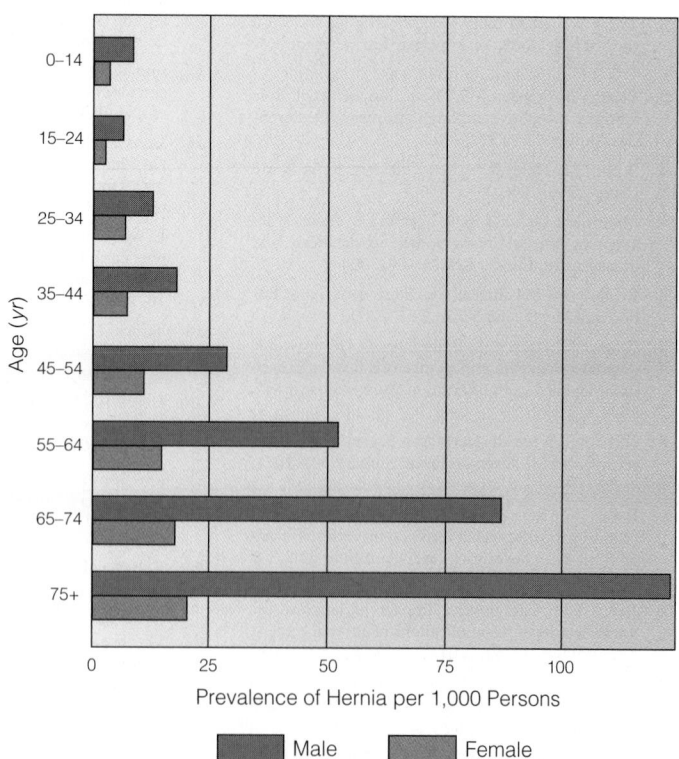

Figure 1 **Illustrated is the prevalence of abdominal wall hernia in the United States per 1,000 population, by age and sex.**[4]

Table 1 Nyhus Classification System for Groin Hernias

Type	Description
1	Indirect hernia with normal internal abdominal ring. This type is typically seen in infants, children, and small adults.
2	Indirect hernia in which internal ring is enlarged without impingement on the floor of the inguinal canal. Hernia does not extend to the scrotum.
3A	Direct hernia. Size is not taken into account.
3B	Indirect hernia that has enlarged enough to encroach upon the posterior inguinal wall. Indirect sliding or scrotal hernias are usually placed in this category because they are commonly associated with extension to direct space. This type also includes pantaloon hernias.
3C	Femoral hernia.
4	Recurrent hernia. Modifiers A, B, C, and D are sometimes added to type 4, corresponding to indirect, direct, femoral, and mixed, respectively.

Categorization of ventral abdominal wall hernias is not as critical as categorization of inguinal hernias, because there are so many different types of ventral hernias; however, Zollinger has proposed a classification scheme for these hernias that is frequently used [*see Table 2*]. Of the ventral hernias, incisional hernias are common enough to warrant their own discrete classification system. The scheme most often used for categorizing incisional hernias [*see Table 3*] represents the results of a 1998 consensus conference held in conjunction with the European Hernia Society's annual congress.[7] This system is important in that it affords investigators a reliable means of comparing results between one procedure and another or between one center and another.

Table 2 Zollinger Classification System for Ventral Abdominal Wall Hernias

Type	Examples
Congenital	Omphalocele Gastroschisis Umbilical (infant)
Acquired	Midline Diastasis recti Epigastric Umbilical (adult, acquired, paraumbilical) Median Supravesical (anterior, posterior, lateral) Paramedian Spigelian Interparietal
Incisional	Midline Paramedian Transverse Special operative sites
Traumatic	Penetrating, autopenetrating* Blunt Focal, minimal injury Moderate injury Extensive force or shear Destructive

*Penetration from host tissue such as bone.

Abdominal Wall Anatomy

The skin of the lower anterior abdominal wall is innervated by anterior and lateral cutaneous branches of the ventral rami of the seventh through 12th intercostal nerves and by the ventral rami of the first and second lumbar nerves. These nerves course between the lateral flat muscles of the abdominal wall and enter the skin through the subcutaneous tissue.

The first layers encountered beneath the skin are Camper's and Scarpa's fasciae in the subcutaneous tissue. The only significance of these layers is that when sufficiently developed, they can be reapproximated to provide another layer between a repaired inguinal floor and the outside. The major blood vessels of this superficial fatty layer are the superficial inferior and superior epigastric vessels, the intercostal vessels, and the superficial circumflex iliac vessels (which are branches of the femoral vessels).

The external oblique muscle is the most superficial of the great flat muscles of the abdominal wall [*see Figure 2*]. This muscle arises from the posterior aspects of the lower eight ribs and interdigitates with both the serratus anterior and the latissimus dorsi at its origin. The posterior portion of the external oblique muscle is oriented vertically and inserts on the crest of the ilium. The anterior portion of the muscle courses inferiorly and obliquely toward the midline and the pubis. The muscle fibers themselves are of no interest to the inguinal hernia surgeon until they give way to form its aponeurosis, which occurs well above the inguinal region. The obliquely arranged anterior inferior fibers of the aponeurosis of the external oblique muscle fold back on themselves to form the inguinal ligament, which attaches laterally to the anterior superior iliac spine. In most persons, the medial insertion of the inguinal ligament is dual: one portion of the ligament inserts on the pubic tubercle and the pubic bone, whereas the other portion is fan-shaped and spans the distance between the inguinal ligament proper and the pectineal line of the pubis. This fan-shaped portion of the inguinal ligament is called the lacunar ligament. It blends laterally with Cooper's ligament (or, to be anatomically correct, the pectineal ligament). The more medial fibers of the aponeurosis of the external oblique muscle divide into a medial crus and a lateral crus to form the external or superficial inguinal ring, through which the spermatic cord (or the round ligament) and branches of the ilioinguinal and genitofemoral nerves pass. The rest of the medial fibers insert into the linea alba after contributing to the anterior portion of the rectus sheath.

Beneath the external oblique muscle is the internal abdominal oblique muscle. The fibers of the internal abdominal oblique muscle fan out following the shape of the iliac crest, so that the superior fibers course obliquely upward toward the distal ends of the lower three or four ribs while the lower fibers orient themselves inferomedially toward the pubis to run parallel to the external oblique aponeurotic fibers. These fibers arch over the round ligament or the spermatic cord, forming the superficial part of the internal (deep) inguinal ring.

Beneath the internal oblique muscle is the transversus abdominis. This muscle arises from the inguinal ligament, the inner side of the iliac crest, the endoabdominal fascia, and the lower six costal cartilages and ribs, where it interdigitates with the lateral diaphragmatic fibers. The medial aponeurotic fibers of the transversus abdominis contribute to the rectus sheath and insert on the pecten ossis pubis and the crest of the pubis, forming the falx inguinalis. Infrequently, these fibers are joined by a portion of the internal oblique aponeurosis; only when this occurs is a true conjoined tendon formed.[8]

Aponeurotic fibers of the transversus abdominis also form the structure known as the aponeurotic arch. It is theorized that con-

Table 3 Classification System for Incisional Hernias

Parameter	Categories

Location	Vertical
	    Midline, above or below umbilicus
	    Midline, including umbilicus
	    Paramedian
	Transverse
	    Above or below umbilicus
	    Crosses midline
	Oblique
	    Above or below umbilicus
	    Combined

Size*	< 5 cm 5–10 cm > 10 cm
Recurrence	Primary Multiply recurrent Stratification for type of previous repair

Reducibility	Yes
	    Obstruction
	    No obstruction
	No
	    Obstruction
	    No obstruction

Symptoms	Asymptomatic Symptomatic

*Difficult to measure consistently.

traction of the transversus abdominis causes the arch to move downward toward the inguinal ligament, thereby constituting a form of shutter mechanism that reinforces the weakest area of the groin when intra-abdominal pressure is raised. The area beneath the arch varies. Many authorities believe that a high arch, resulting in a larger area from which the transversus abdominis is by definition absent, is a predisposing factor for a direct inguinal hernia. The transverse aponeurotic arch is also important because the term is used by many authors to describe the medial structure that is sewn to the inguinal ligament in many of the older inguinal hernia repairs.

The rectus abdominis forms the central anchoring muscle mass of the anterior abdomen. It arises from the fifth through seventh costal cartilages and inserts on the pubic symphysis and the pubic crest. It is innervated by the seventh through 12th intercostal nerves, which laterally pierce the aponeurotic sheath of the muscle. The semilunar line is the slight depression in the aponeurotic fibers coursing toward the muscle. In a minority of persons, the small pyramidalis muscle accompanies the rectus abdominis at its insertion. This muscle arises from the pubic symphysis. It lies within the rectus sheath and tapers to attach to the linea alba, which represents the conjunction of the two rectus sheaths and is the major site of insertion for three aponeuroses from all three lateral muscle layers. The line of Douglas (i.e., the arcuate line of the rectus sheath) is formed at a variable distance between the umbilicus and the inguinal space because the fasciae of the large flat muscles of the abdominal wall contribute their aponeuroses to the anterior surface of the muscle, leaving only transversalis (or transverse) fascia to cover the posterior surface of the rectus abdominis.

The innervation of the anterior wall muscles is multifaceted. The seventh through 12th intercostal nerves and the first and second lumbar nerves provide most of the innervation of the lateral muscles, as well as of the rectus abdominis and the overlying skin.

The nerves pass anteriorly in a plane between the internal oblique muscle and the transversus abdominis, eventually piercing the lateral aspect of the rectus sheath to innervate the muscle therein. The external oblique muscle receives branches of the intercostal nerves, which penetrate the internal oblique muscle to reach it. The anterior ends of the nerves form part of the cutaneous innervation of the abdominal wall. The first lumbar nerve divides into the ilioinguinal nerve and the iliohypogastric nerve [*see Figure 3*]. These important nerves lie in the space between the internal oblique muscle and the external oblique aponeurosis. They may divide within the psoas major or between the internal oblique muscle and the transversus abdominis. The ilioinguinal nerve may communicate with the iliohypogastric nerve before innervating the internal oblique muscle. The ilioinguinal nerve then passes through the external inguinal ring to run parallel to the spermatic cord, while the iliohypogastric nerve pierces the external oblique muscle to innervate the skin above the pubis. The cremaster muscle fibers, which are derived from the internal oblique muscle, are innervated by the genitofemoral nerve. There can be considerable variability and overlap.

The blood supply of the lateral muscles of the anterior wall comes primarily from the lower three or four intercostal arteries, the deep circumflex iliac artery, and the lumbar arteries. The rectus abdominis has a complicated blood supply that derives from the superior epigastric artery (a terminal branch of the internal thoracic [internal mammary] artery), the inferior epigastric artery (a branch of the external iliac artery), and the lower intercostal arteries. The lower intercostal arteries enter the sides of the muscle after traveling between the oblique muscles; the superior and

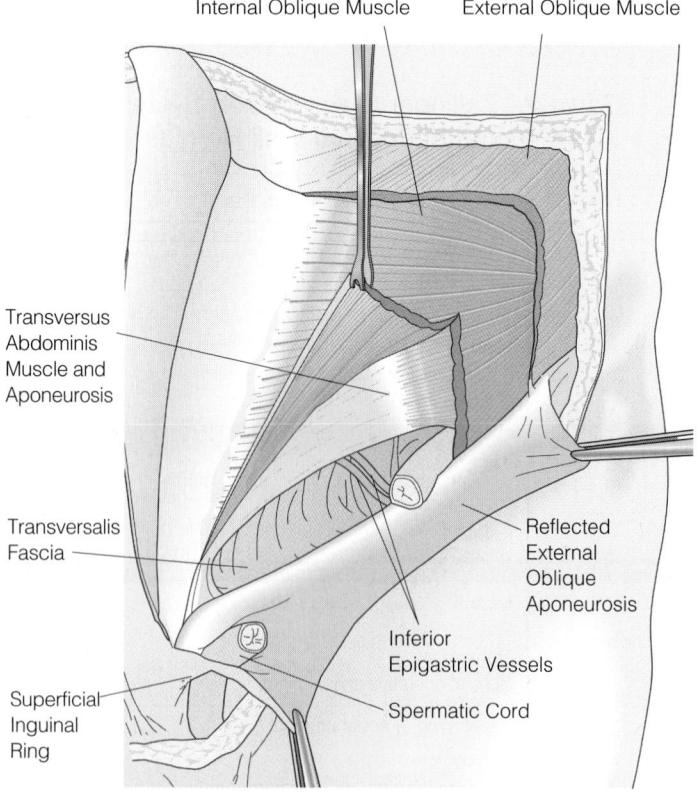

Figure 2 **Depicted is the relationship of the great flat muscles of the abdominal wall to the groin.**

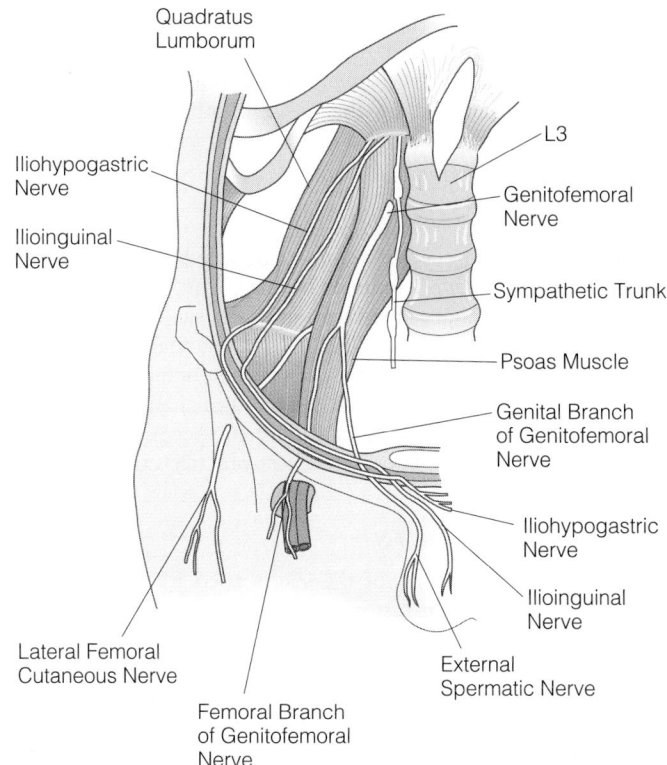

Quadratus
Lumborum

Iliohypogastric
Nerve

Ilioinguinal
Nerve

L3

Genitofemoral
Nerve

Sympathetic Trunk

Psoas Muscle

Genital Branch
of Genitofemoral
Nerve

Iliohypogastric
Nerve

Ilioinguinal
Nerve

Lateral Femoral
Cutaneous Nerve

External
Spermatic Nerve

Femoral Branch
of Genitofemoral
Nerve

Figure 3 **Shown are the important nerves of the lower abdominal wall.**

the inferior epigastric arteries enter the rectus sheath and anastomose near the umbilicus.

The endoabdominal fascia is the deep fascia covering the internal surface of the transversus abdominis, the iliacus, the psoas major and minor, the obturator internus, and portions of the periosteum. It is a continuous sheet that extends throughout the extraperitoneal space and is sometimes referred to as the wallpaper of the abdominal cavity. Commonly, the endoabdominal fascia is subclassified according to the muscle being covered (e.g., iliac fascia or obturator fascia).

The transversalis fascia is particularly important for inguinal hernia repair because it forms anatomic landmarks known as analogues or derivatives. The most significant of these analogues for hernia surgeons are the iliopectineal arch, the iliopubic tract, the crura of the deep inguinal ring, and Cooper's ligament (i.e., the pectineal ligament). The superior and inferior crura form a "monk's hood"–shaped sling around the deep inguinal ring. This sling has functional significance, in that as the crura of the ring are pulled upward and laterally by the contraction of the transversus abdominis, a valvular action is generated that helps preclude indirect hernia formation. The iliopubic tract is the thickened band of the transversalis fascia that courses parallel to the more superficially located inguinal ligament. It is attached to the iliac crest laterally and inserts on the pubic tubercle medially. The insertion curves inferolaterally for 1 to 2 cm along the pectineal line of the pubis to blend with Cooper's ligament, ending at about the midportion of the superior pubic ramus. Cooper's ligament is actually a condensation of the periosteum and is not a true analogue of the transversalis fascia.

Hesselbach's inguinal triangle is the site of direct inguinal hernias. As viewed from the anterior aspect, the inguinal ligament forms the base of the triangle, the edge of the rectus abdominis

forms the medial border, and the inferior epigastric vessels form the superolateral border. (It should be noted, however, that Hesselbach actually described Cooper's ligament as the base.)

Below the iliopubic tract are the critical anatomic elements from which a femoral hernia may develop. The iliopectineal arch separates the vascular compartment that contains the femoral vessels from the neuromuscular compartment that contains the iliopsoas muscle, the femoral nerve, and the lateral femoral cutaneous nerve. The vascular compartment is invested by the femoral sheath, which has three subcompartments: (1) the lateral, containing the femoral artery and the femoral branch of the genitofemoral nerve; (2) the middle, containing the femoral vein; and (3) the medial, which is the cone-shaped cul-de-sac known as the femoral canal. The femoral canal is normally a 1 to 2 cm blind pouch that begins at the femoral ring and extends to the level of the fossa ovalis. The femoral ring is bordered by the superior pubic ramus inferiorly, the femoral vein laterally, and the iliopubic tract (with its curved insertion onto the pubic ramus) anteriorly and medially. The femoral canal normally contains preperitoneal fat, connective tissue, and lymph nodes (including Cloquet's node at the femoral ring), which collectively make up the femoral pad. This pad acts as a cushion for the femoral vein, allowing expansion such as might occur during a Valsalva maneuver, and serves as a plug to prevent abdominal contents from entering the thigh. A femoral hernia exists when the blind end of the femoral canal becomes an opening (the femoral orifice) through which a peritoneal sac can protrude.

Between the transversalis fascia and the peritoneum is the preperitoneal space. In the midline behind the pubis, this space is known as the space of Retzius; laterally, it is referred to as the space of Bogros. The preperitoneal space is of particular importance for surgeons because many of the inguinal hernia repairs (see below) are performed in this area. The inferior epigastric vessels, the deep inferior epigastric vein, the iliopubic vein, the rectusial vein, the retropubic vein, the communicating rectusioepigastric vein, the internal spermatic vessels, and the vas deferens are all encountered in this space.[9]

Inguinal Herniorrhaphy: Choice of Procedure

The major indication for a surgeon to choose any one inguinal hernia repair over another is personal experience with a particular operation. Thus, in theory, any patient can be considered a candidate for any of these procedures. Some general guidelines are useful, however. The overriding consideration should be the need to tailor the operation to the patient's particular hernia. For example, a simple Marcy repair would be completely adequate for a pediatric patient with a Nyhus type 1 hernia but not for an elderly patient who has an indirect hernia in conjunction with extensive destruction of the inguinal floor. The conventional anterior prosthetic repairs are particularly useful in high-risk patients because they can easily be performed with local anesthesia. On the other hand, giant prosthetic reinforcement of the visceral sac (GPRVS), especially when bilateral, necessitates general or regional anesthesia and thus is best for patients with bilateral direct or recurrent hernias or, perhaps, for patients with connective tissue disorders that appear to be associated with their hernia. If surgery has previously been done in either the anterior or the preperitoneal space, the surgeon should choose a procedure that uses the undissected space. If local or systemic infection is present, a nonprosthetic repair is usually considered preferable, though the newer biologic prosthesis now being evaluated may eventually change this view. Uncorrected coagulopathy is a contraindication to elective repair.

Inguinal Herniorrhaphy: Conventional Anterior Nonprosthetic Repairs

ANESTHESIA

Local anesthesia is entirely adequate, especially when combined with I.V. infusion of a rapid-acting, short-lasting, amnesic, and anxiolytic agent such as propofol. This is the approach most commonly employed in specialty hernia clinics. In general practice, general anesthesia is preferred. This approach is reasonable in fit patients but is associated with a higher incidence of postoperative urinary retention.[10] If general anesthesia is used, a local anesthetic should be given at the end of the procedure as an adjuvant to reduce immediate postoperative pain. Spinal or epidural anesthesia can also be used but is less popular.

OPERATIVE TECHNIQUE

The various anterior nonprosthetic herniorrhaphies have a number of initial technical steps in common; they differ primarily with respect to the specific details of the actual repair.

Step 1: Administration of Local Anesthetic

Generally, we use a solution containing 50 ml of 0.5% lidocaine with epinephrine and 50 ml of 0.25% bupivacaine with epinephrine; the epinephrine is optional and may be omitted in patients who have a history of coronary artery disease. In an adult of normal size, 70 ml of this solution is injected before preparation and draping: 10 ml is placed medial to the anterior superior iliac spine to block the ilioinguinal nerve, and the other 60 ml is used as a field block along the orientation of the eventual incision in the subcutaneous and deeper tissues. Care is taken to ensure that some of the material is injected into the areas of the pubic tubercle and Cooper's ligament, which are easily identified by tactile sensation (except in very obese patients). Intradermal injection is unnecessary because by the time the surgeon is scrubbed and the patient draped, anesthesia is complete. The remaining 30 ml is reserved for discretionary use during the procedure. With this technique, endotracheal intubation is avoided and the patient can be aroused from sedation periodically to perform Valsalva maneuvers to test the repair.

Step 2: Initial Incision

Traditionally, the skin is opened by making an oblique incision between the anterior superior iliac spine and the pubic tubercle. For cosmetic reasons, however, many surgeons now prefer a more horizontal skin incision placed in the natural skin lines. In either case, the incision is deepened through Scarpa's and Camper's fasciae and the subcutaneous tissue to expose the external oblique aponeurosis. The external oblique aponeurosis is then opened through the external inguinal ring.

Step 3: Mobilization of Cord Structures

The superior flap of the external oblique fascia is dissected away from the anterior rectus sheath medially and the internal oblique muscle laterally. The iliohypogastric nerve is identified at this time; it can be either left in situ or freed from the surrounding tissue and isolated from the operative field by passing a hemostat under the nerve and grasping the upper flap of the external oblique aponeurosis. Routine division of the iliohypogastric nerve along with the ilioinguinal nerve is practiced by some surgeons but is not advised by most. The cord structures are then bluntly dissected away from the inferior flap of the external oblique aponeurosis to expose the shelving edge of the inguinal ligament and the iliopubic tract. The cord structures are lifted en masse

with the fingers of one hand at the pubic tubercle so that the index finger can be passed underneath to meet the ipsilateral thumb or the fingers of the other hand. Mobilization of the cord structures is completed by means of blunt dissection, and a Penrose drain is placed around them so that they can be retracted during the procedure.

Step 4: Division of Cremaster Muscle

Complete division of the cremaster muscle has been common practice, especially with indirect hernias. The purposes of this practice are to facilitate identification of the sac and to lengthen the cord for better visualization of the inguinal floor. Almost always, however, adequate exposure can be obtained by opening the muscle longitudinally, which reduces the chances of damage to the cord and prevents testicular descent. Accordingly, the latter approach should be considered best practice unless there are extenuating circumstances.

Step 5: High Ligation of Sac

The term high ligation of the sac is used frequently in discussing hernia repair; its historical significance has ingrained it in the descriptions of most of the older operations. For our purposes in this chapter, high ligation of the sac should be considered equivalent to reduction of the sac into the preperitoneal space without excision. The two methods work equally well and are highly effective. Some surgeons believe that sac inversion results in less pain (because the richly innervated peritoneum is not incised) and may be less likely to cause adhesive complications. To date, however, no randomized trials have been done to determine whether this is so.[11] Sac eversion in lieu of excision does protect intra-abdominal viscera in cases of unrecognized incarcerated sac contents or sliding hernia.

Step 6: Management of Inguinal Scrotal Hernial Sacs

Some surgeons consider complete excision of all indirect inguinal hernial sacs important. The downside of this practice is that the incidence of ischemic orchitis from excessive trauma to the cord rises substantially. The logical sequela of ischemic orchitis is testicular atrophy, though this presumed relationship has not been conclusively proved. In our view, it is better to divide an indirect inguinal hernial sac in the midportion of the inguinal canal once it is clear that the hernia is not sliding and no abdominal contents are present. The distal sac is not removed, but its anterior wall is opened as far distally as is convenient. Contrary to the opinion commonly voiced in the urologic literature, this approach does not result in excessive postoperative hydrocele formation.

Step 7: Repair of Inguinal Floor

Methods of repairing the inguinal floor differ significantly among the various repairs and thus are described separately [see Details of Specific Repairs, below].

Step 8: Relaxing Incision

A relaxing incision is made through the anterior rectus sheath and down to the rectus abdominis, extending superiorly from the pubic tubercle for a variable distance, as determined by the degree of tension present. Some surgeons prefer to "hockey-stick" the incision laterally at the superior end. The posterior rectus sheath is strong enough to prevent future incisional herniation. This relaxing incision works because as the anterior rectus sheath separates, the various components of the abdominal wall are displaced laterally and inferiorly.

Step 9: Closure

Closure of the external oblique fascia serves to reconstruct the superficial (external) ring. The external ring must be loose enough to prevent strangulation of the cord structures yet tight enough to ensure that an inexperienced examiner will not confuse a dilated ring with a recurrence. A dilated external ring is sometimes referred to as an industrial hernia, because over the years it has occasionally been a problem during preemployment physical examinations. Scarpa's fascia and the skin are closed to complete the operation.

Details of Specific Repairs

Marcy repair The Marcy repair is the simplest nonprosthetic repair performed today. Its main indication is for treatment of Nyhus type 1 hernias (i.e., indirect inguinal hernias in which the internal ring is normal). It is appropriate for children and young adults in whom there is concern about the long-term effects of prosthetic material. The essential features of the Marcy repair are high ligation of the sac and narrowing of the internal ring. Displacing the cord structures laterally allows the placement of sutures through the muscular and fascial layers [*see Figure 4*].

Bassini repair Edoardo Bassini (1844–1924) is considered the father of modern inguinal hernia surgery. By combining high ligation of a hernial sac with reconstruction of the inguinal floor and taking advantage of the developing disciplines of antisepsis and anesthesia, he was able to reduce morbidity and mortality substantially. Before Bassini's achievements, elective herniorrhaphy was almost never recommended, because the results were so bad. Bassini's operation, known as the radical cure, became the gold standard for inguinal hernia repair for most of the 20th century.

The initial steps in the procedure are essentially as already described (see above). Bassini felt that the incision in the external oblique aponeurosis should be as superior as possible while still allowing the superficial external ring to be opened,[12] so that the

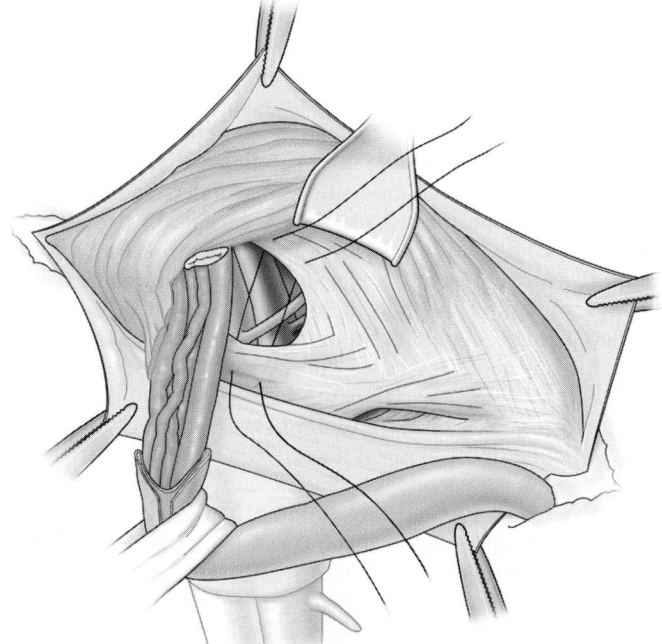

Figure 4 **Inguinal herniorrhaphy: Marcy repair. The deep inguinal ring is narrowed medially with several sutures that approximate the transverse aponeurotic arch to the iliopubic tract.**

reapproximation suture line created later in the operation would not be directly over the suture line of the inguinal floor reconstruction. Whether this technical point is significant is debatable. Bassini also felt that lengthwise division of the cremaster muscle followed by resection was important for ensuring that an indirect hernial sac could not be missed and for achieving adequate exposure of the inguinal floor.

After performing the initial dissection and the reduction or ligation of the sac, Bassini began the reconstruction of the inguinal floor by opening the transversalis fascia from the internal inguinal ring to the pubic tubercle, thereby exposing the preperitoneal fat, which was bluntly dissected away from the undersurface of the superior flap of the transversalis fascia [*see Figure 5a*]. This step allowed him to properly prepare the deepest structure in his famous "triple layer" (comprising the transversalis fascia, the transversus abdominis, and the internal oblique muscle).

The first stitch in Bassini's repair includes the triple layer superiorly and the periosteum of the medial side of the pubic tubercle, along with the rectus sheath. In current practice, however, most surgeons try to avoid the periosteum of the pubic tubercle so as to decrease the incidence of osteitis pubis. The repair is then continued laterally, and the triple layer is secured to the reflected inguinal ligament (Poupart's ligament) with nonabsorbable sutures. The sutures are continued until the internal ring is closed on its medial side [*see Figure 5b*]. A relaxing incision was not part of Bassini's original description but now is commonly added.

Concerns about injuries to neurovascular structures in the preperitoneal space as well as to the bladder led many surgeons, especially in North America, to abandon the opening of the transversalis fascia. The unfortunate consequence of this decision is that the proper development of the triple layer is severely compromised. In lieu of opening the floor, a forceps (e.g., an Allis clamp) is used to grasp tissue blindly in the hope of including the transversalis fascia and the transversus abdominis. The layer is then sutured, along with the internal oblique muscle, to the reflected inguinal ligament as in the classic Bassini repair. The structure grasped in this modified procedure is sometimes referred to as the conjoined tendon, but this is not correct because of the variability in what is actually grasped in the clamp. This imprecise "good stuff to good stuff" approach almost certainly accounts for the inferior results achieved with the Bassini procedure in the United States.

Maloney darn The Maloney darn gets its name from the way in which a long nylon suture is repeatedly passed between the tissues to create a weave that one might consider similar to a mesh. After initial preparation of the groin (see above), a continuous nylon suture is used to oppose the transversus abdominis, the rectus abdominis, the internal oblique muscle, and the transversalis fascia medially to Poupart's ligament laterally. The suture is continued into the muscle around the cord and is woven in and out to form a reinforcement around the cord. On the lateral side of the cord, it is sutured to the inguinal ligament and tied. The darn is a second layer. The sutures are placed either parallel or in a crisscross fashion and are plicated well into the inguinal ligament below. The darn must be carried well over the medial edge of the inguinal canal. Once the darn is complete, the external oblique muscle is closed over the cord structures. The Maloney darn can be considered a forerunner of the mesh repairs, in that the purpose of the darn is to provide a scaffold for tissue ingrowth.[13]

Shouldice repair Steps 1 through 6 are performed essentially as previously described (see above). Particular importance

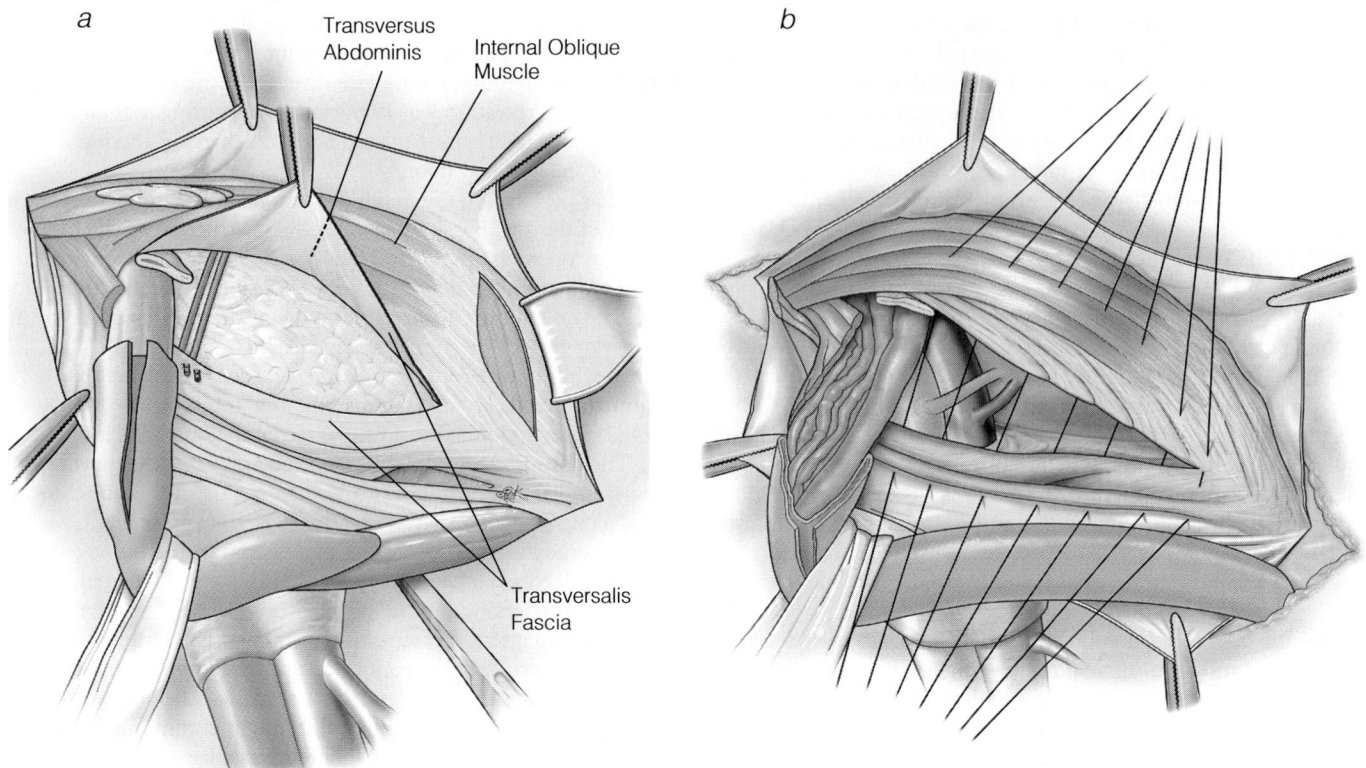

a

Transversus
Abdominis

Internal Oblique
Muscle

Transversalis
Fascia

b

Figure 5 **Inguinal herniorrhaphy: Bassini repair. (*a*) The transversalis fascia has been opened and the preperitoneal fat stripped away to prepare the deepest structure in Bassini's triple layer (comprising the transversalis fascia, the transversus abdominis, and the internal oblique muscle). (*b*) The triple layer superiorly is approximated to the inguinal ligament, beginning medially at the pubic tubercle and extending laterally until the deep inguinal ring is sufficiently narrowed.**

is placed on freeing of the cord from its surrounding adhesions, resection of the cremaster muscle, high dissection of the hernial sac, and division of the transversalis fascia during the initial steps of the procedure.[14] A continuous nonabsorbable suture (typically of monofilament steel wire) is used to repair the floor. The Shouldice surgeons believe that a continuous suture distributes tension evenly and prevents potential defects between interrupted sutures that could lead to recurrence.

The repair is started at the pubic tubercle by approximating the iliopubic tract laterally to the undersurface of the lateral edge of the rectus abdominis [*see Figure 6a*]. The suture is continued laterally, approximating the iliopubic tract to the medial flap, which is made up of the transversalis fascia, the internal oblique muscle, and the transversus abdominis. Eventually, four suture lines are developed from the medial flap. The continuous suture is extended to the internal ring, where the lateral stump of the cremaster muscle is picked up to form a new internal ring. Next, the direction of the suture is reversed back toward the pubic tubercle, approximating the medial edges of the internal oblique muscle and the transversus abdominis to Poupart's ligament, and the wire is tied to itself and then to the first knot [*see Figure 6b*]. Thus, two suture lines are formed by the first suture.

A second wire suture is started near the internal ring, approximating the internal oblique muscle and the transversus abdominis to a band of external oblique aponeurosis superficial and parallel to Poupart's ligament—in effect, creating a second, artificial Poupart's ligament. This third suture line ends at the pubic crest. The suture is then reversed, and a fourth suture line is constructed in a similar manner, superficial to the third line. At the

Shouldice clinic, the cribriform fascia is always incised in the thigh, parallel to the inguinal ligament, to make the inner side of the lower flap of the external oblique aponeurosis available for these multiple layers. In general practice, however, this step is commonly omitted.

The results at the Shouldice clinic have been truly outstanding and continue to be so today. For a time, the Shouldice repair was the gold standard against which all newer procedures were compared. The major criticism of this operation is that it is difficult to teach because surgeons have problems understanding what is really being sewn to what. Unless one is specifically trained at the Shouldice clinic and has the opportunity to work with the surgeons there, one may find it hard to identify the various layers in the medial flap reliably and reproducibly—a step that is crucial for developing the multiple suture lines. To compound the difficulty, modifications developed outside the Shouldice clinic have given rise to different versions of the procedure. For example, some surgeons use three continuous layers instead of four for reconstruction of the inguinal floor.

McVay Cooper's ligament repair This operation is similar to the Bassini repair, except that it uses Cooper's ligament instead of the inguinal ligament for the medial portion of the repair. Interrupted sutures are placed from the pubic tubercle laterally along Cooper's ligament, progressively narrowing the femoral ring; this constitutes the most common application of the repair—namely, treatment of a femoral hernia [*see Figure 7*]. The last stitch in Cooper's ligament is known as a transition stitch and includes the inguinal ligament. This stitch has two purposes: (1) to com-

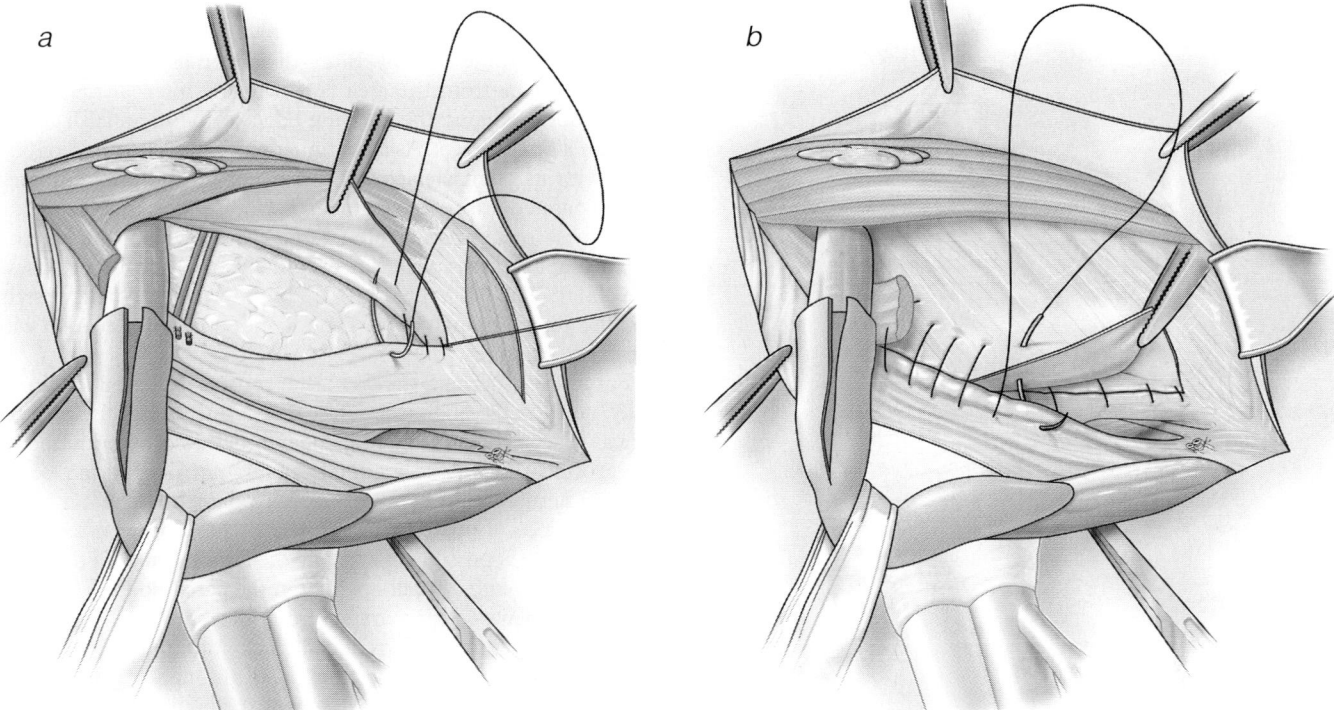

Figure 6 **Inguinal herniorrhaphy: Shouldice repair. (*a*) The first suture line starts at the pubic tubercle by approximating the iliopubic tract laterally to the undersurface of the lateral edge of the rectus abdominis. The suture is continued laterally, approximating the iliopubic tract to the medial flap (made up of the transversalis fascia, the internal oblique muscle, and the transversus abdominis). (*b*) The second suture line begins after the stump of the divided cremaster muscle has been picked up. The direction of the suture is reversed back toward the pubic tubercle, approximating the medial edges of the internal oblique muscle and the transversus abdominis to Poupart's ligament. Two more suture lines will be constructed by approximating the internal oblique muscle and the transversus abdominis to a band of the inferior flap of the external oblique aponeurosis superficial and parallel to Poupart's ligament—in effect, creating a second and a third artificial Poupart's ligament.**

plete the narrowing of the femoral ring by approximating the inguinal ligament to Cooper's ligament, as well as to the medial tissue, and (2) to provide a smooth transition to the inguinal ligament over the femoral vessel so that the repair can be continued laterally (as in a Bassini repair). Given the considerable tension required to bridge such a large distance, a relaxing incision should always be used. In the view of many authorities, this tension results in more pain than is noted with other herniorrhaphies and predisposes to recurrence. For this reason, the McVay repair is rarely chosen today, except in patients with a femoral hernia or patients with a specific contraindication to mesh repair.

Subinguinal femoral hernia repair Femoral hernias in females can easily be approached via a groin incision with dissection into the fossa ovalis beneath the inguinal ligament without the external oblique fascia being opened. The defect can be either closed with sutures or bridged with a mesh plug prosthesis [*see Figure 8*]. Larger femoral hernias in females and all femoral hernias in males are better treated with a McVay Cooper's ligament repair.

Pediatric hernia repair Children and young adults commonly present with an indirect sac only, with no discernible destruction of the inguinal floor. An extensive repair is not indicated: nearly all such patients are cured with sac ligation or eversion alone. A Marcy repair is the most extensive procedure that should be considered in this population.

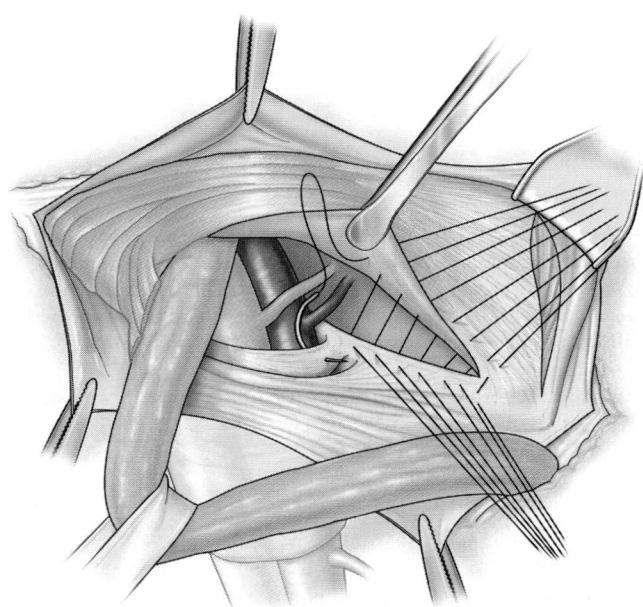

Figure 7 **Inguinal herniorrhaphy: McVay Cooper's ligament repair. The lateral stitch is the transition stitch to the femoral sheath and the inguinal ligament.**

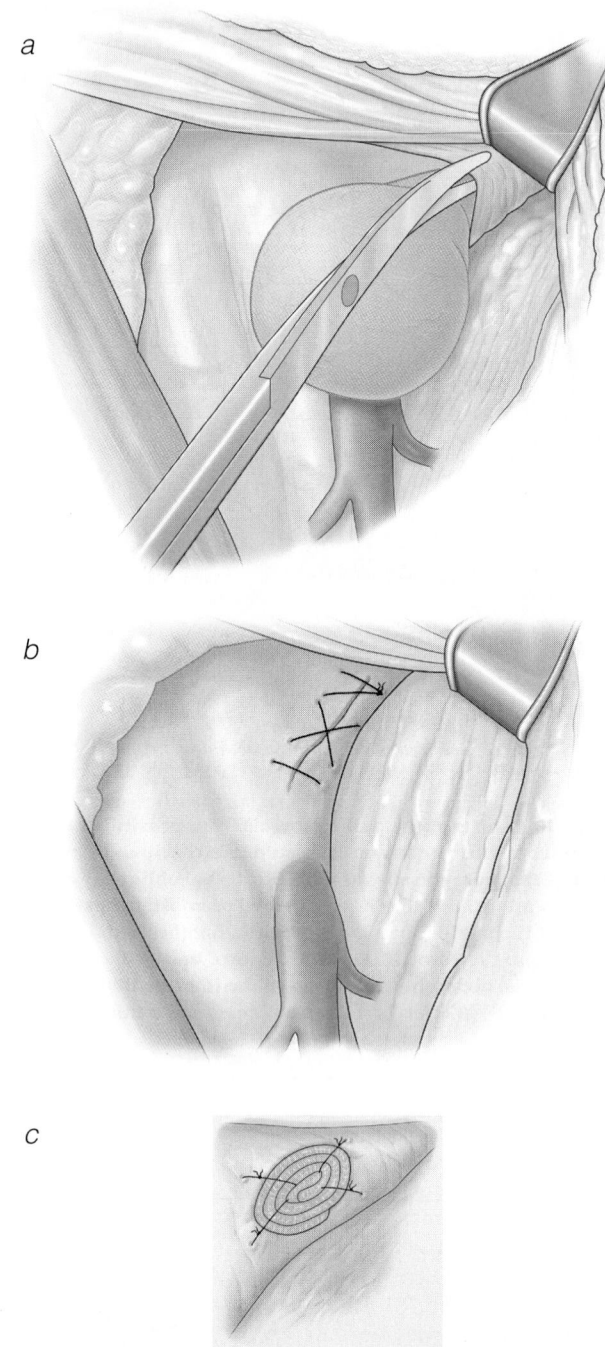

Figure 8 **Inguinal herniorrhaphy: femoral hernia repair in females. The femoral canal is opened by dividing the inguinal ligament, the lacunar ligament, or both to facilitate reduction of the contents of the hernia. (*a*) The repair is then accomplished with either a continuous suture (*b*) or a mesh plug (*c*).**

Inguinal Herniorrhaphy: Conventional Anterior Prosthetic Repairs

LICHTENSTEIN REPAIR

Steps 1 through 6

The first six steps of a Lichtenstein repair are very similar to the first six steps of a conventional anterior nonprosthetic repair [*see* Inguinal Herniorrhaphy: Conventional Anterior Nonprosthetic Repairs, *above*], but there are certain technical points that are worthy of emphasis. The external oblique aponeurosis is generously freed from the underlying anterior rectus sheath and internal oblique muscle and aponeurosis in an avascular plane from a point at least 2 cm medial to the pubic tubercle to the anterior superior iliac spine laterally. Blunt dissection is continued in this avascular plane from the area lateral to the internal ring to the pubic tubercle along the shelving edge of the inguinal ligament and the iliopubic tract. As a continuation of this same motion, the cord with its cremaster covering is swept off the pubic tubercle and separated from the inguinal floor. Besides mobilizing the cord, these maneuvers create a large space beneath the external oblique aponeurosis that can eventually be used for prosthesis placement. The ilioinguinal nerve, the external spermatic vessels, and the genital branch of the genitofemoral nerve all remain with the cord structures.

For indirect hernias, the cremaster muscle is incised longitudinally, and the sac is dissected free and reduced into the preperitoneal space. Theoretically, this operation could be criticized on the grounds that if the inguinal floor is not opened, an occult femoral hernia might be overlooked. To date, however, an excessive incidence of missed femoral hernias has not been reported. In addition, it is possible to evaluate the femoral ring via the space of Bogros through a small opening in the canal floor.

Direct hernias are separated from the cord and other surrounding structures and reduced back into the preperitoneal space. Dividing the superficial layers of the neck of the sac circumferentially—which, in effect, opens the inguinal floor—usually facilitates reduction and helps maintain it while the prosthesis is being placed. This opening in the inguinal floor also allows the surgeon to palpate for a femoral hernia. Sutures can be used to maintain reduction of the sac, but they have no real strength in this setting; their main purpose is to allow the repair to proceed without being hindered by continual extrusion of the sac into the field, especially when the patient strains.

Step 7: Placement of Prosthesis

A mesh prosthesis is positioned over the inguinal floor. For an adult, the prosthesis should be at least 15 × 8 cm. The medial end is rounded to correspond to the patient's particular anatomy and secured to the anterior rectus sheath at least 2 cm medial to the pubic tubercle. A continuous suture of either nonabsorbable or long-lasting absorbable material should be used. Wide overlap of the pubic tubercle is important to prevent the pubic tubercle recurrences all too commonly seen with other operations. The suture is continued laterally in a locking fashion, securing the prosthesis to either side of the pubic tubercle (not into it) and then to the shelving edge of the inguinal ligament. The suture is tied at the internal ring.

Step 8: Creation of Shutter Valve

A slit is made at the lateral end of the mesh in such a way as to create two tails, a wider one (approximately two thirds of the total width) above and a narrower one below. The tails are positioned around the cord structures and placed beneath the external oblique aponeurosis laterally to about the anterior superior iliac spine, with the upper tail placed on top of the lower. A single interrupted suture is placed to secure the lower edge of the superior tail to the lower edge of the inferior tail—in effect, creating a shutter valve. This step is considered crucial for preventing the indirect recurrences occasionally seen when the tails are simply reapproximated. The same suture incorporates the shelving edge of the inguinal ligament so as to create a domelike buckling effect over the direct space, thereby ensuring that there is no tension, especially when the patient assumes an upright postion. The Lichtenstein group has now developed a customized prosthesis with a built-in domelike configuration, which, in their view, makes suturing the approximated tails to the inguinal ligament unnecessary.

Step 9: Securing of Prosthesis

A few interrupted sutures are placed to attach the superior and medial aspects of the prosthesis to the underlying internal oblique muscle and rectus fascia [see Figure 9]. On occasion, the iliohypogastric nerve, which courses on top of the internal oblique muscle, penetrates the medial flap of the external oblique aponeurosis. In this situation, the prosthesis should be slit to accommodate the nerve. The prosthesis can be trimmed in situ, but care should be taken to maintain enough laxity to allow for the difference between the supine and the upright positions, as well as for possible shrinkage of the mesh.

Step 10: Repair of Femoral Hernia

If a femoral hernia is present, the posterior surface of the mesh is sutured to Cooper's ligament after the inferior edge has been attached to the inguinal ligament, thereby closing the femoral canal.

Step 11: Closure

Closure is accomplished in the same manner as in a conventional anterior nonprosthetic repair.

PLUG-AND-PATCH REPAIR

The mesh plug technique was first developed by Gilbert and subsequently modified by Rutkow and Robbins, Millikan, and others [see Figure 10].[15-17] The groin is entered via a standard

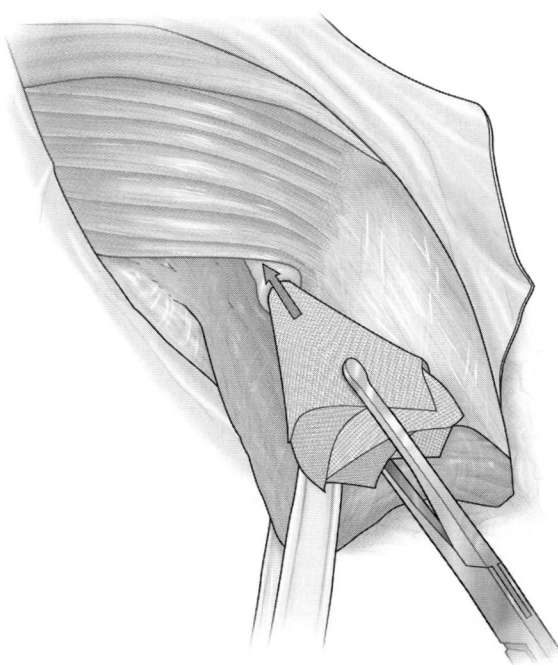

Figure 10 Inguinal herniorrhaphy: Gilbert repair. Depicted is the mesh plug technique for repair of an inguinal hernia. A flat sheet of polypropylene mesh is rolled up like a cigarette or formed into a cone (as shown here), inserted into the defect, and secured to either the internal ring (for an indirect hernia) or the neck of the defect (for a direct hernia) with interrupted sutures. Prefabricated mesh plugs are now available.

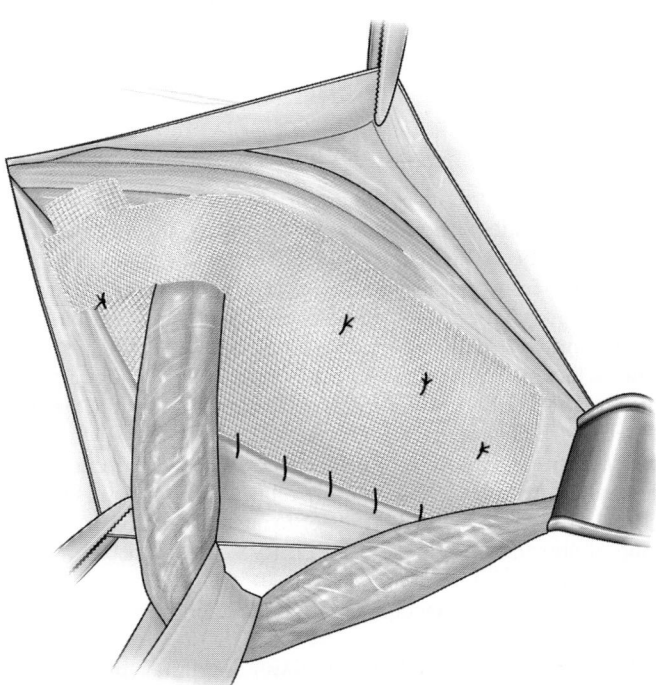

Figure 9 Inguinal herniorrhaphy: Lichtenstein repair. A mesh prosthesis is positioned over the inguinal floor and secured to the rectus sheath with a continuous suture. A slit is made in the mesh to accommodate the cord structures, and the two tails are secured to each other and to the shelving edge of the inguinal ligament with a single interrupted suture. The superior and medial aspects of the prosthesis are secured to the internal oblique muscle and the rectus fascia with a few interrupted sutures.

anterior approach. The hernial sac is dissected away from surrounding structures and reduced into the preperitoneal space. A flat sheet of polypropylene mesh is rolled up like a cigarette, tied, inserted in the defect, and secured with interrupted sutures to either the internal ring (for an indirect hernia) or the neck of the defect (for a direct hernia).

A prefabricated prosthesis that has the configuration of a flower is commercially available and is recommended by Rutkow and Robbins. This prosthesis is tailored to each patient's particular anatomy by removing some of the "petals" to avoid unnecessary bulk. Many surgeons consider this step important for preventing erosion into surrounding structures (e.g., the bladder); indeed, such complications have been reported, albeit rarely.

Millikan further modified the procedure by recommending that the inside petals be sewn to the ring of the defect. For an indirect hernia, the inside petals are sewn to the internal oblique portion of the internal ring, which forces the outside of the prosthesis underneath the inner side of the defect and makes it act like a preperitoneal underlay. For direct hernias, the inside petals are sewn to Cooper's ligament and the shelving edge of the inguinal ligament is sewn to the conjoined tendon, which, again, forces the outside of the prosthesis to act as an underlay.

The patch portion of the procedure is optional and involves placing a flat piece of polypropylene in the conventional inguinal space so that it widely overlaps the plug, much as in a Lichtenstein repair. The difference with a plug-and-patch repair is that only one or two sutures—or even, perhaps, no sutures—are used to secure the flat prosthesis to the underlying inguinal floor. Some surgeons, however, place so many sutures that they have in effect performed a Lichtenstein operation on top of the plug—a procedure sometimes referred to as a "plugstenstein."

To the credit of its proponents, the plug-and-patch repair, in all of its varieties, has been skillfully presented and has rapidly taken a significant share of the overall inguinal hernia market. It is not only fast but also extremely easy to teach, which has made it popular in both private and academic centers.

Inguinal Herniorrhaphy: Preperitoneal Nonprosthetic Repairs

A key technical issue in a preperitoneal hernia repair is how the surgeon chooses to enter the preperitoneal space. In fact, within this general class of repair, the method of entry into this space constitutes the major difference between the various procedures.

Many approaches to the preperitoneal space have been described. For example, the space can be entered either anteriorly or posteriorly. If an anterior technique is to be used, the initial steps of the operation are similar to those of a conventional anterior herniorrhaphy. If a posterior technique is to be used, any of several incisions (lower midline, paramedian, or Pfannenstiel) will allow an extraperitoneal dissection. The preperitoneal space can also be entered transabdominally. This is useful when the patient is undergoing a laparotomy for some other condition and the hernia is to be repaired incidentally. Of course, the transabdominal preperitoneal laparoscopic repairs described elsewhere [see 70 Laparoscopic Hernia Repair], by definition, enter the preperitoneal space from the abdomen.

Reed credits Annandale as being the first surgeon to describe the anterior method of gaining access to the preperitoneal space.[18] Bassini's operation, as classically performed, is technically an anterior preperitoneal operation, but it is never discussed in this group, because in the American variant of the procedure, the preperitoneal space is not entered. Cheatle suggested the posterior approach to the preperitoneal space for repair of an inguinal hernia but used a laparotomy to do it.[19] Cheatle and Henry subsequently modified the operation so as to render it entirely extraperitoneal (the so-called Cheatle-Henry approach), which made the procedure more acceptable to surgeons.[20]

The preperitoneal nonprosthetic method remained popular into the second half of the 20th century, championed by proponents such as Nyhus and Condon, who emphasized the importance of the iliopubic tract as the inferior border in primary closures of direct or indirect hernia defects.[21] Today, however, these operations are of little more than historical significance, because it is now universally agreed that better results are obtained in this space when a prosthesis is used. Indeed, after 1975, Nyhus and Condon began routinely placing a 6 × 14 cm piece of polypropylene mesh to buttress the primary repair in all patients with recurrent hernias.[22] When contraindications to a prosthesis are present [see Table 4], most surgeons would opt for a conventional anterior herniorrhaphy (e.g., a Bassini or Shouldice repair) rather than a preperitoneal nonprosthetic herniorrhaphy.

Inguinal Herniorrhaphy: Preperitoneal Prosthetic Repairs

The most important step in any preperitoneal prosthetic repair is the placement of a large prosthesis in the preperitoneal space on the abdominal side of the defect in the transversalis fascia. The theoretical advantage of this measure is that whereas in a conventional repair abdominal pressure might contribute to recurrence, in a preperitoneal repair, the abdominal pressure would actually help fix the mesh material against the abdominal wall, thereby adding strength to the repair. The hernia defect itself may or may not be closed, depending on the preference of the surgeon. The strength of the repair depends on the prosthesis rather

Table 4 Contraindications to Use of Prosthesis for Herniorrhaphy	
Local infection*[52]	Allergy
Systemic infection	Patient preference

*The newer biological prostheses made of human cadaver skin or of submucosa from porcine small intestine may be acceptable.

than on closure of the defect; however, such closure may decrease the seroma formation that inevitably occurs at the site of the undisturbed residual sac. Although these seromas almost always are self-limited and disappear with time, they can be confused with recurrences by both patients and referring physicians. Accordingly, some surgeons prefer to take every step possible to prevent them.

ANTERIOR APPROACH

Read-Rives Repair

The initial part of a Read-Rives repair, including the opening of the inguinal floor, is much like that of a classic Bassini repair. The inferior epigastric vessels are identified and the preperitoneal space completely dissected. The spermatic cord is parietalized by separating the ductus deferens from the spermatic vessels. A 12 × 16 cm piece of mesh is positioned in the preperitoneal space deep to the inferior epigastric vessels and secured with three sutures placed in the pubic tubercle, in Cooper's ligament, and in the psoas muscle laterally. The transversalis fascia is closed over the prosthesis and the cord structures replaced. The rest of the closure is accomplished much as in a conventional anterior prosthetic repair.

POSTERIOR APPROACH

Stoppa-Rignault-Wantz Repair (Giant Prosthetic Reinforcement of Visceral Sac)

GPRVS has its roots in the important contribution that Henri Fruchaud made to herniology. In describing the myopectineal orifice that bears his name [see Figure 11], Fruchaud, who was Stoppa's mentor, popularized a different approach to the etiology of inguinal hernias.[23] Instead of subdividing hernias into direct, indirect, and femoral and then examining their specific causes, he emphasized that the common cause of all inguinal hernias was the failure of the transversalis fascia to retain the peritoneum. This concept led Stoppa to develop GPRVS, which reestablishes the integrity of the peritoneal sac by inserting a large permanent prosthesis that entirely replaces the transversalis fascia over the myopectineal orifice of Fruchaud with wide overlapping of surrounding tissue. With GPRVS, the exact type of hernia present (direct, indirect, or femoral) is unimportant, because the abdominal wall defect is not addressed.

Step 1: skin incision A lower midline, inguinal, or Pfannenstiel incision can be used, depending on the surgeon's preference. The inguinal incision is placed 2 to 3 cm below the level of the anterior superior iliac spine but above the internal ring; it is begun at the midline and extended laterally for 8 to 9 cm.[24]

Step 2: preperitoneal dissection The fascia overlying the space of Retzius is opened without violation of the peritoneum. A combination of blunt and sharp dissection is continued later-

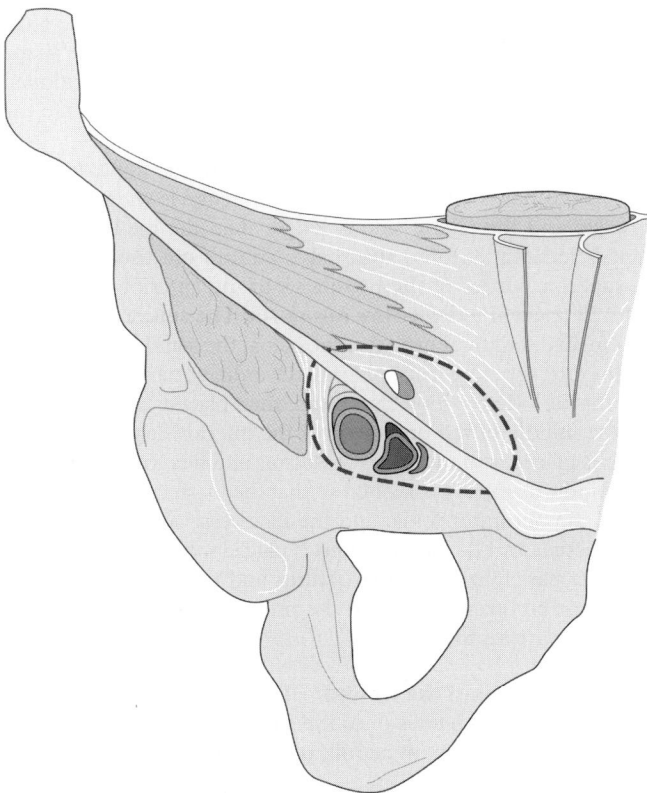

Figure 11 **Inguinal herniorrhaphy. Depicted is the myopectineal orifice of Fruchaud. The area is bounded superiorly by the internal oblique muscle and the transversus abdominis, medially by the rectus muscle and sheath, laterally by the iliopsoas muscle, and inferiorly by Cooper's ligament. Critical anatomic landmarks (e.g., the inguinal ligament, the spermatic cord, and the femoral vessels) are contained within this structure.**

the cord structures and reduced back into the peritoneal cavity. Large sacs may be difficult to mobilize from the cord without undue trauma if an attempt is made to remove the sac in its entirety. Accordingly, large sacs should be divided, with the distal portion left in situ and the proximal portion dissected away from the cord structures. Division of the sac is most easily accomplished by opening the sac on the side opposite the cord structures. A finger is placed in the sac to facilitate its separation from the cord. Downward traction is then placed on the cord structures to reduce any excessive fatty tissue (so-called lipoma of the cord) back into the preperitoneal space. This step prevents the "pseudorecurrences" that may occur if the abnormality palpated during the preoperative physical examination was not a hernia but a lipoma of the cord.

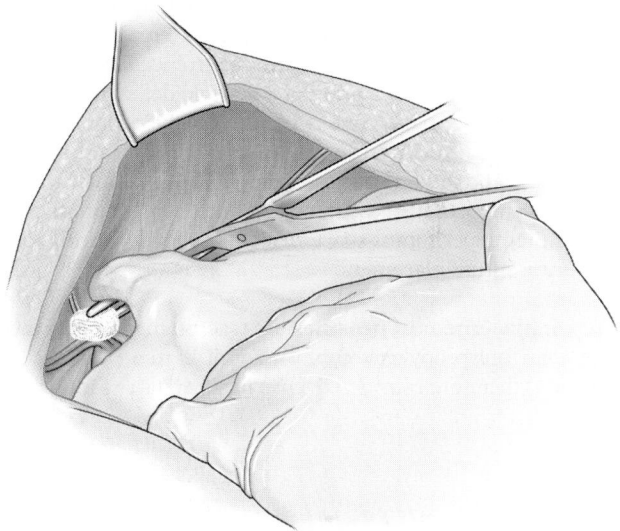

Figure 12 **Inguinal herniorrhaphy: preperitoneal repair. The preperitoneal space is widely dissected from the pubic tubercle to the anterior superior iliac spine. Shown here is isolation of an indirect hernial sac.**

ally posterior to the rectus abdominis and the inferior epigastric vessels. The preperitoneal space is completely dissected to a point lateral to the anterior superior iliac spine [*see Figure 12*]. The symphysis pubis, Cooper's ligament, and the iliopubic tract are identified. Inferiorly, the peritoneum is generously dissected away from the vas deferens and the internal spermatic vessels to create a large pocket, which will eventually accommodate a prosthesis without the possibility of rollup. In the inguinal approach, the anterior rectus sheath and the oblique muscles are incised for the length of the skin incision. The lower flaps of these structures are retracted inferiorly toward the pubis. The transversalis fascia is incised along the lateral edge of the rectus abdominis, and the preperitoneal space is entered; dissection then proceeds as previously indicated.

Step 3: management of hernial sac Direct hernial sacs are reduced during the course of the preperitoneal dissection. Care must be taken to stay in the plane between the peritoneum and the transversalis fascia, allowing the latter structure to retract into the hernia defect toward the skin. The transversalis fascia can be thin, and if it is inadvertently opened and incorporated with the peritoneal sac during reduction, a needless and bloody dissection of the abdominal wall is the result.

Indirect sacs are more difficult to deal with than direct sacs are, in that they often adhere to the cord structures. Trauma to the cord must be minimized to prevent damage to the vas deferens or the testicular blood supply. Small sacs should be mobilized from

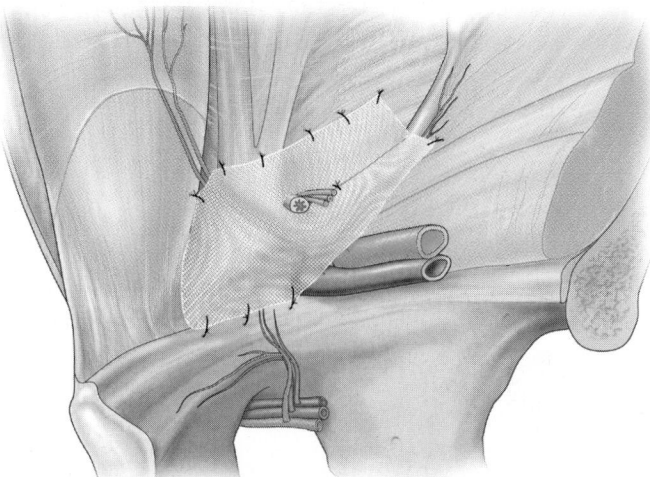

Figure 13 **Inguinal herniorrhaphy: preperitoneal repair. Illustrated is the placement of a mesh prosthesis in the preperitoneal space. The prosthesis is sewn to Cooper's ligament inferiorly and to the transverse fascia well above the hernia defect anteriorly, in the fashion described by Nyhus.**

Step 4: management of abdominal wall defect   It is this step that varies most from one author to another. In Nyhus's approach, the defect is formally repaired, and only then is a tailored mesh prosthesis sutured to Cooper's ligament and the transversalis fascia for reinforcement [*see Figure 13*]. In Rignault's approach, the defect is loosely closed to prevent an unsightly early postoperative bulge.[25] In Stoppa's and Wantz's approaches, the defect is usually left alone, but the transversalis fascia in the defect is occasionally plicated by suturing it to Cooper's ligament to prevent the bulge caused by a seroma in the undisturbed sac.

Step 5: parietalization of spermatic cord   The term parietalization of the spermatic cord, popularized by Stoppa, refers to a thorough dissection of the cord aimed at providing sufficient length to permit lateral movement of the structure [*see Figure 14*]. In Stoppa's view, this step is essential, in that it allows a prosthesis to be placed without having to be split laterally to accommodate the cord structures; the keyhole defect created when the prosthesis is split has been linked with recurrences. In Rignault's view, on the other hand, creation of a keyhole defect in the mesh to encircle the spermatic cord is preferable, the rationale being that this gives the prosthesis enough security to allow the surgeon to dispense with fixation sutures or tacks. Minimizing fixation in this area is important because of the numerous anatomic elements in the preperitoneal space that can be inadvertently damaged during suture placement.

Step 6: placement of prosthesis   Dacron mesh, being more pliable than polypropylene, conforms well to the preperitoneal space and is therefore considered particularly suitable for GPRVS.

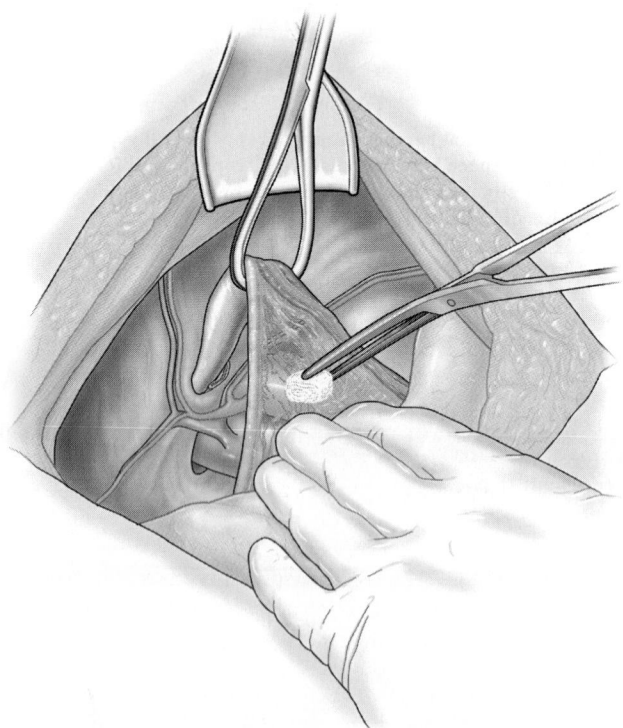

Figure 14   **Inguinal herniorrhaphy: preperitoneal repair. Illustrated is the parietalization of the spermatic cord. The spermatic vessels and the vas deferens are mobilized so that they move laterally. This step is carried out so that the surgeon can place a large prosthesis that widely overlaps the myopectineal orifice without having to slit the prosthesis to accommodate the cord structures.**

Stoppa's technique is most often associated with a single large prosthesis for bilateral hernias. The prosthesis is cut in the shape of a chevron [*see Figure 15a*], and eight clamps are positioned strategically around the prosthesis to facilitate placement into the preperitoneal space [*see Figure 15b*].

Unilateral repairs require a prosthesis that is approximately 15 × 12 cm but is cut so that the bottom edge is wider than the top edge and the lateral side is longer than the medial side. In Wantz's technique, three absorbable sutures are used to attach the superior border of the prosthesis to the anterior abdominal wall well above the defect [*see Figure 16*]. The sutures are placed from medial to lateral near the linea alba, the semilunar line, and the anterior superior iliac spine. A Reverdin suture needle facilitates this task. Three long clamps are then placed on each corner and the middle of the prosthesis of the inferior flap. The medial clamp is placed into the space of Retzius and held by an assistant. The middle clamp is positioned so that the mesh covers the pubic ramus, the obturator fossa, and the iliac vessels and is also held by the assistant. The lateral clamp is placed into the iliac fossa to cover the parietalized cord structures and the iliopsoas muscle. Care must be taken to prevent the prosthesis from rolling up as the clamps are removed.

Step 7: closure of the wound   The surgical wound is closed along anatomic guidelines once the surgeon is assured that there has been no displacement or rollup of the prosthesis.

KUGEL AND UGAHARY REPAIRS

The Kugel and Ugahary repairs were developed to compete with laparoscopic repairs. They require only a small (2 to 3 cm) skin incision placed 2 to 3 cm above the internal ring.[26,27] In Kugel's operation, the incision is oriented obliquely, with one third of the incision lateral to a point halfway between the anterior superior iliac spine and the pubic tubercle and the remaining two thirds medial to this point. The incision is deepened through the external oblique fascia, and the internal oblique muscle is bluntly spread apart. The transversalis fascia is opened vertically for a distance of about 3 cm, but the internal ring is not violated. The preperitoneal space is entered and a blunt dissection performed. The inferior epigastric vessels are identified to confirm that the dissection is being done in the correct plane. These vessels should be left adherent to the overlying transversalis fascia and retracted medially and anteriorly. The iliac vessels, Cooper's ligament, the pubic bone, and the hernia defect are identified by palpation. Most hernial sacs are simply reduced; the exceptions are large indirect sacs, which must sometimes be divided, with the distal sac left in situ and the proximal sac closed. To prevent recurrences, the cord structures are thoroughly parietalized to allow adequate posterior dissection.

The key to Kugel's procedure is a specially designed 8 × 12 cm prosthesis made of two pieces of polypropylene with a single extruded monofilament fiber located near its edge. The construction of the prosthesis allows it to be deformed so that it can fit through the small incision; once inserted, it springs open to regain its normal shape, providing a wide overlap of the myopectineal orifice. The prosthesis also has a slit on its anterior surface, through which the surgeon places a finger to facilitate positioning.

Ugahary's operation is similar to Kugel's, but it does not require a special prosthesis. In what is known as the gridiron technique, the preperitoneal space is prepared through a 3 cm incision, much as in a Kugel repair. The space is held open with a narrow Langenbeck retractor and two ribbon retractors. A 10 × 15 cm piece of polypropylene mesh is rolled onto a long forceps

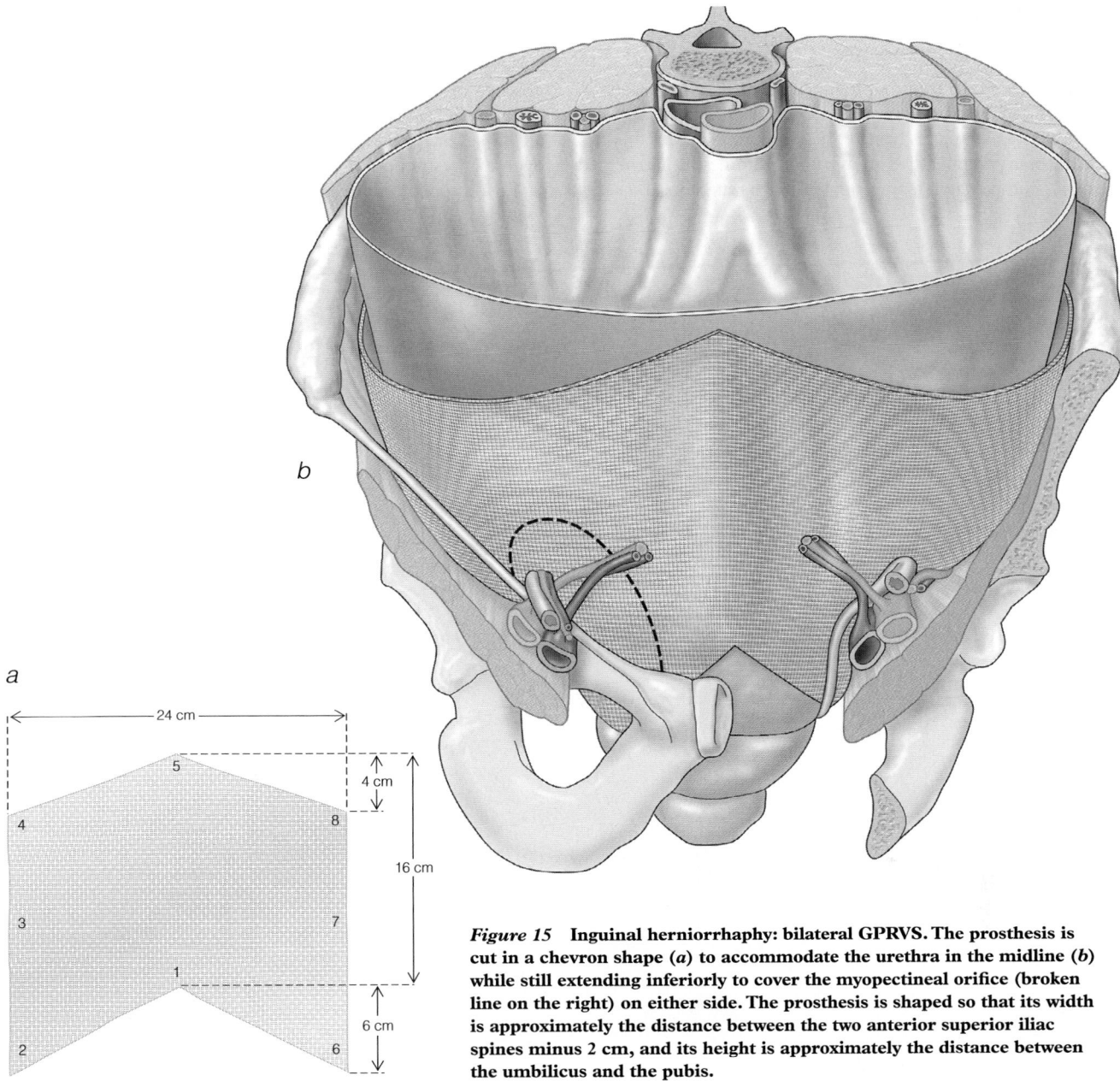

Figure 15 **Inguinal herniorrhaphy: bilateral GPRVS. The prosthesis is
cut in a chevron shape (*a*) to accommodate the urethra in the midline (*b*)
while still extending inferiorly to cover the myopectineal orifice (broken
line on the right) on either side. The prosthesis is shaped so that its width
is approximately the distance between the two anterior superior iliac
spines minus 2 cm, and its height is approximately the distance between
the umbilicus and the pubis.**

after the edges have been rounded and sutures placed to correspond to various anatomic landmarks. The forceps with the rolled-up mesh on it is introduced into the preperitoneal space, and the mesh is unrolled with the help of clamps and specific movements of the ribbon retractors.

Both operations have been very successful in some hands and have important proponents. However, because they are essentially blind repairs, considerable experience with them is required before the surgeon can be confident in his or her ability to place the patch properly.

COMBINED ANTERIOR-POSTERIOR APPROACH

Bilayer Prosthetic Repair

The bilayer prosthetic repair involves the use of a dumbbell-shaped prosthesis consisting of two flat pieces of polypropylene mesh connected by a cylinder of the same material. The purpose of this design is to allow the surgeon to take advantage of the pre-

sumed benefits of both anterior and posterior approaches by placing prosthetic material in both the preperitoneal space and the extraperitoneal space.

The initial steps are identical to those of a Lichtenstein repair. Once the conventional anterior space has been prepared, the preperitoneal space is entered through the hernia defect. Indirect hernias are reduced, and a gauze sponge is used to develop the preperitoneal space through the internal ring. For direct hernias, the transversalis fascia is opened, and the space between this structure and the peritoneum is developed with a gauze sponge. The deep layer of the prosthesis is deployed in the preperitoneal space, overlapping the direct and indirect spaces and Cooper's ligament. The superficial layer of the device occupies the conventional anterior space, much as in a Lichtenstein repair. It is slit laterally or centrally to accommodate the cord structures and then affixed to the area of the pubic tubercle, the middle of the inguinal ligament, and the internal oblique muscle with three or four interrupted sutures.

Inguinal Herniorrhaphy: Complications

POSTHERNIORRHAPHY GROIN PAIN

It is generally recognized that inguinal herniorrhaphy results in greater morbidity than was previously appreciated. Now that modern hernioplasty techniques have reduced recurrence rates to a minimum, chronic postoperative groin pain syndromes have emerged as the major complication facing inguinal hernia surgeons. In a crit-

ical review of inguinal herniorrhaphy studies between 1987 and 2000, the incidence of some degree of long-term groin pain after surgery was as high as 53% at 1 year (range, 0% to 53%).[28] In the absence of a standard raw database, it was somewhat difficult to extrapolate from these data, but the best estimate was that moderate to severe pain occurred in about 10% of patients and some degree of restriction of activity in about 25%.

Various postherniorrhaphy groin pain syndromes may develop,

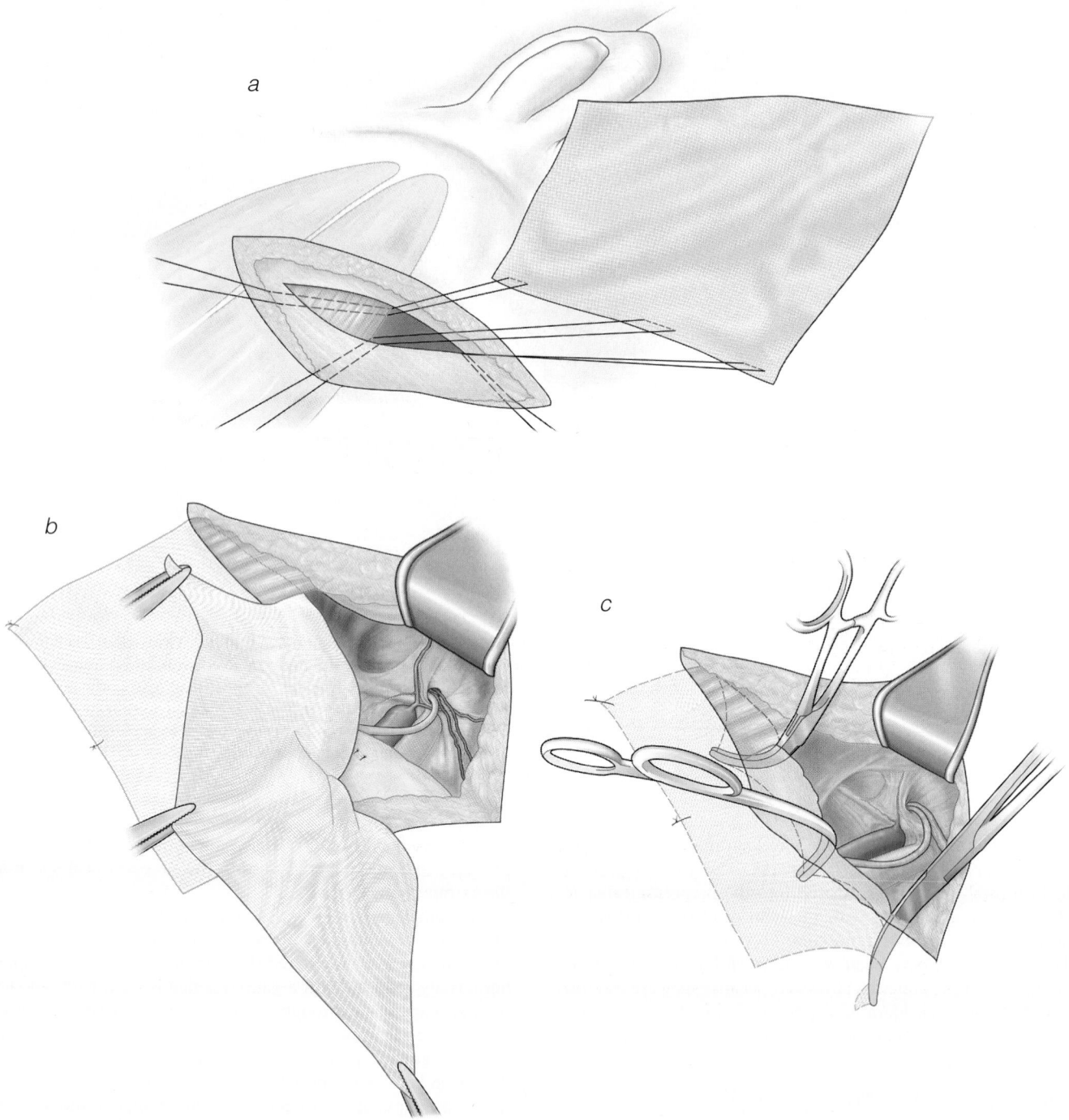

Figure 16 Inguinal herniorrhaphy: unilateral GPRVS (Wantz technique). The prosthesis is cut so that the inferior edge is wider than the superior edge by 2 to 4 cm and the lateral side is longer than the medial side. The width at the superior edge is approximately the distance between the umbilicus and the anterior superior iliac spine minus 1 cm, and the height is approximately 14 cm. Anteriorly, three sutures are placed—near the linea alba, near the semilunar line, and near the anterior superior iliac spine—from medial to lateral to fix the superior border (*a*). Three long clamps on the inferior edge (*b*) are used to implant the prosthesis deep into the preperitoneal space (*c*) with the peritoneal sac retracted cranially.

usually as a consequence of scarring, reaction to prosthetic material, or incorporation of a nerve in staples or suture material during the repair. Chronic postoperative groin pain occurs without regard to the type of repair performed. It can be classified into three general types, as follows:

1. Somatic (nociceptive) pain, the most common form, includes ongoing preoperative pathologic states that were the real causes of patients' pain preoperatively, usually related to ligament or muscle injury; new ligament or muscle injury caused by the operation; scar tissue; osteitis pubis; and reaction to prosthetic material.
2. Neuropathic pain is related to direct nerve damage. Accurate diagnosis is important because if the cause of pain is incorporation of a nerve in staples or sutures, effective surgical treatment is available. The nerves usually involved are the ilioinguinal nerve, the iliohypogastric nerve, the genital and femoral branches of the genitofemoral nerve, and the lateral cutaneous nerve of the thigh. The first two nerves are especially likely to be injured during a conventional herniorrhaphy, whereas the latter two are more likely to be damaged during a preperitoneal herniorrhaphy. Femoral nerve injury, fortunately, is extremely rare and is usually the result of a gross technical misadventure. Neuropathy is generally signaled by pain or paresthesia in the injured nerve's distribution; however, there is significant overlap in the distributions of these nerves, and as a result, it is frequently difficult to determine exactly which nerve is damaged.
3. Visceral pain is related to specific visceral functions; common examples are pain with urination and the dysejaculation syndrome.

Perhaps the most important single issue in dealing with postherniorrhaphy pain is whether the current pain is the same as or different from the pain that brought the hernia to the attention of the physician in the first place. If the latter is the case, efforts must be made to determine which of the numerous potential causative conditions is responsible. Computed tomography, ultrasonography, herniography, laparoscopy, and magnetic resonance imaging all are of diagnostic value in this setting. Of these, MRI has emerged as the most useful because of its ability to differentiate between muscle tears, osteitis pubis, bursitis, and stress fracture. A strain of the adductor muscle complex (comprising the adductor longus, the adductor brevis, the adductor magnus, and the gracilis) is a commonly overlooked cause of pain.

Treatment is difficult and often fails entirely. The difficulty is compounded when workers' compensation issues cloud the picture. The first possibility that must be ruled out is a recurrent hernia. As a rule, all three types of pain are best treated initially with reassurance and conservative treatment (e.g., anti-inflammatory medications and local nerve blocks); frequently, the complaint resolves spontaneously. The only exception to this rule might be the patient who complains of severe pain immediately (i.e., in the recovery room), who might be best treated with immediate reexploration before scar tissue develops. Otherwise, we scrupulously avoid reexploration in the first year after the procedure to allow for the possibility of spontaneous resolution. When groin exploration is required, neurectomy and neuroma excision, adhesiolysis, muscle or tendon repair, and foreign-body removal are all possibilities. The results are often less than satisfying.

ISCHEMIC ORCHITIS AND TESTICULAR ATROPHY

Orchitis or atrophy may result if the testicular blood supply is compromised during herniorrhaphy. Orchitis is defined as postoperative inflammation of the testicle occurring within the first 2 postoperative days. Patients experience painful enlargement and hardening of the testicle, usually associated with a low-grade fever; the pain is severe and may last several weeks. Ischemic orchitis is most likely attributable to thrombosis of the veins draining the testicle, caused by dissection of the spermatic cord. It may progress over a period of months and eventually result in testicular atrophy. This latter development is not inevitable, however. In fact, the occurrence of testicular atrophy is quite unpredictable, in that most patients with this condition have no history of any testicular problems associated with the index herniorrhaphy. Overall, the vast majority of patients who experience testicular problems as an immediate complication of herniorrhaphy go on to recover without atrophy. Bendavid, in a study of the incidence of testicular atrophy at the Shouldice Hospital, found that this complication occurred in only 19 (0.036%) of 52,583 primary inguinal hernia repairs and in only 33 (0.46%) of 7,169 recurrent inguinal hernia repairs.[29]

HEMORRHAGE

Postherniorrhaphy bleeding—usually the result of delayed bleeding from the cremasteric artery, the internal spermatic artery, or branches of the inferior epigastric vessels—can produce a wound or scrotal hematoma. Injuries to the deep circumflex artery, the corona mortis, or the external iliac vessels may result in a large retroperitoneal hematoma.

OSTEITIS PUBIS

Osteitis pubis has diminished in frequency since surgeons began to realize the importance of not placing sutures through the periosteum. In laparoscopic repairs, staples are used to attach the mesh to Cooper's ligament, which may cause osteitis in some cases.

PROSTHESIS-RELATED COMPLICATIONS

The increasingly liberal use of prosthetic material in conventional herniorrhaphy and the routine use of such material in laparoscopic herniorrhaphy make the discussion of complications related directly to foreign material a timely one. Tissue response, which is variable from person to person, can be so intense that the prosthetic material is deformed by contraction. Erosion can result in intestinal obstruction or fistulization, especially if there is physical contact between intestine and prosthesis.[30,31] Erosion into the cord structures has also been reported.[32]

INFECTION

The prostheses used for inguinal herniorrhaphies, unlike those used for ventral herniorrhaphies, rarely become infected. The reasons why the groin is apparently a protected area are unclear. When infections do occur in the groin, they can occasionally be successfully treated with drainage and prolonged antibiotic therapy; more often, however, the prosthesis must be removed. Rejection of the prosthesis because of an allergic response is possible but extremely rare. What patients call rejection in their histories is usually the result of infection.

Incisional Herniorrhaphy

Incisional hernias occur as a complication of previous surgery. They may be caused by poor surgical technique, rough handling of tissues, use of rapidly degraded absorbable suture materials for closing the abdomen, closure of the abdomen under tension, and infection (with or without clinical wound dehiscence).[33] Male sex, advanced age, morbid obesity, abdominal distention, cigarette smoking, pulmonary disease, and hypoalbuminemia have all been incriminated as associated predisposing conditions, but the exact nature of these associations has never been studied in well-controlled trials. Most authorities believe that the best way of preventing incisional hernias is to close abdominal wounds with continuous nonabsorbable monofilament sutures. This is a contentious issue among surgeons, because some feel that the new longer-lasting absorbable sutures are just as good and are less likely to cause suture sinus formation, which is reported in as many as 9% of patients whose abdomens are closed with a nonabsorbable suture.[34]

In 2000, a systematic review and meta-analysis of randomized controlled trials was published that used the MEDLINE and Cochrane Library databases in an effort to determine which suture material and technique best reduced the risk of incisional hernia.[35] The incidence of incisional hernia was significantly lower when nonabsorbable sutures were used in a continuous closure; however, the incidence of suture sinus formation and that of wound pain were significantly higher. The incidence of wound dehiscence or wound infection was not affected by suture material or closure method. Subgroup analyses of individual sutures showed no significant difference in incisional hernia rates between polydioxanone and polypropylene; however, rates were noticeably higher with polyglactin. The authors concluded that surgical practice in this area depended far more on tradition than on high-quality level I scientific evidence.

Continuous suturing is faster, and there has never been convincing evidence that it is inferior to interrupted fascial closure; accordingly, it is favored by most surgeons. In a continuous closure, stitches should be placed 1 cm away from the edge and 1 cm apart from each other. To prevent excessive tension, the length of the suture should be four times the length of the wound.[36] The abdominal wall may be closed with a mass technique, whereby the peritoneum and the anterior and posterior muscle sheaths are fused as a single layer.[37] Alternatively, a multilayered approach may be considered.

The incidence of incisional herniation depends on how the condition is defined. The best definition is any abdominal wall gap, with or without a bulge, that is perceptible on clinical examination or imaging by 1 year after the index operation. If a visible bulge is made part of the definition, the incidence will be underestimated. In the literature, the incidence of incisional herniation after a midline laparotomy ranges from 3% to 20% and doubles if the index operation was associated with infection.

Herniation is most common after midline and transverse incisions but is also well documented after paramedian, subcostal, appendectomy (gridiron), and Pfannenstiel incisions.[38] A 1995 analysis of 11 publications addressing ventral hernia incidence after various types of incisions found the risk to be 10.5%, 7.5%, and 2.5% for midline, transverse, and paramedian incisions, respectively.[34] Upper midline incisions are most likely to lead to ventral hernia formation; transverse and oblique incisions are the least likely. Muscle-splitting incisions probably are associated with a lower incidence of herniation, but they restrict access to the abdominal cavity. Males and females are at roughly equal risk, but early evisceration is more common in males. Most cases are detected within 1 year of surgery, and the basic cause is thought to be separation of aponeurotic edges in the early postoperative period. Incarceration and strangulation occur with significant frequency, and recurrence rates after operative repair approach 50%.

OPERATIVE TECHNIQUE

Simple Nonprosthetic Repair

Simple nonprosthetic repair of an incisional hernia is reserved for only the least complicated defects, because in large series of

unselected patients, the recurrence rate ranges from 25% to 55%.[7] If there is a solitary defect 3 cm or less in diameter, primary closure with nonabsorbable suture material is appropriate. Some surgeons perform a simple edge approximation after flaps are developed on either side of the defect. Others use a Mayo "vest-over-pants" repair. Various advancement and darn procedures have also been described.

A more substantial repair for these defects was popularized by Ramirez.[39] In this operation, known as the component separation technique, fascial planes are incised between muscle groups, so that, in effect, the abdominal wall is lengthened by allowing the muscle to separate on either side of a defect. The hernia can then be repaired primarily with less tension on the repair. This procedure is especially useful at contaminated hernia sites.

A similar procedure is the keel operation of Maingot, which was popular in the middle of the 20th century. The anterior rectus sheath is incised longitudinally, and the medial edge is allowed to rotate behind the rectus abdominis. This, in effect, lengthens the posterior rectus sheath, allowing it to be closed under less tension. The lateral edges of the incised rectus sheath on each side are then approximated to each other.

Onlay Prosthetic Repair

In this technique, a prosthetic onlay is placed over any of a wide variety of simple repairs. Large series of selected patients have documented acceptable results with onlay prosthetic repair, but most surgeons feel that this technique offers little advantage over the simple repair that the prosthesis overlies.[7]

Prosthetic Bridging Repair

Prosthetic bridging repair became popular in the 1990s, in keeping with the tension-free concept for inguinal herniorrhaphy. The basic principle underlying this technique is that for a prosthetic repair to be effective, the defect should be bridged. Although this repair is theoretically attractive, it has not been nearly as successful for incisional hernias as for inguinal hernias. The recurrence rate is especially high in obese patients.

When a hernia defect is bridged with a mesh prosthesis, every attempt should be made to isolate the material from the intra-abdominal viscera to prevent erosion and subsequent fistula formation or adhesive bowel obstruction. This can be accomplished by means of a peritoneal flap constructed from the peritoneal sac or omentum. When contact with intra-abdominal organs cannot be avoided, expanded polytetrafluoroethylene (e-PTFE) should be strongly considered for the prosthesis. Most authorities feel that complications are less likely with e-PTFE, though this has not been unequivocally shown to be the case.

Combined Fascial and Mesh Closure

The issue of contact between the intra-abdominal viscera and the prosthesis has been further addressed by techniques that combine features of the component separation technique with the tension-free concept. The posterior fascia is closed primarily, but the anterior fascia is allowed to remain open, so that there is no tension at all. The anterior fascia is then bridged with a prosthesis.

Sublay Prosthetic Repair

Sublay prosthetic repair, sometimes referred to as the retromuscular approach, is characterized by the placement of a large prosthesis in the space between the abdominal muscles and the peritoneum [*see Figure 17*]. It was popularized by Velamenta, Stoppa, and Wantz and is particularly suitable for large and multiply recurrent hernias when most of the abdominal wall must be

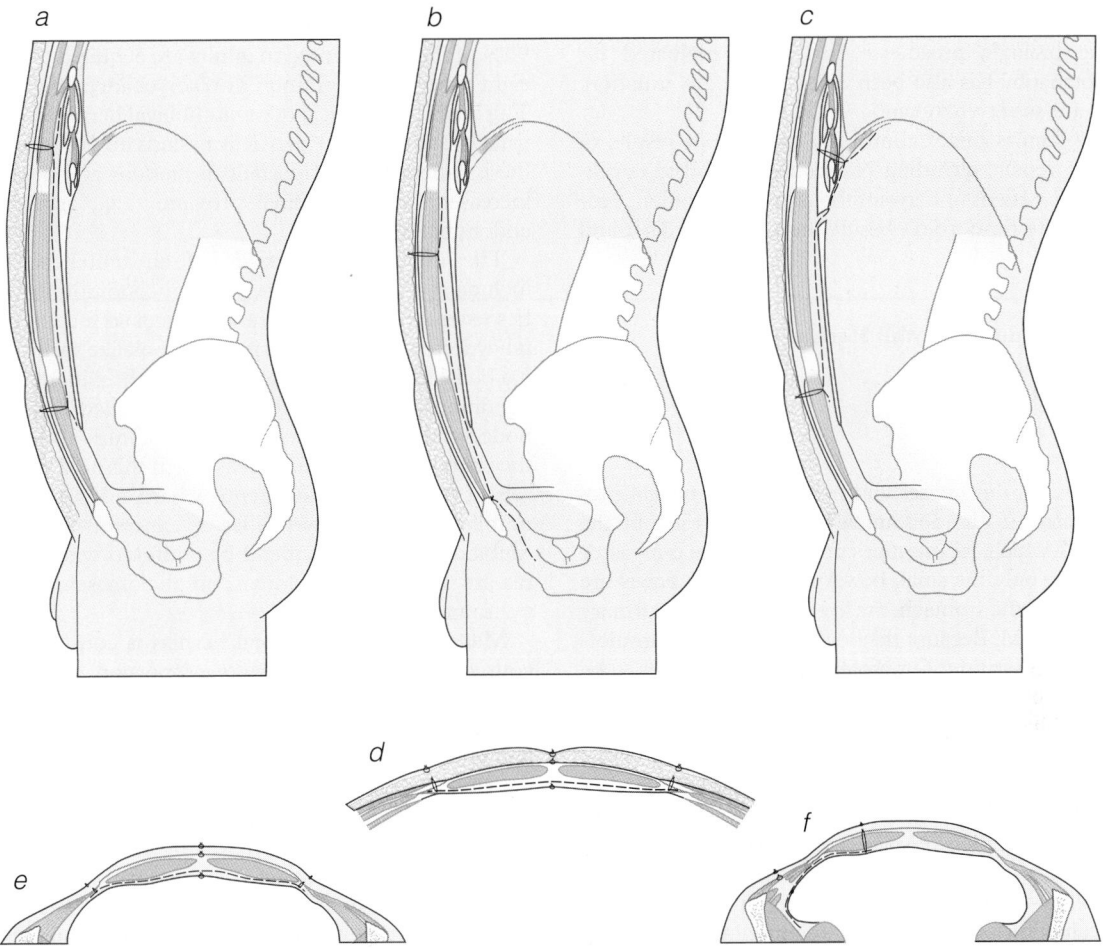

Figure 17 **Incisional herniorrhaphy: sublay prosthetic repair. The lateral views show sites of prosthesis implantation (broken lines) and suture fixation for incisional hernias in (*a*) the upper midline, (*b*) the lower midline, and (*c*) the subcostal region. The cross-sectional views show the same things for incisional hernias in (*d*) the upper midline, (*e*) the lower midline, and (*f*) the right lower quadrant (after appendectomy).**

reconstructed.[40-42] It is considered the most effective conventional incisional hernia repair and therefore the one against which other procedures must be measured.

The posterior rectus sheath is opened on each edge of the hernia defect and dissected away from the undersurface of the recti for a distance of 10 to 15 cm. The posterior rectus sheaths are then approximated to each other primarily. A large mesh prosthesis (composed of e-PTFE if the approximation of the posterior rectus sheath is inadequate) is then placed in this space outside the repaired posterior sheath but beneath the recti. The mesh is secured in this position with several sutures that are placed with a suture passer through small stab incisions at the periphery of the prosthesis and tied in the subcutaneous tissue above the fascia. The laparoscopic incisional herniorrhaphy discussed elsewhere [*see 70 Laparoscopic Hernia Repair*] was designed with the principles of this operation in mind.

COMPLICATIONS

Although prosthesis-related infection is rare with prosthetic inguinal herniorrhaphies, it remains a major problem with prosthetic incisional herniorrhaphies. It occurs in about 5% of repairs and can delay healing for prolonged periods. Risk factors for prosthesis infection include preexisting infection or ulceration of the skin overlying the hernia, obesity, incarcerated or obstructed

bowel within the hernia, and perforation of the bowel during hernia repair. Seromas are common, especially when a large prosthesis is required or there has been extensive flap dissection of the subcutaneous layer from the fascia. Untreated seromas commonly become infected secondarily. Suction drains can be useful but are likely to result in prosthesis infection if left in place too long. Strategies for preventing and managing seromas are largely based on empiricism and personal opinion; objective data are virtually nonexistent. It is not always necessary to remove the mesh prosthesis if infection develops. A trial of local wound care after opening the incision and debriding the infected area is warranted. As noted, some authorities believe that e-PTFE is less prone to infection. Nevertheless, once infection is established, e-PTFE prostheses (unlike mesh prostheses) usually have to be removed.

A dilemma arises when a patient has a large incisional hernia and the wound is contaminated either by skin infection or by injury to the bowel during mobilization. In this situation, a nonabsorbable mesh would have a significant chance of becoming infected, and an enterocutaneous fistula could complicate matters further. For these situations, an absorbable mesh made of polyglycolic acid is recommended to prevent evisceration. Granulation tissue forms over the mesh, making skin grafting possible. The mesh itself is absorbed in about 3 weeks, leaving no permanent foreign body to serve as a persistent focus of infection.

Unfortunately, however, recurrence of the incisional hernia is inevitable. The biologic prosthesis now being evaluated for inguinal herniorrhaphy has also been employed in this situation, but the results are as yet unknown.

Several other factors might contribute to the poor results of incisional hernia repair, including preexisting comorbid conditions for which the patient underwent the original operation, cancer-related debilitation, morbid obesity, the use of steroids, and chemotherapy.

Repair of Other Abdominal Wall Hernias

PERIUMBILICAL HERNIA

Gastroschisis

Gastroschisis is seen in fetuses and neonates. The typical presentation is a defect in the abdominal wall to the right of the umbilicus through which the intestines protrude. There is no associated sac. Usually, only the small bowel and the large bowel are eviscerated; however, the stomach, the liver, and the genitourinary system may be involved. Because the bowel is exposed to amniotic fluid, the maternal serum α-fetoprotein (AFP) level tends to be elevated, and the bowel may become thickened and dilated as a result. Bowel complications (e.g., malrotation and segmental atresia) are present in approximately 15% of cases of gastroschisis; however, other anomalies are uncommon. Gastroschisis occurs sporadically and is not associated with chromosome abnormalities, though some familial occurrences are reported.

After the presence of gastroschisis is confirmed, serial ultrasonographic follow-up is indicated for measurement of fetal growth and evaluation of bowel status. Counseling of a couple expecting a baby with gastroschisis should include assessment of the prognosis, description of the surgical and medical support the newborn is likely to need, and discussion with both the neonatologist and the pediatric surgeon.

Omphalocele (Exomphalos)

Omphalocele also is seen in fetuses and neonates. In this condition, a midline defect of the abdominal wall results in herniation of the bowel and intra-abdominal contents into the umbilical cord; the coverings of the hernia are therefore the coverings of the umbilical cord. The defect may be categorized according to whether the liver is present in the omphalocele sac. If the liver is present in the sac, the omphalocele is extracorporeal; if not, the omphalocele is intracorporeal. Omphalocele differs from gastroschisis in that the bowel contents are contained in a membrane, and thus, maternal serum AFP levels generally are not elevated. Often, ascites develops within the omphalocele sac.

Amniocentesis is indicated when an omphalocele is identified in a fetus, because approximately 30% of fetuses with an omphalocele have a chromosome abnormality. The most common such abnormalities are trisomies 18, 13, and 21; Turner syndrome (45, X); and triploidy. Beckwith-Wiedemann syndrome may also be associated with omphalocele. Approximately 67% to 88% of fetuses with an omphalocele have other anomalies as well. These associated anomalies often determine the prognosis.

Umbilical and Paraumbilical Hernia

An umbilical hernia is the result of improper healing of an umbilical scar, which leads to a fascial defect that is covered by skin. If the defect is to one side, it is called a paraumbilical hernia; this variant is more common in adults. The vast majority of umbilical hernias presenting in children are congenital, whereas 90% of those diagnosed in adults are acquired. These hernias are eight times more common in black children than in white ones. The onset of umbilical or paraumbilical hernia in older patients is usually sudden, and the defect tends to be relatively small. In these patients, it is important to look for an underlying cause of increased intra-abdominal pressure (e.g., ascites or an intra-abdominal tumor).

The differential diagnosis of an umbilical hernia should include so-called caput medusae, a condition in which varicosities extend radially from the umbilicus as a consequence of portal hypertension. These varicosities look like varicose veins, exhibit a bluish discoloration, and fill when the patient strains. Another condition to be considered is the so-called Sister Mary Joseph node, which is a metastatic deposit of intra-abdominal cancer at the umbilicus. The cancer cells reach this area via lymphatic vessels in the falciform ligament. A hard nodule is palpable at the umbilicus, and biopsy verifies its cancerous nature. Other periumbilical masses that might be confused with an umbilical hernia are umbilical granulomas, omphalomesenteric duct remnant cysts, and urachal cysts.

Management of umbilical hernias is conservative in children younger than 2 years. A large proportion of these defects heal spontaneously. Consequently, the usual practice is to observe the hernia until the child has reached 2 years of age, by which point about 80% of defects will have healed. Umbilical hernias persisting after the age of 2 years probably will not heal spontaneously and therefore must be treated surgically. The customary recommendation is to repair the hernia by the time the child reaches 5 years of age, so that he or she is not subjected to psychological trauma when participating in normal school sports activities.

In young patients, compression of the hernia with a bandage or a coin is commonly attempted. This practice probably has no real effect but has gained acceptance by parents; the high rate of spontaneous closure fuels the perception (or misperception) of efficacy. In patients who do require surgery—namely, children older than 2 years and adults—the repair used depends on the size of the hernia. Most of the defects are small and can therefore be closed by simple suturing. Alternatively, the Mayo technique may be used. A subumbilical semilunar incision is made, the hernial sac is opened, the contents of the sac are reduced into the abdomen, and the sac is excised. An overlapping or waistcoating technique is then employed, in which the upper edge of the linea alba is placed so as to overlap the lower and fixed in place with a nonabsorbable mattress suture. This technique is controversial: some surgeons argue that the overlapping layers serve only to increase the tension on the repair, thus inviting recurrence.

For larger hernias, particularly those in adults, a popular approach is to dissect the sac away from the undersurface of the skin of the umbilicus and reduce it into the preperitoneal space. The fascial defect is then bridged with a prosthesis without fear of contact with the intra-abdominal viscera. The prosthesis is sutured circumferentially to the defect; alternatively, it can be sutured to the undersurface of the posterior rectus sheath and the linea alba above the peritoneal closure. If the peritoneum cannot be kept intact beneath the defect, omentum should be tacked to the peritoneum circumferentially to isolate the abdominal viscera from the prosthesis at least to some degree.

EPIGASTRIC HERNIA

Epigastric hernias occur through a defect in the linea alba. In most patients with these hernias, as well as those with umbilical hernias, only a single decussation of the fibers of the linea alba is present, as opposed to the triple decussation seen in most persons; this abnormality is the cause of the defect in the midline.

The reported incidence of epigastric hernia ranges from less than 1% to as high as 5%. They are two to three times more common in men than in women, and 20% of them are multiple. Most defects are less than 1 cm long and contain only incarcerated preperitoneal fat, with no peritoneal sac. For this reason, they generally cannot be visualized laparoscopically. The usual complaint is a painful nodule in the upper midline. As a rule, reduction of the preperitoneal fat and simple closure of the defect resolves the complaint. Given the relatively high recurrence rate (up to 10%), however, some surgeons prefer to place a postage stamp–sized piece of prosthetic material in the preperitoneal space to reinforce the repair. Others bridge the defect by suturing the prosthesis circumferentially. Some authorities recommend exposure of the entire linea alba because of the incidence of multicentricity. We believe that this practice leads to unnecessary morbidity. Instead, we make a small incision with the patient under local anesthesia and explain to him or her that additional repairs may be required later.

Left untreated, an epigastric hernia can become large enough to develop a peritoneal sac into which intra-abdominal contents can protrude. Usually, however, the sac is wide, and serious complications are infrequent.

DIASTASIS RECTI

In diastasis recti, the two recti abdominis are separated quite widely, and the linea alba area is stretched and protrudes like a fin. Although the protrusion is easily reducible and almost never produces complications, many patients find it unsightly and request treatment. Surgical therapy would involve removing a strip of the weakened linea alba and reapproximating it; however, this approach could result in tension, which in turn might lead to recurrence. The alternative would be a mesh repair.

PARASTOMAL HERNIA

Parastomal hernia is one of the most common complications of stoma formation. Its incidence is much higher than is generally appreciated. There is good evidence to suggest that more than 50% of patients will eventually be found to have a paracolostomy hernia if followed for longer than 5 years.[43] The rate of herniation with small bowel stomas is also discouraging, though less so than that with colostomies. The results of parastomal hernia repair are particularly dismal, with recurrence being the rule rather than the exception.

Some parastomal hernias can be accounted for by poor site selection or technical errors (e.g., making the fascial opening too large or placing a stoma in an incision), but the overall incidence is too high to be explained by these causes alone. Placement of the stoma lateral to the rectus sheath is widely touted as a cause of parastomal hernia, but this claim is not universally accepted. Obesity, malnutrition, advanced age, collagen abnormalities, postoperative sepsis, abdominal distention, constipation, obstructive uropathy, steroid use, and chronic lung disease are also contributing factors.[44,45]

Newer techniques for stomal construction (e.g., extraperitoneal tunneling) have had little impact on the incidence of parastomal hernia. Fortunately, patients tolerate these hernias well, and life-threatening complications (e.g., bowel obstruction or strangulation) are rare. Routine repair, therefore, is not recommended; repair is appropriate only when there is an absolute or relative indication [see Table 5]. If repair is considered, patients

must be informed that there is a significant chance that the hernia will recur.

Three general types of parastomal hernia repairs are currently performed: (1) fascial repair, (2) stomal relocation, and (3) prosthetic repair. Fascial repair involves local exploration around the stoma site, with primary closure of the defect. This approach should be considered of historical interest only because the results are so miserable. Stomal relocation yields much better results and is considered the procedure of choice by many surgeons. This approach is especially appropriate for patients who have other stomal problems (e.g., skin excoriation or suboptimal stomal construction). The use of a prosthesis with stomal relocation is not generally recommended because of the inherent danger of contamination. In the past few years, the popularity of stomal relocation has waned because of the realization that many patients who undergo this procedure ultimately end up with three hernias instead of one: incisional hernias develop in the old stoma site and the laparotomy incision, while a paracolostomy hernia develops at the new site.

Prosthetic repair appears to be the most promising approach, but it is necessary to accept the complications inherent in the placement of a foreign body. The stomal exit site must be isolated from the surgical field to lower the risk of prosthesis-related infection. The prosthesis can be placed extraperitoneally by making a hockey-stick incision around the stoma, taking care to ensure that the incision is outside the periphery of the stomal appliance. Once the subcutaneous tissue is divided, dissection proceeds along the fascia until the sac is identified and removed. The defect is then closed and an overlying prosthesis buttress sutured in place. Alternatively, the fascial defect is bridged with the prosthesis for a "tension-free" repair.

The extraperitoneal prosthetic approach seems logical but can be very technically demanding, in that it is sometimes difficult to define the entire extent of the hernia defect. Moreover, the considerable undermining involved can lead to seroma formation and eventual infection. As an alternative, an intra-abdominal prosthetic approach has also been described that is theoretically attractive because it avoids the local complications of the extraperitoneal operation and incorporates the mechanical advantage gained by placing the prosthesis on the peritoneal side of the abdominal wall.[46,47] Intra-abdominal pressure then serves to fuse the prosthetic material to the abdominal wall rather than being a factor in recurrence. Either e-PTFE or polypropylene mesh can be used. The detractors of the intra-abdominal approach argue that the risk of complications (e.g., adhesive bowel obstruction and fistula formation resulting from the intra-abdominal placement of the prosthesis) outweighs the advantages. The intra-abdominal approach is particularly well suited for laparoscopic repair, and several techniques have been described.[48,49]

SPIGELIAN HERNIA

The Flemish anatomist Adriaan van der Spieghel was the first to describe the semilunar line, which defines the lower limit of the posterior rectus sheath. A spigelian hernia protrudes through an area of weakness just lateral to the rectus sheath and just below this line.[50] The hernia usually is interparietal and rarely penetrates the external oblique fascia; consequently, it can be difficult to appreciate. Spigelian hernias are unusual, with fewer than 750 cases described in the literature to date; however, given that they are so easily diagnosed laparoscopically, it is possible that the incidence will increase. These hernias tend to occur more often in elderly female patients. It is difficult to explain precisely why

Table 5 Indications for Repair of
Parastomal Hernia

Absolute indications	Obstruction Incarceration with strangulation
Relative indications	Incarceration Prolapse Stenosis Intractable dermatitis Difficulty with appliance management Large size Cosmesis Pain

spigelian hernias develop; there is no area of weakness in the abdominal wall caused by the passage of blood vessels through the abdominal wall in this position. Undoubtedly, childbirth and various other events that stretch the abdominal wall contribute to their development.

Spigelian hernias are usually small (about 1 to 2 cm in diameter), though large ones (up to 14 cm in diameter) have been described. Omentum, small bowel, or large bowel may enter the sac. Incarceration and strangulation are common complications. The usual clinical presentation is a lower abdominal swelling just lateral to the lateral border of the rectus abdominis. In many cases, however, pain and tenderness are the only signs. Plain x-rays may show a bowel shadow in this area, and of course, CT scanning visualizes the defect and the hernia well.

The standard treatment for a spigelian hernia is operative repair. A transverse incision is centered over the mass. The external oblique aponeurosis is split to reveal the protrusion. If there is a large sac, it is divided and sutured. The aponeurotic defect is triangular, with the base located at or near the lateral border of the rectus abdominis. The defect is closed by joining the separated transversus abdominis and internal oblique muscle layers. Recurrence is uncommon.

SUPRAVESICAL HERNIA

Supravesical hernias develop anterior to the urinary bladder as a consequence of failure of the integrity of the transversus abdominis and the transversalis fascia, both of which insert into Cooper's ligament.[51] The preperitoneal space is continuous with the retropubic space of Retzius, and the hernial sac protrudes into this area. The sac is directed laterally and emerges at the lateral border of the rectus abdominis in the inguinal region, the femoral region, or the obturator region. It also may be associated with an inguinal hernia, a femoral hernia, or an obturator hernia. Treatment of a supravesical hernia involves prompt recognition of the defect at the time of groin exploration and appropriate reinforcement of the area of the defect.

A variant of this hernia, known as an internal supravesical hernia, may also arise. Internal supravesical hernias are classified according to whether they cross in front of, beside, or behind the bladder. Bowel symptoms predominate in patients with these defects, and urinary tract symptoms develop in as many as 30%. Treatment is surgical and is accomplished transperitoneally via a low midline incision. The sac can usually be reduced without difficulty; the neck of the sac should be divided and closed.

INTERPARIETAL HERNIA

With an interparietal hernia, the hernial sac lies between the

layers of the abdominal wall. It may be either preperitoneal (between the peritoneum and the transversalis fascia) or interstitial (between the muscle layers of the abdominal wall). Most interparietal hernias are of the latter type and occur in the groin; accordingly, they are designated inguinal interstitial hernias. When the sac passes behind the inguinal ligament in the region of the femoral ring, the resulting defect is known as an inguinocrural hernia.

The cause of interparietal hernias appears to be related to congenital abnormalities (e.g., maldescent of the testis, congenital pouches, absence of the cremaster muscle, and absence of the external abdominal ring). Diagnosis is difficult because there is no obvious swelling of the abdominal wall unless the hernia is large. In many cases, pain is the only symptom; therefore, it is not unusual for patients to present with intestinal obstruction secondary to incarceration. CT, ultrasonography, and laparoscopy can facilitate the diagnosis. Not infrequently, the correct diagnosis is made only at operation. Treatment starts by addressing the intestinal obstruction that is so often the presenting symptom. The defect itself is then repaired in accordance with the same principles followed in inguinal or incisional herniorrhaphy.

RICHTER'S HERNIA

In a Richter's hernia, part of the bowel wall herniates through the defect and may become ischemic and gangrenous, but intestinal obstruction does not occur. The overlying skin may be discolored. The herniated bowel wall is exposed by opening the sac, and the neck of the sac is enlarged to allow delivery of the bowel into the wound. The gangrenous patch is excised and the bowel wall reconstituted. The hernia is then repaired.

LUMBAR HERNIA

The lumbar region is the area bounded inferiorly by the iliac crest, superiorly by the 12th rib, posteriorly by the erector spinae group of muscles, and anteriorly by the posterior border of the external oblique muscle as it extends from the 12th rib to the iliac crest. There are three varieties of lumbar hernia:

1. The superior lumbar hernia of Grynfelt. In this variety, the defect is in a space between the latissimus dorsi, the serratus posterior inferior, and the posterior border of the internal oblique muscle.
2. The inferior lumbar hernia of Petit. Here, the defect is in the space bounded by the latissimus dorsi posteriorly, the iliac crest inferiorly, and the posterior border of the external oblique muscle anteriorly.
3. Secondary lumbar hernia. This hernia develops as a result of trauma—mostly surgical (e.g., renal surgery)—or infection. In the past, it was encountered relatively frequently as a consequence of spinal tuberculosis with paraspinal abscesses; however, it is less common today. Surgical repair is discouraged because the natural history is more consistent with that of a diastasis recti than that of a true hernia. Denervation appears to play a significant role in the pathogenesis. In other words, this "hernia" really reflects a weakness in the abdominal wall more than it does a dangerous hernia defect. Therefore, appropriate repair is commonly followed by gradual eventration, which is perceived by the patient as a recurrence.

Lumbar hernias should be repaired if they are large or symptomatic. A prosthesis or a tissue flap of some kind is usually required for a successful repair. A rotation flap of fascia lata can be used for inferior lumbar hernias.

References

1. Bay-Nielsen M, Kehlet H, Strand L, et al: Quality assessment of 26,304 herniorrhaphies in Denmark: a prospective nationwide study. Lancet 358: 1124, 2001

2. Rutkow IM: Epidemiologic, economic, and sociologic aspects of hernia surgery in the United States in the 1990s. Surg Clin North Am 78:941, 1998

3. McIntosh A, Hutchinson A, Roberts A, et al: Evidence-based management of groin hernia in primary care—a systematic review. Fam Pract 17:442

4. Gaster J: Hernia one day repair. Hafner Publishing Co, Darien, Connecticut, 1970

5. Fitzgibbons RJ, Jonasson O, Gibbs J, et al: The development of a clinical trial to determine if watchful waiting is an acceptable alternative to routine herniorrhaphy for patients with minimal or no hernia symptoms. J Am Coll Surg 196:737, 2003

6. Zollinger RM Jr: Classification of ventral and groin hernias. Nyhus and Condon's Hernia, 5th ed. Fitzgibbons RJ Jr, Greenburg AG, Eds. Lippincott Williams & Wilkins, Philadelphia, 2002, p 71

7. Korenkov M, Paul A, Sauerland S, et al: Classification and surgical treatment of incisional hernia: results of an experts' meeting. Langenbecks. Arch Surg 386:65, 2001

8. Condon RE: The anatomy of the inguinal region and its relation to groin hernia. Hernia. Nyhus LM, Condon RE, Eds. JB Lippincott, Philadelphia, 1995, p 31

9. Bendavid R: The space of Bogros and the deep inguinal venous circulation. Surg Gynecol Obstet 174:355, 1992

10. Kozol RA, Mason K, McGee K: Post-herniorrhaphy urinary retention: a randomized prospective study. J Surg Res 52:111, 1992

11. Smedgerg SGG, Broome AEA, Gullmo A: Ligation of the hernia sac? Surg Clin North Am 64:299, 1984

12. Castrini G, Pappalardo G, Trentino P, et al: The original Bassini technique in the surgical treatment of inguinal hernia. Int Surgery 71:141, 1986

13. Lifschutz H: The inguinal darn. Arch Surg 121:717, 1986

14. Bendavid R: The Shouldice technique: a canon in hernia repair. Can J Surg 40:199, 1997

15. Gilbert AI: Sutureless repair of inguinal hernia. Am J Surg 163:331, 1992

16. Millikan KW, Cummings B, Doolas A: The Millikan modified mesh-plug hernioplasty. Arch Surg 138:525, 2003

17. Rutkow IM, Robbins AW: "Tension-free" inguinal herniorrhaphy: a preliminary report on the "mesh plug" technique. Surgery 114:3, 1993

18. Reed RC: Annandale's role in the development of preperitoneal groin herniorrhaphy. Hernia 1:111, 1997

19. Cheatle GL: An operation for the radical cure of inguinal and femoral hernia. Br Med J 2:68, 1920

20. Henry AK: Operation for femoral hernia by a midline extraperitoneal approach, with a preliminary note on the use of this route for reducible inguinal hernia. Lancet 1:531, 1936

21. Condon RE, Nyhus LM: Complications of groin hernia and of hernial repair. Surg Clin North Am 51:1325, 1971

22. Nyhus LM: Iliopubic tract repair of inguinal and femoral hernia: the posterior (preperitoneal) approach. Surg Clin North Am 73:487, 1993

23. Stoppa RE: The midline preperitoneal approach and prosthetic repair of groin hernias. Nyhus and Condon's Hernia, 5th ed. Fitzgibbons RJ Jr, Greenburg AG, Eds. Lippincott Williams & Wilkins, Philadelphia, 2002, p 199

24. Wantz GE, Fischer E: Unilateral giant prosthetic reinforcement of the visceral sac. Nyhus and Condon's Hernia, 5th ed. Fitzgibbons RJ Jr, Greenburg AG, Eds. Lippincott Williams & Wilkins, Philadelphia, 2002, p 219

25. Rignault DP: Properitoneal prosthetic inguinal hernioplasty through a Pfannenstiel approach. Surg Gynecol Obstet 163:465, 1986

26. Kugel RD: Minimally invasive, nonlaparoscopic, preperitoneal, and sutureless, inguinal herniorraphy. Am J Surg 178:298, 1999

27. Ugahary F: The gridiron hernioplasty. Hernias of the Abdominal Wall: Principles and Management. Bendavid R, Abrahamson J, Arregui M, et al, Eds. Springer-Verlag, New York, 2001, p 407

28. Poobalan AS, Bruce J, Smith WC, et al: A review of chronic pain after inguinal herniorrhaphy. Clin J Pain 19:48, 2003

29. Bendavid R: Complications of groin hernia surgery. Surg Clin North Am 78:1089, 1998

30. Gray MR, Curtis JM, Elkington JS: Colovesical fistula after laparoscopic inguinal hernia repair. Br J Surg 81:1213, 1994

31. Miller K, Junger W: Ileocutaneous fistula formation following laparoscopic polypropylene mesh hernia repair. Surg Endosc 11:772, 1997

32. Silich RC, McSherry CK: Spermatic granuloma: an uncommon complication of the tension-free hernia repair. Surg Endosc 10:537, 1996

33. Ellis H, Bucknall TE: Abdominal incisions and their closure. Curr Probl Surg 22:41, 1985

34. Carlson MA, Ludwig KA, Condon RE: Ventral hernia and other complications of 1,000 midline incisions. South Med J 88:450, 1995

35. Hodgson NC, Malthaner RA, Ostbye T: The search for an ideal method of abdominal fascial closure: a meta-analysis. Ann Surg 231:436, 2000

36. Israelsson LA, Jonsson T, Knutsson A: Suture technique and wound healing in midline laparotomy incisions. Eur J Surg 162:605, 1996

37. Weiland DE, Bay C, Delsordi S: Choosing the best abdominal closure by meta-analysis. Am J Surg 176:666, 1998

38. Bucknall TE, Cox PJ, Ellis H: Burst abdomen and incisional hernia: a prospective study of 1129 major laparotomies. Br Med J 284:931, 1982

39. Ramirez OM, Girotto JA: Closure of chronic abdominal wall defects: the component separation technique. Hernias of the Abdominal Wall: Principles and Management. Bendavid R, Abrahamson J, Arregui M, et al, Eds. Springer-Verlag, New York, 2001, p 487

40. Temudon T, Saidati M, Sarr MG: Repair of complex giant or recurrent ventral hernias by using tension-free intraparietal prosthetic mesh (Stoppa technique): lessons learned from our initial experience (50 patients). Surgery 120:738, 1996

41. Flament JB, Palot JP, Burde A, et al: Treatment of major incisional hernias. Probl Gen Surg 12:151, 1995

42. Wantz GE: Incisional hernioplasty with Mersilene. Surg Gynecol Obstet 172:129, 1991

43. Rubin MS, Schoetz DJ Jr, Matthews JB: Parastomal hernia. Is stoma relocation superior to fascial repair? Arch Surg 129:413, 1994

44. Sugerman HJ, Kellum JM, Reines HD, et al: Greater risk of incisional hernia with morbidly obese than steroid dependent patients and low recurrence with prefascial polypropylene mesh. Am J Surg 171:80, 1996

45. Pearl RK: Parastomal hernias. World J Surg 13: 569, 1989

46. Byers JM, Steinberg JB, Postier RG: Repair of parastomal hernias using polypropylene mesh. Arch Surg 127:1246, 1992

47. Sugarbaker PH: Peritoneal approach to prosthetic mesh repair of paraostomy hernias. Ann Surg 201: 344, 1985

48. Bickel A, Shinkarevsky E, Eitan A: Laparoscopic repair of paracolostomy hernia. J Laparoendosc Adv Surg Tech A 9:353, 1999

49. Porcheron J, Payan B, Balique JG: Mesh repair of paracolostomy hernia by laparoscopy. Surg Endosc 12:1281, 1998

50. Spangen L: Spigelian hernia. Surg Clin North Am 64:351, 1984

51. Skandalakis JE: Internal and external supravesical hernia. Am Surg 42:142, 1976

52. Franklin ME Jr, Gonzalez JJ Jr, Michaelson RP, et al: Preliminary experience with new bioactive prosthetic material for repair of hernias in infected fields. Hernia 6:171, 2002

Acknowledgments

Supported by a Grant from the United States Agency for Healthcare Research and Quality (5 R01 HS09860-03) and the Department of Veterans Affairs Cooperative Studies Research and Development Program (CSP #456).

Figures 2 through 17   Tom Moore.

Liane S. Feldman, M.D., F.A.C.S., Marvin J. Wexler, M.D., F.A.C.S., and Shannon A. Fraser, M.D.

Since its first description in 1990,[1] laparoscopic inguinal herniorrhaphy has shown a great deal of promise; however, concurrently with its development, open anterior herniorrhaphy has evolved into a tension-free, mesh repair that is easily performed with the patient under local anesthesia and that is also associated with rapid recovery and low recurrence rates [*see 69 Open Hernia Repair*].[2,3] Thus, the key question about laparoscopic inguinal hernia repair at present is whether it provides a significant advantage over the tension-free open repair now in use.

The two most common techniques for laparoscopic inguinal hernia repair involve the insertion of mesh into the preperitoneal space; one makes use of a transabdominal preperitoneal (TAPP) approach, the other a totally extraperitoneal (TEP) approach. Both approaches would appear to offer potential advantages, such as reduced postoperative pain, shortened recovery, quicker and more accurate assessment and repair of bilateral groin hernias simultaneously, and, in the case of recurrent hernia, avoidance of previously dissected and technically difficult scarred areas. In practice, however, the advantages are not invariably realized; a laparoscopic approach is not always minimally invasive, and various disadvantages accrue from the current requirement for general anesthesia, the need to traverse the abdominal cavity in the TAPP technique, and the increase in operating room time and costs.[4]

Meticulous attention to surgical technique is essential. Because surgeons may be unfamiliar with inguinal anatomy as viewed from inside the abdomen and because the potential for complication necessitating laparotomy is increased with the laparoscopic approach, surgeons must be proficient in laparoscopic techniques and must have a precise knowledge of anatomic relations in the region of the groin as seen from the peritoneal surface.

Since the late 1990s, laparoscopic video techniques have also been increasingly applied to the repair of incisional hernias.[5-9] Laparoscopic repair of large incisional hernias resembles open repair in that mesh is inserted to cover the defect in the abdominal wall fascia [*see 69 Open Hernia Repair*]. A laparoscopic approach is theoretically attractive because an open approach usually necessitates a large incision as well as extensive and tedious wide dissection to expose the abdominal wall defect, resulting in considerable postoperative pain and a risk of wound complications—problems that a laparoscopic approach to the defect from within might minimize.

It may be many more years before the true safety and efficacy of laparoscopic herniorrhaphy can be determined and the correct indications for its use established. In the meantime, every repair performed should be subjected to careful classification, documentation, and quality-of-life assessment. Surgeons should not perform laparoscopic herniorrhaphy simply because it is relatively new or potentially economical; they should perform it only when convinced that it is anatomically and physiologically correct and logical.

In what follows, we discuss laparoscopic repair of both inguinal and incisional hernias. In addition to describing current operative techniques, we address inguinal surgical anatomy, preoperative planning, and complications. Finally, we review selected trials measuring the results of laparoscopic repair against those of open repair and comparing the outcomes of TAPP repair with those of TEP repair.

Laparoscopic Inguinal Hernia Repair

ANATOMIC CONSIDERATIONS

To most surgeons, inguinal anatomy as viewed through the laparoscope appears unfamiliar. This is particularly true for the TEP approach, in which the preperitoneal space must be developed. The surgical perspective on the pelvic anatomy from the intraperitoneal view has been elegantly described by Skandalakis and coworkers[10] and has been elegantly demonstrated in cadaver dissections by Spaw and colleagues,[11] whose work forms the basis of the descriptions we present in this chapter. Excellent descriptions of the preperitoneal space by Wantz[12] and Condon[13] are also worthy of review.

During laparoscopic herniorrhaphy, a number of structures that are usually visible during open herniorrhaphy (e.g. the inguinal ligament, the pubic tubercle, the lacunar ligament, and the ilioinguinal and iliohypogastric nerves) are not seen initially. Conversely, a number of structures that are visible only after significant dissection in the open approach are easily viewed through the laparoscope [*see Figure 1*]. Identification of the iliopubic tract, Cooper's ligament, and the transversus abdominis arch is mandatory to ensure proper coverage by the prosthetic material used in the repair.

During a TAPP repair, four important landmarks should be seen at initial laparoscopic inspection of the inguinal region [*see Figure 2*]: the spermatic vessels, the obliterated umbilical artery (also referred to as the medial umbilical ligament or the bladder ligament), the inferior epigastric vessels (also referred to as the lateral umbilical ligament), and the external iliac vessels. During a TEP repair, once the preperitoneal space has been established, the first easily identified landmarks are Cooper's ligament and the inferior epigastric vessels; identification of these structures is helpful in guiding early dissection.

Spermatic Vessels

The testicular artery and vein descend from the retroperitoneum, travel directly over and slightly lateral to the external iliac artery, and enter the internal spermatic ring posteriorly. These vessels are covered only by the peritoneum and are usually well visualized as flat structures in the abdominal cavity that assume a cordlike appearance when joined by the vas deferens immediately before entering the internal spermatic ring. If no hernia is present, a mere dimple will be seen [*see Figure 2*]. In the TAPP approach, an indirect hernia, if present, will be immediately apparent and will have an obvious opening. In the TEP approach, the indirect sac will be seen later, after dissection of the tissue on the anterior abdominal wall. The vas deferens is best identified where it joins the spermatic vessels. From there, the vas can be traced back medially as it courses over the

a

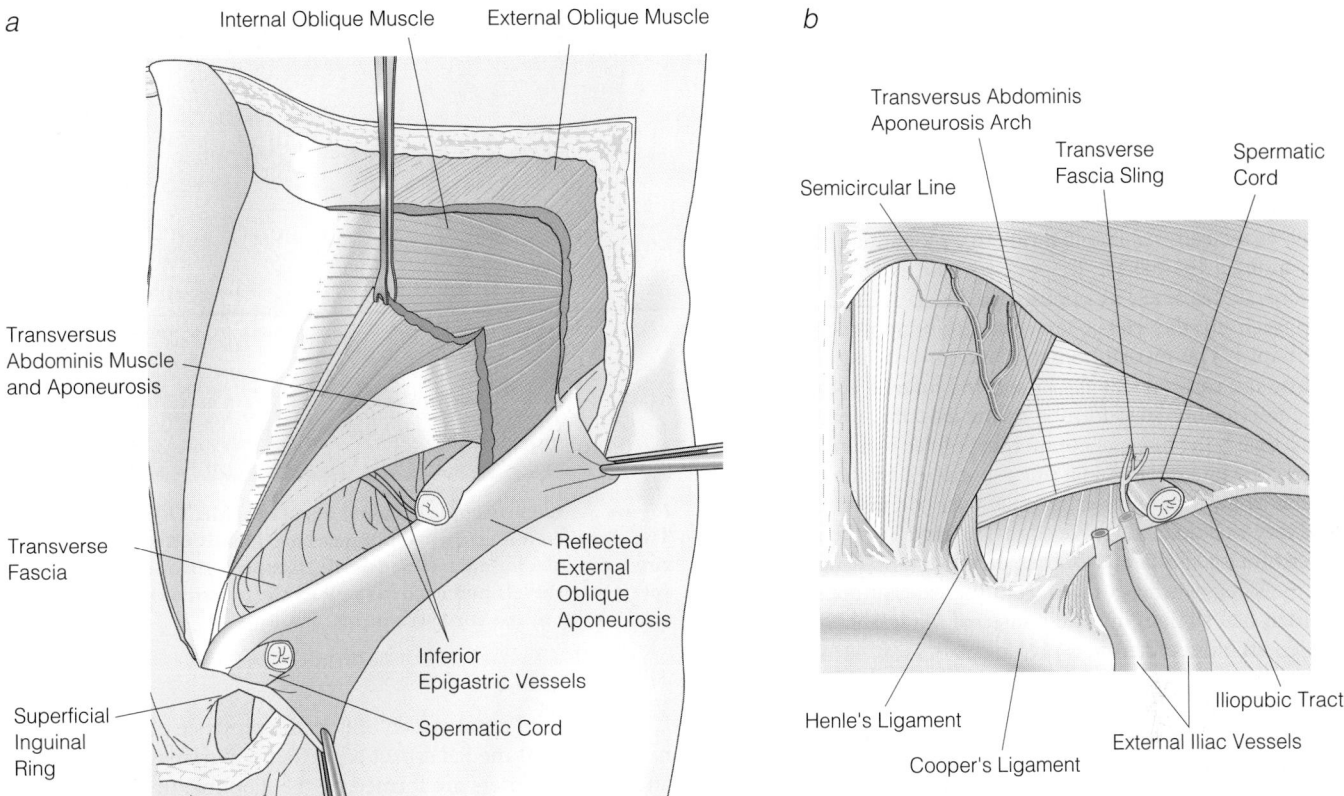

b

Figure 1 Laparoscopic inguinal hernia repair. Shown are (*a*) the anatomy of the left groin region as seen from the traditional anterior approach to herniorrhaphy and (*b*) the anatomy of the right groin from the posterior, or peritoneal, approach. The inguinal canal floor is covered by transverse fascia alone, and a large space separates the transversus abdominis aponeurosis from the inguinal ligament (*a*). A preperitoneal view of the groin region shows the distance between the transversus abdominis tendon and Cooper's ligament, the iliopubic tract, and the inguinal ligament (*b*).

pelvic brim and falls into the pelvis and behind the bladder. There is a small artery that runs with the vas deferens and is not well seen or known. It is white and cordlike in appearance and can usually be seen just beneath the peritoneum.

Obliterated Umbilical Artery

The obliterated umbilical artery is an unfamiliar but sometimes prominent structure that is seen in the TAPP approach. It courses along the anterior abdominal wall toward the umbilicus, often with an apparent mesentery. It is most prominent in the region of the medial inguinal space. This ligament is most readily identified when the umbilical laparoscope is directed toward the pelvic midline, where the ligament's bilateral structure is best seen as it is oriented toward the umbilicus. Medial retraction of this structure is usually necessary for full exposure of the medial aspect of the inguinal canal.

Inferior Epigastric Vessels

The inferior epigastric artery and vein lie in the medial aspect of the internal inguinal ring and ascend the inferior surface of the rectus abdominis. In the TAPP approach, these vessels may be difficult to visualize, particularly in obese patients. They are best identified by locating the internal inguinal ring at the junction of the vas deferens and the testicular artery and vein. At this location, the vessels exit the medial margin of the internal ring. However, they can quickly fade from view as they travel superiorly and medially along the anterior abdominal wall. In the TEP approach, early identification of the inferior epigastric vessels helps guide lateral dissection

and identification of the internal ring [*see Figure 3*]. However, dissection in the incorrect plane when the preperitoneal space is initially established may strip these vessels off the abdominal wall.

External Iliac Vessels

The lateral spermatic vessels and the medial vas deferens merge at the internal inguinal ring and enter the inguinal canal, where they form the apex of the so-called triangle of doom [*see Figure 4a, insert*]. Beneath this triangle lie the external iliac artery and the external iliac vein. More laterally, the femoral nerve can be found. The external iliac vessels are often difficult to visualize, though in an elderly patient, a calcified pulsating artery may be prominent. Extreme care must be taken not to dissect within the triangle of doom, because such dissection can result in serious bleeding.

Cooper's Ligament

Cooper's ligament is a condensation of the transversalis fascia and the periosteum of the superior pubic ramus lateral to the pubic tubercle. It can be seen only in the preperitoneal space and is the first landmark that should be identified during a TEP repair. In the initial stages of a TAPP repair, with the peritoneum intact, it is often easier to palpate the ligament than to see it, but once the ligament has been identified and cleaned, its glistening white fibers are apparent. Care must be taken during dissection to avoid the tiny branches of the obturator vein that often run along the ligament's surface. The iliopubic tract inserts into the superior ramus of the pubis just lateral to Cooper's ligament, blending into it.

Internal Inguinal Ring

In the TAPP approach, the internal inguinal ring is normally identified by a slight indentation of the peritoneum at the junction of the vas deferens and the spermatic vessels. When an indirect hernia is present, however, a true ring or opening is easily identified, and by rotating a 30° laparoscope, the surgeon can look directly into the hernial sac or insert the laparoscope into the sac, which often allows the external inguinal ring to be identified more medially. An indirect hernial sac lies anterior and lateral to the spermatic cord at this level, as opposed to the familiar medial cord position seen in the classic exterior groin approach to open herniorrhaphy. The medial border of the internal inguinal ring is formed by the transversalis fascia and the inferior epigastric vessels. The inferior border is formed by the iliopubic tract, a distinct structure that is the internal counterpart of the inguinal ligament. Anteriorly, the internal inguinal ring is bordered by the transversus abdominis arch, which passes laterally over the internal ring and forms a very well defined visible edge. The layers of the abdominal wall constituting the lateral border of the internal inguinal ring appear the same as when viewed from the exterior approach, and this border, like all margins of the internal inguinal ring, is visible only when an indirect hernia is present.

Iliopubic Tract

The iliopubic tract originates laterally from the anterior superior spine of the ilium and courses medially, forming the inferior margin of the internal inguinal ring and the roof of the femoral canal before inserting medially into the superior pubic ramus. This tract is formed by the condensation of the transversalis fascia with the most inferior portion of the transversus abdominis muscle and aponeurosis, and it is usually sturdy along its entire course. All inguinal hernia defects lie above the iliopubic tract, either anterior or superior to it. Conversely, femoral hernias occur below the tract, either posterior or inferior to it. Fibers of the iliopubic tract extend into Cooper's ligament medially, where they become the medial margin of the femoral canal. The iliopubic tract is frequently confused with the inguinal ligament. This ligament, though nearby, is part of the superficial musculoaponeurotic layer, which is not seen laparoscopically, whereas the iliopubic tract is part of the deep layer.

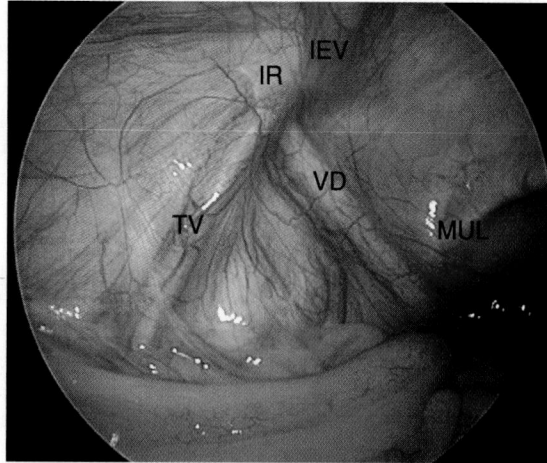

Figure 2 Laparoscopic inguinal hernia repair. Shown is a laparoscopic view of the anatomy of the left groin with the peritoneum intact in a patient without a hernia. (IEV—inferior epigastric vessels; IR—internal ring; MUL—medial umbilical ligament; TV—testicular vessels; VD—vas deferens)

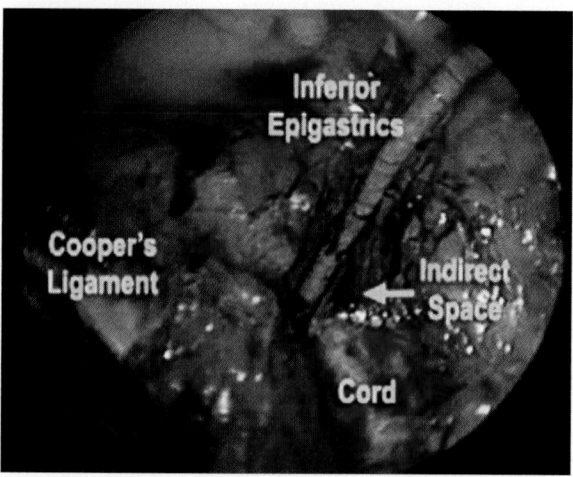

Figure 3 Laparoscopic inguinal hernia repair: TEP approach. The significant anatomic landmarks are identified at the internal ring: the inferior epigastric vessels, Cooper's ligament, and the spermatic vessels and cord, as well as the potential indirect space seen lateral to the cord structures.

Femoral Canal

The femoral canal is seen only in the presence of a femoral hernia in the most medial aspect of the femoral triangle. The anterior and medial borders are formed by the iliopubic tract, the posterior border is formed by the pectineal fascia, and the lateral border is formed by the femoral sheath and vein.

Trapezoid of Disaster

Another area worthy of careful attention is the so-called trapezoid of disaster, containing the genitofemoral, ilioinguinal, iliohypogastric, and lateral cutaneous nerves of the thigh, which innervate the spermatic cord, the testicle, the scrotum, and the upper and lateral thigh, respectively. A detailed knowledge of the anatomic courses of the nerves and careful avoidance of these structures during dissection are essential [*see Figure 4*].

Genitofemoral nerve The genitofemoral nerve arises from the first and second lumbar nerves; pierces the psoas muscle and fascia at its medial border opposite L3 or L4; descends under the peritoneum, on the psoas major; and divides into a medial genital and a lateral femoral branch. The femoral branch descends lateral to the external iliac artery and spermatic cord, passing posteroinferior to the iliopubic tract and into the femoral sheath to supply the skin over the femoral triangle. The genital branch crosses the lower end of the external iliac artery and enters the inguinal canal through the internal inguinal ring with the testicular vessels. This branch supplies the coverings of the spermatic cord down to the skin of the scrotum. The genitofemoral nerve is the most visible of the cutaneous nerves and is sometimes confused with the testicular vessels if the latter are not well appreciated in their more medial position.

Ilioinguinal and iliohypogastric nerves When dissected from the anterior position, the ilioinguinal and iliohypogastric nerves lie between the external oblique and the internal oblique muscles above the internal inguinal ring and descend with the spermatic cord. In the abdomen, the ilioinguinal and iliohypogastric nerves arise from the 12th thoracic and first lumbar nerve roots, are more laterally located, and run subperitoneally, emerging from the lateral psoas border to pierce the transversus abdominis near the iliac crest, then piercing and coursing between the

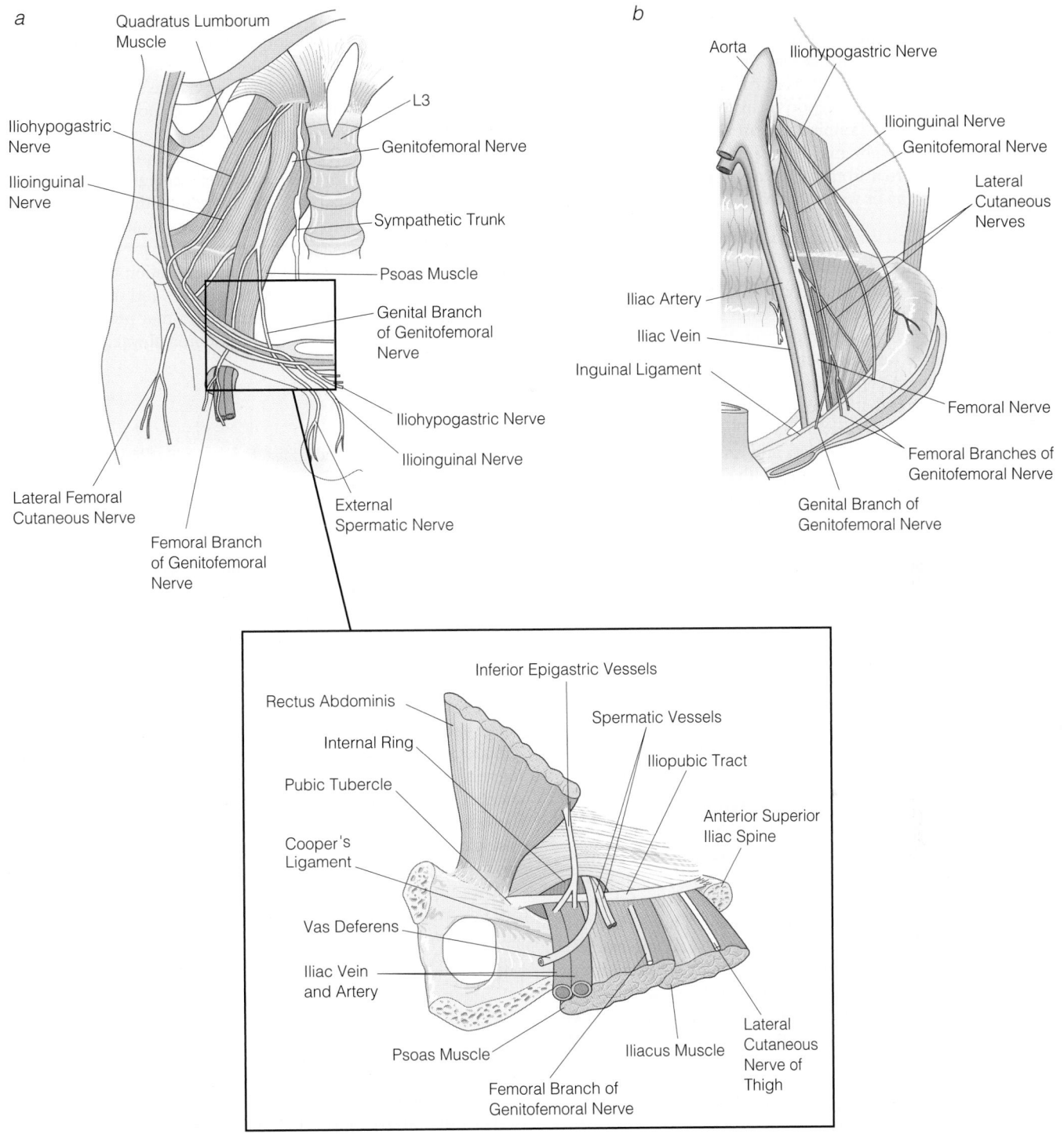

Figure 4 **Laparoscopic inguinal hernia repair. Shown are the courses of the genitofemoral and ilioinguinal nerves of the right groin (*a*) and of the left groin (*b*). Inset shows the preperitoneal anatomy of the right groin, as seen by the laparoscopic surgeon.**

internal oblique and the external oblique muscles close to the internal inguinal ring. Aberrant branches sometimes descend with the genital nerve. The ilioinguinal nerve supplies a small cutaneous area near the external genitals.

Lateral cutaneous nerve of thigh Supplying the front and lateral aspect of the thigh, the lateral cutaneous nerve of the thigh arises from the second and third lumbar nerves and emerges at the lateral border of the psoas. There, it descends deep to the peri-

toneum on the iliac muscle and only comes to lie in a superficial position 3 cm below the anterosuperior iliac spine.

PREOPERATIVE EVALUATION

History and Physical Examination

Preoperative assessment is necessary to determine whether a patient is a suitable candidate for laparoscopic herniorrhaphy. A careful surgical history, including both previous hernia repairs and other procedures (particularly those involving the lower abdomen), should be elicited. A cardiovascular history should also be obtained and risk factors for general anesthesia determined.

Physical examination should confirm the presence of an inguinal hernia. If the patient reports a history of a bulge but no hernia is felt on physical examination, an occult hernia may be presumed. Ultrasonography may be helpful for distinguishing an incarcerated groin hernia from other causes of inguinal swelling (e.g., lymphadenopathy or venous varix).

Selection of Patients

Indications With the evolution of the open anterior approach to tension-free prosthetic mesh repair, determining which patients will benefit significantly from laparoscopic herniorrhaphy has become increasingly important. In 2003, the Cochrane Database of Systemic Reviews[4] published an update to its original 2000 report on laparoscopic versus open techniques for hernia repair, which indicated that whereas laparoscopic repairs (TAPP and TEP) generally took longer and had a higher rate of more serious complications (bowel, bladder, and vascular injuries) than open repairs, they also were associated with shorter recovery times and a lower incidence of persistent pain and numbness.[14] Reduced hernia recurrence was related to the use of mesh rather than to operative technique. The overall risk of recurrence with the laparoscopic approach may be related to the surgeon's level of experience.[15] We believe that patients are best served when a surgeon has several approaches at his or her command that can be applied to and, if necessary, modified for individual circumstances.

Currently, we treat primary unilateral hernias with an open anterior mesh repair, preferably with the patient under local or regional anesthesia; possible exceptions include manual laborers and athletes who desire a rapid return to vigorous physical activity. We generally reserve laparoscopic inguinal herniorrhaphy for the following clinical situations:

1. Recurrent hernia after previous anterior repair. In such cases, a laparoscopic approach allows the surgeon to avoid the scar tissue and distorted anatomy present in the anterior abdominal wall by performing the repair through unviolated tissue, thereby potentially reducing the risk of damage to the vas deferens or the testicular vessels. This is especially true when mesh has previously been placed anteriorly.
2. Bilateral hernias or a unilateral hernia when the presence of a contralateral hernia is strongly suspected. In such cases, a laparoscopic approach allows the surgeon to repair the two hernias simultaneously (and perhaps more rapidly) without having to make additional incisions.
3. Repair of an inguinal hernia concurrent with another laparoscopic procedure, provided that there is no contamination of the peritoneal cavity.

The choice of laparoscopic technique depends on the patient's history and on the type of hernia present. In general, we favor TEP repair for most patients because it does not involve entry into the abdominal cavity. The TEP approach reduces the risk of complications affecting intra-abdominal structures, theoretically decreases the risk of adhesions, maintains an intact peritoneal layer between the mesh and the intra-abdominal contents, and allows the mesh to be placed without the use of fixation. However, it has a steeper learning curve than TAPP does, and it may not be feasible in patients who have undergone lower abdominal procedures.

Contraindications We do not treat acutely incarcerated hernias laparoscopically. In patients to whom general anesthesia may pose an increased risk, we prefer open anterior repair using local or regional anesthesia. In infants and young children with indirect hernias, for whom repair of the posterior canal wall is unnecessary, we recommend high ligation of the sac via the anterior approach.

Previous lower abdominal surgery, though not an absolute contraindication, may make laparoscopic dissection difficult. In particular, with respect to TEP repair, previous lower abdominal wall incisions may make it impossible to safely separate the peritoneum from the abdominal parietes for entry into the extraperitoneal plane, and conversion to a TAPP repair or an open repair may be required. Previous surgery in the retropubic space of Retzius, as in prostatic procedures, is a relative contraindication that is associated with an increased risk of bladder injury[16] and other complications.[17] Similarly, previous pelvic irradiation may preclude safe dissection of the peritoneum from the abdominal wall.[18]

OPERATIVE PLANNING

Preparation

General anesthesia is administered routinely. Prophylactic antibiotics are unnecessary.[19] The patient is instructed to void before surgery, which renders bladder catheterization unnecessary.

Patient Positioning

The patient is placed in the supine position with both arms tucked against the sides. The anesthesia screen is placed as far toward the head of the table as possible to allow the surgeon a wide range of mobility with the laparoscope. The skin is prepared and draped so as to allow exposure of the entire lower abdomen, the genital region, and the upper thighs because manipulation of the hernial sac and the scrotum may be necessary. After the laparoscope has been introduced, the patient is placed in a deep Trendelenburg position so that the viscera will fall away from the inguinal areas. Further bowel manipulation is rarely necessary, except to reduce hernial contents. Rotation of the table to elevate the side of the hernia can provide additional exposure, if necessary. A single video monitor is placed at the foot of the bed, directly facing the patient's head.

The surgeon usually begins the repair while standing on the side contralateral to the defect; the assistant surgeon stands opposite the surgeon, and the nurse stands on the ipsilateral side [see Figure 5]. A two-handed operating technique provides a distinct technical advantage.

Equipment

Because inguinal hernias occur in the anterior abdominal wall, visualization through the umbilicus requires that the laparoscope be angled close to the horizontal plane. The view is paralleled anteriorly by the surface of the lower abdominal wall, which may make visualization with a 0° laparoscope difficult. In addition, an indirect hernia is a three-dimensional tubular defect that can be well visualized in its entirety only with an angled lens. For these reasons, we recommend routine use of an oblique, forward-viewing 30° or 45° laparoscope. Excellent laparoscopes are currently available in 10 mm and 5 mm sizes. For the TAPP repair, one 10/12 mm and two 5 mm trocars are used. The dissection is performed with a dissector and scissors, to which an electrocautery may be attached. For mesh fixation, we currently use a spiral tacker (e.g., TACKER; U.S. Surgical Inc., Norwalk, Connecticut).

In a TEP repair, besides the equipment needed for a TAPP repair, a balloon-tipped blunt trocar is used to gain access to the preperitoneal space. We usually develop the preperitoneal space with a balloon system [see Operative Technique, Totally Extraperi-

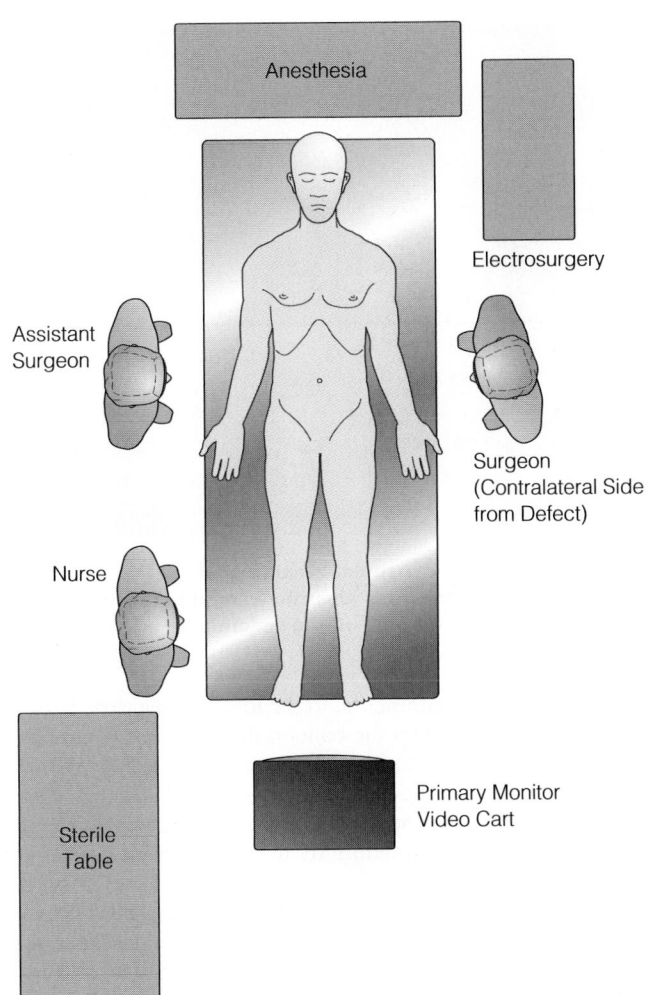

Figure 5 Laparoscopic inguinal hernia repair. Shown is one of several possible OR setups. The surgeon stands on the side contralateral to the defect, with a nurse on the ipsilateral side. The assistant surgeon stands opposite the surgeon. This positioning may vary, depending on the surgeon's preference and handedness, the visibility of the defect, and the type of defect present, as well as on the prominence of the medial umbilical ligament and the need for its retraction

toneal Repair, *below*], but this can also be done with blunt dissection if the surgeon prefers. Two additional 5 mm trocars are placed. The dissection is performed with two blunt-tipped dissectors.

OPERATIVE TECHNIQUE

Totally Extraperitoneal Repair

The extra-abdominal preperitoneal approach to laparoscopic hernia repair, developed by McKernan,[20,21] attempts to duplicate the open preperitoneal repair described by Stoppa[22-24] and Wantz.[12,25] In a TEP repair, the trocars are placed preperitoneally in a space created between the fascia and the peritoneum. Ideally, the dissection remains in the extra-abdominal plane at all times, and the peritoneum is never penetrated.

Step 1: creation of preperitoneal space With the patient in the Trendelenburg position, the anterior rectus fascia is opened through a 1 cm infraumbilical transverse incision placed slightly toward the side of the hernia, which helps prevent inadvertent opening of the peritoneum. An index finger is inserted on the medial aspect of the exposed rectus abdominis and slid over the posterior rectus sheath. In this plane, a preperitoneal tunnel between the recti abdominis and the peritoneum is created in the midline by inserting a Kelly forceps (with the tips up) and performing gentle blunt dissection to the level of the symphysis pubis. A blunt 10/12 mm trocar is then secured in the preperitoneal space with fascial stay sutures.

A 30° or 45° operating laparoscope is inserted into the trocar for visualization of the development of the correct plane while insufflation of the preperitoneal space is begun, with the recti abdominis seen anteriorly and the peritoneum posteriorly. Maximal inflation pressure is 10 to 12 mm Hg to prevent disruption of the peritoneum or development of extensive subcutaneous emphysema. Blunt gentle dissection with the laparoscope is employed to develop the space sufficiently to allow placement of additional trocars.

An alternative approach to dissection of the preperitoneal space—one that is especially helpful early in a surgeon's experience—is to employ a preperitoneal distention balloon system (e.g., PDB; U.S. Surgical Inc., Norwalk, Connecticut). This system consists of a trocar with an inflatable balloon at its tip, which is used to develop the preperitoneal space by atraumatically separating the peritoneum from the abdominal wall. The balloon is

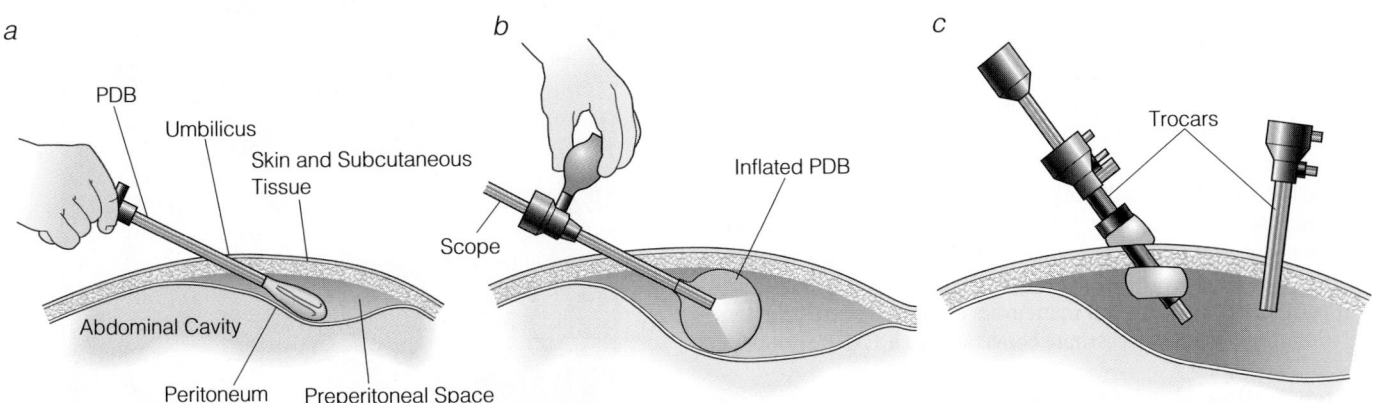

Figure 6 Laparoscopic inguinal hernia repair: TEP approach. Shown is the preperitoneal distention balloon (PDB) system. The PDB is introduced into the preperitoneal space (*a*). As it is tunneled inferiorly toward the pubis, the PDB is inflated under laparoscopic vision (*b*). Once the preperitoneal space is created, the PDB is removed and replaced with a blunt-tip trocar. The preperitoneal space is insufflated under low pressure, additional trocars are placed, and the repair is completed (*c*).

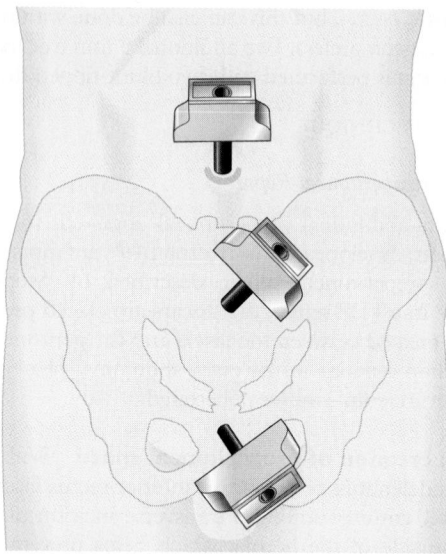

Figure 7 Laparoscopic inguinal hernia repair: TEP approach. Shown is standard trocar placement for TEP repair. As in TAPP repair, three trocar sites are used. One trocar is placed in the umbilicus; the second is placed in the midline, midway between the umbilicus and the pubis; and the third is placed above the pubic arch. The trocars should not penetrate the peritoneum.

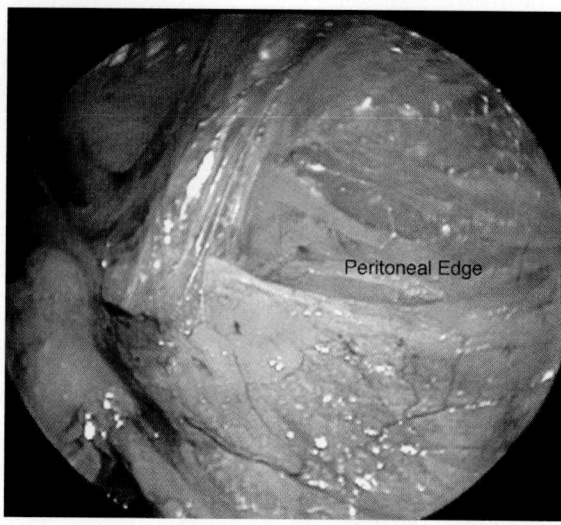

Figure 8 Laparoscopic inguinal hernia repair: TEP approach. The edge of the peritoneum is identified lateral to the internal ring and is dissected cephalad off the abdominal wall.

inserted into the preperitoneal space below the umbilicus by means of an open Hasson technique and is tunneled inferiorly toward the pubis until the bone is felt with the tip of the balloon trocar. With the laparoscope in the trocar, the preperitoneal working space is developed by gradual inflation of the balloon to a volume of 1 L; the transparency of the balloon permits constant laparoscopic visualization throughout the distention process. Once the working space is created, the PDB is removed and replaced with a blunt sealing trocar. S-retractors are used to elevate the rectus and help ensure correct positioning of the trocar above the posterior fascia. The preperitoneal space is then reinsufflated to a pressure of 10 to 12 mm Hg [*see Figure 6*].

Step 2: trocar placement   After the peritoneum is dissected away from the rectus abdominis, a midline 5 mm trocar is inserted under direct vision three fingerbreadths below the infraumbilical port. A second 5 mm trocar is then inserted another three fingerbreadths below the first 5 mm trocar. Placement of the working trocars away from the pubis facilitates mesh placement, in that the bottom port is not covered by the top of the mesh and thereby rendered nonfunctional [*see Figure 7*]. Care must be taken not to penetrate the peritoneum during trocar placement. If the peritoneum is penetrated, the resulting pneumoperitoneum can reduce the already limited working space. If the working space is compromised to the point where the repair cannot continue (which is not always the case), the surgeon can either try to repair the rent with a suture or place a Veress needle in the upper abdominal peritoneal cavity. If such maneuvers are unsuccessful, the loss of working space may necessitate conversion to a TAPP approach.

Step 3: dissection of hernial sac   Wide dissection of the preperitoneal space is then undertaken with blunt graspers in a two-handed technique by bluntly dividing the avascular areolar tissue between the peritoneum and the abdominal wall [*see Figure 8*]. The pubis, Cooper's ligament, and the inferior epigastric vessels are located first and used to orient the dissection. If

a direct hernia is present medial to the inferior epigastric vessels, it will often be reduced by the balloon dissector [*see Figure 9*]. If not, the sac and the preperitoneal contents are carefully dissected away from the fascial defect and swept cephalad as far as possible. Gentle traction is applied to expose and dissect away the attachment of the peritoneum to the transversalis fascia [*see Figure 10*].

The indirect space is then exposed by sweeping off the tissue lateral to the inferior epigastric vessels until the peritoneum is found. If a lipoma of the cord is present, it will be lateral to and covering the peritoneum and should be dissected out of the internal ring in a cephalad direction to prevent it from displacing the mesh.[18] If there is no indirect hernia, the peritoneum will be found cephalad to the internal ring. To ensure secure mesh placement, the peritoneum is bluntly dissected off the cord structures and placed as far cephalad as possible.

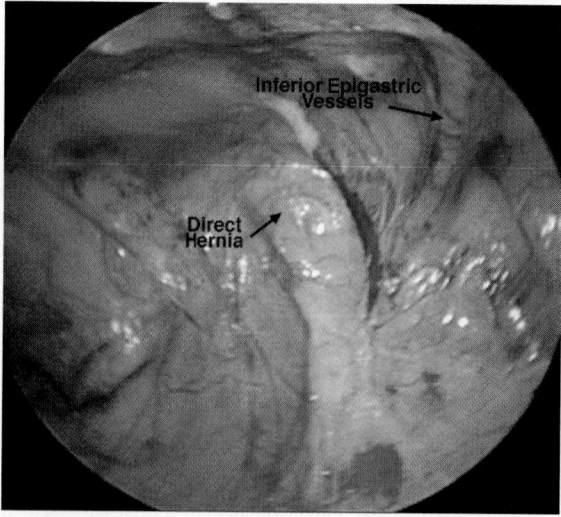

Figure 9 Laparoscopic inguinal hernia repair: TEP approach. Shown is a right-side direct hernia, with the inferior epigastric vessels lateral to the defect, as visualized after initial gas insufflation and before dissection of preperitoneal fat.

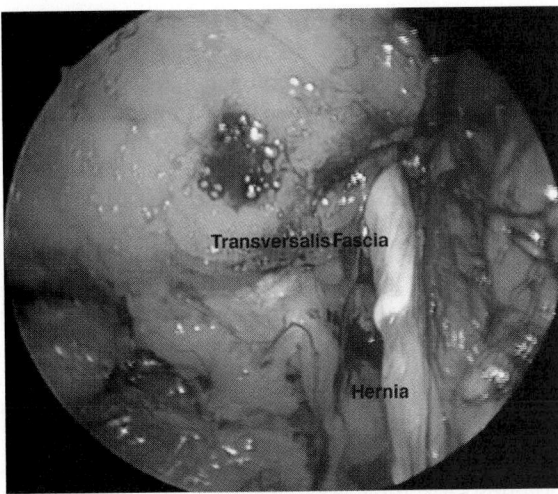

Figure 10 **Laparoscopic inguinal hernia repair: TEP approach. The transversalis fascia is seen adherent to the hernial sac. The sac must be separated from the fascia and dissected cephalad to the level of the umbilicus.**

If an indirect hernia is present, the sac will be lateral and anterior to the cord structures. A small indirect hernial sac is bluntly dissected off the spermatic cord with a hand-over-hand technique and reduced until an area sufficient for mesh placement is created [*see Figure 11*]. To prevent early recurrence, all attachments of the peritoneum should be dissected cephalad to where the inferior edge of the mesh will be. If a large indirect sac is not easily reduced from the scrotum, it may be transected in its superolateral edge, dissected off the cord structures, and closed with an endoscopic ligating loop. The distal sac is then left in place and not ligated.

Unlike a TAPP repair, in which any indirect hernia present is readily apparent at first inspection, a TEP repair always requires that the space lateral to the inferior epigastric vessels be dissected to make sure that there is no indirect component. This dissection should be done even if a direct or femoral hernia is identified. The medial border of dissection is the iliac vein or its overlying fat, and the lateral border of dissection is the psoas muscle. Superiorly, dissection should reach the level of the umbilicus.

Step 4: placement of mesh As a rule, we use a large (10.8 × 16 cm) piece of polypropylene mesh shaped to the contours of the inguinal region. A number of different products can also be used for this purpose, including various forms of polypropylene and several types of polyester. A marking suture is placed at the superior edge of the mesh on the concave side, which is to be apposed to the peritoneum. The mesh is wrapped around a grasper in a tubular fashion, then inserted through the umbilical trocar into the preperitoneal space. Once in the preperitoneal space, the mesh is manipulated to cover the pubic tubercle, the internal ring, Cooper's ligament, the femoral canal, and the rectus abdominis superiorly [*see Figure 12*]. Tacks or sutures are not usually needed for fixation, but if they are used, they should be placed into Cooper's ligament and the anterior abdominal wall; to prevent nerve injury, no tacks should be placed inferior to the iliopubic tract lateral to the internal ring. Some surgeons believe that with direct hernias, there is a risk that the mesh may migrate into a large defect. Accordingly, they place several tacks into Cooper's ligament to prevent this occurrence. For bilateral hernias, two identical repairs are done, and two mesh patches are used.

Step 5: closure The operative site is inspected for hemostasis. The trocars are removed under direct vision. The insufflated CO_2 is slowly released so that the mesh may be visualized as the preperitoneal fat and contents collapse back onto the mesh. The fascia at trocar sites 10 mm or larger is closed with 2-0 polydioxanone sutures, and the skin is closed with subcuticular sutures.

Transabdominal Preperitoneal Repair

Step 1: placement of trocars Pneumoperitoneum is established through a small infraumbilical incision. We generally prefer an open technique, in which a blunt-tipped 12 mm trocar is inserted into the peritoneal cavity under direct vision. CO_2 is then insufflated into the abdomen to a pressure of 12 to 15 mm Hg. The angled laparoscope is introduced, and both inguinal areas are inspected. Two 5 mm ports are placed, one at the lateral border of each rectus abdominis at the level of the umbilicus, to allow placement of the camera and the instruments [*see Figure 13*]. The 5 mm lateral ports may be replaced with 10 mm ports if only a 10 mm laparoscope is available.

Step 2: identification of anatomic landmarks The four key anatomic landmarks mentioned earlier [*see* Laparoscopic Inguinal Hernia Repair, Anatomic Considerations, *above*]—the spermatic vessels, the obliterated umbilical artery (medial umbilical ligament), the inferior epigastric vessels (lateral umbilical ligament), and the external iliac vessels—are identified on each side.

In the presence of an indirect hernia, the internal inguinal ring is easily identified by the presence of a discrete hole lateral to the junction of the vas deferens, the testicular vessels, and the inferior epigastric vessels. Identification of a direct hernia can be more difficult. Sometimes, a direct hernia appears as a complete circle or hole; at other times, it appears as a cleft, medial to the vas deferens–vascular junction; and at still other times, it is completely hidden by preperitoneal fat and the bladder and umbilical ligaments. Visualization can be particularly difficult in obese patients, who may have considerable lipomatous tissue between the peritoneum and the transversalis fascia, or in patients whose hernia consists of a weakness and bulging of the entire inguinal floor rather than a distinct sac. For adequate definition of this type of hernia and deeper anatomic structures, the peritoneum must be opened, a peritoneal flap developed, and the underlying fatty layer dissected.[26] Direct hernial defects are often situated

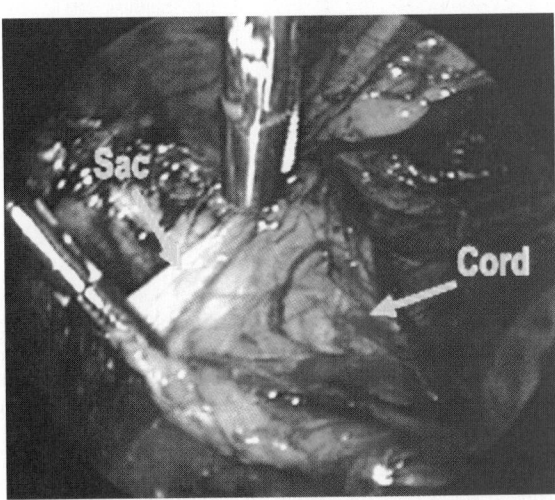

Figure 11 **Laparoscopic inguinal hernia repair: TEP approach. Shown is an indirect hernial sac retracted laterally, with cord structures visualized medially.**

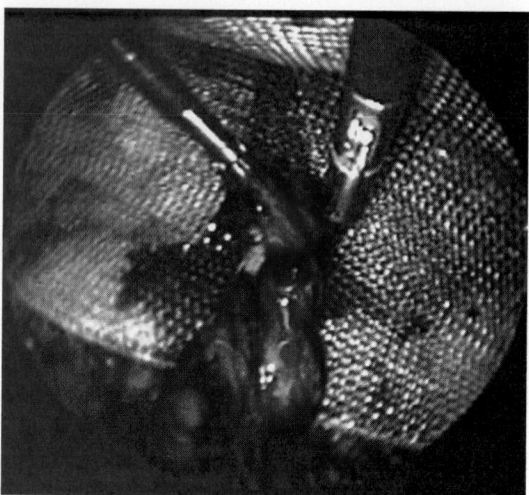

Figure 12 Laparoscopic inguinal hernia repair: TEP approach. The mesh is oriented so as to cover the indirect, direct, and femoral spaces (inguinal floor). The dissected hernial sac is placed over the top of the mesh to reduce the risk that the sac will slide underneath the mesh and cause a recurrence of the hernia.

medial to the ipsilateral umbilical ligament, and retraction or even division of this structure is sometimes necessary. Division of this structure has no negative sequelae; however, the surgeon should be aware that the obliterated umbilical artery may still be patent and that use of the electrocautery or clips may be necessary. Traction on the ipsilateral testicle can demonstrate the vas deferens when visualization is obscured by overlying fat or pressure from the pneumoperitoneum.

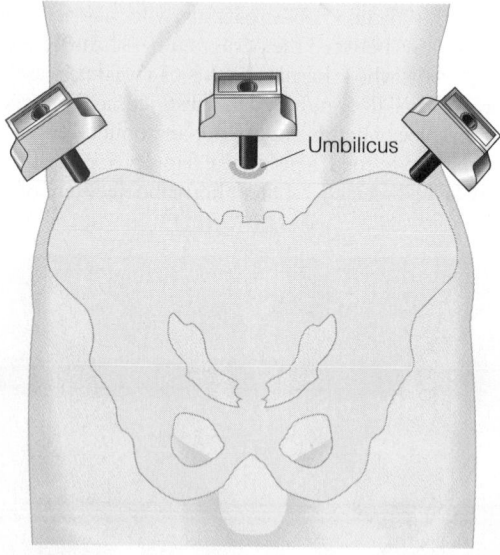

Figure 13 Laparoscopic inguinal hernia repair: TAPP approach. Shown is standard trocar placement for TAPP repair. Usually, three trocar sites are used. The laparoscope is inserted through the umbilical trocar, and two additional trocars are placed in the right and the left midabdomen. To ensure that the first trocar is not placed too close to the surgical field, the first trocar should be placed either in the umbilicus or immediately above it. The two lateral trocars should be placed lateral to the rectus sheath to prevent bleeding and postoperative muscle spasms. At least one trocar must be 10/12 mm to allow insertion of the mesh.

Step 3: creation of peritoneal flap The curved scissors or the hook cautery is used to create a peritoneal flap by making a transverse incision along the peritoneum, beginning 2 cm above the upper border of the internal inguinal ring and extending medially above the pubic tubercle and laterally 5 cm beyond the internal inguinal ring [*see Figure 14*]. Extreme care must be taken to avoid the inferior epigastric vessels. Bleeding from these vessels can usually be controlled by cauterization, but application of hemostatic clips may be necessary on occasion. Another solution is to pass percutaneously placed sutures above and below the bleeding point while applying pressure to the bleeding vessel so as not to obscure the field of vision. If the monopolar cautery is used to create the peritoneal flap, the entire uninsulated portion of the instrument must be visible at all times to ensure that inadvertent bowel injury does not occur.

The incised peritoneum is grasped along with the attached preperitoneal fat and the peritoneal sac and is dissected cephalad with blunt and sharp instruments to create a lower peritoneal flap [*see Figure 15*]. Dissection must stay close to the abdominal wall. A significant amount of preperitoneal fat may be encountered, and this should remain with the peritoneal flap so that the abdominal wall is cleared. When the correct preperitoneal plane is entered, dissection is almost bloodless and is easily carried out.

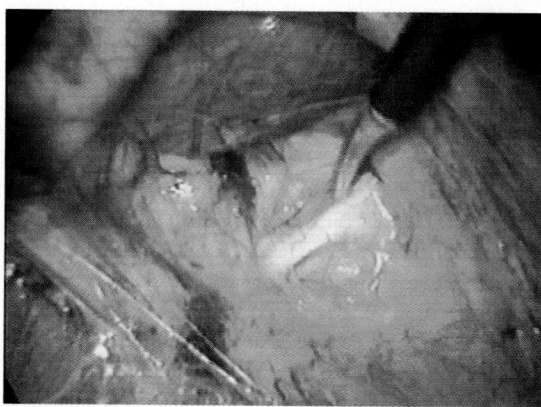

Figure 14 Laparoscopic inguinal hernia repair: TAPP approach. Shown is dissection of a left direct inguinal hernia. The hernial sac is inverted and the peritoneum incised superior to the sac.

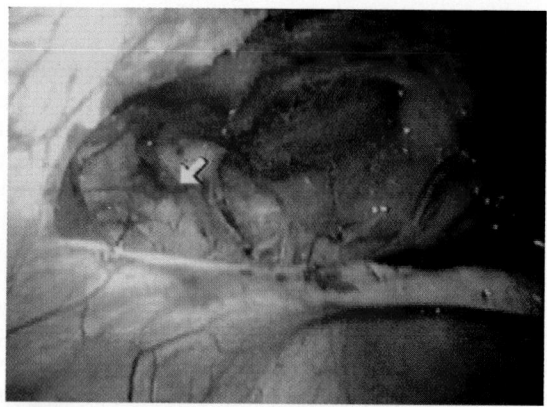

Figure 15 Laparoscopic inguinal hernia repair: TAPP approach. A flap of peritoneum is dissected downward, revealing a hernial defect and the inferior epigastric vessels (arrow) on the left side.

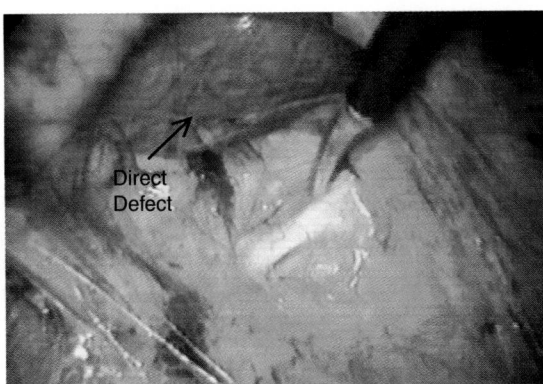

Figure 16 Laparoscopic inguinal hernia repair: TAPP approach. Dissection of the preperitoneal space on the left side allows identification of the anatomic landmarks. The dissector points to the iliopubic tract inferior to the direct hernial defect.

Step 4: dissection of hernial sac The hernial sac, if present, is removed from Hesselbach's triangle or the spermatic cord and surrounding muscle through inward traction, countertraction, and blunt dissection with progressive inversion of the sac until the musculofascial boundary of the internal inguinal ring and the key deep anatomic structures are identified. In most cases, the hernial sac can be slowly drawn away from the transversalis fascia or the spermatic cord. The sac is grasped at its apex and pulled inward, thus being reduced by inversion. The indirect sac may be visualized more easily if it is grasped and retracted medially; this step facilitates its dissection away from the cord structures.

Spermatic cord lipomas usually lie posterolaterally and are extensions of preperitoneal fat. In the presence of an indirect defect, such lipomas should be dissected off the cord along with the peritoneal flap to lie cephalad to the internal inguinal ring and the subsequent repair so that prolapse through the ring can be prevented.

A large indirect hernial sac can be divided at the internal ring if it cannot be readily dissected away from the cord structures. This step may prevent the type of cord injury that can result from extensive dissection of a large indirect sac. Division of a large indirect sac is best accomplished by opening the sac on the side opposite the spermatic cord, then completing the division from the inside.[16]

Step 5: reidentification and exposure of landmarks Once the peritoneal flap has been created, the key anatomic landmarks mentioned earlier [*see* Laparoscopic Inguinal Hernia Repair, Anatomic Considerations, *above*] must be reidentified and exposed so that neurovascular structures can be protected from injury and the tissues required for reliable mesh fixation can be located. The pubic tubercle is often more easily felt than seen. Cooper's ligament is initially felt and subsequently seen along the pectineal prominence of the superior pubic ramus as dissection continues laterally and fatty tissue is swept off to expose the glistening white structure. Care must be taken to avoid the numerous small veins that often run on the surface of the ligament, as well as to avoid the occasional aberrant obturator artery. The iliopubic tract is initially identified at the inferior margin of the internal inguinal ring, with the spermatic cord above, and is then followed in both a medial and a lateral direction. Minimal dissection is carried out inferior to the iliopubic tract so as not to injure the genital femoral nerve, the femoral nerve, and the lateral cutaneous nerve of the thigh [*see Figure 16*].

Step 6: placement of mesh A 10 × 6 cm sheet of polypropylene mesh is rolled into a tubular shape and introduced into the abdomen through the 10/12 mm umbilical trocar. Prolene is preferable to Marlex in this application because it is less dense, conforms more easily to the posterior inguinal wall, and has larger pores, which facilitate visualization and subsequent securing with staples or tacks. The inherent elasticity and resiliency of Prolene mesh allow it to unroll easily while maintaining its form. The mesh is used to cover the direct space (Hesselbach's triangle), the indirect space, and the femoral ring areas (i.e., the entire inguinal floor). We do not make a slit in the mesh for the cord.

It is our practice with the TAPP technique to tack the mesh to prevent any migration. We use an endoscopic multifire spiral tacker to secure the mesh, beginning medially and proceeding laterally. The upper margin is first tacked to the rectus abdominis and the transversus abdominis fascia and arch, with care taken to stay 1 to 2 cm above the level of the internal inguinal ring and to avoid the inferior epigastric vessels, up to a point several centimeters lateral to the internal inguinal ring or the indirect hernial defect. Extending mesh fixation to the anterior iliac spine is neither necessary nor desirable. A two-handed technique is recommended for tack placement: one hand is on the tacker, and the other is on the abdominal wall, applying external pressure to place the wall against the tacker. The tacker itself is frequently pushed against the tissues and used as a spreader and palpator. However, it must not be forced too deeply into the abdominal wall superolateral to the spermatic cord; doing so might lead to inadvertent entrapment of the sensory nerves. The tacker can be moved from the left to the right port, depending on which position more readily allows placement of the staples perpendicular to the mesh and the abdominal wall.

Once the superior margin is fixed, fixation of the inferior margin is accomplished, beginning at the pubic tubercle and moving laterally along Cooper's ligament. The mesh is lifted frequently to ensure adequate visualization of the spermatic cord. Care is taken to avoid the adjacent external iliac vessels, which lie inferiorly. Lateral to the cord structures, all tacks are placed superior to the iliopubic tract to prevent subsequent neuralgias involving the lateral cutaneous nerve of the thigh or the branches of the genitofemoral nerve. If the surgeon can palpate the tacker through the abdominal wall with the nondominant hand, the tacker is above the iliopubic tract. The mesh should lie flat at the end of the procedure.

Step 7: closure of peritoneum The peritoneal flap, including the redundant inverted hernial sac, is placed over the mesh, and the peritoneum is reapproximated with the tacker [*see Figure 17*]. Reduction of the intra-abdominal pressure to 8 mm Hg, coupled with external abdominal wall pressure, facilitates a tension-free reapproximation. Alternatively, the peritoneum may be sutured over the mesh, but in most surgeons' hands, this closure takes longer.

Step 8: closure of fascia and skin The peritoneal repair is inspected to ensure that there are no major gaps that might result in exposure of the mesh and subsequent formation of adhesions. The trocars are then removed under direct vision, and the pneumoperitoneum is released. The fascia at the 10/12 mm port sites is closed with 2-0 polydioxanone sutures to prevent incisional hernias. The skin is closed with 4-0 absorbable subcuticular sutures.

POSTOPERATIVE CARE

Patients are observed in the recovery room until they are able to ambulate unassisted and to void; if they are unable to void at the time of discharge, in-and-out catheterization is performed. Patients are advised to resume their usual activities as they see fit; driving a car is permitted when pain is minimal. Outpatient prescriptions for acetaminophen, naproxen, and oxycodone are given, and follow-up visits in the surgical clinic are scheduled for postoperative day 7 to 14. Patients who live alone, have had intraoperative complications, have significant nausea or vomiting, or experience unexplained or inordinate pain are admitted overnight.

DISADVANTAGES AND COMPLICATIONS

Disadvantages

Need for general anesthesia The need for pneumoperitoneum and thus for general anesthesia in laparoscopic herniorrhaphy is sometimes considered a major disadvantage. Nausea, dizziness, and headache are more common in the recovery room after TAPP repair than after Lichtenstein repair.[27] It is not necessarily true, however, that local or regional anesthesia is safer than general anesthesia.[28] Anesthesiology studies critically appraising anesthetic techniques for hernia surgery have shown the choice of general anesthesia over local or regional anesthesia to be safe and, in many cases, advantageous, particularly in patients who are in poor health. Furthermore, TEP repair has been successfully done with patients under epidural and local anesthesia.[14,29,30]

Lower cost-effectiveness A study comparing costs at North American teaching hospitals found that TEP repair cost US$852 more than Lichtenstein repair; however, this study could not quantify the cost savings arising from faster recuperation and earlier reentry into the workforce.[31] Some studies have demonstrated economic savings with the use of a laparoscopic approach, in the form of fewer days of work missed and reduced worker's compensation costs.[32,33] Operating costs can also be reduced by avoiding the use of disposable instruments.[34] In addition, operating time has been shown to decrease as the surgeon's experience with the procedure increases.[15,35,36]

Complications

Most randomized trials comparing laparoscopic repair with open mesh repair have found the overall complication rate to be comparable between groups.[14,15] In general, however, the rate of serious perioperative complications, though still low, is increased with the laparoscopic approach.[15]

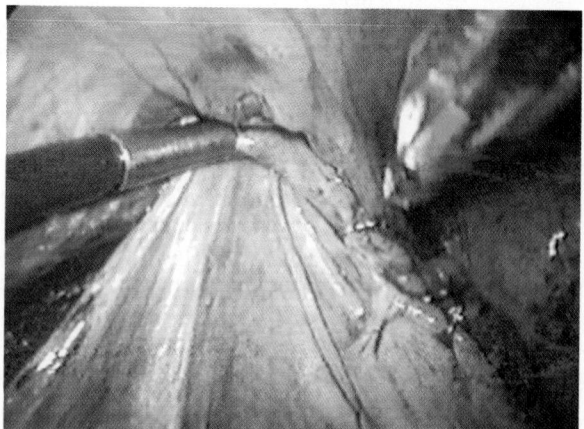

Figure 17 **Laparoscopic inguinal hernia repair: TAPP approach. The peritoneum is stapled over the mesh.**

Complications of access to peritoneal cavity A TAPP repair exposes the patient to several potentially serious risks related to the choice of the transabdominal route. Trocar injuries to the bowel, the bladder, and the vascular structures can occur during the creation of the initial pneumoperitoneum or the subsequent insertion of the trocars.[14,37] Visceral injury rates reported for the laparoscopic approach, though quite low, are still about 10 times those reported for the open approach.[14] Another complication related to trocar placement is incisional hernia,[14] which can lead to postoperative bowel obstruction[14,15,38]; however, this complication can be minimized by using 5 mm trocars and a 5 mm laparoscope instead of the larger 10/12 mm instruments.

Complications of dissection Injuries occurring during dissection are often linked to inexperience with laparoscopic inguinal anatomy. If serious enough, they can necessitate laparotomy. Fortunately, such conversion is rare (< 3%).[14] The most common vascular injuries occurring during laparoscopic inguinal herniorrhaphy are those involving the inferior epigastric vessels and the spermatic vessels.[14] The external iliac, circumflex iliac, profunda, and obturator vessels are also at risk. A previous lower abdominal operation is a risk factor.[16] The source of any abnormal bleeding during the procedure must be quickly identified. All vessels in the groin can be ligated except the external iliac vessels, which must be repaired.[16]

Injuries to the urinary tract may also occur. Four bladder injuries necessitating repair were documented in a collected series of 762 laparoscopic repairs by different surgical groups.[37,39,40] Bladder injuries are most likely to occur when the space of Retzius has been previously dissected (e.g., in a prostatectomy). Renal and ureteral injuries identified intraoperatively should be repaired immediately. Often, however, these injuries are not apparent until the postoperative period, when they present as lower abdominal pain, renal failure, ascites, dysuria, or hematuria—all of which should be investigated promptly. Although indwelling catheter drainage may constitute sufficient treatment of a missed retroperitoneal bladder injury, intraperitoneal injuries are best treated by direct repair via either laparoscopy or laparotomy.

Complications related to mesh Complications related to the use of mesh include infection, migration, adhesion formation, and erosion into intraperitoneal organs. Such complications usually become apparent weeks to years after the initial repair, presenting as abscess, fistula, or small bowel obstruction.

Mesh infection is very rare. In the 2003 Cochrane review of antibiotic prophylaxis for nonmesh hernia repairs,[19] the overall infection rate was 4.69% in the control group and 3.08% in the treatment group. Thus, to prevent one infection in 30 days, 50 patients would have to be treated, and these patients would then be at risk for antibiotic-associated complications. Laparoscopic repairs were excluded from this review; however, in a meta-analysis comparing postoperative complications after laparoscopic inguinal hernia repair with those after open repair, superficial infection was less frequent in the laparoscopic groups.[14] Deep mesh infection was rare in both groups. Mesh infection usually responds to conservative treatment with antibiotics and drainage. On rare occasions, the mesh must be removed; this may be accomplished via an external approach. It is noteworthy that removal of the mesh does not always lead to recurrence of the hernia, a finding that may be attributable to the resulting fibrosis.[41]

Mesh migration may lead to hernia recurrence. In a TAPP repair, appropriate stapling of the mesh should reduce this possibility. In a TEP repair, stapling does not appear to be necessary to prevent migration.[35,42]

The risk that adhesions to the mesh will form is augmented if the mesh is left exposed to the bowel. The long-term durability and effectiveness of the sometimes flimsy peritoneal coverage employed in the TAPP approach have been questioned. Even in the TEP approach, small tears in the peritoneum may expose the bowel to the mesh.

Urinary complications   Injuries to the urinary tract aside [see Complications of Dissection, above], urinary retention, urinary tract infection, and hematuria are the most common complications. Avoidance of bladder catheterization reduces the incidence of these complications, but urinary retention still occurs in 1.5% to 3% of patients.[15] General anesthesia and the administration of large volumes of I.V. fluids may also predispose to retention.

Vas deferens and testicular complications   Wantz[43] believed that the most common cause of postoperative testicular swelling, orchitis, and ischemic atrophy is surgical trauma to the testicular veins (i.e., venous congestion and subsequent thrombosis). Because spermatic cord dissection is minimized with the laparoscopic approach, the risk of groin and testicular complications resulting from injury to cord structures and adjacent nerves may be reduced.[15]

Most testicular complications, such as swelling, pain and epididymitis, are self-limited. Testicular pain occurs in about 1% of patients after laparoscopic repair,[33] an incidence comparable to that seen after open repair.[15,44] A similar number of patients experience testicular atrophy,[37] for which there is no specific treatment.

The risk of injury to the vas deferens appears to be much the same in laparoscopic repair as in open repair.[14] If fertility is an issue, the cut ends should be reapproximated if the injury is recognized intraoperatively.

Postoperative groin and thigh pain   Unlike patients who undergo open anterior herniorrhaphy, in whom discomfort or numbness is usually localized to the operative area, patients who undergo laparoscopic repair occasionally describe unusual but specific symptoms of deep discomfort that are usually positional and are often of a transient, shooting nature suggestive of nerve irritation. The pain is frequently incited by stooping, twisting, or movements causing extension of the hip and can be shocklike. Although these symptoms can frequently be elicited in the early postoperative period, they are usually transient. If tacks or staples were used and neuralgia is present in the recovery room, prompt reexploration is the best approach.[16]

Persistent pain and burning sensations in the inguinal region, the upper medial thigh, or the spermatic cord and scrotal skin region occur when the genitofemoral nerve or the ilioinguinal nerve is stimulated, entrapped, or unintentionally injured. When these symptoms persist, they may result in severe morbidity.[45] A more worrisome symptom is lateral or central upper medial thigh numbness, which is reported in 1% to 2% of patients and often lasts several months or longer. Whether this numbness is related to staple entrapment, fibrous adhesions, cicatricial neuroma, or mesh irritation is unknown. Numbness and paresthesia of the lateral thigh are less frequent and are related to the involvement of fibers of the lateral cutaneous nerve. These problems can be prevented by paying careful attention to anatomic detail and technique.[46] Anatomic study, based on cadaveric dissections, suggests that both the genitofemoral nerve and the lateral cutaneous nerve of the thigh will be protected in all cases if no staples are placed further than 1.5 cm lateral to the edge of the internal ring.[47]

A great deal of attention has rightly been focused on the risk of nerve injury with laparoscopic hernia repair, as well as on ways of preventing it. At the same time, it is important to note that pain and numbness, including thigh numbness, can also occur after open repair and may in fact be more common in that setting than was previously realized. In one study, persistent groin pain was present in 9.5% of patients after Lichtenstein repair versus 5.5% of patients after TAPP.[48] In the Cochrane meta-analysis, persistent pain and numbness 1 year after surgery were found to be significantly reduced with either TEP or TAPP repair.[14] This finding was confirmed by a 2004 study that reported a 9.8% incidence of neuralgia or other pain at 2 years in patients who underwent laparoscopic repair, compared with a 14.3% incidence in open repair patients.[15]

Miscellaneous complications   Laparoscopic repair apparently reduces the incidence of hematomas while increasing that of seromas.[14] Lipomas of the spermatic cord, if left unreduced in patients with indirect hernias, may produce a persistent groin mass and a cough impulse that mimic recurrence, especially to an uninitiated examiner. These lipomas are always asymptomatic.

OUTCOME EVALUATION

Although there is a large body of literature on laparoscopic inguinal hernia repair—including a variety of randomized, controlled trials—the benefits of the laparoscopic approach have not yet been clearly defined or widely accepted. Given the low morbidity and relatively short recovery already associated with the conventional operation, demonstration of any significant differences between the open mesh and laparoscopic techniques requires large study samples. The previously cited meta-analysis done by the Cochrane collaboration addressed this question.[14] Forty-one trials were included in this meta-analysis, ranging in size from 38 to 994 randomized patients. The duration of follow-up ranged from 6 weeks to 36 months. The results of the meta-analysis suggested that whereas operating times were longer and the risk of rare but serious complications higher in the laparoscopic groups, recovery was quicker and persistent pain and numbness less frequent. Recurrence rates did not differ significantly.

In addition, a large randomized, multicenter Veterans Affairs (VA) study published in 2004 compared open mesh repair with laparoscopic mesh repair (TEP, 90%; TAPP, 10%) in 2,164 patients.[15] Patients with previous mesh repairs were excluded. In this study, the laparoscopic approach was associated with a higher risk of complications and, in contrast to the findings of the meta-analysis, a higher overall recurrence rate at 2 years after operation. Pain was reduced and recovery time shortened in the laparoscopic group.

Thus, there remains a degree of controversy regarding the ideal approach to and outcome for inguinal hernia repair. Accordingly, we will briefly review the salient outcomes of a number of studies that compare laparoscopic inguinal herniorrhaphy with open mesh repair.

Laparoscopic Repair versus Open Mesh Repair

Operating time   The Cochrane meta-analysis suggested that overall, the average operating time was 15 minutes longer with the laparoscopic approach; however, for bilateral hernias, laparoscopic repair required no more time than open repair.[14] The surgeon's level of experience with laparoscopic technique was not explicitly stated in all of these studies, which made it difficult to assess the impact of this variable on operating time. It has been shown that with more experience and greater specialization, the differences in operating time between laparoscopic and open repair tend to decrease and become clinically unimportant.[35,49]

Recovery time The most significant short-term outcome measure after hernia repair is recovery time, defined as the time required for the patient to return to normal activities. One of the most frequently cited benefits of laparoscopic herniorrhaphy is the patient's rapid return to unrestricted activity, including work. The Cochrane meta-analysis revealed that recovery time was significantly shorter after laparoscopic repair than after open mesh repair.[14] In a cost comparison between TEP repair and Lichtenstein repair, recovery time was 15 days after the former, compared with 34 days after the latter.[31] In the 2004 VA study, laparoscopic repair patients returned to their normal activities 1 day earlier.[15]

Postoperative pain After laparoscopic repair, most patients experience minimal immediate postoperative pain and have little or no need for analgesics after postoperative day 1. Patients are able to perform some exercises better after laparoscopic repair than after Lichtenstein repair.[48] That patients experience less postoperative pain after laparoscopic repair than after open mesh repair has been reported in several randomized studies.[27,32,40,44,50,51] In the Cochrane meta-analysis, persistent pain and numbness 1 year after surgery was significantly less after either TEP or TAPP repair than after open repair.[14] In a 2003 report describing a 5-year follow-up of 400 patients treated with either Lichtenstein open mesh repair or TAPP repair, the incidence of permanent paresthesia and groin pain was lower with the TAPP approach.[52] Moreover, all of the patients with pain and paresthesia significant enough to affect their daily lives were in the open repair group. A later study that evaluated postoperative neuralgia in 400 patients who underwent either TAPP repair or Lichtenstein repair reported similar findings.[48]

Quality of life The studies that have assessed quality of life immediately after hernia repair have tended to favor the laparoscopic approach, albeit marginally. Using the SF-36 (a widely accepted general health-related quality-of-life questionnaire), one group found that at 1 month, greater improvements from baseline were apparent in the laparoscopic group in every dimension except general health; however, by 3 months, the differences between the two groups were no longer significant.[27] Another group also found no differences in any SF-36 domains at 3 months after operation.[37] Yet another study, however, using the Sickness Impact Profile, found some benefit to the laparoscopic approach.[53] In contrast, no postoperative differences in SF-36 domains were found in the VA study.[15]

Bilateral hernias Laparoscopy allows simultaneous exploration of the abdominal cavity (TAPP) and diagnosis and treatment of bilateral groin hernias, as well as coexisting femoral hernias (which are often unrecognized preoperatively), potentially without added risk or disability. Bilateral hernias accounted for 9% of the hernias reviewed in the Cochrane database.[14] Operating time was longer in the laparoscopic groups than in the open groups; however, recovery time, the incidence of persistent numbness, and the risk of wound infection were significantly reduced in the former. These results are consistent with those of a prospective, randomized, controlled trial from 2003 that compared TAPP repair with open mesh repair for bilateral and recurrent hernias.[54] In this study, TAPP repair not only was less painful and led to an earlier return to work but also was associated with a shorter operating time. Further prospective, randomized trials designed to compare simultaneous bilateral open tension-free repair with bilateral TEP laparoscopic repair should be undertaken.

Recurrent hernias Approximately 10% of patients undergoing hernia repair present with recurrent inguinal hernia.[54] Patients with recurrent hernias may potentially derive greater benefits from a laparoscopic approach through an undisturbed plane of dissection, rather than a second groin exploration via an open technique, dissecting through scar tissue and potentially causing significant tissue trauma. This is especially true when mesh was used for the previous open repair.

Open mesh repair has been associated with long-term recurrence rates of 1% or less, even when not performed by hernia specialists.[2,55] If the laparoscopic approach is to be a viable alternative to open repair, it should have comparable results. With respect to short-term results, prospective, randomized trials suggest that hernia recurrence rates are comparable in laparoscopic repair and open mesh repair groups.[14] However, the Cochrane meta-analysis found that reductions in hernia recurrence were effected primarily by the use of mesh rather than by any specific placement technique.[14] This finding is consistent with the Cochrane meta-analysis of open mesh inguinal hernia repair versus open nonmesh repair, which indicated that tension-free mesh repair led to a significant reduction in hernia recurrence.[3] In a 5-year follow-up study from 2004, the recurrence rate after laparoscopic mesh repair still was not significantly different from that after open mesh repair.[34] In the VA study, the hernia recurrence rate at 2 years was higher in the laparoscopic group (10%) than in the open mesh repair group (4%) for primary, unilateral hernias.[15] In both groups, the recurrence rates were higher than generally expected. However, these rates were found to be affected by the surgeon's level of experience: those who had performed more than 250 laparoscopic repairs reported a recurrence rate of 5%.

Most reported recurrences after laparoscopic herniorrhaphy come at an early stage in the surgeon's experience with these procedures and arise soon after operation.[56] The majority can be attributed to (1) inadequate preperitoneal dissection; (2) use of an inadequately sized patch, which may migrate or fail to support the entire inguinal area, including direct, indirect, and femoral spaces; or (3) staple failure with TAPP repair.

Transabdominal Preperitoneal Repair (TAPP) versus Totally Extraperitoneal Repair (TEP)

The TAPP approach is easier to learn and perform than the TEP approach, and even experienced laparoscopic hernia surgeons report more technical difficulties with the latter.[15,57] Nonetheless, there is a growing body of literature to suggest that TEP repair, by avoiding entry into the peritoneal cavity, has significant advantages over TAPP repair.[4] In particular, the TEP approach should reduce the risk of trocar site hernias, small bowel injury and obstruction, and intraperitoneal adhesions to the mesh. In a study that included 426 patients, TAPP repairs were performed in 339 and TEP repairs in 87, and the patients were followed for a mean of 23 and 7 months, respectively.[58] Time off work was shorter after TEP. A total of 15 major complications were noted, including one death, two bowel obstructions, one severe neuralgia, three trocar site hernias, one epigastric artery hemorrhage, and seven recurrences. With the exception of the epigastric artery hemorrhage, all of these complications occurred in the TAPP group. It is possible, however, that these results can be partly explained by the learning curve, in that the TAPP repairs were all done before the TEP repairs. That six TAPP recurrences occurred in the first 31 cases, whereas only one occurred in the subsequent 395 cases, lends support to this possibility.

In a study comparing 733 TAPP repairs with 382 TEP repairs, 11 major complications occurred in the TAPP group (two recurrences, six trocar site hernias, one small bowel obstruction, and two small bowel injuries), whereas only one recurrence and no intraperitoneal complications occurred in the TEP group.[59] Seven TEP procedures were converted to TAPP procedures. Time off work was equal in the two groups but was prolonged in patients receiving compensation. As in the study cited above,[58] the TAPP patients were followed longer than the TEP patients, and the TAPP cases occupied the first part of the learning curve. To avoid this type of selection bias would require a randomized study.

Not all surgeons are convinced that TEP repair is the laparoscopic procedure of choice. A 1998 study compared 108 TAPP repairs with 100 TEP repairs.[57] Although the TEP repairs were done only by surgeons who were already familiar with TAPP repair, many of the surgeons still encountered technical difficulties and problems with landmark identification. Overall, complications did not occur significantly more frequently in either group, but they seemed more severe in the TAPP group: four trocar site hernias, one bladder injury, and six seromas were noted in the TAPP group, compared with one cellulitis and six seromas in the TEP group. The authors concluded that because TAPP repair is easier and does not increase complications significantly, it is an "adequate" procedure. The sample size may have been too small to permit detection of small differences in complication rates.

Regardless of any individual preference for one technique or the other, laparoscopic hernia surgeons ideally should be capable of performing both TEP and TAPP well. For example, a planned TEP repair may have to be converted to a TAPP repair, or a TAPP approach may be required if the surgeon is doing another intraperitoneal diagnostic or therapeutic procedure.

Laparoscopic Incisional Hernia Repair

Incisional hernias develop in approximately 2% to 11% of patients undergoing laparotomy.[60,61] It has been estimated that 90,000 ventral hernia repairs are done in the United States every year.[5] When prosthetic mesh is not used, repair of large incisional hernias is associated with recurrence rates as high as 63% after 10 years, compared with 32% when mesh is used.[62] In addition to these high recurrence rates, even with the use of mesh, open incisional hernia repair may be associated with significant complications and a substantial hospital stay.

Initially described in 1992,[9] laparoscopic repair of incisional hernias has evolved from an investigational procedure to one that can safely and successfully be used to repair ventral hernias. Taking a laparoscopic approach allows the surgeon to minimize abdominal wall incisions, avoid extensive flap dissection and muscle mobilization, and eliminate the need for drains in proximity to the mesh, thereby potentially achieving reductions in pain, recovery time, and duration of hospitalization, as well as lower rates of surgical site infection (SSI).[8,63,64] In addition, the improved visualization of the abdominal wall associated with the laparoscopic view may result in better definition of the defect, the discovery of unrecognized hernia sites, and improved adhesiolysis. Improved visualization permits more precise and accurate placement and tailoring of the mesh, as is suggested by the reduced recurrence rates (9% to 12%) reported up to 5 years after laparoscopic incisional herniorrhaphy.[64-66]

PREOPERATIVE EVALUATION

Selection of Patients

Laparoscopic incisional hernia repair may be considered for any ventral hernia in which mesh will be used for the repair. This cat-

Table 1 Meshes Used for Incisional Hernia Repair

Manufacturer	Product Name	Composition
Gore	Dualmesh	Dual-sided ePTFE
	Dualmesh Plus	Dual-sided ePTFE, antibiotic-impregnated
Bard/Davol	Composix	Polypropylene/ePTFE laminate
	Composix E/X	Polypropylene/ePTFE laminate
	Composix Kugel	Polypropylene/ePTFE laminate
	Visilex	Polypropylene
	Dulex	Dual-sided ePTFE
	Reconix	Dual-sided ePTFE
Genzyme	Sepramesh	Polypropylene/HA/CMC laminate
Sofradim	Parietex	Polyester/type I collagen hydrophilic film laminate
Brennen Medical	Glucamesh	Polypropylene/β-glucan laminate
	Glucatex	Polyester/β-glucan laminate
Ethicon Endo-Surgery	Proceed	Polypropylene/oxidized regenerated cellulose
Cook	Surgisis	Porcine intestinal submucosa
	Surgisis Gold	

ePTFE—expanded polytetrafluoroethylene HA/CMC—hyaluronate/carboxymethylcellulose

egory includes virtually all incisional hernias, in that even small (< 10 cm²) defects are known to carry a significant risk of recurrence.[62] Both upper abdominal and lower abdominal incisions are amenable to a laparoscopic approach, although hernias at the extremes of the abdominal wall—abutting the pubis, the xiphoid, or the costal margins—pose a technical challenge for effective mesh fixation. The so-called Swiss cheese hernia, which comprises multiple small defects, is particularly well suited to this approach; open repair would necessitate a large incision for access to the multiple fascial defects, and small defects might not be appreciated. Incarcerated hernias can also be approached laparoscopically; however, the suspected presence of compromised bowel is a contraindication. An abdomen that has undergone multiple operations and contains dense adhesions presents a challenge in terms of both access to the abdominal cavity and access to the hernia site. If the surgeon cannot obtain safe access to the peritoneal cavity for insufflation, a laparoscopic approach is contraindicated.

Contraindications Laparoscopic incisional herniorrhaphy is contraindicated in patients with suspected strangulated bowel or loss of domain. Hernias in which the fascial edges extend lateral to

Table 2 Devices Used for Mesh Fixation in Incisional Hernia Repair

Manufacturer	Device Name	Fixation Method
U.S. Surgical (AutoSuture)	TACKER	Steel spiral tacks
Ethicon Endo-Surgery	EndoANCHOR	Nitinol anchors
Sofradim	Pariefix	Polyglycolic T-fasteners
Onux Medical	Salute	Wire loop deployment

the midclavicular line may make trocar placement lateral to the defect impossible. Defects in close proximity to the bony margins of the abdomen, especially those near the xiphoid, pose significant challenges for mesh fixation, though this is also true with open incisional herniorrhaphy. Patients who have undergone multiple previous operations, with or without mesh, may have dense adhesions. Patients in whom polypropylene mesh has previously been placed in an intra-abdominal position may have dense adhesions to the underlying viscera. Whether such patients are approached laparoscopically should be determined by the surgeon's expertise.

OPERATIVE PLANNING

Preparation

The procedure is performed with the patient under general anesthesia. Mechanical bowel preparation is not routinely used; however, it may be considered if incarcerated colon is suspected. If the defect is in the lower abdomen, a three-way Foley catheter is placed in the bladder. Sequential compression stockings are applied. Patients are routinely given heparin, 5,000 U subcutaneously, and prophylactic antibiotics.[67]

Positioning

The patient is placed in the supine position with both arms tucked. If the hernia is in the midline, the surgeon can stand on either side of the patient, with the monitor directly opposite. If the hernia extends significantly to one side, initial trocar placement is done on the opposite side. Initially, the assistant stands on the same side as the surgeon; however, he or she may later have to move to the opposite side to help with dissection and stapling. A second monitor on the opposite side of the table is useful. If the defect is subcostal, the surgeon may prefer to operate from between the patient's legs, with a monitor at the head of the bed.

Equipment

As the wide variety of mesh materials currently available suggests, there is no one ideal mesh. Meshes may be divided into two categories: (1) polymeric meshes and (2) meshes made of specially prepared connective tissue (animal or human) [*see Table 1*]. The polymeric meshes are biocompatible materials made of either polypropylene, polyester, expanded polytetrafluoroethylene (ePTFE), or laminates of these. Most ePTFE meshes are engineered so that one side is porous to encourage tissue ingrowth and the other is smooth to resist adhesion formation. They may also be coated with an adhesion-resisting absorbable material.

Because laparoscopic incisional hernia repair leaves the mesh exposed to the intraperitoneal cavity, concerns have been expressed about the risk of adhesion formation and fistulization if polypropylene mesh is used. Polytetrafluoroethylene (PTFE) mesh has been demonstrated to have a reduced propensity for adhesion formation.

Additional special equipment used for incisional hernia repair includes a suture passer, a 5 mm spiral tacker (or other tacking device), and 2-0 monofilament sutures. Several tacking devices and suture placement devices have been developed to facilitate mesh fixation [*see Table 2*]. All work in essentially the same manner. A Keith or similar needle may also be used. Atraumatic bowel instruments are required to manipulate the bowel if lysis of adhesions is needed.

OPERATIVE TECHNIQUE

In essence, the repair consists of the intraperitoneal placement of a large piece of mesh so that it overlaps the defect in the fascia

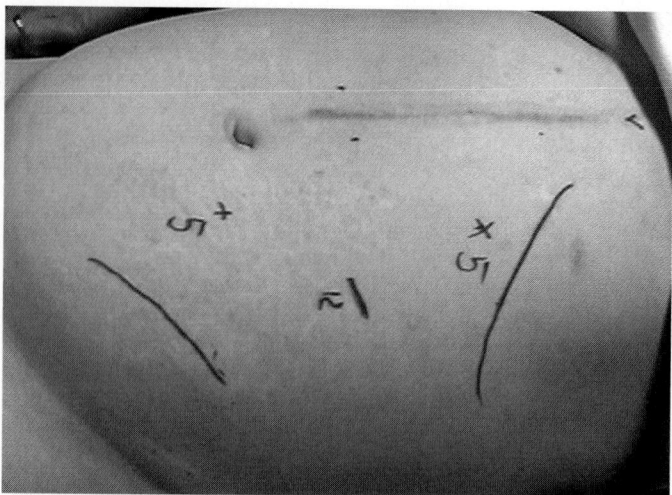

Figure 18 **Laparoscopic incisional hernia repair. Shown is an external view of incisional hernia trocar site placement. Open insertion of a blunt 10/12 mm trocar at the left lateral midabdomen site is performed, with subsequent placement under direct vision of two 5 mm trocars above and below the initial trocar.**

and the abdominal wall. The defect is not closed. The mesh is anchored with a minimum of four subcutaneously tied transfascial sutures placed at the four corners and is further secured between the sutures with intraperitoneally placed tacks and additional sutures as needed.

Step 1: placement of trocars Because of the probability of extensive intra-abdominal adhesions, we begin with open insertion of a blunt 12 mm trocar. Although open insertion necessitates an often tedious dissection through several layers of the abdominal wall, it has the advantage of allowing early diagnosis and repair of any iatrogenic bowel injury. Nevertheless, good results have also been reported with insertion of a Veress needle, usually in the left upper quadrant (where adhesions are presumed to be minimal). Ultimately, trocar position is determined by the location of the hernia. For midline hernias, we usually begin on the left side of the patient and insert the first trocar lateral to the edges of the defect, about midway between the costal margin and the iliac crest.

CO_2 is then insufflated to a pressure of 12 to 15 mm Hg, and a 5 mm 30° scope is inserted. As in laparoscopic inguinal hernia repair, an angled scope is essential because dissection and repair are done on the undersurface of the anterior abdominal wall, which cannot be adequately visualized with a 0° scope. The hernial defect is visually identified, and two additional 5 mm trocars are placed on the same side under direct vision, with their precise placement dependent on the size and contours of the defect and on the locations of any adhesions. If possible, these trocars are placed superior and inferior to the initial trocar, as far laterally as possible, with care taken to ensure that the downward movement of the instruments is not limited by the iliac crest or the thigh. Lateral placement is necessary to optimize exposure of the abdominal wall [*see Figure 18*].

Step 2: exposure of hernial defect The edges of the hernial defect are exposed by reducing the contents of the hernia into the abdominal cavity. All adhesions from bowel or omentum to the abdominal wall in the vicinity of the defect and along the full length of the previous incision should be divided. Complete adhesiolysis of abdominal wall adhesions facilitates the identification of

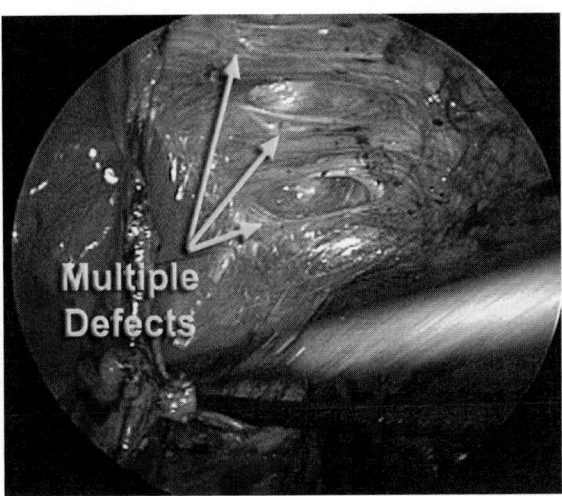

Figure 19 **Laparoscopic incisional hernia repair. Multiple small hernial defects (so-called Swiss cheese hernia) may be seen.**

Swiss cheese defects [*see Figure 19*]. Starting in the upper abdomen may be easier, in that bowel adhesions are less likely to be encountered. External pressure may also help reduce hernial contents and facilitate identification of the hernial sac. Placing the patient head down or head up and rotating the table will also aid in exposure.

If dense adhesions are present, it is preferable to divide the sac or the fascia, so as not to risk bowel injury [*see Figure 20*]. Sharp dissection with scissors is recommended to prevent thermal injury to the bowel, which may not be immediately recognized. If incarcerated bowel cannot be reduced with laparoscopic techniques, an incision is made over the area of concern, and the bowel is freed under direct vision. Once this incision is closed, laparoscopic mesh placement can proceed, and there may be no need for full conversion to an open operation. Strategies for avoidance and treatment of bowel injury are discussed in more detail elsewhere [*see* Complications, Bowel Injury, *below*].

Step 3: selection of mesh The contours of the hernial defect are marked as accurately as possible on the exterior abdominal wall; the edges may be delineated with a combination of palpation and visualization. All Swiss cheese defects are marked. The defect is measured after pneumoperitoneum is released to ensure

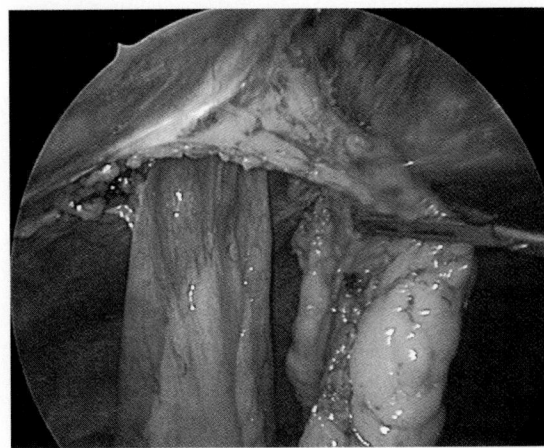

Figure 20 **Laparoscopic incisional hernia repair. Shown is dissection of incarcerated small bowel and omentum from an incisional hernia.**

that its size is not overestimated [*see Figure 21*]. Ideally, the prosthesis should overlap the defect by at least 3 cm on all sides. Coverage of all of the defects with a single sheet of mesh is preferred, but more than one sheet may be needed, depending on the locations of the defects and the size of the patient. The mesh sheet is laid on the abdominal wall in a position that approximates its eventual intra-abdominal position, and its four corners and those of its representation on the abdominal wall are numbered clockwise from 1 through 4 for later orientation [*see Figure 22*]. A mark is made on the inner side of the mesh sheet so that the surgeon can easily determine which side is to face the peritoneum once the mesh is inserted into the peritoneal cavity. If a dual-sided mesh is being used, the smooth side must be the one facing the bowel. A 2-0 monofilament suture is tied in each corner of the mesh, and both ends of each suture are left about 15 cm long.

The mesh swatch is rolled as tightly as possible around a grasping forceps and introduced into the peritoneal cavity. Small swatches can be inserted through a 12 mm trocar; for larger pieces, we remove a large trocar and insert the mesh directly into the abdomen. The trocar is then repositioned and insufflation of CO_2 recommenced.

Step 4: fixation of mesh Once the mesh swatch has been introduced into the abdomen, it is unfurled and spread out, with the previously placed corner sutures facing the fascia and oriented so that the four numbered corners are aligned with the numbers marked on the abdominal wall. Small skin incisions are then made with a No. 11 blade. Through each of these incisions, a suture passer is inserted to grasp one tail of the previously placed anchoring suture and pull it out through the abdominal wall, then reintroduced through the incision at a slightly different angle to pull out the second tail. This is done for each of the four anchoring sutures, and the mesh is unfurled under appropriate tension (with care taken to avoid excessive tension and stretching). Initially, the corner sutures are held with hemostats and not tied; some adjustment to achieve optimal positioning of the mesh is often required, especially early in the surgeon's experience.

Once the mesh is in a satisfactory position, each suture is tied and buried in the subcutaneous tissue to anchor the mesh swatch to the fascia and maintain its proper orientation [*see Figure 23*]. With large defects, it is usually necessary to place one or more additional 5 mm trocars contralateral to the initial ports to aid in mesh fixation. A tacker is then employed to tack the mesh circumferentially at 1 cm intervals along its edge. A two-handed technique is used, in which the second hand applies external pressure to the abdominal wall to ensure that the tacks obtain the best possible purchase on the mesh and the abdominal wall [*see Figure 24*]. Care should be taken to place the tacks flush because they can cause bowel injury if left protruding.[68] Additional sutures are then passed at 5 cm intervals directly through the mesh with either the suture passer and a free suture or a suture on a Keith needle. Sutures should be tied taut but not tight, so as not to cause necrosis of the intervening tissue.

Step 5: closure The pneumoperitoneum is released. The fascia at any trocar site 10 mm in diameter or larger is closed. Careful closure of the site used for open insertion of the first trocar is mandatory to prevent trocar site hernia. The skin is then closed with subcuticular sutures.

POSTOPERATIVE CARE

The Foley catheter is removed at the end of the procedure. Unless adhesiolysis was minimal, patients are admitted to the hos-

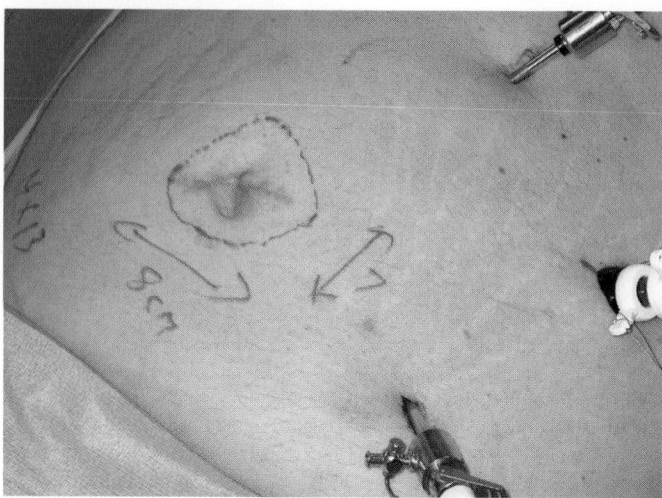

Figure 21 Laparoscopic incisional hernia repair. The contours of the incisional hernial defect are marked on the abdomen, as measured after gas insufflation has been released (here, 8 × 7 cm). Ideally, the mesh should overlap the defect by 3 cm on all sides, meaning that it should be at least 14 × 13 cm.

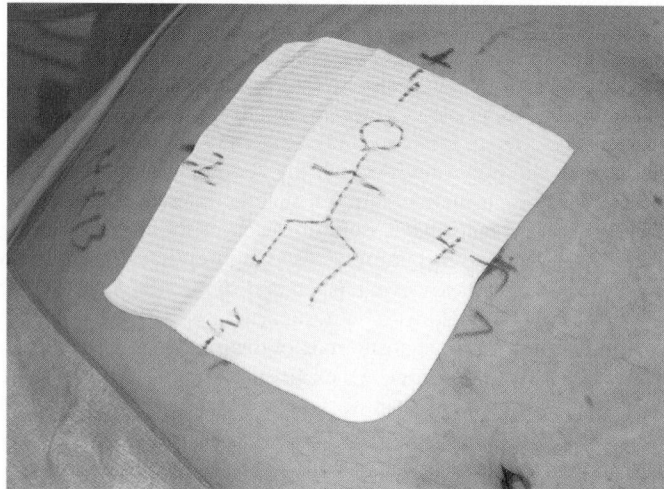

Figure 22 Laparoscopic incisional hernia repair. Shown is an external view of the orientation of a two-sided mesh swatch overlying the marked hernial defect. The sites of suture placement are numbered.

pital. Oral intake is begun immediately. Patients are discharged when oral intake is tolerated and pain is controlled with oral medication. Patients are informed that fluid will accumulate at the hernia site and are asked to report any fever or redness. Finally, patients are instructed to resume all regular activities as soon as they feel capable.

SPECIAL SITUATIONS

Suprapubic Hernia

For hernial defects that extend to the pubic bone, a three-way Foley catheter is inserted. After adhesiolysis, the patient is placed in the Trendelenburg position, and the bladder is distended with methylene blue in saline. The bladder is dissected off the pubic bone until Cooper's ligament is reached. The mesh is then abpaced so that it extends behind the bladder and is tacked to the pubic bone, to Cooper's ligament, or to both.

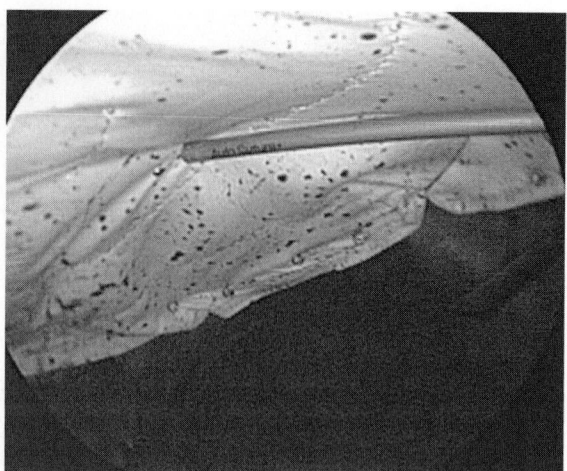

Figure 23 Laparoscopic incisional hernia repair. Shown is an internal view of a two-layer mesh covering the hernial defect and fixed to the abdominal wall with sutures and spiral tacks.

Subxiphoid or Subcostal Hernia

A hernia in which there is no fascia between the hernia and the ribs or the xiphoid (e.g., a poststernotomy hernia) poses significant challenges for fixation. Because of the risk of intrathoracic injury, the mesh is not tacked to the diaphragm. Although some surgeons perform mesh fixation to the ribs, this measure is often associated with significant postoperative pain and morbidity. In these situations, we take down the falciform ligament and lay the mesh along the diaphragm above the liver, placing tacks and sutures up to but not above the level of the costal margin. Taking down the falciform ligament may be a helpful step for all upper abdominal wall hernia repairs. The recurrence rates for subxiphoid and subcostal hernias are higher than those for hernias at other locations.[69]

Parastomal Hernias

As many as 50% of stomas are complicated by parastomal hernia formation,[70-72] and 10% to 15% will require operative intervention for obstruction, pain, difficulty with stoma care, or unsatisfactory cosmesis. Three methods of repair have been described:

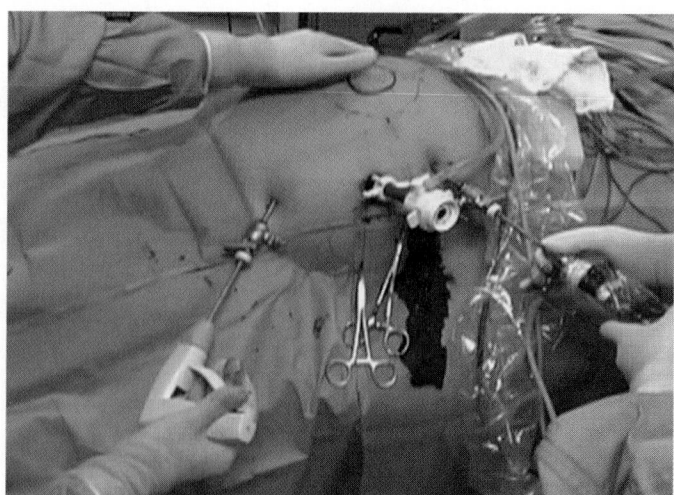

Figure 24 Laparoscopic incisional hernia repair. Shown is two-handed tacking.

primary fascial repair, repair with mesh, and stoma relocation [*see 69 Open Hernia Repair*]. Repair via a laparoscopic approach that uses ePTFE mesh has shown promising short-term results.[72,73] The technique that currently seems to be the most successful is the one described by LeBlanc and Bellanger.[73] Rather than lateralizing the intestine (as in the technique described by Sugarbaker[74]), this method centralizes the intestine in the mesh by cutting an appropriately sized hole in the middle of the mesh sheet, along with a slit to allow it to be placed around the intestine. This step is repeated on a second piece of mesh, but with the slit oriented to the opposite side. The mesh is fixed with sutures and tacks in such a way that it overlaps the defect by at least 3 cm (more commonly, 5 cm) on all sides, as in other ventral hernia repairs. This method appears to minimize the risk of mesh prolapse and bowel herniation alongside the stoma. The authors reported no recurrences within their 3- to 11-month follow-up period and no morbidity. In contrast, a subsequent study reported recurrences within 12 months in five of nine patients who underwent a variation of this repair, in which a slit in the mesh (instead of a central defect) was created and only one mesh sheet (instead of two) was used to cover the defect.[71]

Laparoscopic parastomal hernia repair appears to be a viable alternative to laparotomy or stoma relocation, but long-term multicenter evaluation is necessary for full assessment of this technique's value in this setting.

COMPLICATIONS

Overall, fewer complications are reported after laparoscopic incisional herniorrhaphy than after open mesh repair.[8,63,75-77] There are, however, several specific complications that are of particular relevance in laparoscopic procedures (see below).

Bowel Injury

A missed bowel injury is a potentially lethal complication. The overall incidence of bowel injury does not differ significantly between open repair and laparoscopic repair and is generally low with either approach (1% to 5% when serosal injuries are included). It should be noted, however, that pneumoperitoneum may hinder the recognition of bowel injury at the time of operation. There have also been several reports of late bowel perforation secondary to thermal injury with laparoscopic repair.[65,76-79] One study reported two bowel injuries that were not discovered until sepsis developed; these late discoveries resulted in multiple operations, removal of the mesh, prolonged hospital stay, and, in one patient, death. The incidence of bowel injury is likely to be higher with less experienced surgeons[80] and in patients who require extensive adhesiolysis. In one series describing a surgeon's first 100 cases, four of six inadvertent enterotomies were made in the first 25 cases.[81]

To reduce the risk of bowel injury, we strongly discourage the use of electrocauterization and ultrasonic dissection. The visualization afforded by the pneumoperitoneum, which helps place adhesions between the abdominal wall and the bowel under tension, and the magnification afforded by the laparoscope facilitate identification of the least vascularized planes. As far as possible, we avoid grasping the bowel itself, preferring simply to push it or to grasp the adhesions themselves to provide countertraction. External pressure on the hernia may also help. Larger vessels in the omentum or adhesions are controlled with clips. Some degree of oozing from the dissected areas is tolerated; such oozing almost always settles down without specific hemostatic measures.

As noted, if dense adhesions are present, it is preferable to divide the sac or the fascia rather than risk injury to bowel. In the case of densely adherent polypropylene mesh, it may be better to excise it from the abdominal wall rather than attempt to separate it from the serosa of the bowel. If there is reason to suspect that bowel injury may have occurred, immediate and thorough inspection should be carried out; if this is not done, it may be difficult or impossible to find the exact site of injury later, once the bowel has been released after being freed of its attachments. If an injury to the bowel is recognized, the extent of the injury and the surgeon's level of comfort with laparoscopic suture repair will determine the best approach. If there is no or minimal spillage of bowel contents, the injury may be treated with either laparoscopic repair or open repair; the latter usually can be carried out through a several centimeter counterincision over the injured area. Whether a mesh prosthesis will be placed depends on the degree of contamination. If there has been minimal or no contamination, any small open incision is closed, and laparoscopic lysis of adhesions and mesh placement can continue. If the contamination is more significant, adhesiolysis is completed, but the patient is brought back for mesh placement at another date. More significant bowel injuries may necessitate conversion to open repair.

Chronic Pain

In about 5% of patients, the transfascial fixation sutures used to secure the mesh cause pain that lasts more than 2 months. In most cases, postoperative pain decreases over time; if it does not, injection of local anesthetic into the area around the painful suture may be helpful.[82]

Seroma

Seroma formation is one of the most commonly reported complications: it occurs immediately after operation in virtually all patients, to some extent.[65,80,83] Patients sometimes mistake a tense seroma for recurring incisional hernia, but appropriate preoperative discussion should provide them with significant reassurance on this point. Seroma formation seems not to be related to particular mesh types or to the use of drains.[80] Virtually all seromas resolve spontaneously over a period of weeks to months, with fewer than 5% persisting for more than 8 weeks.[64] They are rarely clinically significant. Aspiration may increase the risk of mesh infection.[84]

Infection

Overall wound complication rates have been shown to be lower with laparoscopic incisional herniorrhaphy than with open repair.[65,79,80,85] In particular, SSIs appear to be reduced with the laparoscopic approach.[65,79,80,85] SSI rates for open incisional repair range from 5% to 20%,[63,79,80,83] whereas those for laparoscopic repair range from 1% to 8%.[5,65,72,79] Mesh infection extensive enough to necessitate mesh removal is rare (incidence ~ 1%); however, SSI after laparoscopic repair, especially when PTFE is used, more frequently results in seeding of the mesh.[65,80] Because this type of mesh does not become well incorporated, antibiotic treatment alone is ineffective.[80]

OUTCOME EVALUATION

Several studies have demonstrated improvements in outcome measures—such as decreased postoperative pain, shorter length of stay, earlier return to work,[86] and reduced blood loss—with the laparoscopic approach to incisional hernia repair.[5,8,63,64,76,84,87-89] The only randomized trial published to date compared 30 laparoscopic incisional hernia repairs with 30 open repairs.[6] The mean operating time was significantly shorter in the laparoscopic group (87 minutes versus 111.5 minutes), as was the postoperative length of stay (2.2 days versus 9.1 days). Another study compared 56 prospective laparoscopic incisional hernia repairs with 49 open incisional hernia repairs assessed through retrospective chart review.[8] The laparoscopic and open groups were comparable in terms of patient characteristics and hernia size. Although the mean operating time was longer in the laparoscopic group (95.4 minutes versus 78.5 minutes), the postoperative length of stay was significantly shorter after laparoscopic repair (3.4 days versus 6.5 days). In contrast, some studies have found the operating time to be 30 to 40 minutes shorter with laparoscopic repair.[63,76]

The recurrence rate—the primary long-term outcome measure of interest—is reported to be reduced after laparoscopic repair. In studies comparing laparoscopic and open incisional hernia repair with mesh, the recurrence rates after the laparoscopic repairs ranged from 0% to 11%, whereas those after the open repairs ranged from 5% to 35%.[6,8,78,86,88] In expert hands, recurrence rates are low after laparoscopic repair. For example, in a multicenter series of 850 laparoscopic incisional hernia repairs, mostly followed prospectively, the recurrence rate after a mean follow-up period of 20 months was 4.7%.[77] One group found no recurrences in the laparoscopic group and two in the open group after a minimum follow-up period of 18 months.[76] Another group, however, reported a recurrence rate of 18%,[90] which approached that reported after open mesh repair. Recurrence has been associated with lack of suture fixation, prostheses that overlap the defect by less than 2 to 3 cm, postoperative complications, and previous repairs.[64,65,77,91]

The surgeon's level of experience plays a significant role in patient outcome, as demonstrated by a group that compared the outcomes for their first 100 laparoscopic incisional hernia repair patients with those for their second 100.[84] Recurrence rates after a mean follow-up period of 36 months dropped from 9% in the first 100 patients to 4% in the second 100. In addition, the second set of patients were an average of 9 years older, had a higher percentage of recurrent hernias, and exhibited more comorbidities, yet despite these added challenges, operating time was not lengthened, length of stay was similarly short, and the complication rate was no different. Another group reported similar findings for their laparoscopic incisional hernia repair learning curve.[92] Operating times and complication rates in the first 32 patients were comparable to those in the second 32; however, bowel injuries were more common in the first 32.

Although the results of large randomized trials are not available yet, the evidence to date suggests that the laparoscopic approach to the repair of large incisional hernias is highly promising. The laparoscopic approach seems to be safe and compares favorably with the open operation in terms of complication and recurrence rates.

References

1. Ger R, Monroe K, Duvivier R, et al: Management of indirect hernias by laparoscopic closure of the neck of the sac. Am J Surg 159:370, 1990
2. Robbins AW, Rutkow IM: Mesh plug repair and groin hernia surgery. Surg Clin North Am 78:1007, 1998
3. Scott NW, McCormack K, Graham P, et al: Open mesh versus non-mesh for groin hernia repair (Cochrane Review). Cochrane Database Syst Rev (4):CD002197, 2002
4. Crawford DL, Phillips EH: Laparoscopic repair and groin hernia surgery. Surg Clin North Am 78:1047, 1998
5. Toy FK, Bailey RW, Carey S, et al: Prospective, multicenter study of laparoscopic ventral hernioplasty: preliminary results. Surg Endosc 12:955, 1998
6. Carbajo MA, Martin del Olmo JC, Blanco JI, et al: Laparoscopic treatment vs. open surgery in the solution of major incisional and abdominal wall hernias with mesh. Surg Endosc 13:250, 1999
7. Franklin ME, Dorman JP, Glass JL, et al: Laparoscopic ventral hernia repair. Surg Laparosc Endosc 8:294, 1998
8. Park A, Birch DW, Lovrics P: Laparoscopic and open incisional hernia repair: a comparison study. Surgery 124:816, 1998
9. LeBlanc KA, Booth WV: Laparoscopic repair of incisional abdominal hernias using expanded polytetrafluoroethylene: preliminary findings. Surg Laparosc Endosc 3:39, 1992
10. Skandalakis JE, Gray SW, Skandalakis LJ, et al: Surgical anatomy of the inguinal area. World J Surg 13:490, 1989
11. Spaw AT, Ennis BW, Spaw LP: Laparoscopic hernia repair: the anatomic basis. J Laparoendosc Surg 1:269, 1991
12. Wantz GE: Atlas of Hernia Surgery. Raven Press, New York, 1991
13. Condon RE: The anatomy of the inguinal region and its relation to groin hernia. Hernia, 3rd ed. Nyhus LM, Condon RE, Eds. JB Lippincott Co, Philadelphia, 1989, p18
14. McCormack K, Scott NW, Go PM, et al: Laparoscopic techniques versus open techniques for inguinal hernia repair. Cochrane Database Syst Rev (1):CD001785, 2003
15. Neumayer L, Giobbie-Hurder A, Jonasson O, et al: Open mesh versus laparoscopic mesh repair of inguinal hernia. N Engl J Med 350:1819, 2004
16. Memon MA, Fitzgibbons RJ: Laparoscopic inguinal hernia repair: transabdominal (TAPP) and totally extraperitoneal (TEP). The SAGES Manual. Scott-Connor CEH, Ed. Springer, New York, 1999
17. Ramshaw BJ, Tucker JG, Conner T, et al: A comparison of the approaches to laparoscopic herniorrhaphy. Surg Endosc 10: 29, 1996
18. Felix EL: Laparoscopic extraperitoneal hernia repair. Mastery of Endoscopic and Laparoscopic Surgery. Eubanks WS, Swanstrom LL, Soper NJ, Eds. Lippincott Williams & Williams, Philadelphia, 2000
19. Sanchez-Manuel FJ, Seco-Gil JL: Antibiotic prophylaxis for hernia repair. Cochrane Database Syst Rev (4):CD003769, 2004
20. McKernan JB, Laws HL: Laparoscopic repair of inguinal hernias using a totally extraperitoneal prosthetic approach. Surg Endosc 7:26, 1993
21. McKernan JB: Extraperitoneal inguinal herniorrhaphy. Operative Laparoscopy and Thoracoscopy. MacFayden BV, Ponsky JL, Eds. Lippincott-Raven, Philadelphia, 1996
22. Stoppa R, Warlaumont C, Verhaeghe P, et al: Dacron mesh and surgical therapy of inguinal hernia. Chir Patol Sper 34:15, 1986
23. Stoppa R, Warlaumont CR: The preperitoneal approach and prosthetic repair of groin hernias. Hernia, 3rd ed. Nyhus LM, Condon RE, Eds. JB Lippincott Co, Philadelphia, 1989
24. Stoppa R: The treatment of complicated groin and incisional hernias. World J Surg 13:545, 1989
25. Wantz GE: Giant prosthetic reinforcement of the visceral sac. Surg Gynecol Obstet 169:408, 1989
26. Arregui ME: Transabdominal retroperitoneal inguinal herniorrhaphy. Operative Laparoscopy and Thoracoscopy. MacFayden BV, Ponsky JL, Eds. Lippincott-Raven, Philadelphia, 1996
27. Wellwood J, Sculpher MJ, Stoker D, et al: Randomized clinical trial of laparoscopic versus open mesh repair for inguinal hernia: outcome and cost. BMJ 317:103, 1998
28. Amado WJ: Anesthesia for hernia surgery. Surg Clin North Am 73:427, 1993
29. Ferzli G, Sayad P, Hallak A, et al: Endoscopic extraperitoneal hernia repair: a 5-year experience. Surg Endosc 12:1311, 1998
30. Ferzli G, Sayad P, Vasisht B: The feasibility of laparoscopic extraperitoneal hernia repair under local anesthesia. Surg Endosc 13:588, 1999
31. Schneider BE, Castillo JM, Villegas L, et al: Laparoscopic totally extraperitoneal versus Lichtenstein herniorrhaphy: cost comparison at teaching hospitals. Surg Laparosc Endosc Percutan Tech 3:261, 2003
32. Heikkinen T, Haukipuro K, Leppälä J, et al: Total costs of laparoscopic and Lichtenstein inguinal hernia repairs: a prospective study. Surg Lap Endosc 7:1, 1997
33. Heikkinen TJ, Haukipuro K, Halkko A: A cost and outcome comparison between laparoscopic and Lichtenstein hernia operations in a day-case unit: a randomized prospective study. Surg Endosc 12: 1199, 1998
34. Heikkinein TJ, Bringman S, Ohtonen P, et al: Five-year outcome of laparoscopic and Lichtenstein hernioplasties. Surg Endosc 18:518, 2004
35. Leim MSL, van Steensel CJ, Boelhouwer RU, et al: The learning curve for totally extraperitoneal laparoscopic inguinal hernia repair. Am J Surg 171:281, 1997
36. Pawanindra L, Kajla RK, Chander J, et al: Randomized controlled study of laparoscopic total extraperitoneal vs. open Lichtenstein inguinal hernia repair. Surg Endosc 17:850, 2003

37. Laparoscopic versus open repair of groin hernia: a randomized comparison. MRC Laparoscopic Groin Hernia Trial Group. Lancet 354:185, 1999

38. Phillips EH, Arregui ME, Carroll BJ, et al: Incidence of complications following laparoscopic hernioplasty. Surg Endosc 9:16, 1995

39. MacFayden BV Jr, Arregui M, Corbitt J, et al: Complications of laparoscopic herniorrhaphy. Surg Endosc 7:155, 1993

40. Johansson B, Hallerbäck B, Glise H, et al: Laparoscopic mesh versus open preperitoneal mesh versus conventional technique for inguinal hernia repair: a randomized multicenter trial (SCUR hernia repair study). Ann Surg 230:225, 1999

41. Avtan L, Avci C, Bulut T, et al: Mesh infections after laparoscopic inguinal hernia repair. Surg Laparosc Endosc 7:192, 1997

42. Ferzli GS, Frezza EE, Pecorato AM Jr, et al: Prospective randomized study of stapled versus unstapled mesh in a laparoscopic preperitoneal inguinal hernia repair. J Am Coll Surg 188:461, 1999

43. Wantz GE: Ambulatory surgical treatment of groin hernia: prevention and management of complications. Problems in General Surgery 3:311, 1986

44. Wright DM, Kennedy A, Baxter JN, et al: Early outcome after open versus extraperitoneal endoscopic tension-free hernioplasty: a randomized clinical trial. Surgery 119:552, 1996

45. Starling JR, Harms BA: Diagnosis and treatment of genitofemoral and ilioinguinal neuralgia. World J Surg 13:586, 1989

46. Kraus MA: Nerve injury during laparoscopic inguinal hernia repair. Surg Laparosc Endosc 3:342, 1993

47. Rosen A, Halevy A: Anatomical basis for nerve injury during laparoscopic hernia repair. Surg Laparosc Endosc 7:469, 1997

48. Bueno J, Serralta A, Planells M, et al: Inguinodynia after two inguinal herniorrhaphy methods. Surg Laparosc Endosc Percutan Tech 14:210, 2004

49. Bringman S, Rael S, Keikkinen T, et al: Tension-free inguinal hernia repair: TEP versus mesh plug versus Lichtenstein: a prospective randomized controlled trial. Ann Surg 237:142, 2003

50. Champault GG, Rizk N, Catheline J-M, et al: Inguinal hernia repair: totally preperitoneal laparoscopic approach versus Stoppa operation: randomized trial of 100 cases. Surg Lap Endosc 7:445, 1997

51. Khoury N: A randomized prospective controlled trial of laparoscopic extraperitoneal hernia repair and mesh-plug hernioplasty: a study of 315 cases. J Laparoendosc Surg 8:367, 1998

52. Douek M, Smith G, Oshowo A, et al: Prospective randomized controlled trial of laparoscopic versus open inguinal hernia mesh repair: five year follow up. BMJ 326:1012, 2003

53. Filipi CJ, Gaston-Johansson F, McBride PJ, et al: An assessment of pain and return to normal activity: laparoscopic herniorrhaphy vs. open tension-free Lichtenstein repair. Surg Endosc 10:983, 1996

54. Mahon D, Decadt B, Rhodes M: Prospective randomized trial of laparoscopic (transabdominal preperitoneal) vs. open (mesh) repair for bilateral and recurrent inguinal hernia. Surg Endosc 17:1386, 2003

55. Lichtenstein IL, Shulman AG, Amid PK: The cause, prevention, and treatment of recurrent groin hernia. Surg Clin North Am 73:529, 1993

56. Fitzgibbons RJ Jr, Camps J, Cornet DA, et al: Laparoscopic inguinal herniorrhaphy: results of a multicenter trial. Ann Surg 221: 3, 1995

57. Cohen RV, Alvarez G, Roll S, et al: Transabdominal or totally extraperitoneal laparoscopic hernia repair? Surg Laparosc Endosc 8:264, 1998

58. Kald A, Anderber B, Smedh K, et al: Transperitoneal or totally extraperitoneal approach in laparoscopic hernia repair: results of 491 consecutive herniorrhaphies. Surg Laparosc Endosc 7:86, 1997

59. Felix El, Michas CA, Gonzalez MH Jr: Laparoscopic hernioplasty: TAPP vs. TEP. Surg Endosc 9:984, 1995

60. Hesselink VJ, Luijendik RW, de Wilt JHW, et al: An evaluation of risk factors in incisional hernia recurrence. Surg Gynecol Obstet 176:228, 1993

61. Santora TA, Roslyn JJ: Incisional hernia. Surg Clin North Am 73:557, 1993

62. Burger J, Luijendijk R, Hop W, et al: Long-term follow-up of a randomized controlled trial of suture versus mesh repair of incisional hernia. Ann Surg 240:578, 2004

63. Ramshaw BJ, Esartia P, Schwab J, et al: Comparison of laparoscopic and open ventral herniorrhaphy. Am Surg 65:827, 1999

64. Heniford TB, Park A, Ramshaw BJ, et al: Laparoscopic repair of ventral hernias: nine years' experience with 850 consecutive hernias. Ann Surg 238:319, 2003

65. Chu UB, Adrales GL, Schwartz RW, et al: Laparoscopic incisional hernia repair: a technical advance. Curr Surg 2003

66. Moreno-Egea A, Torralba JA, Girela E, et al: Immediate, early and late morbidity with laparoscopic ventral hernia repair and tolerance to composite mesh. Surg Laparosc Endosc Percutan Tech 14:130, 2004

67. Abramov D, Jeroukhimov I, Yinnon AM, et al: Antibiotic prophylaxis in umbilical and incisional hernia repair: a prospective randomized study. Euro J Surg 162:955, 1996

68. Ladurner R, Mussack T: Small bowel perforation due to protruding spiral tackers: a rare complication in laparoscopic incisional hernia repair. Surg Endosc 18:1001, 2004

69. Landau O, Raziel A, Matz A, et al: Laparoscopic repair of poststernotomy subxiphoid epigastric hernia. Surg Endosc 15:1313, 2001

70. Cheung MT, Chia NH, Chiu WY: Surgical treatment of parastomal hernia complicating sigmoid colostomies. Dis Colon Rectum 44:266, 2001

71. Safadi B: Laparoscopic repair of parastomal hernias. Surg Endosc 18:676, 2003

72. Berger DB, Bientzle MB, Müller AM: Technique and results of the laparoscopic repair of parastomal hernias. Surg Endosc 17(suppl):S3, 2003

73. LeBlanc KA, Bellanger DE: Laparoscopic repair of paraostomy hernias: early results. J Am Coll Surg 194:232, 2002

74. Sugarbaker PH: Peritoneal approach to prosthetic mesh repair of paraostomy hernias. Ann Surg 201:344, 1985

75. Goodney PP, Birkmeyer CM, Birkmeyer JD: Short-term outcomes of laparoscopic and open ventral hernia repair—a meta-analysis. Arch Surg 137:1161, 2002

76. Carbajo MA, del Olmo JC, Blanco JI, et al: Laparoscopic treatment of ventral abdominal wall hernias: preliminary results in 100 patients. J Soc Laparoendosc Surg 4:141, 2000

77. Heniford BT, Park A, Ramshaw BJ, et al: Laparoscopic ventral and incisional hernia repair in 407 patients. J Am Coll Surg 190:645, 2000

78. Wright BE, Niskanen BD, Peterson DJ, et al: Laparoscopic ventral hernia repair: are there comparative advantages over traditional methods of repair? Am Surg 68:291, 2002

79. McGreevy JM, Goodney PP, Birkmeyer CM, et al: A prospective study comparing the complication rates between laparoscopic and open ventral hernia repairs. Surg Endosc 17:1778, 2003

80. Salameh JR, Sweeney JF, Gravis EA, et al: Laparoscopic ventral hernia repair during the learning curve. Hernia 6:182, 2002

81. Ben-Haim M, Kuriansky J, Tal R, et al: Pitfalls and complications with laparoscopic intraperitoneal expanded polytetrafluoroethylene patch repair of postoperative ventral hernia. Lessons from the first 100 consecutive cases. Surg Endosc 16:785, 2002

82. Carbonell AM, Harold KL, Mahmutovic AJ, et al: Local injection for the treatment of suture site pain after laparoscopic ventral hernia repair. Am Surg 69:688, 2003

83. Berger D, Bientzle M, Müller A: Postoperative complications after laparoscopic incisional hernia repair. Surg Endosc 16:1720, 2002

84. LeBlanc KA, Whitaker JM, Bellanger DE, et al: Laparoscopic incisional and ventral hernioplasty: lessons learned from 200 patients. Hernia 7:118, 2003

85. Robbins AB, Pofahl WE, Gonzalez RP: Laparoscopic ventral hernia repair reduces wound complications. Am Surg 67:896, 2001

86. Raftopoulos I, Vanuno D, Khorsand J, et al: Comparison of open and laparoscopic prosthetic repair of large ventral hernias. JSLS 7:227, 2003

87. Roth JS, Park AE, Witzke D, et al: Laparoscopic incisional/ventral herniorrhaphy. Hernia 3:209, 1999

88. DeMaria EJ, Moss JM, Sugerman HJ: Laparoscopic intraperitoneal polytetrafluoroethylene (PTFE) prosthetic patch repair of ventral hernia: prospective comparison to open prefascial polypropylene mesh repair. Surg Endosc 14:326, 2000

89. Franklin ME, Gonzalez JJ Jr, Glass JL, et al: Laparoscopic ventral and incisional hernia repair: an 11-year experience. Hernia 8:23, 2004

90. Rosen M, Brody F, Ponsky J, et al: Recurrence after laparoscopic ventral hernia repair—a five year experience. Surg Endosc 17:123, 2003

91. Koehler RH, Voeller G: Recurrences in laparoscopic incisional hernia repairs: a personal series and review of the literature. J Soc Laparoendosc Surg 3:293, 1999

92. Bencini L, Sanchez LJ: Learning curve for laparoscopic ventral hernia repair. Am J Surg 187:378, 2004

Acknowledgments

The authors thank Dr. Dennis Klassen for providing information on available bioprosthetic meshes and fixation devices.
Figures 1, 4, 5, 6, 7, 13   Tom Moore.

71 INTESTINAL ANASTOMOSIS

Julian Britton, M.S., F.R.C.S.

Intestinal obstruction, peritonitis from a perforated bowel, abdominal trauma, and disease of the bowel are common surgical problems throughout the world. These problems usually must be treated operatively; hence, it is frequently necessary to join two sections of bowel together. Unlike joining two areas of skin, where there is a powerful evolutionary incentive to achieve rapid healing, joining two segments of bowel so as to restore intestinal function without leakage of intestinal contents is not easy. Over time, the basic principles crucial for obtaining successful results have been defined [*see Table 1*]. Accurate approximation of the bowel without tension and with a good blood supply to both of the structures being joined are obviously fundamental. Surgical technique is equally important: between two given surgeons, rates of anastomotic breakdown can vary by as much as a factor of 60.[1]

Failure of an anastomosis with leakage of intestinal contents is still, regrettably, a common surgical experience. Reported failure rates range from 1.5%[2] to 2.2%,[3] depending on what type of anastomosis was performed and whether the operation was an elective or an emergency procedure. A leaking anastomosis greatly increases the morbidity and mortality associated with the operation: it can double the length of the hospital stay and increase the mortality as much as 10-fold.[4] Dehiscence, when it occurs, has been associated with one fifth to one third of all postoperative deaths in patients who underwent an intestinal anastomosis.[5]

Unfortunately, anastomotic dehiscence can occur even in ideal circumstances. This unwelcome fact has stimulated a great deal of debate regarding the reliability of various methods and approaches. With the aim of clarifying the debate, I will address certain fundamental technical issues in the performance of an intestinal anastomosis and attempt to summarize what is known about how these issues relate to the reliability of the various anastomotic techniques in current use. I will then outline operative approaches to performing three common intestinal anastomoses in somewhat greater detail [*see* Operative Techniques for Selected Anastomoses, *below*].

Intestinal Anastomotic Healing

Most of the strength of the bowel wall resides in the submucosa[6]; however, for the purpose of suturing bowel segments together, it is important to keep in mind that the serosa (i.e., the visceral peritoneum) holds sutures better than either the longitudinal or the circular muscle layer [*see Figure 1*]. The absence of a peritoneal layer makes suturing of the thoracic esophagus and the rectum below the peritoneal reflection technically more difficult than suturing the intraperitoneal segments of the intestine. In addition, the stomach and the small bowel possess a richer blood supply than the esophagus and the large bowel and consequently tend to heal more readily.

The process of intestinal anastomotic healing mimics that of wound healing elsewhere in the body in that it can be arbitrarily divided into an acute inflammatory (lag) phase, a proliferative phase, and, finally, a remodeling or maturation phase. The strongest component of the bowel wall, the submucosa, owes most of its strength to the collagenous connective tissue it contains. Collagen is thus the single most important molecule for determining intestinal strength, which makes its metabolism of particular interest for understanding anastomotic healing.

Collagen is secreted from fibroblasts in a monomeric form called tropocollagen; this is a large, stiff molecule that can be visualized by electron microscopy. Collagen itself can be divided into subtypes on the basis of compositional differences (i.e., different combinations of α_1 and α_2 chains). Type I collagen predominates in mature organisms; type II is found primarily in cartilage; and type III is associated with type I in remodeling tissue and in elastic tissues such as the aorta, the esophagus, and the uterus. Synthesis of collagen is an intracellular process that occurs on polysomes. A critical stage in collagen formation is the hydroxylation of proline to produce hydroxyproline; this process is believed to be important for maintaining the three-dimensional triple-helix conformation of mature collagen, which gives the molecule its structural strength. The amount of collagen found in a tissue is indirectly determined by measuring the amount of hydroxyproline, though no significant statistical correlation between hydroxyproline content and objective measurements of anastomotic strength has ever been demonstrated.[7] Vitamin C deficiency results in impaired hydroxylation of proline and the accumulation of proline-rich, hydroxyproline-poor molecules in intracellular vacuoles.

The degree of fiber and fibril cross-linking relates to the maturity of the collagen and is probably important in determining the overall strength of the scar tissue. Of equal importance is the orientation of the fibers and their weave. The bursting pressure of anastomoses has often been used to gauge the strength of the healing process. This pressure has been found to increase rapidly in the early postoperative period, reaching 60% of the strength of the surrounding bowel by 3 to 4 days and 100% by 1 week.[8,9]

Collagen synthesis is a dynamic process that depends on the balance between synthesis and collagenolysis. Degradation of mature collagen begins in the first 24 hours and predominates for

---

Table 1 **Principles of Successful Intestinal Anastomosis**

Well-nourished patient with no systemic illness

No fecal contamination, either within the gut or in the surrounding peritoneal cavity

Adequate exposure and access

Well-vascularized tissues

Absence of tension at the anastomosis

Meticulous technique

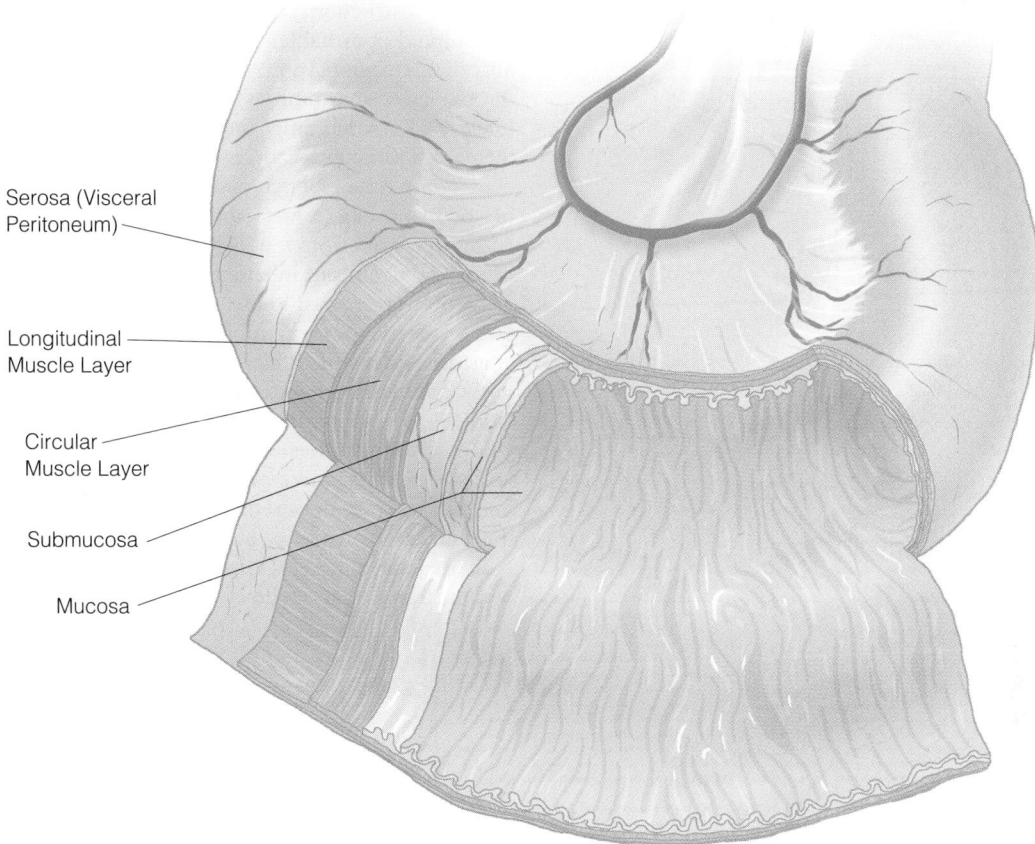

Serosa (Visceral
Peritoneum)

Longitudinal
Muscle Layer

Circular
Muscle Layer

Submucosa

Mucosa

Figure 1 **Shown are the tissue layers of the jejunum. Most of the bowel wall's strength is provided by the submucosa.**

the first 4 days. By 1 week, collagen synthesis is the dominant force, particularly proximal to the anastomosis. After 5 to 6 weeks, there is no significant increase in the amount of collagen in a healing wound or anastomosis, though turnover and thus synthesis are extensive. The strength of the scar continues to increase for many months after injury. Local infection increases collagenase activity and reduces levels of circulating collagenase inhibitors.[10,11]

Collagen synthetic capacity is relatively uniform throughout the large bowel but less so in the small intestine: synthesis is significantly higher in the proximal and distal small intestine than in the midjejunum. Overall collagen synthetic capacity is somewhat less in the small intestine. Although no significant difference has been found between the strength of ileal anastomoses and that of colonic anastomoses at 4 days, colonic collagen formation is much greater in the first 48 hours.[12] It is noteworthy that the synthetic response is not restricted to the anastomotic site but appears to be generalized to a significant extent.[13]

Various attempts have been made to improve the healing of intestinal anastomoses. A 2002 animal study concluded that locally applied charged particles improved the healing of colonic anastomoses.[14]

Technical Options for Fashioning Anastomoses

Sewing bowel segments together with various suture materials, ranging from catgut to stainless steel wire, has been a standard surgical technique for more than 150 years. Staplers, though first developed early in the 20th century, only began to have a significant impact on GI surgery within the past three decades. Staplers certainly

appeal to the technically minded, and most studies suggest that they save a small amount of operating time[15]; however, they remain relatively expensive, and it is still unclear whether the results are any better than can be achieved with suturing. Accordingly, it is worthwhile to examine the technical aspects of the two approaches to bowel anastomosis and to compare their respective merits.

SUTURING: TECHNICAL ISSUES

Choice of Suture Material

Sutures act as foreign bodies in the anastomosis and thus produce an inflammatory reaction.[7] One study that examined the relative efficiency of absorbable and nonabsorbable material concluded that the strength of the anastomosis, expressed as a percentage of normal tissue strength, was essentially the same regardless of the type of suture used. Other studies that examined the amount of inflammation induced at the anastomosis by various types of sutures found that polypropylene (Prolene), catgut, and polyglycolic acid (Dexon) were equivalent in this regard.[16,17] Silk, however, produced a significantly greater cellular reaction at the anastomosis, and the reaction persisted for as long as 6 weeks.[17] A 1975 study reported on a series of 41 patients who underwent low anterior resection involving a primary side-to-end colorectal anastomosis with 5-0 stainless steel wire.[18] The investigators considered this material ideal because of its strength and relative inertness within the tissues, and they supported their claims with a relatively low clinical leakage rate (7.3%).

The ideal suture material—one that causes minimal inflammation and tissue reaction while providing maximum strength during the lag phase of wound healing—is yet to be discovered.

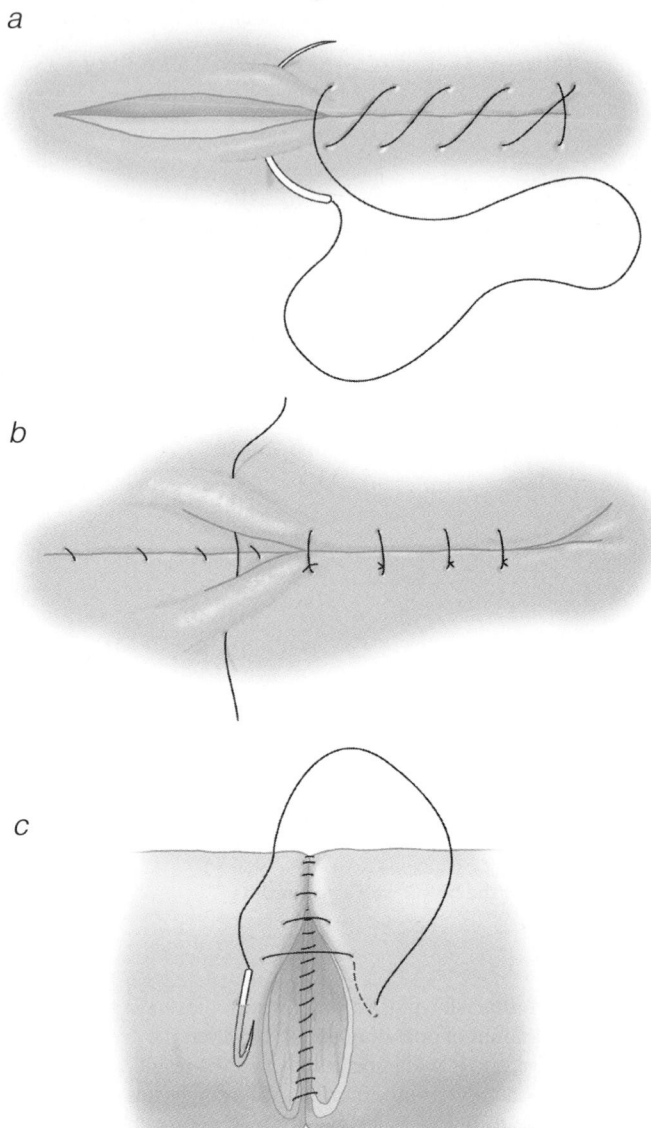

Figure 2 **Shown are stitches commonly used in fashioning intestinal anastomoses: (*a*) the continuous over-and-over suture, (*b*) the interrupted Lembert suture, and (*c*) the Connell suture.**

Clearly, however, monofilament and coated braided sutures represent an advance beyond silk and other multifilament materials.

Continuous versus Interrupted Sutures

Both continuous and interrupted sutures are commonly used in fashioning intestinal anastomoses [*see Figure 2*]. No randomized trials have addressed the question of whether interrupted sutures have a significant advantage over continuous sutures in a single-layer anastomosis; however, retrospective reviews have not revealed any such advantage.[19-21] Animal studies, on the other hand, indicated that perianastomotic tissue oxygen tension was significantly less with continuous sutures than with interrupted sutures.[22] This finding was correlated with an increased anastomotic complication rate and impaired collagen synthesis and healing with continuous sutures in a rat model.[23]

Single-Layer versus Double-Layer Anastomoses

Double-layer anastomoses were described in the literature before single-layer ones. All such anastomoses are of essentially similar construction, consisting of an inner layer of continuous or interrupted absorbable sutures and an outer layer of interrupted absorbable or nonabsorbable sutures [*see Figure 3*]. Traditionally, double-layer anastomoses have been considered more secure; however, for some time, single-layer anastomoses have been performed in difficult locations (e.g., low in the pelvis or high in the chest) or in difficult circumstances (e.g., in a patient who is unstable or has multiple intra-abdominal injuries) with good results. Moreover, work from the 1980s suggests that the single-layer technique has significant inherent advantages.[23-26]

Double-layer anastomoses were long believed to be essential for safe healing; however, subsequent pathologic analysis of these anastomoses revealed microscopic areas of necrosis and sloughing of the tissues incorporated in the inner layer as a result of strangulation.[27] Animal studies confirmed that single-layer anastomoses take less time to create,[28] cause less narrowing of the intestinal lumen,[24-29] foster more rapid vascularization[23] and mucosal healing, and increase the strength of the anastomosis (as measured by the bursting pressure) in the first few postoperative days.[28] Nonetheless, although clinical studies have fairly consistently demonstrated that single-layer anastomoses are associated with

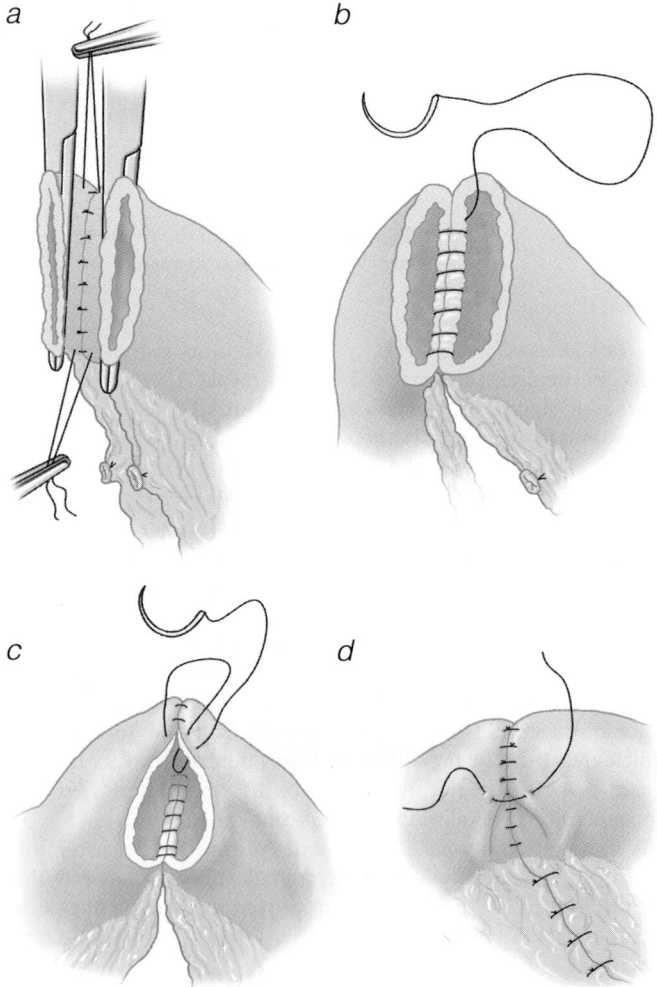

Figure 3 **Double-layer end-to-end anastomosis. (*a*) Interrupted Lembert stitches are used to form the posterior outer layer. (*b*) A full-thickness continuous over-and-over stitch is used to form the posterior inner layer. (*c*) A Connell stitch is used to form the anterior inner layer. (*d*) Interrupted Lembert stitches are used to form the anterior outer layer.**

improved postoperative return to normal bowel function (as measured by bowel sounds, passage of flatus, and return to oral intake),[30,31] nonrandomized studies of anastomotic leakage rates have not shown any differences between single- and double-layer anastomoses in this regard.[32-34]

Some authors still favor double-layer anastomoses when the tissues are very edematous or friable, are under minimal tension, or lie in highly vascular areas (e.g., the stomach). There are no data to indicate that this practice yields superior results.

STAPLING: TECHNICAL ISSUES

Choice of Stapler

Surgical stapling devices were first introduced in 1908 by Hültl; however, they did not gain popularity at that time and for some time afterward because the early instruments were cumbersome and unreliable. The development of reliable, disposable instruments over the past 25 years has changed surgical practice dramat-

ically. With modern devices, technical failures are rarer, the staple lines are of more consistent quality, and anastomoses in difficult locations are easier to construct.

Three different types of stapler are commonly used for fashioning intestinal anastomoses. The transverse anastomosis (TA) stapler is the simplest of these. This device places two staggered rows of B-shaped staples across the bowel but does not cut it: the bowel must then be divided in a separate step. The gastrointestinal anastomosis (GIA) stapler places two double staggered rows of staples and simultaneously cuts between the double rows. The circular, or end-to-end anastomosis (EEA), stapler places a double row of staples in a circle and then cuts out the tissue within the circle of staples with a built-in cylindrical knife. All of these staplers are available in a range of lengths or diameters. Staplers may be used to create functional or true anatomic end-to-end anastomoses as well as side-to-side anastomoses. The original staplers were all designed for use in open procedures, but there are now a number of instruments (mostly of the GIA type) available for use in laparo-

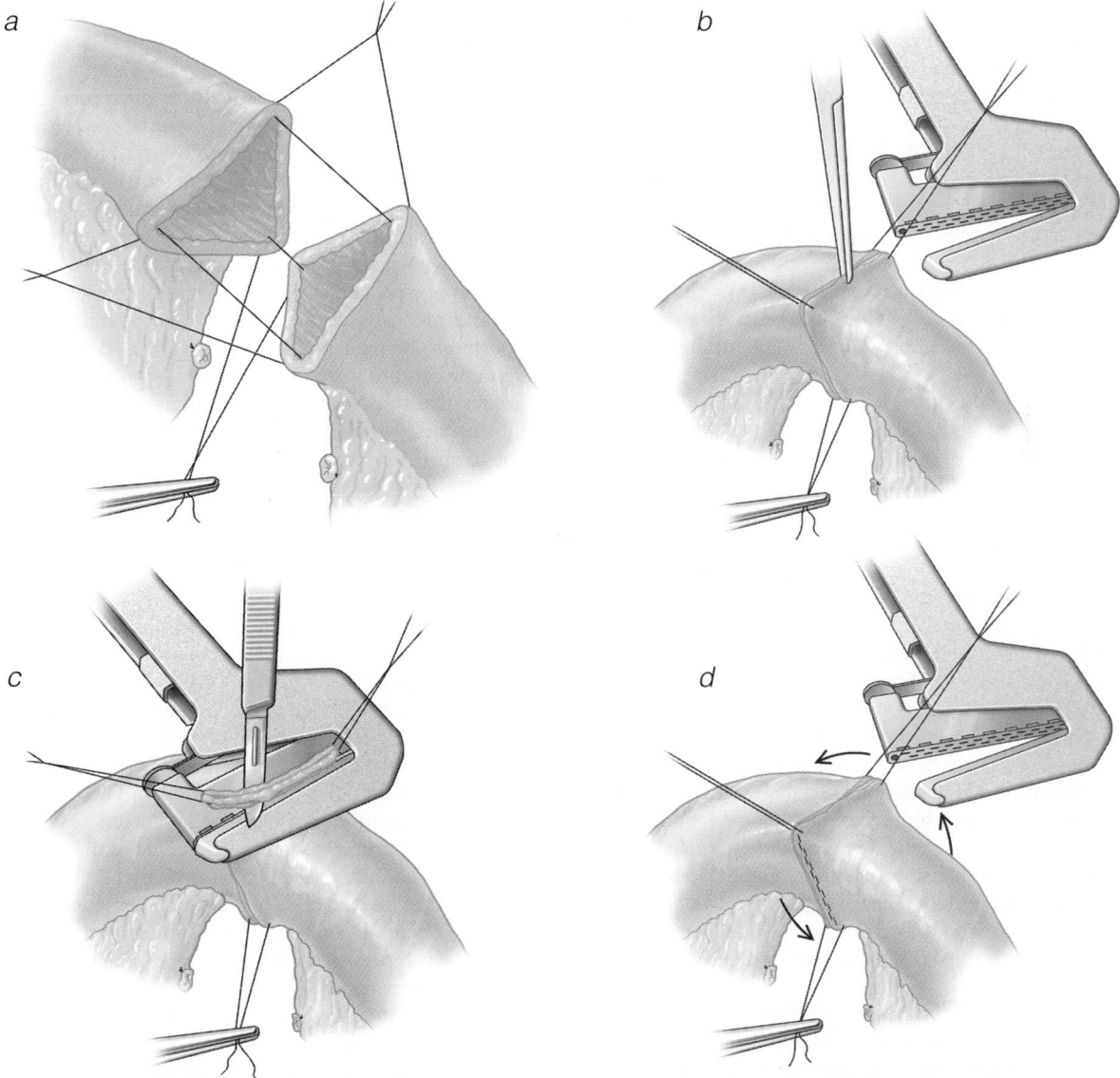

Figure 4 **End-to-end anastomosis with linear noncutting stapler. (*a*) The bowel ends are triangulated with three traction sutures. (*b*) A noncutting linear stapler (TA) is placed between two of the sutures. (*c*) The stapler is closed and the excess tissue excised. (*d*) The bowel is rotated, and steps *b* and *c* are repeated twice more to close the remaining two sides of the triangle.**

scopic procedures. The staples themselves are all made of titanium, which causes little tissue reaction. They are not magnetic and do not cause subsequent difficulties with MRI scanning.

In a functional end-to-end anastomosis, two cut ends of bowel (either open or stapled closed) are placed side by side with their blind ends beside each other. If the bowel ends are closed, an enterotomy must be made in each loop of bowel to allow insertion of the stapler. A cutting linear (GIA) stapler is then used to fuse the two bowel walls into a single septum with two double staggered rows of staples and to create a lumen between the two bowel segments by dividing this septum between the rows. A noncutting linear (TA) stapler is then used to close the defect at the apex of the anastomosis where the GIA stapler was inserted. An alternative, and cheaper, method of closing the defect is to use a continuous suture. The cut and stapled edges of the bowel should be inspected for adequacy of hemostasis before the apex is closed. Some authors suggest cauterizing these edges to ensure hemostasis[35]; however, given that electrical current may be conducted along the metallic staple line to the rest of the bowel, it is probably easier and safer simply to underpin bleeding vessels with a fine absorbable suture. It is also important to offset the two inverted staple lines before closing the apex.[36]

True anatomic end-to-end stapled anastomoses may be fashioned with a linear stapler by triangulating the two cut ends and then firing the stapler three times in intersecting vectors to achieve complete closure [see Figure 4]. The potential drawback of this approach is that the staple lines are all everted. It is often easier to join two cut ends of bowel with an EEA stapler, which creates a directly apposed, inverted, stapled end-to-end anastomosis. However, circular staplers can be more difficult to use at times because of the need to invert a complete circle of full-thickness bowel wall. In addition—at least at locations other than the anus—they typically require closure of an adjacent enterotomy.

Staple Height

TA and GIA staplers are available with a variety of inserts containing several different types of staples. These inserts vary with respect to width, the height (or depth) of the closed staple, and the distance between the staples in the rows. They are designed for use in specific tissues, and it is important to choose the correct stapler insert for a given application. In particular, inserts designed for closing blood vessels should not be used on the bowel, and vice versa. With TA and EEA staplers, it is possible to vary the depth of the closed staples by altering the distance between the staples and the anvil as the instrument is closed. The safe range of closure is usually indicated by a colored or shaded area on the shaft of the instrument. Thus, if full closure would cause excessive crushing of the intervening tissues, the stapler need not be closed to its maximum extent.

A 1987 comparison of anastomotic techniques that used blood flow to the divided tissues as a measure of outcome found that the best blood flow to the healing site was provided by stapled anastomoses in which the staple height was adjusted to the thickness of the bowel wall.[37] The next best blood flow was provided by double-layer stapled and sutured anastomoses, followed by double-layer sutured anastomoses and tightly stapled anastomoses, in that order.

Single-Stapled versus Double-Stapled Anastomoses

To accomplish many of these anastomoses, intersecting staple lines are created. Initially, some concern was expressed about the security of these areas and about the ability of the blade in the cutting staplers to divide a double staggered row of staples. Animal studies, however, demonstrated that even though nearly all (> 90%) of the staple lines that were subsequently transected by a second staple line contained bent or cut staples, the integrity of the anastomosis was not compromised in any way, nor was healing adversely affected.[38,39]

HAND-SEWN VERSUS STAPLED ANASTOMOSES

Stapled anastomoses are said to heal by primary intention, whereas sutured anastomoses are said to heal by secondary intention, though further experimentation is needed to confirm this distinction.[40] Titanium staples are ideal for tissue apposition at anastomotic sites because they provoke only a minimal inflammatory response and provide immediate strength to the cut surfaces during the weakest phase of healing. Initially, tissue eversion at the stapled anastomosis was a major concern, given that everted hand-sewn anastomoses had previously been shown to be inferior to inverted ones; however, the greater support and improved blood supply to the healing tissues associated with stapling tend to counteract the negative effects of eversion. In fact, one study found that bursting strength for canine colonic end-to-end anastomoses was six times greater when the procedure was performed with an EEA stapler than when it was done with interrupted Dacron sutures.[41] Another study demonstrated a significantly reduced radiographic anastomotic leakage rate with staples applied by an EEA stapler as opposed to a double layer of sutures.[42] Various prospective, randomized trials have demonstrated no differences in clinical and subclinical leakage rates, length of hospital stay, or overall morbidity.[15,39,43-46] Even when the anastomosis had to heal under adverse conditions (e.g., carcinomatosis, malnutrition, previous chemotherapy or radiation therapy, bowel obstruction, anemia, or leukopenia), no significant differences were apparent between stapled and hand-sewn anastomoses. Stapling did, however, shorten operating time, especially for low pelvic anastomoses.

Cancer recurrence rates at the site of the anastomosis have been reported to be higher or lower depending on the technique used. Certainly, suture materials engender a more pronounced cellular proliferative response than titanium staples do, particularly with full-thickness sutures as opposed to seromuscular ones,[47] and malignant cells have been shown to adhere to suture materials.[48] Two studies suggested that stapling anastomoses after resection for cancer reduces anastomotic recurrence by 40% and cancer-specific mortality by 50%.[47,49]

UNUSUAL TECHNIQUES

In 1892, Murphy introduced his button, which consisted of a two-part metal stud that was designed to hold the bowel edges in apposition without suturing until adhesion had occurred.[50] Thereafter, the stud was voided via the rectum. Several modifications of this technique have been described since then, primarily focusing on the composition of the rings or stents. In particular, dissolvable polyglycolic acid systems have been developed. These so-called biofragmentable anastomotic rings leave a gap of 1.5, 2.0, or 2.5 mm between the bowel ends to prevent ischemia of the anastomotic line.

The use of adhesive agents such as methyl-2-cyanoacrylate to approximate the divided ends of intestinal segments has been studied as well.[51] There was only a moderate inflammatory response at the wound, which persisted for 2 to 3 weeks. Leakage rates were high, however, and many technical problems remained (e.g., how to stabilize the bowel edges while they underwent adhesion).

Fibrin glues have also been employed in this setting. Although these substances are not strong enough to hold two pieces of bowel in apposition, they have been used to coat a sutured bowel anastomosis in an effort to reduce the risk of anastomotic failure. So far, no controlled clinical trials have confirmed that this approach is worthwhile.

Factors Contributing to Failure of Anastomoses

TYPE AND LOCATION OF ANASTOMOSIS

As a rule, for any given technique, the location of the anastomosis seems not to influence the overall leakage rate. There are two exceptions to this general rule. First, low anterior rectal anastomoses are associated with leakage rates ranging from 4.5% to an incredible 70%.[52,53] Second, esophageal anastomoses are associated with leakage rates of about 5%.[54]

Animal studies demonstrated improved transmission of the intestinal migrating myoelectric complex across hand-sewn end-to-end anastomoses, compared with stapled or sewn side-to-side or end-to-side anastomoses or stapled functional end-to-end anastomoses.[55] This improvement may be significant for patients with diseases affecting small bowel motility, but in ordinary surgical practice, there is no difference between the two methods of anastomosis with respect to return of intestinal function.[56]

PATIENT PREPARATION

Many intestinal anastomoses are constructed in an emergency setting. In this context, careful preoperative preparation, including adequate fluid resuscitation, is important and should be carried out to the extent possible. Elective patients should be as fit as is feasible, and any other active coexisting illnesses should be stabilized or controlled as well as possible. To maximize the chances that the anastomosis will heal uneventfully, patients should be well nourished and not anemic. Adequate preoperative antibiotic prophylaxis has been shown to reduce the risk of postoperative infection in all types of bowel surgery and must be given at the start of the operation [see 5 Prevention of Postoperative Infection]. Some patients require additional steroids perioperatively [see 125 Endocrine Problems].

For elective operations on the colon, it is traditional to empty the bowel before surgery. Some studies, however, have suggested that mechanical bowel preparation may not be essential for successful healing.[57,58] In one such study, a series of 72 patients underwent elective colonic anastomosis without any mechanical bowel preparation and with a single preoperative dose of I.V. antibiotics.[57] Anastomotic dehiscence was not observed, nor were any differences in wound infection rates (8.3%) or overall mortality (2.7%) noted in comparison with published reports of series of patients who underwent full bowel preparation. On the other hand, a 1989 study reported significantly increased anastomotic bursting pressure and reduced anastomotic dehiscence rates in dogs that underwent mechanical bowel cleansing before low anterior resection.[52] This observation was further supported by a study showing that adding oral erythromycin and kanamycin to bowel preparation led to significantly increased bursting pressure at 7 days after operation.[59] In a number of published clinical series, inadequate bowel preparation increased the incidence of anastomotic complications.[53,60] However, there are also several papers in which mechanical bowel preparation yielded no demonstrable benefit.[61]

Whatever the advantages or disadvantages of preoperative bowel preparation from a postoperative point of view, most surgeons would agree that it is much easier to operate on an empty bowel. Several methods of bowel preparation are in current use, including oral laxatives (e.g., magnesium sulfate and sodium picosulfate), enemas, washouts, and various combinations of these. It is advisable for patients to stop eating solid food 24 hours before the operation. The evidence that adding oral antibiotics is beneficial is inconclusive, but many trials have confirmed the benefits of one, two, or three doses of I.V. antibiotics over the perioperative period. Prophylaxis of thromboembolism [see 85 Venous Thromboembolism] is mandatory in all patients scheduled to undergo intestinal anastomosis.

ASSOCIATED DISEASES AND SYSTEMIC FACTORS

Anemia, diabetes mellitus, previous irradiation or chemotherapy, malnutrition with hypoalbuminemia, and vitamin deficiencies are all associated with poor anastomotic healing. Some of these factors can be corrected preoperatively. Malnourished patients benefit from nutritional support delivered enterally or parenterally before and after operation [see 137 Nutritional Support]. Well-nourished patients appear not to derive similar benefits from such support.[62]

Resections for Crohn disease appear to carry a significant risk of anastomotic dehiscence (12% in one prospective study) even when macroscopically normal margins are obtained.[3] Strictureplasty has therefore become an attractive alternative to resectional management of Crohn disease even in the presence of moderately long strictures, diseased tissue, or sites of previous anastomoses.

The glucocorticoid response to injury may attenuate physiologic responses to other mediators whose combined effects could be deleterious to the organism.[63] In animal experiments, wound healing, as measured by bursting pressure of an ileal anastomosis 1 week after operation, was optimal at a plasma corticosterone level that maintained maximal nitrogen balance and corresponded to the mean corticosterone level of normal animals.[64] Both supranormal and subnormal cortisol levels resulted in significantly impaired wound healing, probably through different mechanisms. It is believed that slow protein turnover is responsible for delayed anastomotic healing in adrenalectomized animals,[65] whereas negative nitrogen metabolic balance is responsible for increased protein breakdown and delayed healing in animals with excess glucocorticoid activity.[64] Nonsteroidal anti-inflammatory drugs (NSAIDs) may help increase anastomotic bursting pressure by decreasing perianastomotic inflammation,[66,67] but this effect has not been well studied.

Controversial Issues in Intestinal Anastomosis

INVERSION VERSUS EVERSION

The question of the importance of inversion (as described by Lembert in the early 1800s) versus eversion of the anastomotic line has long been a controversial one. It has been argued that the traditional inverting methods ignore the basic principle of accurately opposing clean-cut tissues. In the late 19th century, Halsted proposed an interrupted extramucosal technique, which has since been assessed in retrospective[1] and prospective[3] reviews and found to have a low leakage rate (1.3% to 6.0%) in a wide variety of circumstances. A 1969 study reported greater anastomotic strength, less luminal narrowing, and less edema and inflammation with everted small intestinal anastomoses in dogs.[67] Subsequent laboratory and clinical studies have not confirmed these findings and, in fact, have often yielded quite the opposite results: lower bursting pressure,[68] slower healing,[69] and more severe inflammation[31] have all been associated with an everted suture line. Another argument in favor of inversion is an aesthetic one: an inverted anastomosis always looks neater.

NASOGASTRIC DECOMPRESSION

Routine nasogastric decompression in patients undergoing a procedure involving an intestinal anastomosis remains controversial. In retrospective[70] and prospective,[71] randomized, controlled trials, routine use of a nasogastric tube conferred no significant advantage. In fact, there was a trend toward an increased incidence of respiratory tract infections after routine gastric decompression.[72] Nonetheless, one study found that nearly 20% of patients required insertion of a gastric tube in the early postoperative period.[71] If the choice is made not to place a nasogastric tube routinely, it is important to remain alert to the potential for gastric dilatation, which can develop suddenly and without warning.

ABDOMINAL DRAINS

There has been a great deal of disagreement regarding the ability of abdominal drainage to "protect" an anastomosis. Even before World War I, the old dictum "when in doubt, drain" was called into question by Yates, who wrote that the peritoneal cavity could not be effectively drained because of adhesions and rapid sealing of the drain tract.[73] Six decades later, one study showed a dramatic increase in the incidence of anastomotic dehiscence (from 15% to 55%) after the placement of perianastomotic drains in dogs.[74] This increase was associated with a significant increase in mortality. A 1999 study of pelvic drainage after a rectal or anal anastomosis showed that prophylactic drainage did not improve outcome or reduce complications.[75] Yet another study reported the severe inflammatory reaction caused by drains at anastomoses.[76]

These findings to the contrary, many surgeons elect to place an intra-abdominal drain to the pelvis after an anterior resection or a coloanal anastomosis because of the higher than usual risk that a fluid collection will develop. Drainage is rarely helpful, or indeed easy, after a gastric or small bowel anastomosis. Drains are indicated, however, after emergency operations for peritonitis or trauma in which it was necessary to close or anastomose damaged or inflamed bowel. Rectal tubes are commonly employed after subtotal colectomy for acute colitis and after two-stage pelvic pouch procedures.

Operative Techniques for Selected Anastomoses

In what follows, I outline the essential preliminary steps before a bowel anastomosis and then describe three generic operations involving the small and large bowel. These procedures illustrate many of the general principles previously discussed (see above).

PATIENT POSITIONING AND INCISION

Patients must be positioned on the operating table in a manner that is appropriate for the planned operation. Most abdominal operations are performed through a midline incision of adequate length with the patient supine. For pelvic procedures, the patient is placed in the lithotomy position to allow access to the abdomen and the anus; care must be taken to position the legs and feet in the stirrups correctly, without excessive flexion or abduction and with sufficient padding to prevent pressure ulceration, thrombosis, and neurapraxia. For esophageal procedures, the patient is positioned lying on the appropriate side, and the incision of choice is a lateral thoracotomy [see 34 Open Esophageal Procedures]. Occasionally, the patient must be shifted to a different position during the course of an operation.

Gravity can be useful for moving structures out of the way. Accordingly, it is often helpful to alter the axis of the operating table. For example, a 30° head down or Trendelenburg position facilitates pelvic operations.

EXPOSURE, MOBILIZATION, AND DISSECTION

The incision should be held open with a suitable retractor. In addition, sophisticated mechanical systems are available that attach to the operating table and can be positioned to expose the area of the surgeon's attention, thereby reducing the need for surgical assistants. Constructing such systems and adjusting them for specific patients takes some time and skill, but the effort is usually well rewarded. Adequate exposure of the operative field is an essential preliminary to any operation. Given that most intestinal operations are performed inside the body cavity, packing away structures that are not required for the procedure being done is an important skill. In a pelvic operation, for example, the small bowel should be packed into the upper abdomen and retained there with a suitable retractor; in an esophageal resection, the lung should be deflated and held well away.

In the absence of adhesions or tethering caused by disease, the small bowel is usually sufficiently mobile to allow the relevant segment to be brought out of the abdomen. Doing so makes the operation easier and allows the remainder of the bowel to be kept warm and tension free inside the abdominal cavity. Sometimes, the transverse colon and the sigmoid colon are mobile enough to be brought to the surface. More commonly, however, as with the other sections of the large bowel, the peritoneum must be divided along the lateral border of the colon and the retroperitoneal structures reflected posteriorly. Tension is rarely a problem during small bowel anastomosis, but for colonic or esophageal anastomoses, it is absolutely vital that the two ends of bowel to be joined lie together easily. For a large bowel anastomosis, this means that the splenic flexure or the hepatic flexure—or, sometimes, both—must be adequately mobilized.

Classically, the tissues around the bowel are divided with a scissors, whereas the mesentery is divided between clamps and tied with a suitable thread. Recognized tissue planes are separated by means of blunt dissection with either the fingers or a swab. Minor bleeding points are occluded with a coagulating electrocautery, though this approach is often relatively ineffective on mesenteric or omental vessels. The disadvantages of this dissection technique are that oozing from raw surfaces can be a nuisance and that the tissues beyond a tie are often bulky and leave dead tissue within the body that may act as a focus for infection and adhesions. Newer methods of dissection that make use of the ultrasonic scalpel or the bloodless bipolar electrocautery prevent these problems by coagulating a small section of tissue between the jaws of the instrument and simultaneously occluding all blood vessels up to a certain size within the tissues. Consequently, bleeding is reduced, fewer (or no) ties are needed, and only a small quantity of dead tissue results at each point. Becoming skilled in the use of these instruments often takes a little time, but the time is well spent, in that it is now possible to perform an intestinal resection without resort to a single tie.

BOWEL RESECTION

The precise techniques involved in resecting specific bowel segments will not be discussed in great detail here. (Colonic resection, for example, is covered elsewhere [see 76 Segmental Colon Resection].) The following discussion outlines only the general principles.

Preparation

The segment of bowel to be removed must be isolated with an adequate resection margin. To this end, all surrounding adhesions are divided. Next, the mesentery is divided. The key consideration in this step is to preserve the blood supply to the two remaining ends of bowel while still achieving adequate excision of the diseased bowel. This is more easily accomplished in the small bowel than in the large bowel, thanks to the ample blood supply of the former; even so, transillumination of the mesentery and careful division of the vascular arcade are vital. In the colon, the surrounding fat and the appendices epiploicae should be cleared from the remaining bowel ends so that subsequent suture placement is straightforward.

Care should be taken to avoid two common problems. First, ties placed close to the bowel can bunch tissues excessively and thereby cause angulation or distortion of the free edge of the intestine, which can make the anastomosis difficult and threaten the blood supply. Second, because mesenteric vessels are usually tied very close to their ends, the arteries sometimes slip back beyond the ties. Such slippage results in a hematoma within the leaves of the mesentery, which can itself threaten the viability of the bowel. Generally, the bleeding vessel can be secured with a fine stitch; sometimes, however, a limited further bowel resection is the only safe course of action. Both of these problems can be avoided by using the ultrasonic scalpel or the bipolar coagulating electrocautery.

Division of Bowel

If staplers are not available, the bowel segment to be removed is isolated between noncrushing clamps placed across the intestinal lumen some distance away from the resection margin so as to limit the amount of bowel contents that can escape into the wound. Crushing clamps are then placed on the specimen side of the diseased segment at the point of the resection, and the bowel is divided with a knife just proximal and distal to the clamps. Thus, the lumen of the diseased segment is never open within the abdominal wound. Even so, the contents of the bowel between the open ends and the noncrushing clamps can leak into the wound. To minimize this problem, it is usual to isolate the working area with abdominal packs, which are sometimes soaked in an antiseptic (e.g., povidone-iodine).

One advantage of using staplers for anastomosis is that in most instances, division of the bowel can be accomplished without opening the lumen. A linear cutting stapler (e.g., GIA) transects the bowel and seals the two cut ends simultaneously. Unfortunately, in the pelvis, it is usually necessary to employ an angulated noncutting linear stapler (e.g., TA) so as to obtain as much length as possible distal to the lesion. The proximal rectum is then clamped with a crushing bowel clamp, and a long knife is used to transect the rectum above the staple line. Even so, there remains the potential for leakage of a small amount of fecal material, which must then be suctioned away.

SIMPLE BOWEL CLOSURE

There are many cases in which simple closure of a hole in the bowel is required, as with a perforated duodenal ulcer, a gunshot wound, or the inadvertent perforation of the small bowel during the division of dense peritoneal adhesions. Most surgeons close such holes with two layers of soluble suture material (e.g., 2-0 polyglycolic acid). My own preference is for an inner continuous layer inverted with outer seromuscular interrupted sutures, but there are many perfectly satisfactory alternatives.

Special mention should be made of the technique of strictureplasty, which is used for a number of benign small bowel strictures (especially those resulting from Crohn disease) as a means of avoiding small bowel resection and anastomoses. In this procedure, the bowel is opened longitudinally and closed transversely with a single layer of 2-0 polyglycolic acid sutures in a Connell stitch. Excellent functional results have been achieved with this technique despite its reputation for fistula formation, which is associated with Crohn disease.

SINGLE-LAYER SUTURED EXTRAMUCOSAL SIDE-TO-SIDE ENTEROENTEROSTOMY

A side-to-side anastomosis [see Figure 5] may be performed when no resection is done, as a bypass procedure (e.g., a gastroen-

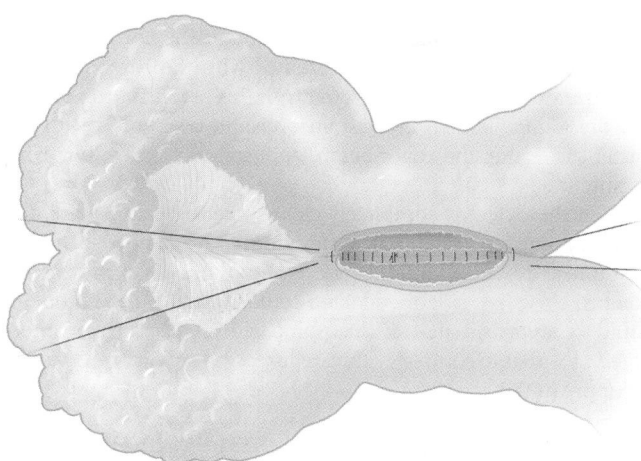

Figure 5 **Single-layer sutured extramucosal side-to-side enteroenterostomy. A full-length suture is started in the back wall and run through the seromuscular and submucosal layers in the direction of the surgeon; the corners of the enterotomy are approximated with a baseball stitch, and a single Connell stitch is used to invert the anterior layer. A second suture is started at the same spot on the posterior wall and run in the opposite direction, again through all layers except the mucosa; the corners of the enterotomies are approximated with a baseball stitch, and the suture is continued in either the Connell stitch or the over-and-over stitch to complete the anterior wall of the anastomosis.**

terostomy); after a small bowel resection; when there is a discrepancy in the diameter of the two ends to be anastomosed (e.g., an ileocolic anastomosis after a right hemicolectomy); or when the anatomy is such that the most tension-free position for the anastomosis is with the two bowel segments parallel (as in a Finney strictureplasty).

Two stay sutures of 3-0 polyglycolic acid are placed approximately 8 cm apart on the inner aspect of the antimesenteric border. A 5 cm enterotomy is made on each loop with an electrocautery or a blade on the inner aspect of the antimesenteric border. If electrocautery is used, care must be taken not to injure the mucosa of the posterior wall during this maneuver; placement of a hemostat into the enterotomy to lift the anterior wall usually prevents this problem. Hemostasis of the cut edges is ensured, and the remaining enteric contents are gently suctioned out. A swab soaked in povidone-iodine may be used at this point to cleanse the lumen of the bowel in the perianastomotic region.

A full-length seromuscular and submucosal stitch of 4-0 polyglycolic acid is placed and tied on the inside approximately 5 to 10 mm from the far end of the enterotomies. The stitch is not passed through the mucosa: to do so would add no strength to the anastomosis and would hinder epithelialization by rendering the tissue ischemic. A hemostat is placed on the short end of the tied suture, and the assistant applies continuous gentle tension to the long end of the suture. An over-and-over stitch is started in the direction of the surgeon; small bites are taken, and proper inversion of the suture line is ensured with each pass through tissue. When the proximal ends of the enterostomies are reached, this so-called baseball stitch is continued almost completely around to the anterior wall of the anastomosis. A single Connell stitch may be used to invert this anterior layer.

Another full-length seromuscular and submucosal suture of 4-0 polyglycolic acid is then inserted and tied at the same location in the posterior wall as the first. If the two sutures are placed close enough together, the short ends need not be tied together and may simply be cut off. The remainder of the posterior wall is sewn away from the surgeon in the same manner as the portion already sewn, and the corners are approximated with the baseball stitch. The anterior wall is then completed with this second suture, either with the Connell stitch or with an over-and-over stitch with the assistant inverting the edges before applying tension to the previous stitch.

When the defect is completely closed, the two sutures are tied across the anastomotic line. The stay sutures are removed, and the anastomosis is carefully inspected. Often, there is no mesenteric defect to close in a side-to-side anastomosis, but if there is one, it should be approximated at this point with continuous or interrupted absorbable sutures, with care taken not to injure the vascular supply to the anastomosis.

DOUBLE-LAYER SUTURED END-TO-SIDE ENTEROCOLOSTOMY

In this procedure, the end of the ileum is joined to the side of the transverse colon [see Figure 6]. The distal colon is divided with a cutting stapler so that a blind end is left. Some surgeons underpin or bury this staple line, though this practice is probably unnecessary. The proximal cut end of the intestine is similarly closed either with staples after division with a cutting linear stapler or with a crushing bowel clamp. This proximal end is brought into apposition with the side of the distal bowel segment at a point no farther than 2.5 to 5 cm from the blind end of the distal segment; this proximity to the cut end is important for prevention of the blind loop syndrome.

Stay sutures of 3-0 polyglycolic acid are placed between the serosa of the proximal limb, about 10 to 15 mm from the clamp, and the serosa of the distal limb. Interrupted seromuscular sutures of 3-0 polyglycolic acid are then placed between these stay sutures, spaced about three to six to the centimeter. These stitches

may be tied sequentially or snapped and tied once they are all in place. It is crucial not to apply excessive tension, which could cut the seromuscular layer or render it ischemic. Suction is then readied. The staple line or crushed tissue on the proximal limb is cut off with a coagulating electrocautery or a knife; this maneuver opens the lumen of the proximal limb. All residual intestinal content is gently suctioned.

An enterotomy or colotomy is created on the distal limb opposite the open lumen of the proximal bowel. A full-thickness suture of 3-0 polyglycolic acid is inserted in the posterior wall at a point close to the far end of the enterotomy and run in an over-and-over stitch back toward the surgeon. The corner is rounded with the baseball stitch, and when the anterior wall is reached, the Connell stitch is used. A second full-length 3-0 suture is started at the same point on the posterior wall as the first, and the short ends of the two sutures are tied together and cut. This second suture is then run away from the surgeon to complete the posterior wall, and the anterior wall is completed with the Connell stitch. The two sutures are then tied across the anastomotic line.

A second series of interrupted seromuscular stitches is then placed anteriorly in the same fashion as the seromuscular stitches placed in the posterior wall. It is important not to narrow either lumen excessively by imbricating too much of the bowel wall into this second layer. The lumen of the anastomosis is palpated to confirm patency, and the mesenteric defect is closed if possible with either continuous or interrupted absorbable sutures.

DOUBLE-STAPLED END-TO-END COLOANAL ANASTOMOSIS

Resection of the distal sigmoid colon and the rectum is a common procedure. In the past, it often resulted in a permanent colostomy because of the technical difficulties associated with a hand-sewn

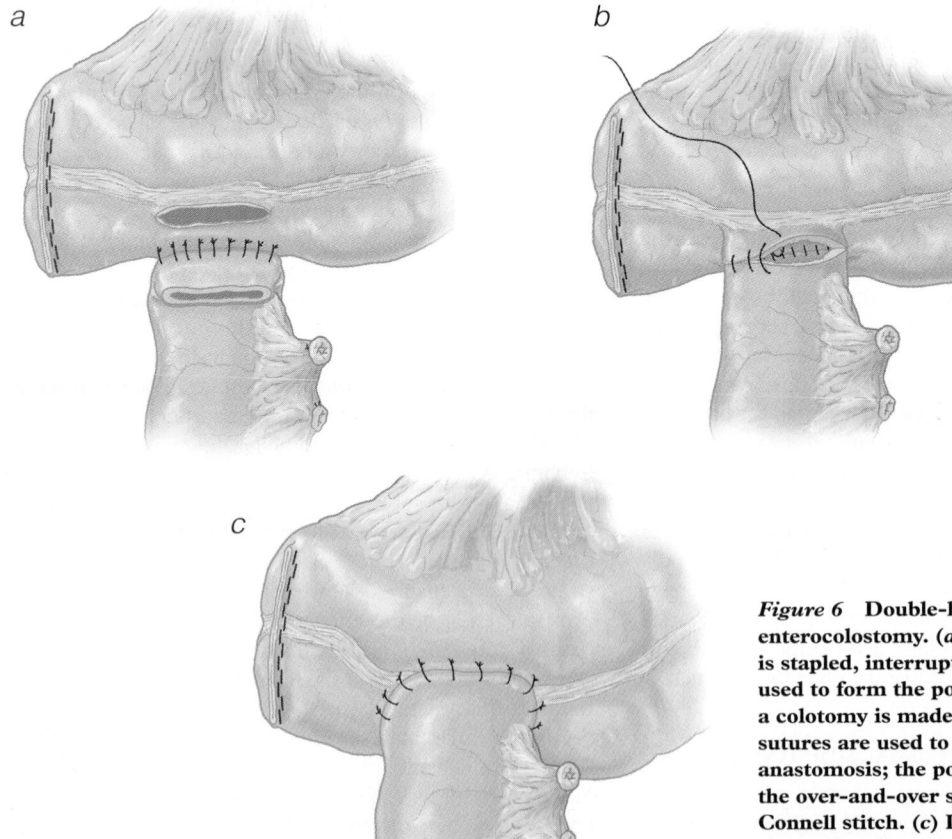

Figure 6 **Double-layer sutured end-to-side enterocolostomy. (*a*) The proximal bowel end is stapled, interrupted Lembert stitches are used to form the posterior outer layer, and a colotomy is made. (*b*) Two continuous sutures are used to form the inner layer of the anastomosis; the posterior portion is done with the over-and-over stitch, the anterior with the Connell stitch. (*c*) Interrupted Lembert stitches are used to form the anterior outer layer.**

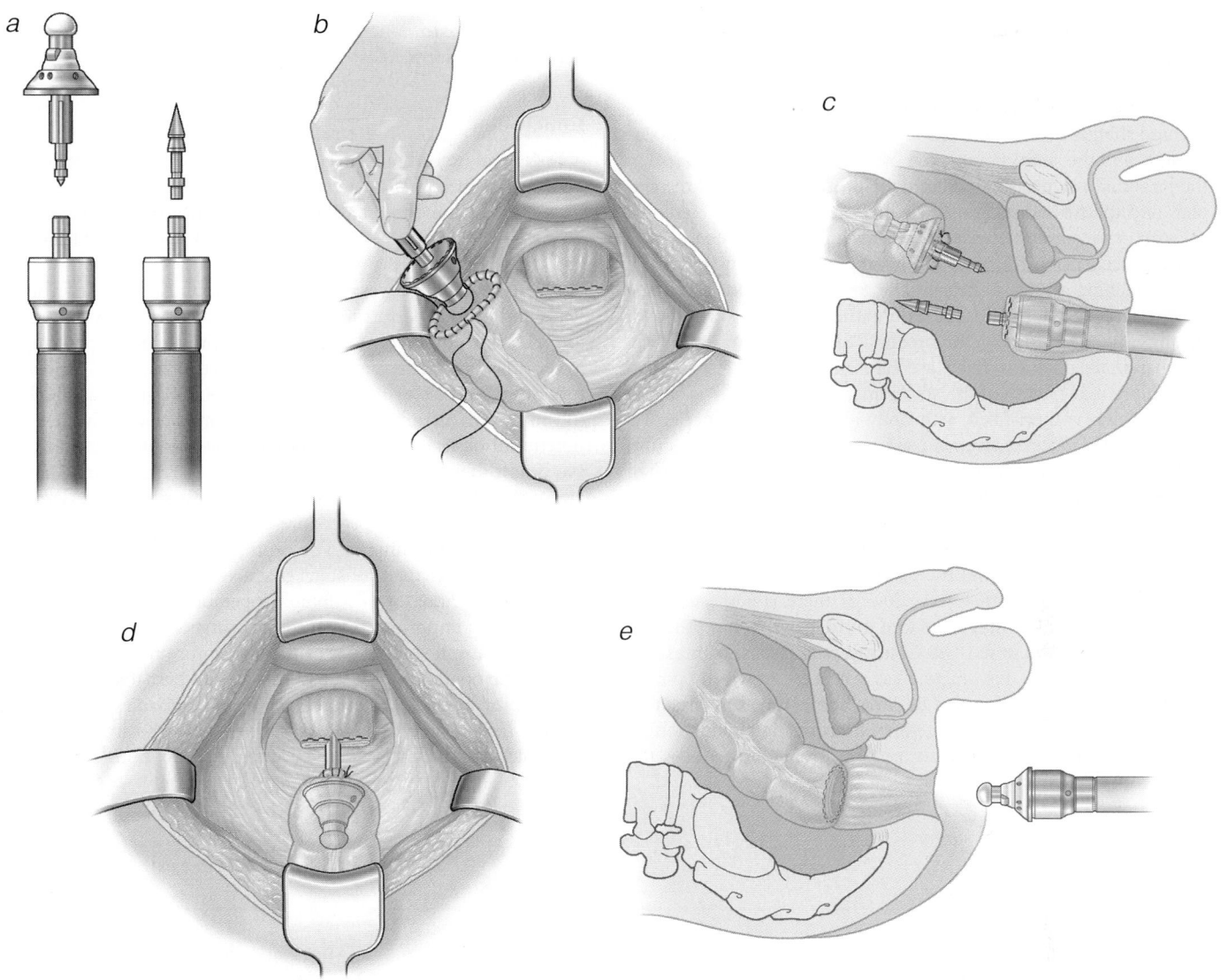

Figure 7 **Double-stapled end-to-end coloanal anastomosis. (*a*) The C-EEA stapler comes with both a standard anvil (left) and a trocar attachment (right). (*b*) The rectal stump is closed with an angled linear noncutting stapler. A purse-string suture is placed around the colotomy, and the anvil of the stapler is placed in the open end and secured. (*c*) The stapler, with the sharp trocar attachment in place, is inserted into the anus, and the trocar is made to pierce the rectal stump at or near the staple line, after which the trocar is removed. (*d*) The anvil in the proximal colon is joined with the stapler in the rectal stump, and the two edges are slowly brought together. (*e*) The stapler is fired and then gently withdrawn.**

anastomosis deep in the pelvis. The development of circular staplers reduced the technical difficulty of the operation and made possible anastomoses as far down as the anus [*see Figure 7*].

Proper preparation of the patient and the bowel is essential before resection of the rectum. The patient is placed in the lithotomy position with the head tilted down, and the small bowel is packed away in the upper abdomen. This positioning gives the surgeon the best access to the pelvis.

The splenic flexure and all of the distal large bowel are fully mobilized along with the rectum. The proximal resection margin is determined and cleared of serosal fat, and the bowel is divided either with a GIA stapler or between crushing bowel clamps. An angled TA stapler is fired across the distal rectal resection margin, and another bowel clamp is placed proximal to it. The rectum is divided with a long-handled knife, with care

taken to avoid plunging the blade into the pelvic sidewall, which could cause significant neurovascular damage. The specimen is removed and the stapler withdrawn. Adequate pelvic hemostasis is ensured.

Once the surgeon is satisfied that the bowel is sufficiently mobilized, a noncrushing bowel clamp is placed on the colon 10 to 15 cm proximal to the margin, and the crushing clamp is removed. At this stage, it is usual to create an 8 to 10 cm colonic J pouch; this measure typically yields a substantially improved functional outcome, especially in the early postoperative period in older patients.[77] A whip-stitch (or purse-string suture) of 2-0 polypropylene is placed around the colotomy, and the anvil from the appropriately sized curved EEA stapler is inserted into the open end and secured in place by tying the suture [*see Figure 7*]. The proximal bowel clamp is removed. The assistant—who may also, if desired, gently wash out the rectal stump with a dilute povidone-iodine solution—performs a digital rectal examination.

The stapler, with its trocar attachment in place, is then inserted into the anus under the careful guidance of the surgeon. The pointed shaft is brought out through or adjacent to the linear staple line, and the sharp point is removed. The peg from the anvil in the proximal colon is snapped into the protruding shaft of the stapler, and the two edges are slowly brought together. The colonic mesentery must not be twisted, and the ends must come together without any tension whatsoever. The stapler is fired, and a distinctive crunching sound is heard. The anvil is then loosened the appropriate amount, and the entire mechanism is withdrawn through the anus. Finally, the proximal and distal rings of tissue, which remain on the stapler, are carefully inspected to confirm circumferential closure of the staple line.

The pelvis is then filled with body-temperature saline, and a Toomey or bladder syringe is used to insufflate the neorectum with air. The surgeon watches for bubbling in the pelvis as a sign of leakage from the anastomosis. If there is a leak, additional soluble sutures must be placed to close the defect and another air test performed. A rectal tube may then be inserted by the assistant or may be placed at the end of the procedure.

When the anastomosis is very low or there is some concern about healing, a drain may be placed in the pelvis behind the staple line; however, as noted [see Controversial Issues in Intestinal Anastomosis, above], this practice has not been shown to be beneficial and may in fact impair healing. Some surgeons prefer to protect the anastomosis with a temporary proximal defunctioning stoma. There is some evidence that such protection reduces the risk of an anastomotic leak, but it is unclear whether a loop ileostomy or a loop colostomy is better for this purpose.[78-82]

Conclusion

A general note about the cosmetic aspect of these procedures is appropriate here. After any of these operations, a close visual inspection of the entire circumference of the anastomosis should be performed. As a rule, if the divided ends appear well apposed, then the anastomosis is probably sound.

Over the past 200 years, our understanding of how the bowel heals and how to perform intestinal anastomoses safely and effectively has improved considerably. This improvement is reflected in lower anastomotic leakage and dehiscence rates, lower operative morbidity, and lower mortality. Some would argue that much of the improved outcome is attributable to improved anesthesia, more potent antibiotics, and better postoperative monitoring and care. No doubt there is a good deal of truth to this argument. There is also no doubt, however, that one of the most significant determinants of outcome after procedures that include intestinal anastomosis is surgical technique. The central importance of meticulous technique means that constant practice and careful attention to detail are essential for all surgeons operating on the GI tract. In addition, it is important that academic surgeons in particular continue to research such issues as the best suture material or stapler for specific operations, the most suitable and best-tolerated type of bowel preparation, the mechanisms and variables involved in wound healing and collagen deposition, and the importance of local and systemic factors in determining overall outcome.

References

1. Smith SRG, Connolly JC, Crane PW: The effect of surgical drainage materials on colonic healing. Br J Surg 69:153, 1982

2. Matheson NA, McIntosh CA, Krukowski ZH: Continuing experience with single layer appositional anastomosis in the large bowel. Br J Surg 72(suppl):S104, 1985

3. Carty NJ, Keating J, Campbell J, et al: Prospective audit of an extramucosal technique for intestinal anastomosis. Br J Surg 78:1439, 1991

4. Debas HT, Thompson FB: A critical review of colectomy with anastomosis. Surg Gynecol Obstet 135:747, 1973

5. Schrock TR, Deveney CW, Dunphy JE: Factors contributing to leakage of colonic anastomoses. Ann Surg 177:513, 1973

6. Halsted W: Circular suture of the intestine—an experimental study. Am J Med Sci 94:436, 1887

7. Hastings JC, Van Winkle W, Barker E, et al: Effects of suture materials on healing of wounds of the stomach and colon. Surg Gynecol Obstet 140:701, 1975

8. Wise L, McAlister W, Stein T, et al: Studies on the healing of anastomoses of small and large intestines. Surg Gynecol Obstet 141:190, 1975

9. Hesp F, Hendriks T, Lubbers E-J, et al: Wound healing in the intestinal wall: a comparison between experimental ileal and colonic anastomoses. Dis Colon Rectum 24:99, 1984

10. Hawley PJ, Hunt TK, Dunphy JE: Aetiology of colonic anastomotic leaks. Proc R Soc Med 63:28, 1970

11. Hawley PJ, Faulk WP: A circulating collagenase inhibitor. Br J Surg 57:900, 1970

12. Martens M, Hendriks T: Postoperative changes in collagen synthesis in intestinal anastomoses of the rat: differences between small and large bowel. Gut 32:1482, 1991

13. Martens M, deMan B, Hendriks T, et al: Collagen synthetic capacity throughout the uninjured and anastomosed intestinal wall. Am J Surg 164:354, 1992

14. Guler M, Kologlu M, Kama NA, et al: Effect of topically applied charged particles on healing of colonic anastomoses. Arch Surg 137:813, 2002

15. Fingerhut A, Hay J-M, Elhadad A, et al: Supraperitoneal colorectal anastomosis: hand-sewn versus circular staples—a controlled clinical trial. Surgery 118:479, 1995

16. Koruda MJ, Rolandelli RH: Experimental studies on the healing of colonic anastomoses. J Surg Res 48:504, 1990

17. Munday C, McGinn FP: A comparison of polyglycolic acid and catgut sutures in rat colonic anastomoses. Br J Surg 63:870, 1976

18. Khubchandani IT: Low end-to-side rectoenteric anastomosis with single-layer wire. Dis Colon Rectum 18:308, 1975

19. Irvin T, Goligher J: Aetiology of disruption of intestinal anastomoses. Br J Surg 60:461, 1973

20. Olsen GB, Letwin E, Williams HTG: Clinical experience with the use of a single-layer intestinal anastomosis. Can J Surg 56:771, 1969

21. Sarin S, Lightwood RG: Continuous single-layer gastrointestinal anastomosis: a prospective audit. Br J Surg 76:493, 1989

22. Shandall A, Lowndes R, Young HL: Colonic anastomotic healing and oxygen tension. Br J Surg 72:606, 1985

23. Jiborn H, Ahonen J, Zederfeldt B: Healing of experimental colonic anastomoses: the effect of suture technique on collagen metabolism in the colonic wall. Am J Surg 139:406, 1980

24. Khoury GA, Waxman BP: Large bowel anastomosis: I. The healing process and sutured anastomoses: a review. Br J Surg 70:61, 1983

25. Abramowitz H: Everting and inverting anastomoses: an experimental study of comparative safety. Rev Surg 28:142, 1971

26. Polglase AL, Hughes ESR, McDermott FT, et al: A comparison of end-to-end staple and suture colorectal anastomosis in the dog. Surg Gynecol Obstet 152:792, 1981

27. O'Neil P, Healey JEJ, Clark RI, et al: Nonsuture intestinal anastomosis. Am J Surg 104:761, 1962

28. Orr NWM: A single layer intestinal anastomosis. Br J Surg 56:77, 1969

29. Templeton JL, McKelvey STD: Low colorectal anastomoses: an experimental assessment of two sutured and two stapled techniques. Dis Colon Rectum 28:38, 1985

30. Goligher J, Morris C, McAdam W: A controlled trial of inverting versus everting intestinal suture in clinical large-bowel surgery. Br J Surg 57:817, 1970

31. Brunius U, Zederfeldt B: Effects of antiinflammatory treatment on wound healing. Acta Chir Scand 129:462, 1965

32. Fielding LP, Stewart Brown S, Blesowsky L, et al: Anastomotic integrity after operations for large bowel cancer: a multicentre study. Br Med J 282:411, 1980

33. Leob MJ: Comparative strength of inverted, everted and endon intestinal anastomoses. Surg Gynecol Obstet 125:301, 1967

34. Undre AR: Enteroplasty: a new concept in the management of benign strictures of the intestine. Int Surg 68:73, 1983

35. Chassin JL, Rifkind KM, Turner JW: Errors and pitfalls in stapled gastrointestinal tract anastomoses. Surg Clin North Am 64:441, 1984

36. Ravitch MM: Intersecting staple lines in intestinal anastomoses. Surgery 97:8, 1985

37. Chung RS: Blood flow in colonic anastomoses: effect of stapling and suturing. Ann Surg 206:335, 1987

38. Julian TB, Ravitch MM: Evaluations of the safety of end-to-end stapling anastomoses across linear stapled closure. Surg Clin North Am 64:567, 1984

39. Brennan SS, Pickford IR, Evans M, et al: Staples or sutures for colonic anastomosis—a controlled clinical trial. Br J Surg 69:722, 1982

40. O'Donnell AF, O'Connell PR, Royston D, et al: Suture technique affects perianastomotic colonic crypt cell production and tumour formation. Br J Surg 78:671, 1991

41. Greenstein A, Rogers P, Moss G: Doubled fourth-day colorectal anastomotic strength with complete retention of intestinal mature wound collagen and accelerated deposition following full enteral nutrition. Surgery Forum 29:78, 1978

42. Bubrick MP: Effects of technique on anastomotic dehiscence. Dis Colon Rectum 24:232, 1981

43. Lafreniere R, Ketcham AS: A single layer open anastomosis for all intestinal structures. Am J Surg 149:797, 1985

44. Beart RW, Kelly KA: Randomized prospective evaluation of the EEA stapler for colorectal anastomoses. Am J Surg 141:143, 1981

45. Kracht M, Hay J-M, Fagniez P-L, et al: Ileocolonic anastomosis after right hemicolectomy for carcinoma: stapled or hand-sewn. Int J Colorect Dis 8:29, 1993

46. Valverde A, Hay JM, Fingerhut A, et al: Manual versus mechanical esophagogastric anastomosis after resection for carcinoma: a controlled trial. French Association for Surgical Research. Surgery 120:476, 1996

47. Akyol AM, McGregor JR, Galloway DJ, et al: Recurrence of colorectal cancer after sutured and stapled large bowel anastomoses. Br J Surg 78:1297, 1991

48. O'Dwyer P, Ravikumar TS, Steele G: Serum dependent variability in the adherence to tumour cells to surgical sutures. Br J Surg 72:466, 1985

49. Everett WG, Friend PJ, Forty J: Comparison of stapling and hand-suture for left-sided large bowel anastomosis. Br J Surg 73:345, 1986

50. Murphy JB: A contribution to abdominal surgery, ideal approximation of abdominal viscera without suture. North American Practitioner 4:481, 1892

51. Ballantyne GH: The experimental basis of intestinal suturing: effect of surgical technique, inflammation and infection on enteric wound healing. Dis Colon Rectum 27:61, 1984

52. O'Dwyer PJ, Conway W, McDermott EWM, et al: Effect of mechanical bowel preparation on anastomotic integrity following low anterior resection in dogs. Br J Surg 76:756, 1989

53. Goligher JC, Graham NG, DeDombal FT: Anastomotic dehiscence after anterior resection of the rectum and sigmoid. Br J Surg 57:109, 1970

54. Fok M, Ah-Chong AK, Cheng SWK, et al: Comparison of a single layer continuous hand-sewn method and circular stapling in 580 esophageal anastomoses. Br J Surg 78:342, 1991

55. Hocking M, Carlson R, Courington K, et al: Altered motility and bacterial flora after functional end-to-end anastomosis. Surgery 108:384, 1990

56. West of Scotland and Highland Anastomosis Study Group: Suturing or stapling in gastrointestinal surgery: a prospective randomized study. Br J Surg 78:337, 1991

57. Irving AD, Scrimgeour D: Mechanical bowel preparation for colonic resection and anastomosis. Br J Surg 74:580, 1987

58. Hughes ESR: Asepsis in large bowel surgery. Ann R Coll Surg Engl 51:347, 1972

59. LeVeen HH, Wapnicks S, Falk D: Effects of prophylactic antibiotics on colonic healing. Am J Surg 131:47, 1976

60. Irvin T, Goligher J, Johnston D: A randomized prospective clinical trial of single-layer and two-layer inverting intestinal anastomoses. Br J Surg 60:457, 1973

61. van Geldere D, Fa-Si-Oen P, Noach LA, et al: Complications after colorectal surgery without mechanical bowel preparation. J Am Coll Surg 194:40, 2002

62. Bozetti F: Perioperative nutrition of patients with gastrointestinal cancer. Br J Surg 89:1201, 2002

63. Munck A, Guyre M, Holbrook N: Physiological functions of glucocorticoids in stress and their relation to pharmacological actions. Endocrinol Rev 5:25, 1984

64. Matsusue S, Walser M: Healing of intestinal anastomoses in adrenalectomized rats given corticosterone. Am J Physiol 263:R164, 1992

65. Quan Z, Walser M: The effect of corticosterone administration at varying levels on leucine oxidation and whole body protein synthesis and breakdown in adrenalectomized rats. Metabolism 40:1263, 1991

66. Gadacz T, Menguy RB: Effects of anti-inflammatory drug oxyphenbutazone on the rate of wound healing and the biochemical composition of wound tissue. Surgery Forum 18:58, 1967

67. Getzen L: Intestinal anastomoses. Curr Probl Surg, August 1969, p 3

68. Kratzer GL, Onsanit T: Single layer steel wire anastomosis of the intestine. Surg Gynecol Obstet 139:93, 1974

69. Ravitch MM, Steichen FM: Techniques of staple suturing in the gastrointestinal tract. Ann Surg 175:815, 1972

70. Burg R, Geigle C, Faso J, et al: Omission of routine gastric decompression. Dis Colon Rectum 21:98, 1978

71. Reasbeck P, Rice M, Herbison G: Nasogastric intubation after intestinal resection. Surg Gynecol Obstet 158:354, 1984

72. Argov S, Goldstein I, Barzilai A: Is routine use of a nasogastric tube justified in upper abdominal surgery? Am J Surg 139:849, 1980

73. Yates JL: An experimental study of the local effects of peritoneal drainage. Surg Gynecol Obstet 1:473, 1905

74. Berliner SD, Burson LC, Lear PE: Use and abuse of intraperitoneal drains in colon surgery. Arch Surg 89:686, 1964

75. Merad F, Hay JM, Fingerhut A, et al: Is prophylactic pelvic drainage useful after elective rectal or anal anastomosis? A multicentre controlled randomized trial. French Association for Surgical Research. Surgery 125:529, 1999

76. Manz CW, LaTendresse C, Sako Y: The detrimental effects of drains on colonic anastomoses. Dis Colon Rectum 13:17, 1970

77. Sailer M, Fuchs K-H, Fein M, et al: Randomized clinical trial comparing quality of life after straight and pouch coloanal reconstruction. Br J Surg 89:1108, 2002

78. Gorfine SR, Gelernt IM, Bauer JJ, et al: Restorative proctocolectomy without diverting ileostomy. Dis Colon Rectum 38:188, 1995

79. Grobler SP, Hosie KB, Keighley MR: Randomized trial of loop ileostomy in restorative proctocolectomy. Br J Surg 79:903, 1992

80. Dehni N, Schlegel RD, Cunningham C, et al: Influence of a defunctioning stoma on leakage rates after low colorectal anastomosis and colonic J pouch-anal anastomosis. Br J Surg 85:1114, 1998

81. Law WL, Chu KW, Choi HK: Randomized clinical trial comparing loop ileostomy and loop transverse colostomy for fecal diversion following total mesorectal excision. Br J Surg 89:704, 2002

82. Edwards DP, Leppington-Clarke A, et al: Stoma-related complications are more frequent after transverse colostomy than loop ileostomy: a randomized prospective clinical trial. Br J Surg 88:360, 2001

Acknowledgments

Figures 1 through 7 Tom Moore.

Portions of this chapter are based on a previous iteration written for *ACS Surgery* by Zane Cohen, M.D., and Barry Sullivan, M.D. The author wishes to thank Drs. Cohen and Sullivan.

J. Graham Williams, M.Ch., F.R.C.S.

Formation of an intestinal stoma is frequently a component of surgical intervention for diseases of the small bowel and the colon. The most common intestinal stomas are the ileostomies (end and loop) and the colostomies (end and loop); the less common stomas, such as cecostomy and appendicostomy, have limited applications and thus are not considered further in this chapter.

For optimal results, it is essential that stoma creation be considered an integral part of the surgical procedure, not merely an irritating and time-consuming addendum at the end of a long operation. Accordingly, the potential requirement for a stoma should be appropriately addressed in the planning of an intestinal procedure. A great effort should be made to counsel the patient before operation as to whether a stoma is likely to be needed, what stoma creation would involve, where the stoma would be situated, and whether the stoma is likely to be permanent or temporary.

Operative Planning

PREOPERATIVE COUNSELING

Ideally, as soon as surgical intervention that may involve a stoma is contemplated, the enterostomal nursing service should become involved—though this may not be possible in an emergency setting. Patients often have misconceptions about the effects stoma will have on their quality of life and consequently may experience considerable anxiety. Adequate preoperative counseling helps correct these misconceptions and reduce the attendant anxiety. Enough time should be set aside to allow the counselor to explore the patient's knowledge of the disease and understanding of why a stoma may be required. This process involves reviewing the planned operation, describing what the stoma will look like, and explaining how the stoma will function. Visual aids (e.g., videos, CD-ROMs, and booklets) can be very useful in this regard and should be freely available to patients and their families. As simple a measure as showing the patient a stoma appliance and attaching it to the abdominal wall before the procedure can be helpful in preparing the patient for a stoma. Many patients facing the prospect of stoma surgery also derive great benefit from meeting patients of similar age and background who have a stoma.

CHOICE OF PROCEDURE

A number of common indications for stoma formation have been identified [*see Table 1*]. These indications are usually associated with particular types of stoma, but the association is not always a simple or automatic one. In many situations, more than one option exists, and it can be difficult to select the best available option for a particular patient.

Loop Ileostomy versus Loop Colostomy

Defunctioning of a distal anastomosis after rectal excision and anastomosis may be achieved with either a loop ileostomy or a loop transverse colostomy. A number of nonrandomized studies[1-3] and randomized control trials[4-7] have been performed in an effort to determine which of these two approaches is superior.

Both types of stoma effectively defunction the distal bowel; however, loop ileostomy appears to be associated with a lower incidence of complications related to stoma formation and closure, though it may also carry a higher risk of postoperative intestinal obstruction.[6] The two types of stoma are comparable with respect to patient quality of life, and the degree of subsequent social restriction is influenced more by the number and type of complications than by the type of stoma formed.[8]

SELECTION OF STOMA SITE

A poorly sited stoma will cause considerable morbidity and adversely affect quality of life. For this reason, great emphasis should be placed on selecting the best site for the stoma on the abdominal wall. In many instances [*see Table 1*], it may not be possible to decide beforehand whether a colostomy or an ileostomy is to be performed. An example would be the case of a patient with a tumor in the lower rectum in which the surgeon's intention is to perform a restorative resection covered by a loop ileostomy. In such a case, the surgeon sometimes finds that restorative resection is not technically possible and elects to perform an abdominoperineal resection or a low Hartmann resection with an end colostomy instead.

A stoma should be brought out through a separate opening in the abdominal wall, not through the main incision: there is a high incidence of wound infection and incisional hernia formation if the main incision is used as a stoma site. In general, ileostomies are sited in the right iliac fossa, sigmoid colostomies (loop or end) in the left iliac fossa, and transverse loop colostomies in either the right or the left upper quadrant. These positions are preferred because they are conveniently close to the particular bowel segments to be used for creating the various stomas. At need, however—as when finding a suitable site proves difficult because of previous scars or deformity—both the ileum and the colon can be mobilized to provide sufficient length to reach most sites on the abdominal wall.

In selecting and marking a stoma site, the following key considerations should be taken into account:

1. A flat area of skin is required for adequate adhesion of the appliance.
2. The patient should be able to see the stoma.
3. Skin creases, folds, previous scars, and bony prominences should be avoided.
4. The stoma site should not be located at the beltline.
5. The site should be identified with the patient lying, sitting, and standing.
6. Preexisting disabilities should be taken into account.

According to received wisdom, the stoma should be brought out of the abdomen through the rectus abdominis, so that the emerging stoma will be supported and the incidence of parastomal hernia reduced. Several studies, however, have shown that this approach is not always ideal and that the optimum site for a stoma should be selected without regard to its position in relation to the rectus abdominis.[9-11] Once selected, the site is marked with an indelible pen or tattooed with India ink and a fine needle.

Table 1 Indications for Different Types of Intestinal Stomas

Disease	Presentation	Indication	Stoma Type	Intention
Colorectal cancer	Perforation	Defunctioning of bowel	Loop or end colostomy	Temporary, often permanent
	Obstruction	Relief of obstruction	Loop or end colostomy	Temporary
	Rectal cancer	Low tumor (abdominoperineal resection)	End colostomy	Permanent
		Defunctioning of low anastomosis	Loop ileostomy or colostomy	Temporary
Diverticular disease	Perforation	Resolution of sepsis; defunctioning of bowel	Colostomy	Temporary, sometimes permanent
	Obstruction	Relief of obstruction	Loop or end colostomy	Temporary, sometimes permanent
	Elective resection for fistula	Protection of anastomosis	Loop ileostomy or colostomy	Temporary
Ulcerative colitis	Acute colitis	Defunctioning of bowel	End ileostomy (after subtotal colectomy)	Temporary or permanent
	Chronic colitis	Eradication of disease	End ileostomy (after panproctocolectomy)	Permanent
		Ileoanal pouch procedure	Loop ileostomy	Temporary
Crohn disease	Crohn colitis	Defunctioning of bowel	Loop or split ileostomy	Temporary, sometimes permanent
		Defunctioning of bowel after excision	End ileostomy or colostomy	Temporary, often permanent
	Small bowel disease	Defunctioning of bowel	Loop, end, or split ileostomy	Temporary, sometimes permanent
	Perianal disease	Defunctioning of bowel	Loop or split ileostomy	Temporary, often permanent
		Excision of disease	Ileostomy (after panproctocolectomy)	Permanent
			Colostomy (after rectal excision)	
	Elective resection for septic complications	Defunctioning of bowel	Loop or divided loop ileostomy	Temporary
Trauma	Colon injury	Defunctioning of bowel	Colostomy or loop ileostomy	Temporary, sometimes permanent
	Rectal injury	Defunctioning of bowel	Colostomy	Temporary, sometimes permanent
Functional disorders	Fecal incontinence	Defunctioning of anus	End colostomy	Permanent
	Sphincter repair	Defunctioning of bowel	Loop ileostomy or colostomy	Temporary

Operative Technique

GENERAL PRINCIPLES

Most abdominal stomas are formed at the end of an open operation performed to resect bowel, drain an infectious focus, or relieve obstruction. In this setting, a midline incision is generally the most appropriate choice for gaining access to the abdominal cavity because it leaves the areas to either side of the midline available for stoma placement. Other incisions may be used as well, but more careful operative planning will be required.

A defunctioning stoma can be created without opening the abdomen by making a trephine hole and using retractors and forceps to identify the relevant bowel loop from which the stoma will be formed. I generally avoid this approach, for two reasons. First, the trephine hole invariably ends up larger than is ideal, and the greater size leads to an increased risk of parastomal hernia. Second, it is often difficult to be sure that the correct bowel loop has been identified and the correct end opened as a stoma. These disadvantages can be overcome by taking a laparoscopic approach. One port is placed though the previously marked site. A tissue forceps is passed down this port and used to grasp and orient the relevant bowel segment. If necessary, the bowel can be mobilized by means of laparoscopic dissection. The colon is then divided with a linear stapler, and the proximal end is brought out through a small trephine hole made at the port site.

The fundamental concept in stoma formation is that a stoma is simply an anastomosis between a piece of bowel and the skin of the abdominal wall. For this reason, the same basic principles that apply to intestinal anastomosis also apply to stoma formation—namely, maintaining an adequate blood supply to both sides of the anastomosis, ensuring that the anastomosis is performed without tension, and avoiding any preexisting infection. In accordance with these principles, the bowel segment used should have as much of its blood supply as possible preserved during mobilization, and mobilization should be sufficient to allow the bowel to be brought through the abdominal wall without tension and without occlusion of the blood supply at the fascial level by a too-small hole in the abdominal wall. If these criteria are not met, then either the bowel should be mobilized further or a new bowel segment should be selected. It is important to make the best possible technical choices at the time of initial stoma formation. If the correct principles are not followed at the beginning of the procedure, it is generally futile to hope that the situation will improve thereafter; the usual result is a poor stoma that requires surgical revision.

Creation of Stoma Aperture

It is wise to leave formation of the hole for the stoma until the end of the procedure because unforeseen events during the operation may necessitate a change in the type or the site of the stoma. A circular incision 2.5 cm in diameter is made at the marked site, and the skin is excised. The subcutaneous fat is parted with scissors and small retractors until the fascia of the abdominal wall is reached. The fat need not be excised: it supports the emerging stoma, and its absence would leave a potential dead space. A cruciate incision is made in the rectus sheath, initially no more than

2 cm in each direction. The muscle fibers of the underlying rectus abdominis are split in the direction of their fibers with an arterial clamp or the tips of heavy scissors. The small retractors are inserted deeper to keep the muscle fibers apart, and a small cruciate incision is made in the posterior rectus sheath with an electrocautery. A swab held against the peritoneum at the stoma site will protect the intra-abdominal organs and the assistant's fingers from being injured by the electrocautery point.

On occasion, the epigastric vessels, which lie between the rectus abdominis and the posterior sheath, are injured. Should this occur, the simplest way of dealing with the problem is to open the posterior sheath from inside the abdominal cavity and suture-ligate the bleeding point.

COLOSTOMY

End

The typical site for an end colostomy is the left iliac fossa, and either the sigmoid or the descending colon is used for the stoma. If the rectum has been excised, the inferior mesenteric vessels will have been divided, and the blood supply to the distal colon will come from the middle colic vessels via the marginal artery. It is not usually necessary to take down the splenic flexure to mobilize the colon adequately; however, if there is any concern regarding tension on the stoma, full splenic flexure mobilization should be performed. For a simple defunctioning end colostomy, only a few small vessels in the mesentery will have to be divided.

The colon is divided at the relevant site with either crushing clamps or a linear intestinal stapler. The adequacy of the vascular supply is checked by inspection. A nontraumatic bowel clamp or a Babcock tissue forceps is passed through the hole in the abdominal wall and used to grasp the closed-off end of the colon. Care is taken when drawing the colon through the abdominal wall to keep from twisting the colon and damaging the small vessels in the supporting mesentery. The end of the colon should sit 2 cm above the skin surface. To prevent wound contamination, the colostomy is constructed only after the skin incision has been fully closed and dressed. The closed-off end of the colon is excised with a sharp knife, and the colostomy is constructed with a small spout by everting the bowel wall. The spout helps the patient position the stoma appliance but should not protrude more than 0.5 to 1 cm above the surface of the skin. The anastomosis is performed with interrupted absorbable sutures that take bites of the full thickness of the end of the colon and the subcuticular layer of the skin. Small bites are also taken of the seromuscular layer of the emerging colon at the level of the skin [*see Figure 1*].

This technique is sometimes modified by closing the lateral space between the abdominal wall and the colon with absorbable sutures in an effort to prevent internal herniation of the small bowel. An alternative approach is to tunnel the colostomy to the hole in the abdominal wall via an extraperitoneal route. This approach may prevent herniation and colostomy prolapse,[9] but the stoma may be slow to function and difficult to mobilize if a reversal or revision operation is performed.

Loop

A loop colostomy is usually performed as a quick and temporary method of relieving acute colonic obstruction or to cover an anastomosis in the distal colon or rectum. Whenever possible, I avoid using loop colostomies, for the following reasons.

1. Because of the need to accommodate two pieces of bowel, a loop colostomy requires a larger hole in the abdominal wall

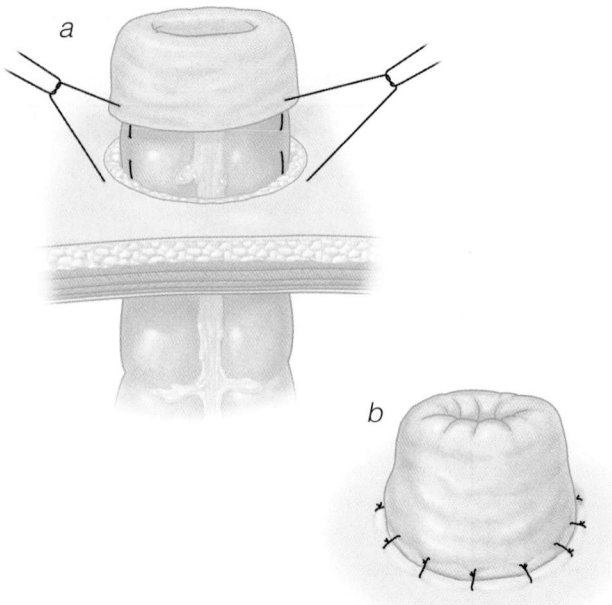

Figure 1 **End colostomy. (*a*) The end of the colon sits 1 to 2 cm above skin level. Four absorbable sutures are placed, one in each quadrant of the stoma. Each suture takes a full-thickness bite of the end of the colon, a seromuscular bite of the emerging colon at skin level, and a subcutaneous bite of the edge of the skin opening. (*b*) The stoma is completed by filling in the gaps between the four quadrant sutures with interrupted sutures that take full-thickness bites of the end of the colon and subepidermal bites of the skin edge. The stoma should have a small (0.5 to 1 cm) lip, which facilitates accurate positioning of the colostomy bag.**

than an end colostomy does. This is a particular concern in emergency situations, where the colon may be greatly dilated.
2. The larger hole predisposes to formation of a parastomal hernia, which can be a problem if the stoma is not reversed.
3. Loop colostomies are more prone to prolapse than end colostomies are, possibly as a conseqence of parastomal hernia formation.
4. The effluent from the transverse colon can be highly liquid, and the absence of a spout with loop colostomy may lead to difficulties with appliance leakage.
5. When a loop colostomy is used to defunction a distal anastomosis, there is a theoretical risk of damage to the marginal artery, which may be the only vessel supplying the distal side of the anastomosis.

The usual site for a loop colostomy is either the right upper quadrant (using the proximal transverse colon) or the left iliac fossa (using the left colon). The colon segment that will be used to form the stoma is identified, and peritoneal attachments are divided to provide sufficient length to reach the desired site on the abdominal wall without tension. If the transverse colon is to be used, the omentum is removed. Care is taken not to damage the marginal artery, which, if occluded, may compromise vascular supply to the distal bowel.

A trephine hole is made at the marked site as described [*see Operative Technique, General Principles, above*]. The hole is usually larger than it would be in an end colostomy; the bowel loop to be brought out is often bulky, especially when the colon is obstructed. A small window is made in the mesentery immediately adjacent to the colon wall, and a Jacques catheter is passed through this aperture. The Jacques catheter is used as a handle by

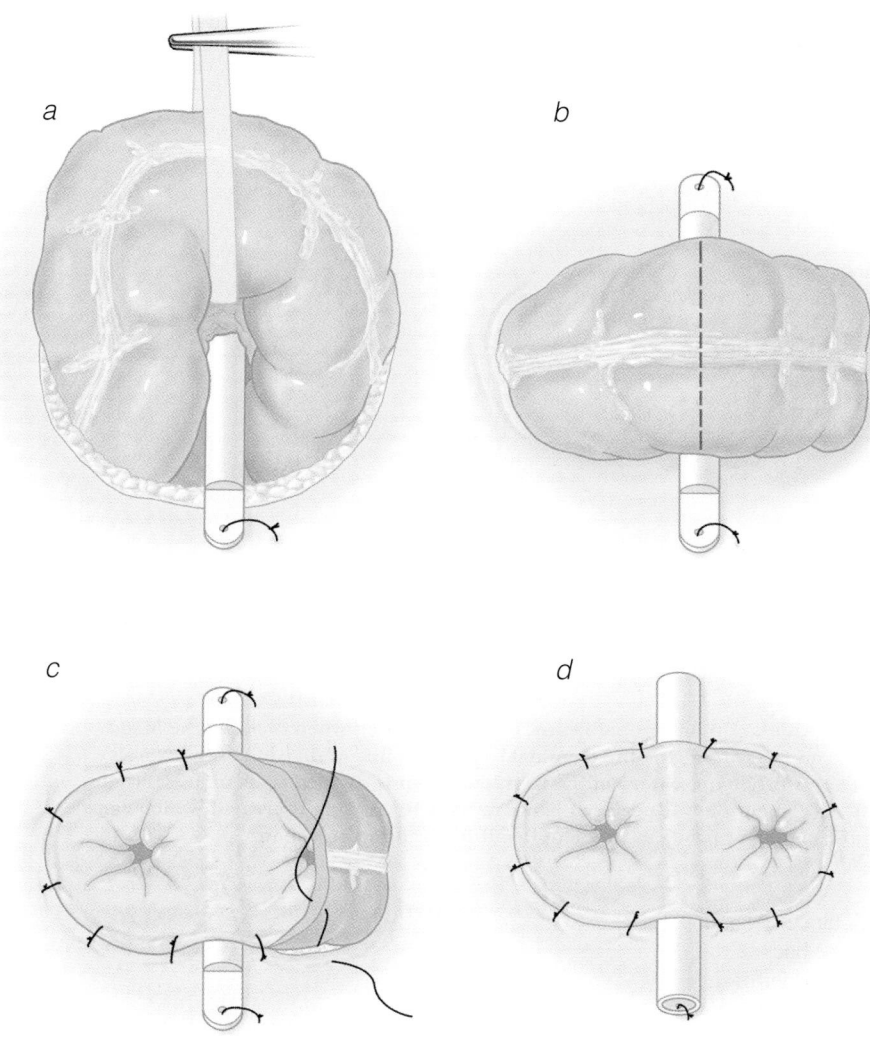

Figure 2 Loop colostomy. (*a*) A soft catheter or a length of nylon tape is passed through a small window made in the mesentery of the colon, and the prepared loop of colon is eased through the hole in the abdominal wall with the aid of the catheter. The catheter or tube is replaced by a supporting colostomy rod. (*b*) A transverse incision is made across the apex of the colon loop. (*c*) The cut edges of the colon are everted and sutured to the skin edge of the stoma hole with interrupted absorbable sutures that take full-thickness bites of the colon and subepidermal bites of the skin. (*d*) The rod is left in place for 5 days to support the loop stoma during the early phase of healing.

which the colon loop is drawn through the trephine hole in the abdominal wall, with care taken to maintain the orientation of the colon and avoid twisting [*see Figure 2a*]. The catheter is then replaced by a plastic or glass stoma rod, which supports the loop at the level of the skin.

The main incision is closed, and the stoma is matured. A transverse incision is made in the apex of the bowel loop [*see Figure 2b*], and the two edges are peeled back and sutured to the skin edge of the trephine hole to produce a double opening [*see Figure 2c, d*]. The bridge remains in place for 5 days, by which time the stoma is usually beginning to function properly. The rod can then be removed because by this point, the stoma is fixed in place and unable to retract into the abdominal cavity.

Double-Barrel

At one time, there was a vogue for creating a double-barrel colostomy to defunction the colon. Although the height of the vogue has passed, this type of stoma still has a place in the management of colorectal trauma. After resection of a damaged segment of the colon, the proximal and distal ends of the colon are tacked together along the antimesenteric surfaces with interrupted absorbable sutures. The resulting double end is then brought out through a trephine incision at the relevant site. The double-barrel configuration makes the colostomy easier to close: closure can be performed after mobilization by resection and a sutured anastomosis or via a double-stapled technique.

ILEOSTOMY

End

End ileostomy is most frequently performed after colectomy for inflammatory bowel disease. The most distal segment of the ileum is used (i.e., that immediately proximal to the ileocecal valve), the reason being that it is important to preserve intestinal length, both for nutritional reasons and to allow for the possibility that an ileoanal pouch may have to be fashioned in the future. In certain instances, it is necessary to create an end ileostomy from a more proximal segment of the ileum.

The terminal ileum is mobilized, a large avascular window is opened between the ileocolic vessels and the ileal branches of the superior mesenteric vessels, and the ileocolic vessels are divided where they branch from the superior mesenteric vessels. The terminal ileum is usually supplied by two arcades of vessels, which join the ileocolic vessels adjacent to the cecum. These arcades must be divided as close to the ileocolic vessels as possible to preserve the blood supply to the terminal ileum [*see Figure 3*]. The ileocecal fold (Treves's fold) is dissected away from the terminal ileum, which can then be divided flush with the ileocecal valve, either with a linear stapler or with a knife between bowel clamps.

The trephine incision is created at the previously marked site, and a Babcock tissue forceps is passed into the abdominal cavity and used to grasp the divided end of the ileum. The terminal ileum and the supporting mesentery are gently eased through the aperture, with the mesenteric surface oriented superiorly, until 5

a

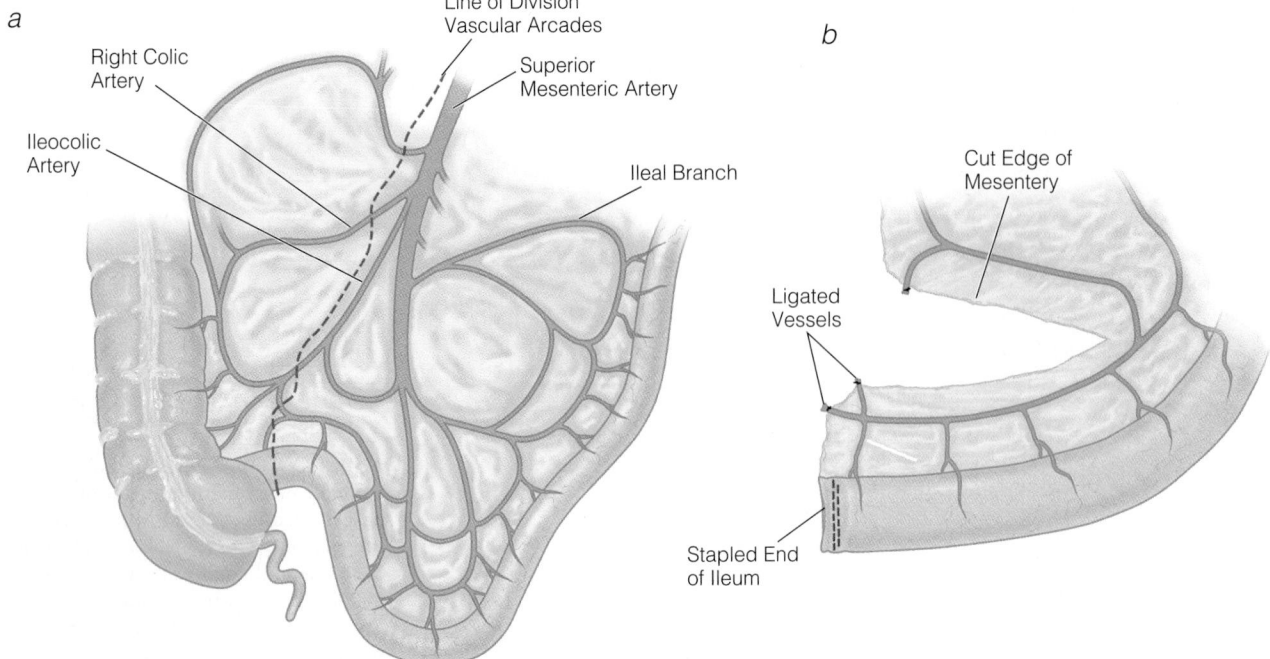

Right Colic Artery

Ileocolic Artery

Line of Division Vascular Arcades

Superior Mesenteric Artery

Ileal Branch

b

Cut Edge of Mesentery

Ligated Vessels

Stapled End of Ileum

Figure 3 **End ileostomy. Shown is preparation of the terminal ileum. (*a*) Care is taken when dividing the blood supply of the right colon to preserve the arcades supplying the terminal ileum. The line of division of the vessels and the mesentery is shown (dashed line). (*b*) The mesentery of the terminal ileum is divided so as to preserve the vascular arcade adjacent to the ileum. A segment of well-perfused ileum at least 10 cm long is created, which can be brought through the abdominal wall opening to provide sufficient ileum for creation of a spout.**

cm of ileum protrudes above the abdominal skin. The cut edge of the ileal mesentery is secured to the peritoneum of the back of the anterior abdominal wall, along the line of the lateral border of the rectus abdominis, with an absorbable suture. This measure helps stabilize the stoma and is thought to prevent stoma prolapse, volvulus, and internal herniation around the stoma.

The stapled end of the ileum is excised to produce a fresh bleeding end. The emerging ileum is then everted to yield a spout about 2.5 cm long. This is accomplished by placing a suture on either side of the mesentery and a third suture on the antimesenteric side, which lies inferiorly. The superior sutures take bites of the serosa of the emerging ileum, 5 cm from the cut end of the bowel, and the inferior suture includes a serosal bite 4 cm from the cut edge [*see Figure 4*]. When the sutures are tied, an everted spout is created that points downward into the ileostomy appliance.[12] The mucocutaneous anastomosis is then completed with a series of interrupted absorbable sutures.

Loop

A loop ileostomy is employed to rest the distal bowel or to protect an anastomosis. The ileal loop used should be as distal as possible while still maintaining adequate mobility; if there is any tension, a more proximal loop may be required. The technique of loop ileostomy formation is similar to that of loop colostomy formation. A Jacques catheter is used to draw the loop through the abdominal wall trephine hole, ideally with the proximal limb in the lower position [*see Figure 5a*]. Care is taken to distinguish the proximal and distal limbs of the loop and to keep from rotating the loop during its passage through the abdominal wall. A marking suture is useful for identifying the proximal side of the loop. A supporting rod may be used, but it is not necessary, and it can hinder the fitting the stoma appliance.

The ileostomy is created by making a circumferential incision around 80% of the distal limb at the level of the skin, with the

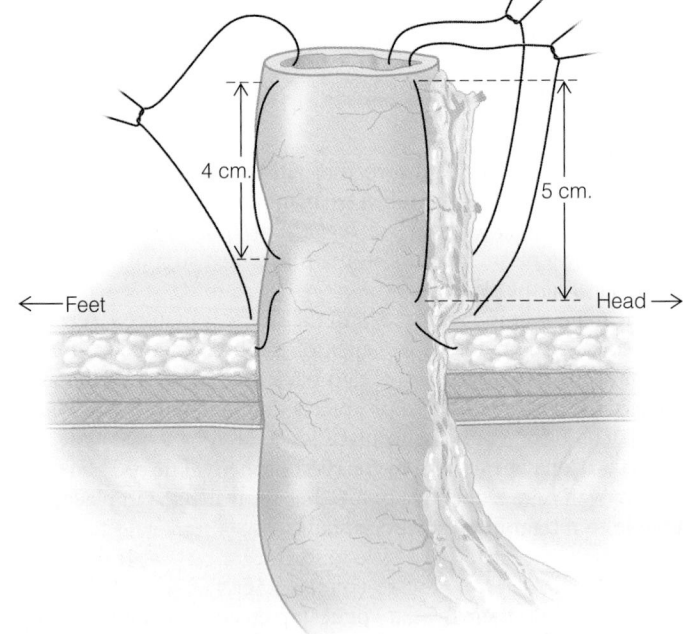

4 cm.

5 cm.

←— Feet

Head —→

Figure 4 **End ileostomy. The ileum having been brought through the abdominal wall, the ileostomy is created by everting the end of the ileum. Three sutures are placed: one on the antimesenteric side and one to each side of the mesentery. Each suture takes a full-thickness bite of the cut edge of the ileum, a seromuscular bite of the emerging ileum at skin level, and a subepidermal bite of the skin edge. The spout is created when these sutures are tied. A nontoothed forceps or a Babcock tissue forceps is sometimes helpful for everting the ileum. Gaps between the three sutures are filled in with further absorbable sutures, which include only the end of the ileum and the skin edge.**

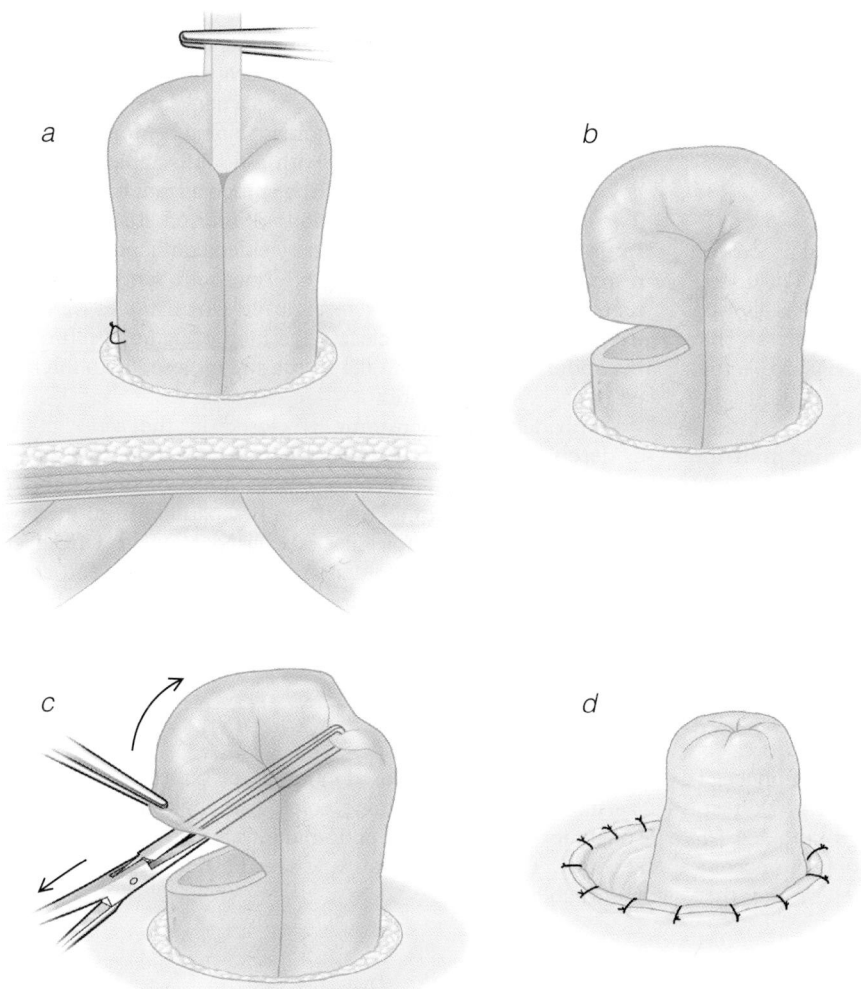

Figure 5 **Loop ileostomy. (*a*) A soft catheter or a length of nylon tape is passed through a small window made in the mesentery of the ileum, and the ileal loop to be used for the stoma is eased through the hole in the abdominal wall and left protruding a few centimeters above skin level. A suture is placed to mark the distal limb. (*b*) A semilunar incision is made in the mesenteric border of the distal limb at skin level, extending around most of the circumference of the ileum. (*c*) A Babcock tissue forceps is inserted into the loop and used to grasp the wall of the proximal limb. The cut edge of the ileum is peeled back to evert the bowel wall and create a spout from the proximal limb of the loop. (*d*) The stoma is completed by placing interrupted absorbable sutures between the cut edge of the ileum and the subepidermal layer of the skin. A few of these sutures also take a seromuscular bite of the emerging ileum at skin level.**

mesenteric side preserved [*see Figure 5b*]. The cut edge of the proximal limb is then everted to create a spout for the ileostomy [*see Figure 5c*]. A Babcock tissue forceps is sometimes used to apply gentle traction to the mucosal side of the proximal limb. The cut edge of the ileum is anastomosed to the skin with a series of interrupted subcuticular absorbable sutures. The distal limb is sutured flush with the skin. On the proximal side, several sutures take bites of the serosa of the emerging ileum at skin level. The corners of the incision in the ileum are drawn around the proximal limb of the ileostomy to accentuate the spout effect and create a thin, semilunar distal limb opening [*see Figure 5d*].

An alternative approach is to create a divided loop ileostomy, which some consider superior to a conventional loop stoma.[13] The construction technique for this stoma is similar to that of its conventional counterpart. The distal limb of the ileostomy is divided with a linear cutting stapler after the loop is brought through the abdominal wall. The closed distal end is tacked to the side of the emerging spout of the proximal end below skin level, and the proximal end is fashioned into an everted spout as in a conventional end ileostomy. A divided loop ileostomy is slightly more difficult and expensive to construct than a conventional loop ileostomy, but it has the advantage of achieving complete defunctioning of the distal bowel (because there is no chance that the ileostomy contents will spill over).

Loop-End

A loop-end ileostomy can be useful in cases where the ileum and its supporting mesentery are grossly thickened and the sur-

geon is encountering difficulty in preparing a sufficient length of well-vascularized ileum for a conventional end ileostomy. In a loop-end ileostomy, the ileum is prepared as in a conventional end ileostomy, but the vascular arcades are left undisturbed. A small window is made in the mesentery 5 to 10 cm proximal to the closed end of the ileum, and a nylon tape or a Jacques catheter is used to draw this distal ileal loop through the abdominal wall. The stapled closed end of the ileum lies just within the abdominal cavity. The ileostomy is then constructed in essentially the same manner as a conventional loop ileostomy.

Split

A split ileostomy is created by bringing out the two cut bowel ends at different sites. The proximal end is usually terminal ileum, but the distal end may be either ileum or colon, depending on the indication for stoma formation. This procedure forms a mucous fistula, and only a small stoma appliance is usually required. The distal end can be either included in the closure of the abdominal wound or brought out through a separate trephine hole on the opposite side of the abdomen from the ileostomy. The advantage of a split ileostomy is that it completely defunctions the bowel without the risk of intra-abdominal leakage from a closed distal stump. The disadvantage is that it is more difficult to close: closure usually necessitates reopening of the main incision.

Continent

A continent ileostomy involves formation of a reservoir and placement of a nonreturn nipple valve, which is emptied regularly via a catheter, so that the patient need wear only a small cap appliance. The surgical technique is demanding and beyond the scope of this chapter; it is described more fully elsewhere.[14]

STOMA CLOSURE

Loop Ileostomy

Closure of a loop ileostomy is usually a simple local procedure that does not require the main incision to be opened. The operation is easier to perform if a period of at least 12 weeks is allowed to elapse between formation of the stoma and closure so that there is time for edema and inflammatory adhesions to settle. Dissection is facilitated by injecting epinephrine (1:100,000 solution) into the subcutaneous plane around the stoma.

An incision is made in the peristomal skin 2 mm from the mucocutaneous junction [*see Figure 6a*]. The incision is deepened into the subcutaneous fat until the serosa of the emerging bowel appears. Sharp dissection is continued circumferentially in this plane, dividing the fine adhesions between the bowel and its mesentery and the subcutaneous fat [*see Figure 6b*]. Blunt dissection should be avoided because it can easily lead to serosal tears. Some difficulty may be encountered at the fascial level, and care must be taken with the dissection if adhesions are particularly dense. Eventually, the peritoneal cavity is entered, and the remaining adhesions are identified with a finger and divided.

The emerging ileal loop is withdrawn from the abdominal cavity, and the mucocutaneous junction and the rim of skin are excised. The everted proximal end of the stoma is unfolded [*see Figure 6c*]; some sharp dissection is usually required to accomplish this. The freshened edges of the enterotomy are then approximated with interrupted seromuscular absorbable sutures [*see Figure 6d*]. Sometimes, a limited ileal resection is required if the stoma site is in poor condition, and a conventional end-to-end anastomosis is performed to restore intestinal continuity. It is possible to close a loop ileostomy with a double-stapled technique; however, there does not appear to be much advantage in doing so. Two randomized trials and a nonrandomized study comparing suture closure with stapled closure yielded conflicting results with respect to complication rates,[15-17] but both randomized trials reported that extra costs were incurred when staples were used. Once the enterotomy is closed, the loop of ileum is returned to the abdominal cavity, and the stoma site is closed with interrupted nonabsorbable sutures.

A divided loop ileostomy is closed in the same manner as described above. Care should be taken to identify the closed distal end and to fully mobilize both limbs of the ileum from the abdomen. The closed distal end is separated from the proximal limb, and the staple line is excised to yield a fresh end. The proximal end is unfolded and a simple end-to-end anastomosis is performed with interrupted sutures. There may be a significant size discrepancy between the two limbs. Again, a double-stapled technique may be employed as an alternative closure method.

Loop Colostomy

A loop colostomy is closed in much the same manner as a loop ileostomy after the emerging colon is mobilized away from the subcutaneous fat and the abdominal wall by means of sharp dissection. Transverse closure is achieved with interrupted absorbable sutures.

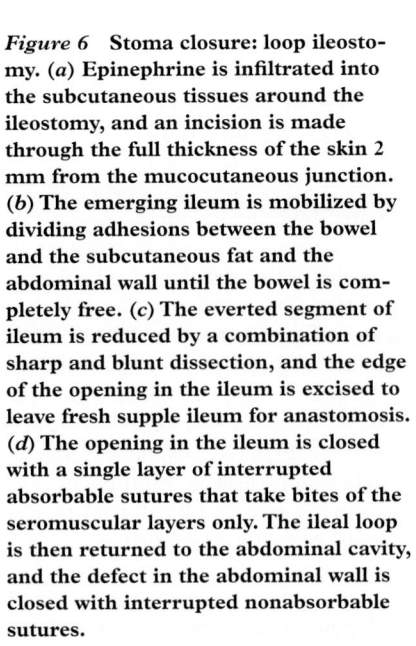
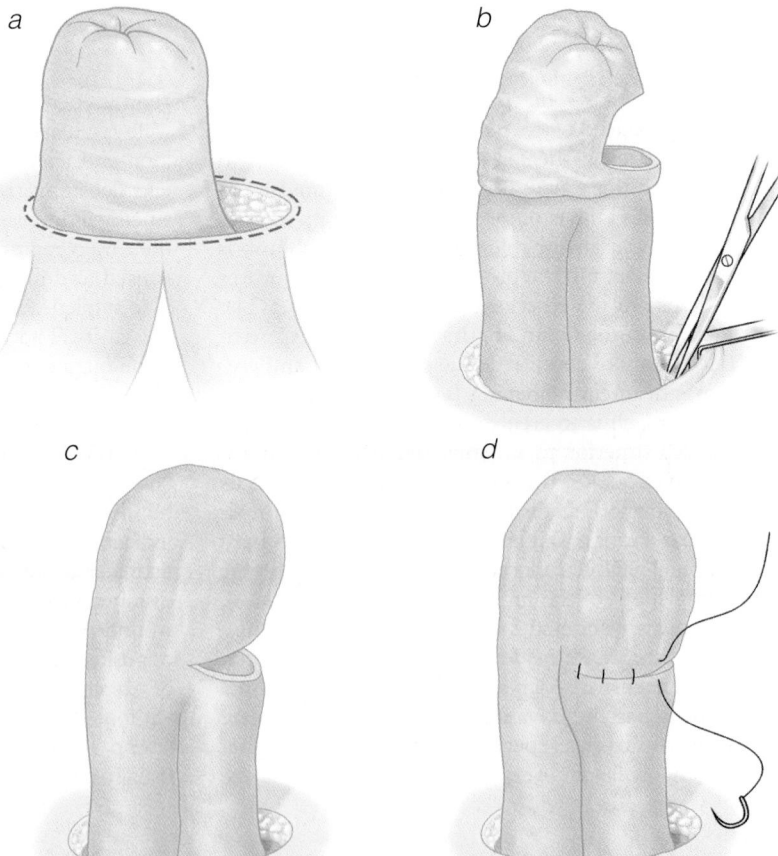

Figure 6 **Stoma closure: loop ileostomy. (*a*) Epinephrine is infiltrated into the subcutaneous tissues around the ileostomy, and an incision is made through the full thickness of the skin 2 mm from the mucocutaneous junction. (*b*) The emerging ileum is mobilized by dividing adhesions between the bowel and the subcutaneous fat and the abdominal wall until the bowel is completely free. (*c*) The everted segment of ileum is reduced by a combination of sharp and blunt dissection, and the edge of the opening in the ileum is excised to leave fresh supple ileum for anastomosis. (*d*) The opening in the ileum is closed with a single layer of interrupted absorbable sutures that take bites of the seromuscular layers only. The ileal loop is then returned to the abdominal cavity, and the defect in the abdominal wall is closed with interrupted nonabsorbable sutures.**

Postoperative Care

A clear stoma appliance is cut to the proper size and placed on the stoma before the patient leaves the operating room. A degree of edema is to be expected in the first week. In addition, the stoma may appear somewhat dusky; this is a sign that the aperture in the abdominal wall is the correct size. It often happens that the patient becomes alarmed at the initial appearance of the stoma and requires reassurance that the stoma will look better as time passes.

When the stoma starts to function, the clear appliance is changed for the chosen appliance, and the patient is instructed in how and when to empty the pouch. When confident with this aspect of stoma management, the patient is instructed in how to cut the plate to the correct size and how to change the stoma bag or flange (if he or she is using a two-piece appliance). An ileostomy works throughout the day, often showing an increase in activity after meals. The appliance will therefore require regular emptying, a task that some patients find inconvenient. A loop transverse colostomy may be as unpredictable as an ileostomy in this regard; however, a sigmoid colostomy may have a more predictable activity, similar to the frequency of normal bowel movements. Some patients find that quality of life is improved by irrigating the colostomy with water instilled via a special appliance. This procedure induces a full colonic clearout and allows the patient to wear a less obtrusive cap appliance for 24 to 48 hours, until irrigation is repeated.

Detailed discussion of stoma care is beyond the scope of this chapter. A key role is played by the enterostomal therapist, who is an important point of contact for the patient, providing advice, instruction, and emotional support in the postoperative period. Skin complications are common, and most can be managed by the enterostomal therapist. Many such complications result from contact between the peristomal skin and digestive enzymes; common causes include poor appliance fit and stoma retraction. Skin problems can usually be resolved by means of simple measures such as switching to a different appliance, using a convex flange, applying barrier cream, or filling dips in the peristomal skin with stoma paste. Given that surgical complications such as fistula formation and parastomal hernia may present as skin problems, it is important that the surgeon and the enterostomal therapist work closely together in addressing these problems.

Troubleshooting

Wound infection after stoma closure is common. Drainage of the incision with a small corrugated drain can help reduce the incidence of such infection. Some surgeons leave the stoma site open and allow it to heal by second intention.

Incisional hernia can develop in the stoma site, and its incidence is increased by wound infection in the postoperative period. Because the defect is relatively narrow, the hernia can lead to significant symptoms. Repair is usually necessary.

Breakdown of the anastomosis lying beneath the incision will lead to a fecal fistula, with discharge from the stoma site. If the fistula is simple and there is no distal obstruction, it is likely to heal spontaneously. Expert nursing is required to manage the fistula effluent while healing occurs to prevent damage to the surrounding skin.

If there is a complex inflammatory mass at the closure site, spontaneous healing is less likely. Laparotomy may be required, with resection of the stoma site and reanastomosis or further stoma formation, depending on the patient's condition.

Table 2 Incidence of Common Complications of Intestinal Stomas

Complication	Ileostomy Patients[18] (N = 150) No. (%)*	Colostomy Patients[46] (N = 126) No. (%)†	Colostomy Patients[9] (N = 203) No. (%)‡
Skin problems	44 (34)	17 (14)	24 (17.4)
Obstruction	27 (23)	9 (7)	11 (13.7)
Retraction	19 (17)	—	3 (1.5)
Hernia	16 (16)	14 (11)	43 (36.7)
Prolapse	12 (11)	4 (3)	11 (11.8)
Fistula	11 (12)	3 (2)	2 (1.0)
Stenosis	6 (5)	11 (9)	10 (7.3)
Necrosis	1 (1)	—	—

* All complications recorded at clinic review. Complication rate expressed as cumulative probability from life-table analysis.
†Retrospective review of all patients who underwent end colostomy formation.
‡All complications recorded at clinic review. Complication rate expressed as cumulative probability from life-table analysis.

Complications

Complications after stoma formation are frequent and varied [see Table 2] and can adversely affect quality of life. The complication rate has been reported to be about 25% after a colostomy formation and as high as 57% after an end ileostomy[18] and 75% after a loop ileostomy.[19] Cumulative complication rates at 20 years have reached 76% in patients undergoing ileostomy for ulcerative colitis and 56% in those undergoing ileostomy for Crohn disease.[20] As noted [see Postoperative Care, above], many complications can be successfully managed with enterostomal care.[18] This is fortunate because the results of surgical correction are often unsatisfactory, with many patients requiring further surgical revision of their stomas.[21]

Careful assessment is warranted when a patient presents with stomal complications. Such complications may be interrelated or may have a different cause from what initial examination suggests. For example, skin damage may be a result of a poorly fitting appliance, but the poor fit may itself be caused by a parastomal hernia or a flush ileostomy. Furthermore, stomal complications may arise from renewed activity of the underlying disease (e.g., recrudescence of Crohn disease[21-23] or recurrence of cancer).

ISCHEMIA

Mild ischemia of the stoma is common in the early postoperative period but usually resolves within a few days. More profound ischemia can result in necrosis of all or part of the circumference of the bowel end used to form the stoma. Satisfactory healing of the stoma depends on an adequate blood supply. Problems with the blood supply are more common with end stomas than with loop stomas; likely causes include excessive division of mesenteric blood vessels, tension on the stoma from inadequate mobilization, and a too-narrow aperture through the abdominal wall that constricts the vessels at the fascial level. It is a good idea to prepare the relevant bowel segment for use in a stoma some time before the end of the operation so that any problems with the blood supply will be evident before the stoma is fashioned. An obviously ischemic stoma should be revised at the time of operation. Such revision may include mobilization of a more proximal bowel segment.

Patchy necrosis that is confined to the mucosa can be managed expectantly and usually heals by second intention. Complete necrosis of an ileostomy is an indication for urgent revision. Necrosis of a colostomy may not necessitate revision if the segment is short. However, a fistula may form at the fascial level, or stenosis may develop as the necrotic segment heals.

STENOSIS

Stenosis of the stoma is a consequence of postoperative ischemia. Mild stenosis can be managed with simple dilatation and may not cause many symptoms, particularly if the effluent is liquid. Substantial stenosis of a colostomy can lead to subacute obstruction that must be managed with surgical revision. Sometimes, revision can be accomplished as a local procedure. A disk of skin that includes the stenosed stoma site is excised. The distal colon is mobilized and sutured to the new skin opening. In most instances, however, it is not possible to mobilize sufficient length with this approach, and laparotomy is required for adequate mobilization.

PROLAPSE

Prolapse may occur with any type of stoma but is most common with loop colostomy. Patients with loop colostomies usually have a degree of parastomal hernia, which allows adequate space for prolapse of the emerging bowel. Appearances are often alarming, and symptoms are usually related to difficulties with fitting an appliance or to leakage. The best treatment option is to close the stoma (if appropriate). Another option is to divide the loop stoma, thus creating an end colostomy, and then to return the closed distal end to the abdomen. Amputation of the prolapsed

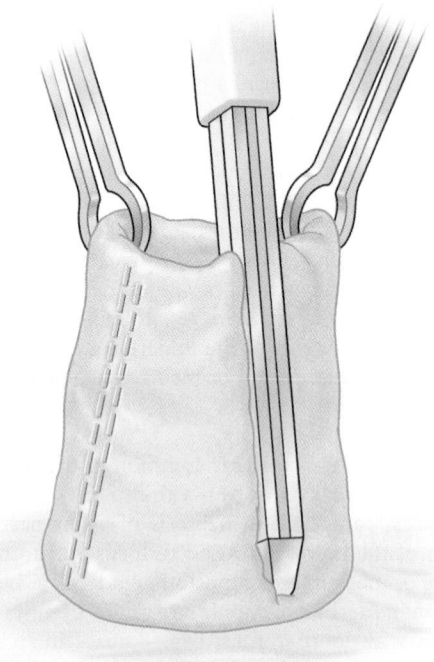

Figure 7 **Illustrated is an alternative method of stabilizing a retracted ileostomy. The ileostomy is everted to its full extent with a Babcock tissue forceps. The site of the mesentery is identified. A noncutting linear stapler is inserted with the anvil in the stoma, with care taken to avoid the mesentery. The stapler is fired several times to fix the two walls of the ileum together.**

stoma corrects the problem in the short term, but the prolapse often recurs quickly. Repairing a coexisting parastomal hernia can lower the risk of recurrence, but it involves a more extensive operation [*see* Parastomal Hernia, *below*]. Neither ensuring that the emerging stoma is brought through the rectus abdominis nor fixing the mesentery to the abdominal wall appears to prevent stoma prolapse.[20]

RETRACTION

Stoma retraction is more of a concern with an ileostomy than with a colostomy because of the possibility of leakage from the appliance. Retraction generally results from poor adhesion between the serosal surfaces of the everted stoma but may also reflect the presence of a parastomal hernia. If the retracted ileostomy is fixed in position, laparotomy will probably be required to correct the problem, though it is worthwhile to attempt local mobilization of the stoma after incising the mucocutaneous junction. If the retracted ileostomy is mobile, the problem can be corrected by inserting a series of interrupted absorbable sutures through the full thickness of the everted stoma to fix the walls together. A similar effect can be obtained by pulling the retracted stoma upward with tissue forceps, then fixing the walls together with several firings of a noncutting linear stapler inserted into the ileostomy, with care taken to avoid the mesentery [*see Figure 7*].[24]

PARASTOMAL HERNIA

Formation of an abdominal stoma necessarily involves creating a defect in the abdominal wall to accommodate the emerging bowel. Such defects may become enlarged as a result of tangential force applied to the edge of the opening, and this enlargement may lead to hernia formation. The tangential force is related to the radial force and the radius of the opening; in turn, the radial force is related to the intra-abdominal pressure and the radius of the abdominal cavity.[25] Consequently, tangential forces are greater in larger openings in obese patients, who are thus at greater risk for parastomal hernia. Patients undergoing emergency procedures in which dilated bowel is used to form a stoma are also likely to be at increased risk for hernia formation. Care must be taken to make an opening that is just large enough for the emerging bowel. An incision that admits only two fingers is appropriate for most elective indications.

Several authors have addressed the problem of enlargement of the stoma opening by reinforcing the opening with a prosthetic ring or a sheet of Marlex mesh.[25,26] One randomized trial compared the incidence of parastomal hernia in patients undergoing conventional end colostomy with the incidence in patients undergoing colostomy with insertion of a partially absorbable lightweight mesh between the posterior rectus sheath and the rectus abdominis.[27] At 12 months, eight of the 18 patients with a conventional colostomy showed evidence of parastomal hernia formation, compared with none of the 16 with a mesh-reinforced colostomy.[27]

There remains some controversy over the issue of where the stoma site should be located in relation to the rectus abdominis. Some authors claim that hernia formation is less frequent when the stoma emerges through the rectus abdominis[28-30]; however, other authors dispute this claim,[9-11] and a clinical and radiologic study of paraileostomy hernia found no differences in incidence between stomas brought out through the rectus abdominis and stomas brought out more laterally.[31]

The incidence of parastomal hernia formation varies widely among published studies [*see Table 3*]. This wide variation reflects both differences in length of follow-up and differences in the

Table 3 Incidence of Parastomal Hernia Formation

Author(s)	Date	Stoma Type	Duration of Follow-up (yr)	Total No. of Patients	Patients with Hernia (No. [%])
Watts et al[47]	1966	Ileostomy	3.4 (mean)	119	3 (2.5)
Burns[48]	1970	Colostomy*	1–21	307	16 (5.2)
Saha et al[49]	1973	Colostomy*	1–6	200	2 (1.0)
Kronborg et al[50]	1974	Colostomy†	1–10	362	42 (11.6)
Harshaw et al[51]	1974	Colostomy‡	1–7	99	9 (9.1)
Marks and Richie[52]	1975	Colostomy‡	1–6	227	23 (32.6§)
Burgess et al[53]	1984	Colostomy†	1–10	124	6 (4.8)
von Smitten et al[54]	1986	Colostomy	8	54	26 (48)
Carlstedt et al[55]	1987	Ileostomy‖	1–26	203	3 (1.5)
Weaver et al[22]	1988	Ileostomy	NA	111	9 (8.1)
Sjödahl et al[30]	1988	All stomas¶	1–36	130	9 (6.9)
Porter et al[46]	1989	Colostomy‡	< 8	130	14 (10.8)
Williams et al[31]	1990	Ileostomy**	1–16	46	13 (28.2)
Hoffman et al[56]	1992	Colostomy‡	< 10	111	5 (4.5)
Leong et al[10]	1994	Ileostomy†	< 20	150	16 (16.0§)
Martin et al[57]	1994	All stomas¶	NA	242	15 (6.2)
Londono-Schimmer et al[9]	1994	Colostomy‡	10	203	43 (36.7§)
Carlsen and Bergan[58]	1995	Ileostomy	2.6 (mean)	224	4 (1.8)
Mäkelä et al[59]	1997	Colostomy	8	80	9 (11.3)
Cheung et al[60]	2001	Colostomy	7	322	126 (39.1)

* Details of method of follow-up not provided. †Prospective follow-up of patients undergoing stoma construction. ‡Retrospective study of patients undergoing stoma construction. §Figure represents cumulative rate, based on life-table analysis. ‖Incidence based on reoperation rate. ¶Patients presenting to a specialist stoma clinic. **Patients specifically reviewed for hernia formation.

methods used to identify parastomal hernias. Given that many hernias are small and asymptomatic, the true incidence of hernia formation may well be higher than the reported figures. It is generally accepted, however, that paracolostomy hernias are more common than paraileostomy hernias. It is unclear why this is so, but the reason is likely to involve the size of the opening in the abdominal wall.

Parastomal hernias are often asymptomatic, and in obese patients, they may not be apparent on clinical examination. Patients usually present with an unsightly bulge at the stoma site, but they may also have other symptoms, such as leakage around the stoma appliance, skin problems, or difficulty in irrigating a colostomy. Rarer presenting symptoms include intestinal obstruction and strangulation of the bowel loop within the hernia. Clinical examination usually suffices for making the diagnosis, particularly when performed with the patient standing. Small hernias in obese patients can be a challenge to diagnose; in this setting, computed tomographic scanning limited to the stoma area can be helpful.[31]

Surgical repair of a parastomal hernia often yields disappointing results and should be considered only if the patient's symptoms are troublesome. Many patients manage reasonably well by wearing a suitably adapted appliance and a support belt. When surgical repair is indicated, it follows one of three possible approaches:

1. Local repair. This approach to hernia repair is the simplest of the three but also the least successful.[32-34] The stoma is mobilized, and the sac is identified and removed. The defect in the fascia of the abdominal wall is narrowed around the emerging bowel with a series of interrupted nonabsorbable sutures. The repair is completed by recreating the mucocutaneous anastomosis.

2. Repair with prosthetic mesh. Mesh repairs have become increasingly popular as different meshes have become available and as surgeons have become aware of the advantages of these materials in hernia surgery. The mesh can be inserted intra-abdominally,[35,36] in the preperitoneal plane [see Figure 8],[32,37] or in the subcutaneous plane.[38,39] Regardless of where the mesh is inserted, the basic principle is the same—namely, to achieve and maintain a narrowing of the stoma site by surrounding the emerging bowel with a sheet of mesh in which a hole is cut to accommodate the stoma.

3. Stoma relocation. The stoma can be moved to a fresh site on the abdominal wall without reopening the main incision. The stoma is fully mobilized, and a new hole is made in the abdominal wall. A plane is developed between the peritoneum and the abdominal contents by means of blunt finger dissection between the existing stoma site and the new one. The mobilized stoma is then passed through the new hole.[40] If difficulties are encountered, a laparotomy will be required. An alter-

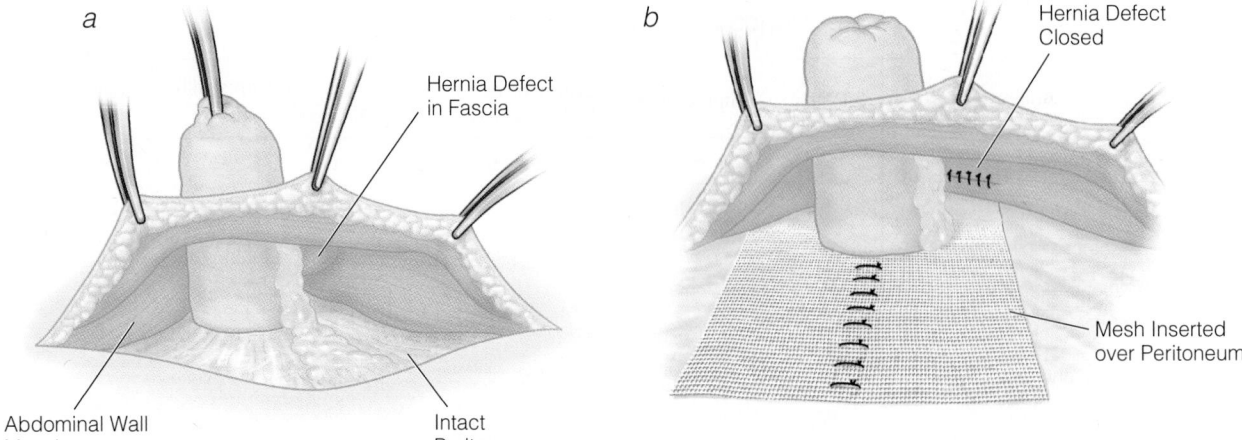

Figure 8 **Depicted is preperitoneal mesh repair of parastomal hernia. (*a*) The midline incision is reopened without disturbing the stoma. The space between the peritoneum and the muscles of the abdominal wall is opened widely, with care taken not to damage the bowel as it emerges from the abdominal cavity. The contents of the hernia are returned to the abdominal cavity, and the defect in the peritoneum is repaired with absorbable sutures. (*b*) A piece of nonabsorbable mesh is cut to shape to cover the defect in the abdominal wall and to just accommodate the emerging bowel. The mesh swatch is placed round the bowel on the intact peritoneum, and the two tails of the swatch are sutured together so as to encircle the bowel. The defect in the muscle layer is closed with a few interrupted nonabsorbable sutures.**

native approach is to reroute the stoma through a new fascial defect while maintaining the existing skin aperture. The original fascial defect is repaired with mesh.[41]

The best method of repair has not been established.[42] Most published studies have included relatively few patients who were followed for a relatively short time. With longer follow-up, recurrence rates as high as 76% have been reported. Local repair is associated with the highest recurrence rate,[43] and stoma relocation carries an increased morbidity (from incisional hernia at the original stoma site).[44] Nor is mesh repair free of problems: intra-abdominal placement of mesh is associated with a significant risk of adhesions to the mesh and of small bowel obstruction.[45] The risk of mesh infection is highest when the mesh is placed in a superficial position through a parastomal incision.

At present, the best approach is to tailor repair to the individual patient's condition and situation. For more specific recommendations, randomized trials of the different methods of parastomal hernia repair will be required. There is a growing amount of evidence in favor of inserting prosthetic mesh at the time of stoma formation in an effort to reduce the incidence of this complication.

OBSTRUCTION

Conditions that may cause intestinal obstruction after stoma formation include stenosis of the stoma, parastomal hernia, postoperative adhesions, and recurrent disease (e.g., Crohn disease in the proximal ileum or recurrent cancer). Management depends on the cause of the obstruction. Retrograde contrast studies are useful for identifying the site and determining the likely cause of obstruction.

FISTULA

A fistula may form adjacent to a stoma as a consequence of inadvertent full-thickness placement of a suture through both walls of the stoma during formation, pressure necrosis at skin level from a tightly fitting stoma appliance, or recurrent disease, especially Crohn disease in the ileum proximal to the stoma. Surgical treatment usually involves laparotomy and reformation of the stoma at a new site.

OTHER COMPLICATIONS

Other, less common complications arising after stoma formation include bleeding, perforation, skin ulceration, and the development of cancer [*see Table 4*].

Table 4 Additional Complications Arising after Stoma Formation

Complication	Cause	Differential Diagnosis	Treatment
Bleeding	Trauma Inflammatory polyps	Portal hypertension Recurrent disease	Review of stoma appliance and technique
Perforation	Traumatic (irrigation) Recurrent disease	Stercoral (constipation)	Laparotomy and revision of stoma
Skin ulceration	Contact dermatitis	Pyoderma gangrenosum	Review of stoma appliance and technique
Cancer formation	Recurrence at stoma site De novo cancer formation	Inflammatory polyps	Resection

References

1. Fasth S, Hulten L, Palselius I: Loop ileostomy—an attractive alternative to a temporary transverse colostomy. Acta Chir Scand 146:203, 1980

2. Sakai Y, Nelson H, Larson D, et al: Temporary transverse colostomy vs loop ileostomy in diversion: a case-matched study. Arch Surg 136:338, 2001

3. Rullier E, Le Toux N, Laurent C, et al: Loop ileostomy versus loop colostomy for defunctioning low anastomoses during rectal cancer surgery. World J Surg 25:274, 2001

4. Williams NS, Nasmyth DG, Jones D, et al: Defunctioning stomas: a prospective controlled trial comparing loop ileostomy with loop transverse colostomy. Br J Surg 73:566, 1986

5. Gooszen AW, Geelkerken RH, Hermans J, et al: Temporary decompression after colorectal surgery: randomized comparison of loop ileostomy and loop colostomy. Br J Surg 85:76, 1998

6. Law WL, Chu KW, Choi HK: Randomized clinical trial comparing loop ileostomy and loop transverse colostomy for faecal diversion following total mesorectal excision. Br J Surg 89:704, 2002

7. Edwards DP, Leppington-Clarke A, Sexton R, et al: Stoma-related complications are more frequent after transverse colostomy than loop ileostomy: a prospective randomized clinical trial. Br J Surg 88:360, 2001

8. Gooszen AW, Geelkerken RH, Hermans J, et al: Quality of life with a temporary stoma: ileostomy vs. colostomy. Dis Colon Rectum 43:650, 2000

9. Londono-Schimmer EE, Leong APK, Phillips RKS: Life table analysis of stomal complications following colostomy. Dis Colon Rectum 37:916, 1994

10. Leong APK, Londono-Schimmer EE, Phillips RKS: Life-table analysis of stomal complications following ileostomy. Br J Surg 81:727, 1994

11. Ortiz H, Sara MJ, Armendariz P, et al: Does the frequency of paracolostomy hernias depend on the position of the colostomy in the abdominal wall? Int J Colorect Dis 9:65, 1994

12. Hall C, Myers C, Phillips RKS: The 554 ileostomy. Br J Surg 82:1385, 1995

13. Fonkalsrud EW, Thakur A, Roof L: Comparison of loop versus end ileostomy for fecal diversion after restorative proctocolectomy for ulcerative colitis. J Am Coll Surg 190:418, 2000

14. Peiser JG, Cohen Z, McLeod RS: Surgical treatment of ulcerative colitis—continent ileostomy. Inflammatory Bowel Diseases. Allan RN, Rhodes JM, Hanauer SB, et al, Eds. Churchill Livingstone, New York, 1997, p 753

15. Bain IM, Patel R, Keighley MRB: Comparison of sutured and stapled closure of loop ileostomy after restorative proctocolectomy. Ann R Coll Surg Engl 78:555, 1996

16. Hasegawa H, Radley S, Morton DG, et al: Stapled versus sutured closure of loop ileostomy: a randomized controlled trial. Ann Surg 231:202, 2000

17. Hull TL, Kobe I, Fazio VW: Comparison of hand-sewn with stapled loop ileostomy closures. Dis Colon Rectum 39:1086, 1996

18. Phillips R, Pringle W, Evans C, et al: Analysis of a hospital-based stomatherapy service. Ann R Coll Surg Engl 67:37, 1985

19. Park JJ, Del Pino A, Orsay CP, et al: Stoma complications: the Cook County Hospital experience. Dis Colon Rectum 42:1575, 1999

20. Leong APK, Londono-Schimmer EE, Phillips RKS: Life-table analysis of stomal complications following ileostomy. Br J Surg 81:727, 1994

21. Andromanakos N, Williams JG, Alexander-Williams J: Ileostomy revision for stomal complications in inflammatory bowel disease. Dig Surg 13:26, 1996

22. Weaver RM, Alexander-Williams J, Keighley MRB: Indications and outcome of reoperation for ileostomy complications in inflammatory bowel disease. Int J Colorect Dis 3:38, 1988

23. Ecker KW, Gierend M, Kreissler-Haag D, et al: Reoperations at the ileostomy in Crohn's disease reflect inflammatory activity rather than stoma complications alone. Int J Colorect Dis 16:76, 2001

24. Winslet MC, Alexander-Williams J, Keighley MRB: Ileostomy revision with a GIA stapler under intravenous sedation. Br J Surg 77:647, 1990

25. de Ruiter P, Bijnen AB: Successful local repair of paracolostomy hernia with a newly developed prosthetic device. Int J Colorect Dis 7:132, 1992

26. Bayer I, Kyser S, Chaimoff C: A new approach to primary strengthening of colostomy with Marlex mesh to prevent parastomal hernia. Surg Gynecol Obstet 163:579, 1986

27. Jänes A, Cengiz Y, Israelsson LA: Randomized clinical trial of the use of a prosthetic mesh to prevent parastomal hernia. Br J Surg 91:280, 2004

28. Goligher JC: Surgery of the Anus, Rectum and Colon, 5th ed. Baillière Tindall, London, 1984, p 702

29. Rosin JD, Bonardi RA: Paracolostomy hernia repair with marlex mesh: a new technique. Dis Colon Rectum 20:229, 1977

30. Sjödahl R, Anderberg B, Bolin T: Parastomal hernia in relation to site of the abdominal stoma. Br J Surg 75:339, 1988

31. Williams JG, Etherington R, Hayward MWJ, et al: Paraileostomy hernia: a clinical and radiological study. Br J Surg 77:1355, 1990

32. Devlin HB: Management of Abdominal Hernias. Butterworths, London, 1988, p 177

33. Allen-Mersh T, Thomson JPS: Surgical treatment of colostomy complications. Br J Surg 75:416, 1988

34. Horgan K, Hughes LE: Para-ileostomy hernia: failure of a local repair technique. Br J Surg 73:439, 1986

35. Byers JM, Steinberg JB, Postier RG: Repair of parastomal hernias using polypropylene mesh. Arch Surg 127:1246, 1992

36. Sugarbaker PH: Peritoneal approach to prosthetic mesh repair of paraostomy hernias. Ann Surg 201:344, 1985

37. Kasperk R, Klinge U, Schumpelick V: The repair of parastomal hernia using a midline approach and a prosthetic mesh in the sublay position. Am J Surg 179:186, 2000

38. Leslie D: The parastomal hernia. Surg Clin North Am 64:407, 1984

39. Amin SN, Armitage NC, Abercrombie JF, et al: Lateral repair of parastomal hernia. Ann R Coll Surg Engl 83:206, 2001

40. Kaufman JJ: Repair of parastomal hernia by translocation of the stoma without laparotomy. J Urol 129:278, 1983

41. Stephenson BM, Phillips RKS: Parastomal hernia: local resiting and mesh repair. Br J Surg 82:1395, 1995

42. Carne PWG, Robertson GM, Frizelle FA: Parastomal hernia. Br J Surg 90:784, 2003

43. Mellbring G, Fazio VW, Lavery IC, et al: The results of surgery for parastomal hernia (abstr). Presented at the annual meeting of the American Society of Colon and Rectal Surgeons, Anaheim, California, 1988

44. Rubin MS, Schoetz DJ, Matthews JB: Parastomal hernia. Is stoma relocation superior to fascial repair? Arch Surg 129:413, 1994

45. Morris-Stiff G, Hughes LE: The continuing challenge of parastomal hernia: failure of a novel polypropylene mesh repair. Ann R Coll Surg Engl 80:184, 1998

46. Porter JA, Salvati EP, Rubin RJ, et al: Complications of colostomies. Dis Colon Rectum 32:299, 1989

47. Watts JM, de Dombal FT, Goligher JC: Long-term complications and prognosis following major surgery for ulcerative colitis. Br J Surg 53:1014, 1966

48. Burns FJ: Complications of colostomy. Dis Colon Rectum 13:448, 1970

49. Saha SP, Rao N, Stephenson SE: Complications of colostomy. Dis Colon Rectum 16:515, 1973

50. Kronberg O, Kramhöft J, Backer O, et al: Late complications following operations for cancer of the rectum and anus. Dis Colon Rectum 17:750, 1974

51. Harshaw DH, Gardner B, Vives A, et al: The effect of technical factors upon complications from abdominal perineal resections. Surg Gynecol Obstet 139:756, 1974

52. Marks CG, Ritchie JK: The complications of synchronous combined excision for adenocarcinoma of the rectum at St Mark's Hospital. Br J Surg 62:901, 1975

53. Burgess P, Matthew VV, Devlin HB: A review of terminal colostomy complications following abdominoperineal resection for carcinoma. Br J Surg 71:1004, 1984

54. von Smitten K, Husa A, Kyllönen I: Long-term results of sigmoidostomy in patients with anorectal malignancy. Acta Chir Scand 152:211, 1986

55. Carlstedt A, Fasth S, Hultén L, et al: Long-term ileostomy complications in patients with ulcerative colitis and Crohn's disease. Int J Colorect Dis 2:22, 1987

56. Hoffman MS, Barton DPJ, Gates J, et al: Complications of colostomy performed on gynecology cancer patients. Gynecol Oncol 44:231, 1992

57. Martin L, Foster G: Parastomal hernia. Ann R Coll Surg Engl 78:81, 1996

58. Carlsen E, Bergan A: Technical aspects and complications of end-ileostomies. World J Surg 19:632, 1995

59. Mäkelä JT, Turku PH, Laitinen ST: Analysis of late stomal complications following ostomy surgery. Ann Chir Gynecol 86:305, 1997

60. Cheung MT, Chia NH, Chiu WY: Surgical treatment of parastomal hernia complicating sigmoid colostomies. Dis Colon Rectum 44:266, 2001

Acknowledgment

Figures 1 through 8   Tom Moore.

73 APPENDECTOMY

Hung S. Ho, M.D., F.A.C.S.

First depicted in anatomic drawings in 1492 by Leonardo da Vinci, the vermiform appendix was described as an anatomic structure in 1521 by Jacopo Berengari da Carpi, a professor of human anatomy at Bologna. Appendicitis became recognized as a surgical disease when the Harvard University pathologist Reginald Heber Fitz read his analysis of 257 cases of perforating inflammation of the appendix and 209 cases of typhlitis or perityphlitis at the 1886 meeting of the Association of American Physicians. In this landmark report, Fitz correctly pointed out that the frequent abscesses in the right iliac fossa were often due to perforation of the vermiform appendix, and he referred to the condition as appendicitis.[1] Among his classic observations of the disease was his emphasis on the "vital importance of early recognition" and its "eventual treatment by laparotomy." It was not until 1894 that Charles McBurney first described the surgical incision that bears his name and the technique of appendectomy that was to become the gold standard for appendectomy throughout the 20th century and into the 21st.[2]

Although appendectomy has traditionally been done—and largely continues to be done—as an open procedure, there has been increasing interest in laparoscopic appendectomy since the beginning of the 1990s. At present, however, the only patients for whom laparoscopic appendectomy appears to offer significant advantages are women of childbearing age, obese patients, and patients with an unclear diagnosis [*see Figure 1*]. Accordingly, the gold standard for surgical treatment of acute appendicitis remains open appendectomy as described by McBurney. The occasional patient with chronic appendicitis should be electively treated with the laparoscopic approach.

Operative Technique

OPEN APPENDECTOMY

With the patient in the supine position, general anesthesia is induced and the abdomen is prepared and draped in a sterile fashion so as to expose the right lower quadrant. The skin incision is made in an oblique direction, crossing a line drawn between the anterior superior iliac spine and the umbilicus at nearly a right angle at a point about 2 to 3 cm from the iliac spine. This point, McBurney's point, is approximately one third of the way from the iliac spine to the umbilicus [*see Figure 2*]. The subcutaneous fat and fascia are incised to expose the external oblique aponeurosis. A slightly shorter incision is made in this aponeurosis; first, a scalpel is used, and then, the incision is extended with scissors in the direction of the fibers of the muscle and its tendon in such a way that the fibers are separated but not cut.

The fibers of the internal oblique muscle and the transversus abdominis are separated with a blunt instrument at nearly a right angle to the incision on the external oblique aponeurosis. The parietal peritoneum is lifted up, with care taken not to include the underlying viscera, and is opened in a transverse fashion with a scalpel. This incision is then enlarged transversely with scissors. When greater exposure is required, the lateral edge of the rectus sheath is incised and the rectus abdominis is

retracted medially without being divided [*see Figure 3*].

A foul smell or the presence of pus on entry into the peritoneum is an indication of advanced or perforating appendicitis. The free peritoneal fluid is collected for bacteriologic analysis. The appendix is located by following the cecal taeniae distally. The inflamed appendix usually feels firm and turgid. The appendix, together with the cecum, is delivered into the surgical incision and held with a Babcock tissue forceps. If this step proves difficult, the appendix can sometimes be swept into the field with the surgeon's right index finger as gentle traction is maintained on the cecum with a small, moist gauze pad held in the left hand [*see Figure 4*]. Care should be taken at this point not to avulse the friable and possibly necrotic appendix. To deliver a retrocecal appendix, it may be necessary to mobilize the ascending colon partially by dividing the peritoneum on its lateral side, starting from the terminal ileum and proceeding toward the hepatic flexure.

The mesoappendix, containing the appendicular artery, is divided between clamps and ligated with 3-0 absorbable sutures [*see Figure 5*]. The appendix is held up with a Babcock tissue forceps, and its base is crushed with a straight mosquito arterial forceps. The mosquito forceps is then opened, moved up the appendix, and closed again. The base of the appendix is doubly ligated with 2-0 absorbable sutures at the point where it was crushed, so that a cuff of about 3 mm is left between the forceps and the tie.

The appendix is divided by running a scalpel along the underside of the forceps. The mucosa of the appendiceal stump is fulgurated with the electrocautery. The stump is not routinely invaginated into the cecum. In those rare cases in which the viability of the appendiceal base is in question, a 2-0 absorbable purse-string suture is placed in the cecum, and the stump is invaginated as the suture is tied; if this is done, palpation for a patent ileocecal valve is indicated. The operative field is then checked for hemostasis. In cases of perforating appendicitis, the right paracolic gutter and pelvis are irrigated and thoroughly aspirated to ensure that any collected pus or particulate material is removed.

The peritoneum is then closed with a continuous 3-0 absorbable suture. The fibers of the transversus abdominis and the internal oblique muscle fall together readily, and their closure can be completed with two interrupted 3-0 absorbable ligatures. The external oblique aponeurosis is closed from end to end with a continuous 2-0 absorbable suture. Scarpa's fascia is approximated with interrupted 3-0 absorbable sutures, and the skin is closed with a continuous subcuticular 4-0 absorbable suture and reinforcing tapes (Steri-Strips).

If the wound has been grossly contaminated, the fascia and muscles are closed as described, but the skin is loosely approximated with Steri-Strips, which can easily be removed after the procedure if surgical site infection or abscess develops. An alternative approach is to leave the skin and the subcutaneous tissue open but dressed with sterile nonadherent material and then to perform delayed primary closure with Steri-Strips on postoperative day 4 or 5. A meta-analysis of 27 studies involving 2,532 patients with gangrenous or perforating appendicitis concluded that the risk of surgical site infection was no higher with primary closure than with delayed primary closure.[3]

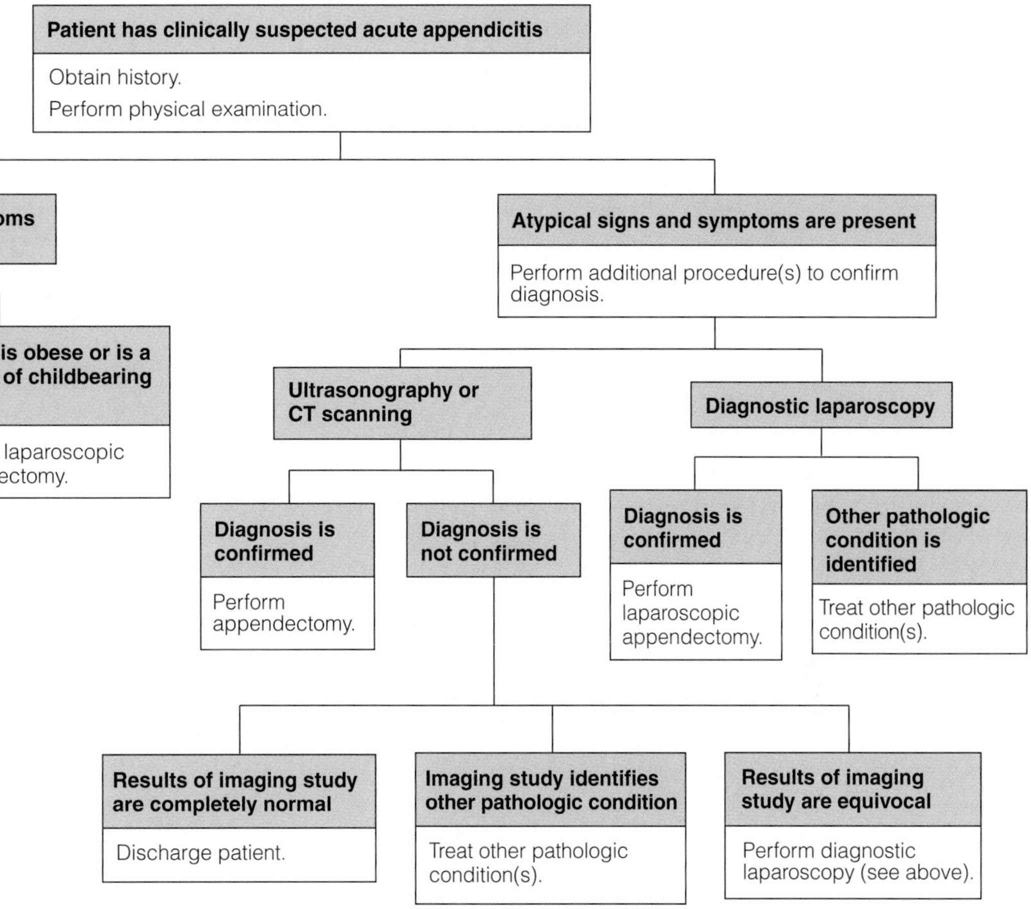

Patient has clinically suspected acute appendicitis

Obtain history.
Perform physical examination.

Typical signs and symptoms are present

Atypical signs and symptoms are present

Perform additional procedure(s) to confirm diagnosis.

Patient is not obese and is not a woman of childbearing age

Perform open appendectomy.

Patient is obese or is a woman of childbearing age

Perform laparoscopic appendectomy.

Ultrasonography or CT scanning

Diagnostic laparoscopy

Diagnosis is confirmed

Perform appendectomy.

Diagnosis is not confirmed

Diagnosis is confirmed

Perform laparoscopic appendectomy.

Other pathologic condition is identified

Treat other pathologic condition(s).

Figure 1 Shown is an algorithm for choosing between treatment options for patients with suspected acute appendicitis.

Results of imaging study are completely normal

Discharge patient.

Imaging study identifies other pathologic condition

Treat other pathologic condition(s).

Results of imaging study are equivocal

Perform diagnostic laparoscopy (see above).

LAPAROSCOPIC APPENDECTOMY

The patient is placed in the supine position, with both arms tucked along the sides, and general anesthesia is induced. Decompression with an orogastric tube should be routine, as should placement of a urinary Foley catheter and use of lower-extremity sequential compression devices. The surgeon should stand on the patient's left side, with the assistant (who operates the camera) near the patient's left shoulder [*see Figure 6*]. The monitors are placed on the opposite side of the operating table so that both the surgeon and the assistant can view the procedure at all times.

The abdomen is prepared and draped in a sterile fashion so as to expose the entire abdomen. A three-port approach is routinely used [*see Figure 6*]. All skin incisions along the midline are made vertically to allow a more cosmetically acceptable conversion to laparotomy, should this become necessary. The suprapubic port must be large enough to accommodate the laparoscopic stapler (usually 12 mm); the other two ports can be smaller (e.g., 5 or 10 mm). The ports are placed as far away from the operative field as possible to permit the application of a two-handed dissection technique. The use of a 30° angled scope facilitates operative viewing and dissection.

With the patient pharmacologically relaxed and in the Trendelenburg position, a Veress needle is inserted into the peritoneal cavity at the base of the umbilical ligament. Aspiration and the saline-drop test are performed to ensure that the tip of the needle is correctly positioned. Pneumoperitoneum is established by insufflating CO_2 to an intra-abdominal pressure of 14 mm Hg. The first port is placed at the infraumbilical skin incision, the laparoscope is inserted, and a complete diagnostic laparoscopy is

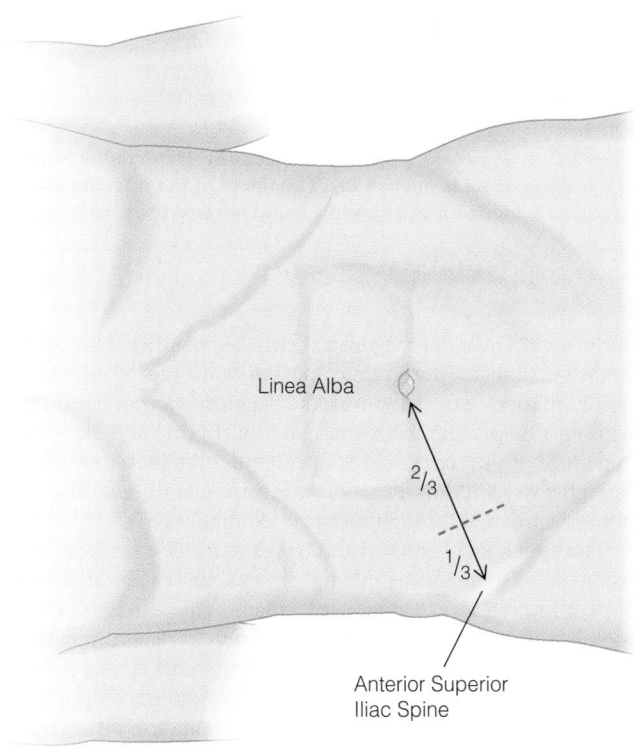

Linea Alba

$^2/_3$

$^1/_3$

Anterior Superior Iliac Spine

Figure 2 **Open appendectomy. Shown are McBurney's point and McBurney's incision.**

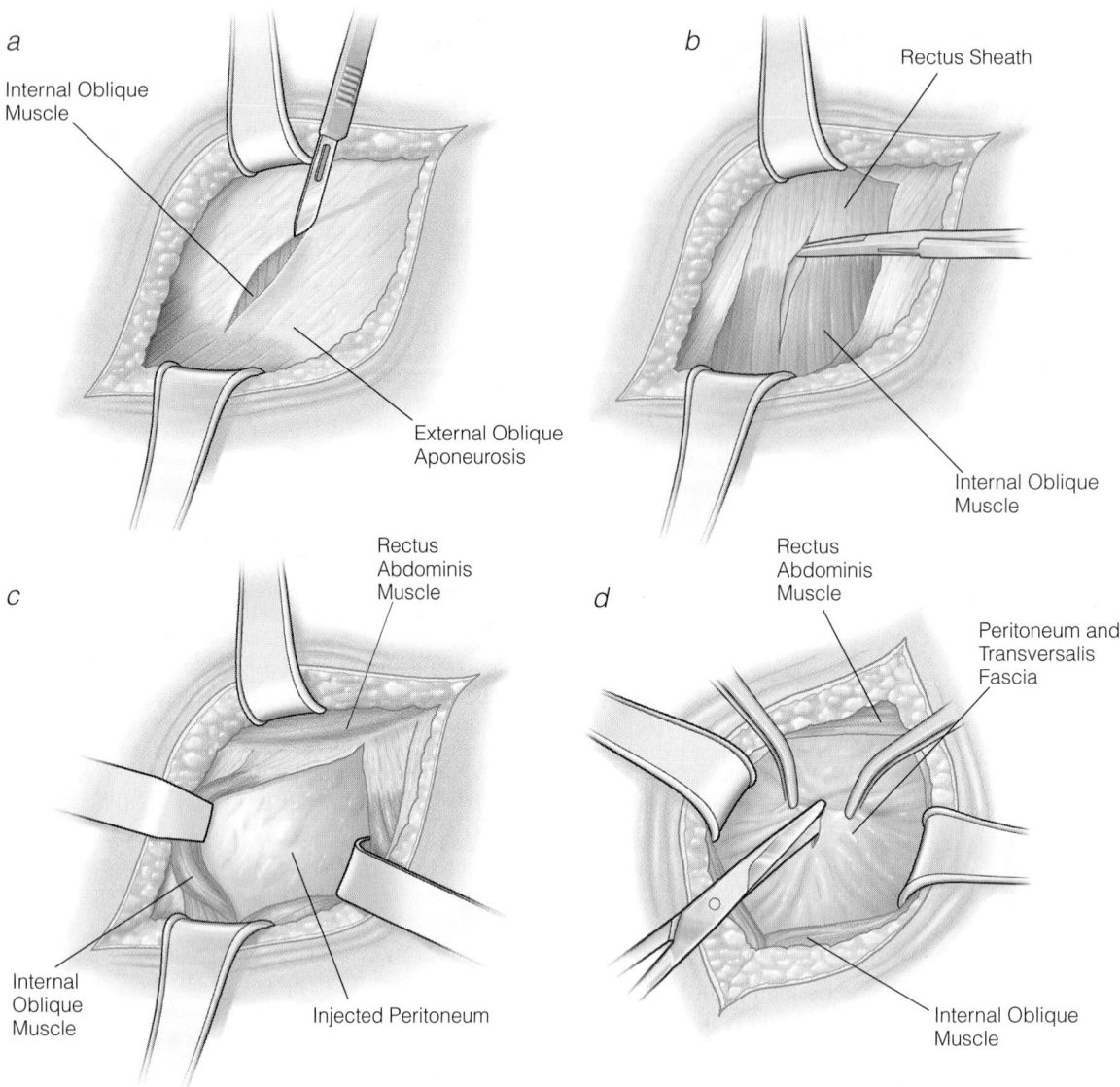

Figure 3   **Open appendectomy. Depicted is exposure of the abdominal cavity. The external oblique aponeurosis is opened (a). The fibers of the internal oblique muscle are separated bluntly (b). The parietal peritoneum is exposed (c) and opened transversely (d).**

performed. Once the diagnosis of acute appendicitis is confirmed by inspection, the two remaining ports are placed under direct vision. In many cases, however, the diagnosis cannot be confirmed without first placing the second and third ports and exposing the appendix. If purulent fluid is encountered, it should be carefully aspirated dry without irrigation to ensure that the infected fluid is not disseminated throughout the abdominal cavity.

The appendix is exposed and traced to its base on the cecum by using an atraumatic retracting forceps. In cases of retrocecal appendix or severe appendiceal inflammation, it is best first to mobilize the cecum completely by taking the lateral reflection of the peritoneum around the terminal ileum and up the ascending colon with an ultrasonic scalpel (e.g., the Harmonic Scalpel; Ethicon Endo-Surgery, Inc., Cincinnati, Ohio). Surrounding structures, such as the iliac and gonadal vessels and the ureter, should be clearly identified to minimize the risk of injury. Dissection of the appendix can then begin.

The tip of the appendix is grasped and retracted anteriorly toward the anterior abdominal wall and slightly toward the pelvis; the mesoappendix is thus exposed in a triangular fashion. A window between the base of the appendix and the blood supply is created with a curved dissecting forceps. The mesoappendix is divided either with hemostatic clips and scissors or with a laparoscopic gastrointestinal anastomosis (GIA) stapler loaded with a vascular cartridge [*see Figure 7*]. If a window on the mesoappendix cannot be safely created because of intense inflammation, antegrade dissection of the blood supply is necessary. The ultrasonic scalpel is a handy (albeit expensive) instrument for this purpose. Endoscopic hemostatic clips usually suffice to control the small branches of the appendicular artery during the course of this dissection.

The base of the appendix is then cleared circumferentially of any adipose or connective tissue and is divided with a laparoscopic GIA stapler loaded with an intestinal cartridge [*see Figure 8*]. To ensure an adequate closure away from the inflamed appendiceal wall, a

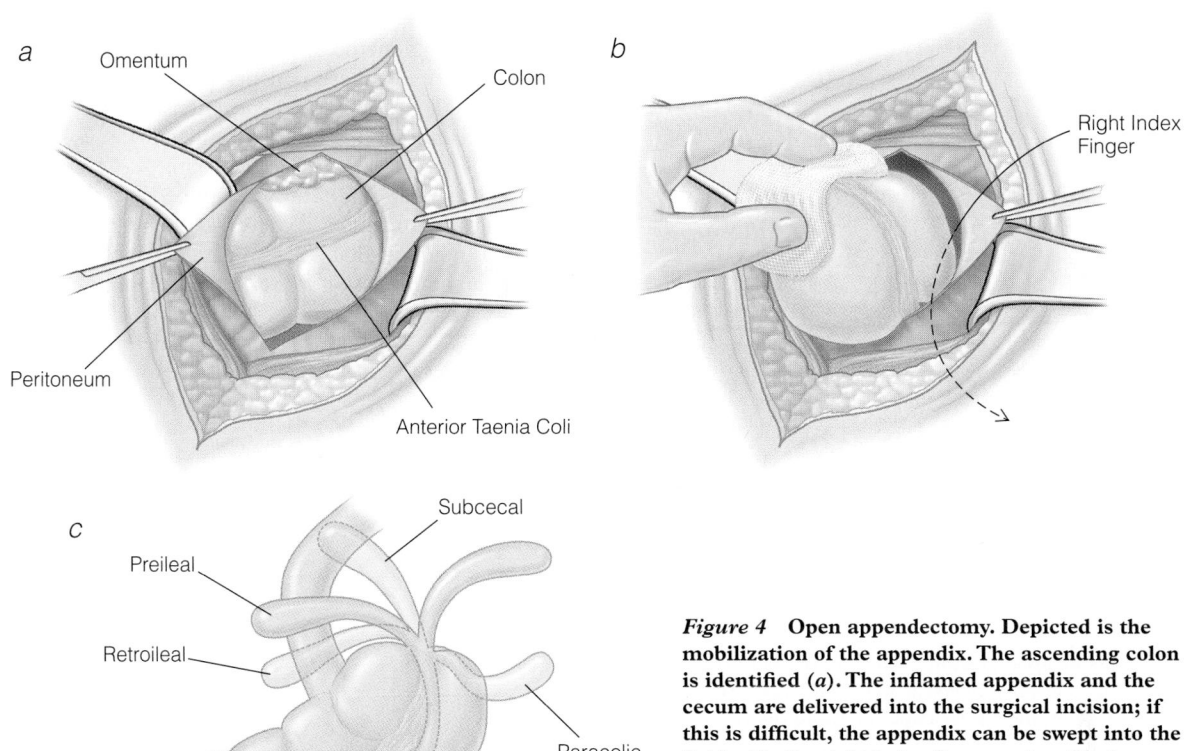

Figure 4 Open appendectomy. Depicted is the mobilization of the appendix. The ascending colon is identified (*a*). The inflamed appendix and the cecum are delivered into the surgical incision; if this is difficult, the appendix can be swept into the field with the right index finger as traction is maintained on the cecum with a gauze pad (*b*). The appendix may be seen to occupy any of a number of potential locations (*c*).

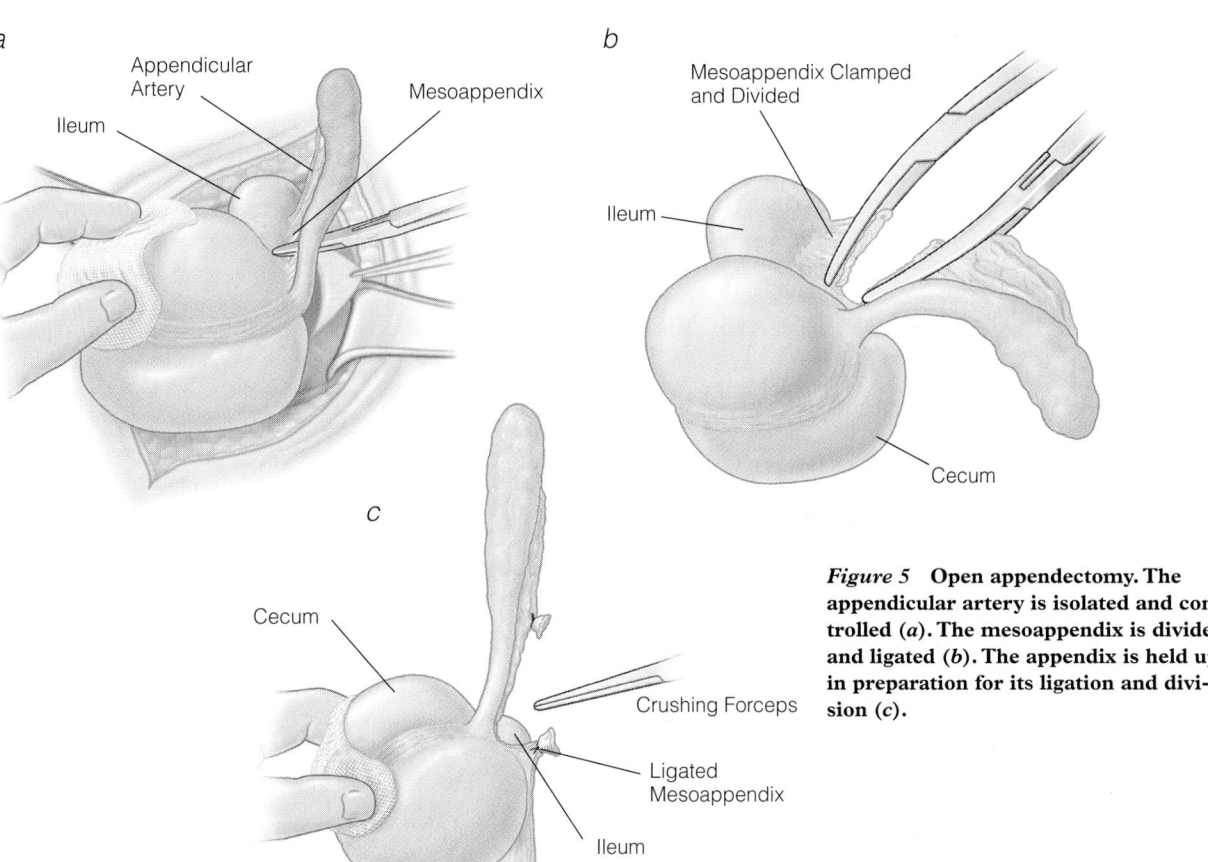

Figure 5 Open appendectomy. The appendicular artery is isolated and controlled (*a*). The mesoappendix is divided and ligated (*b*). The appendix is held up in preparation for its ligation and division (*c*).

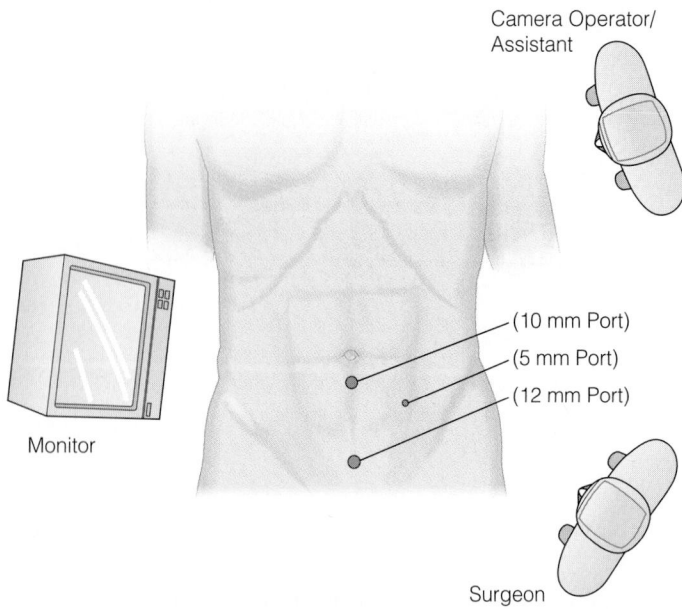

Figure 6 **Laparoscopic appendectomy. Shown are the positioning and placement of the operative ports, as well as the recommended positions for the surgeon, the camera operator, and the video monitor.**

small portion of the cecum may have to be included within the stapler. To ensure proper placement of the stapler and to prevent injury to the right ureter or the adjacent small bowel, the tips of the stapler must be clearly visualized before the instrument is closed. The use of an angled scope and an articulated rotating laparoscopic GIA stapler (e.g., Roticulator; AutoSuture, Norwalk, Connecticut) will facilitate this maneuver. A noninflamed or minimally inflamed appendix can be ligated with sutures, as described earlier [*see* Open Appendectomy, *above*]. The appendix is removed from the abdominal cavity, with care taken to avoid direct contact with the abdominal wall. A mildly inflamed appendix can be delivered through one of the larger ports; a severely inflamed appendix is often too big and hence should be delivered in a specimen retrieval bag [*see Figure 9*].

The operative field is irrigated and aspirated dry. Hemostasis is confirmed, and the cecum is inspected to ensure proper closure of the appendiceal stump. The ports are removed under direct vision, the absence of back-bleeding from the port sites is confirmed, and the abdomen is completely decompressed. All fascial defects larger than 5 mm are closed with 0 absorbable sutures. The skin incisions are reapproximated with a subcuticular 4-0 absorbable suture and reinforcing Steri-Strips.

Special Considerations

HISTOLOGICALLY NORMAL APPENDIX

Acute appendicitis is the most common cause of an acute surgical abdomen in the United States, and it remains one of the most challenging diagnoses to make in the emergency department. Although the use of advanced diagnostic imaging modalities (e.g., ultrasonography and computed tomography) has led to more accurate diagnosis of acute appendicitis in research settings, it has not been shown to reduce the rate of misdiagnosis of acute appendicitis in the general population.[4]

The incidence of histologically normal appendix in patients with clinical signs and symptoms of acute appendicitis ranges from

8% to 41%.[5-14] Nonetheless, appendectomy relieves symptoms in the vast majority of these patients. When extensive sectioning is done on histologically normal specimens, it often happens that a focus of inflammation is found in only a few serial sections. This condition is known as focal appendicitis—so called because the polymorphonuclear infiltration is confined to a single focus, while the remaining appendix is devoid of any polymorphonuclear cells.[15] It is not clear that all cases of acute appendicitis arise from this focal inflammation; however, such inflammatory foci may be

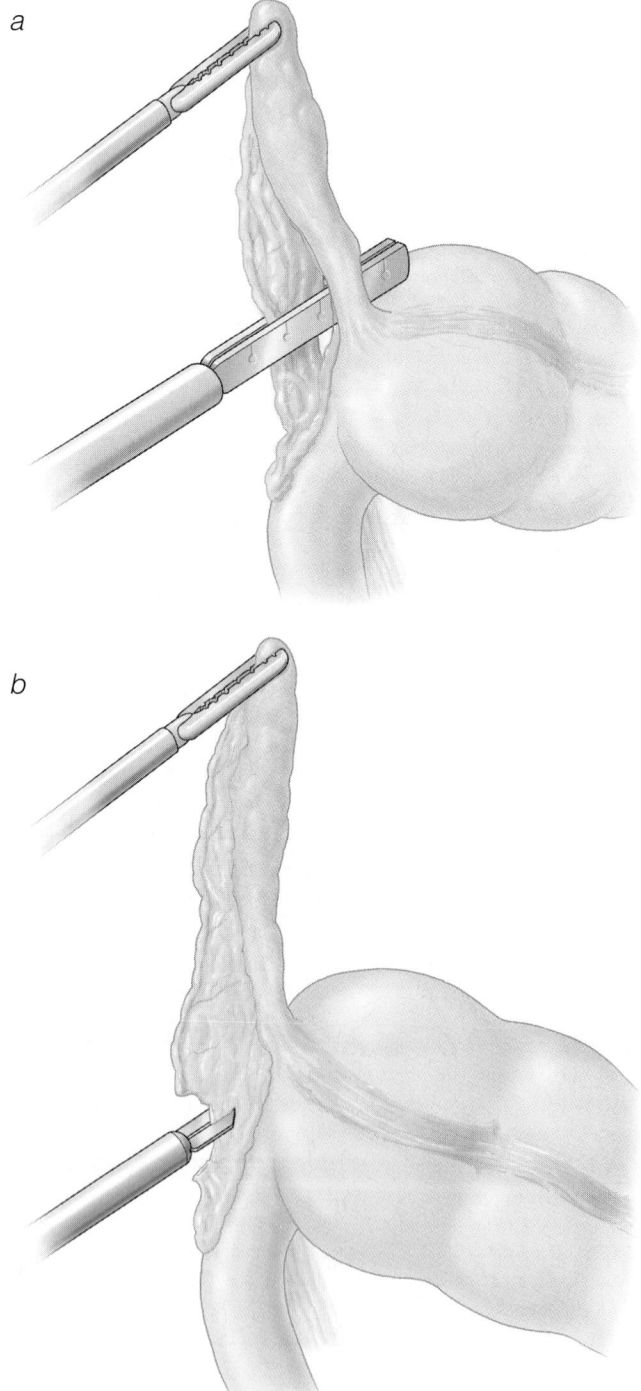

Figure 7 **Laparoscopic appendectomy. The mesoappendix is divided either with a laparoscopic GIA stapler (*a*) or with hemostatic clips and scissors (*b*).**

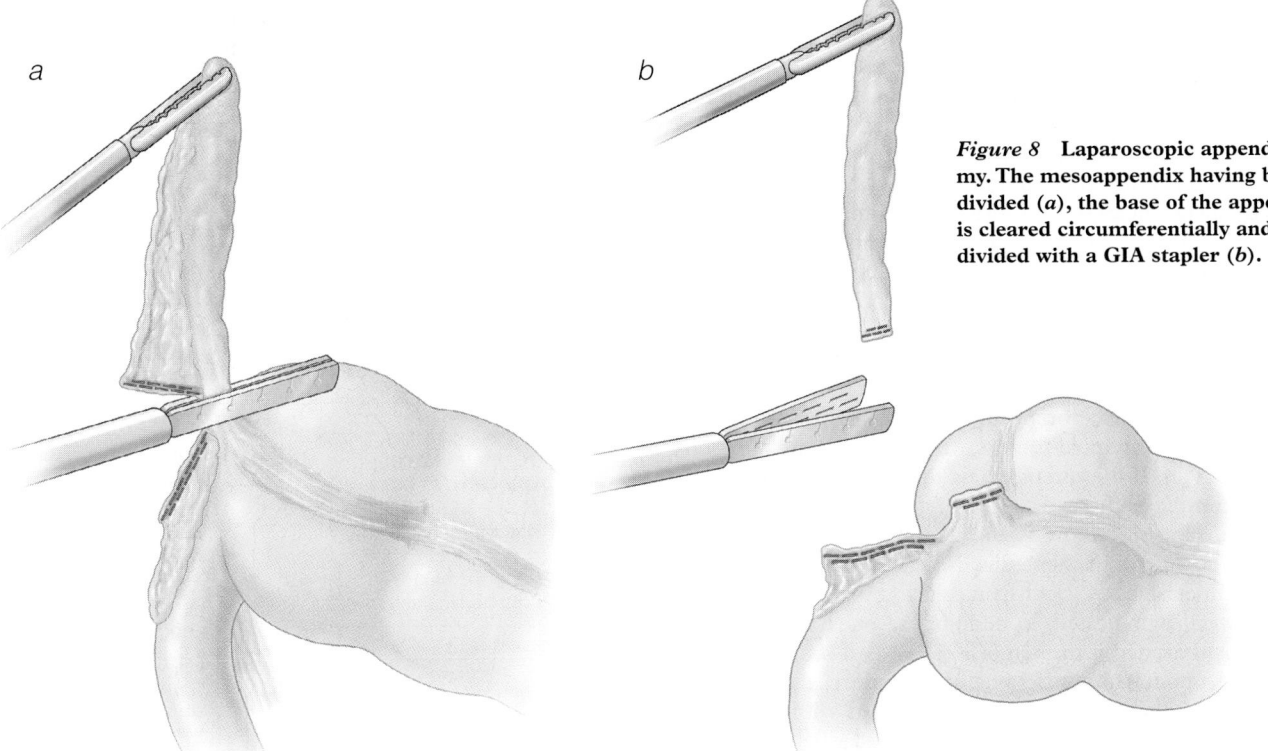

Figure 8 **Laparoscopic appendectomy. The mesoappendix having been divided (*a*), the base of the appendix is cleared circumferentially and divided with a GIA stapler (*b*).**

the earliest recognizable manifestations of appendicitis in some so-called negative appendectomies. Furthermore, a substantial proportion of histologically normal appendices removed from patients with clinical signs and symptoms of acute appendicitis exhibit significantly increased expression of tumor necrosis factor–α and interleukin-2 messenger RNA (a sensitive marker of inflammation in appendicitis) in germinal centers, the submucosa, and the lamina propria.[16] Therefore, appendectomy is recommended in patients with clinically suspected acute appendicitis even when the appendix does not appear inflamed during exploration.[17]

Laparoscopic appendectomy has not been shown to reduce the incidence of negative exploration in patients with clinically suspected acute appendicitis [*see* Complications and Outcome Evaluation, Open versus Laparoscopic Appendectomy, *below*].

APPENDICEAL NEOPLASM

Neoplastic lesions of the appendix are found in as many as 5% of specimens obtained with routine appendectomy for acute appendicitis.[18-21] Most are benign. Preoperative detection of such conditions is rare, and intraoperative diagnosis is made in fewer than 50% of cases. Appendectomy alone may be curative for appendiceal mucocele, localized pseudomyxoma peritonei, most appendiceal carcinoids, and other benign tumors. Definitive management of an appendiceal mass unexpectedly encountered during exploration for clinically suspected acute appendicitis depends on whether the tumor is carcinoid, its size and location, the presence or absence of metastatic disease, and histologic and immunohistochemical findings [*see Figure 10*].

Benign neoplasms of the appendix include mucosal hyperplasia or metaplasia, leiomyomas, neuromas, lipomas, angiomas, and other rare lesions. Appendiceal adenomas tend to be diffuse and to have a predominant villous character. Mucus-producing cystadenomas predispose to appendiceal mucocele, sometimes accompanied by localized pseudomyxoma peritonei. These lesions are

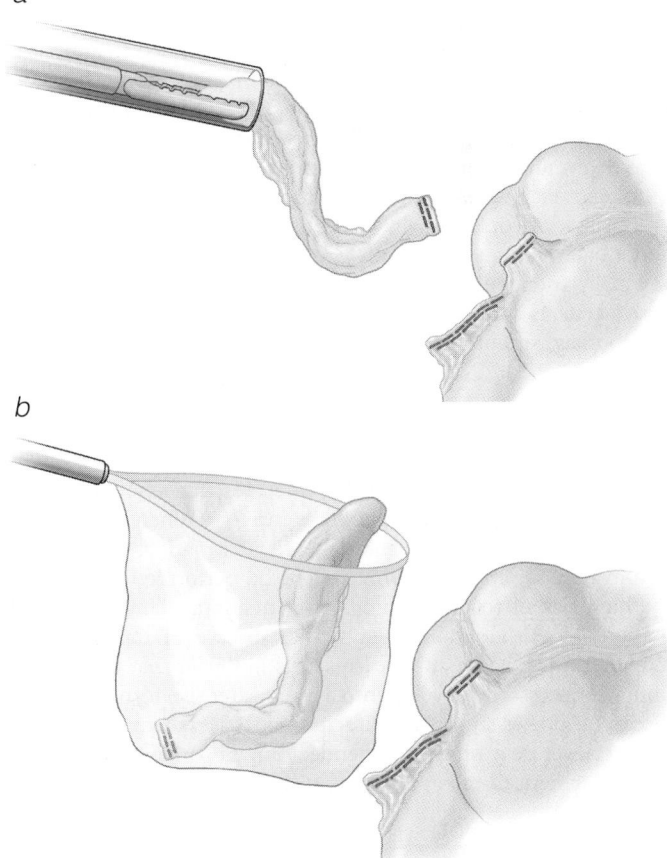

Figure 9 **Laparoscopic appendectomy. The specimen is delivered either through one of the larger ports (*a*) or in a specimen retrieval bag (*b*).**

rarely symptomatic and are often encountered incidentally during operation; however, they may also be clinically manifested as acute appendicitis, torsion, intussusception, ureteral obstruction, or another acute condition. If the base of the appendix is free of disease, appendectomy alone is sufficient treatment.

Malignant tumors of the appendix primarily consist of carcinoids and adenocarcinomas; all together, they account for 0.5% of all GI malignancies.[22] The incidence of malignancy in the appendix is 1.35%.[18] Metastasis to the appendix is rare. Carcinoids are substantially more common than adenocarcinomas in the appendix: as many as 80% of all appendiceal masses are carcinoid tumors. Overall, carcinoid tumors are found in 0.5% of all appendiceal specimens, and appendiceal carcinoid tumors account for 18.9% of all carcinoid lesions.[23] These tumors are predominantly of neural cellular origin and have a better prognosis than all other intestinal carcinoid tumors, which typically are of mucosal cellular origin. If the tumor is less than 2 cm in diameter, is located within the body or the tip of the appendix, and has not metastasized, appendectomy is the treatment of choice. If the lesion is at the base of the appendix, is larger than 2 cm in diameter, or has metastasized, right hemicolectomy [*see 76 Segmental Colon Resection*] is indicated. In addition, secondary right hemicolectomy is indicated if the tumor is invasive, if mucin production is noted, or if the tumor is found to be of mucosal cellular origin at final pathologic examination.[24,25] Patients with metastatic appendiceal carcinoid tumors appear to have a far better prognosis than those with other types of metastatic cancers.[24] Therefore, hepatic debulking for symptomatic control is indicated and justified in cases of liver metastasis.

Primary adenocarcinoma of the appendix is rare, and as yet there is no firm consensus regarding prognosis, treatment of choice, and outcome.[26] Currently, the recommended treatment is right hemicolectomy: a 1993 study found that this approach resulted in an overall 5-year survival rate of 68%, compared with a rate of 20% when appendectomy alone was performed.[25] The prognosis is determined by the degree of tumor differentiation and by the histologic stage. As many as one third of these patients have a second primary neoplasm, which will be located within the GI tract about half the time.

Finally, nonepithelial appendiceal tumors, though extremely rare, occur as well. Such lesions include malignant and Burkitt lymphomas, smooth muscle tumors, granular cell tumors, ganglioneuromas, and Kaposi sarcoma.

INFLAMMATORY BOWEL DISEASE

The appendix is frequently involved in Crohn disease and ulcerative colitis (25% and 50% of cases, respectively), but isolated Crohn disease of the appendix is rare.[27-30] When a histologically normal appendix is encountered in a patient with active Crohn disease, appendectomy should be performed because of the high risk of recurrent right lower quadrant pain, fever, and tenderness. Although isolated Crohn disease of the appendix may present as acute appendicitis, it is not clear that this condition will necessarily develop into a more extensive form of Crohn disease. Appendectomy is safe in such cases because fistulas almost never develop after appendectomy in patients with isolated involvement of the appendix.

GYNECOLOGIC CONDITIONS

It is clear that the presentation of right lower quadrant pain in a woman remains a challenge to the treating physician. Frequently, the causes can be identified by means of proper blood work or ultrasonography, but often they can be revealed only through sur-

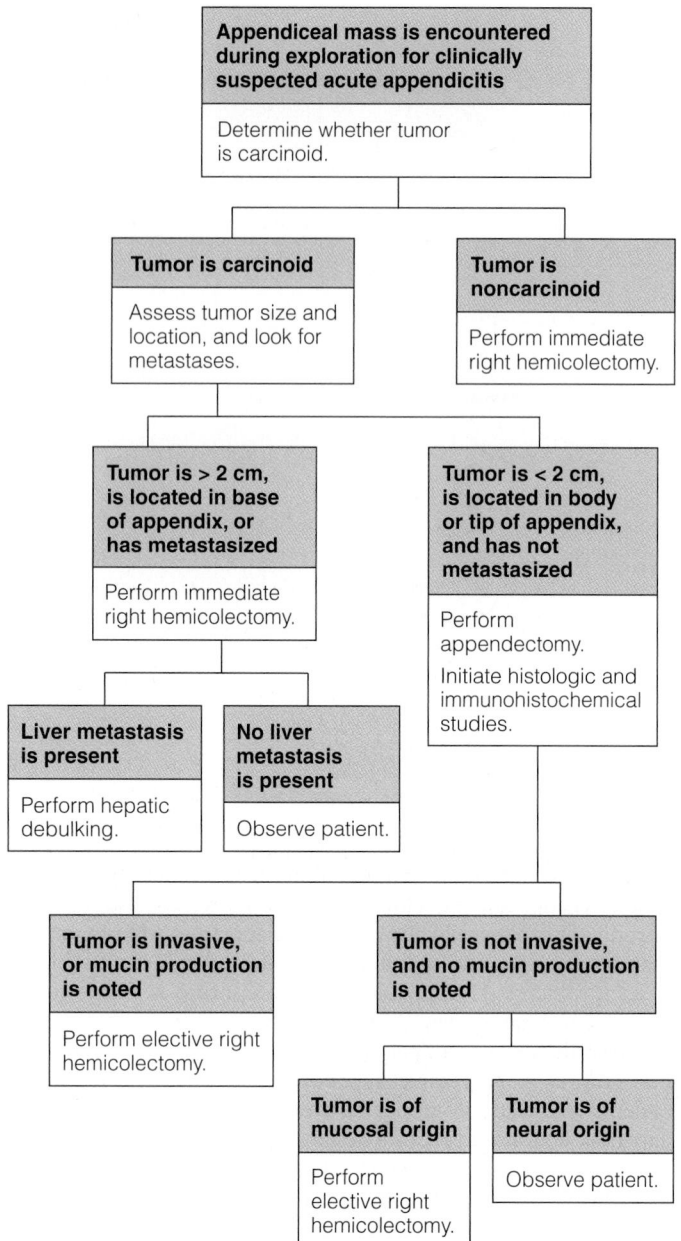

Figure 10 Shown is an algorithm for the management of an appendiceal mass encountered during exploration for clinically suspected acute appendicitis.

gical exploration. In such cases, diagnostic laparoscopy provides an excellent view of the pelvic organs, and it offers the potential for easy continuation on to laparoscopic treatment. Ovarian cysts found in premenopausal women include unilocular clear fluid cysts (e.g., follicular cysts and corpus luteum cysts), dermoid cysts, and endometrial cysts. They can be removed by making an incision on the ovary and separating the cyst from the ovarian cortex. Dermoid cysts should be removed in toto to prevent chemical peritonitis. Endometrial cysts are best evaporated with the laser: complete removal is very difficult and sometimes impossible. Torsion of the fallopian tube or the ovary can be reversed by gentle detorsion of the organ with atraumatic forceps. If there is no evidence of ischemia, no further therapy is indicated. If there is gangrene with no indication of recovery, resection is indicated. If the organ shows partial recovery within 10 minutes after the pedicle is untwisted, a

Table 1 Results of 31 Prospective, Randomized Trials Comparing Laparoscopic Appendectomy with Open Appendectomy[31-61]

Variable	Laparoscopic Appendectomy (N=2,194)		Open Appendectomy (N=2,158)	
	No.	Range	No.	Range
Negative appendix	314 (14.3%)	7.7%–36.0%	319 (14.8%)	0%–35.5%
Conversion to open procedure	223 (10.2%)	0%–23.9%	NA	NA
Surgical site infection	77 (3.5%)	0%–18.3%	144 (6.7%)	0%–17.3%
Intra-abdominal abscess	55 (2.5%)	0%–7.4%	24 (1.1%)	0%–4.6%
Days in hospital	2.7	1–4.9	3.2	1.2–5.3

second-look laparoscopy is indicated in 24 hours. Pelvic inflammatory disease should be treated on an individualized basis in accordance with the degree of inflammation, the patient's age and desire to have children, and the microbiologic findings.

Complications and Outcome Evaluation

OPEN VERSUS LAPAROSCOPIC APPENDECTOMY

To date, 31 reports of randomized, controlled trials comparing laparoscopic appendectomy with open appendectomy have been published as full manuscripts in English [see Table 1].[31-61] These reports involved a total of 4,352 patients, of whom 2,194 underwent laparoscopic appendectomy and 2,158 underwent open appendectomy. The incidence of histologically normal appendix was similar in the two groups (14.3% with laparoscopic appendectomy versus 14.8% with open appendectomy). The conversion rate from laparoscopic appendectomy to open appendectomy was 10% (range, 0% to 23%). Laparoscopic appendectomy was associated with a lower incidence of postoperative wound infection than open appendectomy was (3.5% versus 6.7%), but it was also associated with a higher incidence of postoperative intra-abdominal abscess (2.5% versus 1.1%). The length of stay was slightly shorter after laparoscopic appendectomy (1 to 4.9 days; average, 2.7 days) than after open appendectomy (1.2 to 5.3 days; average, 3.2 days). Randomized, controlled trials carried out within the past 5 years have not led to any significant changes in the statistical picture.

In men and children with suspected acute appendicitis, laparoscopic appendectomy has no major advantage over open appendectomy.[37] In women of childbearing age and in equivocal cases, laparoscopy may be valuable as a diagnostic tool, but the practice of not removing a normal-looking appendix during exploration for right lower quadrant pain is controversial. Laparoscopic appendectomy appears to offer the potential benefit of less postoperative adhesion formation, but the evidence is inconclusive in the light of the short follow-up times reported in these trials, and the higher incidence of intra-abdominal abscess formation remains cause for concern. To date, unfortunately, there have been no studies designed specifically to address reduced adhesion formation as a primary end point.

Although laparoscopic appendectomy is being performed with increased frequency, it continues to be used selectively. The laparoscopic version of the procedure is at least as safe as the corresponding open procedure, but it is undeniably more time-consuming and more costly. Moreover, it remains questionable whether the benefits of laparoscopic appendectomy—reduced postoperative pain, earlier resumption of oral feeding, shortened hospital stay, quicker return to normal preoperative activities, and lower incidence of surgical site infection—outweigh the doubled incidence of postoperative intra-abdominal abscess formation. Further randomized clinical studies focusing on the efficacy of laparoscopic appendectomy as a diagnostic tool and on the incidence of postoperative intra-abdominal abscess and adhesion formation are needed, as are additional cost analyses.

References

1. Fitz RH: Perforating inflammation of the vermiform appendix with special reference to its early diagnosis and treatment. Trans Assoc Am Physicians 1:107, 1886

2. McBurney C: The incision made in the abdominal wall in cases of appendicitis, with a description of a new method of operating. Ann Surg 20:38, 1894

3. Rucinski J, Fabian T, Panagopoulos G, et al: Gangrenous and perforated appendicitis: a meta-analytic study of 2532 patients indicates that the incision should be closed primarily. Surgery 127:136, 2000

4. Flum DR, Morris A, Koepsell T, et al: Has misdiagnosis of appendicitis decreased over time? a population-based analysis. JAMA 286:1748, 2001

5. Chang AR: An analysis of the pathology of 3,003 appendices. Aust NZ J Surg 51:169, 1981

6. Knight PJ, Vassy LE: Specific diseases mimicking appendicitis in childhood. Arch Surg 116:744, 1981

7. Pieper R, Kager L, Nasman P: Acute appendicitis: a clinical study of 1,018 cases of emergency appendectomy. Acta Chir Scand 148:51, 1982

8. Arnbjornsson E, Asp NG, Westin SI: Decreasing incidence of acute appendicitis, with special reference to the consumption of dietary fiber. Acta Chir Scand 148:461, 1982

9. Blind PJ, Dahlgren ST: The continuing challenge of the negative appendix. Acta Chir Scand 152:623, 1986

10. Lau WY: Correlation between gross appeareance of the appendix and histological examination. Ann R Coll Surg Edinb 70:336, 1988

11. Budd JS, Armstrong CP: The correlation between gross appearance at appendix and histological examination. Ann R Coll Surg Edinb 70:395, 1988

12. Blair PM, Bugis PS, Turner LJ, et al: Review of the pathologic diagnosis of 2,216 appendectomy specimens. Am J Surg 165:618, 1993

13. Dahlstom JE, MacArthur EB: Enterobius vermicularis: a possible cause of symptoms resembling appendicitis. Aust NZ J Surg 64:692, 1994

14. Pearl RH, Hale DA, Molloy M, et al: Pediatric appendectomy. J Pediatr Surg 30:173, 1995

15. Truji M, Puri P, Reen DJ: Characterization of the local inflammatory response in appendicitis. J Pediatr Gastroenterol Nutr 16:43, 1993

16. Wang Y, Reen DJ, Puri P: Is a histologically normal appendix following emergency appendicectomy always normal? Lancet 347:1076, 1996

17. Grunewald B, Keating J: Should the 'normal' appendix be removed at operation for appendicitis? J R Coll Surg Edinb 38:158, 1993

18. Collins DC: 71,000 human appendix specimens: a final report, summarizing 40 years' study. Am J Proctol 14:265, 1963

19. Chan W, Fu KH: Value of routine histopathological examination of appendices in Hong Kong. J Clin Pathol 40:429, 1987

20. Lenriot JP, Hugier M: Adenocarcinoma of the appendix. Am J Surg 155:470, 1988

21. Gupta SC, Gupta AK, Keswani NK, et al: Pathology of tropical appendicitis. J Clin Pathol 42:1169, 1989

22. Thomas RM, Sobin LH: Gastrointestinal cancer. Cancer 75:154, 1995

23. Modlin IM, Sandor A: An analysis of 8305 cases of carcinoid tumors. Cancer 79:813, 1997

24. Moertel CG, Weiland LH, Nagorney DM, et al: Carcinoid tumor of the appendix: treatment and prognosis. N Engl J Med 317:1699, 1987

25. Gouzi JL, Laigneau P, Delalande JP, et al: Indications for right hemicolectomy in carcinoid tumors of the appendix. Surg Gynecol Obstet 176:543, 1993

26. Nitecki SS, Wolff BG, Schlinkert R, et al: The natural history of surgically treated primary adenocarcinoma of the appendix. Ann Surg 219:51, 1994

27. Yang SS, Gibson P, McCaughey RS, et al: Primary Crohn's disease of the appendix. Ann Surg 189:334, 1979

28. Jahadi MR, Shaw ML: The pathology of the appendix in ulcerative colitis. Dis Colon Rectum 19:345, 1976

29. Ruiz V, Unger SW, Morgan J, et al: Crohn's disease of the appendix. Surgery 107:113, 1990

30. Goldblum JR, Appelman HD: Appendiceal involvement in ulcerative colitis. Mod Pathol 5:607, 1992

31. Attwood SEA, Hill ADK, Murphy PG, et al: A prospective randomized trial of laparoscopic versus open appendectomy. Surgery 112:497, 1992

32. Tate JJT, Dawson JW, Chung SCS, et al: Laparoscopic versus open appendectomy: prospective randomised trial. Lancet 342:633, 1993

33. Kum CK, Ngoi SS, Goh PMY, et al: Randomized controlled trial comparing laparoscopic and open appendicectomy. Br J Surg 80:1599, 1993

34. Frazee RC, Roberts JW, Symmonds RE, et al: A prospective randomized trial comparing open versus laparoscopic appendectomy. Ann Surg 219:725, 1994

35. Ortega AE, Hunter JG, Peters JH, et al: A prospective, randomized comparison of laparoscopic appendectomy with open appendectomy. Am J Surg 169:208, 1995

36. Martin LC, Puente I, Sosa JL, et al: Open versus laparoscopic appendectomy: a prospective randomized comparison. Ann Surg 222:256, 1995

37. Hansen JB, Smithers BM, Schache D, et al: Laparoscopic versus open appendectomy: prospective randomized trial. World J Surg 20:17, 1996

38. Mutter D, Vix M, Bui A, et al: Laparoscopy not recommended for routine appendectomy in men: results of a prospective randomized study. Surgery 120:71, 1996

39. Cox MR, McCall JL, Toouli J, et al: Prospective randomized comparison of open versus laparoscopic appendectomy in men. World J Surg 20:263, 1996

40. Lejus C, Dellie L, Plattner V, et al: Randomized, single-blinded trial of laparoscopic versus open appendectomy in children. Anesthesiology 84:801, 1996

41. Williams MD, Collins JN, Wright TF, et al: Laparoscopic versus open appendectomy. South Med J 89:668, 1996

42. Hart R, Rajgopal C, Plewes A, et al: Laparoscopic versus open appendectomy: a prospective randomized trial of 81 patients. Can J Surg 39:457, 1996

43. Reiertsen O, Larsen S, Trondsen E, et al: Randomized controlled trial with sequential design of laparoscopic versus conventional appendicectomy. Br J Surg 84:842, 1997

44. Laine S, Rantala A, Gullichsen R, et al: Laparoscopic appendectomy—is it worthwhile? A prospective, randomized study in young women. Surg Endosc 11:95, 1997

45. Macarulla E, Vallet J, Abad JM, et al: Laparoscopic versus open appendectomy: a prospective randomized trial. Surg Laparosc Endosc 7:335, 1997

46. Kazemier G, de Zeeuw GR, Lange JF, et al: Laparoscopic versus open appendectomy: a randomized clinical trial. Surg Endosc 11:336, 1997

47. Minne L, Varner D, Burnell A, et al: Laparosopic versus open appendectomy: prospective randomized study of outcomes. Arch Surg 132:708, 1997

48. Hay SA: Laparoscopic versus conventional appendectomy in children. Pediatr Surg Int 13:21, 1998

49. Klinger A, Henle KP, Beller S, et al: Laparoscopic appendectomy does not change the incidence of postoperative infectious complications. Am J Surg 175:232, 1998

50. Hiekkinen TJ, Haukipuro K, Hulkko A: Cost-effective appendectomy: open or laparoscopic? A prospective randomized study. Surg Endosc 12:1204, 1998

51. Hellberg A, Rudberg C, Kullman E, et al: Prospective randomized multicentre study of laparoscopic versus open appendicectomy. Br J Surg 86:48, 1999

52. Ozmen MM, Zulfikaroglu B, Tanik A, et al: Laparoscopic versus open appendectomy: prospective randomized trial. Surg Laparosc Endosc Percutan Tech 9:187, 1999

53. Pedersen AG, Petersen OB, Wara P, et al: Randomized clinical trial of laparoscopic versus open appendicectomy. Br J Surg 88:200, 2001

54. Lavonius MI, Liesjarvi S, Ovaska J, et al: Laparoscopic versus open appendectomy in children: a prospective randomised study. Eur J Pediat Surg 11:235, 2001

55. Long KH, Bannon MP, Zietlow SP, et al: A prospective randomized comparison of laparoscopic appendectomy with open appendectomy: clinical and economic analyses. Surgery 129:390, 2001

56. Lintula H, Kokki H, Vanamo K: Single-blind randomized clinical trial of laparoscopic versus open appendicectomy in children. Br J Surg 88:510, 2001

57. Huang MT, Wei PL, Wu CC, et al: Needlescopic, laparoscopic, and open appendectomy: a comparative study. Surg Laparosc Endosc Percutan Tech 11:306, 2001

58. Little DC, Custer MD, May BH, Blalock SE, Cooney DR: Laparoscopic appendectomy: An unnecessary and expensive procedure in children? J Pediatr Surg 37:310, 2002

59. Milewczyk M, Michalik M, Ciesielski M: A prospective, randomized, unicenter study comparing laparoscopic and open treatments of acute appendicitis. Surg Endosc 17:1023, 2003

60. Ignacio RC, Burke R, Spencer D, et al: Laparoscopic vs open appendectomy: what is the real difference? Results of a prospective randomized double-blinded trial. Surg Endosc 18:334, 2004

61. Katkhouda N, Mason RJ, Towfigh S, Gevorgyan A, Essani R: Laparoscopic versus open appendectomy: a prospective randomized double-blind study. Ann Surg 242:439, 2005

Acknowledgments

Figures 1 and 10   Marcia Kammerer.
Fgures 2 through 9   Tom Moore.

74 PROCEDURES FOR DIVERTICULAR DISEASE

Jeffrey L. Cohen, M.D., F.A.C.S., F.A.S.C.R.S., and John P. Welch, M.D., F.A.C.S.

Preoperative Evaluation

The extent of the preoperative evaluation received by patients undergoing surgical treatment of diverticular disease is dictated predominantly by the urgency of the situation. Whereas patients with recurrent symptoms will undergo repeated assessments with myriad diagnostic tests before the decision is made to proceed with surgical intervention, patients with perforated diverticulitis may have only a chest x-ray documenting free air before they are taken to the operating room. Given the varied complications of diverticular disease and the numerous options for surgical treatment, we believe it is most convenient to divide the relevant operations into emergency procedures and elective procedures. Such a division facilitates discussion of technical issues, preoperative evaluation, and management of complications.

As noted, in the emergency setting, a demonstration of pneumoperitoneum may be the only workup performed. In fact, in most patients with perforated diverticulitis, pneumoperitoneum is the initial presentation.[1,2] In patients who present with massive lower GI hemorrhage, angiographic demonstration of the bleeding site is known to reduce operative mortality, even if therapeutic superselective embolization is unsuccessful in controlling the bleeding.[3,4] The other complication of diverticular disease that may necessitate an emergency operation is colonic obstruction. A careful history may reveal progressive obstructive symptoms, but if the patient presents with complete obstruction and cecal dilatation, urgent decompression is required. In this setting, retrograde administration of a water-soluble enema may be very helpful—at least for delineating the level of the obstruction, if not the specific cause.[1,5] Communication with the radiologist should be maintained to prevent both overly forceful instillation of the contrast material and the use of barium, which may cause problems if the agent cannot be evacuated.

When surgical treatment of diverticular disease is to be performed in the elective setting, a detailed preoperative evaluation is imperative [see 54 Diverticulitis]. The key point here is that objective evidence of diverticulitis must be obtained at some point in the care of the patient. Too often, symptoms of irritable bowel syndrome are confused with those of diverticulitis, with the result that the patient carries an incorrect diagnosis.[6-9] In the most common scenario, computed tomographic scanning is performed when a patient is experiencing left-side pain, possibly associated with fever, nausea, anorexia, or abdominal distention. A finding of pericolonic inflammation in an area of diverticulosis is the definitive radiographic presentation.[10,11] Preoperative endoscopic evaluation of the colon, whenever feasible, is extremely valuable not only for confirming the presence of diverticulosis but also for ruling out inflammatory bowel disease or even a neoplastic lesion.

It is possible to expend a great deal of effort on trying to demonstrate a diverticular fistula. In many circumstances, however, this task proves difficult to accomplish. In our view, demonstration of a diverticular fistula should not be considered a mandatory precondition for operative treatment. A strong history of either a colovaginal or a colovesical fistula with suggestive findings on CT scans (e.g., air in the bladder or pericolonic inflammation contiguous with either the bladder or the vagina) constitutes a sufficient indication for surgical resection.[12,13]

Operative Planning

In planning the operative approach to a patient with diverticular disease, the major decision is whether to perform a one-stage or a two-stage procedure. Traditionally, an emergency operation for perforation, obstruction, or massive bleeding includes a temporary stoma procedure to eliminate the risk of anastomotic leakage.[14,15] The operation most commonly performed in this setting is the Hartmann procedure [see Emergency Procedures, Hartmann Procedure, below], named after Henri Hartmann, who first described the use of this operation to treat colon cancer in 1923.[16] The obvious advantage of the Hartmann procedure is that it removes the inflammatory focus without putting the compromised patient at risk for anastomotic leakage. Unfortunately, to restore intestinal continuity after this procedure, it is necessary to perform a potentially difficult second operation; as many as one third of patients never undergo reversal of their colostomy.[17,18]

Another therapeutic option is to perform a primary anastomosis with a diverting loop ileostomy instead of a colostomy. In this situation, the risk of anastomotic leakage with possible fecal peritonitis is still avoided, but only a relatively minor second procedure is necessary to reverse the ileostomy.[19] Occasionally, it may be appropriate to perform on-table colonic lavage with a primary anastomosis. This approach is most useful in the setting of colonic obstruction secondary to a diverticular stricture in a patient who is otherwise hemodynamically stable but has a large fecal load proximal to the intended anastomosis.[20,21]

Laparoscopic intestinal surgery has shown tremendous development of late, benefited both by significant technological improvements and by growing surgical experience with advanced laparoscopic procedures.[22,23] Newer approaches (e.g., hand-assisted techniques) have markedly reduced the learning curve and shortened the operating time.[24,25] Consequently, minimal access surgery is rapidly becoming the approach of choice in the management of uncomplicated diverticular disease.[26-29]

Emergency Procedures

Patient setup and positioning are similar for all emergency operations. The patient is placed in a modified lithotomy position to facilitate access to the rectum. Urinary drainage with a Foley catheter and temporary gastric decompression with a nasogastric tube are performed. When feasible, the stoma is marked by an enterostomal therapist before operation.

HARTMANN PROCEDURE

Step 1: Incision and Initial Exploration

A lower midline incision is made and extended above the umbilicus as necessary. The abdomen is thoroughly explored to confirm the diagnosis of diverticular disease and to wash out any gross fecal spillage. A self-retaining retractor (e.g., a Bookwalter retractor) is placed, with care taken to pad the abdominal wall.

Step 2: Mobilization and Division of Sigmoid Colon

The patient is placed in the Trendelenburg position, with the small bowel carefully retracted into the upper abdomen. The sigmoid colon is mobilized away from the lateral peritoneal attachments. Mobilization is continued into the pelvis lateral to the upper portion of the rectum.

Troubleshooting If a severe phlegmon is stuck to the pelvic sidewall, it may be helpful at some point in the mobilization to dissect cephalad from below the mass so as to isolate the area from above and below.

Step 3: Identification of Ureter

As the sigmoid colon is retracted medially, the ureter can usually be identified where it crosses over the bifurcation of the iliac vessels. The gonadal vessels are usually identified first; the ureter lies slightly medial and deep to them [see Figure 1].

Step 4: Division of Sigmoid Colon

The proximal sigmoid colon is divided through noninflamed tissue with a linear cutting stapler [see Figure 2a]. The sigmoid vessels are sequentially divided (with attention paid to their relation to the left ureter) up to the rectosigmoid junction, which is identified by the loss of the taeniae coli. The rectum is then transected through noninflamed tissue with a linear stapler [see Figure 2b].

Troubleshooting The top of the rectal stump can be marked with a nonabsorbable suture to facilitate subsequent identification.

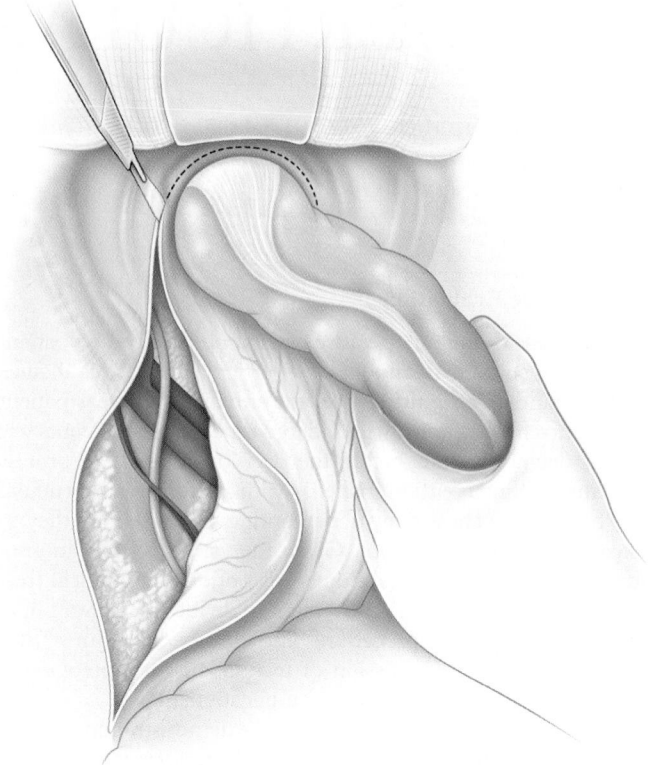

Figure 1 **Hartmann procedure. Illustrated is the relation of the ureter to other structures in the left lower quadrant.**

Step 5: Construction of Colostomy

The proximal colon is delivered through the previously marked stoma site in the left lower quadrant with a muscle-splitting incision in the rectus abdominis (with care taken not to twist it on its mesentery), and a colostomy is created [see 72 Intestinal Stomas].

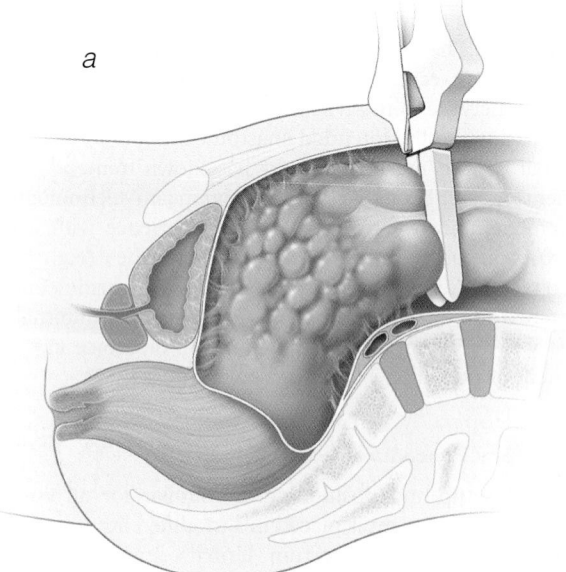

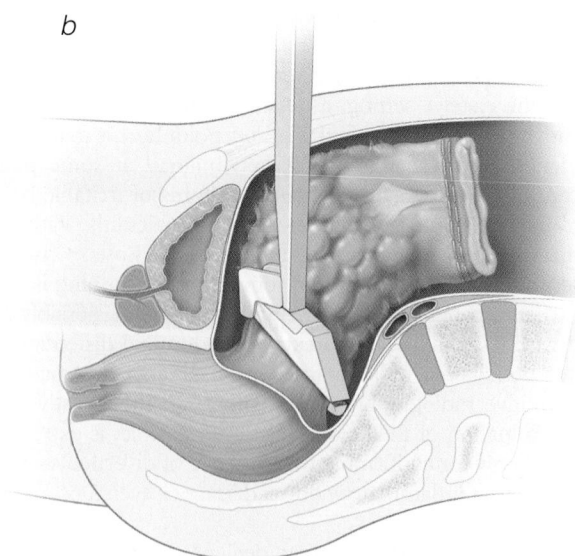

Figure 2 **Hartmann procedure. (*a*) The colon is divided above the level of the inflammatory mass. (*b*) The rectum is divided below the inflammatory mass; division must be through normal tissue.**

Step 5—Alternative (Primary Anastomosis with Diverting Ileostomy): Creation of Colorectal Anastomosis

As an alternative to a colostomy, the surgeon may elect to perform a primary colorectal anastomosis with a diverting ileostomy. (Such an anastomosis is described in more detail elsewhere [see 77 *Procedures for Rectal Cancer*].) The anvil of a circular stapler is positioned in the proximal colon, and a purse-string suture is placed around it. If there is any gaping of the tissue around the shaft of the anvil, a second suture may be added for reinforcement.

The stapler is inserted through the anus, with the shaft being brought out either through the anterior wall of the rectum or through the top of the rectal stump, adjacent to the staple line. The stapler is then engaged, with care taken to ensure that no extraneous tissue is caught between the body of the stapler and the anvil and that the proximal bowel is not twisted on its mesentery. The stapler is fired to create the anastomosis, and the integrity of the anastomosis is tested by occluding the proximal bowel and placing the anastomotic area under water while air is insufflated into the rectum via a rigid proctoscope.

Troubleshooting It is helpful to divide the mesentery where it is draped over the anvil. This measure diminishes the risk of bleeding from the circular staple line while also providing a greater length of colon for the anastomosis. If there is any question regarding possible tension on the anastomosis, the splenic flexure should be fully mobilized.

Step 6—Alternative (Primary Anastomosis with Diverting Ileostomy): Construction of Loop Ileostomy

A loop ileostomy is created in the right lower quadrant, using a muscle-splitting incision in the rectus abdominis [see 72 *Intestinal Stomas*]. Loop ileostomies can usually be designed to be diverting; however, stapling the distal end and leaving it at skin level will ensure complete diversion.

Troubleshooting If there is a column of stool between the ileostomy and the anastomosis, it should be washed out before the ileostomy is completed.

ON-TABLE COLONIC LAVAGE

Steps 1 through 4

Steps 1, 2, 3, and 4 of on-table colonic lavage are the same as the first four steps of the Hartmann procedure.

Step 5: Mobilization of Flexures

After the sigmoid resection, the hepatic flexure and the splenic flexure are carefully mobilized to facilitate the washout process.

Step 6: Placement of Tubing

Corrugated anesthesia tubing is placed in the colon proximal to the resected segment and secured in place with umbilical tape. The distal end of the tubing is passed off the operating table and is connected to a device that collects the effluent [see Figure 3].

Step 7: Construction of Appendicostomy

An appendicostomy is performed, a Foley catheter is placed, and a purse-string suture is tied around the tube with the balloon inflated. If the patient has previously undergone appendectomy, the terminal ileum is used instead.

Step 8: Irrigation of Colon

The colon is washed with an irrigant until the effluent is relatively clear. It may be necessary to manipulate the colon so as to initiate flushing of formed stool.

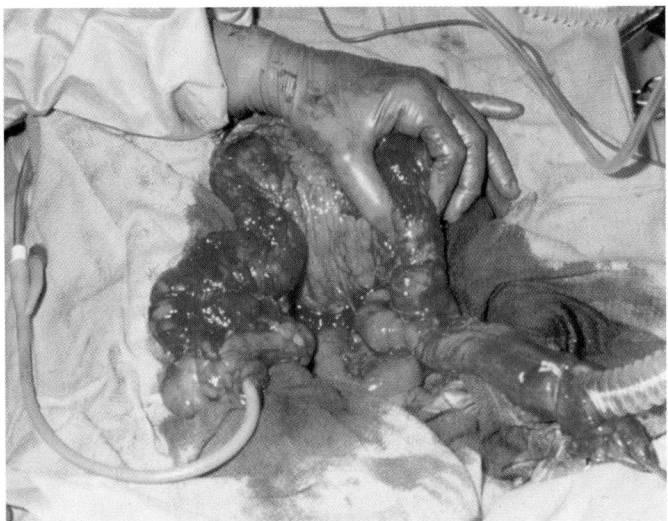

Figure 3 **On-table colonic lavage. Shown is full mobilization of the colon, with corrugated anesthesia tubing secured in the colon and connected to a collection system. A Foley catheter is inserted through an appendicostomy into the base of the cecum.**

Step 9: Excision of Appendix and Creation of Colorectal Anastomosis

A formal appendectomy is performed [see 73 *Appendectomy*]. The corrugated anesthesia tubing is removed from the colon, and a colorectal anastomosis is performed, usually with a circular stapler.

Elective Procedures

OPEN RESECTION

Open resection in the elective setting consists of steps 1 through 4 of the Hartmann procedure, followed by creation of a primary colorectal anastomosis and a diverting loop ileostomy (alternative steps 5 and 6) [see Emergency Procedures, Hartmann Procedure, *above*].

LAPAROSCOPIC RESECTION

The patient is placed in a low lithotomy position with minimal hip flexion. The right arm is well padded and tucked at the side because both surgeons will be operating from the right side of the table. Video monitors are placed on both sides of the table. It is beneficial to place the patient on a bean bag because a significant portion of the operation will be performed with the patient in extremes of positioning.

Step 1: Placement of Trocars

The first port is placed at a periumbilical location by means of an open Hasson approach, and a 30° laparoscope is inserted. After pneumoperitoneum is achieved, the other ports are placed under direct vision: 5 and 12 mm ports are placed in the right lower quadrant, and an optional 5 mm port may be placed in the midepigastrium [see Figure 4]. The midepigastric port facilitates mobilization of the left colon and is essential for mobilization of the splenic flexure.

Step 2: Mobilization of Sigmoid Colon

After the abdomen has been explored, the patient is placed in a steep Trendelenburg position, with the right side tilted down. This

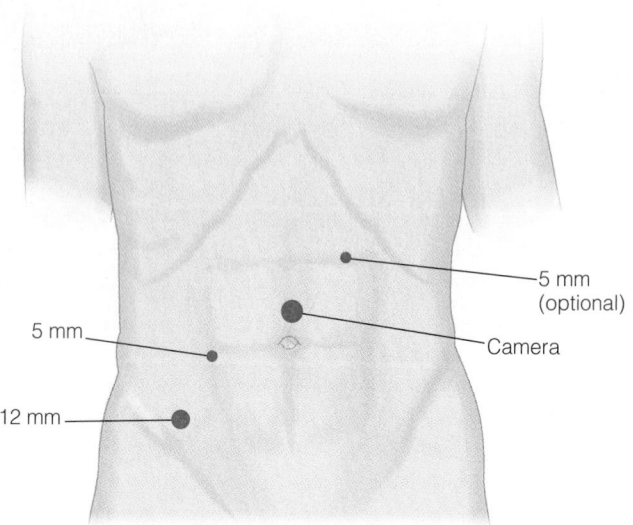

Figure 4 **Laparoscopic sigmoid resection. Shown is recommended port placement. The midepigastric 5 mm port is essential for mobilization of the splenic flexure.**

position allows gravity to retract the small bowel into the upper abdomen. The sigmoid colon is mobilized from its lateral peritoneal attachments, and the colon is thereby converted to a midline structure. Mobilization is extended superiorly along the descending colon and inferiorly to the pelvic cul-de-sac. The left ureter is then identified and swept laterally away from the base of the mesentery.

Alternative approach to colonic mobilization and division In place of the conventional approach (see above), a medial-to-lateral approach can be undertaken. In this approach, the initial dissection proceeds from the right side of the colon, mobilizing the superior rectal vessels from the sacral promontory. The left ureter is then visualized through the window thus created before the sigmoid mesentery is divided. Division of the sigmoid mesentery is performed in a proximal-to-distal direction, with the inferior mesenteric vessels generally divided first. Once the sigmoid mesentery has been completely divided, the bowel is transected with staplers at the rectosigmoid junction.

The advantage of the traditional approach is that surgeons are more familiar with it from corresponding open procedures. In our view, given the difficulty of mastering laparoscopic colon surgery, the medial-to-lateral approach to colonic mobilization only increases the steepness of the learning curve without affording any significant benefit.

Step 3: Division of Rectum and Sigmoid Mesentery

An incision is made in the peritoneum along the right side of the rectosigmoid mesentery and extended inferiorly to the pelvic cul-de-sac. A window is created between the upper rectum and its mesentery and enlarged to allow insertion of an endoscopic gastrointestinal anastomosis (GIA) stapler [*see Figure 5*]. The stapler is then fired once or twice to divide the rectosigmoid bowel. The mesentery of the sigmoid colon is sequentially divided with staplers, clips, an ultrasonic scalpel, or the LigaSure system (Valleylab, Boulder, Colorado).

Step 4: Exteriorization of Sigmoid Colon

Once the colon is mobilized and the blood supply divided, either a left lower quadrant muscle-splitting incision or a Pfannenstiel incision is made to exteriorize the bowel, which is then divided proximally. The anvil of a circular stapler is inserted in the proximal colon and secured with a purse-string suture. The bowel is then replaced into the abdomen, and the incision is closed.

Step 5: Creation of Colorectal Anastomosis

After pneumoperitoneum is recreated, the circular stapler is inserted transanally. The shaft is brought out either through the top of the rectal stump or through the anterior wall of the rectum [*see Figure 6*]; the former is preferred if bowel length is an issue. After the stapler is engaged but before it is fired, the proximal colon is inspected to confirm that it is not twisted. The stapler is

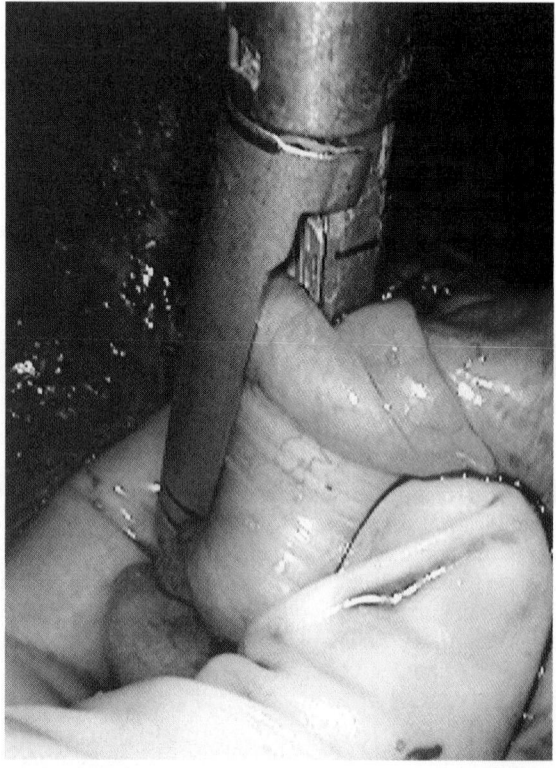

Figure 5 **Laparoscopic sigmoid resection. Shown is division of the rectum with the endoscopic stapler.**

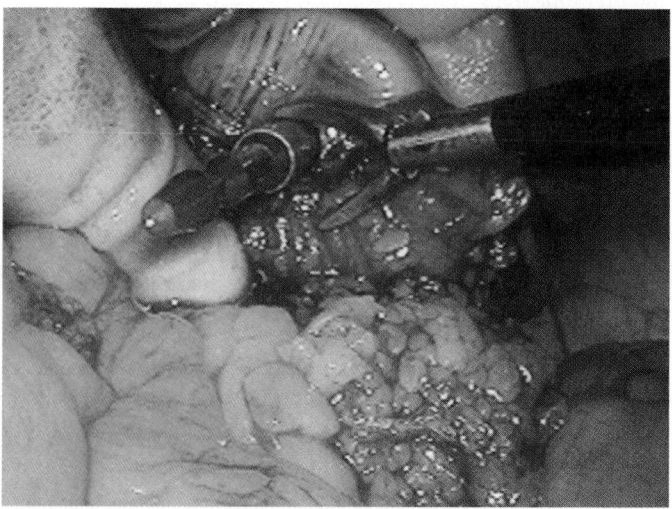

Figure 6 **Laparoscopic sigmoid resection. The shaft of the circular stapler is guided through the top of the rectal stump by applying countertraction with a laparoscopic instrument.**

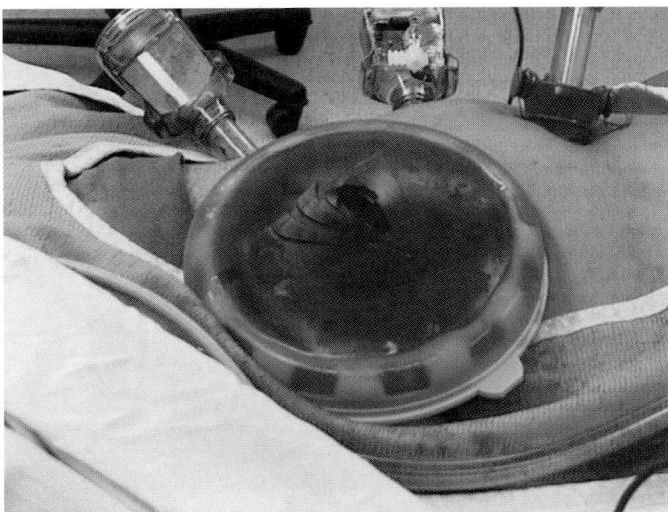

Figure 7 **Hand-assisted laparoscopic resection. Shown is the placement of one of the hand devices through which the surgeon's hand is advanced into the pelvis.**

then fired, and the anastomosis is then tested under water to confirm the absence of an air leak.

HAND-ASSISTED LAPAROSCOPIC RESECTION

Steps 1 and 2

The first two steps of a hand-assisted laparoscopic resection are identical to steps 1 and 2 of a full laparoscopic resection.

Step 3: Placement of Hand Device

A 6 to 8 cm muscle-splitting incision is made in the left lower quadrant, and the hand device is placed [*see Figure 7*]. The surgeon's left hand is placed through this device into the abdomen.

Step 4: Division of Rectum and Sigmoid Mesentery

The surgeon's left hand is used to facilitate creation of a window between the rectum and the underlying mesentery. An endoscopic GIA stapler is safely guided through this window, and the bowel is divided [*see Figure 8a*]. The hand is then used to isolate segments of the mesentery for division [*see Figure 8b*], as well as to help control vessels that continue to bleed despite having been divided.

Steps 5 and 6

Steps 5 and 6 are identical to steps 4 and 5 of a full laparoscopic resection.

Troubleshooting Having the surgeon's hand in the pelvis greatly facilitates engagement of the circular stapler and makes its closure safer by protecting the surrounding structures [*see Figure 9*]. Furthermore, the presence of the hand in the pelvis not only assists in testing the anastomosis but also helps the surgeon better assess the degree of tension (if any) on the anastomosis. Given that the size of the hand port is similar to that of the extraction site in a full laparoscopic resection, we prefer the hand-assisted technique on the basis of its greater safety and its ability to restore a measure of tactile sense and proprioception to the surgeon.

LAPAROSCOPIC HARTMANN CLOSURE

Step 1: Placement of Trocars

A port is placed by means of the Hasson technique at an upper midline location, cephalad to the previous incision if possible. A 30° laparoscope is inserted through this port. After pneumoperitoneum is achieved, two 5 mm ports are placed in the right lower quadrant to facilitate dissection of pelvic and midline adhesions as necessary.

Step 2: Mobilization of Colostomy and Rectal Stump

All adhesions and attachments should be cleared away from the intra-abdominal portions of the colostomy [*see Figure 10*]. In addition, the top of the Hartmann pouch should be cleared of all adherent small bowel or adjacent structures. Occasionally, other ports may have to be placed to facilitate takedown of adhesions, especially those from the original midline incision. The colostomy is detached from the skin circumferentially. The anvil of a circular stapler is then placed in the proximal bowel after the exposed portion of the colostomy has been resected.

Step 3: Placement of Hand and Completion of Anastomosis

The colostomy site is enlarged slightly so that the surgeon's left hand can be placed in the abdomen. The stapler is engaged and fired while the surgeon's hand keeps any extraneous tissue away from the anastomotic area. The anastomosis is then tested by placing it under water and insufflating air via a proctoscope.

Troubleshooting It is often easier to bring out the shaft of

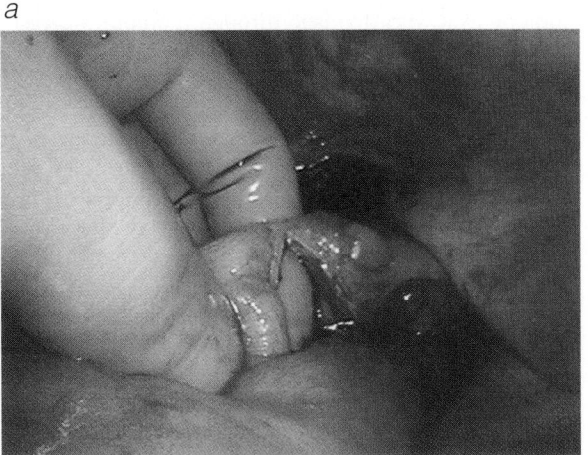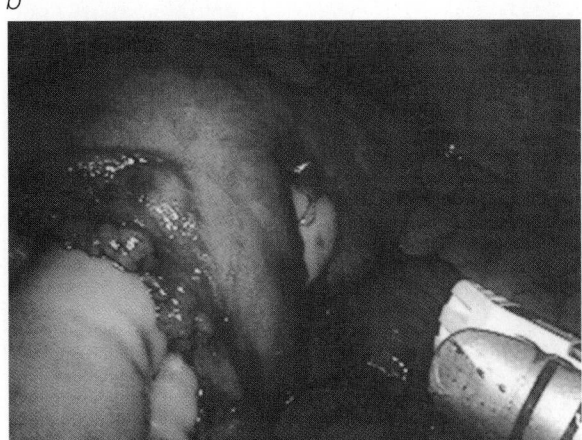

Figure 8 **Hand-assisted laparoscopic resection. (*a*) Placement of the surgeon's hand intracorporeally facilitates division of the rectum. (*b*) The surgeon's hand isolates mesenteric vessels for subsequent division.**

a

b

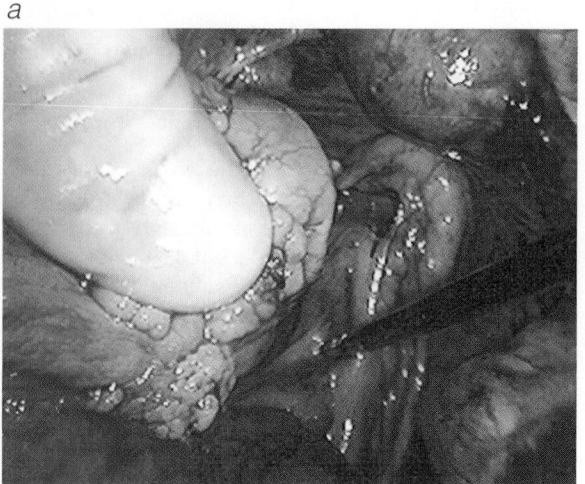
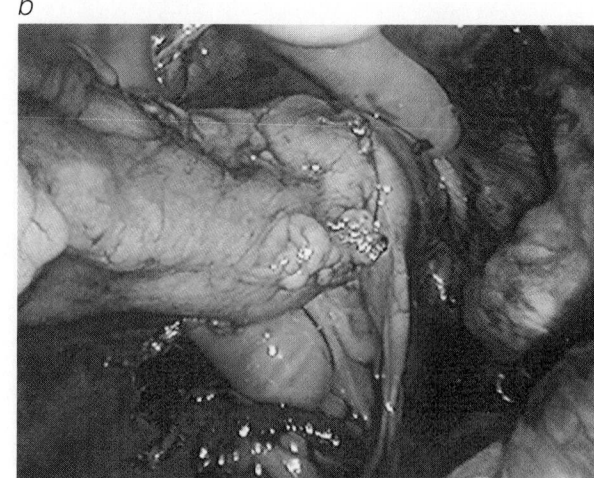

Figure 9 **Hand-assisted laparoscopic resection. (*a, b*) The surgeon's hand guides engagement of the circular stapler, protecting surrounding pelvic structures.**

the stapler through the anterior wall of the rectum, especially if there has been a significant inflammatory response around the area of the Hartmann pouch.

Complications

Operative management of diverticular disease poses distinct challenges, the level of which is proportional to the degree of inflammation present and to the urgency of the procedure. Whereas many of the complications encountered are not specific to this setting but are common to all abdominal procedures, there are several that warrant particular attention in the context of surgical treatment of diverticular disease.

ANASTOMOTIC LEAKAGE

The most serious and potentially life-threatening complication of procedures for diverticular disease is the development of an anastomotic leak. Many factors contribute to the maintenance of anastomotic integrity, ranging from the surgeon's technical ability to the patient's comorbidities. Of these factors, however, the single most important one is probably the setting in which the operation is carried out. Patients undergoing emergency procedures are at four

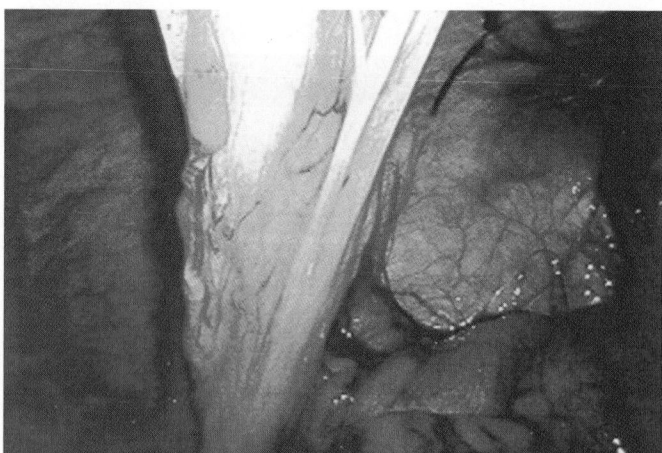

Figure 10 **Laparoscopic Hartmann closure. Shown is a laparoscopic view of the colostomy after intra-abdominal adhesions have been divided.**

times higher risk for anastomotic leakage than those undergoing elective procedures.[30,31] Furthermore, mortality is 13% in patients presenting with purulent peritonitis and 43% in those presenting with feculent peritonitis; these figures suggest that performing an anastomosis in these settings is unwise.[14,15,32,33]

As with any anastomosis, the long-established basic technical principles—using healthy, uninflamed tissue; ensuring an adequate blood supply; and avoiding tension on the anastomosis—should be strictly adhered to. If any of these principles cannot be followed, then either the patient should undergo proximal diversion or (preferably) the problem with the anastomosis should be corrected. For instance, in a situation where the sigmoid inflammatory process extends into the rectal mesentery, attempts should be made to resect below the level of the inflammation, even if the process is reaching well into the rectum itself. Another technical point worth mentioning involves preserving the superior rectal vessels, though no randomized, prospective study has yet been performed to determine whether this measure has any significant positive effect.

RECURRENT DISEASE

It is unusual for a recurrent diverticular fistula to develop after takedown with resection of the involved colon. Much more likely than the persistence of a diverticular fistula is the development of a recurrent colovesical or colovaginal fistula secondary to an anastomotic leak with drainage through the point of least resistance (i.e., the anastomosis).

There is some question as to whether a recurrence of diverticulitis after sigmoid resection is actually a complication of the procedure. Although it has been shown that resection of all diverticulum-bearing colon is not required for successful treatment of the disease process, it does appear that the location of any remaining diverticulosis influences the recurrence of the disease. Studies have demonstrated that if a sigmoid resection with a colorectal anastomosis is performed, the recurrence rate is 5%, whereas if the anastomosis is performed to the distal sigmoid colon, the recurrence rate rises to 12%.[34,35] When recurrent diverticulitis develops, it is important to reexamine the histologic findings from the original operation to rule out the possibility that the patient was misdiagnosed. Occasionally, diverticulosis and Crohn disease coexist; recurrence of Crohn disease is much more common than recurrence of diverticulosis and, given a long enough follow-up period, is actually to be expected.

URETERAL INJURY

Ureteral injuries occur in as many as 1% of patients undergoing diverticular resection.[36] Because of the inflammatory process associated with severe diverticular disease, it may be difficult to identify the ureter as it crosses the bifurcation of the iliac vessels; however, it is always possible to identify the ureter more proximally and then follow it down to the inflamed area. If a difficult dissection is anticipated or if technical difficulties are encountered intraoperatively, ureteral stents may be placed. These stents do not prevent injuries from occurring, but they can facilitate early identification of developing problems. Ureteral injuries should always be repaired at the time of operation, in consultation with the urologist.

References

1. Hughes LE: Complications of diverticular disease: inflammation, obstruction and bleeding. Clin Gastroenterol 4:147, 1975

2. Dawson JL, Hanon I, Roxburgh RA: Diverticulitis complicated by diffuse peritonitis. Br J Surg 52:354, 1965

3. Browder W, Cerise EJ, Litwin MS: Impact of emergency angiography in massive lower intestinal bleeding. Ann Surg 204:530, 1986

4. Pennoyer WP, Vignati PV, Cohen JL: Mesenteric angiography for lower GI hemorrhage: are there predictors for positive study? Dis Colon Rectum 49:1014, 1997

5. King DW, Lubowski DZ, Armstrong AS: Sigmoid stricture at colonoscopy—an indication for surgery. Int J Colorectal Dis 5:161, 1990

6. Thompson WG: Do colonic diverticula cause symptoms? Am J Gastroenterol 81:613, 1986

7. Goy JA, Eastwood MA, Mitchell WD, et al: Fecal characteristics contrasted in the irritable bowel syndrome and diverticular disease. Am J Clin Nutr 29:1480, 1976

8. Littlewood ER, Ornstein MH, McLean Baird I, et al: Doubts about diverticular disease. BMJ 283:1524, 1981

9. Francis CY, Whorwell PJ: The irritable bowel syndrome. Postgrad Med J 73:1, 1997

10. Hulnick DH, Megibow AJ, Balthazar EJ, et al: Computed tomography in the evaluation of diverticulitis. Radiology 152:491, 1984

11. Neff CC, van Sonnenberg E: CT of diverticulitis: diagnosis and treatment. Radiol Clin North Am 27:743, 1989

12. Woods RJ, Lavery IC, Fazio VW, et al: Internal fistulas in diverticular disease. Dis Colon Rectum 31:591, 1988

13. Kurtz DI, Mazier P: Diverticular fistulas. Semin Colon Rectal Surg 1:93, 1994

14. Krukowski ZH, Koruth NM, Matheson NA: Evolving practice in acute diverticulitis. Br J Surg 82:684, 1985

15. Hinchey GC, Schall GH, Richards MB: Treatment of perforated diverticulitis of the colon. Adv Surg 12:85, 1978

16. Hartmann H: Nouveau procédé d'ablation des cancers de la partie terminale du cólon pelvien. Cong Franc Chir 30:411, 1923

17. Haas PA, Haas GP: A critical evaluation of the Hartmann's procedure. Am Surg 54:381, 1988

18. Roe AM, Prabhu S, Ali A, et al: Reversal of Hartmann's procedure: timing and operative technique. Br J Surg 78:1167, 1991

19. Hackford AW, Schoetz DJ, Coller JA, et al: Surgical management of complicated diverticulitis: the Lahey Clinic experience 1967 to 1982. Dis Colon Rectum 28:317, 1985

20. Murray JJ, Schoetz DJ, Coller JA, et al: Intra-operative colonic lavage and primary anastomosis in nonelective colon resection. Dis Colon Rectum 34:527, 1991

21. Stewart J, Diament RH, Brennan TG: Management of obstructing lesions of the left colon by resection, on-table lavage and primary anastomosis. Surgery 114:502, 1933

22. Ramos JM, Beart RW Jr, Goes R, et al: Role of laparoscopy in colorectal surgery: a prospective evaluation of 200 cases. Dis Colon Rectum 38:494, 1995

23. Ortega AE, Beart RW Jr, Steele GD Jr, et al: Laparoscopic bowel surgery registry: preliminary results. Dis Colon Rectum 38:681, 1995

24. Mooney MJ, Elliott PL, Galapon DB, et al: Hand-assisted laparoscopic sigmoidectomy for diverticulitis. Dis Colon Rectum 41:630, 1998

25. Eijsbouts QA, de Haan J, Berends F, et al: Laparoscopic elective treatment of diverticular disease: a comparison between laparoscopic-assisted and resection-facilitated techniques. Surg Endosc 14:726, 2000

26. Berthou JC, Charbonneau P: Elective laparoscopic management of sigmoid diverticulitis. Surg Endosc 13:457, 1999

27. Trebuchet G, Lechaux D, Lecalve JL: Laparoscopic left colon resection for diverticular disease. Surg Endosc 16:18, 2002

28. Kockerling F, Schneider C, Reymond MA, et al: Laparoscopic resection of sigmoid diverticulitis. Surg Endosc 13:567, 1999

29. Senagore AJ, Duepree HJ, Delaney CP, et al: Cost structure of laparoscopic and open sigmoid colectomy for diverticular disease. Dis Colon Rectum 45:485, 2002

30. Irvin TT, Goligher JC: Aetiology and disruption of intestinal anastomosis. Br J Surg 60:461, 1973

31. Krukowski ZH, Matheson NA: Emergency surgery for diverticular disease complicated by generalized fecal peritonitis: a review. Br J Surg 71:921, 1984

32. Shepard A, Keighley MR: Audit of complicated diverticular disease. Ann R Coll Surg Engl 68:8, 1986

33. Sarin S, Poulos PB: Evaluation of current surgical management of acute inflammatory diverticular disease. Ann R Coll Surg Engl 73:278, 1991

34. Benn PL, Wolff BC, Ilstrup DM: Level of anastomosis and recurrent colonic diverticulitis. Am J Surg 151:269, 1986

35. Bell AM, Wolff BG: Progression and recurrence after resection for diverticulitis. Semin Colon Rectal Surg 1:99, 1990

36. Fry DE, Milholen L, Harbrecht PJ: Iatrogenic ureteral injury. Arch Surg 118:454, 1983

Acknowledgments

Figures 1 and 2   Dragonfly Media Group.
Figure 4   Tom Moore.

75 PROCEDURES FOR ULCERATIVE COLITIS

Robert R. Cima, M.D., F.A.C.S., F.A.S.C.R.S., Tonia Young-Fadok, M.D., M.S., F.A.C.S., F.A.S.C.R.S., and John H. Pemberton, M.D., F.A.C.S., F.A.S.C.R.S.

Chronic ulcerative colitis (CUC) is one of the two main categories of inflammatory bowel disease (Crohn disease being the other). CUC is characterized by contiguous inflammation of the mucosa, beginning in the rectum and progressing for variable distances proximally within the colon. Its cause is unknown. Patients typically experience intermittent exacerbations of the disease, which are notable for bloody diarrhea associated with urgency and tenesmus. In a minority of patients, the first episode of the disease is a fulminant presentation that may be fatal without prompt surgical intervention.

Medical therapy for CUC is aimed at controlling symptoms or managing the underlying inflammatory process; it does not cure either the intestinal or the extraintestinal manifestations of CUC. The intestinal manifestations of CUC and the associated risk of malignancy can, however, be effectively cured by surgical intervention, which involves removal of the entire large intestine. In what follows, we discuss the indications for surgical treatment of CUC and describe the surgical options.

Preoperative Evaluation

INDICATIONS FOR OPERATION

Surgical treatment of CUC is indicated in a variety of situations. The easiest classification scheme divides these indications into two broad categories: indications for emergency operation and indications for elective operation.

Emergency Operation

The main conditions calling for emergency operative treatment of CUC are fulminant colitis, toxic megacolon, and massive hemorrhage. In these situations, the primary surgical strategy is to remove the bulk of the diseased colon to allow the patient's medical condition to improve; an important secondary consideration is to perform an operation that will not preclude a future restorative procedure.

Fulminant colitis   Although as a rule, CUC is a chronic disease that allows deliberate and coordinated care, approximately 10% of patients initially present with severe disease.[1] Fulminant colitis is characterized by the sudden onset of severe and frequent (> 10/day) bloody bowel movements, abdominal pain, dehydration, and anemia. Diagnostic criteria for fulminant colitis (originally described by Truelove and Witts in 1955) include the above signs and symptoms and at least two of the following: tachycardia, body temperature higher than 38.6° C (101.5° F), leukocytosis (> 10,500/mm³), and hypoalbuminemia.[2]

Patients with fulminant colitis are extremely ill and require rapid, aggressive medical therapy, including fluid resuscitation, correction of electrolyte abnormalities, and, in some cases, blood transfusions. A nihil per os (NPO) regimen is indicated. Naso-

gastric tube decompression may be required if colonic distention is a component of the presentation. If CUC is known to be present, high-dose intravenous steroid administration should be initiated, and stool cultures should be obtained. If no diagnosis of CUC has yet been made, endoscopic evaluation of the colon should be carried out expeditiously, with the aim not of assessing the entire colon but only of visualizing the rectal and distal colonic mucosa. If the results of the endoscopic examination are obviously consistent with CUC, the endoscope can be withdrawn; the remainder of the colon need not be evaluated.

If the patient is clinically stable, antibiotic therapy is not indicated. If, however, the patient is very ill or has a high fever or leukocytosis, administration of appropriate broad-spectrum antibiotics should be initiated after cultures are obtained. The patient should be observed closely for 24 to 48 hours while on maximal medical therapy. If there is no improvement or if the patient's condition deteriorates, surgical treament is recommended. If there is evidence of peritonitis, hemodynamic instability, or perforation, the patient should be operated on immediately.

Toxic megacolon   Toxic megacolon may be the initial presentation of ulcerative colitis or may represent a flare in a patient with long-standing disease. Either the entire colon or an isolated segment of the colon (usually the transverse or the left colon) is involved. Although a radiographic definition of toxic megacolon exists (i.e., greater than 5.5 cm dilatation of the transverse colon on a supine abdominal film), toxic megacolon is truly a clinical diagnosis.

Medical treatment of toxic megacolon is similar to that of fulminant colitis—namely, an NPO regimen, nasogastric tube decompression, correction of fluid deficits and electrolyte abnormalities, administration of high-dose steroids, and initiation of antibiotic therapy if there is fever or an elevated leukocyte count. Emergency surgical management is indicated if the patient's clinical or radiographic status worsens, if there is evidence of perforation, or if there is no improvement 24 to 36 hours after aggressive medical therapy is begun. Delaying the operation increases the risk of perforation, which raises mortality from less than 5% to nearly 30%.[1] Fortunately, fewer patients are now seen with severe complications of CUC than was once the case, primarily because of improved medical therapies and a general trend toward earlier surgical intervention for CUC.

Other surgical emergencies   Colonic perforation without megacolon should raise concern that the actual diagnosis might be Crohn disease or that there might be another cause for the perforation (e.g., a gastric or duodenal ulcer related to steroid use). Whatever the cause of the perforation, there is no role for conservative therapy, and the patient should immediately undergo surgical exploration.

Hemorrhage severe enough to result in hemodynamic instability is an unusual complication of CUC. Decisions regarding intervention are made after consultation with the treating gastroenterologist. Initial treatment should consist of aggressive fluid and blood-product resuscitation. Any electrolyte or clotting deficiencies should be corrected. Upper GI endoscopy should be done to exclude the possibility that a gastric or duodenal ulcer is causing the bleeding. The timing of operation is determined by the clinical situation. If the patient is hemodynamically unstable even after effective resuscitation, emergency operation is indicated because medical therapy would take too long to decrease the mucosal inflammation responsible for the bleeding. If there is slow but continuing hemorrhage that does not cause hemodynamic instability or symptoms, high-dose steroid therapy may be tried for 48 to 72 hours before surgical intervention is considered.

Elective Operation

Given the chronic nature of CUC, the indications for elective operation may occur early in the course of a patient's disease or may arise after years of relatively mild disease. The major indications for elective surgical treatment of CUC are failure of medical management to control symptoms (intractability) and the presence of mucosal dysplasia, dysplasia-associated lesion or mass (DALM), or malignancy. Elective surgical treament may also be indicated in patients with extraintestinal manifestations of CUC and children with growth retardation.

Intractable symptoms Intractability is a clinically defined condition that can occur in either the acute or the chronic state of CUC. In an acute flare, intractability refers to the inability to control a patient's symptoms with maximal medical therapy; in the chronic state, it refers to either the inability to taper steroids to a reasonable maintenance dose or the development of severe drug-related side effects.

In most cases, medical management of an acute CUC flare consists of I.V. steroid therapy for 5 to 10 days. If this approach does not bring about clinical improvement, elective operation is advisable. One study recommended I.V. or oral cyclosporine therapy for patients who are experiencing an acute flare of CUC that does not respond to I.V. steroid therapy[3]; however, a subsequent report involving a larger number of patients and a longer follow-up period showed that nearly 50% of all patients treated in this manner required colectomy within 1 year.[4] During the treatment period for acute disease, it is important that the patient receive adequate nutritional support (often in the form of total parenteral nutrition). If the patient's nutritional status declines significantly, a three-stage procedure may be necessary to improve surgical outcome.[5]

Dysplasia or malignancy The development of malignancy in the setting of CUC has been well described. The risk of colon cancer in a CUC patient has been estimated to be anywhere from 2% at 20 years after onset of CUC to 43% at 35 years.[6] A patient's individual risk level for colon cancer appears to increase when there is evidence of high-grade dysplasia on random colon biopsies or if there is a DALM. The presence of low-grade dysplasia on random biopsy is a more difficult clinical situation. Traditionally, most clinicians have recommended increases in the frequency of surveillance colonoscopies rather than surgery. There are, however, some preliminary reports suggesting that the presence of any degree of dysplasia not associated with a mass lesion should be viewed with a very high degree of suspicion and that surgery should be recommended[7]; this has

become our practice. In addition, any colonic stricture significant enough to cause obstructive symptoms, even if it appears benign on endoscopy, should be considered to be potentially harboring a malignancy and should be treated surgically.

When there is a suspected or known colonic or rectal malignancy, the surgical options should be driven by oncologic principles. In most patients, except for those with low rectal cancers or metastatic disease, total colectomy with ileal pouch–anal anastomosis (IPAA) is an acceptable surgical treatment modality. There is a particular concern regarding the performance of an IPAA in the setting of a rectal cancer, in that the required irradiation may severely compromise pouch function. Stage for stage, the prognosis for patients with malignancies who have CUC is generally similar to that of patients with malignancies who do not have CUC. CUC patients who have undergone surgical treatment, particularly with an IPAA procedure, tolerate chemotherapy as well as patients without CUC do.[8-10] As a rule, if oncologic principles are not compromised, an IPAA procedure can be performed without any deleterious impact on oncologic outcome or long-term IPAA function.

Operative Planning

CHOICE OF PROCEDURE

Currently, there are two widely accepted surgical options for the treatment of CUC: total proctocolectomy with end (Brooke) ileostomy and total proctocolectomy with IPAA. A third option, total abdominal colectomy with ileorectal anastomosis, may be considered in highly select groups of patients—namely, those who have relatively mild disease and who have a contraindication to an ostomy (e.g., portal hypertension or ascites) and those in whom an ileal pouch procedure would be technically impossible and who refuse an ileostomy. Previously, a fourth option, proctocolectomy with construction of a continent ileostomy (or Kock pouch), was employed; however, this procedure was associated with such a high rate of pouch dysfunction (requiring surgical correction in the majority of patients) that it is no longer performed. For this reason, as well as because the IPAA procedure has yielded outstanding functional results, the continent ileostomy is now of historical interest only and thus will not be discussed further.

The choice of surgical procedure is individualized on the basis of the patient's underlying physical and medical condition, as well as of his or her social and psychological situation. At present, proctocolectomy with IPAA (first described in 1978[11,12]) is the preferred operation for most patients because it removes the diseased colon while preserving fecal continence and nearly normal defecation through the anus. Construction of the ileal pouch is the key to the success of this operation: the pouch provides a fecal reservoir that is adequate to allow voluntary defecation, albeit at a higher (but still manageable) daily frequency than is seen in patients with an intact rectum. In almost all series, the majority of IPAA patients report good functional results and a high degree of satisfaction with quality of life, and these findings remain stable over time. The decision to proceed with operations other than IPAA is based on individual patient circumstances or on the presence of preexisting medical or physiologic conditions that are contraindications to this type of restorative procedure.

In patients who require emergency surgery or are in poor medical condition as a consequence of their underlying disease, a three-stage procedure is performed. Stage I consists of total abdominal colectomy with a Hartmann closure and an end ileostomy. The majority of the diseased colon is removed, the patient's clinical condition is improved, and any immunosuppressive medications the patient has been receiving can be tapered. Once the patient has recovered and is clinically ready for another operation, stage II—entailing either a completion proctectomy with end ileostomy or an IPAA with diverting loop ileostomy—is carried out. If the latter alternative is chosen, the patient must subsequently undergo stage III, which involves reversal of the ileostomy.

The reason why a proctectomy is not performed in an emergency setting is that if the rectum is left in place, a restorative operation can be performed later without the dissection planes in the pelvis having been disturbed. In addition, emergency proctectomy is associated with a higher risk of bleeding and injury to the nerves of the pelvic floor, the bladder, and the genitalia. Usually, the small amount of diseased tissue left behind does not present a clinical problem.

Special Considerations in Patient Selection

Age Most CUC patients are relatively young and thus, unless there are unusual circumstances, should be offered proctocolectomy and IPAA. However, CUC is known to have a bimodal age distribution, and significant numbers of older CUC patients are being referred for surgical evaluation. Although many institutions have reported their long-term results with IPAA, few have regularly performed IPAA in elderly patients. In a Mayo Clinic survey of 1,386 patients who underwent IPAA, the median age at the time of operation was 32 years (range, 5 to 65 years)[13]; only 16% were older than 45 years, and none were older than 65 years. Functional outcomes—determined on the basis of nocturnal stool frequency, daytime and nocturnal incontinence, and need for constipating medications—were significantly worse in patients who were older than 45 years at the time of the IPAA.

Results such as those of this Mayo survey have often led gastroenterologists and surgeons not to recommend IPAA for elderly patients. Another study, however, came to somewhat different conclusions.[14] The investigators evaluated their experience with IPAA patients from the age of 50 years to past the age of 70 years. Twenty-eight of 227 patients were older than 50 years when the IPAA was performed; of those 28, 10 were between 60 and 70 years of age and five were between 70 and 80. When the elderly patients were compared with younger patients with CUC, there were no significant differences between the groups with respect to the major complications (i.e., pelvic sepsis, pouch-related fistula, and anastomotic leakage); however, pouch-anal stenosis was significantly more common in the older patient group. In regard to functional outcome—determined on the basis of frequency of daytime and nighttime bowel movements, use of pads, and incontinence episodes—there were no significant differences. Overall, advanced age is not an absolute contraindication to IPAA. The data suggest that in healthy older patients with good sphincter tone, functional results may be comparable to those in younger patients.

Fertility and fecundity Given that most patients diagnosed with CUC are in their childbearing years, the possible impact of surgery on fertility is obviously an important consideration when surgical management is being discussed with a young woman. A number of studies have evaluated fertility and the course of subsequent pregnancy after surgical treatment of CUC.[15-19] Patients who have undergone proctocolectomy with an end ileostomy or a Kock pouch can expect to have a normal pregnancy and delivery; the type of delivery chosen (vaginal or cesarean section) should depend on obstetric issues. Although pregnancies and deliveries may be uneventful, patients often experience temporary stoma or Kock pouch dysfunction.[17] Studies documented similar dysfunction in post-IPAA patients, who reported a slight increase in stool frequency, incontinence, and pad usage during pregnancy,[19,20] though they returned to baseline pouch function after delivery. These studies noted a higher rate of cesarean sections in post-IPAA patients than was seen in other studies that reported on modes of fetal delivery in patients with Kock pouches and end ileostomies. It is unclear, however, whether this increase was due to uncertainty about how these patients would fare after vaginal deliveries, because fewer than 50% of these cesarean sections were performed for obstetric indications. Overall, there appeared to be no contraindication to vaginal delivery, though the authors suggested that women who have a scarred, stiff perineum might be best advised to avoid vaginal delivery.

Although various studies have examined the course of pregnancy and the development of complications after IPAA, the specific issue of fecundity (the ability to become pregnant) after IPAA has not been thoroughly investigated. One analysis of the rate of pregnancy after IPAA reported a significant reduction in postoperative fertility.[18] In a subsequent study, the same authors examined young women with familial adenomatous polyposis and found that fecundity was significantly lower in those with an ileal pouch than in those with an iliorectal anastomosis.[21] The basis of the decrease in fertility with IPAA is unknown, but it has been suggested that anatomic changes in the pelvis may contribute to the problem. Until further studies are done to confirm and clarify these findings, women considering undergoing IPAA should be informed of the possibility of decreased fertility.

TECHNICAL CONTROVERSIES

The two main controversies regarding the technical aspects of the IPAA procedure revolve around the choice of anastomotic technique and the question of whether a diverting ileostomy is needed.

Ultimately, the choice of anastomotic technique depends on the patient's clinical situation and the surgeon's preference. Currently, most authorities believe that the double-stapled technique is easier to perform than a mucosectomy with a handsewn anastomosis and yields superior functional results in terms of episodes of incontinence or soiling.[22,23] Those surgeons who advocate the double-stapled pouch-anal anastomosis at the level of the pelvic floor believe that leaving 1.5 to 2.0 cm of anal mucosa proximal to the dentate line improves the functional result by enhancing anal canal sensation. Not all investigators have found this to be the case, however. In a prospective trial from the Mayo Clinic in which 41 patients with CUC were randomly selected to undergo either mucosectomy and handsewn IPAA or double-stapled IPAA, there was no significant difference between the groups with respect to functional outcome (determined on the basis of stool frequency or episodes of fecal incontinence) at 6 months after ileostomy closure.[24] However, the double-stapled IPAA group generally had higher resting sphincter pressures (as measured by manometry) and tended to experience less nocturnal incontinence. Although proponents of mucosectomy with a handsewn anastomosis believe that this operation removes all of the anal canal mucosa at risk, analyses of the fate of the anal canal mucosa after mucosectomy indicate that even after mucosectomy, islands of residual rectal mucosa remain.[25,26] Taken as a whole, the evidence available at present suggests that double-stapled IPAA might yield slightly better functional results than handsewn IPAA.

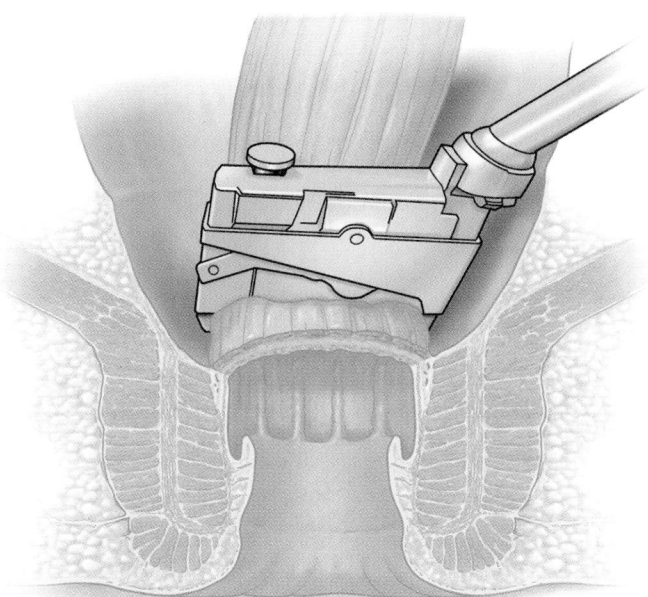

Figure 1 **Open proctocolectomy and IPAA. Once the rectum has been dissected down to the level of the pelvic floor, it is divided with a stapler. The stapler is positioned 1 to 2 cm above the dentate line and fired. This positioning ensures that the final pouch-anal anastomosis is within the anal canal and not in the rectum.**

The need for a temporary ileostomy has been questioned in several quarters. In most large series, the IPAA procedure has included a temporary ileostomy to divert the fecal stream from the pouch while the pouch staple line and the anastomosis heal.[13,27-29] Proponents of this approach believe that the diverting ileostomy decreases the rate of pelvic sepsis, which is known to result in worse long-term functional results. Supporters of a one-stage procedure, on the other hand, believe that an IPAA can be performed without an increased risk of pelvic sepsis.[30-35] In addition to avoiding an ileostomy, a one-stage procedure renders a second hospitalization and operation unnecessary, lowers the total cost, results in a shorter hospital stay, and perhaps even decreases the incidence of small bowel obstruction. In one large single-institution study, there were no differences in complication rate and functional outcome between patients who had not undergone diversion and those who had, nor was there any correlation between diversion and steroid use.[27] Others have reported similar findings.[32,36] Although there might be no significant difference in the rate of complications without a diverting ileostomy, one study suggested that complications might be more severe in patients who lack a protecting ileostomy.[37] Our view is that in properly selected patients who are undergoing uncomplicated procedures performed by experienced surgeons, a one-stage IPAA might be appropriate. However, the surgeon and the patient care team must be vigilant for the early signs of pelvic sepsis, aggressively investigate any possibility of leakage from the pouch or the anastomosis, and intervene as needed.

Operative Technique

Since its introduction, proctocolectomy with IPAA has continued to evolve, especially with the application of new technologies such as laparoscopy.[37-39] Conceptually, the operation can be divided into four phases: (1) removal of the intra-abdominal colon; (2) dissection and removal of the rectum, with the pelvic nerves and

the anal sphincter mechanism spared; (3) construction of an ileal reservoir (pouch); and (4) anastomosis of the ileal reservoir to the anal canal. The following descriptions illustrate the general open and laparoscopic approaches by which these phases are carried out at the Mayo Clinic.

OPEN PROCTOCOLECTOMY AND ILEAL POUCH–ANAL ANASTOMOSIS

A complete bowel preparation is performed on the evening before operation. After induction of anesthesia, the patient is placed in the modified lithotomy position, which allows easy access to both the abdomen and the perineum.

Step 1: Initial Incision and Exploration of Abdomen

The abdomen is entered through a midline vertical incision, and the abdomen is thoroughly explored to determine whether there are any technical or pathologic contraindications to the planned procedure.

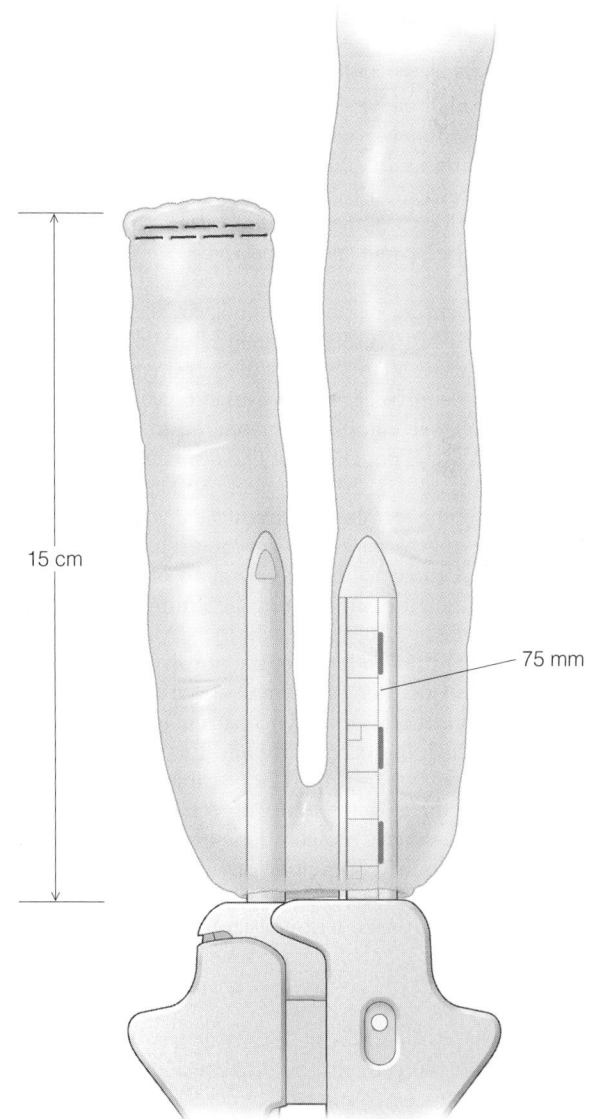

15 cm

75 mm

Figure 2 **Open proctocolectomy and IPAA. The ileal pouch is constructed by dividing the common wall of the afferent and efferent limbs of the distal ileum by means of multiple firings of a linear cutting stapler.**

Step 2: Mobilization and Division of Colon

The entire colon is mobilized away from its retroperitoneal attachments. The transverse colon is freed from the greater omentum, which is preserved if it is of good quality and quantity. Once the intra-abdominal colon has been mobilized, the terminal ileum is divided from the right colon adjacent to the ileocecal junction with a linear stapler. The mesentery is divided as close to the right colon as possible so as not to injure the ileocolic vessels supplying the terminal ileum. Once the right colon has been mobilized, the remainder of the colon is divided from its mesentery.

Step 3: Dissection and Division of Rectum

When the intra-abdominal colon has been fully mobilized and the mesentery has been divided, the patient is placed in a steep Trendelenburg position to facilitate the pelvic dissection of the rectum. The rectum is freed down to the pelvic floor. Great care is taken to avoid the pelvic nerves that lie in the interface between the mesorectum and the presacral fascia. The rectum is divided at the pelvic floor with a stapler [*see Figure 1*]. The colon and the rectum are then sent in their entirety for pathologic evaluation.

Step 4: Construction of Ileal Pouch

After the colon has been removed, the ileal reservoir is constructed. The small bowel mesentery is completely mobilized from the retroperitoneum up to the inferior border of the pancreas; this mobilization is crucial for ensuring that there is adequate small bowel length to allow the ileal pouch to reach the pelvic floor. To increase the length further, the visceral peritoneum should be scored along the right side of the superior mesenteric vessel.

Once the mesentery has been mobilized, the pouch is fashioned. Our practice is to use a J-shaped reservoir (J pouch) constructed from the last 30 to 35 cm of the terminal ileum. J pouches are simpler to construct, use less small bowel length, and are associated with fewer complications related to pouch-emptying problems than W or S pouches are. The ultimate reservoir capacity of the pouch should be approximately 400 ml. Construction is begun by folding the terminal ileum into a J shape. The hook of the J should be approximately 15 cm long. This efferent limb of the J is loosely secured to the afferent limb of the small bowel. The reservoir is then formed by firing a 75 mm linear cutting stapler twice from the apex of the pouch, thereby dividing the common wall between the two limbs of the pouch [*see Figure 2*].

Whether an adequate length of small bowel is available must be determined before the reservoir is constructed. To confirm that the pouch will reach the pelvic floor and the region of the anastomosis without tension, it should be possible to pull the apex of the pouch 3 to 5 cm below the upper aspect of the pubic symphysis. If, after full mesenteric mobilization and scoring of the visceral peritoneum, the pouch does not easily reach the pelvic floor, it may be necessary to divide either the ileocolic vessel or one of the proximal branches of the superior mesenteric vessels. When there is a concern that a J pouch will not reach the pelvic floor satisfactorily, an S or a W pouch may be constructed instead.

Step 5: Construction of Ileal Pouch–Anal Anastomosis

Before the pouch is brought down to the anus, one must verify that the small intestine from the ligament of Treitz to the ileal pouch is not twisted. At this point in the operation, there are, as noted [*see* Operative Planning, Technical Controversies, *above*], two options for performing the anastomosis. The first is to secure the pouch to the anal canal by means of a double-stapled technique. The head of an end-to-end anastomosis (EEA) stapler is

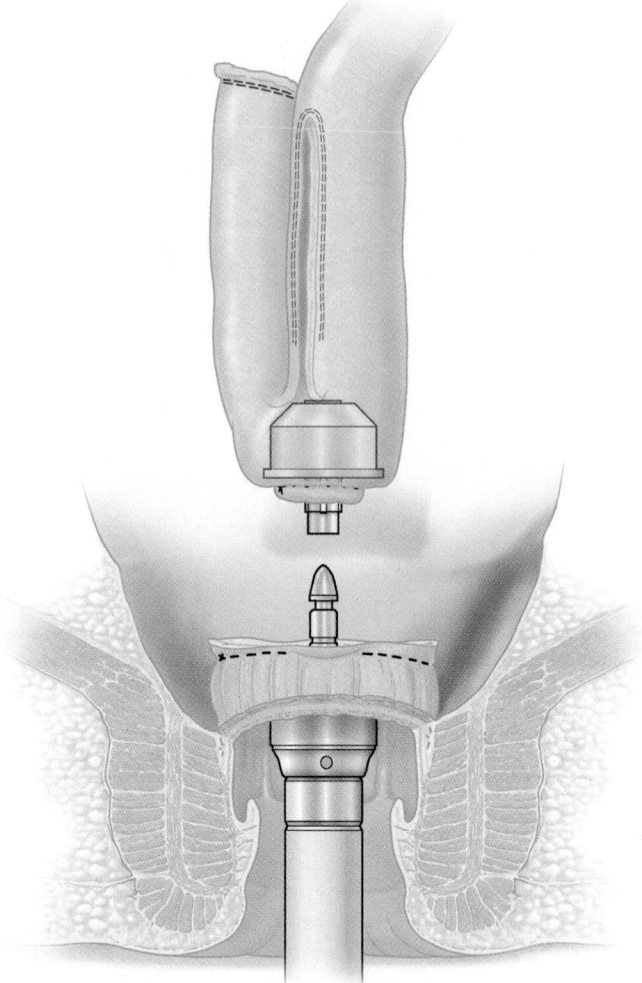

Figure 3   **Open proctocolectomy and IPAA. After the pouch is constructed, the head of an EEA stapler is secured in the apex of the pouch and connected to the pin of the stapler, which was placed upward through the anus.**

secured in the apex of the pouch with a purse-string suture [*see Figure 3*]. The stapler is then advanced into the anus, and the attachment pin is placed adjacent to the staple line marking the point where the rectum was divided at the level of the pelvic floor. The pouch is brought down into the pelvis, with proper orientation maintained, the head of the stapler is fitted onto the pin, and the stapler is fired to anastomose the pouch to the anus [*see Figure 4*].

The second option is to perform a mucosectomy of the anal canal and the lower rectal remnant. The dentate line area is exposed with the help of a self-retaining retractor. A dilute solution of epinephrine is injected into the submucosa to facilitate circumferential excision of the anal canal mucosa; the muscularis propria is left intact. The excision is extended proximally to the level of the stapled rectum. Once the staple line is reached, the full thickness of the rectal wall is divided, and the intact lower rectal remnant and the anal canal mucosa are removed. A long Babcock clamp is placed into the pelvis through the anal opening, and the apex of the pouch is drawn down to the level of the dentate line. A side-to-end handsewn anastomosis between the apex of the pouch and the dentate line is performed with absorbable interrupted sutures. Once the anastomosis is completed, one or two closed suction drains are placed behind the pouch and brought out of separate left abdominal stab wounds. In the majority of patients, a loop ileostomy is constructed in the right lower abdomen.

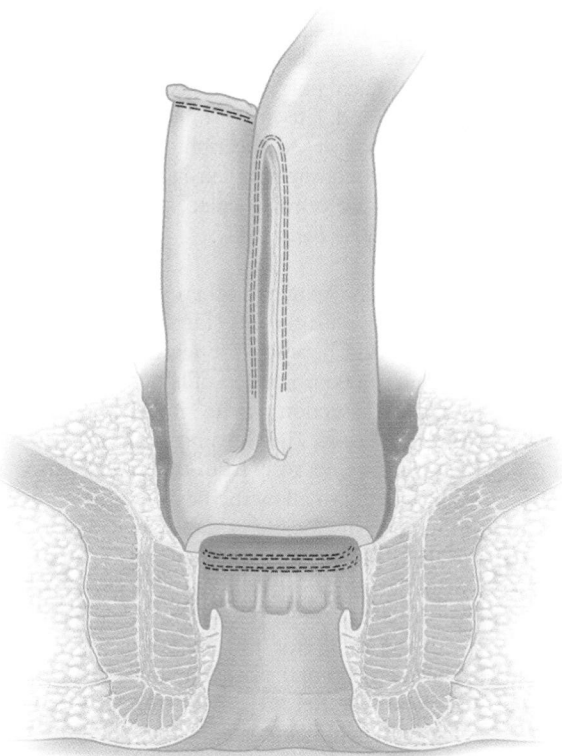

Figure 4 **Open proctocolectomy and IPAA. Shown is the completed ileal J pouch with the circular stapled anastomosis within the anal canal, just above the dentate line.**

Step 6: Later Reversal of Loop Ileostomy

Approximately 3 months after the original operation, a barium study through the anus is performed to determine whether the pouch has healed. If the reservoir and the anastomosis have healed completely, the loop ileostomy can be reversed during a second operation. Often, the ileostomy can be closed by mobilizing it through a small transverse biconvex incision around the stoma. The loop of ileum is then fully mobilized, and an end-to-end handsewn anastomosis or a stapled side-to-side functional end-to-end anastomosis can be done.

LAPAROSCOPIC PROCTOCOLECTOMY AND ILEAL POUCH–ANAL ANASTOMOSIS

Laparoscopic approaches to IPAA were developed to reduce the impact of the procedure on patients who are already physiologically stressed. Initial descriptions of laparoscopic IPAA, however, were not encouraging. In a comparison of five open cases with five laparoscopic cases, operating time was markedly longer in the laparoscopic group, as were hospital stay and the duration of postoperative ileus.[40] The study did, however, show that the procedure was feasible. The procedure described in the initial reports was complex, using seven incisions—five for the ports, a separate Pfannenstiel incision for rectal dissection, and another incision for the ileostomy. Other early series also reported very long operating times, in the range of 380 to 710 minutes,[41-43] as well as high complication rates.[44,45] A 2000 study, however, documented benefits from a minimally invasive approach, with a reduction in hospital stay from 8 days to 7 days ($P = 0.02$), though operating times were still significantly longer than with open IPAA (330 minutes versus 225 minutes).[46]

The technical issues surrounding laparoscopic IPAA have been addressed by developing a simplified version of the procedure, based on lessons learned from segmental procedures.[47] The sim-

plified operation differs from the original version in several key respects: only four ports are placed [*see Figure 5*], the right and the left colon are dissected in a lateral-to-medial direction, the rectum is mobilized intracorporeally, a 4 to 5 cm periumbilical incision is employed for specimen extraction, and the right lower quadrant port site is used for the ileostomy.

As work proceeds in different quadrants of the abdomen and the pelvis, the monitors are moved between the patient's shoulders and ankles, in line with the surgeon's field of view. An instrument stand is placed above the head, and a larger instrument table is placed behind the scrub nurse. The patient's arms are tucked adjacent to the body, and the thighs are kept level with the abdomen to prevent interference with the instruments placed in the lower ports. Because steep position changes are used, the patient is carefully secured (e.g., with padded straps or a bean bag). The bladder is decompressed with a urinary catheter, and the stomach is decompressed with an orogastric tube, which is removed at the end of the procedure. In general, the first assistant stands opposite the surgeon, and the camera-holder stands next to the surgeon.

Step 1: Placement of Trocars and Exploration of Abdomen

A 12 mm blunt port is placed above the umbilicus via cutdown; this port is used for a 30° laparoscope. After abdominal exploration, three additional trocars are placed so as to form a diamond shape with the first trocar [*see Figure 5*]. One 5 mm trocar is placed in the left lower quadrant, and another in the suprapubic midline. If a loop ileostomy is planned, an appropriate site in the right lower quadrant is marked before operation, and a 12 mm trocar is placed at this location. This trocar is used for passage of the stapler, and its site does not require closure, because it becomes the stoma site. A disk of skin and subcutaneous fat is excised from the planned stoma site before the trocar is placed directly through the fascia.

Step 2: Mobilization of Intra-abdominal Colon

Left colon The patient is placed in the Trendelenburg posi-

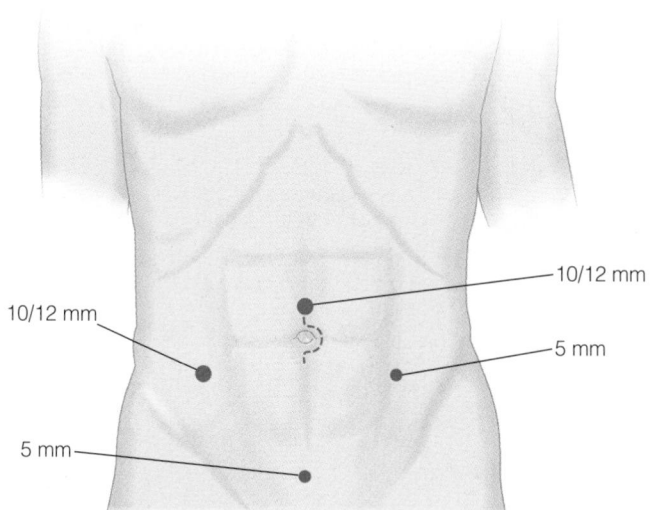

Figure 5 **Laparoscopic proctocolectomy and IPAA. Four trocars are placed in a diamond-shaped pattern: a 12 mm trocar is placed supraumbilically for the camera, another 12 mm trocar is placed in the right lower quadrant, a 5 mm trocar is placed in the left lower quadrant, and another 5 mm trocar is placed above the pubis. A disk of skin and fat is excised for the ileostomy.**

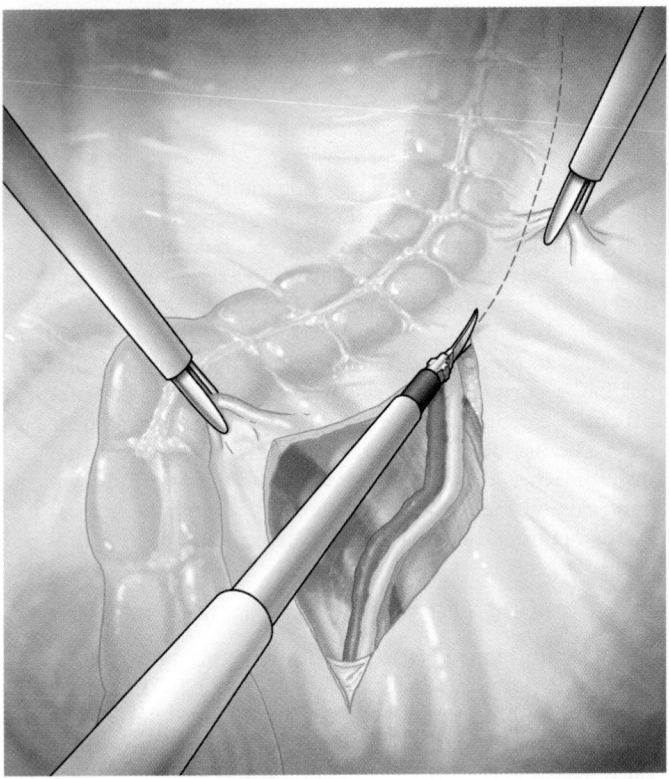

Figure 6 **Laparoscopic proctocolectomy and IPAA. Illustrated is mobilization of the left colon. With the patient in the Trendelenburg position and the left side tilted up, the left lateral peritoneal reflection is opened and the left ureter identified. The descending colon and the sigmoid colon are mobilized medially.**

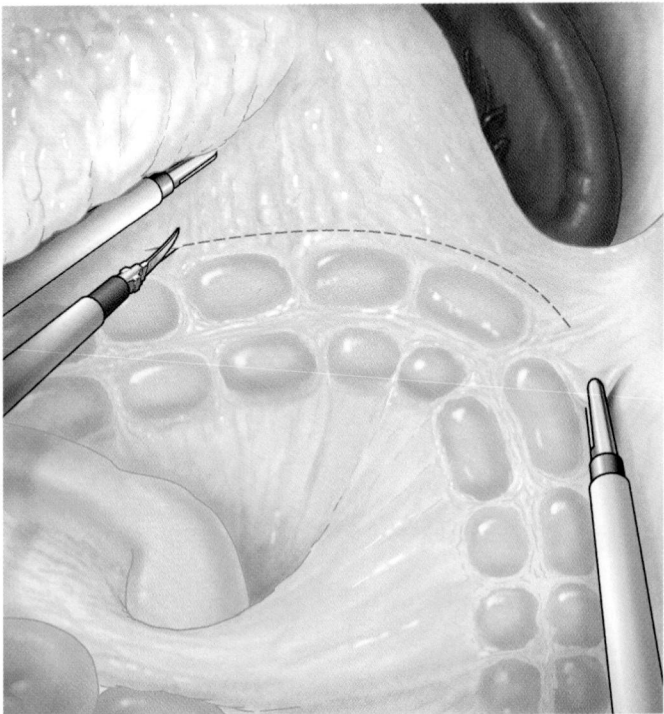

Figure 7 **Laparoscopic proctocolectomy and IPAA. Illustrated is mobilization of the splenic flexure. With the patient in the reverse Trendelenburg position and the left side tilted up, the splenic flexure is mobilized off the retroperitoneum and the omentum dissected off the distal transverse colon.**

tion, with the left side tilted up. Gravity moves the omentum and the small bowel away from the operative site. With the laparoscope in the supraumbilical port, the surgeon faces the left colon, using the suprapubic and left lower quadrant ports. The first assistant provides retraction via the right lower quadrant port. The left ureter is identified after the left lateral peritoneal reflection is opened, and the descending colon and the sigmoid colon are mobilized medially [*see Figure 6*].

Splenic flexure The patient is then placed in the reverse Trendelenburg position, with the left side still tilted up. The surgeon moves to a position between the legs. Mobilization of the splenic flexure requires a combination of lateral dissection off the retroperitoneum and dissection of the omentum off the distal transverse colon [*see Figure 7*]. The first assistant elevates the omentum, which is dissected away from the medial aspect of the splenic flexure sufficiently to allow the flexure to reach below the level of the umbilicus; this facilitates subsequent exteriorization [*see* Step 4, *below*].

Right colon The patient is returned to the Trendelenburg position, but with the right side tilted up. In slim patients, the right ureter is identified before the peritoneum is opened; in heavier patients, it is identified after the peritoneum has been opened. The correct retroperitoneal plane is entered by scoring the peritoneum around the base of the cecum and the terminal ileum. The ascending colon is mobilized medially after the right lateral peritoneal reflection is opened [*see Figure 8*]. Medially, the peritoneal attachments of the terminal ileum are divided up to the inferior border of the duodenum to ensure that the terminal ileum is sufficiently mobilized.

Hepatic flexure The patient is again placed in the reverse Trendelenburg position, but with the right side still tilted up. The attachments of the hepatic flexure are exposed. From the point where the previous dissection ended, the gastrocolic ligament is grasped immediately cephalad to the transverse colon and elevated. The duodenum is identified and protected as dissection proceeds medially [*see Figure 9*]. When the hepatic flexure can be brought down to the level of the umbilicus, it is sufficiently mobilized.[43]

Step 3: Pelvic Dissection

The patient is once more moved into the Trendelenburg position, but tilted neither to the left nor to the right. The surgeon may stand on either the right or the left, in either case performing the dissection on the near side of the pelvis and exposing the planes for the assistant during dissection of the far side. The presacral space is entered by scoring the left pararectal peritoneum, and the plane is developed posteriorly and laterally. The right pararectal peritoneum is similarly scored, the presacral space is entered, and the plane is developed so as to join the previous dissection. Anteriorly, in male patients, care is taken to identify the seminal vesicles and the prostate. To obtain anterior exposure in female patients, the uterus is suspended either with two sutures passed through the abdominal wall or with a fan retractor (which would require an additional port). The rectum is circumferentially dissected down to the pelvic floor, where digital rectal examination confirms the level of the dissection [*see Figure 10*]. The rectum is transected at the pelvic floor with a laparoscopic articulated linear stapler introduced through the 12 mm right lower quadrant port. If mucosectomy is indicated, it is performed at this point.

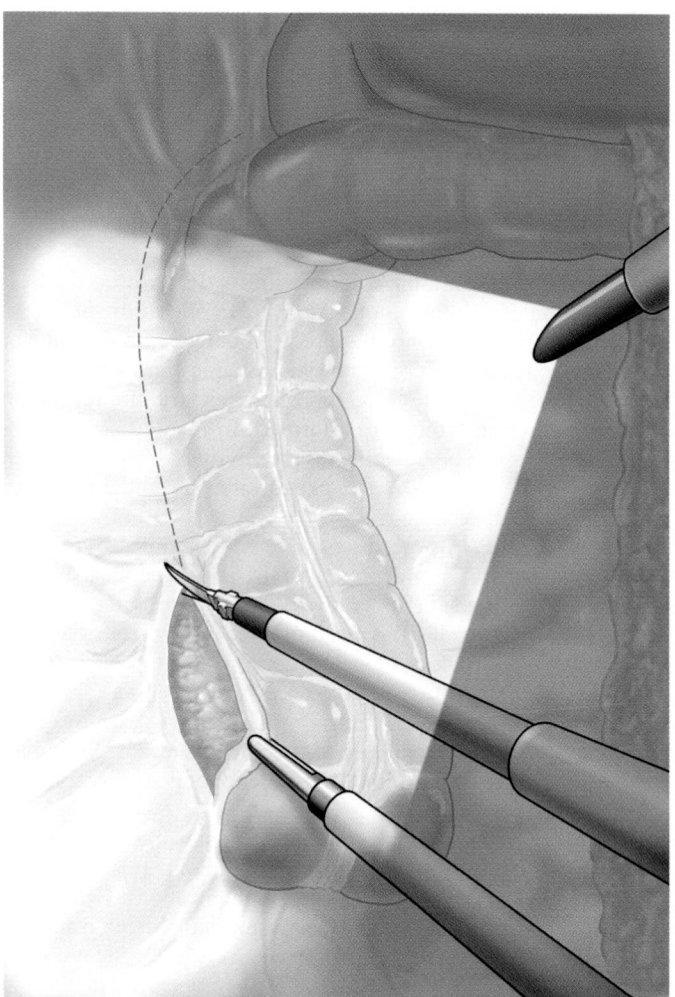

Figure 8 **Laparoscopic proctocolectomy and IPAA. Illustrated is mobilization of the right colon. With the patient in the Trendelenburg position and the right side tilted up, the peritoneum around the cecum and the terminal ileum is scored to enter the correct retroperitoneal plane.**

Step 4: Exteriorization and Resection of Colon and Rectum; Creation of Pouch

The supraumbilical trocar incision is enlarged around the umbilicus to a length of 4 to 5 cm. The specimen is exteriorized from the terminal ileum to the transected distal rectum; the omentum may be preserved or removed with the specimen. The mesentery is divided and ligated; the ileocolic pedicle may be preserved if desired. In lean patients (body mass index [BMI] < 25), the mesenteric vessels are divided at their origin, but in heavier patients, the vessels must be divided closer to the colon. (This is not a critical consideration in the setting of benign disease.) Alternatively, the mesentery may be divided intracorporeally; however, the method we describe here is faster, safer (because bleeding is readily controlled), and cheaper (because multiple clips or stapler applications are unnecessary).

The terminal ileum is divided with a linear stapler. The small bowel is exteriorized to allow inspection for Crohn disease, then replaced into the abdomen, with care taken to maintain the correct orientation of the cut edge of the small bowel mesentery. A standard 15 cm J pouch is constructed, and the head of a circular stapler is secured in the apex of the pouch. The pouch is

returned to the abdomen, which is then irrigated. The midline incision is closed with interrupted sutures, two of which are used to secure the blunt port in the incision. Pneumoperitoneum is reestablished.

Step 5: Construction of Ileal Pouch–Anal Anastomosis

The circular stapler is inserted into the anus, and the spike is brought out adjacent to the staple line. The pouch mesentery is traced from the pouch to the duodenum to confirm correct orientation. The pouch and the anvil are then placed onto the handle of the stapler, which is approximated and fired. A drain is left adjacent to the pouch and brought out through the suprapubic port site.

To create an ileostomy, an appropriate point on the ileum is identified and brought up through the right lower quadrant trocar site after the anterior and posterior rectus fasciae have been incised in a cruciate fashion. The ileostomy is drawn through the site under direct vision to ensure correct orientation. The remaining trocars are removed, the sites are inspected for hemostasis, the skin incisions are closed, and the stoma is matured.

Postoperative Care

On postoperative day 1, clear liquids are started if the patient is not experiencing nausea and if the abdomen is not distended. A

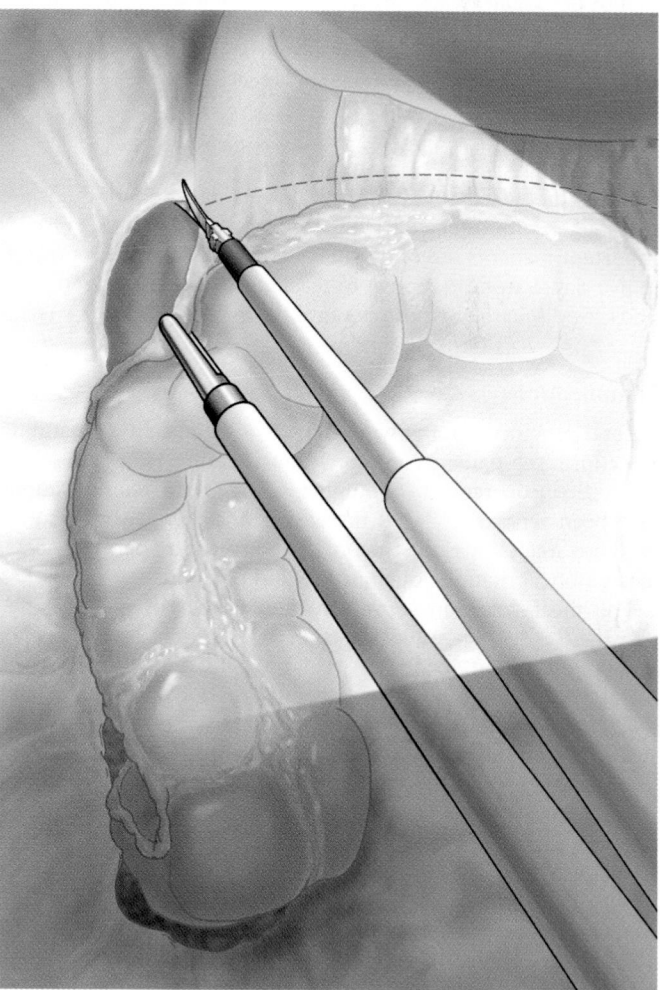

Figure 9 **Laparoscopic proctocolectomy and IPAA. Illustrated is mobilization of the hepatic flexure. With the patient in the reverse Trendelenburg position and the right side tilted up, the gastrocolic ligament is elevated.**

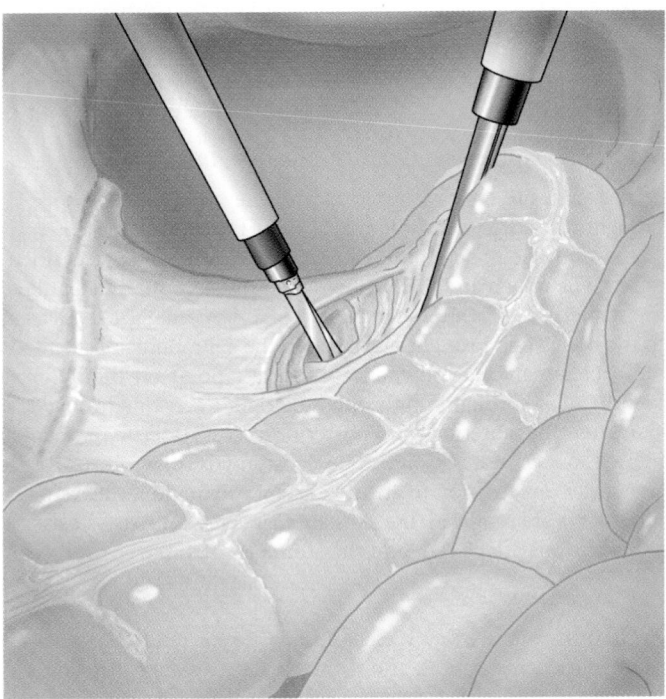

Figure 10 **Laparoscopic proctocolectomy and IPAA. Illustrated is mobilization of the rectum. With the patient in the Trendelenburg position and the table tilted neither to the left nor to the right, the left pararectal peritoneum is scored and the presacral space entered.**

low-fiber diet is instituted on the following day if clear liquids are tolerated. Communication with the enterostomal therapist is important: patients are often sufficiently comfortable on postoperative day 1 to be receptive to teaching, and some patients are ready for discharge by postoperative day 3.

Complications

Total proctocolectomy with IPAA is a technically demanding procedure: the patient commonly must endure two, and sometimes three, operations. A number of significant complications have been reported.[48-52] Of these, the most frequently encountered are small bowel obstruction, pouch leakage, pelvic abscess, anastomotic stricture, pouch fistula, and pouchitis.

The most common short-term and long-term complication after IPAA is small bowel obstruction. In a series of 1,310 patients who underwent an open IPAA at the Mayo Clinic, the incidence of this complication in the perioperative period was 15%,[48] and 24% of patients required early reoperation to resolve the obstruction. Other groups have reported similar incidences, albeit with generally lower rates of reoperation.[27,50] The long-term incidence of small bowel obstruction is also relatively high: one review of the literature on late small bowel obstruction after IPAA reported incidences of 18% at 1 year, 27% at 5 years, and 31% at 10 years.[50] The majority of patients responded to conservative management, but the rate of operative treatment increased from 2.7% at 1 year to 7.5% at 10 years. The most common operative findings in patients who required exploration for relief of the obstruction were pelvic adhesions (32%) and adhesions to the ileostomy closure site (20%).

Pouch leakage and the associated pelvic sepsis are potentially devastating complications after IPAA. The reported incidence of such complications ranges from 5% to 14%.[36,48,53] In the Mayo Clinic study just cited (see above), sepsis occurred in 74 (6%) of 1,310 patients, 73 of whom had pelvic sepsis as the result of the pouch procedure.[48] The majority (63%) of these patients required operative intervention; the remainder were treated with either antibiotics or a combination of antibiotics and CT-guided drainage. In this series and others, the rate of pouch leaks and episodes of pelvic sepsis declined as experience with the procedure increased.

Another fairly common complication of IPAA procedures is the formation of an anastomotic stricture. In one study, 42 (37%) of the 114 patients who required reoperative treatment for pouch-related complications had symptomatic anastomotic strictures.[54] There is no clear correlation between stricture formation and the type of anastomosis performed. In many cases, anastomotic strictures can be treated with intermittent dilatation, which can often be performed by the patient after an initial operative dilatation.

Fistulas after IPAA procedures are extremely difficult to treat. Pouch-vaginal fistulas and, more rarely, pouch-perineal fistulas can occur either in the perioperative period or years later. An early pouch fistula is generally the result of a technical error or a complication of a pouch leak or pelvic abscess. A late pouch fistula raises the possibility of Crohn disease. Most fistulas are low and originate at the level of the anastomosis. They appear to occur equally frequently with handsewn anastomoses and with double-stapled anastomoses. The reported incidence of pouch-vaginal fistulas ranges from 4% to 12%.[27,55-59]

The most important considerations in managing a postpouch fistula are to rule out Crohn disease and to initiate treatment by a surgeon experienced in treating these complications. Before any surgical treatment of a fistula, the patient should be examined under anesthesia and biopsies performed to rule out the presence of Crohn disease. The basic principles of management are (1) local control of any septic process and (2) repair of the fistula by interposing healthy tissue between the pouch and the vagina or the perineal opening. Pouch-vaginal fistulas have been repaired via transanal, transvaginal, transperineal, and transabdominal approaches, with rates of successful closure ranging from 10% to 78%[55,56,58,59]; however, both these fistulas and pouch-perineal fistulas can often be successfully managed with simple interventions, such as seton fistulotomy.[55] Severely symptomatic patients may eventually require pouch diversion or complete pouch excision with end ileostomy.

Pouchitis is a late complication of IPAA. It is an acute inflammatory process of the pouch. In a minority (< 10%) of patients, however, pouchitis can become a chronic process. Chronic pouchitis may eventually lead to pouch failure that necessitates excision of the pouch; fortunately, this is a quite rare event. Pouchitis occurs more frequently in patients who have extraintestinal manifestations of CUC than in those who do not.[60] Measuring the exact incidence of pouchitis is difficult because of variations in presentation and differences in diagnostic criteria, but most series report figures between 12% and 50%.[13,48,61] Pouchitis should be suspected in any patient who experiences abdominal cramps, increased stool frequency, watery or bloody diarrhea, and flulike symptoms. Although many patients are treated on clinical grounds alone, accurate diagnosis requires endoscopic visualization of the pouch, as well as histologic evaluation.

The exact cause of pouchitis is unclear, but the observation that antibiotic therapy (particularly with metronidazole) can successfully treat acute and chronic pouchitis lends support to the theory that interaction between pouch bacteria levels and the mucosal immune system plays an important role in pathogenesis. In cases of chronic pouchitis, immunosuppressive agents may have to be added to achieve control of symptoms. Fewer than 8% of patients who undergo an IPAA procedure experience chronic severe pouchitis, and about half of these require pouch excision.[13,60]

Outcome Evaluation

Perhaps surprisingly, given the complexity of the IPAA procedure and the often debilitated condition of the patients, quite similar functional results have been obtained by many different surgeons and many different institutions.[13,27,30,31,36,48-50,61] Most patients report good to excellent pouch function. The most commonly used markers of pouch function are the number of diurnal and nocturnal bowel movements, the number of episodes of soiling, the number of episodes of incontinence, and the extent to which medications are required to control bowel activity. In the Mayo Clinic series of open IPAA patients cited earlier [*see* Operative Planning, Choice of Procedure, Special Considerations in Patient Selection, *above*], the average number of diurnal bowel movements at the time of discharge after closure of the ileostomy was six, and the average number of nocturnal bowel movements was one.[13,48] Nearly 80% of patients had complete diurnal continence, whereas 19% had occasional episodes of incontinence and 2% had frequent episodes. Occasional nocturnal incontinence occurred in 49% of patients. Nearly 50% of patients were discharged on some type of medication to slow their bowels or provide dietary bulk. In patients who had had an ileal pouch for longer than 10 years, stool frequency and continence remained remarkably stable over time. When all patients were considered, however, episodes of incontinence increased slightly, with 73% of patients reporting complete continence at 10 years (a modest decrease from the initial 80%). Many groups have reported similarly stable functional results.[61-63]

A number of studies have investigated patients' quality of life after surgical treatment of CUC. One group found that quality of life after IPAA is comparable to the norms for the general healthy population in the United States.[64] Others reported that quality-of-life measures yielded better results after an IPAA than after an end or continent ileostomy.[65-67] These results do not, however, mean that the IPAA is the treatment of choice for all CUC patients or that CUC patients who either request an end ileostomy or are unable to have an IPAA will necessarily have a poorer postoperative quality of life. Several reports have shown that quality of life improves after operation regardless of what procedure is performed, probably as a consequence of eradication of the underlying disease.[68-70]

It is generally accepted that avoiding an abdominal stoma improves a patient's body image, but it is unclear whether the route of bowel emptying (i.e., through a pouch or through a stoma) has any real effect on quality of life. A study in which patients were asked to place a monetary value on the disability they believe themselves to be experiencing as a result of their condition found no difference between ileostomy patients and IPAA patients.[71] In fact, when patients were asked to rank the impact of altered bowel emptying on quality of life and disability, those with pelvic pouches considered altered bowel emptying a significantly worse problem than those with stomas did. These findings suggest, again, that the choice of operation for CUC must be individualized on the basis of various health and personal factors specific to each patient.

LAPAROSCOPIC IPAA

Laparoscopic proctocolectomy with IPAA has been performed in more than 70 CUC patients since the initial pilot study involving seven patients.[72] The indications for operative intervention [*see* Preoperative Evaluation, Indications for Operation, *above*] are the same for the laparoscopic approach as for the open approach. In a case-matched series of 40 patients undergoing laparoscopic IPAA, each of whom was matched to two open IPAA patients (with disease, age, gender, BMI, and date of operation controlled for), the laparoscopic group experienced significant benefits with respect to time to clear liquid ingestion (1 versus 3 days; $P < 0.001$), time to resumption of regular diet (3 versus 4 days; $P < 0.001$), and time to restoration of bowel function (2 versus 3 days; $P < 0.001$).[73] The duration of narcotic use was shorter in the laparoscopic group ($P < 0.001$), and length of stay was reduced as well (4 versus 7 days; $P < 0.001$). Operating time was longer in the laparoscopic group (270 versus 192 minutes; $P < 0.001$), but it decreased as the surgeon gained experience with the procedure, reaching an average of 3 to 3.5 hours. Other authors are reporting similar advantages.[39,74]

References

1. Becker JM: Surgical therapy for ulcerative colitis and Crohn's disease. Gastroenterol Clin North Am 28:371, 1999

2. Truelove SC, Witts LF: Cortisone in ulcerative colitis: final report on a therapeutic trial. Br Med J 2:1041, 1955

3. Actis GC, Ottobrelli A, Pera A, et al: Continuously infused cyclosporine at low dose is sufficient to avoid emergency in acute attacks of ulcerative colitis without the need for high-dose steroids. J Clin Gastroenerol 17:10, 1993

4. Gurudu SR, Griffel LH, Gialanell RJ, et al: Cyclosporine therapy in inflammatory bowel disease: short-term and long-term results. J Clin Gastroenterol 29:151, 1999

5. Fearon KC, Luff R: The nutritional management of surgical patients: enhanced recovery after surgery. Proc Nutr Soc 62:807, 2003

6. Lewis JD, Deren JJ, Lichenstein GR: Cancer risk in patients with inflammatory bowel disease. Gastroenterol Clin North Am 28:459, 1999

7. Gorfine SR, Bauer JJ, Harris MT, et al: Dysplasia complicating chronic ulcerative colitis: is immediate colectomy warranted? Dis Colon Rectum 43:1575, 2000

8. Taylor TA, Wolff BG, Dozois RR, et al: Ileal pouch–anal anastomosis for chronic ulcerative colitis and familial polyposis coli complicated by adenocarcinoma. Dis Colon Rectum 31:358, 1988

9. Radice E, Nelson H, Devine RM, et al: Ileal pouch–anal anastomosis in patients with colorectal cancer: long-term functional and oncologic outcomes. Dis Colon Rectum 41:11, 1998

10. Remzi FH, Preen M: Rectal cancer and ulcerative colitis: does it change the therapeutic approach? Colorectal Dis 5:483, 2003

11. Parks AG, Nichols RJ: Proctocolectomy without ileostomy for ulcerative colitis. Br Med J 2:85, 1978

12. Parks AG, Nichols RJ, Belliveau P: Proctocolectomy with ileal reservoir and anal anastomosis. Br J Surg 67:533, 1980

13. Farouk R, Pemberton JH, Wolff BG, et al: Functional outcomes after ileal pouch-anal anastomosis for chronic ulcerative colitis. Ann Surg 231:919, 2000

14. Tan HT, Connolly AB, Morton D, et al: Results of restorative proctocolectomy in the elderly. Int J Colorectal Dis 12:319, 1997

15. Metcalf AM, Dozois RR, Kelly KA: Sexual function after proctocolectomy. Ann Surg 204:624, 1986

16. Anderson JB, Turner GM, Williamson RC: Fulminant ulcerative colitis in late pregnancy and the puerperium. J R Soc Med 80:492, 1987

17. Gopal KA, Amshel AL, Shonberg IL, et al: Ostomy and pregnancy. Dis Colon Rectum 28:912, 1985

18. Olsen Ko, Joelsson M, Laurberg S, et al: Fertility after ileal pouch–anal anastomosis in women with ulcerative colitis. Br J Surg 86:493, 1999

19. Juhasz ES, Fozard B, Dozois RR, et al: Ileal pouch-anal anastomosis function following childbirth: an extended evaluation. Dis Colon Rectum 38:159, 1995

20. Nelson H, Dozois RR, Kelly KA, et al: The effect of pregnancy and delivery on the ileal pouch-anal anastomosis functions. Dis Colon Rectum 32:384, 1989

21. Olsen KO, Juul S, Bulow S, et al: Female fecundity before and after operation for famillial adenomatous polyposis. Br J Surg 90:227, 2003

22. Gemlo BT, Belmonte C, Wiltz O, et al: Functional assessment of ileal pouch–anal anastomotic techniques. Am J Surg 169:137, 1995

23. Saigusa N, Kurahashi T, Nakamura T, et al: Functional outcome of stapled ileal pouch–anal canal anastomosis versus handsewn pouch–anal anastomosis. Surg Today 30:575, 2000

24. Reilly WT, Pemberton JH, Wolff BG, et al: Randomized prospective trial comparing ileal pouch-anal anastomosis performed by excising the anal mucosa to ileal pouch–anal anastomosis performed by preserving the anal mucosa. Ann Surg 225:666, 1997

25. Heppell J, Weiland LH, Perrault J, et al: Fate of the rectal mucous after rectal mucosectomy and ileoanal anastomosis. Dis Colon Rectum 26:768, 1983

26. O'Connell PR, Pemberton JH, Weiland LH, et al: Does rectal mucous regenerate after ileoanal anastomosis? Dis Colon Rectum 30:1, 1987

27. Fazio VW, Ziv Y, Church JM, et al: Ileal pouch-anal anastomoses complications and function in 1005 patients. Ann Surg 222:120, 1995

28. Pemberton JH, Kelly KA, Beart RW, et al: Ileal pouch–anal anastomosis for chronic ulcerative colitis: long-term results. Ann Surg 206:504, 1987

29. Becker JM, McGrath KM, Meager MP, et al: Late functional adaptation after colectomy, mucosal proctectomy, ileal pouch–anal anastomosis. Surgery 110:718, 1991

30. Sugerman HJ, Sugerman EL, Meador JG, et al: Ileal pouch anal anastomosis without ileal diversion. Ann Surg 232:530, 2000

31. Heuschen UA, Hinz U, Allemeyer EH, et al: One- or two-stage procedure for restorative proctocolectomy: rationale for a surgical strategy in ulcerative colitis. Ann Surg 234:788, 2001

32. Hosie KB, Grobler SP, Keighley MR: Temporary loop ileostomy following restorative proctocolectomy. Br J Surg 79:33, 1992

33. Tjandra JJ, Fazio VW, Milsom JW, et al: Omission of temporary diversion in restorative proctocolectomy—is it safe? Dis Colon Rectum 36:1007, 1993

34. Matikainen M, Santavirta J, Hiltunen K: Ileoanal anastomosis without a covering ileostomy. Dis Colon Rectum 33:384, 1990

35. Sugerman HJ, Newsome HH, Decosta G, et al: Stapled ileoanal anastomosis for ulcerative colitis and familial polyposis without a temporary diverting ileostomy. Ann Surg 213:606, 1991

36. Cohen Z, McLeod RS, Stephen W, et al: Continuing evolution of the pelvic pouch procedure. Ann Surg 216:506, 1992

37. Williamson MER, Lewis WG, Sagar PM, et al: One-stage restorative proctocolectomy without temporary ileostomy for ulcerative colitis: a note of caution. Dis Colon Rectum 40:1019, 1997

38. Kienle P, Weitz J, Benner A, et al: Laparoscopically assisted colectomy and ileoanal pouch procedure with and without protective ileostomy. Surg Endosc 17:716, 2003

39. Ky AJ, Sonoda T, Milsom JW: One-stage laparoscopic restorative proctocolectomy: an alternative to the conventional approach? Dis Colon Rectum 45:207, 2002

40. Wexner SD, Johansen OB, Nogueras JJ, et al: Laparoscopic total abdominal colectomy: a prospective trial. Dis Colon Rectum 35:651, 1992

41. Liu CD, Rolandelli R, Ashley S, et al: Laparoscopic surgery for inflammatory bowel disease. Am Surg 61:1054, 1995

42. Thibault C, Paulin EC: Total laparoscopic proctocolectomy and laparoscopy assisted proctocolectomy for inflammatory bowel disease: operative technique and preliminary report. Surg Laparosc Endosc 5:472, 1995

43. Hasegawa H, Watanabe M, Baba H, et al: Laparoscopic restorative proctocolectomy for patients with ulcerative colitis. J Laparoendoscop Adv Surg Tech 12:403, 2002

44. Reissman P, Salky BA, Pfeifer J, et al: Laparoscopic surgery in the management of inflammatory bowel disease. Am J Surg 171:47, 1996

45. Pace DE, Seshadri PA, Chiasson PM, et al: Early experience with laparoscopic ileal pouch–anal anastomosis for ulcerative colitis. Surg Lap Endosc Perc Tech 12:337, 2002

46. Marcello PW, Milsom JW, Wong SK, et al: Laparoscopic restorative proctocolectomy: case-matched comparative study with open restorative proctocolectomy. Dis Colon Rectum 43:604, 2000

47. Young-Fadok TM, Nelson H: Laparoscopic right colectomy: five step procedure. Dis Colon Rectum 43:267, 2000

48. Meagher AP, Farouk R, Dozois RR, et al: J ileal pouch–anal anastomosis for chronic ulcerative colitis: complications and long-term outcome in 1310 patients. Br J Surg 85:800, 1998

49. Dayton MT, Larsen KP: Outcomes of pouch–related complications after ileal pouch–anal anastomosis. Am J Surg 174:728, 1997

50. Maclean AR, Cohen Z, MacRae HM, et al: Risk of small bowel obstruction after the ileal pouch–anal anastomosis. Ann Surg 235:200, 2002

51. Korsgen S, Keighley MRB: Causes of failure and life expectancy of the ileoanal pouch. Int J Colorectal Dis 12:4, 1997

52. Romanos J, Samarasekera DN, Stebbing JF, et al: Outcomes of 200 restorative proctocolectomy operations: the John Radcliffe Hospital experience. Br J Surg 84:814, 1997

53. Marcello PW, Robert PL, Schoetz DJ Jr, et al: Long-term results of ileoanal pouch procedure. Arch Surg 128:500, 1993

54. Galandiuk S, Scott NA, Dozois RR, et al: Ileal pouch-anal anastomosis: reoperation for pouch-related complications. Ann Surg 212:446, 1990

55. Keighly MRB, Gobler SP: Fistula complicating restorative proctocolectomy. Br J Surg 80:1065, 1993

56. Wexner SD, Rothenberger DA, Jensen L, et al: Ileal pouch vaginal fistulas: incidence, etiology, and management. Dis Colon Rectum 32:460, 1989

57. Paye F, Penna C, Chiche L, et al: Pouch-related fistulas following restorative proctocolectomy. Br J Surg 83:1574, 1996

58. Groom JS, Nicholls RJ, Hawley PR, et al: Pouch-vaginal fistulas. Br J Surg 80:936, 1993

59. Lee PY, Fazio VW, Church JM, et al: Vaginal fistula following restorative proctocolectomy. Dis Colon Rectum 40:752, 1997

60. Lohmuller JL, Pemberton JH, Dozois RR, et al: Pouchitis and extraintestinal manifestations of inflammatory bowel disease after ileal pouch–anal anastomosis. Ann Surg 211:622, 1990

61. Bullard KM, Madoff RD, Gemlo BT: Is ileoanal pouch function stable with time? Results of a prospective audit. Dis Colon Rectum 45:299, 2002

62. Brunel M, Penna C, Tiret E, et al: Restorative proctocolectomy for distal ulcerative colitis. Gut 45:542, 1999

63. Martin A, Dinca M, Leone L, et al: Quality of life after proctocolectomy and ileo-anal anastomosis for severe ulcerative colitis. Am J Gastroenterol 93:166, 1998

64. Fazio VW, O'Riordan MG, Lavery IC, et al: Long-term functional outcome and quality of life after stapled restorative proctocolectomy. Ann Surg 230:575, 1999

65. Kohler LW, Pemberton JH, Zinsmeister AR, et al: Quality of life after proctocolectomy: a comparison of Brooke ileostomy, Kock pouch, ileal pouch–anal anastomosis. Gastroenterology 101:679, 1991

66. Pemberton JH, Phillips SF, Ready RR, et al: Quality of life after Brooke ileostomy and ileal pouch–anal anastomosis: comparision of performance status. Ann Surg 209:620, 1989

67. Pezim ME, Nicholls RJ: Quality of life after restorative proctocolectomy with pelvic ileal reservoir. Br J Surg 72:31, 1985

68. Jimmo B, Hyman NH: Is ileal pouch–anal anastomosis really the procedure of choice for patients with ulcerative colitis? Dis Colon Rectum 41:41, 1998

69. McLeod RS, Churchill DN, Lock AM, et al: Quality of life of patients with ulcerative colitis preoperatively and postoperatively. Gastroenterology 101:1307, 1991

70. Weinryb RM, Gustavsson JP, Liljeqvist L, et al: A prospective study of the quality of life after pelvic pouch operation. J Am Coll Surg 180:589, 1995

71. O'Bichere A, Wilkinson K, Rumbles S, et al: Functional outcomes after restorative panproctocolectomy for ulcerative colitis decreases an otherwise enhanced quality of life. Br J Surg 87:802, 2000

72. Young-Fadok TM, Dozois ED, Sandborn WJ, et al: A case-matched study of laparoscopic proctocolectomy and ileal pouch–anal anastomosis (IPAA) versus open IPAA for ulcerative colitis (abstract). Gastroenterology A-452, 2001

73. Hahnloser D, Young-Fadok TM: Earlier postoperative spontaneous diuresis in laparoscopic versus open total proctocolectomy and ileal pouch–anal anastomosis. Surg Endosc 17:S238, 2003

74. Kienle P, Weitz J, Benner A, et al: Laparoscopically assisted colectomy and ileoanal pouch procedure with and without protective ileostomy. Surg Endosc 17:716, 2003

Acknowledgment

Figures 1 through 10   Tom Moore.

Toyooki Sonoda, M.D., and Jeffrey W. Milsom, M.D., F.A.C.S.

Segmental (or partial) resections of the colon are commonly performed throughout the world to treat both benign and malignant disease. Benign conditions that may be treated with these procedures include polyps, inflammatory bowel disease, diverticulitis, hemorrhage, ischemia, trauma, and redundancy (e.g., volvulus, constipation, or rectal prolapse). However, malignant conditions, as a group, constitute the most common indication for colon resection. Adenocarcinoma is the neoplasm for which segmental colectomy is most commonly performed in most Western countries, but there are a number of other neoplasms (e.g., carcinoid tumor, lymphoma, leiomyoma, and leiomyosarcoma) for which such treatment may also be indicated. Detailed knowledge of the relevant surgical anatomy and a systematic approach to colonic mobilization are essential to the performance of a safe and oncologically sound segmental colectomy.

Operative Planning

BENIGN VERSUS MALIGNANT DISEASE

The differences between segmental colon resections done to treat benign disease and those done to treat malignancies are fundamentally important and may have a substantial effect on outcome. Accordingly, before specific techniques are described, it is worthwhile to review these differences, paying particular attention to the basic principles of and justifications for oncologic resections.

Resections for Benign Disease

For patients with benign colon disease, removal of the diseased portion of the bowel in such a way as to leave uninvolved, healthy, and well-vascularized margins should be sufficient treatment. When indicated, the proximal and distal ends are anastomosed to restore continuity of the bowel. In these benign cases, dissection of the mesentery should be performed where it is easiest and most convenient. To this end, the major named branches are usually divided in their midportions: if the mesentery is divided within a few centimeters of the bowel wall, many of the small mesenteric branches will have to be ligated, which is inconvenient and time-consuming [*see Figure 1*].

Modern electrosurgical devices, such as the LigaSure vessel sealing system (Valleylab, Boulder, Colorado), can reliably seal mesenteric vessels as large as 7 mm in diameter without the traditional clamping and tying, and they can reduce operating times during more extensive colon resections (whether laparoscopic or open). The LigaSure Atlas and the LigaSure V use bipolar current and have a built-in knife that allows the surgeon to seal and divide the vessel in a single maneuver.

Certain inflammatory conditions (e.g., Crohn disease and diverticulitis) may result in such severe pericolic inflammation and thickening that dissection of the mesentery close to the bowel wall may not be possible. In these cases, it may be necessary to perform a more radical mesenteric dissection in an area where the mesentery is softer. Severe inflammatory adhesions may cause the bowel

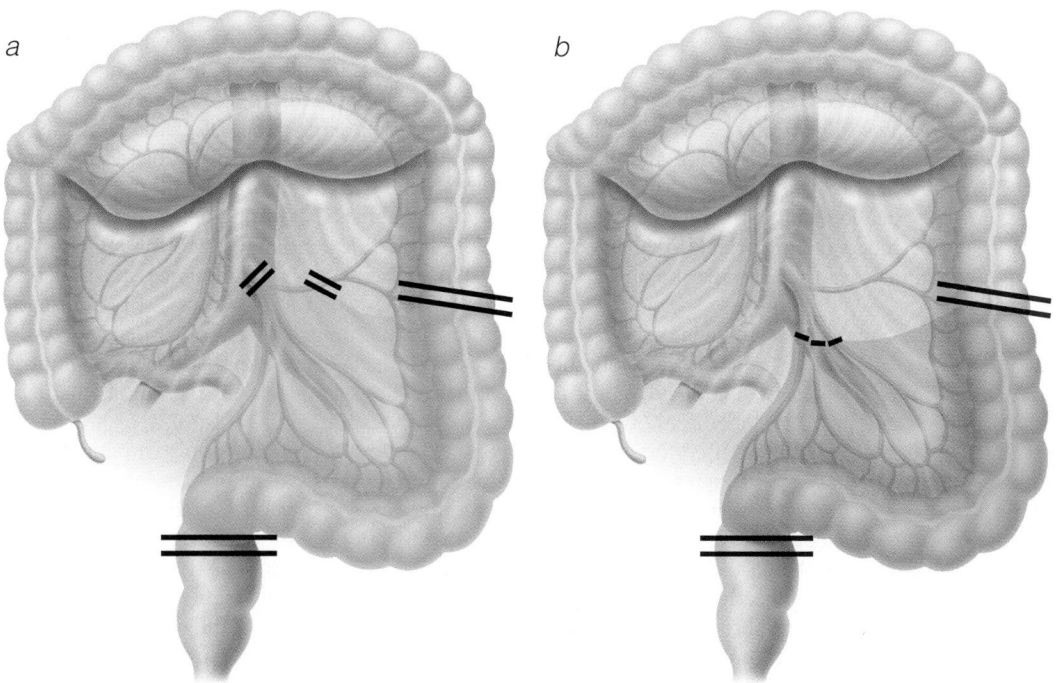

a   *b*

Figure 1 **Illustrated is the difference between (*a*) malignant and (*b*) benign resections of the sigmoid colon.**

to be stuck to the retroperitoneum, making the usual lateral mobilization of the colon nearly impossible. In these cases, early division of the mesentery (i.e., medial-to-lateral mobilization of the colon) may provide easier access to the proper plane of dissection, where the tissues are soft (i.e., in the retromesenteric plane anterior to Toldt's retroperitoneal fascia [*see Figure 2*]). This approach may help minimize the risk of injury to retroperitoneal organs (e.g., the ureter).

Resections for Malignant Disease

Colon resections for malignancy should include radical en bloc removal of the draining lymphovascular complex, with bowel margins wide enough to limit intraluminal and pericolic (lymphatic) recurrence. The drainage of the lymphatic system mirrors that of the vascular system. In the case of colon carcinomas, there are two possible directions for lymphatic drainage: (1) paraintestinal (along the intestine) and (2) central (along named mesenteric vessels). To prevent regional lymphatic recurrence, the major draining mesenteric vessel should be divided at the point of origin, together with the accompanying lymphatic network. If the tumor is equidistant from two named mesenteric vessels, both vessels should be ligated proximally.

Although, in most cases, intramural spreading of cancer should not exceed 2 cm,[1,2] an oncologic resection of the abdominal colon should aim at achieving proximal and distal margins of at least 5 to 10 cm to ensure adequate procurement of the epicolic and pericolic lymph nodes.[3,4] The two exceptions to this rule are in resection of rectal cancer, where a margin of 1 to 2 cm is accepted as part of a sphincter-saving operation, and in resection of a cecal carcinoma, where the ileum can be divided close to the ileocecal valve without compromising the oncologic outcome, provided that the lymphatic vessels along the ileocolic pedicle are removed. The ultimate length of the resected bowel segment is dictated by the lymphovascular resection. Large adenomatous polyps may harbor cancer, especially when they are villous, and resections for this indication should also include wide mesenteric clearance.

Oncologic principles   There is increasing evidence that the quality of the operation done to treat colorectal carcinoma is directly correlated with the quality of the oncologic outcome. To date, the bulk of this evidence has come from studies of rectal carcinoma, but the correlation appears to hold true for colon cancer as well. In an excellent study carried out by the German Colon Cancer Study Group, the treating surgeon and the treating institution were found to be independent variables that affected both survival and locoregional recurrence after colon cancer resections.[5]

The concept that surgical technique may influence survival was first popularized in the 1960s. In a classic study (that has nonetheless been criticized for its uncontrolled methodology), Turnbull and associates retrospectively compared the outcomes of patients who underwent resections for malignancy that used the no-touch isolation technique with the outcomes of patients who underwent more traditional resections performed by other surgeons.[6] The patients who underwent no-touch oncologic resections had a better 5-year survival. In the no-touch isolation technique, draining mesenteric vessels are ligated at their origin early in the dissection, and the bowel is divided proximal and distal to the lesion before the tumor is mobilized; as a result, the tumor is effectively isolated from intraluminal and hematogenous spillage during manipulation. This operative technique makes sense in the light of reports suggesting that malignant cells may be shed into the portal circu-

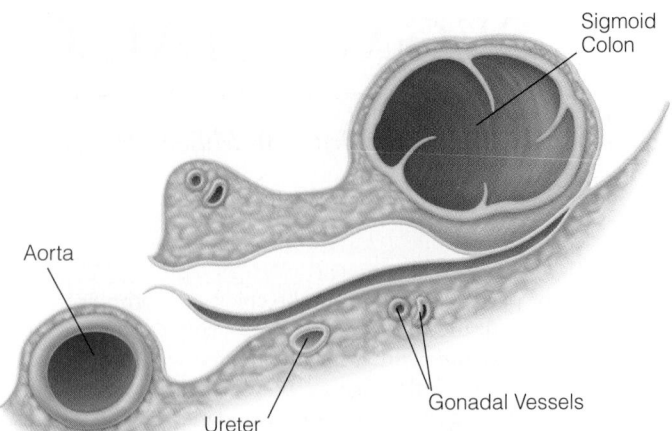

Sigmoid Colon

Aorta

Ureter

Gonadal Vessels

Figure 2   **In patients with severe inflammatory conditions of the colon, early division of the mesentery provides access to the retromesenteric plane medially.**

lation during colon cancer operations (though the evidence for this phenomenon is still inconclusive).[7-9]

To date, only one randomized, prospective trial has compared the no-touch isolation technique with conventional techniques for the curative treatment of colon cancer. In this trial, which involved 236 patients, there was no significant difference in 5-year survival between the no-touch group and the conventional group, though there was a trend toward better cancer-related survival in the former.[10] Fewer liver metastases were observed in the no-touch group, and those that were observed seemed to develop later. This study was criticized on the grounds that the mean numbers of lymph nodes harvested were only 3.8 and 4.8 for conventional and no-touch operations, respectively, which raised questions about the quality of the oncologic resections. However, the authors pointed out that the study was designed to analyze only the effects of early lymphovascular isolation and that extensive lymphadenectomies were not performed.

Another randomized, prospective trial compared extended resections with segmental resections for treatment of carcinoma of the left colon. In this trial, 260 patients with cancer between the distal transverse colon and the rectosigmoid were randomly assigned to undergo either left hemicolectomy or segmental colectomy.[11] The lymphadenectomy done as part of the left hemicolectomy extended to the origin of the inferior mesenteric artery (IMA), whereas that done as part of the segmental colectomy was more limited, extending only to the region of the left colic artery (LCA). There was no difference in survival between the two groups, even when Dukes class C (TNM stage III) cancers were compared. Although a few retrospective studies have suggested that a more extensive lymphadenectomy improves survival, there remains some disagreement regarding whether true high ligation accomplishes this goal.[12-14] Intuitively, it would seem that high ligation should affect survival only in patients who have malignant lymph node involvement up to—but not past—the origin of the draining vessel. However, an adequate lymphadenectomy is undoubtedly important for accurate staging, and the current recommendation is that at least 13 lymph nodes should be harvested to ensure a high degree of staging accuracy.[15]

Although the quality of the operation does appear to affect the oncologic outcome, routine use of no-touch isolation for curative treatment of colon cancer is not currently an evidence-based practice. We believe that the risk of locoregional recurrences can be minimized by maintaining the following principles:

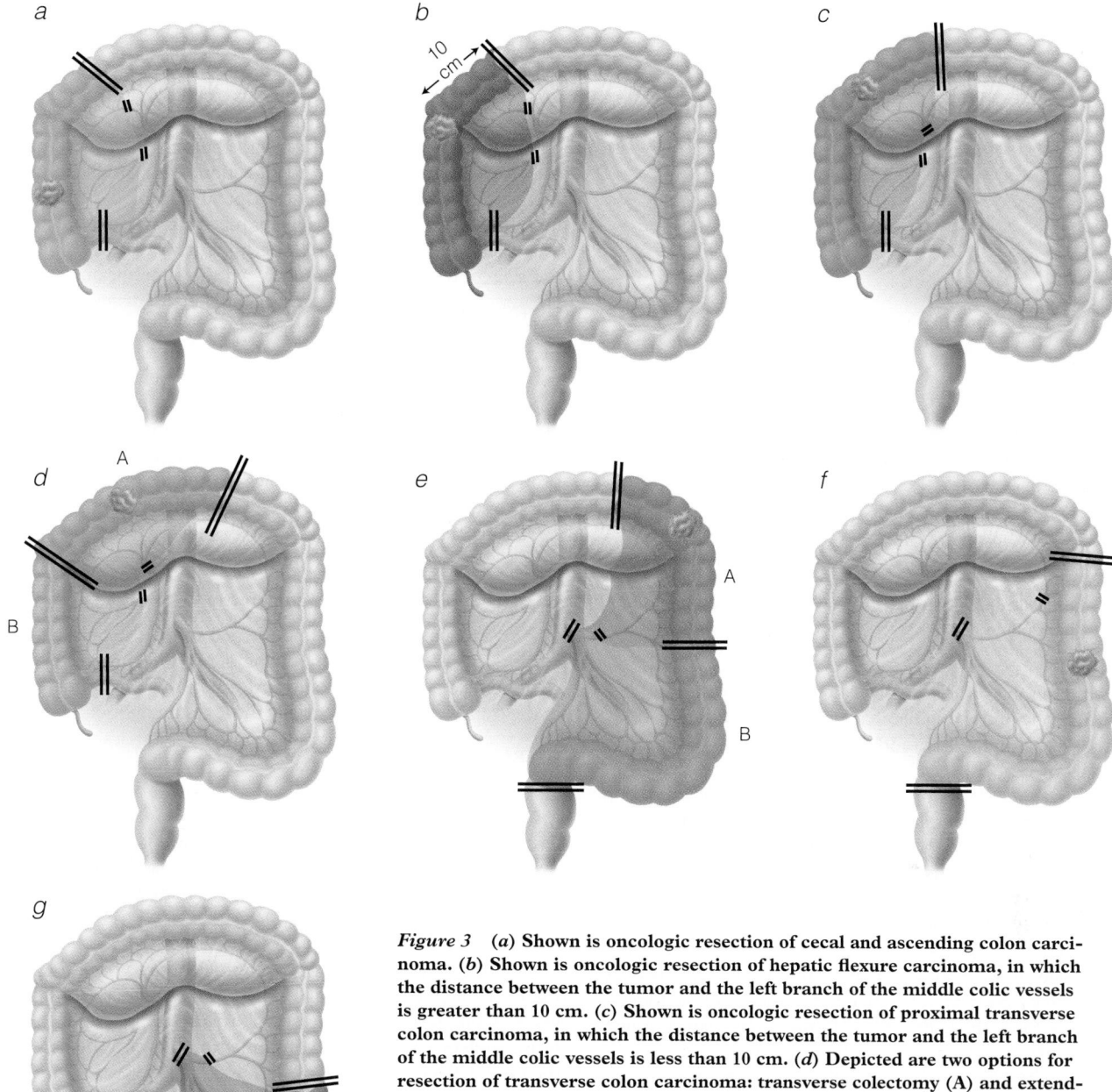

Figure 3 (*a*) Shown is oncologic resection of cecal and ascending colon carcinoma. (*b*) Shown is oncologic resection of hepatic flexure carcinoma, in which the distance between the tumor and the left branch of the middle colic vessels is greater than 10 cm. (*c*) Shown is oncologic resection of proximal transverse colon carcinoma, in which the distance between the tumor and the left branch of the middle colic vessels is less than 10 cm. (*d*) Depicted are two options for resection of transverse colon carcinoma: transverse colectomy (A) and extended right hemicolectomy (A plus B). (*e*) Depicted are two options for resection of splenic flexure carcinoma: splenic flexure resection (A) and left hemicolectomy (A plus B). (*f*) Shown is oncologic resection of descending colon carcinoma. (*g*) Shown is oncologic resection of sigmoid colon carcinoma.

1. Wide mesenteric clearance, including high ligation of all draining mesenteric vessels.
2. Minimization of trauma to the tumor during mobilization.
3. Adequate proximal and distal bowel margins.
4. Wide clearance of tumor in cases of contiguous organ invasion.
5. Complete and accurate intraoperative exploration.

It can be argued that the no-touch isolation technique is an important component of oncologic surgical principles. Certainly, this technique adds little to the difficulty of the operation and can be performed without causing additional morbidity. We continue to employ the no-touch technique in the resection of

colon carcinomas. Recommended resections of the abdominal colon for cancer depend on the location of the tumor [*see Figure 3*].

LAPAROSCOPIC VERSUS OPEN RESECTION

Laparoscopic surgical treatment of colorectal disease has been slow to gain acceptance, primarily because the techniques are difficult to master, the operations are longer, and the ileus response is still not eliminated after the procedure. At present, the overwhelming majority of colon resections in the United States are still being performed by conventional means.

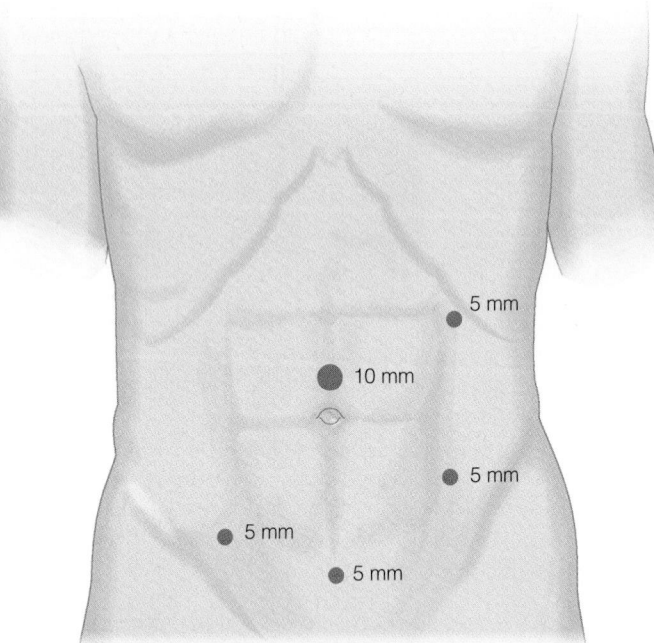

Figure 4 **Laparoscopic right hemicolectomy. Illustrated is recommended port placement.**

A growing number of reports have described short-term benefits of laparoscopy in treating benign conditions of the colon (e.g., diverticulitis, Crohn disease, and ulcerative colitis). Controlled studies performed by experienced surgeons have found laparoscopy to have advantages over open resection in terms of resolution of ileus, duration of hospitalization, level of postoperative pain, recovery of pulmonary function, and complication rates.[16-20] Even some cost analyses favor laparoscopic colectomy over conventional surgery, finding that the higher costs of the surgical instruments and the potentially longer operating times are outweighed by the shorter duration of hospitalization.[21-24] There also appears to be a lower incidence of surgical site complications after laparoscopy than after open surgery, as well as a lower incidence of postoperative adhesions (and thus, possibly, of subsequent small bowel obstruction).[25,26]

Fear of port-site recurrences initially kept laparoscopy from being widely accepted in the treatment of colorectal carcinoma, but several randomized, controlled studies reported that the wound recurrence rates with laparoscopic resections were no different from those with open resections.[27-31] Particularly significant were the long-awaited results of the randomized, prospective trial carried out by the Clinical Outcomes of Surgical Therapy (COST) Study Group, which found the oncologic outcomes of open and laparoscopic surgery to be similar after a median follow-up period of 4.4 years.[31] Also noteworthy was a randomized, prospective trial from Barcelona, which reported that cancer-related survival was actually better after laparoscopic surgery for colon cancer than after open surgery.[29] Further randomized trials are under way in Europe and Australia. These studies have helped lift the virtual moratorium on laparoscopic treatment of colorectal cancer, but surgeons must be reminded that they must first gain adequate laparoscopic experience with benign conditions of the colon before attempting laparoscopy for malignant disease.

APPROACHES TO MOBILIZATION OF COLON

The development of laparoscopy has given prominence to the concept of medial-to-lateral mobilization of the colon, as opposed to the lateral mobilization employed in most open colectomies. In all, there are four main approaches to mobilizing the colon. With the lateral approach, the lateral attachment of the colon is divided first, and the retromesenteric plane is then developed in a lateral-to-medial fashion. With the medial-to-lateral approach, the mesenteric vessels are isolated first, and the retromesenteric plane is then developed in an outward direction, with the lateral attachments of the colon left alone to suspend the colon during medial mobilization. With the inferior approach (as in right colectomy), the ileal attachment to the retroperitoneum is dissected initially in the direction of the duodenum. With the superior approach, the greater omentum and the transverse colon are dissected first.

It is quite possible—indeed, likely—that during the mobilization of a given colon segment, several or all of these approaches may be used sequentially. One approach may suit a particular patient better than another one does, and it is not uncommon for one approach to be abandoned in favor of another in the middle of the operation. Accordingly, it is important that surgeons achieve proficiency with all four approaches to mobilization. Provided that the proper dissection plane is entered, all four approaches will eventually converge.

Laparoscopic Right Hemicolectomy

A right hemicolectomy is performed to treat neoplasms of the cecum, the ascending colon, or the hepatic flexure. An extended right hemicolectomy is usually performed to treat tumors located in the transverse colon, especially those to the right of the midline.

OPERATIVE TECHNIQUE

Step 1: Placement of Ports

The patient is placed in a modified lithotomy position. Four 5 mm ports and one 10 mm port are placed [*see Figure 4*]. The surgeon can stand either between the patient's legs or on the patient's left.

Step 2: Isolation of Ileocolic Pedicle

The patient is moved into the Trendelenburg position, with the right side tilted up. The greater omentum is raised above the transverse colon, and the transverse colon is retracted superiorly. The terminal ileum is allowed to drop inferiorly toward the pelvis, and the proximal small bowel loops are swept to the patient's left. The

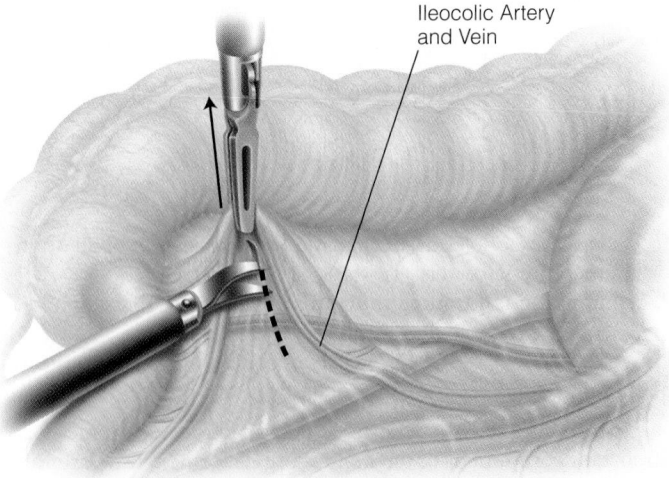

Ileocolic Artery
and Vein

Figure 5 **Laparoscopic right hemicolectomy. The ileocolic pedicle is dissected in the direction of its origin and isolated.**

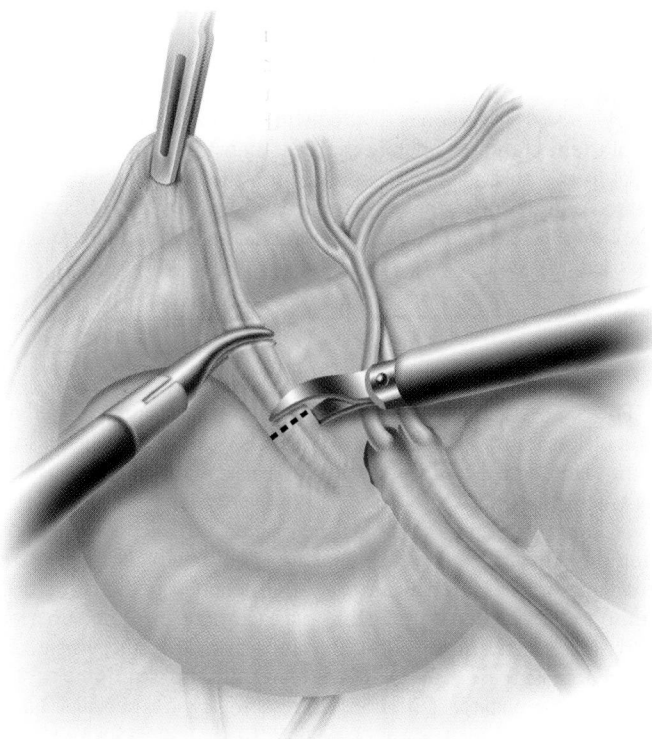

Figure 6 **Laparoscopic right hemicolectomy. The right colic vein and the artery accompanying it to the hepatic flexure are isolated and divided.**

duodenum is initially identified through the mesentery, just to the right of the superior mesenteric vessels at the angle between the transverse mesocolon and the right colonic mesentery. With anterolateral traction placed on the ileocecal junction, the ileocolic pedicle can be seen "bowstringing" through the mesentery, just inferior to the duodenum. Studies of arterial anatomy show that the ileocolic artery (ICA) is a constant structure and that, in almost

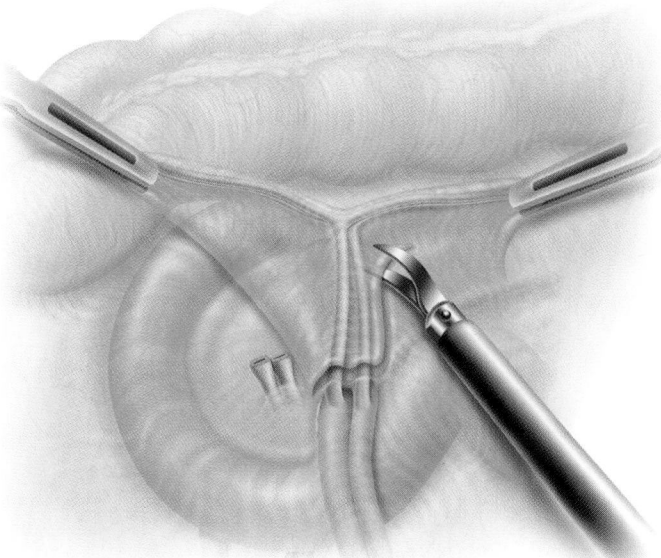

Figure 7 **Laparoscopic right hemicolectomy. The main trunk of the middle colic artery is most easily accessed via a plane created to the left of the vessel.**

90% of cases, the right colic artery (RCA) branches off from the ICA, not from the superior mesenteric artery (SMA). A window is made in the mesentery inferior and superior to the ileocolic pedicle, and the pedicle is dissected in the direction of its origin and ligated [*see Figure 5*]. Ligation can be accomplished by means of clips, vascular staplers, or the LigaSure Atlas; unless clips are used, the ICA and the ileocolic vein (ICV) can be ligated together.

Step 3: Dissection of Middle Colic Vessels

Next, the thin cut edge of the transverse mesocolon overlying the duodenum is grasped, and the duodenum is carefully swept down in a posterior direction. This measure initiates the medial-to-lateral mobilization of the transverse colon. The head of the pancreas is bluntly dissected, with care taken not to avulse the right colic vein or a branch of the inferior pancreaticoduodenal vein. A plane is gently developed to the right of the middle colic vessels. If this dissection proves difficult, the planned medial-to-lateral mobilization approach should be abandoned in favor of superior mobilization, and the omentum should be dissected off the transverse colon. In this way, access behind the middle colic artery (MCA) is facilitated.

The first vessel encountered to the right of the middle colic vessels is a venous branch to the right colic flexure. This branch converges with the right gastroepiploic vein (GEV) to form Henle's gastrocolic trunk, which empties into the superior mesenteric vein (SMV). The right colic vein (RCV) should be divided proximally so as to spare the right GEV. In some cases, an artery accompanies the RCV to the hepatic flexure; if present, this artery should be divided proximally, together with the vein [*see Figure 6*]. The peritoneum overlying the middle colic vasculature is then opened from right to left, and the right branch of the MCA is isolated and divided at its origin, with care taken to preserve the left branch. The anatomy of the MCA is quite variable, and the classic pattern of a single trunk that bifurcates into right and left branches occurs in only 46% of cases. Instead, one, two, or even three vessels may arise from the SMA to supply the transverse colon.

In the case of an extended right hemicolectomy, the main trunk of the MCA should be divided at its takeoff from the SMA at the base of the pancreas. To this end, the peritoneum overlying the base of the middle colic vessels is opened from right to left, and a dissection plane is created to the left of the MCA [*see Figure 7*]. Access behind the middle colic vessels is best gained by proceeding from left to right, with the surgeon operating from the patient's left side. The middle colic vessels are isolated and divided at the appropriate level. After ligation of the middle colic vessels, an area of the transverse colon is chosen as the distal transection line, and the transverse mesocolon is divided in the direction of the bowel wall.

Step 4: Medial-to-Lateral Mobilization of Right Colon

The transverse mesocolon is then lifted anteriorly, and blunt medial-to-lateral dissection of the colon is performed, extending the previous dissection plane above the duodenum to the patient's right [*see Figure 8*]. Care should be taken to ensure that the dissection plane remains anterior to Toldt's retroperitoneal fascia (the white line of Toldt). The dissection is extended underneath the hepatic flexure, then underneath the right colon and the cecum. The right ureter should remain safely underneath an intact retroperitoneal fascia.

Step 5: Inferior Mobilization of Ileum and Lateral Mobilization of Right Colon

Next, the terminal ileum is retracted out of the pelvis. With strong traction applied anteriorly and cephalad, the ileal attach-

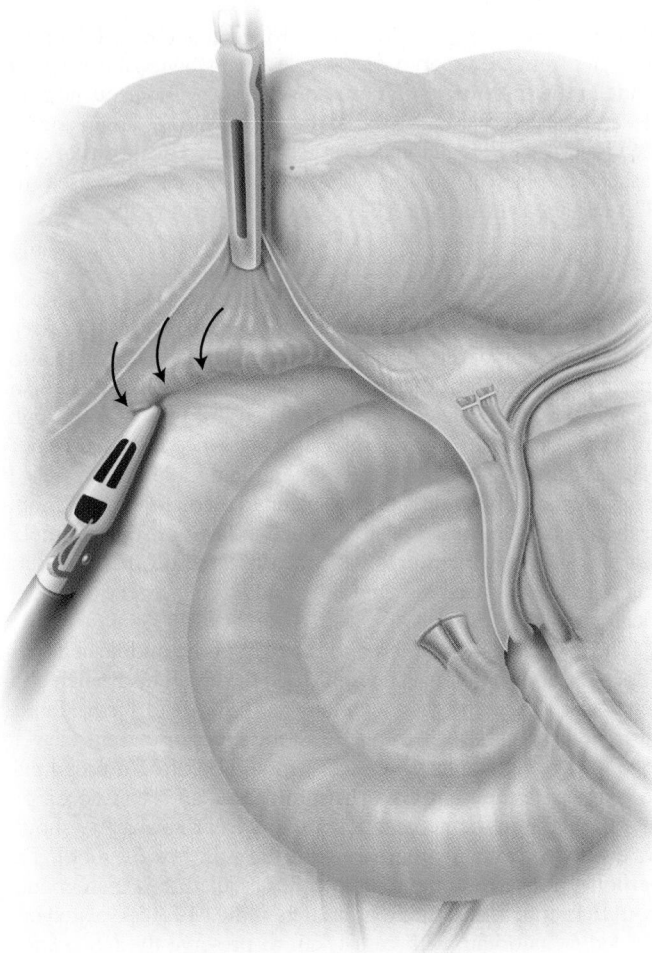

Figure 8 **Laparoscopic right hemicolectomy. The right colon undergoes medial-to-lateral retromesenteric dissection, with the lateral attachments remaining untouched.**

ment to the retroperitoneum is exposed and the peritoneum incised. If the medial dissection was adequate, this attachment will be thin; if not, the retroperitoneum may remain adherent to the cecum, in which case it will be necessary to identify the right ureter as it crosses over the right iliac vessels to ensure that it is not injured during mobilization. After the dissection has met the previous medial dissection plane, it is continued around the appendix and the cecum, and the lateral attachments of the right colon are taken down [*see Figure 9*]. Dissection of the hepatic flexure will become difficult with this approach. To resolve the difficulty, the patient is taken out of the Trendelenburg position, and the surgeon moves to the patient's left. The omentum is further dissected off the proximal transverse colon from left to right, and the takedown of the hepatic flexure is completed via this approach.

Step 6: Exteriorization, Resection, and Anastomosis

The appendix is grasped with a bowel clamp. A minilaparotomy is made, either as a midline extension of the umbilical port incision or in the epigastrium, depending on the transverse colon reach. It is usually about 5 cm long, but the size may be adjusted, depending on the size of the tumor. A wound protector is inserted to keep the surgical site from being contaminated by tumor. The mobilized right colon is then exteriorized.

Extracorporeally, the terminal ileum is cleaned and divided proximal to the ileocecal valve with a linear stapler. The ileal

mesentery is dissected from the divided ileum toward the cut edge of the ileocolic pedicle, and the ileal and accessory ileal branches are ligated. The marginal artery of the transverse colon is ligated, and the transverse colon is divided with a linear stapler 5 to 10 cm distal to the tumor to liberate the specimen.

As in the equivalent open procedure, the anastomosis is then created extracorporeally with either handsewn stitches or staples. The bowel is replaced into the abdomen, and the minilaparotomy is closed.

TROUBLESHOOTING

Injury to Superior Mesenteric Vessels

The SMV is fragile and is susceptible to sharp injury, as well as to avulsion injury at the origin of the ICV caused by aggressive blunt dissection. Accordingly, the area around this vessel must be dissected with particular care. To prevent sharp injury to the SMV, the peritoneum overlying the origin of the ileocolic pedicle should be dissected first; this measure should help clarify the vascular anatomy. During ligation of the ileocolic pedicle, a small stump should be left to prevent encroachment into the superior mesenteric vessels. If bleeding develops from the cut pedicle, an absorbable 2-0 tie can be placed around the stump with an Endoloop applicator (Ethicon Endo-Surgery, Somerville, New Jersey).

Injury to Inferior Pancreaticoduodenal Vein or Right Gastroepiploic Vein

The head of the pancreas is susceptible to significant venous bleeding, especially when a branch of the inferior pancreaticoduodenal vein is torn during aggressive blunt mobilization. The right GEV is also at risk for division or injury with proximal ligation of the RVC. Any blunt dissection at the pancreatic head must be performed gently. It should be kept in mind that the RCV converges with the right GEV at the head of the pancreas. To prevent injury to the right GEV, the transverse colon should be lifted anteriorly, and only the vein or veins traveling to the colon should be divided; any veins traveling underneath the colon toward the stomach should be spared.

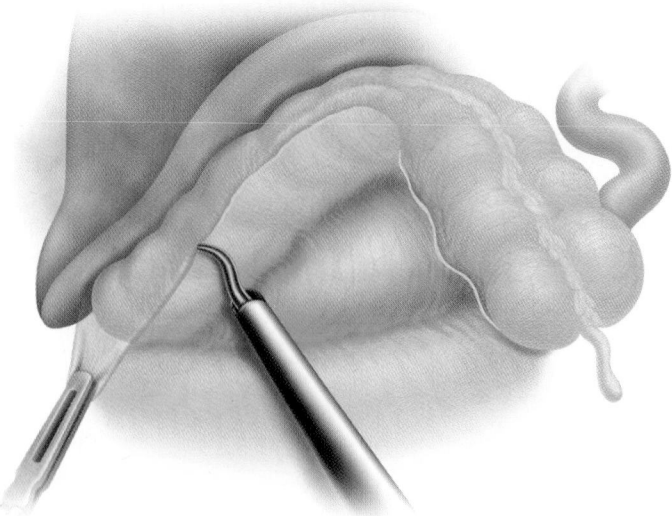

Figure 9 **Laparoscopic right hemicolectomy. The right colon is mobilized laterally.**

Injury to Duodenal Sweep

Because the origin of the ileocolic pedicle is always in close proximity to the duodenal sweep, the latter structure is at risk for injury during dissection of the former. Accordingly, during the mobilization and division of the ileocolic pedicle, the duodenum should be identified and bluntly swept away to ensure that it is not subjected to sharp injury or accidental cauterization.

Injury to Right Ureter

As a rule, in a properly performed laparoscopic right hemicolectomy, the ureter should remain underneath Toldt's retroperitoneal fascia, and thus, the surgeon should be able to complete the operation without seeing a skeletonized right ureter. However, injury to the right ureter remains a risk. If Toldt's fascia cannot be clearly visualized via a medial approach and the dissection plane is unclear during the isolation of the ileocolic pedicle, it is advisable to switch to an inferior approach and mobilize the ileum off the retroperitoneum, identifying the right ureter and tracing it toward the duodenum before dividing the pedicle. Right ureter injury most commonly occurs over the right iliac vessels during cecal mobilization; accordingly, care should be taken to make sure that the dissection plane is not too posterior.

Mobilization Posterior to Gerota's Fat

In some patients, Gerota's fat is fused to the posterior aspect of the right colon mesentery. When this is the case, there is a risk that Gerota's fat will be entered during either medial or lateral mobilization—or, worse, that dissection will take place posterior to the kidney during lateral mobilization. To minimize this risk, one must carefully look for Toldt's retroperitoneal fascia during both medial and lateral mobilization, then make sure to push down this fascia and remain anterior to it.

Twisting of Ileum during Anastomosis

During anastomosis, the terminal ileum (or, less commonly, the transverse colon) can be twisted 360° around its mesentery. The twisting tends to occur after division of the ileum, while the surgeon is concentrating on the transverse colon; often, it is not visible through a minilaparotomy and consequently goes unnoticed. To prevent this complication, two seromuscular stay sutures, one proximal and one distal, may be placed into the ileum after the right colon is exteriorized and the terminal ileum and the mesentery are divided. These stay sutures are clamped individually and are never crossed. Once the anastomosis has been created, a final look through the laparoscope can confirm that the mesenteric orientation is correct.

Open Right Hemicolectomy

The major elements of open right hemicolectomy are essentially the same as those of the corresponding laparoscopic procedure [see Laparoscopic Right Hemicolectomy, above]: (1) vascular isolation, (2) bowel division, (3) mobilization, and (4) anastomosis. The length of the resected specimen should be the same for the open version of the operation as for the laparoscopic version. In what follows, we describe the no-touch isolation technique, which is our preferred approach.

OPERATIVE TECHNIQUE

Step 1: Incision

Although the operation is technically feasible through either a transverse incision or a midline incision, we prefer to use a midline incision. Superiorly, the incision should extend about two thirds of the distance between the umbilicus and the xiphoid; inferiorly, it should extend about one third of the distance between the umbilicus and the pubic symphysis. The abdomen is explored for metastatic disease, and an abdominal retractor is inserted. A simple retractor, such as a Balfour or Alexis wound retractor, will usually suffice, though some additional manual retraction may be necessary. Some surgeons prefer to use a Thompson or Omni retractor, either of which will be more cumbersome to set up than a Balfour or Alexis retractor but will allow a wider field of retraction.

Step 2: Division of Ileocolic Pedicle

The tumor is identified but is not extensively manipulated. The omentum and the transverse colon are retracted superiorly, and any obvious lymph node enlargement is addressed along the ileocolic and middle colic vessels, the right gastroepiploic vessels, and the superior mesenteric vessels. If malignant involvement is suspected, a central lymph node may be sampled and evaluated by frozen-section examination. The ileocolic pedicle is identified as in a laparoscopic right hemicolectomy. A mesenteric window is made superior and inferior to the ileocolic pedicle, and the pedicle is isolated between two fingers. Both the artery and the vein are dissected in the direction of their origin from the superior mesenteric vessels, and the pedicle is clamped, divided, and tied.

Step 3: Dissection of Middle Colic Vessels

Next, the duodenum and the head of the pancreas are gently mobilized posteriorly and are bluntly swept away from the posterior aspect of the transverse mesocolon to expose the right side of the middle colic vessels. A dissecting clamp is placed underneath the peritoneum at the superior aspect of the divided ileocolic pedicle, and the peritoneum is incised just to the right of the superior mesenteric vessels in the direction of the trunk of the middle colic vessels. The peritoneum is then further incised along the right side of the middle colic trunk past the bifurcation of the middle colic vessels. (Delineation of these vessels can be facilitated by transillumination of the transverse mesocolon from the superior aspect.)

The right branches of the middle colic vessels are then carefully isolated and divided at their origins; the left branches are spared. The dissection is extended back toward the pancreas, and the RCV is divided at its origin, with the right GEV spared [see Laparoscopic Right Hemicolectomy, above]. The transverse mesocolon is dissected outward toward the transverse colon wall, where the marginal artery is divided and tied. The omentum is dissected away from the right half of the transverse colon, and the transverse colon is transected with a linear cutting stapler (for a stapled anastomosis) or divided between clamps (for a handsewn anastomosis).

If, during any part of this dissection, the anatomy of the middle colic vessels is unclear, it is advisable to switch to a superior approach. In this approach, the omentum is dissected away from the right half of the transverse colon and the mesocolon, and the transverse colon is cleaned off and divided at the appropriate level. The transverse mesocolon is then dissected in a central direction. The marginal artery is divided, and the mesentery is divided with the electrocautery in the direction of the bifurcation of the middle colic vessels. At this point, the right branch of the middle colic system should be easily identifiable. After the right branch is divided, the RCV is identified and divided near the head of the pancreas—again, with the right GEV spared.

Step 4: Division of Ileum and Ileal Mesentery

Next, the terminal ileum is retracted forcefully out of the pelvis and dissected free of the retroperitoneal structures along Toldt's

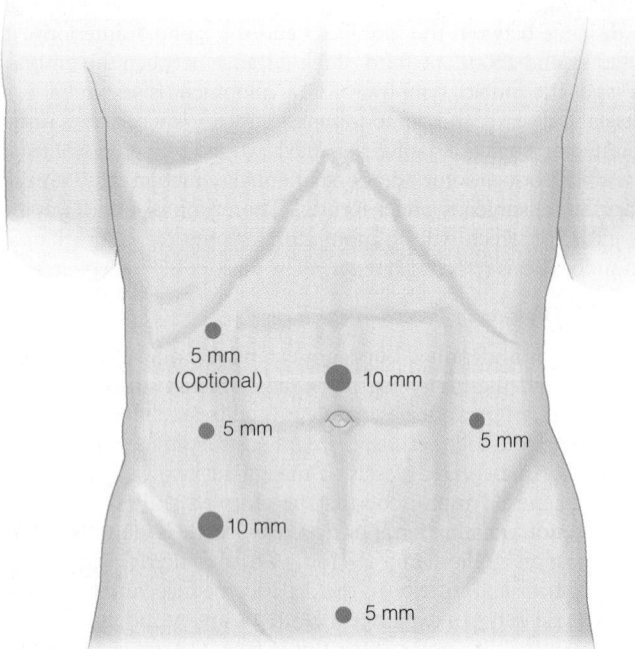

Figure 10 **Laparoscopic sigmoid colectomy. Illustrated is recommended port placement.**

retroperitoneal fascia. The terminal ileum is cleaned off and divided about 5 cm proximal to the ileocecal valve, either with a linear cutting stapler or between clamps. The ileal mesentery is then divided in the direction of the cut ileocolic pedicle. The marginal artery and the ileal and accessory ileal branches are divided. This step completes the isolation of the tumor before any manipulation of the cancer-bearing segment.

Step 5: Mobilization of Right Colon

The rest of the bowel mobilization is carried out via the lateral approach. With the ileocecal region retracted cephalad, the peritoneum is incised around the cecum along the white line of Toldt. A finger is passed through the peritoneal defect, and the cecum is retracted away from the retroperitoneum to facilitate this dissection. It is important that the dissection remain anterior to the right

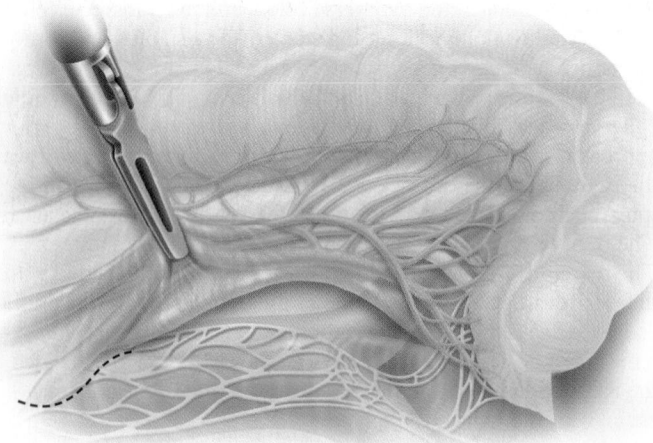

Figure 11 **Laparoscopic sigmoid colectomy. A wide peritoneal window is created to provide access to the avascular plane posterior to the inferior mesenteric vessels.**

ureter and the gonadal vessels. Dissection is continued around the cecum, and the right colon is mobilized along the white line of Toldt in the direction of the hepatic flexure. Some degree of fusion may be present between Toldt's retroperitoneal fascia and the mesentery, causing the mobilization to stray posterior to Gerota's fascia or even the right kidney; however, the correct dissection plane always remains anterior to the retroperitoneal fascia. A finger is passed underneath the peritoneal layers of the hepatic flexure, and the flexure is mobilized with the electrocautery.

As the right colon is peeled away from the retroperitoneal fascia, the duodenum is identified. The duodenal attachments to the mobilized right colon are divided to free the specimen.

Step 6: Anastomosis

The anastomosis between the ileum and the transverse colon can be created with any of several handsewn or stapled techniques (e.g., end-to end, end-to-side, side-to-side, or functional end-to-end). Basic anastomotic techniques are discussed in greater detail elsewhere [*see 71 Intestinal Anastomosis*]. For present purposes, it is sufficient to note that all of the various approaches to intestinal anastomosis, if constructed well, should yield essentially equal results in terms of postoperative function and rate of leakage. Whichever approach is adopted, it is essential that the cut ends of the bowel be well perfused. If bowel perfusion is in doubt, one should check for bleeding from the cut bowel edge or assess the marginal artery for pulses or bleeding. The mesenteric window need not be closed after creation of the anastomosis, because it is usually large and a mesenteric hernia with incarceration is exceedingly rare.

Laparoscopic Sigmoid Colectomy

Step 1: Placement of Ports

The patient is placed in a modified lithotomy position. Three or four 5 mm ports, one 10 mm port, and one 12 mm port are placed [*see Figure 10*]. When addressing the left lower quadrant, the surgeon stands to the patient's right, with the assistant standing to the patient's left. When mobilizing the splenic flexure, the surgeon stands between the patient's legs, with the assistant standing to the patient's right.

Step 2: Isolation and Division of Inferior Mesenteric Vessels

The patient is moved into a steep Trendelenburg position, with the left side tilted up. With the medial-to-lateral approach to mobilization, the IMA is first approached medially. The sigmoid colon is retracted strongly out of the pelvis, and the sigmoid mesocolon is placed on anterolateral traction by the assistant. The initial dissection plane is just posterior to the IMA, where there is a clear avascular space, and the dissection is best begun at the sacral promontory. A wide peritoneal incision is made in the sigmoid mesentery [*see Figure 11*]. The right and left hypogastric nerves are swept away from the inferior mesenteric vessels in a posterior direction. The dissection plane is then extended laterally toward the abdominal wall, staying anterior to Toldt's retroperitoneal fascia. The left ureter must be identified before the next step is initiated; if it cannot be identified, it should be sought on the superior aspect of the LCA, or the approach should be changed to a lateral one. The IMA is isolated at its takeoff from the aorta and divided. The IMV is then isolated and divided proximally.

Next, Toldt's retroperitoneal fascia is bluntly swept away from the posterior aspect of the left colon mesentery in a medial-to-lateral direction as far as the lateral abdominal wall. If the dissection

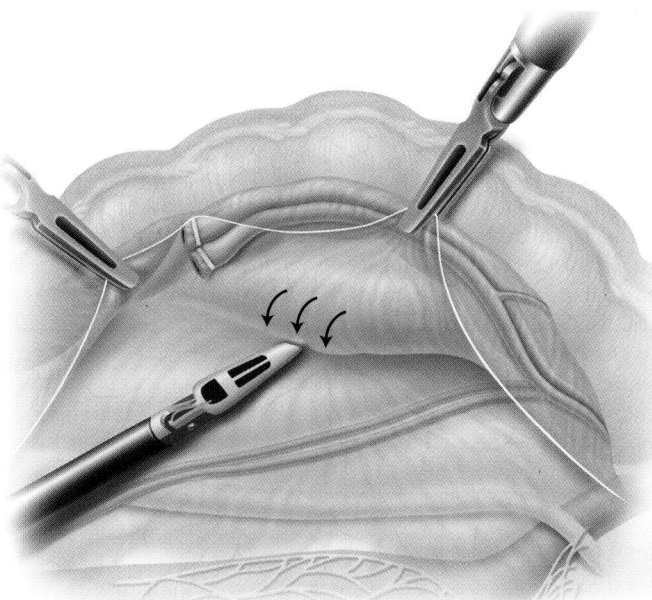

Figure 12 **Laparoscopic sigmoid colectomy. In a medial-to-lateral retromesenteric dissection, the correct dissection plane is anterior to Toldt's retroperitoneal fascia.**

is carried out in the correct plane, Gerota's fat will remain safely underneath Toldt's retroperitoneal fascia, as will the left ureter and the left gonadal vein [*see Figure 12*]. This retromesenteric dissection is then continued toward the upper pole of the kidney until it becomes difficult, at which point it is extended inferiorly toward the left psoas muscle and the iliac vessels.

Step 3: Lateral Mobilization of Left Colon and Takedown of Splenic Flexure

The sigmoid colon is retracted medially, and its attachment to the lateral abdominal wall is taken down. If the medial mobilization was adequately done underneath the sigmoid colon, the lateral attachment should be thin [*see Figure 13*]. The lateral ligament is divided cephalad, toward the splenic flexure. The attachments of the splenic flexure are complex; eventually, the splenocolic ligament, the so-called renocolic ligament (which is actually more a fusion of tissues than it is a ligament), and the omental attachments are mobilized. The inferior border of the pancreas has

attachments to the transverse mesocolon, and this area should be dissected carefully so as not to injure the pancreatic tail, which sometimes, at first viewing, is difficult to distinguish from omental fat. A LigaSure Atlas or an ultrasonic dissector works especially well for limiting blood loss during takedown of the splenic flexure. The greater omentum is dissected off the distal transverse colon from right to left, the lesser sac is entered, and mobilization is continued laterally until it meets the previous dissection, at which point the flexure is completely mobilized.

Step 4: Distal Division, Exteriorization, and Proximal Division of Sigmoid Colon

The mesentery of the rectosigmoid is then mobilized, and the line of distal transection is determined. The hypogastric nerves should be assessed again to confirm that they are not stuck to the mesentery in this area. The upper mesorectum, including the superior hemorrhoidal vessels, is divided until the rectosigmoid wall is cleaned off. A laparoscopic linear stapler is inserted through the 12 mm port in the lower abdomen, and the rectosigmoid is divided. Division may require one or two firings and is facilitated by the use of an articulated rotating stapler. The cut end of the rectosigmoid is grasped with a bowel grasper placed through the right lower quadrant port.

A minilaparotomy is then created, either as an extension of the left lower quadrant port incision or as an extension of the umbilical port incision. As in a right hemicolectomy, the length of the minilaparotomy is tailored to the size of the tumor. A wound protector is inserted to prevent implantation of tumor cells, and the cut end of the specimen is exteriorized through the minilaparotomy [*see Figure 14*]. The sigmoid colon is brought out of the wound until at least 15 cm proximal to the tumor has been exteriorized. The colon is then divided so as to leave an adequate proximal margin, and the marginal artery is ligated at this level to liberate the specimen.

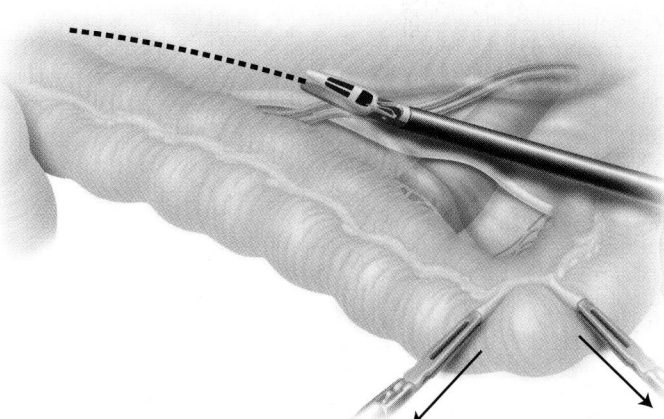

Figure 13 **Laparoscopic sigmoid colectomy. The left colon is mobilized laterally.**

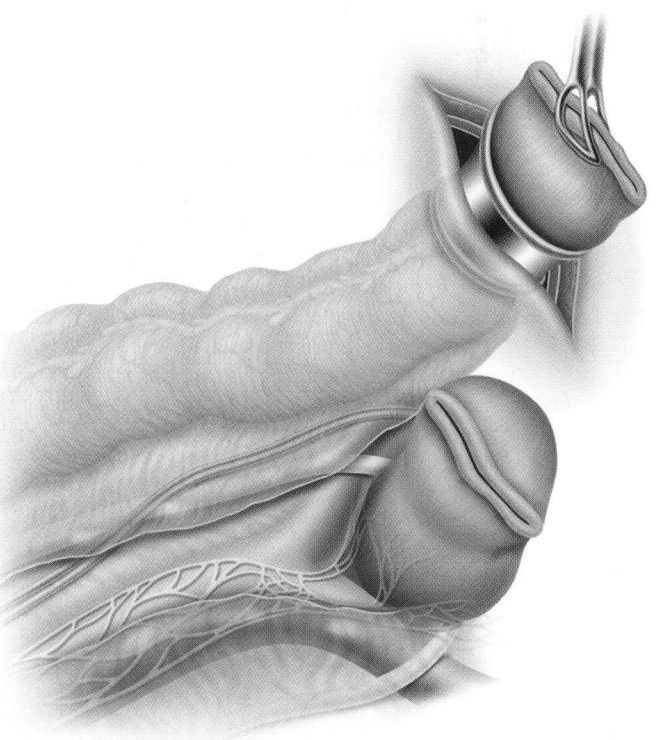

Figure 14 **Laparoscopic sigmoid colectomy. After distal transection, the sigmoid colon is exteriorized.**

Step 5: Anastomosis

Next, the colon is prepared for anastomosis. A purse-string suture is placed into the open mouth of the colon, and the center rod and the anvil of a circular end-to-end anastomosis (EEA) stapler are inserted. The colon is placed back into the abdomen, and the minilaparotomy is closed.

Pneumoperitoneum is reestablished, and under laparoscopic visualization, a stapled circular anastomosis is fashioned between the proximal cut end and the rectosigmoid stump. A leak test is performed by instilling normal saline into the pelvis, occluding the bowel proximal to the anastomosis, and injecting air through a rigid proctoscope or a flexible sigmoidoscope. A final exploration is performed to confirm that the small bowel has not migrated underneath the left colon mesentery.

TROUBLESHOOTING

Difficulty Identifying IMA

Especially in obese patients, initial identification of the IMA can be difficult from the medial approach (with dissection either too posterior or too anterior), leading to a bloody and confusing mobilization. The problem can be minimized by first retracting the sigmoid colon strongly out of the pelvis, then retracting it anterolaterally. This action pulls the IMA pedicle anteriorly away from the surface of the aorta. The next step is to feel for the sacral promontory with laparoscopic instruments and start the dissection there; this site affords the easiest entry into the avascular plane posterior to the IMA. If the bony promontory cannot be palpated, the colon has not been adequately retracted. If the correct plane still cannot be identified, it is advisable to switch to the lateral approach.

Injury to Hypogastric Nerve Plexus

The right and left hypogastric nerves travel along the anterior surface of the aorta and over the aortic bifurcation, then spread out toward the pelvic sidewall. Branches of these nerves—and sometimes the main trunks—adhere to the posterior aspect of the inferior mesenteric pedicle and consequently may be transected when the IMA is divided. To keep this from occurring, these nerves must be visualized and swept away in a posterior direction. The initial mesenteric window should be made wide enough for adequate visualization. The surface of the aorta and its bifurcation should not be skeletonized.

Injury to Left Ureter

With the medial approach, it is easy to dissect too deeply, extending the plane underneath the left ureter and the left gonadal vein. Care should therefore be taken to search for Toldt's retroperitoneal fascia and stay anterior to it. Ideally, the left ureter should be identified before the IMA is ligated. If this is not possible, it is advisable to switch to the lateral approach and mobilize the sigmoid colon accordingly.

Tearing of Splenic Capsule during Splenic Flexure Mobilization

Avulsion of the splenic capsule is usually caused by traction. The capsule is most vulnerable to injury when the colon is in close proximity to the spleen. The risk of splenic injury may be reduced by either (1) early (posterior) dissection of the renocolic ligament before lateral mobilization of the splenic flexure or (2) dissection of the flexure close to the colonic wall. The early separation of the left kidney from the left colonic mesentery (with the dissection plane remaining anterior to the retroperitoneal fascia) causes the flexure to drop down, which widens the distance between the colon and the spleen. During mobilization of the splenocolic liga-

ment and the greater omentum, it is important that the dissection not wander away from the colonic wall; if it does, the anatomy can become even more confusing.

Positive Anastomotic Leak Test

When a leak test yields positive results, the anastomosis must be repaired or revised. If the site of the bubbling from the anastomosis can be identified and is on the anterior aspect of the colon, sutures may be placed laparoscopically for repair, and the leak test should be repeated. If the site of the leak is hard to identify, the rectum distal to the anastomosis may be dissected and divided and the anastomosis refashioned; however, this can be a difficult procedure. In cases where laparoscopic repair is not feasible, a small laparotomy (either a Pfannenstiel incision or a low midline incision) may be made, and the problem may be addressed by means of open techniques.

Open Sigmoid Colectomy

The major elements of open sigmoid colectomy, like those of open right hemicolectomy, are similar to those of its laparoscopic counterpart [see Laparoscopic Sigmoid Colectomy, above]: (1) vascular isolation, (2) bowel division, (3) mobilization, and (4) anastomosis. The excellent visualization afforded by the laparoscope allows the use of the no-touch isolation technique for laparoscopic resection of left colon malignancies, but it is difficult to employ a true no-touch technique for open left colon resections. Because it is hard to ligate the IMA as the initial step, the sigmoid colon is usually mobilized via a lateral approach, which facilitates isolation and ligation of the inferior mesenteric vessels.

OPERATIVE TECHNIQUE

Step 1: Incision

A midline incision is made from a point halfway between the xiphoid and the umbilicus down to the level of the pubis. The abdomen is explored, and a wound retractor is inserted.

Step 2: Mobilization of Sigmoid Colon

The sigmoid colon is strongly retracted in an anteromedial direction, and the white line of Toldt is incised to allow the sigmoid colon to be mobilized in a medial direction. With care taken not to dissect into the retroperitoneal structures, the dissection proceeds cephalad toward the splenic flexure along the line of fusion between the left colon and Toldt's retroperitoneal fascia, remaining anterior to the fascia at all times. The left gonadal vessels and the left ureter are identified and swept away from the sigmoid mesentery. Eventually, the undersurface of the IMV is identified in the midline. The left hypogastric nerve fibers are bluntly swept away in a posterior direction, and a finger is inserted underneath the inferior mesenteric vessels toward the patient's right. The sigmoid mesentery from the medial side is then opened widely, and the right hypogastric nerve fibers are preserved by sweeping them away from the IMA in a posterior direction.

Step 3: Division of Inferior Mesenteric Artery and Vein

The IMA is dissected in the direction of its takeoff from the aorta, isolated, and divided. If the IMA is not fully skeletonized, the left ureter should be checked to make sure that it has not been inadvertently clamped together with the IMA before transection of the vessel. The IMV, located just lateral to the IMA at this location, is isolated and divided in the direction of the inferior border of the pancreas. The mesenteric dissection is then continued back toward the LCA, which is divided at its origin to preserve a secondary arcade that will perfuse the proximal aspect of the anastomosis.

Step 4: Mobilization of Left Colon and Splenic Flexure

The splenic flexure should be mobilized via an inferior rather than a lateral approach. With the sigmoid colon retracted anteriorly and superiorly, a broad white line is apparent, delineating the fusion of Toldt's retroperitoneal fascia with the left colon mesentery (i.e., the renocolic ligament). The retroperitoneal fascia overlying the left kidney is bluntly swept away from the posterior aspect of the left colonic mesentery toward the base of the pancreas. When the upper pole of the left kidney is reached, the colon is returned to its original position, and the splenic flexure is approached.

Early mobilization of the splenic flexure posteriorly allows the flexure to drop down, increasing the distance between it and the capsule of the spleen in most cases. A finger is inserted underneath the peritoneum overlying the splenic flexure, staying close to the colon wall, and this splenocolic ligament is divided with the electrocautery. Any omental attachments to the flexure that are present are divided close to the colonic wall until the dissection becomes difficult. Takedown of the splenic flexure is easiest when dissection is done from both the right and the left. The omentum is dissected away from the distal transverse colon in a right-to-left direction as the colon both distal to and proximal to the flexure is simultaneously retracted inferiorly (the so-called omega maneuver). The final attachments of the splenic flexure are taken down with the electrocautery.

Step 5: Proximal and Distal Division of Bowel

With the left colon fully mobilized, the proximal resection line is chosen, with care taken to ensure that the proximal margin is adequate and that the remaining bowel will be able to reach down to the pelvis without undue tension. The left colon mesentery is divided from the cut edge of the LCA toward the bowel wall, and the marginal artery is divided. The bowel is transected between clamps.

Distally, the rectosigmoid colon and the mesentery are mobilized, and the hypogastric nerves are swept away from the specimen. The mesentery of the rectosigmoid is dissected, and the superior hemorrhoidal vessels are divided. The rectosigmoid wall is then cleaned off and divided either between clamps or with a linear stapler (for a double-stapled anastomosis) to liberate the specimen.

Step 6: Anastomosis

A colorectal anastomosis is created between the proximal and distal cut edges of the bowel. For a double-stapled anastomosis [see 71 Intestinal Anastomosis], a purse-string suture is placed into the open mouth of the proximal bowel, the center rod and the anvil of a circular EEA stapler are inserted, and the purse-string suture is tied. The body of the stapler is advanced into the rectal stump, and the spike is pushed through the rectal wall. Once the proximal bowel has been checked to confirm that it is not twisted, the stapler is engaged and fired. A leak test of the anastomosis is then performed by instilling saline into the pelvis and gently infusing air into the bowel with a rigid proctoscope or a flexible sigmoidoscope while occluding the bowel proximally.

The anastomosis can also be created by means of a handsewn technique or a single-stapled technique (in which purse-string sutures are placed in both the proximal bowel and the distal bowel); these alternatives are described in more detail elsewhere [see 71 Intestinal Anastomosis]. In many cases, handsewn and stapling techniques may be equally suitable; however, for anastomoses fashioned lower in the pelvis, staples should be favored over sutures.

References

1. Williams NS, Dixon MF, Johnston D: Reappraisal of the 5 centimetre rule of distal excision for carcinoma of the rectum: a study of distal intramural spread and of patients' survival. Br J Surg 70:150, 1983

2. Hughes TG, Jenevein EP, Poulos E: Intramural spread of colon carcinoma: a pathologic study. Am J Surg 146:697, 1983

3. Morikawa E, Yasutomi M, Shindou K, et al: Distribution of metastatic lymph nodes in colorectal cancer by the modified clearing method. Dis Colon Rectum 37:219, 1994

4. Hida JI, Okuno K, Yasutomi M, et al: Optimal ligation level of the primary feeding artery and bowel resection margin in colon cancer surgery: the influence of the site of primary feeding artery. Dis Colon Rectum 48:2232, 2005

5. Kessler H, Mansmann U, Hermanek P, et al: Study Group Colo-Rectal Carcinoma. Does the surgeon affect outcome in colon carcinoma? Seminars in Colon and Rectal Surgery 9:233, 1998

6. Turnbull RB, Kyle K, Watson FR, et al: Cancer of the colon: the influence of the no-touch isolation technique on survival rates. Ann Surg 166:420, 1967

7. Griffiths JD, Mc Kinna JA, Rowbotham HD, et al: Carcinoma of the colon and rectum: circulating malignant cells and five-year survival. Cancer 31:226, 1973

8. Garcia-Olmo D, Ontanon J, Garcia-Olmo DC, et al: Experimental evidence does not support use of the "no-touch" isolation technique in colorectal

cancer. Dis Colon Rectum 42:1449, 1999

9. Hayashi N, Egami H, Kai M, et al: No-touch isolation technique reduces intraoperative shedding of tumor cells into the portal vein during resection of colorectal cancer. Surgery 125:369, 1999

10. Wiggers T, Jeekel J, Arends JW, et al: No-touch isolation technique in colon cancer: a controlled prospective trial. Br J Surg 75:409, 1988

11. Rouffet F, Hay JM, Vacher B, et al: Curative resection for left colonic carcinoma: hemicolectomy vs. segmental colectomy. A prospective, controlled, multicenter trial. Dis Colon Rectum 37:651, 1994

12. Tagliacozzo S, Tocchi A: Extended mesenteric excision in right hemicolectomy for carcinoma of the colon. Int J Colorect Dis 12:272, 1997

13. Toyota S, Ohta H, Anazawa S: Rationale for extent of lymph node dissection for right colon cancer. Dis Colon Rectum 38:705, 1995

14. Enker WE, Laffer UT, Block GE: Enhanced survival of patients with colon and rectal cancer is based upon wide anatomic resection. Ann Surg 190:350, 1979

15. Scott KW, Grace RH: Detection of lymph node metastasis in colorectal carcinoma before and after fat clearance. Br J Surg 76:1165, 1989

16. Gonzalez R, Smith CD, Mattar SB, et al: Laparoscopic vs. open resection for the treatment of diverticular disease. Surg Endosc 18:276, 2004

17. Faynsod M, Stamos MJ, Arnell T, et al: A case-control study of laparoscopic versus open sigmoid colectomy for diverticulitis. Am Surg 66:841, 2000

18. Milsom JW, Hammerhofer KA, Bohm B, et al:

Prospective, randomized trial comparing laparoscopic vs. conventional surgery for refractory Crohn's disease. Dis Colon Rectum 44:1, 2001

19. Marcello PW, Milsom JW, Wong SK, et al: Laparoscopic restorative proctocolectomy: case-matched comparative study with open restorative proctocolectomy. Dis Colon Rectum 43:604, 2000

20. Marcello PW, Milsom JW, Wong SK, et al: Laparoscopic total colectomy for acute colitis: a case control study. Dis Colon Rectum 44:1441, 2001

21. Senagore AJ, Duepree HJ, Delaney CP, et al: Cost structure of laparoscopic and open sigmoid colectomy for diverticular disease: similarities and differences. Dis Colon Rectum 45:485, 2002

22. Dwivedi A, Chahin F, Agrawal S, et al: Laparoscopic colectomy vs. open colectomy for sigmoid diverticular disease. Dis Colon Rectum 45:1309, 2002

23. Young-Fadok TM, Hall-Long K, McConnell EJ, et al: Advantages of laparoscopic resection for ileocolic Crohn's disease. Improved outcomes and reduced costs. Surg Endosc 15:450, 2001

24. Delaney CP, Kiran RP, Senagore AJ, et al: Case-matched comparison of clinical and financial outcome after laparoscopic or open colorectal surgery. Ann Surg 238:67, 2003

25. Duepree HJ, Senagore AJ, Delaney CP, et al: Does means of access affect the incidence of small bowel obstruction and ventral hernia after bowel resection? Laparoscopy versus laparotomy. J Am Coll Surg 198:177, 2003

26. Gutt CN, Oniu T, Achemmer P, et al: Fewer adhesions induced by laparoscopic surgery? Surg Endosc 18:898, 2004

27. Stage JG, Schulze S, Moller P, et al: Prospective randomized study of laparoscopic versus open colonic resection for adenocarcinoma. Br J Surg 84: 391, 1997

28. Milsom JW, Bohm B, Hammerhofer KA, et al: A prospective, randomized trial comparing laparoscopic versus conventional techniques in colorectal cancer surgery: a preliminary report. J Am Coll Surg 187:46, 1998

29. Lacy AM, Garcia-Valdecasas JC, Delgado S, et al: Laparoscopy-assisted colectomy versus open colectomy for treatment of non-metastatic colon cancer: a randomized trial. Lancet 359:2224, 2002

30. Leung KL, Kwok SP, Lam SC, et al: Laparoscopic resection of rectosigmoid carcinoma: prospective randomized trial. Lancet 363:1187, 2004

31. Clinical Outcomes of Surgical Therapy Study Group: A comparison of laparoscopically assisted and open colectomy for colon cancer. N Eng J Med 350:2050, 2004

Acknowledgment

Figures 1 through 3, 5 through 9, and 11 through 14 Alice Y. Chen.

Figures 4 and 10   Tom Moore.

77 PROCEDURES FOR RECTAL CANCER

David A. Rothenberger, M.D., F.A.C.S., F.A.S.C.R.S., and Rocco Ricciardi, M.D.

Rectal cancer is a common and lethal malignancy that is diagnosed in more than 42,000 persons in the United States each year.[1] In treating this condition, the goals are to cure or control the primary cancer, to maintain or restore bowel continuity with normal anal continence, to preserve sexual and bladder function, and to minimize other treatment-associated morbidity and mortality. A variety of rectal cancer treatment regimens are now available, spanning the spectrum from simple polypectomy to prolonged and potentially morbid multimodality regimens involving neoadjuvant chemoradiation therapy, radical extirpative surgery, and adjuvant chemotherapy.

Choosing the optimal therapy for rectal cancer is a complex process. Although physicians from different disciplines are often involved, it is the colorectal surgeon who generally directs the process of evaluation and treatment. As new knowledge has been acquired and new therapies and techniques have been developed, management of rectal cancer has changed dramatically. In this chapter, we examine the surgeon's unique and critical role in the preoperative decisions leading to choice of therapy, review the intraoperative decisions influencing the course of surgical therapy, and address key technical aspects of the operations performed to treat rectal cancer.

Preoperative Evaluation

Evaluation of the patient with rectal cancer includes the following: (1) visualization of the tumor and biopsy to determine the precise location of the lesion and confirm the diagnosis of adenocarcinoma; (2) accurate staging of the neoplasm by determining the extent of bowel wall penetration (T stage), the presence of metastases to local lymph nodes (N stage), and the presence of metastatic spread to distant sites (M stage); (3) colonoscopy to exclude synchronous lesions or other pathologic conditions of the colon; and (4) a thorough medical assessment to determine operative risk. A standardized workup facilitates staging and decision making.

HISTORY AND PHYSICAL EXAMINATION

A thorough history and a careful physical examination must be done to assess operative risk so that therapeutic options can be tailored to fit the comorbidities and desires of the patient. In modern series, mortality after radical resection of the rectum ranges from 2% to 6%,[2,3] with the most common causes of death being myocardial infarction, pneumonia, venous thromboembolism (deep vein thrombosis and pulmonary embolism), anastomotic leakage, and stroke.[4] Factors associated with increased mortality include impaired sensorium, low albumin level, elevated blood urea nitrogen concentration, and prolonged prothrombin time.[3]

The history focuses on gaining information that might alter the treatment plan or identify preexisting conditions worth addressing before an elective procedure. Essential information to be elicited includes a personal history of colorectal polyps or cancers; previous operations (especially those involving the digestive or genitourinary organs); previous irradiation of the pelvis; baseline bowel and anal sphincter function; smoking status; use of alcohol or other drugs; medical comorbidities; and current medications. In particular, a family history suggestive of a hereditary cancer syndrome should be sought because such a history might call for additional diagnostic testing or affect the extent of bowel resection.

During the physical examination, the surgeon should be alert to the presence of liver enlargement, abdominal tenderness or masses, lymphadenopathy, and abdominal scars or ventral hernias from previous operations. The integrity and function of the anal sphincter are carefully assessed by means of digital rectal examination. A patient with preexisting fecal incontinence or sphincter injury may be best served by a local procedure or abdominoperineal resection (APR) rather than a well-intentioned but ill-conceived heroic effort to save the anal sphincter.

DETERMINATION OF EXTENT OF LOCAL DISEASE

Evaluation of the extent of the primary rectal cancer is essential for planning appropriate therapy. An easily palpable distal rectal malignancy that directly invades the anal sphincters usually is treated with APR. A large, fixed cancer that invades adjacent organs, the pelvic sidewalls, or the sacrum usually is treated with neoadjuvant chemoradiation followed by resection or palliative measures. A small, mobile, and readily accessible lesion may be amenable to local therapy.

Determination of the extent of local disease involves clinical examination, endoscopic assessment, and diagnostic imaging. Digital rectal examination, combined with proctoscopy, endorectal ultrasonography (ERUS), or magnetic resonance imaging, can determine the morphology of the lesion, the percentage of the rectal circumference involved, and the quadrants affected, as well as the degree of fixation, the adjacent organs invaded, and the presence of lymph nodes or extrarectal masses. The level of the lesion in relation to the anal sphincters is best assessed by means of digital rectal examination and ERUS or endorectal MRI. The distance of the lesion from the dentate line or the anal verge is assessed more accurately with rigid proctoscopy than with flexible endoscopy. Biopsy is required to confirm the suspected diagnosis of adenocarcinoma and to ascertain whether any unfavorable histologic features (e.g., mucin production, lymphovascular invasion, or signet cell histology) are present.

ERUS and MRI with endorectal coil are the two most useful methods of determining the T and N stages of rectal cancer. In a combined review of 1,966 patients evaluated with ERUS, staging accuracy averaged 88%.[5] ERUS was highly (80% to 90%) accurate in predicting the extent of bowel wall involvement but was somewhat less (70% to 80%) accurate in identifying lymph node metastases.[6] Currently, MRI with endorectal coil, though promising, is accurate in only 40% to 60% of cases; accordingly, it has not replaced ERUS for staging the extent of local disease.[7,8] Newer MRI approaches that employ stronger magnets and do not require insertion of an endorectal coil may prove more accurate. ERUS has the added advantage of offering a convenient and accurate means of performing image-directed biopsies of suspicious areas.

Pelvic computed tomographic scanning is not very accurate in determining the depth of bowel wall involvement or the presence of lymph node metastases: the highest accuracy reported for CT in this setting is approximately 76%,[9] and most studies report much lower figures. Pelvic CT scanning is, however, useful for detecting extrarectal pelvic spread from rectal cancer. Presacral stranding, obliteration of normal landmarks lateral to the rectum, direct invasion of the sacrum or the pelvic sidewalls, invasion into the bladder or the vagina, and evidence of hydronephrosis are all signs of extensive pelvic disease.

SEARCH FOR DISTANT METASTASES

Evaluation of the patient with rectal cancer must also include a search for metastatic disease because the approach to the primary lesion may change if metastases are present. Few data are available on the utility of palliative rectal cancer surgery in the setting of metastatic disease; however, it is generally accepted that patients who present with asymptomatic or minimally symptomatic distant metastases but who have major local symptoms resulting from the primary rectal cancer may benefit from some form of palliative operation. As a rule, the least morbid procedure that will relieve the local symptoms is preferred. Often, the chosen procedure is palliative proctectomy, but sometimes, a less invasive local procedure (e.g., stenting) is an option. Patients who present with advanced and highly symptomatic distant metastases but who have an asymptomatic primary rectal cancer are usually best served by therapy directed toward the symptomatic metastases. The presence of extensive but minimally symptomatic metastases and a minimally symptomatic primary cancer of the rectum may mandate use of nonoperative, palliative treatment regimens.

Distant metastases arise most frequently in the liver and the lungs and are often asymptomatic; accordingly, routine evaluation for distant disease focuses on assessment of these two sites. If patients have specific symptoms suggestive of possible metastases to other organs or sites, additional imaging studies are ordered to explore this possibility. Chest x-ray and CT scanning are the modalities most commonly employed to identify pulmonary metastases; CT and MRI scanning are the ones most commonly employed to identify liver metastases. An alternative modality, positron emission tomography (PET), has proved highly (96%) sensitive in detecting the primary cancer but is of limited value in detecting local pelvic lymph node metastases.[10] Some advocate using PET to detect other organ metastases or involvement of lymph nodes at distant sites. At present, however, there is little evidence to justify routine use of PET scanning in the workup of rectal cancer. Its major current uses are (1) to clarify equivocal findings on other scans and (2) to minimize the risk of missing a distant metastasis to an unusual site in a patient being considered for a highly morbid resection of an extensive primary or recurrent rectal cancer.

ASSESSMENT OF SYNCHRONOUS COLORECTAL NEOPLASMS

Total colonoscopy is recommended to exclude or remove synchronous lesions (e.g., polyps and other cancers). It is estimated that 5% to 10% of rectal cancer patients have synchronous cancers and 30% have additional adenomatous polyps. The significance of these other lesions is highlighted by a study of 98 patients with rectal cancers who underwent full colonoscopic surveillance before operation; in this study, surgical treatment was altered in 33% of cases.[11] If colonoscopy is incomplete, a double-contrast barium enema or virtual colonoscopy with CT colography is a suitable alternative. If preoperative surveillance of the proximal colon is not possible, intraoperative or postoperative colonoscopy should be done.

Operative Planning

PRETREATMENT DECISIONS

In general, the surgeon is responsible for deciding what the intent of therapy will be (curative or palliative) and which treatment or treatments will be employed. To make these decisions, he or she must carefully consider the clinical staging information in the light of the anticipated operative technical challenges, the likely functional results, and the patient's level of operative risk, comorbidities, previous treatments, and specific needs.

Clinical staging is based on integration of information obtained from several sources, including clinical evaluation, imaging studies (e.g., ERUS, CT, MRI, and PET), colonoscopy, and histopathologic examination of the specimen obtained via biopsy or local excision. Because the information on which it is based is obtained before institution of definitive treatment, clinical staging is necessarily a less than perfect means of assessing the extent of disease. Nonetheless, it usually suffices to allow the surgeon to decide whether the intent of treatment will be curative or palliative and whether a local procedure, a radical procedure, or multimodality therapy will be indicated.

A history of previous cancer treatment may influence the choice of therapy, as may the presence of synchronous lesions, metastatic disease, extensive local spread, or unfavorable histopathology. Not infrequently, the ideal treatment is not feasible—either because of patient risk factors and comorbidities or because the patient refuses to accept the proposed treatment and its associated morbidity (e.g., a permanent colostomy)—and the treatment eventually chosen represents a compromise. The experienced surgeon can counsel the patient about therapeutic options, realistic expectations, and likely prognosis and obtain informed consent to proceed with a treatment protocol that is individualized to the specifics of a given case.

TREATMENT PROTOCOLS AND MULTIMODALITY THERAPY

Because treatment of rectal cancer is so highly individualized, it is difficult to be dogmatic about what constitutes optimal therapy. Nonetheless, there are certain generally accepted treatment guidelines for curative-intent treatment of rectal cancer, based primarily on pretreatment stage of disease, that are useful for the practicing surgeon [see Table 1].[12,13] Curative-intent treatment of rectal cancer involves resection or ablation of all neoplastic tissue, which almost always necessitates surgical intervention, usually in the form of a radical resection. In highly select cases, local therapy may be indicated. Currently, multimodality therapy that combines operative treatment with perioperative chemoradiation is increasingly being employed to overcome the persistent problem of local recurrence.

Clinical trials designed to assess the efficacy of postoperative adjuvant pelvic irradiation in treating advanced cancers of the rectum demonstrated that appropriate doses of radiation can reduce local recurrence and even improve survival, especially when administered in conjunction with radiation-sensitizing chemotherapy and postoperative adjuvant chemotherapy.[14-17] In the United States, most centers administer 45 to 54 Gy of radiation to the rectal cancer and the pelvis over a period of 4 to 6

Table 1 Rectal Neoplasms: Curative-Intent Therapy

Pretreatment Stage	Preferred Treatment	Acceptable Treatment
Stage 0 Tis N0 M0	Local therapy if technically feasible (excision is preferred to ablation for obtaining pathologic confirmation of T stage)	Radical resection (APR rarely indicated for Tis N0 M0 lesion) if local therapy is not feasible or safe
Stage I T1 N0 M0 (favorable features*)	Local therapy ± chemoradiation for distal-third lesions or high-risk patients; radical resection for proximal lesions in good-risk patients	Radical resection
T1 N0 M0 (unfavorable features)	Radical resection	Local therapy plus chemoradiation
T2 N0 M0	Radical resection (especially if unfavorable features are present and for proximal lesions in good-risk patients)	Local therapy plus chemoradiation
Stage II T3 N0 M0	Preoperative chemoradiation, radical resection, and adjuvant chemotherapy	Radical resection, postoperative chemoradiation, and adjuvant chemotherapy if pathologically appropriate (no adjuvant therapy if lesion is early T3 N0 M0)
T4 N0 M0	Preoperative chemoradiation, radical resection with en bloc resection of involved organs, and adjuvant chemotherapy	Radical resection, postoperative chemoradiation, and adjuvant chemotherapy
Stage III Tany N+ M0	Preoperative chemoradiation, radical resection, and adjuvant chemotherapy	Radical resection, postoperative chemoradiation, and adjuvant chemotherapy

*Lesions with favorable features are those that are exophytic, moderately or well differentiated, nonmucinous, non–signet cell, without lymphovascular invasion, extending around one quarter or less of the circumference of the rectum or no more than 3 cm in diameter, and located so that local therapy options are technically feasible and safe.

weeks. A 1990 National Institutes of Health consensus conference endorsed postoperative multimodality treatment of all stage II and III rectal cancers.[18]

Several researchers have assessed the use of preoperative neoadjuvant chemoradiation in treating advanced-stage rectal cancers.[19,20] It was argued that because preoperative irradiation treats undisturbed, well-oxygenated rectal cancers, it should be more effective than postoperative irradiation, resulting in improved local control and better survival. In addition, it was argued that by decreasing the size of bulky rectal cancers, preoperative irradiation should increase the rate of curative resection and the rate of sphincter preservation.[21] It was also thought that this neoadjuvant approach should diminish the incidence of the radiation injury seen after postoperative irradiation when small bowel is adherent to the pelvic operative site.[22] Whereas centers in the United States tended to employ a prolonged course of irradiation both preoperatively and postoperatively, many European centers, especially in Scandinavia, preferred to use a protocol of preoperative short-course, high-dose, hypofractionation irradiation, which usually delivered 25 Gy over a period of 1 week.[23]

There is now considerable evidence that chemoradiation can decrease local recurrence rates after radical procedures for rectal cancer and that it may improve survival and decrease the need for a permanent colostomy. To date, most studies have used 5-fluorouracil–based chemotherapy for radiation sensitization; studies using newer agents may be able to obtain further improvements in outcome.[17] The success achieved by employing perioperative chemoradiation in conjunction with radical surgery has led to the use of perioperative chemoradiation with local excision in several centers. These promising results must be weighed against the short- and long-term morbidity associated with chemoradiation. At present, the main controversies in the selection of multimodality therapy for rectal cancer are (1) the tumor selection criteria, (2) the timing of therapy (preoperative or postoperative), (3) the dosing and course of radiation therapy, and (4) the use of chemoradiation in conjunction with local therapy. Discussion of these controversies and other issues surrounding the application of chemoradiation and adjuvant chemotherapy in the setting of rectal cancer is beyond the scope of this chapter.

PATHOLOGY-BASED STAGING AND POSTTREATMENT DECISIONS

Clinical staging that is based on pretreatment assessment must be distinguished from pathology-based staging that relies on information obtained by means of gross and microscopic examination of the resected rectal tumor and the surrounding mesorectum after radical excision. The classic pathology-based staging system developed by Dukes correlated patient survival with depth of rectal cancer invasion and local lymph node metastases.[24] Many modifications to the Dukes staging system were proposed, but it remained the most widely used system until 1987, when the American Joint Committee for Cancer Staging and End Results Reporting (now the American Joint Committee on Cancer [AJCC]) developed a new classification methodology that incorporated both relevant clinical information and pathology-based information.[25] The AJCC's proposed TNM classification system, which has been adopted by the International Union Against Cancer, is clinically useful, simple to use, and accepted worldwide [*see Tables 2 and 3*].

An important principle in managing patients with rectal cancer is to compare the pretreatment clinical stage with the final pathology-based stage to confirm the appropriateness of the proposed treatment protocol or to adjust therapy on the basis of new information. There is some evidence to indicate that patients who undergo radical procedures immediately after local excision of a tumor with unfavorable pathologic characteristics survive longer than those who undergo radical resection after a local recurrence.[26] The finding of a more advanced T stage after local therapy may induce the surgeon to proceed with radical resection or to add postoperative chemoradiation to the treatment protocol. The finding of a less advanced T stage after local therapy may induce the surgeon to recommend observation rather than risk the morbidity associated with planned chemoradiation. The presence of unsuspected multiple lymph node metastases in the mesorectum after radical resection of a T2 cancer may dictate use of postoperative chemoradiation. Whether a complete clinical response to neoadjuvant preoperative chemoradiation therapy for advanced-stage rectal cancer obviates radical resection is an issue that remains to be resolved.

Table 2 American Joint Committee on Cancer TNM Clinical Classification of Colorectal Cancer[76]

Stage	Description*
Primary tumor (T)	Tis Carcinoma in situ T1 Invades submucosa T2 Invades muscularis propria T3 Invades serosa T4 Invades peritoneal cavity or adjacent organ through serosa
Regional lymph nodes (N)	NX Nodes cannot be assessed N0 No regional node metastases N1 1–3 positive nodes N2 4 or more positive nodes N3 Positive central nodes
Distant metastasis (M)	MX Cannot assess metastases M0 No distant metastases M1 Distant metastases present

*Suffix "m" is used to indicate primary tumors in a single site; prefix "y," to indicate cancers classified after pretreatment; prefix "r," to indicate tumors that have recurred; and prefix "a," to indicate staging at autopsy.

CHOICE OF PROCEDURE

Local Procedures

The benefits of local procedures for treatment of rectal cancer include minimal morbidity and mortality and rapid postoperative recovery. Such procedures allow preservation of genitourinary function and cause only minimal disturbance of anal continence. In some cases, local therapy is the only alternative to permanent colostomy. The major disadvantage of local procedures is that employing them inappropriately will result in high local recurrence rates and compromised survival. Local procedures may be used as curative-intent therapy for rectal cancer or as compromise therapy for patients who might not tolerate a radical procedure or who refuse a recommended radical resection (usually because of the potential for a permanent colostomy). Local therapy may also be used in select cases for palliation of symptomatic but incurable rectal cancers.

Curative-intent local therapy is usually restricted to treatment of highly favorable, accessible rectal cancers that do not invade the anal sphincter, are confined to the rectal wall, and are small enough to be totally removed or ablated. Any spread to local lymph nodes or distant sites is a contraindication to curative-intent local therapy. In theory, preoperative selection of such favorable T1–2 N0 M0 cancers for local treatment should result in minimal morbidity, excellent function, and long-term cancer-free survival.

Critics of local therapy note that on the basis of final pathology-based staging after radical resection, as many as 12% of patients with T1 cancers and 22% of those with T2 cancers have node-positive disease that would not have been treated by local procedures.[27-32] These critics suggest that imaging studies cannot reliably distinguish node-negative from node-positive T1 and T2 rectal cancers and that treating all T1 and T2 rectal cancers with local therapy would result in dramatic increases in local recurrence rates and unacceptable decreases in survival rates. Thus, they argue that using local therapy as the only form of curative-intent treatment is inappropriate even for presumed early rectal cancer. Some authorities maintain that curative-intent local therapy should be employed only in conjunction with multimodality therapy, even for favorable T1 lesions.

Proponents of curative-intent local therapy suggest that it is possible to restrict such therapy to select T1 and T2 rectal cancers that do not have associated lymph node metastases. It is known that the incidence of lymph node metastases correlates most closely with the depth of rectal wall invasion and is especially high if the cancer extends through the wall. These proponents argue that preoperative staging with ERUS or MRI can differentiate intramural (T1–2) cancers from transmural (T3) cancers with a high degree of accuracy[33] and can distinguish most of the T1 and T2 cancers in which lymph node metastases are present. In addition, they note that poorly differentiated tumors recur three times more often than well-differentiated to moderately differentiated tumors[34] and that lymph node metastases are more common if preoperative biopsy reveals poor differentiation, lymphovascular invasion, mucin production, or signet cell histology. Accordingly, they recommend avoiding curative-intent local therapy if any of these unfavorable histologic characteristics are present, if imaging studies suggest involvement of lymph nodes, or if the cancer is transmural, arguing that occult lymph node metastases are rarely present if such stringent selection criteria are used. Furthermore, advocates of curative-intent local therapy suggest that close post-treatment follow-up will detect any local cancer development arising from occult nodal disease at a point where salvage therapy can still be instituted.

It was hoped that by using these strict criteria for initiating curative-intent local therapy, T1–2 N0 M0 lesions amenable to such therapy could be reliably identified. Unfortunately, this hope has not been realized [*see* Local Procedures, Operative Technique, Local Excision, *below*]. The poor outcomes reported after local excision of select T1 and T2 cancers of the rectum have prompted several centers (including our own) to limit the use of curative-intent local therapy by restricting it to favorable T1 tumors as staged by ERUS or MRI. Some surgeons recommend further subdividing T1 lesions on the basis of submucosal invasion and employing local therapy only for those lesions that extend into the superficial third or the middle third of the submucosa.[35,36] Ideally, strictly limiting the indications for local therapy should retain the advantages (e.g., low morbidity) while minimizing the disadvantages (e.g., high local recurrence rates), but further studies are needed to determine whether this will be an effective strategy. Clearly, the key to more appropriate use of local therapy lies in finding better means of predicting the precise TNM stage and biologic behavior of rectal cancers before initiating therapy.

Table 3 American Joint Committee on Cancer Staging System for Colorectal Cancer[76]

Stage	T	N	M
Stage 0	Tis	N0	M0
Stage I	T1, T2	N0	M0
Stage IIA	T3	N0	M0
Stage IIB	T4	N0	M0
Stage IIIA	T1, T2	N1	M0
Stage IIIB	T3, T4	N1	M0
Stage IIIC	Any T	N2	M0
Stage IV	Any T	Any N	M1

Radical Procedures

The majority of patients with operable rectal cancer require a radical proctectomy. The primary goal of radical resection is to remove the rectal cancer, the rectosigmoid mesentery, and the mesorectum with clear margins. Curative-intent radical resections may be classified on the basis of the final pathologic assessment as follows: R0 if all margins are clear, R1 if microscopic tumor is present at the margin, and R2 if gross disease is present.

For the first half of the 20th century, APR with permanent colostomy was accepted as the treatment of choice for most rectal cancers. Improvements in perioperative care, anesthesia, and surgical technique; the development of reliable bowel-stapling devices; and improved understanding of the extent and nature of the spread of rectal cancer led to reductions in operative and cancer-related mortality and made anal sphincter–sparing operations increasingly reliable and popular. Gradually, anterior resection with colorectal anastomosis became the preferred procedure for proximal rectal and midrectal cancers.

Radical extirpation, with or without colorectal anastomosis, remained the only treatment option for most rectal cancers until the last quarter of the 20th century, when multimodality therapy was proved to be effective. Currently, surgeons frequently combine chemoradiation with radical resection and increasingly perform restorative procedures even for distal rectal cancers. Despite these improvements, local recurrence and poor function continue to be major sources of morbidity and mortality after radical resection.

Local Procedures

Local procedures used to treat rectal cancer include polypectomy, excision, fulguration, and endocavitary radiation. Polypectomy and excision have the advantage of providing a biopsy specimen that can be examined to determine the depth of tumor invasion and thereby confirm or change the preoperative T stage. If microscopic examination of the specimen shows involvement of the circumferential or deep margins or if the pathologic T stage is more advanced than the preoperative clinical T stage, radical surgery or chemoradiation may be employed to improve local control. It is not clear whether this approach—excisional biopsy with subsequent additional therapy depending on final pathologic examination of the specimen—compromises survival in comparison with a more aggressive initial approach. Obviously, this approach is not feasible if local ablative techniques (e.g., endocavitary radiation or fulguration) are employed, because the primary lesion is destroyed and thus unavailable for pathologic study.

Endocavitary radiation has the distinct advantage of being performed in the outpatient setting with local anesthesia with sedation; however, it requires special equipment and expertise and is not widely available. Fulguration is now used primarily for palliation. Its main advantage is that it controls bleeding from incurable rectal cancers with minimal morbidity. None of the local therapy techniques include removal of the mesorectum; thus, lymph nodes are not assessed, and it is impossible for the pathologist to confirm or alter the preoperative N stage.

OPERATIVE TECHNIQUE

Polypectomy

Snare polypectomy is most often done during colonoscopic examination of the entire colon with the assumption that the rectal polyp is benign. Polyps larger than 1.0 cm, polypoid villous adenomas, and polyps with firm ulcerated areas are more likely to harbor invasive cancer. With such lesions, it is occasionally helpful to use a large-diameter rigid proctoscope to facilitate snare polypectomy. The goal is to remove the polyp in one piece and provide the pathologist with a properly oriented specimen. If the endoscopist has any suspicion that the polyp may harbor a malignancy, the polypectomy site should be marked by means of submucosal injection and the precise level of the lesion recorded in the procedure note.

Benign-appearing sessile polyps of the rectum are generally best removed in one piece by means of transanal local submucosal or full-thickness operative excision rather than piecemeal by means of endoscopic snare excision. This approach provides the pathologist with a single specimen that can be properly oriented for histologic examination to assess the depth of tissue invasion. It also avoids the difficulties that arise when an unsuspected invasive cancer is identified microscopically but inability to orient the multiple pieces of tissue removed by piecemeal excision precludes accurate assessment of the T stage.

Snare polypectomy by itself is adequate for treating cancer arising in a rectal polyp if the lesion is noninvasive (i.e., confined to the mucosa) or if an invasive cancer is confined to the head, neck, or stalk of a pedunculated polyp and the margins are clear. If tumor is present within 2 mm of the margin or if the cancer extends into the submucosa of a pedunculated or sessile polyp, additional therapy is usually indicated. Various options are available for such therapy, including transanal excision of the rectal wall along with the base of the polyp (for accurate determination of the T stage), chemoradiation, and radical resection. The factors that determine whether local therapy is sufficient for cancers arising in a polyp or whether radical resection or adjuvant therapy is indicated are reviewed elsewhere.[37]

Local Excision

The goal of local excision procedures is to perform a full-thickness resection of the primary rectal cancer with a 1.0 cm margin. Local excision is most often accomplished via an endoanal (transanal) approach under direct vision or by means of transanal endoscopic microsurgery (TEM). The endoanal approach is generally suitable for more distal tumors up to 10 cm from the anal verge, whereas TEM is appropriate for more proximal cancers.

Posterior approaches to excision are rarely necessary. Occasionally, it is helpful to expose the anorectum via a parasacral incision so as to facilitate local excision of a rectal cancer that is otherwise difficult to access. Currently, transsacral and transperineal approaches are infrequently used because of the significant associated morbidity (i.e., wound infections, bowel fistulas, and impaired continence). Tumors closer to the anal verge may involve the anal sphincter; such involvement is a contraindication to local excision unless the patient is unfit for a more aggressive option.

Endoanal local excision Because of its relative simplicity and excellent safety record, transanal excision is the most commonly performed local procedure [see Figure 1]. Full mechanical bowel preparation is recommended to reduce the possibility of postoperative impaction and to maintain optimal visualization. The procedure can be performed with the patient in either the lithotomy or the prone jackknife position. The prone position has the advantages of providing easier access for an assistant surgeon and of being suitable for rectal cancers in any quadrant; the lithotomy position is most suitable for distal posterior tumors. The use of headlights or lighted retractors is highly recommended. A Lone Star self-retaining retractor or Gelpi retractors may be used to efface the anus, and a handheld bivalve retractor, a Ferguson-Hill

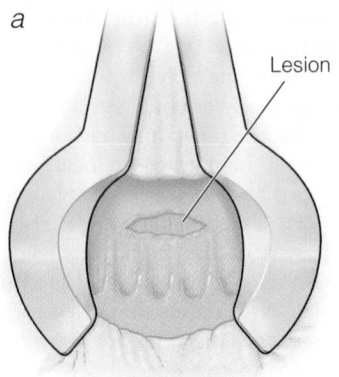
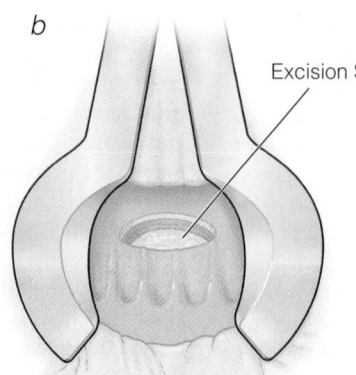
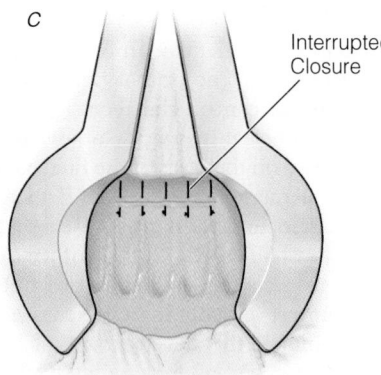

Figure 1 Local excision. (*a*) The rectal lesion is exposed with a bivalve retractor. (*b*) Full-thickness excision of the lesion is performed. (*c*) The defect is closed with interrupted sutures.

retractor, or a Parks anoscope may be used to provide endoanal exposure of the lesion. Deep retractors (e.g., narrow Deaver retractors) are often helpful for exposing more proximal cancers.

Dissection may be facilitated by injecting saline or a local anesthetic with epinephrine solution into the rectal wall near the lesion. It is sometimes helpful to place a traction suture 2 cm distal to the lesion to facilitate prolapse of the rectal wall before dissection is begun. An electrocautery with a needle tip is generally employed to perform a full-thickness excision of the cancer with a 1.0 cm margin, but surgeons are increasingly using laparoscopic instruments to facilitate local excision. Hemostasis and orientation must be maintained. If desired, the defect in the rectal wall may be closed as the dissection progresses. Each suture can be used for traction to keep the lesion in view. Innovative techniques making use of laparoscopic or conventional staplers have also been developed and have yielded good results.

Once the specimen has been resected, it is inspected to confirm that adequate margins have been obtained, then marked for orientation and pinned out for fixation before histologic examination. The operative site may be irrigated with sterile water or tumoricidal agents to minimize the risk that viable tumor cells will be left in the rectal wall. If the rectal wall defect is extraperitoneal, it may be left open to heal secondarily; however, many prefer to close all rectal wounds primarily.[38] If the defect is intraperitoneal, closure is essential and is usually performed with a durable absorbable suture. Care must be taken to prevent stricture formation. This is an especially critical concern if large or circumferential lesions are removed. In such cases, a sleeve closure with a handsewn anastomosis after advancement of the proximal rectal wall to the more distal rectum is often the best option. Once the defect is closed, the surgeon should perform proctoscopy to ensure that the rectal lumen has not been compromised.

Results. The data currently available suggest that local recurrence rates are unacceptably high and that survival may be compromised even when curative-intent local therapy is restricted to patients who have small, accessible intramural cancers with no signs of suspicious lymph nodes on preoperative imaging studies and no unfavorable histologic features on the pretreatment biopsy. The risk of local recurrence after local excision of selected, presumably favorable lesions is 18% for T1 cancers and 37% to 47% for T2 cancers.[27-32] Salvage surgery is often possible if follow-up shows progression of pelvic cancer. No prospective studies directly comparing the results of local excision with those of more radical extirpative procedures have yet been done, and it is unlikely

that such trials will ever be successfully completed. Studies involving short-term follow-up have not demonstrated any impact on cancer-free survival for T1 cancers but have indicated that survival is compromised if T2 cancers are treated with local excision alone. More information is needed before definitive therapeutic recommendations can be made.

Local recurrence rates after local excision can be lowered by adding adjuvant radiation therapy, with or without chemotherapy. Estimated local recurrence rates after adjuvant therapy range from 0% to 9% for T1 tumors and from 0% to 24% for T2 tumors.[39-41] Reliable long-term survival data are unavailable. To date, only three small retrospective series have evaluated a promising newer approach: neoadjuvant therapy followed by local excision of early-stage, favorable rectal cancers. Clinical trials aimed at studying this approach are being developed.

Transanal endoscopic microsurgery TEM is a novel technique that has found a niche in local treatment of sessile polyps and of favorable T1 cancers in the middle to upper rectum. It may be used in combination with chemoradiation to treat more advanced cancers of the middle and upper rectum, especially in high-risk patients who cannot tolerate an anterior resection. More proximal lesions of the rectum that are not amenable to transanal excision or to endoscopic removal may be best treated by TEM, with low morbidity and mortality.

TEM begins with insufflation of CO_2 into the rectum via a 4 cm operating rectoscope. Endoscopic instruments are then inserted and used under magnification to perform the local resection. The principles of resection are the same as for endoanal excision (see above).

Results. The largest review of TEM results to date included 137 patients and reported an 8% minor morbidity rate, a 2% major morbidity rate, and a combined 5% recurrence rate for T1 to T3 tumors over a period of 6 months.[21] These results are promising, but the follow-up period is too short for definitive conclusions to be drawn.

Posterior approach to local excision Local excision of rectal cancers can be performed via either a transsacral or a transsphincteric approach with the patient in the prone jackknife position. The Kraske procedure takes a transsacral approach. An incision is made in the midline of the sacrum to expose the posterior rectum by excising the coccyx and the last two sacral vertebrae. Either a short segmental resection of the rectum with primary anastomosis or a proctotomy to expose and locally excise an intraluminal lesion is performed. In closing the rectal wall defect, care is taken not to compromise the lumen and create a stricture.

The York-Mason procedure takes a transsphincteric approach to expose the posterior rectum without resection of the sacrum. Instead, the pelvic floor muscles are divided in the posterior plane, and the resection then proceeds as in the Kraske procedure. The sphincter muscles must be carefully reconstructed. Unfortunately, morbidity is relatively high (e.g., a 20% incidence of fecal fistula) after both procedures.[42]

Fulguration (Electrocoagulation)

Fulguration, or electrocoagulation, involves destroying a cancer with an electrode inserted into the wall of the lesion. As coagulum builds up, it is debrided to allow additional coagulation until the lesion and a circumferential rim of normal tissue have been ablated. The disadvantages of this procedure include postoperative fever, the lack of a surgical specimen for staging, the requirement for repeated procedures, and the need to convert to more radical procedures in a large number of patients.[43]

Fulguration has often been used as curative-intent treatment, with reported 5-year survival rates reaching 58%, but it is now used primarily for palliative purposes. Fulguration may be optimal for patients with bulky bleeding rectal cancers who are too ill to undergo radical resection.

Endocavitary Radiation (Papillon Technique)

Endocavitary radiation involves high-dose contact (superficial) radiotherapy delivered via a specially designed proctoscope. A total radiation dose of 9 to 15 Gy is delivered in several sessions, usually over a period of 60 days. This modality is appropriate for small noncircumferential lesions located within 10 cm of the anal verge. The reported 5-year survival rate is 76%, with a local recurrence rate of 8.3% and a mortality of 7.7%.[44]

Radical Procedures

OPERATIVE PLANNING

Preoperative Preparation

The possibility that a permanent or temporary stoma may be necessary should prompt a consultation with an enterostomal therapy nurse for the purpose of counseling the patient and marking the abdominal wall at the appropriate location for a colostomy or temporary ileostomy [see 72 Intestinal Stomas].

Generally, full mechanical and antibiotic bowel preparation is performed on an outpatient basis the day before operation. An antibiotic is administered intravenously just before induction of anesthesia. General anesthesia is employed, and an epidural catheter is often inserted to provide postoperative analgesia. If there is a large, bulky rectal tumor or an associated inflammatory mass, ureteral stents may be placed to facilitate intraoperative identification and protection of the ureters. A bladder catheter is inserted, and the patient is placed in a modified lithotomy position with the legs in stirrups. Pneumatic compression stockings and compression devices are used routinely, with or without heparin. Digital rectal examination and rigid proctoscopy are performed to empty the rectum and reassess the rectal cancer. The degree of involvement of the anal sphincter or other organs, the level of the distal edge of the tumor, and the response of the tumor to chemoradiation are noted.

A number of instruments are required to facilitate the conduct of radical extirpative procedures. Headlights and lighted retractors allow visualization deep in the pelvis. Self-retaining retractors (e.g., Balfour or Bookwalter retractors) are necessary. The St. Mark pelvic retractor and the Wylie renal vein retractor facilitate deep pelvic dissection. Long instruments are essential, and a variety of staplers should be available. The presence of an experienced second surgeon or a highly trained assistant is invaluable.

Intraoperative Decision Making

The surgeon always has a plan in place for the operation before laparotomy, but it often happens that intraoperative findings necessitate a change in the plan. Thus, the surgeon must be flexible and willing to alter the planned operation in accordance with the situation.

After a midline incision is made, a thorough abdominal exploration is performed. At this point, the surgeon can confirm or revise the operative plan. Most often, the choice between a sphincter-sparing approach and a sphincter-sacrificing approach has been made before operation, but for distal rectal cancer, it is not always possible to determine whether a restorative anastomosis is feasible until the rectum has been fully mobilized. In such cases, the choice between sphincter-sparing and sphincter-sacrificing proctectomy must be based on assessment of the adequacy of the distal margin [see Anterior Resection, Operative Technique, Step 4, below].

Neoadjuvant therapy can reduce the size of a tumor so that it is amenable to low anterior resection instead of requiring APR.[45] After full rectal mobilization, the surgeon assesses the possibility of obtaining clean radial and distal margins, then decides to proceed with either resection and anastomosis or APR. The desire to perform an anastomosis must not be allowed to compromise oncologic outcome. Occasionally, circumstances arise in which the cancer is larger than anticipated or is extending into the sacrum or other pelvic structures. In such circumstances, a more extensive operation than was originally planned is appropriate if curative resection can be achieved. Alternatively, the surgeon may be forced to perform a palliative operation.

ANTERIOR RESECTION

Operative Technique

All curative-intent radical resections for rectal cancer use the same technique for mobilizing the rectum and achieving proximal, lateral, and radial margin clearance. Anterior resections are classified as high, low, or extended low, depending on the extent of rectal mobilization and resection and on the level of the restorative anastomosis.

Step 1: mobilization of colon After abdominal exploration, the small bowel is packed into the upper abdomen, and the patient is placed in a slight Trendelenburg position. The rectosigmoid is retracted to the right, and the peritoneal attachments to the left of the sigmoid colon are incised along the avascular plane. The left ureter and gonadal vessels are identified and preserved by using sharp and gentle blunt dissection to separate the retroperitoneal tissues from the sigmoid mesentery. The peritoneum is incised along the left side of the descending colon as far as the splenic flexure. Adhesions to the spleen are divided, and the splenic flexure is taken down. The colon mobilization extends proximally to the left transverse colon.

Step 2: ligation of inferior mesenteric artery The mobilized rectosigmoid is retracted anteriorly and to the left to expose

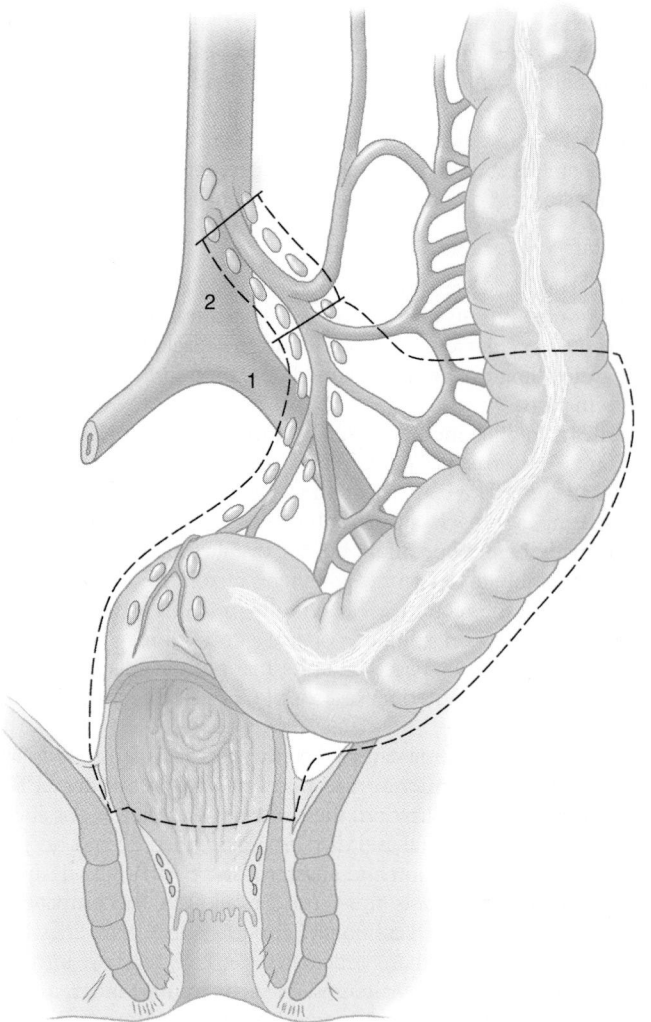

Figure 2 **Anterior resection. Illustrated is the tissue excised during anterior resection. The surgeon may perform either a low ligation of the IMA (1), with preservation of the ascending branch, or a high ligation (2), where the IMA branches from the aorta.**

the inferior mesenteric artery (IMA). Transillumination of the mesentery facilitates identification of an avascular space adjacent to the IMA at the base of the mesentery. The peritoneum overlying this space is incised on either side of the IMA. Some surgeons prefer a high ligation of the IMA where it branches from the aorta, suggesting that this measure provides a more complete lymph node harvest. Others prefer a low ligation of the IMA just distal to the left colic artery, suggesting that this approach ensures better blood supply to the proximal colon and prevents nerve injury at the base of the IMA [*see Figure 2*]. At present, there is not enough evidence to recommend one approach over the other. After ligation of the IMA, it is convenient to divide the colon at the descending-sigmoid junction with a linear stapler.

Step 3: total mesorectal excision and preservation of autonomic nerves The rectosigmoid is retracted anteriorly and inferiorly toward the pubis to expose the avascular plane posterior to the rectum. Sharp incision of this avascular plane while traction is placed on the rectosigmoid typically allows air to enter the areolar tissue posterior and lateral to the rectum. The surgeon follows the air, sharply dividing the loose areolar tissue posteriorly and laterally [*see Figure 3*].

During the retrorectal dissection, the hypogastric nerves are identified at the sacral promontory. These nerves descend in the presacral space in a wishbone shape and must be preserved to maintain postoperative sexual and urinary function. In the 1940s, sexual dysfunction after proctectomy was reported in 95% of male patients.[46] If attention is given to nerve preservation during proctectomy, however, 86% of male patients younger than 60 years retain sexual function.[47] Posteriorly, the rectosacral fascia is divided under direct vision, and the dissection proceeds distally to the level of the coccyx. In mobilizing the rectum, it is helpful to dissect in a posterior-to-lateral direction, with care taken to maintain the integrity of the endopelvic fascial envelope encasing the bilobed mesorectum. The nervi erigentes are identified and preserved on the lateral pelvic sidewalls. When the middle rectal artery is present as a distinct vessel, it can generally be fulgurated during the lateral dissection; occasionally, however, the vessel is large enough that ligation is necessary.

The final attachments are divided anterolaterally, and the anterior pelvis is exposed. Exposure may be facilitated by reducing the angle of the Trendelenburg position or even shifting the patient to a reverse Trendelenburg position. The cul-de-sac is opened, and Denonvillier's fascia is incised. Deep pelvic retractors are placed to protect the seminal vesicles and prostate (in males) or the vagina (in females) as the dissection continues distally.

Step 4: assessment of distal margin At this point in the operation, the rectum has been fully mobilized via the abdominal approach, and the surgeon must decide whether a sphincter-preserving anastomosis is possible or whether a sphincter-sacrificing resection with construction of a permanent colostomy is necessary. Because all radical resections for rectal cancer use the same proximal, lateral, and radial dissection technique, the decision to perform an anastomosis is based primarily on the ability to obtain a clear distal margin.

There are two components to the distal margin: intramural and mesorectal. At one time, a 5.0 cm intramural margin was recommended; however, subsequent studies demonstrated that a 2.0 cm intramural margin was adequate for curative resection. Margins smaller than 1.0 cm were associated with increased local recurrence rates and decreased survival.[48-50] Considerable emphasis is now being placed on ensuring adequate mesorectal clearance. It was observed that local recurrence after radical resection correlated not just with the stage of the disease but also with the surgeon performing the operation. Careful analysis suggested that some surgeons did not remove the mesorectum completely and that tumor deposits in the mesorectum distal to the rectal cancer were responsible for high recurrence rates.[51] Total mesorectal excision (TME) was recommended as a means of minimizing local recurrences. The current view is that a 5.0 cm mesorectal clearance is essential to prevent local recurrence in the pelvis.

If distal clearance (both intramural and mesorectal) is adequate and if anal sphincter function justifies proceeding with an anastomosis, a right-angle clamp is placed distal to the tumor, and the distal rectum is irrigated with sterile water or a tumoricidal agent. A second right-angle clamp is then placed distally, and the rectum is divided between the two clamps. This technique is used if an open purse-string suture is to be placed in the distal rectal cuff. If a double-stapled reconstruction is planned instead, a transverse anastomosis (TA) stapler is placed distal to the right-angle clamp. The stapler is fired and the rectum divided, leaving a closed rectal cuff for subsequent anastomosis.

The surgeon should then examine the resected specimen to assess the radial and distal margins and evaluate the integrity of the mesorectal dissection. If the margins are inadequate or the mesorectum has been violated, local recurrence is a major concern. The treatment plan may have to be altered to reduce the risk of recurrence.

Step 5: creation of anastomosis Several reconstructive options are available for restoring bowel continuity after radical proctectomy. An end-to-end anastomosis is the traditional choice, but alternative anastomoses are acceptable options in some situations [see Alternative Anastomoses, *below*].

A straight or an end-to-side colorectal anastomosis (the Baker technique) is appropriate after resection of most cancers in the proximal half of the rectum. The anastomosis can be handsewn, but most surgeons prefer to use a circular stapler. Functional results after such proximal anastomoses are generally good. As surgeons developed reliable means of performing lower colorectal and coloanal anastomoses, functional results were often suboptimal: patients reported urgency, frequency, seepage, and incontinence. To overcome these problems, surgeons devised newer techniques aimed at increasing rectal reservoir capacity (e.g., the colonic J pouch and coloplasty).

Double-stapled end-to-end anastomosis. The double-stapled technique was devised to eliminate the need for a purse-string suture on the rectal cuff and to prevent fecal contamination. A purse-string suture is placed in the cut edge of the distal descending colon [see Figure 4a]. The anvil of a circular stapler is inserted into the descending colon, and the purse-string is tied.

The integrity of the stapled distal rectal stump is checked by insufflating air into the rectum via a proctoscope while the rectal stump is covered with saline. If no air leaks are noted, the circular

stapler, without the anvil but with a trocar attachment, is inserted through the anus and advanced proximally to the apex of the closed stump [see Figure 4b]. The stapler is opened to drive the trocar through the apex of the rectal stump adjacent to the staple line. The trocar attachment is removed, and the mobilized descending colon, with the anvil in place, is mated to the stapler [see Figure 4c]. The stapler is closed and fired, resulting in an end-to-end anastomosis [see Figure 4d]. The integrity of the anastomosis is assessed by insufflating air into the rectum with a proctoscope while the anastomosis is under water [see Figure 5].

Purse-string end-to-end anastomosis. The alternative to the double-stapled technique is to place purse-string sutures on both the proximal and the distal end of the bowel to be anastomosed. A continuous 2-0 purse-string suture is placed in the proximal end of the open rectal cuff, and a second purse-string suture is placed in the descending colon [see Figure 6]. The circular stapler is placed through the anus, and the anastomosis is fashioned and checked for leaks as in the double-stapled technique.

Handsewn end-to-end anastomosis. The alternative to a stapled anastomosis is a handsewn colorectal end-to-end anastomosis, which may be done in one or two layers with interrupted or continuous sutures. Handsewn colorectal anastomoses are typically performed from the abdominal field. It is often easiest to place all of the sutures first, then "parachute" the proximal bowel down to the rectal cuff as the sutures are tied. The knots are generally tied on the inside to produce mucosal inversion.

Alternatively, if the distal cuff cannot be visualized from the abdominal field, a handsewn anastomosis may be performed transanally. This is generally more easily accomplished with the patient in the prone jackknife position.

Alternative anastomoses. Three alternative reconstruction procedures have been devised to facilitate restoration of bowel continuity deep in the pelvis. The colonic J pouch and the Baker technique involve an end-to-side anastomosis, an approach that some surgeons believe offers a more reliable blood supply than the traditional end-to-end anastomosis. The colonic J pouch and coloplasty were designed to overcome the poor functional outcomes frequently observed after straight coloanal or low colorectal anastomoses by increasing the capacity of the neorectum.

A colonic J pouch is considered only for low anastomoses less than 5 cm from the anal verge; if the procedure is performed more proximally than 8 cm from the anal verge, it offers no functional advantages over a straight colorectal anastomosis.[52] Patients with a colonic J pouch anastomosis 4 cm or less from the anal verge demonstrate the greatest functional improvements.[52]

To create a colonic J pouch, the splenic flexure is mobilized to provide adequate bowel length, and a well-vascularized segment of the colon is selected for the pouch. The distal descending colon is then folded into a J configuration [see Figure 7a]. It is essential that the hook (i.e., the efferent limb) of the J be no longer than 5 to 6 cm, because longer limb lengths are associated with difficulty in evacuation.[53] A linear cutting stapler is inserted through a colotomy on the antimesenteric surface of the inferior aspect of the J pouch, then closed and fired. Once the linear staple line has been checked for bleeding, the anvil of a circular stapler is placed in the colotomy of the J pouch and secured in place with a 2-0 nonabsorbable suture. The J pouch–anal anastomosis is then performed with the circular stapler [see Figure 7b].

Approximately 25% of patients are not suitable candidates for a colonic J pouch because of a narrow pelvis or obesity.[54] For

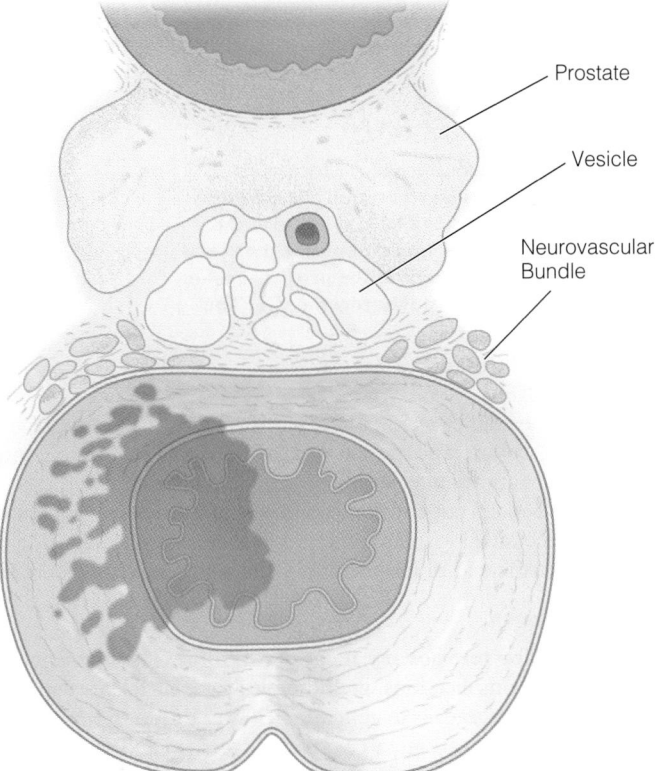

Figure 3 **Anterior resection. Shown is a schematic depiction of total mesorectal excision, highlighting the endopelvic fascial dissection plane.**

Prostate

Vesicle

Neurovascular Bundle

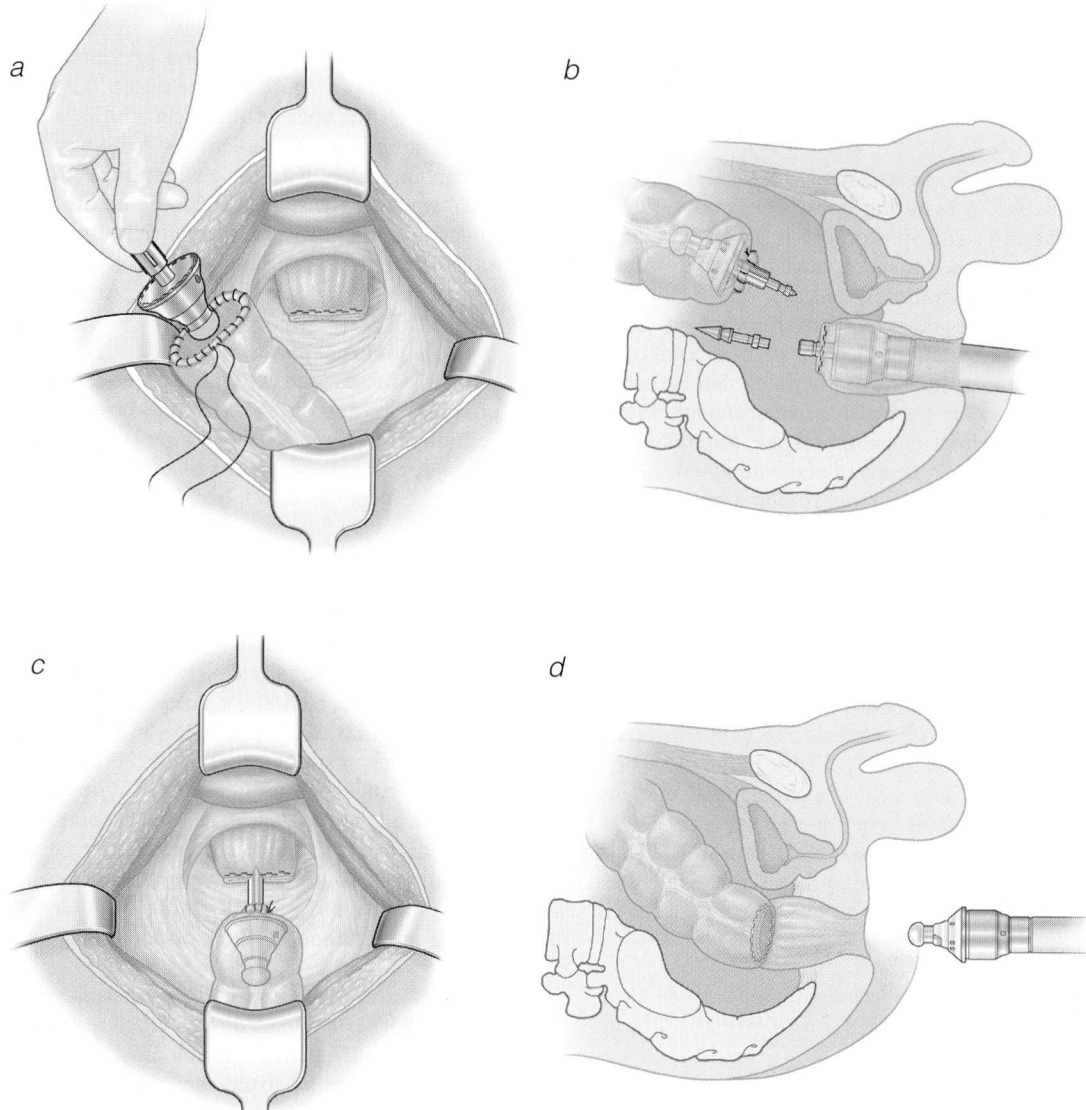

Figure 4 Anterior resection. Shown is a double-stapled end-to-end anastomosis. (*a*) The rectal stump is closed with a linear noncutting stapler. A purse-string suture is placed around the colotomy, and the anvil of the circular stapler is placed in the open end and secured. (*b*) The stapler, with the sharp trocar attachment in place, is inserted into the anus, and the trocar is made to pierce the rectal stump at or near the staple line, after which the trocar is removed. (*c*) The anvil in the proximal colon is joined with the stapler in the rectal stump, and the two edges are slowly brought together. (*d*) The stapler is fired and then gently withdrawn.

these patients, coloplasty is an alternative. Coloplasty is similar to Heineke-Mikulicz pyloroplasty. An 8 to 10 cm long antimesenteric colotomy is initiated at a point 5 to 6 cm from the cut end of the descending colon and extended proximally [*see Figure 8a*]. The anvil of a circular stapler is placed in the colon and brought out the end of the colon before closure of the coloplasty. The colotomy is closed in a transverse direction, perpendicular to the antimesenteric border, with either absorbable sutures or a linear stapler [*see Figures 8b and 8c*]. An end-to-end anastomosis is then performed with the circular stapler [*see Figure 8d*]. This procedure has not been accepted by most surgeons because of the long longitudinal colotomy along the antimesenteric border.

Although the end-to-side (Baker) anastomosis is not a new technique, it is gaining popularity as an alternative to the more difficult and time-consuming pouch procedures. After the rectal resection, the stapler anvil is inserted through the cut end of the descending colon. The trocar end of the anvil is brought out through the antimesenteric side of the colon approximately 3 to 4 cm from the distal cut end. The open end of the descending colon is closed. A circular stapler is then used to anastomose the side of the colon to the end of the rectum or the anal canal [*see Figure 9*].

Troubleshooting

Criteria for temporary fecal diversion The incidence of anastomotic complications, including leakage, correlates with the level of the anastomosis: in general, the lower the anastomosis, the higher the complication rate. Other factors, including previous radiation therapy, immunosuppression, and underlying vascular insufficiency or diabetes, may also increase the risk of anastomotic complications.

The consequences of a leaking anastomosis remain a major

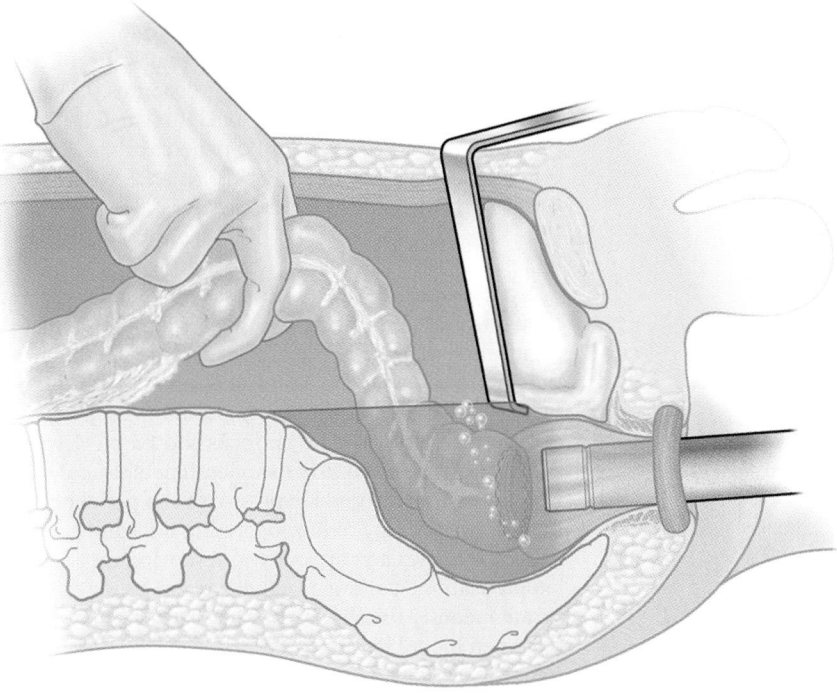

Figure 5 **Anterior resection. The integrity of the anastomosis is assessed by holding it under water and insufflating air via a proctoscope while the bowel is clamped.**

source of morbidity and death after surgical resection of rectal cancer. Consequently, many surgeons perform routine temporary fecal diversion for patients undergoing low anastomoses, especially for those subjected to preoperative irradiation or receiving steroid treatment. Loop ileostomy is the most commonly performed temporary diversion, though some surgeons prefer proximal loop colostomy [see 72 Intestinal Stomas]. Proximal fecal diversion does not protect against anastomotic leakage or prevent anastomotic complications, but it does diminish the morbidity resulting from leakage and reduce the likelihood of an emergency operation.[55] Our practice is to perform diversion for all patients with a colorectal or coloanal anastomosis within 5 cm of the anus, especially if they have undergone preoperative radiation therapy or are immunosuppressed.

Outcome Evaluation

Information is now available on functional outcome and quali-

ty of life after coloanal or colorectal reconstruction. The data indicate that the functional advantages of coloplasty and colonic J pouches are most discernible in the first 2 years after operation. Measures of function—including urgency, frequency, nocturnal stooling, and continence—all show significant improvements in patients who undergo colonic J pouch or coloplasty reconstruction[56]; quality-of-life indicators and physiologic measures show significant improvements as well.[57] A 2002 trial from Singapore found the incidence of anastomotic leaks to be higher after coloplasty reconstruction than after colonic J pouch reconstruction.[58] Although this finding has tempered the enthusiasm for coloplasty reconstruction, the procedure remains a viable option in the patient with a narrow pelvis.

The functional and surgical results seen with end-to-side anastomoses are similar to those seen with colonic pouch anastomoses.[59] More data are needed to determine which reconstructive technique is best in which setting.

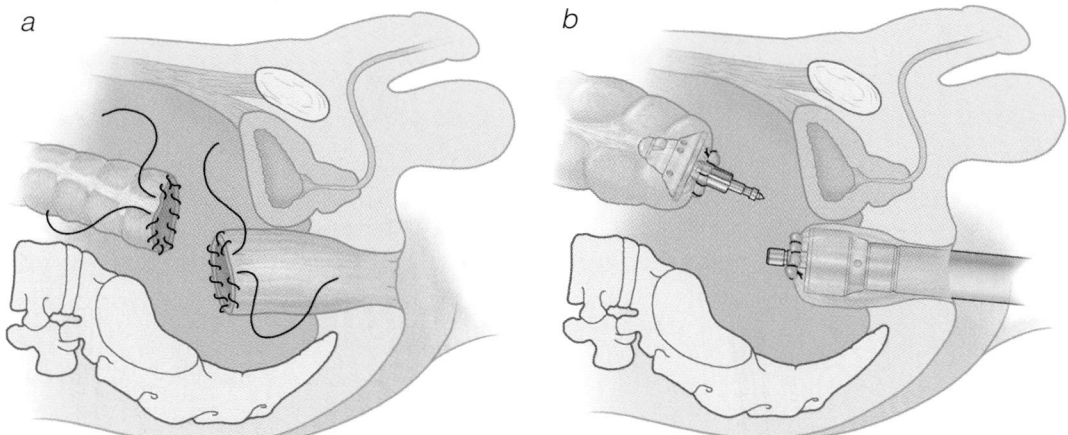

Figure 6 **Anterior resection. Shown is a purse-string end-to-end anastomosis. (*a*) Purse-string sutures are placed on the rectum and on the proximal bowel. (*b*) The anvil of a circular stapler is placed in the proximal bowel, and the stapler is placed through the anus. The anvil is joined with the body of the stapler, and the stapler is fired to complete the anastomosis.**

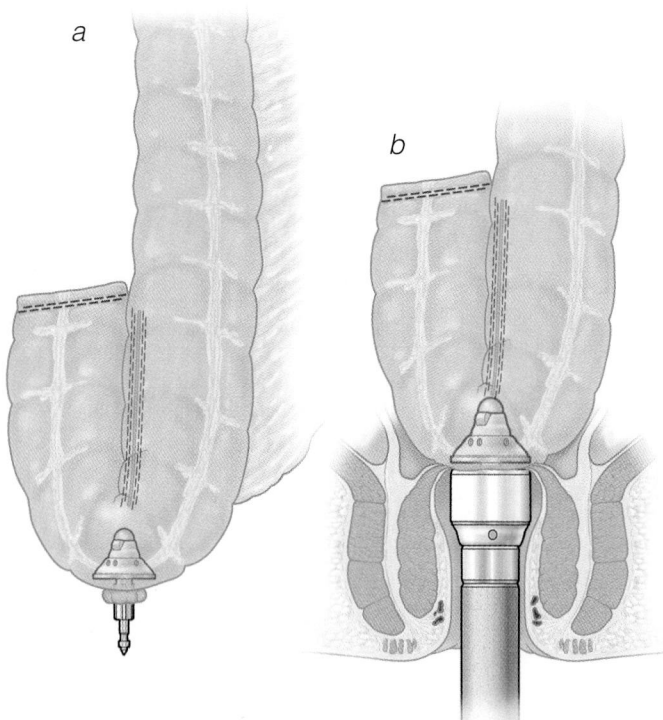

Figure 7 **Anterior resection. Shown is the creation of a coloanal anastomosis with a colonic J pouch. (*a*) The proximal bowel is stapled closed and folded into a J shape, with the hook of the J being about 5 to 6 cm long. A colotomy is made in the base of the J, and a J pouch is formed by inserting and firing a linear stapler. The anvil of a circular stapler is placed in the base of the pouch. (*b*) The J pouch is brought down to the anus, and the circular stapler is used to create the coloanal anastomosis.**

ABDOMINOPERINEAL RESECTION

APR involves en bloc resection of the rectosigmoid, the rectum, and the anus along with the surrounding mesentery, mesorectum, and perianal soft tissues [*see Figure 10*]. Current efforts to perform

more restorative anastomoses after radical resection of rectal cancer are based on data suggesting that APR offers no survival advantage over sphincter-sparing procedures.[17] Nevertheless, APR is still performed in an estimated 30% to 60% of rectal cancer patients. A large review of 7,400 patients in the United States documented a 58% rate of APR performance.[60] The reasons for this persistently high APR rate are unclear.

Operative Planning

Synchronous APR APR, as the name suggests, may be thought of as comprising two phases: an abdominal phase and a perineal phase. The perineal phase of the operation may be done synchronously with the abdominal phase, with the patient maintained in a modified lithotomy position. Proper positioning and exposure are critical. The buttocks should be elevated with a pad extending over the edge of the operating table and should be taped laterally to provide good exposure of the perineum. The synchronous approach may reduce operating time and is useful if the surgeon anticipates any difficulty in removing the rectum because of lateral fixation. Working from above and below the area of fixation simultaneously usually allows the proctectomy to be safely completed en bloc. This approach demands the presence of two experienced surgeons: performing the perineal phase with the patient in the lithotomy position can be very demanding technically, especially if the patient is obese.

Sequential APR Alternatively, the perineal phase may be performed with the patient in the prone jackknife position after completion of the abdominal phase. This approach is generally preferred because it provides excellent visualization for the perineal dissection and is especially useful if the tumor is fixed anteriorly. In addition, it has the advantage of providing more room for an assistant.

Operative Technique

Steps 1 through 4 The abdominal phase of APR, including TME and nerve preservation, is identical to steps 1 through 4 of an anterior resection [*see* Anterior Resection, Operative Technique, *above*].

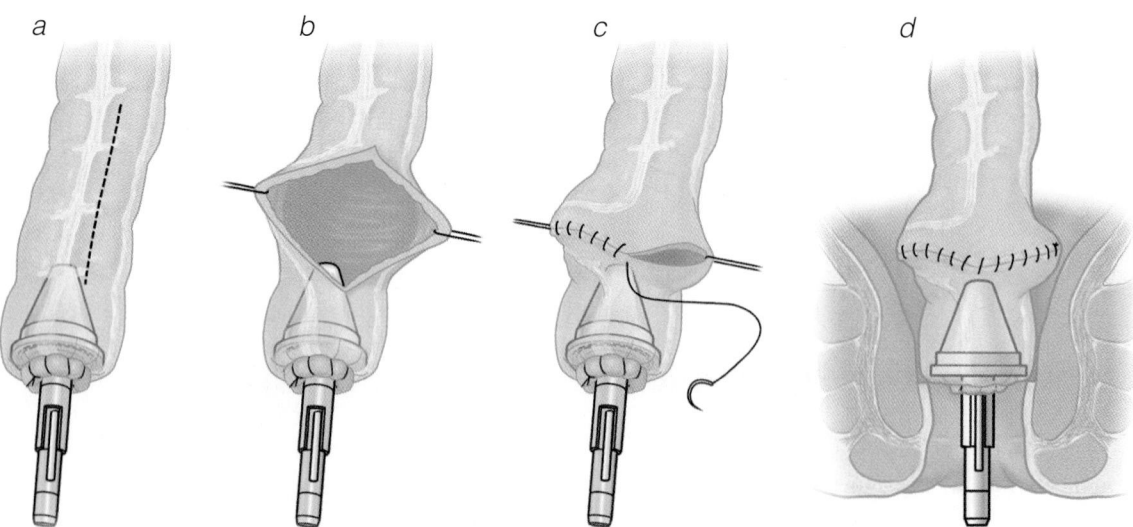

Figure 8 **Anterior resection. Illustrated is the coloplasty technique. (*a*) A longitudinal colotomy is made in the antimesenteric side of the colon. (*b*) Sutures are placed on either side of the incision and used to apply traction transversely. (*c*) The colotomy is closed in a transverse direction. (*d*) An end-to-end anastomosis to the anus is performed.**

is completed anteriorly, the specimen is inspected and sent for pathologic examination. The pelvis is irrigated and hemostasis secured. Some surgeons prefer to place a mobilized pedicle of omentum into the pelvis to facilitate healing and reduce the risk of small-bowel adhesions in the depths of the pelvis. The perineal incision is closed in several layers with absorbable sutures. A transabdominal drain is placed in the pelvis.

Step 6: creation of colostomy An end colostomy [*see 72 Intestinal Stomas*] is created before the perineal dissection if sequential APR is performed but may be created simultaneously with the perineal resection if a two-team synchronous APR is performed. A 2 cm circular incision is made in the skin and subcutaneous tissues overlying the premarked stoma site, which is usually in the left lower quadrant of the abdomen. A cruciate incision is made in the anterior fascia, the rectus abdominis is split, and a second cruciate incision is made in the posterior fascia. The mobilized colon is passed through this site and fixed to the skin with 3-0 or 4-0 absorbable sutures. Because many enterostomal therapists and patients find it easier to pouch an elevated left-side colostomy, an eversion technique is used to mature the stoma.

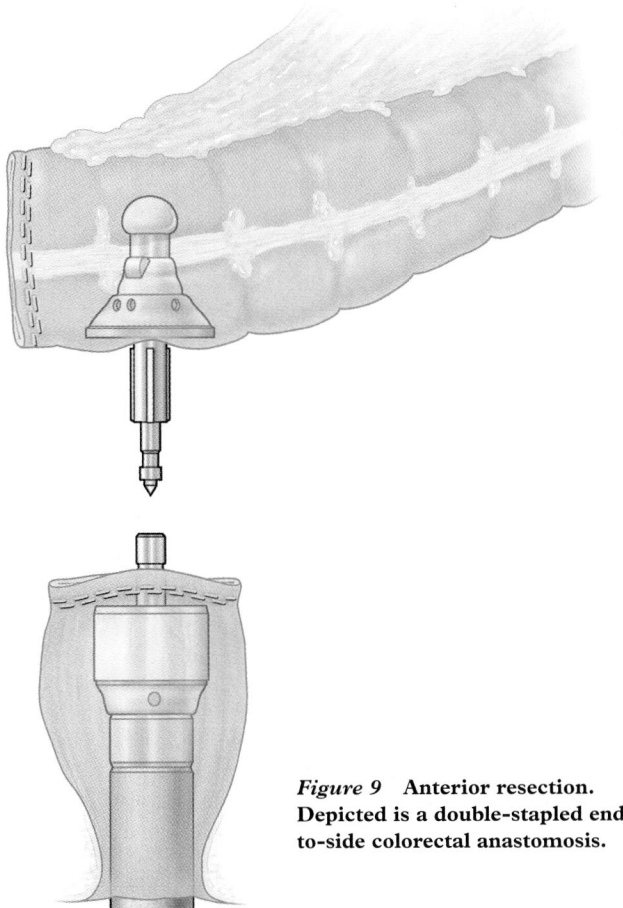

Figure 9 **Anterior resection. Depicted is a double-stapled end-to-side colorectal anastomosis.**

Step 5: perineal resection The perineal phase of APR is performed with the patient in either the lithotomy or the prone jackknife position, depending on whether the synchronous or the sequential approach is followed. The perineum is exposed with the aid of self-retaining retractors [*see Figure 11*]. The anus is closed with a heavy purse-string suture to minimize the risk of spillage of feces or tumor. An alternative means of accomplishing this goal is to make the initial elliptical incision around the anus and then approximate the perianal skin edges with sutures or Kocher clamps. The elliptical incision should extend from the perineal body anteriorly to the coccyx posteriorly. Laterally, the incision should overlie the ischium. The incision is deepened into the ischioanal fossa bilaterally with the electrocautery. The anococcygeal ligament is divided posteriorly. The perineal surgeon can then insert an index finger into the pelvis to guide division of posterolateral soft tissue with the electrocautery. An appendectomy retractor or springs may be used to improve retraction during deeper dissection into the perineum. The dissection is continued laterally and anterolaterally. When an ample aperture is created, the proximal end of the specimen is passed between the coccyx and the anus.

Traction is applied to the everted specimen to help the surgeon develop the anterior dissection plane. In a female patient, an anterior lesion may necessitate a posterior-wall vaginectomy to ensure adequate margins. In a male patient, anterior dissection may lead to injury to the urethra or excessive bleeding from the prostate capsule; to minimize the risk of the former, it is helpful to palpate the Foley catheter during anterior dissection. Once the dissection

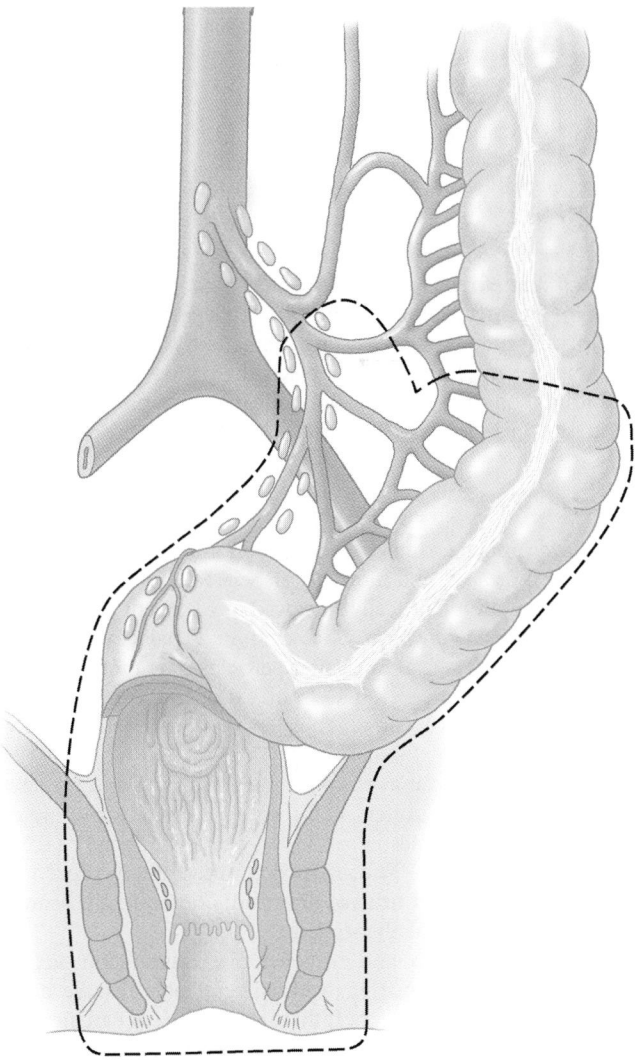

Figure 10 **Abdominoperineal resection. Illustrated is the tissue excised during APR.**

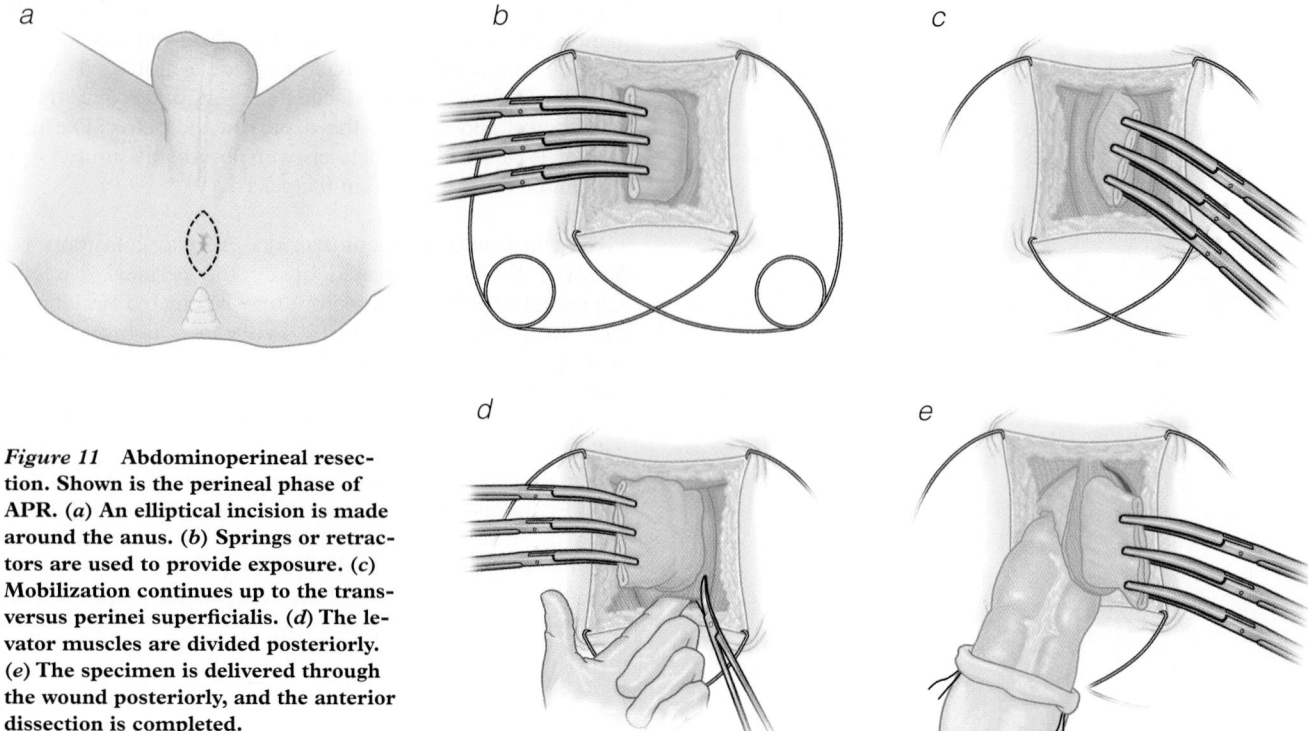

Figure 11 **Abdominoperineal resection. Shown is the perineal phase of APR. (*a*) An elliptical incision is made around the anus. (*b*) Springs or retractors are used to provide exposure. (*c*) Mobilization continues up to the transversus perinei superficialis. (*d*) The levator muscles are divided posteriorly. (*e*) The specimen is delivered through the wound posteriorly, and the anterior dissection is completed.**

OTHER RADICAL PROCEDURES

Hartmann Procedure

The Hartmann procedure [*see 74 Procedures for Diverticular Disease*] is a seldom-used option that plays only a limited role in the treatment of rectal cancer. It may be a good choice if the likelihood of local recurrence is high (as with a perforated cancer) or if the patient manifests preexisting sphincter dysfunction. In these situations, perineal dissection subjects the patient to unnecessary morbidity. The distal rectum or anal canal is stapled closed and left in situ in the pelvis. The end colostomy is performed as in APR.

Pelvic Exenteration and Sacrectomy

The indications for pelvic exenteration are limited by the relatively high morbidity and mortality associated with the procedure. Pelvic exenteration for locally advanced or recurrent rectal cancer has been shown to have oncologic and palliative benefits. Reported 5-year survival rates after pelvic exenteration for locally recurrent rectal cancer range from 20% to 30%.[61] Primary advanced rectal cancer, however, is less often amenable to pelvic exenteration.

Pelvic exenteration may involve resection of the anus, the rectum, the bladder, the ureters, and the pelvic reproductive organs. Sacrectomy is sometimes necessary as well if the rectal cancer is invading posteriorly.[62] Reconstruction after these procedures involves both fecal and urinary diversion; consequently, a multidisciplinary team is usually needed.

Detailed preoperative and intraoperative examination is essential to verify the presence of localized resectable disease before proceeding with exenteration. If there is evidence of carcinomatosis, liver metastases, pelvic sidewall invasion, bilateral ureteral obstruction, or aortic node metastases, curative exenteration cannot be performed. Invasion of the upper sacral vertebra is a con-

traindication to sacrectomy because in this setting, the procedure would result in unacceptably high morbidity and functional sequelae. In the setting of advanced disease, the surgeon should consider comfort care or additional adjuvant therapy before performing palliative exenteration. Other treatment modalities (e.g., intraoperative radiotherapy, brachytherapy, and further chemoradiation) may be useful in this population.

Outcome Evaluation

FOLLOW-UP REGIMENS

The primary purpose of surveillance after treatment of rectal cancer is to detect early recurrence so that salvage therapy can be instituted. A secondary purpose is to prevent development of a metachronous cancer by identifying and removing new polyps. Symptoms of pain, pressure, weight loss, or bowel dysfunction should be investigated. In addition to the physical examination, various laboratory studies, endoscopic procedures, and imaging modalities are used to detect or exclude recurrences. Although survival is improved after resection of recurrent lesions, especially in the setting of hepatic metastases, few data exist on the utility of close follow-up. Some studies have questioned the utility of follow-up protocols.[63,64] A survey of the American Society of Colon and Rectal Surgeons and the Society of Surgical Oncology found that practice patterns were highly variable and that there was no clear consensus on what constitutes appropriate follow-up after treatment of rectal cancer.[65]

Most follow-up regimens include a routine history and physical examination, carcinoembryonic antigen (CEA) testing, CT scanning, and routine colonoscopic evaluation. The roles of MRI, PET, and other imaging studies have not been defined. Our practice is to follow good-risk rectal cancer patients who have undergone curative-intent therapy every 4 months with ERUS and rigid proctoscopy for the first 3 years, then every 6 months for 2 more years. Data on the efficacy of such regimens are limited. A meta-analysis of 3,000 patients revealed a 9% increase in 5-year survival in patients who underwent intensive investigation with routine CEA testing and aggressive resection. Unfortunately, this meta-analysis involved patients enrolled in nonrandomized trials.[66] Patients with limited lifespans or multiple medical problems were probably more likely to opt out of close surveillance.

RECURRENT DISEASE

Recurrence of rectal cancer after treatment may be classified as either local (if it arises at the anastomosis or in the pelvis) or systemic (if it develops in distant sites). One autopsy series found local recurrence in one quarter of patients, distant metastases in one quarter, and combined local and distant recurrence in one half.[67] Patients with systemic recurrences generally are not candidates for extensive surgical procedures. Instead, they should be evaluated by a multidisciplinary team that includes a surgeon, a radiation oncologist, and a medical oncologist. A multimodality approach comprising chemotherapy, irradiation, and, if the disease becomes more manageable, surgery is individualized on the basis of each patient's needs and condition.[68] The 5-year survival rate for patients treated with this aggressive approach ranges from 12% to 27%.[69-71]

Recurrence after Local Resection

Recurrence rates after local resection vary, depending on the extent of the primary disease. Positive margins, transmural bowel wall invasion, and lymphovascular invasion are associated with an increased risk of local recurrence.[72] One quarter of patients with recurrent disease after local excision have local recurrences that can be managed with surgical extirpation or other treatments.[73] Recurrences after local resection in patients who have metastatic disease or comorbidities that make them poor candidates for radical surgery are best managed with palliative procedures. Good surgical candidates with isolated local recurrences are best treated with a combination of radical surgery and adjuvant therapy. Repeat local procedures are rarely recommended for these patients.

Recurrence after Radical Resection

In the past, reported local recurrence rates after radical proctectomy reached 30% to 40%. Currently, however, with the general acceptance of TME techniques, reported local recurrence rates are as low as 3% to 5%.[74] Recurrence rates are primarily a reflection of the stage of the original disease at the time of initial treatment. Approximately 7% to 20% of patients with local nonhepatic colorectal recurrences can undergo repeat resection.[75] Recurrence is more likely to manifest as a surgically correctable lesion after low anterior resection than after APR.[61] Recurrence at the anastomosis after high anterior resection may be amenable to treatment with either curative repeat resection and a lower anastomosis or APR. The surgical options available for treating recurrence after APR are usually limited to exenteration and sacrectomy; the likelihood that an isolated local perineal recurrence amenable to local excision will be identified after APR is small.

Patients scheduled for repeat resection should undergo an extensive workup with modalities such as CT, MRI, and PET to exclude any extrapelvic recurrence. Before committing to a potentially morbid repeat resection, the surgeon should carry out an extensive operative exploration to confirm that a curative-intent resection is feasible. If preoperative imaging and abdominal exploration reveal no contraindications to repeat resection, the surgeon may proceed cautiously with anterior resection, APR, or pelvic exenteration. Alternatively, in the palliative setting, local control may be obtained with chemoradiation, fulguration, or local excision techniques rather than procedures that call for a major laparotomy.

References

1. Jemel A, Murray T, Samuels A: Cancer statistics 2003. CA Cancer J Clin 53:5, 2003

2. Philips RKS, Hittinger R, Blesovsky L, et al: Local recurrence following curative surgery for large bowel cancer: the overall picture. Br J Surg 71:12, 1984

3. Longo WE, Virgo KS, Johnson FE, et al: Outcome after proctectomy for rectal cancer in Department of Veterans Affairs hospitals. Ann Surg 228:64, 1998

4. Wiggers T, Arends JW, Volovics A: Regression analysis of prognostic factors in colorectal cancer after curative resections. Dis Colon Rectum 31:33, 1988

5. Marohn MR: Endorectal ultrasound. Postgraduate course syllabus. Society of American Gastrointestinal and Endoscopic Surgeons, 1997

6. Hunerbein M: Endorectal ultrasound in rectal cancer. Colorectal Dis 5:402, 2003

7. Meyenberger C, Boni RAH, Bertschinger P, et al: Endoscopic ultrasound and endorectal MR imaging: a prospective comparative study for preoperative staging and follow-up for rectal cancer. Endoscopy 27:469, 1995

8. Thaler W, Watzka S, Martin F, et al: Preoperative staging of rectal cancer by endoluminal ultrasound vs. MR imaging: preliminary results of a prospective comparative study. Dis Colon Rectum 37:1189, 1994

9. Billingham RP: Conservative treatment of rectal cancer: extending the indications. Cancer 70:1355, 1992

10. Mukai M, Sadahiro S, Yasuda S, et al: Preoperative evaluation by whole body 18F-fluorodeoxyglucose positron emission tomography in patients with primary colorectal cancer. Oncol Rep 7:85, 2000

11. Isler JT, Brown PC, Lewis FG, et al: The role of preoperative colonoscopy in colorectal cancer. Dis Colon Rectum 30:435, 1987

12. Practice parameters for the treatment of rectal carcinoma. The American Society of Colon and Rectal Surgeons. Dis Colon Rectum 36:989, 1993

13. Rectal cancer clinical practice guidelines in oncology. Journal of the National Comprehensive Cancer Network 1:54, 2003

14. Kapiteijn E, Marijen CA, Nagtegaal ID, et al: Preoperative radiotherapy combined with total mesorectal excision for resectable rectal cancer. N Engl J Med 345:638, 2001

15. Camma C, Giunta M, Fiorica F, et al: Preoperative radiotherapy for respectable rectal cancer: a meta-analysis. JAMA 284:1008, 2000

16. Colorectal Cancer Collaborative Group: Adjuvant radiotherapy for rectal cancer: a systematic overview of 8507 patients from 22 randomized trials. Lancet 358:1291, 2001

17. Wolmark N, Weiand HS, Hyams DM, et al: Randomized trial of postoperative adjuvant chemotherapy with or without radiotherapy for carcinoma of the rectum. National Surgical Adjuvant Breast and Bowel Project, protocol R-02. J Natl Cancer Inst 92:388, 2000

18. NIH consensus conference. Adjuvant therapy for patients with colon and rectal cancer. JAMA 19:1444, 1990

19. Chari RS, Tyler DS, Anscher MS, et al: Preoperative radiation and chemotherapy in the treatment of adenocarcinoma of the rectum. Ann Surg 221:778, 1995

20. Gerard JP, Chapet O, Nemoz C, et al: Preoperative concurrent chemoradiotherapy in locally advanced rectal cancer with high-dose radiation and oxaliplatin containing regimen: the Lyon R0-04 phase II trial. J Clin Oncol 21:1119, 2003

21. Guerrieri M, Feliciotti F, Baldarelli M, et al: Sphincter-saving surgery in patients with rectal cancer treated by radiotherapy and transanal endoscopic microsurgery: 10 years' experience. Dig Liver Dis 35:876, 2003

22. Sauer R: Adjuvant versus neoadjuvant combined modality treatment for locally advanced rectal cancer: first results of the German Rectal Cancer Study (CAO/ARO/AIO-94). Int J Radiat Oncol Biol Phys 57:S124, 2003

23. Glimelius B, Pahlman L: Preoperative radiotherapy for rectal cancer: hypofractionation with multiple fractions (15-25 Gy). Ann Ital Chir 72:539, 2001

24. Dukes CE: The classification of cancer of the rectum. J Pathol Bacteriol 25:323, 1932

25. Nogueras JJ, Rothenberger DA: The ABC's of colorectal cancer staging systems. Perspectives in Colon and Rectal Surgery 4:185, 1991
26. Baron PL, Enker WE, Zakowski MF, et al: Immediate vs. salvage resection after local treatment for early rectal cancer. Dis Colon Rectum 38:177, 1995
27. Blumberg D, Paty PB, Guillem JG, et al: All patients with small intramural rectal cancers are at risk for lymph node metastasis. Dis Colon Rectum 42:881, 1992
28. Mellgren A, Sirivongs P, Rothenberger DA, et al: Is local excision adequate therapy for early rectal cancer? Dis Colon Rectum 43:1064, 2000
29. Brodsky JT, Richard GK, Cohen AM, et al: Variables correlated with the risk of lymph node metastasis in early rectal cancer. Cancer 69:322, 1992
30. Sitzler PJ, Seow-Choen F, Ho YH, et al: Lymph node involvement and tumor depth in rectal cancers: an analysis of 805 patients. Dis Colon Rectum 40:1472, 1997
31. Garcia-Aguilar J, Mellgren A, Sirivongs P, et al: Local excision of rectal cancer without adjuvant therapy: a word of caution. Ann Surg 23:345, 2000
32. Paty PB, Nash GM, Baron P, et al: Long-term results of local excision for rectal cancer. Ann Surg 236:522, 2002
33. Garcia-Aguilar J, Pollack J, Lee SH, et al: Accuracy of endorectal ultrasonography in preoperative staging of rectal tumors. Dis Colon Rectum 45:10, 2002
34. Graham RA, Garnsey L, Jessup JM: Local excision of rectal adenocarcinoma. Am J Surg 160:306, 1990
35. Kikuchi R, Takano M, Takagi K, et al: Management of early invasive colorectal cancer: risk of recurrence and clinical guidelines. Dis Colon Rectum 38:1286, 1995
36. Nivatvongs S: Surgical management of malignant colorectal polyps. Surg Clin North Am 82:959, 2002
37. Rothenberger DA and Garcia-Aguilar J: Management of cancer in a polyp. Colorectal Cancer: Multimodality Management. Saltz LB, Ed. Humana Press, Totowa, New Jersey, 2002, p 325
38. Ramirez JM, Aguilella V, Arribas D, et al: Transanal full-thickness excision of rectal tumours: should the defect be sutured? A randomized controlled trial. Colorectal Dis 4:51, 2002
39. Bleday R, Breen E, Jessup JM, et al: Prospective evaluation of local excision for small rectal cancers. Dis Colon Rectum 40:388, 1997
40. Steele GD Jr, Herndon JE, Bleday R, et al: Sphincter sparing treatment for distal rectal adenocarcinoma. Ann Surg Oncol 6:433, 1999
41. Wagman R, Minsky BD, Cohen AM, et al: Conservative management of rectal cancer with local excision and postoperative adjuvant therapy. Int J Radiat Oncol Biol Phys 44:841, 1999
42. Christiansen J: Excision of mid-rectal lesions by the Kraske sacral approach. Br J Surg 67:651, 1980

43. Salvatti EP, Rubin RJ, Eisenstat TE, et al: Electrocoagulation of selected carcinoma of the rectum. Surg Gynecol Obstet 166:393, 1988
44. Papillon J, Berard P: Endocavitary radiation in the conservative treatment of adenocarcinoma of the low rectum. World J Surg 16:451, 1992
45. Rouanet P, Dravet F, Dubois JB, et al: Proctectomy and colo-anal anastomosis after high-dose irradiation of cancers of the lower third of the rectum: functional and oncological results. Ann Chir 48:512, 1994
46. Jones TE: Complications of onstage abdominoperineal resection of the rectum. JAMA 120:104, 1942
47. Havenga K, Enker WE, McDermott K, et al: Male and female sexual and urinary function after total mesorectal excision with autonomic nerve preservation for carcinoma of the rectum. J Am Coll Surg 182:495, 1996
48. Paty PB, Enker WE, Cohen AM, et al: Treatment of rectal cancer by low anterior resection with coloanal anastomosis. Ann Surg 219:365, 1994
49. Shirouza K, Isomoto H, Kakegawa T: Distal spread of rectal cancer and optimal margin of resection for sphincter preserving surgery. Cancer 76:388, 1995
50. Vernava AM, Moran M: A prospective evaluation of distal margins in carcinoma of the rectum. Surg Gynecol Obstet 175:333, 1992
51. Heald RJ: A new approach to rectal cancer. Br J Hosp Med 22:277, 1979
52. Hida J, Yasutomi M, Maruyama T, et al: Indications for colonic J pouch reconstruction after anterior resection for rectal cancer: determining the optimal level of anastomosis. Dis Colon Rectum 41:558, 1998
53. Lazorthes F, Gamagami R, Chiotasso P, et al: Prospective randomized study comparing clinical results between small and large colonic J-pouch following coloanal anastomosis. Dis Colon Rectum 40:1409, 1997
54. Harris GJC, Lavery IJ, Fazio VW: Reasons for failure to construct to colonic J pouch: what can be done to improve the size of the neorectal reservoir should it occur? Dis Colon Rectum 45:1304, 2002
55. Marusch F, Koch A, Schmidt HD, et al: Value of protective stoma in low anterior resections for rectal carcinoma. Dis Colon Rectum 45:1164, 2002
56. Mantyh CR, Hull TL, Fazio VW: Coloplasty in low colorectal anastomosis: manometric and functional comparison with straight and colonic J pouch anastomosis. Dis Colon Rectum 44:37, 2001
57. Sailer M, Fuchs HK, Fein M, et al: Randomized clinical trial comparing quality of life after straight and pouch coloanal reconstruction. Br J Surg 89:1108, 2002
58. Ho YH, Brown S, Heah SM, et al: Comparison of J-pouch and coloplasty pouch for low rectal cancers. Ann Surg 236:49, 2002
59. Machado M, Nygren J, Goldman S, et al: Similar outcome after colonic pouch and side-to-end anastomosis in low anterior resection for rectal cancer: a prospective randomized trial. Ann Surg 238:214, 2003

60. Beart RW, Steele GD, Menck HR, et al: Management and survival of patients with adenocarcinoma of the colon and rectum: a national survey of the commission on cancer. J Am Coll Surg 181:225, 1995
61. Avradopoulos KA, Vezeridis MP, Wanebo HJ: Pelvic exenteration for recurrent rectal cancer. Adv Surg 29:215, 1996
62. Sugerbaker PH: Partial sacrectomy for en-bloc excision of rectal cancer with posterior fixation. Dis Colon Rectum 25:708, 1982
63. Bohm B, Schwenk W, Hoche HP, et al: Does methodological long-term follow-up affect survival after curative resection of colorectal carcinoma? Dis Colon Rectum 36:280, 1993
64. Ohlsson B, Bleland V, Ekberg H, et al: Follow-up after curative surgery for colorectal carcinoma: randomized comparison with no follow-up. Dis Colon Rectum 38:619, 1995
65. Johnson FE, Novell LA, Coplin MA, et al: How practice patterns in colon cancer patient follow-up are affected by surgeon age. Surg Oncol 5:127, 1996
66. Bruinvels DJ, Stiggelbout AM, Kievit J, et al: Follow-up of patients with colorectal cancer: a meta-analysis. Ann Surg 219:174, 1994
67. Welch JP, Donaldson GA: The clinical correlation of an autopsy study of recurrent colorectal cancer. Ann Surg 189:496, 1979
68. Kendal WS, Cripps C, Viertelhausen S, et al: Multimodal management of locally recurrent colorectal cancer. Surg Clin North Am 82:1059, 2002
69. Alektiar KM, Zelefsky MJ, Paty PB, et al: High dose rate intra-operative brachytherapy for recurrent colorectal cancer. Int J Radiat Oncol Biol Phys 48:219, 2000
70. Haddock MG, Gunderson LL, Nelson H, et al: Intraoperative irradiation for locally recurrent colorectal cancer in previously irradiated patients. Int J Radiat Oncol Biol Phys 49:1267, 2001
71. Lindel K, Willet CG, Shellito PC, et al: Intraoperative radiation therapy for locally advanced recurrent rectal or rectosigmoid cancer. Radiother Oncol 58:83, 2001
72. Bouvet M, Milas M, Giacco GG, et al: Predictors of recurrence after local excision and postoperative chemoradiation therapy of adenocarcinoma of the rectum. Ann Surg Oncol 6:26, 1999
73. Killingback M: Local excision of carcinoma of the rectum: indications. World J Surg 16:437, 1992
74. Heald RJ, Ryall RD: Recurrence and survival after total mesorectal excision for rectal cancer. Lancet 1:1479, 1986
75. Turk PS, Wanebo HJ: Results of surgical treatment of nonhepatic colorectal metastases. Cancer 71(suppl):4267, 1993
76. Greene FL, et al: AJCC Cancer Staging Manual, 6th ed. Springer-Verlag, New York, 2002

Acknowledgment

Figures 1 through 11   Tom Moore.

78 PROCEDURES FOR RECTAL PROLAPSE

Steven D. Wexner, M.D., F.A.C.S., F.A.S.C.R.S., and Susan M. Cera, M.D.

Rectal prolapse is an intussusception of the rectum, which may be categorized as occult (internal), mucosal, or complete. Occult rectal prolapse does not extend beyond the anal canal and often is not associated with any symptoms; it may be a precursor to complete prolapse. Mucosal prolapse involves protrusion of the mucosa only, with the muscular layers of the rectum remaining in place. Complete rectal prolapse, or rectal procidentia, involves full-thickness protrusion of the rectum through the anus [see Figure 1].

Whereas the exact pathophysiology of rectal prolapse remains unclear, several factors have been associated with its development, including constipation, female sex, postmenopausal status, and previous anorectal surgical procedures. The constipation frequently arises from conditions such as colonic inertia, neurologic disease, psychiatric illness, and obstructed defecation. Obstructed defecation is also referred to as anismus, spastic pelvic floor, and paradoxical or nonrelaxing puborectalis syndrome. Patients with this condition experience significant pain and have difficulty passing stool; digital compression or any of a variety of perineal maneuvers may be necessary to relieve the functional obstruction.

Chronic constipation and straining are thought to lead to herniation of the rectum through the muscular aperture of the pelvic floor, much as occurs with a hiatal or ventral hernia. As herniation progresses, the mesorectum lengthens and the lateral and rectosigmoid attachments stretch. Weakened pelvic floor muscles (from aging and the postmenopausal state) contribute to the herniation process, as do sphincter defects and pudendal neuropathy from previous anorectal operations or obstetric injuries.

Initially, prolapse occurs only with straining; later in the course of the disease, it occurs with any increase in intra-abdominal pressure or may develop into a chronic condition. Chronic prolapse results in the development of a patulous anus and incontinence. The incontinence may derive from direct sphincteric stretching, from traction injury of the pudendal nerves caused by straining, or from continuous stimulation of the rectoinhibitory reflex by the intussusception, which results in chronic reflexive relaxation of the internal anal sphincter and inappropriate leakage of stool and mucus.

The anatomic abnormalities resulting from rectal prolapse include a deep cul-de-sac, a redundant rectosigmoid, an elongated mesorectum, diastasis of the levator ani, perineal descent, a patulous anus, and loss of support of the uterus and the bladder [see Table 1]. Rectal prolapse also is frequently associated with other anatomic defects of the pelvic floor, such as rectoceles, enteroceles, cystoceles, and uterine and vaginal prolapse. Recognition of how the functional pathology of the pelvic floor results in the anatomic abnormalities seen with rectal prolapse is essential to understanding the various operative approaches and determining appropriate long-term management. Patients with rectal prolapse, like most patients with pelvic floor dysfunction, frequently require postoperative bowel retraining with fiber therapy, laxatives, or biofeedback to address the functional component of this disease and thereby prevent recurrence once the prolapse has been surgically corrected.

More than 120 operations for treating rectal prolapse have been described. A detailed description of all available options is clearly beyond the scope of this chapter. Instead, we focus on a few key procedures that currently are freqently employed and enjoy widespread acceptance. For present purposes, we have excluded a number of procedures that, though popular in certain regions of the world, are not universally accepted.

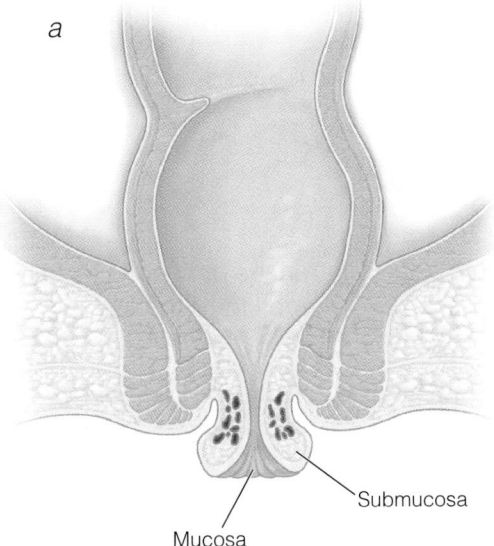
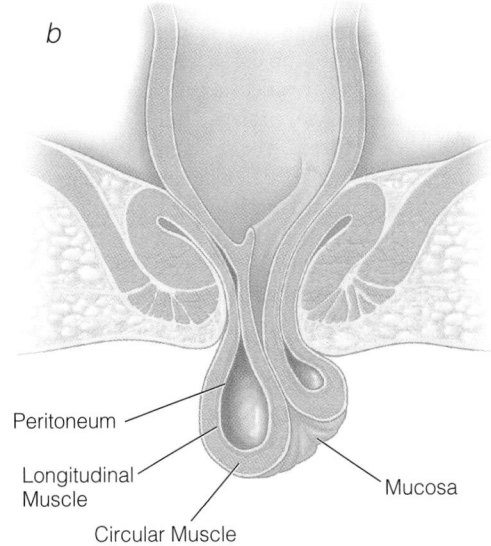

a

b

Submucosa

Mucosa

Peritoneum

Longitudinal Muscle

Circular Muscle

Mucosa

Figure 1 In mucosal prolapse (*a*), only the mucosa protrudes, whereas in complete rectal prolapse (*b*), the full thickness of the rectal wall protrudes.

Table 1 Anatomic Abnormalities Associated with Rectal Prolapse

Deep cul-de-sac	Herniation of pelvic organs through pelvic funnel
Redundant rectosigmoid colon	
Elongated mesorectum	Patulous anus
Diastasis of levator ani	Loss of support of uterus and bladder
Perineal descent	

Preoperative Evaluation

Because of the protrusion of tissue through the anus and the frequent bloody discharge, most patients initially mistake rectal prolapse for hemorrhoids [see Table 2]. Such patients often present with a complaint of "persistent hemorrhoids" after a recent hemorrhoid operation. Similarly, many patients mistake incarcerated rectal prolapse for thrombosed hemorrhoids. Consequently, a high level of suspicion and careful physical examination are required to differentiate hemorrhoids from rectal procidentia [see Table 3].

The diagnosis is most easily made with the patient straining while seated on the toilet. If the prolapse cannot be reproduced in the office setting, administration of a phosphate enema may reveal it. The appearance of circumferential, concentric folds of rectal mucosa serves to differentiate rectal prolapse from hemorrhoids, in which the folds (sulci) occur in a radial pattern, yielding three discrete anatomic bundles [see Figure 2]. In addition, close inspection of a full-thickness rectal prolapse reveals a circumferential sulcus between the anus and rectum, and palpation reveals a double rectal wall. The prolapse should be easily reducible unless incarcerated.

Chronic prolapse leads to inflammation, edema, and ulceration of the rectal mucosa. Biopsy of these areas should be undertaken to determine whether there is a neoplastic lesion acting as the source of the intussusception. In addition, complete colonoscopy is performed to search for lesions elsewhere in the colon, which may affect the surgical approach to the proplapse. Occasionally, a solitary rectal ulcer in the anterior rectum is seen in a patient with obstructed defecation caused by ischemia of the rectal wall from chronic straining. Barium enemas may induce strangulation and thus should be avoided; however, water-soluble contrast enemas may be of some use in identifying pathologic conditions in the remainder of the colon. Defecography is useful when occult intussusception or mucosal prolapse is suspected or when the patient has a history of prolapse but is unable to reproduce the prolapse in the office. If the prolapse is associated with conditions arising from pelvic floor defects (e.g., urinary incontinence, rectocele, enterocele, cystocele, and uterine and vaginal prolapse), consultation with a gynecology team for combined surgical intervention is warranted.[1,2]

About 50% of patients with prolapse have a history of constipation.[1,3] Possible causes of the underlying constipation—such as electrolyte (calcium) imbalance, hormonal (thyroid) dysfunction, obstructed defecation, and colonic inertia—should be investigated. Surface electromyography may be used to diagnose paradoxical contraction of the puborectalis muscle. In patients with severe constipation, a colonic transit study using ingested radiopaque markers aids in diagnosing colonic inertia, which may necessitate inclusion of subtotal colectomy as part of surgical management.

Fecal incontinence is a presenting symptom in 30% to 80% of patients with rectal prolapse.[3,4] For these patients, anal ultra-sonography, manometry, electromyography, and pudendal nerve terminal motor latency testing are indicated to help guide the choice of surgical procedure to treat the prolapse.

Operative Planning

CHOICE OF PROCEDURE

Because the etiology and pathophysiology of rectal prolapse are not well understood and appear to vary, it has not proved possible to identify any individual procedure as the optimal surgical approach to this condition. The current focus in the literature is on developing criteria by which specific patients can be matched to the specific operations that are most appropriate for them. The choice of operation is determined by the patient's age, sex, level of operative risk, associated pelvic floor defects, degree of incontinence, and history of constipation, as well as by the surgeon's experience. The goal is to correct the greatest number of anatomic problems (including the prolapse and any associated functional disorders) safely and efficiently while minimizing both perioperative morbidity and postoperative recurrence.

The procedures performed for repair of rectal prolapse may be divided into two broad categories: perineal and abdominal [see Table 4]. The perineal operations include anal encirclement (the Thiersch wire procedure), mucosal sleeve resection (the Delorme procedure), and perineal rectosigmoidectomy (the Altemeier procedure). In the original description of the Thiersch wire procedure, silver wire was placed in the subcutaneous tissues surrounding the anus through two small incisions, then tied around the assistant's finger to narrow the anal aperture.[5] It was believed that this operation controlled the prolapse by reinforcing the anal sphincter and fixing the rectum to surrounding structures through induction of tissue reaction to the foreign material. The simplicity of the operation was offset by many problems, including breakage of the wire, sloughing of the overlying skin, perineal sepsis, and fecal impaction. Various other, more compliant materials (e.g., Marlex mesh and Silastic rods) have since been used in place of the silver

---

Table 2 Symptoms of Rectal Prolapse

Sensation of protrusion of tissue through anus	Incontinence
"Persistent hemorrhoids"	Incomplete evacuation
Mucoid or bloody discharge	Perineal pressure
Constipation	Excoriation of perianal skin

Table 3 Differences between Rectal Prolapse and Hemorrhoids

	Rectal Prolapse	Hemorrhoids
Tissue folds	Circumferential	Radial
Sulcus between prolapse and rectum	Circumferential	None
Abnormality on palpation	Double rectal wall	Hemorrhoidal plexus
Resting and squeeze pressure	Decreased	Normal

a

b

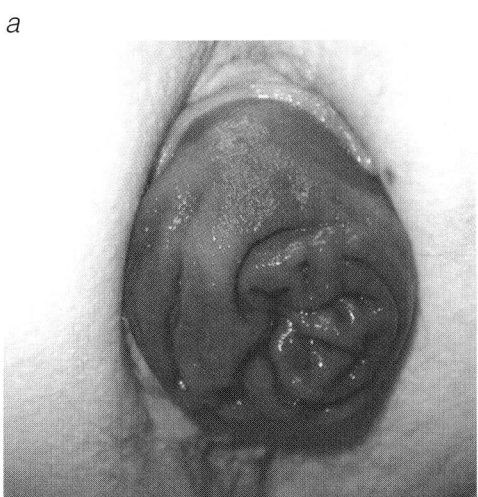
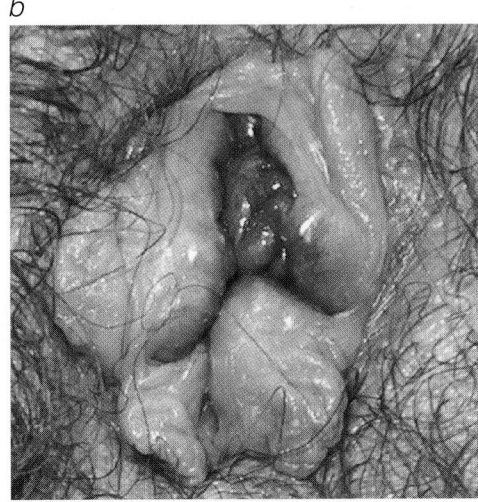

Figure 2 **Rectal prolapse can be differentiated from hemorrhoids on the basis of physical appearance. (*a*) Rectal prolapse is distinguished by concentric mucosal folds. (*b*) Hemorrhoids are distinguished by radial sulci and discrete hemorrhoidal bundles.**

wire, but none of these modifications have proved successful. In addition, better anesthetic techniques and improved perioperative medical management have made it possible to employ other perineal or abdominal procedures safely in most patients. Consequently, anal encirclement remains an option only for those patients who would be at unacceptably high risk with other types of procedures.

Mucosal sleeve resection, as described by Delorme in 1900, involves stripping the mucosa from the redundant rectum and plicating the denuded rectal wall with sutures to create bulk and thus prevent future prolapse.[6] Perineal rectosigmoidectomy, originally described by Mikulicz[7] and subsequently modified by Altemeier,[8] involves transanal amputation of the prolapsed rectum coupled with a coloanal anastomosis.

The various abdominal operations may be performed as either open or laparoscopic procedures, and they differ with respect to how far rectal mobilization extends, whether the lateral ligaments are divided, whether the rectum is fixed anteriorly or posteriorly, what fixation material is used (sutures, mesh, or sponge), and whether sigmoid resection is included. At present, the operation most commonly performed to treat rectal prolapse in the United States is suture rectopexy, with sigmoid resection added (the Frykman-Goldberg procedure) if constipation is a significant presenting complaint. The various posterior rectopexies with sutures or mesh are more popular than the procedures involving anterior fixation with mesh or posterior placement of a polyvinyl alcohol (Ivalon) sponge. Anterior fixation of the rectum using a sling was proposed by Ripstein and Lantern as a way of restoring the natural contour of the rectum and preventing intussusception.[9] Originally, fascia lata was used for the sling; subsequently, various artificial materials (e.g., Teflon, Marlex, and Gore-Tex mesh) came to be used instead. The Ivalon sponge operation (the Wells procedure) entails placement of the sponge posterior to the rectum to create an inflammatory reaction and a consequent rectopexy.[10] Because of the risks imposed by the foreign materials (including infection, erosion, and stenosis), few surgeons now perform either anterior fixation or foreign body placement.

Laparoscopic resection rectopexy involves a laparoscopic-assisted approach with intracorporeal mobilization of the sigmoid colon and the rectum, division of the mesenteric vessels, and distal transection of the bowel. The bowel is then exteriorized through a small incision (often, a Pfannenstiel incision), and the proximal transection is performed. The rectopexy sutures are placed by means of an open technique, and the anastomosis is created with a transanally placed circular stapler. Laparoscopic suture rectopexy without resection is performed entirely laparoscopically, with intracorporeal mobilization and suture placement.

Perineal Procedures

MUCOSAL SLEEVE RESECTION (DELORME PROCEDURE)

Both mucosal sleeve resection and perineal rectosigmoidectomy may be performed with the patient under either general or spinal anesthesia. Preoperatively, the patient undergoes mechanical and antibiotic bowel preparation. Such preparation consists of oral administration of 45 ml of sodium phosphate solution, followed by three 8 oz glasses of water, at 4 P.M. and 9 P.M., and administration of 1 g of neomycin with 500 mg of metronidazole at 7 P.M. and 11 P.M. Before the procedure, the patient receives prophylactic antibiotics, and subcutaneous heparin is used in conjunction with sequential compression devices to prevent venous thromboembolism.

Table 4 Operations Performed to Treat Rectal Prolapse

Perineal procedures	Anal encirclement (Thiersch wire procedure) Mucosal sleeve resection (Delorme procedure) Perineal rectosigmoidectomy (Altemeier procedure)

Transabdominal procedures	Rectopexy
	  Suture
	  Anterior sling (Ripstein procedure)
	  Ivalon sponge (posterior rectopexy)
	  Posterior sling (modified Ripstein procedure)
	Resection
	Suture rectopexy with resection (Frykman-Goldberg procedure)
	Laparoscopic repairs
	  Resection rectopexy
	  Suture rectopexy
	  Rectopexy with mesh

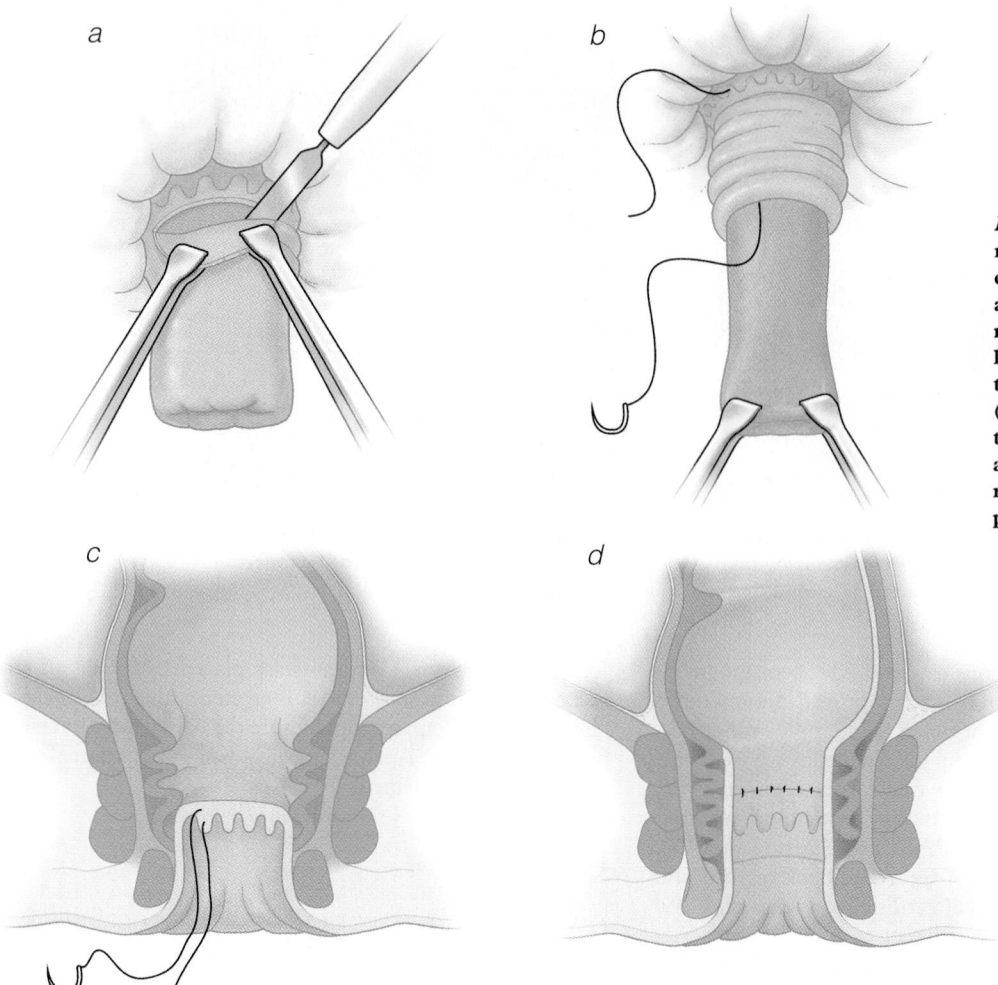

Figure 3 Mucosal sleeve resection. (*a*) With the rectum everted, the mucosa is incised and dissected away from the muscular tube. (*b*) The muscular tube is plicated with sutures to form a muscular pessary. (*c*) A mucosa-to-mucosa anastomosis is fashioned. (*d*) The anastomosis spontaneously reduces into its anatomic position.

After induction of anesthesia or administration of intravenous sedation, a bladder catheter is inserted, and the patient is placed in the prone jackknife position with a Kraske roll beneath the hips and the buttocks abducted with tape. A self-retaining retractor may be used to evert the anus. The muscular stripping can be undertaken with the prolapse either everted or reduced. Our preference is to evert the prolapse, and the following technical description embodies that preference.

Operative Technique

Step 1: eversion of rectum The rectal prolapse is everted by placing gentle traction on the rectal wall with Babcock tissue forceps passed through the anus. As the prolapsed tissue emerges, the Babcock forceps are repositioned more proximally on the rectal wall to provide a better grasp and facilitate delivery of the prolapse through the anus and into the operative field.

Step 2: submucosal injection of anesthetic Once the rectum has been everted, a local anesthetic solution containing 0.25% bupivacaine, 0.5% lidocaine, and epinephrine (in a 1:400,000 dilution) is circumferentially injected 1 to 1.5 cm above the dentate line to minimize bleeding.

Step 3: circumferential incision of mucosa The rectal mucosa is incised at this level with a conventional diathermy, and four clamps are placed on the proximal mucosal edge for traction [*see Figure 3*].

Step 4: dissection of mucosa from muscle Gentle traction is placed on the clamps, and the mucosa is dissected away from the muscle with the electrocautery. A finger is placed inside the muscular tube to facilitate traction and help prevent full-thickness injury. Resection of the mucosal sleeve is continued until resistance prevents further dissection. A tube of redundant muscular tissue then remains.

Step 5: plication of rectal muscle The muscular tube is plicated by placing eight reefing sutures circumferentially in the wall.

Step 6: resection of mucosa and anastomosis The excess mucosa is transected in a superior-to-inferior direction, and the two cut edges of mucosa are approximated with sutures. Transection is continued on one side for a quarter of the circumference, at which point a second suture is placed. With traction applied to these two sutures, two additional sutures are placed at 90° intervals to establish four quadrants. Transection and anastomosis are serially performed in each of the four quadrants until the mucosa is completely excised and the anastomosis has been completed. With the removal of the retractor, the anastomosis should spontaneously reduce into its anatomic position.

Postoperative care Because the patients are often elderly, 1 to 3 days of observation may be indicated. The bladder catheter is removed on the following morning, and the patient is advanced to a regular diet as soon as he or she can tolerate it. The patient is sent home on a regimen of fiber supplementation and sitz baths as soon as medical stability is ensured and appropriate social circumstances arranged.

Troubleshooting

The Delorme procedure prevents rectal intussusception by resecting redundant mucosa and by removing laxity in the rectal wall through plication of the muscular redundancy. The key to success is to continue the sleeve resection until some resistance is met and the dissection cannot proceed further. Sometimes, the anterior wall is longer than the posterior wall or vice versa, but such discrepancies should not affect the repair. The anastomosis is performed one quadrant at a time to prevent retraction of the transected mucosa into the proximal bowel.

PERINEAL RECTOSIGMOIDECTOMY

Operative Technique

Anesthesia and positioning are the same for perineal rectosigmoidectomy as for mucosal sleeve resection.

Steps 1 and 2 Steps 1 and 2 of this procedure are the same as steps 1 and 2 of mucosal sleeve resection (see above).

Step 3: circumferential incision through rectal wall With the rectum everted, the prolapse consists of two tubes of rectal wall, with the inner tube consisting of rectum attached to the sigmoid and the outer tube consisting of rectum attached to the dentate line. The mucosa is circumferentially scored with a standard diathermy 1 to 1.5 cm cephalad to the dentate line [see Figure 4]. The incision should be made at the top of the anal columns to preserve the entire transition zone, which is important for nocturnal continence. The incision is deepened through all layers of the outer rectal tube until perirectal fat is encountered and the mesorectum is identified on the superior aspect of the prolapse with the patient prone.

Step 4: mobilization of rectum and division of mesentery Rectal mobilization is accomplished by clamping, ligating, and dividing the vessels of the mesorectum. As the mesorectum is divided, tension on the rectum delivers more of the prolapse into the operative field. Division of the mesorectum is continued close to the bowel wall until no more bowel can be delivered. During this phase, the sliding hernia of peritoneum (cul-de-sac) anterior to the rectum (on the inferior aspect of the prolapse with the patient prone) may be opened to allow palpation of the intraperitoneal contents and determination of whether the colon is straight in the pelvis.

A finger may be inserted into the pelvis alongside the rectum to facilitate assessment of the redundancy of or the tension on the remaining rectum and sigmoid. If redundancy is still encountered, more mesorectum is divided to allow further mobilization

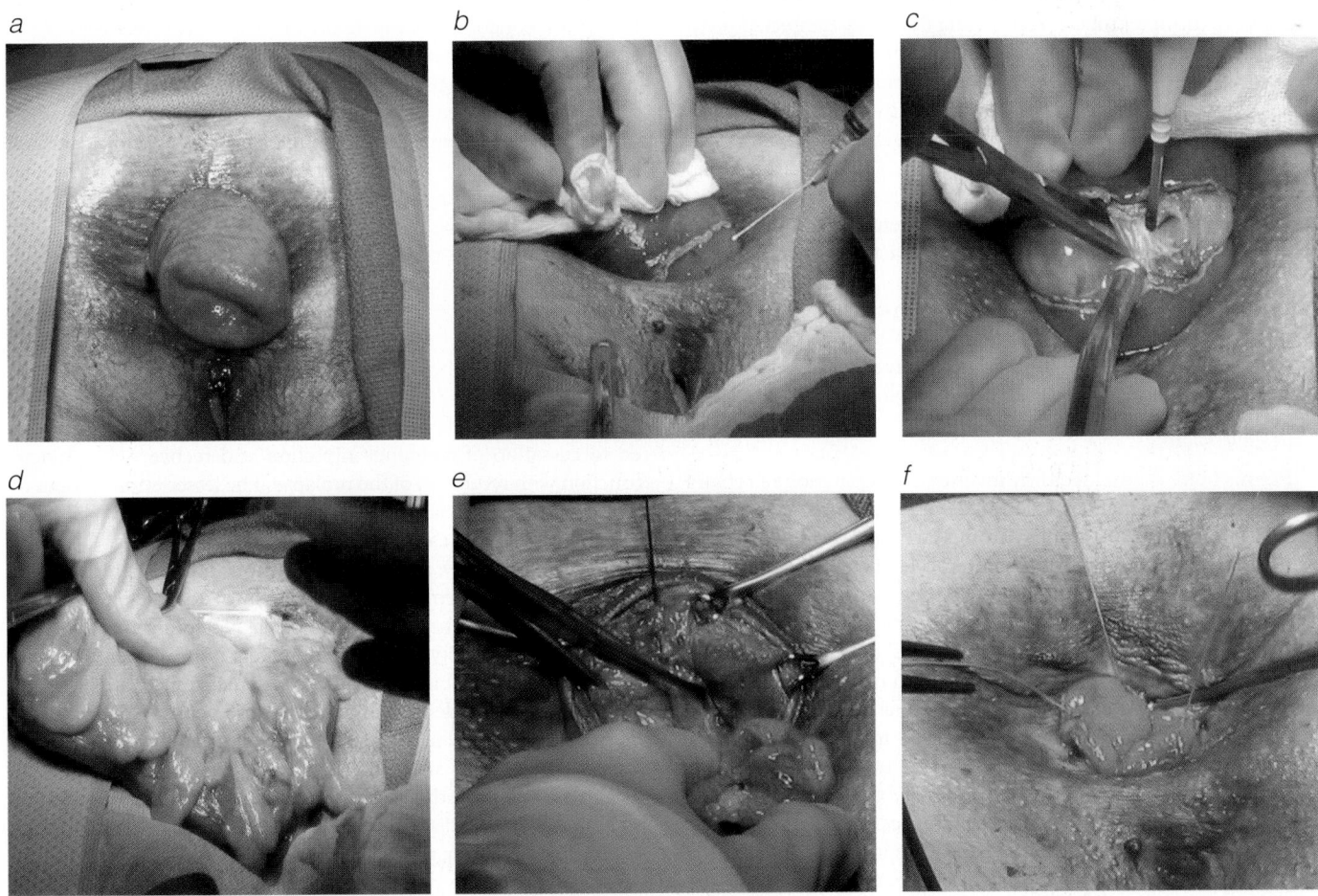

Figure 4 **Perineal rectosigmoidectomy. (*a*) The rectum is everted. (*b*) The anesthetic is injected submucosally. (*c*) A circumferential incision is made and deepened through the outer rectal tube until perirectal fat is encountered. (*d*) The rectum and the sigmoid are mobilized with division of the mesentery; levatorplasty is then done. (*e*) The first suture of the anastomosis is placed. (*f*) The remaining sutures are placed.**

of the bowel through the anus. Careful control of the mesentery with ligatures is advised to prevent retraction of bleeding vessels into the pelvis.

Step 5: ligation of hernia sac Once the redundant rectum and sigmoid have been adequately mobilized, the hernia sac of peritoneum is sutured closed. Care is taken to resect any redundant hernia sac to prevent future anterior intussusception; this step is similar to the high ligation performed for other types of hernias.

Step 6: levatorplasty Levatorplasty is then performed to restore the appropriate angles of the pelvic floor muscles, to aid in treatment of incontinence, and to narrow the aperture through which herniation occurs and thereby prevent recurrence. It can be performed anterior to the rectum, posterior to the rectum, or both. A narrow retractor is employed to expose the outer tube of rectum and uncover the levator muscles. Interrupted 2-0 nonabsorbable sutures are placed through the levator muscles on each side and secured loosely enough to allow a finger to be inserted alongside the rectum.

Step 7: proximal transection of rectum and anastomosis
The point at which the redundant rectum is to be transected is identified at the level at which the mesorectum is divided. The bowel wall is circumferentially cleared of appendages in preparation for transection and anastomosis. Transection is begun by dividing a small area of the bowel wall superiorly and placing a suture through the edge of the outer tube of rectum and the newly transected proximal edge of the bowel. Transection is continued inferiorly on one side for a quarter of the circumference, and a second suture is placed. With traction on these two sutures, two additional sutures are placed around the remaining circumference to mark four quadrants. Transection and anastomosis are serially performed in each of the four quadrants until the rectum is completely transected. When the anastomosis is complete, it retracts into the pelvis, where it may be inspected with a bivalve retractor.

Postoperative care Patients are often observed in the hospital for 1 to 3 days. Their diet is advanced as tolerated, and the bladder catheter is removed on postoperative day 1. Patients are sent home on a regimen of fiber supplementation and sitz baths.

Troubleshooting

Perineal rectosigmoidectomy involves a combination of repairs of anatomic abnormalities associated with rectal prolapse. Rectal mobilization yields a rectopexy from scarring; resection removes redundant bowel; ligation of the enterocele obliterates the hernia sac; and levatorplasty provides reconstruction of the pelvic floor. Each step requires that attention be paid to appropriate planes of dissection and that meticulous hemostasis be maintained. For example, transection of the outer rectal wall may lead to inadvertent division of the mesentery before vascular control is obtained; if this occurs, traction should be placed on the inner wall to expose the proximal mesentery and allow the surgeon to regain vascular control. In addition, transection of the outer rectal wall may lead to inadvertent simultaneous transection of both walls; if this occurs, clamps should be placed on the inner wall to prevent retraction into the pelvis and to facilitate rectal mobilization and division of the mesorectum [see Step 4, above].

To help prevent recurrence, all redundant bowel should be resected once mobilization of the rectum and division of the mesentery are complete. If, at the start of the procedure, only a short segment of prolapse is produced or the patient is found to have only a mucosal prolapse, a Delorme operation may be performed instead.

COMPLICATIONS

Partial separation of the mucosal anastomosis after mucosal sleeve resection is not uncommon and usually does not warrant intervention. After perineal rectosigmoid resection, anastomotic separation may lead to leakage and pelvic sepsis, which must be treated with bowel rest and antibiotics or, in extreme cases, with debridement, repair, and stoma formation.

Early postoperative bleeding from the mucosal edges or, in the case of the perineal rectosigmoidectomy, from the presacral space may be observed. Late postoperative bleeding may result from tearing of the sutures through the mucosa or from separation of the anastomosis. All significant bleeding should be evaluated and controlled in the OR, with the source of the bleeding dictating the type of repair required.

Anastomotic strictures may occur after either mucosal sleeve resection or perineal rectosigmoidectomy. They are treated with serial dilations either at home or in the OR.

OUTCOME EVALUATION

The advantages of the perineal procedures include (1) the option to use spinal anesthesia, (2) avoidance of peritoneal adhesions, (3) short hospital stays (1 to 4 days), (4) a lower risk of injury to the pelvic nerves, (5) reduced pain, and (6) the opportunity for concomitant repair of other anorectal problems (e.g., sphincter defects, hemorrhoids, rectoceles, cystoceles, and vaginal prolapse). The disadvantages include (1) a higher recurrence rate and (2) reduced improvement of any fecal incontinence.

Reported recurrence rates for the perineal approaches range from 5% to 21%[11-13] and are higher than those for the abdominal approaches; however, the perineal repairs can be performed multiple times in the same patient as necessary.[14] Because they are less invasive, perineal procedures generally carry a lower morbidity than abdominal procedures do, with the majority of the complications being medical in nature.[11,12] Whereas constipation is neither exacerbated nor alleviated by the perineal procedures, continence is significantly improved, though not as much as it is improved by the abdominal procedures.[15,16] The improvement in continence seen after both abdominal and perineal procedures for rectal prolapse is related to cessation of rectoanal inhibition and recovery of sphincter function with reduction of the prolapse. The lesser improvement reported after perineal procedures may be related to sphincter stretching or, in the case of perineal rectosigmoidectomy, to loss of the rectal reservoir. A comparison of various perineal procedures—including the Delorme procedure, perineal rectosigmoidectomy, and rectosigmoidectomy with levatorplasty—found that the addition of a levatorplasty yielded the greatest improvement in continence, the least morbidity, and the lowest recurrence rate.[16]

Because the incidence of rectal prolapse peaks in the sixth and seventh decades of life, patients undergoing these procedures frequently are elderly and have significant comorbid conditions.[17] The perineal procedures are economically and physiologically advantageous in the short term and are therefore ideal for elderly patients or for any patients with multiple comorbid conditions, as well as for those who are at high operative risk or who need combined intervention from various pelvic surgical specialists. In these patients, who generally have limited life expectancies, the high risk of recurrence associated with the perineal procedures may be irrelevant. Perineal operations may also be indicated for

a   *b*

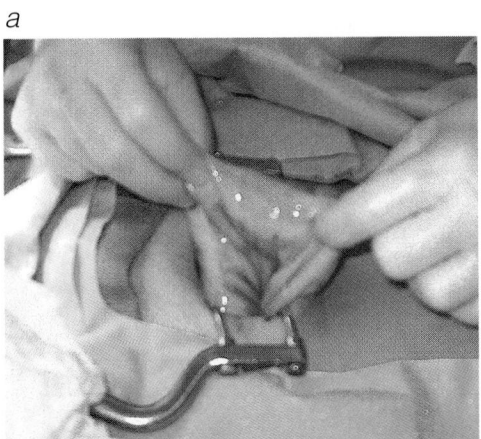
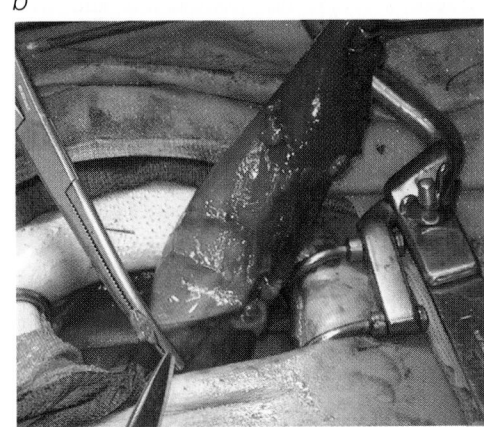

Figure 5 **Open resection rectopexy. (*a*) The redundant sigmoid is mobilized through the abdominal wound. (*b*) The proximal sigmoid is transected, and the sigmoid mesentery is clamped, ligated, and divided.**

patients who have undergone multiple previous abdominal operations and are likely to have dense adhesions, as well as for young men who do not wish to risk impairment of sexual function.

Abdominal Procedures

OPEN RECTOPEXY

Resection Rectopexy (Frykman-Goldberg Procedure)

Just as with perineal procedures, patients undergo mechanical and antibiotic bowel preparation on the day before surgery. Before operation, parenteral antibiotics and subcutaneous heparin are administered, and sequential compression devices are placed on the legs.

After induction of general anesthesia, the patient is placed in the modified lithotomy position with the legs in padded stirrups. If there is a history of one or more previous pelvic operations, bilateral ureteral stents are placed by a urologist, and a urinary catheter is inserted. The rectum is irrigated with saline through a transanally placed mushroom catheter until the effluent is clear, after which point additional irrigation is undertaken with a povidone-iodine solution. The catheter is left in place for the initial portion of the procedure, and the extra effluent is allowed to drain into a plastic bag secured to the catheter. The surgeon stands on the patient's left side.

Operative technique   *Step 1: initial incision and exploration.* A low midline or Pfannenstiel incision is made, the pelvis is explored, a Balfour or Buchwalter retractor is placed, and the small bowel is packed into the upper abdomen.

Step 2: mobilization of sigmoid.   The sigmoid colon is mobilized away from the left lateral wall by incising the lateral peritoneal reflection [*see Figure 5a*]. The gonadal vessels and the ureter are identified and swept posteriorly. The peritoneal incision is continued to the left of the rectum, curving anteriorly in the rectouterine or rectovesical sulcus. The peritoneum at the base of the sigmoid mesentery on the right is also incised, and this incision is continued to the right of the rectum to unite with the previous incision at the anterior rectum.

Step 3: proximal transection of sigmoid colon and placement of stapler anvil.   Once the entire sigmoid is mobilized, the proximal

point of transection is chosen by finding an area of colon that easily falls into the pelvis but includes all of the redundant sigmoid colon. This level of the colon, the sigmoid-descending portion, is circumferentially cleaned of surrounding tissue. A straight clamp is placed proximally and an adjacent bowel clamp distally. The bowel is divided with a knife along the straight clamp. The straight clamp is released, and three Babcock forceps are placed to hold open the lumen. A purse-string suture of 2-0 Prolene is placed, and the head of a 33 mm circular stapler is secured in the lumen. Alternatively, a purse-string clamp may be used.

Step 4: division of sigmoid mesentery.   The mesentery of the sigmoid is clamped, ligated, and divided close to the colon [*see Figure 5b*]. The superior rectal vessels are carefully preserved.

Step 5: mobilization of rectum and division of lateral ligaments.   A Babcock clamp is placed on the rectal stump and lifted upward. The avascular plane of areolar tissue between the mesorectum and the presacral fascia is identified and divided with the electrocautery. A St. Mark's retractor is placed behind the rectum to provide traction, then advanced with dissection distally along the rectum to the level of the coccyx.

Dissection of the right side of the rectum is performed with the surgeon standing to the patient's left. The left hand places traction on the rectum, while the right hand uses the electrocautery to divide the lateral stalk in a posterior-to-anterior direction. The St. Mark's retractor is used to retract the tissues of the sidewall away from the rectum.

Dissection of the left side of the rectum is performed with the surgeon on the patient's right. Again, the left hand places traction on the rectum, while the right hand performs the dissection in a posterior-to-anterior direction.

Dissection anterior to the rectum is performed by using the retractor to place traction on either the uterus (in women) or the bladder (in men), then proceeding anterior to the rectum down to the level of the lower third of the vagina (in women) or below the seminal vesicles (in men). The lower one third to one half of the lateral stalks may be preserved, though the overlying peritoneum should be incised.

Step 6: placement of sutures for rectopexy.   With upward traction applied to the rectal stump, horizontal mattress sutures of 2-0 Prolene are placed to perform the rectopexy. Starting on one side, a suture is placed through the peritoneum and the endopelvic fascia adjacent to the rectum, with care taken not to penetrate the rectal wall. The suture is guided through the presacral fascia and the periosteum to the side of the midline and approximately 1 cm below the level of the sacral promontory. It is then completed by passing it back through the peritoneum and the endopelvic fascia. One or two sutures are placed on each side; they are left untied and are tagged with hemostats.

Step 7: transection of bowel at upper rectum. The rectosigmoid junction is identified on the basis of the splaying of the taeniae coli, the absence of appendices epiploicae, and the proximity to the sacral promontory. This junction marks the site of distal transection. Proctoscopic examination is helpful for determining the appropriate location. Transection may be performed with a stapler, a purse-string suture clamp, or a knife followed by a handsewn purse-string suture.

Step 8: completion of colorectal anastomosis. The circular stapler is advanced through the anus to the rectal stump. Under the manual and visual guidance of the abdominal and perineal operating surgeons, the trocar is advanced and the anvil engaged. The circular stapler is closed and fired. The stapler is then gently removed, and the "doughnuts" are checked for integrity. The anastomosis is tested for leaks by filling the pelvis with irrigant, clamping the colon proximal to the anastomosis, and insufflating air into the rectum. Air bubbles from the anastomosis indicate a leak that requires suture reinforcement. The rectopexy sutures are secured snugly to complete the procedure, and the abdomen is irrigated and closed in the usual fashion.

An alternative approach to this step is to perform endoscopic visualization of the anastomosis while simultaneously insufflating air through either the rigid proctoscope or the flexible sigmoidoscope. This method allows reliable confirmation of mucosal viability and anastomotic integrity. Moreover, if any supplemental anastomotic reinforcement sutures are needed, they can be placed much more easily at this time than after the rectopexy sutures have been secured. Sheets of sodium hyaluronate–based bioresorbable membrane are placed before closure of the fascia to help minimize postoperative adhesion formation; at our institution, these sheets are routinely used during most laparotomies.[18] The abdominal incision is closed in the usual fashion.

Postoperative care. After operation, the patient is started on a clear liquid diet, then advanced to a regular diet when bowel function returns. The bladder catheter is removed on postoperative day 1, when ambulation also begins.

Troubleshooting Either suture rectopexy or sigmoid resection can be performed alone by following some of the steps just outlined (see above). Circumferential mobilization of the rectum to the level of the coccyx posteriorly and the upper third of the vagina anteriorly, with division of the lateral ligaments, is advocated to minimize recurrence. Division of the lateral ligaments increases the risk of postoperative constipation; however, inadequate distal mobilization or posterior mobilization performed without lateral ligament division results in laxity of the rectum and the attachments below the level of sacral fixation, which increases the risk of early recurrence. During the sigmoid resection, it is important to remove all redundant bowel; however, it is equally important to ensure that the anastomosis is tension free and well vascularized. During both rectal mobilization and sigmoid resection, careful attention should be paid to preserving the superior rectal artery and the sacral nerves.

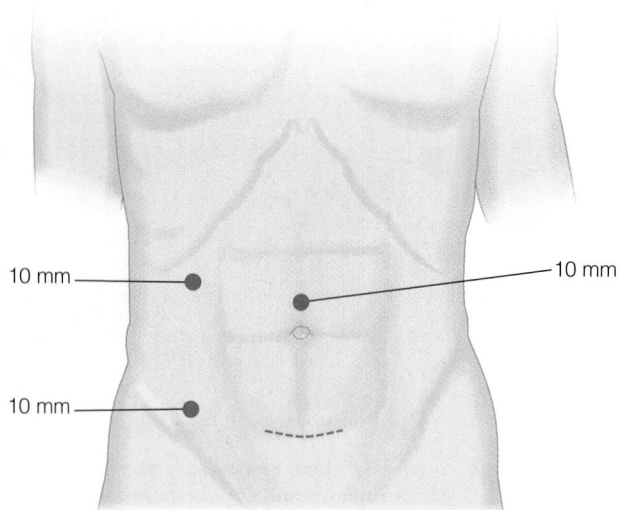

Figure 6 **Laparoscopic resection rectopexy. Shown is the recommended port placement. A 10 mm trocar is placed in the periumbilical region by means of an open technique. Two 10 mm trocars are then placed in the right abdomen.**

Complications Presacral bleeding may result from placement of sutures in the presacral fascia and consequent injury to the presacral veins. It may be controlled by tying down the sutures and applying direct manual pressure. For persistent bleeding, thumbtacks may be required.

Injury to the pelvic nerves and consequent impotence are possibilities with any procedure in which the rectum is mobilized. Performing the dissection close to the bowel wall minimizes the chances that these complications will occur.

Suturing the rectum too close to the sacrum may compress the lumen. This problem may be corrected by removing and replacing the sutures. Any uncertainty about rectal compression can be resolved by means of intraoperative proctoscopy.

The incidence of abdominal sepsis from an anastomotic leak can be minimized by ensuring a well-vascularized and tension-free anastomosis.

LAPAROSCOPIC RECTOPEXY

Laparoscopic Resection Rectopexy

Preoperative management includes full mechanical bowel preparation and both oral and parenteral antibiotic preparation. In addition, cefotetan, 2 g I.V., is administered along with heparin, 5,000 units subcutaneously, at the start of the operation.

After the induction of general anesthesia, the patient is placed in the modified lithotomy position with the legs in pneumatic compression stockings and padded stirrups. The arms are tucked at the sides, and extra care is taken to secure the patient to the bed because of the rotation and tilting required during operation. Two or more monitors are placed on opposite sides of the operating table. The rectum is irrigated with saline through a transanally placed mushroom catheter until the effluent is clear, at which point additional irrigation is initiated with a povidone-iodine solution. The catheter is left in place for the initial portion of the procedure, and the extra effluent is allowed to drain into a plastic bag secured to the catheter. If requested, lateral ureteral stents are placed by a urologist, and a urinary catheter and an orogastric tube are inserted. The abdomen is shaved, prepared with povodone-iodine solution, and appropriately draped.

Operative technique *Step 1: placement of ports.* A 10 mm trocar is placed infraumbilically or supraumbilically (depending on patient size) by means of the open Hasson technique; this port will be used for the camera. Pneumoperitoneum is established, and two additional 10 mm trocars are placed along the lateral edge of the rectus abdominis in the right midabdomen and the right iliac fossa [*see Figure 6*]. If necessary, one or two additional trocars may be placed laterally on the left of the abdomen to assist with sigmoid retraction.

Step 2: mobilization of sigmoid and rectum. The operating table is tilted to the patient's right to facilitate medial retraction of the left colon, which is gently grasped with a Babcock forceps. An ultrasonic scalpel is placed through the right lower port and used to mobilize the sigmoid colon and the descending colon away from the left lateral side wall. Early identification of retroperitoneal structures, including the left ureter and the gonadal and iliac vessels, is achieved. The extent of mobilization is limited because the goal is to resect only the redundant portion of the colon. Laparoscopic resection rectopexy is the only type of left-side resection in which the splenic flexure is deliberately not mobilized in order to prevent redundancy and therefore recurrence of the prolapse. Dissection is extended into the pelvis, and the upper lateral rectal attachments are divided. With cephalad traction applied to the rectum, the mesorectum is circumferentially divided to the level of the coccyx.

Step 3: division of mesenteric vessels. The peritoneum of the left mesocolon is scored to permit identification and preparation of the vessels for transection. A 30 mm linear vascular cutting stapler is inserted through the right iliac fossa port, and the vessels are individually transected. The use of endoscopic hemostatic clips or endoscopic vessel loops is the most expedient option for managing imperfections of hemostasis. The location of the ureter is reconfirmed before each application of the stapler.

Step 4: intracorporeal transection of rectum at rectosigmoid junction. At the point where the taeniae coli coalesce, the rectosigmoid junction is divided with a laparoscopic linear stapler passed through the right lower quadrant port.

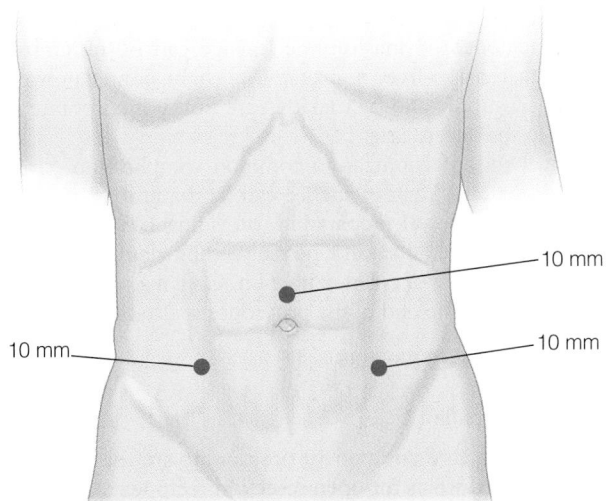

Figure 7 **Laparoscopic suture or mesh rectopexy. A 10 mm trocar is placed in the periumbilical region. Two additional 10 mm trocars are then placed, one in each lower quadrant.**

Step 5: extracorporeal transection of proximal bowel. A small (4 to 5 cm) Pfannenstiel incision is made, a wound protector drape is inserted, and the sigmoid is delivered through the wound. Transection of the proximal bowel is performed in an area of the colon that easily reaches the sacral promontory without redundancy. A purse-string suture is placed in the edge of the proximal bowel, and the anvil of a 33 mm circular stapler is inserted and secured. The bowel is then placed back into the abdomen.

Step 6: placement of rectopexy sutures. Via the Pfannenstiel incision, mattress sutures of nonabsorbable material are passed through the peritoneum and fascia on the lateral rectum, through the presacral fascia just off the midline and 1 cm below the sacral promontory, and back through the lateral tissue. One or two sutures are placed on each side but are not secured until the anastomosis has been created.

Step 7: creation of anastomosis. The circular stapler is inserted transanally to the level of the rectal stump, and its trocar is carefully advanced. The anvil is engaged on the trocar, the surgeon confirms that there is no inclusion of extraneous tissue and no rotation of the bowel or its mesentery, and the stapler is closed. The locations of the ureters and the vagina are reconfirmed to ensure that these structures are not incorporated into the staple line. The stapler is fired, and the tissue doughnuts are inspected to verify circumferential integrity. The anastomosis should be tension free and well vascularized. Its integrity is tested by insufflating air into the rectum with the anastomosis submerged in fluid, and any leaks identified are reinforced with sutures. As with open rectopexy, endoscopic visualization can be a useful alternative; this is in fact our preferred approach for all circular stapled anastomoses. Insufflation of air during visualization completes the assessment.

Finally, the rectopexy sutures are tied and the abdominal and port site incisions closed.

Postoperative care. Patients are immediately started on a clear liquid diet and advanced to a solid diet when bowel function returns. The bladder catheter is removed on postoperative day 1.

Laparoscopic Suture or Mesh Rectopexy

Patient preparation, positioning, and placement of ureteral stents are the same for laparoscopic suture or mesh rectopexy as for laparoscopic resection rectopexy.

Operative technique *Step 1: placement of ports.* An infraumbilical or supraumbilical port is placed, followed by two additional ports in the lower abdomen (one in each quadrant), positioned so that the camera and the needle holders can be exchanged to afford access to both sides of the rectum [*see Figure 7*]. The surgeon stands to the patient's left.

Step 2: mobilization of rectum. Two bowel graspers are used to retract the rectosigmoid junction and the midrectum upwards. An ultrasonic scalpel is employed to perform the presacral dissection and to divide the upper half to two thirds of the lateral ligaments.

Step 3: intracorporeal placement of sutures or mesh. With upward traction applied to the rectum, sutures are passed through the lateral rectal fascia and peritoneum, through the presacral fascia just off the midline and 1 cm below the sacral promontory, and back through the lateral tissue. Two sutures are placed on each side and tied with the laparoscopic needle holders. The port sites are closed in the usual fashion.

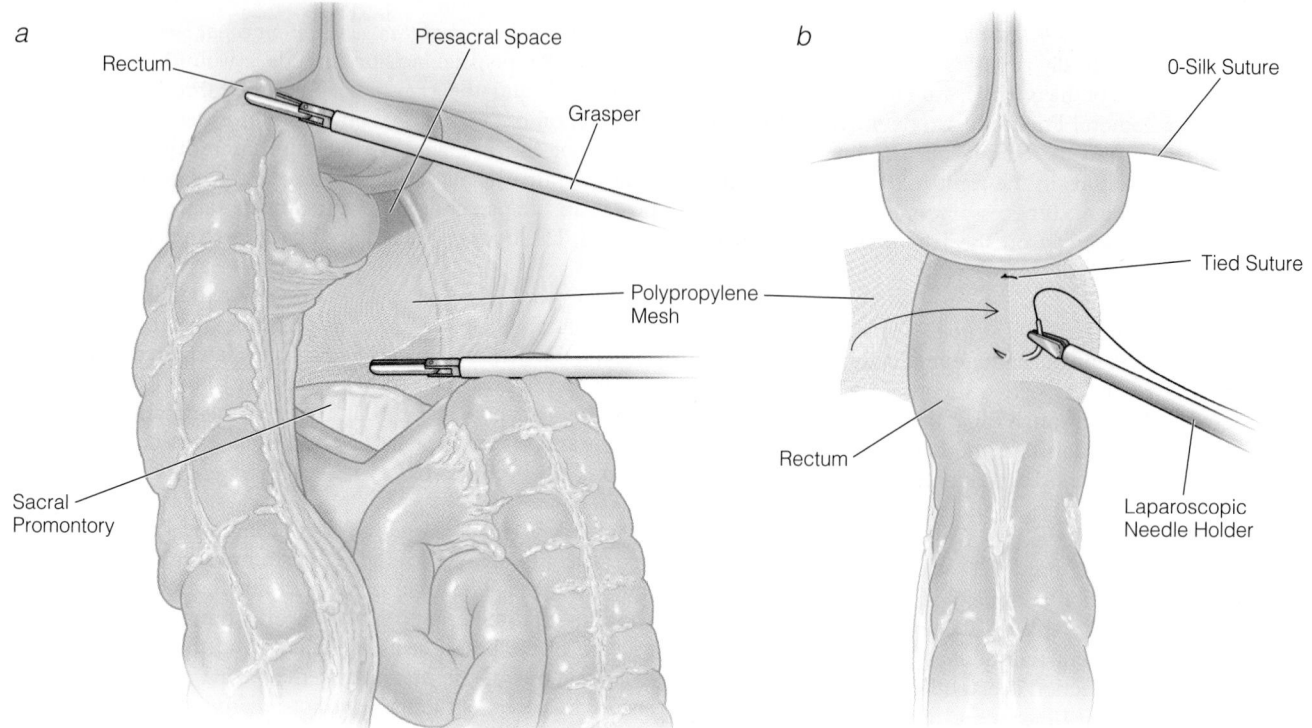

Figure 8 Laparoscopic mesh rectopexy. (*a*) A piece of mesh is inserted into the abdomen through a port, then stapled to the sacrum. (*b*) The lateral edges of the mesh are wrapped around three quarters of the rectal circumference and sutured to the rectal wall.

Alternatively, a piece of mesh is rolled up and inserted through a port. The mesh is tacked to the sacrum with a laparoscopic stapler, and the lateral edges of wrapped mesh are secured to the rectal wall with sutures [*see Figure 8*]. This type of posterior mesh sling procedure is also known as the modified Ripstein procedure.

Postoperative care. The patient is started on a clear liquid diet and advanced to a regular diet on the morning of postoperative day 1. The bladder catheter is also removed at this time.

Troubleshooting

Laparoscopic repair of rectal prolapse follows the same basic principles as open repair. There are multiple variant forms of laparoscopic rectopexy, differing not only with respect to technical details (e.g., resection versus no resection and suture versus mesh) but also with respect to whether the procedure contains an open component or is fully laparoscopic. The essential steps, however, are the same in all of the variants and include adequate mobilization of the rectum, careful placement of sutures, and appropriate resection with healthy anastomosis of the segments. For example, in the approach to laparoscopic resection rectopexy we describe (see above), most of the mobilization is performed laparoscopically, with resection, anastomosis, and suture placement performed in an open fashion, whereas in laparoscopic rectopexy performed without resection, sutures are placed and tied (or mesh secured) intracorporeally. The modified Ripstein procedure (see above) can be performed in a totally laparoscopic fashion if desired.

Complications

Intraoperative complications of laparoscopic rectopexy include inadvertent enterotomy or colotomy, ureteral injury, and organ injury from trocar placement. Most of these injuries are associated with the presence of adhesions and can usually be prevented by careful intra-abdominal dissection in appropriate planes. The

incidence of ureteral injury can be minimized by early identification of these structures, which may be facilitated by the use of ureteral catheters.

Vascular injury can occur at several different points of the operation. Injury to the epigastric vessels during port placement is usually avoided by transilluminating the abdominal wall with the camera to identify the vessels. The iliac and gonadal vessels are retroperitoneal structures, which, like the ureter, can be avoided with careful dissection and identification. The mesenteric vessels must be properly identified and controlled with graspers before the mesocolon is transected. The use of endoscopic clips as the sole means of vascular control before transection is discouraged; the calcified vessels commonly encountered in this mainly elderly population lead to clip slippage and incomplete hemostasis.

The incidence of anastomotic leakage can be minimized by ensuring a tension-free, nonrotated, airtight connection with a good blood supply and by making sure not to incorporate diverticula into the suture line.

Surgical site infections are a common complication of all colorectal resections. Their incidence can be minimized by performing appropriate bowel preparation, providing I.V. antibiotic prophylaxis before operation, and, possibly, employing a plastic wound protector at the site of colon extraction. Copious wound irrigation before closure at the end of the procedure is also helpful.

MESH AND SPONGE REPAIRS

Ripstein Procedure

Preoperative care and patient positioning are the same for the Ripstein procedure as for open resection rectopexy.

Operative technique   *Step 1: initial incision and exploration.* Step 1 in the Ripstein procedure is identical to step 1 in resection rectopexy.

a

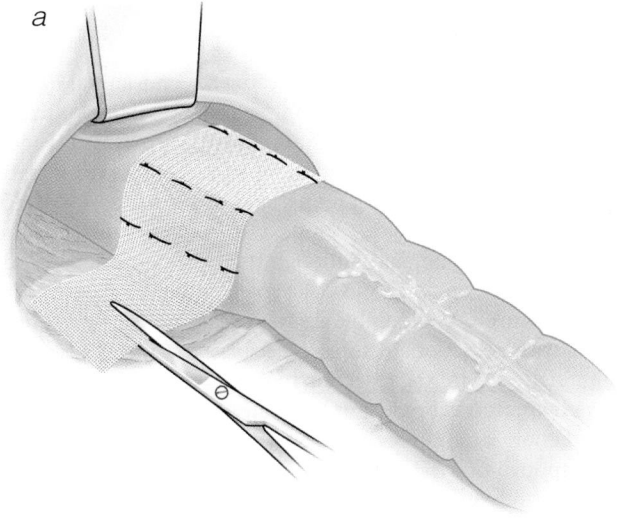

b

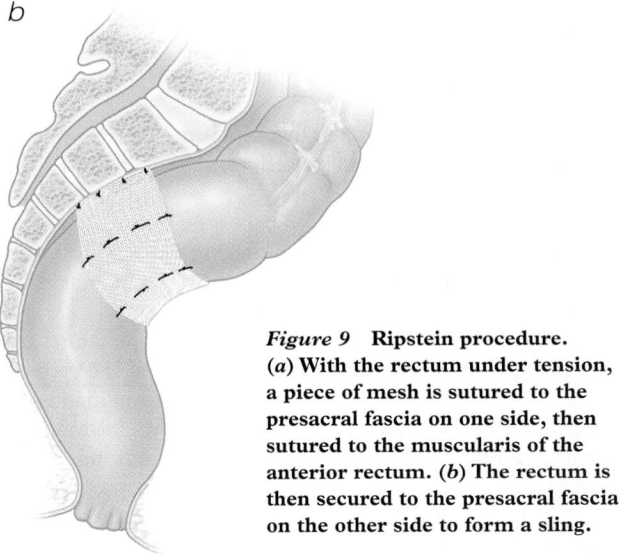

Figure 9 **Ripstein procedure. (a) With the rectum under tension, a piece of mesh is sutured to the presacral fascia on one side, then sutured to the muscularis of the anterior rectum. (b) The rectum is then secured to the presacral fascia on the other side to form a sling.**

Step 2: mobilization of rectum. The lateral peritoneal folds of the rectum in the pelvis are incised from the rectosigmoid junction to the anterior midline on each side. With the St. Mark's retractor used to supply traction, the rectum is dissected away from the sacrum with the electrocautery down to the level of the coccyx. Anterior dissection separates the rectum from the vagina or the seminal vesicles. The upper one third to two thirds of the lateral stalks are divided to facilitate mesh placement.

Step 3: placement of mesh. A 5 cm rectangle of mesh is placed around the anterior rectum at the level of the peritoneal reflection and firmly sutured to the presacral fascia on one side, 5 cm

below the promontory [*see Figure 9a*]. The rectum is pulled taut with upward traction, partial-thickness nonabsorbable sutures are placed in rows along the anterior rectum to hold the mesh in place, and the mesh is sutured to the presacral fascia on the other side [*see Figure 9b*]. The sling is left loose enough to allow two fingers to pass between the bowel and the sac.

Because of the high risk of constipation and even obstipation after anterior mesh encirclement, a modified version of the Ripstein procedure was developed that involved posterior fixation of mesh to the sacrum, leaving the anterior rectal wall free of any potential constriction. In this modified approach, the mesh is tacked to the sacrum first. The lateral edges of the mesh are then wrapped around three quarters of the circumference of the rectum and sutured anterolaterally to the rectal wall. Intraoperative rigid proctoscopy may be helpful for ensuring that the positioning of the mesh does not result in obstruction.

Step 4: closure of peritoneum. The peritoneal reflection is closed so that the mesh is excluded from the peritoneal cavity and the small bowel is prevented from migrating into the pelvis on top of the mesh. The abdomen is irrigated and closed in the usual fashion.

Postoperative care. The patient is started on a clear liquid diet and advanced to a solid diet with resumption of bowel function. The bladder catheter is removed 2 days after operation.

Ivalon Sponge Repair (Wells Procedure)

Preoperative care and positioning are the same for the Wells procedure as for open resection rectopexy.

Operative technique *Steps 1 and 2.* Steps 1 and 2 are the same as in the Ripstein procedure.

Step 3: placement of sponge. A rectangular piece of sterilized and moistened Ivalon sponge is secured in place with mattress sutures passed through the sponge, through the presacral fascia, and back through the sponge. Careful hemostasis is ensured to prevent purulent collections in the area of the sponge. The rectum is retracted cephalad, and the lateral edges of the sponge are folded around it for approximately three fourths of its circumference. The edges are secured to the anterior portion of the rectum with seromuscular sutures [*see Figure 10*].

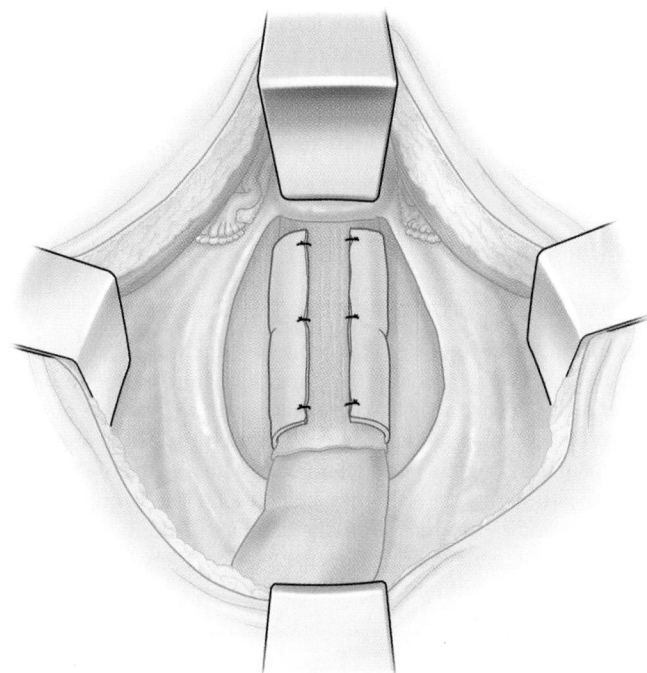

Figure 10 **Ivalon sponge repair (Wells procedure). The sponge is anchored to the sacrum. With the rectum under tension, the edges of the sponge are brought around three quarters of the rectal circumference and sutured to the muscularis of the anterior rectum.**

Step 4: closure of peritoneum. The pelvic peritoneum is closed to exclude the small bowel from the pelvis and thus prevent it from coming in contact with the sponge.

Postoperative care. Postoperative care is the same for the Wells procedure as for the Ripstein procedure.

Complications

Fecal impaction may result from making the sling too tight or from severe constipation caused by leaving a redundant rectosigmoid colon above the level of the repair.

Presacral bleeding may result from placement of sutures in the presacral fascia and consequent injury to the veins. If bleeding occurs, the sutures should be immediately secured and manual pressure applied. If these measures fail, thumbtacks may be required.

Strictures may result at the site of the sling and may be diagnosed by means of barium enema or sigmoidoscopy. If the mesh is wrapped anteriorly, revision may involve laterally transecting the mesh where it is not fused to the rectum, removing the mesh, or resecting the portion of the rectum where stricture occurs. To minimize the risk of this complication, either the mesh should be placed posteriorly (see above) without a circumferential wrap or, if an anteriorly based sling is employed, care should be taken not to encircle the rectum too tightly.

Sepsis may result when placement of full-thickness sutures or erosion into the bowel wall leads to mesh or sponge infection. Pelvic abscesses and fistulas are treated by removing the mesh or sponge and, in some circumstances, by performing a diverting colostomy. Preventive measures include giving perioperative antibiotics, placing seromuscular sutures, and ensuring that the synthetic material is not too tightly wrapped.

Adhesions to the mesh may be associated with small bowel obstruction. This complication can be prevented by reperitonealizing the pelvis to prevent migration of the small bowel onto the foreign substances. Placement of Seprafilm beneath the fascial closure helps reduce adhesions.

OUTCOME EVALUATION

Overall, abdominal operations yield better results than perineal operations with respect to recurrence rates (which range from 0% to 8%) and functional outcome.[19] The abdominal approach allows the rectum to be maximally mobilized and fixed to the sacrum. In addition, transabdominal procedures can be tailored to the presence or absence of functional disorders (e.g., constipation or incontinence) through the addition or omission of sigmoid resection. Morbidity, however, is greater with abdominal procedures than with perineal procedures. In planning surgical treatment of rectal prolapse, therefore, it is essential to consider risk factors for complications in addition to likelihood of cure.

For many surgeons, posterior rectopexy is the procedure of choice because of its low morbidity and recurrence rates.[13,20,21] Some 50% to 88% of patients show improved continence,[22-24] but as many as 53% experience either new-onset constipation or exacerbation of preexisting constipation.[22] The constipation is thought to be attributable to rectal denervation resulting from division of the lateral ligaments; however, preservation of these ligaments is associated with a significantly higher (> 50%) recurrence rate.[25,26] The type of material used to perform the rectopexy has no effect on recurrence: recurrence rates are the same for suture repairs as for mesh repairs.[27] Suture repairs, however, carry a lower risk of associated pelvic sepsis and luminal constriction, especially when compared with repairs involving mesh wrapped around the anterior rectum. Our practice, therefore, is to resect the upper one third to one

half of each lateral stalk in an attempt to balance functional outcome against cure of the prolapse.

The constipation produced by rectopexy and lateral ligament division may be overcome by adding sigmoid resection to the procedure. Several prospective randomized trials revealed a reduction in postoperative constipation when resection was added to rectopexy in patients with preoperative constipation.[28,29] Recurrence rates after resection rectopexy were comparable to those after rectopexy alone, and although the resection imposed additional risks (i.e., anastomotic leakage and wound infection), morbidity rates were comparable as well. Continence rates are improved with resection rectopexy because the rectal reservoir is maintained (by limiting resection to the portion of the large bowel above the peritoneal reflection). Because of the risk of pelvic sepsis, resection is only combined with suture rectopexy, not with Ivalon sponge or mesh repairs.

Isolated resection of the sigmoid colon is an effective method of preventing recurrence permanently; limiting the length of the bowel definitively inhibits the mobility of the rectum.[30] Recurrence rates are the same for this procedure as for other abdominal procedures, and morbidity is determined by the level of the anastomosis. Patients with constipation secondary to colonic inertia associated with rectal procidentia may require an extended resection that includes subtotal colectomy with ileorectal anastomosis.[31]

Disadvantages of the open abdominal procedures for rectal prolapse include a significant incidence of peritoneal adhesions, the need for general anesthesia, a longer hospital stay, greater morbidity, and possible compromise of sexual function. Certain disadvantages (e.g., more extensive intra-abdominal invasion, scarring, and longer recovery time) are reduced when the laparoscopic approach is employed. Controlled studies of laparoscopic rectopexy revealed recurrence rates and morbidity comparable to those of open approaches.[32,33] A subsequent study comparing laparoscopic resection rectopexy with the corresponding open approach found that with the former, though longer operating times were noted, less time was required for return of bowel function, toleration of a regular diet, and hospital stay.[34] Another study found that continence improved to a significant extent after laparoscopic rectopexy without significant changes in postoperative constipation.[35]

Special Situations

INCARCERATION, STRANGULATION, AND GANGRENE

On rare occasions, a rectal prolapse becomes incarcerated. If the bowel is viable, sedation and gentle manual reduction in the emergency department usually suffice. Sprinkling table sugar on the prolapse helps reduce edema.[36] If such measures are unsuccessful, paralyzing the perianal muscles with an anal block or general anesthesia in the OR may help resolve the problem. If the incarceration is irreducible or the viability of the bowel is questionable, emergency perineal rectosigmoidectomy should be performed, with or without fecal diversion.[37]

RUPTURED PROLAPSE

Rupture of the prolapse usually involves opening of the hernia sac and exposure of the small bowel to the perineum. Emergency transabdominal repair is indicated, with closure of the peritoneal hernia sac and suture rectopexy constituting the safest and most efficient repair.

PROLAPSE IN MALE PATIENTS

Prolapse in male patients, though relatively rare, may occur at any age. Rectal mobilization should be modified so as to preserve the presacral nerves, keep from damaging Denonvillier's fascia, and avoid division of one of the lateral ligaments.[38] Lateral pararectal tissues carry parasympathetic fibers and are important in normal ejaculatory function. Consideration should be given to taking a perineal approach or performing resection alone.

RECURRENT PROLAPSE

Rectal prolapse is the anatomic consequence of an underlying functional disorder of the colon and the rectum. Although surgical intervention corrects the anatomic abnormalities present, the functional disorder often persists, resulting in a tendency for the prolapse to recur.[39] Recurrence rates differ among the various types of procedures but are generally higher with the perineal operations than with the abdominal operations. In most cases, the cause of the recurrence cannot be identified, though early recurrences (those occurring less than 2 years after operation) are thought to be related to technical factors associated with the original procedure.[39]

The initial operation for rectal prolapse is chosen on the basis of several different factors, but the choice of operation for recurrent prolapse is based primarily on the procedure chosen for initial man-agement. Some authorities advocate an abdominal procedure for the second operation, regardless of what the initial operation was, because of the superior rates of success with such procedures[39]; however, care must be taken in performing repeat resectional procedures (e.g., anterior resection after perineal rectosigmoidectomy, or vice versa) because of the risk of bowel ischemia between the two anastomoses. In our view, unless the previous anastomosis can be resected in the second procedure, repeat resectional procedures should be avoided.[39,40] Perineal rectosigmoidectomies are an exception to this broad rule: they can be safely repeated because the recurrent prolapse contains the previous anastomosis.[41] Recurrence rates and morbidity after operative treatment of recurrent rectal prolapse are essentially the same as those after operative treatment of primary rectal prolapse.[42]

RECTAL PROLAPSE WITH SOLITARY RECTAL ULCER SYNDROME

As many as 80% of patients with solitary rectal ulcer syndrome (SRUS) have an associated rectal prolapse,[43,44] a finding that indicates a close relationship between these two entities. In cases of symptomatic SRUS associated with asymptomatic prolapse, a trial of medical therapy is warranted[45]; if such therapy fails, surgical intervention with procedures used for rectal prolapse should be considered.[46] In cases of symptomatic prolapse associated with asymptomatic SRUS, healing of the ulcer can be demonstrated in one third of patients undergoing operation for the prolapse.[46]

References

1. Madden MV, Kamm MA, Nicholls RJ, et al: Abdominal rectopexy for rectal prolapse: prospective study evaluating changes in symptoms and anorectal function. Dis Colon Rectum 35:48, 1992

2. Boutsis C, Ellis H: The Ivalon-sponge wrap operation for rectal prolapse: an experience with 26 patients. Dis Colon Rectum 17:21, 1974

3. Madoff RD, Williams JG, Wong WD, et al: Long term functional results of colon resection and rectopexy for overt rectal prolapse. Am J Gastroenterol 87:101, 1992

4. Keighley MR, Shouler PJ: Abnormalities of colonic function in patients with rectal prolapse and fecal incontinence. Br J Surg 71:892, 1984

5. Goldman J: Concerning prolapse of the rectum with special emphasis on the operation by Thiersch. Dis Colon Rectum 31:154, 1988

6. Classic articles in colonic and rectal surgery. Edmond Delorme 1847–1929. On the treatment of total prolapse of the rectum by excision of the rectal mucous membranes or recto-colic. Dis Colon Rectum 28:544, 1985

7. Mikulicz J: Zur operativen Behandlung des prolapsus recti et coli invaginati. Verhandlung der Deutschen Gesellschaft für Chirurgie 17:294, 1888

8. Altemeier WA, Culbertson WR, Schwengerdt C, et al: Nineteen years' experience with the 1-stage perineal repair of rectal prolapse. Ann Surg 173:993, 1971

9. Ripstein CB, Lanter B: Etiology and surgical therapy of massive prolapse of the rectum. Ann Surg 157:259, 1963

10. Wells C: New operation for rectal prolapse. Proc R Soc Med 52:602, 1959

11. Johanson OB, Wexner SD, Daniel N, et al: Perineal rectosigmoidectomy in the elderly. Dis Colon Rectum 36:767, 1993

12. Lechaux JP, Lechaux D, Perez M: Results of the Delorme procedure for rectal prolapse: advantage of a modified technique. Dis Colon Rectum 38:301, 1995

13. Ripstein CB: Surgical treatment of rectal prolapse. Pac Med Surg 75:329, 1967

14. Fengler SA, Pearl RK, Prasad ML, et al: Management of recurrent rectal prolapse. Dis Colon Rectum 40:832, 1997

15. Williams JG, Rothenberger DA, Madoff RD, et al: Treatment of rectal prolapse in the elderly by perineal rectosigmoidectomy. Dis Colon Rectum 35:830, 1992

16. Agachan F, Reissman P, Pfeifer J, et al: Comparison of three perineal procedures for the treatment of rectal prolapse. South Med J 90:925, 1992

17. Agachan F, Daniel N, Wexner SD: The outcome of rectal prolapse surgery in the elderly. Is long-term follow up possible? Coloproctology 18:41, 1996

18. Becker JM, Dayton MT, Fazio VW, et al: Prevention of post-operative abdominal adhesions by a sodium hyaluronate-based bioresorbable membrane: a prospective, randomized, double-blind multicenter study. J Am Coll Surg 183:297, 1996

19. Beck DE, Wexner SD: Rectal prolapse and intussusception. Fundamentals of Anorectal Surgery, 2nd ed. 1998, p 102

20. Duthie GS, Bartolo G: Abdominal rectopexy for rectal prolapse: a comparison of techniques. Br J Surg 79:107, 1992

21. Madoff RD, Mellgren A: One hundred years of rectal prolapse surgery. Dis Colon Rectum 42:441, 1999

22. Aitola PT, Hiltunen KM, Matikainen MJ: Functional results of operative treatment of rectal prolapse over an 11 year period: emphasis of the transabdominal approach. Dis Colon Rectum 42:655, 1999

23. Madden MV, Kamm MA, Nicholls RJ: Abdominal rectopexy for complete rectal prolapse: prospective study evaluating changes in symptoms and anorectal function. Dis Colon Rectum 35:48, 1992

24. McCue IL, Thompson JPS: Clinical and functional results of abdominal rectopexy for complete rectal prolapse. Br J Surg 78:921, 1991

25. Scaglia M, Fasth S, Hallgren T, et al: Abdominal rectopexy for rectal prolapse: influence of surgical technique on functional outcome. Dis Colon Rectum 37:805, 1994

26. Speakman CT, Madden MV, Nicholls RJ, et al: Lateral ligament division during rectopexy causes constipation but prevents recurrence: results of a prospective randomized study. Br J Surg 78:1431, 1991

27. Brazelli M, Bachoo P, Grant A: The Cochrane Database of Systemic Reviews: Surgery for complete rectal prolapse in adults. The Cochrane Library, Vol 3, 2003

28. McKee RF, Lauder JC, Poon FW, et al: A prospective randomized of abdominal rectopexy with and without sigmoidectomy in rectal prolapse. Surg Gynecol Obstet 174:145, 1992

29. Lukkenon P, Mikkonen U, Jarvinen H: Abdominal rectopexy with sigmoidectoy versus rectopexy alone for rectal prolapse: a prospective,

randomized study. Int J Colorect Dis 7:219, 1992

30. Schlinkert RT, Beart RW Jr, Wolff BG, et al: Anterior resection for complete rectal prolapse. Dis Colon Rectum 28:409, 1985

31. Watts JD, Rothenberger DA, Buls JG, et al: The management of procidentia: 30 years' experience. Dis Colon Rectum 28:96, 1985

32. Solomon MJ, Young CJ, Eyers AA, et al: Randomized clinical trial of laparoscopic versus open abdominal rectopexy for rectal prolapse. Br J Surg 89:35, 2002

33. Boccasanta P, Venturi M, Reitano MC, et al: Laparotomic versus laparoscopic rectopexy in complete rectal prolapse. Dig Surg 16:415, 1999

34. Kairaluoma MV, Viljakka MT, Kellokumpu IH: Open versus laparoscopic surgery for rectal prolapse: a case-controlled study assessing short-term outcome. Dis Colon Rectum 46:353, 2003

35. Boccasanta P, Rosati R, Venturi M, et al: Comparison of laparoscopic rectopexy with open technique in the treatment of complete rectal prolapse. Surg Lap Endosc 8:460, 1998

36. Myers JO, Rothenberger DA: Sugar in the reduction of incarcerated prolapsed bowel: report of two cases. Dis Colon Rectum 34:416, 1991

37. Ramanujam PS, Venkatesh KS: Management of acute, incarcerated rectal prolapse. Dis Colon Rectum 35:1154, 1992

38. Abou-Enein: Prolapse of the rectum in young men: treatment with a modified Rascoe Graham operation. Dis Colon Rectum 22:117, 1978

39. Hool GA, Hull TL, Fazio VW: Surgical treatment of recurrent complete rectal prolapse. Dis Colon Rectum 40:270, 1997

40. Fengler SA, Pearl RK, Prasad ML, et al: Management of recurrent rectal prolapse. Dis Colon Rectum 40:832, 1997

41. Williams JG, Rothenberger DA, Madoff RD, et al: Treatment of recurrent rectal prolpase in the elderly by perineal rectosigmoidectomy. Dis Colon Rectum 35:830, 1992

42. Pikarsky AJ, Joo JS, Wexner SD, et al: Recurrent rectal prolapse: what is the next good option? Dis Coln Rectum 43:1273, 2000

43. Mackle EJ, Manton Mills JO, Parks TG: The investigation of anorectal dysfunction in the solitary rectal ulcer syndrome. Int J Colorectal Dis 5:21, 1990

44. Mahieu PH: Barium enema and defecography in the diagnosis and evaluation of the solitary rectal ulcer syndrome. Int J Colorectal Dis 1:85, 1986

45. van den Brandt-Gradel V, Huibregtse K, Tytgat GNJ: Treatment of the solitary rectal ulcer syndrome with high fiber diet and abstention of straining at defecation. Dig Dis Sci 29:1005, 1984

46. Tjandra JJ, Fazio VW, Church JM, et al: Ripstein procedure is an effective treatment for rectal prolapse without constipation. Dis Colon Rectum 36:501, 1993

Acknowledgment

Figures 1, 3, and 6 through 10   Tom Moore.

79 ANAL PROCEDURES FOR BENIGN DISEASE

Ira J. Kodner, M.D., F.A.C.S., F.A.S.C.R.S.

Operative Management of Hemorrhoids

The frequency of hemorrhoid surgery continues to diminish. More patients seem to be achieving adequate symptomatic relief by means of bowel control medications and improved diet (e.g., increased intake of fiber, fruit, vegetables, and grain) [*see 59 Benign Rectal, Anal, and Perineal Problems*]. It is probable that both for these reasons and because more and better patient information is available, fewer patients today have hemorrhoids that progress to a stage advanced enough to necessitate operative treatment for relief of symptoms.

OPERATIVE PLANNING

It is important to distinguish between internal and external hemorrhoids [*see Figure 1*]. Internal hemorrhoids are treated to relieve specific symptoms, including prolapse and bleeding, not simply because hemorrhoidal tissue was seen on routine examinations. Prolapsing tissue occasionally results in maceration of the perianal skin that may not be clearly evident at the time of examination, especially if the patient is in the prone position. External hemorrhoids are treated because they thrombose and cause pain. There are no other symptoms of the anorectum that should be attributed to the presence of hemorrhoids [*see Table 1*]; in particular, difficulties with bowel movements (e.g., straining, the need for digital evacuation of the rectum, and cramping abdominal pain) must not be ascribed to hemorrhoids.

Accordingly, the ability to recognize and diagnose the spectrum of pelvic floor abnormalities (of which rectal prolapse is the most florid manifestation), especially obstructed defecation, is critical to the decision whether to correct hemorrhoids surgically. Attempting to alleviate nonhemorrhoidal symptoms by means of hemorrhoid surgery is likely to yield unsatisfactory results for both patient and surgeon. It is not uncommon for anal fissure/ulcer disease to coexist with hemorrhoids, in which case the chances of a good operative result can be increased by performing a posterior lateral internal sphincterotomy at the time of hemorrhoid surgery.

Before embarking on the surgical treatment of hemorrhoids, one must always rule out neoplastic disease, compromise of the immune system, and defective clotting mechanisms. Patients with a personal or family history of colorectal cancer and those 50 years of age or older should undergo colonoscopy to eliminate the possibility of polyps or cancer before surgical treatment of hemorrhoids is initiated. The patient's general health status and ability to tolerate pain and an operative procedure should also be taken into account. The postoperative response to anorectal surgery varies enormously among patients. For example, young men tend to strain to have bowel movements after anorectal procedures, and this tendency can lead to bleeding and disruption of postoperative healing. These patients often benefit from the administration of parenteral pain medication for the first 12 to 24 hours after operation, which usually requires hospitalization. Elderly patients, on the other hand, prefer not to be in the hospital. For these patients, single elastic ligation of individual clusters of internal hemorrhoids is performed in the outpatient office.

The next step is to determine the appropriate procedure for the patient. The options include (1) elastic ligation of internal hemorrhoids, (2) excision of thrombosed external hemorrhoids, (3) complete excisional hemorrhoidectomy, and (4) elastic ligation of internal hemorrhoids combined with excision of external hemorrhoids. One should always consider whether complete sigmoidoscopy, rigid or flexible, will be necessary at the time of the procedure and

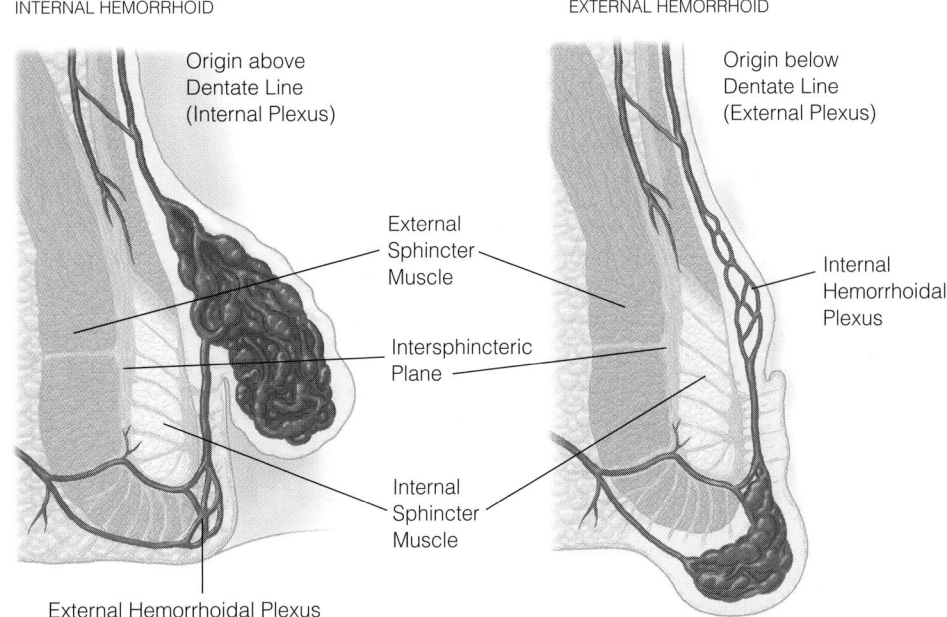

INTERNAL HEMORRHOID

EXTERNAL HEMORRHOID

Origin above Dentate Line (Internal Plexus)

Origin below Dentate Line (External Plexus)

External Sphincter Muscle

Intersphincteric Plane

Internal Hemorrhoidal Plexus

Internal Sphincter Muscle

External Hemorrhoidal Plexus

Figure 1 **Operative management of hemorrhoids. A key issue is the differentiation of internal hemorrhoids from external hemorrhoids. Internal hemorrhoids (left) originate from the internal hemorrhoidal plexus, above the dentate line. External hemorrhoids (right) originate from the external hemorrhoidal plexus, below the dentate line.**

Table 1 Anal Symptoms Mistakenly Attributed to Hemorrhoids

Symptoms	Cause
Pain and bleeding after bowel movement	Ulcer/fissure disease
Forceful straining to have bowel movement	Pelvic floor abnormality (paradoxical contraction of anal sphincter)
Blood mixed with stool	Neoplasm
Drainage of pus during or after bowel movement	Abscess/fistula, inflammatory bowel disease
Constant moisture	Condyloma acuminatum
Mucous drainage and incontinence	Rectal prolapse
Anal pain with no physical findings	*Caution:* possible psychiatric disorder

whether anal sphincterotomy will be indicated, especially in young men with a history of straining. This second consideration is important because many patients are treated for hemorrhoids when in fact their primary disease is anal ulcer/fissure disease, the symptoms of which are pain and some bleeding at defecation. These are not symptoms that can be attributed to hemorrhoids. If a patient undergoes hemorrhoid surgery when the primary disease is anal fissure, proper healing will be impeded.

Finally, one should explain the procedure and its attendant risks to the patient in the outpatient office because in most cases, given the restrictions imposed by health care insurers and managed care administrators, one will not see the patient again until arriving at the day of operation. Specific complications to be discussed preoperatively include urinary retention, bleeding, and infection. In the event that several symptomatic hemorrhoids are present, surgeon and patient should jointly decide between multiple small procedures done in the office and a single larger procedure done in the OR. Individual economic concerns, as well as employment and lifestyle, should be considered.

Special Situations

Acute thrombosed external hemorrhoids This condition is signaled by acute pain and a swelling blood clot within the skin-covered external hemorrhoid. Often, the clot is eroding through the skin, causing bleeding that may be frightening to the patient but is typically insignificant. If I encounter this problem days after its onset, I generally treat it with bowel control and topical medications as the process resolves. If the hemorrhoid is acutely painful or the clot is eroding, the best therapy is surgical excision of the external hemorrhoid, with the anoderm left intact; this is best done with the patient under adequate local anesthesia. Mere evacuation of the clot is rarely appropriate.

Postpartum hemorrhoids The postpartum rosette of acute thrombosed external (and, often, prolapsed internal) hemorrhoidal tissue is appropriately treated with hemorrhoidectomy (see below), carried out as soon after delivery as is convenient. The risk of infection is minimal, and I know of no good reason to send a new mother home with hemorrhoids in addition to a new baby and a healing episiotomy.

OPERATIVE TECHNIQUE

Step 1: Positioning

Operative treatment of hemorrhoids, like the vast majority of anorectal procedures, should be done with the patient in the prone-flexed position [*see Figure 2*]. The transporting stretcher should be kept in the room. The patient will be given I.V. narcotics to allow painless injection of local anesthetics, and if any respiratory compromise results because of the prone-flexed position, the patient can quickly be returned to the supine position on the stretcher until respiration resumes without difficulty.

Step 2: Intravenous Sedation and Local Anesthesia

Before administering a local anesthetic, I usually give the following drugs for sedation: midazolam, 2 to 5 mg, given in the holding area for sedation and amnesia; alfentanil, 0.5 to 1 mg, or fentanyl, 50 to 100 mg, for analgesia to help alleviate the discomfort of the local anesthetic injection; and propofol, 20 to 50 mg, or methohexital, 20 to 50 mg, to achieve patient cooperation with the injection. Sedation is followed by the injection into perianal tissue of 40 ml of bupivacaine (0.5%) along with a buffer that is added immediately before injection (0.5 ml of 8.4% sodium bicarbonate [1 mEq/ml] added to 50 ml of local anesthetic). If resection is anticipated, epinephrine (1:200,000) is usually included with the local anesthetic. To achieve adequate local anesthesia, 5 ml of bupivacaine is injected into the subcutaneous tissue in each quadrant of the tissue immediately surrounding the anus [*see Figure 3a*]. Next, 10 ml of local anesthetic is injected deep into the sphincter mechanism on each side of the anal canal [*see Figure 3b*].

Step 3: Anoscopy or Sigmoidoscopy

Anoscopy, sigmoidoscopy, or both should be performed at this point if neither procedure was done before the operation.

Step 4: Sphincterotomy

As noted, sphincterotomy should always be considered, especially if a hypertrophic band of the lower third of the internal sphincter muscle persists after the local anesthetic has been injected and an anoscope has been inserted. It is always best to obtain permission to do this beforehand on the operative consent form.

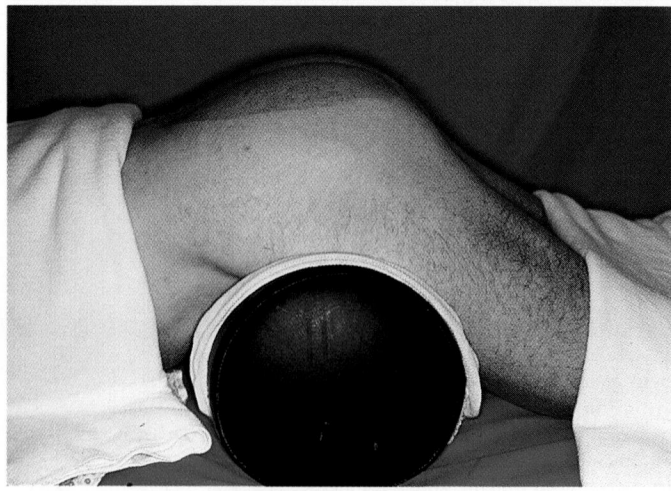

Figure 2 **Operative management of hemorrhoids. The patient is positioned on the operating table in the prone-flexed position, with a soft roll under the hips.**

a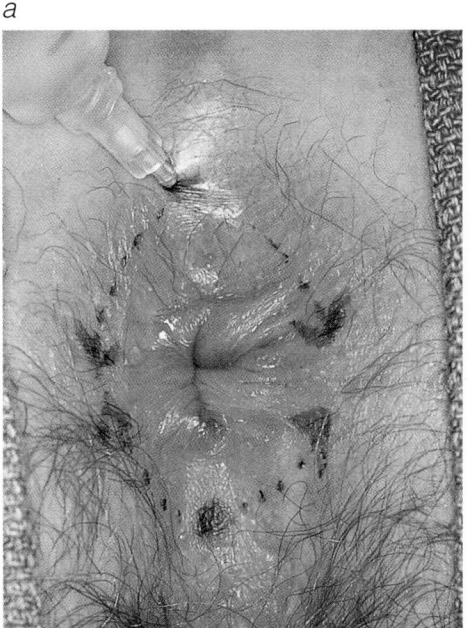

b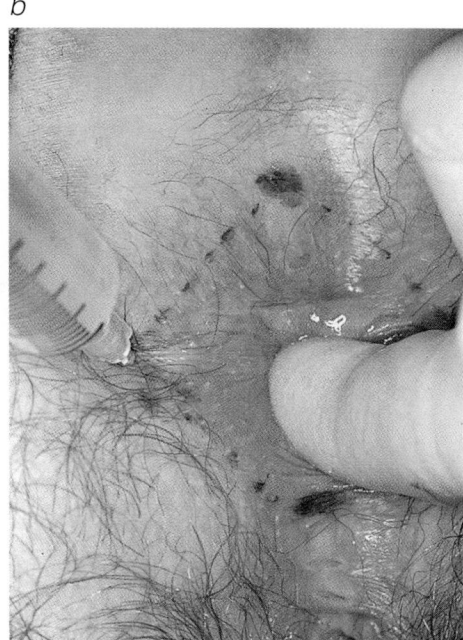

Figure 3 **Operative management of hemorrhoids. (*a*) Five milliliters of bupivacaine is injected into subcutaneous tissue. (*b*) Ten milliliters of local anesthetic is injected deep into the sphincter muscle on each side of the anal canal.**

Step 5: Treatment of Hemorrhoids

Elastic ligation of internal hemorrhoids   This is a very safe operation because by the nature of the banding procedure [*see Figure 4*], bridges of normal mucosa are maintained between treated clusters of hemorrhoids. Any clusters of tissue with squamous metaplasia and obviously friable internal hemorrhoids can be treated in this manner. I find that these tissue clusters are not always confined to the three classic positions identified for hemorrhoids and that in many cases it is necessary to band three or four clusters. If the bands do not stay on, then the tissue probably need not be treated and no further action need be taken.

I use two rubber bands on each cluster. If one of them breaks, bleeding is unlikely to occur, because the tissue rapidly becomes edematous and necrotic. It is important that the placement of the rubber band be proximal to the mucocutaneous junction; if it is not, the procedure will be too painful, given the extensive innervation of the skin. On the other hand, the band should not be placed so proximally as to incorporate the full thickness of the rectal wall; to do so can be risky for patients in whom difficulties with bowel movements indicate the presence of intussusception or some other pelvic floor abnormality. Occasionally, the friable tissue gives rise to a suspicion of cancer. If this is the case, rub-

a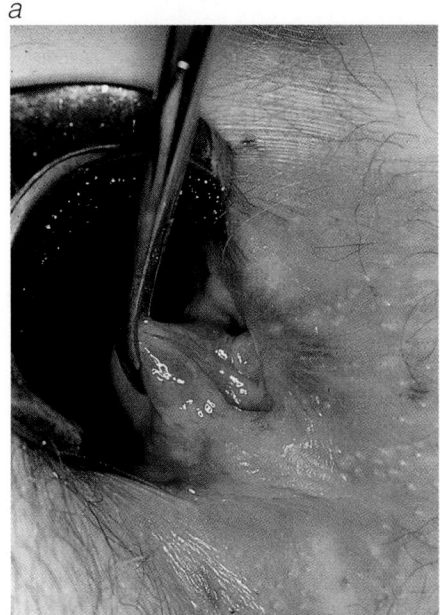

b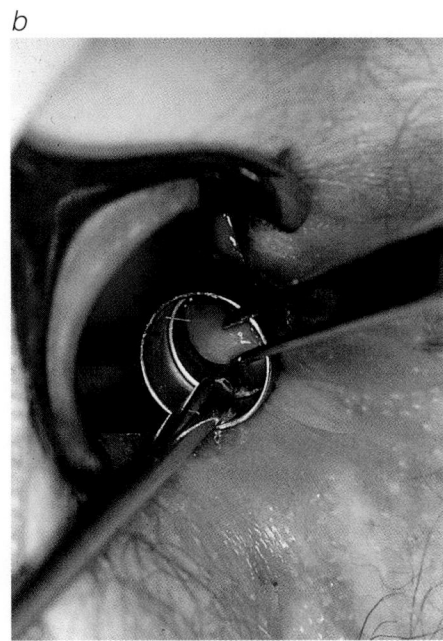

c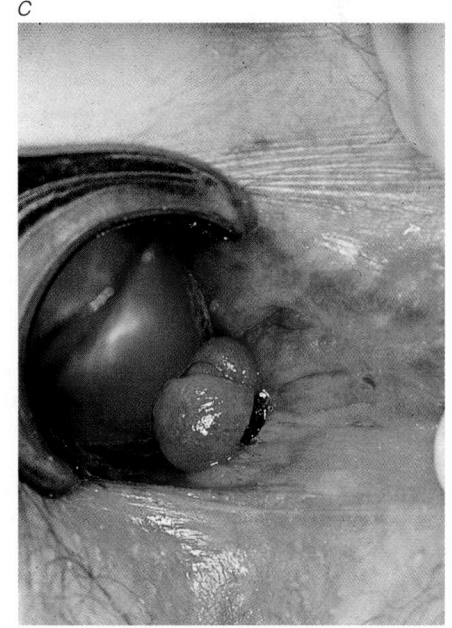

Figure 4   **Operative management of hemorrhoids. Shown is the elastic ligation technique for internal hemorrhoids. (*a*) The hemorrhoidal tissue is identified. (*b*) The hemorrhoid is grasped and pulled through the drum. (*c*) The elastic band is applied to the base of the hemorrhoid.**

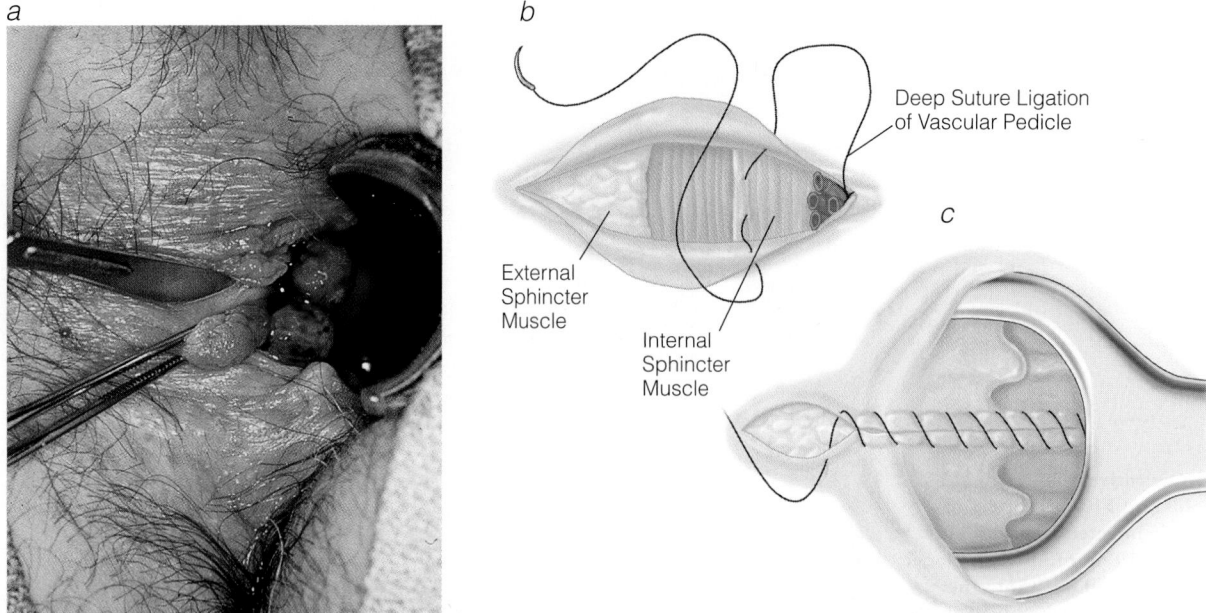

Figure 5 **Operative management of hemorrhoids. Shown is an excisional hemorrhoidectomy. (*a*) An elliptical incision is made in the perianal skin. (*b*) A continuous suture is used in a three-point placement in such a way as to incorporate skin edges and muscle. (*c*) The elliptical defect is closed and the dead space obliterated.**

ber bands may be placed at the base, and the tip may be excised for biopsy.

Excision of residual external hemorrhoids Residual external hemorrhoids are rarely treated as a primary problem: true symptoms are few, and the main indication for treatment is maintenance of hygiene. In addition, I find that much of the external tissue is pulled in when the internal hemorrhoids are ligated. Accordingly, I do the internal ligation first and then excise any residual symptomatic external tissue. An elliptical incision is made in the perianal skin, with care taken to protect the underlying sphincter muscle and avoid the previously placed elastic band [*see Figure 5a*]. Although the perianal skin is very forgiving, it is essential to protect the anoderm; this is achieved through careful placement of the rubber band. The elliptical defect is then closed with a continuous absorbable suture in a three-point placement to obliterate the underlying dead space [*see Figures 5b and 5c*]. The suture is tied loosely to allow for swelling. There is no need for separate ligation or coagulation of the small bleeding vessels; this problem is obviated by the continuous suture. It is important not to use slowly absorbable suture material, because it may give rise to infection in this highly susceptible tissue. I prefer to use 3-0 chromic catgut on an exaggeratedly curved needle.

Complete excisional hemorrhoidectomy This procedure is indicated in patients who have large combined internal and external hemorrhoids, patients who are receiving anticoagulants, and patients who have massive edema and thrombosis, as seen in the postpartum rosette of tissue [*see Figure 6*]. I find that even massive edema generally resolves after the local anesthetic is injected and the muscle is allowed to relax. Resolution of edema then permits identification of the specific clusters of hemorrhoids, which can be isolated with a forceps and excised via an elliptical incision. Care must be taken to preserve the underlying muscle, especially in the anterior region in women. I use 3-0 chromic catgut with a deep stitch at the apex and a continuous three-point suture that is extended on the perianal skin [*see Figure*

5*b*]. It is important to preserve a bridge of anoderm between the areas of excision. I know of no indications for a radical circumferential procedure (the so-called Whitehead procedure); in fact, I see numerous patients who are seeking a remedy for the stenosis and ectropion that frequently occur after this radical operation [*see Figure 7*].

A newer technique, in which a circumferential band of anorectal mucosa is excised with a special circular stapler, is currently under investigation. This technique is intended for patients who have profound prolapsing internal hemorrhoids without much of

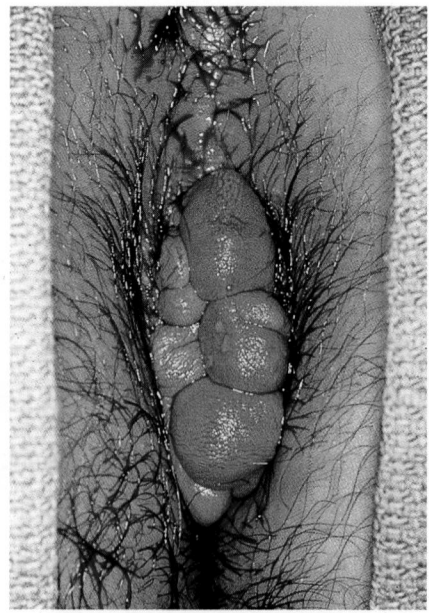

Figure 6 **Operative management of hemorrhoids. Massive edema and thrombosis, as seen in the postpartum rosette of tissue, can be reduced after a local anesthetic is injected and the muscle is allowed to relax.**

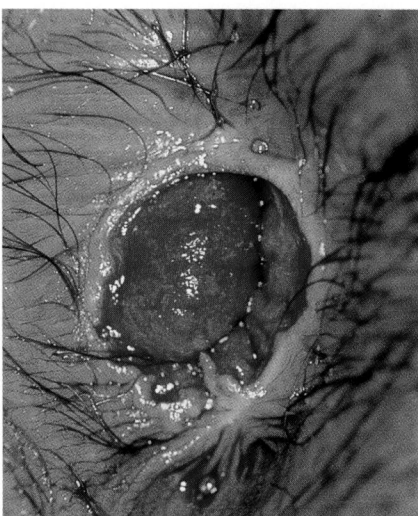

Figure 7 **Operative management of hemorrhoids. Stenosis and ectropion often result from radical circumferential (Whitehead) procedures.**

an external component. Its proponents claim that it results in minimum postoperative discomfort; however, special training with the instrument is required. European centers have reported excellent success rates, and trials have now been completed in the United States. There appears to be some advantage to this procedure, in that patients tend to experience less immediate postoperative pain; however, the long-term results seem no better than those achieved with more conventional approaches, and the rate of recurrent tissue prolapse may in fact be higher than that noted after standard excisional hemorrhoidectomy.[1] In addition, the circumferential stapling procedure has not yet been compared with rubber band ligation, which is now used almost routinely. Perhaps the greatest disadvantage of the new procedure is the finding that there is a significant incidence of serious postoperative complications. At present, given the results available to date, it is difficult to advocate routine use of this modality.

There also exist various forms of nonsurgical treatment for grade 1 and early grade 2 internal hemorrhoids. These entail some form of local tissue destruction (e.g., with infrared coagulation or injection of a sclerosing agent). I do not use these modalities myself, because I find that the symptoms they are used to treat can be managed just as easily, and more safely, by means of dietary changes, bulk-forming agents, and stool softeners.

Step 6: Postoperative Care

Immediately after the procedure—in fact, after any anorectal procedure—antibiotic ointment and a gauze pad are applied. Pressure dressings are unnecessary. Only a very small amount of adhesive tape should be used, so as to prevent traction avulsion of the perianal skin, an event for which we surgeons too often avoid responsibility by ascribing it to a "tape allergy" on the part of the patient.

TROUBLESHOOTING

The most fundamental way of preventing problems is to make an accurate diagnosis. Surgical treatment of hemorrhoids in a patient whose main disease process is Crohn's disease, a pelvic floor abnormality, or ulcer/fissure disease inevitably yields inferior results. It is especially important to recognize the anal pain and spasm of ulcer/fissure disease because in patients with this condi-

tion, excision of hemorrhoidal tissue without sphincterotomy leads to increased postoperative pain and poor wound healing.

I prefer to operate with the patient in the prone-flexed position, using local anesthesia supplemented by I.V. medication. I have found over the years that with this approach, patients retain no unpleasant memories of the OR experience, and good pain control is achieved in the immediate postoperative period.

In the postoperative period, efforts must be made to minimize straining on the part of the patient. To accomplish this, pain must be kept at a low level. I prefer to give only parenteral pain medication, in relatively high doses, on the first night. The patient and the nursing staff must be cautioned that the first sensation of pain, especially after elastic ligation of hemorrhoids, is the urge to defecate. This urge is an indication that pain medication should be given. The patient must not sit on the toilet and strain; to do so is likely to result in extrusion of the recently ligated tissue.

At least 20% of patients experience some degree of urinary retention. If this occurs, an indwelling catheter should be placed. In-and-out straight catheterization is contraindicated. No bladder stimulants should be given: such agents encourage straining and increase the risk of complications.

Bulk-forming agents and stool softeners are started in the immediate postoperative period. I encourage patients to take warm soaks, either in a bathtub or in a shower, rather than try to squeeze into the disposable sitz-bath mechanisms provided by the hospitals, which are often too small. I also encourage patients to sit on soft cushions rather than the rubber rings marketed for postoperative care; the rings seem to cause more dependent edema and pain.

COMPLICATIONS

Bleeding

Either immediate or delayed bleeding may occur after hemorrhoid surgery. Bleeding within the first 12 to 24 hours after the operation represents a technical error. The only management is to return the patient to the OR, with good anesthesia and adequate visualization, so that the bleeding site can be suture ligated. Frequently, spinal or epidural anesthesia is necessary because the patient is too uncomfortable, and the tissue perhaps too edematous, to allow local anesthesia. Bleeding within 5 to 10 days after the operation usually results from sloughing of the eschar created by suturing or elastic ligation. This delayed bleeding is usually minimal, and the patient is encouraged to rest and to take stool softeners. If the bleeding is significant, examination with adequate anesthesia is indicated to allow cauterization or suture ligation of the bleeding site.

It is important to discourage patients from taking aspirin-containing compounds in the postoperative period, and it is especially important to follow patients taking systemic anticoagulants closely. I prefer to treat these patients with excisional hemorrhoidectomy so that sutures can be placed; in this way, I avoid the risk that the elastic-ligated tissue will slough after 5 to 10 days.

Infection

Infection is unusual after hemorrhoidectomy because perianal tissue is normally well vascularized and extremely resistant to infection despite constant bombardment by bacteria. When it does occur, it is most likely to be in an immunocompromised patient—that is, one who has a blood dyscrasia, diabetes, or AIDS or has recently undergone chemotherapy. In my view, it is imperative to obtain at least a complete blood count and a chemistry profile before embarking on anorectal procedures; if the results are abnormal, elective hemorrhoid surgery is contraindicated.

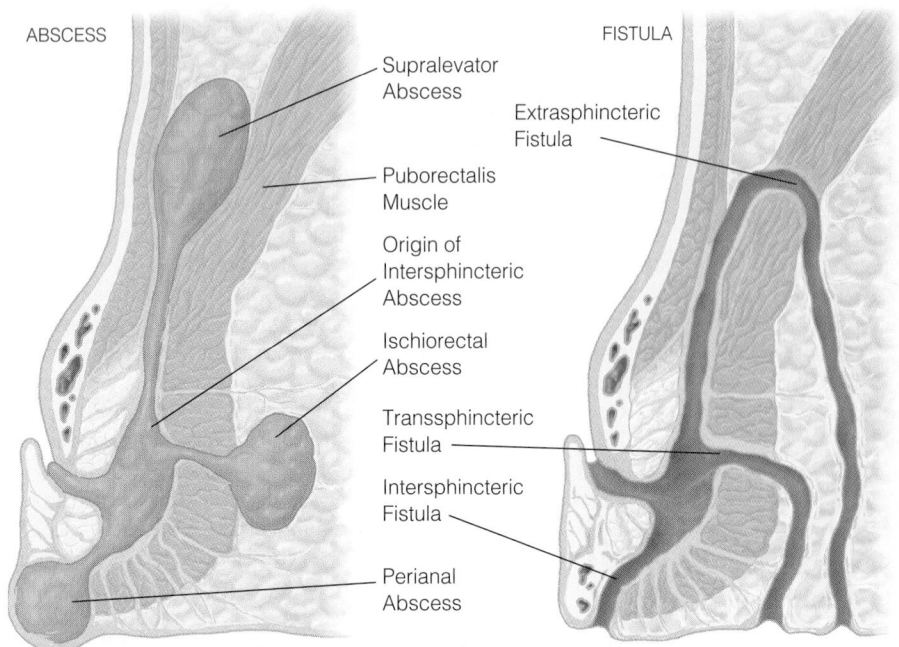

ABSCESS   FISTULA

Supralevator Abscess

Extrasphincteric Fistula

Puborectalis Muscle

Origin of Intersphincteric Abscess

Ischiorectal Abscess

Transsphincteric Fistula

Intersphincteric Fistula

Perianal Abscess

Figure 8 **Abscess and fistula are, respectively, the acute aspect and the chronic aspect of a single disease process. Acute inflammation can lead to different types of abscesses (left), depending on the direction in which the inflammation extends. Chronic inflammation leads to communication of the abscess sites with the surface—that is, fistula tracts (right).**

Any local focus of infection noted in the postoperative period must be drained. I have seen this complication only when slowly absorbable suture material was used, which is the reason why I have returned to using 3-0 chromic catgut. Postoperative perianal infection can be severe and life-threatening, and it is therefore critically important to be familiar with its symptoms and to treat it intensively. Frequently, such infection is initially manifested by pain that is greater than anticipated, urinary retention, and fever. These symptoms have occasionally been reported after elastic ligation of hemorrhoids. In this event, it is critical that the patient be seen on an emergency basis, the elastic bands removed, the patient hospitalized, and parenteral administration of antibiotics begun. In retrospect, I find that all such patients whom I have seen had preoperative symptoms of a pelvic floor abnormality with difficulty in defecation—not clear symptoms of hemorrhoids.

Urinary Retention

Urinary retention is apparently caused by reflex spasm of the pelvic musculature, which may not become evident until the local anesthesia wears off. Often, a patient still under the influence of local anesthesia seems to be doing exceedingly well for the first few hours after operation, only to go into urinary retention later that night. It may be helpful to reduce the fluid load in the perioperative period. When a patient has trouble urinating, an indwelling urinary catheter should be placed and left in place for at least 12 hours. This, in my view, is one of the major reasons for in-hospital observation after treatment of more than one cluster of hemorrhoids. Placement of the indwelling catheter is of particular importance for the patient's well-being, even if it is not looked on with favor by managed care administrators. Urinary retention is a frightening experience for the patient to undergo at home. What is more, if placement of an indwelling catheter is postponed for 12 to 24 hours, recovery may be delayed. Again, it is important to remember that urinary retention may be an early sign of pelvic infection.

Stricture

Stricture, with or without ectropion, results from circumferential excision of hemorrhoids. I mention this point only to discourage the performance of this procedure.

OUTCOME EVALUATION

Because hemorrhoids are treated only when symptoms—bleeding, prolapse, pain, and difficulty with hygiene—are present, success is determined simply by the extent to which the symptoms are alleviated. If other symptoms were present before operation and persist after the procedure, the primary diagnosis should be called into question. Many elderly patients with a single prolapsing hemorrhoid that causes bleeding or maceration of the perianal skin are well served by outpatient ligation; occasionally, there is a second cluster that requires treatment some months later.

The basic point is that any patient treated surgically for hemorrhoids should experience symptomatic relief. With newer surgical techniques and improved methods of postoperative management, there is no reason for the patient to experience the severe pain described by those who have undergone extensive excisional procedures.

Operative Management of Abscess and Fistula

The conditions that cause suppurative processes in the anoperineum are cryptoglandular abscess and fistula, Crohn's disease, and hidradenitis suppurativa [see 59 Benign Rectal, Anal, and Perineal Problems]. Accurate diagnosis is essential for proper surgical management. Although these conditions may appear similar at times, each one is managed somewhat differently.

OPERATIVE PLANNING

The most important initial step is to determine the activity and severity of the disease process and the immune status of the patient. For example, a large, fluctuant abscess surrounded by erythema, induration, and superficial necrosis of the skin in an insulin-dependent diabetic is a surgical emergency. On the other hand, a chronic abscess or fistula that drains periodically over a matter of months is not nearly as urgent a problem. Multiple fistula tracts to the perineum in a patient with Crohn's disease require that one perform an adequate study of the intestinal tract and the sphincter mechanism before attempting definitive surgical treatment. It is important to determine the etiology of the process whenever possible. Unfortunately, the determination cannot always be made without examination under anesthesia, during which treatment as well as diagnosis could be accomplished, and this complicates the obtaining of informed consent and the choice of anesthesia.

It is also important to gain as accurate a picture as possible of the complexity of the disease process; this facilitates the planning of the procedure, the choice of anesthesia, and the selection of the information given to patient and family before treatment. For example, in the absence of other significant health problems, a small, well-localized, low intersphincteric abscess often can be easily drained with the patient under local anesthesia if an internal opening can be seen preoperatively on anoscopy, although on occasion even this procedure calls for spinal or epidural anesthesia. (It should be remembered that use of the prone-flexed position [*see Figure 2*], which is my preference, makes general anesthesia more difficult.) Multiple infected tracts associated with undrained infectious foci in a case of rectal Crohn's disease necessitate examination with the patient under spinal or epidural anesthesia. The treating surgeon should perform careful anoscopy and sigmoidoscopy and conservative temporary drainage procedures until consultation with a specialist can be arranged. Severe destruction and suspected deep tissue necrosis, especially in immunocompromised patients, may necessitate extensive resection of tissue and perhaps a completely diverting colostomy.

Bowel preparation should include mechanical cleansing and antibiotics but may not be possible when the situation is urgent (as is most often the case). Appropriate antibiotic coverage (i.e., agents effective against gram-negative organisms and anaerobes) is indicated for all but the simplest cases, with special consideration given to patients who require prophylaxis because of cardiac disease or the presence of prosthetic material.[2] Usually, a urinary catheter should be inserted before operation, especially if the infectious process is located in the anterior region in a man, where the urethra is at risk for injury.

OPERATIVE TECHNIQUE

Many technical elements are common to all operations for conditions that cause suppurative processes in the perineum. The patient should be in the prone-flexed position, with the buttocks taped apart. Conduction anesthesia (spinal, caudal, or epidural) is usually required. The perineum should be examined carefully with an eye to areas of abscess or external drainage sites. Endoscopic examination of the anus, the rectum, and the vagina should be undertaken to search for primary inflammatory bowel disease, internal openings of the fistula, or vaginal openings of the fistula.

Cryptoglandular Abscess and Fistula

The abscess must be located and characterized because drainage will depend on the location of the abscess, the course of the fistula tract, and any related infectious processes [*see Figure 8*].[3] It is important not to create a fistula through the levator plate of the pelvic floor. This means that an abscess with a low origin must be drained low, with care taken to avoid iatrogenic perforation of the rectum, and an abscess with a high origin (e.g., a high intersphincteric abscess) must be drained high by incising the mucosa and the longitudinal (internal sphincter) muscle of the rectal wall (not a procedure for the occasional rectal surgeon). The internal opening—that is, the crypt where the abscess originated—must be sought; this is best done by means of anoscopy, very careful probing, and sigmoidoscopy to rule out a high source (e.g., Crohn's disease). If the internal opening is found, the abscess can be drained or a fistulotomy can be performed [*see Figure 9*]. With a fistulotomy, determination of safety is a paramount concern. Careful consideration must be given to which

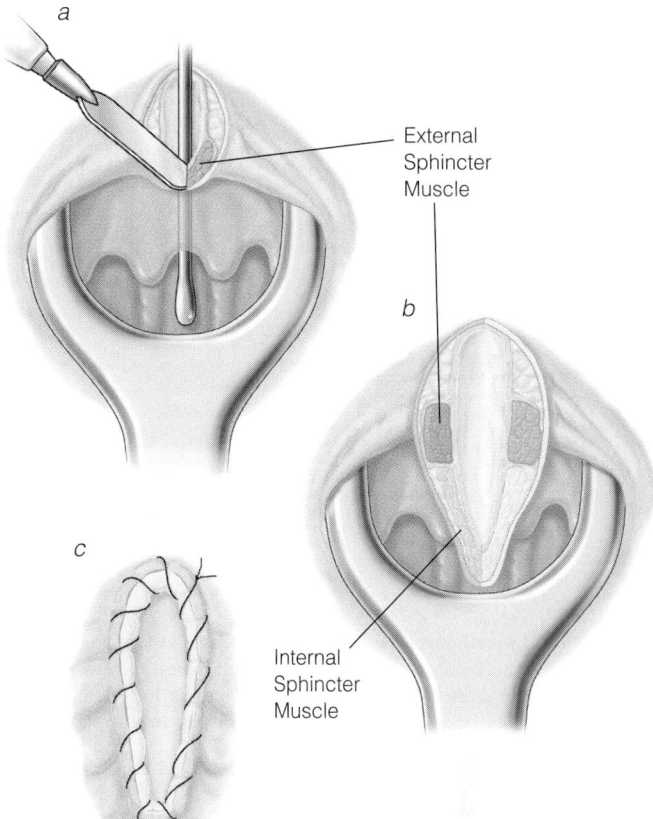

Figure 9 Operative management of abscess and fistula. Shown is a fistulotomy in a patient with cryptoglandular abscess/fistula. (*a*) The fistula tract is carefully probed, a decision is made about which muscle and how much muscle to cut, and the tract is incised. (*b*) Once the tract is open, the involved crypt is excised. (*c*) The defect is marsupialized by sewing skin to the tract.

muscle—and how much of the muscle—is to be cut. The anterior location in a woman is especially precarious. If the fistula involves a significant amount of muscle, or any muscle in the anterior region in a woman, either a seton should be placed or a drain should be placed without disruption of the muscle, in preparation for advancement flap closure of the internal opening.

If the internal opening is not found, one should not make one by probing. The abscess should be drained with a mushroom-tipped catheter [*see Figure 10*]; in my experience, this is preferable to unroofing and eliminates painful packing. The catheter can be left in place for an extended period, and it permits subsequent injection of dye or contrast material. Once the mushroom catheter is in place in the OR, the surgeon can inject diluted methylene blue to search again for internal openings, which, if found, allow one to consider fistulotomy. The drain is usually sutured in place. The patient should be seen a few days after the operation to confirm that the abscess is adequately drained.

After 2 weeks, the patient is seen in the office, and povidone-iodine is injected through the drain while the inside of the anal canal is inspected via an anoscope. If an internal opening is seen, then fistulotomy is planned. If no internal opening is seen (as is the case in about 50% of patients), the drain should be removed 1 week later. This allows any irritant effect of the povidone-iodine to resolve and prevents the abscess from recurring.

If the fistula tract is known to have an external opening and fistulotomy is planned, the following approach should be considered. First of all, fistulectomy is never indicated. Fistulotomy is

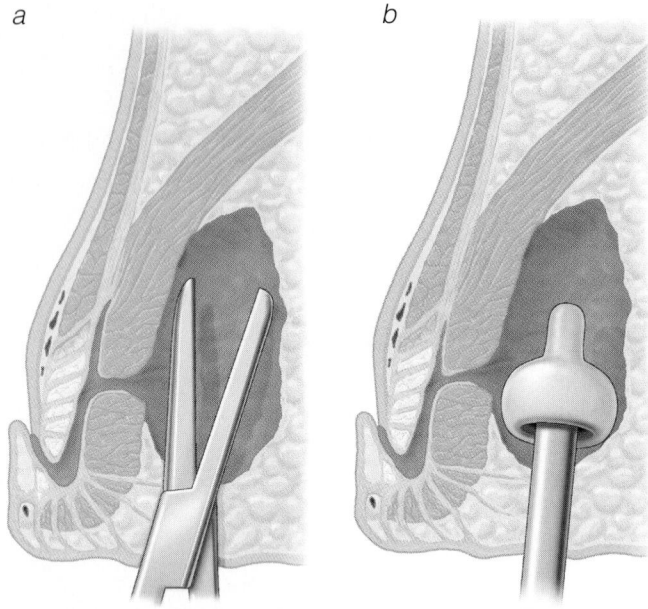

Figure 10 **Operative management of abscess and fistula. Shown is drainage of an ischiorectal abscess. Such abscesses may be palpated above the anorectal ring, even though their location is more inferior. (*a*) The abscess is incised. (*b*) A mushroom-tipped catheter is placed.**

performed rarely and with great caution in the face of Crohn's disease. To perform the fistulotomy, one must first find the internal opening. In this regard, Goodsall's rule is often helpful: external fistula openings anterior to the midanal line are usually connected to internal openings via short, straight tracts, whereas external openings posterior to this line usually follow a curved course to internal openings in the posterior midline. Dilute meth-

ylene blue is injected through the external opening, often via a plastic I.V. catheter.

Careful probing, perhaps with a lacrimal duct probe, is then carried out. If the internal opening still cannot be found, a drain is placed so that the surgeon can return at another time to search for the internal opening. If the internal opening is found, a probe is passed and an effort is made to determine how much muscle and which muscle must be transected to accomplish the fistulotomy and how much muscle will remain to maintain continence [*see Figure 11*].

If the surgeon is not sure of the extent of muscle involvement or of how safe a fistulotomy would be, the infectious process should be drained, and either the patient should be referred to a specialist, or plans should be made for an advancement flap procedure to close the internal opening. If a fistulotomy is done, a biopsy specimen should be obtained from the infected tract, and the tract should be marsupialized to prevent premature healing of the superficial aspect.

It is important to keep in mind that the sphincter mechanism is innervated by a branch of the pudendal nerve that enters the sphincter from the posterolateral aspect. Accordingly, extreme caution must be exercised when a deep fistulotomy is required in the posterolateral perianal quadrants.

There is a growing body of evidence suggesting that injection of commercially available fibrin glue is effective for treatment of fistulas in perianal tissue. Longer tracts appear to respond better to this modality than shorter tracts do. The long-term efficacy of this approach remains to be proved.

Special problems A cryptoglandular abscess that extends into the posterior anal and posterior rectal spaces is often missed as a source of infection. Diagnosis of such abscesses typically involves bidigital examination, often with the patient under anesthesia; needle aspiration may be required as well. Fistulotomy in this area often

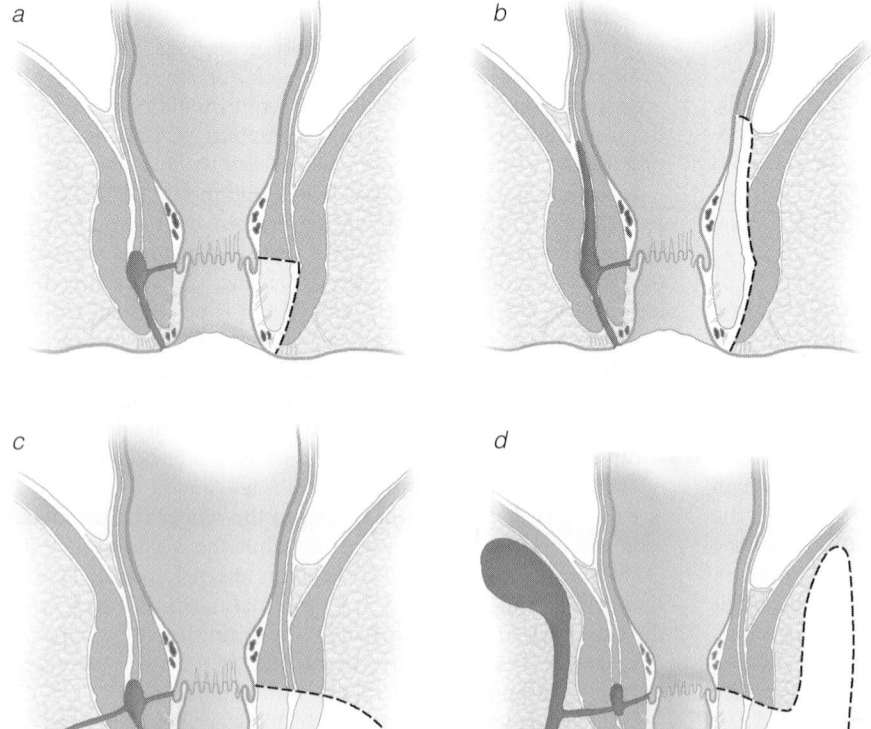

Figure 11 **Operative management of abscess and fistula. Shown are examples of the different types of fistulotomies indicated for some of the many types of fistulas: intersphincteric fistula with a simple low tract (*a*), intersphincteric fistula with a high blind tract (*b*), uncomplicated transsphincteric fistula (*c*), and transsphincteric fistula with a high blind tract (*d*). In each image, the left half of the drawing shows the disease process, and the right half illustrates the recommended operation.**

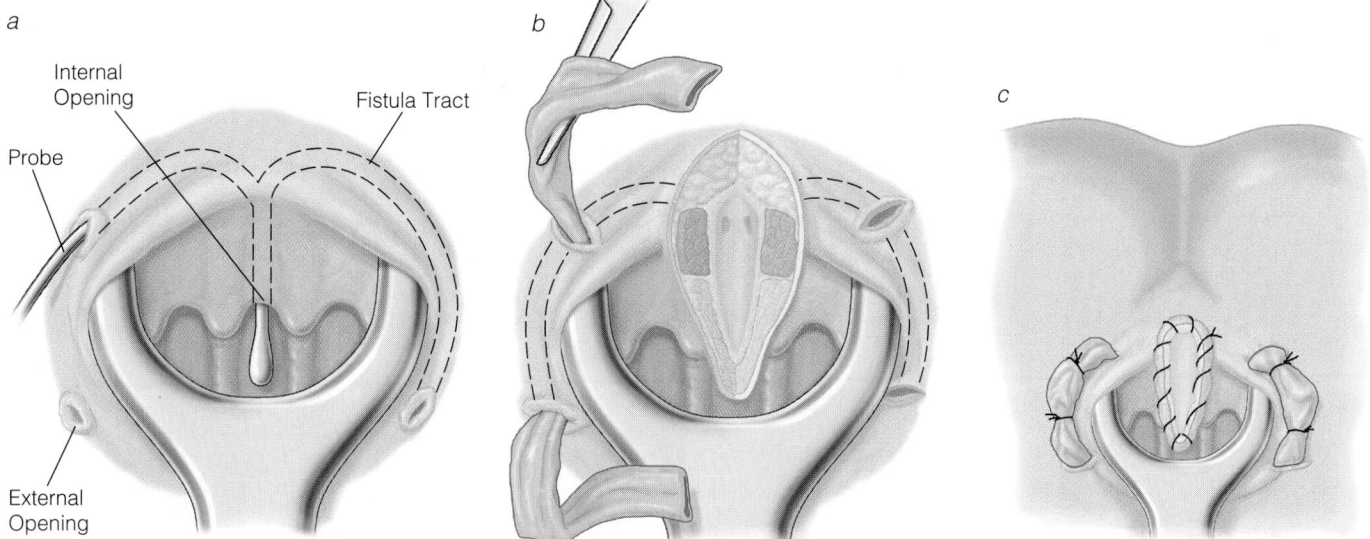

Figure 12 **Operative management of abscess and fistula. Shown is the surgical treatment of a horseshoe fistula. (*a*) The main posterior tract of the fistula is identified by probing. (*b*) The posterior tract is opened, and drains are placed laterally. (*c*) The posterior tract is marsupialized.**

necessitates opening large amounts of tissue, including partial transection of the sphincter muscle; the tract may also have to be marsupialized. If one is unsure of the anatomy or has never done the procedure before, the abscess should be drained as simply as possible and the patient referred to a specialist.

The so-called horseshoe abscess [*see Figure 12*] results from an undiagnosed posterior-space abscess that has dissected laterally and may have been drained several times through the lateral extension into one or both ischiorectal fossae. This condition is cured by opening the posterior space and placing a long-term lateral drain, after which healing proceeds by secondary intention (the so-called Hanley procedure). The drain should not be removed until there is solid healing in the posterior midline; this may take weeks or even months.

Abscess and Fistula Associated with Crohn's Disease

The goals of treatment are to drain and control the focus of infection, to preserve sphincter function, to plan and implement a staged approach to preservation of anorectal function, and to make the correct diagnosis. To these ends, careful identification of the location and course of the abscess and any associated fistulas is essential; this is accomplished via endoscopic dye injection, probing, and vaginoscopy.

The safest approach, in my view, is to place mushroom catheters in abscesses and complicated fistula tracts or, in some cases, to use setons to allow drainage of the fistulas (not to cut through the tissue, which is often the intended result of seton placement) [*see Figure 13*]. For optimal resolution of inflammation at the site of the internal opening in anticipation of a possi-

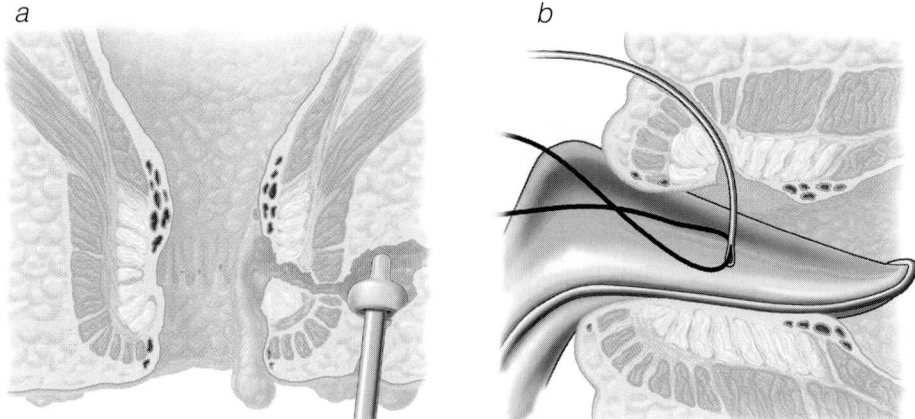

Figure 13 **Operative management of abscess and fistula. Shown are alternatives for treating abscess or fistula associated with Crohn's disease. In Crohn's disease, multiple perianal and perineal fistulas and abscesses may be seen, often in atypical locations. (*a*) Abscesses may be drained by placing a small mushroom-tipped catheter as close to the anus as possible. A Malecot catheter should not be used. (*b*) In some settings, it is appropriate to place a seton between internal and external openings. This seton may then be left in situ for a time for drainage and for prevention of further disease progression.**

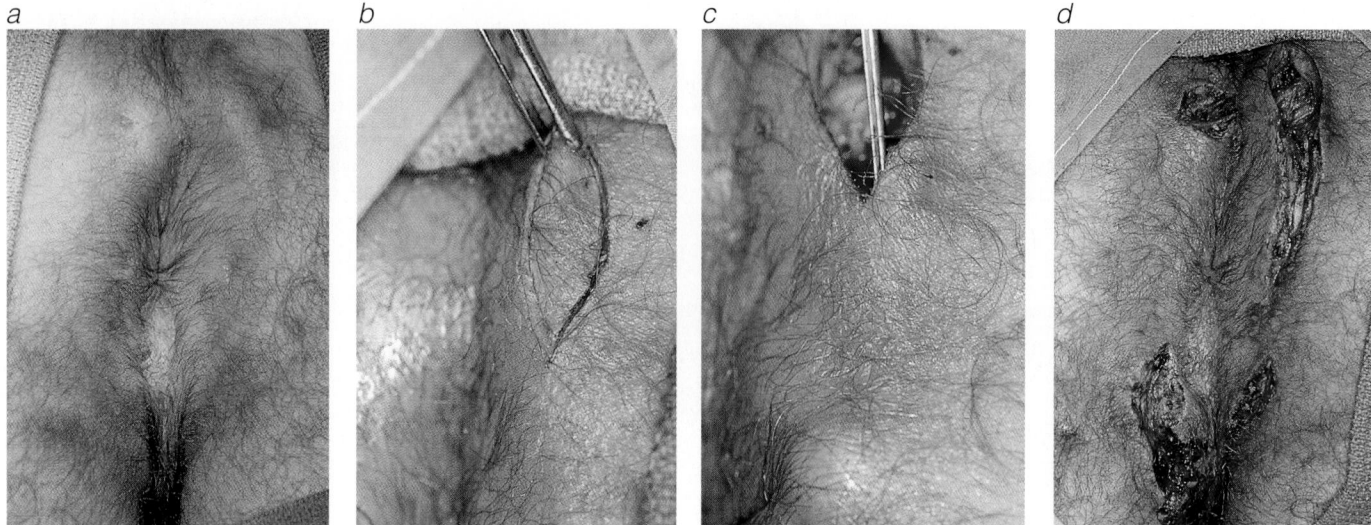

Figure 14 **Operative management of abscess and fistula. In this patient, the causative condition is hidradenitis suppurativa. (*a*) Multiple openings of sinus tracts can be seen and extensive indurated tracts palpated. (*b*) Abscesses are unroofed. (*c*) Indurated tracts are probed. (*d*) All tracts are identified and incised.**

ble advancement flap procedure, perirectal mushroom catheters are preferable to setons placed through the internal opening. Superficial fistula tracts may occasionally be managed with fistulotomy if the Crohn's disease is otherwise inactive. Sphincterotomy is never indicated in a patient with Crohn's disease if severe infection is present or the disease is active. When a patient is known or believed to have Crohn's disease, biopsy of the edematous external skin tags that are often present can be a good way of finding granulomatous tissue to confirm the diagnosis.

The newer forms of medical treatment of Crohn's disease, in which a monoclonal antibody to tumor necrosis factor (infliximab) is given either by itself or in combination with immunosuppressive agents, seem to display some of their most beneficial results in patients with complicated anoperineal fistulas. In my view, a good way of managing abscess and fistula associated with Crohn's disease is for the surgeon to drain and control the suppurative process and for the gastroenterologist then to employ the latest medical regimen to force the disease into remission.

Hidradenitis Suppurativa

Patients with infected fistula tracts or abscesses secondary to hidradenitis suppurativa must be positioned in such a way as to allow visualization of and access to all tracts. This is crucial because some of the tracts may extend into the scrotum, the labia, the inguinal areas, or the suprapubic area. Conduction anesthesia is important in that it covers broad areas of the perineum; adequate local anesthesia is impossible unless one is dealing with very small, isolated tracts.

The definitive therapeutic surgical procedure is incision (rather than excision) of these often extensive inflammatory tracts [*see Figure 14*]. The surgeon should do as much as possible at one time, with the understanding that it is not unusual to leave a few tracts undrained or to return later to address new areas of dissection. Because the primary disease process does not involve the sphincter, intestinal diversion is rarely indicated. Biopsy is indicated because on rare occasions, these long infected tracts exhibit malignant changes or result from an anal malignancy. The perineal skin can tolerate the extensive incisions necessary to cure the process. Special precautions must be taken not only to pre-

serve the sphincter itself but also to avoid damaging the neurovascular bundle that enters the anus from the posterolateral aspect. In male patients, efforts must be made to avoid the urethra during incision in the anterior midline; to this end, a Foley catheter should always be placed before the surgical procedure is begun. Because so many incised skin edges remain after treatment of extensive hidradenitis, it is imperative to achieve adequate hemostasis. The disposable suction cautery units currently available can be especially helpful for this purpose. The wounds may be either left open or loosely packed until good granulation tissue forms.

Bathing the perineum, especially after a bowel movement, is helpful. Often, showers are better for this purpose than the portable minuscule sitz baths commonly used. For patients who have undergone extensive procedures, twice-daily trips to a whirlpool bath (often located in the physical therapy department) are helpful. Despite the multiple lengthy incisions, there is usually little pain, and most of the postoperative care can be done at home. Adequate follow-up is necessary to treat residual or new areas of disease before the dissection becomes extensive again. Care must be taken, especially in the OR, to search for the infected tracts, which may contain little pus and may be apparent only as indurated cords within the perineal skin.

TROUBLESHOOTING

Most of the important steps for avoiding problems have already been described in the course of addressing preoperative planning and operative technique (see above). The goals in the treatment of all of the processes associated with anorectal abscess and fistula in ano are to preserve sphincter function, to control acute infection, and to eliminate the source of the infection. If it is likely that sphincter function will be compromised at all, a baseline level of sphincter function (including the status of muscles and nerves) must be determined before any surgical procedure is initiated. One should never hesitate to perform an examination with the patient under anesthesia and to inject dilute methylene blue to delineate the extent and location of the infectious process.

Anyone embarking on surgical management of such processes must keep in mind the option of performing an advancement flap procedure to close the internal opening, especially in the anterior region and most particularly in women. If such a procedure is planned, initial drainage should be done external to the rectum with a mushroom catheter rather than through the internal opening with a seton. Simple 3-0 chromic catgut should be used to marsupialize fistula tracts because employing the newer, less quickly absorbable materials may lead to a chronic nidus that gives rise to ongoing infection. Patients should be watched closely in the immediate postoperative period to ensure that all infection is controlled. Not uncommonly, a superficial collection is drained, but a deeper abscess remains that must be sought more aggressively.

One should always take into account the risk of anoperineal infection in immunocompromised patients. Given that the anatomy of the anal tissue planes is complex and can be rendered even more so by multiple surgical procedures, one should not venture beyond one's level of expertise. One should never hesitate to drain an infectious focus with a simple mushroom-tipped catheter and, if appropriate, refer the patient to a colon and rectal surgical specialist who is trained to manage complex anoperineal suppurative processes safely and definitively.

COMPLICATIONS

Complications occur if one or more of the goals just mentioned (see above) have not been achieved. Persistent or recurrent infection is seen with some frequency. In patients with cryptoglandular abscess or fistula, infection usually results from failure to locate the internal opening or to discover a deep posterior midline abscess; such failure is often seen in patients with a horseshoe abscess, in whom repeated lateral drainage procedures may have been undertaken without the primary cavity in the posterior anal or posterior rectal space being discovered and dealt with.

In patients with Crohn's disease, infection can persist if a deeper pocket or extension has gone undiscovered or if the disease has recurred, leading to further penetration and infection in the anoperineum or the perirectal tissue. Extensive examination with the patient under anesthesia, including transrectal ultrasonography or CT scanning, may be required to determine the source and extent of the infection. It is always possible that the infection derives from a superlevator abscess secondary to intestinal disease; consequently, a detailed evaluation of the intestinal tract is indicated in patients with Crohn's disease.

In patients with hidradenitis suppurativa, the most common problems are residual undrained tracts and recurrent disease. Again, examination with the patient under anesthesia and repeated drainage are called for. Because this disease process does not originate in the rectum, care must be taken not to enter the rectum or to cut any of the nerves entering the anus from the posterolateral aspect. It has been reported anecdotally that very chronic or persistent fistula tracts may eventually exhibit malignant changes (squamous cell carcinoma); for this reason, such tracts should be biopsied.

OUTCOME EVALUATION

No sophisticated surveillance is necessary: if drainage persists or some degree of incontinence develops, the patient usually will volunteer the information freely. Either of these complaints could be an indication for a detailed examination, including a sophisticated evaluation of sphincter function.

Operative Management of Ulcer/Fissure Disease

Ulcer and fissure are two aspects of a single anorectal disease process with an unclearly defined pathophysiology [see Figure 15]. Accurate diagnosis is crucial [see 59 Benign Rectal, Anal, and Perineal Problems]. Not uncommonly, patients are treated for hemorrhoids when the true primary condition is ulcer/fissure disease.

OPERATIVE PLANNING

Fundamental concerns in planning the operation—besides confirming the diagnosis—are to verify that there are no other conditions that could threaten complete healing of an incision in the anal tissue and to make sure that there is no significant incontinence before the sphincterotomy.

For example, a history of diarrhea compatible with the presence of inflammatory bowel disease indicates the need for further evaluation to eliminate the possibility of Crohn's disease; if Crohn's disease is present, the risk of poor healing is greater, and it will be necessary to preserve all of the available sphincter function of the anus for a long period. As another example, a woman who has borne children by vaginal delivery and has any degree of incontinence should undergo manometry, ultrasonography, and perhaps electromyography to confirm that the sphincter is not compromised by a mechanical or neurologic deficiency. Yet another example is a patient with irritable bowel syndrome or a pelvic floor abnormality who experiences a multitude of difficulties with bowel movements. It is important to recognize such conditions and to advise the patient of the need for special attention to maintain adequate bowel function in the postoperative period.

It is essential to clearly explain the nature of the operative procedure (i.e., the incision of a portion of the internal sphincter mechanism) to the patient and to warn him or her that minor incontinence or flatus may persist for as long as a few months postoperatively. To be fair, significant incontinence is highly unusual: in fact, most patients experience very rapid relief of their often distressing symptoms. One should also advise the patient that any other anal procedures that may be indicated (e.g., elastic ligation of internal hemorrhoids or excision of symptomatic external hemorrhoids) can and should be accomplished at the time of sphincterotomy, with or without excision of the anal ulcer, and that he or she should take 3 to 5 days off from work. The risk of urinary retention, pain, and bleeding must also be discussed. In planning the operative procedure and immediate postoperative care, one must take into account the

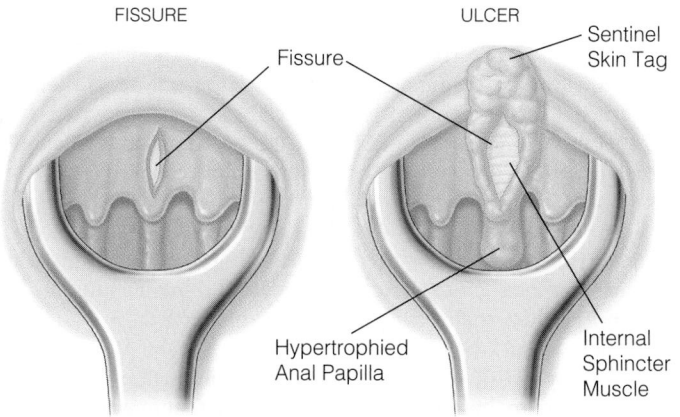

Figure 15 **Operative management of ulcer/fissure disease. Anal fissure (left) and anal ulcer (right) are, respectively, the acute aspect and the chronic aspect of a single disease process.**

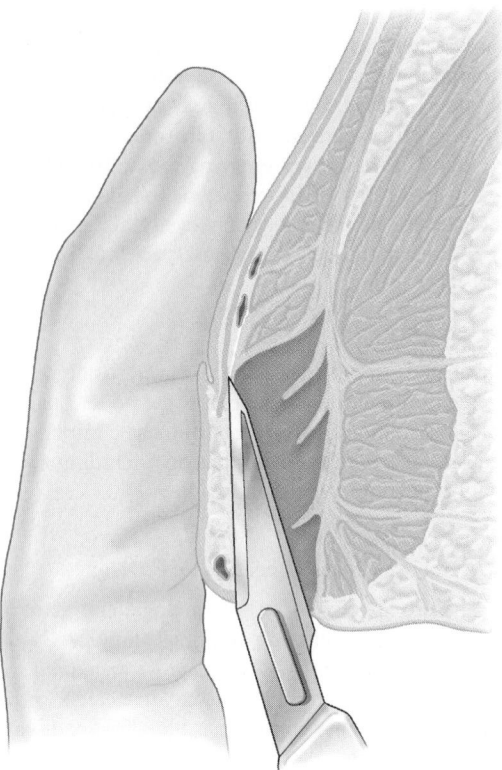

Figure 16 Operative management of ulcer/fissure disease. Shown is the closed approach to posterior lateral internal sphincterotomy. A No. 11 blade is inserted in the intersphincteric groove and moved upward to the level of the dentate line. Medial movement of the blade divides a portion of the internal sphincter muscle. The anoderm and the other anal muscles are not divided.

patient's specific needs, idiosyncrasies, and home environment. Some patients are comfortable undergoing the procedure completely on an outpatient basis, whereas others clearly need to be admitted for short-term observation and parenteral administration of pain medication.

When possible, I keep patients on a liquid diet for 24 hours before operation and use small, self-administered enemas to empty the rectum immediately before the procedure. I advise patients to discontinue any aspirin-containing products and any other anticoagulants, if possible, at least 10 days beforehand.

OPERATIVE TECHNIQUE

Operative treatment of ulcer/fissure disease consists of a posterior lateral internal anal sphincterotomy, in which the internal sphincter is divided but the external sphincter, the anoderm, and the longitudinal muscle remain intact. I generally prefer to place the patient in the prone-flexed position with the buttocks taped apart and adequate local anesthesia in place. The operation can then be performed in one of three ways: (1) as a closed procedure involving the use of a No. 11 blade and digital palpation of the muscle [*see Figure 16*], (2) as an open procedure without direct visualization of the muscle, or (3) as an open procedure with clear identification of the muscle before its transection. The third option is the one I prefer.

An open procedure with visualization of the muscle is done as follows [*see Figure 17*]. The first step is anoscopy, preferably with a medium Hill-Ferguson instrument. The hypertrophied band of the lower third of the internal sphincter muscle is clearly identified. If this band is not a distinctly identifiable entity, sphincterot-

omy should not be performed. The ulcer or fissure itself need not be present, because the disease may be in a relatively inactive state at the time of surgery.

Rigid or flexible sigmoidoscopy should then be performed if it was not done in the immediate preoperative period. The primary purpose of this step is to make sure that no features of Crohn's disease are visible in the rectum. When the endoscopic examination is complete, I usually repeat the preparation of the anal opening.

A 1 cm incision is made in the posterior lateral aspect of the perianal skin, hemostasis is obtained, and a delicate dissection is done with a curved hemostat in the intersphincteric plane. The posterior midline is avoided because healing in this position may result in scar tissue that interferes with perfect continence (the so-called keyhole deformity). The white hypertrophied band of muscle is then elevated into the wound with a curved hemostat. If a rent is made in the anal mucosa, it must be repaired with 3-0 chromic catgut. The band of muscle is then incised with the electrocautery, and pressure is maintained for a few minutes to ensure hemostasis. Digital examination confirms adequate transection of the band. The skin is left open.

Attention is then directed to the ulcer, which may be excised sharply in an elliptical fashion so as to incorporate the entire triad of the ulcer (i.e., the ulcer itself, the sentinel hemorrhoidal tag, and the hypertrophied anal papilla) while avoiding additional transection of the underlying muscle. If I excise the ulcer complex, I usually close the wound with a continuous three-point suture of 3-0 chromic catgut to obliterate any dead space and thus to lower the risk of postoperative infection.

Any additional anal surgery required is then completed, the surgical site is covered with antibiotic ointment, and a very light gauze bandage is applied with a minimum of tape and traction on the perianal skin.

TROUBLESHOOTING

To perform this simple procedure well, one must have a clear understanding of the surgical anatomy of the anal canal and must be able to clearly identify the internal sphincter, the intersphincteric groove, and the external sphincter muscle. The hypertrophied band of muscle must be accurately identified and cleanly transected. No attempt should be made to extend or amplify the procedure by stretching the anal canal and thus bursting the muscle. Although the procedure and anatomy are simple, the best way of learning the operation is to watch an experienced surgeon perform it. I do not believe this procedure can be learned through reading alone.

COMPLICATIONS

Because the internal sphincter muscle is responsible for resting, involuntary continence, injury to this structure can lead to nocturnal incontinence. Again, special caution is advised with respect to the anterior aspect of the anoperineum in women. On the other hand, incising the posterior midline can also lead to the keyhole deformity, which may cause prolonged anal seepage because of the configuration of the scar tissue; a good analogy is a bent rim on a tubeless tire. It is tempting to close the tiny skin incision at the site of sphincterotomy, but I think it should be left open to reduce the already low risk of infection.

There should be very little postoperative pain. If the patient does complain of significant pain, especially in the presence of fever or urinary hesitancy, one must assume that infection is present in the anoperineum, a structure that is normally highly resistant to microbial invasion. Urgent evaluation, removal of sutures, antibiotic therapy, bowel rest, placement of a urinary catheter, and very close observation in the hospital are indicated.

a   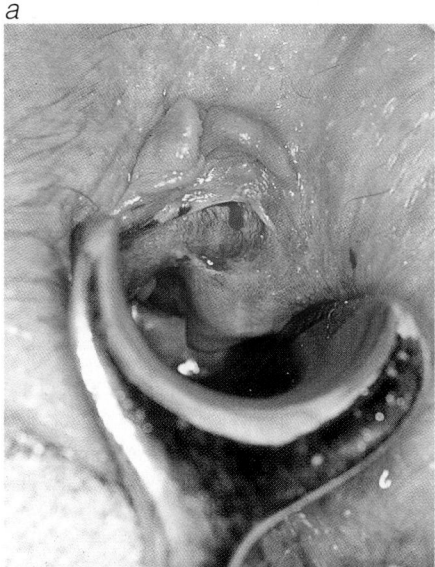   *b*   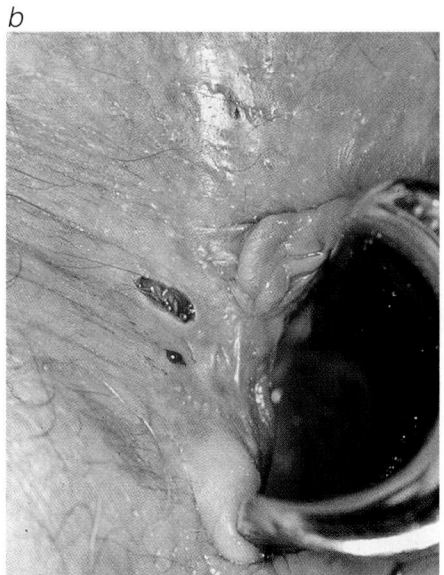   *c*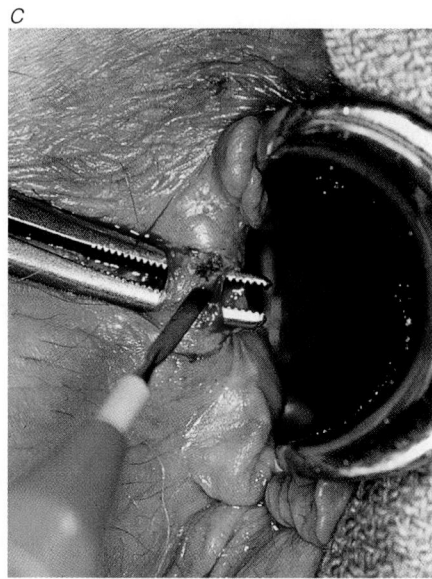

Figure 17   **Operative management of ulcer/fissure disease. Shown is the open approach to posterior lateral internal sphincterotomy. (*a*) The triad of the ulcer complex is visualized. (*b*) Once the hypertrophied band of internal sphincter muscle is identified, a 1 cm incision is made in the posterolateral aspect of the perianal skin. (*c*) The hypertrophied band is elevated into the wound and divided with the electrocautery.**

The major causes of complications are incorrect diagnosis of the disease process (especially overlooking the presence of Crohn's disease) and failure to fully understand the anatomy of the continence mechanism of the anal canal. If too much of the internal sphincter muscle is cut, if this muscle is already compromised, or if the external sphincter muscle is transected by mistake, the patient will be rendered incontinent. On the other hand, if not enough of the internal muscle is transected, the ulcer will not heal and the symptoms will persist.

Overall, the single most common cause of complications that I have observed is the failure even to suspect, much less diagnose, ulcer/fissure disease as the source of a patient's symptoms. I frequently see patients who seem to have failed to heal months after a hemorrhoidectomy. When their symptoms are reviewed and a thorough examination performed, it becomes apparent that the underlying disease process was always ulcer/fissure disease rather than hemorrhoids and that the hemorrhoidectomy only intensi-

fied the anal pain and bleeding. These patients are finally cured when an adequate sphincterotomy is performed.

In very rare instances, drainage continues at the site of the sphincterotomy. If drainage persists for weeks, the patient should be examined under appropriate anesthesia, and the focus of infection should be opened. This is essentially equivalent to a very superficial fistulotomy.

OUTCOME EVALUATION

Again, no sophisticated surveillance is necessary: when the patient returns 2 weeks after the procedure, free of pain and bleeding and able to have bowel movements without difficulty, one may be sure that an acceptable outcome has been achieved. Digital rectal examination should confirm good healing and normal sphincter tone (both while resting and while contracting). For additional confirmation, I have patients continue to take bulk-forming agents and stool softeners and then examine them 1 month later to verify that healing is complete.

References

1. Presented at the annual meeting of the American Society of Colon and Rectal Surgeons, Dallas, Texas, May 8–13, 2004

2. Practice parameters for antibiotic prophylaxis to prevent infective endocarditis or infected prosthesis during colon and rectal endoscopy. Standards Practice Task Force, American Society of Colon and Rectal Surgeons. Dis Colon Rectum 35:277, 1992

3. Kodner IJ, Fry RD, Fleshman JW, et al: Colon, rectum and anus. Principles of Surgery, 6th ed. Schwartz SI, Ed. McGraw-Hill, New York, 1994

Recommended Reading

Corman ML: Colon and Rectal Surgery, 3rd ed. JB Lippincott Co, Philadelphia, 1993

Fry RD, Kodner IJ: Anorectal disorders. Clin Symp 37:6, 1985

Gordon PH, Nivatvongs S: Principles and Practice of Surgery for the Colon, Rectum and Anus. Quality Medical Publishers, St. Louis, 1992

Keighley MRB, Williams NS: Surgery of the Anus, Rectum and Colon, Vols 1 and 2. WB Saunders, London, 1993

Kodner IJ: Differential diagnosis and management of benign anorectal diseases. Gastrointestinal Diseases Today 5:8, 1996

Standards Practice Task Force, American Society of Colon and Rectal Surgeons: Practice parameters for treatment of fistula-in-ano. Dis Colon Rectum 39:1361, 1996

Acknowledgment

Figures 1, 5b, 5c, 8 through 13, 15, 16   Tom Moore. Adapted from original illustrations by John Craig.

80 STROKE AND TRANSIENT ISCHEMIC ATTACK

Thomas S. Maldonado, M.D., and Thomas S. Riles, M.D., F.A.C.S.

Assessment and Management of Stroke and TIA

Stroke is defined as any damage to the central nervous system caused by interruption of the blood supply. Ischemic strokes result from the failure of oxygen and nutrients to reach the affected brain. Transient ischemic attacks (TIAs) are defined as transient neurologic deficits lasting no longer than 24 hours; longer-lasting deficits are considered to be indicative of a cerebral infarction ("brain attack").

Infarction from ischemia is typically confined to a vascular territory, at whose center can be found the injured or obstructed artery supplying that parenchyma. The full extent of a stroke may not become apparent until days or weeks later, when the tenuous peripheral watershed zone, or penumbra, either survives or succumbs to cell death. Smaller infarcts, adequate collateral circulation, and prompt intervention and resuscitation are associated with improved outcome.

Hemorrhagic stroke damages the brain by cutting off connecting pathways and causing localized or generalized pressure injury. Brain edema and hydrocephalus after hemorrhagic stroke may also be deleterious. In some cases, hemorrhagic stroke can lead to ischemia as a consequence of vasospasm, as is seen in the setting of subarachnoid hemorrhage (SAH). Likewise, some ischemic strokes can undergo hemorrhagic transformation.

Incidence and Risk Factors

Stroke is the third leading cause of death in the United States: about 168,000 stroke-related deaths are reported each year.[1] Approximately 500,000 first-time strokes are reported annually. In addition, stroke is the leading cause of serious long-term disability in the United States and poses a substantial economic burden. For 2003, U.S. expenditure on stroke-related medical costs and disability payments amounted to roughly $51 billion. Although a sharp decline in stroke incidence and mortality was noted throughout most of the 20th century, the decline leveled off in the early 1990s, and stroke incidence and mortality are now rising for the first time since 1915.[2,3]

Numerous population studies and stroke registries have been designed to examine the incidence, risk factors, and natural history of stroke.[4-10] Some of the independent risk factors that have been identified—such as age (> 55 years), sex (male), race (African American and Asian), and genetic predisposition—cannot be modified and therefore carry a fixed level of stroke risk. The Rochester (Minnesota) population study demonstrated a marked progressive incidence of cerebral infarction with advancing age, as well as a nearly 1.5 times greater risk of stroke in males.[4] The Lausanne Stroke Registry data confirmed the overall higher incidence of stroke in males, though it also demonstrated a female preponderance in very young (< 30 years) and very old (> 80 years) patients. These latter findings may be attributable to the high frequency of oral contraceptive use in young women in that

study, as well as to the lower life expectancy of men, especially those with vascular risk factors.[9] Race and genetic predisposition are also considered independent risk factors, with African Americans more than twice as likely to die of stroke as whites.[10] The underlying mechanism of stroke appears to vary with race as well: intracranial occlusive disease tends to occur more frequently in African and Asian Americans than in whites or in males as a whole.[11,12] The importance of hereditary risk for stroke has long been recognized. In the Framingham Study, both paternal and maternal histories of stroke were associated with an increased risk of stroke.[10,13]

There are, however, certain risk factors for stroke that are clearly modifiable, including hypertension, smoking, hyperlipidemia, asymptomatic high-grade carotid stenosis, and atrial fibrillation (AF).[14-16] Other purported modifiable risk factors for stroke (e.g., obesity, diabetes, oral contraceptive use, and alcohol intake) are more controversial.[17-20] Hypertension (systolic as well as diastolic) is perhaps the most prominent modifiable risk factor for stroke and is associated with a substantial risk of atherothrombotic, lacunar, or subarachnoid hemorrhage. The Systolic Hypertension in the Elderly Program (SHEP) study demonstrated that treating systolic hypertension in patients 60 years of age or older can reduce the incidence of stroke by as much as 36%.[21] Prompt diagnosis and intervention for stroke may be critical, but many authorities feel that primary prevention is the true cornerstone of therapy for this lethal disease.

Clinical Evaluation

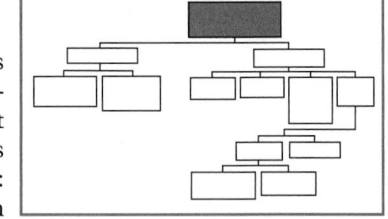

When assessing patients who present with a neurologic deficit, clinicians must immediately ask themselves the following two questions: (1) what is the mechanism of the deficit (i.e., ischemic or hemorrhagic), and (2) where is the lesion (e.g., cerebral lacunae, the territory around a large vessel, or a watershed region)? A thorough history and physical examination, in conjunction with brain imaging studies, usually suffice to guide initial management. Nonvascular conditions that can mimic stroke (e.g., hypoglycemia, migraine, a postictal state, encephalopathy, trauma, and brain tumors or abscesses) must be excluded. Although these syndromes can all cause focal findings, they usually lack the abrupt onset of symptoms consistently seen with stroke.

Ischemic and hemorrhagic stroke must be differentiated early in the course of an acute stroke because a number of therapeutic interventions that are beneficial for some subtypes of stroke are potentially catastrophic for others. Approximately 71% of all strokes are ischemic and 26% hemorrhagic; the remaining 3% are of unknown origin [see Table 1].[22] Hemorrhagic strokes result from subarachnoid or intracerebral bleeding, whereas ischemic strokes result from systemic hypoperfusion, cardioembolism, or atherothrombosis. Although various different laboratory and radiographic tests are available and should be performed, the diagnosis of stroke is primarily a clinical one.

HISTORY

A patient who has suffered a stroke typically presents with a history of sudden onset of a focal brain deficit and a clinical syndrome on neurologic examination. A medical history should elicit any of a number of risk factors associated with either ischemic or hemorrhagic stroke. For example, hypertension is often associated with deep infarcts and hemorrhages, whereas cigarette smoking and hyperlipidemia are more commonly associated with ischemic infarcts resulting from atherosclerosis.[9] (Hypertension can, however, be associated with infarcts caused by hypertensive arteriolopathy.) The presence of atrial fibrillation, a recent myocardial infarction (MI) (< 6 weeks old), or a prosthetic heart valve suggests a possible cardioembolic mechanism.

The onset and course of the neurologic deficit may also be telling. A steady onset is suggestive of hemorrhage, whereas symptoms that progress in a stepwise fashion are more likely to derive from ischemia. Likewise, accompanying signs are frequently useful in differentiating stroke mechanism subtypes. Headache, vomiting, and loss of consciousness constitute the classic picture of hemorrhagic stroke, whereas a focal deficit preceded by TIAs is more suggestive of ischemic stroke.[23] Although the clinical manifestations are generally helpful in differentiating stroke subtypes, it sometimes happens that large infarcts mimic the classic picture of hemorrhage or that lobar or small deep hemorrhages resemble infarction resulting from atherosclerosis. Analysis of 1,000 consecutive patients from the Lausanne Stroke Registry who experienced their first stroke confirmed that the classic hemorrhagic picture (headaches, progressive neuralgic deficits, and decreased level of consciousness) was indeed more common in patients with hemorrhage but found that only one third of patients with hemorrhagic strokes had this clinical triad.[9]

PHYSICAL AND NEUROLOGIC EXAMINATION

A general physical and neurologic examination should detect vascular and cardiac abnormalities, as well as localize the process within the CNS. Heart size and sounds, irregular rhythms or dis-

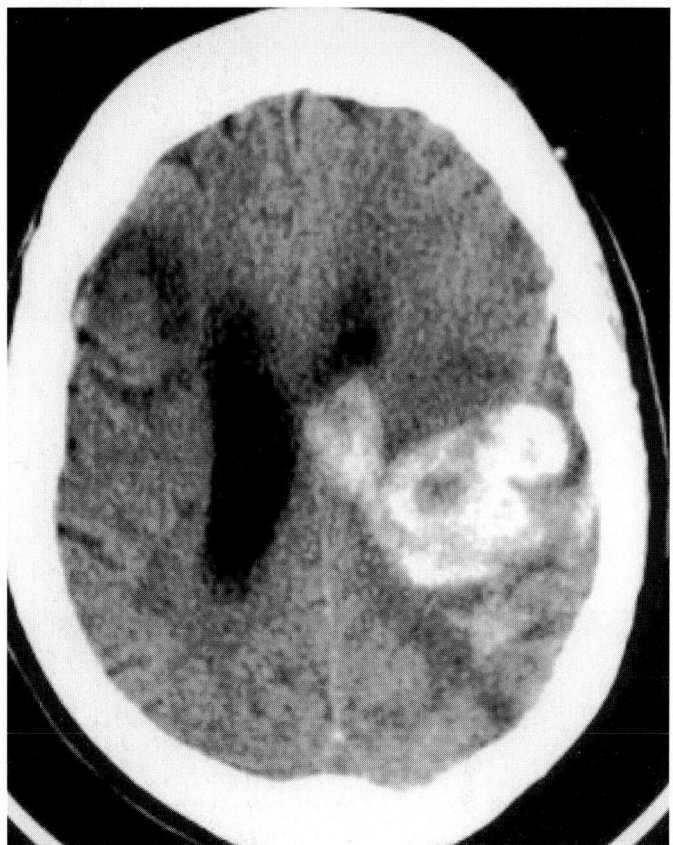

Figure 1 Shown is a CT image of an acute hemorrhagic infarct, with intraparenchymal bleeding apparent.

crepant pulse exams, and carotid bruits should all be noted. Careful examination of the extremities is essential, in that peripheral vascular disease is highly correlated with the presence of atherosclerosis of the carotid and vertebral arteries.[6,24] An ophthalmologic examination should detect subhyaloid hemorrhages, as well as cholesterol emboli (Hollenhorst plaques).

Besides localizing the lesion anatomically, the neurologic examination should be able to identify a probable cause. The absence of major focal neurologic signs is often consistent with SAH; focal deficits localized to the superficial cortex are often attributable to thromboembolism or ischemia. A number of well-described lacunar syndromes also exist; these typically suggest small-vessel disease.

Investigative Studies

IMAGING

Imaging is a mandatory and integral part of evaluation for acute stroke and should be performed expeditiously. Computed tomography is the initial test of choice; it is readily available in most hospitals and is well tolerated by critically ill patients.[25] CT can promptly identify nonvascular causative conditions (e.g., masses) and can readily diagnose intracerebral hemorrhage (ICH) [see Figure 1]. Diagnosis of SAH without I.V. contrast can be more difficult, especially if bleeding is minor or occurred more than 1 day before; the accuracy of CT in detecting SAH decreases after 24 hours.[26] SAH should appear as an increased density in the CSF. If SAH is clinically suspected, lumbar puncture may be necessary for definitive diagnosis.

Table 1 Causes of Stroke as Recorded in NINCDS Data Bank[22]	
Cerebral ischemia	**71%**
Atherosclerosis	10%
Larger-artery stenosis	6%
Tandem arterial lesions	4%
Lacunae	19%
Cardioembolism	14%
Infarct of undetermined cause	27%
Cerebral hemorrhage	**26%**
Parenchymatous	13%
Subarachnoid	13%
Other	**3%**

NINCDS—National Institute of Neurological and Communicative Disorders and Stroke

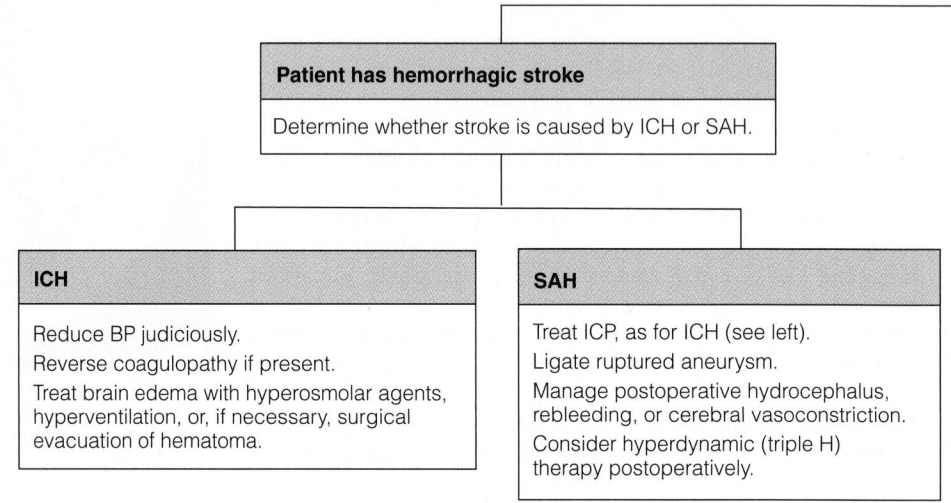

Patient has hemorrhagic stroke

Determine whether stroke is caused by ICH or SAH.

ICH

Reduce BP judiciously.

Reverse coagulopathy if present.

Treat brain edema with hyperosmolar agents, hyperventilation, or, if necessary, surgical evacuation of hematoma.

SAH

Treat ICP, as for ICH (see left).

Ligate ruptured aneurysm.

Manage postoperative hydrocephalus, rebleeding, or cerebral vasoconstriction.

Consider hyperdynamic (triple H) therapy postoperatively.

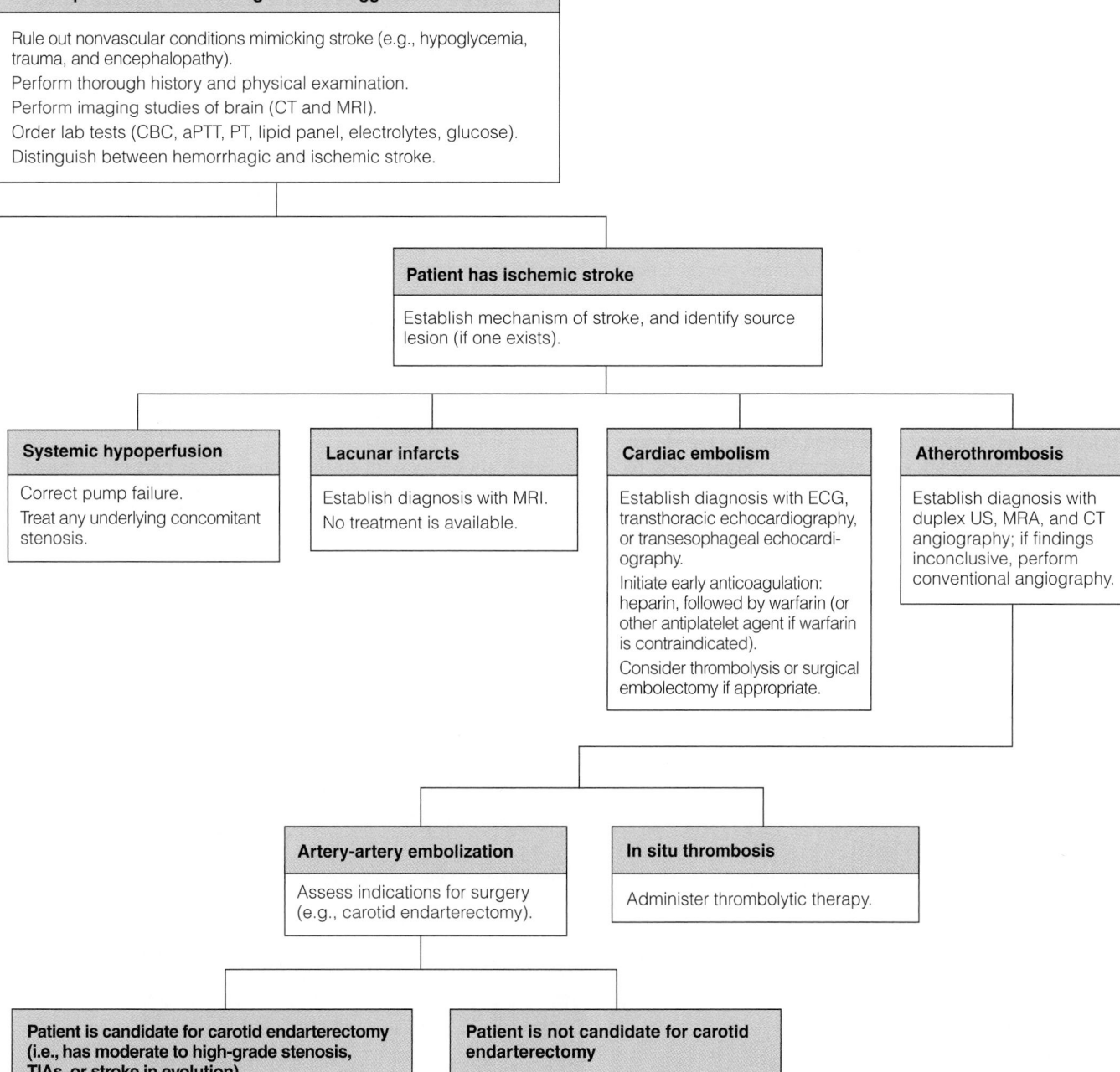

Patient presents with neurologic deficit suggestive of stroke

Rule out nonvascular conditions mimicking stroke (e.g., hypoglycemia, trauma, and encephalopathy).
Perform thorough history and physical examination.
Perform imaging studies of brain (CT and MRI).
Order lab tests (CBC, aPTT, PT, lipid panel, electrolytes, glucose).
Distinguish between hemorrhagic and ischemic stroke.

Patient has ischemic stroke

Establish mechanism of stroke, and identify source lesion (if one exists).

Systemic hypoperfusion

Correct pump failure.
Treat any underlying concomitant stenosis.

Lacunar infarcts

Establish diagnosis with MRI.
No treatment is available.

Cardiac embolism

Establish diagnosis with ECG, transthoracic echocardiography, or transesophageal echocardiography.
Initiate early anticoagulation: heparin, followed by warfarin (or other antiplatelet agent if warfarin is contraindicated).
Consider thrombolysis or surgical embolectomy if appropriate.

Atherothrombosis

Establish diagnosis with duplex US, MRA, and CT angiography; if findings inconclusive, perform conventional angiography.

Artery-artery embolization

Assess indications for surgery (e.g., carotid endarterectomy).

In situ thrombosis

Administer thrombolytic therapy.

Patient is candidate for carotid endarterectomy (i.e., has moderate to high-grade stenosis, TIAs, or stroke in evolution)

Perform carotid endarterectomy. (Alternatively, consider carotid angioplasty and stenting.)
Administer antiplatelet therapy.

Patient is not candidate for carotid endarterectomy

Consider embolectomy or thrombolysis.
Administer antiplatelet therapy.

In cases of acute ischemic stroke, diagnosis of infarction by means of CT can be more difficult. I.V. contrast CT is of limited value in this setting. Signs of infarction can be absent or subtle in the first few hours after the stroke. A lesion may appear as a slight hypodensity within the infarcted zone or as a loss of definition between gray and white matter.[27] Newer CT scanners may be better at delineating these nuances.[28,29] In the days following an ischemic stroke, an infarct may first appear round or oval and then as a hypodense, dark, or wedge-shaped lesion on CT.

Magnetic resonance imaging is more expensive and time-consuming than CT and is less well tolerated by critically ill patients. Nonetheless, MRI is more sensitive than CT in detecting early ischemic changes after a stroke. It can be used to distinguish an old stroke from a new one and to assess the size and location of a lesion, especially when the lesion is adjacent to bony structures [see Figure 2].[30] The size of the infarct as determined by MRI may be of great importance for prognosis. Although lesion size may not correlate with severity of clinical presentation, larger infarcts in the same vascular territory are associated with more severe deficits than smaller infarcts in similar anatomic locations are.

MRI is especially useful for diagnosing lacunar infarcts. In a review of 227 patients with lacunar infarcts, 44% were diagnosed by CT and 78% by MRI.[31] Infarction appears as dark, hypodense areas on T_1-weighted sequences and as bright areas on T_2-weighted sequences. Edema usually develops around the infarct within the first few days and is readily apparent on MRI as a low-density area surrounding the lesion with mass effect. Sometimes, the infarct is small but is still associated with substantial edema. Such edema may be insignificant in an older patient with an atrophied brain whose cranium is able to accommodate a mass effect but may be life-threatening in a younger patient with little intracranial room to spare.

The high sensitivity of MRI in detecting infarction has been demonstrated in studies evaluating patients experiencing TIAs. When patients without signs or symptoms of infarction underwent brain imaging after a TIA, 27% were found to have evidence of so-called silent infarcts on CT and 73% on MRI.[32]

Diagnosis of ICH can be a more delicate task with MRI than with CT. Careful scrutiny by an experienced observer using different acquisition techniques is required. The appearance of a cerebral hematoma on T_1- and T_2-weighted sequences varies as the lesion matures and edema resolves. Acute hematomas are black on T_1-weighted images, and chronic hematomas are white on T_1- and T_2-weighted images.

Normal neuroimaging findings are not uncommon in patients presenting with neurologic deficits suggestive of acute stroke. A patient with a neurologic deficit and a negative CT scan should undergo further cerebral imaging with MRI. The absence of ischemic infarction and hemorrhage on both CT and MRI may suggest transient ischemia or persistent ischemia without infarction. In such cases, one may have to rely on signs and symptoms to localize the ischemic lesion responsible for the stroke. Alternatively, electroencephalography (EEG), positron emission tomography (PET), single-photon emission CT (SPECT), or xenon-enhanced CT (XeCT) may be employed to help localize ischemic foci.[33,34]

LABORATORY TESTS

Blood should be sent to the laboratory as part of the initial assessment of a patient with an acute stroke. Measurement of serum electrolyte and glucose levels is essential to rule out nonvascular conditions mimicking stroke (e.g., hypoglycemia and dehydration). A complete blood count (CBC), an activated partial thromboplastin time (aPTT), a prothrombin time (PT), and a

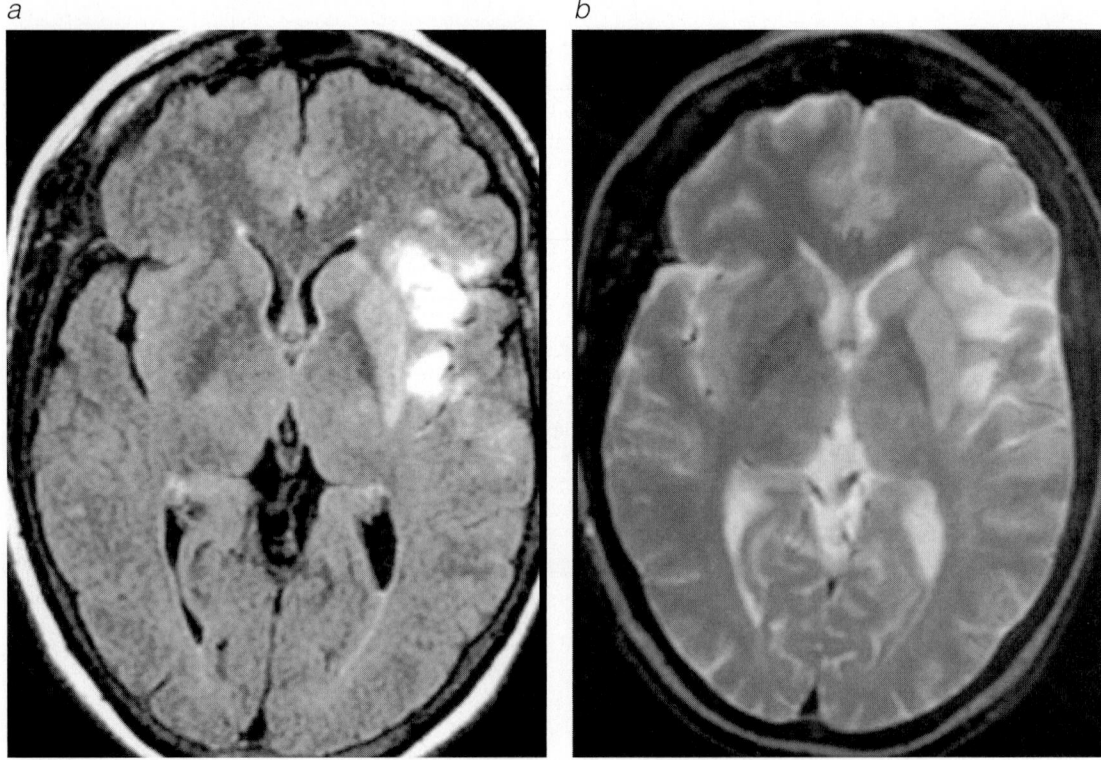

Figure 2 Shown are (*a*) a fluid-attenuated inversion-recovery (FLAIR) MRI image and (*b*) a T_2-weighted MRI image of an acute ischemic infarct in the left middle cerebral artery distribution.

lipid panel are likewise essential components of the initial assessment. Severe anemia has the potential to exacerbate or precipitate cerebral ischemia in stroke; though this is an uncommon occurrence, it should be considered and, if present, corrected.[35] Additional laboratory blood tests (e.g., a cardiac injury panel to rule out myocardial infarction or an erythrocyte sedimentation rate to assess the possibility of vasculitis) may be helpful.

Screening should be performed for hematologic disorders that result in hypercoagulable states, including homocystinuria,[36] antiphospholipid antibody syndrome, protein C and S deficiency, antithrombin deficiency, and activated protein C resistance from factor V Leiden mutation [see 85 Venous Thromboembolism].[37,38] Hemoglobinopathies (e.g., sickle cell disease and thalassemia) can also lead to altered blood flow, hypercoagulability, and stroke.[39] Finally, hyperviscosity syndromes (e.g., polycythemia vera, thrombocytosis, and myeloproliferative disorders) should be included in the differential diagnosis. If a hyperviscosity syndrome is recognized in the setting of acute stroke, hemodilution therapy may be warranted. Experimental and clinical trials have shown hemodilution to increase blood flow in the ischemic brain; however, other studies have failed to show improvement of neurologic status.[40,41] Hemodilution remains indicated in stroke patients who have a high hematocrit or are in a hyperviscosity state; however, close monitoring is required in patients with heart disease or cerebral edema.

Recognition and Management of Specific Stroke Subtypes

HEMORRHAGIC STROKE

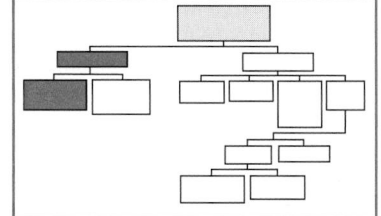

Hemorrhagic stroke can result from ICH or SAH. The consequences of cerebral bleeding can progress rapidly from neurologic deficit to coma to death in a significant number of patients.

Intracerebral Hemorrhage

ICH accounts for approximately 10% to 15% of all strokes in the United States and Europe.[22,42] Potential causative mechanisms include hypertension, trauma, arteriovenous malformations, cerebral amyloid angiopathy, brain tumors, blood dyscrasias, and medications (e.g., anticoagulants and thrombolytics). Of these, hypertensive arteriopathy is most commonly responsible for nontraumatic ICH.[22,43] Hypertensive brain hemorrhages are usually deep and are typically located in the lateral ganglionic region, the subcortex, the thalamus, the caudate nucleus, the pons, or the cerebellum. As early as the 1870s, Charcot and Bouchard correctly postulated that such events were the result of microaneurysmal disease of arteries and arterioles penetrating deep into the brains of hypertensive patients.[44,45] These discrete hemorrhages go on to compress neighboring capillary networks, causing them to burst and bringing about a rapid enlargement of the intracerebral hematoma. Indeed, such enlargement is not uncommon: one prospective study found that 38% of patients with ICH had a hematoma that was enlarged at 3 hours in comparison with its size on baseline CT after the initial bleeding event.[46]

Patients presenting with sizable ICH often rely on a marked compensatory elevation of blood pressure to maintain a pressure gradient in the setting of acute increases in intracranial pressure (ICP). It is vital to resist the impulse to lower blood pressure aggressively in these patients: a rapid drop in blood pressure may induce

brain ischemia. Short-acting antihypertensives should be administered only when the systolic blood pressure is persistently higher than 180 to 200 mm Hg or when there is evidence of active bleeding or an enlarging hematoma. Other medical treatment of hemorrhagic stroke from ICH includes reversal of coagulopathies with transfusions of fresh frozen plasma and platelets when appropriate.

Mortality from ICH has plummeted from 90% before the 1970s to less than 50% in the first decade of the 21st century.[2,22,47] This precipitous decline probably reflects improved antihypertensive therapy, as well as a decreased prevalence of hypertension.[48] Death from ICH most commonly occurs secondary to herniation from the hematoma itself coupled with brain edema, which can develop within the first hours after ICH.[47,49] Thus, treatment of brain edema is the main focus of treatment. Corticosteroids, though indicated for reducing cerebral edema in patients with tumors or abscesses, are contraindicated in patients with ICH because they are not beneficial and may in fact be injurious, predisposing patients to infection and worsening diabetes.[50] Hyperosmolar agents (e.g., mannitol or glycerol solutions) may be more useful for reducing cerebral edema rapidly.[51] Alternatively, in cases of severe brain edema, hyperventilation may reduce ICP by inducing diffuse vasoconstriction in the brain. Any physiologic perturbation that might increase cerebral blood volume (e.g., hypercarbia, hypoxia, or vasodilation) or reduce cerebral perfusion (e.g., hypotension) should be avoided. Finally, surgical evacuation of a hematoma, though controversial, may be employed as a last resort for decompression after ICH.[52]

Subarachnoid Hemorrhage

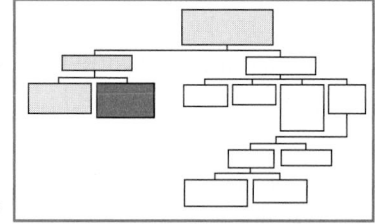

Rupture of saccular or berry aneurysms with subsequent SAH carries significant morbidity and mortality, depending largely on the patient's age, the extent of the hemorrhage, and the presence and severity of rebleeding, cerebral vasospasm, and surgical complications.[53] SAH accounts for 6% to 10% of all strokes and 22% to 25% of all deaths from cerebrovascular accidents.[54] The reported incidence of incidental aneurysms discovered in autopsy studies ranges from 0.8% to 18%.[55-57] SAH tends to occur more often in patients 50 to 60 years of age than in younger or older patients and in women more often than in men (12.3% versus 7.9%).[58] The pathogenesis of saccular aneurysms has not been fully explicated, but the risk factors are well described and include a family history of SAH,[59] hypertension, pregnancy,[60] and black race.[61]

SAH presents with warning signs in as many as 20% of patients within the 3 months preceding a major rupture, presumably because a minor leak develops before the rupture. Such warning signs include a so-called sentinel headache, oculomotor symptoms, nausea and vomiting, and loss of consciousness.[62] The rupture itself is accompanied by sudden severe headache, nuchal rigidity, back pain, nausea, vomiting, photophobia, lethargy, loss of consciousness, and seizure.[60,63]

Medical management of SAH includes tranquil bed rest with the head elevated 30°, stool softeners, antiemetics, and analgesics, as well as deep vein thrombosis (DVT) prophylaxis using pneumatic compression boots [see 85 Venous Thromboembolism]. Management of ICP in SAH patients is similar to that in ICH patients (see above). Furthermore, one must be vigilant for signs of hypothalamic dysfunction manifesting as cardiac dysrhythmias or the syndrome of inappropriate antidiuretic hormone secretion (SIADH).

The timing of microsurgical clip ligation of aneurysms after SAH is somewhat controversial. The International Cooperative Study on the Timing of Aneurysm Surgery showed no overall differences in outcome between early surgery (0 to 3 days after SAH) and delayed surgery (11 to 14 days after SAH).[64] Nonetheless, patients who were alert preoperatively did better with early surgery and demonstrated significantly better rates of good recovery.

Three major neurologic complications affect outcome after surgery for SAH: hydrocephalus, rebleeding, and cerebral vasoconstriction. Hydrocephalus may develop acutely as a result of obstruction of CSF outflow. Ventricular drainage can lead to immediate reduction of ICP and improvement in neurologic symptoms. The risk of rebleeding peaks on postoperative day 1; it is as high as 20% in the first 2 weeks and rises to 50% within 6 months if the aneurysm is not treated.[53] Unlike rebleeding, vasospasm manifests itself gradually over hours to days; it may be associated with up to a threefold increase in mortality during the 2 weeks after SAH.[65-67] The diagnosis is initially made via angiography and followed via transcranial Doppler sonography.[68,69]

Hyperdynamic, or triple H, therapy consists of keeping patients hyperdynamic (to increase cardiac output), hypervolemic-hypertensive (to augment cerebral perfusion pressure), and hemodiluted (to improve cerebral microcirculation by decreasing viscosity). Because of the risk that the aneurysm will rerupture before operation, triple H therapy is reserved for postoperative patients.[70,71] Calcium blockers may also reduce the incidence of symptoms secondary to vasospasm, though they most likely have little effect on spasm per se.[72]

ISCHEMIC STROKE

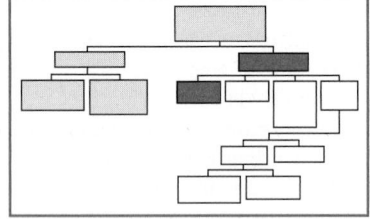

If hemorrhagic stroke is ruled out and ischemic stroke is diagnosed, the next step is to establish the mechanism of the stroke and identify the source lesion responsible (if one exists). Systemic hypoperfusion, cardiac embolism, large-artery atherosclerosis, and small-vessel disease should be systematically considered as potential causes.

Systemic Hypoperfusion

Only a small fraction of all ischemic strokes are attributable to systemic hypoperfusion. A quick assessment of vital signs and symptoms may provide the first clues that a patient is suffering from cerebral ischemia secondary to systemic hypoperfusion. Patients are characteristically either unconscious on arrival in the emergency department or awake but exhibiting neurologic symptoms resembling near-syncope.[73] Generally, they are pale, diaphoretic, and hypotensive. Neurologic signs and symptoms are varied and are explained by ischemia in the border zone (or watershed) between two or three adjacent arterial territories. Difficulty in reading or identifying visual stimuli (or even frank blindness) may be observed; this may be attributed to ischemia between the middle and posterior cerebral arteries. Bilateral arm weakness or cognitive difficulty may suggest ischemia between the middle and anterior cerebral arteries. Global symptoms usually arise from bilateral border-zone infarcts, which can develop in association with prolonged cardiogenic shock, dysrhythmias, or cardiac arrest.[74,75] Alternatively, symptoms may be asymmetrical if they derive from inadequate perfusion distal to a site of severe stenosis or occlusion of major feeding cerebral vessels.

Treatment should focus primarily on correcting the pump failure. Certain patients with concomitant underlying stenosis proximal to border-zone ischemic territories may benefit from treatment of the flow-limiting lesions to eliminate the hemodynamic impairment and thus may do better than patients with systemic hypoperfusion.[76]

Lacunar Infarcts

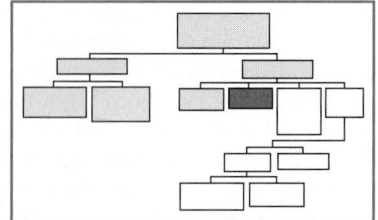

Neurologic examination of a patient believed to have experienced an acute ischemic stroke should be attentive to the possibility of lacunar infarcts, manifested by pure motor hemiparesis, pure sensory syndrome, sensorimotor syndrome, ataxic hemiparesis, and dysarthria–clumsy hand syndrome.[77,78] Lacunae are small (1 to 2 cm) subcortical lesions that result from small-vessel disease deep in the brain. They can occur either alone or in groups and may be present in as many as 23% of persons over the age of 65 years. Lacunar infarcts, unlike other forms of stroke, do not present with headache and are associated with hypertension and diabetes.[79] Although they are asymptomatic (silent) in as many as 89% of patients, their benignity is currently in some doubt: there is evidence to suggest that they may increase the risk of dementia and cognitive decline.[80,81] Lacunar syndromes are characteristic and highly predictive of the presence of lacunae, but they may be less reliable for excluding other mechanisms of stroke. A review of the Northern Manhattan Stroke Study experience demonstrated that as many as 25% of patients presenting with radiographically confirmed lacunar infarcts were ultimately found to have other mechanisms of ischemic stroke.[82] Thus, MRI should be used to confirm or exclude the presence of lacunar infarcts, as well as to screen for nonlacunar mechanisms of stroke.

At present, there is no treatment for lacunar infarcts, but the prognosis is quite good. The survival rate is high, the recurrence rate is low (mean annual stroke rate, 4% to 7%), and patients generally achieve relatively good functional recovery, with as many as 74% experiencing mild or no disability at 1 year.[83-86]

Cardiac Embolism

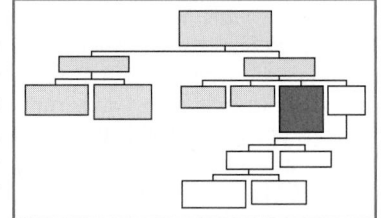

Embolism of cardiac origin accounts for approximately 14% of ischemic strokes [see Table 1]. Given that many infarcts of undetermined cause are probably of cardioembolic origin, this figure may in fact be an underestimate.[22] Whereas clinical suspicion for cardioembolism may be high in the setting of acute stroke, confirming the diagnosis can be more difficult. In most instances, cardioembolic stroke can be diagnosed on the basis of the history, the physical examination, and electrocardiography. A number of conditions are known to predispose to cardioembolism, including AF or atrial flutter, recent MI (< 6 weeks old), placement of a prosthetic valve, disease of the aortic or mitral valves, and paradoxical emboli (usually from DVT).[87] Key clinical manifestations include sudden onset with rapid progression to maximal deficit, infarcts in different arterial territories, rapid regression of symptoms, and decreased consciousness at onset.[88-90] Headache and seizure activity are not specific for cardioembolic stroke. The rapid regression of symptoms—also known as the spectacular shrinking deficit (SSD)—is thought to result from rapid recanalization or fragmentation and migration of cardioembolus downstream.[91] Ironically, the very mechanism purported to result in rapid regression of symptoms may trigger the hemorrhagic transformation seen in as many as 70% of cardioembolic strokes.[92,93] The vast majority of hemorrhagic transformations are caused by cardioembolism. A 2001 study found that delayed recanalization occurring less than 6 hours after an acute cardioembolic stroke developed in 52.8% of patients and was an independent risk factor for hemorrhagic transformation.[93] Other risk factors for such transformation are severe strokes, decreased alertness, and absence of collateral flow.[94]

Atrial fibrillation may or may not be detected on ECG, especially if it is paroxysmal; it remains an elusive but increasingly important risk factor for cardioembolic strokes in older patients.[95] Holter monitoring and electrophysiologic testing may be especially useful for diagnosing paroxysmal AF.[96] Likewise, transthoracic echocardiography and transesophageal echocardiography are useful for detecting mural thrombus caused by AF or another cardiomyopathy, as well as for detecting valvular diseases, vegetations, tumors, and patent foramina ovalia.

In the presence of nonrheumatic AF, the overall incidence of stroke is nearly five times higher, rising from 1.5% in persons 50 to 59 years of age to 23.5% in those 80 to 89 years of age.[97] Moreover, data from the International Stroke Trial indicate that mortality is twice as high in patients with AF as in those without AF (17% versus 7.5% at 2 weeks).[98] It is noteworthy that noncardioembolic strokes are estimated to account for about one third of the strokes that occur in AF patients. A 1997 autopsy study of 82 consecutive patients with symptomatic stroke and nonrheumatic AF demonstrated that 29 (35%) of the infarctions in patients with nonrheumatic AF were in fact of noncardioembolic origin.[95]

As a rule, acute ischemic stroke of cardioembolic origin is best treated with early anticoagulation to prevent recurrent brain embolism. Numerous studies have shown that recurrent embolism to the brain occurs within 2 weeks in 6% to 12% of patients after an initial ischemic infarct from a cardioembolic source.[99-101] A 1999 meta-analysis of 16 AF trials indicated that the overall risk of stroke could be reduced by an average of 62% with anticoagulation.[102] Thus, once a hemorrhagic stroke has been ruled out, heparinization and treatment with warfarin are indicated. Patients with ischemic stroke of cardioembolic origin who are at increased risk for hemorrhage or who have a contraindication to warfarin may be treated with aspirin or another antiplatelet agent; however, such agents are less effective than warfarin in secondary prevention of cardioembolic ischemic stroke.[103,104] Finally, despite the clear benefits of early anticoagulation in stroke patients with cardioembolism, such therapy has not been shown to be advantageous in the general stroke population.

For patients who suffer ischemic strokes of noncardioembolic origin, warfarin appears to offer no additional benefit over aspirin in preventing stroke recurrence.[105] Furthermore, most authorities would agree that patients with acute ischemic stroke who present within 48 hours of the onset of symptoms should be given aspirin, 160 to 325 mg/day, to reduce mortality and morbidity from stroke.[106,107]

Atherothrombosis

Roughly 10% of acute ischemic strokes are believed to occur secondary to large-vessel atherosclerosis, thrombosis, or artery-to-artery distal embolization.[22] Smoking and age are the most important contributors to the development of carotid atheroma.[108]

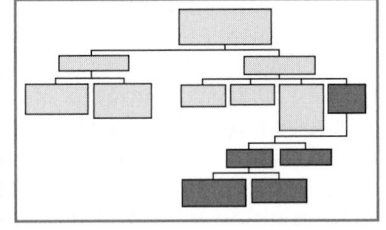

Unlike cardioembolism, carotid atheroemboli and thrombosis are more likely to be associated with TIAs. Moreover, TIAs of carotid arterial origin tend to occur in the same vascular territory, whereas TIAs of cardioembolic origin are more haphazard in location.[88,90] Once the history, the physical examination, and brain imaging studies are complete, duplex ultrasonography should be performed to search for extracranial atherosclerosis of the carotid arteries. Duplex examination of the carotid arteries may also identify ulceration and assess plaque echolucency, both of which may increase the level of risk.[109,110] Other important diagnostic modalities commonly used to assess extracranial sources for atherothrombotic-embolic mechanisms of stroke are magnetic resonance angiography (MRA) and CT angiography. We routinely use these modalities to corroborate the findings of duplex ultrasonography. In patients with carotid arterial stenosis, conventional angiography is usually limited to cases in which duplex ultrasonography disagrees with MRA or CT angiography; in patients with vertebral arterial stenosis, angiography is mandatory before any attempt is made at reconstruction.

Diagnosis of symptomatic carotid artery lesions in the setting of acute ischemic stroke is critical because this subtype of stroke patient stands to benefit significantly from surgical intervention. The results of three prospective randomized trials from the early 1990s comparing medical with surgical treatment of symptomatic carotid arterial stenosis demonstrated that carotid endarterectomy (CEA) had a significant advantage over medical treatment (aspirin).[111-113] Perhaps the most convincing of the three studies was the North American Symptomatic Carotid Endarterectomy Trial (NASCET), which was terminated prematurely because of the clear superiority of the results in the surgical arm.[111] In NASCET, the cumulative risk of ipsilateral stroke was 9% with surgical treatment and 26% with medical treatment at 2-year follow-up, for an absolute risk reduction of 17% and a relative risk reduction of 65.4%. Patients with carotid arterial stenosis of less than 50% did not benefit from CEA. Conversely, studies have shown that patients who have a completely occluded carotid artery in the setting of an acute stroke should not undergo CEA either. Emergency CEA in an acutely occluded artery can result in conversion of an ischemic infarct to a hemorrhagic cerebral infarct, with potentially catastrophic results.[114]

Indications for and Timing of Therapy

SURGICAL THERAPY

Carotid Endarterectomy

CEA [see 88 Surgical Treatment of Carotid Artery Disease] should be performed only when a low (< 5%) morbidity and mortality from stroke can be expected.[111,115] When a symptomatic patient with moderate or high-grade stenosis presents with TIAs or a mild stroke, the decision to perform a CEA is relatively straightforward. Patients who have suffered devastating infarcts, however, usually are not appropriate surgical candidates. Generally speaking, the extent to which neurologic function is spared, the presence and severity of medical comorbidities, and the patient's life expectancy should all be assessed before the decision is made to embark on CEA.

The timing of CEA after an acute stroke continues to be a subject of controversy. According to some authorities, the risk that an ischemic infarct will undergo hemorrhagic transformation after urgent CEA is a contraindication to early surgery.[116,117] ICH after endarterectomy is most likely the result of postoperative hyperperfusion. The combination of hypertension (which is common after stroke) and diminished vasomotor regulation in the penumbra may predispose small vessels in this region to hemorrhage. Other authorities, however, argue that delaying surgery exposes the patient to a substantial risk of recurrent stroke or carotid occlusion and that early intervention is therefore warranted.[118] Although it would probably be generally agreed that waiting an obligatory 30 days before surgery is prudent, there are numerous small series in the literature supporting the idea that early CEA after an acute ischemic stroke is indeed safe and may be indicated.[119,120] Furthermore, documentation of the location and size of the lesions may help identify infarcts that are at increased risk for hemorrhagic transformation after CEA.[120] Ultimately, the optimal timing of surgery after an acute ischemic stroke must be determined on the basis of prospective, randomized clinical trials.

Stroke in evolution A patient with neurologic deficits that worsen progressively in a stuttering fashion is considered to have a stroke in evolution. This state is associated with the highest level of risk, whether it is treated medically or surgically.[121] A patient with a stroke in evolution should promptly undergo CT to rule out hemorrhagic stroke, followed immediately by systemic anticoagulation with heparin and urgent operation. In a 1981 study of patients with stroke in evolution or crescendo TIAs that compared medical treatment (N=31) with urgent CEA (N=24), nonoperative management of stroke in evolution yielded a significantly higher mortality than surgical management (15% versus 6%).[122] Furthermore, 70% of the patients who underwent CEA achieved complete or near-complete recovery, compared with 19% of those managed medically.

Carotid Angioplasty and Stenting

In keeping with the continuing growth of minimally invasive surgery, carotid angioplasty and stenting (CAS) has come to play an emerging role in the management of both symptomatic and asymptomatic carotid stenosis [see 89 Carotid Angioplasty and Stenting]. The advent of neuroprotection techniques using balloon occlusion and aspiration of debris, filter wires placed distal to the culprit lesion, or reversal-of-flow technology has allowed interventionalists to perform CAS more safely, with complication rates approximating those of CEA.[123,124] Nevertheless, the precise role of carotid artery stenting in treatment or prevention of stroke has not yet been defined. The two primary questions that remain unresolved are (1) which patients benefit most from carotid stenting as opposed to open surgery, and (2) are the immediate and long-term results of CAS as good as those of CEA? Determination of the part CAS will eventually play in the management of cerebrovascular disease awaits the results of ongoing clinical trials comparing CAS with CEA.

Selection of patients Initially, CAS was considered a procedure that would be most beneficial for high-risk patients—for example, patients who were poor surgical candidates because of substantial medical comorbidities and patients with so-called hostile anatomy (such as an extremely high or low bifurcation or a neck that had previously been irradiated or operated on). Indeed, one clear benefit of CAS over CEA is that the risk of nerve injury for patients undergoing the former procedure is 0%. A precise definition of a high-risk patient, however, has proved elusive. One study reviewed CEAs that were performed in 228 patients who, because of their increased level of risk, would not have met the NASCET inclusion criteria.[125] This study was unable to demonstrate that these supposedly high-risk patients actually had inferior outcomes with CEA. A subsequent study that included more than

13,000 CEAs found that cardiopulmonary comorbid conditions did not increase the risk of perioperative stroke, death, or cardiac events.[126] Finally, though many investigators have considered patients over the age of 80 (who were ineligible for NASCET and the Asymptomatic Carotid Atherosclerosis Study [ACAS]) to be at increased risk with open surgery, the interim results from the lead-in phase of the Carotid Revascularization Endarterectomy versus Stent Trial (CREST), which is currently in progress, indicated that the risk of periprocedural stroke and death for patients undergoing CAS, surprisingly, was substantially higher (12.1%) in the 99 patients who were over the age of 80.[127] The reason for this increasing risk in older patients is not clear; the CREST results were not affected by adjustment for potential confounding factors such as symptomatic status, the use of antiembolic devices, gender, the degree of carotid stenosis, or the presence of distal arterial tortuosity.

The goal of reliably predicting which patients may be at high risk with either stenting or open surgery has impelled some investigators to develop risk stratification scales for CAS. A 2006 prospective study of 606 consecutive patients who underwent CAS identified the following independent risk factors: diabetes mellitus with inadequate glycemic control (hemoglobin A_{1c} level > 7%), advanced age (80 years), ulceration of the carotid artery stenosis, and a significant contralateral stenosis (50%). Patients with two or more of these risk factors had an 11% risk of a periprocedural complication, whereas patients with none or only one had a 2% risk.[128]

Assessment of results The results of various clinical trials comparing CAS with CEA, some already completed and some still under way, will help determine whether there is clinical equipoise between the two procedures.[127,129-133] The SAPPHIRE (Stenting and Angioplasty with Protection in Patients at HIgh Risk for Endarterectomy) trial randomly compared CAS with CEA in 334 patients with coexisting conditions that potentially increased the risk associated with endarterectomy.[130] Analysis of 30-day and 1-year outcomes (including death, stroke, and MI) found that CAS was not inferior to CEA. However, the overall risk levels were disturbingly high in both arms of this trial: 12.2% for CAS patients and 20.1% for CEA patients. The CaRESS (Carotid Revascularization using Endarterectomy or Stenting Systems) trial was a multicenter prospective study that compared the two techniques in 397 patients on a nonrandom basis.[132] The results indicated that both the 30-day risk and the 1-year risk of death, stroke, or MI were essentially the same in CAS patients as in CEA patients. The Carotid And Vertebral Artery Transluminal Angioplasty Study (CAVATAS) randomly assigned 504 patients to the two treatments.[131] The incidence of major stroke or death in the 30 days following the procedure did not differ significantly between the two groups: 6.4% for CAS patients and 5.9% for CEA patients. At 1 year, severe carotid restenosis was noted more frequently in the CAS group (14% versus 4%). Finally, the Stent-supported Percutaneous Angioplasty of the Carotid artery versus Endarterectomy (SPACE) trial randomly assigned 1,200 patients with symptomatic carotid artery stenosis to undergo either CAS or CEA. At 30 days, the incidence of stroke or death was 6.9% in the CAS group and 6.3% in the CEA group.[133] The investigators concluded (1) that the results failed to prove the noninferiority of CAS in comparison with CEA and (2) that the results did not justify the widespread use of CAS in the short term for the treatment of carotid artery stenosis.

MEDICAL THERAPY

Thrombolysis

Any patient who presents with an acute ischemic stroke, regardless of subtype, is potentially a candidate for thrombolytic therapy. However, ICH documented on the initial head CT is a clear absolute contraindication to I.V. thrombolysis. Other considerations affecting the decision whether to administer thrombolytic agents include a history of GI or urologic hemorrhage, recent major surgery, and rapidly improving neurologic signs, any of which may constitute a clinical contraindication to medical treatment. Vigilant monitoring of the aPTT, the PT (or the international normalized ratio [INR]), the platelet count, and the fibrinogen level is essential throughout the course of thrombolytic treatment.

It has been suggested that maximal benefit is derived from I.V. thrombolytic therapy for acute ischemic stroke when it is delivered within a "golden 3-hour window" starting from the onset of symptoms. The National Institute for Neurological Disorders and Stroke (NINDS) trial (parts 1 and 2) randomly assigned 624 patients to receive either recombinant tissue plasminogen activator (rt-PA), 0.9 mg/kg I.V. to a maximum of 90 mg/kg, or placebo.[134] Patients with all types of ischemic stroke were eligible, provided that they could be treated within 3 hours of the onset of symptoms. Outcome at 3 months was better with rt-PA than with placebo on each of the four outcome measures studied. The odds ratio for a favorable outcome in the rt-PA group was 1.7. The overall rate of symptomatic hemorrhage was 6.4% in the rt-PA group and 0.6% in the placebo group. The beneficial effects of rt-PA were similar for all stroke subtypes and persisted for up to 12 months after the stroke.[135] Patients treated with rt-PA were at least 30% more likely to have minimal or no disability at 12 months than patients treated with placebo were. Mortality at 1 year was comparable in the two groups.

Other randomized, double-blind, placebo-controlled trials of rt-PA for treatment of acute ischemic stroke have examined the effect of thrombolytic therapy given within the first 6 hours after the onset of symptoms. The European Cooperative Acute Stroke Study (ECASS) found no significant differences in functional outcome measures at 90 days between placebo and rt-PA in an intention-to-treat analysis.[136] Similarly, the Alteplase ThromboLysis for Acute Noninterventional Therapy in Ischemic Stroke (ATLANTIS) trial reported no benefit in patients treated with rt-PA within 3 to 5 hours of the onset of symptoms.[137,138] However, patients treated within the golden 3-hour window were more likely to have a favorable outcome at 90 days than patients treated with placebo (60.9% versus 26.3%).

Unfortunately, most patients are ineligible for I.V. rt-PA because of delays in obtaining treatment. Indeed, studies show that only 1% to 2% of ischemic stroke patients receive I.V. rt-PA.[139,140]

Compared with I.V. thrombolysis, intra-arterial thrombolytic therapy ought, in theory, to be able to deliver a higher local concentration of the agent where it is needed while minimizing the systemic concentration. Proponents of intra-arterial thrombolysis hope that it may lengthen the 3-hour treatment window. The PROACT II trial provided the best evidence to date that intra-arterial thrombolysis can improve patient outcomes.[141] This randomized, open-label, multicenter study with blinded follow-up randomly assigned 180 patients with stroke of less than 6 hours' duration to receive either heparin with recombinant prourokinase (r-proUK), 9 mg intra-arterially, or heparin alone. Intra-arterial thrombolysis resulted in significantly better recanalization rates than heparin alone did (66% versus 18%). In addition, more of the r-proUK group had no neurologic deficit or only a slight deficit at 90 days (40% versus 25%). However, intra-arterial thrombolysis did result in significantly increased rates of ICH (35% versus 13%). Symptomatic ICH with neurologic deterioration within 24 hours occurred in 10% of r-proUK patients and 2% of control patients. Patients who experienced ICH after r-proUK therapy had a high mortality (83%).[142] It is noteworthy that only 2% (180/12,333) of the screened patients in the PROACT II trial were randomized according to inclusion criteria, which suggests that intra-arterial thrombolysis may be of limited applicability. Finally, intra-arterial thrombolyis requires an experienced staff capable of performing cerebral angiography and navigating a microcatheter to the clot. At present, I.V. thrombolysis is certainly more practical than intra-arterial thrombolysis; more important, it can be done earlier in the course of the stroke.

References

1. Association AS Stroke Facts 2003: All Americans. CDC/NCHS 2001–2003

2. Broderick JP, Phillips SJ, Whisnant JP, et al: Incidence rates of stroke in the eighties: the end of the decline in stroke? Stroke 20:577, 1989

3. Gillum RF, Sempos CT: The end of the long-term decline in stroke mortality in the United States? Stroke 28:1527, 1997

4. Matsumoto N, Whisnant JP, Kurland LT, et al: Natural history of stroke in Rochester, Minnesota, 1955 through 1969: an extension of a previous study, 1945 through 1954. Stroke 4:20, 1973

5. Sacco RL, Wolf PA, Kannel WB, et al: Survival and recurrence following stroke: the Framingham study. Stroke 13:290, 1982

6. Wolf PA, D'Agostino RB, Belanger AJ, et al: Probability of stroke: a risk profile from the Framingham Study. Stroke 22:312, 1991

7. Sobel E, Alter M, Davanipour Z, et al: Stroke in the Lehigh Valley: combined risk factors for recurrent ischemic stroke. Neurology 39:669, 1989

8. Mohr JP, Caplan LR, Melski JW, et al: The Harvard Cooperative Stroke Registry: a prospective registry. Neurology 28:754, 1978

9. Bogousslavsky J, Van Melle G, Regli F: The Lausanne Stroke Registry: analysis of 1,000 consecutive patients with first stroke. Stroke 19:1083, 1988

10. Sacco RL, Benjamin EJ, Broderick JP, et al: American Heart Association Prevention Conference: IV. Prevention and rehabilitation of stroke. Risk factors. Stroke 28:1507, 1997

11. Wong KS, Huang YN, Gao S, et al: Intracranial stenosis in Chinese patients with acute stroke. Neurology 50:812, 1998

12. Caplan LR, Gorelick PB, Hier DB: Race, sex and occlusive cerebrovascular disease: a review. Stroke 17:648, 1986

13. Kiely DK, Wolf PA, Cupples LA, et al: Familial aggregation of stroke: the Framingham Study. Stroke 24:1366, 1993

14. Amarenco P: Blood pressure and lipid lowering in the prevention of stroke: a note to neurologists. Cerebrovasc Dis 16(suppl 3):33, 2003

15. Leys D, Deplanque D, Mounier-Vehier C, et al: Stroke prevention: management of modifiable vascular risk factors. J Neurol 249:507, 2002

16. Goldstein LB, Adams R, Becker K, et al: Primary prevention of ischemic stroke: a statement for healthcare professionals from the Stroke Council of the American Heart Association. Stroke 32:280, 2001

17. Jorgensen H, Nakayama H, Raaschou HO, et al: Stroke in patients with diabetes. The Copenhagen Stroke Study. Stroke 25:1977, 1994

18. Tegos TJ, Kalodiki E, Daskalopoulou SS, et al: Stroke: epidemiology, clinical picture, and risk factors (part I of III). Angiology 51:793, 2000

19. Stadel BV: Oral contraceptives and cardiovascular disease (first of two parts). N Engl J Med 305:612, 1981

20. Gill JS, Zezulka AV, Shipley MJ, et al: Stroke and alcohol consumption. N Engl J Med 315:1041, 1986

21. Prevention of stroke by antihypertensive drug treatment in older persons with isolated systolic hypertension: final results of the Systolic Hypertension in the Elderly Program (SHEP). SHEP Cooperative Research Group. JAMA 265:3255, 1991

22. Foulkes MA, Wolf PA, Price TR, et al: The Stroke Data Bank: design, methods, and baseline characteristics. Stroke 19:547, 1988

23. Gorelick PB, Hier DB, Caplan LR, et al: Headache in acute cerebrovascular disease. Neurology 36:1445, 1986

24. Kannel WB, McGee DL: Diabetes and cardiovascular disease. The Framingham study. JAMA 241:2035, 1979

25. Welch KM, Levine SR, Ewing JR: Viewing stroke pathophysiology: an analysis of contemporary methods. Stroke 17:1071, 1986

26. Adams HP Jr, Kassell NF, Torner JC, et al: CT and clinical correlations in recent aneurysmal subarachnoid hemorrhage: a preliminary report of the Cooperative Aneurysm Study. Neurology 33:981, 1983

27. von Kummer R, Nolte PN, Schnittger H, et al: Detectability of cerebral hemisphere ischaemic infarcts by CT within 6 h of stroke. Neuroradiology 38:31, 1996

28. Hunter GJ, Hamberg LM, Ponzo JA, et al: Assessment of cerebral perfusion and arterial anatomy in hyperacute stroke with three-dimensional functional CT: early clinical results. AJNR Am J Neuroradiol 19:29, 1998

29. von Kummer R, Allen KL, Holle R, et al: Acute stroke: usefulness of early CT findings before thrombolytic therapy. Radiology 205:327, 1997

30. Maeda M, Abe H, Yamada H, et al: Hyperacute infarction: a comparison of CT and MRI, including diffusion-weighted imaging. Neuroradiology 41:175, 1999

31. Arboix A, Marti-Vilalta JL, Garcia JH: Clinical study of 227 patients with lacunar infarcts. Stroke 21:842, 1990

32. Nicolaides AN PK, Grigg M, et al: Amaurosis Fugax. Springer, New York, 1988

33. Kilpatrick MM, Yonas H, Goldstein S, et al: CT-based assessment of acute stroke: CT, CT angiography, and xenon-enhanced CT cerebral blood flow. Stroke 32:2543, 2001

34. Green JB, Bialy Y, Sora E, et al: High-resolution EEG in poststroke hemiparesis can identify ipsilateral generators during motor tasks. Stroke 30:2659, 1999

35. Kim JS, Kang SY: Bleeding and subsequent anemia: a precipitant for cerebral infarction. Eur Neurol 43:201, 2000

36. Eikelboom JW, Hankey GJ, Anand SS, et al: Association between high homocyst(e)ine and ischemic stroke due to large- and small-artery disease but not other etiologic subtypes of ischemic stroke. Stroke 31:1069, 2000

37. Kenet G, Sadetzki S, Murad H, et al: Factor V Leiden and antiphospholipid antibodies are significant risk factors for ischemic stroke in children. Stroke 31:1283, 2000

38. Madonna P, de Stefano V, Coppola A, et al: Hyperhomocysteinemia and other inherited prothrombotic conditions in young adults with a history of ischemic stroke. Stroke 33:51, 2002

39. Brass LM, Prohovnik I, Pavlakis SG, et al: Middle cerebral artery blood velocity and cerebral blood flow in sickle cell disease. Stroke 22:27, 1991

40. Asplund K: Haemodilution for acute ischaemic stroke. Cochrane Database Syst Rev (4): CD000103, 2002

41. Strand T: Evaluation of long-term outcome and safety after hemodilution therapy in acute ischemic stroke. Stroke 23:657, 1992

42. Sivenius J, Heinonen OP, Pyorala K, et al: The incidence of stroke in the Kuopio area of East Finland. Stroke 16:188, 1985

43. Wityk RJ, Caplan LR: Hypertensive intracerebral hemorrhage: epidemiology and clinical pathology. Neurosurg Clin North Am 3:521, 1992

44. Cole FM, Yates P: Intracerebral microaneurysms and small cerebrovascular lesions. Brain 90:759, 1967

45. Caplan L: Intracerebral hemorrhage revisited. Neurology 38:624, 1988

46. Brott T, Broderick J, Kothari R, et al: Early hemorrhage growth in patients with intracerebral hemorrhage. Stroke 28:1, 1997

47. Schuetz H, Dommer T, Boedeker RH, et al: Changing pattern of brain hemorrhage during 12 years of computed axial tomography. Stroke 23:653, 1992

48. Ueda K, Hasuo Y, Kiyohara Y, et al: Intracerebral hemorrhage in a Japanese community, Hisayama: incidence, changing pattern during long-term follow-up, and related factors. Stroke 19:48, 1988

49. Silver FL, Norris JW, Lewis AJ, et al: Early mortality following stroke: a prospective review. Stroke 15:492, 1984

50. Poungvarin N, Bhoopat W, Viriyavejakul A, et al: Effects of dexamethasone in primary supratentorial intracerebral hemorrhage. N Engl J Med 316:1229, 1987

51. Steiner T, Ringleb P, Hacke W: Treatment options for large hemispheric stroke. Neurology 57(5 suppl 2):S61, 2001

52. Ziai WC, Port JD, Cowan JA, et al: Decompressive craniectomy for intractable cerebral edema: experience of a single center. J Neurosurg Anesthesiol 15:25, 2003

53. Kassell NF, Torner JC, Haley EC Jr, et al: The International Cooperative Study on the Timing of Aneurysm Surgery: part 1. Overall management results. J Neurosurg 73:18, 1990

54. Sacco RL, Wolf PA, Bharucha NE, et al: Subarachnoid and intracerebral hemorrhage: natural history, prognosis, and precursive factors in the Framingham Study. Neurology 34:847, 1984

55. McCormick WF, Acosta-Rua GJ: The size of intracranial saccular aneurysms: an autopsy study. J Neurosurg 33:422, 1970

56. Inagawa T, Hirano A: Autopsy study of unruptured incidental intracranial aneurysms. Surg Neurol 34:361, 1990

57. Dell S: Asymptomatic cerebral aneurysm: assessment of its risk of rupture. Neurosurgery 10:162, 1982

58. Kojima M, Nagasawa S, Lee YE, et al: Asymptomatic familial cerebral aneurysms. Neurosurgery 43:776, 1998

59. Nakagawa T, Hashi K, Kurokawa Y, et al: Family history of subarachnoid hemorrhage and the incidence of asymptomatic, unruptured cerebral aneurysms. J Neurosurg 91:391, 1999

60. Dias MS, Sekhar LN: Intracranial hemorrhage from aneurysms and arteriovenous malformations during pregnancy and the puerperium. Neurosurgery 27:855, 1990

61. Broderick JP, Brott T, Tomsick T, et al: The risk of subarachnoid and intracerebral hemorrhages in blacks as compared with whites. N Engl J Med 326:733, 1992

62. Bassi P, Bandera R, Loiero M, et al: Warning signs in subarachnoid hemorrhage: a cooperative study. Acta Neurol Scand 84:277, 1991

63. Hart RG, Byer JA, Slaughter JR, et al: Occurrence and implications of seizures in subarachnoid hemorrhage due to ruptured intracranial aneurysms. Neurosurgery 8:417, 1981

64. Haley EC Jr, Kassell NF, Torner JC: The International Cooperative Study on the Timing of Aneurysm Surgery: the North American experience. Stroke 23:205, 1992

65. Pasqualin A: Epidemiology and pathophysiology of cerebral vasospasm following subarachnoid hemorrhage. J Neurosurg Sci 42(1 suppl 1):15, 1998

66. Corsten L, Raja A, Guppy K, et al: Contemporary management of subarachnoid hemorrhage and vasospasm: the UIC experience. Surg Neurol 56:140, 2001

67. Torner JC, Kassell NF, Wallace RB, et al: Preoperative prognostic factors for rebleeding and survival in aneurysm patients receiving antifibrinolytic therapy: report of the Cooperative Aneurysm Study. Neurosurgery 9:506, 1981

68. Sloan MA, Burch CM, Wozniak MA, et al: Transcranial Doppler detection of vertebrobasilar vasospasm following subarachnoid hemorrhage. Stroke 25:2187, 1994

69. Newell DW, Winn HR: Transcranial Doppler in cerebral vasospasm. Neurosurg Clin North Am 1:319, 1990

70. Tommasino C, Picozzi P: Physiopathological criteria of vasospasm treatment. J Neurosurg Sci 42(1 suppl 1):23, 1998

71. Treggiari MM, Walder B, Suter PM, et al: Systematic review of the prevention of delayed ischemic neurological deficits with hypertension, hypervolemia, and hemodilution therapy following subarachnoid hemorrhage. J Neurosurg 98:978, 2003

72. Feigin VL, Rinkel GJ, Algra A, et al: Calcium antagonists in patients with aneurysmal subarachnoid hemorrhage: a systematic review. Neurology 50:876, 1998

73. Caplan LR: Diagnosis and treatment of ischemic stroke. JAMA 266:2413, 1991

74. Torvik A: The pathogenesis of watershed infarcts in the brain. Stroke 15:221, 1984

75. Angeloni U, Bozzao L, Fantozzi L, et al: Internal borderzone infarction following acute middle cerebral artery occlusion. Neurology 40:1196, 1990

76. Bogousslavsky J, Regli F: Borderzone infarctions distal to internal carotid artery occlusion: prognostic implications. Ann Neurol 20:346, 1986

77. Mori E, Tabuchi M, Yamadori A: Lacunar syndrome due to intracerebral hemorrhage. Stroke 16:454, 1985

78. Fisher CM: A lacunar stroke: the dysarthria-clumsy hand syndrome. Neurology 17:614, 1967

79. Mast H, Thompson JL, Lee SH, et al: Hypertension and diabetes mellitus as determinants of multiple lacunar infarcts. Stroke 26:30, 1995

80. Longstreth WT Jr, Bernick C, Manolio TA, et al: Lacunar infarcts defined by magnetic resonance imaging of 3660 elderly people: the Cardiovascular Health Study. Arch Neurol 55:1217, 1998

81. Vermeer SE, Prins ND, den Heijer T, et al: Silent brain infarcts and the risk of dementia and cognitive decline. N Engl J Med 348:1215, 2003

82. Gan R, Sacco RL, Kargman DE, et al: Testing the validity of the lacunar hypothesis: the Northern Manhattan Stroke Study experience. Neurology 48:1204, 1997

83. Clavier I, Hommel M, Besson G, et al: Long-term prognosis of symptomatic lacunar infarcts: a hospital-based study. Stroke 25:2005, 1994

84. Salgado AV, Ferro JM, Gouveia-Oliveira A: Long-term prognosis of first-ever lacunar strokes: a hospital-based study. Stroke 27:661, 1996

85. Gandolfo C, Moretti C, Dall'Agata D, et al: Long-term prognosis of patients with lacunar syndromes. Acta Neurol Scand 74:224, 1986

86. Hier DB, Foulkes MA, Swiontoniowski M, et al: Stroke recurrence within 2 years after ischemic infarction. Stroke 22:155, 1991

87. Special report from the National Institute of Neurological Disorders and Stroke Classification of cerebrovascular diseases III. Stroke 21:637, 1990

88. Arboix A, Oliveres M, Massons J, et al: Early differentiation of cardioembolic from atherothrombotic cerebral infarction: a multivariate analysis. Eur J Neurol 6:677, 1999

89. Timsit SG, Sacco RL, Mohr JP, et al: Brain infarction severity differs according to cardiac or arterial embolic source. Neurology 43:728, 1993

90. Kittner SJ, Sharkness CM, Sloan MA, et al: Infarcts with a cardiac source of embolism in the NINDS Stroke Data Bank: neurologic examination. Neurology 42:299, 1992

91. Minematsu K, Yamaguchi T, Omae T: 'Spectacular shrinking deficit': rapid recovery from a major hemispheric syndrome by migration of an embolus. Neurology 42:157, 1992

92. Hornig CR, Bauer T, Simon C, et al: Hemorrhagic transformation in cardioembolic cerebral infarction. Stroke 24:465, 1993

93. Molina CA, Montaner J, Abilleira S, et al: Timing of spontaneous recanalization and risk of hemorrhagic transformation in acute cardioembolic stroke. Stroke 32:1079, 2001

94. Alexandrov AV, Black SE, Ehrlich LE, et al: Predictors of hemorrhagic transformation occurring spontaneously and on anticoagulants in patients with acute ischemic stroke. Stroke 28:1198, 1997

95. Yamanouchi H, Nagura H, Mizutani T, et al: Embolic brain infarction in nonrheumatic atrial fibrillation: a clinicopathologic study in the elderly. Neurology 48:1593, 1997

96. Peters NS, Schilling RJ, Kanagaratnam P, et al: Atrial fibrillation: strategies to control, combat, and cure. Lancet 359:593, 2002

97. Wolf PA, Abbott RD, Kannel WB: Atrial fibrillation as an independent risk factor for stroke: the Framingham Study. Stroke 22:983, 1991

98. Saxena R, Lewis S, Berge E, et al: Risk of early death and recurrent stroke and effect of heparin in 3169 patients with acute ischemic stroke and atrial fibrillation in the International Stroke Trial. Stroke 32:2333, 2001

99. Immediate anticoagulation of embolic stroke: a randomized trial. Cerebral Embolism Study Group Stroke 14:668, 1983

100. Cardiogenic brain embolism. Cerebral Embolism Task Force Arch Neurol 43:71, 1986

101. Cardiogenic brain embolism. The second report of the Cerebral Embolism Task Force Arch Neurol 46:727, 1989

102. Hart RG, Benavente O, McBride R, et al: Antithrombotic therapy to prevent stroke in patients with atrial fibrillation: a meta-analysis. Ann Intern Med 131:492, 1999

103. Warfarin versus aspirin for prevention of thromboembolism in atrial fibrillation: Stroke Prevention in Atrial Fibrillation II Study. Lancet 343:687, 1994

104. Petersen P, Boysen G, Godtfredsen J, et al: Placebo-controlled, randomised trial of warfarin and aspirin for prevention of thromboembolic complications in chronic atrial fibrillation. The Copenhagen AFASAK study. Lancet 1:175, 1989

105. Mohr JP, Thompson JL, Lazar RM, et al: A comparison of warfarin and aspirin for the prevention of recurrent ischemic stroke. N Engl J Med 345:1444, 2001

106. CAST: randomised placebo-controlled trial of early aspirin use in 20,000 patients with acute ischaemic stroke. CAST (Chinese Acute Stroke Trial) Collaborative Group Lancet 349:1641, 1997

107. The International Stroke Trial (IST): a randomised trial of aspirin, subcutaneous heparin, both, or neither among 19435 patients with acute ischaemic stroke. International Stroke Trial Collaborative Group Lancet 349:1569, 1997

108. Lees RS: The natural history of carotid artery disease. Stroke 15:603, 1984

109. Kardoulas DG, Katsamouris AN, Gallis PT, et al: Ultrasonographic and histologic characteristics of symptom-free and symptomatic carotid plaque. Cardiovasc Surg 4:580, 1996

110. el-Barghouty N, Nicolaides A, Bahal V, et al: The identification of the high risk carotid plaque. Eur J Vasc Endovasc Surg 11:470, 1996

111. Beneficial effect of carotid endarterectomy in symptomatic patients with high-grade carotid stenosis. North American Symptomatic Carotid Endarterectomy Trial Collaborators N Engl J Med 325:445, 1991

112. MRC European Carotid Surgery Trial: interim results for symptomatic patients with severe (70–99%) or with mild (0–29%) carotid stenosis. European Carotid Surgery Trialists' Collaborative Group Lancet 337:1235, 1991

113. Mayberg MR, Wilson SE, Yatsu F, et al: Carotid endarterectomy and prevention of cerebral ischemia in symptomatic carotid stenosis. Veterans Affairs Cooperative Studies Program 309 Trialist Group. JAMA 266:3289, 1991

114. Blaisdell WF, Clauss RH, Galbraith JG, et al: Joint study of extracranial arterial occlusion. IV. A review of surgical considerations. JAMA 209:1889, 1969

115. Easton JD, Sherman DG: Stroke and mortality rate in carotid endarterectomy: 228 consecutive operations. Stroke 8:565, 1977

116. Bruetman M, Fields W, Crawford E, et al: Cerebral hemorrhage in carotid artery surgery. Arch Neurol 9:458, 1963

117. Wylie E, Hein M, Adams J: Intracranial hemorrhage following surgical revascularization for treatment of acute strokes. J Neurosurg 21:212, 1964

118. Dosick SM, Whalen RC, Gale SS, et al: Carotid endarterectomy in the stroke patient: computerized axial tomography to determine timing. J Vasc Surg 2:214, 1985

119. Whittemore AD, Ruby ST, Couch NP, et al: Early carotid endarterectomy in patients with small, fixed neurologic deficits. J Vasc Surg 1:795, 1984

120. Toni D, Fiorelli M, Bastianello S, et al: Hemorrhagic transformation of brain infarct: predictability in the first 5 hours from stroke onset and influence on clinical outcome. Neurology 46:341, 1996

121. Moore WS, Mohr JP, Najafi H, et al: Carotid endarterectomy: practice guidelines. Report of the Ad Hoc Committee to the Joint Council of the Society for Vascular Surgery and the North American Chapter of the International Society for Cardiovascular Surgery. J Vasc Surg 15:469, 1992

122. Mentzer RM Jr, Finkelmeier BA, Crosby IK, et al: Emergency carotid endarterectomy for fluctuating neurologic deficits. Surgery 89:60, 1981

123. Ohki T, Veith FJ, Grenell S, et al: Initial experience with cerebral protection devices to prevent embolization during carotid artery stenting. J Vasc Surg 36:1175, 2002

124. Parodi JC, Ferreira LM, Sicard G, et al: Cerebral protection during carotid stenting using flow reversal. J Vasc Surg 41:416, 2005

125. Gasparis AP, Ricotta L, Cuadra SA, et al: High-risk carotid endarterectomy: fact or fiction. J Vasc Surg 37:40, 2003

126. Stoner MC, Abbott WM, Wong DR, et al: Defining the high-risk patient for carotid endarterectomy: an analysis of the prospective National Surgical Quality Improvement Program database. J Vasc Surg 43:285, 2006

127. Hobson RW 2nd, Howard VJ, Roubin GS, et al: Carotid artery stenting is associated with increased complications in octogenarians: 30-day stroke and death rates in the CREST lead-in phase. J Vasc Surg 40:1106, 2004

128. Hofmann R, Niessner A, Kypta A, et al: Risk score for peri-interventional complications of carotid artery stenting. Stroke 37:2557, 2006

129. Gray WA, Hopkins LN, Yadav S, et al: Carotid stenting in high-surgical-risk patients: the ARCHeR results. J Vasc Surg 44:258, 2006

130. Yadav JS, Wholey MH, Kuntz RE, et al: Protected carotid-artery stenting versus endarterectomy in high-risk patients. N Engl J Med 351:1493, 2004

131. Endovascular versus surgical treatment in patients with carotid stenosis in the Carotid and Vertebral Artery Transluminal Angioplasty Study (CAVATAS): a randomised trial. Lancet 357:1729, 2001

132. Carotid revascularization using endarterectomy or stenting systems (CARESS): phase I clinical trial. J Endovasc Ther 10:1021, 2003

133. The SPACE Collaborative Group: 30 day results from the SPACE trial of stent-protected angioplasty versus carotid endarterectomy in symptomatic patients: a randomized non-inferiority trial. Lancet, epub ahead of print, August 10, 2006

134. Tissue plasminogen activator for acute ischemic stroke. The National Institute of Neurological Disorders and Stroke rt-PA Stroke Study Group. N Engl J Med 333:1581, 1995

135. Kwiatkowski TG, Libman RB, Frankel M, et al: Effects of tissue plasminogen activator for acute ischemic stroke at one year. National Institute of Neurological Disorders and Stroke Recombinant Tissue Plasminogen Activator Stroke Study Group. N Engl J Med 340:1781, 1999

136. Hacke W, Kaste M, Fieschi C, et al: Intravenous thrombolysis with recombinant tissue plasminogen activator for acute hemispheric stroke. The European Cooperative Acute Stroke Study (ECASS). JAMA 274:1017, 1995

137. Clark WM, Albers GW, Madden KP, et al: The rtPA (Alteplase) 0- to 6-hour acute stroke trial, part A (276g): results of a double-blind, placebo-controlled, multicenter study. Thrombolytic Therapy in Acute Ischemic Stroke Study Investigators. Stroke 31:811, 2000

138. Clark WM, Wissman S, Albers GW, et al: Recombinant tissue-type plasminogen activator (Alteplase) for ischemic stroke 3 to 5 hours after symptom onset. The ATLANTIS Study: a randomized controlled trial. Alteplase Thrombolysis for Acute Noninterventional Therapy in Ischemic Stroke. JAMA 282:2019, 1999

139. Hacke W, Brott T, Caplan L, et al: Thrombolysis in acute ischemic stroke: controlled trials and clinical experience. Neurology 53(7 suppl 4):S3, 1999

140. Katzan IL, Furlan AJ, Lloyd LE, et al: Use of tissue-type plasminogen activator for acute ischemic stroke: the Cleveland area experience. JAMA 283:1151, 2000

141. Furlan A, Higashida R, Wechsler L, et al: Intra-arterial prourokinase for acute ischemic stroke. The PROACT II study: a randomized controlled trial. Prolyse in Acute Cerebral Thromboembolism. JAMA 282:2003, 1999

142. Kase CS, Furlan AJ, Wechsler LR, et al: Cerebral hemorrhage after intra-arterial thrombolysis for ischemic stroke: the PROACT II trial. Neurology 57:1603, 2001

81 ASYMPTOMATIC CAROTID BRUIT

Claudio S. Cinà, M.D., Sp.Chir. (It.), M.Sc., F.R.C.S.C., Catherine M. Clase, M.B., B.Chir., M.Sc.,
and Aleksandar Radan, M.D., B.Sc.

Assessment of Asymptomatic Carotid Bruit

The term bruit refers to any noise detected on auscultation in the neck. The conventional method of auscultation is to use the bell of the stethoscope and listen over an area extending from the upper end of the thyroid cartilage to just below the angle of the jaw.[1-3] The principal reason why bruits in the neck are matters of some concern is that they may reflect underlying occlusive carotid artery disease, which carries an increased risk of stroke.

In what follows, we outline a problem-oriented approach to the workup of patients found to have cervical bruits at the time of routine or focused vascular examination.

Clinical Evaluation

CAROTID BRUITS VERSUS OTHER CERVICAL SOUNDS

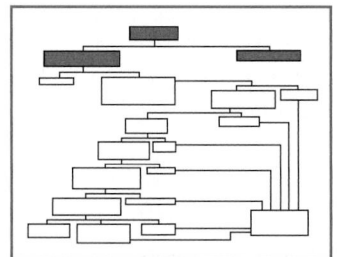

Clinical assessment begins with evaluation of the character of the bruit and examination of the precordium and the cervical structures. Carotid bruits must be distinguished from other sounds heard in the neck. Venous hums are relatively common, being reported in 27% of young adults.[4] They tend to have a diastolic component, are louder when the patient sits or turns the head away from the side of auscultation, and disappear when the patient lies down or when the Valsalva maneuver is performed.[4] Ejection systolic murmurs of cardiac origin may radiate into the neck, but generally, they are bilateral, are louder within the chest, and are less audible distally in the neck[5]; the same is true of bruits arising in other intrathoracic vessels.[6,7] No definitive clinical sign has yet been identified that clearly differentiates bruits from transmitted cardiac murmurs. On occasion, a bruit may be heard over the thyroid gland; however, this finding is extremely rare and is usually accompanied by thyromegaly and other features of autoimmune thyroid disease.[5] In dialysis patients, a bruit may be generated by the increased flow resulting from the creation of an arteriovenous fistula in the forearm.[8]

SYMPTOMATIC VERSUS ASYMPTOMATIC CAROTID BRUITS

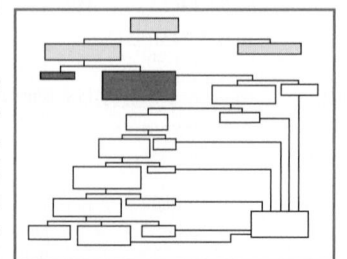

Transient ischemic attacks (TIAs) are defined as brief episodes of focal loss of brain function that can usually be localized to a specific portion of the brain supplied by a single vascular system.[9] By arbitrary convention, such an ischemic episode is considered a TIA if it lasts less than 24 hours; a similar episode, in the absence of evidence of trauma or hemorrhage, is considered an ischemic stroke if it lasts more than 24

hours or causes death.[9] Amaurosis fugax is a transient (< 24 hours) loss of vision in one eye or a portion of the visual field.[9] If a patient with a carotid bruit has a history of any of these conditions in the ipsilateral eye or brain, then the bruit is regarded as neurologically symptomatic, and the relevant question at that point is whether the patient has significant carotid stenosis and may be a candidate for carotid endarterectomy on that basis. Given the substantial differences between the management of patients with symptomatic bruits and those with asymptomatic bruits, the distinction between these two patient groups is crucial.

The history is of critical importance in the diagnosis of TIA because most TIAs last less than 4 hours,[10] which means that patients typically are not seen by physicians during the period of neurologic deficit.[11] Patients should be specifically asked about transient focal problems with vision, language, facial paresis, dysarthria, and arm or leg numbness or weakness. A 1984 study reported good interobserver agreement ($\kappa = 0.65$) [*see Table 1*] between clinicians diagnosing previous ischemic episodes.[12] Assigning a probable neurologic territory to a TIA or stroke, however, proved more difficult: for TIAs, the interobserver agreement between two independent neurologists asked to distinguish between carotid and vertebrobasilar events was relatively poor ($\kappa = 0.31$).[12] There is some evidence that using a standardized protocol for the diagnosis of previous ischemic episodes might improve this low interobserver agreement (e.g., to $\kappa = 0.65$[12] or $\kappa = 0.77$[13]). Similar difficulties attend diagnosis of stroke by means of history and physical examination.[14]

Many patients with a possible TIA or stroke will have undergone neurologic imaging. Such imaging is unhelpful if it yields negative results; however, in some cases, it reveals the presence of an infarct, thereby confirming the ischemic nature of the event and establish-

Table 1 Quantification of Interobserver Agreement*

$\kappa^\dagger$	Strength of Agreement
≤ 0.2	Poor
> 0.2, ≤ 0.4	Fair
> 0.4, ≤ 0.6	Moderate
> 0.6, ≤ 0.8	Good
> 0.8, ≤ 1	Very good

*Reliability (how closely an assessment agrees with another similar assessment on a second occasion or by a second observer) and validity (how closely the assessment agrees with another criterion or a gold standard) are the key properties of any assessment. When agreement between two observers is poor, the assessment in question, whether it is a physical finding, a clinical diagnosis, or an interpretation of a diagnostic test, is lacking in reliability; if more reliable methods are available, they should be considered instead. In clinical medicine, however, more reliable methods are not always available. When this is the case, the physician must use a relatively unreliable assessment as the best available alternative, while remaining aware of its limitations.[118]

$^\dagger\kappa$ is a statistical measure used to quantify agreement between two or more observers. It takes a value between 0 and 1, where 0 represents agreement no better than that expected by chance alone and 1 represents perfect agreement.[118]

ing its location. For a bruit to be regarded as symptomatic on the basis of imaging studies, at least one infarct must be seen in the appropriate ipsilateral anterior vasculature.

It is evident that distinguishing between symptomatic and asymptomatic bruits on clinical grounds may be difficult; nonetheless, it is worthwhile to make the effort because the risk of stroke in the asymptomatic population is quite different from that in the symptomatic population. For example, whereas the Asymptomatic Carotid Atherosclerosis Study (ACAS), which included patients believed on clinical grounds to be neurologically asymptomatic, reported an overall stroke rate of 6.2% at 2.7 years in its medically managed group,[15] the North American Symptomatic Carotid Endarterectomy Trial (NASCET), which included patients assessed as neurologically symptomatic (i.e., with a history of amaurosis fugax, TIA, or minor stroke), reported a stroke rate of 26% at 3 years in its medically managed group.[16]

In determining whether a unilateral bruit is symptomatic or asymptomatic, the physician should concentrate primarily on ischemic deficits in the ipsilateral hemisphere (i.e., those causing focal contralateral motor or sensory deficits) and ipsilateral amaurosis fugax. However, symptoms referable to the contralateral carotid artery, even if no bruit is heard on that side, might prompt evaluation of the patient for symptomatic carotid stenosis on the contralateral side. The absence of a bruit by no means excludes the diagnosis: carotid bruits are absent in 20% to 35% of patients with high-grade stenosis of the internal carotid artery.[17] In the NASCET subgroup in which the physical finding of a carotid bruit was compared with angiographic imaging of the carotid system, the presence of a focal ipsilateral carotid bruit had a sensitivity of 63% and a specificity of 61% for high-grade (70% to 99%) stenosis; the absence of a bruit did not significantly change the probability of significant stenosis in this population (pretest 52%, posttest 40%).[18]

Workup of patients with symptomatic bruits is beyond the scope of this chapter. Accordingly, the ensuing discussion focuses on assessment of patients with asymptomatic bruits.

VASCULAR RISK ASSESSMENT

Vascular diseases and other vascular risk factors are common in patients with asymptomatic carotid bruits. Hypertension is twice as common in patients who have bruits as in those who do not[19]; smoking, ischemic heart disease, and peripheral vascular disease are also more prevalent.[20,21] Consequently, detection of a bruit should prompt a thorough vascular risk assessment. Standard vascular risk factors—hypertension, hyperlipidemia, diabetes, and smoking—can be integrated into risk profiles for particular patients by using either the New Zealand risk tables (http://www.nzgg.org.nz/library/gl_complete/bloodpressure/appendix.cfm) or the formula and spreadsheets provided by Anderson et al.[22,23] The probability of stroke for various follow-up periods may be quantified by using the Framingham stroke-risk profile.[24] From age, systolic blood pressure, diabetes, smoking, cardiovascular disease, atrial fibrillation, and left ventricular hypertrophy, probability of stroke may be calculated for men and women according to a point system.[24]

Smoking cessation should be recommended to all patients,[25-27] and hypertension should be controlled (BP < 140/90).[28-31] Depending on a patient's individual risk profile, dietary and pharmacologic management of hyperlipidemia may also be warranted.[32-34] Diabetic control should be optimized.[35,36]

Patients should be asked specifically about any concurrent vascular disease—in particular, symptoms suggestive of ischemic heart disease or of claudication or rest pain. In patients with established vascular disease, the risk that future vascular events (e.g., coronary-related death, myocardial infarction [MI], new angina, stroke, TIA, new con-

Table 2 Annual Risk of Stroke

Patient Population	Annual Risk of Stroke
Population without bruits, age > 60 yr[19,43,44]	0.86% (95% CI, 0.8–0.9)
Population with bruits, age > 60 yr[19,20,43]	2.1% (95% CI, 0.6–8.5)
Male population without bruits, age > 60 yr[19,24]	0.9% (95% CI, 0.1–3.0)
Male population with bruits, age > 60 yr[19]	8.0% (95% CI, 0.2–38.0)
Female population without bruits, age > 60 yr[24]	2.0% (95% CI, 0.8–4.2)
Female population with bruits, age > 60 yr[19]	2.4% (95% CI, 0.7–5.5)

gestive heart failure, or peripheral vascular syndrome) will occur in the next 5 years is greater than 20%.[22,37] In such patients, consultation of formulas or tables is unnecessary, and all modifiable risk factors should be aggressively managed (target BP < 140/90; target ratio of total cholesterol to high-density lipoprotein [HDL] cholesterol < 4).[22]

A meta-analysis of randomized, controlled trials showed that aspirin reduced the risk of subsequent stroke, MI, and death from vascular events for patients who had previously experienced a cerebrovascular event, MI, or unstable angina.[38] Other meta-analyses of randomized, controlled trials[39,40] were unable to confirm the effectiveness of aspirin in preventing cerebrovascular events in asymptomatic patients or in patients with TIAs or strokes of noncardiac (and presumably vascular) origin[41]; however, one randomized, controlled trial involving hypertensive patients at modest vascular risk found that aspirin reduced the risk of vascular events, if not the risk of stroke.[42] In the absence of contraindications, we recommend that aspirin be considered for all patients who have established vascular disease elsewhere and for all patients who have a bruit in association with any vascular risk factors.

INDICATIONS FOR SURGICAL INTERVENTION

The absolute risk of stroke is increased in the presence of a carotid bruit. In population-based studies, the annual risk of stroke was 2.1% (95% confidence interval [CI], 0.6 to 8.5)[19,20,43,44] for persons who had a carotid bruit and 0.86% (95% CI, 0.8 to 0.9) for those who did not.[19,43,44] These figures represent an absolute risk increase for stroke of 1.24% a year and a relative risk for stroke of 2.4. The mean patient age in these studies was approximately 65 years, and sex distribution and prevalence of risk factors for atherosclerotic disease were similar in patients with bruits and those without bruits. Even after adjustment for age, sex, and the presence of hypertension, the presence of a carotid bruit remained an independently significant variable, with a relative risk of 2.0.[19]

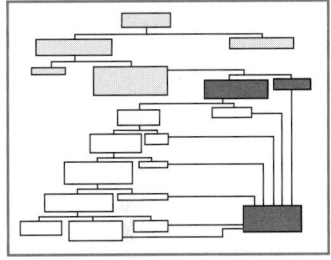

Table 3 Prevalence of Carotid Stenosis in Patients with Bruits and in Healthy Volunteers

Patient Population	Prevalence of Carotid Stenosis
Overall population with cervical bruits	
> 35% stenosis[20,56-58,119]	58% (95% CI, 55–60)
> 60%–75% stenosis[56-58]	21% (95% CI, 18–24)
Healthy volunteers*	
Age > 70 yr[89]	5.1% (95% CI, 2.6–9.0)
Age ≤ 70 yr[89]	1.5% (95% CI, 0.2–5.3)

*In healthy volunteers, the incidence of asymptomatic carotid stenosis is significantly correlated with age ($P < 0.01$) and with the presence of hypertension ($P < 0.005$).

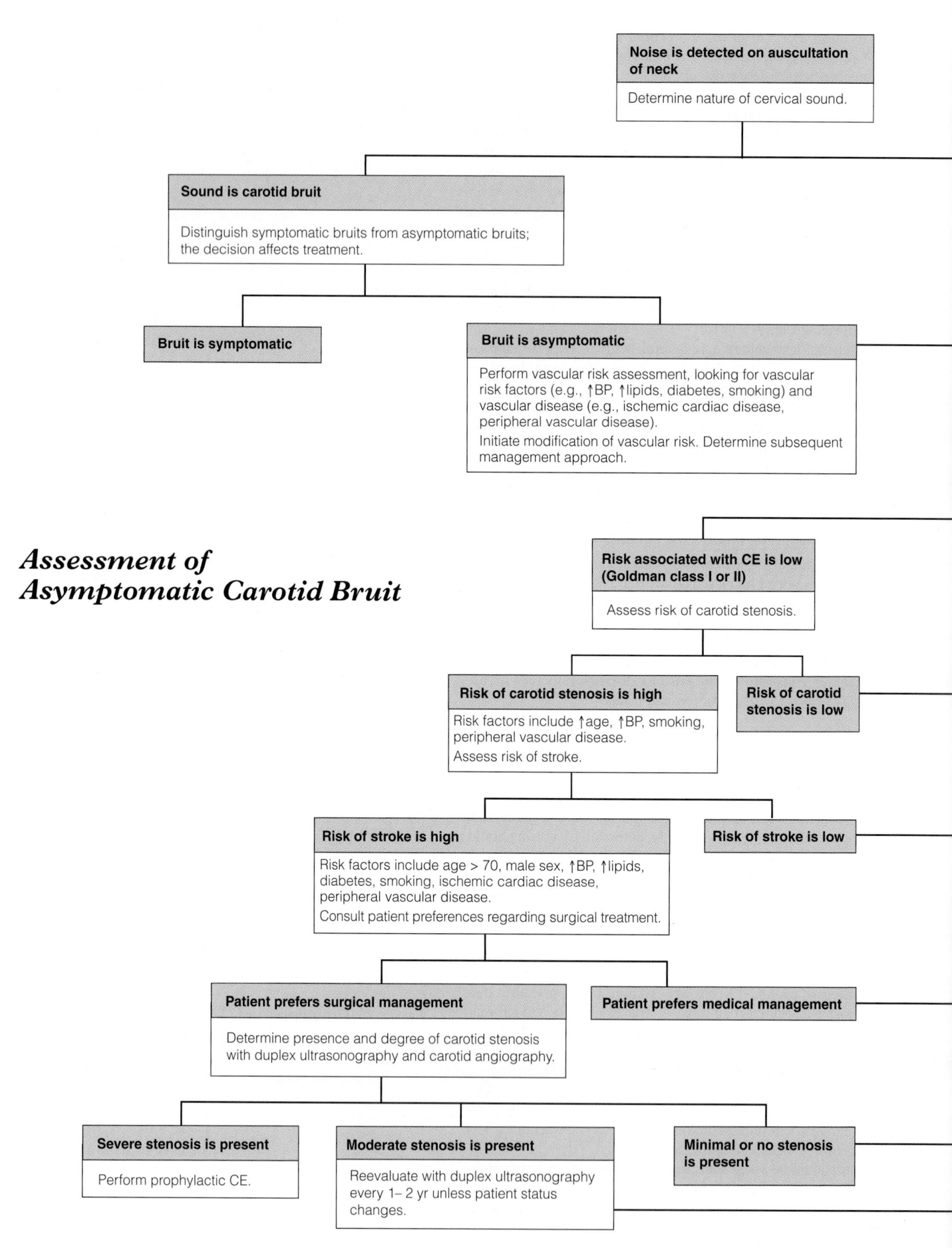

Assessment of Asymptomatic Carotid Bruit

Noise is detected on auscultation of neck

Determine nature of cervical sound.

Sound is carotid bruit

Distinguish symptomatic bruits from asymptomatic bruits; the decision affects treatment.

Bruit is symptomatic

Bruit is asymptomatic

Perform vascular risk assessment, looking for vascular risk factors (e.g., ↑BP, ↑lipids, diabetes, smoking) and vascular disease (e.g., ischemic cardiac disease, peripheral vascular disease).

Initiate modification of vascular risk. Determine subsequent management approach.

Risk associated with CE is low (Goldman class I or II)

Assess risk of carotid stenosis.

Risk of carotid stenosis is high

Risk factors include ↑age, ↑BP, smoking, peripheral vascular disease.

Assess risk of stroke.

Risk of carotid stenosis is low

Risk of stroke is high

Risk factors include age > 70, male sex, ↑BP, ↑lipids, diabetes, smoking, ischemic cardiac disease, peripheral vascular disease.

Consult patient preferences regarding surgical treatment.

Risk of stroke is low

Patient prefers surgical management

Determine presence and degree of carotid stenosis with duplex ultrasonography and carotid angiography.

Patient prefers medical management

Severe stenosis is present

Perform prophylactic CE.

Moderate stenosis is present

Reevaluate with duplex ultrasonography every 1–2 yr unless patient status changes.

Minimal or no stenosis is present

Sound is venous hum, radiating cardiac
murmur or intrathoracic bruit, or thyroid bruit

Patient is to be assessed as candidate for
carotid endarterectomy (CE)

Determine level of risk associated with procedure.

Patient is to be managed
conservatively

Risk associated with CE is
high (Goldman class ≥ III)

Continue modification of vascular risk.
Educate patient regarding symptoms and
signs of stroke.
Carry out nonsurgical follow-up.
Re-refer patient promptly if he or she ever
becomes symptomatic.

Table 4 Necessary Criteria for Offering an Interventional Approach to Selected Patients with Carotid Bruits

Center-specific criteria
Either
DUS is documented to have a > 90% PPV for stenosis > 50% on angiography and is used alone
or
DUS has a lower PPV and is used as a screening test only, and angiography in patients with cerebrovascular disease has a documented complication (stroke or death) rate of around 1%
Surgeon-specific criterion
Perioperative rate of stroke or death is < 3% for carotid endarterectomy

DUS—duplex ultrasonography   PPV—positive predictive value

Given the low absolute risk of stroke in asymptomatic patients with bruits [*see Table 2*], the low prevalence of surgically relevant stenosis in patients with bruits [*see Table 3*], and the small (and only marginally statistically significant) absolute benefit of carotid endarterectomy in patients with asymptomatic stenosis,[45,46] we and others[47-51] do not believe that further investigation with a view to carotid endarterectomy is mandatory in the asymptomatic population. Many surgeons may prefer to manage these patients conservatively, reevaluating them promptly if they become symptomatic [*see Discussion, below*]. Other surgeons may wish to pursue a more interventional strategy with selected patients, in which case further evaluation with an eye to surgical treatment depends on the presence of the following key findings in a given patient: (1) low risk associated with carotid endarterectomy, (2) relatively high risk of carotid stenosis, and (3) high risk of stroke if carotid stenosis is documented. In addition, the patient's preferences should be consulted: no patient should be subjected to further evaluation who is not prepared to undergo surgical treatment if such management is recommended. Patients who, on the basis of any of these criteria, are not suitable candidates for intervention will not benefit from imaging studies and should be managed medically.

Finally, surgeons and centers who are contemplating offering prophylactic carotid endarterectomy for asymptomatic stenosis should be able to document that their rates of stroke or perioperative death for this procedure are lower than 3% [*see Table 4*]. When complication rates exceed this threshold, the value of carotid endarterectomy becomes negligible, and surgeons may find themselves doing more harm than good.[45,46]

Low Risk Associated with Carotid Endarterectomy

In NASCET and ACAS, patients were excluded if they had coexisting medical disease likely to produce significant mortality and morbidity (e.g., cardiac valvular or rhythm disorders, uncontrolled hypertension or dia-

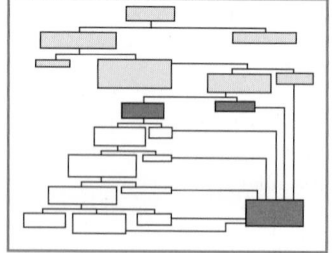

betes, unstable angina pectoris, or MI in the previous 4 months)[16]; accordingly, the results of these trials are not generalizable to patients who have such conditions. Further evidence for the impact of operative risk on outcomes is provided by a retrospective review of 562 patients who underwent carotid endarterectomy for symptomatic and asymptomatic disease in a large community hospital.[52] For patients in Goldman class I or II,[53] the overall rate of death or

nonfatal MI was 2% (95% CI, 1.1 to 3.9), whereas for patients in class III or IV, the corresponding figure was 21% (95% CI, 9.2 to 39.9) [*see Table 5*]. Given that 50 prophylactic carotid endarterectomies would have to be performed to prevent one stroke over the subsequent 3-year period (i.e., the number needed to treat [NNT] is 50), it is clearly unacceptable to perform this procedure in a population facing a 21% incidence of MI or death, in which for every 5 patients undergoing the operation, one would experience an MI or die (i.e., the number needed to harm [NNH] is only 5). Further consideration of prophylactic carotid endarterectomy in patients for whom the procedure carries a high risk is not warranted.

High Risk of Carotid Stenosis

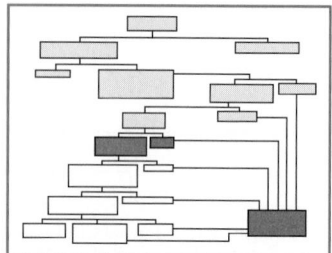

Cohort[45,54-60] and population-based[19,61,62] studies suggest that patients with asymptomatic carotid bruits are more likely to have significant carotid stenosis if they are older, are hypertensive, smoke, or have advanced peripheral vascular disease. In one study, hemodynamically significant stenosis (i.e., > 50%) was found by means of ultrasonography in 32% of patients scheduled to undergo peripheral vascular procedures but in only 6.8% of those scheduled to undergo coronary artery bypass grafting (CABG).[63] (All figures for degree of stenosis in this chapter are determined according to the formula used in NASCET [*see Table 6 and Figure 1*].)

Further consideration of carotid endarterectomy may be warranted in patients with vascular risk factors or known peripheral vascular disease; in the absence of these findings, the risk of significant carotid stenosis is low. Further evaluation is unnecessary for patients who are younger, do not smoke, are not hypertensive or diabetic, and are not known to have peripheral vascular disease.

High Risk of Stroke

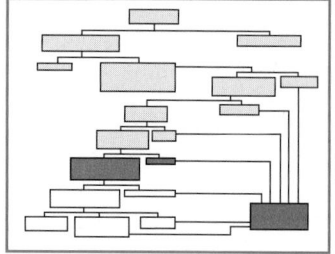

Within the group of patients with asymptomatic carotid stenosis, there is only limited direct evidence for the existence of subgroups of patients at higher risk for stroke. Men seem to be at higher risk for stroke than women are: in the medical arm of ACAS, the incidence of stroke or death at 2.7 years was 7.0% (95% CI, 4.9 to 9.4) for men and 4.9% (95% CI, 2.7 to 8.0) for women. Gender-related differences aside, however, identification of other subgroups at higher risk relies on extrapolation of data from other populations at risk for artery-to-artery embolism. Data from NASCET indicate that for symptomatic patients with greater than 70% carotid stenosis, the presence of a higher number of identifiable clinical risk factors (age > 70 years; male sex; systolic or diastolic hypertension; the occurrence of a cerebrovascular event within the preceding 31 days; the occurrence of a more serious cerebrovascular event, namely, stroke rather than a TIA or amaurosis fugax; smoking; MI; congestive heart failure; diabetes; intermittent claudication; or hyperlipidemia) was associated with a higher annual stroke risk. For patients with zero to three risk factors, the annual stroke risk was 6.6%; for those with four or five, 9.2%; and for those with six or more, 15.8%. Data from the same study indicate that among patients with a contralateral asymptomatic stenosed carotid artery, patients with zero to three risk factors have an annual stroke risk of 1.4% in the territory of the asymptomatic stenosis; those with four or five, 2.8%; and those with six or more, 3.8%.[64]

Obesity is another risk factor for stroke.[49,50] Some 60% of patients who experience a stroke before 65 years of age have a body mass index greater than 24 kg/m².[49] This finding, in conjunction with a history of smoking, was found to predict 60% of strokes in men in this age group.[50]

Patients with carotid bruits who do not have significant systemic risk factors or other vascular disease are at low absolute risk for stroke and are unlikely to benefit from carotid endarterectomy; hence, further investigation is not warranted.[5,18,49] Patients with numerous (i.e., six or more) clinical risk factors [see Table 7] are at relatively high risk for stroke, and it is in this population that most of the benefit from carotid endarterectomy is likely to be concentrated.

Patient Preference for Surgical Intervention

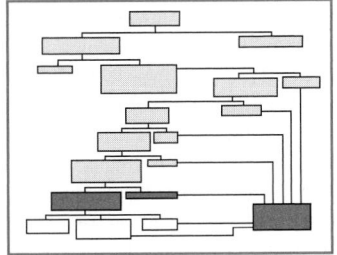

Before pursuing the diagnosis of carotid stenosis with imaging techniques, the surgeon must discuss prophylactic surgical intervention with the patient. The essential question is, if significant stenosis is documented, will the patient wish to undergo carotid endarterectomy? It should be remembered that at this point in the workup, we are considering only those patients (1) for whom the cardiac risk associated with the procedure is acceptably low and (2) who are considered to be at relatively high risk for stroke if carotid stenosis is demonstrated.

Patients should be informed that if they are found to have significant carotid stenosis, their risk of stroke is 6.3% over the ensuing 2.7 years if they do not undergo operation and 4.0% over the same period if they do.[15] They should also be informed that these figures take into account a 3% risk of perioperative stroke or death (2.7% risk of stroke and 0.3% risk of death).[15] The 2.3% absolute risk reduction associated with surgical treatment translates into an NNT of 43, meaning that 43 patients would have to undergo endarterectomy to prevent one stroke over the next 2.7 years.

Given the front-loaded risks of surgery, some patients will prefer a simple risk-modification strategy to a strategy including both risk modification and surgical intervention. In such cases, carotid imaging is not necessary, because knowledge of the degree of stenosis will not affect subsequent management.

Investigative Studies

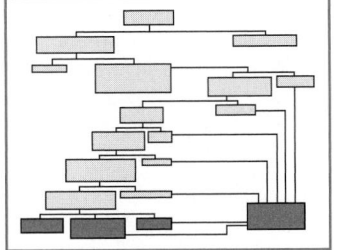

The purpose of investigation of asymptomatic neck bruits is to identify persons with significant carotid stenosis who are at increased risk for cerebrovascular disease[65,66] and who are likely to benefit from carotid endarterectomy. In the absence of other significant findings, cervical bruits are not sufficiently predictive of significant carotid stenosis or ischemic stroke to be useful in selecting candidates for noninvasive imaging.[51] Noninvasive testing is a reasonable step in patients with the characteristics listed above, but routine screening of all patients with asymptomatic carotid bruits is not warranted.[51]

DUPLEX ULTRASONOGRAPHY

Duplex ultrasonography (DUS) should be performed bilaterally. A meta-analysis conducted in 1995 found that for detecting greater

Table 5 Cardiac Risk Assessment*

Parameter	Weighted Score on Cardiac Risk Index		
	Goldman	Detsky	Eagle
Age > 70 yr	5	5	1
MI			1
< 6 mo	10	10	
> 6 mo		5	
Angina			1
Class III		10	
Class IV		20	
Unstable		10	
Diabetes			1
Operation			
Emergency	4	10	
Aortic, abdominal, or thoracic	3		
CHF	11		1
< 1 wk		10	
> 1 wk		5	
ECG			
Rhythm other than sinus	7	5	
> 5 PVCs/min	7	5	
Poor medical status†	3	5	

Risk of Perioperative Cardiac Events

Low	0–12 (class I, II)	0–15	0
Intermediate	13–25 (class III)	16–30	1–2
High	> 25 (class IV)	> 30	≥ 3

*The Goldman cardiac risk index[53] is a multifactorial index of cardiac risk in patients undergoing noncardiac surgery. Modifications have been proposed by Detsky,[121-123] who included angina and institution-specific perioperative cardiac event rates in the model. The Eagle index[124-126] is another risk index based on five clinical variables. Despite the lack of consensus regarding the relative merits of these tools for preoperative cardiac risk assessment, stratification of patients into risk categories is helpful in assessing the risk and benefits of a procedure such as carotid endarterectomy.

†$P_{a}O_2$ < 60 mm Hg; $P_{a}CO_2$ > 50 mm Hg; K^+ < 3 mmol/L; serum HCO_3 < 20 mmol/L; serum urea > 18 mmol/L; creatinine > 260 μmol/L; abnormal ALT; signs of chronic liver disease; bedridden from cardiac causes.

CHF—congestive heart failure   MI—myocardial infarction   PVC—premature ventricular contraction

than 50% stenosis (determined by means of angiography, the gold standard), DUS had a sensitivity of 91% (95% CI, 89 to 94) and a specificity of 93% (95% CI, 88 to 95).[67] Given a disease prevalence of approximately 41% in patients referred for DUS, these findings translate into a positive predictive value of 90% and an accuracy of 92%.[67] A subsequent prospective study of patients (both symptomatic and asymptomatic) in whom carotid endarterectomy was being considered reported a sensitivity of 100% and a specificity of 98% for greater than 60% stenosis, with a positive predictive value of 99%.[68]

At centers where DUS has been internally validated in comparison with angiography and where this level of performance has been documented, the surgeons may choose to proceed to surgery without angiography.[68-70] At centers where DUS is less reliable, however, it should be regarded as a screening test, and angiography should be performed when DUS suggests greater than 50% stenosis.

CAROTID ANGIOGRAPHY

As an invasive procedure, carotid angiography carries a significant risk of morbidity and mortality. All centers performing carotid angiography for cerebrovascular disease should audit their stroke rates

Table 6   Conversion between Different Methods of Measuring
Degree of Carotid Stenosis

Method	Severity of Disease				
	Minimal	Moderate		Severe	Occlusion
ECST*	24%–57%	58%–69%	70%–81%	82%–99%	100%
NASCET	0%–29%	30%–49%	50%–69%	70%–99%	100%
CC method†	35%–56%	57%–61%	62%–80%	81%–99%	100%

*Conversion from ECST to NASCET was done according to the following formula: ECST % stenosis = 0.6(NASCET % stenosis) + 40.[127]
†The relation of the NASCET method to the CC method is linear, with a ratio of 0.62 between the distal internal carotid diameter and the common carotid diameter.[117]

periodically. Since 1990, four prospective studies[71-74] have addressed the question of the risks associated with angiography in patients with atherosclerotic cerebrovascular disease. When the data from these studies were pooled, the risk of permanent neurologic deficit or death was 1.1% (95% CI, 0.6 to 2.0).[75] In ACAS, the 1.2% of patients in the intervention arm who experienced stroke or died after angiography accounted for 40% of the strokes and deaths attributable to surgical intervention.[15] Angiographic complication rates significantly worse than these will adversely impact the risk-benefit ratio associated with surgical intervention. Centers that consistently record relatively high angiographic complication rates should not offer evaluation for and surgical treatment of asymptomatic carotid disease.

Management

CAROTID ENDARTERECTOMY

At this point in management, it is reasonable to offer surgical treatment of asymptomatic disease to patients with greater than 50% stenosis. ACAS[15] and two meta-analyses[45,46] that included other trials of surgical therapy for asymptomatic carotid stenosis documented a small and marginally statistically significant benefit from prophylactic carotid endarterectomy in asymptomatic patients with greater than 50% to 60% carotid stenosis. Because the absolute benefit is small, we do not consider it obligatory to pursue the diagnosis or to follow an invasive strategy in patients identified solely on the basis of an asymptomatic bruit; however, patients possessing all the characteristics listed earlier [*see* Indications for Surgical Intervention, *above*] probably constitute a group that is particularly able to benefit from surgical intervention. Patients with higher degrees of stenosis are at higher risk for stroke and are therefore most likely to benefit.[76-79]

The degree of stenosis and the presence or absence of plaque ulceration may modify the final decision for or against operative management [*see* Discussion, Subgroup Analyses for Potential High-Risk Factors, *below*].

In May 2004, the United Kingdom Medical Research Council Asymptomatic Carotid Surgery Trial (ACST) collaborative group reported the results of a prospective, randomized trial of carotid endarterectomy in asymptomatic patients.[80] More than 3,000 patients were randomly assigned either to undergo immediate carotid endarterectomy or to be placed on indefinite deferral. In the patients referred for immediate carotid endarterectomy, one half underwent endarterectomy within 1 month of referral; 88% underwent endarterectomy within 1 year. Combining the rate of perioperative events and nonperioperative strokes, the 5-year results indicate a stroke rate of 6.4% in the group undergoing immediate carotid endarterectomy, as compared with 11.8% in the deferral group. These findings are strikingly similar to the ACAS findings. However, the ACST found a similar benefit for women. In addition, in the ACST, no difference was found in the degree of stenosis and the benefit of surgery—an interesting observation, because one would expect that

greater degrees of stenosis would be associated with greater risk of stroke. This finding may be explained either by the fact that duplex ultrasound was the sole imaging criterion or that plaque morphology plays a greater role in determining stroke risk than degree of stenosis. Furthermore, unlike previous studies, many of the patients in the ACST were receiving lipid-lowering drugs and other antiplatelet agents. As Barnett pointed out in his discussion of the ACST article, the perioperative stroke rate must be low for the results of this study to be generalized.[81] In the ACST, the risk of stroke or death within 30 days of undergoing carotid endarterectomy was 3.1%.

Technical details of carotid endarterectomy are discussed elsewhere [*see* 88 Surgical Treatment of Carotid Artery Disease].

PATIENT EDUCATION

All patients with asymptomatic carotid bruits, whether they are undergoing prophylactic endarterectomy or not, should be carefully advised regarding the symptoms and signs of stroke, TIAs, and amaurosis fugax and should be strongly encouraged to seek urgent medical attention if such problems arise. Patients who experience one of these untoward events should undergo full reevaluation for stroke risk factors (e.g., hypertension, hyperlipidemia, diabetes, smoking, and atrial fibrillation); in the absence of atrial fibrillation (which

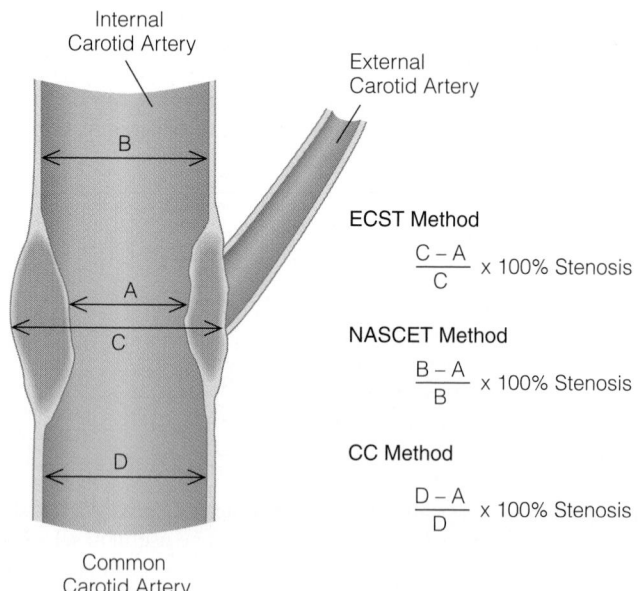

ECST Method

$$\frac{C - A}{C} \times 100\% \text{ Stenosis}$$

NASCET Method

$$\frac{B - A}{B} \times 100\% \text{ Stenosis}$$

CC Method

$$\frac{D - A}{D} \times 100\% \text{ Stenosis}$$

Figure 1   **Carotid angiography remains the gold standard for determining the extent of carotid arterial disease. Several methods of reporting angiographically defined stenosis have been described in the literature.[115] The most commonly used methods are those adopted by the NASCET and ECST investigators, though the so-called common carotid (CC) method has its advocates as well.[116,117]**

Table 7 Risk Factors for Stroke[128,129]

Age > 70 yr	Smoking (or history of smoking)
Male sex	> 80% carotid stenosis
Hypertension*	Presence of ulceration
Hyperlipidemia	Ischemic heart disease†
Diabetes	Peripheral vascular disease

*Defined as systolic BP > 160 mm Hg or diastolic BP > 90 mm Hg.
†MI or CHF.

should prompt consideration of prophylactic anticoagulation[82-84], a change in antiplatelet therapy should be considered. Both ticlopidine[85] and clopidogrel[86] are more effective than aspirin in preventing stroke. (Ticlopidine is associated with reversible but severe neutropenia in fewer than 1% of cases; accordingly, monitoring for this complication is indicated.)

If a patient who is a surgical candidate experiences a TIA or stroke as a result of an ischemic event in the carotid region in the absence of atrial fibrillation, he or she must be promptly referred back to the vascular surgeon. This possibility should be clearly explained to patients once the initial evaluation is complete and they have been referred back to their primary care physicians. Patients referred back to a vascular surgeon under these circumstances should then be regarded as having symptomatic carotid disease. A subgroup analysis of patients with symptomatic stenosis reported that carotid endarterectomy performed soon after a nondisabling stroke was not associated with a significantly higher operative complication rate than endarterectomy performed 30 days or longer after a stroke.[75] Performing endarterectomy early reduces

the risk period for recurrent stroke and may therefore increase the potential benefit of the intervention; the usual approach is to perform the procedure within a week or two of a patient's first neurologic event.

Management of cardiovascular risk factors and concurrent vascular disease should continue. In the absence of concurrent vascular disease, patients may be referred back to the family practitioner, internist, or cardiologist in place of specific surgical follow-up.

FOLLOW-UP OF PATIENTS WITH LOWER-GRADE STENOSIS

Carotid stenosis progresses in about one quarter of patients with asymptomatic carotid stenosis monitored with DUS over a 2-year period.[87] In a population of asymptomatic patients with bruits who were referred to a vascular laboratory, 282 stenotic carotid arteries (average stenosis, 50%) were followed for 38 ± 18 months. Progression of stenosis, defined as an increase in degree of stenosis to 80% or beyond, occurred in 17% of arteries, and 2% became completely occluded. Progression was associated with an increase in stroke risk of 4.9% at 1 year, 16.7% at 3 years, and 26.5% at 5 years. In comparison, the estimated stroke risk in an asymptomatic population of patients with 50% to 79% stenosis was 0.85%, 3.6%, and 5.4% for the same three periods (P = 0.001).[76]

Although carotid stenosis, once identified, tends to progress over time,[20,54,76,88] the data are currently insufficient to permit recommendation of routine ultrasonographic or other surveillance for all patients with neck bruits outside a research setting. In our view, reevaluation every 1 to 2 years with noninvasive diagnostic tests is a reasonable approach to patients (1) who are already known to have greater than 50% stenosis, (2) who do not undergo surgery, and (3) who are at high risk for stroke, are surgical candidates, and are not averse to surgery.

Discussion

Epidemiology

In cross-sectional and population-based studies, the overall prevalence of greater than 75% carotid stenosis has been low. A 1992 study reported a 2.3% prevalence in men and a 1.1% prevalence in women; there was a significant (P < 0.0001) increase with age with each decade from 65 years to beyond 85 years, but there were no significant differences between men and women.[62] In the Framingham study population, the incidence of greater than 50% stenosis was 8% (95% CI, 6.5 to 9.8).[61] In a study of healthy volunteers, the incidence of greater than 50% stenosis was 5.1% (95% CI, 2.6 to 9.0) in patients 70 years of age or older and 1.5% (95% CI, 0.2 to 5.3) in younger patients.[89]

The pooled risk of greater than 60% to 75% stenosis in patients with carotid bruits referred for noninvasive vascular evaluation at an average age of 65 years is reported to be 21% (95% CI, 18 to 24),[56-58] which is three to four times the prevalence expected on the basis of population-based studies. Thus, five persons with neck bruits must be screened to detect one patient with moderate to severe carotid stenosis. The absolute benefit of surgery is small and of borderline statistical significance. In ACAS, as noted (see above), the relative risk reduction for an ipsilateral major stroke or perioperative death over a 2.7-year period was 36.5% (95% CI, 27.5 to 47.1), the absolute risk reduction was 2.3% (95% CI, 0.2 to 7.0), and the NNT was 43 (95% CI, 14 to 500); the number of patients that would have to be screened with DUS to prevent one stroke over a 3-year follow-up period was 250 (95% CI, 70 to 2,500).

Economic Considerations

A cogent argument in favor of pursuing a surgical strategy in at least some patients was made by a 1997 economic analysis,[90] which demonstrated that although prophylactic endarterectomy in patients with asymptomatic carotid stenosis did not reduce societal costs appreciably, it was nonetheless, at a cost of $8,000/quality-adjusted life year (QALY), within the range of many interventions considered by society to be cost-effective. It should be pointed out, however, that this economic analysis addressed only carotid endarterectomy in patients with identified carotid stenosis, not screening strategies for patients with bruits, and consequently did not consider costs associated with investigation and follow-up to the point of recommendation for or against carotid endarterectomy in the broader group of patients with bruits. These costs would alter the economic analysis substantially, and if they are included, it is far from clear whether the resulting overall cost/QALY would still be acceptable. To date, no trial or economic analysis of a screening strategy has been published.

Screening Issues

For the reasons previously discussed, we do not feel justified in recommending routine screening for patients with asymptomatic carotid bruits. Given the available evidence, we believe that such patients may reasonably be managed in either of two ways. One choice is simply to conclude that screening patients with carotid bruits as possible candidates for carotid endarterectomy has not been proved to be a useful intervention and to concentrate instead on general vascular risk reduction. The other, which is appropriate in centers where noninvasive or invasive diagnostic tests reach acceptable standards with an acceptable degree of risk and where the procedure is done by surgeons whose documented perioperative stroke and death rates are less than 3%, is to take a selective approach that addresses various issues related to stroke risk, cardiac risk, and patient preferences before noninvasive tests are ordered.

Subgroup Analyses for Potential High-Risk Factors

Given the small absolute risk reduction reported by ACAS[15] and by the two meta-analyses of all asymptomatic carotid stenosis trials,[45,46] it would be useful to be able to identify one or more high-risk groups within the broader group of patients identified as having stenosis.

SEX

ACAS included a subgroup analysis addressing the effect of sex on ability to benefit from surgery: the absolute reduction in the risk of perioperative stroke or death or ipsilateral stroke at 2.7 years was 3.6% (95% CI, 1.1 to 9.9) for men and 0.5% (95% CI, 0.01 to 2.7) for women.

DEGREE OF STENOSIS

In asymptomatic patients stratified according to their ultrasonographically determined degree of stenosis, the risk of stroke is low both for patients with less than 30% stenosis (4% cumulative event rate at 3 years) and for those with 30% to 74% stenosis (9% cumulative event rate at 3 years); it is highest for those with greater than 75% stenosis (21% cumulative event rate at 3 years).[20] The European Carotid Surgery Trialists (ECST) study,[47] using angiographic data from the asymptomatic carotid arteries of 2,295 patients, reported that the Kaplan-Meyer estimate of stroke risk at 3 years was only 2% and remained low (< 2%) when patients with less than 79% stenosis were considered; stroke risk increased to 9.8% for patients with 70% to 79% stenosis and to 14.4% for those with 80% to 99% stenosis. In a population of patients referred to a vascular laboratory with asymptomatic carotid stenosis on DUS who were followed for a mean of 38 months, the incidence of stroke was 2.1% in patients with 50% to 79% stenosis and 10.4% in those with greater than 80% stenosis.[76]

In ACAS, there were too few strokes to permit subgroup analysis of the effect of degree of stenosis on ability to benefit from carotid endarterectomy. In both ECST[79] and NASCET,[75,77,78,91] however, higher degrees of stenosis in symptomatic patients were consistently observed to be associated with higher stroke risk as well as with greater ability to benefit from surgical treatment [see Table 8].

PLAQUE ULCERATION AND PLAQUE STRUCTURE

At present, there are no subgroup analyses examining the effect of plaque ulceration on the ability of asymptomatic patients to benefit from surgical treatment. In NASCET, however, when symptomatic patients with 70% to 99% stenosis were considered, those with angiographic evidence of plaque ulceration were at higher risk for stroke than those without ulceration[92] and derived greater benefit from surgery.[75] Angiography had a sensitivity of 46% and a specificity of 74% in the detection of ulcerated plaques, with a positive predictive value of 72%.[93] A 1994 study reported that when ulceration was detected with B-mode imaging in patients with asymptomatic carotid stenosis, the incidence of silent cerebral infarction detected by magnetic resonance imaging was 75%, compared with an incidence of 25% when ulceration was absent.[94]

It has also been suggested that carotid plaques of differing structures may have differing embolic potentials.[95] DUS can distinguish between fibrous plaques (which are highly echogenic) and plaques with high concentrations of lipid and necrotic material (which are echolucent). Echolucent plaques are more frequently associated with neurologic symptoms and computed tomography–proven cerebral infarction.[95-97] Interobserver reliability for plaque echostructure, however, seems to be highly variable, ranging from good (κ = 0.79) for greater than 70% stenosis[95] to average (κ = 0.51) for greater than 40% stenosis[98] to poor (κ = 0.29) for greater than 80% stenosis.[99] A 1994 report found no correlation between the presence or type of symptoms and plaque structure as determined by DUS.[100] The true importance of carotid plaque echomorphology and surface characteristics as predictors of cerebrovascular events remains to be defined.

CONTRALATERAL DISEASE

It has been suggested that the presence of contralateral carotid disease is a risk factor for future cerebrovascular events. In NASCET patients with greater than 70% stenosis,[101] contralateral occlusion significantly increased the benefit of surgery with respect to the incidence of stroke or death, but contralateral high-grade stenosis did not.[75]

ASYMPTOMATIC CEREBRAL INFARCTION

The presence of areas of asymptomatic cerebral infarction ipsilateral to the area of carotid stenosis on head CT may identify patients who would benefit from surgery.[102] In asymptomatic patients with carotid stenosis, the incidence of silent strokes demonstrated by CT has been reported to be 10% in patients with 35% to 50% stenosis on DUS, 17% in those with 50% to 75% stenosis, and 30% in those with greater than 75% stenosis.[103] The incidence of silent cerebral infarctions demonstrated by MRI in the same type of population has been reported to be 42%, increasing to 75% for greater than 50% stenosis.[94] Use of CT and MRI of the brain in risk strati-

Table 8 Effectiveness of Surgery by Degree of Stenosis in Patients with Symptomatic Carotid Stenosis[75]

Degree of Stenosis	Relative Risk Reduction or Increase	Absolute Risk Reduction or Increase	Number Needed to Treat or Harm
70%–99%	RRR, 48% (95% CI, 27–63)	ARR, 6.7% (95% CI, 3.2–10)	NNT, 15 (95% CI, 10–31)
50%–69%	RRR, 27% (95% CI, 5–44)	ARR, 4.7% (95% CI, 0.8–8.7)	NNT, 21 (95% CI, 11–125)
≤ 49%	RRI, 20% (95% CI, 0–44)	ARI, 2.2% (95% CI, 0–4.4)	NNH, 45 (95% CI, 22–∞)

ARI—absolute risk increase   ARR—absolute risk reduction   NNH—number needed to harm   NNT—number needed to treat
RRI—relative risk increase   RRR—relative risk reduction

fication of patients with asymptomatic carotid stenosis is controversial and currently is not advised.

CONCLUSIONS

Although only limited data on patients with asymptomatic stenosis are available, we believe that consideration of sex, degree of stenosis, and possibly the presence of plaque ulceration may be helpful in making the final decision on whether to offer carotid endarterectomy to these patients; at present, plaque morphology is insufficiently reliable to be a useful guide to clinical management.

Special Situations

RESTENOSIS OR PREVIOUS CAROTID SURGERY

Patients who have previously undergone carotid surgery have been excluded from most studies of asymptomatic patients; when they have been included in trials addressing symptomatic stenosis, they have experienced increased rates of perioperative complications.[16,50] Patients in whom restenosis occurs after an earlier carotid endarterectomy should be advised against surgery while they remain asymptomatic.[15] It is therefore unnecessary to follow patients with ultrasonography after carotid endarterectomy if no symptoms develop.

PREOPERATIVE ASSESSMENT FOR CORONARY ARTERY BYPASS GRAFTING

Some 20% to 30% of patients undergoing assessment for CABG are found to have carotid bruits,[49,104] and 5% to 20% have greater than 50% stenosis on DUS[105-107] or ocular plethysmography.[108] In asymptomatic patients with carotid stenosis who are undergoing CABG, there is no direct evidence favoring prophylactic carotid endarterectomy either before or in conjunction with CABG. Cohort studies including symptomatic and asymptomatic carotid stenosis indicate that patients undergoing CABG and carotid endarterectomy in the same operation have a stroke rate of 6% (95% CI, 4.6 to 7.8), an MI rate of 4.6% (95% CI, 3.1 to 6.5), and a mortality of 4.7% (95% CI, 3.4 to 6.4).[109] For cohorts in which carotid endarterectomy was performed before CABG, the stroke rate is 3.2% (95% CI, 2.1 to 4.5), the MI rate is 5.2% (95% CI, 3.6 to 6.9)—a nonsignificant increase—and the mortality is 4.7% (95% CI, 3.4 to 6.4).[109] For cohorts in which CABG was done first and carotid stenosis was treated on its own after the cardiac procedure, the stroke rate is 3.5% (95% CI, 1.0 to 9.0), the MI rate is 2% (95% CI, 0.2 to 6.0), and the mortality is 0.8% (95% CI, 0.02 to 4.8).[110-112]

We recommend against a combined surgical approach in patients with asymptomatic carotid stenosis. Given the equivalent stroke rate and the lower MI rate and mortality, we believe that the preferred strategy in patients with bruits is first to proceed with CABG if indicated and then to determine whether the patient should be further evaluated as a candidate for carotid endarterectomy in the same manner as other elective patients would be.

Effect of Center-Specific Variations on Risk-to-Benefit Ratio

In ACAS, 1.2% of the overall 2.7% perioperative stroke rate was accounted for by strokes occurring after angiography. Centers where ultrasonography has been documented to have high predictive values may avoid this risk by proceeding directly from ultrasonography to surgery. If these complications had been avoided in ACAS, the absolute risk reduction would have been more substantial: 3.43% (95% CI, 1.1 to 9.9), corresponding to an NNT of 29 (95% CI, 1 to 80). The true perioperative combined stroke and death rate achieved in this study was 1.5%, a result that is definitive of excellence in the surgical management of carotid endarterectomy and that constitutes a useful quality assurance measure for centers and individual surgeons.

Issues for the Future

It is possible, perhaps likely, that in the future, magnetic resonance angiography[67] and three-dimensional CT angiography,[113,114] together with DUS, will replace angiography as preferred imaging methods for diagnosing internal carotid artery stenosis. As for surgical treatment and screening, further data on patients with asymptomatic carotid stenosis are necessary before definitive recommendations can be made.

References

1. Chambers BR, Norris JW: Clinical significance of asymptomatic neck bruits. Neurology 35:742, 1985

2. Harrison MJ: Cervical bruits and asymptomatic carotid stenosis. Br J Hosp Med 32:80, 1984

3. Ratcheson RA: Clinical diagnosis of atherosclerotic carotid artery disease. Clin Neurosurg 29:464, 1982

4. Jones FL: Frequency, characteristics and importance of the cervical venous hum in adults. N Engl J Med 267:658, 1962

5. Sauve JS, Laupacis A, Ostbye T, et al: Does this patient have a clinically important carotid bruit? JAMA 270:2843, 1993

6. Caplan LR: Carotid artery disease. N Engl J Med 315:886, 1986

7. Thompson JE, Patman RD, Talkington CM: Asymptomatic carotid bruit: long term outcome of patients having endarterectomy compared with unoperated controls. Ann Surg 188:308, 1978

8. Messert B, Marra TR, Zerofsky RA: Supraclavicular and carotid bruits in hemodialysis patients. Ann Neurol 2:535, 1977

9. National Institute of Neurological Disorders and Stroke: Special Report from the National Institute of Neurological Disorders and Stroke. Classification of Cerebrovascular Diseases III. Stroke 21:637, 1990

10. Werdelin L, Juhler M: The course of transient ischemic attacks. Neurology 38:677, 1988

11. Albers GW, Hart RG, Lutsep HL, et al: AHA Scientific Statement. Supplement to the guidelines for the management of transient ischemic attacks: a statement from the Ad Hoc Committee on Guidelines for the Management of Transient Ischemic Attacks, Stroke Council, American Heart Association. Stroke 30:2502, 1999

12. Kraaijeveld CL, van Gijn J, Schouten HJ, et al: Interobserver agreement for the diagnosis of transient ischemic attacks. Stroke 15:723, 1984

13. Koudstaal PJ, van Gijn J, Staal A, et al: Diagnosis of transient ischemic attacks: improvement of interobserver agreement by a check-list in ordinary language. Stroke 17:723, 1986

14. von Arbin M, Britton M, de Faire U, et al: Validation of admission criteria to a stroke unit. J Chronic Dis 33:215, 1980

15. Toole JF, Baker WH, Castaldo JE, et al: Endarterectomy for asymptomatic carotid artery stenosis. JAMA 273:1421, 1995

16. North American Symptomatic Carotid Endarterectomy Trial Collaborators (NASCET): Beneficial effect of carotid endarterectomy in symptomatic patients with high-grade carotid stenosis. N Engl J Med 325:445, 1991

17. Davies KN, Humphrey PRD: Do carotid bruits predict disease of the internal carotid arteries? Postgrad Med J 70:433, 1994

18. Sauve JS, Thorpe KE, Sackett DL, et al: Can bruits distinguish high-grade from moderate symptomatic carotid stenosis? The North American Symptomatic Carotid Endarterectomy Trial. Ann Intern Med 120:633, 1994

19. Heyman A, Wilkinson WE, Heyden S, et al: Risk of stroke in asymptomatic persons with cervical arterial bruits: a population study in Evans County, Georgia. N Engl J Med 302:838, 1980

20. Chambers BR, Norris JW: Outcome in patients with asymptomatic neck bruits. N Engl J Med 315:860, 1986

21. Meissner I, Wiebers DO, Whisnant JP, et al: The natural history of asymptomatic carotid artery occlusive lesions. JAMA 258:2704, 1987

22. Anderson KM, Odell PM, Wilson PW, et al: Cardiovascular disease risk profiles. Am Heart J 121(1 pt 2):293, 1991

23. Anderson KM, Wilson PW, Odell PM, et al: An updated coronary risk profile: a statement for health professionals. Circulation 83:356, 1991

24. Wolf PA, D'Agostino RB, Belanger AJ, et al: Probability of stroke: a risk profile from the Framingham Study. Stroke 22:312, 1991

25. Wolf PA, D'Agostino RB, Kannel WB, et al: Cigarette smoking as a risk factor for stroke. The Framingham Study. JAMA 259:1025, 1988

26. Wannamethee SG, Shaper AG, Whincup PH, et al: Smoking cessation and the risk of stroke in middle-aged men. JAMA 274:155, 1995

27. Shinton R, Beevers G: Meta-analysis of relation between cigarette smoking and stroke. BMJ 298:789, 1989

28. Prevention of stroke by antihypertensive drug treatment in older persons with isolated systolic hypertension: final results of the Systolic Hypertension in the Elderly Program (SHEP). SHEP Cooperative Research Group. JAMA 265:3255, 1991

29. Sutton-Tyrrell K, Alcorn HG, Herzog H, et al: Morbidity, mortality, and antihypertensive treatment effects by extent of atherosclerosis in older adults with isolated systolic hypertension. Stroke 26:1319, 1995

30. Sutton-Tyrrell K, Wolfson SK Jr, Kuller LH: Blood pressure treatment slows the progression of carotid stenosis in patients with isolated systolic hypertension. Stroke 25:44, 1994

31. Collins R, Peto R, MacMahon S, et al: Blood pressure, stroke, and coronary heart disease. Part 2, Short-term reductions in blood pressure: overview of randomised drug trials in their epidemiological context. Lancet 335:827, 1990

32. Randomised trial of cholesterol lowering in 4444 patients with coronary heart disease: the Scandinavian Simvastatin Survival Study (4S). Lancet 344:1383, 1994

33. Furberg CD: Lipid-lowering trials: results and limitations. Am Heart J 128(6 pt 2):1304, 1994

34. Furberg CD, Adams HP Jr, Applegate WB, et al: Effect of lovastatin on early carotid atherosclerosis and cardiovascular events. Asymptomatic Carotid Artery Progression Study (ACAPS) Research Group. Circulation 90:1679, 1994

35. The effect of intensive treatment of diabetes on the development and progression of long-term complications in insulin-dependent diabetes mellitus. The Diabetes Control and Complications Trial Research Group. N Engl J Med 329:977, 1993

36. Intensive blood-glucose control with sulphonyl-ureas or insulin compared with conventional treatment and risk of complications in patients with type 2 diabetes (UKPDS 33). UK Prospective Diabetes Study (UKPDS) Group [published erratum appears in Lancet 354:602, 1999]. Lancet 352:837, 1998

37. Anderson KM, Wilson PW, Odell PM, et al: An updated coronary risk profile: a statement for health professionals. Circulation 83:356, 1991

38. Collaborative overview of randomised trials of antiplatelet therapy—I. Prevention of death, myocardial infarction, and stroke by prolonged antiplatelet therapy in various categories of patients. Antiplatelet Trialists' Collaboration [published erratum appears in BMJ 308:1540, 1994]. BMJ 308:81, 1994

39. Hart RG, Halperin JL, McBride R, et al: Aspirin for the primary prevention of stroke and other major vascular events: meta-analysis and hypotheses. Arch Neurol 57:326, 2000

40. Kronmal RA, Hart RG, Manolio TA, et al: Aspirin use and incident stroke in the cardiovascular health study. CHS Collaborative Research Group. Stroke 29:887, 1998

41. Barnett HJM, Eliasziw M, Meldrum HE: Drugs and surgery in the prevention of ischemic stroke. N Engl J Med 332:238, 1995

42. Hansson L, Zanchetti A, Carruthers SG, et al: Effects of intensive blood-pressure lowering and low-dose aspirin in patients with hypertension: principal results of the Hypertension Optimal Treatment (HOT) randomised trial. HOT Study Group. Lancet 351:1755, 1988

43. Wiebers DO, Whisnant JP, Sandok BA, et al: Prospective comparison of a cohort with asymptomatic carotid bruit and a population-based cohort without carotid bruit. Stroke 21:984, 1990

44. Shorr RI, Johnson KC, Wan JY, et al: The prognostic significance of asymptomatic carotid bruits in the elderly. J Gen Intern Med 13:86, 1998

45. Benavente OR, Moher D, Pham B: Carotid endarterectomy for asymptomatic carotid stenosis: a meta-analysis. BMJ 317:1477, 1998

46. Chambers BR, You RX, Donnan GA: Carotid endarterectomy for asymptomatic carotid stenosis. Cochrane Database Syst Rev (2):CD001923, 2000

47. European Carotid Surgery Trialists' Collaborative Group: Risk of stroke in the distribution of an asymptomatic carotid artery. Lancet 345:209, 1995

48. Gorelick PB: Carotid endarterectomy: where do we draw the line? (editorial) Stroke 30:1745, 1999

49. Gorelick PB, Sacco RL, Smith DB, et al: Prevention of a first stroke: a review of guidelines and a multidisciplinary consensus statement from the National Stroke Association. JAMA 281:1112, 1999

50. Feinberg RW: Primary and secondary stroke prevention. Curr Opin Neurol 9:46, 1996

51. Lee TT, Solomon NA, Heidenreich PA, et al: Cost-effectiveness of screening for carotid stenosis in asymptomatic persons. Ann Intern Med 126:337, 1997

52. Musser DJ, Nicholas GG, Reed JF III: Death and adverse cardiac events after carotid endarterectomy. J Vasc Surg 19:615, 1994

53. Goldman L, Caldera DL, Nussbaum SR, et al: Multifactorial index of cardiac risk in noncardiac surgical procedures. N Engl J Med 297:845, 1977

54. Roederer GO, Langlois YE, Jager KA, et al: The natural history of carotid arterial disease in asymptomatic patients with cervical bruits. Stroke 15:605, 1984

55. Fowl RJ, Marsh JG, Love M, et al: Prevalence of hemodynamically significant stenosis of the carotid artery in an asymptomatic veteran population. Surg Gynecol Obstet 172:13, 1991

56. Zhu CZ, Norris JW: Role of carotid stenosis in ischemic stroke. Stroke 21:1131, 1990

57. AbuRahma AF, Robinson PA: Prospective clinico-pathophysiologic follow-up study of asymptomatic neck bruit. Am Surg 56:108, 1990

58. Lusiani L, Visonà A, Castellani V, et al: Prevalence of atherosclerotic lesions at the carotid bifurcation in patients with asymptomatic bruits: an echo-Doppler (duplex) study. Angiology 36:235, 1985

59. Kartchner MM, McRae LP: Noninvasive evaluation and management of the "asymptomatic" carotid bruit. Surgery 82:840, 1977

60. Clagett GP, Youkey JR, Brigham RA, et al: Asymptomatic cervical bruit and abnormal ocular pneumoplethysmography: a prospective study comparing two approaches to management. Surgery 96:823, 1984

61. Wilson PWF, Hoeg JM, D'Agostino RB, et al: Cumulative effects of high cholesterol levels, high blood pressure, and cigarette smoking on carotid stenosis. N Engl J Med 337:516, 1997

62. O'Leary DH, Polak JF, Kronmal RA, et al: Distribution and correlates of sonographically detected carotid artery disease in the Cardiovascular Health Study. The CHS Collaborative Research Group. Stroke 23:1752, 1992

63. Hennerici M, Aulich A, Sandmann W, et al: Incidence of asymptomatic extracranial arterial disease. Stroke 12:750, 1981

64. Barnett HJ, Eliasziw M, Meldrum HE, et al: Do the facts and figures warrant a 10-fold increase in the performance of carotid endarterectomy on asymptomatic patients? Neurology 46:603, 1996

65. Warlow C: Endarterectomy for asymptomatic carotid stenosis? Lancet 345:1254, 1995

66. Amarenco P, Cohen A, Tzourio C, et al: Atherosclerotic disease of the aortic arch and the risk of ischemic stroke. N Engl J Med 331:1474, 1994

67. Blakeley DD, Oddone EZ, Hasselblad V, et al: Noninvasive carotid artery testing: a meta-analytic review. Ann Intern Med 122:360, 1997

68. Ballotta E, DaGiau G, Abbruzzese E, et al: Carotid endarterectomy without angiography: can clinical evaluation and duplex ultrasonographic scanning alone replace traditional arteriography for carotid surgery workup? A prospective study. Surgery 126:20, 1999

69. Wolf RK, Williams EL II, Kistler PC: Transbrachial balloon catheter tamponade of ruptured abdominal aortic aneurysms without fluoroscopic control. Surg Gynecol Obstet 164:463, 1987

70. Baird RN: Should carotid endarterectomy be purchased? treatment avoids much morbidity. BMJ 310:316, 1995

71. Hankey GJ, Warlow CP, Molyneux AJ: Complications of cerebral angiography for patients with mild carotid territory ischaemia being considered for carotid endarterectomy. J Neurol Neurosurg Psychiatry 53:542, 1990

72. Heiserman JE, Dean BL, Hodak JA, et al: Neurologic complications of cerebral angiography. AJNR Am J Neuroradiol 15:1401, 1994

73. Davies KN, Humphrey PR: Complications of cerebral angiography in patients with symptomatic carotid territory ischaemia screened by carotid ultrasound. J Neurol Neurosurg Psychiatry 56:967, 1993

74. Grzyska J, Freitag J, Zeumer H: Selective cerebral intraarterial DSA: Complication rate and control of risk factors. Neuroradiology 32:296, 1990

75. Cinà CS, Clase CM, Haynes RB: Refining indications for carotid endarterectomy in patients with symptomatic carotid stenosis: a systematic review. J Vasc Surg 30:606, 1999

76. Rockman CB, Riles TS, Lamparello PJ, et al: Natural history and management of the asymptomatic, moderately stenotic internal carotid artery. J Vasc Surg 25:423, 1997

77. Cina CS, Clase CM, Haynes RB: Carotid endarterectomy for symptomatic carotid stenosis. Cochrane Database Syst Rev (2):CD001081, 2000

78. Rothwell PM, Slattery J, Warlow CP: Clinical and angiographic predictors of stroke and death from carotid endarterectomy: systematic review. BMJ 315:1571, 1997

79. European Carotid Surgery Trialists' Collaborative Group: Randomized trial of endarterectomy for recently symptomatic carotid stenosis: final results of the MRC European Carotid Surgery Trial. Lancet 351:1379, 1998

80. Halliday A, Mansfield A, Marro J, et al: Prevention of disabling and fatal strokes by successful carotid endarterectomy in patients without recent neurological symptoms: randomised controlled trial. MRC Asymptomatic Carotid Surgery Trial (ACST) Collaborative Group. Lancet 363:1491, 2004

81. Barnett JHM: Commentary: Carotid endarterectomy. Lancet 363:1486, 2004

82. Stroke Prevention in Atrial Fibrillation Study: Final results. Circulation 84:527, 1991

83. Warfarin versus aspirin for prevention of thromboembolism in atrial fibrillation: Stroke Prevention in Atrial Fibrillation II Study. Lancet 343:687, 1994

84. Go AS, Hylek EM, Phillips KA, et al: Implications of stroke risk criteria on the anticoagulation decision in nonvalvular atrial fibrillation: the Anticoagulation and Risk Factors in Atrial Fibrillation (ATRIA) study. Circulation 102:11, 2000

85. Hass WK, Easton JD, Adams HP Jr, et al: A randomized trial comparing ticlopidine hydrochloride with aspirin for the prevention of stroke in high-risk patients. Ticlopidine Aspirin Stroke Study Group. N Engl J Med 321:501, 1989

86. Creager MA: Results of the CAPRIE trial: efficacy and safety of clopidogrel. Clopidogrel versus aspirin

in patients at risk of ischaemic events. Vasc Med 3:257, 1998

87. Bornstein NM, Chadwick LG, Norris JW: The value of carotid Doppler ultrasound in asymptomatic extracranial arterial disease. Can J Neurol Sci 15:378, 1988

88. Bornstein NM, Norris JW: Management of patients with asymptomatic neck bruits and carotid stenosis. Neurol Clin 10:269, 1992

89. Colgan MP, Strode GR, Sommer JD, et al: Prevalence of asymptomatic carotid disease: results of duplex scanning in 348 unselected volunteers. J Vasc Surg 8:674, 1988

90. Cronenwett JL, Birkmeyer JD, Nackman GB, et al: Cost-effectiveness of carotid endarterectomy in asymptomatic patients. J Vasc Surg 25:298, 1997

91. Barnett HJ, Taylor DW, Eliasziw M, et al: Benefit of carotid endarterectomy in patients with symptomatic moderate or severe stenosis. North American Symptomatic Carotid Endarterectomy Trial Collaborators (NASCET). N Engl J Med 339:1415, 1998

92. Eliasziw M, Streifler JY, Fox AJ, et al: Significance of plaque ulceration in symptomatic patients with high-grade carotid stenosis. North American Symptomatic Carotid Endarterectomy Trial. Stroke 25:304, 1994

93. Streifler JY, Eliasziw M, Fox AJ, et al: Angiographic detection of carotid plaque ulceration. comparison with surgical observations in a multicenter study. North American Symptomatic Carotid Endarterectomy Trial. Stroke 25:1130, 1994

94. Hougaku H, Matsumoto M, Handa N, et al: Asymptomatic carotid lesions and silent cerebral infarction. Stroke 25:566, 1994

95. Sabetai MM, Tegos TJ, Nicolaides AN, et al: Hemispheric symptoms and carotid plaque echomorphology. J Vasc Surg 31(1 pt 1):39, 2000

96. Meairs S, Hennerici M: Four-dimensional ultrasonographic characterization of plaque surface motion in patients with symptomatic and asymptomatic carotid artery stenosis. Stroke 30:1807, 1999

97. Kessler C, von Maravic M, Bruckmann H, et al: Ultrasound for the assessment of the embolic risk of carotid plaques. Acta Neurol Scand 92:231, 1995

98. de Bray JM, Baud JM, Delanoy P, et al: Reproducibility in ultrasonic characterization of carotid plaques. Cerebrovasc Dis 8:273, 1998

99. Albers GW: Expanding the window for thrombolytic therapy in acute stroke: the potential role of acute MRI for patient selection. Stroke 30:2230, 1999

100. Hill SL, Donato AT: Ability of the carotid duplex scan to predict stenosis, symptoms, and plaque structure. Surgery 116:914, 1994

101. Gasecki AP, Eliasziw M, Ferguson GG, et al: Long-term prognosis and effect of endarterectomy in patients with symptomatic severe carotid stenosis and contralateral carotid stenosis or occlusion: results from nascet. North American Symptomatic Carotid Endarterectomy Trial (NASCET) group. J Neuro-

surg 83:778, 1995

102. Findlay JM, Tucker WS, Ferguson GG, et al: Guidelines for the use of carotid endarterectomy: current recommendations from the Canadian Neurosurgical Society. Can Med Assoc J 157:653, 1997

103. Norris JW, Zhu CZ: Silent stroke and carotid stenosis. Stroke 23:483, 1992

104. Halliday AW, Thomas D, Mansfield A: The Asymptomatic Carotid Surgery Trial (ACST): rationale and design. Steering Committee. Eur J Vasc Surg 8:703, 1994

105. Ricotta JJ, O'Brien MS, DeWeese JA: Carotid endarterectomy for non-hemispheric ischaemia: long-term follow-up. Cardiovasc Surg 2:561, 1994

106. Faggioli GL, Curl GR, Ricotta JJ: The role of carotid screening before coronary artery bypass. J Vasc Surg 12:724, 1990

107. Courbier R, Jausseran JM, Poyen V: Current status of vascular grafting in supraaortic trunks. Personal experience. Int Surgery 73:210, 1988

108. Pillai L, Gutierrez IZ, Curl GR, et al: Evaluation and treatment of carotid stenosis in open-heart surgery patients. J Surg Res 57:312, 1994

109. Borger MA, Fremes SE, Weisel RD, et al: Coronary bypass and carotid endarterectomy: does a combined approach increase risk? A metaanalysis. Ann Thorac Surg 68:14, 1999

110. Rosenthal D, Caudill DR, Lamis PA, et al: Carotid and coronary arterial disease: a rational approach. Am Surg 50:233, 1984

111. Newman DC, Hicks RG, Horton DA: Coexistent carotid and coronary arterial disease. Outcome in 50 cases and method of management. J Cardiovasc Surg (Torino) 28:599, 1987

112. Ennix CL Jr, Lawrie GM, Morris GC Jr, et al: Improved results of carotid endarterectomy in patients with symptomatic coronary disease: an analysis of 1,546 consecutive carotid operations. Stroke 10:122, 1979

113. Sameshima T, Miyao J, Oda T, et al: [Effects of allopurinol on renal damage following renal ischemia.] Masui—Japan J Anesthesiol 44:349, 1995

114. Cinat ME, Pham H, Vo D, et al: Improved imaging of carotid artery bifurcation using helical computed tomographic angiography. Ann Vasc Surg 13:178, 1999

115. Fox AJ: How to measure carotid stenosis (editorial). Radiology 186:316, 1993

116. Rothwell PM, Gibson RJ, Slattery J, et al: Equivalence of measurements of carotid stenosis: a comparison of three methods on 1001 angiograms. European Carotid Surgery Trialists' collaborative group. Stroke 25:2435, 1994

117. Eliasziw M, Smith RF, Singh N, et al: Further comments on the measurement of carotid stenosis from angiograms. North American Symptomatic Carotid Endarterectomy Trial (NASCET) group. Stroke 25:2445, 1994

118. Landis R, Koch G: The measurement of observer agreement for categorical data. Biometrics 33:159, 1997

119. Floriani M, Giulini SM, Anzola GP, et al: Predictive value of cervical bruit for the detection of obstructive lesions of the internal carotid artery: data from 2000 patients. Ital J Neurol Sci 10:321, 1989

120. Thiele BL, Jones AM, Hobson RW, et al: Standards in noninvasive cerebrovascular testing. Report from the Committee on Standards for Noninvasive Vascular Testing of the Joint Council of the Society for Vascular Surgery and the North American Chapter of the International Society for Cardiovascular Surgery. J Vasc Surg 15:495, 1992

121. Detsky AS, Abrams HB, Forbath N, et al: Cardiac assessment for patients undergoing noncardiac surgery. Arch Intern Med 146:2131, 1986

122. Detsky AS, Abrams HB, McLaughlin JR, et al: Predicting cardiac complications in patients undergoing non-cardiac surgery. J Gen Intern Med 1(July–August):211, 1986

123. Wong T, Detsky AS: Preoperative cardiac risk assessment for patients having peripheral vascular srugery. Ann Intern Med 116:743, 1992

124. Eagle K, Brundage B, Chaitman B, et al: Guidelines for perioperative cardiovascular evaluation for noncardiac surgery: report of the American College of Cardiology/American Heart Association Task Force on Practice Guidelines (Committee on Perioperative Cardiovascular Evaluation for Noncardiac Surgery). J Am Coll Cardiol 27:910, 1996

125. Eagle K, Froelich J: Reducing cardiovascular risk in patients undergoing noncardiac surgery (editorial). N Engl J Med 335:1761, 1996

126. Eagle KA, Coley CM, Newell JB, et al: Combining clinical and thallium data optimizes preoperative assessment of cardiac risk before major vascular surgery. Ann Intern Med 110:859, 1989

127. Rothwell PM, Gibson RJ, Slattery J, et al: Prognostic value and reproducibility of measurements of carotid stenosis: a comparison of three methods on 1001 angiograms. European Carotid Surgery Trialists' collaborative group. Stroke 25:2440, 1994

128. NASCET: Clinical alert: benefit of carotid endarterectomy for patients with high-grade stenosis of the internal carotid artery. national institute of neurological disorders and stroke stroke and trauma division. North American Symptomatic Carotid Endarterectomy Trial (NASCET) investigators. Stroke 22:816, 1991

129. NASCET: North American Symptomatic Carotid Endarterectomy Trial. Methods, patient characteristics, and progress. Stroke 22:711, 1991

Acknowledgment

Figure 1 Laurie Grace.

82 PULSATILE ABDOMINAL MASS

Timothy A. Schaub, M.D., and Gilbert R. Upchurch, Jr., M.D., F.A.C.S.

Assessment of a Pulsatile Abdominal Mass

When a pulsatile abdominal mass is found on physical examination, the location of the mass and the symptoms associated with it become essential clinical clues. The underlying condition may range in severity from benign to life threatening. Further evaluation is imperative; in certain clinical settings, immediate transport to the operating room is indicated. Because inappropriate treatment can be catastrophic, it is important to base one's approach to assessment and management of a pulsatile abdominal mass as firmly as possible on the available evidence. In what follows, a clinical approach based on relevant evidence is outlined.

Clinical Evaluation

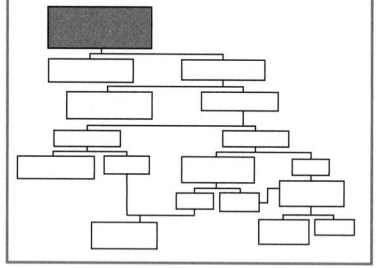

The most feared cause of a pulsatile abdominal mass is an abdominal aortic aneurysm (AAA). In the United States, AAAs are present in 3% to 9% of the population, resulting in approximately 15,000 fatalities each year.[1] In 1999, AAAs were the 15th leading cause of death in the United States.[2] Deaths from AAA declined in subsequent years,[3] but with the overall aging of the U.S. population, this disease remains a major threat to public health.

PRESENTATION

Asymptomatic AAAs are considerably more common than symptomatic AAAs and are often discovered on abdominal or pelvic scans done for other indications (e.g., back pain or renal cysts) rather than on physical examination.[4,5] Plain films of the lumbar region, routinely obtained in patients with back pain, may show a calcified shell of the aorta [*see Figure 1*]. In one review of 31 patients with surgically proven ruptured AAAs, 65% had calcification of the aneurysm that was visible on a plain abdominal radiograph.[6] In addition, ultrasonography and computed tomography are nearly 100% sensitive in detecting AAAs.[7] In elderly patients, evaluation of the aorta should be routinely included in abdominal ultrasonography; scanning of the aorta adds, on average, only 43 seconds to the study.[8] If an AAA is unexpectedly found, either the patient is followed or the aneurysm is repaired, depending on the clinical situation and the size of the aneurysm (see below).

Ruptured AAAs, on the other hand, give rise to pronounced symptoms, and the patient's condition may range from hemodynamic stability to class IV shock. When the patient is unstable, further workup is unnecessary and emergency repair is indicated. The situation is less clear when the patient is stable. The traditional presentation of a ruptured AAA is a triad comprising hypotension, back or abdominal pain, and a pulsatile abdominal mass. Unfortunately, this traditional presentation occurs less than half of the time. In a study of 116 patients with ruptured AAAs, 45% were hypotensive, 72% had pain, and 83% had a pulsatile abdominal mass.[9] Accordingly, it is essential not to be lulled into a false sense of security when evaluating a hemodynamically stable patient with a pulsatile abdominal mass. Although a ruptured AAA is an uncommon event in a patient with a stable blood pressure and no abdominal pain, the absence of these symptoms does not rule out the possibility.

Symptomatic or ruptured aneurysms can mimic many other acute medical conditions and therefore are part of multiple differential diagnoses. The following conditions all may be confused with ruptured AAAs: (1) perforated viscus, (2) mesenteric ischemia, (3) strangulated hernia, (4) ruptured visceral artery aneurysm, (5) acute cholecystitis, (6) acute pancreatitis, (7) ruptured appendix, (8) ruptured necrotic hepatobiliary cancer, (9) lymphoma, and (10) diverticular abscess. Fortunately, misdiagnosis of a ruptured AAA is rare. Moreover, most patients who do undergo an operation for a misdiagnosis either benefit from or at

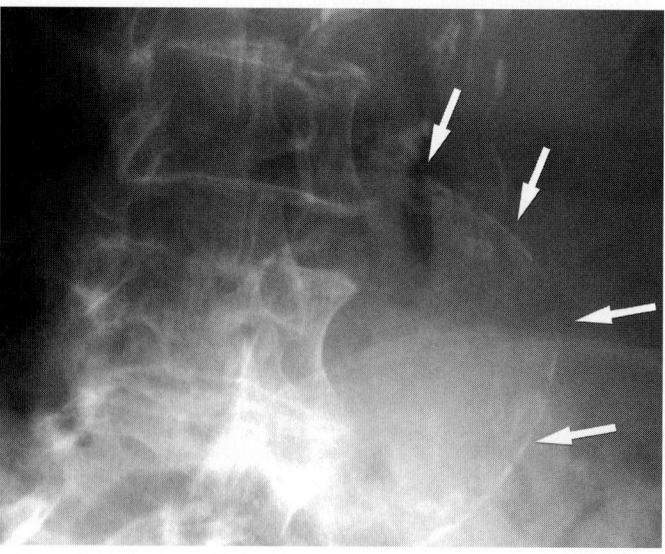

Figure 1 Shown is a plain film of the abdomen (anterior-posterior view) in an elderly woman who presented complaining of vague abdominal pain. The patient was found to have an AAA, diagnosed by plain film and believed to be approximately 5 cm in size. Arrows follow the course of calcium outlining her aorta.

Table 1 Risk Factors Associated with AAA Development

Factors Positively Associated with Development of AAA	Factors Negatively Associated with Development of AAA
Increased age	Female sex
Increased height	Black race
Coronary artery disease	Presence of diabetes
Any atherosclerosis	
High cholesterol levels	
Hypertension	
Smoking	
Male sex	
Family history (first-degree relative)	

least are not harmed by the operation, which should alleviate some potential concerns about taking an aggressive approach to a suspected ruptured AAA.[10] Conversely, AAAs can mimic other disease processes: in one study, nearly one in five patients with symptomatic AAAs in an emergency department were originally diagnosed as having nephroureterolithiasis.[11] Patients who have urologic symptoms but whose urinalysis is normal may benefit from an AAA workup; radiologic evidence of ureteric involvement is present in as many as 71% of AAAs.[12]

HISTORY

The medical history may be helpful in determining the patient's level of risk for an AAA. Even in the absence of clinical symptoms, knowledge of the risk factors may facilitate earlier diagnosis. The Aneurysm Detection and Management Veterans Affairs Cooperative Study Group trial (commonly referred to as the ADAM trial) found a number of factors to be associated with increased risk for AAA: advanced age, greater height, coronary artery disease (CAD), atherosclerosis, high cholesterol levels, hypertension, and, in particular, smoking.[13] The risk was lower in women, African Americans, and diabetic patients.

AAAs occur almost exclusively in the elderly and are rarely seen in patients younger than 50 years. In a 2001 study, the mean age of patients undergoing repair for AAAs in the United States was 72 years.[14] Male patients outnumber female by a factor of 4 to 6, depending on the study cited.[14-18] Family members of AAA patients are also at significant risk: 12% to 19% of persons undergoing AAA repair have a first-degree relative with an AAA.[19-21] Accordingly, screening is recommended in all men and women older than 50 years who have a family history of AAA.[22] AAAs are over seven times more likely to develop in smokers than in nonsmokers, with the duration of smoking, rather than total number of cigarettes smoked, being the key variable [see Table 1].[23]

Of particular importance is identification of risk factors for rupture. The United Kingdom Small Aneurysm (UKSA) trial reported 103 AAA ruptures in 2,257 patients over a period of 7 years, with an annual rupture rate of 2.2%.[23] The factors found to be significantly and independently associated with an increased risk of rupture were female sex, a larger initial AAA diameter, a lower forced expiratory volume in 1 second (FEV_1), a current smoking habit, and a higher mean blood pressure.[23,24] Women are two to four times more likely to experience rupture of an AAA than men are.[24,25] AAAs in cardiac and abdominal transplant patients also appear to have high expansion and rupture rates.[26]

The patient's surgical history is also crucial, particularly in that it can shorten the differential diagnosis at presentation by ruling out disease processes (e.g., appendicitis and cholecystitis). In addition, the nature and extent of any previous abdominal procedures may influence the surgeon's operative approach to the AAA repair. When a pulsatile abdominal mass is discovered in a patient who previously underwent open repair of an AAA, it is important to remember that anastomotic pseudoaneurysms[27] or synchronous lesions (e.g., iliac artery aneurysms[28]) can occur at sites remote from the previous repair.

Patients who have undergone endovascular AAA repair may also present with symptoms in the presence [see Figure 2] or absence of an endoleak. In a 2002 review, most ruptures after endovascular AAA repair occurred with type I endoleaks in the tube endograft configuration.[29] This clinical scenario is well described and can present as a pulsatile abdominal mass.[29-31] The risk of rupture after endovascular repair is small,[29] but the long-term outcome of this relatively new approach remains to be determined. Overall mortality after rupture in patients with previous endografts approaches 50%, and the operative mortality is 41%.[29]

PHYSICAL EXAMINATION

Before the advent of modern radiologic tests, the abdominal examination was the key to detecting an AAA. *Gray's Anatomy*, first published in 1858, noted that AAAs formed "a pulsating tumour, that presents itself in the left hypochondriac or epigastric regions."[32] The abdominal aorta begins at the level of the diaphragm and the 12th thoracic vertebra and runs in the retroperitoneal space just anterior to and slightly to the left of the spine. At approximately the level of the umbilicus and the 4th lumbar vertebra, it bifurcates into the right and left common iliac arteries. In young, thin individuals, the abdominal aorta runs close to the surface of the abdomen and thus can often be palpated during a normal physical examination. Palpation of an AAA is safe and has not been reported to precipitate rupture. A 1997 report found, however, that only 31% of the AAAs studied

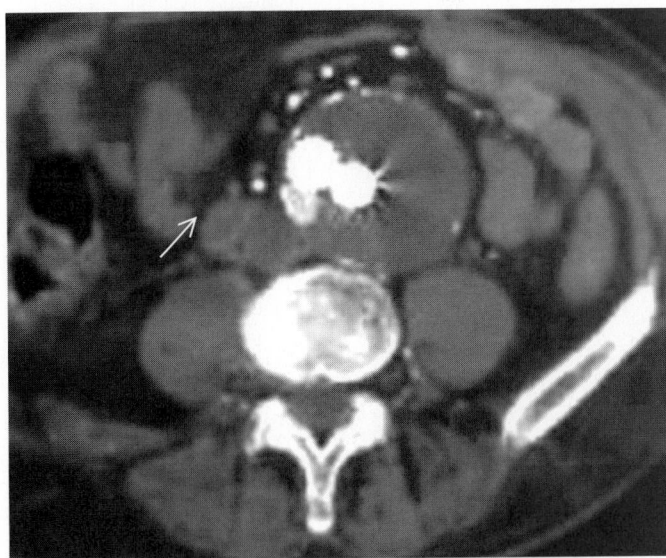

Figure 2 Shown is a CT scan of a patient who presented to the emergency room with increasing back pain 2 years after an endovascular AAA. The patient was found to have a type II endoleak (arrow), which was treated with coil embolization of a lumbar artery.

Patient presents with pulsatile abdominal mass

Perform clinical evaluation.
- *Presenting signs and symptoms:* presence or absence of pain, location, associated symptoms.
- *Medical and surgical history:* risk factors for development or rupture of AAA, previous operations, other surgical disease.
- *Physical examination:* vital signs, abdominal palpation (safe but poor at screening and detection).

Assess stability of patient.

Patient is unstable

Assume ruptured aneurysm until proven otherwise.

Perform emergency repair. Standard of care is open repair, but endovascular repair may be possible in certain circumstances.

No aneurysm is found

Search for other possible causes of complaints.

If aortic diameter is normal and patient > 60 yr, no further screening is indicated.

If aorta is enlarged, rescreen in 5–8 yr or if symptoms develop.

Pain is absent

Base subsequent treatment on aneurysm size.

Aneurysm ≥ 5.5 cm

Risk of rupture in 1 yr is greater than risk of operative repair.

Consider elective AAA repair [*see Figure 4*].

Aneurysm < 5.5 cm

Risk of rupture in 1 yr is less than risk of operative repair.

Optimize medical management.

Perform follow-up US in 6 mo.

If aneurysm grows by > 0.4 cm in 12 mo or becomes symptomatic, offer repair.

Educate patient to signs/symptoms of AAA development and rupture.

Assessment of a Pulsatile Abdominal Mass

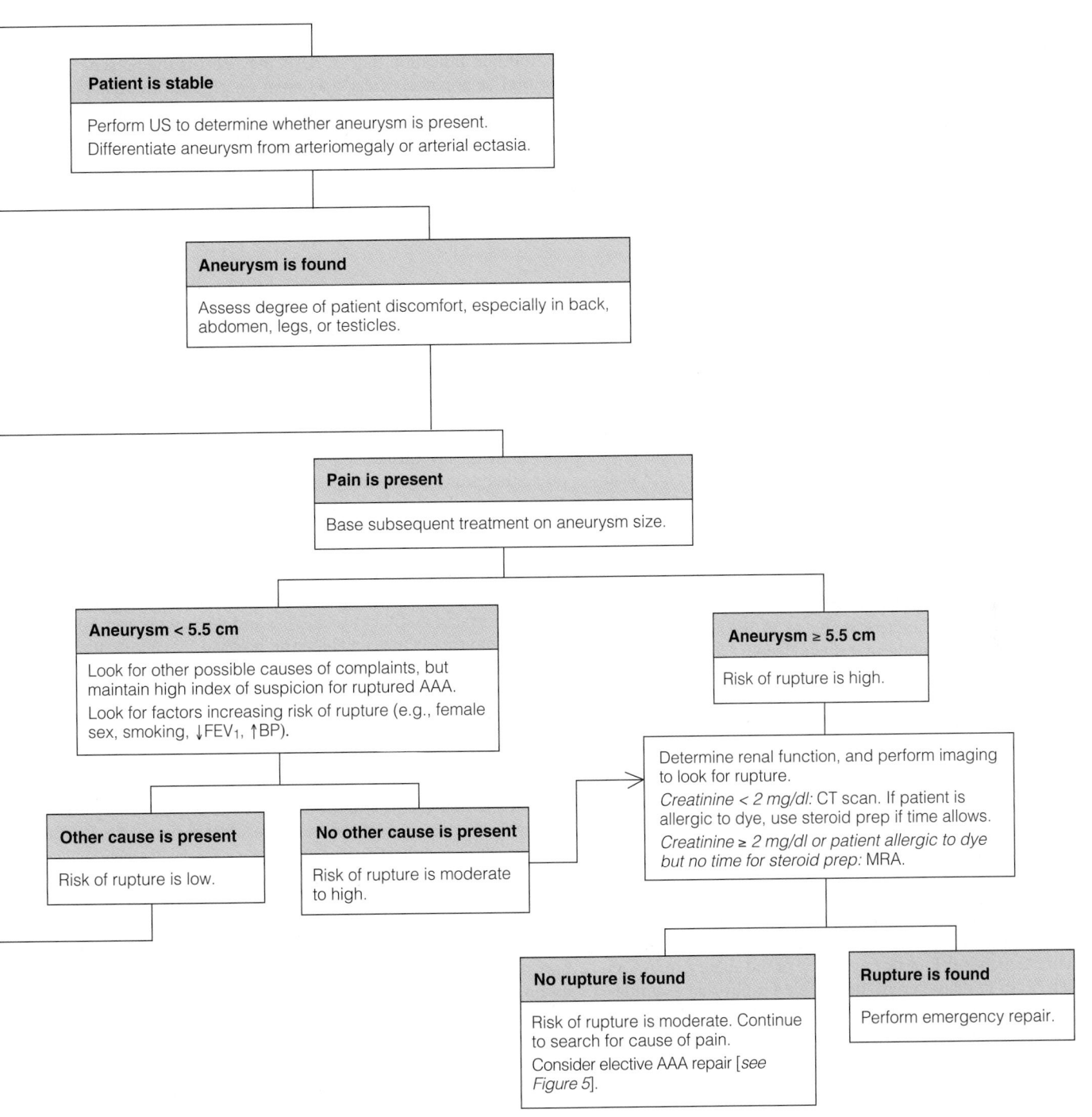

Patient is stable

Perform US to determine whether aneurysm is present.
Differentiate aneurysm from arteriomegaly or arterial ectasia.

Aneurysm is found

Assess degree of patient discomfort, especially in back, abdomen, legs, or testicles.

Pain is present

Base subsequent treatment on aneurysm size.

Aneurysm < 5.5 cm

Look for other possible causes of complaints, but maintain high index of suspicion for ruptured AAA.
Look for factors increasing risk of rupture (e.g., female sex, smoking, ↓FEV$_1$, ↑BP).

Aneurysm ≥ 5.5 cm

Risk of rupture is high.

Determine renal function, and perform imaging to look for rupture.
Creatinine < 2 mg/dl: CT scan. If patient is allergic to dye, use steroid prep if time allows.
Creatinine ≥ 2 mg/dl or patient allergic to dye but no time for steroid prep: MRA.

Other cause is present

Risk of rupture is low.

No other cause is present

Risk of rupture is moderate to high.

No rupture is found

Risk of rupture is moderate. Continue to search for cause of pain.
Consider elective AAA repair [*see Figure 5*].

Rupture is found

Perform emergency repair.

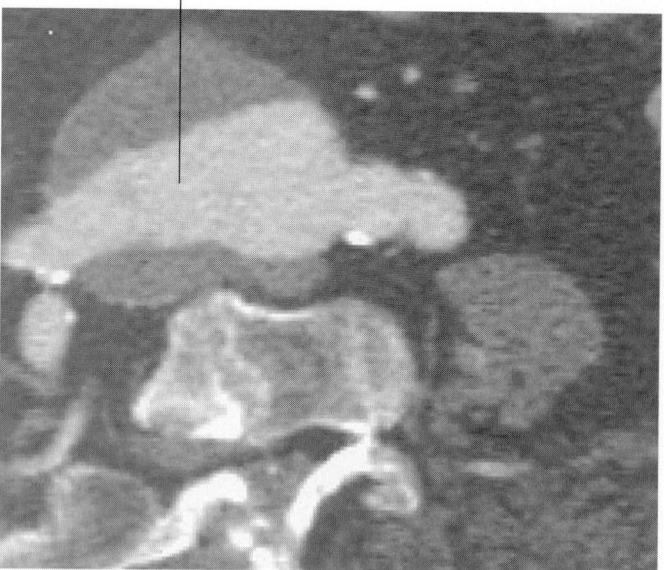

Large Right Common
Iliac Artery Aneurysm

Figure 3 **Shown is a CT scan of a patient presenting with an abdominal mass who, in addition to having a small AAA, was found to have a large right common iliac artery aneurysm, palpable in the right lower quadrant of the abdomen.**

at a major teaching institution were initially detected by physical examination.[33] Nonaneurysmal common iliac arteries also are often difficult to palpate, even in thin individuals.

There are several methods of conducting a proper physical examination of the abdominal aorta. Our preferred approach resembles that of Lederle and Simel[34]:

1. Have the patient lie supine with the knees raised. Encourage the patient to relax the abdomen. A relaxed abdomen is often obtainable with passive exhalation after a deep inhalation.
2. Beginning a few centimeters cephalad to the umbilicus and just to the left of the midline, palpate deeply for the pulsation of the aorta.
3. To confirm that the aorta is being palpated, place both hands on the abdomen with the palms down in such a way that the pulsation is between the tips of the index fingers. The index fingers should move apart with each heartbeat.
4. Once it is certain that the index fingers are bracketing the aorta, estimate the diameter of the aorta by measuring the distance between the fingertips, taking into account the thickness of the overlying tissue.

Unfortunately, physical examination is not very accurate in detecting AAAs: in one study, approximately 62% of known AAAs were missed.[35] Whether an AAA is detectable on physical examination alone depends primarily on the size of the aneurysm. AAAs more than 5 cm in diameter are detectable on physical examination in 76% of the population, whereas those 3 to 3.9 cm in diameter are detectable in only 29%. Palpation of an AAA 3.0 cm in diameter or larger has a positive predictive value of only 43%.[34] In addition, detection of AAAs is significantly limited by truncal obesity.[36,37] Thus, physical examination is clearly insufficient for ruling out or screening for AAAs.[34,36]

In the past, it was considered important to measure the abdominal aorta accurately by means of physical examination. Several studies have been published comparing ultrasonography, the currently preferred screening method, with physical examination.[37,38] One such study found that abdominal palpation had a poor (14.7%) positive predictive value for detecting AAAs greater than 3.5 cm in diameter.[38] At present, with the wide availability of ultrasound screening, physical examination is playing a smaller role in AAA detection.

Although most AAAs appear supraumbilically, not all pulsatile abdominal masses appear there. In some patients, the abdominal aorta becomes more tortuous and elongated with age. As a result, an AAA may appear infraumbilically or to one side of the abdomen or the other. The common iliac arteries may become aneurysmal and palpable in one of the lower abdominal quadrants as well [*see Figure 3*].[39]

Another indication that an AAA may exist is the presence of a femoral or popliteal artery aneurysm on physical examination. A patient with a femoral artery aneurysm has an 85% chance of having a concomitant AAA, and a patient with a popliteal artery aneurysm has a 62% chance.[40,41] Conversely, in a study evaluating 251 patients with documented AAAs, 14% had either a femoral or a popliteal artery aneurysm.[42] There is a significant male predominance, for unknown reasons.[15,42,43]

Indications for Emergency Repair versus Further Workup

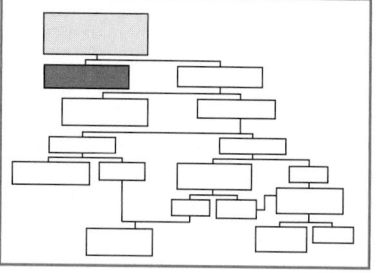

PATIENT IS UNSTABLE

If a patient presents with a pulsatile abdominal mass and is medically unstable, no further study or workup is necessary: the diagnosis, until proved otherwise, is a ruptured AAA. The only cure for a ruptured AAA is an emergency operation. Indeed, when all patients experiencing a ruptured AAA are taken into account, including both those who arrive at the hospital alive and those who do not, overall mortality is still between 77% and 94%, with over 50% of patients expiring before reaching the hospital.[44,45] Most ruptured AAAs leak into the left retroperitoneum, which may serve to confine the bleeding.[46] However, AAAs that rupture freely into the abdominal cavity usually result in death, either at home or en route to the hospital. Even if the patient makes it to the OR, the expected mortality exceeds 50%[47] (though values as low as 15% and as high as 90% have been noted[48]). Mortality after a ruptured AAA has declined since the middle of the 20th century by approximately 3.5% per decade; however, the most recent estimate, for the year 2000, is still 41%.[48]

Although some physicians suggest that patients with predictably high morbidity and mortality from a ruptured AAA may not benefit from attempted repair,[49] most would still maintain that even in this population, this presentation necessitates operative intervention.[50] The high cost of repair and the substantial operative mortality notwithstanding, surgical repair of ruptured AAAs appears to be cost-effective in comparison with no intervention.[51] Thus, cost should not be considered in the management of patients with AAAs.

Open repair of ruptured AAAs is the current standard of care [*see 90 Repair of Infrarenal Abdominal Aortic Aneurysms*]. There is evidence, however, that endovascular approaches may come to play a more significant role. A 2003 study described endovascular repair of 29 ruptured AAAs and reported a mortality of only 11%.[52]

PATIENT IS STABLE

If a patient with a pulsatile abdominal mass is medically stable, further workup is called for. As noted, ultrasound imaging is significantly more accurate in detecting an AAA than physical examination alone is.[38] Duplex ultrasonography is used extensively as a primary screening tool for evaluating the size of an abdominal aorta because of certain advantages it possesses over other, more extensive modalities, such as CT, magnetic resonance angiography (MRA), and conventional angiography. Its main advantages are that (1) it is noninvasive, (2) it is relatively inexpensive, (3) it does not require exposure to radiation, (4) it is portable, and (5) it is as reliable as the other modalities in determining aortic anterior-posterior (AP) diameter. Ultrasound-derived measurements are reproducible to within 3 to 5 mm,[53] and the interobserver variability is less than 5 mm in 84% of AP measurements.[54] In about 75% of cases, ultrasonography underestimates the size of the aorta. A comparison study found that AAA diameter measurements were consistently and significantly larger with CT than with ultrasound (5.69 ± 0.89 cm versus 4.74 ± 0.91 cm).[55] It appears that when radiologists take more care with their measurements (e.g., by using magnifying glasses and calipers), the results correlate better.[56]

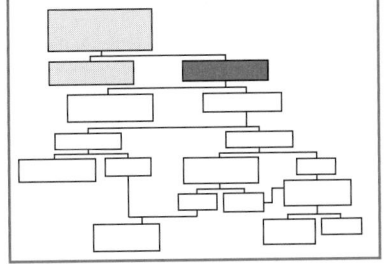

Ultrasonographic measurement of the infrarenal aorta and the common iliac arteries has been evaluated in patients with no known vascular disease. In one study of patients older than 50 years (the age group in which abdominal aortic and iliac artery aneurysms are most common), the aorta measured 1.68 ± 0.29 cm in men and 1.46 ± 0.19 cm in women (P < 0.001).[57] The common iliac arteries measured 1.01 ± 0.20 cm in men and 0.92 ± 0.13 cm in women. An aneurysm is commonly defined as a permanent localized or focal expansion of an artery to 1.5 times its expected diameter.[46] Thus, an infrarenal AAA would be considered to be approximately 3 cm in diameter. It must be remembered, however, that infrarenal aortic diameter is affected by height, age, race, body surface area, and sex.[58-60] An aneurysm should be differentiated from arteriomegaly and from arterial or aortic ectasia. Arteriomegaly is a diffuse enlargement of an artery by an amount that is at least 50% of the normal diameter; ectasia

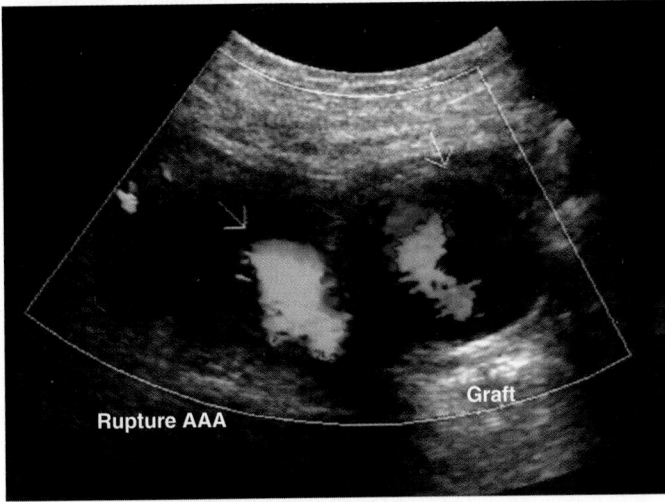

Figure 4 Depicted is rare ultrasonographic documentation of a ruptured AAA proximal to an old aortic tube graft.

is an enlargement of an artery by an amount that is less than 50% of the normal diameter.[61]

The main limitations of ultrasonography are that (1) the results are highly technician dependent and (2) resolution is dependent on body habitus and intestinal gas.[46] Another limitation is that it is unreliable in detecting rupture [see Figure 4]. Because ultrasonography does not provide an accurate picture of the aorta proximal to the renal arteries and because it is subject to the limitations already mentioned, it cannot be routinely used to differentiate a ruptured AAA from a symptomatic intact AAA. If ultrasonography is inconclusive in the evaluation of a palpable abdominal mass, then either CT or MRA (see below) is the next step [see Table 2].

Management

STABLE PATIENT WITHOUT ANEURYSM

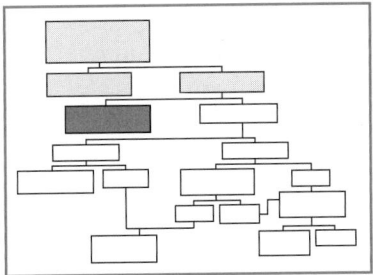

If ultrasonography indicates that a patient with a pulsatile abdominal mass does not have an aneurysm, the risk of aortic or common iliac artery rupture is very low. Consequently, if symptoms (e.g., abdominal pain) persist, another causative condition must be considered.

If arteriomegaly is found to be the cause of the pulsatile abdominal mass and there are no symptoms of occlusion, then no specific treatment is required. Routine ultrasonographic follow-up is indicated because the risk of rupture still applies as the aorta continues to expand. In one study, an aneurysm was present in 1.6% of aortas with arteriomegaly.[62] If aortic ectasia (by most standards, an aorta measuring 2.5 to 3 cm) is found to be the cause, follow-up ultrasonography in 5 to 8 years is recommended.[61,63] It has been suggested that for a 65-year-old man with a normal aortic diameter (defined as less than 2.6 cm), the risk that a significantly dilated aneurysm will develop during the remainder of his life is essentially zero.[64] The distinction between a normal and an ectatic aorta remains something of a gray area, and the preferred follow-up period remains controversial. In general, ectatic infrarenal aortas expand slowly and are not associated with rupture.[61]

In the ADAM trial, independent and significant predictors of a new aneurysm on follow-up ultrasonography included (1) current smoking (odds ratio, 3.09), (2) coexisting CAD (1.81), and, in a separate model with composite variables, (3) any atherosclerosis (1.97).[63] Accordingly, when a patient has any of these risk factors, a lower threshold for follow-up ultrasonography and a shorter period between examinations may be practical.

STABLE PATIENT WITH ANEURYSM

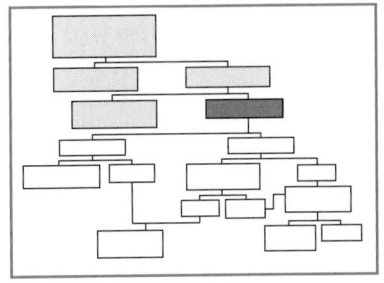

Once the diagnosis of an aneurysm is made in a stable patient, the subsequent course of action is determined by the clinical presentation and the size of the pulsatile abdominal mass. It must be emphasized that if the patient becomes hemodynamically unstable at any point during evaluation, operative intervention is necessary—unless the patient has a terminal condition or has indicated that nothing further should be done to prolong life.

Table 2 Advantages and Disadvantages of Aortic Imaging Techniques

Imaging Modality	Advantages	Disadvantages
Ultrasonography	Noninvasive Relatively inexpensive Does not require radiation exposure Portable Comparable in reliability to other modalities in determining aortic AP diameter	Highly technician dependent Resolution dependent on body habitus and intestinal gas Unreliable in detecting AAA rupture Achieves poor visualization of aorta proximal to renal arteries and of iliac arteries
CT	Yields highly precise measurements Defines proximal and distal extent of AAAs precisely Delineates anatomy of iliac arteries Evaluates AAA wall integrity (notes location and amount of calcification and thrombus) Effective at discovering venous anomalies, retroperitoneal blood, aortic dissection, inflammatory aneurysms, and other intra-abdominal pathology and anomalies	Requires radiation exposure Requires iodinated contrast Expensive
MRA	Comparable to CT in preoperative evaluation Uses nonnephrotoxic contrast agent (gadolinium) Highly sensitive and specific in detecting stenoses of splanchnic, renal, and iliac arteries	Not widely available Very expensive May cause claustrophobia in select patients Requires longer scan time Contraindicated in patients with certain metal foreign bodies
Angiography	Superior in evaluating intraluminal characteristics of aorta Superior in determining visceral branch involvement Superior in delineating variations in vascular anatomy	More expensive than spiral CT Associated with multiple risks (e.g., infection, arterial thrombosis, distal embolization, groin hematoma, local arterial dissection, and risk of renal failure secondary to contrast)

If the patient is experiencing no discomfort and is otherwise stable, the risk of active rupture can be considered extremely low. If, however, the patient is experiencing significant pain or discomfort, especially in the back, the abdomen, the legs, or the testicles, AAA rupture should remain a strong diagnostic possibility.

Pain Is Absent

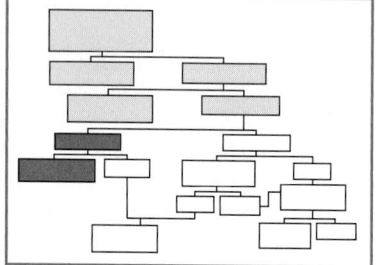

A patient with a pulsatile abdominal mass who has a known AAA and who is hemodynamically stable without complaints of pain should be further categorized on the basis of the size of the aneurysm. This categorization is traditionally based on the physics of an expanding aneurysm and on the association between increased risk of rupture and increased aneurysm size. The key considerations in these patients are (1) whether the risk associated with AAA repair exceeds the risk of rupture in a given period and (2) what other factors are present that may affect this decision.

Indications for operative intervention The physics of aneurysm expansion and rupture are probably best understood via the law of Laplace,[8] according to which the tangential stress (τ) placed on a cylinder filled with fluid (e.g., a blood vessel) is determined by the equation

$$\tau = Pr/\delta$$

where P is the pressure (dynes/cm^2) exerted by the fluid, r is the internal radius (cm) of the cylinder, and δ is the thickness (cm) of the cylinder wall. When the aorta expands, its radius increases while its wall thickness decreases; thus, there is a geometric increase in tangential stress. As an aneurysm grows from 2 cm in diameter to 4 cm, tangential pressure increases not twofold but

fourfold. When the increased tangential stress exceeds the elastic capacity of the wall, rupture occurs. Elastic tissue in the abdominal aorta becomes attenuated as a result of age and of certain acquired and genetic factors; thus, a modest degree of expansion over time is not uncommon. An abnormal rate of expansion is usually considered to be 5 mm/yr or greater. Documentation of an accelerated aneurysm growth rate should cause the surgeon to give serious consideration to operative intervention [*see 90 Repair of Infrarenal Abdominal Aortic Aneurysms*].[46]

Multiple studies have examined aneurysm diameter, usually indicated by the greatest AP diameter of the aorta, as a risk factor for rupture; several studies have documented that increased AP diameter is in fact the greatest predictor of rupture. This conclusion has been challenged, however, by studies using three-dimensional CT scanning to evaluate wall stress via a mathematical technique called finite element analysis.[65-67] In these studies, maximal wall stress was a better predictor of rupture than maximal AP diameter was. For example, one patient with a ruptured 4.8 cm aneurysm had a wall stress equivalent to that of a patient with an electively repaired 6.3 cm AAA.[66] Future management of AAAs may be based on actual wall stress in addition to maximum AP diameter.

In a 2001 study addressing open operative repair of intact AAAs, increased mortality was associated with increased patient age, female sex, cerebral vascular occlusive disease, preoperative renal insufficiency, and the presence of more than three comorbid conditions before operation.[14] In the UKSA trial, the 30-day mortality in patients undergoing elective open AAA repair was 5.8%.[68] The point at which the risk of elective repair became acceptable in relation to the risk of rupture with medical management and serial ultrasonographic follow-up was an aneurysm diameter of 5.5 cm. The investigators suggested that in patients with AAAs less than 5.5 cm in diameter, medical management is the best course of action. The operative mortality reported in this study is considered high, in that many single-center series have documented mortalities of 1% to 3% after open repair of intact AAAs.[69-71] The ADAM investigators also found that survival was not improved when AAAs smaller than 5.5 cm were repaired electively, even if a low operative mortality was associated with the procedure.[70]

Hospital volume may have a significant effect on patient outcome after elective AAA repair. A 2002 study found that mortality after this procedure was 56% higher at low-volume hospitals than at high-volume hospitals.[72] Moreover, mortality after repair of an intact AAA exhibited a ninefold variation that could be attributed to hospital volume, sex, and age alone. Thus, when a patient is being evaluated for AAA repair, it is important to take into account not only the size of the aneurysm but also age, sex, comorbidities, and hospital volume. In turn, more than half of the effect of hospital volume on operative mortality in elective AAA repair appears to be mediated by surgeon volume.[73] Surgeon specialty also appears to affect operative mortality after elective AAA repair.[74]

Given the various possible complicating factors, it is clear that no single aortic diameter can serve as a definitive indication for operative intervention in every patient. It is well known that ruptures can occur unpredictably at aneurysm diameters smaller than 5.5 cm.[75] Therefore, the timing of AAA repair must be individualized, with the 5.5 cm figure serving as a general guideline in the counseling of patients.

Advanced age, terminal conditions, and various end-of-life issues may deter patients from wishing to proceed with operative intervention. In addition, severe coexisting diseases significantly affect the morbidity and mortality associated with AAA repair.[47,76] Accordingly, older patients with multiple comorbidities may be preferentially offered endovascular AAA approach in place of open repair.[30] The surgeon must, however, consider the possibility that any operative intervention will be too risky in this population or that other interventions must be carried out before AAA repair can be attempted. These issues should be addressed via appropriate preoperative evaluation [*see Figure 5*].

Small AAAs (< 5.5 cm): medical management and follow-up

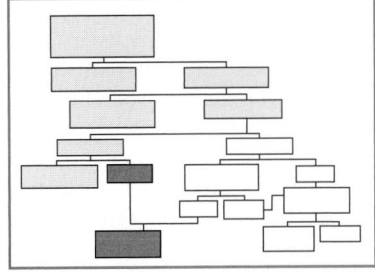

When a patient with stable vital signs and no abdominal pain is diagnosed as having a small AAA (i.e., < 5.5 cm), serial ultrasonography and optimization of medical management are indicated.[77,78] Small AAAs usually do not rupture.[24,79] Most small AAAs continue to grow, however, typically by 0.2 to 0.4 cm in diameter per year.[70,77,80] Small AAAs can also expand rapidly with unpredictable frequency. A rapidly expanding AAA is at high risk for rupture, regardless of how small it may be.[68,70,80,81]

Many risk factors have been identified that may affect the risk of small aneurysm expansion and rupture. For example, one study suggested that diastolic hypertension and chronic obstructive pulmonary disease (COPD) increased the risk that a small AAA would rupture,[75] whereas another found advanced age, severe cardiac disease, previous stroke, and a history of cigarette smoking to be risk factors for rapid expansion.[80] AAAs smaller than 5.5 cm may rupture more frequently in women than in men. A 2002 study found that in almost one quarter of women with ruptured AAAs, the diameter of the aneurysm was less than 5.5 cm at the time of rupture.[44] Currently, the safest and easiest method of following small AAAs is serial ultrasonography.[11,82] When the diameter of an AAA approaches 5.5 cm, a more detailed study (e.g., CT or MRA) is indicated if repair is being considered.[46]

Over the past several decades, the number of AAAs (especially smaller AAAs) detected has increased.[83] This increase has been attributed to two causes: (1) increased serendipitous detection in the course of scans done for other indications and (2) the "graying" of the population.[46,83] With the potential advent of a screening program for AAA in the near future, thanks to growing evidence that such screening is cost-effective,[22,84] it is likely that even more AAAs will be detected yearly. This prospect raises an interesting issue, in that at present, the only proven treatment for AAAs is operative; current medical therapy is notably limited. Clearly, there is a need to find medical therapies that can prevent, reduce, or stabilize the growth of AAAs. To that end, a better understanding of how AAAs develop is essential.

Basic science studies have helped elucidate the etiology of AAAs in greater detail. In particular, current research is focusing on (1) evaluating the role various proteolytic enzymes, such as matrix metalloproteinases (MMPs), play in processes involving the structural elements in the aortic wall; (2) investigating the importance of the immune system, specifically the macrophage, in the development of AAAs; (3) determining how hemodynamic and biomechanical stress affects aortic wall remodeling; and (4) identifying molecular genetic variables that contribute to AAA development.[85]

Proteolytic enzymes are currently being evaluated as potential predictors of the course of AAA growth.[86] Doxycycline, which decreases MMPs in animal aneurysm models independently of its antibiotic properties, was evaluated in a prospective, randomized

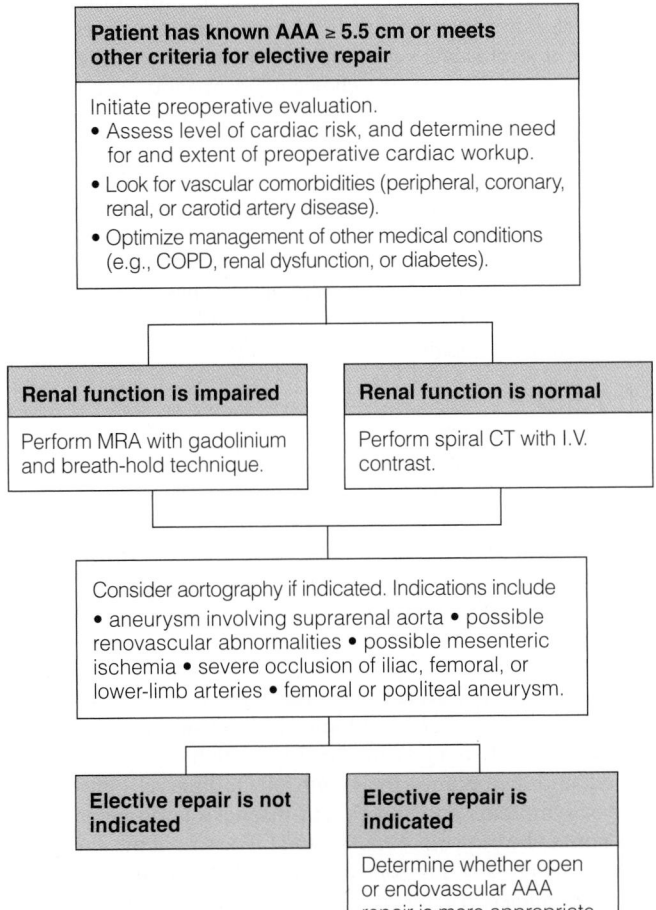

Patient has known AAA ≥ 5.5 cm or meets other criteria for elective repair

Initiate preoperative evaluation.
- Assess level of cardiac risk, and determine need for and extent of preoperative cardiac workup.
- Look for vascular comorbidities (peripheral, coronary, renal, or carotid artery disease).
- Optimize management of other medical conditions (e.g., COPD, renal dysfunction, or diabetes).

Renal function is impaired

Perform MRA with gadolinium and breath-hold technique.

Renal function is normal

Perform spiral CT with I.V. contrast.

Consider aortography if indicated. Indications include
- aneurysm involving suprarenal aorta • possible renovascular abnormalities • possible mesenteric ischemia • severe occlusion of iliac, femoral, or lower-limb arteries • femoral or popliteal aneurysm.

Elective repair is not indicated

Elective repair is indicated

Determine whether open or endovascular AAA repair is more appropriate.

Figure 5 **Shown is an algorithm that may be used to guide the preoperative workup of a patient who is to undergo elective AAA repair.**

phase II trial published in 2002.[87] Although it did not exert a significant effect on aneurysm growth over the short study period (6 months), doxycycline significantly reduced serum levels of MMP-9, a gelatinase that plays a central role in degrading elastin and collagen in the abdominal aortic wall. Few side effects were noted, and most of them were easily reversible. These findings, though not conclusive, suggest that the use of doxycycline may one day prove to be a viable medical means of slowing AAA growth.

Control of hypertension would seem to be an obvious approach to medical control of aneurysms, in that hypertension is a significant risk factor for both development and rupture of AAAs.[24,75,79,88] To this end, various antihypertensive agents, including beta blockers, calcium channel blockers, and angiotensin-converting enzyme (ACE) inhibitors, have been evaluated in patients with AAAs.[23] The results have been somewhat equivocal.

Beta blockers have been shown to reduce the expansion rate of large AAAs (≥ 5 cm) but not that of smaller AAAs.[89,90] Some of them (e.g., propranolol) may be poorly tolerated at high doses.[90] In addition, beta blockers are often contraindicated in patients with severe COPD, though as many as 11% of COPD patients have AAAs.[24] A 1999 study suggested that receiving a calcium channel blocker was an independent risk factor for the presence of an AAA (odds ratio, 2.6).[23] The same study also noted, however, that patients receiving calcium channel blockers had stiffer aortic walls. ACE inhibitors, in contrast, were associated with decreased aortic wall stiffness and increased collagen turnover, whereas diuretics and beta blockers had no effect on aortic wall stiffness. None of the medications examined were found to affect the growth rate of AAAs. Aortic stiffness appears to be an important variable: increased aortic wall distensibility is associated with an increased risk of AAA rupture, and it is almost as powerful a predictor of rupture as actual AAA diameter.[91]

A link between COPD and AAAs is suggested by the presence of a common development pathway: both conditions are associated with elastin breakdown and smoking. A 1999 study argued, however, that the strong association between AAAs and COPD was most likely attributable to coexisting cardiovascular disease and medications.[24] In this study, the average annual aortic diameter expansion rate was 4.7 mm in patients who used oral steroids but only 2.6 mm in those who did not. The use of beta-adrenergic agonists was also a positive predictor of aneurysm expansion. Thus, oral steroids and beta agonists must be used cautiously in COPD patients who have AAAs. If an AAA patient must use one of these medications, close follow-up is indicated to monitor the expansion rate of the aneurysm.

Atherosclerosis is associated with AAAs but is currently believed to be a secondary phenomenon, with inflammation and matrix-degrading enzymes being the primary factors in AAA development.[92] Lipoprotein (a) has been found to be an independent risk factor for atherosclerosis and is elevated in patients with AAAs independently of the patients' cardiovascular risk factors or the extent of atherosclerosis.[93] It seems reasonable that lowering lipid levels would decrease the development of atherosclerosis of the abdominal aorta. This is a potentially important effect because patients with small atherosclerotic AAAs often experience thrombotic complications involving the lower extremities.[94] Levels of apolipoprotein-AI and high-density lipoproteins have also been found to be significantly lower in patients with AAAs.[95] Overall, however, lipids appear to play only a minor role in AAA progression.[96] An animal study suggested that regression of plaque by lowering serum lipid levels after atherosclerotic aneurysm formation may result in increased aneurysm dilation in the abdominal aorta.[97] A subsequent study, however, demonstrated

that statins reduce the production of MMPs in the wall of AAAs.[98] The role of lipid-lowering medications in the treatment of AAAs remains to be clarified. Elevated levels of homocysteine in the blood are a recognized independent risk factor for atherosclerosis, and a study of AAA patients has found significantly higher levels of plasma homocysteine, along with lower levels of vitamin B_{12}.[99] Given this finding, and the possible role of vitamin B_{12} in homocysteine regulation, use of supplemental vitamins may theoretically modify AAA progression.[99]

Smoking is an independent risk factor for AAA development,[63,88] expansion,[80,96] and rupture.[24] Current smokers are 7.6 times more likely to have an AAA than nonsmokers are, and ex-smokers are three times more likely to have an AAA.[23] The duration of smoking is the key variable[13,23,88]: the relative risk of AAA development is increased by 4% for each year of smoking.[23] The ADAM trial noted that a longer interval since the cessation of smoking was significantly associated with a decreased risk of AAA formation[13]; however, the decline in risk appears to be slow.[23] The UKSA trial showed that former smokers were at lower risk for death from AAA repair than current smokers were.[68] A 2002 study found that there was an independent association between smoking and high-grade tissue inflammation in AAAs,[100] lending support to the idea that smoking is an initiating event in AAA formation.

At present, intriguing possibilities notwithstanding, few definitive recommendations can be made regarding the use of medical therapy to reduce AAA growth. The indications for perioperative beta blockade are primarily cardioprotective. Administration of antihypertensives may be beneficial from a practical perspective, but current level I data supporting this practice are lacking. If an antihypertensive is given, the choice of agent should be based on associated clinical data (e.g., the presence of coexisting medical conditions, such as angina or renal insufficiency, whose management must be optimized). The administration of lipid-lowering drugs to patients with AAAs also requires further study, though the utility of such agents in the presence of CAD, which is found in almost 50% of AAA patients,[101] is well documented, and long-term statin use after successful AAA surgery has been associated with reduced mortality (both all-cause and cardiovascular).[102] Finally, smoking cessation is clearly mandatory.

Pain Is Present

When a patient presenting with a pulsatile abdominal mass is hemodynamically stable but complains of pain in the abdomen, the back, the testicles, or the femoral region, the index of suspicion must be high for a symptomatic or rup- 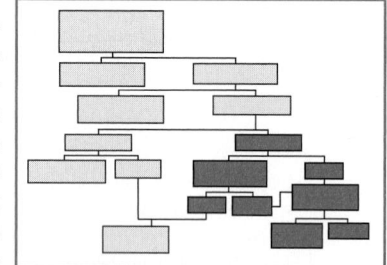 tured AAA. Other possible causes should be considered as well. As noted (see above), many abdominal processes may mimic an AAA; however, it is important that recognition of an AAA not be delayed unduly, because the length of the interval between the onset of symptoms and subsequent diagnosis and operation can have a direct bearing on overall survival. The size of the aneurysm, as determined by ultrasonography, is helpful for identifying patients at highest risk for rupture. Ultrasonography is sometimes able to detect a ruptured aneurysm, but it should not be relied on to rule out rupture. In one study, ultrasonography demonstrated extraluminal blood in only 4% of ruptured AAAs in the emergency department.[103]

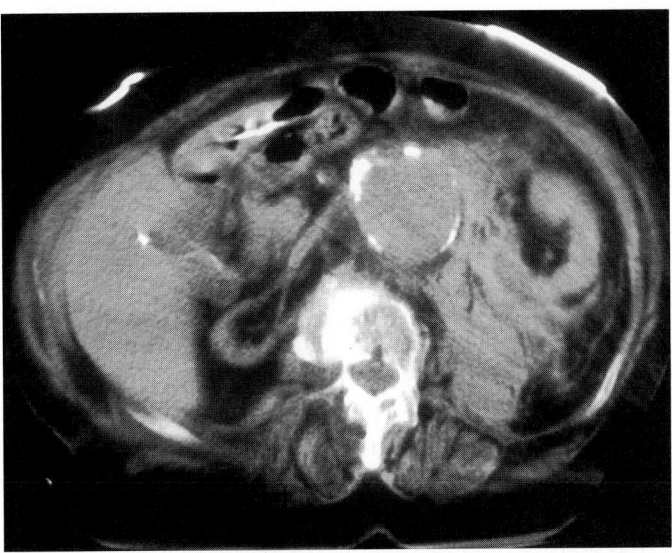

Figure 6 Shown is a CT scan of a patient presenting with a pulsatile abdominal mass and dull, aching back pain. The scan was obtained before contrast administration and demonstrates free extravasation of blood into the retroperitoneum.

In stable patients with AAAs larger than 5.5 cm who are experiencing pain, either CT or MRA may be used to detect AAA rupture; the choice typically depends on the patient's medical history [*see Table 2*]. After ultrasound evaluation, if an aneurysm smaller than 5.5 cm was found and no associated risk factors for rupture were identified, a search for other possible causes of the pain is reasonable, provided that it is performed expeditiously.

If no other cause for the pain can be found, possible rupture should remain a prime consideration, and the next step in evaluation—namely, spiral CT or MRA—should be implemented. Missing or delaying the diagnosis of a ruptured AAA can be disastrous. If retroperitoneal blood is noted, then the study need not be completed, and the patient should be taken to the OR [*see Figure 6*]. If the aneurysm is not ruptured, repair should be undertaken urgently (i.e., within the next 24 hours), with the patient's medical condition optimized to the extent possible [*see 90 Repair of Infrarenal Abdominal Aortic Aneurysms*]. Precipitous repairs of nonruptured symptomatic AAAs have an operative mortality five times that of elective repairs,[104] for reasons yet unknown.

Preoperative Evaluation of Nonemergency AAA Repair Candidates

Evaluation of a patient before elective AAA repair begins with assessment of the expected benefit of repair in relation to the estimated risk. If the decision is made to operate, the history and the physical examination should be completed as described earlier [*see Clinical Evaluation, above*]. The clinical findings, in conjunction with ECG and routine laboratory test results, provide most of the information that is needed for evaluating a patient's candidacy for AAA repair.

COMORBID CONDITIONS

CAD is common in patients with AAAs and is the leading cause of early and late mortality after AAA repair.[105] Renal insufficiency, COPD, and diabetes mellitus also may influence morbidity and mortality after AAA repair. Accordingly, when any of these disease entities is present, further evaluation before repair may be benefi-

cial. Optimization of perioperative medications is also important for maximizing risk reduction. Finally, adequate preoperative imaging is essential. The decision regarding which type of repair is most appropriate in an AAA patient should be based on the preoperative evaluation.

Coronary Artery Disease

Before AAA repair, it is important to identify patients who are at high risk for a perioperative cardiac event and who need a preoperative cardiac intervention. It is also important to identify patients who are at low risk, so that they are not subjected to unneeded testing. A report from the American College of Cardiology/American Heart Association (ACC/AHA) Task Force on Practice Guidelines provided useful guidelines for pre-

Table 3 ACC/AHA Guidelines for Preoperative Cardiac Evaluation in Patients Undergoing Elective High-Risk Vascular Procedures[110]

1. Revascularization in the past 5 years?	If **yes**, without recurrence of signs or symptoms of ischemia, then further cardiac testing is not indicated. Proceed with surgery. If **no**, go to 2.
2. Coronary evaluation in the past 2 years?	If **yes**, findings are favorable on adequate test without onset of new symptoms, or symptoms change, proceed with surgery. If **no** or findings are unfavorable, go to 3.

3. Major clinical predictor of risk present?	Major clinical predictors include
	  Unstable coronary syndromes
	  Decompensated CHF
	  Significant arrhythmias
	  Severe valvular disease
	Presence of these predictors cancels or delays intervention until they are ameliorated. Implement medical management. Consider coronary angiography. Go to 4.

4. Intermediate clinical predictor of risk present?	Intermediate clinical predictors include
	  Mild angina pectoris
	  Prior MI
	  Compensated or prior CHF
	  Diabetes mellitus
	  Renal insufficiency
	When these indicators are present, performance of noninvasive testing in AAA repair candidates is indicated, especially if 2 or more are present. If, after noninvasive testing, patient is determined to be low risk, continue with operation. If risk is high, consider coronary angiography. If **no** predictors are present, go to 5.

5. Minor or no clinical predictors present?	Minor clinical predictors include
	  Advanced age
	  Abnormal ECG
	  Nonsinus rhythm
	  Low functional capacity
	  Previous stroke
	  Uncontrolled systemic hypertension
	If minor or no clinical predictors are present and patient can attain 4 METs or more, proceed with surgery. Consider noninvasive testing when < 4 METs are attained, especially in presence of multiple minor clinical predictors; then go to 6.

6. Risk after noninvasive testing?	Low risk: proceed with operation. High risk: consider coronary angiography.

ACC—American College of Cardiology AHA—American Heart Association
CHF—congestive heart failure MET—metabolic equivalent MI—myocardial infarction

Table 4 Estimated Energy Required
for Various Activities[110,137]

Activity Level	METs*	Sample Activities
Mild	1–3	Eating; playing a musical instrument; walking at 2 mph; getting dressed; golfing (with cart)
Moderate	3–5	Calisthenics without weights; climbing a flight of stairs; housework; golfing (without cart); running a short distance
Vigorous	4–12+	Chopping wood; strenuous sports such as football, basketball, singles tennis, karate, or jogging (10 min mile or faster)

*1 MET = 3.5 ml · kg^{-1} · min^{-1} oxygen uptake.

operative cardiac evaluation in patients undergoing noncardiac vascular surgery [*see Table 3*], with the express goal of limiting the use of perioperative cardiac procedures in patients at moderate and high risk for complications.[106] Use of these guidelines and permutations thereof has proved both safe and effective at reducing resource use and overall costs.[107-109] According to the ACC/AHA guidelines, patients needing urgent or elective AAA repair are stratified first by whether coronary revascularization was done within the past 5 years. If so, and symptoms have not recurred, the patient is cleared for operation. If the patient never underwent coronary revascularization, underwent revascularization more than 5 years before, or is experiencing recurrent symptoms or signs of cardiac ischemia, further evaluation of clinical predictors is necessary.

Clinical predictors of major perioperative cardiovascular risk—defined as myocardial infarction (MI), congestive heart failure, or death—may be divided into three categories[106]: major, intermediate, and minor. The presence of a major predictor requires that the symptom or disease be managed appropriately before nonemergency surgery. The presence of an intermediate predictor is associated with an increased risk of perioperative cardiac complications and requires that current status be fully investigated. The presence of a minor predictor is indicative of cardiovascular disease but has not been shown to independently increase the risk of perioperative cardiovascular complications.

Once the clinical predictors have been evaluated, additional predictive factors, involving the patient's ability to perform various activities (ranging from minor activities of daily living to strenuous

Table 5 ECG Findings as Clinical Predictors of Increased Perioperative Cardiovascular Risk[136]

Major predictors
  High-grade atrioventricular block
  Symptomatic ventricular arrhythmias in the presence of underlying heart disease
  Supraventricular arrhythmias with uncontrolled ventricular rate
Intermediate predictor
  Pathologic Q wave indicating previous myocardial infarction
Minor predictors
  Left ventricular hypertrophy
  Left bundle-branch block
  ST-T abnormalities
  Rhythm other than sinus (e.g., atrial fibrillation)

sports), are assessed. The energy required to perform an activity is quantified in terms of metabolic equivalents (METs). The number of METs of which a patient is capable directly correlates with the ability to perform specific tasks [*see Table 4*]. Patients who are unable to attain 4 METs are considered to be at high risk for perioperative cardiac events and long-term complications. Finally, the inherent risk of the procedure to be performed is evaluated. AAA repair is considered high-risk.

The original ACC/AHA recommendations for supplemental preoperative testing were updated in a 2002 statement.[110] Currently, it is generally agreed that preoperative testing should be limited to patients in whom the results have the potential to alter the current course of management. The following noninvasive tests may be considered.

1. 12-lead ECG. This test is recommended. Certain ECG abnormalities are clinical predictors of perioperative and long-term cardiac risks in patients undergoing high-risk operative procedures [*see Table 5*].
2. Transthoracic echocardiography to evaluate resting left ventricular function. This test is indicated in the presence of heart failure. If it was previously done and demonstrated severe left ventricular dysfunction, repeat evaluation is unnecessary. It may be of benefit in patients with prior heart failure and those with dyspnea of unknown etiology. Routine use is not beneficial in the absence of heart failure.
3. Exercise or pharmacologic stress testing. Such testing is useful for diagnosing CAD in patients with an intermediate pretest probability of CAD, but its value is less well established in those with a high or low pretest probability. It is a good prognosticator for patients with suspected or proven CAD who are undergoing initial evaluation, for patients whose clinical disposition has changed significantly, and for those who have experienced an acute coronary syndrome. Stress testing is also recommended for demonstrating the presence of myocardial ischemia before coronary revascularization and for evaluating the efficacy of medical therapy. It may be useful in patients whose subjective assessment of exercise tolerance is unreliable and in whom evaluation in terms of METs is therefore impossible. Less clear are the following indications for stress testing: (1) diagnosis of CAD in patients who have resting ST depression of less than 1 mm, are on digitalis, or show evidence of left ventricular hypertrophy on ECG, and (2) detection of restenosis in high-risk patients who have recently (i.e., within the past few months) undergone percutaneous transluminal coronary angioplasty (PTCA). Exercise stress testing should not be done (1) to diagnose patients with ECG findings that would prevent adequate assessment, (2) in patients with severe comorbidities that would preclude coronary revascularization, (3) for routine screening of asymptomatic patients, or (4) to evaluate young patients with isolated ectopic beats on ECG.

Coronary angiography, if indicated, may be performed next. Current indications in patients scheduled to undergo AAA repair include (1) high-risk status after noninvasive testing, (2) continued angina despite adequate medical therapy, (3) unstable angina, and (4) an equivocal result on noninvasive testing in high-risk patients. Coronary angiography may be beneficial in patients with multiple intermediate clinical risk factors. If noninvasive testing reveals moderate-sized to large areas of ischemia in a patient without high-risk criteria and a lower left ventricular ejection fraction, or if testing is nondiagnostic in a patient at intermediate clinical risk, coronary angiography may also be indicated. The indication for coronary angiography is more controversial in patients who have experienced a perioperative MI. Coronary angiography is not indicated in patients who are asymptomatic after coronary revascularization and who are capable of at least 7 METs.

Both coronary artery bypass grafting (CABG) and PTCA have been employed to treat CAD before AAA repair. CABG is usually done in this setting only if it has been decided that the patient needs the intervention regardless of the current status of the abdominal aorta. Such patients have a high-risk coronary anatomy and have a long-term prognosis that may improve if coronary revascularization is performed. The combination of AAA repair and CABG has been evaluated, and there are some data to support its use in highly select patients.[111,112]

To date, no controlled trials have evaluated the efficacy of PTCA against that of medical therapy before noncardiac aortic surgery. Although some small observational studies have indicated a low cardiac mortality when preoperative PTCA is performed in this setting, complications after PTCA are not infrequent and include the need for emergency CABG. One retrospective review found that patients who underwent prophylactic PTCA before noncardiac surgery were twice as likely to have an adverse cardiac outcome as healthy patients were.[113] This study did not control for CAD severity, medical management, or comorbidities. A later study concluded that both CABG and PTCA offered only modest protection against adverse cardiac events after major arterial surgery (CABG, < 5 years; PTCA, < 2 years).[114] General indications for PTCA use are outlined in the 2001 revision of the 1993 ACC/AHA Guidelines for Percutaneous Coronary Intervention.[115] It is recommended that patients wait at least 2 weeks—preferably, 4 to 6 weeks—after PTCA before undergoing AAA repair; this delay allows the plaque to stabilize after stenting and permits full treatment with antiplatelet agents.

Pulmonary Disease

Between 7% and 11% of patients with COPD have an AAA.[24] Traditionally, when such patients are to undergo AAA repair, room air arterial blood gas values are determined and pulmonary function tests performed to assess the extent of COPD. If COPD is severe, formal pulmonary consultation may be necessary for prediction of short- and long-term prognoses and optimization of treatment. Several studies have reported that COPD is an independent predictor of operative mortality.[14,71,116] A 2001 study of Veterans Affairs (VA) patients, however, found no significant correlation between the presence of COPD and increased operative mortality (though morbidity was notably higher).[117] A 2003 study evaluating morbidity and mortality after AAA repair in patients with COPD showed that the preoperative factors significantly associated with a poor outcome included (1) suboptimal COPD management, as evidenced by fewer inhalers used, (2) a lower preoperative hematocrit, (3) preoperative renal insufficiency, and (4) the presence of CAD.[118] It is noteworthy that abnormal preoperative pulmonary function tests and arterial blood gas values were not predictive of a poor outcome. Thus, COPD by itself is not a contraindication to AAA repair.

Renal Failure

Preoperative renal insufficiency [see 122 Acute Renal Failure] is known to be a risk factor for a poor outcome after AAA repair[14,71,117,118] and thus should be evaluated and corrected if possible. In certain patients with AAAs, renal artery stenosis may be contributing to impaired renal function; if so, it may be corrected either

noninvasively, before AAA repair, or in the course of the repair.[46]

Diabetes Mellitus

Whether diabetes mellitus is truly an independent risk factor for morbidity or mortality after aortic surgery is controversial. Several studies have shown that the risk of death is not increased in diabetic patients, but the risk of perioperative complications may be.[119-121] Most of these studies had small study groups and thus lacked the statistical power needed to demonstrate that diabetes had a significant influence. A 2002 study of patients at VA medical centers who underwent major vascular procedures found that diabetic patients were indeed at higher risk for death and cardiovascular complications.[122] When examined separately, however, patients undergoing AAA repair did not have higher rates of cardiovascular complications or death than patients undergoing other procedures.

PERIOPERATIVE MEDICATIONS

Multiple studies have addressed optimization of medical management in patients with AAAs. Beta blockers, alpha$_2$-adrenergic agonists, nitrates, and calcium channel blockers have all been evaluated in this setting. Other agents used in the treatment of cardiovascular disease (e.g., aspirin) have not been specifically evaluated in regard to reduction of perioperative cardiac complications in patients undergoing aortic surgery.[123]

A review of the literature supporting perioperative beta blockade was published in 2002.[124] Five randomized, controlled trials were evaluated, and the results suggested that this measure had a beneficial effect on perioperative cardiac morbidity. The number needed to treat to prevent one MI was 2.5 to 6.7 patients; the number needed to treat to produce a significant effect on cardiac or all-cause mortality was 3.2 to 8.3 patients. All but one of the studies reported a significant reduction in postoperative MIs after beta blocker use, with the effect being most obvious in high-risk patients. Thus, it appears that perioperative beta blockade is most likely beneficial for patients at high risk for cardiac events who are to undergo AAA repair, unless it is otherwise contraindicated (e.g., by COPD). The therapeutic goal should be to attain a resting heart rate of 60 beats/min or lower before operation.[123]

Alpha$_2$-adrenergic agonists (e.g., clonidine) have not been shown to reduce MI rates or mortality from cardiac causes. In one study, mivazerol did not exert a significant overall effect in patients undergoing major vascular or orthopedic procedures but was associated with a significant reduction in MI rates and mortality from cardiac causes in patients with known CAD.[125] Therefore, when perioperative beta blockade is contraindicated, administration of alpha$_2$-adrenergic agonists may be of benefit in high-risk patients.

To date, studies evaluating the perioperative use of nitroglycerin and diltiazem to lower the risk of cardiac events have not found this practice to be beneficial in this regard. It may be best to reserve these agents for patients who need them for angina or ischemic symptoms and for those who have myocardial ischemia after operation.[123]

It is widely accepted that aspirin is beneficial in reducing the risks associated with CAD.[126] Its continued use throughout the perioperative period is controversial, however, as is the use of clopidogrel, because of the potential complications associated with decreased platelet function. Indications for the use of these antiplatelet agents may be patient dependent.[127] Traditionally, aspirin is discontinued at least 1 week before aortic surgery.

FURTHER IMAGING

The main methods used to evaluate the aortic anatomy before AAA repair are ultrasonography, CT, MRA, and aortography.

Which method is employed in a given situation depends largely on the clinical presentation, the history, the comorbid conditions present, and the availability of equipment and expertise. Each has its advantages and disadvantages [see Table 2].

Ultrasonography

Further ultrasonographic evaluation of the aortic anatomy, if indicated, is performed in accordance with the approach described earlier [see Patient Is Stable, above].

CT Scanning

The current standard for preoperative imaging of AAAs is contrast-enhanced CT scanning. This modality is more accurate than aortography at measuring AAA diameter and determining the presence of rupture.[53] With spiral CT, it is possible to obtain a three-dimensional view of the abdominal aorta. CT scanning is highly accurate, with measurements reproducible to within 2 mm. Measurement variations as great as 5 mm are sometimes seen, however, occurring 9% to 17% of the time.[54,56] Such variations may be reduced by standardizing measurements, reducing the number of radiologists reading the images, and using calipers and magnification for greater accuracy.[56]

The advantages of CT over ultrasonography include (1) more precise definition of the proximal and distal extent of AAAs, (2) better delineation of the iliac arterial anatomy, (3) the ability to evaluate AAA wall integrity, noting the location and amount of calcification within vessel walls, and (4) the ability to identify venous anomalies, retroperitoneal blood, aortic

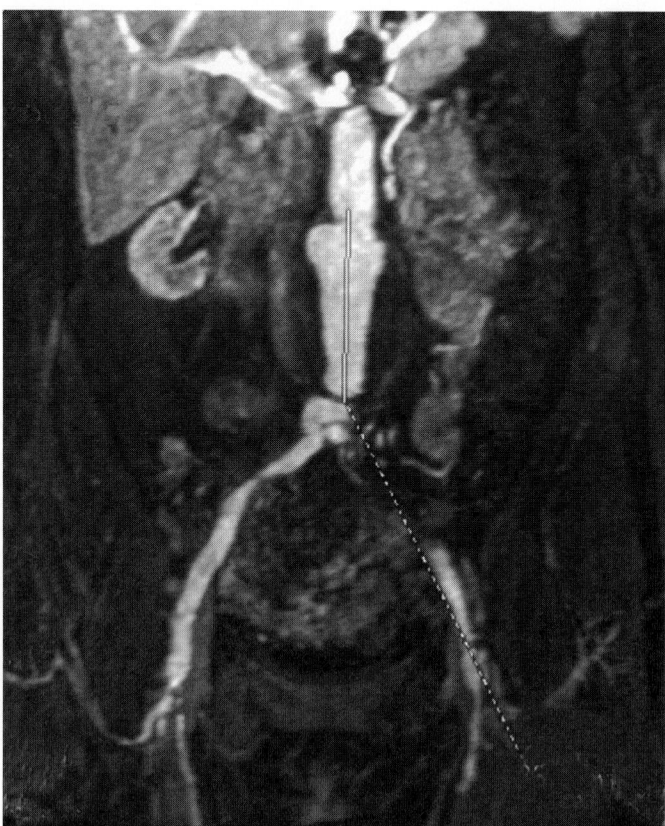

Figure 7 Shown is an MRA of a patient who had undergone both open infrarenal AAA repair and aortobifemoral bypass off the terminal aorta. The AAA grew between the two previous repairs and was subsequently managed endovascularly.

dissection, inflammatory aneurysms, and other intra-abdominal pathologic conditions and anomalies (e.g., horseshoe kidney). Therefore, CT is the study of choice for excluding AAA rupture in stable but symptomatic patients.[1,53,128] Thin-cut helical/spiral CT arteriography with multiplanar reconstruction is a recommended study for evaluating patients before endovascular AAA repair; CT arteriography is also preferred for determining whether an endoleak has occurred after endovascular AAA repair.[129] In the near future, ultrasonography may supplant CT for these applications.

The main drawbacks associated with CT scanning are (1) radiation exposure and (2) the requirement for iodinated contrast material, which cannot be used in patients with dye allergies or renal insufficiency. In addition, spiral CT with three-dimensional reconstruction is relatively expensive at present. Allergic reactions to the contrast agent can usually be prevented by giving a standard steroid-diphenhydramine preparation. Alternatively, CT scanning may be done without contrast to determine whether there is a large retroperitoneal hematoma, which would be indirectly suggestive of a ruptured AAA. If the patient has renal insufficiency, MRA may be more appropriate.

MRA

In patients with renal insufficiency who are scheduled for AAA repair, MRA with gadolinium and the breath-hold technique may be the preoperative study of choice; it is comparable to CT scanning in evaluating elective AAA repair candidates [see Figure 7].[86,130] The main advantages of MRA are that (1) it does not require the use of nephrotoxic agents or radiation and (2) it is highly sensitive and specific in detecting stenoses of the splanchnic, renal, and iliac arteries.[85] Its main drawbacks are that (1) it is not widely available, (2) it is expensive, (3) it may cause claustrophobia in select patients, and (4) it takes longer to perform than CT scanning. MRA is contraindicated in patients with pacemakers, metallic foreign bodies in the eye, cochlear implants, and certain berry aneurysm clips. Over time, however, as MRA becomes faster, more widely available, and less expensive, its advantages may make it a more attractive alternative in the preoperative workup of patients with AAAs.

Aortography

Preoperative digital subtraction aortography is not routinely used for diagnosis but rather as an adjunct to other studies in preparation for AAA repair. Being an invasive test, it carries an added risk over other imaging modalities. Aortography is currently indicated in the preoperative evaluation of an AAA when (1) the extent of the aneurysm may include the juxtarenal or suprarenal aorta, (2) the clinical history is indicative of lower-extremity arterial occlusive disease (i.e., claudication or rest pain), (3) renovascular disease may be present, as evidenced by uncontrolled hypertension or azotemia, or (4) the patient has previously undergone arterial reconstruction.[82] Aortography is superior at evaluating the intraluminal characteristics of the aorta, determining visceral-branch involvement, and delineating variations in the vascular anatomy.[11]

Aortography has a number of important limitations in comparison with CT or MRA. In particular, it is associated with multiple risks that are not incurred with CT or MRA, such as infection, arterial thrombosis necessitating emergency thrombectomy and repair, distal embolization, groin hematoma, and local arterial dissection.[131] There is also a 10% risk of renal failure in patients with elevated creatinine levels (≥ 2.5 mg/dl)[131]; this can often be pre-

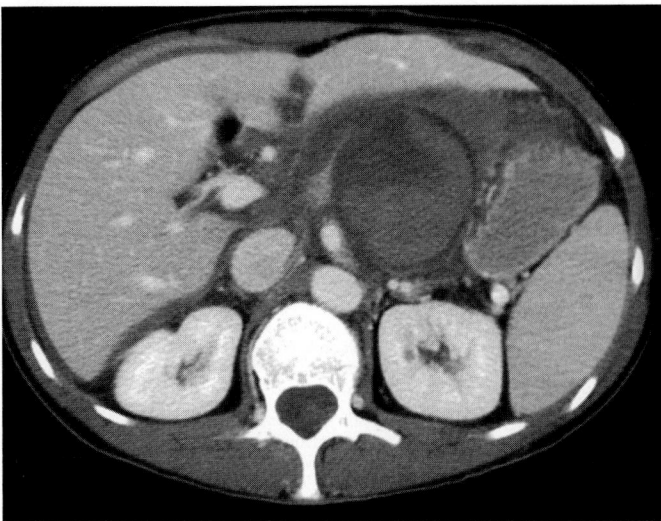

Figure 8 **CT scan of a patient with Marfan syndrome who presented with increasing abdominal pain reveals a large hematoma along the lesser curvature of the stomach. The hematoma was localized via angiography and was found to be consistent with a ruptured left gastric artery aneurysm.**

ic as well. In certain instances, ruptured AAAs may form a continuous luminal connection with a surrounding structure. High-output cardiac failure may result from an arteriovenous shunt between the aorta and the inferior vena cava, which occurs in as many as 2% to 4% of patients with ruptured AAAs.[133,134] AAA patients with intermittent GI bleeding may present with a so-called herald bleed from a primary aortoenteric fistula. Most such fistulas occur in the third or fourth part of the duodenum.[135] Aorta–inferior vena cava shunts and aortoenteric fistulas are medical emergencies that demand immediate operative attention.

AAAs may also give rise to distal lower-extremity atheroemboli [*see 84 Pulseless Extremity and Atheroembolism*]. Small AAAs appear to be the most common sources: infrarenal AAAs with mean diameters of 3.5 cm have been linked to lower-extremity atheroemboli.[136] Thrombosis of an AAA also occurs; if it develops acutely, severe ischemia of the entire lower torso may result, manifested by a bilateral lack of femoral pulses, a drop in skin temperature beginning at the level of the upper thigh, and a change in skin color beginning at the level of the knees.[135] Recognizing these symptoms as potential complications of AAAs can facilitate diagnosis.

vented with adequate hydration before the study. Finally, the cost of aortography is three to four times that of spiral CT, which gives health care providers an incentive to replace aortography with spiral CT whenever possible.[132]

Complications of AAAs

Rupture of an AAA obviously is often life threatening, but erosion of an aneurysm into adjacent structures may be catastroph-

Rare Causes of Pulsatile Abdominal Mass

Finally, when a patient presents with a pulsatile abdominal mass that is suggestive of aneurysmal disease, the most likely diagnosis is an infrarenal AAA, in that 80% of aortic aneurysms are found in this location. It is important to keep in mind, however, that various less common types of aneurysms may also present as a pulsatile abdominal mass, including (but not limited to) iliac artery aneurysms [*see Figure 3*], traumatic pseudoaneurysms, and visceral artery aneurysms [*see Figure 8*].

References

1. Upchurch GR Jr, Wakefield TW, Williams DM, et al: Abdominal aortic aneurysms. Practical Cardiology: Evaluation and Treatment of Common Cardiovascular Disorders. Eagle KA, Baliga RR, Eds. Lippincott Williams & Wilkins, Philadelphia, 2003

2. Hoyert DL, Arias E, Smith BL, et al: National Vital Statistics Reports: Deaths: Final Data for 1999. Division of Vital Statistics, Centers for Disease Control and Prevention. National Center for Health Statistics, vol 49, no 8 (September 21, 2003) http://www.cdc.gov/nchs/data/nvsr49/nvsr49_08.pdf

3. Kochanek KD, Smith BL: National Vital Statistics Reports: Deaths: Preliminary Data for 2002. Division of Vital Statistics, Centers for Disease Control and Prevention. National Center for Health Statistics, vol 52, no 13 (February 11, 2004) http://www.cdc.gov/nchs/data/nvsr52/nvsr52_13.pdf

4. Huber TS, Ozaki CK, Seeger JM: Abdominal aortic aneurysms. Surgery: Scientific Principles and Practice, 3rd ed. Greenfield LJ, Mulholland MW, Oldham KT, et al, Eds. Lippincott Williams & Wilkins, Philadelphia, 2001, p 1803

5. Shames ML, Thompson RW: Abdominal aortic aneurysms: surgical treatment. Cardiol Clin 20:563, 2002

6. Loughran CF: A review of the plain abdominal radiograph in acute rupture of abdominal aortic aneurysms. Clin Radiol 37:383, 1986

7. LaRoy LL, Cormier PJ, Matalon TA, et al: Imaging of abdominal aortic aneurysms. AJR Am J Roentgenol 152:785, 1989

8. Davies AJ, Winter RK, Lewis MH: Prevalence of abdominal aortic aneurysms in urology patients referred for ultrasound. Ann R Coll Surg Engl 81:235, 1999

9. Wakefield TW, Whitehouse WM, Wu S, et al: Abdominal aortic aneurysm rupture: statistical analysis of factors affecting outcome of surgical treatment. Surgery 91:586, 1982

10. Valentine RJ, Barth MJ, Myers SI, et al: Nonvascular emergencies presenting as ruptured abdominal aortic aneurysms. Surgery 113:286, 1993

11. Borrero E, Queral LA: Symptomatic abdominal aortic aneurysms misdiagnosed as nephroureterolithiasis. Ann Vasc Surg 2:145, 1988

12. Hodgson KJ, Webster DJ: Abdominal aortic aneurysm causing duodenal and ureteric obstructions. J Vasc Surg 3:364, 1986

13. Lederle FA, Johnson GR, Wilson SE, et al: The aneurysm detection and management study screening program: validation cohort and final results. Aneurysm Detection and Management

(ADAM) Veterans Affairs Cooperative Study Group. Ann Intern Med 160:1425, 2000

14. Huber TS, Wang JG, Derrow AE, et al: Experience in the United States with intact abdominal aortic aneurysm repair. J Vasc Surg 33:304, 2001

15. Johnston KW and the Canadian Society for Vascular Surgery Aneurysm Study Group: Influence of sex on the results of abdominal aortic aneurysm repair. J Vasc Surg 20:914, 1994

16. Vardulaki KA, Walker NM, Day NE, et al: Quantifying the risks of hypertension, age, sex and smoking in patients with abdominal aortic aneurysm. Br J Surg 87:195, 2000

17. Singh K, Bonaa KH, Jacobsen BK, et al: Prevalence of and risk factors for abdominal aortic aneurysms in a population-based study: the Tromso Study. Am J Epidemiol 154:236, 2001

18. Steckmeier B: Epidemiology of aortic disease: aneurysm, dissection, occlusion. Radiologe 41:624, 2001

19. Darling RC III, Brewster DC, Darling RC, et al: Are familial aortic aneurysms different? J Vasc Surg 10:39, 1989

20. Johansen K, Kopsell T: Familial tendency for abdominal aortic aneurysms. JAMA 256:1934, 1986

21. van Vlijmen-van Keulen CJ, Pals F, Rauwerda JA: Familial abdominal aortic aneurysm: a systematic

review of a genetic background. Eur J Vasc Endovasc Surg 24:105, 2002

22. Kent KC, Zwolak RM, Jaff MR, et al: Screening for abdominal aortic aneurysm: a consensus statement. J Vasc Surg 39:267, 2004

23. Wilmink TB, Quick CR, Day NE: The association between cigarette smoking and abdominal aortic aneurysms. J Vasc Surg 30:1099, 1999

24. Brown LC, Powell JT: Risk factors for aneurysm rupture in patients kept under ultrasound surveillance. U.K. Small Aneurysm Trial Participants. Ann Surg 230:289, 1999

25. Brown PM, Zelt DT, Sobolev B: The risk of rupture in untreated aneurysm: the impact of size, gender, and expansion rate. J Vasc Surg 37:280, 2003

26. Englesbe MJ, Wu AH, Clowes AW, et al: The prevalence and natural history of aortic aneurysms in heart and abdominal organ transplant patients. J Vasc Surg 37:27, 2003

27. Hallett JW Jr, Marshall DM, Petterson TM, et al: Graft-related complications after abdominal aortic aneurysm repair: reassurance from a 36-year population-based experience. J Vasc Surg 25:277, 1997

28. Brunkwall J, Hauksson H, Bengtsson H, et al: Solitary aneurysms of the iliac arterial system: an estimate of their frequency of occurrence. J Vasc Surg 10:381, 1989

29. Bernhard VM, Mitchell RS, Matsumura JS, et al: Ruptured abdominal aortic aneurysm after endovascular repair. J Vasc Surg 35:1155, 2002

30. Faries PL, Brener BJ, Connelly TL, et al: A multicenter experience with the Talent endovascular graft for the treatment of abdominal aortic aneurysms. J Vasc Surg 35:1123, 2002

31. Pearce WH: What's new in vascular surgery. J Am Coll Surg 196:253, 2003

32. Gray H: Anatomy: Descriptive and Surgical, 15th ed. Pick TP, Howden R, Eds. Chancellor Press, London, 1994, p 526

33. Kiev J, Eckhardt A, Kerstein MD: Reliability and accuracy of physical examination in detection of abdominal aortic aneurysms. Vasc Surg 31:143, 1997

34. Lederle FA, Simel DL: Does this patient have abdominal aortic aneurysm? JAMA 281:77, 1999

35. Chervu A, Clagett GP, Valentine RJ, et al: Role of physical examination in detection of abdominal aortic aneurysms. Surgery 117:454, 1995

36. Lederle FA, Walker JM, Reinke DB: Selective screening for abdominal aortic aneurysms with physical examination and ultrasound. Arch Intern Med 148:1753, 1988

37. Fink HA, Lederle FA, Roth CS, et al: The accuracy of physical examination to detect abdominal aortic aneurysm. Arch Intern Med 160:833, 2000

38. Beede SD, Ballard DJ, James EM, et al: Positive predictive value of clinical suspicion of abdominal aortic aneurysm: implication for efficient use of abdominal ultrasonography. Arch Intern Med 150:549, 1990

39. Feinberg RL, Trout HH: Isolated iliac artery aneurysm. Current Therapy in Vascular Surgery, 4th ed. Ernst CB, Stanley JC, Eds. Mosby, St Louis, 2001, p 313

40. Graham LM, Zelenock GB, Whitehouse WM Jr, et al: Clinical significance of arteriosclerotic femoral artery aneurysms. Arch Surg 115:502, 1980

41. Whitehouse WM Jr, Wakefield TW, Graham LM, et al: Limb-threatening potential of arteriosclerotic popliteal artery aneurysms. Surgery 83:694, 1983

42. Diwan A, Sarkar R, Stanley JC, et al: Incidence of femoral and popliteal artery aneurysms in patients with abdominal aortic aneurysms. J Vasc Surg 31:863, 2000

43. Lawrence PF, Wallis C, Dobrin PB, et al: Peripheral aneurysms and arteriomegaly: is there a familial pattern? J Vasc Surg 28:599, 1998

44. Heikkinen M, Salenius J-P, Auvinen O: Ruptured abdominal aortic aneurysm in a well-defined geographic area. J Vasc Surg 36:291, 2002

45. Chew HF, You CK, Brown MG, et al: Mortality, morbidity, and costs of ruptured and elective abdominal aortic aneurysm repairs in Nova Scotia, Canada. Ann Vasc Surg 17:171, 2003

46. Ernst CB: Abdominal aortic aneurysm. N Engl J Med 328:1167, 1993

47. Cowan JA Jr, Dimick JB, Wainess RM, et al: Ruptured thoracoabdominal aortic aneurysm treatment in the United States: 1988 to 1998. J Vasc Surg 38:319, 2003

48. Bown MJ, Sutton AJ, Bell PRF, et al: A meta-analysis of 50 years of ruptured abdominal aortic aneurysm repair. Br J Surg 89:714, 2002

49. Johansen K, Kohler TR, Nicholls SC, et al: Ruptured AAA: the Harborview experience. J Vasc Surg 13:240, 1991

50. Gloviczki P, Pairolero PC, Mucha P Jr, et al: Ruptured abdominal aortic aneurysms: repair should not be denied. J Vasc Surg 15:851, 1992

51. Patel ST, Korn P, Haser PB, et al: The cost-effectiveness of repairing ruptured abdominal aortic aneurysms. J Vasc Surg 32:247, 2000

52. Veith FJ, Ohki T, Lipsitz EC, et al: Treatment of ruptured abdominal aneurysms with stent grafts: a new gold standard? Semin Vasc Surg 16:171, 2003

53. Nowygod R: Ultrasonography and computed tomography in the evaluation of abdominal aortic aneurysm. Current Therapy in Vascular Surgery, 4th ed. Ernst CB, Stanley JC, Eds. Mosby, St Louis, 2001, p 221

54. Jaakkola P, Hippelainen M, Farin P, et al: Interobserver variability in measuring the dimensions of the abdominal aorta: comparison of ultrasound and computed tomography. Eur J Vasc Endovasc Surg 12:230, 1996

55. Sprouse LR 2nd, Meier GH 3rd, Lesar CJ, et al: Comparison of abdominal aortic aneurysm diameter measurements obtained with ultrasound and computed tomography: Is there a difference? J Vasc Surg 38:466, 2003

56. Lederle FA, Wilson SE, Johnson GR, et al: Variability in measurement of abdominal aortic aneurysms. Abdominal Aortic Aneurysm Detection and Management Veterans Administration Cooperative Study Group. J Vasc Surg 21:945, 1995

57. Pedersen OM, Aslaksen A, Vik-Mo H: Ultrasound measurement of the luminal diameter of the abdominal aorta and iliac arteries in patients without vascular disease. J Vasc Surg 17:596, 1993

58. Pearce WH, Slaughter MS, LeMaire S, et al: Aortic diameter as a function of age, gender, and body surface area. Surgery 144:691, 1993

59. Lederle FA, Johnson GR, Wilson SE, et al: Relationship of age, gender, race, and body size to infrarenal aortic diameter. Aneurysm Detection and Management (ADAM) Veterans Administration Cooperative Study Group. J Vasc Surg 26:595, 1997

60. da Silva ES, Rodrigues AJ, Castro de Tolosa EM, et al: Variation of infrarenal aortic diameter: a necropsy study. J Vasc Surg 29:920, 1999

61. d'Audiffret A, Santilli S, Tretinyak A, et al: Fate of the ectatic infrarenal aorta: expansion rates and outcomes. Ann Vasc Surg 16:534, 2002

62. Hollier CH, Stenson AW, Gloviczki P, et al: Arteriomegaly: classification and morbid implications of diffuse aneurismal disease. Surgery 93:700, 1983

63. Lederle FA, Johnson GR, Wilson SE, et al: Yield of repeated screening for abdominal aortic aneurysm after a 4-year interval. Aneurysm Detection and Management Veterans Affairs Cooperative Study Investigation. Arch Intern Med 160:1117, 2000

64. Crow P, Shaw E, Earnshaw JJ, et al: A single normal ultrasonographic scan at age 65 years rules out significant aneurysm disease for life in men. Br J Surg 88:941, 2001

65. Vorp DA, Raghavan ML, Webster MW: Mechanical wall stress in abdominal aortic aneurysm: influence of diameter and asymmetry. J Vasc Surg 27:632, 1998

66. Fillinger MF, Raghavan ML, Marra SP, et al: In vivo analysis of mechanical wall stress and abdominal aortic aneurysm rupture risk. J Vasc Surg 36:589, 2002

67. Fillinger MF, Marra SP, Raghavan ML, et al: Prediction of rupture risk in abdominal aortic aneurysm during observation: wall stress versus diameter. J Vasc Surg 37:724, 2003

68. Brady AR, Brown LC, Fowkes FGR, et al: Long-term outcomes of immediate repair compared with surveillance of small abdominal aortic aneurysms. United Kingdom Small Aneurysm Trial. N Engl J Med 346:1445, 2002

69. Cruz CP, Drouilhet JC, Southern FN, et al: Abdominal aortic aneurysm repair. Vasc Surg 35:335, 2001

70. Lederle FA, Wilson SE, Johnson GR, et al: Immediate repair compared with surveillance of small abdominal aortic aneurysms. Aneurysm Detection and Management Veterans Affairs Cooperative Study Group. N Engl J Med 346:1437, 2002

71. Hertzer NR, Mascha EJ, Karafa MT, et al: Open infrarenal abdominal aortic aneurysm repair: the Cleveland Clinic experience from 1989 to 1998. J Vasc Surg 35:1145, 2002

72. Dimick JB, Stanley JC, Axelrod DA, et al: Variation in death rate after abdominal aortic aneurysmectomy in the United States: impact of hospital volume, gender, and age. Ann Surg 235:579, 2002

73. Birkmeyer JD, Stukey TA, Siewers AE, et al: Surgeon volume and operative mortality in the United States. N Engl J Med 349:2117, 2003

74. Dimick JB, Cowan JA, Stanley JC, et al: Surgeon specialty and provider volumes are related to outcomes of intact abdominal aortic aneurysm repair in the United States. J Vasc Surg 38:739, 2003

75. Cronenwett JL, Murphy TF, Zelenock GB, et al: Actuarial analysis of variables associated with rupture of small abdominal aortic aneurysm. Surgery 98:472, 1985

76. Menard MT, Chew DKW, Chan RK, et al: Outcome in patients at high risk after open surgical repair of abdominal aortic aneurysm. J Vasc Surg 37:285, 2003

77. Biancari F, Mosorin M, Antilla V, et al: Ten-year outcome of patients with very small abdominal aortic aneurysm. Am J Surg 183:53, 2002

78. Powell JT, Greenhalgh RM: Clinical practice. Small abdominal aortic aneurysms. N Engl J Med 348:1895, 2003

79. Santilli SM, Littooy FN, Cambria RA, et al: Expansion rates and outcomes for the 3.0-cm to the 3.9-cm infrarenal abdominal aortic aneurysm. J Vasc Surg 35:666, 2002

80. Chang JB, Stein TA, Liu JP, et al: Risk factors associated with rapid growth of small abdominal aortic aneurysms. Surgery 121:117, 1997

81. Scott RAP, Tisi PV, Ashton HA, et al: Abdominal aortic aneurysm rupture rates: a 7-year follow-up of the entire abdominal aortic aneurysm population detected by screening. J Vasc Surg 28:124, 1998

82. Beebe HG, Kritpracha B: Screening and preoperative imaging of candidates for conventional repair of abdominal aortic aneurysm. Semin Vasc Surg 12:300, 1999

83. Hallett JW Jr: Management of abdominal aortic aneurysms: concise review for clinicians. Mayo

Clin Proc 75:395, 2000

84. Multicentre aneurysm screening study (MASS): cost effectiveness analysis of screening for abdominal aortic aneurysms based on four year results from randomized controlled trial. Multicentre Aneurysm Screening Study Group. BMJ 325: 1135, 2002

85. Wassef M, Baxter T, Chisholm RL, et al: Pathogenesis of abdominal aortic aneurysms: a multidisciplinary research program supported by the National Heart, Lung, and Blood Institute. J Vasc Surg 34:730, 2001

86. Lindholt JS, Vammen S, Fasting H, et al: The plasma level of matrix metalloproteinase 9 may predict the natural history of small abdominal aortic aneurysms: a preliminary study. Eur J Vasc Endovasc Surg 20:281, 2000

87. Baxter BT, Pearce WH, Waltke EA, et al: Prolonged administration of doxycycline in patients with small asymptomatic abdominal aortic aneurysms: report of a prospective (phase II) multicenter study. J Vasc Surg 36:1, 2002

88. Vardulaki KA, Walker NM, Day NE, et al: Quantifying the risks of hypertension, age, sex and smoking in patients with abdominal aortic aneurysm. Br J Surg 87:195, 2000

89. Gadowski GR, Pilcher DB, Ricci MA: Abdominal aortic aneurysm expansion rate: effect of size and beta-adrenergic blockade. J Vasc Surg 19:727, 1994

90. Propranolol for small abdominal aortic aneurysms: results of a randomized trial. Propranolol Aneurysm Trial Investigators. J Vasc Surg 35:72, 2002

91. Wilson KA, Lee AJ, Lee AJ, et al: The relationship between aortic wall distensibility and rupture of infrarenal abdominal aortic aneurysm. J Vasc Surg 37:112, 2003

92. Grange JJ, Davis V, Baxter BT: Pathogenesis of abdominal aortic aneurysm: an update and look toward the future. Cardiovasc Surg 5:256, 1997

93. Schillinger M, Domanovits H, Ignatescu M, et al: Lipoprotein (a) in patients with aortic aneurismal disease. J Vasc Surg 36:25, 2002

94. Keen RR, McCarthy WJ, Shireman PK, et al: Surgical management of atheroembolization. J Vasc Surg 21:773, 1995

95. Simoni G, Gianotti A, Ardia A, et al: Screening study of abdominal aortic aneurysm in a general population: lipid parameters. Cardiovasc Surg 4:445, 1996

96. Lindholdt JS, Heegaard NH, Vammen S, et al: Smoking, but not lipids, lipoprotein(a) and antibodies against oxidized LDL, is correlated to the expansion of abdominal aortic aneurysms. Eur J Vasc Endovasc Surg 21:51, 2001

97. Zarins CK, Xu CP, Glasgov S: Aneurysmal enlargement of the aorta during regression of experimental atherosclerosis. J Vasc Surg 15:90, 1992

98. Nagashima H, Aoka Y, Sakomura Y, et al: A 3-hydroxy-3-methylglutaryl coenzyme A reductase inhibitor, cerviastatin, suppresses production of matrix metalloproteinase-9 in human abdominal aortic aneurysm wall. J Vasc Surg 36:158, 2002

99. Warsi AA, Davies B, Morris-Stiff G, et al: Abdominal aortic aneurysm and its correlation to plasma homocysteine, and vitamins. Eur J Vasc Endovasc Surg 27:75, 2004

100. Rasmussen TE, Hallett JW Jr, Tazelaar HD, et al: Human leukocyte antigen class II immune response genes, female gender, and cigarette smoking as risk and modulating factors in abdominal aortic aneurysms. J Vasc Surg 35:988, 2002

101. Hertzer NR, Beven EG, Young JR, et al: Coronary artery disease in peripheral vascular patients: a classification of 1000 coronary angiograms and

results of surgical management. Ann Surg 199:223, 1984

102. Kertai MD, Boersma E, Westerhout CM, et al: Association between long-term statin use and mortality after successful abdominal aortic aneurysm surgery. Am J Med 116:296, 2004

103. Sheeman WP: Suspected leaking abdominal aortic aneurysm: use of sonography in the emergency room. Radiology 168:117, 1988

104. Sullivan CA, Rohrer MJ, Cutler BS: Clinical management of the symptomatic but unruptured abdominal aortic aneurysm. Surgery 11:799, 1990

105. Roger VL, Ballard DJ, Hallett JW, et al: Influence of coronary artery disease on morbidity and mortality after abdominal aortic aneurysmectomy: a population-based study 1971–1987. J Am Coll Cardiol 14:1245, 1989

106. Eagle KA, Brundage BH, Chaitman BR, et al: Guidelines for perioperative cardiovascular evaluation for noncardiac surgery: report of the American College of Cardiology/American Heart Association Task Force on Practice Guidelines (Committee on Perioperative Cardiovascular Evaluation for Noncardiac Surgery). J Am Coll Cardiol 27:910, 1996

107. Froehlich JB, Karavite D, Russman PL, et al: American College of Cardiology/American Heart Association preoperative assessment guidelines reduce resource utilization before aortic surgery. J Vasc Surg 36:758, 2002

108. Samain E, Farah E, Leseche G, et al: Guidelines for perioperative cardiac evaluation from the American College of Cardiology/American Heart Association task force are effective for stratifying cardiac risk before aortic surgery. J Vasc Surg 31:971, 2000

109. Bartels C, Bechtel JFM, Hossmann V, et al: Cardiac risk stratification for high-risk vascular surgery. Circulation 95:2473, 1997

110. Eagle KA, Berger PB, Hugh C, et al: ACC/AHA guideline update for perioperative cardiovascular evaluation for noncardiac surgery: executive summary: a report of the American College of Cardiology/American Heart Association Task Force on Practice Guidelines (Committee to update the 1996 Guidelines on Perioperative Cardiovascular Evaluation for Noncardiac Surgery). Circulation 105:1257, 2002

111. Falk V, Walther T, Mohr FW: Abdominal aortic aneurysm repair during cardiopulmonary bypass: rationale for a combined approach. Cardiovasc Surg 5:271, 1997

112. Morimoto K, Taniguchi I, Miyasaka S, et al: Usefulness of one-stage coronary artery bypass grafting on the beating heart and abdominal aortic aneurysm repair. Ann Thorac Cardiovasc Surg 10:29, 2004

113. Posner KL, Van Norman GA, Chan V, et al: Adverse cardiac outcomes after noncardiac surgery in patients with prior percutaneous transluminal coronary angioplasty. Anesth Analg 89:553, 1999

114. Back MR, Stordahl N, Cuthbertson D, et al: Limitations in the cardiac risk reduction provided by coronary revascularization prior to elective vascular surgery. J Vasc Surg 36:526, 2002

115. Smith SC Jr, Dove JT, Jacobs AK, et al: ACC/AHA guidelines for percutaneous coronary intervention: executive summary and recommendations: a report of the American College of Cardiology/American Heart Association Task Force on Practice Guidelines Committee to Revise the 1993 Guidelines for Percutaneous Transluminal Coronary Angioplasty. J Am Coll Cardiol 37:2215, 2001

116. Johnston KW: Multicenter prospective study of nonruptured abdominal aortic aneurysm: part II. Variables predicting morbidity and mortality. J Vasc Surg 9:437, 1989

117. Axelrod DA, Henke PK, Wakefield TW, et al: Impact of chronic obstructive pulmonary disease on elective and emergency abdominal aortic aneurysm repair. J Vasc Surg 33:72, 2001

118. Upchurch GR Jr, Proctor MC, Henke PK, et al: Predictors of severe morbidity and death after elective abdominal aortic aneurysmectomy in patients with chronic obstructive pulmonary disease. J Vasc Surg 37:594, 2003

119. Berry AJ, Smith RB III, Wintraub WS, et al: Age versus comorbidities as risk factors for complications after elective abdominal aortic reconstructive surgery. J Vasc Surg 33:345, 2001

120. Dardik A, Lin JW, Gordon TA, et al: Results of elective abdominal aortic aneurysm repair in the 1990's: a population based analysis of 2335 cases. J Vasc Surg 30:985, 1999

121. Treiman GS, Treiman RI, Foran RF, et al: The influence of diabetes mellitus on the risk of abdominal aortic surgery. Am Surg 60:436, 1994

122. Axelrod DA, Upchurch GR Jr, DeMonner S, et al: Perioperative cardiovascular risk stratification of patients with diabetes who undergo elective major vascular surgery. J Vasc Surg 35:894, 2002

123. Fleisher LA, Eagle KA: Lowering cardiac risk in noncardiac surgery. N Engl J Med 345:1677, 2001

124. Auerbach AD, Goldman L: β-Blockers and reduction of cardiac events in noncardiac surgery: scientific review. JAMA 287:1435, 2002

125. Oliver MF, Goldman L, Julian DG, et al: Effect of mivazerol on perioperative cardiac complication during non-cardiac surgery in patients with coronary heart disease: the European Mivazerol Trial (EMIT). Anesthesiology 91:951, 1999

126. Willard JE, Lange RA, Hillis LD: The use of aspirin in ischemic heart disease. N Engl J Med 327:175, 1992

127. Ehlers R, Eagle KA: Lowering cardiac risk in noncardiac surgery (letter). N Engl J Med 346:1096, 2002

128. Cronenwett JL, Krupski WC, Rutherford RB: Abdominal aortic and iliac aneurysms. Vascular Surgery, 5th ed. Rutherford RB, Ed. WB Saunders Co, Philadelphia, 2000, p 1246

129. Geller SC, Society of Interventional Radiology Device Forum: Imaging guidelines for abdominal aortic aneurysm repair with endovascular stent grafts. J Vasc Interv Radiol 14:S263, 2003

130. Petersen MJ, Cambria RP, Kaugman JA, et al: Magnetic resonance angiography in the preoperative evaluation of abdominal aortic aneurysms. J Vasc Surg 21:891, 1995

131. Baker KD, Bandyk DF, Back MR: Arteriography in the evaluation of abdominal aortic aneurysm. Current Therapy in Vascular Surgery, 4th ed. Ernst CB, Stanley JC, Eds. Mosby, St Louis, 2001, p 215

132. Rubin GD, Armerding MD, Dake MD, et al: Cost identification of abdominal aortic aneurysm imaging by using time and motion analyses. Radiology 215:63, 2000

133. Duong C, Atkinson N: Review of aortoiliac aneurysms with spontaneous large vein fistula. Aust N Z J Surg 71:52, 2001

134. Rajmohan B: Spontaneous aortocaval fistula. J Postgrad Med 48:203, 2002

135. Connolly JE, Kwaan JH, McCart PM, et al: Aortoenteric fistula. Ann Surg 194:402, 1981

136. Messina LM, Sarkar R: Peripheral arterial embolism. Surgery: Scientific Principles and Practice, 3rd ed. Greenfield LJ, Mulholland MW, Oldham KT, et al, Eds. Lippincott Williams & Wilkins, Philadelphia, 2001, p 1568

137. Fletcher GF, Baledy G, Froelicher VF, et al: Exercise standards: a statement for healthcare professionals from the American Heart Association. Circulation 91:580, 1995

Melina R. Kibbe, M.D., and Heitham T. Hassoun, M.D.

Diagnosis and Management of Acute Bowel Ischemia

Acute mesenteric ischemia is an uncommon life-threatening clinical entity that ultimately leads to death unless it is diagnosed and treated appropriately. Despite diagnostic and therapeutic advances and an improved understanding of the pathophysiology, the morbidity and mortality associated with acute mesenteric ischemia remain high, having changed relatively little over the past several decades. Accordingly, the index of suspicion for this disease should be high whenever a patient presents with acute-onset severe abdominal pain that is out of proportion to the physical findings. Once the diagnosis is made, prompt intervention is required to minimize morbidity and mortality.

Acute mesenteric ischemia can result from any of four distinct processes: (1) embolic occlusion of the mesenteric circulation (usually the superior mesenteric artery [SMA]); (2) acute thrombosis of the mesenteric circulation; (3) intense splanchnic vasoconstriction—so-called nonocclusive mesenteric ischemia (NOMI)—which is usually associated with a low-flow state or profound hypovolemia; or (4) mesenteric venous thrombosis (MVT).

Clinical Evaluation

HISTORY AND PHYSICAL EXAMINATION

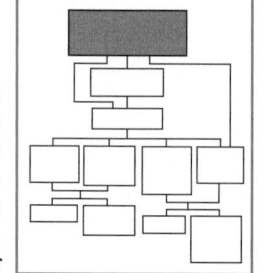

The classic presentation for patients with embolic disease of the mesenteric vessels is sudden-onset midabdominal pain that is described as being out of proportion to the physical findings and is associated with immediate bowel evacuation. In fact, only about one third of patients present with the triad of abdominal pain, fever, and heme-positive stools. A study that considered all causes of acute mesenteric ischemia found that 95% of patients presented with abdominal pain, 44% with nausea, 35% with vomiting, and 35% with diarrhea[1]; only 16% presented with blood per rectum.

Patients with thrombotic mesenteric occlusion also present with sudden-onset severe midabdominal pain that is out of proportion to the physical findings, but unlike patients with acute embolic occlusion, they typically have a history of chronic postprandial abdominal pain and significant weight loss.

Patients with NOMI present somewhat differently. The pain reported is usually not as sudden as that noted with embolic or thrombotic occlusion: it is generally more diffuse and tends to wax and wane (unlike the pain associated with embolic or thrombotic disease, which tends to get progressively worse).

Patients with MVT often present with various nonspecific abdominal complaints; accordingly, this diagnosis may be especially challenging. Common complaints include nausea, vomiting, diarrhea, abdominal cramping, and nonlocalized abdominal pain. As a rule, these symptoms are not acute. A study of MVT patients found that 84% presented with abdominal pain.[2] Of those 84%, only 16% presented with peritoneal signs, whereas

68% presented with vague abdominal pain. Other presenting symptoms included diarrhea (42%), nausea and vomiting (32%), malaise (16%), and upper GI bleeding (10%).[2]

In addition to the clinical presentation, risk factors provide essential clues for correct identification of these disease processes. Certain general risk factors for acute mesenteric ischemia have been identified. In one study, 78% of the patients presented with a history of hypertension, 71% with a history of tobacco use, 62% with a history of peripheral vascular disease, and 50% with a history of coronary artery disease (CAD).[1]

There are also more specific risk factors for individual causes of acute mesenteric ischemia. Patients with embolic occlusion of the mesenteric circulation typically have a history of recent cardiac events (e.g., myocardial infarction, atrial fibrillation, mural thrombus, mitral valve disease, or left ventricular aneurysm) or previous embolic disease. In the study just cited, 50% of the patients who presented with embolic occlusive disease had atrial fibrillation.[1] Patients with acute mesenteric ischemia secondary to thrombotic occlusive disease typically have other manifestations of diffuse atherosclerotic disease (e.g., CAD, peripheral artery disease, and carotid stenosis). The risk factors for NOMI are slightly different. This condition usually occurs during severe low-flow states and represents extreme mesenteric vasoconstriction. It is much more common among severely ill patients in an intensive care unit who require vasopressors and among patients undergoing dialysis with excessive fluid removal. The risk factors for MVT include a history of previous venous thrombosis or pulmonary embolism, a known or suspected hypercoagulable state, oral contraception, and estrogen supplementation. In a study of 31 patients who presented with MVT at Northwestern University, 13 (42%) were diagnosed with a hypercoagulable state, six (19%) had a history of previous thrombotic episodes, and four (13%) had a history of cancer.[2]

Investigative Studies

Although there are no basic laboratory or radiographic studies that are diagnostic for acute mesenteric ischemia, such studies can help confirm the diagnosis when it is suspected on the basis of the history and the physical examination.

LABORATORY TESTS

In most cases, the white blood cell count is elevated. In a study from the Mayo Clinic, 98% of patients who presented with acute mesenteric ischemia were found to have an elevation of the leukocyte count, and 50% were found to have counts higher than 20,000/mm[3].[1] Lactate is another nonspecific indicator of mesenteric bowel ischemia. In the same Mayo Clinic study, approximately 91% of patients had elevated lactate levels, with 61% having levels higher than 3 mmol/L.[1] In addition, 71% of patients presented with an elevated AST, whereas 52% presented with an abnormal base deficit.[1]

Diagnosis and Management of Acute Bowel Ischemia

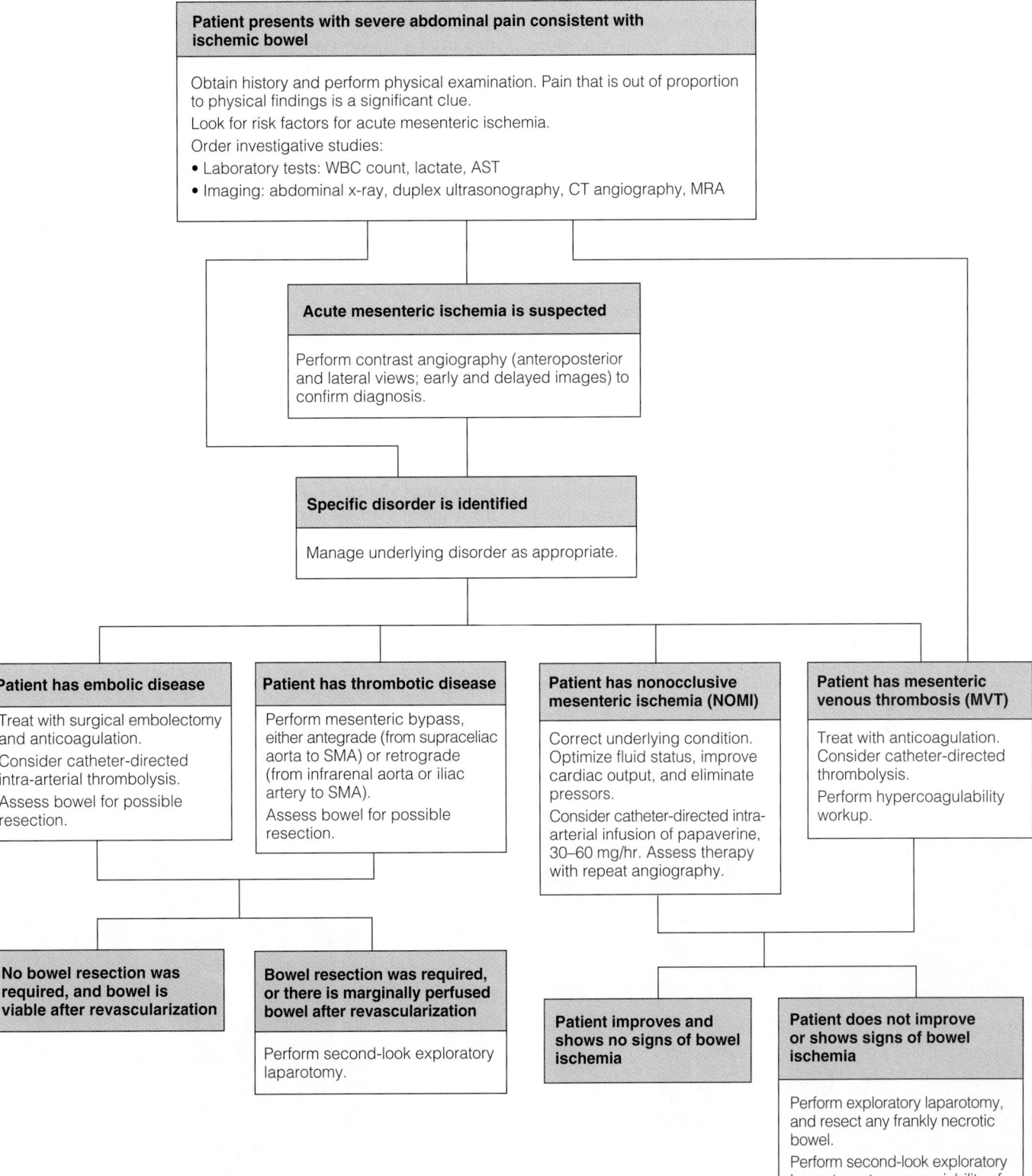

Patient presents with severe abdominal pain consistent with ischemic bowel

Obtain history and perform physical examination. Pain that is out of proportion to physical findings is a significant clue.
Look for risk factors for acute mesenteric ischemia.
Order investigative studies:
- Laboratory tests: WBC count, lactate, AST
- Imaging: abdominal x-ray, duplex ultrasonography, CT angiography, MRA

Acute mesenteric ischemia is suspected

Perform contrast angiography (anteroposterior and lateral views; early and delayed images) to confirm diagnosis.

Specific disorder is identified

Manage underlying disorder as appropriate.

Patient has embolic disease

Treat with surgical embolectomy and anticoagulation.
Consider catheter-directed intra-arterial thrombolysis.
Assess bowel for possible resection.

Patient has thrombotic disease

Perform mesenteric bypass, either antegrade (from supraceliac aorta to SMA) or retrograde (from infrarenal aorta or iliac artery to SMA).
Assess bowel for possible resection.

Patient has nonocclusive mesenteric ischemia (NOMI)

Correct underlying condition. Optimize fluid status, improve cardiac output, and eliminate pressors.
Consider catheter-directed intra-arterial infusion of papaverine, 30–60 mg/hr. Assess therapy with repeat angiography.

Patient has mesenteric venous thrombosis (MVT)

Treat with anticoagulation.
Consider catheter-directed thrombolysis.
Perform hypercoagulability workup.

No bowel resection was required, and bowel is viable after revascularization

Bowel resection was required, or there is marginally perfused bowel after revascularization

Perform second-look exploratory laparotomy.

Patient improves and shows no signs of bowel ischemia

Patient does not improve or shows signs of bowel ischemia

Perform exploratory laparotomy, and resect any frankly necrotic bowel.
Perform second-look exploratory laparotomy to assess viability of any marginally perfused bowel.

1017

IMAGING

Abdominal X-rays

Although abdominal radiographic films can neither establish nor exclude the diagnosis of acute mesenteric ischemia, they may reveal signs that are consistent with bowel ischemia. If obtained early, abdominal plain films should show no abnormalities. If obtained late in the presentation, however, they may reveal edematous bowel with thumbprinting. In severe cases, abdominal plain films may reveal gas in the bowel wall and the portal vein. More commonly, however, they reveal a pattern consistent with ileus or are completely unremarkable. In a study of patients operated on for acute mesenteric ischemia, mortality was 29% in patients with normal plain radiographic films, compared with 78% in those with abnormal films.[3] Nevertheless, it must be emphasized that the primary role of abdominal plain radiographic films in this setting is to exclude other identifiable causes of abdominal pain (e.g., obstruction and perforation with free air).

Duplex Ultrasonography

Duplex ultrasonography plays only a limited role in the management of acute mesenteric ischemia—not surprisingly, given the acute nature of the presentation, the accompanying ileus with excessive bowel gas and bowel edema (which hinders visualization of the mesenteric vessels), and the reduced access to the vascular laboratory during off hours. Furthermore, duplex ultrasonography, though capable of imaging stenotic and occlusive lesions at the origin of a mesenteric vessel, is of no value in detecting emboli beyond the proximal portion of the vessel. Similarly, it has no role in the diagnosis of NOMI.

Duplex ultrasonography does have a definite and well-defined role in the diagnosis of chronic mesenteric ischemia. Well-accepted published criteria exist for the diagnosis of celiac artery and SMA stenosis on the basis of velocity measurements.[4] In the diagnosis of acute mesenteric ischemia, however, where the primary goal is to determine whether there is an acute occlusion of the celiac artery or the SMA, the aforementioned technical limitations of this diagnostic modality limit its application.

CT Angiography

Computed tomographic angiography and magnetic resonance angiography (MRA) are more commonly used to confirm the diagnosis of acute mesenteric ischemia than duplex ultrasonography is. Both CT and MRA have undergone significant advances over the past decade. Traditional CT scanning can evaluate arterial patency and anatomy and detect calcifications and aneurysms. In addition, it can evaluate the status of the bowel and help identify other causes of abdominal pain (e.g., pancreatitis, bowel perforation, and bowel obstruction). However, it was not until the advent of helical (spiral) CT scanning—and, subsequently, of multislice, multiarray helical CT scan technology with maximum-intensity projection—that the visceral arterial anatomy could be visualized with three-dimensional spatial resolution [*see Figure 1*]. This technology allows much more rapid acquisition of data and thereby improves the quality of vascular imaging tremendously. A study comparing spiral CT angiography with conventional contrast angiography found that the former had a sensitivity of 75% and a specificity of 100% for the detection of greater than 75% stenosis of the celiac artery.[5] Furthermore, spiral CT angiography had a sensitivity of 100% and a specificity of 91% for the detection of SMA stenosis.

Although CT technology has become much more sophisticated and the image clarity and definition have improved greatly, there are still limits to what can be determined by means of CT in the setting of acute embolic or thrombotic disease. The origins of the celiac artery and the SMA are well visualized with CT, but secondary, tertiary, and smaller branches are less well defined; for visualizing these branches, contrast angiography remains the gold standard [*see* Contrast Angiography, *below*]. Another limitation of current CT scanning technology is the need to administer intravenous contrast agents, which can be nephrotoxic or, in some patients, trigger contrast allergies. CT angiography also tends to overestimate the degree of critical stenosis when compared with conventional angiography; however, this limitation appears to be less of an issue with the advent of multiarray or multidetector technology, which is more sensitive in detecting arterial stenosis. Finally, significant calcification at the origin of the vessel can make it difficult to determine the true degree of stenosis with CT scanning.

In contrast to its relatively limited role in the diagnosis of acute mesenteric ischemia of embolic or thrombotic origin, CT plays a valuable role in diagnosing MVT and is the preferred diagnostic imaging modality in patients presenting with abdominal pain who have a history of deep vein thrombosis (DVT) or a known hypercoagulable disorder.[6] CT scanning can readily reveal thrombosis

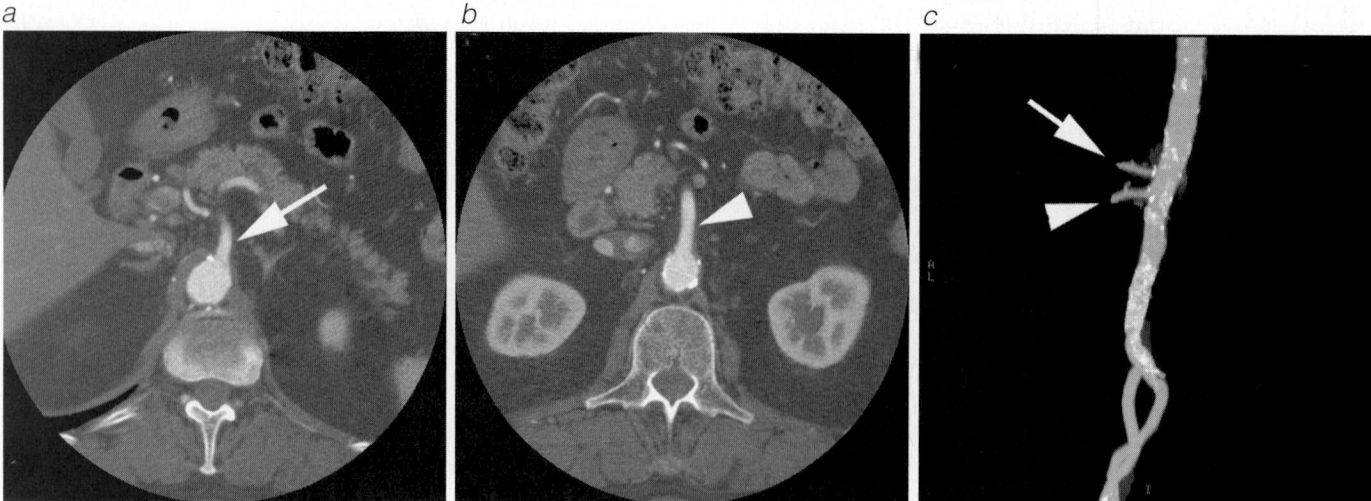

Figure 1 Shown are CT scans of mesenteric vessels: (*a*) transaxial image of celiac artery (arrow); (*b*) transaxial image of SMA (arrowhead); and (*c*) three-dimensional reconstruction of aorta and origins of celiac artery (arrow) and SMA (arrowhead).

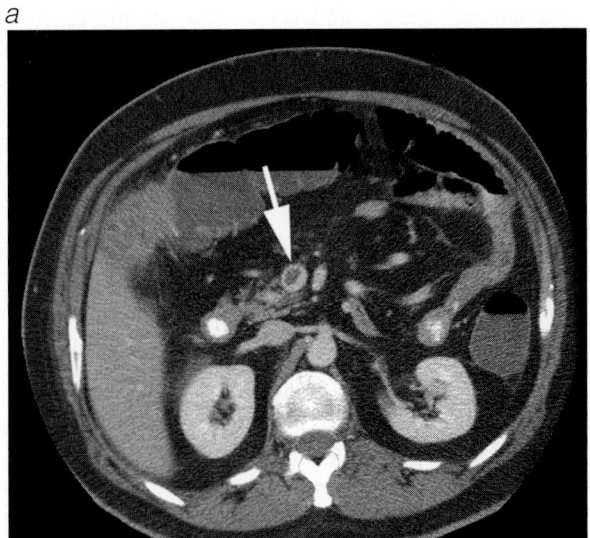
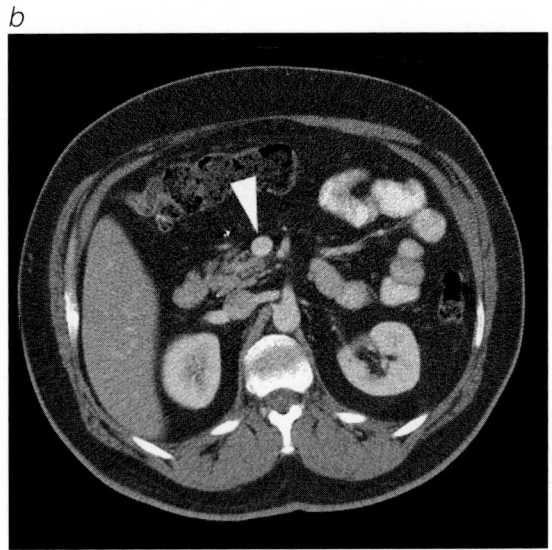

Figure 2 (*a*) CT scan shows partially occluding thrombus in SMV (arrow). (*b*) CT scan obtained 4 months later reveals complete resolution of thrombus (arrowhead).

of the superior mesenteric vein (SMV), with or without associated bowel abnormalities [*see Figure 2*]. In fact, CT scans of SMV thrombosis in asymptomatic patients have provided useful information on the pathophysiology of MVT and broadened our understanding of the wide spectrum of this disease entity. In a study from the Mayo Clinic, CT scanning correctly identified 100% of patients who presented with acute MVT and 93% of those who presented with chronic venous thrombosis.[7] In a subsequent study from our institution (Northwestern University), CT scanning identified 100% of MVT patients who presented with vague abdominal pain or diarrhea and 90% of MVT patients who underwent a CT scan.[2] In contrast, conventional angiography correctly diagnosed MVT in only five of nine patients.[2]

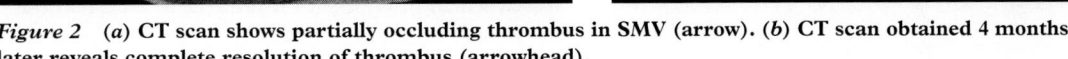

Figure 3 Shown are contrast-enhanced three-dimensional MRAs of aorta and mesenteric vessels. (*a*) Anterior projection shows celiac artery (arrow) and SMA (arrowhead). (*b*) Lateral projection shows celiac artery (arrow) and SMA (arrowhead).

Magnetic Resonance Angiography

Advances in magnetic resonance technology—in particular, the development of contrast-enhanced three-dimensional MRA—have made MRA imaging of visceral vessels much more practical than was once the case. Fast imaging techniques using I.V. administration of gadolinium over a single breath-hold can provide high-quality three-dimensional images [*see Figure 3*] in axial, sagittal, or oblique planes. An advantage MRA has over CT angiography is that gadolinium is significantly less nephrotoxic than the contrast agents used for CT scans. Like CT angiography, however, MRA does not adequately assess the distal branches of the mesenteric vessels. One study compared contrast-enhanced breath-hold MRA with conventional digital subtraction angiography in 33 patients.[8] There was excellent agreement between the two studies for the celiac artery and the SMA; however, there was poor agreement for the distal branches of the SMA, as well as for the intrahepatic branches of the hepatic artery.

Given the current state of imaging technology, it is possible to confirm the diagnosis of acute mesenteric ischemia with either CT angiography or MRA. If the cause of the ischemia is confirmed—and, in the case of SMA thrombosis, if distal targets are identified for revascularization—it is conceivable that the patient could be explored in the OR without undergoing conventional angiography. Many institutions, however, do not have ready access to all the latest imaging technology. In such situations, the best imaging modality for evaluation of the mesenteric vasculature remains contrast angiography.

Contrast Angiography

Contrast angiography has long been considered the gold standard for imaging the visceral vessels. This modality can visualize the aorta and the main trunks of the mesenteric vessels and can adequately assess several orders of distal branches. The images obtained with contrast angiography are superior to those obtained with CT angiography or

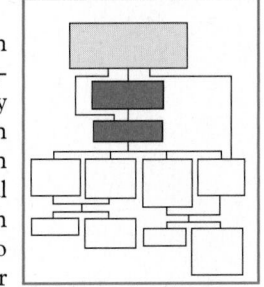

MRA. The procedure is performed in a transfemoral manner by means of the Seldinger technique, with infusion of approximately 60 to 100 ml of contrast material. Arteriography should include

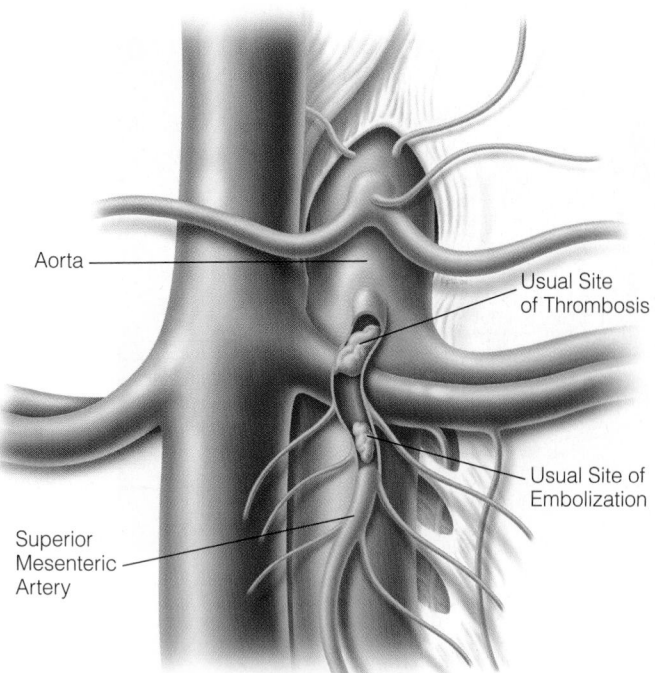

Figure 4 **Schematic drawing demonstrates usual site for SMA thrombosis versus that for SMA embolus.**

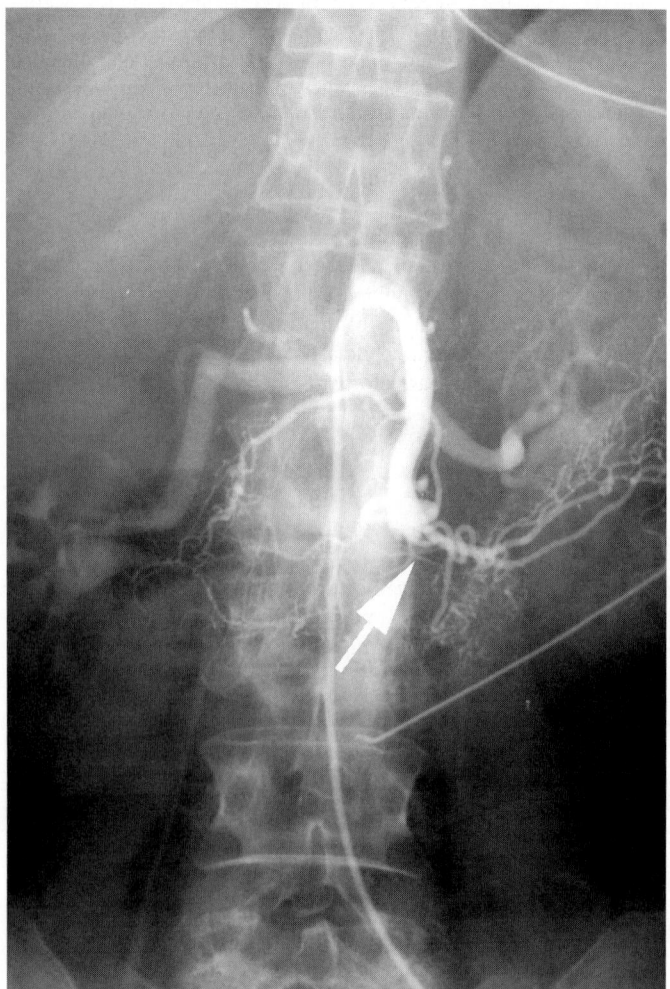

Figure 5 **Selective angiogram of SMA in anterior projection demonstrates embolus within vessel (arrow) at typical location.**

both anteroposterior and lateral views of the celiac artery, the SMA, and the inferior mesenteric artery (IMA). The origins of the celiac artery and the SMA are best seen on the lateral view, whereas the middle and distal SMA and the IMA are best seen on the anteroposterior view. Delayed views are useful in evaluating a patient for NOMI.

There are classic angiographic patterns that serve to distinguish mesenteric ischemia of embolic origin from that of thrombotic origin [*see Figure 4*]. Of the three mesenteric vessels, the SMA is most likely to be the site of embolic lodgment because it takes off from the main axis of the aorta at a less sharp angle than the celiac artery and the IMA, which arise from the aorta more perpendicularly. When emboli lodge in the SMA, they usually lodge distal to the middle colic branch and the jejunal branch [*see Figure 5*]. In thrombotic disease, the thrombus usually forms at the atherosclerotic plaque, which, for most patients, is usually at the origin of the mesenteric vessel. Consequently, the angiogram typically demonstrates complete absence of flow in the mesenteric vessel, which often makes it difficult to ascertain the location of the vessel's origin [*see Figure 6*].

Patients with NOMI typically exhibit angiographic evidence of SMA vasospasm. A small SMA trunk is visualized, with very few branching vessels visible, and the branches that are visualized show a characteristic tapering of the vessel to the point of occlusion [*see Figure 7a*]. These patterns are best seen on the anteroposterior projection.

Angiography is less useful for the diagnosis of MVT. Typically, MVT is diagnosed on the venous phase of the selective arterial contrast injection; however, as noted [*see CT Angiography, above*], conventional angiography is less sensitive and specific for MVT than the diagnostic imaging modality of choice—namely, CT.

Besides providing superior image quality, contrast angiography enables the surgeon to perform selective injection of any of the mesenteric vessels and to perform therapeutic intervention. In patients with NOMI, for example, the SMA may be selectively catheterized and papaverine infused directly into the vessel [*see Figure 7b*]. In a stable patient with acute mesenteric ischemia from a partially occluding embolus but no peritoneal signs, selective catheterization of the SMA allows the institution of catheter-directed intra-arterial thrombolytic therapy [*see Figure 8*]. Thus, contrast angiography not only represents the gold standard for diagnostic imaging but also provides important therapeutic options.

Management

TREATMENT OF SPECIFIC DISORDERS

Embolic Occlusion of Mesenteric Vessels

The goals in the surgical treatment of acute mesenteric ischemia are (1) to restore normal pulsatile flow to the SMA and (2) to resect any nonviable intestine. In general, revascularization

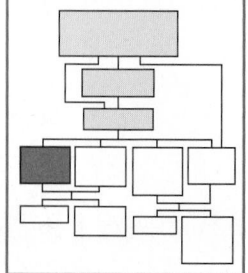

precedes resection. The therapeutic approach varies, depending on the specific underlying cause. For embolic disease of the SMA, the standard treatment is surgical embolectomy; this procedure is described in more detail elsewhere [*see 93 Mesenteric Revascularization Procedures*].

Percutaneous interventional treatment of acute SMA occlusion has also been described in the literature. At present, however, the applicability of this approach is limited, in that most patients present with symptoms that warrant an exploratory laparotomy for evaluation of intestinal viability. In patients who present with abdominal pain, have no peritoneal signs that would necessitate an exploratory laparotomy, and are found to have a partially occluding embolus in the SMA, catheter-directed intra-arterial thrombolytic therapy is worth considering. We have treated such patients in this manner at our institution. This route should be used cautiously, however, and if intra-arterial thrombolytic therapy is instituted, the patient should be closely monitored in the ICU with serial abdominal examinations. Even if thrombolytic therapy does restore blood flow to the ischemic intestine, the patient may still experience pain sufficient to necessitate exploration. For these reasons, our use of thrombolytic therapy is highly selective.

Thrombotic Occlusion of Mesenteric Vessels

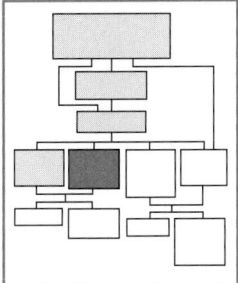

Acute mesenteric ischemia secondary to thrombotic disease occurs in patients with long-standing atherosclerotic disease of the mesenteric vessels. In this situation, the entire midgut is usually involved. Surgical treatment consists of a bypass procedure [see 93 Mesenteric Revascularization Procedures], which may be done in either an antegrade or a retrograde manner. The conduit of choice is a reversed autologous greater saphenous vein graft. Synthetic graft material should be avoided in the setting of acute bowel ischemia, given the high risk of transmural bowel infarction and perforation.

There are several different inflow options for revascularizing the SMA that must be considered carefully. The main choices for inflow are the supraceliac aorta, the infrarenal aorta, and the iliac artery. In cases of acute mesenteric ischemia where time is of the essence and prompt revascularization of the bowel is required, it is often easier to perform a retrograde bypass from the infrarenal aorta or iliac artery, in that the exposure is relatively simple and readily familiar to all vascular surgeons. Furthermore, a retrograde bypass yields less hemodynamic compromise because it avoids supraceliac clamping and the associated mesenteric and renal ischemia. Accordingly, retrograde bypass is the preferred approach in our institution. In cases of acute mesenteric ischemia where the suprarenal aorta is easily approachable and not calcified, however, an antegrade vein graft from the suprarenal aorta to the SMA will lie better because it is less susceptible to kinking than a retrograde graft once the bowel is restored to its correct anatomic position.

Nonocclusive Mesenteric Ischemia

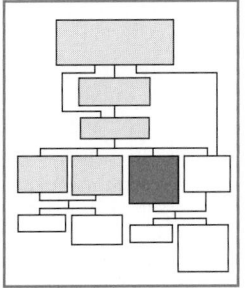

Management of NOMI is largely nonoperative. Once the diagnosis has been established with angiography [see Figure 7], treatment of the underlying precipitating cause is the key therapeutic intervention. Optimization of fluid resuscitation, improvement of cardiac output, and elimination of vasopressors are the measures that have the greatest impact on outcome. Selective catheterization of the SMA with direct intra-arterial infusion of papaverine (30 to 60 mg/hr) may be employed as adjunctive therapy. The infusion is continued for at least 24 hours, with repeat angiography performed at regular intervals to determine the effectiveness of this therapy.

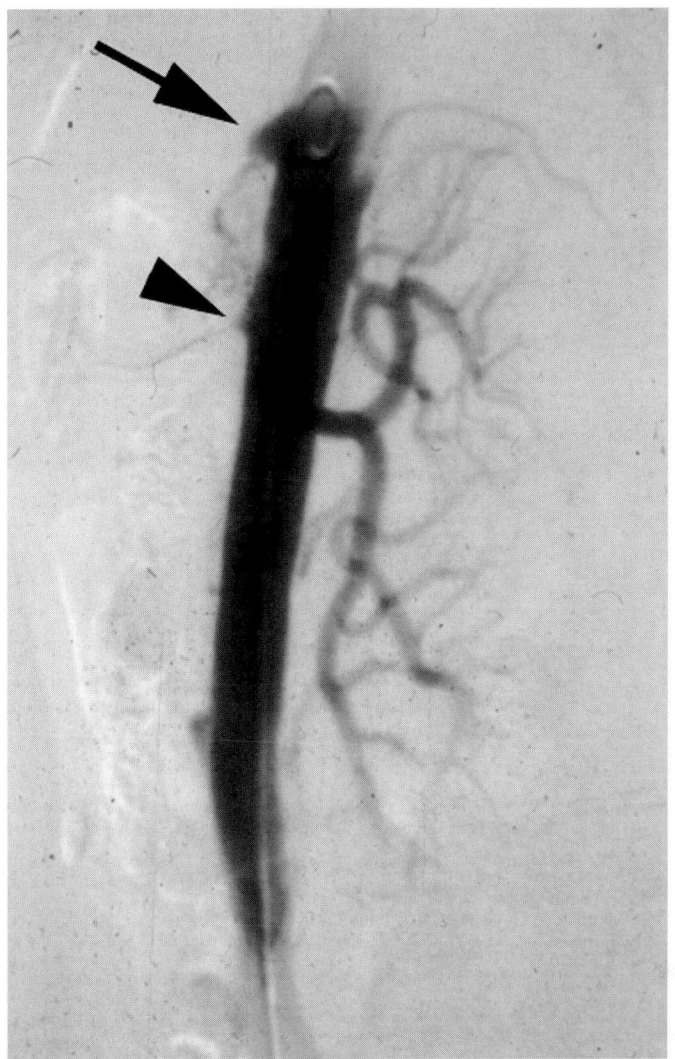

Figure 6 Lateral contrast angiogram of aorta demonstrates complete occlusion of both celiac artery (arrow) and SMA (arrowhead) at their origins, consistent with in situ thrombosis. Lack of collaterals suggests an acute process.

If the patient presents with peritoneal signs on physical examination, an exploratory laparotomy will be required for resection of frankly necrotic or gangrenous bowel. If an intra-arterial infusion of papaverine has been initiated, it should be continued throughout the exploratory laparotomy. Given the known propensity of this disease process for waxing and waning, a second-look laparotomy is also imperative [see Second-Look Laparotomy, below].

Mesenteric Venous Thrombosis

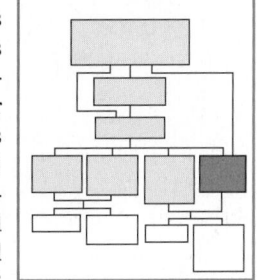

Once mesenteric venous thrombosis is diagnosed, the mainstay of therapy is anticoagulation. If the patient's condition does not improve or worsens after anticoagulation or if signs or symptoms of bowel ischemia (e.g., peritonitis) develop, abdominal exploration is warranted. Typically, the bowel is dusky and edematous. All frankly necrotic bowel should be resected. Within 24 to 48 hours, a second-look laparotomy should be done to evaluate the viability of any marginally perfused bowel [see Second-Look

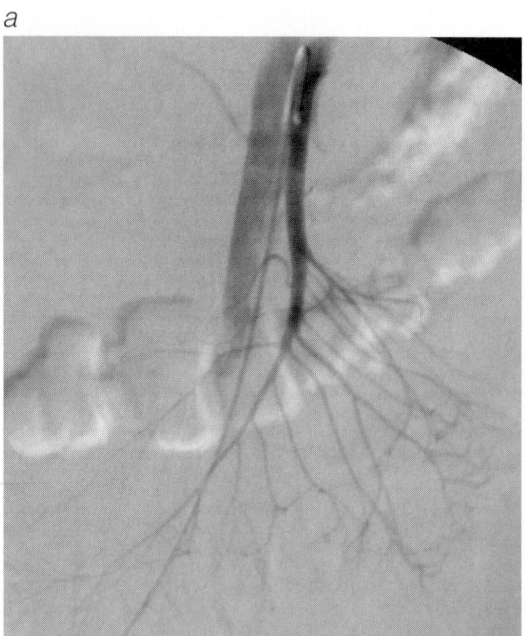
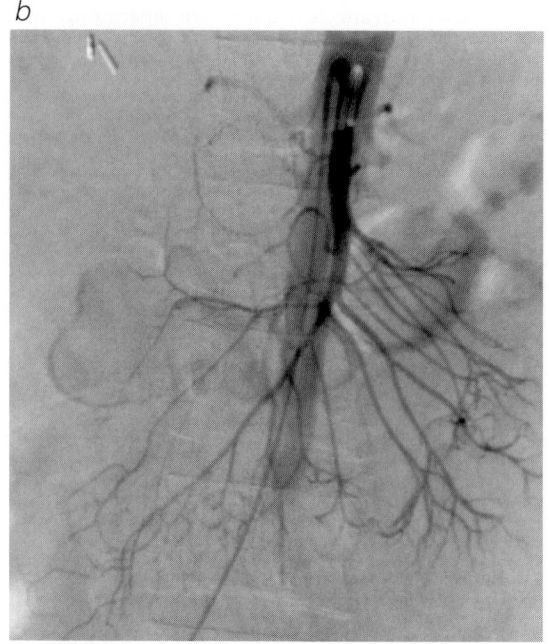

a   *b*

Figure 7   **Shown are contrast angiograms of aorta and mesenteric vessels in a patient with NOMI.** (*a*) **Selective angiogram (anterior projection) of SMA demonstrates distal spasm of SMA.** (*b*) **Selective angiogram (anterior projection) of SMA after intra-arterial papaverine infusion demonstrates improved filling of distal branches of SMA.**

Laparotomy, *below*]. In a study of 31 MVT patients from our institution,[2] the majority were successfully treated with anticoagulation alone and experienced complete resolution of their symptoms; however, 32% did require small bowel resection. Perioperative mortality was 23%. Among those who survived operation, the long-term survival rate was 88%; all of these survivors were symptom free at last follow-up.

Thrombolytic therapy has also been employed to treat MVT. The catheter may be directed into the SMA for lysis of portal vein thrombus.[2] Alternatively, it may be directed into the SMV or the portal vein intraoperatively.[9]

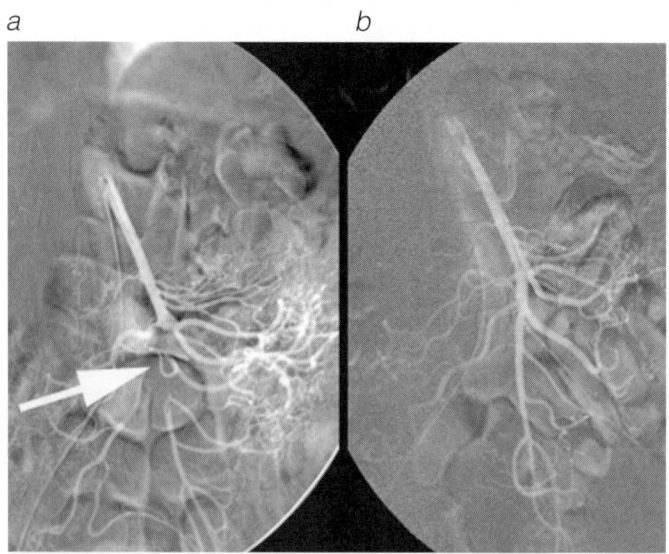

a   *b*

Figure 8   (*a*) **Selective angiogram of SMA demonstrates partially occluding embolus in distal vessel (arrow).** (*b*) **Selective angiogram after catheter-directed intra-arterial thrombolytic therapy shows resolution of embolus.**

Once the diagnosis of MVT has been established, a hypercoagulability workup should be performed in an effort to identify the underlying cause. If the cause is found to be a hematologic hypercoagulable state, lifelong anticoagulation is recommended. If the cause is reversible, anticoagulation may be discontinued after 3 to 6 months.

SECOND-LOOK LAPAROTOMY

Second-look laparotomy is an essential part of the management of acute mesenteric ischemia. No matter which adjunctive method is used intraoperatively to assess bowel perfusion and viability, second-look laparotomy is the most reliable means of determining the viability of marginally perfused bowel after revascularization. A second-look 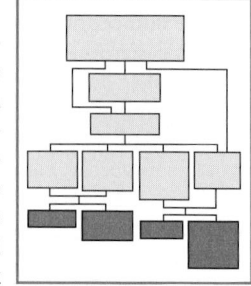 laparotomy should be preceded by adequate fluid resuscitation and correction of the acid-base imbalance. Furthermore, the decision to perform a second-look laparotomy should be made during the first operation and adhered to no matter what the patient's condition is 24 to 48 hours later. Occasionally, even though the patient is in better physical condition 24 to 48 hours later—largely because of aggressive fluid resuscitation and correction of the acid-base imbalance—there is still some necrotic bowel that must be resected. Accordingly, we adhere to a strict policy of planned reexploration for acute mesenteric ischemia patients who require bowel resection during the initial operation or who have areas of marginally viable bowel after revascularization.

Intraoperative Consultation

Vascular surgeons are frequently consulted intraoperatively to evaluate a patient for acute mesenteric ischemia. Often, the patient has been taken to the OR on an emergency basis for acute abdominal pain with peritoneal signs or hemodynamic

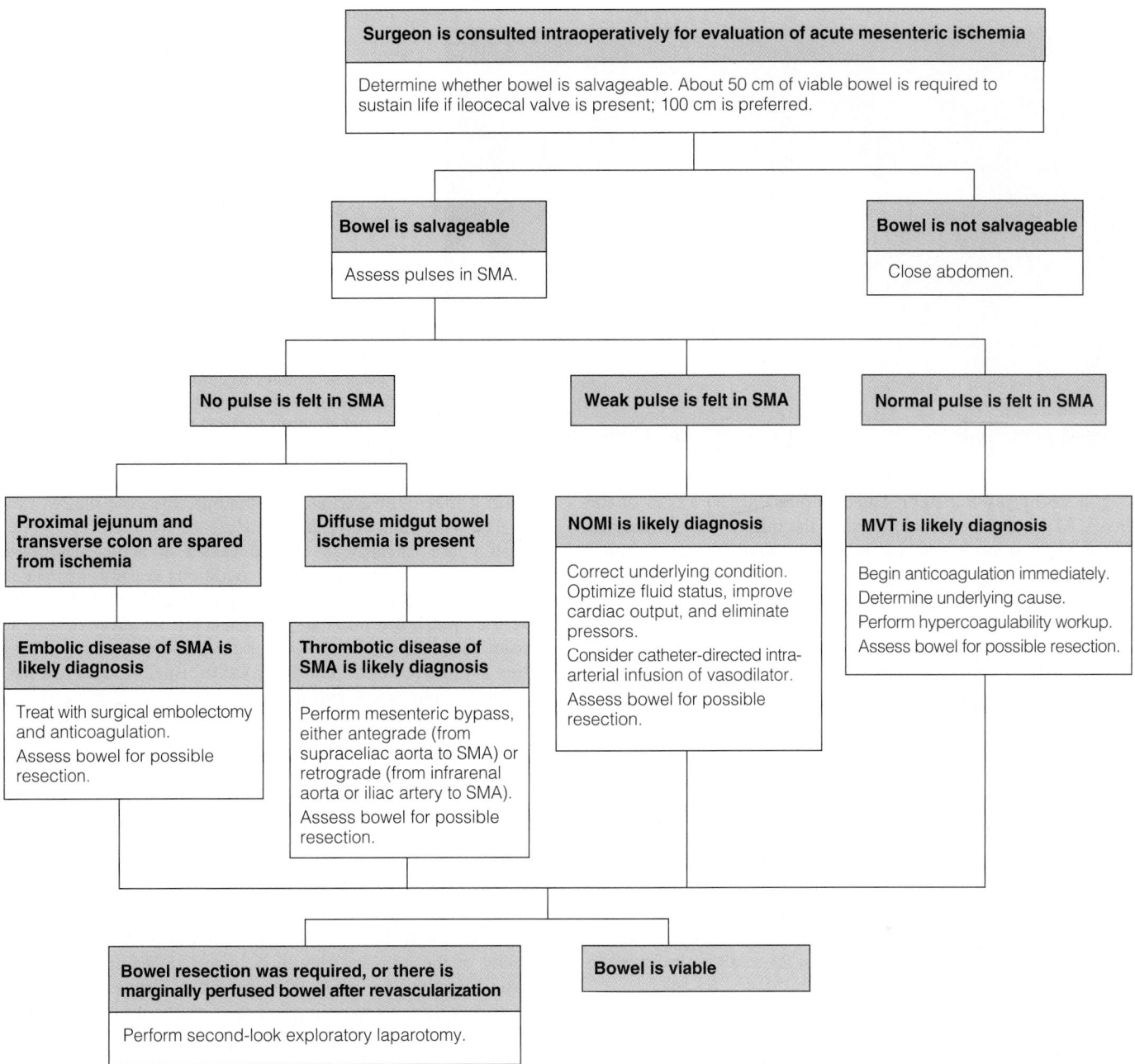

Figure 9 Algorithm illustrates intraoperative determination of bowel salvageability, evaluation of SMA pulses, and assessment of bowel viability after revascularization.

instability [*see Figure 9*]. In the OR, acute mesenteric ischemia typically presents as diffuse bowel ischemia. The first decision point in the evaluation is the determination of whether the bowel is salvageable.

DETERMINATION OF BOWEL SALVAGEABILITY

If diffuse bowel necrosis exists and the bowel is not salvageable, it is best to close the abdomen without attempting further therapy. Approximately 50 cm of viable bowel is required to sustain life if the ileocecal valve is present, and 100 cm is preferable.[10] Therefore, if it is obvious that no bowel can be preserved, further intervention is pointless. If the bowel is salvageable, blood flow to the bowel must be evaluated by assessing the pulses in the SMA. If no pulse can be detected in the SMA, it is imperative that revascularization be undertaken before bowel resection.

INTRAOPERATIVE EVALUATION OF SUPERIOR MESENTERIC ARTERY

SMA pulses are assessed by palpating the root of the mesentery. The transverse colon is reflected superiorly, and the small bowel is reflected to the patient's right. The SMA is then palpated by placing four fingers of the hand behind the root of the mesentery, with the thumb opposite and anterior to the root. The SMA can also be identified by following the middle colic artery proximally until it enters the SMA. Alternatively, a handheld Doppler device may be employed to listen to the quality and character of the arterial signal at the root of the mesentery. Intraoperative angiography may also be used for evaluation, but it is often difficult to perform in the OR if there has not been adequate preparation and setup ahead of time, and it may not be feasible in some institutions.

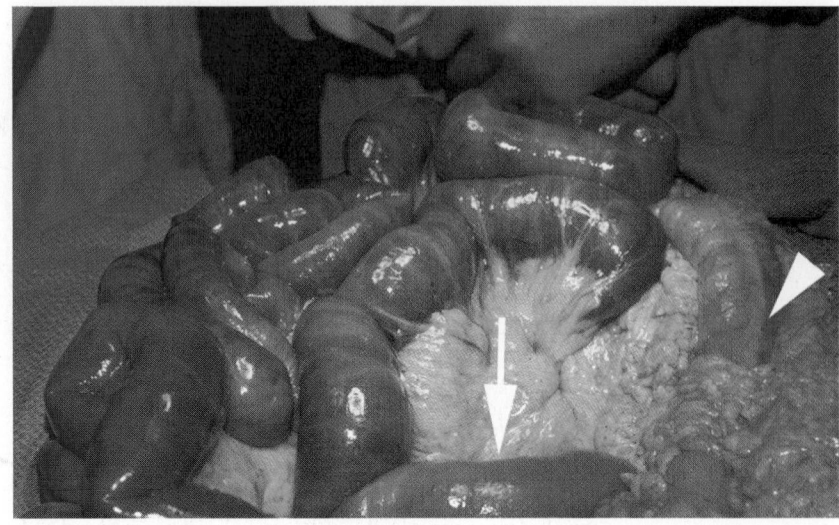

Figure 10 **Intraoperative photograph of patient who presented with acute mesenteric ischemia secondary to embolus of SMA shows diffuse bowel ischemia with classic sparing of proximal jejunum (arrow) and transverse colon (arrowhead).**

If a strong pulse is appreciated throughout the length of the SMA, MVT is the probable cause of the diffuse bowel ischemia. Once MVT is suspected, I.V. administration of heparin should immediately follow. If the bowel is viable, the patient should be observed closely for signs or symptoms of deterioration. If the patient's condition appears to be deteriorating, reexploration is indicated, with resection of any frankly necrotic bowel; thrombolytic therapy should be considered, and a second-look laparotomy should be performed. It is important to palpate the SMA pulse distally as well as proximally to ensure that the patient does not have an embolus to the distal SMA.

If the SMA pulse is weak, the diagnosis of NOMI should be entertained. The mainstay of therapy for NOMI is treatment of the underlying cause, which typically involves fluid resuscitation, administration of inotropes and calcium channel blockers, and cessation of vasoconstrictors. Catheter-directed intra-arterial infusion of papaverine for 24 to 48 hours may be beneficial as well. If bowel resection proves necessary at the time of exploration, it is best to plan on performing a second-look laparotomy, regardless of the patient's clinical status 24 to 48 hours after the initial exploration.

If there is no SMA pulse at the root of the mesentery, the most likely diagnosis is in situ thrombosis from chronic mesenteric arterial disease [*see Figure 4*]. If the SMA pulse is palpable proximally but not several centimeters distally, the likely diagnosis is an embolus to the SMA [*see Figure 4*]. Distinguishing between these two conditions is important because their surgical treatments differ significantly. To make this distinction correctly, the surgeon should be aware of how the patient presented, whether the patient experienced postprandial abdominal pain for an extended period before the acute presentation, and whether the patient has other risk factors of arterial occlusive disease [*see* Clinical Evaluation, *above*]. In addition, the surgeon should be aware of the specific pattern of bowel ischemia present.

DIFFERENTIATION OF PATTERNS OF BOWEL ISCHEMIA

The different causes of acute mesenteric ischemia are associated with different classic patterns of bowel ischemia, which must be distinguished from one another. The basic distinction between arterial and venous pathologic conditions is relatively simple. In mesenteric ischemia resulting from venous disease, the bowel typically is diffusely edematous, congested, and dilated. In mesenteric ischemia resulting from arterial disease, the small bowel is typically contracted during the early phase of presentation, though it may be dilated and edematous when the patient presents late with frank bowel necrosis.

Within the category of arterial causes of acute mesenteric ischemia, the various underlying conditions are also associated with distinct patterns of bowel ischemia. Typically, in embolic disease, the small bowel and the proximal colon are affected, and the proximal jejunal segment and the transverse colon are spared [*see Figure 10*]; the reason is that the embolus usually lodges just past the middle colic artery and the jejunal branches of the SMA. If the entire small bowel is diffusely affected, as well as the ascending and transverse colon, the origin of the SMA is probably occluded; this disease pattern is consistent with thrombotic occlusion of the vessel by underlying atherosclerotic lesions. In NOMI, the entire small bowel may be affected, but the pattern of ischemia tends to be patchy, with segmental areas of involvement.

INTRAOPERATIVE ASSESSMENT OF BOWEL VIABILITY AFTER REVASCULARIZATION

Approximately 10 to 20 minutes after revascularization, the viability of the intestine should be assessed. Waiting until after revascularization to assess the extent of irreversible bowel ischemia or necrosis requiring resection makes it possible to preserve more bowel length. After restoration of flow, the bowel may contain frankly necrotic areas, normal areas, and marginally perfused areas. Obviously, clearly necrotic or nonviable bowel must be resected at the time of the operation. Determination of the viability of marginally perfused bowel is more difficult.

Intraoperatively, the color, motility, and integrity of the bowel should be evaluated. The characteristic appearance of ischemic bowel includes loss of the normal sheen, dull-gray discoloration, and lack of peristalsis. Determination of the character and quality of the pulses in the antimesenteric border and the mesenteric arcades may help determine which areas of the bowel will remain viable once revascularization has been performed. Intraoperative Doppler assessment of bowel perfusion may be performed with a sterilized continuous-wave Doppler ultrasound flow detector. The probe is placed on the antimesenteric border of the intestine to detect pulsatile Doppler signals. Even in the best of hands, however, this technique remains unreliable in predicting subsequent bowel viability.

Other diagnostic options include I.V. administration of fluorescein, transcutaneous oxygen measurement, and second-look exploratory laparotomy. All of these measures are relatively simple to perform, but each has its limitations.

Discussion

Mesenteric Ischemia and Reperfusion

Although acute mesenteric ischemia is initially managed surgically, significant morbidity and mortality remain after treatment, largely resulting from local and systemic inflammation and the subsequent development of multiple organ dysfunction syndrome (MODS). Mesenteric ischemia-reperfusion promotes local synthesis and release of various inflammatory mediators that exacerbate gut injury and prime circulating neutrophils for enhanced superoxide anion production and subsequent remote (i.e., pulmonary and hepatic) injury.[11] At the cellular level, mesenteric ischemia-reperfusion activates a cascade of oxidative stress-sensitive protein kinases that converge on specific transcriptional factors to regulate expression of proinflammatory genes. These gene products include enzymes (e.g., inducible nitric oxide synthase [iNOS], cyclooxygenase, and phospholipase A_2), cytokines (e.g., tumor necrosis factor–α [TNF-α] and interleukin-1 [IL-1]), chemokines (e.g., IL-8), and adhesion molecules (e.g., intercellular adhesion molecule–1 [ICAM-1]).[12-18] Excessive gene activation leads to a maladaptive systemic inflammatory response syndrome that can trigger early MODS. Alternatively, this hyperinflammatory state can cause local gut dysfunction, characterized by histologic evidence of mucosal injury, increased intestinal epithelial and microvascular permeability, and impaired motility; patients become more susceptible to bacteremia and endotoxemia and, eventually, to late MODS.[19]

Experimental work suggests that mesenteric ischemia-reperfusion triggers protein phosphorylation cascades that converge on specific transcription factors to regulate the pattern, timing, and magnitude of expression of not only proinflammatory but also anti-inflammatory gene products.[19] Presumably, this process is mediated by alterations in the cellular redox state induced by the conversion of xanthine dehydrogenase to xanthine oxidase during ischemia, with subsequent production of reactive oxygen metabolites and H_2O_2 during reperfusion.[20] Alterations in the cellular redox state activate families of stress-sensitive protein kinases, such as the nonreceptor tyrosine kinases c-Src and Syk, PI3-kinase/Akt, and the mitogen-activated protein kinases. These parallel kinase cascades phosphorylate nascent transcription factors (e.g., nuclear factor–κB [NF-κB] and AP-1), which target genes that encode proteins involved in mediator synthesis.[19,21]

Therapies directed at attenuating these pathways have been successful in laboratory models of mesenteric ischemia-reperfusion and may eventually be able to affect outcome in patients presenting with acute intestinal ischemia.[22-26] However, clinical trials investigating the efficacy of pharmacologic blockade of individual mediators (e.g., TNF-α, IL-1, and iNOS) have found this approach to be largely unsuccessful and sometimes even deleterious in treating patients with sepsis and MODS.[22] The reasons for the failure of these trials are probably multifactorial, but it appears that both the redundancy and breadth of the inflammatory cascade and the poor timing of therapy (i.e., the inability to target early inflammatory events) are major contributing factors. Nonetheless, it is likely that to achieve any meaningful improvements in our ability to treat patients with acute mesenteric ischemia, we will have to expand our knowledge of the early molecular pathways involved in the activation and proliferation of both local and systemic inflammation.

Outcome after Surgical Treatment

Most studies that include a large number of patients with acute mesenteric ischemia report perioperative mortalities ranging from 32% to 69% and 5-year survival rates ranging from 18% to 50%.[1,27,28] One group performed a systematic review of survival after acute mesenteric ischemia according to underlying cause by evaluating available data from the period between 1966 and 2002.[29] The investigators examined a total of 45 observational studies, which included 3,692 patients with acute mesenteric ischemia. They reported that mortality varied substantially according to the cause of the acute mesenteric episode. Overall mortality was lower with ischemia of venous origin (i.e., MVT) than with ischemia of arterial origin. Within the category of arterial causes, mortality was 54.1% after treatment of arterial embolic disease, 77.4% after treatment of arterial thrombotic disease, and 72.7% after treatment of NOMI. The difference in mortality between embolic and thrombotic disease may be accounted for by the tendency of thrombosis to occur more proximally and thus to be associated with a greater degree of bowel infarction than embolic disease is.

A 2003 study reviewed the institutional experience at Wake Forest University between 1990 and 2000.[27] A total of 76 patients were treated for acute mesenteric ischemia, of whom 42% had embolic disease and 58% had thrombotic disease. Various surgical treatment options were employed, including exploration alone, bowel resection alone, and revascularization with or without bowel resection. Overall perioperative mortality was 62%. When mortality was examined in relation to the cause of ischemia, however, patients with embolic disease tended to fare better: overall perioperative mortality was 62% to 70% for patients with thrombotic disease and 50% for those with embolic disease. None of the patients who underwent exploration alone survived; 33% of those who underwent intestinal resection alone survived. In contrast to perioperative mortality, morbidity was higher in the embolic disease group than in the thrombotic disease group (69% versus 46%). The 5-year survival rates were dismal in both groups (18%). Peritonitis and bowel necrosis at presentation were found to be independent predictors of death or survival dependent on total parenteral nutrition.

In a 10-year institutional review from the Mayo Clinic,[1] a total of 58 patients were treated for acute mesenteric ischemia. Overall 30-day mortality was 32%; however, when the data were further analyzed according to the cause of ischemia, it was found that mortality from embolic disease was 31%, mortality from thrombotic disease was 32%, and mortality from NOMI was 80%. Multiple organ failure was the most frequent cause of death. The 1-year and 3-year cumulative survival rates were 43% and 32%, respectively. Independent predictors of survival included age less than 60 years, bowel resection, and the absence of a recent major cardiovascular procedure.

From these studies, it is apparent that acute mesenteric ischemia is a lethal disease that carries a high morbidity and mortality. The only way to reduce the morbidity and mortality associated with this disease process is to diagnose and treat it early, before irreversible signs of bowel ischemia develop.

References

1. Park WM, Gloviczki P, Cherry KJ Jr, et al: Contemporary management of acute mesenteric ischemia: factors associated with survival. J Vasc Surg 35:445, 2002

2. Morasch MD, Ebaugh JL, Chiou AC, et al: Mesenteric venous thrombosis: a changing clinical entity. J Vasc Surg 34:680, 2001

3. Ritz JP, Runkel N, Berger G, et al: [Prognostic factors in mesenteric infarct]. Zentralbl Chir 122:332, 1997

4. Moneta GL, Yeager RA, Dalman R, et al: Duplex ultrasound criteria for diagnosis of splanchnic artery stenosis or occlusion. J Vasc Surg 14:511, 1991

5. Cikrit DF, Harris VJ, Hemmer CG, et al: Comparison of spiral CT scan and arteriography for evaluation of renal and visceral arteries. Ann Vasc Surg 10:109, 1996

6. Boley SJ, Kaleya RN, Brandt LJ: Mesenteric venous thrombosis. Surg Clin North Am 72:183, 1992

7. Rhee RY, Gloviczki P, Mendonca CT, et al: Mesenteric venous thrombosis: still a lethal disease in the 1990s. J Vasc Surg 20:688, 1994

8. Ernst O, Asnar V, Sergent G, et al: Comparing contrast-enhanced breath-hold MR angiography and conventional angiography in the evaluation of mesenteric circulation. AJR Am J Roentgenol 174:433, 2000

9. Kaplan JL, Weintraub SL, Hunt JP, et al: Treatment of superior mesenteric and portal vein thrombosis with direct thrombolytic infusion via an operatively placed mesenteric catheter. Am Surg 70:600, 2004

10. Thompson JS, Langnas AN, Pinch LW, et al: Surgical approach to short-bowel syndrome. Experience in a population of 160 patients. Ann Surg 222:600, 1995

11. Moore EE, Moore FA, Franciose RJ, et al: The postischemic gut serves as a priming bed for circulating neutrophils that provoke multiple organ failure. J Trauma 37:881, 1994

12. Welborn MB III, Douglas WG, Abouhamze Z, et al: Visceral ischemia-reperfusion injury promotes tumor necrosis factor (TNF) and interleukin-1 (IL-1) dependent organ injury in the mouse. Shock 6:171, 1996

13. Tamion F, Richard V, Lyoumi S, et al: Gut ischemia and mesenteric synthesis of inflammatory cytokines after hemorrhagic or endotoxic shock. Am J Physiol 273:G314, 1997

14. Panes J, Granger DN: Leukocyte–endothelial cell interactions: molecular mechanisms and implications in gastrointestinal disease. Gastroenterology 114:1066, 1998

15. Hassoun HT, Weisbrodt NW, Mercer DW, et al: Inducible nitric oxide synthase mediates gut ischemia/reperfusion-induced ileus only after severe insults. J Surg Res 97:150, 2001

16. Sonnino RE, Pigatt L, Schrama A, et al: Phospholipase A2 secretion during intestinal graft ischemia. Dig Dis Sci 42:972, 1997

17. Turnage RH, Kadesky KM, Bartula L, et al: Splanchnic PGI2 release and "no reflow" following intestinal reperfusion. J Surg Res 58:558, 1995

18. Salzman AL: Nitric oxide in the gut. New Horiz 3:352, 1995

19. Hassoun HT, Kone BC, Mercer DW, et al: Postinjury multiple organ failure: the role of the gut. Shock 15:1, 2001

20. Granger DN, Hollwarth ME, Parks DA: Ischemia-reperfusion injury: role of oxygen-derived free radicals. Acta Physiol Scand Suppl 548:47, 1986

21. Yeh KY, Yeh M, Glass J, et al: Rapid activation of NF-kappaB and AP-1 and target gene expression in postischemic rat intestine. Gastroenterology 118:525, 2000

22. Huber TS, Gaines GC, Welborn MB III, et al: Anticytokine therapies for acute inflammation and the systemic inflammatory response syndrome: IL-10 and ischemia/reperfusion injury as a new paradigm. Shock 13:425, 2000

23. Hassoun HT, Zou L, Moore FA, et al: Alpha-melanocyte-stimulating hormone protects against mesenteric ischemia-reperfusion injury. Am J Physiol Gastrointest Liver Physiol 282:G1059, 2002

24. Attuwaybi BO, Kozar RA, Moore-Olufemi SD, et al: Heme oxygenase-1 induction by hemin protects against gut ischemia/reperfusion injury. J Surg Res 118:53, 2004

25. Tadros T, Traber DL, Heggers JP, et al: Effects of interleukin-1alpha administration on intestinal ischemia and reperfusion injury, mucosal permeability, and bacterial translocation in burn and sepsis. Ann Surg 237:101, 2003

26. Zou L, Attuwaybi B, Kone BC: Effects of NF-kappa B inhibition on mesenteric ischemia-reperfusion injury. Am J Physiol Gastrointest Liver Physiol 284:G713, 2003

27. Edwards MS, Cherr GS, Craven TE, et al: Acute occlusive mesenteric ischemia: surgical management and outcomes. Ann Vasc Surg 17:72, 2003

28. Klempnauer J, Grothues F, Bektas H, et al: Long-term results after surgery for acute mesenteric ischemia. Surgery 121:239, 1997

29. Schoots IG, Koffeman GI, Legemate DA, et al: Systematic review of survival after acute mesenteric ischaemia according to disease aetiology. Br J Surg 91:17, 2004

Acknowledgment

Figure 4   Alice Y. Chen.

84 PULSELESS EXTREMITY AND ATHEROEMBOLISM

Vicken N. Pamoukian, M.D., and Cynthia K. Shortell, M.D., F.A.C.S.

Approach to the Acutely Ischemic Limb

Pulseless Extremity

Acute limb ischemia (ALI) is a sudden reduction in limb perfusion that poses a potential threat to the viability of an extremity. The incidence of ALI in the general population is approximately 1.7/10,000 per year.[1] The clinical presentation ranges from subtle to dramatic. Management of ALI is challenging and is complicated by the myriad comorbid conditions typically seen in conjunction with ALI.

In the early 1970s, a study comprising more than 3,000 patients with ALI from 35 centers documented a mortality of 26% and an amputation rate of 37%.[2] Substantial improvements in surgical management approaches, techniques, and instruments have been achieved since then, but morbidity and mortality remain high, with death rates around 15% and amputation rates between 10% and 30%.[3]

Cardiac risk assessment with the Goldman index allows rapid evaluation of the level of physiologic risk patients face. Again, the major cause of morbidity in ALI patients is the associated medical conditions typically present [*see Table 1*].

Given the general frailty of ALI patients and the multiplicity of available therapeutic options, it is important to take a logical, methodical approach to the treatment of this condition. In particular, the use of algorithms, decision trees, or clinical pathways for patient care helps the clinician visualize and evaluate multiple potential avenues for management and select the path likely to yield the best outcome.

CLINICAL EVALUATION

History

A thorough history should be taken. Generally, the dominant symptoms are related to pain or loss of function. The onset and duration of symptoms should be determined, and the location and the intensity of any changes should be established. The pain of ALI is not well 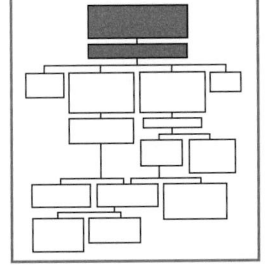 localized and is not affected by gravity. Pain of sudden onset suggests that an embolic cause is likely, whereas long-standing pain before the acute event suggests a thrombotic cause [*see Discussion, Etiology of ALI, below*].

It is imperative to ask whether the patient experienced pain before the current ischemic episode and whether the current episode is the first. It is also important to ask about previous surgical revascularization as well as previous or current cardiac disease (e.g., myocardial infarction [MI], atrial fibrillation, or valvular disease), aneurysmal disease, or vasculitis. Finally, inquiries should be made about previous atherosclerotic disease, current risk factors for atherosclerosis (e.g., hypertension, smoking, diabetes, tobacco abuse, hyperlipidemia, and stroke), and previous clotting episodes.

Physical Examination

The characteristic signs and symptoms of ALI may be summarized as the six Ps: *P*ulselessness, *P*ain, *P*allor, *P*oikilothermia, *P*aresthesia, and *P*aralysis.

- Pulses should be palpated and documented. Any previous documentation should be noted.
- Pain should be documented with regard to severity, area, and progression.
- Pallor may be seen in the early stages, followed by cyanosis.
- Poikilothermia may propagate the ischemic cascade through its vasoconstrictive effects. The level of coolness and pallor is typically one level below the point of occlusion on the arterial tree, and it should correlate with the pulses or signals found. As always, baseline documentation should be done so that the progression or resolution of the process can be tracked.
- Paresthesia is an essential finding. The earliest sign of tissue loss is the loss of light touch, two-point discrimination, vibratory perception, and proprioception, especially in the first dorsal web space of the foot.
- Paralysis, if present, is an indication of advanced limb-threatening ischemia. The extent of paralysis must be determined. The intrinsic muscles of the foot are affected by ischemia of the vessels around the ankle. Dorsiflexion and plantar flexion of the foot are functions of muscles that rely on blood supplied by the popliteal and superficial femoral arteries. Loss of dorsiflexion and plantar flexion indicates that blood flow is cut off at a higher level and signals that more tissue may be at risk.

Peripheral Pulses

Careful assessment of peripheral pulses will help localize the area of arterial obstruction. When clot is fresh, its soft, semiliquid consistency allows the pulse to be translated at the level of obstruction. Only when the thrombus becomes organized and densely compacted is the pulse lost at the site of occlusion. As an example, in a patient with obstruction at the popliteal artery, popliteal pulses remain palpable in the earlier stages of the process, but distal pulses are lost [*see Table 2*].

Staging of Limb Ischemia

A prime goal of clinical evaluation is to determine the severity of the disease process so that appropriate management can be rapidly instituted. To this end, the key question that must be

Approach to the Acutely Ischemic Limb

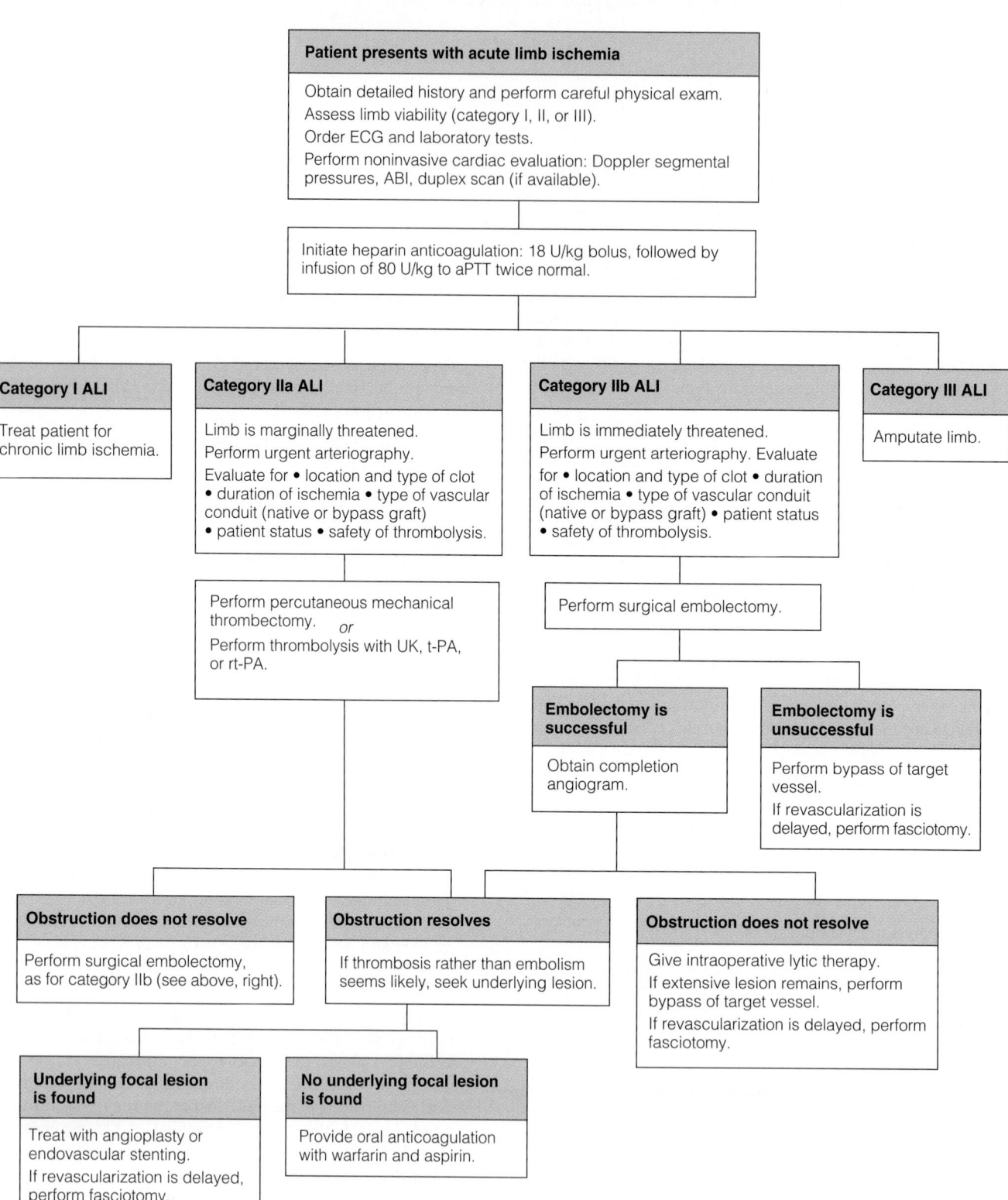

Patient presents with acute limb ischemia

Obtain detailed history and perform careful physical exam.
Assess limb viability (category I, II, or III).
Order ECG and laboratory tests.
Perform noninvasive cardiac evaluation: Doppler segmental pressures, ABI, duplex scan (if available).

Initiate heparin anticoagulation: 18 U/kg bolus, followed by infusion of 80 U/kg to aPTT twice normal.

Category I ALI

Treat patient for chronic limb ischemia.

Category IIa ALI

Limb is marginally threatened.
Perform urgent arteriography.
Evaluate for • location and type of clot • duration of ischemia • type of vascular conduit (native or bypass graft) • patient status • safety of thrombolysis.

Perform percutaneous mechanical thrombectomy.   *or*
Perform thrombolysis with UK, t-PA, or rt-PA.

Category IIb ALI

Limb is immediately threatened.
Perform urgent arteriography. Evaluate for • location and type of clot • duration of ischemia • type of vascular conduit (native or bypass graft) • patient status • safety of thrombolysis.

Perform surgical embolectomy.

Embolectomy is successful

Obtain completion angiogram.

Embolectomy is unsuccessful

Perform bypass of target vessel.
If revascularization is delayed, perform fasciotomy.

Category III ALI

Amputate limb.

Obstruction does not resolve

Perform surgical embolectomy, as for category IIb (see above, right).

Obstruction resolves

If thrombosis rather than embolism seems likely, seek underlying lesion.

Obstruction does not resolve

Give intraoperative lytic therapy.
If extensive lesion remains, perform bypass of target vessel.
If revascularization is delayed, perform fasciotomy.

Underlying focal lesion is found

Treat with angioplasty or endovascular stenting.
If revascularization is delayed, perform fasciotomy.

No underlying focal lesion is found

Provide oral anticoagulation with warfarin and aspirin.

Table 1 Incidence of Medical Comorbidities in Patients Presenting with ALI[97]

Comorbidity	Incidence (%)			
	Rochester Trial (N = 114)	TOPAS-1 Trial (N = 213)	TOPAS-2 Trial (N = 544)	Total (N = 871)
Cerebrovascular disease	NR	15.4	11.5	11.6
Congestive heart failure	NR	15.5	12.5	13.3
Coronary artery disease	56.1	47.1	42.5	45.4
Diabetes mellitus	28.1	36.7	29.0	30.8
Hypercholesterolemia	31.6	29.6	23.5	26.0
Hypertension	63.2	60.9	69.6	60.3
Malignancy	NR	11.9	11.5	11.6
Tobacco history	51.8	79.3	77.5	74.6

NR—not reported TOPAS—Thrombolysis Or Peripheral Arterial Surgery

answered is whether the limb is viable or not. In 1997, the Joint Council of the Society for Vascular Surgery and the North American Chapter of the International Society for Cardiovascular Surgery developed reporting standards for ALI and stratified it into three distinct categories on the basis of the severity of the disease process [*see Table 3*].[4]

In category I ALI, patients present with acute occlusion of an artery that is chronically narrowed. Therefore, abundant collaterals can be found, and the limb is viable. In category II ALI, the ischemic limb is threatened but may be salvaged without the need for an amputation if adequate revascularization can be achieved. This category is further subdivided into categories IIa and IIb. Category IIa includes patients with mild forefoot numbness or any lesion for which prompt revascularization of the limb achieves a good result. Category IIb includes patients with diminished sensation of the entire foot and weakness of calf muscles whose limb is still salvageable but who require immediate revascularization. In category III, ischemia is irreversible and amputation is required. Clinical features include permanent tissue loss, anesthesia, and paralysis of the limb.

INVESTIGATIVE STUDIES

In addition to the clinical evaluation, a full battery of diagnostic tests should be performed. An electrocardiogram should be obtained, and if a cardiac source is suspected, a transesophageal echocardiogram should be obtained as well. A full set of laboratory tests, including a complete blood count and a platelet count,

blood chemistries, and coagulation profiles, should be ordered. In addition, chest and abdominal x-rays should be done to look for obvious calcifications. If it appears that a hypercoagulable state may be causing thrombosis, a hypercoagulability profile should be ordered [*see 85 Venous Thromboembolism*].

Evaluation of Arterial Tree

An objective evaluation of the arterial tree should be performed when feasible. If ischemia is particularly severe and long-lasting, a full angiographic evaluation may not be possible; however, noninvasive Doppler studies and, if time permits, angiography should be considered strongly in this setting.

Doppler segmental pressures and ankle-brachial index Examination should begin at the level of the ankle and should include assessment of arterial signals and venous hums. When arterial signals are found, the ankle-brachial index (ABI) should be measured.

The ABI is derived from the ankle systolic pressure and the brachial systolic pressure and is determined as follows. The systolic pressure is measured in each arm, and the higher of the two measurements is taken to be the brachial systolic pressure. A cuff is then placed on each calf, and the examiner listens to signals in the dorsalis pedis and posterior tibial arteries. The cuff is inflated until the signal is no longer heard. At this point, the cuff is slowly released, and the systolic pressure is recorded at the point where the signal is once again audible. Again, the higher of the two systolic measurements is taken to be the ankle systolic pressure. The systolic ankle

Table 2 Localization of Arterial Obstruction through Palpation of Peripheral Pulses[97]

Palpable Pulses			Location of Obstruction	Possible Causes
Femoral	Popliteal	Pedal		
−	−	−	Aortoiliac segment	Aortoiliac atherosclerosis; embolus to common iliac bifurcation
+	−	−	Femoral segment	Thrombosis, femoral atherosclerosis; common femoral embolus
+	++	−	Distal popliteal ± tibials	Popliteal aneurysm with embolization
+	+	−	Distal popliteal ± tibials	Popliteal embolus; popliteal/tibial atherosclerosis, diabetes

Table 3 Clinical Categorization of ALI[4]

Category	Findings			Doppler Signals	
	Description/Prognosis	Sensory Loss	Muscle Weakness	Arterial	Venous
I. Viable	Not immediately threatened	None	None	Audible	Audible
IIa. Marginally threatened	Salvageable if promptly treated	Minimal (toes) or none	None	(Often) inaudible	Audible
IIb. Immediately threatened	Salvageable with immediate revascularization	More than toes, associated with rest pain	Mild, moderate	(Usually) inaudible	Audible
III. Irreversible*	Major tissue loss or permanent nerve damage inevitable	Profound, anesthetic	Profound, paralysis (rigor)	Inaudible	Inaudible

*When presenting early, category IIb and category III may be difficult to differentiate.

pressure is then divided by the brachial systolic pressure to yield the ABI. An ABI in the range of 1 is normal; however, the ABI can be falsely elevated if the distal arteries are not compressible. When the ABI falls below 0.6, there is a significant difference in blood pressure between the proximal arterial tree and the distal extremity, which usually denotes an occlusive process. Next, segmental pressures are obtained by placing cuffs at the ankle, below the knee, above the knee, and on the thigh. Systolic blood pressures are measured at each location, and any pressure drop greater than 15 mm Hg is considered significant.

When the venous Doppler signal or hum is lost in addition to the arterial Doppler signal, the ischemia is severe. In addition, when a Doppler signal is present, intervention may be delayed slightly. However, the absence of signals does not always signify an irreversibly threatened limb.

Duplex ultrasonography   Duplex scanning can be valuable for localizing the site of occlusion, especially in bypass grafts. Unfortunately, it is not always a practical option in acute circumstances, both because the machine is often unavailable in the emergency setting and because the results of scanning are highly operator dependent. However, in specialized centers where a duplex ultrasound machine is readily available and personnel are experienced in its use, a quick look at the suspected site may yield helpful information.[5] In stenotic regions, the velocities measured across the lesion are greatly increased.[6,7] In addition, duplex ultrasonography can be used to visualize plaque morphology, stenoses, dissections, and thrombi. In some centers of excellence, duplex ultrasound technology has obviated the need for lengthy arteriograms and has benefited patients by reducing ischemia time.

Arteriography   Arteriography remains the gold standard for diagnosis of ALI and may even be a primary tool in its management. It should not, however, be performed if doing so would keep a critically ischemic leg from receiving prompt surgical therapy. Arteriography should be reserved for patients with viable limbs who can tolerate the additional delay before revascularization.

Arteriography should be performed from a site remote from the point of concern. Thus, if lytic therapy is to be administered, entry-site bleeding will be minimized. A complete angiogram that includes the runoff vessels in the foot should be performed to establish the baseline degree of arterial disease and delineate the inflow and outflow anatomy. This information facilitates subsequent planning for revascularization, should this step prove necessary. Digital subtraction angiography is preferred in that it allows a reduced contrast load and lowers the incidence of contrast-associated renal injury.[8,9] If the patient is allergic to the contrast agent

or has renal insufficiency, CO_2^- or gadolinium-based angiography may be performed instead. These two modalities have the advantage of possessing minimal to no nephrotoxicity, but they yield poorer suprainguinal arterial visualization than standard contrast angiography does.[10,11]

The arteriogram can provide useful clues for differentiating emboli from thrombi. In a patient with arterial embolism, there is often an identifiable source, there is rarely a history of claudication, contralateral and proximal pulses are normal, cutoff is sharp, atherosclerosis is minimal, a few collateral vessels are present, and a discrete clot is clearly visible on contrast studies. In a patient with arterial thrombosis, the thrombus has no identifiable source, there is a history of claudication with evidence of peripheral vascular disease, diffuse atherosclerotic vessel wall disease is present, cutoff is tapered and irregular, and there is ample collateral circulation.

TREATMENT

Until the middle of the 20th century, when revascularization techniques were developed, amputation was the only treatment for acute lower-extremity ischemia [*see* 99 *Lower-Extremity Amputation for Ischemia*]. Today, however, the vascular surgeon possesses an immense armamentarium for the treatment of this condition, ranging from emergency bypass to embolectomy to thrombolytic therapy.

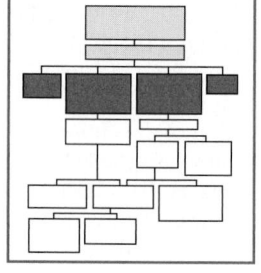

The treatment of ALI is an emergency situation. Rapid restoration of flow to the extremity substantially reduces morbidity and mortality. Accordingly, the clinician must be thoroughly familiar with the therapeutic modalities available and capable of making an appropriate choice among them without undue delay. Whichever therapeutic modality is chosen for a given patient, several primary measures should be undertaken to protect and optimize the status of the extremity. Full systemic heparinization should not be delayed. The extremity should be placed in a dependent position, with care taken to avoid extrinsic pressure on the limb. Temperature fluxes should be minimized: cold induces vasoconstriction, and heat increases tissue demand and metabolic and circulatory demands. Finally, tissue oxygenation should be maximized via transfusion, improvement of cardiac function, and restoration of intravascular volume.

Laboratory tests, radiologic studies, and a cardiology evaluation are required. The ABI should be documented. Abnormalities in blood counts, electrolyte concentrations, and coagulation profiles should be corrected. The duration of ischemia should be noted and any comorbid conditions identified so that the examiner can determine the appropriate degree of monitoring required (e.g., arterial line or pulmonary arterial catheter). Proper and timely preoperative preparation is crucial for preventing rapid deterioration of the patient's condition.

Anticoagulation

Heparin administration should be started as soon as the diagnosis of ALI is entertained. Numerous studies have shown that this measure decreases the morbidity and mortality associated with ALI and increases the limb salvage rate. Heparin impedes the propagation of clots and, in the instance of embolism, may help prevent additional events.

Heparin acts at multiple sites in the normal coagulation system, inhibiting reactions that lead to the clotting of blood and the formation of fibrin clots both in vitro and in vivo. Small amounts of heparin, in combination with antithrombin (heparin cofactor), can inhibit thrombosis by inactivating activated factor X and inhibiting the conversion of prothrombin to thrombin.[12] Once active thrombosis has developed, larger amounts of heparin can inhibit further coagulation by inactivating thrombin and preventing the conversion of fibrinogen to fibrin. Heparin also prevents the formation of a stable fibrin clot by inhibiting the activation of fibrin-stabilizing factor.[12-14]

Heparin does not have fibrinolytic activity and therefore does not lyse existing clots. Heparin therapy can be complicated by thrombocytopenia, which has a reported incidence of 0% to 30%.[15] If the thrombocyte count falls below 100,000/mm³ or if recurrent thrombosis develops, heparin should be discontinued.[16,17] Patients receiving heparin may experience new thrombus formation, either early or late, in association with this thrombocytopenic phenomenon as a consequence of irreversible heparin-induced platelet aggregation (the so-called white clot syndrome). This process may lead to severe thromboembolic complications, including skin necrosis, gangrene of the extremities, MI, pulmonary embolism, stroke, and, possibly, death.[16,18,19] Accordingly, if new thrombosis develops in association with thrombocytopenia, heparin should be promptly discontinued.

Periodic platelet counts, hematocrits, and tests for fecal occult blood are recommended during the entire course of heparin therapy, regardless of the route of administration.

Bleeding time is usually unaffected by heparin. Clotting time is prolonged by full therapeutic doses of heparin, but in most cases, it is not measurably affected by low doses.

Thrombolysis

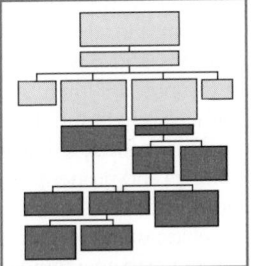

The use of thrombolysis to treat chronic and acute arterial insufficiency dates back to the 1970s, when it was popularized by Dotter.[20] Systemic fibrinolytic therapy has not proved effective and consequently has been supplanted by intra-arterial (catheter-directed) thrombolysis, which yields significantly better results. Still, the role of thrombolytic therapy for ALI is somewhat controversial. In addition, such therapy requires a skilled team with considerable clinical expertise, typically including a vascular surgeon, an interventional radiologist, and a well-trained ancillary staff. The benefits of pharmacologic clot lysis must always be weighed against those of surgical intervention and the risk of bleeding associated with fibrinolysis.

Despite the use of fibrin-specific agents and catheter-directed infusion, thrombolytic agents still exert systemic effects, most of which are dose related. About 10% of patients receiving throm-

bolytic therapy experience significant bleeding, including bleeding from both puncture and remote sites. Absolute contraindications to the use of lytic agents include recent surgery, recent stroke or brain tumor, pregnancy, a bleeding diathesis, recent trauma, and active bleeding [see Table 4].

Thrombolysis versus surgical treatment   Three prospective, randomized trials—the University of Rochester trial,[21] the Surgery versus Thrombolysis for Ischemia of the Lower Extremity (STILE) trial,[22] and Thrombolysis Or Peripheral Arterial Surgery (TOPAS) trial[23,24]—addressed the differences between thrombolytic therapy and traditional surgery.

Rochester trial. This randomized, controlled single-center trial compared urokinase (UK) with surgery in patients with ischemia of less than 7 days' duration.[21] At the end of 1 year, overall mortality was lower in the thrombolysis group (25%) than in the surgery group (48%). The amputation rates were similar in the two groups. Total hospital charges were comparable as well, which suggests that at initial treatment, thrombolytic therapy is as costly as surgery. Major bleeding was encountered in 11% of patients.

STILE trial. This randomized, controlled multicenter trial compared surgery with recombinant tissue plasminogen activator (rt-PA) and with UK.[22] It was stopped early because of an increase in the number of patients with ongoing ischemia in the thrombolysis groups. An ad hoc committee later determined that the reason for this increase was the inclusion of chronically symptomatic patients in the study. In any case, the study clearly demonstrated that patients with less than 14 days of ischemia had a lower amputation rate when treated with thrombolysis (11% versus 30%; $P = 0.02$) but that patients with more than 14 days of ischemia had a lower amputation rate when treated with surgery.

TOPAS trial. This randomized, controlled multicenter trial compared surgery with recombinant urokinase (r-UK) thrombolysis in patients with ischemic symptoms of less than 14 days' duration.[23,24] At the end of 1 year, the amputation rates in the two groups were similar. Bleeding complications were seen only in patients undergoing thrombolysis, four of whom had intracranial

---

Table 4   Contraindications to Thrombolytic Therapy[98]

Absolute contraindications
   Established cerebrovascular event (including TIAs) within past 2 mo
   Active bleeding diathesis
   GI bleeding within past 10 days
   Neurosurgery (intracranial, spinal) within past 3 mo
   Intracranial trauma within past 3 mo

Major relative contraindications
   Cardiopulmonary resuscitation within past 10 days
   Major nonvascular surgery or trauma within past 10 days
   Uncontrolled hypertension: systolic BP > 180 mm Hg, diastolic BP > 110 mm Hg
   Puncture of noncompressible vessel
   Intracranial tumor
   Recent eye surgery

Minor relative contraindications
   Hepatic failure, particularly in patients with coagulopathy
   Bacterial endocarditis
   Pregnancy
   Diabetic hemorrhagic retinopathy

TIA—transient ischemic attack

hemorrhage. When additional end points were considered, the thrombolysis group was found to require significantly fewer major interventions at the time of discharge and at 12 months.

A prospective, randomized multicenter trial evaluated local thrombolysis with either rt-PA or urokinase in 234 patients with thrombotic occlusions (223 native femoral or popliteal arteries, 11 bypass grafts).[25] Complete reperfusion occurred in 62% of the patients treated with rt-PA and in 50% of the patients treated with urokinase ($P = 0.18$). However, bleeding was observed in 12.8% of rt-PA–treated patients (including one instance of cerebral hemorrhage) and in 9.1% of UK-treated patients (none of whom experienced cerebral bleeding).

Current data suggest, but do not prove, that thrombolytic therapy is effective as initial therapy for patients with acute arterial and graft occlusions and no sensorimotor deficits. Such an approach, however, is not suitable for patients with common femoral artery emboli, which should be treated surgically, and there are certain patients with sensorimotor deficits (e.g., those without any runoff) for whom the potential benefits of thrombolysis outweigh the risks of delay.

At present, acute thrombotic arterial occlusion in an occluded bypass graft is the area where intra-arterial fibrinolysis may be most useful, permitting better planning of the subsequent operation and resulting in a less extensive procedure. Such therapy, however, does not necessarily yield improvements in major long-term end points. It is important to remember that thrombosis of femoropopliteal or similar bypasses is related to early or late surgical stenosis and atherosclerosis and that restoring flow usually does not suffice to ensure continued patency.

Logistics of thrombolysis In patients with mild or no sensory deficits, angiography is performed first. Depending on the location of the obstruction, the type of clot present, and the level of patient risk, the patient may be offered thrombolysis as initial therapy.

In our practice, the patient is taken from the emergency department to the angiography suite. Informed consent is obtained for diagnostic and therapeutic angiography, including the use of stents, balloon angioplasty, stent grafts and thrombolysis, and finally the requirement for an emergency surgical procedure. A discussion is undertaken with the patient to outline the course of treatment and to explain that indwelling catheters may have to be placed and that a stay in the ICU may be required.

Access to the arterial system is gained via a single-wall puncture technique; the risk of posterior-wall bleeding associated with a double-wall technique is thereby avoided. Access should be obtained from a site as remote from the intervention site as possible. Generally, this is accomplished by starting from the contralateral counterpart of the target artery and going up and over the aortic bifurcation, then back to the ipsilateral artery. By removing the puncture site from the site of catheter-directed thrombolysis, the incidence of bleeding and formation of hematomas or pseudoaneurysms is reduced.

After completion of the angiogram and delineation of the pathology, a guide wire is passed into the occluded area. We use a 0.035 in. hydrophilic guide wire, which has a slippery, wet coating that enables it to cross nonhydrophilic lesions. Once in place, the wire is guided through the clot. A multiple-sidehole catheter is placed through the clot, and a hand-injection angiogram is performed to confirm that the catheter tip is in the true lumen. The guide wire is then left within the catheter to occlude the tip, so that the lytic agent is infused through the sideholes preferentially. This graded "coaxial" infusion technique allows the agent to reach the greatest possible surface area, maximizes the length of infusion, and enables the surgeon to treat some of the longest bypass grafts.

In many cases, mechanical thrombus removal, with or without pulse spray, is employed initially, followed by continuous infusion of a thrombolytic agent. In addition to lytic therapy, administration of heparin is started (200 to 400 units I.V. or via sheath) to prevent pericatheter thrombosis. Serial laboratory evaluation is carried out to verify that the patient is not bleeding and that the fibrinogen level is higher than 100 mg/dl. Serial follow-up arteriograms are performed to monitor progress. It is critically important that successful thrombolysis be followed by treatment, whether endovascular or open, of any lesions uncovered during thrombolysis; if it is not, reocclusion is inevitable. At the conclusion of thrombolysis and before intervention, the patient must be kept on a heparin drip to prevent the formation of a new thrombus. The rate of successful reperfusion is approximately 90% to 95% in most studies.

An important advantage of this selective approach is that it allows simultaneous angiographic definition of the nature of the occlusion (i.e., embolic versus thrombotic) and of any vessel wall abnormalities that would lead to rethrombosis if not corrected by surgery or balloon angioplasty. A major drawback to this approach is that arterial catheterization is required for prolonged periods (20 hours, on average), leading to major bleeding and thromboembolic complications in 6% to 20% of patients. Therefore, the end points of thrombolytic therapy are (1) resolution and reconstitution of flow through the obstruction, (2) absence of change in the occlusion of the vessel on angiography, and (3) bleeding complications. If it is determined that thrombolysis is not progressing, it should be abandoned and surgical intervention undertaken.

Thrombectomy

Percutaneous aspiration thrombectomy This technique uses a large, thin-walled catheter and a large syringe to remove an embolus or thrombus from a vascular conduit, whether native vessel or graft. The catheter is placed as previously described [*see* Logistics of Thrombolysis, *above*] and is parked immediately by the clot. Aspiration of the clot with the syringe is then attempted. If the clot is new, success is likely, but an old clot that is organized will not be as amenable to removal. Percutaneous aspiration thrombectomy is most effective as an adjunct to catheter-directed thrombolysis.[26,27]

Percutaneous mechanical thrombectomy Percutaneous mechanical thrombectomy (PMT) functions on the basis of a hydrodynamic circulation. The basic concept is that a hydrodynamic vortex is created around the tip of the PMT catheter. Thrombectomy is accomplished with the introduction of a pressurized saline jet stream through the directed orifices in the distal tip of the catheter. The jets generate a localized low-pressure zone via the Bernoulli effect, which entrains and macerates thrombus. The saline and the fragmented thrombus are then sucked back into the exhaust lumen of the catheter and out of the body for disposal.

This technique has proved beneficial when used in appropriate settings and properly selected patients. Its efficiency relies on the age of the clot. Fresh thrombus is readily treated with PMT, but older clots are much less amenable to this technique and may have to be treated with an adjunctive catheter-based modality (e.g., angioplasty, intra-arterial thrombolysis, or atherectomy).[28-31]

Surgical Embolectomy and Revascularization

When a patient has significant sensory and motor deficits related to a profoundly ischemic limb, immediate surgical revascularization is indicated. The decision whether to accomplish this percutaneously or surgically should be made expeditiously. OR availability should be determined, the method of anesthesia should be chosen, and the technical details of the procedure should be planned [*see 96*

Infrainguinal Arterial Procedures]. Heparin administration should be started before the patient enters the OR. General anesthesia is the preferred method of anesthesia.

For lower-extremity emboli, access to the femoral vessels should be obtained rapidly. The common, deep, and superficial femoral arteries are controlled proximally and distally with tape, and the common femoral artery is opened transversely. Catheter embolectomy of the superficial femoral, deep femoral, common femoral, and external iliac arteries is then performed. Differently sized embolectomy catheters are used, depending on the size of each artery. In our experience, a No. 3 catheter is usually suitable for the deep femoral artery, a No. 4 for the superficial femoral artery, and a No. 5 for the common femoral and external iliac arteries. The extracted clot is sent for pathologic evaluation. When the clot is believed to be in the distal vessels of the lower extremity, control of the popliteal artery and its trifurcation is obtained via a popliteal incision. A No. 3 catheter should be adequate at this site.

For upper-extremity emboli, a curvilinear incision is made that starts on the medial aspect of the upper arm, extends transversely across the antecubital fossa, and ends halfway down the middle of the lower arm. This incision allows control of the brachial, radial, and ulnar arteries. A No. 3 embolectomy catheter is typically used here.

Several passes are done in each vessel until no more clot can be seen and there is brisk back-bleeding from the vessel. When no further clot can be retrieved, a completion angiogram is done to visualize the distal vessels and elucidate any anatomic pathology in the native vessels. If distal clot is still present after the completion angiogram, intraoperative thrombolysis can be employed for a brief period to soften the clot. The multiple-sidehole catheter is advanced distally to the location of the clot, the guide wire is passed through the lesion, and the catheter is passed over the wire into the substance of the clot. Infusion of the lytic agent is then started.

Repeat angiograms indicate whether the clot has dissolved or is still present. If the clot is still apparent, repeat embolectomy is attempted. If thrombosis rather than embolism is suspected, an underlying lesion must be sought. In performing the embolectomy, attention should be paid to the tactile sensations felt as the balloon is withdrawn. Such sensations give the operator a sense of the disease process. When several deflations are needed and the withdrawal path of the balloon feels rough, a long-standing process (e.g., an atherosclerotic calcified vessel with anatomic discrepancies) is likely.

If there appears to be no residual clot after embolectomy, then a completion angiogram is sufficient and the artery can be closed primarily. Heparin is continued, and the patient is eventually switched to warfarin, which is continued for at least 6 months postoperatively. Finally, the location from which the embolus originated is sought and appropriately treated. When an underlying lesion is identified, a decision must be made as to whether it can be treated with angioplasty or stenting or whether a formal bypass is required to correct the problem and salvage the limb.

Key to the final management of these patients is assessment of the lower extremities, especially the calves, for compartment syndrome. To minimize the chances that an otherwise successful surgical operation may fail as a consequence of this syndrome, we typically perform intraoperative fasciotomies on the extremity if profound ischemia has been present for several hours.

Cost Considerations

A retrospective study published in 1995 compared thrombolysis with surgical thrombectomy as first-line therapy for ALI.[32] Only the costs of the initial admission were documented. The average charge for the two treatments ranged from $20,000 to $26,000. Economic analysis confirmed that the total economic impact of thrombolysis approximated that of initial operative therapy. The conclusion of the study was that there was no difference between an endovascular approach and an operative approach with respect to cost. Thus, when acute treatment of ALI is being considered, cost should not be factored into the decision-making process.[32,33]

Atheroembolism

Atheroembolism is a condition in which microscopic cholesterol-laden debris travels from proximal arteries until it reaches the most distal arterial segments, typically in the skin of the lower extremities and in the end-organs.[34-37] This debris usually originates from unstable plaque found at inflection points in the arterial tree, especially in the aorta.[38,39] It may also originate from aneurysmal sacs either in the aorta or in the peripheral arteries.

CLINICAL EVALUATION

Patients with atheroembolism usually present with focal toe ischemia—the so-called blue-toe syndrome—in conjunction with palpable pulses in the distal extremity [*see Figure 1*]. Acute pain of sudden onset is typically noted in the affected area. This pain can often establish the exact timing of embolization. Cyanosis is present either on the toe or over a more extensive area if the atheroemboli were circulated throughout the extremity.[40,41] When both lower extremities are involved, an aortic source of the microemboli is commonly found.

A complete vascular examination should be performed and pulses documented. Although a patent arterial tree is the rule, emboli that are sufficiently small may travel through collateral channels. Palpation should be done to detect any aneurysmal disease. A massive proximal atheroembolic event may affect the entire abdominal wall and both extremities, giving the appearance of livedo reticularis. As the source of the atheroemboli ascends in the arterial tree, more vital organs (e.g., the kidneys and the GI tract) may be damaged.

Manipulation of an intra-arterial catheter or clamping or surgical manipulation of the arterial tree can also result in plaque disruption. In these cases, the adverse effects are usually apparent immediately after the procedure.

INVESTIGATIVE STUDIES

Doppler examination may visualize unstable ulcerated plaques or aneurysmal disease. Doppler segmental pressures may be used to identify the responsible lesion by localizing a significant drop in pressure and determining where the plaque is. Duplex imaging with noncolor flow can also provide clues to the morphology of a plaque. This is only true, however, in the extremity arteries. When the aorta is the suspected source of the emboli, computed tomography, magnetic resonance imaging, or magnetic resonance angiography is performed; these modalities provide better visualization of intraluminal disease. Arteriography also plays a useful role in identifying intraluminal pathology along the entire vascular tree. In addition, intravascular ultrasonography may be performed with the guide wire in place and may help delineate the extent of the underlying disease.

TREATMENT

If the atheroembolic events are minor and solitary, conservative medical management is recommended. If, however, the emboli are recurrent or massive, a thorough evaluation should be initiated, followed by urgent treatment.

Medical management of atheroembolism consists primarily of antiplatelet therapy. Given that most patients with atheroemboli are already receiving aspirin, addition of clopidogrel or ticlopidine

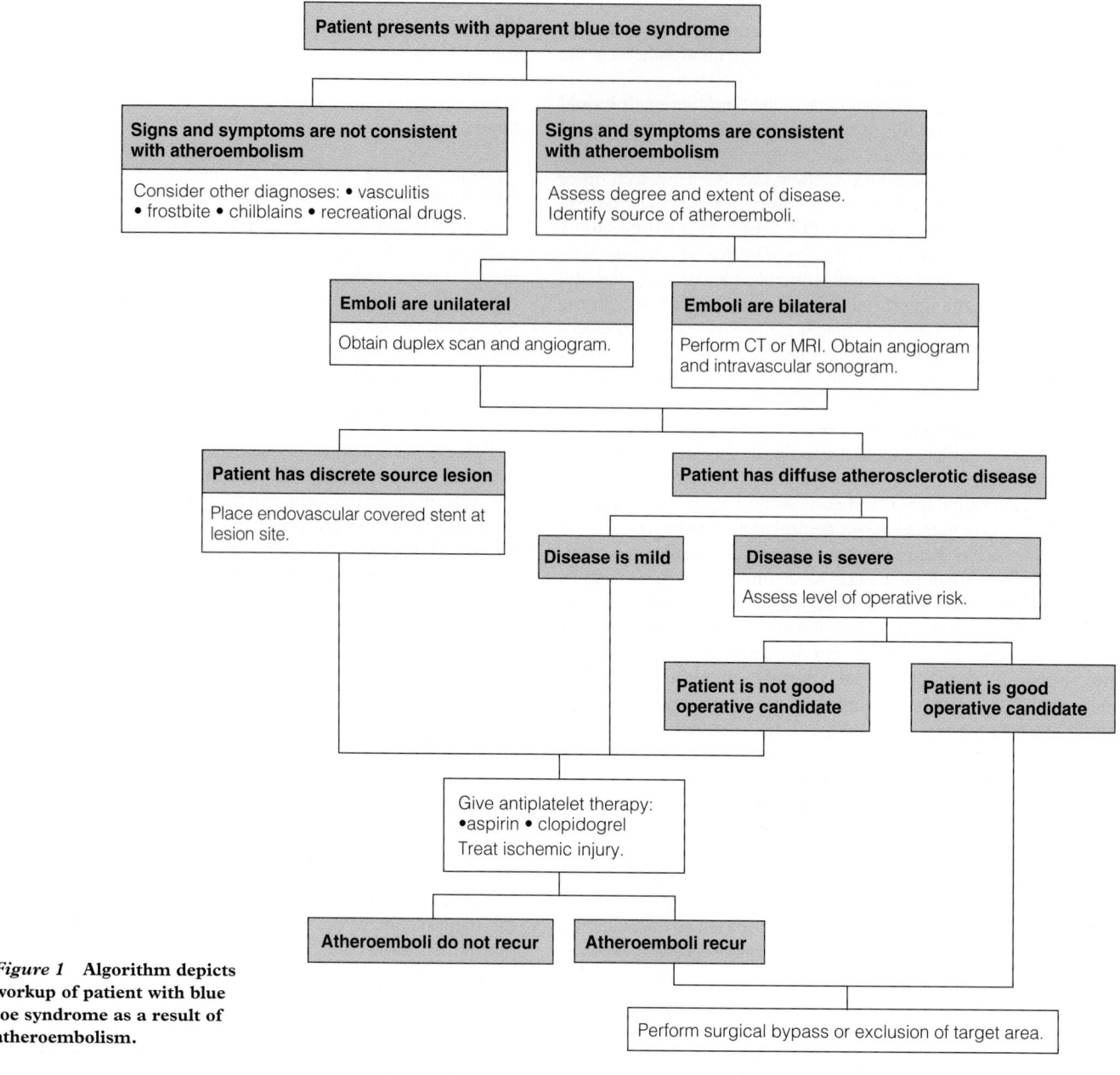

Figure 1 Algorithm depicts workup of patient with blue toe syndrome as a result of atheroembolism.

is appropriate. The optimal agents for preventing recurrence of atheroembolism may prove to be lipid-lowering drugs, particularly statins. At present, direct evidence from randomized trials supporting the use of statins to prevent atheroembolism is lacking, but the hypothesis remains under investigation.

The role of warfarin therapy in treating atheroembolic disease has not been established with certainty. Such therapy may even aggravate the disease process by causing intraplaque hemorrhage and increased embolization. The Warfarin Aspirin Recurrent Stroke Study (WARSS), a randomized multicenter study that included 2,206 patients who had recently experienced an ischemic stroke, found no evidence that warfarin is superior to aspirin for preventing recurrent ischemic stroke or death within 2 years.[42] Nor was there a significant difference in bleeding risk between warfarin-treated patients and aspirin-treated patients.

For patients with diffuse atherosclerotic disease, the mainstay of therapy is an antiplatelet regimen. Traditionally, an atheroembolic source has been treated by surgical excision or by exclusion of the disease process with a bypass graft, either of which provides a good

degree of safety from further embolization.[43] With the advent of endovascular surgery, however, the use of covered stents, placed securely and precisely at the site of the offending lesion, appears to be an increasingly effective and popular option [see Table 5].[44,45]

Table 5 Surgical Management of Atheroembolism

Source of Emboli	Treatment
Upper extremity	Bypass of subclavian or axillary artery First rib or cervical rib resection
Aorta	Focal disease: covered aortic stent Diffuse disease: aortobifemoral bypass
Iliac artery	Covered iliac stent
Popliteal artery	Ligation and bypass of popliteal artery

Our current approach to treating atheroembolism may be summarized as follows. The source lesion is first identified by means of the modalities already discussed. If embolization is minor, aspirin and clopidrogel are started. If embolization is recurrent or massive, an endovascular approach is attempted, involving the placement of a covered stent over the lesion. This approach is indicated for segments of the arterial tree where there are no collaterals, so that vital blood flow to organs is not hindered. If aneurysmal disease is present, either conventional or endovascular therapeutic approaches may be applied to exclude any source of emboli. In the case of thoracic aortic disease, covered stents may be placed to push the plaque against the wall and prevent further embolization. If suprarenal plaque cannot be treated with a stented graft, aortic ligation with an axillo-bifemoral bypass may be performed [see 91 Aortoiliac Reconstruction]. Such treatment does not, however, protect the renal and visceral vessels, and these patients require lifelong strict antiplatelet therapy.

Discussion

Pathophysiology of ALI

The course of ALI usually begins with occlusion of a peripheral artery or bypass graft. It can then develop either slowly, over an extended period, or quickly, over a few hours. A protracted course leading to thrombosis allows collateral vessels to form, and the onset of symptoms is gradual. When occlusion is acute, however, as in embolization or acute thrombosis of a vessel or a bypass graft, signs and symptoms of acute ischemia may become rapidly apparent, including excruciating pain, mottling, cyanosis, and, commonly, sensorimotor changes. Patients typically are seen in an emergency setting within hours after the onset of such symptoms.

With the advent of aggressive surgical management of peripheral vascular disease, more and more patients are being treated with bypass grafts. As a result, graft occlusions now outnumber thromboses of native arteries by a ratio of 1.3 to 1. Thrombotic occlusions outnumber embolic events by a ratio of 6 to 1.

The pathophysiology of limb ischemia is related to the progression of tissue infarction and irreversible cell death. The lower extremity comprises different tissues with different metabolic rates. The extent to which each cell type can tolerate ischemia depends on its metabolic rate. Bone and skin are the most resistant to ischemia, nervous tissue is the least resistant, and muscle is somewhere in between. For muscle and nerve cells, 6 hours is the approximate upper limit of ischemic tolerance; nervous tissue is affected well before this point.[46] Knowledge of the varying degrees of ischemic tolerance helps in determining the viability of the limb.

HYPOPERFUSION-REPERFUSION STATE

Hypoperfusion leads to ischemic infarcts via various mechanisms. During the hypoperfusion state, three major physiologic events occur. First, movement of blood through the vessels is slowed. As a result, the thrombus is able to grow and propagate, occluding collateral vessels and further decreasing blood flow. Second, ischemic cells swell and accumulate water. The resulting increase in pressure within a fixed space between fascial structures creates a compartment syndrome that further decreases flow and exacerbates the injury. Third, the precapillary arteriolar cells swell, narrowing the lumina of distal arterioles, capillaries, and venules and again reducing blood flow.

The reperfusion state that results when flow is restored can be as detrimental to the ischemic extremity as the hypoperfusion state was. During reperfusion, highly active oxygen metabolites are produced by neutrophils.[47] These free radicals destroy cells by attacking the unsaturated bonds of fatty acids within the phospholipid membrane, thereby disrupting the cell membrane, allowing water to enter the cell, and eventually causing cell lysis. Free radical scavengers (e.g., mannitol and superoxide dismutase) have a slight protective effect against reperfusion injury when given before large-scale release of these radicals.[48,49] In addition, myoglobin from injured muscle cells is released into the circulation and is cleared via the renal system. Myoglobin may cause renal failure through its direct toxic effect on the renal tubules and through the accumulation of casts in the tubules.

Creatinine phosphokinase levels may also increase to dramatic levels once perfusion is reestablished. High concentrations of lactic acid, potassium, thromboxane, and cellular enzymes are secreted as a consequence of the rhabdomyolysis; these substances accumulate in the ischemic limb and are released into the systemic circulation upon reperfusion.[50] In one study that measured the venous effluent from a series of patients with limb ischemia, the pH was 7.07 and the mean potassium level 5.7 mEq/L 5 minutes after surgical embolectomy.[51]

Detrimental physiologic changes are seen when toxic oxygen metabolites are released systemically. Depression of myocardial function, an increase in cardiac dysrhythmias, and loss of vascular tone may induce shock and even death.[52]

Etiology of ALI

The etiology of ALI can be divided into two distinct categories: thrombosis and embolism. A thorough evaluation must be performed to elucidate the precise cause of ischemia in each individual patient.

The two categories are each associated with specific symptoms and signs [see Table 6]. Knowledge of these associations helps direct the clinician toward the most appropriate means of accomplishing limb salvage in a given situation.

Thrombosis of a native vessel or bypass graft almost always develops in conjunction with an underlying lesion in the vessel or graft. The lesion usually has been present for some time, and the throm-

Table 6 Differentiation of Embolism from Thrombosis

Variable	Embolism	Thrombosis
Identifiable source	Frequently detected	None
Claudication	Rare	Frequent
Physical findings	Proximal and contralateral pulses normal	Evidence of ipsilateral and contralateral peripheral vascular disease
Angiographic findings	Minimal atherosclerosis; sharp cutoff; few collaterals; multiple occlusions	Diffuse atherosclerotic disease; tapered and irregular cutoff; well-developed collateral circulation

bosis occurs as a result of it. In contrast, embolic events occur in nondiseased vessels that become resting places for emboli.

THROMBOSIS

Native Artery Thrombosis

Native artery thrombosis is usually the end stage of a long-standing disease process of atheromatous plaque formation at specific sites in the arterial tree. Atherosclerotic plaque begins with the slow deposition of lipids in the intima of the vessel and continues with the deposition of calcium, resulting in an atherosclerotic core.[53] This core is a highly thrombogenic surface that encourages platelet aggregation, which results in disturbances of blood flow.[54] The flow disturbances create a zone of separation, stagnation, turbulence, and distorted velocity vectors. These factors cause low shear rates at inflection points in the arterial tree, and endothelial damage ensues. The endothelial damage activates a repair process that results in intimal hyperplasia, which causes further attraction of platelets and eventual thrombus formation. The process by which occlusion develops from an atheromatous plaque may be more important than the degree of stenosis within the lumen. This would explain why acute occlusion occurs in vessels with minimal (< 50%) stenosis: the contact between the atherosclerotic core and the bloodstream leads to platelet aggregation and hence to eventual thrombosis.

Occasionally, thrombosis of a native artery occurs without any obvious underlying pathologic condition. In such cases, a thorough investigation should be initiated into other causes of thrombosis (e.g., hypovolemia, malignancy, hypercoagulable states, and blood dyscrasias).

Bypass Graft Thrombosis

Aggressive management of patients with peripheral vascular disease has led to an increase in bypass graft procedures. As a result, graft thrombosis has become the leading cause of acute lower-extremity ischemia. In patients with native conduits, intimal hyperplasia and valvular hyperplasia are the two leading causes of graft failure.[55] The situation is different in the prosthetic graft population, where the inherent thrombogenicity of the graft material and kinking of the graft from crossing joints are the leading causes. These patients often have graft occlusions without any definable underlying lesion.

EMBOLISM

Peripheral arterial embolization results in the sudden onset of extreme ischemia as the absence of collateral vessels compounds the reduction in flow to the extremity. The heart is by far the predominant source of spontaneous arterial emboli. As the population ages, the number of patients with significant cardiac disease increases and the incidence of embolic phenomena increases. Over the past 20 years or so, the incidence of embolization has doubled, from 23 to 51 per 100,000 admissions. Atherosclerotic heart disease currently accounts for as many as 60% to 70% of all cases of arterial embolism,[56,57] and atrial fibrillation and rheumatic valvular disease account for the remaining 30% to 40%.[56,58]

With respect to peripheral emboli in particular, atrial fibrillation is currently associated with two thirds to three quarters of cases. Transthoracic echocardiography is notoriously insensitive in visualizing atrial clots, especially in the left atrial appendage, which is the most common cardiac source of emboli.[59,60] Transesophageal echocardiography, however, offers significantly better imaging of all four chambers and hence is considered the superior diagnostic test for suspected cardiac embolic sources.[61-64]

MI is the next most important cause of peripheral emboli. A 1986 study of 400 patients found that MI was a causative factor in 20%.[58]

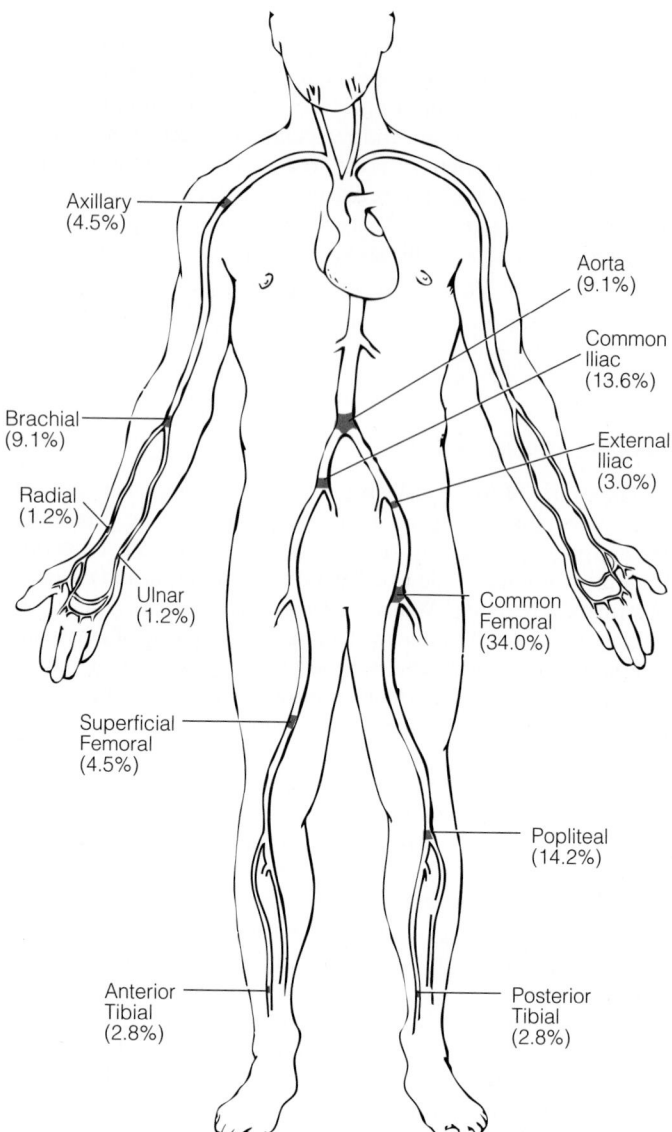

Figure 2 **Depicted are the most common sites of arterial embolic occlusions.**

Labels on figure:
Axillary (4.5%)
Aorta (9.1%)
Common Iliac (13.6%)
Brachial (9.1%)
External Iliac (3.0%)
Radial (1.2%)
Ulnar (1.2%)
Common Femoral (34.0%)
Superficial Femoral (4.5%)
Popliteal (14.2%)
Anterior Tibial (2.8%)
Posterior Tibial (2.8%)

After an MI, a left ventricular wall thrombus is often seen, with[65] or without[66-68] a left ventricular wall aneurysm; however, only 5% of such thrombi embolize and cause a problem.[66-68] Other studies suggest that the period in which the risk of embolization is highest for an intracardiac thrombus is that between day 3 and day 28.[69]

The ring portions of prosthetic cardiac valves are major intracardiac embolic sources before anticoagulation,[70] as are biologic xenovalves, which do not require anticoagulation.[71] Finally, tumors (e.g., atrial myxomas) are occasional sources of peripheral emboli.[69] Cardiac vegetations from bacterial or fungal endocarditis should be considered as possible sources of peripheral emboli when I.V. drug abuse is suspected in a patient with no previous history of cardiac disease.[72,73]

Noncardiac sources account for 5% to 10% of peripheral emboli. The majority of these involve downstream atherosclerotic arterial disease (e.g., aneurysms or unstable plaques).[74-77] Foreign objects (e.g., missiles[78,79]) and tumors (e.g., melanoma[80,81]) can also embolize if they gain access to the arterial tree. So-called paradoxical embolization occurs when a venous thrombus crosses from right to left via an atrial or ventricular route, gains access to the arterial side, and becomes an arterial embolus.[82-84] About 5% to 10% of emboli remain unidentified despite a thorough diagnostic evaluation[85,86]; some of these are now being attributed to hypercoagulable states.[87]

Incidence

As a consequence of the ongoing growth in the number of endovascular interventions being performed, overall incidence patterns for embolism are shifting yet again, with a greater number of emboli now arising from intravascular handling. A 1996 study found that 45% of all atheroemboli were iatrogenic and that the majority of these originated during manipulation of the abdominal aorta, the iliac artery, or the femoropopliteal artery, with the remainder originating during surgery.[88] Emboli usually lodge at arterial bifurcations and consequently impair blood flow to more than one vessel. Axial limb vessels account for 60% to 80% of clinically significant embolic events,[58,69,89] with the remainder divided between cerebral vessels (20%) and upper-extremity vessels (10% to 20%). The most common site for embolic lodgment is the common femoral bifurcation [see Figure 2]. The aortoiliac region is the next most common site, followed closely by the popliteal artery.[52,57,58,69,90,91]

The presence of normal pulses in the contralateral leg in a patient with an ischemic leg should elicit an aggressive workup to rule out cardiac sources for the emboli and may be a clue that the occlusive event is more likely to be embolic than thrombotic.

Upper-Extremity Emboli

Acute ischemia of the upper extremity is usually caused by embolism, usually deriving from an intracardiac source. Subclavian aneurysms, arteriovenous fistulae, upper-extremity arterial bypasses, and iatrogenic manipulation of the arteries are rare causes.[92] As noted (see above), emboli lodge at inflection points of the arterial tree. In the upper extremity, the bifurcation of the brachial artery into the radial and ulnar arteries is the most common lodgment site, followed by the takeoff of the deep brachial artery. Adequate exposure of all three arteries can be obtained via an elongated S-shaped incision that runs medially to laterally across the elbow joint.

Other Causes

Sepsis and cardiogenic shock bring about a low-flow state that places patients at high risk for thrombosis. Certain vasoconstrictors and recreational drugs are also associated with lower-extremity thrombosis.[93,94] Patients with these conditions usually present with bilateral extremity ischemia. Vasculitides (e.g., Takayasu) may also cause extremity ischemia.[95]

The hypercoagulable states (e.g., antithrombin deficiency, antiphospholipid syndrome, protein C and S deficiencies, factor V Leiden mutation, and hyperprothrombinemia) are the most common disorders associated with acute arterial thrombosis.[96] The consequences are usually devastating.

References

1. Davies B, Braithwaite BD, Birch PA, et al: Acute leg ischaemia in Gloucestershire. Br J Surg 84:504, 1997

2. Blaisdell FW, Steele M, Allen RE: Management of acute lower extremity arterial ischemia due to embolism and thrombosis. Surgery 84:822, 1978

3. Dormandy J, Heeck L, Vig S: Acute limb ischemia. Semin Vasc Surg 12:148, 1999

4. Rutherford RB, Baker JD, Ernst C, et al: Recommended standards for reports dealing with lower extremity ischemia: revised version. J Vasc Surg 26:517, 1997

5. Katzenschlager R, Ahmadi A, Atteneder M, et al: Colour duplex sonography-guided local lysis of occlusions in the femoro-popliteal region. Int Angiol 19:250, 2000

6. Mazzariol F, Ascher E, Hingorani A, et al: Lower-extremity revascularisation without preoperative contrast arteriography in 185 cases: lessons learned with duplex ultrasound arterial mapping. Eur J Vasc Endovasc Surg 19:509, 2000

7. Ascher E, Mazzariol F, Hingorani A, et al: The use of duplex ultrasound arterial mapping as an alternative to conventional arteriography for primary and secondary infrapopliteal bypasses. Am J Surg 178:162, 1999

8. Kim D, Porter DH, Brown R, et al: Renal artery imaging: a prospective comparison of intra-arterial digital subtraction angiography with conventional angiography. Angiology 42:345, 1991

9. Lindholt JS: Radiocontrast induced nephropathy. Eur J Vasc Endovasc Surg 4:296, 2003

10. Kerns SR, Hawkins IFJ, Sabatelli FW: Current status of carbon dioxide angiography. Radiol Clin North Am 33:15, 1995

11. Waver FA, Pentecoast MJ, Yellin AE, et al: Clinical applications of carbon dioxide/digital subtraction arteriography. J Vasc Surg 13:266, 1991

12. Bjork I, Lindahl U: Mechanism of the anticoagulant action of heparin. Mol Cell Biochem 48:161, 1982

13. Hirsh J, Dalen Je, Deykin D, et al: Heparin, mechanism of action, pharmacokinetics, dosing consideration, monitoring, efficacy and safety. Chest 102:337S, 1992

14. Salzman EW, Deykin D, Shapiro RM, et al: Management of heparin therapy: controlled prospective trial. N Engl J Med 292:1046, 1976

15. Walenga JM, Frenkel EP, Bick RL: Heparin-induced thrombocytopenia, paradoxical thromboembolism, and other adverse effects of heparin-type therapy. Hematol Oncol Clin North Am 7:259, 2003

16. Warkentin TE, Bernstein RA: Delayed-onset heparin-induced thrombocytopenia and cerebral thrombosis after a single administration of unfractionated heparin. N Engl J Med 348:1067, 2003

17. Kelton JG: Heparin-induced thrombocytopenia: an overview. Blood Rev 16:77, 2002

18. Rice L, Attisha WK, Drexler A, et al: Delayed-onset heparin-induced thrombocytopenia. Ann Intern Med 136:210, 2002

19. Visentin GP: Heparin-induced thrombocytopenia: molecular pathogenesis. Thromb Haemost 82:448,1999

20. Dotter C: Selective clot lysis with low-dose streptokinase. Radiology 111:31, 1974

21. Ouriel K, Shortell C, DeWeese JA, et al: A comparison of thrombolytic therapy with operative revascularization in the initial treatment of acute peripheral arterial ischemia. J Vasc Surg 19:1021, 1994

22. Weaver FA, Camerota AJ, Youngblood M, et al: Surgical revascularization versus thrombolysis for non-embolic lower extremity native artery occlusions: results of a prospective randomized trial. The STILE investigators: Surgery versus Thrombolysis for Ischemia of the Lower Extremity. J Vasc Surg 24:513, 1996

23. Ouriel K, Veith FJ, Sasahara AA: Thrombolysis or peripheral arterial surgery: phase I results. TOPAS investigators. J Vasc Surg 23:64, 1996

24. A comparison of recombinant urokinase with vascular surgery as initial treatment for acute arterial occlusion of the legs. Thrombolysis or Peripheral Arterial Surgery (TOPAS) investigators. N Engl J Med 338:1105, 1998

25. Mahler F, Schneider E, Hess H: Recombinant tissue plasminogen activator versus urokinase for local thrombolysis of femoropopliteal occlusions: a prospective, randomized multicenter trial. J Endovasc Ther 8:638, 2001

26. Morgan R, Belli AM: Percutaneous thrombectomy: a review. Eur Radiol 12:205, 2002

27. Zehnder T, Birrer M, Do DD, et al: Percutaneous catheter thrombus aspiration for acute or subacute arterial occlusion of the legs: how much thrombolysis is needed? Eur J Vasc Endovasc Surg 20:41, 2000

28. Crain MR: Percutaneous mechanical thrombolysis and thrombectomy. Tech Vasc Interv Radiol 1:235, 1998

29. Demin VV, Zeienin VV, Zheludkov AN, et al: Initial experience of transcutaneous rheolytic thrombectomy for peripheral major arterial lesions. Angiol Vasc Surg 5:1, 1999

30. Dick A, Neuerburg J, Schmitz-Rode T, et al: Declotting of embolized temporary vena cava filter by ultrasound and the AngioJet: comparative experimental in vitro studies. Invest Radiol 33:91, 1998

31. Douek PC, Gandjbakhche A, Leon MB, et al: Functional properties of a 'prototype rheolytic thrombectomy catheter' for percutaneous thrombectomy—in vitro investigations. Invest Radiol 29:547, 1994

32. Ouriel K, Kolassa M, DeWeese JA, et al: Economic implications of thrombolysis or operation as the initial treatment modality in acute peripheral arterial occlusion. Surgery 118:810, 1995

33. Korn P, Khilnani NM, Fellers JC, et al: Thrombolysis for native arterial occlusions of the lower extremities: clinical outcome and cost. J Vasc Surg 33:1148, 2001

34. Carvajal JA, Anderson WR, Weiss L, et al: Atheroembolism: an etiologic factor in renal insufficiency, gastrointestinal hemorrhages, and peripheral vascular diseases. Arch Intern Med 119:593, 1967

35. Karmody AM, Jordan FR, Zaman SM: Left colon gangrene after acute mesenteric artery occlusion. Arch Surg 111:972, 1976

36. Gore L, Collins DP: Spontaneous atheromatous embolization: review of the literature and a report of 16 additional cases. Am J Clin Pathol 33:416, 1960

37. Ramirez G, O'Neill WM, Lambert R, et al: Cholesterol embolization: a complication of angiography. Arch Intern Med 118:534, 1966

38. Williams GM, Harrington D, Burdick J, et al: Mural thrombus of the aorta: an important, frequently neglected cause of large peripheral emboli. Ann Surg 194:737, 1981

39. Khatibzadeh M, Mitusch R, Stierle U, et al: Aortic atherosclerotic plaques as a source of systemic embolization. J Am Coll Cardiol 27:664, 1996

40. Falanga V, Fine MJ, Kapoor WN: The cutaneous manifestations of cholesterol crystal embolization. Arch Dermatol 122:1194, 1986

41. Karmody AM, Powers SR, Monaco VJ, et al: "Blue toe syndrome": an indication for limb salvage surgery. Arch Surg 111:1263, 1976

42. Mohr JP, Thompson JL, Lazar RM, et al: A comparison of warfarin and aspirin for the prevention of recurrent ischemic stroke. N Engl J Med 345:1444, 2001

43. Keen RR, McCarthy WJ, Shireman PK, et al: Surgical management of atheroembolism. J Vasc Surg 21:773, 1995

44. Dougherty MJ, Calligaro KD: Endovascular treatment of embolization of aortic plaque with covered stents. J Vasc Surg 36:727, 2002

45. Kumins NH, Owens EL, Oglevie SB, et al: Early experience using the Wallgraft in the management of distal microembolism from common iliac artery pathology. Ann Vasc Surg 16:181, 2002

46. Blebea J, Kerr JC, Franco CD, et al: Technetium 99m pyrophosphate quantitation of skeletal muscle ischemia and reperfusion injury. J Vasc Surg 8:117, 1998

47. Quinones-Baldrich WJ, Chervu A, Hernandez JJ, et al: Skeletal muscle function after ischemia: "no reflow" versus reperfusion injury. J Surg Res 51:5, 1991

48. Ricci MA, Graham Am, Corbisiero R, et al: Are free radical scavengers beneficial in the treatment of compartment syndrome after acute arterial ischemia? J Vasc Surg 9:244, 1989

49. Ouriel K, Smedira NG, Ricotta JJ: Protection of the kidney after temporary ischemia: free radical scavengers. J Vasc Surg 2:49, 1985

50. Mathieson MA, Dunham BM, Huval WV, et al: Ischemia of the limb stimulates thromboxane production and myocardial depression. Surg Gynecol Obstet 157:500, 1983

51. Fischer R, Fogarty T, Morrow A: A clinical and biochemical observation of the effect of transient femoral artery occlusion in man. Surgery 68:233, 1970

52. Green RM, DeWeese J, Rob CG: Arterial embolectomy before and after the Fogarty catheter. Surgery 77:24, 1975

53. Stary HC, Chandler AB, Dinsmore RE, et al: A definition of advanced types of atherosclerotic lesions and a histological classification of atherosclerosis: a report from the committee on vascular lesions of the council on arteriosclerosis, American Heart Association. Circulation 92:1355, 1995

54. Fernandez-Ortiz A, Badimon JJ, Falk E, et al: Characterization of the relative thrombogenicity of atherosclerotic plaque components: implications for consequences of plaque rupture. J Am Coll Cardiol 23:1562, 1994

55. Ouriel K, Shortell CK, Green RM, et al: Differential mechanisms of failure of autogenous and non-autogenous bypass conduits: an assessment following successful graft thrombolysis. Cardiovasc Surg 3:469, 1995

56. Abbott W, Maloney R, McCabe C et al: Arterial embolism a 44 year perspective. Am J Surg 143:460, 1982

57. Fogarty T, Daily P, Shumway N, et al: Experience with balloon catheter technique for arterial embolectomy. Am J Surg 122:231, 1971

58. Paneta T, Thomson J, Talkington C, et al: Arterial embolectomy: a 34 year experience with 400 cases. Surg Clin North Am 66:339, 1986

59. Shresta N, Moreno F, Narcisco F, et al: Two dimensional echocardiographic diagnosis of left atrial thrombus in rheumatic heart disease: a clinicopathologic study. Circulation 67:341, 1983

60. Schweizer P, Bardos F, Erbel R: Detection of left atrial thrombi by echocardiography. Br Heart J 45:148, 1981

61. Daniel W, Mugge A: Transesophageal echocardiography. N Engl J Med 332:1268, 1995

62. Husain A, Alter M: Transesophageal echocardiography in diagnosing cardioembolic stroke. Clin Cardiol 18:705, 1995

63. Seward J, Khandheria B, Oh J, et al: Transesophageal echocardiography: technique, anatomic correlations, implementation, and clinical applications. Mayo Clin Proc 63:649, 1988

64. Rubin B, Barzilai B, Allen B, et al: Detection of the source of arterial emboli by transesophageal echocardiography: a case report. J Vasc Surg 15:573, 1992

65. Loop F, Effler D, Navia J, et al: Aneurysms of the left ventricle: survival and results of a ten-year surgical experience. Ann Surg 178:399, 1973

66. Hellerstein H, Martin J: Incidence of thromboembolic lesions accompanying myocardial infarction. Am Heart J 33:443, 1947

67. Keely E, Hillis L: Left ventricular mural thrombus after acute myocardial infarction. Clin Cardiol 19:83, 1996

68. Asinger R, Mikell F, Elsperger J: Incidence of left ventricular thrombosis after acute transmural myocardial infarction. N Engl J Med 305:297, 1981

69. Darling R, Austen W, Linton R: Arterial embolism. Surg Gynecol Obstet 124:106, 1967

70. Perier P, Bessou J, Swanson J, et al: Comparative evaluation of aortic valve replacement with Starr, Bjork, and porcine valve prostheses. Circulation 72:140, 1985

71. Pipkin R, Buch W, Fogart T: Evaluation of aortic valve replacement with porcine xenograft without long-term anticoagulation. J Thorac Cardiovasc Surg 71:179, 1976

72. Kitts D, Bongard F, Klein S: Septic embolism complicating infective endocarditis. J Vasc Surg 14:1480, 1991

73. Freischlag J, Asburn H, Sedwitz M, et al: Septic peripheral embolization from bacterial and fungal endocarditis. Ann Vasc Surg 3:318, 1989

74. Lord J Jr, Rossi G, Daliana M, et al: Unsuspected abdominal aortic aneurysm as the cause of peripheral arterial occlusive disease. Ann Surg 177:767, 1973

75. Kempczynski R: Lower extremity emboli from ulcerating atherosclerotic plaque. JAMA 241:807, 1979

76. Kwaan J, Vander Molen R, Stemmer E, et al: Peripheral embolism resulting from unsuspected atheromatous plaques. Surgery 78:583, 1975

77. Machleder H, Takiff H, Lois J, et al: Aortic mural thrombus: an occult source of arterial thromboembolism. J Vasc Surg 4:473, 1986

78. Shannon J, Nghia M, Stanton P Jr, et al: Peripheral arterial missile embolization: a case report and a 22 year review of the literature. J Vasc Surg 5:773, 1987

79. Symbas P, Harlaftis N: Bullet emboli in the pulmonary and systemic arteries. Ann Surg 185:318, 1977

80. Harriss R, Andros G, Dulawa L, et al: Malignant melanoma embolus as a cause of acute aortic occlusion: report of a case. J Vasc Surg 3:550, 1986

81. Morasch MD, Shanik GD: Tumor embolus: a case report and review of the literature. Ann Vasc Surg 17:210, 2003

82. Ward R, Jones D, Haponik E: Paradoxical embolism: an underrecognized problem. Chest 108:549, 1995

83. Katz S, Andros G, Kohl R, et al: Arterial emboli of venous orign. Surg Gynecol Obstet 174:17, 1992

84. Gazzaniga A, Dalen J: Paradoxical embolism: its pathophysiology and clinical recognition. Ann Surg 171:137, 1970

85. Hight D, Tilney N, Couch N: Changing clinical trends in patients with peripheral emboli. Surgery 79:172, 1976

86. Thompson J, Sigler L, Raut P, et al: Arterial embolectomy: a 20 year experience. Surgery 67:212, 1970

87. Eason J, Mills J, Beckett W: Hypercoagulable states in arterial thromboembolism. Surg Gynecol Obstet 174:211, 1992

88. Sharma P, Babu P, Shah P, et al: Changing patterns of atheroembolism. Cardiovasc Surg 4:573, 1996

89. Elliott J, Hageman J, Szilagyi D: Arterial embolization: problems of source, multiplicity, recurrence, and delayed treatment. Surgery 88:833, 1980

90. Elliott JP Jr, Hageman J, Szilagyi D, et al: Arterial embolization: problems of source, multiplicity, recurrence and delayed treatment. Surgery 88:883, 1980

91. Dale W: Differential management of acute peripheral ischemia. J Vasc Surg 1:269, 1984

92. Banis JC Jr, Rich N, Whelan TJ Jr: Ischemia of the upper extremity due to noncardiac emboli. Am J Surg 134:131, 1977

93. Balbir-Gurman A, Braun-Moscovici Y, Nahir AM: Cocaine-induced Raynaud's phenomenon and ischaemic finger necrosis. Clin Rheumatol 20:376, 2001

94. Disdier P, Granel B, Serratrice J, et al: Cannabis arteritis revisited—ten new case reports. Angiology 52:1, 2001

95. Ishikawa K: Patterns of symptoms and prognosis in occlusive thromboarthropathy (Takayasu's disease). J Am Coll Cardiol 8:1401, 1986

96. Mira Y, Todoli T, Alonso R, et al: Factor V Leiden and prothrombin G20210A in relation to arterial and/or vein rethrombosis: two cases. Clin Appl Thromb Hemost 7:234, 2001

97. Ouriel K: Acute ischemia and its sequelae. Vascular Surgery, 5th ed. Rutherford RB, Ed. WB Saunders Co, Philadelphia, 2000

98. Thrombolysis in the management of lower limb peripheral arterial occlusion—a consensus document. Working Party on Thrombosis in the Management of Limb Ischemia. J Vasc Interv Radiol 14(9 Pt 2):5337, 2003

John T. Owings, M.D., F.A.C.S.

Deep vein thrombosis (DVT) (deep thrombophlebitis) occurs in approximately 2.5 million people in the United States each year.[1] The incidence of DVT in surgical patients varies widely depending on the method of study: in eight series, the incidence of DVT verified by venography or autopsy ranged from 18% to 90% (average, 42%).[2]

Reviews suggest that pulmonary embolism (PE) occurs in approximately 700,000 people in the United States each year, of whom about 200,000 will die as a result.[3,4] In the absence of prophylaxis, fatal PE occurs in 4% to 7% of hip surgery patients and in 0.1% to 0.8% of general surgery patients.[3,5] In 40% to 60% of patients who die of PE, the diagnosis is not made clinically. PE may be responsible for as many as 5% of postoperative deaths, and it may occur in as many as 25% of patients admitted to the hospital.[6,7] Pulmonary infarction occurs in about 10% of PE patients.[8]

Significant PE is believed, as a rule, to arise from thrombosis of the deep veins of the thigh and the pelvis. Most studies of thromboembolism use DVT as a surrogate end point for PE. The only major study of thromboembolism prophylaxis to date that successfully used death from PE as an end point required more than 5,000 patients to reach statistical significance.[9] Accordingly, the National Institutes of Health has concluded that using DVT as a surrogate for PE is a valid approach.[10]

The optimal treatment of thromboembolism is prevention, particularly in persons at high risk [*see Table 1*].[11,12] Risk factors for venous thromboembolism include increased age ($\geq$ 30 years in some studies),[13] major trauma (Injury Severity Score of 15 or greater or the presence of a pelvic or lower-extremity long bone fracture), morbid obesity, major operation, prolonged immobility, thrombophilia, and previous thromboembolism.

Prophylaxis against Thromboembolism

In evaluating the effectiveness of the methods used to prevent thromboembolic complications, it is important to consider the specific population of patients studied. Within the surgical patient population, there is one reasonable division: between (1) patients who have an ongoing pathologic process that affects coagulation when first encountered and (2) elective patients for whom the surgical insult is the inciting risk factor. For the first group, the typical patient is the polytrauma patient; for the second, the patient undergoing elective hip or knee replacement.

The key distinction between these two groups lies in whether prophylaxis can be given before the inciting insult. Several techniques for prophylaxis of thromboembolism that are effective when employed before the inciting event are completely ineffective if employed afterward. This point can be illustrated by comparing elective colorectal surgery patients with trauma patients. In a 2001 study, elective colorectal surgery patients who were given their first dose of unfractionated heparin before operation and then were given additional doses of unfractionated heparin (5,000 units subcutaneously three times daily) after operation were as well protected against DVT as comparable patients receiving low-molecular-weight heparin (LMWH) and were at lower risk for bleeding.[14] In a 1996 study, however, trauma patients who were given unfrac-

tionated heparin subcutaneously as prophylaxis against DVT fared no better than those treated with placebo.[15] Subsequent work has shown that effective DVT prophylaxis can be achieved in this population by using the LMWH enoxaparin.

COMPRESSION TECHNIQUES

Elastic stockings have long been used as prophylaxis for thromboembolism. Most commercial stockings, however, do not fit adequately or provide adequate compression and thus probably offer little or no benefit.[4] Low-molecular-weight dextran, which lowers blood viscosity and inhibits platelet aggregation, may be helpful in certain instances, but data showing greater efficacy as compared with current techniques are lacking.[12]

Pneumatic devices that compress the venous plexuses of the lower extremities are popular because they do not require anticoagulation and thus are not associated with increased bleeding risk. Intermittent pneumatic compression is capable of intermittently increasing venous flow velocities in the femoral and pelvic veins.[16] It has been argued that some of the benefit might derive from the known tourniquet effect of enhancing fibrinolytic activity, attributed both to an increase in tissue plasminogen activator (t-PA) and to a decrease in plasminogen activator inhibitor (PAI). This argument seems to be valid for up to 24 hours of continuous use,[17] but after that point, the effect is exhausted.[16] Intermittent pneumatic compression is a safe, albeit somewhat uncomfortable, method of preventing clots in patients immobilized for prolonged periods. It is particularly useful in critical care units, where other forms of prophylaxis are inapplicable or contraindicated.[11]

Several different pneumatic compression devices have been developed. The first to gain widespread acceptance was the full-length (calf and thigh) sequential compression stocking, which proved effective in a number of settings, including trauma.[18]

Table 1 **Risk Factors for the Development of Venous Thromboembolism**

Hypercoagulability
   Congenital hypercoagulability
   Malignancy
   Oral contraceptives
   Polycythemia
   Thrombocytosis
Venous stasis
   Immobility
   Varicose veins
   Advanced age
   Congestive heart failure
   Obesity
Endothelial injury
   Trauma
   Recent surgery
   Severe infection

Because some injured patients were unable to wear the device, various modified compression devices were developed, including a calf-only device and a foot pump designed to compress the plantar venous plexus. Several studies have demonstrated that the various compression devices are not all equally effective in preventing thromboembolism. This is an important point because many of the devices are marketed solely on the basis of compliance data rather than efficacy data; those that are marketed without published evidence of efficacy often use cost advantages to gain market share.

The effectiveness of pneumatic compression devices is based on their ability to increase peak venous flow velocity in the large vessels of the thigh and the pelvis. Because some units create higher peak flow velocities, it would be logical to assume that these units would be more effective in reducing DVT. Support was lent to this assumption by a 2000 study in which more than 300 patients undergoing elective knee surgery were treated with different compression devices.[19] Devices applying asymmetrical compression (which results in higher peak venous flow velocity) were compared with traditional compression devices, and calf-only devices were compared with calf-and-thigh devices. The two calf-and-thigh units studied proved superior to the calf-only unit, and the calf-and-thigh asymmetrical sequential compression device that generated higher peak flow velocities was superior to the traditional calf-and-thigh device. Similar results were obtained in a 2004 study that compared knee-high compression devices.[20]

It is therefore important to recognize that although compliance is a critical component of compression devices, differences in efficacy must be taken into account. Given the absence of efficacy data for many of the compression devices now in use, great caution should be exercised in considering whether these products should be adopted, regardless of anticipated cost savings.

PROPHYLACTIC ANTICOAGULATION

A major study of thromboembolic prophylaxis in hip surgery patients found that subcutaneous administration of 5,000 units of heparin two or three times daily before, during, and after the operation substantially reduced thromboembolic complications without increasing bleeding.[5] This low-dose protocol has been criticized as being insufficiently individualized for specific high-risk patients. Low-dose heparin acts by markedly augmenting the antithrombotic effect of antithrombin[21]; therefore, it may be ineffective if antithrombin levels are reduced, and higher doses may be more appropriate in such settings.

Because of these pitfalls, an adjusted-dose technique was devised in the mid-1980s.[22] In this method, heparin is given (either subcutaneously or I.V.) in sufficient doses to elevate the activated partial thromboplastin time (aPTT) by 2 to 5 seconds, thereby compensating for depleted antithrombin levels in high-risk patients. This technique is superior to the low-dose method for preventing venous thromboembolism,[22] and for practical purposes, it should replace the latter as the standard prophylactic dosing technique for unfractionated heparin.[22,23]

LMWH possesses the same antithrombin-potentiating pentasaccharide chain that unfractionated heparin does. Consequently, it is similarly ineffective if antithrombin levels are depleted. The main advantage of LMWH over unfractionated heparin is that it has a more dependable half-life and bioavailability. Thus, it can be given without monitoring of drug effect or plasma heparin level.

Most of the clinical trials documenting the efficacy of LMWH evaluated patients undergoing elective hip[24,25] or knee operations. A few, however, addressed other patient populations (e.g., trauma patients).[15] In these studies, the incidence of DVT in patients receiving unmonitored LMWH therapy was generally lower than that in patients receiving placebo[24] or low-dose heparin.[15,25] LMWH therapy and adjusted-dose heparin therapy were of roughly equal efficacy.

In the light of these data, it appears that LMWH can be recommended over low-dose unfractionated heparin in elective, emergency, and trauma patients. Whether it is superior to adjusted-dose unfractionated heparin therapy remains uncertain, though it is clearly simpler to manage. Where compliance with monitoring and

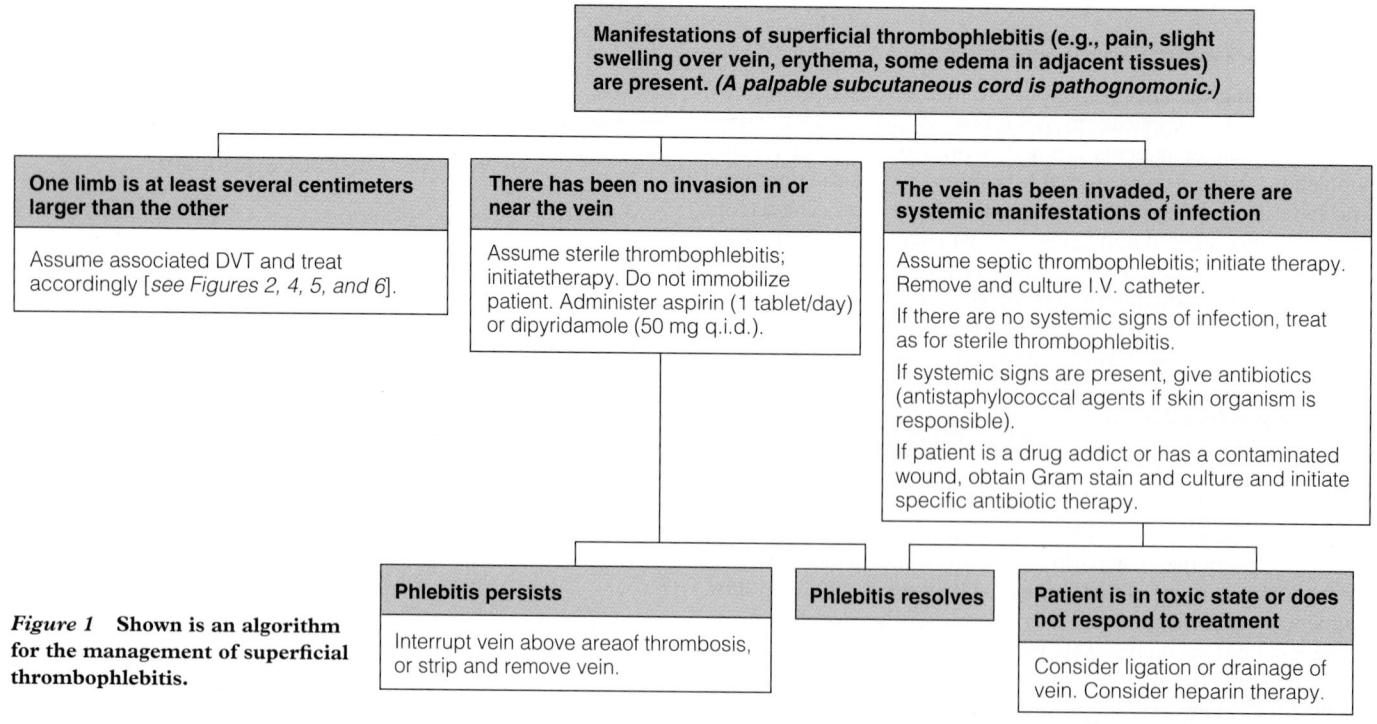

Figure 1 **Shown is an algorithm for the management of superficial thrombophlebitis.**

Manifestations of superficial thrombophlebitis (e.g., pain, slight swelling over vein, erythema, some edema in adjacent tissues) are present. *(A palpable subcutaneous cord is pathognomonic.)*

One limb is at least several centimeters larger than the other

Assume associated DVT and treat accordingly [*see Figures 2, 4, 5, and 6*].

There has been no invasion in or near the vein

Assume sterile thrombophlebitis; initiate therapy. Do not immobilize patient. Administer aspirin (1 tablet/day) or dipyridamole (50 mg q.i.d.).

The vein has been invaded, or there are systemic manifestations of infection

Assume septic thrombophlebitis; initiate therapy. Remove and culture I.V. catheter.

If there are no systemic signs of infection, treat as for sterile thrombophlebitis.

If systemic signs are present, give antibiotics (antistaphylococcal agents if skin organism is responsible).

If patient is a drug addict or has a contaminated wound, obtain Gram stain and culture and initiate specific antibiotic therapy.

Phlebitis persists

Interrupt vein above area of thrombosis, or strip and remove vein.

Phlebitis resolves

Patient is in toxic state or does not respond to treatment

Consider ligation or drainage of vein. Consider heparin therapy.

dose-adjusting protocols is an issue, unmonitored LMWH therapy may well be preferable.

Fondaparinux, a synthetic form of the specific pentasaccharide that interacts with antithrombin to potentiate its effect, has been approved by the Food and Drug Administration. This agent is smaller than the LMWHs and seems to have the same advantages over these substances that they have over unfractionated heparin—namely, increased bioavailability, longer half-life, and a more consistent effect. As the molecular weight of the antithrombin potentiator decreases, the antithrombotic effect focuses more sharply on inhibiting factor X (as opposed to factors II, IX, XII, etc.).

Before fondaparinux is uniformly adopted for thromboembolism prophylaxis, the supporting evidence should be carefully considered. The initial findings are quite promising. In a prospective, randomized trial that included approximately 1,700 hip fracture patients, fondaparinux was superior to enoxaparin with respect to the incidence of venographically identified DVT[26]; however, the enoxaparin dosage (40 mg once daily) was lower than the dosage shown to be effective in trauma patients by previous investigators (30 mg twice daily).[15] No significant difference in bleeding rates was observed. In another trial, which included approximately 700 patients undergoing elective knee surgery, fondaparinux, 2.5 mg once daily, proved superior to enoxaparin, 30 mg twice daily.[27] In this study, the bleeding rate was significantly higher with fondaparinux.

Ultimately, with regard to prophylactic anticoagulation, simple logic applies. The more potent the anticoagulant used, the lower the risk of PE and the higher the risk of serious bleeding. It is therefore appropriate to base one's selection of an anticoagulant regimen on a careful weighing of the expected benefits against the anticipated bleeding risk.

In some patients (e.g., those undergoing major gynecologic procedures), warfarin may be used instead of heparin.[12,28] A low-dose regimen (as little as 1 mg/day) may offer some prophylactic benefit.[28] Warfarin anticoagulation must be started 3 or 4 days before the surgical procedure. The international normalized ratio (INR) [see General Principles of Anticoagulation and Lytic Therapy, below] should be kept below 3.0 to prevent excessive bleeding. Warfarin is not as easy to regulate as heparin is. In addition, the therapeutic effect takes several days to be realized and several more days to wear off. Frequently, postoperative patients are unable to resume a normal stable diet. Because warfarin interferes with the clotting factors in the vitamin K pathway, dosage management in the immediate postoperative period is challenging. Because the risk of intracranial bleeding is greater with warfarin than with heparin, great care should be taken in using warfarin for immediate perioperative prophylaxis.

PROPHYLACTIC VENA CAVAL INTERRUPTION

Prophylactic vena caval interruption or filter placement provides prophylaxis only against PE, not against DVT, and thus is discussed elsewhere [see Pulmonary Embolism, Minor, Vena Cava Filters, below]. There is evidence that placement of a vena cava filter in fact increases the likelihood of DVT.[29]

Superficial Thrombophlebitis

Characteristic clinical manifestations of superficial thrombophlebitis [see Figure 1] include pain and slight swelling of the extremity, with most of the edema over the course of the involved vein. Unless the patient is obese, a palpable, tender subcutaneous cord is usually found (a pathognomonic finding). Erythema may be present in the overlying skin. The differential diagnosis includes cellulitis and streptococcal lymphangitis. For both conditions, there should be a proximal source (e.g., an open wound). If there is overt limb swelling in a patient who appears to have superficial phlebitis, DVT should be assumed and appropriate treatment [see Deep Vein Thrombosis, below] initiated.

Superficial thrombophlebitis is largely benign but is often overtreated out of fear that infection may be contributing to phlebitis. It is therefore important to differentiate between sterile and septic superficial thrombophlebitis.

STERILE

If there is no invasion in or near the superficial vein involved, sterile thrombophlebitis can be assumed with minimal risk of misdiagnosis. It is best treated simply by giving aspirin (one tablet daily) or dipyridamole (50 mg four times daily).

If superficial phlebitis of the saphenous vein extends to the saphenofemoral junction, interruption of the vein may be appropriate. The choice of treatment is between interrupting the vein above the area of palpable thrombosis and stripping the vein. The second alternative carries a higher morbidity but can be effective when there are associated varicosities. Stripping of the channels above and below the phlebitic process as well as the phlebitic area itself removes the risk of extension and subsequent recurrence. Several authors have explored medical management of patients with above-the-knee superficial thrombophlebitis, using an approach similar to that used for DVT. Therapeutic-dose heparin (unfractionated heparin or LMWH) is given initially, followed by long-term oral anticoagulation. The incidence of extension may be higher than with surgical management, but the operative risks are avoided.[30]

SEPTIC

If there are systemic manifestations of severe infection, septic thrombophlebitis is likely. In addition, the induration, tenderness, and redness over and along the course of the vein are usually more extensive than with sterile thrombophlebitis.

Septic thrombophlebitis associated with an I.V. catheter can be detected by removing the device and culturing the tip. Antibiotics should be administered. In most cases, antistaphylococcal drugs are appropriate. If the patient is a drug addict or phlebitis is associated with a contaminated wound, blood samples for culture and Gram staining should be obtained by aspirating the vein. Specific antibiotic therapy directed toward the organisms identified should then be instituted.

If the patient is in a toxic state from presumed septic thrombophlebitis in a subcutaneous vein or is not responding to treatment, it may be appropriate to ligate the vein, to drain it by cutting down on the phlebitic process with the patient under local or general anesthesia and laying the vein open, or to combine ligation with drainage. Moist compresses are then applied, the area is immobilized, and antibiotics are administered. Heparin may occasionally be of value, particularly when the process appears to be extending into the deep venous system.

Deep Vein Thrombosis

DVT can involve either obstructive clots, which affect drainage of venous blood from an extremity, or nonobstructive clots, which are relatively asymptomatic. The latter may be more dangerous because such clots are not circumferentially attached to the vein wall and thus are more likely to embolize. DVT may be divided into three main forms: nonocclusive, occlusive, and phlegmasia cerulea dolens (massive, limb-threatening DVT).

NONOCCLUSIVE

Nonocclusive DVT is common in postoperative and trauma patients but all too often is not suspected until an embolic complication occurs.[31] There may be absolutely no manifestations of clot on clinical examination, or there may be nonspecific swelling in an extremity; rarely is there sufficient pain or tenderness to suggest DVT. Consequently, it is essential to be aware of the major risk factors [see Table 1].

When DVT develops in an outpatient, every effort should be made to determine the cause [see Figure 2]. Apparent spontaneous onset is often the manifestation of an underlying malignancy or even a congenital clotting tendency that will necessitate lifelong treatment [see Hypercoagulability States, below]. Conversely, when risk factors for DVT are identified in a hospitalized patient, it can be assumed that the cause is acquired and that the clotting tendency will be reversed upon recovery.

Before therapy is begun, the diagnosis should be verified. The differential diagnosis includes muscle contusion, plantar or gastrocnemius muscle rupture, ruptured Baker's cyst, popliteal artery aneurysm, arthritis of the knee or the ankle, cellulitis, and myositis. The gold standard for diagnosis of DVT is ascending venography. However, study of the entire lower-extremity venous system often involves injection of dye not only at the foot or ankle level [see Figure 3] but also at the groin level for visualization of the iliac and femoral veins. This approach is uncomfortable and is associated with morbidity; in critically ill ICU patients, it may not be feasible. Accordingly, noninvasive evaluation techniques are favored.

The presence of intravascular clot can be confirmed by detecting D-dimer, a product formed when cross-linked fibrin is broken down by the fibrinolytic system. Both qualitative and quantitative assays are in current use. The various quantitative assays available have differing negative predictive values. The gold standard is the enzyme-linked immunosorbent assay (ELISA) method. Generally, 500 µg/L (in fibrin-equivalent units) or 250 µg/L (in standard units) is an acceptable threshold for a positive result. The latex agglutination test, though inexpensive, has an unacceptably low sensitivity and is the one quantitative method that should not be used. Because some amount of physiologic intravascular clot (e.g., at a wound site) is to be expected in many, if not most, patients at risk for DVT, a positive D-dimer assay is of little diagnostic value. D-dimer assay is therefore unsuitable for screening. In patients suspected of having DVT or PE, however, a negative D-dimer assay can, for the most part, rule out DVT and, by extension, PE.[32-34]

Various forms of plethysmography (e.g., impedance plethysmography) have been used to identify nonocclusive DVT.[35,36] These techniques are accurate only when there is at least 50% obstruction of the lumen of a deep vein. The presence of large collateral vessels may result in a false-negative test result as well. Doppler ultrasonography can be performed quickly and easily, though interpretation of the results requires considerable experience. It has essentially the same drawbacks as plethysmography.[35]

Real-time B-mode (duplex) ultrasonography can be valuable in this setting.[35,37,38] It can actually visualize thrombus within a vessel. Inability to obliterate the vein with probe compression is additional evidence of thrombus. Often, experienced users can even differentiate between new and old thrombi on the basis of echogenicity. Duplex ultrasonography is quite sensitive and specific in patients with suspected DVT, and its diagnostic qualities can be further enhanced by the addition of color flow imaging. It has in fact become the noninvasive procedure of choice for assessment of clot in the neck and the extremity vessels. Unfortunately, it is less specific proximal to the axilla and the inguinal ligament, where compression of the vessels is difficult or impossible. Duplex ultrasonography is particularly valuable for detecting associated conditions that may confuse the diagnosis (e.g., muscle hematomas or a Baker's cyst).[38]

Ultimately, ascending venography is the most accurate method of diagnosing DVT.[39,40] If a good contrast study fails to demonstrate the presence of clot, DVT is conclusively ruled out.

Once nonocclusive DVT is diagnosed, the treatment of choice is initial therapeutic-dose heparin therapy followed by warfarin therapy. If the patient is responsible and reasonably well educated, initial heparin anticoagulation can be done on an outpatient basis with subcutaneous LMWH.[41,42] If this approach is not appropriate, inpatient therapeutic-dose I.V. heparin anticoagulation is employed. After 3 or 4 days, depending on the response, heparin is replaced with warfarin.

OCCLUSIVE

Lower Extremity

Lower-extremity occlusive DVT [see Figure 4] is usually associated with swelling; however, if good collateral circulation or duplicate veins are present, especially in the thigh, only local inflammation may be apparent. Typical findings include pain and tenderness

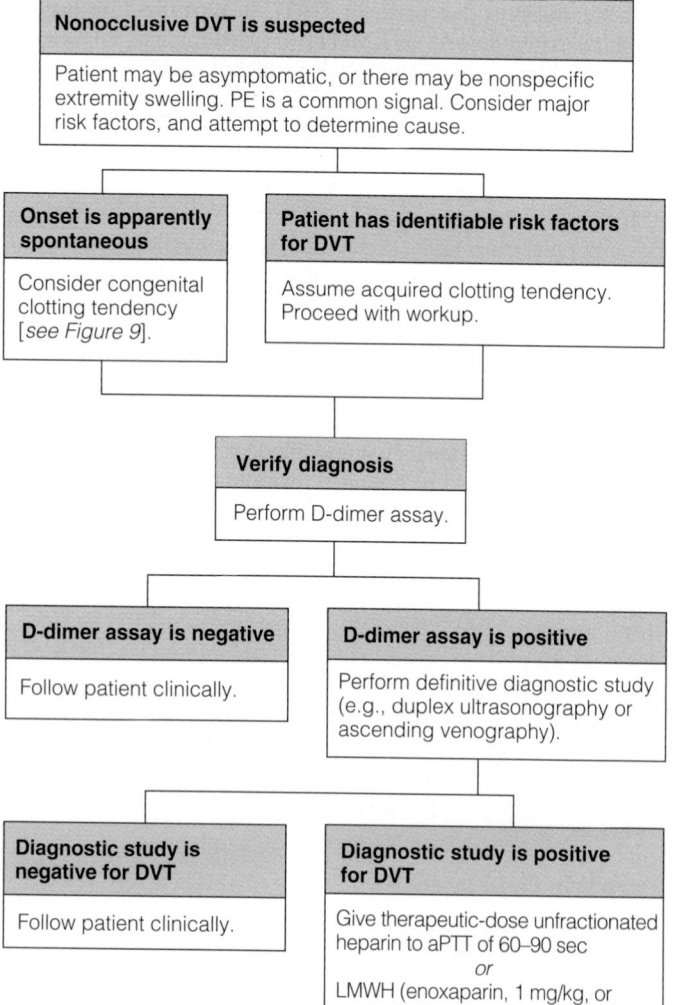

Figure 2 Shown is an algorithm for the management of nonocclusive DVT.

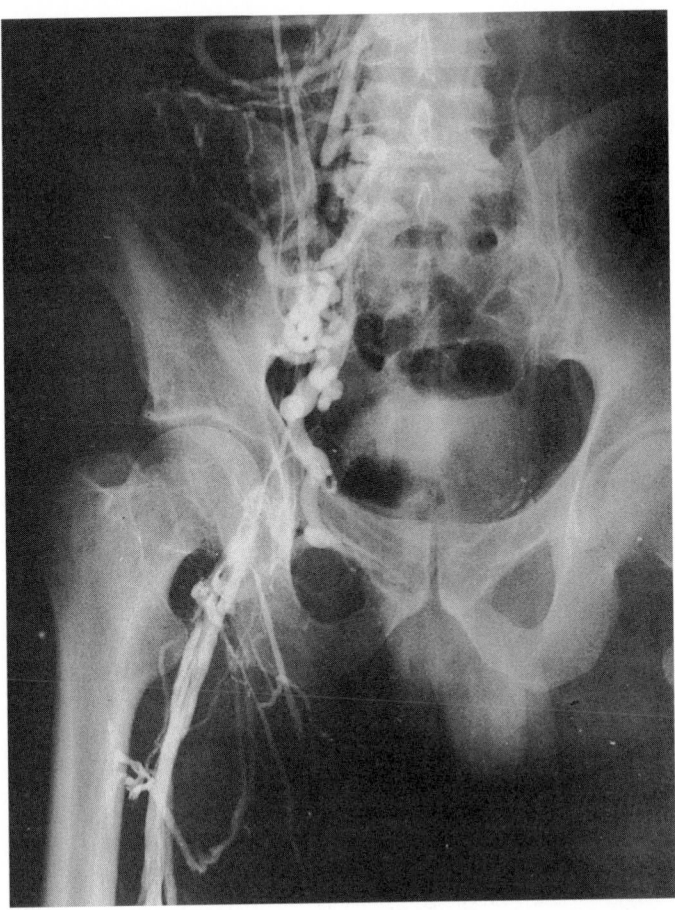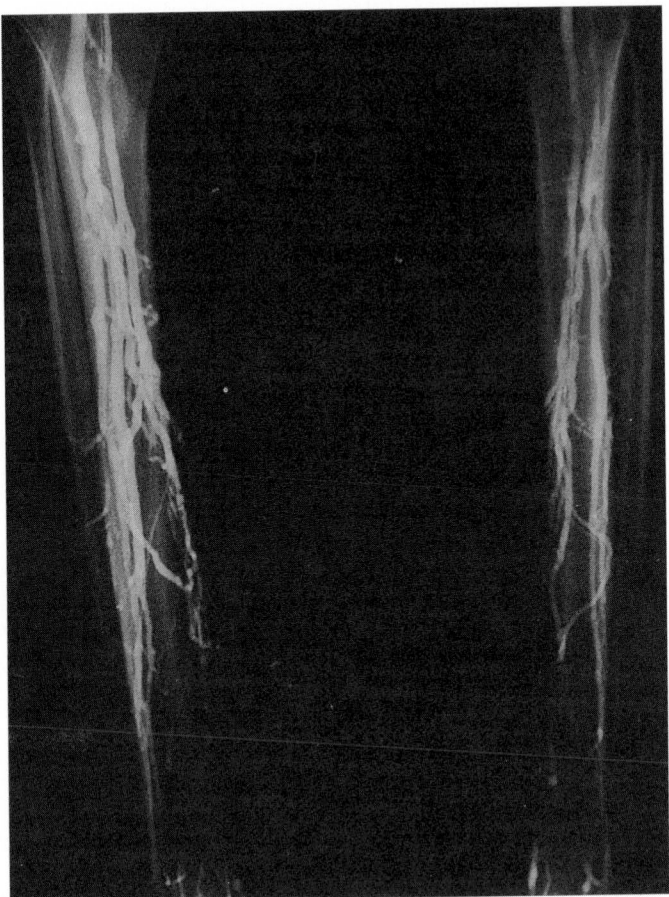

Figure 3 Injection of dye into dorsal foot veins demonstrates occlusion of iliac veins with excellent pelvic collateral circulation.

over the involved veins as well as swelling in the distal limb (which may be minimal with the patient supine). The differential diagnosis is essentially the same as for nonocclusive DVT. In addition, lower-extremity DVT can be associated with PE: free-floating clot may occur in conjunction with occlusive clot.

If both legs are swollen, the proximal extent of the thrombus is likely in the vena cava. If one entire leg is swollen, the proximal extent must be in the iliac veins. If the swelling is limited to the lower leg below the knee, the thrombus is probably in the superficial femoral vein. If the only manifestations are minimal swelling and calf tenderness, the thrombus is probably limited to the sural vein, the gastrocnemius vein, or both.

If the patient has a history of DVT, is hospitalized, and is at risk for recurrence, heparin therapy may be started before test results are available (provided that there is no contraindication to anticoagulation). If the patient is an outpatient, is hospitalized but lacks risk factors for DVT, or has a contraindication to anticoagulation, a D-dimer assay should be performed. If the assay is negative, an alternative diagnosis should be sought. If it is positive, the diagnostic workup of DVT should proceed. If diagnostic studies yield equivocal results and venography is difficult or impossible, treatment should proceed as if the diagnosis had been confirmed.

The treatment of choice is immobilization in bed, elevation of the limb (with or without elastic compression), and therapeutic-dose heparin (unfractionated heparin or LMWH), followed by 3 to 6 months of warfarin therapy. If the episode is mild, recovery is usually prompt. If pain and swelling do not respond promptly to anticoagulation, either the diagnosis is wrong or anticoagulation is inadequate. Lytic therapy combined with heparin anticoagulation may be superior to heparin anticoagulation alone, leading to better clearance of clot from the valves with improved function and less risk of postphlebitic syndrome.[43]

Upper Extremity

For all practical purposes, upper-extremity DVT [*see Figure 5*] involves only the axillary, the subclavian, or the innominate vein (or a combination thereof). Involvement of the superior vena cava is rare, mainly occurring in chronic conditions (e.g., long-term venous catheterization). Arm thrombophlebitis is characterized by pain and swelling with tenderness over the involved vein. Often, it is relatively asymptomatic: because of the excellent collateral circulation in the arm, thrombosis must be extensive to produce marked swelling.

Spontaneous onset of axillary or subclavian vein thrombosis can occur in association with thoracic compression syndromes (effort thrombosis) or as a complication of so-called Saturday night palsy, in which an alcoholic sleeps with the axilla compressed by the arm of a chair. If a potential mechanical cause is not apparent, other possible causes must be explored. The onset of swelling, tenderness, or fever in a patient with a central venous catheter is an indication for removal of the catheter. If there is no bacteremia or fever, if there has been a catheter in the vein, and if the problem developed spontaneously, sterile thrombophlebitis may be assumed. In these cases, once the catheter is removed, anticoagulation is unnecessary.[44]

Subclinical nonocclusive clot is probably of little significance because documented PE from the upper extremity is quite rare.

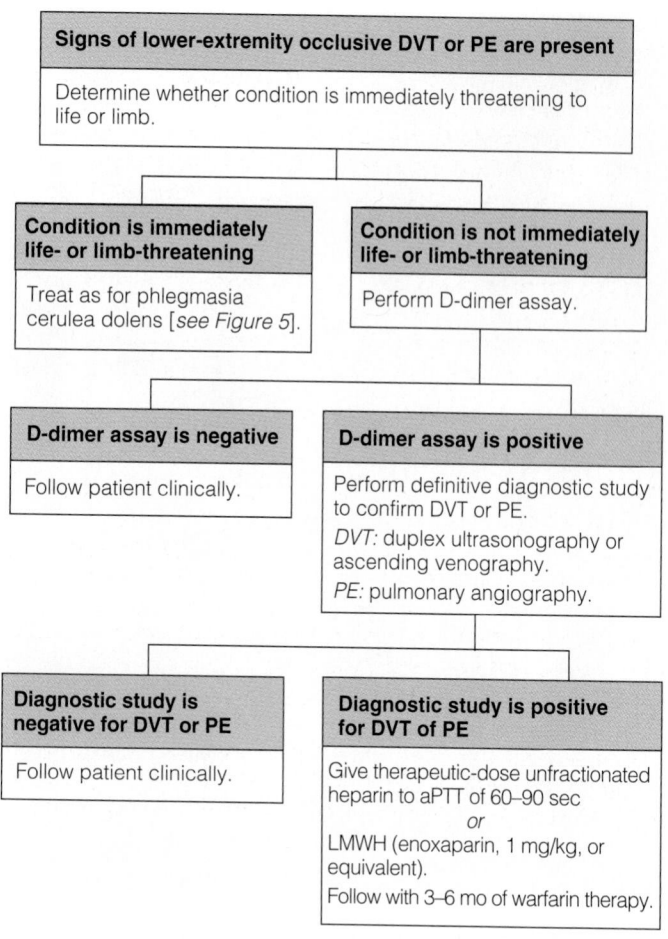

Signs of lower-extremity occlusive DVT or PE are present

Determine whether condition is immediately threatening to life or limb.

Condition is immediately life- or limb-threatening

Treat as for phlegmasia cerulea dolens [see Figure 5].

Condition is not immediately life- or limb-threatening

Perform D-dimer assay.

D-dimer assay is negative

Follow patient clinically.

D-dimer assay is positive

Perform definitive diagnostic study to confirm DVT or PE.
DVT: duplex ultrasonography or ascending venography.
PE: pulmonary angiography.

Diagnostic study is negative for DVT or PE

Follow patient clinically.

Diagnostic study is positive for DVT of PE

Give therapeutic-dose unfractionated heparin to aPTT of 60–90 sec
or
LMWH (enoxaparin, 1 mg/kg, or equivalent).
Follow with 3–6 mo of warfarin therapy.

Figure 4 **Shown is an algorithm for the management of lower-extremity occlusive DVT.**

Noninvasive tests [*see* Nonocclusive, *above*] typically yield positive results when the upper extremity is involved.[39] Moreover, distal vein catheterization is easy, and phlebography is relatively uncomplicated. These techniques should be used whenever the diagnosis is in doubt.

The morbidity of occlusive upper-extremity DVT can be substantial. Thus, if the patient presents with massive swelling of the upper limb, therapeutic-dose heparin anticoagulation should be initiated immediately, and consideration should be given to lytic therapy.[43] If phlebography shows compression of arm veins at the thoracic inlet after lytic therapy or spontaneous recovery from the thrombotic process, resection of rib 1 may be indicated, particularly if positional morbidity is present.[45,46]

Septic DVT is more common in the upper extremity than in the lower, primarily because upper-extremity veins are more frequently catheterized and more often used for injection of illicit drugs. If phlebitis occurs in a catheterized vein with fever and sepsis, the catheter should be removed immediately, the tip cultured, and Gram staining done on any clot present. Broad-spectrum antibiotics should be administered until more specific antibiotic therapy can be instituted. Heparin anticoagulation is the primary treatment unless contraindicated.

Ligation and drainage are not as practical for deep veins as for superficial veins, but either may be indicated on rare occasions if the process does not respond to conventional therapy within 3 or 4 days and marked swelling and fever persist. Drainage is done on the most accessible portion of the phlebitic process. For ligation, the proximal end of the process should be identified via surgery or phlebography and the vein then ligated proximally.

MASSIVE (PHLEGMASIA CERULEA DOLENS)

Phlegmasia cerulea dolens [*see Figure 6*] is most apt to occur in dehydrated, cachectic patients and is usually superimposed on another critical illness. It can involve either the upper or the lower extremity but more commonly affects the lower. In the lower

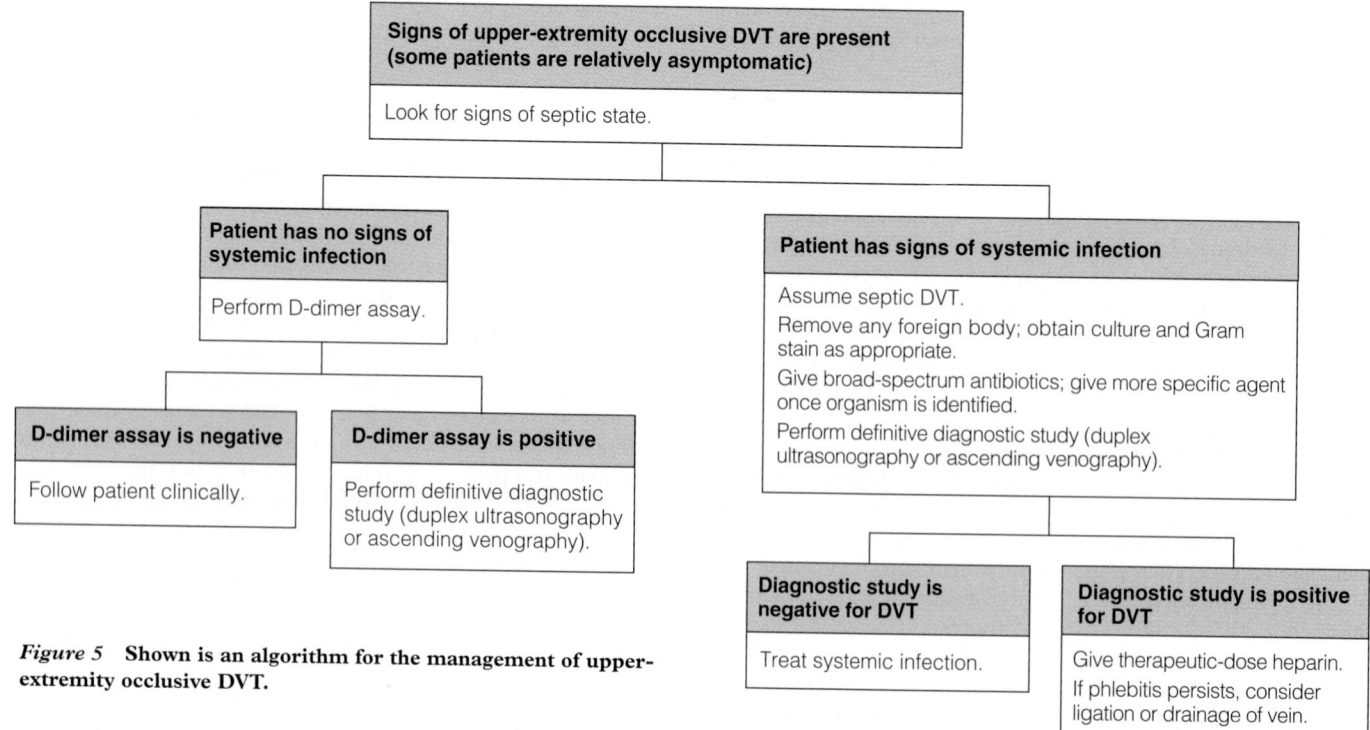

Signs of upper-extremity occlusive DVT are present (some patients are relatively asymptomatic)

Look for signs of septic state.

Patient has no signs of systemic infection

Perform D-dimer assay.

Patient has signs of systemic infection

Assume septic DVT.
Remove any foreign body; obtain culture and Gram stain as appropriate.
Give broad-spectrum antibiotics; give more specific agent once organism is identified.
Perform definitive diagnostic study (duplex ultrasonography or ascending venography).

D-dimer assay is negative

Follow patient clinically.

D-dimer assay is positive

Perform definitive diagnostic study (duplex ultrasonography or ascending venography).

Diagnostic study is negative for DVT

Treat systemic infection.

Diagnostic study is positive for DVT

Give therapeutic-dose heparin.
If phlebitis persists, consider ligation or drainage of vein.

Figure 5 **Shown is an algorithm for the management of upper-extremity occlusive DVT.**

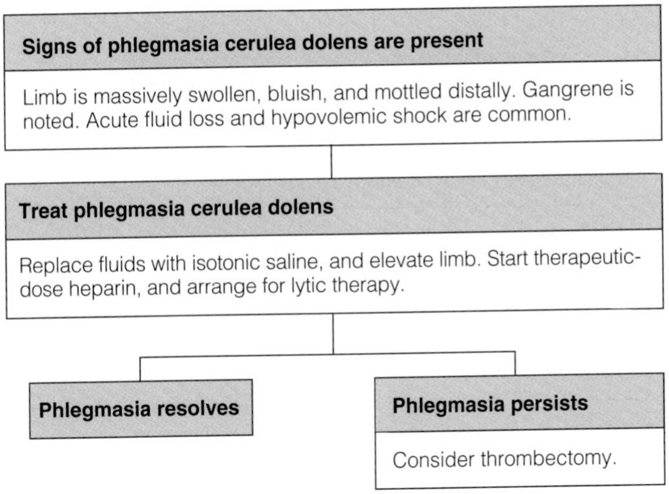

Signs of phlegmasia cerulea dolens are present
Limb is massively swollen, bluish, and mottled distally. Gangrene is noted. Acute fluid loss and hypovolemic shock are common.

Treat phlegmasia cerulea dolens
Replace fluids with isotonic saline, and elevate limb. Start therapeutic-dose heparin, and arrange for lytic therapy.

Phlegmasia resolves	Phlegmasia persists
	Consider thrombectomy.

Figure 6 **Shown is an algorithm for the management of massive DVT (phlegmasia cerulea dolens).**

extremity, there is usually simultaneous thrombosis of the iliac, femoral, common femoral, and superficial femoral veins. The limb is massively swollen, bluish, and mottled. Eventually, it becomes nonviable as arterial flow stops because of arterial spasm associated with venous outflow obstruction. The problem is compounded by acute massive fluid loss into the limb, which can result in hypovolemic shock.

Treatment involves rapid and aggressive fluid replacement, elevation of the limb, and aggressive heparin anticoagulation or catheter-directed lytic therapy.[47,48] If the patient does not respond, thrombectomy may be considered, provided that the associated disease does not carry a fatal prognosis.[49] The procedure is best done transfemorally with a limited incision so that anticoagulation can be continued postoperatively. If anticoagulation cannot be continued, thrombophlebitis will recur immediately.

Pulmonary Embolism

It is widely agreed that PE is grossly underdiagnosed.[3,4,50,51] Most episodes (up to 90%) are unsuspected,[52,53] and only a minority (10% to 25%) of fatal episodes are diagnosed before death. Clinical manifestations include dyspnea, hemoptysis, pleurisy, heart failure, and cardiovascular collapse; however, each of these is also associated with other conditions [see Table 2]. Risk factors for PE are similar to those for DVT [see Table 1].

PE should be distinguished from pulmonary infarction. Of the approximately 10% of all pulmonary emboli that are recognized clinically, only 10% are associated with pulmonary infarction.[8] Because the lung has excellent collateral circulation, obstruction of the larger pulmonary arteries rarely leads to death of lung tissue. When pulmonary infarction does occur, the diagnosis is usually obvious; hemoptysis, pleuritic chest pain, and a wedge-shaped density on chest x-ray are the classic manifestations. In most PE patients (i.e., those without pulmonary infarction), these findings are absent, and the chest x-ray may even be normal.

For the purposes of clinical diagnosis and treatment, PE is best classified as minor (or suspected), moderate, or catastrophic [see Figure 7].

MINOR

Manifestations of minor PE [see Figure 7a] may include transient tachypnea (with perhaps a slight change in blood gas values)

and cardiac irritability (with frequent premature beats or tachyarrhythmias).[54-56] These changes may resolve in moments, and the patient may then appear perfectly normal. In these circumstances, the embolus probably either is small or is composed of relatively fresh clot that produces only transient obstruction when it enters the pulmonary vascular tree.

It was long believed that after operation, hospitalization, or injury, the earliest PE might occur was 4 to 7 days after the insult. A 1997 study of previously healthy trauma patients, however, found that approximately 25% of the PE episodes occurred in the first 4 days after injury.[57] Accordingly, the presence of clinical signs and symptoms consistent with PE in a patient with risk factors calls for appropriate workup, regardless of how soon after the insult they appear.

The differential diagnosis includes acute respiratory distress syndrome (ARDS), aspiration, atelectasis, heart failure, pneumonia, and systemic infection. If the diagnosis is not obvious but the risk of PE is substantial and there is no contraindication to anticoagulation, heparin therapy (therapeutic-dose unfractionated heparin or LMWH) may be instituted while diagnostic tests are being selected and performed.

If PE is unlikely, the risk from anticoagulation is high, or other serious diagnostic possibilities cannot be ruled out, specific studies (e.g., intravascular coagulation, spiral computed tomography, or pulmonary angiography) should be ordered before anticoagulation.

In a stable patient with suspected PE, a blood D-dimer level should be obtained. If the result is negative, PE can be excluded and further diagnostic studies canceled. As with DVT, a positive

Table 2 Clinical Features of Pulmonary Embolism: Differential Diagnosis

Clinical Feature	Other Conditions Associated with Feature
Dyspnea	Aspiration Atelectasis Pneumonia Pneumothorax Pulmonary edema Systemic infection
Heart failure	Cardiac tamponade Intracardiac injury Myocardial contusion Myocardial infarction
Hemoptysis	Bronchial injury Pulmonary contusion Tracheal erosion Unsuspected neoplasm
Pleurisy	Chest wall injury Pneumonia Pneumothorax Subphrenic inflammation
Cardiovascular collapse	Air embolism Cardiac tamponade Hypovolemia Myocardial infarction Severe hypoxemia Systemic infection Tension pneumothorax

a

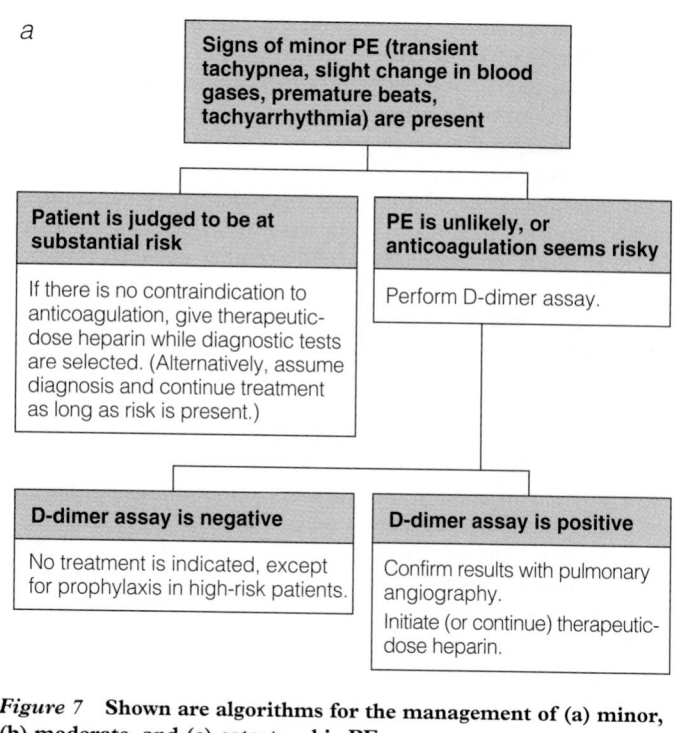

Signs of minor PE (transient tachypnea, slight change in blood gases, premature beats, tachyarrhythmia) are present

Patient is judged to be at substantial risk

If there is no contraindication to anticoagulation, give therapeutic-dose heparin while diagnostic tests are selected. (Alternatively, assume diagnosis and continue treatment as long as risk is present.)

PE is unlikely, or anticoagulation seems risky

Perform D-dimer assay.

D-dimer assay is negative

No treatment is indicated, except for prophylaxis in high-risk patients.

D-dimer assay is positive

Confirm results with pulmonary angiography.
Initiate (or continue) therapeutic-dose heparin.

b

Signs of moderate PE (transient hypotension, tachycardia or other arrhythmias, tachypnea, ↓ Po₂ and Pco₂, apprehension, symptoms and signs of pulmonary infarction) are present

Perform D-dimer assay.

D-dimer assay is negative

Seek alternative explanation for signs.

D-dimer assay is positive

Assess risk of anticoagulation and likelihood of PE.

PE is likely

Give therapeutic-dose heparin.
Consider lytic therapy for acute episodes.

PE is unlikely, or anticoagulation seems risky

Attempt to make specific diagnosis via pulmonary angiography.

Diagnosis is not confirmed

If patient is at risk for embolism and anticoagulation is not contraindicated, give prophylactic-dose heparin.

Diagnosis is confirmed

If anticoagulation is not contraindicated, give therapeutic-dose heparin. If it is, consider vena caval interruption.

Figure 7 **Shown are algorithms for the management of (a) minor, (b) moderate, and (c) catastrophic PE.**

c

Signs of catastrophic PE (cardiac arrest, circulatory collapse, bradyarrhythmia, severe hypotension, left heart failure) are present

Give 100% O_2 by ET tube. Give cardiotonic agents and massive doses of heparin. Consider Trendelenburg's procedure or cardiopulmonary bypass.

Provide further treatment as needed

If patient survives emergency treatment and improves, continue therapeutic-dose heparin and consider lytic therapy or a caval filter.

D-dimer assay does not confirm DVT or PE. The negative predictive value of the assay for DVT and PE is between 90% and 100% when an appropriate assay with an appropriate cutoff value is used.[31-33] If a patient is experiencing a life-threatening respiratory event consistent with PE, the D-dimer assay should be skipped, therapy instituted, and formal diagnostic studies performed.

Noninvasive evaluation of the legs may establish the presence of DVT necessitating anticoagulation. This circuitous way of establishing the diagnosis of PE has severe limitations. When noninvasive assessment aimed at detecting clot in the major leg veins is done before documented PE, it yields positive results in only 33% to 45% of cases.[58] Venography is more sensitive than duplex ultrasonography. When it is used to diagnose venous thrombosis, as many as 30% to 40% of patients with PE are found not to have clot in the major veins of the leg or the abdomen. If the duplex scan or venogram is positive for DVT and there are no contraindications, anticoagulation may be begun. If, on the other hand, a patient is suspected of having PE but is sent for a duplex scan in place of a pulmonary arteriogram, and the duplex scan is negative, workup must continue. It is unacceptable in such cases to assume that the negative result excludes PE.

The initial enthusiasm for the use of lung scans to diagnose or screen for PE has diminished.[59,60] Current thinking about the use of scans for this purpose may be summarized as follows. If a scan is read as high probability, there is roughly an 85% chance that the diagnosis is correct. If a scan is read as normal, there is roughly a 5% chance that the patient had PE. If a scan is read as low or intermediate probability (the most likely scenario), the likelihood that the diagnosis is correct is little better than random chance.

As a result of the dramatic improvements in CT imaging, many proposed replacing pulmonary angiography with CT. There were several good arguments for this proposal. First, CT scanning is less invasive than pulmonary angiography. Second, it does not require the immediate presence of a radiologist. Third, it is less costly at most institutions. Finally, CT scanning is usually more easily obtained than pulmonary angiography. The initial results

from CT scanning for PE were quite promising.[61]

In the past few years, CT has undergone rapid increases in sophistication. Specifically, as CT technology has moved from single-detector to multiple-detector (light-speed) scanners, the sensitivity achievable with this modality has skyrocketed. As a result, the negative predictive value of CT in this setting—that is, the degree to which a negative CT pulmonary angiogram can be relied on to rule out PE—has risen dramatically.[62] For most institutions, the result of this technologic improvement is that CT angiography is now the primary radiologic diagnostic study for excluding PE. It has been argued that CT angiography cannot yet replace pulmonary angiography altogether, because thrombolytic therapy (if required) may be provided during pulmonary angiography, whereas it typically cannot be provided during CT angiography. This argument probably applies only to the sickest PE patients, who are the ones most likely to benefit from thrombolytic therapy and least likely to be able to tolerate a second load of dye (as when pulmonary angiography is done for treatment purposes after CT angiography).

For critically ill patients, who tolerate diagnostic testing poorly, pulmonary angiography is a more appropriate initial study [see Figure 8].[3,50,63] If the angiogram is obtained immediately after the clinical episode, particularly if the patient is still symptomatic, a negative result rules out PE. However, if the patient improves or recovers before angiography, the angiogram may be falsely negative, implying that the clot was minimal or was disposed of by natural lytic processes. Thus, a negative angiogram in such a patient does not unequivocally rule out PE.[64] The pulmonary angiogram does, however, establish the degree of patency of the pulmonary vasculature, which affects prognosis.

PE can occur even immediately after injury in previously healthy persons.[57] These early emboli are generated from fresh clot and thus are more easily fragmented and broken down. They are much more likely to be found in the periphery.[65] For these reasons, CT is less sensitive in detecting them.[65] Accordingly, patients with suspected PE shortly after injury or operation should undergo pulmonary arteriography.

If all diagnostic tests for PE yield negative results, therapeutic anticoagulation is not indicated; however, if risk factors are present, prophylaxis is indicated. If test results are suggestive or indicative of PE, therapeutic heparin anticoagulation should be continued.

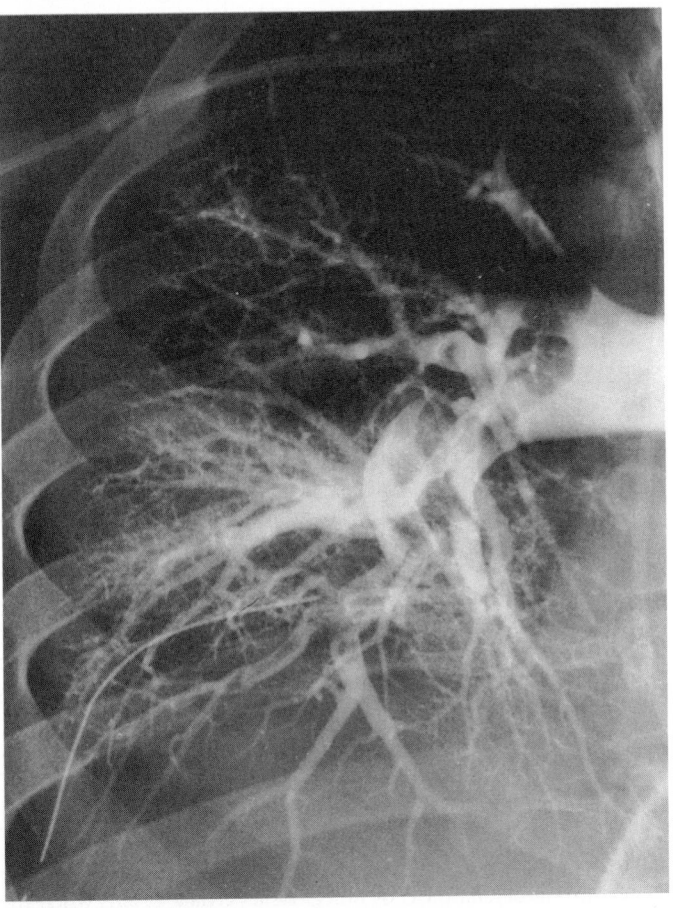

Figure 8 Pulmonary angiogram shows unequivocal filling defects in multiple arteries.

MODERATE

Manifestations of moderate PE [see Figure 7b] include transient hypotension, tachycardia or other cardiac dysrhythmias, tachypnea with a significant fall in arterial oxygen and carbon dioxide tension, apprehension, and symptoms or signs of pulmonary infarction[54,56]; there may be signs of right heart failure as well. Electrocardiography is rarely helpful in the differential diagnosis. Acute right axis deviation, new incomplete right bundle branch block, and changes in S_1, Q_3, or T_3 are thought to characterize this disorder but are found in only a small percentage of patients with proven PE.

If the diagnosis is probable and there are no likely alternatives, heparin therapy should be initiated. Lytic therapy is of debatable utility in these patients: compared with standard heparin therapy, it appears not to reduce mortality or pulmonary dysfunction significantly, yet it carries a higher risk of bleeding.[3,66] Moreover, lytic therapy is often contraindicated because of recent surgery, injury, or vascular punctures.

If there is a relative contraindication to anticoagulation (e.g., an acute surgical wound, a previous bleeding episode, or an allergic reaction to heparin) or alternative diagnoses are likely, specific diagnosis is required, ideally via pulmonary angiography. Peripheral noninvasive venous studies may be helpful because if they show significant venous obstruction, the likelihood of PE increases and the need for therapy is documented. Ventilation-perfusion scanning, again, is valuable only if strongly positive.

If there is no contraindication to heparin therapy and the diagnosis is strongly suspected but not confirmed, therapeutic-dose heparin anticoagulation should be started.[67,68] Treatment is continued if the diagnosis is verified and stopped if the diagnosis is excluded.[69-72]

Vena Caval Filters

Vena caval interruption has often been recommended for patients with documented PE despite apparently adequate systemic anticoagulation, but many authorities now advocate vena caval filter placement even in patients who do not have documented thromboembolism but are at high risk and in whom anticoagulation is contraindicated.[73-75] Supporting data come largely from studies with historical controls. In the one prospective, randomized, controlled trial involving patients with thromboembolic disease, there was no reduction in mortality at any time, nor was there even a reduction in PE at 2 years; however, there was an increased incidence in DVT over that period.[29] These findings suggest that vena cava filters should be reserved for patients with documented DVT, a contraindication to anticoagulation, and a high risk of subsequent PE.

In 2005, an 8-year follow-up analysis of the patients enrolled in the aforementioned prospective, randomized trial[29] was published.[76] Over the 8-year period, the incidence of PE was lower in the group that received inferior vena cava filters than in the group that did not; however, there was an increased rate of recurrent DVT in the filter group. Overall, there was no significant difference in mortality between the two groups. The authors reiterated their recommendation that vena cava filters be used with restraint.

If vena caval interruption is considered necessary, it should be done percutaneously via either the jugular or the femoral route. If it is done by the latter route, phlebography (from the insertion site through the vena cava) should be performed first to document the absence of clot along the planned route. A number of different vena caval filters are currently on the market. Each is slightly different from the others, but none has demonstrated clear superiority in preventing PE or reducing caval thrombosis. Surgeons should be aware of the advantages and disadvantages of the types available at their institutions.

Removable filters are now widely available. Several have been approved by the FDA and are in clinical use. Because these devices were approved comparatively recently, data on long-term efficacy and complication rates are not yet available.

One of the most critical questions that remains unanswered is, what will be the long-term consequences when the damage caused by the venotomy required for filter removal is superimposed on the endothelial damage caused by the filter? This question should be kept in mind, as should the reservations expressed by the authors of the only prospective, randomized trial of inferior vena caval filters published to date.[29,76] Still, it appears that removable vena caval filters are likely to have a role to play in this setting. They should be considered in patients who are at extremely high risk for PE, who have an absolute contraindication to anticoagulation for a finite period, and in whom anticoagulation can be instituted upon removal of the filter.

CATASTROPHIC

Catastrophic PE [see Figure 7c] is most apt to be superimposed on a critical illness or a major operation. The peak incidence is 7 to 10 days after the procedure or the onset of clinical illness, though emboli may occur at any time.[54] The reason for this apparent delay is that for the clot to remain intact after embolization to the pulmonary vasculature, it must mature in the vascular system, a process that takes several days. Fresh clot breaks up readily and dissipates promptly, whereas older clot is resistant to lysis. The manifestation of early embolization of fresh clot to the pulmonary vasculature is ARDS. Embolization of older clot can produce acute pulmonary obstruction and acute right heart failure, making radiologic diagnosis of PE relatively easy.[54] Occlusion of large portions of the vasculature is associated with hemodynamic catastrophe.

Typically, the clinical onset of catastrophic PE comes when a patient, having just been mobilized, performs a vigorous Valsalva maneuver in the course of his or her first postoperative bowel movement. The great abdominal veins distend, and any clot present tends to be stripped loose. If a large clot embolizes, immediate collapse and cardiac arrest may result; in some cases, bradyarrhythmia or severe hypotension precedes the actual arrest. Immediate emergency treatment comprises intubation and administration of 100% oxygen, heparin anticoagulation, and, if cardiac arrest occurs, cardiopulmonary resuscitation. A Swan-Ganz catheter should be inserted as soon as possible so that the effects of therapy can be monitored. Cardiotonic agents (e.g., dopamine, 2.0 to 5.0 µg/min, or dobutamine, 2.5 to 10.0 µg/kg/min) should be administered to strengthen myocardial function. If sudden arrest occurs in circumstances that permit emergency thoracotomy, Trendelenburg's procedure can be performed; however, it is rarely indicated and even more rarely successful. If the patient survives initial emergency treatment and improves, high-dose heparin therapy should be continued and lytic therapy considered.[71,77]

General Principles of Anticoagulation and Lytic Therapy

HEPARIN ANTICOAGULATION

Therapeutic Dose

Heparin therapy may be instituted with either unfractionated heparin or LMWH. In either case, the key is to give enough heparin soon enough to have a beneficial effect. Both types of heparin exert their effect by potentiating antithrombin; thus, if a patient's anti-

thrombin stores are depleted, progressively higher heparin doses will be required to achieve the same degree of anticoagulation.

Unfractionated heparin therapy is also frequently referred to as conventional anticoagulation.[78-80] Before therapy is begun, a clotting battery should be performed, consisting of the aPTT, the INR, the platelet count, and levels of fibrinogen, antithrombin, and D-dimer. High fibrinogen levels and platelet counts are seen in patients with chronic clotting syndromes,[81] probably representing overcompensation for increased utilization. Elevated D-dimer levels suggest intravascular clotting with activation of the fibrinolytic system.

In the average patient, therapeutic-dose heparin anticoagulation begins with administration of 5,000 to 10,000 units, followed by continuous I.V. infusion at a rate sufficient to double or triple the aPTT—typically, 1,000 to 2,000 units/hr. When dosages higher than 2,000 units/hr are required, antithrombin depletion is highly probable.

Tight control of the aPTT change as a result of heparin therapy is not as important as monitoring for evidence of bleeding and platelet depletion. Clinical evidence of bleeding is not necessarily a contraindication to anticoagulation. Minimal amounts of blood may be lost in the urine or through the GI tract; if the patient has a clearly identifiable need for anticoagulation, such minor blood loss should be accepted. Only when transfusion is indicated to maintain the hematocrit should discontinuance of heparin be considered. At that point, if the risks of bleeding seem to outweigh the benefits of anticoagulation, heparin infusion can be stopped or reduced to prophylactic levels. It is important to watch for falls in the hematocrit indicative of significant bleeding. The most common sites for hemorrhagic complications are surgical wounds and the retroperitoneum. Retroperitoneal bleeding is generally asymptomatic until the patient progresses to hemorrhagic hypovolemic shock.

As a rule, the therapeutic dose of LMWH is twice the prophylactic dose. The various LMWHs currently on the market all have slightly different activities and half-lives. Enoxaparin may be taken as prototypical. The accepted prophylactic dose for enoxaparin is 30 mg twice daily, and the therapeutic dose is 60 mg (or 1 mg/kg) twice daily.

A major benefit of using LMWHs to treat DVT and PE is that therapeutic doses can be given subcutaneously.[41,42] As a result, patients may be treated as outpatients both in the acute phase of the disease and in the subacute phase, during the transition to oral anticoagulants. This approach requires that patients be clinically stable and able to follow dosing instructions. Because there are no validated methods of monitoring LMWH therapy, an initial assessment of antithrombin activity is appropriate. If this is low, unfractionated heparin therapy in conjunction with aPTT monitoring is probably preferable.

High Dose

High-dose heparin therapy is reserved for patients who are dying of PE or are at risk for immediate limb loss from phlegmasia cerulea dolens. Such therapy consists of administering a large enough dose of heparin to elevate the aPTT off the scale. The maximum aPTT that can be measured by our laboratory is 150 seconds; high-dose heparin treatment should therefore yield an aPTT higher than this value. Theoretically, given that a fully anticoagulated patient should not form clot at all, the aPTT should be infinite. This method of treatment may be used in patients with immediately life-threatening PE or phlegmasia cerulea dolens when the more conventional technique, catheter-directed thrombolytic therapy, is unavailable.

In most patients, high-dose therapy begins with a 20,000 unit I.V. bolus, followed by infusion of 5,000 units/hr I.V.[82-86] The end point of therapy is clinical evidence of improvement. In patients being treated for PE, pulmonary function should improve.

Because complete anticoagulation is the essential principle of high-dose heparin therapy, there is no need to be concerned about an upper limit for the dosage: if the patient cannot clot, doubling or even tripling the dosage should not increase the risk of bleeding. Moreover, because the incidence of bleeding is very low in the first 2 or 3 days of therapy, regardless of the dosage,[85,86] high initial dosages do not carry an unacceptable bleeding risk. After heparin has been observed to have an effect and a prolonged aPTT documented, the high dosage should be continued for at least 24 hours, then decreased by 500 to 1,000 units/hr over the next 24 hours. If the clinical effect is maintained and improvement continues, the dosage can be decreased by another 500 to 1,000 units/hr over the following 24 hours. In theory, once all clotting stops, natural antithrombin levels should recover, allowing lower dosages of heparin to be effective. After 3 or 4 days of therapy, the dosage may be reduced to more conventional levels [see Therapeutic Dose, above].

If the initial improvement is lost, the dosage should be restored to its previous high level and maintained there for several days before any attempt is made to reduce it again. The platelet count and the hematocrit should be carefully monitored, the latter at least four times a day. Heparin should be discontinued or the dosage reduced only when the risks of bleeding and transfusion exceed the benefits of anticoagulation. In a monitored environment, patients very rarely die of hemorrhage; rather, they die of the consequences of clotting.

Complications

The most devastating hemorrhagic risk of heparin therapy—fortunately, a rare one—is intracranial bleeding. The risk of major hemorrhage ranges from 4% to 9% and is directly affected by how tightly the INR is controlled.[87] The risk is greatest in elderly patients, particularly women,[79] but it is still small in comparison with the obvious risks posed by the clotting episode. Nevertheless, the existence of this risk makes it appropriate to use high-dose heparin primarily in life-threatening conditions.

A more common complication of full heparin anticoagulation is retroperitoneal bleeding. This problem is accentuated in elderly patients. Because aging is associated with loss of connective tissue elasticity, bleeding into retroperitoneal connective tissue that would normally be insignificant can become life-threatening. Usually, this is not a serious problem if the hematocrit is followed, heparin dosing adjusted, and lost blood replaced. When the perceived risk of bleeding outweighs the thrombotic risk, heparin should be discontinued.

Two forms of acute heparin-induced thrombocytopenia (HIT) have been reported.[88-91] Mild HIT occurs in 2% to 5% of patients 2 to 15 days after the initiation of therapy. The platelet count usually remains at about 100,000/mm³, and treatment can be continued without undue risk of bleeding or thrombosis. Severe HIT is much less frequent. It usually occurs about 7 to 14 days after the initiation of heparin therapy and is reversible once the drug is discontinued. It is not dependent on the heparin dose given. Clinical manifestations include a substantial (at least 50%) drop in the platelet count followed by a thrombotic episode (frequently both arterial and venous). An ELISA directed at the platelet factor 4–heparin complex is generally accepted for laboratory confirmation of the diagnosis. Treatment consists of discontinuance of heparin. If the patient still requires anticoagulation, a different anticoagulant must be used. The most widely accepted agent for this purpose is lepirudin (a direct thrombin inhibitor).[92] Other direct thrombin inhibitors (e.g., argatroban) and heparinoids (e.g., danaproid) have also been successfully used to provide anticoagulation in patients with HIT. None of the LMWHs are acceptable in this setting, and at present, the FDA does not allow use of the pentasaccharide in severe HIT.

Unlike warfarin, heparin does not cross the placenta and has not been associated with fetal malformations; thus, it is preferred for thrombotic complications of pregnancy. Heparin can be administered subcutaneously in an outpatient setting for 3 to 6 months. Long-term administration can lead to osteoporosis and spontaneous vertebral fractures.[93]

Very rarely, heparin therapy can lead to adrenal hemorrhage and consequent adrenal insufficiency.[79] If acute adrenal insufficiency is suspected, anticoagulant therapy should be discontinued and high-dose steroid therapy (preferably with hydrocortisone) initiated. Treatment should not await laboratory confirmation. CT scanning may be useful. Heparin may suppress aldosterone synthesis, especially with prolonged use.[79]

Reversal of Heparin Effect

The anticoagulant effect of heparin disappears within hours after discontinuance. If the effect must be reversed quickly, the patient should receive protamine sulfate I.V. This agent binds the heparin and prevents it from activating antithrombin. Protamine sulfate should be given in the smallest dosages that still evoke the desired result—typically, about 1 mg for every 100 units of heparin remaining in the patient. It should be administered slowly over 5 to 10 minutes; rapid infusion can cause shortness of breath, flushing, bradycardia, hypotension, or anaphylaxis. On rare occasions, patients previously sensitized to protamine may experience massive platelet aggregation, as manifested by catastrophic arterial thrombosis. Patients particularly likely to manifest this adverse reaction include diabetics and persons with fish allergies. Protamine has little or no capacity for reversing either LMWH or fondaparinux. Research aimed at developing specific protamines to inactivate the LMWHs is now being carried out, but at present, no such agents are available in the United States.

ORAL ANTICOAGULATION

Warfarin is the prototypical oral anticoagulant; the agents in this class have much the same effects, differing primarily with respect to potency and duration of action.[79,80] Warfarin is also available in an I.V. form; however, in view of its mechanism of action, caution should be exercised when it is given parenterally.

Dosage

Historically, warfarin dosage has been regulated by monitoring the prothrombin time (PT), with a PT 1.5 to 2.5 times normal (11 or 12 seconds) generally considered to represent the optimal level. In response to the wide variations in PT reported by different laboratories, the World Health Organization (WHO) has recommended substituting the INR for the PT ratio so that all laboratory assessments will be comparable.[94] An INR of 2.0 to 3.0 corresponds to a PT that is 1.3 to 1.5 times normal (moderate dose); an INR of 3.0 to 4.5 corresponds to a PT that is 1.5 to 2.0 times normal (high dose). Lower INRs are recommended for all but extremely high-risk patients (e.g., those with mechanical heart valves) [see Table 3].[94]

Initially, the daily dose of warfarin required to increase the INR to between 2.0 and 3.0 is estimated and administered. The INR is then checked every morning. If it suddenly overshoots the target

Table 3 Recommendations for Use of Varying Dosages of Warfarin

The dosage of warfarin is regulated by monitoring the INR. A less intense therapeutic range (INR = 2.0 to 3.0, corresponding to a PT 1.3 to 1.5 times normal with a WHO-designated thromboplastin) is appropriate for the following applications:

1. The prevention of venous thromboembolism in high-risk patients.

2. The treatment of venous thrombosis and PE after an initial course of heparin.

3. The prevention of systemic embolism (a) in patients with tissue heart valves, (b) in selected patients with atrial fibrillation, (c) in patients with acute anterior wall myocardial infarction, and (d) in patients with valvular heart disease.

A more intense therapeutic range (INR = 3.0 to 4.5, corresponding to a PT 1.5 to 2.0 times normal with a WHO-designated thromboplastin) is appropriate for patients with mechanical prosthetic valves and patients with recurrent systemic embolism.

INR—international normalized ratio   PT—prothrombin time   WHO—World Health Organization

range, the warfarin dosage is reduced. If the INR has not reached or surpassed 1.5 after the third dose, the dosage is increased. The maintenance dosage averages about 5 mg/day but may range from 1 to 10 mg/day.

While the maintenance dosage is being determined, the INR should be checked daily. Once the patient stabilizes, the INR can be checked less often: twice weekly for the first few weeks, once weekly for the next several months, and once monthly thereafter if the patient is stable. The patient should be cautioned about drug interactions. If the dosages of other medications are changed, the impact on the INR should be investigated and the warfarin dosage adjusted as appropriate.

Duration

There is no general agreement on how long oral anticoagulant therapy should be continued after a thromboembolic event. Current data suggest that the duration of therapy should be based on the level of underlying risk rather than on the severity of the event. For patients with a limited risk period (e.g., a young patient with a femur fracture and no other risk factors), an 8- to 12-week course is as efficacious as a longer course.[95] For patients with a life-long risk (e.g., a patient with a congenital hypercoagulability syndrome or cancer), a therapeutic dosage for 3 to 6 months, followed by a low dosage for the remainder of the patient's life, is indicated.[87] Lengthening the duration of full anticoagulant therapy in patients with long-term risk factors appears only to delay the recurrence of thromboembolism, not to prevent it.

Drug Interactions

Response to warfarin is affected not only by various bodily factors but also by drug interactions [see Table 4]. Such interactions are most dangerous when drugs administered in parallel are taken intermittently.[79,80] Increased metabolic clearance of the drug can result from administration of barbiturates, rifampin, or phenytoin; long-term use of alcohol; ingestion of large amounts of vitamin K; and rich foods. Elevated levels of coagulation factors during pregnancy also decrease warfarin's effectiveness.

Decreased metabolism or displacement from protein-binding sites caused by phenylbutazone, sulfinpyrazone, metronidazole, disulfiram, allopurinol, cimetidine, amiodarone, or acute intake of ethanol can elevate the INR and increase the risk of hemorrhage. Relative vitamin K deficiency, resulting from inadequate diet or the

elimination of the intestinal flora by antimicrobial agents, may have similar effects. For these reasons, warfarin should be used with great caution in patients who are receiving antibiotics or who cannot tolerate a regular diet.

There are some serious interactions that increase the risk of bleeding without altering the INR. These include inhibition of platelet function by drugs such as aspirin and gastritis or gastric ulceration induced by anti-inflammatory drugs. Obviously, when placing a patient on more than one anticoagulant simultaneously, great care must be taken.

Complications

Bleeding is the major complication of oral anticoagulation. Tight control of warfarin therapy is essential for minimizing this complication.[87] Bleeding is rare when the INR is kept below 3.0. When bleeding does occur, a preexisting lesion is likely. If the bleeding is minor, the warfarin dosage should be adjusted; if it is major, the drug may have to be discontinued. The risk of intracerebral or subdural hematoma is greater with warfarin than with heparin, particularly in patients older than 50 years. If there is any sign of hemorrhage, the next anticoagulant dose should be withheld and the INR measured. For continued or serious bleeding, 5 to 10 mg of vitamin K_1 oxide (phytonadione) I.V. is effective. Several hours may pass before hemostasis improves significantly, and 24 hours or longer may be needed for maximal effect. If immediate restoration of hemostatic competence is necessary, levels of vitamin K–dependent coagulation factors can be raised by giving fresh frozen plasma, 10 to 20 ml/kg body weight, or prothrombin complex concentrate.[96]

Administration of warfarin during pregnancy can cause birth defects and abortion and therefore is contraindicated. Warfarin-induced skin necrosis is a rare complication of oral anticoagulant therapy.[90] This syndrome, characterized by the appearance of skin lesions shortly after initiation of treatment, may be the result of a

Table 4 Factors Influencing Response to Warfarin

Factors Leading to Increased Response	Factors Leading to Decreased Response
Drugs	Drugs
Allopurinol	Barbiturates
Amiodarone	Cholestyramine
Aspirin	Diuretics
Cephalosporins	Ethanol (chronic use)
Cimetidine	Phenytoin
Clofibrate	Rifampin
Disulfiram	Vitamin K
Ethanol (acute intoxication)	Foods
Heparin	Green leafy vegetables
Metronidazole	Bodily factors
Sulfinpyrazone	Hereditary resistance
Trimethoprim-sulfamethoxazole	Hypometabolic states
Bodily factors	Pregnancy
Age	Uremia
Congestive heart failure	
Dietary inadequacy	
Hypermetabolic states	
Intestinal flora loss	
Liver disease	

Table 5 Characteristics of Current Thrombolytic Agents

Agent	Abbreviation	Half-life (min)	Fibrin-Specific	Antigenic	FDA-Approved Indication	Comments	Current Trials
Streptokinase	SK	30	No	Yes	AMI, PE, DVT, PAO, AV cannulae	Systemic plasminogen activator	—
Urokinase	UK	15	No	No	AMI, PE, catheter occlusion	Systemic plasminogen activator	—
Alteplase	t-PA	4–8	Yes	No	AMI, acute stroke, PE	Sometimes termed accelerated t-PA	GUSTO TIMI
Reteplase	rt-PA	14–18	Yes	No	AMI	Increased fibrin specificity; increased resistance to PAI-1	ASSENT-II In-Time II
Tenecteplase	TNK-tPA	11–20	Yes	No	AMI	Resistance to plasmin cleavage; increased effectiveness on arterial thrombi	ASSENT-II
Anistreplase	APSAC	40–70	No	No	AMI	Not commonly used, Lys-plasminogen complex with streptokinase	—
Lanoteplase	n-PA	23–37	No	No	—	Increased resistance to PAI-1, less fibrin specificity	In-TIME II
Saruplase	rpro-UK	7–9	No	No	—	Recombinant urokinase-type plasminogen activator without immunogenicity	PROACT III
Staphylokinase	SakSTAR rSak	6	Selectively	Yes	—	Reduction in antigenicity with variants, fibrin-bound is not inhibited by α_2–antiplasmin	CAPTORS II
Pamiteplase	YM866	30–47	No	No	—	Resistance to plasmin cleavage	—
Desmoteplase	Bat-PA b-PA DSPA DSPAα1	t½α:1 t½β:17	Yes	Minimally	—	Vampire bat PA; greater fibrin specificity than tissue plasminogen activator	DEDAS
Monteplase	E6010	23	No	Unlikely	—	—	COMA

AMI—acute myocardial infarction ASSENT— Assessment of the Safety and Efficacy of a New Thrombolytic Agent AV—arteriovenous CAPTORS—Collaborative Angiographic Patency Trial of Recombinant Staphylokinase COMA—Combining Monteplase with Angioplasty DEDAS—Dose Escalation study of Desmoteplase in Acute Ischemic Stroke DVT—deep vein thrombosis In-TIME—Intravenous n-PA for Treatment of Infarcting Myocardium Early PA—plasminogen activator PAI—plasminogen activator inhibitor PAO—peripheral arterial occlusion PE—pulmonary embolism PROACT—Prolyse in Acute Cerebral Thromboembolism

transient hypercoagulable state caused by depletion of the natural anticoagulants (proteins C and S) before the onset of warfarin's effect. To mitigate the initial hypercoagulable state, some advocate starting warfarin therapy only after initial heparinization.

Investigational Oral Anticoagulant

A newer oral anticoagulant, the direct thrombin inhibitor ximelagatran, has been approved for use in Europe and has been widely studied; however, it has not been approved by the FDA for use in the United States. Initial studies of this agent yielded promising results, raising hopes that there might be an effective oral anticoagulant that is safer and easier to administer than warfarin.

In a prospective, double-blind study from 2003, more than 1,800 patients undergoing knee surgery were randomly assigned to receive either ximelagatran or warfarin.[97] Venography was performed on day 7. Warfarin was given in standard dosages, with a target INR of 2.0 to 3.0. Ximelagatran was given in two different doses (as a dosing trial), without monitoring. The authors observed a significantly lower incidence of DVT in the ximelagatran group, with no significant difference in bleeding. After the publication of this study, several reports of adverse reactions (specifically, liver failure) were reported to the FDA.

In a subsequent study, almost 4,000 patients with atrial fibrilla-

tion were randomly assigned to receive either warfarin or ximelagatran for stroke prophylaxis.[98] The authors found no significant differences in the rates of stroke, embolism, or death but did note a significantly higher incidence of bleeding in the warfarin group. They also found that a significant percentage of the patients in the ximelagatran group had increases in their hepatic enzymes that were correlated with administration of the drug. In addition, there were cases of fatal hepatic failure that could have been associated with the drug.

Thus, ximelagatran appears to hold great promise, but it is unclear whether it will be approved for the American market.

LYTIC THERAPY

A number of different lytic agents have been studied [*see Table 5*]. At present, however, lytic therapy is generally understood to refer to administration of streptokinase, urokinase, or t-PA,[79,80,99-102] all of which act on the endogenous fibrinolytic system to convert plasminogen to plasmin. Streptokinase combines with plasminogen to form streptokinase-plasminogen complexes that are converted to streptokinase-plasmin complexes, which then convert residual plasminogen to plasmin.[79,102] Urokinase directly cleaves a peptide bond in the plasminogen molecule to form plasmin. t-PA binds to fibrin via lysine binding sites at the N-terminal.

Lytic therapy is most effective when it can be initiated within hours. It is worth attempting when the clot has been present for less than 1 week, particularly if it has been present for less than 3 days. When lytic therapy is begun, heparin therapy usually is temporarily discontinued because of the theoretical possibility of increased bleeding risk; it may be resumed immediately upon completion of lytic therapy. If, however, the problem is immediately life-threatening (e.g., myocardial infarction or massive PE), anticoagulation should probably be done in parallel with lytic therapy to prevent rethrombosis.

Indications and Contraindications

The indications for lytic therapy are being extended.[96] Urokinase, t-PA, and, to a much lesser degree, streptokinase are being used for venous thrombotic conditions, such as symptomatic obstruction of major upper-extremity veins. The morbidity of axillary vein thrombosis can be considerable; clearance of clot may not only help restore patency but also help identify the underlying cause. In the lower extremities, more thorough clearance of clot should, in theory, help restore valve function and prevent so-called postphlebitic syndrome.[101,103]

Contraindications to lytic therapy include surgery in the previous 10 days, serious GI bleeding in the previous 3 months, a history of hypertension, an active bleeding or hemorrhagic disorder, a previous cerebrovascular accident, and an active intracranial process. As with heparin, the risk of intracranial bleeding is increased in older patients; the risk appears to be higher with t-PA than with streptokinase or urokinase.

Agents

Streptokinase Streptokinase is a 47 kd protein produced by β-hemolytic streptococci. Because it is not endogenous, circulating antibodies to it (from previous streptococcal infections) often are already present in plasma. When streptokinase is infused, a loading dose must be given to overcome these antibodies. Once the antibodies are depleted, the half-life of streptokinase is about 80 minutes. Achievement of the desired therapeutic effects is confirmed by documenting a rise in the thrombin time (TT), a fall in the fibrinogen level, or an abrupt rise in the D-dimer level. Because streptokinase may deplete circulating plasminogen after a few hours, the optimal approach may be to administer it for 6 hours by continuous infusion every 24 hours for 2 or 3 days, then to administer heparin in the intervals between infusions.

Urokinase Urokinase is a 34 kd globulin originally found in human urine and now isolated from cultured human cells. It has a half-life of 15 minutes and is metabolized by the liver. It was removed from the U.S. market for several years as a result of concerns expressed by the FDA, but it subsequently was reintroduced after these concerns were satisfactorily addressed. For catheter clearance, a solution containing 5,000 units/ml should be infused into the obstructed tubing. Urokinase is not fibrin-specific and therefore produces a systemic lytic state. Its primary disadvantage is that it costs far more than streptokinase.

t-PA Tissue plasminogen activator is an enzymatic glycoprotein composed of 527 amino acids that is produced from a human melanoma cell line by means of recombinant DNA technology. Its half-life is approximately 4 minutes; it is metabolized by the liver, and approximately 80% of the dose is excreted in the urine within 18 hours. It is not antigenic and does not promote antibody formation. Theoretically, t-PA should be somewhat more specific for fibrin clot than urokinase or streptokinase. In practice, however, its

effects are clinically indistinguishable from those of urokinase. Like urokinase, t-PA is extremely expensive.

Technique of Administration

The traditional method of administering lytic therapy, venous infusion, is widely used to treat coronary artery thrombosis[104]; however, it is only modestly effective against peripheral arterial occlusion and is associated with a high rate of hemorrhagic complications.[105] Current methods focus more closely on the site of occlusion, particularly with the development of intra-arterial infusion techniques.

Lytic therapy for acute PE has attractive theoretical benefits; however, the FDA currently approves this approach only for patients with so-called massive PE (i.e., PE resulting in both shock and heart failure). Clinical trials demonstrated that in patients who were hemodynamically unstable as a result of PE, thrombolysis achieved greater improvements in intermediate end points (e.g., right ventricular function) than heparin alone did, though survival was not improved.[106] Subsequent studies evaluated recombinant t-PA in patients with so-called submassive PE, with similar results.[66]

Monitoring

Although monitoring of lytic therapy is less standardized than monitoring of anticoagulant therapy, several principles should be followed. The effects must be monitored from both a clinical and a laboratory perspective. Clinical monitoring involves following improvements on the angiograms. Laboratory monitoring has three components. First, D-dimer levels should be measured; a marked increase signals that cross-linked fibrin is undergoing breakdown. Second, adequate stores of plasminogen should be documented; without plasminogen, none of the thrombolytic drugs are effective. Third, fibrinogen levels should be followed to prevent exhaustion of native clotting; most authorities recommend that lytic therapy be discontinued once fibrinogen levels fall below 50 mg/dl. Previously, the TT was used for monitoring thrombolysis; today, however, given the recommendation for concurrent use of heparin,[104] the TT is considered to be of little value in this setting.

Complications

The major toxicity of all three major lytic agents is hemorrhage, resulting from (1) lysis of physiologic thrombi occurring at vascular injury sites and (2) a systemic lytic state caused by the systemic formation of plasmin. The incidence of bleeding is many times higher after lytic therapy than after anticoagulant therapy and is dependent on both the dosage and the duration of lytic therapy. Careful administration of lytic agents can keep the incidence of major hemorrhage below 5% and the incidence of intracranial hemorrhage below 1%.[102]

A potential major complication is distal embolism of partially lysed clot. In theory, this possibility should rule out lytic therapy for treating thrombus in the heart or in the cerebrovascular system.[102] Surprisingly, however, dislodgment of intracardiac clot as a result of lytic therapy is rare.

Streptokinase causes several adverse reactions that urokinase and t-PA do not. When first produced, streptokinase was associated with a very high incidence of antigenicity and severe pyrogenic reactions. The current purified formulation is relatively free of pyrogens and has a reduced incidence of allergic side effects, but it is still antigenic and may still cause allergic reactions or, in rare instances, anaphylaxis. Streptokinase may also induce the formation of additional antibodies that make re-treatment impossible. In contrast, retreatment with urokinase may be carried out as often as necessary with minimal risk of allergic reactions.

Hypercoagulability States

Certain patients seem to have a tendency to clot spontaneously. So-called hypercoagulability states were long thought to exist, but they were difficult to document except on clinical grounds. Currently, however, these clotting tendencies are better understood,[107] thanks in large part to recognition of the role of antithrombins. If an antithrombin deficiency exists and clotting goes unchecked, activation of a clotting cascade could theoretically progress to clotting throughout the entire vasculature. Another important development was the recognition that deficiencies of certain natural clot-removing substances in the blood may lead to a clinical thrombotic tendency. Both types of deficiency can be either acquired or congenital.

SCREENING

When the etiology of a clotting episode is unclear, the family history should be reviewed for evidence of a congenital disorder. Even if the history is negative, the patient should be screened for both acquired and congenital disorders [see Figure 9].

Acquired Clotting Conditions

Screening for acquired clotting conditions [see Table 6] is based on the history, physical examination, and laboratory assessment. The history should include medications, diseases, and surgical procedures or other injuries.[108-110] Examination may disclose causes of hypercoagulability.[111] Soft tissue injury, for example, is a potent activator of the coagulation system. If the injury is severe enough, it may be capable of causing a severe acquired coagulopathy. The problem is usually obvious, but on occasion, detailed study may be necessary to identify tissue damage or ischemic injury to bowel or extremities. Hypovolemia—especially hypovolemic shock—markedly reduces clotting time: blood from a patient in profound shock may clot instantaneously in the syringe as it is being drawn. The breakdown of red cells in a hemolytic transfusion reaction can cause clotting. Severe infection, especially from gram-negative organisms, is a potent activator of coagulation.[112]

Of the acquired hypercoagulability syndromes, Trousseau syndrome is a particularly important condition for surgeons to recognize because it occurs in the surgical population (cancer patients) and must be treated with heparin (it is unresponsive to warfarin). It occurs when an adenocarcinoma secretes a protein recognized by the body as tissue factor, resulting in multiple episodes of venous thromboembolism over time (migratory thrombophlebitis). Simple depletion of vitamin K–dependent factors is ineffective. Patients should receive therapeutic-dose heparin indefinitely or until the cancer is brought into remission.[113]

Laboratory screening may facilitate diagnosis. A complete blood count may document the presence of polycythemia or leukemia. Thrombocythemia may be a manifestation of a hypercoagulable disorder, and thrombocytopenia after the administration of heparin raises the possibility of intravascular platelet aggregation. A prolonged aPTT is suggestive of lupuslike anticoagulant. Increased levels of D-dimers, fibrin degradation products (FDPs), or fibrin monomers in the plasma may reflect low-grade intravascular coagulation.

Congenital Clotting Conditions

Congenital clotting tendencies can result from deficiencies in inhibitors of thrombosis (antithrombin, proteins C and S, and possibly heparin cofactor II), dysfibrinogenemias, or dysfibrinolysis [see Table 7]. Most congenital clotting defects are transmitted as an autosomal dominant trait. A negative family history does not preclude inherited thrombophilia, because the defects have a low penetrance, and fresh mutations may have occurred.

INITIAL LABORATORY ASSESSMENT

Initial evaluation of a patient with an unexplained thrombotic episode should be directed at the most common causes of hypercoagulability. Acquired causes of clotting are more commonly seen by surgeons than congenital causes and therefore must be excluded first. If a clotting disorder is determined to be congenital, a laboratory workup should be undertaken. Several of the relevant assays (see below)—specifically, the functional assays—should be performed after the acute phase of the disorder has passed. If they are performed during the acute phase, levels of several antithrombotics (e.g., antithrombin and proteins C and S) will be misleadingly low—not because deficiencies of these substances caused the underlying thrombotic process but because they were consumed in that process.

SPECIFIC CAUSES OF THROMBOTIC TENDENCY

The most common congenital causes of accelerated clotting are mutations of prothrombin (prothrombin G20210A mutation) and factor V (Leiden mutation, or activated protein C resistance).[114-116] The prevalence of each of these ranges from 1% to 5% in the general population and may be much higher in specific ethnic subpopulations.[117] Each mutation may be identified conclusively by means of polymerase chain reaction (PCR) techniques. Detection of these mutations, unlike assays for antithrombin and proteins C and S, is not dependent on the patient's current inflammatory state. It must be remembered that the presence of one of these mutations, especially in the heterozygous form, does not imply that it is the sole cause of thrombosis. In many patients, a second precipitating factor must be present for the pathologic genetic thrombotic potential to be manifested.

Prothrombin G20210A Mutation

The prothrombin G20210A mutation is known to involve a single amino acid substitution in the prothrombin gene, but precisely how this increases the risk of venous thromboembolism is unclear. The one apparent manifestation of the mutation is a 15% to 40% increase in circulating prothrombin. Regardless of the mechanism at work, patients who are at least heterozygous for the trait are at two- to sixfold greater risk for venous thromboembolism than those without the mutation.[118]

Resistance to Activated Protein C (Factor V Leiden)

Resistance of human clotting factors to inactivation by activated protein C is believed to be the most common inherited procoagulant disorder.[114] Normally, activated factor V is degraded by activated protein C in the presence of membrane surface as part of normal regulation of thrombosis. Activated protein C resistance is caused by a single substitution mutation in the factor V gene, which is passed in an autosomal dominant fashion. The mutant factor V that results, termed factor V Leiden, is resistant to inactivation by activated protein C and thus has a greater ability to activate thrombin and accelerate clotting.

Two techniques are commonly used to diagnose this disorder. The first is a functional assay that compares a standard aPTT to one performed in the presence of exogenous activated protein C. If the latter aPTT does not exhibit significant prolongation, the patient is probably resistant to activated protein C. The results of this assay must be interpreted with caution if the patient is still in the acute phase of the illness. The second technique, which is more reliable, involves direct detection of the mutation via PCR analysis of DNA.

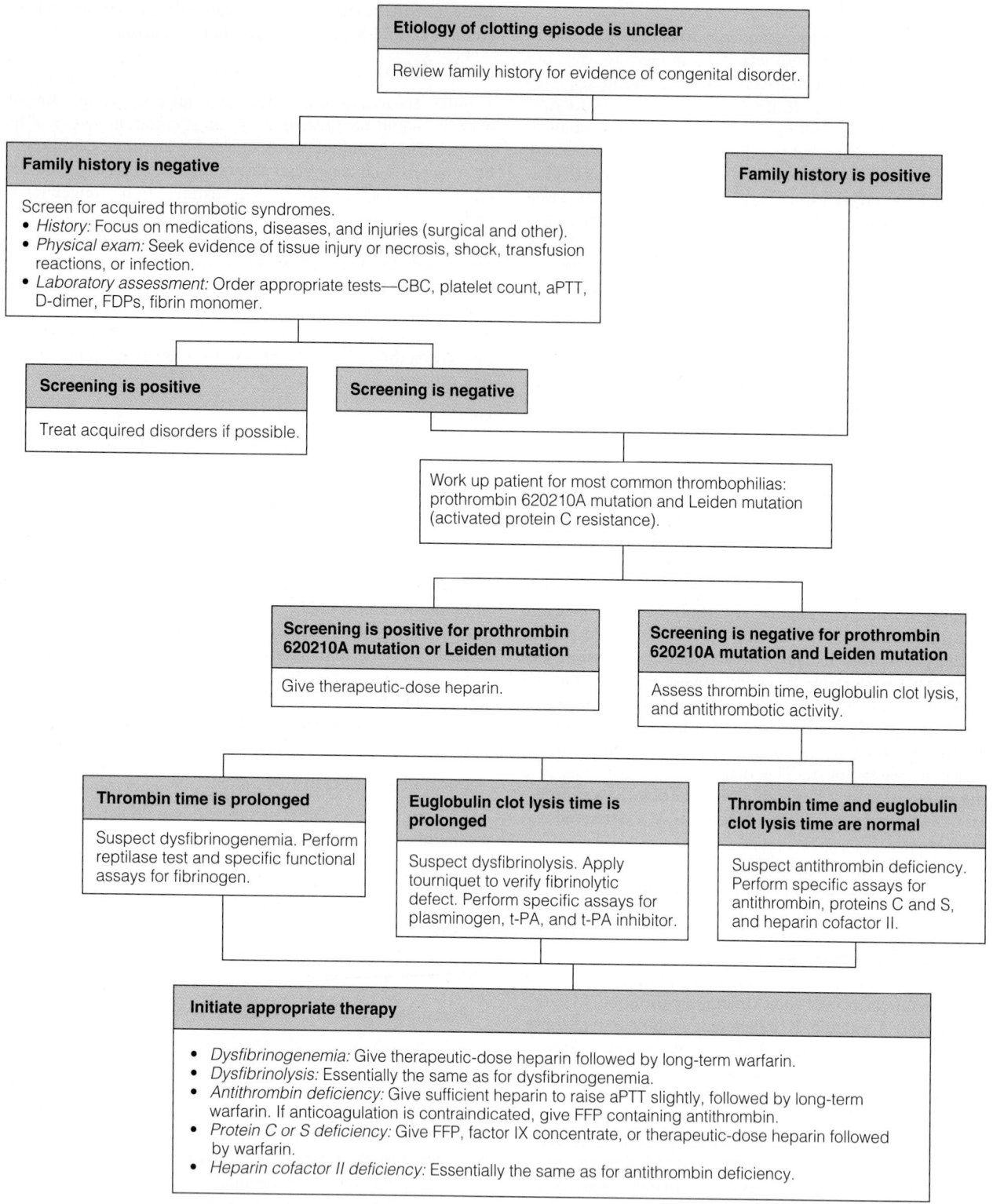

Etiology of clotting episode is unclear

Review family history for evidence of congenital disorder.

Family history is negative

Screen for acquired thrombotic syndromes.
- *History:* Focus on medications, diseases, and injuries (surgical and other).
- *Physical exam:* Seek evidence of tissue injury or necrosis, shock, transfusion reactions, or infection.
- *Laboratory assessment:* Order appropriate tests—CBC, platelet count, aPTT, D-dimer, FDPs, fibrin monomer.

Family history is positive

Screening is positive

Treat acquired disorders if possible.

Screening is negative

Work up patient for most common thrombophilias: prothrombin 620210A mutation and Leiden mutation (activated protein C resistance).

Screening is positive for prothrombin 620210A mutation or Leiden mutation

Give therapeutic-dose heparin.

Screening is negative for prothrombin 620210A mutation and Leiden mutation

Assess thrombin time, euglobulin clot lysis, and antithrombotic activity.

Thrombin time is prolonged

Suspect dysfibrinogenemia. Perform reptilase test and specific functional assays for fibrinogen.

Euglobulin clot lysis time is prolonged

Suspect dysfibrinolysis. Apply tourniquet to verify fibrinolytic defect. Perform specific assays for plasminogen, t-PA, and t-PA inhibitor.

Thrombin time and euglobulin clot lysis time are normal

Suspect antithrombin deficiency. Perform specific assays for antithrombin, proteins C and S, and heparin cofactor II.

Initiate appropriate therapy

- *Dysfibrinogenemia:* Give therapeutic-dose heparin followed by long-term warfarin.
- *Dysfibrinolysis:* Essentially the same as for dysfibrinogenemia.
- *Antithrombin deficiency:* Give sufficient heparin to raise aPTT slightly, followed by long-term warfarin. If anticoagulation is contraindicated, give FFP containing antithrombin.
- *Protein C or S deficiency:* Give FFP, factor IX concentrate, or therapeutic-dose heparin followed by warfarin.
- *Heparin cofactor II deficiency:* Essentially the same as for antithrombin deficiency.

Figure 9 **Shown is an algorithm for screening for acquired and congenital thrombotic syndromes.**

Antithrombin Deficiency

Antithrombin (once termed antithrombin III) is a 65 kd protein that decelerates the coagulation system by inactivating activated factors—primarily factor Xa and thrombin but also factors XII, XI, and IX.[119,120] Antithrombin therefore acts as a scavenger of activated clotting factors. Its activity is enhanced 100-fold by the presence of heparans on the endothelial surface and 1,000-fold by administration of exogenous heparin.

Congenital antithrombin deficiency occurs in approximately 0.01% to 0.05% of the general population and 2% to 4% of patients with venous thrombosis.[119] The trait is passed on as an autosomal dominant trait, with the heterozygous genotype being incompatible with life. Antithrombin-deficient patients are at increased risk for thromboembolism when their antithrombin activ-

Table 6 Etiology of Acquired Hypercoagulability

Tissue and cellular damage
  Shock
  Trauma
  Surgery
  Tissue necrosis
  Transfusion necrosis
Drugs
  Estrogens
  Drug reactions and interactions
  Heparin platelet antibody
  Warfarin
Disease
  Blood dyscrasias
  Cancer
  Diabetes
  Homocystinuria
  Hyperlipidemia
  Presence of lupuslike anticoagulant
  Severe infection
Pregnancy

ity falls below 70% of normal.[121]

Patients with congenital antithrombin deficiency frequently present after a stressful event. They usually have DVT but sometimes have PE. If anticoagulation is not contraindicated, the treatment of choice is heparin at a dosage sufficient to raise the aPTT to the desired level, followed by warfarin. If anticoagulation is contraindicated (as it is during the peripartum period), antithrombin concentrate should be given to raise the antithrombin activity to 80% to 120% of normal during the period when anticoagulants cannot be given.

Acquired antithrombin deficiency is a well-recognized entity. In most patients undergoing severe systemic stress, antithrombin levels fall below normal.[122] Patients with classic risk factors for venous thromboembolism tend to have the lowest levels.

Protein C and Protein S Deficiency

Protein C is a 62 kd glycoprotein with a half-life of 6 hours. Because it is vitamin K dependent, a deficiency will develop in the absence of vitamin K. Acquired protein C deficiency is seen in liver disease, malignancy, infection, the postoperative state, and disseminated intravascular coagulation.[49] Protein C deficiency occurs in approximately 4% to 5% of patients younger than 40 to 45 years who present with unexplained venous thrombosis.[123] It is transmitted as an autosomal dominant trait, and the family history is usually positive for a clotting tendency. Protein C levels range from 70% to 164% of normal in patients without a clotting tendency; levels below 70% of normal are associated with a thrombotic tendency. The most appropriate tests for screening are functional assays; there are cases of dysfunctional protein C deficiency in

Table 7 Congenital Clotting Disorders

Prothrombin G20210A mutation
Activated protein C resistance (Leiden V mutation)
Antithrombin deficiency
Proteins C and S deficiency
Dysfibrinogenemias
Dysfibrinolysis
  Hypoplasminogenemia
  Impaired release of t-PA
  High levels of t-PA inhibitor
  Factor XII deficiency

which protein C antigen levels are normal but protein C activity is low, and these would not be detected by the usual immunoassays.

Protein S is a vitamin K–dependent protein that acts as a cofactor for activated protein C by enhancing protein C–induced inactivation of activated factor V. The incidence of protein S deficiency is similar to that of protein C deficiency.[123] It is transmitted as a dominant trait, and the family history is often positive for a thrombotic tendency.

Hyperhomocysteinemia

Although hyperhomocysteinemia is more commonly associated with cardiac disease and arterial thrombosis, it may also be associated with an increased incidence of venous thromboembolism.[124] This association is not as strong as those already discussed (see above). Accordingly, anticoagulation of asymptomatic patients with elevated homocysteine levels is not currently recommended.

Dysfibrinogenemia

More than 100 qualitative abnormalities of fibrinogen (dysfibrinogenemias) have been reported.[125] Dysfibrinogenemias are inherited in an autosomal dominant manner, with most patients being heterozygous. Most patients with dysfibrinogenemia have either no clinical symptoms or symptoms of a bleeding disorder; a minority (about 11%) have clinical features of a recurrent thromboembolic disorder.[126,127] Congenital dysfibrinogenemias associated with thrombosis account for about 1% of cases of unexplained venous thrombosis occurring in young people. The most commonly observed functional defect in such dysfibrinogenemias is abnormal fibrin monomer polymerization combined with resistance to fibrinolysis. Decreased binding of plasminogen and increased resistance to lysis by plasmin have been noted.

In addition to a prolonged TT, patients who have dysfibrinogenemia associated with thromboembolism may have a prolonged INR. The diagnosis is confirmed if the reptilase time is also prolonged. Measured with clotting techniques, fibrinogen levels may be slightly or moderately low; measured immunologically, levels may be normal or even increased.

Dysfibrinolysis

Fibrinolysis can be impaired by inherited deficiencies of plasminogen, defective release of t-PA from the vascular endothelium, and high plasma levels of regulatory proteins (e.g., t-PA inhibitors).[127,128] In addition, factor XII (contact factor) deficiency may induce failure of fibrinolysis activation.

Inherited plasminogen deficiency is probably only rarely responsible for unexplained DVT in young patients. It is transmitted as an autosomal dominant trait. In heterozygous persons with a thrombotic tendency, plasminogen activity is about one half normal (3.9 to 8.4 μmol/ml). The euglobulin clot lysis time is prolonged. Functional assays should be carried out, and there should be full transformation of plasminogen into plasmin activators.

The important role of t-PA inhibitors I and II in the regulation of fibrinolysis is well defined.[128,129] In normal plasma, t-PA inhibitor I is the primary inhibitor for both t-PA and urokinase. Release of t-PA inhibitor I by platelets results in locally increased concentrations where platelets accumulate. The ensuing local inhibition of fibrinolysis may help stabilize the hemostatic plug. t-PA inhibitor II is present in and secreted by monocytes and macrophages.

Factor XII deficiency is a rare cause of impaired fibrinolysis. Initial contact activation of factor XII not only results in activation of the clotting cascade and of the inflammatory response but also leads to plasmin generation. This intrinsic activation of fibrinolysis requires factor XII, prekallikrein, and high-molecular-weight kininogen. Patients with factor XII deficiencies can be identified by a prolonged aPTT in the absence of clinical bleeding.[107,130]

TREATMENT

Treatment of a clinical hypercoagulable state involves both prophylaxis [see Prophylaxis against Thromboembolism, above] and specific treatment.[131] Prophylaxis in postoperative patients consists primarily of maintaining good hydration, ensuring normal cardiac output, and early mobilization. Low-dose heparin, intermittent pneumatic compression, low-molecular-weight dextran, or some combination of these may also be appropriate.

Patients with activated protein C resistance who present with venous thrombosis should be treated with heparin in the standard fashion. They also should receive genetic counseling and refrain from using oral contraceptives.

Treatment of antithrombin deficiency associated with active clotting involves initiating heparin anticoagulation at a dosage sufficient to ensure a significant rise in the aPTT. Warfarin is the drug of choice for long-term prophylaxis and should be given at a dosage sufficient to maintain an INR of 2.0 to 3.0. When anticoagulation is contraindicated, a purified form of antithrombin may be administered directly. Patients with acquired antithrombin deficiency should receive prophylaxis in the form of heparin at a dosage sufficient to raise the aPTT 5 seconds above the upper limit of the normal laboratory value.

Treatment of clotting states related to protein C or protein S deficiency involves administering fresh frozen plasma or factor IX concentrate. Therapeutic-dose heparin followed by warfarin may be appropriate for long-term treatment.

Treatment of thromboembolism associated with dysfibrinogenemia involves therapeutic-dose heparin followed by long-term warfarin. Treatment of thromboembolic disorders associated with dysfibrinolysis is essentially the same as that of dysfibrinogenemia. Some patients with these qualitative plasminogen defects and acute massive thrombotic events may not respond to fibrinolytic treatment with urokinase or streptokinase.

References

1. Dunmire SM: Pulmonary embolism. Emerg Med Clin North Am 7:339, 1989
2. Shackford SR, Moser KM: Deep venous thrombosis and pulmonary embolism in trauma patients. J Intensive Care Med 3:87, 1988
3. Hirsh J, Hull RD: Venous Thromboembolism: Natural History, Diagnosis, and Management. CRC Press, Boca Raton, Florida, 1988
4. Bergqvist D: Postoperative Thromboembolism: Frequency, Etiology, Prophylaxis. Springer-Verlag, New York, 1983
5. Kakkar VV, Stringer MD: Prophylaxis of venous thromboembolism. World J Surg 14:670, 1990
6. Bell WR, Simon TL: Current status of pulmonary thromboembolic disease: pathophysiology, diagnosis, prevention and treatment. Am Heart J 103:239, 1982
7. Sabiston DC Jr: Pathophysiology, diagnosis and management of pulmonary embolism. Am J Surg 138:384, 1979
8. Dalen JE, Haffajee CI, Alpert JS 3rd, et al: Pulmonary embolism, pulmonary hemorrhage and pulmonary infarction. N Engl J Med 296:1431, 1977
9. Kakkar VV, Corrigan TP, Fossard DP, et al: Prevention of fatal postoperative pulmonary embolism by low doses of heparin: reappraisal of results of international multicentre trial. Lancet 1:567, 1977
10. Prevention of venous thrombosis and pulmonary embolism. NIH Consensus Development. JAMA 256:744, 1986
11. Blaisdell FW: Preventing postoperative thromboembolism. West J Med 151:188, 1989
12. Reilly DT: Prophylactic methods against thromboembolism. Acta Chir Scand Suppl 550(suppl): 115, 1989
13. Knudson MM, Lewis FR, Clinton A, et al: Prevention of venous thromboembolism in trauma patients. J Trauma 37:480, 1994
14. McLeod RS, Geerts WH, Sniderman KW, et al: Subcutaneous heparin versus low-molecular-weight heparin as thromboprophylaxis in patients undergoing colorectal surgery: results of the Canadian colorectal DVT prophylaxis trial: a randomized, double-blind trial. Ann Surg 233:438, 2001
15. Geerts WH, Jay RM, Code KI, et al: A comparison of low-dose heparin with low-molecular-weight heparin as prophylaxis against venous thromboembolism after major trauma. N Engl J Med 335:701, 1996

16. Christen Y, Wutschert R, Weimer D, et al: Effects of intermittent pneumatic compression on venous haemodynamics and fibrinolytic activity. Blood Coagul Fibrinol 8:185, 1997
17. Comerota AJ, Chouhan V, Harada RN, et al: The fibrinolytic effects of intermittent pneumatic compression: mechanism of enhanced fibrinolysis. Ann Surg 226:306, 1997
18. Elliott CG, Dudney TM, Egger M, et al: Calf-thigh sequential pneumatic compression compared with plantar venous pneumatic compression to prevent deep-vein thrombosis after non–lower extremity trauma. J Trauma 47:25, 1999
19. Howard A, Zaccagnini D, Ellis M, et al: Randomized clinical trial of low molecular weight heparin with thigh-length or knee-length antiembolism stockings for patients undergoing surgery. Br J Surg 91:842, 2004
20. Lachiewicz PF, Kelley SS, Haden LR: Two mechanical devices for prophylaxis of thromboembolism after total knee arthroplasty. A prospective, randomised study. J Bone Joint Surg Br 86:1137, 2004
21. Rosenberg RD: Action and interactions of antithrombin and heparin. N Engl J Med 292:145, 1975
22. Leyvraz PF, Richard J, Bachmann F, et al: Adjusted versus fixed-dose subcutaneous heparin in the prevention of deep-vein thrombosis after total hip replacement. N Engl J Med 309:954, 1983
23. Owings JT, Blaisdell FW: Low-dose heparin thromboembolism prophylaxis. Arch Surg 131: 1069, 1996
24. Turpie AG, Levine MN, Hirsh J, et al: A randomized controlled trial of a low-molecular-weight heparin (enoxaparin) to prevent deep-vein thrombosis in patients undergoing elective hip surgery. N Engl J Med 315:925, 1986
25. Levine MN, Hirsh J, Gent M, et al: Prevention of deep vein thrombosis after elective hip surgery: a randomized trial comparing low molecular weight heparin with standard unfractionated heparin. Ann Intern Med 114:545, 1991
26. Eriksson BI, Bauer KA, Lassen MR, et al: Fondaparinux compared with enoxaparin for the prevention of venous thromboembolism after hip-fracture surgery. Steering Committee of the Pentasaccharide in Hip-Fracture Surgery Study. N Engl J Med 345:1298, 2001
27. Bauer KA, Eriksson BI, Lassen MR, et al: Fondaparinux compared with enoxaparin for the preven-

tion of venous thromboembolism after elective major knee surgery. Steering Committee of the Pentasaccharide in Major Knee Surgery Study. N Engl J Med 345:1305, 2001
28. MacCallum PK, Thomson JM, Poller L: Effects of fixed minidose warfarin on coagulation and fibrinolysis following major gynaecological surgery. Thromb Haemost 64:511, 1990
29. Decousus H, Leizorovicz A, Parent F, et al: A clinical trial of vena caval filters in the prevention of pulmonary embolism in patients with proximal deep-vein thrombosis. N Engl J Med 338:409, 1998
30. Belcaro G, Nicolaides AN, Errichi BM, et al: Superficial thrombophlebitis of the legs: a randomized, controlled, follow-up study. Angiology 50: 523, 1999
31. Geerts WH, Code KI, Jay RM, et al: A prospective study of venous thromboembolism after major trauma. N Engl J Med 331:1601, 1994
32. Owings JT, Gosselin RC, Battistella FD, et al: Whole blood D-dimer assay: an effective non-invasive method to rule out pulmonary embolism. J Trauma 48:795, 2000
33. Owings JT, Gosselin RC, Anderson JT, et al: Practical utility of the whole blood D-dimer assay for excluding thromboembolism in severely injured trauma patients. J Trauma 51:425, 2001
34. Gosselin RC, Owings JT, Jacoby RC, et al: Evaluation of a new automated quantitative D-dimer, Advanced D-Dimer, in patients suspected of venous thromboembolism. Blood Coag Fibrinol 13:323, 2002
35. Bergqvist D, Bergentz SE: Diagnosis of deep vein thrombosis. World J Surg 14:679, 1990
36. Hirsh J: Reliability of non-invasive tests for the diagnosis of venous thrombosis (editorial). Thromb Haemost 65:221, 1991
37. Krupski WC, Bass A, Dilley RB, et al: Propagation of deep venous thrombosis identified by duplex ultrasonography. J Vasc Surg 12:467, 1990
38. Lensing AW, Prandoni P, Brandjes D: Detection of deep-vein thrombosis by real-time B-mode ultrasonography. N Engl J Med 320:342, 1989
39. Haire WD, Lynch TG, Lund GB: Limitations of magnetic resonance imaging and ultrasound directed (duplex) scanning in the diagnosis of subclavian vein thrombosis. J Vasc Surg 13:391, 1991
40. Barnes RW, Nix ML, Barnes CL: Perioperative asymptomatic venous thrombosis: role of duplex

scanning versus venography. J Vasc Surg 9:25, 1989

41. Simonneau G, Sors H, Charbonnier B, et al: A comparison of low-molecular-weight heparin with unfractionated heparin for acute pulmonary embolism. The THE-SEE Study Group. Tinzaparine ou Heparine Standard: Evaluations dans l'Embolie Pulmonaire. N Engl J Med 337:663, 1997

42. Low-molecular-weight heparin in the treatment of patients with venous thromboembolism. The Columbus Investigators. N Engl J Med 337:657, 1997

43. Hirsh J, Turpie AG: Use of plasminogen activators in venous thrombosis. World J Surg 14:688, 1990

44. Sakakibara Y, Shigeta O, Ishikawa S, et al: Upper extremity vein thrombosis: etiologic categories, precipitating causes, and management. Angiology 50:547, 1999

45. DiFelice GS, Paletta GA Jr, Phillips BB, et al: Effort thrombosis in the elite throwing athlete. Am J Sports Med 30:708, 2002

46. Schmacht DC, Back MR, Novotney ML, et al: Primary axillary-subclavian venous thrombosis: is aggressive surgical intervention justified? Vasc Surg 35:353, 2001

47. Wells PS, Forster AJ: Thrombolysis in deep vein thrombosis: is there still an indication? Thromb Haemost 86:499, 2001

48. Patel NH, Plorde JJ, Meissner M: Catheter-directed thrombolysis in the treatment of phlegmasia cerulea dolens. Ann Vasc Surg 12:471, 1998

49. Lord RS, Chen FC, DeVine TJ, et al: Surgical treatment of acute deep venous thrombosis. World J Surg 14:694, 1990

50. LeClerk JR: Venous Thromboembolic Disorders. Lea & Febiger, Philadelphia, 1991, p 54

51. Smith GT, Dammin GJ, Dexter L: Postmortem arteriographic studies of the human lung in pulmonary embolization. JAMA 188:143, 1964

52. Goldhaber SZ, Hennekens CH, Evans DA, et al: Factors associated with correct antemortem diagnosis of major pulmonary embolism. Am J Med 73:822, 1982

53. Karwinski B, Svendsen E: Comparison of clinical and postmortem diagnosis of pulmonary embolism. J Clin Pathol 42:135, 1989

54. Moser KM, Hull R, Saltzman HA, et al: Recent advances in diagnosis of pulmonary embolism and deep venous thrombosis. Am Rev Respir Dis 138:1046, 1988

55. Coon WW: Risk factors in pulmonary embolism. Surg Gynecol Obstet 143:385, 1976

56. Boneu B, Bes G, Pelzer H, et al: D-dimers, thrombin antithrombin III complexes and prothrombin fragments 1 + 2 diagnostic value in clinically suspected deep vein thrombosis. Thromb Haemost 65:28, 1991

57. Owings JT, Kraut EJ, Battistella FD, et al: Timing of the occurrence of pulmonary embolism in trauma patients. Arch Surg 132:862, 1997

58. Killewich LA, Nunnelee JD, Auer AI: Value of lower extremity venous duplex examination in the diagnosis of pulmonary embolism. J Vasc Surg 17:934, 1993

59. PIOPED Investigators: Value of ventilation/perfusion scan in acute pulmonary embolism: results of prospective investigation of pulmonary embolism diagnosis (PIOPED). JAMA 263:2753, 1990

60. Hull RD, Hirsh J, Carter CJ, et al: Diagnostic value of ventilation-perfusion lung scanning in patients with suspected pulmonary embolism. Chest 88:819, 1985

61. Remy-Jardin M, Remy J, Deschildre F, et al: Diagnosis of pulmonary embolism with spiral CT: comparison with pulmonary angiography and scintigraphy. Radiology 200:699, 1996

62. Prologo JD, Gilkeson RC, Diaz M, et al: The effect of single-detector CT versus MDCT on clinical

outcomes in patients with suspected acute pulmonary embolism and negative results on CT pulmonary angiography. AJR Am J Roentgenol 184:1231, 2005

63. Hull RD, Raskob GE, Hirsh J: The diagnosis of clinically suspected pulmonary embolism: practical approaches. Chest 89:4175, 1986

64. Ferris EJ, Holder JC, Lim WN, et al: Angiography of pulmonary emboli: digital studies and balloon-occlusion cineangiography. Am J Roentgenol 142:369, 1984

65. Anderson JT, Jeng T, Bain M, et al: Diagnosis of post traumatic pulmonary embolism: is chest computed tomographic angiography acceptable? J Trauma 54:472, 2003

66. Konstantinides S, Geibel A, Heusel G, et al: Management Strategies and Prognosis of Pulmonary Embolism-3 Trial Investigators. Heparin plus alteplase compared with heparin alone in patients with submassive pulmonary embolism. N Engl J Med 347:1143, 2002

67. Atik M, Broghamer WL Jr: The impact of prophylactic measures on fatal pulmonary embolism. Arch Surg 114:366, 1979

68. Collins R, Scrimgeour A, Yusuf S, et al: Reduction in fatal pulmonary embolism and venous thrombosis by perioperative administration of subcutaneous heparin: overview of results of randomized trials in general, orthopedic, and urologic surgery. N Engl J Med 318:1162, 1988

69. Geerts WH: Pulmonary embolism. Conn's Current Therapy 1992. Rakel RE, Ed. WB Saunders Co, Philadelphia, 1992, p 179

70. Moser KM: State of the art: pulmonary embolism. Am Rev Respir Dis 115:829, 1977

71. Thomas DP: Therapeutic role of heparin in acute pulmonary embolism. Curr Ther Res 18:21, 1975

72. Silver D: Pulmonary embolism: prevention, detection and nonoperative management. Surg Clin North Am 54:1089, 1974

73. Rohrer MJ, Scheidler MG, Wheeler HB, et al: Extended indications for placement of an inferior vena cava filter. J Vasc Surg 10:44, 1989

74. Fink JA, Jones BT: The Greenfield filter as the primary means of therapy in venous thromboembolic disease. Surg Gynecol Obstet 172:253, 1991

75. Wells I: Inferior vena cava filters and when to use them. Clin Radiol 40:11, 1989

76. PREPIC Study Group: Eight-year follow-up of patients with permanent vena cava filters in the prevention of pulmonary embolism: the PREPIC (Prevention du Risque d'Embolie Pulmonaire par Interruption Cave) randomized study. Circulation 112:416, 2005

77. Schmitz-Rode T, Janssens U, Duda SH, et al: Massive pulmonary embolism: percutaneous emergency treatment by pigtail rotation catheter. J Am Coll Cardiol 36:375, 2000

78. Rooke TW: Deep venous thrombosis of the extremities. Conn's Current Therapy 1992. Rakel RE, Ed. WB Saunders Co, Philadelphia, 1992, p 289

79. Majerus PW, Broze GJ Jr, Miletich JP, et al: Anticoagulant, thrombolytic and antiplatelet drugs. Goodman & Gilman's The Pharmacological Basis of Therapeutics. Goodman AG, Rall TW, Nies AS, et al, Eds. Pergamon Press, New York, 1990, p 1311

80. USP DI, Drug Information for the Health Care Professional vol IB. The United States Pharmacopeial Convention, Inc, Rockville, Maryland, 1992, pp 1505, 2357, 2658

81. Owen CA Jr, Bowie EJ, et al: Chronic intravascular coagulation syndromes: a summary. Mayo Clin Proc 49:673, 1974

82. Blaisdell FW, Graziano CJ, Effeney DJ: In vivo assessment of anticoagulation. Surgery 82:827, 1977

83. Blaisdell FW, Steele M, Allen RE: Management of

acute lower extremity arterial ischemia due to embolism and thrombosis. Surgery 84:822, 1978

84. Blaisdell FW, Graziano CJ: Assessment of clotting by the determination of fibrinogen catabolism. Am J Surg 135:436, 1978

85. Conti S, Daschbach M, Blaisdell FW: A comparison of high-dose versus conventional-dose heparin therapy for deep vein thrombosis. Surgery 92:972, 1982

86. Kashtan J, Conti S, Blaisdell FW: Heparin therapy for deep venous thrombosis. Am J Surg 140:836, 1980

87. Ridker PM, Goldhaber SZ, Danielson E, et al: for the PREVENT Investigators: Long-term, low-intensity warfarin therapy for the prevention of recurrent venous thromboembolism. N Engl J Med 348:1425, 2003

88. Silver D, Kapsch DN, Tsoi EK: Heparin induced thrombocytopenia, thrombosis and hemorrhage. Ann Surg 198:301, 1983

89. Becker PS, Miller VT: Heparin-induced thrombocytopenia. Stroke 20:1449, 1989

90. Celoria GM, Steingart RH, Banson B, et al: Coumarin skin necrosis in a patient with heparin-induced thrombocytopenia: a case report. Angiology 39:915, 1988

91. Walker AM, Jick H: Predictors of bleeding during heparin therapy. JAMA 244:1209, 1980

92. Mudaliar JH, Liem TK, Nichols WK, et al: Lepirudin is a safe and effective anticoagulant for patients with heparin-associated antiplatelet antibodies. J Vasc Surg 34:17, 2001

93. Ginsberg JS, Kowalchuk G, Hirsh J, et al: Heparin effect on bone density. Thromb Haemost 64:286, 1990

94. Hirsh J, Poller L, Deykin D, et al: Optimal therapeutic range for oral anticoagulants. Chest 95(2 suppl):5s, 1989

95. Pinede L, Ninet J, Duhaut P, et al: Investigators of the 'Duree Optimale du Traitement AntiVitamines K' (DOTAVK) Study. Comparison of 3 and 6 months of oral anticoagulant therapy after a first episode of proximal deep vein thrombosis or pulmonary embolism and comparison of 6 and 12 weeks of therapy after isolated calf deep vein thrombosis. Circulation 103:2453, 2001

96. Yasaka M, Minematsu K, Naritomi H, et al: Predisposing factors for enlargement of intracerebral hemorrhage in patients treated with warfarin. Thromb Haemost 89:278, 2003

97. Francis CW, Berkowitz SD, Comp PC, et al: Comparison of ximelagatran with warfarin for the prevention of venous thromboembolism after total knee replacement. N Engl J Med 349:1703, 2003

98. Albers GW, Diener HC, Frison L, et al: Ximelagatran vs warfarin for stroke prevention in patients with nonvalvular atrial fibrillation: a randomized trial. JAMA 293:690, 2005

99. Blaisdell FW: Hemostasis and thrombosis. Vascular Surgery: A Comprehensive Review, 2nd ed. Moore WS, Ed. Grune & Stratton, New York, 1986, p 909

100. Meyerovitz MF, Goldhaber SZ, Reagan K, et al: Recombinant tissue-type plasminogen activator versus urokinase in peripheral arterial and graft occlusions: a randomized trial. Radiology 175:75, 1990

101. Turpie AG: Thrombolytic agents in venous thrombosis. J Vasc Surg 12:196, 1990

102. Marder VJ, Sherry S: Thrombolytic therapy: current status. N Engl J Med 318:1585, 1988

103. Goldhaber SZ, Buring JE, Lipnick RJ, et al: Pooled analyses of randomized trials of streptokinase and heparin in phlebographically documented acute deep venous thrombosis. Am J Med 76:393, 1984

104. The effects of tissue plasminogen activator, streptokinase, or both on coronary-artery patency, ventricular function, and survival after acute myocardial infarction. The GUSTO Angiographic Inves-

tigators. N Engl J Med 329:1615, 1993

105. Amery A, Deloof W, Vermylen J, et al: Outcome of recent thromboembolic occlusions of limb arteries treated with streptokinase. Br Med J 4:639, 1970

106. Meyer GJ, Sors H, Charbonnier B, et al: Effects of intravenous urokinase versus alteplase on total pulmonary resistance in acute massive pulmonary embolism: a European multicenter double-blind trial. The European Cooperative Study Group for Pulmonary Embolism. J Am Coll Cardiol 19:239, 1992

107. Schafer AI: The hypercoagulable states. Ann Intern Med 102:814, 1985

108. Baehner RL: Alterations in blood coagulation with trauma. Pediatr Clin North Am 22:289, 1975

109. Jansson IG, Hetland O, Rammer LM, et al: Effects of phospholipase C, a tissue thromboplastin inhibitor, on pulmonary microembolism after missile injury of the limb. J Trauma 28:S222, 1988

110. Effeney DJ, McIntyre KS, Blaisdell FW, et al: Fibrinogen kinetics in major human burns. Surg Forum 29:56, 1978

111. Blaisdell FW: Acquired and congenital clotting syndromes. World J Surg 14:664, 1990

112. Hauptman JG, Hassouna HI, Bell TG, et al: Efficacy of antithrombin III in endotoxin induced disseminated intravascular coagulation. Circ Shock 25:111, 1988

113. Callander N, Rapaport SI: Trousseau's syndrome. West J Med 158:364, 1993

114. Dahlbäck B, Carlsson M, Svensson PJ: Familial thrombophilia due to a previously unrecognized mechanism characterized by poor anticoagulant response to activated protein C: prediction of a cofactor to activated protein C. Proc Natl Acad Sci USA 90:1004, 1993

115. Bertina RM, Reitsma PH, Rosendaal FR, et al: Resistance to activated protein C and factor V Leiden as risk factors for venous thrombosis. Thromb Haemost 74:449, 1995

116. De Stefano V, Martinelli I, Mannucci PM, et al: The risk of recurrent deep venous thrombosis among heterozygous carriers of both factor V Leiden and the G20210A prothrombin mutation. N Engl J Med 341:801, 1999

117. Hessner MJ, Luhm RA, Pearson SL, et al: Prevalence of prothrombin G20210A, factor V G1691A (Leiden), and methylenetetrahydrofolate reductase (MTHFR) C677T in seven different populations determined by multiplex allele-specific PCR. Thromb Haemost 81:733, 1999

118. Marder VJ, Matei DE: Hereditary and acquired thrombophilic syndromes. Hemostasis and Thrombosis. Colman, Hirsch, Marder, et al, Eds. Lippincott Williams & Wilkins, Philadelphia, 2001

119. Egeberg O: Inherited antithrombin deficiency causing thrombophilia. Thromb Diath Haemorrhag 13:516, 1965

120. High KA: Antithrombin-III, protein-C, and protein-S: naturally occurring anticoagulant proteins. Arch Pathol Lab Med 112:28, 1988

121. Bauer KA, Goodman TL, Kass BL, et al: Elevated factor Xa activity in the blood of asymptomatic patients with congenital antithrombin deficiency. J Clin Invest 76:826, 1985

122. Owings JT, Bagley M, Gosselin R, et al: Effect of critical injury on plasma antithrombin activity: low antithrombin levels are associated with thromboembolic complications. J Trauma 41:396, 1996

123. Gladson CL, Scharrer I, Hach V, et al: The frequency of type I heterozygous protein-S and protein-C deficiency in 141 unrelated young patients with venous thrombosis. Thromb Haemost 59:18, 1988

124. den Heijer M, Koster T, Blom HJ, et al: Hyperhomocysteinemia as a risk factor for deep-vein thrombosis. N Engl J Med 334:759, 1996

125. Rocha E, Paramo JA, Aranda A, et al: Congenital dysfibrinogenemias: a review. Ric Clin Lab 15:205, 1985

126. Liu Y, Lyons RM, McDonagh J: Plasminogen San Antonio: an abnormal plasminogen with a more cathodic migration, decreased activation and associated thrombosis. Thromb Haemost 59:49, 1988

127. Nilsson IM, Ljungner H, Tengborn L: Two different mechanisms in patients with venous thrombosis and defective fibrinolysis: low concentration of plasminogen activator or increased concentration of plasminogen activator inhibitor. Br Med J 290:1453, 1985

128. Kruithof EK, Gudinchet A, Bachmann F: Plasminogen activator inhibitor 1 and plasminogen activator inhibitor 2 in various disease states. Thromb Haemost 59:7, 1988

129. Juhan-Vague I, Roul C, Alessi MC, et al: Increased plasminogen activator inhibitor activity in non insulin dependent diabetic patients—relationship with plasma insulin. Thromb Haemost 61:370, 1989

130. Rodgers GM, Shuman MA: Congenital thrombotic disorders. Am J Hematol 21:419, 1986

131. Blaisdell FW: What's new in clotting and anticoagulation. Progress in Vascular Surgery. Najarian JS, Delaney JP, Eds. Year Book Medical Publishers, Chicago, 1988, p 75

86 DIABETIC FOOT

Cameron M. Akbari, M.D., F.A.C.S., and Frank W. LoGerfo, M.D., F.A.C.S.

Evaluation and Management of the Diabetic Foot

Surgeons caring for diabetic patients are faced with a diverse spectrum of foot disease.[1,2] The clinical presentation may range from the asymptomatic patient who requires nothing more than preventive foot care to the unstable and critically ill patient in whom both loss of limb and death are imminent threats. This wide range of disease severity, coupled with inappropriate and untimely use of diagnostic testing, contributes to the clinical confusion that often leads to delays in diagnosis and treatment and, ultimately, to limb loss. It is important, therefore, that surgeons caring for diabetic patients develop a simple but comprehensive and orderly approach to diabetic foot problems that (1) can be implemented for any such problem, (2) recognizes the pathogenic roles of neuropathy, ischemia, and infection, and (3) emphasizes the initial clinical assessment at the bedside.[3]

Clinical Evaluation

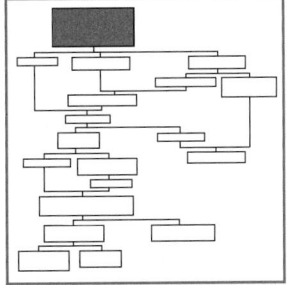

Evaluation of any diabetic foot problem begins with a complete history and a careful physical examination. Broadly speaking, such evaluation should address the healing potential of the foot, the details of the foot problem (e.g., ulcer, gangrene, infection, or osteomyelitis), the systemic consequences of diabetes, and any immediate threats to life or limb. With this information in hand, the surgeon can usually make an accurate diagnosis and start a comprehensive treatment plan without having to order further diagnostic tests, which are liable to be both costly and time-consuming.

HISTORY

The history of the foot problem can yield valuable insights into the potential for healing, the presence of coexisting infection or arterial occlusive disease, and the need for further treatment. Whenever a patient presents with a foot ulceration or gangrene, possible underlying arterial insufficiency should immediately be suspected, even if neuropathy or infection is present. It is helpful to be aware of the event that incited the foot problem. In a patient with diabetes and arterial insufficiency, the inciting event for a foot ulcer may be a seemingly benign action, such as cutting a toenail, soaking the foot in a warm bath, or applying a heating pad. Unfortunately, because of the broad microneurovascular and macrovascular abnormalities associated with diabetes, these relatively innocuous actions can progress to a nonhealing ulcer and gangrene. Similarly, failure to heal after any podiatric procedure is strongly suggestive of underlying unrecognized arterial insufficiency.

The duration of the ulcer also provides important clues, in that a long-standing, nonhealing ulcer is strongly suggestive of ischemia. Certainly, an ulcer or gangrenous area that has been present for several months is unlikely to heal without some further treatment, whether it be offloading of weight-bearing areas, treat-

ment of infection, or, most commonly, correction of arterial insufficiency. In some cases, the present ulcer has already healed at least once, and the current episode represents a relapse. A history of intermittent healing followed by relapse raises the possibility of underlying untreated infection (e.g., recurrent osteomyelitis) or an uncorrected architectural abnormality (e.g., a bony pressure point or a varus deformity).

In view of the many vague and unsupported therapies advocated for the diabetic foot, it is helpful to know the type and duration of any treatments the patient has already undergone for the current problem. For example, a patient with an ischemic ulceration may have completed several different courses of antibiotics without success. Thus, if antibiotic therapy is contemplated for a current infection, possible antibiotic resistance must be taken into account in choosing the appropriate agent. It is also helpful to know which treatments were not previously offered to the patient and to look critically at why they were not offered. For example, many diabetic patients with correctable foot ulceration and limb ischemia are told that their only option is limb amputation, usually because of the physician's inherited pessimism or his or her inadequate knowledge of the advances made in limb and foot salvage. No patient should be denied an opportunity for limb salvage on the basis of a previous medical or surgical opinion without a new comprehensive evaluation being performed.

Inquiries should be made about any previous foot and limb problems—for instance, whether the patient had other ulcers on the same foot that healed spontaneously, how long such healing took, and whether foot surgery was ever performed on that side. A history of recent ipsilateral ulceration or foot surgery that healed in a timely and uncomplicated manner suggests, but does not prove, that the arterial supply is adequate. Problems and procedures more remote in time, however, are less useful indicators. A history of previous leg revascularization (including percutaneous therapies) is also an important clue to possible underlying arterial insufficiency. Because of the predilection for mirror image–type atherosclerotic occlusive disease, the contralateral leg must be considered as well: previous revascularization in the opposite leg is often associated with arterial insufficiency on the affected side. Other cardiovascular risk factors, such as cigarette smoking and hyperlipidemia, must also be taken into account: their presence increases the likelihood that ischemia is contributing to the current foot problem.

Although claudication and rest pain have traditionally been associated with vascular disease, they may be obscured by diabetic neuropathy; hence, their absence in the diabetic patient certainly does not rule out ischemia. Because even moderate ischemia precludes healing in the diabetic foot, the absence of rest pain is not a reliable indicator of an adequate arterial blood supply; moreover, many patients may not be walking long enough distances for vasculogenic claudication to develop. Conversely, some patients with true ischemic rest pain are dismissed for years as having "painful neuropathy."

Evaluation and Management of the Diabetic Foot

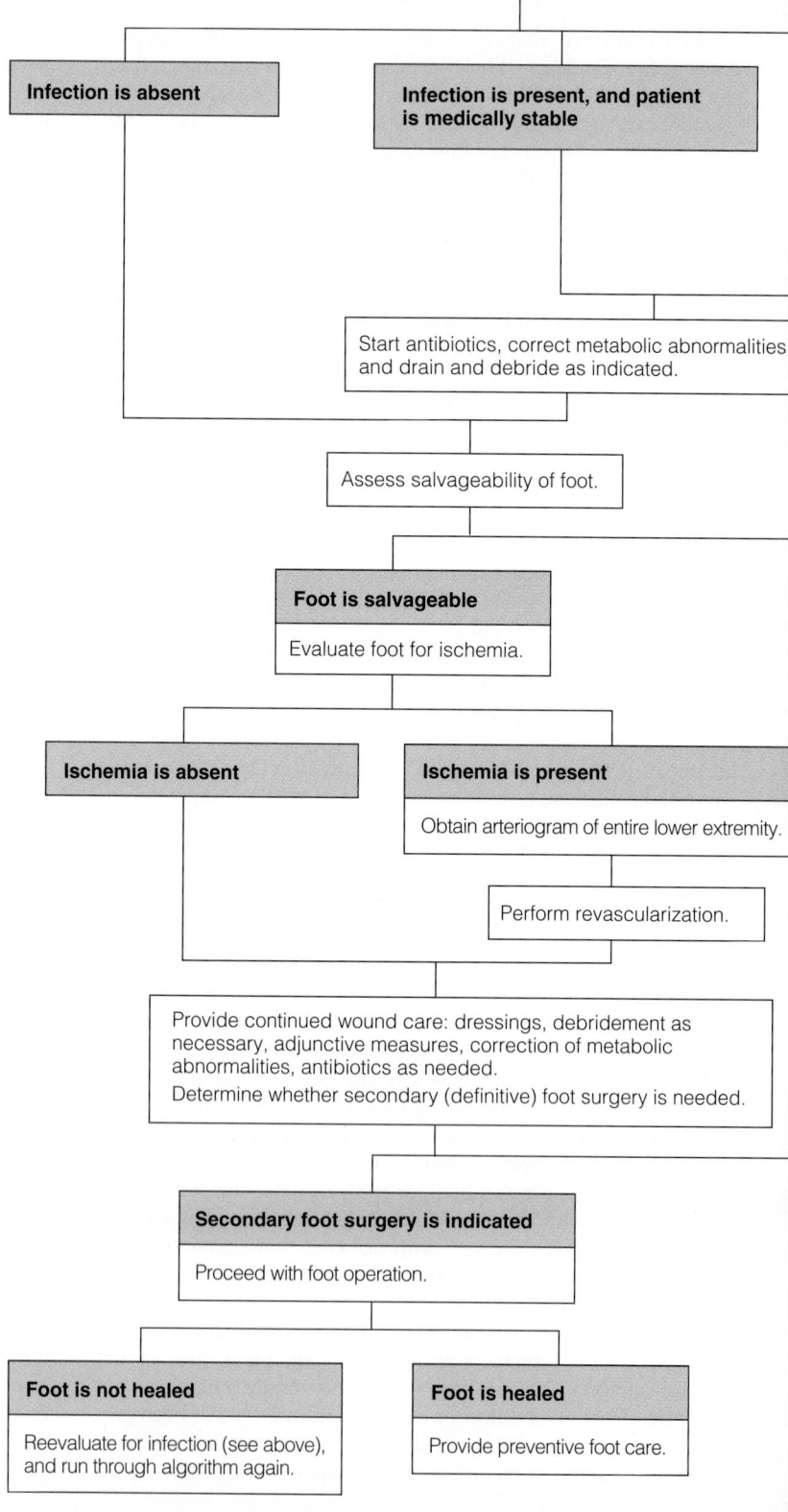

Diabetic patient has foot problem

Obtain history: inciting event, duration, healing, previous treatment (including surgery), vascular disease and risk factors, overall health, functional status.

Perform physical examination: signs of infection, diabetic neuropathy, pulses, arterial perfusion.

Assess clinical findings to determine direction of subsequent workup and treatment.

Infection is absent

Infection is present, and patient is medically stable

Start antibiotics, correct metabolic abnormalities, and drain and debride as indicated.

Assess salvageability of foot.

Foot is salvageable

Evaluate foot for ischemia.

Ischemia is absent

Ischemia is present

Obtain arteriogram of entire lower extremity.

Perform revascularization.

Provide continued wound care: dressings, debridement as necessary, adjunctive measures, correction of metabolic abnormalities, antibiotics as needed.

Determine whether secondary (definitive) foot surgery is needed.

Secondary foot surgery is indicated

Proceed with foot operation.

Foot is not healed

Reevaluate for infection (see above), and run through algorithm again.

Foot is healed

Provide preventive foot care.

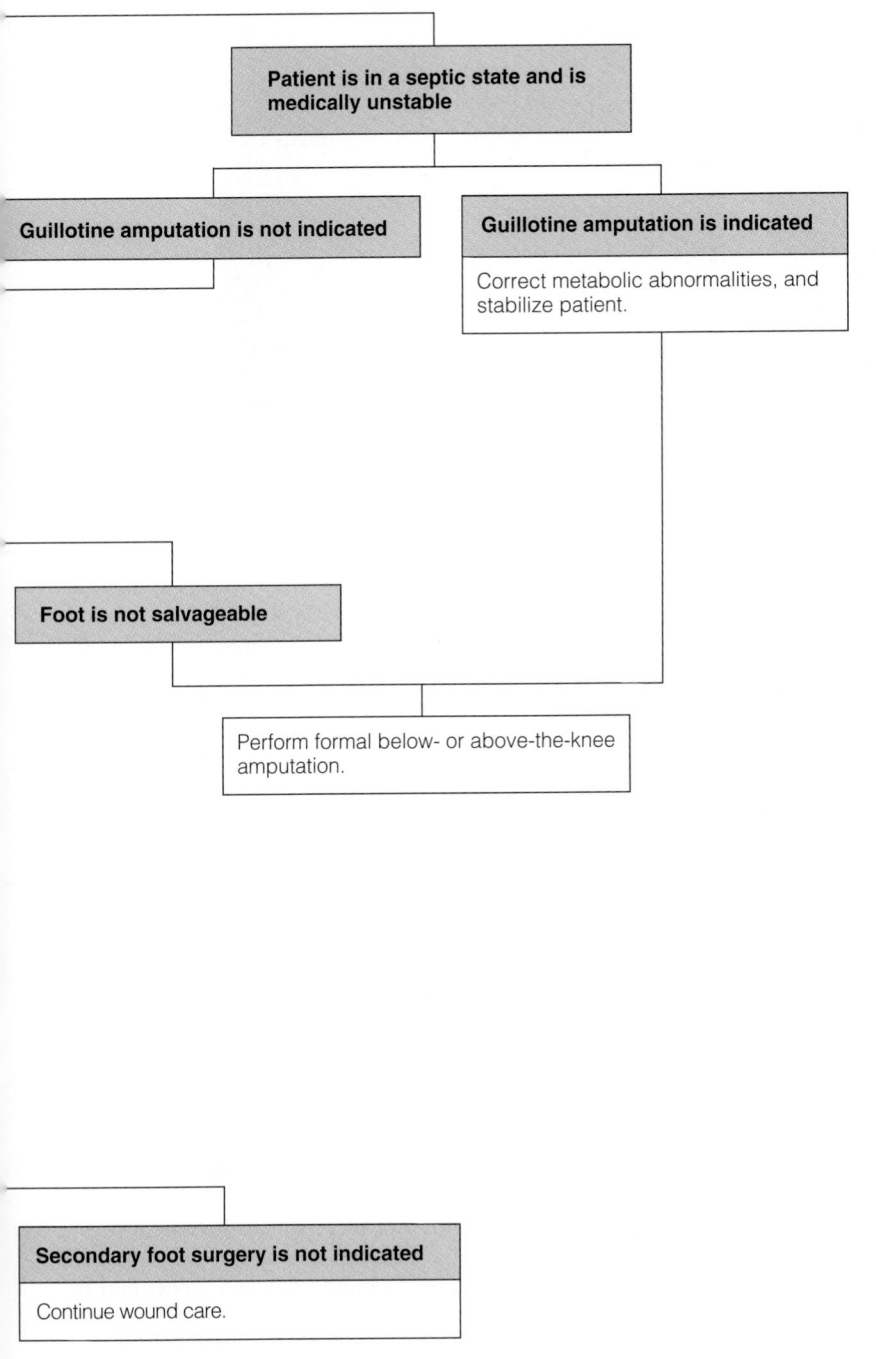

Patient is in a septic state and is medically unstable

Guillotine amputation is not indicated

Guillotine amputation is indicated

Correct metabolic abnormalities, and stabilize patient.

Foot is not salvageable

Perform formal below- or above-the-knee amputation.

Secondary foot surgery is not indicated

Continue wound care.

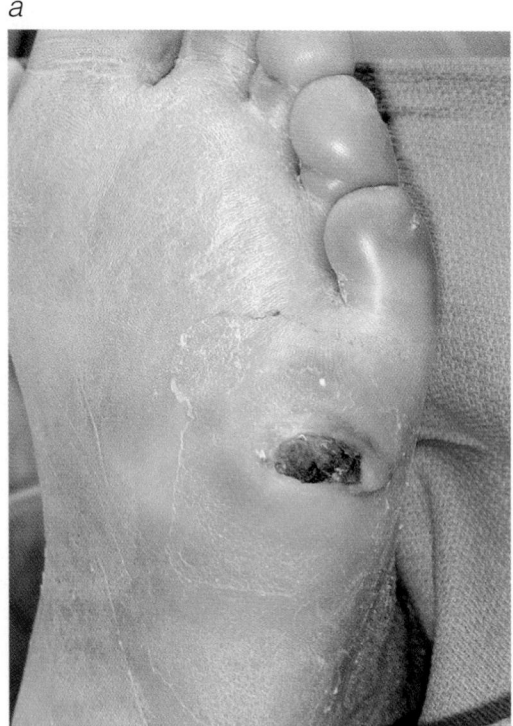
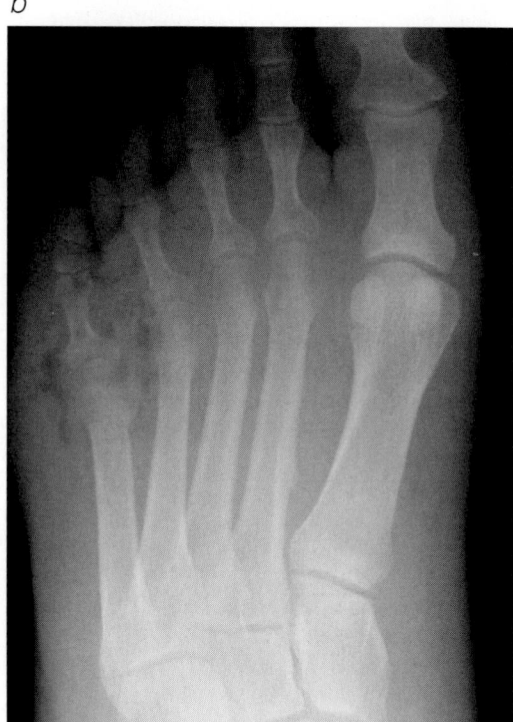

a

b

Figure 1 Shown is a benign-appearing gangrenous eschar (*a*) on the foot of a diabetic patient. Plain x-ray (*b*) reveals extensive subcutaneous air in soft tissue, consistent with severe necrotizing fasciitis.

Both the systemic effects of the foot problem and the systemic consequences of diabetes itself should be assessed. Because unrecognized infection in the diabetic patient may rapidly progress to a life-threatening condition, attention should be directed toward detecting the subtle manifestations of an infected foot ulcer. The patient should be asked about worsening hyperglycemia, recent erratic blood glucose control, and higher insulin requirements. As a consequence of the microvascular and neuropathic abnormalities in the diabetic foot, classic symptoms of infection (e.g., chills and pain) are often absent, and hyperglycemia is often the sole presenting symptom of undrained infection. Faced with ongoing infection and hyperglycemia, the surgeon should strongly suspect impending ketoacidosis or nonketotic hyperglycemic hyperosmolar coma, with the attendant symptoms of weakness, confusion, and altered mental status.

Because a patient with a diabetic foot problem often needs some type of operative intervention, the history should also include a comprehensive assessment of overall health status to help stratify perioperative risk. For example, knowledge of previous cardiac events (e.g., myocardial infarction or revascularization) and current cardiac status (e.g., New York Heart Association [NYHA] class or anginal severity) can help determine whether perioperative cardiac monitoring or preoperative cardiac testing is indicated and what form such monitoring or testing should take. Similarly, in a patient with suspected infection and ischemia, a history of worsening renal function or impending need for hemodialysis can help determine the choice and dosage of antibiotics and may alter plans for standard contrast arteriography. The essential point to be understood regarding patient evaluation in this setting is that diabetes may affect virtually every organ system, often in an indolent pattern; thus, in the evaluation of any diabetic patient with foot disease, attention must be paid to all of these systems.

Functional status also becomes an important consideration at this point, and the history should carefully determine the patient's ambulatory and rehabilitative potential. Many different methods of quantifying functional status have been suggested. One simple approach is to classify functional status as a point on a continuum. One end of the continuum might be a fully ambulatory patient; almost all surgeons would recognize that such a patient should be offered every attempt at limb salvage. The other end might be a completely bedridden patient with multiple comorbid conditions; most surgeons would adopt a far less aggressive approach to such a patient. In practice, many patients fall somewhere between these two extremes, in which case a more thorough evaluation of functional and social status becomes imperative before any firm decisions can be made regarding limb salvage.

PHYSICAL EXAMINATION

Fever and tachycardia are strongly suggestive of deep or undrained infection, with hypotension being a late manifestation of ongoing sepsis. It is important to remember, however, that these signs may be absent in diabetic patients with impending or progressive infection. A focused cardiopulmonary examination helps confirm the presence or absence of congestive heart failure, valvular abnormalities, or rhythm disturbances, which must be recognized in diabetic patients with poor underlying medical reserve.

Evaluation of the diabetic foot ulcer should include a strong suspicion of infection and a thorough search for it. In a patient with cellulitis, the entire foot, including the web spaces and the nail beds, should be examined for any potential portals of entry, such as a puncture wound or an interdigital ("kissing") ulcer. Encrusted and heavily calloused areas over the ulceration should be unroofed and the wound thoroughly inspected to determine the extent of involvement. A benign-appearing dry gangrenous eschar often hides an undrained infectious collection [*see Figure 1*]. Cultures should be taken from the base of the ulcer; superficial swabs may yield only colonizing organisms.

Findings consistent with infection include purulent drainage, crepitus, tenderness, mild erythema, and sinus formation [*see Figure 2*], though these findings may be entirely absent in the neuropathic foot. With more advanced and deep infection, edema may be present as a result of elevated pressures within one or more of the plantar compartments [*see Figure 3*]. If left untreated, this process may spread proximally along tendon sheaths to involve the ankle or even the calf. Close inspection of the ulcer and the use of a sterile probe may also confirm the presence of osteomyelitis, which occurs commonly even in conjunction with benign-appearing ulcers. If bone is detected with gentle probing, osteomyelitis is presumed present.

Because of its prevalence and its causative role in diabetic foot ulceration and limb loss, neuropathy should be assessed in every diabetic patient, and appropriate preventive measures should be taken to guard against foot ulceration in the high-risk neuropathic foot. Protective sensation may be evaluated by pressing a Semmes-Weinstein 5.07 monofilament against the skin; inability to feel the monofilament correlates well with an increased risk of foot ulceration. Advanced sensorimotor neuropathy will lead to the presence of a so-called claw foot (from gradual atrophy of the intrinsic muscles) or to Charcot degeneration with bone and joint destruction at the midfoot. Both of these conditions give rise to abnormal pressure points on the plantar prominences and the potential for foot ulceration.

Assessment of the arterial perfusion in the diabetic foot is a fundamental consideration, in that the diabetic foot needs maximal perfusion to heal. In the presence of ischemia, all efforts at limb salvage will fail. Therefore, the physical examination must include a systematic approach to the assessment of arterial insufficiency. Simple inspection of the leg and foot, including the ulcer, often provides suggestive clues. For example, distal ulceration (on the

tip of a digit), ulceration unassociated with an exostosis or a weight-bearing area, and gangrene are all strongly consistent with underlying ischemia [*see Figure 4*]. The presence of multiple ulcerations or gangrenous areas on the foot, the absence of granulation tissue, and the lack of bleeding with debridement of the ulcer should immediately be taken as signals of possible underlying arterial insufficiency. Other signs suggestive of ischemia are pallor with elevation, fissures (particularly at the heel), and the absence of hair growth. Poor skin condition and hyperkeratosis, though not always good indicators of arterial disease, should be noted because they may help confirm initial clinical impressions.

The pulse examination, including the status of the foot pulses, is the single most important component of the physical examination. In the absence of a palpable pulse, ischemia is always presumed to be present. Although an accurate pulse examination of the lower extremities is not difficult, it is an acquired skill, and time should be devoted to practicing and perfecting the technique.

The femoral pulse is palpated midway between the superior iliac spine and the pubic tubercle, just below the inguinal ligament. The popliteal pulse is palpated with both hands and with the knee flexed no more than 15°. Palpation of the foot pulses is somewhat more demanding, requiring close attention and a good knowledge of the usual locations of the native arteries. The dorsalis pedis is located between the first and second metatarsal bones, just lateral to the extensor hallucis longus tendon, and its pulse is palpated with the pads of the fingers as the hand is partially wrapped around the foot [*see Figure 5*]. If the pulse cannot be palpated, the fingers may be moved a few millimeters in each direction; the dorsalis pedis occasionally follows a slightly aberrant course. A common mistake is to place a single finger at one location on the dorsum of the foot. The posterior tibial artery is typically located in the hollow curve just behind the medial malleolus,

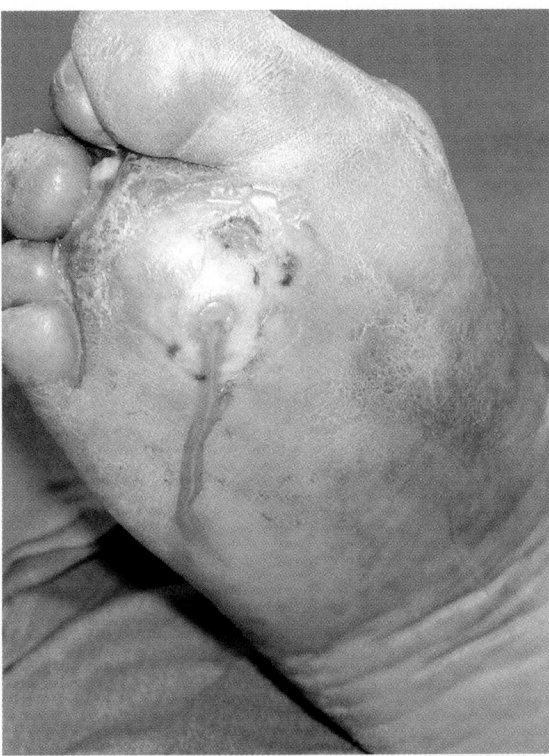

Figure 2 Purulent drainage is seen from a submetatarsal ulcer on the plantar surface of the foot of a diabetic patient.

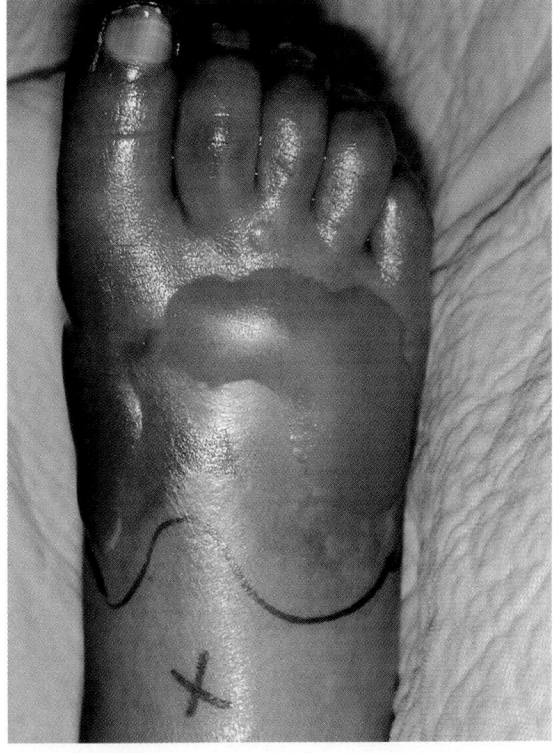

Figure 3 Shown is wet gangrene with edema and undrained severe infection in the foot of a diabetic patient presenting with hyperglycemia and ketoacidosis.

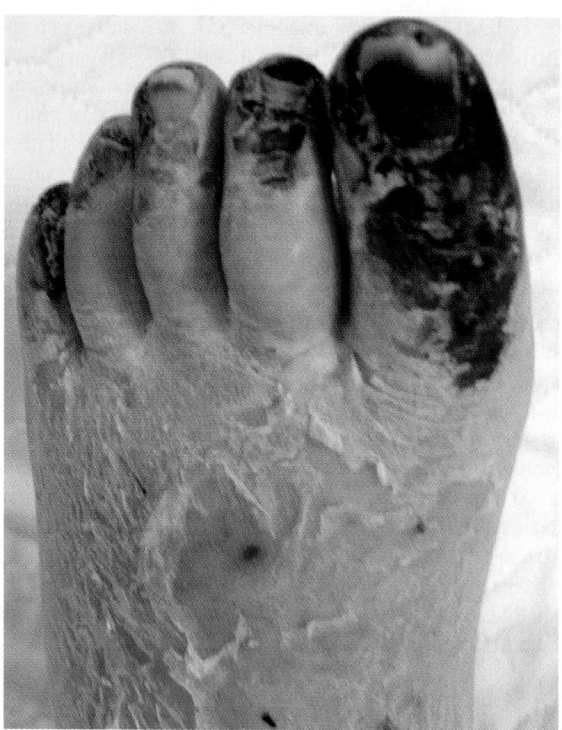

Figure 4 Shown is dry gangrene of several toes in a diabetic patient with femoropopliteal and tibial arterial occlusive disease.

approximately halfway between the malleolus and the Achilles tendon. The examiner's hand should be contralateral to the examined foot (i.e., the right hand should be used to palpate the left foot, and vice versa), so that the curvature of the hand naturally follows the contours of the ankle [*see Figure 6*].

Assessment of Clinical Findings

Once the clinical evaluation is complete, the next step is to assess the findings from the history and the physical examination so as to determine the course and urgency of the subsequent workup and treatment. This assessment is made at the bedside, focusing on three main concerns: (1) the presence and severity of infection, (2) the salvageability of the limb, and (3) the presence of ischemia.

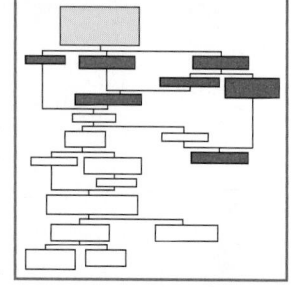

PRESENCE OF INFECTION

Evaluation for and treatment of infection is the first priority in the management of any diabetic foot problem.[4,5] Although radiographic tests may confirm initial clinical suspicions, the determination of the severity of infection is almost always made on the basis of clinical findings. Infection in the diabetic foot may range from a minimal superficial infection to fulminant sepsis with extensive necrosis and destruction of foot tissue. Accordingly, the treatment plan should address the choice of antibiotic (which requires knowledge of the microbiology), the need for drainage, the option of local or even guillotine amputation, and the patient's overall medical condition.

The microbiology of the diabetic foot varies according to the depth and severity of the infection and the nature of the patient's

environment (e.g., hospitalized or outpatient). Certain general assumptions can be made about likely causative organisms. Mild localized and superficial ulcerations, particularly in outpatients, are usually caused by aerobic gram-positive cocci (e.g., *Staphylococcus aureus* and streptococci). In contrast, deeper ulcers and generalized limb-threatening infections are usually polymicrobial. In addition to gram-positive cocci, potential causative organisms include gram-negative bacilli (e.g., *Escherichia coli, Klebsiella, Enterobacter aerogenes, Proteus mirabilis,* and *Pseudomonas aeruginosa*) and anaerobes (e.g., *Bacteroides fragilis* and peptostreptococci). Enterococci may also be isolated from the wound, notably in hospitalized patients; in the absence of other cultured virulent organisms, they should probably be considered pathogenic.

Currently, it is clear that resistant organisms, particularly methicillin-resistant *S. aureus* (MRSA), are playing a growing role in the development of skin and soft tissue infections. Traditionally arising in patients who had previously been hospitalized and those who had previously received antibiotic therapy, MRSA-associated infections are now frequently encountered in outpatient settings. Indeed, in many U.S. cities, these so-called community-acquired MRSA infections are the most common skin and soft tissue infections seen in patients presenting to the emergency department.[6] Accordingly, in both outpatient and inpatient settings, it is advisable to assume that MRSA is present in a patient with a diabetic foot infection until the culture data suggest otherwise. Awareness of the increasing prevalence of resistant organisms is critical for current management of diabetic foot infections, especially with respect to the initiation of antibiotic coverage.

Initially, the choice of antibiotics is made empirically on basis of these general assumptions. When the results of the initial cultures become available, antibiotic coverage may be broadened or narrowed as appropriate. In a compliant patient with a small ulcer and no evidence of deep space involvement or systemic infection, treatment may be delivered on an outpatient basis. A dual-antibiotic regimen (pending culture results) is instituted, typically consisting of a cephalosporin or a β-lactam antibiotic (for activity against staphylococci and streptococci) and trimethoprim-sulfamethoxazole or a tetracycline (for activity against MRSA). A dual regimen consisting of fluoroquinolone and linezolid is an acceptable alternative that also provides adequate coverage. In addition, the patient is instructed to offload weight from the

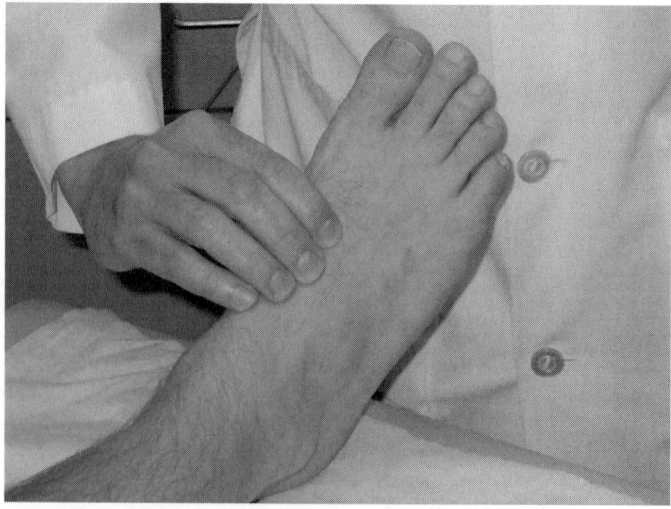

Figure 5 Illustrated is the correct technique for palpation of the dorsalis pedis pulse.

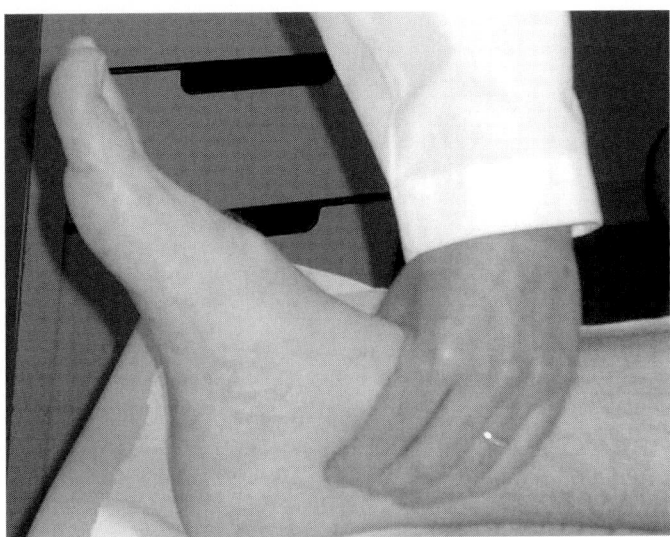

Figure 6 **Illustrated is the correct technique for finding the posterior tibial pulse.**

involved extremity and is taught appropriate methods for changing wound dressings. Frequent follow-up is vital, and guidelines should be imparted by which improvement or worsening of the lesion can be determined.

A more common presentation, unfortunately, is a patient with ulceration or gangrene who has a deep infection affecting tendon or bone and possible systemic involvement. For such patients, immediate hospitalization is indicated, including bed rest with elevation of the infected foot, correction of any systemic abnormalities, and broad-spectrum I.V. antibiotic therapy (which may be focused more tightly once culture results are complete). Because the clinical findings of impending sepsis may be subtle, these patients should undergo a complete laboratory workup aimed at detecting and correcting electrolyte and acid-base imbalances.

The choice of antibiotic agent and the duration of therapy are dependent on the extent of the infection. For patients with deep or chronic recurrent ulcers, which are typically polymicrobial, or

those with limb-threatening or life-threatening infections, appropriate empirical antibiotic options include (1) vancomycin plus a β-lactam antibiotic with a β-lactamase inhibitor (e.g., piperacillin-tazobactam) and (2) vancomycin plus metronidazole plus a quinolone (in cases of penicillin allergy). Subsequent culture results then dictate further antibiotic coverage, if any. In the absence of osteomyelitis, antibiotics should be continued until the wound appears clean and all surrounding cellulitis has resolved (typically, 10 to 14 days). If osteomyelitis is present, treatment should include both surgical debridement and a prolonged (4- to 6-week) course of antibiotic therapy (though the course may be abbreviated if the entire infected bone has been removed, as with digital or transmetatarsal amputation). Heel lesions often present with some degree of calcaneal destruction, and determination of osteomyelitis may be made by clinical examination either alone or in conjunction with other radiographic tests (e.g., magnetic resonance imaging) [*see Figure 7*].

In the presence of an abscess or deep space infection, immediate incision and drainage of all infected tissue planes is mandatory. Incisions should be chosen with an eye to the normal anatomy of the foot (including the various compartments) and the need for subsequent secondary (foot salvage) procedures [*see Figure 8*]. Drainage should be complete, with incisions placed to allow for dependent drainage, and all necrotic tissue must be debrided. Repeat cultures (including both aerobes and anaerobes) should be obtained from the deep tissues. Drainage incisions on the dorsum of the foot should be avoided. Abscesses in the medial, central, or lateral compartment should be drained via longitudinal incisions made in the direction of the neurovascular bundle and extending the entire length of the abscess. The medial and central compartments are drained through a medial incision, and the lateral compartment is drained through a lateral incision; both of these incisions are made just above the plantar surface of the forefoot [*see Figure 9*]. Web space infections may be drained similarly through the plantar aspect of the foot. In some instances, open amputation of the foot (e.g., an open toe or transmetatarsal amputation) may be necessary to allow complete drainage and resection of necrotic tissue. Strict adherence to textbook amputations may lead to unnecessary soft tissue removal and possibly to a higher amputa-

a

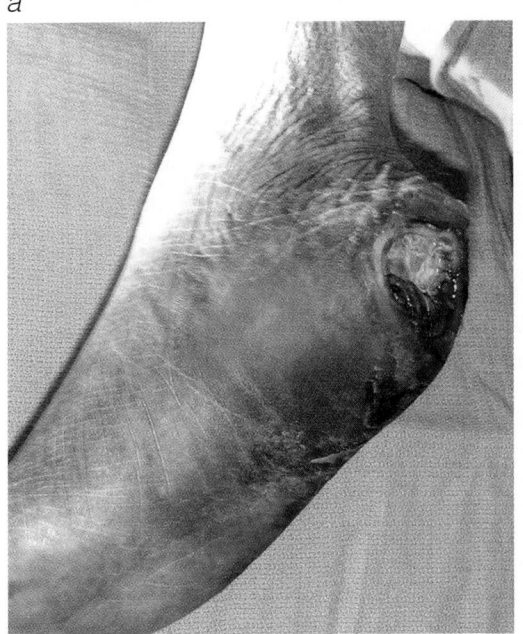

b

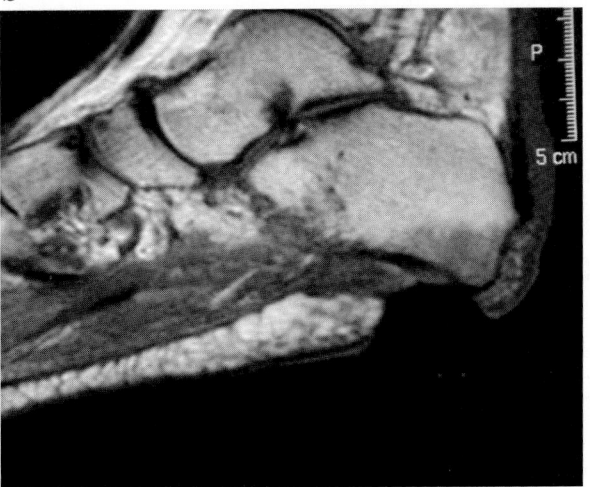

Figure 7 **Shown is heel ulceration with eschar (*a*) in a diabetic patient. MRI findings (*b*) are consistent with calcaneal osteomyelitis.**

tion during future closure; therefore, all viable tissue should be conserved.

A patient with an ongoing undrained infection may present with an unsalvageable foot and fulminant sepsis, manifested by hemodynamic instability, bacteremia, and severe acid-base and electrolyte abnormalities. Such patients should undergo prompt open (guillotine) below-the-knee amputation [*see 99 Lower-Extremity Amputation for Ischemia*]. This type of amputation is usually performed at the ankle level, with the aim of removing the septic source while allowing for revision and closure at a later date. Administration of I.V. antibiotics, correction of dehydration and electrolyte abnormalities, and continuous cardiac monitoring are absolutely essential throughout treatment.

Once the infection has been drained and tissues debrided, continued wound inspection and management are essential. Ongoing necrosis should raise the possibility that undrained infection or untreated ischemia is present, in which case further debridement and treatment may be necessary. Avoidance of weight-bearing should be continued. Neither whirlpool therapy nor soaks are beneficial.

Medical Stabilization

Concomitant with the measures outlined above to control infection, medical stabilization of the diabetic patient must be carried out, and the surgeon must be directly involved in this process. Hyperglycemia is almost always seen when infection is present; it should be gradually corrected. More advanced hyperglycemia leads to ketotic or nonketotic hyperosmolar states, which carry a 10% to 25% mortality. Serum concentrations of electrolytes, magnesium, and creatinine should be obtained and osmolality determined at frequent intervals; any abnormalities should be corrected [*see 123 Acid-Base Disorders*]. Dehydration is common in hyperglycemic patients and should be corrected. A urinary catheter is mandatory to help guide the response to fluid therapy; in unstable patients, a central venous pressure catheter or a pulmonary arterial catheter may be needed [*see 119 Cardiovascular Monitoring*]. Continuous cardiac monitoring is essential in patients with the hyperglycemic hyperosmolar syndrome or ketoacidosis.

SALVAGEABILITY OF LIMB

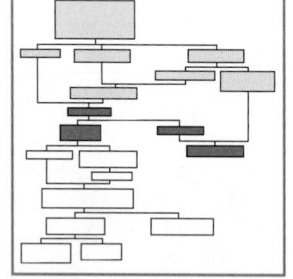

While the infection is being treated and controlled, the surgeon should determine whether limb salvage is feasible. This determination is based largely on the patient's functional status and the degree of foot destruction. For example, primary limb amputation may be considered in a nonambulatory, bedridden patient or in a patient with severe Charcot destruction and degeneration, for whom no further reconstructive foot surgery is possible. Poor medical condition, by itself, is not necessarily an indication for primary limb amputation, given the high perioperative morbidity associated with amputation. Moreover, it is often possible to improve the patient's overall medical status while he or she is being treated for infection and evaluated for ischemia.

Assessment of limb salvageability should be carried out simultaneously with treatment of infection because appropriate drainage and antibiotics can dramatically change the appearance and viability of the foot. If limb salvage is not deemed possible, the patient should undergo formal below-the-knee or above-the-knee amputation [*see 99 Lower-Extremity Amputation for Ischemia*].

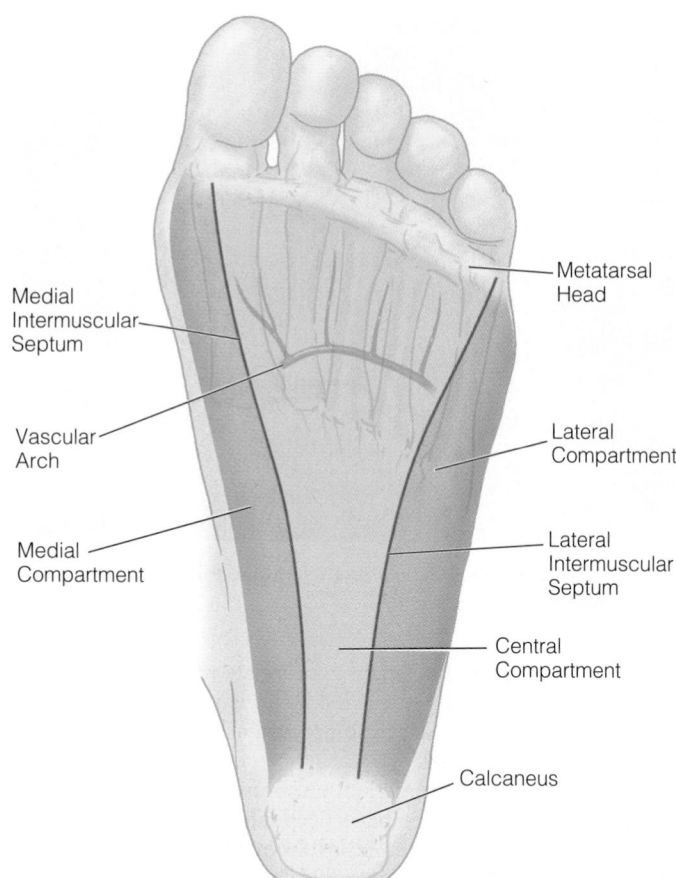

Figure 8 **The foot has three plantar compartments: medial, central, and lateral. The intrinsic muscles of the great toe are in the medial compartment, and those of the fifth toe are in the lateral compartment. The central compartment contains the intrinsic muscles of the second through fourth toes, the extensor flexor tendons of the toes, the plantar nerves, and the plantar vascular structures. The floor of each compartment is the rigid plantar fascia; the roof is composed of the metatarsal bones and interosseous fascia. The medial and central compartments are separated by the medial intermuscular septum, which extends from the medial calcaneal tuberosity to the head of the first metatarsal. The lateral and central compartments are separated by the lateral intermuscular septum, which extends from the calcaneus to the head of the fifth metatarsal.**

PRESENCE OF ISCHEMIA

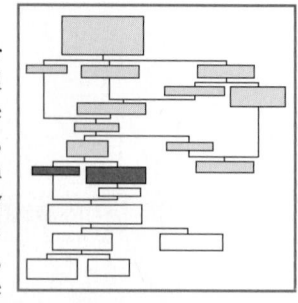

Evaluation of the diabetic foot for ischemia begins with the history and the physical examination. By the conclusion of the clinical evaluation, the surgeon can usually make an accurate assessment of the adequacy of the arterial circulation to the foot. As noted [*see* Clinical Evaluation, Physical Examination, *above*], the absence of a palpable foot pulse strongly suggests ischemia unless proved otherwise.

Noninvasive arterial testing plays only a limited role in the assessment of diabetic patients with foot ulceration and should not be employed in place of the bedside evaluation. Certainly, for patients with poor healing or gangrene and absent foot pulses, noninvasive testing adds little additional useful information to the initial clinical evaluation and typically serves only to further delay vascular reconstruction. For selected patients, however, noninvasive testing, in conjunction with the clinical findings, may be useful. Patients who might benefit from such testing include those with absent foot pulses who have a superficial ulcer with evidence of healing or a previous history of a healed foot ulcer and those without any foot lesions who are scheduled to undergo elective foot surgery.

The presence of diabetes imposes limitations on all of the noninvasive arterial tests currently available. Medial arterial calcinosis occurs frequently and unpredictably in patients with diabetes and can result in noncompressible arteries and artificially elevated segmental systolic pressures and ankle-brachial indices. Because calcification levels tend to be lower in the toe vessels, toe systolic pressures are sometimes obtained, but their value is often limited by the proximity of the foot ulcer to the cuff site. Segmental Doppler waveforms and pulsed volume recordings are unaffected by medial calcification, but evaluation of these waveforms is primarily qualitative rather than quantitative. In addition, the quality of the waveforms is affected by peripheral edema, and cuff placement is commonly affected by the presence of ulceration. Regional transcutaneous oximetry measurements are also unaffected by medial calcinosis, and this modality appears to be reliable for predicting ulcer healing and amputation levels. However, transcutaneous oximetry measurements are actually higher in patients with diabetes and foot ulcers than in nondiabetic patients, possibly because of the effects of arteriovenous shunting. Other limitations, including lack of equipment standardization, user variability, and a large gray area in the interpretation of the measurements, further limit the ability of this test to predict ischemia. Therefore, although these measurements have been used to predict healing in patients without diabetes, high values may not correlate with healing potential in the presence of diabetes.

When a patient presents with absent foot pulses in conjunction with gangrene, nonhealing ulceration, or significant tissue loss, it can be assumed that ischemia is present and must be corrected if the limb is to be salvaged. In such patients, arteriography of the entire lower extremity should be performed. The decision to perform arteriography and vascular reconstruction should be made as soon as infection has started to resolve and signs of systemic toxicity have disappeared; prolonged delays in making this decision may result in further tissue loss and make salvage impossible. For a complete assessment, the arteriogram should include the foot vessels in both lateral and anterior views.

Concern over possible contrast-induced renal failure should not be considered a contraindication to high-quality angiography of the entire lower extremity. The incidence of contrast nephropathy is not higher in diabetic patients without preexisting renal disease, even when ionic contrast agents are employed. Selective use of magnetic resonance angiography (MRA), carbon dioxide angiography, and duplex scanning may help minimize the contrast dye load.

In patients with preexisting renal disease, use of a nonionic contrast agent, in conjunction with appropriate hydration and judicious administration of kidney-protecting agents, should minimize the risk of contrast-induced nephrotoxicity. *N*-acetylcysteine, 600 mg twice daily, should be started on the day before the arteriogram and continued for 48 hours, and 0.45 N saline should be given I.V. at a rate of 1 mg/kg/hr, beginning 12 hours before the scheduled arteriogram.[7]

Management

REVASCULARIZATION

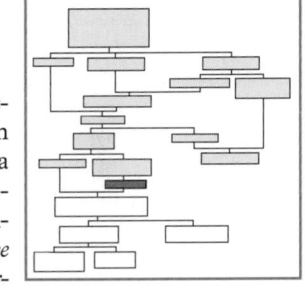

The goals of arterial reconstruction are to restore maximal perfusion to the foot and, ideally, to restore a palpable foot pulse. Possible approaches include endovascular techniques (angioplasty and stenting) [*see 98 Endovascular Procedures for Lower-Extremity Disease*], bypass grafting (with autogenous or prosthetic grafts), and some combination of the two. Ultimately, the choice of procedure in any given case is based on the individual patient's anatomy, the comorbid conditions present, and the results of the preoperative assessment, with the aim being to provide the most

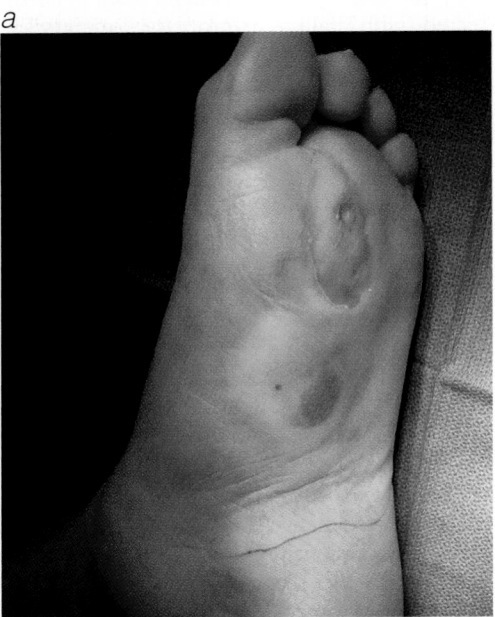

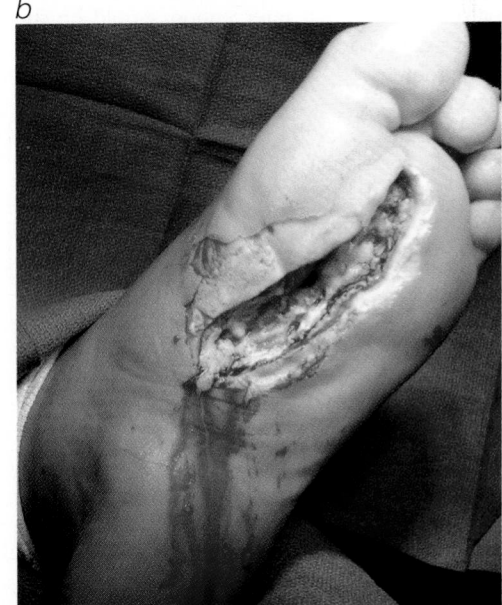

Figure 9 Shown is an infection in the central compartment of the foot from a submetatarsal ulcer that has extended proximally to include the medial compartment (*a*). A plantar incision through the ulcer and both compartments (including the septum) allows complete dependent drainage (*b*).

durable procedure with the least risk. For example, in rare patients with isolated iliac artery stenoses, angioplasty may be effective by itself, but in patients with multilevel disease, it may have to be combined with an infrainguinal bypass [*see 96 Infrainguinal Arterial Procedures*]. In patients who have previously undergone surgical revascularization, careful consideration should be given to the availability of an autogenous conduit (e.g., an arm vein or the lesser saphenous vein), given the superiority of autogenous vein over prosthetic grafts.

As a rule, arterial bypass grafting is required for restoration of the foot pulse.[8] Proximal bypass to either the popliteal artery or the tibial and peroneal arteries may restore foot pulses, and preference should be given to these vessels if they are in continuity with the foot. Often, however, because of the presence of more distal obstructive disease, bypass grafting to the popliteal or even the tibial artery will not restore the foot pulse. In such cases, restoration of pulsatile flow to the foot may be accomplished with autogenous vein bypass grafts to the paramalleolar or inframalleolar arteries (e.g., the dorsalis pedis). The vein graft can be prepared as an in situ graft, a reversed graft, or a nonreversed graft, without any significant difference in outcome; the choice of approach should be based on the patient's particular vascular anatomy.

As noted (see above), the absence of an ipsilateral greater saphenous vein is not a contraindication to pedal bypass: comparable results may be obtained by using arm vein or lesser saphenous vein grafts. Prosthetic material should seldom, if ever, be used for dorsalis pedis or other extreme distal (inframalleolar) bypass grafts. Active infection in the foot is not a contraindication to pedal bypass, provided that the proximal dorsum of the foot is free of infection and that incisions can be placed in clean tissue planes. The foot should be free of cellulitis, lymphangiitis, and edema before any inframalleolar bypass.

Current advances in endovascular therapy are allowing this approach to be used more frequently and successfully in the peripheral vasculature. Lesions determined to be favorable on the basis of arteriography (e.g., short-segment stenoses) may be treated with angioplasty and, possibly, stenting. Similarly, endovascular therapy may be preferred to surgical bypass grafting in high-risk patients and patients who have no suitable autogenous conduit. Ultimately, the goal of endovascular intervention should be the same as that of bypass grafting: to restore the foot pulse and maximal blood flow to the foot.

CONTINUED WOUND CARE

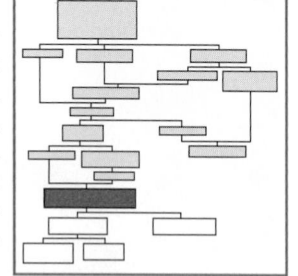

Once the foot is fully revascularized—or once it is clear that the foot was adequately perfused to begin with—care of the foot wound should be continued. Revascularization of a severely ischemic foot ulcer may result in an immediate paradoxical worsening of the infection, and frequent inspection is mandatory postoperatively. New-onset cellulitis, hyperglycemia, or fever should prompt concern regarding potential worsening of the foot infection. Frequent debridement to healthy, bleeding tissue is required more often than not.

Wounds should be kept moist, with wet-to-dry dressings avoided in favor of normal saline wet-to-wet dressings. Various adjunctive wound treatments are available, including chemical enzymatic debriding agents, growth factors, and hyperbaric oxygen therapy. Some of these may offer a slight additional benefit in terms of improved healing, but they are expensive; blanket use of these costly modalities is therefore discouraged. Failure of wound healing in the diabetic foot is usually attributable to unrecognized ischemia, ongoing infection, or poor conventional wound care—not, as a rule, to the absence of more sophisticated wound therapy.

Hyperglycemia and malnutrition are common in hospitalized diabetic patients with foot ulceration, and both adversely affect wound healing. Correction of these abnormalities should begin early and continue throughout the wound-healing period. Attention should also be directed toward preventing new foot lesions (e.g., decubitus ulcers on the heel from prolonged bed rest). Heel splints, air mattresses, and leg pillows are all valuable in this regard.

SECONDARY FOOT PROCEDURES

After successful revascularization, secondary procedures on the foot may be performed for maximal foot salvage, with the aim of addressing both the acute problem and the underlying cause. The basic goals of such procedures are (1) to remove infected bone (if present), (2) to restore functional stability, and (3) to reduce the risk of subsequent ulceration.

In the forefoot, digital, single metatarsal (ray), or transmetatarsal amputation [*see 99 Lower-Extremity Amputation for Ischemia*] may be performed, depending on the location of the ulcer. Tissue should be handled gently, forceps should not be used, and incisions should be carefully placed. Care must be taken to prevent dead spaces along tendon sheaths, bone splintering, and areas of residual necrosis, all of which can lead to failure of the procedure. If there is persistent infection or an abscess, the wound should be left open. Every effort, however, should be made to perform a closed amputation so as to avoid the time and cost associated with open wound care. This is a particularly important consideration in the occasional diabetic patient with unreconstructible foot ischemia, because open amputations rarely heal in the presence of ischemia.

Underlying bony structural abnormalities in the diabetic foot are often the cause of ulceration. Such abnormalities may be corrected with hallux arthroplasty, metatarsal head resection, metatarsal osteotomy, or sesamoidectomy; if ulceration is present, these procedures may be combined with ulcer excision. Similarly, ulceration on a previous transmetatarsal amputation may be the result of an equinovarus deformity (from disrupted tendons and a decrease in calcaneal inclination). This problem should be treated with revision of the transmetatarsal amputation (perhaps in conjunction with ulcer excision) and biomechanical correction (e.g., Achilles tendon lengthening or, in more severe cases, posterior tibial tendon release).

Heel lesions are particularly formidable, and there is considerable confusion regarding how best to manage them. Generally, dry eschars with no evidence of deep infection or abscess may be treated with offloading alone so as to allow healing beneath the eschar in the fully revascularized foot. In patients with chronic ulceration or osteomyelitis, partial calcanectomy may be considered. The presence of calcaneal osteomyelitis may be determined by means of probing or adjunctive studies such as MRI [*see Figure 7*]. Primary closure is occasionally possible, but given the relatively fixed nature of the heel, either secondary healing or some type of flap coverage is usually indicated. Both local and free flaps may be used in the fully revascularized foot.

After any type of surgery of the diabetic foot, frequent postoperative observation of the wound is mandatory. Delays in healing or wound breakdown should immediately raise the possibility of infection or unrecognized ischemia and should trigger the appropriate workup.

PREVENTIVE FOOT CARE

Once the foot has healed, preventive measures should be initiated to prevent future ulceration. Foremost among these measures is patient education, focusing on general hygiene (e.g., daily washing and moisturizer use) and daily inspection of the feet. Walking barefoot, employing heat pads, wearing thong

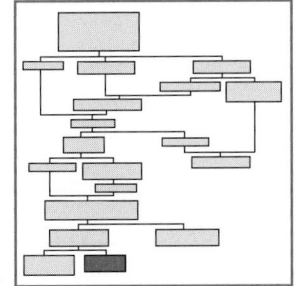

sandals, and using caustic over-the-counter foot medications should all be strongly discouraged.

Neuropathy continues to be the most common cause of diabetic foot ulceration, and its presence is a strong predictor of the likelihood of future ulceration. As noted (see above), inability to feel a Semmes-Weinstein 5.07 monofilament when it is pressed to the skin correlates well with an increased risk of foot ulceration. In addition, abnormal pressure points (secondary to mechanical deformity of the foot and motor neuropathy) can be identified by means of pedobarography, a procedure in which plantar pressure is measured on specialized contour plots as the patient walks on a pressure-sensitive platform. Identification of any high-pressure areas can facilitate the construction of specific, custom-molded orthotics and insoles to help in offloading.

References

1. LoGerfo FW, Coffman JD: Vascular and microvascular disease of the foot in diabetes. N Engl J Med 311:1615, 1984
2. Akbari CM, LoGerfo FW: Diabetes and peripheral vascular disease. J Vasc Surg 30:373, 1999
3. Caputo GM, Cavanagh PR, Ulbrecht JS, et al: Assessment and management of foot disease in patients with diabetes. N Engl J Med 331:854, 1994
4. Fox HR, Karchmer AW: Management of diabetic foot infections, including the use of home intravenous antibiotic therapy. Clin Podiatr Med Surg 13:671, 1996
5. Joshi N, Caputo GM, Weitekamp MR, et al: Infections in patients with diabetes mellitus. N Engl J Med 341:1906, 1999
6. Moran GJ, Krishnadasan A, Gorwitz RJ, et al: Methicillin-resistant *S. aureus* infections among patients in the emergency department. N Engl J Med 355:666, 2006
7. Tepel M, van der Giet M, Schwarzfeld C, et al: Prevention of radiographic-contrast-agent-induced reductions in renal function by acetylcysteine. N Engl J Med 343:180, 2000
8. Akbari CM, LoGerfo FW: Distal bypasses in the diabetic patient. Current Techniques in Vascular Surgery. Yao JST, Pearce WH, Eds. McGraw-Hill, New York, 2001, p 285

Acknowledgment

Figure 8   Tom Moore.

87 FUNDAMENTALS OF ENDOVASCULAR SURGERY

Jon Matsumura, M.D., F.A.C.S., and Joseph Vijungco, M.D.

Endovascular techniques are now an important part of vascular surgery. Ongoing technological advances have made it possible to treat the majority of vascular diseases by minimally invasive means. To perform these new therapeutic techniques, it is necessary to possess certain basic endovascular skills. In this chapter, we describe some of the fundamental techniques that a skilled vascular interventionalist must master.

Choice of Vascular Access Site

The initial step in endovascular surgery is selection of the vascular access site. Several choices are available. The ideal access vessel is large, close to the treatment site, free of disease, and only minimally tortuous. Such a vessel is least likely to be associated with complications.[1] For most endovascular interventions, the femoral artery is the preferred choice, though the axillary, brachial, subclavian, common carotid, and iliac arteries may also be used. Occasionally, the aorta is accessed via direct puncture, laparotomy, or thoracotomy.

Before puncture, the vessel undergoes evaluation, including palpation to assess the strength of the pulse in comparison with the opposite side. A weak pulse suggests disease at or proximal to the area, and the vessel should therefore be used with caution. Preoperative assessment may include noninvasive imaging (e.g., duplex ultrasonography, computed tomography, or magnetic resonance angiography) to visualize significant lesions. Finally, with any endovascular procedure, it is helpful to assess and document the peripheral pulses and the ankle-brachial index (ABI) beforehand to provide reference points for possible subsequent complications.

Puncture of Artery

GENERAL TECHNICAL PRINCIPLES

Once the skin site has been prepared and draped, 1% lidocaine is infiltrated into the skin and the perivascular tissue. Besides providing anesthesia to the area, lidocaine helps prevent vasospasm.[2] The pain and discomfort from intradermal injection of lidocaine is caused by the low pH of commercially available preparations and can be reduced by adding sodium bicarbonate (1 ml of a 1 mEq/ml $NaHCO_3$ solution in 10 ml of 1% lidocaine).[3] A small nick should be made in the skin about 1 to 2 cm beyond the intended site of arterial entry, and the subcutaneous tissue should be gently dissected with a clamp; this measure allows smoother entry of the needle, the guide wire, the sheath, and the catheter. Access needles are available in different sizes, of which the two most common are the 18-gauge thin-walled needle, which accepts a 0.035-in. guide wire, and the 21-gauge needle, which accepts an 0.018-in. guide wire. The latter is used for micropuncture techniques and is favored for brachial approaches. Longer needles are used for translumbar puncture.

There are two main methods of cannulating the artery with the needle [see Figure 1]: double-wall entry and single-wall entry.

Certain principles apply to both methods. The needle is advanced at an angle of 45° to 60°. When it is within the subcutaneous tissue, it should proceed in a straight line: the needle tip is sharp, and side-to-side movement may cause inadvertent laceration of a neurovascular structure. When a needle must be repositioned, it should be withdrawn into the subcutaneous tissue superficial to the intended target and redirected along another course. If the needle becomes dulled as a result of contact with bone or other hard surfaces, it should be discarded and a new one used.

The double-wall entry method involves a through-and-through puncture of both the anterior wall and the posterior wall of the vessel. A multipart needle with an inner trochar may be helpful. After the needle is advanced through both walls of the artery, the inner trocar is removed. The needle is then slowly withdrawn until arterial pulsation is noted. The needle is stabilized, and a guide wire is advanced through it into the artery. Once the guide wire is in place, the needle is removed.

In the single-wall entry method, the needle is slowly moved toward the anterior wall of the vessel. The arterial pulsation can be felt through the shaft of the needle. Gentle pressure is applied, and the needle is advanced through the anterior wall only. It may be helpful to think of the arterial pulse wave as pushing the anterior arterial wall onto the needle. The appearance of pulsatile flow confirms entry into the arterial lumen. The needle may be rotated or deflected slightly to optimize pulsatile back-bleeding. A guide wire is then passed into the needle, and the needle is removed.

Pulsations should be transmitted through the needle shaft in an anterior-to-posterior manner. If the needle is either medial or lateral to the artery, the pulsations may deflect the needle from side to side.[2] Once the needle is in the vessel, the flow pattern should be observed. A forceful but irregular spraying flow may indicate arterial stenosis in the vicinity of the needle. A barely pulsatile flow may signal occlusive disease, a subintimal location of the needle, or a venous puncture.[2] If the guide wire cannot be passed with minimal resistance after access is obtained, the needle tip may be against the wall or against plaque, or (if the needle tip has already entered the wall) a dissection may have been started. Often, the situation can be remedied by making a small change in the needle's insertion angle or by withdrawing the needle slightly.

FEMORAL ARTERY PUNCTURE

As noted, the common femoral artery (CFA) is the vessel most commonly used for arterial access. It is generally quite well suited to this purpose, being readily accessible, fairly large, and easily compressible. CFA puncture facilitates study and treatment of a number of key structures, including the lower-extremity arteries, the abdominal aorta and its branches, the thoracic aorta, the brachiocephalic vessels, the coronary arteries, and the left ventricle. In addition, it is associated with a lower complication rate than puncture of other arteries.[1] The CFA should, however, be avoided when the patient is known to have severe iliofemoral occlusive disease, a local infection, a femoral artery aneurysm, or marked tortuosity of the iliac arteries that would preclude catheter placement or manipulation.

The CFA runs lateral to the common femoral vein (CFV) and beneath the inguinal ligament. It may be localized by palpation just proximal to its bifurcation into the superficial femoral artery (SFA) and the profunda femoris (PF). The inguinal ligament, which runs from the anterior superior iliac spine to the pubic tubercle, is a convenient landmark for localization of the CFA, but these bony landmarks provide only a rough approximation of the location of the inguinal ligament. The CFA typically lies about two fingerbreadths lateral to the pubic tubercle along the line of the inguinal ligament. The artery should be punctured over the middle of the medial third of the femoral head in the posterior-anterior projection [see Figure 2]. The window available for safe CFA puncture is small—only 3 to 5 cm.

There are several methods that can be used to localize the CFA in patients with difficult anatomy (e.g., those who have previously undergone groin surgery, those who are obese, and those who have a pulseless artery). The bony landmarks are even less reliable guides to the location of the inguinal ligament in these patients. According to a 1993 anatomic study, in the majority of cases, the position of the inguinal ligament is about 1 to 2 cm below where palpation would suggest it to be, and the average position of the ligament is approximately 1.5 cm superior to the midfemoral head.[4]

Fluoroscopy may help localize the CFA over the medial third of the femoral head. The chances of hitting the artery are maximized by aiming for the middle (craniocaudal) portion of the medial third of the femoral head. To minimize parallax errors, the femoral head should be centered in the image intensifier. The

anatomic relations of the arteries in this area vary little with body habitus, gender, or age. A 1999 anatomic study showed that the CFA bifurcates into the SFA and the PF approximately 2 cm below the femoral head.[5] Occasionally, calcifications in the arteries may serve as landmarks for locating the CFA.

Another localization approach involves palpation of anatomic landmarks; this approach may be especially useful when the artery is pulseless.[6] With a finger placed immediately lateral to the pubic tubercle and inferior to the inguinal ligament, palpation is carried out to locate the point allowing the greatest degree of posterior depression. Anatomically, this point of maximal depression lies between the iliopsoas muscle laterally and the pectineus muscle medially. The CFV lies in the floor of this depression, and the CFA lies 1.5 cm lateral to the depression.[6]

Ultrasonography has also proved useful for finding the CFA. The projection of choice with real-time ultrasonography is the transverse plane. The nonpalpable CFA is identified lateral to the compressible CFV. Occasionally, the artery can be identified on the basis of sonographic shadowing from calcified atheromatous plaques.[7] A second ultrasonographic technique involves the use of a so-called smart needle, which has an ultrasound probe at its tip. The needle emits a signal as it approaches the artery, thereby giving notice of proximity to the vessel.

Another method of localizing and puncturing a pulseless CFA involves performing a contralateral femoral artery puncture, obtaining a diagnostic angiogram, and roadmapping. A similar method that is useful in patients who may be moving or who cannot receive additional contrast material is to pass a guide wire over the aortic

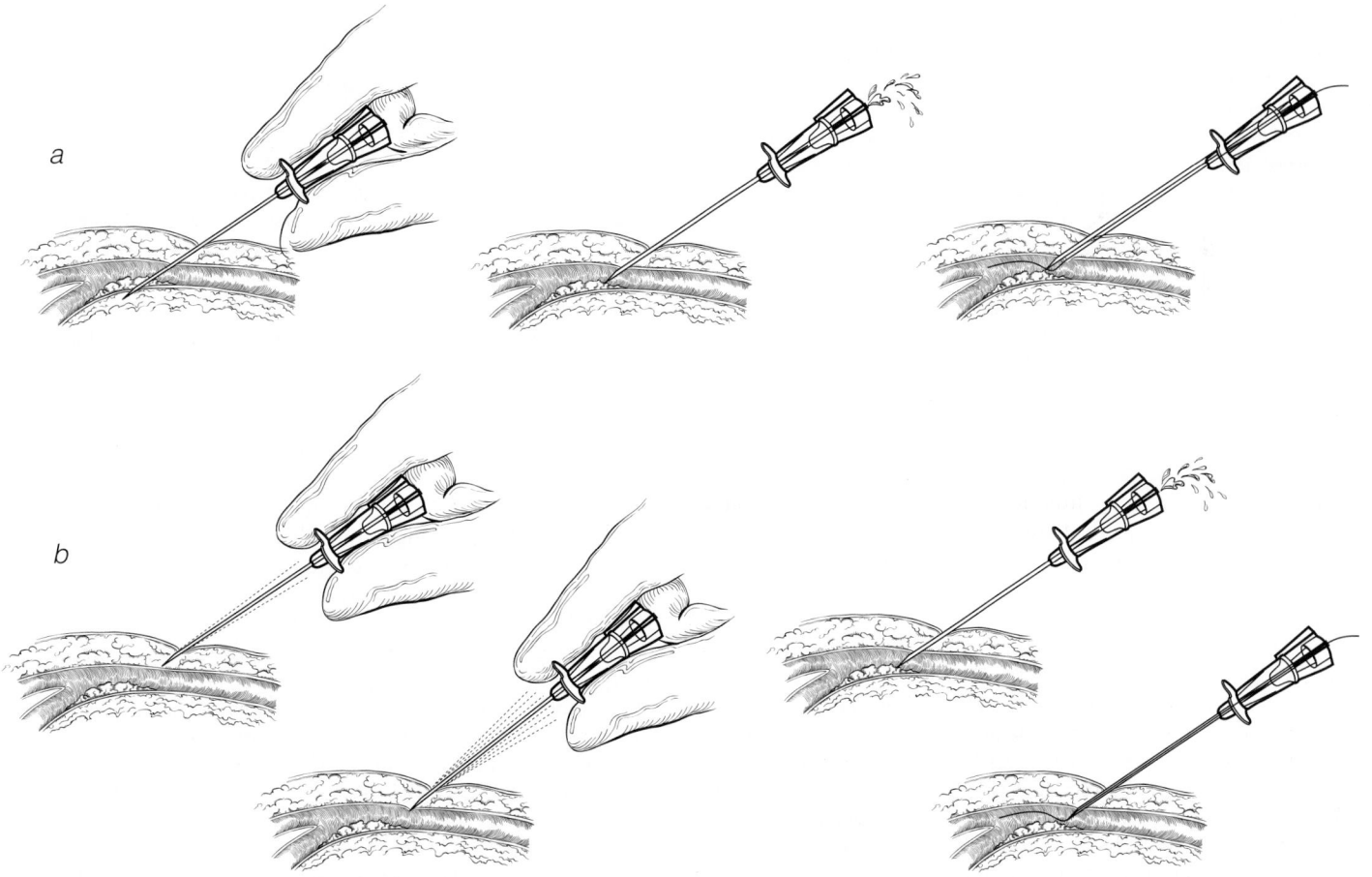

Figure 1 Shown are the two methods of entry into an artery: (*a*) through-and-through puncture of both walls and (*b*) puncture of the anterior wall only.

bifurcation and then antegrade through the iliac artery into the target femoral artery.[8] Under fluoroscopy, the guide wire becomes a visible target for introduction of the needle into the CFA.

Troubleshooting

The CFA is typically described as lateral to the CFV; however, one study showed that attempts to puncture the CFA frequently result in puncture of the CFV, signaled by the appearance of dark, nonpulsatile venous blood. If this occurs, one should note the position of the original puncture, move the needle 1 to 1.5 cm laterally, and reinsert the needle. At times, especially in emergency procedures, arterial blood may be dark and may resemble venous blood. If it is unclear whether the blood is coming from an artery or a vein, a small amount of a contrast agent should be gently injected into the needle by hand; the source of the blood should then be easily identifiable. When contrast is injected in the femoral sheath outside the artery, the resulting tubular "filling defect" can be used to identify the femoral artery.

If the puncture is done too high (in the external iliac artery), the inguinal ligament and the deeper location of the external iliac artery may make adequate compression of the vessel impossible. Many closure systems will not work in the external iliac artery. High puncture is associated with retroperitoneal bleeding, which should be suspected in any patient with an unexplained drop in the hematocrit, hypotension, or flank pain. To minimize this problem, the artery should be entered caudal to the inguinal ligament at a site where it can be compressed against the femoral head.[9]

If the puncture is done too low (in the SFA or the PF), there is a greater incidence of hematoma, pseudoaneurysm, arteriovenous fistula, and catheter-related thrombosis.[4,10] The reason for this increased incidence may be that it is harder to compress the SFA and the PF adequately than it is to compress the CFA, which lies over bone for most of its length. The CFA is larger in diameter than either the SFA or the PF and thus is better suited for the passage of large catheters and sheaths.

Experience is critical for achieving easy and complication-free femoral artery access. Although standard learning points are helpful in the accumulation of this experience, veteran interventionalists typically develop their own individual procedural algorithms, based on what is most familiar to and works best for them. Routine use of femoral arteriography and ultrasonography can shorten the learning period by visually demonstrating the nuances of the anatomy in tandem with the tactile learning. Thoughtful study of failed or complicated access cases, including observing the vascular anatomy when surgical repair becomes necessary, can also help develop experience more rapidly. In such cases, exploration often reveals altered femoral anatomy, side-wall punctures, low and high punctures, and posterior wall dissection. For even the most masterful interventionalist, femoral puncture complications are an ever-present risk, despite his or her best efforts.

BRACHIAL ARTERY PUNCTURE

The brachial artery is typically the second choice for arterial access after the femoral artery. This vessel is located in the lower third of the upper arm, anteromedial to the humerus. The median nerve lies just medial to the brachial artery at this level, and the radial nerve lies posterior to the artery. Even though the brachial artery is best palpated in the lower middle third of the arm, some clinicians prefer to puncture it in the high brachial position because complications may be less frequent with this approach.

The patient's arm is extended and supinated. The upper portion of the brachial artery is entered several fingerbreadths distal to the axillary crease, over the proximal humeral shaft. The middle por-

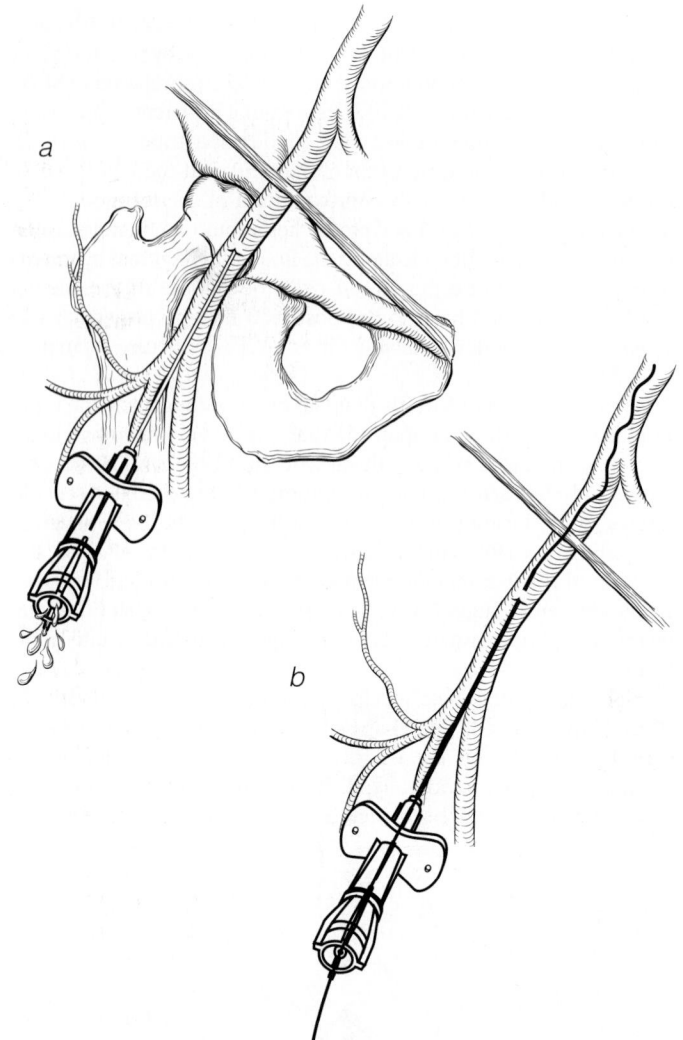

Figure 2 Puncture of common femoral artery. (*a*) The needle enters the CFA. (*b*) **The guide wire is passed through the needle.**

tion of the brachial artery is entered just above the antecubital fossa. Because this vessel is very mobile, it may be advisable to fix it between the surgeon's middle and index fingers before puncture.

Troubleshooting

The brachial artery is typically smaller than the CFA and more prone to thrombosis. Accordingly, the needles, guide wires, catheters, and sheaths used for brachial artery puncture must be smaller as well. Occasionally, the median nerve or the radial nerve may be damaged by the puncture. Any distal neurologic symptoms (e.g., median nerve distribution paresthesias or pain or weakness of the opponens muscle) that arise are evaluated on an urgent basis; on occasion, emergency exploration proves necessary. Frequently, there is no palpable hematoma, and the symptoms are attributable to a very small hematoma adjacent to the nerve. Not uncommonly, the brachial artery goes into spasm after puncture. Intra-arterial injection of papaverine, tolazoline, or nitroglycerin may reduce the risk of spasm.

AXILLARY ARTERY PUNCTURE

The axillary artery is divided into three parts on the basis of its relation to the overlying pectoralis minor. The third portion of the artery lies lateral to the pectoralis minor, and its most distal portion extends beyond the pectoralis major, at which location it is very superficial.[2] The axillary artery is typically used for vascular access when neither the femoral nor the brachial artery is available. The use of this approach may be restricted in patients who have subclavian artery occlusive disease or aneurysmal disease. A physical examination should be performed before the procedure to look for a blood pressure differential between the two arms, as well as to auscultate for the presence of a supraclavicular bruit. A blood pressure differential greater than 20 mm Hg suggests the presence of hemodynamically significant arterial stenosis in the arm with the lower pressure.

Axillary artery puncture is useful in patients with a steeply downward-coursing (caudal) mesenteric or renal artery, patients with infrarenal aortic or bilateral iliac occlusion, and patients with a history of embolization from infrarenal aortic catheterization.[3] However, access at this site poses an added risk, in that the artery is located near the brachial plexus, which may be damaged by direct trauma or compression from a hematoma. In addition, access via the axillary artery is relatively uncomfortable for both patient and physician. Generally, for access to the descending thoracic aorta, the abdominal aorta, and the lower-extremity vessels, the left axillary artery may be preferred, whereas for access to the ascending aorta and the coronary vessels, the right axillary artery may be preferred.

The arm can be placed in either of two positions: (1) abducted 90° or (2) maximally abducted with the patient's hand placed under the head. The second position stretches the artery and fixes it in place. The artery is palpated along the lateral axillary fold over the proximal humerus at the neck so that the underlying bone provides support during compression.[11] The vessel is then entered over the proximal humeral shaft just distal to the axillary fold. Like the brachial artery, the axillary artery is relatively mobile. It may be compressed along its length between the index and middle fingers to fix it in place for subsequent puncture.

Troubleshooting

Thrombosis and pseudoaneurysm formation are more common with the axillary artery approach.[3] In addition, the median and ulnar nerves run along with the axillary and proximal brachial arteries in a fascial sheath, so that a small hematoma can cause nerve compression. If a sensory or motor deficit develops, surgical decompression may be required. Cerebral embolization occurs in as many as 4% of cases of axillary artery puncture.[3]

TRANSLUMBAR PUNCTURE

Translumbar puncture of the aorta is indicated when femoral, axillary, and brachial methods are all relatively unsuitable. It is frequently used in patients who have abdominal aneurysms after endovascular repair.

An upper translumbar approach is indicated if visualization of the visceral and renal arteries is required. The patient is placed in a prone position. The 12th thoracic vertebra is located either by palpating the 12th rib or, more accurately, by means of fluoroscopy. The skin is entered 1 to 2 cm below the level of the 12th rib and 8 to 10 cm to the left, lateral to the posterior spinous process of the 12th vertebra. The needle is aimed ventrally and cephalad toward the level of the middle to lower portion of the body of T12 until the needle strikes the vertebra. Care must be taken to keep the needle below the diaphragm so that it does not hit the lung and the pleura. Particular care must also be taken to avoid the renal arteries inferiorly. After striking T12, the needle is withdrawn several centimeters and aimed laterally and ventrally until the pulsations of the aorta are felt. When the needle hits the aorta, slight resistance

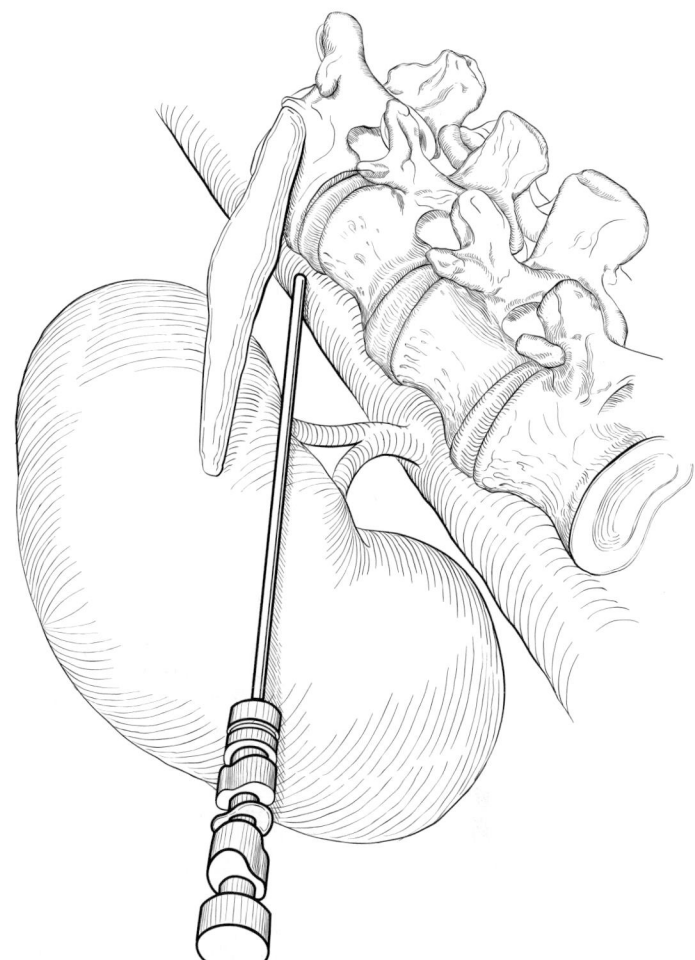

Figure 3 Translumbar puncture of aorta. The vessel is approached at the level of T12.

will be felt, followed by release of tension and a very slight give or "pop" when the needle enters the aorta. Only the proximal wall should be punctured. The needle is then advanced about 3 to 5 mm to the middle of the lumen [see Figure 3].

A lower translumbar approach may be used to access an aortic aneurysm sac after endovascular repair. The puncture site is located via fluoroscopy of radiopaque markers on the device already in place. With the patient in the prone position, the needle is introduced 8 to 10 cm lateral to the spinous process of L2 and directed anterior to the lumbar spine. Often, careful review of the CT images suggests a specific target and tract. As with an upper translumbar puncture, a "pop" can be felt when the needle enters the aneurysm sac; alternatively, the needle can be visualized entering a calcified wall.

Troubleshooting

The high translumbar technique is limited by its inability to deliver the contrast material at the bifurcation of the aorta or to perform selective catheterization of vessels. Too high a puncture (e.g., at T11) can lead to inadvertent puncture of the lung and cause a hemothorax or a pneumothorax. If the needle moves with the respiratory diaphragmatic movements of the patient, it may be in the thoracic cavity. If the initial needle stick is too medial, only the lateral wall of the aorta is reached. If the needle stick is too lateral, the needle passes between the vertebral body and the aorta. If the needle is advanced at too shallow an angle, it may enter the spinal canal.[2] If resistance is felt when the guide wire is placed, the wire may have entered the renal, celiac, or superior mesenteric artery. Small retroperitoneal hematomas develop in most patients who undergo translumbar puncture, but the incidence of major complications is only 3%.

Placement of Guide Wires

Once vascular access has been obtained through arterial puncture, it is maintained through placement of a guide wire. Most guide wires consist of a soft tip and a stiffer main body. The flexibility of the soft tip allows the surgeon to manipulate the guide wire past stenoses while minimizing the risk of perforation or dissection. For best results, the guide wire must be suitable for the intended procedure in terms of (1) tip configuration, (2) diameter, and (3) length. Sometimes, multiple wires are used at different stages of the procedure.

Guide wires come in several different tip configurations, including straight, angled, and J-shaped. Straight-tipped wires are used in vessels that are relatively straight and free of disease. J-tipped guide wires are sometimes preferred for atherosclerotic vessels because the shape of the tip reduces the likelihood that the wire will pass subintimally and cause unintentional dissection. Many specialty wires are available for specific uses (e.g., crossing chronic total occlusions).

Guide wires also come in a variety of diameters, typically ranging from 0.014 to 0.052 in. The diameters most commonly used for endovascular procedures are 0.035 and 0.014 in. Larger guide wires are typically stiffer, which makes it easier to deliver sheaths and catheters over them. Smaller wires are typically used for endovascular work involving the carotid, renal, or infragenicular vessels. In choosing the diameter of the wire, the interventionalist must keep in mind the gauge of the needle that was used to access the vessel. The guide wire should fit the needle yet be large enough to allow delivery of interventional devices.

The length of the guide wire is an important concern because choosing an appropriate length facilitates exchange of catheters or interventional devices without loss of access across a remote lesion. A general rule for determining optimal guide wire length is as follows[12]:

Optimal guide wire length = Length from outer edge of sheath or insertion site to lesion + length of longest catheter or interventional device + at least 10 cm

In an average adult, the wire used for selective angiography is typically about 145 to 180 cm long. Longer wires (260 to 300 cm) are used for exchanging long over-the-wire vascular devices. Occasionally, a 450 cm long wire is needed for combined brachial-femoral access.

Once arterial access is obtained, several safety measures should be undertaken. The needle should have its bevel facing upward to optimize conditions for wire advancement; a downward-facing bevel may cause the sharp edge of the needle to damage or even sever the wire. The floppy end of the wire should be used for initial introduction into the needle and the vessel; the stiff end may damage the vessel if used for initial entry. Caution should be exercised in introducing the guide wire if there is unexpected poor flow from the needle.

After entry into the lumen, the guide wire is advanced about 15 to 20 cm. The needle is then removed, and a catheter or an introducer sheath is placed over the wire. Further advancement of the wire is done under fluoroscopic guidance. Once placed, the guide wire should be carefully monitored and kept in place (pinned)

whenever any other devices are manipulated. As a general rule, the guide wire is not removed until the very end of the procedure. After removal, guide wires are rinsed and loosely coiled for storage (in case they are needed later).

TROUBLESHOOTING

The guide wire should never be forcefully introduced into the vessel. If significant resistance is encountered, the end of the needle may be against the vessel wall or partially within the wall. In this situation, the needle should be repositioned slightly and another attempt made to pass the wire. Occasionally, the guide wire may pass easily for several centimeters before encountering resistance to further advancement. Such resistance may be secondary to stenosis or tortuosity of the vessel. Placement of a different wire with a different tip configuration or insertion of a guide catheter may be necessary to advance the wire further.

Wiping the guide wire with heparinized saline minimizes thrombus formation on the wire. If thrombus is allowed to build up, friction will increase during catheter exchange, making the exchange more difficult. Some hydrophilic-coated guide wires require constant wetting to maintain their characteristics. Other guide wire coatings swell after prolonged wetting and thus may inhibit catheter exchanges. Hydrophilic wires should not be used for initial cannulation through the access needle, because they may be sheared off by the needle tip when withdrawn. Damaged or kinked guide wires should be exchanged for new undamaged wires when this can be done safely.

Placement of Sheaths

Once guide wire access is achieved, a sheath or guide is typically placed over the guide wire to maintain a stable pathway for catheter exchange or for placement of a device. Before the sheath is placed, dilators are first passed over the guide wire to create a smooth tract through the soft tissue into the vessel. Whereas sheaths are measured according to their inner circumference (1 mm circumference = 1 French), guides are measured according to their outer circumference; thus, a 6 French guide fits inside a 6 French sheath. Dilators are also measured according to their outer circumference. Therefore, when a 5 French sheath is to be placed in scarred fibrous tissue, a 6 French dilator must be placed to create a similarly sized tract. Most commonly, a dilator and a sheath of the same size are pinned and placed together.

Most introducer sheaths have hemostatic valves and side ports. Guide catheters can be effectively converted to sheaths by adding a Touhy-Borst valve apparatus. These valves seal around a smaller catheter and reduce back-bleeding. The side port can be used for continuous infusion of heparinized saline to reduce the risk of thrombus formation. The sheath can also be used to straighten tortuous arteries (e.g., the iliac arteries). For example, when a guide wire has been passed through the iliac artery and into the abdominal aorta, the sheath can be advanced over the wire into the abdominal aorta. Passage of a sheath through the tortuous iliac vessel facilitates subsequent passage of catheters and devices.

Once properly placed, sheaths should be secured in position (i.e., pinned or sutured) so that they are not inadvertently advanced without the introducer or accidentally withdrawn.

Insertion of Catheters

There are many differentiating characteristics by which various types of catheters can be distinguished from one other, including size, shape, stiffness, coating, radiopacity, and side-hole configura-

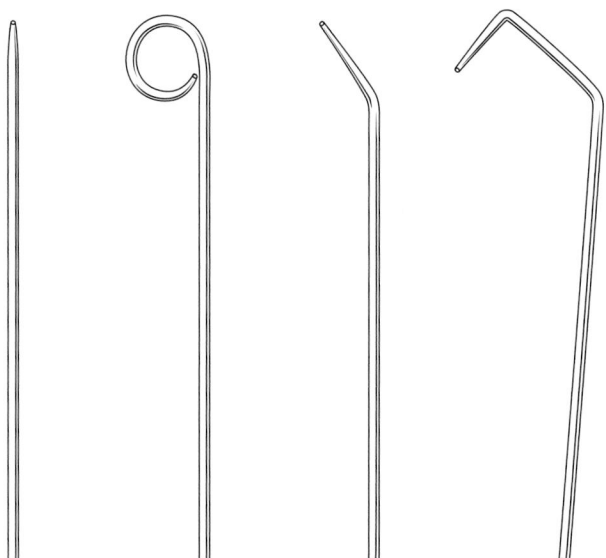

Figure 4 **Catheters come with various tip configurations. Shown are straight, pigtail, angled, and double-angled tips (left to right).**

tion. As a rule, catheters are sized according to their outer diameter (French) and their length (cm). Numerous tip shapes are available [*see Figure 4*] (e.g., straight, cobra, headhunter, angled, shepherd's hook, reverse curve, pigtail, and racquet). The initial catheter shape is selected on the basis of the specific requirements of the procedure and the individual patient anatomy. Generally, within the abdominal aorta, the angle of the primary curve of the catheter tip should be similar to that of the vessel takeoff. In some cases, multiple catheters may be needed, used either in sequence or coaxially to perform superselective catheterizations. A variety of complex catheter shapes may be used to select vessels that have steep angles of origin. The use of coatings (e.g., hydrophilic surfaces and Teflon) can facilitate advancement of the catheter in tortuous vessels. Specialty catheters may come with radiopaque tips or with multiple radiopaque markers placed at 1 cm intervals for reference during vessel sizing. Multi–side-hole catheters have a spiraling set of holes that allow more even distribution of a large volume of contrast or other infusate; they are typically used to opacify large vessels with high flows. Generally, opacification of smaller vessels requires a smaller dose of contrast material administered at a slower rate; for this purpose, an end-hole catheter suffices.

Before contrast is injected, the catheter should be aspirated to remove any air bubbles and to verify intraluminal location by means of free-flowing back-bleeding. A small test injection is useful for checking the catheter's position. Depending on the clinical circumstances, the patient may undergo anticoagulation to reduce the risk of thrombus formation on the outside of the catheter. Periodically, the catheter may be flushed with heparinized saline to prevent thrombus formation within it. When a stiffer catheter is advanced forward, it is usually advanced over a guide wire; however, a softer catheter can be used in the same way as a guide wire. Some complex curved catheters may have to be removed over a wire to reduce the risk that the catheter will scrape the vessel wall.

TROUBLESHOOTING

There are several areas in the handling of catheters where attention to detail and good technique can help optimize results. Two common errors of selective catheterization are (1) looking for a specific artery in the wrong location (e.g., as a consequence of

misidentification of bone landmarks) and (2) failing to recognize when the appropriate vessel has been entered (particularly in patients with anomalous vessels or postoperative changes).[13] These errors can be prevented by first performing roadmapping with nonselective catheterization and angiography; often, repeated roadmapping in multiple projections is required. Another potential problem is accidental loss of guide wire access, which may be more common with inexperienced operators who are not pinning the guide wire in place while a catheter is being pulled out. There are many advanced techniques for handling catheters and guide wires, but these are outside the scope of this discussion.

Use of Balloon Catheters

The purpose of a balloon catheter is to exert a radial force on the luminal surface of a blood vessel to dilate a stenotic lesion. As the balloon inflates, the media and adventitia of the artery stretch, causing a longitudinal fracture of the plaque. Minor arterial dissection is expected with this technique. Thus, the compression of the plaque is not the principal means of increasing the cross-sectional area of the vessel.

Several features are considered in selecting a balloon catheter for a specific intervention, including balloon diameter and length, catheter size and length, trackability, balloon type (e.g., compliant, noncompliant, cutting, or trilobed), and catheter profile [*see Figure 5*]. Typically, balloons range from 1.5 to 40 mm in diameter and from 1.5 to 10 cm in length. The vessel should be slightly overdistended when the balloon is inflated. Thus, measuring the diameter of the normal vessel distal to the lesion will help determine an appropriate balloon diameter. If the operator is unsure of the proper balloon diameter, it is best to choose a smaller-diameter balloon and then move to a larger balloon if necessary. The shortest balloon length that spans the entire lesion with a slight extension into the normal artery should be chosen, so that the shoulder of the balloon dilates as little as possible of the normal portion of the vessel. If the balloon is too short and is not centered, it may be squeezed away from the stenosis during inflation (the so-called watermelon seed effect). Balloon catheters typically range from 70 to 150 cm in length. The shortest catheter length that reaches the lesion from the access site is preferred because a shorter catheter is easier to manipulate. The diameter (or profile) of the catheter depends on the type and size of the balloon and typically ranges from 3 to 14 French. Sometimes, a smaller-profile balloon may be used if a smaller-diameter guide wire provides enough support for treatment of the lesion. If the balloon catheter is smaller than the sheath, contrast injection is possible when the balloon is in position; this allows the balloon's position to be fine-tuned immediately before inflation.

The balloon catheter is advanced over the guide wire through the sheath to the lesion, and the balloon is centered over the lesion. The balloon is inflated with a dilute contrast solution so that its expansion can be monitored fluoroscopically. Guidelines for inflation and deflation techniques vary with respect to speed and duration of inflation, number of dilatations, and balloon pressure. Typically, the balloon is inflated to a pressure that results in a smooth parallel profile of the balloon walls, held for 20 to 60 seconds, and then deflated. In most clinical circumstances, the inflation pressure should not exceed rated burst pressures. After dilatation, the balloon catheter is removed, with the guide wire left in place across the lesion (in case stenting proves necessary). Completion angiography is performed for evaluation of the results, including assessment of distal vascular beds.

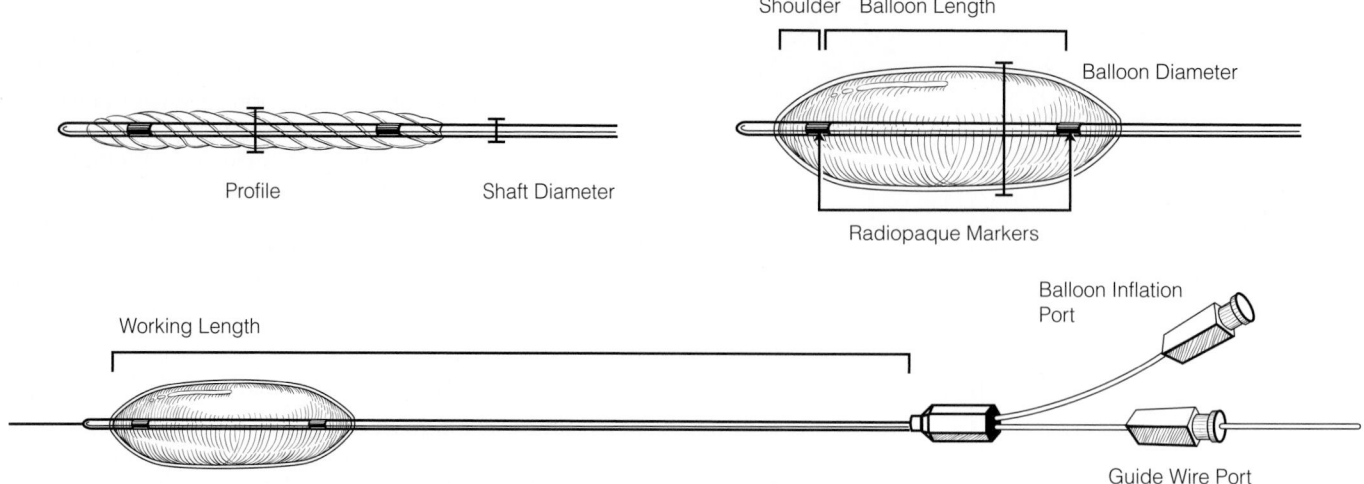

Figure 5 **Shown is a balloon angioplasty catheter.**

Dilatation may be considered successful if (1) flow-limiting dissection is absent, (2) residual luminal diameter stenosis is less than 30%, and (3) the systolic pressure gradient is less than 5 to 10 mm Hg. Vasodilators can unmask a significant gradient.

TROUBLESHOOTING

Complications associated with the use of balloon catheters include thrombosis, vessel rupture, embolization, and dissection. The incidence of these complications is influenced by patient selection and by the nature of the lesion being treated. For example, complications may be more likely with treatment of stenoses adjacent to aneurysms, long segments of occlusion, tandem lesions, lesions near major branches, and calcified eccentric plaques. Even though some degree of dissection is expected after balloon angioplasty, larger flow-limiting dissections may call for further management. This problem can often be solved by placing a stent over the dissection.

Most patients feel discomfort and mild pain during balloon inflation. If a patient experiences severe pain that persists after deflation of the balloon, the possibility of vessel rupture must be considered. If the vessel ruptures, the balloon may be reinflated over the injury to tamponade it. Prolonged balloon inflation often closes the leak, but at the risk of causing thrombosis. If the vessel continues to leak, a covered stent may be placed over the injury, or open vascular repair may be necessary.

If inflation of the balloon fails to dilate the vessel completely, it may be helpful to use a larger-diameter balloon or a higher inflation pressure. Higher inflation pressures may be cautiously attempted, but the vessel may simply recoil after dilatation.[14] A stent is often useful in this scenario.

If the balloon crosses the lesions only partially, it should not be inflated. The position of the guide wire should be checked: the wire may be in a subintimal location. If the stenosis is very tight, the lesion may be predilated with a smaller-profile balloon catheter.

Placement of Vascular Stents

Intravascular stents are commonly used in endovascular surgery, particularly after failed percutaneous transluminal angioplasty. Placement of an iliac artery stent is indicated when there is significant residual stenosis, flow-limiting dissection, or a persistent pressure gradient. Although angioplasty is often successful, it may fail when there is elastic recoil of the arterial wall or when the lesion is resistant to dilatation because of heavy calcification.

Stenting can often remedy these situations by providing physical support to keep the vessel open. Many physicians now regard primary stenting (i.e., routine use of stents) as a preferred approach for many vascular lesions.

CHOICE OF STENT TYPE

Stents are divided into two categories: balloon-expandable stents and self-expanding stents. They may also be described as being covered (with a graft material), coated (with a therapeutic compound), absorbable, or radioactive. Stent types differ with respect to hoop strength (for resisting arterial recoil), cell size, cell structure, shape (e.g., tapered or nontapered), radiopacity, longitudinal flexibility (for crossing tortuous vessels), radial elasticity (for resisting repeated external compression), and profile. Stents come in many different lengths and expanded diameters on a wide variety of deployment catheters.

Balloon-Expandable Stents

Balloon-expandable stents come either premounted on balloon catheters or unmounted; unmounted stents must be manually crimped onto a balloon to be delivered. With unmounted stents, a smaller inventory can be maintained, and a wider range of stent-balloon combinations is available. Premounted stents, however, tend to be more solidly mounted and less likely to be lost during delivery. Once the stent is at the desired lesion, the balloon is inflated and the stent expanded.

The main advantage balloon-expandable stents have over self-expanding stents is that they have greater hoop strength, which means that they can better resist the recoil of the vessel after full expansion of the stent. In addition, many interventionalists feel that balloon-expandable stents can be more precisely placed than self-expanding stents and thus are preferable when accuracy is of high clinical importance. However, older balloon-expandable stents are less flexible than current models, and navigating such older devices in a tortuous vessel can be difficult.

Self-Expanding Stents

Self-expanding stents are placed within a delivery catheter and rely on a self-expansion mechanism for full deployment. A common deployment mechanism involves the use of an outer jacket and a plunger: the jacket is withdrawn while the stent is held in position by the plunger, and the stent then expands to its predetermined diameter. Commonly, a balloon is employed to ensure that the stent is fully expanded and impacted into the plaque.

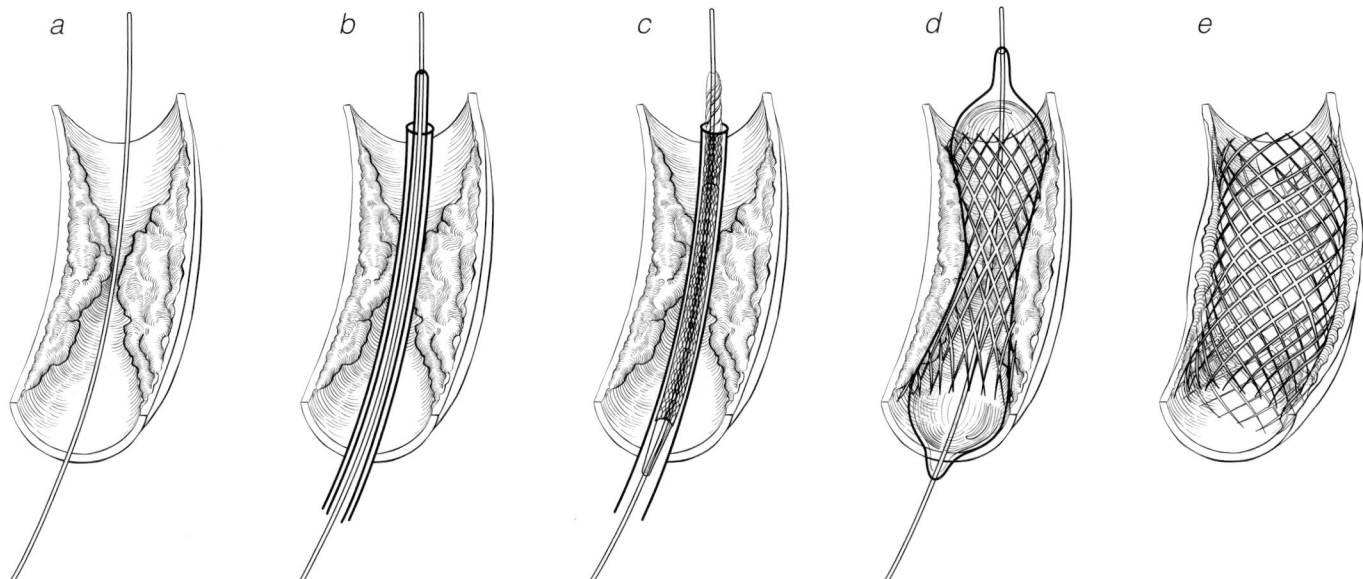

Figure 6 Deployment of a balloon-expandable stent. (*a*) The guide wire is passed across the lesion. (*b*) The sheath-dilator combination is passed over the guide wire across the lesion. (*c*) The dilator is removed, and the balloon-expandable stent is advanced. (*d*) The sheath is retracted and the balloon inflated. (*e*) The balloon is deflated and withdrawn, leaving the stent fully deployed.

An advantage self-expanding stents have over balloon-expandable stents is that they offer a greater degree of longitudinal flexibility and thus are more easily tracked into position. Self-expanding stents come in lengths of up to 20 cm, which means that fewer overlap zones and fewer stents are required in the treatment of long lesions. In addition, they may be delivered by catheters with smaller profiles, which may reduce arterial-access complications. Self-expanding stents may also be placed in regions of the body where they are subject to crushing forces (e.g., the carotid artery) because they are capable of recovering from the deformation and maintaining the arterial lumen.[15] As noted, however, self-expanding stents have less hoop strength than the balloon-expandable stents.

Covered Stents

Stents may be covered with polyester, polytetrafluoroethylene, or other materials. Currently, covered stents are being used more frequently for treating occlusive lesions, but they are more commonly employed for treating aneurysms, arterial rupture, and arteriovenous fistulas.[15,16]

GENERAL TECHNICAL PRINCIPLES

Conceptually, stent placement is very similar to balloon angioplasty [*see Figure 6*]. Preoperatively, the patient is often given an antiplatelet agent, which may be continued for 4 weeks or longer postoperatively to reduce the risk of thrombosis. In general, the diameter of the fully deployed stent should slightly exceed that of the vessel, though many interventionalists do not fully dilate stents in the aorta and the carotid bifurcation.[11] If occlusion makes the exact diameter of the artery difficult to measure, the vessel's contralateral counterpart can be used as a guide.[16] The stent should also be slightly longer than the lesion to ensure that the entire lesion is covered. In this way, good wall apposition can be achieved and stent migration prevented.

The classic approach is to advance a guide (or a long sheath) across the stenosis over the previously placed guide wire; the vascular stent is then passed through the guide and positioned at the lesion, the guide is withdrawn, and the stent is deployed. With newer stent delivery systems, the leading tip often allows the stent to be delivered without precrossing the lesion with a guide or sheath. Multiple stents are sometimes required to complete the procedure.

TROUBLESHOOTING

It is often helpful to place the leading end of a self-expanding stent slightly beyond the lesion, then draw it back. This measure removes loaded tension from the system; it also allows the stent to be pulled back slightly after the initiation of deployment, at which point various forces sometimes cause the stent to move forward. However, the partially deployed struts of the stent can injure the vessel wall if moved too much or advanced forward. It is also important to keep in mind the potential for foreshortening of the stent during deployment. Failure to cover the entire lesion with the stent results in residual disease after the procedure, which can cause subsequent thrombosis and necessitate the placement of an additional stent. To prevent restenosis, multiple stents should generally be placed so as to overlap one another, but doing so may increase the risk of fatigue fractures. Clearly, the nuances of stent deployment vary according to the system being used; frequent use of a particular system will enhance the interventionalist's familiarity with the behavior of the device and improve the subsequent clinical results.

Postprocedural Management of Arterial Access Site

After any endovascular procedure, the arterial access site must be addressed. Manual compression is still the most common method of hemostasis and is effective in most instances. The artery often must be compressed for longer than 20 minutes to prevent bleeding complications. If the patient is receiving anticoagulant therapy, it may be necessary to wait until the coagulation parameters have normalized before pulling out the sheath. This can be done when the patient is out of the OR or the interventional suite and in the recovery room or when the patient has been moved onto the hospital floor. After hemostasis has been achieved at the access site, the patient should refrain from walking for about 6 hours, after which period the puncture site generally is sufficiently stable. After therapeutic procedures involving relatively large devices, use of an arterial closure device may be advantageous. Several such closure devices are now commercially available. These devices are improving in quality and are certain to be used more frequently in the future.

Summary: Basic Steps in Endovascular Procedures

1. Before operation, assess the patient with respect to renal function, allergies, active infections, anticoagulant management, and skin condition (in cases of planned access). Consider prescribing antiplatelet agents.
2. Monitor and sedate the patient as necessary.
3. Prepare and drape the selected arterial access site or sites.
4. Infiltrate a local anesthetic at the selected site.
5. Use a scalpel to nick the skin at the planned needle entry site, a few centimeters distal to the intended arterial puncture site.
6. Cannulate the artery with the entry needle.
7. Pass the guide wire into the needle for at least 20 to 25 cm. Use fluoroscopy to follow the guide wire as indicated.
8. Remove the needle while pinning the guide wire in place.
9. Apply manual compression during exchanges to prevent hematoma formation around the artery.
10. Use dilators to create an appropriate tract while pinning the guide wire.
11. Pass a sheath over the pinned guide wire. Often, with small sheaths and minimal scarring, the dilator and the sheath are placed simultaneously. Remove the dilator.
12. Administer anticoagulation as indicated.
13. Manipulate the guide wire to the appropriate position past the lesion (in cases of nonselective catheterization).
14. Pass the catheter over the guide wire and through the sheath. Manipulate the catheter to select the branches for guide wire cannulation.
15. Perform angiography through the catheter or the sheath to clarify the anatomy.
16. Remove the catheter while pinning the guide wire.
17. Pass the balloon catheter over the guide wire. Advance the balloon across and center it over the lesion. If indicated, primary stenting may be performed.
18. Inflate the balloon.
19. Deflate the balloon.
20. Remove the balloon catheter while pinning the guide wire.
21. Perform angiography.
22. If necessary, pass the vascular stent over the guide wire and advance it across the lesion.
23. Deploy the stent.
24. Perform completion angiography.
25. If the angiogram is satisfactory, remove the guide wire, the catheter, and the sheath.
26. Apply manual compression to the access site, or use a closure device.

Dr. Matsumura has received grants, research support, or consulting fees from Abbott Laboratories; C. R. Bard, Inc.; Cook Biotech Inc.; Cordis Corp.; ev3 Inc.; W. L. Gore and Associates; and Medtronic, Inc.

References

1. Tortorici M: Fundamentals of Angiography. CV Mosby Co, St Louis, 1982
2. Johnsrude I, Jackson D, Dunnick N: A Practical Approach to Angiography, 2nd ed. Little, Brown & Co, Boston, 1987
3. Valji K: Vascular and Interventional Radiology. WB Saunders Co, Philadelphia, 1999
4. Rupp SB, Vogelzang RL, Nemcek AA, et al: Relationship of the inguinal ligament to pelvic radiographic landmarks: anatomic correlation and its role in femoral arteriography. J Vasc Intervent Radiol 4:409, 1993
5. Baum PA, Matsumoto AH, Teitelbaum GP, et al: Anatomic relationship between the common femoral artery and vein: CT evaluation and clinical significance. Cardiovasc Radiol 173:775, 1999
6. Millward SF, Burbride BE, Luna G: Puncturing the pulseless femoral artery: a simple technique that uses palpation of anatomic landmarks. J Vasc Intervent Radiol 4:415, 1993
7. Jaques PF, Mauro MA, Keefe B: US guidance for vascular access: technical note. J Vasc Intervent Radiol 3:427, 1992
8. Khangure MS, Chow KC, Christensen MA: Accurate and safe puncture of a pulseless femoral artery. Radiology 144:927, 1982
9. Spijkerboer AM, Scholten FG, Mali WPTM, et al: Antegrade puncture of the femoral artery: morphologic study. Radiology 176:57, 1990
10. Grier D, Hartnell G: Percutaneous femoral artery puncture: practice and anatomy. Br J Radiol 63:602, 1990
11. Kandarpa K, Aruny JE: Handbook of Interventional Radiologic Procedures. Lippincott Williams & Wilkins, Philadelphia, 2002
12. Moore WS, Ahn SS: Endovascular Surgery, 3rd ed. WB Saunders Co, Philadelphia, 2001
13. Neiman HL, Yao JST: Angiography of Vascular Disease. Churchill Livingstone, New York, 1985
14. Hood DB, Hodgson KJ: Percutaneous transluminal angioplasty and stenting for iliac artery occlusive disease. Surg Clin North Am 79:575, 1999
15. Nicholson T: Stents: an overview. Hosp Med 60:571, 1999
16. Henry M, Clonaris C, Amor M, et al: Which stent for which lesion in peripheral interventions? Texas Heart Inst J 27:119, 2000

Acknowledgment

Figures 1 through 6   Alice Y. Chen.

SURGICAL TREATMENT OF CAROTID ARTERY DISEASE

Wesley S. Moore, M.D., F.A.C.S.

The rationale for operating on patients with carotid artery disease is to prevent stroke. It has been estimated that in 50% to 80% of patients who experience an ischemic stroke, the underlying cause is a lesion in the distribution of the carotid artery, usually in the vicinity of the carotid bifurcation. It would follow, then, that appropriate identification and intervention could significantly reduce the incidence of ischemic stroke.

Carotid endarterectomy (CEA) for both symptomatic and asymptomatic carotid artery stenosis has been extensively evaluated in prospective, randomized trials. Symptomatic patients have been studied in the North American Symptomatic Carotid Endarterectomy Trial (NASCET),[1] the European Carotid Stenosis Trial (ECST),[2] and the symptomatic carotid stenosis trial from the Veterans Affairs (VA) Cooperative Studies Program.[3] The results of all three trials conclusively demonstrate that symptomatic patients with greater than 50% stenosis on arteriography are at substantially lower risk for stroke after CEA than control subjects receiving medical management alone. Asymptomatic patients with hemodynamically significant stenosis also benefit from surgical treatment: the Asymptomatic Carotid Atherosclerosis Study (ACAS)[4] and the asymptomatic carotid stenosis trial from the VA Cooperative Studies Program[5] show that the risk of both transient ischemic attacks (TIAs) and stroke is markedly lower in patients treated with CEA and best medical management than in control subjects treated with best medical management alone. The Medical Research Council study of the Asymptomatic Carotid Stenosis Trial (ACST) confirmed the findings of these two studies, citing results virtually identical to those originally reported by ACAS.[6]

Surgical reconstruction of the carotid artery yields the greatest benefits when done by surgeons who can keep complication rates to an absolute minimum. The majority of complications associated with carotid arterial procedures are either technical or judgmental; accordingly, in what follows, I emphasize the procedural details that I consider particularly important for deriving the best short- and long-term results from surgical intervention.

Preoperative Evaluation

PATIENT SELECTION

Indications for carotid artery surgery can be divided into two major categories: (1) asymptomatic critical stenosis and (2) symptomatic hemodynamically significant stenosis.[7]

Asymptomatic Critical Stenosis

The VA asymptomatic carotid stenosis study, ACAS, and ACST all found that in patients with diameter-reducing stenosis of 60% or greater on angiography, CEA resulted in fewer fatal and nonfatal strokes over a 5-year period than nonoperative treatment with best medical management alone. It is important to keep in mind that there are several different ways of measuring stenosis [*see 81 Asymptomatic Carotid Bruit*]. The 60% figure cited by ACAS and the VA study was determined according to the North American

method rather than the European method. Moreover, it was determined by means of contrast angiography rather than duplex ultrasonography (DUS) or magnetic resonance imaging. If the decision for CEA is to be based on DUS, some conversion of values is required. A patient who has an 80% to 99% stenosis on DUS can generally be assumed to have a diameter-reducing stenosis of at least 60% on angiography; a stenosis that is less than 80% on DUS may fall short of a 60% diameter-reducing stenosis on angiography.

Symptomatic Hemodynamically Significant Carotid Stenosis

Both NASCET and ECST found that symptomatic patients with hemodynamically significant stenoses experienced fewer fatal and nonfatal strokes after CEA combined with best medical management than after best medical management alone, provided that the perioperative morbidity and mortality from stroke was 6.0% or less. Thus, patients with monocular or hemispheric TIAs are good candidates for CEA. Global ischemic attacks have also been used as an indication for CEA. This practice has not been evaluated in clinical trials; it is usually justified on the basis of the ACAS data alone.

Patients who have previously experienced a hemispheric stroke but who are not disabled and have made a reasonable recovery are also good candidates for CEA if they have a hemodynamically significant stenosis.

IMAGING

Identification of a carotid lesion that can be treated with endarterectomy usually begins with a carotid duplex scan. Indications for carotid duplex scanning fall into three main categories: symptoms, signs, and risk factors. Symptoms include classic TIAs and strokes that give rise to clinical suspicion of carotid bifurcation disease. The primary sign is the presence of a carotid bruit on auscultation. Risk factors include cigarette smoking, hypertension, diabetes mellitus, hypercholesterolemia, peripheral vascular disease, and coronary artery disease. As the number of risk factors present increases, the likelihood of associated carotid bifurcation disease increases exponentially.

Patients who present with focal ischemic symptoms are likely to have associated carotid bifurcation disease; however, other pathologic conditions (e.g., emboli of cardiac origin, aortic arch disease, intracranial vascular disease, coagulopathy, and brain tumors) can also be responsible for focal symptoms. Accordingly, a complete workup of a symptomatic patient should include cardiac evaluation as well as intracranial imaging.

The accuracy of carotid duplex scanning is highly dependent on the technician performing it and on the laboratory where it is done. A carefully performed carotid duplex scan is often the most accurate indicator of carotid bifurcation disease; however, a hastily or carelessly performed scan can result in overestimation of the extent of the carotid bifurcation disease. For this reason, additional imaging studies (e.g., magnetic resonance angiography, computed tomographic angiography, and, when there is serious doubt, contrast angiography) may be indicated.

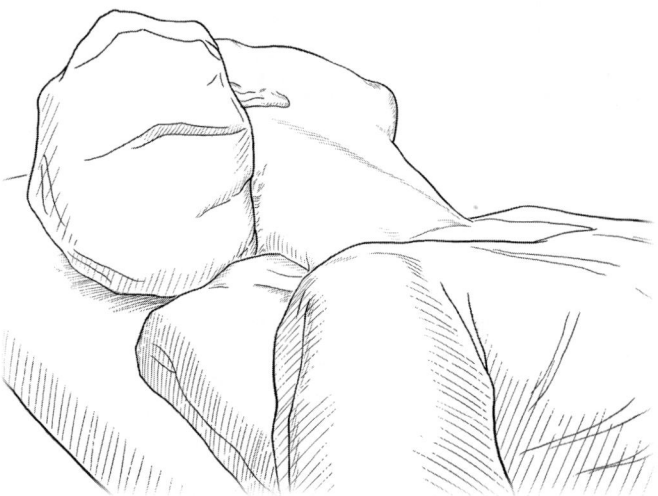

Figure 1 **Carotid arterial procedures. Shown is the recommended patient positioning.**

Operative Planning

Before operation is scheduled, the general health of the patient must be assessed, with particular attention paid to cardiac and pulmonary status. Given that many patients with carotid artery disease are hypertensive or diabetic, good preoperative control of diabetes mellitus and blood pressure is mandatory. In addition, to reduce the risk of thromboembolic complications, patients should receive antiplatelet drugs (e.g., aspirin) up to and on the day of operation. Finally, it is well documented that the risk of perioperative cardiac complications can be materially reduced by placing patients on a combination regimen that includes a statin and a beta blocker.

ANESTHESIA

Surgery on the cervical portion of the carotid artery may be performed with the patient under either general or cervical block anesthesia. Both techniques have their advocates, their advantages, and their disadvantages.

The advantages of general anesthesia include a quiet operative field, maximal patient comfort, and good airway control. In addition, general anesthesia may lead to improved cerebral blood flow and give better protection against reduced blood flow during carotid clamping. The disadvantages of general anesthesia include blood pressure swings during induction and the inability to monitor the patient's conscious response to carotid clamping. Some reports also suggest that the incidence of cardiac complications is higher during general anesthesia than during cervical block anesthesia.

The main advantage of cervical block anesthesia is the ability to monitor cerebral function during carotid clamping: an awake patient can be engaged in conversation and can be asked to carry out motor activities of the extremities. The disadvantages of cervical block anesthesia include possible patient discomfort, restlessness, and intolerance of the longer operations that are sometimes necessary for technical reasons. Another disadvantage is that on occasion, a patient cannot tolerate carotid clamping and demonstrates an immediate neurologic deficit with clamp application. Such an occurrence heightens the anxiety level of the surgical team, thereby increasing the risk that they will commit technical errors in the rush to place an internal shunt.

Besides considering the inherent advantages and disadvantages of these two anesthetic techniques with respect to the patient, it is important to consider their advantages and disadvantages with re- spect to individual surgical practice. A given

surgeon may well work better and achieve better results with one technique or the other.

Whichever anesthetic approach is used, all patients should have a radial arterial line in place to allow continuous blood pressure monitoring and to provide access for determining blood gas levels. As a rule, there is no need to place a central venous line or a right heart catheter, except in patients with marginal cardiac function.

PATIENT POSITIONING

Proper positioning of the patient is necessary to provide optimal exposure of the neck from the clavicle up to the mastoid process on the side of the proposed operation [*see Figure 1*]. The patient is placed in the supine position with a folded sheet under the shoulders to induce a mild degree of neck extension. Excessive neck extension should be avoided, however, because it places tension on the artery and actually hinders rather than facilitates exposure. This potential problem can be addressed by placing one or more towels under the head to adjust the neck to the optimal degree of extension. The patient's head is then turned away from the side of the operation to improve cervical exposure further. Finally, the table top may be rotated slightly away from the side of the operation so as to provide a flat surgical field. The head of the table may be elevated slightly if the patient's blood pressure is adequate; this step helps lower venous pressure and reduce venous bleeding during the operation [*see Figure 1*].

Operative Technique

STEP 1: INITIAL INCISION

Either of two incisions may be used for exposure of the cervical carotid artery. The more common choice is a vertical incision placed along an imaginary line that extends from the sternoclavicular junction to the mastoid process, paralleling the anterior margin of the sternocleidomastoid muscle as well as the course of the carotid artery and the contents of the carotid sheath [*see Figure 2*]. The incision is centered over the presumed location of the

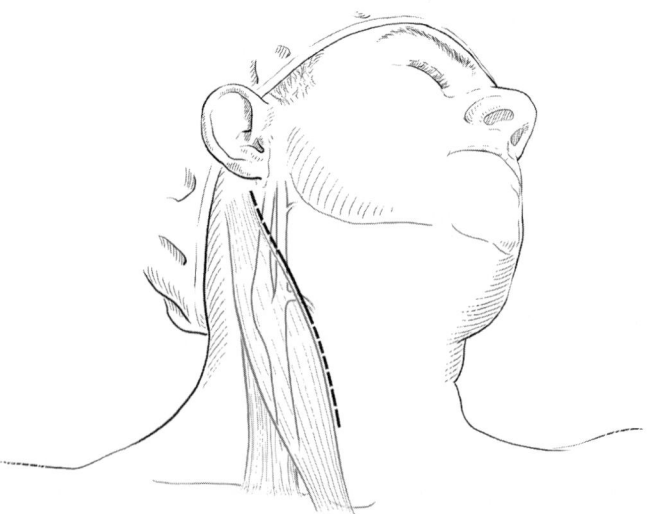

Figure 2 **Carotid arterial procedures. The incision most commonly used to expose the cervical carotid artery is a vertical one placed along the anterior margin of the sternocleidomastoid muscle and centered over the presumed location of the carotid bifurcation. It may be extended proximally or distally, depending on where the carotid bifurcation turns out to be.**

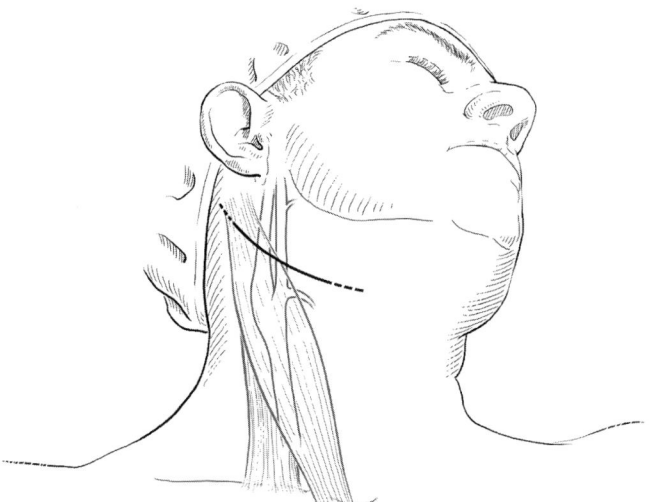

Figure 3 **Carotid arterial procedures. An alternative incision to the vertical incision is a transverse incision along a skin crease in the vicinity of the carotid bifurcation.**

carotid bifurcation. The advantage of this incision is that it provides optimal exposure of the cervical carotid artery and can readily be extended either proximally or distally along the aforementioned imaginary line to give additional exposure when needed (e.g., when the carotid bifurcation is unusually high). The disadvantage of this incision is that it runs against Langer's lines; thus, if a keloid occurs, it is likely to be in an unsightly position. In most patients, the incision heals to a fine line, and it usually is not noticeable once healing is complete.

The alternative to the vertical incision is a transverse incision that is placed in a skin crease on the anterior portion of the neck and then curved toward the mastoid process posteriorly [see Figure 3].

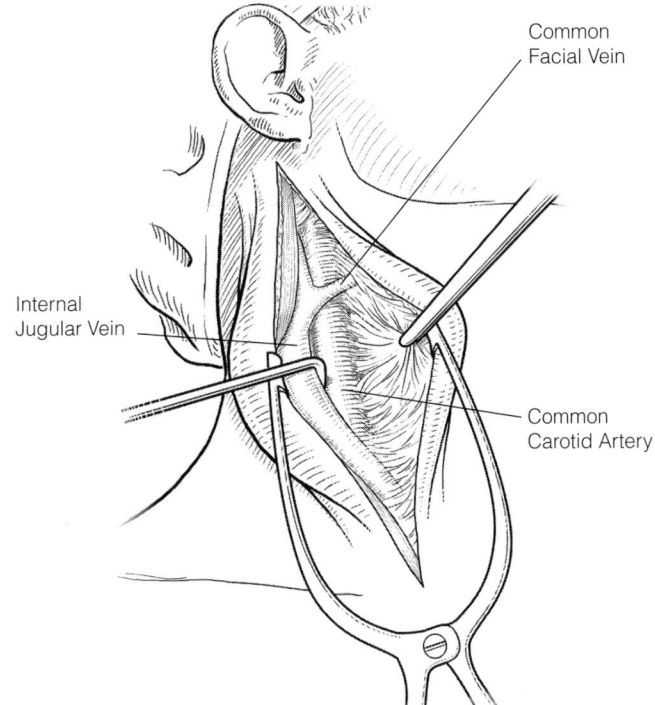

Figure 4 **Carotid arterial procedures. After the sternocleidomastoid muscle is mobilized off the carotid sheath, the jugular vein is identified. The perivascular plane along the jugular vein is opened until the common facial vein is exposed.**

Skin flaps are raised in a subplatysmal layer, and the incision is deepened along the anterior border of the sternocleidomastoid muscle. The advantage of this alternative incision is that it may be more cosmetically acceptable; however, its inferior portion frequently crosses the neck anteriorly, which may make it more visible than an incision confined to the line of the sternocleidomastoid muscle would be. The disadvantage of this incision is that it requires the raising of skin flaps, which takes additional time and may limit the extent of any proximal exposure that may be required.

STEP 2: EXPOSURE OF CAROTID ARTERY

Once the incision through the platysmal layer has been completed, an avascular areolar plane is developed along the anterior border of the sternocleidomastoid muscle for the full length of the incision so as to expose the carotid sheath. The internal jugular vein is usually the most visible vessel, and the carotid sheath is opened along this vessel's anterior border. The common facial vein, which drains into the internal jugular vein, is a relatively constant landmark. Because the common facial vein is the venous analogue of the external carotid artery, it can generally be used as a guide to the position of the carotid bifurcation [see Figure 4]. On occasion, a patient has several accessory facial veins instead of a single common facial vein. The common facial vein or the accessory facial veins are then divided between ligatures so that the jugular vein can be retracted laterally. The common carotid artery and the carotid bifurcation lie immediately beneath the divided facial veins.

At this point, care must be taken to look for the vagus nerve. This nerve is usually located posterior to the common carotid artery, but it is sometimes rotated into a more superficial position. Another important neurologic structure in this area is the ansa cervicalis, which is formed by the junction of fibers from the hypoglossal (12th cranial) nerve and fibers from the first cervical nerve and which continues inferiorly as a single trunk, providing innervation to the strap muscles. This nerve should be spared if possible, but it can be divided without significant sequelae if it interferes with optimal exposure of the carotid bifurcation. One convenient method of separating the nerve from the artery is to divide the fibers running from the first cervical nerve to the ansa cervicalis; when this is done, the nerve is readily mobilized and retracted anteriorly away from the carotid artery.

The perivascular plane of the common carotid artery is then entered, and the common carotid artery is circumferentially mobilized. The common carotid artery is palpated against a right-angle clamp to determine the proximal extent of the atherosclerotic plaque. If possible, the common carotid artery should be mobilized proximal to the plaque until a circumferentially soft portion of that vessel is reached. During mobilization, the vagus nerve should be identified in its usual location posterior to the vessel and carefully protected; this nerve sometimes spirals anterior to the carotid artery as the vessel is dissected distally.

Dissection is then extended distally toward the carotid bifurcation and continued along both the internal and external carotid arteries. Excessive manipulation of the area around the carotid bifurcation must be avoided. In particular, it is important to be careful around the bulb of the internal carotid artery: this is where the majority of the plaque will be located, and manipulation can easily dislodge plaque or thromboembolic material. With exposure of the carotid bifurcation, the hypoglossal nerve may come into view. Care should be taken not to injure this nerve, though it may have to be mobilized to permit sufficient distal exposure of the internal carotid artery.

Common Facial Vein

Internal Jugular Vein

Common Carotid Artery

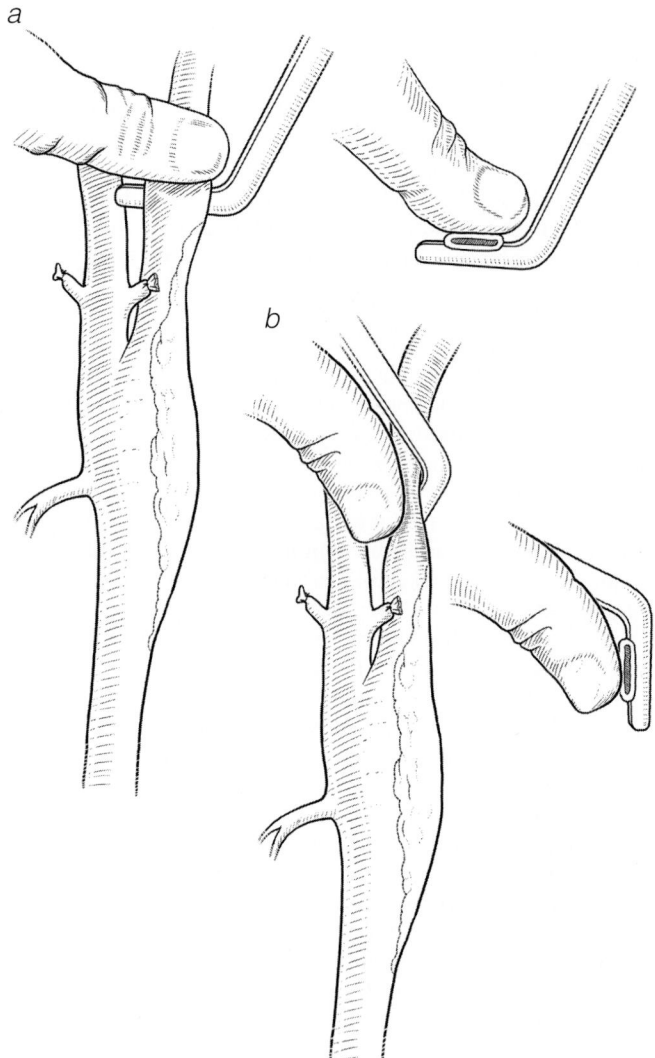

Figure 5 Carotid arterial procedures. After the common carotid artery and the internal and external carotid arteries have been mobilized, the internal carotid artery is palpated against a right-angle clamp in at least two planes (*a, b*) to confirm that the artery has been freed beyond the end point of the plaque.

Next, dissection is continued distally beyond the bulb of the internal carotid artery to a point where the internal carotid artery is normal. At this point, the relevant portion of the vessel is circumferentially mobilized and palpated against a right-angle clamp in at least two planes to confirm that the atheromatous plaque does not reach up to the level of the proposed clamping [*see Figure 5*]. Once this is accomplished, the external carotid artery is mobilized beyond the end point of plaque extension in a similar manner.

If the patient has a high carotid bifurcation or if the plaque in the internal carotid artery extends further distally than usual, a more extensive exposure of the carotid bifurcation, the internal carotid artery, or both is required. To provide such exposure, the skin incision is extended all the way to the mastoid process. The sternocleidomastoid muscle is fully mobilized up to the mastoid process, with care taken to look for the spinal portion of the accessory (11th cranial) nerve as it enters the sternocleidomastoid muscle on the medial surface. With the sternocleidomastoid muscle fully mobilized and retractors in place, the internal carotid artery can then be further exposed.

The jugular vein is mobilized up toward the base of the skull, with care taken to look for additional accessory facial branches, which must be divided between ligatures so that the jugular vein can be fully mobilized and moved posteriorly. The perivascular plane of the internal carotid artery is carefully defined, and the artery is gently mobilized; the more distal portion of the internal carotid artery can then be mobilized downward. If the vessel is still insufficiently mobile, then the nerve to the carotid body and the ascending pharyngeal artery within the crotch between the internal and external carotid arteries are mobilized and divided between ligatures. These two structures often serve as a de facto suspensory ligament for the carotid bulb; dividing them allows the carotid bifurcation to drop down and permits further downward traction of the internal carotid artery as the vessel is gently mobilized distally [*see Figure 6*].

Once the internal carotid artery is further exposed distally and the hypoglossal nerve is mobilized along its vertical portion and moved anteriorly, the posterior belly of the digastric muscle is encountered. An areolar plane is developed posteriorly and superiorly along the inferior margin of the posterior belly of the digastric muscle, allowing the muscle to be mobilized anteriorly to yield additional exposure of the internal carotid artery. If the

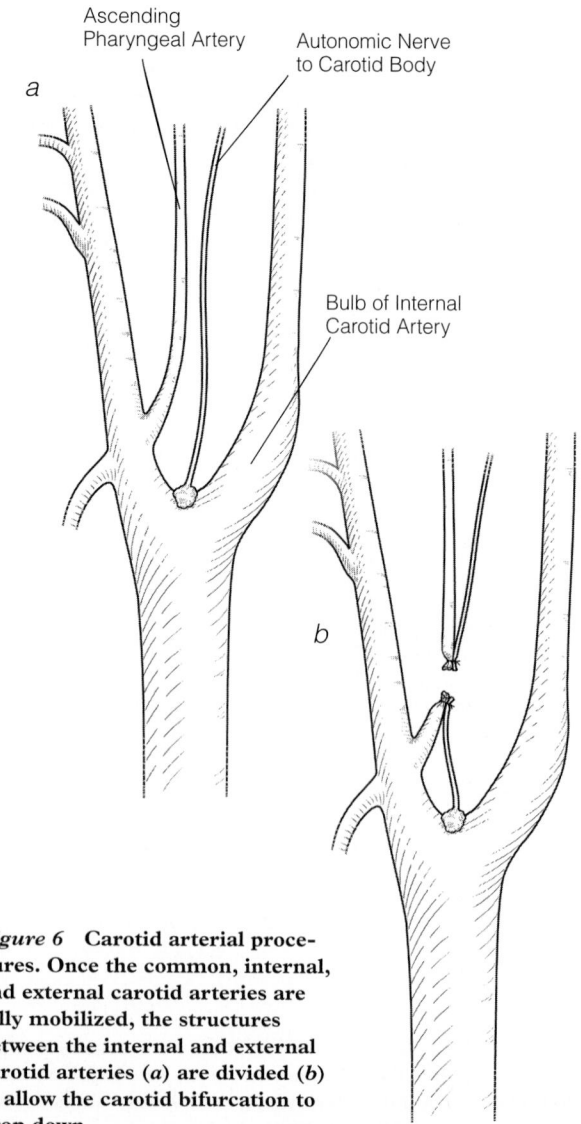

Figure 6 Carotid arterial procedures. Once the common, internal, and external carotid arteries are fully mobilized, the structures between the internal and external carotid arteries (*a*) are divided (*b*) to allow the carotid bifurcation to drop down.

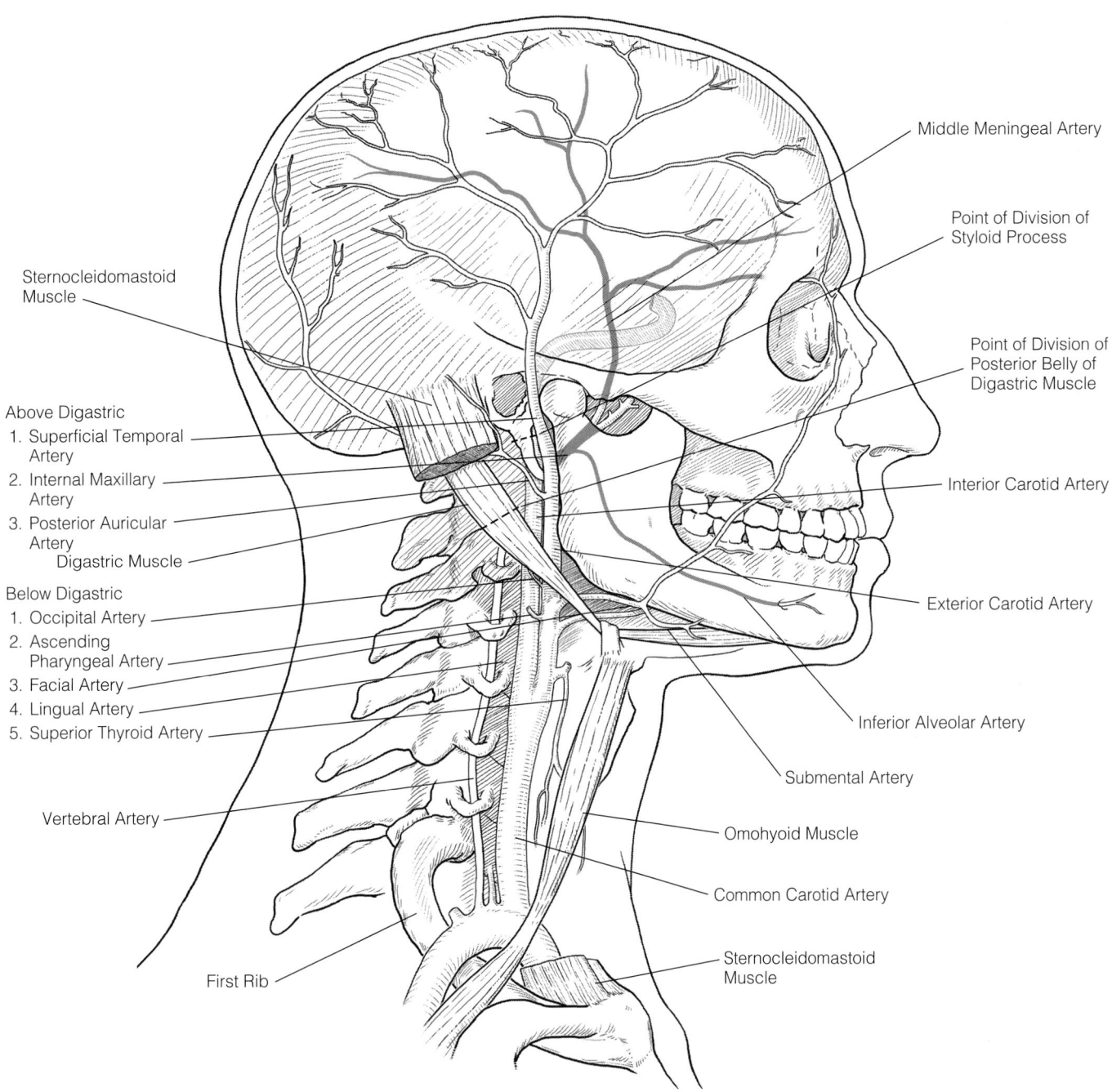

Figure 7 **Carotid arterial procedures. Division of the posterior belly of the digastric muscle yields additional exposure of the internal carotid artery. If the internal carotid artery must be mobilized all the way to the base of the skull, further distal exposure is obtained by separating the attachments of the ligaments to the styloid process and dividing the styloid process.**

resulting exposure is not sufficient, the muscle may be carefully encircled with a right-angle clamp and divided [*see Figure 7*]. In those relatively uncommon cases in which even further distal exposure is required, the styloid process is palpated and the muscular and ligamentous attachments to the styloid process divided, so that the styloid process can be exposed with a periosteal elevator. Once the styloid process has been completely freed of its muscular and ligamentous attachments and the cranial nerves in the vicinity have been identified and carefully protected, the styloid process is cut close to the base of the skull [*see Figure 7*]. This step yields optimal exposure of the internal carotid artery all the way to the base of the skull.

Additional adjunctive measures for more extensive exposure of the internal carotid artery have been described. These include subluxation or dislocation of the mandible,[8] wiring of the mandible into a subluxed position, and division of the ramus of the mandible with rotation of the mandible away from the base of the skull. In my view, these measures are unnecessary, provided that the sternocleidomastoid muscle and the jugular vein have been adequately mobilized, the plane around the internal carotid artery has been developed, and the carotid bifurcation has been released.

A significant risk associated with extended exposure of the internal carotid artery is possible injury to the vagus nerve, the accessory nerve, or the hypoglossal nerve. Retraction of the vagus nerve may produce either temporary or permanent vocal cord palsy, and extensive retraction of or injury to the hypoglossal nerve causes denervation of the ipsilateral side of the tongue, manifested by tongue deviation to the ipsilateral side on protrusion or difficulty with mastication or swallowing. In addition, posterior exposure of a high carotid bifurcation may result in injury to branches of the glossopharyngeal (ninth cranial) nerve.

A common error in carotid artery mobilization is failure to recognize that the plaque in the internal carotid artery extends beyond the upper limit of the arterial exposure. It is far better to anticipate this problem before clamping and opening the artery than to discover it afterward and be forced to mobilize the vessel after it has been clamped. Once the common carotid and internal carotid arteries have been mobilized sufficiently, they are encircled with umbilical tapes; Rumel tourniquets are used if an internal shunt is required or desired.

STEP 3: CEREBRAL CIRCULATORY SUPPORT

Clamping of the carotid artery necessarily results in interruption of blood flow through the vessel. Patients who have good collateral circulation via the contralateral carotid artery or the vertebral arteries generally (though not always) tolerate the temporary interruption of flow through the clamped artery well.[9] Patients who have inadequate collateral blood flow require cerebral circulatory support, usually in the form of placement of an internal shunt. There are three basic approaches to shunt use: (1) routine use of an internal shunt, (2) selective use of an internal shunt, and (3) routine avoidance of shunting in an attempt to minimize clamp time.

Shunting Options

Routine shunting In approximately 10% of patients undergoing carotid artery surgery, collateral blood flow is inadequate and temporary use of an indwelling shunt is necessary to prevent brain damage. In the remaining 90%, collateral blood flow is adequate and clamping generally well tolerated, and shunting is therefore unnecessary. Clearly, routine use of an internal shunt takes care of the 10% of patients who require shunts. Its disadvantage is that it is an additional procedure that carries its own complications, to which not only the 10% of patients who require shunting but also the 90% who do not are subjected. The potential complications associated with placement of a shunt include intimal injury (including the raising of an intimal flap), atheroma embolization (if atheromatous material is scooped up during shunt placement), and air embolization (if air bubbles are trapped within the shunt and not recognized).

Selective shunting Selective placement of a shunt has an advantage over routine placement in that the procedure and its potential complications are limited to the 10% of patients who actually require a shunt. Its main disadvantage is that the methods used to identify patients who require shunting may not be entirely reliable.

Selective identification of patients who require shunting can be accomplished in several ways. The most direct—and perhaps safest—method is to employ local or cervical block anesthesia so that the effect of temporary carotid clamping can be assessed in a conscious patient; if clamping leads to a neurologic deficit, then the patient clearly requires an internal shunt. Other methods of identifying patients who require a shunt make use of techniques such as continuous electroencephalographic monitoring, measurement of somatosensory evoked potential, and monitoring of middle cerebral blood flow with transcranial Doppler ultrasonography.

A useful method of determining the adequacy of collateral cere-

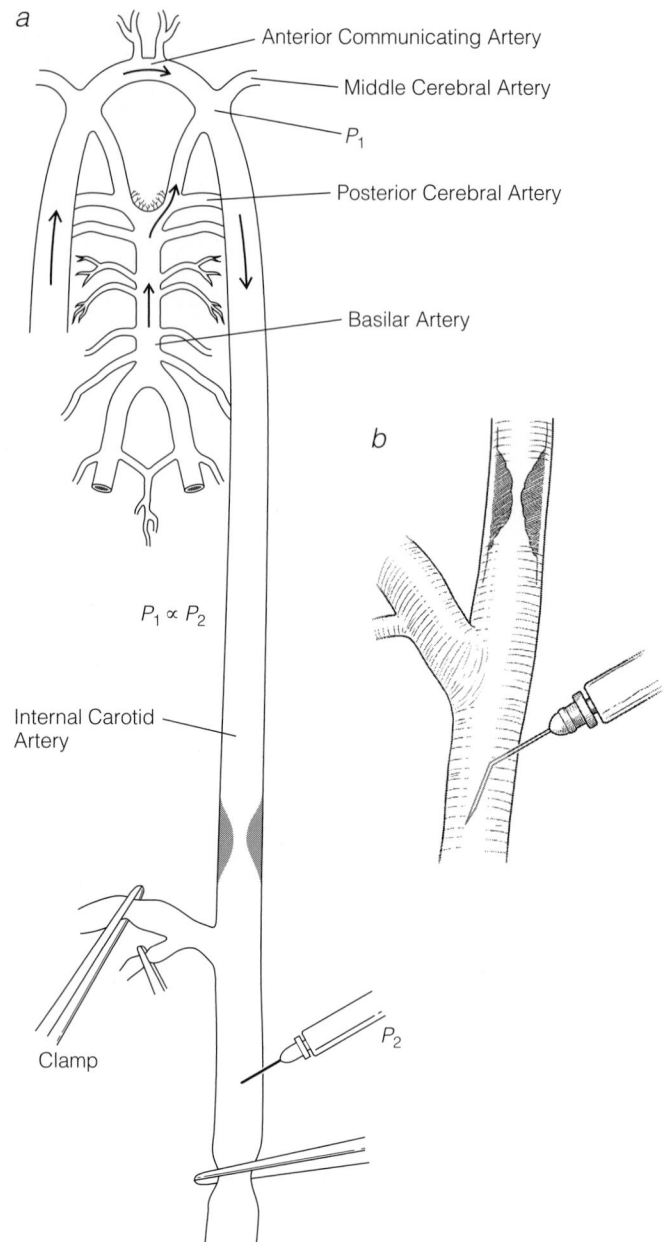

Figure 8 Carotid arterial procedures. (*a*) Shown is a graphic representation of the measurement of internal carotid artery back-pressure. (*b*) The needle is bent at a 45° angle before being inserted into the common carotid artery.

bral blood flow is measurement of back-pressure in the internal carotid artery.[10] Back-pressure has been shown to be a good index of the adequacy of collateral blood flow, and it correlates well with the safety of temporary clamping and thus with the necessity of placing an internal shunt. Back-pressure is measured by placing into the common carotid artery a needle that is connected to pressure tubing and a pressure transducer. The tip of the needle is bent at a 45° angle. Systemic blood pressure is measured, and clamps are placed on the common carotid artery proximal to the needle and on the external carotid artery. The residual pressure in the common carotid artery, which is in continuity with the internal carotid artery, is then allowed to equilibrate; the resulting pressure reading represents internal carotid artery back-pressure [*see Figure 8*]. It has been determined that patients with back-pressures high-

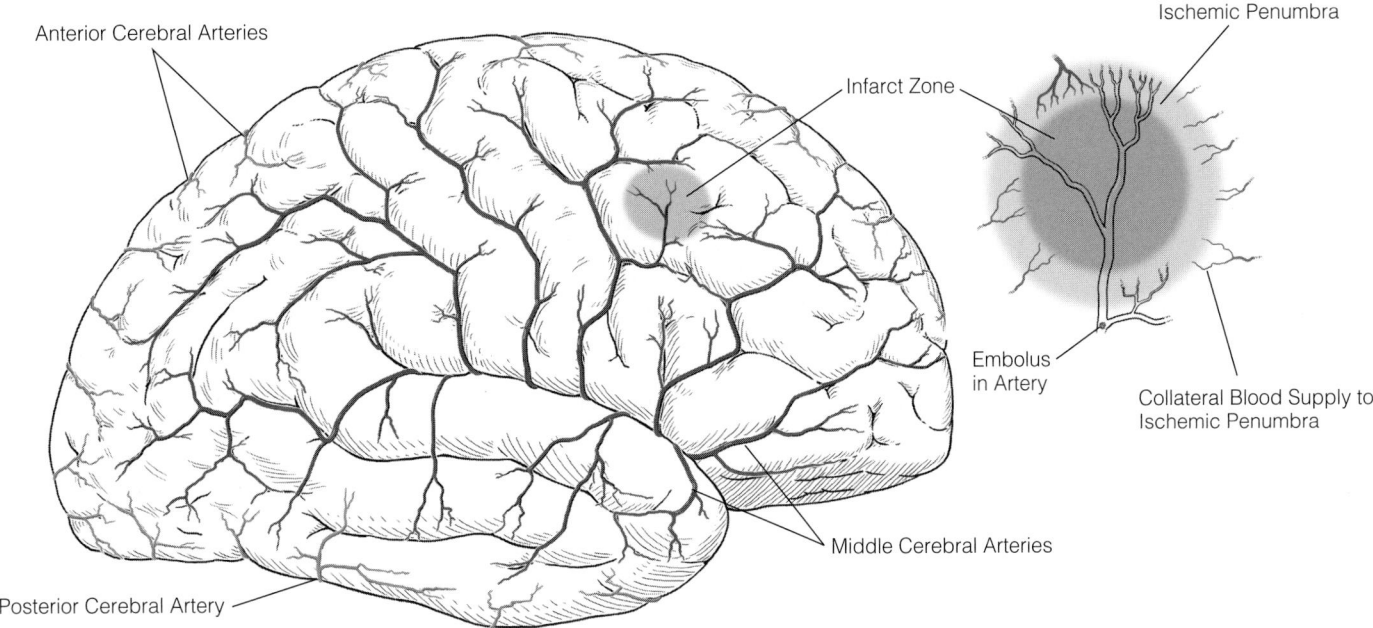

Figure 9 **Carotid arterial procedures. When a thromboembolic fragment occludes a cortical arterial branch, a central infarct zone develops, surrounded by an ischemic zone that derives some residual blood supply from collateral vessels. In this zone, known as the ischemic penumbra, the residual blood supply is sufficient to maintain viability.**

er than 25 mm Hg can tolerate temporary clamping without incurring brain damage.

The utility of selective shunting in appropriate settings notwithstanding, routine shunting is recommended for patients who have previously had a stroke, regardless of the degree of neurologic recovery. In these patients, a central area of cerebral infarction is surrounded by a zone of relatively ischemic tissue—the so-called ischemic penumbra. The ischemic penumbra is made up of live and potentially functional brain tissue, but its viability is highly dependent on maximization of cerebral perfusion pressure through collateral channels. Accordingly, any interruption of carotid circulation, regardless of the degree of collateral circulation present, may threaten the ischemic penumbra and extend the infarct [*see Figure 9*]. In my opinion, all CEA patients with prior strokes should receive shunts on a routine basis.

Routine avoidance of shunting The advantage of routinely avoiding the use of shunts is that the technical issues and potential complications associated with the additional procedure are avoided entirely. The disadvantage is that unshunted patients with poor collateral blood flow may sustain ischemic brain damage, particularly if the clamp time turns out to be longer than was anticipated.

Technique of Shunt Placement

Internal shunts must be placed with great care if shunt-associated complications are to be avoided. Of the various shunts currently available, I prefer the Javid shunt, which is tapered, has smooth leading edges, and possesses external bulbous circumferential extensions that permit it to be held in place with a circumferential Rumel tourniquet, thereby minimizing the chances of inadvertent dislodgment. Optimal placement of an internal shunt may be achieved by means of the following steps [*see Figure 10*].

After the patient has been adequately heparinized and the artery clamped and opened, the distal portion of the internal shunt is placed into the internal carotid artery. A clamp is placed

on the shunt and briefly opened to allow back-bleeding; good back-bleeding confirms that the shunt is lying free in the lumen of the internal carotid artery. The shunt is then secured by tightening a Rumel tourniquet, and the bulbous portion of the shunt is engaged to prevent dislodgment.

Next, the proximal portion of the shunt is placed into the common carotid artery. As this is done, the clamp is removed from the shunt so that backflow from the shunt will dislodge any loose material and air within the common carotid artery. The shunt is then reclamped, and the clamp is removed from the common carotid artery as the proximal portion of the shunt is passed into that vessel.

When the proximal portion of the shunt is in the proper position in the common carotid artery, it is secured by tightening a Rumel tourniquet on the vessel. The clamp on the shunt is then slowly opened so that the surgeon can observe flow through the translucent device and thus verify that no solid particles or air bubbles are passing through it. Because the shunt is relatively long, the surgeon has a reasonable amount of time in which to observe flow. If any particles or air bubbles are identified, the shunt can be quickly clamped, removed from the common carotid artery, and back-bled, and the procedure can then be repeated.

Once the shunt is secured in place and open, its length and redundancy allow it to be easily manipulated medially and laterally; endarterectomy can then be performed without the encumbrance of an inlying shunt.

STEP 4: RECONSTRUCTION OPTIONS

There are four principal reconstructions involving the common carotid artery and the carotid bifurcation: (1) conventional open CEA with either patch angioplasty or primary closure, (2) eversion endarterectomy, (3) reconstruction for proximal lesions of the common carotid artery, and (4) reconstruction for recurrent stenosis with resection of the carotid bifurcation and grafting.

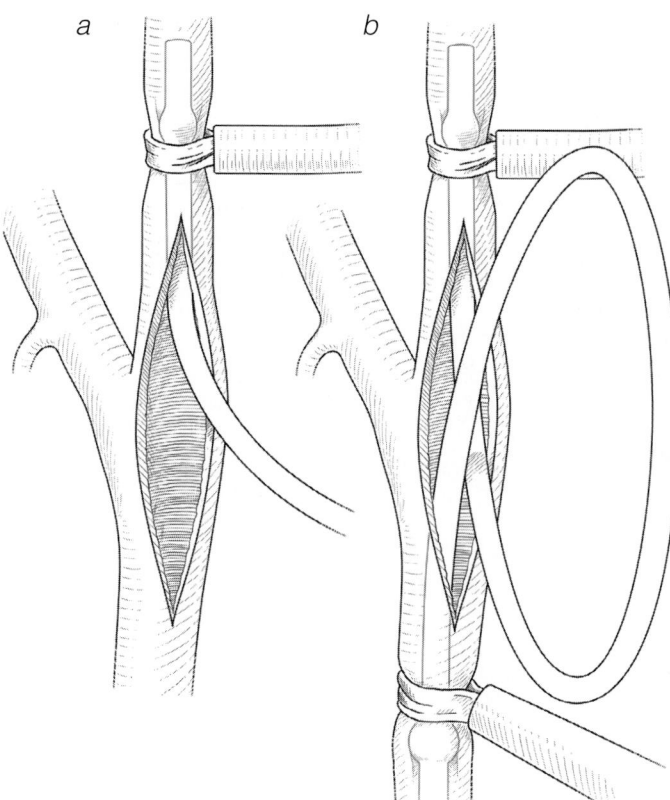

Figure 10 **Carotid arterial procedures. Shown is the technique of shunt placement, first distally (*a*) and then proximally (*b*).**

Open Carotid Endarterectomy

Once the carotid bifurcation has been fully mobilized both proximal and distal to the lesion, systemic anticoagulation with heparin is initiated. I generally give 5,000 units, an amount that is sufficient to produce adequate anticoagulation for the duration of carotid clamping but is not large enough to necessitate heparin reversal on completion of the operation. If the patient has been receiving clopidogrel—particularly if clopidogrel was given in combination with aspirin—the heparin dose must be reduced to allow adequate hemostasis to be achieved after reconstruction. In these cases, I usually limit the heparin dose to 3,000 units. If internal carotid artery back-pressure is to be used to determine whether the patient requires an internal shunt, then it is measured at this time. If cerebral electrical activity is to be the determinant, then the internal, external, and common carotid arteries are clamped and electrical activity is monitored (e.g., via EEG) with the clamps in place. If electrical changes are noted with clamping, an internal shunt is required.

Arteriotomy The common carotid artery and the carotid bifurcation are rotated so as to be positioned for an arteriotomy that begins on the common carotid artery and extends through the bulb of the internal carotid artery to a point 180° opposite the flow divider [see Figure 11]. This incision effectively bivalves the carotid bulb, thus making possible a more accurate primary or patch closure. The arteriotomy continues through the plaque and extends well up into the internal carotid artery, beyond the visible end point of the atherosclerotic plaque.

Plaque removal A dissection plane separating the atherosclerotic intima from the media and the adventitia is then developed with a sharp-bladed dissector. As a rule, it is easiest to begin

the endarterectomy at the point where the plaque is bulkiest. At this point, the medial fibers are usually gone, but as the dissection continues both proximally and distally, more normal medial tissue may be seen. It is important to develop the dissection plane between the intima and the media if possible because doing so permits the creation of a feathered end point distally as dissection proceeds into a relatively normal portion of the internal carotid artery [see Figure 12]. If the dissection plane is between the media and the adventitia, a feathered end point is much harder to achieve. Failure to achieve a feathered end point often results in a sharp shelf at the internal carotid artery level, which increases the risk of subsequent intimal dissection when blood flow is restored.

Once the dissection plane is complete on one side of the arteriotomy at the level of the common carotid artery, a right-angle clamp is gently inserted into the plane and advanced through it to the opposite side of the arteriotomy, thereby separating the plaque from the arterial wall around the entire circumference of the vessel. The clamp is then gently spread and brought downward to complete the circumferential dissection of the plaque proximally. The proximal end point of plaque dissection is obtained by cutting the intima with a No. 15 blade.

With the same depth of dissection now existing on both sides of the open common carotid artery, dissection then continues distally up to the carotid bifurcation. At this point, the plaque within the external carotid artery is carefully separated in a circumferential fashion. This is usually done by using a sharp mosquito clamp until all of the plaque has been separated from the vessel wall and dissection has reached normal intima. The freed plaque is gently grasped with the opened mosquito clamp, traction is applied, and

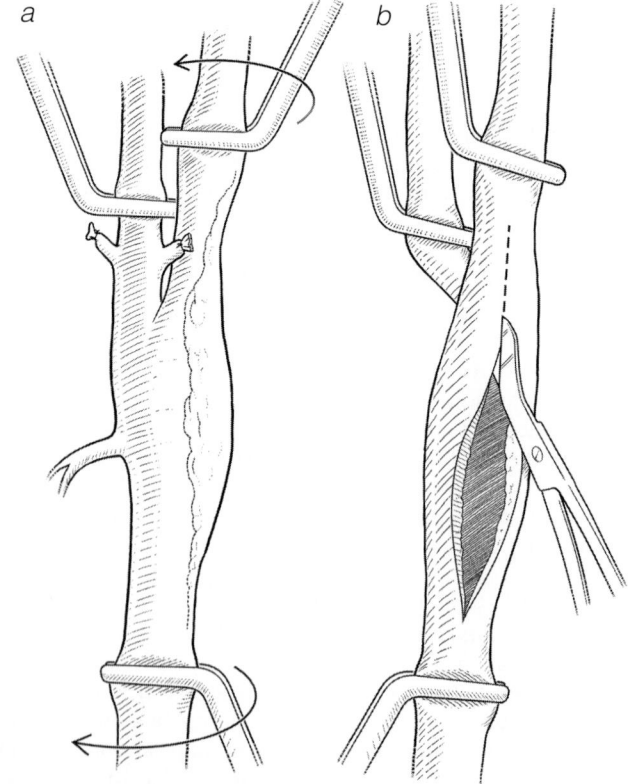

Figure 11 **Carotid arterial procedures: open endarterectomy. Clamps are applied to the common, internal, and external carotid arteries, and the structures are rotated (*a*) so that an arteriotomy can be made in the common carotid artery 180° opposite the flow divider (*b*).**

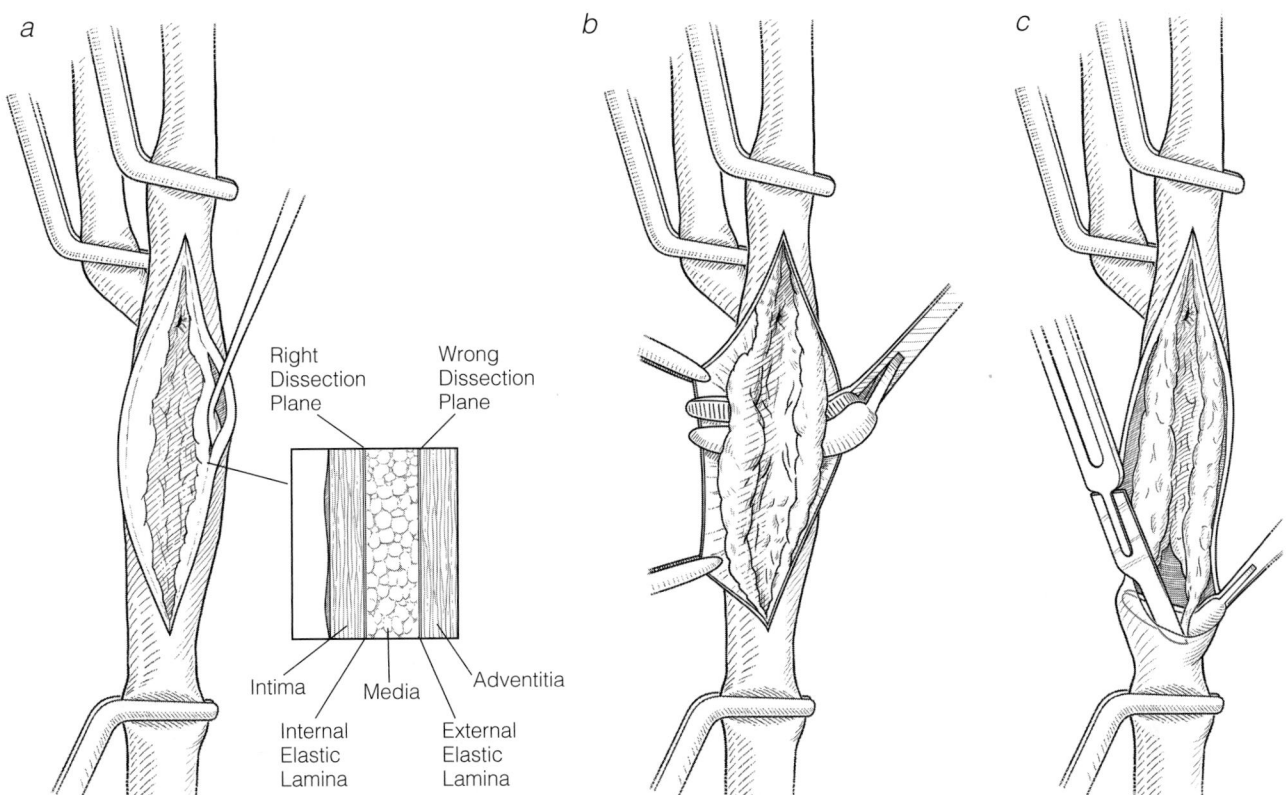

Figure 12 Carotid arterial procedures: open endarterectomy. (*a*) Dissection is started where plaque is thickest. Often, medial fibers are completely gone here. Dissection proceeds both proximally and distally along one side, and more normal medial tissue may be found. Development of a plane between intima and media, if possible, is valuable for creating a feathered end point distally. (*b*) Once dissection is complete on one side, the same plane is established on the opposite side. (*c*) The end point of proximal dissection is established by sharp division of plaque against the clamp.

the distal end point of plaque dissection in the external carotid artery is obtained.

Dissection then continues up the internal carotid artery, with care taken to leave normal intima behind. Often, the plaque becomes a relatively narrow tongue of atheroma on the posterior wall of the internal carotid artery. If the edge of the atheromatous plaque is followed to its end, a tapered, feathered end point can be achieved.

Irrigation and clearing of debris   After removal of the specimen, the intimectomized surface is vigorously irrigated with heparinized saline. Any medial debris present is carefully removed. The distal end point is irrigated to determine whether there is a residual flap that might lead to subsequent intimal dissection; if there is a flap, it is carefully removed. If there is a sharp shelf at the distal end point, it is usually an indication that the endarterectomy has not been carried far enough distally. When this is the case, the arteriotomy should be lengthened so that the endarterectomy can be extended to a point where the intima is completely normal. If the patient has a very high carotid bifurcation, very distal plaque, or both and further dissection is impeded by the base of the skull, it may be necessary to secure the distal end point with tacking sutures. Tacking sutures should be used only in exceptional circumstances because their use may lead to healing abnormalities or to the presence of platelet aggregate material that can cause thromboembolic or occlusive complications.

Once the intimectomized surface is completely clear of debris, the lumen of the external carotid artery should be visually inspect-

ed to confirm that all overlying dissected intima has been cleared. Any residual dissected intima can be gently teased out with a mosquito clamp. Once the vessel is completely clear, preparation is made for closure of the arteriotomy.

Closure of arteriotomy   If the arteriotomy is relatively short and extends only up to the central portion of the bulb of the internal carotid artery, it can usually be closed primarily with a continuous 6-0 polypropylene suture. Placing very small stitches close together in the internal carotid artery should minimize the risk of vessel narrowing.

If the vessel is relatively small or the arteriotomy was extended well up on the internal carotid artery to ensure a complete endarterectomy, the arteriotomy should be closed with a patch angioplasty. Of the several patch options available, the basic choice is between a prosthetic patch and an autogenous patch composed of a segment of saphenous vein obtained from an extremity. The relative merits of autogenous and prosthetic patches have been extensively debated in the literature, but no definitive conclusions have been reached. One of the disadvantages of an autogenous patch is that surgeons tend to use the entire open portion of the saphenous vein, which then dilates further under arterial pressure, leading to an artery of aneurysmal proportions. Another disadvantage is the potential for patch blowout, which, though rare, has been reported in several series. The main disadvantage of a prosthetic patch is the risk of infection, but this is extremely low.

At present, it would appear that a prosthetic patch is at least as acceptable as an autogenous patch, and the prosthetic patch has

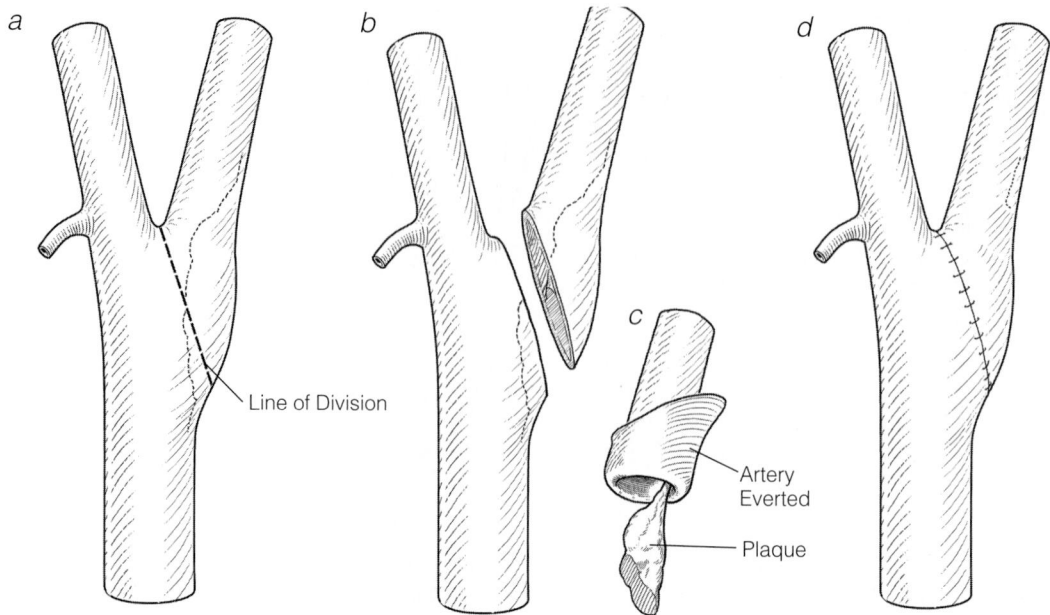

Figure 13 **Carotid arterial procedures: eversion endarterectomy. (*a, b*) The internal carotid artery is divided from the common carotid artery in an oblique line. (*c*) The divided internal carotid artery is everted on itself so that it can be separated from the underlying plaque. Eversion proceeds distally until the plaque end point is encountered, and the plaque is removed from the internal carotid artery. Proximal endarterectomy of the common carotid artery and endarterectomy of the external carotid artery are then carried out. (*d*) Once all of the plaque has been removed, the internal carotid artery is reverted and an end-to-side anastomosis is fashioned between the common carotid artery opening and the internal carotid artery.**

an additional advantage in that there is no need to remove a normal saphenous vein segment from an extremity. Prosthetic patches can be composed of either fabric or polytetrafluoroethylene (PTFE). Fabric patches now come impregnated with either collagen or gelatin to make them leakproof; PTFE patches do not leak on the surface, but they are prone to leakage at suture needle puncture sites.

Patch size is a crucial consideration: it is important that the patch be neither too wide nor too narrow. If the patch is too narrow, it will not provide the additional material needed to restore the carotid bifurcation to a normal diameter. If the patch is too wide, it will provide too much additional material and create what virtually amounts to a carotid aneurysm; this would represent a significant disadvantage to the patient in terms of flow dynamics and the risk of producing laminated thrombus in the most dilated portion of the carotid bulb. My preference is to use a 6.0 mm wide collagen-impregnated fabric patch for patch angioplasty.

Whichever patch is selected is cut to length, beveled at each end, and sewn in place with a continuous 6-0 polypropylene suture.

Before completion of the closure, the internal carotid artery and the external carotid artery are back-bled and the common carotid artery flushed. The arteriotomy is then completely closed. Removing the clamp on the internal carotid artery allows blood flow to fill the carotid bulb and permits one last internal flush. The origin of the internal carotid artery is then occluded with a vascular forceps, and the clamps are removed first from the external carotid artery and then from the common carotid artery to allow resumption of blood flow. After several heartbeats, the forceps on the origin of the internal carotid artery is removed, and blood flow through the internal carotid artery is restored. There may be some leakage of blood along the suture line, which can usually be controlled with the placement of thrombin-soaked absorbable gelatin

sponge. If any obvious defect is noted between sutures, an additional stitch should be placed.

Eversion Endarterectomy

Eversion endarterectomy was designed and developed to eliminate the need for a suture line on the internal carotid artery, in the hope that doing so would reduce the incidence of myointimal hyperplasia and consequent restenosis. There is evidence to suggest that the use of eversion endarterectomy has led to some reduction in the incidence of myointimal hyperplasia, but the data are controversial and certainly are not conclusive. Nonetheless, the technique may well have merit, and it should be a part of the vascular surgeon's armamentarium.

Besides the avoidance of a suture line on the internal carotid artery, the advantages of eversion endarterectomy include the simple end-to-side anastomotic closure and the possibility of managing a redundant internal carotid artery by moving it down the common carotid artery. One disadvantage is the potential difficulty of achieving an end point in cases in which the bifurcation is high or plaque extends well up the internal carotid artery toward the base of the skull. Another disadvantage arises with patients who require an internal shunt, in that it is not possible to keep an internal shunt in place for the entire duration of an eversion endarterectomy. Yet another disadvantage is that the distal end point cannot be viewed as clearly as it can in open endarterectomy. A fourth disadvantage is that eversion endarterectomy is poorly suited to cases in which the internal carotid artery is relatively small and contracted and thus better treated with patch angioplasty.

Eversion and plaque dissection After the carotid bifurcation is fully mobilized, the internal, external, and common carotid arteries are clamped. A circumferential incision is placed in an oblique fashion at the junction of the common carotid artery and the bulb of the internal carotid artery to permit division of the bulbous portion of the internal carotid artery from the common carotid [see Figure 13]. The edges of the adventitia of the bulb of the internal carotid artery are grasped, and the outer layers of the vessel wall are gradually everted away from the plaque within the artery. Eversion continues cephalad until it reaches the distal end point of the atherosclerotic lesion, which is marked by the presence of a thin, filmy intima that clearly separates with the specimen, leaving normal vessel behind. The plaque in the common carotid artery and the external carotid artery is then removed in the traditional manner; the opening in the common carotid artery may be extended proximally to facilitate this portion of the endarterectomy.

Reversion and reanastomosis The internal carotid artery is then reverted to its normal anatomic position, and an anastomosis between the end of the divided bulb of the internal carotid artery and the common carotid artery is fashioned with a continuous 6-0 polypropylene suture. If the internal carotid artery is redundant [see Special Considerations, below], the arteriotomy on the common carotid artery is extended proximally and the arteriotomy on the medial aspect of the bulb of the internal carotid artery is extended distally so that the carotid bifurcation may be advanced between the internal and common carotid arteries to eliminate the redundancy.

Reconstruction for Proximal Lesions of Common Carotid Artery

Lesions at the origin of the common carotid artery, either at the level of the aortic arch (in the case of the left common carotid artery) or at the innominate bifurcation (in the case of the right common carotid artery), are relatively rare but do occur. Such lesions may arise either in isolation or in combination with carotid bifurcation disease. They can be managed by dividing the common carotid artery and transposing it to the adjacent subclavian artery, provided that there is no occlusive disease in the ipsilateral subclavian artery.

Exposure and mobilization If the lesion at the origin of the common carotid artery is the only one being treated, both the common carotid artery and the subclavian artery should be exposed through a supraclavicular incision that parallels the clavicle. If a carotid bifurcation lesion is present in conjunction with the lesion at the origin of the common carotid artery, the supraclavicular incision is supplemented with a vertical incision along the sternocleidomastoid muscle to permit exposure of the carotid bifurcation. Exposure of the bifurcation has already been addressed (see above); accordingly, I focus here on exposure of the subclavian artery and the proximal common carotid artery.

A supraclavicular incision is placed approximately 1.5 fingerbreadths above the clavicle and centered over the lateral head of the sternocleidomastoid muscle. The lateral head of the sternocleidomastoid muscle is divided, and the scalene triangle is defined. The scalene fat pad is mobilized off the anterior scalene muscle. The phrenic nerve is identified, mobilized off the scalene muscle, and gently retracted. A plane is developed with gentle dissection between the posterior portion of the anterior scalene muscle and the underlying subclavian artery, and the anterior scalene muscle is divided. Division of the muscle exposes the underlying subclavian artery, a sufficient length of which can then be mobilized in the perivascular plane to permit an anastomosis.

The jugular vein is identified at the medial aspect of the incision and mobilized anteriorly and medially to expose the common

carotid artery. The vagus nerve is identified and carefully protected. The common carotid artery is then mobilized both proximally and distally; proximal mobilization should extend as far behind the sternoclavicular junction as the surgeon can comfortably manage.

Transection and anastomosis The common carotid artery is clamped proximally and distally, then divided; the proximal portion of the vessel is oversewn. The transected common carotid artery is brought posterior to the jugular vein in the vicinity of the subclavian artery. The subclavian artery is clamped proximally and distally, a longitudinal arteriotomy is made, and a small ellipse of subclavian arterial tissue is removed. The end of the common carotid artery is then sewn to the side of the subclavian artery with a continuous 6-0 polypropylene suture.

Before completion, the vessels are back-bled and flushed. Once the anastomosis is complete, blood flow is restored, first to the distal subclavian artery and then to the common carotid artery.

Reconstruction for Recurrent Carotid Stenosis

For an initial recurrence of carotid stenosis that primarily results from myointimal hyperplasia, conversion to a patch angioplasty is generally the best treatment. For second or third recurrences or for recurrences that develop in spite of patch angioplasty, resection of the carotid bifurcation with interposition grafting between the common carotid artery and the normal distal internal carotid artery is the best treatment.

Exposure and mobilization Exposure of a carotid bifurcation for treatment of recurrent carotid stenosis can be challenging. The initial skin incision is reopened, and dissection is carried down through the scar tissue to the common carotid artery. The common carotid artery is sharply dissected from the surrounding scar tissue, with the dissection plane kept close to the adventitia to minimize the risk of injury to the vagus nerve and the hypoglossal nerve. Once the common carotid artery has been adequately mobilized, dissection is carried distally to include the carotid bifurcation and the internal carotid artery. In the course of distal dissection, care must be taken to watch for the hypoglossal nerve, which may be incorporated into the scar tissue; this structure must be carefully dissected away from the artery and protected.

Distal dissection continues beyond the end point of the previous closure of the internal carotid artery. Beyond this end point, it is usually possible to enter a previously undissected plane of the internal carotid artery; from here onward, the artery typically is soft around its circumference and is not involved in the recurrent stenosis. The external carotid artery is then mobilized sufficiently to allow the surgeon to control back-bleeding.

Conversion to patch angioplasty If the artery was originally closed primarily, an arteriotomy is made through the old suture line and carried distally through the area of stenosis and onto a relatively normal area of the internal carotid artery. Exploration of the luminal surface usually reveals a smooth, glistening neointima, and observation of the cut section of the artery reveals an area where a whitish, firm thickening of the intimal wall has occurred as a result of myointimal hyperplasia. No attempt should be made to reendarterectomize the stenotic area, because the intimal lesion is not, in fact, plaque but scar tissue. If the intima is removed, the cascade of events that led to the myointimal hyperplasia will simply be reinitiated. Accordingly, the healed intimal surface should be carefully protected. A patch angioplasty across the stenotic area, extending from the common carotid artery proximally to a relatively normal portion of the internal carotid artery distally, is usually sufficient to treat the lesion.

Resection of carotid bifurcation with interposition grafting If the stenosis is recurring for the second or third time or the artery was originally closed with a patch, the surgeon should proceed with resection and interposition grafting. In most cases, it is necessary to sacrifice the external carotid artery and oversew its origin. The internal carotid artery is divided distal to the intimal hyperplastic lesion, the common carotid artery is divided proximally, and the diseased specimen is removed.

I prefer to use 6.0 mm thin-walled PTFE for the interposition graft. The internal carotid artery distally and the common carotid artery proximally are spatulated by making vertical incisions approximately 6.0 mm in length. The PTFE graft is appropriately beveled both proximally and distally, and beveled or spatulated end-to-end anastomoses are performed, first to the internal carotid artery and then to the common carotid artery.

Before completion, the vessels are back-bled and flushed; once the anastomoses are complete, blood flow is reestablished.

Some surgeons may be tempted to use autogenous saphenous vein for the interposition graft. To use such grafts would appear, on the face of it, to be a good idea; in fact, it is a mistake. For reasons not clearly understood, the use of autogenous saphenous vein in the neck has an extremely poor track record, yielding unacceptably high rates of recurrent stenosis and occlusion in comparison with the use of prosthetic grafts.

Special Considerations

Fibromuscular dysplasia of internal carotid artery Fibromuscular dysplasia of the internal carotid artery is a congenital or acquired lesion that has been subdivided into four pathologic varieties, of which the most common is medial fibroplasia. On contrast angiography, medial fibroplasia has a characteristic appearance, resembling a string of beads in the extracranial portion of the internal carotid artery [*see Figure 14*]. A common initial manifestation is a relatively loud bruit in the neck of a young woman. Fibromuscular dysplasia can cause symptoms of monocular or hemispheric TIAs, or it may go on to cause a stroke, usually as a consequence of a dissection resulting in thrombotic occlusion. If symptoms develop, they can generally be controlled by means of antiplatelet drugs. Currently, the only indication for surgical intervention is the persistence of symptoms despite antiplatelet therapy.

Treatment of fibromuscular dysplasia has evolved over the years. The first attempts at surgical repair involved a total resection of the internal carotid artery coupled with interposition of a graft (usually composed of saphenous vein). This technique has largely been abandoned because of the extensive surgical dissection required and the substantial risk of cranial nerve injury; its only remaining application is in cases where there is associated aneurysmal dilatation in the dysplastic segment that calls for resection and graft interposition. At present, the two most popular modes of therapy both involve intraluminal dilatation with disruption of the small septa within the artery. One mode achieves intraluminal dilatation via an open approach, and the other achieves the same end via a percutaneous approach that includes balloon angioplasty. Dilatation and fracturing of the intraluminal septa often result in the release of particles of septal tissue, which in turn can lead to cerebral embolization and infarction. Consequently, an open approach, which enables the surgeon to flush out the disrupted segments, or balloon angioplasty with cerebral embolic protection is usually favored.

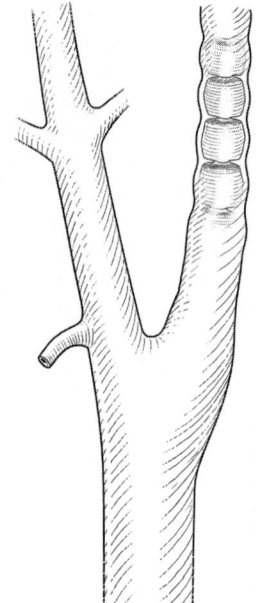

Figure 14 **Carotid arterial procedures: repair of fibromuscular dysplasia. Depicted is the so-called string of beads deformity of the cervical portion of the internal carotid artery, which is characteristic of medial fibroplasia.**

In symptomatic patients with fibromuscular dysplasia, the carotid bifurcation may be exposed in the usual manner. If there is significant redundancy of the internal carotid artery, as documented by preoperative imaging, the artery should be mobilized relatively extensively so that it can be straightened by downward traction before intraluminal dilatation is begun. If, on the other hand, the artery is relatively straight, only minimal mobilization is required. It should be kept in mind that approximately 25% of patients with fibromuscular dysplasia have associated atheromatous disease of the carotid bifurcation that must be dealt with at the time of operation. In addition, about the same number of

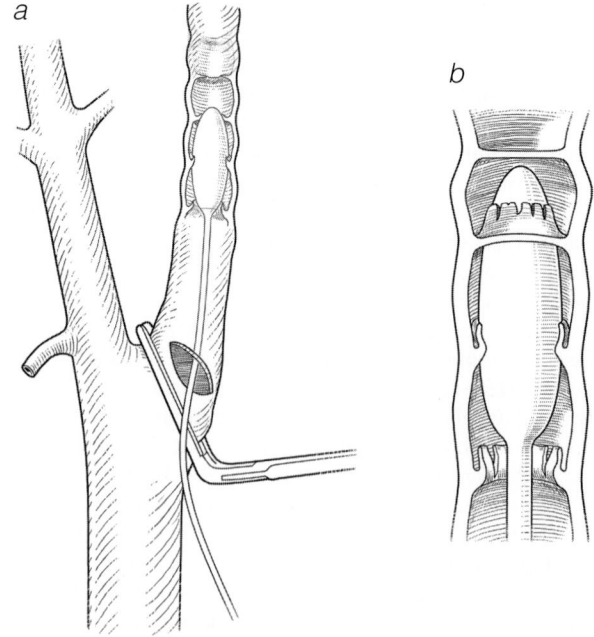

Figure 15 **Carotid arterial procedures: repair of fibromuscular dysplasia. (*a*) The proximal portion of the internal carotid bulb is clamped, a transverse arteriotomy is made, and a coronary dilator is passed into the internal carotid artery and advanced up the vessel to the base of the skull. (*b*) The small septa in the internal carotid artery are disrupted by the advancing probe.**

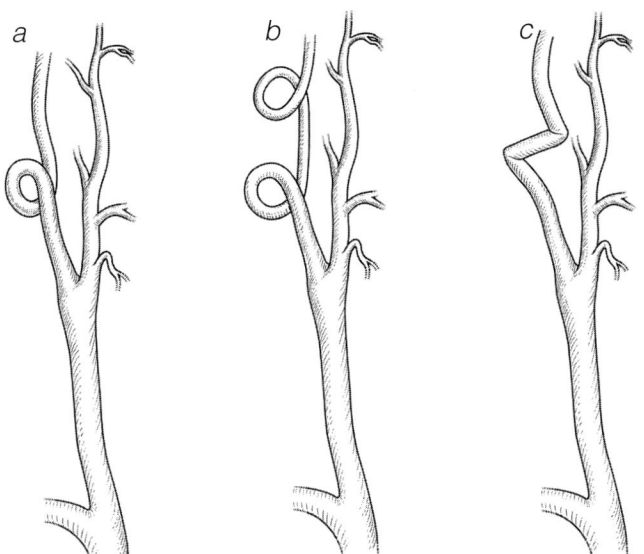

Figure 16 **Carotid arterial procedures: repair of coiling or kinking of the internal carotid artery. (*a*, *b*) Redundancy of the internal carotid artery can result in one or more 360° coils in the vessel. (*c*) Degenerative atheromatous changes of the internal carotid artery can cause elongation with associated kinking or buckling.**

patients have associated intracranial aneurysms that should be checked for by means of intracranial imaging studies.

Once the carotid bifurcation has been suitably mobilized and it has been established that no associated atheromatous plaque is present, a small transverse incision is made on the bulb of the internal carotid artery, with flow being maintained between the common and external carotid arteries. Serial intraluminal dilatations are then performed with coronary artery dilators of progressively increasing diameter [*see Figure 15*]. The first dilator (usually 2.5 mm in diameter) is passed up the carotid artery to the base of the skull under digital control. The dilator is then withdrawn, and the artery is back-bled to flush out any fractured segments. The next larger dilator (3.0 mm in diameter) is passed in a similar fashion. Dilatation is repeated with progressively larger dilators (3.5, 4.0, and possibly 4.5 mm in diameter) to complete the procedure.

The transverse arteriotomy is closed with 6-0 polypropylene suture material and flow is reestablished. A completion angiogram verifies that the dysplastic segment is fully restored.

Coiling or kinking of internal carotid artery Redundancy of the internal carotid artery, often resulting in a 360° coil of the high cervical portion of the internal carotid artery, is usually thought to be developmental in origin [*see Figure 16a*]. Elongation of the internal carotid artery, which often results in kinking of the vessel, is believed to be related to the degenerative changes that occur with aging and atherosclerosis [*see Figure 16b*]. Both of these phenomena, in and of themselves, are usually asymptomatic; exceptions occur when an atheromatous plaque develops at the apex of the coil or when kinking of the internal carotid artery is accentuated with changes in head position in a patient who depends on relatively normal blood flow through that vessel. Redundancy of the internal carotid artery often becomes a technical consideration during standard surgical treatment of a carotid bifurcation atheroma. When redundancy occurs, it must be appropriately dealt with to prevent postoperative complications.

Anticipated redundancy of the internal carotid artery at the time of carotid bifurcation endarterectomy can usually be managed with a patch angioplasty. Provided that the arteriotomy extends beyond the apex of the kink, the patch should smooth out the curvature of the redundant vessel and eliminate the kink. If it appears that internal carotid artery redundancy is greater than can be corrected by an elongated patch, then detachment of the internal carotid artery followed by eversion endarterectomy and reimplantation is indicated.

If the arteriotomy has already been closed when it becomes apparent that a kink is present, the problem may be dealt with by mobilizing the external carotid artery sufficiently and then resecting a segment of the common carotid artery and pulling down on the carotid bifurcation with a new end-to-end anastomosis to straighten the redundant internal carotid artery [*see Figure 17*]. Segmental resection of the internal carotid artery itself combined with end-to-end repair has also been described; this approach is less desirable, being more technically demanding and hence more subject to technical error.

Patients with coiling of the internal carotid artery may present a more difficult problem. If the atheromatous plaque involves only the first portion of the internal carotid artery and the vessel beyond that first portion is relatively normal up to the point where coiling begins, the surgeon can simply avoid the problem by leaving the smooth coil in place and not carrying out an extensive distal dissection. If, on the other hand, it appears that there may be plaque in the coil, then the entire coil must be dissected free, and the patient is left with a very redundant internal carotid artery that must be dealt with. Once again, the best method of managing the problem is to resect the redundant segment of the internal carotid artery, with or without eversion endarterectomy, and to reimplant the internal carotid artery onto the distal common carotid artery at the point of transection.

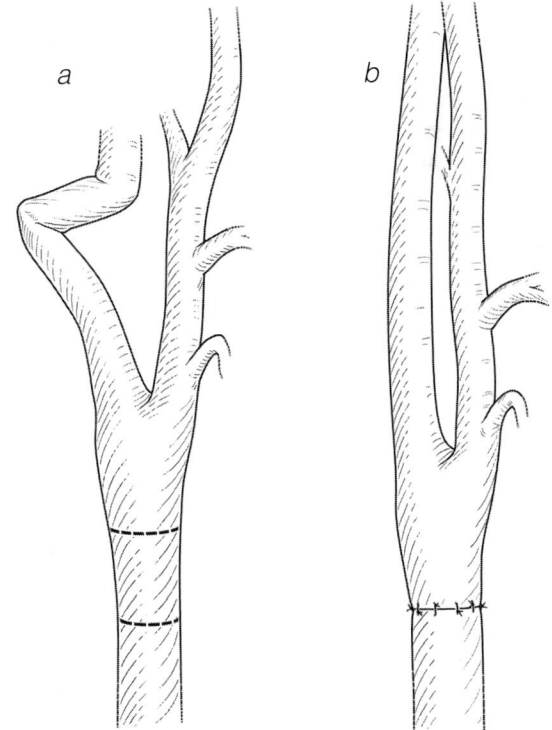

Figure 17 **Carotid arterial procedures: repair of coiling or kinking of the internal carotid artery. Kinking or redundancy of the internal carotid artery can be managed by mobilizing the external carotid artery, then resecting a segment of the common carotid artery (*a*). The surgeon can then draw down the carotid bifurcation for a new primary anastomosis (*b*).**

Upon completion of the reconstruction, a completion angiogram should be obtained to verify that the coiling or kinking has been adequately treated.

STEP 5: COMPLETION IMAGING

Given that the majority of neurologic complications after carotid artery surgery are attributable to technical error, it is imperative that the technical accuracy of the reconstruction be confirmed before the incision is closed and the patient is sent to the recovery room. There are two principal methods of determining the technical quality of the reconstruction: on-table angiography and direct-contact duplex scanning of the carotid artery. To perform either of these techniques routinely in all patients adds relatively little time to the surgical procedure and offers significant advantages to both the patient and the surgeon.[11,12]

My preferred method of confirming the quality of the reconstruction is completion angiography using a C-arm with digital imaging. For this reason, the operation is done on a table that has angiographic capability, and the radiology technician and the equipment are called for at the beginning of the arteriotomy closure. A 10 ml syringe is connected to flexible tubing, and a 20-gauge needle is attached to the end of the tubing and bent at a 45° angle. Air bubbles are carefully evacuated from the tubing and the needle. Placing the needle into the artery or, in the case of a patched artery, into the midportion of the patch in a retrograde fashion will provide good stability for the needle, which lies in the lumen of the artery in an axial position. Once the C-arm is in place and the fluoroscopy unit turned on, the contrast material is injected by hand. The resulting image of the carotid bifurcation can be continuously replayed until maximal radiographic opacity of the carotid bifurcation and the intracranial circulation has been attained. The image is then carefully inspected for defects at the end points in the internal and external carotid arteries.

Intimal defects in the internal carotid artery are unusual, though not rare. Defects in the external carotid artery are more common because the endarterectomy is essentially done in a blind or closed manner. Defects in the external carotid artery are matters of concern because they may lead to thrombus formation in this vessel; if the thrombus propagates proximally, it may embolize up the internal carotid artery and cause a stroke.[13] For this reason, if a defect is found in the external carotid artery, it is repaired at the time of the operation. To accomplish the repair, clamps are placed on the external carotid artery proximally at its origin and distally beyond the intimal flap. A transverse arteriotomy is made in the external carotid artery to permit identification and removal of the intimal flap. Once the flap has been carefully removed, the transverse arteriotomy is closed with two or three interrupted 6-0 polypropylene sutures and flow is restored.

Completion angiography also has the advantage of permitting the surgeon to image the intracranial circulation. Now that many operations are being performed on the basis of preoperative carotid duplex scanning, intracranial imaging is typically unavailable beforehand, which means that the status of the intracranial circulation with respect to atherosclerotic lesions in the area of the siphon or the middle cerebral artery or with respect to intracranial aneurysms is usually unknown at the start of the procedure. A completion angiogram gives the surgeon the opportunity to rule out these lesions by looking not only at the area around the reconstruction but also at the intracranial circulation.

An alternative to completion angiography is intraoperative DUS. DUS can be a highly satisfactory way of examining the area of reconstruction, provided that the operating room has duplex scanning capability and that a technologist is available to operate the equipment. Standard B-mode imaging, in conjunction with Doppler ultrasonography, can accurately identify patent or compromised internal and external carotid arteries.

Once the surgeon has confirmed that a good technical reconstruction has been achieved, preparations can be made for closure.

STEP 6: CLOSURE

The dissected area around the reconstructed carotid artery is carefully irrigated with an antibiotic solution, and the wound is meticulously inspected for hemostasis. Even when good hemostasis has been achieved, it is my practice to place a drain overnight—specifically, a 7.0 mm Jackson-Pratt drain brought out through a small separate stab wound. The platysmal layer is closed with a continuous 3-0 absorbable suture, and the skin is closed with a continuous 4-0 subcuticular absorbable suture. A clear adhesive plastic dressing is applied to the skin, and the patient is sent to the recovery room.

Postoperative Care

The main patient variables to be evaluated in the postoperative period are neurologic status, blood pressure, and wound stability.

On awakening from anesthesia, the patient is carefully observed with a view to determining gross cerebral function on the basis of response to commands and movement of extremities. When the patient is fully awake, vagus nerve and hypoglossal nerve function can be tested.

Blood pressure monitoring is of critical importance after CEA. It is essential first to decide on an acceptable blood pressure range for the patient and then to ensure that this pressure is maintained: neither hypertension nor hypotension is acceptable. Patients with severe carotid bifurcation disease who have undergone CEA temporarily lose autoregulation on the side of the operation; therefore, hypertension can result in reperfusion injury to that side of the brain, ranging all the way from simple headache to fatal intracerebral hemorrhage.

The surgical site should be carefully observed for possible wound expansion resulting from hematoma formation. Even when good hemostasis is achieved and a drain is in place, there is still the possibility of delayed bleeding leading to hematoma and airway compromise. If an expanding hematoma is noted, the safest response is to return the patient to the OR so that the hematoma can be evacuated and a bleeding site sought. The earlier this is done, the better.

If the patient is neurologically intact, blood pressure is well controlled, and there is no evidence of an expanding hematoma, then the remaining postoperative care can be provided in a regular hospital room. It is seldom necessary to observe the patient in the intensive care unit, as was once standard practice.

Follow-up

Periodic follow-up examination is essential. There are two major areas of concern: (1) the possibility of recurrent stenosis on the side that was operated on and (2) the possibility of disease developing or progressing in the contralateral carotid artery. It is my practice to see the patient approximately 3 weeks after CEA. In that visit, the patient is examined for quality of wound healing and the presence or absence of a carotid bruit on both the operated side and the contralateral side, and a carotid duplex scan is performed. If at this time there are no grounds for concern about the contralateral side, scanning is done only on the side of the operation. The scan serves to establish the new baseline and confirms that the carotid reconstruction is satisfactory. The new baseline is then used as the basis for assessing patient status during subsequent follow-up.

The next patient visit takes place 6 months after operation, at which time a bilateral carotid duplex scan is performed. If the operated side continues to be normal and there are no major problems on the contralateral side, the patient is seen again at the 1-year anniversary of the procedure. If examinations yield satisfactory results at this time, the patient may thereafter be seen at 1-year intervals, with bilateral carotid duplex scanning done at each visit.

Alternatives to Direct Carotid Reconstruction

Carotid angioplasty with stenting (CAS) has been investigated as a therapeutic alternative to CEA for carotid artery stenosis [see 89 Carotid Angioplasty and Stenting]. In the Wallstent trial (an industry-supported prospective, randomized study), patients with stenosis of 60% to 99%, which was angiographically confirmed according to the North American method of measurement, were randomly assigned to undergo either CAS or CEA.[14] Initially, it was proposed that the study would include 700 patients with symptomatic lesions; however, the trial was stopped by the safety-monitoring committee after 219 patients were randomized. The results were reported at the 26th International Stroke Conference in February 2001.

Of the 219 patients, 107 were entered into the CAS arm and 112 into the CEA arm. Patients were well matched with respect to age, gender, symptoms, degree of stenosis, and median follow-up. The primary end point was ipsilateral stroke, procedure-related death, or vascular death within 1 year. At approximately 1 year, the primary end-point rate was 12.1% in the CAS group and 3.6% in the CEA group. The 30-day stroke morbidity and mortality was 12.1% in the CAS group and 4.5% in the CEA group. Upon cessation of the study, the investigators concluded that CAS was not equivalent to CEA for treatment of symptomatic carotid stenosis.

In the SAPPHIRE (Stenting and Angioplasty with Protection in Patients at High-Risk for Endarterectomy) trial, which was also an industry-sponsored study, CAS with the use of a cerebral antiembolism device was compared with CEA.[15] Nonrandomized patients were entered into either a stent registry or a surgical reg-istry, but the important part of the study was a randomized, multicenter trial involving 307 patients at 29 investigational sites. Of these 307 patients, 156 were entered into the CAS–cerebral protection arm and 151 into the CEA arm. The primary end points were (1) death, any stroke, or nonfatal myocardial infarction (MI) within 30 days after the procedure and (2) 30-day major morbidity plus death and ipsilateral stroke between 31 days and 12 months after the procedure. Secondary end points included (1) patency (defined by restenosis < 50%), (2) disabling stroke between 30 days and 6 months, and (3) a composite of major adverse clinical events at 6 months, 1 year, 2 years, and 3 years.

At 30 days, there were no statistically significant differences between the two study arms when the individual parameters—death, stroke, and nonfatal MI—were considered separately. When these events were viewed in the aggregate, their composite incidence was 5.8% in the CAS–cerebral protection group and 12.6% in the CEA group. When death and stroke were considered together, however, the incidence was 4.5% in the CAS–cerebral protection group and 6.6% in the CEA group. Thus, it is apparent that the major benefit of CAS over CEA lies in reducing the incidence of nonfatal MI.

In November 2006, the results of a large French trial that compared CAS with CEA in good-risk symptomatic patients were published.[16] The study design called for the prospective randomization of 872 patients so as to yield a statistical power of 80%, the aim being to determine whether CAS was not inferior to CEA. After the inclusion of 527 patients, the trial was stopped prematurely for reasons of unsafety and futility. The 30-day incidence of any stroke or death was 3.9% after CEA and 9.6% after CAS. At 6 months, the incidence of stroke or death was 6.1% after CEA and 11.7% after CAS.[16]

On the basis of the evidence accumulated to date, the Medicare guidelines are still appropriate. CAS is indicated only for (1) symptomatic patients in whom CEA, in the opinion of a vascular surgeon, poses unacceptable risks or (2) patients who are willing to participate in an approved clinical trial (e.g., CREST [Carotid Revascularization Endarterectomy versus Stenting Trial]). CEA remains the treatment of choice for patients with suitable lesions of the carotid bifurcation.

References

1. Beneficial effect of carotid endarterectomy in symptomatic patients with high-grade carotid stenosis. North American Symptomatic Carotid Endarterectomy Trial Collaborators. N Engl J Med 325:445, 1991

2. MRC European Carotid Surgery Trial: interim results for symptomatic patients with severe (70-99%) or with mild (0-29%) carotid stenosis. European Carotid Trialists' Collaborative Group. Lancet 337:1235, 1991

3. Mayberg MR, Wilson SE, Yatsu F, et al: Carotid endarterectomy and prevention of cerebral ischemia in symptomatic carotid stenosis. Veterans Affairs Cooperative Studies Program 309 Trialist Group. JAMA 266:3332, 1991

4. Endarterectomy for asymptomatic carotid artery stenosis. Executive Committee for the Asymptomatic Carotid Atherosclerosis Study. JAMA 273:1421, 1995

5. Hobson RW II, Weiss DG, Fields WS, et al: Efficacy of carotid endarterectomy for asymptomatic carotid stenosis. The Veterans Affairs Asymptomatic Cooperative Study Group. N Engl J Med 328:221, 1993

6. Asymptomatic Carotid Surgery Trial Collaborators. The MRC Asymptomatic Carotid Surgery Trial (ACST). Carotid endarterectomy prevents disabling and failed carotid territory strokes. Lancet 363:1491, 2004

7. Moore WS, Barnett HJM, Beebe HG, et al: Guidelines for carotid endarterectomy—a multidisciplinary consensus statement from the Ad Hoc Committee, American Heart Association. Circulation 91:566, 1995

8. Fisher DF Jr, Clagett GP, Parker JI, et al: Mandibular subluxation for high carotid exposure. J Vasc Surg 1:727, 1984

9. Moore WS, Yee JM, Hall AD: Collateral cerebral blood pressure—an index of tolerance to temporary carotid occlusion. Arch Surg 106:520, 1973

10. Moore WS, Hall AD. Carotid artery back pressure—a test of cerebral tolerance to temporary carotid occlusion. Arch Surg 99:702, 1969

11. Blaisdell FW, Lim R Jr, Hall AD: Technical results of carotid endarterectomy: arteriographic assessment. Am J Surg 114:239, 1967

12. Schwartz RA, Peterson GJ, Noland KA, et al: Intraoperative duplex scanning after carotid recon-struction: a valuable tool. J Vasc Surg 7:260, 1988

13. Moore WS, Martello JY, Quiñones-Baldrich WJ, et al: Etiologic importance of the intimal flap of the external carotid artery in the development of postcarotid endarterectomy stroke. Stroke 21:1497, 1990

14. Alberts MJ: Results of a multicenter prospective randomized trial of carotid artery stenting vs. carotid endarterectomy (abstr). Stroke 32:325d, 2001

15. Yadav J, for the SAPPHIRE Investigators: Stenting and angioplasty with protection in patients at high risk for endarterectomy: the SAPPHIRE study (abstr). Circulation 106:2986a, 2002

16. Mas J-L, Chantellier G, Beyssen B, et al: Endarterectomy versus stenting in patients with symptomatic severe carotid stenosis. N Engl J Med 355:1660, 2006

Acknowledgment

Figures 1 through 17   Tom Moore.

Timothy M. Sullivan, M.D., F.A.C.S.

Choice between Carotid Endarterectomy and Carotid Angioplasty and Stenting

OPERATIVE RISK AND PATIENT SELECTION

For most patients with high-grade carotid lesions, whether symptomatic or asymptomatic, surgical endarterectomy [*see 88 Surgical Treatment of Carotid Artery Disease*], rather than best medical therapy (i.e., risk factor reduction and antiplatelet agents), is the treatment of choice for stroke prophylaxis, as the North American Symptomatic Carotid Endarterectomy Trial (NASCET) and the Asymptomatic Carotid Atherosclerosis Study (ACAS) have shown.[1,2] In NASCET, the risk of disabling stroke or death after carotid endarterectomy (CEA) was 1.9%, and the risk of minor stroke was 3.9%. In ACAS, the risk of major stroke or death was 0.6% when the 1.2% risk of stroke caused by diagnostic arteriography was excluded. These findings have led to the performance of CEA in increasing numbers of patients.

In the past few years, however, despite the proven efficacy of CEA in preventing ischemic stroke, great interest has been generated in carotid angioplasty and stenting (CAS) as an alternative to surgical therapy, and CEA has again come under attack.[3] Proponents of CAS have suggested that the results of NASCET and ACAS are not achievable in general practice outside selected centers of excellence. Both ACAS and NASCET included patients who were determined to be good operative risks on the basis of reasonable life expectancy (so that they would be available for follow-up) and the absence of other potential causes of stroke (e.g., atrial fibrillation) [*see Table 1*].

A number of investigators have examined the results of CEA in high-risk subsets, albeit using several different ways of defining high risk [*see Tables 2 and 3*].[4-8] In one study, involving 776 consecutive CEAs performed at the Mayo Clinic in Rochester, Minnesota, procedures were categorized as high risk according to the patient inclusion and exclusion criteria employed by the Stenting and Angioplasty with Protection in Patients at HIgh Risk for Endarterectomy (SAPPHIRE) trial of CAS with cerebral embolic protection.[4] Of the 776 CEAs, 323 (42%) were considered high risk. The clinical presentation was similar in the high-risk and low-risk groups. The overall postoperative stroke rate was 1.4% (symptomatic, 2.9%; asymptomatic, 0.9%), and there was no statistical difference in stroke rate between the high-risk group and the low-risk group. Patients at significantly increased stroke risk were those who underwent cervical radiation therapy, those who had class III or IV angina, those who were symptomatic at presentation, and those who were 60 years of age or younger. Overall mortality was 0.3% (symptomatic, 0.5%; asymptomatic, 0.2%), and there was no significant difference between the high-risk group (0.6%) and the low-risk group (0.0%). Myocardial

Table 1 High-Risk Carotid Endarterectomy as Defined by Major Exclusion Criteria for NASCET and ACAS

Study	Exclusion Criteria						
	Age	History	Comorbidities				Anatomic Criteria
			Cardiac	Pulmonary	Renal	Other	
NASCET[1]	> 79 yr	Contralateral CEA < 4 mo Major surgical procedure < 1 mo Stroke in evolution	Unstable angina Atrial fibrillation Valvular heart disease Symptomatic CHF MI < 6 mo	Pulmonary failure	Renal failure	Uncontrolled hypertension Uncontrolled diabetes mellitus Hepatic failure Cancer with < 50% chance of 5-yr survival	Previous ipsilateral CEA Tandem lesion > target stenosis
ACAS[2]	> 79 yr	Major surgical procedure < 1 mo Stroke in evolution	Unstable angina Atrial fibrillation Valvular heart disease Symptomatic CHF	Pulmonary failure with impact on 5-yr survival	SCr > 3 mg/dl	> 180 mm Hg systolic BP, > 115 mm Hg diastolic BP Fasting glucose > 400 mg/dl Hepatic failure Cancer with < 50% chance of 5-yr survival Active ulcer disease Warfarin anticoagulation	Previous ipsilateral CEA Tandem lesion > target stenosis Cervical radiation treatment

ACAS—Asymptomatic Carotid Atherosclerosis Study   BP—blood pressure   CEA—carotid endarterectomy   CHF—chronic heart failure   MI—myocardial infarction   NASCET—North American Symptomatic Carotid Endarterectomy Trial   SCr—serum creatinine concentration

Table 2   High-Risk Carotid Endarterectomy as Defined by Major Inclusion Criteria for Selected Studies

Study	Inclusion Criteria						Anatomic Criteria
	Age	History	Comorbidities				
			Cardiac	Pulmonary	Renal	Other	
Ouriel (2001)[5]			PTCA or CABG < 6 mo History of CHF	Severe COPD	SCr > 3 mg/dl		
Jordan (2002)[6]		Major vascular procedure < 1 mo	Coronary procedure < 1 mo CABG < 6 wk Angina NYHA class III or IV EF < 30% MI < 4 wk	FEV₁ < 1 L Home oxygen			Previous ipsilateral CEA Cervical radiation treatment Contralateral carotid occlusion High cervical lesion Lesion below clavicle
Gasparis (2003)[7]	≥ 80 yr		NYHA functional class III or IV Heart failure Canadian class III or IV CABG < 6 mo	Steroid dependence Oxygen dependence	SCr > 3 mg/dl		Previous ipsilateral CEA Cervical radiation treatment Contralateral carotid occlusion High cervical lesion
SAPPHIRE[8]	> 80 yr		Open heart surgery < 6 wk MI < 4 wk Angina CCS class III or IV CHF class III or IV EF < 30% Abnormal cardiac stress test result				Previous ipsilateral CEA Severe tandem lesion Cervical radiation treatment Contralateral carotid occlusion High cervical lesion (at least C2) Lesion below clavicle Contralateral laryngeal palsy

CABG—coronary artery bypass graft   CCS—Canadian Cardiovascular Society   CEA—carotid endarterectomy   CHF—congestive heart failure   COPD—chronic obstructive pulmonary disease   EF—ejection fraction   FEV₁—forced expiratory volume in 1 sec   MI—myocardial infarction   NYHA—New York Heart Association   PTCA—percutaneous transluminal coronary angioplasty   SAPPHIRE—Stenting and Angioplasty with Protection in Patients at High Risk for Endarterectomy   SCr—serum creatinine concentration

infarction (MI) was more frequent in the high-risk group (3.1%) than in the low-risk group (0.9%); notably, all of the MIs reported in this series were nontransmural (non-Q). A composite cluster of adverse clinical events (death, stroke, and MI) was more frequent in the symptomatic high-risk group (9.3% versus 1.6%), but not in the asymptomatic cohort. There was a trend toward a higher incidence of major cranial nerve injuries in patients with local risk factors (e.g., high carotid bifurcation, reoperation, and cervical radiation therapy) (4.6% versus 1.7%). In 121 patients who were excluded on the basis of synchronous or immediate subsequent operations (and who would also have been excluded from SAPPHIRE), the overall rates of stroke (1.65%), death (1.65%), and MI (0.83%) were not significantly different from those in the study population. The authors concluded that SAPPHIRE-eligible high-risk patients could undergo CEA with stroke and death rates that were well within accepted standards and that patients with local risk factors were at higher risk for cranial nerve injuries but not necessarily for stroke. These conclusions call into question the application of CAS as an alternative to CEA, even in high-risk patients.

Although these studies do not support the premise that operative risk is higher in patients who would be excluded by NASCET and ACAS criteria, there may in fact be categories of patients for whom CEA is not optimal therapy. A 2001 study from the Cleveland Clinic attempted to identify a subgroup of patients who, on retrospective analysis, were at increased risk for CEA and therefore might be better served by CAS.[5] A total of 3,061 carotid endarterectomies were examined from a prospective database covering a 10-year period. A high-risk cohort was identified on the basis of the presence of severe coronary artery disease, a history of congestive heart failure (CHF), the presence of severe chronic obstruc-

tive pulmonary disease (COPD), or the development of renal insufficiency [*see Table 2*]. For the composite end point of stroke, death, and MI, the rate was 3.8% in the group as a whole (stroke, 2.1%; MI, 1.2%; death, 1.1%); however, the rate was 7.4% in high-risk patients, compared with only 2.9% in low-risk patients. High-risk patients were further subdivided into those who underwent CEA alone and those who underwent CEA combined with coronary artery bypass grafting (CABG). Not surprisingly, the incidence of the composite end point was greater in the latter subgroup than in the former. Among patients who underwent CEA

Table 3   SAPPHIRE Exclusion Criteria for Defining High-Risk Carotid Endarterectomy[8]

Acute stroke (≤ 48 hr)
Staged elective procedure (within 30 days after CEA)
  Elective percutaneous intervention
  Contralateral CEA
  Other elective operation
Synchronous operation
  CCA angioplasty/stenting or bypass
  Cardiac operation
  Noncardiac operation
Intracranial pathology
  Intracranial mass
  Aneurysm > 9 mm
  Arteriovenous malformation
  Ventriculoperitoneal shunt

CCA—common carotid artery   CEA—carotid endarterectomy

Table 4 Indications for Carotid Angioplasty and Stenting in High-Risk Patients

Severe cardiac disease
   Requirement for PTCA or CABG
   History of CHF
Severe chronic obstructive pulmonary disease
   Requirement for home oxygen
   $FEV_1 < 20\%$ of predicted
Severe chronic renal insufficiency
   Serum creatinine concentration > 3.0 mg/dl
   Patient currently on dialysis
Previous CEA (restenosis)
   Contralateral vocal cord paralysis
Surgically inaccessible lesions
   Lesion at or above C2
   Lesion inferior to clavicle
Radiation-induced carotid stenosis
Previous ipsilateral radical neck dissection

alone, the risk of death was significantly greater in the high-risk group. Notably, although the risk of the combined end point was greater in the high-risk group, the difference was not statistically significant. In addition, the rates of the individual end points of MI and stroke did not differ statistically between the high-risk group and the low-risk group.

These data appear to support the notion that the patients enrolled in the multicenter trials of CEA (i.e., NASCET and ACAS) were probably similar to the Cleveland Clinic's low-risk group and that the patients in the Clinic's high-risk group might not have had such stellar outcomes if they had been included in those multicenter endarterectomy trials. Subsequent clinical investigations have therefore focused on medically compromised, high-risk patients who may benefit from alternatives to CEA (e.g., CAS).

INDICATIONS FOR CAROTID ANGIOPLASTY AND STENTING

The basic indications for CAS are essentially the same as those for standard open CEA:

1. Asymptomatic lesions that fall within the high-grade stenosis (typically, 80% to 99%) range on duplex ultrasonography, which correlates with a stenosis of at least 60% on angiography [see 81 Asymptomatic Carotid Bruit]. Most clinical trials of CAS in asymptomatic patients require an angiographic stenosis of at least 80% for study inclusion.
2. Symptomatic lesions (e.g., hemispheric transient ischemic attack [TIA], amaurosis fugax, or stroke with minimal residua) with a stenosis of at least 70% on angiography [see 80 Stroke and Transient Ischemic Attack]. Symptomatic patients who have greater than 50% stenoses with ulceration may benefit from endarterectomy; however, this finding has not yet been extrapolated to carotid intervention.

At present, there is a paucity of data on the safety and efficacy of CAS from well-controlled studies. Accordingly, my use of CAS to date has been limited to treatment of patients judged to be at high risk for CEA. Such patients account for 10% to 20% of all patients undergoing intervention (open or endovascular) for carotid disease in the Division of Vascular Surgery at the Mayo Clinic. Symptomatic patients with greater than 50% angiographic stenosis and asymptomatic patients with greater than 80% angiographic stenosis are considered for intervention, either surgical or percutaneous.

Reasonable criteria for patients at increased risk for CEA have been developed, and these criteria may serve as a general guide for those embarking on a program of carotid stenting [see Table 4]. Relative contraindications to CAS have also been determined [see Table 5]. CAS should be performed by physicians with a thorough knowledge of the pathophysiology and natural history of carotid disease and by those with current expertise in peripheral, cardiac, or neurointerventional procedures. If a physician is unable to participate in FDA-approved trials, the procedure should be performed as part of a local Institutional Review Board (IRB)–approved protocol with dispassionate oversight, independent preprocedural and postprocedural neurologic examination, and prospective case review. In addition, development of a carotid stenting program may facilitate cooperation among the various specialists who may desire to participate in this high-profile arena. A team of experienced personnel should be assembled (including one or two physicians and a technician) to ensure patient safety, maximize exposure within a small cadre of operators, and avoid duplication of effort. All patients considered for CAS should have provided informed consent, should receive counseling regarding the risks and benefits vis-à-vis CEA and best medical therapy, and should possess a clear understanding of the investigational nature of the procedure. In addition, patients must agree to regular and careful follow-up examinations.

Anatomic Considerations

A solid grasp of the anatomy of the cerebral circulation is crucial for the planning of CAS. Several anatomic considerations are particularly germane. The first important anatomic issue to address is the configuration of the aortic arch. With advancing age, the apex of the arch tends to become displaced further distally. This displacement makes selective catheterization of the brachiocephalic vessels more challenging and influences the choice of a catheter. The interventionalist should become familiar with a variety of selective catheters; I prefer the Simmons II catheter, which allows deep cannulation of the common carotid artery (CCA) and thus facilitates eventual passage of a guide wire for delivery of a sheath. As the level of the vessel's origin becomes farther from the dome of the arch, the task of obtaining guide-wire and sheath access becomes more difficult. Cannulation of a left CCA arising from a common brachiocephalic trunk (bovine arch) may be particularly

Table 5 Limitations of and Contraindications to Carotid Angioplasty and Stenting

Inability to obtain femoral artery access
Unfavorable aortic arch anatomy
Severe tortuosity of CCA or ICA
Severely calcified or undilatable stenoses
Lesions containing fresh thrombus
Large amount of laminated thrombus at site of patch angioplasty
   (previous CEA) on duplex ultrasonography
Extensive stenoses (> 2 cm)
Critical (≥ 99%) stenoses
Lesions adjacent to carotid artery aneurysms
Contrast-related issues
   Chronic renal insufficiency
   Previous life-threatening contrast reaction
Preload-dependent states (e.g., severe aortic valvular stenosis)

difficult to accomplish. Problematic arch configurations should be identified on preprocedural contrast studies or magnetic resonance angiography (MRA) of the aorta. Especially at the beginning of an operator's experience with these interventions, a complete study that includes the aortic arch and the origins of the brachiocephalic trunks is essential.

Another important issue is the presence of any tandem lesions along the course of the cerebral circulation. If a proximal CCA lesion is present, intervention may be required before revascularization of the internal carotid artery (ICA) to provide safe access to the ICA. A third concern is the tortuosity of the ICA. Fortunately, most ICAs are relatively straight; however, some patients do have extremely tortuous ICAs, which may preclude safe passage of a guide wire or protection device and thus render safe intervention impossible. The anatomic configuration of the external carotid artery (ECA) typically is not an important consideration in carotid intervention, even when this vessel is affected by stenosis of iatrogenic origin or is covered with a bare stent.

Finally, the collateral circulation (or lack thereof) through the circle of Willis is an important consideration that may profoundly influence procedural strategy. The status of the contralateral ICA, the vertebral-basilar system, and the intracranial collaterals may affect the type of embolic protection to be used. Anatomic variations in the circle of Willis are actually the rule rather than the exception: a complete circle is present in fewer than 50% of all cases. Common variations include a hypoplastic (10%) or absent A1 segment of the anterior cerebral artery and a plexiform (10% to 33%) or duplicated (18%) anterior communicating artery. Anomalies of the posterior portion of the circle of Willis, including a hypoplastic (33%) or absent posterior communicating artery, occur in about 50% of all cases. During preprocedural angiography or intracranial MRA, careful attention should be paid to the anterior and posterior communicating arteries. Patients with limited collateral circulation may exhibit reversible neurologic symptoms during inflation of a protective balloon or angioplasty of the target lesion. They may also be at higher risk for permanent neurologic deficits because their limited collateral blood supply is less likely to be able to compensate for any iatrogenic arterial occlusions that may complicate the procedure.

Preoperative Evaluation

For those with limited experience in carotid intervention, diagnostic angiography of the arch, the carotid arteries, and the cerebral arteries (done well in advance of the proposed intervention) is suggested; high-quality MRA that includes the aortic arch is an acceptable substitute. This measure allows the interventionalist to make a careful, unhurried evaluation of the aortic arch and the brachiocephalic origins, which is essential for determining the ease or difficulty of sheath or guide access to the CCAs—an issue that has a direct bearing on the success of the procedure. If the brachiocephalic trunk (i.e., the innominate artery) or the left CCA originates in a location more than two CCA diameters (approximately 2 cm) below the dome of the aortic arch, some difficulty with access should be anticipated. In addition, the length of the lesion, the maximum degree of stenosis, and the diameters of the CCA and the ICA can be determined by placing a radiopaque marker of known diameter in the field of view; ball bearings of progressively increasing diameter (2 through 7 mm) are ideal for this purpose. These measurements facilitate preprocedural selection of appropriately sized balloons and stents and make performance of the procedure smoother

and more efficient, thereby serving the main goals of therapy—patient safety and exemplary results.

In all cases, a thorough history should be taken and a careful physical examination performed, with close attention paid to comorbid medical conditions and femoral pulses. A complete neurologic examination should be performed by a certified neurologist. In addition to preprocedural arteriography or MRA, duplex ultrasonography should be performed in an accredited vascular laboratory—ideally, the same laboratory where the follow-up examinations will be performed. In my practice, patients receive aspirin, 325 mg daily for at least 1 week before the procedure, and clopidogrel, 75 mg daily for at least 3 days beforehand. All patients receive antibiotics (typically cefazolin, 1 g I.V.) immediately before the procedure.

Operative Planning

Regardless of the exact physical location at which the procedure is performed, access to high-quality imaging equipment is mandatory; portable C-arms are less than ideal for this purpose. I perform CAS in a neuroradiology suite, which has the advantage of offering biplane imaging. With this arrangement, duplication of effort and equipment is avoided, and the room is staffed by knowledgeable personnel, including a certified registered nurse anesthetist (CRNA), who monitors the patient with continuous electrocardiography, blood pressure, and pulse oximetry readings. Patients are placed in a supine position, and both groins are prepared. The head is placed in a cradle and gently secured to minimize patient motion during critical portions of the procedure. The procedure is generally performed with the patient awake, though minimal sedation is acceptable if the patient is particularly anxious.

Operative Technique

The technique of CAS has evolved over time. In its current iteration, the procedure is performed in the following steps, with few exceptions. Although it is, of course, essential to be able to adjust the technical approach to deal with unanticipated situations, it is nonetheless desirable to standardize the procedure as much as possible.

Basic principles of endovascular surgery are discussed more fully elsewhere [see 87 Fundamentals of Endovascular Surgery]; the following steps focus primarily on the procedural elements specific to CAS.

STEP 1: SECURING OF ARTERIAL ACCESS

Retrograde femoral access is obtained, and a 5 French sheath is inserted. Full heparin anticoagulation (typically 100 mg/kg body mass) is instituted after arterial access is secured and before manipulation of catheters in the aortic arch and the brachiocephalic vessels.

STEP 2: SELECTIVE CAROTID CATHETERIZATION AND ARTERIOGRAPHY

After selective catheterization of the midportion of the ipsilateral CCA (typically with a Simmons II catheter), a selective arteriogram of the carotid bifurcation is obtained, with care taken to choose a view that yields minimal overlapping of the ICA and the ECA and maximal visualization of the target lesion. A complete cerebral arteriogram, if not previously obtained, is obtained at this point to serve as a baseline and to identify any intracranial pathologic conditions (e.g., aneurysms and arteriovenous communications) that may be present.

STEP 3: ADVANCEMENT OF SHEATH AND DILATOR INTO COMMON CAROTID ARTERY

Two techniques have been employed to advance a sheath into the CCA. The first technique—which I prefer—is to place an exchange-length guide wire into the terminal branches of the ECA. I generally use a stiff, angled glide wire (keeping in mind that sheath exchange over this highly slippery wire can be tricky). The diagnostic catheter and the 5 French sheath are removed (with constant visualization of the guide wire in the ECA maintained all the while). A long (70 to 90 cm, depending on patient body habitus) 6 French sheath is then advanced, along with its dilator, into the CCA. If larger (> 8 mm in diameter) stents are required, a 7 French sheath may be necessary to allow contrast injection around the stent delivery system. Care must be taken to identify the tip of the dilator (which is not radiopaque) because it may extend a significant distance from the end of the sheath, depending on the brand of sheath used. Obviously, inadvertently advancing the dilator into the carotid bulb may have disastrous consequences. In patients with short CCAs or low bifurcations, the sheath can be advanced over the dilator once the sheath edge (a radiopaque marker) is past the origin of the CCA.

The second technique is to advance the long sheath into the transverse arch over a guide wire. The dilator is removed, and an appropriate selective diagnostic catheter is advanced into the CCA. This catheter must be substantially longer than the sheath, typically more than 100 cm long. A stiff guide wire is then advanced into the ECA. Both the wire and the catheter are pinned at the groin to provide support, and the sheath (without the dilator) is advanced into the CCA. This technique may be advantageous in so-called hostile arches, in that the catheter and the wire provide more support than a wire alone would; however, without the protection of the sheath dilator, there is a risk of "snowplowing" the edge of the sheath at the junction of the aortic arch and the innominate artery or the left CCA, which can cause dissection or distal embolization.

The importance of gaining and maintaining sheath access to the distal CCA should not be underestimated: once the 0.035 in. guide wire is removed (and, eventually, exchanged for a 0.014 in. wire), support for angioplasty and stent placement is provided solely by the sheath. If the sheath backs up into the aortic arch during the interventional procedure, it is virtually impossible to advance it into the CCA over a 0.014 in. guide wire or protection device. Appropriate patient selection and accurate recognition of which arches to avoid are essential for success. In particularly difficult arches, deep inspiration or expiration may facilitate sheath advancement by subtly changing the configuration of the brachiocephalic origins once guide-wire access has been obtained. Alternatively, when a sheath cannot be advanced into the CCA, a preshaped guide catheter can be seated in the proximal CCA. Although this maneuver may facilitate an otherwise impossible intervention, it should be kept in mind that guide catheters provide a less stable support platform than sheaths do and should be used only if there is no other reasonable alternative.

Troubleshooting

In patients with an occluded ECA, sheath access to the CCA may be difficult to obtain. Two techniques may be employed to overcome this difficulty. The first is to place a stiff 0.035 in. wire with a preshaped J into the distal CCA, taking care to avoid the bulb and the bifurcation. The J configuration keeps the guide wire from crossing the lesion. A stiff wire with a shapable tip can be used to the same end.

The second technique is to use a variable-diameter wire (0.018 in. at the tip, enlarging to 0.035 in. more proximally) to cross the internal carotid lesion, providing additional guide-wire support to facilitate sheath advancement. This approach is a reasonable option, but it ultimately necessitates crossing the target lesion twice.

STEP 4: REMOVAL OF GUIDE WIRE AND DILATOR AND SELECTIVE ARTERIOGRAPHY OF CAROTID BIFURCATION

Once the sheath is in place, the guide wire and the dilator are removed. The sheath sidearm may be attached to a slow, continuous infusion of heparin-saline solution to keep blood from stagnating in the sheath. Selective angiography of the carotid bifurcation is then performed through the sheath, again demonstrating the area of maximal stenosis, the extent of the lesion, and the normal ICA and CCA above and below the lesion. Roadmapping, if available, is helpful in crossing the lesion with an embolic protection device or guide wire [see Step 6, below]. The overwhelming majority of procedures are now performed with the aid of an embolic protection device, typically a filter [see Figure 1].

STEP 5: MEASUREMENT OF ACTIVATED CLOTTING TIME

It is advisable to measure the activated clotting time (ACT) before crossing the lesion and performing CAS. If balloon occlusion of the ICA is being used for embolic protection, an ACT longer than 300 seconds is desirable. If a filter-type device or a standard guide wire is being used, an ACT longer than 250 seconds is probably sufficient. The interventional team should discuss, in detail, all the subsequent steps to be performed so that all members are on the same page. Balloons are flushed and prepared, and special care should be taken to remove all air from the system as a protective measure against the unlikely event of balloon rupture. The stent is opened and placed on the table, and the crossing guide wire or embolic protection device is prepared. For de novo lesions, I typically administer atropine (0.5 to 1.0 mg I.V.) as prophylaxis against bradycardia during balloon inflation in the carotid bulb; for restenoses after CEA, this measure may not be necessary. The monitoring nurse or CRNA should be alerted that balloon inflation may cause significant hemodynamic instability.

STEP 6: ADVANCEMENT OF GUIDE WIRE ACROSS LESION

The guide wire or embolic protection device (0.014 in.) is advanced across the lesion with the aid of roadmapping (if available). Care should be taken when the device is inserted through the sheath valve because the tip can be damaged at this juncture. If a protection device is being used, it should be deployed into the distal extracranial ICA, just before the horizontal petrous segment. For balloon-occlusion devices, absence of flow in the ICA must be demonstrated. For filter devices, apposition of the device to the ICA must be documented, along with flow in the ICA through the device; these should also be documented after each subsequent step of the intervention to detect possible occlusion of the filter by debris.

STEP 7: PREDILATION OF LESION

The lesion is predilated with a 5.0 mm angioplasty balloon, typically on a monorail or rapid-exchange platform. To save time, the balloon can be advanced into the distal CCA before the lesion is crossed with the guide wire or protection device. In most cases, the desired balloon profile can be achieved with relatively low inflation pressures (4 to 6 mm Hg). After the predilation balloon is removed, another bifurcation angiogram is performed through the sheath (unless distal balloon occlusion is employed, in which case

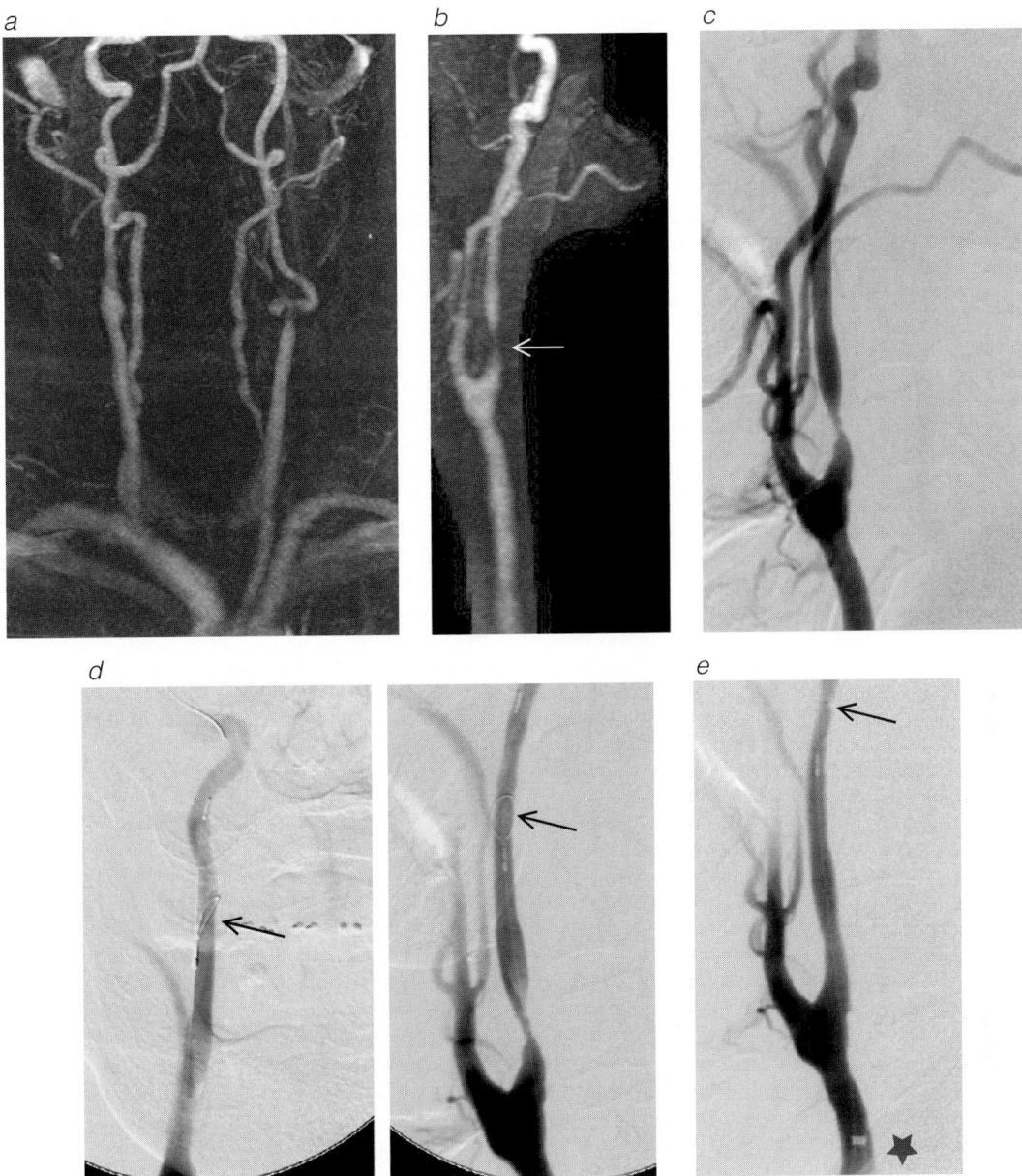

Figure 1 Carotid angioplasty and stenting. In this example, a filter device is used for cerebral protection. (*a*) MRA shows aortic arch and cervical carotid and vertebral arteries. (*b*) MRA shows recurrent (postendarterectomy) high-grade stenosis of right ICA. (*c*) Selective angiogram shows right carotid bifurcation. (*d*) FilterWire EX (Boston Scientific, Natick, Massachusetts) is deployed within ICA; angiographic assessment is performed in two planes (left, right) to confirm adequate apposition of filter to vessel wall (arrows). (*e*) Shown is vessel after angioplasty and placement of self-expanding nitinol stent. Sheath is properly positioned in distal CCA (star). Spasm may be seen at site of filter (arrow).

the ICA will not be visualized and the distal stent must be placed according to predetermined bony landmarks and the location of the CCA bifurcation).

STEP 8: DEPLOYMENT OF STENT

Once correct positioning has been confirmed, the stent is deployed. Currently, I prefer to use nitinol stents, most commonly extending an 8 to 10 mm × 30 mm stent from the ICA into the CCA and covering the origin of the ECA. Nitinol stents exhibit a tendency to "jump" distally when deployed rapidly (despite manufacturers' claims to the contrary), and this jump may cause the operator to miss the target lesion. To counter this tendency, I typically expose and deploy two or three stent rings, then wait for 5 to 7 seconds, allowing the distal stent to become fully expanded, well apposed to the ICA, and attached to the vessel wall above the lesion. I can then deploy the remainder of the stent more rapidly, with little worry that it will migrate.

The diameter of the stent is determined by the diameter of the largest portion of the vessel, which is typically the distal CCA (not the ICA). It is important that there be no unapposed stent in the CCA: any part of the stent that is not apposed to the vessel wall may become a nidus for thrombus formation. The diameter of the unconstrained stent should be at least 10% (approximately 1 to 2 mm) larger than the maximum diameter of the CCA. On occasion, the lesion is limited to the ICA well above the carotid bifurcation; in such cases, a shorter stent confined to the ICA may be used.

STEP 9: POSTDILATION OF LESION

If necessary, the lesion is postdilated with a 5 or 5.5 mm balloon; larger balloons are rarely necessary. As noted [see Step 7, above], I currently prefer to use a relatively large balloon (5 mm) for predilation so as to obviate postdilation if possible. A residual stenosis of 10% or so is completely acceptable; the goal of the intervention is protection from embolic stroke, not necessarily a perfect angiographic result.

STEP 10: COMPLETION ARTERIOGRAPHY

A completion angiogram of the carotid bulb and bifurcation and the distal extracranial ICA is obtained before wire removal to verify that no dissection or occlusion has occurred. Severe vasospasm may be encountered (sometimes mimicking dissection); watchful waiting, coupled on occasion with administration of vasodilators through the sheath (e.g., nitroglycerin in 100 μg aliquots), usually resolves this problem. Sometimes, the wire must be removed before vasospasm will resolve completely, but this should be done only after dissection is excluded. After the wire is removed, completion angiography of the carotid and intracranial circulation is performed in two views.

STEP 11: ACCESS-SITE HEMOSTASIS

Heparin anticoagulation typically is not reversed. Access-site hemostasis is achieved with a percutaneous closure device.

Postoperative Care

After the procedure, the patient is monitored in the recovery area for approximately 30 minutes, then transferred to a monitored floor; admission to an intensive care unit generally is not necessary. In 2 to 3 hours, patients are allowed to ambulate if a closure device was used and are allowed to resume a regular diet. Some patients experience prolonged hypotension from carotid sinus stimulation; this problem can be managed with judicious fluid administration, pharmacologic treatment of bradycardia, and, occasionally, I.V. infusion of a vasopressor (e.g., dopamine). Rarely, a patient experiences prolonged hypotension that must be treated with an oral agent (e.g., phenylephrine or midodrine).

A duplex ultrasonogram is obtained before hospital discharge as a baseline study; the criteria for stenosis and restenosis change after placement of a metal stent in the carotid artery. Subsequent ultrasound examinations are performed at 6 weeks, 6 months, and 1 year, then yearly thereafter. Neurologic evaluation is performed according to the same schedule as the duplex studies. Patients are treated with aspirin for life and with clopidogrel for 4 to 6 weeks.

As with carotid endarterectomy, proper patient selection, procedural standardization, and meticulous attention to detail are mandatory for a successful procedure, regardless of the exact technique used for CAS.

Special Considerations

CEREBRAL PROTECTION

Ischemic stroke remains the most devastating complication of procedures directed at the extracranial carotid artery, whether open or endovascular. A number of different causes of stroke have been described, but the majority of strokes are attributable to cerebral embolization of atheromatous debris or thrombus. Even when cerebral emboli do not produce a major stroke, they may cause substantial cognitive impairment. A prospective study of 100 patients monitored with transcranial Doppler ultrasonography (TCD) during CEA found that microemboli were detected during 92% of procedures.[9] Although most of the emboli were air emboli (and were not associated with adverse clinical events), there were more than 10 particulate emboli whose presence was correlated with significant deterioration of postoperative cognitive function.

A subsequent study evaluated 70 patients who underwent cardiac surgery with cardiopulmonary bypass, measuring cognitive function at 1 week, 2 months, and 6 months after operation; elderly patients who underwent urologic surgery served as the control group.[10] TCD detected more than 200 emboli in 40 patients, principally during aortic clamping and release, when bypass was initiated, and during defibrillation. Emboli were associated with significant memory loss. In addition, cognitive function deteriorated more in the study group than in the control group, though it recovered by 2 months after operation.

A study using a rat model examined the effect of atheroemboli of varying sizes on neuronal cell death.[11] The animals exposed to particles less than 200 μm in diameter showed no evidence of brain injury at 1 and 3 days, whereas those exposed to particles between 200 and 500 μm showed a scattered pattern of neuronal cell death at necropsy. At 7 days after embolization, however, both groups showed evidence of cell death. These findings suggest that whereas the brain may have a substantial tolerance for small emboli in the acute setting, even particles smaller than 200 μm may cause neuronal ischemia at a later point.

Angioplasty and Carotid Embolization

Various studies have assessed the embolic potential of carotid plaques in ex vivo models. One such study, which used specimens of human atherosclerotic plaque in a flow chamber to model CAS, found that substantial numbers of particles were released from the lesions during angioplasty and that most of these particles were captured by an experimental filter device.[12] The filter device itself produced very few particles, thanks to its low crossing profile.

A subsequent study also addressed the embolic potential of human carotid plaques during experimental angioplasty.[13] An average of 133 emboli per angioplasty were measured, and there was a positive correlation between lesion severity and the maximum size of the embolic particles. A notable finding was that patients who had been placed on statin therapy more than 4 weeks before operation had significantly fewer and smaller emboli.

A clinical study that employed a distal balloon-occlusion system during CAS found that the median number of particles, their maximum diameter, and their maximum area were all significantly higher in patients with periprocedural neurologic complications.[14] Three procedural steps are associated with an increased risk of embolization: predilation, stent deployment, and postdilation [see Operative Technique, Steps 7, 8, and 9, above].[15]

Devices for Cerebral Embolic Protection

The use of embolic protection in large numbers of patients has been described with respect to the coronary vascular bed, where interventional procedures performed on diseased aortocoronary saphenous vein grafts carry a 20% risk of periprocedural complications, largely related to distal embolization of atheromatous debris. The Saphenous vein graft Angioplasty Free of Emboli Randomized (SAFER) trial was the first multicenter randomized

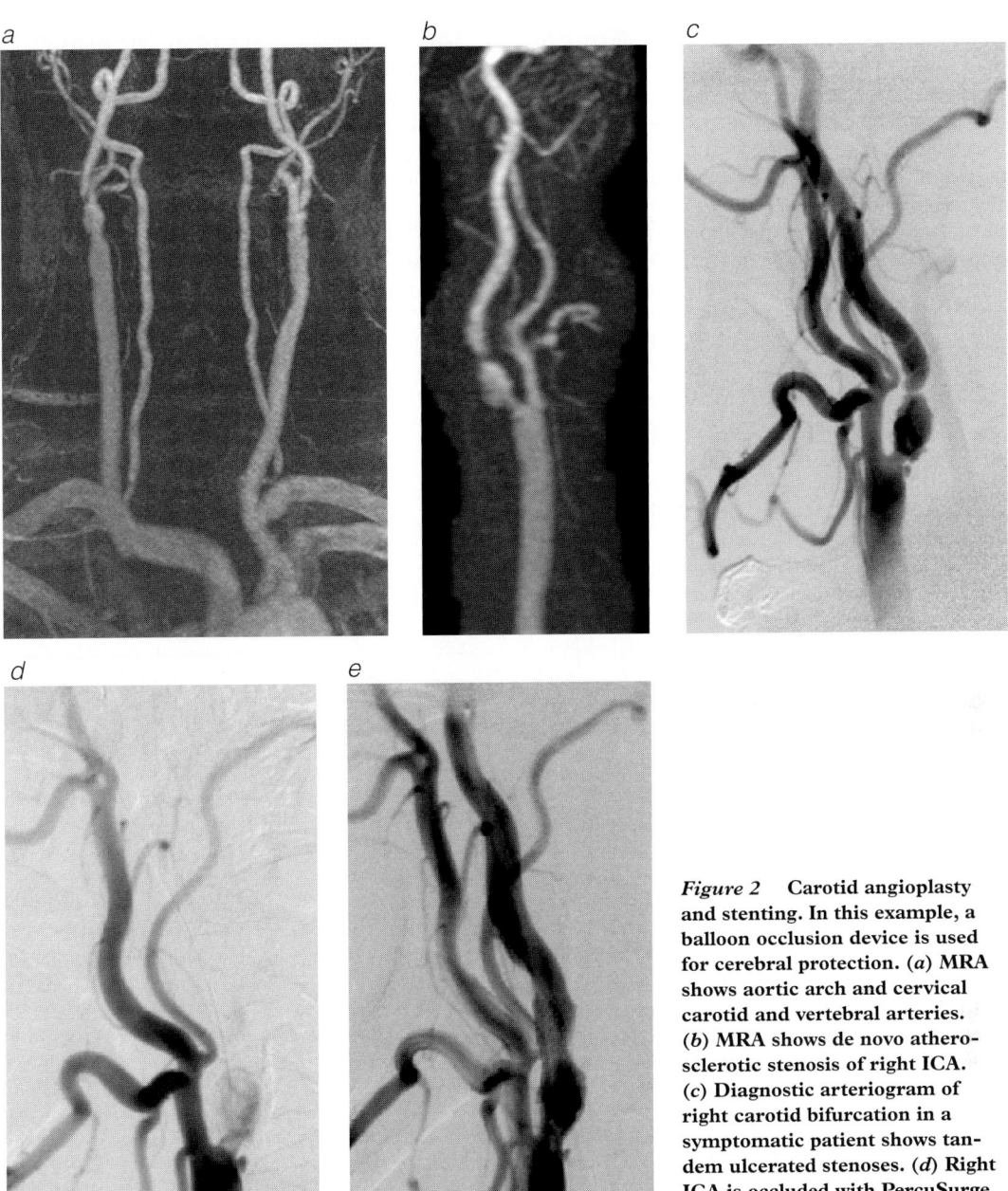

Figure 2   **Carotid angioplasty and stenting. In this example, a balloon occlusion device is used for cerebral protection. (*a*) MRA shows aortic arch and cervical carotid and vertebral arteries. (*b*) MRA shows de novo atherosclerotic stenosis of right ICA. (*c*) Diagnostic arteriogram of right carotid bifurcation in a symptomatic patient shows tandem ulcerated stenoses. (*d*) Right ICA is occluded with PercuSurge GuardWire device. (*e*) Shown is vessel after angioplasty and placement of nitinol stent.**

study to evaluate the use of distal embolic protection during saphenous vein graft interventions.[16] Of the 801 eligible patients, 406 were randomly assigned to angioplasty and stenting with distal balloon protection and 395 to angioplasty and stenting over a conventional guide wire. The composite primary end point (death, MI, emergency coronary bypass, target lesion revascularization) was reached in 16.5% of the control group and 9.6% of the study group; the differences between the two groups were largely driven by decreases in MI and distal embolization. These dramatic results suggest that patients with lesions of high embolic potential (e.g., those at the carotid bifurcation) may benefit from some type of embolic protection. A 2000 study using an ex vivo model of angioplasty confirmed the findings of other investigators that emboli occur at several stages of carotid intervention and stressed that cerebral protection techniques should be effective from the earliest stages of the procedure.[17]

Three types of embolic protection—distal balloon occlusion, distal filter protection, and reversal of ICA flow—are currently available for use in the carotid artery, either as part of an FDA-approved clinical trial or as an "off-label" application of a device approved for noncarotid use. A 1987 study was the first to report on the use of an angioplasty technique involving temporary occlusion of the internal carotid artery during manipulation of ulcerated plaques.[18] The same investigators subsequently reported on the use of a triple-coaxial catheter system for angioplasty with cerebral protection in 13 patients[19]; cholesterol crystals ranging in size from 600 to 1,200 μm were aspirated at the time of intervention. The PercuSurge GuardWire (Medtronic AVE, Santa Rosa, California), which is approved for aortocoronary saphenous vein graft intervention, has been used in the MAVERIC trial of carotid intervention and has been employed extensively for off-label carotid intervention outside FDA-approved clinical trials [*see Figure 2*]. The advantages of this device include its low profile (which allows it to cross the target lesion easily), its procedural simplicity, and its ability to aspirate large debris particles after intervention. The disadvantages include the potential for incomplete occlusion of the ICA in patients with particularly large arteries (because the device can be inflated only from 3 mm to 6 mm in diameter) and the device's inability to aspirate exceptionally large particles into the suction catheter after intervention.[14] In addition, as flow is diverted into the ECA, emboli may travel by this route and into the ipsilateral middle cerebral artery via periorbital and ophthalmic artery collaterals.[20] Finally, a small percentage of patients with an incomplete circle of Willis and an isolated cerebral hemisphere may be intolerant of even temporary ICA occlusion. A 2002 study that evaluated the PercuSurge device in 75 CAS procedures found that four patients (5%) experienced transient neurologic symptoms during balloon occlusion that resolved with deflation and restoration of internal carotid flow.[21] Embolic material was aspirated from the ICA in all patients; no patients had suffered major or minor stroke at 30 days after the intervention.

Filter protection devices have been the object of a great deal of interest in the past few years. Such devices are designed to be able to trap large particulate debris while maintaining flow in the ICA, thereby not only providing continued cerebral perfusion during intervention but also allowing angiography of the target vessel during various phases of the procedure. All of the currently available filters have pores larger than 100 μm, which means that they allow passage of smaller particles that may not cause clinically significant neurologic events but may nonetheless cause silent neuronal injury. These filters also have higher physical profiles than balloon occlusion devices and thus may be difficult to pass across particularly severe stenoses. Filters that are not completely apposed to the vessel wall may allow emboli to pass around the device and into the distal cerebral circulation. A 2001 study described CAS performed in 86 lesions with three different filter devices.[22] In three cases, the filter could not be advanced across the lesion. However, more than half of the successfully deployed filters contained macroscopic embolic material, and only one patient (1.2%) experienced a neurologic complication (a minor stroke).

Finally, a device has been developed that induces reversal of flow in the ICA through balloon occlusion of the CCA and the ECA and creation of a temporary arteriovenous shunt between the ICA and the femoral vein.[23] This device, though potentially more cumbersome than other protection devices, may produce virtually complete protection by preventing any emboli from traveling to the intracranial circulation.

A 2004 report summarized one group of operators' experience with 1,202 CAS procedures between 1994 and 2002.[24] In 33% of the patients studied, a cerebral protection device was used during the procedure. The overall stroke rate was 4.4%; the risk of stroke reached its height (9.1%) during the period extending from September 1996 to September 1997 and reached its nadir (0.6%) during the final year of the study. The authors concluded that improvements in technique, equipment, and pharmacotherapy, as well as the use of neuroprotection, contributed significantly to improvements in results. In an earlier series, 46 patients were treated with CAS, of whom 25 received cerebral protection.[25] Two neurologic events (9.5%) occurred in the unprotected cohort; no events occurred in the protected group. Although the small numbers of patients prevented meaningful statistical analysis, the authors concluded that cerebral protection was technically feasible and effective in preventing neurologic complications during CAS.

The evidence accumulated to date suggests that most, if not all, CAS procedures should be performed with a cerebral embolic protection device. In time, more such devices will be approved by the FDA and will be available outside the setting of clinical trials.

Outcome Evaluation

The short-term results of CAS depend largely on the presence or absence of cerebral embolization. It is therefore not surprising that the addition of cerebral protection to CAS appears to have reduced the stroke risk associated with the procedure. Admittedly, however, ongoing technological developments have created something of a moving target, making evaluation of the results of CAS difficult at best. Nevertheless, the available literature is sufficient

Table 6 Results of Carotid Angioplasty and Stenting

Study	Arteries (N)	Symptomatic Vessels (%)	Cerebral Protection	Combined Stroke-Death Rate (%)
Diethrich (1996)[28]	117	28	No	7.3
Yadav (1997)[29]	126	59	No	7.9
Henry (1998)[30]	174	35	Mixed	2.9
Teitelbaum (1998)[31]	25	68	No	27.3
Bergeron (1999)[32]	99	44	No	2
Shawl (2000)[33]	192	61	No	2.9
Malek (2000)[34]	28	100	No	3.6
Roubin (2001)[26]	604	52	Mixed	7.4
Ahmadi (2001)[35]	298	38	Mixed	3.0
CAVATAS (2001)[36]	251	96	No	10
Brooks (2001)[37]	53	100	No	0
d'Audiffret (2001)[38]	68	30	Mixed	5.8
Chakhtoura (2001)[39]	50	39	No	2.2
Leger (2001)[40]	8	38	No	0
Dietz (2001)[41]	43	100	Yes	5
Baudier (2001)[42]	50	98	Mixed	6
Reimers (2001)[22]	88	36	Yes	2.3
Pappada (2001)[43]	27	93	Mixed	3.7
Paniagua (2001)[44]	69	16	No	5.6
Criado (2002)[27]	135	40	Mixed	2
Guimaraens (2002)[45]	194	92	Yes	2.6
Al-Mubarak (2002)[46]	164	48	Yes	2
Bonaldi (2002)[47]	71	100	Mixed	5.6
Kao (2002)[48]	118	75	No	4.2
Whitlow (2002)[21]	75	56	Yes	0
Qureshi (2002)[49]	73	37	Mixed	4.1
Macdonald (2002)[50]	50	84	Yes	6
Stankovic (2002)[51]	102	37	Mixed	0
Kastrup (2003)[52]	100	63	Mixed	5
Cremonesi (2003)[53]	442	57	Yes	1.1
Terada (2003)[54]	87	80	Yes	2.3
Bowser (2003)[55]	52	60	No	5.7
Wholey (2003)[56]	12,392	53	Mixed	4.75
Becquemin (2003)[57]	114	33	Mixed	7.0
Dabrowski (2003)[58]	73	Not stated	Mixed	5.5
Cernetti (2003)[59]	104	26	Yes	4
Bush (2003)[60]	51	29	No	2
Gable (2003)[61]	31	69	No	3
Lal (2003)[62]	122	45	Mixed	3.3
SAPPHIRE (2004)[8]	167	30	Yes	5.5
Total	17,087			4.7

to provide a reasonably accurate picture of the current status of the procedure [see Table 6].[8,21,22,26-62]

In a study from the University of Alabama at Birmingham and Lenox Hill Hospital in New York,[26] a total of 604 arteries were treated in 528 consecutive patients over a 5-year period. CAS was performed both with balloon-expandable stents and with self-expanding stents and both with and without cerebral protection devices. The overall 30-day combined stroke-death rate was 8.1% (minor stroke, 5.5%; major stroke, 1.6%; nonneurologic death, 1%). On a year-by-year basis, the risk of stroke and death reached its maximum (12.5%) in the period ending in September 1997 and fell to its minimum (3.2%) the following year. This rather dramatic change in results from one year to the next probably is attributable to technical advances (e.g., in protection devices, stents, and guide wires), as well as to improvements in the investigators' ability to select appropriate patients for intervention.

A subsequent report describes the authors' experience with CAS in a vascular surgery practice.[27] During a 40-month period from 1997 to 2001, 135 procedures were performed in 132 patients, most (60%) of whom were asymptomatic. The rate of complications was acceptable (2%), and only one patient had a significant restenosis at follow-up (mean follow-up interval, 16 months). Perhaps more important, these 132 patients represented 41% of all patients being treated for carotid disease in this practice. This percentage seems extraordinarily high, but it may simply be a bellwether of things to come in the practice of vascular surgery, and it underscores the importance of multispecialty involvement in this new technology.

The results of the SAPPHIRE trial of CAS in high-risk patients were published in 2004.[8] To date, this trial, which included 334 patients randomly assigned to either CAS (N = 167) or CEA (N = 167), is the only industry-sponsored FDA-approved trial that was actually randomized. A separate registry of nonrandomized patients was compiled that included those who were felt to be at unacceptably high risk for CEA and therefore underwent CAS (N = 406), as well as those who were not suitable candidates for CAS and therefore underwent CEA (N = 7). The goal of the SAPPHIRE trial was to evaluate the combined end point of major adverse events (stroke, death, and MI). Inclusion and exclusion criteria for the study are listed more fully elsewhere [see Tables 2 and 3]. Patients were independently evaluated by a certified neurologist before and after the procedure. The majority of the randomized patients were asymptomatic: in the CAS group, only 30% were symptomatic, and in the CEA group, only 28% were symptomatic. A key point to keep in mind is that this trial was designed to test the idea that CAS was not inferior to CEA, not to establish that CAS was superior to CEA or CEA to CAS. At 30 days, the risk of stroke was not significantly different in the two groups (CAS, 3.6%; CEA 3.1%). Two patients in the CAS group (1.2%) and four patients in the CEA group (2.5%) died within 30 days; this difference did not reach statistical significance (P = 0.39). More patients experienced periprocedural MI in the CEA group (6.1%) than in the CAS group (2.4%), a difference that did not reach statistical significance on the basis of intent to treat. Notably, most of the MIs were non-Q MIs, identified by routine postprocedural laboratory studies. The incidence of the combined end point (stroke-death-MI) was higher in the CEA group (9.8%) than in the CAS group (4.8%), but this difference was statistically insignificant as well. These results have been used to support FDA approval of the stent and filter protection device used in this important study.

Lesions of the proximal CCA are relatively uncommon in comparison with lesions of the carotid bifurcation, but they can also be effectively treated with CAS. In my experience, most are treated with common carotid cutdown, retrograde angioplasty, and placement of a balloon-expandable stent. Of 14 consecutive CCA interventions performed at the Cleveland Clinic,[63] one was converted to carotid-subclavian transposition after iatrogenic dissection, and two resulted in stroke secondary to ICA thrombosis. In both of the interventions resulting in stroke, which were performed in conjunction with redo bifurcation endarterectomies, the CCA was patent at the time of surgical reexploration and ICA thrombectomy. Although the carotid stent procedure is unlikely to have played a role in causing these strokes, it is nonetheless advisable to exercise caution when performing these combined procedures.

References

1. North American Symptomatic Carotid Endarterectomy Trial Collaborators: Beneficial effect of carotid endarterectomy in symptomatic patients with high-grade carotid stenosis. N Engl J Med 325:445, 1991

2. Executive Committee for the Asymptomatic Carotid Atherosclerosis Study: Endarterectomy for asymptomatic carotid artery stenosis. JAMA 273:1421, 1995

3. Menzoian JO: Presidential address: carotid endarterectomy, under attack again! J Vasc Surg 37:1137, 2003

4. Mozes G, Sullivan T, Torres-Russotto D, et al: Carotid endarterectomy in SAPPHIRE-eligible 'high-risk' patients: implications for selecting patients for carotid angioplasty and stenting. J Vasc Surg 39:958, 2004

5. Ouriel K, Hertzer NR, Beven EG, et al: Preprocedural risk stratification: identifying an appropriate population for carotid stenting. J Vasc Surg 33:728, 2001

6. Jordan WD Jr, Alcocer F, Wirthlin DJ, et al: High-risk carotid endarterectomy: challenges for carotid stent protocols. J Vasc Surg 325:16, 2002

7. Gasparis AP, Ricotta L, Cuadra SA, et al: High-risk carotid endarterectomy: fact or fiction. J Vasc Surg 37:40, 2003

8. Yadav JS, Wholey MH, Kuntz RE, et al: Stenting and Angioplasty with Protection in Patients at High Risk for Endarterectomy Investigators. Protected carotid-artery stenting versus endarterectomy in high-risk patients. N Engl J Med 351:1493, 2004

9. Gaunt ME, Martin PJ, Smith JL, et al: Clinical relevance of intraoperative embolization detected by transcranial Doppler ultrasonography during carotid endarterectomy: a prospective study of 100 patients. Br J Surg 81:1435, 1994

10. Fearn SJ, Pole R, Wesnes K, et al: Cardiopulmonary support and physiology. J Thorac Cardiovasc Surg 121:1150, 2001

11. Rapp JH, Pan XM, Sharp FR, et al: Atheroemboli to the brain: size threshold for causing acute neuronal cell death. J Vasc Surg 32:68, 2000

12. Ohki T, Marin ML, Lyon RT, et al: Ex vivo human carotid artery bifurcation stenting: correlation of lesion characteristics with embolic potential. J Vasc Surg 27:463, 1998

13. Bicknell CD, Cowling MG, Clark MW, et al: Carotid angioplasty in a pulsatile flow model: factors affecting embolic potential. Eur J Vasc Endovasc Surg 26:22, 2003

14. Tübler T, Schlüter M, Dirsch O, et al: Balloon-protected carotid artery stenting: relationship of periprocedural neurological complications with the size of particulate debris. Circulation 104:2791, 2001

15. Al-Mubarak N, Roubin GS, Vitek JJ, et al: Effect of the distal-balloon protection system on macroembolization during carotid stenting. Circulation 104:1999, 2001

16. Baim DS, Wahr D, George B, et al: Randomized trial of a distal embolic protection device during percutaneous intervention of saphenous vein aorto-coronary bypass grafts. Circulation 105:1285, 2002

17. Coggia M, Goëau-Brissonière, Duval J-L, et al: Embolic risk of the different stages of carotid bifurcation balloon angioplasty: an experimental study. J Vasc Surg 31:550, 2000

18. Theron J, Raymond J, Casasco A, et al: Percutaneous angioplasty of atherosclerotic and postsurgical stenosis of carotid arteries. Am J Neuroradiol 8:495, 1987

19. Theron J, Courtheoux P, Alachkar F, et al: New triple coaxial catheter system for carotid angioplasty with cerebral protection. Am J Neuroradiol 11:869, 1990

20. Al-Mubarak N, Vitek JJ, Iyer S, et al: Embolization via collateral circulation during carotid stenting with the distal balloon protection system. J Endovasc Ther 8:354, 2001

21. Whitlow PL, Lylyk P, Londero H, et al: Carotid artery stenting protected with an emboli containment system. Stroke 22:1308, 2002

22. Reimers B, Corvaja N, Moshiri S, et al: Cerebral protection with filter devices during carotid artery stenting. Circulation 104:12, 2001

23. Ohki T, Parodi J, Veith FJ, et al: Efficacy of a proximal occlusion catheter with reversal of flow in the prevention of embolic events during carotid artery stenting: an experimental analysis. J Vasc Surg 33:504, 2001

24. New G, Roubin GS, Iyer SS, et al: Outcomes from carotid artery stenting in over 1,000 cases from a single group of operators. J Am Coll Cardiol 41(suppl A):868, 2003

25. Parodi JC, LaMura R, Ferriera LM, et al: Initial evaluation of carotid angioplasty and stenting with three different cerebral protection devices. J Vasc Surg 32:1127, 2000

26. Roubin GS, New G, Iyer SS, et al: Immediate and late clinical outcomes of carotid artery stenting in patients with symptomatic and asymptomatic carotid artery stenosis: a 5-year prospective analysis. Circulation 103:532, 2001

27. Criado FJ, Lingelbach JM, Ledesma DF, et al: Carotid artery stenting in a vascular surgery practice. J Vasc Surg 35:430, 2002

28. Diethrich EB, Ndiaye M, Reid DB: Stenting in the carotid artery: initial experience in 110 patients. J Endovasc Surg 3:42, 1996

29. Yadav JS, Roubin GS, Iyer S, et al: Elective stenting of the extracranial carotid arteries. Circulation 95: 376, 1997

30. Henry M, Amor M, Masson I, et al: Angioplasty and stenting of the extracranial carotid arteries. J Endovasc Surg 5:293, 1998

31. Teitelbaum GP, Lefkowitz MA, Giannotta SL: Carotid angioplasty and stenting in high-risk patients. Surg Neurol 50:300, 1998

32. Bergeron P, Becquemin JP, Jausseran JM, et al: Percutaneous stenting of the internal carotid artery: the European CAST I Study. Carotid Artery Stent Trial. J Endovasc Surg 6:155, 1999

33. Shawl F, Kadro W, Domanski MJ, et al: Safety and efficacy of elective carotid artery stenting in high-risk patients. J Am Coll Cardiol 35:1721, 2000

34. Malek AM, Higashida RT, Phatouros CC, et al: Stent angioplasty for cervical carotid artery stenosis in high-risk symptomatic NASCET-ineligible patients. Stroke 31:3029, 2000

35. Ahmadi R, Willfort A, Lang W, et al: Carotid artery stenting: effect of learning curve and intermediate-term morphological outcome. J Endovasc Ther 8: 539, 2001

36. Endovascular versus surgical treatment in patients with carotid stenosis in the Carotid and Vertebral Artery Transluminal Angioplasty Study (CAVATAS): a randomised trial. Lancet 357:1729, 2001

37. Brooks WH, McClure RR, Jones MR, et al: Carotid angioplasty and stenting versus carotid endarterectomy: randomized trial in a community hospital. J Am Coll Cardiol 38:1589, 2001

38. d'Audiffret A, Desgranges P, Kobeiter H, et al: Technical aspects and current results of carotid stenting. J Vasc Surg 33:1001, 2001

39. Chakhtoura EY, Hobson RW 2nd, Goldstein J, et al: In-stent restenosis after carotid angioplasty-stenting: incidence and management. J Vasc Surg 33:220, 2001

40. Leger AR, Neale M, Harris JP: Poor durability of carotid angioplasty and stenting for treatment of recurrent artery stenosis after carotid endarterectomy: an institutional experience. J Vasc Surg 33:1008, 2001

41. Dietz A, Berkefeld J, Theron JG, et al: Endovascular treatment of symptomatic carotid stenosis using stent placement: long-term follow-up of patients with a balanced surgical risk/benefit ratio. Stroke 32:1855, 2001

42. Baudier JF, Licht PB, Roder O, et al: Endovascular treatment of severe symptomatic stenosis of the internal carotid artery: early and late outcome. Eur J Vasc Endovasc Surg 22:205, 2001

43. Pappada G, Marina R, Fiori L, et al: Stenting of atherosclerotic stenoses of the extracranial carotid artery. Acta Neurochir (Wien) 143:1005, 2001

44. Paniagua D, Howell M, Strickman N, et al: Outcomes following extracranial carotid artery stenting in high-risk patients. J Invasive Cardiol 13:375, 2001

45. Guimaraens L, Sola MT, Matali A, et al: Carotid angioplasty with cerebral protection and stenting: report of 164 patients (194 carotid percutaneous transluminal angioplasties). Cerebrovasc Dis 13:114, 2002

46. Al-Mubarak N, Colombo A, Gaines PA, et al: Multicenter evaluation of carotid artery stenting with a filter protection system. J Am Coll Cardiol 39:841, 2002

47. Bonaldi G: Angioplasty and stenting of the cervical carotid bifurcation: report of a 4-year series. Neuroradiology 44:164, 2002

48. Kao HL, Lin LY, Lu CJ, et al: Long-term results of elective stenting for severe carotid artery stenosis in Taiwan. Cardiology 97:89, 2002

49. Qureshi AI, Suri MF, New G, et al: Multicenter study of the feasibility and safety of using the memotherm carotid arterial stent for extracranial carotid artery stenosis. J Neurosurg 96:830, 2002

50. Macdonald S, Venables GS, Cleveland TJ, et al: Protected carotid stenting: safety and efficacy of the MedNova NeuroShield filter. J Vasc Surg 35:966, 2002

51. Stankovic G, Liistro F, Moshiri S, et al: Carotid artery stenting in the first 100 consecutive patients: results and follow up. Heart 88:381, 2002

52. Kastrup A, Skalej M, Krapf H, et al: Early outcome of carotid angioplasty and stenting versus carotid endarterectomy in a single academic center. Cerebrovasc Dis 15:84, 2003

53. Cremonesi A, Manetti R, Setacci F, et al: Protected carotid stenting: clinical advantages and complications of embolic protection devices in 442 consecutive patients. Stroke 34:1936, 2003

54. Terada T, Tsuura M, Matsumoto H, et al: Results of endovascular treatment of internal carotid artery stenoses with a newly developed balloon protection catheter. Neurosurgery 53:617, 2003

55. Bowser AN, Bandyk DF, Evans A, et al: Outcome of carotid stent-assisted angioplasty versus open surgical repair of recurrent carotid stenosis. J Vasc Surg 38:432, 2003

56. Wholey MH, Al-Mubarek N, Wholey MH: Updated review of the global carotid artery stent registry. Catheter Cardiovasc Interv 60:259, 2003

57. Becquemin JP, Ben El Kadi H, Desgranges P, et al: Carotid stenting versus carotid surgery: a prospective cohort study. J Endovasc Ther 10:687, 2003

58. Dabrowski M, Bielecki D, Golebiewski P, et al: Percutaneous internal carotid artery angioplasty with stenting: early and long-term results. Kardiol Pol 58:469, 2003

59. Cernetti C, Reimers B, Picciolo A, et al: Carotid artery stenting with cerebral protection in 100 consecutive patients: immediate and two-year follow-up results. Ital Heart J 4:695, 2003

60. Bush RL, Lin PH, Bianco CC, et al: Carotid artery stenting in a community setting: experience outside of a clinical trial. Ann Vasc Surg 17:629, 2003

61. Gable DR, Bergamini T, Garrett WV, et al: Intermediate follow-up of carotid artery stent placement. Am J Surg 185:183, 2003

62. Lal BK, Hobson RW 2nd, Goldstein J, et al: In-stent recurrent stenosis after carotid artery stenting: life table analysis and clinical relevance. J Vasc Surg 38:1162, 2003

63. Sullivan TM, Gray BH, Bacharach JM, et al: Angioplasty and primary stenting of the subclavian, innominate, and common carotid arteries in 83 patients. J Vasc Surg 28:1059, 1998

90 REPAIR OF INFRARENAL ABDOMINAL AORTIC ANEURYSMS

Frank R. Arko, M.D., Stephen T. Smith, M.D., and Christopher K. Zarins, M.D., F.A.C.S.

An arterial aneurysm is defined as a permanent localized enlargement of an artery to a diameter more than 1.5 times its expected diameter. Aneurysms are classified according to morphology, etiology, and anatomic site. The most common morphology is a fusiform, symmetrical, circumferential enlargement that involves all layers of the arterial wall. A saccular morphology is also seen, in which aneurysmal degeneration affects only part of the arterial circumference.

The most common cause of an arterial aneurysm is atherosclerotic degeneration of the arterial wall. The pathogenesis is a multifactorial process involving genetic predisposition, aging, atherosclerosis, inflammation, and localized activation of proteolytic enzymes. Most aneurysms occur in elderly persons, and the prevalence rises with increasing age. Aneurysms also occur in genetically susceptible individuals with Ehlers-Danlos syndrome or Marfan syndrome. Other causes include tertiary syphilis and localized infection resulting in a mycotic aneurysm.

Aneurysms of the infrarenal aorta are by far the most common arterial aneurysms encountered in clinical practice today: they are three to seven times more common than thoracic aneurysms and affect four times as many men as women.[1] Abdominal aortic aneurysms (AAAs) have a tendency to enlarge and rupture, causing death. In the United States, AAAs result in approximately 15,000 deaths each year and are thus the 13th leading cause of death.[2,3] The only way to reduce the death rate is to identify and treat aortic aneurysms before they rupture [*see 82 Pulsatile Abdominal Mass*].

The relationship between aneurysm size and risk of rupture is well known. The annual risk of rupture is 1% to 2% for aneurysms less than 5 cm in diameter, 10% for aneurysms 5 to 6 cm in diameter, and 25% or higher for aneurysms larger than 6 cm.[4] Although large aneurysms are much more likely to rupture than small aneurysms, small aneurysms can and do rupture on occasion.

The exact size at which an asymptomatic small AAA should be treated remains unsettled. This issue was the subject of two prospective, randomized clinical trials: the United Kingdom Small Aneurysm Trial[5] and the Aneurysm Detection And Management (ADAM) Veterans Affairs (VA) Cooperative Study.[6] Both trials randomly assigned low-risk patients with small (4.0 to 5.4 cm) AAAs to either open surgical repair or ultrasound surveillance. Patients in the surveillance groups were closely monitored with serial ultrasound examinations and underwent open surgical repair if the aneurysm enlarged, became tender to palpation, or became symptomatic. With respect to the primary end point—overall survival—the two trials came to similar conclusions: there was no difference in overall survival between the surgery group and the surveillance group.[5,6] There was, however, a late survival benefit in the surgery group in the U.K. Small Aneurysm Trial.[7]

Aneurysm rupture rates were low (1%) in both trials, leading many clinicians to conclude that aneurysms smaller than 5.5 cm need not be treated, because the risk of rupture is so low. Closer examination of the data, however, reveals that more than 60% of the patients in the surveillance groups underwent open surgical repair during the two trials: 81% of patients with 5.0 to 5.4 cm aneurysms in the ADAM trial underwent surgery, and almost all patients in the U.K. trial ultimately required surgical management. Thus, it is likely that the reason for the low rupture risk in these trials was that surgical treatment of the aneurysm was provided when clinically indicated. This conclusion is supported by data from a prospective study of patients from the VA hospitals involved in the ADAM trial who were not eligible for randomization and did not undergo operative repair. In these patients, the 1-year risk of rupture for slightly larger (5.5 to 5.9 cm) aneurysms was 9.4%.[8] Furthermore, very close surveillance with ultrasound examinations every 3 to 6 months did not prevent aneurysm rupture in 1% of patients. Thus, the decision whether to treat an aneurysm is based on assessment of the risk of aneurysm rupture relative to the risk associated with treatment rather than on an absolute size criterion or a surveillance protocol.

Open Repair

PREOPERATIVE EVALUATION

Identification of Risk Factors

For successful surgical reconstruction of AAAs, any significant comorbidities that would increase the risk of operative repair must be identified and managed at an early stage. Patients undergoing the procedure usually are elderly and often have coexisting cardiac, pulmonary, cerebrovascular, renal, or peripheral vascular disease. The major anesthetic risk factors for elective resection of AAAs are similar to those for other major intra-abdominal operations; in particular, they include inadequate cardiopulmonary and renal function. Patients with unstable angina or angina at rest, a cardiac ejection fraction of less than 25%, a serum creatinine concentration higher than 3 mg/dl, or pulmonary disease (manifested by arterial oxygen tension < 50 mm Hg, elevated arterial carbon dioxide tension, or both on room air) are considered to be at high risk.[9,10]

Myocardial ischemia is the most common cause of perioperative morbidity and mortality after arterial reconstruction of the aorta. Optimization of preoperative medical management, perioperative invasive monitoring, and long-term risk-factor modification are all facilitated by an accurate preoperative cardiac evaluation. Such evaluation may include transthoracic echocardiography, exercise stress testing, myocardial scintigraphy, stress echocardiography, and coronary angiography; each test has its own merits and limitations with regard to clinical risk assessment.

There has been considerable controversy over the potential benefit of preoperative coronary revascularization in this setting. This issue was addressed by a clinical trial in which patients requiring AAA or peripheral vascular surgery who had high-risk cardiac disease were randomly assigned to undergo either vascular surgery without preoperative coronary revascularization or coronary revascularization followed by vascular surgery.[11] There was no differ-

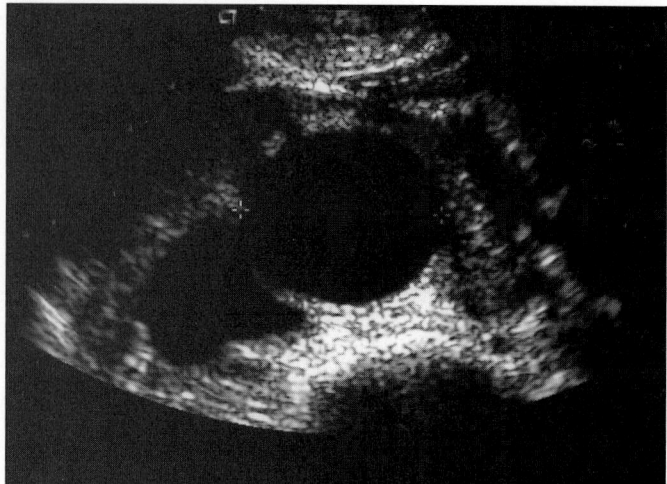

Figure 1 **Duplex ultrasonography may be used as a screening test and to determine the actual size of the aneurysm.**

ence between the two groups with respect to the incidence of postoperative MI or overall mortality. The investigators concluded that patients with stable coronary disease do not benefit from preoperative coronary revascularization. Patients with unstable severe coronary disease may benefit from invasive cardiac evaluation and preliminary coronary intervention.

To reduce the mortality associated with resection of AAAs, it is necessary not only to identify high-risk groups but also to institute appropriate preoperative, intraoperative, and postoperative alterations in patient care. With intensive perioperative monitoring and support in place, resection of AAAs has been successfully performed even in high-risk patients, with operative mortalities of less than 6%.[12-14]

Confirmation of Diagnosis and Determination of Aneurysm Size

Physical examination suffices for detection of most large aneurysms. To determine the exact size of the aneurysm and to identify smaller aneurysms, however, more objective methods are available and should be used. Determination of the size of the aneurysm is extremely important because size is the most important determinant of the likelihood of rupture and plays a crucial role in subsequent management decisions. Imaging modalities commonly employed to diagnose and measure aneurysms include duplex ultrasonography (DUS), aortography, computed tomography, and magnetic resonance imaging.

The main advantages of DUS are its ready availability in both inpatient and outpatient settings, its low cost, its safety, and its good performance; many studies have documented the ability of DUS to establish the diagnosis and accurately determine the size of AAAs [*see Figure 1*].[15-17] The primary limitations of DUS are that imaging of the thoracic and suprarenal aorta is poor, that the quality of the images is considerably lower in the presence of obesity or large amounts of intestinal gas, and that it must be performed by a skilled imaging technician.

Aortography yields excellent images of the contours of the aortic lumen, but it is not a reliable method for determining the diameter of an aneurysm or even for establishing its presence, because the mural thrombus within the aneurysm tends to reduce the lumen to near-normal size. Nonetheless, aortography can be helpful in determining the extent of an aneurysm (especially when there is iliac or suprarenal involvement), defining associated arterial lesions involving the renal and visceral arteries, and detecting

lower-extremity occlusive disease. There are risks associated with aortography that place some restrictions on its use. Among these risks are the potential renal toxicity resulting from the use of contrast agents. In addition, manipulation of catheters through the laminated mural thrombus increases the risk of distal embolization. Finally, local arterial complications may arise at the arterial puncture site.

CT provides reliable information about the size of the entire aorta, thereby allowing accurate determination of both the size and the extent of the AAA [*see Figure 2*]. Spiral CT scanning permits identification of the visceral and renal arteries and their relationship to the aneurysm. The administration of I.V. contrast material allows assessment of the aortic lumen, the amount and location of mural thrombus, and the presence or absence of retroperitoneal hematoma [*see Figure 3*]. Overall, spiral CT is currently the most useful imaging method for evaluation of the abdominal aorta.

MRI is also useful in the preoperative evaluation of aortic aneurysms.[18,19] It employs radiofrequency energy and a magnetic field to produce images in longitudinal, transverse, and coronal planes. The advantages of MRI over CT are that no ionizing radiation is administered, multiplane images can be obtained, and no nephrotoxic contrast agents are used.

Classification of Patients for Elective or Urgent Repair

Patients may usefully be classified into three categories according to how they present for repair: (1) elective patients, (2) symptomatic patients, and (3) patients with ruptured aneurysms.

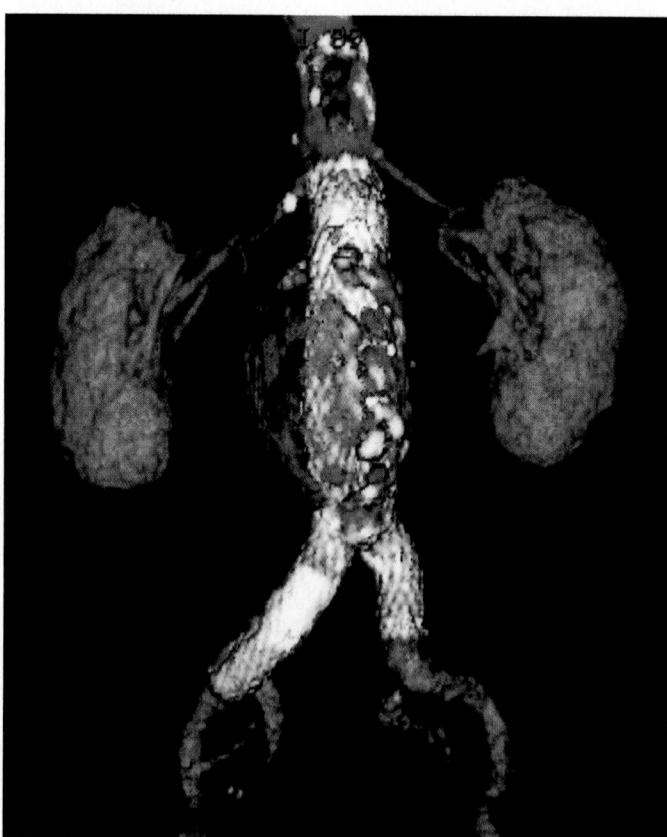

Figure 2 **Shown is a CT angiogram providing a three-dimensional reconstruction of an infrarenal AAA after endovascular repair. Of particular interest is the relation of the graft to the renal arteries and the hypogastric arteries distally.**

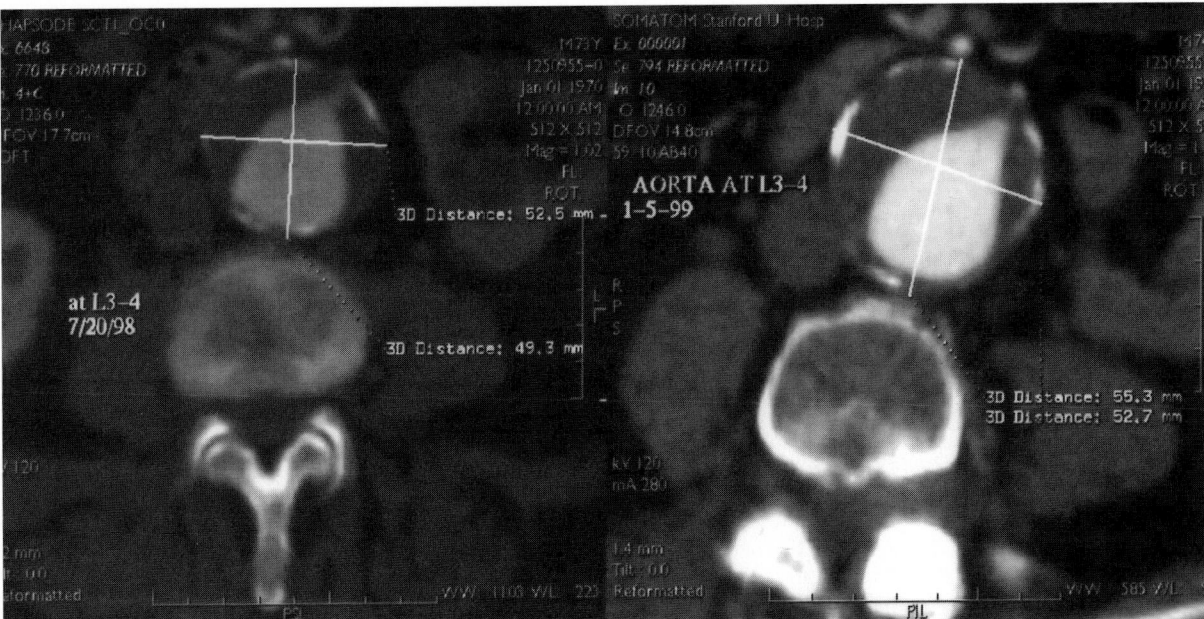

Figure 3 CT scanning assesses the size of the aneurysm, the amount of mural thrombus present, and the relation of other intra-abdominal structures to the aneurysm.

Elective aneurysm repair is recommended for asymptomatic patients who have aneurysms 5.0 cm in diameter or larger, who have an acceptable level of operative risk, and who have a life expectancy of 1 year or more. Furthermore, elective operation should be considered for patients with aneurysms smaller than 5.0 cm who are not at high operative risk if they are hypertensive or live in a remote area where proper medical care is not readily available. Repair is also appropriate for aneurysms that are between 4.0 and 5.0 cm in diameter and have shown growth of more than 0.5 cm on serial images in less than 6 to 12 months. Peripheral embolization originating from the aneurysm is an indication for repair, regardless of the size of the aneurysm.

Urgent operation is indicated for patients with symptomatic aneurysms, regardless of the size of the aneurysm. Such patients typically present with abdominal or back pain. Sometimes, the back pain radiates to the groin, much as in ureteral colic; this pain may be elicited by palpating the aneurysm. In most cases, DUS, CT, and MRI will reliably detect the presence of periaortic blood; however, the absence of this finding should not delay operation, because actual rupture of the aneurysm can occur at any time.

Emergency operation is indicated for almost all patients with known or suspected rupture of an aneurysm.

OPERATIVE PLANNING

Preoperative planning is essential for a successful outcome after repair of an infrarenal AAA. Like the choice between elective and urgent or emergency repair, operative planning is governed by the presentation of the patient. In patients with ruptured aneurysms, diagnosis is immediately followed by operative repair. In patients with symptomatic aneurysms, the amount of preoperative imaging done is balanced against the risk of impending rupture. In patients presenting for elective repair, it is generally possible to perform extensive imaging to determine whether the repair is best done via an endovascular approach [see Endovascular Repair, *below*] or a standard open approach. Current preoperative imaging methods utilizing CT angiography (CTA) obviate several common pitfalls. The availability of endovascular techniques for excluding an aneurysm should not alter the patient selection criteria for aneurysm repair. Consideration of endovascular aneurysm repair (EVAR) does introduce certain morphologic criteria into the process of patient selection, in that stent grafting is appropriate only for patients in whom the infrarenal neck and the iliac arteries are suitable.

Given that the long-term outcome of endovascular grafting is currently unknown, younger patients who are at low operative risk and are expected to survive into the long term are typically better served with open surgical repair. In addition, patients who require additional abdominal or pelvic revascularization procedures, who have small or diseased access vessels, or who have short (< 10 mm) or tortuous infrarenal necks are not candidates for endovascular grafting and should undergo open surgical repair instead.

Preoperative preparation to optimize cardiopulmonary function, administration of preoperative antibiotics, and intraoperative hemodynamic monitoring with appropriate fluid management can significantly reduce the risks associated with AAA repair. Before aortic cross-clamping, appropriate volume loading, combined with vasodilatation, is carried out to help prevent declamping hypotension.

OPERATIVE TECHNIQUE

Step 1: Initial Incision and Choice of Approach

Open surgical repair of infrarenal AAAs is performed through a transperitoneal or retroperitoneal exposure of the aorta with the patient under general endotracheal anesthesia. The aneurysm may be exposed through either a long midline incision (for the transperitoneal approach) or an oblique flank incision (for the retroperitoneal approach) [see Figure 4a]. An upper abdominal transverse incision may also be used for either retroperitoneal or transperitoneal exposure. The results with the two exposures are equivalent. The transperitoneal approach is preferred when exposure of the right renal artery is required and when access to the distal right iliac system or to intra-abdominal organs is necessary. The retroperitoneal exposure offers advantages when extensive peritoneal adhesions, an intestinal stoma, or severe pulmonary disease is present and when there is a need for suprarenal exposure. Use of the retroperitoneal approach has been associated with a shorter

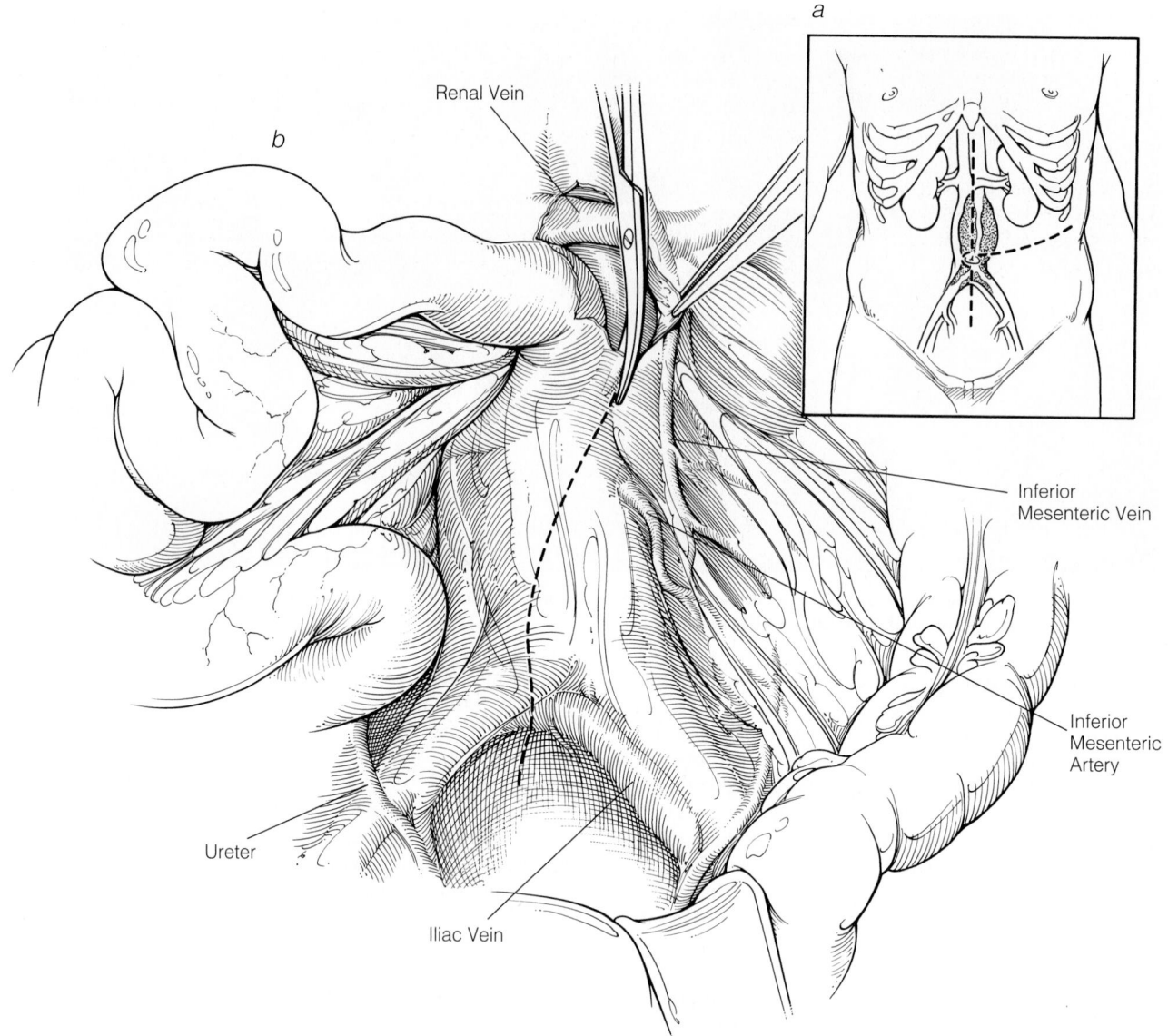

Figure 4 Open repair of infrarenal AAAs. (*a*) For the transabdominal approach to the abdominal aorta, a midline or transverse incision is appropriate. For the retroperitoneal approach, an oblique flank incision may be used. (*b*) The small intestine (including the duodenum) is retracted laterally after the ligament of Treitz is mobilized, and the retroperitoneum is incised in the midline. The left renal vein is the landmark for the infrarenal neck.

duration of postoperative ileus, a lower incidence of pulmonary complications, and a reduction in length of stay in the ICU.

Step 2 (Transperitoneal Approach): Exposure and Control of Aorta and Iliac Arteries

When the transperitoneal approach is taken, the small bowel (including the duodenum) is retracted to the right, and the retroperitoneum overlying the aneurysm is divided to the left of the midline [*see Figure 4b*]. The duodenum is completely mobilized, and the left renal vein is identified and exposed. The normal infrarenal neck, which is just below the left renal vein, is then exposed and encircled for proximal control. Both common iliac arteries are mobilized and controlled, with care taken to avoid the underlying iliac veins and ureters that cross over at the iliac bifurcation [*see Figure 5*]. If the common iliac arteries are aneurysmal, then both the internal and the external iliac arteries are controlled. The inferior mesenteric artery is then dissected out and controlled for possible reimplantation into the graft after the aneurysm has been repaired.

Step 2 (Retroperitoneal Approach): Exposure and Control of Aorta and Iliac Arteries

When the retroperitoneal approach is taken, a transverse left abdominal or flank incision is made, and the peritoneum is reflected anteriorly. The left kidney usually is left in place but may be mobilized anteriorly to expose the posterolateral aorta. Exposure of the right iliac system can be achieved by dividing the inferior mesenteric artery early in the course of dissection. The aorta and the iliac arteries are controlled in essentially the same fashion regardless of the type of incision used.

Step 3: Opening of Aneurysm and Creation of Proximal Anastomosis

Systemic anticoagulation with I.V. heparin is then performed. After sufficient time (3 to 5 minutes) has elapsed to permit adequate circulation, the infrarenal neck and the iliac arteries are clamped. To prevent distal embolization, the distal clamps should be applied before the proximal aortic clamp. The aneurysm is then opened longitudinally, the mural thrombus is removed, and back-bleeding lumbar arteries are oversewn. Depending on its degree of backflow and on the patency of the hypogastric arteries, the inferior mesenteric artery may be either ligated or clamped and left with a rim of aortic wall for subsequent reimplantation [see Troubleshooting, below].

The aortic neck is then partially or completely transected, and an appropriately sized tubular or bifurcated graft is sutured to the aorta with a continuous nonabsorbable monofilament suture [see Figure 6]. When the proximal aortic neck is very short, suprarenal aortic

clamping may be required for performance of the proximal anastomosis. If suprarenal clamping is necessary, the security of the proximal anastomosis should be verified, and the clamp should then be moved onto the graft below the renal arteries as soon as possible to minimize renal ischemia. If the aorta is especially weak or friable, the anastomosis may be supported with Teflon-felt pledgets.

Step 4: Creation of Distal Anastomosis

When the aneurysm is confined to the aorta, the distal anastomosis is performed by suturing a straight tube graft to the aortic

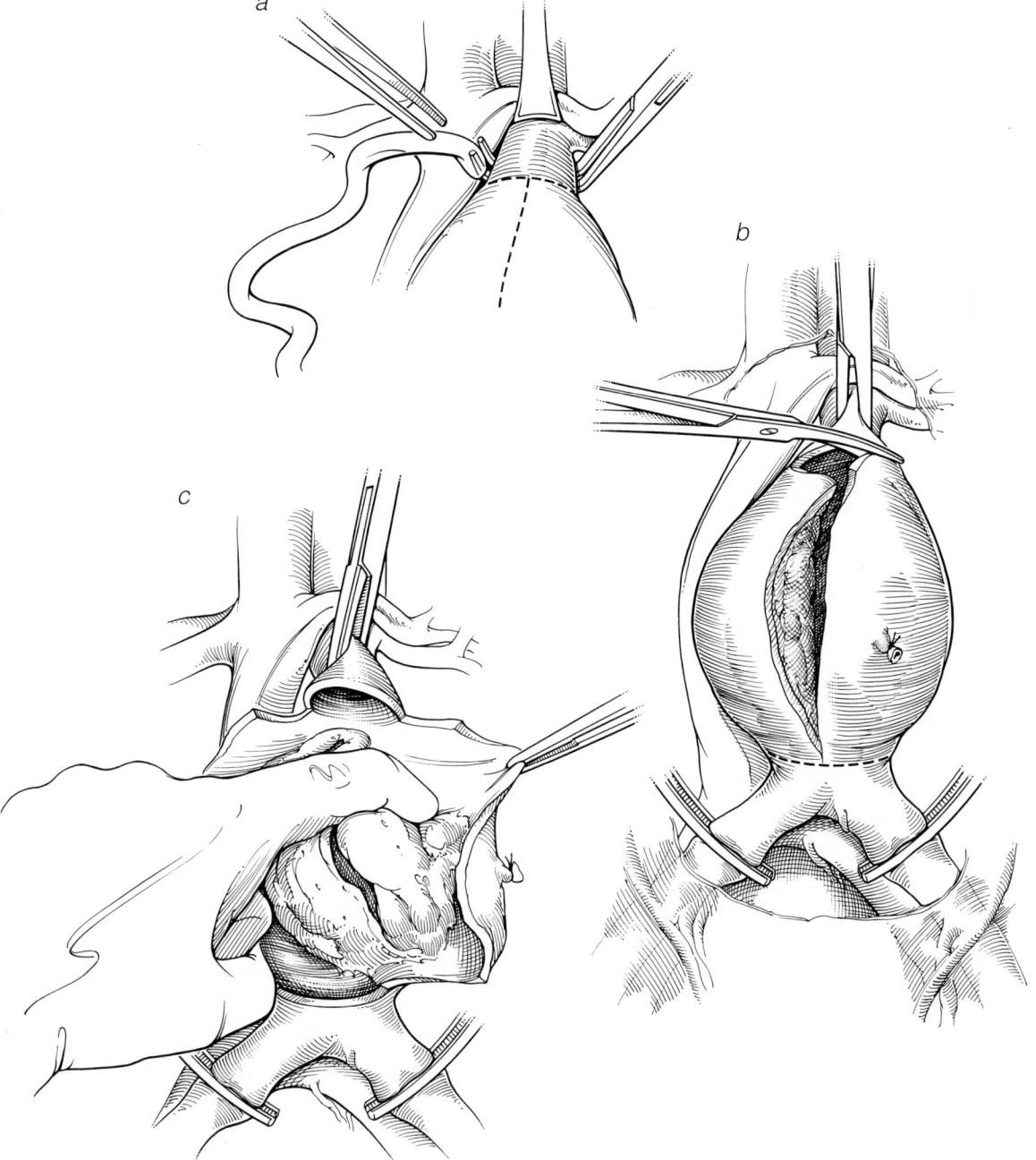

Figure 5 **Open repair of infrarenal AAAs. (*a*) Once the aneurysm is exposed, proximal control is obtained by encircling the proximal neck with an umbilical tape or heavy Silastic. The inferior mesenteric artery is identified and then either clamped or ligated for possible reimplantation at the end of the procedure. (*b*) The iliac arteries are dissected free, systemic heparin anticoagulation is instituted, and distal control is obtained, followed by proximal control to prevent distal embolization. The aneurysm sac is then opened longitudinally. (*c*) All mural thrombus is removed, and the proximal and distal necks of the aorta are incised.**

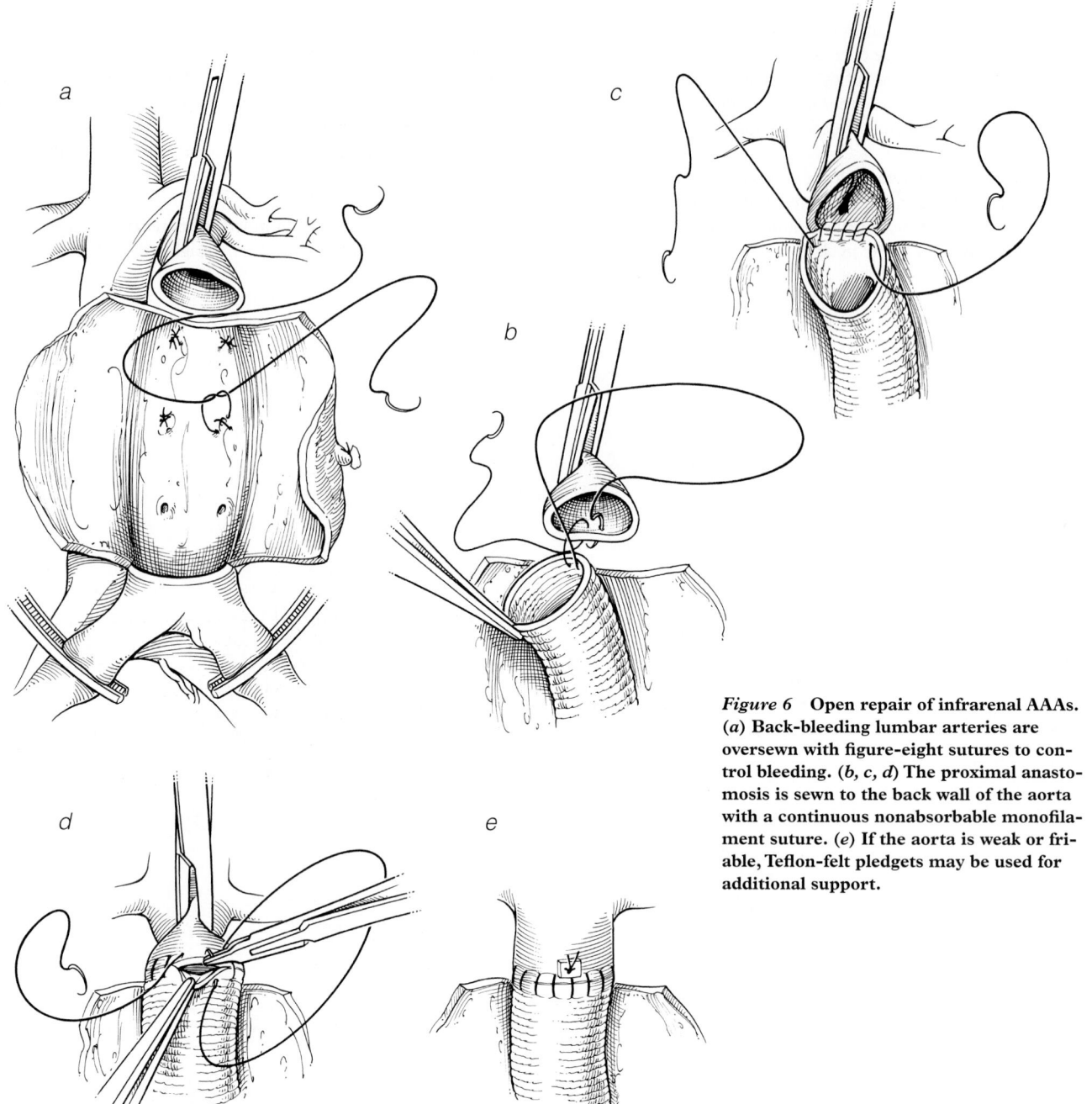

Figure 6 **Open repair of infrarenal AAAs. (*a*) Back-bleeding lumbar arteries are oversewn with figure-eight sutures to control bleeding. (*b, c, d*) The proximal anastomosis is sewn to the back wall of the aorta with a continuous nonabsorbable monofilament suture. (*e*) If the aorta is weak or friable, Teflon-felt pledgets may be used for additional support.**

bifurcation [*see Figure 7*]; straight tube graft reconstructions are used about 30% of the time. Distally, the dissection should avoid the fibroareolar tissue overlying the left common iliac artery because this tissue contains branches of the inferior mesenteric artery and the autonomic nerves that control sexual function in men.

When the aneurysm extends into the common iliac arteries, the distal anastomosis is accomplished by suturing a bifurcated graft to the distal common iliac arteries or, in the case of significant occlusive disease, to the common femoral arteries. In these situations, control of the iliac arteries is best achieved by mobilizing the external and internal arteries and clamping them individually [*see Figure 8*]. It is sometimes easier to control iliac artery back-bleeding by using intraluminal balloon catheters and oversewing the common iliac arteries from within the opened aortic or iliac aneurysms. Care must be taken not to injure the accompanying venous structures or the ureters, which cross anterior to the iliac bifurcation.

Every effort should be made to ensure perfusion of at least one hypogastric artery to help minimize the risk of postoperative left colon ischemia.

Declamping hypotension may occur after reperfusion of the lower extremities. It is essential to maintain communication with the anesthesiologist so that blood and fluid replacement can be adjusted in anticipation of lower-extremity reperfusion. Even though the graft and vessels are flushed and back-bled before distal flow is reestablished, it is preferable first to establish flow into one of the hypogastric arteries so as to minimize the chances of distal embolization to the legs.

Before the abdomen is closed, adequate perfusion of the lower extremities and the left colon should be ensured via either direct inspection or noninvasive monitoring. The open aneurysm sac is then sutured closed over the aortic graft to separate the graft from the duodenum and the viscera [*see Figure 9*]. This step reduces the risk of aortoenteric fistula.

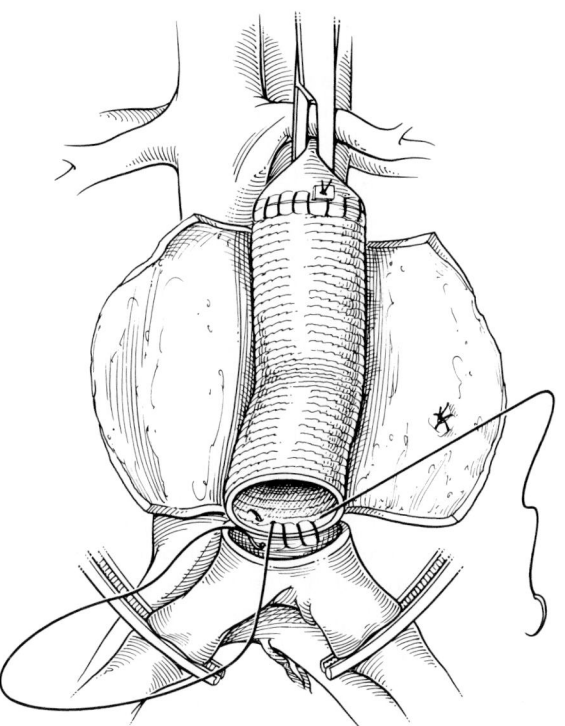

Figure 7 **Open repair of infrarenal AAAs. When the aneurysm does not extend into the iliac arteries, a straight tube graft is used. The distal anastomosis is completed with a continuous suture. Before completion of the anastomosis, the graft is flushed by back-bleeding the iliac arteries and flushing the proximal anastomosis.**

Troubleshooting

If the inferior mesenteric artery is small and back-bleeding is adequate, it may be ligated [*see Figure 10a*]; however, if the vessel is large or back-bleeding is meager, it should be reimplanted. Reimplantation of the inferior mesenteric artery can be accomplished with relative ease by using the Carrel patch technique. After the graft has been completely sewn to the aorta, a partial occluding clamp is placed on the main body of the graft or on one of the limbs. An opening in the graft is then created, and an end-to-side anastomosis [*see Figure 10b*]—with an interposition graft added if necessary [*see Figure 10c*]—is used to reconstruct the inferior mesenteric artery. This anastomosis is created with a continuous monofilament suture.

SPECIAL CONSIDERATIONS

Concurrent Disease Processes

At times, a concurrent disease process complicates repair of an AAA. The most common problems encountered are hepatobiliary, pancreatic, gastrointestinal, gynecologic, and genitourinary disorders. Careful evaluation of the situation is necessary to determine whether to treat the two disease entities concurrently. As a rule, the more life-threatening disorder is treated first.

There are three key points that should be remembered in the management of patients with AAAs and concurrent diseases. First, a careful preoperative diagnostic workup usually detects any concomitant disease processes. Second, in emergency situations such as ruptured or symptomatic aneurysms, the aneurysm always takes priority unless the other condition is life-threatening and the aneurysm clearly is not the cause of the critical symptoms. Finally, many concomitant intra-abdominal problems can be avoided by taking an endovascular approach.

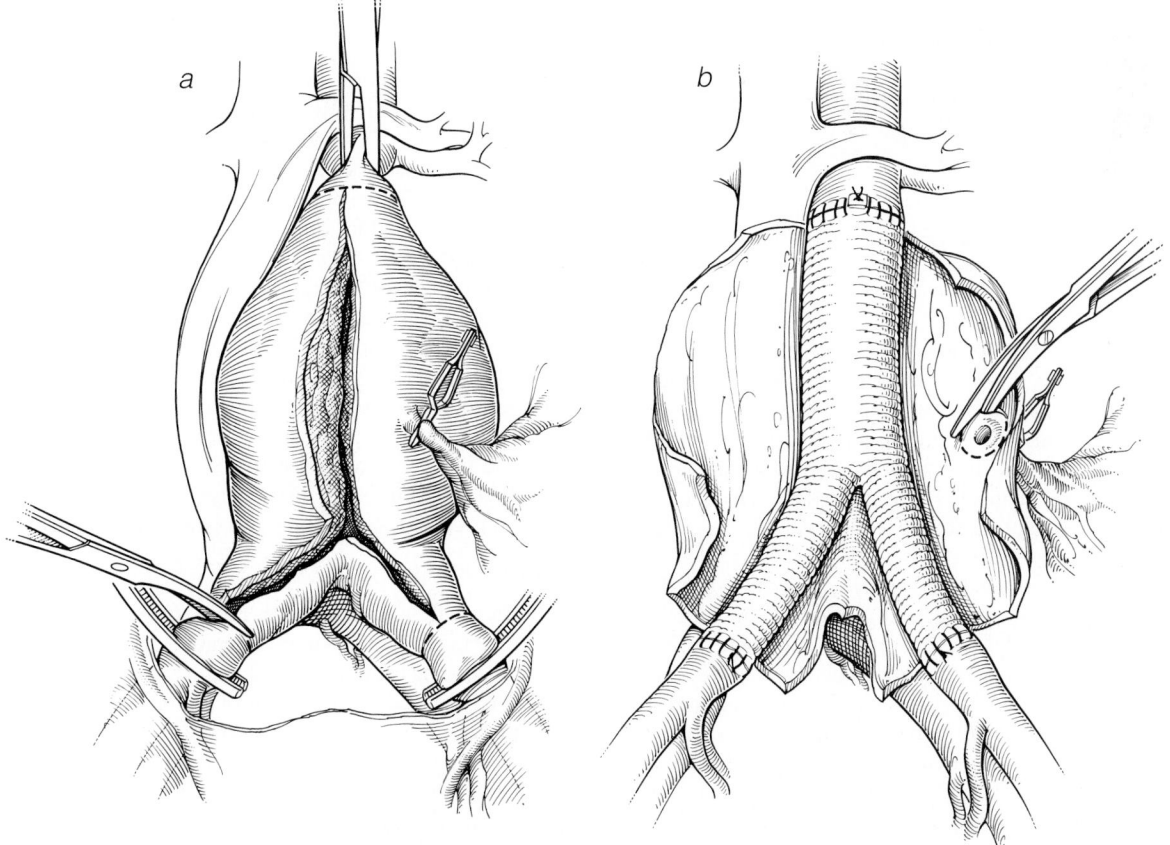

Figure 8 **Open repair of infrarenal AAAs. When the common iliac arteries are aneurysmal, both the internal and the external iliac arteries must be clamped individually (*a*), and a bifurcated graft is sewn to the iliac arteries bilaterally (*b*).**

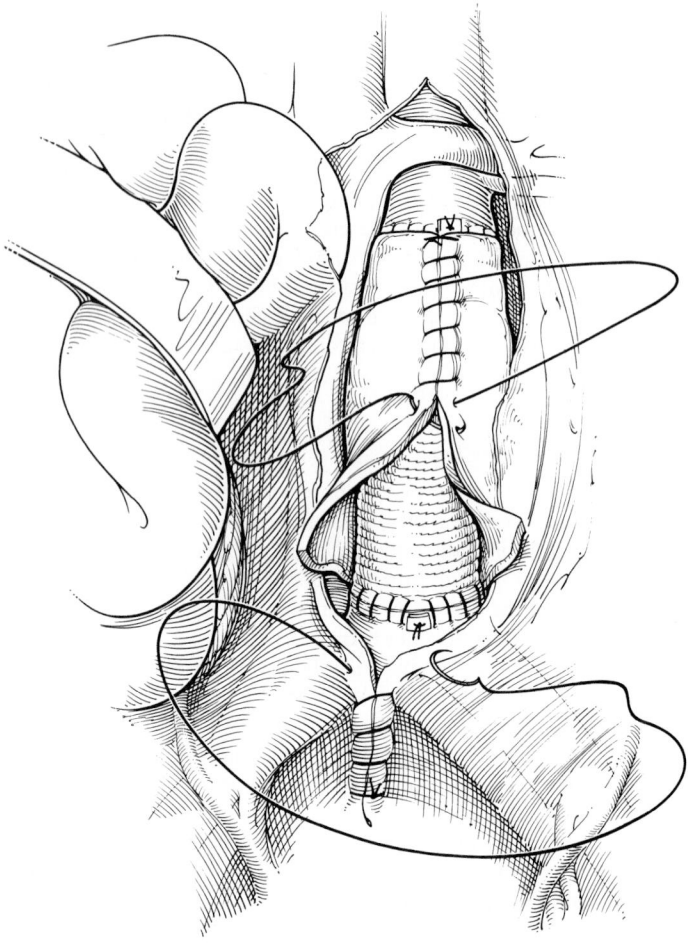

Figure 9 **Open repair of infrarenal AAAs. Once the anastomoses have been completed and adequate flow to the lower extremities and the left colon has been confirmed, the open aneurysm sac is sutured closed over the aortic graft.**

Anatomic Variants

Several anatomic variants may be encountered during repair of AAAs, including horseshoe kidney, accessory renal arteries, and venous anomalies.

Horseshoe kidney The incidence of horseshoe kidney in the general population is less than 3%. Most patients with horseshoe kidneys have between three and five renal arteries.[20] To preserve renal function, renal arteries arising from the aneurysm should be reimplanted. In patients with horseshoe kidneys who have more than five renal arteries, there often are multiple small accessory arteries, some of which originate from the aneurysm, the iliac arteries, or both.

The presence of a horseshoe kidney may complicate—but does not preclude—an anterior approach to repair of an infrarenal AAA.[21] In such cases, the left retroperitoneal approach provides excellent exposure of the infrarenal aorta. This approach requires that the surgeon dissect the space between the aneurysm and the left portion and isthmus of the kidney; the kidney can then be reflected to the right and the aneurysm fully exposed. The left ureter crosses the iliac arteries from the right in this position, and duplication of ureters may be noted.

Venous anomalies A number of different venous anomalies may be observed in the course of AAA repair; however, the overall

incidence is quite low. Left renal vein variants, such as retroaortic left renal veins and circumaortic venous rings, are the most commonly seen venous anomalies.[22] Azygous continuation of the inferior vena cava and bilateral inferior vena cava have also been noted. Unnecessary bleeding can be prevented by means of careful dissection and meticulous technique.

Inflammatory Aneurysm

Approximately 5% of infrarenal AAAs are inflammatory.[23] These AAAs have a dense fibroinflammatory rind that typically adheres to the fourth portion of the duodenum; they may also involve the inferior vena cava, the left renal vein, or the ureters. Patients with inflammatory AAAs typically experience abdominal or flank pain and may present with weight loss. The erythrocyte sedimentation rate is usually elevated as well. Inflammatory aneurysms rarely rupture, because most are symptomatic and consequently are treated before rupture can occur. Repair of inflammatory aneurysms poses technical problems because of the involvement of adjacent structures. A retroperitoneal approach is usually advocated for these aneurysms.

Ruptured Aneurysm

Infrarenal AAAs can rupture freely into the peritoneal cavity or into the retroperitoneum. Free rupture into the peritoneal cavity is usually anterior and is typically accompanied by immediate hemodynamic collapse and a very high mortality. Retroperitoneal ruptures are usually posterior and may be contained by the psoas muscle and adjacent periaortic and perivertebral tissue. This type of rupture may occur without significant blood loss initially, and the patient may be hemodynamically stable.

When an aortic aneurysm ruptures, immediate surgical repair is indicated. If the patient is unstable and either an abdominal aortic aneurysm was previously diagnosed or a palpable abdominal mass is present, no further evaluation is necessary and the patient should be taken directly to the OR. If the patient is stable and the diagnosis is questionable, CT scanning may be performed to confirm the presence of an aneurysm and determine its extent, the site of the rupture, and the degree of iliac involvement. Bedside ultrasonography may also be used for quick confirmation of the presence of an AAA.

Surgical repair of ruptured aneurysms is performed via a transperitoneal approach. In cases of contained rupture, supraceliac control should be achieved before infrarenal dissection; once the neck of the aneurysm has been dissected free, the aortic clamp may be moved to the infrarenal level. In cases of free rupture, efforts to obtain vascular control may include compression of the aorta at the hiatus and infrarenal control with a clamp or an intraluminal balloon. Once proximal and distal control have been achieved, the operation is conducted in much the same way as an elective repair.

OUTCOME EVALUATION

The mortality associated with repair of AAAs has been greatly reduced by improvements in preoperative evaluation and perioperative care: leading centers currently report death rates ranging from 0% to 5%.[24] Mortality after repair of inflammatory aneurysms and after emergency repair of symptomatic nonruptured aneurysms continues to be somewhat higher (5% to 10%), primarily as a consequence of less thorough preoperative evaluation.

Overall morbidity after elective aneurysm repair ranges from 10% to 30%. The most common complication is myocardial ischemia, and MI is the most common cause of postoperative death. Mild renal insufficiency is the second most frequent com-

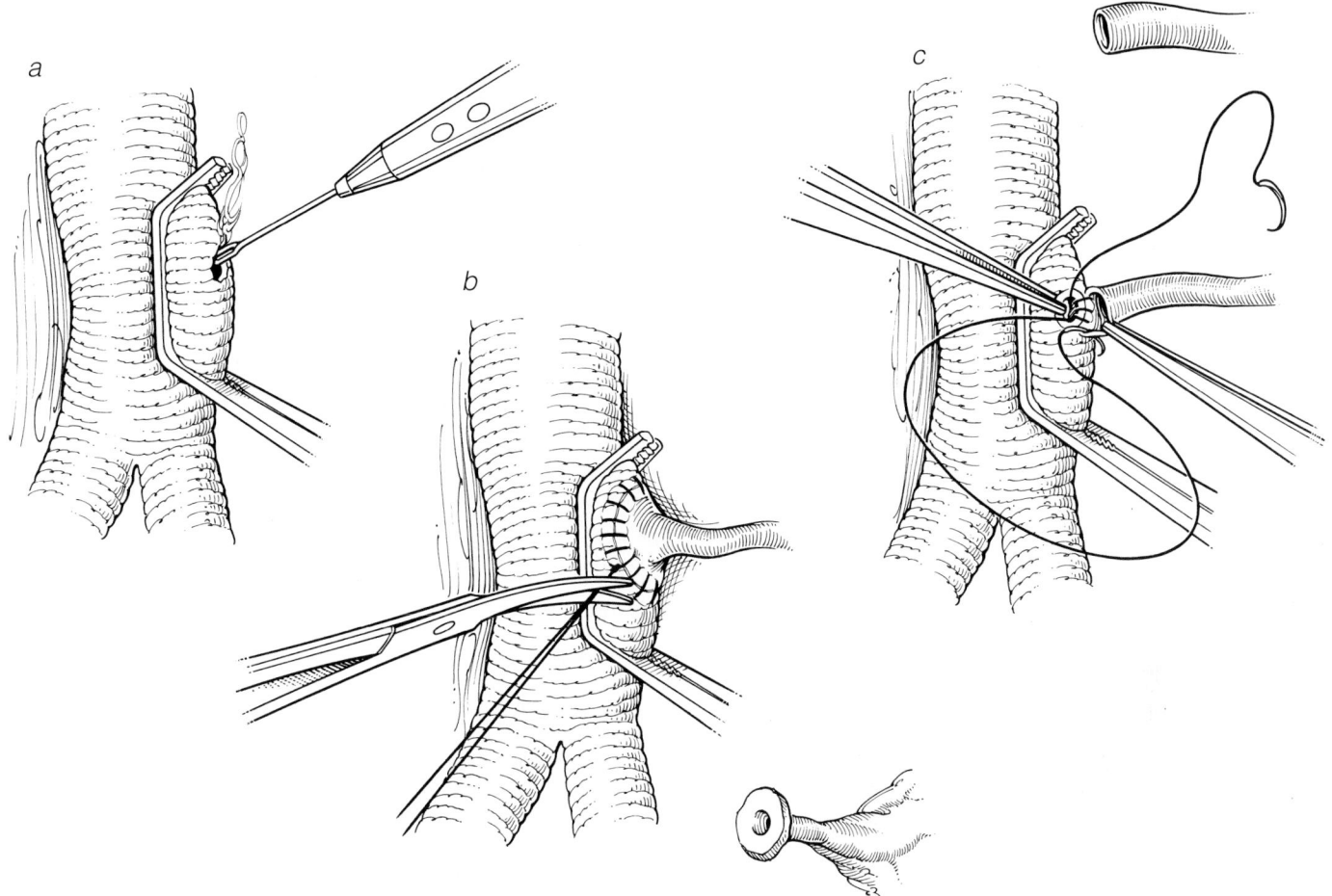

Figure 10 **Open repair of infrarenal AAAs. (*a*) A small, adequately back-bleeding inferior mesenteric artery may be ligated. (*b*) A large or meagerly back-bleeding inferior mesenteric artery should be reimplanted. A side-biting clamp is applied to the graft, and an end-to-side anastomosis is created with a fine monofilament suture. (*c*) If the inferior mesenteric artery is not long enough for a direct anastomosis, an interposition graft—either a segment of a vein or a prosthetic graft—may be used for added length.**

plication, occurring after 6% of elective aneurysm repairs; however, severe renal failure necessitating dialysis is rare in this setting. The third most common complication is pulmonary disease; the incidence of postoperative pneumonia is approximately 5%.

Postoperative bleeding may occur as well. Common sources of such bleeding include the anastomotic suture lines, inadequately recognized venous injuries, and coagulopathies resulting from intraoperative hypothermia or excessive blood loss. Any evidence of ongoing bleeding is an indication for early exploration.

Lower-extremity ischemia may occur as a result of either emboli or thrombosis of the graft and may necessitate reoperation and thrombectomy. So-called trash foot may also develop when diffuse microemboli are carried into the distal circulation.

Colon ischemia develops after 1% of elective aneurysm repairs. Patients usually present with bloody diarrhea, abdominal pain, a distended abdomen, and leukocytosis. The diagnosis is confirmed by sigmoidoscopy, which reveals mucosal sloughing. In cases of transmural colonic necrosis, colon resection and exteriorization of stomas are warranted.

Paraplegia is rare after repair of infrarenal AAAs: the incidence is only 0.2%. Most instances of paraplegia occur after repair of a ruptured aneurysm or when the pelvis has been devascularized. The majority of patients recover at least some degree of neurologic function.

Late complications (e.g., pseudoaneurysms at the suture lines,

graft or graft limb thrombosis, and graft infection) may occur but are extremely rare. Graft infection may be associated with graft-enteric fistula and is notoriously difficult to diagnose and treat.

Long-term survival in patients who have undergone successful AAA repair is reduced in comparison with that in the general population. The 5-year survival rate after AAA repair is 67% (range, 49% to 84%), compared with 80% to 85% in age-matched control subjects, and the mean duration of survival after AAA repair is 7.4 years. Part of the difference in survival can be attributed to associated coronary disease in patients with aneurysms. Late deaths result primarily from cardiac causes.

Endovascular Repair

Endovascular repair was introduced during the 1990s as a less invasive approach to treating infrarenal AAAs. In this approach, a stent-graft is placed endoluminally via bilateral groin incisions; thus, there is no need for a major abdominal incision and aortic clamping. The results to date have been promising: blood loss is decreased, hospital stay is shortened, and earlier return to function is achieved. Not all patients are candidates for endovascular repair, however. In September 1999, the Food and Drug Administration approved two stent-graft devices for use in surgical management of AAAs: the Ancure device (Guidant, Indianapolis, Indiana), which is a balloon-expandable one-piece bifurcated stent-graft, and the

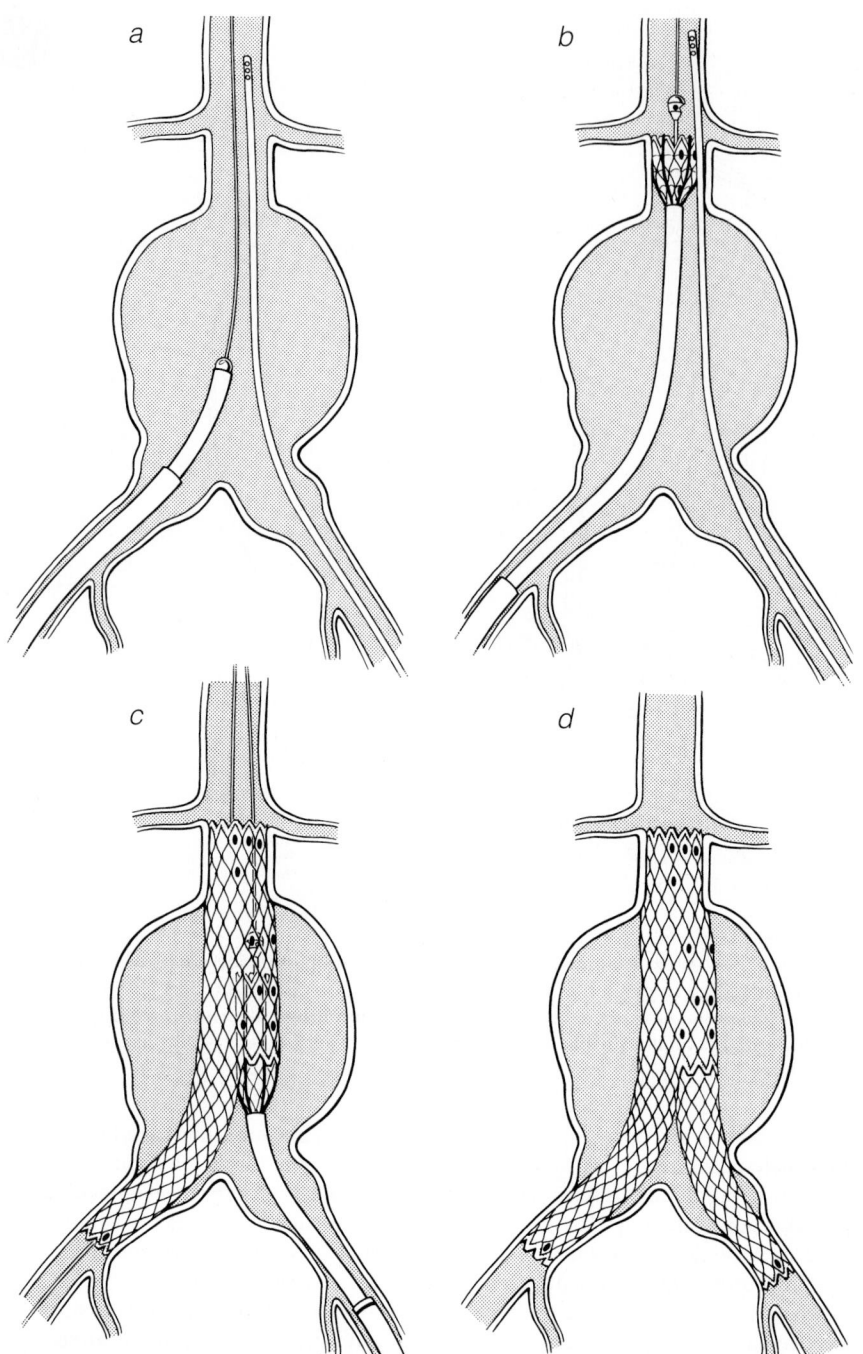

Figure 11 **Endovascular repair of infrarenal AAAs. (*a*) The main bifurcated stent-graft is advanced through the aortoiliac system under fluoroscopic guidance. (*b*) The sheath over the stent-graft is retracted under fluoroscopic guidance. Controlled deployment allows the graft to be gradually positioned directly below the renal arteries. (*c*) With the main body of the stent-graft deployed, the contralateral limb is cannulated. Once this is done, the contralateral limb is positioned within the junction gate and the common iliac artery. (*d*) Shown is proper deployment of the stent-graft within the aortoiliac system, with good proximal and distal fixation of the stent to the arterial wall.**

AneuRx device (Medtronic AVE, Santa Rosa, California), which is a self-expanding bifurcated modular device that is fully supported externally by a nitinol stent. Subsequently, the FDA approved three more devices for endovascular repair of AAAs: the Excluder Bifurcated Endoprosthesis (W. L. Gore and Associates, Flagstaff, Arizona), in November 2002, the Zenith AAA Endovascular Graft (Cook Incorporated, Bloomington, Indiana), in May 2003, and the Endologix Powerlink System (Endologix Incorporated, Irvine, California), in November 2004. The Ancure device is no longer available.

PREOPERATIVE PREPARATION

Precise preoperative evaluation that yields accurate measurements will result in proper planning and effective prevention of problems. Both CTA and contrast biplane angiography are used for this purpose. Of the two, spiral CTA is currently preferred. This imaging modality is capable of obtaining high-quality images of the vascular anatomy and reconfiguring them into detailed three-dimensional images. For optimal evaluation, images should be obtained at 1.5 to 3 mm intervals from the celiac artery to the femoral arteries. Spiral CTA accurately defines the proximal and distal characteristics of the AAA, as well as detects any significant renal, visceral, or iliac occlusive disease. It is particularly helpful in defining the infrarenal neck between the renal arteries and the proximal portion of the aneurysm.

Angiography is employed as a complement to spiral CTA in this setting. An arteriogram is useful in that it helps define renal, mesenteric, and distal arterial anatomy; helps characterize tortuosity, calcification, and stenoses in access arteries; and helps determine the angles between the aorta, the proximal neck, and the aneurysm.

Intravascular ultrasonography (IVUS) is a useful intraoperative imaging adjunct in the process of sizing and selecting endograft components. It can be used to measure vessel diameters and landing zone lengths, as well as to determine the amount of mural thrombus in the aneurysm neck. In patients with severe renal insufficiency, IVUS is used primarily to identify the renal and hypogastric arteries, allowing the endograft to be deployed with minimal or no resort to angiography.

Proper patient selection is mandatory for successful outcome. The common femoral arteries must be large enough to accept a delivery system larger than 21 French. The proximal infrarenal aortic neck must be suitable for device implantation—that is, its diameter must be between 16 and 28 mm, and its length should be at least 15 mm. The common iliac artery implantation should be carried out as close to the iliac bifurcation as possible to increase the columnar strength of the implanted device. The iliac artery diameter must be between 8 and 20 mm. In patients with iliac artery aneurysms, it is possible to land the end of the stent in the external iliac artery and thereby exclude one internal iliac artery. Exclusion of both internal iliac arteries should be avoided so as to prevent ischemic sequelae (e.g., buttock claudication, colon ischemia, and erectile dysfunction). Coil embolization may be performed in conjunction with EVAR to treat internal iliac aneurysms. However, a waiting period of several weeks between coil embolization of a hypogastric artery on one side and the same procedure on the other side should be considered to allow recruitment of collateral vessels and reduce the incidence of pelvic ischemia.

TECHNIQUE

The methods and technical principles we briefly describe here derive from the personal experience of two surgeons (F.R.A and C.K.Z) with more than 1,000 modular implants. The ensuing technical description is not intended to be exhaustive, nor is it meant as a substitute for the instructions provided by any of the manufacturers.

The patient is placed under epidural or general anesthesia. Bilateral femoral artery cutdowns are performed through transverse groin incisions to allow exposure of the common femoral artery from the inguinal ligament to the femoral bifurcation. Proximal control of the femoral arteries is obtained with umbilical tapes. Systemic anticoagulation with I.V. heparin is instituted to prolong the activated clotting time (ACT) to greater than 250 seconds. The ACT is monitored and maintained at this level throughout the procedure, and additional heparin is given as needed.

The femoral arteries are cannulated with an 18-gauge needle, and 0.035-in. guide wires are placed bilaterally under fluoroscopic guidance; 10 French sheaths are then placed over the two guide wires and advanced into the aneurysm under fluoroscopic guidance. A superstiff 0.035-in. guide wire 260 cm in length is inserted into the thoracic aorta, usually from the right limb. In the contralateral iliac artery, a pigtail catheter is placed just above the level of the renal arteries, and an initial roadmapping aortogram is obtained. The 10 French sheath in the right femoral artery is then exchanged for the device, which is placed over the superstiff guide wire and carefully advanced into the proximal infrarenal aorta under fluoroscopic guidance, then into the perirenal aorta [see Figure 11a]. A second aortogram is performed to verify the position of the renal arteries. Under fluoroscopic guidance, the stent-graft is then gradually deployed by retracting the outer sheath and allowing the graft to expand, and it is positioned directly below the level of the renal arteries [see Figure 11b].

Once the main bifurcation module has been deployed, the 10 French sheath in the contralateral iliac artery is pulled back, and a 0.035-in. angled hydrophilic wire and a guide catheter are inserted into the contralateral limb of the bifurcation module. The hydrophilic wire is then exchanged for a superstiff guide wire, over which the contralateral limb is then advanced through the sheath into the contralateral vessel and deployed [see Figure 11c]. A final aortogram is then performed to confirm that a satisfactory technical result has been achieved [see Figure 11d]. Proximal and distal extender cuffs may be placed if necessary. The femoral arteriotomies are repaired, and lower-extremity perfusion is reestablished.

OUTCOME EVALUATION

EVAR is significantly less invasive than open surgical repair and consequently is associated with a significant reduction in major procedure-related morbidity. Prospective clinical trials comparing open AAA repair with EVAR have consistently found that patients undergoing the latter experience less intraoperative blood loss, need less postoperative ICU care, have shorter lengths of stay, and regain normal function earlier.[25,26] Procedure-related mortality after EVAR is 1% to 2%, which is essentially equivalent to that reported after open repair in prospective clinical trials but lower than the 5% mortality reported after open repair in most multicenter studies.[27,28]

In the past few years, two randomized, controlled trials comparing EVAR with open AAA repair have been published. The Dutch Randomized Endovascular Aneurysm Management (DREAM) trial found EVAR to have a significant advantage in the first 30 days, with reduced mortality and a lower incidence of severe complications.[29] This survival advantage was not sustained, however, and at 1 year, there was no difference between EVAR and open AAA repair. The EVAR 1 trial, carried out in the United Kingdom, found EVAR to yield a similar reduction in 30-day mortality.[30] Again, this survival advantage was not sustained, and at 4 years, there was no difference between EVAR and open repair in terms of overall mortality or health-related quality of life. EVAR did, however, have a significant advantage over open AAA repair with regard to 4-year aneurysm-related mortality. The impact of this advantage will continue to be assessed as this trial's follow-up period lengthens.

On occasion, EVAR fails to exclude blood flow from the aneurysm sac completely. This condition, known as endoleak, may arise from an incomplete seal at the site where the endograft is affixed to the aortic neck or the iliac arteries (type I endoleak), from retrograde flow into the aneurysm from the inferior mesenteric artery or the lumbar arteries (type II endoleak), or from the graft or modular junction site (type III endoleak). Type I and type

III endoleaks call for secondary treatment to prevent possible aneurysm rupture. The significance of type II endoleaks is less certain. There is no clear evidence that type II endoleaks lead to aneurysm rupture; however, most such endoleaks are treated if they are associated with aneurysm enlargement.

Although numerous studies have shown that endovascular AAA repair results in less morbidity and perioperative mortality than open repair,[31-34] reports describing endograft migration over time, aneurysm enlargement, and occasional aneurysm rupture have raised questions about the long-term durability of the procedure.[35,36] These adverse events, though uncommon, serve as reminders that EVAR is still a new technology, one whose long-term outcome is unknown. Accordingly, close patient monitoring and follow-up surveillance are warranted, and secondary treatments may be required (e.g., additional endovascular procedures or, possibly, open surgical repair). New endovascular devices are currently being designed and evaluated in clinical trials, and endovascular treatment strategies continue to evolve and improve.

Clinical follow-up of patients treated during the initial prospective clinical trials now extends to more than 7 years, and EVAR continues to show favorable results. The largest multicenter endovascular clinical trial to date, involving 1,193 patients who were followed for as long as 6 years, found that prevention of aneurysm rupture (the primary objective) was achieved in 99% of patients, whereas procedure-, aneurysm-, or graft-related death was avoided in 97%.[37,38] These results are consistent with the favorable overall outcomes reported from a European registry of EVAR using a variety of endovascular devices.[39] Thus, the midterm results of EVAR are favorable and support the consideration of this approach for most patients who are candidates for the procedure.

References

1. Taylor LM, Porter JM: Basic data related to clinical decision-making in abdominal aortic aneurysms. Ann Vasc Surg 1:502, 1980

2. Bickerstaff LK, Hollier LH, Van Peenen HJ, et al: Abdominal aortic aneurysm: the changing natural history. J Vasc Surg 1:6, 1984

3. Melton L, Bickerstaff L, Hollier LH, et al: Changing incidence of abdominal aortic aneurysms: a population based study. Am J Epidemiol 120:379, 1984

4. Finlayson SRG, Birkeyer JD, Fillinger MF, et al: Should endovascular surgery lower the threshold for abdominal aortic aneurysms? J Vasc Surg 29:973, 1999

5. The UK Small Aneurysm Trial Participants: Mortality results for randomized controlled trial of early elective surgery or ultrasonographic surveillance for small abdominal aortic aneurysms. Lancet 352:1649, 1998

6. Lederle FA, Wilson SE, Johnson GR, et al: Immediate repair compared with surveillance of small abdominal aortic aneurysms. N Engl J Med 346:1437, 2002

7. The United Kingdom Small Aneurysm Trial Participants: Long-term outcomes of immediate repair compared with surveillance for small abdominal aortic aneurysms. N Engl J Med 346:1445, 2002

8. Lederle FA, Johnson GR, Wilson SE, et al: Rupture rate of large abdominal aortic aneurysms in patients refusing or unfit for elective repair. JAMA 287:2968, 2002

9. Darling RC, Messina CR, Brewster DC, et al: Autopsy study of unoperated aortic aneurysms. Circulation 56(suppl 2):161, 1977

10. Thurmond AS, Semler JH: Abdominal aortic aneurysm: incidence in a population at risk. J Cardiovasc Surg 27:457, 1986

11. McFalls EO, Ward HB, Moritz TE, et al: Coronary-artery revascularization before elective major vascular surgery. N Engl J Med 351:2795, 2004

12. Whittemore AD, Clowes AW, Hechtman HB, et al: Aortic aneurysm repair reduced operative mortality associated with maintenance of optimal cardiac performance. Ann Surg 120:414, 1980

13. Pairolero PC: Repair of abdominal aortic aneurysms in high-risk patients. Surg Clin North Am 69:755, 1989

14. Stokes J, Butcher HR: Abdominal aortic aneurysms: factors influencing operative mortality and criteria of operability. Arch Surg 107:297, 1973

15. Quill DS, Colgan MP, Summer DS: Ultrasonic screening for the detection of abdominal aortic aneurysms. Surg Clin North Am 69:713, 1989

16. Bluth EI: Ultrasound of the abdominal aorta. Arch Intern Med 144:377, 1994

17. Gomes MN, Choyke PL: Preoperative evaluation of abdominal aortic aneurysms: ultrasound or computed tomography? J Cardiovasc Surg 28:159, 1987

18. Amparo EG, Hoddick WK, Hricak H, et al: Comparison of magnetic resonance imaging and ultrasonography in the evaluation of abdominal aortic aneurysms. Radiology 154:451, 1985

19. Lee JKT, Ling D, Heiken JP, et al: Magnetic resonance imaging of abdominal aneurysms. Am J Roentgenol 143:1197, 1984

20. Papin E: Chirurgie du rein. Anomalies du rein. Paris, G. Doin, 1928, p 205

21. Zarins CK, Gewertz BL: Atlas of Vascular Surgery. New York, Churchill Livingstone, 1988, p 56

22. Trigaux JP, Vandroogenbroek S, De Wispelaere JF, et al: Congenital anomalies of the inferior vena cava and left renal vein: evaluation with spiral CT. J Vasc Interv Radiol 9:339, 1998

23. Crawford JL, Stowe CL, Safi HJ, et al: Inflammatory aneurysms of the aorta. J Vasc Surg 2:133, 1985

24. Crawford ES, Saleh SA, Babb JW 3rd, et al: Infrarenal abdominal aortic aneurysm: factors influencing survival after operation performed over a 25-year period. Ann Surg 193:699, 1981

25. Zarins CK, White RA, Schwarten D, et al: AneuRx stent graft vs. open surgical repair of abdominal aortic aneurysm: multicenter prospective clinical trial. J Vasc Surg 29:292, 1999

26. Makaroun MS: The Ancure endografting system: an update. J Vasc Surg 33:S129, 2001

27. Nonruptured abdominal aortic aneurysm: six-year follow-up results from the multicenter prospective Canadian aneurysm study. Canadian Society for Vascular Surgery Aneurysm Study Group. J Vasc Surg 20:163, 1994

28. Zarins CK, Harris EJ: Operative repair of aortic aneurysms: the gold standard. J Endovasc Surg 4:232, 1997

29. Prinssen M, Verhoeven ELG, Buth J, et al: A randomized trial comparing conventional and endovascular repair of open abdominal aortic aneurysms. N Engl J Med 351:1607, 2004

30. EVAR trial participants. Endovascular aneurysm repair versus open repair in patients with abdominal aortic aneurysm (EVAR trial 1): randomised controlled trial. Lancet 365:2179, 2005

31. Arko FR, Lee WA, Hill BB, et al: Aneurysm-related death: primary endpoint analysis for comparison of open and endovascular repair. J Vasc Surg 36:297, 2002

32. Moore WS, Kashyap VS, Vescera CL, et al: Abdominal aortic aneurysm: a 6 year comparison of endovascular versus transabdominal repair. Ann Surg 230:298, 1999

33. Adriansen MEAPM, Bosch JL, Halpern EF, et al: Elective endovascular versus open surgical repair of abdominal aortic aneurysms: systematic review of short-term results. Radiology 224:739, 2002

34. Arko FR, Hill BB, Olcott C, et al: Endovascular repair reduces early and late morbidity compared to open surgery for abdominal aortic aneurysm. J Endovasc Ther 9:711, 2002

35. Cao P, Verzini F, Zannetti S, et al: Device migration after endoluminal abdominal aortic aneurysm repair: analysis of 113 cases with a minimum follow-up period of 2 years. J Vasc Surg 35:229, 2002

36. Torsello GB, Klenk E, Kasprzak B, et al: Rupture of abdominal aortic aneurysm previously treated by endovascular stent graft. J Vasc Surg 28:184, 1998

37. Zarins CK, White RA, Moll FL, et al: The AneuRx stent graft: four-year results and worldwide experience 2000. J Vasc Surg 33:S135, 2001

38. The U.S. AneuRx Clinical Trial: 6-year clinical update 2002. AneuRx Clinical Investigators. J Vasc Surg 37:904, 2003

39. Harris PL, Vallabhaneni SR, Desgranges P, et al: Incidence and risk factors of late rupture, conversion, and death after endovascular repair of infrarenal aneurysms: the Eurostar experience. J Vasc Surg 32:739, 2000

Acknowledgment

Figures 4 through 11 Susan Brust, C.M.I.

91 AORTOILIAC RECONSTRUCTION

Mark K. Eskandari, M.D., F.A.C.S.

Symptomatic aortoiliac occlusive disease is the consequence of a diffuse atherosclerotic process that is exacerbated by smoking, hypertension, hypercholesterolemia, and diabetes.[1-4] The resultant narrowing of the aorta and the iliac vessels impairs circulation into the pelvis and the lower extremities, thereby causing myriad patient complaints. Manifestations range from impotence, claudication (in the buttock, the thigh, or the calf), and rest pain (in the forefoot) to ulceration or gangrene.

Hemodynamically significant obstruction of blood flow arising from aortoiliac occlusion may be either segmental or diffuse. Fortunately, there are a number of different vascular reconstructions that can be performed to reestablish sufficient flow to the lower body. The choice of a surgical revascularization approach is based on two factors: (1) anatomic constraints and (2) comorbid conditions. Regardless of which technique is selected, preoperative workup and planning are essentially the same.

Preoperative Evaluation

Once it has been established that a patient's symptoms (e.g., claudication, rest pain, or a nonhealing wound) are attributable to hemodynamically significant aortoiliac occlusive disease, a thorough preoperative evaluation is initiated. Such evaluation typically includes obtaining objective physiologic documentation of the extent of occlusive disease by measuring lower-extremity blood flow with arterial waveforms and ankle-brachial indices. An imaging study is also required to guide revascularization. Percutaneous diagnostic angiography is widely used for this purpose; however, technological advancements may allow magnetic resonance angiography (MRA) to supplant traditional contrast arteriography.[5-7] If an extra-anatomic bypass is anticipated, ancillary tests, including bilateral arm blood pressure measurements and computed tomography scans of the chest, abdomen, or pelvis, may be necessary. A standard cardiac risk assessment is mandatory before any form of revascularization, and the extent of testing is tailored to the level of cardiac risk.

Operative Technique

AORTOILIAC ENDARTERECTOMY

Although localized aortoiliac endarterectomy is less commonly performed today than it once was, it remains useful for a subgroup of patients with focal aortic bifurcation disease. The classic candidate for this procedure has minimal disease of the infrarenal abdominal aorta and the external iliac arteries but a severely diseased and narrowed aortic bifurcation.

Step 1: Incision and Approach

A standard lower midline transperitoneal incision allows rapid, direct access. Usually, the incision can be made below the umbilicus and extended to the pubis.

Step 2: Exposure and Control of Aorta and Iliac Arteries

Upon entry into the abdominal cavity, exposure of the aortic bifurcation is achieved by retracting the small bowel cephalad. A self-retaining retractor, such as an Omni (Omni-Tract Surgical, Minneapolis, Minnesota) or a Bookwalter (Cardinal Health, V. Mueller, McGaw Park, Illinois), is often helpful. The retroperitoneum overlying the aortic bifurcation is then incised in the midline, and the aorta is exposed to the level of the inferior mesenteric artery [*see 90 Repair of Infrarenal Abdominal Aortic Aneurysms*]. Both common iliac arteries are exposed, with care taken not to damage the underlying iliac veins and the overlying ureters, which normally cross at the iliac bifurcation.

Given that this procedure is best suited for treatment of localized disease, exposure beyond the iliac bifurcation is rarely necessary. If it appears that the disease process extends into the external iliac arteries or more proximally in the infrarenal aorta, another form of treatment, such as aortobifemoral bypass (see below), may be indicated.

Step 3: Aortoiliac Endarterectomy

Once the aorta and the iliac vessels are exposed, I.V. heparin is given for systemic anticoagulation. The vessels are then controlled with vascular clamps. As a rule, the iliac vessels should be clamped first to reduce the risk of distal embolization during placement of the aortic cross-clamp. These vessels should be clamped only enough to prevent retrograde bleeding. They must not be repeatedly clamped and unclamped, because they are prone to the development of flow-limiting intimal flaps or fractured atherosclerotic plaques.

Next, the aorta is incised longitudinally from a point just above the bifurcation (where the aorta is soft) down into the common iliac artery in which the disease process extends further. Sometimes, the middle sacral or lower lumbar arteries must be oversewn to control back-bleeding. A dissection plane is developed between the media and the adventitia, and a standard endarterectomy of the infrarenal aorta and the more diseased iliac artery is performed. The endarterectomy of the contralateral iliac artery is performed by means of eversion through the aortotomy [*see Figure 1*]. If the distal termination points in the iliac vessels are irregular or have a significant step-off, the plaque should be tacked down with two or three 6-0 polypropylene sutures, with the knots tied on the outside of the vessel wall.

Troubleshooting Occasionally, endarterectomy results in a very thin residual wall, or the distal termination points are too steep to fix with tacking sutures alone. In such cases, the best recourse is to replace this section of the aorta and the common iliac vessels with a short standard bifurcated prosthetic interposition graft. Proximally, the graft is sewn to the infrarenal aorta in an end-to-end fashion. Distally, the two limbs are sewn to the two common iliac arteries in the same manner.

Step 4: Repair of Arteriotomy

The arteriotomy can be closed either primarily or with a patch, depending on the size of the aorta and the iliac vessels. Primary closure is preferred, but if it appears that such closure will significantly narrow the aorta or the iliac artery, a patch (either prosthetic or autogenous) should be used instead. Before closure is completed, the vessels should be flushed and back-bled to diminish the risk of distal embolization to the legs upon reestablishment of inline flow. The adequacy of the repair is confirmed pri-

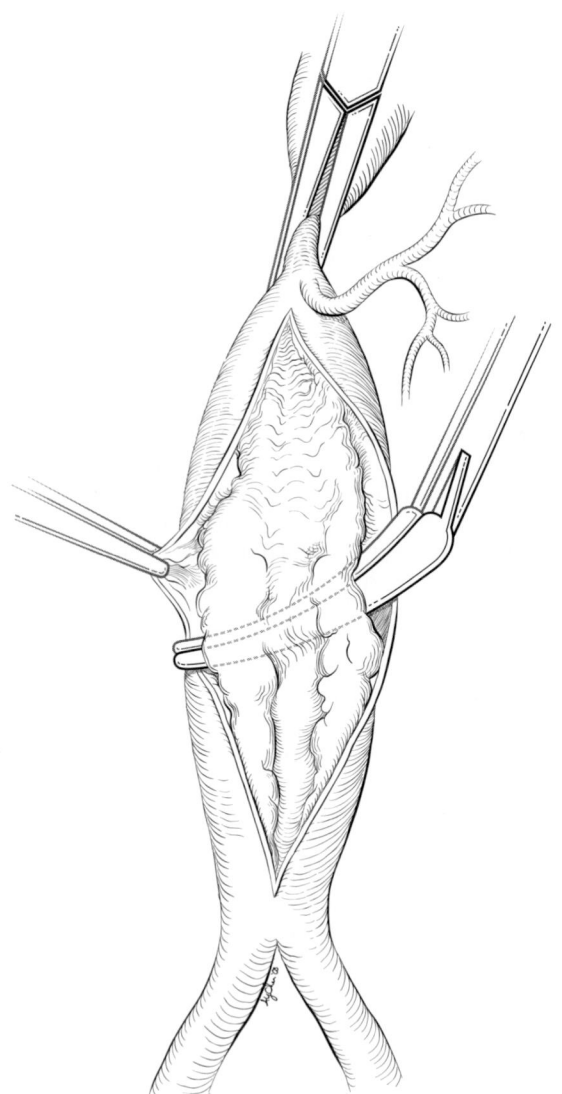

Figure 1 **Aortoiliac endarterectomy. Plaque is removed through a longitudinal aortotomy.**

marily by the palpation of normal femoral pulses in the groins.

Step 5: Closure of Retroperitoneum

Before abdominal closure, the retroperitoneum is closed with an absorbable suture so as to isolate the repair from the GI tract. This step reduces the risk of an aortoenteric fistula.

ILIOFEMORAL BYPASS

Iliofemoral bypass, already an uncommon procedure, has now largely been supplanted by advances in percutaneous endoluminal techniques. Nevertheless, it is still used on occasion and thus is worth knowing. One limitation on the application of iliofemoral bypass is that aortoiliac occlusive disease typically causes diffuse aortic and bilateral iliac artery narrowing. For this operation to be successful, there must be a relatively disease-free common iliac artery that can provide unimpeded inflow. Accordingly, iliofemoral bypass is most suitable for those rare patients who have isolated unilateral external iliac artery disease.

Step 1: Incision and Approach

The patient is placed in the supine position, and two incisions are made [see Figure 2]. The common iliac artery is approached through a lower-quadrant retroperitoneal incision positioned medial to the lateral border of the rectus muscle. The femoral artery is approached through a standard vertical groin incision.

Step 2: Exposure of Iliac and Femoral Arteries

Once the retroperitoneum is entered, the visceral contents and the ureter are bluntly dissected away from the psoas muscle medially. This dissection, which takes place through a mostly bloodless field, yields full exposure of the targeted common iliac artery and its bifurcation into the external and internal iliac arteries. It should proceed far enough to allow control of the arteries with vascular clamps. Care must be taken not to damage the underlying iliac veins. In particular, no attempt should be made to isolate these vessels circumferentially, which can lead to troublesome bleeding.

The vertical incision in the groin permits full exposure of the common femoral artery and its bifurcation into the superficial femoral artery and the profunda femoris. Unlike the iliac arteries, the femoral artery and its branches may be circumferentially dissected.

Step 3: Tunneling of Bypass Graft

Once the inflow and outflow vessels are adequately exposed, the bypass graft is tunneled from the retroperitoneum to the groin, passing beneath the ureter and the inguinal ligament. During tunneling, care must be taken not to avulse the bridging epigastric vein found just cephalad and posterior to the inguinal ligament. Typically, a prosthetic graft 6 to 8 mm in diameter is used; however, autogenous material (e.g., a segment of the greater saphenous vein) may be used if desired.

Step 4: Proximal Anastomosis to Iliac Artery

With the bypass graft in position, the patient undergoes systemic anticoagulation with I.V. heparin. The common, external, and internal iliac arteries are controlled with vascular clamps. The proximal anastomosis is then performed to the selected common iliac artery. If practicable, the anastomosis should be an end-to-side one so as to preserve antegrade flow into the internal iliac artery.

Troubleshooting Occasionally, the common iliac artery is too diseased to clamp or to use as an inflow source. In such cases, the infrarenal aorta may be clamped instead or used as the site of the proximal anastomosis.

Step 5: Distal Anastomosis to Femoral Artery

Vascular clamps are placed on the common femoral artery and its branches, and the distal anastomosis is performed in an end-to-side manner. The configuration of the longitudinal arteriotomy depends on the presence and extent of disease in the femoral arteries. If both the superficial femoral artery and the profunda femoris are relatively free of disease, the arteriotomy should extend from the common femoral artery into the superficial femoral artery. If, however, the superficial femoral artery is occluded or heavily diseased, the arteriotomy should extend down into the profunda femoris [see Figure 3]. In either case, an end-to-side anastomosis is fashioned. Before completion of the bypass, the inflow vessel is flushed and the outflow vessel backbled to reduce the risk of distal embolization to the legs.

AORTOFEMORAL BYPASS

Before the application of percutaneous balloon angioplasty and stenting, aortofemoral bypass grafting was the revascularization operation of choice for patients with diffuse aortoiliac occlusive disease. This operation is still favored by many, and it yields excellent long-term patency.

Step 1: Incision and Approach

Typically, the patient is placed in the supine position, and the operation is performed through a midline laparotomy and two longitudinal groin incisions. A self-retaining retractor is recommended to facilitate exposure of the infrarenal aorta.

Alternatively, the infrarenal aorta may be exposed via a left retroperitoneal incision extending obliquely from the lateral border of the rectus muscle, at the level of the umbilicus, to the tip of the 11th rib. For this approach, the patient is placed in a right semilateral decubitus position with the assistance of an inflatable beanbag. The hips are rotated so that they are flat on the bed, providing easy access to the groins.

Step 2: Exposure of Aorta

Upon entry into the abdominal cavity, the fourth portion of the duodenum is dissected free of its retroperitoneal attachments, and the small bowel is retracted to the right of the aorta. The self-retaining retractor may then be placed to facilitate exposure. Next, the retroperitoneum overlying the infrarenal aorta is incised in the midline to expose the vessel, ideally in a location that is not heavily diseased or calcified. Unlike the dissection required in a localized endarterectomy [see Aortoiliac

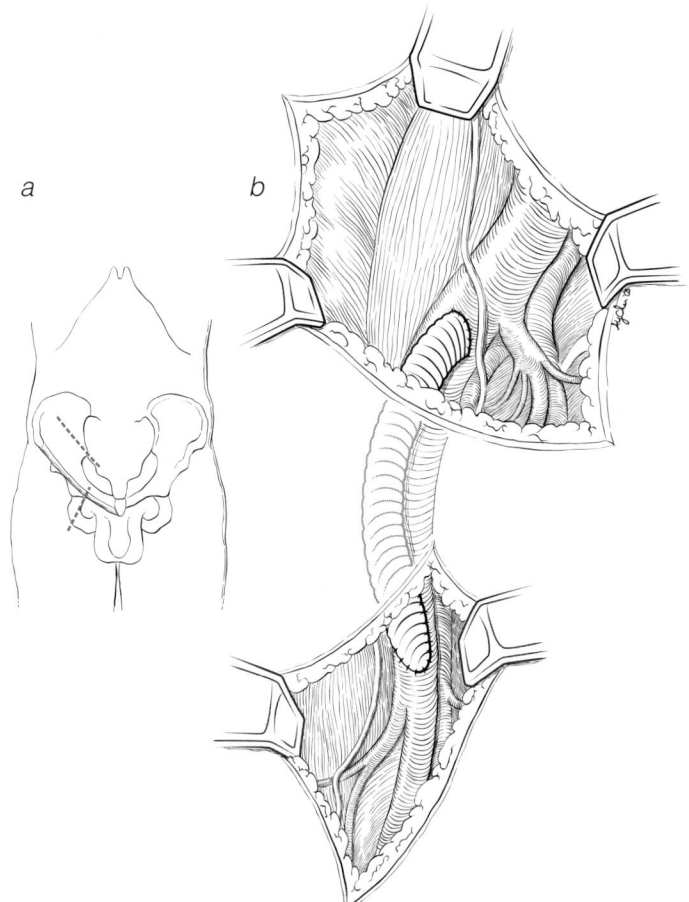

Figure 2 **Iliofemoral bypass. (*a*) A low retroperitoneal incision and an ipsilateral groin incision are made for exposure of the inflow and outflow bypass vessels. (*b*) The graft is tunneled beneath the ureter and the inguinal ligament.**

Endarterectomy, *above*], this dissection is primarily between the renal arteries and the inferior mesenteric artery. In most cases, the dissection need not be extended downward below the aortic bifurcation into the iliac arteries.

When this operation is performed through a left retroperitoneal incision, the external and internal oblique muscles and the transversus abdominis are divided, and the retroperitoneum is entered. Complete exposure of the infrarenal aorta is obtained by mobilizing the abdominal contents, the left kidney, and the left ureter medially after blunt dissection along the anterior border of the psoas muscle.

Troubleshooting In those cases in which aortofemoral bypass is being done for a patient with complete infrarenal aortic occlusion, the operative approach is modified to allow placement of a vascular clamp above the renal arteries. The dissection is carried cephalad by retracting the small bowel mesentery and the superior mesenteric artery to the right. The left renal vein is found anterior to the aorta at the level of the renal arteries. Generally, this vein need not be divided to expose the suprarenal aorta. Rather, it should be thoroughly dissected and encircled with a vessel loop so that it can be retracted cephalad and caudad. Sometimes, an adrenal or gonadal vein draining into the left renal vein must be ligated and divided to give the renal vein added mobility. With the left renal vein retracted caudad, the suprarenal aorta is dissected.

Step 3: Exposure of Femoral Artery

A vertical groin incision provides full exposure of the common femoral artery and its bifurcation into the superficial femoral artery and the profunda femoris. The femoral artery and its branches should be circumferentially dissected to give the surgeon an unobstructed view for placement of the vascular clamps.

Step 4: Tunneling of Bypass Graft

Once the inflow and outflow vessels are adequately exposed, the bypass graft—typically, a bifurcated prosthetic graft measuring 14 × 7 mm or 16 × 8 mm—is tunneled from the abdomen to the groins. Its course should pass beneath the ureter and the inguinal ligament. To create the tunnel, one index finger, oriented so that its dorsum faces the vessel wall, is inserted in the midline incision and advanced caudad down to the groin. Simultaneously, the other index finger, oriented so that its volar aspect faces the common femoral artery, is inserted into a groin incision and advanced cephalad until the two fingers meet. As with an iliofemoral bypass graft, care must be taken not to avulse the bridging epigastric vein found just cephalad and posterior to the inguinal ligament. With one of the two fingers held in place, a Silastic tube or vessel loop is passed through the tunnel. The limbs of the graft are attached to the tube or loop and passed through the tunnel down to the groins.

Step 5: Proximal Anastomosis to Aorta

The proximal aortic anastomosis can be done in either an end-to-end or an end-to-side configuration. An end-to-side beveled anastomosis is preferable for (1) patients with a small (< 1.5 cm) infrarenal aorta and (2) patients with severe occlusive disease of both external iliac arteries in whom it is desirable to preserve flow into the pelvic circulation via the internal iliac arteries. An end-to-end anastomosis is preferable for (1) patients with occlusive iliac disease and a concomitant aortic aneurysm and (2) patients undergoing revascularization for chronic total aortic occlusion. The latter configuration is also less bulky and easier to cover and

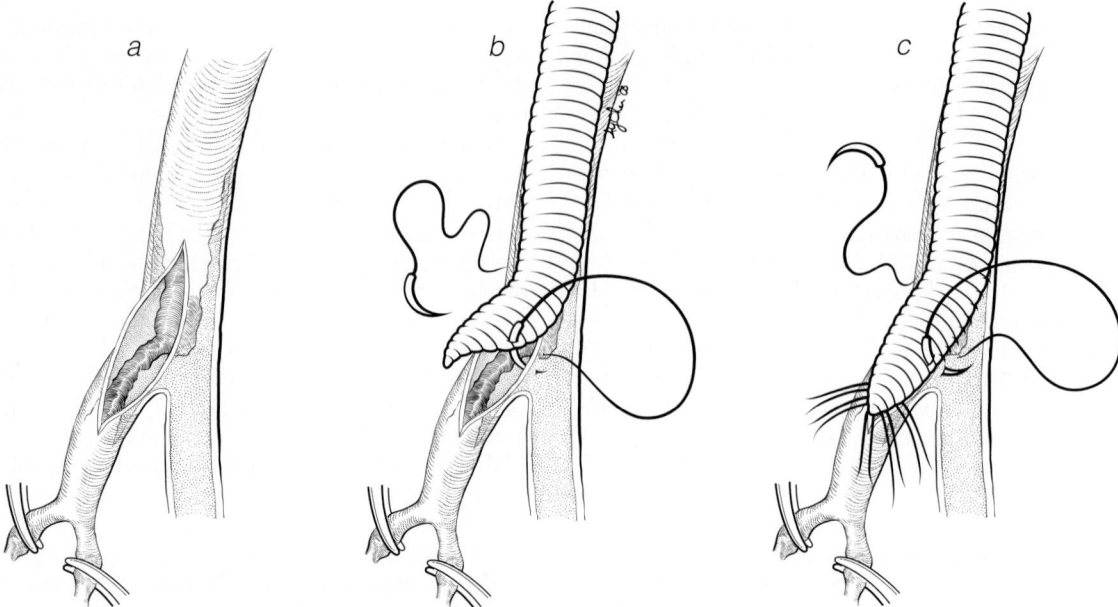

a   *b*   *c*

Figure 3   Iliofemoral bypass. (*a*) When concomitatnt superficial femoral artery disease is present, the distal anastomosis is performed to a longitudinal arteriotomy that extends onto the proximal profunda femoris. (*b*) The heel of the hood of the graft is anastomosed to the common femoral artery. (*c*) The tip of the graft is extended down the profunda femoris.

isolate from the GI tract at the conclusion of the operation.

Once a configuration for the anastomosis has been chosen, I.V. heparin is given for systemic anticoagulation. The graft is trimmed so that its bifurcation lies close to the proximal anastomosis. The infrarenal aorta is controlled, most commonly with vascular clamps above and below the site of the intended anastomosis. Control of the aorta with a partially occluding vascular clamp may be attempted, but the size of the vessel and the coexistence of aortic disease typically make this difficult or impossible to accomplish.

If an end-to-side anastomosis is to be performed, a longitudinal aortotomy is made and the graft sewn in place in a spatulated fashion. The toe of the graft is oriented cephalad [*see Figure 4*]. The anastomosis should be spatulated steeply so that it is not too bulky in the retroperitoneum and can be covered at the end of the procedure. Before completion of the anastomosis, the graft is flushed and back-bled.

If an end-to-end anastomosis is to be performed, a small portion of the aorta is resected to allow the graft to fit neatly into the retroperitoneum. In some cases, back-bleeding lumbar arteries in the region of the resected aorta must be oversewn. The distal stump is oversewn with 2-0 or 3-0 polypropylene in two rows; the first row is done with a continuous suture in a horizontal mattress stitch, the second with a continuous suture in a baseball stitch [*see Figure 5*].

Troubleshooting   Vascular control of the aorta is achieved differently when chronic infrarenal aortic occlusion is present. In this setting, placement of a vascular clamp just below the renal arteries may squeeze atherosclerotic debris up into the renal arteries. To prevent this, the vascular clamp should be placed between the superior mesenteric artery and the renal arteries. Once the distal clamp is in place, the aorta is opened below the renal arteries and the atherosclerotic plug removed. The suprarenal clamp can then be moved to just below the renal arteries, and the proximal anastomosis can be fashioned as already described (see above).

A heavily calcified infrarenal aorta encountered at the time of

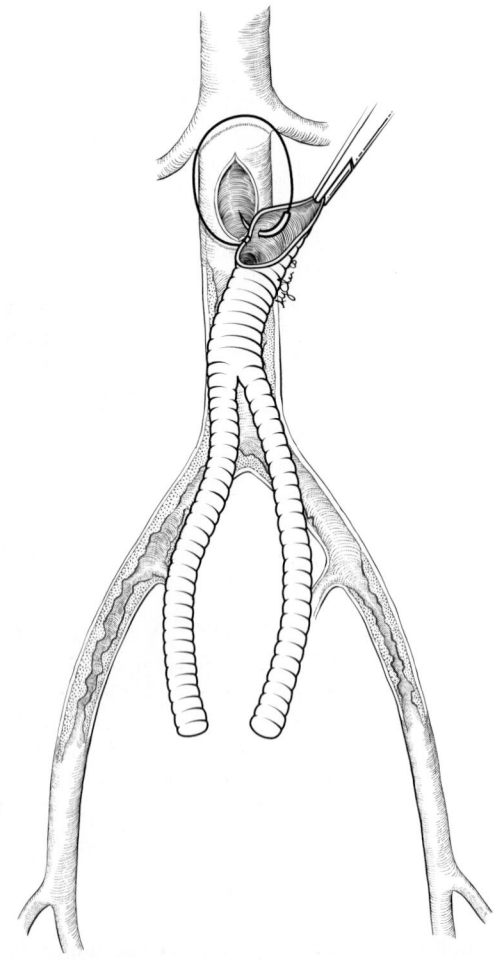

Figure 4   Aortofemoral bypass. Shown is an end-to-side proximal anastomosis.

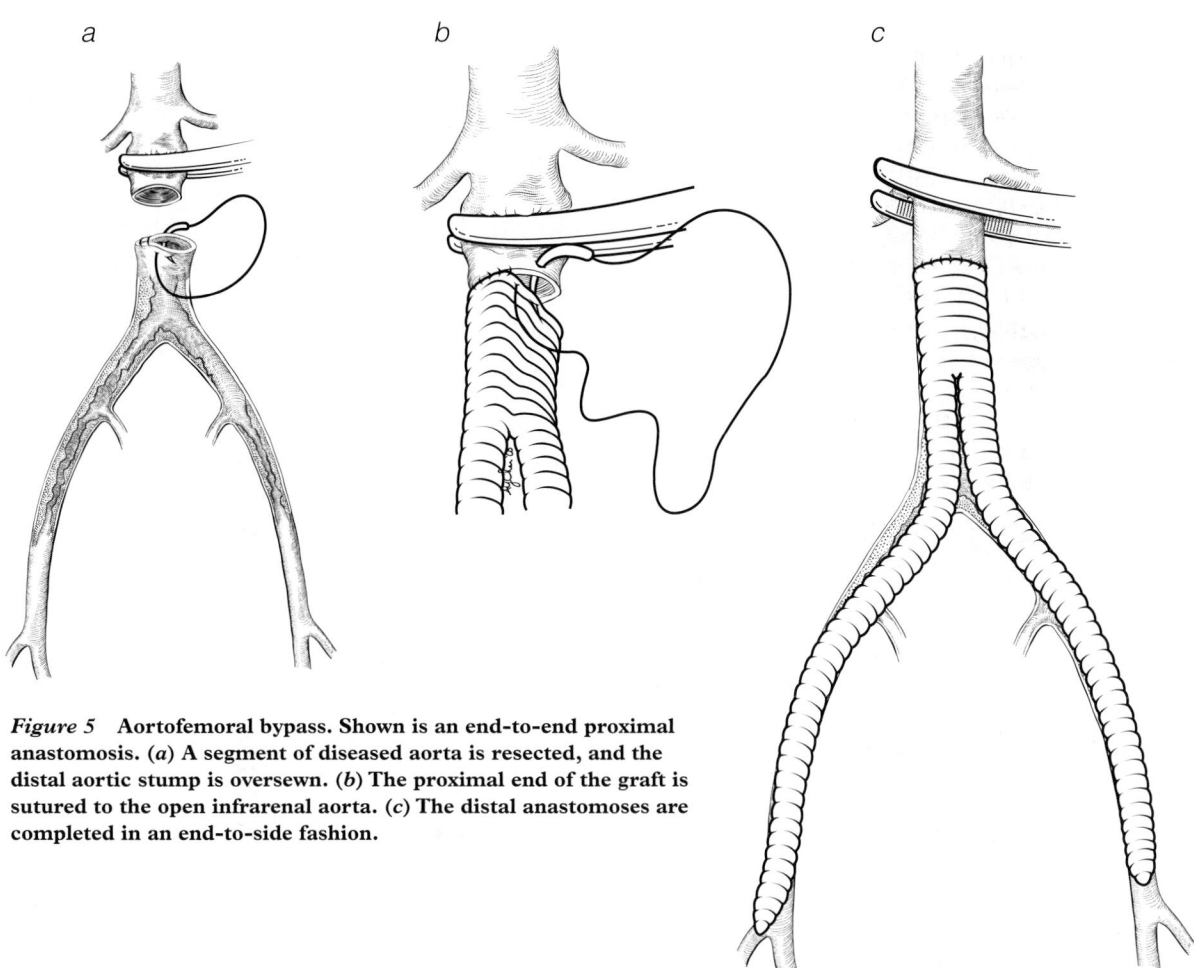

a   *b*   *c*

Figure 5 **Aortofemoral bypass. Shown is an end-to-end proximal anastomosis. (*a*) A segment of diseased aorta is resected, and the distal aortic stump is oversewn. (*b*) The proximal end of the graft is sutured to the open infrarenal aorta. (*c*) The distal anastomoses are completed in an end-to-side fashion.**

operation presents a difficult problem. In most cases, the infrarenal aorta can still be used, but the proximal anastomosis should be performed in an end-to-end configuration. Even in the most calcified aortas, the region 1 to 2 cm below the renal arteries is often soft enough to allow an anastomosis to be fashioned. If this is not the case, there are two alternatives: (1) suprarenal aortic control and endarterectomy of the infrarenal aorta just below the renal ostia before the proximal anastomosis and (2) conversion to a thoracofemoral bypass graft [*see* Thoracofemoral Bypass, *below*].

Step 6: Distal Anastomosis to Femoral Artery

Vascular clamps are placed on the common femoral artery and its branches, and the distal anastomosis is performed. As with an iliofemoral bypass, the configuration of the longitudinal arteriotomy depends on the existence of disease in the femoral arteries. If both the superficial femoral artery and the profunda femoris are relatively free of disease, the arteriotomy should extend from the common femoral artery into the superficial femoral artery. If, however, the superficial femoral artery is occluded or heavily diseased, the arteriotomy should extend downward into the profunda femoris. In either case, an end-to-side anastomosis is indicated. Before completion of the bypass, the inflow vessel is flushed and the outflow vessel back-bled to diminish the risk of distal embolization to the legs.

Step 7: Closure of Retroperitoneum

Before abdominal closure, the retroperitoneum is closed with an absorbable suture to isolate the repair from the GI tract and reduce the risk of an aortoenteric fistula. The ureters should be

visualized and preserved. Careless closure of the retroperitoneum can lead to laceration or entrapment of the ureter, particularly the right ureter. Every attempt should be made to cover the graft. If the retroperitoneum is too thin or the graft too bulky, an omental pedicle flap may be used.

THORACOFEMORAL BYPASS

A thoracofemoral bypass is ideal for a small subgroup of patients, comprising (1) those with an occluded old aortofemoral bypass graft, (2) those with a so-called lead-pipe calcified infrarenal aorta that is unusable as an inflow source, and (3) those with a so-called hostile abdomen (i.e., those with an ileal conduit, an ileostomy or colostomy, or a previous aortic graft infection). Candidates for this procedure must have adequate pulmonary reserve and be able to tolerate a thoracotomy. They must also be informed of and accept the low but real risk of paralysis.

The patient is placed in a right semilateral decubitus position so that the hips are nearly flat on the table and the torso is slightly rotated to the patient's right [*see* Figure 6]. An axillary roll and an inflatable beanbag will help maintain this position. Because single-lung ventilation will be necessary when the proximal anastomosis is done, either a double-lumen endotracheal tube or a bronchial blocker must be used. Placement of an orogastric tube to decompress the stomach helps keep the diaphragm down during exposure of the descending thoracic aorta.

Step 1: Incision and Exposure of Descending Thoracic Aorta

The descending thoracic aorta is approached through a left posterior lateral thoracotomy at the level of the 7th or 8th interspace. Additional exposure can be gained by resecting part of the rib and using a self-retaining table-mounted retractor. With the left lung decompressed, the parietal pleura overlying the descending thoracic aorta is incised. The aorta is cleanly dissected, with care taken not to damage the esophagus, which lies medially. Having an orogastric tube in place is advantageous in this regard: the esophagus can easily be located by palpating the tube. Any intercostal vessels in the region of the anticipated aortotomy can be preserved and controlled at the time of the anastomosis.

Step 2: Exposure of Femoral Artery

Full exposure of the common femoral artery and its bifurcation into the superficial femoral artery and the profunda femoris is obtained via a standard groin incision.

Step 3: Tunneling of Bypass Graft

The tunnel for the prosthetic graft has two components: (1) a left retroperitoneal tunnel and (2) a subcutaneous tunnel over the pubis. Usually, a tube prosthetic graft is sutured to a bifurcated graft before being tunneled through the retroperitoneum. The retroperitoneal tunnel is started in the chest by making a 1 cm hole in the posterior lateral aspect of the left diaphragm. An index finger is inserted through this hole and advanced caudad into the retroperitoneum as far as it can go. The other index finger is inserted through the left groin incision, oriented directly over the external iliac artery, and advanced cephalad into the retroperitoneum [see Figure 7]. Care is taken not to avulse the bridging epigastric vein found posterior and inferior to the inguinal ligament. In most cases, the left retroperitoneal tunnel must then be completed by using a long, hollow metal tunneling device such as the Gore Tunneler (W. L. Gore & Associates, Inc., Tempe, Ariz.). Once this tunnel is completed, the graft is passed through it in such a way that the bifurcated limbs are brought caudad down into the left groin wound.

Next, the subcutaneous tunnel from the left groin to the right groin is bluntly fashioned anterior to the pubis. It should not be oriented superior to the pubis because of the risk of injury to an overdistended bladder. To minimize this risk, an indwelling urinary catheter is advocated. The subcutaneous tunnel is used to pass the right limb of the graft over to the right groin. It is not uncommon for the bifurcation of the prosthetic graft to lie just cephalad to the left groin wound.

Step 4: Proximal Anastomosis to Descending Thoracic Aorta

Once the graft has been tunneled, the patient undergoes systemic anticoagulation with I.V. heparin. The descending thoracic aorta is controlled either with a side-biting clamp or with two completely occluding aortic clamps placed in close proximity to each other. In the latter case, one or two intercostal arteries may have to be temporarily controlled as well. A longitudinal aortotomy is then made along the left lateral aspect of the thoracic aorta, and a beveled end-to-side anastomosis is fashioned. Exposure can be enhanced by ventilating the right lung and attaching the orogastric tube to suction to decompress the stomach. Before completion of the anastomosis, the aorta is flushed and back-bled.

Troubleshooting Partial aortic control with a side-biting vascular clamp is successful in most cases, but it is not recommended when the descending thoracic aorta is heavily diseased and calcified or when preoperative imaging studies show thrombus in this location. If an intercostal artery cannot be temporarily controlled with clamps, it can be oversewn from the inside of the aorta to prevent nuisance back-bleeding.

Step 5: Distal Anastomosis to Femoral Artery

Vascular clamps are placed on the common femoral artery and its branches, and an end-to-side anastomosis is fashioned distally. Again, the configuration of the longitudinal arteriotomy depends on the existence of disease in the femoral arteries. If both the superficial femoral artery and the profunda femoris are relatively free of disease, the arteriotomy should extend from the common femoral artery into the superficial femoral artery. If, however, the superficial femoral artery is occluded or heavily diseased, the arteriotomy should extend downward into the profunda femoris. Before completion of the bypass, the inflow vessel is flushed and the outflow vessel back-bled.

Step 6: Closure of Chest

Once the proximal anastomosis is complete, the left lung is reinflated. At the conclusion of the operation, the chest is closed in a standard fashion over two chest tubes. The proximal anastomosis should be covered with either a prosthetic patch or bovine pericardium to diminish the risk of an aortopulmonary fistula.

AXILLOFEMORAL BYPASS

Axillofemoral bypass is ideally suited to elderly patients who cannot tolerate an aortic operation. The hemodynamic changes occurring during the operation are minimal, and recovery from the three small incisions used is substantially quicker than that from a laparotomy or a thoracotomy.

Because hemodynamically significant occlusive disease is less common in the right innominate artery than in the left subclavian artery, the right axillary is more often used as the inflow vessel than the left axillary artery is. Such occlusion can easily be identified preoperatively by measuring blood pressure in both arms. The sterile field includes both groins, the appropriate side of the chest (usually the right) up to the neck, and the appropriate flank (again, usually the right). It need not include the entire inflow arm; however, the arm should be abducted 90° and positioned on an arm board.

Step 1: Incision and Exposure of Axillary Artery

The patient is placed in the supine position. The axillary artery is approached through a horizontal 6 cm infraclavicular incision placed approximately 2 cm below the inferior border of the clavicle. Dissection is carried through the subcutaneous tissue, the fascia overlying the pectoralis major is incised, and the muscle is bluntly dissected along the length of its fibers. The dissection plane should remain medial to the pectoralis minor.

Next, the axillary vein is encountered and retracted caudad, and the underlying axillary artery is visualized. The axillary artery is cleanly dissected, with care taken not to retract or damage the brachial plexus lying deep and superior to the artery. For full exposure of the axillary artery, the thoracoacromial artery may have to be ligated at its origin. For easier retraction, the axillary artery may be encircled with vessel loops.

Step 2: Exposure of Femoral Artery

The femoral artery and its bifurcation into the superficial femoral and profunda femoris arteries are approached through a standard groin incision.

Step 3: Tunneling of Bypass Graft

Once the inflow and outflow vessels are adequately exposed, a prosthetic graft 80 to 100 cm long and 8 or 10 mm in diameter is tunneled from the axillary incision, beneath the pectoralis

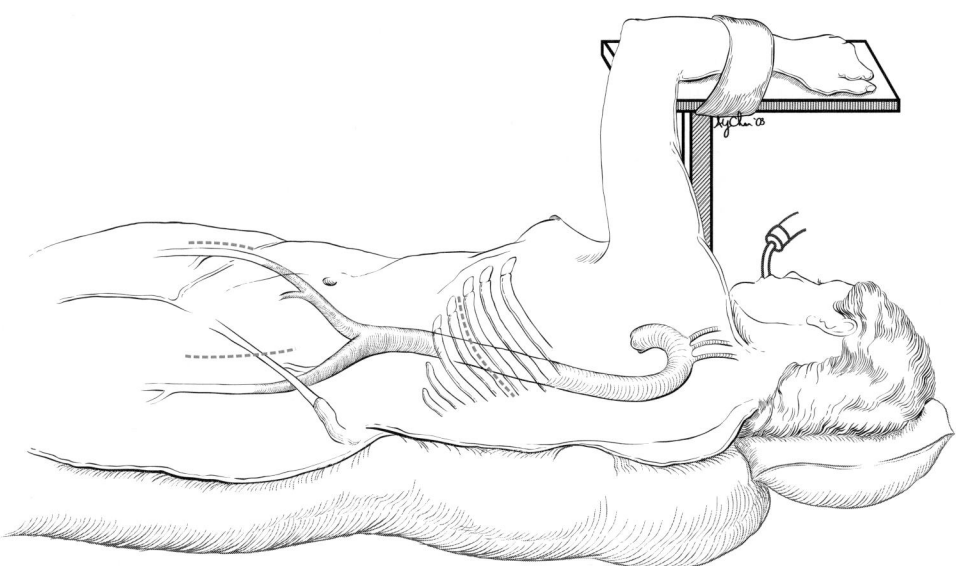

Figure 6 **Thoracofemoral bypass. The patient is positioned so that the hips are flat but the torso is slightly rotated to the patient's right. Three incisions are made: a left postero-lateral thoracotomy and two groin incisions.**

minor, and down to the flank. The use of a long, hollow metal tunneler is recommended at this point. To facilitate tunneling, a single counterincision is made in the midaxillary line over the sixth or seventh intercostal space. From this counterincision, the graft is tunneled along the flank, over the iliac crest, anterior to the anterior superior iliac process, and into the ipsilateral groin wound. Except for the portions in the axilla and the groin, the entire graft should lie in a subcutaneous plane.

Next, a subcutaneous tunnel from the ipsilateral groin to the contralateral groin is bluntly fashioned anterior to the pubis to allow passage of a second prosthetic graft (a short crossover graft 8 mm in diameter). This tunnel should not be oriented superior to the pubis because of the risk of injury to an overdistended bladder.

Step 4: Proximal Anastomosis to Axillary Artery

With the long graft in place, I.V. heparin is given for systemic anticoagulation. The pectoralis minor may be retracted laterally

to provide additional exposure. The axillary artery is controlled with vascular clamps, with care taken not to include any part of the brachial plexus lying nearby. A longitudinal arteriotomy is made along the length of the axillary artery. The proximal anastomosis is then fashioned in an end-to-side configuration. The anastomosis must lie medial to the pectoralis minor. This is critical for preventing avulsion of the graft from the axillary artery when the patient fully abducts the arm. Before the anastomosis is completed, it is flushed and back-bled. Once blood flow to the arm is reestablished, the graft should be positioned so that it lies parallel to the axillary artery for a length of 2 to 3 cm before diving deep and caudad.

Step 5: Distal Anastomosis to Femoral Artery

The distal anastomosis to the femoral arteries is performed as described earlier [*see* Thoracofemoral Bypass, *above*]. There remains some controversy over the formation of the short crossover

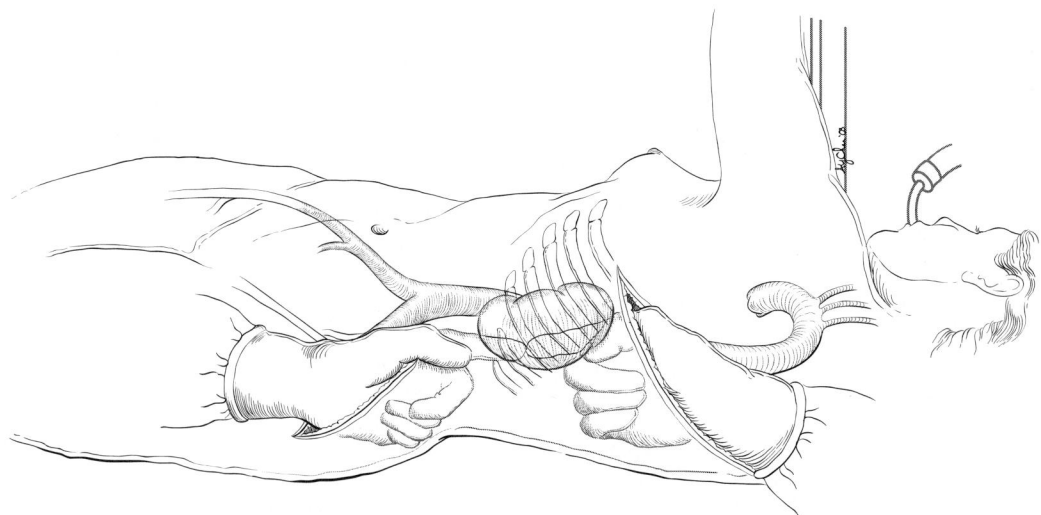

Figure 7 **Thoracofemoral bypass. A left retroperitoneal tunnel is fashioned for passage of the prosthetic graft downward to the groin. (The right arm of the graft is subsequently passed to the right groin via a subcutaneous tunnel anterior to the pubis.)**

graft from the axillary bypass graft to the contralateral femoral artery. My practice is to place the proximal anastomosis of the crossover femorofemoral anastomosis on the hood (or distal anastomosis) of the axillofemoral bypass graft [see Figure 8]. Others prefer to use a commercially available bifurcated axillofemoral prosthetic graft or to place the crossover graft more proximally along the length of the axillofemoral graft.

FEMOROFEMORAL BYPASS

A femorofemoral crossover bypass is well suited to patients who have unilateral complete occlusion or a diffusely diseased iliac system but have a relatively normal contralateral iliac system. It is performed with the patient supine and is conducted in essentially the same fashion as an axillofemoral bypass, but without the axillary anastomosis.

ENDOVASCULAR THERAPY

The use of percutaneous balloon angioplasty and stenting for the treatment of peripheral vascular disease has grown exponentially since its introduction in the 1990s. As regards short-term results, patients clearly experience less pain, recover more quickly, and regain function earlier. Initially, there was some question about the durability of stenting; however, data from longer follow-up periods indicate that this approach is an acceptable alternative for patients with focal aortoiliac occlusive disease.[8-10]

Complications

Certain complications are associated with all of the revascularization procedures discussed, such as bleeding, distal embolization, graft thrombosis, and graft infection. Late graft infection, recurrent disease, and pseudoaneurysm formation are known long-term complications as well. In addition, the following complications are unique to one or more of the procedures but do not arise with the others.

1. Injury to the ureters, resulting from their position overlying the iliac vessels (aortoiliac endarterectomy, iliofemoral bypass, axillofemoral bypass).
2. Impotence, resulting from damage to the autonomic nerve fibers around the origin of the left common iliac artery (aortoiliac endarterectomy, iliofemoral bypass, axillofemoral bypass).
3. Bleeding or deep venous thrombosis, related to trauma to the underlying iliac venous structures (all).
4. Paraplegia, resulting from the sacrifice of intercostal vessels supplying the anterior spinal artery (thoracofemoral bypass).
5. Colonic ischemia or infarction, resulting from hindered primary flow via the inferior mesenteric artery or collateral vessels from the hypogastric arteries (axillofemoral bypass).
6. Buttock claudication, resulting from disruption of inline flow to the pelvic circulation (axillofemoral bypass).
7. Aortoduodenal fistula, resulting from incomplete coverage of an aortic graft (axillofemoral bypass).
8. Renal failure, resulting from acute tubular necrosis or embolization when a suprarenal aortic clamp is used (thoracofemoral bypass, axillofemoral bypass).
9. Arm paralysis, resulting from injury to the deep and superiorly oriented brachial plexus (axillofemoral bypass).
10. Respiratory failure resulting from effusion or hemothorax after a left thoracotomy or from inadvertent pneumothorax

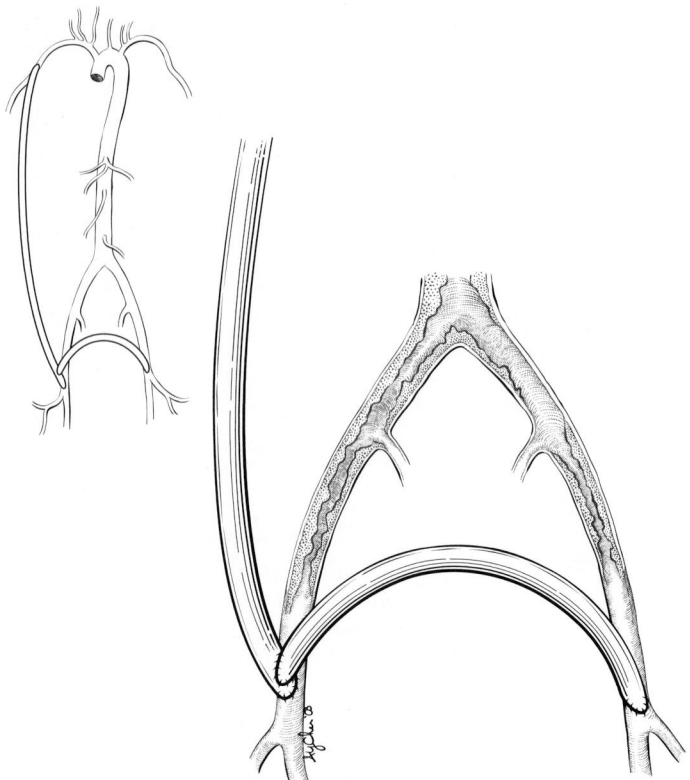

Figure 8 **Axillofemoral bypass. Shown is the recommended configuration for the short femorofemoral crossover graft originating from the long axillofemoral graft. The femorofemoral graft originated from the hood of the axillofemoral graft.**

during exposure of the axillary artery (thoracofemoral bypass, axillofemoral bypass).

Outcome Evaluation

Regardless of which operation is performed to treat aortoiliac occlusive disease, the subsequent outcome should be immediate relief of presenting symptoms—for example, reduced claudication, resolution of rest pain, or improved distal wound healing. Unfortunately, overall long-term survival in patients with symptomatic aortoiliac occlusive disease is not improved by operative management and is typically 10 to 15 years less than that in a normal age-matched group. Not surprisingly, by far the most significant long-term cause of death in these patients is atherosclerotic cardiac disease, which underscores the importance of a thorough preoperative cardiac evaluation.

In general, direct aortoiliac reconstructions (i.e., endarterectomy, aortofemoral bypass, and thoracofemoral bypass) have an expected patency rate of 85% to 90% at 5 years and 70% to 75% at 10 years.[11-13] When these operations are performed at experienced centers on patients who are considered to be good risk candidates, mortality is typically less than 3%.[14,15] Femorofemoral bypass and axillobifemoral bypass have expected 5-year patency rates of 70% to 75% and 60% to 85%, respectively.[16-19] Coexistent superficial femoral artery disease in the recipient vessels has a detrimental effect on the long-term patency of these bypasses.[20] Long-term anticoagulation may improve the patency for an axillobifemoral bypass graft.

References

1. Witteman JC, Grobbee DE, Valkenburg HA, et al: Cigarette smoking and the development and progression of aortic atherosclerosis: a 9-year population-based follow-up study in women. Circulation 88:2156, 1993

2. McGill HC Jr, McMahan CA, Malcom GT, et al: Effects of serum lipoproteins and smoking on atherosclerosis in young men and women. The PDAY Research Group. Pathobiological determinants of atherosclerosis in youth. Arterioscler Thromb Vasc Biol 17:95, 1997

3. Van Der Meer IM, De Maat MP, Hak AE, et al: C-reactive protein predicts progression of atherosclerosis measured at various sites in the arterial tree: the Rotterdam study. Stroke 33:2750, 2002

4. Faries PL, LoGerfo FW, Hook SC, et al: The impact of diabetes on arterial reconstructions for multilevel arterial occlusive disease. Am J Surg 181:251, 2001

5. Morasch MD, Collins J, Pereles FS, et al: Lower extremity stepping-table magnetic resonance angiography with multilevel contrast timing and segmented contrast infusion. J Vasc Surg 37:62, 2003

6. Loewe C, Schoder M, Rand T, et al: Peripheral vascular occlusive disease: evaluation with contrast-enhanced moving-bed MR angiography versus digital subtraction angiography in 106 patients. AJR Am J Roentgenol 179:1013, 2002

7. Pandharipande PV, Lee VS, Reuss PM, et al: Two-station bolus-chase MR angiography with a stationery table: a simple alternative to automated-table techniques. AJR Am J Roentgenol 179:1583, 2002

8. Back MR, Novotney M, Roth SM, et al: Utility of duplex surveillance following iliac artery angioplasty and primary stenting. J Endovasc Ther 8:629, 2001

9. Sanchez LA, Wain RA, Veith FJ, et al: Endovascular grafting for aortoiliac occlusive disease. Semin Vasc Surg 10:297, 1997

10. Gray BH, Sullivan TM: Aortoiliac occlusive disease: surgical versus interventional therapy. Curr Interv Cardiol Rep 3:109, 2001

11. Kalman PG: Thoracofemoral bypass: proximal exposure and tunneling. Semin Vasc Surg 13:65, 2000

12. Nash T: Aortoiliac occlusive vascular disease: a prospective study of patients treated by endarterectomy and bypass procedures. Aust N Z J Surg 49:223, 1979

13. Brewster DC: Clinical and anatomical considerations for surgery in aortoiliac disease and results of surgical treatment. Circulation 83:I42, 1991

14. de Vries SO, Hunink MG: Results of aortic bifurcation grafts for aortoiliac occlusive disease: a meta-analysis. J Vasc Surg 26:558, 1997

15. Passman MA, Taylor LM, Moneta GL, et al: Comparison of axillofemoral and aortofemoral bypass for aortoiliac occlusive disease. J Vasc Surg 23:263, 1996

16. Martin D, Katz SG: Axillofemoral bypass for aortoiliac occlusive disease. Am J Surg 180:100, 2000

17. Taylor LM Jr, Moneta GL, McConnell D, et al: Axillofemoral grafting with externally supported polytetrafluoroethylene. Arch Surg 129:588, 1994

18. Rutherford RB, Patt A, Pearce WH: Extra-anatomic bypass: a closer view. J Vasc Surg 6:437, 1987

19. Naylor AR, Ah-See AK, Engeset J: Axillofemoral bypass as a limb salvage procedure in high risk patients with aortoiliac disease. Br J Surg 77:659, 1990

20. Criado E, Burnham SJ, Tinsley EA Jr, et al: Femorofemoral bypass graft: analysis of patency and factors influencing long-term outcome. J Vasc Surg 18:495, 1993

Acknowledgment

Figures 1 through 8   Alice Y. Chen.

92 SURGICAL TREATMENT OF THE INFECTED AORTIC GRAFT

Victor J. D'Addio, M.D., F.A.C.S., and G. Patrick Clagett, M.D., F.A.C.S.

In dealing with an infected aortic graft, the primary goal of treatment is to save life and limb. This goal is best accomplished by eradicating all infected graft material and maintaining adequate circulation with appropriate vascular reconstruction. Secondary goals are to minimize morbidity, to restore normal function, and to maintain long-term function without the need for repeated intervention or amputation.

Before definitive reconstruction, all infected graft material must be debrided, along with any grossly infected vascular tissue and surrounding soft tissue. Once debridement is complete, there are several options for reconstruction, including (1) extra-anatomic bypass, (2) use of an arterial allograft, (3) placement of vascular prostheses treated with or soaked in antibiotic solutions, and (4) in situ replacement with a femoral-popliteal vein (FPV) graft. The choice among these options is made on the basis of the specific clinical situation present. The primary focus of the technical description in this chapter, however, will be on the fourth option [see Operative Technique, *below*].

Choice of Procedure

EXTRA-ANATOMIC BYPASS

Extra-anatomic bypass, usually performed as an axillobifemoral bypass [see *Figure 1 and 91 Aortoiliac Reconstruction*], is a good option for treatment of an infected aortic graft when groin infection is absent and lower-extremity runoff is good. The primary advantages of extra-anatomic bypass are that it minimizes lower-extremity ischemic time and that it is less of a physiologic insult than an aorta-based bypass procedure (mainly because it is typically done in a staged fashion). The primary disadvantages are that long-term patency is poor and that there is a significant risk of reinfection. In addition, if groin infection is present, the bypass is compromised even further by the need to use vessels such as the profunda femoris artery or the popliteal artery for distal targets. Bilateral axillofemoral bypasses are often required in this situation. Because of these factors, the durability of an extra-anatomic bypass may be limited despite aggressive antithrombotic treatment.

Extra-anatomic bypasses are plagued by sudden thrombotic occlusion, and amputation rates are high. In one large series, one third of patients required a major amputation during long-term follow-up.[1] Reinfection also is a major concern when prosthetic grafts are employed in patients with ongoing infection: it occurs in 10% to 20% of such patients and often proves lethal. A final major concern in patients who undergo excision of an infected aortic graft and extra-anatomic bypass is the possibility of blowout of the aortic stump. This is an infrequent occurrence (incidence < 10%) but one that is typically fatal.

AORTIC ALLOGRAFT

In situ aortic allografting has been employed to treat aortic graft infections, with somewhat mixed results. In one report, a 20%

mortality was associated with this method of treatment.[2] In addition, many survivors experience significant problems, including early or late allograft rupture and late aortic graft dilation.[3] Reinfection of allografts may also occur and usually proves fatal when it does. Complications may be reduced by using cryopreserved allografts instead of fresh ones, but at present, the data are insufficient to determine whether one type of allograft is clearly superior to the other overall. Currently, aortic allografts are available in the United States only on a limited basis; accordingly, this technique is not a useful option in emergency situations.

ANTIBIOTIC-TREATED PROSTHETIC GRAFT

Use of antibiotic-treated prosthetic graft material for reconstruction has the advantage of permitting an expeditious reconstruction that leaves no aortic stump.[2,4-8] However, the reinfection rate is high and unpredictable, and patients must undergo lifelong antibiotic therapy. Typically, the new prosthetic graft is soaked in rifampin, 60 mg/ml, for 15 minutes before implantation.[6,7]

IN SITU AUTOGENOUS RECONSTRUCTION

Dissatisfaction with the long-term patency of extra-anatomic bypass led to the development of in situ autogenous venous reconstruction.[9-11] Early reconstructive attempts that made use of greater saphenous vein grafts proved unsuccessful because the small caliber of the venous conduit resulted in low patency rates. Subsequent attempts that made use of larger-caliber FPV grafts, however, proved highly successful.

FPV grafts have excellent long-term patency and are resistant to reinfection. In addition, they are ideal conduits for patients with extensive multilevel occlusive disease, in whom venous grafts theoretically would have better patency than prosthetic grafts. (An analogy would be the superior durability of venous grafts for femoropopliteal bypass in comparison with prosthetic grafts.) The 5-year patency rates for aortoiliac/aortofemoral reconstructions using FPV grafts range from 85% to 100%.[11,12] Long-term amputation rates are correspondingly low.

The primary disadvantage of reconstruction with FPV grafts is that the procedure is time consuming and technically demanding. In our experience, the mean operating time is about 8 hours. The lower-extremity ischemic time is longer than that in patients undergoing extra-anatomic bypass, but it can be minimized by sequencing the operation so as to shorten cross-clamp time and by using a two-team approach. An additional disadvantage of using FPV grafts is the associated short-term venous morbidity. Approximately 20% of patients who undergo FPV harvesting will require fasciotomy, typically performed at the time of the harvest. The fasciotomy rate is highest in patients who undergo concurrent greater saphenous vein harvesting and in those who have severe lower-extremity ischemia (ankle-brachial index [ABI] < 0.4).[13] Long-term venous morbidity appears to be low, with no known cases of venous ulceration or venous claudication.[14] Mild to moderate chronic edema develops in approximately 30% of

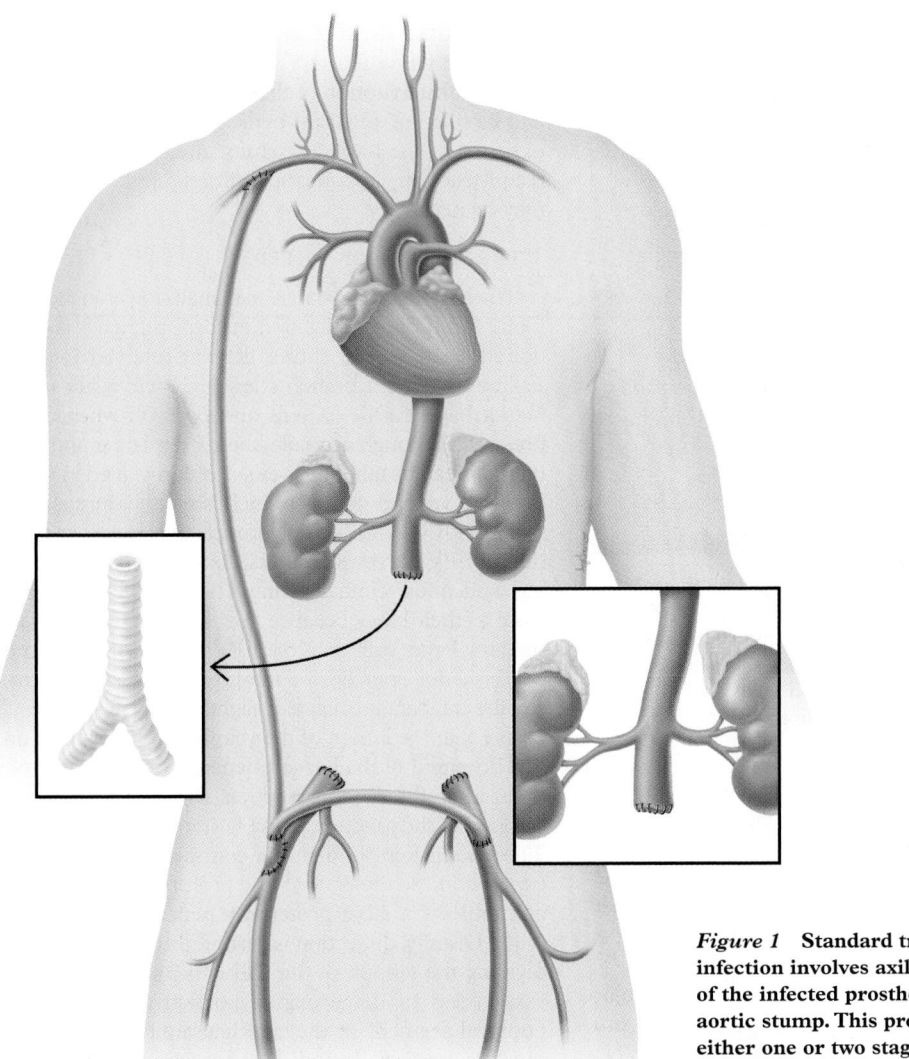

Figure 1 **Standard treatment of aortic graft infection involves axillobifemoral bypass, removal of the infected prosthesis, and oversewing of the aortic stump. This procedure can be performed in either one or two stages. It is most useful in patients who do not have infection extending into the femoral area.**

patients. Aneurysmal degeneration of the vein grafts is a theoretical risk, but in practice, it is rare.

Preoperative Evaluation

The preoperative workup should assess the extent of infection, look for concomitant occlusive disease (indicating a possible need for infrainguinal, visceral, or renal reconstruction), and determine whether there are other associated infectious complications that must be treated surgically (e.g., a psoas abscess, an entrapped ureter with hydronephrosis, or duodenal erosion necessitating duodenal repair). In patients who have previously undergone prosthetic aortofemoral bypass, infection may be limited to one limb of the graft, and it may be treatable by replacing only that limb. In patients who have previously undergone prosthetic infrainguinal bypass, the prosthetic graft may have to be removed and replaced with an autogenous graft.

Traditionally, the mainstay of the preoperative workup was arteriography complemented by computed tomography, but currently, the workup is increasingly being performed with CT angiography alone. CT angiography is often capable of evaluating the extent of infection, visualizing the sites of previous prosthetic anastomoses, and delineating the arterial anatomy. Magnetic reso-

nance angiography can also be a helpful adjunct, particularly in patients with renal insufficiency.

When autogenous reconstruction with deep vein grafts is being considered, preoperative assessment of the adequacy of the vein segments must also be performed. This is accomplished by means of venous duplex ultrasonography. Duplex examination of the lower-extremity venous system establishes the diameter and the available length of the deep veins. In addition, the duplex scan can evaluate acute or chronic thrombosis of the deep veins, any recanalization changes, the congenital absence or duplication of venous segments, and unusually small deep veins. When the FPV is small (< 5 mm), absent, or incomplete, a dominant profunda femoris vein is usually present. This vein courses posteriorly through the thigh to connect with the popliteal vein and can also be used as a venous autograft. Duplex vein mapping of the greater saphenous system is also routinely performed and may provide useful information in the event that concomitant infrainguinal reconstruction is planned or may have to be performed unexpectedly.

Operative Planning

Removal of an infected aortic graft and autogenous reconstruction require prolonged exposure of large portions of the body sur-

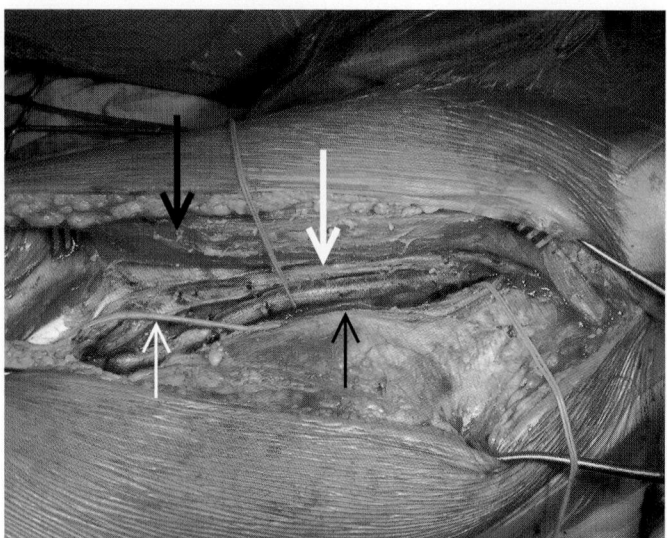

Figure 2 **The FPV (thin black arrow), the superficial femoral artery (thick white arrow), and the saphenous nerve (thin white arrow) lie deep to the sartorius (thick black arrow) in the subsartorial canal. The sartorius is reflected medially to expose these structures. The adductor magnus tendon is divided to expose these structures as they traverse Hunter's canal.**

face. Significant drops in core body temperature, combined with blood loss and resuscitation, may lead to metabolic acidosis, coagulopathy, cardiac dysrhythmia, and immune compromise. Accordingly, core body temperature should be kept above 36° C (96.8° F) by applying heated-air warming blankets to the upper body, using warmed fluid for resuscitation, and maintaining a warm ambient temperature in the operating room.

To minimize ischemic time with cross-clamping, the major tasks involved in excision of an infected aortic graft and in situ autogenous reconstruction should be sequenced as follows: (1) dissection of FPVs, which are left in situ until needed; (2) isolation and control of the femoral vessels; (3) entry into the abdomen and control of the aorta; (4) removal of the infected prosthesis; and (5) reconstruction with the deep vein grafts.[15]

Operative Technique

STEP 1: THIGH INCISION AND EXPOSURE OF FEMORAL VESSELS

The patient is placed in the supine position with the legs "frog-legged" and supported under the thighs. An incision is made on the thigh along the lateral border of the sartorius muscle. This lateral incision not only facilitates vein harvesting but also allows the surgeon to expose the femoral vessels while avoiding the infected femoral incision medially in the groins.

The sartorius is reflected medially so as to preserve the medial segmental blood supply. The subsartorial canal is entered, and the femoral vessels are exposed. The femoral vein is usually located posterior to and slightly medial or lateral to the artery at this level. The deep venous system is then exposed from the distal common femoral vein downward, including the proximal profunda femoris vein through Hunter's canal to the mid-popliteal level [*see Figure 2*]. The saphenous nerve is located in this canal and is intimately associated with the femoral vessels. Care must be taken not to injure this nerve either directly or through excessive traction; such injury will cause irritating postoperative saphenous neuralgia.

Care must also be taken to preserve major branches of the superficial femoral artery when this vessel is occluded or severely diseased. Interruption of these branches, which may supply collateral circulation to distal beds, may result in unexpected critical ischemia of the lower extremity after completion of the proximal reconstruction, and further infrainguinal arterial reconstruction may be necessary.

STEP 2: DISSECTION OF FPV

The FPV has many large and small side branches. Careful, meticulous and unhurried ligation of these branches is critical. Most are doubly ligated, with suture ligation reserved for the larger ones. Failure to ligate a branch adequately will result in exsanguinating hemorrhage if a tie loosens and pops off when exposed to aortic pressure. Although as a rule, the FPV is larger and sturdier than the typical greater saphenous vein, it is thin-walled in some areas where branches are present. If a branch is avulsed during dissection, suture repair with 6-0 or 7-0 polypropylene is necessary. Branch ligation during FPV harvesting differs from the typical branch ligation during saphenous vein harvesting. The branches of the FPV are ligated close to their bases because this is where the vein wall tends to be thin; the larger caliber of the FPV makes this technique possible. In contrast, the branches of the greater saphenous vein, which is of smaller caliber, are ligated slightly away from the vessel wall to ensure that the lumen of the vein is not encroached on.

The extent of the harvest depends on the length of venous conduit required for reconstruction. Proximally, dissection extends to the level of the junction of the femoral and profunda femoris veins. These veins join to form the common femoral vein, which is also exposed in the dissection. The profunda femoris vein is easily recognizable as a large posteriorly penetrating vein in the proximal thigh. Distally, dissection is carried through the adductor hiatus by dividing the tendon of the adductor magnus; this measure allows easy access to the proximal portion of the popliteal vein. The popliteal segment of the vein has multiple large branches, which must be carefully ligated. The dissection can easily be taken down to the level of the knee joint. The veins are left in situ until the required length of conduit can be determined.

STEP 3: DISSECTION AND CONTROL OF FEMORAL VESSELS

The femoral vessels can usually be dissected by extending the vein harvest incision cephalad along the lateral border of the sartorius to

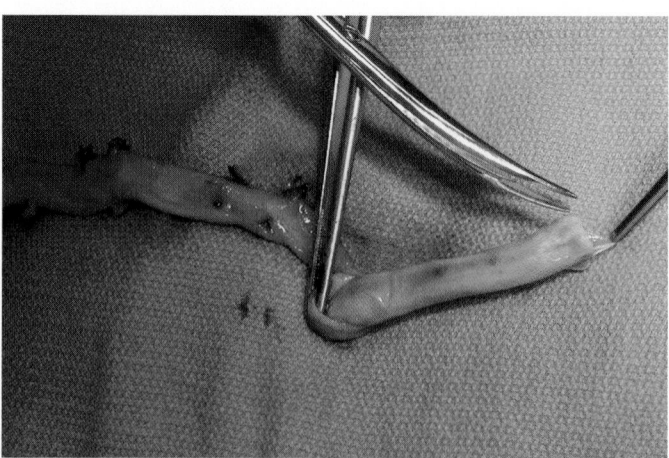

Figure 3 **Use of a valvulotome typically results in incomplete valve lysis. It is preferable to evert the entire venous graft and excise the valves (which usually number 3 or 4) completely with scissors.**

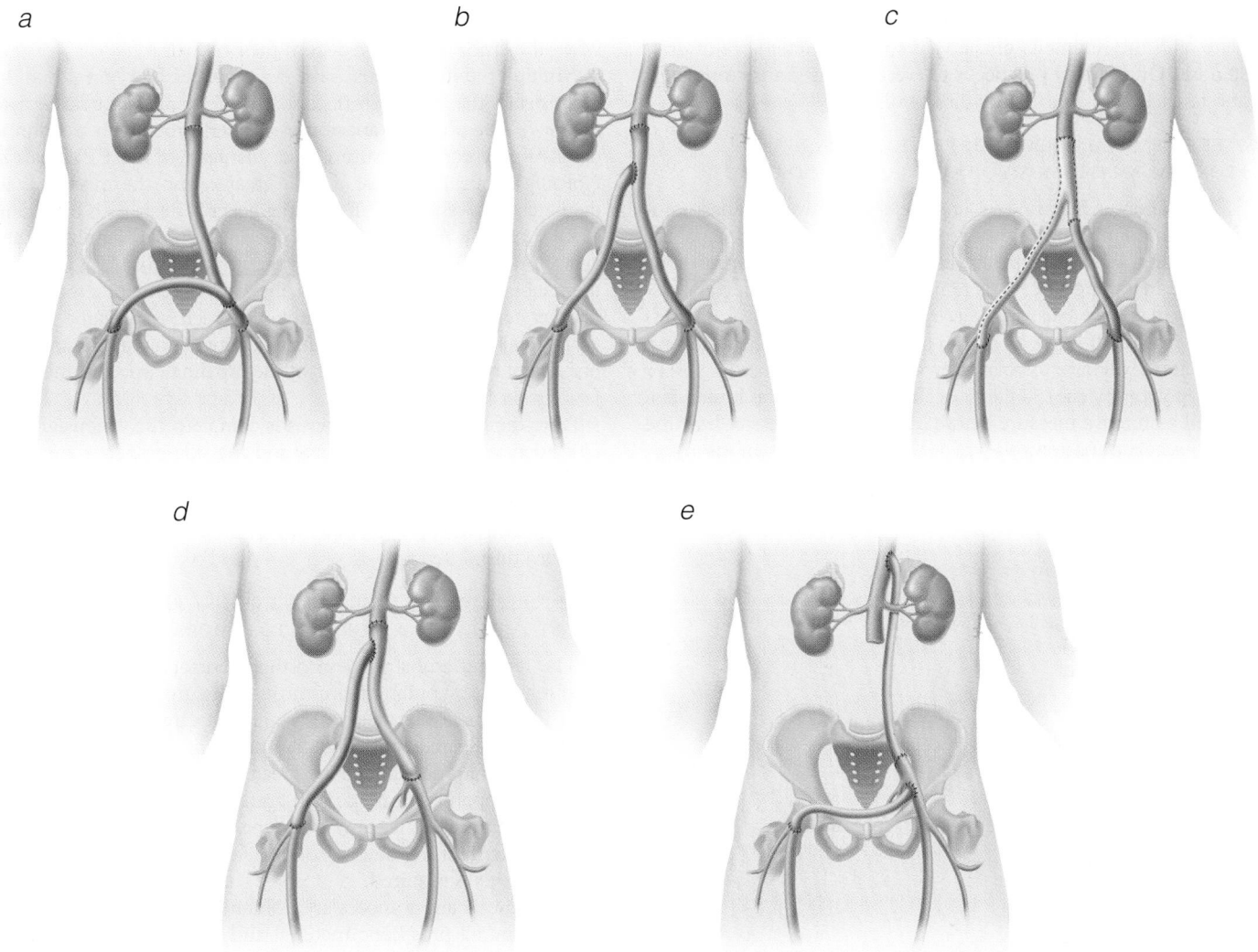

Figure 4 **Multiple anatomic reconstructions have been used to recreate the aorto-iliac-femoral anatomy. (*a*) Shown is an aortounifemoral bypass with a femorofemoral crossover. (*b*) Instead of a femorofemoral bypass, the second limb may be brought off the midportion of the first limb in an end-to-side manner. (*c*) If infection is limited to one limb of an aortofemoral bypass, an FPV graft may be used to replace only the infected portion. (*d*) One segment of vein may be used to replace both segments of an aortoiliac or aortofemoral graft. (*e*) In some instances, it may be easier to approach the paraceliac aorta via a retroperitoneal approach for the proximal anastomosis.**

the level of the anterior superior iliac spine. Through this incision, control of the superficial femoral, profunda femoris, and common femoral vessels is gained. In addition, the distal limbs of the existing aortofemoral graft can be controlled. Occasionally, control is difficult to obtain from a position lateral to the sartorius, in which case the medial aspect of the muscle may be dissected from the subcutaneous tissue to afford improved exposure. Only rarely is a more medial incision required. As noted [*see* Step 1, *above*], the lateral approach allows the surgeon to avoid entering the previous incision, where there may be a draining sinus or cellulitis.

STEP 4: ABDOMINAL INCISION AND DISSECTION OF AORTA

The abdomen is then entered either through a midline abdominal incision or via a retroperitoneal approach; the latter is particularly helpful in avoiding tedious abdominal adhesions. Dissection for control of the aorta above the aortic anastomosis is performed. The anastomosis may be near the level of the renal arteries, in which case suprarenal or supraceliac aortic control may be required.

STEP 5: REMOVAL AND PREPARATION OF VENOUS GRAFTS

Before cross-clamping, the vein grafts are removed and prepared. The length of the grafts is determined by measuring from the aortic anastomosis to the femoral anastomoses on both sides. The femoral vein is divided flush with the profunda femoris vein and oversewn with a 5-0 polypropylene suture. This creates a smooth transition point from the profunda femoris vein to the common femoral vein and leaves no stump in which blood can stagnate and create thrombus. The grafts are then distended in a 4° C solution containing lactated Ringer solution (1 L), heparin (5,000 U), albumin (25 g), and papaverine (60 mg). Any leaks are repaired either with additional silk ties or with figure-eight fine polypropylene sutures. Any adventitial bands that distort the lumen are lysed.

Next, the valves in the grafts must be lysed. This is a critical step because the grafts are placed in a nonreversed fashion to optimize size matching with the aorta for the proximal anastomosis. Valvulotomes have been used for valve lysis in these large-caliber veins, but the results have been unsatisfactory: lysis is often incomplete, and the remnants of the valves may become sites of graft stenosis. Our current practice is to evert venous grafts completely and to excise all valves under direct vision [*see Figure 3*].

STEP 6: REMOVAL OF BODY OF PREVIOUS GRAFT AND PROXIMAL ANASTOMOSIS OF NEW GRAFT TO AORTA

The patient is heparinized, and the aorta above the anastomosis and both limbs of the graft are cross-clamped. The body of the graft is then excised, with the limbs left in place. All prosthetic material, including sutures, is removed. The previous aortic anastomosis may have been done in either an end-to-end or an end-to-side fashion. If it was an end-to-side anastomosis, the distal end of the aorta will have to be oversewn with a large suture (e.g., 0 or No. 1 polypropylene). Balloon occlusion of the distal lumen is a helpful adjunctive measure before ligation. Regardless of how the previous aortic anastomosis was done, the new anastomosis is typically constructed in an end-to-end fashion. The distal limbs of the existing graft are left in place while the aortic anastomosis is per-

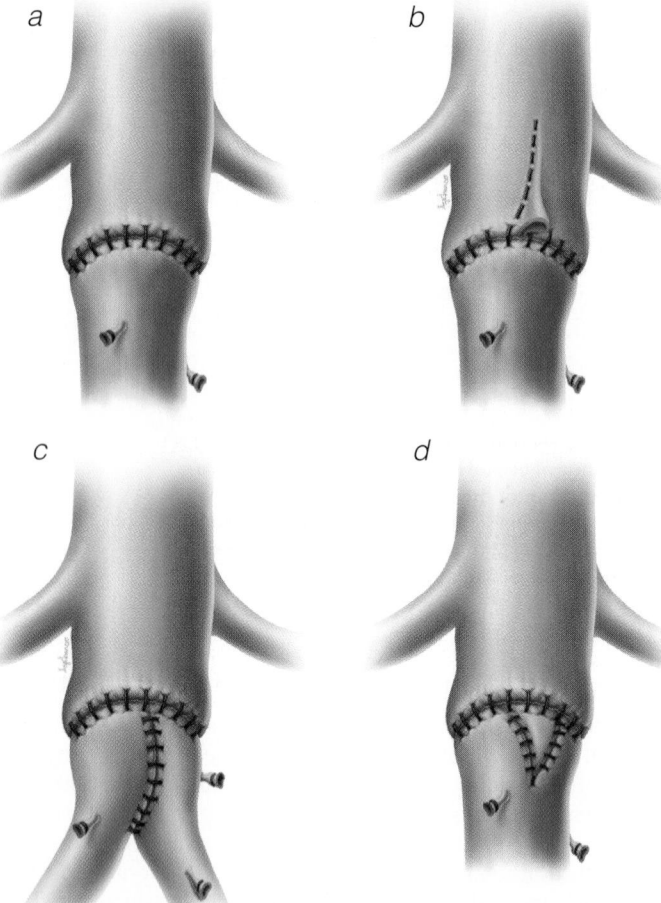

a

b

c

d

Figure 5 (*a*) An end-to-end proximal anastomosis is usually possible if the diameter of the FPV graft is large enough and the aorta is of normal size. (*b*) If the end of the aorta is significantly larger in diameter than the venous graft, plication of the aorta can be performed. (*c*) A pantaloon technique may also be used to deal with a size mismatch between the aorta and the FPV graft. This technique effectively doubles the circumference of the vein. (*d*) The proximal anastomosis can also be facilitated by incorporating a wedge-shaped portion of vein into the proximal end of the graft.

formed so as to cut down on the blood loss that typically occurs when the limbs are removed from their tunnels.

Multiple configurations have been successfully employed to reconstruct the distal aortic and iliac-femoral vasculature [*see Figure 4*]. The proximal anastomosis is performed with a continuous 4-0 polypropylene suture. The diameter of the FPV graft is typically about 1.5 cm or a little greater, and the mismatch in diameter between the graft and the aorta is dealt with by taking slightly more advancement (i.e., placing sutures slightly farther apart) on the aortic wall than on the graft wall [*see Figure 5a*]. If the caliber discrepancy between the two structures is too large, another technique must be employed, such as plication of the aorta, joining of the venous grafts in a pantaloon configuration, or placement of a triangular patch at the proximal aspect of the graft [*see Figures 5b through 5d*].

After the proximal anastomosis is complete, the venous graft is distended under aortic pressure, and the side branches are carefully examined to confirm that all ligatures are securely placed. Any questionable areas are repaired. Anastomotic leakage is also repaired with the aorta clamped to ensure that the venous graft is not torn during repair.

STEP 7: REMOVAL OF LIMBS OF PREVIOUS GRAFT AND DISTAL ANASTOMOSES OF NEW GRAFTS TO FEMORAL ARTERIES

The femoral limbs of the prosthetic aortobifemoral grafts are then removed by pulling them through the groin incisions. When the FPV grafts are tunneled to the groins, care must be taken to ensure that ligated side branches are not torn or dislodged. Because it may be difficult to create new tunnels through the scarred retroperitoneum, the vein grafts may be tunneled through the existing tunnels. In many cases, the existing tunnels are smaller in caliber than the new vein grafts, and careful digital dilation of the tunnels is required.

The femoral anastomoses are fashioned in a standard manner. Once again, all prosthetic material and all surrounding infected tissue must be debrided from the groins. On occasion, profundaplasty or reimplantation of the profunda femoris may be required. If possible, the femoral anastomoses should be done in an end-to-side manner to preserve retrograde pelvic perfusion.

Perfusion of the extremities must be assessed before the leg wounds are closed. If Doppler arterial signals are absent at the level of the ankle, a femoropopliteal or distal bypass may be necessary [*see 96 Infrainguinal Arterial Procedures*]. Because the popliteal artery is exposed during FPV harvesting, adjunctive femoropopliteal bypass is easily accomplished in this setting.

STEP 8: CLOSURE

After reversal of heparinization, the thigh wounds are copiously irrigated and closed over closed suction drains. Placement of drains prevents postoperative seromas and subsequent wound complications. Even though these wounds are contaminated as a consequence of the proximity of the infected graft in the groin wound, infection is rare. Often, there are draining sinuses medial to the vein harvest incisions, which are debrided and left open.

Postoperative Care

Parenteral antibiotics are continued for 5 to 7 days, and antibiotic coverage is modified on the basis of intraoperative cultures of the graft material and wound swabs. Intermittent pneumatic compression and low-dose subcutaneous heparin (5,000 U every 8 to 12 hours) are employed for prevention of deep vein thrombosis. Thrombosis of the residual popliteal vein is common, and aggressive prophylaxis may prevent extension of the thrombus into the calf veins. With the FPV absent, the risk of pulmonary embolism is low.

Complications

The incidence of chronic venous morbidity after FPV harvesting is low, but the fasciotomy rate is approximately 20%. In our practice, the decision to perform a fasciotomy is based primarily on clinical examination of the legs. We specifically assess progressive compartment swelling and firmness on serial examination after reperfusion of the lower extremities. We also consider risk factors in making this decision. Two specific risk factors for fasciotomy are (1) a low preoperative ABI (< 0.4) and (2) concurrent greater saphenous vein harvesting.[13] Other factors may also help determine the need for fasciotomy, including the indication for operation, the length of vein harvested, the duration of arterial cross-clamping, and the amount of fluid administered intraoperatively.

References

1. Quinones-Baldrich WJ, Hernandez JJ, Moore WS: Long-term results following surgical management of aortic graft infection. Arch Surg 126:507, 1991

2. Speziale F, Rizzo L, Sbarigia E, et al: Bacterial and clinical criteria relating to the outcome of patients undergoing in situ replacement of infected abdominal aortic grafts. Eur J Vasc Endovasc Surg 13:127, 1997

3. Kieffer E, Gomes D, Chiche L, et al: Allograft replacement for infrarenal aortic graft infection: early and late results in 179 patients. J Vasc Surg 39:1009, 2004

4. Bandyk DF, Novotney ML, Back MR, et al: Expanded application of in situ replacement for prosthetic graft infection. J Vasc Surg 32:451, 2000

5. Walker WE, Cooley DA, Duncan JM, et al: The management of aortoduodenal fistula by in situ replacement of the infected abdominal aortic graft. Ann Surg 205:727, 1987

6. Hayes PD, Nasim A, London NJM, et al: In situ replacement of infected aortic grafts with rifampin-bonded prostheses: the Leicester experience (1992 to 1998). J Vasc Surg 30:92, 1999

7. Young RM, Cherry KJ, Davis PM, et al: The results of in situ prosthetic replacement for infected aortic grafts. Am J Surg 178:136, 1999

8. Batt M, Magne JL, Alric P, et al: In situ revascularization with silver-coated polyester grafts to treat aortic infection: early and midterm results. J Vasc Surg 38:983, 2003

9. Clagett GP, Bowers BL, Lopez-Viego MA, et al: Creation of a neo-aortoiliac system from lower extremity deep and superficial veins. Ann Surg 218:239, 1993

10. Nevelsteen A, Lacroix H, Suy R: Autogenous reconstruction with the lower extremity deep veins: an alternative treatment of prosthetic infection after reconstructive surgery for aortoiliac disease. J Vasc Surg 22:129, 1995

11. Clagett GP, Valentine RJ, Hagino RT: Autogenous aortoiliac/femoral reconstruction from superficial femoral-popliteal veins: feasibility and durability. J Vasc Surg 25:255, 1997

12. Jackson M, Ali A, Bell C, et al: Aortofemoral bypass in young patients with premature atherosclerosis: is superficial femoral vein superior to Dacron? J Vasc Surg 40:17, 2004

13. Modrall JG, Sadjadi J, Ali A, et al: Deep vein harvest: predicting need for fasciotomy. J Vasc Surg 39:387, 2004

14. Wells JK, Hagino RT, Bargmann KM, et al: Venous morbidity after superficial femoral-popliteal vein harvest. J Vasc Surg 29:282, 1999

15. Clagett GP: Treatment of aortic graft infection. Current Therapy in Vascular Surgery, 4th ed. Ernst CB, Stanley JC, Eds. CV Mosby, Philadelphia, 2001, p 422

Acknowledgment

Figures 1, 4, and 5 Alice Y. Chen.

Scott E. Musicant, M.D., Gregory L. Moneta, M.D., F.A.C.S., and Lloyd M. Taylor, Jr., M.D., F.A.C.S.

Mesenteric ischemia is encountered infrequently. To date, there have been no randomized, controlled trials comparing treatment modalities for either acute or chronic mesenteric ischemia. Consequently, decisions on how to treat this condition must be based on a few large case series in which a variety of operations were used.

Overall evaluation and management of acute mesenteric ischemia are addressed more fully elsewhere [see 83 Acute Mesenteric Ischemia]. In what follows, we focus specifically on the operative techniques used to treat mesenteric ischemia (whether chronic or acute) and discuss the available literature supporting their use. The appropriate technique for a particular patient varies according to the individual anatomy and the particular intraoperative findings.

The relevant surgical procedures may be conveniently divided into those employed for chronic mesenteric ischemia and those employed for acute ischemia.

Procedures for Chronic Intestinal Ischemia

PREOPERATIVE EVALUATION

J. E. Dunphy, in 1936, was the first to suggest that timely diagnosis and intervention for mesenteric artery occlusive disease may prevent intestinal infarction.[1] It is now clear that optimal treatment of mesenteric ischemia depends on prompt diagnosis and that a high index of suspicion is vital.

Patients with chronic intestinal ischemia generally, but not always, report experiencing colicky, dull, or aching abdominal pain, primarily located in the epigastrium but occasionally radiating to the back. Symptoms typically begin 15 to 30 minutes after eating and may last as long as 3 hours. Peritonitis is not a characteristic of reversible intestinal ischemia; rather, it is indicative of intestinal infarction. Chronic postprandial abdominal symptoms result in markedly reduced food intake (so-called food fear),[2] which generally leads to weight loss.

Physical examination often yields no significant abdominal findings. Abdominal bruits may be audible, but they are a nonspecific sign. Patients often, but not always, show evidence of atherosclerotic disease in other vascular territories. Bowel habits vary, ranging from normal elimination to diarrhea or constipation.

Useful diagnostic tests include duplex ultrasonography, contrast angiography, and magnetic resonance angiography (MRA). Duplex scanning is effective in detecting visceral artery stenosis [see Figure 1] and may allow earlier detection of visceral artery stenosis associated with chronic mesenteric ischemia.[3,4] By itself, however, it is not sufficient for planning a mesenteric revascularization procedure.

Arteriography is the primary imaging procedure employed in planning mesenteric revascularization for chronic intestinal ischemia [see Figures 2 and 3]. Lateral and anteroposterior views of the aorta are required for full evaluation of the severity of vis-

ceral stenosis or occlusion and the extent of collateral development. In most cases, a transfemoral Seldinger technique is suitable, though in the setting of iliofemoral occlusive disease, a transaxillary approach is occasionally required. Between 60 and 100 ml of contrast material is required for appropriate lateral and anteroposterior views of the abdominal aorta. Visceral artery lesions are usually ostial but may extend beyond the orifice of the vessel as a posterior plaque, especially in the superior mesenteric artery (SMA). Selective catheterization of the main intestinal arteries is rarely necessary and may be dangerous. Appropriate magnification views generally allow characterization of the proximal SMA beyond its origin, even without selective catheterization of the SMA. Intra-arterial digital subtraction techniques are usually adequate for lateral views, and they require less contrast material than other techniques. Arteriography also demonstrates coexisting lesions of the aorta and of the renal and iliac arteries that may be important in planning revascularization.

OPERATIVE PLANNING

Essentially all patients with peripheral artery disease have concomitant coronary artery disease (CAD). Although no symptoms of CAD may be evident, care must still be taken to provide perioperative cardiac protection. Perioperative beta blockade and antiplatelet therapy should be routinely employed in all patients undergoing elective procedures.

If the patient is undergoing a bypass procedure, the choice of graft material should be addressed. In general, prosthetic grafts

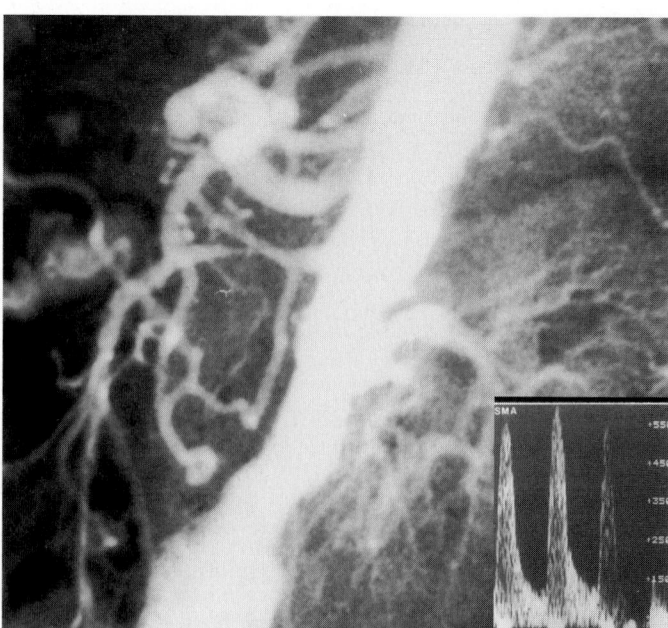

Figure 1 **Example of duplex spectral waveform with comparative arteriogram in patient with SMA stenosis.**

A more versatile endarterectomy technique is transaortic endarterectomy.[7] This procedure involves a posterolateral approach to the aorta, in which the aorta is exposed transperitoneally with medial visceral rotation. Alternatively, a completely retroperitoneal approach may be taken. The main disadvantage of the retroperitoneal approach is that it restricts the surgeon's ability to assess the bowel at the completion of revascularization.

Transaortic endarterectomy *Step 1: incision and initial approach.* A midline incision is recommended. A complete medial visceral rotation is performed, with the left kidney left in its bed.

Step 2: exposure. The lateral aorta is exposed, and the celiac artery and the SMA may be identified anteriorly; the left renal artery lies posteriorly.

Step 3: endarterectomy. A trapdoor incision is made in the aortic wall in such a way as to encompass the orifices of the SMA and the celiac artery. Partial occlusion of the aorta with a clamp is sometimes possible, but in most cases, complete aortic occlusion is required. If necessary, the aortotomy can be extended distally and posteriorly to include the renal artery orifices as well.

Among the advantages of this operation are that it permits simultaneous endarterectomy of the aorta and all visceral vessel orifices and that it does not require the use of prosthetic material [*see Figure 3*]. The disadvantages include the potential risks associated with suprarenal clamping (e.g., cardiac overload, renal and lower-extremity embolization, and ischemia). Because of

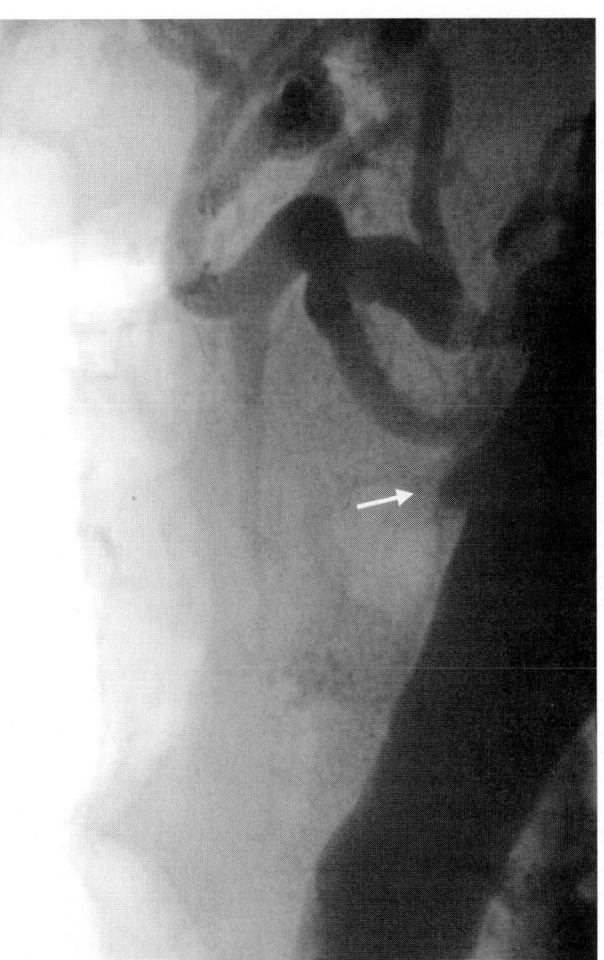

Figure 2 **Lateral aortogram clearly shows moderate stenosis of proximal celiac artery and occlusion of SMA (arrow) in patient with intestinal ischemia.**

work well for mesenteric artery bypass. However, the entire abdomen and both legs should still be included in the operative field in case autologous vein proves necessary for the bypass conduit. Autologous vein is often required in cases involving bowel resection and may also be preferable for bypasses to smaller visceral vessels. If an autologous vein bypass procedure is planned, preoperative duplex scanning of the greater saphenous and femoral veins is recommended to facilitate selection of the best available vein for the conduit.

OPERATIVE TECHNIQUE

Visceral Endarterectomy

Visceral endarterectomy for treatment of mesenteric ischemia was first described in 1958 by Shaw and Maynard,[5] who performed endarterectomy of the SMA in a blind retrograde fashion through a distal arteriotomy. At present, retrograde endarterectomy cannot be recommended.

The SMA can be approached directly once control of the suprarenal aorta has been obtained.[6] A longitudinal incision is made across the origin of the SMA, and an endarterectomy is performed. In most patients, the exposure is limited. This direct approach may be considered when the SMA is widely separated from the renal arteries and the visceral aorta is relatively free of disease; however, this scenario is uncommon.

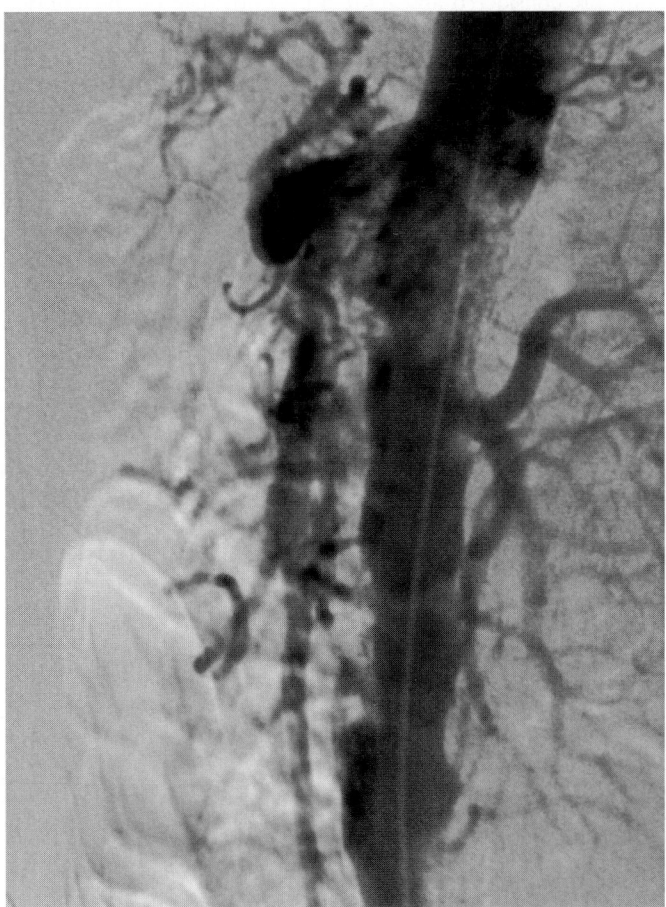

Figure 3 **Lateral aortogram showing so-called coral reef atheroma involving visceral aorta with occlusion of origin of SMA.**

these risks, the need for more extensive dissection, and the unfamiliarity of most surgeons with this procedure, arterial bypass procedures are generally preferred for treatment of chronic mesenteric ischemia.

Mesenteric Arterial Bypass

Technical considerations *Single-vessel versus multiple-vessel revascularization.* There are two schools of thought on the extent of revascularization for chronic mesenteric ischemia. Proponents of so-called complete revascularization advocate revascularization of both the celiac artery and the SMA and suggest that this approach makes recurrent ischemia less likely should one graft or graft limb undergo thrombosis.[8] In a 1992 study, overall graft patency and survival were better in patients who underwent multiple-vessel bypass than in those who underwent single-vessel bypass. The investigators concluded that multiple-vessel bypass patients were likely to remain asymptomatic because of the presence of additional grafts or graft limbs that remained patent.[8]

Others maintain that the critical vessel involved in chronic mesenteric ischemia is the SMA and argue that bypass to the SMA alone is a relatively simple procedure that relieves symptoms of mesenteric ischemia. In a 2000 study evaluating 49 patients who underwent bypass to the SMA alone, the 9-year primary assisted graft patency rate was 79% and the 5-year survival rate was 61%[9]—results equivalent to those noted in contemporary studies of multiple-vessel revascularization for chronic intestinal ischemia.[10]

Antegrade versus retrograde bypass. Mesenteric bypass grafts may originate either above or below the renal arteries. Bypass grafts are considered antegrade if they originate on the anterior surface of the abdominal aorta cephalad to the celiac artery, retrograde if they originate from the infrarenal aorta or a common iliac artery. Antegrade bypass from the supraceliac aorta, using either prosthetic material or autologous vein, has certain advantages, including a straight graft configuration that minimizes turbulence and graft kinking and, typically, reduced atherosclerotic calcification in the supraceliac aorta.[11] The disadvantages of antegrade bypass are similar to those of visceral endarterectomy and derive from the need to clamp the supraceliac aorta for the proximal anastomosis. As with visceral endarterectomy, partial occlusion clamping is theoretically possible but not always practical. Clamping of the supraceliac aorta may increase the risk of cardiac events, visceral or renal emboli, and ischemia. One prerequisite for use of the supraceliac aorta in an antegrade bypass is that the vessel must be angiographically normal to ensure that it can safely be clamped. It should also be kept in mind that reoperation on the supraceliac aorta is difficult: once this site has been used, reexposure generally is not safe.

Antegrade bypass *Step 1: incision and initial approach.* Supraceliac aorta–visceral artery bypass is performed through an upper midline incision. Self-retaining retractors are helpful.

Step 2: exposure. The dissection begins with division of the gastrohepatic ligament and retraction of the left lobe of the liver to the right, followed by incision of the diaphragmatic crus and exposure of the anterior aspect of the aorta.

Step 3: choice of graft. In clean cases with no intestinal necrosis or perforation, we use woven Dacron bifurcated grafts. If a single-vessel bypass is to be performed, a single limb is cut from the bifurcated graft. Autologous vein grafts are usually reserved for

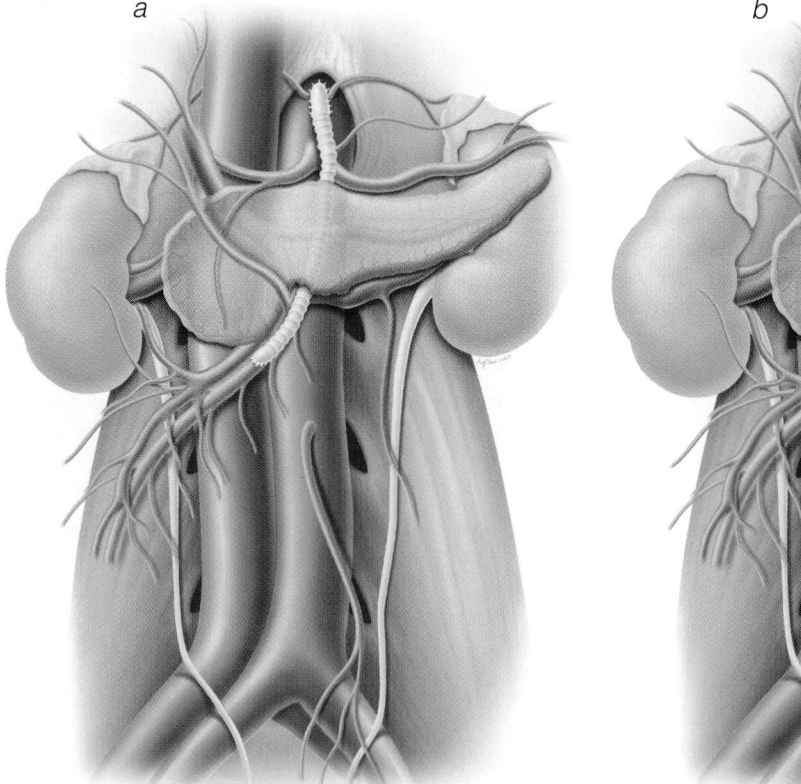
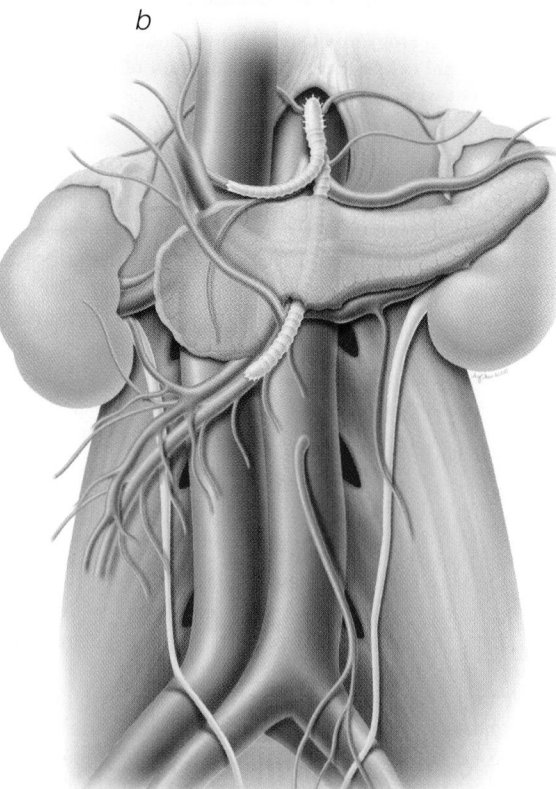

a   *b*

Figure 4 **Arterial bypass: antegrade. Shown is bypass from supraceliac aorta to SMA alone (*a*) or to hepatic artery and SMA (*b*).**[28]

contaminated cases. The femoral vein is an excellent autogenous conduit for mesenteric arterial bypass.

Step 4: anastomosis of graft to supraceliac aorta and visceral artery. If the celiac artery alone is to be revascularized, the usual procedure is to perform an end-to-side proximal anastomosis to the aorta, followed by an end-to-side distal anastomosis to the common hepatic artery. If the SMA alone is to be revascularized, it is generally necessary to tunnel the graft beneath the pancreas to the inferior border of the pancreas, then perform an end-to-side anastomosis to the SMA at that level [*see Figure 4a*]. Extreme care must be exercised in developing the retropancreatic tunnel. If this area appears too narrow or is scarred as a result of previous pancreatic inflammation, the graft should be tunneled anterior to the pancreas to ensure that it is not compressed and to avoid causing bleeding from disrupted pancreatic veins.[12] If a prepancreatic tunnel is required, an autogenous conduit should be considered because the graft will be lying adjacent to the posterior wall of the stomach. If both the celiac artery and the SMA are to be revascularized from the supraceliac aorta, a bifurcated prosthetic graft is attached to the supraceliac aorta proximally, with one distal limb anastomosed to the hepatic artery and the other to the SMA [*see Figure 4b*].

Retrograde bypass In a retrograde bypass, the infrarenal aorta or a common iliac artery is used as the inflow vessel. One clear advantage of this procedure is that the approach to the infrarenal aorta is more familiar to most surgeons. Another is that dissection and clamping of the infrarenal aorta are less risky than dissection and clamping of the supraceliac aorta. Yet another is that the surgeon can work within a single operative field. Once the self-retaining retractor is placed, the operation on the infrarenal aorta and the SMA can be performed without further adjustment of the retractor.

Step 1: incision and initial approach. Here too, a midline incision and a transperitoneal approach are preferred. The transverse mesocolon is retracted upward, and the ligament of Treitz is divided.

Step 2: exposure. After division of the ligament of Treitz, the duodenum and the small bowel are retracted to the right. The SMA may then be identified arising from beneath the inferior border of the pancreas. The retroperitoneum is divided distally along the aorta to a point just beyond the level of the aortic bifurcation. The distal aorta and both common iliac arteries are assessed to allow determination of the proper location for the proximal anastomosis.

Step 3: choice of graft. As a rule, grafts made of Dacron or of ringed, reinforced expanded polytetrafluoroethylene (ePTFE) are preferred. Problems may arise when retrograde bypasses are performed with autologous vein grafts, in that such grafts are prone to kinking when the viscera are replaced. When a retrograde vein bypass is performed, the graft may be brought straight up from the right iliac artery so that it lies between the aorta and the duodenum, then anastomosed to the posteromedial wall of the SMA.

Step 4: anastomosis to infrarenal aorta or common iliac artery and SMA. Our preference is to use the area near the junction of the aorta with the right common iliac artery for the proximal anastomosis. (Short grafts originating from the midportion of the infrarenal aorta, though commonly used, are prone to kinking when the viscera are returned to their normal position.) The graft

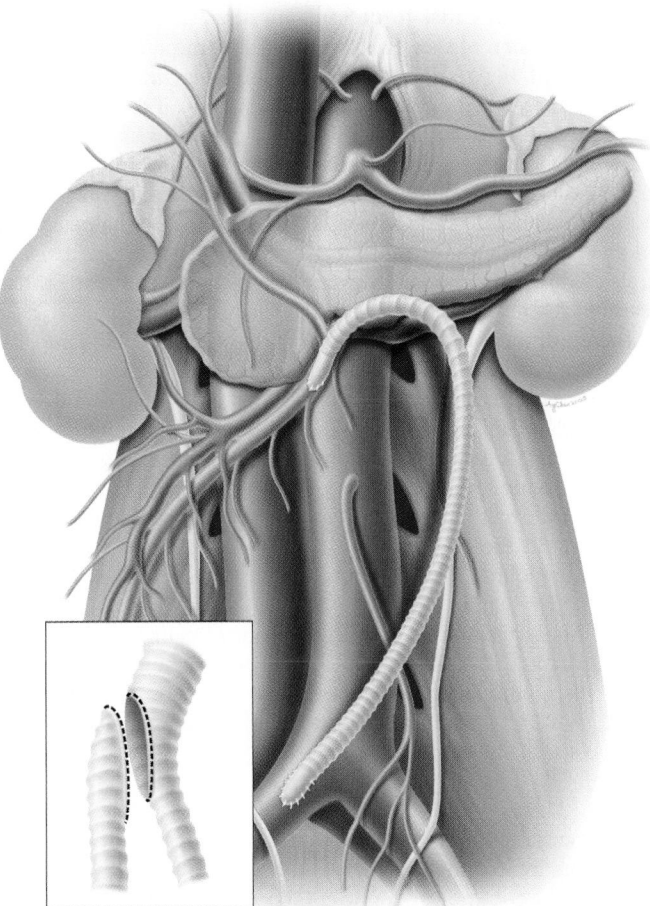

Figure 5 **Arterial bypass: retrograde. Shown is bypass from iliac artery to SMA.**[28]

to the SMA is passed cephalad, turned anteriorly and inferiorly 180°, and anastomosed to the anterior wall of the SMA just beyond the inferior border of the pancreas.[12] In this manner, a gentle C loop is formed that, if placed correctly, keeps the graft from kinking when the viscera are restored to their anatomic position after retractor removal [*see Figure 5*]. The ligament of Treitz and the parietal and mesenteric peritoneum are closed over the graft to exclude it from the peritoneal cavity.

Endovascular Techniques

Early reports describing the use of percutaneous transluminal angioplasty (PTA) to treat visceral atherosclerotic lesions indicated that initial technical success rates were as high as 80% but that recurrence rates ranged from 20% to 40%.[12,13] In a 1996 study of PTA in 19 patients who were considered high risk, the initial success rate was 95%, and the recurrence rate was 20% at 28 months.[14] In a subsequent study of 25 patients who underwent angioplasty and stenting of the celiac artery or the SMA for chronic visceral ischemia, the initial technical success rate was 96%, and the initial clinical response rate was 88%.[15] At 6 months, 92% of the stents remained patent.

COMPLICATIONS

Technical

The main technical complication of mesenteric bypass is acute graft thrombosis. This event is rare, but when it occurs, prompt recognition is essential to prevent intestinal infarction. Kinking and compression of the graft are the most common causes of this condition. If the retrograde graft is too long, the redundancy makes it more susceptible to kinking. Similarly, if the graft is not positioned so as to form a gentle C loop, it is at risk for kinking when the viscera are returned to their normal position. An antegrade graft that is too long is equally at risk for kinking and occlusion. When an antegrade bypass is tunneled behind the pancreas, an adequate amount of space must be present to ensure that the graft is not compressed. In general, prosthetic grafts are more resistant to kinking and compression than vein grafts are.

Identification of perioperative graft occlusion is hindered by postoperative incisional pain, fluid shifts, fever, and leukocytosis, all of which are common in the postoperative period and may mask signs of intestinal ischemia. Patients with chronic mesenteric ischemia often have symptoms only when eating and thus may be asymptomatic in the postoperative period until they resume oral feeding. For these reasons, we advocate evaluating the graft early in the postoperative period with either conventional contrast angiography or computed tomographic angiography [see Outcome Evaluation, below].

Additional technical complications may occur as a result of clamp placement. Clamping of the supraceliac aorta can lead to renal atheroemboli or ischemia. These problems can be minimized by using a supraceliac clamp only on an angiographically normal aorta.

Systemic

Myocardial infarction is the most common cause of mortality in patients treated for mesenteric ischemia. Pulmonary compromise is also a common systemic complication of mesenteric revascularization. Renal failure after mesenteric revascularization is more common in patients with preoperative renal insufficiency.[16] Mortality is markedly increased when renal failure occurs postoperatively.[16] Postoperative renal insufficiency can be minimized by administering mannitol, furosemide, and, possibly, vasodilators intraoperatively.

Patients who undergo mesenteric revascularization occasionally experience a profound reperfusion syndrome manifested by acidosis, pulmonary compromise, and coagulopathy. We recommend administering sodium bicarbonate (to minimize the effects of metabolic acidosis) and mannitol (for its free radical–scavenging properties) before restoring intestinal perfusion.

OUTCOME EVALUATION

Restoration of pulsatile flow to the small bowel usually results in immediate active peristalsis and intestinal edema. The technical success of surgical revascularization is assessed intraoperatively through visual examination of the intestine and continuous-wave Doppler examination of the distal mesenteric vasculature and the bowel wall. Doppler signals should be heard along the antimesenteric border, and pulses should be palpable in the mesentery. Intraoperative duplex scanning may also be used to visualize anastomotic sites directly.[17]

Electromagnetic flow measurements can be helpful in evaluating the adequacy of mesenteric revascularization. Such measurements must be made after all packs and retractors have been removed. In most cases, the flow rate through the graft should be between 500 and 800 ml/min, but flow rates as high as 1,000 ml/min may be recorded.[12]

To confirm technical success after mesenteric revascularization, we advocate routine postoperative imaging of the graft. Ideally, this is done early in the postoperative period. Catheter-based contrast angiography is optimal for evaluating the bypass graft and the distal vasculature, allowing identification of anastomotic stenoses, kinking, or, in the case of autologous grafts, narrowing caused by valves [see Figure 6a]. If a technical defect is discovered, reoperation and correction are required to ensure prolonged patency. In the past few years, we have started evaluating selected patients perioperatively with CT angiography. This modality is less invasive than traditional contrast angiography, but it still requires administration of contrast material and exposure to radiation [see Figure 6b].

Duplex ultrasonography has been used for postoperative graft surveillance after mesenteric revascularization.[18] At present, there are no validated criteria for determining what constitute normal velocities within a mesenteric bypass graft. Undoubtedly, duplex-derived peak systolic velocities and end-diastolic velocities depend on the caliber of the graft, whether the graft supplies both the celiac artery and the SMA, and the length of the graft. The lack of validating data notwithstanding, we routinely use postoperative duplex scanning to establish baseline values and to permit comparisons for follow-up evaluation of graft patency. If markedly elevated, focal peak systolic velocities are recorded—especially if they increase on serial examinations—a contrast angiogram should be obtained to confirm graft stenosis. Duplex scanning can be difficult in the early postoperative period because of incisional tenderness and the increased intra-abdominal gas associated with postoperative ileus.

Procedures for Acute Intestinal Ischemia

PREOPERATIVE EVALUATION

As in the evaluation of patients with possible chronic mesenteric ischemia, a high index of suspicion is of primary importance in the evaluation of patients with possible acute mesenteric ischemia [see 83 Acute Mesenteric Ischemia]. Most cases of acute intestinal ischemia result either from thrombosis of a preexisting stenotic lesion or from embolization[19] (most frequently to the SMA). Cardiac emboli are the most common variety, though tumor emboli[20] and atheroemboli are seen as well. Atheroemboli generally result from iatrogenically induced cholesterol embolization caused by aortic catheterization. The prognosis for acute intestinal ischemia of embolic origin is more favorable than that for ischemia of thrombotic origin. Emboli typically lodge distally in the SMA distribution, and therefore, the proximal intestine is still partially perfused.[19] In contrast, thrombotic occlusion occurs at the origin of the vessel, resulting in complete interruption of midgut perfusion.

Acute, severe abdominal pain that is out of proportion to the physical findings is the classic manifestation and is strongly suggestive of intestinal ischemia. The duration of symptoms does not appear to correlate with the degree of intestinal infarction.[21] Peritonitis is initially absent, but vomiting and diarrhea may be present, and occult gastric or rectal bleeding may be identified in as many as 25% of patients.[21]

There are no reliable serum markers for acute intestinal ischemia. Leukocytosis, hyperamylasemia, or elevated lactate levels may be present, but these findings are insensitive and inconsistent. Abdominal radiographs may reveal dilated bowel loops and, occasionally, thickened bowel wall, but these findings are similarly inconsistent. In theory, duplex ultrasonography may be helpful, but in practice, its applicability is often limited by the gaseous visceral distention frequently associated with acute intestinal ischemia.

a

b

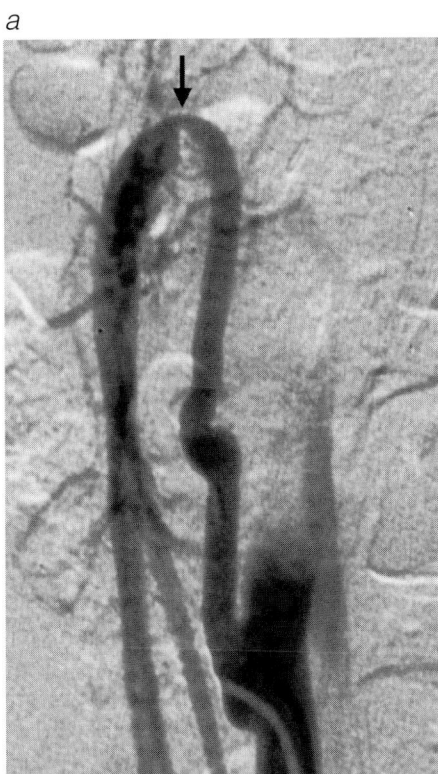
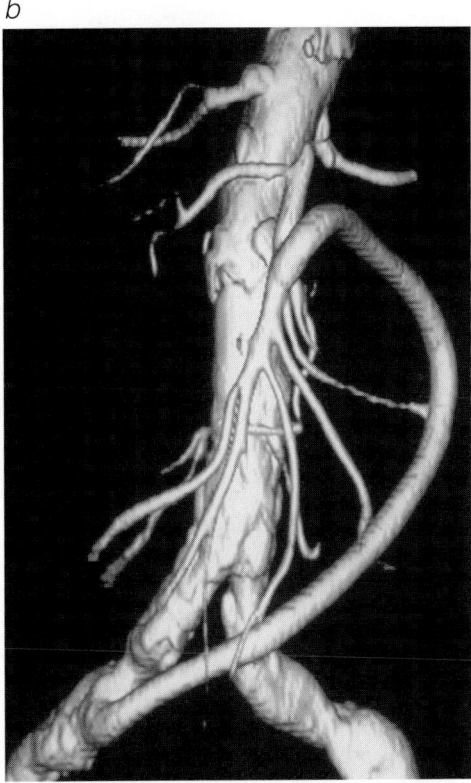

Figure 6 Routine postoperative imaging is performed to confirm technical success after revascularization. (*a*) Postoperative arteriogram shows iliac artery–SMA saphenous vein graft with kink (arrow). This problem was asymptomatic and was corrected by reoperation on postoperative day 5. (*b*) Postoperative CT arteriogram shows retrograde iliac artery–SMA prosthetic graft. C (hook) configuration of distal anastomosis provides antegrade flow into SMA.

The use of preoperative arteriography to diagnose acute ischemia is controversial. Acute intestinal ischemia is a true surgical emergency, and delaying treatment to perform arteriography could result in further intestinal infarction. Angiography may be considered in patients who have abdominal pain without any other signs or symptoms of systemic illness [*see Figure 7*]. In patients who have rebound tenderness, rigidity, or evidence of toxicity or shock, emergency exploration is indicated.

OPERATIVE PLANNING

Patients with acute intestinal ischemia who present with evidence of toxicity must be resuscitated expeditiously to ensure that surgical intervention is not delayed. Once it is determined that surgery is indicated, no further delay is justified. The patient is placed supine on the operating table, and the entire abdomen and both legs are prepared. As in operative treatment of chronic intestinal ischemia, the possibility that autologous vein will be needed for bypass grafting must be anticipated.

OPERATIVE TECHNIQUE

Intraoperative Considerations

Mesenteric revascularization and bowel resection The goals of surgical therapy are to restore normal pulsatile inflow, to ensure that questionably viable bowel is adequately perfused, and to resect any clearly nonviable bowel. During abdominal exploration, the viability of the intestine and the status of the blood flow to the SMA are assessed with an eye to determining the appropriate treatment. The surgeon should be prepared to perform both intestinal revascularization and intestinal resection. Seg-

ments of clearly viable bowel are often interspersed with segments of marginally viable bowel and segments of necrotic bowel. Acutely ischemic bowel that is not yet necrotic may appear deceptively normal. Mildly to moderately ischemic bowel may exhibit

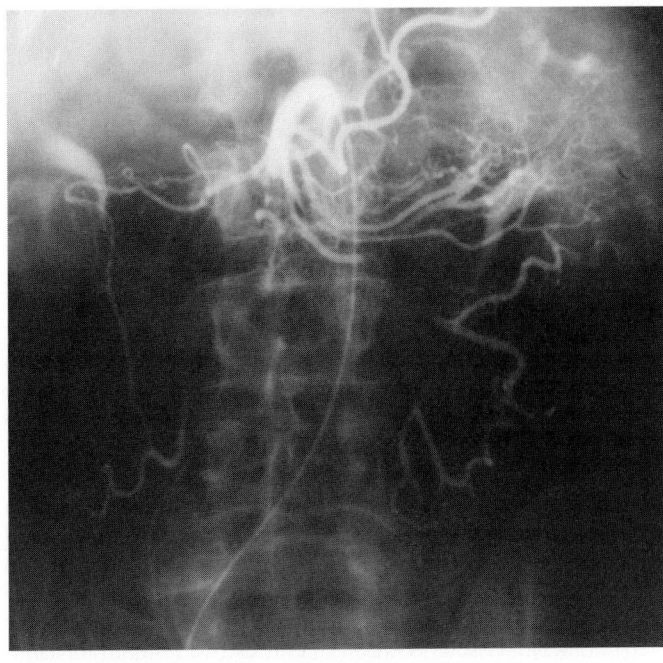

Figure 7 Preoperative arteriogram shows embolic occlusion of SMA distal to its origin.

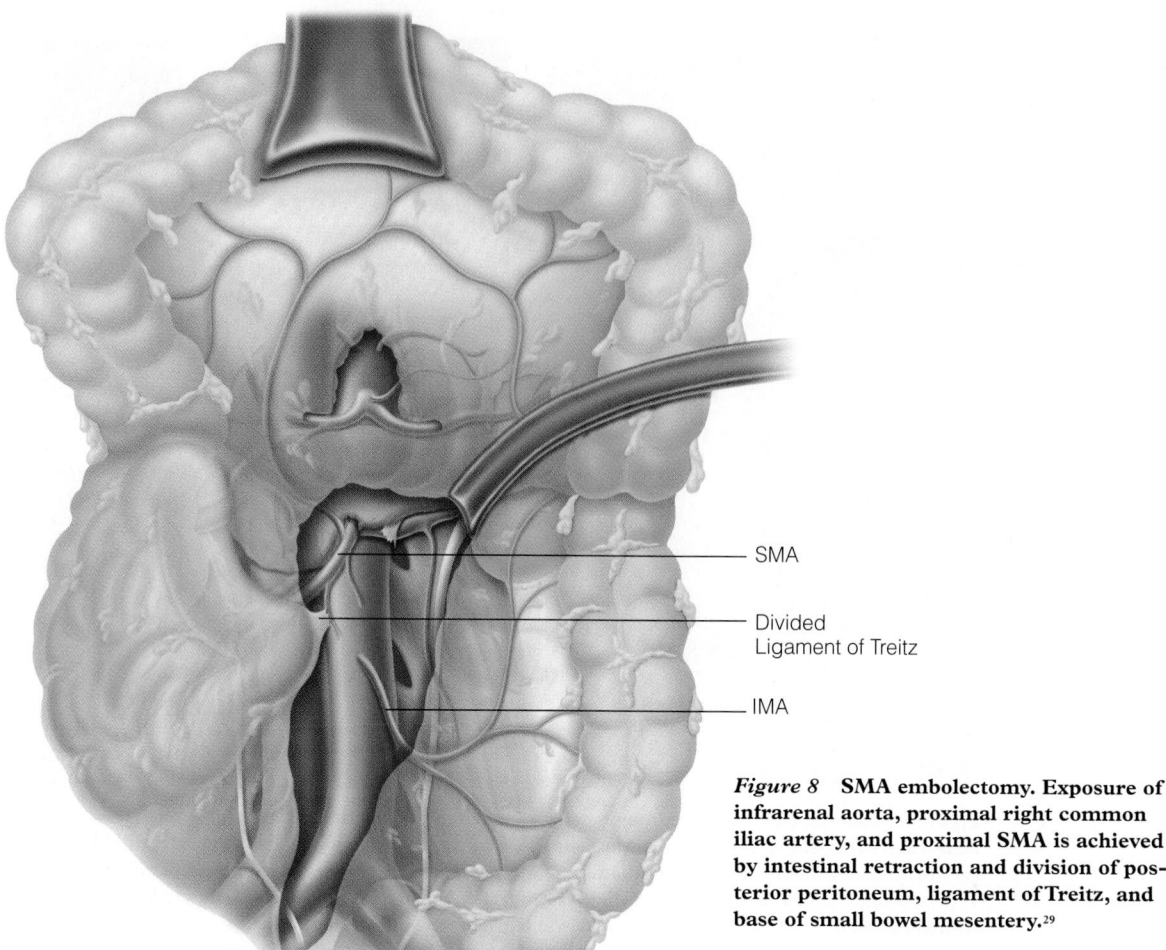

— SMA

— Divided
Ligament of Treitz

— IMA

Figure 8 **SMA embolectomy. Exposure of infrarenal aorta, proximal right common iliac artery, and proximal SMA is achieved by intestinal retraction and division of posterior peritoneum, ligament of Treitz, and base of small bowel mesentery.**[29]

loss of normal sheen, absence of peristalsis, and dull-gray discoloration. Other objective signs of ischemia are the absence of a palpable pulse in the SMA or in its distal branches, the absence of visible pulsations in the mesentery, and the absence of flow on continuous-wave Doppler examination of the vessels of the bowel wall. The small bowel may be deeply cyanotic yet still viable. In most cases, if there is any doubt, bowel resection should not be performed until after revascularization.

The distribution of ischemic changes provides valuable information about the cause of the ischemia. SMA thrombosis often results in ischemia to the entire small bowel, with the stomach, the duodenum, and the distal colon spared; in severe cases, the entire foregut may be ischemic. In contrast, ischemia secondary to SMA embolism generally spares the stomach, the duodenum, and the proximal jejunum because the emboli tend to lodge at the level of the middle colic artery rather than at the origin of the SMA. The choice of operation for revascularizing the bowel depends on the underlying causative condition. Embolectomy is indicated for arterial embolism, whereas bypass is indicated for thrombotic occlusion.

Revascularization of the acutely ischemic intestine In patients with very advanced intestinal ischemia, widespread bowel necrosis may be obvious. This situation invariably proves fatal, and thus, revascularization is not indicated. In many patients, however, substantial portions of the bowel are ischemic but not frankly necrotic. Whether such bowel segments can be restored to viability cannot be accurately predicted. In most instances, therefore, revascularization should precede resection.

Restoration of normal flow to the SMA can produce remarkable changes in an ischemic bowel. Because these changes do not always occur immediately, it is often necessary to preserve questionably viable portions of the bowel initially and then perform a second-look laparotomy within 12 to 36 hours. If the questionably viable bowel is not in significantly better condition at the time of the second-look operation, it should be resected. Occasionally, however, even a third look is prudent. Revascularized intestine that was profoundly ischemic may swell dramatically. Temporary abdominal closure with mesh may permit tension-free abdominal closure, prevent abdominal compartment syndrome, and perhaps even improve intestinal perfusion by reducing intra-abdominal pressure.

Superior Mesenteric Artery Embolectomy

Step 1: incision and initial approach Again, a midline incision is made, and a transperitoneal approach is taken.

Step 2: exposure of SMA at root of mesentery The SMA is exposed after division of the ligament of Treitz at the base of the transverse colon mesentery. The duodenum and the small bowel are retracted to the right [*see Figure 8*]. The visceral peritoneum is incised above the ligament of Treitz, just cephalad to the third portion of the duodenum. The SMA should be readily palpable in this location as it crosses over the third portion of the duodenum. The dissection is continued to obtain sufficient proximal and distal control of the vessel. Heparin is administered, and the vessel is clamped proximally and distally.

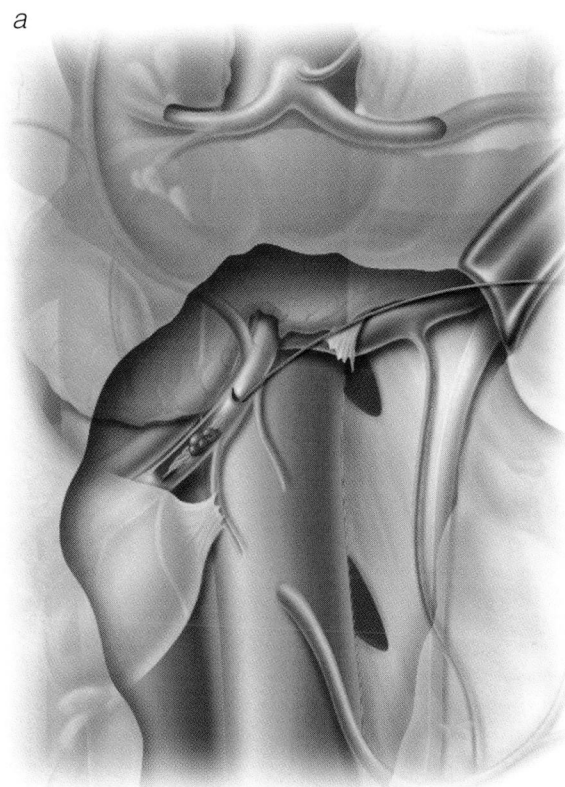

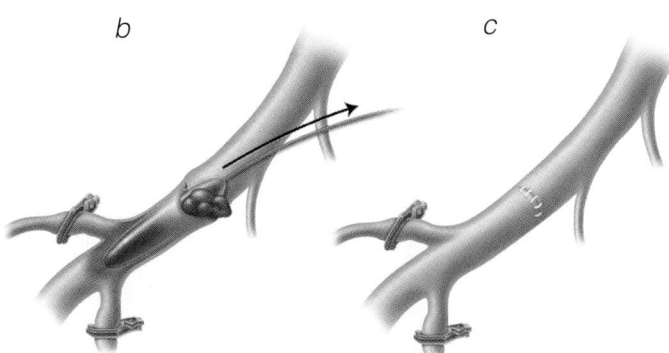

Figure 9 **SMA embolectomy. (***a***) Location of embolus within SMA is identified. (***b***) Transverse (as shown) or longitudinal arteriotomy is performed, and embolus is extracted with balloon catheter. (***c***) Arteriotomy is closed. Primary closure (as shown) suffices for transverse arteriotomy, but vein patch is usually required for closure of longitudinal arteriotomy.**[29]

Step 3: arteriotomy An arteriotomy is then made in the SMA. The incision may be either transverse or longitudinal. We prefer to perform a longitudinal arteriotomy if there is any possibility that a bypass graft may be needed. The arteriotomy should be made approximately 2 to 3 cm distal to the origin of the SMA, though alternative placements may be appropriate on occasion, depending on the anatomy and the estimated location of the occlusion [*see Figures 9a, b*].

Step 4: embolectomy Proximal embolectomy should be performed first to ensure adequate inflow. A 3 or 4 French balloon catheter is sufficient in most cases. If very good pulsatile inflow is not achieved after embolectomy, then thrombosis of a stenotic lesion is likely to be the underlying cause of the acute intestinal ischemia, and a bypass graft should be placed. Even when inflow is apparently adequate, a bypass should be strongly considered if the proximal SMA is palpably abnormal.

The narrowness and fragility of the distal SMA and its branches can make distal embolectomy particularly challenging. It is best to use a 2 French embolectomy catheter for this procedure. The catheter must be passed gently, without undue force.

Step 5: closure Once all possible thrombus has been removed, the arteriotomy is closed. A transverse arteriotomy may be closed primarily with interrupted monofilament sutures [*see Figure 9c*]; however, a longitudinal arteriotomy frequently must be closed with an autologous vein patch. If adequate flow is not restored after the clamps are removed, the arteriotomy is used as the distal anastomotic site of a bypass graft.

Superior Mesenteric Artery Bypass

Patients with SMA thrombosis who are seen early enough and who have no intestinal necrosis may undergo SMA bypass grafting with a prosthetic conduit. At exploration, many of these patients have fluid within the peritoneal cavity. This finding is not, in itself, a contraindication to the use of a prosthetic graft. However, if the patient has necrotic bowel that must be resected or if perforation has occurred, a prosthetic graft should not be used. In these situations, an autologous vein graft is preferred. A good-quality vein is mandatory; if the saphenous vein is inadequate, the femoral vein may be used instead.

The techniques of mesenteric bypass for acute intestinal ischemia are identical to those for chronic intestinal ischemia. Because these patients are often acutely ill, it is vital to perform the operation rapidly and efficiently. In the acute setting, bypass to the SMA alone is strongly preferred [*see Figure 10*]. As a rule, a retrograde approach, using the infrarenal aorta or a common iliac artery for inflow, is best; the supraceliac aorta is used for inflow only if the infrarenal vessels are unsuitable for this purpose. Even highly calcified iliac arteries can be used for inflow, provided that there is no significant pressure gradient and that the surgeon is familiar with intraluminal balloon occlusion techniques for proximal and distal control.

Endovascular Techniques

It would seem reasonable that endovascular therapies might come to play a role in the treatment of acute intestinal ischemia, given that a preoperative angiogram is usually feasible in stable patients. Several groups have reported treating acute arterial embolism with intra-arterial thrombolysis[22,23]; others have reported treating acute embolism, as well as thrombotic occlusion, with PTA.[24,25] Although a degree of anecdotal success with these techniques has been achieved in selected cases, it should be kept in mind that reliance on endovascular therapy alone for presumed acute intestinal ischemia runs the risk of missing bowel necrosis. After endovascular therapy, frequent clinical reevaluation is necessary to identify patients with persistent intestinal ischemia. Abdominal exploration should be very strongly considered in

a

b

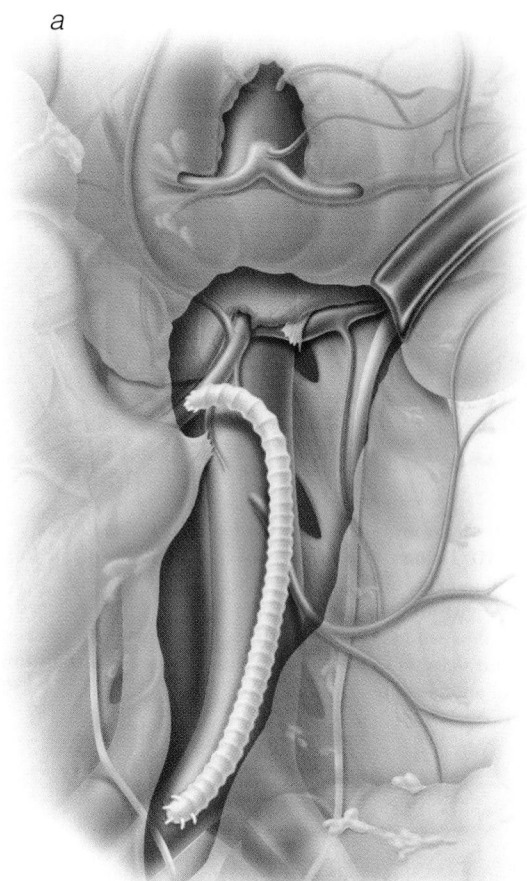

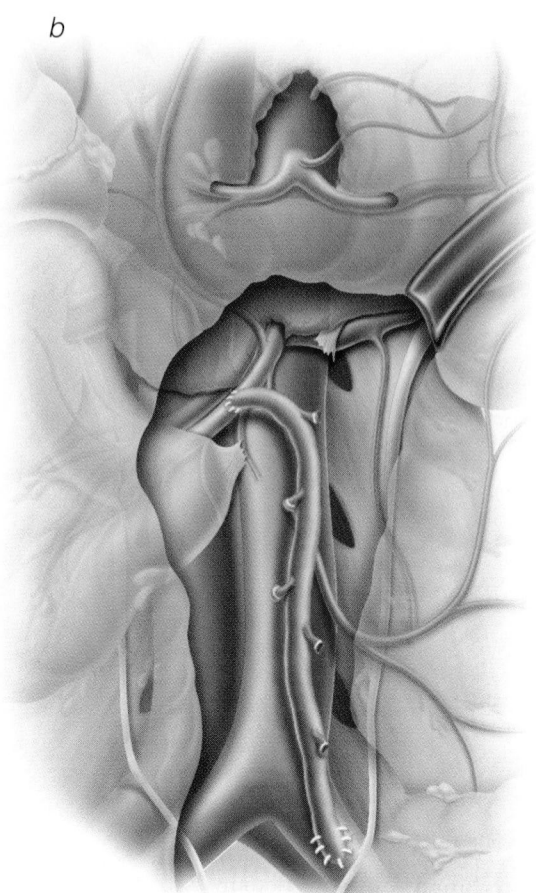

Figure 10 **SMA bypass. (*a*) Iliac artery–SMA bypass with prosthetic graft is suitable for cases in which SMA thrombosis produces ischemic but salvageable bowel. (*b*) Iliac artery–SMA bypass with saphenous vein is suitable for cases in which some segments of necrotic or perforated bowel must be resected.**[29]

most cases, even if the angiographic result of endovascular treatment is good.

TROUBLESHOOTING

Occasionally, patients present with emboli that have lodged in the small arterial branches of the SMA. These vessels are often too small to allow the passage of embolectomy catheters, and bypass beyond the point of obstruction frequently is not possible. In these situations, resection of marginally viable bowel is the best option.

As noted (see above), avoidance of graft kinking is crucial for preventing early graft failure. Graft failure can have an even greater adverse effect on bowel viability in the setting of acute ischemia than in the setting of chronic intestinal ischemia.

Recovery after revascularization is often prolonged. Early and prolonged parenteral nutrition may be necessary in patients with extensive bowel infarction. Only rarely, however, is lifelong parenteral nutrition required.

OUTCOME EVALUATION

The techniques employed to evaluate the success of mesenteric revascularization for acute ischemia include clinical inspection, continuous-wave Doppler ultrasonography, and I.V. administration of fluorescein. Clinical inspection entails visual assessment of pulsatile flow in the mesenteric arcades, peristalsis, bleeding from cut surfaces, and, of course, color. In one study, clinical parameters were found to be 82% sensitive and 91% specific for bowel viability.[26]

We routinely use a sterile continuous-wave Doppler ultrasound flow detector to evaluate pulsatile flow on the bowel surface. Grossly discolored bowel with no Doppler signal after a period of observation should be resected; marginal bowel with no Doppler signal is an indication for second-look laparotomy.

With the fluorescein fluorescence method, 10 to 15 mg/kg of fluorescein is injected intravenously, and the intestine is inspected with a Wood lamp. A complete absence of fluorescence is diagnostic of nonviability; rapid, confluent, bright fluorescence is diagnostic of viability. There is, however, a large gray area between these two extremes in which interpretation is subjective. In one study, the I.V. fluorescein method was found to be 100% sensitive and specific for detecting nonviable bowel.[27] The disadvantages of this technique are that it requires special equipment and that it exposes the critically ill patient to the risk of an adverse reaction to the dye. Other assessment methods (e.g., surface oximetry, infrared photoplethysmography, and laser Doppler velocimetry) are available, but at present, they are mostly experimental and are not in general use for evaluation of bowel viability.

References

1. Dunphy JE: Abdominal pain of vascular origin. Am J Med Sci 192:109, 1936

2. Moneta GL: Diagnosis of intestinal ischemia. Vascular Surgery. Rutherford RB, Ed. WB Saunders Co, Philadelphia, 2000, p 1501

3. Moneta GL, Yeager RA, Dalman R, et al: Duplex ultrasound criteria for diagnosis of splanchnic artery stenosis or occlusion. J Vasc Surg 14:511, 1991

4. Nicholls SC, Kohler TR, Martin RL, et al: Use of hemodynamic parameters in the diagnosis of mesenteric insufficiency. J Vasc Surg 3:507, 1986

5. Shaw RS, Maynard EP III: Acute and chronic thrombosis of the mesenteric arteries associated with malabsorption: a report of two cases successfully treated by thromboendarterectomy. N Engl J Med 258:874, 1958

6. Hansen HJB: Abdominal angina: results of arterial reconstruction in 12 patients. Acta Chir Scand 142:319, 1976

7. Stoney RJ, Ehrenfeld WK, Wylie EJ: Revascularization methods in chronic visceral ischemia. Ann Surg 186:468, 1977

8. McAfee MK, Cherry KJ, Naessens JM, et al: Influence of complete revascularization on chronic mesenteric ischemia. Am J Surg 164:220, 1992

9. Foley MI, Moneta GL, Abou-Zamzam AM, et al: Revascularization of the superior mesenteric artery alone for treatment of intestinal ischemia. J Vasc Surg 32:37, 2000

10. Park WM, Cherry KJ, Chua HK, et al: Current results of open revascularization for chronic mesenteric ischemia: a standard for comparison. J Vasc Surg 35:853, 2002

11. Murray SP, Ramos TK, Stoney RJ: Surgery of the celiac and mesenteric arteries. Haimovici's Vascular Surgery. Ascher E, Ed. Blackwell Publishing, Malden, Massachusetts, 2004, p 861

12. Taylor LM, Moneta GL, Porter JM: Treatment of chronic visceral ischemia. Vascular Surgery. Rutherford RB, Ed. WB Saunders Co, Philadelphia, 2000, p 1532

13. Odurny A, Sniderman KW, Colapinto RF: Intestinal angina: percutaneous transluminal angioplasty of the celiac and superior mesenteric arteries. Radiology 167:59, 1988

14. Allen RC, Martin GH, Rees CR, et al: Mesenteric angioplasty in the treatment of chronic intestinal ischemia. J Vasc Surg 24:415, 1996

15. Sharafuddin MJ, Olson CH, Sun S, et al: Endovascular treatment of celiac and mesenteric artery stenoses: applications and results. J Vasc Surg 38:692, 2003

16. Mateo RB, O'Hara PJ, Hertzer NR, et al: Elective surgical treatment of symptomatic chronic mesenteric occlusive disease: early results and late outcomes. J Vasc Surg 29:821, 1999

17. Leke MA, Hood DB, Rowe VL, et al: Technical consideration in the management of chronic mesenteric ischemia. Am Surg 68:1088, 2002

18. Nicoloff AD, Williamson WK, Moneta GL, et al: Duplex ultrasonography in evaluation of splanchnic artery stenosis. Surg Clin North Am 77:339, 1997

19. Taylor LM, Moneta GL, Porter JM: Treatment of acute intestinal ischemia caused by arterial occlusions. Vascular Surgery. Rutherford RB, Ed. WB Saunders Co, Philadelphia, 2000, p 1512

20. Low DE, Frenkel VJ, Manley PN, et al: Embolic mesenteric infarction: a unique initial manifestation of renal cell carcinoma. Surgery 106:925, 1989

21. Ottinger LW: The surgical management of acute occlusion of the superior mesenteric artery. Ann Surg 188:72L, 1978

22. Calin GA, Calin S, Ionescu R, et al: Successful local fibrinolytic treatment and balloon angioplasty in superior mesenteric arterial embolism: a case report and literature review. Hepatogastroenterology 50:732, 2003

23. Michel C, Laffy P, Leblanc G, et al: Intra-arterial fibrinolytic therapy for acute mesenteric ischemia. J Radiol 82:55, 2001

24. Yilmaz S, Gurkan A, Erdogan O, et al: Endovascular treatment of an acute superior mesenteric artery occlusion following failed surgical embolectomy. J Endovasc Ther 10:386, 2003

25. Brountzos EN, Critselis A, Magoulas D, et al: Emergency endovascular treatment of a superior mesenteric artery occlusion. Cardiovasc Intervent Radiol 24:57, 2001

26. Bulkley GB, Zuidema GD, Hamilton SR, et al: Intraoperative determination of small bowel viability following ischemic injury: a prospective, controlled trial of two adjuvant methods (Doppler and fluorescein) compared with standard clinical judgment. Ann Surg 193:628, 1981

27. Carter MS, Fantini GA, Sammartano RJ, et al: Qualitative and quantitative fluorescein fluorescence in determining intestinal viability. Am J Surg 147:117, 1984

28. Taylor LM Jr, Porter JM: Treatment of chronic intestinal ischemia. Semin Vasc Surg 3:186, 1990

29. Kazmers A: Operative management of acute mesenteric ischemia. Ann Vasc Surg 12:187, 1998

Acknowledgment

Figures 4, 5, 8, 9, and 10   Alice Y. Chen.

94 UPPER-EXTREMITY REVASCULARIZATION PROCEDURES

John Byrne, M.CH., F.R.C.S.I.(Gen), Philip S. K. Paty, M.D., F.A.C.S., and R. Clement Darling III, M.D., F.A.C.S.

Vascular surgeons are commonly called on to treat patients with acute arm ischemia. Elective arm revascularization is an infrequently performed procedure, one that usually prompts surgeons to resort to reference texts. Even in busier centers, elective arm reconstructions currently account for only 3.2% of elective limb revascularizations. Balloon angioplasty has largely replaced surgical bypass in the treatment of subclavian occlusions; however, the very growth of endoluminal approaches to arm revascularization has led to a paradoxical increase in the need for so-called prophylactic carotid-subclavian bypass in patients with thoracic aneurysms. In addition, the rising incidence of diabetes and the longer survival times reported in patients with renal impairment have led to increased use of distal bypass procedures in the arm (analogous to pedal bypass procedures in the leg [*see 96 Infrainguinal Arterial Procedures*]). Finally, the growing number of dialysis access procedures performed has led to an increased incidence of arm ischemia resulting from these operations.

In this chapter, we describe the technical aspects of the procedures employed for emergency and elective arm revascularization. We also touch on pharmacologic alternatives to elective revascularization and briefly consider the potential role of minimally invasive techniques (e.g., thoracoscopic sympathectomy).

Procedures for Acute Arm Ischemia

Acute arm ischemia accounts for one fifth of all episodes of acute limb ischemia. It occurs twice as often in females as in males. Brachial embolectomy is the most common treatment. After successful brachial embolectomy, 95% of patients are symptom free[1]; however, the operative mortality may be as high as 12%.[2] Most reports that address acute arm ischemia include only those patients who are treated surgically. In fact, between 9% and 30% of patients who present to vascular surgeons with acute arm ischemia are managed conservatively, either because they are unfit for surgery or because they have minimal symptoms. These conservatively managed patients are probably underrepresented in the literature. In the few reported series, assessment of symptoms and disability has been largely inconsistent. However, in a 1964 series that included 95 patients, 32% of those who were managed conservatively were left with abnormal function in the arm after treatment.[3] In a 1977 report, 75% of the conservatively managed patients had poor functional outcomes.[4] In a 1985 study, 50% of the conservatively managed patients had persistent forearm claudication.[5] The conclusion to be drawn is that although conservative management is appropriate for some patients with acute arm ischemia, every effort should be made to restore blood flow in patients who have a reasonable life expectancy.

BRACHIAL EMBOLECTOMY

Preoperative Evaluation

Patients with acute arm ischemia tend to be slightly older at presentation than patients with leg ischemia (74 years versus 70 years).[6] Usually, there is an underlying embolic source (e.g., cardiac dysrhythmia). Most arm emboli (75%) are of cardiac origin. The brachial artery is the most common site of emboli (60% of cases), followed by the axillary artery (26%). In situ thrombosis accounts for 5% of episodes of arm ischemia.[7]

Selection of patients All patients with acute-onset arm ischemia are candidates for embolectomy. Conservative management should be considered only for patients who are terminally ill or unfit for surgical intervention.

Alternative therapy Some authors have achieved good results by using thrombolysis to treat acute occlusion of the axillary artery or the brachial artery.[8] However, in a 2001 series that included 38 patients with 40 occlusions treated with thrombolysis, the success rate of this approach was only 55%, and eight patients had to undergo surgical thrombectomy after thrombolysis failed.[9] Excellent outcomes have also been reported for the treatment of acute arm ischemia with rotational thrombectomy devices (e.g., Rotarex; Straub Medical, Wangs, Switzerland). To date, however, no large published studies have evaluated these devices, and clinical experience with them is currently limited to case reports.[10]

Operative Planning

In most patients with acute arm ischemia, diagnosis is straightforward and surgical treatment relatively easy. Some instances of acute arm ischemia, however, are caused by an inflow lesion in the subclavian artery (SA) (e.g., from ulcerated plaques, a thrombosed SA aneurysm, or an arterial thoracic outlet syndrome). In such situations, even a technically perfect embolectomy will fail to restore normal hand perfusion.

The majority of brachial embolectomies are performed with local anesthesia, with or without monitored conscious sedation.

Operative Technique

The origins of the ulnar and radial arteries are exposed by means of a so-called lazy S incision [*see Figure 1a*], which prevents the elbow contracture that can occur with a vertical incision. The skin and the subcutaneous tissues are divided. Care is taken to preserve the superficial veins, especially the median antecubital vein, which may be needed to patch the brachial artery. The bicipital fascia is incised, and the brachial artery is found between the tendon of the biceps laterally and the median nerve medially [*see Figure 1b*]. Dissection is continued distally until the ulnar and radial arteries are encountered. The radial artery is a continuation of the brachial artery; the ulnar artery comes off the brachial artery medially and, within 2 to 3 cm of its origin, dives beneath the pronator and epitrochlear muscles. It is important to expose the origins of both forearm arteries because the embolectomy catheter must be passed down each vessel. If the catheter is blindly passed down the brachial artery, it will probably travel down the radial artery.

An arteriotomy (usually vertical) is made in the brachial artery. Clot may be encountered at the bifurcation; if so, it is readily

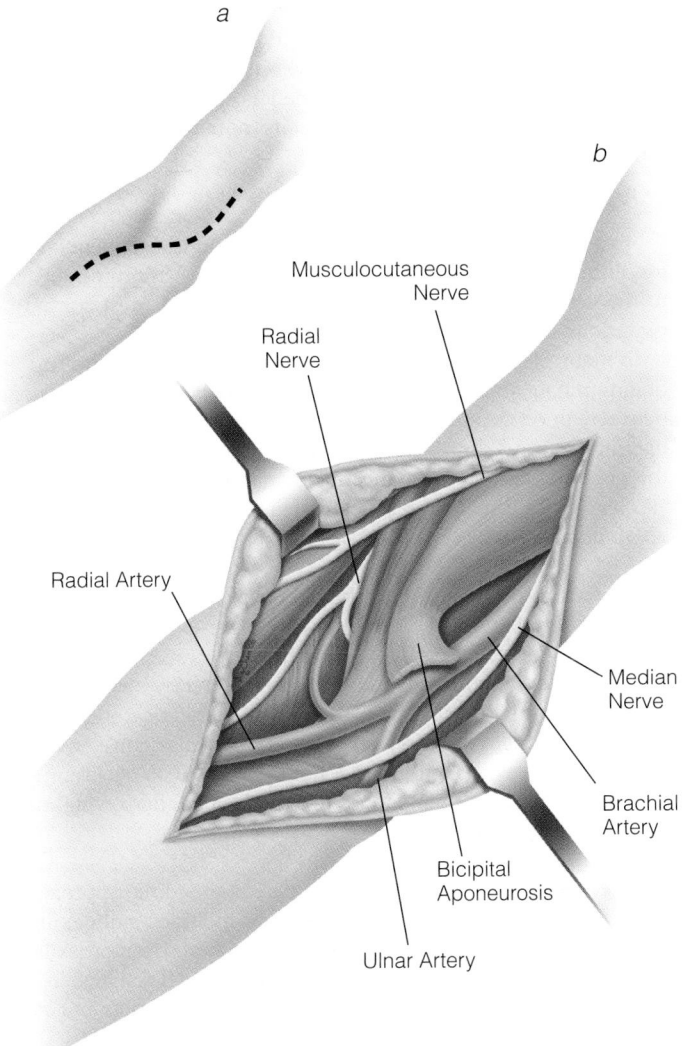

Figure 1 **Brachial embolectomy. Shown are (*a*) a lazy S skin incision and (*b*) the main nerves and vessels exposed.**

Labels in figure:
- *a*
- *b*
- Musculocutaneous Nerve
- Radial Nerve
- Radial Artery
- Median Nerve
- Brachial Artery
- Bicipital Aponeurosis
- Ulnar Artery

removed. In some cases, the brachial artery is pulseless, which indicates that the embolus is lodged more proximally. Once inflow is established, a size 2 or 3 embolectomy catheter is passed distally down each forearm artery. The arteriotomy is then closed either primarily or with a vein patch. A segment of vein may be harvested from the antecubital fossa. Adequate flow in the radial and ulnar arteries is confirmed by means of an intraoperative Doppler probe.

Occasionally, the hand continues to appear ischemic even after an adequate embolectomy. This persistent ischemia is caused either by an unrecognized inflow lesion or by embolization to the digital arteries that has been occurring over an extended period. In these patients, an arch aortogram with selective views of the affected arm should be performed immediately after operation. Any lesion in the SA or the innominate artery can be treated with angioplasty and stenting.

Postoperative Care

The mainstay of postoperative management is adequate anticoagulation. Embolization recurs after successful embolectomy in one third of patients if systemic anticoagulation is not instituted. It may recur even in the face of oral anticoagulation: in a 1989 study, 11% of patients given warfarin after embolectomy sus-

tained a further embolic episode, and all had ongoing atrial fibrillation.[6] Patients are routinely followed up by means of noninvasive studies 4 to 6 weeks after operation.

FOREARM FASCIOTOMY

Unlike calf fasciotomies, which are commonly necessary for leg ischemia, forearm fasciotomies are rarely required for acute arm ischemia. They are more commonly required for traumatic injuries to the arm (e.g., crush injuries or supracondylar fractures of the humerus) or for iatrogenic injuries (e.g., inadvertent infusion of fluid into the muscle compartments of the forearm). Forearm fasciotomies are immediately effective when they are performed, and the incisions, though extensive, usually heal quickly.

Preoperative Evaluation

The forearm muscles are typically tense and tender, though the diagnosis can be difficult to make. One option for assessment is to test compartment pressures with a needle and a transducer; if the intracompartmental pressure is higher than 30 mm Hg, fasciotomy may be indicated. Another option is insonation of the radial and ulnar arteries; if the signal is absent or severely obstructed, fasciotomy may be indicated. Neither of these techniques, however, is reliable. As with lower-extremity ischemia, even the finding of a pulse does not eliminate the need for fasciotomy. The decision whether to perform the procedure is made on clinical grounds.[11] The relevant dictum is "If one is thinking about a fasciotomy, it is probably indicated."

Selection of patients Awareness of the diagnosis is crucial. Any patient with the traumatic or iatrogenic conditions previously mentioned (see above) should be considered to be at risk for compartment syndrome.

Alternative therapy There is no alternative to fasciotomy. Failure to recognize the problem or undue delay in performing adequate fasciotomies will lead to forearm muscle ischemia and a Volkmann's ischemia contracture, resulting in a useless hand.

Operative Planning

Because this procedure is rarely performed, the surgeon may find it useful to mark the incisions on the skin with an indelible pen before operation. The operation is generally performed with general anesthesia, but if the patient is profoundly ill, it may be performed with local anesthesia instead.

Operative Technique

Both a volar and a dorsal incision are required [*see Figure 2*]; there is no single-incision option, as there is for leg fasciotomy. On the volar aspect of the arm, a curvilinear incision is made to allow decompression of the flexor compartment. Because this compartment is supplied by a single vessel (the interosseous artery) and lacks any collateral circulation, it is particularly susceptible to ischemia. On the dorsal aspect, a vertical incision is made to release the dorsal compartment. Because of its deep location in the forearm, the median nerve is especially susceptible to compartment syndrome. At the level of the elbow, the bicipital aponeurosis is divided so that it can be decompressed. At the wrist, the flexor retinaculum is divided in much the same way as in a carpal tunnel decompression. In severe cases, the deep intramuscular fascia enveloping the flexor digitorum superficialis, the flexor digitorum profundus, and the flexor pollicis longus may be opened as well. As a rule, the skin incisions are loosely approximated to facilitate later closure. In any case, the incisions usually heal very well.

Postoperative Care

Regular dressings are applied to the area. Often, delayed primary closure of the fasciotomy sites may be performed once the muscle edema has resolved. Further pressure measurements may be performed to confirm that all muscle compartments have been released.

Procedures for Chronic Arm Ischemia

The etiology of chronic arm ischemia is diverse. Although atherosclerosis is still the major cause, other potential causes (including thoracic outlet syndrome and iatrogenic injury, as well as rarer causes such as Takayasu arteritis, giant cell arthritis, and radiation-induced injury) must also be considered. Initial assessment is carried out by means of noninvasive studies (e.g., pulse-volume recordings [PVRs] and duplex ultrasonography), followed by magnetic resonance angiography (MRA) or computed tomographic angiography (CTA). Confirmation of the findings obtained from these studies may be obtained by means of arch and arm angiography. As a rule, any occlusive lesions found will be in the innominate, subclavian, axillary, or forearm arteries. Each location calls for a different treatment stratagem.

AORTOSUBCLAVIAN BYPASS AND EXTRATHORACIC OPTIONS FOR INNOMINATE ARTERY OCCLUSION

Innominate artery reconstruction is a major surgical procedure. In one major series, the reported operative mortality was 5.4%.[12] Currently, innominate artery bypass is rarely performed, having been largely supplanted by balloon angioplasty and stenting. Nevertheless, there are still some patients who, for technical

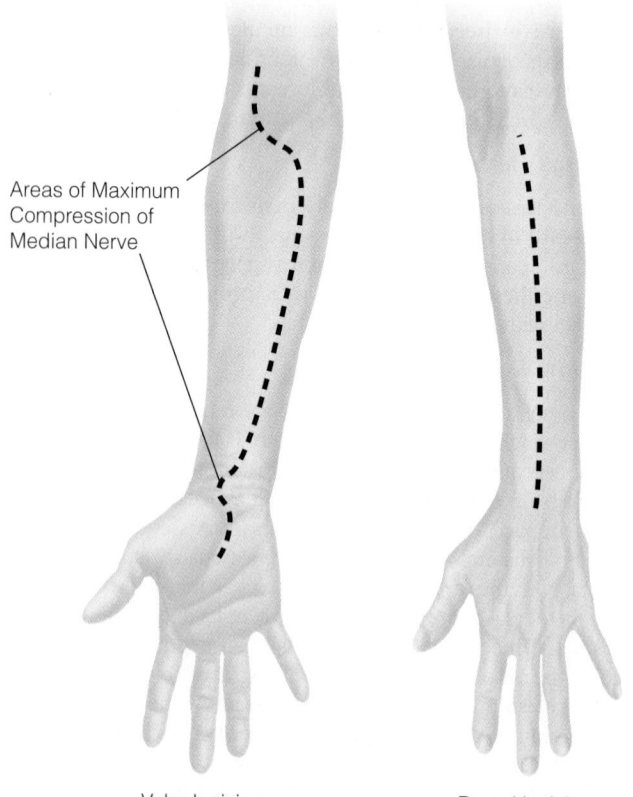

Areas of Maximum Compression of Median Nerve

Volar Incision   Dorsal Incision

Figure 2 **Forearm fasciotomy. Shown are (*a*) a volar incision and (*b*) a dorsal incision in the forearm.**

reasons, may not be candidates for endovascular procedures (e.g., those with an occluded stent and those in whom the anatomy is unsuitable). In patients for whom it is indicated, innominate artery bypass has durable beneficial effects and thus is an option worth considering, despite its potential for significant morbidity.

Preoperative Evaluation

Arm ischemia is the typical presentation for patients with innominate artery occlusion. Cerebrovascular symptoms related to the vertebral or carotid arteries are the second most common presentation.

In many patients, noninvasive imaging yields the first indication of innominate artery stenosis. It is difficult, however, to distinguish between an occlusion in the proximal SA and one in the innominate artery on a duplex ultrasonogram. Contrast angiography is the gold standard for making this distinction. As with all major vascular procedures, standard cardiac investigations and clearance are mandatory.

Selection of patients Innominate artery bypass is the operative standard for selected patients with upper-extremity ischemia. In patients who are at particularly high risk, however, extrathoracic options (e.g., carotid-carotid bypass or, rarely, axilloaxillary crossover grafting) should be considered. We prefer carotid-carotid crossover for higher-risk patients. Cerebrovascular considerations (e.g., asymptomatic high-grade lesions [i.e., > 70% occlusion] or ulcerated plaques with greater than 50% luminal narrowing) may also warrant intervention.

Alternative therapy Indirect or extra-anatomic approaches to innominate artery reconstruction include axilloaxillary crossover grafting, carotid-carotid crossover, and femoroaxillary bypass. In general, these approaches are reserved for higher-risk patients in whom endovascular therapy is not an option.

Operative Planning

Operative planning must take into account relevant anatomic details. It is important to keep in mind that the anatomy of the aortic arch is not invariable: in 30% of patients, there are variations in the arch anatomy that may make innominate artery bypass more difficult. The most common variation is an innominate artery that branches into a right common carotid artery (CCA) and a right SA, with the right CCA and the right SA coming directly off the arch. In 16% of patients, however, the innominate artery and the right CCA may have a common ostium. In 8% of patients, the left CCA comes off the innominate artery, leaving the left SA as the only other artery coming off the arch. In 6% of patients, the left vertebral artery comes off the arch between the left CCA and the left SA. In fewer than 1% of patients, the right SA comes off the descending aorta as the last arch branch, then travels behind the esophagus (as the retroesophageal right SA) to reach the right supraclavicular fossa.[13]

Operative Technique

The innominate artery is approached via a median sternotomy.[14] A sternal retractor is placed and opened. The thymus is divided along its midline with the electrocautery, and the inferior thymic vein is ligated and divided. The brachiocephalic vein is identified as it crosses the innominate artery, then mobilized and placed in a vessel sling. The pericardium is opened from the ventricular surface to a point just below the origin of the innominate artery. It is held away from the operative field with stay sutures.

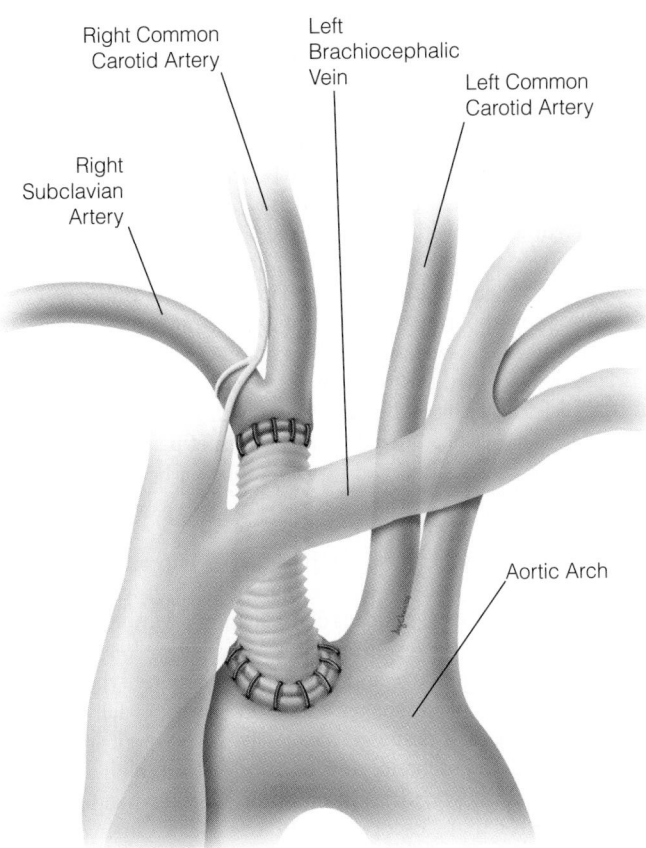

Right Common Carotid Artery

Left Brachiocephalic Vein

Left Common Carotid Artery

Right Subclavian Artery

Aortic Arch

Figure 3 **Innominate artery bypass. One end of the graft is sewn to the aorta in an end-to-side fashion, and the other is sewn to the common ostium of the right SA and the right CCA in an end-to-end fashion.**

The ascending aorta is then exposed. Fat and visceral pericardium are cleared from the anterior and lateral walls of the aorta to allow placement of a partial exclusion clamp.

The brachiocephalic vein is retracted downwards, and dissection is continued distally along the innominate artery toward the origins of the right SA and the right CCA. Care must be taken to keep from injuring any major nerves, particularly the right recurrent laryngeal nerve.

Some authors have employed a partial median sternotomy approach to the innominate artery, which is useful when access to the distal half of the innominate artery is required and access to the ascending aorta is not required. The advantage of this approach is that it preserves the lower sternum, thereby enhancing the stability of the chest and reducing postoperative pain. The incision extends only to the fourth intercostal space.

After heparinization, a partial exclusion clamp is placed on the ascending aorta, and an arteriotomy is made. An 8 mm graft is sutured to the aorta in an end-to-side fashion with 3-0 or 4-0 polypropylene. If the innominate artery is occluded, the right CCA and the right SA are clamped, and the innominate artery is divided and oversewn. The graft is then sewn to the common ostium of the SA and the CCA in an end-to-end fashion [*see Figure 3*]. Flow is confirmed with a Doppler probe, as with all the reconstructions we describe in this chapter.

Postoperative Care

After the operation, patients are observed in the intensive care unit. In general, anticoagulation is not indicated. After recovery, patients are followed by means of noninvasive graft surveillance.

CAROTID-SUBCLAVIAN BYPASS OR TRANSPOSITION

Most patients with SA stenosis or occlusion require no treatment. In many cases, overt symptoms are absent, and the diagnosis is made serendipitously when a reduced pulse pressure is encountered in one arm. For patients with symptomatic lesions, balloon angioplasty with stent insertion is currently the treatment of choice, having been shown to be a durable and effective therapy.[15,16] Elective bypass is typically reserved for lesions that are not amenable to balloon angioplasty. As stenting of thoracic aortic aneurysms becomes more common, however, stents are increasingly being applied across the origin of the left SA to facilitate proximal fixation, which means that a carotid-subclavian transposition or bypass is required to maintain flow. Thus, the growth of endovascular surgical treatment of thoracic aortic aneurysms has, paradoxically, created a growing population of patients who require a carotid-subclavian bypass. It is important, therefore, that this procedure remain part of the armamentarium of all vascular surgeons.

Preoperative Evaluation

A healthy CCA is an excellent inflow source for an SA bypass procedure. Before operation, the CCA should be evaluated with duplex ultrasonography, supplemented by arteriography. Aortic arch anomalies (e.g., the presence of a bovine aortic arch) should be identified. In patients with contrast allergies or renal impairment, MRA may be employed. In the future, CTA may prove to be the modality of choice.

Selection of patients   It is important to confirm that arm symptoms are in fact caused by subclavian disease. In young patients, the possibility of thoracic outlet syndrome should be considered. In older patients, the differential may include cervical disc problems or osteoarthritis. In patients with thoracic aortic aneurysms, our threshold for treatment is a diameter of 5 cm. Given the complexity of the anatomy and the potential for nerve injury, some surgeons are reluctant to perform carotid-subclavian bypass or transposition, instead favoring axilloaxillary crossover grafting. However, axilloaxillary crossover has a lower patency rate than carotid-subclavian bypass or transposition, and its subcutaneous placement and prominence make it less acceptable to most patients. In addition, instances of erosion through the skin have been reported.

Alternative therapy   Subclavian artery balloon angioplasty is less invasive than surgical bypass and is a durably effective procedure that is well tolerated by most patients.[17] However, patients who have recurrent stenosis or whose lesions are too close to the vertebral arteries may not be candidates for angioplasty. For such patients, prosthetic bypass or reimplantation of the subclavian artery is an ideal option. The temptation to perform a lesser procedure (e.g., axilloaxillary bypass) should be resisted.

Operative Planning

The two key considerations in the planning of the operation are (1) whether to perform a bypass or a transposition and (2), if a bypass is chosen, whether to use autologous vein or synthetic material as the conduit. For a bypass, prosthetic grafts, being short and of large caliber, are generally considered preferable to autologous vein grafts[18,19]: they are less likely to become kinked or give rise to intrinsic disease, and the long-term patency of prosthetic reconstructions is excellent.

Transposition of the SA is an excellent alternative to carotid-subclavian bypass, with long-term patency rates approaching 100%.[20] Preoperative consent should include acknowledgment of the potential for injury to the phrenic nerve or the brachial plexus.

Operative Technique

The patient is placed in the supine position, with a towel roll placed between the scapulae. The neck is tilted toward the contralateral shoulder. A transverse incision is made 1 cm superior to the clavicle. The underlying platysma and the lateral portion of the sternocleidomastoid muscle are divided in the line of the incision. The underlying omohyoid muscle and the external jugular veins are divided, and the scalene fat pad is mobilized and retracted laterally and cephalad. Minor lymphatic vessels are identified and ligated. The internal jugular vein is visible medially in the carotid sheath, and the carotid artery is usually situated posteriorly. Every effort should be made to keep from injuring the vagus nerve and the thoracic duct on the left; the risk of thoracic duct injury may be minimized by not dividing the lymphatic tissue lying between the phrenic nerve and the lateral border of the internal jugular vein. The anterior scalene muscle is divided as far caudad as possible to reveal the SA; care must be taken to avoid the overlying phrenic nerve, which courses diagonally in a lateral-to-medial direction along the anterior surface of the muscle.

A bypass from the CCA to the SA is then performed in an end-to-side fashion with a 6 mm or 8 mm prosthetic graft [*see Figure 4*]. The graft is usually tunneled under the internal jugular vein. Often, the graft-SA anastomosis is constructed first. A clamp is placed on the proximal graft, and the anastomosis to the CCA is constructed. The CCA is mobilized so that once two straight vascular clamps are placed and rotated anteriorly, the graft-CCA anastomosis may be performed more easily. Once the bypass has been completed, flow is restored—first to the arm, then to the proximal SA, and finally to the distal CCA, so as to minimize the carriage of embolic debris to the brain. Flow should then be assessed with a pencil Doppler probe.

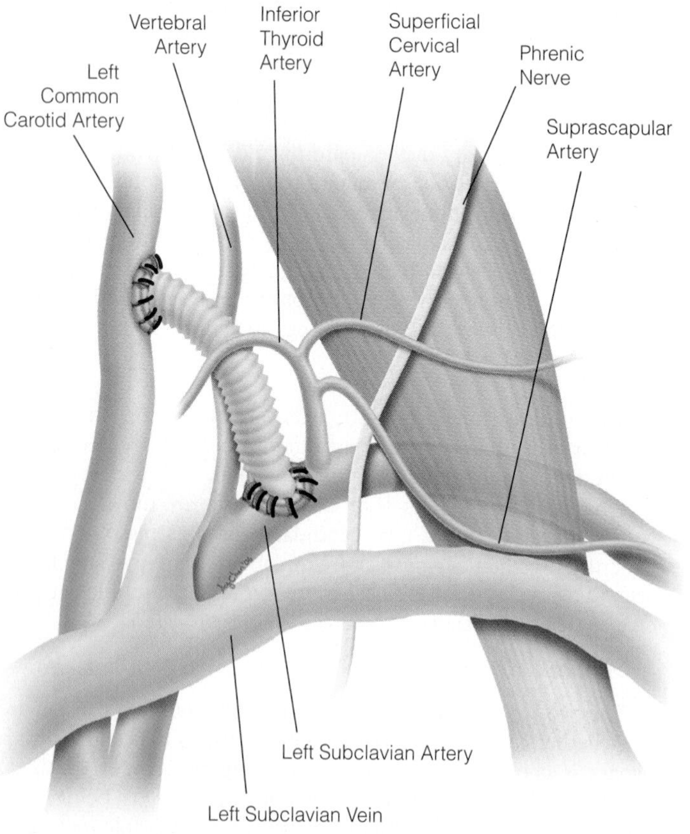

After completion of the bypass, the scalene fat pad is tacked to its former medial and inferior attachments; failure to do so may leave a visible defect in this area. The wound is drained with a closed suction apparatus. An upright chest x-ray is obtained to rule out pneumothorax or hemidiaphragmatic elevation secondary to phrenic nerve injury. Postoperative evaluation of bypass patency is accomplished by physical examination with palpation of pulses at the wrist. Further objective documentation of patency is obtained by means of PVRs, duplex ultrasonography, or both.

Postoperative Care

The major postoperative complication is phrenic nerve injury and resulting paralysis of the hemidiaphragm [*see 33 Paralyzed Diaphragm*]. Another significant complication is lymphatic leakage, which may occur as a result of either minor or major duct injury. Adequate wound drainage and prompt recognition of the lymphatic leak are the keys to management. Minor leaks usually seal with adequate drainage. If drainage is excessive, the patient will have to be maintained on parenteral nutrition with a formula that includes medium-chain triglycerides. On occasion, thoracic duct ligation via thoracotomy or thoracoscopy may be necessary. Other complications include pneumothorax, brachial plexus injury, and stroke.

Patients are followed with serial PVRs of the arm and duplex ultrosonography of the grafts.

AXILLOBRACHIAL BYPASS

Axillobrachial bypass may be performed to treat severe occlusive disease in the axillary or proximal brachial arteries. It is infrequently performed for chronic ischemia and more frequently performed for shoulder trauma. In the latter setting, it is often associated with brachial plexus injuries.

Preoperative Evaluation

Axillobrachial bypass is not commonly performed on an elective basis. The axillary and proximal brachial arteries seem to be remarkably impervious to the effects of systemic atherosclerosis. In those rare cases in which this procedure is indicated, preoperative evaluation of the affected arm with selective angiography is appropriate. Vein mapping should be performed. It is important to confirm that the patient's symptoms derive from arm ischemia and not from other conditions (e.g., neuropathy).

Alternative therapy   If arm ischemia is truly symptomatic at this level, sympathectomy may be considered [*see Alternative Therapies for Chronic Arm Ischemia, below*]. Angioplasty may be an option for axillary artery lesions, but it is infrequently performed in this setting, and data on its effectiveness and durability are relatively sparse.

Operative Planning

Autogenous vein is the conduit of choice for axillobrachial bypass. Prosthetic bypasses have lower patency rates than venous bypasses in this setting and should therefore be avoided. The greater saphenous vein is the preferred source of the venous conduit, though the use of the cephalic vein in situ has also been described.

Figure 4   **Carotid-subclavian bypass. One end of the graft is sewn to the left SA in an end-to-side fashion, and the other is sewn to the left CCA in an end-to-side fashion.**

Labels in figure:
Left Common Carotid Artery
Vertebral Artery
Inferior Thyroid Artery
Superficial Cervical Artery
Phrenic Nerve
Suprascapular Artery
Left Subclavian Artery
Left Subclavian Vein

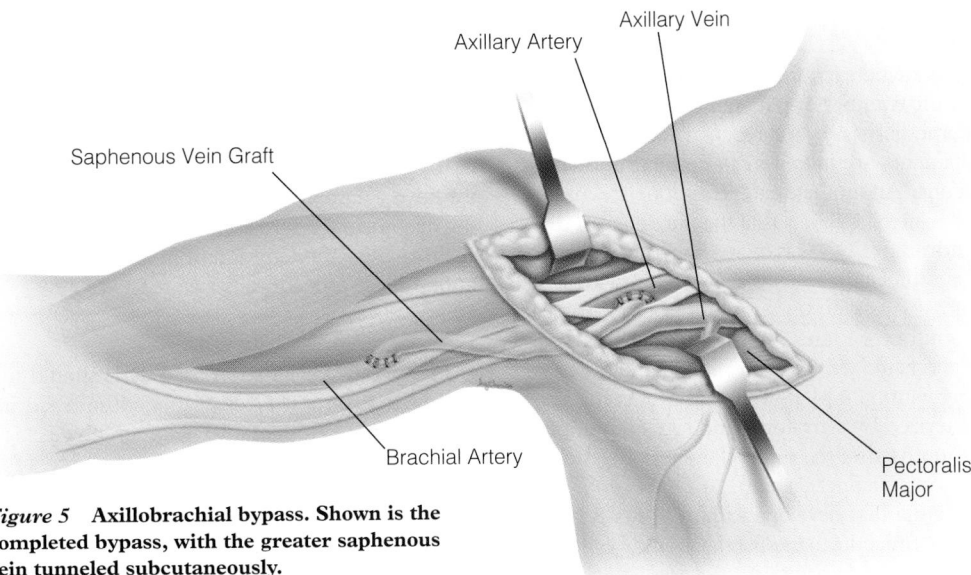

Saphenous Vein Graft

Axillary Artery

Axillary Vein

Brachial Artery

Pectoralis Major

Figure 5 **Axillobrachial bypass. Shown is the completed bypass, with the greater saphenous vein tunneled subcutaneously.**

Operative Technique

The patient is placed in the supine position, and the arm is draped circumferentially. A previously mapped leg is draped in preparation for vein harvesting. The axillary artery is approached via a transverse incision placed 2 cm below the middle third of the clavicle. The underlying pectoralis major is divided in the line of the decussation between its sternocostal and clavicular portions. Despite the assurances of most operative texts, the decussation is not always readily apparent. Division of the pectoralis major exposes the clavipectoral fascia, which is then divided. The axillary artery is identified cephalad to the axillary vein and is carefully dissected, with care taken not to injure the surrounding branches of the brachial plexus. The second part of the axillary artery is exposed by dividing the pectoralis minor.

If necessary, the distal third of the axillary artery may be exposed. An oblique incision is made along the lateral margin of the pectoralis major with the arm abducted 90° relative to the thorax. Once the subcutaneous tissue is divided, the axillary sheath is located near the posteroinferior border of the coracobrachialis. Care should be taken to keep from injuring the medial and lateral cords of the brachial plexus medially and the median and ulnar nerves laterally.

By preference, bypasses originating from the axillary artery are tunneled anatomically along the axis of the axillary and brachial arteries. Alternatively, they may be positioned subcutaneously; however, subcutaneous bypasses are more susceptible to distraction injuries caused by forcible abduction of the shoulder. Accordingly, some degree of redundancy should be built into a subcutaneous bypass.

The middle or the distal portion of the brachial artery is exposed as necessary. The proximal or the middle third of the vessel is exposed by making a medial incision over the bicipital groove, with care taken to keep from injuring the basilic vein and the cutaneous nerves located within the subcutaneous tissue. Traction on or transection of the median antebrachial cutaneous nerve may lead to hyperesthesia or anesthesia along the medial dorsal surface of the forearm; these problems occasionally occur after dialysis access procedures (e.g., basilic vein transposition) and can be highly debilitating, sometimes even rendering the fistula unusable. The brachial sheath is then incised longitudinally. The median nerve is the most superficial structure encountered

within the sheath. It is gently mobilized and retracted to afford access to the brachial artery. Any venous branches that cross the artery should be divided carefully, and every effort should be made to keep from injuring the posteriorly located ulnar nerve.

In contrast, the distal third of the brachial artery and its bifurcation are exposed in the antecubital fossa. A lazy S or sigmoid incision [*see Figure 1a*] is made to expose the brachial artery while avoiding wound contracture. The bicipital aponeurosis is then incised to expose the brachial artery, which is sandwiched between the biceps tendon laterally and the median nerve medially. Further dissection exposes the origins of the ulnar and radial arteries.

After systemic heparinization, the venous conduit is harvested, and its side branches are ligated with fine polypropylene suture ligatures or silk ties. The vein is distended with a solution containing dextrose 70 (500 ml I.V.), heparin (1,000 U), and papaverine (120 mg). The excised conduit may be employed in either a reversed or an orthograde (nonreversed) orientation, depending on the taper of the conduit. If the orthograde orientation is used, the proximal anastomosis is performed, the conduit is distended, and the valves are lysed with a retrograde Mills valvulotome. In either case, the conduit is tunneled anatomically wherever possible; in this way, it will be less prone to movement, distraction, or distortion. After tunneling, the distal anastomosis is constructed [*see Figure 5*]. Immediately upon completion of the bypass, patency and augmentation of flow are assessed with a pencil Doppler probe.

Major potential complications include injuries to the brachial plexus, the median nerve, or the ulnar nerve. Such injuries usually are caused by traction and may be minimized by careful dissection during operative exposure. The median and ulnar nerves and the brachial plexus are also vulnerable to direct thermal injury; accordingly, dissection with the electrocautery should be avoided.

Postoperative Care

Postoperatively, the patency of the bypass is documented by surveillance with noninvasive studies. In general, duplex ultrasonography is valuable for determining the patency of the reconstruction and for detecting any early flow abnormalities in the venous conduit. Graft infection should be watched for and appropriately treated if found.

DISTAL REVASCULARIZATION–INTERVAL LIGATION AND REVISION USING DISTAL INFLOW

The rising incidence of diabetes in the United States has led to a corresponding rise in the number of patients in whom vascular access is required for hemodialysis.[21,22] As reconstructions become more complex, these patients are increasingly coming under the care of vascular surgeons. An unfortunate consequence of the growing number of upper-arm fistulas is that the incidence of dialysis-associated steal syndrome (DASS) is increasing as well. DASS is rare after Cimino or radiocephalic fistula procedures,[23] but it occurs in 6% to 8% of patients who undergo upper-arm brachial artery–based fistula or graft procedures.[24,25] DASS may present in either an acute form (characterized by severe rest pain and obvious ischemia developing within 24 to 48 hours after operation) or a chronic form (characterized by symptoms and signs developing several weeks or even months after the original operation), each of which is managed in its own distinct fashion.

In cases of acute ischemia that develops within 24 to 48 hours after an upper-arm fistula procedure, the fistula should be ligated to restore flow down the native arteries. In cases of chronic ischemia, however, the aim is to preserve the fistula and avoid ligation. To this end, there are two main surgical options that should be considered. The first option is distal revascularization–interval ligation (DRIL), which involves the creation of a venous bypass from the proximal portion of the brachial artery to the distal portion of the vessel [see Figure 6]. The brachial artery distal to the origin of the fistula is ligated, flow to the distal arm is restored, and the fistula is preserved.[26] The second option is revision using distal inflow (RUDI), which involves ligation of the fistula at its origin, followed by reestablishment of the fistula by means of a venous bypass from the radial or the ulnar artery.[27] By using a smaller distal artery as the inflow source, RUDI lengthens the fistula and preserves antegrade flow in the brachial artery.

Of the two options, DRIL is better established and more widely used at present. It is our preferred option and thus is the primary focus of the ensuing description. Nevertheless, there are aspects of the DRIL procedure that many vascular surgeons find counterintuitive—namely, the ligation of a healthy artery and the bypassing of a normal arterial segment with a venous conduit. There does seem to be a good argument in favor of RUDI. Long-term evaluation of this procedure is awaited.

Preoperative Evaluation

Preoperative evaluation for DRIL should follow the same pattern as that for any elective procedure performed to treat arm or leg ischemia. Preoperative angiography is performed with vein mapping to identify an adequate source of a venous conduit. Cardiac clearance is obtained.

Selection of patients DRIL is generally reserved for patients with chronic arm ischemia in whom a fistula has been established that must be preserved. If the option of creating a new fistula in the other arm is available, DRIL is probably a less appropriate choice than simply ligating the original fistula.

Alternative therapy Besides simple ligation of the offending fistula, which is an option that should always at least be considered in these patients, there are two techniques that deserve mention as alternatives to DRIL. The first technique is aimed at preventing steal from an upper-arm fistula (always a laudable aim). In this technique, the fistula is formed by extending the cephalic vein or the basilic vein down the arm and anastomosing it to the proximal ulnar artery or the radial artery just below the brachial bifurcation so as to preserve part of the blood supply to the hand. The median cubital vein may also be used.[28]

The second technique is RUDI [see Figure 7]. This procedure differs from DRIL in that it is the fistula, not the native arterial supply, that is placed at risk by the surgical revision, so that in the event of graft failure, the fistula is lost but the arm is not endangered.

Operative Planning

We do not use prosthetic grafts for this procedure; we prefer to use autogenous vein for the graft, usually a segment of the greater saphenous vein from the leg. As a rule, the operation is performed with the patient under general anesthesia.

Operative Technique

A vertical incision is made in the upper arm at the level of the proximal brachial artery. The skin and the subcutaneous fat are divided, and the proximal brachial artery is sharply dissected free. The portion of the brachial artery distal to the origin of the fistula is also dissected free. An adequately long segment of vein is obtained and prepared. Anticoagulation is initiated, and a proximal end-to-side anastomosis is fashioned with 6-0 polypropylene. The vein graft is tunneled subcutaneously, and a distal end-to-end anastomosis to the distal brachial artery is created. Some surgeons prefer an end-to-side distal anastomosis with ligation of the brachial artery proximal to the anastomosis. Adequate flow is confirmed by means of intraoperative Doppler ultrasonography.

Postoperative Care

Postoperative anticoagulation is generally not warranted; however, a postoperative graft surveillance protocol is initiated. If the

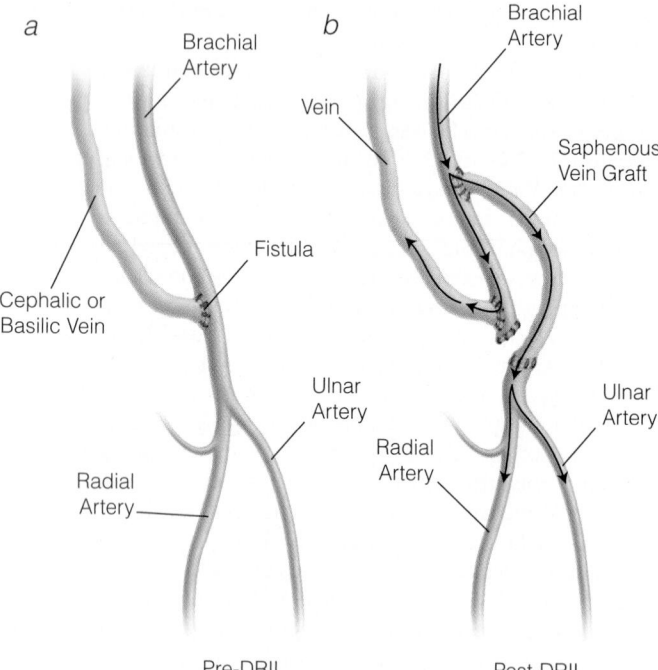

Figure 6 **Distal revascularization–interval ligation (DRIL). In patients with a brachial artery–based fistula (*a*), chronic ischemia may develop weeks or months after the procedure. The best established surgical treatment option is DRIL (*b*), which preserves the fistula by creating a venous bypass between the proximal brachial artery (above the origin of the fistula) and the distal brachial artery.**

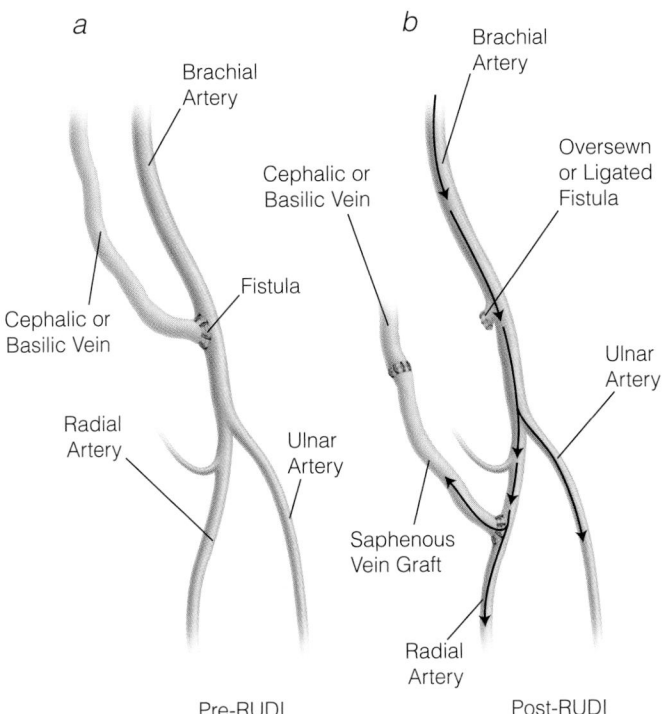

Figure 7 **Revision using distal inflow (RUDI). Another option for patients with a brachial artery–based fistula (*a*) is RUDI (*b*), which involves ligating the fistula at its origin, lengthening the original venous graft with an additional vein segment, and reestablishing the fistula by anastomosing the lengthened graft to the radial artery (as shown) or the ulnar artery.**

venous graft becomes occluded, the fistula is ligated. This step frequently leads to resolution of the symptoms of arm ischemia.

HAND REVASCULARIZATION

Patients with rest pain in the hands and digital ulcers often have significant comorbid conditions (e.g., collagen vascular or rheumatologic disorders, end-stage renal disease, or hypercoagulable states). In addition, patients who have received organ transplants and are taking immunosuppressive medications may experience severe occlusion of forearm or palmar arteries. Younger patients with hand ischemia are often manual laborers who have hypothenar hammer syndrome. Patients with established signs and symptoms of hand ischemia have little to lose by undergoing revascularization: there are few viable therapeutic alternatives.

Aggressive treatment of hand ischemia is worthwhile, in that it achieves rapid relief of symptoms and offers the opportunity for hand and limb salvage. The techniques resemble those employed for distal bypass in the leg [*see 96 Infrainguinal Arterial Procedures*]. Early results from several centers indicate that hand bypass procedures can be performed with low morbidity and good long-term patency.[29,30] Postoperative life expectancy, however, is often limited by the comorbid conditions present.

Preoperative Evaluation

Preoperative evaluation for hand bypass should follow the same protocol as that for any elective revascularization: preoperative angiography to delineate anatomy with vein mapping to identify a venous conduit.

Many patients with hand ischemia have intractable pain from ulcerative lesions, gangrene, or both. Their main requirement is adequate relief of pain; improved hand function is a secondary

consideration. Vascular reconstruction offers a chance to gain both. The alternative to attempted arm salvage is amputation.

Selection of patients At our institution (Albany Medical Center), all patients with rest pain, digital necrosis, or nonhealing ulcers are evaluated for possible palmar artery reconstruction, provided that they are surgical candidates. Reconstruction is feasible in approximately half of the patients who have renal disease or diabetes.

Alternative therapy Sympathectomy, in various incarnations, has been employed in the treatment of hand ischemia. Isolated reports of success notwithstanding, the experience of most vascular surgeons with sympathectomy in this setting has not been favorable.

Operative Planning

Fortunately, exposure of the palmar vessels beyond the wrist is not as difficult as might be imagined [*see* Operative Technique, *below*]. Nevertheless, because hand bypass procedures are relatively new territory for many vascular surgeons, operative planning may benefit from a brief review of the normal anatomy. The hand is supplied with blood by the superficial and deep palmar arches. The superficial palmar arch is supplied by a branch of the radial artery and by the ulnar artery. The deep palmar arch is supplied by the radial artery itself and by a deep branch of the ulnar artery.

Venous grafts are preferred to prosthetic grafts for hand bypasses. All venous grafts are tunneled anatomically. In a radial artery reconstruction, the graft is tunneled over the anatomic snuff box onto the dorsum of the hand, between the thumb and the index finger, to join the deep palmar arch. In an ulnar artery reconstruction, the venous graft takes a less circuitous course, passing superficial to the flexor retinaculum at the wrist to join the superficial palmar arch.

Operative Technique

The donor limb that will provide the venous graft is prepared. The brachial artery is exposed as described previously [*see* Procedures for Acute Arm Ischemia, Brachial Embolectomy, Operative Technique, *above*].

The course of the radial artery in the forearm follows an oblique line from the brachial artery pulse medial to the biceps tendon to the styloid process of the radius. In the midforearm, the radial artery is medial to the brachioradialis and lateral to the flexor carpi radialis. A lateral longitudinal incision is made, and the muscles are separated to reveal the radial artery. At the wrist, the radial artery is exposed by making a longitudinal incision between the tendon of the flexor carpi radialis and the tendon of the brachioradialis. This is the site of the radial artery pulse in normal persons. Here, the artery is superficial, and exposure is relatively straightforward. Care must, however, be taken not to injure the superficial branch of the radial nerve, which is often located near the lateral aspect of the artery. Injury to this nerve branch can result in troublesome paresthesia along the lateral aspect of the thumb.

The course of the ulnar artery runs from the medial epicondyle of the humerus to the pisiform bone. In the midforearm, the ulnar artery lies beneath the deep fascia between the belly of the flexor digitorum laterally and the belly of the flexor carpi ulnaris medially. The ulnar nerve joins the artery on its lateral aspect for the distal two thirds of the vessel's length; this nerve may be injured if not carefully identified and preserved. At the wrist, the ulnar artery is lateral to the tendon of the flexor carpi ulnaris. It is exposed by locating this tendon (which is the most medial tendon palpable at

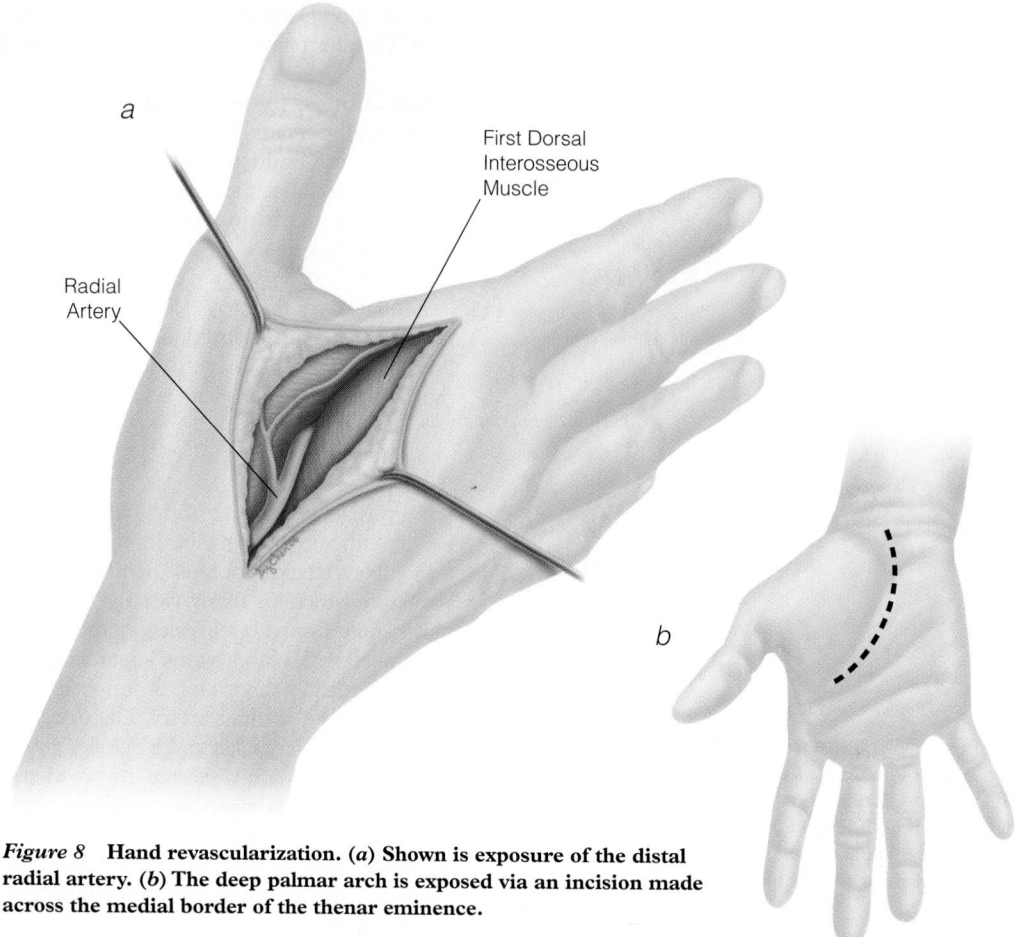

Figure 8 **Hand revascularization. (*a*) Shown is exposure of the distal radial artery. (*b*) The deep palmar arch is exposed via an incision made across the medial border of the thenar eminence.**

the wrist) and making a vertical skin incision lateral to it. Although the ulnar artery lies deeper than the radial artery at the wrist, it is just as easily exposed. Superficial to the ulnar artery, palmar cutaneous branches of the ulnar nerve may be identified; these should also be preserved.

Grafts originating from the brachial artery are tunneled in the subcutaneous plane. Subcutaneous tunneling facilitates physical examination to determine the patency of the bypass, as well as surveillance of the bypass with duplex ultrasonography. Alternatively, if good-quality basilic or cephalic veins are present, an in situ bypass may be performed.

Exposure of radial artery and deep palmar arch Exposure of the radial artery is relatively straightforward. Generally, it may be accomplished as previously described (see above). Alternatively, it may be accomplished by making a vertical incision over the anatomic snuff box (which lies between the extensor pollicis longus tendon posteriorly and the tendons of the extensor pollicis brevis and the abductor pollicis longus anteriorly). This incision is then deepened through the subcutaneous tissues to expose the radial artery in the floor of the snuff box [*see Figure 8a*]. This area contains no significant nerves and thus is often chosen as a site for hemodialysis access.

The deep palmar arch is much less accessible than the radial artery. Consequently, exposure of this vascular structure is considerably more difficult than exposure of the radial artery. The deep palmar arch extends across the palm, level with the proximal border of the outstretched thumb. To expose it, an incision is made along the medial border of the thenar eminence [*see Figure 8b*]. Extensive dissection of the superficial and deep flexor tendons of

the hand and division of the oblique head of the adductor pollicis are then required to provide access to the origin of the deep palmar arch.

Exposure of ulnar artery and superficial palmar arch Like exposure of the radial artery, exposure of the ulnar artery and the superficial palmar arch is fairly straightforward. In reality, these vessels are no smaller than the tibial and pedal vessels in the leg. A curved incision is made along the lateral border of the hypothenar eminence [*see Figure 9a*]. The aponeurotic layer is divided, and the artery is exposed in the upper part of the palm at the origin of the superficial palmar arch. There are no major nerves in the vicinity, and it usually is not difficult to expose a reasonable length of artery for an arterial anastomosis [*see Figure 9b*]. Alternatively, the superficial palmar arch may be exposed in the palm by making an incision along one of the larger vertical or oblique skin creases.

Postoperative Care

As with all venous grafts, postoperative graft surveillance is essential. Routine postoperative anticoagulation generally is not warranted.

Alternative Therapies for Chronic Arm Ischemia

THORACOSCOPIC SYMPATHECTOMY AND DIGITAL SYMPATHECTOMY

Our experience with sympathectomy in the treatment of patients with critical hand ischemia or digital ulceration has been, frankly, disappointing. When we do perform sympathectomy, we

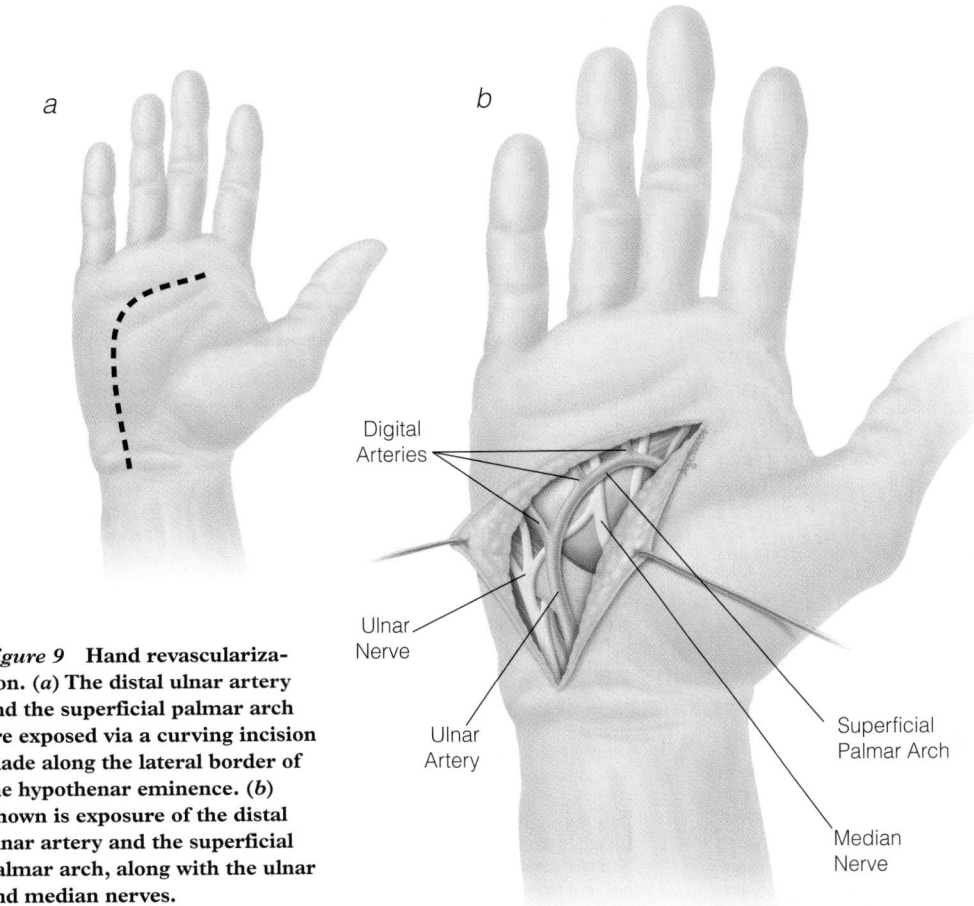

Figure 9 **Hand revasculariza-tion. (*a*) The distal ulnar artery and the superficial palmar arch are exposed via a curving incision made along the lateral border of the hypothenar eminence. (*b*) Shown is exposure of the distal ulnar artery and the superficial palmar arch, along with the ulnar and median nerves.**

prefer the thoracoscopic approach to the traditional cervical route. Either way, however, the results have been discouraging; any improvements noted prove to be only temporary. Sympathectomy may help alleviate pain in these patients, but even in this regard, the results are, at best, unpredictable. A review of the literature seems to support this conclusion. Admittedly, the available data on thoracoscopic sympathectomy for digital ischemia are sparse: to date, only three reports encompassing 21 patients have been published.[31-33] In contrast, there is a wealth of data on thoracoscopic sympathectomy for hyperhidrosis.

An alternative technique has been devised in which a very distal sympathectomy is performed at the level of the origin of the proper digital arteries. The sympathectomy site is exposed via a palmar approach, and a 3 to 4 mm length of the adventitia is removed from the proper digital arteries distal to the junction of the distal perforating artery with the common digital artery. This procedure appears to be well tolerated, and data from small series attest to its value in selected patients with digital ulcers.[34]

PROSTACYCLINS

The prostacyclin analogue iloprost has been used in Europe to treat patients with hand ischemia. Although iloprost therapy appears to be reasonably effective in patients with vasospastic disorders, such as Raynaud syndrome,[35] the results in patients with peripheral ischemia are less encouraging. At present, iloprost is mainly used to treat patients with digital ulcers caused by systemic sclerosis, systemic lupus erythematosus, mixed connective tissue disease, or cutaneous polyarteritis nodosa. There are no good data on its use to treat patients with digital ulcers caused by diabetes mellitus, atherosclerosis, or renal impairment; however, a study of iloprost therapy for arterial leg ulcers found that the success rate was lower than 50%.[36]

GUANETHIDINE BLOCKS

Transvenous regional guanethidine blocks have also been employed to treat critical digital ischemia. Patients receive a single block, with 5 mg of guanethidine in 60 ml of normal saline injected into a superficial vein of the affected hand under 30 minutes of arterial arrest. In successful cases, hyperemia is induced in the treated upper limb, and blood flow to the fingers improves. The effects of these blocks are said to persist for up to 1 month. Patients who have finger ulcers, however, appear to be less responsive than those whose only symptom is pain. The advantages of this treatment approach are that it is free of side effects and that it can be repeated for as long as necessary[37]; the disadvantage is that it *must* be repeated at monthly intervals for as long as necessary.

References

1. Hernandez-Richter T, Angele MK, Helmberger T, et al: Acute ischemia of the upper extremity: long-term results following thromboembolectomy with the Fogarty catheter. Langenbecks Arch Surg 386:261, 2001

2. Wirsing P, Andriopoulos A, Botticher R: Arterial embolectomies in the upper extremity after acute occlusion: report on 79 cases. J Cardiovasc Surg (Torino) 24:40, 1983

3. Baird RJ, Lajos TZ: Emboli to the arm. Ann Surg 160:905, 1964

4. Savelyev VS, Zatevakhin II, Stepanov NV: Artery embolism of the upper limbs. Surgery 81:367, 1977

5. Galbraith K, Collin J, Morris PJ, et al: Recent experience with arterial embolism of the limbs in a vascular unit. Ann R Coll Surg Engl 67:30, 1985

6. Stonebridge PA, Clason AE, Duncan AJ, et al: Acute ischaemia of the upper limb compared with acute lower limb ischaemia; a 5-year review. Br J Surg 76:515, 1989

7. Eyers P, Earnshaw JJ: Acute non-traumatic arm ischaemia. Br J Surg 85:1340, 1998

8. Widlus DM, Venbrux AC, Benenati JF, et al: Fibrinolytic therapy for upper-extremity arterial occlusions. Radiology 175:393, 1990

9. Cejna M, Salomonowitz E, Wohlschlager H, et al: rt-PA thrombolysis in acute thromboembolic upper-extremity arterial occlusion. Cardiovasc Intervent Radiol 24:218, 2001

10. Zeller T, Frank U, Burgelin K, et al: Treatment of acute embolic occlusions of the subclavian and axillary arteries using a rotational thrombectomy device. Vasa 32:111, 2003

11. Dente CJ, Feliciano DV, Rozycki GS, et al: A review of upper extremity fasciotomies in a level I trauma center. Am Surg 70:1088, 2004

12. Kieffer E, Sabatier J, Koskas F, et al: Atherosclerotic innominate artery occlusive disease: early and long-term results of surgical reconstruction. J Vasc Surg 21:326, 1995

13. Daseler EH, Anson BJ: Surgical anatomy of the subclavian artery and its branches. Surg Gynecol Obstet 108:149, 1959

14. Berguer R: Supraaortic trunks. Vascular Surgical Approaches. Branchereau A, Berguer R, Eds. Futura Publishing Co, New York, 1999, p 93

15. Woo EY, Fairman RM, Velazquez OC, et al: Endovascular therapy of symptomatic innominate-subclavian arterial occlusive lesions. Vasc Endovascular Surg 40:27, 2006

16. Brountzos EN, Petersen B, Binkert C, et al: Primary stenting of subclavian and innominate artery occlusive disease: a single center's experience. Cardiovasc Intervent Radiol 27:616, 2004

17. De Vries JP, Jager LC, Van den Berg JC, et al: Durability of percutaneous transluminal angioplasty for obstructive lesions of proximal subclavian artery: long-term results. J Vasc Surg 41:19, 2005

18. Law MM, Colburn MD, Moore WS, et al: Carotid-subclavian bypass for brachiocephalic occlusive disease. Choice of conduit and long-term follow-up. Stroke 26:1565, 1995

19. AbuRahma AF, Robinson PA, Jennings TG: Carotid-subclavian bypass grafting with polytetrafluoroethylene grafts for symptomatic subclavian artery stenosis or occlusion: a 20-year experience. J Vasc Surg 32:411, 2000

20. Cina CS, Safar HA, Lagana A, et al: Subclavian carotid transposition and bypass grafting: consecutive cohort study and systematic review. J Vasc Surg 35:422, 2002

21. National Diabetes Surveillance System: State-specific estimates of diagnosed diabetes among adults. U.S. Department of Health and Human Services, Centers for Disease Control and Prevention, National Center for Chronic Disease Prevention and Health Promotion, Atlanta, Georgia http://www.cdc.gov/diabetes/statistics/prev/state/Methods.htm, accessed April 2006

22. U.S. Renal Data System, USRDS 2005 Annual Data Report: Atlas of end-stage renal disease in the United States. National Institutes of Health, National Institute of Diabetes and Digestive and Kidney Diseases, Bethesda, Maryland, 2005

23. Zibari GB, Rohr MS, Landreneau MD, et al: Complications from permanent hemodialysis vascular access. Surgery 104:681, 1988

24. Revanur VK, Jardine AG, Hamilton DH, et al: Outcome for arterio-venous fistula at the elbow for haemodialysis. Clin Transplant 14:318, 2000

25. Wolford HY, Hsu J, Rhodes JM, et al: Outcome after autogenous brachial-basilic upper arm transpositions in the post-National Kidney Foundation Dialysis Outcomes Quality Initiative era. J Vasc Surg 42:951, 2005

26. Mwipatayi BP, Bowles T, Balakrishnan S, et al: Ischemic steal syndrome: a case series and review of current management. Curr Surg 63:130, 2006

27. Minion DJ, Moore E, Endean E: Revision using distal inflow: a novel approach to dialysis-associated steal syndrome. Ann Vasc Surg 19:625, 2005

28. Ehsan O, Bhattacharya D, Darwish A, et al: 'Extension technique': a modified technique for brachio-cephalic fistula to prevent dialysis access-associated steal syndrome. Eur J Vasc Endovasc Surg 29:324, 2005

29. Chang BB, Roddy SP, Darling RC 3rd, et al: Upper extremity bypass grafting for limb salvage in end-stage renal failure. J Vasc Surg 38:1313, 2003

30. Nehler MR, Dalman RL, Harris EJ, et al: Upper extremity arterial bypass distal to the wrist. J Vasc Surg 16:633, 1992

31. Grigorovici A, Gavrilovici V, Popa R: Thoracoscopic sympathectomy for upper limb ischemic disease. Rev Med Chir Soc Med Nat Iasi 106:817, 2002

32. De Giacomo T, Rendina EA, Venuta F, et al: Thoracoscopic sympathectomy for symptomatic arterial obstruction of the upper extremities. Ann Thorac Surg 74:885, 2002

33. Ishibashi H, Hayakawa N, Yamamoto H, et al: Thoracoscopic sympathectomy for Buerger's disease: a report on the successful treatment of four patients. Surg Today 25:180, 1995

34. el-Gammal TA, Blair WF: Digital periarterial sympathectomy for ischaemic digital pain and ulcers. J Hand Surg [Br] 16:382, 1991

35. Rademaker M, Cooke ED, Almond NE, et al: Comparison of intravenous infusions of iloprost and oral nifedipine in treatment of Raynaud's phenomenon in patients with systemic sclerosis: a double blind randomized study. BMJ 298:561, 1989

36. Mirenda F, La Spada M, Baccellieri D, et al: Iloprost infusion in diabetic patients with peripheral arterial occlusive disease and foot ulcers. Chir Ital 57:731, 2005

37. Stumpflen A, Ahmadi A, Attender M, et al: Effects of transvenous regional guanethidine block in the treatment of critical finger ischemia. Angiology 51:115, 2000

Acknowledgment

Figures 1 through 9   Alice Y. Chen.

95 REPAIR OF FEMORAL AND POPLITEAL ARTERY ANEURYSMS

Amir Kaviani, M.D., and Patrick J. O'Hara, M.D., F.A.C.S.

Femoral and popliteal artery aneurysms constitute the majority of peripheral aneurysms. Recognition of these aneurysms is increasing, perhaps because of better surveillance of the aging population, as well as improvements in and more widespread use of vascular imaging modalities.[1] Femoral and popliteal aneurysms rarely rupture, but they have a significant potential for limb-threatening complications such as embolization and thrombosis. Large aneurysms can also exert a mass effect and thereby cause compression of veins or nerves.

In general, with both femoral and popliteal aneurysms, elective repair and reconstruction tend to be associated with significantly better postoperative outcomes than is emergency repair undertaken after a limb-threatening complication. Specific treatment decisions may be influenced by the presence or absence of symptoms of aneurysmal disease. There is little disagreement regarding optimal management of symptomatic femoral or popliteal aneurysms, but there is some controversy regarding optimal management of aneurysms that are asymptomatic when detected, especially if they are small. The extent of aneurysmal disease may also influence management choices. For example, a more extensive and complex reconstruction is required for treatment of diffuse arteriomegaly than is necessary for treatment of a focal femoral or popliteal aneurysm.

Lower extremity aneurysms may be either true aneurysms, in which the degenerative process involves all three layers of the arterial wall, or pseudoaneurysms, which result from trauma, anastomotic disruption, or infection. The pathogenesis of true (i.e., degenerative) lower extremity aneurysmal disease has not been definitively established, but it is known that the disease is much more common in men than in women; in fact, men with true femoral or popliteal aneurysms may outnumber women with such lesions by more than 30 to 1.[2,3] One of the factors proposed as a possible contributor to aneurysm formation is turbulent flow beyond a relative stenosis. At the groin, the inguinal ligament may act as a constricting band, and at the popliteal level, the tendinous hiatus, the heads of the gastrocnemius, and the popliteal ligament may compress the artery in certain susceptible individuals. In addition, there is evidence for the existence of a genetic predisposition to true aneurysm formation in the femoral and popliteal arteries, in view of the demonstrated association of femoral and popliteal aneurysms with abdominal aortic aneurysms.[4] Accordingly, all patients presenting with femoral or popliteal aneurysms should be carefully evaluated for other aneurysms, especially in the aortoiliac segment and in the contralateral limb.

Regardless of the underlying cause of disease, repair of peripheral artery aneurysms follows the same basic principles applicable to repair of aneurysms in other locations. Specifically, the objectives of treatment are (1) to eliminate the embolic source, (2) to minimize the risk of rupture, (3) to eliminate the mass effect produced by the aneurysm (if present), (4) to restore adequate distal limb perfusion, and (5) to accomplish all of the preceding objectives in a durable fashion. In what follows, we describe key components of the management of femoral and popliteal artery aneurysms, with specific attention to preoperative planning and intraoperative exposure and technique.

Repair of Femoral Artery Aneurysms

True (degenerative) aneurysms of the femoral artery are relatively unusual. They are generally confined to the common femoral artery, but in approximately 50% of cases, they extend to the femoral artery bifurcation. According to a classification scheme proposed by Cutler and Darling in 1973, femoral artery aneurysms are classified as type I if they are confined to the common femoral artery and as type II if they involve the orifice of the profunda femoris artery.[5] This classification scheme is convenient for the discussion of operative repair, in that type II aneurysms frequently necessitate more extensive surgical reconstruction than type I aneurysms do.

Like peripheral aneurysms elsewhere, true femoral artery aneurysms are frequently associated with abdominal aortic aneurysms, as well as with aneurysms in other locations. In a large series of patients with multiple aneurysms, 95% of patients with a femoral artery aneurysm had a second aneurysm, 92% had an aortoiliac aneurysm, and 62% had an aneurysm in the contralateral femoral artery.[6] The natural history of these lesions is not fully understood; it may be relatively benign unless they are symptomatic or large at presentation.

Femoral pseudoaneurysms, on the other hand, are increasingly encountered after trauma (e.g., iatrogenic catheter injury) or after arterial reconstruction. These lesions, especially those arising from disrupted anastomoses, are thought to have a more ominous course if untreated. Aneurysms confined to the superficial femoral artery or the profunda femoris artery alone are distinctly unusual and are often of mycotic or traumatic origin.

PREOPERATIVE EVALUATION

Asymptomatic patients may present with a smooth, fusiform, nontender, pulsatile mass discovered either during physical examination or incidentally on imaging studies done for other reasons. Symptoms may result from local compression of the femoral nerve, which causes pain in the groin or the anterior thigh, or compression of the femoral vein, which may be associated with lower extremity edema and skin changes suggestive of venous stasis. Arterial symptoms (e.g., claudication or lower extremity ischemia) may be present in as many as 40% of patients with femoral artery aneurysms. Atheroemboli originating from the aneurysm can cause painful ischemic lesions; however, such lesions may also be partly a result of concomitant atherosclerotic occlusive disease rather than a direct result of the aneurysm itself.[6]

Complications of femoral artery aneurysms include thrombosis, embolization, and rupture. In one series of 45 patients with 63 aneurysms, nearly one half (47%) of the patients had experienced a complication by the time of initial presentation.[4] Acute thrombo-

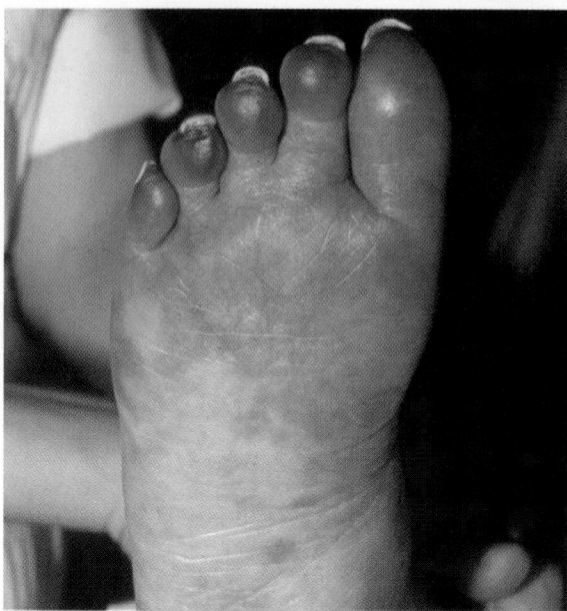

Figure 1 Shown is an example of extensive atheroembolization to the foot. The source of the atheromatous debris may be a proximal aneurysm or an ulcerating atherosclerotic lesion.

sis, because it involves compromise of both the profunda femoris artery and the superficial femoral artery, may result in a critically threatened limb that initially exhibits sensory or motor deficits and eventually manifests frank gangrene. Acute thrombosis secondary to a femoral artery aneurysm is associated with substantial morbidity: limb loss is reported to occur in more than 28% of cases.[6] Patients with gradual or chronic thrombosis, who have had time to develop collateral circulation, may present with claudication.

Embolization from a femoral artery aneurysm may be clinically silent or, if extensive, may present as the so-called blue toe syndrome [see 84 Pulseless Extremity and Atheroembolism]. Embolic debris originating in the aneurysm may lodge in the digital arteries or obstruct the microcirculation, leading to characteristic painful distal ischemic lesions, despite the presence of palpable distal pulses [see Figure 1]. In more severe cases, obstruction of

the outflow bed may compromise blood flow to the entire limb, resulting in limb-threatening ischemia. Rupture of a femoral pseudoaneurysm is not unusual, especially if the lesion is enlarging. Rupture of a true femoral artery aneurysm, however, is a relatively uncommon event, with reported rupture rates ranging from 1% to 12%, and is accompanied by severe groin pain, ecchymosis, and swelling.[3,6]

Femoral artery aneurysms can usually be diagnosed by means of physical examination alone. Ultrasonography is a useful adjunctive measure for delineating the aneurysm, as well as for screening patients for associated popliteal or aortoiliac aneurysms [see Figure 2a]. CT and MRI scans can be helpful in delineating the extent and morphology of the aneurysm, as well as the status of the adjacent arteries, especially in obese patients [see Figure 2b]. Once the diagnosis has been made, angiography should be performed to establish the extent of aneurysmal and associated occlusive or embolic disease by providing detailed information about the inflow and outflow vessels [see Figure 3]. In selected circumstances (e.g., the presence of recent thrombosis of the outflow bed), arteriography may provide the opportunity for a trial of thrombolytic therapy to improve outflow. Good judgment must be exercised, however, in that there may not be enough time for adequate thrombolysis if the limb is severely ischemic.

Finally, preoperative evaluation should include careful assessment and optimization of comorbid medical conditions often present in patients with femoral artery aneurysms. Because cardiac complications are a major source of early postoperative and late morbidity in this population, special emphasis should be placed on evaluating patients for associated coronary artery disease by means of cardiac stress testing or coronary angiography and on following evaluation with appropriate treatment when indicated. Similarly, imaging of the contralateral limb and the aortoiliac vessels is prudent to detect associated aneurysms and establish treatment priorities.

OPERATIVE PLANNING

Repair is clearly indicated for all symptomatic femoral aneurysms, irrespective of cause. Patients who present with limb-threatening complications require expeditious intervention. Asymptomatic femoral pseudoaneurysms should also be repaired once the diagnosis is established because they are often associated with

a

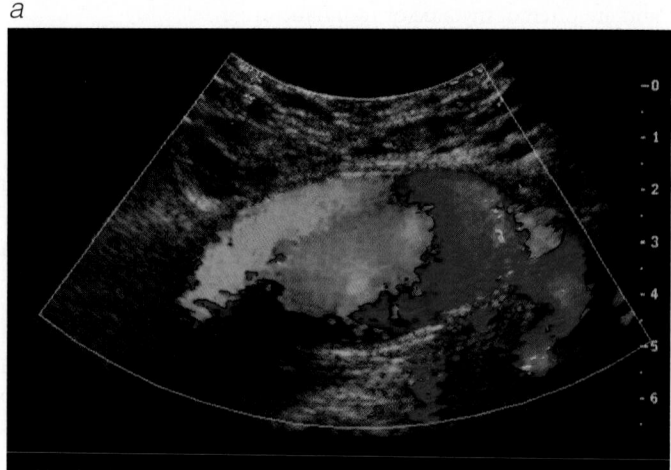

b

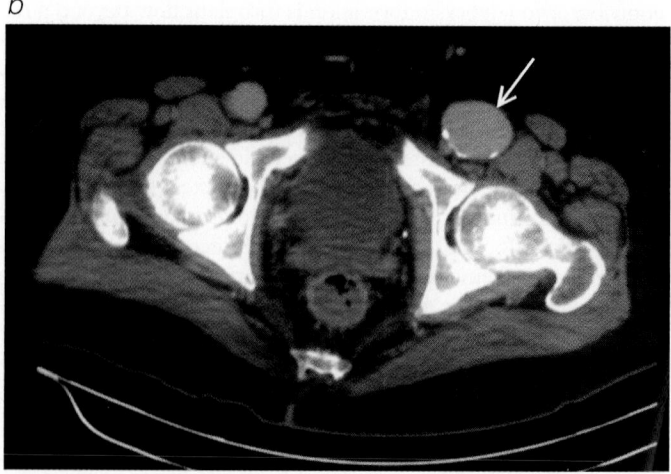

Figure 2 (*a*) Shown is a duplex ultrasonogram of a left common femoral artery aneurysm (sagittal view). (*b*) Shown is a CT scan of a left common femoral aneurysm (arrow). In practice, multiple slices are used to delineate the proximal and distal extent of the aneurysm.

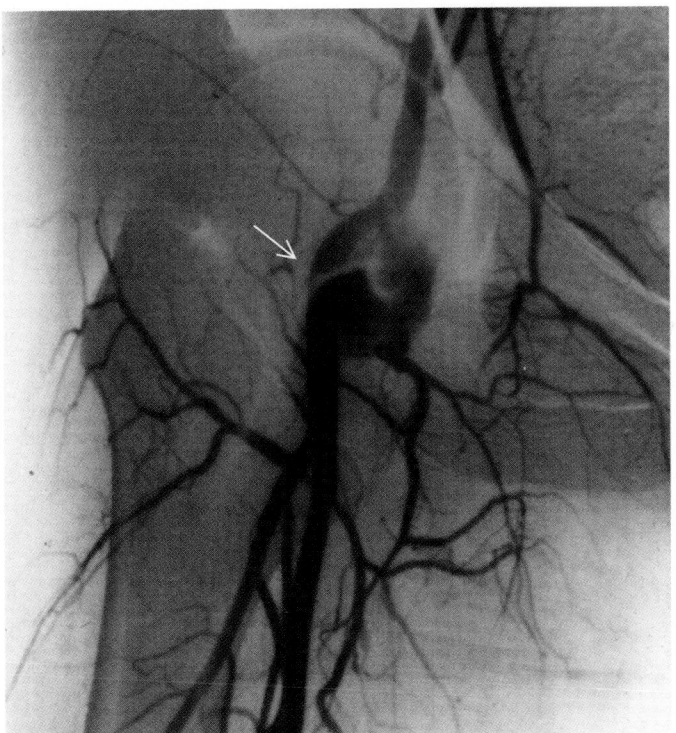

Figure 3 **Anteroposterior arteriogram demonstrates a localized common femoral artery aneurysm (arrow).**

complications. Currently, however, there is no firm consensus on the indications for treatment of asymptomatic true femoral aneurysms, because the natural history of these lesions is not known with certainty and is thought to be relatively benign. Furthermore, no specific aneurysm size has been identified at which the incidence of complications increases dramatically, though it

appears that symptomatic lesions tend to be larger than asymptomatic ones. Most surgeons, however, would probably agree that true femoral artery aneurysms larger than 2.5 cm in diameter should be repaired in good-risk patients, especially if the aneurysm is known to have enlarged. Smaller asymptomatic true femoral artery aneurysms, particularly in high-risk patients, should be followed, with intervention reserved for cases in which symptoms develop or the lesion enlarges significantly. On occasion, it may also be necessary to repair a small asymptomatic true femoral aneurysm in conjunction with an aortofemoral or femoropopliteal bypass graft procedure in order to avoid performing an anastomosis to a diseased artery.

OPERATIVE TECHNIQUE

At present, endovascular approaches to definitive treatment of femoral artery aneurysms are limited because the femoral artery crosses the groin crease and is subject to repeated flexion and extension stresses in this location. Current endoprostheses are likely to fail at this site because of kinking, migration, or metal fatigue. Furthermore, the femoral incision required for standard surgical repair is not extensive and is usually well tolerated by most patients. Consequently, the potential advantages of an endovascular approach are less apparent with respect to the repair of femoral artery aneurysms than they are with respect to repair of abdominal or thoracic aneurysms.

Small femoral pseudoaneurysms arising after catheter diagnostic or interventional procedures may resolve over time or, sometimes, may be managed with ultrasound-guided compression or thrombin injection at the time of diagnostic imaging. Surgical repair is usually reserved for pseudoaneurysms that enlarge, become symptomatic, or do not resolve spontaneously [*see Figure 4*]. A potential advantage of open repair of large pseudoaneurysms is the capacity for decompression of large hematomas, which may be especially important if continued anticoagulation is likely to be required.

The common femoral artery may be approached through

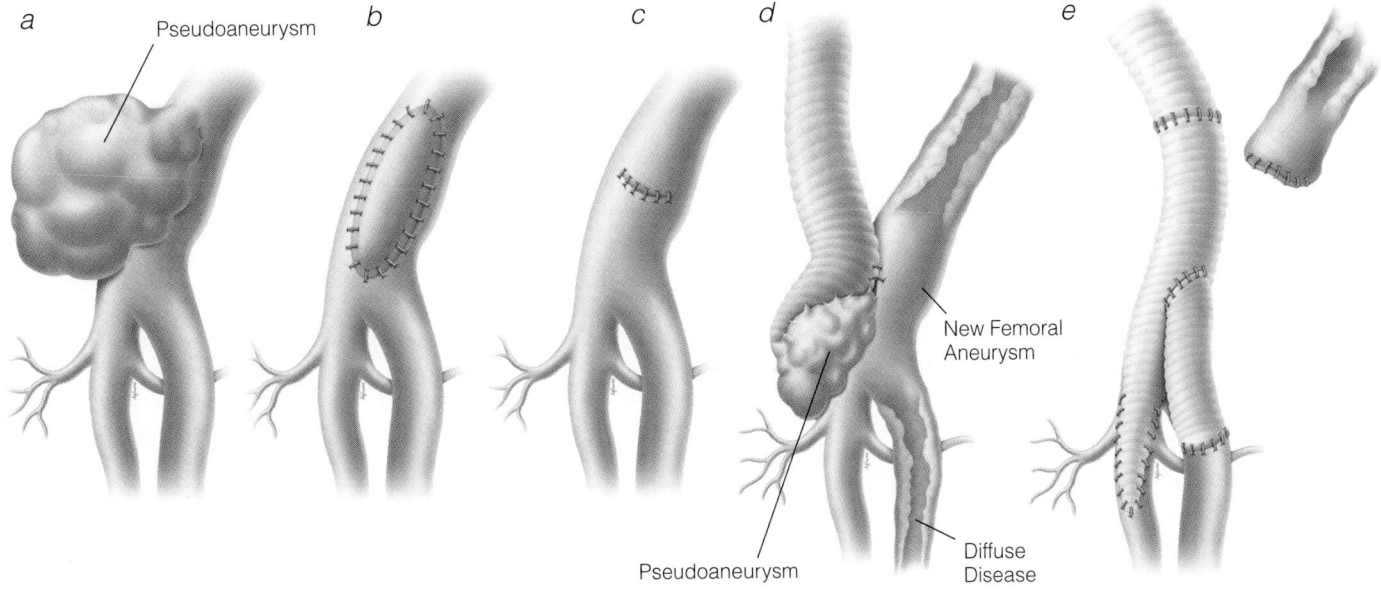

Figure 4 **Repair of femoral artery aneurysms (pseudoaneurysms) (*a*). Depicted are commonly employed options for repair of femoral artery pseudoaneurysms: (*b*) primary closure and (*c*) patch angioplasty with either autogenous or synthetic patch material. Also depicted is repair of anastomotic femoral pseudoaneurysms (*d*). An interposition graft is placed to the profunda femoris (*e*), and a jump graft is placed to the superficial femoral artery.**

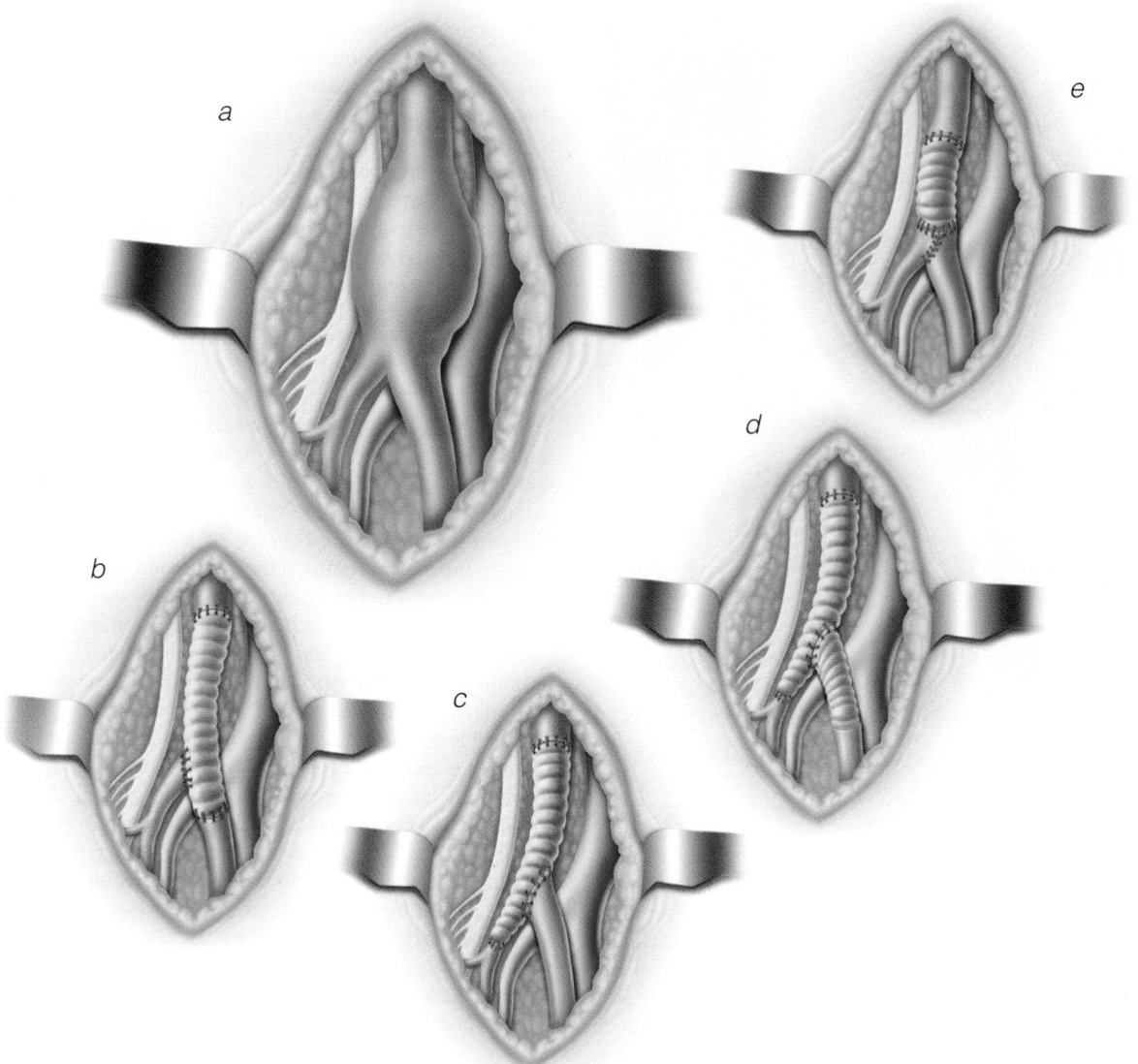

Figure 5 **Repair of femoral artery aneurysms (type II true aneurysms) (*a*). Depicted are commonly employed options for repair of true femoral artery aneurysms involving the origins of the profunda femoris and superficial femoral arteries (type II femoral aneurysms). (*b*) The profunda femoris artery may be implanted into an interposition graft placed to the superficial femoral artery. (*c*) The superficial femoral artery may be implanted into an interposition graft placed to the profunda femoris artery. (*d*) An interposition graft may be placed to the profunda femoris artery, with a jump graft to the superficial femoral artery. Alternatively, the superficial femoral artery may be reimplanted into the interposition graft if there is sufficient length to allow the reconstruction to be performed without tension. (*e*) Syndactylization of the profunda femoris and superficial femoral arteries may be done to form a common outflow channel for a synthetic interposition graft originating from the common femoral artery or the distal external iliac artery.**

either a longitudinal or an oblique incision over the femoral artery. The usual preference, however, is a longitudinal incision angled approximately 20° medially, which permits exposure of the distal profunda femoris artery without the creation of a skin flap. Both the distal extent of the femoral aneurysm and the degree of associated occlusive disease may influence the configuration of open surgical repair [*see Figure 5*]. Type I aneurysms, which spare the origins of the profunda femoris and superficial femoral arteries, are usually managed by constructing a short interposition graft with the proximal anastomosis at the level of the distal external iliac artery or the proximal common femoral artery [*see Figure 6*]. Occasionally, if proximal control of the retroperitoneal iliac artery is required, a flank incision may be needed. When it is necessary to repair additional proximal or distal aneurysms, the short femoral interposition graft may also act as the recipient of an aortofemoral or iliofemoral graft [*see 91 Aortoiliac Reconstruction*]

or as the origin of a femorodistal bypass graft [*see 96 Infrainguinal Arterial Procedures*].

If the femoral aneurysm is more extensive, a bypass from the common femoral artery to the profunda femoris artery with a jump graft to the superficial femoral artery is usually preferred [*see Figures 5d and 7*]. This approach allows the surgeon to work sequentially from the deep tissue planes to the more superficial ones.

Alternatively, some surgeons favor implantation of the distal profunda femoris artery into an interposition graft placed between the common femoral artery and the superficial femoral artery [*see Figure 5b*]. Others have described joining the superficial and deep femoral arteries at their bifurcation to form a common outflow tract that serves as the distal anastomotic end point for the interposition graft, a technique sometimes referred to as syndactylization [*see Figure 5e*]. Application of these two methods

a

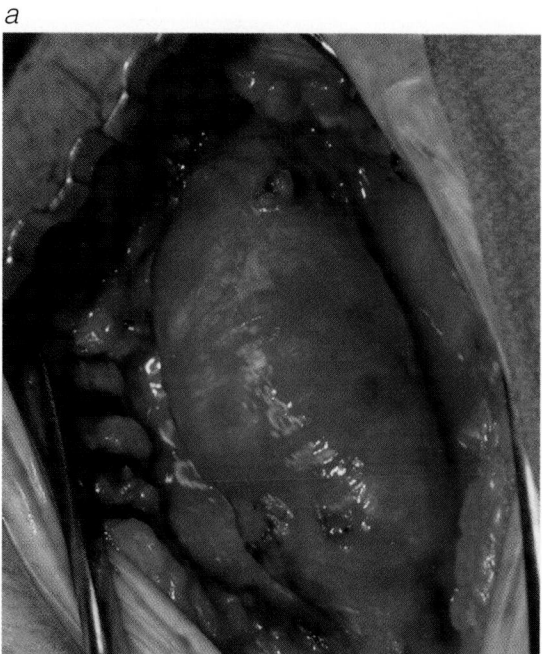

b

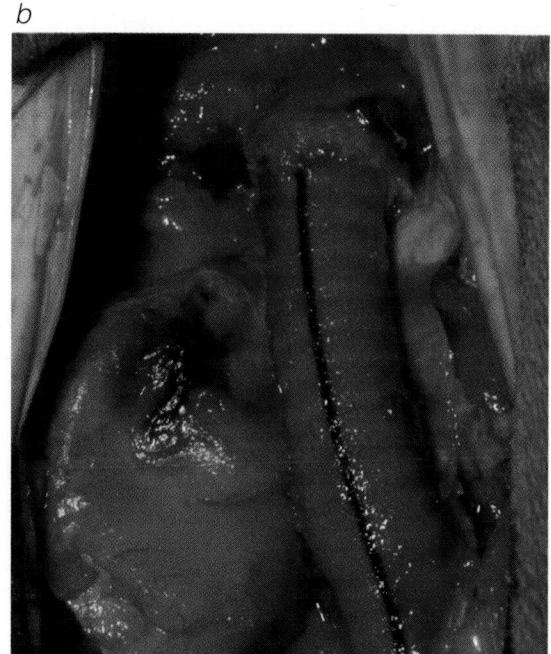

Figure 6 **Repair of femoral artery aneurysms (type I true aneurysms). Shown is a type I true aneurysm of the common femoral artery (*a*) before and (*b*) after reconstruction with a Dacron interposition graft.**

may be hampered by the presence of associated occlusive disease, which is frequently present. Nevertheless, the surgeon should be familiar with all of the available options for reconstruction and should be prepared to adapt his or her choice of reconstruction method to the details of the local anatomy.

For treatment of noninfected femoral aneurysms, especially anastomotic pseudoaneurysms, synthetic grafts have been used with good results; they usually offer a better size match with the native femoral arteries [*see Figure 4d*]. If local infection is present or the potential for wound complications is high, autogenous grafts are preferred.

OUTCOME EVALUATION

The results of operative repair of femoral artery aneurysms are generally excellent. In published series, the perioperative mortali-

Figure 7 **Repair of femoral artery aneurysms (type II true aneurysms). Shown is the repair of a type II femoral artery aneurysm with a Dacron interposition graft to the profunda femoris artery and a polytetrafluoroethylene (PTFE) jump graft to the superficial femoral artery.**

ty ranges from 0 (for isolated asymptomatic femoral aneurysm repair) to approximately 4% (if aneurysm repair is combined with more extensive aortic procedures).[5-7] The reported 5-year patency rate for saphenous vein and Dacron interposition grafts used for repair of isolated femoral artery aneurysms is 80% to 83%.[5,7] In general, patients who are operated on before they show evidence of impaired limb perfusion fare better than those presenting with lower extremity complications.[6]

Repair of Popliteal Artery Aneurysms

Aneurysms of the popliteal artery are the most commonly encountered peripheral aneurysms. Unlike femoral aneurysms, popliteal aneurysms are more likely to be true (i.e., degenerative) aneurysms than pseudoaneurysms. True popliteal aneurysms typically occur in men in their fifth and sixth decades. Their clinical importance lies in their propensity to cause limb-threatening complications. When true popliteal aneurysms are left untreated, the future incidence of thromboembolic events in initially asymptomatic patients is high. In one series of patients who were managed conservatively, only 32% had no complications at 5 years' follow-up.[8] Multiple aneurysms are common in this population, and it has been reported that nearly 50% of patients presenting with a popliteal aneurysm have associated abdominal aortic aneurysms and that 40% may also have coexisting femoral artery aneurysms.[4,8,9] In the largest reported series, 70% of these patients had a popliteal artery aneurysm in the contralateral extremity.[10] The clear link between the presence of popliteal aneurysms and the presence of other associated aneurysms underscores the importance of careful investigation of all patients who present with a newly diagnosed popliteal artery aneurysm. In approximately 50% of cases, popliteal artery aneurysms are confined to the popliteal artery itself; in the remaining cases, aneurysmal degeneration may extend proximally to involve the superficial femoral artery or distally down to the level of the tibioperoneal trunk.[9]

PREOPERATIVE EVALUATION

Popliteal artery aneurysms may be asymptomatic on initial presentation. The diagnosis is usually suspected on the basis of the detection of a prominent pulsatile mass behind the knee during physical examination. The mass is often best felt with the knee in a slightly flexed position. Small aneurysms may be more difficult to detect during physical examination, especially if thrombosis has already occurred. A high index of suspicion, usually based on recognition of an aneurysm in another location, is helpful in identifying these lesions.

The most frequent initial presentation of a symptomatic popliteal aneurysm is the development of acute limb-threatening ischemia as a consequence of arterial occlusion from thrombosis of the aneurysm or distal embolization.[9,11] Early manifestations (i.e., those occurring before complete occlusion of the popliteal artery itself) may be limited to painful petechial hemorrhages or localized gangrenous changes in the digital arteries that result from microembolization [see Figure 1]. In some series, claudication has been a presenting symptom in 40% to 75% of patients with popliteal aneurysms.[9] Rupture is a distinctly unusual event: fewer than 5% of patients present with this complication.[9] In rare instances, patients with very large popliteal aneurysms may present with symptoms resulting from compression of adjacent structures, such as paresthesias or neuropraxia involving the lower leg (from direct popliteal nerve compression) or deep vein thrombosis, superficial varicosity formation, and phlebitis (from popliteal vein compression).

Plain radiographs of the knee may demonstrate calcium in the aneurysm wall; however, once the diagnosis is suspected, it is best confirmed by means of ultrasonography [see Figure 8], computed tomography, or magnetic resonance imaging. These imaging modalities are particularly helpful in distinguishing popliteal aneurysms from other space-occupying lesions of the popliteal fossa (e.g., Baker's cyst).

Angiography is less useful for the diagnosis of popliteal artery aneurysms: it demonstrates only the flow channel of the vessel, and any intramural thrombus that is present may obscure the presence of the popliteal aneurysm. Nevertheless, angiography plays a valuable role in the planning of operative reconstruction because

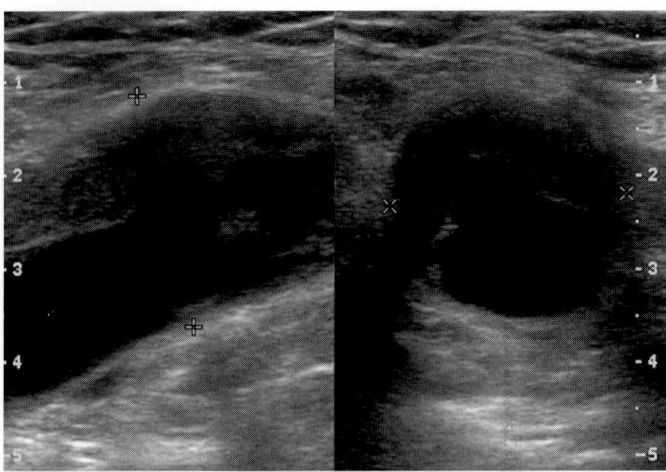

Figure 8 **Repair of popliteal artery aneurysms. Ultrasonographic examination of the right popliteal artery demonstrates a 2.6 cm right popliteal artery aneurysm, shown in both sagittal (left) and transverse (right) views.**

it can delineate the extent of aneurysmal involvement of the popliteal and adjacent arteries and detect the presence of associated occlusive disease [see Figure 9]. In addition, as noted (see above), it may facilitate the use of adjunctive thrombolytic therapy, which may be particularly beneficial if the outflow bed has been severely compromised by distal thrombosis or embolization. The goal of thrombolysis of occluded outflow vessels is to uncover a suitable target vessel that can be used to provide outflow for a surgical bypass; this modality is particularly useful in this setting, in that intraoperative balloon thromboembolectomy sometimes cannot clear sufficient thrombus from small vessels to maintain long-term graft patency. In one study of selected patients with poor outflow, thrombolytic therapy followed by surgical repair yielded results that compared favorably with those of isolated surgical repair, and the combined approach was associated with lower amputation rates.[12] It should be kept in mind, however, that thrombolytic therapy is more rapid and effective if thrombosis is recent and the volume of thrombus is not large. If limb ischemia

a

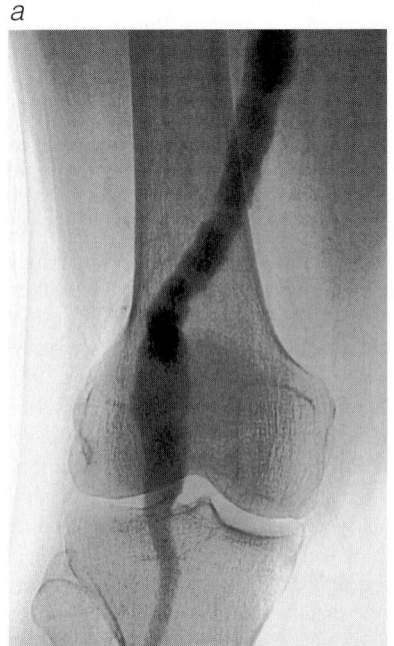

b

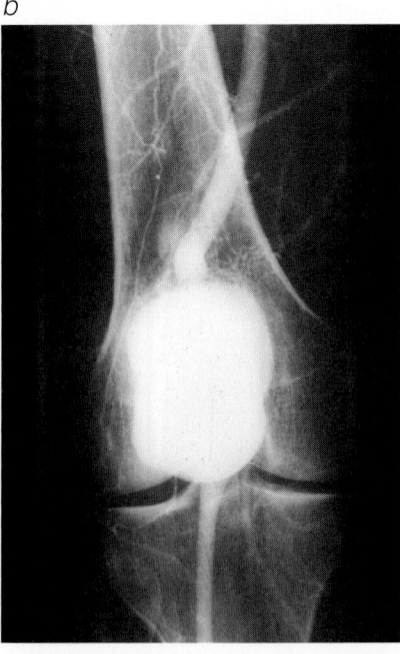

Figure 9 **Repair of popliteal artery aneurysms. Preoperative arteriograms illustrate two common varieties of popliteal artery aneurysm. Extent of disease influences choice of reconstruction. (*a*) The aneurysm is localized to the popliteal artery. (*b*) Arteriomegaly extends proximally to involve the superficial femoral artery.**

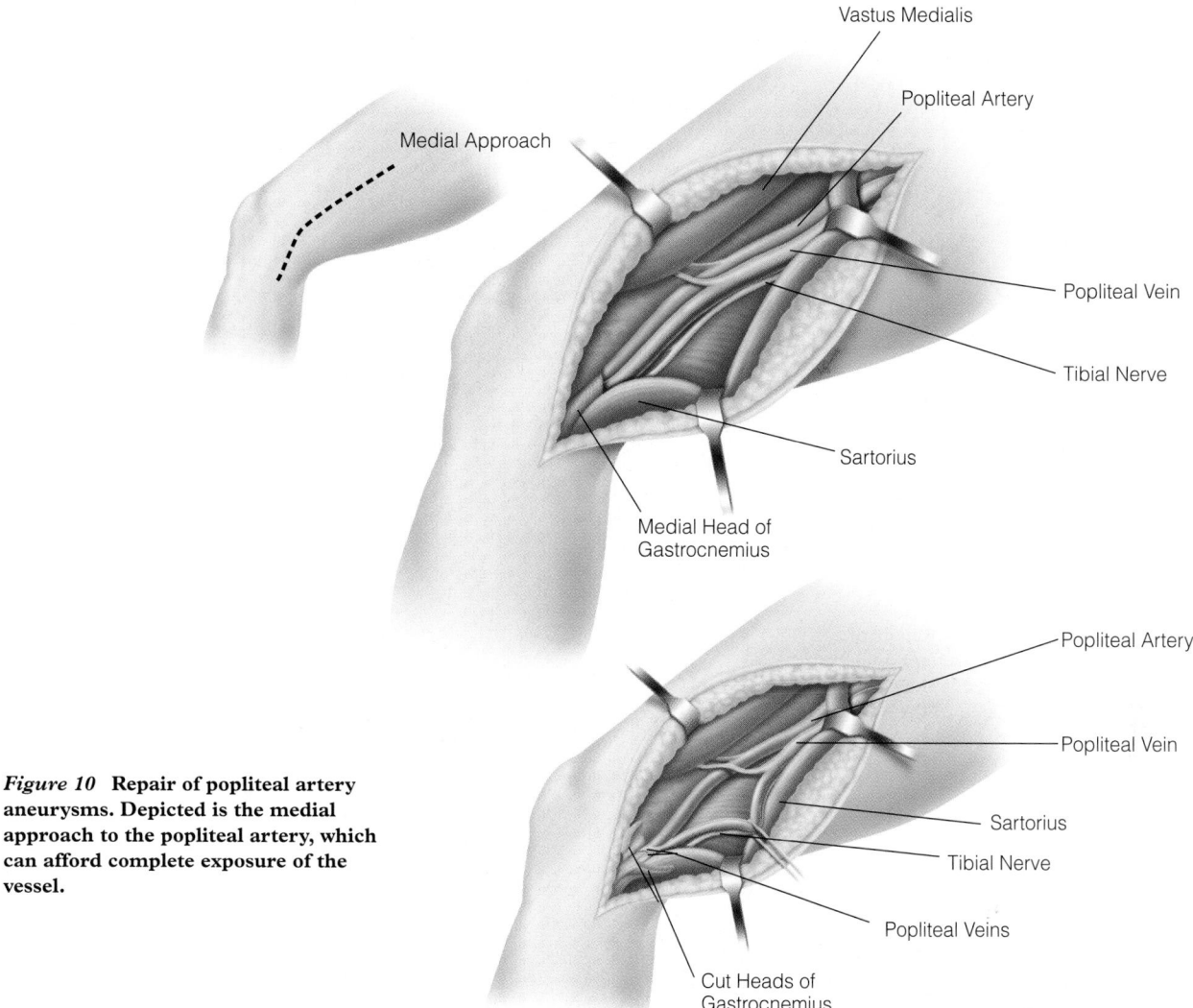

Figure 10 **Repair of popliteal artery aneurysms. Depicted is the medial approach to the popliteal artery, which can afford complete exposure of the vessel.**

is severe, the length of time required to establish reperfusion may be prohibitive, and it may be best to proceed with direct surgical intervention before irreversible tissue loss occurs.

In patients with popliteal artery aneurysms, as in those with femoral artery aneurysms, there is a high incidence of associated atherosclerotic disorders: nearly 50% have some degree of myocardial dysfunction, and nearly two thirds are hypertensive.[13] Consequently, preoperative evaluation of patients under consideration for popliteal aneurysm repair should include careful optimization of associated coexisting medical conditions, especially associated coronary artery disease.

OPERATIVE PLANNING

There is a consensus that all patients with symptomatic popliteal aneurysms should undergo expeditious operative repair; conservative management in these cases is associated with a substantial risk of limb loss, especially in the presence of limb-threatening ischemia. There is also general agreement that asymptomatic popliteal aneurysms should be repaired upon diagnosis; such lesions are associated with the development of limb-threatening complications in a substantial number of patients. In a series of 94 patients with asymptomatic popliteal artery aneurysms who were followed for nearly 7 years, 18% of the limbs with aneurysms eventually became symptomatic (25% acutely and 75% chronically), and 4% had to be amputated.[14] In this cohort, aneurysm size

greater than 2 cm, the presence of mural thrombus, and poor distal lower extremity runoff were significant predictors of the development of symptoms. In a meta-analysis of the published literature that encompassed nearly 2,500 popliteal artery aneurysms, nearly 35% of the patients who were treated conservatively eventually experienced ischemic complications, and 25% of the patients who required surgical treatment for an ischemic complication eventually required amputation.[15] Given these results, most surgeons would agree that surgical repair of asymptomatic popliteal artery aneurysms is indicated for all but extremely high risk patients.

Although the likelihood that popliteal aneurysms will give rise to complications does not appear to be related to the size of the aneurysms, optimal management of small asymptomatic popliteal aneurysms remains controversial—in part because of problems with their definition, especially in the presence of generalized arteriomegaly. Factors believed to be associated with the eventual development of ischemic complications include size greater than 2 cm, deformation of the artery itself, and the existence of intraluminal thrombus. The presence of these factors, especially if the popliteal aneurysm is localized, makes a case for operative repair.

OPERATIVE TECHNIQUE

The primary therapeutic objectives of popliteal artery aneurysm repair are (1) to eliminate the aneurysm as a source of emboli or thrombosis and (2) to maintain distal perfusion in a dur-

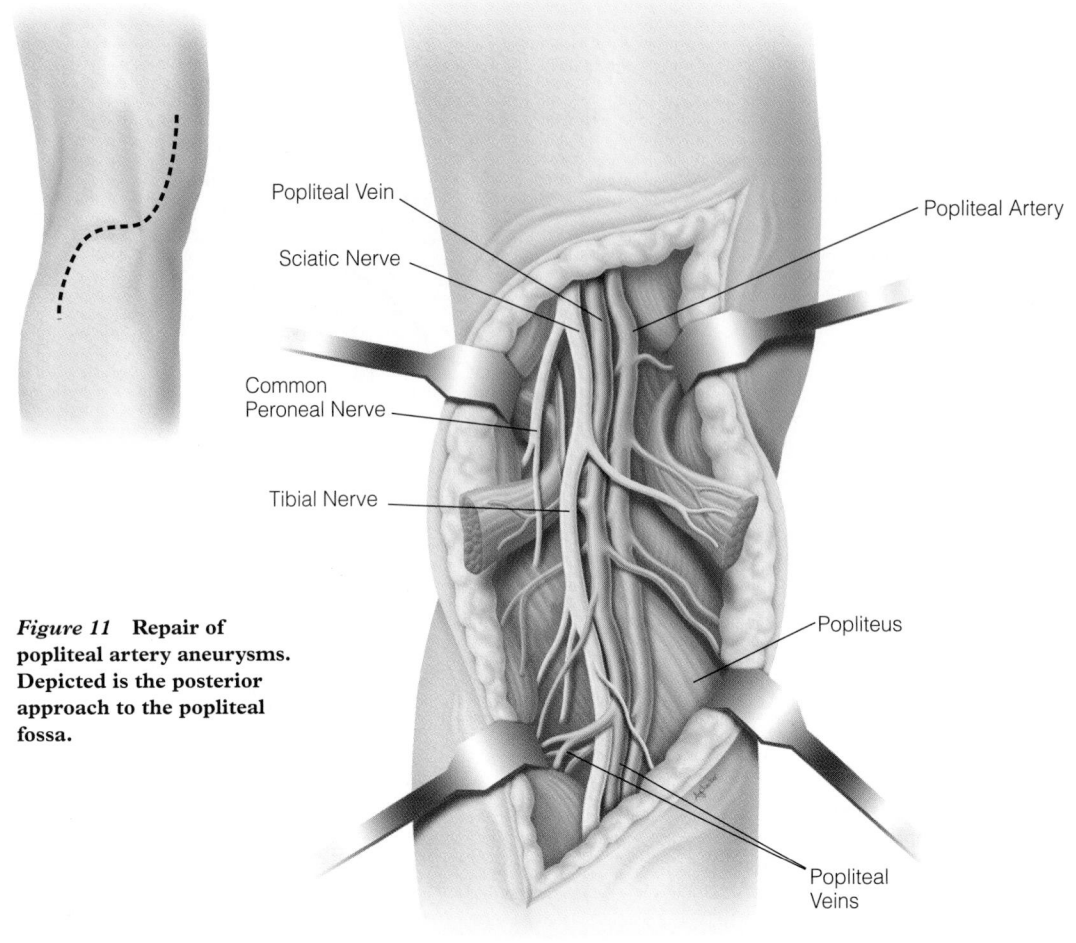

Popliteal Vein

Sciatic Nerve

Common
Peroneal Nerve

Tibial Nerve

Popliteal Artery

Popliteus

Popliteal
Veins

Figure 11 **Repair of
popliteal artery aneurysms.
Depicted is the posterior
approach to the popliteal
fossa.**

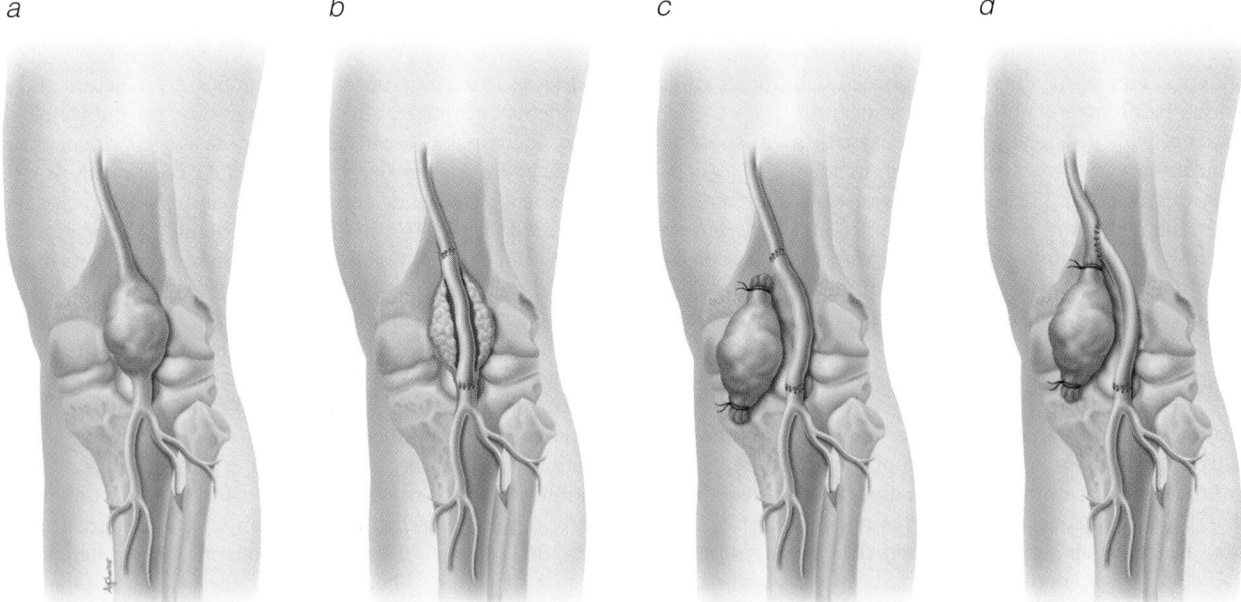

a　　　　*b*　　　　*c*　　　　*d*

Figure 12 **Repair of popliteal artery aneurysms (*a*). Depicted are various bypass configurations that can be employed
for repair of popliteal aneurysms. (*b*) An interposition graft may be placed within a large aneurysm. (*c*) If the graft and
the artery are sufficiently well matched in terms of size, ligation and bypass of the aneurysm with end-to-end proximal
and distal anastomoses may be employed. (*d*) If there is a significant size mismatch between the graft and the artery,
ligation and bypass of the aneurysm with an end-to-side proximal anastomosis may be employed.**

a

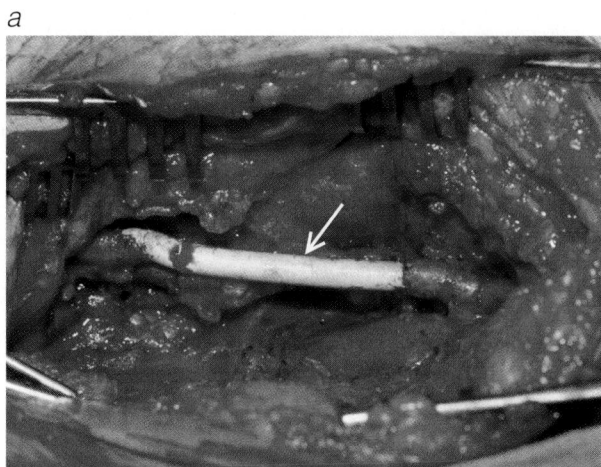

b

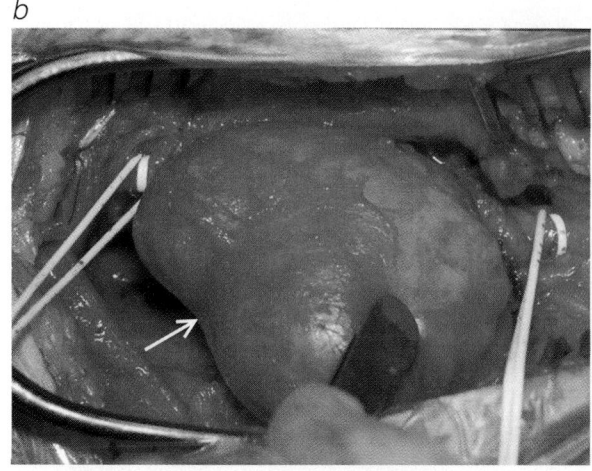

Figure 13 Repair of popliteal artery aneurysms. (*a*) Operative photograph shows a large popliteal aneurysm (arrow) exposed via the medial approach. (*b*) A PTFE interposition graft (arrow) is placed within the aneurysm sac, which has been decompressed. Saphenous vein is the preferred graft material, but a synthetic conduit may be required if the autogenous conduit is unavailable or inadequate. Collateral inflow into the sac has been interrupted.

able fashion. Other objectives are to prevent hemorrhage resulting from rupture, to eliminate the mass effect exerted by large aneurysms, and to prevent recurrence. Several reports have evaluated endovascular treatment of popliteal aneurysms with covered stents delivered under fluoroscopic guidance[16,17]; however, to date, the results have been inferior to those of open surgical treatment. At present, endovascular treatment of popliteal aneurysms remains investigational and should be confined to those patients who are considered to be at unacceptable risk with standard surgical therapy. If endovascular therapy is employed, close late follow-up is necessary to detect fracture or migration of the stent, as well as expansion or thrombosis of the aneurysm.

The two most important factors influencing the surgical approach to popliteal aneurysm repair and the configuration of the reconstruction used are (1) the extent of the aneurysmal disease and (2) the size of the aneurysm. In most settings, the medial approach with the patient in the supine position is preferred. This approach allows exposure of the entire popliteal artery, if necessary, through division of the semimembranosus, semitendinosus, and gastrocnemius tendons, which can be repaired at the time of closure. In addition, it offers the most flexibility for expanding the reconstruction if the aneurysm is large, extensive, or multilobed [*see Figure 10*]. The posterior approach to the popliteal artery, which is favored by some surgeons, can also provide adequate exposure of localized popliteal aneurysms, but it requires that the patient be prone [*see Figure 11*]. Although it is well tolerated, the posterior approach precludes exposure of the common and superficial femoral arteries or the greater saphenous vein and offers less flexibility for proximal or distal extension. Familiarity with both approaches permits the vascular surgeon to choose the one that best suits the given clinical situation.

A small, localized popliteal artery aneurysm with few side branches may be treated with simple proximal and distal ligation of the aneurysm sac, accompanied by construction of a bypass graft with a short segment of autologous saphenous vein. The venous graft may be tunneled in the anatomic position, deep to the medial head of the gastrocnemius muscle. The proximal and distal anastomoses are fashioned in either an end-to-end or an end-to-side configuration, depending on the compatibility of the graft's diameter with that of the artery [*see Figure 12*].

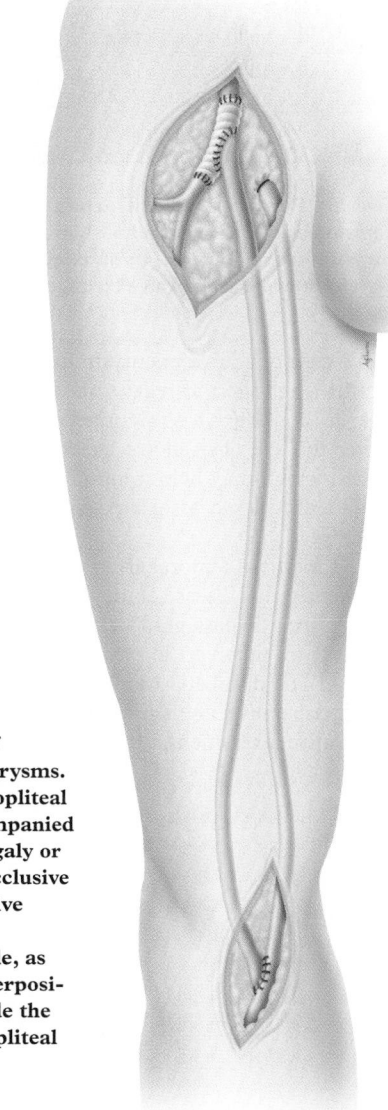

Figure 14 Repair of popliteal artery aneurysms. When femoral and popliteal aneurysms are accompanied by diffuse arteriomegaly or associated arterial occlusive disease, more extensive reconstructions are required. For example, as shown, a femoral interposition graft may provide the inflow for an infrapopliteal bypass.

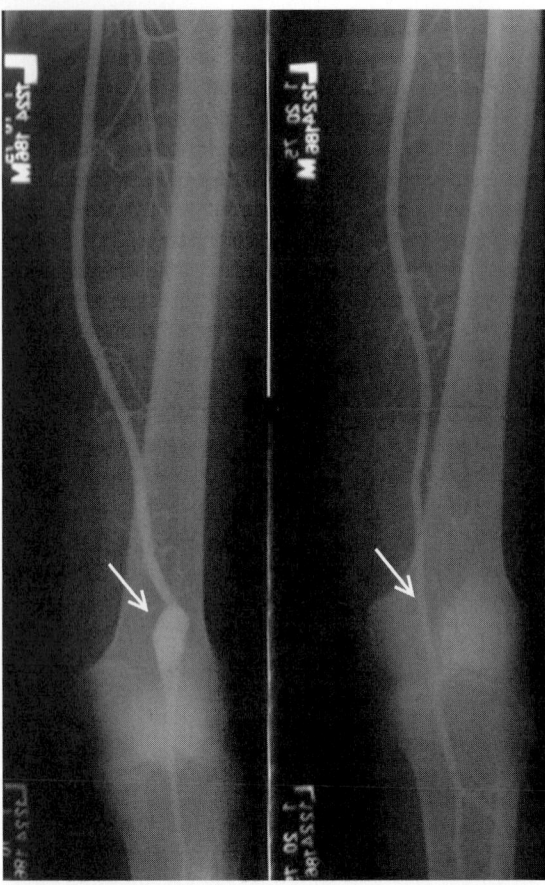

Figure 15 **Repair of popliteal artery aneurysms. Preoperative and postoperative arteriograms show a localized popliteal artery aneurysm (arrow, left) and its subsequent repair with a saphenous vein interposition graft (arrow, right).**

In the case of a large aneurysm for which evacuation of mural thrombus is required to relieve mass effect symptoms, it may be feasible to construct a short interposition graft [*see Figure 13*]. Opening the sac also allows ligation of the feeding geniculate branches, which may help minimize the risk of late enlargement of the aneurysm sac associated with recurrence of mass effect symptoms.

If the superficial femoral artery is severely involved with occlusive or aneurysmal disease, it may be necessary to construct a long saphenous vein bypass graft originating from the common femoral artery, in either an in situ or a reversed configuration [*see Figure 14*]. The distal anastomotic site is determined on the basis of the preoperative angiographic findings, in conjunction with intraoperative assessment.

As a rule, grafts constructed from autogenous vein are preferred, but synthetic grafts may be required if the autogenous vein is unavailable or inadequate. An effort should be made to keep graft length to the minimum necessary to treat the aneurysmal disease. Intraoperative completion angiography is recommended to allow detection and correction of technical problems with the reconstruction before closure [*see Figure 15*].

OUTCOME EVALUATION

In a study from the Cleveland Clinic that described the surgical management of 110 popliteal aneurysms, there were eight (7.3%) early postoperative deaths.[9] Six (75%) of the eight early postoperative deaths were attributable to cardiac complications—an observation that highlights the need for careful cardiac evaluation, when feasible, before the treatment of popliteal artery aneurysms.

The presence of symptoms, the adequacy of the outflow bed on presentation, and the choice of autogenous graft material for reconstruction are the main factors that influence limb salvage and graft patency rates after repair of popliteal artery aneurysms. In one study, the 5-year patency rate for saphenous vein grafts was 92% for patients who had asymptomatic popliteal aneurysms and in whom good outflow vessels were identified, compared with 66% for a matched cohort with known occlusive disease.[18] In other studies that included similar patients, the 10-year patency rate was in excess of 80%, and the limb salvage rate was approximately 95%.[9,19]

Patients who undergo urgent surgical treatment of popliteal aneurysms that were symptomatic on presentation have less favorable outcomes. In one study, when thrombosis of the popliteal aneurysm was apparent on presentation or distal outflow was poor, the 5-year patency rate was approximately 50%, and the limb salvage rate was only 60%.[20] Several studies documented the influence of the choice of conduit graft material on bypass durability; each demonstrated that patency rates were nearly four times higher with saphenous vein grafts than with nonvenous alternative grafts.[8,14,21] Limb salvage rates were also higher with autogenous saphenous vein grafts. For example, in one report, 23% (7/31) of the popliteal artery bypasses performed with a prosthetic conduit resulted in limb loss, whereas only 2% (1/42) performed with a saphenous vein graft resulted in amputation.[14]

In the past few years, instances of continued expansion of the popliteal aneurysm sac despite ligation and bypass have been reported.[22] This phenomenon may result from inadequate ligation of the aneurysm sac, but it may also result from retrograde perfusion of the sac via patent geniculate collateral vessels. Consequently, it seems advisable to ligate all large collateral vessels feeding the aneurysm sac at the time of the initial aneurysm repair. If the aneurysm is large, it may be necessary to perform the ligation from within the evacuated sac.

References

1. Lawrence PF, Lorenzo-Rivero S, Lyon JL: The incidence of iliac, femoral, and popliteal artery aneurysms in hospitalized patients. J Vasc Surg 22:409, 1995

2. Dawson I, Sie R, van Baalen JM, et al: Asymptomatic popliteal aneurysm: elective operation versus conservative follow-up. Br J Surg 81:1504, 1994

3. Dawson I, Sie RB, van Bockel JH: Atherosclerotic popliteal aneurysm. Br J Surg 84:293, 1997

4. Dent TL, Lindenauer SM, Ernst CB, et al: Multiple arteriosclerotic arterial aneurysms. Arch Surg 105:338, 1972

5. Cutler BS, Darling RC: Surgical management of arteriosclerotic femoral aneurysms. Surgery 74:764, 1973

6. Graham LM, Zelenock GB, Whitehouse WM Jr, et al: Clinical significance of arteriosclerotic femoral artery aneurysms. Arch Surg 115:502, 1980

7. Sapienza P, Mingoli A, Feldhaus RJ, et al: Femoral artery aneurysms: long-term follow-up and results of surgical treatment. Cardiovasc Surg 4:181, 1996

8. Vermilion BD, Kimmins SA, Pace WG, et al: A review of one hundred forty-seven popliteal aneurysms with long-term follow-up. Surgery 90:1009, 1981

9. Anton GE, Hertzer NR, Beven EG, et al: Surgical management of popliteal aneurysms: trends in presentation, treatment, and results from 1952 to 1984. J Vasc Surg 3:125, 1986

10. Szilagyi DE, Schwartz RL, Reddy DJ: Popliteal arterial aneurysms: their natural history and management. Arch Surg 116:724, 1981

11. Whitehouse WM Jr, Wakefield TW, Graham LM, et al: Limb-threatening potential of arteriosclerotic popliteal artery aneurysms. Surgery 93:694, 1983

12. Wyffels PL, DeBord JR, Marshall JS, et al: Increased limb salvage with intraoperative and postoperative ankle level urokinase infusion in acute lower extremity ischemia. J Vasc Surg 15:771, 1992

13. Bouhoutsos J, Martin P: Popliteal aneurysm: a review of 116 cases. Br J Surg 61:469, 1974

14. Lowell RC, Gloviczki P, Hallett JW Jr, et al: Popliteal artery aneurysms: the risk of nonoperative management. Ann Vasc Surg 8:14, 1994

15. Dawson I, van Bockel JH, Brand R, et al: Popliteal artery aneurysms: long-term follow-up of aneurysmal disease and results of surgical treatment. J Vasc Surg 13:398, 1991

16. Henry M, Amor M, Ethevenot G, et al: Initial experience with the Cragg Endopro System 1 for intraluminal treatment of peripheral vascular disease. J Endovasc Surg 1:31, 1994

17. Henry M, Amor M, Beyar R, et al: Clinical experience with a new nitinol self-expanding stent in peripheral arteries. J Endovasc Surg 3:369, 1996

18. Upchurch GR Jr, Gerhard-Herman MD, Sebastian MW, et al: Improved graft patency and altered remodeling in infrainguinal vein graft reconstruction for aneurysmal versus occlusive disease. J Vasc Surg 29:1022, 1999

19. Roggo A, Brunner U, Ottinger LW, et al: The continuing challenge of aneurysms of the popliteal artery. Surg Gynecol Obstet 177:56, 1993

20. Lilly MP, Flinn WR, McCarthy WJ 3rd, et al: The effect of distal arterial anatomy on the success of popliteal aneurysm repair. J Vasc Surg 7:653, 1988

21. Hagino RT, Fujitani RM, Dawson DL, et al: Does infrapopliteal arterial runoff predict success for popliteal artery aneurysmorrhaphy? Am J Surg 168:652, 1994

22. Ebaugh JL, Morasch MD, Matsumura JS, et al: Fate of excluded popliteal artery aneurysms. J Vasc Surg 37:954, 2003

Acknowledgment

Figures 4, 5, 10, 11, 12, and 14   Alice Y. Chen.

96 INFRAINGUINAL ARTERIAL PROCEDURES

William D. Suggs, M.D., F.A.C.S., and Frank J. Veith, M.D., F.A.C.S.

Since the early 1980s, there have been enormous advances in the treatment of lower-extremity ischemia secondary to infrainguinal arteriosclerosis. Effective interventional management strategies have been developed for virtually all patterns of arteriosclerosis underlying limb-threatening ischemia.[1,2] Bypasses to the infrainguinal arteries using segments of autologous vein have become routine for limb salvage. As this technique has evolved, the distal limits of revascularization have been extended. Bypasses to arteries near the ankle or in the foot can now be offered to patients who have no patent arteries suitable for more proximal bypasses. In addition, bypasses to distal tibial or tarsal vessels may be performed in some patients whose popliteal arteries are patent but who have three-vessel distal occlusive disease and forefoot gangrene.[3,4] Frequently, patients who require very distal bypasses have already undergone vascular reconstruction; these patients may be candidates for alternative approaches, such as a popliteal-distal bypass or a tibiotibial bypass.[5-7]

Patients with limbs threatened by distal tibial occlusive disease present an ongoing challenge to the vascular surgeon. Provided that careful attention is paid to obtaining high-quality preoperative angiograms and that the surgeon is willing to consider alternative approaches, it is generally possible to achieve good results from limb salvage procedures.

It should be kept in mind that only patients with threatened limbs—manifested by rest pain, frank gangrene, or nonhealing ulcers—should be considered candidates for infrainguinal bypass. Patients who have gangrene that extends into the deeper tarsal region of the foot, who have a severe organic mental syndrome, or who are nonambulatory are not candidates for limb salvage surgery and should be treated with primary amputation instead.[1,2]

Preoperative Evaluation

HISTORY AND PHYSICAL EXAMINATION

A careful history and a thorough physical examination are crucial for accurate assessment of the extent of the patient's atherosclerotic disease. In the course of the history, the examiner should pay particular attention to distinguishing true rest pain from other causes of pain (e.g., arthritis and neuritis). Significant ischemic pain is usually associated not only with decreased pulses but also with other manifestations of ischemia (e.g., atrophy, decreased skin temperature, marked rubor, and pain that is relieved when the foot is dangled). In the course of the physical examination, the examiner should look for and assess the extent of any underlying infection and should closely examine any surgical scars for clues to the nature and extent of any previous vascular operations involving the use of the saphenous vein. In addition, a careful pulse examination should be performed to assess the patient's baseline arterial status; these baseline measurements provide a basis for comparison if the disease subsequently progresses and may help determine the approach to be used to salvage the threatened limb.

NONINVASIVE TESTING

Noninvasive tests are helpful in that they provide semiquantitative assessment of the circulation and help confirm the diagnosis made on the basis of the history and the physical examination. Such test measurements include the ankle-brachial index (ABI) and pulse volume recordings (PVRs).

The ABI is determined by dividing the ankle pressure in each lower limb by the higher of the two brachial pressures. Normal circulation typically yields an ABI of 1.0 to 1.2; claudication, an ABI of 0.40 to 0.95; and limb-threatening ischemia, an ABI of 0 to 0.5. It is vital to remember, however, that lower-extremity pressure measurements are less reliable in patients with heavily calcified vessels (e.g., diabetics and patients with end-stage renal disease). In these patients, ABIs are falsely elevated as a result of the higher cuff pressures required to occlude calcified vessels, which in some cases are not occluded even with pressures higher than 300 mm Hg.

PVRs are obtained by means of calibrated air-cuff plethysmography. Standard blood pressure cuffs are placed at different levels of the lower extremity, and the increases in pressure within the cuffs resulting from the volume increase during systole are recorded as pulse waves. Tracings exhibiting a brisk rise during systole and a dicrotic notch are characterized as normal, those exhibiting loss of the notch and a more prolonged downslope are characterized as moderately abnormal, and those exhibiting a flattened wave are characterized as severely abnormal. Absolute amplitudes on PVRs are not directly comparable between patients; however, serial PVRs from a single patient are highly reproducible and thus are quite useful for following the course of severe peripheral vascular disease in individual cases.[4] One disadvantage of PVRs is that they cannot differentiate proximal femoral disease from iliac occlusive disease.[8]

IMAGING

Duplex Scanning

Duplex scanning is a useful noninvasive method of assessing the aortoiliac and infrainguinal arterial systems. Several studies have evaluated the ability of duplex scanning to predict iliac artery stenosis. A 1987 trial found that duplex scanning was highly sensitive (89%) and specific (90%) in predicting iliac stenosis of 50% or greater.[9] Three subsequent trials corroborated these findings, reporting sensitivities ranging from 81% to 89% and specificities ranging from 88% to 99%.[10-12] This noninvasive modality may be especially useful for improving evaluation of diabetic patients before invasive procedures (e.g., angiography and angioplasty).[10]

Duplex scanning has also been used to allow infrapopliteal bypasses to be performed without preoperative angiography. In one study, a limb salvage rate of 86% was achieved with this approach, and completion arteriography matched the runoff status predicted by duplex scanning in 96% of cases.[13] In a study from our own institution, we were able to perform femoropopliteal bypasses without preoperative arteriography and were able to perform distal bypasses with confirmatory arteriograms at the time of operation.[14]

Magnetic Resonance Angiography

Magnetic resonance angiography (MRA), a noninvasive modality that does not require contrast agents, often yields good arterial images and may, in fact, be more sensitive than angiography in imaging distal lower-extremity runoff vessels.[15,16] More recently, developments such as gadolinium enhancement, multistation examination, and the floating table technique have further improved the resolution of MRA,[17-19] to the point where many institutions that use current forms of MRA no longer routinely obtain preoperative angiograms. MRA, in combination with arterial duplex scanning, has the potential to replace contrast arteriography in the assessment of patients with distal arterial occlusive disease.

Arteriography

Until MRA and duplex scanning become more widely available, contrast angiography will remain the gold standard for the evaluation of patients with distal arterial occlusive disease. A complete evaluation of the existing arterial disease from the aorta to the pedal vessels is necessary for diabetic patients, who frequently have multilevel occlusive disease. Obtaining intraarterial pressure measurements at the time of angiography significantly improves detection of clinically significant stenosis. The systolic pressure gradient across the lesion should also be measured: gradients greater than 15 mm Hg are considered hemodynamically significant.[20]

In the general population, arteriography has a complication rate of only 1.7% to 3.3%.[21] Elderly patients with severe aortoiliac or infrainguinal disease must be carefully evaluated before the procedure because they are more likely to experience local and systemic complications than patients in the general population are. For the majority of patients, the transfemoral approach is the safest; however, for patients with weak or nonpalpable femoral pulses, other approaches (e.g., translumbar, transbrachial, or transaxillary) may be preferable. These alternative approaches are associated with higher rates of local complications, including hematomas, pseudoaneurysms, dissections, thrombosis, and embolization.

Renal insufficiency is an important complication of angiography: 6.5% to 8.2% of patients who undergo arteriography experience some degree of impairment associated with contrast agents.[22,23] Patients who have preexisting azotemia and whose baseline creatinine concentrations exceed 2.0 mg/dl are at highest risk for renal complications after angiography. Elderly patients typically have lower creatinine clearances for a given serum creatinine level and thus should always be considered at higher risk for nephrotoxicity. All possible precautions should be taken to limit the renal insult. There is some evidence to suggest that the use of low-osmolar contrast agents can decrease the incidence of renal impairment,[24,25] but the data are not unanimous on this point.[26] Adequate hydration and administration of oral acetylcysteine before arteriography are highly effective in diminishing the risk of contrast nephropathy. Administration of mannitol, which has an osmotic diuretic effect, helps prevent contrast toxicity as well. These measures, coupled with judicious use of contrast agents, should minimize renal impairment associated with arteriography.

Femoropopliteal Bypass

Patients whose limbs are clearly threatened and who have undergone arteriographic examination should undergo femoropopliteal bypass when the superficial femoral artery or the popliteal artery is occluded and when arteriography indicates that a patent popliteal artery segment distal to the occlusion has luminal continuity with any of its three terminal branches (even if one or more of these branches ends in an occlusion anywhere in the leg). Even if the popliteal artery segment into which the graft is to be inserted is occluded distally, femoropopliteal bypass to this segment can be considered.[27,28] If the isolated popliteal segment is shorter than 7 cm or if there is extensive gangrene or infection in the foot, a femorodistal artery bypass or a sequential bypass is sometimes performed in one or two stages.

OPERATIVE TECHNIQUE

Femoropopliteal bypass may be carried out either above or below the knee.

Above-the-Knee Bypass

For above-the-knee bypass, the patient is placed in the supine position with the thigh externally rotated and the knee flexed approximately 30°. This position affords easy exposure of the femoral and popliteal arteries as well as of the saphenous vein.

Harvesting of saphenous vein The greater saphenous vein is harvested through intermittent skip incisions starting in the groin and proceeding distally toward the knee [*see Figure 1*]. Multiple short skin incisions heal better than a single long one and are less likely to result in skin necrosis.

Dissection of the saphenous vein begins at the groin. This proximal incision is also used for exposure of the femoral artery. The saphenofemoral junction is carefully mobilized, and the tributaries are ligated with fine silk close to where they enter the main trunk, with care taken not to impinge on the wall of the trunk. As dissection continues distally, the main trunk of the saphenous vein is progressively elevated, and all tributaries are identified and ligated. The vein is then removed from its bed and

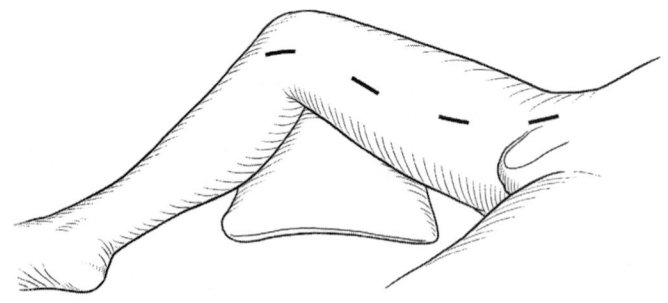

Figure 1 **Femoropopliteal bypass: above knee. Shown is the appropriate position of the leg. Interrupted skin incisions are made in the thigh and upper leg to permit harvesting of the saphenous vein.**

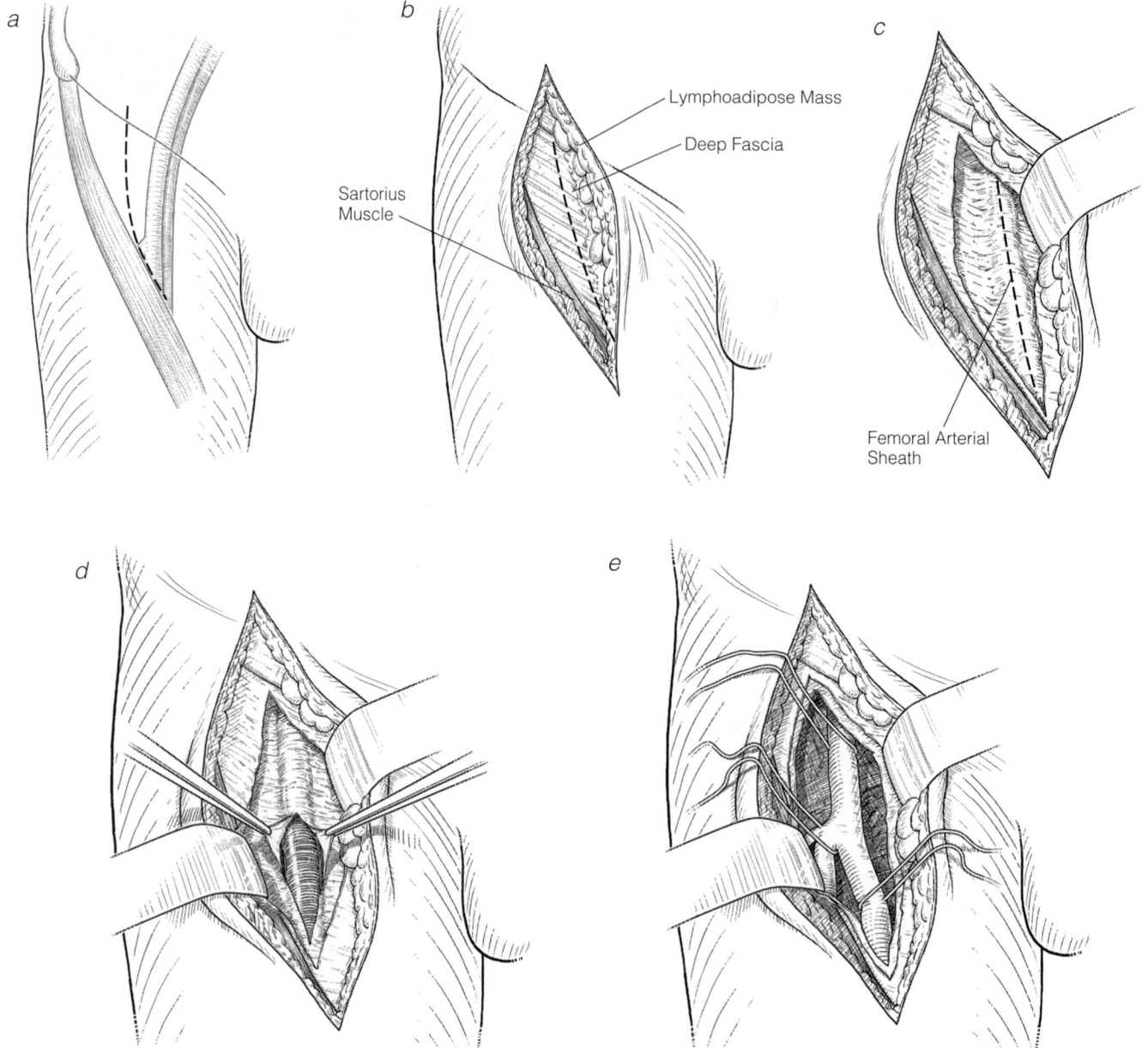

Figure 2 Femoropopliteal bypass: above knee. Depicted is exposure of the femoral artery. (*a*) A curved 4 to 5 in. skin incision is made slightly lateral to the pulsation of the femoral artery. (*b*) Lymphoadipose tissue is retracted to expose the deep fascia overlying the course of the femoral artery. (*c*) The deep fascia is incised, exposing the femoral arterial sheath, which is then opened along its axis (*d*). (*e*) The common and superficial femoral arteries are mobilized and encircled with Silastic vessel loops.

immediately placed into a basin containing heparinized saline (or heparinized whole blood) at a temperature of 4° C or cold Hanks solution. A small cannula is passed through the distal end of the divided vein, and the vessel is irrigated with cold Hanks solution to expel any liquid blood or clot and to locate any leaks. If a leak is found, it is repaired with 6-0 Prolene.

Step 1: exposure of femoral artery A slightly curved skin incision, with the concavity facing the medial aspect, is made starting at a point slightly above the inguinal crease and extending distally for 10 to 12.5 cm [*see Figure 2a*]. The incision should be slightly lateral to the pulsation of the femoral artery so as to avoid the lymphatics as much as possible. Any minor bleeding or

divided lymphatic vessels should be controlled with electrocoagulation or fine ligatures. Self-retaining retractors are placed both proximally and distally in the wound, and the lymphoadipose tissue is gently retracted medially [*see Figure 2b*].

The deep fascia is opened along the femoral artery [*see Figure 2c*], and the sheath of the artery is opened along its axis [*see Figure 2d*]. The common and superficial femoral arteries are mobilized, and Silastic loops are placed around them [*see Figure 2e*]. These vessels are then elevated slightly, and the origin of the deep femoral artery comes into view lateral and posterior to the common femoral artery and just proximal to the superficial femoral artery. Dissection of the origin of the deep femoral artery must be done carefully so as not to injure the collateral

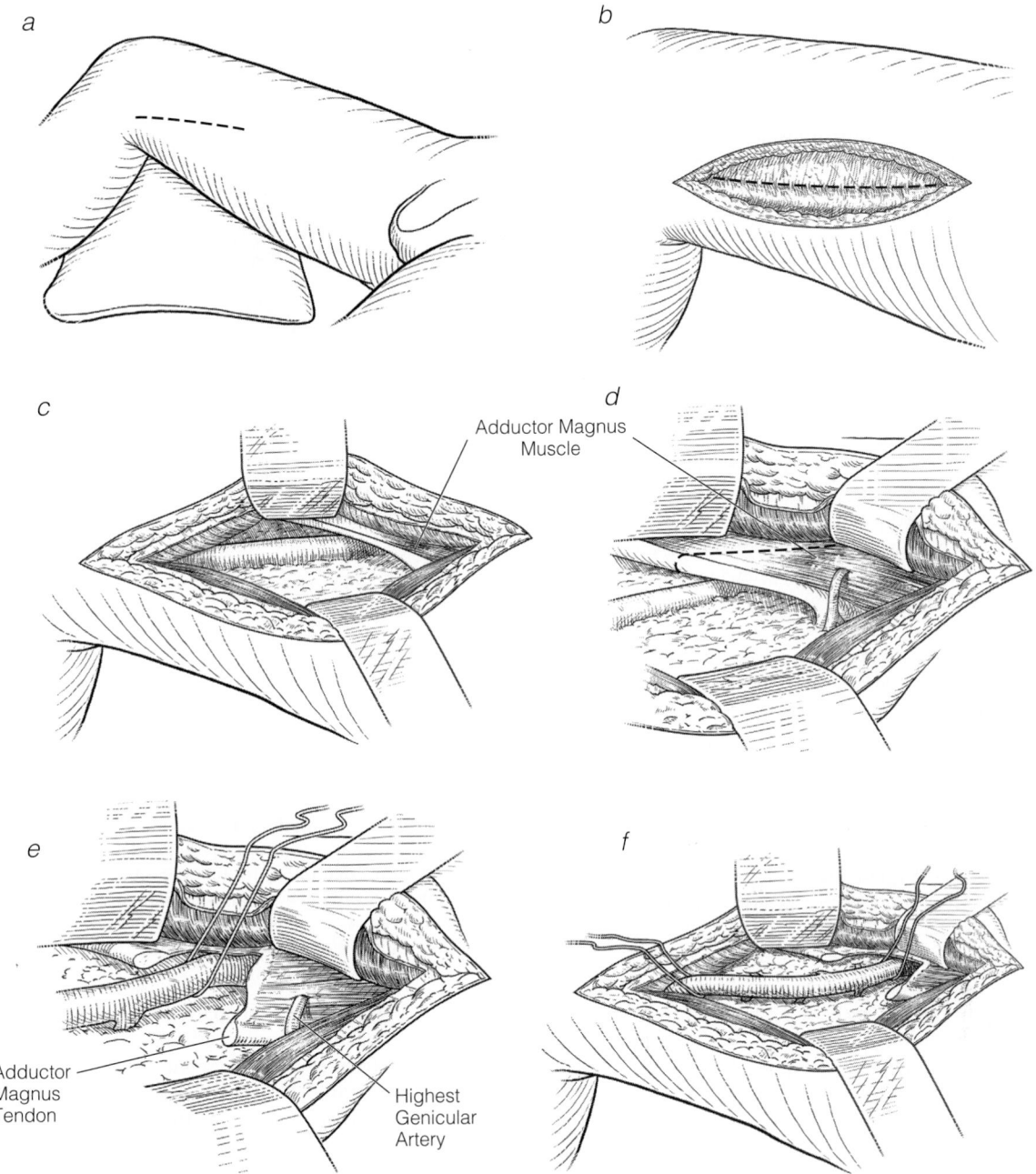

Figure 3 Femoropopliteal bypass: above knee. Depicted is medial exposure of the proximal popliteal artery. (*a*) An incision is made in the lower third of the thigh, anterior to the sartorius muscle. (*b*) The deep fascia is incised, and the sartorius muscle is retracted posteriorly, allowing the popliteal artery to be readily palpated. (*c*) The popliteal arterial sheath is opened, exposing the vessel and its surrounding venules. The adductor magnus tendon may be seen covering the proximal end of the artery (*d*), and it may have to be divided (*e*) to provide better exposure of the artery. (*f*) The popliteal artery, freed of the venous plexus, is mobilized between two vessel loops.

vessels coming off the artery at that level and the one or two branches of the satellite veins that cross the anterior portion of its initial segment. If mobilization of the deep femoral artery proves difficult, the satellite vein branches can be divided and ligated.

Step 2: exposure of proximal popliteal artery For the approach to the popliteal artery, the surgeon moves to the opposite side of the table. An incision is made in the lower third of the thigh anterior to the sartorius muscle and is extended close to the medial aspect of the knee [*see Figure 3a*]. The deep fascia anterior to the sartorius muscle is opened, and the sartorius

muscle is detached from the vastus medialis muscle and retracted posteriorly. The popliteal artery is identified by palpation; it is the most superficial structure palpable through this exposure [*see Figure 3b*]. The overlying fascia is incised, and the adipose tissue usually present at this level is dissected until the vascular bundle is reached.

The sheath of the artery is opened [*see Figure 3c*]. At this level, there is almost always a network of venules surrounding the artery, which must be carefully dissected away from the arterial wall. Division of the adductor magnus tendon may be required to yield adequate exposure of the proximal portion of the popliteal artery [*see Figures 3d and 3e*]. The venous network is separated from the arterial adventitia, and the various branches are divided and ligated. The popliteal vein is then separated from the artery—a process that, because of the intimate connection between the two vessels, is sometimes quite difficult. In separating the vein from the artery, care must be taken not to injure any of the genicular branches of the artery. The popliteal artery is freed for a length of approximately 1.5 to 2 in., and vessel loops are placed around it [*see Figure 3f*].

If the proximal popliteal artery appears markedly sclerotic and unsuitable for anastomosis to the graft, the exposure must be extended to the middle portion of the artery. To achieve this extended exposure, the hamstring muscles and their tendons are mobilized and retracted posteriorly, and the medial head of the gastrocnemius muscle is divided close to the medial condyle of the femur.

Next, the sheath of the popliteal artery is opened farther distally, and the tributaries of the veins surrounding the artery are further dissected away from it. Dissection of the middle portion of the popliteal artery may be facilitated by flexing the knee; this measure relaxes the artery, thereby allowing it to be readily drawn closer to the superficial level of the exposure.

Step 3: creation of tunnel Implantation of the graft may be started in either the popliteal artery or the femoral artery; the former is our usual preference. Before the anastomoses are constructed, a tunnel is created under the sartorius muscle by means of either a tunneler or an aortic clamp with a red rubber catheter attached to it to mark the tunnel.

Step 4: construction of distal anastomosis to popliteal artery Heparin is routinely administered before the vascular clamps are applied. A longitudinal arteriotomy is made in the anterior wall of the artery with a sharp No. 15 knife blade. This arteriotomy is then enlarged with a scalpel or a Potts angled scissors. The length of the opening in the artery should be approximately twice the diameter of the vessel. If the edges of the arteriotomy are calcified and the atheromatous intima overlaps the cut edge, the diseased intima should be excised with arteriotomy scissors.

The saphenous vein segment is then brought into the field. It is reversed so that its proximal end becomes the distal end for the anastomosis. This distal end is then enlarged with a longitudinal incision in its posterior wall, and the right-angle tips of the two sides of the divided posterior wall are cut away. Double-armed sutures are placed through the proximal angle (or heel) of the graft, with the needles going from the outside of the arteriotomy to the inside and then from the inside to the outside. Next, a similar double-armed suture is passed through the distal angle (or toe) of the graft from the outside to the inside and then from the inside to the outside through the end of the arteriotomy.

The edge of the vein is then approximated to that of the arteriotomy with a continuous suture starting at the toe of the graft and proceeding toward the heel [*see Figure 4*]. When half of the anastomosis has been completed, the edge of the vein graft is separated from the edge of the opposite side of the arteriotomy to permit inspection of the arterial lumen and the completed suture. The other half of the anastomosis is then completed by placing a second continuous suture, starting at the heel and proceeding toward the toe. Finally, the two sutures are tied together midway between the heel and the toe to complete the popliteal anastomosis.

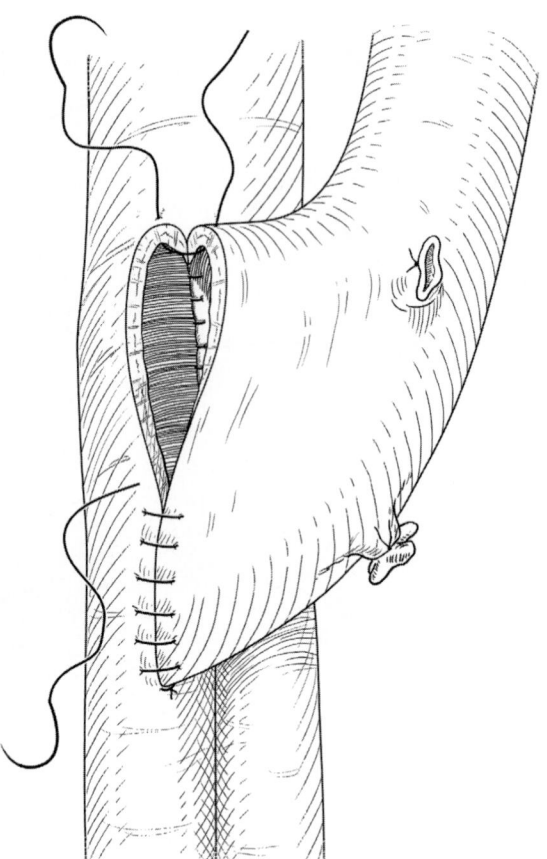

Figure 4 **Femoropopliteal bypass: above knee. Shown are details of the anastomotic suturing, which is begun at the distal end and continued to the middle portion of each side of the anastomosis of the artery and the saphenous vein graft. Equal bites of all layers of each vessel are included in each stitch, all of which are placed under direct vision.**

Step 5: placement of graft in tunnel The graft is distended by injecting heparinized saline solution into it to test for leaks either from the vein segment itself or from the anastomotic site. The graft is then marked to ensure that it does not become twisted when brought through the tunnel. The graft is brought through the tunnel either by using an aortic clamp or by attaching it to the previously placed red rubber catheter.

Step 6: construction of proximal anastomosis to femoral artery Before the proximal anastomosis is begun, the proper length of the graft should be determined to ensure that there is no redundancy. The proximal end of the graft is split and enlarged in the same fashion as the distal end, and the resulting right-angle corners are similarly trimmed. The graft is then anastomosed to the arteriotomy made in the femoral artery (which, like the popliteal arteriotomy, should be at least twice as long as the vessel is wide). The graft is attached by double-armed needles at its proximal angle and then in a similar fashion at its distal angle. The anastomosis is then completed from each end toward the center, just as the popliteal anastomosis was.

Below-the-Knee Bypass

When occlusion or marked stenosis renders the proximal and middle portions of the popliteal artery unsuitable for graft implantation, the lower portion of the vessel, which is often relatively free of atherosclerosis, may be used for the distal anastomosis instead.

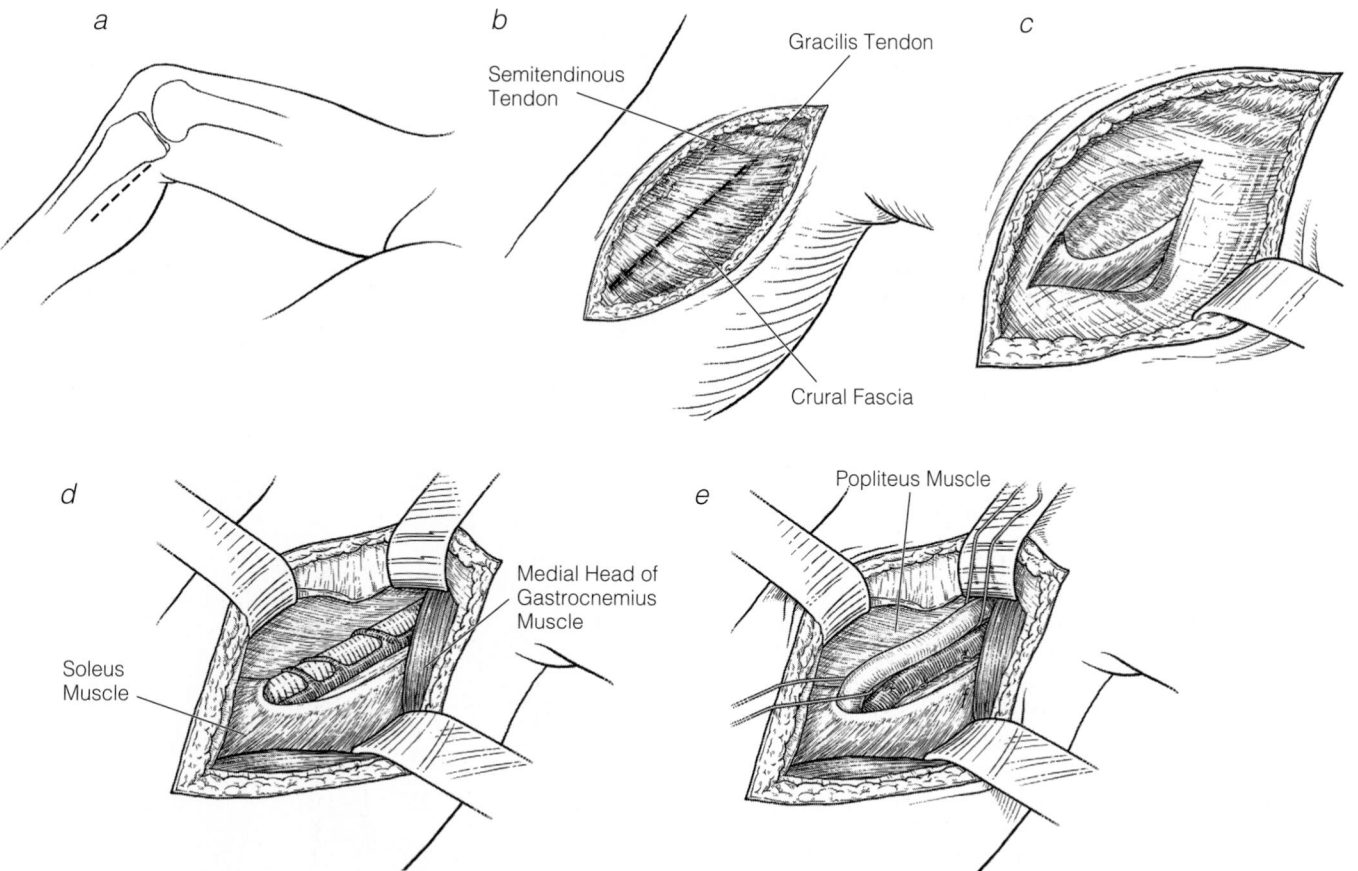

Figure 5 **Femoropopliteal bypass: below knee. Depicted is medial exposure of the distal popliteal artery.**
(*a*) An incision is made just behind the posteromedial surface of the tibia. (*b*) The crural fascia is exposed.
(*c*) The fascia is incised, exposing the vascular bundle. (*d*) The medial head of the gastrocnemius muscle is
retracted posteriorly, exposing the distal popliteal vessels and the arcade of the soleus muscle. (*e*) The distal
popliteal artery is freed and mobilized between vessel loops.

Step 1: exposure of popliteal artery With the knee moderately flexed and supported by a rolled sheet placed under it, a vertical skin incision is made just behind the posteromedial surface of the tibia [*see Figure 5a*], exposing the crural fascia [*see Figure 5b*]. Care must be taken to avoid injury to the greater saphenous vein during the skin incision. When a saphenous vein graft is to be used, the same incision can serve both for harvesting of the vein and for exposure of the artery.

The crural fascia is opened along its fibers [*see Figure 5c*], its distal attachments are separated from the semitendinosus and gracilis tendons, and the two tendons are mobilized proximally and, if necessary, divided. The medial head of the gastrocnemius muscle is retracted posteriorly [*see Figure 5d*] to expose the popliteal artery and vein and the posterior tibial nerve as these structures cross the popliteus muscle posteriorly [*see Figure 5e*].

It should be noted that (1) the distal popliteal artery has few branches below the inferior geniculate arteries, (2) atheromatous plaques are rarely present at this level, and (3) the arterial wall is often more suitable for graft implantation in this portion of the popliteal wall than it is above the knee.

Step 2: exposure of femoral artery This exposure is accomplished in essentially the same way as it would be in an above-the-knee bypass.

Step 3: creation of tunnel Tunneling for a below-the-knee femoropopliteal bypass is carried out through Hunter's canal, through the upper popliteal space, and finally through the region behind the popliteus muscle.

Steps 4 through 6 Steps 4, 5, and 6 of a below-the-knee femoropopliteal bypass—the distal anastomosis of the vein graft to the distal popliteal artery, the placement of the graft in the tunnel, and the proximal anastomosis to the femoral artery—are carried out in much the same way as the corresponding steps in an above-the-knee bypass. A completion angiogram should be obtained to confirm the adequacy of the distal anastomosis and verify the position of the graft in the tunnel [*see Figure 6*].

OUTCOME EVALUATION

Femoropopliteal bypasses performed with segments of the greater saphenous vein are associated with 4-year primary patency rates ranging from 68% to 80% and limb salvage rates ranging from 75% to 80%.[29] Femoropopliteal bypasses performed with polytetrafluoroethylene (PTFE) grafts yield comparable patency and limb salvage rates above the knee but are significantly less successful below the knee.[30]

Newer vein harvesting techniques may help improve outcome further. The use of endoscopic vein harvesting methods has been shown to reduce the incidence of wound complications associated with femoropopliteal bypass.[31] This approach allows above-the-knee bypasses to be performed through two incisions.

Infrapopliteal Bypass

Bypasses to the small arteries beyond the popliteal artery are performed only when femoropopliteal bypass is contraindicated according to accepted criteria [see Femoropopliteal Bypass, above]. Infrapopliteal bypasses are performed to the posterior tibial artery, the anterior tibial artery, or the peroneal artery, in that order of preference. As a rule, a tibial artery is used only if its lumen runs without obstruction into the foot, though bypasses to isolated tibial artery segments and other disadvantaged outflow tracts have been performed and have remained patent for more than 4 years.[2,3] Generally, the peroneal artery is used only if it is continuous with one or two of its terminal branches, which communicate with foot arteries [see Figure 7]. Neither the absence of a plantar arch nor vascular calcification is considered a contraindication to a reconstruction.[2,7] With both femoropopliteal and infrapopliteal bypasses, stenosis of less than 50% of the diameter of the vessel is acceptable at or distal to the site chosen for the distal anastomosis.

OPERATIVE TECHNIQUE

Bypasses to tibial arteries should be performed with autogenous vein grafts, and either the reversed technique (as previously described [see Femoropopliteal Bypass, above]) or the in situ technique [see In Situ Bypass, below] may be used. Placement of a tourniquet above the knee allows the distal anastomosis to be performed without extensive dissection of the tibial vessels or the application of clamps.[32] Exposure of the inflow vessel (i.e., the femoral artery or the popliteal artery) is achieved in the same way as in femoropopliteal bypass. Accordingly, bypasses to tibial and

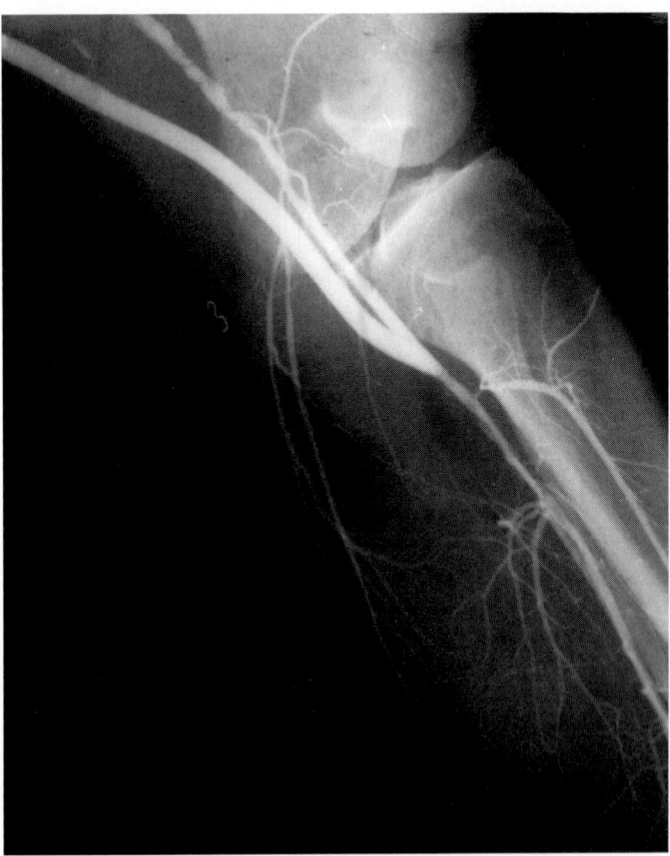

Figure 6 Femoropopliteal bypass: below knee. A completion arteriogram from a patient who underwent below-the-knee femoropopliteal bypass for a nonhealing toe amputation site shows runoff through all three tibial vessels.

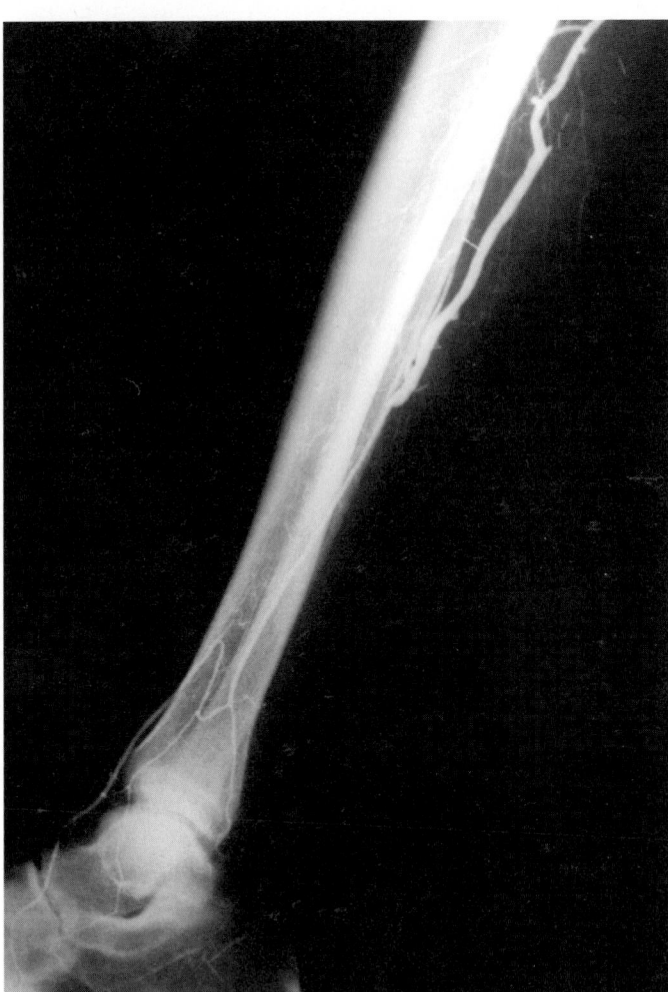

Figure 7 Infrapopliteal bypass. An arteriogram from a 65-year-old female with rest pain in the right foot who underwent in situ bypass to the middle portion of the peroneal artery shows communication of the peroneal artery with foot arteries and reconstitution of the dorsalis pedis artery.

peroneal arteries are best described in terms of the approaches required for exposure of these vessels and the tunnels required for routing the bypass conduits.

Exposure of Posterior Tibial Artery

The very proximal portion of the posterior tibial artery is aproached via a below-the-knee popliteal incision. The deep fascia is incised, and the popliteal space is entered. The gastrocnemius muscle is retracted posteriorly, and the soleus muscle is separated from the posterior surface of the tibia. The distal portion of the posterior tibial artery is approached via a medial incision along the posterior edge of the tibia [see Figure 8]; deepening this incision along the posterior tibialis muscle and the posterior surface of the tibia allows exposure of the posterior tibial artery. The tunnel from the popliteal fossa to the distal posterior tibial artery is made just below the muscle fascia, ideally with a long, gently curved clamp.

Exposure of Anterior Tibial Artery

To expose the proximal portion of the anterior tibial artery, an anterolateral incision is made in the leg midway between the tibia and the fibula over the appropriate segment of patent artery [see

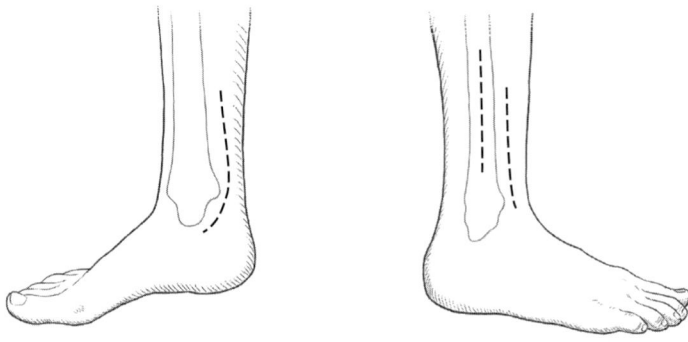

Figure 8 Infrapopliteal bypass: posterior tibial artery. Shown are incisions for bypasses to the distal regions of the leg.

Figure 9a]. Additional small medial incisions are also required for tunneling. The anterior incision is carried through the deep fascia, and the fibers of the anterior tibial muscle and the extensor digitorum longus muscle are separated to reveal the neurovascular bundle. The accompanying veins are mobilized and their branches divided to allow visualization of the anterior tibial artery, which can then be carefully mobilized [*see Figure 9b*]. With the artery mobilized, further posterior dissection can be performed, and the interosseous membrane can then be visualized and incised in a cruciate fashion.

Careful blunt finger dissection via the anterior incision and from the popliteal fossa via the medial incision facilitates creation of a tunnel without injury to the numerous veins in the area [*see*

Figure 9c]. Alternatively, the tunnel for the bypass may be placed lateral to the knee in a subcutaneous plane.

The distal anterior tibial artery is approached via an anterior incision placed midway between the tibia and the fibula [*see Figure 8*]. A tunnel is made from the distal popliteal fossa across the interosseous membrane (like the tunnel to the peroneal artery) and beneath the deep fascia to a point 5 to 7 cm above the lateral malleolus. Once the distal anastomosis is complete and the graft has been drawn through the tunnel, any tendons that may be distorting or compressing the graft in its course around the tibia are divided; this measure proves necessary in most low anterior tibial bypasses.

Exposure of Peroneal Artery

The peroneal artery is usually approached via the same incision as the posterior tibial artery [*see* Exposure of the Posterior Tibial Artery, *above*]. The artery is located and isolated just medial to the medial edge of the fibula. In its distal third, however, and in patients with stout calves and ankles, the peroneal artery should be approached via a lateral incision [*see Figure 8*], followed by excision of the fibula.

For lateral exposure of the peroneal artery, a long segment of fibula is freed from its muscle attachments with a combination of blunt and sharp dissection; particular care should be taken in dissecting along the medial edge of the bone because the peroneal vessels run just below this edge and are easily injured by instruments. Next, a finger is passed around the fibula [*see Figure 10a*]; once this is done, the free edge of bone is further developed by

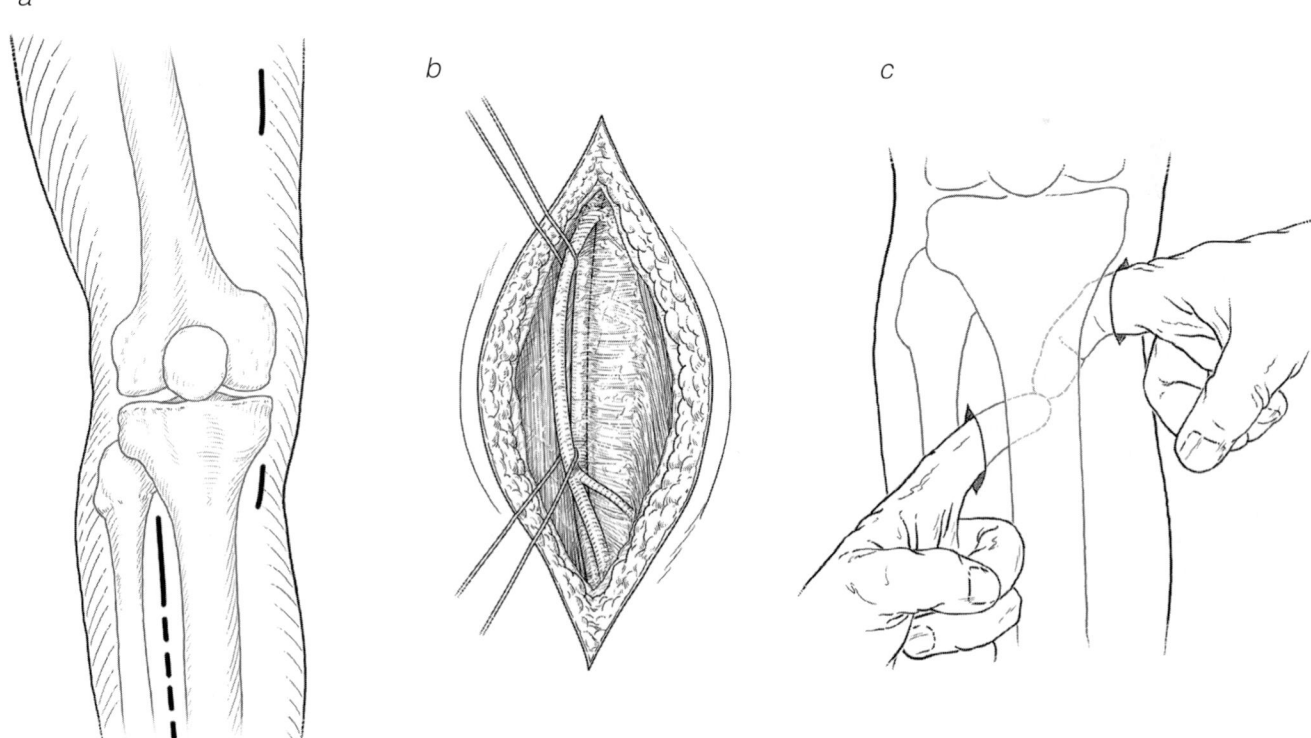

Figure 9 Infrapopliteal bypass: anterior tibial artery. (*a*) **An anterolateral incision is made midway between the tibia and the fibula over the artery; small medial incisions are also made for tunneling. (*b*) The anterior incision is carried through the deep fascia, the anterior tibial and extensor digitorum longus muscles are separated, the accompanying veins are mobilized and divided, and the anterior tibial artery is mobilized. (*c*) A tunnel is created with careful blunt finger dissection.**

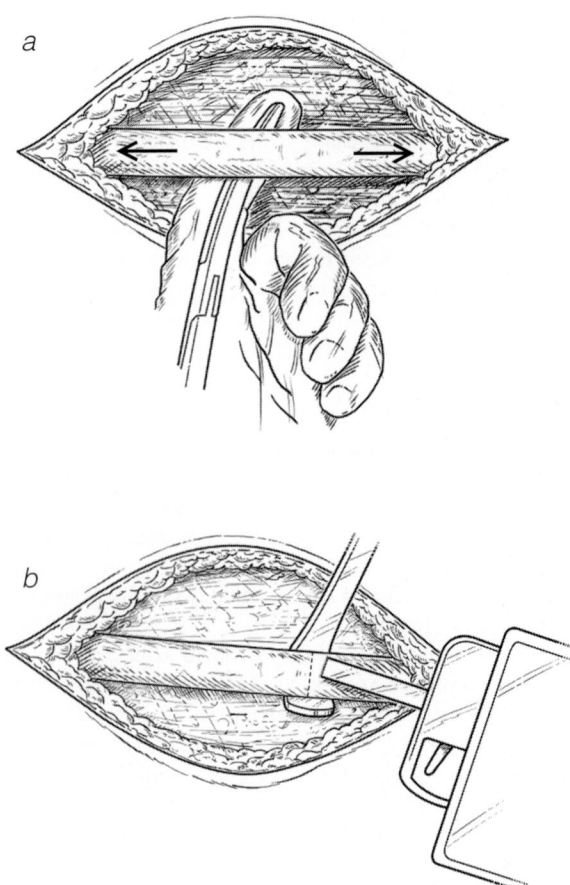

Figure 10 **Infrapopliteal bypass: lateral exposure of peroneal artery. Lateral exposure of the peroneal artery typically requires excision of part of the fibula; this is done by (*a*) passing a finger behind the fibula, developing the free bone edge further with a right-angle clamp, (*b*) passing a right-angle retractor behind the fibula, and dividing the bone with a power saw.**

forcefully pushing a right-angle clamp inferiorly and superiorly [*see Figure 10b*]. A right-angle retractor is passed behind the bone, and the fibula is divided with a power saw. The peroneal artery can then be dissected free from surrounding veins and used in the construction of the distal anastomosis.

Gentle blunt finger dissection is required to develop a tunnel from this lateral wound to the distal popliteal fossa, and great care should be taken to avoid injury to the numerous veins in the area. Because the peroneal artery is the least accessible of the three leg arteries used for infrapopliteal bypasses and normally has the poorest connections with the arteries of the foot, we recommend that it be used as a distal implantation site only when the anterior and posterior tibial arteries are not suitable.

Exposure of Dorsalis Pedis Artery

When no more proximal procedure is possible, a bypass to the ankle region or the foot may be performed. The dorsalis pedis artery is easily approached via a lateral incision on the dorsum of the foot [*see Figure 11a*]. The incision is curved slightly and a flap raised so that the incision will not be directly over the anastomosis [*see Figure 11b*]. If the artery must be approached at the ankle, the extensor retinaculum must be divided. Otherwise, the operation is performed in much the same fashion as a distal anterior tibial bypass [*see Figure 12*]. The posterior tibial artery can be

approached down to a point several centimeters below the medial malleolus.

In Situ Bypass

In situ bypass is an acceptable alternative to reversed vein bypass. Minimally invasive techniques have been developed to reduce the wound complications encountered when in situ bypass is performed with long incisions.

With the help of a side-branch coil occlusion system, in situ bypass can be performed through the two arterial access incisions. The angioscopic coil device is passed through the proximal greater saphenous vein, and the coils are placed into the side branches under angioscopic guidance [*see Figure 13*]. As the device is advanced more distally through the vein, the valves are lysed with a flexible valvulotome.

Another approach to side-branch occlusion involves the use of an endoscopic vein harvesting system. Three skin incisions are made: two incisions for arterial access and one 2 cm incision above the knee for insertion of an endoscopic device to locate and clip the side branches of the saphenous vein. Once the proximal anastomosis is complete, the valves are lysed with a flexible valvulotome passed through the distal end of the vein. Completion cineangiography is then performed to confirm side-branch occlusion and to assess the entire reconstruction.[33]

OUTCOME EVALUATION

Infrapopliteal bypasses should have 5-year primary patency rates ranging from 60% to 67% and limb salvage rates ranging from 70% to 75% whether they are done with the reversed-vein technique or with the in situ technique.[34,35] For all such grafts, close patient follow-up and graft surveillance improve secondary

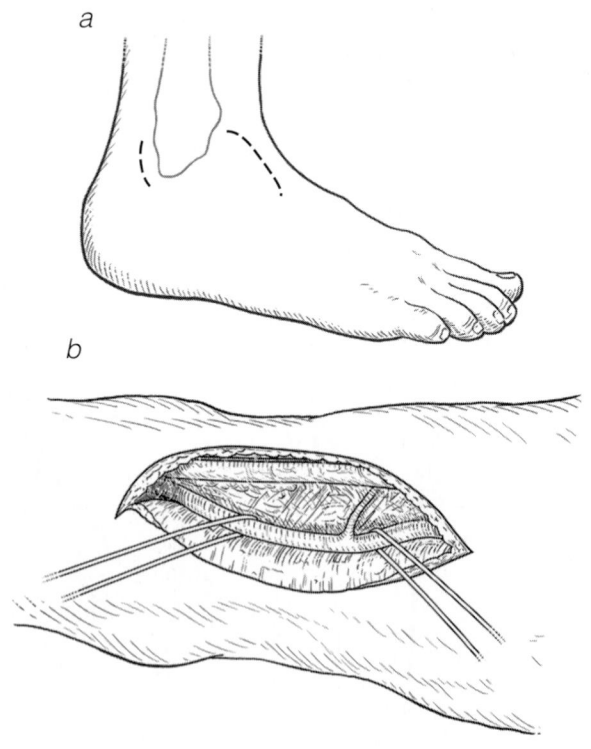

Figure 11 **Infrapopliteal bypass: dorsalis pedis artery. (*a*) The dorsalis pedis artery is approached via an incision on the dorsum of the foot. (*b*) The incision is curved and a flap raised so that the incision is not directly over the anastomosis.**

patency rates. Reduced complications and decreased length of stay have been reported for patients undergoing distal in situ bypasses using either the endoscopic or the coil occulsion approach.[36,37]

Plantar Bypass

Extension of the standard approaches to limb salvage has led to the performance of bypasses to vessels below the ankle joint [see Figures 14 and 15]. Such bypasses are indicated when the more proximal tibial vessels are occluded, which frequently occurs secondary to failure of a more proximal bypass. The technique required for performing bypasses to secondary branches in the foot is essentially the same as that required for performing bypasses to major infrapopliteal vessels.

Optimal illumination by means of head lamps is important for achieving technical success with plantar bypass, and loupe magnification is helpful when the vessel is less than 1.5 mm in diameter. In addition, visualization of perimalleolar and inframalleolar arteries requires excellent preoperative imaging studies.

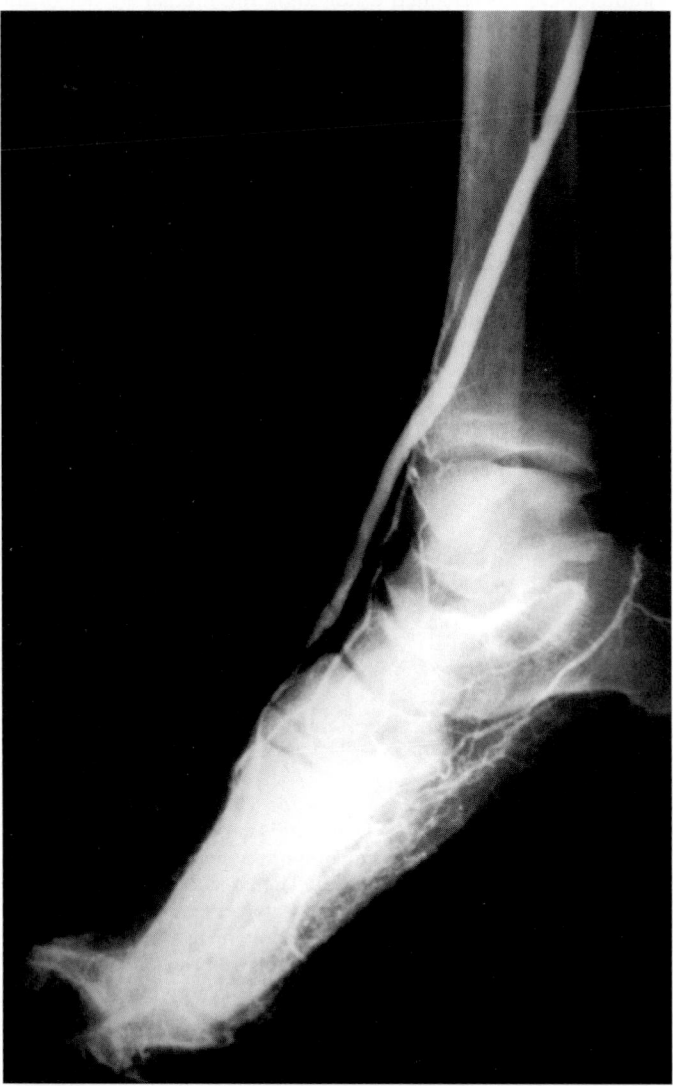

Figure 12 Infrapopliteal bypass: dorsalis pedis artery. Shown is an arteriogram from a 72-year-old diabetic patient who underwent a popliteal artery–dorsalis pedis artery bypass with a reversed saphenous vein graft for a nonhealing great toe amputation.

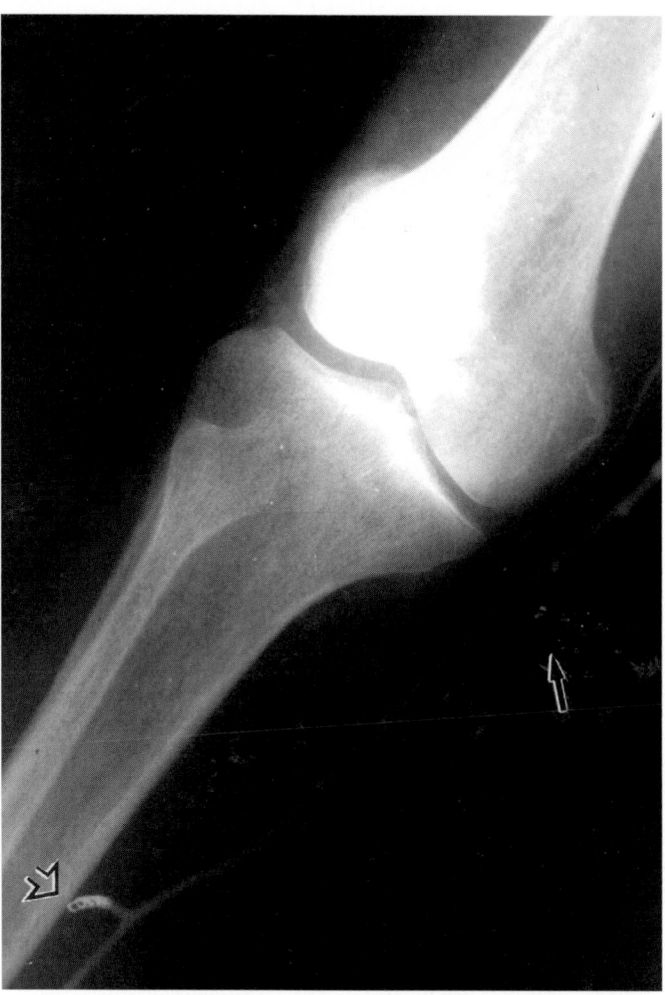

Figure 13 Infrapopliteal bypass: in situ technique. A completion arteriogram from a patient who underwent an in situ bypass with coil occlusion of the side branches shows the two coils (arrows), which have successfully occluded the side-branch veins.

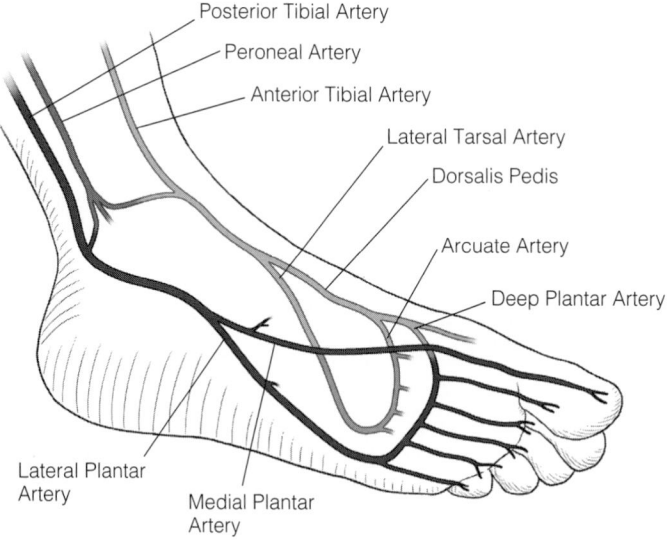

Figure 14 Plantar bypass. Shown are the major arteries of the foot, including the two major branches of the posterior tibial artery.[3] The lateral plantar artery is usually the larger and ends in the deep plantar arch.

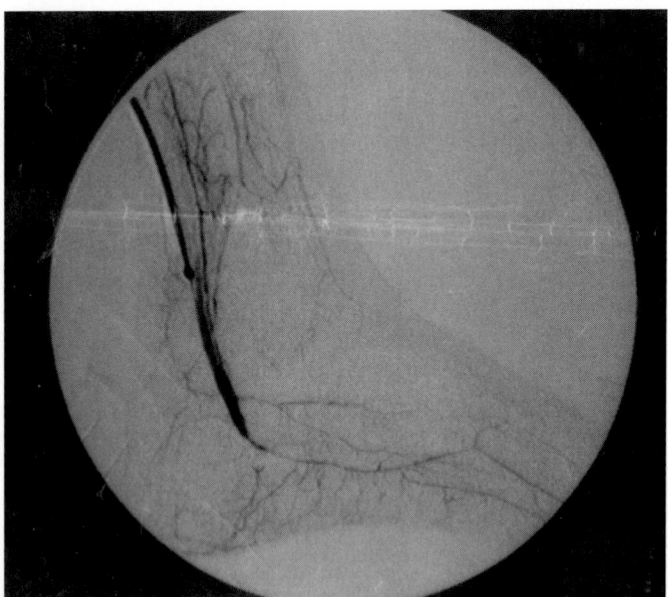

Figure 15 **Plantar bypass. A completion arteriogram from a 62-year-old diabetic with nonhealing toe ulcers who underwent a popliteal artery–medial plantar artery bypass with a reversed saphenous vein graft shows the distal anastomosis, with flow visible through a small but patent medial plantar artery.**

These very distal bypasses offer a viable alternative to a major amputation. Like infrapopliteal bypasses, they are best described in terms of the anatomic approaches to the distal branch vessels. In what follows, we outline exposure of the plantar and tarsal arteries; exposure of the dorsalis pedis artery is outlined elsewhere [*see* Infrapopliteal Bypass, *above*].

OPERATIVE TECHNIQUE

Exposure of Lateral and Medial Plantar Arteries

The lateral and medial plantar branches are the continuation of the posterior tibial artery in the foot [*see* Figure 16]. The lat-

eral plantar artery forms the deep plantar arch and is larger than the medial plantar artery. If the lateral branch is occluded, the medial branch may enlarge and feed the plantar arch through collateral vessels.

The initial incision is made over the termination of the posterior tibial artery below the malleolus. The artery is isolated, and the incision is extended inferiorly and laterally onto the sole. A direct approach to the individual branches is difficult, for several reasons. First, because the skin of the sole is not easily retracted, adequate exposure of the lateral and medial plantar arteries is hard to obtain if the incision does not follow their course exactly. Second, because these arteries are small in diameter and lie deep within the foot, they can be quite difficult to locate. Third, it is sometimes hard to distinguish the lateral plantar artery from the medial plantar artery. Dissection of the termination of the posterior tibial artery can help the surgeon make this distinction. The lateral branch is usually located inferiorly when the foot is externally rotated on the operating table.

Exposure of the proximal 2 to 3 cm of the plantar branches is accomplished by incising the flexor retinaculum and the adductor muscle of the great toe. More distal exposure of these branches can be obtained by dividing the medial border of the plantar aponeurosis and the extensor digitorum brevis muscle.

Exposure of Deep Plantar Artery and Lateral Tarsal Artery

The deep plantar artery and the lateral tarsal artery are branches of the dorsalis pedis artery. The deep plantar artery originates at the metatarsal level, where it descends into a foramen bounded proximally by the dorsal metatarsal ligament, distally by the dorsal interosseous muscle ring, and medially and laterally by the bases of the first and second metatarsal bones. As the deep plantar artery exits from this tunnel, it connects with the lateral plantar artery to form the deep plantar arch [*see* Figure 17].

A slightly curved longitudinal 3 to 4 cm incision is made over the dorsum of the middle portion of the foot, and the dorsalis pedis artery is dissected distally down to its bifurcation into the deep plantar and first dorsal metatarsal branches. The extensor hallucis brevis muscle is retracted laterally—or, if necessary,

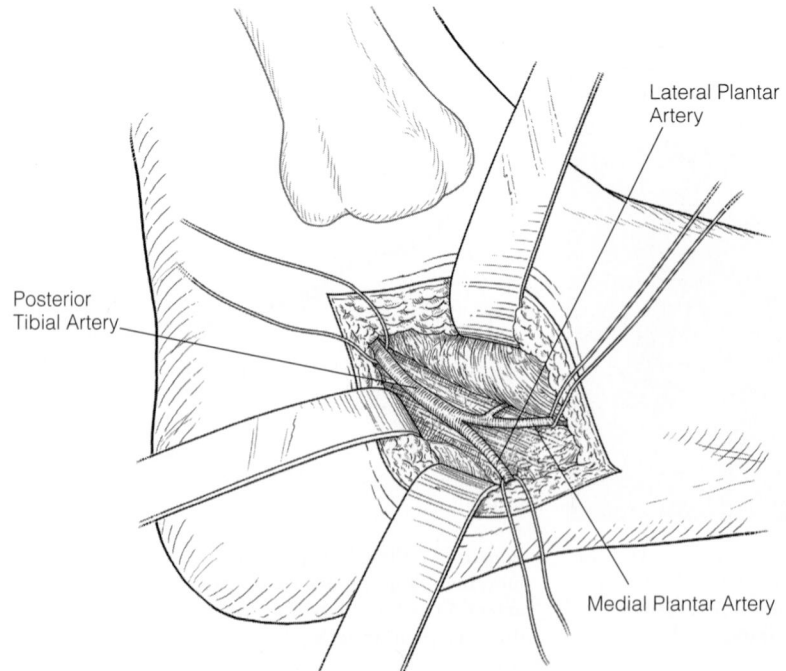

Lateral Plantar Artery

Posterior Tibial Artery

Medial Plantar Artery

Figure 16 **Plantar bypass. Depicted is exposure of the distal portion of the posterior tibial artery. The lateral and medial plantar arteries branch from this vessel and lie beneath the flexor retinaculum and the abductor hallucis muscle, which can be incised.**

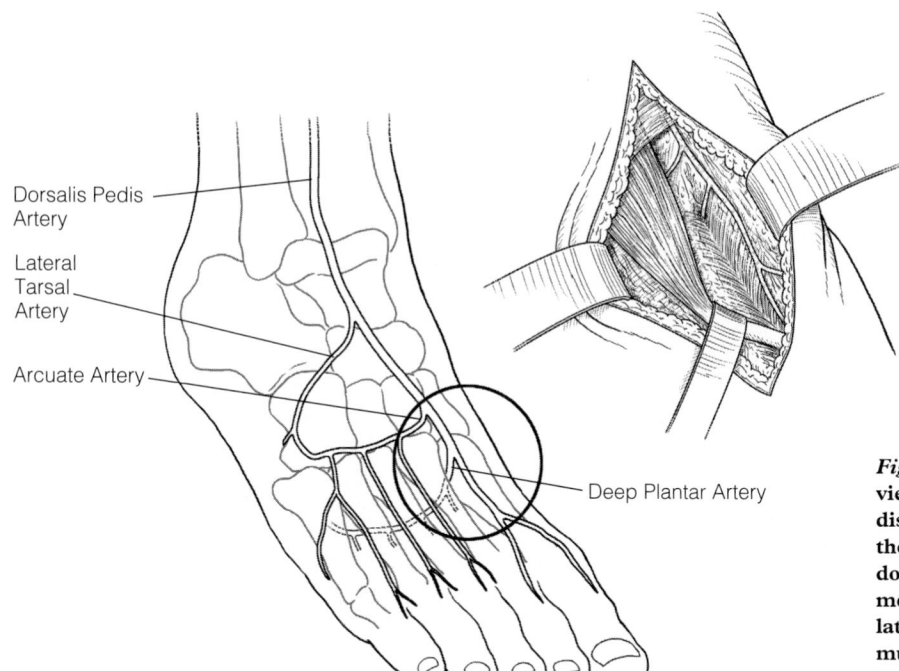

Dorsalis Pedis
Artery

Lateral
Tarsal
Artery

Arcuate Artery

Deep Plantar Artery

Figure 17 **Plantar bypass. Shown is a dorsal view of the arteries of the foot. Exposure of the distal dorsalis pedis artery (insert) highlights the origin of the deep plantar artery and its downward course between the first and second metatarsal bones. This exposure is facilitated by lateral retraction of the extensor hallucis brevis muscle.**

transected—and the dorsal interosseous muscle ring is split to allow better exposure of the proximal portion of the deep plantar artery. The periosteum of the proximal portion of the second metatarsal bone is then incised and elevated. A fine-tipped rongeur is used to excise enough of the metatarsal shaft to permit ample exposure of the deep plantar artery.

OUTCOME EVALUATION

Bypasses to the dorsalis pedis artery and its branches have yielded results comparable to those of bypasses to more proximal tibial vessels, with 3-year primary patency rates ranging from 58% to 60% and limb salvage rates ranging from 75% to 95%.[38-40] In one review, patency rates were higher in patients who had an intact plantar arch than in those who did not; however, failure to visualize the plantar arch on preoperative arteriograms does not preclude the performance of these bypasses for limb salvage. With careful follow-up, the assisted primary patency rates for these grafts have been substantially improved.[41] The available reports emphasize the need to repair failing grafts because their secondary patency was much better than that of failed grafts. In one study, patients who required shorter bypasses or had lower preoperative C-reactive protein levels experienced significantly better outcomes.[42] In some patients, occlusion of the distal tibial vessel necessitates performance of a tibiotibial bypass to achieve wound healing.[7]

Bypasses to plantar or tarsal vessels performed with vein grafts yield 2-year patency rates ranging from 65% to 75% and limb salvage rates higher than 80%.[4,5] In one report, the primary patency rate for these grafts was 74% at 1 year and 67% at 2 years, and the limb salvage rate was 78% at 2 years.[3]

Alternative Bypasses Using More Distal Inflow Vessels

Traditionally, the femoral artery has been the inflow site of choice for infrainguinal bypasses. Since the early 1980s, the superficial femoral, deep femoral, popliteal, and tibial arteries have all been used as inflow sources when these vessels were relatively disease free or when the amount of autologous vein available was limited. Currently, the superficial femoral artery and the popliteal artery are preferentially used for primary bypasses when they are free of disease.

The strategy of utilizing more distal inflow sources is particularly applicable to inframalleolar bypasses, in which very long vein segments would be required to reach the dorsalis pedis or other pedal arteries from the usual more proximal inflow sites. Two studies from the latter half of the 1980s reported that the patency rates in bypasses originating from the superficial femoral and popliteal arteries were comparable to those in bypasses originating from the common femoral artery.[43,44] In a review of our own experience with popliteal-distal vein graft bypasses,[5] we reported a patency rate of 65% at 4 years—a figure comparable to rates reported for femorodistal bypasses with reversed or in situ vein grafts (67% and 69%, respectively).[34] Given these results, surgeons should not hesitate to employ either the popliteal artery or the superficial femoral artery as an inflow source. Use of these more distal inflow sites results in shorter grafts and allows portions of saphenous vein to be preserved for other purposes.

An increasing number of limb salvage procedures are secondary interventions. These secondary procedures are generally more difficult to perform because the access routes to the arteries have been previously dissected and because there frequently is little good autologous vein left. In some cases, patients present with gangrene developing below a functioning bypass or after a previous failed bypass. Some of these patients need nothing more than a short distal extension of their functioning bypass; others have only enough vein left to make up a short graft. For such patients, a tibiotibial bypass may be an effective alternative revascularization approach.

In 1994, our group reported our 11-year experience with tibiotibial bypasses, comprising 42 procedures in 41 patients.[7] Ten of these bypasses were performed because previous bypasses failed; the remainder were performed because the amount of autologous vein available was limited. Approximately 50% of the bypasses were to pedal or tarsal vessels. At 5 years, the patency rate for these grafts was 65%, and the limb salvage rate was 73%.[7] A subsequent study reported comparable results.[45]

References

1. Veith FJ, Gupta SK, Wengerter KR, et al: Changing arteriosclerotic disease patterns and management strategies in lower-limb–threatening ischemia. Ann Surg 212:402, 1990

2. Veith FJ, Gupta SK, Samson RH, et al: Progress in limb salvage by reconstructive arterial surgery combined with new or improved adjunctive procedures. Ann Surg 194:386, 1981

3. Ascer E, Veith FJV, Gupta SK: Bypasses to plantar arteries and other tibial branches: an extended approach to limb salvage. J Vasc Surg 8:434, 1988

4. Andros G: Bypass grafts to the ankle and foot: a personal perspective. Surg Clin North Am 75:715, 1995

5. Wengerter KR, Yang PM, Veith FJ, et al: A twelve-year experience with the popliteal-to-distal artery bypass: the significance and management of proximal disease. J Vasc Surg 15:143, 1992

6. Veith FJ, Gupta SK, Samson RH, et al: Superficial femoral and popliteal arteries as inflow site for distal bypasses. Surgery 90:980, 1981

7. Lyon RT, Veith FJ, Marsan BU, et al: Eleven-year experience with tibiotibal bypass: an unusual but effective solution to distal tibial artery occlusive disease and limited autologous vein. J Vasc Surg 17:1128, 1994

8. Baker JD, Dix D: Variability of Doppler ankle pressures with arterial occlusive disease: an evaluation of ankle index and brachial-ankle pressure gradient. Surgery 79:134, 1976

9. Kohler TR, Nance DR, Cramer MM, et al: Duplex scanning for diagnosis of aortoiliac and femoropopliteal disease—a prospective study. Circulation 76:1074, 1987

10. Langsfeld M, Nupute J, Hershey FB, et al: The use of deep duplex scanning to predict hemodynamically significant aortoiliac stenosis. J Vasc Surg 7:395, 1988

11. Moneta GL, Yeager RA, Antonovic R, et al: Accuracy of lower extremity arterial duplex mapping. J Vasc Surg 15:275, 1992

12. Legemate DA, Teeuwen C, Hoenveld H, et al: Value of duplex scanning compared with angiography and pressure measurement in the assessment of aortoiliac lesions. Br J Surg 78:1003, 1991

13. Ascer E, Mazzariol F, Hingorani A, et al: The use of duplex ultrasound arterial mapping as an alternative to conventional arteriography for primary and secondary infrapopliteal bypasses. Am J Surg 178:162, 1999

14. Wain RA, Berdejo GL, Delvalle WN, et al: Can duplex scan arterial mapping replace contrast arteriography as the test of choice before infrainguinal revascularization? J Vasc Surg 29:100, 1999

15. Owens RS, Carpenter JP, Baum RA, et al: Magnetic resonance imaging of angiographically occult runoff vessels in peripheral arterial occlusive disease. N Engl J Med 326:1577, 1992

16. Carpenter JP, Owen RS, Baum RA, et al: Magnetic resonance angiography of peripheral runoff vessels. J Vasc Surg 16:807, 1992

17. Earls JP, Patel NH, Smith PA, et al: Gadolinium-enhanced three-dimensional MR angiography of the aorta and peripheral arteries: evaluation of a multistation examination using two gadopentetate dimeglumine infusions. AJR Am J Roentgenol 171:599, 1998

18. Fellner F, Janka R, Fellner C, et al: Post occlusion visualization of peripheral arteries with "floating table" MR angiography. Magn Reson Imaging 17:1235, 1999

19. Fenlon HM, Yucel EK: Advances in abdominal, aortic, and peripheral contrast-enhanced MR angiography. Magn Reson Imaging Clin North Am 7:319, 1999

20. Brewster DC, Waltman AC, O'Hara PJ, et al: Femoral artery pressure measurement during aortography. Circulation 60:120, 1979

21. Hessel SJ, Adams DF, Abrams HL: Complications of angiography. Radiology 138:273, 1981

22. Gomes AS, Baker JD, Martin-Paredero V, et al: Acute renal dysfunction after major arteriography. AJR Am J Roentgenol 145:1249, 1985

23. Martin-Paredero V, Dixon SM, Baker JD, et al: Risk of renal failure after major angiography. Arch Surg 118:1417, 1983

24. Nikonoff T, Skau T, Berglund J, et al: Effects of femoral arteriography and low osmolar contrast agents on renal function. Acta Radiol 34:88, 1993

25. Katholi RE, Taylor GJ, Woods WT, et al: Nephrotoxicity of nonionic low-osmolality versus ionic high osmolality contrast media: a prospective double-blind randomized comparison in human beings. Radiology 186:183, 1993

26. Lautin EM, Freeman NJ, Schoenfeld AH, et al: Radiocontrast-associated renal dysfunction: a comparison of lower-osmolality and conventional high-osmolality contrast media. AJR Am J Roentgenol 157:59, 1991

27. Kram HB, Gupta SK, Veith FJ, et al: Late results of two hundred seventeen femoropopliteal bypasses to isolated popliteal artery segments. J Vasc Surg 14:386, 1991

28. Veith FJ, Gupta SK, Daly V: Femoropopliteal bypass to the isolated popliteal segment: is polytetrafluoroethylene graft acceptable? Surgery 89:296, 1981

29. Taylor LM, Edwards JM, Porter JM: Present status of reversed vein bypass grafting: five-year results of a modern series. J Vasc Surg 11:193, 1990

30. Veith FJ, Gupta SK, Ascer E, et al: Six year prospective multicenter randomized comparison of autologous saphenous vein and expanded polytetrafluoroethylene grafts in infrainguinal arterial reconstructions. J Vasc Surg 3:104, 1986

31. Jordan WD, Voellinger DC, Schroeder PT, et al: Video-assisted saphenous vein harvest: the evaluation of a new technique. J Vasc Surg 26:405, 1997

32. Wagner WH, Treiman RL, Cossman DV, et al: Tourniquet occlusion technique for tibial artery reconstruction. J Vasc Surg 18:637, 1993

33. Suggs WD, Sanchez LA, Woo D, et al: Endoscopically assisted in situ lower extremity bypass: a preliminary report of a new minimally invasive technique. J Vasc Surg 34:668, 2001

34. Bergamini TM, Towne JB, Bandyk DF, et al: Experience with in situ saphenous vein bypasses during 1981 to 1989: determinant factors of long-term patency. J Vasc Surg 13:137, 1991

35. Wengerter KR, Veith FJ, Gupta SK, et al: Prospective randomized multi center comparison of in situ and reversed vein infrapopliteal bypasses. J Vasc Surg 13:189, 1991

36. Rosenthal D, Arous EJ, Friedman SG, et al: Endovascular-assisted versus conventional in situ saphenous vein bypass grafting: cumulative patency, limb salvage, and cost results in a 39-month multi center study. J Vasc Surg 21:60, 2000

37. Piano G, Schwartz LB, Foster L, et al: Assessing outcomes, costs, and benefits of emerging technology for minimally invasive saphenous vein in situ distal arterial bypasses. Arch Surg 133:613, 1998

38. Schneider JR, Walsh DB, McDaniel MD, et al: Pedal bypass versus tibial bypass with autogenous vein: a comparison of outcome and hemodynamic results. J Vasc Surg 17:1029, 1993

39. Harrington EB, Harrington ME, Schanzer H, et al: The dorsalis pedis bypass: moderate success in difficult situations. J Vasc Surg 15:409, 1992

40. Panayiotopoulos YP, Tyrrell MR, Arnold FJ, et al: Results and cost analysis of distal [crural/pedal] arterial revascularization for limb salvage in diabetic and nondiabetic patients. Diabet Med 14:214, 1997

41. Rhodes JM, Gloviczki P, Bower TC, et al: The benefits of secondary interventions in patients with failing or failed pedal bypass grafts. Am J Surg 178:151, 1999

42. Biancari F, Alback A, Kantonen I, et al: Predictive factors for adverse outcome of pedal bypasses. Eur J Vasc Endovasc Surg 18:138, 1999

43. Cantelmo NL, Snow JR, Menzoian JO, et al: Successful vein bypass in patients with an ischemic limb and a palpable popliteal pulse. Arch Surg 121:217, 1986

44. Rosenbloom JS, Walsh JJ, Schuler JJ, et al: Long-term results of infragenicular bypasses with autogenous vein originating from the distal superficial femoral and popliteal arteries. J Vasc Surg 7:691, 1988

45. Plecha EJ, Lee C, Hye RJ: Factors influencing the outcome of paramalleolar bypass grafts. Ann Vasc Surg 10:356, 1996

Acknowledgment

Figures 1 through 17   Tom Moore.

John F. Golan, M.D., F.A.C.S., Donald M. Glenn, P.A.-C., John J. Bergan, M.D., F.A.C.S., and Luigi Pascarella, M.D.

Varicose veins are a common problem, accounting for approximately 85% of the venous conditions treated. Over the past decade, management options for varicose veins and venous insufficiency of the lower extremity have become more diverse. Operative vein stripping is rapidly being replaced with a variety of endovenous techniques, ranging from laser vein obliteration to radiofrequency (RF) closure to foam sclerotherapy. Conventional surgical stripping has a poor image with the public, being associated with large unsightly incisions, severe postoperative pain, and a significant risk of recurrence. Current evidence indicates that patients experience less pain and return to work more quickly after endovenous treatment of varicosities than after surgical vein stripping.[1] In addition, the elimination of the word stripping from the technical description has facilitated the public's growing preference for endovenous therapy over conventional surgical therapy (even though the basic therapeutic principles are essentially similar for the two approaches).

As a consequence of the minimally invasive nature of endovenous therapy, treatment of vein disease is moving from the hospital to the office. This shift has allowed a diverse group of physicians (e.g., dermatologists, gynecologists, and cardiologists) to enter a field that previously had been left to surgeons. Accordingly, to remain up to date with respect to the treatment of vein disease, it is essential for surgeons to acquire the knowledge and skills required to use the new endovenous techniques. In this chapter, we review the procedures, results, and complications associated with endovenous therapy, as well as traditional surgical techniques.

Terminology

All physicians treating lower-extremity venous disease should be familiar with the current names for the veins of the thigh and leg, as specified in the 2001 revision of the official terminologia anatomica by the International Interdisciplinary Consensus Committee on Venous Anatomical Terminology.[2] Failure to employ current standardized terminology can hinder data exchange in translated research studies. In addition, retention of the traditional nomenclature can result in potentially dangerous clinical scenarios. For instance, ultrasonographically diagnosed thrombosis of the superficial femoral vein might, because of the term used for the vein, be erroneously interpreted as superficial thrombophlebitis instead of true deep vein thrombosis (DVT). To prevent these and other errors, a more accurate delineation of the branches of the common femoral vein is required. Thus, the terms femoral vein (instead of superficial femoral vein) and deep femoral vein (instead of profunda femoris) are now employed.

Of particular significance for the purposes of this chapter is that the greater (long) saphenous vein is now referred to as the great saphenous vein (GSV), and the lesser (short) saphenous vein is now referred to as the small saphenous vein (SSV). In addition, the terms saphenofemoral junction and saphenopopliteal junction have been accepted into the official nomenclature—a change that is especially relevant to endovenous treatment of varicose veins. Various other changes in the names of lower-extremity and pelvic veins were also

recommended in the Committee's consensus statement; however, these changes have little bearing on the current discussion and thus are not addressed further here.

Indications for Varicose Vein Surgery

The indications for surgical treatment of varicose veins are well established [*see Table 1*]. Although many physicians believe that varicose veins are nothing more than a cosmetic nuisance, this is in fact true only for some men. Women, for the most part, have specific symptoms (e.g., aching, burning pain, and heaviness) that are related to their varicose veins and are exacerbated by the presence of progesterone. Such symptoms develop with prolonged standing or sitting and reach maximal levels on the first day of the menstrual period, when progesterone levels are at their peak. Men, lacking progesterone, have few such symptoms until the varicose veins progress with aging to the point where they press on somatic nerves. In general, the severity of the symptoms bears no relation to the size of the vessels being treated. Telangiectasias can produce symptoms identical to those of varicose veins, and such symptoms can be relieved by simple sclerotherapy.

Longitudinal studies have shown that large varicose veins can produce venous ulcerations within 15 years. Given that the incidence of venous ulceration is 20% in patients who are first seen with large varicose veins, large varicosities constitute an indication for surgery. Various skin changes characteristic of chronic venous insufficiency precede the development of venous ulceration.

Varicose thrombophlebitis is followed by recurrent varicose thrombophlebitis in nearly every case, at intervals ranging from a few weeks to many months. Nevertheless, superficial thrombophlebitis, which can be quite disabling, can be prevented by removing varicose vein clusters.

It is true that for many women, the undesirable appearance of varicose veins is a major reason for seeking surgical treatment. When questioned, however, such patients often admit to having symptoms such as pain, heaviness, and fatigue. Typically, they do not relate these symptoms to the varices themselves but instead attribute them to prolonged standing during daily work.

Table 1 Indications for Varicose Vein Surgery

Pain: leg aching, leg heaviness
Patchy burning (venous neuropathy)
Swelling: foot, ankle, leg
Dermatitis: focal, extensive
Lipodermatosclerosis
Ulceration: present or healed
Superficial thrombophlebitis
External hemorrhage
Appearance

Preoperative Evaluation

DUPLEX MAPPING

Over the years, surgical treatises have devoted a great deal of space to clinical examination of the patient with varicose veins. Numerous clinical tests have been described, many of which carry the names of famous persons interested in venous pathophysiology. This august history notwithstanding, the Trendelenburg test, the Schwartz test, the Perthes test, and the Mahorner and Ochsner modifications of the Trendelenburg test are, for the most part, useless in preoperative evaluation of patients today.[3] There is no doubt that clinical evaluation can be improved by using handheld Doppler devices. In our view, however, preoperative evaluation is best performed by combining duplex scanning with physical examination.[4] Duplex mapping defines individual patient anatomy with considerable precision and provides valuable information that supplements the physician's clinical impression. This information allows the physician to develop a strategy that will treat abnormal refluxing veins while leaving normal portions of the venous system in place, thereby minimizing operative trauma and reducing long-term recurrence.

A protocol for duplex mapping of incompetent superficial veins has been published.[4] In essence, the examination consists of interrogating specific points of reflux with the patient standing [*see Table 2*]. Forward flow is produced with muscular compression, and reverse flow is then assessed in the crucial areas that are important to subsequent procedural planning.

The patient is placed in an upright position so that the leg veins are maximally dilated. No clothing is worn on the lower extremities from the waist down, except for nonconstricting underwear. The patient is instructed to inform the sonographer of any sensation of light-headedness, faintness, dizziness, or nausea. These symptoms seem to be associated with the overall atmosphere of the room and the presence of Doppler velocity signals; they appear to be less likely to occur when the examination itself is performed silently. If a tendency to fainting because of vagovagal reflux is encountered, the examination may have to be modified so that the patient is in a semiupright position instead.

Examination should include both lower extremities, though post-treatment examinations may target a single extremity or a single area of an extremity. The full length of the axial venous system from ankle to groin is examined. The probe is aligned transversely so that specific named veins can be identified and their relations to other limb structures determined. The veins are scanned by moving the probe up and down along their courses. Double segments, sites of tributary confluence, and large perforating veins (along with their deep venous connections) are identified. (Perforating veins are those that course from the subcutaneous tissue through deep fascia to anastomose with one of the named deep venous structures; communicating veins are those that anastomose with one another within a single anatomic plane.) Varicose veins are often arranged in multiple parallel channels. It is unnecessary to follow reflux into all of the varicose clusters, because these are obvious to the treating physician. Augmentation of flow (distal compression) is done sharply, quickly, and aggressively, and pressure is applied to the calf to activate the gastrocnemius-soleus pump. When a color or pulsed-wave Doppler device is used, the probe is angled to provide an insonation angle of 60° or less.

For the anterior examination, the patient faces the sonographer with his or her weight borne on the lower extremity that is not being examined. The non–weight-bearing extremity is then evaluated. The common femoral vein and the saphenofemoral junction are assessed with the Valsalva maneuver and with distal compression and release. If reflux is present, the diameter of the refluxing GSV is noted

---

Table 2 Interrogation Points in the Venous Reflux Examination

Common femoral vein
Femoral vein
  Upper third
  Distal third
Popliteal vein
Sural veins
Saphenofemoral junction*
Saphenous vein, above the knee
Saphenous vein, below the knee
Saphenopopliteal junction†
Mode of termination, lesser saphenous vein

*Record diameter of refluxing long saphenous vein.
†Record distance from floor.

---

ed for subsequent use in selecting the proper endovenous catheter during saphenous ablation.

The GSV is identified on the basis of its relation to the deep and superficial fascia that ensheathe it to form the saphenous compartment. High-resolution B-mode ultrasonographic imaging of the superficial fascia in the transverse plane has shown that this structure reflects ultrasound strongly, yielding a characteristic image of the GSV known as the saphenous eye [*see Figure 1*]. The saphenous eye is a constant marker that is clearly demonstrable in transverse sections of the medial aspect of the thigh and that readily differentiates the GSV from varicose tributaries and other superficial veins. Casual examination of the thigh often reveals an elongated, dilated vein that is incorrectly assumed to be the GSV. This mistaken assumption can be corrected by means of ultrasound scanning with the saphenous eye as an anatomic marker.

Venous reflux can be elicited manually by calf muscle compression and release, by the Valsalva maneuver, or by pneumatic tourniquet release. In terms of efficacy, there is no difference between pneumatic tourniquet release and manual compression and release. However, pneumatic tourniquet release is cumbersome and requires two vascular sonographers, which makes the manual compression and release method very attractive by comparison. If saphenofemoral reflux lasting longer than 0.5 second is present, the diameter of the GSV is recorded 2.5 cm distal to the saphenofemoral junction.

The examination continues distally along the GSV, with distal augmentation of flow performed at intervals to check for reflux. Reflux frequently ends in the region of the knee. The point at which reflux stops is recorded in terms of distance from the floor in centimeters. The femoral vein (i.e., the vessel formerly termed the superficial femoral vein) is checked at midthigh for reflux and vein wall irregularities.

The posterior examination is also done on the non–weight-bearing lower extremity, with attention paid to reflux in the popliteal vein, the saphenopopliteal junction, and the SSV. The Valsalva maneuver may be used to stimulate reflux, as may distal augmentation and release. Valsalva-induced reflux is halted by competent proximal valves. The SSV is followed from its retromalleolar position on the lateral aspect of the ankle proximally to the saphenopopliteal junction, and augmentation maneuvers are performed every few centimeters.

The termination of the SSV is noted. If the vein terminates proximally in the vein of Giacomini, the femoropopliteal vein, or another vein, a specific check is made for a connection to the popliteal vein. If the SSV shows reflux, the distance from the sapheno-popliteal junction to the floor is measured and recorded.

A search for incompetent perforating veins is necessary only in limbs with chronic venous insufficiency (CVI) manifested by hyper-pigmentation, atrophie blanche, woody edema, scars from healed ulceration, or actual open ulcers. Incompetent perforating veins in limbs without CVI are associated with varicose veins and can be controlled with varicose phlebectomy. Identification of perforating veins in the lower extremity can be difficult even for the experienced sonographer.

Procedural Planning

For varicose vein treatment to be successful, two goals must be met: (1) reflux must be ablated from the deep veins to the superficial veins, and (2) all branch varicosities must be removed. Reflux must be eliminated from all major problem areas, including the saphenofemoral junction, the saphenopopliteal junction, and the midthigh Hunterian perforator vein. To identify these problem areas, careful preoperative duplex mapping of major superficial venous reflux is essential. All varicose vein clusters are meticulously marked before operation; they may be difficult to identify during the procedure, when the patient is supine.

At present, three techniques are approved for the elimination of axial reflux in the GSV and the SSV: (1) traditional surgical stripping, (2) laser vein ablation (i.e., endovenous laser therapy [EVLT]), and (3) radiofrequency (RF) ablation. Regardless of which technique is employed, the principal goals of treatment (see above) are the same. In addition, the procedure must be done in a manner that optimizes cosmetic results and minimizes complications.

Endovenous Procedures

Current endovenous techniques for treating varicose veins are based on three major developments: (1) the availability of laser and RF probes that deliver heat endovenously, (2) the introduction of tumescent anesthesia, and (3) the evolution of duplex ultrasonography. Tumescent anesthesia allows physicians to use large volumes (500 ml) of dilute (0.1%) lidocaine in a single session while achieving anesthesia levels equivalent to those achieved with 1% lidocaine. In this way, the entire thigh portion of the GSV can be safely anes-

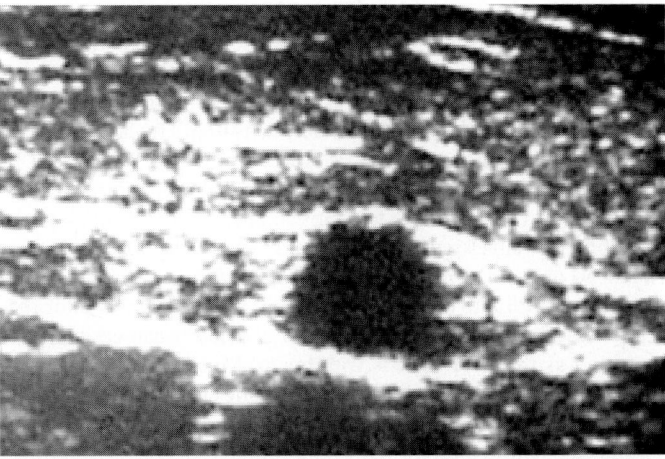

Figure 1 Shown is an ultrasonographic image of the so-called saphenous eye. Correct identification of this marker is crucial to correct performance of the preoperative ultrasonographic reflux examination.

thetized (and consequently obliterated) at one time. Epinephrine can be added to the solution to improve postoperative hemostasis, increase venous contraction around the heat-generating catheter, and lengthen the duration of postprocedural analgesia. A common formula for the tumescent anesthesia solution is 450 ml of normal saline mixed with 50 ml of 1% lidocaine with epinephrine (1:100,000 dilution) and 10 ml of sodium bicarbonate to buffer the acidity of the lidocaine.

Duplex ultrasonography has revolutionized treatment of varicose veins. It dramatically enhances physicians' ability to evaluate the cause of varicosities and to tailor treatment so that only the diseased vein segments are ablated while the normal segments are preserved. It also serves to guide placement of sheaths and heat-generating catheter tips, allowing these devices to be situated very precisely within the vein.

TECHNIQUE

Laser Vein Ablation

Laser vein ablation [*see Figure 2*] may be performed either in the office or in the hospital. Reimbursement issues make in-office treatment advantageous for most physicians. Neither conscious sedation nor noninvasive monitoring is required. On occasion, a nervous patient may benefit from administration of an oral anxiolytic agent 1 to 2 hours before the procedure.

Standard surgical preparation and draping are indicated, including the use of sterile gowns, masks, drapes and aseptic technique. Depending on the results of the preoperative physical examination and duplex ultrasonography, the GSV, the SSV, the anterior accessory saphenous vein, or the posterior accessory saphenous vein may be treated, either alone or in combination with other vessels as necessary. The GSV is usually treated from the upper third of the calf to the saphenofemoral junction. If the calf portion of the GSV is to be treated, tumescent anesthesia should be liberally employed to reduce the risk of saphenous nerve injury. The SSV is treated from the distal third of the calf to the point where it angles toward the popliteal vein in the popliteal fossa. The relation of the sural nerve to the distal third of the SSV precludes safe treatment of this portion of the vein, and the proximity of the popliteal nerve to the SSV in the popliteal fossa precludes safe treatment of the most proximal portion of the vein. The procedure does not allow flush ligation of the saphenofemoral junction, but current evidence suggests that this measure may not be indicated: flush ligation eliminates normal venous drainage from the saphenofemoral junction and may increase the risk of neovascularization of the saphenofemoral junction and recurrence of varicosities.

The saphenous vein being treated is accessed with a micropuncture system after a small amount of lidocaine (sufficient to raise a small skin wheal) is injected into the dermis. The position of the 0.015-in. wire in the saphenous vein is confirmed by means of ultrasonography. A 4 French catheter is then passed over the wire, allowing the placement of a 0.035-in. wire for access to the proximal portion of the saphenous vein. Next, the 0.035-in. wire is positioned at the appropriate saphenous junction, and a 5 French vascular sheath is advanced over the wire to the junction. The sheath is positioned either just below the superior epigastric vein or 1 to 2 cm distal to the junction of the GSV; if the SSV is being treated, the tip is positioned 2 to 3 cm below the junction at the point where the vein makes its transition from an oblique course to a parallel path under the fascia of the leg. The 600 μm laser fiber is then passed to the tip of the sheath, which is pinned and pulled to expose the tip of the laser fiber. The rigidity and sharpness of the laser fiber makes advancing its tip dangerous. Most laser systems allow the fiber to be locked to the sheath, so that the

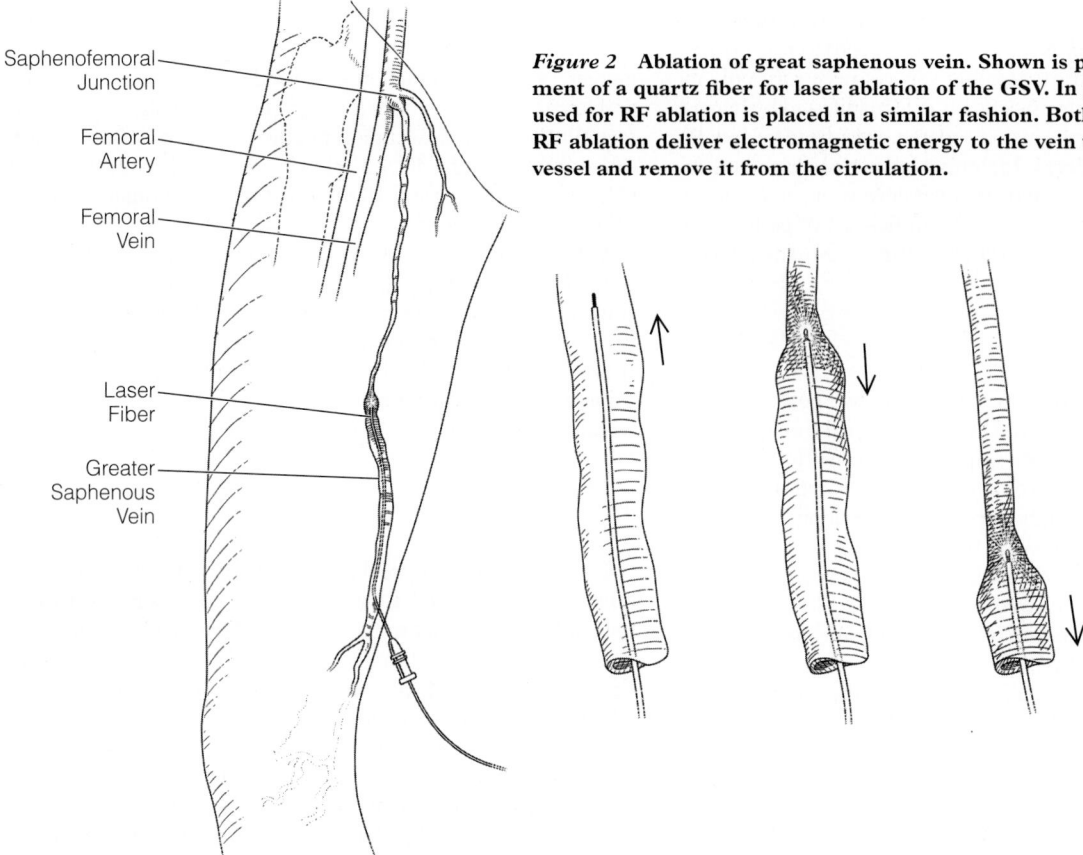

Saphenofemoral Junction

Femoral Artery

Femoral Vein

Laser Fiber

Greater Saphenous Vein

Figure 2 Ablation of great saphenous vein. Shown is percutaneous placement of a quartz fiber for laser ablation of the GSV. In practice, the catheter used for RF ablation is placed in a similar fashion. Both laser ablation and RF ablation deliver electromagnetic energy to the vein wall to destroy the vessel and remove it from the circulation.

two devices can be advanced and positioned as a single unit.

To this point in the procedure, no anesthesia other than the initial dermal injection has been employed. The next step, accordingly, is to initiate tumescent anesthesia, with or without epinephrine, along the saphenous compartment. The addition of epinephrine to the anesthetic solution results in improved constriction of the vein around the laser sheath, particularly when a saphenous vein larger than 12 mm in diameter is being treated; it also prolongs the analgesic effect of lidocaine, providing pain relief for as long as 6 to 8 hours after the procedure. A particular benefit of tumescent anesthesia is that the large volume of the injectate constitutes a heat sink that absorbs the heat created by the laser, thereby eliminating injury to surrounding soft tissue structures (e.g., nerves, fat, and skin). Further protection against injury is provided by rapid pullback of the laser fiber. As a result, the reported incidence of thermal skin or nerve injuries with laser vein ablation is almost zero.

Administration of the tumescent anesthesia solution starts at the sheath entry site and continues proximally until the entire vein segment to be treated exhibits a circumferential zone of echolucence. The vein is generally treated in the saphenous compartment between the superficial and deep fasciae of the leg. The anesthetic is administered via a 22-gauge needle with a 20 ml syringe or, alternatively, via a 10 ml autofill syringe or a Klein pump (both of which have the advantage of allowing more rapid administration with less risk of needle-stick injury to the staff). The needle is kept in a static position during administration, and the fluid is allowed to dissect up and down the fascial compartment.

Besides providing pain relief, tumescent anesthesia serves to move the saphenous vein being treated away from any structure that might be injured by the heat produced by the laser (e.g., the skin and the femoral vein). A 1 cm distance between the skin and the laser fiber is optimal. More liberal amounts of tumescent anesthesia

solution are administered when the vein being treated lies in close proximity to one or more nerves (e.g., the SSV and the calf portion of the GSV). As a rule, we prefer not to treat the subdermal portions of the GSV with laser ablation; the presence of an inflamed and tender vein just beneath the dermis is likely to lead to increased postoperative pain and noticeable skin discoloration. The superficial segments of the GSV are best treated with phlebectomy at the time of laser ablation.

When administration of the tumescent anesthesia solution is complete, the position of the laser fiber's tip is again confirmed. As the vein constricts, it also shortens, and this process may advance the tip of the laser fiber into the saphenofemoral or saphenopopliteal junction. If the tip is found to have moved in this manner, it is withdrawn until it is again 1 to 2 cm below the junction. A quick scan down the vein is done to confirm that the entire vein is surrounded by the anesthetic solution and is at least 1 cm from the skin.

At this point, the laser may be safely activated. The laser is always used in the continuous mode. The power setting may range from 10 to 12 W, depending on the physician's personal preference. We typically employ a 10 W setting for veins smaller than 10 mm and a 12 W setting for veins larger than 10 mm. The essential point is that between 50 and 100 J must be delivered to each centimeter of vein treated; according to one study, 70 J/cm is the ideal amount for reliable long-term vein obliteration.[5] Energy delivery can easily be determined as the laser fiber is withdrawn. Most laser sheaths have markings 1 cm apart, and the laser machines have digital readouts that indicate the total amount of energy (J) delivered in real time. A simple calculation after 10 cm of the catheter has been withdrawn provides instant feedback on the energy delivered per centimeter of vein. On the 12 W power setting, delivery of the recommended amount of energy generally necessitates a pullback rate of 1 cm every 4 to 5 seconds (2.0 to 2.5 mm/sec). One group has advocated delivery of 140 J/cm proximally (pullback rate of 1 mm/sec) and roughly 70 J/cm distally (pullback rate of 3 mm/sec), theorizing that for long-term success, more energy is required proximally.[6] At the completion of the procedure, the laser is deactivated before the fiber is withdrawn from the skin. Ultrasonography is then performed to confirm that the common femoral vein and the superficial epigastric vein are patent and that the GSV is occluded.

An adhesive strip (e.g., Steri-Strip; 3M, St. Paul, Minnesota) covered by a transparent surgical adhesive dressing is applied over the entry site. The patient is then placed in a prescription compression stocking, which is worn for 1 to 2 weeks after the procedure. Whereas most physicians use a class 2 (30 to 40 mm Hg) compression stocking, we have switched to using a class 1 (20 to 30 mm Hg) stocking without observing any changes in complications (e.g., postoperative pain and swelling) or results. This switch has enhanced patient satisfaction, in that a class 1 stocking is easier to don and more comfortable to wear.

A 2003 study that followed 499 limbs over 2 years demonstrated a varicosity recurrence rate of less than 7% after ablation of the GSV with an 810 nm diode laser.[7] This rate is comparable to or lower than those reported after traditional surgical stripping, RF ablation, and ultrasound-guided sclerotherapy. Several smaller studies documented similar outcomes, making it evident that laser vein ablation is both effective and safe when compared to other means of treating varicose veins [see Table 3].[1,6,8-11]

At present, the question of how to manage residual varicosities after laser ablation remains controversial. The two main options are (1) to perform phlebectomy simultaneously with laser vein ablation and (2) to perform laser ablation alone, then observe the patient for spontaneous regression of varicosities. When the residual varicosities are left untreated, 10% to 20% of patients show sufficient regression to render further intervention unnecessary; however, 5% to 10% of patients experience superficial thrombophlebitis in the residual varicosities as a consequence of stasis from altered venous drainage. If delayed treatment of residual varicosities proves necessary, it may be accomplished with either phlebectomy or sclerotherapy, depending on the physician's preference. Our treatment of choice is laser vein ablation with concurrent phlebectomy. This approach adds only 10 to 20 minutes to the length of the procedure while offering the patient a more rapid and complete resolution of visible varicose veins and greatly reducing the risk of secondary thrombophlebitis.

Radiofrequency Ablation

In an attempt to minimize postoperative discomfort while main-

taining the benefits of saphenous vein ablation, RF alternating current has been employed to effect rapid thermic electrocoagulation of the vein wall and its valves. This approach is exemplified by the Closure procedure (VNUS Medical Technologies, Inc., San Jose, California). Prolonged exposure to the high-frequency energy results in total loss of vessel wall architecture, disintegration, and carbonization.[12] Ultrasonographic follow-up shows that treated saphenous veins disappear after the 2-year point. Clinical observations suggest that patients are much more comfortable after RF ablation than after surgical stripping.[13]

The technique of RF ablation is somewhat similar to that of laser ablation [see Figure 2] but differs in several important respects [see Laser Vein Ablation, above]. After percutaneous access is obtained, either a 6 or an 8 French RF radiofrequency catheter is placed 1 to 2 cm from the saphenofemoral junction, and tumescent anesthesia is instituted. The probe is connected to the RF generator box, the tines of the probe are exposed, and the unit is activated. The catheter is pulled back slowly (1 cm every 30 seconds) while its temperature and impedance are monitored. In the procedure as originally performed, the catheter was heated to 85° C, but current approaches often involve heating the catheter to 90° or 95° C with the aim of shortening the pullback time (to compete with the shorter pullback times characteristic of laser ablation). In general, however, pullback times are still somewhat longer with RF ablation than with laser ablation, allowing more dissemination of heat to surrounding tissue; postprocedural paresthesia continues to be reported in about 12% of cases.[14] The technical results of RF ablation are excellent: with the Closure procedure, the closure rate at 4 years is 89%.[14] However, the continued occurrence of paresthesias and the slower pullback times associated with RF ablation still appear to make laser vein ablation a safer and more rapid procedure.

The issue of recurrent varicosities after obliteration of the GSV without disconnection of the saphenofemoral junction tributaries is unsettled at present. It does appear, however, that endovenous RF ablation of the GSV (e.g., with the Closure procedure) prevents subsequent neovascularization in the groin. Many centers have reported that neovascularization does not occur in the absence of a groin incision.

The specific goal of endoluminal treatment of venous reflux is obliteration of the saphenous vein. Follow-up to 4 years shows that RF ablation with the Closure procedure accomplishes this goal.[14]

OUTCOMES AND COMPLICATIONS

Both EVLT and RF ablation have proved to be effective and safe

Table 3 Complications of Laser Vein Ablation and Radiofrequency (RF) Ablation in Selected Studies[15]

Ablation Method	Study	Limbs Treated (N)	Skin Burn (%)	Paresthesia (%)	Phlebitis (%)	DVT (%)	Recanalization (%)
Laser	Navarro[43]	40	0	0	0	0	0
	Proebstle[44]	109	0	0	10	0	10
	Min[7]	504	0	0	5	0	2
	Perkowski[45]	154	0	0	0	0	3
RF	Weiss[46]	140	0	4	0	0	10
	Merchant[47]	318	4	15	2	1	15
	Hingorani[48]	73	0	0	0.3	16	4
	Merchant[14]	1,078	2	12	3	0.5	11

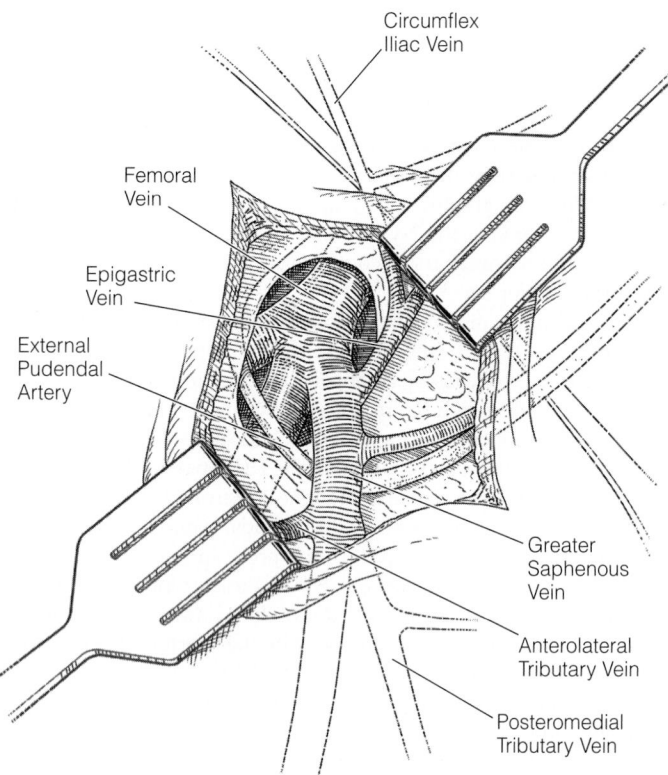

Circumflex
Iliac Vein

Femoral
Vein

Epigastric
Vein

External
Pudendal
Artery

Greater
Saphenous
Vein

Anterolateral
Tributary Vein

Posteromedial
Tributary Vein

Figure 3 **Shown are a typical saphenofemoral junction and the most important tributary vessels. The classic surgical approach dictates total disconnection of all tributaries at this junction.**

for the treatment of venous reflux disease. Several studies that followed treated limbs for 2 years or longer have shown that with respect to efficacy, these modalities are equivalent or superior to standard surgical techniques.[7,11,15,16] It is noteworthy that neovascularization seems to be almost nonexistent with endovenous procedures; this result appears to be related exclusively to standard ligation surgery.

Multiple studies have reported similar end-point results for EVLT and RF ablation: long-term occlusion of the GSV is consistently achieved at rates approaching or exceeding 90%. In general, EVLT has somewhat better long-term success rates, ranging from 92% to 95%; RF ablation generally yields success rates between 85% and 91%. The incidence of DVT (which is more accurately described as extension of thrombus from the treated vein into the deep venous system) is low with both procedures but is slightly higher with RF ablation. No cases of life-threatening pulmonary embolism have been reported with either EVLT or RF ablation, and both are associated with only negligible rates of superficial thrombophlebitis, cellulitis, (excessive) pain, and transient paresthesias.

A 2006 study stressed the importance of treating the posterior thigh circumflex vein so as to lower the incidence of recanalization.[15] A large posterior thigh circumflex vein can drain cool blood into the segment being ablated, thus inhibiting proper heating of the refluxing segment and making adequate closure more difficult. Accordingly, the authors recommended ablating any posterior thigh circumflex veins larger 4 mm in tandem with the primary procedure.

Surgical Vein Stripping

Ligation of the GSV at the saphenofemoral junction [*see Figure 3*] has been widely practiced in the belief that it would control gravitational reflux while preserving the vein for subsequent arterial bypass.

It is true that the GSV is largely preserved after proximal ligation[17]; however, reflux continues, and hydrostatic forces are not controlled.[18] Recurrent varicose veins are more frequent after saphenous ligation than after stripping.[19] Varicosities also recur more frequently after ligation and sclerotherapy than after stripping and sclerotherapy.[20] A prospective, randomized trial that compared proximal GSV ligation and stab avulsion of varices with stripping of the thigh portion of the GSV and stab avulsion of varices showed the latter approach to be superior.[21,22] Routine GSV stripping reduces the rate of recurrent varicosities and the need for reoperation for recurrent saphenofemoral incompetence.

Although it can be argued that the GSV should be retained for possible use in arterial bypass grafting, the relatively high (> 20%) reoperation rate makes this strategy undesirable. Almost three quarters of limbs that undergo GSV ligation alone have an incompetent GSV on follow-up duplex imaging. Until studies show a clear advantage to retaining the GSV in defined patient populations, surgical stripping should remain a routine part of primary GSV surgery. In several studies, preservation of the patency of the GSV and continuing reflux in this vein were found to be the factors most frequently associated with recurrence of varicosities.[23-25] In one study of patients who underwent reoperation for relief of recurrent variceal symptoms, two thirds of the patients required removal of the GSV as part of the procedure.[23]

Over the past 100 years, ankle-to-groin stripping of the GSV has been the dominant approach to treatment of varicose veins.[26-28] It has been argued, however, that routine stripping of the leg (i.e., ankle-to-knee) portion of the GSV is inadvisable. One argument against this practice is that there is a significant risk of concomitant saphenous nerve injury [*see Figure 4*].[19] Another argument is that whereas the objective of GSV removal is detachment of perforating veins emanating from the GSV in the thigh, the perforating veins in the leg are actually part of the posterior arch vein system rather than of the saphenous vein system. This latter argument notwithstanding, preoperative ultrasonography often demonstrates that the leg portion of the GSV is in fact directly connected to perforating veins. It is clear, however, that elimination of the refluxing thigh portion of the GSV frequently eliminates reflux in the calf portion of the vein, even when the calf portion is left behind. Therefore, removal of the GSV from ankle to knee generally is not necessary. If reflux subsequently becomes a problem in this portion of the vein, it can usually be controlled with sclerotherapy.

OPERATIVE TECHNIQUE

The surgical approach to vein stripping must be tailored to the individual patient and the individual limb being treated. As a rule, general or spinal anesthesia is required, though the procedure can also be performed with tumescent anesthesia. Groin-to-knee stripping of the GSV should be considered in every patient requiring surgical intervention.[29] In nearly all patients, this measure is supplemented by removal of the varicose vein clusters via stab avulsion or some form of sclerotherapy [*see Table 4*].

Step 1: Placement of Incisions

Preoperative marking, if correctly performed, will have documented the extent of varicose vein clusters and identified the clinical points where control of varices is required. Incisions can then be planned. As a rule, incisions in the groin and at the ankle should be transverse and should be placed within skin lines. In the groin, an oblique variation of the transverse incision may be appropriate. This incision should be placed high enough to permit identification of the saphenofemoral junction [*see Figure 3*]. The use of a portable ultrasound unit in the operating room facilitates placement of the incision directly over the saphenofemoral junction. Generally, throughout the leg and the thigh, the best cosmetic results are obtained with vertical incisions. Transverse incisions are used in the region of the knee, and oblique incisions are appropriate over the patella when the incisions are placed in skin lines.

A major cause of discomfort and occasional permanent skin pigmentation is subcutaneous extravasation of blood during and after saphenous vein stripping. Such extravasation can be minimized by using tumescent anesthesia around the vein to be stripped.

The practice of identifying and carefully dividing each of the tributaries to the saphenofemoral junction has been dominant over the past 50 years. The rationale for this practice is to avoid leaving behind a network of interanastomosing inguinal tributaries. Accordingly, special efforts have been made to draw each of the saphenous tributaries into the groin incision so that when they are placed on traction, their primary and even secondary tributaries can be controlled. The importance of these efforts has been underscored by de-

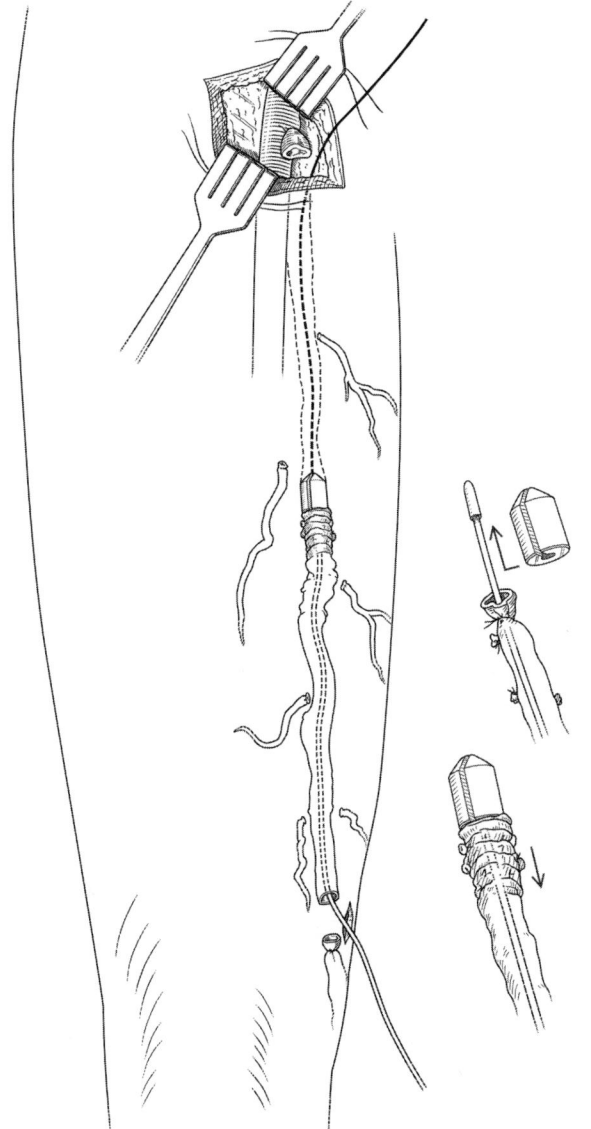

Figure 4 **Surgical stripping of great saphenous vein. Illustrated is an early attempt to minimize distal incisions and prevent saphenous nerve injury at the knee. The stripper and its obturator are pulled to knee level, then retrieved through the groin incision. (Note division of perforating and communicating veins.)**

Table 4 Methods of Variceal Ablation
Formal ligation, division, and excision
Stab avulsion
Sclerotherapy
With liquid sclerosant
With foamed sclerosant
Sclerotherapy aided by transillumination
Sclerotherapy aided by ultrasound guidance

scriptions of residual inguinal networks as an important cause of varicose vein recurrence.[23] Currently, however, this central principle of varicose vein surgery is under challenge, on the grounds that groin dissection can lead to neovascularization and hence to recurrence of varicosities [*see* Outcome Evaluation, *below*].

Step 2: Introduction of Stripping Device

Preoperative duplex studies having already demonstrated incompetent valves in the saphenous system, a disposable plastic Codman stripper can be introduced from above downward; alternatively, an Oesch stripper can be employed.[30] Both of these devices can be used to strip the GSV from groin to knee via the inversion technique [*see Figure 5*]. This approach has been shown to reduce soft tissue trauma in the thigh.[31]

In the groin, the stripper is inserted proximally into the upper end of the divided internal saphenous vein and passed down the main channel through incompetent valves until it can be felt lying distally approximately 1 cm medial to the medial border of the tibia at a point approximately 4 to 6 cm distal to the level of the tibial tubercle. The GSV is anatomically constant in this location, just as it is in the groin and ankle. If the GSV is removed from the groin to this level, both the midthigh perforating vein, which usually enters the GSV, and the most distal incompetent perforating veins, which are in the distal third of the thigh, will be treated.

A small incision is made over the palpable distal end of the stripper. The GSV will subsequently be divided through this incision, and the stripper and the inverted vein will be delivered through it. In exposing the GSV at knee level, the superficial fascia must be incised because the vein lies between this structure and the deep fascia of the thigh.

If the stripper passes unimpeded to the ankle, it can be exposed there with an exceedingly small skin incision placed in a carefully chosen skin line. Passage of the stripper from above downward to the ankle serves to confirm the absence of functioning valves, and stripping of the vein from above downward is unlikely to cause nerve damage. At the ankle, the vein should be carefully and cleanly dissected to free it from surrounding nerve fibers. If this is not done, saphenous nerve injury will result, and the patient will experience numbness of the foot below the ankle.

Step 3: Removal of Saphenous Vein

The previously placed stripper is pulled distally to remove the GSV. Although plastic disposable vein strippers and their metallic equivalents were designed to be used with various-sized olives to remove the GSV, in fact, a more efficient technique is simply to tie the vein to the stripper below its tip so that the vessel can then be inverted into itself and removed distally, usually at knee level.

Phlebectomy for Management of Residual Varicosities

Management of residual varicose veins after vein stripping traditionally has been done at the same time as the surgical procedure.

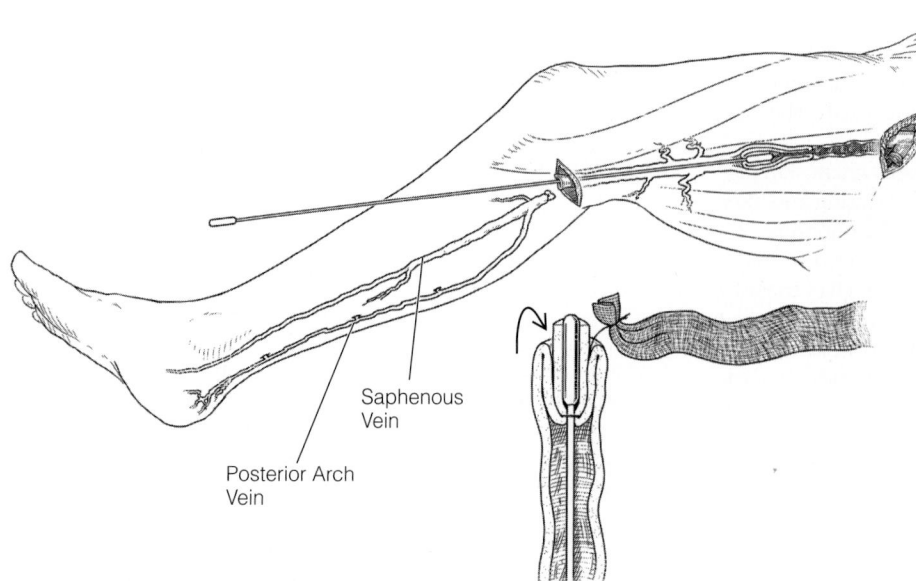

Saphenous
Vein

Posterior Arch
Vein

Figure 5 **Surgical stripping of great saphenous vein. Inversion stripping of the GSV decreases soft tissue trauma in the thigh. However, tearing of the vein occurs on occasion. This problem may be largely prevented by attaching a corner of a 2 in. gauze roll soaked in lidocaine-epinephrine solution to the end of the stripper. As the stripper is pulled, the gauze is drawn into the vein, thereby assisting hemostasis. The gauze can then be left in place for 10 to 20 minutes while the stab wounds from the avulsion part of the procedure are being closed.**

Management of residual varicose veins after vein ablation is more controversial. Currently, many physicians who treat vein disease are not familiar with the surgical technique of phlebectomy and therefore elect to wait for varicosities to regress after vein ablation. In 10% to 20% of cases, enough regression of varicose veins occurs after ablation that no further treatment is required. If delayed treatment proves necessary, it may be accomplished by means of either phlebectomy or sclerotherapy, depending on the physician's preference.

The technique of phlebectomy is easy to learn. A tumescent anesthesia solution is infused between the skin and the superficial fascia of the leg in the area of the previously marked varicosities. The infusion of the anesthetic tends to dissect the GSV away from the surrounding tissue and causes vasoconstriction. Vertical incisions 1 to 3 mm in length are made where appropriate. In the anterior knee and ankle regions, where skin lines are obviously horizontal, incisions are hidden in the lines [*see Figure 6*]. Varicosities are exteriorized by means of hooks or forceps; particularly useful for this purpose are specially designed vein hooks such as the Varady dissector, the Muller hook, and the Oesch hook [*see Figures 7 and 8*].[32] Nothing should penetrate the skin other than the small end of the hook. Usually, the vein is easily distinguished from the surrounding fat by its taut rubber band feel. The vessel is brought out of the skin, then removed proximally and distally by using a hand-over-hand technique with mosquito clamps. Eventually, the vein tears in each direction, but because of the epinephrine in the tumescent anesthesia solution, very little bleeding occurs. The procedure is continued in a proximal-to-distal direction until all varicose clusters have been removed; generally, between 10 and 15 incisions are required for removal of all clusters. Veins of any size can be removed by means of this technique, even in the office setting. In patients who have had superficial phlebitis or have previously undergone sclerotherapy, the veins typically are fibrotic and adherent to the surrounding tissue and cannot be easily removed. If treatment of such veins proves necessary at some point in the future, sclerotherapy is generally the method of choice.

When all phlebectomies have been completed, small elastic strips are used to close the skin incisions. A compressive dressing is applied for 24 hours to minimize bleeding, bruising, and swelling. When the procedure is done properly, the incisions are invisible by 6 to 8 weeks and the patients are very happy with the results. Experienced workers in Europe have achieved marked refinements of phlebectomy techniques for varicose clusters.[33]

COMPLICATIONS

Surgical removal of the GSV on an outpatient basis still requires two incisions, one in the groin and the other near the knee. Postoper-

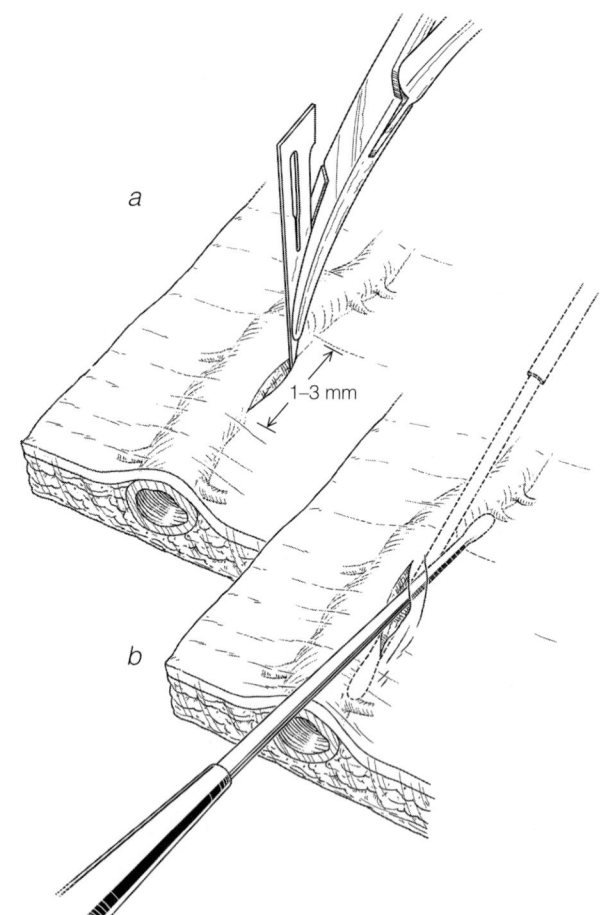

a

1–3 mm

b

Figure 6 **Surgical stripping of great saphenous vein: phlebectomy for residual varicosities. (*a*) Skin incisions for stab avulsion of varicosities are limited with respect to both length and depth. (*b*) The dissector blade facilitates mobilization of the vein before removal.**

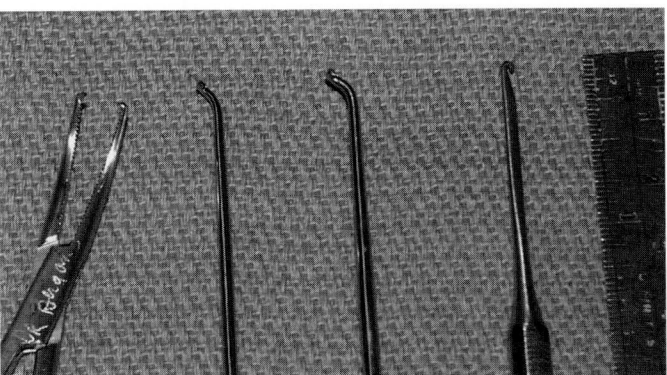

Figure 7 **Surgical stripping of great saphenous vein: phlebectomy for residual varicosities. Shown are tools used for exteriorizing varicosities: a Hartman clamp with its single tooth placed distally, two Muller clamps, and a Varady hook and dissector (left to right).**

ative compression bandaging is standard, and most patients experience little downtime. Some, however, do experience hematoma, pain, and extensive bruising. These three complications are linked; thus, every effort should be made to prevent oozing. The most feared complication of varicose vein surgery is venous thromboembolism, but the incidence of this complication is quite low (probably about 1%). In countries where postoperative immobilization, hospitalization, and delayed ambulation are employed for patients with varicosities, prophylaxis against venous thromboembolism is common. In the United States, however, this measure is generally considered unnecessary in these patients. The most common complication of varicose vein surgery is recurrence of varicosities, which is experienced by 15% to 30% of patients treated.[24]

To speak of permanent removal of varicosities implies that all potential causes of recurrence have been considered and that surgical management has been planned so as to address them. There are four principal causes of recurrence of varicose veins, three of which can be dealt with at the time of the primary operation.

One cause of recurrent varicosities is failure to perform the primary operation correctly. Common errors include missing a duplicated saphenous vein and mistaking an anterolateral or accessory saphenous vein for the GSV. Careful and thorough anatomic identification will help minimize such errors. It has long been held that a second cause of recurrent varicose veins is failure to do a proper groin dissection; however, it is now known that such dissection causes neovascularization in the groin, leading to recurrence of varicose veins [see Outcome Evaluation, below]. A third cause is failure to remove the GSV from the circulation. A reason often cited for this failure is the desire to preserve the GSV for subsequent use as an arterial bypass, but it is clear that the preserved GSV continues to reflux and continues to elongate and dilate its tributaries, thereby producing more varicosities even after primary operative treatment has removed the varicose veins present at the time. A fourth cause of recurrent varicosities is persistence of venous hypertension through nonsaphenous sources—chiefly perforating veins with incompetent valves. Muscular contraction generates enormous pressures that are directed against valves in perforating veins. Venous hypertension induces a leukocyte endothelial reaction, which, in turn, incites an inflammatory response that ultimately destroys the venous valves and weakens the venous wall.[34] The perforating veins most commonly associated with recurrent varicosities are the midthigh perforating vein, the distal thigh perforating vein, the proximal anteromedial calf perforating vein, and the lateral thigh perforating vein, which connects the deep femoral vein to surface varicosities.

In addition to the four principal causes of recurrent varicosities, there is a fifth cause, which is beyond the operating surgeon's control—namely, the genetic tendency to form varicosities. This tendency results in the development of localized or generalized venous wall weakness, localized blowouts of venous walls, or stretched, elongated, and floppy venous valves.[35,36]

OUTCOME EVALUATION

As a rule, when undesirable outcomes occur after surgical saphenous vein stripping, they become evident quite early.[21] As noted (see above), it has long been accepted practice to dissect tributary vessels at the saphenofemoral junction very carefully, taking each of the vessels back beyond the primary and even the secondary tributaries if possible.[31] In practice, however, such dissection appears to cause neovascularization in the groin[37]; surveillance with duplex ultrasonography supports this finding.[38] It has now been amply confirmed that neovascularization causes recurrent varicose veins. Clearly, this is a significant disadvantage of standard surgical treatment of varicosities. This disadvantage has been a major impetus for the development of less invasive alternatives to surgical saphenous vein stripping [see Endovenous Procedures, above, and Foam Sclerotherapy, below]. These alternatives are proving to be effective and may be superior to surgical stripping, if only because they are not followed by groin neovascularization.

Foam Sclerotherapy

The prospect of a rapid, minimally invasive, and durable treatment of varicose veins is an attractive one. Current evidence suggests that these objectives may be achieved without operative intervention by using sclerosant microfoam [see Figure 9]. In 1944 and 1950, E. J. Orbach introduced the concept of a macrobubble air-block technique to enhance the properties of sclerosants in performing macrosclerotherapy.[39,40] At the time, few clinicians evinced much interest in the subject, and the technique languished.

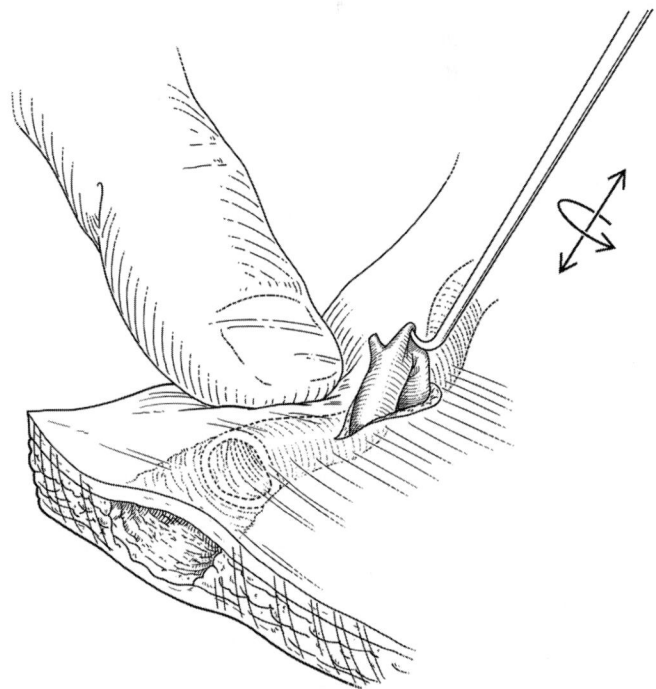

Figure 8 **Surgical stripping of great saphenous vein: phlebectomy for residual varicosities. The varix is exteriorized with a hook, then divided to permit proximal and distal avulsion.**

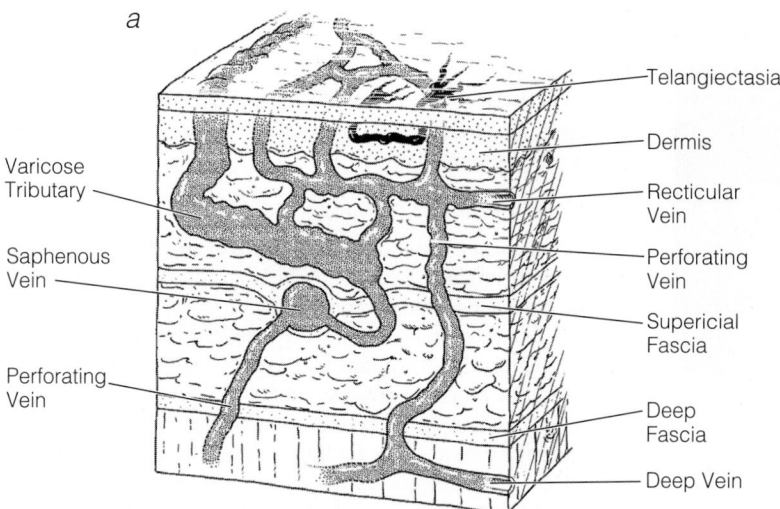

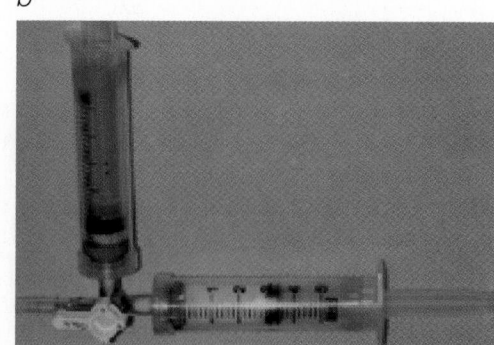

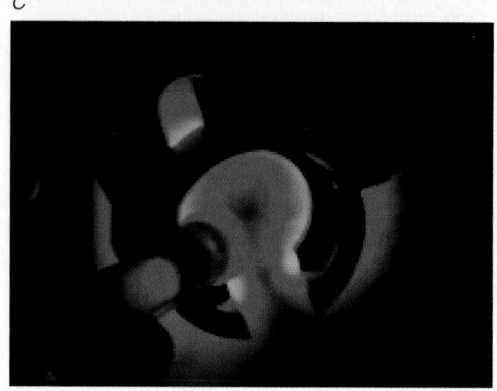

Figure 9 **Microfoam sclerotherapy. (***a***) The relationships among the venous structures in a lower extremity with varicosities explain why microfoam sclerotherapy can succeed. Injections into varices, reticular veins, or perforating veins can place the foam into varicose structures and even into telangiectatic blemishes. (***b***) Sclerosant foam is made by mixing room air with 0.5% sodium tetradecyl sulfate (STS) in a 2:1 ratio via a three-way stopcock. The syringes are emptied 35 times to create a foam that lasts about 5 minutes. (***c***) A halogen light (vein light), as used here during a foam injection, is helpful for treating persistent or recurrent varices along with the GSV in situations where surgery is undesirable.**

Half a century later, the work of Juan Cabrera and colleagues in Granada attracted the attention of some phlebologists and reawakened interest in using foam technology for the treatment of venous insufficiency.[41] These investigators showed that foam sclerotherapy was technically simple and worked well in small to moderate-sized varicose veins, and they demonstrated that the limitations of liquid sclerotherapy could be erased by using microfoam. Their 5-year report represents the longest observation period to date for microfoam sclerotherapy for varicose veins. In most of the cases, a single injection sufficed to treat saphenous veins and varicose tributaries. Extensive vasospasm was seen immediately, but compression was applied after treatment. Complete fibrosis of the saphenous vein was achieved in 81% of cases, and patency with reflux persisted in only 14%. Tributary varicosities disappeared in 96% of cases. Vessels that remained open and were refluxing were successfully closed with retreatment.

A subsequent study demonstrated that even severely affected limbs could be safely and effectively treated by means of foam sclerotherapy combined with compression.[42] In this study, limbs affected by lipodermatosclerosis, atrophie blanche, or even open venous ulcers showed statistically significant improvement after the injection of a foamed sclerosant followed by compression with a medical-grade stocking or an Unna boot. The study results also underscored the importance of applying compression immediately after the injection of the sclerosant. Limbs that underwent foam sclerotherapy and compression healed better and more quickly than limbs that were treated by sclerotherapy alone.

If subsequent work continues to confirm these favorable results, it may be that microfoam sclerotherapy will eventually replace all other methods of varicose vein treatment. As of December 2006, however, foam sclerotherapy had not been approved by the United States Food and Drug Administration, because of concerns about potential air embolization after the injection of the sclerosant.

References

1. Rautio T, Ohinmaa A, Perala J, et al: Endovenous obliteration versus conventional stripping operation in the treatment of primary varicose veins: a randomized, controlled trial with comparison of the costs. J Vasc Surg 35:958, 2002

2. Caggiati A, Bergan J, Gloviczki P, et al: Nomenclature of the veins of the lower limb: extensions, refinements, and clinical application. J Vasc Surg 41:719, 2005

3. Ballard JL, Bergan, JJ, DeLange M: Venous imaging for reflux using duplex ultrasonography. Noninvasive Vascular Diagnosis. AbuRahma AF, Bergan JJ, Eds. Springer-Verlag, London, 2000, p 329

4. Mekenas LV, Bergan JD: Venous reflux examination: technique using miniaturized ultrasound scanning. J Vasc Technol 26:139, 2002

5. Timperman P, Sichlau M, Ryu R: Greater energy delivery improves treatment success of endovenous laser treatment of incompetent saphenous veins. J Vasc Interv Radiol 15:1061, 2004

6. Min R, Khilnani N: Endovenous laser ablation of varicose veins. J Cardiovasc Surg 46:395, 2005

7. Min R, Khilnani N, Zimmet S: Endovenous laser treatment of saphenous vein reflux: long-term results. J Vasc Interv Radiol 14:991, 2003

8. Sadick NS, Wasser S: Combined endovascular laser with ambulatory phlebectomy for the treatment of superficial venous incompetence: a 2-year perspective. J Cosmet Laser Ther 6:44, 2004

9. Disselhoff B, Kinderen D, Moll F: Is there recanalization of the great saphenous vein 2 years after endovenous laser treatment? J Endovasc Ther 12:731, 2005

10. Proebstle T, Gul D, Kargl A, et al: Endovenous laser treatment of the lesser saphenous vein with a 940-nm diode laser: early results. Dermatol Surg 29:357, 2003

11. Puggioni A, Kalra M, Carmo M, et al:

Endovenous laser therapy and radiofrequency ablation of the great saphenous vein: analysis of early efficacy and complications. J Vasc Surg 42:488, 2005

12. Petrovic S, Chandler JG: Endovenous obliteration: an effective, minimally invasive surrogate for saphenous vein stripping. J Endovasc Surg 7:11, 2000

13. Goldman MP: Closure of the greater saphenous vein with endoluminal radiofrequency thermal heating of the vein wall in combination with ambulatory phlebectomy: preliminary 6-month followup. Dermatol Surg 26:105, 2000

14. Merchant RF, Pichot O, Myers KA: Four-year follow-up on endovascular radiofrequency obliteration of great saphenous reflux. Dermatol Surg 31:129, 2005

15. Almeida J, Raines J: Radiofrequency ablation and laser ablation in the treatment of varicose veins. Ann Vasc Surg 20:4, 2006

16. Pannier F, Rabe E: Endovenous laser therapy and radiofrequency ablation of saphenous varicose veins. J Cardiovasc Surg 47:3, 2006

17. Rutherford RB, Sawyer JD, Jones DN: The fate of residual saphenous vein after partial removal or ligation. J Vasc Surg 12:422, 1990

18. McMullin GM, Coleridge Smith PD, Scurr JH: Objective assessment of high ligation without stripping the long saphenous vein. Br J Surg 78:1139, 1991

19. Munn SR, Morton JB, MacBeth WAAG, et al: To strip or not to strip the long saphenous vein? A varicose veins trial. Br J Surg 68:426, 1981

20. Neglen P: Treatment of varicosities of saphenous origin: comparison of ligation, selective excision, and sclerotherapy. Bergan JJ, Goldman MP, Eds. Varicose Veins and Telangiectasias: Diagnosis and Management. Quality Medical Publishing, St Louis, 1993, p 148

21. Sarin S, Scurr JH, Coleridge Smith PD: Assessment of stripping the long saphenous vein in the treatment of primary varicose veins. Br J Surg 79:889, 1992

22. Dwerryhouse S, Davies B, Harradine K, et al: Stripping the long saphenous vein reduces the rate of reoperation for recurrent varicose veins; five-year results of a randomized trial. J Vasc Surg 29:589, 1999

23. Stonebridge PA, Chalmers N, Beggs I, et al: Recurrent varicose veins; a varicographic analysis leading to a new practical classification. Br J Surg 82:60, 1995

24. Darke SG: The morphology of recurrent varicose veins. Eur J Vasc Surg 6:512, 1992

25. Conrad P: Groin-to-knee down stripping of the long saphenous vein. Phlebology 7:20, 1992

26. Mayo CH: Treatment of varicose veins. Surg Gynecol Obstet 2:385, 1906

27. Babcock WW: A new operation for extirpation of varicose veins. NY Med J 86:1553, 1907

28. Keller WL: A new method for extirpating the internal saphenous and similar veins in varicose conditions: a preliminary report. NY Med J 82:385, 1905

29. Goren G, Yellin AE: Primary varicose veins: topographic and hemodynamic correlations. J Cardiovasc Surg 31:672, 1990

30. Goren G, Yellin AE: Invaginated axial saphenectomy by a semirigid stripper: perforate-invaginate stripping. J Vasc Surg 20:970, 1994

31. Bergan JJ: Saphenous vein stripping by inversion: current technique. Surg Rounds 23:118, 2000

32. Bergan JJ: Varicose veins: hooks, clamps and suction: application of new techniques to enhance varicose vein surgery. Semin Vasc Surg 15:21, 2002

33. Ricci S, Georgiev M, Goldman MP: Ambulatory Phlebectomy: a Practical Guide for Treating Varicose Veins. Mosby, St Louis, 1995

34. Ono T, Bergan JJ, Schmid-Schönbein GW, et al: Monocyte infiltration into venous valves. J Vasc Surg 27:158, 1998

35. Thulesius O, Ugaily-Thulesius L., Gjores JE, et al: The varicose saphenous vein, functional and ultrastructural studies, with special reference to smooth muscle. Phlebology 3:89, 1988

36. Rose SS, Ahmed A: Some thoughts on the aetiology of varicose veins. J Cardiovasc Surg 27:534, 1986

37. Jones L, Braithwaite BD, Selwyn D, et al: Neovascularization is the principal cause of varicose vein recurrence: results of a randomized trial of stripping the long saphenous vein. Eur J Vasc Endovasc Surg 12:442, 1996

38. Fischer R, Linde N, Duff C, et al: Late recurrent saphenofemoral junction reflux after ligation and stripping of the greater saphenous vein. J Vasc Surg 34:236, 2001

39. Orbach EJ: Sclerotherapy of varicose veins: utilization of intravenous air block. Am J Surg 66:362, 1944

40. Orbach EJ: Contribution to the therapy of the varicose complex. J Intl Coll Surg 13:765, 1950

41. Cabrera J, Cabrera J, Garcia-Olmedo MA: Treatment of varicose long saphenous vein with sclerosant in microfoam form: long term outcomes. Phlebology 15:19, 2000

42. Pascarella L, Bergan J, Mekenas L: Severe chronic venous insufficiency treated by foam sclerosant. Ann Vasc Surg 20:83, 2006

43. Navarro L, Min RJ, Bone C: Endovenous laser: a new minimally invasive method of treatment for varicose veins—preliminary observations using an 810 nm diode laser. Dermatol Surg 27:117, 2001

44. Proebstle TM, Gul D, Lehr HA, et al: Infrequent early recanalizaion of greater saphenous vein after endovenous laser treatment. J Vasc Surg 38:511, 2003

45. Perkowski P, Ravi R, Gowda RC, et al: Endovenous laser ablation of the saphenous vein for treatment of venous insufficiency and varicose veins: early results from a large single-center experience. J Endovasc Ther 11:132, 2004

46. Weiss RA, Weiss MA: Controlled radiofrequency endovenous occlusion using a unique radio frequency catheter under duplex guidance to eliminate saphenous varicose vein reflux: a 2-year follow-up. Dermatol Surg 20:38, 2002

47. Merchant RF, DePalma RG, Kabnick LS: Endovascular obliteration of saphenous reflux: a multicenter study. J Vasc Surg 35:1190, 2002

48. Hingorani AP, Ascher E, Markevich N, et al: Deep venous thrombosis after radiofrequency ablation of greater saphenous vein: a word of caution. J Vasc Surg 40:500, 2004

Acknowledgments

Figures 2 through 6, 8, and 9a Tom Moore.

98 ENDOVASCULAR PROCEDURES FOR LOWER-EXTREMITY DISEASE

Heather Y. Wolford, M.D., and Mark G. Davies, M.D., Ph.D., F.A.C.S.

Endovascular procedures are increasingly being applied to the treatment of lower-extremity vascular disease: for many common vascular conditions, minimally invasive approaches have become important supplements to (or even supplanted) conventional open surgical approaches.[1] The evolution of these endovascular techniques is likely to result in a corresponding evolution in the therapeutic decision-making process for patients with lower-extremity vascular disease. Research into the long-term outcomes of lower-extremity endovascular procedures will be necessary for a better understanding of the indications for treatment and of the risks and benefits for patients.

Arterial Procedures

Arterial conditions of the lower extremity that may be treated with endoluminal therapy include chronic ischemia, acute ischemia, and aneurysmal disease. The fundamental skill set and the basic techniques employed are the same for all of these conditions. Accordingly, the ensuing discussion first reviews the basics of endovascular therapy and then focuses on specific areas of chronic, acute, and aneurysmal arterial disease of the lower extremity that are amenable to endoluminal intervention.

BASIC ENDOVASCULAR PROCEDURES

Preprocedural Evaluation

Clinical evaluation   The first step in the intervention consists of a thorough history and a careful physical examination. Patients should be specifically asked about chronic renal insufficiency, current or past anticoagulant therapy, and previous vascular and endovascular interventions. Lower-extremity pulses should be assessed, and the degree of ischemia present should be determined [*see Table 1*]. Basic serum biochemical and hematologic data should be obtained and reviewed. The results of any previous imaging studies should also be obtained and reviewed. Patients with serum creatinine concentrations higher than 1.5 mg/dl should be considered for a renal protection protocol [*see Table 2*], and at the time of the procedure, the use of an alternative contrast

agent to decrease total nephrotoxic dye volumes (see below) may be considered. Patients taking oral hypoglycemic agents are asked to stop doing so on the day of the procedure and not to resume for 48 hours after the procedure. In general, to prevent bleeding complications, it is preferred that the international normalized ratio (INR) be lower than 1.6 and the platelet count higher than 50,000/mm³ at the time of intervention.

If a therapeutic intervention is planned, the patient should be given aspirin, 81 mg/day, and clopidogrel, 75 mg/day, for at least 3 days beforehand. If there is not enough time to do this, the patient may be given clopidogrel, 150 to 300 mg, within the 2 hours preceding the procedure.

Investigative studies   Imaging is required before any intervention. Noninvasive vascular ultrasonographic studies document the initial status of the arterial blood supply and allow localization of the culprit lesions. The ankle-brachial index (ABI) (or, in diabetics and patients with incompressible ankle vessels, the toe-brachial index), pulse-volume recordings (PVRs), and segmental pressures quantify arterial perfusion and define areas of stenosis or occlusion within each leg. Duplex ultrasonography is an alternative to PVRs and segmental pressures and provides further diagnostic information that allows the interventionalist to identify involved vessel segments and lesions amenable to percutaneous therapy. These objective measurements serve as a baseline against which postinterventional results may be assessed.

Generally, noninvasive studies provide sufficient information to allow one to proceed with diagnostic angiography and possible endoluminal intervention. In many cases, however, additional studies are required to refine the interventional plan and to reduce the time and resources required. Computed tomographic angiography (CTA) provides two-dimensional images of the arterial system, which are then postprocessed to generate three-dimensional reconstructions. It is particularly effective for imaging tibial vessels. The main drawbacks of CTA are the time necessary to reconstruct the images, the possibility of interference from metal implants, and the contrast load involved. Magnetic resonance angiography (MRA) also provides potentially helpful preprocedural

Table 1   Classification of Critical Ischemia

Grade	Limb Status	Prognosis for Limb	Capillary Refill	Motor Changes	Sensory Loss	Arterial Doppler US	Venous Doppler US
I	Viable	Not threatened	Intact	None	None	+	+
IIa	Threatened	Salvageable	Slow	None	Partial	–	+
IIb	Threatened	Salvageable with emergency intervention	Slow or absent	Diminished function	Partial	–	+
III	Irreversible	Nonsalvageable	Absent	No function	Complete	–	–

US—ultrasonography

Table 2 Renal Protection Strategies

Oral Therapy	Other Strategies
N-acetylcysteine, 600 mg p.o., b.i.d., for total of four doses; first dose given 12 hr before procedure Theophylline, 200 mg I.V., given 30 min before procedure, or 200 mg p.o., b.i.d., starting 24 hr before procedure and continued for 48 hr after procedure	Hydration with normal saline, starting 1 hr before procedure and continued for 3 hr after procedure Sodium bicarbonate drip, 154 mEq/L, starting 1 hr before procedure and continued for 6 hr after procedure Use of alternative contrast agent

information and has the advantage of using gadolinium, which is a relatively low risk contrast agent for patients with renal insufficiency. The main drawbacks of MRA are relatively poor patient tolerance of the machine, the tendency to overestimate lesion severity, the long image acquisition time, and the variability in image quality as one proceeds distally in the leg. Patients with limited arterial access will benefit from a cross-sectional imaging algorithm: such an approach allows one to perform a focused angiogram and to make more efficient use of resources during a therapeutic intervention.

Preprocedural Planning

Choice of arterial access site The common femoral artery (CFA) contralateral to the affected side is the arterial access site most commonly employed. If the patient has an occluded CFA or a "hostile groin," a radial, high brachial, or axillary artery approach may be chosen instead; however, access at these sites is associated with a relatively higher incidence of complications. Ideally, to facilitate manual compression, the access site should lie over a flat bony prominence. An antegrade ipsilateral CFA approach is a useful alternative to contralateral access if there is a contraindication to working from the contralateral side (e.g., significant contralateral iliac disease, a heavily scarred groin, recent application of a vascular closure device, or a bifurcated aortic graft) and if preoperative imaging has demonstrated that there is an adequate working distance (generally, at least 15 to 20 cm) between the CFA access point and the target lesion. If an antegrade approach fails, a retrograde approach may be employed to target ipsilateral iliac arterial disease from the CFA or superficial femoral artery (SFA) disease from the popliteal artery.

Selective Lower-Extremity Angiography

Technique Standard methods of obtaining vascular access for angiography are described in more detail elsewhere [see 87 Fundamentals of Endovascular Surgery]. For selective angiography of the lower extremity, a 4 or 5 French diagnostic sheath is initially placed in the CFA contralateral to the affected extremity. A 4 or

5 French multi–side-hole diagnostic catheter (in a straight, curved, or pigtail configuration) is then placed over a wire into the juxtarenal aorta. After the initial aortic films are obtained in the anteroposterior (AP) projection, the diagnostic catheter is moved down to a point 2 to 3 cm above the aortic bifurcation, and a series of pelvic images are taken in the AP and lateral projections.

The aortic bifurcation is generally traversed with a curved catheter; the curve of the tip should be similar to the angle of the bifurcation. A wire is maneuvered into the iliac system and positioned in the external iliac artery or the CFA, and the curved diagnostic catheter is advanced to the point where its tip lies within the distal external iliac artery and its holes are beyond the ostium of the internal iliac artery.

Once the catheter has been correctly positioned, further contrast injections are performed. Complete lower-extremity images, which should include tibial and pedal vessels (in AP and magnified lateral foot views), are taken before the intervention so that preprocedural status can be compared with postprocedural status and any distal complications can be recognized. Contrast doses commonly employed for digital subtraction arteriography (DSA) depend on the specific arterial segment being addressed [see Table 3].

Alternative contrast agents. Standard angiography is performed with an iodinated nonionic contrast agent. In patients with creatinine concentrations higher than 1.5 mg/dl, an alternative contrast agent may be preferable. Carbon dioxide may be used to image the abdominal aorta, the iliac arteries, and, occasionally, the proximal leg arteries. As the vessels become smaller, however, CO_2 images become less clear. Elevating the legs may help in obtaining adequate imaging to the level of the knees. For CO_2 imaging, a 60 ml syringe is connected to a three-way stopcock, and CO_2 from a tank is loaded into the syringe through the stopcock assembly while the stopcock is submerged in normal saline and manually kept under pressure. The submerged system is flushed with CO_2 several times to purge any residual air. The CO_2-containing syringe is connected to an indwelling catheter, and the CO_2 is then injected forcefully by hand while the fluoroscopy unit is activated. The resulting images must undergo postprocessing to be viewed correctly. CO_2 imaging should not be used above the diaphragm or in the visceral artery segment of the aorta.

Gadolinium may also be used to image the pelvic vessels and the proximal leg arteries. Like CO_2 images, gadolinium images become less clear as the lower-extremity arteries become smaller and more distal. Gadolinium is loaded into the power injector or injected by hand, like standard contrast agents. Doses higher than 0.3 mmol/kg may be nephrotoxic.[2]

Troubleshooting If crossing the aortic bifurcation proves difficult, changing to a hydrophilic wire (e.g., a 0.035-in. soft or

Table 3 DSA Imaging Techniques with Power Injector

Arterial Segment Imaged	View	Contrast Dosage	Delay
Infrarenal aorta	AP	10–20 ml/sec for 2 sec	No
Iliac arteries	AP/oblique	3–10 ml/sec for 2–3 sec	No
CFA and SFA	AP	3–10 ml/sec for 2–3 sec	Flow dependent
Tibial arteries	AP	3–5 ml/sec for 3–4 sec	Yes
Pedal artery	AP/lateral foot	3–6 ml/sec for 3–4 sec	Yes

AP—anteroposterior CFA—common femoral artery SFA—superficial femoral artery stiff glide wire) may help. Occasionally, if one has trouble advancing the 5 French catheter, using a 4 French hydrophilic catheter may mitigate the problem. Attempts at passing the bifurcation should not be abandoned until several different angled catheters have been tried. If all such attempts fail and contralateral access is imperative, ipsilateral puncture with introduction of a snare to grasp the contralateral wire in the abdominal aorta should be considered. Alternatively, DSA may be performed from the aortic bifurcation; however, the contrast loads will be significantly higher in this situation.

Crossing of Lesion

The diagnostic imaging studies and the preliminary angiogram should suffice to identify a lesion that is amenable to endovascular therapy. Once such a lesion is identified, wire access across the target lesion is required to establish a platform for subsequent intervention.

Technique Iliac lesions may be approached either in a retrograde fashion from the ipsilateral CFA or in an antegrade fashion from the contralateral CFA if there is adequate working distance between the bifurcation and the iliac lesion. For more distal lesions, when a contralateral CFA approach is used, a guide sheath is required to stabilize catheters and wires. A wire is placed in the external iliac artery on the affected side (see above), and the diagnostic catheter placed across the bifurcation is replaced with a stiff sheath, such as a 6 French Balkin sheath (Cook Incorporated, Bloomington, Indiana), which has a curve that naturally rests over the bifurcation. Occasionally, it is difficult to get the sheath to cross the bifurcation. In such a situation, the initial wire may be exchanged for a stiffer wire, such as a 0.035-in. Amplatz wire (Cook Urological, Spencer, Indiana), and the sheath may be placed over this wire. The use of a reinforced or stiff guide sheath eliminates the mechanical disadvantage of a wire that moves away from the limb with all manipulations, and it solidifies unilateral limb access for subsequent angiography during the therapeutic portion of the procedure.

Once the sheath is in place, a long, angled end-hole catheter and a glide wire are directed toward the specific vessel segment being treated and carefully manipulated so as to cross the target lesion. Road mapping, fluoroscopy fade, or intermittent puffing of contrast material through the guide catheter can delineate the contours of the vessel, identify the correct path to take, and help keep the wire within the true lumen. In general, a stenosis can be crossed by a curved or J-tip wire, a 0.035-in. hydrophilic glide wire, or a Wholey wire (a 0.035-in. wire with a floppy tip; Mallinckrodt, St. Louis, Missouri). The hydrophilic coating on the glide wire makes it more prone to dissection than the other wires are. With angled catheters, it is essential to use torque devices to direct the tip of the wire in the appropriate direction. In some cases, using a TAD II wire with a 0.018-in. distal tip and a 0.035-in. main body (Mallinckrodt, St. Louis, Missouri) makes access through a tight lesion easier to obtain; in addition, it provides a transition to a larger, more robust wire, which can be a very effective platform. For tibial stenoses, a 0.014-in. or 0.018-in. system is generally employed to cross tighter lesions. To stabilize the 0.014-in. wire, a 3 or 4 French catheter may be used as a guide catheter, placed just proximal to the lesion.

Occlusions can be difficult to cross, particularly when significant calcification is apparent on the plain films obtained before angiography. The techniques employed are the same as those used to cross a stenosis. The goal is to traverse the occlusion and gain access to the true lumen distally; accordingly, a J-tip or Wholey wire may be preferred, in that hydrophilic wires tend to create dissection planes. Often, the occlusion cannot be crossed, and a subintimal plane must be developed. A glide wire is used to gain access near the proximal portion of the lesion at a branch point and allowed to deform in such a way as to form a loop; the wire is then pushed forward, supported by a 4 or 5 French catheter. Often, the true lumen is accessed without any difficulty, and the location of the wire within the lumen is confirmed by contrast injections. Occasionally, however, reentry into the true lumen proves difficult. Various manipulations and techniques may be employed to help with this technical issue. In addition, two systems have been developed with this potential problem in mind. The CrossPoint IVUS catheter (Medtronic, Minneapolis, Minnesota) combines an intravascular ultrasound probe with a puncture needle and allows one to visualize the true lumen, enter it with a hollow needle, and pass a wire to maintain access. The Outback catheter (LuMend, Redwood City, California) has a special tip that microdissects the plaque to facilitate reentry into the true lumen. If these options fail, retrograde puncture and retrograde passage of a wire, with interval snaring to "floss" the occlusion, may be considered.

Troubleshooting In crossing occlusions, the following three points must be emphasized.

1. Care must be taken to ensure that the operator is in the true lumen.
2. To preserve subsequent bypass targets, the next segment of the vessel must not be compromised by an overly aggressive attempt to regain access from a subintimal dissection plane.
3. Wire access across the lesion must be maintained at all times.

A low-dose intravenous bolus of heparin (2,000 to 5,000 IU) must be given before any intervention to help prevent the thrombosis that may result from manipulation and transient occlusion of the lesion.

Angioplasty and Stenting

Technique *Angioplasty.* Angioplasty is the initial treatment for most lower-extremity lesions. It may be the only therapeutic intervention required, or it may be employed as a prelude to stent deployment as a means of ensuring that the arterial lumen is wide enough to allow free passage of a platform. Angioplasty balloons exist in several varieties, which are reviewed in more detail elsewhere [*see 87 Fundamentals of Endovascular Surgery*]. In general, a noncompliant balloon is chosen that is 1 to 2 mm smaller than the normal or anticipated final vessel diameter for the area of the vasculature being addressed. The normal vessel diameter may be estimated on the basis of operator experience, measured with a radiopaque ruler placed alongside the vessel, or quantitated with the calibration software available on most imaging systems.

Once the balloon has been successfully maneuvered into position across the lesion, it is inflated with a manual inflation device to allow controlled delivery of a defined pressure load. Inflation is continued until the waist of the balloon disappears or maximal balloon inflation pressure (8 to 15 atm on most standard balloons) is reached. If an optimally sized balloon or stent will not cross a highly stenotic lesion, preangioplasty dilatation with a lower-profile, smaller-diameter balloon is required.

If the lesion is in close proximity to or involves a bifurcation (e.g., the aortic bifurcation, the femoral bifurcation, or the tibioperoneal trunk), care must be taken to prevent occlusion of the other branching vessel during dilatation of the target lesion. To this end, most interventionalists advocate use of the so-called kissing balloon technique, which involves simultaneous dilatation or

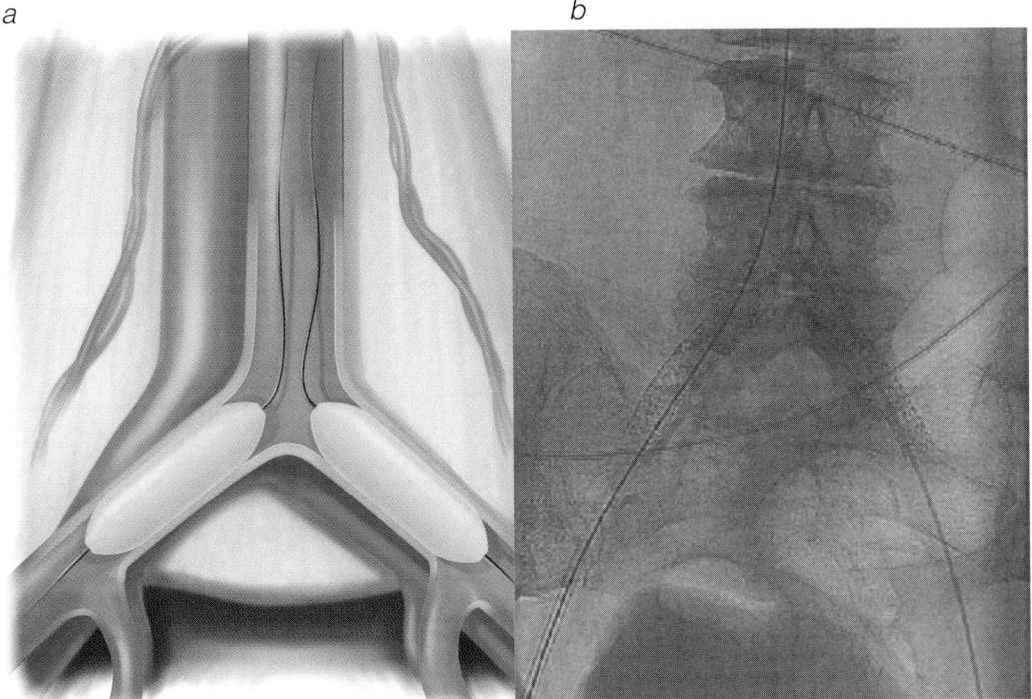

Figure 1 Basic endovascular techniques: angioplasty and stenting. Shown is the so-called kissing balloon technique. The patient presented with bilateral claudication, a decreased ABI on exercise treadmill testing, and a duplex ultrasonogram that suggested iliac occlusive disease. (*a*) Illustration shows two balloons "kissing" in the common iliac arteries. (*b*) Radiograph shows two stents "kissing" in the iliac arteries.

stenting of both branching vessels of the bifurcation to preserve both lumina. This technique is most commonly employed for proximal common iliac artery lesions [*see Figure 1*]. Alternatively, one may place a guard wire in the unaffected vessel and use this wire as a safety measure if there is a danger of luminal compromise, or one may deploy a balloon in the unaffected ostium while the affected ostium is treated.

Stenting. Basic stent choices are discussed more fully elsewhere [*see 87 Fundamentals of Endovascular Surgery*]. Stents may be placed either primarily or as a secondary procedure when initial angioplasty yields inadequate results (generally defined as either greater than 30% residual stenosis or the occurrence of an angioplasty-related complication, such as arterial wall perforation or flow-limiting dissection). Stents are generally sized according to the normal diameter of the adjacent vessel; 10% to 15% oversizing is acceptable. If the stent will be crossing two vessel segments with mismatched diameters (e.g., the common iliac artery and the external iliac artery), it is preferable to use a self-expanding stent, which is better able to adjust to such mismatching. Treatment of specific arteries is discussed more fully in connection with management of chronic lower-extremity ischemia [*see* Procedures for Chronic Lower-Extremity Ischemia, *below*].

Adjuncts to angioplasty and stenting. Over the past few years, several innovative devices have been developed that expand on the basic concepts of angioplasty and stenting in the lower extremities. One such device is the PolarCath cryoplasty balloon (Boston Scientific, Natick, Massachusetts) [*see Figure 2a*]. This device delivers cold thermal energy to the vessel wall in the form of nitrous oxide (–10° C) and is inflated to a pressure of 8 atm. It is presumed that the freezing of the vessel allows a more controlled vessel wall injury

and concomitantly promotes apoptosis and reduces the restenosis response. To date, the PolarCath has been employed mainly in the SFA; it is currently being tested for use in the tibial vessels. In initial reports, anatomic patency rates in the femoropopliteal arteries have exceeded 80% at 1 year for TransAtlantic Inter-Society Consensus (TASC) grade A, B, and C lesions.[3]

Another such device is the Peripheral Cutting Balloon (Boston Scientific, Natick, Massachusetts) [*see Figure 2b*], which is increasingly being used on lower-extremity vascular lesions, particularly those that proved resistant to balloon angioplasty. This device consists of a noncompliant balloon that has four thin blades placed longitudinally around it; it is available in sizes ranging from 2 mm to 8 mm, and it operates over a 0.018-in. platform. The theoretical rationale for its use is that fracturing or cutting the lesion in a controlled pattern may reduce the severity of the vessel injury while achieving a satisfactory luminal response and mitigating the restenosis response. Initial results in stenotic vein grafts have been encouraging, with 95% patency reported at 11 months' follow-up in one small study.[4]

Directional atherectomy devices are being used to treat chronic atherosclerotic leg ischemia in the belief that debulking the lesion will allow greater increases in luminal diameter than the conventional methods of angioplasty and stenting, which merely displace plaque. Multiple different systems are available, all of which appear to be yielding roughly equivalent results. One of the more widely used directional atherectomy devices is the SilverHawk Plaque Excision System (FoxHollow Technologies, Redwood City, California), which consists of a catheter that is compatible with a 0.014-in. wire and that has a rotating blade at the tip. As the blade shaves plaque off the vessel wall, the shavings are stored in the tip of the catheter. When the storage unit in the tip becomes full, the catheter is removed and cleaned, then reinserted. Initial intermediate-term results have been satisfactory; however, wider

a

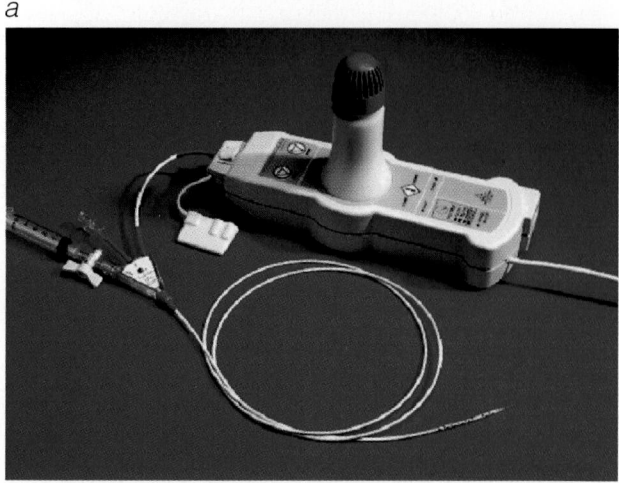

b

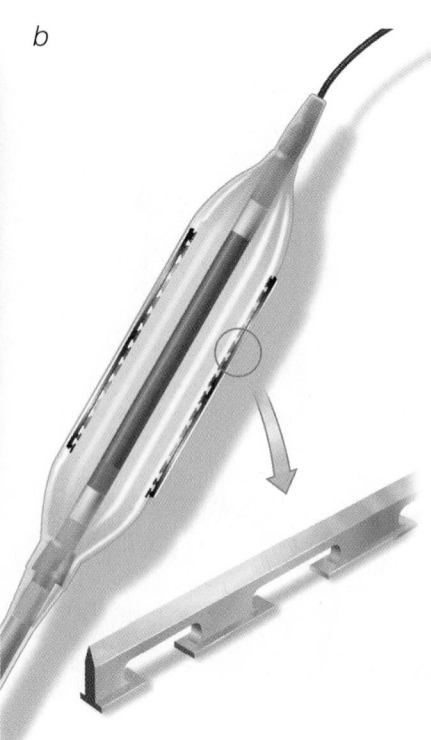

Figure 2 **Basic endovascular techniques: angioplasty and stenting. (*a*) Shown is the PolarCath peripheral dilatation system, comprising an inflation unit, a cryoplasty balloon, a cord attached to a separate power module, and a nitrous oxide cartridge. (*b*) Shown is the Peripheral Cutting Balloon, with an enlarged view of an atherotome. (Images provided courtesy of Boston Scientific, Natick, Massachusetts).**

use of this device will depend on the results of the multicenter TALON registry.[5]

Drug-eluting stents have become popular for use within the coronary circulation, but at present, they are only in the initial stages of investigation for treatment of lower-extremity arterial disease. Initial trials with the sirolimus-coated S.M.A.R.T. stent (Cordis, Miami Lakes, Florida) showed a nonsignificant trend toward decreased restenosis rates.[6]

Troubleshooting Angioplasty can result in either non–flow-limiting or flow-limiting dissections. If dissection occurs, reinflation of the balloon over the dissection for 5 to 10 minutes may anneal the flap to the wall. If balloon reinflation fails and flow is still disrupted, a stent should be placed.

In situ thrombosis of the vessel occasionally occurs after angioplasty or stent placement. If it develops in a patient who underwent angioplasty alone, the thrombosed vessel may be stented open. If this measure fails or if the in situ thrombosis develops after stent placement, a thrombolysis catheter is placed across the lesion and a single bolus of a thrombolytic agent administered. If this approach yields suboptimal results, an indwelling catheter is placed for a 12- to 24-hour infusion [*see* Procedures for Acute Lower-Extremity Ischemia, *below*]. Alternatively, mechanical thrombectomy with a rheolytic catheter may be considered. Finally, restenting with an open or covered stent is an option, but it may result in distal embolization.

Perforation of the vessel can occur during angioplasty or recannulization. Perforations that are small or that occurred during a failed recannulization need not be treated. Perforations associated with persistent extravasation of contrast may be managed primarily with balloon tamponade (20 minutes of inflation, with intermittent deflations to allow distal circulation and reversal of anticoagulation) and secondarily with placement of a covered stent.

Endoluminal intervention to treat plaque can result in distal embolization of cholesterol or plaque or distal dislodgment of thrombi. Mechanical or pharmacologic thrombolysis remains the mainstay option in such cases. If, however, one is concerned about

a possible nonthrombotic embolic event, aspiration or open embolectomy may be required to achieve satisfactory reconstitution of flow.

When a vessel is heavily calcified, a self-expanding stent may be unable to deploy and may be effectively "jailed" in the lesion. In this situation, wire access must be maintained, and a low-profile balloon should be used to enlarge the operating lumen so that a high-pressure balloon can then be introduced. The introduction of a series of balloons with successively larger diameters will eventually allow the stent to be deployed. Balloon perforation often occurs in these cases, and care should be taken to extract the perforated balloon intact.

Unplanned stent dislodgment is rare but not unknown. If it occurs, the errant stent may be fixed in place by placing an additional overlapping stent. Alternatively, a balloon may be inflated distal to the tip of the dislodged stent and used to move the stent to another vessel, where it may be safely deployed.

Complications The most common complications of angioplasty and stenting in the lower extremities are access-related issues, including hematoma, arteriovenous fistula formation, and pseudoaneurysm. The incidence of hematoma can be minimized by using the smallest sheath possible, waiting for normalization of the activated clotting time before pulling the sheath, and holding manual pressure for 30 minutes after the procedure. Devices designed for vessel closure after percutaneous intervention are available but have not been proved to reduce the incidence of access-related complications.[7] With several of these closure devices, it is recommended that access of the groin not be attempted for up to 90 days after insertion.

PROCEDURES FOR CHRONIC LOWER-EXTREMITY ISCHEMIA

Preprocedural Evaluation

Patients presenting with chronic lower-limb ischemia are evaluated as previously outlined [*see* Basic Endovascular Procedures, Preprocedural Evaluation, *above*]. Patients with claudication are

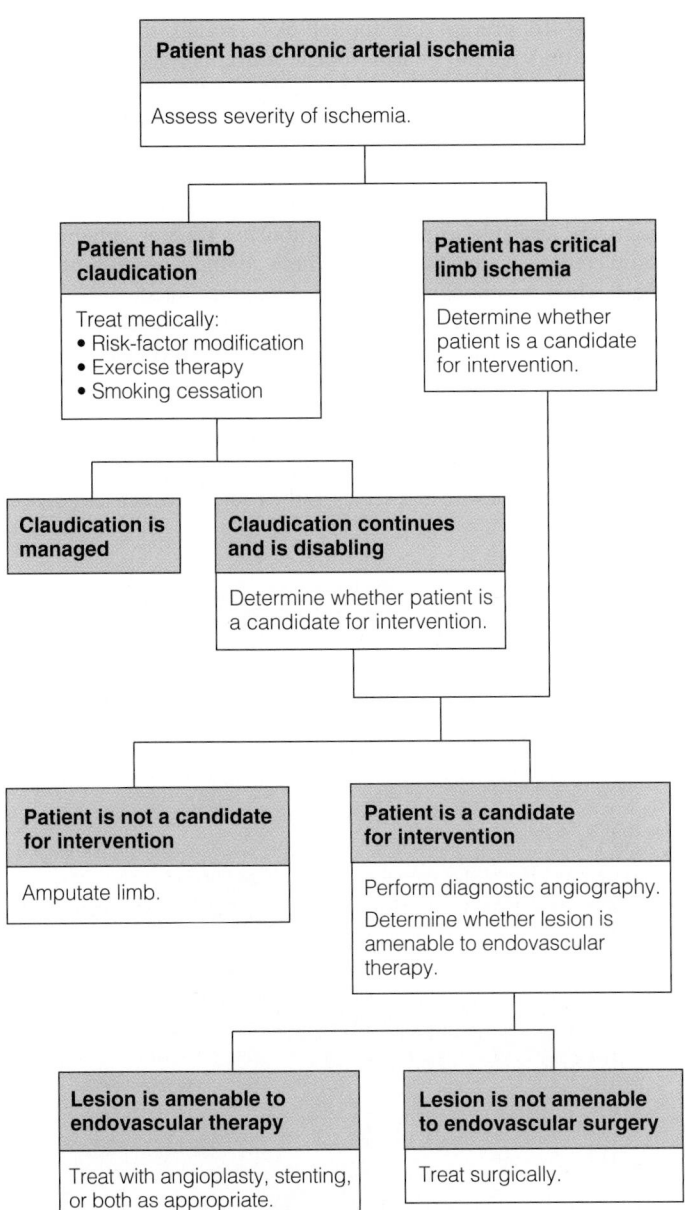

Figure 3 **Algorithm illustrates workup of patients with chronic lower-extremity ischemia.**

managed medically by controlling risk factors, instituting exercise therapy, and providing advice on smoking cessation.[8] In patients with disabling claudication, rest pain, or tissue loss, diagnostic imaging studies are performed with the intent of identifying and subsequently treating any lesion that is amenable to endovascular therapy [*see Figure 3*]. If an intervention is indicated, patients are pretreated with antiplatelet agents as appropriate.

Technique

Techniques and protocols for diagnostic angiography and accessing the target lesion have been outlined [*see Basic Endovascular Procedures, above*]. If it is unclear whether a vessel has a hemodynamically significant stenosis, arterial pressures can be measured across the lesion by connecting an end-hole catheter to a pressure transducer. A drop of more than 10 mm Hg in systolic blood pressure or more than 5 mm Hg in mean arterial pressure across the lesion is considered significant. The area in question should also be subjected to a chemical challenge. Local intra-arterial delivery of a vasodilator (e.g., papaverine, 30 mg; priscoline, 25 mg; or nitroglycerin, 200 µg) will create distal vasodilatation, accentuate the translesional gradient, and, in many cases, unmask a significant lesion that might otherwise be missed.

Iliac lesions may be treated either by means of primary angioplasty, with stenting reserved for cases in which angioplasty yields unsatisfactory results, or by means of primary stenting. Either balloon-expandable or self-expanding stents may be used in the iliac vessels. Highly calcified lesions and lesions in smaller iliac vessels (< 7 mm) generally are best treated with self-expanding stents. Lesions in the external iliac artery or the femoral artery (including the CFA, the profunda femoris [PF], and the SFA) are best treated with angioplasty alone. In these vessels, stents usually are placed only when angioplasty has been unsuccessful or dissection or vessel rupture has occurred. As a rule, stenting for SFA lesions is best done with self-expanding stents, though very focal lesions may be treated with balloon-expandable stents. Stenting is relatively contraindicated in the popliteal artery; the extended range of motion across the nearby joint often leads to stent fracture. At present, stents are not used as primary therapy in infrapopliteal vessels. If stenting is required at infrapopliteal sites, coronary balloon-mounted platforms are the only available choices.

Postprocedural Care

After the procedure, patients require at least 2 to 12 hours of bed rest. Hydration with I.V. infusion of normal saline should be initiated, and appropriate dosages of renal-protective agents should be given. Aspirin, 81 mg/day, should be given on a long-term basis, and clopidogrel, 75 mg/day, should be administered for 30 days.

Outcome Evaluation

In most series, rates of technical success (defined as less than 30% residual stenosis) have exceeded 90%. Secondary patency rates for iliac interventions at 10 years have exceeded 50%.[9] Angioplasty and stenting in the SFA have been studied, for the most part, in a retrospective fashion. Intermediate-term data have suggested patency rates of 70%, 60% and 50% at 1, 3, and 5 years, respectively. The reported clinical benefit has generally exceeded the anatomic patency rates.[10-12] None of the randomized studies published to date have found primary stenting to have any advantage over primary angioplasty in the femoral vessels.[13-16] Factors indicative of a poor prognosis include intervention for more advanced limb ischemia, diabetes, complete occlusion (as opposed to stenosis), lesions longer than 10 cm, and poor distal runoff.[8] The use of TASC criteria to stratify lesions anatomically helps predict which patients are likely to benefit most from endovascular therapy in the SFA.[17] In one study that included almost 400 SFA interventions, patients who had TASC A and B lesions experienced significantly better outcomes than those who had TASC C and D lesions, with an overall 6-year patency rate of 52%.[10] Currently, angioplasty is being evaluated for use in infrapopliteal disease. Some initial success has been reported, though it still appears that this approach is best reserved for patients in whom open surgical management is relatively contraindicated.[18]

PROCEDURES FOR ACUTE LOWER-EXTREMITY ISCHEMIA

Preprocedural Evaluation

The initial decision in managing acute lower-extremity ischemia limb should be whether to proceed directly to surgery or to obtain a diagnostic angiogram and consider endovascular therapy. The Working Party on Thrombolysis developed a consensus

Table 4 Contraindications to Thrombolysis

Relative Contraindications	Absolute Contraindications
Recent surgery (within 2 wk)	Active internal bleeding
Recent trauma (within 1 mo)	Recent stroke (within 2 mo)
History of coagulopathy	Intracranial pathology
Pregnancy or recent delivery	

on how to approach patients with acute arterial ischemia. The main message of this consensus was that classifying patients according to their grade of ischemia is essential to forming treatment plans [*see 84 Pulseless Extremity and Atheroembolism*].[19] Grade IIa and early grade IIb ischemia may be amenable to endoluminal therapy, including thrombolysis. Established grade IIb ischemia is best treated by means of surgical embolectomy or thrombectomy, with intraoperative angiography, intraoperative thrombolysis, and over-the-wire embolectomy as options. Grade III ischemia is non-salvageable and generally necessitates amputation [*see 99 Lower-Extremity Amputation for Ischemia*].

Arterial Thrombolysis

Thrombolysis, either pharmacologic or mechanical, is the mainstay of endovascular therapy for acute arterial ischemia.[20] Relative and absolute contraindications to thrombolytic therapy have been established [*see Table 4*].

Technique An initial diagnostic angiogram of the affected limb is obtained, with care taken to gain arterial access in such a way that thrombolytic therapy is not prevented. The standard approach is from the contralateral groin (see above). To reduce the chances of access site hematoma during administration of a thrombolytic agent, access should be gained at a substantial distance from the occlusion. Crossing the lesion involves identifying the origin of the occlusion. In cases of native vessel occlusion, this is generally a straightforward process. If a bypass graft is occluded, one may be able to visualize a stump of the graft, which will aid in direct management [*see Figure 4*]. The standard methods of crossing a stenosis or an occlusion [*see Basic Endovascular Procedures, Crossing of Lesion, above*] should be employed.

Once the lesion has been crossed securely with a wire, an infusion catheter (e.g., a 3 French multi–side-hole catheter) is advanced over the wire and situated in the occlusion. An infusion wire may also be inserted through the infusion catheter in a coaxial fashion and placed distally to increase the area of direct lysis, to protect the outflow vessel, or to address two separate lesions [*see Figure 5*]. The position of the catheter and the wire are then documented by means of fluoroscopy. With the infusion catheter left securely in place, the thrombolytic infusion is begun. Often, it helps to insert a guide sheath into the contralateral iliac system to prevent dislodgment and facilitate subsequent access.

Pharmacologic agents. The use of thrombolytic drugs has been refined over the past decade. In the United States, urokinase and tissue plasminogen activator (t-PA) have been the most widely used agents. Urokinase was popular in the 1980s and 1990s, but its temporary withdrawal from the market in 1998 because of manufacturing problems allowed physicians to become more comfortable working with t-PA. At present, recombinant t-PA (rt-PA) (e.g., alteplase) is the lytic agent most commonly used in the United States. Reteplase is a newer recombinant agent that is similar to rt-PA but has a longer half-life and a less specific affinity for

fibrin.[21,22] To prevent buildup of clot around the sheath, all patients undergoing pharmacologic thrombolysis also receive heparin in a continuously administered low dosage (200 to 500 U/hr); higher dosages are associated with a substantially increased risk of hemorrhagic complications.

Mechanical adjuncts to thrombolysis. Several mechanical adjuncts are available to reduce thrombolytic time or enhance the completeness of clot dissolution. These adjuncts can also be beneficial when thrombolytic therapy is contraindicated.

Various mechanical thrombectomy systems are commercially available. One such system is the AngioJet system (Possis Medical, Minneapolis, Minnesota). The Angiojet consists of a pump drive unit and a 4 to 6 French catheter, which is passed over a 0.035-in. wire to the target area. The catheter has two lumens: one is used to pulse heparinized normal saline at a pressure of 10,000 psi, and the other contains the wire and serves as the route by which clot debris

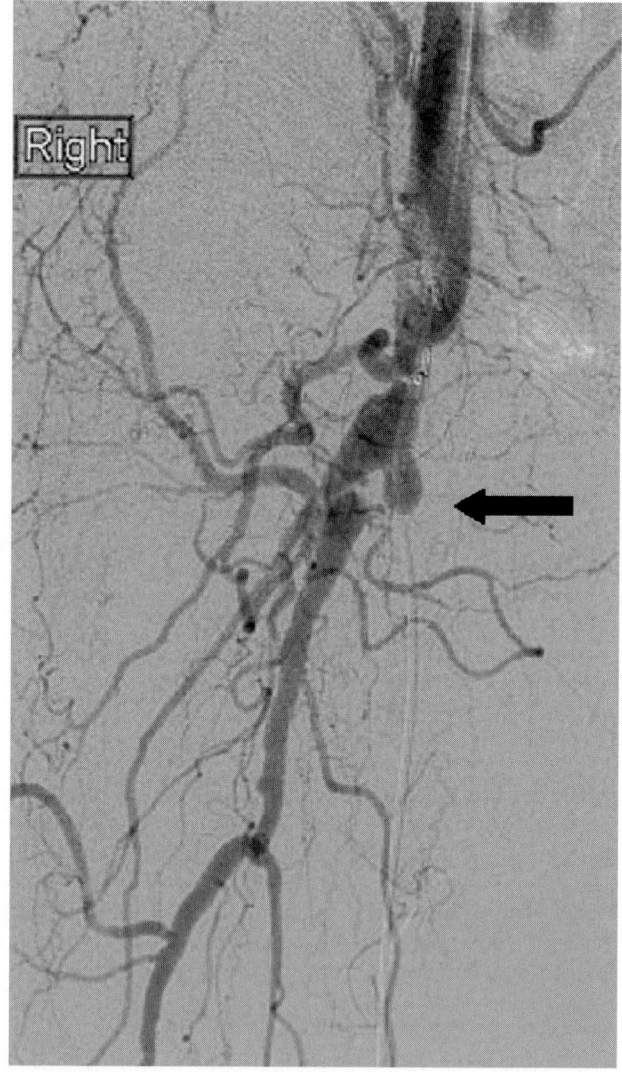

Figure 4 **Arterial thrombolysis. Patient presented with grade IIa ischemia, and duplex ultrasonography showed evidence of an occluded femoropopliteal reverse saphenous vein bypass graft. Angiogram taken from the ipsilateral external iliac artery demonstrating a patent but diseased CFA and a patent PF. The SFA is occluded. The stump of the occluded arterial bypass graft is visible (arrow).**

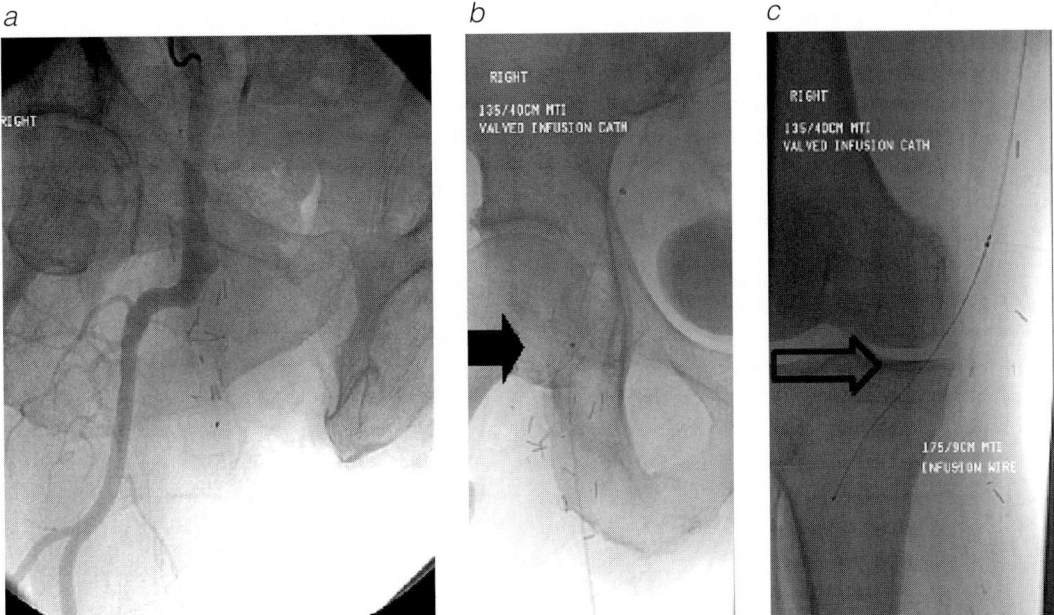

Figure 5 Arterial thrombolysis. Follow-up imaging of the patient in Figure 4 illustrates the use of a thrombolytic infusion catheter. (*a*) Shown is the proximal end of the occluded CFA–popliteal artery bypass graft. (*b*) The infusion catheter (black arrow) is placed. (*c*) The infusion wire rests in the distal bypass graft (hollow arrow), increasing the infusion length for the thrombolytic agent.

is removed. The power pulse spray technique, with rt-PA added to the saline (10 mg in 100 ml) and delivered by the rheolytic catheter directly into the clot, may also be employed to help dissolve clot. In this technique, the system is modified so that the outflow circuit is closed and the unit pulses the saline–rt-PA mixture into the clot, allowing simultaneous lysis and maceration. Once the thrombus has been treated and an additional 15-minute interval has elapsed, conventional catheter therapy is employed to remove the clot and the residual rt-PA. The advantage of this approach is that it permits high-dose lysis while imposing only a low systemic load.[23] If more than 750 ml of saline is used with the AngioJet catheter during a single session, there is a significant risk of acute renal impairment secondary to hemolytic debris.

Also used for mechanical thrombectomy are wall-contact instruments such as the Arrow-Trerotola device (Arrow International, Reading, Pennsylvania). Such devices result in significant endothelial damage and distal clot embolization and thus are better suited for hemodialysis grafts. Another option is the Helix Clot Buster (ev3, Plymouth, Minnesota), which creates a vortex at the catheter tip that macerates the clot into microscopic fragments; it differs from the AngioJet in that it lacks an aspirating port. The Oasis thrombectomy catheter (Boston Scientific, Natick, Massachusetts) also fragments thrombus into small particles. The use of these devices in the setting of acute arterial occlusion was addressed in a comprehensive review published in 2001.[24] All of these devices may be used either in place of or in addition to pharmacologic thrombolysis.

At present, the evidence supporting the use of mechanical thrombectomy devices in the setting of acute limb ischemia is modest. One retrospective study demonstrated successful recanalization in approximately 60% of patients.[25] At our own institution, we have found these devices to be useful in decreasing the clot burden on the second or third t-PA check (24 to 36 hours after commencement of the infusion), after the clot has been softened by the initial pharmacologic lysis. It remains to be seen whether this approach reduces the overall time needed for thrombolytic therapy.

Over-the-wire embolectomy is another mechanical means of removing clot. Newer designs of the standard Fogarty embolectomy catheter have been developed that include an inner lumen, so that the catheter can be passed over a 0.035-in. wire. Use of these devices facilitates fluoroscopically guided embolectomy and ensures that the catheter can be passed to all target vessels. Over-the-wire embolectomy provides an efficient percutaneous method of removing clot without any need for the constant monitoring that pharmacologic thrombolysis requires.

This embolectomy technique may be supplemented by intraoperative catheter-directed thrombolytic therapy when postoperative imaging reveals residual clot or inadequate perfusion. Under fluoroscopic guidance, an end-hole catheter or a multi–side-hole infusion catheter is guided over a wire into the target vessel or vessels, and a thrombolytic agent (e.g., rt-PA, 0.5 mg/kg over 30 minutes) is directly infused with inflow occlusion. Imaging is recommended both before and after thrombolysis. Adjunctive use of an embolectomy catheter may also be beneficial. If, however, there is still no perfusion after adequate thrombolytic therapy and embolectomy, the situation generally is not retrievable, and alternative therapies should be explored. In the clinical trials of perioperative thrombolytic therapy published to date, success rates ranged from 64% to 100%. Bleeding was the most common complication.

Postprocedural care After the intervention, the patient is observed in a monitored unit by personnel trained in the management of thrombolytic therapy. Lower-extremity neurovascular examinations are carried out frequently (every 1 to 2 hours). The patient's clinical status is also monitored for evidence of bleeding, including access-site hematoma, neurologic changes, and hypotension. Repeat angiograms are performed at 12-hour intervals (or sooner if clinical examination reveals significant deterioration) to assess the progress of lytic therapy and to allow changes in catheter positioning. Some physicians recommend following fibrinogen levels and discontinuing the lytic agent if levels fall below 150 mg/dl. Other end points for the thrombolytic therapy are failure to progress, complete lysis of the target thrombus, or significant bleeding complications necessitating discontinuance of lysis.

Once lysis is discontinued, the heparin dosage should be increased to achieve therapeutic levels of anticoagulation. Any lesions unmasked by thrombolytic therapy should be treated, either by endovascular means or with an open procedure. Whether long-term anticoagulation is indicated depends on the patient's circumstances and the specific cause of the thrombosis.

Troubleshooting   Many of the issues raised in connection with basic arterial access techniques arise during attempts at thrombolysis. Occasionally, the interventionalist experiences significant difficulty in accessing an occluded bypass graft. Thrombolysis of these occluded grafts can often be facilitated by employing a double-puncture technique, in which both a retrograde and an antegrade puncture of a bypass graft are performed under ultrasonographic guidance, allowing the infusion catheters to be placed so as to cover the entire length of the graft [see Figure 6].[26] With this approach, there is no need for CFA puncture, which is often made difficult by the presence of scar tissue, and the problem of finding access to the graft takeoff is eliminated. If a lesion cannot be crossed, the thrombolytic agent may be delivered just proximal to the lesion for 2 to 4 hours after initiation of therapy, but the chances of a good outcome with this approach are diminished.

Whereas it is common for clinical findings to worsen slightly (as a result of distal microembolization) before improving—the so-called storm before the calm phenomenon—dramatic worsening of the physical findings calls for urgent angiography. Possible reasons for ischemic progression include propagation of clot (treatable by performing open embolectomy or thrombectomy), displacement of the lysis catheter (treatable by repositioning the catheter), or distal embolization of clot resulting in obstruction of the principal runoff vessels (treatable by advancing the infusion catheter or wire more distally, employing a rheolytic catheter, or performing open embolectomy or thrombectomy).

Complications   General access-site complications—including hematoma, pseudoaneurysm formation, ischemia to the contralateral leg from an occlusive sheath, nerve damage (which is more common with axillary or brachial puncture secondary to an axillary sheath hematoma), arterial dissection of the access vessel, and distal embolization of the clot—are also seen with thrombolyt-

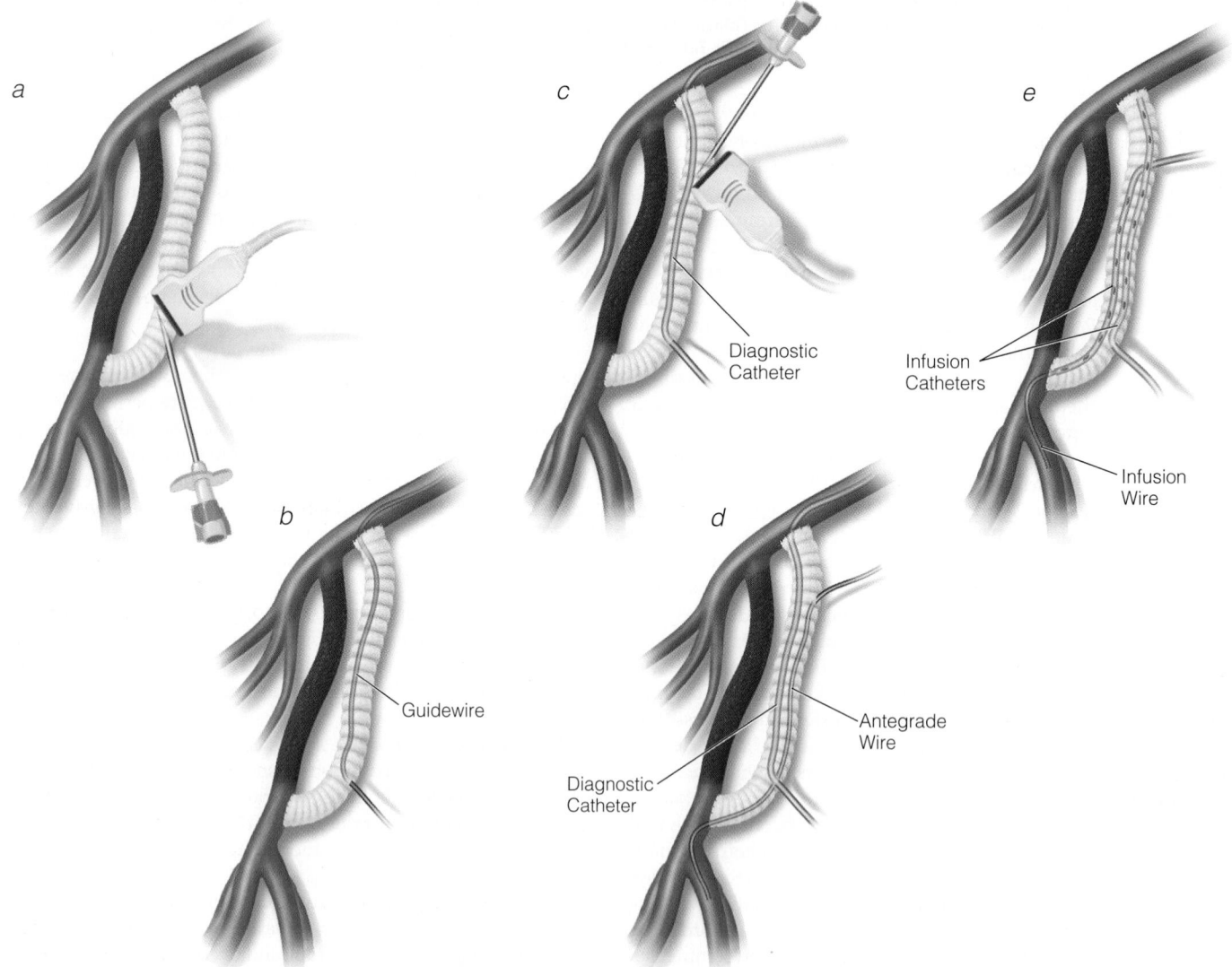

Figure 6   **Arterial thrombolysis. Illustrated is ultrasound-guided double puncture of an arterial bypass graft for thrombolysis.**[26]

Table 5 Prospective, Randomized, Controlled Trials of Arterial Thrombolytic Therapy

Trial (Date)	N	Lytic Agent	Limb Salvage Rate at 1 Yr (Surgery vs. Lytic Therapy)	30-Day Mortality (Surgery vs. Lytic Therapy)	Bleeding Complication Rate with Lytic Therapy
Rochester (1994)[41]	114	Urokinase	82% vs. 82% (NS)	18% vs.12% (NS)	11%
STILE (1994)[27]	393	Urokinase/rt-PA	100% vs. 90%	No difference	5.6%
TOPAS (1996)[42]	213	Urokinase	65% vs. 75% (NS)	5% vs. 3% (NS)	10%

NS—not significant   STILE—Surgery versus Thrombolysis for Ischemia of the Lower Extremity   TOPAS—Thrombolysis Or Peripheral Arterial Surgery

ic therapy. Bleeding complications have presented a significant hurdle for thrombolytic therapy. Early studies that used therapeutic doses of heparin and higher doses of thrombolytics reported unacceptable rates of intracranial hemorrhage and other bleeding complications. Currently, most physicians employ rt-PA doses in the range of 0.25 to 0.50 mg/hr without compromising results. Overall, rates of bleeding complications with urokinase and rt-PA range from 5% to 10%, and the incidence of intracranial hemorrhage is less than 2%.[22] As with open surgical therapy, compartment syndrome can complicate reperfusion of the ischemic limb; this complication should be checked for on serial clinical examinations.

Outcome evaluation The use of thrombolysis to treat acute lower-extremity arterial occlusion has been extensively studied. The results of the major prospective, randomized trials [see Table 5] showed thrombolytic therapy to be equivalent to surgery with respect to limb salvage and mortality and superior with respect to the need for complex surgical intervention. Most of these major trials were performed with urokinase and t-PA. The information gained from them has helped surgeons determine which patients are good candidates for thrombolytic therapy. Factors predictive of successful thrombolysis include symptoms of less than 14 days' duration, prosthetic graft occlusion, and high medical risk for open operation. Factors predictive of a poor outcome include chronic occlusion, native artery occlusion, and a lesion that cannot be crossed with a wire.[27]

PROCEDURES FOR LOWER-EXTREMITY ARTERIAL ANEURYSMS

Ultrasound-Guided Thrombin Injection

Pseudoaneurysms of the CFA are a complication of femoral access for therapeutic procedures and are often amenable to percutaneous therapy. The pseudoaneurysm is visualized with a 7.5-MHz duplex ultrasound probe. Contraindications to injection of the sac are the presence of a wide mouth and no discernible neck, the development of an arteriovenous fistula, compression of adjacent structures by the pseudoaneurysm, and skin changes overlying the pseudoaneurysm. If infection is a possibility, the procedure should not be attempted. The ABI should be determined and duplex ultrasonography of the groin performed before injection.

Once it is certain that the pseudoaneurysm meets the criteria for thrombin injection, the sac is injected in the fundus area, away from the native artery, under direct ultrasonographic visualization and after infiltration of a local anesthetic. Usually, 1,000 units of thrombin is injected, and injection may be repeated one or more times. With multilobar aneurysms, serial injections into each fundus may be required to achieve complete resolution.

Factors associated with successful treatment are a long, narrow pseudoaneurysm neck and a sac diameter smaller than 8 cm.

Overall success rates may exceed 95%. Complications include distal native artery thrombosis and distal embolization, which generally can be treated with I.V. heparin.[28]

Placement of Covered Stent

Treatment of lower-extremity aneurysms with covered stents is currently being studied. Isolated iliac artery and SFA lesions, though rare, lend themselves to endovascular repair [see Figure 7]. Initial data suggest that repair of popliteal aneurysms with covered stents is also feasible in high-risk patients.[29] Newer stents are being developed that are better able to withstand the stresses imposed by the repetitive motion of the knee joint.

Venous Procedures

As endovascular therapy for arterial disease continues to evolve, techniques learned in the arterial tree are increasingly being applied to the venous system. At present, the main venous disease processes being treated with endovascular techniques are iliofemoral deep vein thrombosis (DVT) and superficial reflux of the greater saphenous system causing symptomatic varicose veins.

VENOUS THROMBOLYSIS

Lower-extremity DVT can have a significant impact on patients' quality of life. Multiple studies indicate that approximately 50% of patients experience postthrombophlebitic syndrome (PTS) and that the majority of patients with PTS report that physical and emotional well-being are negatively affected.[30] The goals of venous lysis are to relieve obstruction and to preserve valve function.

Preprocedural Evaluation

If DVT is less than 1 month old, a trial of lytic therapy is appropriate. The ideal candidate for such therapy has a symptomatic clot with lower-extremity swelling, is young and mobile, is not in a hypercoagulable state, and has no contraindications to lysis. Currently, lytic therapy is more commonly employed in active patients, whose quality of life is more likely to be negatively affected by PTS. In cases of unprovoked DVT or recurrent DVT, a hypercoagulability workup is indicated.[31] Venous thrombosis is discussed more fully elsewhere [see 85 Venous Thromboembolism].

Technique

The initial diagnostic venogram can be obtained via almost any venous access site. Our preference is to perform an ipsilateral popliteal vein stick with the patient in the prone position; the posterior tibial vein or the contralateral femoral vein can also be used. The popliteal vein is accessed with a micropuncture needle under ultrasonographic guidance by means of a Seldinger technique.

The micropuncture sheath is then replaced with a 5 French sheath over a 0.035-in. wire. The diagnostic venogram is performed through the sheath or with a straight multi–side-hole diagnostic catheter.

As in arterial thrombolysis [see Arterial Procedures, Procedures for Acute Lower-Extremity Ischemia, Arterial Thrombolysis, above], a 3 French infusion catheter is advanced over the wire and positioned within the clot. Longer lesions can be managed with a coaxial infusion catheter–wire system. The lytic infusion is started, and a low-dose intravenous heparin infusion is initiated through the sheath. Mechanical thrombectomy and power pulse spray thrombectomy can efficiently debulk thrombus and may be beneficial in patients with phlegmasia caerulea dolens.[32] The patient is kept in a monitored floor bed, and repeat venograms are performed every 12 to 24 hours.

In some patients, May-Thurner syndrome (compression of the iliac vein by the overlying iliac artery) develops; it is treated by placing a venous stent in the iliac vein to help reduce the effect of external compression and presumably treat the initiating factor. Venous stents are larger than corresponding arterial stents in a given vascular bed. Because of the increased compliance of the venous wall, self-expanding stents are preferred for use in veins.

Once lysis either is complete or has been continued for 72 hours, the lytic infusion is stopped, and the heparin infusion is increased to therapeutic levels. The patient is placed on warfarin therapy and should be treated in accordance with current algorithms for DVT [see 85 Venous Thromboembolism].

Complications

Reported rates of bleeding complications after venous lysis are higher than those after arterial lysis, typically ranging from 10% to 15%.[33] Pulmonary embolism, though rare in this setting, is known to occur, presumably as a result of partially lysed clot breaking off. To prevent this complication, some authors advocate prophylactic placement of an inferior vena cava (IVC) filter.[34] Ongoing development and wider use of retrievable IVC filters may accelerate the application of this adjunctive technique.

Outcome Evaluation

In a large retrospective study of 312 cases of iliofemoral and femoropopliteal DVT treated with urokinase infusion, greater than 50% lysis was achieved in 83% of the patients; 11% experienced complications, and 1% had pulmonary emboli.[33] Small prospective, randomized trials found that thrombolysis yielded increased patency and decreased venous reflux in comparison with standard anticoagulation therapy.[35] Retrospective studies indicated that this improved venous patency and valve function might translate into better quality of life than would be achieved with anticoagulation alone.[36]

TREATMENT OF SAPHENOFEMORAL VENOUS REFLUX

The application of endovascular techniques to saphenofemoral venous reflux has significantly changed the treatment of this condition.[37] Over the past decade, two minimally invasive approaches have been developed to replace standard high ligation and stripping of the greater saphenous vein (GSV): radiofrequency ablation (RFA) and endolaser obliteration.

Preprocedural Evaluation

Initially, symptomatic varicose veins are treated conservatively, with compression stockings. If conservative methods fail to provide relief, a varicose vein–related complication develops, and there is evidence of significant superficial reflux on duplex ultrasonography, the patient may be considered for endovenous treatment of GSV reflux.

Preprocedural Planning

GSV ablation procedures may be performed either in an office or in an operating or procedure room. If an office setting is chosen, the patient must be able to tolerate a small amount of discomfort with light sedation. The interventionalist must be certified to deliver conscious sedation and must be laser qualified if providing laser therapy. The procedure room, whether in an office or a medical facility, should be equipped with a procedure table capable of a steep Trendelenburg position, a high-resolution duplex ultrasonography device, and the appropriate ablation equipment. For more symptomatic side-branch varicosities, stab avulsions may be needed; as a rule, these are best done in the OR.

Technique

RFA of GSV The development of the Closure system (VNUS Medical Technologies, Sunnyvale, California) has allowed the application of RFA to GSV reflux therapy. Before the procedure, the GSV is mapped by means of ultrasonography. The

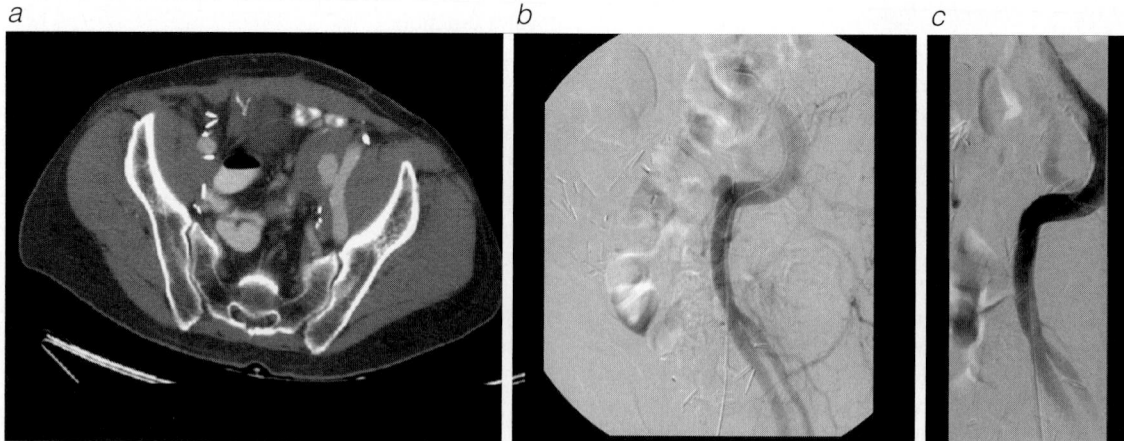

a   *b*   *c*

Figure 7 **Placement of covered stent. Shown is endovascular repair of an external iliac artery aneurysm. The patient presented with left groin pain several months after undergoing urologic surgery. (*a*) CT scan demonstrates a left external iliac artery pseudoaneurysm. (*b*) Angiogram demonstrates the same pseudoaneurysm. (*c*) Shown is the left external iliac artery after covered stent placement successfully excluded the pseudoaneurysm.**

patient is placed in the Trendelenburg position with a tourniquet around the upper thigh. Access to the GSV is obtained at the knee with an introducer needle and a wire threaded into the vein, and the needle is then replaced with a proprietary sheath. The Closure catheter is threaded through the sheath, and the tip is placed under ultrasonographic guidance just proximal to the takeoff of the superficial epigastric vein at the saphenofemoral junction (SFJ). A mixture of normal saline (500 ml), 1% lidocaine with epinephrine (50 ml), and sodium bicarbonate (5 mg) is injected under ultrasonographic guidance through the sheath and into the area surrounding the GSV to provide anesthesia, improve impedance, and protect the overlying tissues from exposure to the heat (so-called tumescent anesthesia).

The Closure device is then connected to the RFA delivery system, deployed, and pulled back at a controlled rate (initially, 1 cm every 30 seconds), with both impedance and temperature checked periodically. Manual compression, particularly in the upper thigh, may help in obtaining optimal numeric values on the RFA unit, as well as increase the efficiency of ablation. After the catheter has been withdrawn into the sheath, it is removed, and ultrasonography is performed to confirm that the GSV has been obliterated.

Endovenous laser treatment of GSV   Access to the GSV is obtained as in RFA (see above), and a wire is advanced under ultrasonographic guidance to a point above the SFJ. A 600 μm laser fiber is placed over the wire and positioned just distal to the SFJ in the GSV. A tumescent anesthetic solution is injected. Laser energy is delivered (e.g., with an 810 nm diode laser) as the laser fiber is pulled back. One advantage endolaser obliteration has over RFA is that the laser wire can be pulled back relatively quickly (up to 18 mm/min).

Complications

The most serious complication associated with any of these endovenous techniques is DVT. There have been several reports of DVT resulting from RFA of the GSV, with incidences as high as 16%.[38] As of September 2005, four instances of pulmonary embolism from these clots had been reported in the United States Food and Drug Administration's Manufacturer and User Facility Device Experience (MAUDE) database (http://www.fda.gov/cdrh/maude.html), with at least one patient dying of a pulmonary embolism after the procedure.

Lower-extremity DVT has also been reported after endovenous laser therapy. Other problems include saphenous nerve paresthesias along the course of the GSV, bruising, skin burns, and superficial phlebitis. If endovenous laser therapy fails to obliterate the GSV, the problem can be remedied by prompt high ligation at the time of ablation. Clot in the common femoral vein can be treated with standard anticoagulation. Clot abutting the common femoral vein can be treated with clopidogrel, 75 mg/day orally for 1 month; serial ultrasonograms should be obtained to confirm that the clot is not propagating.

Outcome Evaluation

Overall, good results are obtained with endovenous treatment of GSV reflux. In one study of patients who underwent RFA of the GSV, 85% of patients had complete occlusion of the GSV at 2 years, and 90% of all patients were free of GSV reflux at that time.[39] In a study of patients who underwent endolaser obliteration, similar results were obtained: ultrasonographic surveillance documented a 93% rate of complete GSV closure at 2 years.[40]

1. Pell JP: Impact of intermittent claudication on quality of life. Eur J Vasc Endovasc 9:469, 1995

2. Spinosa D, Kaufmann JA, Hartwell GD: Gadolinium chelates in angiography

References

and interventional radiology: a useful alternative to iodinated contrast media for angiography. Radiology 223:319, 2002

3. Fava M, Loyola S, Polydorou A, et al: Cryoplasty for femoropopliteal arterial disease: late angiographic results of inital human experience. J Vasc Interv Radiol 15:1239, 2004

4. Kasirajan K, Schneider PA: Early outcome of "cutting" balloon angioplasty for infrainguinal vein graft stenosis. J Vasc Surg 39:702, 2004

5. Zeller T, Rastan A, Schwarzwalder U, et al: Percutaneous peripheral atherectomy of femoropopliteal stenosis using a new-generation device: six-month results from a single-center experience. J Endovasc Ther 11:676, 2004

6. Duda SH, Bosiers M, Lammer J, et al: The SIROCCO II trial: sirolimus-eluting versus bare nitinol stent for obstructive superficial femoral artery disease. J Vasc Interv Radiol 16:331, 2005

7. Nikolsky E, Mehran R, Halkin A, et al: Vascular complications associated with arteriotomy closure devices in patients undergoing percutaneous coronary procedures: a meta-analysis. J Am Coll Cardiol 44:1200, 2004

8. Davies MG, Waldman DL, Pearson TA: Comprehensive endovascular therapy for femoropopliteal arterial atherosclerotic occlusive disease. J Am Coll Surg 201:275, 2005

9. Schurmann K, Mahnken A, Meyer J, et al: Longterm results 10 years after iliac arterial stent placement. Radiology 224:731, 2002

10. Surowiec SM, Davies MG, Lee D, et al: Percutaneous angioplasty and stenting of the superficial femoral artery. J Vasc Surg 41:269, 2005

11. Murphy TP, Khwaja AA, Webb MS: Aortoiliac stent placement in patients treated for intermittent claudication. J Vasc Interv Radiol 9:421, 1998

12. Karch LA, Mattos MA, Henretta JP, et al: Clinical failure after percutaneous transluminal angioplasty of the SFA and popliteal arteries. J Vasc Surg 31:880, 2000

13. Becquemin JP, Allaire E, Qvarfordt P, et al: Surgical transluminal iliac angioplasty with selective stenting: long term results assessed by means of duplex scanning. J Vasc Surg 29:422, 1999

14. Cejna M, Schoder M, Lammer J: PTA versus stent in femoropopliteal obstruction. Radiologie 39:144, 1999

15. Vroegindeweij D, Vos LD, Buth J, et al: Balloon angioplasty combined with primary stenting versus balloon angioplasty alone in femoropopliteal obstructions: a comparative randomized study. Cardiovasc Interv Radiol 20:420, 1997

16. Zdanowski Z, Albrechtsson U, Lundin A, et al: Percutaneous transluminal angioplasty with or without stenting for femoropopliteal occlusions? A randomized controlled study. Int Angiol 18:251, 1999

17. TASC Working Group: Management of peripheral arterial disease (PAD): Transatlantic Inter-Society Consensus (TASC). Eur J Vasc Endovasc Surg 19:S1, 2000

18. Soeder HK, Manninen HI, Jaakkola P, et al: Prospective trial of infrapopliteal artery balloon angioplasty for critical limb ischemia: angiographic and clinical results. J Vasc Interv Radiol 11:1021, 2000

19. Working Party on Thrombolysis in the Management of Limb Ischemia: Thrombolysis in the management

of lower limb peripheral arterial occlusion—a consensus document. Am J Cardiol 81:207, 1998

20. Davies MG, Lee DE, Green RM: Current Spectrum of Thrombolysis, 3rd ed. WB Saunders Co, Philadelphia, 2001

21. Ouriel K: A history of thrombolytic therapy. J Endovasc Ther 11:128, 2004

22. Ouriel K, Kandarpa K: Safety of thrombolytic therapy with urokinase or recombinant tissue plasminogen activator for peripheral arterial occlusion: a comprehensive compilation of published work. J Endovasc Ther 11:436, 2004

23. Allie DE, Herbert CJ, Lirtzman MD, et al: Novel simultaneous combination chemical thrombolysis/rheolytic thrombectomy therapy for acute critical limb ischemia: the power-pulse spray technique. Catheter Cardiovasc Interv 63:512, 2004

24. Kasirajan K, Gray B, Beavers FP, et al: Rheolytic thrombectomy in the management of acute and subacute limb-threatening ischemia. J Vasc Interv Radiol 12:413, 2001

25. Kasirajan K, Haskal ZJ, Ouriel K: The use of mechanical thrombectomy devices in the management of acute peripheral arterial occlusive disease. J Vasc Interv Radiol 12:405, 2001

26. Lee DE, Waldman DL, Sumida RK, et al: Direct graft puncture with use of a crossed catheter technique for thrombolysis of peripheral bypass grafts. J Vasc Interv Radiol 11:445, 2000

27. STILE Investigators: Results of a prospective randomized trial evaluating surgery versus thrombolysis for ischemia of the lower extremity: the STILE trial. Ann Surg 220:251, 1994

28. Powell A, Benenati JF, Becker GJ, et al:

Percutaneous ultrasound-guided thrombin injection for the treatment of pseudoaneurysms. J Am Coll Surg 194:S53, 2002

29. Tielliu IFJ, Verhoeven ELG, Zeebregts CJ, et al: Endovascular treatment of popliteal artery aneurysms: results of a prospective cohort study. J Vasc Surg 41:561, 2005

30. Kahn SR, Hirsch A, Shrier I: Effect of postthrombotic syndrome on health-related quality of life after deep venous thrombosis. Arch Intern Med 162:1144, 2002

31. Weitz JI, Middeldorp S, Geerts W, et al: Thrombophilia and new anticoagulant drugs. Hematology (Am Soc Hematol Educ Program) 1:424, 2004

32. Bush RL, Lin PH, Bates JT, et al: Pharmacomechanical thrombectomy for the treatment of symptomatic lower extremity deep venous thrombosis: safety and feasibility study. J Vasc Surg 40:965, 2004

33. Mewissen MW, Seabrook GR, Meissner MH, et al: Catheter-directed thrombolysis for lower extremity deep venous thrombosis: report of a national multicenter registry. Radiology 211:39, 1999

34. Tarry WC, Makhoul RG, Tisnado J, et al: Catheter-directed thrombolysis following vena cava filtration for severe deep venous thrombosis. Ann Vasc Surg 8:583, 1994

35. Elsharawy M, Elzayat E: Early results of thrombolysis vs. anticoagulation in iliofemoral venous thrombosis: a randomized clinical trial. Eur J Vasc Endovasc Surg 24:209, 2002

36. Comerota AJ, Throm RC, Mathias SD, et al: Catheter-directed thrombolysis for iliofemoral deep venous thrombosis improves health-related quality of life. J Vasc Surg 32:130, 2000

37. Bergan JJ, Kumins NH, Owens EL, et al: Surgical and endovascular treatment of lower extremity venous insufficiency. J Vasc Interv Radiol 13:563, 2002

38. Hingorani AP, Ascher E, Markevich N, et al: Deep venous thrombosis after radiofrequency ablation of greater saphenous vein: a word of caution. J Vasc Surg 40:500, 2004

39. Merchant RF, DePalma RG, Kabnick LS: Endovascular obliteration of saphenous reflux: a multicenter study. J Vasc Surg 35:1190, 2002

40. Min RJ, Khilnani N, Zimmet SE: Endovenous laser treatment of saphenous vein reflux: long term results. J Vasc Interv Radiol 14:1991, 2003

41. Ouriel K, Veith FJ, Sasahara AA: Thrombolysis or peripheral arterial surgery: phase I results. TOPAS investigators. J Vasc Surg 23:64, 1996

42. Ouriel K, Shortell C, DeWeese JA, et al: A comparison of thrombolytic therapy with operative revascularization in the initial treatment of acute peripheral arterial ischemia. J Vasc Surg 19:1021, 1994

Acknowledgment

Figures 1a, 2b, and 6   Tom Moore.

99 LOWER-EXTREMITY AMPUTATION FOR ISCHEMIA

William C. Pevec, M.D., F.A.C.S.

Patients with infected, painful, or necrotic lower extremities can be restored to a better functional level by means of a properly selected and performed amputation. This procedure should be considered reconstructive and restorative. In what follows, I address amputations across the toe, the forefoot, the leg, and the thigh. Because Symes' amputations and hip disarticulations are seldom appropriate on ischemic limbs, I omit discussion of these procedures.

General Preoperative Planning

Selecting the appropriate level of amputation is of primary importance for healing and preservation of function. For an ambulatory patient who has either a palpable pulse over the dorsal pedal or posterior tibial arteries or a functioning infrainguinal arterial bypass graft, amputation on the foot (either toe amputation or transmetatarsal amputation) is appropriate. For an ambulatory patient who has a palpable femoral pulse and a patent profunda femoris artery, whose skin is warm at least to the level of the ankle, and who has no skin lesions on the proposed amputation flaps, amputation below the knee is appropriate. For a nonambulatory patient who has ischemic rest pain, ulceration, or gangrene, amputation above the knee is appropriate. Arterial reconstruction is not indicated if the extremity is nonfunctional. Below-the-knee amputation does not offer nonambulatory patients any functional advantage; moreover, it is less likely to heal and often results in a flexion contracture at the knee that leads to pressure ulceration of the stump. Above-the-knee amputation depends on pulsatile flow into the ipsilateral internal iliac artery for successful healing. Above-the-knee amputation is also necessary for a patient whose skin is cool at or above the midcalf or who has skin lesions at or proximal to the midcalf.

Several adjunctive measurements (e.g., transcutaneous oxygen tension and segmental arterial pressure) have been used to select the level of amputation but have not proved particularly helpful. Generally, these adjuncts can reliably determine a level of amputation at which healing is virtually ensured, but they cannot reliably determine the level at which an amputation will not heal. Consequently, reliance on such measures to select the level of amputation will result in an unnecessarily high percentage of more proximal amputations.

In most cases, definitive amputation can be accomplished in a single stage. Local cellulitis can usually be controlled beforehand with bed rest and systemic administration of antibiotics. Undrained pus or recalcitrant cellulitis, however, must be treated with debridement and drainage in advance of definitive amputation. This can be accomplished with local soft tissue debridement, single-toe amputation, or guillotine amputation across the ankle.

Careful preoperative medical assessment is essential. Lower-extremity amputation for ischemia is associated with a mortality of 4.5% to 16%,[1-6] owing to the poor overall condition of the patient population. Accordingly, optimization of cardiac and pulmonary function and control of systemic infection are mandatory.

Finally, the timing of elective amputation is crucial. Because the loss of a limb is a difficult and frightening thing for a patient to accept, there is a natural tendency to delay amputation for as long as possible. This tendency is understandable but must be weighed against the potential problems associated with delay, such as poor preoperative pain control, which leads to an increased incidence of postamputation phantom limb pain, and extended preoperative immobility, which leads to physical deconditioning and makes prosthetic limb rehabilitation more difficult. A preoperative consultation with a physiatrist can allay some of the patient's anxiety by addressing the expected postoperative course of rehabilitation and thereby removing some of the fear of the unknown.

Toe Amputation

Amputation of the toe can be done either across a phalanx or across a metatarsal bone; the latter procedure is commonly referred to as a ray amputation. Many of the perioperative issues are essentially similar for the two approaches; however, indications and operative details differ somewhat and thus will be described separately.

OPERATIVE PLANNING

As noted (see above), for a toe amputation to heal properly, there must be either a palpable pulse over the dorsal pedal or posterior tibial artery or a functioning bypass graft to an infrapopliteal artery. If tissue necrosis or infection is confined to the distal or middle phalanx, transphalangeal amputation is appropriate; if tissue loss or necrosis involves the proximal phalanx, ray amputation is indicated. If tissue necrosis or infection extends over the metatarsophalangeal joint, either transmetatarsal amputation of the entire forefoot or below-the-knee amputation is usually necessary (see below).

Multiple transphalangeal amputations are functionally well tolerated. If, however, ray amputation of the great toe or of more than one smaller toe is called for, it is preferable to perform a transmetatarsal amputation of the forefoot. Adequate skin coverage is usually difficult to achieve with a great-toe or multiple-toe ray amputation. In addition, ray amputation of more than one of the middle toes often causes central deviation of the remaining outside toes, which can lead to ulcerations secondary to abnormal pressure points. Finally, loss of the first metatarsal head or of several of the other metatarsal heads results in abnormal weight bearing on the remaining metatarsal heads, which may give rise to late ulceration.

OPERATIVE TECHNIQUE

Transphalangeal Amputation

Digital block anesthesia is ideal for transphalangeal amputation. A 25-gauge needle is inserted into the skin over the medial aspect of the dorsum of the proximal phalanx and advanced until the bone is encountered. The needle is then withdrawn slightly, and a small amount of fluid is aspirated to confirm that the tip of the needle is not in a blood vessel. Next, 0.5 to 1.0 ml of lidocaine, 0.5% or 1.0% without epinephrine, is slowly injected. The needle is then carefully advanced medial to the bone until the tip can be felt pressing against (but not puncturing) the plantar skin. Again, the needle is withdrawn slightly, fluid is aspirated, and 0.5 to 1.0 ml of lidocaine is injected. The same technique is repeated on the lateral aspect of the proximal phalanx. In this way, all four digital nerve branches are blocked. If multiple toe amputations are required, an ankle block, epidural anesthesia, spinal anesthesia, or general anesthesia can be used.

An incision is made to create dorsal and plantar skin flaps. Typically, these flaps are equal in length; however, depending on the location of the skin lesion, either the dorsal flap or the plantar flap can be left longer [*see Figure 1*]. Care must be taken not to create excessively long flaps, which may lack sufficient perfusion for healing, or to create undermined bevels with the scalpel [*see Figure 2*], which will lead to epidermolysis of the suture line.

The incision is extended down to the phalanx, and the soft tissues are gently separated from the bone with a small periosteal elevator. All tendons and tendon sheaths are debrided because the poor vascularity of these tissues may compromise the healing of the toe. The phalanx is transected at the level of the apices of the skin incisions [*see Figure 1*]. Care must be taken not to leave the remaining bone segment too long: this places undue tension on the skin flaps and is a primary cause of poor healing. The best way of transecting the phalanx is to use a pneumatic oscillating saw. Manual bone cutters can splinter the bone, and manual saws can cause extensive damage to the soft tissues. The bone is always transected across the shaft: because of the poor vascularity of the articular cartilage, disarticulation across a joint typically leads to poor healing.

Hemostasis is achieved with absorbable sutures and limited use of the electrocautery. Excessive tissue manipulation and electrocauterization should be avoided. The skin edges are carefully approximated with simple interrupted nonabsorbable monofilament sutures; perfect apposition is necessary to maximize the potential for primary healing. The sutures must not be placed too close to the skin edges, because the heavily keratinized skin of the foot is easily lacerated. The final step is the application of a soft dressing.

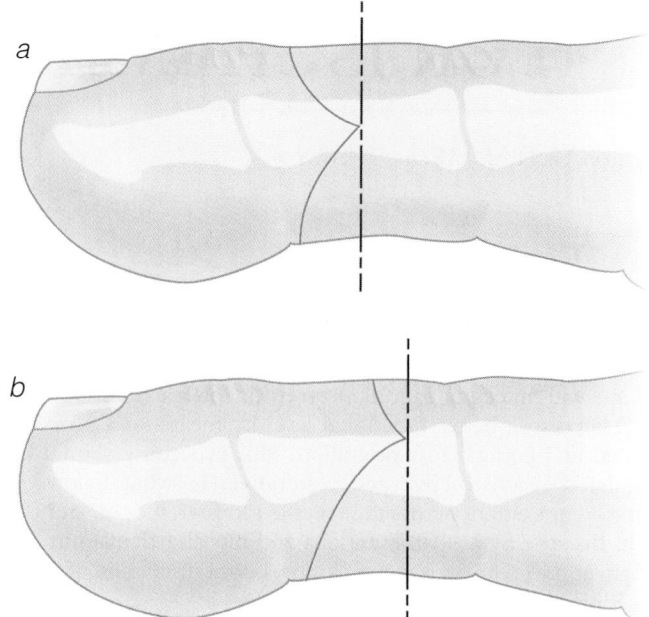

Figure 1 **Toe amputation: transphalangeal amputation. Transphalangeal amputation can be performed either with dorsal and plantar flaps of equal length (*a*) or with a plantar flap that is longer than the dorsal flap (*b*). The phalanx is transected at the level of the apex of the skin flaps (dashed line). The bone is transected through the shaft of the phalanx, never across the joint.**

Ray Amputation

For ray amputation [*see Figure 3*], spinal, epidural, or general anesthesia can be employed. A so-called tennis-racket incision is made—that is, a straight incision along the dorsal surface of the affected metatarsal bone coupled with a circumferential incision around the base of the toe. The goal is to save all available viable skin on the toe; this skin is used to ensure a tension-free closure, and any excess skin can be debrided later, at the time of closure. Again, undermined bevels are avoided. The incision is taken down to the bone, and the soft tissues are separated from the distal metatarsal bone with a periosteal elevator. Dissection must be kept close to the affected metatarsal head to prevent injury to the adjacent metatarsophalangeal joint, which can lead to necrosis of the adjacent toe. The metatarsal bone is transected across the shaft with a pneumat-

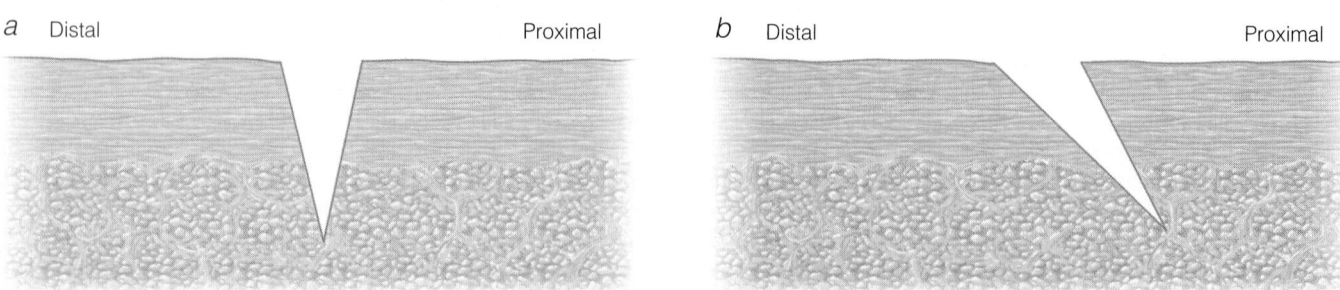

Figure 2 **In a lower-extremity amputation, the skin is always incised perpendicular to its surface (*a*). Given the varying contours encountered during extremity amputation, it can be difficult to maintain the perpendicular orientation of the scalpel; however, an incision that undermines the proximal skin flap (*b*) will devascularize the epidermis and lead to necrosis of the suture line.**

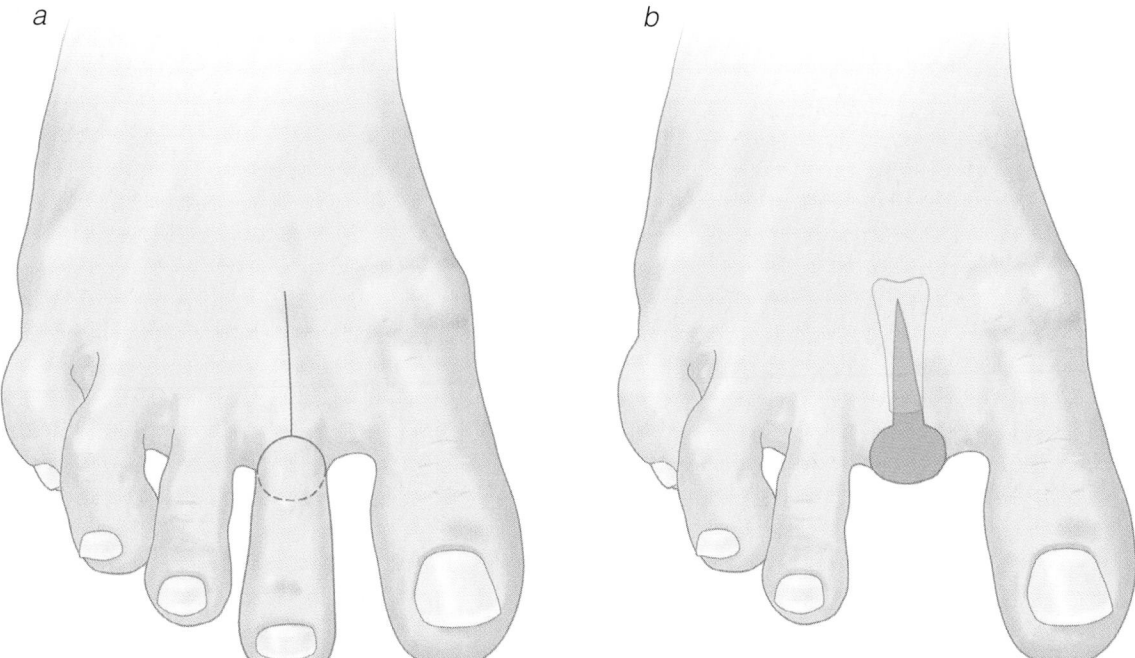

a

b

Figure 3 Toe amputation: ray amputation. (*a*) A longitudinal incision is made along the dorsum of the shaft of the metatarsal bone of the affected toe. A circumferential incision is then made around the phalanx. The circumferential incision should be placed as distal on the toe as there is viable skin so that as much skin as possible is retained for closure of the wound. (*b*) The metatarsal bone is transected across its shaft, proximal to the metatarsal head; the joint is never disarticulated.

ic oscillating saw. The tendons and the tendon sheaths are debrided.

Meticulous hemostasis is achieved with absorbable sutures and limited use of the electrocautery. The skin is approximated with simple interrupted nonabsorbable monofilament sutures [*see Figure 4*]. If sufficient viable skin was preserved, a flap of plantar skin is rotated dorsally, and the incision is closed in the shape of a Y. Alternatively, the medial and lateral edges are shifted (one proximally and the other distally), the corners are trimmed, and the incision is closed in a linear fashion. A soft supportive dressing is applied.

COMPLICATIONS

Complications of toe amputation include bleeding, infection, and failure to heal. Because even a small amount of bleeding under the skin flaps can prevent proper healing, meticulous hemostasis is mandatory. In most cases, infection and failure to heal are attributable to poor patient selection and poor surgical technique; the usual result is a more proximal amputation.

OUTCOME

For optimal healing, there must be an extended period (2 to 3 weeks) during which no weight is borne by the foot that underwent toe amputation. Once healing is complete, the patient should be able to walk normally, with no need for orthotic or assist devices. Beginning ambulation too early can disrupt healing flaps and necessitate more proximal amputation, which lengthens the hospital stay and increases long-term disability. For these reasons, toe amputation in patients with arterial occlusive disease is not an outpatient procedure. Patients are kept on bed rest and instructed in techniques (e.g., use of a wheelchair, a walker, or crutches) that allow them to function without stepping on the foot that was operated on. Hospital discharge is delayed until such techniques are mastered.

Transmetatarsal Amputation

OPERATIVE PLANNING

As noted (see above), transmetatarsal amputation is indicated if there is tissue loss in the forefoot involving the first metatarsal head, two or more of the other metatarsal heads, or the dorsal forefoot. It is contraindicated if there is extensive skin loss on the plantar surface of the foot or on the dorsum proximal to the midshaft of the metatarsal bones. The peroneus longus and the peroneus brevis insert on the proximal portions of the fourth and fifth metatarsal bones; if these insertions are sacrificed, inversion of the foot results, eventually leading to chronic skin breakdown from the side of the foot repeatedly striking the ground during ambulation. Transmetatarsal amputation is also contraindicated if there is a preexisting footdrop (peroneal palsy).

OPERATIVE TECHNIQUE

Spinal, epidural, or general anesthesia may be employed for transmetatarsal amputation. Placement of a tourniquet on the calf is a useful adjunctive measure. This step greatly reduces intraoperative blood loss. More important, the bloodless operative field that results allows more accurate assessment of tissue viability and hence more precise selection of the level of amputation; in a field stained with extravasated blood, it is easy to leave behind nonviable tissue that will doom the amputation. Use of a tourniquet is, however, contraindicated in patients who have a functioning infrapopliteal artery bypass graft.

After sterile preparation and draping, the leg is elevated to help drain the venous blood, and a sterile pneumatic tourniquet is placed around the calf, with care taken to pad the skin under the tourniquet and to position the tourniquet over the calf muscles, where it will not apply pressure over the fibular head (and the common peroneal nerve) or other osseous prominences. The tourniquet is then inflated to a pressure higher than the systolic

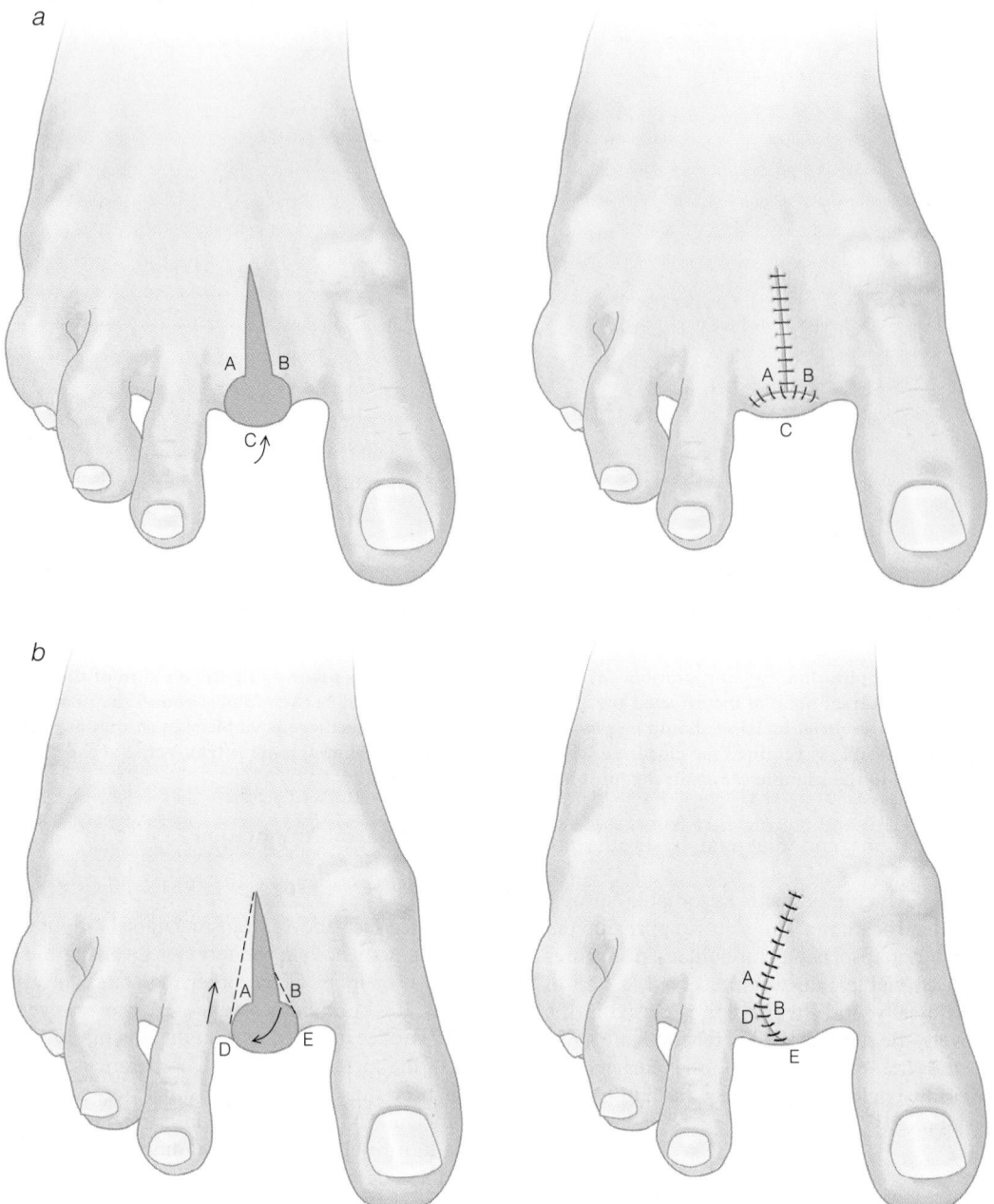

Figure 4 Toe amputation: ray amputation. (*a*) If adequate skin is available, a plantar flap can be rotated dorsally and the skin closed in a Y configuration. This closure is technically easy to perform; however, there is a risk of skin necrosis at corners A and B. (*b*) Alternatively, the skin can be closed in a linear fashion. Corners A and B are gently trimmed. Corner B is shifted distally toward point D as corner A is shifted proximally. A slight dog-ear will result at point E; however, it will diminish with time.

blood pressure. In patients who do not have diabetes mellitus, a tourniquet inflation pressure of 250 mm Hg is typically employed; in patients who have diabetes mellitus and calcified arteries, a pressure of 350 to 400 mm Hg is preferred.

An incision is made across the dorsum of the foot at the level of the middle of the shafts of the metatarsal bones, extending medially and laterally to the level of the center of the first and fifth metatarsal bones, respectively [*see Figure 5*]. The dorsal incision is curved proximally at the medial and lateral edges to ensure that no dog-ears remain at the time of closure. The dorsal incision is continued perpendicularly through the soft tissues on the dorsum down to the metatarsal bones. The plantar incision is extended distally to a point just proximal to the toe crease.

Care is taken not to bevel the skin incisions.

A plantar flap is created by making an incision with the scalpel adjacent to the metatarsophalangeal joints; the incision is then carried more deeply to the level of the midshafts of the metatarsal bones on their plantar surfaces. The periosteum of the first metatarsal bone is scored circumferentially with the scalpel, and the soft tissue is dissected away from the first metatarsal bone with a periosteal elevator to a point about 1 cm proximal to the dorsal skin incision. The first metatarsal bone is then transected perpendicular to its shaft at the level of the dorsal skin incision with a pneumatic oscillating saw. This process is repeated for each individual metatarsal bone, with care taken to follow the normal contour of the forefoot by cutting the lateral metatarsal bones at

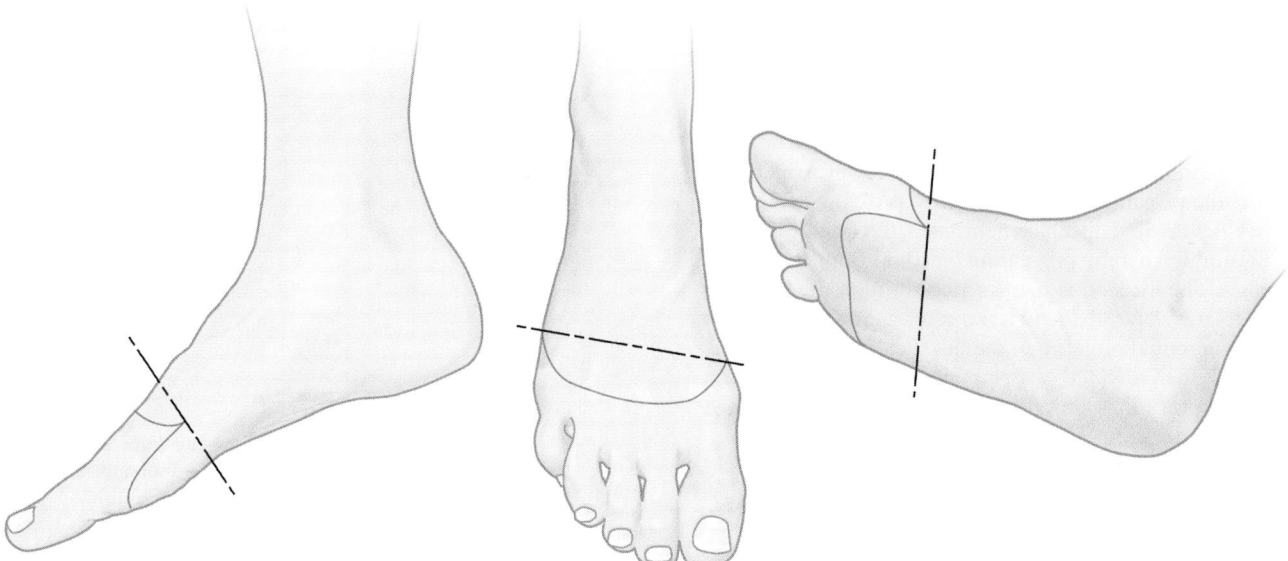

Figure 5 **Transmetatarsal amputation. The skin incisions are shown from various angles. The metatarsal shafts are divided in their midportions (dashed line). The metatarsal bone transection is at the level of the apices of the skin incision, and the lateral metatarsal bones are cut slightly more proximally than the medial metatarsal bones, in a pattern reflecting the normal contour of the forefoot.**

a level slightly proximal to the level at which the more medial bones are transected. All visible digital arteries are clamped and tied with absorbable ligatures. If a tourniquet was used, it is deflated at this time. All tendons and tendon sheaths are debrided from the wound.

Meticulous hemostasis is achieved with absorbable sutures and limited use of the electrocautery. Any sharp edges on the metatarsal bones are smoothed with a rongeur or a rasp. The wound is irrigated to flush out devitalized tissue and thrombus. The plantar flap is trimmed as needed. The dermis is approximated with simple interrupted absorbable sutures, and the knots are buried. Because the edge of the plantar flap is generally longer than the edge of the dorsal flap, the sutures must be placed slightly farther apart on the plantar flap than on the dorsal flap if perfect alignment is to be obtained. It is imperative to achieve the correct skin alignment with the dermal suture layer. Once this is accomplished, the skin edges are gently and perfectly apposed with interrupted vertical mattress sutures of nonabsorbable monofilament material. Finally, a soft supportive dressing with good padding of the heel is applied; casts and splints are avoided because of the risk of ulceration of the heel or over the malleoli.

COMPLICATIONS

If a tourniquet is not used, intraoperative blood loss can be substantial; the blood pools in the sponges and drapes, often out of the anesthesiologist's field of view. Consequently, good communication between the surgeon and the anesthesiologist is crucial for preventing ischemic complications secondary to hemorrhage.

Postoperative complications include bleeding, infection, and failure to heal, all of which are likely to result in more proximal amputation. They can best be prevented by means of careful patient selection and meticulous surgical technique.

OUTCOME

For proper healing, postoperative edema must be avoided and the plantar flap protected against shear forces. To prevent swelling, the patient is kept on bed rest with the foot elevated for

the first 3 to 5 days. This step is particularly important if the transmetatarsal amputation was performed simultaneously with arterial reconstruction, which carries a high risk of reperfusion edema of the foot. After 3 to 5 days, the patient is instructed in techniques for moving in and out of the wheelchair without stepping on the foot. The foot that was operated on should not bear any weight at all for at least 3 weeks; early weight-bearing may disrupt the healing of the plantar flap and necessitate more proximal amputation.

Once healed, patients should be able to walk independently with standard shoes. There is, however, a risk that they may trip over the unsupported toe of the shoe. In addition, the pushoff normally provided by the toes is lost after transmetatarsal amputation, and this change results in a halting, flat-footed gait. These problems can be obviated by using an orthotic shoe with a steel shank (to keep the toe of the shoe from bending and causing tripping) and a rocker bottom (to provide a smooth heel-to-toe motion).

Guillotine Ankle Amputation

OPERATIVE PLANNING

Guillotine amputation across the ankle is indicated when a patient presents with extensive wet gangrene that precludes salvage of a functional foot (e.g., wet gangrene that destroys the heel, the plantar skin of the forefoot, or the dorsal skin of the proximal foot). In such patients, initial guillotine amputation through the ankle is safer than extensive debridement: the operation is shorter, less blood is lost, the risk of bacteremia is reduced, and better control of infection is possible. Guillotine amputation is also indicated in patients with foot infections who have cellulitis extending into the leg. Transection at the ankle, perpendicular to the muscle compartments, tendon sheaths, and lymphatic vessels, allows effective drainage and usually brings about rapid resolution of the cellulitis of the leg, thus permitting salvage of the knee in many cases in which the knee might otherwise be unsalvageable.

OPERATIVE TECHNIQUE

General anesthesia is preferred for guillotine ankle amputation; regional anesthesia is relatively contraindicated for critically ill patients who are in a septic state. Anesthesia is required for no more than 15 to 20 minutes.

A circumferential incision is made at the narrowest part of the ankle (i.e., at the proximal malleoli) regardless of the level of the cellulitis [see Figure 6]. This placement takes the line of incision across the tendons, thereby preventing bleeding from transected muscle bellies. The incision is then carried through the skin and soft tissues to the bone. If the arteries are patent, the assistant applies circumferential pressure to the distal calf. The distal tibia and fibula are then divided with a Gigli saw. Hemostasis is achieved with suture ligation and electrocauterization. A moist dressing is applied.

OUTCOME

After the procedure, the patient is kept on bed rest and given systemic antibiotics. Formal below-the-knee amputation can be performed when the cellulitis resolves, usually within 3 to 5 days. Routine dressing changes are unnecessary—first, because they are painful, and second, because the decision to proceed with formal below-the-knee amputation is based on the extent of the cellulitis in the calf, not on the appearance of the transected ankle.

Below-the-Knee Amputation

OPERATIVE PLANNING

Below-the-knee amputation is indicated when the lower extremity is functional but the foot cannot be salvaged by arterial reconstruction or by amputation of one or more of the toes or the forefoot. Healing can be expected if there is a palpable femoral pulse with at least a patent deep femoral artery, provided that the skin is warm and free of lesions at the distal calf. Before formal below-the-knee amputation, infection should be controlled with antibiotic therapy, debridement, and, if indicated, guillotine amputation. It is advisable to obtain consent to possible above-the-knee amputation beforehand in case unexpected muscle necrosis is encountered below the knee.

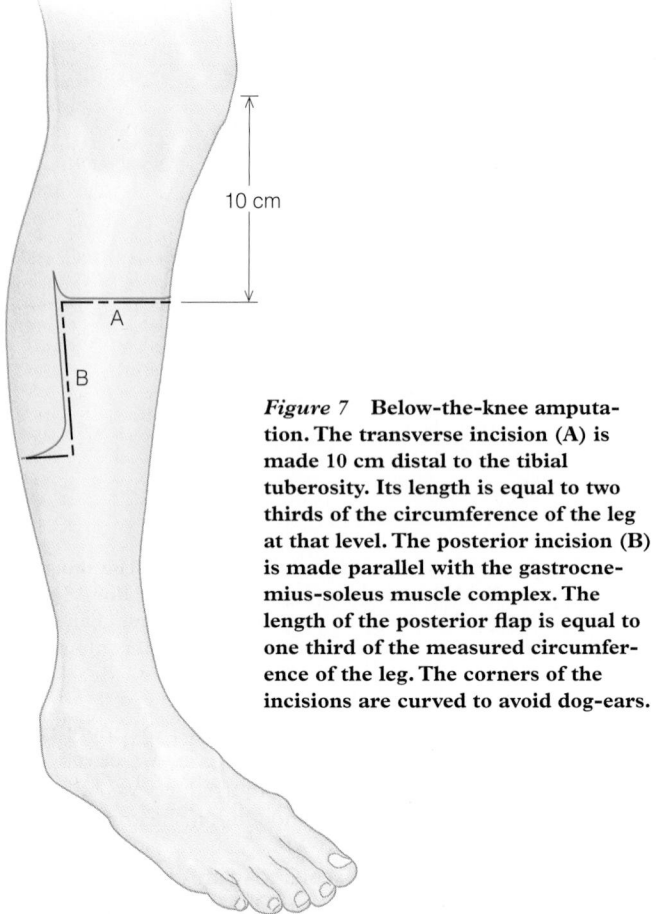

Figure 7 **Below-the-knee amputation. The transverse incision (A) is made 10 cm distal to the tibial tuberosity. Its length is equal to two thirds of the circumference of the leg at that level. The posterior incision (B) is made parallel with the gastrocnemius-soleus muscle complex. The length of the posterior flap is equal to one third of the measured circumference of the leg. The corners of the incisions are curved to avoid dog-ears.**

As with any amputation, the surgeon's preoperative interaction with the patient should be as positive as possible. A constructive perspective to convey is that the amputation, though regrettably necessary, is in fact the first step toward rehabilitation. A well-motivated patient whose cardiopulmonary status is not too greatly compromised can generally be expected to walk again, albeit at an increased energy cost. In this regard, a preoperative discussion with a physiatrist can be very helpful, as can a meeting with an amputee who is doing well with a prosthesis. By inculcating a positive attitude in the patient before the procedure, the surgeon can greatly improve the patient's chances of achieving full rehabilitation, as well as decrease the time needed for rehabilitation.

OPERATIVE TECHNIQUE

Epidural, spinal, or general anesthesia is appropriate for below-the-knee amputation. The lines of incision should be marked on the skin. The primary level of amputation is determined by measuring a distance of 10 cm from the tibial tuberosity [see Figure 7]. The circumference of the leg at this level is then measured by passing a heavy ligature around the leg and cutting the ligature to a length equal to the circumference. The ligature is folded into thirds and cut once more at one of the folds, so that two segments of unequal length remain. The longer segment of the ligature, which is equal in length to two thirds of the leg's circumference 10 cm below the tibial tuberosity, is used to measure the anterior transverse incision; this incision is centered not on the tibial crest but on the gastrocnemius-soleus muscle complex. The shorter segment, which is one third of the leg's circumfer-

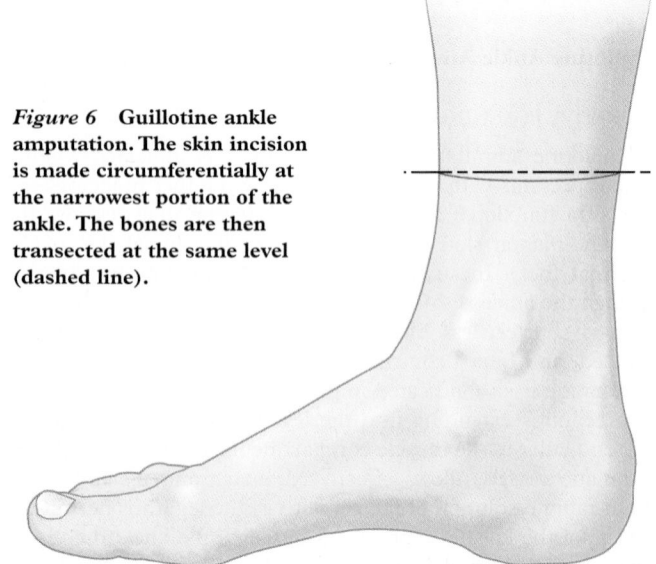

Figure 6 **Guillotine ankle amputation. The skin incision is made circumferentially at the narrowest portion of the ankle. The bones are then transected at the same level (dashed line).**

ence at this level, is used to measure the posterior flap; the line of the posterior incision runs parallel with the gastrocnemius-soleus complex. To prevent dog-ears, the medial and lateral ends of the anterior transverse incision are curved cephalad before meeting the posterior incision, and the distal corners of the posterior incision are curved as well.

Blood loss can be reduced by using a sterile pneumatic tourniquet. A gauze roll is passed around the distal thigh. The leg is elevated to drain the venous blood, and the tourniquet is applied over the gauze roll. The tourniquet is inflated to a pressure of 250 mm Hg (350 to 400 mm Hg if the patient has heavily calcified arteries). The assistant elevates the leg, and the incision on the posterior flap is made first, followed by the anterior transverse incision; this sequence helps prevent blood from obscuring the field while the incisions are being made. The incisions are carried fully through the dermis, and the skin edges are allowed to separate and expose the subcutaneous fat. Care is taken to keep the scalpel perpendicular to the skin so as not to bevel the incision, which can lead to necrosis of the epidermal edges [see Figure 2].

The anterior muscles are transected with the scalpel in a direction parallel to the transverse skin incision. The tibia is scored circumferentially, and a periosteal elevator is used to dissect the soft tissues away from the tibia for a distance of approximately 3 to 4 cm. The tibia is then transected just proximal to the transverse skin incision. Dividing the tibia more than 1 cm proximal to the anterior skin incision will cause the thin skin of the anterior leg to be pulled taut over the cut end of the tibia by the weight of the posterior flap, thereby leading to skin ulcera-

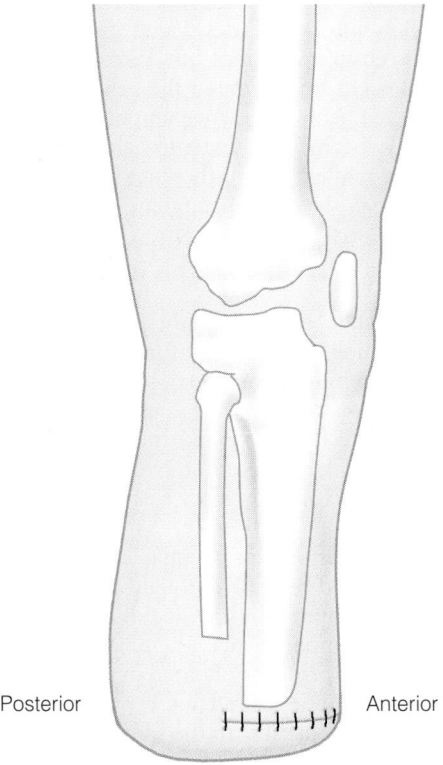

Figure 8 **Below-the-knee amputation. In this lateral view of the right leg, the tibia is beveled anteriorly, and the anterior portion is smoothed with a rasp. The fibula is transected at least 1 cm proximal to the level of transection of the tibia.**

tion. The tibia is transected perpendicularly, with a cephalad bevel of the anterior 1 cm to keep from creating a sharp point at the tibial crest [see Figure 8]. The tibia can be transected with either a Gigli saw or an oscillating saw; because of the unpleasant sound of the power saw, the Gigli saw is preferred if the patient is under regional anesthesia. Sedation should be augmented in awake patients before division of the tibia. Benzodiazepines provide good sedation and amnesia.

The lateral muscles are divided, and the fibula is scored circumferentially. A periosteal elevator is used to dissect the soft tissues away from the fibula to a point 2 to 3 cm cephalad to the level at which the tibia was transected. The fibula is then transected with a bone cutter at least 1 cm cephalad to the tibial transection level. The distal end of the tibia is lifted with a bone hook, and division of the posterior muscles is completed with an amputation knife. The specimen is then handed off the field.

The anterior tibial, posterior tibial, and peroneal arteries and veins are clamped, and the tourniquet is released. Clamps are placed on all other bleeding vessels. The posterior tibial and sural nerves are placed on gentle traction and clamped proximally. The distal nerves are transected, and the proximal nerves are allowed to retract into the soft tissues so as to prevent painful neuromas at the end of the stump. All clamped structures are then ligated with absorbable ligatures. The nerves are ligated because their nutrient vessels can bleed significantly. The distal anterior tip of the tibia is smoothed with a rasp to decrease the risk of skin ulceration over this osseous prominence. The stump is gently irrigated to remove all thrombus and devitalized tissue and to reveal any bleeding sites that may have been missed. Electrocauterization is rarely necessary.

The deep muscle fascia—not the Achilles tendon—is approximated with simple interrupted absorbable sutures, with care taken to align the posterior flap with the anterior incision. The dermis is approximated as a separate layer with simple interrupted absorbable sutures; if correctly placed, the dermal sutures should take all tension off the skin. The skin edges are then accurately apposed with interrupted vertical mattress sutures composed of monofilament nonabsorbable material. A carefully padded posterior splint or cast is applied to prevent flexion contracture.

COMPLICATIONS

The most common complications after below-the-knee amputation are bleeding, infection, and failure to heal, all of which are likely to result in a more proximal amputation, frequently accompanied by loss of the knee. Prevention of these complications depends on careful patient selection, preoperative control of infection, and meticulous surgical technique.

To walk with a prosthetic leg, the patient must be able to fully extend and lock the knee; thus, flexion contracture at the knee is a major complication. Such contractures are usually attributable either to poor pain control or to noncompliance with knee extension exercises. Good perioperative analgesia is of vital importance because knee flexion is the position of comfort and the patient will be unwilling to extend the knee if doing so proves too painful. To maintain knee extension, the patient should be placed in either a cast or a splint in the early postoperative period. Once postoperative pain has abated, the splint or cast can be removed. At this point, the patient must be taught extension exercises, in which the quadriceps muscles are contracted to maintain the length of the hamstring muscles. If a patient spends all of his or her time in a sitting position with the knee flexed, a flexion contracture will quickly develop. Once this happens, the patient may find it very difficult to regain full knee extension, and without full

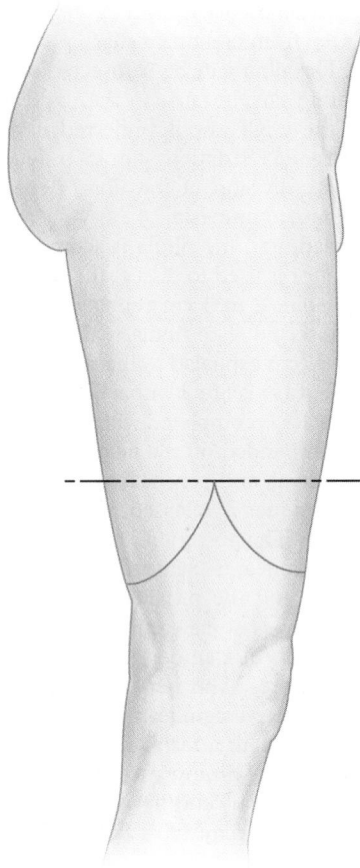

Figure 9 **Above-the-knee amputation. Broadly based anterior and posterior flaps are created. The femur is transected along the dashed line, at the apices of the skin flaps. The skin flaps and the level of transection of the femur can be placed more proximally if clinically indicated.**

knee extension, prosthetic limb rehabilitation is impossible.

Phantom sensation is a common complication after below-the-knee amputation but is rarely of any consequence. Phantom pain, on the other hand, can be devastating. Sometimes, phantom pain develops as a consequence of unintentional suggestions made to the patient by medical personnel who fail to distinguish between the two entities. For example, a patient remarks to a medical attendant that he or she can still feel the amputated foot and toes, and the attendant suggests in response that the patient has phantom pain; the patient then focuses on the sensation and exaggerates the severity of the foot and toe discomfort, setting up a cycle of ever-worsening pain. This scenario is even more likely if the patient has had prolonged ischemic rest pain before the amputation. Phantom pain can be prevented by (1) encouraging early amputation in a patient with a hopelessly ischemic foot (while taking into account the patient's need to come to grips with the prospect of amputation), (2) providing good pain control in the early postoperative period, and (3) assuring the patient that phantom sensation after a below-the-knee amputation is common and that any discomfort in the foot immediately after the operation period will vanish once he or she begins walking again with a prosthetic leg.

Ulceration of the skin over the transected anterior portion of the tibia is another serious complication that may preclude successful prosthetic limb fitting. This complication is also best managed through prevention, which depends on meticulous surgical technique. As noted (see above), the anterior tibial crest must be carefully beveled and smoothed at the level of transection, and the tibia must not be transected more than 1 cm proximal to the anterior skin incision.

With a standard below-the-knee prosthetic leg, weight is borne on the femoral condyles, the patella, and the tibial tuberosity. Breakdown of the stump can occur if weight is borne on the distal portion of the stump. Several decades ago, Jan Ertl described a tibiofibular synostosis designed to allow distal weight-bearing; however, this technique has not been widely adopted.[7]

OUTCOME

Shortly after the amputation, the patient should be encouraged to start working on strengthening the upper body; upper-body strength is critical for making transfers and for using parallel bars, crutches, or a walker. In patients who have preoperative intractable ischemic rest pain, postoperative administration of epidural analgesia can break the cycle of pain. Once postoperative pain is adequately controlled, patients are taught to transfer in and out of a wheelchair. A compression garment is used on the stump once the sutures have been removed and the stump is fully healed.

Prosthetic rehabilitation begins when the stump achieves a conical shape. Unfortunately, a number of patients who have undergone amputation for ischemia are unable to walk with a prosthetic limb because of comorbid medical conditions and general debility. In many cases, however, even if full ambulation is impossible, patients can maintain relative independence if the knee is salvaged by using a combination of a prosthetic leg and a walker for transfers and movement around the house.[6]

Above-the-Knee Amputation

OPERATIVE PLANNING

Above-the-knee amputation is indicated if the lower extremity is unsalvageable and there is no femoral pulse. The presence of pulsatile flow into a well-developed ipsilateral internal iliac artery usually ensures healing, but even when there is more severe arterial occlusive disease in the pelvis, healing can sometimes be achieved. Above-the-knee amputation is also indicated if there is tissue necrosis or uncontrollable infection extending cephalad to the midleg. Above-the-knee amputation is the procedure of choice in the case of gangrene or ulceration of a completely nonfunctional lower extremity.

OPERATIVE TECHNIQUE

Epidural, spinal, or general anesthesia may be used for above-the-knee amputation. For the best functional results, it is desirable to keep the femur as long as possible. A longer stump improves the prognosis for prosthetic limb rehabilitation and provides better balance for sitting and transfers. Healing potential, however, is lower with a longer stump; therefore, if the pelvic circulation is severely compromised, a shorter stump should be fashioned.

Anterior and posterior flaps of equal length are marked on the skin. The flaps should be wide and long [*see Figure 9*], and their apices should be centered on the line dividing the anterior and posterior muscle compartments. The posterior incision is made first to minimize the presence of blood in the operative field. The anterior incision is made second and carried through the anterior muscles in a plane parallel to the skin incision. The skin incisions are carried through the dermis, and the skin edges are allowed to separate and expose the subcutaneous fat; as in other amputations, they should be perpendicular to the skin surface so as not to undermine the skin.

If the superficial femoral artery is patent, the artery and vein are isolated and clamped after the sartorius is divided but before

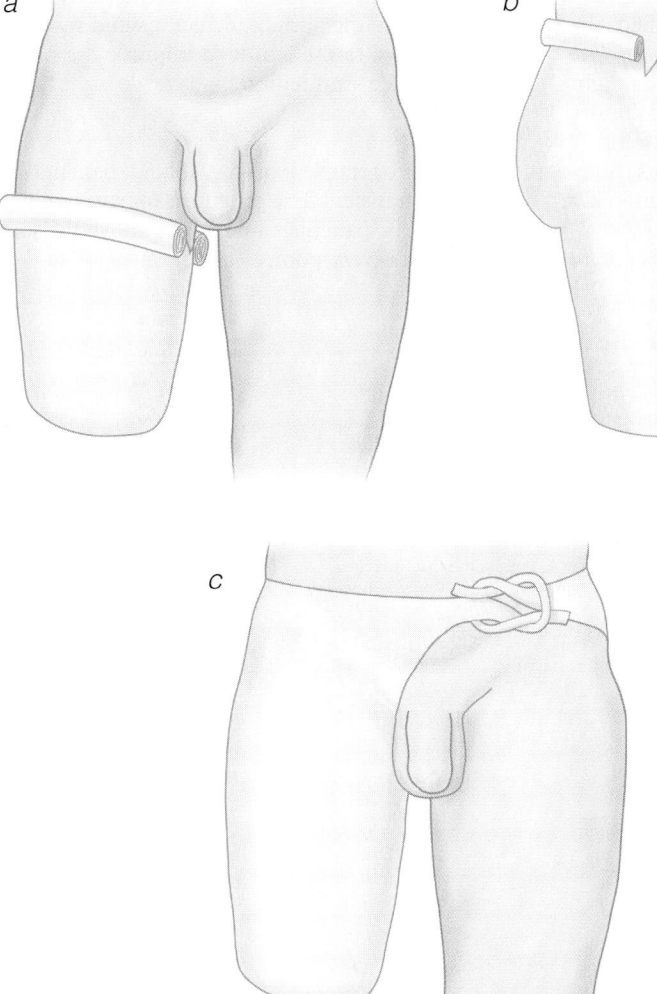

Figure 10 **Above-the-knee amputation. (*a*) After an aerosol tincture of benzoin is applied to the thigh, the hip, and the lower abdomen, a 4 in. wide stockinette is rolled over the amputation stump. The cuff of the stockinette is cut medially at the groin. (*b*) The remainder of the stockinette is then rolled laterally up over the hip, and the cuff is cut on the lateral midline. (*c*) The two resulting strips of cloth are passed around the waist, one anteriorly and one posteriorly, and these strips are tied on the anterior midline to complete the dressing.**

the remainder of the anterior muscles are divided. The femur is scored circumferentially. The soft tissues are dissected away from the femur to the level of the apices of the flaps, and the femur is divided with an oscillating saw at this level. If the end of the resected femur extends beyond the apices of the flaps, the wound cannot be closed without tension. The posterior flap is completed with an amputation knife, and the specimen is handed off the field.

All bleeding points are clamped and tied with absorbable sutures. The sciatic nerve is placed on gentle traction, clamped, divided, and ligated, and the transected nerve is allowed to retract into the muscles. The deep fascia is approximated with interrupted absorbable sutures, with adjustments made for any discrepancy in length between the two flaps. The dermis is approximated with interrupted absorbable sutures; the dermal sutures should take all tension off the skin. The skin edges are then carefully apposed with interrupted vertical mattress sutures.

A nonadherent dressing is placed on the suture line and covered with dry, fluffed gauze bandages. An aerosol tincture of benzoin is sprayed on the thigh, the hip, and the lower abdomen. When the benzoin is dry, a cloth stockinette with a diameter of 4 in. is stretched over the stump [*see Figure 10*]. The cuff of the stockinette is cut medially at the groin, and the stockinette is rolled laterally above the hip, where the cuff is then cut on the midaxillary line. This process yields two strips of cloth, one ante-

rior and one posterior, which are passed around the patient's waist and tied on the anterior midline.

If the patient is a candidate for prosthetic limb rehabilitation, a traction rope is passed through a hole cut in the distal end of the stockinette and tied. The rope is hung over the end of the bed and tied to a 5 lb weight; this step helps prevent flexion contracture at the hip.

The stockinette need not be removed for the wound to be inspected. A window is cut in the distal end of the stockinette, and the gauze is removed. Once the incision has been inspected, fresh gauze is applied, and the window in the stockinette is closed with safety pins.

COMPLICATIONS

Postoperative complications include bleeding, infection, and failure to heal, all of which are likely to result in the need for surgical revision of the amputation stump. Control of preoperative infection and meticulous surgical technique and hemostasis are necessary to prevent these complications.

Flexion contracture of the hip is a major complication of above-the-knee amputation. Such contractures preclude successful prosthetic limb rehabilitation. In dealing with this complication, prevention is far more effective than treatment: once a flexion contracture at the hip becomes fixed, it is very difficult to reverse. If a patient is a candidate for prosthetic limb rehabilitation, the traction weight mentioned earlier (see above) can be very helpful. As soon as postoperative pain is controlled, the patient should be taught to spend three periods daily in a prone position to help extend the hip. He or she should then be taught exercises for maintaining range of motion in the hip before prosthetic limb rehabilitation is initiated. Flexion contracture of the hip is less of a problem in nonambulatory patients; however, it can still lead to wound breakdown and chronic skin ulceration.

Gottschalk noted that loss of the adductor magnus leads to abnormal abduction of the femur. Accordingly, he proposed preservation of the adductor magnus and myodesis of the transected muscles to the femur to improve the biomechanics after above-the-knee amputation.[8,9]

OUTCOME

Once postoperative pain has abated, patients are mobilized to wheelchair transfers. The prognosis for successful prosthetic limb ambulation in patients undergoing above-the-knee amputation for ischemia is very poor.

References

1. Reichle FA, Rankin KP, Tyson RR, et al: Long-term results of 474 arterial reconstructions for severely ischemic limbs: a fourteen year follow-up. Surgery 85:93, 1979

2. Maini BS, Mannick JA: Effect of arterial reconstruction on limb salvage. Arch Surg 113:1297, 1978

3. Ellitsgaard N, Andersson AP, Fabrin J, et al: Outcome in 282 lower extremity amputations: knee salvage and survival. Acta Orthop Scand 61:140, 1990

4. Stewart CPU, Jain AS, Ogston SA: Lower limb amputee survival. Prosthet Orthot Int 16:11, 1992

5. Inderbitzi R, Buttiker M, Pfluger D, et al: The fate of bilateral lower limb amputees in end-stage vascular disease. Eur Vasc Surg 6:321, 1992

6. Nehler MR, Coll JR, Hiatt WR, et al: Functional outcome in a contemporary series of major lower extremity amputations. J Vasc Surg 38:7, 2003

7. Pinzur MS, Pinto MA, Smith DG: Controversies in amputation surgery. Instr Course Lect 52:445, 2003

8. Gottschalk F: Transfemoral amputation: biomechanics and surgery. Clin Orthop 361:15, 1999

9. Gottschalk FA, Stills M: The biomechanics of trans-femoral amputation. Prosthet Orthot Int 18:12, 1994

Acknowledgment

Figures 1 through 10   Tom Moore.

100 INITIAL MANAGEMENT OF LIFE-THREATENING TRAUMA

Frederick A. Moore, M.D., F.A.C.S., and Ernest E. Moore, M.D., F.A.C.S.

Initial Approach to the Critically Injured Patient

Salvage of the critically injured patient is optimized by a coordinated team effort in an organized trauma system. Management of life-threatening trauma must be prioritized according to physiologic necessity for survival—that is, active efforts to support airway, breathing, and circulation (the ABCs) are usually initiated before specific diagnoses are made. In this chapter, we outline a systematic approach to severely injured patients within the so-called golden hour. The discussion is divided into prehospital care and emergency department management; the ED component is further divided into (1) primary survey with initial resuscitation, (2) evaluation and continued resuscitation, and (3) secondary survey with definitive diagnosis and triage.

Prehospital Care

INTERVENTION AT
INJURY SITE

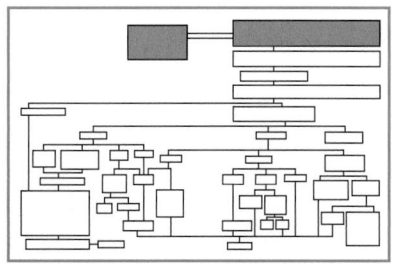

Resuscitation and evaluation of the trauma patient begins at the injury site. The goal is to get *the right patient to the right hospital at the right time* for definitive care. First responders (typically firefighters and police) provide rapid basic trauma life support (BTLS) and are followed by paramedics and flight nurses with advanced trauma life support (ATLS) skills. Medical control is ensured by preestablished field protocols, radio communication with a physician at the base hospital, and subsequent trip audits. Management priorities of BTLS on the scene are (1) to assess and control the scene for the safety of the patient and the prehospital care providers, (2) to tamponade external hemorrhage with direct pressure, (3) to protect the spine after blunt trauma, (4) to clear the airway of obstruction and provide supplemental inspired oxygen, (5) to extricate the patient, and (6) to stabilize long-bone fractures. Whereas the benefits of BTLS are undisputed, the merits of the more advanced interventions remain controversial.[1,2] Airway access, once considered a major asset of the care provided by paramedics and flight nurses, has now been questioned, not only because missed tracheal intubation is a concern but also because unintentional hyperventilation (hypocarbia) is detrimental in the setting of traumatic brain injury (TBI) and during cardiopulmonary resuscitation (CPR).[3-5] Moreover, the value of I.V. fluid administration remains controversial.[6,7]

FIELD TRIAGE

Prehospital trauma scores have been devised to identify critically injured trauma victims, who represent about 10% to 15% of

all injured patients. When it is geographically and logistically feasible, critically injured patients should be taken directly to a designated level I trauma center or to a level II trauma center if a level I trauma center is more than 30 minutes away. The currently available field trauma scores, however, are not entirely reliable for identifying critically injured patients[8]: to capture a sizable majority of patients with life-threatening injuries, a 50% overtriage is probably necessary. Advance transmission of key patient information to the receiving trauma center facilitates the organization of the trauma team and ensures the availability of ancillary services.[9]

DECLARATION OF DEATH AT SCENE

The determination that care is futile during prehospital evaluation is best made on the basis of the cardiac rhythm. Asystole justifies declaration of death at the scene, and recent profound bradycardia (heart rate < 40 beats/min) has been shown to signal an unsalvageable situation.[10-12]

Emergency Department Management

ARRIVAL AT HOSPITAL
UNDER ACTIVE
CARDIOPULMONARY
RESUSCITATION

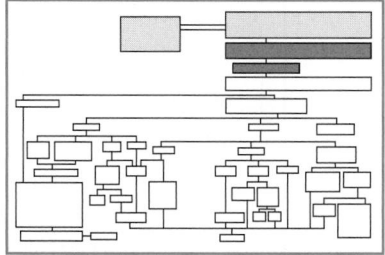

Prehospital pulseless electrical activity (PEA) in injured patients has a dismal prognosis, and it has been proposed that such patients should be declared dead in the field.[13] Unfortunately, most first responders do not use the cardiac rhythm to decide whether to initiate CPR. When a patient arrives in the ED after prehospital CPR has been initiated, the critical question is whether to perform a resuscitative thoracotomy. The prognosis for blunt trauma patients is poor because the major causes of cardiopulmonary arrest after blunt trauma (e.g., massive brain injury, high spinal cord injury, and exsanguination from multiple injuries) are difficult to reverse. In contrast, patients with stab wounds to the heart are frequently salvageable if cardiac arrest occurs because of cardiac tamponade. In most cases, the heart can be resuscitated by simply decompressing the pericardium, given that blood volume is usually maintained. Guidelines for terminating resuscitation are based on the mechanism of injury, the duration of CPR, the presence of signs of life (e.g., pupillary response, respiratory effort, or motor activity), and the presence of asystole documented by cardiac monitoring [*see Table 1*].[14]

Initial Approach to the Critically Injured Patient

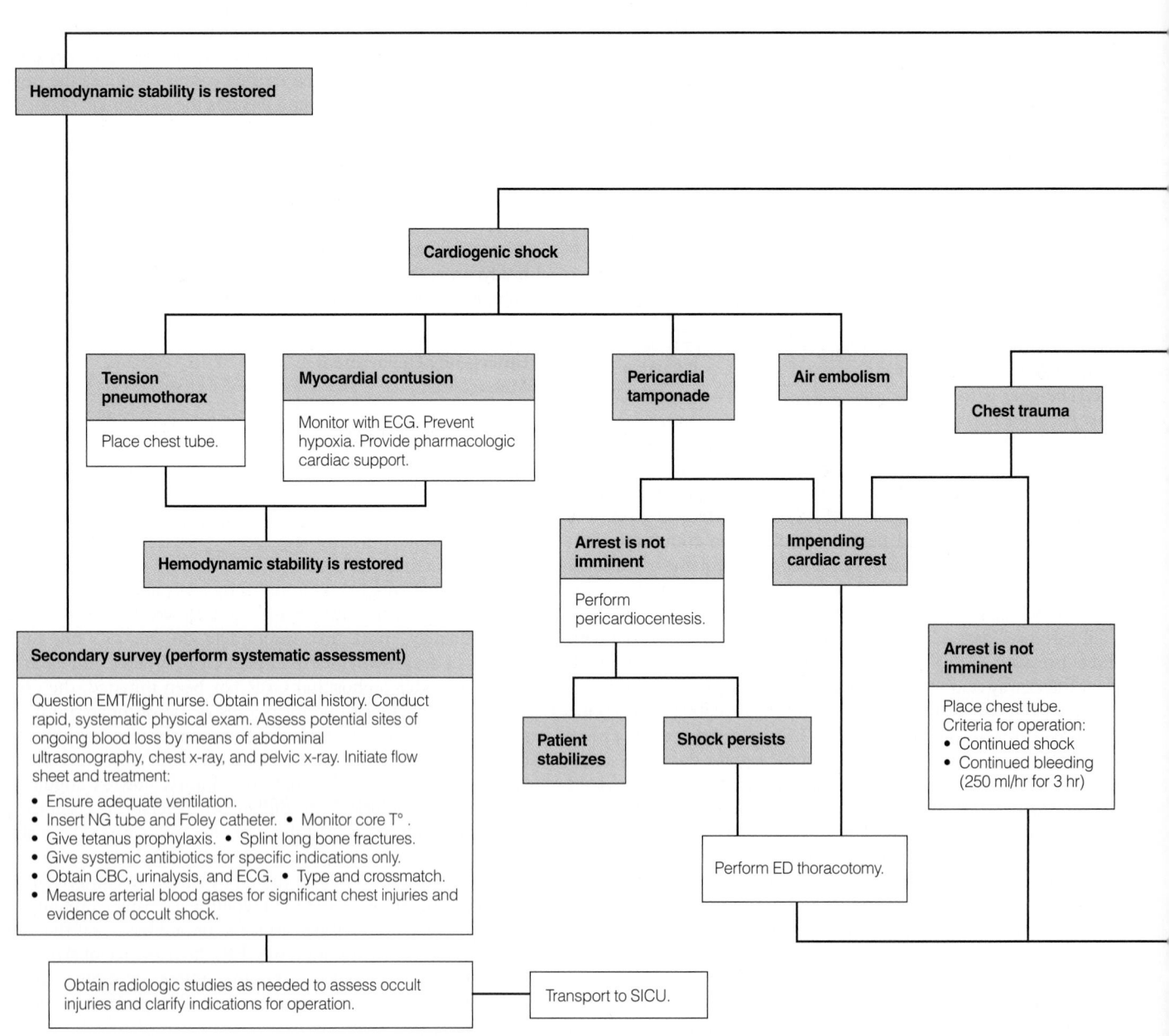

Communicate with base hospital

Field triage: Level I, II, or III facility
Assemble trauma team:
- Trauma surgeon
- ED physician
- Surgical specialist
- Radiology technicians
- Nurses
- Respiratory technicians

Ensure ancillary services:
- OR
- CT scanning
- Blood bank
- Interventional radiology

Hemodynamic stability is restored

Cardiogenic shock

Tension pneumothorax

Place chest tube.

Myocardial contusion

Monitor with ECG. Prevent hypoxia. Provide pharmacologic cardiac support.

Pericardial tamponade

Air embolism

Chest trauma

Hemodynamic stability is restored

Arrest is not imminent

Perform pericardiocentesis.

Impending cardiac arrest

Arrest is not imminent

Place chest tube.
Criteria for operation:
- Continued shock
- Continued bleeding (250 ml/hr for 3 hr)

Secondary survey (perform systematic assessment)

Question EMT/flight nurse. Obtain medical history. Conduct rapid, systematic physical exam. Assess potential sites of ongoing blood loss by means of abdominal ultrasonography, chest x-ray, and pelvic x-ray. Initiate flow sheet and treatment:

- Ensure adequate ventilation.
- Insert NG tube and Foley catheter. • Monitor core T°.
- Give tetanus prophylaxis. • Splint long bone fractures.
- Give systemic antibiotics for specific indications only.
- Obtain CBC, urinalysis, and ECG. • Type and crossmatch.
- Measure arterial blood gases for significant chest injuries and evidence of occult shock.

Patient stabilizes

Shock persists

Perform ED thoracotomy.

Obtain radiologic studies as needed to assess occult injuries and clarify indications for operation.

Transport to SICU.

Urban: < 15 minutes (Rural: > 30 minutes)

Initiate resuscitation and evaluation of trauma patients at the injury scene; communicate with base hospital

Management priorities of basic trauma life support are the following:
- Assess and control the accident scene
- Tamponade external hemorrhage with direct pressure
- Protect the spine after blunt trauma
- Extricate the patient
- Supplement inspired O_2
- Stabilize long bone fractures

Advanced trauma life support may include the following:
- Active airway support
- I.V. fluid administration
- Decompression of thorax for suspected pneumothorax

< 3 Minutes

Primary survey (evaluate and initiate management of airway, breathing, and circulation)

Listen to prehospital report. **Airway:** Clear airway and establish patency; obtain cervical spine x-ray. **Breathing:** Assist ventilation; vent suspected hemopneumothoraces with chest tubes. **Circulation:** Establish I.V. access; infuse fluid (crystalloid); draw blood samples.

Assess chest and abdomen with ultrasonography.
Blunt trauma: obtain x-rays of cervical spine, chest, and pelvis.

< 5 Minutes

Evaluate response to initial resuscitation

Assess response to crystalloid infusion (i.e., BP, heart rate, respiratory rate, mental status). Identify easily reversible causes of shock.

Shock persists

Reassess physical signs. Monitor CVP.
Repeat ultrasonography; consider DPL if ultrasonography is equivocal.

Secondary survey:
Unstable patients: 5 minutes
(Stable patients: up to 30 minutes)

Hypovolemic shock

Neurogenic shock

[*See 118 Shock.*]

Abdominal trauma

Pelvic fracture

Compress with sheet or C-clamp; administer blood.

Impending cardiac arrest

Multisystem trauma

Isolated injury

Hemodynamic stability is restored

Consider pelvic fixation (consult orthopedic surgeon).

Shock persists

Perform ultrasonography or open DPL.

Abdominal ultrasonography is positive

Abdominal ultrasonography is equivocal

Perform DPL.

Ultrasonogram or DPL is grossly positive

DPL is positive by red cell count or negative

Perform angiography and percutaneous embolization, depending on fracture geography. If DPL was negative, transport to ICU. If DPL was positive, evaluate by CT scan.

Perform ED thoracotomy.

DPL is negative

DPL is positive

Transport to OR.

< 30 Minutes

1213

Table 1 Guidelines for Declaring Patients Dead on Arrival

Penetrating trauma	Prehospital CPR for > 15 min with no signs of life Asystole without wound that could cause pericardial tamponade
Blunt trauma	Prehospital CPR for > 5 min with no signs of life Asystole

PRIMARY SURVEY AND INITIAL RESUSCITATION

During initial assessment, an empirical sequence of lifesaving therapeutic and diagnostic procedures is pursued. The ultimate goal is to establish adequate oxygen delivery to the vital organs. This is accomplished by first progressing through the ABCs: airway control with cervical spine precautions, assisted breathing with ventilation, and empirical tube thoracostomy to relieve a pneumothorax if indicated. These maneuvers are carried out to maximize oxygen delivery to the alveoli. Support of the circulation (tamponade of external bleeding and fluid administration) is instituted to restore effective blood volume, thereby enhancing myocardial performance and thus oxygen delivery to the tissues.

Unstable patients fall into two categories: those who respond to initial intervention and those who do not. Early nonresponders are challenging because they require an immediate lifesaving intervention. The challenge is to perform the correct intervention before the patient dies. Patients who respond to initial interventions can be equally challenging because a subset of them have only a finite time window before shock recurs. Multiple diagnoses must be considered before correct definitive triage is possible. The clinician must rapidly formulate a differential diagnosis and then sequentially initiate the appropriate diagnostic tests.

Airway and Breathing

After blunt trauma, airway control should proceed on the assumption that an unstable cervical spine fracture exists; thus, hyperextension of the neck must be avoided. Airway management in the seriously injured victim can usually be accomplished with simple techniques, but it is occasionally challenging. Evaluation begins by asking the patient a question such as "How are you?" A response given in a normal voice indicates that the airway is not in immediate jeopardy; a breathless, hoarse response or no response at all indicates that the airway may be compromised.

Airway obstruction and hypoventilation are the most likely causes of respiratory failure. The critical decision is whether active airway intervention is needed. The first maneuver is to clear the airway of debris and to suction secretions. In the obtunded patient, this procedure is followed by elevation of the angle of the mandible to alleviate pharyngeal obstruction and placement of an oropharyngeal or nasopharyngeal tube to maintain airway patency. Supplemental oxygen is given via a nasal cannula (6 L/min) or a nonrebreathing oxygen mask (12 L/min). Airway patency, however, does not ensure adequate ventilation, nor does a normal arterial oxygen saturation (S_aO_2) on pulse oximetry. Clinical evidence of hypoventilation includes poor air exchange at the nose and mouth, diminished breath sounds, and decreased chest wall excursion; the most likely causes are head injury, spinal cord transection, hemopneumothorax, flail chest, and profound shock.

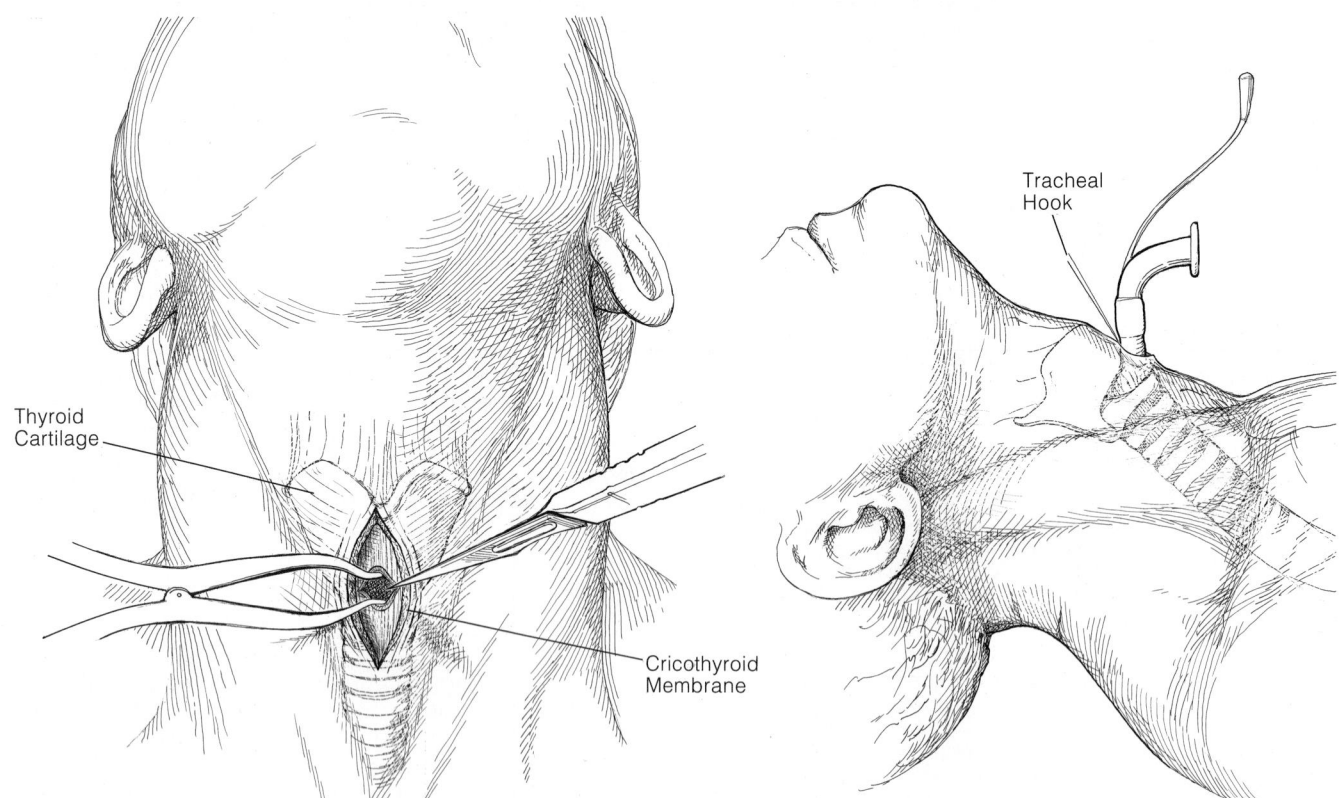

Figure 1 Technique for cricothyrotomy is illustrated here. The larynx is stabilized with one hand, and a 2 cm vertical incision is made over the cricothyroid space. The cricothyroid membrane is palpated and incised horizontally. A Trousseau dilator is inserted and spread vertically for visualization of the subglottic space (left). A tracheal hook is used to retract the inferior border of the thyroid cartilage as a tracheostomy tube with a 6 mm internal diameter is inserted into the trachea (right).

Table 2 10 Steps in Rapid-Sequence Intubation

1. Preparation of equipment and supplies
2. Preoxygenation
3. Sedation to decrease anxiety
4. Premedication to mitigate adverse effects: vecuronium bromide (1 mg) to prevent defasciculations, lidocaine (1.5 mg/kg) to prevent increased ICP with TBI
5. Cricoid pressure
6. Administration of paralytic agent: succinylcholine (1.0–1.5 mg/kg), vecuronium bromide (0.6–1.2 mg/kg) if succinylcholine contraindicated
7. Intubation
8. Confirmation of tube position by auscultation and capnography
9. Securing of airway
10. Chest x-ray

ICP—intracranial pressure   TBI—traumatic brain injury

Suspected hemopneumothoraces should be vented with large-bore chest tubes inserted via the midlateral thorax.

Cervical spine protection is integral to airway management but should not be allowed to delay necessary intervention. The majority of significant spinal injuries in adults arriving alive at the ED are at the C5 to C7 levels. In children 8 years old or younger, the most frequent site of spinal injury is between the occiput and the C3 level. Significant spinal cord injury without radiographic abnormalities (i.e., the SCIWORA syndrome) is a relatively rare event (0.5% of patients undergoing radiography), and the data on its relative frequency in children and in adults are conflicting.[15,16] A fractured cervical spine is usually tender to direct palpation in alert patients, but pain may be masked by distracting injuries.[17,18] Even good-quality cross-table lateral cervical spine films may not detect 15% of unstable fractures. Accordingly, in high-risk patients, a cervical collar is left in place until the cervical spine has been radiologically evaluated for bony and ligamentous integrity.[19]

Bag-mask ventilation is an effective temporizing measure, but it consumes the attention of a skilled trauma team member, it may insufflate air into the stomach, and it can be resisted by spontaneously breathing patients. It is also ineffective in the presence of severe maxillofacial trauma. The decision for urgent airway control is made on clinical grounds; there often is no time to obtain a confirmatory arterial blood gas (ABG) analysis.[20] Persistent airway obstruction or signs of inadequate ventilation mandate prompt intervention. Patients with expanding neck hematomas, deteriorating vital signs, or severe head trauma are also best managed with an aggressive airway approach. On the other hand, in equivocal situations, an ABG analysis may be decisive.

The best method of airway control depends on (1) the presence of maxillofacial trauma, (2) possible cervical spine injury, (3) overall patient condition, and (4) the experience of the physician. Patients in respiratory distress with severe maxillofacial trauma warrant operative intervention. Cricothyrotomy is the preferred approach in adults and has virtually replaced tracheostomy in the ED [see Figure 1]; the rare exceptions are in patients with major laryngeal trauma or extensive tracheal disruption. Percutaneous transtracheal ventilation may be safer than both of these surgical procedures for temporary airway management, particularly in children. In all other patients, the current standard approach is rapid sequence intubation (RSI) of the trachea orally with inline immobilization [see Table 2].[21,22] In adults, a large (8 mm internal diameter) cuffed endotracheal tube is inserted to a distance of 23 cm from the incisors. In children, tube size is gauged to equal the diameter of the little finger. The proper depth (in centimeters) to which the tube should be inserted can be estimated by multiplying the tube's internal diameter (in millimeters) by 3. A chest x-ray should be obtained as soon as possible to rule out the possibility of right mainstem intubation.

Intubated patients should be placed on a high fraction of inspired oxygen (F_IO_2), and their S_aO_2 should be monitored by means of pulse oximetry. Generally, a low S_aO_2 is easily treated by increasing the F_IO_2. Patients who do not respond when the F_IO_2 is increased to 100% should be treated with low levels of positive end-expiratory pressure (PEEP) once adequate volume status is assured. Positive-pressure ventilation impedes return of blood to the heart; as a result, emergency intubation of a hypovolemic patient can adversely affect cardiac output. Hyperventilation should be avoided. An ABG analysis should be obtained to assess pH and arterial carbon dioxide tension (P_aCO_2).

Circulation

Once alveolar ventilation is ensured, the next priority is to optimize oxygen delivery by maximizing cardiovascular performance. External hemorrhage is controlled by means of manual compression, and empirical volume loading for presumed hypovolemia via large-bore I.V. cannulas is initiated. The size, number, and sites of I.V. catheters depend on the degree of shock present and on estimates of injury severity. If the patient arrives in shock or has obvious multiple injuries, a short 14 French catheter should be placed in each antecubital vein. When vascular collapse precludes peripheral percutaneous access in an adult, the alternative is cannulation of the femoral or the subclavian vein by means of the Seldinger technique. We have found the supraclavicular subclavian approach to be useful in the ED.[23] Venous access should be avoided in regions with potential penetrating vascular injuries (e.g., lower neck, upper chest, pelvis, or groin).

Intraosseous infusion through a cannula placed in the medullary cavity of a long bone is a safe and efficacious method for emergency vascular access in infants and children younger than 6 years. This procedure is typically performed in the anteromedial aspect of the tibial plateau in an uninjured extremity; the distal femur, the distal tibia, and the sternum are other potential sites. Intraosseous infusion generally allows administration of sufficient fluid to facilitate subsequent cannulation of the venous circulation.[24] If access remains problematic in children, greater saphenous vein cutdown at the groin is the preferred route because inadvertent femoral artery injury with the percutaneous approach may result in limb-threatening vasospasm.

With establishment of the first I.V. line, blood should be drawn for hematocrit, white blood cell (WBC) count, electrolyte concentrations, blood-group typing, coagulation profile, and toxicology screen as indicated.

Isotonic crystalloid is used for initial resuscitation in the ED.[25,26] Lactated Ringer solution (LR) is preferred to normal saline (NS) unless the patient has an obvious brain injury. Excessive early administration of crystalloids has been identified as a risk factor for adverse outcomes; accordingly, the amount infused should be closely monitored.[27] If the patient does not respond to crystalloid infusion at levels exceeding 30 ml/kg, blood should be administered. LR and banked blood should not be infused through the same I.V. line.

Early empirical blood transfusions are indicated in patients who arrive in severe shock or who have injuries associated with significant bleeding (e.g., a vertical shear pelvic fracture or bilateral femur fractures), especially if the patients are elderly. Type-specific blood should be available within 20 minutes. If type-specific blood is not available, reconstituted O-negative packed red blood cells (RBCs) may be used. Micropore filters are not used in blood infusion lines in hemodynamically unstable patients, because they impede infusion capabilities.[28] In the future, hemoglobin-based oxygen carriers may become available, obviating crossmatching. Protocols for massive transfusions should be established with the blood bank to ensure prompt availability of blood products for patients arriving with life-threatening bleeding.[29,30]

EVALUATION AND CONTINUED RESUSCITATION

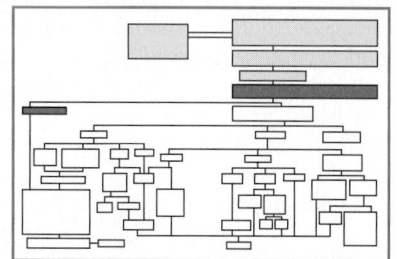

Identification of Hemodynamic Instability

Recognizing the presence of shock and assessing its severity [see 118 Shock] are key factors in early decision making. During the initial ABCs, palpation for the presence of pulses can be used to generate an estimate of systolic blood pressure (SBP). In general, a radial pulse is detected when SBP is higher than 80 mm Hg, a femoral pulse when SBP is above 70 mm Hg, and a carotid pulse when SBP exceeds 60 mm Hg. The initial blood pressure measurement should be made with a manual cuff; automatic cuff BP measurement machines may overestimate SBP in hypovolemic trauma patients.[31] An SBP lower than 90 mm Hg (or an age-adjusted decrease in SBP that exceeds 30 mm Hg) in conjunction with a heart rate higher than 120 beats/min is generally considered indicative of shock. Most patients, however, especially young ones, can compensate for hypovolemia and maintain a normal BP even in the face of significant ongoing hemorrhage. It should be kept in mind that because acute massive blood loss may paradoxically trigger a vagal-mediated bradycardia, the traditional inverse correlation between increased HR and reduced effective blood volume may not hold in the early resuscitation period.[32] The initial hemoglobin level is notoriously misleading, whether because the patient has not yet been volume loaded or because there has not been sufficient time for influx of interstitial fluid into the intravascular space. It may therefore be helpful to measure the hemoglobin level again after initial volume loading for purposes of comparison; a decrease greater than 2 g/dl should be grounds for concern.

The size of the base deficit can be a useful measure of the depth of hemorrhagic shock.[33] Whether the base deficit is persisting or declining is more important than its absolute value, but generally a base deficit smaller than –8 mEq/L is indicative of severe shock.

Figure 2 In acute trauma, a tube thoracostomy is performed through the fourth or fifth interspace at the midaxillary line, well above the diaphragm (*a*). A short subcutaneous tunnel is fashioned over the superior edge of the rib, and the overlying fascia and intercostal muscle are divided sharply. The pleural space is entered by incising the intercostal muscle and the pleura with a heavy scissors (*b*). A gloved finger is then inserted to confirm penetration of the thoracic cavity and to free up intrapleural adhesions (*c*). A large-bore tube (36 French) is directed posteriorly toward the pleural apex; the proximal port must be well inside the chest (*d*). The tube is then secured to the chest wall with No. 5 braided polyethylene suture and connected to a standard collection apparatus.

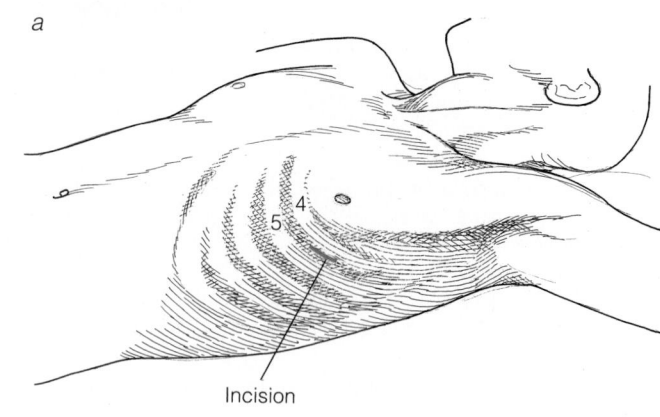

a

Incision

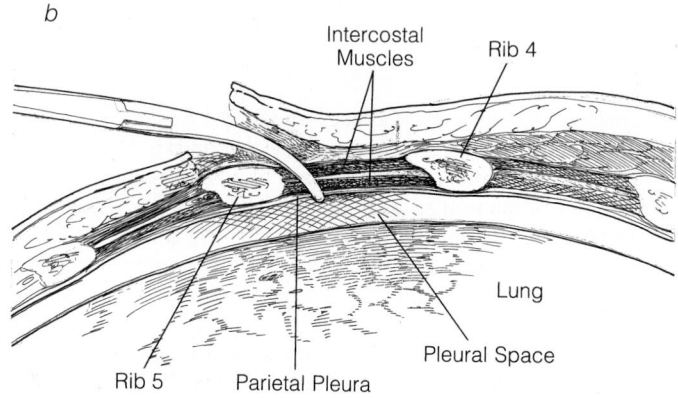

b

Intercostal Muscles
Rib 4
Lung
Pleural Space
Parietal Pleura
Rib 5

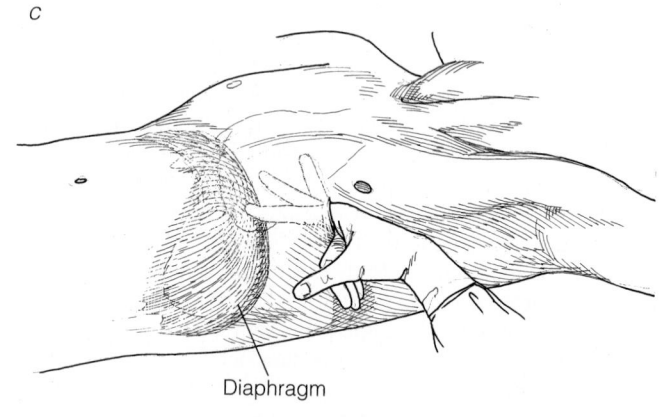

c

Diaphragm

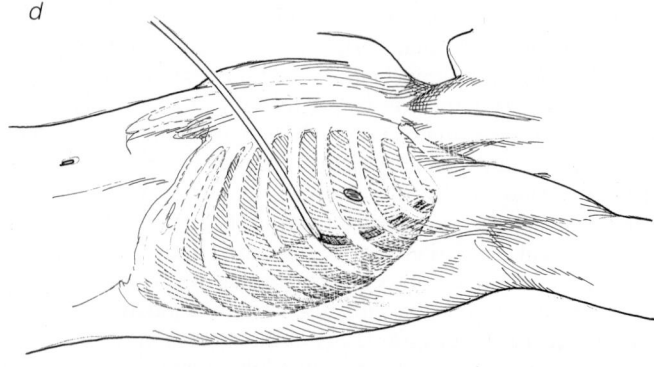

d

Measurement of central venous pressure (CVP) is helpful in identifying severe hypovolemia, and serial CVP measurements can be used to assess response to volume loading. Although arterial lines are of limited value in initial ED management, they become increasingly useful as time passes. The end points of initial resuscitation during the time of critical diagnostic testing and triage are as follows: (1) SBP higher than 90 mm Hg, (2) HR lower than 120 beats/min, (3) hemoglobin concentration equal to or greater than 10 g/dl, and (4) CVP equal to or greater than 10 cm H_2O.

Management of Nonresponsive Unstable Patients

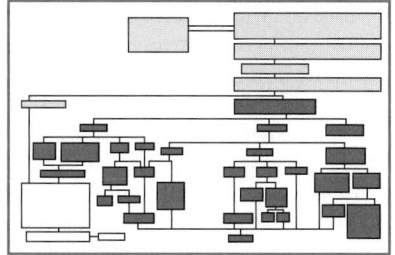

Shock that persists despite initial volume loading may derive from severe hypovolemia, cardiogenic causes, or neurogenic causes. Given that neurogenic shock is fairly well tolerated, the key concern at this point is to quickly distinguish hypovolemic shock from cardiogenic shock because cardiogenic shock may necessitate immediate ED intervention. This distinction can reasonably be made by measuring CVP. In hypovolemic shock, CVP is generally less than 5 mm Hg, whereas in clinically significant cardiogenic shock, CVP usually exceeds 20 mm Hg.

The differential diagnosis of traumatic cardiogenic shock depends on the mechanism of injury and may include (1) tension pneumothorax, (2) pericardial tamponade, (3) myocardial contusion, and (4) air embolism. Except in refractory shock, telltale physical signs are frequently hard to discern in a noisy ED, especially when compounded by persistent hypovolemia. Timely diagnosis requires a high index of suspicion. Tension pneumothorax, the most common cause of cardiogenic shock in both blunt and penetrating trauma, is often first confirmed with emergency chest tube placement [see Figure 2].

In traumatic pericardial tamponade, the classic components of Beck's triad (hypotension, muffled heart sounds, and jugular venous distention) are frequently absent, and pulsus paradoxus is rarely detectable. ED ultrasonography is the first test employed by trauma surgeons in patients with high-risk penetrating wounds.[34] CVP measurements and pericardiocentesis [see Figure 3] are helpful confirmative tests. Occasionally, a blunt trauma patient can be salvaged through timely diagnosis of a blunt atrial tear.

Myocardial contusion should be suspected in any blunt trauma patient with unexplained cardiogenic shock or persistent arrhythmia. Electrocardiographic changes are usually nonspecific.[35,36] Fundamental measures include correction of acidosis, hypoxia, and electrolyte abnormalities; judicious administration of fluid; and pharmacologic suppression of life-threatening arrhythmias.

Bronchovenous air embolism into the left atrium from a pulmonary laceration typically occurs after penetrating trauma and probably is more common than is generally recognized.[37] Hemodynamic instability develops after positive pressure ventilation is initiated, as air is forced from the pulmonary bronchioles into the adjacent open pulmonary veins and, ultimately, into the coronary arteries. ED thoracotomy is essential for pulmonary hilar cross-clamping, air aspiration from the left ventricle, and cardiac massage. The patient is then transferred to the OR for definitive management of the pulmonary lesion before the hilar clamp is released.

ED thoracotomy is an integral part of the initial management of the patient who arrives in extremis and deteriorates to immi-

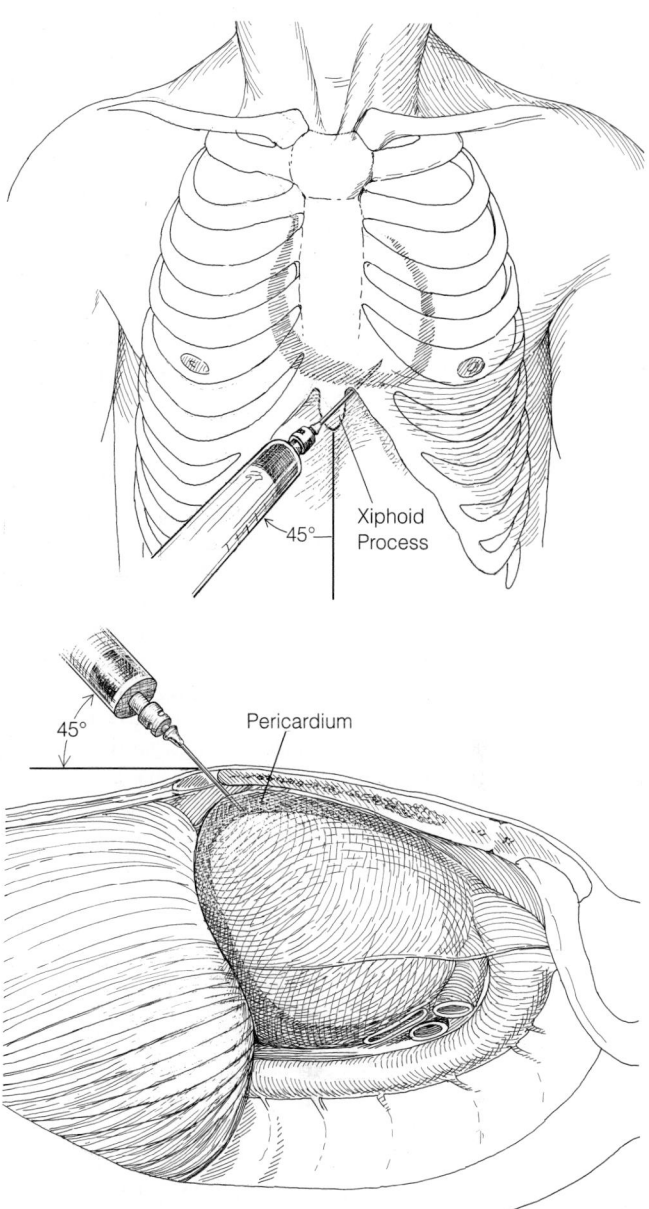

Figure 3 **For pericardiocentesis, an 18-gauge spinal needle is inserted at the left xiphoid-costal junction and inserted toward the inferior tip of the left scapula (angled 45° to the patient's right and 45° from the chest wall). The needle is advanced until blood or air is encountered; a "pop" may be appreciated as the needle tip traverses the pericardium. If air is withdrawn, the needle tip should be directed more toward the patient's midline. If blood is withdrawn, 50 ml should be aspirated and injected onto a sheet so that it can be inspected for clots. As a rule, intraventricular blood will clot, whereas defibrinated pericardial blood will not clot.**

nent cardiac arrest [see Figure 4].[38] The physiologic rationale is to minimize the duration of profound shock. ED thoracotomy permits (1) release of pericardial tamponade, (2) control of intrathoracic blood loss, (3) internal cardiac massage, and (4) crossclamping of the descending thoracic aorta to enhance coronary and cerebral perfusion and to reduce subdiaphragmatic bleeding. Internal cardiac massage should be done bimanually; otherwise, a forceful thumb may rupture the relatively thin right ventricle as it becomes distended. Ventricular lacerations are repaired with pledgeted horizontal mattress sutures, whereas atrial injuries are controlled with a partially occluding vascular clamp and repaired with a continuous suture [*see Figure 5*]. Small left ventricular wounds can be closed without pledgets. For large left ventricular wounds, skin staples are an alternative means of rapid closure.

SECONDARY SURVEY
WITH DEFINITIVE
DIAGNOSIS AND
TRIAGE DECISIONS

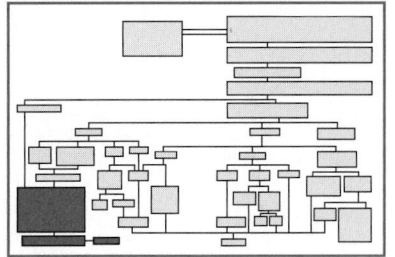

Fortunately, most acutely injured patients arriving in shock can be rendered hemodynamically stable enough to undergo a secondary survey. Diagnosis and treatment proceed simultaneously. Prioritization is imperative and is governed by the severity of shock and its rate of progression. Easily correctable life-threatening injuries should be addressed first before a search is made for occult trauma. Prioritization is also guided by the mechanism of injury. Penetrating trauma typically results in a localized injury, whereas blunt trauma frequently results in multiple injuries involving several body regions. When hemodynamic instability recurs, its cause must be identified and corrected promptly.

The length of time spent in the ED, the decision for urgent operation, and the ordering of special radiologic studies are critical decisions that must take into account the mechanism of injury, the response to resuscitation, and the availability of a staffed operating room or interventional radiology suite. A patient in refractory shock with a central abdominal gunshot wound, for example, clearly should be transported to the OR in a matter of minutes, but the management of a previously unstable victim of a motor vehicle crash who has a positive ultrasonogram combined with altered mental status, a widened mediastinum on chest x-ray, and an unstable pelvic fracture requires a far more complex decision. In general, however, when priorities conflict, the safest arena for managing critically injured patients is the OR.

Penetrating Trauma

Systematic assessment The secondary survey is more focused in cases of penetrating trauma than in cases of blunt trauma. The priorities are (1) to identify all of the wounds, (2) to decide whether an urgent operation is indicated, and (3) to determine whether additional testing is needed to assist with intraoperative management. The decision-making process is driven by hemodynamic stability and the location of the wounds. Efforts should focus not on resuscitating the patient until vital signs are normal but, rather, on obtaining adequate I.V. access, ensuring that blood products are available, and notifying the OR. Hemodynamically unstable patients should be rapidly sent to the OR with minimal or no testing.

Neck Patients who have an obvious life-threatening injury (e.g., a gurgling wound, pulsatile bleeding, or a compromised airway) or are in severe shock should undergo operation promptly. ED management should be limited to airway control, external compression to control bleeding, I.V. access, and chest x-ray. A neurologic examination should be performed and documented.

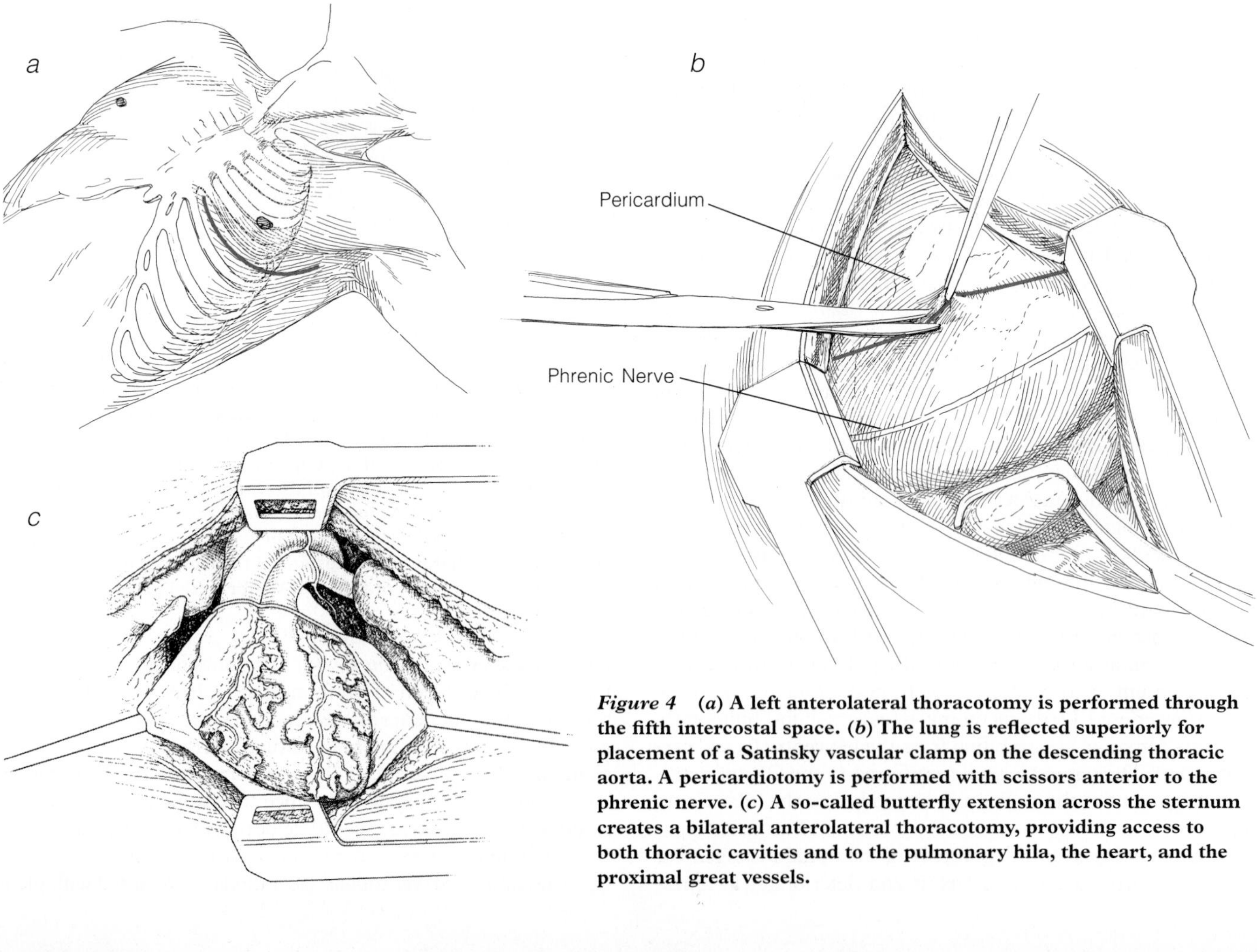

Figure 4 (*a*) A left anterolateral thoracotomy is performed through the fifth intercostal space. (*b*) The lung is reflected superiorly for placement of a Satinsky vascular clamp on the descending thoracic aorta. A pericardiotomy is performed with scissors anterior to the phrenic nerve. (*c*) A so-called butterfly extension across the sternum creates a bilateral anterolateral thoracotomy, providing access to both thoracic cavities and to the pulmonary hila, the heart, and the proximal great vessels.

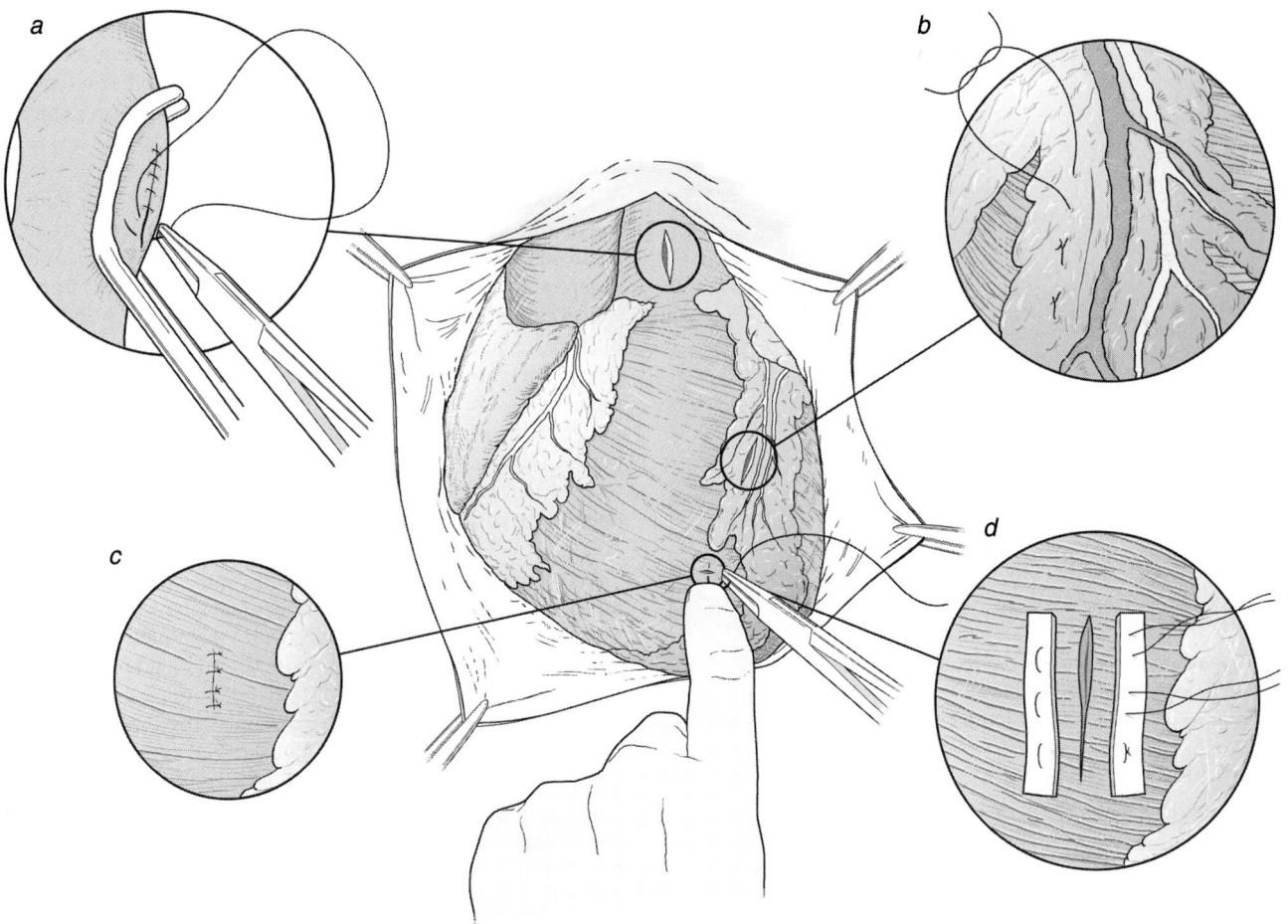

Figure 5 (*a*) **A Satinsky vascular clamp is used to control arterial and major vessel injuries while they are closed with a running suture. (*b*) For wounds close to coronary arteries, horizontal mattress sutures should be used to spare the arteries. (*c*) Small wounds to the thick left ventricle can be closed with interrupted simple sutures. (*d*) Larger wounds should be closed using pledgets; staple closure may be preferred for larger ventricular wounds.**

Management of hemodynamically stable patients without obvious injury is selective.[39] Patients with zone I wounds should undergo CT scanning or angiography to rule out occult vascular injuries. Alert patients with zone II injuries but without significant hematoma, crepitance, dysphonia, or dysphagia may be managed expectantly. A missed esophageal injury is associated with significant morbidity. If there is reason to suspect such an injury, both esophagoscopy and esophagography should be performed. Although individually these tests have false negative rates ranging from 10% to 15%, their combined sensitivity approaches 100%.[40] Asymptomatic patients with zone III injuries should undergo CT scanning or angiography if there is any suspicion of an occult vascular injury.

Chest In unstable patients with thoracic injuries, a chest tube should be placed into the wounded hemithorax, followed by a chest x-ray to confirm tube placement, lung expansion, hemothorax evacuation, and the presence of foreign bodies. If a cardiac wound is suspected, ED ultrasonography should be performed.[34] Persistent instability without evidence of intrathoracic bleeding or pericardial tamponade should raise the suspicion of intra-abdominal bleeding. Occasionally, a high spinal cord injury contributes to hemodynamic instability.

The challenge in this setting is to quickly identify those patients who require an urgent operation. Patients who have wounds close to the heart (i.e., in the so-called mediastinal box), ultrasono-graphically documented hemopericardium, and persistent tachycardia should undergo pericardiocentesis to relieve any ongoing subendocardial ischemia even if SBP is normal [*see Figure 3*]. Patients who exhibit persistent signs of pericardial tamponade despite negative results from ultrasonography or pericardiocentesis should be transported to the OR for creation of a subxiphoid pericardial window. In approximately 15% of cases, the results of pericardial aspiration for acute hemopericardium are falsely negative because the blood in the pericardial sac is clotted and cannot be aspirated.

If the patient is in extremis, ED thoracotomy should be performed promptly [*see Figure 4*]. Most patients experiencing intrathoracic bleeding without pericardial tamponade stabilize after tube thoracostomy and modest volume loading. Urgent thoracotomy is indicated for (1) so-called caked hemothorax [*see Figure 6*], (2) an initial chest tube output higher than 20 ml/kg, (3) a persistent output higher than 3 ml/kg/hr for 2 consecutive hours, or (4) a 12-hour output exceeding 30 ml/kg. Patients with an initial chest tube output higher than 10 ml/kg should be closely observed for hemodynamic instability in the ICU. Abrupt cessation of chest tube output may be deceptive; if hypotension persists or recurs, a second chest tube should be inserted and another chest x-ray obtained.

Patients with large air leaks, massive subcutaneous emphysema, or a persistent pneumothorax should undergo bronchoscopy to exclude a tracheobronchial injury. Patients with transmediastinal

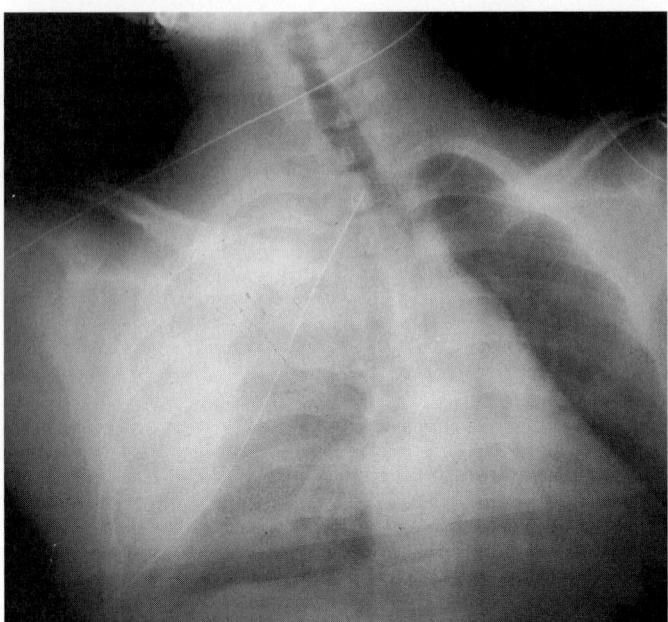

Figure 6 **ED chest x-ray shows a massive hemothorax. If the chest tube fails to evacuate the blood, this is a so-called caked hemothorax, which is an indication for emergency thoracotomy in the OR.**

gunshot wounds (GSWs) or penetrating wounds close to the great vessels should undergo CT angiography, formal angiography, or both.[41]

Lower chest. Wounds located below the nipples anteriorly or the tips of the scapulas posteriorly may penetrate the diaphragm and cause significant intra-abdominal or retroperitoneal injuries. Such penetration occurs in 10% of stab wounds and 30% of GSWs.[42] If the patient is unstable, tube thoracostomy, chest x-ray, and abdominal ultrasonography are indicated. If instability persists, the patient should be transported to the OR. If the patient stabilizes after tube thoracostomy, additional testing must be done to exclude associated injuries. Diagnostic peritoneal lavage (DPL) is a good screening test for intra-abdominal injuries. The RBC threshold for abdominal exploration is lowered to 10,000/mm³ because isolated diaphragmatic injuries may not bleed. An intermediate RBC count (1,000 to 10,000/mm³) warrants further evaluation with thoracoscopy or laparoscopy because DPL may contribute this degree of RBC contamination.[43] CT scanning may assist in diagnosing occult retroperitoneal injuries, but it is not reliable for excluding penetrating diaphragmatic injuries.[44]

Anterior abdomen Unstable patients should be transported to the OR with minimal resuscitation and testing. Biplanar abdominal x-rays are often helpful in clarifying bullet trajectories; entrance and exit wounds should be marked with radiopaque objects. Intravenous pyelography (IVP) is not indicated, because it takes too much time. Management of stable patients depends on the mechanism of injury. Laparotomy is indicted for GSWs that violate the peritoneal cavity. DPL or laparoscopy is indicated for suspicious tangential GSWs. Laparotomy is indicated in patients with overt peritonitis after a stab wound. In other patients, the stab wound should be explored. If there is no violation of the anterior fascia, the patient can safely be discharged. If the fascia is violated, DPL is indicated; an RBC count higher than 100,000/mm³ mandates laparotomy. Furthermore, an elevated WBC count, amylase level, alkaline phosphatase level, or bilirubin concentration in the lavage fluid may identify hollow viscus injury (HVI); however, threshold values for these measurements have not been established.[45,46]

Flank, back, and pelvis Unstable patients with injuries to the flank, the back, or the pelvis should undergo immediate laparotomy. Stable patients are difficult to evaluate. With the exception of blood on rectal examination, the findings from physical examination are unreliable. Gross hematuria is indicative of bladder or kidney injury. Triple-contrast CT scanning may be helpful in patients with high-risk wounds.[44,47] Most retroperitoneal HVIs are identified on the basis of extraluminal gas or fluid rather than of contrast extravasation. Sigmoidoscopy should be performed if a rectal injury is suspected. High-risk wounds should be explored to ensure that retroperitoneal HVIs are not missed; delayed diagnosis is associated with significant morbidity.

Extremities Unstable patients with isolated penetrating injuries to the extremities should be managed with external compression to control bleeding (not with tourniquets or direct vessel clamping), I.V. access with modest volume loading, and prompt triage to the OR for exploration and definitive treatment. Management of stable patients with penetrating extremity injuries begins with a search for "hard" signs of arterial injury (e.g., a large, expanding, or pulsatile hematoma; absent distal pulses; a palpable thrill; an audible bruit; and signs of distal ischemia).[48] Presence of any of these hard signs prompts further evaluation. If signs of distal ischemia exist, the patient should be taken to the OR, where an on-table angiogram can be performed. If knowledge of the patient's specific vascular anatomy is needed and no signs of ischemia exist, a formal angiogram is reasonable. If "soft" signs of vascular injury are present, distal blood pressures should be measured in the injured extremity, the contralateral extremity, and, often, the brachial artery. If either the ratio of the BP in the injured extremity to that in the contralateral extremity or the ratio of the BP in the injured ankle to that in the brachial artery is 0.90 or higher, arterial injury is excluded and no additional testing is needed. These ratios are not, however, reliable for excluding arterial injuries in the axilla or the groin. The presence of a good Doppler signal does not exclude a vascular injury.

Blunt Trauma

Systematic assessment The goal is to identify all potentially life- and limb-threatening injuries. A comprehensive assessment is crucial to facilitate triage from the ED to the OR, the CT scanning suite, the interventional radiology suite, or the ICU. The details of the patient's medical history, as well as the details specifically related to the injury, are critical. The prehospital emergency medical technicians are encouraged to provide a comprehensive account of the event and a thorough patient assessment. A minimal review of the patient's medical history should include preexisting medical illnesses, current medications (and when they were most recently ingested), allergies, tetanus immunization status, and the time of the last meal. A rapid, systematic physical examination is done, literally from head to toe. Patients are completely disrobed and, once spinal injury is excluded, rolled from side to side so that the back and the flanks can be inspected. A rectal examination is done to look for blood and to evaluate sphincter tone; the perineum and the axillae are inspected; and neurologic function and peripheral pulses are assessed.

The cervical spine is rigidly immobilized, and long-bone frac-

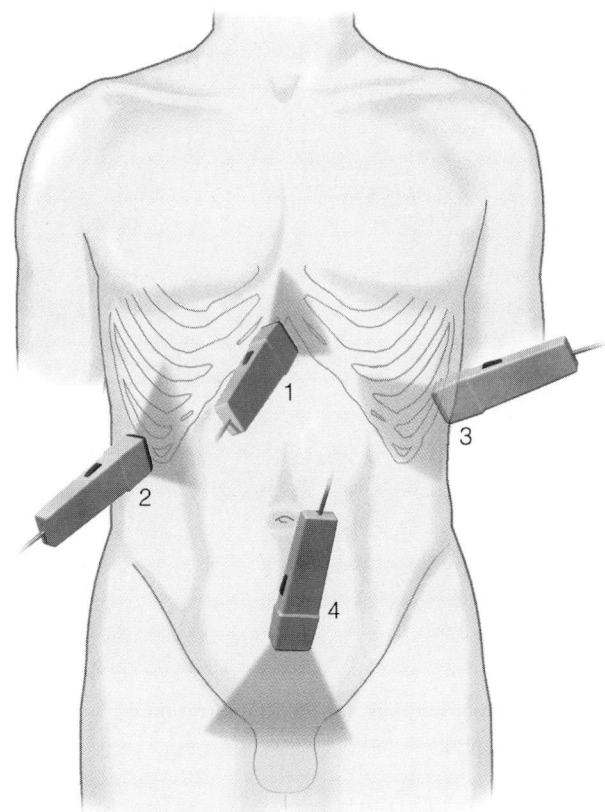

Figure 7 **Shown are four transducer positions in the FAST (*f*ocused *a*ssessment for *s*onographic evaluation of the *t*rauma patient): (1) pericardial area, (2) right upper quadrant, (3) left upper quadrant, and (4) pelvis.**

tures are splinted to minimize pain, blood loss, and soft tissue damage. Insertion of a nasogastric tube decompresses the stomach and reduces the risk of pulmonary aspiration, but because maxillofacial injury may provide a pathway into the cranial vault,[49] the tube should be placed orally when midfacial fractures are present. Blood in the gastric aspirate may be the only sign of an otherwise occult injury to the stomach or the duodenum.

Placement of a Foley catheter empties the bladder, may disclose hematuria, and permits the physician to monitor urinary output. The Foley catheter should not, however, be inserted until abdominal ultrasonography is completed, and it should not be placed on an urgent basis in male patients with suspected urethral injuries (i.e., those with blood at the meatus, a perineal hematoma, a high-riding prostate, or an extensively displaced anterior pelvic fracture). If urethral injury is suspected, a retrograde urethrogram, followed by a cystogram (to exclude bladder injury) is obtained, prioritized in accordance with the given setting. In females, the urethra is shorter and better protected and thus is rarely injured.

Routine x-rays performed simultaneously with the ABCs include lateral cervical spine, anteroposterior chest, and pelvic films. Once life-threatening injuries have been addressed, thoracic and lumbar spine films should be obtained in patients who complain of back pain, those with neurologic deficits, and those with high-risk mechanisms of injury in whom physical examination is unreliable. X-rays of extremities with suspected fractures (including the joint above and the joint below) should also be obtained.

Given that trauma victims are uniquely susceptible to hypothermia, a rectal or bladder temperature probe is essential in those

who have been exposed to a cold environment or who require massive volume replacement. A core temperature reading lower than 32° C (89.6° F) should be confirmed with an esophageal probe, and rewarming measures appropriate for the degree of hypothermia should be initiated.[50] Tetanus prophylaxis is routine. Systemic antibiotics should be withheld until a specific indication arises. An electrocardiogram is obtained after blunt chest trauma, and an ABG analysis is done in select patients to confirm adequate ventilation and metabolic balance. In any patient with evidence of hypovolemia, a blood sample should be sent for blood-group typing and coagulation studies if urgent blood transfusion is required.

Rapid hemorrhage control Blunt trauma patients who arrive in shock and remain hemodynamically unstable pose difficult triage decisions. Initial screening must be directed at identifying life-threatening bleeding that necessitates immediate OR intervention. Most hospitals do not have an interventional radiology suite immediately available; early notification is crucial in assembling the team. At our institutions, after normal working hours, this process consumes about 1 hour.

Initial screening focuses on the chest, the abdomen, and the pelvis. A chest x-ray is the most reliable screening test for intrathoracic bleeding; it also confirms the location of endotracheal, nasogastric, and thoracostomy tubes, as well as that of the central venous catheter. The presence of pleural fluid may be difficult to confirm on a supine chest x-ray: 1 L of blood may produce only a hazy appearance in a hemithorax. Hemothoraces should be drained promptly via tube thoracostomy [*see Figure 2*]. Continued bleeding must be monitored carefully by measuring chest tube output, obtaining serial chest films to detect retained intrapleural blood, and observing vital signs. The criteria used to decide when thoracotomy is indicated are similar to those used in cases of penetrating trauma, but far fewer blunt trauma patients meet these criteria, and intrathoracic bleeding is rarely a reason for immediate OR triage.[51]

The abdomen is notoriously difficult to evaluate and is much more likely than the chest to harbor occult life-threatening bleeding. The peritoneal cavity may sequester as much as 3 L of blood with only minimal abdominal distention. Head injury or intoxication frequently alters the patient's response to acute injury, and pain from associated fractures may overshadow peritoneal irritation secondary to bleeding. Ultrasonography [*see Figures 7 and 8*] is the most rapid method of identifying free blood, but it may yield false negative results in as many as 15% of patients on initial examination.[52,53] DPL [*see Figure 9*] remains the most reliable method of identifying significant intraperitoneal hemorrhage: in patients with life-threatening bleeding, its sensitivity approaches 100%.[54] A grossly positive aspirate (> 10 ml of blood) mandates emergency laparotomy.

Assessment of bony stability by means of physical examination and plain films of the pelvis is crucial for the early identification of major pelvic fractures. Life-threatening hemorrhage occurs most commonly with fracture patterns involving the posterior columns [*see Figure 10*].[30,55] Appropriate initial management of unstable patients who have a high-risk pelvic fracture on initial pelvic x-ray includes blood volume replacement (including early blood and fresh frozen plasma [FFP]) and application of a pelvic binder; wrapping with a sheet is also effective [*see Figure 11*].

The next step is to evaluate the response to initial resuscitation and then perform ultrasonography or DPL to determine whether significant intra-abdominal bleeding is present.[56,57] An unstable patient with clearly positive findings from ultrasonography or DPL should undergo laparotomy because of the high probability

a

b

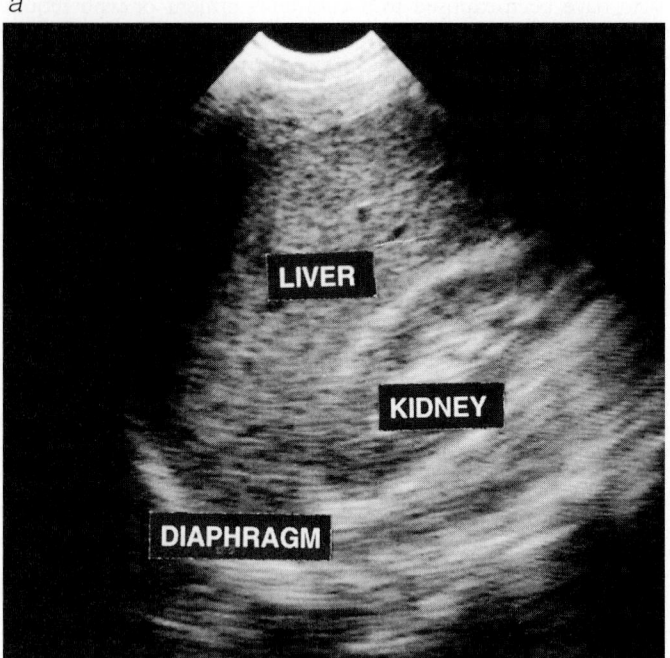
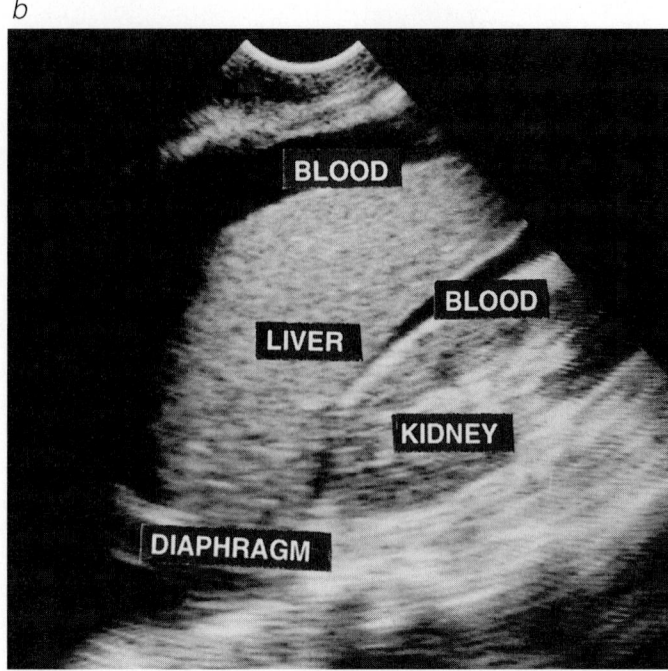

Figure 8 (*a*) Sagittal ultrasound image of liver, kidney, and diaphragm yields normal findings. (*b*) Sagittal ultrasound image of right upper quadrant shows blood between liver and kidney and between liver and diaphragm.

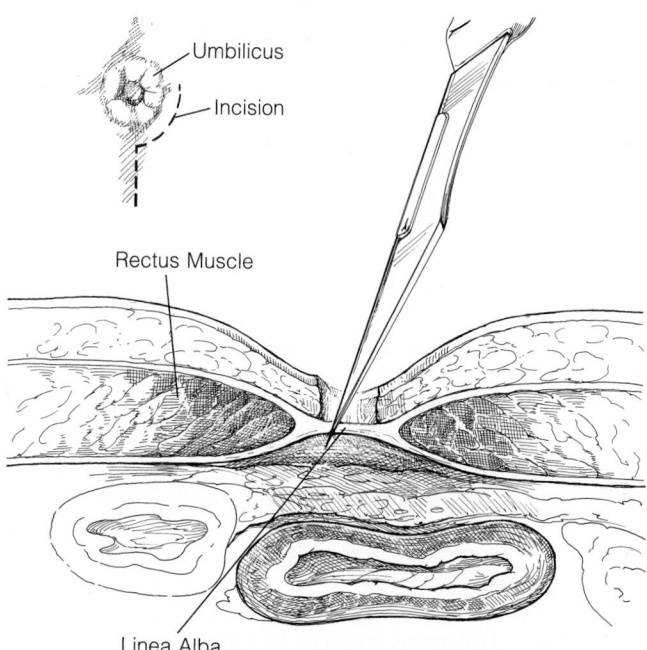
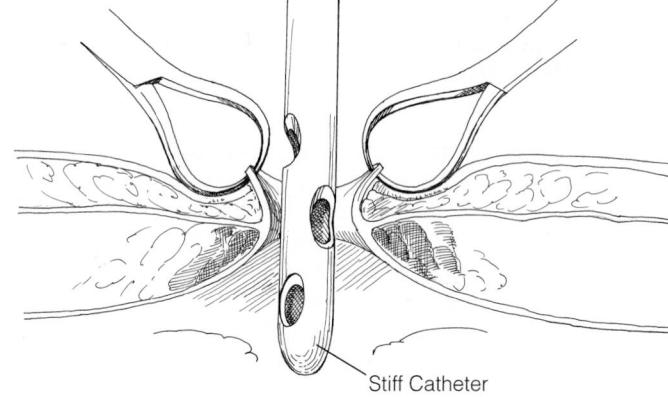
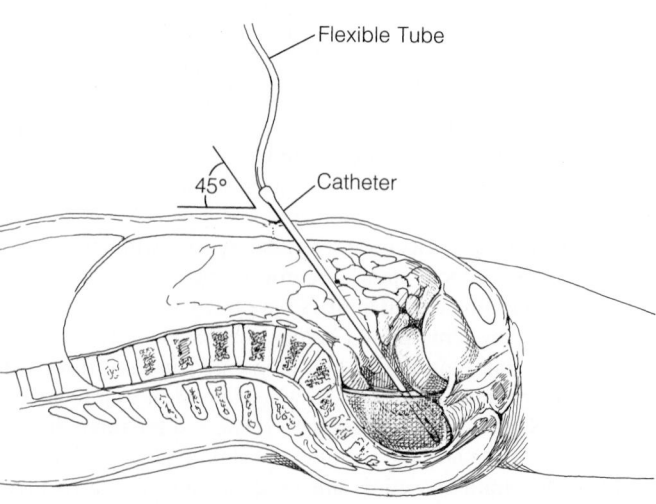

Figure 9 Illustrated here is the semiopen technique for peritoneal lavage. A 3 to 4 cm incision is made over the infraumbilical ring, and the linea alba is incised vertically for 1 cm. The fascial edges are grasped with towel clips and elevated. A standard peritoneal dialysis catheter is introduced into the peritoneum at a 45° angle and then advanced into the pelvis without use of the trocar. If 10 ml of gross blood is aspirated, the study is considered to be positive. Otherwise, 1 L of normal saline (10 ml/kg for children) is infused. The lavage fluid is retrieved by gravity siphonage; the empty saline bag is dropped to the floor. Ultrasonography is helpful for confirming intraperitoneal fluid infusion. A 50 ml sample of the fluid is submitted for laboratory analysis.

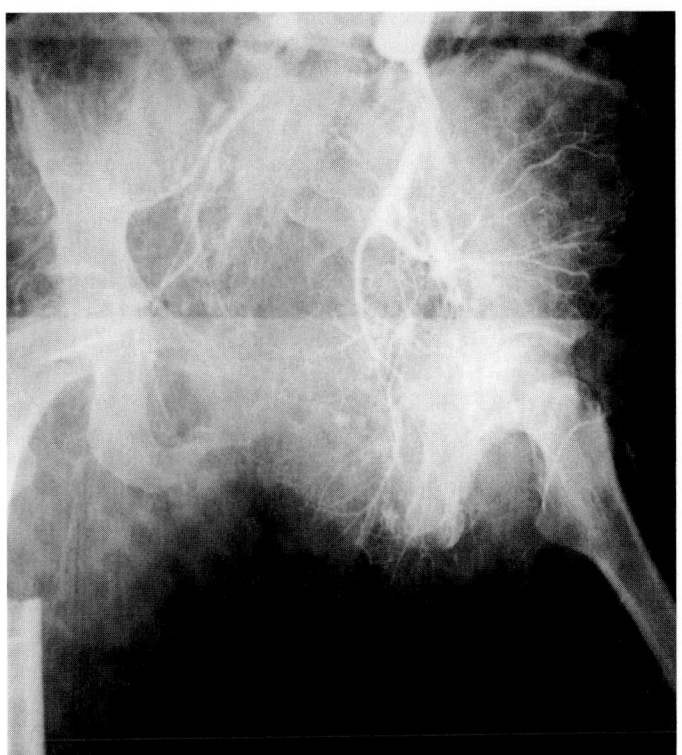

Figure 10 **Pelvic angiography with selective embolization may be an integral component in the early management of a major pelvic crush injury with continuing hemorrhage.**

of major hepatic, splenic, or mesenteric bleeding. If there is a large pelvic hematoma at the time of laparotomy and the patient is unstable, embolization of the internal iliac artery may be performed with a slurry of autogenous clot, microfibrillar collagen, thrombin, and calcium chloride.[58] A hemodynamically unstable patient in whom the ultrasonogram is normal and DPL yields confirmatory negative results should undergo prompt pelvic arteriography for selective embolization.[59]

Fast track CT scanning to refine triage   In unstable patients who respond to initial interventions, the priorities are as follows: (1) identify and quantitate ongoing sources of bleeding, (2) identify TBI, especially in those patients who require immediate craniotomy, and (3) identify any other injuries that call for urgent intervention (e.g., thoracic aortic injury [TAI]) or special precautions (e.g., spine fractures). With the widespread availability of multidetector CT scanners, rapid whole-body imaging is now feasible, permitting accurate triage for these competing priorities. The important question is whether the patient is stable enough to survive for the time such imaging takes. At our institutions, preparation, transport, and scanning take, in all, roughly 40 minutes. The decision to order CT scanning is made early, while the ABCs are being addressed and ultrasonography and initial plain x-rays are being performed, and depends on the age of the patient, any obvious injuries identified, and the patient's hemodynamic stability. The decision is less clear-cut in the common situation in which a previously unstable patient has a positive abdominal ultrasonogram. The key issue here is which injuries identified by CT scanning would alter the decision to perform an urgent laparotomy.

Identification of abdominal injuries   The decision to perform an urgent laparotomy in a patient with a positive ultrasono-

gram depends on the patient's hemodynamic stability. A CT scan can be helpful in refining triage by identifying extravasation of I.V. contrast (i.e., a blush) and in diagnosing HVIs. A blush should prompt consideration of angiography. Early angiography is a helpful adjunct in managing liver and kidney injuries, though its role in managing acute splenic injuries remains to be established.[60-64] HVIs are notoriously difficult to diagnose; extravasation of oral contrast is rare.[65,66] When all signs (e.g., unexplained free fluid, bowel wall thickening, mesenteric streaking, and free air) are considered, however, the sensitivity of CT in making the diagnosis approaches 90%. In questionable cases of HVI in stabilized patients, we advocate delayed DPL to search for elevations in WBC count, amylase level, and alkaline phosphatase level.

Identification of traumatic brain injury   Approximately 20% of blunt trauma patients who arrive in shock have a TBI.[67] During initial evaluation, it is important to identify TBI patients who might benefit from an emergency craniotomy. The neurologic examination is of utmost importance. The initial Glasgow Coma Scale (GCS) score in the field should be confirmed with prehospital personnel, and short-acting sedatives/paralytics should then

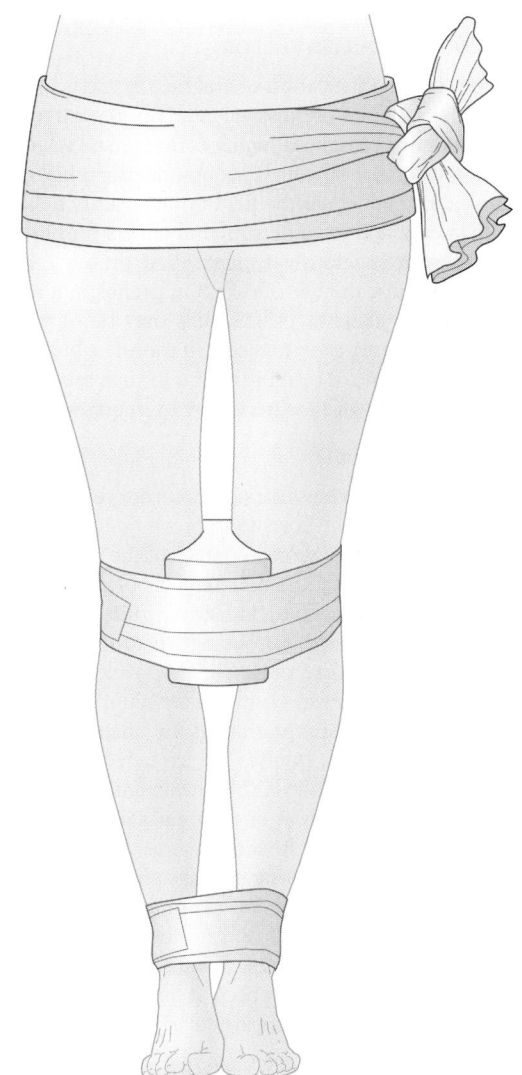

Figure 11   **Shown is the wrapping technique currently used for support of a mechanically unstable pelvic fracture.**

be given sparingly. A GCS score lower than 8 and a lateralizing neurologic examination indicate a significant risk that emergency craniotomy will be needed and, therefore, justify obtaining a CT scan of the head if hemodynamic stability permits.[68,69]

Identification of thoracic aortic injury Initial plain films should be examined for evidence of TAI. We use the overpenetrated mediastinal view and specifically look for evidence of a mediastinal hematoma. In the multi-institutional study from the American Association for the Surgery of Trauma (AAST), however, 7% of patients with TAI had a normal ED chest x-ray. We therefore obtain a chest CT scan on the basis of the mechanism of injury.[70] At our institutions, CT scanning has replaced angiography for the diagnosis of TAI. An occasional angiogram is done to confirm the diagnosis of great vessel injury or to clarify the vascular anatomy before thoracotomy.

The management of TAI has changed markedly over the past decade. Traditionally, a diagnosis of TAI mandated urgent thoracotomy.[71] Currently, however, antihypertensive therapy and ICU monitoring allow delayed repair in patients with significant associated injuries.[72] Delayed repair is safe but is associated with increased infectious complications and longer ICU stays.[73]

Identification of limb ischemia The absence of distal pulses in a fractured or dislocated extremity should be addressed urgently. Fractures and dislocations should be reduced, and the extremity should be closely examined for signs of ischemia. Distal SBP measurements comparing injured limbs with noninjured limbs (i.e., the ankle-ankle index [AAI] or the ankle-brachial index [ABI]) should be obtained. If the ABI or AAI is less than 0.90 after reduction, CT angiography or formal angiography should be performed to exclude the presence of a vascular injury.[74,75] A pulseless extremity is best evaluated in the OR by means of on-table angiography. Delayed diagnosis as a result of waiting for formal angiography is a preventable cause of limb amputation.

Discussion

Prehospital Care

ADVANCED TRAUMA LIFE SUPPORT

The growing sophistication of emergency medical services has expanded the scope of prehospital care, but the extent of prehospital interventions remains a highly controversial issue.[1,2] In trauma, advocates of the so-called scoop-and-run philosophy argue that resuscitative efforts in the field unnecessarily delay provision of definitive care and have detrimental effects on physiology and survival when overzealously applied.[3,5] At present, there is little evidence to support the use of ATLS in prehospital management of urban trauma patients. ATLS skills may be of value in rural areas where transport time exceeds 30 minutes, but unfortunately, the limited volume of serious trauma in such areas makes it difficult to gain the experience necessary to maintain this expertise.

Airway Management

The goal of initial resuscitation is to restore adequate oxygen delivery to vital organs. Efforts to improve tissue perfusion will be unproductive unless the oxygen content of the circulating blood is sufficient. Airway patency and maintenance of adequate ventilation are thus the initial priorities. However, intubation and positive pressure ventilation inhibit venous return to the heart and detrimentally decrease cardiac output in hypovolemic patients.[76] In addition, emergency airway control after blunt trauma should be performed with the assumption that an unstable cervical spine fracture exists until such injuries are excluded radiologically, but this policy does not preclude RSI. The current recommendation—orotracheal intubation with in-line manual stabilization of the head and neck—has proved safe in clinical series to date. When orotracheal intubation fails, the laryngeal mask airway (LMA) is a rapid, safe, and effective technique for maintaining temporary airway control until definitive medical care becomes available.[77] For patients with extensive maxillofacial trauma that precludes oral intubation, cricothyrotomy has been the traditional alternative, but this procedure has some risks, particularly in children.

Prehospital Intubation of Patients with TBI

Because hypoxia has been associated with increased mortality in patients with TBI, aggressive prehospital airway protocols that include RSI have been instituted. This practice may, however, be associated with worse outcomes.[3] Patients intubated in the field are routinely hyperventilated, and this state has adverse physiologic consequences. Increased intrathoracic pressure obstructs venous return to the heart, impairs venous drainage from the brain, and, in hypovolemic patients, decreases cardiac output. Additionally, a low P_aCO_2 causes cerebral vasoconstriction. Routine end-tidal capnometry for TBI patients undergoing field intubation has been proposed as the standard of care for preventing excessive hyperventilation.[4]

Prehospital Volume Resuscitation

A provocative 1994 clinical trial found that for hypotensive patients with penetrating torso injuries, survival improved when fluid resuscitation was delayed until surgical intervention had controlled the source of hemorrhage.[6] A subsequent subset analysis, however, revealed that survival was improved only in patients who had sustained cardiac injuries, not in patients who had sustained major vascular, abdominal solid organ, or noncardiac thoracic injuries.[78] Although this clinical trial had some methodologic flaws, it is important because it emphasizes that source control of hemorrhage is an overriding priority in hemodynamically unstable patients.

Whether fluid resuscitation should be withheld until control of hemorrhage is achieved is doubtful; such an approach is clearly not the current standard of care. The point at issue is whether it is preferable to administer fluids to restore oxygen delivery to tissue, thus potentially causing hemodilution and disruption of early hemostatic clots, or to withhold fluid resuscitation, thus prolonging cellular shock to the point where it may be irreversible by the time operative control is accomplished. At present, the rational compromise between these two approaches is hypotensive resuscitation with moderate volume loading.[79,80] Whereas this approach is becoming the standard of care for penetrating trauma, its application to blunt trauma is not as clear. Some 20% of patients with major torso trauma have a serious concomitant TBI; if they are inadequately resuscitated, reduced cerebral perfusion pressure may lead to devastating secondary brain injury. The anticipated availability of hemoglobin-based oxygen carriers may further confound the hypotensive resuscitation debate.

Resuscitation with Hypertonic Saline

Small-volume hypertonic saline (HS) has been shown to be as effective as large-volume crystalloid in expanding plasma volume and enhancing cardiac output.[81] Furthermore, HS increases perfusion of the microcirculation, presumably by inducing selective arteriolar vasodilation and by reducing the swelling of RBCs and endothelium[82]; however, this improved microcirculation could lead to increased bleeding. The resuscitative effectiveness of HS can be further enhanced by combining it with dextran (hypertonic saline dextran [HSD]).[83]

In view of the small volumes needed to achieve the desired effects, there has been great interest in employing these fluids for field resuscitation in both military and civilian settings. A number of trials investigating the use of HS and HSD have been performed. Individually, these trials reported inconsistent results in terms of improved survival; however, collectively, the trials did confirm that a bolus of either HS or HSD was safe.[84] Meta-analysis of the data suggested that HS was no better than the current standard of care (isotonic crystalloid fluids) but that HSD might be better.[83] Subgroup analysis of the data showed that the patients who benefited most from HSD were those who presented with shock and concomitant severe TBI. The results of this analysis agreed with laboratory data showing that in comparison with isotonic crystalloid, both HS and HSD raised cerebral perfusion pressure, lowered intracranial pressure, and reduced brain edema.[85]

The argument in favor of HS resuscitation is even more compelling with the recognition that this approach markedly reduces the inflammatory response (specifically, neutrophil cytotoxicity) in animal models of hemorrhagic shock, ischemia and reperfusion, and sepsis. However, one well-executed trial that tested HS for field resuscitation of TBI patients in shock did not demonstrate any benefits.[86]

Emergency Department Management

EMERGENCY DEPARTMENT RESUSCITATIVE THORACOTOMY

ED thoracotomy is an integral part of the initial management of trauma patients who arrive in extremis.[87] When blood volume is depleted or pericardial tamponade is present, closed-chest compression is ineffective in maintaining systemic blood flow,[88] whereas open cardiac massage maintains coronary and cerebral perfusion for as long as half an hour. Adjunctive thoracic aorta occlusion enhances both coronary and cerebral perfusion by maintaining aortic diastolic pressure and increasing carotid systolic pressure. Aortic cross-clamping also decreases subdiaphragmatic bleeding in the event of associated abdominal injury.[89] These benefits are obtained at the expense of increased myocardial oxygen demand and poor perfusion of the lower torso. Clinical experience suggests that 30 minutes is the limit for prevention of splanchnic ischemic sequelae.

The possibility of patient salvage is largely determined by the mechanism of injury, as well as by the patient's condition at the time of thoracotomy. Success rates approach 50% in patients arriving in shock from a penetrating cardiac wound and 20% in patients with penetrating wounds as a whole. On the other hand, patient outcome is dismal when ED thoracotomy is performed in the setting of blunt trauma; it is now considered futile in patients lacking cardiac activity. Adding laparotomy in the emergency department for definitive control of abdominal hemorrhage has not improved outcomes.[90]

BLOOD VOLUME RESTITUTION

Crystalloid versus Colloid

Resuscitation with isotonic crystalloids has been the standard of care in the United States since the late 1960s. A number of clinical trials were performed in the 1970s and 1980s that compared isotonic crystalloid resuscitation with colloid resuscitation. Individually, these trials were underpowered and reported conflicting results. When subjected to meta-analysis, they yielded no consistent differences in overall outcome.[91] When the same data were subjected to subgroup analysis, however, the use of isotonic crystalloids in trauma patients appeared to be associated with improved survival. A large clinical trial published in 2004 found no differences in outcome between crystalloid and colloid resuscitation in ICU patients, but again, subgroup analysis demonstrated improved outcomes in trauma patients receiving crystalloids.[92] Although these subgroup analyses are not definitive, they are consistent with the early laboratory studies, which indicated that survival in hemorrhagic shock is optimized by administering isotonic crystalloids and blood in a 3:1 ratio. Subsequent animal studies suggested that the optimal ratio rises to 8:1 in severe shock.[93,94] However, several current reports suggest that "damage control" surgery combined with aggressive ICU resuscitation appears to be saving the lives of many patients who previously would have exsanguinated, but it also appears to be causing adverse edema in the brain (increased ICP), the lung (worsened pulmonary edema), and the gut (the abdominal compartment syndrome).[27]

Choice of Crystalloid

The selection of a crystalloid engenders less controversy than the choice between crystalloid and colloid. Although newer formulations (e.g., Ringer's ethyl pyruvate) are being tested clinically,[95] NS and LR remain the most commonly used fluids. In theory, LR is preferable to NS because it provides a better buffer for metabolic acidosis, but to date, investigators have not documented any important differences in outcome.[96,97] One laboratory study found that NS and LR were equivalent in the setting of moderate hemorrhagic shock but that, in the setting of massive hemorrhage, NS was associated with greater physiologic derangement (e.g., hyperchloremic acidosis) and higher mortality.[25] Clinical experience confirms the adverse effects of iatrogenic hyperchloremia.[98] NS is preferred, however, when blood is being transfused simultaneously.[99] There is some concern that the calcium in LR could exceed the chelating capabilities of the citrate in the stored blood, resulting in the formation of clots that could enter the circulation and compromise the microcirculation, but at present, there is no hard evidence that this is a significant issue.

Transfusion Trigger

The optimal hemoglobin level continues to be a subject of lively debate.[100] Early laboratory studies demonstrated that survival was improved when the hemoglobin concentration was maintained in the range of 12 to 13 g/dl.[101] Subsequent studies using isovolemic hemodilution models, however, indicated that the optimal level for maintaining oxygen delivery was 10 g/dl, and until relatively recently, this value represented the recommended level for critically ill patients.[102,103] Currently, there is a growing recognition that administration of stored packed RBCs can adversely affect outcome by modulating the inflammatory response (amplifying early proinflammation and aggravating late immunosuppression) and by impairing tissue perfusion (limiting access to or obstructing the microcirculation as a consequence of reduced RBC deformability).[104-106] A 1999 randomized trial found that patients who received transfusions according to a restrictive policy (i.e., transfusion when the hemoglobin concentration fell below 7 g/dl) did as well as, and possibly better than, patients who received transfusions on a more liberal basis (i.e., transfusion when the hemoglobin concentration fell below 10 g/dl).[107] Admittedly, this study was done in a select group of euvolemic patients; thus, it is not clear precisely how applicable the results are to severely injured trauma patients requiring resuscitation from shock. In addition, if blood transfusions are to be restricted during acute resuscitation, it is not clear which alternative fluids should be used.

Choice of Blood Product

Fully crossmatched blood is rarely available for ED trauma resuscitation. Uncrossmatched type-specific whole blood or packed RBCs can be safely administered,[108,109] and either alternative is available in most hospitals within 20 minutes. If type-specific blood is unavailable, reconstituted O-negative packed RBCs should be used. Type O-negative blood has no cellular antigens; therefore, the risk of major hemolytic reactions caused by patient antibodies attacking donor RBC antigens is minimal. When O-negative packed RBCs are unavailable, O-positive packed red blood cells may be used. The patient will become sensitized to the Rh factor, which is significant for women of childbearing age.

Blood Substitutes

As a consequence of the limited supply of stored blood and the recognition that transfusions contribute to adverse patient outcomes, there has been a resurgence of interest in blood substitutes. Hemoglobin-based oxygen carriers date back to 1933, when it was shown that hemolysates could transport oxygen in mammals.[110] Unfortunately, when these solutions were infused into humans, they had excessively toxic effects (i.e., vasoconstriction, acute renal failure, and abdominal pain), which were attributed to stromal contamination. Although the next generation of carrier solutions was stroma-free, toxic effects persisted and were attributed to the instability of the hemoglobin tetramer, which spontaneously dissociates into dimers and monomers.[111]

One formulation of stabilized tetramer, diaspirin cross-linked hemoglobin, was authorized for a phase III study in trauma patients.[112] However, the trial was prematurely stopped because of the unexpectedly high mortality in the treatment group (24/52 [46%], compared with 8/46 [17%] in the control group). Although this event was judged a major setback for clinical implementation of hemoglobin-based oxygen carriers, the product used had already been shown to increase pulmonary and systemic vascular resistance in animals. Tetrameric hemoglobin extravasates from the vascular space, binds nitric oxide within the vessel wall, and thereby results in unopposed vasoconstriction. This issue has been effectively addressed by polymerizing the hemoglobin tetramer. The additional benefit of these larger moieties is that they exert less colloid osmotic activity, which means that a higher dose can be administered.

A further limitation of earlier hemoglobin-based oxygen carriers was that because of the loss of 2,3-diphosphoglycerate, oxygen affinity was greatly increased; the partial pressure of oxygen required to produce 50% saturation (P_{50}) decreased from the normal 26 mm Hg to 12 mm Hg. This problem was addressed by pyridoxylation of the hemoglobin tetramer, which raised the P_{50} to 29 mm Hg. One such polymerized hemoglobin solution has

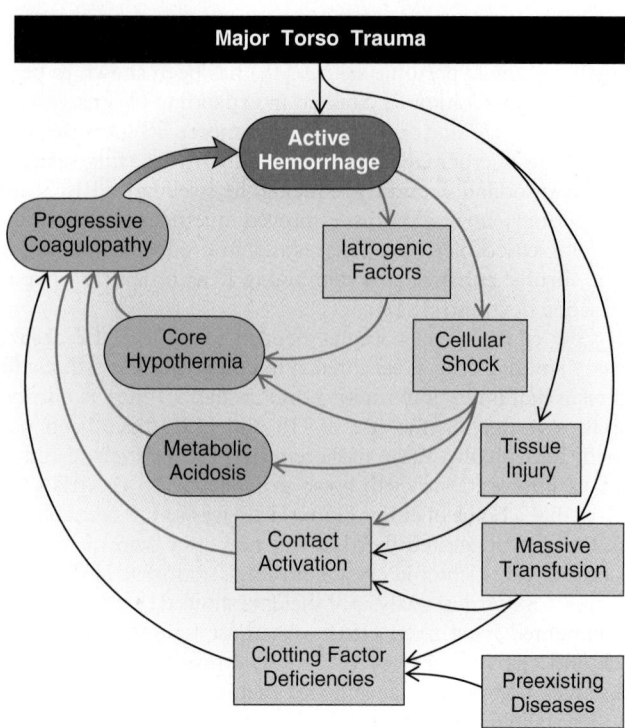

Figure 12 **The so-called bloody vicious cycle is a syndrome that has a multifactorial pathogenesis. The usual manifestations include coagulopathy, hypothermia, and metabolic acidosis.**[118]

been tested extensively in phase I and phase II trials in trauma patients and has proved to be safe and effective.[113,114] A phase III prehospital trial is under way.

EARLY IDENTIFICATION OF NONRESPONDERS

BP and HR are the current standard-of-care monitors of shock resuscitation in the field and in the ED. Both, however, are insensitive markers of early compensated shock; alternative monitors are badly needed for assessing the adequacy of tissue perfusion with a view to avoiding both underresuscitation and overresuscitation. Near-infrared spectroscopy (NIRS), a simple technique that monitors oxygen saturation in tissue, has been shown to track oxygen delivery reasonably well during shock resuscitation and is being tested as an ED monitor.[115] Transcutaneous oxygen tension ($P_{tc}O_2$) monitoring and central venous oxygen saturation ($S_{cv}O_2$) monitoring have also shown promising results in the ED environment.[116]

The challenge is to identify as early as possible those patients who are not responding to early interventions. Blind and aggressive volume loading in the hope of normalizing BP and HR, without appropriate emphasis on control of hemorrhage, sets the stage for the so-called bloody vicious cycle or the abdominal compartment syndrome.

BLOODY VICIOUS CYCLE

Among the most devastating complications of massive blood and fluid resuscitation is a bleeding diathesis. Paradoxically, although clotting is accelerated at the capillary level because of shock and tissue damage, the circulating blood becomes hypocoagulable.[117-119] The pathogenesis of this bloody vicious cycle is complex [*see Figure 12*]. Factors predictive of a severe coagulopathic state include (1) massive rapid blood transfusion (10 units/4 hr), (2) persistent cellular shock (oxygen consumption index < 110 ml/min/m²; lactate concentration > 5 mmol/L), (3) progressive metabolic acidosis (pH < 7.20; base deficit > 14 mEq/L), and (4) refractory core hypothermia (< 34° C).[120]

Stored blood is deficient in factors V and VIII and platelets but replete with fibrin split products and vasoactive substances. Timely administration of FFP and platelets will minimize the risk of coagulopathy after massive transfusion.[29,30] Presumptive factor replacement, though not usually indicated in the early resuscitation phase, is appropriate in patients with massive hemorrhage caused by unstable pelvic fracture.

Also germane to the initial period of massive blood transfusion are the potential complications of acidosis, hypothermia, and hypocalcemia. Moderate hypothermia (< 32° C) causes platelet sequestration and inhibits the release of platelet factors that are important in the intrinsic clotting pathway. In addition, it has consistently been associated with poor outcome in trauma patients.[121] Core temperature often falls insidiously because of exposure at the scene and in the ED and because of administration of resuscitation fluids stored at ambient temperature. The first step is to prevent further heat loss by covering the body (including the head) and infusing warm blood and fluid. Another simple technique is to heat and aerosolize ventilator gases. Active external rewarming with heating blankets and increased room temperature should also be employed. These techniques are not, however, very effective in reversing established hypothermia.

The use of bicarbonate in the treatment of systemic acidosis remains controversial. Moderate acidosis (pH < 7.20) impairs coagulation,[122] myocardial contractility,[123] and oxidative metabolism.[124] Acidosis in the trauma patient is caused primarily by a rise in lactic acid production secondary to tissue hypoxia and usually resolves when the volume deficit has been corrected. Administration of sodium bicarbonate may cause a leftward shift of the oxyhemoglobin dissociation curve, reducing tissue oxygen extraction, and it may worsen intracellular acidosis caused by carbon dioxide production.[119] On the other hand, adrenergic receptors may become desensitized with protracted acidosis. Studies indicate that vasopressin may be more effective than epinephrine as hemorrhagic shock approaches irreversibility.[125,126] Bicarbonate infusion, therefore, should be limited to persons with protracted shock.

Hypocalcemia caused by citrate binding of ionized calcium does not occur until the blood transfusion rate exceeds 100 ml/min (1 U/5 min). Decreased serum levels of ionized calcium depress myocardial function before impairing coagulation.[127,128] Calcium gluconate (10 mg/kg I.V.) should be reserved for cases in which there is ECG evidence of QT interval prolongation or, in rare instances, for cases of unexplained hypotension during massive transfusion.

ABDOMINAL COMPARTMENT SYNDROME

Abdominal compartment syndrome has emerged as a virtual epidemic in busy trauma centers that practice damage-control surgery and goal-oriented ICU resuscitation.[129] This syndrome is an early event, and its clinical trajectory can be accurately predicted within 3 to 6 hours after ED admission.[27] At admission to the ICU, high-risk patients have significant intra-abdominal hypertension and are in persistent shock. Contrary to conventional wisdom, they do not respond well to preload-directed resuscitation.[130] In fact, continued aggressive resuscitation precipitates the full-blown syndrome [see Figure 13].

Fundamental changes are needed in pre-ICU resuscitation. Failure to recognize ongoing bleeding, indiscriminate crystalloid infusion, and failure to prioritize definitive measures for hemorrhage control have been identified as key issues in the ED.[131] We share the belief that colloids may reduce the incidence of abdominal compartment syndrome, but in our view, this possible benefit must be weighed against the potentially detrimental effects of colloids. In severe hemorrhagic shock, the permeability of capillary membranes increases, allowing the entry of colloids into the interstitial space, which can then exacerbate edema and impair tissue oxygenation. The theory that these high-molecular-weight agents plug capillary leaks that occur during neutrophil-mediated organ injury has not been proved.[132,133] Furthermore, it has been suggested that resuscitation with albumin induces renal failure and impairs pulmonary function.[134]

Similarly, hydroxyethyl starch (Hetastarch; Baxter Healthcare, Deerfield, Illinois) has been shown to induce renal dysfunction in patients with septic shock and in recipients of kidneys from brain-dead donors.[135] Hetastarch also has a limited role in massive resuscitation because it causes coagulopathy and hyperchloremic acidosis as a result of its high chloride content. Another hydroxyethyl starch preparation (Hextend; BioTime, Berkeley, California) has been developed that purportedly does not cause these adverse effects, but it has not been studied in the setting of massive resuscitation.[136,137]

In addition, alternative crystalloid solutions are being developed that not only expand the intravascular space and replenish the extracellular fluid but also have anti-inflammatory properties (e.g., Ringer's ethyl pyruvate).[95] The data currently available suggest that crystalloid administration should be restrained. Alternative means of enhancing tissue oxygen delivery may involve earlier use of inotropic or vasoactive agents.

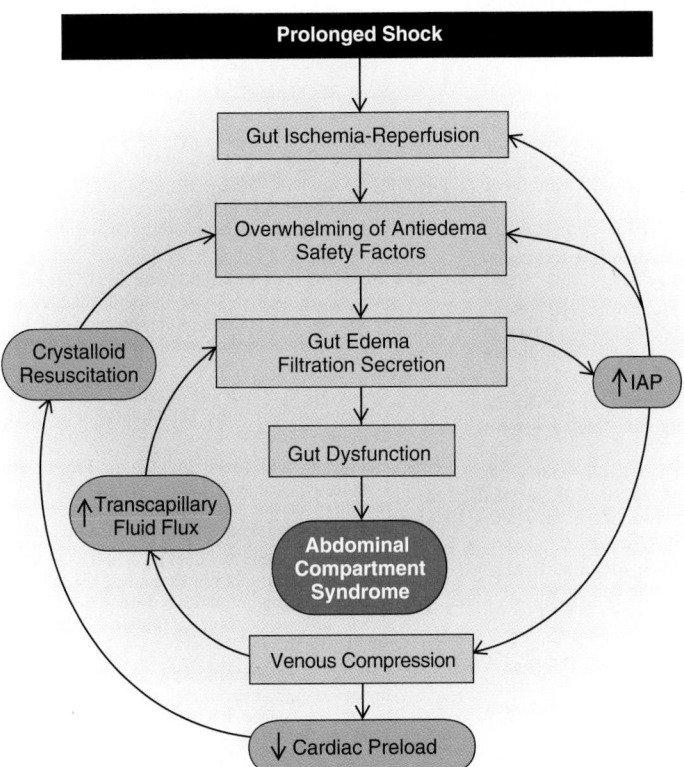

Figure 13 **Depicted is the so-called saltwater vicious cycle, which results in the development of abdominal compartment syndrome. The term filtration secretion refers to the process by which increasing gut edema causes interstitial pressure to rise to high levels, leading to disruption of the interstitial matrix. Ultimately, as a result, the villus tips spring leaks, through which interstitial fluid passes into the gut lumen. (IAP—intra-abdominal pressure)**

References

1. Stiel IG, Wells GA, Field B, et al: Advanced cardiac life support in out-of-hospital cardiac arrest. N Engl J Med 351:647, 2004

2. Liberman M, Mulder D, Lavoie A, et al: Multicenter Canadian study of prehospital trauma care. Ann Surg 237:153, 2003

3. Davis DP, Hoyt DB, Ochs M, et al: The effect of paramedic rapid sequence intubation on outcome in patients with severe traumatic brain injury. J Trauma 54:444, 2003

4. Davis DP, Dunford JV, Ochs M, et al: The use of quantitative end-tidal capnometry to avoid inadvertent severe hyperventilation in patients with head injury after paramedic rapid sequence intubation. J Trauma 56:808, 2004

5. Aufderheide TP, Sigurdsson G, et al: Hyperventilation during cardiopulmonary resuscitation. Circulation 109:1960, 2004

6. Bickell WH, Wall MJ Jr, Pepe PE, et al: Immediate versus delayed fluid resuscitation for hypotensive patients with penetrating torso injuries. N Engl J Med 331:1105, 1994

7. Burris D, Rhee P, Kaufman C, et al: Controlled resuscitation for uncontrolled hemorrhagic shock. J Trauma 46:216, 1999

8. Esposito TJ, Offner PJ, Jurkovich GJ, et al: Do prehospital trauma center triage criteria identify major trauma victims? Arch Surg 130:171, 1995

9. Norwood SH, McAuley CE, Berne JD, et al: A prehospital Glasgow Coma Scale score ≤ 14 accurately predicts the need for full trauma team activation and patient hospitalization after motor vehicle collisions. J Trauma 53:503, 2002

10. Battistella FD, Nugent W, Owings JT, et al: Field triage of pulseless trauma patients. Arch Surg 56:96, 1999

11. Stockinger ZT, McSwain NE Jr: Additional evidence in support of withholding or terminating cardiopulmonary resuscitation for trauma patients in the field. J Am Coll Surg 198:227, 2004

12. NAEMSP Standards and Clinical Practice Committee and the ACS Committee on Trauma: Guidelines for withholding or termination of resuscitation in prehospital traumatic cardiopulmonary arrest. J Am Coll Surg 196:106, 2003

13. Martin SK, Shatney CH, Sherck JP, et al: Blunt trauma patients with prehospital pulseless electrical activity (PEA): poor ending assured. J Trauma 53:876, 2002

14. Powell DW, Moore EE, Cothren CC, et al: Is emergency department resuscitative thoracotomy futile care for the critically injured patient requiring prehospital cardiopulmonary resuscitation? J Am Coll Surg 199:211, 2004

15. Pang D, Pollack IF: Spinal cord injury without radiographic abnormality in children—the SCIWORA syndrome. J Trauma 29:654, 1989

16. Hendey GW, Wolfson AB, Mower WR, et al: Spinal cord injury without radiographic abnormality: results of the National Emergency X-Radiography Utilization Study in Blunt Cervical Trauma. J Trauma 53:1, 2002

17. Ullrich A, Hendey GW, Geiderman J, et al: Distracting painful injuries associated with cervical spinal injuries in blunt trauma. Acad Emerg Med 8:25, 2001

18. Hoffman JR, Mower WR, Wolfson AB, et al: Validity of a set of clinical criteria to rule out injury to the cervical spine in patients with blunt trauma. N Engl J Med 343:94, 2000

19. Davis JW, Phreaner DL, Hoyt DB, et al: The etiology of missed cervical spine injuries. J Trauma 34:342, 1993

20. Danne PD, Hunter M, MacKillip AOF: Airway control. Trauma, 5th ed. Moore EE, Feliciano DV, Mattax RL, Eds. McGraw-Hill, New York, 2004

21. Norwood S, Myers MB, Butler TJ: The safety of emergency neuromuscular blockade and orotracheal intubation in the acutely injured trauma patient. J Am Coll Surg 179:646, 1994

22. Vijayakumar E, Bosscher H: The use of neuromuscular blocking agents in the emergency department to facilitate tracheal intubation in the trauma patient: help or hindrance? J Crit Care 13:1, 1998

23. Nevarre DR, Domingo OH: Supraclavicular approach to subclavian catheterization: review of the literature and results of 178 attempts by the same operator. J Trauma 42:305, 1997

24. Sawyer RW, Bodai BI, Blaisdell FW, et al: The current status of intraosseous infusion. J Am Coll Surg 179:353, 1994

25. Healey MA, Davis RE, Liu FC, et al: Lactated Ringer's is superior to normal saline in a model of massive hemorrhage and resuscitation. J Trauma 45:894, 1998

26. Moore FA, McKinley BA, Moore EE: The next generation in shock resuscitation. Lancet 363:1988, 2004

27. Balogh Z, McKinley BA, Holcomb JB, et al: Both primary and secondary abdominal compartment syndrome can be predicted early and are harbingers of multiple organ failure. J Trauma 54:848, 2003

28. Durtschi MB, Haisch CE, Reynolds L, et al: Effect of micropore filtration on pulmonary function after massive transfusion. Am J Surg 138:8, 1979

29. Hirshberg A, Dugas M, Banez EI, et al: Minimizing dilutional coagulopathy in exsanguinating hemorrhage: a computer simulation. J Trauma 54:454, 2003

30. Biffl WL, Smith WR, Moore EE, et al: Evolution of a multidisciplinary clinical pathway for the management of unstable patients with pelvic fractures. Ann Surg 233:843, 2001

31. Davis JW, Davis IC, Bennink LD, et al: Are automated blood pressure measurements accurate in trauma patients? J Trauma 55:860, 2003

32. Vayer JS, Henderson JV, Bellamy RF, et al: Absence of a tachycardic response to shock in penetrating intraperitoneal injury. Ann Emerg Med 17:227, 1988

33. Davis JW, Kaups KL: Base deficit in the elderly: a marker of severe injury and death. J Trauma 45:873, 1998

34. Rozycki GS, Feliciano DV, Ochsner MG, et al: The role of ultrasound in patients with possible penetrating cardiac wounds: a prospective multicenter study. J Trauma 46:543, 1999

35. Biffl WL, Moore FA, Moore EE, et al: Cardiac enzymes are irrelevant in the patient with suspected myocardial contusion. Am J Surg 169:523, 1994

36. Illig KA, Swierzewski MJ, Feliciano DV, et al: A rational screening and treatment strategy based on the electrocardiogram alone for suspected cardiac contusion. Am J Surg 162:537, 1991

37. King MW, Aitchison JM, Nel JP: Fatal air embolism following penetrating lung trauma: an autopsy study. J Trauma 24:753, 1984

38. Biffl WL, Moore EE, Johnson JC: Emergency department thoracotomy. Trauma, 5th ed. Moore EE, Feliciano DV, Mattox KL, Eds. McGraw-Hill, New York, 2004

39. Britt LD: Neck Injuries: evaluation and management. Trauma, 5th ed. Moore EE, Feliciano DV, Mattox KL, Eds. McGraw-Hill, New York, 2004

40. Weigelt JA, Thal ER, Snyder WH, et al: Diagnosis of penetrating cervical esophageal injuries. Am J Surg 154:619, 1987

41. Stassen NA, Lukan JK, Spain DA, et al: Reevaluation of diagnostic procedures for transmediastinal gunshot wounds. J Trauma 53:635, 2002

42. Moore JB, Moore EE, Thompson JS: Abdominal injuries associated with penetrating trauma in the lower chest. Am J Surg 140:724, 1980

43. Uribe RA, Pachon CE, Frame SB, et al: A prospective evaluation of thoracoscopy for the diagnosis of penetrating thoracoabdominal trauma. J Trauma 37:650, 1994

44. McAllister E, Perez M, Albrink MH, et al: Is triple contrast computed tomographic scanning useful in the selective management of stab wounds to the back? J Trauma 37:401, 1994

45. Feliciano DV, Bitondo-Dyer CG: Vagaries of the lavage white blood cell count in evaluating abdominal stab wounds. Am J Surg 168:680, 1994

46. McAnena OJ, Marx JA, Moore EE: Peritoneal lavage enzyme determinations following blunt and penetrating abdominal trauma. J Trauma 31:1161, 1991

47. Easter DW, Shackford SR, Mattrey RF: A prospective, randomized comparison of computed tomography with conventional diagnostic methods in the evaluation of penetrating injuries to the back and flank. Arch Surg 126:1115, 1991

48. Frybert ER, Schino MA: Peripheral vascular injury. Trauma, 5th ed. Moore EE, Feliciano DV, Mattox KL, Eds. McGraw-Hill, New York, 2004

49. Fremstad JD, Martin SH: Lethal complication from insertion of nasogastric tube after severe basilar skull fracture. J Trauma 18:820, 1978

50. Reed RL, Gentilello LM: Temperature-associated injuries and syndromes. Trauma, 5th ed. Moore EE, Feliciano DV, Mattox KL, Eds. McGraw-Hill, New York, 2004

51. Mansour MA, Moore EE, Moore FA, et al: Exigent postinjury thoracotomy analysis of blunt versus penetrating trauma. Surg Gynecol Obstet 175:97, 1992

52. Rozycki GS, Ochsner MG, Schmidt JA, et al: A prospective study of surgeon-performed ultrasound as the primary adjuvant modality for injured patient assessment. J Trauma 39:492, 1995

53. Dolich M, McKenney MG, Varela J, et al: 2,576 Ultrasounds for blunt abdominal trauma. J Trauma 50:108, 2001

54. Henneman PL, Marx JA, Moore EE, et al: Diagnostic peritoneal lavage: accuracy in predicting necessary laparotomy following blunt and penetrating trauma. J Trauma 30:1345, 1990

55. Eastridge BJ, Starr A, Minei JP, et al: The importance of fracture pattern in guiding therapeutic decision-making in patients with hemorrhagic shock and pelvic ring disruptions. J Trauma 53:446, 2002

56. Latenser BA, Gentilello LM, Tarver AA, et al: Improved outcome with early fixation of skeletally unstable pelvic fractures. J Trauma 31:28, 1991

57. Riemer BL, Butterfield SL, Diamond DL, et al: Acute mortality associated with injuries to the pelvic ring: the role of early patient mobilization and external fixation. J Trauma 35:671, 1993

58. Saueracker AJ, McCroskey BL, Moore EE, et al: Intraoperative hypogastric artery embolization for life-threatening pelvic hemorrhage: a preliminary report. J Trauma 27:1127, 1987

59. Panetta T, Sclafani SJA, Goldstein AS, et al: Percutaneous transcatheter embolization for massive bleeding from pelvic fractures. J Trauma

25:1021, 1985

60. Hagiwara A, Murata A, Matsuda T, et al: The efficacy and limitations of transarterial embolization for severe hepatic injury. J Trauma 52:1091, 2002

61. Richardson JD, Franklin GA, Lukan JK, et al: Evolution in the management of hepatic trauma: a 25-year perspective. Ann Surg 232:324, 2000

62. Davis KA, Fabian TC, Croce MA, et al: Improved success in nonoperative management of blunt splenic injuries: embolization of splenic artery pseudoaneurysms. J Trauma 44:1008, 1998

63. Hagiwara A, Sakaki S, Goto H, et al: The role of interventional radiology in the management of blunt renal injury: a practical protocol. J Trauma 51:526, 2001

64. Haan JM, Biffl W, Knudson MM, et al: Splenic embolization revisited: a multicenter review. J Trauma 56:542, 2004

65. Allen GS, Moore FA, Cox CS, et al: Hollow visceral injury and blunt trauma. J Trauma 45:69, 1998

66. Fakhry SM, Watts DD, Luchette FA: Current diagnostic approaches lack sensitivity in the diagnosis of perforated blunt small bowel injury: analysis from 275,557 trauma admissions from the EAST multi-institutional HVI trial. J Trauma 54:295, 2003

67. Wade CE, Grady JJ, Kramer GC, et al: Individual patient cohort analysis of the efficacy of hypertonic saline/dextran in patients with traumatic brain injury and hypotension. J Trauma 42:S61, 1997

68. Wisner DH, Victor NS, Holcroft JW: Priorities in the management of multiple trauma: intracranial versus intra-abdominal injury. J Trauma 35:271, 1993

69. Winchell RJ, Hoyt DB, Simons RK: Use of computed tomography of the head in the hypotensive blunt-trauma patient. Ann Emerg Med 25:737, 1995

70. Fabian TC, Richardson JD, Croce MA, et al: Prospective study of blunt aortic injury: multicenter trial of the American Association for the Surgery of Trauma. J Trauma 42:374, 1997

71. Sweeney MS, Young DF, Frazier OH, et al: Traumatic aortic transections: eight-year experience with the "clamp-sew" technique. Ann Thorac Surg 64:374, 1997

72. Fabian TC, Davis KA, Gavant ML, et al: Prospective study of blunt aortic injury: helical CT is diagnostic and antihypertensive therapy reduces rupture. Ann Surg 227:666, 1998

73. Hemmila MR, Arbabi S, Rowe SA, et al: Delayed repair for blunt thoracic aortic injury: is it really equivalent to early repair? J Trauma 56:13, 2004

74. Miranda FE, Dennis JW, Veldenz HC, et al: Confirmation of the safety and accuracy of physical examination in the evaluation of knee dislocation for injury of the popliteal artery: a prospective study. J Trauma 52:247, 2002

75. Mills WJ, Barei DP, McNair P: The value of the ankle-brachial index for diagnosing arterial injury after knee dislocation: a prospective study. J Trauma 56:1261, 2004

76. Pepe PE, Raedler C, Lurie KG, et al: Emergency ventilatory management in hemorrhagic states: elemental or detrimental? J Trauma 54:1048, 2003

77. Martin SE, Ochsner MG, Jarman RH, et al: Use of the laryngeal mask airway in air transport when intubation fails. J Trauma 47:352, 1999

78. Wall MJ, Granchi T, Liscum K, et al: Delayed versus immediate resuscitation in patients with penetrating trauma: subgroup analysis. J Trauma 39:173, 1995

79. Mapstone J, Roberts I, Evans P: Fluid resuscitation strategies: a systematic review of animal trials. J Trauma 55:571, 2003

80. Rafie AD, Rath PA, Michell MW, et al: Hypotensive resuscitation of multiple hemorrhages using crystalloid and colloids. Shock 22:262, 2004

81. Moore EE: Hypertonic saline dextran for postinjury resuscitation: experimental background and clinical experience. Aust N Z J Surg 61:732, 1991

82. Mazzoni MC, Borgstrom P, Intaglietta M, et al: Luminal narrowing and endothelial cell swelling in skeletal muscle capillaries during hemorrhagic shock. Circ Shock 29:27, 1989

83. Wade CE, Kramer GC, Grady JJ, et al: Efficacy of hypertonic 7.5% saline and 6% dextran-70 in treating trauma: a meta-analysis of controlled clinical studies. Surgery 122:609, 1997

84. Vassar MJ, Perry CA, Holcroft JW: Analysis of potential risks associated with 7.5% sodium chloride resuscitation of traumatic shock. Arch Surg 125:1309, 1990

85. Doyle JA, Davis DP, Hoyt DB, et al: The use of hypertonic saline in the treatment of traumatic brain injury. J Trauma 50:367, 2001

86. Cooper DJ, Myles PS, McDermott FT, et al: Prehospital hypertonic saline resuscitation of patients with hypotension and severe traumatic brain injury. JAMA 291:1350, 2004

87. Rhee PM, Acosta J, Bridgeman A, et al: Survival after emergency department thoracotomy: review of published data from the past 25 years. J Am Coll Surg 190:288, 2000

88. Sanders AB, Kern KB, Ewy GA, et al: Improved resuscitation from cardiac arrest with open-chest massage. Ann Emerg Med 13:672, 1984

89. Ledgerwood AM, Kazmers M, Lucas CE: The role of thoracic aortic occlusion for massive hemoperitoneum. J Trauma 16:610, 1976

90. Mattox KL, Allen MK, Feliciano DV: Laparotomy in the emergency department. JACEP 8:180, 1979

91. Choi PT-L, Yip G, Quinonez LG, et al: Crystalloids vs colloids in fluid resuscitation: a systematic review. Crit Care Med 27:200, 1999

92. The SAFE Study Investigators: A comparison of albumin and saline for fluid resuscitation in the intensive care unit. N Engl J Med 350:2247, 2004

93. Cervera AL, Moss G: Progressive hypovolemia leading to shock after continuous hemorrhage and 3:1 crystalloid replacement. Am J Surg 129:670, 1975

94. Healey MA, Samphire J, Hoyt DB, et al: Irreversible shock is not irreversible: a new model of massive hemorrhage and resuscitation. J Trauma 50:826, 2001

95. Sims CA, Wattanasirichaigoon S, Menconi MH, et al: Ringer's ethyl pyruvate solution ameliorates ischemia/reperfusion-induced intestinal mucosal injury in rats. Crit Care Med 29:1513, 2001

96. Lowery BD, Cloutier CT, Carey LC: Electrolyte solutions in resuscitation in human hemorrhagic shock. Surg Gynecol Obstet 133:273, 1971

97. Todd SR, Malinoski D, Muller PJ, et al: Lactated Ringer's is superior to normal saline in the resuscitation of uncontrolled hemorrhage shock. J Trauma (in press)

98. Prough DS, Bidani A: Hyperchloremic metabolic acidosis is a predictable consequence of intraoperative infusion of 0.9% saline. Anesthesiology 90:1247, 1999

99. Lorenzo M, Davis JW, Negin S, et al: Can Ringer's lactate be used safely with blood transfusions? Am J Surg 175:308, 1998

100. Mann DV, Robinson MK, Rounds JD, et al: Superiority of blood over saline resuscitation from hemorrhagic shock: a 31P magnetic resonance spectroscopy study. Ann Surg 226:653, 1997

101. Crowell JW, Ford TG, Lewis VM: Oxygen transport in hemorrhagic shock as a function of the hematocrit ratio. Am J Phys 196:1033, 1959

102. Weiskopf RB, Viele MK, Feiner J, et al: Human cardiovascular and metabolic response to acute, severe isovolemic anemia. JAMA 279:271, 1998

103. Czer LSC, Shoemaker WC: Optimal hematocrit value in critically ill postoperative patients. Surg Gynecol Obstet 147:262, 1978

104. Silliman CC, Moore EE, Johnson JL, et al: Transfusion of the injured patient: proceed with caution. Shock 21:291, 2004

105. Parthasarathi K, Lipowsky HH: Capillary recruitment in response to tissue hypoxia and its dependence on red blood cell deformability. Am J Physiol 277:Y2145, 1999

106. Simchon S, Jan KM, Client C: Influence of reduced red cell deformability on regional blood flow. Am J Physiol 253:H898, 1987

107. Hebert PC, Wells G, Blajchman MA, et al: A multicenter, randomized, controlled clinical trial of transfusion requirements in critical care. N Engl J Med 340:409, 1999

108. Blumberg N, Bove JR: Uncrossmatched blood for emergency transfusion: one year's experience in a civilian setting. JAMA 240:2057, 1978

109. Gervin AS, Fischer RP: Resuscitation of trauma patients with type-specific uncrossmatched blood. J Trauma 24:327, 1984

110. Moore EE: Blood substitutes: the future is now. J Am Coll Surg 196:1, 2003

111. Gould SA, Moss GS: Clinical development of human polymerized hemoglobin as a blood substitute. World J Surg 20:1200, 1996

112. Sloan EP, Koenigsberg M, Gens D, et al: Diaspirin cross-linked hemoglobin (DCLHb) in the treatment of severe traumatic hemorrhagic shock: a randomized controlled efficacy trial. JAMA 282:1857, 1999

113. Gould SA, Moore EE, Moore FA, et al: Clinical utility of human polymerized hemoglobin as a blood substitute after acute trauma and urgent surgery. J Trauma 43:325, 1997

114. Gould SA, Moore EE, Hoyt DB, et al: The first randomized trial of human polymerized hemoglobin as a blood substitute in acute trauma and emergent surgery. J Am Coll Surg 187:113, 1998

115. McKinley BA, Marvin RG, Cocanour CS, et al: Tissue hemoglobin O_2 saturation during resuscitation of traumatic shock monitored using near infrared spectrometry. J Trauma 48:637, 2000

116. Rivers E, Nguyen B, Havstad S, et al: Early goal-directed therapy in the treatment of severe sepsis and septic shock. N Engl J Med 345:1368, 2001

117. Hardaway RM, Chun B, Rutherford RB: Coagulation in shock in various species including man. Acta Chir Scand 130:157, 1965

118. Collins JA: Problems associated with the massive transfusion of stored blood. Surgery 75:274, 1974

119. Miller RD, Robbins TO, Tong MJ, et al: Coagulation defects associated with massive blood transfusions. Ann Surg 174:794, 1971

120. Cosgriff N, Moore EE, Sauaia A, et al: Predicting life-threatening coagulopathy in the massively transfused trauma patient: hypothermia and acidoses revisited. J Trauma 42:857, 1997

121. Jurkovich GJ, Greiser WB, Luterman A, et al: Hypothermia in trauma victims: an ominous predictor of survival. J Trauma 27:1019, 1987

122. Dunn EL, Moore EE, Breslich DJ, et al: Acidosis-induced coagulopathy. Forum on Fundamental Surgical Problems 30:471, 1979

123. Clowes GHA Jr, Sabga GH, Konitaxis A, et al: Effects of acidosis on cardiovascular function in surgical patients. Ann Surg 154:524, 1961

124. Fry DE, Ratciffe DJ, Yates JR: The effects of acidosis on canine hepatic and renal oxidative phosphorylation. Surgery 88:269, 1980

125. Douglas ME, Downs JB, Mantini EL, et al: Alteration of oxygen tension and oxyhemoglobin saturation: a hazard of sodium bicarbonate administration. Arch Surg 114:326, 1979

126. Haas T, Voelckel WG, Wiedermann F, et al: Successful resuscitation of a traumatic cardiac arrest victim in hemorrhagic shock with vasopressin: a case report and brief review of the literature. J Trauma 57:177, 2004

127. Morales D, Madigan J, Cullinane S, et al: Reversal by vasopressin of intractable hypotension in the late phase of hemorrhagic shock. Circulation 100:226, 1999

128. Stulz PM, Scheidegger D, Drop LJ, et al: Ventricular pump performance during hypocalcemia: clinical and experimental studies. J Thorac Cardiovasc Surg 78:185, 1979

129. Trunkey D, Carpenter MA, Holcroft J: Calcium flux during hemorrhagic shock in baboons. J Trauma 16:633, 1976

130. Balogh Z, McKinley BA, Cox CS, et al: Abdominal compartment syndrome: the cause or effect of multiple organ failure? Shock 20:483, 2003

131. Balogh Z, McKinley BA, Cocanour CS, et al: Patients with impending abdominal compartment syndrome do not respond to early volume loading. Am J Surg 186:602, 2003

132. Ley K: Plugging the leaks. Nat Med 7:1105, 2001

133. Conhaim RL, Watson KE, Potenza BM, et al: Pulmonary capillary sieving of Hetastarch is not altered by LPS-induced sepsis. J Trauma 46:800, 1999

134. Lucas CE: The water of life: a century of confusion. J Am Coll Surg 192:86, 2001

135. Schortgen F, Lacherade JC, Bruneel F, et al: Effects of hydroxyethyl starch and gelatin on renal function in severe sepsis: a multicenter randomized study. Lancet 357:911, 2001

136. Gan TJ, Bennett-Guerrero E, Phillips-Bute B, et al: Hextend, a physiologically balanced plasma expander for large volume use in major surgery: a randomized phase III clinical trial. Anesth Analg 88:992, 1999

137. Boldt J, Haisch G, Suttner S, et al: Effects of a new modified, balanced hydroxyethyl starch preparation (Hextend) on measures of coagulation. Br J Anaesth 89:722, 2002

Acknowledgments

Figures 1 and 3   Carol Donner, revised by Tom Moore.

Figures 2, 4a, 4b, and 9   Carol Donner.

Figures 4c, 5, and 11   Tom Moore.

Figure 12   Seward Hung.

101 INJURIES TO THE CENTRAL NERVOUS SYSTEM

Marike Zwienenberg-Lee, M.D., Kee D. Kim, M.D., and J. Paul Muizelaar, M.D., Ph.D.

It is estimated that each year, two million patients present to physicians with a primary or secondary diagnosis of head injury. Of these patients, approximately 400,000 are admitted and 70,000 die, most of traumatic brain injury. Thus, brain injury can be considered epidemic. Neurosurgeons, who number 4,000 in the United States, are probably best trained to manage patients with severe head injuries, but initial resuscitation and stabilization are usually performed by emergency department physicians, general surgeons, and trauma surgeons. These professionals are the ones who can make a difference for patients: current understanding of the pathophysiology of traumatic brain injury indicates that treatment during the first few hours is critical and often determines outcome.

Nonetheless, the importance of care immediately after resuscitation and in the ensuing days is not to be underestimated. Patients with multiple system injuries often receive care in surgical intensive care units under the supervision of a general surgeon. Less than optimal management at an early stage has a greater impact overall because of the larger number of patients involved, but less than optimal management at later stages, even in mildly injured patients, has a much more dramatic impact. Initial recovery, followed by relentless decline attributable to insufficient cerebral perfusion, is not an expected outcome. Although we cannot promote healing of the brain by pharmacologic means, we can prevent secondary injury to the brain by ensuring adequate cerebral circulation and oxygenation.

The reported incidence of spinal cord injury in the United States ranges from 29 to 53 per million.[1-3] About 50% of the injuries are related to motor vehicle accidents, 15% to 20% to falls, 15% to 20% to interpersonal violence, and the remaining 15% to 20% to sports and recreational activity. In general, the group at highest risk is between 16 and 30 years of age, not unlike the group at highest risk for head injuries. Most of those injured are males: several studies report that the percentage is approximately 75%.[4] Between 45% and 50% of patients with spinal cord injury have other injuries that seriously affect their prognosis.[5]

The cervical spine is most often involved in spinal cord injury. A major study of trauma outcome, conducted from 1982 to 1989, revealed that the cervical spinal cord was involved in 55% of cases of acute injury, the thoracic spinal cord in 30%, and the lumbar spinal cord in 15%.[6] In an analysis of 358 patients with spinal cord injury, complete neurologic injury occurred in 78% of the 71 cases of thoracic injury, 60% of the 202 cases of cervical injury, and 65% of the 85 cases of thoracolumbar injury.[7] Average direct costs of spinal cord injury (including hospitalization, rehabilitation, residence modification, and long-term care) are tremendous. In 1992, it was estimated that lifetime costs (in 1989 dollars) were $210,379 for a paraplegic and $571,854 for a quadriplegic.[8]

Initial resuscitation and evaluation of injured patients are discussed more fully elsewhere [*see 100 Initial Management of Life-Threatening Trauma*]. In this chapter, we outline approaches to the management of severe head injury and acute spinal cord injury. In addition, we address the pathophysiology of such injuries to provide the reader with the understanding required for making appropriate decisions about diagnosis and treatment of injured patients [*see* Discussion, *below*].

Head Injury

EMERGENCY DEPARTMENT MANAGEMENT

Because hypoxia and hypotension interfere with cerebral oxygenation, complete and rapid physiologic resuscitation is the highest priority for patients with head injuries. A large study from the Traumatic Coma Data Bank demonstrated that a single observation of systolic blood pressure below 90 mm Hg in the field or hypoxia (arterial oxygen tension [P_aO_2] < 60 mm Hg) was a major predictor of poor outcome.[9] A multidisciplinary team should provide the patient with an adequate airway and ventilation (intubation, ventilation, and detection of hemothorax or pneumothorax) and restore and maintain hemodynamic stability (with adequate fluid replacement and detection and treatment of any bleeding), all according to the principles developed by the Advanced Trauma Life Support system.[10] The ABCs of emergency care (*A*irway, *B*reathing, and *C*irculation) take precedence, irrespective of neurologic injuries. The initial neurologic assessment, which should take no more than a few seconds, consists of rating the patient's level of consciousness on the Glasgow Coma Scale (GCS) [*see Table 1*] and assessing the width and reactivity of the pupils. Although the same assessment is made after resuscitation as a guide for prognosis and therapy, it should also be made (and recorded) before resuscitation to permit evaluation of the effect of

Table 1 Glasgow Coma Scale

Test	Response	Score
Eye opening (E)	Spontaneous	4
	To verbal command	3
	To pain	2
	None	1
Best motor response (arm) (M)	Obedience to verbal command	6
	Localization of painful stimulus	5
	Flexion withdrawal response to pain	4
	Abnormal flexion response to pain (decorticate rigidity)	3
	Extension response to pain (decerebrate rigidity)	2
	None	1
Best verbal response (V)	Oriented conversation	5
	Disoriented conversation	4
	Inappropriate words	3
	Incomprehensible sounds	2
	None	1
Total (E + M + V)		3–15

resuscitative measures and differentiation between primary and secondary neurologic injury.

Early orotracheal intubation and ventilation are recommended for patients with a GCS score of 8 or lower or a motor score of 4 or lower. Other indications for immediate intubation are loss of protective laryngeal reflexes and ventilatory insufficiency, as manifested by hypoxemia ($P_aO_2 < 60$ mm Hg), hypercarbia (arterial carbon dioxide tension [P_aCO_2] > 45 mm Hg), spontaneous hyperventilation (causing $P_aCO_2 < 26$ mm Hg), and respiratory arrhythmia. Indications for intubation before transport are deteriorating consciousness (even if the patient is not in a coma), bilateral fractured mandible, copious bleeding into the mouth (as occurs with fracture of the base of the skull), and seizures. An intubated patient must also be ventilated ($P_aCO_2 \approx$ 35 mm Hg).

Fluid replacement should be performed with isotonic solutions such as normal saline, lactated Ringer solution, or packed red blood cells when appropriate. Glucose-based solutions should be avoided in the acute phase. The patient should be examined rapidly and thoroughly for any concomitant life-threatening injuries.

Patients with spinal cord injury above T5 may have severe hypotension as a result of vasogenic spinal shock. Aggressive treatment is indicated, including volume resuscitation and administration of alpha-adrenergic vasopressors. Intracranial hypertension should be suspected if there is rapid neurologic deterioration. Clinical evidence of intracranial hypertension, manifested by signs of herniation, includes unilateral or bilateral dilatation of the pupils, asymmetrical pupillary reactivity, and motor posturing.

Intracranial hypertension should be treated aggressively. Hyperventilation, which does not interfere with volume resuscitation and results in rapid reduction of intracranial pressure (ICP), should be established immediately in cases of pupillary abnormalities. It has been demonstrated that unilateral or bilateral pupillary abnormalities do not result only from compression of the third cranial nerves, as was previously thought, but also derive from compression of the brain stem, with resulting brain stem ischemia.[11] Therefore, administration of mannitol is effective because it not only decreases ICP but also increases cerebral blood flow (CBF) through modulation of viscosity. Because mannitol is not used to dehydrate the body, all fluid losses through diuresis must be replaced immediately or even preventively, especially in patients suffering shock as a result of blood loss. Arterial hypertension occurring after a severe head injury may reflect intracranial hypertension (Cushing's phenomenon), especially when accompanied by bradycardia; it should not be treated, because it may be the sole mechanism permitting the brain to maintain perfusion despite increasing ICP.

In the absence of signs of herniation, sedation should be used when required for safe and efficient transport of the patient. Transport time should be kept to a minimum because transport is often accompanied by secondary insults (e.g., hypoxia or hypotension). Pharmacologic paralysis, which interferes with neurologic examination, should be used only if sedation alone is inadequate for safe and effective transport and resuscitation. When pharmacologic paralysis is used, short-acting agents are preferred. Prophylactic hyperventilation, which may exacerbate early ischemia, is not recommended for these patients. Guidelines for the resuscitation and initial treatment of patients with severe head injuries have been established that facilitate management [see Figure 1].

Minimal radiologic evaluation consists of a lateral cervical spine film or a swimmer's view [see Spinal Cord Injury, below]. After hemodynamic stability is achieved, unenhanced computed to-

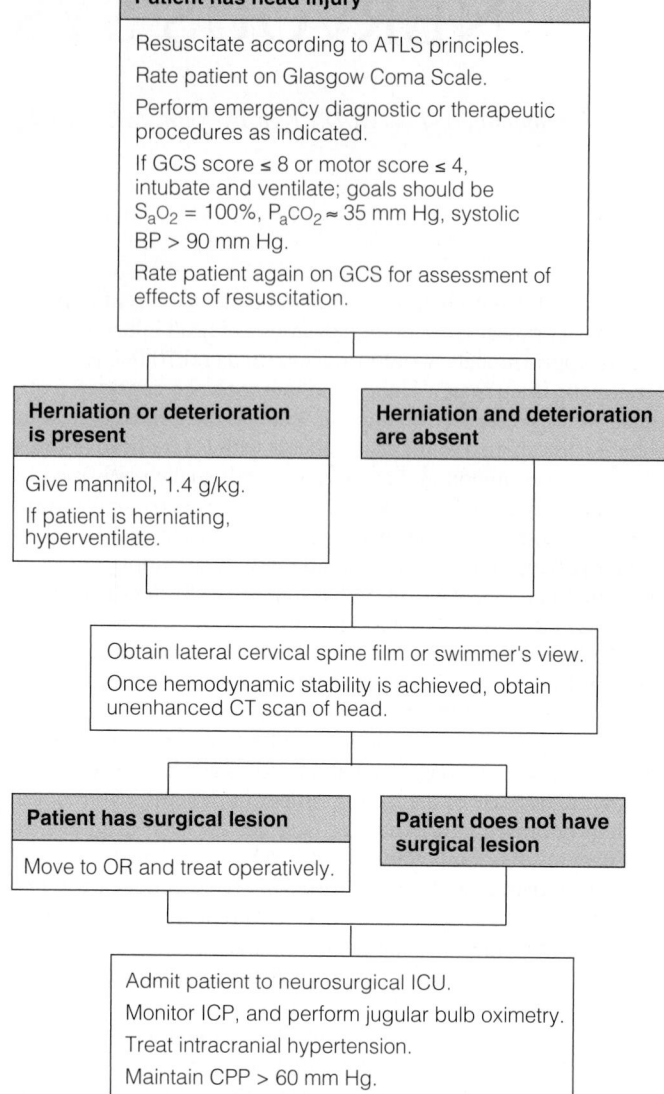

Figure 1 **Shown is an algorithm for initial management of the patient with a severe head injury.**

mography of the head should be performed in all patients with persistent impairment of consciousness. In patients with a GCS of 14 or 15 who have experienced transient loss of consciousness or have posttraumatic amnesia, head CT is probably necessary only in the presence of certain specific signs and symptoms [see Table 2].[12]

OPERATIVE MANAGEMENT

Rapid evacuation of mass lesions decreases ICP and consequently improves cerebral perfusion pressure (CPP) and CBF; reversal of ischemia soon after removal of a subdural hematoma has been documented.[13] In addition, ICP may be extremely high in the presence of a subdural hematoma, and this pressure elevation can be rapidly reversed after decompression.[14] Subdural hematomas call for emergency evacuation by a neurosurgeon; evacuation performed within 4 hours of injury has been shown to result in a better outcome.[15]

An epidural hematoma, which is a life-threatening neurosurgical emergency, should be evacuated urgently. In cases of temporal fracture and rapid clinical deterioration, a temporal craniectomy can be performed. If there is no temporal fracture, an unenhanced CT scan should be obtained instead of searching for a lesion with multiple bur holes. In cases of progressive deterioration, moderate hyperventilation ($P_aCO_2 \approx 30$ mm Hg) should be initiated and mannitol (1.4 g/kg) given while the patient is being readied for surgery.[16,17]

Posterior fossa hematomas, which are rare, also require urgent evacuation, because obstructive hydrocephalus and brain stem compression can result in rapid neurologic deterioration. An intracerebral hematoma causing a midline shift larger than 5 mm is an indication for operative treatment, but surgery can usually be delayed for a few hours.

ICU MANAGEMENT

A GCS score of 8 or lower after resuscitation is an indication for admission to a neurosurgical ICU. The focus of ICU management is prevention of secondary injury and maintenance of adequate cerebral oxygenation. To ensure optimal cerebral oxygenation, CPP, hemoglobin concentration, and oxygen saturation should be optimized; vessel diameter should be maximized; and viscosity should be in the low range. Admission to an ICU does not eliminate the occurrence of secondary insults.[18] In a series of 124 patients admitted to a neurosurgical ICU, more than one episode of hypotension occurred in 73% of all patients, and more than one episode of hypoxia occurred in 40%.[19] In another study, online monitoring of CPP, jugular venous oxygen saturation ($S_{jv}O_2$), local CBF, and local tissue oxygenation was performed in 14 patients who had sustained a severe head injury; 37% of the episodes involving decreased CBF, CPP, and saturation were related to clinical and nursing procedures.[20]

Monitoring

A variety of bedside devices are currently available for monitoring ICP, local CBF, and local and global cerebral oxygenation.[18,20,21]

ICP monitoring Monitoring of ICP has never been subjected to a prospective, randomized clinical trial designed to assess its efficacy in improving patient outcome. Nevertheless, many clinical studies indicate that ICP monitoring is useful for early detection of intracranial mass lesions; that it allows calculation of CPP, an important clinical indicator of CBF; that it limits the indiscriminate use of potentially harmful therapies for control of ICP; that it helps determine prognosis; and that it may improve outcome. ICP monitoring is indicated in patients with a GCS score of 3 to 7 after resuscitation and in selected patients with a GCS score of 8 to 12 and an abnormal CT scan at the time of admission. In patients with a GCS score of 8 to 9 and a normal CT scan, ICP monitoring is indicated if the patient is

Table 3 Jugular Desaturation* and Outcome in 116 Patients with Severe Head Injuries[22]

Jugular Desaturations (No.)	Outcome		
	Good Recovery/ Moderate Disability (%)	Severe Disability/ Vegetative (%)	Deceased (%)
0	45	39	16
1	26	32	42
>1	10	20	70

*Defined as jugular venous oxygen saturation < 50% for longer than 15 min.

older than 40 years, has a systolic BP below 90 mm Hg, and exhibits unilateral or bilateral motor posturing.[21]

Jugular bulb oximetry CBF is an important determinant of neurologic outcome, and the arterial–jugular venous oxygen difference (A-VDO$_2$) is an important indicator of the adequacy of CBF. Monitoring of therapy by measuring CBF and A-VDO$_2$ would be ideal, but there is no practical way of doing this directly and continuously.

An estimate of global A-VDO$_2$ can be obtained from simultaneous monitoring of arterial oxygen saturation (S_aO_2) and $S_{jv}O_2$. Jugular venous oxygen saturation is monitored by percutaneous retrograde insertion of a fiberoptic catheter in the internal jugular vein, with the tip of the catheter located in the jugular bulb. The catheter is usually inserted into the jugular vein with the dominant cerebral venous drainage (the right jugular vein in 80% to 90% of the population), but some prefer to insert the catheter at the site of the most significant brain damage. A-VDO$_2$ is calculated according to the following formula:

$$A\text{-}VDO_2 = (S_aO_2 - S_{jv}O_2) \times 1.34 \times Hb + [(P_aO_2 - P_{jv}O_2) \times 0.0031]$$

The contribution of the variables within the brackets, which is small, is usually ignored for practical purposes. Because calculation of A-VDO$_2$ requires the drawing of blood samples, it can be done only intermittently.

For continuous monitoring, $S_{jv}O_2$, the result of arterial oxygen input and cerebral extraction, is used. In normal individuals, $S_{jv}O_2$ ranges from 50% to 70%. If $S_{jv}O_2$ values below 50% last for more than 15 minutes, they are considered desaturations, resulting from insufficient arterial oxygenation (S_aO_2), inadequate oxygen-carrying capacity (Hb concentration), or, when arterial saturation and oxygen-carrying capacity are normal, from inadequate CBF. A 1994 study described a relation between the occurrence of desaturations and neurologic outcome in patients with severe head injuries [see Table 3].[22] Without desaturation, mortality was 16%; with one documented desaturation, 42%; and with multiple desaturations, 70%. High $S_{jv}O_2$ values indicate low oxygen extraction, which is the case when the cerebral metabolic rate of oxygen (CMRO$_2$) is low.

The limitations of jugular bulb oximetry should be kept in mind when $S_{jv}O_2$ values are interpreted.[23,24] Because $S_{jv}O_2$ represents global oxygenation, regional ischemia may go undetected if the ischemic region is too small to be represented in the total hemispheric $S_{jv}O_2$ value. Ischemia may also occur in a part of the brain being drained by the opposite jugular vein. In addition, extracerebral veins drain into the internal jugular vein approximately 2 cm below the jugular bulb. With low flow values, significant extracere-

Table 2 Constitutional Signs and Symptoms Necessitating Follow-up Nonenhanced Head CT Scan in Patients with Loss of Consciousness and GCS Score of 14 or 15

Headache
Somnolence
Mental-status changes or confusion
Nausea or vomiting
Seizure

Perseveration
Neurologic deficit
Blurred or double vision
Vertigo
Hemotympanum

bral contamination may occur, resulting in deceptively high $S_{jv}O_2$ values. Finally, artifactual readings are often encountered as a result of reduced light intensity when the catheter lodges against the vessel wall. Technical improvements in catheters, however, have markedly reduced the number of artifacts observed.

Tissue oxygen monitoring Tissue oxygen monitoring has been employed for years in Europe to treat patients with brain injuries but was not approved by the Food and Drug Administration for use in the United States until relatively recently. Tissue oxygen tension ($P_{ti}O_2$) in the brain is measured via a fiberoptic monitor locally inserted through a separate bur hole.[25] The oxygen pressure recorded thus reflects a combination of oxygen supply and cerebral oxygen extraction, which makes interpretation of the values less than straightforward. Nevertheless, several investigators have demonstrated a relation between low local tissue O_2 values and poor outcome and have documented improved cerebral oxygenation after introduction of resuscitative measures (e.g., optimization of CPP and blood oxygenation).[25] In normal persons, $P_{ti}O_2$ ranges from 25 to 30 mm Hg. Critical thresholds for $P_{ti}O_2$ values include prolonged and repeated episodes below 10 to 15 mm Hg and any episode below 5 mm Hg.[26]

Management of Cerebral Perfusion Pressure

The rationale behind CPP therapy is expressed in Poiseuille's law [see Discussion, Pathophysiology, below]. Although the effect of CPP therapy has not been investigated in a randomized, controlled clinical trial, several studies suggest that a CPP of 70 to 80 mm Hg may be the clinical threshold below which mortality and morbidity increase.[27-29] In addition, there are now class II data (not yet published as of December 2003) indicating that maintenance of a CPP higher than 60 mm Hg is sufficient to ensure optimal cerebral perfusion and oxygenation (personal communication, American Brain Injury Consortium).

CPP therapy involves manipulation of both arterial BP and ICP, but its objective is the reduction of ICP. If ICP reduction does not achieve a CPP of 60 mm Hg, arterial hypertension is instituted. Mean arterial BP should be raised first by optimizing volume status: ample fluids, including albumin (25 to 30 ml/hr), are administered to maintain central venous pressure at 5 to 10 mm Hg. A pulmonary arterial catheter is suggested for patients older than 50 years and for individuals with known cardiac disease, multiple trauma (particularly chest or abdominal injuries), or a need for vasopressors or high-dose barbiturates. Pulmonary arterial wedge pressure (PAWP) should be maintained between 10 and 14 mm Hg. If necessary, an alpha-adrenergic drug (e.g., phenylephrine, 80 mg in 250 or 500 ml of normal saline) can be combined with the fluids.

Management of Intracranial Pressure

Because ICP is a determinant of CPP, treatment of ICP inevitably affects CPP. Given that the goal is maintenance or improvement of CBF, measures for treating ICP should be evaluated in the light of their effect on CBF. It is not possible to establish an arbitrary threshold for treatment of elevated ICP that would be applicable in all situations. Any interpretation of ICP must be combined with assessment of clinical features and evaluation of CT scan findings. It is possible, for example, to have transtentorial herniation with an ICP of 15 mm Hg in the presence of a mass lesion. Conversely, with diffuse brain swelling, adequate CPP can be maintained despite an ICP as high as 30 mm Hg. As a general rule, ICP values between 20 and 25 mm Hg indicate that therapy should be initiated.

The recommended regimen for treatment of ICP starts with drainage of CSF through a ventriculostomy-ICP catheter and continues as necessary in a stepwise fashion with sedation, paralysis, osmotic therapy, hyperventilation, induction of a metabolic coma, and decompressive surgery [see Figure 2].

Although drainage of CSF has no documented deleterious side effects, it does have the potential to aggravate brain shift. Therefore, only a minimal amount should be drained, sufficient to bring the ICP below 20 mm Hg.

Sedation with morphine sulfate, 2 to 5 mg/hr I.V., is standard treatment; fentanyl, lorazepam, and midazolam are commonly used alternatives. In some centers, propofol is now used for routine sedation. Propofol has a short half-life, which is advantageous for the purposes of neurologic evaluation, but it is expensive and can have deleterious side effects after prolonged use (i.e., > 48 to 72 hours).[30]

Muscular paralysis is employed by many clinicians as the next step in therapy. Its major downside is that it renders neurologic examination pointless, except for assessment of the pupillary response. In addition, the risk of respiratory complications is increased with neuromuscular blockade.

Mannitol is usually administered in I.V. boluses of 0.25 to 1 g/kg over 10 to 15 minutes until either ICP is controlled or serum osmolarity reaches 320 mOsm/L. It now appears, however, that higher doses (e.g., 1.4 g/kg) may be more effective.[16,17] Because volume depletion is an important side effect of mannitol therapy, urine losses should be replaced. Hypertonic saline (3% to 10%) may be used in place of mannitol: it appears to be just as effective as or even more effective than mannitol for ICP control, especially in higher concentrations (e.g., 7.5%).[31] In addition, hypertonic saline is not associated with volume depletion but actually increases intravascular volume. The effect probably is not purely osmotic but is partly related to viscosity, as is the case with mannitol.[32]

As noted, hyperventilation reduces ICP (by vasoconstriction) and CBF, which may be at ischemic levels in certain parts of the brain. Therefore, hyperventilation (P_aCO_2 < 30 mm Hg) should not be instituted prophylactically but should be reserved for acute decompensation and employed as a short-term temporizing measure until more definitive therapy can be instituted. If P_aCO_2 must be reduced to extremely low levels, hyperventilation can be combined with mannitol, thereby improving CBF by reducing blood viscosity. Jugular bulb oximetry is recommended in these situations because it will determine how much the cerebral vessels can be constricted.

Hemoglobin, Hematocrit, and Blood Viscosity

The hematocrit and viscosity are inversely related, and a balance must be established to optimize oxygenation. If the hematocrit is too high, viscosity increases; if the hematocrit is too low, the oxygen-carrying capacity of blood decreases. Maintaining the hematocrit between 0.30 and 0.35 is recommended: below 0.30, oxygen-carrying capacity falls without a significant change in viscosity, and above 0.35, viscosity increases out of proportion to oxygen-carrying capacity.[33] Preferably, blood that has been banked for less than 2 weeks should be used for transfusion. There are some data indicating that the effect of transfusion on cerebral oxygenation is linearly related to the duration of storage of packed red cells.[34]

Brain Protection

When oxygen delivery cannot be sufficiently improved, the brain can be protected by decreasing $CMRo_2$. Barbiturates appear to protect the brain and lower ICP through several mechanisms,

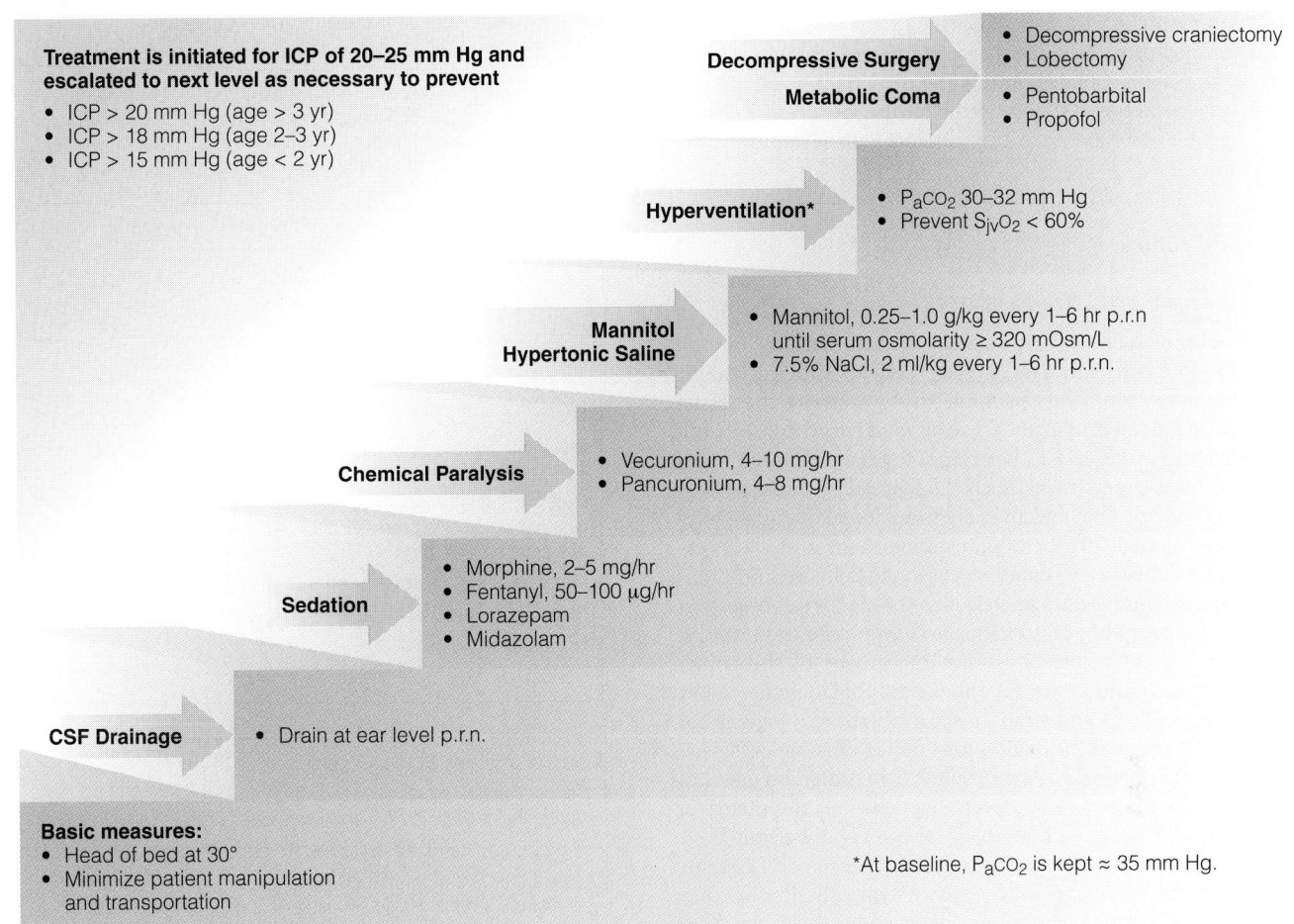

Figure 2 Illustrated is a stepwise approach to the management of ICP.

including alteration of vascular tone, suppression of metabolism, and inhibition of free radical lipid peroxidation. The most important effect may involve coupling of CBF to regional metabolic demands, so that the lower the metabolic requirements, the lower the CBF and the related cerebral blood volume (CBV), with subsequent beneficial effects on ICP and global cerebral perfusion. Barbiturate therapy (usually pentobarbital to a blood level of 4 mg/L) is instituted when other measures to control ICP fail. In one series of 25 patients with an ICP higher than 40 mm Hg, barbiturates not only controlled ICP but also improved outcome.[35] Of the patients whose ICP was controlled by barbiturates, 50% had a good recovery; of the patients whose ICP was not controlled, 83% died. In another trial, prophylactic barbiturate therapy failed to improve neurologic outcome.[36] Of the barbiturate-treated patients, 54% were hypotensive, compared with 7% of the control subjects; however, this trial was conducted before the present emphasis on maintaining CPP was recognized.

Etomidate, a rapidly acting agent with hypnotic properties similar to those of barbiturates, has fewer adverse effects on systemic BP or ICP. However, it suppresses adrenocortical function, and its solvent, propylene glycol, can cause renal insufficiency.[37]

Propofol is a sedative hypnotic with a rapid onset and a short duration of action.[38,39] It depresses $CMRo_2$, but not as effectively as barbiturates and etomidate do. Studies of patients with head injuries have demonstrated that ICP decreases with administration of propofol, but systemic BP usually decreases as well, resulting in a net decrease in CPP. Blood lactate levels do not increase

when propofol is administered, indicating that cerebral oxygenation is adequate. If propofol is used, correction of hypovolemia is recommended to prevent hypotension associated with bolus injection. Finally, because of its preservative-free, lipid-base vehicle, there is an increased risk of bacterial or fungal infection, and the high caloric content (1 kcal/ml) may be problematic during a prolonged infusion.

Hypothermia produces a balanced reduction in energy production and utilization, decreasing $CMRo_2$ and CBF proportionally. Protocols for hypothermia include cooling to 32° to 33° C (89.6° to 91.4° F) within 6 hours of injury and maintenance of this temperature for 24 to 48 hours. Hypothermia to 33° C has been shown to be effective for the control of refractory high ICP. Two pilot clinical trials reported improved neurologic outcome,[40,41] but a multicenter randomized clinical trial failed to demonstrate any overall improvement.[42] Side effects of therapy, which in this case mainly included medical complications in the elderly patients, resulted in the absence of a treatment effect. In addition, rewarming of patients who were hypothermic on admission appeared to be detrimental. However, a subgroup of patients who were already hypothermic on admission (i.e., those younger than 45 years) did benefit from continued treatment with hypothermia, and these patients were subsequently enrolled in a second phase III trial (NABISH-II).

The main side effects of hypothermia are cardiac arrhythmias and coagulation disorders, reported after cooling to 32° to 33° C. Other drawbacks of hypothermia include the difficulty of detecting infection because of the lack of warning signs (e.g., spiking and elevated temperature) and the need for specialized equipment (e.g., rotor beds with cooling control) and personnel to induce and maintain the condition. A body temperature between 35° and 35.5° C may be optimal for treating patients with severe traumatic brain injury.[43]

Spinal Cord Injury

DIAGNOSIS AND INITIAL MANAGEMENT

In the field, all patients with significant trauma, any trauma patients who lose consciousness, and any patients suffering minor trauma who have complaints referable to the spine or the spinal cord should be treated as if they had a spinal cord injury until proven otherwise [see Figure 3]. If cardiopulmonary resuscitation is necessary, it takes precedence [see 100 Initial Management of Life-Threatening Trauma]. The objectives are to maintain adequate oxygenation and maintain BP by administering fluids and vasopressors. The main concerns of management in the field are immobilization before and during extrication from a vehicle (or removal from the scene of another type of accident) and immobilization during transport to prevent active or passive movement of the spine. Subsequently, the patient may require a rigid Philadelphia collar, support from sandbags and straps, a spine board, or a log-roll for turning. A brief motor examination may detect possible deficits.

When the patient arrives at the hospital, care should be taken to provide adequate oxygenation, prevent hypotension, and maintain immobilization. Patients with an injury above C4, who may have respiratory paralysis, may need ventilatory assistance. Lesions above T5 may be accompanied by loss of sympathetic tone and consequently by significant venous pooling and arterial hypotension. Because paralytic ileus is common, usually lasting several days, a nasogastric tube should be placed to prevent vomiting and aspiration. Urinary retention is also a common occurrence, and a Foley catheter should therefore be inserted. Vasomotor paralysis may cause poikilothermia (uncontrolled temperature regulation), and normothermia should therefore be maintained.

A detailed neurologic examination is required to determine whether the injury is complete or incomplete and at what level of the spinal cord the injury occurred. If possible, a history should determine the mechanism of injury (e.g., hyperflexion, extension, axial loading, or rotation). The American Spinal Injury Association (ASIA) (www.asia-spinalinjury.org) has developed a protocol for sensory and motor examination of patients with spinal cord injuries that is precise and relatively easy to follow [see Figure 4].

Spinal shock consists of loss of all or most motor, sensory, and autonomic function below the level of the lesion. It usually develops in the setting of a severe spinal cord injury that occurs over a brief period, and it is most commonly witnessed immediately after the injury (though it may also appears hours later in cases of progressive injury). As originally defined, the term spinal shock referred to arterial hypotension resulting from loss of sympathetic tone after spinal cord injury. Currently, however, most authors use the term to refer to the complex of symptoms associated with the loss of spinal reflex activity below the level of the lesion, which may or may not include arterial hypotension.[44] The motor component of spinal shock may consist of paralysis, flaccidity, and areflexia. The sensory component may involve both spinothalamic and dorsal column sensory function, and the autonomic component may include systemic hypotension, bradycardia, skin hyperemia, and warmth.

Spinal shock should be differentiated from spinal concussion. Spinal concussion is a poorly understood phenomenon. It is de-

---

Patient has apparent spinal cord injury

(In the field, all patients with significant trauma, any trauma patient who loses consciousness, and any patient with minor trauma who has complaints referable to the spine or the spinal cord should be treated as having spinal cord injury until proven otherwise.)

Resuscitate according to ATLS principles.

Immobilize spine, and use spine board, cervical orthosis, sandbags, straps, log-roll, and tape on forehead as necessary.

Perform trauma evaluation.

Perform emergency diagnostic or therapeutic procedures as indicated.

Maintain oxygenation; intubate and ventilate as needed.

Maintain systolic BP > 90 mm Hg with volume replacement (isotonic fluids), MAST, vasopressors (dopamine, 2–10 µg/kg/min), and, if bradycardia (< 45 beats/min) occurs, atropine, 0.5–1.0 mg I.V.

Place NG tube to prevent vomiting and aspiration.

Place Foley catheter to prevent urinary retention.

Normalize T°.

Perform detailed neurologic examination.

Evalute axial skeleton, and obtain x-rays of spine.

Cervical spine: lateral view showing craniocervical and C7–T1 junctions, followed by AP and odontoid views.

Thoracic and lumbosacral spine: AP and lateral views.

Urgent MRI is indicated if (1) there is an incomplete lesion with normal alignment, (2) deterioration occurs, (3) fracture level ≠ deficit level, or (4) a bony injury cannot be identified.

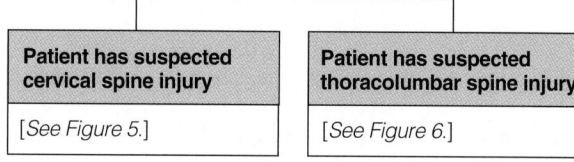

Patient has suspected cervical spine injury	**Patient has suspected thoracolumbar spine injury**
[See Figure 5.]	[See Figure 6.]

Figure 3 **Shown is an algorithm for management of the patient with an acute spinal cord injury.**

---

fined as partial spinal cord sensory or motor deficits that resolve completely within 24 to 72 hours and that are never associated with permanent spinal cord injury. Spinal concussion is rare and has never been described in conjunction with spinal shock.

All patients with possible spine injuries should be examined radiologically. Roentgenography of the cervical spine with the patient is in a rigid collar includes a lateral view showing both the craniocervical and the cervicothoracic (C7-T1) junction. If the lateral view is normal and the patient is coherent and has no neck tenderness or neurologic deficit, the collar can be removed for anteroposterior and odontoid views. If the lower cervical spine or the cervicothoracic junction is not well visualized, a lateral view with caudal traction on the arms, or a swimmer's view, is required. If areas of the spine are still not visualized or if there is a neurologic deficit, a CT scan with sagittal reconstruction should be obtained through the poorly visualized levels.

The use of flexion-extension films (i.e., testing of the active range of motion of the cervical spine from maximal anterior-posterior flexion to extension) is typically limited to patients who are awake and able to cooperate.[45] Although spinal instability is probably best demonstrated with this type of imaging, it should be noted that in patients with neck pain, muscle spasm can limit range of motion and thereby mask a subluxation. Accordingly, it is recommended that patients with posttraumatic neck pain who are neurologically intact, whose plain radiographs are normal, and who are capable of limited flexion and extension effort (i.e., < 30° of motion) be placed in a rigid cervical collar and reevaluated 1 to 2 weeks later. In comatose patients, dynamic films are sometimes obtained under direct fluoroscopic guidance, though magnetic resonance imaging appears to render such studies unnecessary.

CT is particularly helpful in the further evaluation of fractures diagnosed on plain films: it shows bone in greater detail and at higher resolution than plain films do, it achieves better visualization of fixed subluxations, and it allows more accurate assessment of the central bony canal and the neuronal foramina. CT is highly accurate in visualizing body fractures, Jefferson (C1) and hangman (C2) fractures, and bilateral locked facets. It appears to be less accurate, however, in visualizing transverse C2, posterior ele-

ment, and nondisplaced spinous process fractures. Moreover, it sometimes misses superior articular process fractures.[46]

MRI of the cervical spine is the study of choice for evaluating injury to the soft tissues and ligaments. Intrinsic cord damage (e.g., edema, hematoma, or contusion) and injury to the surrounding ligaments, disks, and paravertebral soft tissues are well visualized. In addition, MRI is helpful in the assessment of brachial plexus injury, though a series of special coronal images is usually required. A fat-suppression image usually identifies ligamentous injury to the posterior elements quite well, and fine-cut gradient echo (GRE) imaging of the transverse ligament of C2 is extremely sensitive in detecting disruption.[47] The major drawbacks of MRI are the length of the imaging time, which may be a problem in the critically ill trauma patient, the susceptibility to movement artifacts, and the need for MRI-compatible monitoring devices and traction equipment. Moreover, in this setting, it is often difficult to obtain an adequate medical history with regard to implanted medical devices or old bullet fragments, both of which preclude MRI. Radiologic evaluation and clearance of the cervical spine can be facilitated by the use of an established protocol [see Figure 5].

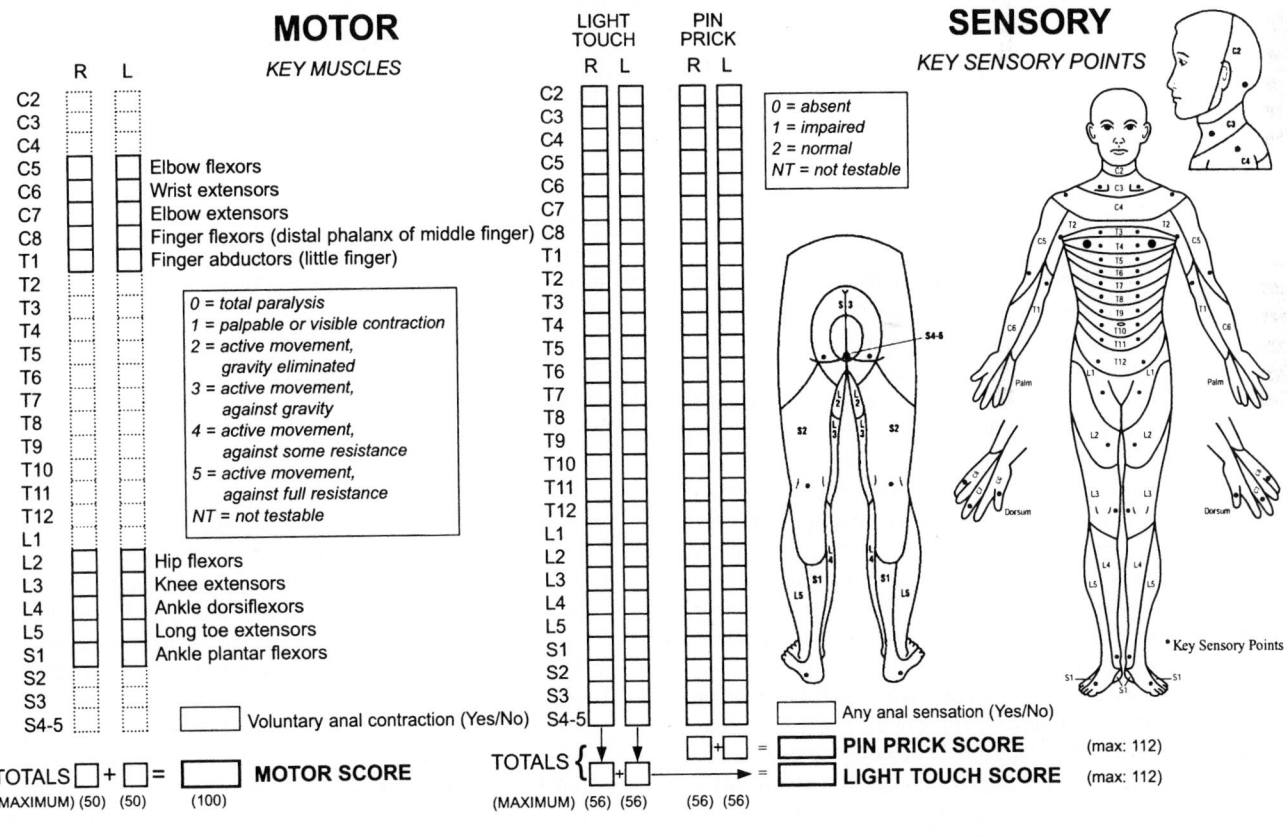

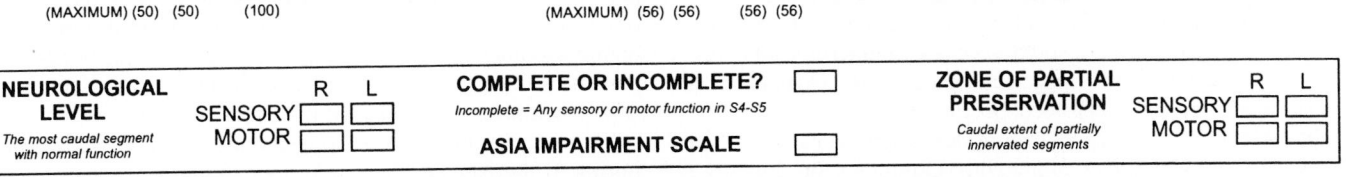

Figure 4 Shown is a form developed by the American Spinal Injury Association to record the principal information about motor, sensory, and sphincter function required for accurate neurologic classification of spinal cord injury. For the motor examination, 10 key muscles are tested (left). For the sensory examination, 28 key dermatomes are tested (right).

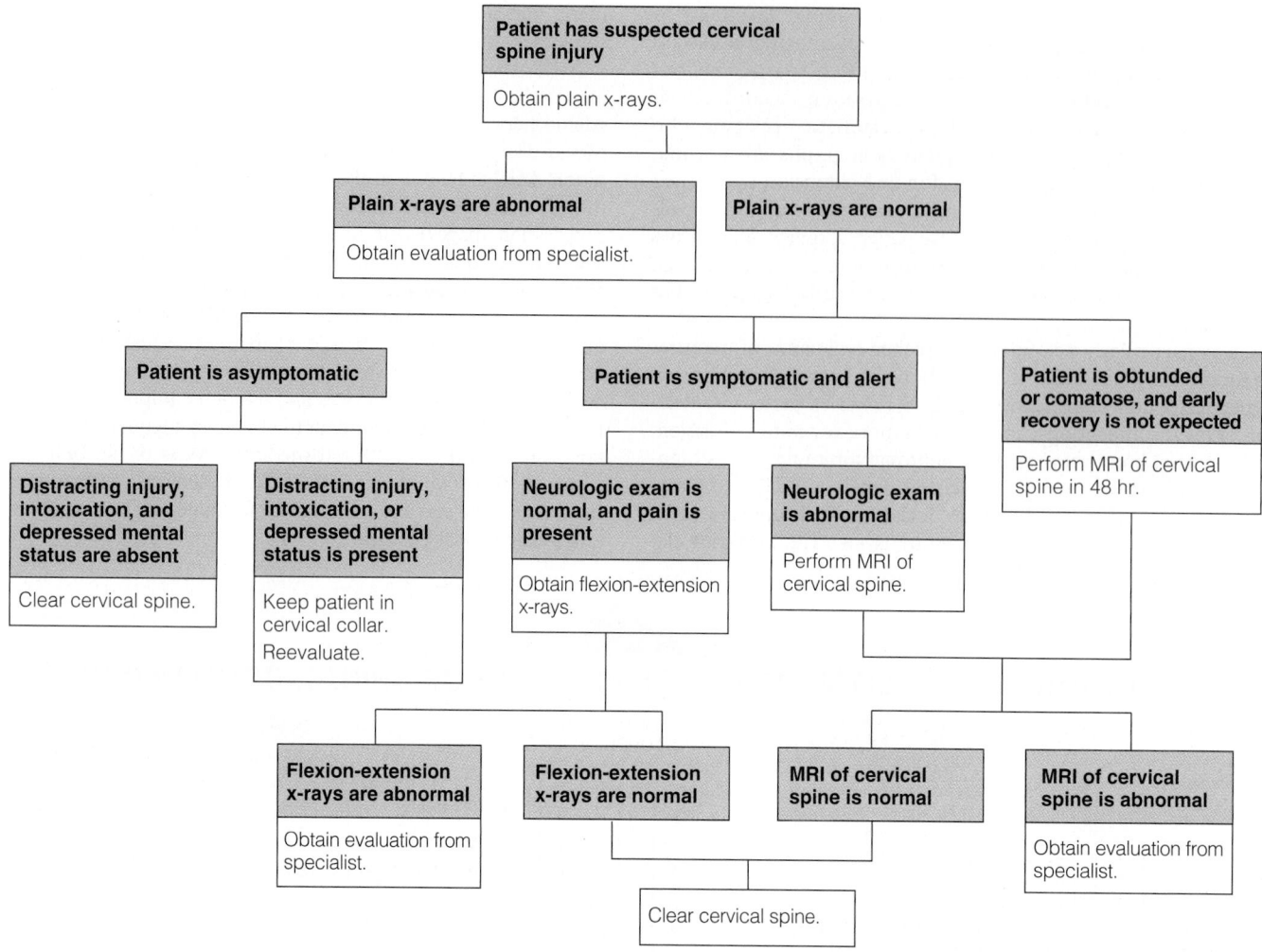

Figure 5 Shown is an algorithm depicting the protocol for radiologic evaluation and clearance of cervical spinal cord injury.

Anteroposterior and lateral views of thoracic and lumbosacral vertebrae should be obtained for all trauma patients who were thrown from a vehicle or fell more than 2 m to the ground, complain of back pain, are unconscious, cannot reliably describe back pain or have altered mental status preventing adequate examination, or have an unknown mechanism of injury or other injuries that suggest the possibility of spinal injury. If a fracture or subluxation is found on the plain films, a CT with sagittal reconstruction extending from one level above the fracture/subluxation to one level below it is recommended.

Indications for urgent MRI include the following: an incomplete lesion with normal alignment (to rule out the possibility of compression); deterioration (worsening deficit or rising level); a fracture level different from the level of deficit; and inability to identify a bony injury (to rule out the possibilities of soft tissue compression, disk herniation, or hematoma that would necessitate surgery). Radiologic evaluation of patients with suspected thoracolumbar spine injuries is also facilitated by use of a protocol [see Figure 6].

In most patients, the spine can be cleared on the basis of plain x-rays and neurologic examination. Obtunded or comatose patients whose plain x-rays are normal but who are at high risk for spine injury (e.g., those injured in high-speed motor vehicle accidents or by falls from great heights) should be evaluated by a spine specialist before spine clearance.

TREATMENT

Traction

The objectives of craniocervical traction are to reduce fracture-dislocations, to maintain normal alignment or immobility of the cervical spine, to prevent further injury, to decompress the spinal cord and roots, and to facilitate bone healing. A common technique is placement of Gardner-Wells tongs, a U-shaped device with pins that are anchored to the skull just above the pinna. Traction is applied with the patient in supine position by adding weights to the traction ring. Alternatively, traction may be applied with the patient in a halo ring. A special traction triangle is then added to the ring. The advantage of this approach is that the patient can be stabilized in a halo vest as soon as reduction is obtained. Furthermore, the halo vest is helpful in dealing with a highly unstable spine that requires instrumentation because the patient can be easily turned onto the operating table without the risk of significant movement of the spine.

Traction should always be applied under strict neurologic monitoring. If the patient's condition deteriorates when the weight is increased, the additional weight should be removed and the patient should immediately undergo imaging (e.g., with plain films, MRI, or both). In the case of a highly unstable fracture, traction should be guided by fluoroscopy rather than serial x-rays.

Pharmacologic Treatment

A number of drugs are known to interfere with the processes of secondary injury. The challenge is to identify the most effective treatment or combination of treatments with the fewest severe side effects—a task requiring many experiments for each treatment tested. Methylprednisolone (MP), thought to act by scavenging free radicals, has been reported to be neuroprotective in patients with spinal cord injuries.[48-50] Considerable controversy remains, however, regarding the clinical benefit of MP administration after acute spinal cord injury.

Three multicenter, randomized, controlled clinical trials carried out in the United States evaluated MP in this setting: National Spinal Cord Injury Study (NASCIS) I, NASCIS II, and NASCIS III.[48-50] In NASCIS I, reported in 1984, the administration of a 100 mg MP bolus followed by 100 mg/day for 10 days was compared with administration of a 1,000 mg MP bolus followed by 1,000 mg/day for 10 days. There was no placebo group. No difference was noted between the two MP groups with respect to motor or sensory outcome at 6 weeks, 6 months, and 1 year.

Because data from animal studies suggested that the MP doses used in NASCIS I were too low to yield a significant difference in outcome, NASCIS II was initiated in 1985. In this trial, administration of high-dose MP (i.e., a 30 mg/kg bolus followed by 5.4 mg/kg/hour for 23 hours) was compared with administration of naloxone (a 5.4 mg/kg bolus followed by 4 mg/kg/hour for 23 hours) and with placebo. Neurologic outcome was graded by evaluating sensory and motor function at 6 weeks and 6 months after

injury. A total of 14 muscle groups were examined and graded on a scale of 0 to 5. The scores were added, with a total score of 0 indicating no motor activity below the level of the lesion and a total score of 70 representing normal motor function. For sensory assessment, 29 spinal cord segments were similarly evaluated and graded on a scale of 1 to 3. A total score of 29 indicated no response in any segment, and a total score of 87 indicated that all sensory segments were normal. The authors reported a statistically significant mean motor and sensory improvement after MP administration. In the MP group, there was a mean improvement of 16.0 in the motor score, compared with a mean improvement of 11.2 in the placebo group. The mean changes in sensory scores were 11.4 (MP) and 6.6 (placebo) for sensation to pinprick and 8.9 (MP) and 4.3 (placebo) for sensation.

In NASCIS III, patients who received a 24-hour regimen of MP (a 30 mg/kg bolus followed by 5.4 mg/kg/hour), a similar 48-hour regimen, or a 48-hour regimen of tyrilazad mesylate (2.5 mg/kg every 6 hours) were evaluated. There was no placebo group. No differences in sensory or motor recovery were observed between groups. In a subgroup analysis, it was noted that in patients whose treatment was initiated more than 3 hours after injury, motor function improved more with the 48-hour MP regimen than with the 24-hour regimen. The Functional Independence Measurement (FIM) did not show any statistically significant differences between groups.

NASCIS II and III have been criticized for flaws in research design and data analysis. For example, patients with a normal motor examination and patients with a combined conus-cauda injury were included. Furthermore, only motor and sensory scores from the right side of the body were reported. Moreover, in the statistical analysis, the only statistically significant results were the result of a post hoc analysis.

A 2000 study presented a statistical reanalysis of the NASCIS II and III data.[51] In this reanalysis, no difference in neurologic recovery between the placebo, 24-hour MP, and 48-hour MP groups was found, but an increased mortality was documented in the 48-hour MP group—a finding that was not reported in the NASCIS studies. Current guidelines take the position that the available medical evidence does not conclusively establish the existence of a significant clinical benefit from administration of MP for either 24 or 48 hours and that the harmful side effects may actually outweigh any clinical benefits.[52] MP administration is therefore considered a treatment option to be used at the discretion of the treating physician.

The calcium channel blocker nimodipine causes significant increases in blood flow in the spinal cord,[53,54] but, paradoxically, the dosage necessary to exert this effect is accompanied by significant systemic hypotension. Administration of GM_1 ganglioside, a compound that occurs naturally in the membranes of mammals and is particularly abundant in the CNS, has been shown to have short-term neuroprotective effects and long-term regenerative effects in animal models. In a prospective, placebo-controlled, double-blind study, some improvement in motor, sensory, and bladder function was seen in patients treated with GM_1 ganglioside, but no overall improvement in neurologic outcome was noted.[55] This agent is currently an optional treatment for patients with spinal cord injuries. Treatment with GM_1 ganglioside is started after the completion of MP therapy and continued for 56 days.

Surgical Treatment

The role of neurosurgery in the treatment of spinal fractures and spinal cord injury remains controversial. There is considerable disagreement as to whether surgery should be performed, what type of surgery should be done, and when should it be done. The

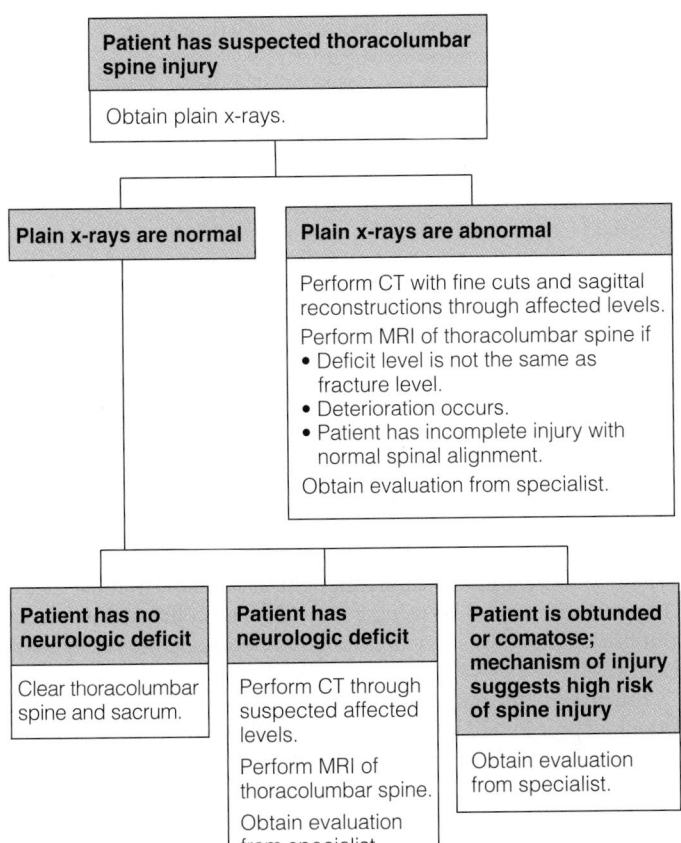

Figure 6 Shown is an algorithm depicting the protocol for radiologic evaluation and clearance of thoracolumbar spinal cord injury.

primary goals of treatment are to decompress and protect under-lying neural structures, to restore spinal stability and alignment, to facilitate early mobilization and rehabilitation, and to maximize neurologic recovery.

There is general agreement among physicians that immobilization of the patient to prevent further injury and early stabilization of fractures and dislocations of the spine are necessary. The single widely accepted indication for early urgent surgical treatment is ongoing neurologic deterioration in the presence of spinal canal compromise from bone and disk fragments, hematoma, or unre-duced subluxation. Surgical indications still under debate include incomplete spinal cord injury (with persistent spinal cord com-pression) and complete spinal cord injury with the possibility of some neurologic recovery.

In some studies, early surgical intervention has been associated with an increased risk of systemic complications (especially pul-monary complications) and neurologic deterioration. One group of investigators found that one third of all cases of neurologic dete-rioration could be attributed directly to surgical intervention; four of 26 patients who underwent spinal surgery within 5 days expe-rienced deterioration, whereas none of the patients treated after 5 days had any neurologic sequelae.[56]

Other studies, however, have not found an increased risk of deteri-oration with early intervention. One study evaluated 110 patients with cervical spinal cord injury, of whom 88 underwent surgery for spinal stabilization; in the 39 patients treated within 24 hours, the in-cidence of systemic complications was reduced by 50% in compari-son with the incidence in the 49 patients treated 24 hours to 3 weeks after injury.[57] In addition, the incidence of neurologic deterioration was 0% in the early-stabilization group compared with 2.5% in the late-stabilization group. Data from NASCIS II showed improved outcome in patients undergoing surgery within 24 hours of injury compared with patients treated after 200 hours, but the difference was not statistically significant.[58]

We adhere to the following protocol in treating patients with cervical spine fracture-dislocations. After systemic stabilization, patients are placed in a halo ring and traction as soon as possible. We prefer to set up traction in the neurologic ICU, but this can be done in the emergency department when necessary. Closed reduc-tion is attempted under the guidance of fluoroscopy or serial x-rays, depending on the degree of spinal cord compromise or expected instability. Patients are then secured in their halo vests and undergo MRI evaluation, regardless of whether reduction attempts succeeded or failed. Patients with reduced and realigned injuries and no cord compromise are kept in their halo vests and offered nonurgent surgical stabilization, depending on the nature of the injury. Patients with irreducible fractures or continued com-promise of the neural elements are taken to the OR promptly for urgent surgical decompression and fixation, regardless of whether the neurologic injury is complete or incomplete.

The efficacy of early surgical decompression in patients with thoracolumbar fractures is not established, except in cases where the neurologic examination reveals deterioration. Most surgeons, however, advocate urgent decompression in patients who have canal compromise and an incomplete injury; patients who do not fall into this category can be kept on strict spinal precautions, with definitive therapy instituted on a nonurgent basis.

Diagnosis and Treatment of Specific Fractures and Dislocations

Cervical spine Injuries to the cervical spine include atlas fractures, axis fractures, fractures of the lower cervical spine, and atlanto-occipital and atlantoaxial dislocations. Atlanto-occipital

dislocation (AOD) is rare, occurring in approximately 1% of pa-tients with cervical spine injuries. Many of these patients die im-mediately after trauma as a result of brain stem injury and respi-ratory arrest. Since the 1980s, advances in emergency patient management in the field, reduced transport time, and better recognition of the condition have improved the survival rate after AOD. Nevertheless, since 1966, fewer than 100 survivors of AOD have been reported in the literature. Patients who survive AOD often have neurologic deficits, such as lower cranial neuropathies, unilateral or bilateral weakness, and quadriplegia. Some 20% of patients, however, exhibit no abnormalities on neurologic exami-nation at presentation. AOD is difficult to diagnose and is often missed on the initial cervical radiograph. Accordingly, a high index of suspicion for this condition should be maintained, particularly when signs such as prevertebral soft tissue swelling on the plain cervical radiograph or subarachnoid hemorrhage at the craniover-tebral junction on CT are present. Additional investigation with MRI may be necessary.

Because AOD mostly involves ligamentous injury, treatment generally consists of operative fusion. Traction is rarely employed, because even a small weight may cause distraction injury with these highly unstable dislocations.

Atlantoaxial dislocations are often fatal as well. Like AODs, they are highly unstable lesions associated with severe ligamentous injury.

Atlas (Jefferson, or C1) fractures, which represent 5% to 10% of all cervical spine fractures, result from axial loading. Because of the large diameter of the spinal canal and the tendency of fragments to move outward, these fractures usually are not accompanied by sig-nificant neurologic injury. However, 40% of patients with an atlas fracture have another cervical fracture as well (usually involving C2). The integrity of the transverse ligament largely determines whether the fracture is stable.[47] Injuries that involve the midportion of the transverse ligament or the periosteal insertion (e.g., types Ia and Ib) will not heal spontaneously and must be treated with surgical fixa-tion of the C1-C2 complex. In contrast, type II injuries (e.g., avul-sion injuries or comminuted lateral mass fractures) will usually heal in a rigid external orthosis (e.g., a halo vest). Most other atlas frac-tures can be managed in a rigid cervical collar, except for widely dis-placed or comminuted fractures, which also require that the patient be immobilized in a halo vest.

Axis (C2) fractures account for 10% to 20% of all cervical spine fractures in adults and 70% of cervical fractures in children. The odontoid process is the part of C2 that is most commonly frac-tured (accounting for 60% of axis fractures). The management of odontoid fractures remains controversial: only class III data are available, which are insufficient to establish practice guidelines.[59]

Three different types of odontoid fractures are recognized. Fractures of the tip of the odontoid process (avulsion fracture, type I) are uncommon but are thought to be stable in most cases. They can be treated by using a hard cervical collar with or with-out preceding cervical traction or by immobilizing the patient in a halo vest.

Fractures of the neck (type II) and fractures at the junction of the odontoid process and the axis body (type III) are more common (ac-counting for 65% to 80% and 20% to 35% of odontoid fractures, re-spectively). Management of type II fractures depends on the degree to which the dens is displaced: fractures with more than 5 mm of dis-placement are typically managed surgically, whereas fractures with less than 5 mm of displacement can be treated nonsurgically with a halo vest or a semirigid orthosis (e.g., a sterno-occipito-mandibular immobilizer [SOMI] brace).[60] The management of type II fractures also depends on the age and general medical condition of the patient. Halo-vest immobilization is associated with a significantly increased risk of pulmonary complications and death in elderly patients and thus should be used with caution in this population. Surgical stabilization and fusion is recommended for type II fractures in patients older than 50 years.[60]

The type IIa subcategory of odontoid fracture warrants special mention. These fractures have either anterior or posterior chip-fracture fragments at the base of the dens and are considered unstable. They are often widely displaced and have a nonunion rate of 75% to 85% with halo-vest immobilization. Accordingly, surgical management is recommended. The integrity of the transverse ligament should be evaluated in patients with type II injuries; fixation with an odontoid screw is contraindicated, and C1-C2 fixation should be performed instead.

Most type III odontoid fractures will fuse with rigid external mobilization (i.e., either cervical traction followed by placement in a rigid cervical collar or placement in a halo vest). Again, more than 5 mm of displacement is an indication for surgical stabilization.[60]

Traumatic spondylolisthesis, or hangman's fracture, accounts for approximately 20% of C2 fractures. Injury usually results from axial compression in combination with hyperextension of the occipito-atlanto-axial complex on the lower spine, resulting in bilateral fracture of the pars interarticularis. Fractures affecting the ring of the axis without C2-C3 angulation are stable and can be treated with immobilization in a Philadelphia collar or a SOMI brace. Halo-vest immobilization is recommended in unreliable patients or patients with both C1 and C2 fractures. The average healing time is 12 weeks. Fractures with angulation, subluxation, or C2-C3 locked facets are treated with halo-vest immobilization if they are adequately reducible and with surgical intervention if they are nonreducible, are associated with disruption of the C2-C3 disk space, or are subject to recurrent subluxation.[47,60]

Approximately 80% of all fractures of the lower cervical spine are produced by indirect forces. The vertebra most commonly involved is C5, and dislocations are most frequent at the C5-C6 level. The following injury mechanisms are observed: flexion and distraction (approximately 40% of cases), flexion and compression (22%), vertical compression (8%), extension and compression (24%), extension and distraction (6%), and lateral flexion (3%).

Flexion and distraction injuries usually result from a blow to the occiput from below. The initial disruption is within the posterior ligamentous complex, leading to facet dislocation and an abnormally large divergence of the spinous processes. Unilateral facet dislocation and facet interlocking result when a rotatory component is involved. Bilateral facet dislocation with anterior translation of the superior vertebra results from severe hyperflexion; the translation is usually at least 50% in such cases. Cord and root involvement vary with the degree of subluxation and translation: 50% of patients with unilateral facet dislocation present with moderate cord and root injury, and 90% of patients with bilateral facet dislocation and a full translation of the vertebral body have a neurologic deficit (most often a complete cord lesion). Teardrop fractures (characterized by a bone chip just beyond the anterior inferior edge of the vertebral body) result from severe hyperflexion injury, and the fractured vertebra is usually displaced posteriorly on the vertebra below; these patients are often quadriplegic.

Flexion and compression injuries, usually observed at the C4-C5 and C5-C6 levels, typically result from a blow to the back of the head. The effect on the anterior vertebral body varies from a moderate rounding or loss of anterior height to a wedge shape with an oblique fracture from the anterior surface to the inferior subchondral plate. Approximately 50% of patients with the latter type of injury have a neurologic deficit. More severe injuries are

accompanied by translation of the inferior posterior margin of the vertebral body into the neural canal. About 75% of patients have neurologic involvement. Translations of more than 3 mm result in a complete spinal cord lesion in most cases.

Extension and compression injuries are usually caused by a blow to the forehead and result in fractures of the posterior complex. About 40% of patients with unilateral vertebral arch fractures (articular process, pedicle, or lamina) have a neurologic deficit (most often a radiculopathy). Bilaminar fractures are accompanied by a complete cord lesion in 40% of cases. Bilateral vertebral arch fractures with complete anterior translation of the vertebral body present with radiculopathy (30% of cases), central cord syndrome (30%), or an incomplete cord lesion (30%). In one series, no complete cord lesions were observed with this type of injury.[61]

Treatment of injuries to the lower cervical spine has not been standardized. As a general rule, severe ligamentous involvement and severe vertical compression call for surgical intervention. Severely comminuted vertebral body fractures may also necessitate surgery because of the high risk of progressive kyphosis. Isolated spinous process fractures and unilateral lamina and pedicle fractures are usually managed conservatively with placement in a rigid cervical collar. If there is a fracture through the transverse foramen above C6, the vertebral artery should be evaluated for dissection by means of magnetic resonance angiography (MRA), CT angiography, or catheter angiography.[45] Surgical intervention should be carefully considered, especially in young trauma victims. In a series from 1988, 87% of patients with distractive flexion injury and 88% of those with compressive flexion injury healed with halo-vest immobilization.[62]

Thoracolumbar spine Approximately 64% of fractures of the spine occur at the T12-L1 junction, and 70% of these fractures are unaccompanied by immediate neurologic injury. Evaluation according to Denis's three-column principle [see Figure 7] is useful for determining whether a fracture is stable, though the precise definition of stability remains controversial.[63] Fractures of the thoracic spine are more stable because of support from the surrounding rib cage and the strong costovertebral ligaments. When two of the three columns are affected, the fracture is considered unstable, and surgical intervention is generally required.

The four major types of thoracolumbar spine injuries are compression fractures, burst fractures, seat-belt fractures (Chance fractures), and fracture-dislocations. These four types of fracture involve the anterior, middle, and posterior columns of the spine in different ways [see Table 4]. Transverse process fractures are rarely unstable and are typically managed conservatively with analgesics or muscle relaxants.

Minimal to moderate compression fractures (< 50% loss of height or < 30° of angulation) with an intact posterior column can be treated with analgesics and bed rest. Ambulation should be started early, and depending on the degree of kyphosis, external immobilization (with a thoracolumbar orthosis or a Boston brace) may or may not be indicated. Severe compression injuries should be treated with external immobilization in extension. If the loss of anterior height of the vertebral body exceeds 50%, there is an increased risk of progressive kyphosis; evaluation with follow-up radiographs is indicated. Occasionally, surgical intervention is required. An anterior injury is considered unstable if it involves more than three adjacent elements or if height loss in a single element exceeds 50% with more than 30° of angulation.[64]

Burst fractures are considered unstable even if there is no initial neurologic deficit. Early ambulation should be avoided because the axial loading may result in progressive collapse or angulation, with concomitant neurologic damage. Indications for the surgical treatment of burst fractures are as follows[64]:

1. Loss of more than 50% of body height.
2. Retropulsed bony fragments narrowing the canal by more than 50%.
3. Kyphotic angulation of 25° or more.

A Chance fracture is a horizontal fracture through all three columns. It occurs most commonly in the lower lumbar spine and is a highly unstable injury. Chance fractures are now less frequent than they once were because of the widespread use of shoulder belts in addition to lap belts, which prevents upper torso flexion during deceleration. Chance fractures are treated with surgical stabilization, and decompression and correction of spinal alignment may be required as well.[64]

Fracture-dislocations, also known as fracture subluxations, are three-column injuries that usually involve disruption of the ligamentous structures or the disk space. Dural lacerations and neurologic injury are common with such injuries. Fracture-dislocations are considered unstable and are treated with surgical decompression and stabilization.

Discussion

Pathophysiology

HEAD INJURY

Cerebral Metabolism

At 1,200 to 1,400 g, the brain accounts for only 2% to 3% of total body weight and does not do any mechanical work; yet it receives 15% to 20% of all cardiac output to meet its high metabolic demands. Of the total energy generated, 50% is used for interneuronal communication and the generation, release, and reuptake of neurotransmitters (synaptic activity); 25% is used for maintenance and restoration of ion gradients across the cell membrane; and the remaining 25% is used for molecular transport, biosynthesis, and other, as yet unidentified, processes.

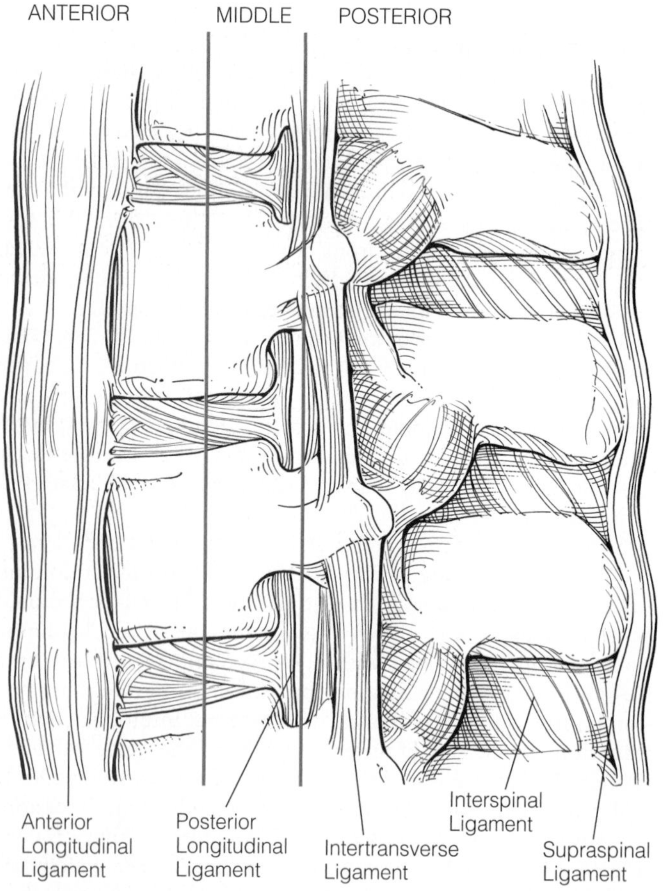

Cell metabolism involves the consumption of adenosine triphosphate (ATP) during work and the ensuing consumption of metabolic substrates to resynthesize ATP from adenosine diphosphate (ADP). ATP is generated both in the cytosol (via glycolysis) and in the mitochondria (via oxidative phosphorylation). Glucose is the sole energy substrate, unless there is ketosis, and 95% of the energy requirement of the normal brain comes from aerobic conversion of glucose to water and CO_2. ATP generation is highly efficient. Glycolysis and subsequent oxidative phosphorylation result in the generation of 38 molecules of ATP for each molecule of glucose:

$$1 \text{ glucose} + 6 \text{ O}_2 + 38 \text{ ADP} + 38 \text{ P}_i \rightarrow 6 \text{ CO}_2 + 44 \text{ H}_2\text{O} + 38 \text{ ATP}$$

In the absence of oxygen, anaerobic glycolysis can proceed, but energy production is much less efficient. Two molecules of ATP and two molecules of lactate are generated for each molecule of glucose:

$$1 \text{ glucose} + 2 \text{ ADP} + 2 \text{ P}_i \rightarrow 2 \text{ lactate} + 2 \text{ ATP}$$

Regulation of Blood Flow

Because the reserves of glucose and glycogen within the astrocytes of the brain are limited and there is no significant storage capacity for oxygen, the brain depends on blood to supply the oxygen and glucose it requires. More specifically, substrate availability is determined by its concentration in blood, flow volume, and the rate of passage across the blood-brain barrier.

Under normal circumstances and with certain physiologic alterations, an adequate supply of substrates can be maintained by regulation of CBF. CBF increases with vasodilatation and decreases with vasoconstriction. Caliber changes take place mainly in cerebral resistance vessels (i.e., arterioles with a diameter of 300 μm down to 15 μm).[65,66] Control of CBF by influencing vessel caliber is commonly referred to as autoregulation of blood flow.

Metabolic autoregulation CBF is functionally coupled to cerebral metabolism, changing proportionally with increasing or decreasing regional or global metabolic demand. Thus, the brain precisely matches local CBF to local metabolic needs. Because 95% of the energy in the normal brain is generated by oxidative metabolism of glucose, CMR_{O_2} is considered to be a sensitive measure of cerebral metabolism. The relation between CBF and metabolism is expressed in the Fick equation:

$$CMR_{O_2} = CBF \times A\text{-}VD_{O_2}$$

ANTERIOR   MIDDLE   POSTERIOR

Anterior Longitudinal Ligament

Posterior Longitudinal Ligament

Intertransverse Ligament

Interspinal Ligament

Supraspinal Ligament

Figure 7 **Illustrated is the three-column concept for assessment of spinal stability. If two or more columns are destroyed or nonfunctional, instability is likely.**

Table 4 Column Failure in the Four Types
of Major Thoracolumbar Spinal Injury[63]

Fracture Type	Anterior Column	Middle Column	Posterior Column
Compression	Compression	Intact	Intact, or distraction if severe
Burst	Compression	Compression	Intact
Seat belt	Intact or mild compression of 10%–20% of anterior vertebral body	Distraction	Distraction
Fracture-dislocation	Compression, rotation, shear	Distraction, rotation, shear	Distraction, rotation, shear

$CMRO_2$, expressed in milliliters per 100 g of brain tissue, is normally about 3.2 ml/100 g/min in awake adults. The average CBF value for mixed cortical flow is 53 ml/100 g/min in a healthy adult. A-VDO$_2$, a measure of cerebral oxygen extraction, can be calculated by subtracting the oxygen content of jugular venous blood (6.7 ml/dl) from that of arterial blood (13 ml/dl), resulting in a value of 6.3 ml/dl; this value can then be corrected for hemoglobin content according to the formula discussed earlier [*see* Head Injury, ICU Management, *above*]. Under conditions of increasing metabolic demand (increased $CMRO_2$), such as seizures or fever, CBF increases proportionally, thus keeping A-VDO$_2$ constant. With decreasing metabolism (anesthesia, deep coma), CBF decreases.

Pressure autoregulation Another important physiologic property of the cerebral circulation is maintenance of a constant supply of substrates at the level set by metabolism. According to Poiseuille's equation,

$$CBF = k \frac{CPP \times d^4}{(8 \times l \times v)}$$

in which k is a constant of proportionality, d is vessel diameter, l is vessel length, and v is blood viscosity, changes in CPP (e.g., arterial hypotension or increases in ICP) are followed by changes in CBF, unless diameter regulation (pressure autoregulation) takes place.[67] In humans, the limits of pressure autoregulation range from 40 to 150 mm Hg of CPP.

Viscosity autoregulation In accordance with Poiseuille's equation, CBF can vary with changes in the viscosity of blood. Blood viscosity changes with variations in hematocrit, γ-globulin, and fibrinogen components of plasma protein. Increased viscosity would increase cerebrovascular resistance ($8 \times l \times v / d^4$). By means of diameter adjustment (viscosity autoregulation), cerebrovascular resistance is decreased and CBF can be kept constant.[68]

CO_2 reactivity Vascular caliber and cerebral blood flow are also responsive to changes in P_aCO_2. Cerebral blood flow changes 2% to 3% for each mm Hg change in P_aCO_2 within the range of 20 to 60 mm Hg. Hypercarbia (hypoventilation) results in vasodilatation and higher CBF, and hypocarbia (hyperventilation) results in vasoconstriction and lower CBF. Autoregulation is a compensatory or adaptive response adjusting CBF to metabolism; with CO_2 variation, vessel caliber changes and CBF follow passively. The vessels respond not to changes in P_aCO_2 but to the pH in the perivascular space. CO_2 can cross the blood-brain barrier freely, thus changing the pH, but over 20 to 24 hours, with a constant new level of P_aCO_2, the pH in blood and in the perivascular space returns to baseline, and the diameter of the cerebral blood vessels also returns to baseline.[69] With CO_2 reactivity, changes in CBF are compensated for by changes in A-VDO$_2$, so that a constant supply of substrates is maintained at the level set by metabolism ($CMRO_2$). A constant A-VDO$_2$ is a common feature of metabolic, pressure, and viscosity autoregulation; because CBF is tuned to metabolism, A-VDO$_2$ can be kept constant.

Cerebral Circulation and Metabolism after Severe Head Injury

Arterial hypoxia and hypotension It is known from eyewitness reports of head injury and experimental studies immediately after the impact that arterial hypotension and interruption of normal respiration, sometimes with a period of prolonged apnea, are common findings. In the days after a head injury, there are many occasions and opportunities for hypoxic and hypotensive insults. Studies have identified hypotension (systolic BP < 90 mm Hg) and hypoxia (P_aO_2 < 60 mm Hg) as major determinants of poor outcome.[9,19,70]

The effect of hypotension on the brain depends on the status of autoregulation. If autoregulation is defective, decreased BP leads directly and linearly to a reduction in CBF. If autoregulation is intact, arterial hypotension can lead to a considerable increase in ICP, which interferes with CBF by decreasing perfusion pressure.

Elevated ICP According to the Monro-Kellie doctrine,[71,72] ICP is governed by three factors within the confines of the skull: brain parenchyma plus cytotoxic edema; CSF plus vasogenic edema; and CBV. When the volume in one compartment increases, ICP increases unless there is a compensatory decrease in volume in the other compartments. The relation between intracranial volume and ICP is expressed in the pressure-volume index (PVI).[73] PVI is defined by the volume that must be added to or withdrawn from the craniospinal axis to raise or decrease ICP 10-fold:

$$PVI = \frac{\Delta V}{\log ICP_i / ICP_o}$$

where ΔV is the change in volume, ICP_o is ICP before the volume change, and ICP_i is ICP after the volume change. PVI is thus a measure for the compliance ($\Delta V / \Delta P$) or tightness of the brain. Under normal circumstances, PVI is 26 ± 4 ml; 26 ml of volume will raise ICP from 1 to 10 mm Hg, but the same volume will also raise ICP from 10 to 100 mm Hg. Conversely, a change in volume of only 6.4 ml is necessary to increase ICP from 10 mm Hg (normal) to the treatment threshold of 20 mm Hg. Thus, small changes in volume have a relatively large effect on ICP. PVI values as low as 5 ml have been reported in patients with head injuries.

Apart from mass lesions, ICP typically increases after severe head injury because of cerebral edema. Initial compensation is by displacement of CSF from the cranium, which is visualized in a CT scan of the head as small ventricles and basal cisterns. Subsequent compensation would be by a decrease in CBV, which can be accomplished by means of vasoconstriction.

Relation between vessel diameter, CBV, and ICP The total diameter of the cerebrovascular bed determines CBV. Cerebral veins contain most of the total blood volume, but their diameter and thus their volume are relatively constant. Approximately 20 ml of blood (i.e., one third of total CBV) is located in the cerebral resistance vessels (which range in diameter from 300 μm down to 15 μm).[69] Because most autoregulatory and CO_2-dependent variations in diameter take place in these vessels, CBV is determined mainly by their diameter. Typically, the diameter ranges from 80% to 160% of baseline, resulting in volume changes between 64% and 256% of baseline. With a baseline value of 20 ml in the resistance vessels, CBV will range from 13 ml (maximal vasoconstriction) to 51 ml (maximal vasodilatation). Given a PVI of 26, change from maximal vasoconstriction to maximal vasodilatation will be accompanied by an almost 29-fold change in ICP.

CBV, ICP, and CBF CBF and CBV are governed by vascular diameter. Thus, depending on other parameters influencing CBF (such as mean arterial BP, ICP, and blood viscosity), changes in vascular caliber also affect CBF.

Hypocarbia reduces ICP by means of vasoconstriction, consequently improving CPP. However, net CBF is decreased because in Poiseuille's equation, vessel diameter is carried to the fourth power. A randomized clinical trial has shown that preventive hyperventilation retards clinical improvement after severe head injury, perhaps through reduction of CBF to ischemic levels.[74] However, its rapid effect on ICP is a great advantage in cases of acute neurologic deterioration (e.g., in the presence of an expanding mass lesion before evacuation can take place) and should be reserved for these situations.

There are two methods of reducing ICP by means of vasoconstriction without affecting CBF. The first is to reduce blood viscosity. As can be deduced from Poiseuille's equation, decreasing the blood viscosity will, by itself, lead to vasoconstriction, provided that viscosity autoregulation is intact. With impaired autoregulation, decreased viscosity will result in an increase in CBF but no decrease in ICP. However, this effect can be used to maintain CBF under vasoconstriction with hypocarbia. The effect of mannitol on ICP is thought to be mediated in part by lowering blood viscosity.[75,76]

The second method of reducing ICP without affecting CBF is to increase CPP, which can be done by raising blood pressure. Again, with intact autoregulation, an increase in CPP will lead to vasoconstriction, with net CBF remaining constant. With impaired autoregulation, CBF will follow CPP passively, and maintenance of normal BP may be indicated in these cases. More important, however, is the avoidance of hypotension under these circumstances; the effect of CPP therapy may be attributable in part simply to prevention of hypotension.[28,77]

Cerebral ischemia Cerebral ischemia, defined as CBF that is inadequate to meet the metabolic demands of the brain, is an important mechanism of secondary injury in patients with severe head injury, and the adequacy of CBF has been associated with neurologic outcome. In autopsy findings from patients dying after severe head injury, histologic damage indicative of cerebral ische-

Table 5 Changes in CBF, CBV, ICP, and A-VDO₂ Associated with Primary Reduction of Selected Variables[81]

Variable Reduced	CBF	CBV (ICP)	A-VDO₂
$CMRO_2$	↓	↓	—
CPP (autoregulation intact)	—	↑	—
CPP (autoregulation defective)	↓	↓	↑
Blood viscosity (autoregulation intact)	—	↓	—
Blood viscosity (autoregulation defective)	↑	—	↓
P_aCO_2	↓	↓	↑
Conductance vessel diameter (vasospasm above ischemia threshold)	↓	↑	↑

A-VDO₂—arteriovenous oxygen content difference   CBF—cerebral blood flow CBV—cerebral blood volume   CMRO₂—cerebral metabolic rate of oxygen   CPP—cerebral perfusion pressure   ICP—intracranial pressure   P₂CO₂—arterial carbon dioxide tension

mia was seen in 80% of cases.[78] One group of investigators found that ischemia (CBF < 18 ml/dl with abnormally high A-VDO₂ values) occurred in 20% to 33% of patients with severe head injuries within 4 to 12 hours of injury and that the ischemia was associated with a poor prognosis.[79] Of the intracranial lesions, acute subdural hematoma and diffuse cerebral swelling were most often associated with ischemia.

The relation between cerebral metabolism and CBF is expressed in the Fick equation [*see* Metabolic Autoregulation, *above*]. The normal brain tends to keep A-VDO₂ constant and to react to changes in metabolism by adjusting blood flow. When CBF decreases in response to metabolism (as with hyperventilation or decreasing CPP with impaired autoregulation), oxygen supply is maintained by increasing oxygen extraction (i.e., A-VDO₂ increases). A rising A-VDO₂ is thus a sensitive marker of insufficient cerebral perfusion. However, the extent to which oxygen extraction can be increased is limited, and this limit is reached when A-VDO₂ is doubled (13.2 ml/dl). Consequently, any further reduction in CBF results in neuronal dysfunction (i.e., $CMRO_2$ decreases). Because 50% of the energy is used for synaptic activity, a reversible and functional loss is usually observed first. Further decline, however, will result in ion pump failure, loss of membrane integrity, consequent cell swelling (cytotoxic edema), and cell death (irreversible infarction). The occurrence of irreversible infarction depends on both the level and the duration of ischemia. When CBF falls to approximately 18 ml/100 g/min for more than 4 hours, it reaches the threshold for irreversible infarction.[80]

Maintenance or improvement of CBF is thus essential to the treatment of severe head injury, and A-VDO₂ is a sensitive marker of the adequacy of therapy. When therapeutic measures fail to sustain CBF, $CMRO_2$ can be decreased to reinstate the match between CBF and metabolism. CNS suppression can be achieved by administering hypnotic agents (e.g., barbiturates or propofol) or inducing hypothermia. Decreasing cell metabolism will result in reduced production of CO_2, lactic acid, or both and (with blood vessels almost always remaining responsive to perivascular pH changes) in vasoconstriction accompanied by reductions in both CBF and ICP. The relations between CMRO₂, CBF, CBV, CPP, and A-VDO₂ are complicated. An overview is available elsewhere [*see* Table 5].[81]

Altered cerebral metabolism Anaerobic metabolism of glucose to the end product lactate is characteristic of cerebral hypoxia/ischemia.[82] Increased lactate production, hyperglycolysis, and low tissue glucose levels have been observed after severe head injury, suggesting an increased turnover of glucose by the anaerobic glycolytic pathway. Increased lactate levels have also been found in the presence of preserved CBF, suggesting impairment not only of oxygen delivery but also of oxidative metabolism (i.e., of mitochondrial function).[83,84] Data from animal and human models indicate that mitochondrial function is impaired after severe head injury, which may explain the poor outcomes despite adequate CBF levels; ATP generation by anaerobic glycolysis is usually insufficient to maintain the metabolic activity of the brain.[85-87] In part, however, such poor outcomes may be attributable to the effects of lactate production (acidosis), because high lactate and hydrogen ion levels interfere with the functional recovery of tissue.

SPINAL CORD INJURY

Spinal cord injury is often viewed as an all-or-nothing event that is irreversible from the moment of injury. By this view, spinal cord injury is classified as either incomplete or complete. This dichotomy is not absolute, however, because some functional recovery occurs even after severe spinal cord injury. NASCIS II revealed that patients with so-called complete loss of neurologic function recovered, on average, 8% of the function they had lost, and patients with an incomplete injury recovered 59%.[88]

An injury classified as complete does not necessarily involve loss of all connections. Several studies have demonstrated that many patients with a clinically complete lesion show evidence of residual connections.[89] A certain number of intact connections is probably necessary for functional recovery. The determinants of functional outcome are complex, however, and probably include not only the extent of axonal loss but also the level of dysfunction of the surviving axons and the plasticity of the spinal cord.

Animal studies have shown that a small number of axons may be sufficient to support functional recovery.[90-92] Animals recover evoked potentials and the ability to walk with as few as 10% of their spinal axons. Nerve sprouting, one of the mechanisms of plasticity, allows a few nerves to carry out the function of many. Finally, animal studies have also shown that many of the axons

surviving traumatic injury are dysfunctional and that many of these axons have lost part or all of their myelin sheath, which is the structural component that improves the reliability and speed of conduction. 4-Aminopyridine, an axon-excitatory drug used for the treatment of multiple sclerosis, has significantly improved conduction in animals and humans with spinal cord injury.[93] Unfortunately, the drug must be given continuously to support axon function, and this is not feasible in humans because of its side effects (seizures, tachycardia, and hyperthermia).

Injury initiates complex responses in the body and the spinal cord. Ischemia is a prominent feature of events occurring after spinal cord injury.[94,95] Within 2 hours of a spinal cord injury, there is a significant reduction in spinal cord blood flow. It is unclear whether this reduction is mechanically or biochemically induced. Like the brain, the spinal cord possesses autoregulatory capacity (pressure autoregulation). When this autoregulation is impaired, blood flow becomes dependent on systemic blood pressure. In a patient with multiple injuries or vasogenic spinal shock (a lesion above T5) complicating the spinal cord injury, severe systemic hypotension may exacerbate the effects of spinal cord injury.

Edema, another prominent feature of spinal cord injury, tends to develop first at the injured site, subsequently spreading to adjacent and sometimes distant segments. The relation between spreading edema and potential worsening of neurologic function is poorly understood. The inflammatory response to injury is mounted in part to scavenge cellular debris and repair tissue. This response is accompanied, however, by the release of toxic substances, which cause further tissue damage, or secondary injury. Processes resulting in secondary injury involve generation of free radicals, excessive calcium influx and excitotoxicity, the release of eicosanoids and cytokines, and programmed cell death.

Some evidence from experimental studies of spinal cord injury suggests that macrophages may play a key role in CNS repair. Administration of stimulated macrophages to the CNS, where the number of macrophages is limited and their activity restricted in comparison with other tissues, has led to partial motor recovery in a completely transected spinal cord in adult rats.[96] Clinical trials have been initiated to evaluate this approach further.

References

1. Fine P, Kuhlemeier K, DeVivo M, et al: Spinal cord injury: an epidemiological perspective. Paraplegia 17:237, 1979
2. Kalsbeek W, McLaurin R, Harris B, et al: The National Head and Spinal Cord Injury Survey: major findings. J Neurosurg 53:S19, 1982
3. Kraus J, Franti C, Riggins R, et al: Incidence of traumatic spinal cord lesions. J Chron Dis 28:471, 1975
4. Kraus J: Epidemiological aspects of acute spinal cord injury: review of incidence, prevalence, causes and outcome. Central Nervous System Trauma Status Report, 1985. Becker D, Poulishock J, Eds. National Institute of Neurological and Communicative Disorders and Stroke, Bethesda, Maryland, 1985, p 313
5. Factsheet No. 2: Spinal cord injury statistical information. National Spinal Cord Injury Association. Woburn, Massachusetts, 1992
6. Burney R, Maio R, Maynard F, et al: Incidence, characteristics, and outcome of spinal cord injury at trauma centers in North America. Arch Surg 128:596, 1992
7. Tator C: Spine-spinal cord relationships in spinal cord trauma. Clin Neurosurg 30:479, 1983
8. Gibson C: An overview of spinal cord injury. Phys Med Rehab Clin North Am 3:699, 1992
9. Chesnut RM, Marshall SB, Piek J, et al: Early and late systemic hypotension as a frequent and fundamental source of cerebral ischemia following severe brain injury in the Traumatic Coma Data Bank. Acta Neurochir Suppl (Wien) 59:121, 1993
10. American College of Surgeons Committee on Trauma Advanced Life Support Course for Physicians, Instructor Manual, 2nd ed. American College of Surgeons, Chicago, 1985
11. Ritter E, Muizelaar J, Barnes T, et al: Brain stem blood flow, pupillary response and outcome in severely head injured patients. Neurosurgery 44:941, 1999
12. Falimirski M, Gonzalez R, Rodriguez A: The need for head computed tomography in patients sustaining loss of consciousness after mild head injury. J Trauma 55:1, 2003
13. Schroder M, Muizelaar J, Kuta A: Documented reversal of global ischemia immediately after removal of a subdural hematoma: report of two cases. J Neurosurg 80:324, 1994
14. Verweij BH, Vinas FC, Muizelaar JP: Hyperacute measurement of intracranial pressure, cerebral perfusion pressure, jugular venous oxygen saturation, and laser Doppler flowmetry, before and during removal of acute subdural hematoma. J Neurosurg 95:569, 2001
15. Seelig J, Becker D, Miller J: Traumatic acute subdural hematoma: major mortality reduction in comatose patients treated within four hours. N Engl J Med 304:1511, 1981
16. Cruz J, Minoja G, Okuchi K: Major clinical and physiological benefits of early high doses of mannitol for intraparenchymal temporal lobe hemorrhages with abnormal pupillary widening: a randomized trial. Neurosurgery 51:628, 2002

17. Cruz J, Minoja G, Okuchi K: Improving clinical outcomes from acute subdural hematomas with the emergency preoperative administration of high doses of mannitol. Neurosurgery 49:864, 2001

18. Andrews P, Piper I, Dearden N, et al: Secondary insults during intrahospital transport of head injured patients. Lancet 335:327, 1990

19. Jones P, Andrews P, Midgley S: Measuring the burden of secondary insults in head-injured patients during intensive care. J Neurosurg Anesthesiol 6:4, 1994

20. Kirkpatrick P, Smielewski P, Czosnyka M, et al: Near-infrared spectroscopy use in patients with severe head injury. J Neurosurg 83:963, 1995

21. Kanter M, Narayan R: Management of head injury: intracranial pressure monitoring. Neurosurg Clin North Am 2:257, 1991

22. Gopinath S, Robertson C, Contant C, et al: Jugular venous desaturation and outcome after severe head injury. J Neurol Neurosurg Psychiatry 57:171, 1994

23. Robertson C, Gopinath SP, Goodman J, et al: $S_{jv}O_2$ monitoring in head-injured patients. J Neurotrauma 12:891, 1995

24. Stochetti N, Paparella A, Bridelli F, et al: Cerebral venous oxygen saturation studied with bilateral samples in the internal jugular veins. Neurosurgery 34:38, 1994

25. van Santbrink H, Maas A, Avezaat CJ: Continuous monitoring of partial pressure of brain tissue oxygen in patients with severe head injury. Neurosurgery 38:21, 1996

26. van den Brink W, van Santbrink H, Avezaat CEA: Monitoring brain oxygen tension in severe head injury: early hypoxia is related to an unfavorable outcome. Neurosurgery 46:868, 2000

27. McGraw C: A cerebral perfusion pressure greater than 80 mm Hg is more beneficial. ICP VII. Hof J, Betz A, Eds. Springer-Verlag, Berlin, 1989, p 839

28. Rosner M, Rosner S, Johnson A: Cerebral perfusion pressure: management protocol and clinical results. J Neurosurg 83:949, 1995

29. Guidelines for cerebral perfusion pressure. J Neurotrauma 17:507, 2000

30. Kelly DF, Goodale DB, Williams J, et al: Propofol in the treatment of moderate and severe head injury: a randomized, prospective double-blinded pilot trial. J Neurosurg 90:1042, 1999

31. Albanese V, Tomachot L, Antonini F: Isovolume hypertonic solutes (sodium chloride or mannitol) in the treatment of refractory posttraumatic intracranial hypertension: 2 ml/kg 7.5% saline is more effective than 2 ml/kg 20% mannitol. Crit Care Med 31:1638, 2003

32. Doyle J, Davis D, Hoyt D: The use of hypertonic saline in the treatment of traumatic brain injury. J Trauma 50:367, 2001

33. Hudak ML, Koehler RC, Rosenberg AA, et al: Effect of hematocrit on cerebral blood flow. Am J Physiol 251(1 pt 2):H63, 1986

34. Smith M, Stiefel M, Magge S, et al: Packed red blood cell transfusion increases local cerebral oxygenation. Neurosurgery (in press)

35. Marshall L, Smith R, Shapiro H: The outcome with aggressive treatment in severe head injuries, part II: acute and chronic barbiturate administration in the management of head injury. J Neurosurg 50:26, 1979

36. Ward J, Becker D, Miller JD, et al: Failure of prophylactic barbiturate coma in the treatment of severe head injury. J Neurosurg 62:383, 1985

37. Levy M, Aranda M, Zelman V, et al: Propylene glycol toxicity following continuous etomidate infusion for the control of refractory cerebral edema. Neurosurgery 37:363, 1995

38. Bullock R, Stewart L, Rafferty C, et al: Continuous monitoring of jugular bulb oxygen saturation and the effect of drugs acting on cerebral metabolism. Acta Neurochir (Wien) 59:113, 1993

39. Pinaud M, Lelasque J, Chetanneau A, et al: Effects of Diprivan on cerebral blood flow, intracranial pressure and cerebral metabolism in head-injured patients. Annales Françaises d'Anesthésie et de Réanimation 10:2, 1991

40. Clifton G, Allen S, Barrodale P, et al: A phase II study of moderate hypothermia in severe brain injury. J Neurotrauma 10:263, 1993

41. Marion D, Obrist W, Carlier P, et al: The use of moderate therapeutic hypothermia for patients with severe head injuries: a preliminary report. J Neurosurg 79:354, 1993

42. Clifton G, Miller E, Choi S: Lack of effect of induction of hypothermia after acute brain injury. N Engl J Med 344:556, 2001

43. Tokutomi T, Morimoto K, Miyagi T: Optimal temperature for the management of severe traumatic brain injury: effect of hypothermia on intracranial pressure, systemic and intracranial hemodynamics, and metabolism. Neurosurgery 52:102, 2003

44. Atkinson PP, Atkinson JLD: Spinal shock. Mayo Clin Proc 71:384, 1996

45. Hadley M, Walters B: Radiographic assessment of the cervical spine in symptomatic trauma patients. Neurosurgery 50 (suppl):S36, 2002

46. Pech P, Kilgore D: Cervical spine fractures: CT detection. Radiology 157:117, 1985

47. Gerber M, Vishteh G, Dickman C, et al: Fractures of the second cervical vertebra. Neurosurgery: Principles and Practice, vol. 2. Batjer H, Loftus C, Eds. Lippincott Williams & Wilkins, Philadelphia, 2003, p 1755

48. Bracken M, Shepard M, Collins W, et al: A randomized controlled trial of methylprednisolone or naloxone in the treatment of acute spinal cord injury. N Engl J Med 322:1405, 1990

49. Bracken M, Shepard M, Collins W, et al: Methylprednisolone or naloxone treatment after acute spinal cord injury: 1-year follow-up data. J Neurosurg 76:23, 1992

50. Bracken M, Shepard M, Holford T, et al: Administration of methylprednisolone for 24 or 48 hours or tirilazad mesylate for 48 hours in the treatment of acute spinal cord injury: results of the Third National Acute Spinal Cord Injury Randomized Controlled Trial. National Acute Spinal Cord Injury Study. JAMA 227:1597, 1997

51. Hurlbert RJ: Methylprednisolone for acute spinal cord injury: an inappropriate standard of care. J Neurosurg 93(1 suppl):1, 2000

52. Apuzzo M: Pharmacological therapy after acute cervical spinal cord injury. Neurosurgery 50 (3 suppl): S63, 2002

53. Guha A, Tator C, Piper I, et al: Increase in rat spinal cord blood flow with the calcium channel blocker nimodipine. J Neurosurg 63:250, 1985

54. Guha A, Tator C, Smith C, et al: Improvement in posttraumatic spinal cord blood flow with a combination of a calcium channel blocker and a vasopressor. J Trauma 29:1440, 1989

55. Geisler F, Coleman W, Grieco G: The Sygen multicenter acute spinal cord injury study. Spine 26:S87, 2001

56. Marshall L, Knowlton S, Garfan S, et al: Deterioration following spinal cord injury: a multi-center study. J Neurosurg 66:400, 1987

57. Wilberger J: Advances in the diagnosis and management of spinal cord trauma. J Neurotrauma 8:75, 1992

58. Wilberger J, Duh M: Surgical treatment of spinal cord injury—the NASCIS II experience.

Presented at the annual meeting of the AANS, Boston, Massachusetts, April 1993

59. Julien T, Frankel B, Traynelis V: Evidence-based analysis of odontoid fracture management. Neurosurg Focus 8(6):article 1, 2000

60. Hadley M, Walters B: Isolated fractures of the axis in adults. Neurosurgery 50 (3 suppl):S125, 2002

61. Allen BL Jr: Recognition of injuries to the lower cervical spine. The Cervical Spine, 2nd ed. The Cervical Spine Research Society, Ed. Philadelphia, JB Lippincott Co, 1989, p 286

62. Lind BL, Nordwall A: Halo-vest treatment of unstable traumatic cervical spine injuries. Spine 13:425, 1988

63. Denis F: The three column spine and its significance in the classification of acute thoracolumbar spinal injuries. Spine 8:817, 1983

64. Patel N, Hahn M, Johnson J: Lumbar fractures. Neurological Surgery: Principles and Practice, vol. 2. Batjer H, Loftus C, Eds. Lippincott Williams & Wilkins, Philadelphia, 2003, p 1776

65. Kontos H, Raper A, Patterson J: Analysis of vasoreactivity of local pH, pCO_2, and bicarbonate on pial vessels. Stroke 8:358, 1977

66. Kontos H, Wei E, Navari R, et al: Responses of cerebral arteries and arterioles to acute hypotension and hypertension. Am J Physiol 234:H371, 1978

67. McHenry LC Jr, West JW, Cooper ES: Cerebral autoregulation in man. Stroke 5:695, 1974

68. Muizelaar J, Wei E, Kontos H, et al: Cerebral blood flow is regulated by changes in blood pressure and in blood viscosity alike. Stroke 17:44, 1986

69. Muizelaar J, Poel H, Li Z, et al: Pial arteriolar vessel diameter and CO_2 reactivity during prolonged hyperventilation in the rabbit. J Neurosurg 69:923, 1988

70. Chesnut R, Marshall L, Klauber MR, et al: The role of secondary brain injury in determining outcome after severe head injury. J Trauma 34:216, 1993

71. Kellie G: On death from cold, and on congestions of the brain: an account of the appearances observed in the dissection of two of three individuals presumed to have perished in the storm of 3rd November 1821; with some reflections on the pathology of the brain. Trans Med Chir Soc Edinburgh 1:84, 1824

72. Monro A: Observations on the structure and function of the nervous system. Creech and Johnson, Edinburgh, 1783

73. Marmarou A, Shulman K, Rosende R: A nonlinear analysis of the cerebral spinal fluid system and intracranial pressure dynamics. J Neurosurg 48:332, 1978

74. Muizelaar JP, Marmarou A, Ward JD, et al: Adverse effects of prolonged hyperventilation in patients with severe head injury: a randomized clinical trial. J Neurosurg 75:731, 1991

75. Muizelaar JP, Lutz HI, Becker D: Effect of mannitol on ICP and CBF and correlation with pressure autoregulation in severely head-injured patients. J Neurosurg 61:700, 1984

76. Muizelaar JP, Wei EP, Kontos H, et al: Mannitol causes compensatory cerebral vasoconstriction and vasodilation in response to blood viscosity changes. J Neurosurg 59:822, 1983

77. Rosner M, Daughton S: Cerebral perfusion management in head injury. J Trauma 30:933, 1990

78. Adams J, Graham D: The pathology of blunt head injury. Scientific Foundation of Neurology. Critchley M, O'Leary J, Jennet B, Eds. Heinemann, London, 1972, p 488

79. Bouma G, Muizelaar JP, Choi S, et al: Cerebral circulation and metabolism after severe traumat-

ic brain injury: the elusive role of ischemia. J Neurosurg 75:685, 1991

80. Jones T, Morawetz R, Crowell R, et al: Thresholds of focal cerebral ischemia in awake monkeys. J Neurosurg 54:773, 1981

81. Muizelaar JP, Schroder M: Overview of monitoring of cerebral blood flow and metabolism after severe head injury. Can J Neurol Sci 21:S6, 1994

82. Hochachka P, Mommsen T: Protons and anaerobiosis. Science 219:1391, 1983

83. Andersen B, Marmarou A: Functional compartmentalization of energy production in neural tissue. Brain Res 585:190, 1992

84. Inao S, Marmarou A, Clarke G, et al: Production and clearance of lactate from brain tissue, CSF and serum following experimental brain injury. J Neurosurg 69:736, 1988

85. Verweij B, Muizelaar J, Vinas F: Impaired cerebral mitochondrial function after traumatic brain injury in humans. J Neurosurg 93:815, 2000

86. Xiong Y, Gu Q, Peterson P, et al: Mitochondrial dysfunction and calcium perturbation induced by traumatic brain injury. J Neurotrauma 14:23, 1997

87. Xiong Y, Peterson PL, Verweij BH, et al: Mitochondrial dysfunction after experimental traumatic brain injury: combined efficacy of SNX-111 and U-101033E. J Neurotrauma 15:531, 1998

88. Young W, Bracken M: The second National Acute Spinal Cord Injury Study. J Neurotrauma 9:S429, 1992

89. Dimitrijevic M, Dimitrijevic M, Faganel J, et al: Residual motor functions in spinal cord injury. Functional Recovery in Neurological Disease. Waxman SE, Ed. Raven Press, New York, 1988

90. Blight A, Decrescito V: Morphometric analysis of experimental spinal cord injury in the cat: the relation of injury intensity to survival of myelinated axons. Neuroscience 19:321, 1986

91. Blight A, Young W: Axonal morphometric correlates of evoked potentials in experimental spinal cord injury. Humana Press, New York, 1990

92. Blight A, Young W: Central axons in injured cat spinal cord recover electrophysiological function following remyelination by Schwann cells. J Neurol Sci 91:15, 1989

93. Hayes K, Blight A, Potter P, et al: Preclinical trial of 4-aminopyridine in patients with chronic spinal cord injury. Paraplegia 31:216, 1993

94. Sandler A, Tator C: Review of the effects of spinal trauma on vessels and blood flow in the spinal cord. J Neurosurg 45:638, 1972

95. Young W: Blood flow, metabolic and neurophysiologic mechanisms in spinal cord injury. Central Nervous System Trauma Status Report, 1985. Becker D, Poulishock J, Eds. National Institute of Neurological and Communicative Disorders and Stroke, Bethesda, Maryland, 1985

96. Schwartz M, Lazarov-Spiegler O, Rapalino O: Potential repair of rat spinal cord injuries using stimulated homologous macrophages. Neurosurgery 5:1041, 1999

Acknowledgments

Figure 2   Seward Hung.

Figure 4   Reprinted courtesy of the American Spinal Injury Association, Chicago, Illinois.

Seth Thaller, M.D., F.A.C.S., and F. William Blaisdell, M.D., F.A.C.S.

Assessment and Management of Maxillofacial Injuries

Tremendous progress has been made in the management of patients with facial injuries. Reconstructive surgeons are treating an increasing number of challenging facial injuries because of excellent advances in the transportation of trauma victims and the regionalization of care in trauma centers. Although severe facial injuries are often associated with devastating cosmetic and functional defects, reconstructive surgeons are achieving better long-term surgical results and are able to repair certain injuries that were once considered nonreconstructible by employing craniofacial surgical techniques developed through the pioneering efforts of Dr. Paul Tessier, of Paris. These techniques include widespread subperiosteal exposure, rigid internal fixation with miniature plates and screws, and widespread primary bone grafting.

Initial Survey

Maxillofacial injuries are secondary to either blunt or penetrating trauma. Motor vehicle accidents remain the most common cause of facial injuries characterized by bony comminution and distraction. However, penetrating injuries, such as knife wounds, can cause extensive soft tissue injuries to skin and underlying nerves, blood vessels, parotid structures, and other structures of the upper aerodigestive system. Gunshot wounds can cause devastating injuries that necessitate extensive flap reconstruction to provide satisfactory soft tissue coverage of the underlying bone.

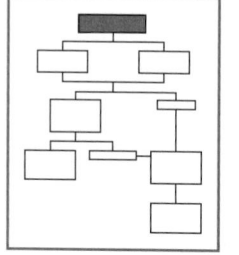

On initial assessment, the physician must always pay special attention to correcting the most life-threatening problems, including an obstructed airway, bleeding, and shock [*see 100 Initial Management of Life-Threatening Trauma, 8 Bleeding and Transfusion, and 118 Shock*]. Patients with facial injuries often have multisystem involvement; priorities in the evaluation and treatment of associated significant injuries are discussed elsewhere. After establishing that the patient is stable, the examiner should quickly make note of lacerations and contusions, extensive bony disruptions, loss of vision, malocclusion, trismus, and bleeding.

In the evaluation of facial injuries, a quick analysis of occlusion provides extremely important diagnostic information that serves as the foundation for future fracture repair. Angle's classification of malocclusion, which is more than 100 years old, remains one of the most commonly used systems. The maxillomandibular relation is determined by the position of the mesiobuccal cusp of the maxillary first molar in relation to the buccal groove of the mandibular first molar. Angle's class I, or neutroclusion, exists when the permanent maxillary first molar is ideally positioned—that is, the buccal cusp of the maxillary first molar and the mesiobuccal groove of the mandibular first molar occlude, resulting in a normal anteroposterior relation of the maxillary and mandibular dentition. Angle's class II, or distoclusion, exists when the maxillary first molar is mesial (i.e., toward the midline) to the corresponding mandibular first molar. Angle's class III, or mesioclusion, exists when the mandibular first molar is mesial to the maxillary first molar.

AIRWAY ASSESSMENT

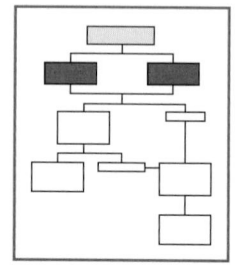

Facial bone fractures, bleeding, loose dentition, debris, and laryngeal injuries can contribute to airway compromise. Accordingly, whenever there is any evidence of maxillofacial injuries, it is essential to monitor the airway status carefully. If the patient is conscious, alert, and breathing at a rate of less than 20 respirations/min, without excessive airway secretions or excessive hemorrhage, it can be assumed that the patient has an adequate airway.

In a comatose patient with compromised vital reflexes (i.e., gag, cough, and swallow), an endotracheal tube must be inserted immediately to prevent aspiration. In the presence of nasopharyngeal bleeding, major maxillofacial injuries, or cerebrospinal fluid leakage, nasal intubation should be avoided because of the potential for intracranial contamination. If there is a possible fracture of the cribriform plate, either an orotracheal tube should be placed or a cricothyrotomy should be performed. In an agitated or restless patient, only a single attempt should be made at inserting an endotracheal or nasotracheal tube; if the attempt is unsuccessful, an emergency cricothyrotomy should be performed [*see 100 Initial Management of Life-Threatening Trauma*]. In slightly more elective circumstances, a deliberate tracheotomy may be the optimal means of ensuring an adequate airway. Cricothyrotomy and tracheotomy must never be taken lightly, because they can lead to significant complications. In addition, because newer treatment modalities using rigid fixation decrease the time required

Assessment and Management
of Maxillofacial Injuries

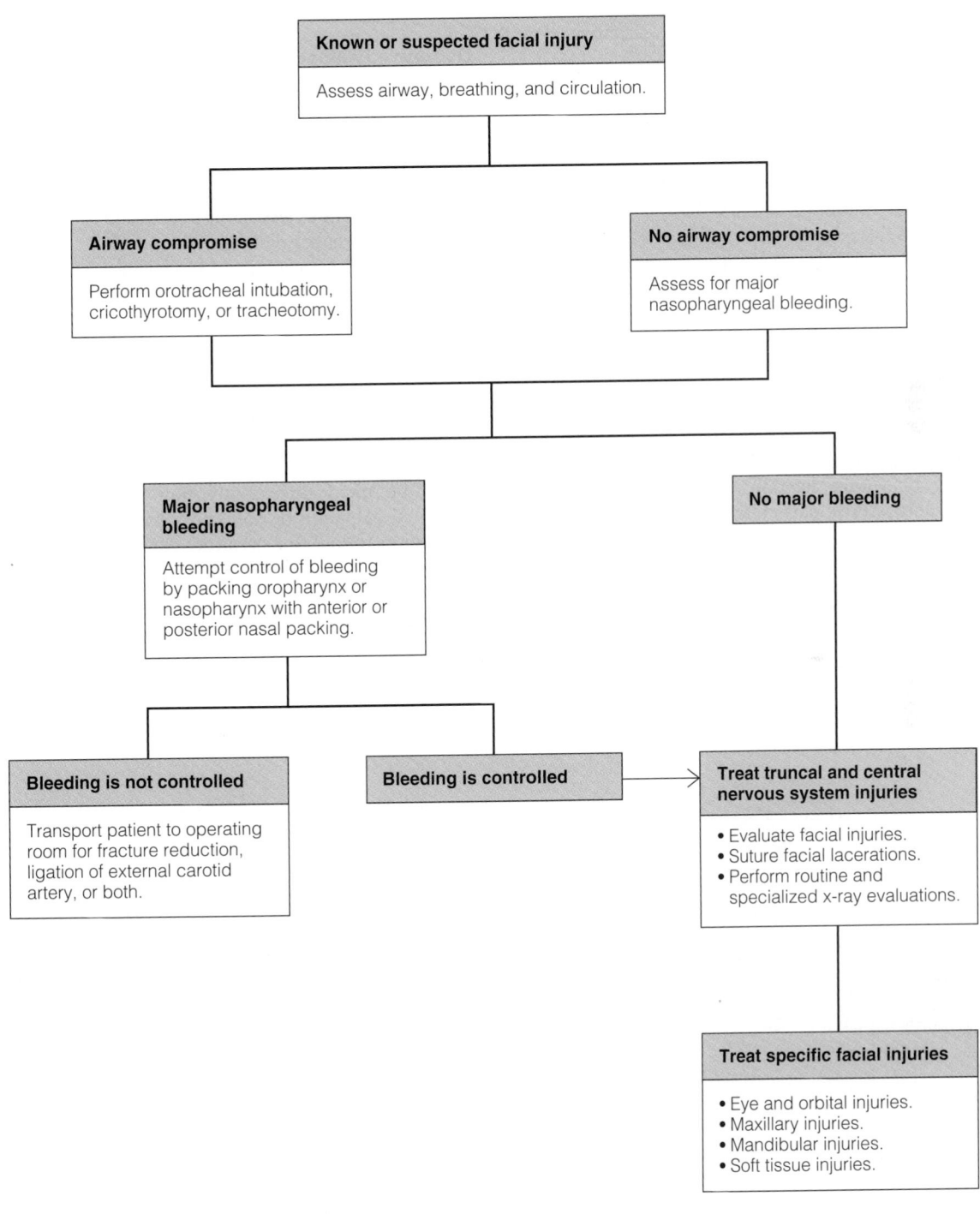

Known or suspected facial injury

Assess airway, breathing, and circulation.

Airway compromise

Perform orotracheal intubation, cricothyrotomy, or tracheotomy.

No airway compromise

Assess for major nasopharyngeal bleeding.

Major nasopharyngeal bleeding

Attempt control of bleeding by packing oropharynx or nasopharynx with anterior or posterior nasal packing.

No major bleeding

Bleeding is not controlled

Transport patient to operating room for fracture reduction, ligation of external carotid artery, or both.

Bleeding is controlled

Treat truncal and central nervous system injuries

- Evaluate facial injuries.
- Suture facial lacerations.
- Perform routine and specialized x-ray evaluations.

Treat specific facial injuries

- Eye and orbital injuries.
- Maxillary injuries.
- Mandibular injuries.
- Soft tissue injuries.

for extensive maxillomandibular fixation, more conservative methods of airway control are often indicated.

If the respiratory rate is higher than 25/min or if there is evidence that the airway is obstructed or compromised, the patient should be carefully monitored. When the respiratory rate increases to 30/min or higher, an immediate assessment of arterial blood gases should be made under close observation. A respiratory rate higher than 35/min is an indication for both intubation and respiratory support unless the cause of the rapid rate can be identified and immediately reversed.

MAXILLOFACIAL BLEEDING

Once the airway has been satisfactorily stabilized, the next priority is to manage maxillofacial bleeding. There is a misconception that patients do not bleed profusely from facial injuries and that facial bleeding can be controlled easily.[1] Unfortunately, this is not necessarily always the case. In addition, because 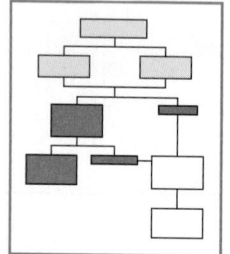 facial injuries themselves can be so striking, associated significant hemorrhage can often be overlooked or underestimated. Firm compression with moist sponges will temporarily stop most arterial and venous bleeding. Careful application of digital pressure or definitive ligation of the bleeding point can often control external bleeding. These procedures are best performed in the operating room, with the patient under general anesthesia.

If the source of hemorrhage is in the depths of a narrow laceration, bleeding can be controlled temporarily by packing. Blind clamping or suture ligation can damage important underlying facial structures, particularly branches of the facial nerve; therefore, such procedures must be avoided. Insertion of an anterior pack moistened with 1:10,000 epinephrine may be used to control nasal bleeding. However, persistent nasopharyngeal hemorrhage will necessitate either placement of a posterior pack or ligation of the internal maxillary artery or the external carotid artery.

In patients with major maxillofacial injuries who are experiencing extensive pharyngeal bleeding, immediate airway access is mandatory, either via an endotracheal tube or by means of cricothyrotomy. Once airway control has been achieved, the patient should be brought to the operating room for reduction of gross bony injuries, which will often stop uncontrollable hemorrhage. In those rare instances when maxillofacial injuries are associated with serious and uncontrollable hemorrhage, it may be necessary to obtain access to the external carotid artery for ligation of the major trunk or a branch if either vessel is the source of bleeding [see 103 Injuries to the Neck].

Definitive Evaluation

When there is no associated airway compromise, facial injuries are a lower priority than potential thoracic, abdominal, or head injuries [see 100 Initial Management of Life-Threatening Trauma]. In fact, in the absence of airway compromise and severe hemorrhage, definitive diagnostic evaluation and management of maxillofacial injuries can be delayed until the more life-threatening injuries have been stabilized and treated.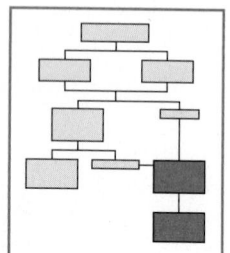

EXAMINATION

Like any other anatomic region, the face must be examined in an orderly fashion, with careful attention paid to gross asymmetry, paralysis, weakness, eye movements, occlusal discrepancies, and ecchymosis. Areas of hypesthesia or anesthesia should be noted. Special attention should be directed toward bimanual palpation of bony prominences within the craniofacial region to look for crepitus, tenderness, irregularities, and step-offs. Palpation should start with the frontal bones and lateral and inferior orbital rims.

The zygomatic arch should be palpated for evidence of depression, and the region of the malar eminence should be evaluated for recession [see Figures 1 through 4]. Fracture of the

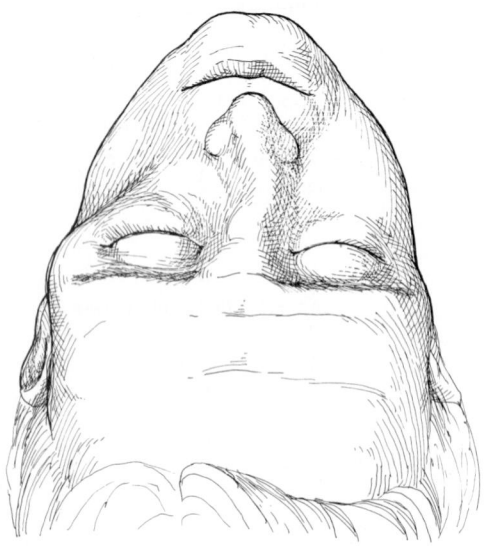

Figure 1 **Broken nose.**

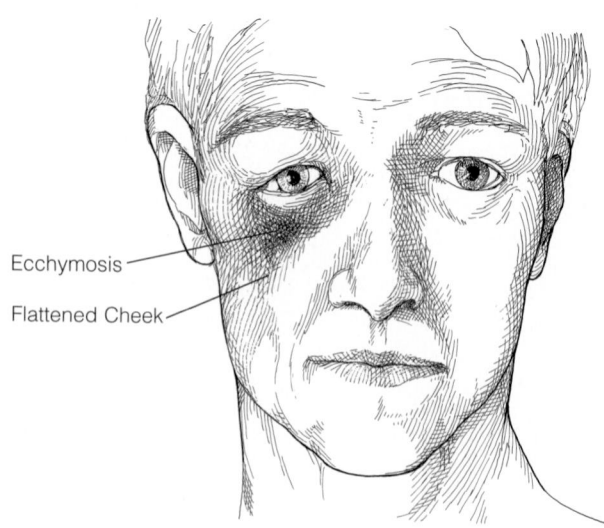

Ecchymosis

Flattened Cheek

Figure 2 **Fractured zygoma.**

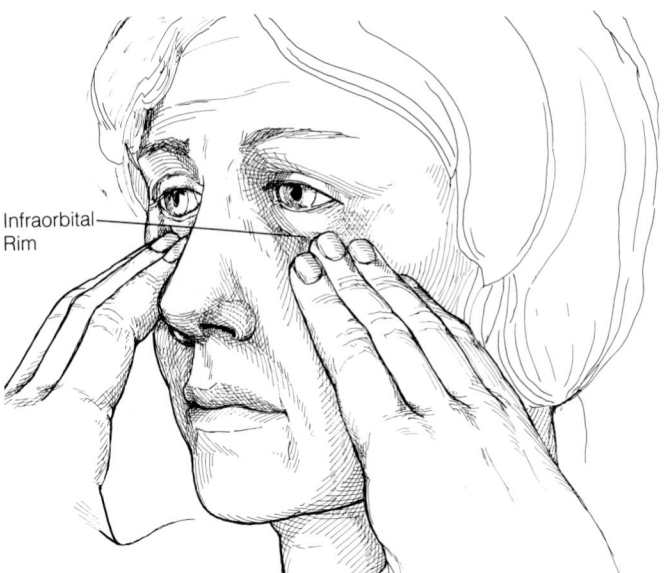

Figure 3 **Infraorbital fracture.**

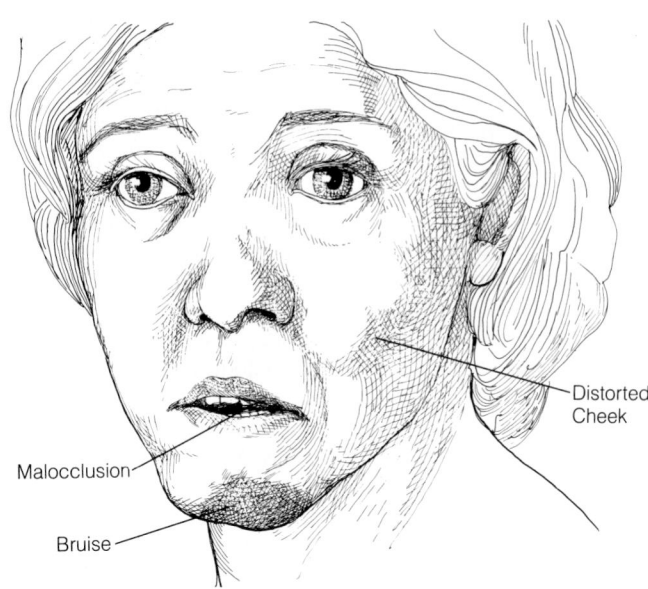

Figure 4 **Fractured mandible.**

zygomatic complex is often identified with an inferiorly displaced lateral canthus, paresthesias of the infraorbital nerve, visual impairment, displacement of the globe, or trismus secondary to impingement of the zygomatic arch on the coronoid process or temporal muscle.

Orbital evaluation is key to the assessment of facial injuries. The nasolacrimal duct should be inspected, and the distance between the medial canthi should be measured for the presence of telecanthus. (The normal intercanthal distance in the average adult is less than 35 mm.) Pupils should be checked for reactivity, and extraocular muscle motion should be assessed. Diplopia secondary to extraocular muscle entrapment should be determined. The position of the globe should also be assessed; orbital floor fractures may cause enophthalmos and severe swelling, and a blow-in type fracture may result in exophthalmos. A visual acuity test must be performed before any surgical intervention for correction of facial fractures. An ophthalmologic consultation is essential if there is any evidence of ocular damage, such as lens displacement, hyphema, retinal detachment, acute visual impairment, or global disruption.

Next, the nose should be gently palpated. Any depression, abnormal motion, or deviation of the nasal bones and cartilages should be noted. The nasal cavity should be examined specifically for the presence of septal deviation, septal hematoma, or leakage of cerebrospinal fluid. A septal hematoma can be ruled out by aspiration with an 18-gauge or 20-gauge needle and syringe; if bleeding is present, an incision and drainage and placement of a drain are necessary. If left untreated, a septal hematoma may lead to the development of a saddle-nose deformity. Flattening of the face, or dish-face deformity, is characteristic of midfacial fractures.

Mobility of the maxilla is determined by placing one hand over the bridge of the nose while the other grasps the palate and upper dentition and moves the maxilla anteriorly and posteriorly, checking for separation of the midfacial structures. The mandible should be palpated carefully with both hands to locate any intraoral mucosal lacerations or lesions. Bimanual palpation of the mandible is accomplished by placing the thumbs over the molar occlusal surfaces and the index fingers externally over the inferior border of the mandible and torquing the bone to check for movement. Any missing or mobile teeth must be recorded. The floor of the mouth should also be examined with bimanual palpation.

The ears should be examined for evidence of lacerations or contusions of the external auditory canal that may be caused by condylar neck fractures. A simple diagnostic method is to insert the fingertip into the external auditory canal on one side; if no movement can be determined with mandibular excursion, a diagnosis of condylar fracture can be made.

FACIAL X-RAYS

A spectrum of available radiologic modalities plays a significant role in the diagnosis and treatment of facial injuries. Appropriate studies are mandatory. In addition, x-rays provide an excellent permanent record for medicolegal purposes. The initial x-rays of patients in the emergency room (the first level for assessment and clarification of maxillofacial injuries) should be performed using conventional films and should consist of a cervical spine series (with all the cervical vertebrae adequately visualized), skull x-rays, and facial x-rays, including the anteroposterior, lateral, Waters, Towne, submentovertex, panorex, and mandibular views. More definitive x-rays can be obtained later for complete evaluation of specific injuries. The Caldwell view defines the orbital walls and the frontal sinus structures. The Waters view is important for determining the bony continuity of the orbit, nose, zygoma, and lateral portion of the maxilla. The lateral skull view is helpful for evaluation of frontal sinus fractures. Oblique views of the orbit are excellent for demonstrating the apex and the medial, lateral, and orbital walls.

The lateral oblique and modified Towne views are used to evaluate the mandible. The lateral oblique is the most common and useful view and provides evaluation of the body, angle of the body, and the ascending ramus. A posteroanterior view is helpful in assessing the symphyseal and body regions as well as the condylar and coronoid processes. Panoramic x-rays are the best screening views for assessing mandibular fractures, especially within the condyles. Associated injuries to the dentition and supporting structures may necessitate dental spot films for more specific information.

OTHER STUDIES

Computed tomographic scanning can be of great value in diagnosing the more complex traumatic injuries, such as craniomaxillofacial injuries and associated central nervous system injuries. Computed tomography is used to evaluate most critically injured patients with craniocerebral trauma, and the studies can easily be extended to include the patient's facial skeleton with little additional risk. Both 3 mm axial and coronal CT cuts of the facial skeleton should be obtained, especially for examination of the orbit. A lateral oblique scan through the midportion of the globe provides additional information regarding the bony architecture of the orbit. This information can be reformatted, and three-dimensional reconstructions can be made for further evaluation. Magnetic resonance imaging is proving to be of benefit in assessing both bony and soft tissue injuries. Arteriography may be needed to evaluate the source of a hemorrhage or to rule out major vascular injuries.

Treatment of Soft Tissue Injuries

Soft tissue injuries are most often the result of penetrating trauma but can also be the result of blunt trauma [see Treatment of Maxillofacial Fractures, below]. Any patients who need general anesthesia, such as a child or a patient with extensive complex lacerations involving deeper structures, should be treated in the operating room after appropriate evaluation of their overall status. Soft tissue injuries can involve nerves, parotid ducts, lacrimal ducts, and other critical facial structures. Abrasions must be thoroughly cleaned, and lacerations should be irrigated with normal saline and conservatively debrided as necessary. With deeply embedded foreign material, debridement and irrigation must be particularly meticulous and extensive to prevent residual cosmetic deformities. Dermabrasion is especially good for large involved areas. Most facial lacerations can be closed primarily with standard suturing procedures [see 11 Acute Wound Care]. Antibiotic coverage is left to individual preferences; however, 24 hours of prophylactic perioperative antibiotic coverage with a cephalosporin is strongly recommended. The examiner must always consider the possibility of underlying injuries, and careful palpation and visualization of important underlying structures should be part of the definitive wound evaluation and treatment.

Local anesthetic agents used in the head and neck region should always contain epinephrine for hemostasis. To decrease pain and discomfort, the local anesthetic should be administered through the margins of the wound rather than through the surrounding skin. Regional nerve blocks are preferred for suture closure of lacerations involving the forehead, cheeks, lips, and chin. The forehead can be blocked by local infiltration of the supraorbital nerve, which is located just superior to the eyebrow. The upper lip, side of the nose, and adjacent skin can be blocked by anesthetizing the infraorbital nerve. Injection of the mental nerve, located between the first and second bicuspids, will anesthetize the lower lip and surrounding chin. Regional blocks also provide the advantage of minimizing tis-

sue damage to already traumatized skin and lead to less scar formation.

NERVE INJURIES

The facial nerve is the nerve most vulnerable to maxillofacial trauma, and its function must be thoroughly evaluated before the administration of any local anesthetic. In addition, facial nerve injuries result in the most serious functional disabilities and aesthetic defects. Sensory nerves, such as the infraorbital and supraorbital nerves, can also be involved in traumatic injures; however, the associated hypesthesia causes only minimal long-term disability.

Whenever the posterior half of the parotid gland suffers a deep laceration, it should be assumed that a major branch of the facial nerve has been divided, and the face should be carefully examined. If there is a clean, sharp division of one of the five major trunks or of the proximal main nerve trunk, it can be repaired immediately with microanastomotic techniques. If there is substantial nerve loss, the nerve ends should be identified and appropriately tagged for future nerve grafting. If a nerve laceration occurs anterior to the region of the lateral canthus, nerve repair is generally unnecessary because there is sufficient crossover from the opposite side. Peripheral branch injury is manifest by inability to raise the eyebrow (frontal branch), inability to close the eyelids (malar), smoothness of the cheek (infraorbital), inability to smile (buccal), and inability to frown (marginal mandibular).

PAROTID DUCT INJURIES

The parotid duct is located between the parotid gland and the oral mucosa, opening opposite the second upper molar. Any deep laceration of the anterior parotid gland can damage this duct. If there is a possibility that the parotid duct is injured, the orifice of Stensen's duct should be probed. Should the probe enter the wound, division of the duct is verified. The proximal cut end of the duct can be located by expressing saliva from the gland. A catheter should then be passed through Stensen's duct and through the area of laceration, and the duct should be repaired over the catheter [see Figure 5].

LACRIMAL DUCT INJURIES

Whenever there is a laceration involving the medial canthal region, a lacrimal duct injury should be assumed. Acute reconstruction of the lacrimal duct is controversial. If both ends of the duct can be easily discerned, the severed ends should be realigned, splinted internally, and repaired. This procedure is best accomplished over a fine Silastic rod. Dissection to locate the residual parts of the duct should be delicate and meticulous, because traumatic dissection can aggravate the injury and result in further permanent damage.

SCALP INJURIES

When scalp injuries are repaired, extensive shaving is unnecessary. Scalp injuries can be associated with profuse bleeding because of the scalp's extensive vascular supply. To obtain adequate control of hemorrhage from the wound margins, closure can be achieved in a single layer with a running, locking 3-0 chromic suture on a large cutting needle. Associated underlying skull fractures are always a possibility, and the skull should be palpated and inspected through any full-thickness scalp wound.

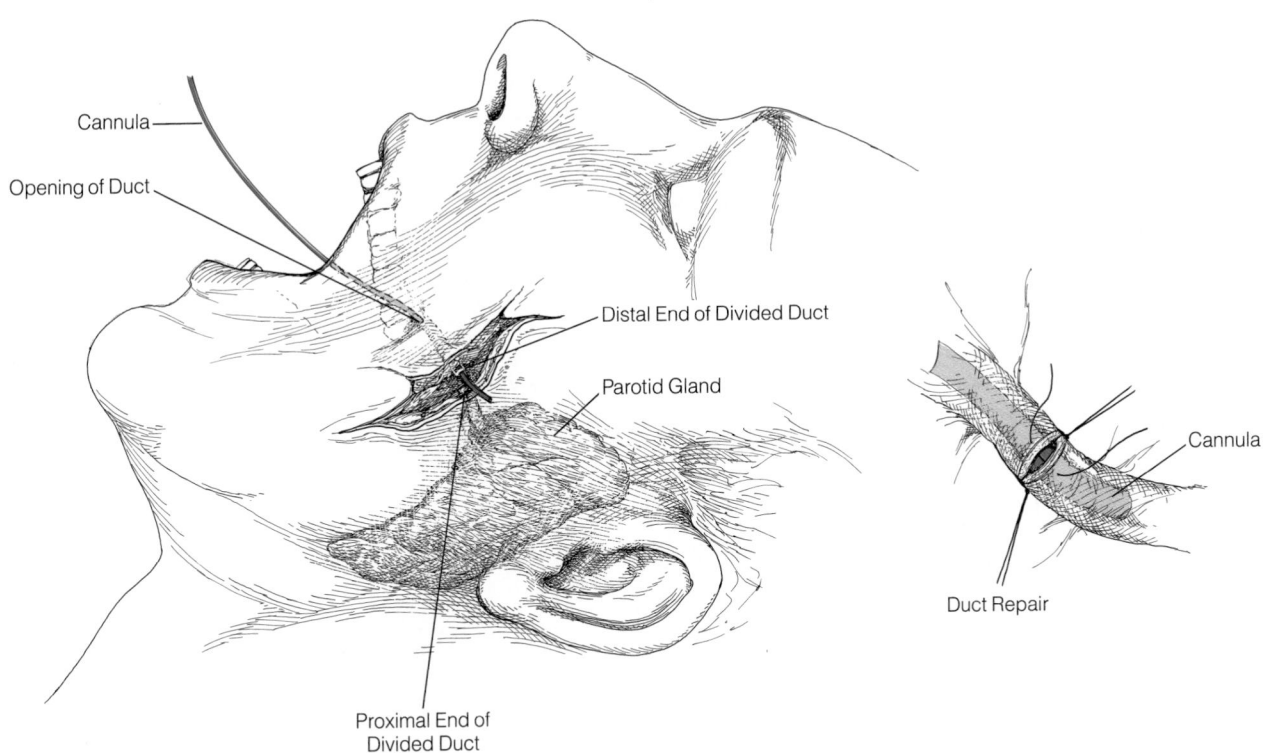

Figure 5 Injuries to the parotid duct are repaired by passing a catheter through Stensen's duct and through the area of laceration and then repairing the parotid duct over the catheter.

EYELID INJURIES

If the patient reports excessive eye pain, the initial examiner must always first rule out an associated ocular injury. In addition, when faced with through-and-through lid lacerations, the examiner must perform a very careful eye examination. Lacerations of the eyelid should be meticulously repaired by approximation of the margins of the lid defect, followed by closure of the laceration in three layers. The conjunctiva may be left unsutured if good apposition can be obtained by closing the tarsal plate and the pretarsal muscles that occupy the middle layer, which is preferably closed with fine absorbable sutures. Fine nonabsorbable skin sutures are employed to close the final layer. All skin sutures should be removed within 48 hours. When there is extensive tissue loss, it may be necessary to use plastic techniques to mobilize sufficient conjunctiva for closure.

EYEBROW INJURIES

For optimal cosmetic results, the eyebrows should be closed meticulously in layers with careful alignment of the eyebrow margins. Lacerations passing through the eyebrow should not be shaved; leaving them intact facilitates good plastic closure. Because the hairs of the eyebrow run obliquely to the surface of the skin, any incision for debridement should follow the line of the eyebrows to avoid further loss of hair.

EXTERNAL-EAR INJURIES

If avulsions of the ear are properly repaired, the chances are good that they will heal because of the highly vascular pedicle. Circulation is maintained if even a small pedicle is present.

Repair of ear wounds should be done in three layers by using fine nonabsorbable sutures to approximate the cartilage and the skin. If the ear is completely detached, the cartilage should be preserved within a subcutaneous pocket in the mastoid region for future reconstruction.

Hematomas can occur secondary to the shearing of the vascular mucoperichondrium from the underlying cartilage. These must be evacuated early, and a conforming pressure dressing should be placed to maintain the normal ear contour.

NASAL INJURIES

Through-and-through lacerations of the nose and near-avulsion injuries are cosmetic problems. Because the nose is extremely vascular, repair of these injuries should be especially meticulous and done in layers. The cartilage and skin should be aligned with fine nonabsorbable interrupted sutures. Absorbable sutures should be employed for repair of the mucosa. Key cosmetic points (i.e., epidermal-mucosal junctions, nasal fold junctions, or critical angles in jagged lacerations) should be sutured first to ensure that no deformity results.

LIP INJURIES

If the margin of the lip has been divided, the vermilion border should be carefully identified and tattooed, and the first sutures should be placed to approximate this critical margin. A common problem in the treatment of lip injuries is that it may become more difficult to identify landmarks when they are obliterated by local anesthetic injections or associated edema.

Treatment of Maxillofacial Fractures

Management of maxillofacial fractures can be extremely challenging. The common maxillofacial fractures include nasal, mandibular, orbital, zygomatic complex, sinus (e.g., maxillary, sphenoid, ethmoid, and frontal), and maxillary fractures (e.g., Le Fort I, II, or III). Management of these fractures often requires sophisticated specialty treatment involving plastic surgeons, ophthalmologists, neurosurgeons, otolaryngologists, or a combination of these.[2-7]

FRONTAL SINUS FRACTURES

The frontal sinus region is prone to injury because of its prominent location and relatively thin anterior bony wall.[8,9] Injuries to the frontal sinus area require comprehensive treatment, often with a team approach. The key to treatment lies in determining the status of the nasofrontal ducts.[10,11] Patients with such injuries also require careful, regular, long-term follow-up care because potentially life-threatening complications, such as meningitis, osteomyelitis, and mucopyocele, may develop.[12-15]

NASAL AND NASO-ORBITO-ETHMOIDAL FRACTURES .

The nasal bone is the most commonly fractured facial bone.[16] Before any treatment is embarked on, it is always helpful to have the patient provide a preinjury photo of himself or herself so that it can be determined whether the nasal deformity is from the acute episode.[17] If a patient is seen almost immediately after injury and the associated swelling and ecchymosis are minimal, closed reduction can be performed at once. Nasal bone fractures can be reduced simply by inserting a scalpel handle or large hemostat into the nostril; the fracture segments can then be elevated and relocated. Usually, the nasal cavity is packed with petroleum jelly gauze to maintain alignment of the fracture and nasal septum, and a malleable splint is taped over the nose to provide counterpressure and assist in maintaining alignment. Packing is removed within 48 hours. However, treatment is generally not urgent and, depending on the individual situation, may be delayed for 7 to 10 days.

Naso-orbito-ethmoidal fractures generally occur secondary to direct force applied over the nasal bridge, resulting in posterior displacement of bony structures and involvement of the medial canthus, lacrimal duct, canaliculi, and sac.[18] Repair of naso-orbito-ethmoidal fractures can be extremely challenging because of the number of important structures involved and their extensive comminution.[19] Satisfactory surgical management should be conducted through a coronal approach, thereby permitting precise three-dimensional reduction and stabilization and extensive primary bone grafting for replacement augmentation.[20] If there is associated CSF rhinorrhea, neurosurgical assistance should be obtained and early fracture reduction done.

ORBITAL FRACTURES

Orbital fractures can occur as isolated events or as a component of more extensive injuries. Orbital fractures, such as lacrimal duct lacerations and injuries to the globe, require highly specialized management with the aid of an ophthalmologist. Naso-orbital fractures with telecanthus should be treated with open reduction and fixation, as should all displaced fractures of the orbital rim and floor.[21,22]

ZYGOMATIC FRACTURES

The zygoma is a tetrapod structure that forms the malar prominence and the inferior and lateral aspects of the orbit. Fractures of the zygomatic complex should be repaired to prevent the development of serious aesthetic and functional deformities. Satisfactory stabilization requires three-point fixation achieved through incisions placed within the regions of the upper and lower lids and the upper buccal sulcus.[23]

MAXILLARY FRACTURES

In 1901, maxillary fractures were classified by René Le Fort into three types.[24] Although the Le Fort classification system remains entrenched in the literature and serves as a basis for both communication and description, it is rare that patients exhibit pure Le Fort fracture patterns. Instead, trauma sur-

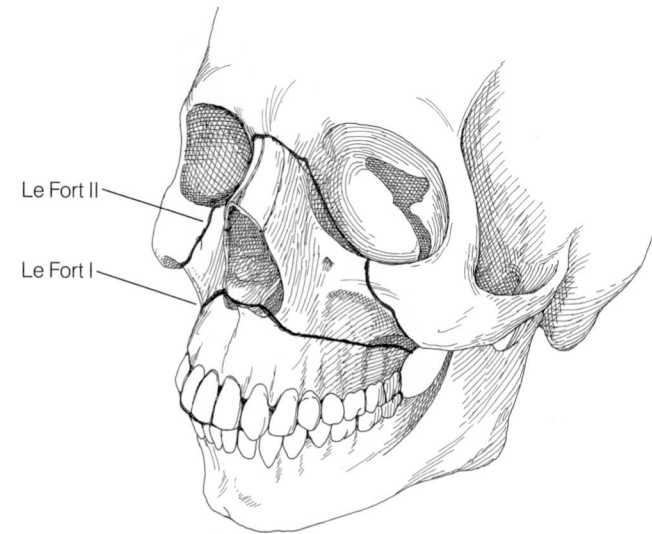

Figure 6 **Le Fort I fractures (black line) affect the upper jaw alone. In Le Fort II fractures (red line), the upper jaw and the central portion of the face are separated from the skull.**

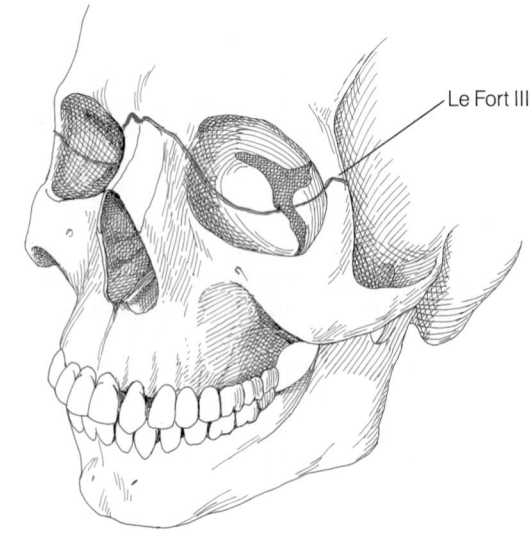

Figure 7 **In Le Fort III fractures, all of the facial bones are separated from the skull.**

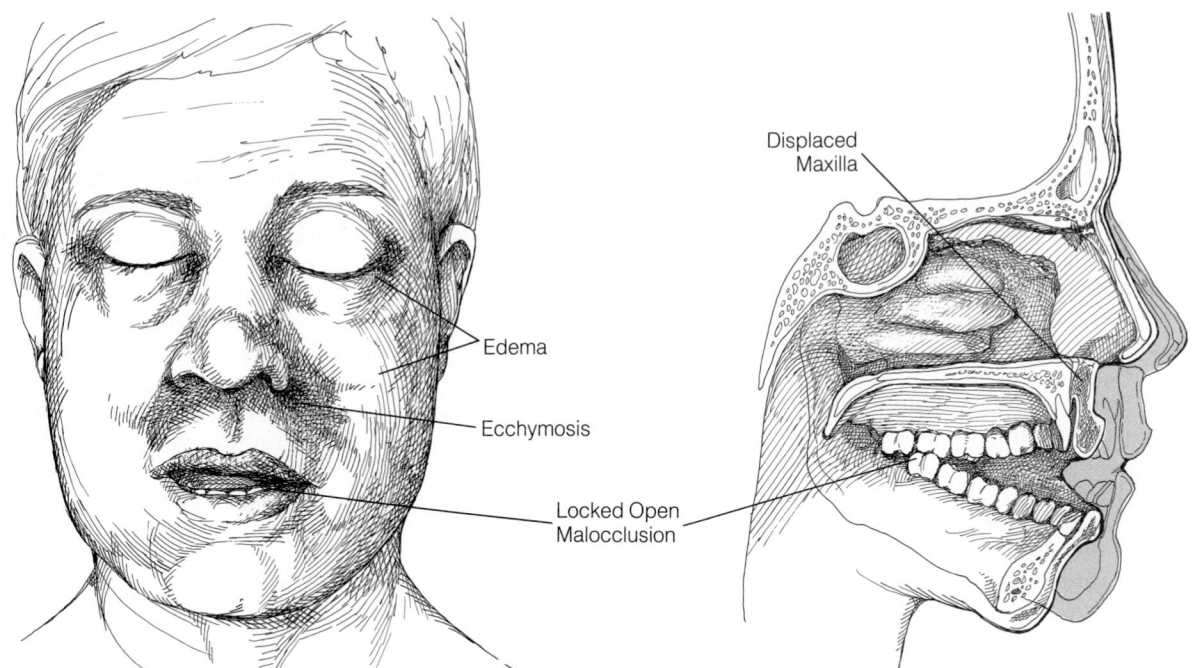

Figure 8 **Findings in patients with Le Fort III maxillary fractures immediately after injury, before obliterative edema develops.**

geons are generally challenged by severe bony comminution and distraction.

Le Fort I, or lower maxillary fractures, are the simplest type of maxillary fracture, consisting of horizontal detachment of the tooth-bearing segment of the maxilla at the level of the nasal floor [*see Figure 6*]. Le Fort II, or central or pyramidal fractures, pass through the central portion of the face, which includes the right and left maxillae, the medial aspect of the antra, the infraorbital rim, the orbital floor, and the nasal bones. Le Fort III, or craniofacial disjunction, is characterized by complete separation of all facial structures from the cranium [*see Figures 7 and 8*]. Le Fort III fractures pass through the upper portions of the orbits as well as through both zygomas.

All Le Fort fractures require highly specialized treatment that involves the use of craniofacial techniques, consisting of exploration and visualization of the entire fracture pattern, precise reduction, and rigid stabilization of bony segments.

MANDIBULAR FRACTURES

Diagnosis of mandibular fractures can usually be made on physical examination. Common findings include malocclusion, intraoral lacerations, and mobility at the fracture site. Radiographs are useful for planning treatment. Fractures of the mandible rarely involve the midline or symphyseal region. Most often, fractures will pass through areas of weakness, including the parasymphyseal region and the angle or neck of the condyle [*see Figure 9*]. The fracture pattern is usually determined by the site and mechanism of injury. Because of the mandible's architectural arrangement, more than one half of mandibular fractures involve multiple sites.

Mandibular fractures are not an emergency, but early defin-

itive treatment results in a decreased number of complications. Preinjury occlusal relations remain the keystone to treatment. Mandibular fractures can be repaired by closed reduction with maxillomandibular fixation or by open reduction and fixation with wire osteosynthesis. However, newer techniques with rigid internal fixation with miniature plates and screws have attained widespread popularity because of increased patient comfort.[25-31] In cooperative patients, a nondisplaced fracture can sometimes be handled conservatively with a dental soft diet and serial x-rays.

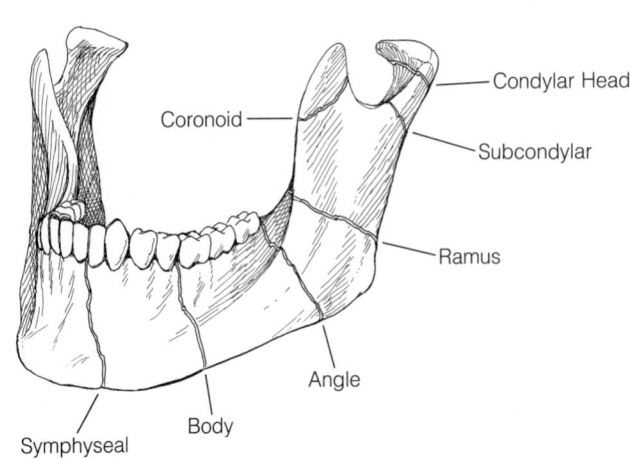

Figure 9 **Mandibular fractures.**

Discussion

Because the face is so thoroughly exposed, it is one of the most frequently injured areas of the body. Facial injuries can occur under a variety of circumstances, such as automobile accidents, altercations, or falls; more specifically, these injuries can be the results of bites, fires, explosions, lacerations, and contact with sharp or blunt objects. In automobile accidents, shards of glass may penetrate the wound, and these shards may not be radiopaque. If abrasions are present, note should be made of the abrading agent, whether it be grease, particles of dirt, gravel from a highway, or other contaminants. Underlying bony injury may or may not be obvious near the wounds. Because such injuries can expose the patient to tetanus or other anaerobic infections, antitetanic agents should be administered as part of the treatment regimen [see 11 Acute Wound Care]. If treatment is delayed for any reason, a systemic prophylactic antibiotic should be administered. Minor lacerations of the face caused by domestic assaults or household accidents can be adequately treated in the emergency department under local anesthesia [see 11 Acute Wound Care]. Lacerations that are contaminated are often best treated in the operating room with the patient under general anesthesia.

Only as much hair should be removed as is necessary for adequate assessment of the wound or for effective suturing. Eyebrows are best left unshaved to facilitate cosmetic repair. Local anesthesia should be induced, and abrasions should be scrubbed with a stiff brush until every particle of dirt is removed. If the dirt is deeply embedded, some tissue may have to be excised; this step can often be accomplished through the use of a fine curette or the point of a No. 11 blade. If dirt is not removed initially, it may be extremely difficult to remove later, and permanent tattooing may result.

Any dead or devitalized tissue should be excised, but there is no place for radical debridement of facial wounds. Tissue can survive on small pedicles. Full-thickness skin loss can be replaced with a free graft, which provides a better cosmetic match than a split-thickness skin graft [see 27 Surface Reconstruction Procedures]. If the wound is so ragged that it cannot be approximated, careful squaring of the edges may be advisable to facilitate a cosmetic closure. Dead or devitalized subcutaneous tissue should be removed conservatively.

Most facial wounds can be closed by simple suturing. Although the deadline for closure of wounds to other sites is usually 6 to 8 hours, facial wounds, unless heavily contaminated, can be closed as long as 24 hours after injury, particularly if meticulous attention is paid to procedural details. Such details include irrigation of the wound, removal of all foreign bodies, excision of devitalized tissue, and accurate approximation of tissue, with minimal dead space and no tension.

If the wound cannot be closed within the first 24 hours, delayed primary closure may be undertaken after 48 hours. In this event, the patient should be given systemic antibiotics, and the wound should be kept moist and protected as much as possible in the interval before closure. For best cosmetic results, the wound should be closed in multiple layers.

Sutures made of fine monofilament nylon, such as 6-0, are ideal for approximating the skin because they are nonreactive. The sutures should be applied loosely so that they do not strangulate tissue.

Key anatomic points should be identified and tattooed, mucosal edges should be approximated, and irregular margins of the skin should be excised and squared to provide the best possible fit. Margins of damaged structures, such as the nose or the ear, should be defined, and the critical margins should be determined and approximated initially. While the wound is being closed, all dead space in the wound should be obliterated and the edges everted. If the needle is passed through the skin at right angles, the edges of the skin will abut and eversion will occur. If, however, the needle is passed through the skin edge obliquely, inversion will result, and healing will be compromised. Subcutaneous or subcuticular sutures should be placed in such a way as to allow the skin edges to be approximated with minimal tension. If this procedure is done, through-and-through sutures can be removed in 3 days, and no marks will be left on the skin.

Any skin defects that require closure should be closed by grafting. No facial wound should be allowed to heal by granulation, because this would lead to excessive scarring. Instead, a temporary cover in the form of a skin graft should be provided to minimize scar formation; any deformity that results from the graft can be repaired at a later date [see 27 Surface Reconstruction Procedures].

The more complex of the maxillofacial fractures, such as major maxillary fractures, orbital fractures, malar fractures, and mandibular fractures [see Treatment of Maxillofacial Fractures, above], must be treated with specialty techniques; therefore, corresponding specialty consultation must be sought. However, in treating these fractures and soft tissue injuries [see Treatment of Soft Tissue Injuries, above], the priorities are to ensure adequacy of the airway and to control immediate bleeding. Once these aims have been achieved, none of the defects described, except for facial lacerations, require emergency treatment; they can be repaired days to even months later, if necessary, without jeopardizing a good cosmetic result.

References

1. Thaller S, Beal S: Maxillofacial trauma: a potentially fatal injury. Ann Plast Surg 27:281, 1991
2. Tung TC, Tseng WS, Chen CT, et al: Acute life-threatening injuries in facial fractures: a review of 1025 patients. J Trauma 49:420, 2000
3. Girotto JA, Gamble WB, Robertson B, et al: Blindness after reduction of facial fractures. Plast Reconstr Surg 104:875, 1999
4. Manson PN, Clark N, Robertson B, et al: Subunit principles in midface fractures: the importance of sagittal buttresses, soft tissue reductions, and sequencing treatment of segmental fractures. Plast Reconstr Surg 104:875, 1999
5. Gruss JS, Whelan MF, Rand RP, et al: Lessons learnt from the management of 1500 complex facial fractures. Ann Acad Med Singapore 28:677, 1999
6. McDonald WS, Thaller SR: Priorities in the treatment of facial fractures for the millennium. J Craniofac Surg 11:97, 2000
7. Mauriello JA, Lee HJ, Nguyen L: CT of soft tissue injury and orbital fractures. Radiol Clin North Am 37:241, 1999
8. Stanley R: Management of frontal sinus fractures. Facial Plast Surg 5:231, 1988
9. Stanley R: Fractures of the frontal sinus. Clin Plast Surg 16:115, 1989

10. Wolfe SA, Johnson P: Frontal sinus injuries: primary care and management of late complications. Plast Reconstr Surg 82:781, 1988

11. Luce E: Frontal sinus fractures: guidelines to management. Plast Reconstr Surg 80:500, 1987

12. Wilson B, Davidson B, Corey J, et al: Comparison of complications following frontal sinus fractures managed with exploration with or without obliteration over 10 years. Laryngoscope 98:516, 1988

13. Shockley W, Stucker F, White L, et al: Frontal sinus fractures: some problems and some solutions. Laryngoscope 98:18, 1988

14. Wallis A, Donald P: Frontal sinus fractures: a review of 72 cases. Laryngoscope 98:593, 1988

15. Rohrich R, Hollier L: Management of frontal sinus fractures. Clin Plast Surg 19:219, 1992

16. Spira M, Hardy S: Management of the injured nose. Tex Med 67:72, 1971

17. Rohrich RJ, Adams WP: Nasal fracture management: minimizing secondary nasal deformities. Plast Reconstr Surg 106:266, 2000

18. Gruss J: Naso-ethmoid-orbital fractures: classification and role of primary bone grafting. Plast Reconstr Surg 75:303, 1985

19. Gruss J, Pollock R, Phillips J, et al: Combined injuries of the cranium and face. Br J Plast Surg 42:385, 1989

20. Manson P, Crawley W, Yaremchuk M, et al: Midface fractures: advantages of immediate extended open reduction and bone grafting. Plast Reconstr Surg 76:1, 1985

21. Koutroupas S, Meyerhoff W: Surgical treatment of orbital floor fractures. Arch Otolaryngol 108:184, 1982

22. Antonyshyn O, Gruss J, Galbraith D, et al: Complex orbital fractures: a critical analysis of immediate bone reconstruction. Ann Plast Surg 22:220, 1989

23. Covington DS, Wainwright DJ, Teichgraeber JF, et al: Changing patterns in the epidemiology of treatment of zygoma fractures: 10-year review. J Trauma 37:243, 1994

24. Le Fort R: Etude expérimentale sur les fractures de la mâchoire supérieure. Rev Chir 23:208, 1901

25. Pogrel M: Compression osteosynthesis in mandibular fractures. Int J Oral Maxillofac Surg 15:521, 1986

26. El-Degwi A, Mathog R: Mandible fractures: economic considerations. Otolaryngol Head Neck Surg 108:213, 1993

27. Eid K, Lynch D, Whitaker L: Mandibular fractures: the problem patient. J Trauma 16:658, 1976

28. Thaller S, Reavie D, Daniller A: Rigid internal fixation with miniplates and screws: a cost-effective technique for treating mandible fractures? Ann Plast Surg 24:469, 1990

29. Bayles SW, Abramson PJ, McMahon SJ, et al: Mandibular fracture and associated cervical spine fracture, a rare and predictable injury: protocol for cervical spine evaluation and review of 1382 cases. Arch Otolaryngol Head Neck Surg 123:1304, 1997

30. Chu L, Gussack GS, Muller T: A treatment protocol for mandible fractures. J Trauma 36:48, 1994

31. Troulis MJ, Kaban LB: Endoscopic approach to the ramus/condyle unit: clinical applications. J Oral Maxillofac Surg 59:503, 2001

Acknowledgment

Figures 1 through 9   Carol Donner.

103 INJURIES TO THE NECK

David H. Wisner, M.D., F.A.C.S., and Robert C. Jacoby, M.D., F.A.C.S.

Assessment and Management of Neck Injuries

Injuries to the neck can be secondary to both blunt and penetrating trauma. Occasionally, blunt trauma to the neck causes injury to the airway, the carotid artery system, or the vertebral artery system. Blunt airway injuries are sometimes surgical emergencies; the approach to these injuries is similar to that of penetrating injuries [*see* Airway Compromise *and* Isolated Laryngotracheal Injuries, *below*].

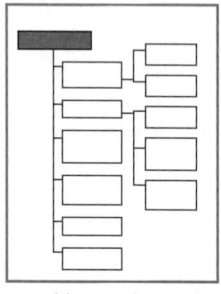

Blunt arterial injuries are almost always discovered by angiography and are usually treated nonoperatively [*see* Discussion, Screening Criteria for and Recommended Management of Blunt Cervical Arterial Injuries, *below*]. In the rare instance of a patient who undergoes operative treatment for a blunt injury to carotid or vertebral arteries, the operative and postoperative principles for penetrating arterial injuries should be applied [*see* Injuries to the Carotid Arteries, Jugular Veins, Pharynx, and Esophagus, *below*].

Patients with penetrating wounds of the neck can be loosely categorized into the following six groups according to the location and nature of the wound:

1. Patients with emergency or impending airway compromise.
2. Patients with an isolated injury to the larynx or trachea.
3. Patients with suspected or known injuries to the carotid arteries, jugular veins, pharynx, or esophagus.
4. Patients with wounds at the base of the neck (particularly when intrathoracic injury is suspected).
5. Patients with known injury to the vertebral arteries.
6. Patients with obviously superficial wounds of the neck.

Division of patients into these groups, though somewhat arbitrary, helps in choosing an incision and determining the initial operative priorities at exploration.

Airway Compromise

Some patients will present with emergency or impending airway compromise. The initial priority should be to ensure an adequate airway. In some patients, this requires orotracheal intubation. In other patients, a surgical airway must be created by means of either cricothyrotomy (in emergency cases) or tracheotomy (in less extreme cases). Nasotracheal intubation is not advisable in most trauma settings.

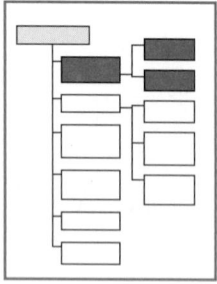

CRICOTHYROTOMY

In true emergencies, a cricothyrotomy should be done. The landmarks of the superior (notched) and inferior borders of the thyroid and the cricoid cartilage should be palpated. For this task, it is helpful to stand on the patient's right side (for a right-handed

surgeon) and to stabilize the cartilaginous framework by holding the thyroid cartilage in place with the left hand. A transverse incision should be made at the level of the cricothyroid membrane and developed rapidly through the subcutaneous tissue [*see 100 Initial Management of Life-Threatening Trauma*]. As with any transversely oriented incision of the anterior neck, the anterior jugular veins are at risk for injury. If such injury occurs, the damaged veins are best controlled with suture ligation after an airway is obtained. In true emergencies when the exact site of injury is unknown, a vertical rather than transverse incision should be used to allow access to as much of the anterior surface of the airway as possible and to decrease the chance of injury to the anterior jugular veins.

After the skin and the subcutaneous tissue have been divided, an incision should be made through the cricothyroid membrane. This is most rapidly done with a No. 11 knife blade. It is important to avoid pushing the knife blade too far and causing injury to the posterior wall of the airway or to the posteriorly located hypopharynx and esophagus. After the incision has been made, the opening should be enlarged by placing the knife handle in the incision and twisting it 90°. At this point, an indwelling endotracheal airway should be placed and secured. In most adults, a No. 6 airway is the largest that can be inserted; a No. 4 or larger airway is adequate for initial placement. Any incisional bleeding from the anterior jugular veins or other vessels should be controlled. Cricothyrotomies should be converted to tracheotomies within 48 to 72 hours as long as the patient's general condition permits [*see* Discussion, Conversion of Cricothyrotomy to Tracheotomy, *below*].

TRACHEOTOMY

In some instances, airway compromise may not be extreme but a surgical airway may still be necessary for safety or subsequent management of a laryngeal injury. In such circumstances, a tracheotomy rather than a cricothyrotomy should be done, because cricothyrotomy is more likely than tracheotomy to make definitive treatment more difficult.

The initial approach for emergency tracheotomy is similar to that for cricothyrotomy, the difference being that a so-called collar incision is made at a point one to two fingerbreadths inferior to the level of the cricothyroid membrane. The incision should be wide enough to provide rapid exposure and should extend as far as the anterior border of the sternocleidomastoid bilaterally. Anteriorly located injuries at the level of the cricoid or the trachea may already have a hole in the airway. In such cases, if the need for a surgical airway is immediate, the wound should be enlarged and used as a route of access to the airway.

On rare occasions, the injury is in the distal cervical or proximal intrathoracic trachea. In such circumstances, access to the trachea may not be possible through a cervical incision alone. Median sternotomy and lateral retraction of the innominate artery and the left internal carotid artery allow exposure of the anterior surface of the trachea at the thoracic inlet. Right thoracotomy provides access to the more distal intrathoracic trachea.

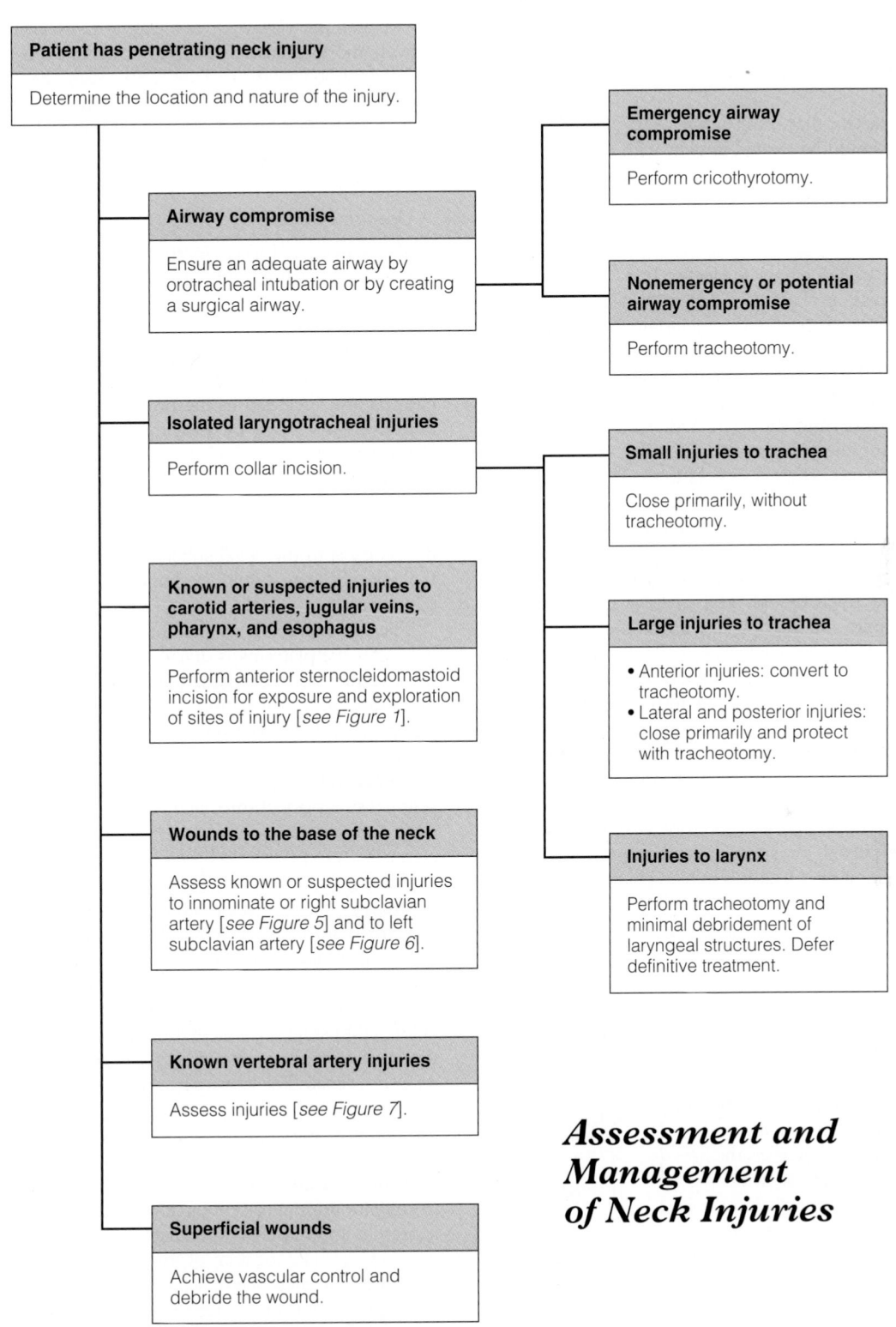

Patient has penetrating neck injury

Determine the location and nature of the injury.

Airway compromise

Ensure an adequate airway by orotracheal intubation or by creating a surgical airway.

Emergency airway compromise

Perform cricothyrotomy.

Nonemergency or potential airway compromise

Perform tracheotomy.

Isolated laryngotracheal injuries

Perform collar incision.

Small injuries to trachea

Close primarily, without tracheotomy.

Large injuries to trachea

- Anterior injuries: convert to tracheotomy.
- Lateral and posterior injuries: close primarily and protect with tracheotomy.

Known or suspected injuries to carotid arteries, jugular veins, pharynx, and esophagus

Perform anterior sternocleidomastoid incision for exposure and exploration of sites of injury [*see Figure 1*].

Injuries to larynx

Perform tracheotomy and minimal debridement of laryngeal structures. Defer definitive treatment.

Wounds to the base of the neck

Assess known or suspected injuries to innominate or right subclavian artery [*see Figure 5*] and to left subclavian artery [*see Figure 6*].

Known vertebral artery injuries

Assess injuries [*see Figure 7*].

Assessment and Management of Neck Injuries

Superficial wounds

Achieve vascular control and debride the wound.

Isolated Laryngotracheal Injuries

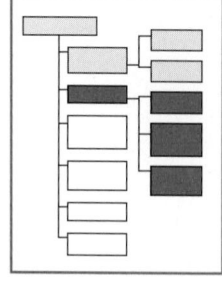

Most commonly, the presence of an isolated laryngotracheal injury is not recognized preoperatively. On occasion, however, isolated injuries to the larynx and trachea are recognized preoperatively on the basis of a suspicious history and the results of diagnostic studies, such as laryngoscopy and bronchoscopy.

Injuries to the larynx that result in airway compromise should be treated initially with a collar incision for the creation of a surgical airway [see Airway Compromise, Tracheotomy, above]; however, definitive treatment should be deferred. Minimal debridement of laryngeal structures should be carried out during the initial operative procedure. Injuries to the larynx should be handled on a semielective basis by otolaryngologists with expertise in laryngeal repair and reconstruction. Further investigation of the larynx, including laryngeal x-rays, laryngoscopy, and computed tomography, may be necessary.

Small injuries of the trachea can be repaired primarily without tracheotomy. Absorbable 3-0 or 4-0 sutures should be placed transversely, if possible, and should include tracheal rings above and below the site of injury. Large anterior defects should be converted to a tracheotomy, whereas defects to the lateral or posterior aspects of the trachea should be closed primarily and protected with a tracheotomy. Tension can be relieved from a repair by mobilizing the trachea proximally and distally. During this mobilization, the recurrent laryngeal nerves are subject to injury if the dissection is carried into the tracheoesophageal groove. Laryngotracheal injuries do not require routine drainage unless there is an associated injury to the pharynx or esophagus [see Injuries to the Carotid Arteries, Jugular Veins, Pharynx, and Esophagus, below].

If a large segment of trachea has been destroyed, primary anastomosis can be accomplished for defects up to five or six tracheal rings in length. Anastomosis requires mobilization of the intrathoracic trachea inferiorly and the laryngeal complex superiorly and is best done electively.[1,2]

Patients with laryngeal injuries should be watched carefully in the postoperative period for signs of mediastinitis, which may result from persistent airway leak or a missed pharyngoesophageal injury. The chest x-ray should also be checked for pneumomediastinum as a sign of continued airway leakage, particularly in patients who remain on positive pressure ventilation.

Injuries to the Carotid Arteries, Jugular Veins, Pharynx, and Esophagus

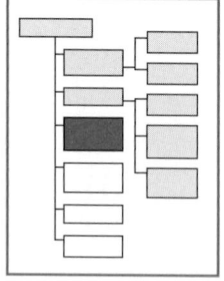

Probably the most common situation in penetrating cervical trauma is the patient with underlying structural injuries, the precise location and nature of which are unknown. An anterior sternocleidomastoid incision provides good access to most of the vital structures in the neck and can be done relatively rapidly.

STERNOCLEIDOMASTOID INCISION

If the location of underlying neck injuries is either unknown or confirmed by preoperative studies to be in the carotid arteries, the jugular veins, the pharynx, or the esophagus, an incision along the anterior border of the sternocleidomastoid muscle should be used [see Figure 1]. The sternocleidomastoid incision is particularly important in patients with a true emergency condition, such as external bleeding, a focal neurologic deficit, coma, or an expanding neck hematoma. When bilateral exploration is necessary, separate sternocleidomastoid incisions should be done.

An anterior sternocleidomastoid incision has several important advantages [see Figure 2]. For example, it can be lengthened to provide more extensive proximal or distal exposure. If a superior extension to below the earlobe is necessary, the incision should be curved posteriorly to avoid injury to the marginal mandibular branch of the facial nerve. Another advantage of the sternocleidomastoid incision is that it provides exposure of the carotid sheath, the pharynx, and the cervical esophagus.

Operative Technique

The patient is placed in the supine position, with the head turned away from the side of exploration and the neck extended. In this regard, it is helpful to clear the cervical spine before operation if possible. If both sides of the neck are to be explored, the head is left in the midposition, facing up. The entire neck and the appropriate side of the face and head are prepared. The anterior chest is also included in the preparation in case a median sternotomy is necessary for proximal control [see Exploration and Exposure, Arteries and Veins, below]. The patient is draped so that the lateral neck is left as the primary field while the chest is kept easily accessible. The lateral chin and the tip of the earlobe are also kept in the field to provide landmarks. If the possibility exists that the injury is to the distal subclavian artery or the axillary artery, the patient's arm should be draped in a way that allows it to be manipulated.

The skin incision is carried through the dermis and the platysma. After the platysma is divided in the direction of the incision, the investing fascia overlying the anterior border of the sternocleidomastoid muscle is incised, and the muscle is retracted laterally and posteriorly to expose the carotid sheath. It is often necessary to divide a venous branch that connects the external jugular vein posterolaterally to the anterior jugular vein anteromedially. This vein lies in a plane immediately deep to the platysma.

Exploration and Exposure

When possible, proximal and distal control should be obtained before exploration of a carotid artery injury. In practice, obtaining proximal control before entering a perivascular hematoma is all that is absolutely necessary. If necessary, distal bleeding can be controlled with digital pressure while the dissection of the injured vessel is completed. Although it is often difficult to obtain control before addressing the area of injury, proximal and distal control of the vessel should be obtained at some point before any attempts at definitive repair. For injuries near the carotid bifurcation, it is necessary to control the common, internal, and external carotid arteries, as well as the proximal branches of the external carotid artery.

Arteries and veins The initial exploration should attempt to rule out arterial or venous injury, unless an overt airway injury is present and requires immediate attention [see Airway Compromise, above]. The location of the carotid artery can then be confirmed by the presence of a pulse. It is often necessary to retract the jugular vein posterolaterally to provide adequate arterial exposure [see Figure 3]. During dissection of the carotid sheath and retraction of the jugular vein, care must be taken to keep from injuring the associated vagus nerve. Jugular vein retraction is facilitated by division of the facial vein, which is superficial to the carotid bifurcation. The severed ends of the facial vein should be suture-ligated to ensure that the ties will not come off with

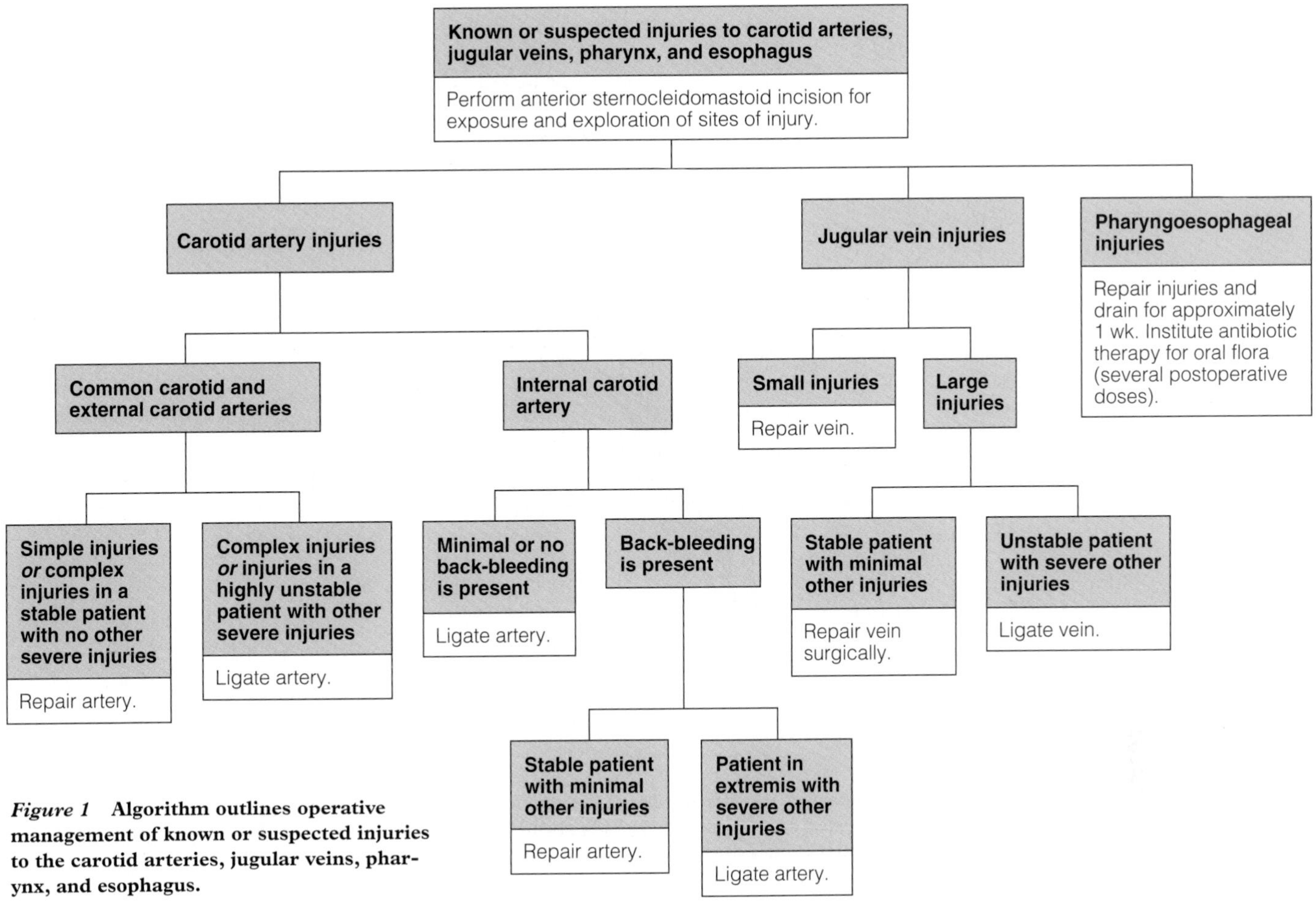

Known or suspected injuries to carotid arteries, jugular veins, pharynx, and esophagus

Perform anterior sternocleidomastoid incision for exposure and exploration of sites of injury.

Carotid artery injuries

Jugular vein injuries

Pharyngoesophageal injuries

Repair injuries and drain for approximately 1 wk. Institute antibiotic therapy for oral flora (several postoperative doses).

Common carotid and external carotid arteries

Internal carotid artery

Small injuries

Repair vein.

Large injuries

Simple injuries or complex injuries in a stable patient with no other severe injuries

Repair artery.

Complex injuries or injuries in a highly unstable patient with other severe injuries

Ligate artery.

Minimal or no back-bleeding is present

Ligate artery.

Back-bleeding is present

Stable patient with minimal other injuries

Repair vein surgically.

Unstable patient with severe other injuries

Ligate vein.

Stable patient with minimal other injuries

Repair artery.

Patient in extremis with severe other injuries

Ligate artery.

Figure 1 **Algorithm outlines operative management of known or suspected injuries to the carotid arteries, jugular veins, pharynx, and esophagus.**

increased intravenous pressure in the postoperative period—for example, secondary to a cough or a Valsalva maneuver.

Exposure of the proximal common carotid artery at the base of the neck is easier after division of the omohyoid muscle at the point where its superior and inferior bellies are joined. Division of the omohyoid muscle results in minimal functional deficit postoperatively. For proximal control of the common carotid artery, it may be necessary to enter the chest via median sternotomy. To minimize blood loss, the decision to do a sternotomy should be made without undue delay. Control of the proximal right common carotid artery via this route is relatively easy and is accomplished by first obtaining control of the innominate artery and then dissecting distally. Proximal control of the left common carotid artery via median sternotomy is more difficult, because its origin from the aortic arch is more posterior than the origin of the innominate artery.

Exposure of the distal internal carotid artery can be very difficult, particularly if there is an injury in that location. As dissection is carried distally on the internal carotid artery, a number of important structures should be identified and protected [*see Figure 4*]. The hypoglossal nerve is usually encountered within several centimeters of the carotid bifurcation and should be dissected free of the internal carotid and retracted upward. This is facilitated by division of the occipital artery, which crosses superficial to the hypoglossal nerve on its course from the external carotid artery toward the occiput. It is also helpful to divide the ansa cervicalis branches that run inferiorly from the hypoglossal nerve to supply the muscles of the neck. Injury to the hypoglossal nerve results in impaired motor function of the tongue and can lead to dysarthria

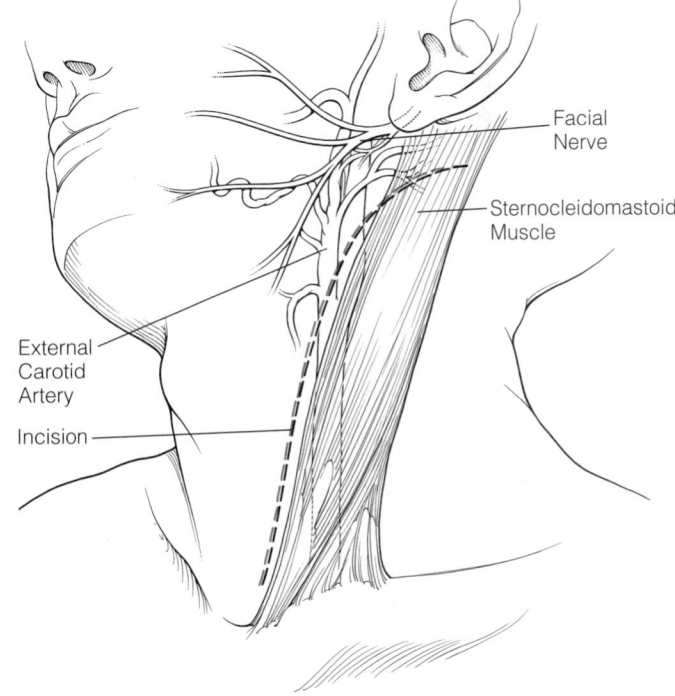

Facial Nerve

Sternocleidomastoid Muscle

External Carotid Artery

Incision

Figure 2 **In general, exposure of structures in the anterior areas of the neck is best done through an incision oriented along the anterior border of the sternocleidomastoid muscle.**

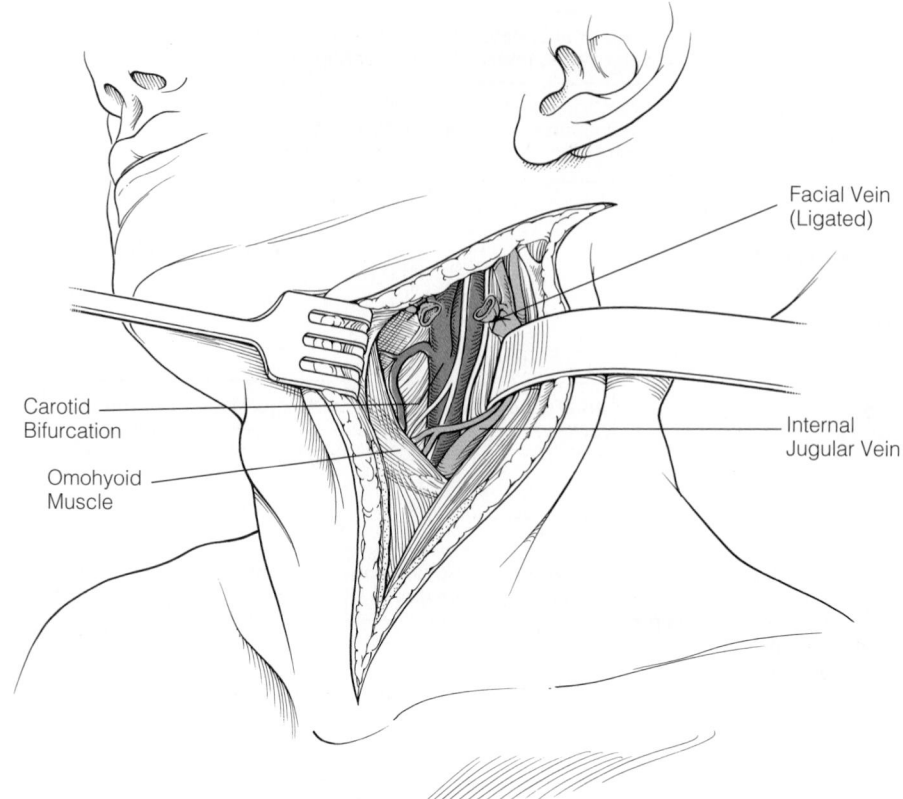

Figure 3   **After a plane along the anterior border of the sternocleidomastoid muscle has been developed, dissection is carried down to the level of the carotid sheath. Suture ligation of the facial vein facilitates this dissection. Lateral retraction of the internal jugular vein improves exposure of the carotid bifurcation.**

and dysphagia. Injury to or sectioning of the ansa cervicalis causes little or no morbidity.

Further distal exposure of the internal carotid artery may require unilateral mandibular subluxation or division of the ascending ramus of the mandible.[3] Such maneuvers are somewhat easier when the patient is nasotracheally intubated. They increase the size of the small area immediately behind the condyle and allow easier division of the stylohyoid ligament and the styloglossus and stylopharyngeus muscles. These three structures can be divided together adjacent to their common origin at the styloid process. If this is done, care should be taken to preserve the facial nerve, which lies superficial to these muscles and must be dissected free of the muscles before they are divided. The underlying glossopharyngeal nerve, which lies deep to these muscles and superficial to the internal carotid artery, should also be protected by dissecting it free of the muscles before their division. Injury to the facial nerve results in loss of function of the muscles of facial expression. If the glossopharyngeal nerve is injured, loss of motor and sensory supply to parts of the tongue and pharynx increases the risk of aspiration.

Once the muscles originating from the styloid process have been divided, the styloid process itself can be resected to gain a further short distance of distal exposure. In very rare instances, it may prove useful to remove portions of the mastoid bone to provide even more distal exposure of the internal carotid artery as it enters the carotid canal. This can generally be accomplished via a cervical incision. For more distal lesions, it is necessary to place a posterolateral scalp incision, reflect a medially based scalp flap, and divide the ipsilateral external auditory canal. This approach results in better exposure of the mastoid process and allows exposure of the intrapetrous portion of the internal carotid after removal of the overlying bone of the mastoid with a high-speed bone drill.

Pharynx and esophagus   The oropharynx, hypopharynx, and cervical esophagus are exposed via the same anterior sternocleidomastoid incision used for arterial and venous injuries. If the patient has a known right-side injury, the incision should be made in the right neck. If the injury is on the patient's left side or if the exact site of injury is unknown, the exposure should be made from the left because the cervical esophagus is located slightly to the left of the midline. After the initial incision, the contents of the carotid sheath are retracted laterally to expose the lateral aspects of the pharynx and the esophagus. This maneuver is made easier if the anesthesiologist places a large colored esophageal dilator through the mouth. The dilator makes identification of the otherwise flat esophagus easier, and the colored tubing of the dilator can sometimes be seen through defects in the esophageal wall.[4]

Sometimes, a pharyngoesophageal injury is suspected but cannot be confirmed preoperatively. In such cases—especially when the injury is more than 1 or 2 hours old—salivary amylase may be present in the wound, giving the surgeon's gloves a greasy feel. The presence of salivary amylase can be a valuable clue to the existence of an otherwise unknown occult injury.

CAROTID ARTERY INJURIES

During dissection of the external carotid artery, the branches should be identified. They can be ligated if necessary but should be preserved if possible (this usually depends on whether they can be temporarily occluded with vessel loops, a looped suture, or

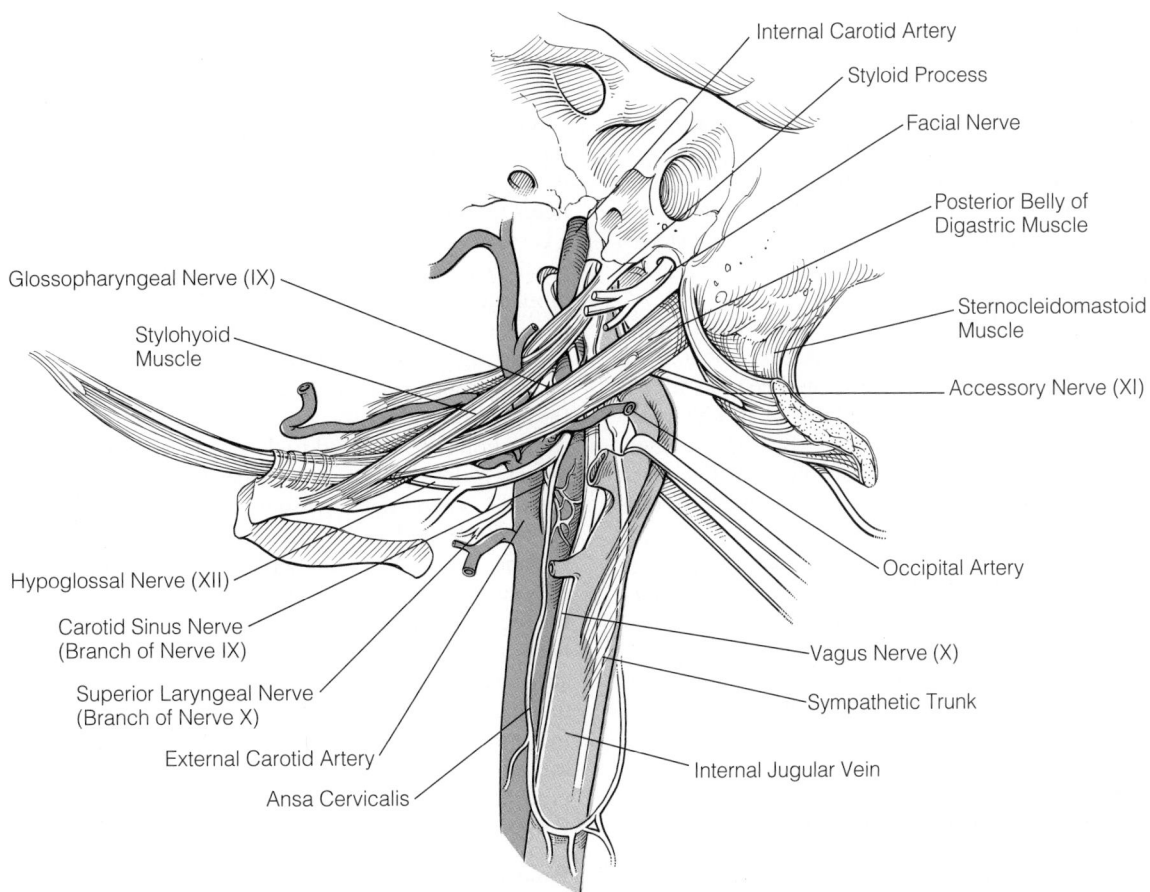

Internal Carotid Artery

Styloid Process

Facial Nerve

Posterior Belly of
Digastric Muscle

Sternocleidomastoid
Muscle

Accessory Nerve (XI)

Glossopharyngeal Nerve (IX)

Stylohyoid
Muscle

Hypoglossal Nerve (XII)

Carotid Sinus Nerve
(Branch of Nerve IX)

Superior Laryngeal Nerve
(Branch of Nerve X)

External Carotid Artery

Ansa Cervicalis

Occipital Artery

Vagus Nerve (X)

Sympathetic Trunk

Internal Jugular Vein

Figure 4 **During distal dissection of the internal and external carotid arteries, a number of important structures are encountered, including the hypoglossal nerve and the occipital artery.**

clips). During dissection around the common and internal carotid arteries, care should be taken to avoid cutting or clamping the posterolaterally located vagus nerve; the recurrent laryngeal nerve runs with the vagus nerve at this level, and damage to the laryngeal nerve can lead to paralysis of the ipsilateral vocal cord.

For wounds of the distal internal carotid artery, distal control may be a problem, particularly in the presence of vigorous ongoing bleeding, in which case a 3 to 5 French Fogarty balloon catheter should be placed through the area of injury or through a proximal arteriotomy. The catheter should be advanced distally, and the balloon should be inflated to provide a dry field for arterial repair. Repair can be done around the catheter; the balloon is deflated near the conclusion of the repair, and the catheter is removed before the final several sutures are tied.

If associated injuries allow, a 5,000 to 10,000 unit bolus of heparin should be given before any of the arteries in the neck are occluded. Because they have no branches, the common and internal carotid arteries can be safely mobilized for some distance from the injury to ensure a tension-free repair.

Management of common or external carotid artery injuries is governed by the extent of injury and the overall status of the patient. Small, simple injuries should be repaired. Complex injuries should be repaired in stable patients and ligated in patients with severe hemodynamic instability or major associated injuries.

Initial management of injuries to the internal carotid artery depends on a determination of the amount of back-bleeding from the artery distal to the site of injury.[5,6] If back-bleeding is minimal or absent, the artery should be ligated. If significant back-bleeding is present, the overall status of the patient and the nature of the

associated injuries should be taken into account [*see* Discussion, Repair versus Ligation of Carotid Arteries, *below*]. If the patient is hemodynamically stable and has minimal or moderate associated injuries, the internal carotid artery should be repaired. If the patient is hemodynamically unstable or has devastating associated injuries, the internal carotid artery should be ligated even when back-bleeding is present.

If a carotid artery injury involves minimal loss of vascular wall, primary repair is straightforward and can be done with either a continuous or an interrupted technique; interrupted sutures will not purse-string the vessel. In younger patients who are still growing, interrupted sutures should be used to prevent later stenosis. As in elective vascular surgery, nonabsorbable sutures should be used; the carotid arteries generally require a 5-0, 6-0, or 7-0 monofilament suture, depending on the location of the injury and the type of suture material employed.

Defects longer than 1 to 2 cm should not be repaired primarily, because this will place excessive tension on the repair. For large defects limited to one surface of the vessel, a patch repair should be done. Either a venous patch or a synthetic patch can be used; when available, a venous patch is preferred for better long-term patency and to avoid placing a foreign body in a potentially contaminated wound. Saphenous vein from the groin is preferable for patches because of its durability; a saphenous vein from the ankle is easiest to harvest when time is of the essence. Although the jugular vein is in the operative field and can be easily harvested, it is better not to interfere with venous outflow in a neck in which the arterial inflow is to undergo repair; in addition, the jugular vein is very thin and difficult to handle.

For repairs near the carotid bifurcation, an alternative to venous patches and synthetic patches is the use of the proximal external carotid artery. This approach is especially appropriate when the origin of the external carotid artery is itself involved in the area of injury. If the injury is to the proximal internal carotid artery and the origin of the external carotid artery is free of injury, it is better to leave the external carotid artery patent and to use a venous patch or a synthetic patch instead; if the repair fails, the external carotid artery provides collateral distribution to the internal carotid artery via the ophthalmic artery.

Repair of circumferential loss of the common or internal carotid arteries is difficult. In this circumstance, if the defect is too long for primary anastomosis and the patient's general and neurologic condition permits, an interposition graft is indicated. As with patch grafts, though either venous or synthetic material can be used, saphenous vein from the groin is generally the donor material of first choice because of its strength. The saphenous vein from the groin is also well suited for reconstruction of the common carotid artery.

Completion angiography should be done after interposition graft placements and complex repairs of the common or internal carotid arteries. In general, patients with carotid artery injuries should be admitted postoperatively to an intensive care unit. ICU observation need not be prolonged but should be continued for at least 12 to 24 hours postoperatively. In the early postoperative period, the patient should be observed for bleeding or for the development of a neck hematoma; large postoperative hematomas may compromise the airway. If a tense hematoma develops postoperatively, the neck should be reexplored. Acute changes in the neurologic examination are a potential sign of thrombosis or embolism from the site of injury and should prompt further investigation or reexploration.

Labile blood pressure—particularly in patients with extensive dissection around the carotid bifurcation—is another potential postoperative problem. It is related to manipulation of the carotid body, and control may require pharmacologic intervention. Labile blood pressure is usually self-limiting and disappears over the first 1 to 3 days after operation, but it is another reason why patients with carotid artery repairs should be monitored initially in the ICU.

Antibiotics should be administered to cover common skin flora and should generally be continued only for one or two postoperative doses.

JUGULAR VEIN INJURIES

Any of the veins in the neck can be ligated when necessary. An exception to this rule is the rare instance when both internal jugular veins have been injured, in which case an attempt should be made to repair one of the veins, if possible. Even in such cases, however, bilateral internal jugular ligation, if necessary, is usually tolerated. It is particularly important to use suture ligatures rather than simple ligatures on the cut ends of the internal jugular vein.

If the injury to the internal jugular is simple, the vein should be repaired. Large jugular vein injuries should be repaired only if the patient's general condition and associated injuries allow; if the patient is hemodynamically unstable or has severe associated injuries, large jugular vein injuries should be treated with ligation.

It is not always necessary to encircle the jugular vein completely both proximal and distal to the site of injury; pressure with a finger or a sponge stick sometimes suffices to control bleeding while simple lateral venorrhaphy is done. In the case of more elaborate repairs, it is better either to encircle and occlude the proximal and distal vein or to place a side-biting vascular clamp for control during repair. Nonabsorbable 4-0 or 5-0 sutures should be used.

PHARYNGOESOPHAGEAL INJURIES

Injuries to the pharynx and the esophagus may be repaired in either one or two layers with either 3-0 or 4-0 absorbable sutures. Attempts should be made to repair nearly all injuries, even when they are severe or their discovery is delayed. In extreme cases of very large injuries or very delayed operative intervention, it may be necessary simply to drain the neck widely and turn the injury into a cervical esophagostomy. Esophageal diversion with distal esophageal ligation is rarely necessary in patients with isolated cervical esophageal injuries, except when the injury is very low in the neck or in the thoracic esophagus.

Pharyngoesophageal injuries should be drained; either closed or Penrose drainage can be used. The drains should be left in place for approximately 1 week, at which time a radiographic contrast study should be obtained to determine whether the repair is competent. If the contrast study is negative for extravasation and the patient's general status permits, feeding can begin. If the feedings are well tolerated, the drains can be removed.

Patients with pharyngoesophageal injuries should receive several postoperative doses of antibiotics appropriate for oral flora. If the repair is inadequate or breaks down, the resultant fistula often heals with nonoperative management, provided that drainage is adequate. A high index of suspicion for mediastinitis should be maintained; the prevertebral space provides a ready route of access from the pharynx and the cervical esophagus into the mediastinum. Missed or inadequately drained injuries may result in profound infection and a septic response.

Wounds at the Base of the Neck

Patients with wounds at the base of the neck should be identified early—particularly when an intrathoracic injury is suspected—so that the appropriate incision and operative approach can be undertaken.

A median sternotomy should be done for unstable patients with injuries at the base of the right neck or patients in whom the superior mediastinum is the most like-

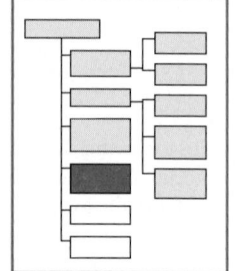

ly site of injury and the most likely arterial injuries are to either the innominate artery or the right subclavian artery [see Figure 5]. Exposure of injuries to the proximal left subclavian artery is extremely difficult via sternotomy because of the artery's posterior location; in patients with such injuries, a left thoracotomy is needed [see Figure 6]. If it appears likely that a left thoracotomy will be necessary, it is helpful to bump up the patient's left hip and shoulder to position the left chest 20° to 30° anteriorly. The head is turned to the right, and the left arm is prepared as far as the elbow and draped so as to allow it free movement. Moving the arm is helpful when proximal exposure and control are obtained through the chest and distal exposure and control are obtained through a supraclavicular incision. It also allows improved exposure of the axillary artery if necessary.

In stable patients with angiographically diagnosed injuries to either subclavian artery, a supraclavicular approach alone can be used, thereby eliminating the need for initial entry into the chest. Because proximal control may not be feasible via this limited incision, the patient should still be positioned, prepared, and draped so that sternotomy or thoracotomy is possible. If the injury is on the right side of the neck and proximal control is not possible, a median sternotomy should be done. If the injury is on the left side of the neck and proximal control is not possible, a left thoracotomy should be performed.

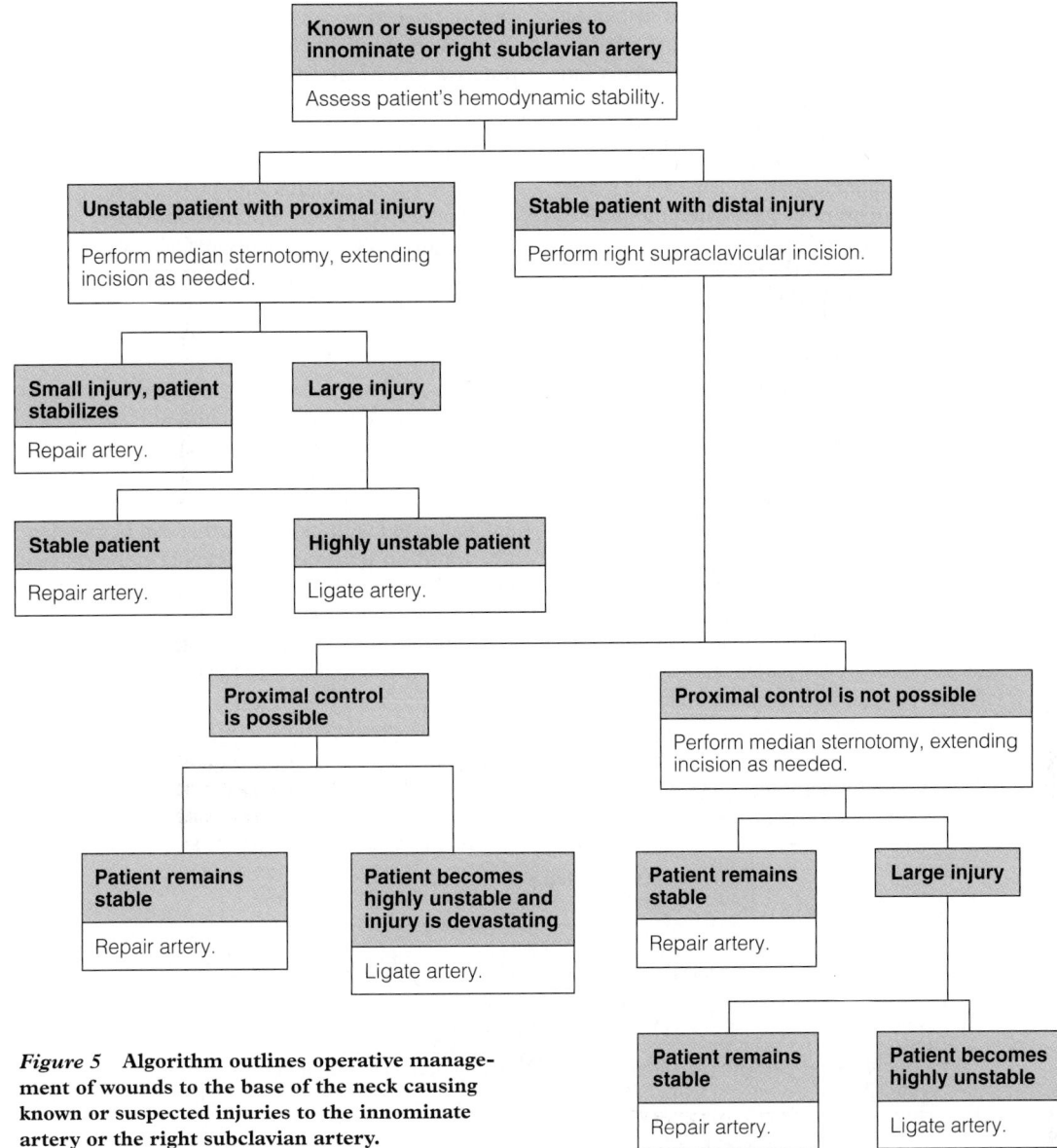

Figure 5 Algorithm outlines operative management of wounds to the base of the neck causing known or suspected injuries to the innominate artery or the right subclavian artery.

If a median sternotomy has been done for exposure of an innominate artery or right subclavian artery injury, it may prove necessary to extend the incision into the right neck to obtain adequate distal control and exposure. Either a right supraclavicular or an anterior sternocleidomastoid extension can be used. Although both are easily accomplished, the anterior sternocleidomastoid extension is the more versatile of the two. If a left thoracotomy is done for proximal control and exposure of the left subclavian artery, the distal subclavian artery should be exposed via a left supraclavicular incision. Improved exposure of the left subclavian artery at the thoracic outlet can be obtained either by resecting the medial one third to one half of the left clavicle or by making a so-called trapdoor incision. The trapdoor incision consists of a superior sternotomy and connection of the medial aspects of the thoracotomy and supraclavicular incisions. We find the trapdoor approach limited and cumbersome and strongly prefer clavicular resection. Medial clavicular resection is accomplished by encircling the midclavicle in the subperiosteal plane via the supraclavicular incision. A Gigli wire saw is passed around the clavicle, and the clavicle is divided. The medial aspect of the divided bone is then grasped with a bone hook or a Kocher clamp, and the dissection is carried medially in the subperiosteal plane to the sternoclavicular joint, which is disarticulated.[7] If necessary, this dissection and resection can be accomplished in a matter of a few minutes.

After adequate exposure and control of innominate or subclavian artery injuries have been obtained, further management is determined by the nature of the injury and the status of the patient. Small injuries should always be repaired. Large injuries are not often seen, because they are usually incompatible with survival to a point where medical attention is available. Nonetheless, such injuries do occur, and their management is influenced by the status of the patient. Attempts at repair should be made for most such injuries, but in highly unstable patients, the artery should be ligated. However, arterial ligation is sometimes associated with severe morbidity and should therefore be avoided if possible.

The wall of the subclavian artery is thin, and extra care should be taken in dissecting around it. Primary repair should be done with either interrupted or continuous nonabsorbable 4-0 or 5-0 sutures, laterally placed. Because of its location and the large number of branches, the subclavian artery is difficult to mobilize extensively. None of the branches are vital, however, and all can be divided as necessary to gain mobility. The origin of the vertebral artery should be preserved if possible, because in rare instances, ligation of the artery can lead to cerebral ischemia. Even with division of arterial branches, only short segments of the subclavian artery can be removed without the need for an interposition graft to prevent an anastomosis under tension. The saphenous vein is usually too small to be used as a graft, even when it is harvested from the groin. Accordingly, a synthetic graft is usually the better choice. Infections in this location are rare, even when the graft is placed in a contaminated field.[8]

Complex injuries of the innominate and subclavian veins should be treated with suture ligation, particularly when the patient has severe associated injuries. Simple injuries can be treated with lateral venorrhaphy. Depending on the circumstances, formal control of the proximal and distal vein can first be obtained, or pressure can be applied proximally and distally to provide for a bloodless field during repair. Another alternative for control of bleeding during venous repair is the use of a side-biting vascular clamp.

Some patients with injuries to the subclavian artery or the subclavian vein require dissection of the supraclavicular area. The supraclavicular fat pad contains a large number of lymph nodes and lymphatic channels, and dissection of the fat pad can result in considerable weeping of lymphatic fluid; these wounds should therefore be drained. Either a closed or an open drain can be used, and the drain should be brought out through a separate stab wound near the incision. After a left-side procedure, persistent milky drainage via either drains or the wound suggests injury to the thoracic duct and may necessitate repeat operative intervention if it persists.

Elevation or paralysis of the hemidiaphragm ipsilateral to the side of dissection can indicate injury to the phrenic nerve, which courses in the field of dissection on the anterior surface of the anterior scalene muscle.

Known Vertebral Artery Injuries

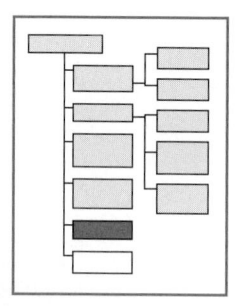

On occasion, patients who present with penetrating cervical wounds and are hemodynamically and neurologically stable are demonstrated on angiographic workup to have an injury to the vertebral artery. In rarer instances, the location of an injury in the posterior triangle of the neck and the presence of ongoing hemorrhage may also indicate the high likelihood of an injury to the distal vertebral artery [see Figure 7].

Most vertebral artery injuries occur in stable patients and are discovered on angiography. Because operative attempts at ligation are associated with blood loss that can be problematic, an alternative approach utilizing angiographic embolization has been developed.[9] In most cases of injury to the distal vertebral artery, the angiographic approach is preferred if available [see Discussion, Angiographic Embolization of Distal Vertebral Artery Injuries, below]. If angiographic expertise is not available and the patient is stable enough for transfer, it is preferable to send the patient to a center with angiographic embolization capability if at all possible. In urgent circumstances, an angiographic approach is not practical, and a direct surgical approach is necessary.[10]

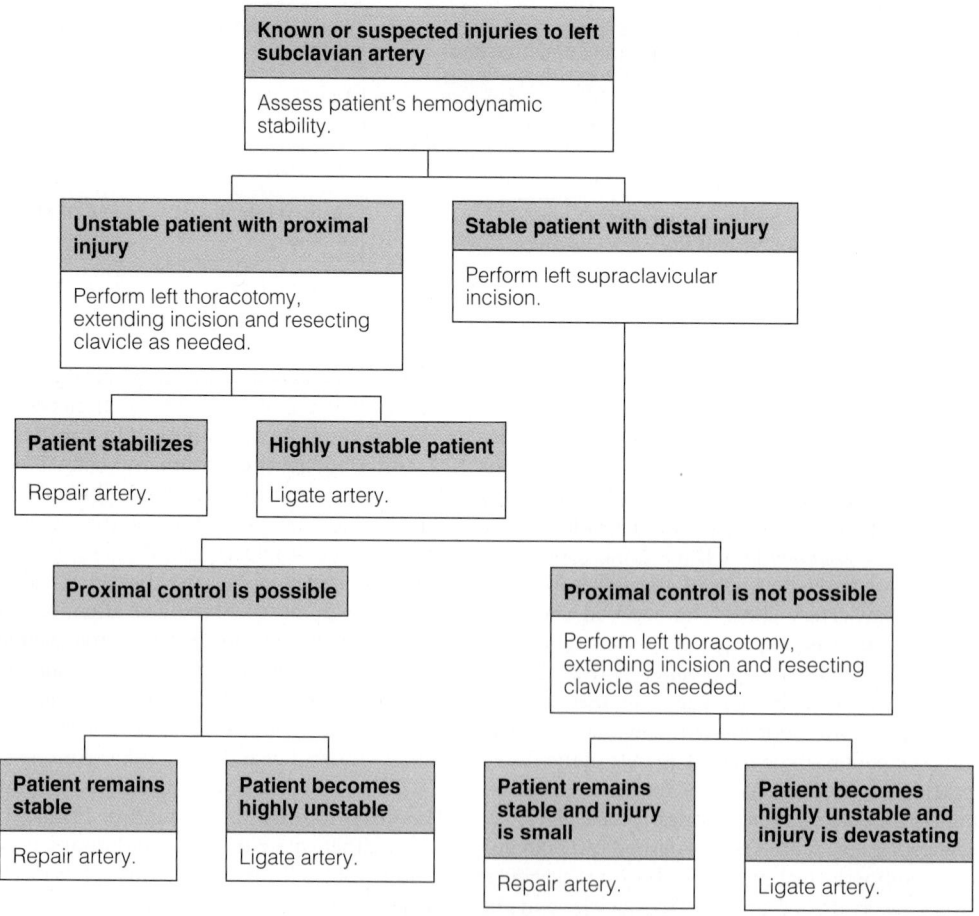

Figure 6 Algorithm outlines operative management of wounds to the base of the neck causing known or suspected injuries to the left subclavian artery.

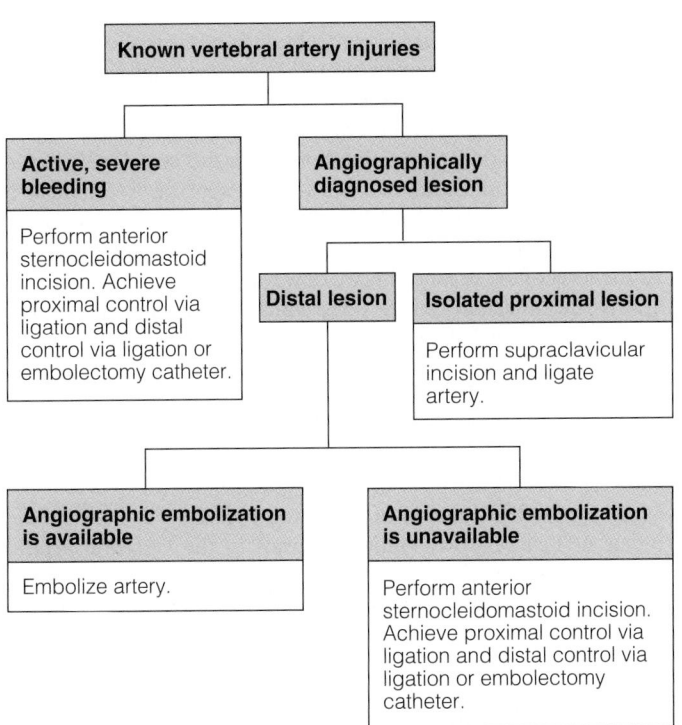

Figure 7 outlines the management algorithm:

Known vertebral artery injuries

- **Active, severe bleeding** — Perform anterior sternocleidomastoid incision. Achieve proximal control via ligation and distal control via ligation or embolectomy catheter.
- **Angiographically diagnosed lesion**
  - **Distal lesion**
    - **Angiographic embolization is available** — Embolize artery.
    - **Angiographic embolization is unavailable** — Perform anterior sternocleidomastoid incision. Achieve proximal control via ligation and distal control via ligation or embolectomy catheter.
  - **Isolated proximal lesion** — Perform supraclavicular incision and ligate artery.

Figure 7 Algorithm outlines management of known injuries to the vertebral artery, which are most often discovered by angiography.

EXPOSURE AND EXPLORATION

In the rare case of a patient who presents with active, severe bleeding and in whom the most likely source of bleeding is the distal vertebral artery, surgical exposure of the vertebral artery is necessary. Such exposure is reviewed more fully elsewhere.[11] Initial exposure should be obtained via an anterior sternocleidomastoid incision [see Injuries to the Carotid Arteries, Jugular Veins, Pharynx, and Esophagus, above]. This approach can be used for exposure of both the proximal and the distal vertebral artery. The incision is developed down to the level of the carotid sheath. The lateral margin of the internal jugular vein is developed sharply, and the internal jugular vein and the other contents of the sheath are retracted medially. After retraction of the carotid sheath, the plane just superficial to the prevertebral muscles is encountered. The ganglia of the cervical sympathetic chain are located here and should be protected, though this is not always possible in emergency circumstances. The anterior longitudinal ligament, located deep in the medial aspect of the wound, is incised longitudinally. The ligament, the underlying periosteum, and the overlying longus colli and longissimus capitis are mobilized anterolaterally with a periosteal elevator [see Figure 8]. The elevation is carried laterally along the lateral margin of the bodies of the cervical vertebrae and along the anterior aspect of the transverse processes of the cervical vertebrae. To avoid injury to the laterally and posteriorly placed cervical nerve roots, the dissection should not be extended laterally beyond the tips of the transverse processes.

After the anterior aspects of the transverse processes of the cervical vertebrae have been exposed, they can be removed with a small rongeur. This should be done distal to the area of injury only; proximal ligation of the vertebral artery can be done in its more easily exposed proximal portion. Although the vertebral artery is also accessible in the spaces between the transverse processes, there are a number of venous branches in these regions, and it is therefore safer to approach the artery within the confines of the bony foramina.

The third and most distal portion of the vertebral artery is most easily approached between the atlas and the axis. The segment of the artery between the transverse processes of these two vertebrae is longer and more exposed than the segments between the other cervical vertebrae and is therefore, in theory, somewhat easier to expose. In practice, rapid exposure of this portion of the vertebral artery is very difficult, particularly in an actively bleeding patient. As with exposures to the second portion of the vertebral artery, lesions requiring this exposure are best treated with angiographic embolization. If angiographic expertise is available, it may prove wisest to pack the wound as a temporizing measure and then take the patient for embolization. If angiographic embolization is not an option, a surgical approach may be necessary.

The standard anterior sternocleidomastoid incision is used but is carried superiorly with a curved extension to a point just below the tip of the ear. Once the plane is developed along the anterior border, the sternocleidomastoid muscle is divided near its origin at the mastoid process. The spinal accessory nerve, which enters the sternocleidomastoid 2 to 3 cm below the tip of the mastoid, is dissected free of the muscle and mobilized anteriorly. After division of the sternocleidomastoid muscle and anterior retraction of the spinal accessory nerve, the transverse process of the atlas is palpable and the prevertebral fascia is visible in the depths of the wound. The fascia is incised in a line with the spinal accessory nerve, and the laterally placed levator scapulae and splenius cervicis are divided as close to the transverse process of the atlas as possible [see Figure 9]. The anterior ramus of the nerve root of C2 is closely associated with the anterior edge of the levator scapulae and should be protected. After division of the levator scapulae and the splenius cervicis, the distal vertebral artery is visible in the medial aspect of the wound. Venous branches associated with the

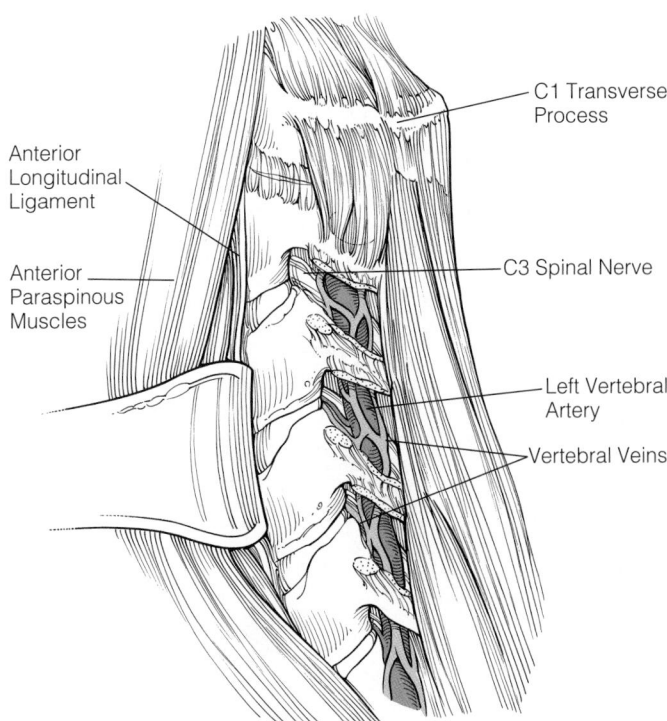

Figure 8 Throughout most of their course, the vertebral artery and the vertebral veins are surrounded by the transverse processes of the cervical vertebrae. Exposure of this portion of the vertebral artery is best done with anterior and lateral mobilization of the longus colli and the longissimus capitis.

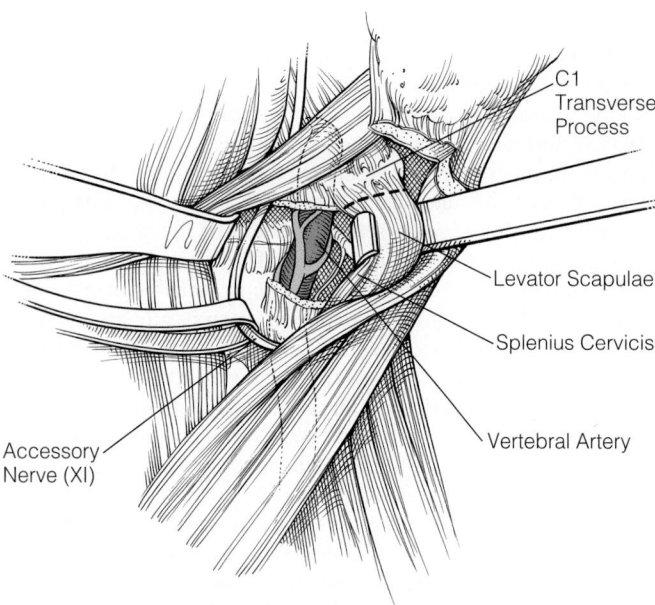

Figure 9 **Exposure of the distal vertebral artery is done via an incision along the anterior border of the sternocleidomastoid muscle. The sternocleidomastoid muscle is then divided near its origin at the mastoid process. The spinal accessory nerve is mobilized anteriorly. The vertebral artery is accessible after division of the levator scapulae and the splenius cervicis.**

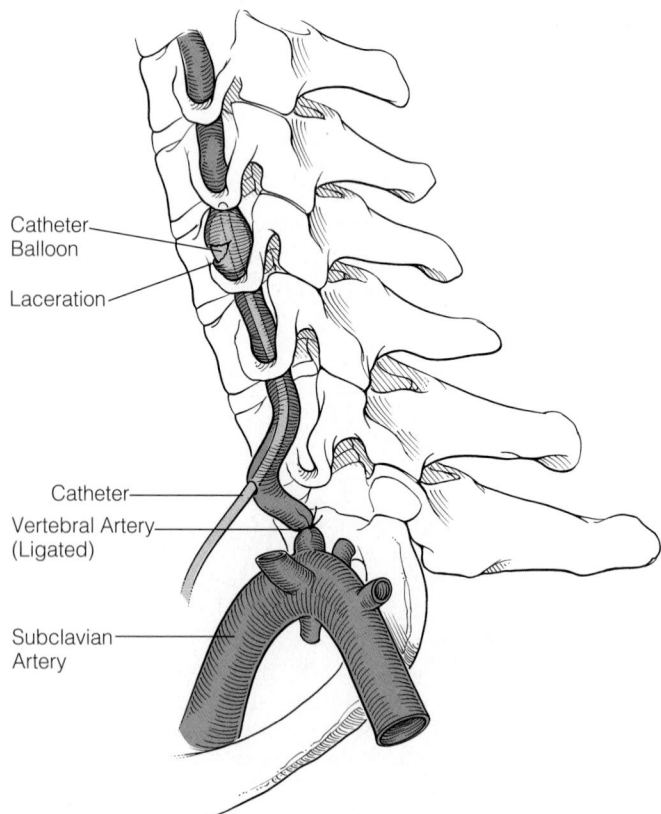

Figure 10 **Bleeding from vertebral artery injuries located within the transverse process of the cervical vertebrae can sometimes be controlled by exposing the proximal vertebral artery at the base of the neck, passing a thrombectomy catheter distally, and inflating the balloon at the site of injury.**

vertebral artery are most likely to be located near the transverse processes; therefore, ligation should be preferentially directed to the middle of the interspace between the transverse processes.

Exposure of the proximal vertebral artery at the base of the neck can also be achieved via an incision along the anterior border of the sternocleidomastoid muscle. Initial exposure is identical to that used for exposure of the carotid arteries [*see* Injuries to the Carotid Arteries, Jugular Veins, Pharynx, and Esophagus, *above*]. At the level of the carotid sheath, however, dissection is carried lateral to the internal jugular vein, which is retracted medially to expose the supraclavicular fat pad. The proximal vertebral artery can then be controlled after dissection deep to the fat pad, as described for the supraclavicular approach to isolated proximal vertebral artery injuries (see below).

TREATMENT

As opposed to injuries of the carotid arteries, in which either repair or ligation is an option, injuries to the vertebral arteries should always be treated with interruption of flow by surgical or other means. Proximal ligation should usually be done at the origin of the vertebral artery because the approach to the artery at this point is easier than the approaches to the more distal segments. The artery should be suture-ligated as close to its origin as possible so as not to create a thrombogenic blind pouch off the subclavian artery. Distal ligation can be accomplished by first exposing the artery (see above) and then ligating with ligatures, suture ligatures, or surgical clips. The use of clips minimizes dissection around the artery, which, in turn, decreases the likelihood of further injury to surrounding veins.

In emergency circumstances, a useful technique is to approach the proximal artery surgically at the base of the neck and pass a thrombectomy catheter distally to the site of injury [*see Figure 10*]. First, the proximal vertebral artery is exposed and ligated at its origin. Next, the thrombectomy catheter is passed distally via an arteriotomy. The catheter balloon is then inflated, and the wound is checked to determine whether bleeding has been controlled. If bleeding has been controlled, the distal end of the catheter is left in place, and the proximal end is brought out through the wound. The catheter is left in situ for approximately 48 hours, at which time the balloon is deflated and the wound is again checked for bleeding. If there is no bleeding for 4 to 6 hours, the catheter can be withdrawn. Use of a thrombectomy catheter can also serve as a bridge to angiographic embolization. If the thrombectomy catheter technique is unsuccessful, a direct surgical approach to the second or third portion of the artery is necessary. A potential disadvantage of a surgical approach, however, is that proximal ligation of the vertebral artery precludes angiographic embolization except via the contralateral vertebral artery. Embolization via the contralateral vertebral artery is extremely difficult and may result in ischemia or uncontrolled embolization.

If the injury is shown by preoperative angiography to be confined to the first portion of the vertebral artery, both proximal and distal ligation may be possible via a supraclavicular incision [*see Figure 11*]. The patient is positioned with the head turned away from the side of the injury, and the chest and ipsilateral neck are prepared and draped. Preparation and draping include the chest so that a left thoracotomy can be done later if necessary for proximal control of the left subclavian artery. In such cases, it is helpful to bump the patient up on the left so that an anterolateral thoracotomy incision can be carried further posteriorly.

The supraclavicular incision is made approximately one fingerbreadth superior to the clavicle and is extended medially to the

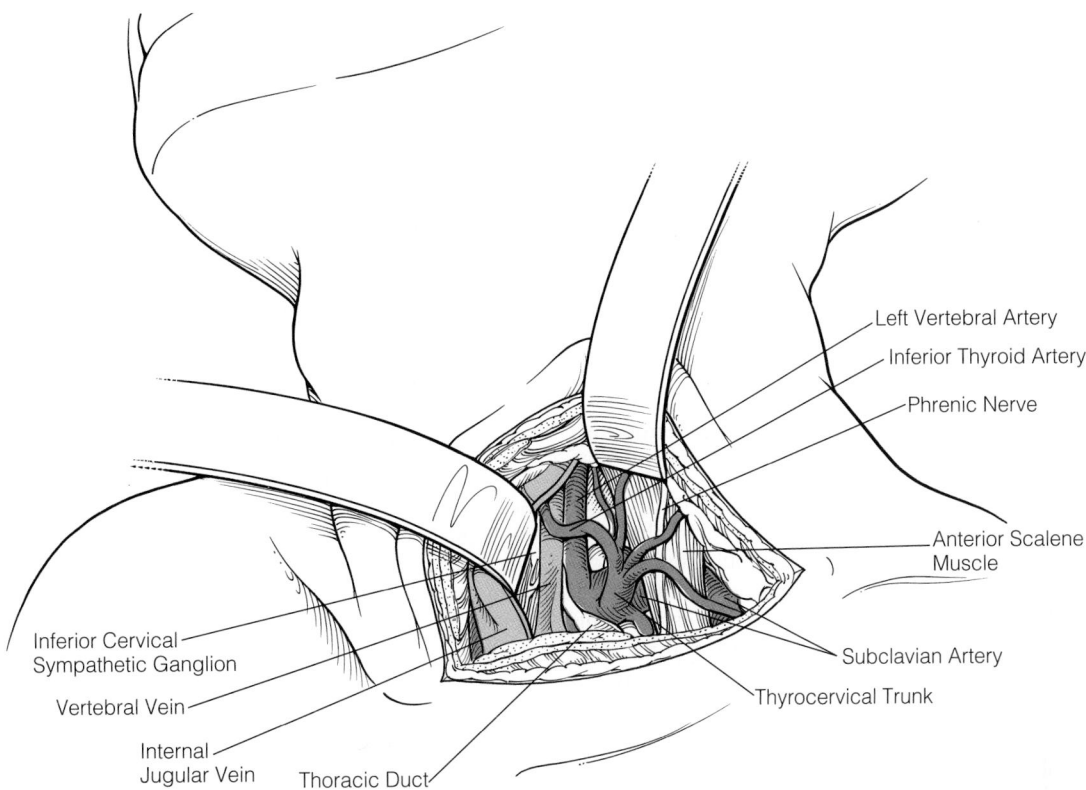

Figure 11 **The proximal vertebral artery can be approached via a supraclavicular incision. Dissection of the supraclavicular fat pad reveals the underlying vertebral artery where it diverges from the subclavian artery. During dissection, care should be taken to avoid injuring the phrenic nerve.**

Labels: Left Vertebral Artery; Inferior Thyroid Artery; Phrenic Nerve; Anterior Scalene Muscle; Subclavian Artery; Thyrocervical Trunk; Inferior Cervical Sympathetic Ganglion; Vertebral Vein; Internal Jugular Vein; Thoracic Duct

midpoint of the sternocleidomastoid insertion and laterally to the juncture of the middle and lateral thirds of the clavicle. The skin, the subcutaneous tissue, and the platysma are incised. The external jugular vein, if in the operating field, is suture-ligated. The clavicular head of the sternocleidomastoid muscle is encountered next, and its lateral aspect is divided with the electrocautery at its insertion on the clavicle. The muscle is then retracted superiorly and medially. In the plane deep to the sternocleidomastoid muscle, the omohyoid muscle is divided in its middle tendinous portion with the electrocautery.

At a level just deep to the sternocleidomastoid and omohyoid muscles, the carotid sheath is encountered in the medial aspect of the wound. The lateral border of the internal jugular vein is dissected free of adjacent tissue and retracted medially. If the operation is on the left, the thoracic duct may be found in the medial portion of the wound. The thoracic duct is easily injured with retraction and should be divided and ligated if it is in the way.

Just lateral to the internal jugular vein at the same depth is the supraclavicular fat pad, which is dissected from the supraclavicular fossa in which it lies. Exposure is further enhanced by dissection and division of the anterior scalene muscle. The phrenic nerve, which is closely applied to the anterior surface of the anterior scalene muscle, is dissected free of the underlying muscle and retracted out of the field with a vessel loop. The anterior scalene muscle is then divided with the electrocautery. During dissection of the supraclavicular fat pad, it may be necessary to divide branches of the thyrocervical and costocervical trunks. The most prominent of these branches is the inferior thyroid artery, which stems from the thyrocervical trunk and courses medially toward the thyroid.

After the supraclavicular fat pad has been dissected, the proximal portion of the vertebral artery is reached. The vertebral vein, which usually lies slightly superficial and medial to the vertebral artery, is divided and suture-ligated to provide better exposure. Care should be taken not to retract the vertebral vein too vigorously before suture ligation so that this vessel is not avulsed from the subclavian vein. At the depth of the vertebral artery, the white, cordlike elements of the brachial plexus are often visible in the superolateral aspect of the wound. If possible, traction should not be placed on the brachial plexus, and use of the electrocautery around the plexus should be minimized. After exposure, the proximal vertebral artery is ligated both proximal and distal to the site of injury. No attempts at repairing the injury should be made.

The use of angiographic embolization, the preferred treatment of angiographically diagnosed injuries of the distal vertebral artery, depends on the availability of equipment for and expertise with the procedure [*see* Discussion, Angiographic Embolization of Distal Vertebral Artery Injuries, *below*]. Stable patients who have angiographically documented injuries to the distal vertebral artery should be transferred to the closest center with cerebral embolization capability. If angiographic embolization is not available, exposure and ligation should be carried out as described (see above).

In cases where angiographic embolization of the vertebral artery has been employed, a postprocedure angiogram should be done several days to weeks after the procedure to ensure that the artery remains occluded and that no arteriovenous fistula has developed between the injured vertebral artery and the surrounding venous plexus. Duplex scanning has also been used to a limited extent for follow-up screening. It can serve as an alternative to angiography, but its sensitivity relative to that of angiography remains to be established.

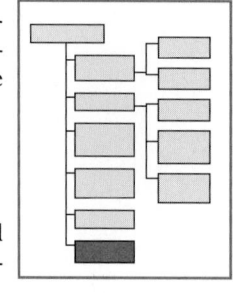

Superficial Wounds

Some wounds are obviously superficial on initial physical examination. Most com-monly, these wounds are slash wounds caused by a knife or other sharp object rather than true stab wounds. Rapid exposure and vascular control are sometimes easily accomplished through these wounds. In such circumstances, the surgical procedure consists of debridement of the neck wound, and deep dissection is not necessary. If greater access and control are needed to rule out further injuries or for definitive repair, a standard anterior sternocleidomastoid incision should be done [*see* Injuries to the Carotid Arteries, Jugular Veins, Pharynx, and Esophagus, *above*].

Discussion

Screening Criteria for and Recommended Management of Blunt Cervical Arterial Injuries

Blunt injuries to cervical arteries, though relatively rare, can be difficult to diagnose and can lead to devastating complications (e.g., stroke and bleeding). Most such injuries result from stretching of the vessels as a consequence of hyperextension of the neck. Motor vehicle collision is the most common mechanism of this sort of stretch injury; chiropractic manipulation and rhythmic flexion and extension of the neck ("head banging") are less common mechanisms.[12,13] Injury may also be caused by direct trauma to the artery or by fracture fragments. Arterial stretching leads to endothelial tearing with subsequent intimal flaps, dissections, or emboli.

The true incidence of blunt cervical vascular injury is unknown. Figures as high as 1.55% of all blunt trauma patients have been reported,[14,15] as have figures an order of magnitude lower. Because many patients with pathologic changes on screening tests are asymptomatic before diagnosis and remain asymptomatic after diagnosis, the reported incidences are likely to depend heavily on the screening criteria used.[16-21]

Many recommendations have been made regarding screening criteria for blunt cervical arterial injuries. Performing four-vessel cervical angiography on all blunt trauma patients would identify nearly all cervical arterial injuries, but the logistical considerations, expense, and potential risks associated with this approach make it unfeasible. When aggressive screening with broad criteria is employed, approximately 3% to 5% of blunt trauma patients undergo workup and approximately 30% of the workups reveal an injury.[14] Even with early and aggressive screening, about a quarter of patients exhibit neurologic signs and symptoms before workup.[16]

Some of the published screening criteria are uncommon and thus, if present, are probably reasonable triggers for diagnostic imaging studies. Such uncommon criteria include arterial bleeding from the ears, nose, or mouth; an expanding cervical hematoma; a cervical bruit in a patient younger than 50 years; evidence of cerebral infarction on CT scanning; Horner syndrome; and basilar skull fracture involving the carotid canal. Other published screening criteria are somewhat more difficult to apply, being either quite common or highly subjective. These more difficult criteria include neurologic symptoms not explained by CT findings; an injury mechanism consistent with severe cervical hyperextension, hyperrotation, or hyperflexion, especially if associated with a displaced facial fracture or complex mandible fracture; closed head injury consistent with diffuse axonal injury of the brain; a near-hanging resulting in cerebral anoxia; seat-belt abrasion or other soft tissue injury to the anterior neck; and cervical vertebral body fracture or distraction injury (isolated spinous process fracture excluded).[22,23]

Four-vessel angiography remains the gold standard for imaging the cervical vasculature. Duplex ultrasonography has not proved sensitive enough for diagnosis of blunt cervical arterial injury, in large part because so many of the lesions are located high in the neck, where accurate ultrasonography is difficult.[18] Magnetic resonance angiography (MRA) also lacks the sensitivity needed to screen trauma patients for blunt cervical arterial injury. MRA imaging relies on signal subtraction related to flow and thus may miss lesions such as pseudoaneurysms, in which flow is diminished. CT angiography has been applied with increasing frequency in attempts to make this diagnosis, with mixed results. Helical CT scanners capable of fewer than 16 slices per rotation probably lack the sensitivity to make a reliable diagnosis, but small series using more sophisticated CT scanners have reported promising results.[24] Large series evaluating current CT angiography technology are lacking at present. CT angiography is particularly attractive in that it is noninvasive, it can be performed relatively rapidly, and it can be done in the course of CT scanning of the head and other parts of the body. Improvements in CT technology and increased use of CT instead of angiography for screening may make widespread radiographic screening for blunt carotid injury much simpler and easier.

Biffl and associates developed a grading scale for blunt cervical arterial injury based on the arteriographic appearance of the lesion.[25] On this scale, grade I and II lesions show less than 25% and greater than 25% luminal narrowing, respectively; grade III lesions are pseudoaneurysms; grade IV lesions demonstrate thrombosis; and grade V lesions are transections with extravasation. Grade I to III lesions may progress to a higher grade. Follow-up imaging should be performed 7 to 10 days after diagnosis.

Treatment of blunt cervical arterial injury depends on the location and grade of the lesion. Grade I injuries, regardless of location, are best treated with anticoagulation.[25] The intimal defect leaves the patient at risk for thromboembolism, and anticoagulation protects against subsequent stroke. Grade II lesions extending to a location that is inaccessible to traditional surgical approaches should also be treated with anticoagulation. Carotid artery pseudoaneurysms (grade III lesions) located at the base of the skull (the usual location) should be treated initially with anticoagulation, then followed up with delayed imaging studies to check for enlargement. Pseudoaneurysms that are enlarged should probably be treated with stenting, though to date, experience with stenting at this location for this indication has been relatively limited. Stenting may also be indicated for lesions that progress and threaten to limit flow despite full anticoagulation, as well as for high grade V lesions.[26] Good results have been obtained with anticoagulation in patients with grade IV injuries.[25] Accessible grade II to V lesions, though rare, should be repaired operatively by means of traditional surgical approaches.

Blunt vertebral artery injuries should be treated nonoperatively for the most part, and the threshold for employing transcatheter embolization should be low. As with carotid artery injuries, small lesions can be treated with anticoagulation. Larger and more distal lesions should be treated with occlusion of the artery by means of interventional radiologic techniques.

The best choice of anticoagulation remains unclear. There is some indication that the use of heparin positively affects patient outcome, but the evidence is not particularly strong.[19,21] The partial thromboplastin time (PTT) should be monitored and maintained within an arbitrary range of 40 to 60 seconds. Patients with a contraindication to heparin therapy (e.g., an intracranial lesion at risk for hemorrhage) can be managed with aspirin. Patients managed with heparin and those managed with aspirin have similar stroke rates; however, the number of patients treated with either drug in published reports is relatively small, and the evidence that anticoagulation of any kind makes a difference is relatively sparse. The safety and efficacy of other antiplatelet treatments are unknown. The optimal duration of treatment is unknown as well, though it appears that 3 to 6 months is adequate in most cases.[21] Therapy may be discontinued when repeat imaging shows that the injury has resolved.

Zones of the Neck and Mandatory versus Selective Neck Exploration for Penetrating Cervical Injuries

One approach to managing penetrating cervical injuries is to categorize them on the basis of their location in the neck. In this schema, the neck is divided into three distinct zones [see Figure 12], and management is determined by the zone in which the patient happens to have wounds in the skin. The idea is that hemodynamically stable patients without any obvious sign of vascular injury (e.g., pulsatile bleeding from the wound, an expanding hematoma, a bruit, or a neurologic deficit) who have wounds to the base of the neck or the upper neck (zones I and III) may have injuries that are problematic with respect to proximal or distal vascular control and thus may require incisions other than the standard sternocleidomastoid approach. Accordingly, these patients undergo imaging studies and endoscopy to rule out injuries to the vasculature or the aerodigestive tract. If the study results are negative for injuries that call for operative repair, the patients are simply observed. Patients with zone II injuries, on the other hand, presumably have underlying injuries to either the vasculature or the aerodigestive tract that are easily accessible via a sternocleidomastoid incision; such patients therefore undergo neck exploration if the wound has violated the platysma.

The concept of mandatory exploration of patients with zone II injuries, though time honored, has a number of problems. Division of the neck into three distinct areas results in extremely small zones I and III, and even zone II, in the middle of the neck, is not very long in most patients. As a result, determining that a given wound is clearly in only one of the zones is often very difficult. Description of a wound as being on the border of zones I and II or on the border of zones II and III is a common and confusing occurrence. Moreover, the location of the skin wound is not a reliable guide to the locations of injuries to underlying structures. This is most obviously true of gunshot wounds, in which the path of the missile is clearly as important as the location of the skin wound. It is also true of knife wounds: a blade that enters the skin in zone II can easily injure structures in zones I or III, depending on the direction in which the knife was thrust after it entered the skin.

A more logical approach to the initial management of penetrat-

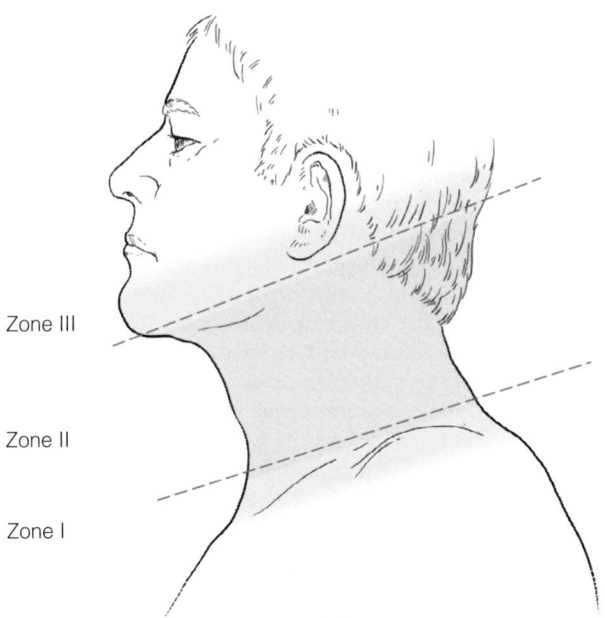

Figure 12 **Depicted is the traditional division of the neck into three separate zones. This division has been used as a basis for decision-making with respect to penetrating cervical injuries.**

ing neck trauma starts by determining the depth of the wound. If the wound did not violate the platysma, injury to major underlying structures can be ruled out. If the wound clearly violated the platysma or its depth cannot be determined, further investigation is warranted. If the patient has any obvious signs of underlying vascular injury, the neck should be explored via the standard sternocleidomastoid incision, and the exploration should be expanded as necessary to obtain proximal or distal control. If the patient is stable and has no obvious signs of underlying vascular injury, a nonoperative workup should be obtained regardless of the location of the skin wound.

Conventional angiography is the gold standard for ruling out vascular injury, but it is somewhat invasive and can be time consuming and resource intensive. As experience with CT in this setting accumulates, this modality is becoming an increasingly valuable imaging adjunct.[27,28] CT can be quite helpful in determining the course that a knife or bullet takes within the neck and detecting the presence of vascular or aerodigestive injury. If CT defines a knife or bullet tract that is clearly remote from major vascular or aerodigestive structures, no further workup is needed. If CT clearly shows an injury that should be repaired, exploration of the neck is indicated. If CT can neither establish nor rule out the presence of vascular or aerodigestive injury, further directed imaging or endoscopic studies should be done. This selective approach reduces the rate of negative neck explorations and decreases the need for invasive, lengthy, and expensive diagnostic modalities.

Repair versus Ligation of Carotid Arteries

Simple injuries to the external carotid artery should be repaired, whereas complex injuries should be ligated.

Injuries to the common carotid artery and the internal carotid artery are more problematic. If the injury is simple and there is no suggestion that flow in the vessel has been interrupted, repair should always be undertaken. An example of such an injury is a simple stab wound of part of the circumference of the artery with an associated pseudoaneurysm and good distal flow. In this circumstance, lateral repair can be done quickly and easily with a short cross-clamp time. After proximal and distal control of the vessel is obtained, a check should be made for back-bleeding. If the back-bleeding from the distal circulation is brisk, as it usually is, repair can be done safely.

If an injury to the common carotid artery or the internal carotid artery has interrupted flow in the vessel, repair creates a theoretical disadvantage. Interruption of flow may lead to focal brain ischemia and partial disruption of the blood-brain barrier. Sudden restoration of blood flow may cause hemorrhage in the area of the ischemia and worsen the extent of brain injury; an anemic, or white, infarct of the brain may be converted to a hemorrhagic, or red, infarct. Whether this pathophysiology is important after traumatic injury is unclear and controversial.

Deciding whether to repair or ligate when flow has been interrupted is often difficult.[5,6] One approach is to base the decision on the patient's preoperative neurologic status. If there is no neurologic deficit, it is presumed that there are no areas of brain ischemia and that repair is safe. Conversely, a focal neurologic deficit is presumed to be related to ischemia, and in such cases, the risk of worsening the patient's neurologic status with restoration of blood flow is increased. Even though this approach is rational, it is not applicable in cases in which a detailed neurologic examination before surgery is not possible. Furthermore, this approach may be applicable only to patients in coma or with severe neurologic deficits. There are indications that milder neurologic deficits respond favorably to revascularization.

Yet another approach is to gauge the appropriateness of repair according to the nature of the injury itself. In this approach, large, complicated injuries requiring involved and lengthy procedures for repair are ligated, whereas simple injuries requiring only simple and quick repairs are repaired. Similarly, repair is not indicated in patients with severe or multiple associated injuries. There is also a difference between the management of injuries of the common carotid artery and management of injuries of the internal carotid artery. Common carotid injuries are more accessible and easier to repair, and repair is generally associated with a good outcome. Continued antegrade flow in the internal carotid artery is more likely after injury to the common carotid artery than after injury to the internal carotid artery because of the possibility of collateral flow via the external carotid artery.

A reasonable way to deal with repair dilemmas is to make the decision on the basis of distal back-bleeding. Interruption of blood flow to the brain is tolerated only for a short time, and restoration of flow is unlikely to be accomplished quickly enough to improve outcome. It is therefore logical to base the decision about revascularization on the state of back-bleeding from the internal carotid artery. If back-bleeding is brisk, the patient is presumed to have good collateral flow, and the chances that there is an area of ischemia are low. Repair rather than ligation is safe in such circumstances. If internal carotid artery back-bleeding is minimal or absent, an ischemic infarct is more likely and restitution of arterial inflow is more dangerous. A corollary to this reasoning is that if back-bleeding is poor, a clot distal to the area of injury may be present, and return of flow with repair may dislodge the clot distally.

Nonoperative Management and Stenting of Carotid Artery Injuries

Some minimal penetrating injuries to the vasculature of the extremities (e.g., small pseudoaneurysms and endothelial injuries) need not be repaired if they do not compromise distal flow, and they usually heal over time without sequelae. It has been hypothe-

sized that minimal injuries to the carotid vasculature can be approached in a similar fashion. The consequences of distal embolization or pseudoaneurysm rupture in the carotid circulation make such an approach somewhat risky.[29,30] Increasing experience with nonoperative management of minor blunt injuries to the cerebral vasculature supports the relative safety of this approach, particularly if the patient can safely undergo anticoagulation to prevent subsequent thromboembolic complications.[31] Experience with nonoperative management of penetrating injuries is more limited, however. Penetrating mechanisms are more likely than blunt mechanisms to involve a full-thickness injury to the vessel, and the presence of a full-thickness injury makes anticoagulation riskier. Furthermore, the apparent degree of vessel injury from penetrating trauma on angiography is often significantly less than the actual degree of injury as seen at exploration. Nonoperative management is currently supported for minor blunt injuries, ideally in conjunction with anticoagulation. Until more experience with nonoperative management of penetrating injuries is reported in the literature, accessible penetrating injuries should be repaired surgically.

There is increasing support for treatment of carotid artery injuries with intraluminal stenting.[32-34] This approach is now commonly used for aneurysms of the thoracic and abdominal aorta, as well as for more distal peripheral vascular lesions. On rare occasions, it has also been applied to the management of traumatic injuries to the thoracic aorta and selected injuries to the peripheral and visceral vasculature. Not surprisingly, stenting has also been used for the management of carotid artery injuries, particularly injuries to the distal internal carotid artery that are not easily approached surgically. Overall, stents are most frequently used in situations where arterial lesions are not surgically accessible or when anticoagulation is contraindicated. The technical success rates have been good in these settings, and there is accumulating (albeit still limited) evidence to suggest that stents in the carotid circulation remain patent for prolonged periods and are not associated with a high thromboembolic complication rate.[25,35-38] Large pseudoaneurysms in inaccessible areas of the distal carotid circulation usually do not heal with time and, when persistent, may reasonably be treated with stenting.[25]

Angiographic Embolization of Distal Vertebral Artery Injuries

Most patients with vertebral artery injuries are stable and experience no external bleeding, and the injury is discovered by angiography. A number of such lesions have been successfully treated with angiographic embolization. Given the difficulties of surgical exposure, lesions of the distal vertebral artery should be treated angiographically when the patient's general condition permits and when the necessary expertise is available. If the patient is bleeding profusely, such an approach is not possible and a rapid surgical approach is indicated, with ligation of the proximal vertebral artery and an attempt at thrombectomy catheter control or packing of the wound until an angiographic approach can be attempted. If this is unsuccessful, the lesion should be approached directly [see Known Vertebral Artery Injuries, above].

If a patient with a distal vertebral artery lesion is stable—particularly when the lesion is otherwise silent and has been detected angiographically—an attempt should be made at angiographic embolization if the necessary expertise is available. If the patient is stable, transfer to the nearest center with cerebral angiographic embolization capability is appropriate. Embolization is done via the ipsilateral proximal vertebral artery. Detachable balloons or coils can be used.

Conversion of Cricothyrotomy to Tracheotomy

Cricothyrotomy is typically reserved for life-threatening airway compromise when the need for a rapid surgical airway is paramount [*see* Airway Compromise, *above, and 100 Initial Management of Life-Threatening Trauma*]. Tracheotomy is preferred if time and a lesser degree of urgency permit. Similarly, in the postoperative period, tracheotomy is preferred to cricothyrotomy. The traditional view, initially promulgated by Chevalier Jackson in 1921, is that cricothyrotomy is more likely than tracheotomy to result in airway stricture or damage to more proximal structures in the larynx. On the basis of this rationale, cricothyrotomies are converted to tracheotomies on a semielective basis within 24 to 48 hours of admission if the patient's general condition permits.[39,40]

The evidence supporting a policy of routine conversion is mixed. Several series document a low but increased incidence of complications to the larynx and trachea from prolonged maintenance of cricothyrotomies. Even though the incidence is low, the complications can be severe and may necessitate extensive reconstructive procedures. Conversely, studies of cardiac patients undergoing routine cricothyrotomy do not demonstrate a significant increase in the incidence of airway complications. Cricothyrotomy is sometimes favored over tracheotomy in these patients because of concerns about the proximity of tracheotomy wounds to the patient's sternotomy incision. The results of studies of routine cardiac patients may be different from results of studies showing an increase in complications after cricothyrotomy, in that the cardiac patients were intubated for shorter periods.

There have been no studies documenting a high incidence of complications in trauma patients who have undergone emergency cricothyrotomy and have remained intubated via the cricothyrotomy for longer than 2 or 3 days. Because complications are potentially so devastating, however, emergency cricothyrotomies should be converted to tracheotomies within 1 to 2 days after admission in stable patients. In a stable patient, the risks of conversion are minimal, and conversion is justified to avoid the possibility of future complications.

References

1. Fuhrman GM, Steig FH III, Buerk CA: Blunt laryngeal trauma: classification and management protocol. J Trauma 30:87, 1990
2. Symbas IN, Hatcher CR Jr, Boehm GAW: Acute penetrating tracheal trauma. Ann Thorac Surg 22:473, 1976
3. Dossa C, Shepard AD, Wolford DG, et al: Distal internal carotid exposure: a simplified technique for temporary mandibular subluxation. J Vasc Surg 12:319, 1990
4. Beal SL, Pottmeyer EW, Spisso JM: Esophageal perforation following external blunt trauma. J Trauma 28:1425, 1988
5. Fabian TC, George SM Jr, Croce MA, et al: Carotid artery trauma: management based on mechanism of injury. J Trauma 30:953, 1990
6. Richardson R, Obeid FN, Richardson JD, et al: Neurologic consequences of cerebrovascular injury. J Trauma 32:755, 1992
7. Wood VE: The results of total claviculectomy. Clin Orthop 207:186, 1986
8. McCready RA, Procter CD, Hyde GL: Subclavian-axillary vascular trauma. J Vasc Surg 3:24, 1986
9. Higashida RT, Halbach VV, Tsai FY, et al: Interventional neurovascular treatment of traumatic carotid and vertebral artery lesions: results in 234 cases. AJR Am J Roentgenol 153:577, 1989
10. Hatzitheofilou C, Demetriades D, Melissas J, et al: Surgical approaches to vertebral artery injuries. Br J Surg 75:234, 1988
11. Anatomic Exposures in Vascular Surgery. Wind G, Valentine R, Eds. Williams & Wilkins, Baltimore, 1991
12. Peters M, Bohl J, Thomke F, et al: Dissection of the internal carotid artery after chiropractic manipulation of the neck. Neurology 45:2284, 1995
13. Jackson MA, Hughes RC, Ward SP, et al: "Head-banging" and carotid dissection. Br Med J (Clin Res Ed) 287:1262, 1983
14. Miller PR, Fabian TC, Croce MA, et al: Prospective screening for blunt cerebrovascular injuries: analysis of diagnostic modalities and outcomes. Ann Surg 236:386, 2002
15. Biffl WL, Ray CE Jr, Moore EE: Treatment-related outcomes from blunt cerebrovascular injuries: importance of routine follow-up arteriography. Ann Surg 235:699, 2002
16. Biffl WL, Moore EE, Ryu RK, et al: The unrecognized epidemic of blunt carotid arterial injuries: early diagnosis improves neurologic outcome. Ann Surg 228:462, 1998
17. Biffl WL, Moore EE, Elliott JP, et al: The devastating potential of blunt vertebral arterial injuries. Ann Surg 231:672, 2000
18. Cogbill TH, Moore EE, Meissner M, et al: The spectrum of blunt injury to the carotid artery: a multicenter perspective. J Trauma 37:473, 1994
19. Fabian TC, Patton JH Jr, Croce MA, et al: Blunt carotid injury: importance of early diagnosis and anticoagulant therapy. Ann Surg 223:513, 1996
20. Prall JA, Brega KE, Coldwell DM, et al: Incidence of unsuspected blunt carotid artery injury. Neurosurgery 42:495, 1998
21. Parikh AA, Luchette FA, Valente JF, et al: Blunt carotid injuries. J Am Coll Surg 185:80, 1997
22. Biffl WL, Ray CE Jr, Moore EE, et al: Noninvasive diagnosis of blunt cerebrovascular injuries: a preliminary report. J Trauma 53:850, 2002
23. Biffl WL, Moore EE: Identifying the asymptomatic patient with blunt carotid arterial injury. J Trauma 47:1163, 1999
24. Berne JD, Norwood SH, McAuley CE, et al: Helical computed tomographic angiography: an excellent screening test for blunt cerebrovascular injury. J Trauma 57:11, 2004
25. Biffl WL, Moore EE, Offner PJ, et al: Blunt carotid arterial injuries: implications of a new grading scale. J Trauma 47:845, 1999
26. Singh RR, Barry MC, Ireland A, et al: Current diagnosis and management of blunt internal carotid artery injury. Eur J Vasc Endovasc Surg 27:577, 2004
27. Munera F, Soto JA, Palacio D, et al: Diagnosis of arterial injuries caused by penetrating trauma to the neck: comparison of helical CT angiography and conventional angiography. Radiology 216:356, 2000
28. Gracias VH, Reilly PM, Philpott J, et al: Computed tomography in the evaluation of penetrating neck trauma. Arch Surg 136:1231, 2001
29. Demetriades D, Asensio JA, Velmahos G, et al: Complex problems in penetrating neck trauma. Surg Clin North Am 76:661, 1996
30. Panetta TF, Sales CM, Marin ML, et al: Natural history, duplex characteristics, and histopathologic correlation of arterial injuries in a canine model. J Vasc Surg 16:867, 1992
31. Cothren CC, Moore EE, Biffl WL, et al: Anticoagulation is the gold standard therapy for blunt carotid injuries to reduce stroke rate. Arch Surg 139:540, 2004
32. Gomez CR, May AD, Terry JB, et al: Endovascular therapy of traumatic injuries of the extracranial cerebral arteries. Crit Care Clin 15:789, 1999
33. Liu AY, Paulsen RD, Marcellus ML, et al: Long-term outcomes after carotid stent placement for treatment of carotid artery dissection. Neurosurgery 45:1368, 1999
34. McArthur CS, Marin ML: Endovascular therapy for the treatment of arterial trauma. Mt Sinai J Med 71:4, 2004
35. Amon YL, Paulsen RD, Marcellus ML, et al: Long-term outcomes after carotid stent placement for treatment of carotid artery dissection. Neurosurgery 45:1368, 1999
36. du Toit DF, Leith JG, Strauss DC, et al: Endovascular management of traumatic cervicothoracic arteriovenous fistula. Br J Surg 90:1516, 2003
37. Coldwell DM, Novak Z, Ryu RK, et al: Treatment of posttraumatic internal carotid arterial pseudoaneurysms with endovascular stents. J Trauma 48:470, 2000
38. Duke BJ, Ryu RK, Coldwell DM, et al: Treatment of blunt injury to the carotid artery by using endovascular stents: an early experience. J Neurosurg 87:825, 1997
39. Milner SM, Bennett JDC: Review article: emergency cricothyrotomy. J Laryngol Otol 105:883, 1991
40. Hawkins ML, Shapiro MB, Cue JI, et al: Emergency cricothyrotomy: a reassessment. Am Surg 61:52, 1995

Acknowledgments

Figure 1 Marcia Kammerer.
Figures 2 through 4 Susan E. Brust, C.M.I.
Figures 5 through 7 Marcia Kammerer.
Figures 8 through 11 Susan E. Brust, C.M.I.
Figure 12 Tom Moore.

104 INJURIES TO THE CHEST

Edward H. Kincaid, M.D., and J. Wayne Meredith, M.D., F.A.C.S.

Most persons who experience torso trauma, whether blunt or penetrating, sustain some degree of associated injury to the chest. Thoracic injuries are a primary or contributing cause of death in nearly half of all cases of torso trauma.[1] Fortunately, many thoracic injuries can be treated effectively, and often definitively, by relatively simple maneuvers that can be learned and performed by most physicians involved in early trauma care. Approximately one in six patients, however, has life-threatening injuries that necessitate urgent operative repair. These extremes in injury severity are unique to the chest and require a correspondingly broad range of knowledge and skills on the part of the treating surgeon.

Initial Evaluation and Management

PRIMARY SURVEY

Initial evaluation and treatment of patients with thoracic injuries are guided by the same principles and priorities as initial evaluation and treatment of patients with other injuries. Evaluation begins with an organized and rapid primary survey aimed at recognizing and treating immediately life-threatening problems.

The first priority is to ensure an adequate airway. An airway often can be established by clearing any blood or debris from the oropharynx and pulling the mandible or the tongue forward. Severely injured patients commonly require nasotracheal or orotracheal intubation, and some, especially those with severe maxillofacial trauma, require cricothyroidotomy or tracheostomy.

The second priority is to ensure adequate ventilation. If the patient is not breathing, he or she must be intubated promptly. If ventilation is inadequate because of open or tension pneumothorax, these problems should be addressed at this stage of care.

The next priority is control of external hemorrhage and restoration of circulation. External hemorrhage is best controlled by direct pressure. Inadequate perfusion generally results from either hypovolemia or pump (i.e., cardiac) problems. Hypovolemia from hemorrhage often must be treated operatively as part of the resuscitative effort. Pump problems are signaled by distended neck veins and are caused by one of four conditions: (1) tension pneumothorax, (2) pericardial tamponade, (3) coronary air embolism, or (4) cardiac contusion or myocardial infarction (MI). These conditions are discussed in detail elsewhere (see below). At this early stage of treatment, they should be addressed sufficiently to ensure adequate perfusion.

In most blunt trauma patients, urgent treatment of thoracic injury is accomplished during the primary survey because the most common blunt chest injuries can be controlled with endotracheal intubation or tube thoracostomy. In this setting, thoracotomy is indicated for cardiac tamponade, a massive hemothorax, or uncontrolled massive air leaks. Neither pulmonary nor cardiac contusions should delay diagnosis or definitive treatment of extrathoracic injuries resulting from blunt trauma.

TUBE THORACOSTOMY: INDICATIONS AND TECHNIQUE

During initial resuscitation, chest tube placement can be both therapeutic and diagnostic. The two most common indications for tube placement in this setting are pneumothorax and hemothorax; however, signs and symptoms of these conditions may not be readily apparent. In addition, when the patient is in shock, the surgeon often cannot afford to take the time to differentiate between various possible causative conditions. Because tube thoracostomy is quick, relatively safe, and simple, it should be liberally used for patients in extremis.

Tension pneumothorax, the most common and easily treated immediately life-threatening thoracic injury, results when blunt or penetrating trauma disrupts the respiratory system and allows air to escape from the lung parenchyma or the tracheobronchial tree into the pleural space, thereby increasing intrathoracic pressure. This increased pressure is transmitted to all the cardiac chambers and retards venous return to the heart, resulting in hypotension. The classic signs of tension pneumothorax—decreased breath sounds, tympany on the ipsilateral side, tracheal shift, and distended neck veins—commonly are absent or are incompletely manifested in a busy emergency department. The diagnosis is often suggested by the presence of shock accompanied by evidence of adequate venous filling on physical examination and recognition of asymmetric motion of the two sides of the chest. Treatment of suspected tension pneumothorax should not be delayed in patients with hemodynamic compromise.

Chest tube placement in the trauma setting is a straightforward procedure. The chest is prepared and draped in a sterile fashion. A local anesthetic (e.g., 1% lidocaine) is not required in unconscious patients but should be used in alert patients. On the midaxillary line in approximately the fifth interspace, a scalpel is used to make a 2 to 3 cm incision, oriented in the direction of the interspace, through all layers of the skin and subcutaneous tissue. A finger or a blunt clamp is inserted to penetrate the intercostal muscles and the parietal pleura. The wound is explored with the index finger (in adults) or the fifth finger (in children) to ensure that the pleural space has been entered and allow local exploration of the chest cavity.

In adults, a 36 French chest tube is then inserted and directed posteriorly and towards the apex for optimally effective drainage of air and blood. The desired tube position is best achieved through appropriate orientation of the skin incision relative to the entrance into the chest cavity: the straight line between these two points defines the direction of the tube once it is in the chest. The tube is then attached to 20 cm of suction with a water seal and a collection chamber. Visual inspection of air passing through the water seal yields an estimate of the size of the air leak—an important consideration with suspected airway injuries.

Collection chambers for hemothoraces should be of the same design. Those associated with autotransfusion devices (e.g., cell savers) have immense theoretical potential for rapid retrieval and processing of shed blood. In practice, however, their utility is limited. For example, with a small to moderate-sized hemothorax (< 1,000 ml), the red-cell yield of an autotransfusion device would be small and not worth the associated time and expense. With a large hemothorax, the most important goal of therapy is control of bleeding, and arranging for autotransfusion could delay or hinder the achievement of this goal. In addition, products of autotransfusion may contain harmful cytokines, damaged cells, and debris, while lacking platelets and other important proteins and coagulation factors.[2]

Antibiotic prophylaxis after tube thoracostomy is controversial.[3] Most clinicians, however, would recommend use of a first-generation cephalosporin for 24 hours, ideally starting before the initial tube placement.

After the primary survey, less dramatic pneumothoraces may be recognized on diagnostic images, along with hemothoraces, on various imaging studies. Treatment of occult pneumothoraces (i.e., those seen only on computed tomography) deserves special mention. In general, patients with occult pneumothoraces who require positive pressure ventilation, those who are hypotensive or have respiratory distress of any etiology, and those who have associated complex injuries or hemothorax should be treated with tube thoracostomy. One group, however, has questioned the need for tube thoracostomy in patients requiring positive pressure ventilation on the basis of findings from a small number of patients.[4] Patients with occult pneumothoraces who are treated without tube thoracostomy should be observed for at least 24 hours.

Retained Hemothorax and Empyema

In treating a hemothorax with tube thoracostomy, the goal is complete removal of blood. Complications such as atelectasis and empyema after chest trauma are clearly related to the presence of residual blood, fluid, and air, as can occur secondary to improper positioning of the tube (i.e., within a fissure), obstruction of the tube, or blood clot or loculated fluid within the chest.

A persistent or clotted hemothorax is suggested by the presence of a persistent opacification in the pleural space in a patient with a known previous hemothorax. This radiodensity can be confused with adjacent pulmonary contusion or atelectasis; chest CT confirms the diagnosis. Because retained blood serves as a nidus for infection and empyema,[5] aggressive attempts at removal are justified. Occasionally, removal can be accomplished by placing more chest tubes, but often, an operative approach is needed. Video-assisted thoracic surgery (VATS) may be useful for managing small, clotted hemothoraces and free-flowing blood in patients who can tolerate single-lung ventilation[6]; however, VATS tends to limit the surgeon's ability to control bleeding and perform definitive repair of injuries. In patients who have ongoing bleeding or large, clotted hemothoraces, posterolateral thoracotomy is generally required.

Empyema thoracis is a relatively common complication after chest trauma, occurring in 5% to 10% of patients.[7,8] Possible causes include retained hemothorax, pneumonia with parapneumonic effusion, persistent foreign body, ruptured pulmonary abscess, bronchopleural fistula, esophageal leakage, and tracking through the intact or injured diaphragm from an abdominal source. Empyema may be difficult to diagnose and must be differentiated from pleural thickening, pulmonary contusion, and an uninfected effusion. Chest CT with intravenous contrast usually demonstrates a fluid collection with loculations or an enhancing rim. Such findings, coupled with a clinical scenario of low-grade sepsis or failure to thrive, are diagnostic. Analysis and culture of fluid obtained at thoracocentesis or chest tube placement typically confirms the diagnosis, but the fluid may be sterile if the patient is already receiving antibiotics.

Antibiotic therapy, either broad-spectrum or specifically directed against cultured organisms (usually gram-positive pathogens), is certainly an important component of therapy for empyema thoracis, but the primary goal is removal of the infection while the fluid is still thin. When this goal is met, a more modest therapeutic procedure can be performed, there is less risk that a restrictive pulmonary peel will develop, and the injured patient recovers faster overall. In the early stages, tube thoracostomy may suffice for treatment; however, if the infected pleural process cannot be completely evacuated via chest tube because of thicker fluid, loculations, or pleural adhesions, a formal thoracotomy with decortication is generally required.

Decortication should not be undertaken in the face of severe sepsis. Instead, antibiotics and chest drainage (via tube thoracostomy, CT-directed catheter placement, or open rib resection) should be employed until sepsis is controlled. In cases of early empyema, VATS has been successfully used for lysis of adhesions and removal of fluid.[9,10] Because of the limited capacity for performing pleurectomy with this procedure, VATS should not be used when thick peel or a trapped lung is present. In adult patients with posttraumatic empyema, there is no proven role for intrapleural fibrinolytic therapy.

EMERGENCY DEPARTMENT THORACOTOMY

ED thoracotomy is a drastic step in the treatment of the injured patient. If possible, the patient should be stabilized and transported to the operating room, where better facilities are available for definitive care.

ED thoracotomy is best reserved for patients who arrive at the ED and deteriorate rapidly and those who have undergone cardiac arrest just before arrival. The results are dismal when it is performed in patients who have undergone cardiac arrest some time before arrival and have required cardiopulmonary resuscitation for more than a few minutes. Blunt trauma victims who have sustained cardiopulmonary arrest at the scene of injury should not be subjected to thoracotomy, either at the scene or in the ED.[11] Similarly, patients who are found at emergency thoracotomy to have no cardiac activity have a dismal prognosis, as do those who do not respond to improvement of systolic blood pressure after aortic occlusion. Overall, the survival rate for patients undergoing ED thoracotomy for blunt trauma is lower than 10%. The reported survival rate for patients undergoing ED thoracotomy for penetrating trauma ranges from 16% to 57%,[11-13] and that for patients with cardiac wounds ranges from 57% to 72%.[11-13]

The technique of ED thoracotomy is straightforward. An antiseptic solution may be splashed on the chest, but skin preparation is not required. An incision is made from the sternal border to the midaxillary line in the fourth intercostal space. A chest retractor is inserted and opened widely. The costochondral junctions of the fifth, the fourth, and sometimes the third rib are divided quickly with the scalpel to provide exposure. Attention is directed first to the injury. If there is exsanguination from a great vessel, the hemorrhage is controlled with pressure. If air embolism is the cause of the arrest, the hilum is clamped and air evacuated from the aorta. Otherwise, the pericardium is opened anterior and parallel to the phrenic nerve. The hemopericardium is evacuated, the cardiac injury is controlled with digital pressure, and a temporary repair is performed.

After the cause of the arrest has been addressed, the descending thoracic aorta is occluded with a vascular clamp or digital pressure and intrathoracic cardiac compression is initiated. The patient's intravascular volume is restored, and electrolyte imbalances are corrected. If the patient can be saved, he or she is transported to the OR for definitive repair and closure.

SECONDARY SURVEY AND DEFINITIVE DIAGNOSIS

The secondary survey should focus on more subtle evidence of injury that may be detected on physical examination and chest x-ray. Simple rib fractures are clinically relevant when associated with pain and are better diagnosed by palpation than by most imaging studies. Pneumothorax and hemothorax often go undetected during the primary survey but are common findings later in the workup.

Echocardiography can be an important adjunct for assessing proximity wounds to the heart or evaluating a new murmur. Because of continuing improvements in CT scanning technology, this modality is increasingly being used in the evaluation of the widened mediastinum.[14] Indeed, CT angiography is now routinely employed for definitive diagnosis of aortic injuries, rendering standard angiography unnecessary in most cases.[15]

Operative Considerations

INDICATIONS FOR OPERATIVE MANAGEMENT

Indications for operative treatment of thoracic injuries fall into five broad categories: (1) hemorrhage, (2) major airway disruption, (3) cardiac and vascular injuries, (4) esophageal disruption, and (5) diaphragmatic disruption. The extent and location of hemorrhage can sometimes be determined from open wounds but are more often established after chest tube insertion. If 1,500 ml of blood or more is obtained initially or ongoing bleeding at a rate of 300 ml/hr or higher for 3 hours is noted, thoracotomy is indicated.[16] Massive air leakage and the presence of gastric or esophageal contents in the chest tube effluent also necessitate surgical intervention. The severity of an air leak can be estimated by examining the amount of air traversing the water seal chamber. Intermittent bubbling signifies a small leak, whereas a continuous stream of bubbles signifies a large leak. A continuous leak seen in conjunction with inability to expand the lung completely or with inadequate tidal volumes is considered a massive air leak. In stable patients with no evidence of bleeding, specific diagnostic measures may be performed to evaluate the thoracic viscera. The likelihood of associated intra-abdominal injuries must not be overlooked.

CHOICE OF INCISION

The choice of thoracic incision obviously depends on many factors, including the indication for operation, the urgency of the situation, the presence of associated injuries, the mechanism of injury, and the results of preoperative studies. For injuries that are suspected or diagnosed preoperatively, the approach to the affected thoracic structure is relatively straightforward [see Table 1]. For exploratory surgery, the choice of incision should depend on the mechanism, the instrument, the location (of the entire injury, not just the entry site), and the symptoms. Stab wounds generally have a lower potential for deep penetration than missile injuries do.

A median sternotomy is one of the more versatile thoracic incisions. It can be opened and closed more quickly than a thoracotomy, is associated with less postoperative pain, and may be less likely to result in contamination of the dependent hemithorax. In gen-

Table 1 Surgical Approaches for Traumatic Injuries to Thoracic Structures

Site of Injury	Incision		
	Sternotomy	Right Thoracotomy	Left Thoracotomy
Right atrium	+++	++	0
Right ventricle	+++	+	+
Left atrium	+++	+	+
Left ventricle	++	0	+++
Superior vena cava	+++	++	0
Azygos vein	++	+++	0
Inferior vena cava	+++	++	0
Aortic root	+++	+	0
Aortic arch	+++	0	++
Right subclavian artery	++	++	0
Proximal right carotid artery	+++	+	0
Innominate artery	+++	++	0
Left subclavian artery	+	0	+++
Proximal left carotid artery	++	0	++
Descending aorta	0	+	+++
Main pulmonary artery	+++	0	++
Right pulmonary artery	++	+++	0
Left pulmonary artery	++	0	+++
Right upper lobe	++	+++	0
Right middle lobe	++	+++	0
Right lower lobe	+	+++	0
Left upper lobe	+	0	+++
Left lower lobe	0	0	+++
Right hilum	++	+++	0
Left hilum	++	0	+++
Pericardium	+++	++	++
Right internal mammary artery	++	+++	0
Left internal mammary artery	++	0	+++
Proximal esophagus	0	+++	0
Distal esophagus	0	++	+++
Proximal trachea	++	+	+
Carina	0	+++	+
Right main stem	0	+++	0
Left main stem	0	++	++
Right hemidiaphragm	+	+++	0
Left hemidiaphragm	+	0	+++
Cardiopulmonary bypass	+++	++	++

+++—preferred ++—acceptable +—site accessible with difficulty
0—site inaccessible

eral, a median sternotomy provides the best exposure of the right-side cardiac chambers, the ascending aorta, the aortic arch, and the arch vessels (excluding the left subclavian artery), and it provides adequate exposure of both lungs and both hemidiaphragms. In the setting of exploratory surgery, a median sternotomy is the best incision for mantle stab wounds and some precordial gunshot wounds whose trajectory can be reliably determined. Its main limitation is that it does not provide exposure of the posterior mediastinal structures.

For exploration of lateral stab or gunshot wounds, a posterolateral thoracotomy on the side of the injury is the incision of choice. Besides being the best incision for exploratory purposes, the fifth interspace thoracotomy is the most versatile approach to ipsilateral pulmonary and mediastinal pathologic states. Exposure can be markedly enhanced by removal of the fifth rib, which yields an incision that is as long as the rib itself and extends as high as the fourth interspace and as low as the sixth interspace. In general, it is unwise to perform an exploratory thoracotomy below the fourth interspace or above the sixth.

A transverse anterior thoracotomy (clamshell incision) is occasionally useful for undetermined or transmediastinal injuries in urgent situations. When exposure of both hemithoraces is required in nonurgent situations, both staged bilateral posterolateral thoracotomies and median sternotomy provide better exposure; one or the other is therefore preferred.

The role of VATS in the trauma setting continues to evolve. In acute situations, VATS is useful for ruling out diaphragm injury and may be preferable to laparoscopy insofar as it is less likely to cause tension pneumothorax. VATS may also have a role to play in the management of persistent intercostal or internal mammary artery bleeding, but this application demands some degree of experience with thoracoscopic surgery. Later after injury, VATS can be employed for evacuation of retained hemothorax and for management of the early stages of empyema.

DAMAGE CONTROL TACTICS

Whereas the concept of damage control is critically important in abdominal trauma, it is less important in thoracic trauma. Although serious bleeding from most thoracic structures is unlikely to be controlled with packing, severe coagulopathy occasionally prevents definitive repair and necessitates abbreviation of surgery and temporary closure of the chest by suturing or stapling the skin incision only.[17] The two most common locations of injury in these scenarios are the lung and the chest wall.

Hemorrhage from lung lacerations in patients with metabolic exhaustion generally should not be treated with formal anatomic resection: stapled wedge resection, tractotomy, or simple suture repair is more appropriate. In patients with persistent chest wall bleeding that is not associated with a major vessel, treatment with lung reexpansion for local tamponade and correction of coagulopathy usually suffices. In rare circumstances, complex esophageal injuries may be associated with extensive loss of tissue, necessitating rapid exclusion and proximal diversion. In most patients with any chance of survival, however, the surgeon should attempt primary closure of the injury, buttressing the repair with autologous tissue, and employing wide drainage. Even with large defects, this approach has a surprisingly high rate of ultimate success.

ANESTHETIC CONCERNS

Airway management can be extremely complex in patients with thoracic injuries, especially when tracheobronchial injury is involved. Whenever operative management is required for a thoracic trauma patient, operative planning should begin with a discussion with the anesthesiology team about airway issues.

In general, double-lumen and bronchial-blocker endotracheal tubes, which allow better exposure by partially or completely deflating a selected lung, should be strongly considered for any thoracic operation. For any given patient, the improved exposure achievable with such tubes must be weighed against the disadvantages—namely, the additional time needed for placement and the requirement that single-lung ventilation be tolerable from a cardiopulmonary standpoint. Hemodynamic stability, therefore, is usually a prerequisite for the use of these devices. The extent of the advantage gained with lung isolation must also be considered. For example, surgery on the mediastinum or the hilum is greatly facilitated by lung deflation, whereas surgery on the chest wall is not. If necessary, these tubes can often be placed in the ED.

If, at presentation, a patient with an otherwise adequate airway has signs of airway injury (e.g., a massive air leak, subcutaneous air, or hemoptysis), further evaluation with bronchoscopy in the OR is indicated before a decision is made to replace the existing adequate airway. In the absence of massive air leakage, bronchial tearing, or hemorrhage into one mainstem bronchus, a double-lumen tube should be advanced into the left mainstem bronchus. Otherwise, the tube should be placed so as to protect the uninjured side.

When a patient with a double-lumen tube in place requires continued intubation after operation, the tube generally must be replaced with a standard endotracheal tube or a tracheostomy because an adequate pulmonary toilet cannot be performed through a double-lumen tube. In contrast, a bronchial-blocker tube may be left in place after surgery because a suction catheter can be passed down it. A disadvantage of the bronchial-blocker tube, however, is that intraoperative lung isolation may be less complete than that obtained with a double-lumen tube.

When a patient requiring a thoracic operation presents with an inadequate airway, specific airway management depends on the nature of the injuries. Most of these patients can be intubated in the standard fashion. If intubation is unsuccessful, however, cricothyroidotomy should be attempted without delay. In cases of tracheal transection, the distal segment must be controlled quickly through a neck incision and selectively intubated through the wound. In cases of known or suspected thoracic airway injuries, an endotracheal tube should be inserted over a bronchoscope past the injury or into an uninjured mainstem bronchus.

Intraoperative management of the airway in patients with complex tracheobronchial injuries can be challenging and is discussed in detail elsewhere [see Tracheobronchial Injuries, below]. Injuries to the thoracic trachea may necessitate placement of temporary tubes within the operative field to provide ventilation [see Figure 1]. After repair of a tracheobronchial injury, the patient should be extubated if at all possible to prevent stress on the repair.

The locations of arterial catheters should be considered as well. In general, radial arterial lines should be placed in the extremity opposite the side of the intended thoracotomy and not (obviously) in vessels distal to anticipated cross-clamps. Placement of an epidural catheter for postoperative pain management [see 10 Postoperative Pain] should also be considered in patients undergoing nonurgent thoracotomy.

Control of body temperature is critical for both operative and nonoperative management. Most thoracic trauma patients are hypothermic and require a warm OR, warm I.V. fluids, and warming blankets. Occasionally, controlled hypothermia is a useful adjunct to procedures involving the thoracic aorta when spinal cord injury and paraplegia are risks. For patients with severe coagulopathy and a core temperature lower than 33.5° C, extracorporeal warming can be lifesaving. This procedure involves placement of a 21 French femoral venous cannula and a 17 French internal jugular cannula and use of a centrifugal pump and a heat exchanger. Heparin is not necessary.

Chest Wall Injuries

BLUNT

The greatest significance of certain chest wall injuries is their frequent association with other, more life-threatening injuries. These so-called sentinel injuries include first rib fractures, scapular fractures, sternal fractures, bilateral rib fractures, and lower rib fractures.

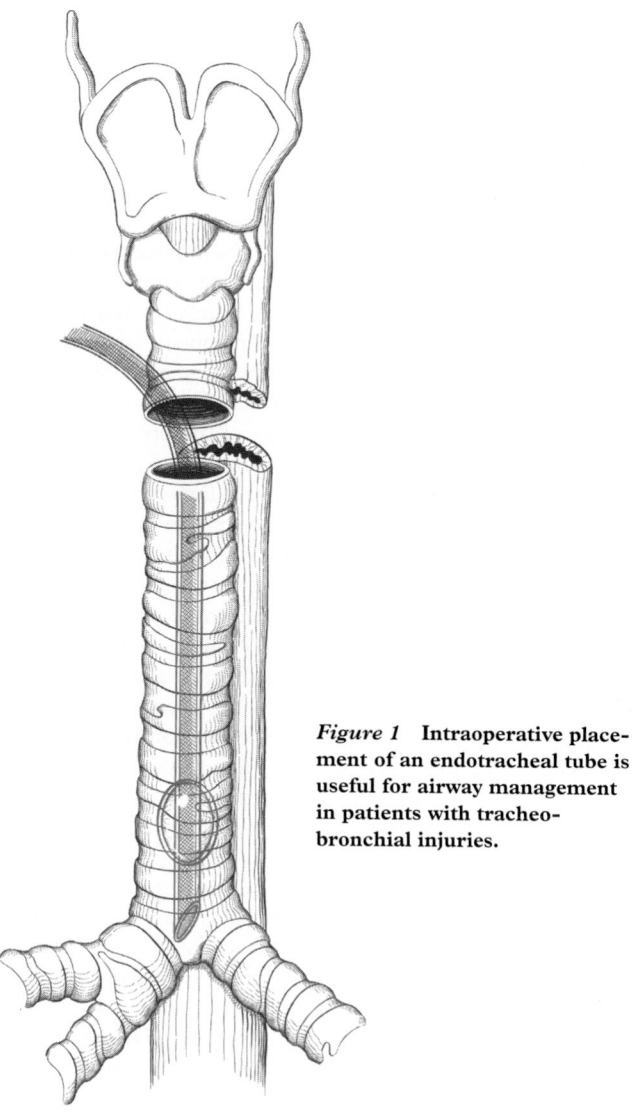

Figure 1 Intraoperative placement of an endotracheal tube is useful for airway management in patients with tracheobronchial injuries.

Simple Rib Fractures

Rib fractures are the most common chest wall injuries resulting from blunt trauma. The main pathophysiologic consequences of rib fractures are pain, splinting, and prevention of adequate cough. The diagnosis should be suspected if pain or splinting occurs on deep inspiration, and it is confirmed by careful physical examination, consisting of anterior-posterior and lateral-lateral manual compression. If an alert patient feels no pain when these maneuvers are done, clinically significant rib fractures can be excluded. Although rib fractures are often identified on routine chest radiographs, they are more likely to be undetectable except on rib-detail films, which are rarely indicated. A variant of rib fracture that falls into the same physiologic category is costochondral or costosternal separation. This condition is usually detected during physical examination but is not seen on routine chest radiographs.

Management Isolated rib fractures can usually be adequately treated by giving oral analgesics and encouraging good pulmonary toilet. We mention chest wall strapping, taping, and bracing only to condemn these practices. Binding devices generally restrict tidal volume and thus promote rather than prevent atelectasis and pulmonary complications. Treatment of multiple rib fractures, costochondral separation, and costosternal separation is described more fully elsewhere [see Flail Chest, *below*].

Special mention should be made of rib fractures in the elderly. The mortality associated with rib fractures is twice as high in patients older than 65 years as in younger patients, and the relative increase in the incidence of pneumonia in older patients is even higher, even after the increased comorbidity is taken into account.[18,19]

Sternal Fractures

The vast majority of sternal fractures result from motor vehicle accidents and are associated with the use of three-point restraints. Isolated sternal fractures in this setting are relatively benign, having a low incidence of associated cardiac, great vessel, and pulmonary injuries. Sternal fractures in unrestrained occupants and victims of crush injuries, however, are commonly associated with underlying visceral injuries, which must be excluded.[20]

The diagnosis of sternal fracture is based on the presence of severe pain, often associated with instability on sternal palpation. In many cases, physical examination can clarify the nature of the fracture. Sternal fractures are almost invariably transverse, with the majority occurring at the sternomanubrial joint or in the midbody of the sternum. They may be characterized as simple (two fragments) or comminuted (multiple fragments), as displaced or aligned, or as stable or unstable. The fragments of an unstable fracture move substantially with activity.

Management Initial management of sternal fracture is directed toward resuscitation and identification or exclusion of other life-threatening injuries. In patients with isolated sternal fractures, a normal electrocardiogram and a normal chest radiograph suggest that associated serious injuries are unlikely. If the pain is controlled with oral analgesics, these fractures can usually be managed on an outpatient basis. Displaced fractures may be reduced by the simple (albeit painful) maneuver of having the patient simultaneously raise his or her head and legs from the bed. Such a position requires contraction of the rectus abdominis, which distracts the caudad segment inferiorly, and the sternocleidomastoid muscles, which retract the cephalad segments superiorly. The physician can then depress the anterior segment and allow the patient to relax. This measure often suffices for alleviation of subsequent pain and sometimes constitutes adequate long-term treatment.

The vast majority of sternal fractures heal with nonoperative management. Those that are unstable or are displaced by more than 1 cm of overlap are more likely to exhibit malunion or nonunion and subsequent chronic pain; they should be treated with open reduction and internal fixation. Occasionally, a patient with a clinically stable, minimally displaced sternal fracture associated with lower extremity injuries who requires crutches for ambulation experiences such disabling sternal pain during ambulation that fracture repair is necessary.

Sternal fractures may be repaired with either of two operative techniques. In both, the sternum is approached via either a vertical midline incision or a sweeping transverse inframammary incision similar to that used for repair of pectus excavatum. The fracture is exposed, and the ends are mobilized and fixed with either reconstruction plates or No. 6 sternal wires. Reconstruction plates provide a more stable and less painful fixation, and they can be used in the management of comminuted and crush fractures. Wire repair is unsatisfactory in patients with comminuted or crush fractures and in many patients requiring crutches for ambulation. Both wire fixation and plate fixation are well tolerated and, in fact, greatly appreciated by properly selected patients.

Flail Chest

Flail chest is the most serious of the blunt chest wall injuries. It is common after any form of blunt thoracic trauma, and though it may occur as an isolated finding, it is usually associated with other significant injuries.[21] Flail chest represents a disruption of the stability and normal respiratory mechanics of the rib cage. It involves fractures of adjacent ribs, each of which is fractured in two or more places, so that a panel of chest wall moves independently of, and in the opposite direction to, the remainder of the chest. When it occurs in conjunction with separation of the costochondral or costosternal joints, the sternum can also be part of the flail segment, and the condition is termed a sternal flail chest.

The following are the three components of the pathophysiology of flail chest:

1. Alteration of chest wall mechanics. The paradoxical motion of a large flail segment occasionally impairs the patient's ability to achieve an adequate tidal volume or an effective cough.
2. Underlying pulmonary contusion. In the vast majority of serious flail chest injuries, this is the most significant physiologic aberration. In the contused portion of the lung, there is extravasation and accumulation of blood and fluid in the alveolar air space, which results in sufficient shunting to produce hypoxemia.
3. Pain. The extreme pain of multiple rib fractures leads to profound splinting and diminution of tidal volume and prevents adequate coughing and pulmonary toilet in most alert patients. The combination of depressed tidal volume and inadequate coughing leads to hypoventilation, atelectasis, and often pneumonia.

The diagnosis is typically suspected on the basis of the presence of numerous adjacent rib fractures on a chest radiograph, but it can be conclusively confirmed only by the presence of a paradoxical motion observed in the involved segment in a spontaneously breathing patient. A flail segment may be overlooked in a patient undergoing positive pressure ventilation because there may be no paradoxical motion without inspiratory effort. Therefore, in an intubated patient, the diagnosis must be sought through careful examination and palpation of the rib cage for instability.

Management Proper management of flail chest hinges on the recognition that the injury is not a static condition but, rather, an evolving process. Frequent reevaluation and timely, appropriate intervention are essential. During the initial assessment, the patency of the airway and the adequacy of ventilation must be established or confirmed. Immediate intubation is rarely required for patients with isolated flail chest injuries. When early intubation is indicated, it is usually for associated injuries, most commonly to the central nervous system.

In virtually all awake and alert patients, management without intubation should be attempted. To this end, early and aggressive pain management is essential. Pain cannot be eliminated entirely, but it usually can be diminished sufficiently to allow an adequate tidal volume and a forceful cough. Oral analgesics rarely suffice for patients with even a small flail segment; stronger agents are required for all but the most stoic of patients. Parenteral narcotics are effective, especially when administered in a patient-controlled analgesia (PCA) device. Intercostal nerve blocks occasionally provide dramatic pain relief, but only for short periods. If the patient is encouraged to cough vigorously during pain relief, intermittent nerve blocks may be helpful, despite the inherent risk of pneumothorax.

The mainstay of pain control in patients with flail chest is thoracic epidural anesthesia, in which a solution containing 0.002% to 0.005% morphine sulfate and 0.075% to 0.2% bupivacaine is infused through a small catheter in the thoracic epidural space at a constant rate of 0.15 to 0.75 mg morphine/hr. At this low dosage, bupivacaine acts synergistically with morphine and does not exert a local anesthetic effect on the spinal cord; in addition, it generally does not give rise to the respiratory depression frequently observed with systemic narcotics. Epidural anesthesia provides immediate comfort, dramatically improves vital capacity and tidal volume, and, most important, enables the patient to produce a forceful cough.[22]

The most common serious adverse effect of epidural anesthesia is transient hypotension at the time of insertion. This complication can be prevented by providing adequate volume resuscitation before creating the chemical sympathectomy. Urinary retention occurs in 30% to 50% of cases; in practical terms, this means that most flail chest patients should not have their urinary catheters removed until the epidural analgesics are no longer required. Patients who have head injuries and are thus at risk for increased intracranial pressure should not undergo epidural catheterization, because an unintentional dural puncture could alter cerebrospinal pressure sufficiently to induce or contribute to cerebral herniation. Relative contraindications to epidural catheter placement include spine fractures and infection; however, fever may be a relative indication if it is thought to be secondary to splinting with atelectasis or pneumonia.

The decision-making process for management of flail chest should begin with assessment of the patient's ability to cough [*see Figure 2*]. If the patient is able to clear tracheal secretions—that is, actually cough them up into the oropharynx—then observation in an acute care setting, in conjunction with small, infrequent doses of narcotics, is appropriate. If the patient has no cough or has a very truncated cough that moves secretions but does not propel them into the oropharynx, an aggressive program to promote pulmonary toilet, including chest physiotherapy and postural drainage, should be instituted. If a sufficiently vigorous cough cannot be achieved and there is no specific contraindication, an epidural catheter is inserted and the patient followed closely with frequent physical examinations in the intensive care unit. Ambulation is encouraged, and frequent coughing is required.

There is no role for antibiotic prophylaxis in the management of flail chest or pulmonary contusion. Pneumonia is common in this setting, occurring in 25% to 50% of flail chest victims, but prophylactic antibiotics do not reduce the incidence of this complication: they simply shift the spectrum of offending organisms to favor drug-resistant bacteria and fungi. Routine administration of steroids also has no role in the treatment of flail chest.

Given adequate pulmonary toilet, many flail chest victims can avoid intubation.[23] However, any patient with flail chest who demonstrates further deterioration of pulmonary function and who becomes hypoxic or hypercarbic should undergo mechanical ventilation aimed at (1) ensuring a tidal volume adequate for establishing normal chest wall excursion and (2) maintaining a respiratory rate adequate for achieving normocarbia. Hypoxia is managed by increasing the fraction of inspired oxygen (F_IO_2) and applying sufficient positive end-expiratory pressure to achieve adequate oxygenation (usually defined as arterial oxygen saturation greater than 90%) with nontoxic levels of F_IO_2.

A few patients with severe disruption of chest wall mechanics as a result of flail chest continue to require positive pressure ventilation even though adequate pain control has been achieved and the pulmonary contusions are beginning to resolve. Some of them

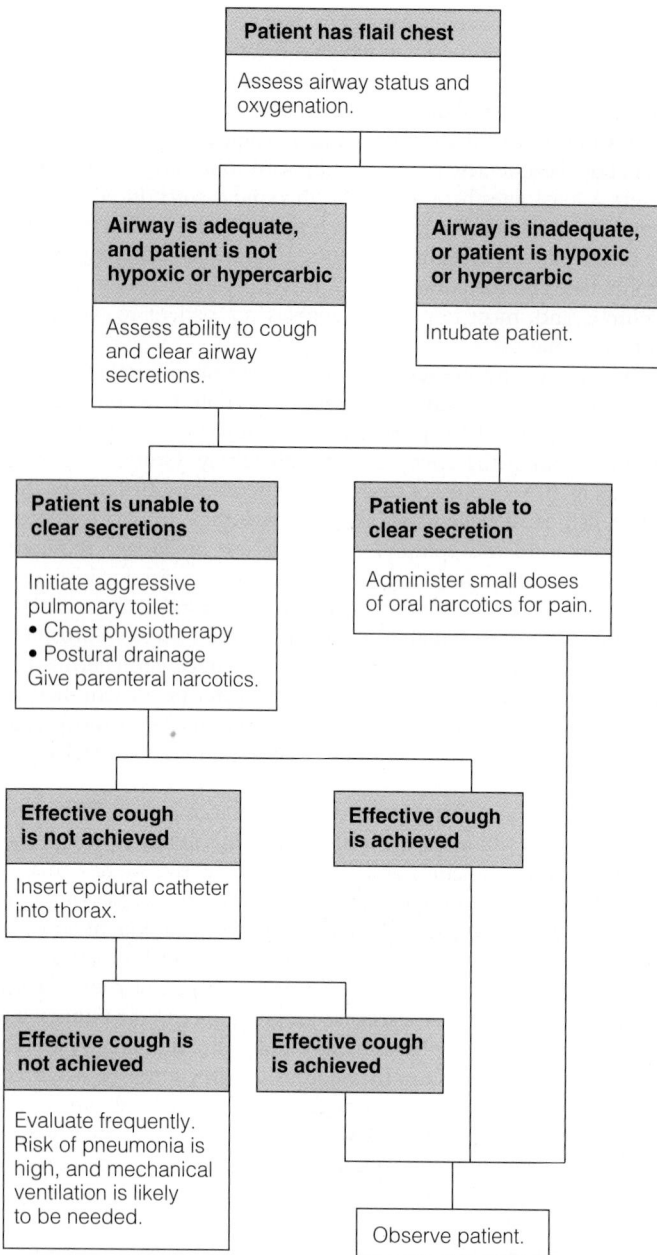

Figure 2 **Algorithm illustrates approach to management of flail chest.**

may benefit from internal fixation of the multiple rib fractures, which restores chest wall stability and eliminates much of the fracture-related pain. In this procedure, the fractured ribs are exposed and a small orthopedic plate is affixed so as to stabilize the ribs and obtain compression osteosynthesis of each fracture site. To date, internal fixation of rib fractures has not been widely studied in the United States, but reports involving a few carefully selected patients suggest that it can provide excellent pain relief. It has also been shown to improve tidal volume and pulmonary mechanics and reduce time spent on the ventilator.[24,25]

PENETRATING

In most cases of penetrating thoracic trauma, the injury to the chest wall is vastly overshadowed by the injury, or potential for injury, to the intrathoracic structures. The notable exceptions to this general rule are hemorrhage and open chest wounds.

Hemorrhage

Stab wounds and low-caliber gunshot wounds to the anterior chest are common in urban areas. Such injuries often can be managed with tube thoracostomy or observation alone, once serious injury to intrathoracic organs has been excluded. Indications for urgent thoracotomy are discussed elsewhere [*see* Operative Considerations, Indications for Operative Management, *above*].

In patients with persistent hemorrhage from chest tubes who require thoracotomy, the most common source of the bleeding is a lacerated internal mammary or intercostal artery. Attempts to control bleeding from these vessels nonoperatively usually fail. Angiography to localize the bleeding vessel is unnecessary and delays definitive care: coupled with embolization of the lacerated vessel, it is more time-consuming than surgical intervention and does not address associated injuries and hemothorax.

Penetrating wounds to the midportion of the pectoral muscle occur with surprising frequency, possibly as a result of an assailant's erroneous conception of the location of the heart. Such injuries often lacerate the pectoral branch of the thoracoacromial artery, which courses along the posterior surface of the pectoral muscle. Control of this troublesome bleeding is extremely difficult to achieve if exploration is attempted directly through an extension of the entrance wound, but it is a straightforward and simple matter if exploration is attempted through an oblique wound along the lateral pectoral margin after entry into the subpectoral plane.

Open Chest Wounds

The diagnosis of an open chest wound is usually obvious, and their treatment depends on the size of the wound and the size of the chest wall defect. Most small open pneumothoraces can be managed initially with occlusive dressings, but there is usually an underlying pulmonary injury with air leakage, which necessitates early tube thoracostomy to prevent tension pneumothorax. Once the patient's condition is stable, the wound can be debrided and closed. Occasionally, primary skin closure must be delayed.

Larger chest wall defects pose a challenging therapeutic problem. Such wounds usually result from high-velocity missiles or shotguns fired at close range. Initial management is directed toward restoration of respiratory mechanics with early intubation and mechanical ventilation.

The next priority is to address any underlying intrathoracic injuries, which may range from mild pulmonary contusion to massive hemorrhage in conjunction with severe lung or hollow viscus injury. When associated intrathoracic injuries are present, the first step in the closure of the defect is to select an appropriate operative approach. Although the primary objective in this situation is to provide excellent exposure for repair of what may be life-threatening injuries, whenever possible, the thoracotomy should be performed in such a way as to preserve the blood supply and muscle mass of the chest wall adjacent to the defect.

After definitive repair of intrathoracic injuries and debridement of devitalized chest wall tissue, the next step is to plan the closure. Such planning requires a degree of familiarity with current and developing techniques and an understanding of pleural drainage, respiratory mechanics, and techniques of tissue transfer. Collaboration with plastic and thoracic surgeons is often helpful. Most chest wall defects can be closed with viable autogenous tissue, usually through rotation of local myocutaneous or myofascial flaps of the pectoral muscle, the latissimus dorsi, or the rectus abdominis.

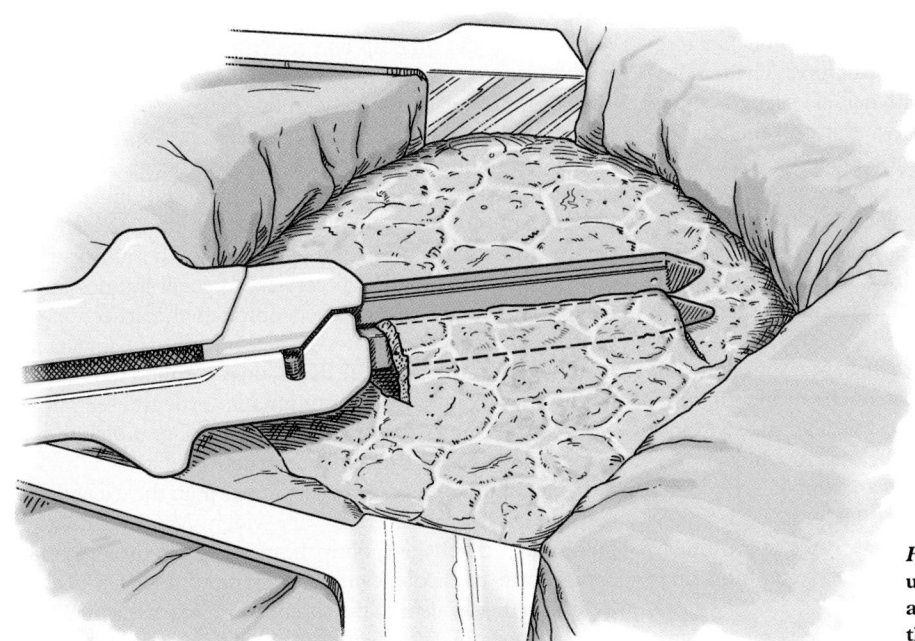

Figure 3 **Pulmonary tractotomy is useful for controlling hemorrhage associated with deep through-and-through injuries to the lungs.**

Pulmonary Injuries

Because of their size, the lungs are commonly injured in cases of thoracic trauma. Mortality from pulmonary lacerations is directly proportional to the amount of blood lost. A 1,500 ml hemothorax, regardless of causative mechanism, should always prompt exploration.

LACERATIONS

Bleeding pulmonary lacerations can be oversewn, resected, or explored via pulmonary tractotomy. Bleeding from small or shallow lacerations can be controlled with an over-and-over repair using a continuous monofilament suture. Bleeding from deeper lacerations is controlled with resection or tractotomy. Most pulmonary resections for trauma should be stapled, nonanatomic resections. Mortality is proportional to the amount of lung tissue resected: with suture repair alone, mortality is 9%; with tractotomy, 13%; with wedge resection, 30%; with lobectomy, 43%; and with pneumonectomy, 50%.[26,27]

Tractotomy is especially useful for deep through-and-through injuries. In this technique, the injury tract is opened with a linear stapler [see Figure 3] or between two aortic clamps. If clamps are used, the cut lung edges are oversewn and the tract left open. Tractotomy exposes bleeding vessels and air leaks inside the tract and permits selective ligation. Occasionally, it exposes an injury to a major vascular or airway structure that must be treated with a formal resection. Because of the risk of exsanguination or excessive devitalization of lung tissue, tractotomy is not indicated when the injury traverses the hilum or when the entire thickness of a lobe will be cut.

Central lung injuries often cause massive hemorrhage. In addition, they may be sources of pulmonary venous air emboli when both a major pulmonary vein and a large airway are disrupted. A common scenario involves an intubated patient on positive pressure ventilation who exhibits sudden deterioration of CNS and cardiac status. Emergency thoracotomy must be performed and the pulmonary hilum clamped. The diagnosis is confirmed by visualizing air in the epicardial coronary arteries. Aspiration of air from the left-side cardiac chambers and elevation of central blood pressure are also useful maneuvers. Most central lung injuries are associated with extensive parenchymal injury in gravely ill patients.

Selective repair of hilar structures is usually impractical in this setting, and lobectomy or pneumonectomy is the salvage procedure of choice.

CONTUSIONS

Pulmonary contusions are bruises to the lung that usually are caused by blunt trauma to the chest but sometimes result from penetrating injury by high-velocity weapons. The contused segment of the lung has a profound ventilation-perfusion mismatch, which produces an intrapulmonary right-to-left shunt and hypoxia. The bruise also may serve later as a source of sepsis. The diagnosis is usually evident on initial chest x-ray or CT, but the bruise often is not fully developed until 12 to 24 hours after injury.

Most pulmonary contusions that are not complicated by excessive attempts at resuscitation or by superinfection resolve over 3 to 5 days. Cardiovascular and, if necessary, ventilatory support must be provided. In general, pulmonary contusion is treated in much the same fashion as flail chest. Patients with rib fractures and painful chest wall excursions must be given sufficient analgesic support to allow them to produce a cough forceful enough to maintain pulmonary toilet. Intubated patients should undergo suctioning frequently. Patients with pulmonary contusions who require substantial volume resuscitation should be considered for pulmonary arterial catheter monitoring. Steroids are not indicated, because they have no effect on the development or resolution of the contusion and because they set the stage for subsequent infection. Diuretics and prophylactic antibiotics are also unnecessary.

Tracheobronchial Injuries

Although tracheobronchial injuries are often lethal, a high index of suspicion for the existence of the injury, a timely diagnosis, and appropriate intervention can improve the chances of a successful outcome. The reported incidence of tracheobronchial injury in blunt chest trauma patients ranges from 0.2% to 8%.[28-30] More than 80% of tracheobronchial ruptures occur within 2.5 cm of the carina. Mainstem bronchi are injured in 86% of patients and distal bronchi in only 9.3%, whereas complex injuries are seen in 8%.

Knowledge of the anatomy of the trachea and the bronchial tree facilitates safe exposure and repair of these structures. The trachea is a tubular structure 10 to 13 cm long, with half of its length in the neck and half in the thorax. The anterior two thirds of the trachea is protected by 18 to 22 U-shaped cartilages. The posterior wall of the trachea is membranous and in intimate contact with the esophagus. The recurrent laryngeal nerve lies adjacent to the esophagus and the trachea in the tracheoesophageal groove. At the level of the fourth thoracic vertebra, the trachea ends and the mainstem bronchi originate. The blood supply to the trachea is segmental and approaches the trachea laterally.

When dissecting and mobilizing the trachea, one should avoid the lateral pedicles and mobilize only one tracheal ring circumferentially so as to maintain an adequate vascular supply. One may resect a substantial length of the trachea (as much as 4 or 5 cm, or half) and still achieve a safe primary anastomosis. Because the trachea is in contact with the esophagus along its entire posterior length and is surrounded by vital structures (e.g., lungs, heart, and great vessels), associated injuries are common and often fatal.

Intrathoracic injury to the tracheobronchial tree is more commonly the result of blunt trauma but may also be caused by bullet wounds. Blunt trauma may injure the trachea and the bronchi via several mechanisms, including direct blows, shear stress, and burst injury. Shear forces on the trachea cause damage at its relatively fixed points—namely, the cricoid and the carina. Burst injury along the tracheobronchial tree often results in rapid anteroposterior compression of the thorax. This compression causes a simultaneous expansion in the lateral thoracic diameter, and the negative intrapleural pressure stretches the lungs laterally along with the chest wall, thereby placing traction on the carina. When the plasticity of the tracheobronchial tree is exceeded, the lungs are pulled apart and the bronchi avulsed. Closure of the glottis before impact may convert the trachea into a rigid tube with increased intratracheal pressure, and as a consequence, the impact may cause a linear tear or blowout of the membranous portion of the trachea or a complex disruption of the trachea and the bronchi. Given the protected nature of these structures, a high degree of energy transfer is usually required to injure them.

Various clinical presentations result after injury to the tracheobronchial tree, generally depending on the severity and the location of the injury. In the neck, airway involvement may create severe respiratory distress that causes death before emergency care can be given. Alternatively, patients with cervical tracheal injuries may present with stridor and severe respiratory distress or with hoarseness, hemoptysis, or cervical subcutaneous emphysema.

The presentation of thoracic tracheobronchial injury depends on whether the injury is confined to the mediastinum or communicates with the pleural space. Thoracic tracheobronchial injuries confined to the mediastinum usually present with a massive pneumomediastinum. Pneumopericardium is occasionally described, but this description is usually mistaken, because air in the pericardial sac is in fact rare. What is actually seen is air in the plane just external to the pericardium, between it and the pleura. Injuries that do extend into the pleural space usually create an ipsilateral pneumothorax that may or may not be under tension. A pneumothorax that persists despite adequate placement of a thoracostomy tube and that leaks air continuously is suggestive of tracheobronchial injury and bronchopleural fistula. Dyspnea may actually worsen after insertion of the chest tube because of the loss of total volume via the tube. Several radiographic clues to possible airway injury may be observed with endotracheal intubation, such as abnormal

migration of the tube tip and distention of the endotracheal tube balloon beyond the normal tracheal diameter.

In only 30% of cases is a definitive diagnosis of tracheobronchial injury made within 24 hours. More often, the diagnosis is made late, when pulmonary collapse and sepsis occur. As many as 10% of tracheobronchial tears give rise to no initial clinical or radiologic signs and are not recognized until months later, after stricture occurs. Immediate intubation of patients with multisystem trauma can mask laryngeal or high cervical tracheal injuries and thereby delay the diagnosis. After tracheobronchial transection, the peribronchial connective tissues sometimes remain intact and allow continued ventilation of the distal lung, in much the same way that perfusion is maintained after traumatic aortic transection. If unrecognized, this injury heals with scarring and granulation tissue and occasionally creates bronchial obstruction.

Concomitant injury is the rule rather than the exception, but the patterns of associated injury vary widely. Major vascular, cardiac, pulmonary, esophageal, bony thoracic, and neurologic injuries are common in tracheobronchial trauma and reflect the site, magnitude, and mechanism of the trauma. The mechanism of injury may alert the examiner to search for specific associated injuries. For example, transcervical and transmediastinal penetrating injuries pose a particular danger to the structures they traverse. The esophagus is the organ most frequently injured in conjunction with tracheal trauma.[31]

The diagnosis is typically suspected on the basis of the clinical history and the characteristic signs and symptoms [see Figure 4]. The advent of spiral CT has led to renewed interest in the use of this modality to evaluate tracheobronchial injury; however, there is, at present, no evidence that CT is adequate to exclude such injury and render diagnostic bronchoscopy unnecessary. Indications for bronchoscopy in this setting include a large pneumomediastinum, a refractory pneumothorax, a large air leak, persistent atelectasis, and possibly marked subcutaneous emphysema.[31] Bronchoscopy is the most reliable means of establishing the diagnosis and determining the site, nature, and extent of the tracheobronchial disruption.

Both rigid and flexible bronchoscopy have been employed in this setting; neither has been conclusively shown to be superior to the other. Rigid bronchoscopy must be performed with the patient under general anesthesia, and it requires a stable ligamentous and bony cervical spine. On the other hand, it permits direct visualization and has the ability to provide ventilation. Flexible bronchoscopy may be performed without general anesthesia and allows controlled insertion of a nasal or orotracheal tube while maintaining cervical stabilization; this maneuver may help prevent the need for emergency tracheostomy and the potential associated morbidity. At the same time, the entire larynx and trachea can be visualized with a flexible bronchoscope, as can the major lobar bronchi.

Whichever type of scope is used, the signs and symptoms should be correlated with the endoscopic findings. The most critical determinant seems to be the endoscopist's level of experience and comfort with the procedure. An experienced bronchoscopist can perform either technique with a high degree of sensitivity, specificity, and accuracy.[29] Often, the lesions are missed initially, or their severity is underestimated, or they evolve into more obvious or severe lesions. For this reason, bronchoscopy should be liberally repeated as needed.

MANAGEMENT

With tracheobronchial injuries, as with all injuries, airway management is the first priority in treatment. If the patient is maintaining his or her own airway and is adequately ventilated, a cau-

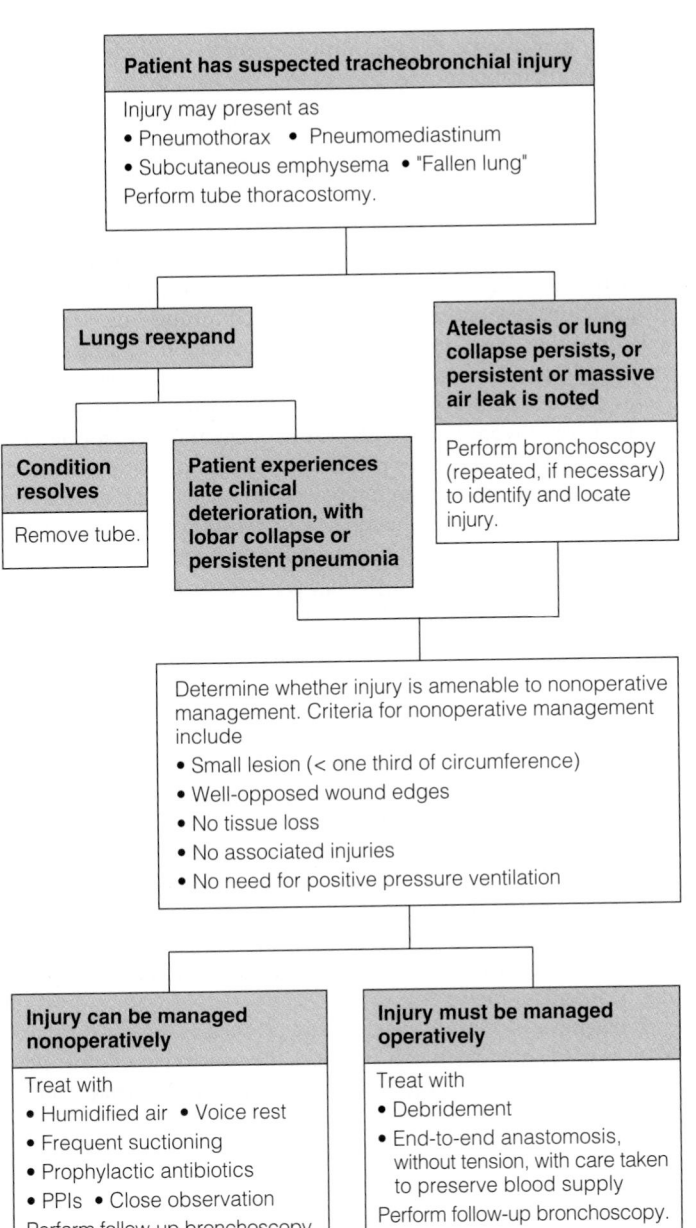

Figure 4 **Algorithm illustrates approach to management of suspected tracheobronchial injury.**

tious noninterventional approach is probably the best initial choice until further diagnostic workup is performed or other life-threatening injuries are stabilized. Careless handling or mishandling of the airway (e.g., inadvertently placing an endotracheal tube through a transected or ruptured airway and into soft tissue) can be disastrous and may compound the injury. ED tracheostomies are difficult and may be dangerous, to say the least.

How best to secure an airway in a patient with neck trauma and possible tracheal injury is a matter of debate. With blind endotracheal intubation, the path of the tube distal to the larynx is unknown, and it is possible to lose the lumen or create a false passage. With intubation over a flexible bronchoscope, the tube can be visualized as it passes beyond the site of injury, and some of the dangers of blind intubation are thereby mitigated; however, some degree of sedation is usually required, and if the patient is oversedated, the airway that was being spontaneously protected may be

lost. Paralytic medications should generally be avoided in this setting, for the same reason. Furthermore, bronchoscopy requires a level of expertise that is not always immediately available in an emergency situation. Urgent tracheostomy or cricothyrotomy, performed in the OR, is advocated by many as the safest and securest way of obtaining airway control. If the trachea is completely transected, the distal trachea can usually be found in the superior mediastinum and grasped for insertion of a cuffed tube. Early tracheostomy may prevent the damage often caused by these hurried, blind attempts at emergency airway control, but inevitably, a number of these tracheostomies will prove to have been unnecessary. The approach taken to airway control must vary with the resources and expertise available at each institution. One must also keep in mind that even after the airway is secured, it may still be possible to exacerbate the injury by means of aggressive ventilation with high airway pressures. Tube thoracostomies should be appropriately placed at this time and connected to suction, even though dyspnea may worsen.

Once the airway is controlled, there is time for orderly identification of concurrent injuries, esophagoscopy, laryngoscopy, arteriography, transport to definitive care areas, and, if necessary, celiotomy.

Nonoperative

On occasion, asymptomatic tracheobronchial tears are found incidentally in the course of bronchoscopy or other imaging procedures. Nonoperative management is reserved for highly selected patients with unsuspected small injuries of this type. Lesions suitable for observation must involve less than one third of the circumference of the tracheobronchial tree. For patients to be candidates for nonoperative care, their lungs should be fully reexpanded with tube thoracostomy, and any air leaks should stop soon after insertion of the tube. There must be no associated injuries and no need for positive pressure ventilation. Prophylactic antibiotics, humidified oxygen, voice rest, frequent suctioning, and close observation for sepsis and airway obstruction are required.

Small penetrating wounds with well-opposed edges and no evidence of loss or devitalization of tracheal tissue may be effectively treated with temporary endotracheal intubation.[32] The cuff of the endotracheal tube should be inflated below the level of injury and left undisturbed for 24 to 48 hours while the wound seals. If a conservatively managed patient's clinical condition deteriorates, bronchoscopy should be liberally repeated. Even small tears may produce substantial amounts of granulation tissue upon healing, which may necessitate late endobronchial excision.

Operative

Like emergency airway management, intraoperative airway management requires close coordination with the anesthesiologist. After the airway is initially secured, manipulation during the repair creates additional challenges. A sterile anesthesia circuit and tube must be available to pass off the table once control of the airway at the level of transection has been regained and the peritracheal connective tissue has been disrupted or entered for repair. If orotracheal intubation is performed, either a single-lumen or a double-lumen endotracheal tube may be used. For proximal levels of rupture, a long single-lumen tube may be passed beyond the area of injury [*see Figure 1*]; for distal injuries, the tube may be advanced into the contralateral mainstem bronchus for single-lung ventilation. Intubation over a flexible bronchoscope improves the safety and diagnostic capability of the procedure.

If a tracheostomy is performed, it should be placed two to three rings caudal to any high tracheal or laryngeal injuries and should be brought out through an incision separate from the surgical repair wound. Tracheostomy proximal to an injury is probably not necessary to protect the suture lines after repair of the thoracic trachea or a major bronchus, and its prophylactic use is discouraged for distal tracheobronchial injuries. Routine use of tracheostomy may result in various complications, including pneumonia, mediastinitis, wound infection, laryngeal and tracheal stenosis, and postoperative dysphonia.

In especially difficult cases, in which airway management is unsatisfactory or the repair is complex, cardiopulmonary bypass or venovenous extracorporeal membrane oxygenation (ECMO) may be instituted. Both of these techniques require systemic anticoagulation, and their potential risks and benefits in multiply injured patients remain to be determined.

Once the repair is complete, the endotracheal tube ideally should be removed immediately after the operation. Occasionally, there is a need for ongoing positive pressure ventilation, which may require the surgeon to employ sophisticated techniques of critical care and ventilation, such as positioning of the endotracheal tube distal to the repair, dual-lung ventilation, high-frequency jet ventilation, and ECMO. Every effort must be made to improve lung compliance by providing good pulmonary toilet, appropriate fluid management, and aggressive treatment of pneumonia.

Intrathoracic tracheal, right bronchial, and proximal left mainstem bronchus injuries are best repaired through a right posterolateral thoracotomy at the fourth or fifth intercostal space because this approach avoids the heart and the aortic arch. Complex or bilateral injuries are also approached through the right chest, for the same reason. Distal left bronchial injuries more than 3 cm from the carina are approached through a left posterolateral thoracotomy in the fifth intercostal space.

Optimal repair includes adequate debridement of devitalized tissue (including cartilage) and primary end-to-end anastomosis of the clean tracheal or bronchial ends. The anastomosis can be accomplished without tension by mobilizing the structures anteriorly and posteriorly, thereby preserving the lateral blood supply.

Tension may also be released with cervical flexion, which can be maintained postoperatively by securing the chin to the chest with a suture. Many investigators recommend performing the anastomosis with interrupted absorbable sutures; however, a continuous absorbable monofilament suture also offers a secure repair, is more readily visible during construction of the anastomosis, and eliminates knots within the tracheal lumen.

The membranous portion may be repaired without tension and then brought together as repair of the cartilaginous portion is begun. Sutures may be placed around or through the cartilage but, in either case, must ensure approximation of mucosa to mucosa. Tying the suture knots on the outside of the lumen also helps prevent suture granulomata and subsequent stricture. To prevent subsequent leakage and fistula formation, the suture line should be reinforced with a patch of pericardium or a vascularized pedicle from the pleura, an intercostal muscle, a strap muscle, or the omentum to protect the repair and assist bronchial healing.

For early repairs, the pleura is too flimsy to be suitable as reinforcement. A vascularized pedicle of intercostal muscle offers both better protection and added healing potential. For this reason, the intercostal muscle should routinely be preserved during thoracotomy, along with the corresponding vein, artery, and nerve. This is accomplished by entering the chest through the bed of the rib; the rib itself may be either preserved or sacrificed. An incision is made directly over the rib, and the periosteum is stripped off. At the superior border of the rib, the incision is carried through the posterior layer of the periosteum to enter the pleural space. The intercostal muscle is then divided from the ribs above and below and used as a flap to be wrapped around and tacked to the trachea. In this manner, viable tissue is placed between the repair and the surrounding vital structures, and the blood supply in the area of the repair is increased, thus facilitating healing [see Figure 5].

If diagnosis is delayed, repair should proceed as soon as the diagnosis is made or as soon as is practical after treatment of other life-threatening injuries. Regardless of the length of the delay, recon-

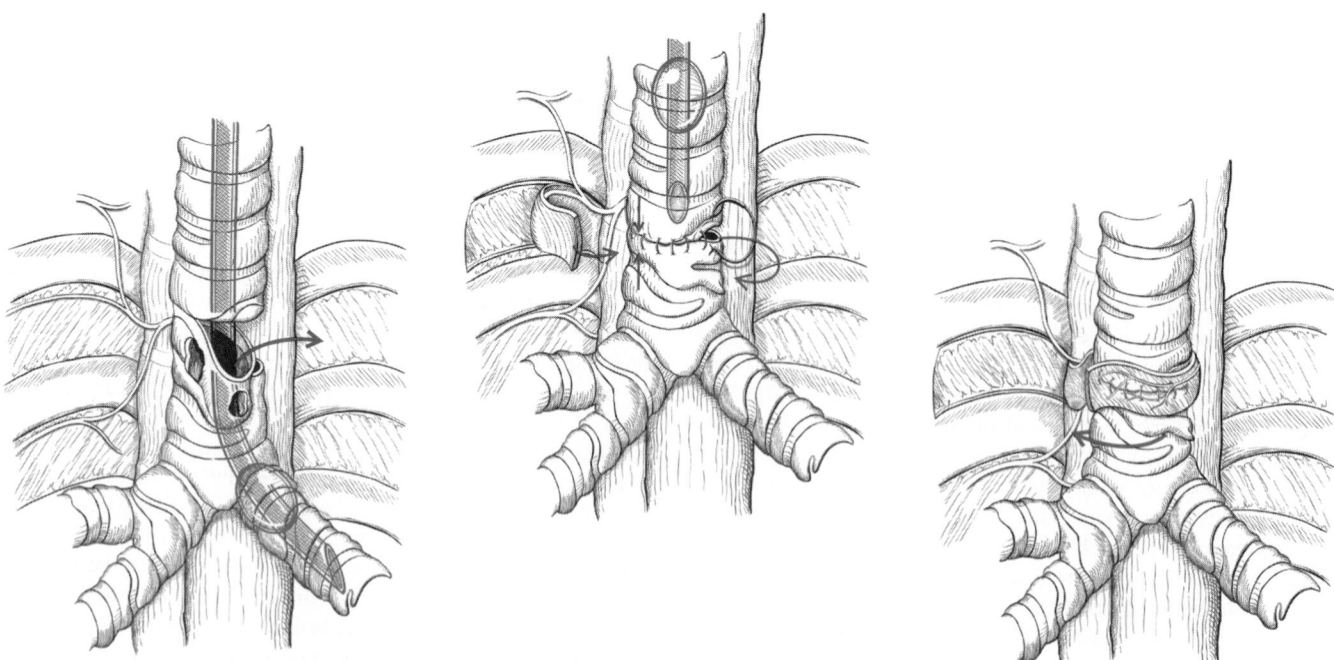

Figure 5 **Tracheal injury may be repaired by means of segmental resection, with the suture line buttressed with an intercostal muscle flap.**

struction of the tracheobronchial tree should be attempted if there is no distal suppuration. Total bronchial disruption often leads to complete occlusion and sterile atelectasis and may be amenable to repair years later. The stenotic segment is resected and repaired in much the same manner as an acute injury or a benign stenosis would be. Incomplete bronchial obstruction ultimately leads to suppuration and irreversible pulmonary parenchymal destruction. Bronchography and sputum culture are useful for determining whether pulmonary resection (pneumonectomy or lobectomy) is necessary for salvage. On occasion, bronchial sleeve resection, lobectomy, or pneumonectomy is urgently required for more extensive or distal injuries to lobar or segmental bronchi.

Although bronchial rupture can be treated successfully in either the acute or the delayed phase, early diagnosis and treatment minimize the risk of infection and resection and shorten hospital stay.

Esophageal Injuries

Injury to the esophagus, though relatively rare, poses particular problems for the treating physician because of the complexity of the presentation, the workup, and the treatment options. Despite diagnostic and therapeutic advances, the morbidity and mortality associated with esophageal injury remain high. Diagnosis and management of esophageal injuries evoke strong, and widely varying, opinions from surgeons. Preoperative evaluation is still a subject of debate, as is the question of mandatory surgical exploration versus selective nonoperative management. Currently, most esophageal injuries are iatrogenic or endoluminal; however, we will concentrate here on injuries specifically related to external trauma—namely, penetrating injury and blunt esophageal rupture.

Whereas the cervical esophagus is relatively unprotected from external trauma, the thoracic esophagus, being surrounded by the bony thorax, is well protected. The esophagus lies in close proximity to the heart, the great vessels, and the entire membranous portion of the trachea. Consequently, simultaneous injury to several of these intrathoracic organs is common, which greatly increases associated morbidity and mortality. The esophagus has no serosal covering; rather, it is entirely surrounded by loose areolar connective tissue, which makes suture placement less secure and increases the overall difficulty of surgical repair. The planes of the paraesophageal and prevertebral spaces communicate freely with the mediastinum. As a result, spillage from the esophagus readily tracks into the mediastinum, leading to mediastinitis, causing sepsis, and accounting for much of the increased morbidity and mortality seen with delayed diagnosis and treatment of esophageal injuries.

The exact incidence of injury of the esophagus caused by external trauma is unknown, but such injury accounts for fewer than 1% of injuries for which patients are admitted to hospitals. Most esophageal injuries result from penetrating trauma. If surgical exploration is performed for all penetrating cervical wounds that violate the platysma, the esophagus is found to be injured approximately 12% of the time. Penetrating intrathoracic esophageal injuries are less common, however, occurring in about 0.7% of all penetrating chest wounds.[33] Blunt esophageal trauma is relatively uncommon; it may develop when the organ suffers a direct blow or when increased intraluminal pressure against a closed glottis causes a burst-type injury.

Intrathoracic esophageal injuries tend to occur just proximal to the esophagogastric junction on the left side, where the esophagus is less well protected. The injury is thought to be the result of increased transmission of intra-abdominal pressure to the stomach, as is seen in postemetic esophageal rupture (Boerhaave syndrome). Gastric contents are widely and violently expelled into the

Table 2 Diagnostic Measures for Evaluating Suspected Esophageal Injuries

Diagnostic Measure	Sensitivity (%)	Specificity (%)	Accuracy (%)
Assessment of clinical signs and symptoms	80	64	72
Contrast esophagography	80–100	94–100	90–95
Rigid esophagoscopy	67–100	89–95	86–94
Flexible esophagoscopy	67–100	67–100	82–97

mediastinum, sepsis ensues, and the resulting mortality is high.

Between 60% and 80% of esophageal injuries give rise to clinical signs or symptoms, the sensitivity and specificity of which depend on the location of the injury, the size of the perforation, the degree of contamination, the length of time elapsed after injury, and the presence of associated injury. Odynophagia, dysphagia, hematemesis, oropharyngeal blood, cervical crepitus, pain and tenderness in the neck or chest, resistance to passive motion, dyspnea, hoarseness, bleeding, cough, and stridor are commonly noted. Fever, subcutaneous emphysema, abdominal tenderness, and mediastinal crunching sounds (Hamman sign) may be observed. Pain is the most common presenting symptom (71% of patients), followed by fever (51%), dyspnea (24%), and crepitus (22%).[34]

Overall, the signs and symptoms associated with esophageal injury are fairly nonspecific, and a high index of suspicion must be maintained to make the diagnosis. As noted (see above), concomitant injuries to structures surrounding the esophagus are common. Of these, tracheal and vascular injuries are most frequently seen, occurring in as many as two thirds of victims. The associated injuries also determine the symptoms seen in patients with esophageal trauma, the course the diagnostic evaluation takes, and the treatment options considered.

Evaluation of potential penetrating trauma to the esophagus is based on the trajectory and path of the missile. For penetrating injuries near the organ, it is necessary to prove that the esophagus is uninjured. Generally, this is done in one of two ways: (1) surgical exploration demonstrates a missile path inconsistent with esophageal injury, or (2) direct examination of the esophagus reveals no injury. If neither option is feasible, proof is obtained through diagnostic testing. Plain x-rays, CT scans, and contrast esophagograms have all been used for this purpose, with varying sensitivity and specificity [*see Table 2*]. Endoscopy may add to the diagnosis, but the results depend on the operator's technique and experience, and there is a risk that it may exacerbate an esophageal tear or further injure an unstable cervical spine.

In an otherwise asymptomatic patient who is awake, alert, and able to cooperate, a simple contrast swallow is usually sufficient to exclude injury. Injuries resulting from low-velocity projectiles and stab wounds do not cause large tissue defects; for these injuries, barium gives superior anatomic detail and is the agent of choice. Injuries from large-caliber or high-velocity projectiles usually cause more damage, and thus, the contrast agent tends to spread more widely throughout the mediastinum during a diagnostic swallow. If contrast studies are indicated in this setting, a water-soluble agent may be used first. Such agents cause pulmonary damage when aspirated, however, and should not be used if tracheoesophageal fistula is suspected.

For patients who are going to the OR for another reason (e.g., vascular repair or laparotomy), it may be most expedient to perform esophagoscopy simultaneously with the operation. If the entire esophagus is well visualized and no injury is identified, no further evaluation is required. If the study is suboptimal for any reason, or if the possibility of an injury persists, a contrast study should be done as soon as the patient's condition permits.

Regardless of the diagnostic studies obtained, evaluation must be carried out expeditiously. Significant delays in management can increase the incidence of esophageal injury–related morbidity by as much as a factor of two.[35]

In cases of blunt trauma, determining when further study is needed is a vexing task. In general, whenever a patient has pneumomediastinum that is extensive or is associated with any of the symptoms of esophageal injury (e.g., odynophagia or blood in the esophagus), the esophagus should be evaluated. Simple pneumomediastinum rarely warrants evaluation of the esophagus. Injury to the thoracic esophagus from blunt trauma is so extremely unusual, compared with the other causes of simple pneumomediastinum,[36] that evaluation for esophageal injury is necessary only in the presence of other suggestive findings, such as pleural effusion, free air, and mediastinitis. In the absence of these suggestive signs and symptoms, pneumomediastinum associated with blunt trauma is much more likely to be from a distal small airway disruption or from a bronchial injury, the evaluation of which should take precedence over evaluation of the esophagus. When esophageal or major airway injury has been ruled out, pneumomediastinum should be treated with observation alone. Chest tubes should be placed only if there is an associated hemothorax or pneumothorax.

MANAGEMENT

Although injuries to the thoracic esophagus caused by external trauma are less common than those to the cervical esophagus, they are more likely to be fatal.[33,37] Trauma to the thoracic esoph-

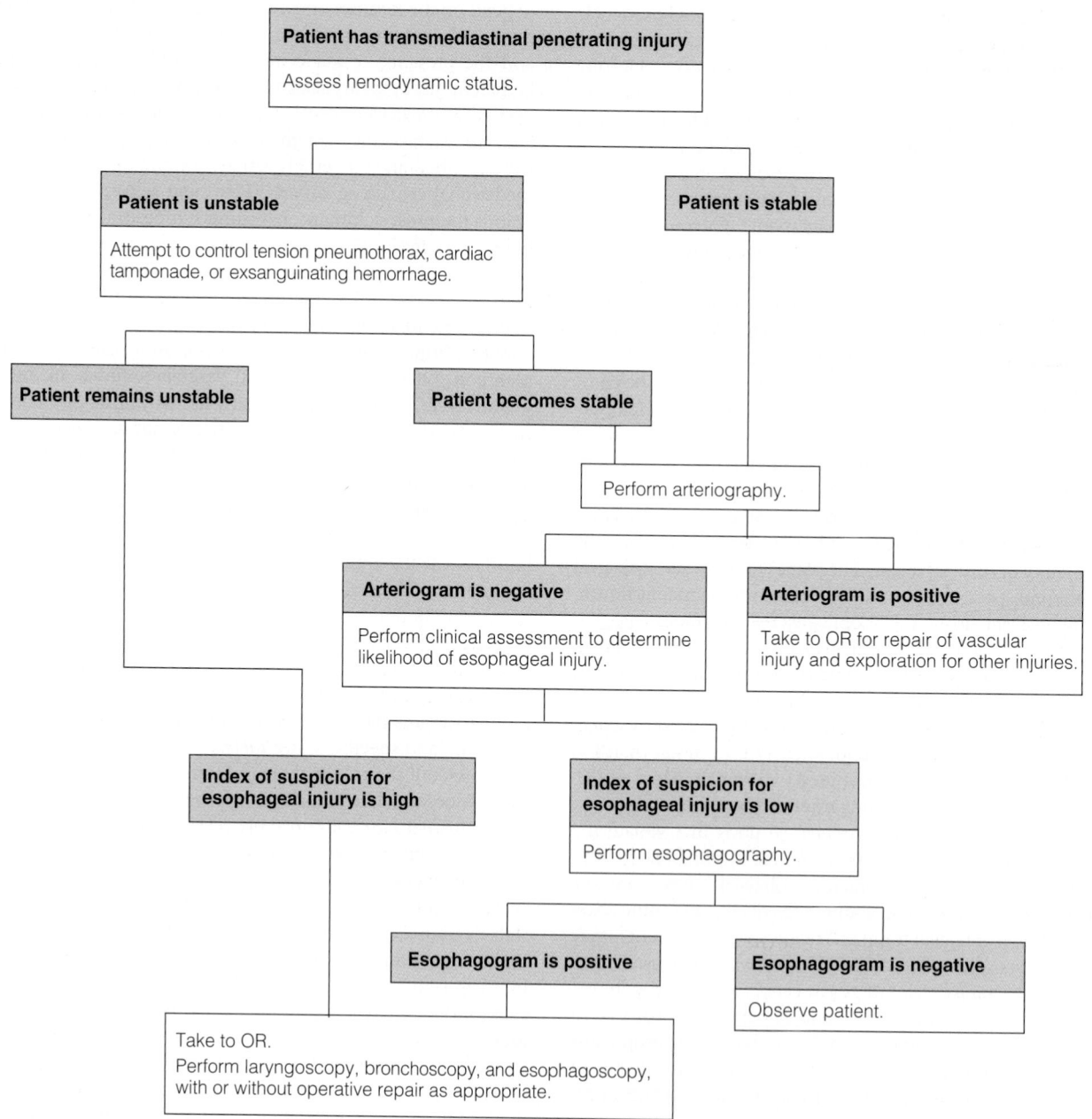

Figure 6 Algorithm illustrates approach to management of transmediastinal penetrating injury.

agus is almost exclusively caused by gunshot wounds; the location of the organ within the chest protects it from most stab wounds. Care of any associated injuries to surrounding structures (e.g., major airways and blood vessels) takes precedence in the management scheme; thus, by necessity, diagnosis and definitive therapy of intrathoracic esophageal injuries are often delayed.

Guidelines have been formulated for the evaluation of transmediastinal penetrating wounds [see Figure 6]. The signs and symptoms of thoracic esophageal injury, besides being nonspecific, often take several hours to develop. As with injuries to all other areas of the esophagus, delays in diagnosis and therapy result in a longer duration of contamination and a higher incidence of mediastinitis, sepsis, and death.

Injuries to the distal third of the thoracic esophagus are most easily approached via the left chest. More proximal injuries are best approached through the right chest or via a combination of chest and cervical incisions. The incision should be made so as to facilitate subsequent buttressing of the repair (e.g., with a pedicle from an intercostal muscle or the latissimus dorsi).

Surgical repair entails local debridement, wide drainage, primary repair of the perforation, and buttressing of the repair with a viable muscle flap. Primary repair can usually be accomplished when the perforation is operated on within 24 hours of occurrence. Many investigators recommend two-layer repair of esophageal injuries; however, a secure single-layer repair performed with a continuous absorbable monofilament suture (e.g., 3-0 polydioxanone) allows excellent visualization of each bite and good mucosa-to-mucosa approximation. There is no evidence that adding a second layer adds any strength or security to the anastomosis. A number of different tissue flaps—free pericardium, pleura, intercostal muscle, diaphragm, rhomboid muscle, lung, and gastric fundus (as in a Thal patch)—have all been used, with varying success. Each of these flaps has its own set of advantages, but the use of any of them (if viable) will yield an improved anastomotic outcome.

Depending on the interval before exploration, the severity of the injury, the degree of contamination, and the extent of the local inflammatory response, primary repair may not be feasible. If this is the case, there are several techniques that may be employed, including esophageal diversion, total esophageal exclusion, esophagectomy, and T tube drainage. Most of the experience with these delayed repairs has been acquired in patients who have perforations caused by instrumentation or by emetogenic esophageal rupture, neither of which is entirely analogous to the injuries seen with external trauma.

In general, even late-presenting esophageal perforations should be treated with an attempt at primary repair with autologous tissue coverage. During the workup and surgical management, esophageal patency must be ascertained. Primary esophageal lesions (e.g., strictures) must be corrected, or the repair is likely to fail. In the absence of distal obstruction, almost all late-presenting esophageal perforations heal after primary repair and tissue flap coverage. Generally speaking, techniques such as esophageal exclusion, diversion, and resection should be needed only when perforation occurs in the setting of a primary esophageal pathologic condition (e.g., cancer); esophageal perforation in this setting is rarely managed by trauma surgeons.

Complications

Complications seen after esophageal repair include esophageal leakage and fistula, wound infection, mediastinitis, empyema, sepsis, and pneumonia. Long-term complications (e.g., esophageal stricture) also occur, but they are more common after iatrogenic

perforation of an already diseased esophagus. Risk factors associated with an increased complication rate include shock, the need for urgent tracheostomy, and associated injuries (especially tracheal disruption and paralysis from spinal cord injuries).

Esophageal anastomotic leakage is the most common complication associated with repair of perforations, occurring in 10% to 28% of repairs.[38] The causes are primarily technical and include inadequate debridement, devascularization, closure under tension, and the presence of associated infection. As many as 50% of these leaks are asymptomatic; in this setting, they are usually associated with prompt flow of oral contrast back into the esophageal or gastric lumen. Continued abstinence from oral intake, supplemental parenteral nutrition, and antibiotic therapy usually suffice for successful treatment.

In patients who have sepsis and esophageal leakage after repair of an esophageal perforation caused by external trauma, treatment should focus on wide local drainage and creation of a controlled fistula, which is usually best accomplished by resecting a segment of a rib posteriorly at the level of the perforation, then packing the wound open. Because there is usually no underlying esophageal or gastric pathologic condition and no forceful distribution of mediastinal contamination, these fistulas generally heal well without resection, diversion, or replacement of the esophagus. Most of these patients also benefit from feeding jejunostomy tubes; healing time is generally measured in weeks.

Thoracic Duct Injuries

Chylothorax after blunt or penetrating chest trauma is rare: only case reports and small case series are found in the literature. Much of the management of this condition is extrapolated from management of iatrogenic thoracic duct injuries, which are much more common. Most patients with traumatic chylothorax show evidence of other axial injuries to the chest, especially spine fractures.[39] The diagnosis is made by finding chylomicrons and high levels of triglycerides in a typically large pleural effusion of milky appearance. Drainage of as much as 1,000 ml/day is not unusual and results in severe nutritional and immunologic derangements, which are the main causes of the high mortality associated with this condition.

MANAGEMENT

Treatment usually begins with limiting oral intake of short- and long-chain triglycerides, which cause increased flow of chyle. Diets high in medium-chain triglycerides must often be given enterally because they are not palatable. Some clinicians recommend instituting total parenteral nutrition with complete abstinence from oral intake. Administration of octreotide may also help decrease chyle production.[40] These modalities, in conjunction with adequate pleural drainage and lung expansion, are successful in approximately 50% of cases after 2 to 6 weeks.

Operative strategies for managing thoracic duct injuries are generally undertaken only after conservative measures fail. Preoperatively, patients are fed cream, with or without dyes such as Sudan black, to increase chyle flow and enhance visualization of the site of injury. The thoracic duct is then ligated above and below the injury; this may be performed by means of VATS on the hemithorax ipsilateral to the effusion.[41] Fibrin glue and talc pleurodesis may be used as adjuncts to ligation. Because there are usually multiple areas of injury and because the thoracic duct is friable by nature, surgical treatment is not always successful. Continued nutritional management and reoperation may be required.

Cardiac Injuries

The incidence of cardiac trauma continues to rise as a consequence of growing urban violence, improved detection of cardiac injuries, and an increase in the percentage of patients with such injuries who arrive at trauma centers alive. Improved prehospital transport, along with the continuing evolution of diagnostic, surgical, and anesthetic techniques, has contributed to an increase in overall survival in this population. Although the overall mortality associated with cardiac trauma remains high, survival rates of 50% to 95% are not uncommon in patients who arrive at the hospital with vital signs.[42-45]

PENETRATING

Patients with penetrating cardiac injuries generally present in one of three ways. In approximately 20% of patients, the injury is clinically silent, at least initially, and is subsequently diagnosed at operation or on diagnostic imaging. In approximately 50%, there is evidence of pericardial tamponade, including one or more of the signs in Beck's triad (hypotension, distended neck veins, and muffled heart sounds). In the remaining patients, hemorrhagic shock develops after free bleeding from an atrial or ventricular wound into one or both hemithoraces.

Diagnosis of penetrating injuries to the heart often requires a high index of suspicion. The locations of entrance and exit wounds, the trajectory and path of the wounding object, and the locations of any retained missiles on radiographs are helpful in predicting heart injuries. Proximity wounds to the heart are defined as those that penetrate the chest wall in the area bounded superiorly by the clavicles, laterally by the midclavicular lines, and inferiorly by the costal margins. Any crossing of the anterior mediastinum by a missile or an instrument is also considered a proximity wound. Because cardiac injuries are present in 15% to 20% of patients who present with proximity wounds, these injuries must be definitively excluded.

Physical examination is often unreliable in detecting pericardial tamponade. It is rare for all three signs in Beck's triad to be found; in fact, only about half of patients with tamponade show even two of the three. Moreover, detection of muffled heart sounds and distended neck veins amid the commotion typical of the trauma bay can be extremely difficult, especially when (as is often the case) the patient is agitated or intoxicated. Accordingly, whenever tamponade is suspected, additional diagnostic modalities should be employed.

As more surgeons become familiar with the use of ultrasonography in the trauma setting, two-dimensional surface echocardiography is gaining acceptance as a means of diagnosing cardiac injuries. When performed by appropriately trained surgeons, this modality detects blood within the pericardial sac with a sensitivity of 96% to 100% and a specificity of 100%—results essentially equivalent to those achieved with a pericardial window.[46] When the requisite equipment is readily available, this test can be performed in approximately 2 minutes. It is of vital importance that the trauma surgeon who is attending to the patient perform and interpret the test: the results will be available sooner, the clinical correlation will be more accurate, and the information obtained will be more rapidly applied to treatment decisions. The main limitations of two-dimensional surface echocardiography are the high cost of the equipment and the specialized training required.

Although cardiac ultrasonography has many advantages, the subxiphoid pericardial window remains the gold standard for diagnosis of cardiac injury. For otherwise stable patients with proximity wounds or suggestive signs and symptoms, a pericardial window should be considered when ultrasonographic findings are equivocal or when ultrasonography is unavailable. This procedure is usually performed in the OR with the patient under general anesthesia, often in combination with abdominal exploration.

A subxiphoid pericardial window is performed through a 10 cm vertical midline incision that is made over the xiphoid, slightly favoring the epigastrium. The xiphoid is grasped with a clamp and dissected away from the abdominal fascia and the diaphragmatic fibers, and the substernal plane is accessed. As the inferior portion of the sternum is being elevated, the prepericardial adipose tissue is dissected to provide exposure of the acute margin of the pericardium. The pericardium is then retracted inferiorly into the wound and incised sharply. The presence of blood or clot within the pericardial sac indicates a positive result, necessitating immediate repair of the injury. A pericardial window can also be accomplished during thoracoscopy of the left hemithorax, and examination of the pericardium can be performed, though less reliably, during laparoscopy via a transdiaphragmatic view.

Some authorities advocate using pericardiocentesis to detect cardiac injuries, especially where rapid access to the OR, trauma surgeons, and anesthesiologists is not available. Drawbacks to this approach include the high rate of false positives and false negatives and the potential for iatrogenic cardiac injuries. Furthermore, pericardiocentesis is of limited use in treating tamponade because blood within the pericardial sac often is clotted and is not amenable to removal through a needle.

Management

Treatment of penetrating cardiac wounds depends on the urgency of the presentation. In patients who are in shock from suspected cardiac injuries, the distinction between the two most likely causes, pericardial tamponade and free hemorrhage, is important. If the patient exhibits distended neck veins and the characteristic plethoric, dusky facial expression, chest tubes should immediately be placed bilaterally. If shock does not then resolve, the diagnosis of tamponade should be made and a pericardial window performed, either in the ED with local or no anesthesia or in the OR as described (see above). If there is a suspicion of free hemorrhage into one or both hemithoraces, which can usually be detected by means of physical examination and chest x-ray, the patient should be transported to the OR for definitive treatment. In patients who are in extremis from either causative condition or who go into cardiac arrest in the ED, an emergency left anterior thoracotomy should be performed.

In planning the surgical approach to the repair of cardiac injuries, the location of the entrance and exit wounds, the path of the wounding object, the type of wound created, the associated signs and symptoms, and the level of suspicion for other thoracic visceral injuries are important considerations. A median sternotomy is a logical extension of a subxiphoid pericardial window and provides access to all four chambers of the heart. It is appropriate for most precordial stab wounds and some low-caliber gunshot wounds. Its main limitations are that it does not allow repair or cross-clamping of the descending aorta or examination or repair of the esophagus and bronchi and that it provides limited exposure of the lower lobes of the lungs and the hemidiaphragms. A left thoracotomy is appropriate for patients who may require cross-clamping of the thoracic aorta and for those with suspected cardiac injuries in conjunction with other complex thoracic visceral injuries. Only occasionally is a right thoracotomy required; this incision generally does not provide adequate exposure of the heart.

Atrial wounds are generally amenable to early control by finger pressure or by exclusion with a vascular clamp and simple oversewing. Right or left ventricular free wall injuries away from the coronary arteries may be treated by applying digital pressure over the entrance wound for hemostasis, then placing horizontal mattress sutures under the wound, reinforced with an epicardial continuous suture along the site of injury. All left ventricular wounds should be repaired with felt-pledgetted or pericardial-pledgetted sutures. Many right ventricular stab wounds can be closed primarily without pledgets if the sutures are tied accurately.

Injuries near coronary arteries must be closed without the coronary artery being incorporated within the suture. This can be accomplished by placing horizontal mattress sutures lateral and deep to the coronary artery across the cardiac laceration. If the sutures are tied with careful attention to the function of the myocardium distal to the injury and equally careful attention to the electrocardiogram, the laceration can be closed without coronary artery occlusion and subsequent ischemia.

An alternative method of repair of cardiac lacerations employs a skin stapler, which is effective in controlling hemorrhage from stab injuries and low-velocity gunshot wounds.[47] The stapler can be used on all chambers of the heart, and in some instances, staple repair can be quicker than suture repair.

With all penetrating cardiac wounds, it is important to recognize the possibility of associated intracardiac injuries. The surgeon should palpate the heart along the pulmonary outflow tract for a thrill that would indicate a traumatic ventricular septal defect. This diagnosis can be confirmed by performing co-oximetry on a sample of blood aspirated from the pulmonary artery and the right atrium and demonstrating a step-up. Digital palpation through atrial wounds should be routinely employed to identify atrioventricular valvular insufficiency or, occasionally, an atrial septal defect. Intraoperative surface echocardiography and transesophageal echocardiography are also excellent at diagnosing intracardiac injuries, but they are not readily available in the urgent trauma setting.

Postoperatively, all patients with cardiac wounds should receive a thorough cardiovascular examination aimed at detecting murmurs or evidence of cardiac failure and should undergo echocardiography if either of these is detected. Repair of intracardiac lesions usually can wait until the patient's condition is stable and cardiac catheterization has been performed, though some patients experience such profound heart failure that immediate operative repair, with cardiopulmonary bypass, must be performed.

BLUNT

Blunt cardiac injuries range from disruption of myocardium, septa, or valvular structures to cardiac contusion. Both cardiac disruption (also known as cardiorrhexia) and cardiac contusion are common; the former is seen most often in patients who die at the scene, the latter in those who survive to reach the hospital.

Blunt cardiac injury typically involves a direct blow to the chest, usually sustained in a motor vehicle collision or a fall. Cardiac injuries generally are associated with sternal or rib fractures, though they may occur in the absence of any chest wall fracture; however, sternal fractures do not predict the presence of blunt cardiac injury. The most common location of blunt cardiac injury is the anterior heart, which consists primarily of the right ventricle. A blow that causes the sternum to exert a direct impact on the myocardium may result in direct injury to myocardial cells, sometimes leading to cell death, mechanical dysfunction, or dysrhythmias.

The diagnosis of myocardial contusion is elusive. Many tests have been proposed, but none have proved definitive, except for direct visualization of the heart at surgery or autopsy. For practical purposes, the clinically significant sequelae of myocardial contusion are myocardial dysrhythmias and pump failure. Both of these sequelae must be treated, regardless of whether the diagnosis of blunt cardiac injury can be made. Guidelines have been proposed that may facilitate the workup of this condition.[48]

As an initial test, a 12-lead ECG should be obtained whenever blunt cardiac injury is suspected. If the ECG is normal, no further workup is required. If there is an ECG abnormality that does not necessitate treatment (e.g., nonspecific ST-T wave changes), the patient should undergo monitored observation for 12 hours, then be discharged if there are no dysrhythmias and the ECG is normal at that time. If there is a more serious ECG abnormality (e.g., dysrhythmia, ST-segment elevation, or heart block), the patient should undergo observation for at least 24 to 48 hours and may require further testing and treatment, depending on the sequelae of the abnormality. In patients with hemodynamic instability and suspected blunt cardiac injury, echocardiography should be performed promptly. There is no role for cardiac enzyme analysis or cardiac troponin assay in this setting. The latter test may detect myocardial injury, but this information does not complement ECG and echocardiographic findings and has no clinical utility. Similarly, there is no role for nuclear medicine studies.

Management

Pump failure associated with cardiac contusion is usually the result of right heart failure, in that most hemodynamically significant cardiac contusions are caused by injury to the anterior right ventricular free wall. Treatment of right heart failure from cardiac contusion consists of inotropic support and reduction of right ventricular afterload. Dysrhythmias secondary to cardiac contusion are treated in the same manner as dysrhythmias of any other etiology.

The commonly repeated adage that cardiac contusion should be treated similarly to MI is incorrect. Therapy for MI is based on the premises that the patient is likely to have concomitant coronary artery disease and that increased myocardial oxygen demand may result in extension of the evolving infarct or the creation of an additional infarct. However, most young trauma patients have normal coronary arteries, and increased myocardial oxygen demand is unlikely to extend cardiac contusion unless the heart sustains an additional blow. Generally, the goal in resuscitation of injured patients is to increase systemic oxygen delivery, which may increase cardiac work. In addition, unlike patients with MI, patients with myocardial contusion appear not to be at increased risk for cardiac complications from general anesthesia and surgery.

In the rare patient with cardiorrhexia who presents to the hospital with signs of life, the most common injury is right atrial perforation. Other lesions seen in patients with vital signs, in order of decreasing incidence, are left atrial perforation, right ventricular perforation, atrial septal perforation, ventricular septal perforation, coronary artery thrombosis, and valvular insufficiency (most commonly involving the tricuspid and mitral valves).[42-45] Patients with cardiac rupture generally present with signs of pericardial tamponade and require rapid decompression. Placement of an intraaortic balloon pump is often an effective temporizing measure while preparations are made for definitive repair.

Patients with blunt cardiac trauma who lose vital signs in the field or who go into cardiac arrest before arrival at the hospital generally should not be subjected to ED thoracotomy, because virtually none of these patients can be saved. Patients admitted with vital signs after suffering blunt cardiac rupture, however, have about a 50% chance of survival, and much of the mortality in these patients is attributable to associated injuries.

Blunt Aortic Injuries

Traumatic rupture of the aorta may account for as many as 10% to 15% of all traffic fatalities, and the majority of such injuries are fatal at the scene. Of those who survive the initial injury, 50% die in the first 24 hours and 90% die within the first month if the aorta is not repaired. Traumatic disruption of the thoracic aorta results from rapid deceleration and is produced by a shearing effect caused by differences in the mobility of the aorta above and below a point where the vessel is fixed. Most thoracic aortic disruptions in survivors occur at the aortic isthmus just distal to the origin of the left subclavian artery, where the aorta is fixed to a significant degree by the ligamentum arteriosum. Autopsy series reveal that as many as 40% of aortic injuries in nonsurvivors are not located at the isthmus, and the injuries tend to be complex.[49]

Suspicion of an aortic injury is most often triggered by abnormal findings on a chest x-ray in a patient with a high-speed mechanism of injury and multiple other injuries. Most patients show no signs or symptoms on physical examination, but some complain of interscapular pain or hoarseness, and some exhibit a difference in blood pressure or pulse fullness between the upper and lower extremities or between the right and left upper extremities. Accordingly, the diagnosis is usually made radiographically, often beginning with the recognition of mediastinal hemorrhage on a screening chest x-ray.

Numerous radiographic signs of a torn thoracic aorta have been described, all of which are manifestations of hemorrhage within the mediastinum that alters or obliterates the shadows seen on a normal chest radiograph. Mediastinal widening is the most frequent indicator of mediastinal hematoma from a torn thoracic aorta. Other important signs are obscuration of the detail of the contour of the aortic knob, opacification of the aortopulmonary window, depression of the left mainstem bronchus, apical cap, deviation of the nasogastric tube, and displacement of the esophagus to the right. These signs may be present in any combination or may be entirely absent.

Currently, high-speed CT scanning with I.V. contrast is being liberally used for diagnosis of thoracic vascular injuries. Appropriately, this modality is employed in virtually all patients with abnormal chest x-rays and in many patients with normal x-rays whose injury mechanisms include a high degree of energy transfer. CT findings that are diagnostic of aortic injury include mediastinal hematoma, periaortic hematoma, intraluminal irregularity (intimal flap), acute coarctation, and abnormal aortic contour [see Figure 7]. Depending on the experience of the interpreting clinician, aortography may be eliminated in most of these patients before surgical repair; the sensitivity and specificity of CT in this setting approach 100%.[15,50,51] Aortography should continue to be used for equivocal cases or cases in which spiral CT is not available.

MANAGEMENT

Essentially all aortic injuries associated with mediastinal hematomas should be repaired. The timing of repair, however, is less urgent than the timing of certain associated maneuvers that must be done, such as attainment of an adequate airway, control of external or cavitary hemorrhage, and evacuation of intracranial mass lesions. In general, if there is active bleeding from a blunt

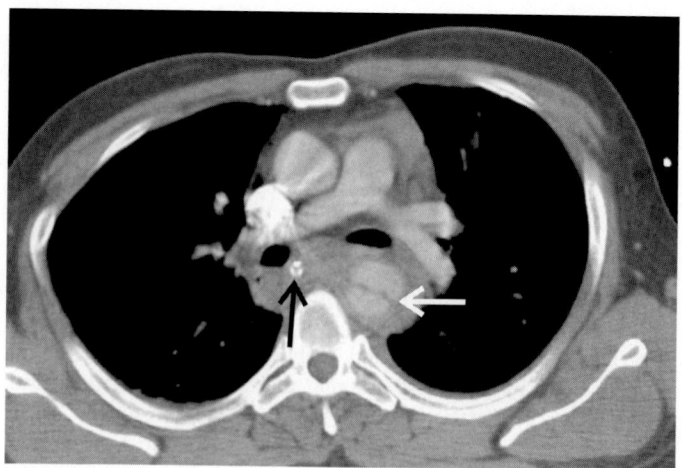

Figure 7 Shown is an injury to the descending thoracic aorta (white arrow). A nasogastric tube can be seen in the esophagus, which is deviated to the right (black arrow).

aortic injury, it will be massive; lesser amounts of bleeding from a chest tube often derive from associated injuries. If intra-abdominal bleeding is present, laparotomy is indicated before repair of the torn thoracic aorta and before aortography. Similarly, in patients with intracranial hemorrhage that necessitates operative evacuation, craniotomy should take precedence over repair of the torn thoracic aorta.

While one is temporizing, stringent efforts must be made to prevent hypertension and reduce shear forces across the injury, ideally by means of I.V. beta blockade. Esmolol, because of its short half-life, is the best agent to use in these patients, who are at risk for sudden hypovolemic episodes of hypotension. The goals of medical therapy are a heart rate lower than 100 beats/min and a systolic blood pressure of approximately 100 mm Hg (in young and middle-aged patients) or 110 to 120 mm Hg (in elderly patients).[15] Nitroprusside may have to be given to achieve these goals, but it should not be used until after adequate beta blockade is achieved, because it can increase intravascular shear forces when used alone. During pharmacologic treatment of aortic injuries, pulmonary arterial catheter monitoring is essential to prevent deleterious reductions in cardiac output and mixed venous oxygen saturation. With careful delayed operative management of aortic injuries, the risk of rupture is low but is not completely eliminated.[15,52]

Traditional repair techniques include exposure of the aorta and arch through a left thoracotomy and direct repair or interposition graft placement. Although excellent results have been obtained with so-called clamp-and-sew techniques, most guidelines recommend use of some form of distal aortic perfusion (e.g., left atrial–distal aortic bypass or partial cardiopulmonary bypass with femoral cannulation). Systemic heparinization is required for cardiopulmonary bypass and has been shown to be safe with respect to hemorrhagic complications.[53,54] The aortic arch is clamped between the common carotid and left subclavian arteries after these vessels and the distal aorta have been controlled. An interposition graft is required for most of these injuries, though 15% to 20% can be treated with suture repair alone. With distal aortic perfusion, the risk of paraplegia is approximately 5% and is independent of clamp time; without distal aortic perfusion, ischemic times longer than 30 minutes are associated with an exponential rise in the incidence of spinal cord injury.

Another potential advantage to using cardiopulmonary bypass is the ability to institute deep hypothermic circulatory arrest if needed. This technique involves cooling to a core temperature lower than 20° C to induce cardiac standstill, turning off the pump, and operating on the unclamped aorta in a relatively dry field. Circulatory arrest can be safely maintained in this setting for approximately 30 to 45 min. This technique may be useful for patients who have previously undergone thoracic aortic surgery or who have complex tears involving the arch.

An evolving modality for the treatment of aortic injury is endovascular stent grafting. The rationale for the insertion of a stent graft in this population is that the aorta above and below the injury is usually normal, which is not the case in the atherosclerotic population. Early results with this method of treatment are encouraging and are in fact superior to those obtained with endovascular repair of aortic aneurysms and dissections.[55] If longer-term follow-up continues to report acceptable outcomes, stent grafts will probably become standard therapy for uncomplicated aortic injuries.

Great Vessel Injuries

Except for tears in the descending aorta, injuries to the thoracic great vessels, by any mechanism, are rarely seen in clinical practice; the best descriptions come from wartime and autopsy series. Indeed, postmortem studies reveal that patients with nonisthmus aortic and great vessel injuries rarely reach the hospital alive.[56] As many as 14% of patients have multiple great vessel injuries. Diagnosis and management of these injuries covers a wide spectrum of possibilities, depending on mechanism of injury, presenting features, and associated injuries.

PENETRATING

Penetrating thoracic great vessel injuries are usually obvious. The presence of an entrance wound at the base of the neck or in the chest should alert the clinician to this possibility. If the patient is in shock, urgent operation is required. If the patient's condition stabilizes with resuscitation, an arteriogram should be performed to localize the injury.

Management

Exposure is most often obtained via a median sternotomy, with or without neck extension as needed for innominate, right subclavian, or carotid arterial injuries [see Table 1]. Exposure of the left subclavian artery can be more difficult, even through a sternotomy with a trap-door extension. For isolated injuries to the proximal subclavian artery, a fourth-interspace left posterolateral thoracotomy is most useful. For injuries to the middle and distal thirds, supraclavicular incisions or deltopectoral incisions—or, occasionally, a combination thereof—are appropriate, provided that inflow control can be achieved. When inflow control may not be achievable, as in cases involving injury at the thoracic outlet or the presence of a large hematoma, endovascular control of the proximal subclavian artery by means of a balloon catheter placed percutaneously through the femoral artery may be necessary. There are also case reports describing total endovascular management of subclavian injuries through stent-graft placement.[57] This technique may be valuable for unstable patients who are already undergoing arteriography and for patients with multiple high-priority injuries.

Most penetrating wounds of the middle and distal segments of the great vessels are amenable to lateral repair or end-to-end anastomosis; injuries involving greater tissue destruction, for which grafts might be indicated, usually prove fatal before the patient arrives at the hospital. The subclavian artery is a notable exception to this general rule because the lack of elastic fibers in its tunica media makes it extremely friable. End-to-end anastomosis of an injured subclavian artery under any tension is doomed to failure. Accordingly, many subclavian injuries should be repaired with an interposition graft. Proximal injuries to the great vessels are best repaired by exclusion and bypass grafting with prosthetic material from the ascending aorta. Because bleeding is usually active, there is rarely enough time to arrange for cardiopulmonary bypass. In any case, cardiopulmonary bypass generally is not needed, except for rare cases of associated ascending or aortic arch injury.

BLUNT

Blunt injuries of the great vessels are typically the result of high speed and rapid deceleration. In postmortem examinations, pedestrians struck by motor vehicles have the highest rate of great vessel injuries. Patients with such injuries are rarely seen in the ED with signs of life.[56] Superior mediastinal hematoma is the most common finding during workup; its presence is an indication for further imaging with spiral CT or angiography. Besides vessel laceration with hematoma, presentations of blunt thoracic great vessel injury include dissection and thrombosis, which may be asymptomatic if localized to the proximal segments. Central neurologic injury may also be present, especially with carotid dissection. Associated stretch injury of the brachial plexus or the cervical nerve roots is common with subclavian artery injuries.

Management

Once the diagnosis is made, virtually all great vessel injuries should be treated surgically, with the possible exception of small intimal defects that are found incidentally. Surgery is contraindicated, however, if neurologic injury is present, the injury is deemed unsurvivable, or a common carotid dissection has extended into the distal internal carotid artery. As with blunt aortic injuries, the timing of surgery should be tailored to the treatment priorities mandated by the associated injuries. When time permits, proximal lesions are best managed with cardiopulmonary bypass and hypothermic circulatory arrest. Arranging for these techniques is mandatory with injuries involving the ascending aorta and the arch.

Mediastinal blood seen on chest CT probably more often derives from mediastinal venous injuries than from arterial injuries. These isolated venous injuries need not be repaired unless they are associated with cardiac tamponade or massive hemorrhage into a pleural space, both of which are uncommon. An exception is injury to the intrapericardial venae cavae, which is usually associated with tamponade. These injuries are caused by tearing of the mobile heart against the relatively fixed veins, particularly the inferior vena cava. In most cases, they can be repaired primarily. Associated venous injuries are commonly encountered during exploration for great vessel arterial injury. If possible, they should be treated with lateral repair or patch venorrhaphy with pericardium or saphenous vein. However, ligation of these veins sometimes proves necessary and is generally well tolerated.

References

1. Kemmerer WT, Eckert WJ, Gathwright JB, et al: Patterns of thoracic injuries in fatal traffic accidents. J Trauma 1:595, 1961

2. Boldt J, Zickmann B, Fedderson B, et al: Six different hemofiltration devices for blood conservation in cardiac surgery. Ann Thorac Surg 51:747, 1991

3. Luchette FA, Barrie PS, Oswanski MF, et al: Practice management guidelines for prophylactic antibiotic use in tube thoracostomy for traumatic hemopneumothorax: the EAST practice management guidelines work group. J Trauma 48:753, 2000

4. Brasel KJ, Stafford RE, Weigelt JA, et al: Treatment of occult pneumothoraces from blunt trauma. J Trauma 46:987, 1999

5. Aguilar MM, Battistella FD, Owings JT, et al: Posttraumatic empyema: risk factor analysis. Arch Surg 132:647, 1997

6. Meyer DM, Jessen ME, Wait MA, et al: Early evacuation of traumatic retained hemothoraces using thoracoscopy: a prospective, randomized trial. Ann Thorac Surg 64:1396, 1997

7. Wilson JM, Boren CH Jr, Peterson SR, et al: Traumatic hemothorax: is decortication necessary? J Thorac Cardiovasc Surg 77:489, 1989

8. Mandal AK, Thadepalli H, Mandal AK, et al: Posttraumatic empyema thoracis: a 24-year experience at a major trauma center. J Trauma 43:764, 1997

9. O'Brien J, Cohen M, Solit R, et al: Thoracoscopic drainage and decortication as definitive treatment for empyema thoracis following penetrating chest injury. J Trauma 36:536, 1994

10. Scherer LA, Battistella FD, Owings JT, et al: Video-assisted thoracic surgery in the treatment of posttraumatic empyema. Arch Surg 133:637, 1998

11. Hopson LR, Hirsh E, Delgado J, et al: Guidelines for withholding or termination of resuscitation in prehospital traumatic cardiopulmonary arrest: joint position statement of the National Association of EMS Physicians and the American College of Surgeons Committee on Trauma. J Am Coll Surg 196:106, 2003

12. Miglietta MA, Robb TV, Eachempati SR, et al: Current opinion regarding indications for emergency department thoracotomy. J Trauma 51:670, 2001

13. Feliciano DV, Bitondo CG, Cruse PA, et al: Liberal use of emergency center thoracotomy. Am J Surg 152:654, 1986

14. Exadaktylos AK, Sclabas G, Schmid SW, et al: Do we really need routine computed tomographic scanning in the primary evaluation of blunt chest trauma in patients with "normal" chest radiograph? J Trauma 51:1173, 2001

15. Fabian TC, Davis KA, Gavant ML, et al: Prospective study of blunt aortic injury: helical CT is diagnostic and antihypertensive therapy reduces rupture. Ann Surg 227:666, 1998

16. Karmy-Jones R, Jurkovich GJ, Nathens AB, et al: Timing of urgent thoracotomy for hemorrhage after trauma: a multicenter study. Arch Surg 136:513, 2001

17. Vargo DJ, Battistella FD: Abbreviated thoracotomy and temporary chest closure: an application of damage control after thoracic trauma. Arch Surg 136:21, 2001

18. Bergeron E, Lavoie A, Clas D, et al: Elderly trauma patients with rib fractures are at greater risk of death and pneumonia. J Trauma 54:478, 2003

19. Bulger EM, Arneson MA, Mock CN, et al: Rib fractures in the elderly. J Trauma 48:1040, 2000

20. Brookes JG, Dunn RJ, Roger IR: Sternal fractures: a retrospective analysis of 272 cases. J Trauma 35:46, 1993

21. Ciraulo DL, Elliot D, Mitchell KA, et al: Flail chest as a marker for significant injuries. J Am Coll Surg 178:466, 1994

22. Mackersie RC, Shackford SR, Hoyt DB, et al: Continuous epidural fentanyl analgesia: ventilatory function improvement with routine use in treatment of blunt chest injury. J Trauma 27:1207, 1987

23. Richardson JD, Adams L, Flint LM: Selective management of flail chest and pulmonary contusion. Ann Surg 196:481, 1982

24. Tanaka H, Yukioka T, Yamaguti Y, et al: Surgical stabilization of internal pneumatic stabilization? a prospective randomized study of management of severe flail chest patients. J Trauma 52:727, 2002

25. Voggenreiter G, Neudeck F, Aufmkolk M, et al: Operative chest wall stabilization in flail chest—outcomes of patients with or without pulmonary contusion. J Am Coll Surg 187:130, 1998

26. Karmy-Jones R, Jurkovich GJ, Shatz D, et al: Management of traumatic lung injury: a WTA multicenter review. J Trauma 51:1049, 2001

27. Cothren C, Moore EE, Biffl WL, et al: Lung-sparing techniques are associated with improved outcome compared with anatomic resection for severe lung injuries. J Trauma 53:483, 2002

28. Barmada H, Gibbons JR: Tracheobronchial injury in blunt and penetrating chest trauma. Chest 106:74, 1994

29. Baumgartner F, Sheppard B, de Virgilio C, et al: Tracheal and main bronchial disruptions after blunt chest trauma: presentation and management. Ann Thorac Surg 50:569, 1990

30. Campbell DB: Trauma to the chest wall, lung, and major airways. Semin Thorac Cardiovasc Surg 4:234, 1992

31. Flynn AE, Thoma AN, Schecter WP: Acute tracheobronchial injury. J Trauma 29:1326, 1989

32. Symbas PN, Justicz AG, Ricketts RR: Rupture of the airways from blunt trauma: treatment of complex injuries. Ann Thorac Surg 54:177, 1992

33. Cornwell EE, Kennedy F, Ayad IA, et al: Transmediastinal gunshot wounds: a reconsideration of the role of aortography. Arch Surg 131:949, 1996

34. Nesbitt JC, Sawyers JL: Surgical management of esophageal perforation. Am Surg 53:183, 1987

35. Asenio JA, Chahwan S, Forno W, et al: Penetrating esophageal injuries: multicenter study of the American Association for the Surgery of Trauma. J Trauma 50:289, 2001

36. Lotz PR, Martel W, Rohwedder JJ, et al: Significance of pneumomediastinum in blunt trauma to the thorax. AJR Am J Roentgenol 132:817, 1979

37. Defore WW, Mattox KL, Hansen HA, et al: Surgical management of penetrating injuries of the esophagus. Am J Surg 134:734, 1977

38. Glatterer MS Jr, Toon RS, Ellestad C, et al: Management of blunt and penetrating external esophageal trauma. J Trauma 25:784, 1985

39. Silen ML, Weber TR: Management of thoracic duct injury associated with fracture-dislocation of the spine following blunt trauma. J Trauma 39:1185, 1995

40. Markham KM, Glover JL, Welsh RJ, et al: Octreotide in the treatment of thoracic duct injuries. Am Surg 66:1165, 2000

41. Fahimi H, Casselman FP, Mariani MA, et al: Current management of postoperative chylothorax. Ann Thorac Surg 71:448, 2001

42. Lancey RA, Monahan TS: Correlation of clinical characteristics and outcomes with injury scoring in blunt cardiac trauma. J Trauma 54:509, 2003

43. Henderson VJ, Smith RS, Fry WR, et al: Cardiac injuries: analysis of an unselected series of 251 cases. J Trauma 36:341, 1994

44. Henderson VJ, Smith RS, Fry WR, et al: Cardiac injuries: analysis of an unselected series of 251 cases. J Trauma 36:341, 1994

45. Fulda G, Brathwaite CE, Rodriquez A, et al: Blunt traumatic rupture of the heart and pericardium: a ten-year experience (1979–1989). J Trauma 31:167, 1991

46. Rozycki GS, Feliciano DV, Ochsner MG, et al: The role of ultrasound in patients with possible penetrating cardiac wounds: a prospective multicenter study. J Trauma 46:543, 1999

47. Macho JR, Markison RE, Schecter WP: Cardiac stapling in the management of penetrating injuries of the heart: rapid control of hemorrhage and decreased risk of personal contamination. J Trauma 34:711, 1993

48. Pasquale MD, Nagy K, Clarke J: Practice management guidelines for screening of blunt cardiac injury. Eastern Association for the Surgery of Trauma Practice Parameter Workgroup for Screening of Blunt Cardiac Injury. http://www.east.org/tpg/chap2.pdf, accessed February 19, 2004

49. Burkhart HM, Gomez GA, Jacobson LE, et al: Fatal blunt aortic injuries: a review of 242 autopsy cases. J Trauma 50:113, 2001

50. Melton SM, Kerby JD, McGiffin D, et al: The evolution of chest computed tomography for the definitive diagnosis of blunt aortic injury: a single-center experience. J Trauma 56:243, 2004

51. Dyer DS, Moore EE, Klke DN, et al: Thoracic aortic injury: how predictive is mechanism and is chest computed tomography a reliable screening tool? a prospective study of 1,561 patients. J Trauma 48:673, 2000

52. Hemmila MR, Arbabi S, Rowe SA, et al: Delayed repair for blunt thoracic aortic injury: is it really equivalent to early repair? J Trauma 56:13, 2004

53. Fabian TC, Richardson JD, Croce MA, et al: Prospective study of blunt aortic injury: multicenter trial of the American Association for the Surgery of Trauma. J Trauma 42:374, 1997

54. Miller PR, Kortesis BG, McLaughlin CA 3rd, et al: Complex blunt aortic injury or repair: beneficial effects of cardiopulmonary bypass use. Ann Surg 237:877, 2003

55. Orford VP, Atkinson NR, Thomson K, et al: Blunt traumatic aortic transection: the endovascular experience. Ann Thorac Surg 75:106, 2003

56. Dosios TJ, Salemis N, Angouras D, et al: Blunt and penetrating trauma of the thoracic aorta and aortic arch branches: an autopsy study. J Trauma 49:696, 2000

57. Althaus SJ, Keskey TS, Harker CP, et al: Percutaneous placement of self-expanding stent for acute traumatic arterial injury. J Trauma 41:145, 1996

Acknowledgments

Figures 1 and 5   Alice Y. Chen.
Figure 3   Tom Moore.

105 OPERATIVE EXPOSURE OF ABDOMINAL INJURIES AND CLOSURE OF THE ABDOMEN

Erwin R. Thal, M.D., F.A.C.S., and Terence O'Keeffe, M.B., Ch.B., F.R.C.S.Ed.

Over the past two decades, the advent of nonoperative management techniques for many solid-organ injuries has led to a significant shift in the care of patients who have sustained abdominal trauma. The ever-improving accuracy of diagnostic modalities (computed tomography in particular) has also contributed to this shift.[1-4] Today, fewer patients require operative intervention for treatment of abdominal injuries. Those who do require such intervention make up a select group who continue to pose a significant challenge to surgeons. In our view, these patients are best managed by following a standardized operative approach, the aim of which is to diagnose, prioritize, and treat the injuries in an expeditious fashion so that the patient is not kept in the operating room any longer than necessary [*see Figure 1*]. Such an approach optimizes patient care by minimizing the risk of missed injuries and ensuring a rapid and efficient response by the members of the surgical team. Naturally, every patient's care should be individualized as necessary. In general, however, a standardized operative approach, complemented by a solid knowledge of a variety of exposures and techniques, should allow the surgeon to deal with virtually any abdominal injury. In this chapter, we outline our recommended approach to operative intervention in patients with abdominal trauma.

Patient Preparation

The key to success in this setting is advance preparation aimed at covering all eventualities. Such preparation involves both the environment and the patient. The room should be warmed to ensure that the patient does not lose too much heat and become hypothermic. The instruments should be open on the back table, and specific instruments should be available when specific injuries are anticipated (e.g., a vascular set should be available when a vascular injury is suspected). A sufficient number of laparotomy pads should be on hand, and a retracting device with which the surgical team is familiar should be employed. Cell saver systems and rapid infusion systems can be useful adjuncts; if desired and available, they should be requested in advance.[5]

Patient preparation begins with the insertion of a nasogastric or orogastric tube and a Foley catheter. Invasive monitoring lines may have to be placed, and resuscitation should continue as the patient is being prepared. A broad-spectrum antibiotic should be administered intravenously before the initial incision is made. When the patient is correctly positioned on the operating table, skin preparation should extend from the sternal notch superiorly to include the anterior thorax. Thus, no further preparation will be required if a thoracic injury is identified or vascular control in the thorax is necessary. Thoracostomy, if required, can also be performed without the drapes being changed. Inferiorly, skin preparation should extend to the upper anterior thighs so that the proximal saphenous veins are available if a vascular reconstruction is required and so that distal vascular control can be achieved without undue delay.

All areas of the body that are not included in the skin preparation should be covered so as to prevent excessive heat loss, and warming devices should be placed if available. Sterile draping should be placed so as to allow access to all potential injuries. If the patient is in extremis and in danger of expiring, however, patient preparation should be limited to a rapid skin cleansing and surgery should commence immediately.

Incision and Initial Exploration

CHOICE OF INCISION

A midline celiotomy is the incision of choice. Its advantages are that it allows rapid and easy access to the abdominal cavity, with good exposure of the majority of the intra-abdominal organs and structures, and that it can be extended into a median sternotomy if necessary. Its main disadvantage is that it may not provide adequate exposure of injuries in the deep recesses of the upper quadrants.

Patients with previous midline incisions pose a challenge to the surgeon. If at all possible, an attempt should be made to enter the abdomen above or below the previous incision, in an area less likely to have adhesions. If this is not possible, an alternative incision, such as a chevron (bilateral subcostal) incision, should be considered. A chevron incision provides entry into the abdomen while avoiding any viscera that are adherent to the undersurface of the previous laparotomy scar. However, this incision takes more time, does not provide ideal exposure, and is associated with a higher morbidity; accordingly, it should be considered only when the circumstances are dire. Paramedian, subcostal, retroperitoneal, and flank incisions are not recommended, for much the same reasons.

INITIAL EXPLORATION

Once the peritoneal cavity has been entered, initial exploration proceeds in an orderly fashion so as to minimize hemorrhage and contamination, prevent iatrogenic injury, and facilitate the expeditious identification of injuries. The intestines are eviscerated, and gross blood is rapidly evacuated. Laparotomy pads are then rapidly placed in all four quadrants to pack the abdomen; the right upper quadrant is packed first, then the left upper quadrant, and finally the lower two quadrants. Care should be taken not to tear the falciform ligament or the fibrous capsule of the liver during this maneuver. Blood pressure may drop when the abdomen is decompressed. Anesthesia should be given the opportunity to catch up with resuscitation efforts at this point.

Once hemodynamic stability has been achieved, the intraperitoneal portion of the exploration is begun. In cases of blunt trauma, the temporary packs (except for those around the solid viscera) may now be carefully removed and any remaining blood evacuated. In cases of penetrating trauma, it is often easier initially to address the site of ongoing hemorrhage via a direct approach. Vascular injuries are controlled manually until proximal and distal

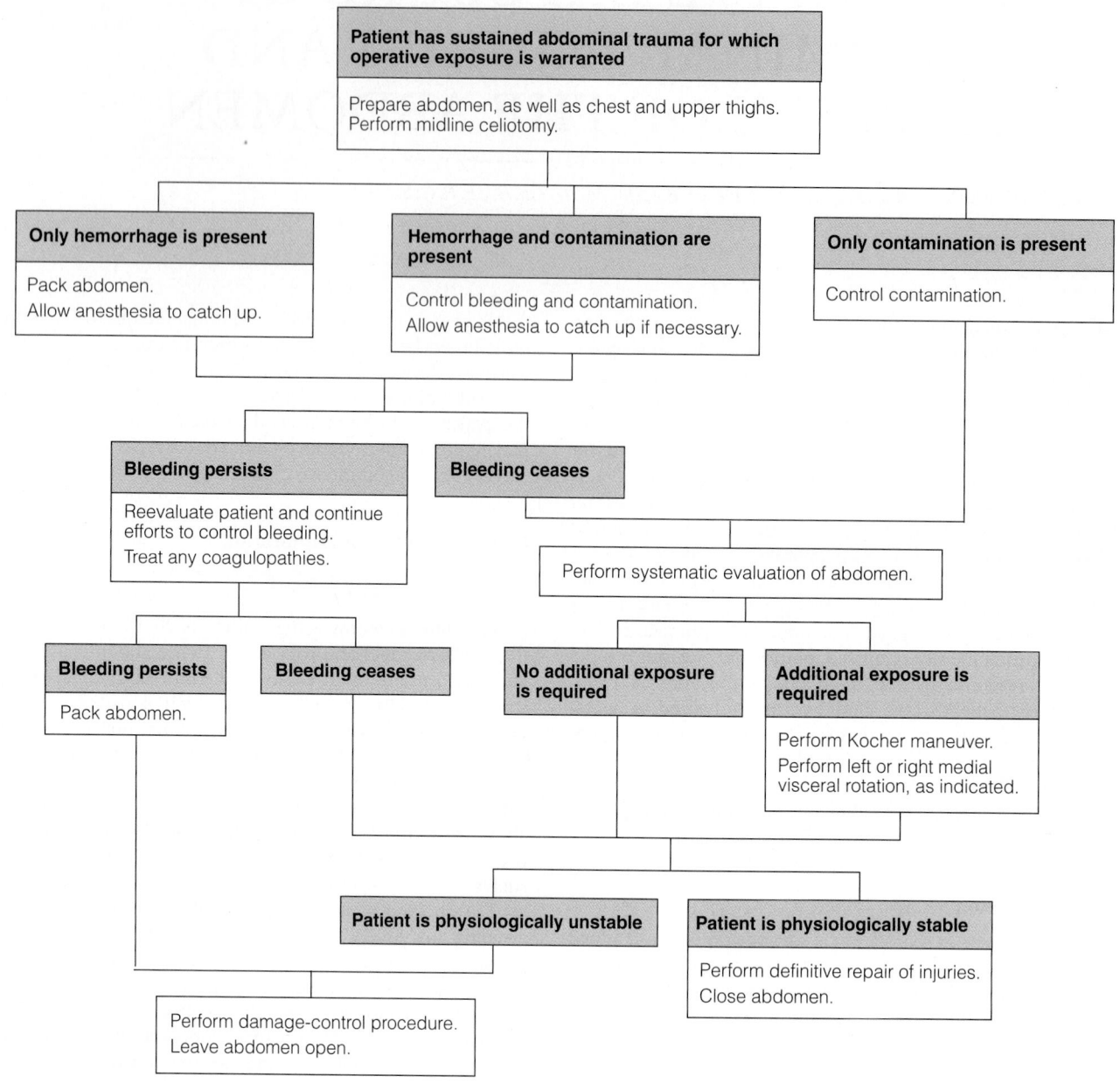

Figure 1 **Algorithm outlines the approach to initial operative exposure in abdominal trauma patients.**

control can be achieved. Mesenteric bleeding sites are clamped. Solid organs are initially packed as for blunt trauma, then treated with directed repair. In either scenario, bleeding that remains uncontrolled by packing requires immediate attention.

The enteric viscera are then examined in an orderly fashion. The anterior aspect of the stomach is inspected from the esophagogastric junction down to the pylorus. If an injury is present or is strongly suspected on the basis of the mechanism of injury or the presence of a hematoma or soilage, the posterior aspect of the stomach is examined by opening the gastrocolic omentum; this measure also permits examination of the anterior surface of the body of the pancreas. The exploration then continues distally along the course of the GI tract. If duodenal or pancreatic injury is a possibility, the duodenum is mobilized fully by means of a Kocher maneuver. The duodenojejunal junction at the ligament of Treitz is then inspected, and the small intestine is inspected all the way to the ileocecal valve. Both sides of the small intestine must

be examined, and particular care must be taken not to miss an injury at the mesenteric border. Careful consideration should also be given to the possibility of mesenteric vascular injuries, which may be manifested as mesenteric hematomas.

Next, the colon is inspected from the cecum to the rectum. If injuries are present or missile tracts are noted in proximity to a portion of the ascending or descending colon, the retroperitoneal portion of the colon is inspected by incising the white line of Toldt (the retroperitoneal reflection) so as to allow access to the posterior surface of the colon. Finally, the laparotomy pads around the solid organs are removed, one organ at a time, to permit inspection for hemorrhage or injury.

Once the peritoneal survey is complete, the retroperitoneum is inspected for potential injuries. Retroperitoneal hematomas are classified on an anatomic basis: zone 1 is the central area, bounded laterally by the kidneys and extending from the diaphragmatic hiatus to the bifurcation of the vena cava and the aorta; zone 2 comprises the lateral area of the retroperitoneum, from the kidneys laterally to the paracolic gutters; and zone 3 is the pelvic portion [*see Figure 2*].Whether exploration is warranted for a retroperitoneal hematoma depends on the mechanism of injury and the location of the hematoma [*see Priorities in Management, Repair of Retroperitoneal Injuries, below, and 109 Injuries to the Great Vessels of the Abdomen*]. A careful evaluation is performed to identify possible occult injuries to organs (e.g., the pancreas, the duodenum, the retroperitoneal colon, the kidneys, and vascular structures).

The initial exploration concludes with a brief pelvic survey aimed at excluding injuries to the rectum or the distal urogenital tract (including the bladder). At the end of the operation, this initial inspection should be repeated, following the same sequence, to confirm that no injuries have been missed.

Operative Exposure

To expose the various organs that may be injured in patients who have sustained abdominal trauma, the surgeon must be familiar with a number of different techniques. In what follows, we detail the operative exposures that enable the surgeon to perform

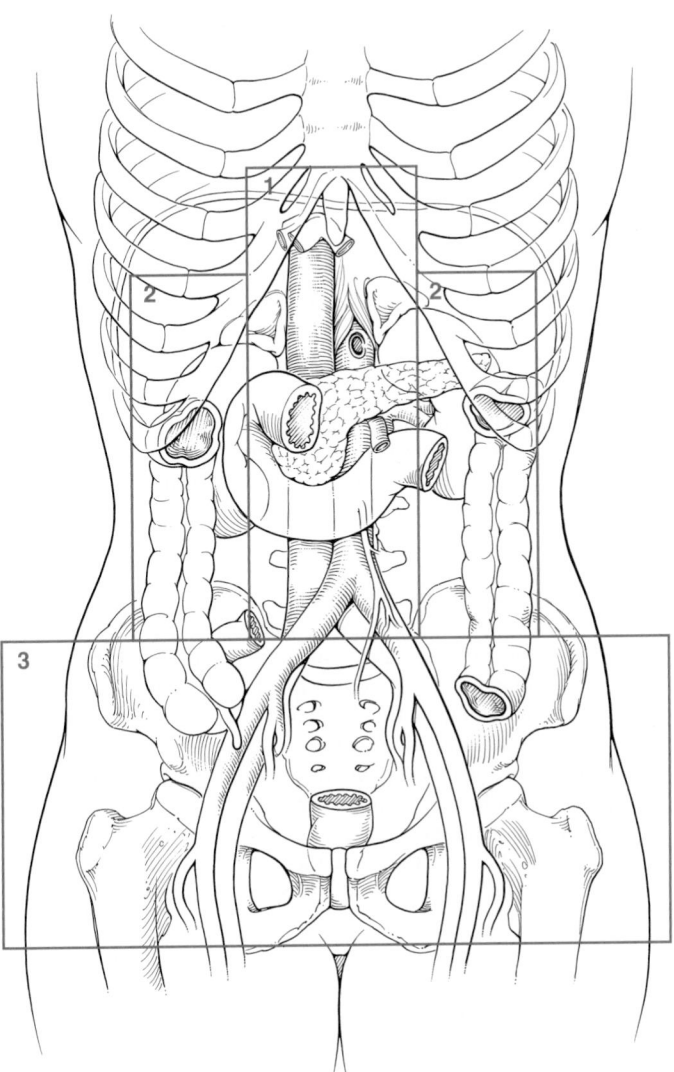

Figure 2 **Shown are the anatomic zones of the retroperitoneum: zone 1 (central), zone 2 (flank), and zone 3 (pelvic).**

the necessary repairs. The repairs themselves are described in greater detail elsewhere [*see 106 Injuries to the Liver, Biliary Tract, Spleen, and Diaphragm; 107 Injuries to the Stomach, Small Bowel, Colon, and Rectum; 108 Injuries to the Pancreas and Duodenum; 109 Injuries to the Great Vessels of the Abdomen; and 110 Injuries to the Urogenital Tract*].

AORTA AND BRANCHES

Control of the aorta can be gained at several different levels, depending on the site of injury. The supraceliac aorta can be exposed by incising the gastrohepatic ligament, retracting the left hemiliver laterally and cephalad, and retracting the stomach caudally. The esophagus and periesophageal fat pad are then mobilized laterally to permit identification of the abdominal aorta at the diaphragmatic hiatus, at which point the aorta can be encircled, clamped, or compressed. This exposure allows control of the aorta, but it is inadequate in terms of providing vascular access for definitive repair. Better exposure of the supraceliac aorta and its branches can be obtained by means of a left medial visceral rotation [*see Figure 3*]. To perform this maneuver, the splenorenal ligament is mobilized with a combination of sharp and blunt dissection. The left peritoneal reflection is incised from the splenocolic flexure down the paracolic gutter to the level of the distal sigmoid colon. The left-side viscera are then gently mobilized to the midline (mostly with blunt dissection) in a plane anterior to Gerota's fascia. This technique allows exploration of the entire length of the abdominal aorta, the origin of the celiac axis, the origin of the superior mesenteric artery, the left iliac system, and the origin of the right common iliac artery. In addition, it facilitates control of the left renal vascular pedicle before exploration of a left-side zone 2 retroperitoneal hematoma. Alternatively, a variation on the standard left medial visceral rotation (the Mattox maneuver[6]) may be employed, in which the left kidney is also included in the organs that are rotated (the plane being anterior only to the muscles of the posterior abdominal wall). This variant may afford better access to the origin of the left renal artery.

If the injury is more distal, the aorta may be approached in a transperitoneal fashion. The small intestine is retracted to the right, the transverse colon is retracted cephalad, and the descending colon is retracted laterally. The peritoneum is then incised directly over the aorta, and the third and fourth portions of the duodenum are mobilized cephalad. The proximal limit of this dissection extends to the left renal vein, which may be divided if necessary to provide more cephalad access to the aorta. If ligation of the left renal vein is called for, it should be done at a point where the gonadal vein will be left intact to drain the kidney. A more limited dissection may suffice to expose the distal infrarenal aorta. Depending on the injury, distal control may or may not be required. Control may be achieved at the level of the distal infrarenal aorta, above the bifurcation.

Once again, if the patient is in extremis, formal dissection may be curtailed and proximal control achieved either by manually compressing the aorta against the spine at the level of the esophagogastric junction or by using an aortic occluder [*see 109 Injuries to the Great Vessels of the Abdomen*].

VENA CAVA AND BRANCHES

Access to the suprahepatic inferior vena cava can be gained only by either incising the central tendon of the diaphragm or by performing a median sternotomy and opening the pericardium. The infrahepatic inferior vena cava is exposed by performing a right medial visceral rotation (the Cattell-Braasch maneuver) [*see Figure*

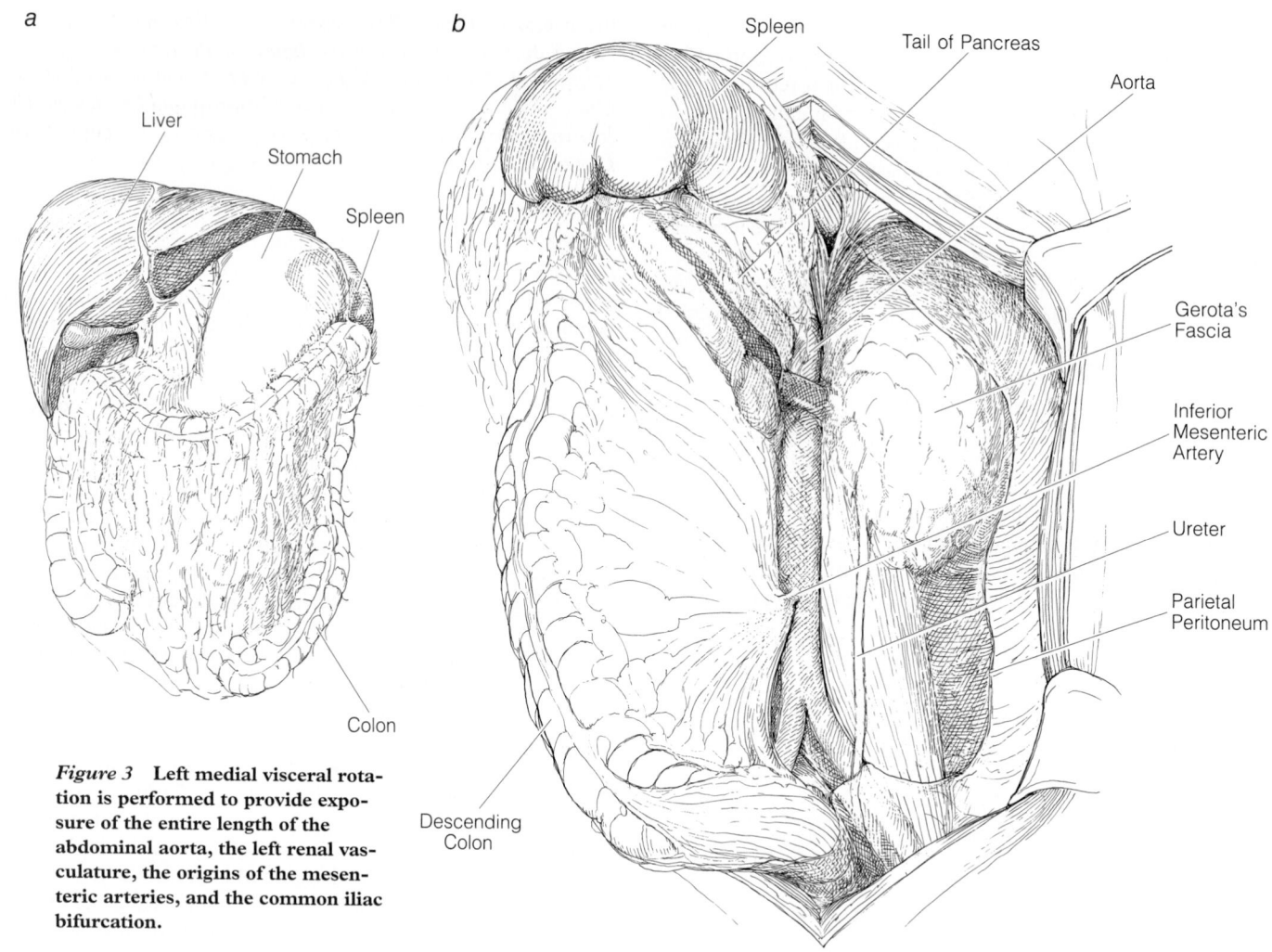

a

Liver

Stomach

Spleen

Colon

b

Spleen

Tail of Pancreas

Aorta

Gerota's Fascia

Inferior Mesenteric Artery

Ureter

Parietal Peritoneum

Descending Colon

Figure 3 **Left medial visceral rotation is performed to provide exposure of the entire length of the abdominal aorta, the left renal vasculature, the origins of the mesenteric arteries, and the common iliac bifurcation.**

4]. The right colon is mobilized by taking down the hepatic flexure and then incising the right peritoneal reflection along the paracolic gutter. The colon is once again reflected medially toward the aorta in a plane anterior to Gerota's fascia with careful blunt dissection. If additional exposure is necessary, the inferior margin of the peritoneal incision may be extended to the root of the mesentery—and even beyond, if the inferior mesenteric vein is sacrificed. This exposure permits visualization of both the aorta below the origin of the superior mesenteric artery and the vena cava below the third portion of the duodenum. Exposure of the portion of the vena cava directly below the liver alone can be achieved by performing a Kocher manuever [*see Figure 5*] with medial mobilization of the duodenum and the head of the pancreas.

LIVER

Mobilization of the liver begins with division of the round ligament (ligamentum teres), followed by takedown of the falciform ligament (to prevent iatrogenic trauma to the liver capsule during exposure and identification of other intraperitoneal injuries). This mobilization may be extended as far cephalad as is necessary. Further mobilization can be achieved by incising the left triangular ligament, with care taken not to injure the suprahepatic inferior vena cava at the diaphragmatic hiatus during the dissection. When visualization of the right hemiliver is required, the falciform ligament should be incised to its most superior extent, and the right triangular ligament should then be carefully divided. This

step is challenging and may have to be performed partly by palpation, with care taken not to injure the inferior vena cava, the hepatic veins, or the phrenic vessels [*see 106 Injuries to the Liver, Biliary Tract, Spleen, and Diaphragm*].

SPLEEN

The spleen can be mobilized into the midline by dividing the phrenicosplenic and splenorenal ligaments with a mixture of sharp and blunt dissection. In cases where the spleen has been injured by blunt trauma, these ligaments often are already disrupted, and this disruption facilitates the dissection. The splenocolic ligament often contains sizeable blood vessels that must be controlled, and the gastrosplenic ligament contains the short gastric arteries. Once the spleen is mobilized into the midline, control of the vascular pedicle can be achieved, the splenic injury can be assessed, and splenorrhaphy or splenectomy can be performed as appropriate [*see 106 Injuries to the Liver, Biliary Tract, Spleen, and Diaphragm and 67 Splenectomy*].

PANCREAS

Intraoperative evidence of a central hematoma, peripancreatic edema, or bile staining in the retroperitoneum or the lesser sac raises the possibility of pancreatic injury. The contents of the lesser sac can be visualized by performing a direct inspection through the gastrohepatic ligament or by dividing the ligament. Alternatively, access can be gained by dividing and ligating two or three gastroepiploic arcades of the gastrocolic ligament. If it proves necessary to explore the pancreas, the stomach is separated from the transverse colon by completing the division of the gastrocolic ligament, and a Kocher maneuver is performed to reflect all portions of the duodenum medially, along with the head of the pancreas. The peritoneum lateral to the duodenum is incised, and careful blunt dissection is employed to mobilize the duodenal loop from the common bile duct superiorly to the superior mesenteric vein inferiorly. This mobilization allows inspection of the anterior and posterior surfaces of the head of the pancreas, as well as the uncinate process. If injury to the body or tail of the pancreas is suspected, the splenorenal and splenocolic ligaments are incised. At this point, the spleen and then the pancreas can be mobilized medially to a position near the level of the superior mesenteric vessels, and the anterior and posterior aspects of the body and tail of the pancreas can be examined [see 108 Injuries to the Pancreas and Duodenum].

KIDNEYS

Operative exposure of the kidneys starts with either a left or a right medial visceral rotation, depending on which kidney is involved. The renal vascular pedicle should be controlled before any hematoma in Gerota's fascia is opened [see 110 Injuries to the Urogenital Tract]. Repair of the kidney may be facilitated by mobilizing the organ out of Gerota's fascia and retracting it medially.

DUODENUM, BILIARY TRACT, AND SMALL INTESTINE

Exposure of the posterior surface of the duodenum is achieved by means of a Kocher maneuver [see Pancreas, above, and Figure 5]. This technique is also used when injury to the distal extrahepatic biliary system is suspected. The proximal extrahepatic biliary tree is visualized by using a Kocher maneuver in conjunction with local exploration of the porta hepatis. In patients with injuries to the distal duodenum or the proximal jejunum, division of the ligament of Treitz may also be necessary for accurate identification of the site of injury. Because of the mobility of the small intestine, injuries to this structure generally are readily identified and repaired without additional mobilization.

COLON AND RECTUM

Evidence of staining, pneumatosis, or hematoma in proximity to a portion of the ascending or descending colon, particularly in the setting of related injuries or missile tracts, should prompt a full evaluation of the colon. Because the colon is a partially retroperitoneal structure, the retroperitoneal reflection must be incised to allow inspection of the posterior surface of the colon. Sometimes, rectal injuries are not accessible via an intraperitoneal approach; in this situation, consideration should be given to a diverting colostomy and presacral drainage [see 107 Injuries to the Stomach, Small Bowel, Colon, and Rectum].[7,8]

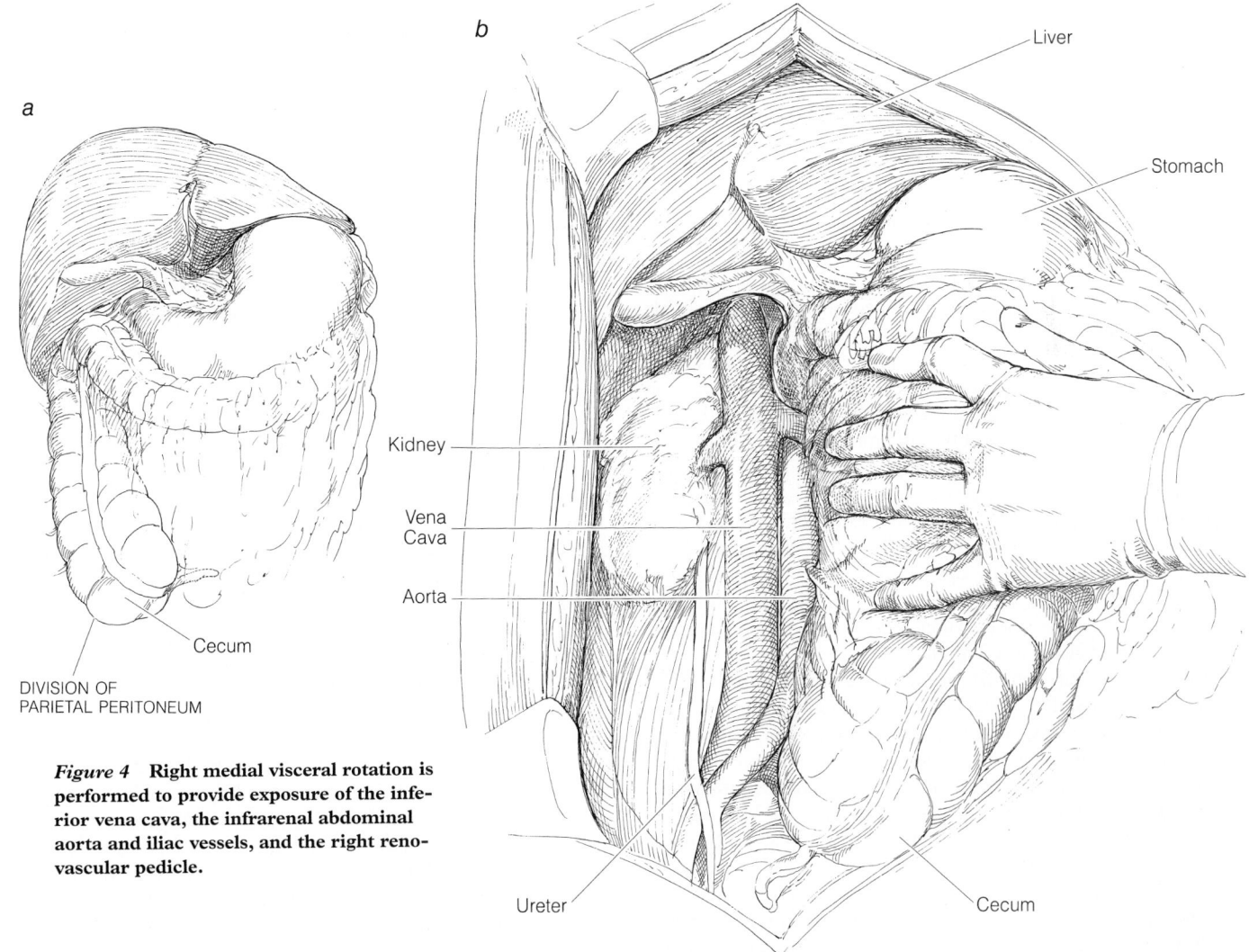

Figure 4 **Right medial visceral rotation is performed to provide exposure of the inferior vena cava, the infrarenal abdominal aorta and iliac vessels, and the right renovascular pedicle.**

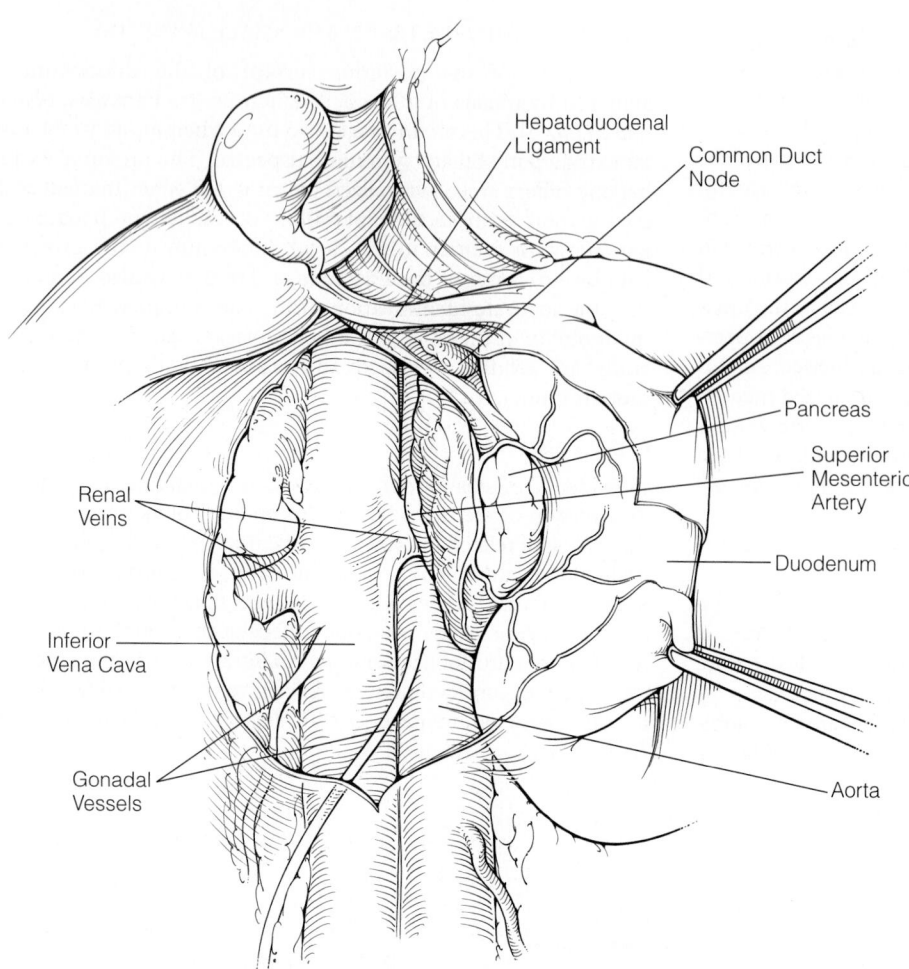

Figure 5 **The Kocher maneuver reflects the duodenum and the pancreatic head from the retroperitoneum, allowing access to the infrahepatic inferior vena cava as well as to the distal common bile duct, the duodenum, and the pancreatic head.**

Priorities in Management

CONTROL OF HEMORRHAGE

In the event that the patient remains hemodynamically unstable because of persistent uncontrolled hemorrhage, the primary focus of the initial exploration is control of bleeding. As noted (see above), the approach to hemorrhage control differs depending on whether the patient sustained blunt trauma or penetrating trauma. In cases of blunt trauma with bleeding from a solid organ, the first thing that should be done is to attempt repeat packing of the specific bleeding site with a sufficient number of laparotomy pads. This is an important skill to master and can be effective as a temporizing measure until either more definitive vascular control can be achieved or coagulopathy can be corrected. In cases of penetrating trauma, bleeding is more effectively managed by means of either vascular control just proximal and distal to the site of injury or direct control at the bleeding site.

When significant hemorrhage is anticipated, control of the injured vessel should be obtained by the operative techniques discussed previously [see Operative Exposure, *above*]. Given the possibility of exsanguinating hemorrhage, the surgeon must be prepared to gain proximal aortic control at the diaphragmatic hiatus or even within the chest via a left lateral thoracotomy. For immediate control, the aorta can be manually compressed at the hiatus; a padded Richardson retractor, an aortic compressor, or an assistant's hand can then take over this function to allow the surgeon to continue the exploration. If a need for prolonged proximal aortic control is anticipated, an atraumatic aortic vascular clamp should be placed. Injuries to the proximal abdominal aorta often necessitate that the vessel be controlled in the chest to permit repair.

In patients who have sustained parenchymal injuries to solid viscera, control of the vascular inflow is crucial as both a diagnostic and a therapeutic maneuver. Gaining control of the splenic hilum effectively arrests further splenic hemorrhage. Similarly, use of the Pringle maneuver [see *106 Injuries to the Liver, Biliary Tract, Spleen, and Diaphragm*] to control the vessels in the porta hepatis (the hepatic artery and the portal vein) helps determine the source of perihepatic hemorrhage. This maneuver is initially performed by digitally compressing the portal structures; if digital compression causes the hemorrhage to diminish, the surgeon's hand is replaced with an atraumatic vascular clamp or a Rumel tourniquet. Although the Pringle maneuver can be maintained for at least 30 to 45 minutes without causing permanent liver damage, the clamp or tourniquet should be removed as soon as is feasible. In the vast majority of cases of liver trauma—aside from those involving an injury to the retrohepatic vena cava—the use of the Pringle maneuver, combined with perihepatic packing, should arrest hemorrhage.

In patients who have sustained injuries to the retrohepatic vena cava, it may be necessary to gain vascular control by performing hepatic exclusion before definitive repair can be attempted [see *106 Injuries to the Liver, Biliary Tract, Spleen, and Diaphragm*]. Hepatic exclusion may be achieved by means of either atriocaval shunting (which is rarely if ever used[9,10]) or occlusion of the inferior vena cava both above and below the liver. The latter may lead to significant hemodynamic instability, particularly in volume-depleted patients; however, it may reasonably be considered in patients whose volume status is adequate. Complete hepatic exclusion involves both (1) atriocaval shunting or clamping of both the infra-hepatic and the suprahepatic inferior vena cava and (2) control of hepatic arterial and portal venous inflow.[11] In general, injuries to the retrohepatic vena cava are best dealt with by means of dam-age-control procedures.

Hepatic parenchymal hemorrhage can be challenging, and any of a number of techniques may be used to control it, depending on the location, type, and degree of bleeding. These techniques range from simple electrocauterization and parenchymal suturing to argon beam cauterization, direct vessel ligation, hepatotomy, and even resection [see 106 Injuries to the Liver, Biliary Tract, Spleen, and Diaphragm].[12,13] In difficult cases, it may be advisable to per-form an abbreviated laparotomy, pack the liver extensively, and transport the patient to the angiography suite, where selective embolization can be performed; the patient can then be transport-ed to the ICU, undergo warming, and have any coagulopathy cor-rected before returning to the OR to have the packs removed.

Mesenteric bleeding can usually be controlled with manual com-pression of the vessel followed by suture ligation. Retroperitoneal hematomas are often harbingers of vascular injury, and proximal and distal vascular control should be obtained before exploration is initiated [see 109 Injuries to the Great Vessels of the Abdomen]. Typi-cally, bleeding from injured hollow viscera is minor and can be controlled by repairing the injury; on occasion, however, tempo-rary hemostatic suturing or stapling may be required.

CONTROL OF CONTAMINATION

Once hemorrhage has been controlled, the next priority is to control contamination. All gross spillage should be removed from the abdomen with suction and laparotomy pads, and fur-ther contamination should be prevented by temporarily closing small enterotomies with Babcock clamps (or, alternatively, with a continuous suture or skin staples). When multiple enteroto-mies are present, suture closure is preferred (to ensure that mul-tiple clamps are not present in the operative field). If the injuries are in close proximity, the preferred method of controlling intestinal spillage is to apply atraumatic bowel clamps at both the proximal and the distal end of the injury site. Alternatively, if the injured segment will have to be resected, rapid control of further spillage can be obtained by firing a GI stapler at each end of the injured segment.

REPAIR OF VASCULAR INJURIES

Once intestinal contamination has been dealt with, the next pri-ority is definitive vascular repair [see 109 Injuries to the Great Vessels of the Abdomen]. If proximal and distal control of the injured ves-sel has not already been obtained, it is obtained at this point. The extent of the vascular injury is determined, dead or devitalized tis-sue is carefully debrided, and vessel continuity is reestablished if possible. If the injury is not amenable to primary repair and the vessel cannot be ligated, autogenous tissue should be obtained (usually from the proximal greater saphenous vein) and used for either patch angioplasty or interposition grafting. If no suitable autogenous venous tissue is available, synthetic material may be considered as an alternative vascular conduit. For aortic or iliac arterial injuries, primary ligation with subsequent extra-anatomic bypass is an acceptable alternative. In cases in which an abbrevi-ated laparotomy is necessary, vascular shunting may serve as a sub-stitute for definitive repair until hypothermia, coagulopathy, and acidosis are corrected.

REPAIR OF DAMAGED OR DEVITALIZED BOWEL

Once vascular injuries have been addressed, the next priority is to repair any enteric injuries [see 107 Injuries to the Stomach, Small Bowel, Colon, and Rectum]. Because the stomach is a large and well-vascularized organ, gastric injuries are usually amenable to prima-ry repair. Injuries to the small intestine that involve less than 50% of bowel circumference after debridement of devitalized edges can be repaired with either a single-layer or a two-layer closure; single-layer closure, being less likely to compromise the lumen of the bowel, is generally preferred. In cases involving multiple enteroto-mies in close proximity or a large area of devitalized tissue, a seg-mental enterectomy with primary anastomosis is preferable. The anastomosis may be either hand-sewn or stapled; the latter tends to be more expeditious but less cost-effective.

Solitary injuries to the colon that do not necessitate resection after debridement and are not associated with multiple transfu-sions or significant gross contamination are managed by means of primary closure. Large or multiple injuries to the right colon are best managed with a right hemicolectomy followed by an imme-diate ileocolic anastomosis. Similar injuries to the left colon are generally treated with resection and proximal diversion. The distal limb may be exteriorized as a mucous fistula, or, if inadequate bowel length renders diversion impossible, a Hartmann procedure may be performed. [14-16]

REPAIR OF RETROPERITONEAL INJURIES

Once all injuries within the peritoneal cavity have been addressed, the next priority is to inspect the retroperitoneum once more, paying particular attention to the possibility of hematoma expansion. The decision whether to explore a retroperitoneal hematoma is based on the mechanism of injury and on the zone in which the injury is located. All zone 1 hematomas should be explored regardless of the injury mechanism: they signal possible aortic, vena caval, duodenal, or pancreatic injury. Zone 2 and 3 hematomas should be explored in cases of penetrating trauma but not, as a rule, in cases of blunt trauma (with the exception of expanding zone 2 hematomas).

Before a retroperitoneal hematoma is opened, proximal vascu-lar control should be obtained so that hemorrhage will be mini-mized once the effect of the tamponade has been lost. Injuries to retroperitoneal organs (e.g., the kidneys, the pancreas, and the adrenal glands) are treated by means of debridement or resection, with drainage as indicated. Vascular injuries are repaired as dis-cussed previously [see Repair of Vascular Injuries, above, and 109 Injuries to the Great Vessels of the Abdomen].

Closure

GENERAL TECHNIQUE

Once the abdominal exploration has been completed, the abdomen is copiously irrigated with an isotonic crystalloid solu-tion. The closure method employed is typically determined on the basis of five main considerations: (1) the degree of blood loss, (2) the volume of resuscitation fluid received, (3) the degree of conta-mination, (4) the patient's perceived nutritional status, and (5) the patient's hemodynamic stability. In cases that necessitate an abbre-viated or damage-control procedure, the speed with which the clo-sure can be performed may be the most important factor. Provided that the risk of subsequent abdominal compartment syndrome (ACS) is considered to be low, every effort should be made to close the fascia. Fascial closure is usually accomplished with a continu-

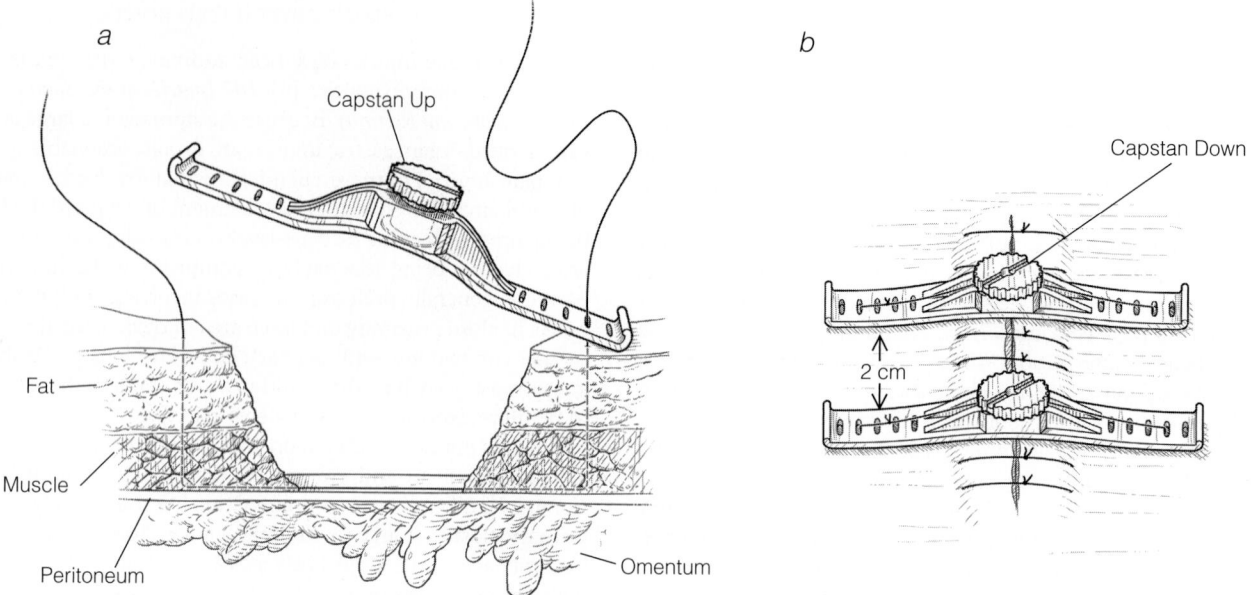

Figure 6 Retention sutures may be used to bolster fascial closure in wounds at high risk for breakdown. (*a*) Sutures are placed in the subfascial plane. (*b*) The defect is approximated, and the sutures are tied over skin bridges.

ous absorbable or nonabsorbable monofilament suture, though it may also be accomplished with interrupted sutures. The rate of fascial dehiscence is essentially the same for the two techniques; however, the extent of dehiscence is more limited when closure is done with interrupted sutures.[17,18] With either technique, it is important not to place excessive tension on the fascial tissues.

In cases where there is a specific reason to be concerned about possible dehiscence (e.g., in patients who are malnourished or obese or are receiving steroid therapy), large monofilament sutures may be placed at intervals within the standard closure to serve as retention sutures. They may be tied over bolsters created from a red rubber catheter or over plastic skin bridges [*see Figure 6*]. If rapid closure is required, the abdomen may be closed with four or five retention sutures of this type that are placed through the abdominal wall and just above the peritoneum. These sutures must be checked daily and should be loosened if there is evidence that they are cutting through the abdominal skin as a consequence of edema creating increased tension on the wound.

SKIN CLOSURE

If the patient has minor injuries without evidence of enteric contamination, the skin may be closed primarily. Stapled closure is most expeditious, but suture closure is also acceptable. A degree of clinical judgment is required in assessing a wound's suitability for closure. If the skin is closed primarily, it should be inspected daily, and the wound should be opened without delay if there is concern about subsequent infection. Alternatively, primary delayed closure may be performed by leaving the wound open, packed with moist gauze. If the wound shows no evidence of infection when examined after 3 to 5 days, it may be closed with Steri-Strips or with interrupted sutures that are placed (without being tied) during the original operation. If intraperitoneal contamination has occurred, either primary delayed closure should be performed or the wound should be packed and left to heal by secondary intention.

ABBREVIATED OR DAMAGE-CONTROL LAPAROTOMY

If a patient remains unstable after surgical bleeding and contamination have been controlled or is cold and coagulopathic, an abbreviated or damage-control procedure is indicated. It may be necessary to perform a rapid abdominal closure—with the proviso that further exploration, as well as definitive repair of injuries that have been temporarily controlled, will be required. The decision to perform a damage-control procedure should be made at an early stage, before the so-called lethal triad (hypothermia, acidosis and coagulopathy) has had time to develop. Damage control has undoubtedly led to improved survival for trauma patients, but it has also led to an increase in the number of patients whose abdomens are left open.[19]

TEMPORARY ABDOMINAL CLOSURE

When a damage-control procedure is required, it is often most expedient to perform a rapid temporary abdominal closure, then to transport the patient to the intensive care unit. This measure may also be necessary in patients whose abdomens cannot be closed because of intestinal and organ edema caused by intraoperative fluid resuscitation. The simplest form of temporary abdominal closure is the use of towel clips to close only the skin [*see Figure 7*], in conjunction with the application of a biooclusive dressing to control fluid loss and contamination. This closure, however, leaves the patient still at risk for subsequent ACS.

The first temporary abdominal dressing described was the so-called Bogotá bag—that is, an empty intravenous fluid bag that was cut in half and sewn to the wound edges. This dressing can still be used in circumstances where no other equipment is available. The so-called vacuum pack technique involves the placement of a sterile plastic drape over the bowel contents and under the fascia, followed by insertion of two or more suction drains, over which sterile towels or open laparotomy pads may be placed. To minimize heat loss and insensible fluid loss, an adherent biooclusive dressing is placed over the entire dressing and the abdominal wall, with the drains attached to suction. Several commercial devices are now available that can be used to facilitate temporary closure of the open abdomen; these include the VAC Abdominal Dressing System (Kinetic Concepts Inc., San Antonio, Texas) and the Wittmann Patch (Star Surgical, Burlington, Wisconsin).[20,21]

MANAGEMENT OF THE OPEN ABDOMEN

Once the patient's physiologic status has stabilized, he or she should be returned to the OR for reexploration and definitive repair of any remaining injuries [see Figure 8], preferably within 48 hours after the first operation. At this juncture, the abdomen should be assessed for the feasibility of closure. In some patients, the fascial edges cannot be approximated, because of edema; in others, reapproximation may cause a significant rise in intra-abdominal pressure, as evidenced by a rise in pulmonary inspiratory pressures. These patients are at risk for ACS, and their abdomens should be left open.

At this point, if temporary abdominal coverage continues to be required, a temporary abdominal dressing should be placed that attempts to prevent fascial retraction and the associated increased risk of nonclosure of the abdomen. Options include dynamic retention sutures, the Suture Tension Adjustment Reel (STAR) (WoundTEK, Inc., Newport, Rhode Island), the Wittmann Patch, nonabsorbable mesh, fascial zippers, and the VAC Abdominal Dressing System.[20-25] Once the dressing is placed, it should be

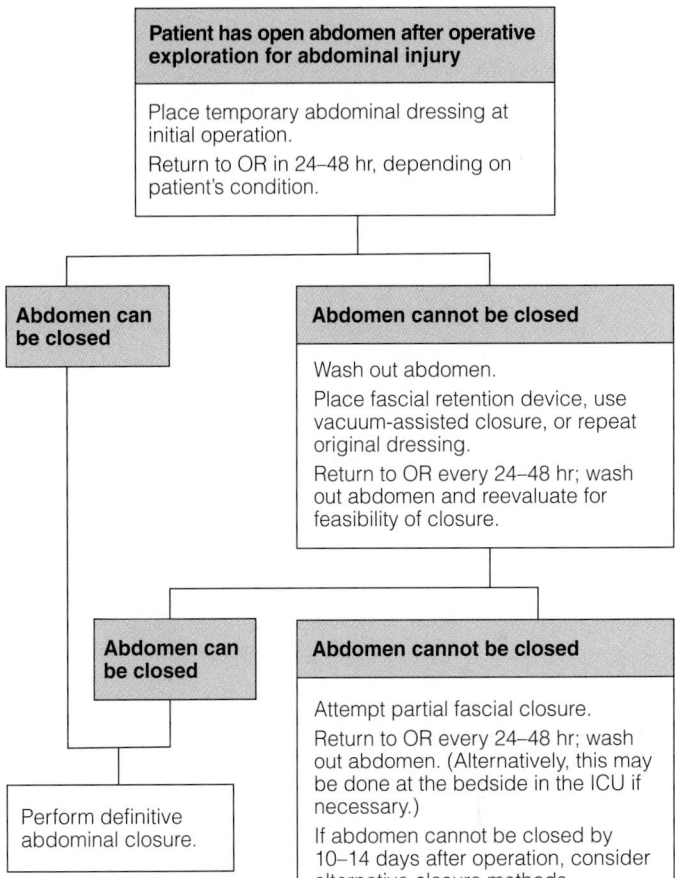

Figure 8 Algorithm outlines the approach to the open abdomen in a patient with abdominal injuries.

examined every 24 to 48 hours, depending on the degree of contamination; this is often best done in the OR, but it may also be done in the ICU if the patient remains unstable. At every subsequent procedure, the fascia should be assessed for the possibility of closure. Partial closure of the incision (i.e., closure of the cephalad and caudad portions) should be considered, even if full closure cannot be accomplished. In approximately 50% of patients, closure of the fascia is not possible; however, there is some evidence to suggest that this figure may be lowered by employing some of the devices now commercially available.[20,26,27]

ABDOMINAL COMPARTMENT SYNDROME

Patients who undergo fascial closure are at risk for ACS as a consequence of ongoing resuscitation efforts and associated bowel and organ edema. ACS is defined as intra-abdominal hypertension greater than 25 mm Hg in conjunction with dysfunction of one or more organ systems (e.g., pulmonary, renal, or cardiac). [28,29] Intra-abdominal pressure is determined indirectly by measuring bladder pressure. Bladder pressure can be measured by using an arterial transducer at the level of the symphysis pubis that is connected to the urinary catheter after 30 to 50 ml of sterile water has been introduced. Alternatively, an idea of the intra-abdominal pressure can be gained by raising the Foley tubing above the bed after instillation of the water, then measuring the column.[30] A rising trend in pressure can be as significant as a single elevated measurement. Patients who have undergone a long operation, have been the object of vigorous resuscitation efforts, or who have sustained mul-

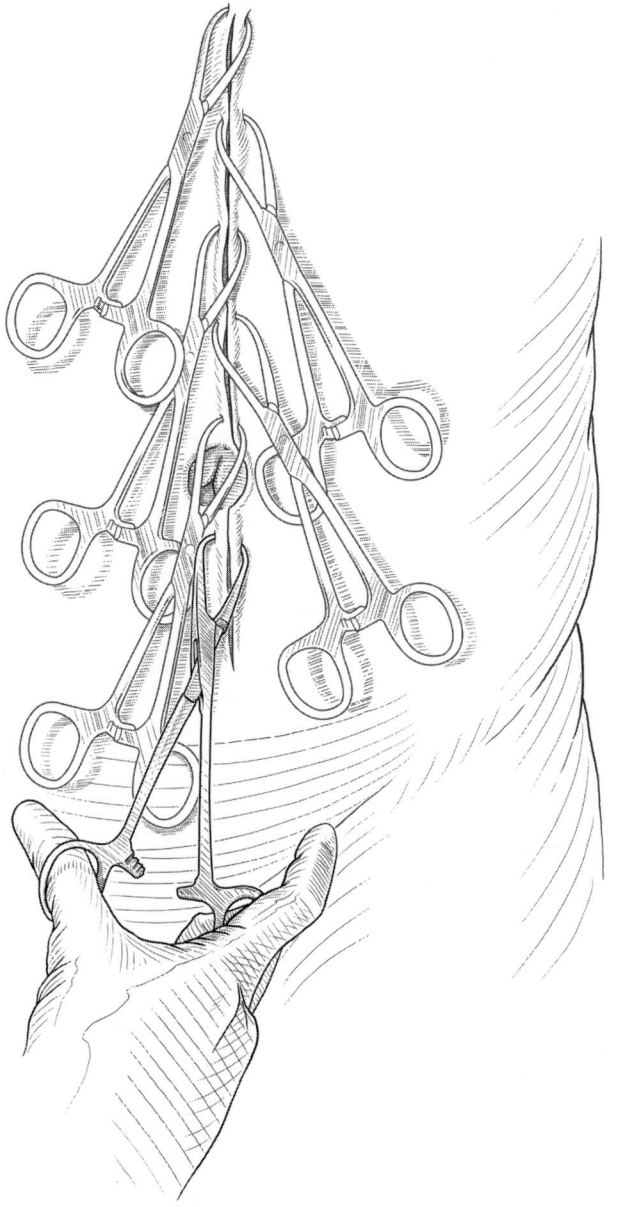

Figure 7 Shown is a "quick out" closure with surgical towel clips.

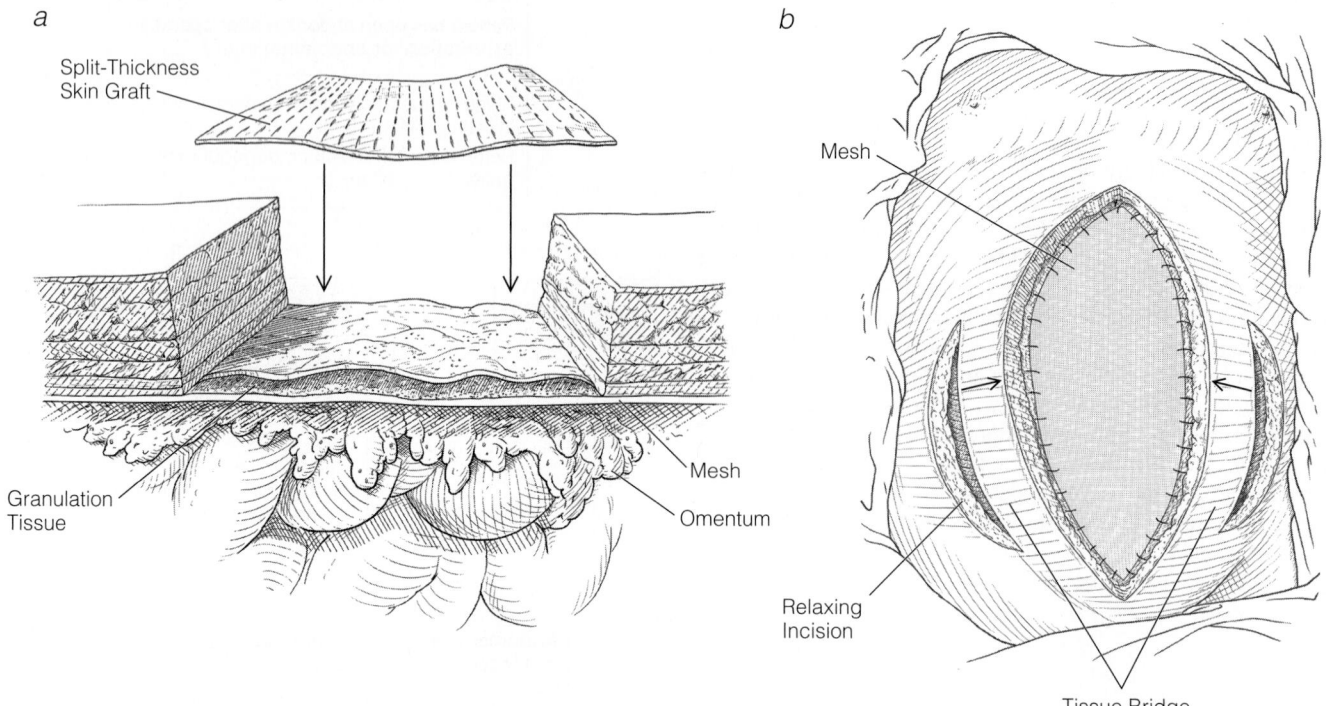

a

Split-Thickness
Skin Graft

Granulation
Tissue

Mesh

Omentum

b

Mesh

Relaxing
Incision

Tissue Bridge

Figure 9 **Mesh may be used for temporary or permanent abdominal closure in patients at risk for increased abdominal pressure. (*a*) Mesh is sutured into the fascial plane, then covered with a split-thickness skin graft. (*b*) The abdominal defect is closed with mesh.**

tiple injuries should be monitored closely for the development of ACS. If the diagnostic criteria for ACS are met, prompt abdominal decompression is indicated. On occasion, this measure may have to be carried out at the bedside in the ICU.

Occasionally, ACS develops in patients who have a temporary abdominal dressing in place (so-called tertiary ACS). Accordingly, it is mandatory to continue to monitor intra-abdominal pressure in these patients.[29]

CLOSURE OF THE OPEN ABDOMEN

It is important to close the abdomen as early as possible: an open abdomen carries an increased risk of desiccation of the intestines and subsequent fistula formation. In certain patients, however, despite aggressive efforts to close the fascia, it proves impossible to accomplish primary closure, even after many days and repeated procedures. There are several techniques that may be employed to obtain final closure in this situation.

The simplest method is to allow granulation tissue to form over the omentum and the exposed intestines and later, when there is a good clean granulation bed with no evidence of infection, to place a split-thickness skin graft. Alternatively, a piece of absorbable mesh may be placed; this helps facilitate dressing changes, provides a modicum of protection to the intestines, and serves to control evisceration [*see Figure 9*]. A skin graft can then be placed in the same fashion, once a granulation bed has developed.

Another option is to employ relaxing incisions, either to allow a skin-only closure or to allow the skin to be closed over absorbable mesh. Open skin wounds should be left open to heal by secondary intention. Unfortunately, the use of relaxing incisions will not prevent the formation of large ventral hernias, which will have to be repaired at a later date.

Abdominal fascial defects may also be closed with sheets of nonincorporable synthetic material (e.g., Gore-Tex; W. L. Gore and Associates, Inc., Newark, Delaware). The advantages of these nonabsorbable materials are that they do not react with tissue and that they are associated with a low incidence of complications (e.g., fistula formation). The disadvantages are that they are expensive and that they must ultimately be removed unless the skin can be closed over them to prevent contamination.

Another option for achieving primary closure of the abdomen is component separation of the rectus sheath. The external oblique aponeurosis is incised and mobilized, along with the rectus sheath, to bring the fascia to the midline. Defects as wide as 14 to 20 cm can be bridged in this fashion, but recurrent hernia rates remain high.[31]

Several biosynthetic materials are now available to be used for bridging abdominal fascial defects. One such material is Surgisis (Cook Biotech Inc., West Lafayette, Indiana), a porcine submucosal matrix that can provide scaffolding for the ingrowth of fibrous tissue while supporting abdominal contents and permitting skin closure.[32] Another is AlloDerm (LifeCell Corp., Branchburg, New Jersey), a denatured human cadaveric product that can be used in a similar fashion to replace denuded fascia or to bridge the fascial gap in cases where primary closure cannot be accomplished.[33,34] At present, long-term follow-up data are lacking for both products, and their use is further limited by their very high cost.

Morbidity is very high in these patients; subsequent complications range from prolonged ventilator dependence to enteric fistulas to massive ventral hernias.[35,36] Major ventral hernias represent a significant technical challenge and should not be repaired until the patient's recovery from injury is complete and his or her nutritional and general status has returned to normal. This may take as long as 12 months from the time of the initial trauma.

References

1. Malhotta AK, Fabian TC, Crou MA, et al: Blunt hepatic injury: a paradigm shift from operative to non-operative management in the 1990's. Ann Surg 231:804, 2000

2. Sharma OP, Oswanski MF, Singer D: Role of repeated computerized tomography in nonoperative management of solid organ trauma. Am Surg 71:244, 2005

3. Fata P, Robinson L, Fakhry SM: A survey of EAST member practices in blunt splenic injury: a description of current trends and opportunities for improvement. J Trauma 59:836, 2005

4. Fernandez L, McKenney MG, McKenney ML, et al: Ultrasound in blunt abdominal trauma. J Trauma 45:841, 1998

5. Jurkovich GJ, Moore EE, Medina G: Autotransfusion in trauma: a pragmatic analysis. Am J Surg 148:782, 1984

6. Mattox KL, McCollum WB, Beall AC, et al: Management of penetrating injuries of the suprarenal aorta. J Trauma 15: 808, 1975

7. Weinberg JA, Fabian TC, Magnotti LJ, et al: Penetrating rectal trauma: management by anatomic distinction improves outcome. J Trauma 60:508, 2006

8. Gonzalez RP, Falimirski ME, Holevar MR: The role of presacral drainage in the management of penetrating rectal injuries. J Trauma 45:656, 1998

9. Kudsk KA, Sheldon GF, Lim RC Jr: Atrial-caval shunting (ACS) after trauma. J Trauma 22:81, 1982

10. Rovito PF: Atrial caval shunting in blunt hepatic vascular injury. Ann Surg 205:318, 1987

11. Klein SR, Baumgartner FJ, Bongard FS: Contemporary management strategy for major inferior vena caval injuries. J Trauma 37:35, 1994

12. Walker ML: The operative and nonoperative management of blunt liver injury. J Natl Med Assoc 86:29, 1994

13. Parks RW, Chrysos E, Diamond T: Management of liver trauma. Br J Surg 86:1121, 1999

14. Tzovaras G, Hatzitheofilou C: New trends in the management of colonic trauma. Injury 36:1011, 2005

15. Nelson R, Singer M: Primary repair for penetrating colon injuries. Cochrane Database Syst Rev (3):CD002247, 2003

16. Herr MW, Gagliano RA: Historical perspective and current management of colonic and intraperitoneal rectal trauma. Curr Surg 62:187, 2005

17. Ceydeli A, Rucinski J, Wise L: Finding the best abdominal closure: an evidence-based review of the literature. Curr Surg 62:220, 2005

18. Carlson MA: Acute wound failure. Surg Clin North Am 77:607, 1997

19. Nicholas JM, Rix EP, Easley KA, et al: Changing patterns in the management of penetrating abdominal trauma: the more things change, the more they stay the same. J Trauma 55:1095, 2003

20. Suliburk JW, Ware DN, Balogh Z, et al: Vacuum-assisted wound closure achieves early fascial closure of open abdomens after severe trauma. J Trauma 55:1155, 2003

21. Cipolla J, Stawicki SP, Hoff WS, et al: A proposed algorithm for managing the open abdomen. Am Surg 71:202, 2005

22. Koniaris LG, Hendrickson RJ, Drugas G, et al: Dynamic retention: a technique for closure of the complex abdomen in critically ill patients. Arch Surg 136:1359, 2001

23. McKenney MG, Nir I, Fee T, et al: A simple device for closure of fasciotomy wounds. Am J Surg 172:275, 1996

24. Howdieshell TR, Proctor CD, Sternberg E, et al: Temporary abdominal closure followed by definitive abdominal wall reconstruction of the open abdomen. Am J Surg 188:301, 2004

25. Bose SM, Kalra M, Sandhu NP: Open management of septic abdomen by Marlex mesh zipper. Aust NZ J Surg 61:385, 1991

26. Stone PA, Hass SM, Flaherty SK, et al: Vacuum-assisted fascial closure for patients with abdominal trauma. J Trauma 57:1082, 2004

27. Kaplan M: Negative pressure wound therapy in the management of abdominal compartment syndrome. Ostomy Wound Management 50(11A suppl):20S, 2004

28. Balogh Z, McKinley BA, Holcomb JB, et al: Both primary and secondary abdominal compartment syndrome can be predicted early and are harbingers of multiple organ failure. J Trauma 54:848, 2003

29. Sugrue M: Abdominal compartment syndrome. Curr Opin Crit Care 11:333, 2005

30. Iberti TJ, Lieber CE, Benjamin E: Determination of intra-abdominal pressure using a transurethral bladder catheter: clinical validation of the technique. Anesthesiology 70:47, 1989

31. de Vries Reilingh TS, van Goor H, Rosman C, et al: "Components separation technique" for the repair of large abdominal wall hernias. J Am Coll Surg 196:32, 2003

32. Pu LL; Plastic Surgery Educational Foundation DATA Committee: Small intestinal submucosa (Surgisis) as a bioactive prosthetic material for repair of abdominal wall fascial defect. Plast Reconstr Surg 115:2127, 2005

33. Scott BG, Welsh FJ, Pham HQ, et al: Early aggressive closure of the open abdomen. J Trauma 60:17, 2006

34. Kolker AR, Brown DJ, Redstone JS, et al: Multilayer reconstruction of abdominal wall defects with acellular dermal allograft (AlloDerm) and component separation. Ann Plast Surg 55:36, 2005

35. Barker DE, Kaufman HJ, Smith LA, et al: Vacuum pack technique of temporary abdominal closure: a 7-year experience with 112 patients. J Trauma 48:201, 2000

36. Miller RS, Morris JA Jr, Diaz JJ Jr, et al: Complications after 344 damage-control open celiotomies. J Trauma 59:1365, 2005

Recommended Reading

Blaisdell FW, Trunkey DD: Abdominal Trauma. Thieme Medical Publishers, New York, 1993

Donovan AJ: Trauma Surgery. Mosby–Year Book Co, St Louis, 1994

Greenfield LJ: Complications in Surgery and Trauma. JB Lippincott Co, Grand Rapids, Michigan, 1990

Hirshberg A, Mattox KL: Top Knife: The Art and Craft of Trauma Surgery. tfm publishing Ltd, Harley, Shropshire, United Kingdom, 2005

Ivatury RR, Cayten CG: The Textbook of Penetrating Trauma. Williams & Wilkins, Baltimore, 1996

Mattox KL: Complications of Trauma. Churchill Livingstone, New York, 1994

Mattox KL, Feliciano DV, Moore EE: Trauma, 4th ed. Appleton & Lange, Stamford, Connecticut, 1998

Maull KI, Rodriguez A, Wiles CE: Complications in Trauma and Critical Care. WB Saunders Co, Philadelphia, 1996

Thal ER, Weigelt JA, Carrico CJ: Operative Trauma Management: An Atlas, 2nd ed. McGraw-Hill, New York, 2002

Wilson RF, Walt AJ: Management of Trauma: Pitfalls and Practice, 2nd ed. Williams & Wilkins, Baltimore, 1996

Acknowledgments

Figures 2 and 5   Susan Brust, C.M.I.

Figures 3 and 4   Carol Donner.

Figures 6, 7, and 9   Tom Moore. Adapted from *Operative Trauma Management: An Atlas*, by C. J. Carrico, E. R. Thal, and J. A. Weigelt. Appleton & Lange, Stamford, Connecticut, 1998.

Jon M. Burch, M.D., F.A.C.S., and Ernest E. Moore, M.D., F.A.C.S.

Injuries to the Liver

ASSESSMENT

The initial step in the management of penetrating abdominal injuries and of blunt abdominal injuries in cases when nonoperative treatment is contraindicated or has failed is exploratory laparotomy [*see 105 Operative Exposure of Abdominal Injuries and Closure of the Abdomen*].

Visualization of the right hemiliver [*see Figure 1*] is hindered by the posterior attachments and by the right lower costal margin. Exposure of the right hemiliver is facilitated by elevating the right costal margin with a large Richardson retractor. Further exposure can be achieved with mobilization, which requires division of the right triangular and coronary ligaments [*see Figure 2*]. In dividing the superior coronary ligament, care must be taken not to injure the lateral wall of the right hepatic vein; in dividing the inferior coronary ligament, care must be taken not to injure the right

adrenal gland (which is vulnerable because it lies directly beneath the peritoneal reflection) or the retrohepatic vena cava. When the ligaments have been divided, the right hemiliver can be rotated medially into the surgical field. Mobilization of the left hemiliver poses no unusual problems other than the risk of injury to the left hepatic vein, the left inferior phrenic vein, and the retrohepatic vena cava.

If optimal exposure of the junction of the hepatic veins and the retrohepatic vena cava is necessary, the midline abdominal incision can be extended by means of a median sternotomy. The pericardium and the diaphragm can then be divided toward the center of the inferior vena cava. This combination of incisions provides superb exposure of the hepatic veins and the retrohepatic vena cava while avoiding injury to the phrenic nerves.

Hepatic injuries are classified according to the grading system developed by the American Association for the Surgery of Trauma Committee on Organ Injury Scaling [*see Table 1 and Figure 3*].[1] The

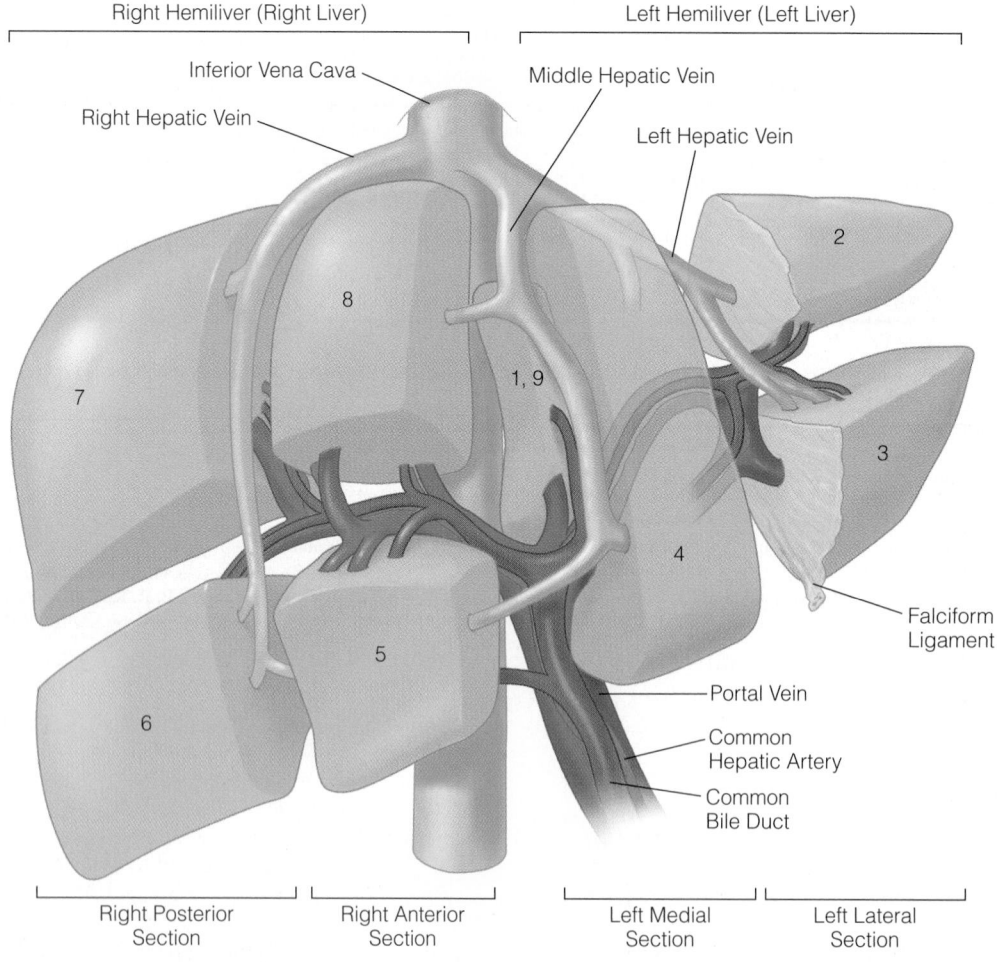

Figure 1 Shown are the anatomic divisions of the liver.

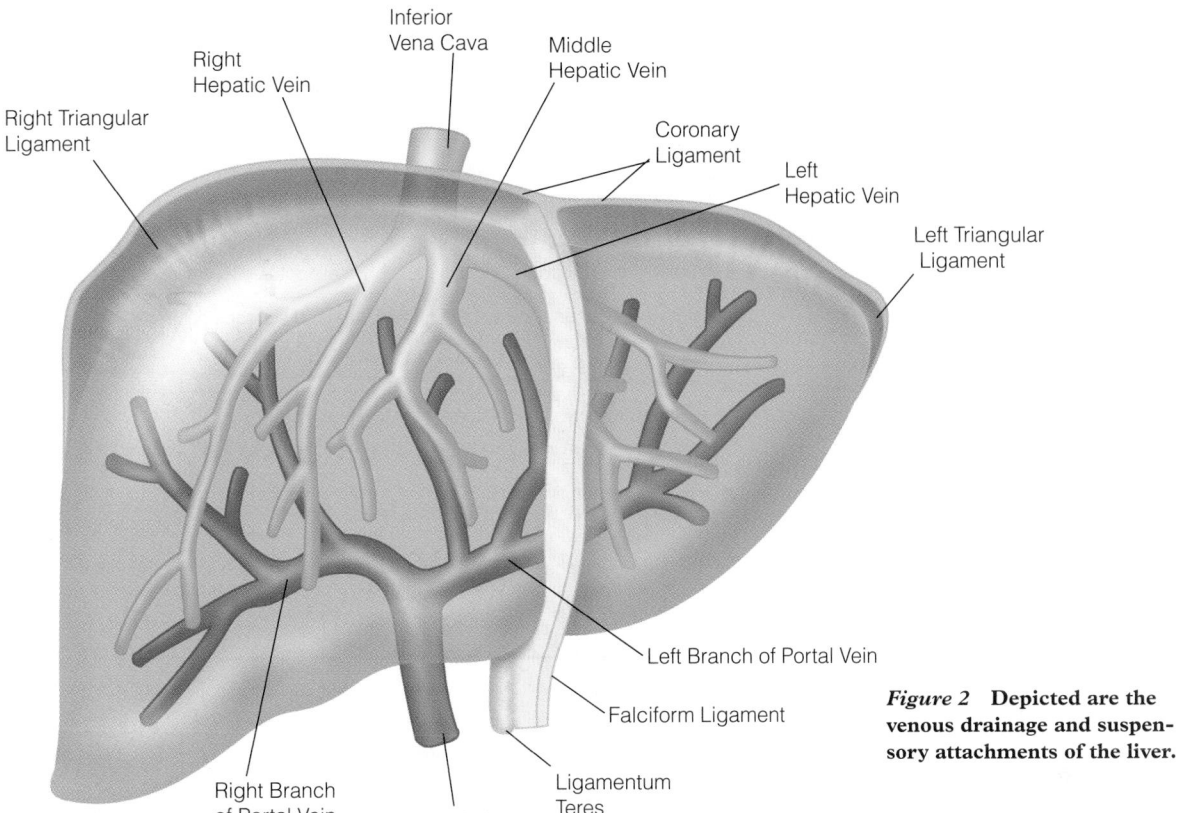

Figure 2 **Depicted are the venous drainage and suspensory attachments of the liver.**

grading scale ranges from I to VI, with I representing superficial lacerations and small subcapsular hematomas and VI representing avulsion of the liver from the vena cava. Isolated injuries that are not extensive (grades I to III) often require little or no treatment; however, extensive parenchymal injuries and those involving the juxtahepatic veins (grades IV and V) may require complex maneuvers for successful treatment, and hepatic avulsion (grade VI) is lethal.

Clamping of the hepatic pedicle—the Pringle maneuver—is helpful for evaluating grade IV and V hepatic injuries [*see Figure 4*]. This maneuver allows one to distinguish between hemorrhage from branches of the hepatic artery or the portal vein, which ceases when the clamp is applied, and hemorrhage from the hepatic veins or the retrohepatic vena cava, which does not. When performing the Pringle maneuver, we prefer to tear open the lesser omentum manually and place the clamp from the patient's left side while guiding the posterior blade of the clamp through the foramen of Winslow with the aid of the left index finger. The advantages of this approach are the avoidance of injury to the structures within the hepatic pedicle, the assurance that the clamp will be properly placed the first time, and the inclusion of a replacing or accessory left hepatic artery between the blades of the clamp.

MANAGEMENT OF INJURIES

Techniques for Temporary Control of Hemorrhage

Temporary control of hemorrhage is essential for two reasons. First, during treatment of a major hepatic injury, ongoing hemorrhage may pose an immediate threat to the patient's life, and temporary control gives the anesthesiologist time to restore the circulating volume before further blood loss occurs. Second, multiple bleeding sites are common with both blunt and penetrating trauma, and if the liver is not the highest priority, temporary control of hepatic bleeding allows repair of other injuries without unnecessary blood loss. The most useful techniques for the temporary control of hepatic hemorrhage are manual compression, perihepatic packing, and the Pringle maneuver.

Periodic manual compression with the addition of laparotomy pads is useful in the treatment of complex hepatic injuries to provide time for resuscitation [*see Figure 5*].[2-4] Hands and pads should be positioned to realign the liver in its normal anatomic position. Perihepatic packing with carefully placed laparotomy pads is capable of controlling hemorrhage from almost all hepatic injuries.[5-9] The right costal margin is elevated, and the pads are strategically placed over and around the bleeding site [*see Figure 6*]. Additional pads may be placed between the liver and the diaphragm and between the liver and the anterior chest wall until the bleeding has been controlled. Ten to 15 pads may be required to control the hemorrhage from an extensive right lobar injury. Packing is not as effective for injuries to the left hemiliver, because with the abdomen open, there is insufficient abdominal and thoracic wall anterior to the left hemiliver to provide adequate compression. Fortunately, hemorrhage from the left hemiliver can be controlled by dividing the left triangular and coronary ligaments and compressing the hemiliver between the hands. Two complications may be encountered with the packing of hepatic injuries. First, tight packing compresses the inferior vena cava, decreases venous return, and reduces left ventricular filling; hypovolemic patients may not tolerate the resultant decrease in cardiac output. Second, perihepatic packing forces the right diaphragm superiorly and impairs its motion; this may lead to increased airway pressures and decreased tidal volume. Careful consideration of the patient's condition is necessary to determine whether the risk of these complications outweighs the risk of additional blood loss.

The Pringle maneuver is often used as an adjunct to packing

Table 1 AAST Organ Injury Scales for Liver, Biliary Tract, Diaphragm, and Spleen

Injured Structure	AAST Grade	Characteristics of Injury	AIS-90 Score
Liver*	I	Hematoma: subcapsular, nonexpanding, < 10% surface area	2
		Laceration: capsular tear, nonbleeding, < 1 cm parenchymal depth	2
	II	Hematoma: subcapsular, nonexpanding, 10%–50% surface area; intraparenchymal, nonexpanding, < 10 cm in diameter	2
		Laceration: capsular tear, active bleeding, 1–3 cm parenchymal depth, < 10 cm in length	2
	III	Hematoma: subcapsular, > 50% surface area, expanding; ruptured subcapsular hematoma with active bleeding; intraparenchymal, > 10 cm or expanding	3
		Laceration: > 3 cm parenchymal depth	3
	IV	Hematoma: ruptured intraparenchymal hematoma with active bleeding	4
		Laceration: parenchymal disruption involving 25%–75% of hepatic lobe or 1–3 Couinaud's segments within a single lobe	4
	V	Laceration: parenchymal disruption involving > 75% of hepatic lobe or > 3 Couinaud's segments within a single lobe	5
		Vascular: juxtahepatic venous injuries (i.e., injuries to retrohepatic vena cava or central major hepatic veins)	5
	VI	Vascular: hepatic avulsion	5
Extrahepatic biliary tree*	I	Gallbladder contusion/hematoma	2
		Portal triad contusion	2
	II	Partial gallbladder avulsion from liver bed; cystic duct intact	2
		Laceration or perforation of gallbladder	2
	III	Complete gallbladder avulsion from liver bed	3
		Cystic duct laceration	3
	IV	Partial or complete right or left hepatic duct laceration	3
		Partial common hepatic duct or common bile duct laceration (< 50%)	3
	V	> 50% transection of common hepatic duct or common bile duct	3–4
		Combined right and left hepatic duct injuries	3–4
		Intraduodenal or intrapancreatic bile duct injuries	3–4
Diaphragm†	I	Contusion	2
	II	Laceration < 2 cm	3
	III	Laceration 2–10 cm	3
	IV	Laceration > 10 cm, with tissue loss < 25 cm²	3
	V	Laceration with tissue loss > 25 cm²	3
Spleen*	I	Hematoma: subcapsular, nonexpanding, < 10% surface area	2
		Laceration: capsular tear, nonbleeding, < 1 cm parenchymal depth	2
	II	Hematoma: subcapsular, nonexpanding, 10%–50% surface area; intraparenchymal, nonexpanding, < 5 cm in diameter	2
		Laceration: capsular tear, active bleeding, 1–3 cm parenchymal depth, not involving a trabecular vessel	2
	III	Hematoma: subcapsular, > 50% surface area or expanding; ruptured subcapsular hematoma with active bleeding; intraparenchymal, > 5 cm or expanding	3
		Laceration: > 3 cm parenchymal depth or involving trabecular vessels	3
	IV	Hematoma: ruptured intraparenchymal hematoma with active bleeding	4
		Laceration: laceration involving segmental or hilar vessels producing major devascularization (> 25% of spleen)	4
	V	Laceration: completely shattered spleen	5
		Vascular: hilar vascular injury that devascularizes spleen	5

*Advance one grade for multiple injuries, up to grade III.
†Advance one grade for bilateral injuries, up to grade III.
AAST—American Association for the Surgery of Trauma

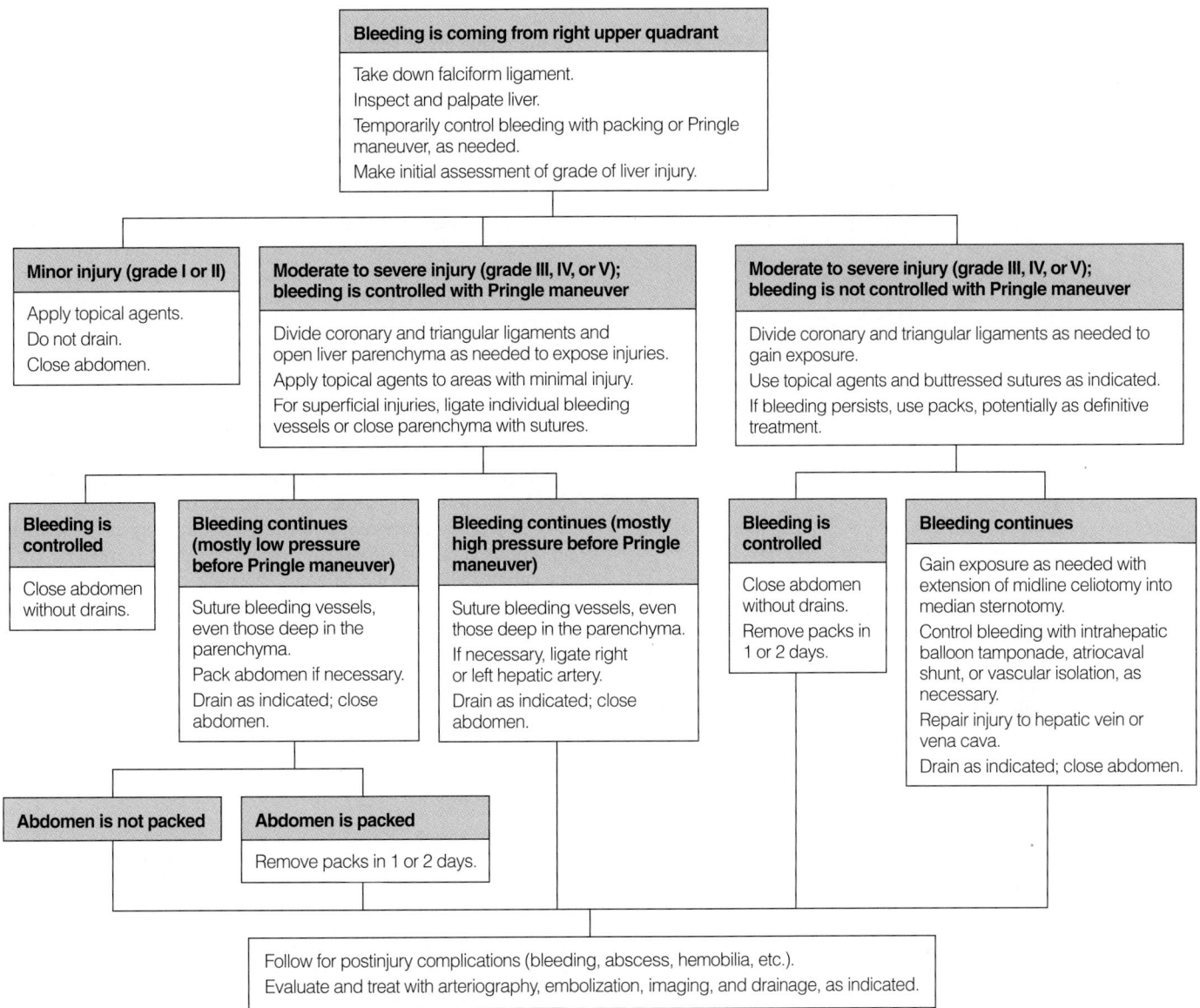

Figure 3 **Shown is an algorithm for the treatment of hepatic injuries.**

for the temporary control of hemorrhage.[3] Over the years, the length of time for which surgeons believe a Pringle maneuver can be maintained without causing irreversible ischemic damage to the liver has increased. Several authors have documented the maintenance of a Pringle maneuver for longer than 1 hour in patients with complex injuries, without appreciable hepatic damage.[4,10] When a life-threatening hepatic injury is encountered on entry into the abdomen, the Pringle maneuver should be performed immediately and perihepatic packs placed. Persistent bleeding in the face of effective inflow occlusion implies that either the retrohepatic vena cava or hepatic vein has been injured. Perihepatic packing is more likely to control bleeding from the retrohepatic vena cava.

Another technique for temporary control of hepatic hemorrhage is the application of a tourniquet or a liver clamp.[11] Once the bleeding hemiliver is mobilized, a 2.5 cm Penrose drain is wrapped around the liver near the anatomic division between the left hemiliver and the right. The drain is stretched until hemorrhage ceases, and tension is maintained by clamping the drain. Unfortunately, tourniquets are difficult to use: they tend to slip off

or tear through the parenchyma if placed over an injured area. An alternative is the use of a liver clamp; however, the application of such devices is hindered by the variability in the size and shape of the liver. We have not had consistent success with either of these methods.

Juxtahepatic venous injuries are technically challenging, difficult to control with packing, and often lethal. Complex procedures may be required for temporary control of these large veins. Of these procedures, the most important are hepatic vascular isolation with clamps, placement of the atriocaval shunt, and use of the Moore-Pilcher balloon.

Hepatic vascular isolation is accomplished by executing a Pringle maneuver, clamping the aorta at the diaphragm, and clamping the suprarenal and suprahepatic vena cava.[12] In patients scheduled for elective procedures, this technique has enjoyed nearly uniform success, but in trauma patients, the results have been disappointing. The relative ineffectiveness of hepatic vascular isolation with clamps in this setting is presumably due to the inability of a patient in shock to tolerate an acute reduction in left ventricular filling pressure; on occasion, sudden death has occurred

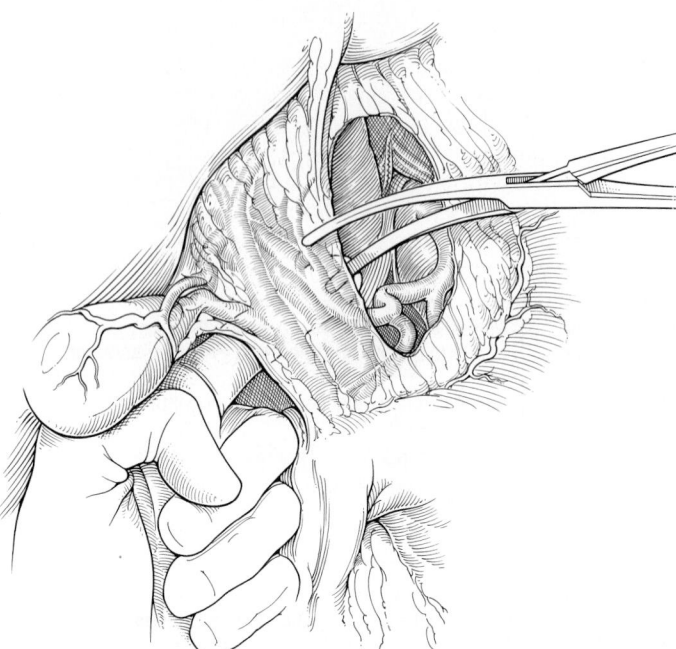

Figure 4   **The Pringle maneuver controls arterial and portal vein hemorrhage from the liver. Any hemorrhage that continues must come from the hepatic veins.**

on placement of the venous clamps.[13] If, however, a trauma patient requiring hepatic vascular isolation has been maintained in a relatively normal physiologic condition, it is reasonable to consider this method.

An alternative approach to exposure of the retrohepatic vena cava and the hepatic veins has been developed in which vascular isolation of the liver is achieved by means of clamping and the suprahepatic vena cava is divided between vascular clamps [*see Figure 7*].[14] The liver and the suprahepatic vena cava are then

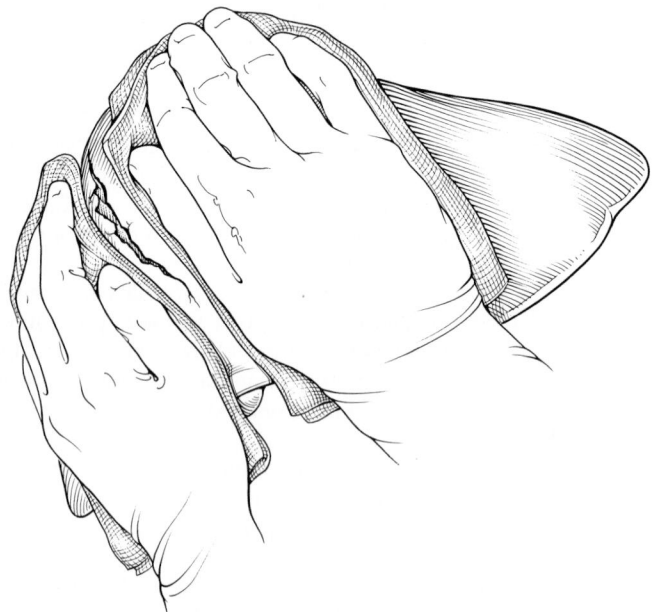

Figure 5   **Manual compression of large hepatic injuries temporarily controls blood loss in hypovolemic patients until the circulating blood volume can be restored.**

rotated anteriorly to provide direct access to the posterior aspect of the retrohepatic vena cava. Anterior injuries of the large veins are repaired through an incision in the posterior aspect of the retrohepatic vena cava.

The atriocaval shunt was designed to achieve hepatic vascular isolation while still permitting some venous blood from below the diaphragm to flow through the shunt into the right atrium.[4] After a few early successes, the initial enthusiasm for the atriocaval shunt declined as high mortalities associated with its use began to be reported.[15-20] Surgeons' lack of familiarity with the technique; the manipulation of a cold, acidotic heart; and poor patient selection have all contributed to the poor overall results.[13] A variation on the original atriocaval shunt has been described in which a 9 mm endotracheal tube is substituted for the usual large chest tube [*see Figure 8*].[21] The balloon of the endotracheal tube makes it unnecessary to surround the suprarenal vena cava with an umbilical tape. This minor change eliminates one of the most difficult maneuvers required for the original shunt procedure: because hemorrhage must be controlled by posterior pressure on the liver during the insertion of the shunt, access to the suprarenal vena cava is severely restricted, and thus, surrounding this vessel with an umbilical tape is almost impossible. A side hole must be cut in the tube to allow blood to enter the right atrium. Care must be taken to avoid damage to the integral inflation channel for the balloon.

An alternative to the atriocaval shunt is the Moore-Pilcher balloon.[21] This device is inserted through the femoral vein and advanced into the retrohepatic vena cava. When the balloon is properly positioned and inflated, it occludes the hepatic veins and the vena cava, thus achieving vascular isolation. The catheter itself is hollow, and appropriately placed holes below the balloon permit

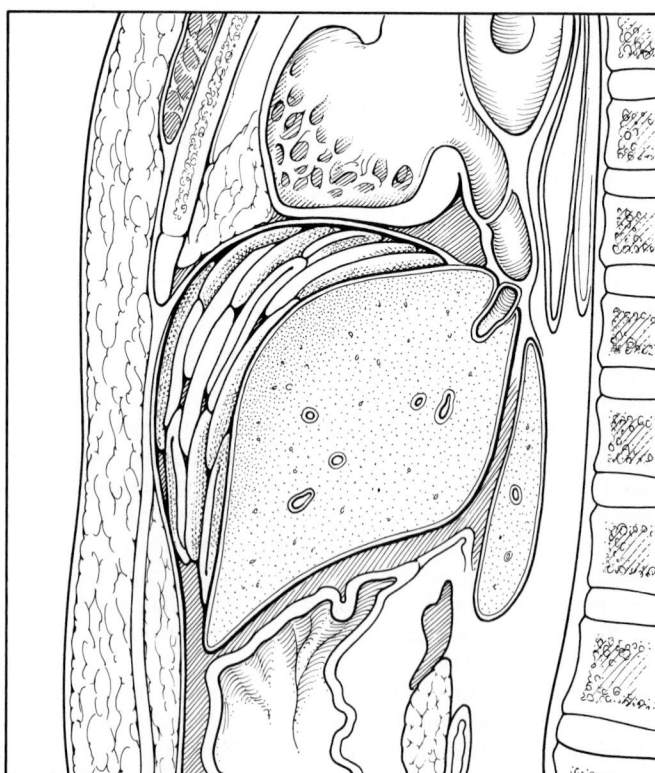

Figure 6   **Perihepatic packing is often effective in managing extensive parenchymal injuries. It has also been successfully employed for grade V juxtahepatic venous injuries.**

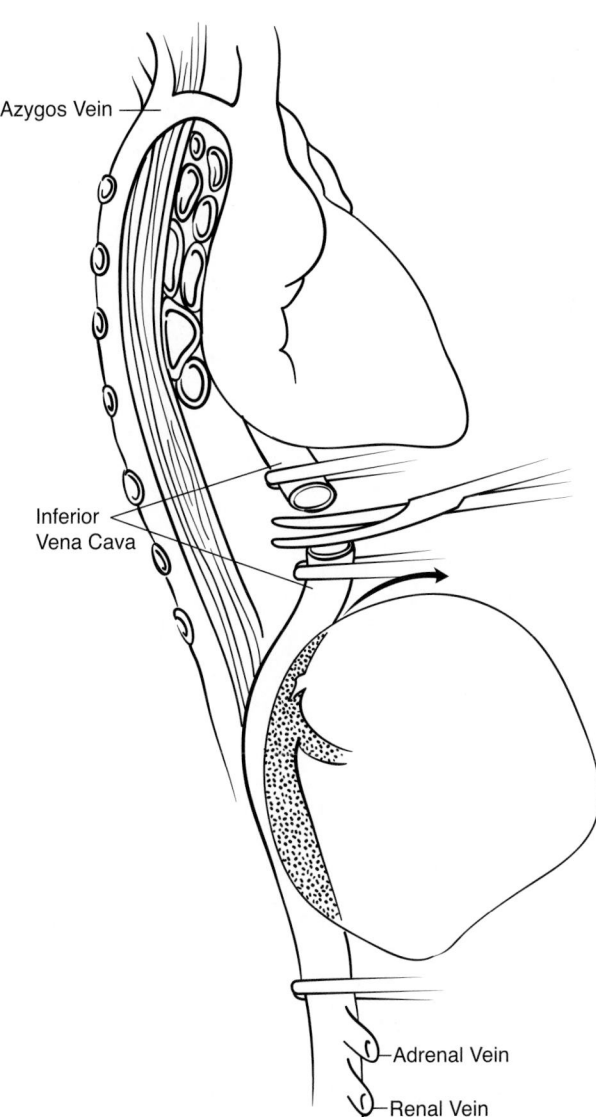

Figure 7 **With hepatic vascular isolation accomplished, the suprahepatic vena cava is divided between clamps, and the liver and the suprahepatic vena cava are rotated anteriorly to afford access to the posterior aspect of the retrohepatic vena cava.**

blood to flow into the right atrium, in much the same way as the atriocaval shunt. At present, the survival rate for patients with juxtahepatic venous injuries who are treated with this device is similar to that for patients treated with the atriocaval shunt.[18]

Surgeons who attempt hepatic vascular isolation should be aware that none of these techniques provide complete hemostasis. Drainage from the right adrenal vein and the inferior phrenic veins and persistent hepatopetal flow resulting from unrecognized replacing or accessory left hepatic arteries contribute to this problem. The relatively small volume of blood that continues to flow after vascular isolation is readily removed by means of suction.

An adjunct to vascular isolation with clamps is venovenous bypass. This technique provides vascular decompression for the small bowel and maintains high cardiac filling pressures, which are often necessary. Venovenous bypass is accomplished by placing a catheter in the inferior vena cava via the femoral vein and a second catheter in the superior mesenteric vein [*see Figure 9*].[22] A centrifugal pump withdraws blood from these veins and pumps it into the superior vena cava through a third catheter placed in the internal jugular vein.

Techniques for Definitive Management of Injuries

Techniques available for the definitive management of hepatic injuries range from manual compression to hepatic transplantation. Grade I or II lacerations of the hepatic parenchyma can generally be controlled with manual compression. If these injuries do not respond to manual compression, they can often be controlled with topical hemostatic measures.

The simplest of these measures is electrocauterization, which can often control small bleeding vessels near the surface of the liver (though the machine's power output may have to be increased). Bleeding from raw surfaces of the liver that does not respond to the electrocautery may respond to the argon beam coagulator. This device imparts less heat to the surrounding hepatic tissue and creates a more consistent eschar, which enhances hemostasis. Also useful in similar situations is microcrystalline collagen in the powdered form. The powder is placed on a clean 10 × 10 cm sponge and applied directly to the oozing surface, with pressure maintained on the sponge for 5 to 10 minutes. Thrombin can also be applied topically to minor bleeding injuries by saturating either a gelatin foam sponge or a microcrystalline collagen pad and pressing it to the bleeding site.

In previous years, there was interest in the use of "bathtub" fi-

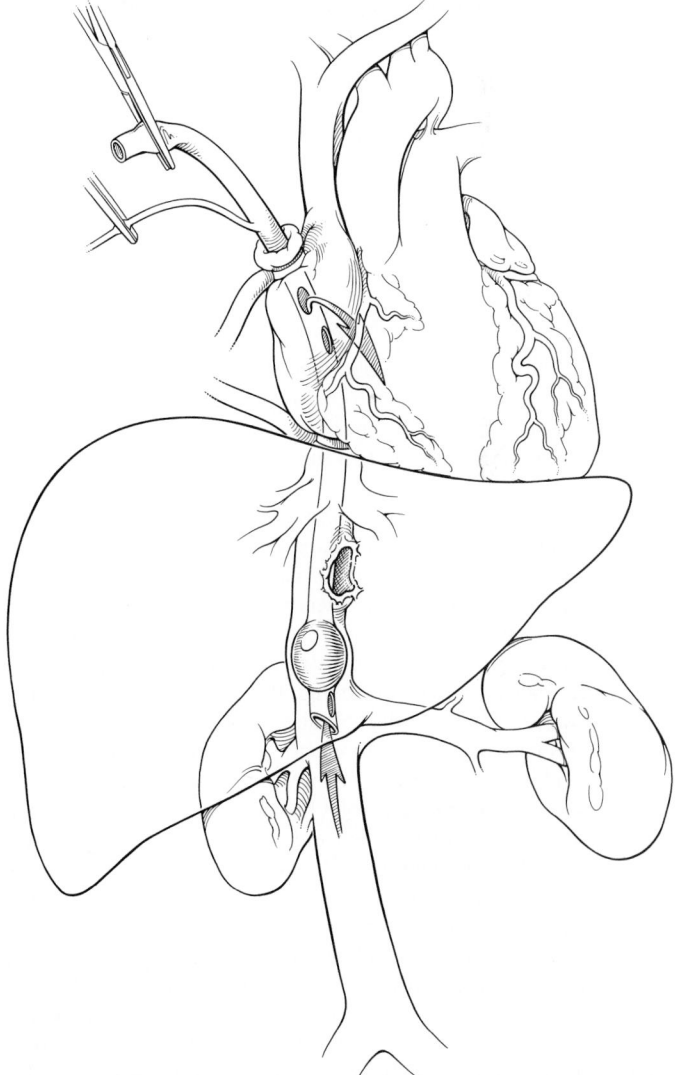

Figure 8 **Shown is a method of achieving hepatic vascular isolation with a 9 mm endotracheal tube.**

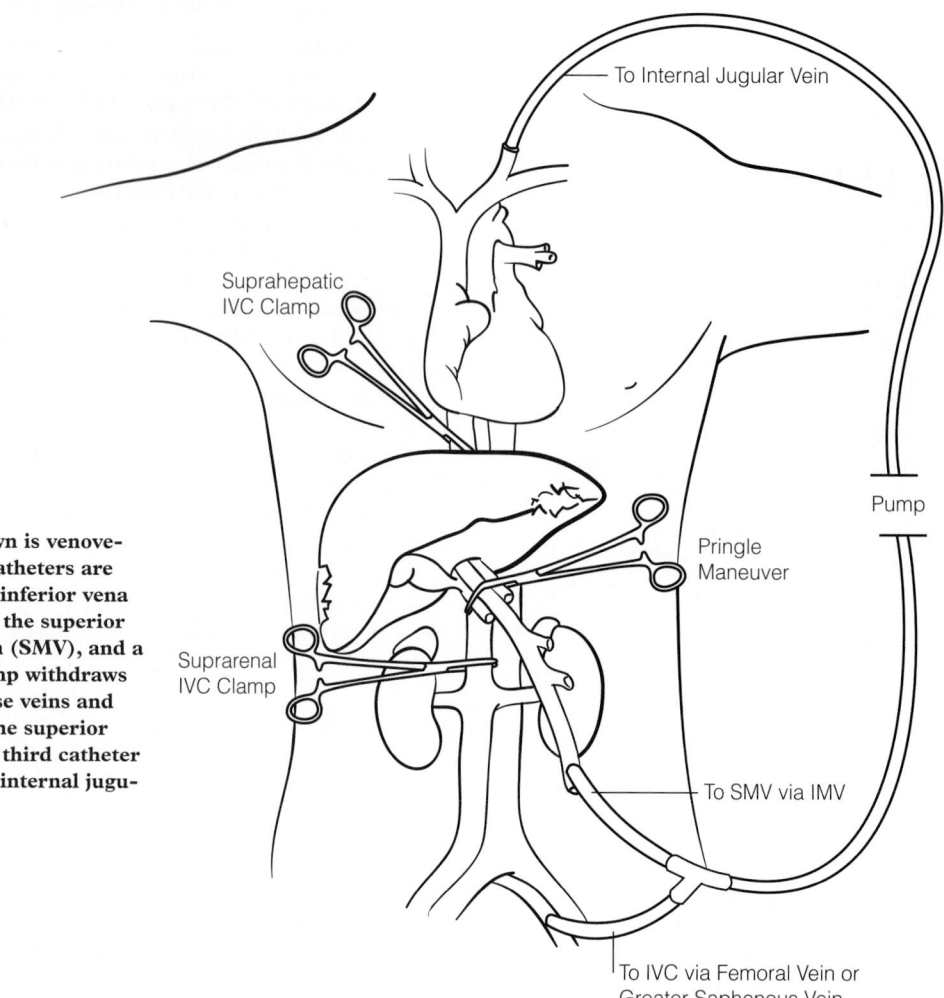

To Internal Jugular Vein

Suprahepatic
IVC Clamp

Pump

Pringle
Maneuver

Suprarenal
IVC Clamp

To SMV via IMV

To IVC via Femoral Vein or
Greater Saphenous Vein

Figure 9 **Shown is venovenous bypass. Catheters are placed into the inferior vena cava (IVC) and the superior mesenteric vein (SMV), and a centrifugal pump withdraws blood from these veins and pumps it into the superior vena cava via a third catheter placed into the internal jugular vein.**

brin glue (made by mixing concentrated human fibrinogen with a solution containing bovine thrombin and calcium) to treat hepatic lacerations.[23,24] This substance has now been rendered obsolete by the commercial availability of numerous glues and sealants [*see Table 2*].

Another relatively new hemostatic adjunct that can be highly useful in the setting of hepatic injury is recombinant activated factor VII (NovoSeven; Novo Nordisk, Copenhagen), which works by promoting coagulation at the lacerated edges of blood vessels. Many trauma surgeons have personally witnessed the abrupt cessation of hemorrhage when factor VII has been administered after other materials have failed. Although this agent seems at times to have an almost magical effect, it does not always work, and it is extremely expensive; furthermore, the only prospective study to date that addressed the use of factor VII in trauma patients reported only a modest decrease in total blood use and failed to demonstrate a survival advantage.[25] For these reasons, many institutions, including ours (University of Colorado Health Sciences Center), have created protocols for the use of factor VII. At our institution, for factor VII to be used, (1) the patient must be salvageable; (2) the patient must have received at least 10 units of packed red blood cells (PRBCs) plus clotting factors; (3) surgical control of hemorrhage must be achieved; and (4) the patient must still be experiencing diffuse hemorrhage. The usual dose is 60 to 90 µg/kg, which may be repeated once. It should be kept in mind that factor VII is not a substitute for fresh frozen plasma and platelets and that adequate amounts of fibrin and platelets must be present for it to work.

Although some grade III and IV lacerations respond to topical measures, many do not. In these instances, one option is to suture the hepatic parenchyma. Although this hemostatic technique has been maligned as a cause of hepatic necrosis, it still is frequently used.[3,4,10,17,26,27] Suturing of the hepatic parenchyma is often employed to control persistently bleeding lacerations less than 3 cm in depth; it is also an appropriate alternative for deeper lacerations if the patient cannot tolerate the further hemorrhage associated with hepatotomy and selective ligation. If, however, the capsule of the liver has been stripped away by the injury, this technique is far less effective.

The preferred suture material is 0 or 2-0 chromic catgut attached to a large, blunt-tipped, curved needle; the large diameter prevents the suture from pulling through Glisson's capsule. For shallow lacerations, a simple continuous suture may be used to approximate the edges of the laceration. For deeper lacerations, interrupted horizontal mattress sutures may be placed parallel to the edges. When tying sutures, one may be sure that adequate tension has been achieved when hemorrhage ceases or the liver blanches around the suture.

Most sources of venous hemorrhage can be managed with parenchymal sutures. Even injuries to the retrohepatic vena cava and the hepatic veins have been successfully tamponaded by closing the hepatic parenchyma over the bleeding vessels.[13,28] Venous hemorrhage caused by penetrating wounds traversing the central portion of the liver may be managed by closing the entrance and exit wounds with interrupted horizontal mattress sutures.

Table 2 Characteristics of Selected Commercially Available Tissue Glues and Sealants

	Tisseel VH*	FloSeal*	CoSeal*	BioGlue†
Contents	Human fibrinogen and thrombin; calcium chloride; bovine aprotinin	Bovine gelatin and thrombin	Polyethylene glycol	Glutaraldehyde; bovine albumin
Method of absorption (time)	Fibrinolysis (10–14 days)	Cell-mediated inflammation (6 wk)	Hydrolysis (30 days)	Not absorbed
Physical properties	Flexible and elastic	Granular; conforms to irregular surfaces	Clear hydrogel; flexible and elastic	Ridged and inelastic
Preparation time	7–15 min	1–2 min	1–2 min	1–2 min
General applications	Tissue sealing and adherence; hemostasis in venous oozing	Hemostasis in wet fields up to arterial pressure	Tissue sealing in dry fields	Tissue sealing in dry fields
Specific applications	Venous oozing; sealing of staple lines; decortication; pleurodesis	Active bleeding	Sealing of small vessels and synthetic grafts; prevention of adhesion in pediatric cardiac surgical patients; sealing of large vessels	Sealing of large vessels
Means of application	Cannula; spray; minimally invasive surgery	Cannula; minimally invasive surgery; 8 cm or 10 cm bulb tip	Flexible cannula; spray; minimally invasive surgery	Cannula
Limiting factors	Arterial pressure	Does not seal	Wet field	Wet field, nerves
Set times	3 min	2 min	1 min	30 sec
Stability	4 hr	2 hr	2 hr	—

*Baxter International, Deerfield, Illinois.
†CryoLife, Inc., Kennesaw, Georgia.

Although this measure may lead to the formation of intrahepatic hematomas that may then become infected, the risk is reasonable compared with the risks posed by an intracaval shunt or a deep hepatotomy. Still, suturing of the hepatic parenchyma is not always successful in controlling hemorrhage, particularly hemorrhage from the larger branches of the hepatic artery. If it fails, one must acknowledge the failure promptly and remove the sutures so that the wound can be explored.

Hepatotomy with selective ligation of bleeding vessels is an important technique that is usually reserved for deep or transhepatic penetrating wounds. Most authorities prefer it to parenchymal suturing[3,4,10,29,30]; some even favor it over placement of an atriocaval shunt for exposure and repair of juxtahepatic venous injuries.[20] The finger-fracture technique is used to extend the length and depth of a laceration or a missile tract until the bleeding vessels can be identified and controlled [see Figure 10]. It should be remembered that considerable blood loss may be incurred with the division of viable hepatic tissue in the pursuit of bleeding from deep penetrating wounds. As an alternative to finger fracture, we have begun to use the LigaSure vessel sealing system (Valleylab, Boulder, Colorado) and have observed significant decreases in blood loss with this device.

An adjunct to parenchymal suturing or hepatotomy is the use of the omentum to fill large defects in the liver and to buttress hepatic sutures. The rationale for this use of the omentum is that it provides an excellent source for macrophages and fills a potential dead space with viable tissue.[31] In addition, the omentum can provide a little extra support for parenchymal sutures, often enough to prevent them from cutting through Glisson's capsule.

Hepatic arterial ligation may be appropriate for patients with arterial hemorrhage from deep within the liver[32]; however, it plays only a limited role in the overall treatment of hepatic injuries,

because it does not stop hemorrhage from the portal and hepatic venous systems.[33] Its primary role is in the management of deep injuries when application of the Pringle maneuver results in the cessation of arterial hemorrhage. If the bleeding from the wound stops once the left or right hepatic artery is isolated and clamped, hepatic arterial ligation is a reasonable alternative to deep hepatotomy. Generally, ligation of the right or left hepatic artery is well tolerated; however, ligation of the proper hepatic artery (distal to the origin of the gastroduodenal artery) may produce hepatic necrosis.

An alternative to suturing the entrance and exit wounds of a transhepatic penetrating injury or to performing an extensive hepatotomy is the use of an intrahepatic balloon.[34] These devices are hand-crafted by the surgeon in the operating room. One method of fashioning such a device is to tie a 2.5 cm Penrose drain to a hollow catheter [see Figure 11]. The balloon is then inserted into the bleeding wound and inflated with a soluble contrast agent. If the hemorrhage is controlled, a stopcock or clamp is used to occlude the catheter and maintain the inflation. (It should be noted that the balloon catheter may not be able to generate sufficient intraparenchymal pressure to tamponade major arterial hemorrhage.) The balloon is left in the abdomen and removed at a subsequent operation after 24 to 48 hours. The hemorrhage may recur when the balloon is deflated.

Resectional debridement is indicated for peripheral portions of nonviable hepatic parenchyma. Except in rare circumstances, the amount of tissue removed should not exceed 25% of the liver. Resectional debridement is performed by means of the finger-fracture technique and is appropriate for selected patients with grade III to grade V lacerations. Because additional blood loss occurs during removal of nonviable tissue, this procedure should be reserved for patients who are in sound physiologic condition and can tolerate additional blood loss.

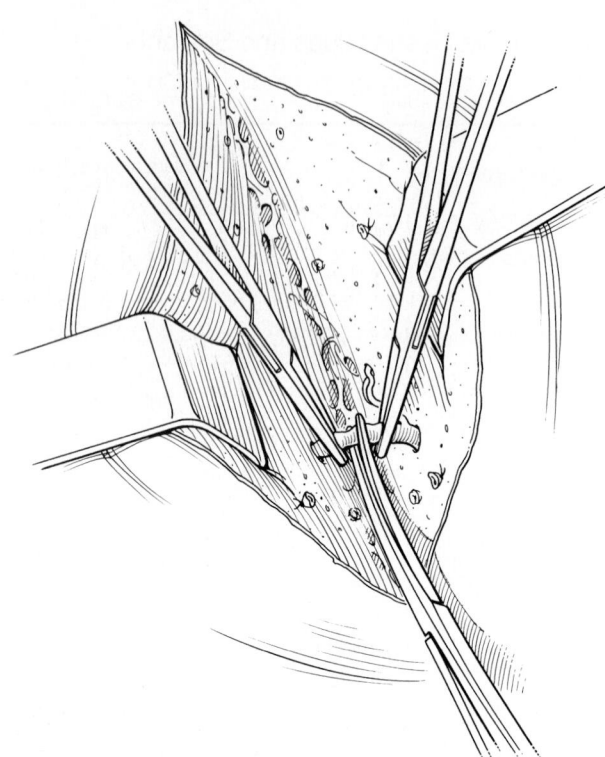

Figure 10 **Hepatotomy with selective ligation is an important technique for controlling hemorrhage from deep (usually penetrating) lacerations. This technique includes finger fracture to extend the length and depth of the wound until vessels or ducts are encountered and controlled.**

Perihepatic packing is the most significant advance in the treatment of hepatic injuries to occur in the past 25 years. The practice of packing hepatic injuries is not a new one, but the concepts and techniques associated with it have changed. In the past, liver lacerations were packed with yards of gauze, and one end of the gauze strip was brought out of the abdomen through a separate stab wound[35]; the remainder of the gauze was then teased out of the wound over a period of days. Unfortunately, this approach often led to abdominal infection and failed to control the hemorrhage, and as a result, it eventually fell from favor. The current approach is not to place packing material in the laceration itself but rather to place it over and around the injury to compress the wound by compressing the liver between the anterior chest wall, the diaphragm, and the retroperitoneum.[5-9] The abdomen is closed, and the patient is taken to the surgical intensive care unit for resuscitation and correction of metabolic derangements. Within 24 hours, the patient is returned to the OR for removal of the packs. Perihepatic packing is indicated for grade IV and V lacerations and for less severe injuries in patients who have a coagulopathy caused by associated injuries.

A technique that may be attempted if packing fails is to wrap the injured portion of the liver with a fine porous material (e.g., polyglycolic acid mesh) after the injured hemiliver has been mobilized.[36,37] Using a continuous suture or a linear stapler, the surgeon constructs a tight-fitting stocking that encloses the injured hemiliver. Blood clots beneath the mesh, which results in tamponade of the hepatic injury. Although this technique is intuitively attractive, to date it has achieved only limited success.

The final alternative for patients with extensive injuries to one hemiliver is anatomic hepatic resection. In elective circumstances, anatomic hemihepatectomies can be performed with excellent results; however, in the setting of trauma, the mortality associated with this procedure exceeds 50% in most series.[26,27,29,38-40] Consequently, hepatic resection is rarely performed in trauma patients, having been largely replaced by perihepatic packing, resectional debridement, and hepatotomy with selective ligation. Nonetheless, there are two circumstances in which anatomic resection may still be a reasonable choice. The first is prompt resection in patients with extensive injuries of the left lateral section of the liver; because hemorrhage from the left hemiliver is easily controlled with bimanual compression, the risk of uncontrolled blood loss is not as high as it is with left or right anatomic hemihepatectomies. The second is delayed anatomic hemihepatectomy in patients whose hemorrhage has been controlled but whose left or right hemiliver is nonviable as a result of ligation or thrombosis of essential blood vessels. Because of the large mass of necrotic liver tissue, there is a high risk of subsequent infection or persistent hyperinflammation, setting the stage for the multiple organ dysfunction syndrome (MODS). The necrotic hemiliver should be removed as soon as the patient's condition permits.

Hepatic transplantation has been successful in several trauma patients with devastating hepatic injuries who required total hepatectomy.[41-44] In each of these five patients, the mean anhepatic period was approximately 24 hours. All five survived the transplantation, though two died of disseminated viral infections within 2 months of the procedure. Two others were alive and well 16 and 17 months after the procedure; no follow-up was reported for the fifth patient. Hepatic transplantation represents the ultimate expression of aggressive trauma care. All other injuries must be well delineated (particularly injuries to the CNS), and the patient must have an excellent chance of survival aside from the hepatic injury. High cost and limited availability of donors restrict the performance of hepatic transplantation for trauma, but it seems probable that this procedure will continue to be performed in extraordinary circumstances.

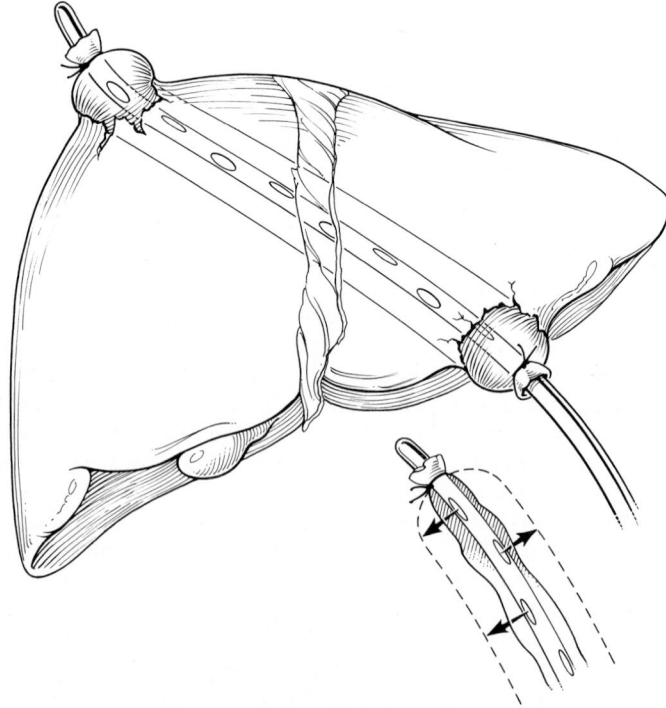

Figure 11 **A handmade balloon from a Robinson catheter and a Penrose drain may effectively control hemorrhage from a transhepatic penetrating wound.**

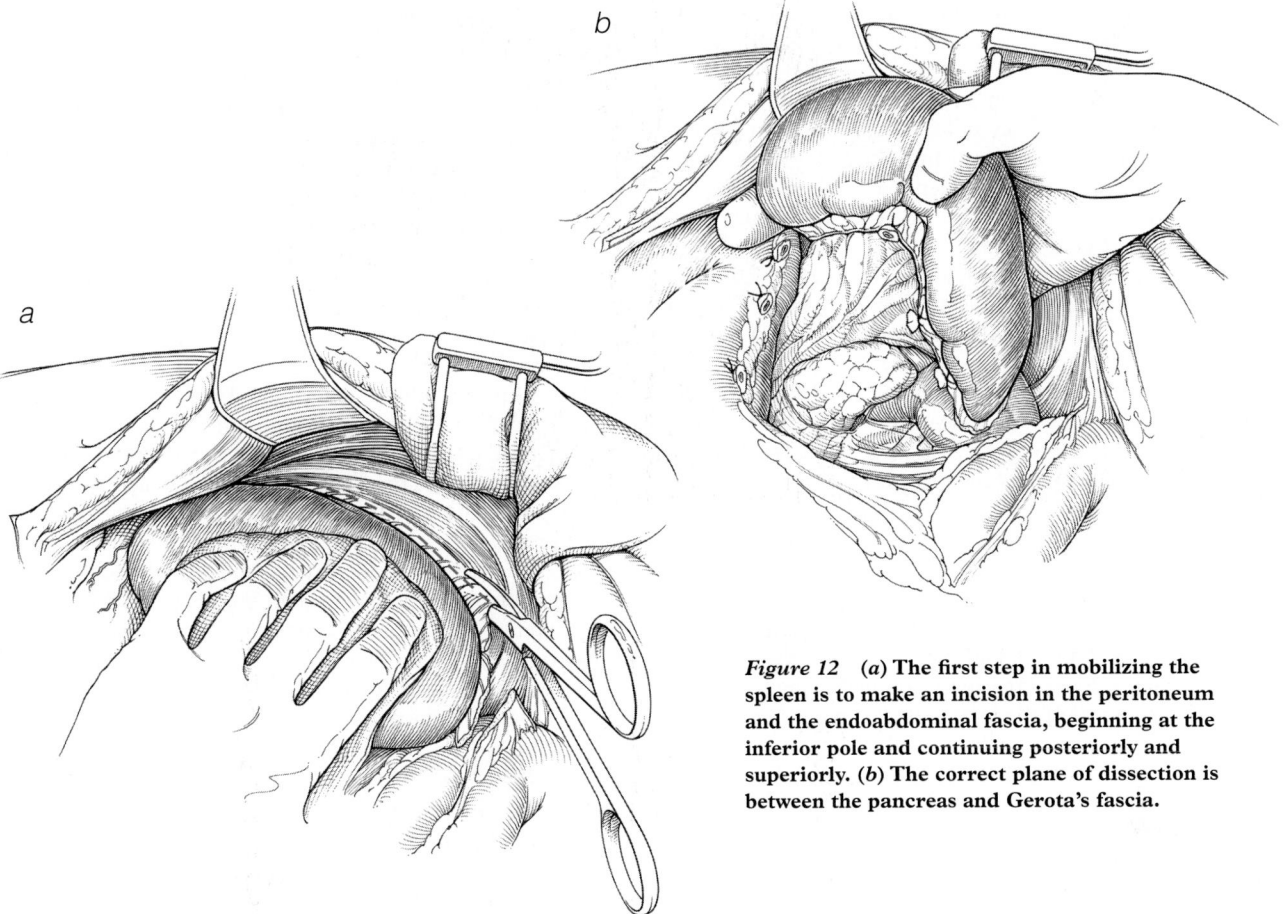

Figure 12 (*a*) **The first step in mobilizing the spleen is to make an incision in the peritoneum and the endoabdominal fascia, beginning at the inferior pole and continuing posteriorly and superiorly.** (*b*) **The correct plane of dissection is between the pancreas and Gerota's fascia.**

Subcapsular Hematoma

An uncommon but troublesome hepatic injury is subcapsular hematoma, which arises when the parenchyma of the liver is disrupted by blunt trauma but Glisson's capsule remains intact. Subcapsular hematomas range in severity from minor blisters on the surface of the liver to ruptured central hematomas accompanied by severe hemorrhage [*see Table 1*]. They may be recognized either at the time of the operation or in the course of CT scanning.

Regardless of how the lesion is diagnosed, subsequent decision making is often difficult. If a grade I or II subcapsular hematoma—that is, a hematoma involving less than 50% of the surface of the liver that is not expanding and is not ruptured—is discovered during an exploratory laparotomy, it should be left alone. If the hematoma is explored, hepatotomy with selective ligation may be required to control bleeding vessels. Even if hepatotomy with ligation is effective, one must still contend with diffuse hemorrhage from the large denuded surface, and packing may also be required. A hematoma that is expanding during operation (grade III) may have to be explored. Such lesions are often the result of uncontrolled arterial hemorrhage, and packing alone may not be successful. An alternative strategy is to pack the liver to control venous hemorrhage, close the abdomen, and transport the patient to the interventional radiology suite for hepatic arteriography and embolization of the bleeding vessels. Ruptured grades III and IV hematomas are treated with exploration and selective ligation, with or without packing.

Perihepatic Drainage

For years, all hepatic injuries were drained via Penrose drains brought out laterally or through the bed of the resected 12th rib; recently, the use of large sump drains and closed suction drains has become increasingly popular. Several prospective and retrospective studies have demonstrated that the use of either Penrose or sump drains carries a higher risk of intra-abdominal infection than the use of either closed suction drains or no drains at all.[45-47] It is clear that if drains are to be used, closed suction devices are preferred. What remains unclear, however, is whether closed suction drains are better or worse than no drains, particularly in view of the advent of percutaneous catheter drainage. Patients who are initially treated with perihepatic packing may also require drainage; however, drainage is not indicated at the initial procedure, given that the patient will be returned to the OR within the next 48 hours.

MORTALITY AND COMPLICATIONS

Overall mortality for patients with hepatic injuries is approximately 10%. The most common cause of death is exsanguination, followed by MODS and intracranial injury. Three generalizations may be made regarding the risk of death and complications: (1) both increase in proportion to the injury grade and to the complexity of repair; (2) hepatic injuries caused by blunt trauma carry a higher mortality than those caused by penetrating trauma; and (3) infectious complications occur more often with penetrating trauma.[48]

Postoperative hemorrhage occurs in a small percentage of patients with hepatic injuries. The source may be either a coagulopathy or a missed vascular injury (usually to an artery). In most instances of persistent postoperative hemorrhage, the patient is best served by being returned to the OR. Arteriography with embolization may be considered in selected patients. If coagulation studies indicate that a coagulopathy is the likely cause of post-operative hemorrhage, there is little to be gained by reoperation until the coagulopathy is corrected.

Perihepatic infections occur in fewer than 5% of patients with significant hepatic injuries. They develop more often in patients with penetrating injuries than in patients with blunt injuries, presumably because of the greater frequency of enteric contamination. An elevated temperature and a higher than normal white blood cell count after postoperative day 3 or 4 should prompt a search for intra-abdominal infection. In the absence of pneumonia, an infected line, or urinary tract infection, an abdominal CT scan with intravenous and upper gastrointestinal contrast should be obtained. Many perihepatic infections can be treated with CT-guided drainage; however, infected hematomas and infected necrotic liver tissue cannot be expected to respond to percutaneous drainage. Right 12th rib resection remains an excellent approach for posterior infections and provides superior drainage in refractory cases.

Bilomas are loculated collections of bile that may or may not be infected. If a biloma is infected, it is essentially an abscess and should be treated as such; if it is sterile, it will eventually be resorbed. Biliary ascites is caused by disruption of a major bile duct. Reoperation after the establishment of appropriate drainage is the prudent course. Even if the source of the leaking bile can be identified, primary repair of the injured duct is unlikely to be successful. It is best to wait until a firm fistulous communication is established with adequate drainage.

Biliary fistulas occur in approximately 3% of patients with major hepatic injuries.[40] They are usually of little consequence and generally close without specific treatment. In rare instances, a fistulous communication with intrathoracic structures forms in patients with associated diaphragmatic injuries, resulting in a bronchobiliary or pleurobiliary fistula. Because of the pressure differential between the biliary tract and the thoracic cavity, most of these fistulas must be closed operatively; however, we know of one pleurobiliary fistula that closed spontaneously after endoscopic sphincterotomy and stent placement.

Hemorrhage from hepatic injuries is often treated without identifying and controlling each bleeding vessel individually, and arterial pseudoaneurysms may develop as a consequence. As the pseudoaneurysm enlarges, it may rupture into the parenchyma of the liver, into a bile duct, or into an adjacent branch of the portal vein. Rupture into a bile duct results in hemobilia, which is characterized by intermittent episodes of right upper quadrant pain, upper GI hemorrhage, and jaundice; rupture into a portal vein may result in portal vein hypertension with bleeding varices. Both of these complications are exceedingly rare and are best managed with hepatic arteriography and embolization.

Injuries to the Bile Ducts and Gallbladder

Injuries to the extrahepatic bile ducts [see Table 1] can be caused by either penetrating or blunt trauma; however, they are rare in either case.[49-53]

The diagnosis is usually made by noting the accumulation of bile in the upper quadrant during laparotomy for treatment of associated injuries. Treatment of common bile duct (CBD) injuries after external trauma is complicated by the small size and thin wall of the normal duct, which render primary repair almost impossible except when the laceration is small and there is no tissue loss. When there is tissue loss or the laceration is larger than 25% to 50% of the diameter of the duct, the best treatment option is a Roux-en-Y choledochojejunostomy [see 64 Procedures for Benign

and Malignant Biliary Tract Disease].[54-57] Treatment of injuries to the left or right hepatic duct is even more difficult—so much so that we question whether repair should even be attempted under emergency conditions. If only one hepatic duct is injured, a reasonable approach is to ligate it and deal with any infections or atrophy of the hemiliver rather than to attempt repair.[58] If both ducts are injured, each should be intubated with a small catheter brought through the abdominal wall. Once the patient has recovered sufficiently, delayed repair is performed under elective conditions. Injuries to the intrapancreatic portion of the CBD are treated by dividing the duct at the superior border of the pancreas, ligating the distal portion, and performing a Roux-en-Y choledochojejunostomy.

The Roux-en-Y choledochojejunostomy is done in a single layer with interrupted 5-0 absorbable monofilament sutures. To prevent ischemia and possible stricture, no circumferential dissection of the duct is performed. A round patch of approximately the same diameter as the CBD is removed from the seromuscular layer of the small bowel, but the mucosa and submucosa are only perforated, not resected. The posterior row of sutures is placed first, with full-thickness bites taken through both the duct and the small bowel. The anterior row is then completed. Finally, three or four 3-0 polypropylene sutures are placed to secure the small bowel around the anastomosis to the connective tissue of the porta hepatis. The only purpose for these sutures is to spare the fragile anastomosis any potential tension. No T tubes or stents are employed. Closed suction drainage is added in the case of injuries to the intrapancreatic portion of the duct or at the surgeon's discretion.

Injuries to the gallbladder [see Table 1] are treated by means of either lateral repair with absorbable sutures or cholecystectomy [see 63 Cholecystectomy and Common Bile Duct Exploration]; the decision between the two approaches depends on which is easier in a given situation. Cholecystostomy is rarely, if ever, indicated.

Injuries to the Spleen

Splenic injuries [see Table 1] are treated operatively by means of splenic repair (splenorrhaphy), partial splenectomy, or resection, depending on the extent of the injury and the condition of the patient.[57,58] The continued enthusiasm for nonoperative management of splenic injuries is driven, in part, by concern about the rare but often fatal complication known as overwhelming postsplenectomy infection (OPSI). OPSI is caused by encapsulated bacteria (e.g., Streptococcus pneumoniae, Haemophilus influenzae, and Neisseria meningitidis) and is very resistant to treatment: mortality may exceed 50%. OPSI occurs most often in young children and immunocompromised adults and is uncommon in otherwise healthy adults. For this reason, splenic salvage is attempted more vigorously in pediatric patients than in adult ones [see Discussion, Nonoperative Management of Blunt Hepatic and Splenic Injuries, below].

To ensure safe removal or repair, the spleen should be mobilized to the point where it can be brought to the surface of the abdominal wall without tension. To this end, the soft tissue attachments between the spleen and the splenic flexure of the colon must be divided. Next, an incision is made in the peritoneum and the endoabdominal fascia, beginning at the inferior pole, 1 to 2 cm lateral to the posterior peritoneal reflection of the spleen, and continuing posteriorly and superiorly until the esophagus is encountered [see Figure 12a]. Care must be taken not to pull on the spleen, so that it will not tear at the posterior peritoneal reflection, causing significant hemorrhage. Instead, the spleen should be rotated counterclockwise, with posterior pressure applied to expose the peritoneal reflection. It is often helpful to rotate the operating table 20° to the patient's right so that the weight of the abdominal viscera facilitates their retraction. A plane is thus established between the spleen and pancreas and Gerota's fascia that can be extended to the aorta [*see Figure 12b*]. With this step, mobilization is complete, and the spleen can be repaired or removed without any need to struggle to achieve adequate exposure.

Splenectomy [*see 67 Splenectomy*] is the usual treatment for hilar injuries or a pulverized splenic parenchyma. It is also indicated for lesser splenic injuries in patients who have multiple abdominal injuries and a coagulopathy, and it is frequently necessary in patients in whom splenic salvage attempts have failed. Partial splenectomy is suitable for patients in whom only a portion of the spleen (usually the superior or inferior half) has been destroyed. Once the damaged portion has been removed, the same methods used to control hemorrhage from hepatic parenchyma can be used to control hemorrhage from splenic parenchyma [*see Figure 13*]. When horizontal mattress sutures are placed across a raw edge, gentle compression of the parenchyma by an assistant facilitates hemostasis; when the sutures are tied and compression is released, the spleen will expand slightly and tighten the sutures further. Drains are never used after completion of the repair or resection.

If splenectomy is performed, vaccines effective against the encapsulated bacteria are administered. The pneumococcal vaccine is routinely given, and vaccines effective against *H. influenzae* and *N. meningitidis* should also be given if available.

Injuries to the Diaphragm

In cases of blunt trauma to the diaphragm, the injury is on the left side 75% of the time, presumably because the liver diffuses some of the energy on the right side. With both blunt and penetrating injuries [*see Table 1*], the diagnosis is suggested by an abnormality of the diaphragmatic shadow on chest x-ray. Many of these abnormalities are subtle, particularly with penetrating injuries, and further diagnostic evaluation may be warranted. The typical injury from blunt trauma is a tear in the central tendon; often, the tear is quite large. Regardless of the cause, acute injuries are repaired

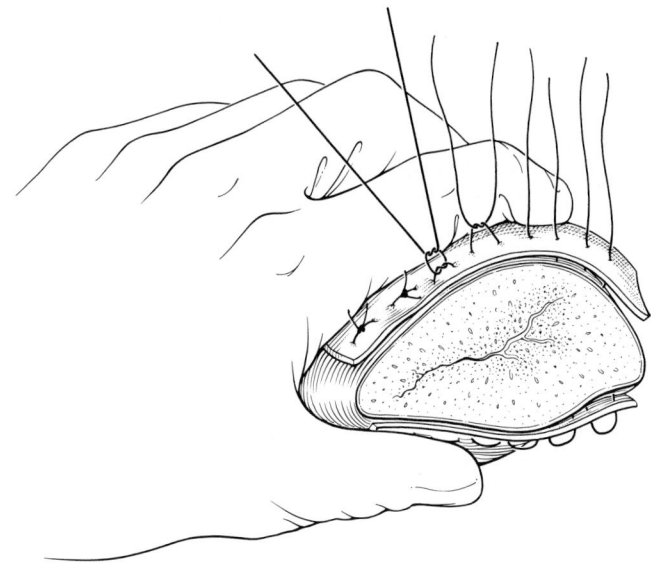

Figure 13 **Methods for controlling hemorrhage from the splenic parenchyma are similar to those for controlling hemorrhage from the hepatic parenchyma. Shown are interrupted mattress sutures across a raw edge of the spleen.**

through an abdominal incision. Because of the concave shape of the diaphragm and the overlying anterior ribs, anterior diaphragmatic injuries may be difficult to suture. Repair is greatly facilitated by using a long Allis clamp to grasp part of the injury and evert the diaphragm. Lacerations are repaired with continuous No. 1 monofilament nonabsorbable sutures. Occasionally, with large avulsions or gunshot wounds accompanied by extensive tissue loss, polypropylene mesh is required to bridge the defect.

The explosive growth of laparoscopic procedures has led to the application of this technology for both diagnostic and therapeutic purposes in trauma patients. In a number of patients with low anterior thoracic stab wounds who otherwise were not candidates for a laparotomy, small diaphragmatic lacerations have been identified and repaired with laparoscopy and stapling.

Discussion

Nonoperative Treatment of Blunt Hepatic and Splenic Injury

Only a few years ago, blunt and penetrating hepatic and splenic injuries were managed in a similar fashion on the basis of a positive diagnostic peritoneal lavage or the probability of peritoneal penetration: a laparotomy was performed, and the injured organs were identified and treated. Currently, although penetrating abdominal injuries are still treated in the same way, nearly all children and 50% to 80% of adults with blunt hepatic and splenic injuries are treated without laparotomy.[59-68] This remarkable change was made possible by the development of the high-speed helical CT scanner, the replacement of diagnostic peritoneal lavage by ultrasonography, and the growth of interventional radiology.

The diagnosis of blunt abdominal trauma is suspected on the basis of the mechanism of injury and the presence of associated injuries (e.g., right or left lower rib fractures). Ultrasonographic examination of the abdomen may reveal a fluid stripe in Morrison's pouch, the left upper quadrant, or the pelvis, which suggests a hemoperitoneum. This observation prompts a CT scan of the abdomen, which establishes the presence or absence of injuries to the liver or the spleen and, to some degree, serves as a means of grading the severity of organ injury. Patients may be observed either in the SICU or on the ward, depending on the apparent severity of the parenchymal injury on the CT scan, the presence and extent of any associated injuries, and the overall hemodynamic status.[69,70]

The primary requirement for nonoperative therapy is hemodynamic stability.[63-72] To confirm stability, frequent assessment of vital signs and monitoring of the hematocrit are necessary. Continued hemorrhage occurs in 1% to 4% of patients.[65,66,68-73] Hypotension may develop, usually within the first 24 hours after hepatic injury but sometimes several days later, especially when splenic injury is present.[71,72] It is often an indication that operative intervention is necessary. A persistently falling hematocrit should be treated with PRBC transfusions. If the hematocrit continues to fall after two or three units of PRBCs, embolization of the liver in the interventional radiology suite should be considered.[66] Overall, nonoperative treatment obviates laparotomy in more than 95% of cases.[59-65]

Out of concern over the risk of delayed hemorrhage or other complications, follow-up CT scans have often been recommended; unfortunately, there is no consensus as to when or even whether they should be obtained. Given that patients with grade I or II hepatic or splenic injuries rarely show progression of the lesion or other complications on routine follow-up CT scans, it is reasonable to omit such scans if patients' hematocrits remain stable and they are otherwise well. Patients with more extensive injuries often have a less predictable course, and CT scanning may be necessary to evaluate possible complications. Routine scanning before discharge, however, is unwarranted. On the other hand, patients who participate in vigorous or contact sports should have CT documentation of virtually complete healing before resuming those activities.

A more convenient and less expensive alternative to follow-up CT scanning is ultrasonographic monitoring of lesions. Ultrasonographic monitoring is particularly useful for following up splenic injuries; however, it may not be useful for following up hepatic injuries, because the technology currently available is incapable of reliably imaging the entire liver.

Other complications of nonoperative therapy for blunt hepatic and splenic injuries occur in 2% to 5% of patients; these include missed abdominal injuries, parenchymal infarction, infection, and bile leakage (a complication associated solely with hepatic injuries).[59,62-64] Aseptic infarcts, infected hematomas, and bile collections are suspected on the basis of a clinical picture suggestive of infection and confirmed by CT-guided aspiration. Aseptic infarction usually does not necessitate operative intervention. Fluid collections are drained, with the method depending on the viscosity of the fluid: CT-guided drainage may be effective in treating thin collections, but operative intervention is required for thicker collections, those with solid components, and those for which percutaneous drainage was attempted without success. Extrahepatic bile collections should be treated with percutaneous drainage under CT guidance. Most biliary fistulas close spontaneously; endoscopic stent placement may hasten closure in recalcitrant cases.[74] Intrahepatic collections of blood and bile are managed expectantly. Complete absorption of large intrahepatic collections may take several months. If a collection becomes infected, CT-guided aspiration is performed and drainage obtained as described.

Missed enteric and retroperitoneal injuries are another cause of failed nonoperative treatment. Such injuries are present in 1% to 4% of patients in whom nonoperative treatment is attempted.[59,61-64] High-quality images and expert interpretation minimize the number of missed injuries on CT scans but cannot eliminate them entirely. Therefore, patients must be watched carefully for the development of peritoneal irritation and other signs of intraabdominal pathology.

References

1. Moore EE, Cogbill TH, Jurkovich GJ, et al: Organ injury scaling: spleen and liver (1994 revision). J Trauma 38:323, 1995

2. Hepatic trauma revisited. Feliciano DV, Pachter HL, Eds. Curr Probl Surg 26, 1986

3. Moore EE: Critical decisions in the management of hepatic trauma. Am J Surg 148:712, 1984

4. Feliciano DV, Mattox KL, Jordan GL, et al: Management of 1000 consecutive cases of hepatic trauma (1979–1984). Ann Surg 204:438, 1986

5. Feliciano DV, Mattox KL, Burch JM, et al: Packing for control of hepatic hemorrhage. J Trauma 26:738, 1986

6. Ivantury RR, Nallathambi M, Gunduz Y, et al: Liver packing for uncontrolled hemorrhage: a reappraisal. J Trauma 26:744, 1986

7. Carmona RH, Peck DZ, Lim RC: The role of packing and planned reoperation in severe hepatic trauma. J Trauma 24:779, 1984

8. Cue JI, Cryer HG, Miller FB, et al: Packing and planned reexploration for hepatic and retroperitoneal hemorrhage: critical refinements of a useful technique. J Trauma 30:1007, 1990

9. Beal SL: Fatal hepatic hemorrhage: an unresolved problem in the management of complex liver injuries. J Trauma 30:163, 1990

10. Pachter HL, Spencer FC, Hofstetter SR, et al: Significant trends in the treatment of hepatic trauma: experience with 411 injuries. Ann Surg 215:492, 1992

11. Murray DH Jr, Borge JD, Pouteau GG: Tourniquet control of liver bleeding. J Trauma 18:771, 1978

12. Heaney JP, Stanton WR, Halbert DS, et al: An improved technic for vascular isolation of the liver. Ann Surg 163:237, 1966

13. Burch JM, Feliciano DV, Mattox KL: The atrio-caval shunt: facts and fiction. Ann Surg 207:555, 1988

14. Buechter KJ, Gomez GA, Zeppa R: A new technique for exposure of injuries at the confluence of the retrohepatic veins and the retrohepatic vena cava. J Trauma 30:328, 1990

15. Schrock T, Blaisdell FW, Matthewson C Jr: Management of blunt trauma to the liver and hepatic veins. Arch Surg 96:698, 1968

16. Bricker DL, Morton JR, Okies JE, et al: Surgical management of injuries to the vena cava: changing patterns of injury and newer techniques of repair. J Trauma 11:725, 1971

17. Yellin AE, Chaffee CB, Donovan AJ: Vascular isolation in treatment of juxtahepatic venous injuries. Arch Surg 102:566, 1971

18. Walt AJ: The mythology of hepatic trauma: or Babel revisited. Am J Surg 125:12, 1978

19. Millikan JS, Moore EE, Cogbill TH, et al: Inferior vena cava injuries: a continuing challenge. J Trauma 23:207, 1983

20. Pachter HL, Spencer FC, Hofstetter SR, et al: The management of juxtahepatic venous injuries without an atriocaval shunt. Surgery 99:569, 1986

21. Pilcher DB, Harman PK, Moore EE: Retrohepatic vena cava balloon shunt introduced via the sapheno-femoral junction. J Trauma 17:837, 1977

22. Biffl WL, Moore EE, Franciose RJ: Venovenous bypass and hepatic vascular isolation as adjuncts in the repair of destructive wounds to the retrohepatic inferior vena cava. J Trauma 45:400, 1998

23. Kram HB, Nathan RC, Stafford FJ, et al: Fibrin glue achieves hemostasis in patients with coagulation disorders. Arch Surg 124:385, 1989

24. Berguer R, Staerkel RL, Moore EE, et al: Warning: fatal reaction to the use of fibrin glue in deep hepatic wounds: case reports. J Trauma 31:408, 1991

25. Boffard KD, Riou B, Warren B, et el: Recombinant factor VIIa as adjunctive therapy for bleeding control in severely injured trauma patients: two parallel randomized, placebo-controlled, double-blind clinical trials. J Trauma 59:8, 2005

26. Ochsner MG, Maniscalco-Theberge ME, Champion HR: Fibrin glue as a hemostatic agent in hepatic and splenic trauma. J Trauma 30:884, 1990

27. Trunkey DD, Shires GT, McClelland R: Management of liver trauma in 811 consecutive patients. Ann Surg 179:722, 1974

28. Levin A, Gover P, Nance FC: Surgical restraint in the management of hepatic injury: a review of Charity Hospital experience. J Trauma 18:399, 1978

29. Lucas CE, Ledgerwood AM: Prospective evaluation of hemostatic techniques for liver injuries. J Trauma 16:442, 1976

30. Camona RH, Lim RC Jr, Clark GC: Morbidity and mortality in hepatic trauma: a 5 year study. Am J Surg 144:88, 1982

31. Moore FA, Moore EE, Seagrave A: Nonresectional management of major hepatic trauma: an evolving concept. Am J Surg 150:725, 1985

32. Stone HH, Lamb JM: Use of pedicled omentum as an autogenous pack for control of hemorrhage in major injuries of the liver. Surg Gynecol Obstet 141:92, 1975

33. Mays ET: Lobar dearterialization for exsanguinating wounds of the liver. J Trauma 12:397, 1972

34. Flint LM, Polk HC: Selective hepatic artery ligation: limitations and failures. J Trauma 19:319, 1979

35. Poggetti RS, Moore EE, Moore FA, et al: Balloon tamponade for bilobar transfixing

hepatic gunshot wounds. J Trauma 33:694, 1992

36. Madding GF, Lawrence KB, Kennedy PA: War wounds of the liver. Tex State J Med 42:267, 1946

37. Reed RL, Merrell RC, Meyers WC, et al: Continuing evolution in the approach to severe liver trauma. Ann Surg 216:524, 1992

38. Jacobson LE, Kirton OC, Gomez GA: The use of an absorbable mesh wrap in the management of major liver injuries. Surgery 111:455, 1992

39. Lim RC Jr, Knudson J, Steele M: Liver trauma: current method of management. Arch Surg 104:544, 1972

40. Donovan AJ, Michaelian MJ, Yellin AE: Anatomical hepatic lobectomy in trauma to the liver. Surgery 73:833, 1973

41. Defore WW, Mattox KL, Jordan GL, et al: Management of 1590 consecutive cases of liver trauma. Arch Surg 111:493, 1976

42. Esquivel CO, Bernardos A, Makowka L, et al: Liver replacement after massive hepatic trauma. J Trauma 27:800, 1987

43. Angstadt J, Jarrell B, Moritz M, et al: Surgical management of severe liver trauma: a role for liver transplantation. J Trauma 29:606, 1989

44. Ringe B, Pichlmayr R, Ziegler H, et al: Management of severe hepatic trauma by two-stage total hepatectomy and subsequent liver transplantation. Surgery 109:792, 1991

45. Jeng LB, Hsu C, Wang C, et al: Emergent liver transplantation to salvage a hepatic avulsion injury with a disrupted suprahepatic vena cava. Arch Surg 128:1075, 1993

46. Fischer RP, O'Farrell KA, Perry JF Jr: The value of peritoneal drains in the treatment of liver injuries. J Trauma 18:393, 1978

47. Noyes LD, Doyle DJ, McSwain NE: Septic complications associated with the use of peritoneal drains in liver trauma. J Trauma 28:337, 1988

48. Kozar RA, Moore FA, Cothren CC, et al: Predicting hepatic-related morbidity associated with nonoperative management of complex blunt hepatic injuries: a multicenter trial. Arch Surg (in press)

49. Jurkovich GJ, Hoyt DB, Moore FA, et al: Portal triad injuries: a multi-institutional study. J Trauma 39:426, 1995.

50. Noyes LD, Doyle DJ, McSwain NE: Septic complications associated with the use of peritoneal drains in liver trauma. J Trauma 28:337, 1988

51. Fabian TC, Croce MA, Stanford GG, et al: Factors affecting morbidity after hepatic trauma. Ann Surg 213:540, 1991

52. Posner MC, Moore EE: Extrahepatic biliary tract injury: operative management plan. J Trauma 25:833, 1985

53. Ivatury RR, Rohman M, Nallathami M, et al: The morbidity of injuries of the extra-hepatic biliary system. J Trauma 25:967, 1985

54. Sheldon GF, Lim RC, Yee ES, et al: Management of injuries to the porta hepatis. Ann Surg 202:539, 1985

55. Feliciano DV, Bitondo CG, Burch JM, et al: Management of traumatic injuries to the extrahepatic biliary ducts. Am J Surg 150:705, 1985

56. Bade PG, Thomson SR, Hirshberg A, et al: Surgical options in traumatic injury to the extrahepatic biliary tract. Br J Surg 76:256, 1989

57. Csendes A, Diaz JC, Burdiles P, et al: Late results of immediate primary end to end repair in accidental section of the common bile duct. Surg Gynecol Obstet 168:125, 1989

58. Howdieshell TR, Hawkins ML, Osler TM, et al: Management of blunt hepatic duct transection by ligation. South Med J 83:579, 1990

59. Barrett J, Sheaff C, Abuabara S, et al: Splenic preservation in adults after blunt and penetrating trauma. Am J Surg 145:313, 1983

60. Feliciano DV, Spjut-Patrinely V, Burch JM, et al: Splenorrhaphy: the alternative. Ann Surg 211:569 1990

61. Cogbill TH, Moore EE, Jurkovich JJ, et al: Nonoperative management of blunt septic trauma: a multicenter experience. J Trauma 29:1312, 1989

62. Meredith JW, Young JS, Bowling J, et al: Nonoperative management of blunt hepatic trauma: the exception or the rule? J Trauma 36:529, 1994

63. Pachter HL, Hofstetter ST: The current status of nonoperative management of adult blunt hepatic injuries. Am J Surg 169:442, 1995

64. Croce MA, Fabian TC, Menke PG, et al: Nonoperative management of blunt hepatic trauma is the treatment of choice for hemodynamically stable patients. Ann Surg 221:744, 1995

65. Boone DC, Federle M, Billiar TR, et al: Evolution of management of major hepatic trauma: identification of patterns of injury. J Trauma 39:344, 1995

66. Pachter HL, Knudson MM, Esrig B, et al: Status of nonoperative management of blunt hepatic injuries in 1995: a multicenter experience with 404 patients. J Trauma 40:31, 1996

67. Powell M, Courcoulas A, Gardner M, et al: Management of blunt splenic trauma: significant differences between adults and children. Surgery 122:654, 1997

68. Richardson JD: Changes in the management of injuries to the liver and spleen. J Am Coll Surg 200:648, 2005

69. Sclafani SJA, Shaftan GW, Scalea TM, et al: Nonoperative salvage of computed tomography–diagnosed splenic injuries: utilization of angiography for triage and embolization for hemostasis. J Trauma 39:818, 1995

70. Malhotra AK, Fabian TC, Crou MA, et al: Blunt hepatic injury: a paradigm shift from operative to nonoperative management in the 1990's. Ann Surg 231:804, 2000

71. Sutyak JP, Chiu WC, D'Amelio LF, et al: Computed tomography is inaccurate in estimating the severity of adult splenic injury. J Trauma 39:514, 1995

72. Croce MA, Fabian TC, Kudsk KA, et al: AAST organ injury scale: correlation of CT-graded liver injuries and operative findings. J Trauma 31:806, 1991

73. Gates JD: Delayed hemorrhage with free rupture complicating the nonsurgical management of blunt hepatic trauma: a case report and review of the literature. J Trauma 36:572, 1994

74. Sugimoto K, Asari Y, Sakaguchi T, et al: Endoscopic retrograde cholangiography in the nonsurgical management of blunt liver injury. J Trauma 35:192, 1993

Acknowledgments

Figure 1   Tom Moore.

Figures 2, 7, and 9   Thom Graves.

Figure 3   Marcia Kammerer.

Figures 4 through 6, 8, and 10 through 13   Susan Brust, C.M.I.

Table 2   Information provided by Baxter International, Deerfield, Illinois.

107 INJURIES TO THE STOMACH, SMALL BOWEL, COLON, AND RECTUM

Jordan A. Weinberg, M.D., F.R.C.S.C., and Timothy C. Fabian, M.D., F.A.C.S.

Hollow viscus injury is most commonly the result of penetrating abdominal trauma. It is relatively infrequent in the setting of blunt trauma: in one multi-institutional analysis, only 1.2% of blunt trauma admissions were associated with a hollow viscus injury.[1] Initial resuscitation of the patient with abdominal trauma is described in detail elsewhere [see 100 Initial Management of Life-Threatening Trauma]. The diagnosis of hollow viscus injury remains a challenge in abdominal trauma patients, and subsequent evaluation is determined by the mechanism of injury. Regardless of the specific injury mechanism, however, the principles of operative management are the same.

Determination of Need for Operation

BLUNT TRAUMA

Hollow viscus injury after blunt trauma, though uncommon, can have serious consequences if the diagnosis is missed or delayed. In a multi-institutional study of 198 patients with blunt small bowel injury, delay of as little as 8 hours in making the diagnosis resulted in increased morbidity and mortality.[2] Mortality increased in parallel with time to operative intervention (< 8 hours to operation, 2% mortality; 8 to 16 hours, 9%; 16 to 25 hours, 17%; > 24 hours, 31%), as did the complication rate.

Particular consideration should be given to lap- and shoulder-restraint injuries, which may be associated with an increased risk of hollow viscus injury. The so-called seat-belt sign (i.e., ecchymosis of the abdominal wall secondary to the compressive force of the lap belt) is associated with a more than doubled relative risk of small bowel injury.[3] Flexion-distraction fractures of the spine (Chance fractures) are also associated with lap-belt use, and the presence of such fractures should raise the index of suspicion for associated hollow viscus injury.

Clinical examination often indicates the need for exploratory laparotomy. Abdominal tenderness after blunt torso trauma is frequently associated with significant intra-abdominal pathology, but the reliability of the examination may be compromised by distracting chest or long bone injury, closed head injury, spinal cord injury, or intoxication. In such scenarios, additional diagnostic tests are necessary.

Ultrasonography is routinely performed early in the evaluation of blunt abdominal trauma. It is highly specific and moderately sensitive in identifying intra-abdominal fluid, the presence of which in a hemodynamically unstable patient is an indication for laparotomy (in that it strongly suggests the presence of significant intra-abdominal hemorrhage).[4] Ultrasonography does not, however, reliably distinguish solid-organ injury from hollow viscus injury—a distinction that is critical for determining subsequent management (i.e., operative versus nonoperative) in a hemodynamically stable patient. Diagnostic peritoneal lavage (DPL) may help differentiate one type of injury from the other (see below).

Helical (spiral) computed tomography is currently the imaging modality of choice in stable patients who have undergone blunt abdominal trauma. Our experience indicates that it is useful for identifying blunt hollow viscus injury. In a review of over 8,000 CT scans performed to evaluate cases of blunt abdominal trauma, we found that the number of abnormal radiologic findings suggesting blunt injury to the bowel, the mesentery, or both [see Table 1] was correlated with the true presence of injury.[5] A CT scan demonstrating a solitary abnormality was associated with a true positive rate of 36%, whereas a scan demonstrating more than one abnormality was associated with a true positive rate of 83%. Unexplained intraperitoneal fluid (i.e., fluid appearing in the absence of solid-organ injury) was the most common radiographic finding associated with blunt bowel or mesenteric injury, but it often proved to be a false positive finding [see Table 1].

On the basis of this experience, we developed an algorithm for the evaluation of blunt hollow viscus injury in patients with unreliable clinical examination results [see Figure 1]. If CT scanning demonstrates no suspicious findings, the patient is observed. No further diagnostic workup of hollow viscus injury is performed, and the duration of the observation period depends on the reliability of the clinical examination. It is worth noting that the 2003 multi-institutional review of 2,457 cases carried out by the Eastern Association for the Surgery of Trauma (EAST) reported a 13% incidence of blunt small bowel injury in patients with an initial negative CT scan. These results indicate that caution should be exercised in dismissing the presence of hollow viscus injury on the basis of a negative scan.[3] This concern is echoed by our own insti-

Table 1 Incidence of Findings Suggestive of Blunt Mesenteric and Bowel Injury in True Positive and False Positive CT Scans[6]

Finding	Incidence	
	True Positive CT Scans (%)	False Positive CT Scans (%)
Unexplained intraperitoneal fluid	74	79
Pneumoperitoneum	28	2
Bowel wall thickening	30	8
Mesenteric fat stranding	9	4
Mesenteric hematoma	19	19
Extravasation of luminal content	4	0
Extravasation of vascular content	9	0

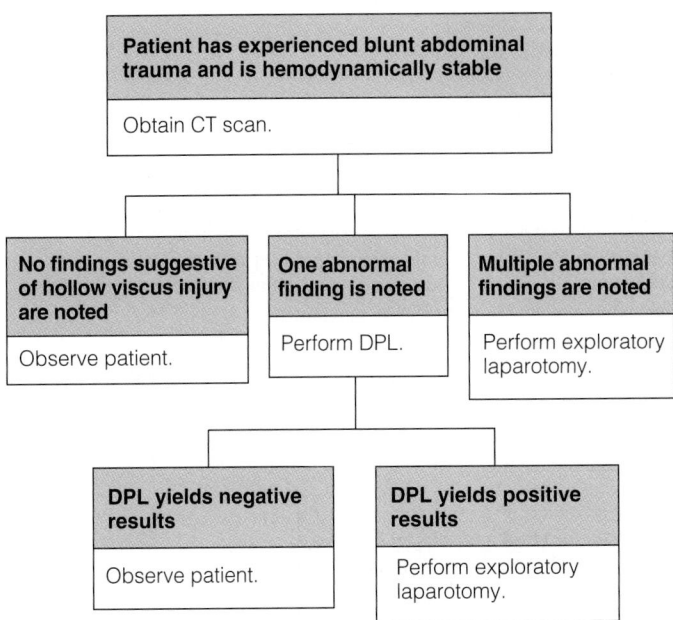

Figure 1 Algorithm outlines the evaluation of blunt injury to a hollow viscus.

tutional experience, in which the incidence of injury in patients with an initial negative CT scan was 12%.[5]

If CT demonstrates a solitary suspicious finding, DPL is performed for further evaluation. If DPL yields positive results (white blood cell [WBC] count > 500 cells/mm³, alkaline phosphatase level > 10 IU/L, or amylase level > 20 IU/L), exploratory laparotomy is performed. It must be kept in mind, however, that DPL results may be falsely negative or equivocal in the early period after trauma.[6] This phenomenon may be attributable to a time lag between the intestinal perforation and the subsequent development of intraperitoneal leukocytosis. If a high degree of suspicion of hollow viscus injury remains even after a negative DPL result, DPL may be repeated. Alternatively, exploratory laparotomy may be performed. The choice between the two options is largely based on the individual surgeon's clinical judgment.

If CT demonstrates multiple abnormalities, DPL is omitted from the workup and exploratory laparotomy is performed.

PENETRATING TRAUMA

Gunshot Wounds

Gunshot wounds to the abdomen generally necessitate exploratory laparotomy, given the high incidence of intra-abdominal injury. The exception to this rule is the case of a tangential wound that is believed to be traversing the soft tissues of the abdominal wall without entering the peritoneal cavity. In this scenario, we usually perform laparoscopy to look for peritoneal penetration. If the peritoneum has been violated, a laparotomy is done to permit systematic evaluation of the peritoneal cavity. If the peritoneum has not been violated, the operation may be terminated and the patient discharged after recovery from anesthesia, provided that there are no other extra-abdominal injuries necessitating hospital admission.

Stab Wounds

Stab wounds to the abdomen are associated with a lower incidence of intra-abdominal injury than gunshot wounds are. Accordingly, there has been a shift toward selective management

algorithms that rely on diagnostic tests, serial abdominal examination, or some combination of the two. When the peritoneum has obviously been penetrated (as with omental or bowel evisceration), we perform a laparotomy to evaluate the entire peritoneal cavity for organ injury. When it is unclear whether the peritoneum has been penetrated, we proceed with a definitive evaluation to rule out peritoneal violation. Anterior wounds (i.e., those anterior to the midaxillary line) are evaluated for fascial penetration by means of local wound exploration. In the emergency department (ED), with sterile technique and local anesthesia, the wound is sharply extended to allow retraction of the subcutaneous tissue and visualization of the anterior fascia. If fascial penetration is evident, laparoscopy is performed in the operating room to look for peritoneal penetration; if peritoneal penetration is confirmed, a laparotomy is then done. In cooperative patients who have no history of abdominal surgery, it is often possible to perform diagnostic laparoscopy with local anesthesia in the ED by establishing pneumoperitoneum through a 5 mm trocar (e.g., Optiview; Ethicon Endo-Surgery, Cincinnati, Ohio) and maintaining a relatively low (7 mm Hg) intra-abdominal pressure to allow visualization of the peritoneum while maintaining patient comfort.

Several centers have reported favorable experiences with expectant management of anterior stab wounds.[7,8] Patients without evidence of peritonitis are admitted and monitored with serial physical examinations. As noted (see above), we prefer to determine the presence of peritoneal penetration at the time of presentation. The rationale for this approach is to avoid any delay in diagnosis of hollow viscus injury and to allow early discharge of patients with no peritoneal violation. Various centers have described both DPL and CT criteria for excluding peritoneal penetration.[9,10]

Wounds to the lower back or the flank (posterior to the midaxillary line), which carry a lower risk of intra-abdominal injury, are evaluated with CT, augmented by intravenous, oral, and rectal contrast studies. CT scanning has proved to be a reliable means not only of identifying posterior intraperitoneal violation but also of evaluating injury to retroperitoneal structures.[11]

Operative Management of Injuries at Specific Sites

When hollow viscus injury is suspected, antibiotics with broad-spectrum aerobic and anaerobic coverage should be administered before the skin incision. If injury is confirmed, the antibiotics should be continued for a 24-hour period. The EAST Practice Management Guidelines Workgroup has reviewed the available evidence regarding perioperative antibiotic use in the trauma setting.[12] Data from prospective studies clearly indicate that prolonging antibiotic administration beyond 24 hours provides no additional protection against surgical site infection (SSI).

Abdominal exploration is generally performed through a midline incision that is sufficiently extensive to permit evaluation of the entire peritoneal cavity. Once initial control of any significant bleeding has been obtained, the next step is to control any contamination from spilled GI contents. Babcock clamps are useful for temporarily controlling contamination from bowel perforations without causing injury to the bowel wall. Inspection commences in a systematic fashion, with any holes in the bowel controlled as they are found. In the setting of penetrating injury, when an odd number of hollow viscus perforations are encountered, a diligent search for an additional perforation is essential. An odd number of perforations implies that one of the wounds is tangential (or that the projectile is intraluminal); this is a diagnosis of exclusion.

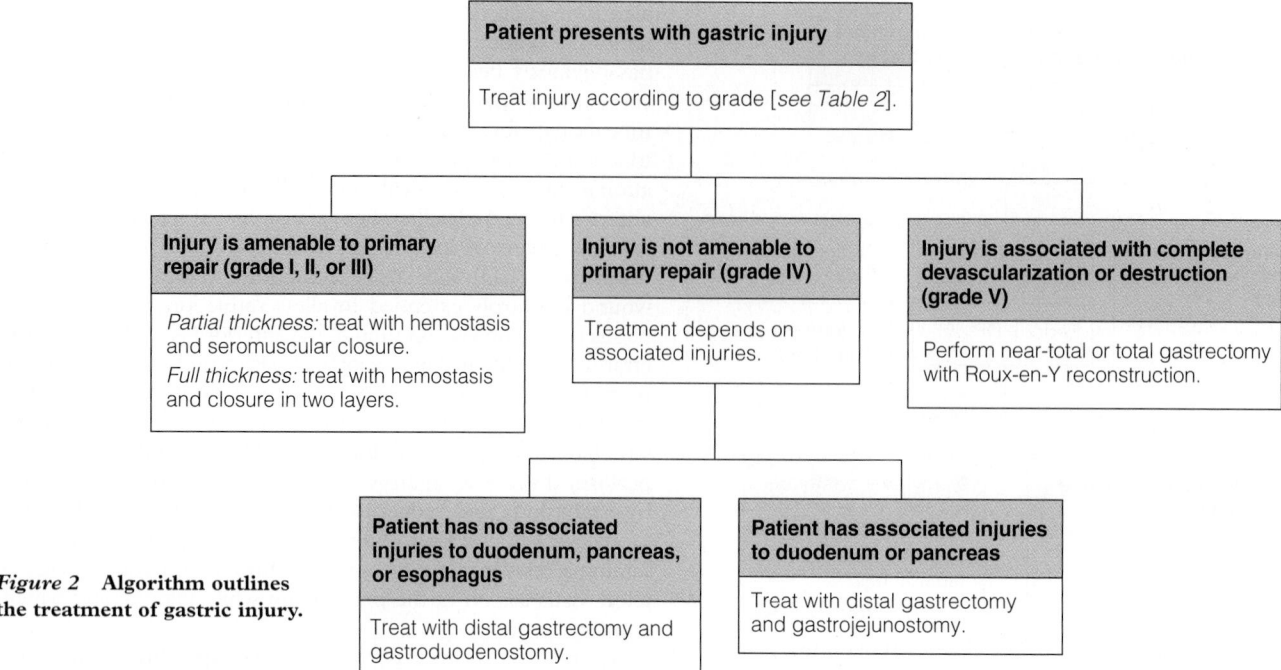

Figure 2 Algorithm outlines the treatment of gastric injury.

INJURIES TO THE STOMACH

Intraoperative evaluation of the stomach begins with full visualization of the anterior gastric surface from the pylorus to the esophagogastric junction. Proximal exposure is facilitated by incising the triangular ligament and retracting the left lateral section of the liver to the patient's right. The posterior aspect of the stomach is assessed by opening the gastrocolic ligament, which provides access to the lesser sac. Care must be taken to avoid injuring the vascular arcade of the greater curvature. While the stomach is elevated superiorly, the transverse colon is retracted inferiorly to expose the posterior gastric wall. Frequently, light adhesions between the posterior gastric wall and the retroperitoneum overlying the pancreas must be freed to provide full exposure. Alternatively, the greater omentum may be detached from its avascular attachment to the transverse colon to afford access to the lesser sac. Care must be taken to avoid placing excess tension on the greater curvature of the stomach and the short gastric vessels so as not to cause iatrogenic injury to the spleen. The greater and lesser curvatures should be closely inspected because the omental attachments may obscure an underlying gastric wound. Such inspection is particularly important in the setting of a small-caliber missile wound: the perforation can be remarkably small, and the serosal tissue damage in such cases is often subtle.

Treatment of a gastric injury is dictated by its severity [*see Figure 2*], which is classified according to the grading system developed by the American Association for the Surgery of Trauma (AAST) [*see Table 2*]. Intramural hematomas (grade I) are managed by means of unroofing and evacuation, followed by seromuscular closure with interrupted sutures. The great majority of gastric perforations are amenable to primary repair (grades II and III). In view of the propensity of the richly vascularized gastric wall to bleed at the site of injury, a two-layer technique is recommended to achieve adequate hemostasis. When the wound involves the pylorus, conversion to pyloroplasty to prevent stenosis is often beneficial. Suture repair of wounds at the cardioesophageal junction is reinforced by gastric fundoplication.

Some extensive wounds are not amenable to primary repair (grades IV and V). Such injuries include significant tissue loss or

gastric devascularization and often are associated with major vascular injury as a consequence of the proximity of the major vessels and the force necessary to cause such a significant injury. Patients with grade IV or V injuries often do not survive long enough to undergo laparotomy, and consequently, these extensive gastric wounds are rarely encountered. Grade IV injuries can usually be managed by means of a partial gastrectomy. Restoration of gastric outflow is accomplished with either a gastroduodenostomy or a gastrojejunostomy; the choice is dictated by the extent of the resection and the presence or absence of an associated duodenal or pancreatic injury. In the exceedingly rare event of complete gastric devascularization or destruction, a total gastrectomy is required; we have yet to encounter such a situation. Occasionally, reconstruction of intestinal continuity after resection should not be performed at the initial operation. Such a damage-control approach is indicated in the presence of the triad of acidosis, hypothermia, and coagulopathy.

In fasting patients, the stomach harbors low numbers of bacteria because of its low pH. In trauma victims, however, who, it seems, often arrive with full stomachs, a more neutral pH and a higher bacterial count can be expected. If a gastric perforation with significant contamination is encountered, secondary or delayed primary skin closure should be performed in view of the increased risk of SSI; this is particularly true when significant hemorrhage or associated injury is present, in which case the rate of intra-abdominal abscess formation may be as high as 24%.[13]

INJURIES TO THE SMALL INTESTINE

Injury to the small intestine is evaluated intraoperatively by "running the bowel": the small bowel and its mesentery are inspected in a systematic and comprehensive fashion from the ligament of Treitz caudad to the ileocecal valve. As active mesenteric bleeding is encountered, it is controlled by isolation and individual ligation of the bleeding vessels rather than by mass ligation of the mesentery, which may produce ischemia. Likewise, as bowel perforations are found, temporary control measures are rapidly initiated in an effort to prevent excessive or ongoing soilage. Once all bowel injuries are accounted for, the decision must be made

Table 2 AAST Organ Injury Scales for Stomach, Small Intestine, Colon, and Rectum

Injured Structure	AAST Grade*	Characteristics of Injury	AIS-90 Score
Stomach	I	Intramural hematoma < 3 cm; partial-thickness laceration	2
	II	Intramural hematoma ≥ 3 cm; small (< 3 cm) laceration	2
	III	Large (> 3 cm) laceration	3
	IV	Large laceration involving vessels on greater or lesser curvature	3
	V	Extensive (> 50%) rupture; stomach devascularized	4
Small bowel	I	Contusion or hematoma without devascularization; partial-thickness laceration	2
	II	Small (< 50% of circumference) laceration	3
	III	Large (≥ 50% of circumference) laceration without transection	3
	IV	Transection	4
	V	Transection with segmental tissue loss; devascularized segment	4
Colon	I	Contusion or hematoma; partial-thickness laceration	2
	II	Small (< 50% of circumference) laceration	3
	III	Large (≥ 50% of circumference) laceration	3
	IV	Transection	4
	V	Transection with tissue loss; devascularized segment	4
Rectosigmoid and rectum	I	Contusion or hematoma; partial-thickness laceration	2
	II	Small (< 50% of circumference) laceration	3
	III	Large (≥ 50% of circumference) laceration	4
	IV	Full-thickness laceration with perineal extension	5
	V	Devascularized segment	5

*Advance one grade for multiple injuries, up to grade III.
AIS-90—Abbreviated Injury Score, 1990 version   AAST—American Association for the Surgery of Trauma

whether to perform primary repair, resection of the injured segment, or some combination of the two. Primary repair of multiple injuries preserves bowel length and is generally preferred. At the discretion of the operating surgeon, resection of a segment containing multiple injuries may be performed to expedite the operation, provided that the amount of bowel to be resected is small enough that its loss would have only a negligible effect on digestive function.

Management of each individual wound is determined by its severity according to the AAST grading system [*see Figure 3 and Table 2*]. Small partial-thickness injuries (grade I) are managed by reapproximating the seromuscular layers with interrupted sutures. Small full-thickness wounds (grade II) are repaired with limited debridement and closure. Closure is performed in either one or two layers (we prefer a single-layer closure), and transverse closure is preferred to avoid luminal narrowing. Larger full-thickness wounds (grade III) may be repaired primarily if luminal narrowing can be avoided; otherwise, resection and anastomosis should be performed. Extensive wounds and wounds associated with devascularization (grades IV and V) are treated with resection and anastomosis. When mesenteric injury is encountered in the absence of bowel injury, the associated bowel must be closely assessed for evidence of vascular compromise. If the bowel appears viable, the rent in the mesentery should be reapproximated after bleeding is controlled to prevent an internal hernia. If there is evidence of vascular compromise, bowel resection and anastomosis are indicated.

Determination of intestinal viability begins with assessment of the bowel's appearance. Adjunctive measures, such as the use of a handheld Doppler device or fluorescein infusion with Wood lamp illumination, may facilitate assessment of perfusion in segments where viability is questionable. We generally prefer to use a handheld Doppler device because it is easy to use and is available at short notice in the OR. A probe applied directly to the antimesenteric side of the bowel wall effectively detects the presence of arterial flow, which reliably demonstrates viability.

Small bowel anastomoses are usually handsewn in one or two layers, though stapling devices may also be employed [*see 71 Intestinal Anastomosis*]. The choice of technique depends largely on surgeon preference. One multicenter retrospective study suggested that in the setting of trauma, stapled anastomoses had a higher complication rate than sutured anastomoses did[14]: overall, 13% of stapled anastomoses were associated with an intra-abdominal postoperative complication, compared with 5% of sutured anastomoses. Because this study did not separate small intestinal anastomoses from colonic anastomoses, it is unclear to what extent the results apply specifically to small bowel anastomoses. It is likely, however, that bowel edema contributes to staple line failure. If bowel edema is evident or anticipated, it may be prudent to perform a sutured anastomosis.

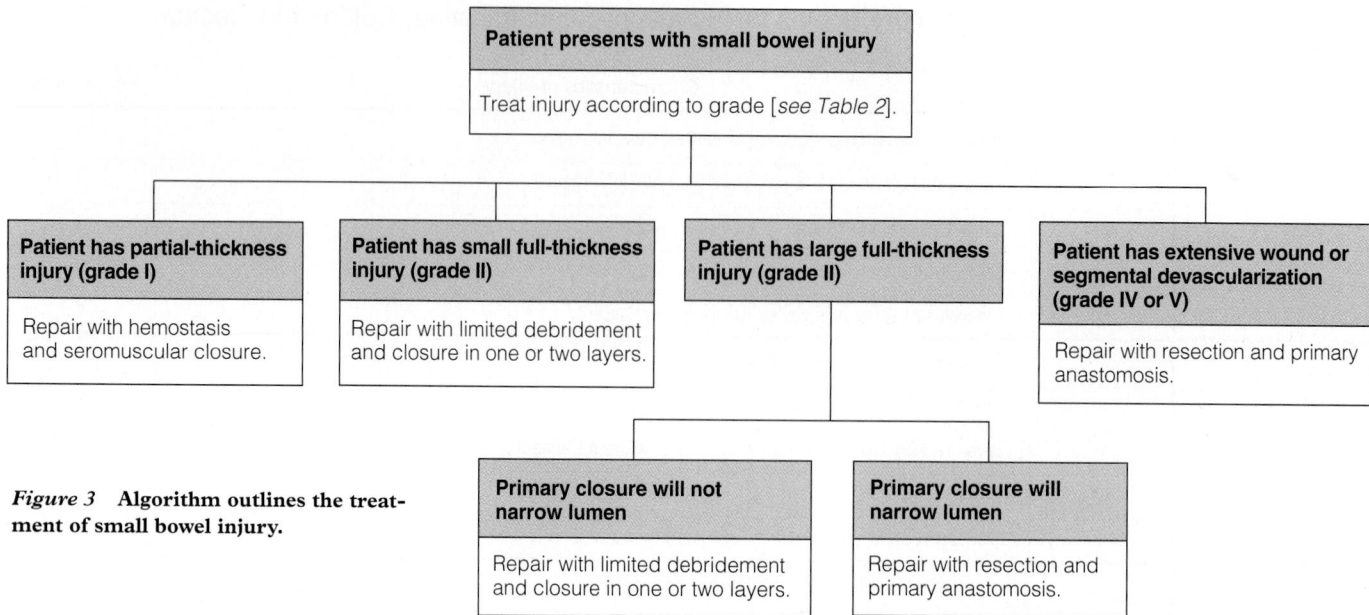

Figure 3 Algorithm outlines the treatment of small bowel injury.

INJURIES TO THE COLON

In World War II, colostomy was mandatory for penetrating colon trauma because of the significant morbidity associated with anastomotic suture line dehiscence.[15] In the ensuing years, experience with primary repair of penetrating colonic injuries in civilian settings suggested that primary repair could be performed safely and perhaps, in select cases, with less morbidity than colostomy.[16,17] This suggestion was confirmed in the late 1970s by a randomized, prospective study that demonstrated significantly lower rates of intra-abdominal infection in patients treated with primary repair than in those treated with colostomy.[18] In that early trial, high-risk patients (i.e., those with shock, hemorrhage, associated injuries, delayed presentation, significant peritoneal soilage, destructive wounds of the colon, or loss of abdominal wall integrity) were excluded from randomization and treated with colostomy. Currently, there is less concern for such risk factors, and primary repair is gaining wider acceptance.[19]

To direct management decisions, it is helpful to categorize penetrating colonic injuries as either nondestructive or destructive [see Figure 4].[20,21] Although blunt colonic injuries are considerably less common, we manage them in a similar fashion.

Nondestructive colonic injuries are defined as wounds that involve less than 50% of the bowel wall without devascularization. Such wounds account for approximately 80% of colon wounds and are amenable to primary suture repair with limited amounts of debridement. Sufficient data have been accumulated over the past 30 years to support primary repair as standard treatment for nondestructive colon wounds in the absence of peritonitis, regardless of associated injuries or comorbid conditions. Evaluation of the available prospective and retrospective data indicates that the suture line failure rate for primary repair is approximately 1%, which is less than the rate generally reported for elective colon and rectal surgery. Mortality associated with suture line failure in this setting is uncommon. The favorable morbidity and mortality profiles, along with the inherent benefits of avoiding colostomy, support primary repair as standard therapy for nondestructive wounds. Partial-thickness lacerations (grade I) are repaired with inverting seromuscular sutures. Full-thickness lacerations (grade II) may be closed in one or two layers.

Destructive colonic injuries are defined as wounds that com-

pletely transect the colon (grade IV) or involve tissue loss and devascularized segments (grade V). Optimal management of such wounds is less certain than optimal management of nondestructive wounds. Data from randomized and prospective trials demonstrate that resection and primary anastomosis can be performed safely.[22-25] It should be kept in mind, however, that these results are derived from a relatively small number of reported cases. The retrospective data indicate a higher incidence of suture line failure and a significant incidence of associated mortality, suggesting that resection and primary anastomosis may not be the optimal treatment for all colonic wounds.[20]

A 1994 report from our institution (University of Tennessee) concluded that patients with destructive colonic injuries who had comorbid medical conditions or transfusion requirements greater

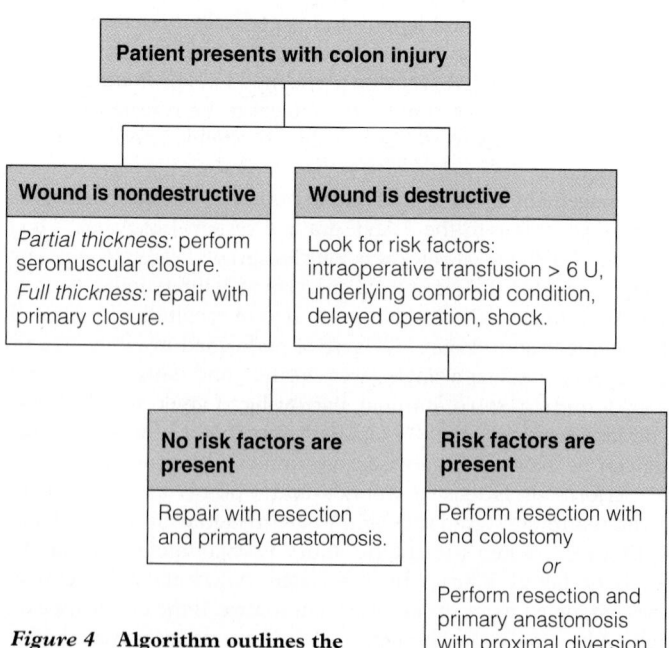

Figure 4 Algorithm outlines the treatment of colon injury.

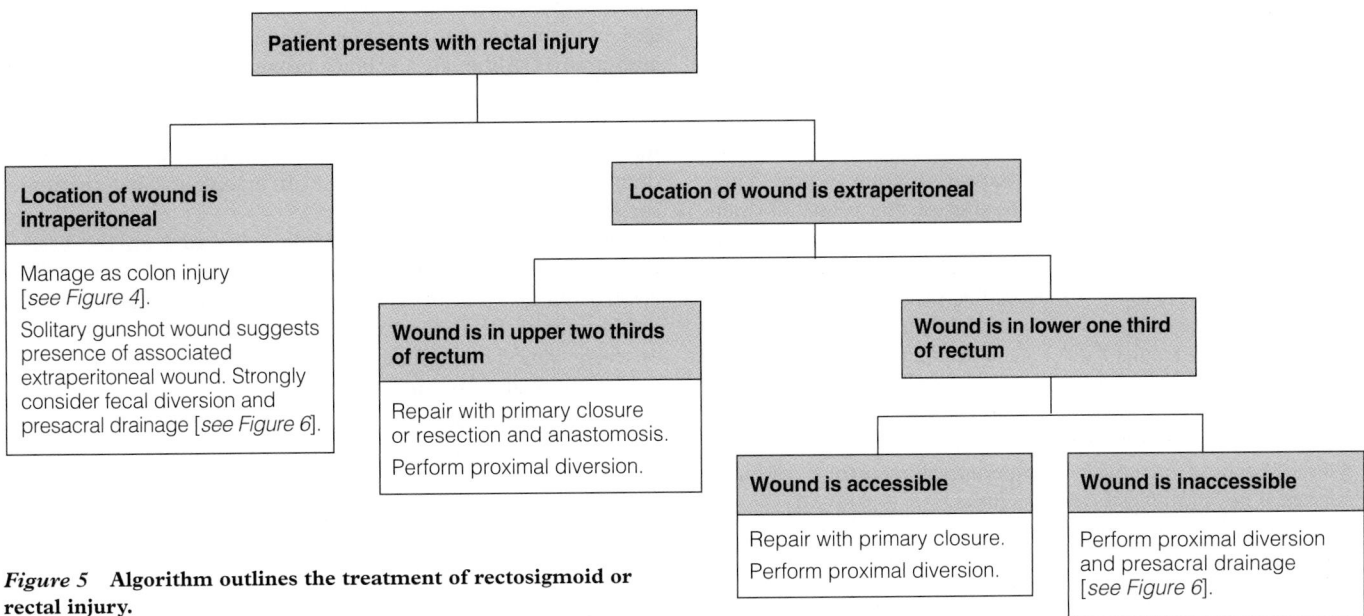

Figure 5 **Algorithm outlines the treatment of rectosigmoid or rectal injury.**

than 6 units of blood were at significantly higher risk for suture line breakdown when the wounds were managed with resection and primary anastomosis.[26] Other reported risk factors that may direct the surgeon toward fecal diversion include a Penetrating Abdominal Trauma Index (PATI) score greater than 25, shock, and a delayed operation.[27] It is our practice to manage these patients as high-risk patients and perform fecal diversion. Diversion may be accomplished by means of either loop colostomy (with an open or closed distal stoma) or end colostomy (with a mucous fistula or closure of the rectal stump) [*see 71 Intestinal Stomas*]. The diversion technique is dictated both by surgeon preference and by the nature of the colonic injury. In most civilian clinical practices, destructive wounds account for approximately 20% of all colon wounds encountered. Between 50% and 75% of destructive wounds do not have risk factors that prompt diversion. Thus, the overall diversion rate ranges from 5% to 10%. In our experience over the past several years, 90% to 95% of all colon wounds have been managed with primary repair or resection and anastomosis.

The potential risk of postoperative SSI associated with colonic injury should be considered at the time of initial laparotomy. Retained bullets or other projectiles that have penetrated the colon or rectum may act as nidi for abscess formation and should be removed when it is technically feasible to do so. Approximately 10% of these retained missiles result in soft tissue infection or osteomyelitis.[28] Delayed primary or secondary skin closure is recommended.

If colostomy is performed, it will eventually have to be closed in most cases. The mortality associated with colostomy closure is low, but the reported morbidity has varied considerably, ranging from 5% to 25% in single-institution studies.[29-31] We typically perform closure 2 to 3 months after hospital discharge to allow time for the resolution of the dense inflammatory adhesions that may form after laparotomy. Before closure, a contrast enema is obtained to confirm that no distal strictures or fistulas are present. Some surgeons maintain that early closure (within 2 weeks) is as safe as the traditional late closure (3 months), with a shorter operating time and less intraoperative blood loss, and suggest that it may also allow colostomy closure during the patient's initial hospitalization.[32] To date, however, this practice has not garnered wide enthusiasm.

Occasionally, blunt abdominal trauma associated with lap-belt use results in a large deserosalization injury to the cecum and ascending colon or to the sigmoid colon. In such cases, the serosa may be reapproximated with interrupted silk sutures in an accordion-type fashion, provided that the lumen is not significantly compromised by the imbrication of the submucosa. It is likely that subclinical luminal narrowing occurs frequently after such repairs, of which we rarely see sequelae. If significant luminal narrowing is anticipated or the serosal disruption is extensive enough to preclude reapproximation, resection of the injured segment with primary anastomosis is indicated.

INJURIES TO THE RECTUM

Recognition of rectal injuries requires diagnostic vigilance. All patients with a penetrating wound to the pelvis, perineum, buttock, or upper thigh should be evaluated for rectal injury. Digital examination for the presence of rectal blood is mandatory, but the absence of blood does not definitively rule out injury. Rigid proctoscopy should be performed whenever there is any suspicion of rectal injury.

It is our practice to classify rectal injuries according to anatomic criteria, which then dictate management [*see Figure 5*].[33] The anterior and lateral sidewalls of the upper two thirds of the rectum are serosalized; injuries in this region are classified as intraperitoneal and are managed in the same manner as colonic injuries [*see Figure 4*]. The upper two thirds of the rectum posteriorly and the lower one third of the rectum circumferentially are not serosalized; injuries in these regions are classified as extraperitoneal.

Extraperitoneal wounds in the upper two thirds are usually amenable to exploration and suture repair. Fecal diversion is also performed as an adjunctive measure and may be accomplished with either loop or end colostomy [*see 71 Intestinal Stomas*]. In select cases in which the wound is primarily intraperitoneal with minimal extraperitoneal involvement, diversion may be omitted.

Extraperitoneal wounds to the lower third of the rectum are usually explored and repaired, provided that the wound is easily accessible without risk to the associated neurovascular and genitourinary structures. Fecal diversion is recommended. Wounds that are difficult to reach are not explored and instead are managed with proximal fecal diversion and presacral drainage. Presacral drainage is performed with the patient in the lithotomy position [see Figure 6]. A curvilinear incision is made in the skin between the coccyx and the anus, and blunt dissection is employed to gain entry into the presacral space. Generally, we place one or two Penrose drains into this space and gradually withdraw them between postoperative days 5 and 7.

Whether presacral drainage is necessary is controversial. There is published prospective evidence to suggest that presacral drainage does not lessen morbidity[34]; however, this study did not make a distinction between accessible and inaccessible extraperitoneal wounds. Our view is that for inaccessible extraperitoneal wounds, presacral drainage is required to prevent retroperitoneal abscess formation, which results from fecal contamination of a relatively closed space and can produce significant morbidity in the form of retroperitoneal infection that may also track downward into the thighs. Accessible extraperitoneal wounds that are explored and repaired become effectively intraperitonealized; thus, presacral drainage is not required for these injuries.

As emphasized (see above), a tangential gunshot wound is a diagnosis of exclusion. This point is of particular importance when the wound involves the rectum, because mobilization and visualization may be limited by a narrow pelvis, a fat-laden mesorectum,

and, in many cases, a patient who is unstable as a result of associated injuries. Although a solitary proximal rectal gunshot wound may truly be tangential (or the projectile may be intraluminal), an associated distal extraperitoneal wound is often present. After primary repair of the proximal wound, fecal diversion and presacral drainage should be performed, as with inaccessible extraperitoneal rectal injuries.

Distal rectal washout was initially advocated on the basis of experience gained during the Vietnam War.[35] In the majority of civilian studies since then, however, distal rectal washout has had no significant effect on morbidity.[33,36-38] It may be useful in cases of severe wound contamination or fecal impaction, but in general, it does not seem to be an important adjunct to the management of rectal injuries. Typically, distal rectal washout involves lavage of the rectum distal to the injury with 3 to 6 L of irrigant via an irrigation tube placed into the distal limb of a loop colostomy. The irrigant may be normal saline, a genitourinary irrigant, or an antiseptic solution. Digital rectal dilatation is performed to facilitate drainage of the irrigant. Care should be taken to protect the midline wound with a polyethylene or similar barrier to reduce the risk of wound contamination during the washout.

Figure 6 **Presacral drainage is provided through a curved incision midway between the anus and the tip of the coccyx. With blunt dissection, two fingers are inserted between the rectum and the hollow of the sacrum. Penrose drains are inserted and sutured to the skin.**

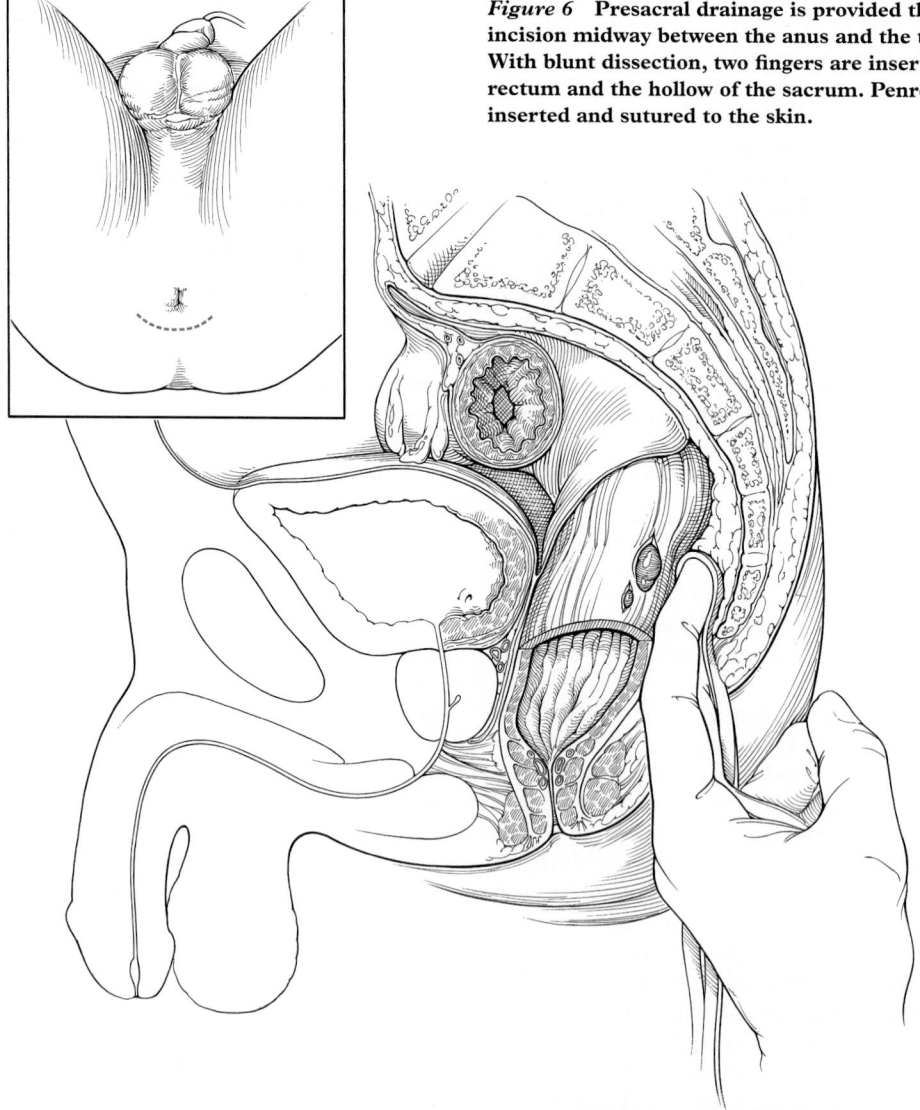

References

1. Watts DD, Fakhry SM: Incidence of hollow viscus injury in blunt trauma: an analysis from 275,557 trauma admissions from the EAST multi-institutional trial. J Trauma 54:289, 2003

2. Fakhry SM, Brownstein M, Watts DD, et al: Relatively short diagnostic delays (< 8 hours) produce morbidity and mortality in blunt small bowel injury: an analysis of time to operative intervention in 198 patients from a multicenter experience. J Trauma 48:408, 2000

3. Current diagnostic approaches lack sensitivity in the diagnosis of perforated blunt small bowel injury: analysis from 275,557 trauma admissions from the EAST multi-institutional HVI trial. EAST Multi-Institutional Hollow Viscus Injury Research Group. J Trauma 54:2956, 2003

4. Rozycki GS, Ballard RB, Feliciano DV, et al: Surgeon-performed ultrasound for the assessment of truncal injuries: lessons learned from 1540 patients. Ann Surg 228:557, 1998

5. Malhotra AK, Fabian TC, Katsis SB, et al: Blunt bowel and mesenteric injuries: the role of screening computed tomography. J Trauma 48:991, 2000

6. Alyono D, Perry JF Jr: Significance of repeating diagnostic peritoneal lavage. Surgery 91:656, 1982

7. Demetriades D, Rabinowitz B: Indications for operation in abdominal stab wounds: a prospective study of 651 patients. Ann Surg 205:129, 1987

8. Leppäniemi AK, Haapiainen RK: Selective nonoperative management of abdominal stab wounds: prospective, randomized study. World J Surg 20:1101, 1996

9. Gonzalez RP, Turk B, Falimirski ME, et al: Abdominal stab wounds: diagnostic peritoneal lavage criteria for emergency room discharge. J Trauma 51:939, 2001

10. Shanmuganathan K, Mirvis SE, Chiu WC, et al: Penetrating torso trauma: triple-contrast helical CT in peritoneal violation and organ injury—a prospective study in 200 patients. Radiology 231:775, 2004

11. Kirton OC, Wint D, Thrasher B, et al: Stab wounds to the back and flank in the hemodynamically stable patient: a decision algorithm based on contrast-enhanced computed tomography with colonic opacification. Am J Surg 173:189, 1997

12. Luchette FA, Borzotta AP, Croce MA, et al: Practice management guidelines for prophylactic antibiotic use in penetrating abdominal trauma:

the EAST Practice Management Guidelines Work Group. J Trauma 48:508, 2000

13. Croce MA, Fabian TC, Patton JH Jr, et al: Impact of stomach and colon injuries on intra-abdominal abscess and the synergistic effect of hemorrhage and associated injury. J Trauma 45:649, 1998

14. Brundage SI, Jurkovich GJ, Hoyt DB, et al: Stapled versus sutured gastrointestinal anastomoses in the trauma patient: a multicenter trial. J Trauma 51:1054, 2001

15. Office of the Surgeon General. Circular Letter No. 178. October 23, 1943

16. Axelrod AJ, Hanley PH: Treatment of perforating wounds of the colon and rectum: a reevaluation. South Med J 60:811, 1967

17. Woodhall JP, Ochsner A: The management of perforating injuries of the colon and rectum in civilian practice. Surgery 29:305, 1951

18. Stone HH, Fabian TC: Management of perforating colon trauma: randomization between primary closure and exteriorization. Ann Surg 190:430, 1979

19. Demetriades D, Murray JA, Chan L, et al: Penetrating colon injuries requiring resection: diversion or primary anastomosis? An AAST prospective multicenter study. J Trauma 50:765, 2001

20. Cayten CG, Fabian TC, Garcia VF, et al: Patient management guidelines for penetrating intraperitoneal colon injuries. Trauma Practice Guidelines. Kurek S Jr, Ed. Eastern Association for the Surgery of Trauma, 1998

21. Miller PR, Fabian TC, Croce MA, et al: Improving outcomes following penetrating colon wounds: application of a clinical pathway. Ann Surg 235:775, 2002

22. Gonzalez RP, Falimirski ME, Holevar MR: Further evaluation of colostomy in penetrating colon injury. Am Surg 66:342, 2000

23. Chappuis CW, Frey DJ, Dietzen CD, et al: Management of penetrating colon injuries: a prospective randomized trial. Ann Surg 213:492, 1991

24. Sasaki LS, Allaben RD, Golwala R, et al: Primary repair of colon injuries: a prospective randomized study. J Trauma 39:895, 1995

25. Falcone RE, Wanamaker SR, Santanello SA, et al: Colorectal trauma: primary repair or anastomosis with intracolonic bypass vs. ostomy. Dis Colon Rectum 35:957, 1992

26. Stewart RM, Fabian TC, Croce MA, et al: Is resection with primary anastomosis following destructive colon wounds always safe? Am J Surg 168:316, 1994

27. Cornwell EE 3rd, Velmahos GC, Berne TV, et al: The fate of colonic suture lines in high-risk trauma patients: a prospective analysis. J Am Coll Surg 187:58, 1998

28. Poret HA 3rd, Fabian TC, Croce MA, et al: Analysis of septic morbidity following gunshot wounds to the colon: the missile is an adjuvant for abscess. J Trauma 31:1088, 1991

29. Crass RA, Salbi F, Trunkey DD: Colostomy closure after colon injury: a low-morbidity procedure. J Trauma 27:1237, 1987

30. Pachter HL, Hoballah JJ, Corcoran TA, et al: The morbidity and financial impact of colostomy closure in trauma patients. J Trauma 30:1510, 1990

31. Bulger EM, McMahon K, Jurkovich GJ: The morbidity of penetrating colon injury. Injury 34:41, 2003

32. Velmahos GC, Degiannis E, Wells M, et al: Early closure of colostomies in trauma patients—a prospective randomized trial. Surgery 118:815, 1995

33. McGrath V, Fabian TC, Croce MA, et al: Rectal trauma: management based on anatomic distinctions. Am Surg 64:1136, 1998

34. Gonzalez RP, Falimirski ME, Holevar MR: The role of presacral drainage in the management of penetrating rectal injuries. J Trauma 45:656, 1998

35. Lavenson GS, Cohen A: Management of rectal injuries. Am J Surg 122:226, 1971

36. Burch JM, Feliciano DV, Mattox KL: Colostomy and drainage for civilian rectal injuries: is that all? Ann Surg 209:600, 1989

37. Thomas DD, Levison MA, Dykstra BJ, et al: Management of rectal injuries: dogma versus practice. Am Surg 56:507, 1990

38. Ivatury RR, Licata J, Gunduz Y, et al: Management options in penetrating rectal injuries. Am Surg 57:50, 1991

Acknowledgment

Figure 6   Susan Brust, C.M.I.

108 INJURIES TO THE PANCREAS AND DUODENUM

Gregory J. Jurkovich, M.D., F.A.C.S.

Pancreatic and duodenal injuries continue to challenge trauma surgeons. The relative rarity of these unforgiving injuries, the difficulty of diagnosing them in a timely manner, and the high morbidity and mortality associated with them justify the anxiety they evoke. Because of the deep, central, and retroperitoneal location of the pancreas and much of the duodenum, trauma to these organs is infrequent; however, this relatively protected anatomic location also is the reason for the diagnostic difficulty and contributes to the high morbidity and mortality. Mortality for pancreatic trauma ranges from 9% to 34%. Duodenal injuries are similarly lethal, with mortality ranging from 6% to 25%. Complications after duodenal or pancreatic injuries are alarmingly frequent, occurring in 30% to 60% of patients.[1,2] If these injuries are recognized early, treatment is straightforward, and morbidity and mortality are low; if they are recognized late, they typically follow a protracted, difficult clinical course, often ending in a devastating outcome.

Injuries to the Pancreas

DIAGNOSIS

The two most important determinants of outcome after pancreatic injury are (1) the status of the main pancreatic duct and (2) the time interval between initial trauma and definitive management of a duct injury. These determinants were probably first recognized and emphasized in 1962 by Baker and associates.[3] Two subsequent reviews of pancreatic trauma cases at the University of Louisville confirmed the importance of determining pancreatic duct status. The first found that resection of distal duct injuries, as opposed to drainage alone, significantly lowered postoperative morbidity and mortality.[4] The second confirmed this observation by noting that pancreatic resection distal to the site of duct injury caused mortality at the University to decrease from 19% to 3%.[5] Experience at my institution (University of Washington School of Medicine) supported this finding, in that accurate determination of the status of the pancreatic duct with intraoperative pancreatography was found to reduce the complication rate from 55% to 15%.[6]

Unfortunately, the cross-sectional body-imaging techniques currently employed in multiply injured patients (e.g., abdominal computed tomography) are not sensitive enough for accurate assessment of duct status, and operation for direct inspection carries its own morbidity. Thus, the main challenge in addressing potential pancreatic trauma is to make an early determination of whether or not a pancreatic duct injury has occurred.

Which diagnostic techniques are most useful in a patient with a possible pancreatic injury depends on the mechanism of injury, the presence or absence of other indications for early laparotomy, and the time that has elapsed since the initial abdominal insult occurred. If the patient has a clear indication for laparotomy, there is little or no need for preoperative evaluation directed at identifying a possible pancreatic injury, because the diagnosis of such injury must be made intraoperatively. If, however, the patient does not require immediate laparotomy for hemorrhage or bowel perforation, establishing the presence of pancreatic injury is a considerable challenge, made more difficult by the knowledge that a missed pancreatic duct injury has dire consequences for the patient.[7-10]

There are isolated reports of patients with complete duct transection who remain asymptomatic for weeks, months, or even years after the initial injury.[5,7,8,11] More commonly, however, patients with pancreatic duct injuries that were initially missed manifest an abdominal crisis within a few days after the injury.[12-14] The reasons why physical signs and symptoms may not develop promptly are related to the retroperitoneal location of the pancreas, the inactivity of pancreatic enzymes after an isolated injury, and the decreased secretion of pancreatic fluid after trauma. Early identification of a subtle pancreatic injury therefore depends on a high index of suspicion, a carefully planned approach, and close observation.

A high index of suspicion is warranted in any patient who has sustained a direct high-energy blow to the epigastrium—for example, from a crushed steering wheel (in an adult) or a bicycle or tricycle handlebar (in a child).[15,16] The energy of impact causes the retroperitoneal structures to be crushed against the spine, and the pancreas is typically transected at this point. The presence of soft tissue contusion in the upper abdomen or disruption of the lower ribs or costal cartilages should suggest possible pancreatic injury. Epigastric pain that is out of proportion to the abdominal examination findings is often another clue to a retroperitoneal injury.

Although the highest concentration of amylase in the human body is in the pancreas, hyperamylasemia is not a reliable indicator of pancreatic trauma. In one series, only 8% of hyperamylasemic patients with blunt abdominal trauma had pancreatic duct injuries.[17] As many as 40% of patients with pancreatic injuries may initially have normal serum amylase levels.[18,19] In addition, there is evidence that isolated brain injury can cause elevated amylase[20] or lipase levels[21] through a central mechanism that remains to be clarified. Nonetheless, the presence of hyperamylasemia should raise the index of suspicion for pancreatic injury. The time between pancreatic duct injury and serum amylase determination may be critical. In a report of 73 patients with documented blunt injury to the pancreas, serum amylase levels were elevated in 61 patients (84%) and normal in 12 (16%).[22] Patients with elevated serum amylase levels were assayed 7 ± 1.5 hours after injury, whereas those with normal levels were assayed 1.3 ± 0.2 hours after injury. The investigators concluded that determination of serum amylase levels within 3 hours after injury did not yield diagnostic results.

Review of the available data suggests that the sensitivity of serum amylase level determination in detecting blunt pancreatic trauma ranges from 48% to 85% and that the specificity ranges from 0% to 81%.[1] The negative predictive value of the serum amylase level after blunt trauma is about 95%.[18,19,23] The sensitivity and the positive predictive value may be increased if the serum amylase level is obtained more than 3 hours after injury. The conclusion to be drawn is that 95% of blunt abdominal trauma patients with normal amylase levels will not have a pancreatic injury.

An elevated amylase level in serum or peritoneal lavage effluent does not necessarily confirm the presence of a pancreatic injury, but it does mandate further evaluation.

Blunt abdominal trauma patients with hyperamylasemia in whom the results of abdominal examination are reliable and benign are carefully observed, and the amylase level is measured again after several hours. Persistent elevation of serum amylase levels or the development of abdominal symptoms is an indication for further evaluation, which may include abdominal CT, endoscopic retrograde cholangiopancreatography (ERCP), or surgical exploration. If the abdominal examination initially yields equivocal or unreliable results in a hemodynamically stable patient with hyperamylasemia, a dual-contrast (i.e., intravenous and oral) abdominal CT scan should be done as part of the initial evaluation. If abdominal symptoms subsequently develop or the amylase level does not return to normal, directed evaluation of the pancreas by means of repeat abdominal CT, ERCP, or surgical exploration is warranted.

Overall, abdominal CT is reported to be 70% to 80% sensitive and specific for diagnosing pancreatic injury, though its accuracy is largely dependent on the experience of the interpreter, the quality of the scanner, and the time elapsed since injury.[24-26] Characteristic CT findings associated with pancreatic injury include direct visualization of a parenchymal fracture, an intrapancreatic hematoma, fluid in the lesser sac, fluid separating the splenic vein and the pancreatic body, a thickened left anterior renal fascia, and a retroperitoneal hematoma or fluid collection. These findings often are subtle and rarely are all present in one patient.[27] If the patient is examined immediately after injury, some of the CT signs of pancreatic injury may not yet be apparent, which may be part of the explanation for the false negative CT scans reported in as many as 40% of patients with significant pancreatic injuries.[28] This possibility is not sufficient grounds for delaying CT evaluation, but it is an argument for repeating CT if symptoms persist.

ERCP has no role in the acute evaluation of hemodynamically unstable patients, but numerous reports over the past decade have indicated that it can be useful in the diagnosis and management of pancreatic trauma. Currently, ERCP is the best available modality for imaging the pancreatic duct and its divisions, but it usually involves anesthesia, and it is not readily or widely available. For the most part, ERCP has been used in the setting of a late or missed diagnosis of pancreatic duct injury, occasionally with transductal stenting to manage the injury, particularly in children.[29-33] Appropriate application of ERCP is an evolving issue that will continue to foster investigations, but any application will continue to be based on the principle of timely diagnosis, recognition, and management of pancreatic duct injury.[4,34] If ERCP is done early and shows intact pancreatic ducts (including the secondary and tertiary radicles) without any extravasation, nonoperative therapy is permissible if no associated injuries are present.[35] The difficulties in this management scheme are determining which patients should undergo ERCP and getting the ERCP accomplished promptly.[36,37]

Magnetic resonance imaging has emerged as a potentially valuable technique for evaluation of the pancreatic duct.[38,39] Although to date, magnetic resonance pancreatography (MRP) has primarily been employed in elective settings, it has also been employed as a noninvasive alternative method of determining the status of the main pancreatic duct in patients with pancreatic injuries. Early reports suggest that MRP is unreliable early after injury but is useful for delayed diagnosis and management.[10] Further study of its sensitivity and specificity in this setting appears warranted.

Intraoperative Evaluation

Careful inspection of the pancreas and classification of injuries [see Management, Classification of Pancreatic Injuries, below] are often complicated by the extent and severity of associated injuries and occasionally hindered by the reluctance of the surgeon to mobilize retroperitoneal structures. Clues suggesting pancreatic injury include the injury mechanisms described (see above), the presence of an upper abdominal wall contusion or abrasion, and concomitant lower thoracic spine fractures. The presence of an upper abdominal central retroperitoneal hematoma, edema around the pancreatic gland and the lesser sac, and retroperitoneal bile staining mandate thorough pancreatic inspection.

Inspection of the pancreas requires complete exposure of the gland. First, the lesser sac is opened through the gastrocolic ligament just outside the gastroepiploic vessels. This exposure is carried far to the patient's left, fully opening the lesser sac and freeing the transverse colon. The transverse colon is then retracted downward and the stomach upward and anteriorly [see Figure 1]. Frequently, there are a few adhesions between the posterior stomach and the anterior surface of the pancreas that must be incised. Next, a complete Kocher maneuver is performed to provide adequate visualization of the pancreatic head and the uncinate process. In addition, mobilization of the hepatic flexure of the colon (a frequently overlooked maneuver) greatly facilitates visualization and bimanual examination of the head and neck of the pancreas. Inspection of the pancreatic tail requires exposure of the splenic hilum. If the injury involves the tail, the peritoneal attachments lateral to the spleen and colon are divided, and the colon, the spleen, and the body and tail of the pancreas are then mobilized forward and medially by creating a plane between the kidney and the pancreas with blunt finger dissection. This maneuver permits bimanual palpation of the pancreas and inspection of its posterior surface.

Injuries to the major pancreatic duct occur in perhaps 15% to 20% of cases of pancreatic trauma. At my institution, of 193 patients with pancreatic injuries managed over a period of 15 years, only 27 (14%) had grade III injuries, and 10 (5%) had grade IV or V injuries.[2] Studies from the 1970s and 1980s observed that penetrating trauma was more likely to cause pancreatic duct injury than blunt trauma was,[40,41] but subsequent reviews did not confirm these observations.[2,42]

The majority of pancreatic duct injuries, regardless of mechanism, can be diagnosed through careful inspection of the injury tract after adequate exposure. All penetrating wounds should be traced from the entry point through the surrounding tissue to the exit point or the end of the tract. If the pancreas was damaged by a knife or a bullet, it is necessary to determine the integrity of the major pancreatic duct. With most penetrating wounds to the margins of the gland, the pancreas can be inspected directly and duct integrity confirmed. With penetrating wounds to the head, neck, or central portion of the pancreas, however, further evaluation is often required. Occasionally, intravenous injection of 1 to 2 μg of cholecystokinin pancreozymin (CCK-PZ) may stimulate pancreatic secretions enough to allow an otherwise unrecognized major pancreatic duct injury to be identified. The remaining few injuries may necessitate the use of more elaborate investigative techniques, including intraoperative pancreatography (see below).

Minor blunt contusions or lacerations of the pancreatic substance usually do not necessitate further evaluation of the pancreatic duct and can be effectively managed with closed suction drainage. The presence of an intact pancreatic capsule, however, does not necessarily rule out complete division of the pancreatic

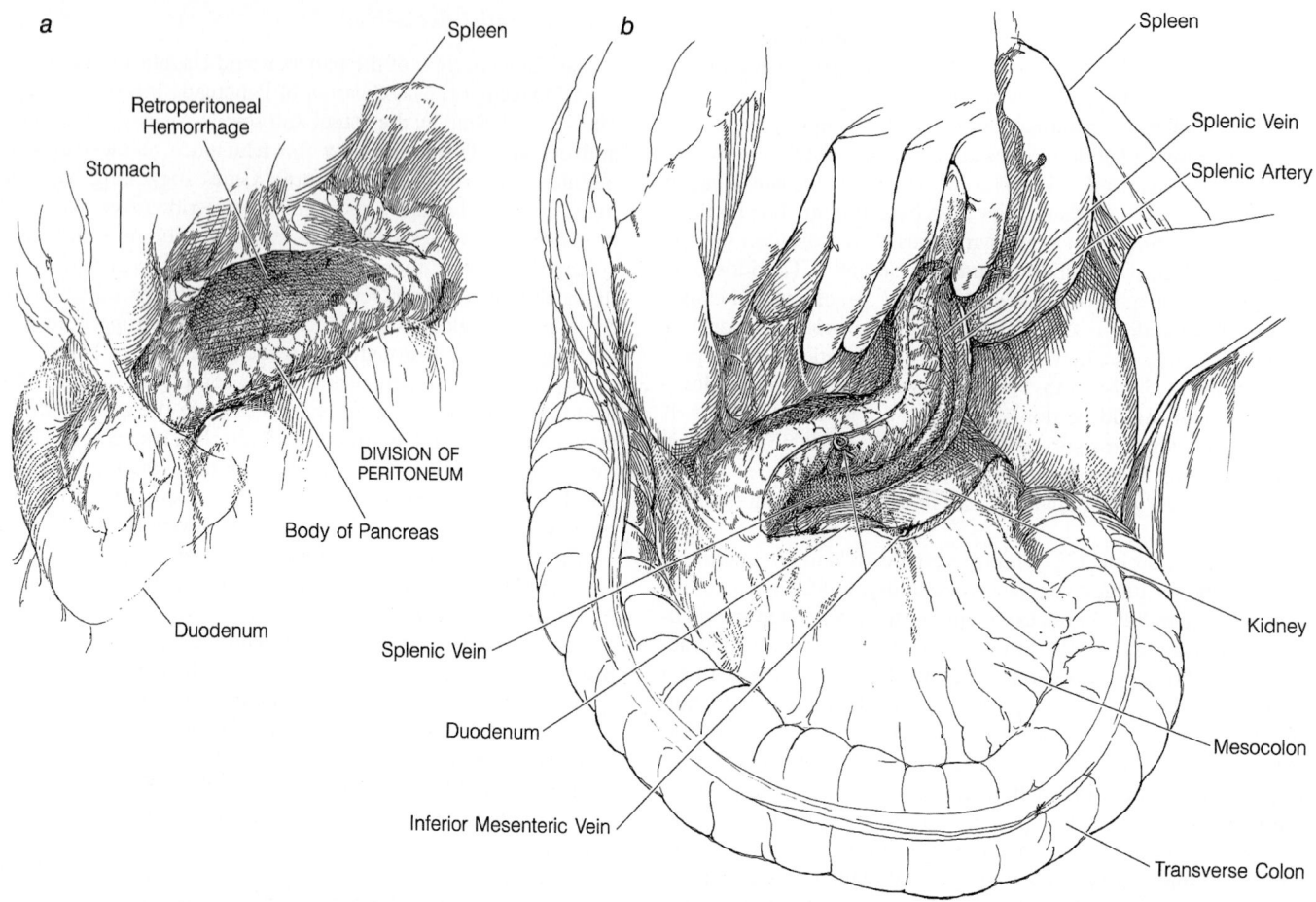

Figure 1 Illustrated is the appearance of a contusion to the body of the pancreas overlying the vertebral column, as seen from the lesser sac (*a*). The pancreas is mobilized to determine whether a fracture is present and to assess the likelihood of a duct injury. This exposure is best accomplished by dissecting along the inferior border of the gland, dividing the inferior mesenteric vein if necessary, and reflecting the pancreas superiorly (*b*).

duct, and on rare occasions, a blunt impact on the pancreas can result in transection of the major duct without complete transection of the gland.[5] Under these circumstances, establishing the status of the major duct system is an essential step in determining therapy and in anticipating late morbidity and mortality. In one study, routine performance of intraoperative pancreatography when proximal pancreatic duct injury was suspected reduced postoperative morbidity from 55% to 15%.[6]

Intraoperative imaging of the pancreatic duct can be performed with ERCP, direct open ampullary cannulation, or needle cholangiopancreatography. Intraoperative ERCP is cumbersome and often difficult to coordinate during an emergency operation, but it has been used in this setting.[43] Duodenotomy and direct ampullary cannulation—or even transection of the tail of the pancreas and distal duct cannulation—have been employed in the past, but as a consequence of advances in perioperative imaging, improvements in exposure and direct visualization of the pancreas, and effective use of wide closed suction drainage and postoperative ERCP, these very invasive diagnostic methods of imaging the pancreatic duct have largely been abandoned.[44] Needle cholecystocholangiopancreatography remains a useful intraoperative adjunct in the evaluation of the pancreatic duct. This technique involves cannulating the gallbladder with an 18-gauge angiocatheter and injecting 30 to 75 ml of three-quarter–strength water-

soluble contrast material under fluoroscopic guidance. It typically yields clear images of the biliary tree, and in one study, it successfully visualized the pancreatic duct in 64% of the patients (7/11).[2] Contracture of the sphincter of Oddi from I.V. morphine administration may enhance the likelihood of pancreatic duct visualization. A cholecystectomy is not necessary after this procedure.

MANAGEMENT

Classification of Pancreatic Injuries

Classification of pancreatic injuries is based on the status of the pancreatic duct and the site of injury relative to the neck of the pancreas. Several different classification systems have been devised to catalogue pancreatic injuries.[39,44,45] At present, the most widely used system is the one devised by the American Association for the Surgery of Trauma (AAST) [*see Table 1*], which addresses the key issues of parenchymal disruption and major pancreatic duct status by focusing on the anatomic location of the injury for the more severe (grade III to V) injuries.[46]

The management alternatives for proximal pancreatic duct injuries differ from those for distal duct and parenchymal injuries [*see Figure 2*]. For parenchymal contusions or lacerations with minimal or no parenchymal tissue loss and no duct injury (grade I or II), the only treatment required is external drainage. For combined

Table 1 AAST Organ Injury Scales for Pancreas and Duodenum

Injured Structure	AAST Grade*	Characteristics of Injury	AIS-90 Score
Pancreas	I	Small hematoma without duct injury; superficial laceration without duct injury	2
	II	Large hematoma without duct injury or tissue loss; major laceration without duct injury or tissue loss	2; 3
	III	Distal transection or parenchymal laceration with duct injury	3
	IV	Proximal† transection or parenchymal laceration involving ampulla	4
	V	Massive disruption of pancreatic head	5
Duodenum	I	Single-segment hematoma; partial-thickness laceration without perforation	2; 3
	II	Multiple-segment hematoma; small (< 50% of circumference) laceration	2; 4
	III	Large laceration (50%–75% of circumference of segment D2 or 50%–100% of circumference of segment D1, D3, or D4)	4
	IV	Very large (75%–100%) laceration of segment D2; rupture of ampulla or distal CBD	5
	V	Massive duodenopancreatic injury; devascularization of duodenum	5

*Advance one grade for multiple injuries, up to grade III.
†Proximal pancreas is to the patient's right of the superior mesenteric vein.
AAST—American Association for the Surgery of Trauma AIS-90—Abbreviated Injury Score, 1990 version CBD—common bile duct

duodenal and pancreatic head injuries that include the major duct or the ampulla, the required treatment is a combined pancreatico-duodenectomy (Whipple procedure). The difficult decisions in managing pancreatic trauma involve patients with parenchymal disruption and major duct injury. By focusing on the anatomic location of duct and parenchymal injury (proximal versus distal), the AAST classification provides a useful management guide.

Grades I and II: Contusions and Lacerations without Duct Injury

Minor pancreatic contusions, hematomas, and capsular lacerations (grade I) account for about 50% of all pancreatic injuries; lacerations of the pancreatic parenchyma without major duct disruption or tissue loss (grade II) account for an additional 25%. These injuries are treated with hemostasis and adequate external drainage.[47] No attempt should be made to repair capsular lacerations, because closure may result in a pancreatic pseudocyst, whereas a controlled pancreatic fistula is usually self-limiting. Soft closed suction drains (Jackson–Pratt) are preferred to Penrose drains or sump drains because intra-abdominal abscess formation is less likely, effluent is more reliably collected, and the skin excoriation at the exit site is significantly less with closed suction drains.[15,48,49] Drains are removed when the amylase concentrations in the drains are lower than the serum concentration, which generally occurs within 24 to 48 hours. An international consensus group has defined pancreatic fistula as the persistence of any measurable volume of drain output on or after postoperative day 3 with an amylase content higher than three times the serum amylase content.[50] This group has also defined three grades of pancreatic fistula complications [see Complications, below]. Drains are generally left in situ until there is no evidence of pancreatic leakage.

Nutrition should be provided via the oral or gastric route as soon as possible. In patients with severe pancreatic injuries, however, prolonged gastric ileus or pancreatic complications may preclude standard gastric feeding. Because most tube-feeding formulas are high in fat and increase pancreatic effluent volume and amylase concentration, elemental diets, which have a lower fat content and a higher pH and tend to be less stimulating to the pancreas, are preferred.[51,52]

Creation of a needle-catheter jejunostomy or a small-feeding-tube jejunostomy at the time of the initial celiotomy should be considered for all patients with grade III to V pancreatic injuries. This measure allows early postoperative enteral nutrition and avoids committing patients who cannot tolerate oral or gastric feedings to total parenteral nutrition (TPN). Surgically placed feeding tubes are, however, associated with some degree of morbidity. In a study from my institution, feeding jejunostomies had a major complication rate of 4% in severely injured patients.[53] Needle-catheter jejunostomies were associated with fewer complications than Witzel-tube jejunostomies—hence my preference for the smaller-caliber feeding tube.

Grade III: Distal Transection or Distal Parenchymal Injury with Duct Disruption

The anatomic distinction between the proximal and the distal pancreas is generally defined by the superior mesenteric vessels passing behind the pancreas at the junction of the pancreatic head and body. In the gland itself, there is no true anatomic distinction between the head, the body, and the tail, but dividing the organ into these three parts is useful for estimating residual pancreatic endocrine and exocrine function. A 1994 study found that a distal pancreatic resection at the portal vein removed an average of 56% of the gland by weight (range, 36% to 69%).[54] Because most blunt-trauma pancreatic injuries occur at the spine, which is just to the patient's left of the portal vein as it crosses behind the pancreas, a distal pancreatectomy in this circumstance involves resecting, on average, 56% of the gland. A resection at the common bile duct (CBD), on the other hand, removes an average of 89% of the gland (range, 64% to 95%). Although there have been reports of normal endocrine and exocrine function after a 90% pancreatectomy, every possible effort should be made to leave at least 20% of the pancreatic tissue in situ to minimize postoperative complications.[55,56]

Distal parenchymal transection, particularly if it involves disruption of the main pancreatic duct, is best treated by means of distal pancreatectomy [see Figure 3]. If there is any concern regarding the status of the remaining proximal main pancreatic duct, intraoperative pancreatography should be performed through the open end of the proximal duct. If the remaining proximal duct is normal, the transected duct should be identified and closed with a direct U stitch ligature using nonabsorbable monofilament suture material.[57] The parenchyma may be closed with a large (4.8 mm) TA-55 stapler[57,58]; however, I find that this crushes the residual pancreas excessively, and I prefer to place mattress sutures through the full thickness of the pancreatic gland from the anterior to the posterior capsule to minimize leakage from the transected parenchyma. Although most surgeons prefer nonabsorbable suture material for pancreatic stump closure, one report found that complication rates were lower when absorbable polyglycolic acid sutures were employed.[34] A small omental patch may be used to buttress the surface, and a drain should be left near the transection line.

Concerns about the possibility of overwhelming postsplenectomy infection (OPSI) and subphrenic abscess formation after splenectomy have prompted several authors to consider distal pancreatectomy without splenectomy. The technical challenge in pancreatectomy with splenic salvage is how to isolate the pancreatic branch vessels off the splenic vein and artery and ligate them without causing injury to the splenic hilum and thrombosis of the splenic vein. Generous mobilization of the entire pancreatic gland and the spleen is a prerequisite. On average, there are 22 tributaries of the splenic vein and seven branches of the splenic artery that must be ligated.[59] One report suggested that this maneuver would increase operating time by an average of 50 minutes (range, 37 to 80 minutes).[60] Another reported splenic salvage in 21 (64%) of the 33 patients who underwent distal pancreatic resection.[13] The increased operating time and the potential blood loss associated with pancreatectomy without splenectomy must be balanced against the slight risk of OPSI. In my view, the balance favors splenic salvage only when the patient is hemodynamically stable and normothermic and when the pancreatic injury is isolated or occurs with only minor associated injuries.

Grade IV: Proximal Transection or Parenchymal Injury with Probable Duct Disruption

Injuries to the pancreatic head represent the most challenging management dilemmas. The key steps in immediate management, in order of importance, are (1) to control bleeding, (2) to halt contamination, and (3) to define the anatomy of the injury. Only when these steps have been carried out is effective management possible.

In particular, it is essential that the surgeon define the anatomy of the pancreatic duct in patients who have sustained proximal pancreatic injuries. This can usually be accomplished through local inspection and exploration of the defect to determine the status of the duct.[61] If local exploration fails to determine the status of the main pancreatic duct, intraoperative pancreatography (see above) is strongly recommended. The only exception to this approach involves hemodynamically unstable patients with hypothermia, acidosis, and coagulopathy, for whom simple damage-control surgery is advised.

Some experienced surgeons have expressed reservations about making a duodenotomy to perform pancreatography. In many cases (64%, according to experience at my institution), needle cholecystocholangiopancreatography can image the pancreatic duct along with the distal CBD.[2] If this technique proves unsuccessful, the best consists of wide external drainage with several closed suction drains in conjunction with planned early postoperative ERCP or MRP. If postoperative ERCP confirms the presence of major proximal pancreatic duct injury, pancreatic duct stenting may be considered as an alternative to near-total pancreatectomy. A growing body of experience suggests that pancreatic duct stenting is a promising approach[30,32,33]; however, at least one report has found it to yield discouraging results, citing long-term stricture development and acute sepsis as particular problems.[10]

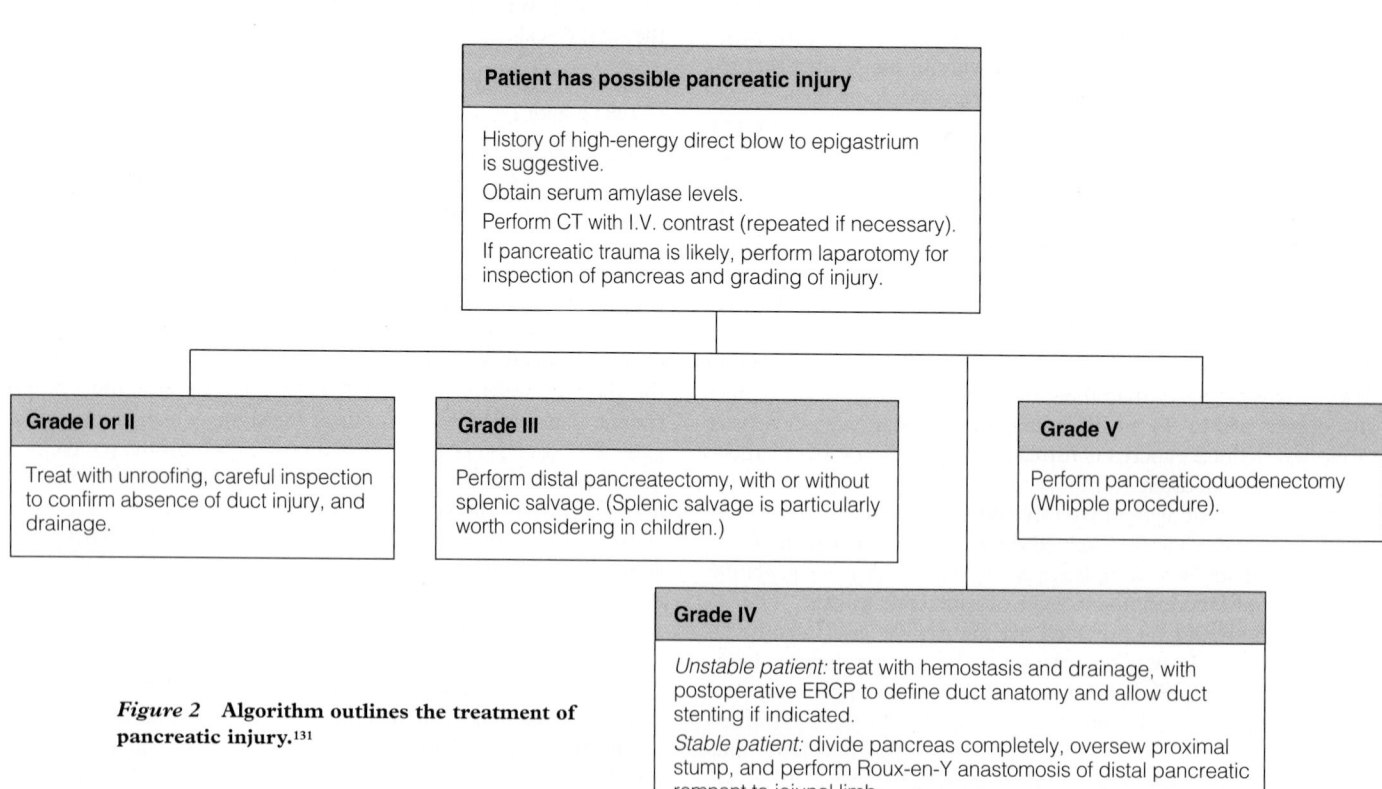

Figure 2 **Algorithm outlines the treatment of pancreatic injury.**[131]

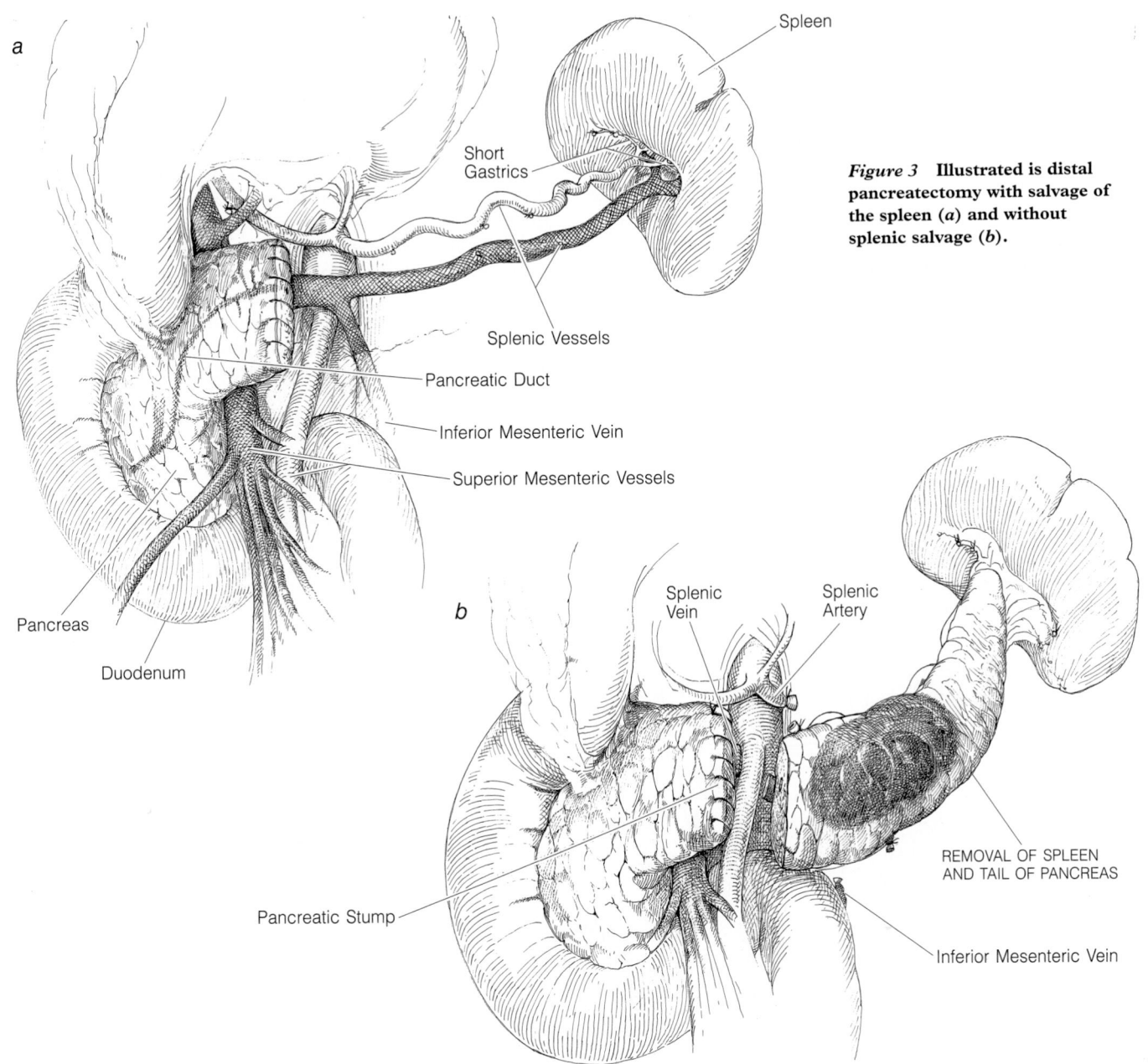

Figure 3 Illustrated is distal pancreatectomy with salvage of the spleen (*a*) and without splenic salvage (*b*).

If the proximal pancreatic duct is injured but the ampulla and the duodenum are spared (a rare scenario), two options are available. The first option is extended distal pancreatectomy, resulting in subtotal removal of the gland. The proximal residual gland should drain into the duodenum in a normal fashion if the duct is intact. Wide external drainage of the residual pancreatic duct surface must be provided. I do not add pyloric exclusion or duodenal defunctionalization or diverticularization [*see* Combined Pancreatic-Duodenal Injuries, *below*] to this procedure, though others advocate the use of such techniques in this circumstance.[51,61] If it appears that the residual proximal pancreatic tissue may be inadequate to provide endocrine or exocrine function, the second option may be applied, which is to preserve the pancreatic tail distal to the injury by performing a Roux-en-Y pancreaticojejunostomy [*see Figure 4*]. This technique involves division of the pancreas at the site of injury, debridement of injured parenchyma, secure closure of the proximal duct and the parenchyma, and anastomosis of the open end of the divided distal pancreas to the Roux-en-Y jejunal limb.

A review of 399 patients with pancreatic injuries from four separate published reports revealed that only two (0.5%) patients underwent Roux-en-Y drainage of the distal segment of a transected pancreatic gland.[13,34,62,63] A report from the University of Tennessee at Memphis is compelling for its findings regarding the effectiveness of drainage alone, without extended pancreatectomy, particularly for proximal pancreatic gland injuries in which the duct status is unclear.[13] A total of 37 patients with proximal pancreatic duct injuries were managed with closed suction drainage alone, and the fistula and abscess rate was a modest 13.5%. Because pancreatography was not performed in these patients, the status of the pancreatic duct was not defined. Thus, it remains unclear whether this technique is truly effective in the presence of a major pancreatic duct injury.

In cases of incomplete pancreatic parenchymal transection, some surgeons have employed an end-to-side jejunopancreatic anastomosis. This technique is not recommended, because of the difficulty of ensuring the integrity of the anastomosis and because of the potential for a high-output pancreatic fistula resulting from the posterior pancreatic wound. A 1981 report illustrated the high complication rate associated with this dated technique: of the seven patients (out of a total of 283 patients) in whom the technique was used, five (71%) had fistulas and three (43%) died.[49]

Again, provisions should be made for early enteral nutritional support in all patients with major pancreatic duct injuries. A measure of foresight in placing a jejunal feeding tube at the time of the initial celiotomy will be amply rewarded by the institution of a simplified and advantageous enteral nutrition regimen.[64] Elemental or short-chain polypeptide feeding formulas are particularly useful in this situation. These formulas may be delivered via a needle-catheter jejunostomy, which is the approach I prefer.[52,53]

Combined Pancreatic-Duodenal Injuries

Severe combined injuries to the pancreatic head and the duodenum are, fortunately, rare. In one study, only 48 (3%) of 1,404 patients with pancreatic duct injuries reported between 1981 and 1990 underwent pancreaticoduodenectomy.[65] These combined injuries are most commonly caused by penetrating trauma and occur in association with multiple other intra-abdominal injuries. In fact, the associated injuries are the primary cause of mortality, a fact that again underscores the importance of hemorrhage control and contamination control in dealing with pancreatic or duodenal injury. Most of the immediate mortality in patients with combined pancreatic and duodenal injuries is attributable to major vascular injury in the vicinity of the head of the pancreas. Provided that immediate control of hemorrhage and adequate resuscitation can be achieved, the Whipple procedure [*see 66 Procedures for Benign and Malignant Pancreatic Disease*] remains the preferred option in the select group of patients who have unreconstructable injuries to the ampulla or the proximal pancreatic duct or who have massive destruction of both the duodenum and the pancreatic head. In these patients, pancreaticoduodenectomy is essentially the completion of surgical debridement of devitalized tissue. For patients with hemodynamic instability, hypothermia, coagulopathy, and acidosis, a staged operative approach (i.e., damage-control surgery) is advocated. First, hemorrhage is controlled; next, bowel and bacterial contamination are managed; and finally, the anatomy of the injury is identified. The patient is then resuscitated in the ICU and returned to the operating room for definitive reconstruction and anastomoses when stabilized (generally, 24 to 48 hours later).

Because of the large number of possible combinations of injuries to the pancreas and the duodenum, no single therapeutic approach is appropriate for all patients. In a review of 129 cases of combined pancreatic-duodenal injuries, 24% of the patients were treated with simple repair and drainage, 50% underwent repair and pyloric exclusion, and only 10% required a Whipple procedure.[61] The best treatment option for a given patient is determined

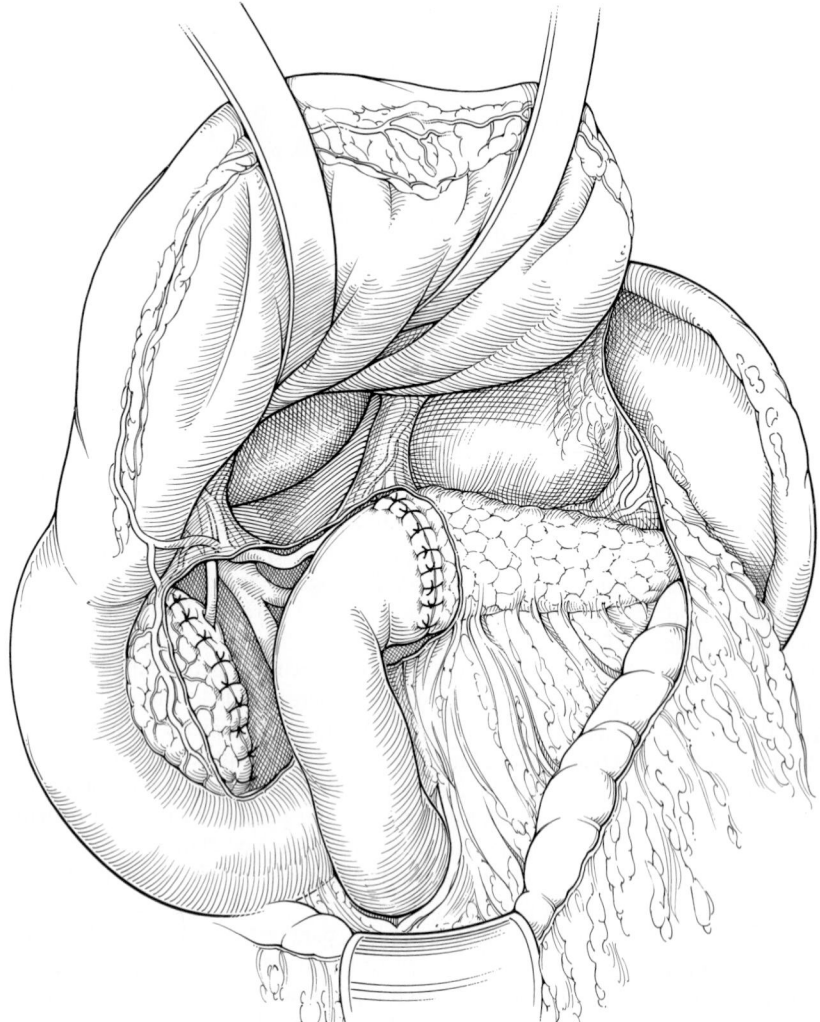

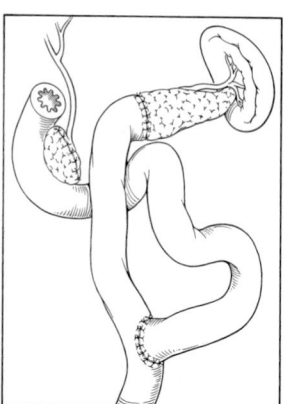

Figure 4 **If a patient has a grade IV injury to the pancreatic head and there is concern regarding whether the proximal residual gland would have adequate endocrine and exocrine function if the distal gland is resected in an extended distal pancreatectomy, an option is to preserve the uninjured portion of the distal gland. This is done by dividing the pancreas at the site of the injury and performing a Roux-en-Y pancreaticojejunostomy to allow the distal pancreas to drain into the jejunal limb.**

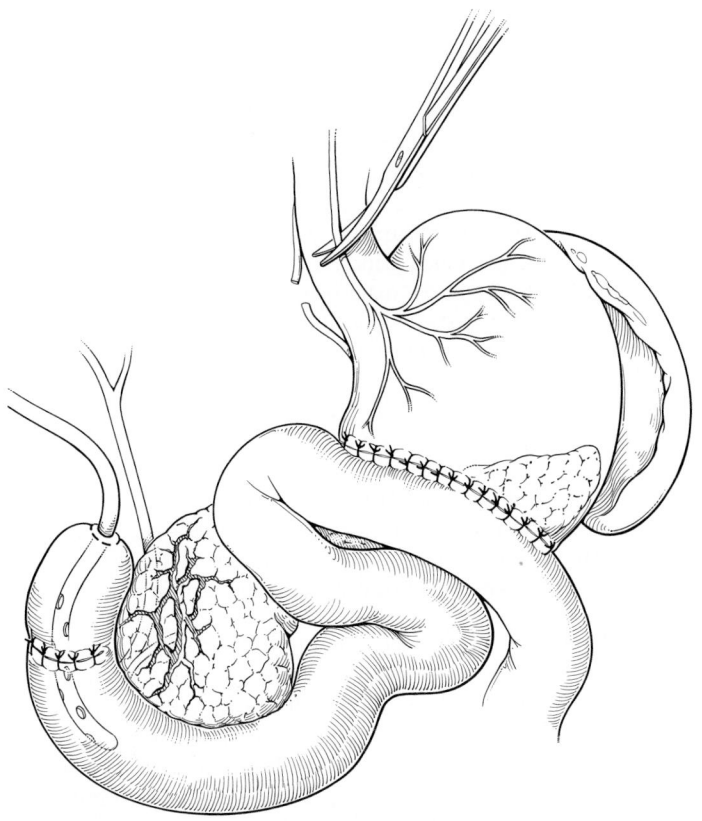

Figure 5 Duodenal diverticularization consists of antrectomy with gastrojejunostomy, tube duodenostomy, vagotomy, and peripancreatic drainage.

by the integrity of the distal CBD and the ampulla, as well as by the severity of the duodenal injury. For this reason, every patient with a combined pancreatic-duodenal injury should undergo cholangiography, pancreatography, and evaluation of the ampulla. If the CBD and the ampulla are intact (as they are in the majority of cases), the duodenum may be closed primarily and the pancreatic duct injury treated as described (see above). If the status of the pancreatic duct cannot be determined intraoperatively, wide external drainage of the pancreatic head with closed suction drains, rather than total pancreatectomy, should be performed, followed by early postoperative ERCP or MRP.

In cases of severe injury to the duodenum, it may be advisable to divert gastric contents away from the duodenal repair. One technique for accomplishing this diversion is duodenal diverticularization, which employs primary closure of the duodenal wound, antrectomy, vagotomy, end-to-side gastrojejunostomy, drainage of the CBD with a T tube, and lateral tube duodenostomy [*see Figure 5*]. The goals are (1) complete diversion of both gastric and biliary contents away from the duodenal injury, (2) provision of enteral nutrition via the gastrojejunostomy, and (3) conversion of a potential uncontrolled lateral duodenal fistula to a controlled fistula.

A less formidable and less destructive alternative technique for diversion of gastric contents is pyloric exclusion, which does not employ antrectomy, biliary diversion, or vagotomy [*see Figure 6*].[51,66-68] This procedure is performed through a gastrotomy and involves grasping the pylorus with a Babcock clamp, suturing the pylorus closed with absorbable size 0 polyglycolic acid or polyglyconate, and constructing a loop gastrojejunostomy. Gastric flow is then diverted away from the duodenum for several weeks while the duodenal and pancreatic duct injuries heal. After a period of 2

weeks to 2 months, the pylorus opens and the gastrojejunostomy functionally closes. One group has described a technical method of controlling the release of the pyloric exclusion knot and thereby timing the opening of the pyloric occlusion.[69] Marginal ulceration at the gastrojejunostomy site has been reported in 5% to 33% of patients in whom a vagotomy was not performed.[67,68,70,71] Pyloric exclusion is generally reserved for severe combined pancreatic head and duodenal injuries for which a Whipple procedure is not required. Few surgeons advocate pyloric exclusion for isolated pancreatic duct injuries.

In patients who have sustained massive injuries of the proximal duodenum and the head of the pancreas, destruction of the ampulla and the proximal pancreatic duct or the distal CBD may preclude reconstruction. In addition, because the head of the pancreas and the duodenum share an arterial supply, it is essentially impossible to resect one structure entirely without making the other ischemic. In this situation, a pancreaticoduodenectomy [*see 66 Procedures for Benign and Malignant Pancreatic Disease*] is required. Between 1961 and 1994, 184 Whipple procedures for trauma were reported; there were 26 operative deaths and 39 delayed deaths, for a 65% overall survival rate.[65] Subsequent experience, however, suggests that with appropriate selection criteria, pancreaticoduodenectomy for trauma can be performed with morbidity and mortality comparable to those of pancreaticoduodenectomy for cancer.[72-74]

Nonoperative Management in Children

Major pancreatic duct injury is rare in children, occurring in only 0.12% of children with blunt abdominal trauma.[75] Most pediatric pancreatic injuries are grade I or II injuries, which do not

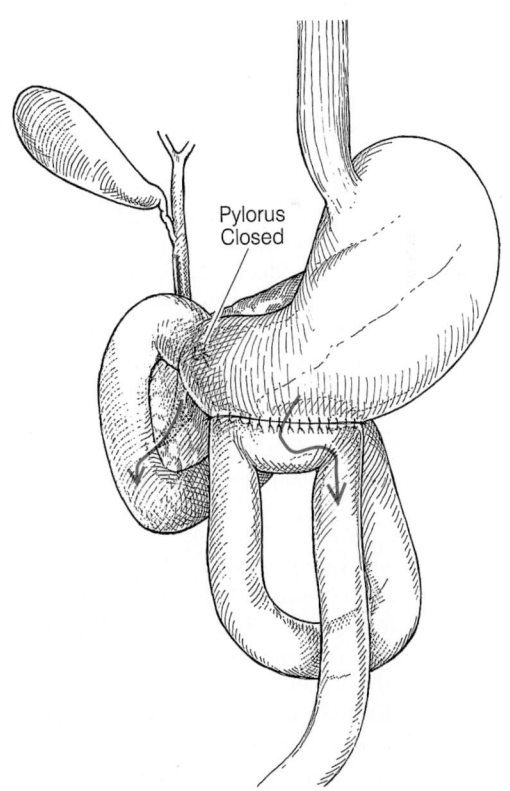

Figure 6 Pyloric exclusion consists of closure of the pylorus from within the stomach, followed by gastrojejunostomy. The procedure eliminates discharge of gastric acid into the duodenum, thus minimizing the stimulation of pancreatic secretion and reducing morbidity if there is breakdown of a repair.

involve major pancreatic duct injury. Accordingly, several authors have advocated managing all blunt pediatric pancreatic injuries nonoperatively with bowel rest, serial abdominal CT scans to watch for pseudocyst formation, and percutaneous drainage as required.[76-79] However, this approach is generally associated with a high morbidity and a prolonged hospital course and therefore may not be justified, given the good recovery reported after distal pancreatectomy with splenic salvage.[80] Pseudocysts develop in 40% to 100% of children with major duct injury,[78,81,82] and recurrent episodes of pancreatitis may arise long after the time of injury.[16,83] ERCP with proximal stenting of duct injuries may be a useful adjunct to care in these patients, but it requires a skilled pediatric endoscopist.

A report from Toronto detailed the management of 35 children with pancreatic trauma over a 10-year period.[78] In 23, the injury was diagnosed early (< 24 hours), whereas in the remaining 12, the diagnosis was initially missed. In all, 28 of the 35 were managed nonoperatively. A subsequent report provided a more detailed examination of 10 patients from this group who had pancreatic duct transections.[79] Pseudocysts developed in 44% and were managed in all cases with percutaneous drainage. Atrophy of the distal pancreatic remnant developed in 75%, but there was no evidence of endocrine or exocrine dysfunction. A report from Japan found that pseudocysts developed in five out of five children with pancreatic duct injuries that were managed nonoperatively.[82] The data suggest that pediatric pancreatic injuries can be successfully managed nonoperatively but also that there is a high incidence of pseudocyst formation necessitating further hospitalization and interventions and that atrophy of the distal remnant is common. Several pediatric surgeons have argued for the benefits of distal pancreatectomy in terms of shortening hospital stay and minimizing intervention.[29,80,84]

Nonoperative management of adults with blunt pancreatic injuries has been less well studied. In one report, patients with grade I and II injuries (confirmed by laparotomy) had a higher morbidity with external drainage than with exploration without drainage.[85] Selection bias might have affected these results, however, in that less severe injuries might not have been drained. Proponents of nonoperative management of grade I and II injuries have advocated early ERCP to identify the presence of any pancreatic duct injuries that would necessitate surgical intervention.[86,87] Proximal stenting of the pancreatic duct has been successful in isolated case reports of duct injuries in adults.[33] Further study is indicated before any recommendations can be made regarding nonoperative management of pancreatic duct injury in adults. For the present, I continue to advocate operative management for known or suspected pancreatic duct injury.

COMPLICATIONS

The complication rate after pancreatic injury remains uncomfortably high. Between 20% and 40% of patients who undergo surgical intervention for a pancreatic duct injury have a complicated postoperative course, and the rate is even higher if both the pancreatic head and the duodenum were injured.[1] The risk of complications is directly and independently related to the injury grade on the AAST scale and to the presence or absence of an associated bowel injury.[2] Although most of the complications of pancreatic duct injury are either self-limiting or treatable, there is a significant risk of sepsis and multiple organ dysfunction syndrome (MODS), which are responsible for nearly 30% of deaths resulting from pancreatic trauma. In some series, as many as one half of the postoperative complications could have been prevent-

ed by careful inspection of the pancreas and accurate determination of the status of the main pancreatic duct.[9]

Fistula

Postoperative pancreatic fistula has been defined as any measurable drain output with an amylase level higher than three times the serum level.[50] It is the most common complication after pancreatic duct injury, occurring in 7% to 20% of patients (and in 26% to 35% of patients with combined pancreatic-duodenal injury).[2,13,40,88,89] Direct suture closure of the main pancreatic duct may help minimize this complication; fibrin sealants appear to be ineffective.[90]

The vast majority of pancreatic fistulas are minor (drain output < 200 ml/day) and spontaneously resolve within 2 weeks after injury, given adequate external drainage. In a multicenter review of distal pancreatectomy for trauma, the postoperative fistula rate was 14% (10/71), and fistulas closed spontaneously in 89% (8/9) of survivors within 6 to 54 days.[63] Extirpation of a residual pancreatic sequestrum was required to facilitate fistula closure in one patient. By way of comparison, a subsequent study reported a 3.3% fistula rate after elective distal pancreatectomy for chronic pancreatitis.[55]

High-output fistulas (drain output > 700 ml/day) are rare. Generally, either more extended external drainage or surgical intervention is required for resolution. If a high-output fistula does not progressively decrease in volume or persists for longer than 10 days, ERCP is indicated to help establish the cause of the persistent fistula and guide further therapy. Nutritional support must be provided throughout this period. At this point, as noted [*see* Management, Grade IV: Proximal Transection or Parenchymal Injury with Probable Duct Disruption, *above*], the surgeon's foresight in placing a feeding jejunostomy at the time of the initial trauma laparotomy is rewarded. Elemental feeding formulas cause less pancreatic stimulation than standard enteral formulas and should therefore be tried before the patient is committed to TPN.[52] The somatostatin analogue octreotide acetate has shown promise in treating prolonged high-output pancreatic fistulas but only when any infection has been eradicated and when pancreatic duct obstruction or stricture is absent.[91]

The use of octreotide as an adjuvant to standard fistula management probably reduces fistula output, but whether it hastens fistula closure remains to be proved.[92] Somatostatin analogues do appear to prevent postoperative complications and fistula formation in patients undergoing elective pancreatic resection. However, nonrandomized studies addressing the efficacy of somatostatin analogues in pancreatic trauma patients have yielded conflicting results.[93,94] Moreover, in the trials demonstrating reductions in postoperative complications with octreotide use in elective pancreatic resection, octreotide administration was initiated in the preoperative period—a time frame that is not applicable to the trauma setting. The octreotide dosage typically starts at 50 μg subcutaneously every 12 hours but may rise as high as 1,000 μg/day. Although octreotide has been included in TPN solutions, this practice remains controversial and is not recommended by the 1997 package insert, because of the formation of glycosyl octreotide conjugates that may reduce the efficacy of the agent.[95] The major potential side effects are unpredictable changes in serum glucose levels, pain at the injection site, and various nonspecific GI complaints.

Abscess

The incidence of abscess formation after pancreatic trauma ranges from 10% to 25%, depending on the number and type of associated injuries present. Early operative or percutaneous decompression or evacuation is critical, though even with these measures, the mortality in this group of patients remains about 25%.[61,96] In most cases, the abscesses are subfascial or peripancreatic; true pancreatic abscesses are unusual and generally result from inadequate debridement of dead tissue or inadequate initial drainage.[40,63,89,97] True pancreatic abscesses often are not amenable or responsive to percutaneous drainage and must be treated with prompt surgical debridement and drainage. Percutaneous decompression may be helpful in distinguishing abscesses from pseudocysts (see below).

Pancreatitis

Transient abdominal pain and a rise in the serum amylase concentration, signaling pancreatitis, may be anticipated in 8% to 18% of postoperative patients.[5,63,98] This type of pancreatitis is treated with nasogastric decompression, bowel rest, and nutritional support and can be expected to resolve spontaneously. A much less common but far more deadly complication is hemorrhagic pancreatitis. The first sign of this complication may be bloody pancreatic drainage or a fall in the serum hemoglobin concentration, with the patient rapidly becoming desperately ill. It is fortunate that this complication occurs in fewer than 2% of operative pancreatic trauma patients: mortality may approach 80%, and there is no effective treatment.[40,56]

Secondary Hemorrhage

Postoperative hemorrhage necessitating blood transfusion may occur in 5% to 10% of pancreatic trauma patients, particularly when external drainage after pancreatic debridement was inadequate or when intra-abdominal infection has developed.[98,99] Generally, reoperation is required to control secondary hemorrhage, though angiographic embolization may be an effective alternative.

Pseudocysts

Blunt pancreatic injuries that were missed or were intentionally managed nonoperatively often result in the formation of a pseudocyst; in one report, 22 pseudocysts developed in 42 blunt pancreatic trauma patients managed nonoperatively.[8] The status of the pancreatic duct is the key determinant of how a pancreatic pseudocyst is treated. If the pancreatic duct is intact, percutaneous drainage of the pseudocyst is likely to be effective. If the pseudocyst is secondary to major disruption of the duct, however, percutaneous drainage will not provide definitive therapy but will convert the pseudocyst to a chronic fistula. ERCP should therefore precede any attempt at percutaneous drainage. If pancreatic duct stenosis or injury is demonstrated, the treatment options are (1) reexploration and partial resection of the gland, (2) internal Roux-en-Y drainage of the distal gland, and (3) endoscopic transpapillary stenting of the pancreatic duct.[32] There is some evidence to suggest that surgical decompression will be required if the pseudocyst is larger than 10 cm.[82]

Exocrine and Endocrine Insufficiency

Exocrine and endocrine insufficiency are unusual after pancreatic trauma. Animal and human studies suggest that a residuum as small as 10% to 20% of the normal pancreatic tissue mass is adequate for pancreatic function.[6] The implication is that any resection distal to the mesenteric vessels should leave an adequate amount of functioning pancreatic tissue. In a multicenter study of 74 cases of distal pancreatic resection, only one case of endocrine deficiency (diet-controlled hyperglycemia after 80% pancreatectomy) was documented, and no instances of exocrine insufficiency were observed.[63] In another study, no cases of pancreatic insufficiency were reported after resection of as much as 90% of the pancreas.[88] By way of contrast, patients with chronic pancreatitis who undergo distal pancreatectomy have an incidence of diabetes ranging from 15% (with 0% to 33% of the gland resected) to 64% (with 50% to 75% of the gland resected).[55]

Injuries to the Duodenum

Duodenal injuries are uncommon. A 6-year statewide review in Pennsylvania found the incidence of blunt duodenal injury to be only 0.2% (206 of 103,864 trauma registry entries), and only 30 of the patients had full-thickness duodenal injuries.[100] About 75% of the patients in published reports of duodenal injury sustained penetrating rather than blunt trauma; however, this figure may primarily reflect the experience of urban trauma centers.[101] Blunt duodenal injuries are the result of a direct blow to the epigastrium, which in adults is usually the result of a steering-wheel injury to an unrestrained driver and in children is usually the result of a direct blow from a bicycle handlebar or similar device. It is well known that the insidious nature of many blunt duodenal injuries makes the initial diagnosis difficult unless a high index of suspicion is maintained. Nevertheless, delays in the diagnosis of duodenal trauma continue to plague trauma surgeons and seriously compromise patient care.[102]

DIAGNOSIS

The radiologic signs of duodenal injury on the initial plain abdominal or upright chest radiograph are often quite subtle. Mild spine scoliosis or obliteration of the right psoas muscle may be visible, in addition to retroperitoneal air, which is often difficult to distinguish from the overlying transverse colon. An early suspicion of retroperitoneal duodenal rupture is best confirmed or excluded by means of either an abdominal CT scan, with both oral and I.V. contrast, or an upper GI series, first with a water-soluble contrast agent and then with barium if the initial examination yields negative results. The findings must be interpreted with a high index of suspicion for injury, and any uncertainty in interpretation is adequate justification for operative exploration.

Even with careful examination, false negative results are known to occur.[103] In one study of the accuracy of CT in diagnosing duodenal and other small bowel injuries, only 10 (59%) of 17 scans were prospectively (i.e., preoperatively) interpreted as suggestive of bowel injury, but 15 (88%) of 17 were suggestive when evaluated retrospectively.[104] The investigators emphasized that using CT to diagnose blunt bowel rupture requires careful inspection and technique to detect the often subtle findings. Abdominal CT findings suggestive of duodenal injury may be difficult to confirm with duodenography.[105] In a series of 96 patients with CT findings suggestive of duodenal injury, duodenography had a sensitivity of 54% and a specificity of 98%. For injuries necessitating operative repair, the sensitivity was only 25%, with a 25% false negative rate. In another study, 83% of patients in whom diagnosis of blunt duodenal injury was delayed had subtle CT findings (e.g., pneumoperitoneum, unexplained fluid, and unusual bowel morphology) that were dismissed.[106] The authors emphasized the point that subtle findings of duodenal injury on abdominal CT should be an indication for laparotomy.

Diagnostic peritoneal lavage (DPL) is unreliable in detecting isolated duodenal and other retroperitoneal injuries. Nevertheless,

Table 2 Factors Determining Severity of Duodenal Injury[108]

Factor	Degree of Injury	
	Mild	Severe
Means of Injury	Stab	Blunt force or missile
Size of Injury	≤ 75% of circumference	> 75% of circumference
Location of injury in duodenum	D3, D4	D1, D2
Interval between injury and repair	≤ 24 hr	> 24 hr
Adjacent injury to CBD	Absent	Present

it is often helpful, in that approximately 40% of patients with a duodenal injury have associated intra-abdominal injuries that will result in a positive DPL result. The presence of amylase or bile in the lavage effluent is a more specific indicator of possible duodenal injury. Serum amylase levels are nondiagnostic as well, but if they are found to be elevated, additional investigation (via CT or celiotomy) for possible pancreatic or duodenal injury is warranted. At celiotomy, the presence of any central upper abdominal retroperitoneal hematoma, bile staining, or air mandates visualization and thorough examination of the duodenum. The technical details of exposure of the entire duodenum and pancreas are well described elsewhere.[107]

MANAGEMENT

Classification of Duodenal Injury

Treatment of duodenal trauma is determined by the severity of the injury and the likelihood of postrepair complications. Approximately 70% to 80% of duodenal wounds can safely be repaired primarily; approximately 20% to 30% call for more complex procedures. A 1980 review of 247 patients treated for duodenal trauma catalogued factors that determined whether a duodenal wound could be primarily repaired.[108] In the 228 patients who survived longer than 72 hours, the overall duodenal fistula rate was 7%, and the mortality was 10.5%. The investigators identified five factors that, in their view, correlated most significantly with the severity of duodenal injury and subsequent morbidity and mortality [see Table 2]. To these five factors should be added a sixth—namely, the presence of a pancreatic injury, which is a significant predictor of late morbidity and mortality. These factors, both individually and in different combinations, have been used to develop a variety of duodenal injury classification systems. One such system is simply to divide injuries into two categories, mild and severe. In the study already mentioned,[108] the investigators reported a 0% mortality and a 2% duodenal fistula rate in patients with mild duodenal trauma, compared with a 6% mortality and a 10% fistula rate in those with severe duodenal trauma. In general, primary repair is satisfactory for mild duodenal injuries without associated pancreatic injuries. More complex treatment strategies may be required for more severe duodenal injuries.

A more contemporary classification system is that developed by the AAST, in which duodenal injuries are graded from I to V in order of increasing severity [see Table 1 and Figure 7].[46] In a multicenter review of 164 duodenal trauma patients to whom the AAST classification scheme was applied, there were 38 grade I, 70 grade II, 48 grade III, 4 grade IV, and 4 grade V injuries. Primary repair was the sole treatment in 71% (117) of all cases.[109] Ninety of the 108 patients with grade I or II injuries underwent either pri-

mary duodenal repair or no duodenal procedure at all. Twenty-six of the 56 patients with grade III to V injuries were treated with more complex duodenal treatment strategies, including pyloric exclusion, duodenoduodenostomy, duodenojejunostomy, and pancreaticoduodenectomy.

Duodenal Hematoma

Duodenal hematoma is generally considered a consequence of childhood play or child abuse. In one report, 50% of cases of duodenal hematoma in children were attributable to child abuse.[110] However, this condition can occur in adults as well. Nearly one third of patients present with obstruction of insidious onset at least 48 hours after injury, presumably resulting from a fluid shift into the hyperosmotic duodenal hematoma. Generally speaking, duodenal hematoma is a nonsurgical injury, in that the best results are obtained with conservative or nonsurgical management.[111] It may be diagnosed by means of either contrast-enhanced CT or an upper GI study. The initial contrast examination should be done with a water-soluble agent (e.g., meglumine diatrizoate), followed by a barium study to provide the greater detail needed for detection of the so-called coiled-spring or stacked-coin sign. This finding is characteristic of intramural duodenal hematoma, but it is present in only about one quarter of patients with hematomas.

Although initial treatment is nonoperative, care must be taken to exclude associated injuries, with particular attention paid to the potential for pancreatic injuries, which occur in 20% of patients.[111] Continuous nasogastric suction should be employed and TPN initiated. If signs of obstruction do not spontaneously abate, the patient should be reevaluated with upper GI contrast studies at 5- to 7-day intervals. Ultrasonography may also be employed to follow a resolving duodenal hematoma.[112] Percutaneous drainage of an unresolving duodenal hematoma has been reported,[113,114] but the usual recommendation is to perform operative exploration and evacuation of the hematoma after 2 weeks of conservative therapy to rule out stricture, duodenal perforation, or injury to the head of the pancreas as factors that might be contributing to the obstruction.[115] In a review of six cases of duodenal and jejunal hematoma resulting from blunt trauma, the hematomas resolved with nonoperative management in five cases; the average hospital stay was 16 days (range, 10 to 23 days), and the average duration of TPN was 9 days (range, 4 to 16 days). In the sixth case, upper GI series showed evidence of complete bowel obstruction, which failed to resolve after 18 days of conservative management. Laparotomy revealed jejunal and colonic strictures with fibrosis, which were successfully resected.[116]

If a duodenal hematoma is incidentally found at celiotomy, a thorough inspection must be done to exclude perforation. Inspection necessitates an extended Kocher maneuver, which usu-

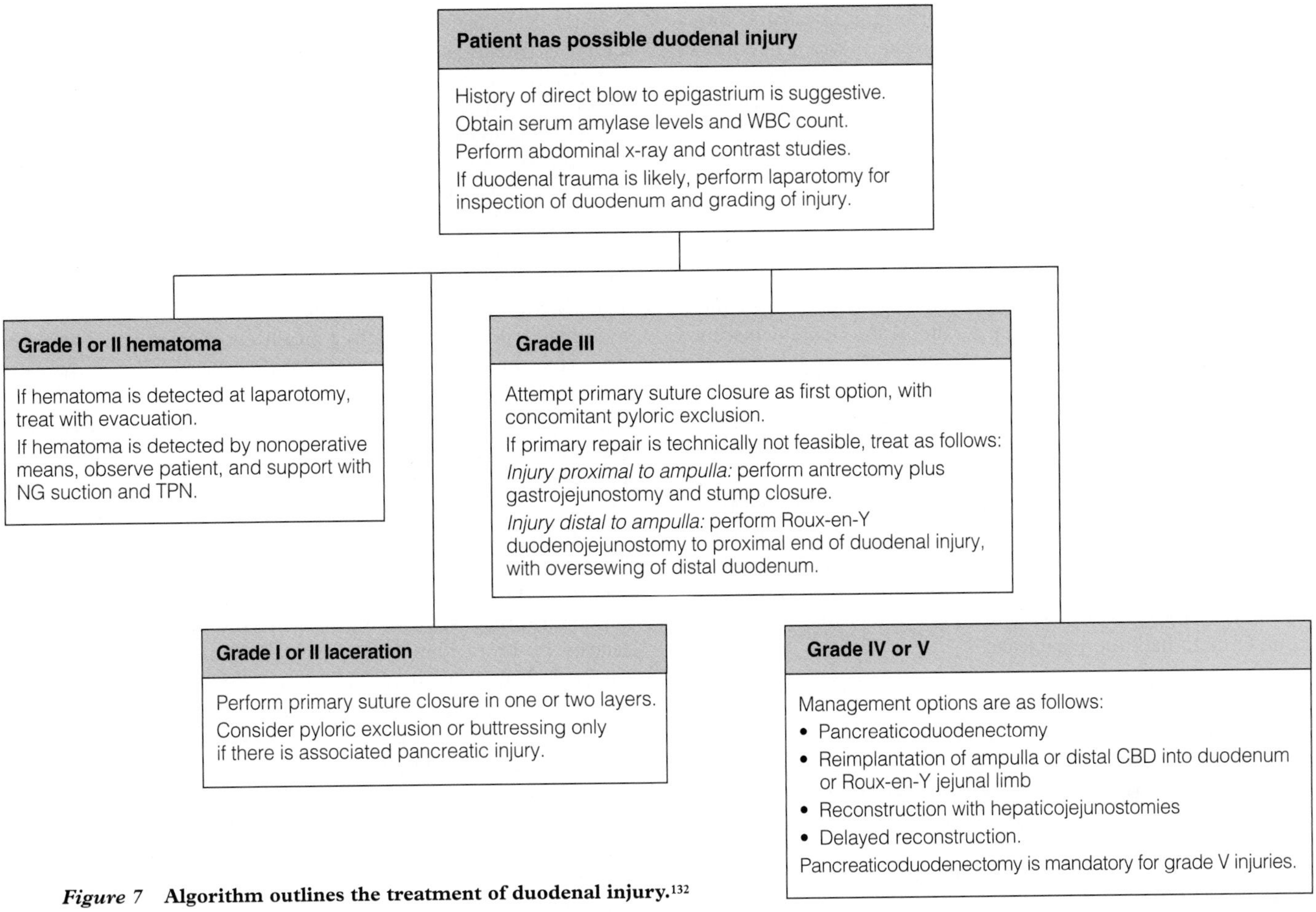

Figure 7 Algorithm outlines the treatment of duodenal injury.[132]

ally successfully drains the subserosal hematoma. It is unclear whether the serosa of the duodenum should intentionally be incised along its extent to evacuate the hematoma or whether doing so would actually increase the likelihood of turning a partial duodenal wall tear into a complete perforation. Because an extended period of gastric decompression will probably be required, a feeding jejunostomy should be placed.

Duodenal Laceration and Transection

For complete transection of the duodenum, primary repair is appropriate if there is little tissue loss, if the ampulla is not involved, and if the mucosal edges can be debrided and closed without tension. If adequate mobilization for a tension-free repair is impossible or if the injury is very near the ampulla and mobilization might result in injury to the CBD, the most reasonable option is a Roux-en-Y jejunal limb anastomosis to the proximal duodenal injury with oversewing of the distal injury. Mucosal jejunal patch repair is rarely, if ever, employed; it was not used in any of the 164 patients in the multicenter trial previously cited,[109] in which only five patients (3%) underwent repair with duodenoduodenostomy or duodenojejunostomy. Pancreaticoduodenectomy is only required for duodenal injuries if there is uncontrollable pancreatic hemorrhage or if duodenal injuries exist in combination with distal CBD or pancreatic duct injuries.

Several techniques may be applied to help protect a tenuous duodenal repair. One option is buttressing the repair with omentum (my preference) or a serosal patch from a loop of jejunum. This approach seems intuitively logical, though its benefits are unproven.[117,118] Another option is diversion of gastric contents, most commonly accomplished by means of pyloric exclusion [see Figure 6].[68] This technique, probably first described by Summers in 1904 as an adjunct to the treatment of duodenal wounds,[119] is less disruptive than true duodenal diverticularization [see Figure 5].[66,120] To date, no prospective, randomized trial has proved that gastric diversion is truly beneficial in the setting of duodenal trauma, but several reports have supported the use of pyloric exclusion and gastrojejunostomy in cases of severe duodenal injury[71,121] or in cases of delayed diagnosis of injury.[67] Potential benefits notwithstanding, the additional operating time and the extra anastomosis required with gastric diversion suggest that this approach should be employed with a good deal of selectivity. Marginal ulceration is a well-described complication of gastric diversion and has prompted some surgeons to add truncal vagotomy to the procedure. Most surgeons, however, do not perform vagotomy with gastric diversion, because nearly all of the pyloric closures open within a few weeks, regardless of the type of suture material used, and the occasional marginal ulcer can be medically managed in the interim.

An alternative or addition to gastric diversion is duodenal decompression via retrograde jejunostomy. In a study of 237 patients with a variety of duodenal injuries treated by means of retrograde jejunostomy tube drainage, the fistula rate was lower than 0.5%, whereas the incidence of duodenal complications was 19.3% when decompression was not performed.[122] Retrograde duodenoduodenal drainage is preferred to lateral duodenostomy. Direct drainage with a tube through the suture line results in a high (23%) rate of dehiscence or fistula. In a 1984 review of the literature on penetrating duodenal trauma and tube duodenostomy,[123] there was an overall mortality of 19.4% and a fistula rate of

11.8% when decompression was not performed, compared with a 9% mortality and a 2.3% fistula rate when it was. The authors concluded that tube drainage should be performed either via the stomach or via a retrograde jejunostomy, noting that these methods were associated with a lower fistula rate and a lower overall mortality than lateral tube duodenostomy was. Nonetheless, there has been no prospective, randomized analysis of the efficacy of tube duodenal drainage techniques, and not all surgeons support the use of decompression in this setting.

Mortality directly related to the duodenal injury is the result of duodenal dehiscence, uncontrolled sepsis, and subsequent MODS. Given the known lethal nature of duodenal dehiscence and duodenal fistula, the operating surgeon may well be strongly tempted to add pyloric exclusion, anastomosis buttressing, and duodenostomy to the repair of grade III or IV duodenal injuries. Concomitant pancreatic injury should be included as a high-risk confounder that might warrant the addition of pyloric exclusion to the duodenal repair. In a report of 40 patients with penetrating duodenal injuries, 14 patients had combined pancreatic-duodenal wounds. Five of these 14 were treated with primary duodenal repair alone, and two of the five had duodenal leaks. Three of the 14 underwent pyloric exclusion in addition to primary repair, and none of them had duodenal leaks.[124]

DETERMINANTS OF OUTCOME

Large series published toward the end of the 20th century documented an average mortality of 18% in patients with duodenal injuries, but the mortalities cited in individual reports showed great variability, ranging from 6% to 29%.[1,71,117,125] Mortality directly related to duodenal injury is much lower—generally, 2% to 5%—and is primarily the result of complications, dehiscence, sepsis, and MODS.[42,108,109,117,121,122,126,127] Morbidity after duodenal injury ranges from 30% to 63%; however, in only about one third of cases is morbidity directly related to the duodenal injury itself.[108,117,125] To a large extent, the variability in morbidity and mortality statistics can be explained by differences in the mechanism of injury, the nature and severity of associated injuries (if present), and the time between initial injury and diagnosis. For example, a review of 100 consecutive penetrating duodenal injuries documented a mortality of 25%,[117] compared with a mortality of 12% to 14% for blunt injuries.[102,108]

Early death from a duodenal injury, particularly a penetrating injury, is usually attributable to exsanguination from associated vascular, hepatic, or splenic trauma.[4,128] The proximity of the duodenum to other vital structures and the high-energy transfer mechanisms involved make isolated duodenal injuries uncommon, though certainly not unheard of. Most late deaths from duodenal trauma are attributable to infection and MODS. In as many as one third of patients who survive the first 48 hours after duodenal injury, a complication related to the injury eventually develops. Common complications include anastomotic breakdown, fistula, intra-abdominal abscess, pneumonia, bloodstream infection, and organ failure. Late deaths typically occur from 1 to 2 weeks or more after the initial duodenal injury; about one third of them are directly attributable to the injury itself.[108,125]

The length of time between injury and definitive treatment has a substantial effect on the development of late complications and subsequent mortality. In one study, 10 patients were identified in whom the diagnosis of duodenal injury was delayed for more than 24 hours; four of the 10 died, and three of the 10 had duodenal fistulas.[129] In a classic report from 1975, the remarkable importance (and frequency) of delays in the diagnosis of duodenal injury was strikingly demonstrated.[130] Diagnosis was delayed by more than 12 hours in 53% of the patients in this report and by more than 24 hours in 28%. In patients whose diagnosis was delayed for more than 24 hours, mortality was 40%; in those who underwent surgery within 24 hours of injury, mortality was 11%. These observations were subsequently confirmed by other studies. In one study, two of the four blunt duodenal trauma patients with delayed diagnoses died, and the other two had duodenal fistulas.[108] In another study, 100% of the deaths directly attributable to duodenal injury occurred in patients with delayed diagnoses.[102]

The implication of these observations is that the first priority in managing duodenal trauma, as in managing pancreatic trauma, should be control of hemorrhage. The second priority should be limiting bacterial contamination from associated colon or other bowel injury, with the aim of preventing late infections. As a rule, if a duodenal injury has occurred, it will be apparent intraoperatively; thus, the next priority should be a diligent search for potential pancreatic injury, with an emphasis on assessing the status of the pancreatic duct.[1,6]

References

1. Jurkovich GJ, Bulger E: Duodenum and pancreas. Trauma, 5th ed. Moore EE, Feliciano DV, Mattox K, Eds. McGraw-Hill, New York, 2004, p 709

2. Kao LS, Bulger EM, Parks DL, et al: Predictors of morbidity after traumatic pancreatic injury. J Trauma 55:426, 2003

3. Baker R, Dippel W, Freeark R: The surgical significance of trauma to the pancreas. Trans Western Drug Assoc 70:361, 1962

4. Heitsch RC, Knutson CO, Fulton RL, et al: Delineation of critical factors in the treatment of pancreatic trauma. Surgery 80:523, 1976

5. Smego DR, Richardson JD, Flint LM: Determinants of outcome in pancreatic trauma. J Trauma 25:771, 1985

6. Berni GA, Bandyk DF, Oreskovich MR, et al: Role of intraoperative pancreatography in patients with injury to the pancreas. Am J Surg 143:602, 1982

7. Carr ND, Cairns SJ, Lees WR, et al: Late complications of pancreatic trauma. Br J Surg 76:1244, 1989

8. Kudsk KA, Temizer D, Ellison EC, et al: Posttraumatic pancreatic sequestrum: recognition and treatment. J Trauma 26:320, 1986

9. Leppaniemi A, Haapiainen R, Kiviluoto T, et al: Pancreatic trauma: acute and late manifestations. Br J Surg 75:165, 1988

10. Lin BC, Chen RJ, Fang JF, et al: Management of blunt major pancreatic injury. J Trauma 56:774, 2004

11. Leppaniemi AK, Haapiainen RK: Risk factors of delayed diagnosis of pancreatic trauma. Eur J Surg 165:1134, 1999

12. Horst H, Bivins B: Pancreatic transection: a concept of evolving injury. Arch Surg 124:1093, 1989

13. Patton JH Jr, Lyden SP, Croce MA, et al: Pancreatic trauma: a simplified management guideline. J Trauma 43:234, 1997

14. Smith D, Stanley R, Rue L: Delayed diagnosis of pancreatic transection after blunt abdominal trauma. J Trauma 40:1009, 1996

15. Anderson CB, Connors JP, Mejia DC, et al: Drainage methods in the treatment of pancreatic injuries. Surg Gynecol Obstet 138:587, 1974

16. Arkovitz MS, Johnson S, Garcia VF: Pancreatic trauma in children: mechanisms of injury. J Trauma 42:49, 1997

17. White P, Benfield J: Amylase in the management of pancreatic trauma. Arch Surg 105:158, 1972

18. Moretz JA 3rd, Campbell DP, Parker DE, et al: Significance of serum amylase level in evaluating pancreatic trauma. Am J Surg 150:698, 1975

19. Olsen W: The serum amylase in blunt abdominal trauma. J Trauma 13:200, 1973

20. Vitale GC, Larson GM, Davidson PR, et al: Analysis of hyperamylasemia in patients with severe head injury. J Surg Res 43:226, 1987

21. Liu KJ, Atten MJ, Lichtor T, et al: Serum amylase and lipase elevation is associated with intracranial events. Am Surg 67:215, 2000

22. Takishima T, Hirata M, Kataoka Y, et al: Pancreatographic classification of pancreatic ductal injuries caused by blunt injury to the pancreas. J Trauma 48:745, 2000

23. Bouwman D, Weaver D, Walt A: Serum amylase and its isoenzymes: a clarification of their implication in trauma. J Trauma 24:573, 1984

24. Ilahi O, Bochicchio GV, Scalea TM: Efficacy of computed tomography in the diagnosis of pancreatic injury in adult blunt trauma patients: a single-institutional study. Am Surg 68:704, 2002

25. Jeffrey R, Federle M, Creass R: Computed tomography of pancreatic trauma. Radiology 147:491, 1983

26. Peitzman AB, Makaroun MS, Slasky BS, et al: Prospective study of computed tomography in initial management of blunt abdominal trauma. J Trauma 26:585, 1986

27. Lane M, Mindelzun R, Jeffrey R: Diagnosis of pancreatic injury after blunt abdominal trauma. Semin Ultrasound CT MRI 17:177, 1996

28. Wilson R, Moorehead R: Current management of trauma to the pancreas. Br J Surg 78:1196, 1991

29. Canty TG Sr, Weinman D: Treatment of pancreatic duct disruption in children by an endoscopically placed stent. J Pediatr Surg 36:345, 2001

30. Huckfeldt R, Agee C, Nichols WK, et al: Nonoperative treatment of traumatic pancreatic duct disruption using endoscopically placed stent. J Trauma 41:143, 1996

31. Kopelman D, Suissa A, Klein Y, et al: Pancreatic duct injury: intraoperative endoscopic transpancreatic drainage of parapancreatic abscess. J Trauma 44:555, 1998

32. Kozarek RA, Ball TJ, Patterson DJ, et al: Endoscopic transpapillary therapy for disrupted pancreatic duct and peripancreatic fluid collections. Gastroenterology 100:1362, 1991

33. Wolf A, Bernhardt J, Patrzyk M, et al: The value of endoscopic diagnosis and the treatment of pancreas injuries following blunt abdominal trauma. Surg Endosc 19:665, 2005

34. Wisner DH, Wold RL, Frey CF: Diagnosis and treatment of pancreatic injuries: an analysis of management principles. Arch Surg 125:1109, 1990

35. Whittwell AE, Gomez GA, Byers P, et al: Blunt pancreatic trauma: prospective evaluation of early endoscopic retrograde pancreatography. South Med J 82:586, 1989

36. Barkin JS, Ferstenberg RM, Panullo W, et al: Endoscopic retrograde cholangiopancreatography in patients with injury to the pancreas. Gastrointest Endosc 34:102, 1988

37. Sugawa C, Lucas C: Editorial: the case for preoperative and intraoperative ERCP in pancreatic trauma. Gastrointest Endosc 34:145, 1988

38. Fulcher AS, Turner MA, Yelon JA, et al: Magnetic resonance cholangiopancreatography (MRCP) in the assessment of pancreatic duct trauma and its sequelae: preliminary findings. J Trauma 48:1001, 2000

39. Soto JA, Alvarez O, Munera F, et al: Traumatic disruption of the pancreatic duct: diagnosis with MR pancreatography. AJR Am J Roentgenol 176:175, 2001

40. Graham J, Mattox K, Jordan G: Traumatic injuries of the pancreas. Am J Surg 136:744, 1978

41. Lucas C: Diagnosis and treatment of pancreatic and duodenal injury. Surg Clin North Am 57:49, 1977

42. Vasquez JC, Coimbra R, Hoyt DB, et al: Management of penetrating pancreatic trauma: an 11-year experience of a level-1 trauma center. Injury 32:753, 2001

43. Laraja RD, Lobbato VJ, Cassaro S, et al: Intraoperative endoscopic retrograde cholangiopancreatography (ERCP) in penetrating trauma of the pancreas. J Trauma 26:1146, 1986

44. Jurkovich GJ, Carrico CJ: Pancreatic trauma. Surg Clin North Am 70:575, 1990

45. Sorensen VJ, Obeid FN, Horst HM, et al: Penetrating pancreatic injuries. Am Surg 52:354, 1986

46. Moore EE, Cogbill TH, Malangoni MA, et al: Organ injury scaling II: pancreas, duodenum, small bowel, colon, and rectum. J Trauma 30:1427, 1990

47. Nowak M, Baringer D, Ponsky J: Pancreatic injuries: effectiveness of debridement and drainage for nontransecting injuries. Am Surg 52:599, 1986

48. Fabian TC, Kudsk KA, Croce MA, et al: Superiority of closed suction drainage for pancreatic trauma: a randomized prospective study. Ann Surg 211:724, 1990

49. Stone HH, Fabian TC, Satiani B, et al: Experiences in the management of pancreatic trauma. J Trauma 21:257, 1981

50. Bassi C, Dervenis C, Butturini G, et al: Postoperative pancreatic fistula: an international study group (ISGPF) definition. Surgery 138:8, 2005

51. Cogbill T, Moore E, Kashuk J: Changing trends in the management of pancreatic trauma. Arch Surg 117:722, 1982

52. Kellum J, Holland G, McNeill P: Traumatic pancreatic cutaneous fistula: comparison of enteral and parenteral feedings. J Trauma 28:700, 1988

53. Holmes JH 4th, Brundage SI, Yuen P, et al: Complications of surgical feeding jejunostomy in trauma patients. J Trauma 47:1009, 1999

54. Innes J, Carey L: Normal pancreatic dimensions in the adult human. Am J Surg 167:261, 1994

55. Hutchins RR, Hart RS, Pacifico M, et al: Long-term results of distal pancreatectomy for chronic pancreatitis in 90 patients. Ann Surg 236:612, 2002

56. Jones W, Finkelstein J, Barie P: Managing pancreatic trauma. Infect Surg 9:29, 1990

57. Fitzgibbons TJ, Yellin AE, Maruyama MM, et al: Management of the transected pancreas following distal pancreatectomy. Surg Gynecol Obstet 154:225, 1982

58. Andersen DK, Bolman RM 3rd, Moylan JA Jr: Management of penetrating pancreatic injuries: subtotal pancreatectomy using the auto suture stapler. J Trauma 20:347, 1980

59. Dawson D, Scott-Conner C: Distal pancreatectomy with splenic preservation: the anatomic basis for a meticulous operation. J Trauma 26:1142, 1986

60. Pachter HL, Hofstetter SR, Liang HG, et al: Traumatic injuries to the pancreas: the role of distal pancreatectomy with splenic preservation. J Trauma 29:1352, 1989

61. Feliciano DV, Martin TD, Cruse PA, et al: Management of combined pancreatoduodenal injuries. Ann Surg 205:673, 1987

62. Ivatury RR, Nallathambi M, Rao P, et al: Penetrating pancreatic injuries: analysis of 103 consecutive cases. Am Surg 56:90, 1990

63. Cogbill TH, Moore EE, Morris JA Jr, et al: Distal pancreatectomy for trauma: a multicenter experience. J Trauma 31:1600, 1991

64. Kudsk KA, Croce MA, Fabian TC, et al: Enteral versus parenteral feeding: effects on septic morbidity after blunt and penetrating abdominal trauma. Ann Surg 215:503, 1991

65. Delcore R, Stauffer JS, Thomas JH, et al: The role of pancreatogastrostomy following pancreatoduodenectomy for trauma. J Trauma 37:395, 1994

66. Berne CJ, Donovan AJ, White EJ, et al: Duodenal "diverticulization" for duodenal and pancreatic injury. Am J Surg 127:503, 1974

67. Buck JR, Sorensen VJ, Fath JJ, et al: Severe pancreatico-duodenal injuries: the effectiveness of pyloric exclusion with vagotomy. Am Surg 58:557, 1992

68. Vaughan GD 3rd, Frazier OH, Graham DY, et al: The use of pyloric exclusion in the management of severe duodenal injuries. Am J Surg 134:785, 1977

69. Fang JF, Chen RJ, Lin BC: Cell count ratio: new criterion of diagnostic peritoneal lavage for detection of hollow organ perforation. J Trauma 45:540, 1998

70. Fang JF, Chen RJ, Lin BC: Controlled reopen suture technique for pyloric exclusion. J Trauma 45:593, 1998

71. Martin TD, Feliciano DV, Mattox KL, et al: Severe duodenal injuries: treatment with pyloric exclusion and gastrojejunostomy. Arch Surg 118:631, 1983

72. Heimansohn DA, Canal DF, McCarthy MC, et al: The role of pancreaticoduodenectomy in the management of traumatic injuries to the pancreas and duodenum. Am Surg 56:511, 1990

73. McKone T, Bursch L, Scholten D: Pancreaticoduodenectomy for trauma: a life saving procedure. Am Surg 54:361, 1988

74. Oreskovich M, Carrico C: Pancreaticoduodenectomy for trauma: a viable option? Am J Surg 147:618, 1984

75. Canty TG Sr, Weinman D: Management of major pancreatic duct injuries in children. J Trauma 50:1001, 2001

76. Bass J, Di Lorenzo M, Desjardins JG, et al: Blunt pancreatic injuries in children: the role of percutaneous external drainage in the treatment of pancreatic pseudocysts. J Pediatr Surg 23:721, 1988

77. Holland AJ, Davey RB, Sparnon AL, et al: Traumatic pancreatitis: long-term review of initial non-operative management in children. J Paediatr Child Health 35:78, 1999

78. Shilyansky J, Sena LM, Kreller M, et al: Nonoperative management of pancreatic injuries in children. J Pediatr Surg 33:343, 1998

79. Wales PW, Shuckett B, Kim PC: Long-term outcome after nonoperative management of complete traumatic pancreatic transection in children. J Pediatr Surg 36:823, 2001

80. Meier DE, Coln CD, Hicks BA, et al: Early operation in children with pancreas transection. J Pediatr Surg 36:341, 2001

81. Burnweit C, Wesson D, Stringer D, et al: Percutaneous drainage of traumatic pancreatic pseudocysts in children. J Trauma 30:1273, 1990

82. Kouchi K, Tanabe M, Yoshida H, et al: Nonoperative management of blunt pancreatic injury in childhood. J Pediatr Surg 34:1736, 1999

83. Gholson CF, Sittig K, Favrot D, et al: Chronic abdominal pain as the initial manifestation of pancreatic injury due to remote blunt trauma of the abdomen. South Med J 87:902, 1994

84. McGahren ED, Magnuson D, Schaller RT, et al: Management of transected pancreas in children. Aust N Z J Surg 65:242, 1995

85. Akhrass R, Yaffe MB, Brandt CP, et al: Pancreatic trauma: a ten-year multi-institutional experience. Am Surg 63:598, 1997

86. Bradley E: Chronic obstructive pancreatitis as a delayed complication of pancreatic trauma. HPB Surg 5:49, 1991

87. Kim HS, Lee DK, Kim IW, et al: The role of endoscopic retrograde pancreatography in the treat-

ment of traumatic pancreatic duct injury. Gastrointest Endosc 54:49, 2001

88. Balasegaram M: Surgical management of pancreatic trauma. Curr Probl Surg 16:1, 1979

89. Jones R: Management of pancreatic trauma. Am J Surg 150:698, 1985

90. Lillemoe KD, Cameron JL, Kim MP, et al: Does fibrin glue sealant decrease the rate of pancreatic fistula after pancreaticoduodenectomy? Results of a prospective randomized trial. J Gastrointest Surg 8:766, 2004

91. Prinz R, Pickleman J, Hoffman J: Treatment of pancreatic cutaneous fistula with a somatostatin analog. Am J Surg 155:36, 1988

92. Martineau P, Shwed JA, Denis R: Is octreotide a new hope for enterocutaneous and external pancreatic fistulas closure? Am J Surg 172:386, 1996

93. Berberat PO, Friess H, Uhl W, et al: The role of octreotide in the prevention of complications following pancreatic resection. Digestion 60:15, 1999

94. Nwariaku FE, Terracina A, Mileski WJ, et al: Is octreotide beneficial following pancreatic injury? Am J Surg 170:582, 1995

95. Seidner D, Speerhas R, Trexler K: Can octreotide be added to parenteral nutrition solutions? Nutr Clin Pract 13:84, 1998

96. Wynn M, Hill DM, Miller DR, et al: Management of pancreatic and duodenal trauma. Am J Surg 150:327, 1985

97. Patton JH Jr, Fabian TC: Complex pancreatic injuries. Surg Clin North Am 76:783, 1996

98. Moore J, Moore E: Changing trends in the management of combined pancreatoduodenal injuries. World J Surg 8:791, 1984

99. Campbell R, Kennedy T: The management of pancreatic and pancreaticoduodenal injuries. Br J Surg 67:845, 1980

100. Ballard RB, Badellino MM, Eynon CA, et al: Blunt duodenal rupture: a 6-year statewide experience. J Trauma 43:229 1997

101. Asensio J, Feliciano DV, Britt LD, et al: Management of duodenal injuries. Curr Probl Surg 11:1021, 1993

102. Cuddington G, Rusnak CH, Cameron RD, et al: Management of duodenal injuries. Can J Surg 33:41, 1990

103. Sherck J, Oakes D: Intestinal injuries missed by computed tomography. J Trauma 30:1, 1990

104. Mirvis S, Gens D, Shanmuganathan K: Rupture of the bowel after blunt abdominal trauma: diagnosis with CT. Am J Roentgenol 159:1217, 1992

105. Timaran CH, Daley BJ, Enderson BL: Role of duodenography in the diagnosis of blunt duodenal injuries. J Trauma 51:648, 2001

106. Allen G, Moore FA, Cox CS Jr, et al: Delayed diagnosis of blunt duodenal injury: an avoidable complication. J Am Coll Surg 187:393, 1998

107. Asensio JA, Demetriades D, Berne JD, et al: A unified approach to the surgical exposure of pancreatic and duodenal injuries. Am J Surg 174:54, 1997

108. Snyder WH 3rd, Weigelt JA, Watkins WL, et al: The surgical management of duodenal trauma: precepts based on a review of 247 cases. Arch Surg 115:422, 1980

109. Cogbill T, Moore EE, Feliciano DV, et al: Conservative management of duodenal trauma: a multicenter perspective. J Trauma 30:1469, 1990

110. Wooley M, Mahour G, Sloan T: Duodenal hematoma in infancy and childhood. Am J Surg 136:8, 1978

111. Jewett TJ, Caldarola V, Karp MP, et al: Intramural hematoma of the duodenum. Arch Surg 123:54, 1988

112. Megremis S, Segkos N, Andrianaki A, et al: Sonographic diagnosis and monitoring of an obstructing duodenal hematoma after blunt trauma: correlation with computed tomographic and surgical findings. J Ultrasound Med 23:1679, 2004

113. Gullotto C, Paulson EK: CT-guided percutaneous drainage of a duodenal hematoma. AJR Am J Roentgenol 184:231, 2005

114. Kortbeek JB, Brown M, Steed B: Percutaneous drainage of a duodenal haematoma. Injury 28:419, 1997

115. Touloukian R: Protocol for the nonoperative treatment of obstructing intramural duodenal hematoma. Am J Surg 145:330, 1983

116. Czyrko C, Weltz CR, Markowitz RI, et al: Blunt abdominal trauma resulting in intestinal obstruction: when to operate? J Trauma 30:1567, 1990

117. Ivatury R, Nallathambi M, Gaudino J, et al: Penetrating duodenal injuries: an analysis of 100 consecutive cases. Ann Surg 202:154, 1985

118. McInnis WD, Aust JB, Cruz AB, et al: Traumatic injuries of the duodenum: a comparison of 1 degrees closure and the jejunal patch. J Trauma 15:847, 1975

119. Summers JJ: The treatment of posterior perforations of the fixed portions of the duodenum. Ann Surg 39:727, 1904

120. Donovan A, Hagen W, Berne D: Traumatic perforations of the duodenum. Am J Surg 111:341, 1966

121. Kashuk J, Moore E, Cogbill T: Management of the intermediate severity duodenal injury. Surgery 92:758, 1982

122. Stone H, Fabian T: Management of duodenal wounds. J Trauma 19:334, 1979

123. Hasson J, Stern D, Moss G: Penetrating duodenal trauma. J Trauma 24:471, 1984

124. McKenney MG, Nir I, Levi DM, et al: Evaluation of minor penetrating duodenal injuries. Am Surg 62:952, 1996

125. Shorr RM, Greaney GC, Donovan AJ: Injuries of the duodenum. Am J Surg 154:93, 1987

126. Flint LM Jr, McCoy M, Richardson JD, et al: Duodenal injury: analysis of common misconceptions in diagnosis and treatment. Ann Surg 191:697, 1980

127. Levison M, Petersen S, Sheldon G: Duodenal trauma: experience of a trauma center. J Trauma 24:475, 1984

128. Sukul K, Lont H, Johannes E: Management of pancreatic injuries. Hepatogastroenterology 39:447, 1992

129. Roman E, Silva Y, Lucas C: Management of blunt duodenal injury. Surg Gynecol Obstet 132:7, 1971

130. Lucas C, Ledgerwood A: Factors influencing outcome after blunt duodenal injury. J Trauma 15:839, 1975

131. Jurkovich GJ: Pancreatic injury. Surgical Decision Making, 5th ed. McIntyre RC Jr, Stiegmann GV, Eiseman B, Eds. WB Saunders Co, Philadelphia, 2004, p 510

132. Jurkovich GJ: Duodenal injury. Surgical Decision Making, 5th ed. McIntyre RC Jr, Stiegmann GV, Eiseman B, Eds. WB Saunders Co, Philadelphia, 2004, p 512

Acknowledgments

Figures 1, 3, and 6   Carol Donner.
Figures 4 and 5   Susan Brust, C.M.I.

109 INJURIES TO THE GREAT VESSELS OF THE ABDOMEN

David V. Feliciano, M.D., F.A.C.S.

In patients who have injuries to the great vessels of the abdomen, the findings on physical examination generally depend on whether a contained hematoma or active hemorrhage is present.[1] In the case of contained hematomas around the vascular injury in the retroperitoneum, the base of the mesentery, or the hepatoduodenal ligament, the patient often has only modest hypotension in transit or on arrival at the emergency center; the hypotension can be temporarily reversed by the infusion of fluids and may not recur until the hematoma is opened at the time of laparotomy. This is usually the situation when an abdominal venous injury is present. In the case of active intraperitoneal hemorrhage, the patient typically has significant hypotension and may have a distended abdomen on arrival. Another physical finding that is occasionally noted in association with an injury to the common or external iliac artery is intermittent or complete loss of a pulse in the ipsilateral femoral artery; this finding in a patient with a transpelvic gunshot wound is pathognomonic of an injury to the iliac artery.

Injuries to the great vessels of the abdomen are caused by penetrating wounds in 90% to 95% of cases; accordingly, they are often accompanied by injuries to multiple intra-abdominal organs, including those in the gastrointestinal tract.[2-5] The general principles governing the sequencing of repairs of injuries to the great vessels and the GI tract are outlined elsewhere [*see 105 Operative Exposure of Abdominal Injuries and Closure of the Abdomen*].

A hematoma [*see Figures 1 and 2*] or hemorrhage associated with an injury to a great vessel of the abdomen occurs in one of the three zones of the retroperitoneum or in the portal-retrohepatic area of the right upper quadrant [*see 105 Operative Exposure of Abdominal Injuries and Closure of the Abdomen*]. The magnitude of injury is usually described according to the Abdominal Vascular Organ Injury Scale, devised in 1992 by the American Association for the Surgery of Trauma [*see Table 1*].[6]

Injuries in Zone 1

SUPRAMESOCOLIC

It is helpful to divide midline retroperitoneal hematomas into those that are supramesocolic and those that are inframesocolic.[1] Hematoma or hemorrhage in the midline supramesocolic area of zone 1 is cause to suspect the presence of an injury to the suprarenal aorta, the celiac axis, the proximal superior mesenteric artery, or the proximal renal artery.

When a hematoma is present in the midline supramesocolic area, one usually has time to perform left medial visceral rotation [*see Figure 3 and 105 Operative Exposure of Abdominal Injuries and Closure of the Abdomen*].[7,8] The advantage of this technique is that it allows visualization of the entire abdominal aorta, from the aortic hiatus of the diaphragm to the common iliac arteries [*see Figure 4*]. Obvious disadvantages include the 4 to 5 minutes required to complete the maneuver when the surgeon is inexperienced; the risk of damage to the spleen, the left kidney, or the

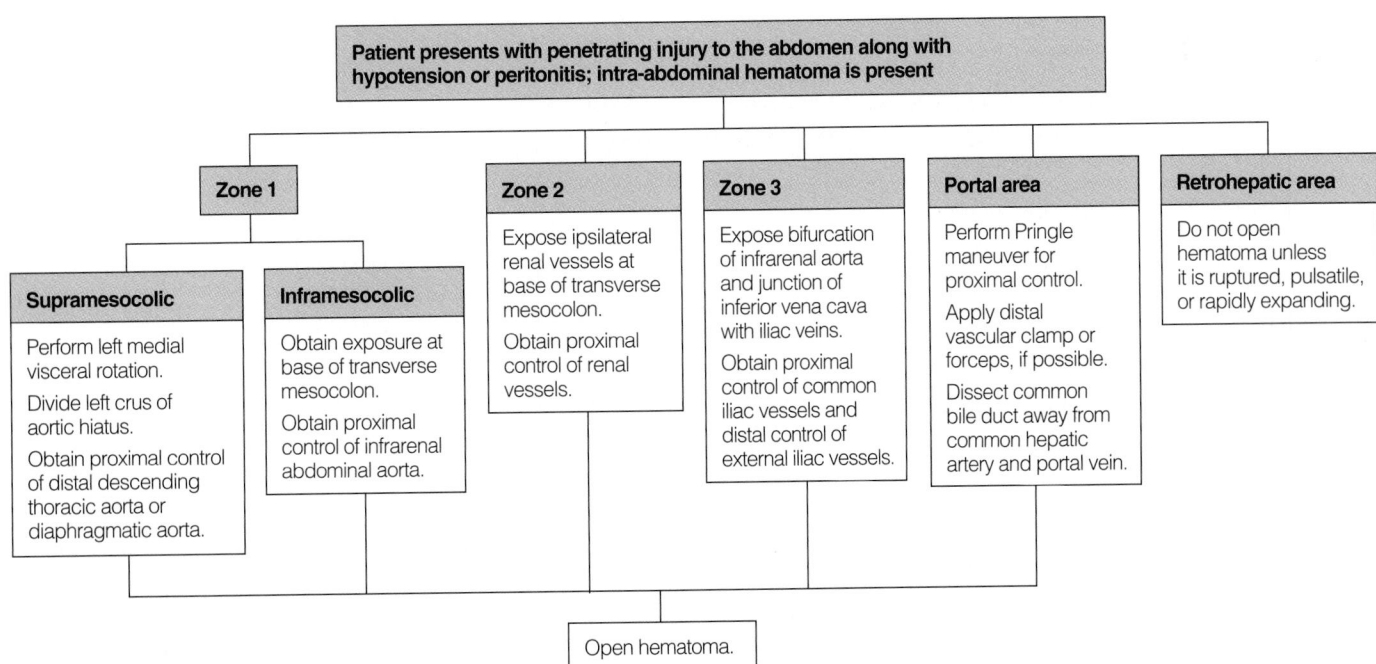

Figure 1 Algorithm illustrates management of intra-abdominal hematoma found at operation after penetrating trauma.

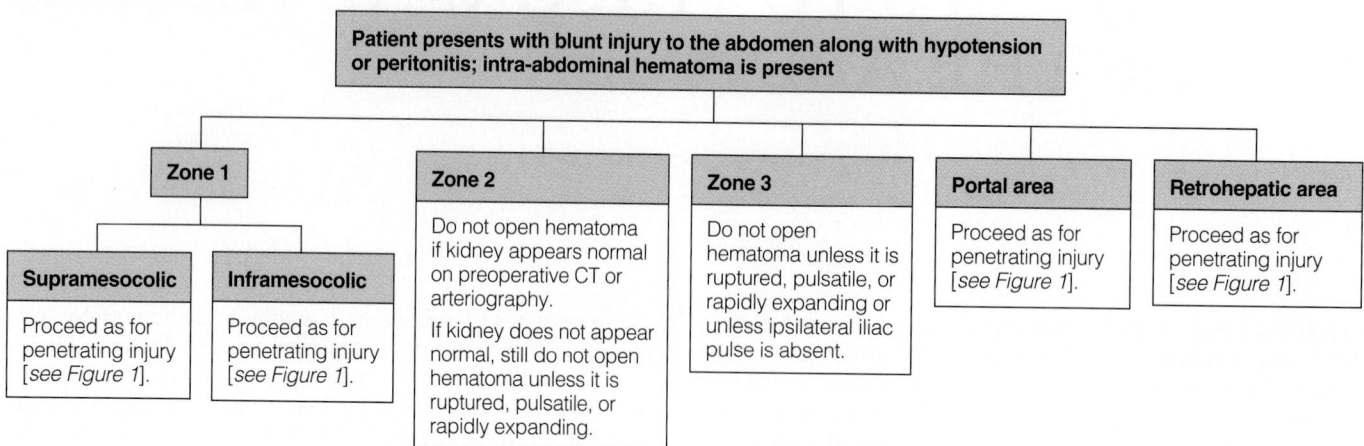

Figure 2 **Algorithm illustrates management of intra-abdominal hematoma found at operation after blunt trauma.**

posterior left renal artery as the maneuver is performed; and the anatomic distortion that results when the left kidney and the left renal artery are rotated anteriorly. When the hematoma is near the aortic hiatus of the diaphragm, it may be advisable to leave the left kidney in its fossa, thereby eliminating potential damage

to the structure as well as the distortion resulting from rotation. Because of the density of the celiac ganglia and nerve plexus and the lymphatic vessels surrounding the upper abdominal aorta, this portion of the aorta is difficult to visualize even when left medial visceral rotation has been performed. It is frequently help-

Table 1 AAST Abdominal Vascular Organ Injury Scale

Grade	Characteristics of Injury	OIS Grade	ICD-9	AIS-90
I	Unnamed superior mesenteric artery or superior mesenteric vein branches	I	902.20/902.39	NS
	Unnamed inferior mesenteric artery or inferior mesenteric vein branches	I	902.27/902.32	NS
	Phrenic artery or vein	I	902.89	NS
	Lumbar artery or vein	I	902.89	NS
	Gonadal artery or vein	I	902.89	NS
	Ovarian artery or vein	I	902.81/902.82	NS
	Other unnamed small arterial or venous structures requiring ligation	I	902.90	NS
II	Right, left, or common hepatic artery	II	902.22	3
	Splenic artery or vein	II	902.23/902.34	3
	Right or left gastric arteries	II	902.21	3
	Gastroduodenal artery	II	902.24	3
	Inferior mesenteric artery, trunk, or inferior mesenteric vein, trunk	II	902.27/902.32	3
	Primary named branches of mesenteric artery (e.g., ileocolic artery) or mesenteric vein	II	902.26/902.31	3
	Other named abdominal vessels requiring ligation or repair	II	902.89	3
III*	Superior mesenteric vein, trunk	III	902.31	3
	Renal artery or vein	III	902.41/902.42	3
	Iliac artery or vein	III	902.53/902.54	3
	Hypogastric artery or vein	III	902.51/902.52	3
	Vena cava, infrarenal	III	902.10	3
IV*†	Superior mesenteric artery, trunk	IV	902.25	3
	Celiac axis, proper	IV	902.24	3
	Vena cava, suprarenal and infrahepatic	IV	902.10	3
	Aorta, infrarenal	IV	902.00	4
V†	Portal vein	V	902.33	3
	Extraparenchymal hepatic vein	V	902.11	3 (hepatic vein) 5 (liver + veins)
	Vena cava, retrohepatic or suprahepatic	V	902.19	5
	Aorta, suprarenal and subdiaphragmatic	V	902.00	4

Note: This classification is applicable to extraparenchymal vascular injuries. If the vessel injury is within 2 cm of the parenchyma of a specific organ, one should refer to the injury scale for that organ.

*Increase grade by I if there are multiple injuries involving > 50% of vessel circumference.

†Reduce grade by I if laceration is < 25% of vessel circumference.

AAST—American Association for the Surgery of Trauma   AIS—Abbreviated Injury Scale   ICD—International Classification of Diseases

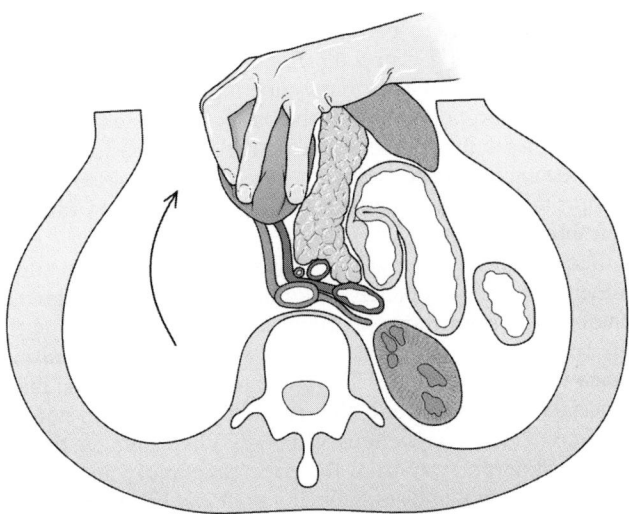

Figure 3 Left medial visceral rotation is performed by means of sharp and blunt dissection with elevation of the left colon, the left kidney, the spleen, the tail of the pancreas, and the gastric fundus.

ful to transect the left crus of the aortic hiatus in the diaphragm at the 2 o'clock position to allow exposure of the distal descending thoracic aorta above the hiatus. Visualization of this portion of the vessel is much easier to achieve than visualization of the diaphragmatic or visceral abdominal aorta below, and an aortic cross-clamp can be applied much more quickly at this level.

Active hemorrhage from the midline supramesocolic area is controlled temporarily by packing with laparotomy pads or using an aortic compression device [*see Figure 5*].[9,10] A definitive approach is to divide the lesser omentum manually, retract the stomach and esophagus to the left, and manually dissect in the area just below the aortic hiatus of the diaphragm to obtain rapid exposure of the supraceliac abdominal aorta.[11] An aortic cross-clamp can then be applied. Distal control of the upper abdominal aorta is difficult to obtain because of the presence of the anteriorly located celiac axis and superior mesenteric artery. In young trauma patients who are

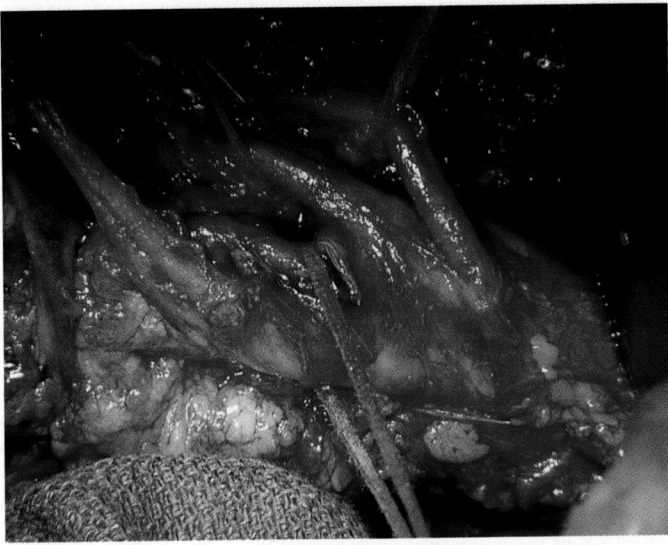

Figure 4 Shown is an autopsy view of the supraceliac aorta and the celiac axis, the proximal superior mesenteric artery, and the medially rotated left renal artery after removal of lymphatic and nerve tissue.

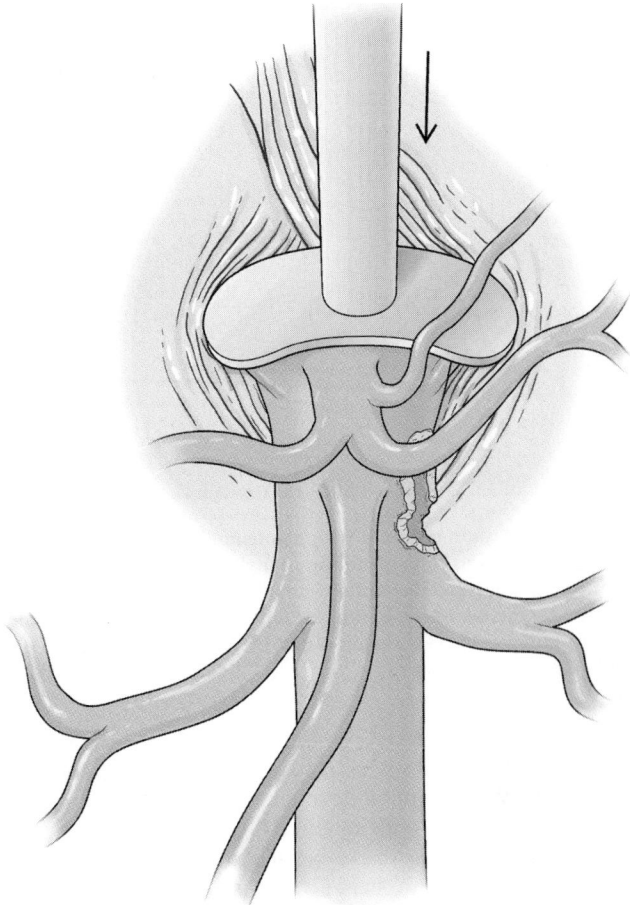

Figure 5 An aortic compression device is used to control hemorrhage from the visceral portion of the abdominal aorta.

otherwise healthy, ligation and division of the celiac axis allow easier application of the distal aortic clamp and better exposure of the supraceliac area for subsequent vascular repair.[12]

Small penetrating wounds to the supraceliac abdominal aorta are repaired with a continuous 3-0 or 4-0 polypropylene suture. If two small perforations are adjacent to each other, they can be connected and the defect closed in a transverse fashion. If closure of a perforation would result in significant narrowing of the aorta or if a portion of the aortic wall is missing, patch aortoplasty with polytetrafluoroethylene (PTFE) is indicated. On rare occasions, in patients with extensive injuries to the diaphragmatic or supraceliac aorta, resection of the area of injury and insertion of a vascular conduit are indicated. Even though many of these patients have associated gastric, enteric, or colonic injuries, the most appropriate prosthesis with such a life-threatening injury is a 12 mm or 14 mm Dacron or PTFE graft [*see Figure 6*].[13] Provided that vigorous intraoperative irrigation is performed after repair of GI tract perforations, that proper graft coverage is ensured, and that perioperative antibiotics are appropriately employed, it is extraordinarily rare for a prosthesis inserted in the healthy aorta of a young trauma patient to become infected.

The aortic prosthesis is sewn in place with a continuous 3-0 or 4-0 polypropylene suture. Both ends of the aorta are flushed before the distal anastomosis is completed, and the distal aortic cross-clamp is removed before the final knot is tied to eliminate air from the system. The proximal aortic cross-clamp is removed very slowly as the anesthesiologist rapidly infuses fluids and intra-

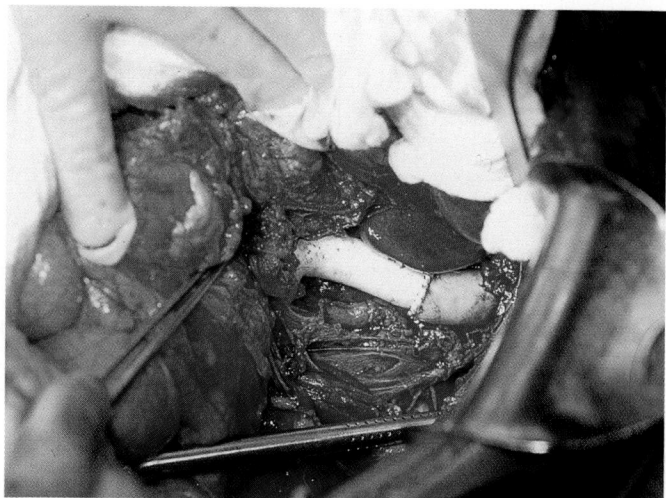

Figure 6 A 22-year-old man with a gunshot wound to the right upper quadrant had injuries to the prepyloric area of the stomach and to the supraceliac abdominal aorta. The aortic injury was managed by means of segmental resection and replacement with a 16 mm polytetrafluoroethylene (PTFE) graft. The patient went home 46 days after injury.

venous bicarbonate to reverse so-called washout acidosis from the previously ischemic lower extremities. The retroperitoneum is then irrigated with an antibiotic solution and closed over the graft in a watertight fashion with an absorbable suture.

Cross-clamping of the diaphragmatic or supraceliac abdominal aorta in a patient with hemorrhagic shock results in severe ischemia of the legs. Restoration of flow through the repaired abdominal aorta may then cause a reperfusion injury in addition to the ischemic edema that develops in the muscle compartments below the knee. In a patient who is hemodynamically stable after repair of the suprarenal abdominal aorta and other injuries, measurement of compartmental pressures below the knees should be performed before the patient is moved from the operating room. Pressures in the range of 30 to 35 mm Hg are likely to rise in the intensive care unit; accordingly, at many centers, bilateral below-the-knee two-incision four-compartment fasciotomies would be performed in this situation.

The survival rate in patients with injuries to the suprarenal abdominal aorta had been 30% to 35% but was lower than 10% in one 2001 review.[4,13]

Injuries to branches of the celiac axis are often difficult to repair because of the amount of dissection required to remove the dense neural and lymphatic tissue in this area. Because most patients have excellent collateral flow in the upper abdomen, major injuries to either the left gastric or the proximal splenic artery generally should be ligated. Because the common hepatic artery may have a larger diameter than either of these two arteries, an injury to this vessel can occasionally be repaired by means of lateral arteriorrhaphy, an end-to-end anastomosis, or the insertion of a saphenous vein graft. One should not worry about ligating the common hepatic artery proximal to the origin of the gastroduodenal artery: there is extensive collateral flow to the liver from the midgut. When the entire celiac axis is injured, it is best to ligate all three vessels and forgo any attempt at repair.

Injuries to the superior mesenteric artery are managed according to the anatomic level of the perforation or thrombosis.[14] On rare occasions, in patients with injuries beneath the neck of the pancreas, one may have to transect the pancreas to obtain proximal control.

Another option is to perform left medial visceral rotation (see above) and apply a clamp directly to the origin of the superior mesenteric artery. Injuries to the superior mesenteric artery in this area or just beyond the base of the mesocolon are often associated with injuries to the pancreas. The potential for a postoperative leak from the injured pancreas near the arterial repair has led numerous authors to suggest that any extensive injury to the artery at this location should be ligated [*see Figure 7*].

Because of the intense vasoconstriction of the distal superior mesenteric artery in patients who have sustained exsanguinating hemorrhage from more proximal injuries treated with ligation, the collateral flow from the foregut and hindgut is often inadequate to maintain the viability of the organs in the distal midgut, especially the cecum and the ascending colon. Therefore, it is safest to place a saphenous vein or PTFE graft on the distal infrarenal aorta, away from the pancreatic injury and any other upper abdominal injuries.[15] Such a graft can be tailored to reach the side or the anterior aspect of the superior mesenteric artery, or it can be attached to the transected distal superior mesenteric artery in an end-to-end fashion without significant tension [*see Figure 8*]. Soft tissue must be approximated over the aortic suture line of the graft to prevent the development of an aortoenteric fistula in the postoperative period.

In patients with severe shock from exsanguination caused by a complex injury to the superior mesenteric artery, damage-control laparotomy is indicated [*see Damage-Control Laparotomy, below*]: the injured area should be resected and a temporary intraluminal Argyle, Javid, or Pruitt-Inahara shunt inserted to maintain flow to the midgut during resuscitation in the surgical intensive care unit.[16]

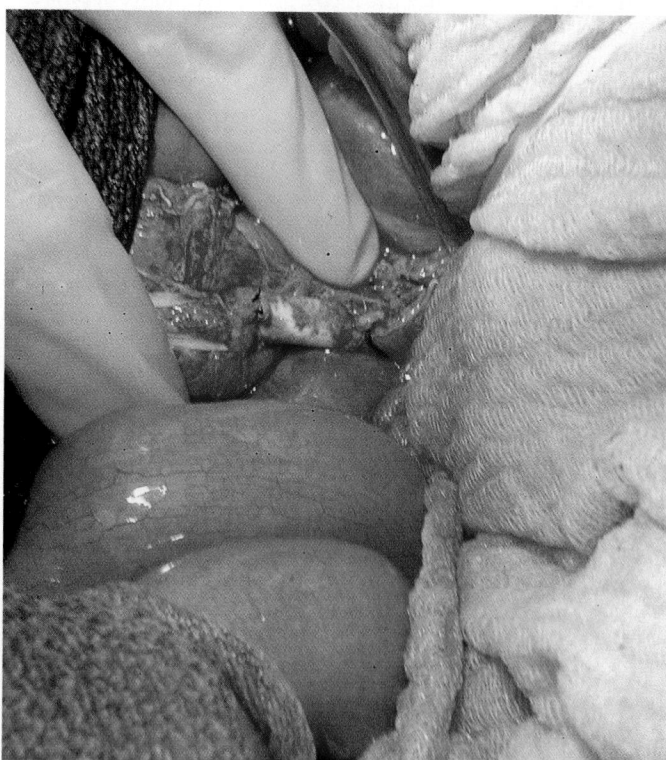

Figure 7 An 18-year-old man experienced a gunshot wound to the head of the pancreas and the proximal superior mesenteric artery. A Whipple procedure was performed, and a 6 mm PTFE graft was placed in the artery. The artery-graft suture line dehisced secondary to a pancreatic leak on day 30 after injury, and the patient died on day 42.

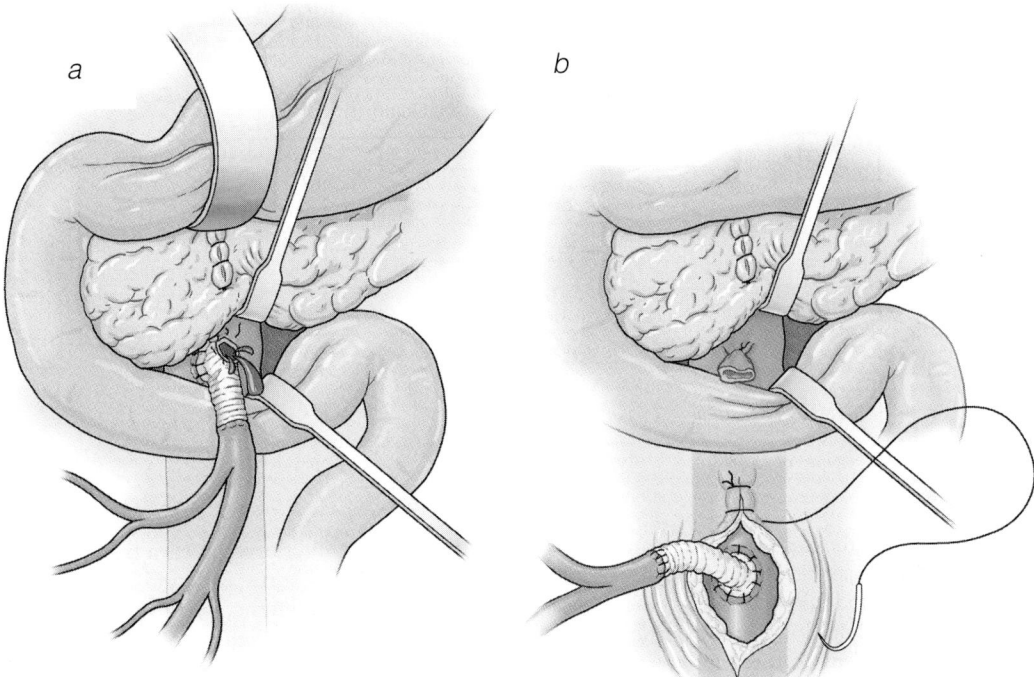

Figure 8 (*a*) **When complex grafting procedures to the superior mesenteric artery are necessary, it may be dangerous to place the proximal suture line near an associated pancreatic injury. (*b*) The proximal suture line should be on the lower aorta, away from the upper abdominal injuries, and should be covered with retroperitoneal tissue.**

When ligation is indicated for more distal injuries to the superior mesenteric artery, segments of the ileum or even the right colon may have to be resected because of ischemia.

The survival rate in patients with penetrating injuries to the superior mesenteric artery is approximately 50% to 55% overall [*see Table 2*] but only 20% to 25% when any form of repair more complex than lateral arteriorrhaphy is necessary.[1-4,15,17]

An injury to the proximal renal artery may also be present under a supramesocolic hematoma or bleeding area. When active hemorrhage is present, control of the supraceliac abdominal aorta in or just below the aortic hiatus must be obtained. When only a hematoma or a known thrombosis of the proximal renal artery is present, proximal vascular control can be obtained by elevating the transverse mesocolon and dissecting the vessel from the lateral aspect of the abdominal aorta. Options for repair of either the proximal or the distal renal artery are described elsewhere [*see Injuries in Zone 2, below*].

The superior mesenteric vein is the other great vessel of the abdomen that may be injured in the supramesocolic or retromesocolic area of the midline retroperitoneum. Because of the overlying pancreas, the proximity of the uncinate process, and the close association of this vessel with the superior mesenteric artery, repair of the superior mesenteric vein is quite difficult. As with injuries to the superior mesenteric artery (see above), one may have to transect the neck of the pancreas between noncrushing vascular or intestinal clamps to gain access to a perforation of the superior mesenteric vein. An injury to this vein below the inferior border of the pancreas can be managed by compressing it manually between one's fingers as an assistant places a continuous 5-0 polypropylene suture to complete the repair. When a penetrating injury to the vein has a posterior component, one must ligate multiple collateral vessels entering the vein in this area to achieve proper visualization.

There is excellent evidence that young trauma patients tolerate ligation of the superior mesenteric vein well when vigorous postoperative fluid resuscitation is performed to reverse the peripheral hypovolemia that results from splanchnic hypervolemia.[18,19] Typically, ligation is followed almost immediately by swelling of the midgut and discoloration suggestive of impending ischemia. In such cases, temporary coverage of the midgut with a silo, followed by early reoperation, may be necessary to reassure the operating surgeon that the ischemia has not become permanent.

The survival rate in patients with injuries to the superior mesenteric vein ranges from 36% to 71%, depending on whether other vascular injuries are present [*see Table 3*].[1-4,18]

INFRAMESOCOLIC

The lower area of the midline retroperitoneum in zone 1 is known as the midline inframesocolic area. Injuries to either the infrarenal abdominal aorta or the inferior vena cava occur in this area.

An injury to the inframesocolic abdominal aorta that is under a hematoma is controlled by performing the same maneuvers used to gain proximal control of an infrarenal abdominal aortic aneurysm. The infrarenal abdominal aorta is exposed by pulling the transverse mesocolon up toward the patient's head, eviscerating the small bowel to the right side of the abdomen, and opening the midline retroperitoneum until the left renal vein is exposed. A proximal aortic cross-clamp is then placed immediately inferior to this vessel [*see Figure 9*]. When the entire inframesocolic area is distorted by the presence of a large pulsatile hematoma, the inexperienced trauma surgeon should remember that the hole in the infrarenal abdominal aorta is under the highest point of the hematoma (the so-called Mt. Everest phenomenon). When there is active hemorrhage from this area, rapid proximal control is obtained in the same fashion or, if necessary because of the need

Table 2 Survival after Injuries to Arteries in the Abdomen

Injured Artery	Asensio et al[2] (2000)		Davis et al[3] (2001)*	Tyburski et al[4] (2001)
	Isolated Injury	With Other Arterial Injury		
Abdominal aorta as a whole	21.7% (10/46)	17.6% (3/17)	39.1% (25/64)	21.1% (15/71)
Pararenal to diaphragm	—	—	—	8.3% (3/36)
Infrarenal	—	—	—	34.2% (12/35)
Superior mesenteric artery	52.4% (11/21)	28.6% (2/7)	53.3% (8/15)	48.8% (20/41)
Renal artery	62.5% (5/8)	33.3% (2/6)	56.2% (9/16)	73.7% (14/19)
Iliac artery				
Common	—	—	55.5% (5/9)	44.7% (17/38)
External	—	—	65.2% (30/46)	62.5% (20/32)

*Excludes patients who exsanguinated before repair or ligation.

to apply compression, by dividing the lesser omentum and applying the cross-clamp just below the aortic hiatus of the diaphragm. Distal control of the infrarenal abdominal aorta is obtained by dividing the midline retroperitoneum down to the aortic bifurcation, taking care to avoid the origin of the inferior mesenteric artery on the left side.

Injuries to the infrarenal aorta are repaired by means of lateral aortorrhaphy, patch aortoplasty, an end-to-end anastomosis, or insertion of a Dacron or PTFE graft. Much as with injuries to the suprarenal abdominal aorta in young trauma patients, it is rarely possible to place a tube graft larger than 12 or 14 mm. Because the retroperitoneal tissue is often thin at this location in young patients, an important adjunctive measure after the aortic repair is to mobilize the gastrocolic omentum, flip it into the lesser sac superiorly, and then bring it down over the infrarenal aortic graft through a hole in the left transverse mesocolon. An alternative is to mobilize the gastrocolic omentum away from the right side of the colon and then swing the mobilized tissue into the left lateral gutter just below the ligament of Treitz to cover the graft. With either technique, it is mandatory to suture the viable omental pedicle superior to the aortic suture line to prevent a postoperative aortoduodenal fistula.[20,21]

The survival rate in patients with injuries to the infrarenal abdominal aorta had been approximately 45% but was 34% in a 2001 review [see Table 2].[1-4]

Injury to the inferior vena cava below the liver should be suspected when the aorta is found to be intact underneath an inframesocolic hematoma, when such a hematoma appears to be more extensive on the right side of the abdomen than on the left, or when there is active hemorrhage coming through the base of the mesentery of the ascending colon or the hepatic flexure. It is certainly possible to visualize the inferior vena cava through the midline retroperitoneal exposure just described (see above); however, most surgeons are more comfortable with visualizing the vessel by mobilizing the right half of the colon and the C loop of the duodenum.[1] With this right medial visceral rotation maneuver, the right kidney is left in situ unless there is an associated injury to the posterior aspect of the right renal vein, to the suprarenal vena cava, or to the right kidney itself. Right medial visceral rotation, in conjunction with the Kocher maneuver, permits visualization of the entire vena caval system from the confluence of the iliac veins to the suprarenal vena cava below the liver [see 105 Operative Exposure of Abdominal Injuries and Closure of the Abdomen]. Local exposure of the iliac vein–vena cava junction in the lower abdomen and of the renal vein–vena cava junction in the upper abdomen is appropriate before completion of right medial visceral rotation. This measure allows rapid application of proximal and distal vascular clamps on the inferior vena cava in the event that exsanguinating hemorrhage results when the caval injury is exposed.

Table 3 Survival after Injuries to Veins in the Abdomen

Injured Vein	Asensio et al[2] (2000)		Davis et al[3] (2001)*	Tyburski et al[4] (2001)
	Isolated Injury	With Other Venous Injury		
Inferior vena cava as a whole	29.3% (12/41)†	22.2% (8/36)†	56% (47/84)	43% (61/142)
Pararenal to diaphragm	—	—	—	40.3% (31/77)
Infrarenal	—	—	—	46.2% (30/65)
Superior mesenteric vein	47.4% (9/19)	35.7% (5/14)	71.4% (15/21)	56.3% (18/32)
Renal vein	—	44.1% (15/34)	70% (21/30)	68.8% (22/32)
Iliac vein (all)	62.2% (23/37)	33.3% (5/15)	—	—
Common	—	—	81% (17/21)	49% (24/49)
External	—	—	74.5% (41/55)	66.7% (16/24)

*Excludes patients who exsanguinated before repair or ligation.
†Excludes retrohepatic vena cava.

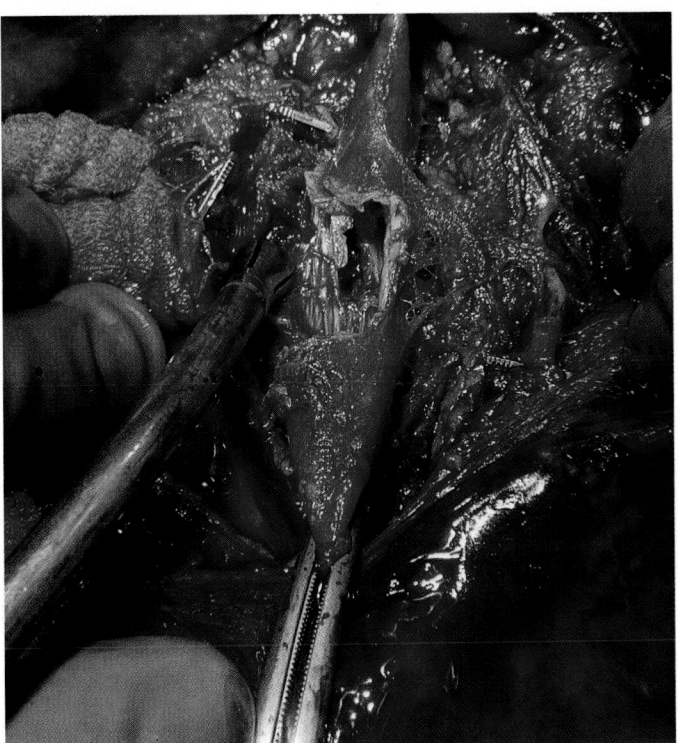

Figure 9 Shown is a gunshot wound to the infrarenal abdominal aorta viewed through standard inframesocolic exposure. Patient's head is at the bottom of the photograph.

For proper exposure of a hole in a large vein such as the inferior vena cava, the loose retroperitoneal fatty tissue must be dissected away from the wall of the vessel. Active hemorrhage coming from the anterior surface of the inferior vena cava is best controlled by applying a Satinsky vascular clamp. If it is difficult to apply this clamp, one should try grasping the area of the perforation with a pair of vascular forceps or several Judd-Allis clamps; this step may facilitate safe application of the Satinsky clamp.[22] When the perforation in the inferior vena cava is more lateral or posterior, it is often helpful to compress the vessel proximally and distally around the perforation, using gauze sponges placed in straight sponge sticks. On occasion, an extensive injury to the inferior vena cava can be controlled only by completely occluding the entire inferior vena cava with large DeBakey aortic cross-clamps. This maneuver interrupts much of the venous return to the right side of the heart and is poorly tolerated by hypotensive patients unless the infrarenal abdominal aorta is cross-clamped simultaneously.

There are two anatomic areas in which vascular control of an injury to the inferior vena cava below the liver is difficult to obtain: (1) the confluence of the common iliac veins and (2) the junction of the renal veins with the inferior vena cava. One interesting approach to an injury to the inferior vena cava at the confluence of the iliac veins is temporary division of the overlying right common iliac artery, coupled with mobilization of the aortic bifurcation to the patient's left.[23] This approach yields a better view of the common iliac veins and the proximal inferior vena cava and makes repair considerably easier than it would be if the aortic bifurcation were left in place. Once the vein is repaired, the right common iliac artery is reconstituted via an end-to-end anastomosis. The usual approach to injuries to the inferior vena cava at its junction with the renal veins involves clamp or sponge-stick compression of the infrarenal and suprarenal vena cava, as

well as control of both renal veins with Silastic loops to facilitate the direct application of angled vascular clamps. As noted, medial mobilization of the right kidney may permit the application of a partial occlusion clamp across the inferior vena cava at its junction with the right renal vein as an alternative approach to an injury in this area. Another useful technique for controlling hemorrhage from the inferior vena cava at any location is to insert a 5 ml or 30 ml Foley balloon catheter into the caval laceration and then inflate it in the lumen.[24, 25] Once the bleeding is controlled, vascular clamps are positioned around the perforation, and the balloon catheter is removed before repair of the vessel.

Anterior perforations of the inferior vena cava are managed by means of transverse repair with a continuous 4-0 or 5-0 polypropylene suture. Much has been written about visualizing posterior perforations by extending anterior perforations, but in my experience, opportunities to apply this approach have been rare. It is often easier to roll the vena cava to one side to complete a continuous suture repair of a posterior perforation. When both anterior and posterior perforations have been repaired, there is usually a significant degree of narrowing of the inferior vena cava, which may lead to slow postoperative occlusion. If the patient's condition is unstable and a coagulopathy has developed, no further attempt should be made to revise the repair. If the patient is stable, there may be some justification for applying a large PTFE patch to prevent this postoperative occlusion [*see Figure 10*].

Ligation of the infrarenal inferior vena cava is appropriate for young patients who are exsanguinating and in whom a complex repair of the vessel would be necessary. After the damage-control abdominal procedure has been completed and a silo has been used to cover the midgut, it is, once again, worthwhile to measure the compartmental pressures below the knees before the patient is moved from the OR. Below-the-knee two-incision four-compartment fasciotomies are performed when pressures exceed 30 to 35 mm Hg. Three-compartment fasciotomies in the thighs have proved necessary in some surviving patients after caval liga-

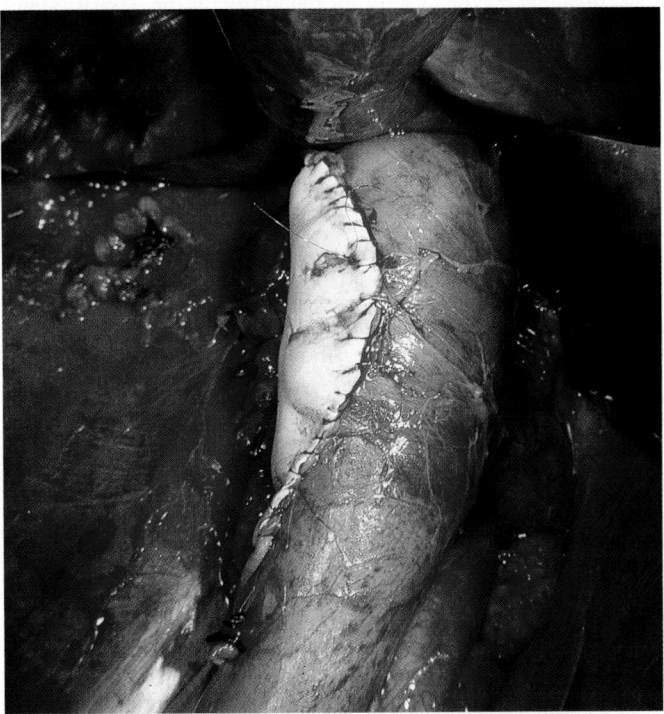

Figure 10 Shown is PTFE patch repair of an injury to the infrarenal inferior vena cava.

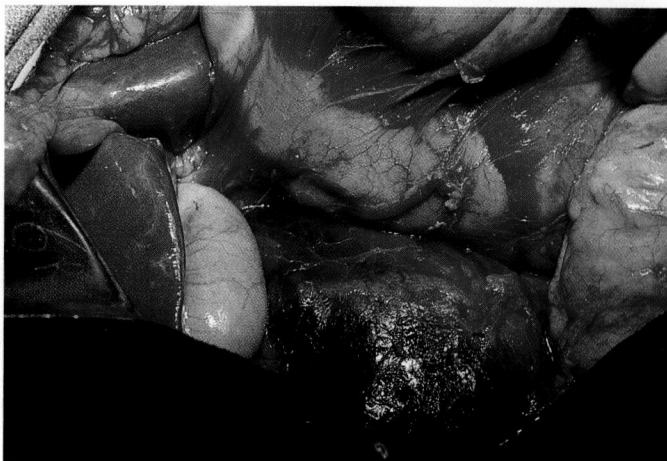

Figure 11 A right perirenal hematoma was not opened at operation, because preoperative abdominal CT documented a reasonably intact kidney.

tion. Patients who have undergone ligation of the infrarenal inferior vena cava require vigorous resuscitation with crystalloid solutions in the postoperative period; in addition, both lower extremities should be wrapped with elastic compression wraps and elevated for 5 to 7 days after operation. Patients who have some residual edema during the later stages of hospitalization despite the elastic compression wraps should be fitted with full-length custom-made support hose. Ligation of the suprarenal inferior vena cava is occasionally necessary when the patient has an extensive injury at this location and appears to be in an irreversible shock state during operation.[26] If the patient's condition improves during a brief period of resuscitation in the SICU, reoperation and reconstruction with an externally supported PTFE graft are usually necessary to prevent renal failure.

The survival rate in patients with injuries to the inferior vena cava depends on the location of the injury; in the past, it ranged from 60% for the suprarenal vena cava to 78% for the infrarenal vena cava but decreased to approximately 33% to 56% if injuries to the retrohepatic vena cava were included. Current studies indicate survival rates of 22% to 56% for inferior vena cava injuries taken as a whole.[1-3,26-28] A 2001 review reported survival rates of 46.1% for the infrarenal inferior vena cava and 40.3% for more superior injuries.[4]

Injuries in Zone 2

Hematoma or hemorrhage in zone 2 is cause to suspect the presence of injury to the renal artery, the renal vein, or the kidney.

In patients who have sustained blunt abdominal trauma but in whom preoperative intravenous pyelography, renal arteriography, or abdominal CT confirms that a reasonably intact kidney is present, there is no justification for opening a perirenal hematoma if one is found at a subsequent operation [see Figure 11].[29]

In highly selected stable patients with penetrating wounds to the flank, there are some data to justify performing preoperative CT. On occasion, documentation of an isolated minor renal injury in the absence of peritoneal findings on physical examination makes it possible to manage such patients nonoperatively.[29] In all other patients with penetrating wounds, when a perirenal hematoma is found during initial exploration, the hematoma should be unroofed and the wound tract explored. If the hematoma is not rapidly expanding and there is no active hemorrhage from the perirenal area,

one may control the ipsilateral renal artery with a Silastic loop in the midline of the retroperitoneum at the base of the mesocolon [see Figure 12].[30,31] Control of the left renal vein can be obtained at the same location; however, control of the proximal right renal vein requires mobilization of the C loop of the duodenum and dissection of the vena cava at its junction with this vessel.

If there is active hemorrhage from the kidney through Gerota's fascia or from the retroperitoneum overlying the renal vessels, no central renal vascular control is necessary. In such a situation, the retroperitoneum lateral to the injured kidney should be opened, and the kidney should be manually elevated directly into the abdominal incision. A large vascular clamp should then be applied directly to the hilar vessels of the elevated kidney to control any further bleeding until a decision is reached on repair versus nephrectomy.

Occasionally, a small perforation of the renal artery can be repaired by lateral arteriorrhaphy or resection with an end-to-end anastomosis.[32] Interposition grafting and replacement of the renal artery with either the hepatic artery (on the right) or the splenic artery (on the left) have been used on rare occasions, but such approaches ordinarily are not indicated unless the injured kidney is the only one the patient has. In patients who have sustained multiple intra-abdominal injuries from penetrating wounds or have undergone a long period of ischemia while other injuries were being repaired, nephrectomy is the appropriate choice for a major renovascular injury, provided that intraoperative palpation has confirmed the presence of a normal contralateral kidney.

The role of renal revascularization in patients who have intimal tears in the renal arteries as a result of deceleration-type trauma remains controversial. If a circumferential intimal tear is noted on preoperative arteriography but flow to the kidney is preserved, the decision whether to repair the artery depends on whether laparotomy is necessary for other injuries and whether the opportunity for anticoagulation is available. If there are no other significant injuries and flow to the kidney is preserved despite the presence of an intimal tear, anticoagulation and a repeat isotope renogram within the first several days may be justified. An alternative approach involves insertion of an endovascular stent in the renal

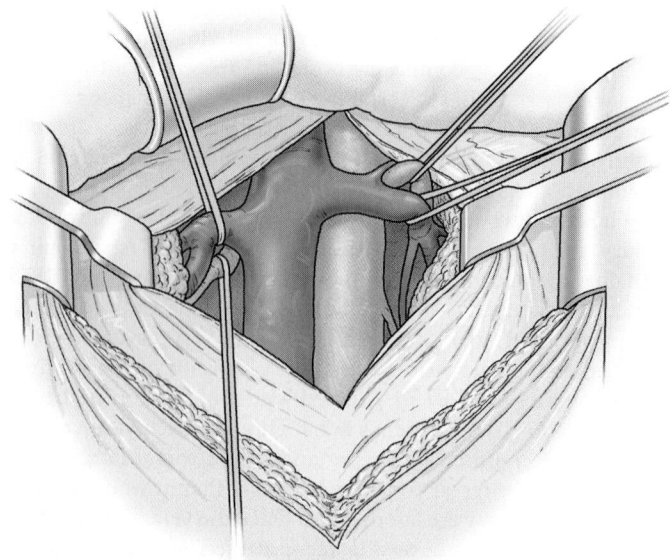

Figure 12 Midline looping of respective renal vessels is performed before entry into any perirenal hematoma.

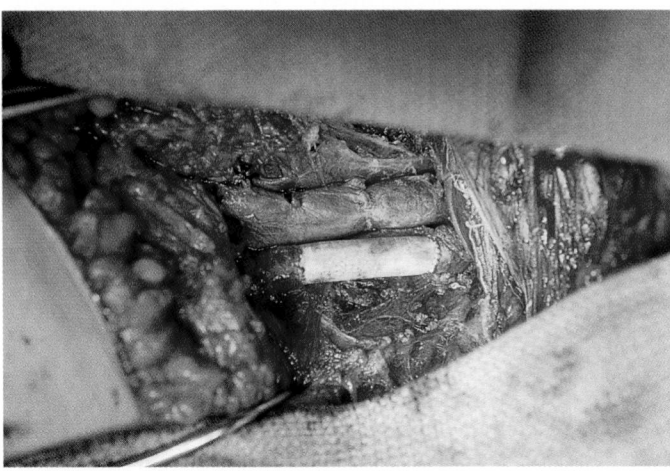

Figure 13 **A 24-year-old man experienced a gunshot wound to the left external iliac artery and vein. The arterial injury was repaired with segmental resection and insertion of an 8 mm PTFE graft; the venous injury was repaired with segmental resection and an end-to-end anastomosis.**

artery, followed by a period of anticoagulation.[33] If occlusion of the proximal renal artery from blunt deceleration-type trauma is documented, the critical factor for renal salvage is the time from occlusion to revascularization. Renal artery occlusion from deceleration-type trauma that is detected within 6 hours of injury may be treated with immediate operation, resection of the area of intimal damage, and an end-to-end anastomosis performed by an experienced vascular trauma team. Given proper exposure and medial mobilization of the kidney, this operation is not technically difficult in a young trauma patient whose renal artery is otherwise normal. In a 1998 review, fewer than 20% of kidneys revascularized in this manner regained any significant degree of function.[34] Hypertension develops in 40% to 45% of patients who undergo observation only after thrombosis is detected.

The survival rate in patients with isolated injuries to the renal arteries ranges from 56% to 74% [*see Table 2*].[1,3,4]

Many patients with penetrating wounds to the renal veins are quite stable as a result of the retroperitoneal tamponade described earlier (see above). Once vascular control is obtained with the direct application of clamps, lateral venorrhaphy is the preferred tech-

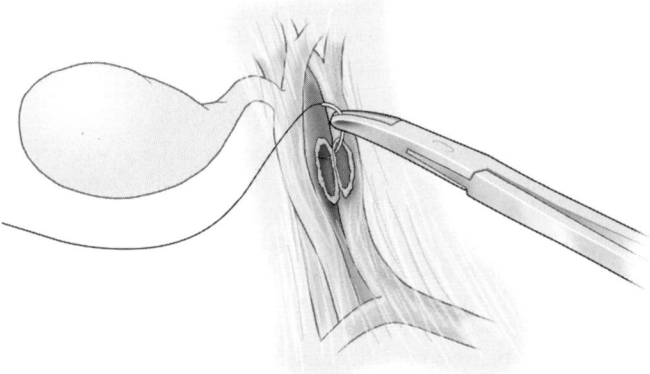

Figure 14 **Failure to properly dissect out the structures in the porta hepatis after a penetrating wound led to the creation of an iatrogenic hepatic artery–portal vein fistula, which was corrected after the arrival of the attending surgeon.**

nique of repair. If ligation of the right renal vein is necessary to control hemorrhage, nephrectomy should be performed, either at initial laparotomy or at reoperation after a damage-control laparotomy; the medial left renal vein may be ligated as long as the left adrenal and gonadal veins are intact. It should be noted, however, that in some series, more postoperative renal complications were noted when this maneuver was used on the left side.[35]

The survival rate in patients with isolated injuries to the renal veins is approximately 70% [*see Table 3*].[1,3,4]

Injuries in Zone 3

Hematoma or hemorrhage in either lateral pelvic area is suggestive of injury to the iliac artery or the iliac vein. When lateral pelvic hematoma or hemorrhage is noted after penetrating trauma, compression with a laparotomy pad or the fingers should be maintained as proximal and distal vascular control is obtained. The proximal common iliac arteries are exposed by eviscerating the small bowel to the right and dividing the midline retroperitoneum over the aortic bifurcation. In young trauma patients, the common iliac artery usually is not adherent to the common iliac vein, and Silastic loops can be passed rapidly around these vessels to provide proximal vascular control. Distal vascular control is most easily obtained where the external iliac artery and vein come out of the pelvis proximal to the inguinal ligament. Even with proximal and distal control of the common or the external iliac artery and vein, there is often continued back-bleeding from the internal iliac artery. Such bleeding is controlled by elevating the Silastic loops on the proximal and distal iliac artery and then either clamping or looping the internal iliac artery, which is the only major branch vessel that descends into the pelvis.

For transpelvic bilateral iliac vascular injuries resulting from a penetrating wound, a technique of total pelvic vascular isolation has been described. Proximally, the abdominal aorta and the inferior vena cava are cross-clamped just above their bifurcations, and distally, both the external iliac artery and the external iliac vein are cross-clamped, with one clamp on each side of the distal pelvis. Back-bleeding from the internal iliac vessels is minimal with this approach.

Ligation of either the common or the external iliac artery in a hypotensive trauma patient leads to a 40% to 50% amputation rate in the postoperative period; consequently, injuries to these vessels should be repaired if at all possible. The standard options for repair—lateral arteriorrhaphy, completion of a partial transection with an end-to-end anastomosis, and resection of the injured area with insertion of a conduit—are feasible in most situations [*see Figure 13*].[36] On rare occasions, it may be preferable either to mobilize the ipsilateral internal iliac artery to serve as a replacement for the external iliac artery or to transpose one iliac artery to the side of the contralateral iliac artery.[37] When a patient is in severe shock from exsanguination caused by a complex injury to the common or the external iliac artery, damage control laparotomy [*see Damage Control Laparotomy, below*] is indicated.[38] The injured area should be resected and a temporary intraluminal Argyle, Javid, or Pruitt-Inahara shunt inserted to maintain flow to the ipsilateral lower extremity during resuscitation in the SICU.[1]

One unique problem associated with repair of the common or the external iliac artery is the choice of technique when significant enteric or fecal contamination is present in the pelvis. In such cases, there is a substantial risk of postoperative pelvic cellulitis, a pelvic abscess, or both, which may lead to blowout of any type of repair. When extensive contamination is present, it is appropriate to divide the common or external iliac artery above the level of injury, close the injury with a double row of continuous 4-0 or 5-0 polypropylene sutures, and bury the stump underneath uninjured retroperitoneum. If a stable patient has obvious ischemia of the ipsilateral lower extremity at the completion of this proximal ligation, one may perform an extra-anatomic femorofemoral crossover bypass with an 8 mm externally supported PTFE graft to restore arterial flow to the extremity.[1] If the patient is unstable, one should take several minutes to perform an ipsilateral four-compartment below-knee fasciotomy; this step will counteract the ischemic edema that inevitably leads to a compartment syndrome and compromises the early survival of the leg. After adequate resuscitation in the SICU, the patient should be returned to the OR for the femorofemoral graft within 4 to 6 hours.

Injuries to the internal iliac arteries are usually ligated even if they occur bilaterally, because young trauma patients typically have extensive collateral flow through the pelvis.

The survival rate in patients with isolated injuries to the external iliac artery exceeds 80% when tamponade is present. If the injury is large and free bleeding has occurred preoperatively, however, the survival rate is only 45%. Current studies report overall survival rates of approximately 45% to 55% for injuries to the common iliac artery and 62% to 65% for injuries to the external iliac artery [see Table 2].[1,3,4,39]

Hemorrhage from injuries to the iliac veins can usually be controlled by means of compression with either sponge sticks or the fingers. As noted, division of the right common iliac artery may be necessary for proper visualization of an injury to the right common iliac vein. Similarly, ligation and division of the internal iliac artery on the side of the pelvis yield improved exposure of an injury to an ipsilateral internal iliac vein.[40]

Injuries to the common or the external iliac vein are best treated by means of lateral venorrhaphy with continuous 4-0 or 5-0 polypropylene sutures. Significant narrowing often results, and a number of reports have demonstrated occlusion on postoperative venography. For patients with narrowing or occlusion, as well as for those in whom ligation was necessary to control exsanguinating hemorrhage, the use of elastic compression wraps and elevation for the first 5 to 7 days after operation is mandatory.[41]

In some centers, once the patient's perioperative coagulopathy has resolved, anticoagulation with a low-molecular-weight heparin is initiated to prevent progression or migration of a venous thrombus. The patient is then discharged on a regimen of oral warfarin sodium, and serial measurement of the international normalized ratio (INR) is continued for 3 months.

The survival rate in patients with injuries to the iliac veins ranges from 33% to 81%, depending on whether associated vascular injuries are present [see Table 3].[1-4,38,42]

Injuries in the Porta Hepatis or Retrohepatic Area

PORTA HEPATIS

Hematoma or hemorrhage in the area of the portal triad in the right upper quadrant is cause to suspect the presence of injury to the portal vein or the hepatic artery or of vascular injury combined with an injury to the common bile duct.

If a hematoma is present, the proximal hepatoduodenal ligament should be occluded with a vascular clamp (the Pringle maneuver [see 106 Injuries to the Liver, Biliary Tract, Spleen, and Diaphragm]) before the hematoma is entered.[43] If the hematoma is centrally located in the porta, one may also be able to apply an angled vascular clamp to the distal end of the portal structures at their entrance into the liver.

If hemorrhage is occurring, compression of the bleeding vessels with the fingers should suffice until the vascular clamp is in place. Once proximal and distal vascular control is obtained, the three structures in the hepatoduodenal ligament must be dissected out very carefully because of the danger of blindly placing sutures in proximity to the common bile duct [see Figure 14].

Injuries to the hepatic artery in this location are occasionally amenable to lateral repair, though ligation without reconstruction is ordinarily well tolerated because of the extensive collateral arterial flow to the liver.[44-47] If an associated hepatic injury calls for extensive suturing or debridement, ligation of the common hepatic artery or artery to the injured lobe will certainly lead to increased postoperative necrosis of the hepatic repair. Moreover, ligation of the common hepatic artery, the right or left hepatic artery supplying the injured lobe, and the portal vein branch to that lobe will lead to necrosis of the lobe and will necessitate hepatectomy. Finally, ligation of the right hepatic artery to control hemorrhage should be followed by cholecystectomy.

Because of the large size of the portal vein and its posterior position in the hepatoduodenal ligament, injuries to this vessel are particularly lethal. Once the Pringle maneuver has been performed, mobilization of the common bile duct to the left and of the cystic duct superiorly, coupled with an extensive Kocher maneuver, allows excellent visualization of any injury to this vein above the superior border of the pancreas. When the perforation extends underneath the neck of the pancreas, it may be necessary to have an assistant compress the superior mesenteric vein below the pancreas and then to divide the pancreas between noncrushing intestinal clamps to obtain exposure of the junction of the superior mesenteric vein and the splenic vein.

The preferred technique for repairing an injury to the portal vein is lateral venorrhaphy with continuous 4-0 or 5-0 polypropylene sutures.[48,49] Complex repairs that have been successful on rare occasions include end-to-end anastomosis, interposition grafting with externally supported PTFE, transposition of the splenic vein, and a venovenous shunt from the superior mesenteric vein to the distal portal vein or the inferior vena cava. Such vigorous attempts at restoration of blood flow are not justified in patients who are in severe hypovolemic shock, for whom ligation of the portal vein is more appropriate. In addition, if a portosystemic shunt is performed in such a patient, hepatic encephalopathy will result because hepatofugal flow will be present in the rerouted or bypassed portal vein. As with ligation of the superior mesenteric vein, it is necessary to infuse tremendous amounts of crystalloids to reverse the transient peripheral hypovolemia that occurs secondary to the splanchnic hypervolemia resulting from ligation of the portal vein.[18,19,49]

Since the early 1980s, the survival rate in patients with injuries to the portal vein has been approximately 50%.[1,3,48,49]

RETROHEPATIC AREA

Retrohepatic hematoma or hemorrhage is cause to suspect the presence of injury to the retrohepatic vena cava, a hepatic vein, or a right renal blood vessel. In addition, hemorrhage in this area may signal injury to the overlying liver [see 106 Injuries to the Liver, Biliary Tract, Spleen, and Diaphragm].

If there is a hematoma that is not expanding or ruptured and clearly has no association with the right perirenal area, a tamponaded injury to the retrohepatic vena cava or a hepatic vein is present. Perihepatic packing around the right lobe of the liver for 24 to 48 hours has been shown to prevent further expansion and should be considered.

If hemorrhage is occurring that does not appear to be coming from the overlying liver, the right lobe of the liver should be compressed posteriorly to tamponade the caval perforation. The Pringle maneuver is then applied, and the surgical and nursing team, the anesthesiologist, and the blood blank are notified. Once the proper instruments and banked blood are in the OR, the overlying injured hepatic lobe or the lobe closest to the presumed site of injury is mobilized by dividing the triangular and coronary ligaments and then lifted out of the subdiaphragmatic area.[50] On occasion, an obvious perforation of the retrohepatic or suprahepatic vena cava or an obvious area where a hepatic vein was avulsed from the vena cava may be grasped with a forceps or a series of Judd-Allis clamps; a Satinsky clamp may then be applied.[4] Because of the copious bleeding that occurs as the liver is lifted and the hole in the vena cava sought, the anesthesiologist should start blood transfusions as the lobe is being mobilized.

If the retrohepatic hemorrhage is not controlled after one or two direct attempts, another technique must be tried. The most common choice is the insertion of a 36 French chest tube or a 9 mm endotracheal tube as an atriocaval shunt [see *105 Operative Exposure of Abdominal Injuries and Closure of the Abdomen and 106 Injuries to the Liver, Biliary Tract, Spleen, and Diaphragm*].[51] The shunt can reduce bleeding by 40% to 60%, but vigorous hemorrhage persists until full control of the perforation is obtained with clamps or sutures. An alternative approach is to isolate the liver and the vena cava by cross-clamping the supraceliac aorta, the porta hepatis, the suprarenal inferior vena cava, and the intrapericardial inferior vena cava.[52] Because profoundly hypovolemic patients usually cannot tolerate cross-clamping of the inferior vena cava, this approach is rarely employed. Some experienced hepatic surgeons have successfully used extensive hepatotomy to expose and repair the retrohepatic vena cava.[53]

The retrohepatic vena cava is repaired with continuous 4-0 or 5-0 polypropylene sutures. When the atriocaval shunt is removed from the heart after the vessel has been repaired, the right atrial appendage is ligated with a 2-0 silk tie.

The survival rate in patients not in cardiac arrest who undergo atriocaval shunting and repair of the retrohepatic vena cava has ranged from 33% to 50%.[51,52]

Damage-Control Laparotomy

Patients with injuries to the great vessels of the abdomen are ideal candidates for damage-control laparotomy[54]: they are uniformly hypothermic, acidotic, and coagulopathic on completion of the vascular repair, and a prolonged operation would lead to their demise. In such patients, packing of minor or moderate injuries to solid organs, packing of the retroperitoneum, stapling and rapid resection of multiple injuries to the GI tract, and consideration of diffuse intra-abdominal packing are all appropriate, as is silo coverage of the open abdomen, in which a temporary silo made from a urologic irrigation bag is sewn to the skin edges with a continuous 2-0 polypropylene or nylon suture.

The patient is then rapidly moved to the SICU for further resuscitation. Priorities in the SICU include rapid restoration of normal body temperature, reversal of shock, infusion of intravenous bicarbonate to correct a persistent pH lower than 7.2, and administration of fresh frozen plasma, platelets, and cryoprecipitate when indicated. It is usually possible to return the patient to the OR for removal of clot and packs, reconstruction of the GI tract, irrigation, and reapplication of silo coverage or application of a vacuum-assisted closure device within 48 to 72 hours.[55,56]

When massive distention of the midgut persists after 7 days of intensive care and use of the vacuum-assisted closure device (15% to 25% of patients), the safest approach is to convert the patient to an open abdomen (i.e., without closure of the midline incision) and cover the midgut with a double-thickness layer of absorbable mesh. With proper nutritional support and occasional use of Dakin solution to minimize bacterial contamination of the absorbable mesh, most patients are ready for the application of a split-thickness skin graft to the eviscerated midgut within 3 to 4 weeks of the original operation for an injury to a great vessel.

Complications

Besides those already mentioned, major complications associated with repair of injuries to the great vessels in the abdomen include thrombosis, dehiscence of the suture line, and infection. Because of the risk of occlusion of repairs in small vasoconstricted vessels (e.g., the superior mesenteric artery), it may be worthwhile to perform a second-look operation within 12 to 24 hours if the patient's metabolic state suggests that ischemia of the midgut is present. Early correction of an arterial thrombosis in the superior mesenteric artery may permit salvage of the midgut.

As noted [see Injuries in Zone 1, *above*], dehiscence of an end-to-end anastomosis or a vascular conduit inserted in the proximal superior mesenteric artery when there is an injury to the adjacent pancreas may be prevented or the incidence lowered by inserting a distal aorta–superior mesenteric artery bypass graft. To prevent adjacent loops of small bowel from adhering to the vascular suture lines, both lines should be covered with soft tissue (retroperitoneal tissue for the aortic suture line and mesenteric tissue for the superior mesenteric arterial suture line). Also as noted [see Injuries in Zone 3, *above*], when an extensive injury to either the common or the external iliac artery occurs in the presence of significant enteric or fecal contamination in the pelvis, ligation and extra-anatomic bypass may be necessary.

On occasion, vascular-enteric fistulas occur after repair of the anterior aorta or the insertion of grafts in either the abdominal aorta or the superior mesenteric artery.[6] In my experience, such fistulas all occur at suture lines; hence, once again, proper coverage of suture lines with soft tissue should eliminate or lower the incidence of this complication.[20,57]

References

1. Feliciano DV: Abdominal vascular injury. Trauma, 5th ed. Moore EE, Feliciano DV, Mattox KL, Eds. McGraw-Hill, New York, 2004

2. Asensio JA, Chahwan S, Hanpeter D, et al: Operative management and outcome of 302 abdominal vascular injuries. Am J Surg 180:528, 2000

3. Davis TP, Feliciano DV, Rozycki GS, et al: Results with abdominal vascular trauma in the modern era. Am Surg 67:565, 2001

4. Tyburski JG, Wilson RF, Dente C, et al: Factors affecting mortality rates in patients with abdominal vascular injuries. J Trauma 50:1020, 2001

5. Wilson RF, Dulchavsky S: Abdominal vascular trauma. Management of Trauma: Pitfalls and Practice. Wilson RF, Walt AJ, Eds. Williams & Wilkins, Baltimore, 1996

6. Moore EE, Cogbill TH, Jurkovich GJ, et al: Organ injury scaling III: Chest wall, abdominal vascular, ureter, bladder, and urethra. J Trauma 33:337, 1992

7. Creech O Jr, DeBakey ME, Morris GS Jr: Aneurysm of thoracoabdominal aorta involving the celiac, superior mesenteric, and renal arteries: report of four cases treated by resection and homograft replacement. Ann Surg 144:549, 1956

8. Elkins R, DeMeester TR, Brawley RK: Surgical exposure of the upper abdominal aorta and its branches. Surgery 70:622, 1971

9. Conn J Jr, Trippel OH, Bergan JJ: A new atraumatic aortic occluder. Surgery 64:1158, 1968

10. Mahoney BD, Gerdes D, Roller B, et al: Aortic compressor for aortic occlusion in hemorrhagic shock. Ann Emerg Med 13:29, 1984

11. Veith FJ, Gupta S, Daly V: Technique for occluding the supraceliac aorta through the abdomen. Surg Gynecol Obstet 151:426, 1980

12. Kavic SM, Atweh N, Ivy ME, et al: Celiac axis ligation after gunshot wound to the abdomen: Case report and literature review. J Trauma 50:738, 2001

13. Accola KD, Feliciano DV, Mattox KL, et al: Management of injuries to the suprarenal aorta. Am J Surg 154:613, 1987

14. Fullen WD, Hunt J, Altemeier WA: The clinical spectrum of penetrating injury to the superior mesenteric arterial circulation. J Trauma 12:656, 1972

15. Accola KD, Feliciano DV, Mattox KL, et al: Management of injuries to the superior mesenteric artery. J Trauma 26:313, 1986

16. Reilly PM, Rotondo MF, Carpenter JP, et al: Temporary vascular continuity during damage control: intraluminal shunting for proximal superior mesenteric artery injury. J Trauma 39:757, 1995

17. Asensio JA, Britt LD, Borzotta A, et al: Multiinstitutional experience with the management of superior mesenteric artery injuries. J Am Coll Surg 193:354, 2001

18. Stone HH, Fabian TC, Turkleson ML: Wounds of the portal venous system. World J Surg 6:335, 1982

19. Donahue TK, Strauch GO: Ligation as definitive management of injury to the superior mesenteric vein. J Trauma 28:541, 1988

20. Bunt TJ, Doerhoff CR, Haynes JL: Retrocolic omental pedicle flap for routine plication of abdominal aortic grafts. Surg Gynecol Obstet 158:591, 1984

21. Nothmann A, Tung TC, Simon B: Aortoduodenal fistula in the acute trauma setting: case report. J Trauma 53:106, 2002

22. Henry SM, Duncan AO, Scalea TM: Intestinal Allis clamps as temporary vascular control for major retroperitoneal venous injury. J Trauma 51:170, 2001

23. Salam AA, Stewart MT: New approach to wounds of the aortic bifurcation and inferior vena cava. Surgery 98:105, 1985

24. Ravikumar S, Stahl WM: Intraluminal balloon catheter occlusion for major vena cava injuries. J Trauma 25:458, 1985

25. Feliciano DV, Burch JM, Mattox KL, et al: Balloon catheter tamponade in cardiovascular wounds. Am J Surg 160:583, 1990

26. Ivy ME, Possenti P, Atweh N, et al: Ligation of the suprarenal vena cava after a gunshot wound. J Trauma 45:630, 1998

27. Wiencek RG, Wilson RF: Abdominal venous injuries. J Trauma 26:771, 1986

28. Klein SR, Baumgartner FJ, Bongard FS: Contemporary management strategy for major inferior vena caval injuries. J Trauma 37:35, 1994

29. Carroll PR, McAninch JW, Klosterman P, et al: Renovascular trauma: risk assessment, surgical management, and outcome. J Trauma 30:547, 1990

30. McAninch JW, Carroll PR: Renal trauma: kidney preservation through improved vascular control—a refined approach. J Trauma 22:285, 1982

31. Gonzalez RP, Falimirski M, Holevar MR, et al: Surgical management of renal trauma: is vascular control necessary? J Trauma 47:1039, 1999

32. Brown MF, Graham JM, Mattox KL, et al: Renovascular trauma. Am J Surg 140:802, 1980

33. Villas PA, Cohen G, Putnam SG III, et al: Wallstent placement in a renal artery after blunt abdominal trauma. J Trauma 46:1137, 1999

34. Haas CA, Dinchman KH, Nasrallah PF, et al: Traumatic renal artery occlusion: a 15-year review. J Trauma 45:557, 1998

35. Rastad J, Almgren B, Bowald S, et al: Renal complications to left renal vein ligation in abdominal aortic surgery. J Cardiovasc Surg 25:432, 1984

36. Landreneau RJ, Lewis DM, Snyder WH: Complex iliac arterial trauma: autologous or prosthetic vascular repair? Surgery 114:9, 1993

37. Landreneau RJ, Mitchum P, Fry WJ: Iliac artery transposition. Arch Surg 124:978, 1989

38. Cushman JG, Feliciano DV, Renz BM, et al: Iliac vessel injury: operative physiology related to outcome. J Trauma 42:1033, 1997

39. Burch JM, Richardson RJ, Martin RR, et al: Penetrating iliac vascular injuries: recent experience with 233 consecutive patients. J Trauma 30:1450, 1990

40. Vitelli CE, Scalea TM, Phillips TF, et al: A technique for controlling injuries of the iliac vein in the patient with trauma. Surg Gynecol Obstet 166:551, 1988

41. Mullins RJ, Lucas CE, Ledgerwood AM: The natural history following venous ligation for civilian injuries. J Trauma 20:737, 1980

42. Wilson RF, Wiencek RG, Balog M: Factors affecting mortality rate with iliac vein injuries. J Trauma 30:320, 1990

43. Busuttil RW, Kitahama A, Cerise E, et al: Management of blunt and penetrating injuries to the porta hepatis. Ann Surg 191:641, 1980

44. Mays ET, Wheeler CS: Demonstration of collateral arterial flow after interruption of hepatic arteries in man. N Engl J Med 290:993, 1974

45. Mays ET, Conti S, Fallahzadeh H: Hepatic artery ligation. Surgery 86:536, 1979

46. Flint LM Jr, Polk HC Jr: Selective hepatic artery ligation: limitations and failures. J Trauma 19:319, 1979

47. Bryant DP, Cooney RN, Smith JS: Traumatic proper hepatic artery occlusion: case report. J Trauma 50:735, 2001

48. Petersen SR, Sheldon GF, Lim RC Jr: Management of portal vein injuries. J Trauma 19:616, 1979

49. Pachter HL, Drager S, Godfrey N, et al: Traumatic injuries of the portal vein. The role of acute ligation. Ann Surg 189:383, 1979

50. Feliciano DV, Mattox KL, Jordan GL Jr, et al: Management of 1000 consecutive cases of hepatic trauma (1979–1984). Ann Surg 204:438, 1986

51. Burch JM, Feliciano DV, Mattox KL: The atriocaval shunt: facts and fiction. Ann Surg 207:555, 1988

52. Yellin AE, Chaffee CB, Donovan AJ: Vascular isolation in treatment of juxtahepatic venous injuries. Arch Surg 102:566, 1971

53. Pachter HL, Spencer FC, Hofstetter SR, et al: The management of juxtahepatic venous injuries without an atriocaval shunt: preliminary clinical observations. Surgery 99:569, 1986

54. Feliciano DV, Moore EE, Mattox KL: Trauma damage control. Trauma, 5th ed. Moore EE, Feliciano DV, Mattox KL, Eds. McGraw-Hill, New York, 2004

55. Feliciano DV, Burch JM: Towel clips, silos, and heroic forms of wound closure. Advances in Trauma and Critical Care. Maull KI, Cleveland HC, Feliciano DV, et al, Eds. Year Book Medical Publishers, Chicago, 1991, vol 6, p 231

56. Tremblay LN, Feliciano DV, Schmidt J, et al: Skin only or silo closure in the critically ill patient with an open abdomen. Am J Surg 182:670, 2001

57. Feliciano DV: Management of infected grafts and graft blowout in vascular trauma patients. Civilian Vascular Trauma. Flanigan DP, Schuler JJ, Meyer JP, Eds. Lea & Febiger, Philadelphia, 1992, p 44

Acknowledgments

Figures 1 and 2   Marcia Kammerer.

Figures 3, 5, 8, 10, 12, and 14   Tom Moore.

Figures 4 and 6   From "Abdominal Vascular Injury," by D. V. Feliciano in *Trauma*, 5th ed., edited by E. E. Moore, D. V. Feliciano, and K. L. Mattox, McGraw-Hill, New York, 2004. Reproduced by permission.

Figure 9   From "Abdominal Vascular Injury," by D. V. Feliciano, J. M. Burch, and J. M. Graham, in *Trauma*, 3rd ed., edited by D. V. Feliciano, E. E. Moore, and K. L. Mattox, Appleton & Lange, Stamford, Connecticut, 1996. Reproduced by permission.

Hunter Wessells, M.D., F.A.C.S.

The World Health Organization (WHO) predicts a dramatic worldwide rise in the burden of disease caused by road traffic accidents and war.[1] This rise will directly influence the incidence of urogenital trauma, in that motor vehicle crashes (MVCs) and firearm injuries are responsible for the overwhelming majority of major renal and pelvic injuries.[2] In one population-based study, the percentage of trauma patients in the United States who had renal injuries was 1.2% (incidence, 4.9 per 100,000 population).[3] Thus, in 1 year, some 14,000 patients with renal injuries are hospitalized nationwide. Approximately 45,000 pelvic fractures occur each year in the United States, 15% to 25% of which are associated with urologic injury. Urogenital injuries, though rarely fatal, can cause profound long-term morbidity and permanently impair quality of life.

Blood in the urine is the hallmark of injury to the urogenital system; however, as an isolated indicator, it is not specific for injury location or severity. In penetrating abdominal trauma, hematuria is a signal that the kidneys, the ureters, and the bladder must be evaluated. Urethral and genital injuries are suspected only in the setting of wounds to the pelvis, the perineum, or the buttocks. When hematuria occurs in association with blunt trauma, the entire urogenital system must be evaluated: the forces associated with high-speed MVCs and falls can cause injuries to both the upper and the lower regions of the urogenital tract.

In what follows, each of the major urogenital organs is treated separately. New imaging modalities and a growing emphasis on nonoperative management of upper and lower urinary tract injuries have dramatically changed the field of urologic trauma. Concomitant injury to both the upper and the lower urinary tract is rare, but extra vigilance must be maintained to detect such injury when it does occur. Evaluation and management of trauma to the female reproductive organs requires special expertise, particularly when the patient is the victim of a sexual assault.

Injuries to the Kidneys

INITIAL EVALUATION

The most reliable sign of injury to the kidney is hematuria [*see Figure 1*], except in patients with renal artery thrombosis or pedicle avulsion, who may have no blood in their urine. However, the degree of hematuria correlates poorly with the severity of renal injury,[4] and as a result, criteria for imaging in these patients must take into account both the mechanism of injury and the probability of severe kidney injury.[5] Accordingly, a Consensus Statement from a Renal Trauma Subcommittee convened by the WHO proposed guidelines for imaging renal injuries [*see Table 1*].[6] As with all guidelines, exceptions exist. A high degree of suspicion for renal trauma is required for patients who do not meet the hematuria criteria for imaging but who have experienced a fall from a height, have sustained a direct blow to the flank, or have other indicators (e.g., persistent flank pain or severe associated injuries).

Computed tomography is the first-line imaging modality for all cases of suspected renal trauma in hemodynamically normal and stable patients. A standard examination includes helical (spiral) CT with a portal venous phase (from the diaphragm to the ischial tuberosities) to visualize active arterial bleeding [*see Figure 2a*], followed after 10 minutes by delayed images (from the kidneys to the ischial tuberosities) to identify urinary contrast extravasation [*see Figure 2b*]. CT should not be used as the primary evaluation method in hemodynamically unstable patients: other diagnostic tests, such as diagnostic peritoneal lavage (DPL) or ultrasonography, should be performed before renal imaging with CT.

The American Association for the Surgery of Trauma (AAST) Organ Injury Scale is used to classify blunt and penetrating renal injuries and corresponds closely to the appearance of the kidney on CT [*see Figure 3 and Table 2*].[7]

MANAGEMENT

Differences in the management of blunt and penetrating renal trauma are a result of the greater instability of the patient after penetrating trauma and the higher likelihood of severe renal injuries after firearm and stab wounds.

Nonoperative

Increasing numbers of renal injuries are being been managed nonoperatively. The accuracy and rapidity of helical CT, combined with the improvements achieved in resuscitation methods, have reduced the number of renal explorations performed.[8] Currently, one half of all penetrating renal injuries and fewer than 5% of blunt injuries necessitate operative management.[3] All grade I and II renal injuries, regardless of the mechanism of injury, can be managed with observation alone because the risk of delayed bleeding is extremely low. Most grade III and IV injuries, including those with devitalized parenchymal fragments and urinary extravasation, can be managed nonoperatively with close monitoring, serial hematocrit measurement, and repeat imaging in selected cases. Active arterial bleeding, in the absence of other associated injuries, can be treated with emergency arteriography and angioembolization.

Thrombosis of the renal artery or its branches is treated expectantly unless the contralateral kidney is absent or injured, in which case emergency revascularization is indicated. Treatment with modalities such as endoluminal stenting and thrombolytic therapy is a promising but still experimental approach.[9-11]

Operative

The only absolute indications for renal exploration are pedicle avulsion, pulsatile or expanding hematoma, and hemodynamic instability resulting from renal injury.[6] Shattered kidneys (grade V) and renal vascular injuries (grades IV and V) call for immediate renal exploration and, usually, nephrectomy [*see Figure 4*].[12,13] In patients who require laparotomy for associated injuries, renal exploration and reconstruction of grade III and IV injuries may reduce the likelihood of delayed complications. Thus, exploration of suspected kidney injuries (as determined by previous imaging or on-table evaluation) in patients undergoing laparotomy for major

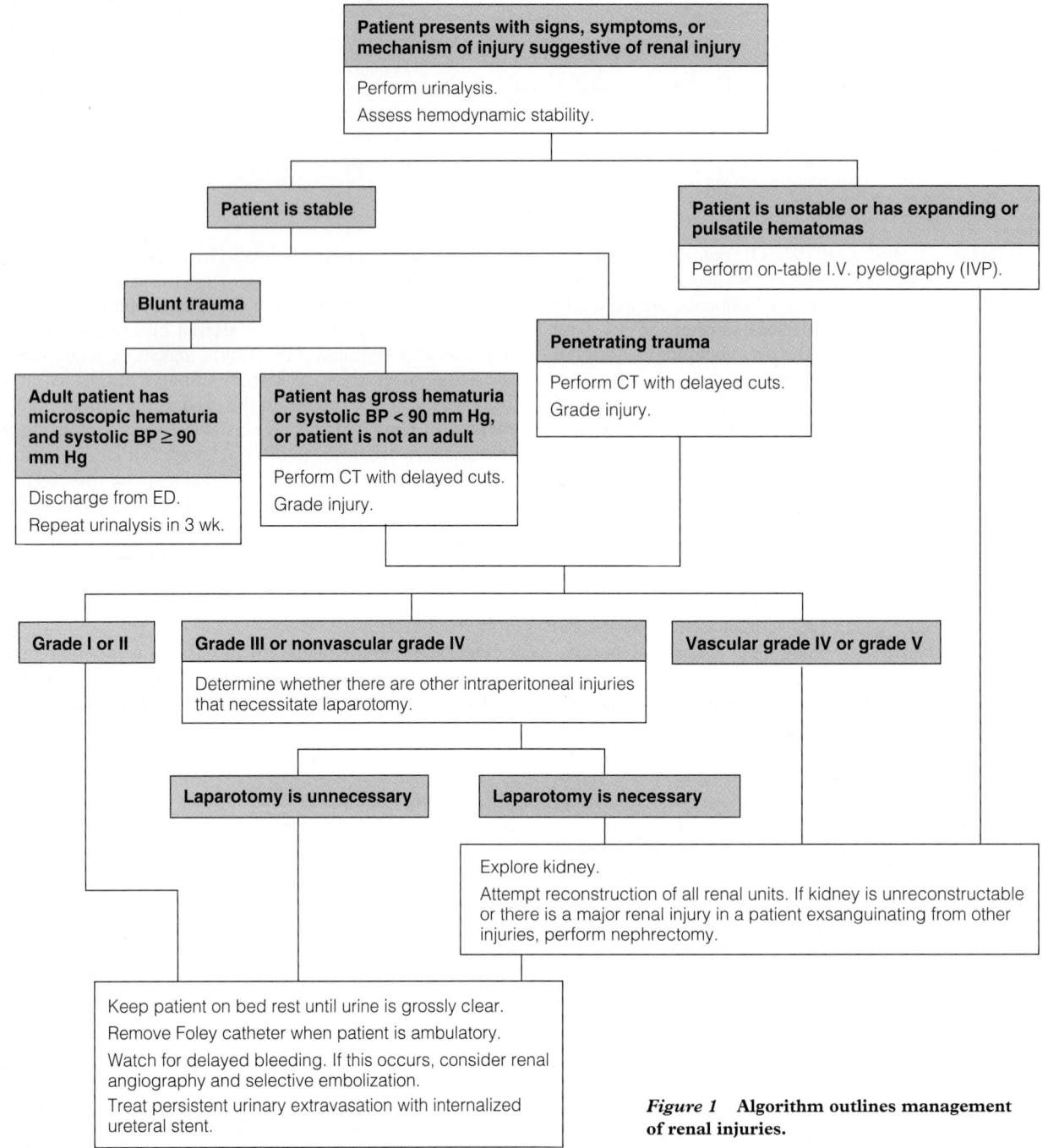

Figure 1 **Algorithm outlines management of renal injuries.**

splenic or bowel injury should be attempted by surgeons experienced in repairing an injured kidney. In reality, the success of nonoperative management for most grade III and IV injuries means that operative intervention in cases of blunt trauma is typically limited to patients with the most severe renal injuries, in whom conservative management fails either because of bleeding or because of ongoing urinary extravasation despite ureteral stenting.[14]

A significant number of patients with a penetrating injury and a minority of those with blunt trauma require immediate laparotomy before radiographic evaluation.[15] Hematuria should alert the surgeon to the possibility of renal injury, and the presence of a perinephric hematoma visible through the mesocolon should prompt further evaluation. If a major renal injury is suspected on the basis of the size of the hematoma or an abnormal intraoperative intravenous pyelogram (IVP), exploration is indicated.

Intraoperative IVP (so-called one-shot IVP) is indicated when exploration of a kidney is planned and no preoperative imaging is available. The main purpose of a one-shot IVP in this setting is to confirm the presence of a contralateral functioning kidney; a potential benefit is the ability to rule out major injury. The plain abdominal film is obtained 10 minutes after injection of a 150 ml bolus of iodinated contrast material. If the injured kidney is adequately imaged and found to be normal, exploration may be omitted[16]; otherwise, the kidney should be explored. In critically ill patients with multiple associated injuries, renal exploration is indicated only if a pulsatile or expanding hematoma is present, in which case expeditious nephrectomy is necessary. If exploration is not done, staging with CT should be completed once the patient is stable; angioembolization and percutaneous drainage can be used to manage bleeding and urinary extravasation, respectively.[17-19]

Table 1 Criteria for Imaging of Renal Injuries

Type of Trauma	Criteria for Imaging
Blunt	Gross hematuria (visibly blood-tinged urine) Adult with microhematuria (defined as ≥ 1 + RBC on dipstick or > 3 RBC/hpf) with a period of hypotension (systolic BP < 90 mm Hg) Child (< 15 yr) with > 50 RBC/hpf
Penetrating	Stable patient with any degree of hematuria and injury near urinary tract

The priorities of operative management for grade III, IV, and V injuries are hemorrhage control and definitive repair of the collecting system. A midline transabdominal incision permits exploration of the kidneys and provides optimal access to the renal hilum. After intraperitoneal sources of bleeding have been controlled, preliminary isolation of the renal artery and vein should be achieved before Gerota's fascia is opened. There is some controversy regarding the value of early vascular control, with one randomized controlled trial showing no benefit from early isolation of the vessels in cases of renal gunshot wounds[20]; however, the weight of the remaining evidence suggests that this technique is still valuable if renal reconstruction is the goal of exploration.[6,21,22] Isolation of the renal vessels is accomplished by opening the posterior peritoneum medial to the inferior mesenteric vein or by reflecting the ipsilateral colon (provided that the perinephric hematoma is left undisturbed).

Once vessel loops have been placed around the renal artery and vein, Gerota's fascia is opened. If massive bleeding occurs when the hematoma is entered, Rumel tourniquets or vascular clamps are applied to occlude the renal artery. If this maneuver does not stop the bleeding, one should suspect a venous injury and occlude the renal vein as well. Surface cooling of the kidney is not advocated, because of time constraints and concerns about possibly exacerbating hypothermia. Total exposure of the kidney by means of sharp and blunt dissection facilitates identification of injury to the parenchyma, the renal pedicle, or the collecting system. The renal capsule should not be pulled off the parenchyma: doing so would complicate subsequent repair.

Renal reconstruction includes sharp debridement of all devitalized tissue, achievement of hemostasis, closure of the collecting system, coverage of the defect, and drainage [*see Figure 5*]. Renal salvage should be possible in nearly 90% of grade III and IV injuries. Nephrectomy is reserved for destroyed kidneys that cannot be reconstructed or for cases of serious renal injury associated with other life-threatening injuries (e.g., vascular or hepatic trauma) in which taking the time required for attempted renal repair would jeopardize the life of the patient.[3,23]

A number of sophisticated products are available for enhancing surgical hemostasis and reducing the need for tedious ligation of individual small arterioles on the parenchymal surface. Such products include a hemostatic bandage applied directly to the cut surface of the kidney,[24] polyethylene glycol–based hydrogels, fibrin glue, and a gelatin matrix–thrombin tissue sealant (FloSeal; Baxter International, Inc., Deerfield, Illinois).[25-28] To date, none of these products have been evaluated in the setting of blunt renal injuries, but results in elective partial nephrectomy models are encouraging.

Once hemostasis is satisfactory, the collecting system is scrutinized for evidence of injury. If the extent of the injury is unclear, 2 to 3 ml of methylene blue is directly injected into the renal pelvis while the ureter is occluded with a vessel loop to identify any openings in the collecting system. Open calyces or infundibula are closed with 4-0 absorbable sutures. Often, the renal capsule can be used to cover exposed renal parenchyma and provide additional hemostasis. The defect in the parenchyma can be filled with folded absorbable gelatin sponges as the capsule is closed over the bolsters. If the capsule has been destroyed, coverage may be obtained with an omental or perinephric fat flap tacked down over the defect, a patch constructed from polyglycolic acid or peritoneum, or an entire sac of polyglycolic acid wrapped around the kidney, with the parenchymal edges kept well apposed.[29]

At the end of the procedure, the kidney is returned to its location within Gerota's fascia, which is not reapproximated. Closed-suction drainage of the renal fossa is recommended only after repair of the collecting system; internalized stents are reserved for complex injuries (e.g., large lacerations of the renal pelvis or the ureteropelvic junction [UPJ]).

a

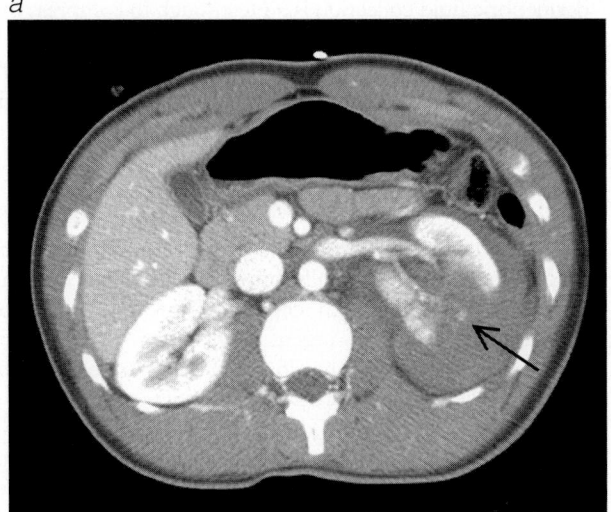

b

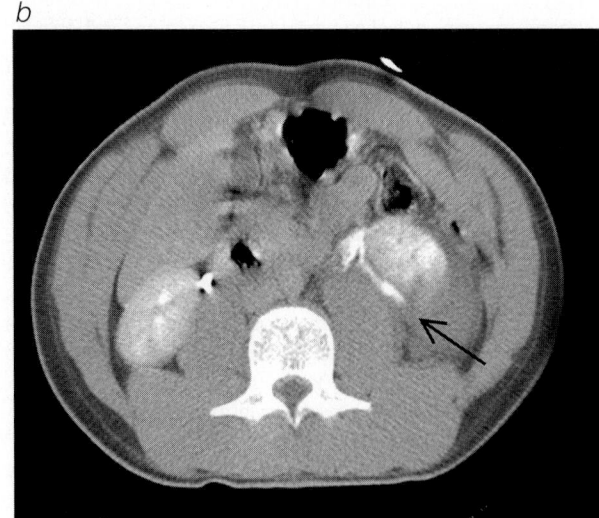

Figure 2 Shown are (*a*) a deep laceration with vascular contrast extravasation (arrow) and (*b*) a deep laceration with urinary contrast extravasation (arrow).

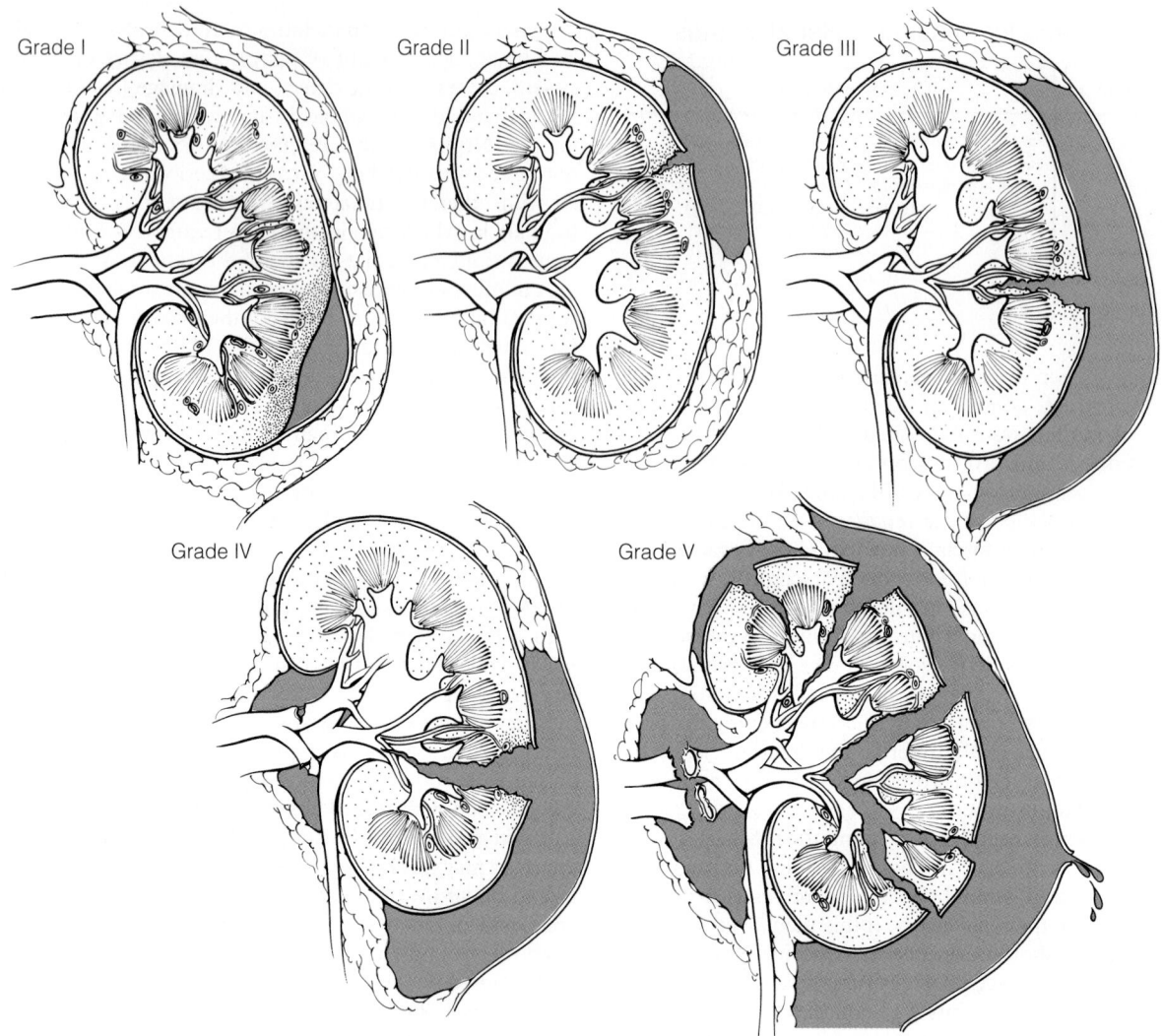

Figure 3 **Illustrated is the AAST classification of renal injuries into grades I through V.**

Postintervention Care

Management of patients after operative or nonoperative intervention for renal trauma depends to a large extent on the presence and severity of associated injuries. The most significant urologic complications are urinary leakage, urinoma formation, and delayed bleeding.

After nonoperative management Bed rest is prescribed until the urine becomes grossly clear. Drainage of the bladder with a Foley catheter is necessary only until other injuries are stable and the patient can void spontaneously. For grade IV injuries with large amounts of urinary extravasation, follow-up imaging 48 to 72 hours after the initial scan is recommended to evaluate the degree of ongoing extravasation. CT is recommended, though in children, protocols that reduce the radiation exposure should be used. If at 72 hours the amount of extravasation has not decreased from that seen on the initial scan, stenting is indicated. Cystoscopy and internal double J stenting allow successful treatment of the small percentage of cases in which the injury does not close spontaneously.[30] When a double J stent is used to manage persistent extravasation, the urinary bladder should be decompressed with a Foley catheter.

Parenchymal fragmentation and arterial thrombosis cause ischemia and often delay resolution of urinary leakage.[31] Nevertheless, internal stenting almost invariably suffices, though

resolution of extravasation can take weeks to months. Ultrasonography is useful for following such collections and for reducing the patient's radiation exposure. For small uninfected collections adjacent to the kidney, no intervention is needed. If a perinephric fluid collection is large enough to compress the ureter or becomes infected, additional percutaneous drainage is indicated [*see Figure 6*]. The drain fluid is tested for creatinine, and if the findings are consistent with a urine leak, the drain is left in place until the collection resolves and leakage can no longer be demonstrated on contrast imaging.

Delayed bleeding is a rare but serious complication of nonoperative management of major lacerations.[32] Pseudoaneurysm formation is the most common cause of delayed bleeding [*see Figure 7*].[33] Gross hematuria usually, but not invariably, accompanies the bleeding. If it is seen in conjunction with hypotension or a decreasing hematocrit, urgent angiography is the best initial approach; selective embolization is an effective treatment that renders exploration unnecessary in most instances.

After operative management Retroperitoneal drains are removed within 48 hours after renal exploration unless the creatinine concentration in the drained fluid is higher than that in the serum. Persistent urinary leakage is best evaluated by means of repeat CT with delayed cuts. As with nonoperative management,

Table 2 AAST Organ Injury Scales for Urinary Tract

Injured Structure	AAST Grade	Characteristics of Injury	AIS-90 Score
Kidney*	I	Contusion with microscopic or gross hematuria, urologic studies normal; nonexpanding subcapsular hematoma without parenchymal laceration	2; 2
	II	Nonexpanding perirenal hematoma confined to renal retroperitoneum; laceration < 1.0 cm parenchymal depth of renal cortex without urinary extravasation	2; 2
	III	Laceration > 1.0 cm parenchymal depth of renal cortex without collecting system rupture or urinary extravasation	3
	IV	Parenchymal laceration extending through renal cortex, medulla, and collecting system; injury to main renal artery or vein with contained hemorrhage	4; 4
	V	Completely shattered kidney; avulsion of renal hilum that devascularizes kidney	5; 5
Ureter*	I	Contusion or hematoma without devascularization	2
	II	< 50% transection	2
	III	≥ 50% transection	3
	IV	Complete transection with < 2 cm devascularization	3
	V	Avulsion with > 2 cm devascularization	3
Bladder†	I	Contusion, intramural hematoma; partial-thickness laceration	2; 3
	II	Extraperitoneal bladder wall laceration < 2 cm	4
	III	Extraperitoneal bladder wall laceration > 2 cm or intraperitoneal bladder wall laceration < 2 cm	4
	IV	Intraperitoneal bladder wall laceration > 2 cm	4
	V	Intraperitoneal or extraperitoneal bladder wall laceration extending into bladder neck or ureteral orifice (trigone)	4
Urethra*	I	Contusion with blood at urethral meatus and normal urethrography	2
	II	Stretch injury with elongation of urethra but without extravasation of urethrography contrast material	2
	III	Partial disruption with extravasation of urethrography contrast material at injury site with visualization in the bladder	2
	IV	Complete disruption with < 2 cm urethral separation and extravasation of urethrography contrast material at injury site without visualization in the bladder	3
	V	Complete transection with ≥ 2 cm urethral separation or extension into the prostate or vagina	4

*Advance one grade for bilateral injuries, up to grade III.
†Advance one grade for multiple injuries, up to grade III.
AAST—American Association for the Surgery of Trauma   AIS-90—Abbreviated Injury Score, 1990 version

internal stenting and percutaneous drainage are the mainstays of treatment for leaks and urinomas, respectively. Postoperative hemorrhage is rare if the injured parenchyma has been adequately debrided and repaired. Angiographic evaluation with embolization is the best approach for postoperative renal bleeding.

Functional imaging Postoperative nuclear imaging is recommended in patients with grade IV and V injuries involving significant parenchymal loss or vascular injury.[34] The goal is to identify patients with significant loss of functioning renal tissue who are at potential risk for chronic renal insufficiency. Patients whose level of residual function in the injured kidney, as determined by radionuclide scintigraphy, is less than 25% should be considered as having a solitary kidney. This information is useful in counseling patients who participate in high-risk sports activities (e.g., skydiving, motocross, and hang gliding). The optimal timing of post-

operative nuclear imaging has not been determined, but by 3 months, the hematoma and inflammation related to the injury usually have resolved.

Hypertension is a rare late complication of renal reconstruction, usually renin-mediated and deriving from an ischemic segment of renal parenchyma. Occasionally, angiography delineates the ischemic segment of the kidney, and excision of the nonperfused segment or complete nephrectomy may be required.

Injuries to the Ureters

INITIAL EVALUATION

Ureteral trauma [see *Table 2*] is rare, accounting for fewer than 1% of genitourinary injuries. Furthermore, the absence of physical signs of injury makes diagnosis difficult, and a delayed presen-

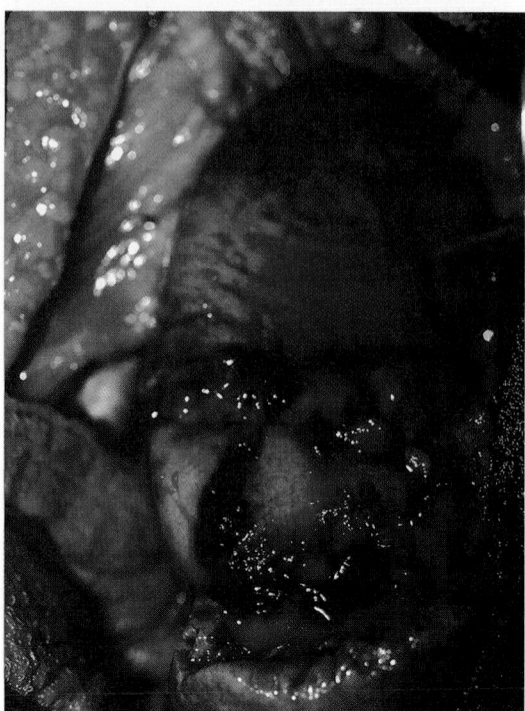

Figure 4 Shown is the intraoperative appearance of a shattered, ischemic, nonviable kidney that was removed (grade V injury).

tation is not uncommon. Gross or microscopic hematuria may be absent in 25% to 70% of patients with ureteral injuries, and as many as one half of all ureteral injuries resulting from blunt trauma are not recognized immediately. A high index of suspicion and a high degree of vigilance are necessary if the diagnosis is to be made early enough to prevent late consequences such as urinoma, sepsis, and nephrectomy.[35-37]

The mechanism of injury has a particular bearing on the diagnosis and management of ureteral injury. Overall, penetrating wounds are the predominant cause of these injuries. CT with delayed cuts should be performed when ureteral injury is suspected and the patient is stable. Imaging is of variable usefulness in the detection of ureteral injuries, but extravasation of the contrast agent is diagnostic.[38] Only 10% to 20% of ureteral injuries are caused by blunt trauma, and within this category, MVCs predominate.[35] In children, ureteral injury at the UPJ often occurs after severe deceleration.[39] Children's ureters are particularly prone to injury at this location because the hyperextensibility of their spines can result in ureteral avulsion at the UPJ.[37,38,40]

MANAGEMENT

All injuries to the ureter should be repaired surgically [*see Figure 8*] unless a delay in diagnosis has resulted in an abscess or a urinoma [*see Figure 9*]. If an abscess or a urinoma is present, drainage by means of percutaneous nephrostomy, coupled with ureteral stenting, allows infection and inflammation to resolve before definitive management; in this setting, an operative approach is likely to result in nephrectomy.

Ureteral Exploration

In stable patients, blunt ureteral injuries are typically identified by preoperative radiographic studies, which allow directed exploration and repair (see below). With penetrating trauma, ureteral injury may not be suspected until the time of laparotomy, when a

hematoma is found near the kidney or ureter. Direct inspection of the entire trajectory of the offending agent requires particular vigilance for direct injury to or contusions of the ureter. Injection of indigo carmine into the collecting system identifies extravasation. Direct injection saves time and ensures that injuries are not missed as a result of low urine output from shock or renal injury. One study found that all penetrating ureteral injuries were detected at laparotomy without previous imaging.[36]

Reconstruction and Repair

Ureteral injuries should undergo surgical reconstruction as soon as they are recognized unless associated injuries prevent such a strategy. For example, gunshot injuries to the iliac vessels or the ureters may necessitate heroic vascular reconstruction. Ligation of the ureter with subsequent nephrostomy tube drainage or exteriorization of a ureteral stent allows elective reconstruction months later. Percutaneous and endoscopic approaches can also be used to establish urinary drainage if ureteral exploration is not feasible.

Reconstructive steps in ureter repair include debridement of devitalized tissue, creation of a spatulated tension-free anastomosis, watertight mucosal approximation, stenting, coverage of the repair with vascularized tissue when feasible, and appropriate drainage.[41] Stab wounds generally cause less tissue damage than gunshot wounds and are more easily repaired; partial transections may be closed primarily.

Upper ureter Disruption or transection of the upper ureter or the UPJ is repaired by means of debridement and primary anastomosis of the renal pelvis and the ureter. Mobilization of the ureter is limited to ensure that the blood supply is not compromised. Interrupted 5-0 or 6-0 absorbable sutures are preferred, and a double J ureteral stent or a nephrostomy tube is inserted before completion of the anastomosis.

Medial ureter Injuries to the abdominal ureter between the UPJ and the pelvic brim are repaired by means of ureteroureterostomy [*see Figure 10*]. After debridement, the ends are spatulated on opposite sides, and an interrupted approximation is completed over a double J stent. In cases of overlying colonic, duodenal, or pancreatic injury, the anastomosis should be covered with omentum or retroperitoneal fat. Large defects in the abdominal ureter may necessitate transureteroureterostomy, in which the injured ureter is passed behind the mesocolon to the contralateral side. Anastomosis of the injured ureter to a 1 to 2 cm opening in the medial side of the normal ureter can be achieved without tension. With transureteroureterostomy, a stent (usually a 5 French pediatric feeding tube) should cross the anastomosis and be brought out through the normal lower ureter or bladder.

Distal ureter Ureteral injuries in the pelvis should be managed with reimplantation into the bladder. The distal stump is ligated, and after the anterior bladder wall is opened, the proximal end of the ureter is brought through a new hiatus on the back wall of the bladder. The ureter is then spatulated and approximated to the bladder mucosa with interrupted chromic sutures. One 3-0 anchoring stitch brings the distal apex of the ureter to the muscle and mucosa; the rest of the sutures approximate the mucosa. A refluxing reimplantation is acceptable in adults. Larger defects can be bridged by performing a vesicopsoas hitch, in which the bladder is sewn to the central tendon of the psoas muscle. The dome is mobilized by dividing the obliterated umbilical arteries bilaterally and, if necessary, the contralateral superior vesical artery. Three interrupted nonabsorbable sutures that enter the detrusor muscle

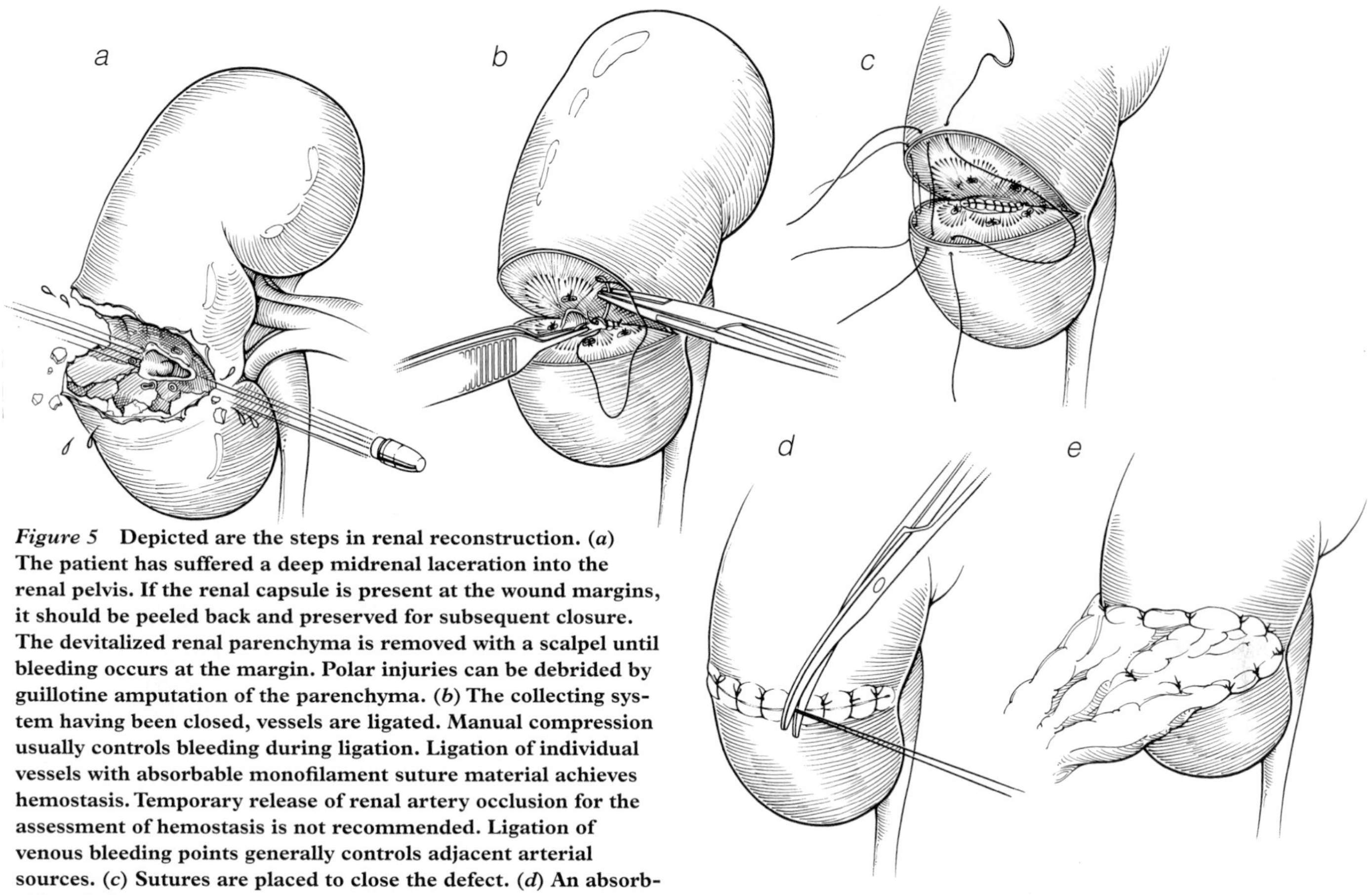

a *b* *c* *d* *e*

Figure 5 **Depicted are the steps in renal reconstruction. (*a*)
The patient has suffered a deep midrenal laceration into the
renal pelvis. If the renal capsule is present at the wound margins,
it should be peeled back and preserved for subsequent closure.
The devitalized renal parenchyma is removed with a scalpel until
bleeding occurs at the margin. Polar injuries can be debrided by
guillotine amputation of the parenchyma. (*b*) The collecting system having been closed, vessels are ligated. Manual compression
usually controls bleeding during ligation. Ligation of individual
vessels with absorbable monofilament suture material achieves
hemostasis. Temporary release of renal artery occlusion for the
assessment of hemostasis is not recommended. Ligation of
venous bleeding points generally controls adjacent arterial
sources. (*c*) Sutures are placed to close the defect. (*d*) An absorbable gelatin sponge is placed. (*e*) Alternatively, the defect may be
closed with an omental pedicle flap.**

(but not the bladder lumen) anchor the dome above the iliac vessels. Complex bladder or vascular injuries in the pelvis make transureteroureterostomy a more attractive option for avoiding further
dissection in the injured area. A ureteral stent should be used in all
ureteral reimplantations. The bladder is closed in two layers with a
continuous 2-0 absorbable suture. Closed-suction retroperitoneal
drainage and Foley catheter decompression of the bladder are
essential.

Postintervention Care

Postoperative care of ureteral trauma relates mainly to the
manipulation of drains and the management of complications.
Retroperitoneal drains may have significant output for several days
but are removed after 2 to 3 days unless output is consistent with
a urine leak as determined by creatinine measurement (see above).
Bladder catheterization is necessary for 7 days after ureteral reimplantation. In combined bladder and ureteral reconstructions, contrast cystography is indicated before catheter removal. Cystoscopic
removal of the double J stent is usually performed with local anesthesia 4 to 6 weeks after operation. CT, IVP, or renal scintigraphy
3 months after removal of the stent rules out the possibility of
asymptomatic obstruction.

Fistula formation, usually the result of distal obstruction or
necrosis of the ureter, should be managed by means of antegrade
or retrograde drainage of the collecting system with percutaneous
or endoscopic techniques. Drainage of periureteral fluid collections may also be necessary. If recognition of an injury or a complication is delayed, reconstruction should be deferred for at least
3 to 6 months until all inflammation has subsided.

Injuries to the Bladder

INITIAL EVALUATION

Bladder injury [*see Table 2*] is most often caused by blunt
injuries, with penetrating trauma accounting for 14% to 33% of
civilian cases. About 9% of patients with a pelvic fracture have an

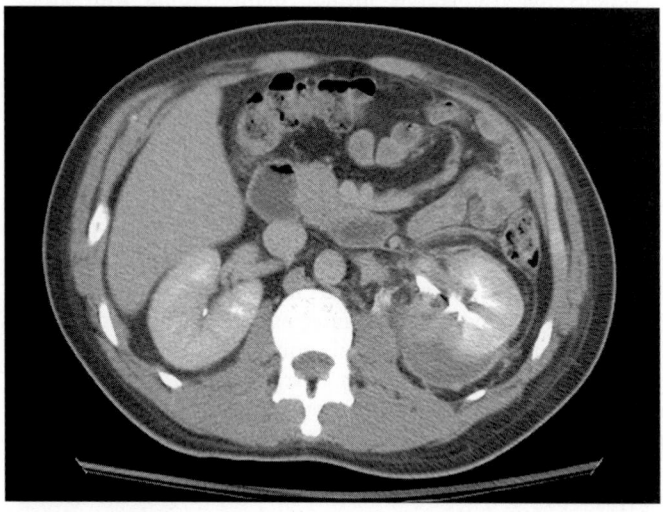

Figure 6 **CT scan shows an infected urinoma in a patient with
left grade IV injury who presented 7 days after injury with fever
and sepsis and subsequently underwent ureteral stenting. The
urinoma was drained percutaneously.**

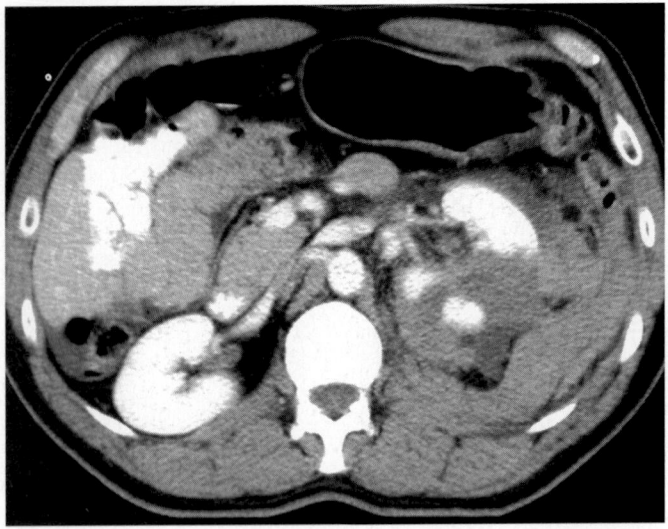

Figure 7 **Shown is a pseudoaneurysm of the left kidney after blunt injury.**

associated injury to the bladder, though there is only a weak association between the type of fracture sustained and the likelihood of bladder injury.[42] Because the fracture type has poor predictive value for the type of associated genitourinary trauma, all patients with pelvic fractures and any degree of hematuria should be suspected of having a bladder injury. Approximately two thirds of bladder injuries are extraperitoneal and one third intraperitoneal, a distinction that has important management ramifications.

The signs and symptoms of bladder injury are generally nonspecific [*see Figure 11*], though 95% of patients with bladder rupture present with gross hematuria. Patients may complain of suprapubic pain, dysuria, or an inability to void. Physical examination may reveal tenderness in the suprapubic region, ileus, or an acute abdomen. The percentage of patients without any hematuria ranges from 0% to 3%.[43,44] Laboratory studies are usually inconclusive unless significant reabsorption of urine causes elevated serum creatinine levels, hyperkalemia, or hyponatremia.[45]

Bladder rupture can be accurately diagnosed with either retrograde CT cystography or plain-film retrograde cystography. The indications for cystography include blunt trauma with gross hematuria in the presence of free abdominal fluid on CT; blunt trauma with a pelvic fracture and any degree of hematuria (> 3 red blood cells [RBCs] per high-power field [hpf]); stable penetrating trauma with any degree of hematuria; and an injury to the pelvis. The appearance of intraperitoneal and extraperitoneal rupture with each modality is characteristic [*see Figure 12*]. Insufficient instillation of the contrast agent can yield false negative results. At one large center, the sensitivity and specificity of CT cystography for bladder rupture caused by blunt trauma were 95% and 100%, respectively.[44] With current patterns of CT usage for trauma evaluation, including imaging of pelvic bony fractures, CT cystography appears to be more efficient than plain-film studies. Furthermore, CT cystography clearly identifies the location of many bladder injuries and may be able to identify bladder neck injuries [*see Figure 12a*]. With penetrating trauma, there must be a higher level of suspicion for bladder injury because the sensitivity and specificity of cystography (CT or conventional) in this setting has not been determined. If bladder injury is associated with a pelvic fracture in a male patient, the possibility of a urethral injury is 10% to 29% and must be excluded.[46] A successfully placed Foley catheter rules out a complete urethral disruption.

MANAGEMENT

Nonoperative

Extraperitoneal bladder injuries caused by blunt trauma are generally managed nonoperatively with 10 days of catheter drainage.[47] Contraindications to nonoperative management include urinary infection; pelvic fractures requiring internal fixation; the presence of bony fragments in the bladder; bladder neck injury, which may compromise continence; rectal injury; and female genital lacerations associated with pelvic fracture. After 10 days, plain-film or CT cystography is performed to document healing. Once the extravasation has resolved, catheter removal can be based on the patient's overall status and mobility. If extravasation persists, cystography is repeated at appropriate intervals until healing occurs.

Operative

All penetrating injuries and all intraperitoneal ruptures of the bladder are managed by means of bladder exploration and repair.

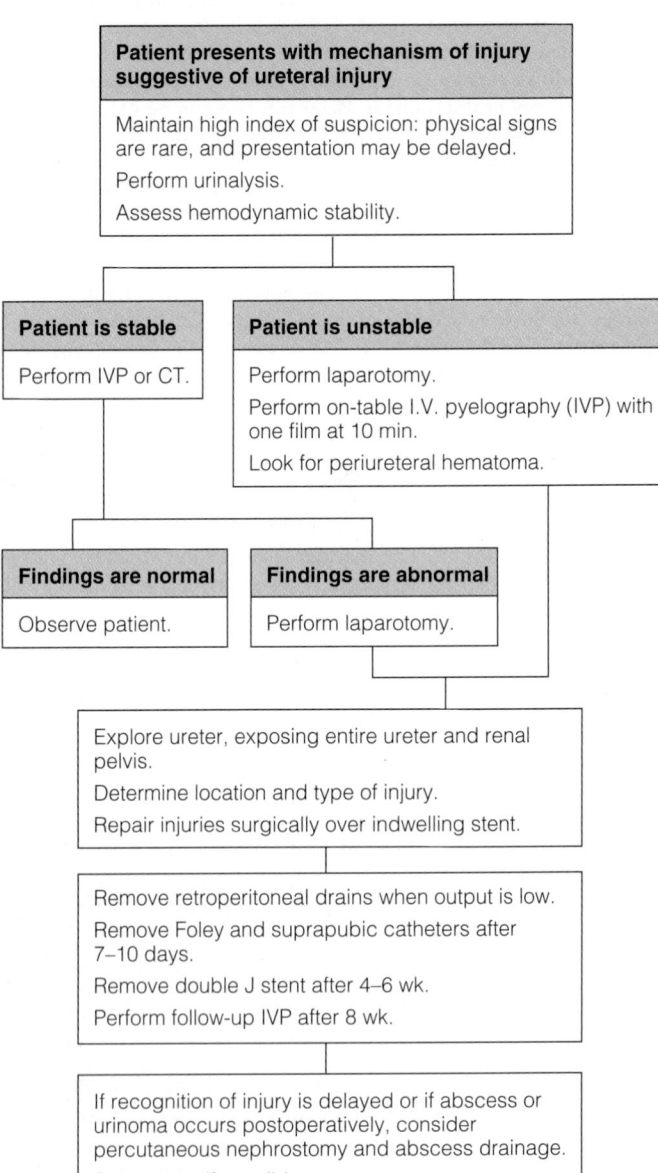

Figure 8 **Algorithm outlines management of ureteral injuries.**

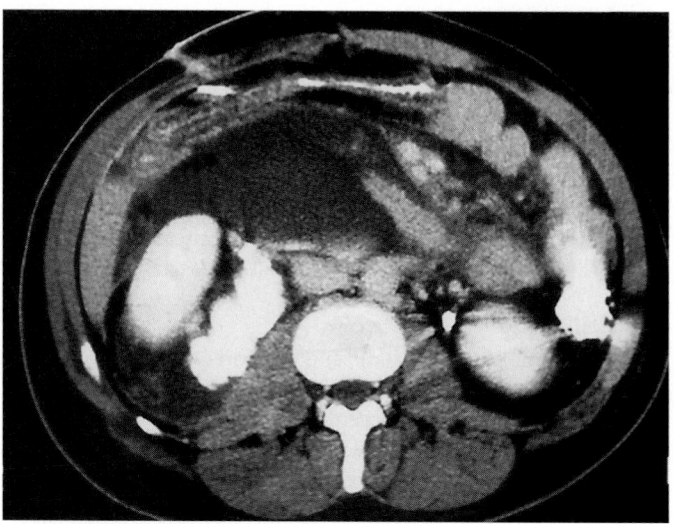

Figure 9 **CT scan shows extravasation and urinoma caused by unrecognized right upper ureteral injury.**

The perivesical drain can be removed after 48 hours unless the creatinine level in the drained fluid indicates ongoing urinary leakage. In the majority of patients with a bladder repair, 7 days of catheter drainage is sufficient to allow healing. Because bladder repair is reliable, any complications of bladder injury are usually related to a delay in diagnosis rather than to postoperative morbidity. Azotemia, ascites, and sepsis can result from an unrecognized intraperitoneal injury. Bladder neck injury, if overlooked, leads to scarring and incompetence of the proximal sphincter mechanism, with resultant incontinence, especially in females.

Injuries to the Urethra

INITIAL EVALUATION

Almost all injuries to the male urethra [*see Table 2*] are caused by blunt trauma. Prostatomembranous urethral distraction

If the patient requires laparotomy for associated injuries and can tolerate the extra operating time, repair of extraperitoneal bladder injuries is also recommended. Conversely, in severely unstable patients, catheter drainage can be used as a temporizing measure until the patient is able to undergo exploration.

Bladder exploration can be performed via an intraperitoneal approach or by entering the extraperitoneal space of Retzius in the anterior pelvis. Intraperitoneal injuries present as a stellate rupture of the dome of the bladder. By enlarging this opening, one can inspect the interior of the bladder to exclude concomitant extraperitoneal injuries, which occur in 8% of cases.[48] In cases involving orthopedic reconstruction of the pelvis, the bladder may be approached extraperitoneally through the incision used to expose the pubic symphysis. Although extensive hemorrhage has been described in this scenario, it is a rare occurrence. Most extraperitoneal bladder injuries associated with pelvic fractures are anteriorly located, small in size, and easily closed without a more extensive bladder exploration.

Penetrating injuries and unrecognized blunt injuries discovered at laparotomy without previous CT cystography call for systematic evaluation. By opening the bladder vertically at the dome or along the anterior surface, one can identify sites of injury intravesically and inspect the ureteral orifices and the bladder neck. Lacerations are closed with 3-0 absorbable sutures, which approximate detrusor muscle and mucosa in one layer and provide hemostasis. In patients with penetrating injuries, entrance and exit sites must be identified. The cystotomy is then closed with two layers of continuous 2-0 slowly absorbable sutures.

Postintervention Care

Adequate urinary drainage is essential to successful healing of the repaired bladder. There is no evidence that suprapubic catheters are superior to urethral catheters in this context.[49,50] However, the catheters placed during trauma resuscitation are not of sufficient caliber to allow easy bladder decompression; therefore, a 20 French urethral catheter should be substituted at the end of the operation. A closed-suction drain near the bladder closure (but not overlying the suture line) is recommended. Cases of severe hematuria resulting from extensive injuries or coagulopathy warrant additional drainage with a suprapubic cystostomy tube to allow irrigation of clots and proper decompression of the bladder.

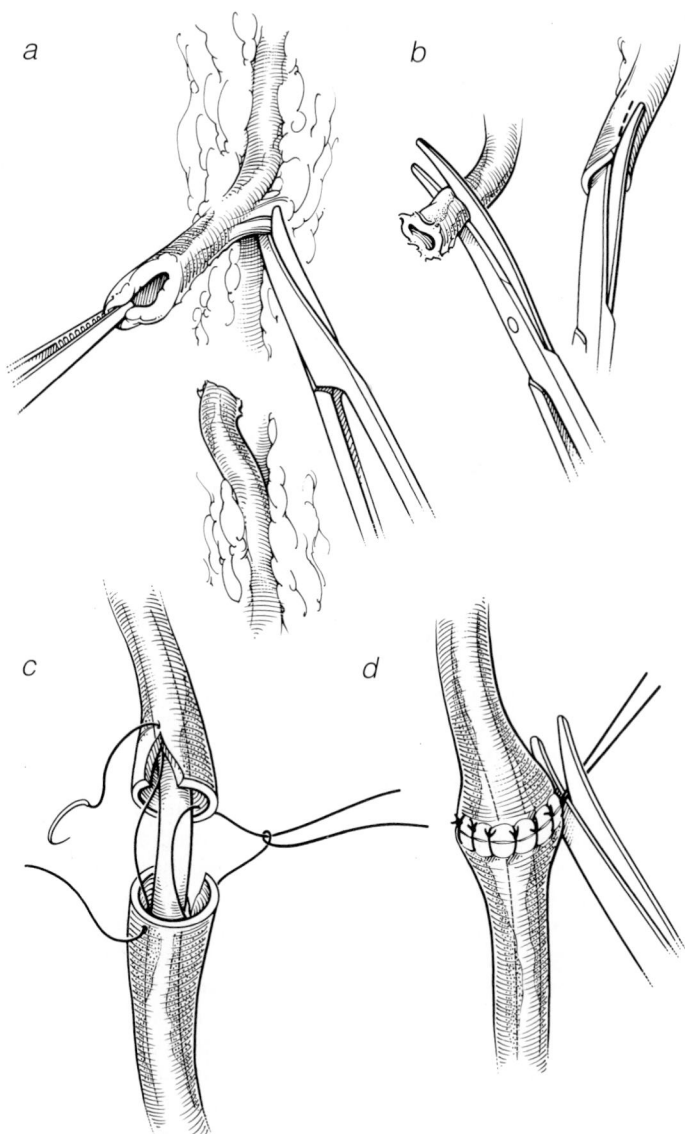

Figure 10 **Depicted are the steps in a ureteroureterostomy. (*a*) The injured ureter is dissected free. (*b*) The ends are debrided and spatulated. (*c*) A stent is placed, and the anastomosis is begun. (*d*) The anastomosis is completed.**

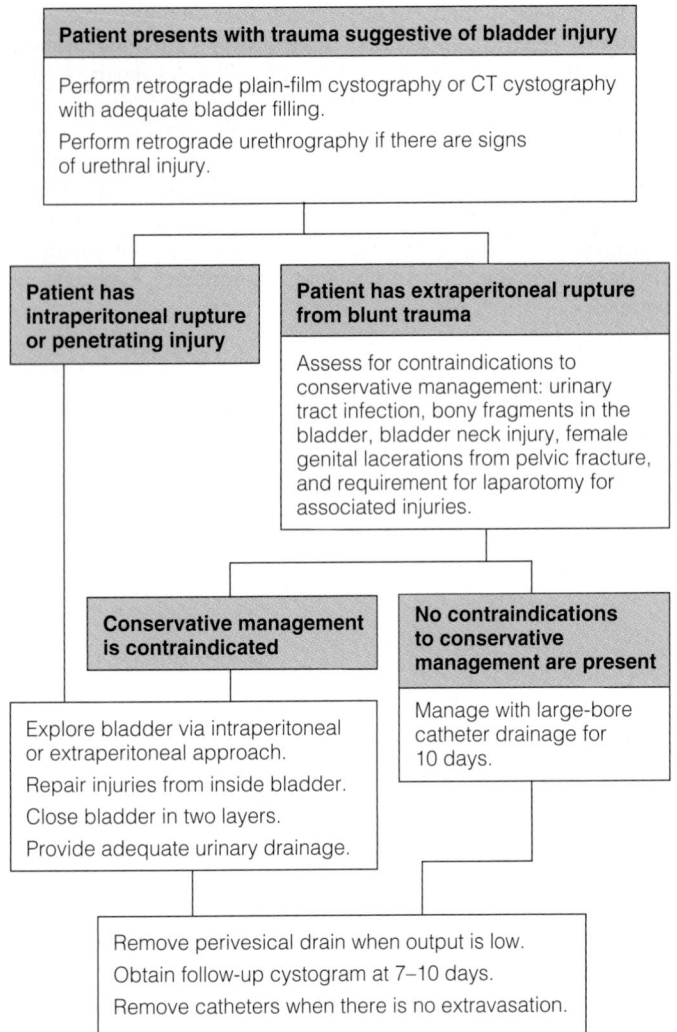

Patient presents with trauma suggestive of bladder injury

Perform retrograde plain-film cystography or CT cystography with adequate bladder filling.

Perform retrograde urethrography if there are signs of urethral injury.

Patient has intraperitoneal rupture or penetrating injury

Patient has extraperitoneal rupture from blunt trauma

Assess for contraindications to conservative management: urinary tract infection, bony fragments in the bladder, bladder neck injury, female genital lacerations from pelvic fracture, and requirement for laparotomy for associated injuries.

Conservative management is contraindicated

No contraindications to conservative management are present

Manage with large-bore catheter drainage for 10 days.

Explore bladder via intraperitoneal or extraperitoneal approach.
Repair injuries from inside bladder.
Close bladder in two layers.
Provide adequate urinary drainage.

Remove perivesical drain when output is low.
Obtain follow-up cystogram at 7–10 days.
Remove catheters when there is no extravasation.

Figure 11   **Algorithm outlines the management of bladder injury.**

injuries in males occur in 5% of pelvic fractures, which are the most common cause of posterior urethral injury. Anterior urethral (penile and bulbar urethral) injuries are commonly caused by straddle injury but may be the result of penile fracture or penetrating injuries to the genitalia. The female urethra is rarely injured, but when such injury occurs, it is usually associated with bladder injury and pelvic fracture.[51]

Blood at the urethral meatus—the classic sign of injury to the male urethra—is an indication for immediate urethrography. Attempts at catheter placement risk converting an incomplete injury to a complete disruption and are to be discouraged if urethral injury is suspected.

Because signs of urethral injury are variable, retrograde urethrography is the essential diagnostic test used for documenting the location, nature, and extent of injury. Extravasation of the contrast agent is evidence of urethral injury [see Figure 13]. In the absence of extravasation, a Foley catheter should be passed. If a catheter has been placed but its position is unclear, contrast injection will confirm its placement in the bladder. In such cases, the catheter should be left in place until a pericatheter contrast study can fully evaluate the urethra. In cases of pelvic fracture and complete posterior urethral injury, bladder injury must be excluded by open bladder exploration or via cystography through a percutaneously placed suprapubic tube.

MANAGEMENT

Traumatic urethral injuries have traditionally been managed by means of suprapubic cystostomy, with reconstruction delayed for 3 to 6 months; however, most urethral trauma patients can undergo immediate realignment, with or without sutured repair. The exception is the patient with a straddle-type crush injury to the bulbar urethra, which should always be treated with urinary diversion and delayed repair. The recommended treatment is based on the location and mechanism of injury [see Figure 14 and Table 3].

Posterior Urethra

Posterior urethral (prostatic and membranous urethral) injuries can be managed with suprapubic cystostomy or early primary urethral realignment. Realignment without sutured repair renders definitive reconstruction unnecessary in a significant percentage of patients.[52] Bladder neck injury and wide separation of the bladder from the urethra warrant immediate surgical intervention.[53] Simultaneous rectal injury often occurs in this setting and necessitates evacuation of the pelvic hematoma, irrigation, placement of drains, and primary realignment of the urethra. Primary realignment is also preferred in cases of open reduction and internal fixation of pelvic fractures because the risk of hardware contamination is considered to be lower with a urethral catheter than with suprapubic cystostomy.[54]

Primary realignment is usually performed through a lower midline abdominal incision, which allows antegrade passage of instruments through the bladder at the same time as retrograde passage of instruments from the urethral meatus. Flexible cystoscopes or magnetic-tipped catheters advanced under fluoroscopic guidance are used to place a wire into the bladder beyond the injury, and a Council-tip Foley catheter is then advanced over the wire. Neither mucosal approximation nor direct anastomosis is the goal. Suprapubic catheter drainage is not required, but a perivesical drain should be left in place for 48 hours.

Anterior Urethra

Immediate surgical reconstruction is preferred for penetrating injuries of the bulbar and penile urethra and for urethral injuries associated with penile fracture. For these grade III and IV injuries, primary repair is associated with a lower stricture rate than simple realignment.[55,56] Wounds accompanied by major tissue loss and defects larger than 2 cm (e.g., grade V injuries) or major associated injuries are best treated with suprapubic tube urinary diversion (see below) and subsequent reconstruction at a tertiary referral center.

Suprapubic Cystostomy

Many centers continue to use suprapubic cystostomy as the primary management of prostatomembranous urethral disruption and straddle injuries to the bulbar urethra. Suprapubic cystostomy, with the tube percutaneously placed under fluoroscopic guidance, allows temporary urinary diversion for initial stabilization and evaluation of the patient. Cystography can then be performed via the suprapubic tube to rule out associated bladder injury. Straddle injuries must be treated with suprapubic diversion unless the urethral disruption is only partial and allows passage of a guide wire or catheter under fluoroscopic guidance. Finally, suprapubic cystostomy is also recommended for penetrating injuries to the anterior urethra if the injuries were caused by high-velocity weapons and are characterized by extensive tissue loss; if serious associated injuries are present; or if bony fractures prevent proper placement of the patient in the lithotomy position.

a

b

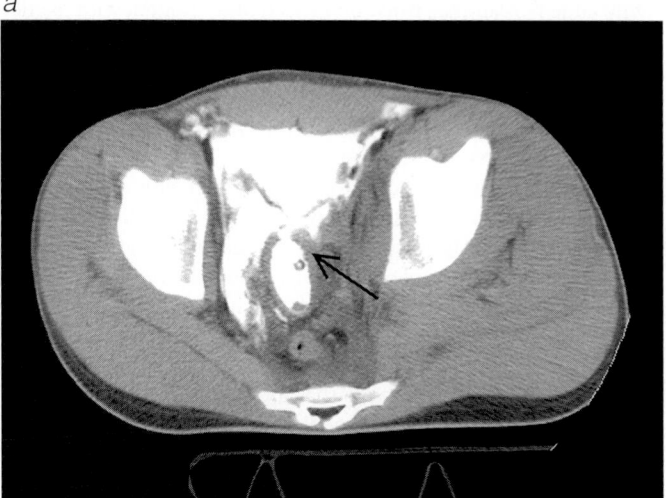

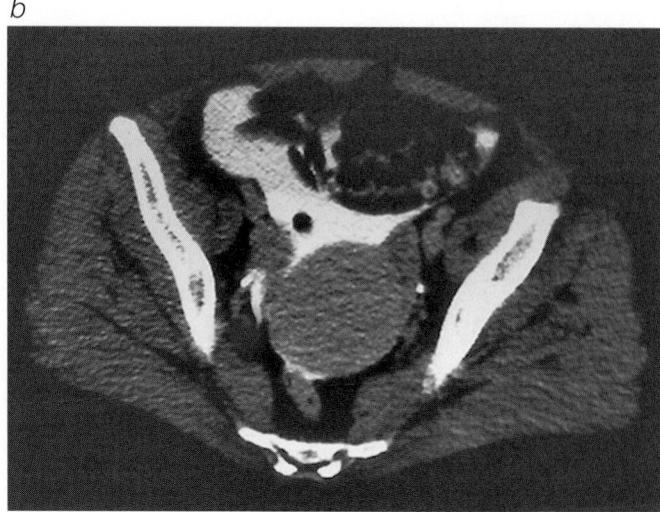

Figure 12 (*a*) **CT cystogram shows extraperitoneal bladder rupture. A definitive discontinuity in the bladder wall is visible (arrow). (*b*) CT cystogram shows intraperitoneal bladder rupture.**

Postintervention Care

Catheter care is of great importance after urethral reconstruction or suprapubic cystostomy. Urethral catheters should be secured to the abdominal wall in the early postoperative period. After immediate reconstruction of the anterior urethra, the Foley catheter should remain in place for 3 weeks, at which time a contrast voiding cystourethrogram should be obtained. If extravasation is present, the catheter should be replaced for 1 week and the study repeated. After primary realignment of urethral injuries, the urethral catheter is left in place for 6 weeks, at which time a pericatheter retrograde urethrogram is obtained, with the expectation that any extravasation will have resolved.

If the patients initially underwent diversion with a suprapubic tube alone, the tube should be changed after a tract has formed (usually about 4 weeks after the procedure) and then monthly until

reconstruction can be performed. Stricture formation or complete obliteration of the urethra may be the final result of this nonoperative approach. Subsequent radiographic studies will indicate whether secondary endoscopic or open procedures are needed.

Injuries to the Vagina, Uterus, and Ovaries

Injuries to the female genitalia [*see Table 4 and Figure 15*] must be regarded as especially morbid because of their association with sexual assault and interpersonal violence, as well as because of the potential medical complications (infection and bleeding). Genital trauma is reported in 20% to 53% of sexual assault victims.[57,58] Blunt unintentional trauma, including pelvic fracture and straddle injuries, often results in perineal and vaginal injuries and, less commonly, cervical and uterine trauma.[59-61] Enlargement of a reproductive organ predisposes that organ to injury.[62] Penetrating

a

b

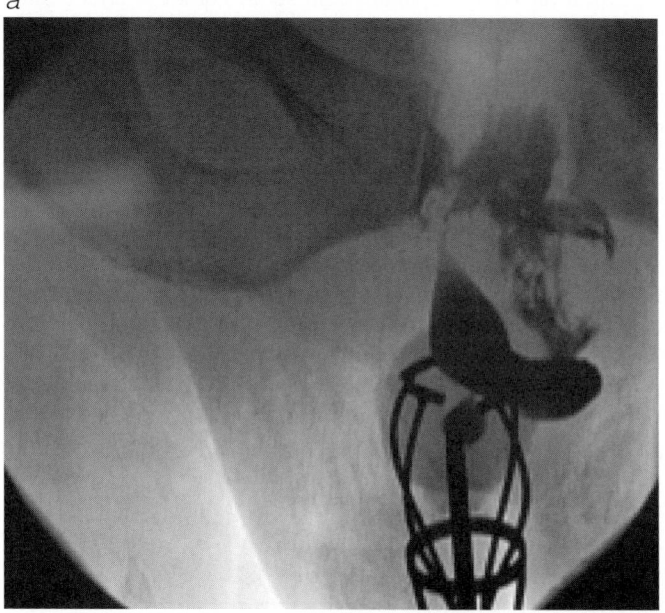

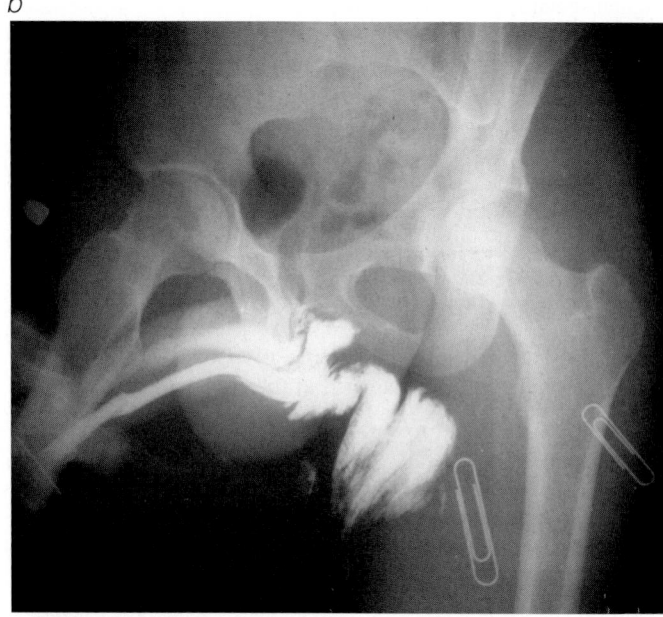

Figure 13 (*a*) **Retrograde urethrogram of a posterior urethral injury after pelvic fracture shows extravasation at the level of the urogenital diaphragm. (*b*) Retrograde urethrogram of an anterior urethral injury caused by a gunshot wound shows extravasation at the level of the bulbar urethra.**

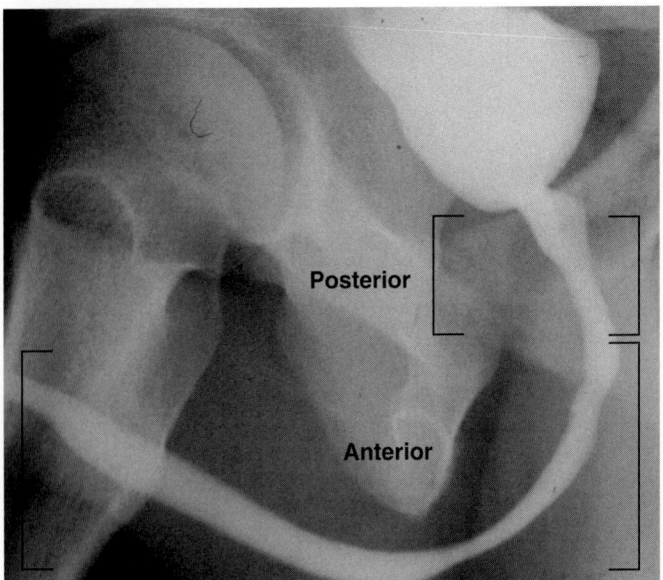

Figure 14 **Shown are the posterior and anterior portions of the urethra. The posterior portion comprises the prostatic urethra and the membranous urethra; the anterior portion comprises the bulbar urethra and the penile urethra. Treatment of urethral injury depends on the location and mechanism of injury.**

injuries account for almost all injuries to the fallopian tubes, the ovaries, and the nongravid uterus.[63]

INITIAL EVALUATION

A history of sexual trauma must be sought; if such a history is elicited, appropriate police and support services must be notified.[64] In addition, if sexual assault has occurred, informed consent for the rest of the patient assessment must be obtained. This assessment includes a history, physical examination, collection of evidence and laboratory specimens, and treatment, as outlined by the American College of Obstetricians and Gynecologists.[65] The percentage of assault victims with identifiable spermatozoa in the vaginal specimens is lower than 50%.[66]

All female patients with evidence of lower urinary tract and urethral injury should undergo examination of the external genitalia, as well as speculum examination of internal organs. The finding of blood implies vaginal laceration. In the presence of pelvic fracture or impalement injury, vaginal laceration warrants complete evaluation (with cystourethrography, proctoscopy, and laparotomy, as indicated) to rule out associated urinary tract and GI tract injuries. Failure to identify vaginal injury associated with pelvic fracture may lead to abscess formation, sepsis, and death.

MANAGEMENT

Perineal lacerations in the absence of associated urinary tract and rectal injury can be managed in the emergency department.

Only large hematomas must be incised and drained, with ligation of vessels. Lacerations of the vulva may be closed primarily after irrigation and debridement. Interrupted absorbable sutures allow any accumulated fluid to drain and eliminate the need for suture removal. Drains are used if there is a large cavity; if hemostasis is suboptimal, the wound may be packed.[61]

Vaginal and cervical lacerations from either blunt or penetrating injury will bleed extensively if the pudendal vessels are injured.[61] If bleeding is not severe, examination and repair with local anesthesia is possible in the ED. If large lacerations are associated with bleeding and hematoma, speculum examination under anesthesia permits more complete assessment and repair of injuries. Vaginal lacerations should be closed with continuous or interrupted absorbable sutures that include mucosal and muscular layers. Antibiotic-soaked vaginal packing should be left in place for 24 hours. Perioperative administration of broad-spectrum antibiotics is sufficient, unless injuries are more complex.

Complex vaginal and perineal lacerations associated with pelvic fracture must be managed much more aggressively to prevent the morbidity and mortality characteristic of open fractures.[67] Evaluation of vaginal injuries with the patient under anesthesia, cystography, and rigid proctoscopy are mandatory. The vaginal laceration should be closed with absorbable sutures. Even in the absence of injury to the bladder or the rectum, diversion of the urinary and fecal streams should be considered to facilitate care of the perineal wound[67]; however, I rarely divert the fecal stream unless the perineal injury extensively involves the rectum or the sphincter.[68] Extraperitoneal bladder rupture associated with vaginal lacerations must be repaired operatively to prevent infection of a pelvic hematoma or formation of a vesicovaginal fistula. Urologic, gynecologic, and orthopedic consultations are necessary for care of associated injuries.

Injury to the pelvic genital organs is rare in a nongravid patient. Penetrating trauma is the most common cause, and the majority of patients have associated injuries necessitating laparotomy.[62] Blunt injury of the nongravid uterus and the pelvic organs occurs in the face of preexisting abnormalities; DPL demonstrates hemoperitoneum in these instances.[63] The uterus, the organ most commonly injured, is repaired with figure-eight sutures or a two-layer closure using slowly absorbable sutures.[62] Avulsion of the uterine artery or extensive blast destruction of the uterus may necessitate hysterectomy.[61] When hysterectomy is necessary for trauma, the vaginal cuff should be left open to allow drainage of the operative bed.[69] Lacerations to the ovary or the fallopian tube are managed by primary closure or salpingo-oophorectomy if contralateral structures are normal.

After hysterectomy or repair of vaginal lacerations, a vaginal pack should remain in place for 24 hours. Hemorrhage caused by uterine injury has been treated with oxytocin, which increases uterine tone and controls bleeding. Fertility after injury to the female reproductive organs is not well documented, but patients must be counseled about the possible adverse consequences of uterine and adnexal trauma.

Table 3 Management of Urethral Trauma

Location of Injury	Mechanism of Injury		
	Blunt	Penetrating	Penile Fracture
Posterior (prostatic and membranous urethra)	Realignment or suprapubic cystostomy	Realignment	NA
Anterior (bulbar and penile urethra)	Suprapubic cystostomy	Surgical repair	Surgical repair

Table 4 AAST Organ Injury Scales for Female Reproductive Tract

Injured Structure	AAST Grade	Characteristics of Injury	AIS-90 Score
Vagina*	I	Contusion or hematoma	1
	II	Superficial laceration (mucosa only)	1
	III	Deep laceration (into fat or muscle)	2
	IV	Complex laceration (into cervix or peritoneum)	3
	V	Injury to adjacent organs (anus, rectum, urethra, bladder)	3
Vulva*	I	Contusion or hematoma	1
	II	Superficial laceration (skin only)	1
	III	Deep laceration (into fat or muscle)	2
	IV	Avulsion (skin, fat, or muscle)	3
	V	Injury to adjacent organs (anus, rectum, urethra, bladder)	3
Nongravid uterus*	I	Contusion or hematoma	2
	II	Superficial laceration (< 1 cm)	2
	III	Deep laceration (≥ 1 cm)	3
	IV	Laceration involving uterine artery	3
	V	Avulsion or devascularization	3
Fallopian tube†	I	Hematoma or contusion	2
	II	Laceration < 50% of circumference	2
	III	Laceration ≥ 50% of circumference	2
	IV	Transection	2
	V	Vascular injury or devascularized segment	2
Ovary†	I	Contusion or hematoma	1
	II	Superficial laceration (depth < 0.5 cm)	2
	III	Deep laceration (depth ≥ 0.5 cm)	3
	IV	Partial disruption of blood supply	3
	V	Avulsion or complete parenchymal destruction	3
Gravid uterus*	I	Contusion or hematoma (without placental abruption)	2
	II	Superficial laceration (< 1 cm) or partial placental abruption (< 25%)	3
	III	Deep laceration (≥ 1 cm) in second trimester or placental abruption > 25% but < 50%; deep laceration in third trimester	3; 4
	IV	Laceration involving uterine artery; deep laceration (≥ 1 cm) with > 50% placental abruption	4; 4
	V	Uterine rupture in second trimester; uterine rupture in third trimester; complete placental abruption	4; 5; 4–5

*Advance one grade for multiple injuries, up to grade III.
†Advance one grade for bilateral injuries, up to grade III.

Injuries to the Penis

Injury to the flaccid penis is rare, occurring mainly as a result of penetrating trauma and machinery accidents.[56,70,71] The increased use of protective armor on the torso has caused a shift in battlefield urologic injuries from renal structures to pelvic and genital organs.[72] Penile fracture is an uncommon injury of the tunica albuginea that occurs only with full penile rigidity.[73-75] Prompt operative treatment allows recovery of erectile function after most penile injuries [*see Table 5*]. Remarkably, in many cases,

penile replantation successfully restores erectile capability.

INITIAL EVALUATION

Missed intromission, acute bending of the penis, and a snapping or popping sound followed by acute pain and immediate detumescence are characteristic of penile fracture. Delayed presentation, attributable to embarrassment, is common. Penetrating injuries to the penis may result from deliberate attempts at mutilation, as well as from accidental firearm injury (typically occurring when a

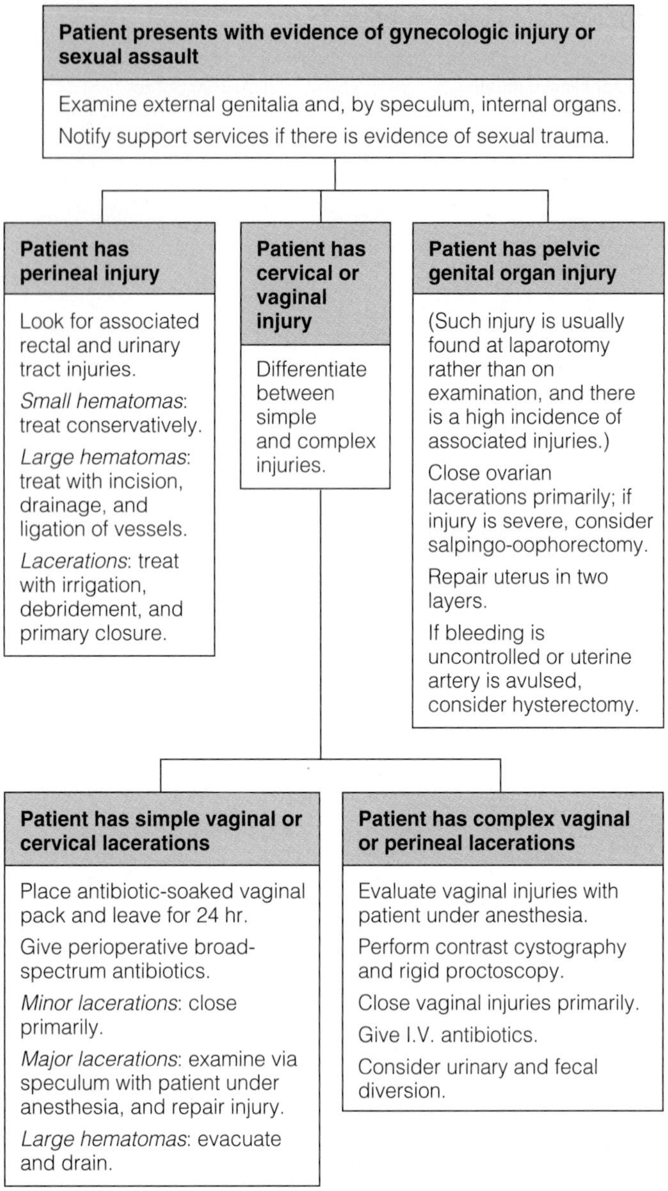

Patient presents with evidence of gynecologic injury or sexual assault

Examine external genitalia and, by speculum, internal organs. Notify support services if there is evidence of sexual trauma.

Patient has perineal injury

Look for associated rectal and urinary tract injuries.

Small hematomas: treat conservatively.

Large hematomas: treat with incision, drainage, and ligation of vessels.

Lacerations: treat with irrigation, debridement, and primary closure.

Patient has cervical or vaginal injury

Differentiate between simple and complex injuries.

Patient has pelvic genital organ injury

(Such injury is usually found at laparotomy rather than on examination, and there is a high incidence of associated injuries.)

Close ovarian lacerations primarily; if injury is severe, consider salpingo-oophorectomy.

Repair uterus in two layers.

If bleeding is uncontrolled or uterine artery is avulsed, consider hysterectomy.

Patient has simple vaginal or cervical lacerations

Place antibiotic-soaked vaginal pack and leave for 24 hr.

Give perioperative broad-spectrum antibiotics.

Minor lacerations: close primarily.

Major lacerations: examine via speculum with patient under anesthesia, and repair injury.

Large hematomas: evacuate and drain.

Patient has complex vaginal or perineal lacerations

Evaluate vaginal injuries with patient under anesthesia.

Perform contrast cystography and rigid proctoscopy.

Close vaginal injuries primarily.

Give I.V. antibiotics.

Consider urinary and fecal diversion.

Figure 15 **Algorithm outlines management of injuries to the female genitalia.**

handgun goes off while in a man's pants pocket). Because of the pliability of the flaccid penis, entry and exit wounds may be complex. Penile swelling is usually limited to the shaft of the penis by Buck's fascia; scrotal and perineal ecchymosis develop if the deep investing fascia of the penis is disrupted. Imaging of the corpora cavernosa with contrast cavernosography has limited sensitivity and specificity and thus is not recommended.[76] Associated urethral, scrotal, bladder, and rectal injuries must be excluded.

Inability to void, gross hematuria, and blood at the meatus all imply urethral injury and warrant further investigation. A uniform policy of exploration for all penile fractures and penetrating injuries will ensure that urethral injuries are identified. Passage of a catheter in the operative field with inspection of the involved urethra allows identification and primary repair of a lacerated or transected urethra.

Penile Amputation

Whether caused by a jealous lover or by self-mutilation, penile amputation is a catastrophic event.[77] Proper preservation of the

amputated organ is critical for successful restoration of function. The amputated part should be placed on saline-soaked gauze inside a clean bag, which should then be sealed and placed inside a second bag containing ice slush.[77] Cold ischemia times longer than 24 hours are acceptable and allow transport of the patient to tertiary centers, where replantation can be performed. Even at normal temperatures, replantation 16 hours after injury has been successful.[78] Microsurgical repair techniques have certain advantages, including better preservation of the penile shaft skin and the possibility of a sensate glans and normal orgasmic function. However, astonishing results have also been reported with the conventional technique of corporal reattachment without microvascular reanastomosis of the dorsal neurovascular structures.

MANAGEMENT

A circumferential subcoronal incision provides exposure after penile fracture and most penetrating injuries of the shaft and permits corporal and urethral repair. The superficial layers and skin are bluntly degloved back to the base of the penis. For deeper injuries, proximal to the suspensory ligament or in the crura, a penoscrotal or perineal incision is required to provide access to the corpus cavernosum. Rupture of the corpus cavernosum as a result of a fracture, a stab wound, or a bullet wound is signaled by the presence of active bleeding and a defect in the fibrous tunica albuginea. Careful exploration and inspection of the corpus spongiosum are mandatory, even if urethrography shows no extravasation. Tunical ruptures caused by fracture are transversely oriented [see Figure 16] and sometimes extend behind the spongiosum; this structure may have to be mobilized and retracted for adequate visualization of the injury.

The tunica albuginea is closed with interrupted 3-0 slowly absorbable sutures. Debridement and curettage have occasionally been used in this setting but generally are reserved for late presentations. Skin closure is possible with most penetrating injuries to the penis. The extensive vascular supply to the skin is rarely compromised. Interrupted chromic sutures provide a cosmetic closure and allow drainage of residual blood between the sutures. A lightly compressive dressing is sufficient; tight wraps are to be avoided because they may lead to necrosis of swollen shaft skin. Catheter drainage is mandatory if urethral injury is present. Sexual intercourse is contraindicated for 1 month after penile injury.

Penile Amputation

Microsurgical replantation differs from simple corporal reattachment in that the neurovascular structures are reanastomosed in addition to the urethra and the tunica albuginea. With corporal reattachment, a spatulated end-to-end urethral anastomosis is performed with interrupted absorbable sutures over a urethral catheter. The adventitia of the corpus spongiosum is reapproximated in a second layer, and the tunica albuginea and its septum are then connected. The restored cavernosal blood flow preserves the distal corpora, the glans, and the urethra. Ischemic skin loss is expected without reanastomosis of the dorsal artery and vein. When microsurgical techniques are available, the dorsal nerves, the dorsal arteries, and the deep dorsal vein are each reanastomosed with fine nonabsorbable sutures. Meticulous closure of the superficial tunica dartos and the skin completes the repair.

Temporary ectopic replantation of the penis has been described in cases where the perineum is heavily contaminated or too extensively damaged for immediate replantation.[79] Postoperative care includes urinary diversion, bed rest, anticoagulation (in selected

Table 5 AAST Organ Injury Scales for Male Genitalia

Injured Structure	AAST Grade	Characteristics of Injury	AIS-90 Score
Scrotum	I	Contusion	1
	II	Laceration < 25% of scrotal diameter	1
	III	Laceration ≥ 25% of scrotal diameter	2
	IV	Avulsion < 50%	2
	V	Avulsion ≥ 50%	2
Testis*	I	Contusion or hematoma	1
	II	Subclinical laceration of tunica albuginea	1
	III	Laceration of tunica albuginea with < 50% parenchymal loss	2
	IV	Major laceration of tunica albuginea with ≥ 50% parenchymal loss	2
	V	Total testicular destruction or avulsion	2
Penis†	I	Cutaneous laceration or contusion	1
	II	Laceration of Buck's fascia (cavernosum) without tissue loss	1
	III	Cutaneous avulsion, laceration through glans or meatus, or cavernosal or urethral defect < 2 cm	3
	IV	Partial penectomy or cavernosal or urethral defect ≥ 2 cm	3
	V	Total penectomy	3

*Advance one grade for bilateral injuries, up to grade III.
†Advance one grade for multiple injuries, up to grade III.

cases), hydration, and monitoring of arterial flow in the distal penis.

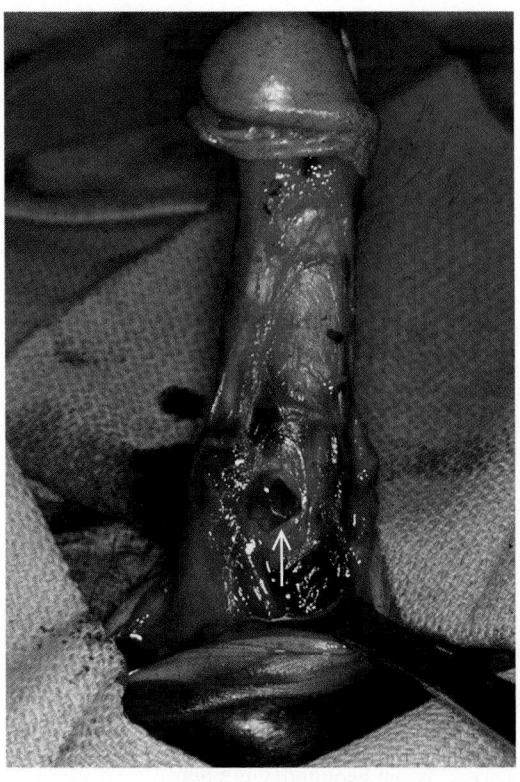

Figure 16 **Shown is a case of penile fracture. A linear tear in the tunica albuginea can be seen (arrow).**

Injuries to the Scrotum and Testes

INITIAL EVALUATION

Scrotal trauma may result in testicular injury or genital skin loss [*see Table 5*]. Because blunt injuries to the testicle are difficult to recognize, high-resolution ultrasonography has become a key element in the evaluation of scrotal trauma [*see Figure 17*]. When a straddle injury or penetrating mechanism suggests the possibility of urethral injury, retrograde urethrography is indicated.

Penetrating scrotal injuries commonly involve not only the testis but also the corpora cavernosa, the urethra, and the spermatic cord. Ultrasonography is useful to ascertain the integrity of the arterial inflow to the testis.[80] The excellent blood supply of the scrotal skin allows most penetrating injuries to be debrided and closed. Even simple bite injuries can be irrigated and closed with appropriate antibiotic coverage. Exceptions to this general rule include complex contaminated human and animal bites, which are left open and are treated with intravenous antibiotics and local wound care (or debridement in cases of severe soft tissue infection).[81]

Rupture of the testicle is often immediately painful, with rapid onset of swelling. Falls, straddle injuries, and direct blows are common mechanisms of injury.[82] However, seemingly minor degrees of trauma may be associated with delayed onset of pain; in this scenario, testicular torsion must be included in the differential diagnosis. Physical signs of rupture include scrotal swelling, tenderness, and ecchymosis. Injury to the scrotal wall or the tunica vaginalis may cause significant swelling without rupture of the tunica albuginea of the testis; pelvic hematoma caused by fracture can result in massive scrotal swelling. For these reasons, blunt injury to the scrotum should be evaluated by ultrasonography unless the findings from the physical examination are normal.

The ultrasonographic characteristics of testicular rupture [*see Figure 18*] include loss of normal homogeneity of the testicular

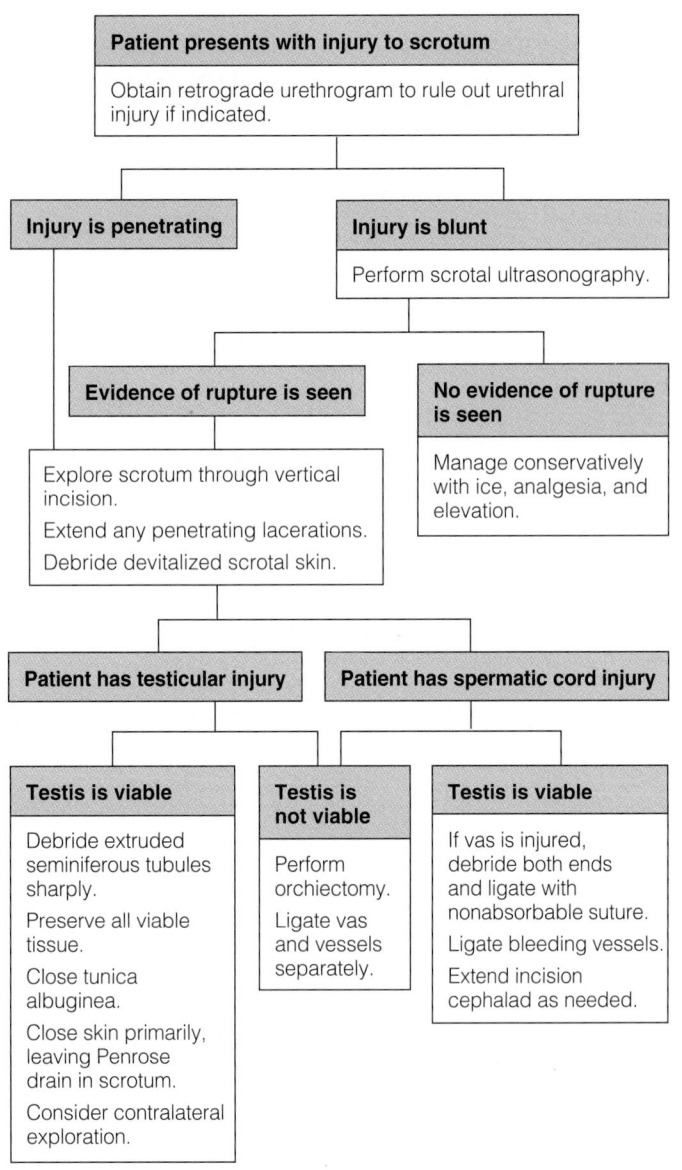

Patient presents with injury to scrotum

Obtain retrograde urethrogram to rule out urethral injury if indicated.

Injury is penetrating

Injury is blunt

Perform scrotal ultrasonography.

Evidence of rupture is seen

No evidence of rupture is seen

Explore scrotum through vertical incision.

Extend any penetrating lacerations.

Debride devitalized scrotal skin.

Manage conservatively with ice, analgesia, and elevation.

Patient has testicular injury

Patient has spermatic cord injury

Testis is viable

Debride extruded seminiferous tubules sharply.

Preserve all viable tissue.

Close tunica albuginea.

Close skin primarily, leaving Penrose drain in scrotum.

Consider contralateral exploration.

Testis is not viable

Perform orchiectomy.

Ligate vas and vessels separately.

Testis is viable

If vas is injured, debride both ends and ligate with nonabsorbable suture.

Ligate bleeding vessels.

Extend incision cephalad as needed.

Figure 17 **Algorithm outlines management of injury to the scrotum or testes.**

parenchyma, loss of continuity of the tunica albuginea, and intra-parenchymal hematoma.[83] A discrete break in the tunica is relatively rare. In cases of pelvic fracture with massive scrotal edema, ultrasonography can document the integrity of the testis and allow conservative management of the swelling. If rupture is not documented, treatment with ice packs, analgesics, and elevation allows resolution of swelling.

MANAGEMENT

Exploration of the scrotum through a vertical incision allows inspection of the scrotal contents; when spermatic cord injury is discovered, the incision can be extended cephalad to the groin. The goal is preservation of testicular parenchyma for endocrine and cosmetic purposes; normal sperm production and transport are not expected after repair of rupture. Clots and extruded seminiferous tubules are debrided with scissors to allow closure of the tunica albuginea over the edematous parenchyma. A continuous 3-0 slowly absorbable suture is sufficient.

When spermatic cord injury is detected, the first priority is determination of the viability of the testis. A small incision into the tunica albuginea should cause some bleeding; if the testis is cyanotic and does not bleed when cut, orchiectomy should be performed. If only the vas deferens or spermatic vessels are injured, the testis will remain viable. Ligation of the spermatic vessels is performed in the standard fashion; if vasal ligation is necessary, use of nonabsorbable suture with long tails enables later identification for reconstruction if infertility ensues.

Scrotal skin lacerations can be closed primarily in most instances. Exceptions arise if there is a prolonged delay between injury and definitive care or if grossly contaminated wounds are associated with rectal injuries. Hemostasis should be meticulous. Interrupted suture closure of the tunica dartos and skin in separate layers, with a Penrose drain brought out through a separate dependent stab wound, limits postoperative hematoma formation. Fluffed gauze should be used for dressing, and a scrotal supporter should be used to keep the scrotum elevated. The Penrose drain is removed on postoperative day 1. There are no major restrictions to activity after scrotal surgery, and patients can be discharged once they have recovered from associated injuries.

Scrotal avulsion can be devastating and must be differentiated from complex lacerations. Skin avulsed by shear forces in MVCs may be suitable for cleansing and preparation for full- or split-thickness grafts; however, when high-speed rotating machinery is

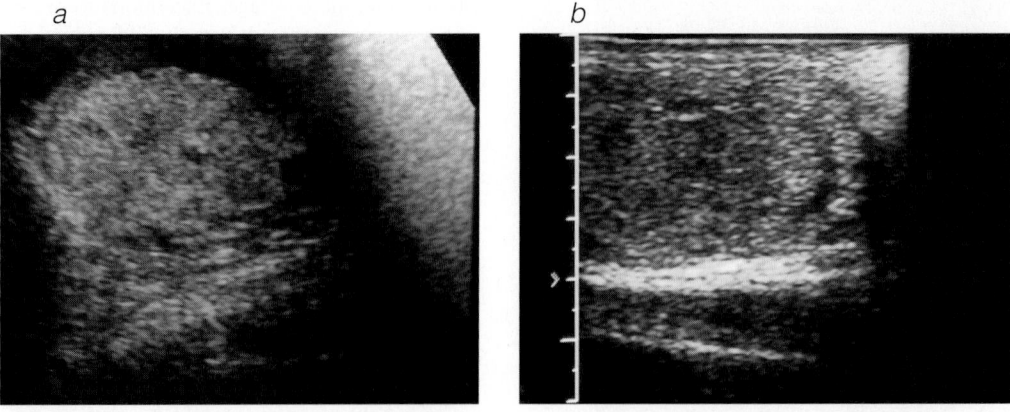

Figure 18 **(a) Ultrasonogram of ruptured testes shows intraparenchymal hematoma and heterogeneous echotexture. (b) Ultrasonogram of ruptured testes shows indistinct testicular contour and abnormal echotexture.**

the mechanism, as when clothing and skin are caught in a power takeoff, this approach is not recommended. The intrinsic microvasculature of the skin is probably damaged. Scrotal skin loss caused by burns or electrical or mechanical injury usually spares the testis, which has a separate blood supply. Conservative debridement is possible if there is no infection, but the demarcation between viable and nonviable tissue should be identified before extensive debridement.[84] Management depends on the amount of skin remaining. Options include primary closure, immediate coverage with meshed split-thickness skin grafts, and placement of the testes in subcutaneous pouches in the thigh.

References

1. World Health Organization: http://www.who.int/ msa/mnh/ems/dalys/table.htm, accessed May 31, 2004

2. American College of Surgeons: National Trauma Data Bank Report. http://www.facs.org/dept/trauma/ntdbannualreport2002.pdf, accessed March 21, 2003

3. Wessells H, Suh D, Porter JR, et al: Renal injury and operative management in the United States: results of a population-based study. J Trauma 54:423, 2003

4. Bright TC, White K, Peters PC: Significance of hematuria after trauma. J Urol 120:455, 1978

5. Miller KS, McAninch JW: Radiographic assessment of renal trauma: our 15 year experience. J Urol 154:352, 1995

6. Santucci RA, Wessells H, Bartsch G, et al: Evaluation and Management of Renal Injuries: Consensus Statement of the Renal Trauma Subcommittee. BJU Int 93:937, 2004

7. Moore EE, Shackford SR, Pachter HL, et al: Organ injury scaling: spleen, liver, kidney. J Trauma 29:1664, 1989

8. Hammer CC, Santucci RA: Effect of an institutional policy of nonoperative treatment of grades I to IV renal injuries. J Urol 169:1751, 2003

9. Villas PA, Cohen G, Putnam SG, et al: Wallstent placement in a renal artery after blunt abdominal trauma. J Trauma 46:1137, 1999

10. Paul JL, Otal P, Perreault P, et al: Treatment of posttraumatic dissection of the renal artery with endoprosthesis in a 15-year-old girl. J Trauma 47:169, 1999

11. Whigham CJ, Jr, Bodenhamer JR, Miller JK: Use of the Palmaz stent in primary treatment of renal artery intimal injury secondary to blunt trauma. J Vasc Intervent Radiol 6:175, 1995

12. DiGiacomo JC, Rotondo MF, Kauder DR, et al: The role of nephrectomy in the acutely injured. Arch Surg 136:1045, 2001

13. Santucci RA, McAninch JW, Safir M, et al: Validation of the American Association for the Surgery of Trauma organ injury severity scale for the kidney. J Trauma 50:195, 2001

14. Cheng DL, Lazan D, Stone N: Conservative management of type III renal trauma. J Trauma 36:491, 1994

15. Sagalowsky AI, McConnel JD, Peters PC: Renal trauma requiring surgery: an analysis of 185 cases. J Trauma 23:128, 1983

16. Morey AF, McAninch JW, Tiller BK, et al: Single shot intraoperative excretory urography for the immediate evaluation of renal trauma. J Urol 161:1088, 1999

17. Hagiwara A, Sakaki S, Goto H, et al: The role of interventional radiology in the management of blunt renal injury: a practical protocol. J Trauma 51:526, 2001

18. Wilkinson AG, Haddock G, Carachi R: Separation of renal fragments by a urinoma after renal trauma: percutaneous drainage accelerates healing. Pediatr Radiol 29:503, 1999

19. Steffens MG, Bode PJ, Lycklama a Nijeholt AA, et al: Selective embolization of pseudo-aneurysms of the renal artery after blunt abdominal injury in a patient with a single kidney. Injury 27:219, 1996

20. Gonzalez RP, Falimirski M, Holevar MR, et al: Surgical management of renal trauma: is vascular control necessary? J Trauma 47:1039, 1999

21. McAninch JW, Carroll PC: Renal trauma: kidney preservation through improved vascular control—a refined technique. J Trauma 22:285, 1982

22. Atala A, Miller FB, Richardson JD, et al: Preliminary vascular control for renal trauma. Surg Gynecol Obstet 172:386, 1991

23. Nash PA, Bruce JE, McAninch JW: Nephrectomy for traumatic renal injuries. J Urol 153:609, 1995

24. Morey AF, Anema JG, Harris R, et al: Treatment of grade 4 renal stab wounds with absorbable fibrin adhesive bandage in a porcine model. J Urol 165:955, 2001

25. Ramakrishna S, Roberts WW, Fugita OE, et al: Local hemostasis during laparoscopic partial nephrectomy using biodegradable hydrogels: initial porcine results. J Endourol 16:489, 2002

26. Richter F, Schnorr D, Deger S, et al: Improvement of hemostasis in open and laparoscopically performed partial nephrectomy using a gelatin matrix-thrombin tissue sealant (FloSeal). Urology 61:73, 2003

27. Richter F, Tullmann ME, Turk I, et al: [Improvement of hemostasis in laparoscopic and open partial nephrectomy with gelatin thrombin matrix (FloSeal)]. Urologe A 42:338, 2003

28. User HM, Nadler RB: Applications of FloSeal in nephron-sparing surgery. Urology 62:342, 2003

29. Lee SS, Cheng CL, Yu DS, et al: Vicryl mesh for repair of severely injured kidneys: an experimental study. J Trauma 34:406, 1993

30. Matthews LA, Smith EM, Spirnak JP: Nonoperative treatment of major blunt renal lacerations with urinary extravasation. J Urol 157:2056, 1997

31. Moudouni SM, Patard JJ, Manunta A, et al: A conservative approach to major blunt renal lacerations with urinary extravasation and devitalized renal segments. BJU Int 87:290, 2001

32. Wessells H, McAninch JW, Meyer A, et al: Criteria for nonoperative treatment of significant penetrating renal lacerations. J Urol 157:24, 1997

33. Lee RS, Porter JR: Traumatic renal artery pseudoaneurysm: diagnosis and management techniques. J Trauma 55:972, 2003

34. Knudson MM, Harrison PB, Hoyt DB, et al: Outcome after major renovascular injuries: a Western trauma association multicenter report. J Trauma 49:1116, 2000

35. Elliott SP, McAninch JW: Ureteral injuries from external violence: the 25-year experience at San Francisco General Hospital. J Urol 170:1213, 2003

36. Digiacomo JC, Frankel H, Rotondo MF, et al: Preoperative radiographic staging for ureteral injuries is not warranted in patients undergoing celiotomy for trauma. Am Surg 67:969, 2001

37. Palmer LS, Rosenbaum RR, Gershbaum MD, et al: Penetrating ureteral trauma at an urban trauma center: 10-year experience. Urology 54:34, 1999

38. Medina D, Lavery R, Ross SE, et al: Ureteral trauma: preoperative studies neither predict injury nor prevent missed injuries. J Am Coll Surg 186:641, 1998

39. Boone TB, Gilling PJ, Husmann DA: Ureteropelvic junction disruption following blunt abdominal trauma. J Urol 150:33, 1993

40. Brandes SB, Chelsky MJ, Buckman RF, et al: Ureteral injuries from penetrating trauma. J Trauma 36:766, 1994

41. Presti JC, Carroll PR, McAninch JW: Ureteral and renal pelvic injuries from external trauma: diagnosis and management. J Trauma 29:370, 1989

42. Aihara R, Blansfield JS, Millham FH, et al: Fracture locations influence the likelihood of rectal and lower urinary tract injuries in patients sustaining pelvic fractures. J Trauma 52:205, 2002

43. Hsieh CH, Chen RJ, Fang JF, et al: Diagnosis and management of bladder injury by trauma surgeons. Am J Surg 184:143, 2002

44. Deck AJ, Shaves S, Talner L, et al: Computerized tomography cystography for the diagnosis of traumatic bladder rupture. J Urol 164:43, 2000

45. Ciftci AO, Tanyel FC, Senocak ME, et al: Biochemical predictors for differentiating intraperitoneal and extraperitoneal bladder perforation. J Pediatr Surg 34:367, 1999

46. Cass AS: Diagnostic studies in bladder rupture: indications and techniques. Urol Clin North Am 16:267, 1989

47. Corriere JN, Sandler CM: Extraperitoneal bladder rupture. Urol Clin North Am 16:275, 1989

48. Peters PC: Intraperitoneal rupture of the bladder. Urol Clin North Am 16:279, 1989

49. Ali MO, Singh B, Moodley J, et al: Prospective evaluation of combined suprapubic and urethral catheterization to urethral drainage alone for intraperitoneal bladder injuries. J Trauma 55:1152, 2003

50. Parry NG, Rozycki GS, Feliciano DV, et al: Traumatic rupture of the urinary bladder: is the suprapubic tube necessary? J Trauma 54:431, 2003

51. Takayama T, Mugiya S, Ohira T, et al: Complete disruption of the female urethra. Int J Urol 6:50, 1999

52. Porter JR, Takayama TK, DeFalco AJ: Traumatic posterior urethral injury and early realignment using magnetic urethral catheters. J Urol 158:425, 1997

53. Webster GD: Perineal repair of membranous urethral stricture. Urol Clin North Am 16:303, 1989

54. Routt ML, Simonian PT, Defalco AJ, et al: Internal fixation in pelvic fractures and primary repairs of associated genitourinary disruptions: a team approach. J Trauma 40:784, 1996

55. Husmann DA, Boone TB, Wilson WT: Management of low velocity gunshot wounds to the ante-

rior urethra: the role of primary repair versus urinary diversion alone. J Urol 150:70, 1993

56. Mohr AM, Pham AM, Lavery RF, et al: Management of trauma to the male external genitalia: the usefulness of American Association for the Surgery of Trauma organ injury scales. J Urol 170:2311, 2003

57. Sugar NF, Fine DN, Eckert LO: Physical injury after sexual assault: findings of a large case series. Am J Obstet Gynecol 190:71, 2004

58. Riggs N, Houry D, Long G, et al: Analysis of 1,076 cases of sexual assault. Ann Emerg Med 35:358, 2000

59. Mandell J, Cromie WJ, Caldamone AA: Sports-related genitourinary injuries in children. Clin Sports Med 1:483, 1982

60. Haefner HK, Andersen HF, Johnson MP: Vaginal laceration following a jet-ski accident. Obstet Gynecol 78:986, 1991

61. Knudson MM, Crombleholme WR: Female genital trauma and sexual assault. Abdominal Trauma. Blaidsell FW, Trunkey DD, Eds. Thieme Medical Publishers, New York, 1993, p 311

62. Quast DC, Jordan GL: Traumatic wounds of the female reproductive organs. J Trauma 4:839, 1964

63. Maull KI, Rozycki GS, Pedigo RE: Injury to the female reproductive system. Trauma. Mattox KL, Moore EE, Feliciano DV, Eds. Appleton-Lange, San Mateo, California, 1988

64. Bottomley CP, Sadler T, Welch J: Integrated clinical service for sexual assault victims in a genitourinary setting. Sex Transm Infect 75:116, 1999

65. American College of Obstetricians and Gynecologists ACOG: Sexual assault. ACOG Educ Bull (242):1, 1997

66. Grossin C, Sibille I, Lorin de la Grandmaison G, et al: Analysis of 418 cases of sexual assault. Forensic Sci Int 131:125, 2003

67. Niemi TA, Norton LW: Vaginal injuries in patients with pelvic fracture. J Trauma 25:547, 1985

68. Woods RK, O'Keefe G, Rhee P, et al: Open pelvic fracture and fecal diversion. Arch Surg 133:281, 1998

69. Shires GT: Trauma. Principles of Surgery. Schwartz SI, Shires GT, Spencer FC, et al, Eds. McGraw-Hill, New York, 1984, p 199

70. Monga M, Moreno T, Hellstrom WJG: A strategy for success: managing gunshot wounds to the male genitalia. Contemp Urol 7:58, 1995

71. Cline KJ, Mata JA, Venable DD, et al: Penetrating trauma to the male external genitalia. J Trauma 44:492, 1998

72. Thompson I, Flaherty SF, Morey AF: Battlefield injuries. J Am Coll Surg 187:139, 1998

73. Eke N: Urological complications of coitus. BJU Int 89:273, 2002

74. Uygur MC, Gulerkaya B, Altug U, et al: 13 years' experience of penile fracture. Scand J Urol Nephrol 31:265, 1997

75. Karadeniz T, Topsakal M, Ariman A, et al: Penile fracture: differential diagnosis, management and outcome. Br J Urol 77:279, 1996

76. Gross H: The role of cavernosography in acute fracture of the penis. Radiology 144:787, 1982

77. Jordan GH, Gilbert DA: Management of amputation injuries of the male genitalia. Urol Clin North Am 16:359, 1989

78. Wei FC, McKee NH, Huerta FJ, et al: Microsurgical replantation of a completely amputated penis. Ann Plast Surg 10:317, 1983

79. Matloub HS, Yousif NJ, Sanger JR: Temporary ectopic implantation of an amputated penis. Plast Reconstr Surg 93:408, 1994

80. Tsai HN, Wu WJ, Huang SP, et al: Bilateral traumatic testicular dislocation—a case report. Kaohsiung J Med Sci 18:95, 2002

81. Wolf JS, Gomez R, McAninch JW: Human bites to the penis. J Urol 147:1265, 1992

82. Gomez R: Genital injuries. Probl Urol 8:279, 1994

83. Wessells H, McAninch JW: Testicular trauma. Urology 47:750, 1996

84. Wessells H: Genital skin loss: unified reconstructive approach to a heterogeneous entity. World J Urol 17:107, 1999

Acknowledgments

The author expresses his thanks to Jack W. McAninch, M.D., F.A.C.S., for guidance and help in preparing earlier versions of this chapter.

Figures 3, 5, and 10 Susan Brust, C.M.I. Adapted from originals by P. Stempen.

Figures 1, 8, 11, 15, and 17 Marcia Kammerer.

111 INJURIES TO THE PELVIS AND EXTREMITIES

J. C. Goslings, M.D., Ph.D., K. J. Ponsen, M.D., and O. M. van Delden, M.D., Ph.D.

Injuries to the pelvis and extremities are common, occurring in approximately 85% of patients who sustain blunt trauma. Improper management can have devastating consequences. Major long bone fractures are a sign that substantial force has been applied to the body, and they are frequently associated with torso injuries. Trauma to the pelvis or the extremities can result in injuries that are potentially life-threatening (e.g., pelvic disruption with hemorrhage, major arterial bleeding, and crush syndrome) or limb-threatening (e.g., open fractures and joint injuries, vascular injuries and traumatic amputation, compartment syndrome, and nerve injury secondary to fracture dislocation). In this chapter, we outline the basic knowledge the general or trauma surgeon requires for initial management of injuries to the pelvis, the extremities, or both.

Evaluation and Assessment

INITIAL PRIORITIES

In the surgical management of musculoskeletal injury, the priorities are (1) to save the patient's life, (2) to save the endangered limb, (3) to save the affected joints, and (4) to restore function; these priorities are pursued in accordance with advanced trauma life support (ATLS) guidelines.[1] The musculoskeletal injury that it is most important to identify during the primary survey is an unstable pelvic injury, which can lead to massive and life-threatening internal bleeding. If manual compression-distraction of the iliac crests elicits abnormal movement or pain, a pelvic fracture is probably present. In this case, a prefabricated splint or sheet wrap is applied around the pelvis to reduce the intrapelvic volume, and the legs are wrapped together to induce internal rotation of the lower limbs. Grossly deformed extremities are reduced by means of manual traction to reduce motion and to enhance the tamponade effect of the muscles. In the initial phase, control of hemorrhage from deep soft tissue lesions and vessel injury is best achieved with direct compression.

During the secondary survey, the rest of the musculoskeletal system is assessed to identify fractures, dislocations, and soft tissue injuries. It is advisable to perform a tertiary survey 24 to 48 hours after admission to detect any missed injuries, especially in multiply injured patients whose condition at admission precluded the completion of a full secondary survey.[2]

IMAGING

Diagnostic imaging usually begins with conventional x-rays. The pelvis is imaged during the primary survey, but x-rays of the extremities typically are obtained only after life-threatening injuries have been corrected and the patient's general condition is such that the surgeon can afford to spend the time necessary to complete extremity and spine imaging (which is often as along as several hours). Conventional x-rays of the affected limb are guided by the injury mechanism, the history, and the physical examination and are always done in two planes (anteroposterior [AP] and lateral). Long bones should be visualized over their entire length, including the adjacent joints. After reduction of fractures and dislocations, x-rays should be repeated, unless no time is available (e.g., because of the presence of limb-threatening vascular injury).

Computed tomographic scanning is frequently used as an adjunct to conventional x-rays, especially in patients with periarticular fractures and dislocations or pelvic fractures. Axial, sagittal, coronal, and three-dimensional reconstructions allow exact determination of the extent of the fracture and the position of fracture fragments. CT scanning also helps in the process of deciding between operative and nonoperative treatment, and it facilitates preoperative planning when a surgical therapy is adopted. In addition, CT scanning may play a role in detecting bleeding sources in the pelvis, though hemodynamic instability or ongoing blood loss in the presence of a pelvic fracture usually is best managed with immediate angiography rather than CT.

Magnetic resonance imaging can be helpful with complex malunions, soft tissue injuries, and certain fracture types (e.g., scaphoid fracture).[3] Bone scintigraphy and ultrasonography are less frequently employed in the setting of pelvic and extremity trauma. Triphasic bone scanning is primarily used to detect osteomyelitis, avascular necrosis, and malignant lesions, whereas ultrasonography is mostly used to assess soft tissue injuries.

CLASSIFICATION OF INJURIES

Fracture

Of the many existing fracture classification systems, the one that is most frequently used is the system developed by two Swiss organizations, the Association for Osteosynthesis (AO) and the Association for the Study of Internal Fixation (ASIF) [see Figure 1].[4] The AO-ASIF fracture classification system serves both as a means of documenting fractures (e.g., for research purposes) and as an aid to the surgeon in assessing the severity of the fracture and determining the appropriate treatment.

In the AO-ASIF system, any given extremity fracture can be described in terms of a five-place alphanumeric designation [see Figure 1a]. The first place represents the bone injured. The second represents the segment affected by the injury (proximal, middle or diaphyseal, or distal, with malleolar a fourth category that is sometimes employed). The third represents the fracture type (A, B, or C). In middle-segment long bone fractures, type A refers to simple fractures with two fragments, type B refers to wedge fractures with contact between the main proximal and distal fragments after reduction, and type C refers to complex fractures without contact between the main fragments after reduction [see Figure 1b]. In proximal and distal long bone fractures, type A refers to extra-articular fractures with the articular surface intact, type B refers to partial articular fractures in which there is some articular involvement but part of the articular surface remains attached to the diaphysis, and type C refers to complete articular fractures in which

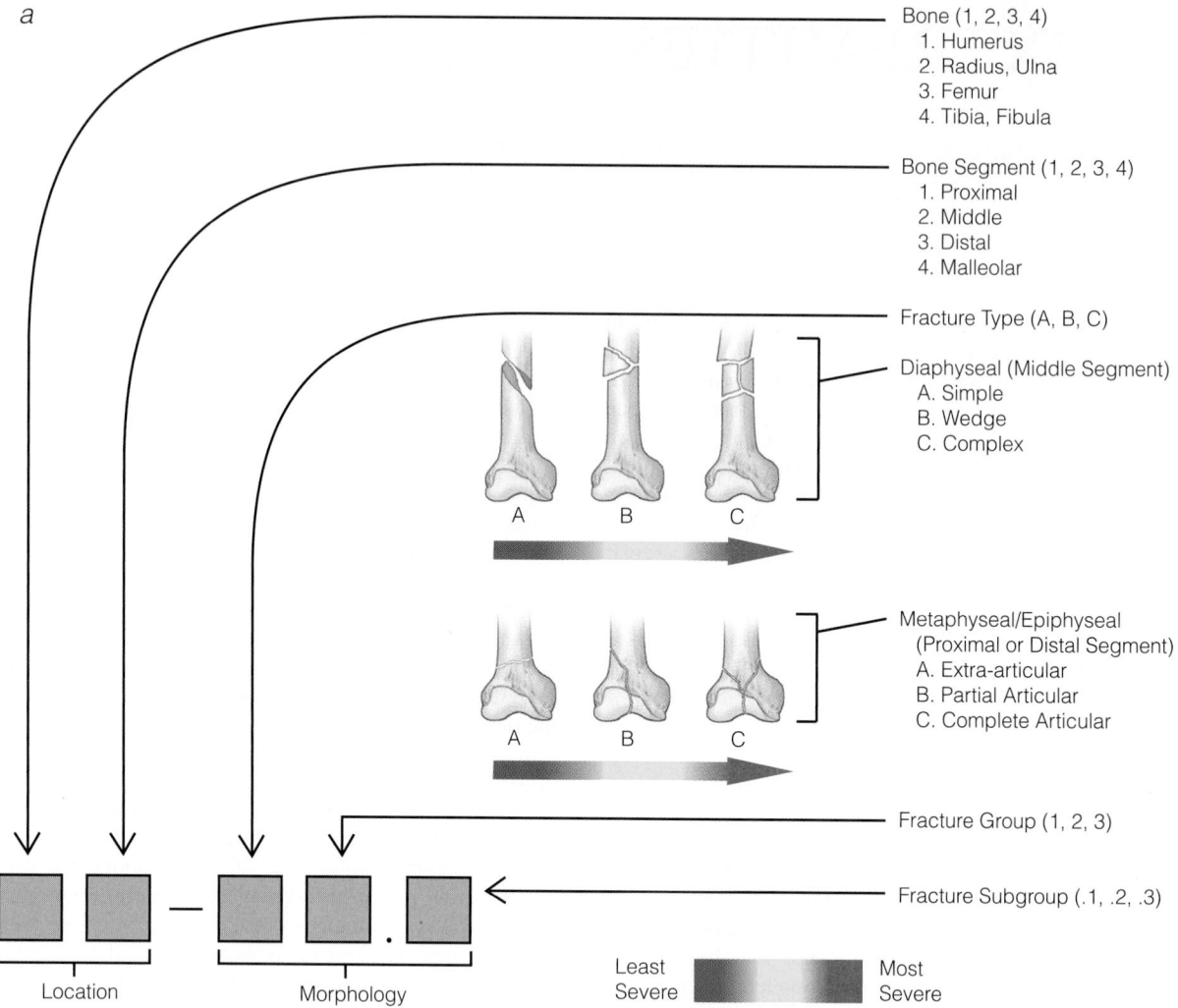

a

Bone (1, 2, 3, 4)
  1. Humerus
  2. Radius, Ulna
  3. Femur
  4. Tibia, Fibula

Bone Segment (1, 2, 3, 4)
  1. Proximal
  2. Middle
  3. Distal
  4. Malleolar

Fracture Type (A, B, C)

Diaphyseal (Middle Segment)
  A. Simple
  B. Wedge
  C. Complex

A   B   C

Metaphyseal/Epiphyseal
  (Proximal or Distal Segment)
  A. Extra-articular
  B. Partial Articular
  C. Complete Articular

A   B   C

Fracture Group (1, 2, 3)

Fracture Subgroup (.1, .2, .3)

Location   Morphology

Least   Most
Severe   Severe

Figure 1 (*a*) **Shown is the AO-ASIF classification system for fractures, as expressed in a five-place alphanumeric designation. (*b*) Illustrated are the three types of diaphyseal long bone fractures, along with the three groups into which each type is divided. (*c*) Depicted are the three types of metaphyseal or epiphyseal long bone fractures.**

the articular surface is disrupted and completely separated from the diaphysis [*see Figure 1c*]. The fracture types are then further subdivided into three groups (1, 2, or 3), represented by the fourth place, and (mainly for scientific purposes) three subgroups (.1, .2, or .3), represented by the fifth place.

For the fracture types, groups, and subgroups, increasing letter and number values represent increasing severity, as determined by the complexity of the fracture, the difficulty of treatment, and the prognosis. Thus, an A1 fracture is the simplest injury with the best prognosis, and a C3 fracture is the most complex injury with the worst prognosis. For practical purposes, the first four places of the AO-ASIF alphanumeric designation are usually sufficient for treatment planning; the fifth (the subgroup) adds little to the process.

Pelvic ring and acetabular fractures are classified in essentially the same fashion [*see Management of Pelvic and Acetabular Injuries, below*].

Soft Tissue Injury

The type of soft tissue injury present and its extent are determined by the type of insult sustained (e.g., blunt, sharp, or crush), the degree and direction of the force applied, the area affected, and the extent of contamination (if any). With closed injuries, the intact skin prevents direct assessment of the subcutaneous tissues, and as a result, soft tissue injuries are frequently underestimated. In the emergency department, a single inspection is made, and the wound is covered by a sterile dressing; at this point, it may be helpful to take pictures with a digital camera. Exact grading of the soft tissue injury is best done in the operating room by an experienced surgeon who can also decide on a treatment plan.

The system most commonly used for classification of open fractures is the one developed by Gustilo and Anderson, which divides these fractures into three types as follows [*see Figure 2*][4,5]:

1. Type I: the wound is smaller than 1 cm and results from an inside-out perforation, with little or no contamination; the fracture type is simple (type A or B).
2. Type II: the skin laceration is larger than 1 cm but is associated with little or no contusion of the surrounding tissues; there is no dead musculature, and the fracture type is moderate to severe (B or C).
3. Type III: extensive soft tissue damage has occurred, with or without severe contamination, frequently in association with compromised vascular status; the fracture is highly unstable (type C) as a result of comminution or segmental defects. Type

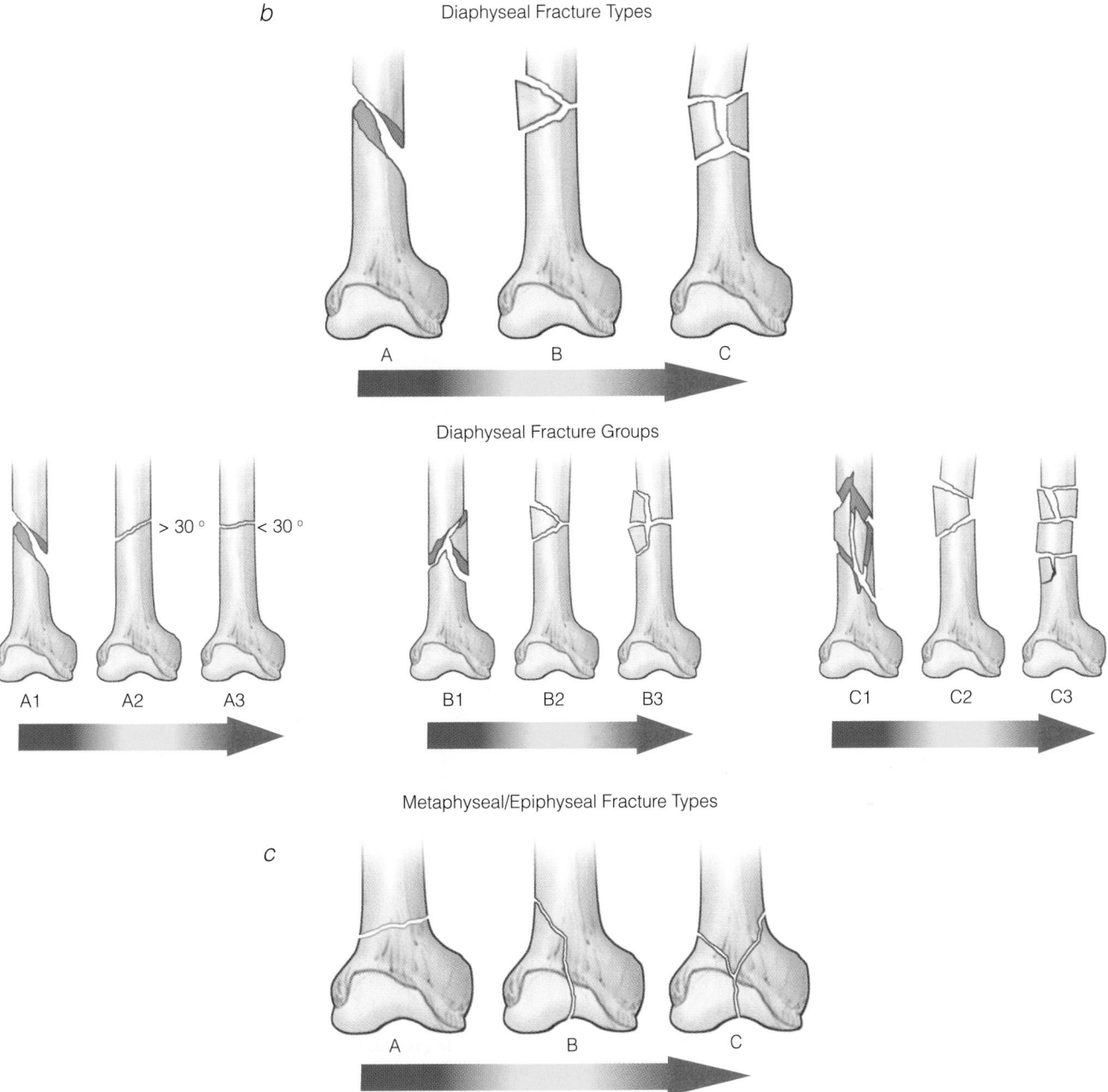

b Diaphyseal Fracture Types

Diaphyseal Fracture Groups

Metaphyseal/Epiphyseal Fracture Types

c

III fractures are further divided into the following three sub-categories:

a. IIIA: adequate soft tissue coverage of the bone is still possible.

b. IIIB: extensive soft tissue loss occurs with periosteal stripping and exposed bone; contamination is usually massive.

c. IIIC: an arterial injury is present that requires repair; any open fracture accompanied by such an injury falls into this category, regardless of fracture type.

Closed fractures are less frequently classified according to the type and extent of soft tissue injury, though this does not mean that such injury is not an important consideration with closed fractures. The classification system most commonly used for closed fractures is that of Tscherne, which recognizes the following four grades:

1. Grade 0: soft tissue injury is absent or minor; the fracture type is simple.

2. Grade I: superficial abrasion or contusion is present as a result

of pressure applied by the fragment from the inside; the fracture type is simple or moderate.

3. Grade II: deep contaminated abrasions and localized skin or muscle contusion are present as a consequence of direct trauma, possibly leading to compartment syndrome; the fracture type is moderate to severe.

4. Grade III: extensive skin contusions, destruction of musculature, and subcutaneous tissue avulsion have occurred; the fracture is severe and mostly comminuted.

Timing and Planning of Intervention

In multiply injured patients, the timing of operative treatment of injuries to the pelvis and extremities depends both on the condition of the patient and on the particular combination of skeletal and soft tissue injuries sustained [*see Table 1*]. In such cases, the threshold for adoption of a damage-control strategy [*see Damage-Control Surgery, below*] to minimize operating time and tissue

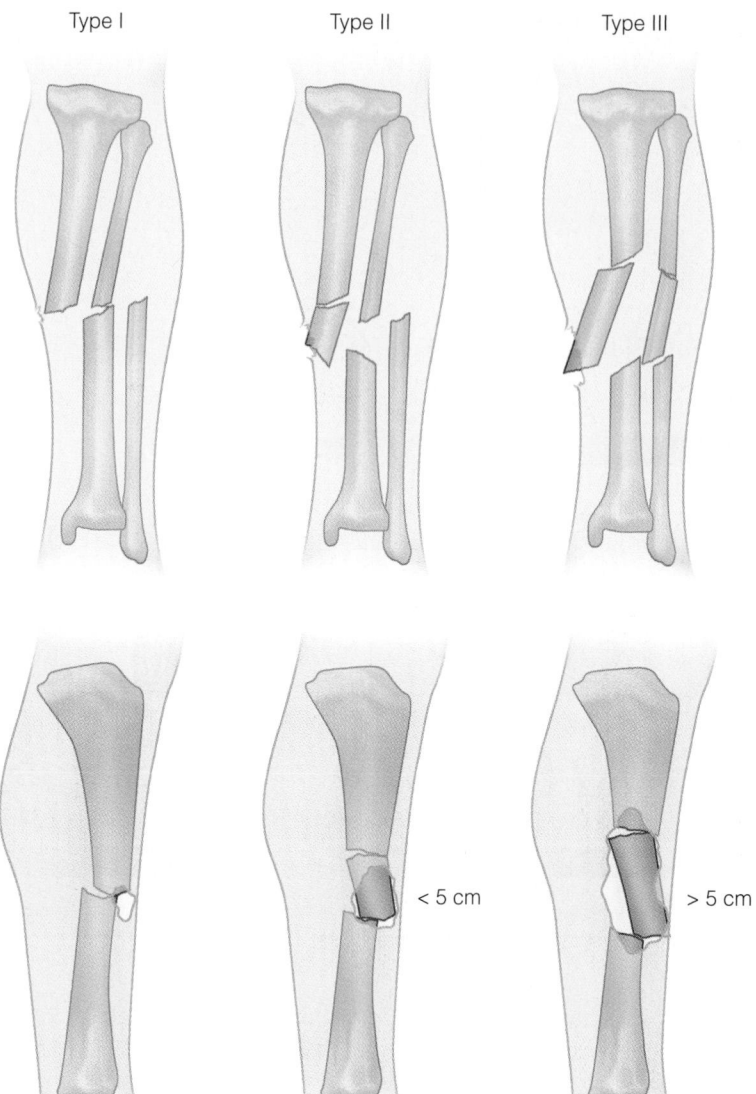

Type I Type II Type III

< 5 cm

> 5 cm

Figure 2 **Illustrated is the Gustilo-Anderson classification system for open fractures.**

insult should be low.[6,7] The performance of multiple definitive osteosyntheses is an option only in patients who have been successfully resuscitated (as indicated by stable hemodynamic status without a need for inotropes; absence of hypoxia, hypercapnia, and acidosis; normothermia; normal coagulation parameters; and normal diuresis).

In other cases, the timing and extent of operative treatment of musculoskeletal injuries may be more complex. Generally, if open reduction and internal fixation are indicated, the sooner the operation is performed, the better. With early operation, fracture surfaces are more easily cleaned of blood clots and other material, and reduction is facilitated by the absence of prolonged dislocation and shortening. After 6 to 8 hours, swelling develops, making both the operation and the subsequent closure more difficult and thereby increasing the risk of infection and other wound complications. There are some cases, however, in which it might be preferable to postpone a complex articular reconstruction in order to ensure that the surgical team is optimally prepared. If, for any reason, significant swelling precludes a definitive operation, it is usually safer to stabilize the fracture temporarily (e.g., with splinting or external fixation), then wait 5 to 10 days for the swelling to subside. Temporary stabilization usually allows the surgeon to achieve a

reasonable provisional reduction; however, complete joint dislocations are not acceptable. Clinically, sufficient reduction of swelling has occurred when the skin has regained its creases and is wrinkled over the operative site. Early definitive surgery may also be contraindicated when abrasion or degloving injury is present at the fracture site on admission.

Swelling is less of a problem with shaft fractures that will be treated with intramedullary nailing. If, however, it is not possible to perform nailing within 24 to 48 hours after the injury, it is better to postpone the operation for 7 to 10 days; patients operated on between days 3 and 7 are at higher risk for the acute respiratory distress syndrome (ARDS).[8,9] If the procedure must be delayed for more than 2 to 3 weeks (e.g., because of sepsis and organ failure), reconstruction of bones and joints will be substantially more difficult. If such delay leads to suboptimal axial alignment and nonanatomic reconstruction of the articular surface, the long-term prognosis will be worse.

Thorough preoperative planning is necessary for any operation done on the musculoskeletal system. Depending on the procedure to be performed, logistical considerations may include availability of the appropriate operating team, availability of the correct operating table, availability of the specific instruments needed, availability of the appropriate implants, and availability of intraoperative imaging. Technical considerations include the operative approach to be followed and the fixation method to be used, which are determined on the basis of an understanding of the extent of the injuries and a detailed knowledge of the anatomy in the area to be exposed. For example, awkward placement of fixator pins could seriously obstruct soft tissue reconstruction if the pins are in the area that should be used for a soft tissue flap. Before operation, the correct operative site is verified (with the patient awake) and marked with a permanent marker pen. A drawing of the planned reduction maneuvers and fixation techniques may be helpful for the surgeon while also serving as an educational tool for the assisting team members. Correct documentation is important for both medical and legal reasons.

DAMAGE-CONTROL SURGERY

Immediate and complete care of all fractures, dislocations, and soft tissue injuries may seem the ideal treatment strategy for patients with musculoskeletal injuries. However, this is not always the case. Major trauma leads to a systemic inflammatory response syndrome (SIRS) characterized by increased capillary leakage, high energy consumption, and a hyperdynamic hemodynamic state. Especially in the setting of severe single-organ injury or multiple injuries, the physiologic and immunologic impact of extend-

Table 2 Goals of and Indications for Damage-Control Surgery in Management of Pelvic and Extremity Trauma

Goals	Control of hemorrhage Control of contamination Removal of dead tissue and prevention of ischemia-reperfusion injury Facilitation of ICU treatment Pain relief

Indications	Clinical parameters
	  Multiple trauma (ISS > 15) and additional chest trauma
	  Pelvic ring injuries with exsanguinating hemorrhage
	  Multiple trauma with abdominal or pelvic injuries and hemorrhagic shock (BP < 90 mm Hg)
	  Radiographic findings indicating (bilateral) lung contusion
	  Femoral fractures in polytrauma patient
	  Polytrauma in geriatric patient
	  Resuscitation, operation, or both expected to last > 90 min
	Physiologic parameters
	  Severe metabolic acidosis (pH < 7.20)
	  Base deficit (< −6 mEq/L)
	  Hypothermia (T° < 35° C)
	  Coagulopathy (PT > 50% of normal)
	  Multiple transfusions

ISS—Injury Severity Score   PT—prothrombin time

Table 1 Time Frames for Operative Treatment of Pelvic and Extremity Trauma*

Category I: immediate	(Imminent) hemodynamic instability (e.g., pelvic fracture) Neurovascular injury with compromised vitality of extremity (Imminent) compartment syndrome
Category II: urgent (within 6–12 hr)	Open fractures (increased risk of infection) Joint dislocations that cannot be reduced in ED Primary stabilization (e.g., external fixation) in multiply injured patients who are hemodynamically stable Femoral neck fractures in patients < 65 yr (to prevent femoral head necrosis) Long bone fractures (to prevent complications and immobilization) Severe soft tissue injury (e.g., degloving caused by rollover accident) Closed fractures with compromised skin Dislocated talar neck fractures
Category III: semiurgent (within 12–24 hr)	Femoral neck, intertrochanteric, and subtrochanteric fractures Closed reduction of fractures in children Treatment of soft tissue injuries (e.g., to tendons of wrist and hand) Closed fractures that benefit from early treatment (e.g., to prevent swelling with ankle fractures) Spine fractures that are unstable or associated with neurologic deterioration Wound debridement and irrigation or washout
Category IV: semielective (within 24–72 hr or delayed)	Achilles tendon ruptures Stable spine fractures Other fractures Revision procedures other than those done for infection

*These time frames are general guidelines and may be modified in accordance with individual patient parameters (e.g., physiologic condition, soft tissue injury, and fracture type) and local preferences.

ed surgical procedures on the patient's general condition can increase the risk of the multiple organ failure syndrome (MODS), ARDS, and other complications. Balanced against this risk is the understanding that early fracture fixation in polytrauma patients is beneficial in terms of mortality and morbidity. Improved understanding of the physiologic response to major trauma over the past decade has led to the approach known as damage-control surgery (DCS) or staged surgery, the purpose of which is to keep the patient from having to deal with the "second hit" imposed by the operation right after experiencing the "first hit" imposed by the initial trauma.

Currently, DCS is widely promoted for management of intra-abdominal, vascular, and musculoskeletal injuries. It can be divided into three main phases: (1) a resuscitative phase, (2) an intensive care phase, and (3) a reconstructive phase.[10] The initial focus is on control of bleeding, contamination, and temporary stabilization of fractures; time-consuming reconstructions and osteosyntheses are avoided at this point. At a later stage, when vital functions have been restored, definitive reconstructions are performed during one or more planned reoperations.

The decision whether to employ DCS should be made before the operation to avoid a scenario in which the patient's general condition of the patient deteriorates seriously during a difficult operation (e.g., a complex femoral nailing procedure) [see Table 2]. An experienced and judicious surgeon will make an appropriate decision about DCS more often than not. If, as sometimes happens despite the surgeon's best efforts, the patient's condition does show serious deterioration unexpectedly during operation, the surgeon should immediately choose a bailout option, usually involving external fixation.

As applied to musculoskeletal trauma, DCS begins with debridement of open wounds and irrigation with pulsed lavage (so-called washout). Amputation of the injured limb or limbs is considered if it appears potentially lifesaving [see Management of Life-Threatening or Limb-Threatening Injuries, Mangled Extremity, below]. During the initial debridement, osteochondral fragments in open joint fractures are retained—provided that they are not severely contaminated—to allow later reconstruction of the joint surface. Dislocations and diaphyseal fractures are reduced and stabilized with simple external fixator frames (if necessary, placed so as to span the adjacent joint or joints), and wounds are provisionally closed. Fixator pins are placed through stab incisions in safe zones. Fractures need not be reduced anatomically under image intensifier control; the only goals at this point are to restore length and align long bone fractures and joints, to reduce contamination, and to enable postoperative wound management in the intensive care unit while definitive treatment is pending. The more complex the fixator frame, the more time-consuming its application usually is. Muscle compartments believed to be at risk for compartment syndrome are widely decompressed.

At all times, the operating surgeon must keep the goals of DCS clearly in mind. The main aim of this strategy is not necessarily a nice-looking postoperative x-ray showing parallel fixator pins and a perfectly reduced tibia; rather, it is the survival of the patient in stable physiologic condition. Depending on the severity of the injuries, the reconstructive procedures likely to be performed, and the availability of specialists or subspecialists, consultation with a plastic surgeon during the initial operation may be advisable to optimize operative and logistical planning.[6,7]

Careful attention must be paid to the logistical aspects of DCS. As soon as the decision for DCS is made, OR personnel should be notified of the type of procedures to be performed and the implants required. It may be helpful to have a dedicated DCS equipment trolley with all the materials and equipment necessary for the first hour.[11] Once the patient and the operating team are in the OR, the injuries sustained, the operative plan, and the injuries (known or suspected) that need special attention (e.g., a small pneumothorax) are written down or sketched on a whiteboard so that all persons present in the OR know what is to be done.

During the operation, the surgeon should stay in close contact with the anesthesiologist regarding the condition of the patient and the procedure currently under way. If operative procedures are required in more than one organ system (e.g., laparotomy and external fixation of the femora), they should, whenever possible, be performed simultaneously by multiple teams working together. The end of the procedure should be announced well ahead of time so that the anesthesiologist can take the precautions necessary for transport of a potentially unstable patient and so that the ICU can be notified of the patient's arrival. In this way, unnecessary waiting times in the OR can be kept to a minimum.

The second phase of DCS is restoration of vital functions in the ICU. This phase is crucial for ensuring that the patient is fit to undergo a second procedure.[10] Close cooperation between surgeon and critical care physician is required to outline an aggressive strategy for ventilation, circulatory support, and reversal of hypothermia, coagulopathy, acidosis, and other abnormalities. Administration of large volumes of fluid will be necessary as a consequence of massive tissue swelling and bowel edema. Cardiac monitoring with central venous access should usually be employed. Application of external fixators allows the nursing staff to place the patient in the position that is most suitable for intensive care of head, chest, and abdominal injuries, while still allowing wound inspection and dressing changes as required. During this phase, imaging studies may be performed (or, if already performed, repeated) to allow planning for repeated washouts and definitive reconstructive procedures.

The third phase in the DCS sequence is the performance of one or more planned reoperations. This usually takes place at least 24

to 48 hours after the initial procedure, when the patient is stable and normothermic and has normal or near-normal coagulation parameters.[10] Subsequent visits to the OR are used to continue wound debridement and coverage and to exchange external fixators for definitive fixation (e.g., with intramedullary nails).[12,13] During these operations, multiple teams can work simultaneously on the repair of abdominal, musculoskeletal, and other injuries. The period from postinjury day 5 to day 10 is often referred to as the window of opportunity for reconstruction of intra-articular or periarticular fractures and of upper-limb fractures.

Management of Life-Threatening or Limb-Threatening Injuries

LIFE-THREATENING PELVIC TRAUMA

Pelvic fractures are frequently associated with significant hemorrhage, not only because of the fracture itself but also because pelvic trauma is often accompanied by serious injuries to other parts of the body (e.g., the chest or the abdomen). Significant arterial hemorrhage is present in approximately 25% of patients with unstable pelvic fractures.[4,5,10,14,15] Bleeding from pelvic trauma can be quite severe: as much as 4 L of blood may accumulate in the retroperitoneal space. Whether hemorrhagic shock is associated with certain fracture types remains a matter of debate, but there is certainly a link between the severity of the pelvic injury and the incidence of hemorrhagic shock. Hemorrhagic shock in patients with pelvic fracture strongly influences outcome and necessitates immediate evaluation and treatment.

Hemorrhage may originate either from within the fractured pelvic bones themselves or from torn arteries and veins in the pelvis, which are in close proximity to the bony structures of the pelvis. In particular, the presacral venous plexus and the internal iliac arteries and side branches may be lacerated. The most commonly injured anterior branches of the internal iliac artery are the internal pudendal artery and the obturator artery, whereas the most commonly injured posterior branches are the superior gluteal artery and the lateral sacral artery.[16,17]

Given that bleeding in pelvic fracture patients can occur in other body compartments besides the pelvis and can be arterial as well as venous, it is of the utmost importance to identify its source and, ideally, determine its nature as soon as possible. This information is crucial in determining what the next steps in management should be [see Figure 3].

The first step after diagnosing a pelvic fracture should be the immediate application of some type of external stabilization device (e.g., a sheet wrap or a device such as the Pelvic Binder [Pelvic Binder Inc., Dallas, Texas]) [see Figure 4].[18] The rationale behind this step is that approximating the fractured bones and thereby decreasing the volume of the pelvis may reduce blood loss, particularly from the fractured bones and the lacerated venous plexus. In addition, stabilization may minimize further damage to blood vessels and prevent dislodgment of recent clots. It is doubtful, however, whether this procedure actually reduces arterial hemorrhage to a significant degree.

In hemodynamically unstable patients with clinical signs of a pelvic fracture, the next step (immediately after—or, preferably, while—x-rays of the chest, the pelvis, and the cervical spine are obtained according to ATLS protocols) should be the FAST (focused assessment for sonographic evaluation of the trauma patient) to rule out a significant intra-abdominal bleeding source. If the FAST is negative and no other obvious sources of hemorrhage (e.g., chest or extremities) are found, the pelvis is the most

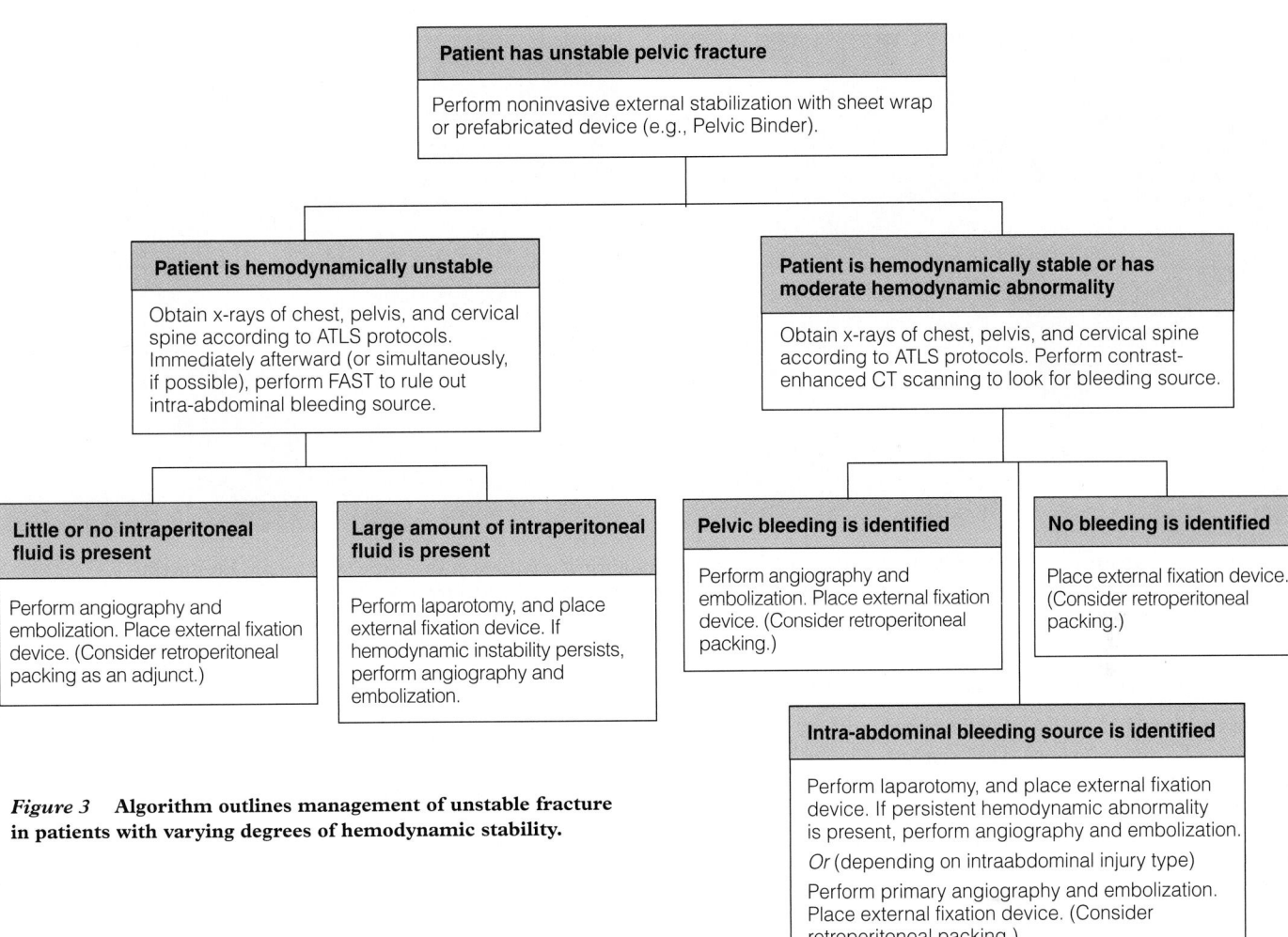

Figure 3   Algorithm outlines management of unstable fracture in patients with varying degrees of hemodynamic stability.

likely source of the bleeding. The question then arises whether the pelvic hemorrhage is predominantly arterial or venous. An arterial bleeding source in the pelvis is found in 73% of hypotensive patients who do not respond to initial fluid resuscitation.[19]

Contrast-enhanced CT scanning is extremely helpful in determining the presence of arterial hemorrhage in cases of pelvic fracture, but it can be performed only if the patient is stable enough to undergo the time-consuming transfer to the imaging suite. If a CT scanner is available in the shock room, it may be possible to extend the use of this modality to unstable patients. Extravasation of contrast medium, a large retroperitoneal hematoma, or abrupt cutoff of an artery on CT indicates that angiographic embolization is necessary. Contrast extravasation (so-called contrast blush) is a particularly good predictor of arterial hemorrhage necessitating embolization, having a sensitivity and specificity of well over 80%.[20] Thus, CT is an ideal means of identifying patients who should be treated with angiographic embolization and ideally should be performed in all pelvic fracture patients who are stable enough to undergo this procedure.

Arterial hemorrhage should preferably be treated by angiographic embolization, which has shown excellent results in current studies [see Table 3].[21,22] Several authors have argued that in unstable patients, angiographic embolization should be done immediately, before operative placement of an external fixation device, because the chance of finding an arterial bleeding source is high and because the duration of the interval between arrival in the ED

and the performance of embolization strongly influences outcome. Angiographic embolization with gel foam or coils can almost always be performed via the common femoral artery approach, even with a sheet wrap or an external fixation device in place. Success rates exceed 90%, and major complication rates are below 5%. This technique does, however, require a skilled, experienced, and permanently available interventional radiology service.

In patients with unstable fractures, venous hemorrhage is treated with operative placement of an external fixation device. This measure requires specific expertise on the part of the trauma surgeon; in experienced hands, it should take no longer than 20 minutes to perform. Patients with more severe pelvic fractures (e.g., AO-Tile type B and C fractures and higher grades of lateral compression and anteroposterior compression fractures [see Management of Pelvic and Acetabular Injuries, Pelvic Ring, below]) probably benefit most from this procedure. Retroperitoneal packing may be employed as an adjunct to external fixator placement.[23] It is unlikely that external fixation has a significant impact on arterial hemorrhage; consequently, it is vital to decide whether angiographic embolization should precede placement of an external fixation device in the OR.

The optimal strategy for controlling bleeding in patients with life-threatening pelvic injuries remains subject to debate.[24,25] We favor a prominent role for CT scanning and angiographic embolization, whereas others favor more liberal use of surgical retroperitoneal packing of the pelvis.

a

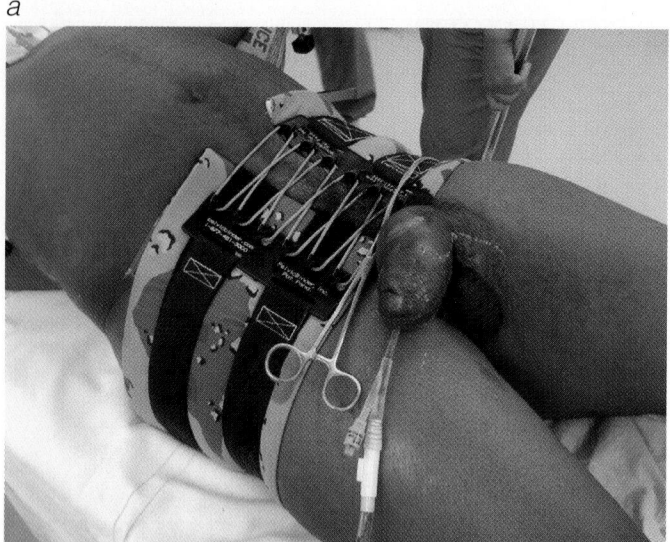

b

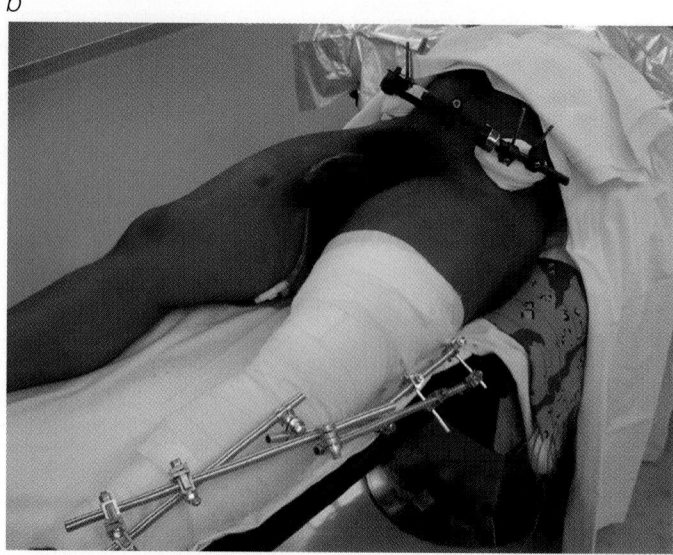

Figure 4   (*a*) **Shown is initial stabilization of pelvic fracture in a patient with severe head injury, life-threatening unstable pelvic fracture, distal femoral fracture, and proximal tibial fracture. (*b*) Shown is the same patient after DCS.**

OPEN FRACTURES AND SOFT TISSUE RECONSTRUCTION

Approximately 3% to 5% of all fractures and 10% to 15% of all long bone fractures are open. The prognosis after an open fracture is very different from that after a closed fracture; treatment of open fractures is much more complex than treatment of simple fractures or traumatic wounds. The existence of an open fracture means that a great deal of energy has been delivered to the bone to produce soft tissue disruption. Accordingly, it can be inferred that there has been considerable stripping of muscle, periosteum, and ligament from the bone, resulting in relative devascularization, and that varying degrees of contusion, crushing, and devascularization of the associated soft tissues have occurred. All of these events greatly influence the rate of healing, the incidence of nonunion, and the risk of infection (most commonly by *Staphylococcus aureus*, *Enterococcus*, or *Pseudomonas*). As noted [*see* Evaluation and Assessment, Classification of Injuries, Fracture, *above*], open fractures are typically classified according to the system formulated by Gustilo and Anderson.[4,5,26]

Management of open fractures in the ED starts with a detailed history that includes the patient's medical condition before the injury, the mechanism of injury, and the time elapsed since the injury. A careful physical examination is then performed, with particular attention paid to neurovascular status, muscle function, and the presence or absence of associated injuries. Compartment syndrome [*see* Management of Life-Threatening or Limb-Threatening Injuries, Mangled Extremity, *below, and 112 Injuries to the Peripheral Blood Vessels*] should be ruled out in patients at risk; as many as 10% of open tibial fractures are associated with compartment syndrome as a result of severe soft tissue injury. If the limb is malaligned, gentle gross reduction should be performed to relieve any vascular compromise. The wound is then inspected, and a sterile dressing is applied. Once this is done, the dressing should not be removed until the patient is in the OR and preparation for operation has begun. The need for repeated inspections by various specialists can be eliminated by taking pictures of the fractured limb with a digital camera. A temporary splint is applied to the limb to relieve pain and prevent further soft tissue injury. X-rays are obtained in two planes, with the adjacent joints included. Antibiotic treatment is started in the ED, and antitetanus measures

are instituted according to local protocols.

The goals of treatment are to prevent infection, achieve adequate soft tissue coverage, allow bone healing, and promote early and full functional recovery. The basic principles of management consist of aggressive debridement, open wound treatment, soft tissue and bone stabilization, and systemic administration of antibiotics.[4,5] These principles have reduced the formerly high mortality associated with open fractures to acceptable levels.

High-velocity gunshot wounds and open fractures must be approached differently from closed fractures because of the force imparted to the soft tissues. Open fractures call for emergency surgical treatment. Ideally, such treatment should begin within 6 hours of injury; the incidence of infection is directly related to in the time elapsed before initiation of treatment. Typically, a second-generation cephalosporin is administered for 48 to 72 hours; prolonged administration is not necessary. For grade III open fractures, gentamicin should be added to cover gram-negative bacteria; for farmyard injuries, which are at risk for contamination with *Clostridium*, penicillin should be added.[27,28]

The first stage of operative treatment consists of thorough irrigation of the wound with 6 L of normal saline; pulsed or jet lavage

---

Table 3   Indications for Angiographic Embolization in Patients with Pelvic Fracture

Hemodynamic instability; FAST negative for intra-abdominal bleeding source; inadequate response to fluid resuscitation

Contrast blush on contrast-enhanced pelvic CT scan

Large retroperitoneal hematoma on CT scan; expanding retroperitoneal hematoma on sequential CT scans

Persistent hemodynamic instability after operative placement of external fixator, laparotomy, or both

Hemodynamic stability with prolonged transfusion requirement (> 3 units of RBCs/24 hr) or other clinical signs of ongoing hemorrhage

---

FAST—focused assessment for sonographic evaluation of the trauma patient
RBCs—red blood cells

can be helpful for this purpose. Cultures are ordered at this time. To determine the true extent of the soft tissue damage, it is frequently necessary to enlarge the skin wound. Foreign contaminants, as well as dead bone and other devitalized tissues, predispose to infection and should therefore be removed. It is good practice to perform a routine second-look operation 48 to 72 hours after the initial debridement; debridement should be repeated until the soft tissues appear healthy and clean.

Although grade I open fractures may sometimes be treated in much the same way as similar closed fractures, grade II and grade III open fractures must be surgically stabilized during the second stage of the initial operation. Restoring of the normal anatomy through reduction and stabilization improves circulation; promotes healing of bone and soft tissue; reduces inflammation, bleeding, and dead space; and increases revascularization of devitalized tissue. It also results in earlier mobilization of multiply injured trauma patients and improves their overall status.

Internal fixation is preferred for most open fractures, with plates and screws mostly used for articular and metaphyseal fractures and intramedullary nailing for femoral and tibial shaft fractures. It is not always necessary, however, to achieve definitive fixation in the first operation. In the case of complex fractures for which additional imaging or a specialized operative team is required, a correctly placed external fixator is a safe and sensible option. External fixation as a temporary bridge to definitive fixation is also frequently used for severely contaminated grade III open fractures. Surgically created wound extensions may be closed; however, the traumatic wound itself should be left wide open. If the wound is small, a portion of the surgical extension should be left open to allow adequate drainage and to prevent the traumatic wound from sealing off prematurely. Every attempt should be made to cover bone, joint surfaces, implants, and sensitive structures (e.g., tendons, nerves, and blood vessels) with available local soft tissue, but such coverage must be achieved without tension. As an alternative to soft tissue coverage, a temporary method of wound coverage may be chosen (e.g., traditional wet dressings, synthetic membranes, allografts, or other skin substitutes).[4,5,29,30]

Because leaving a wound open for prolonged periods increases the risk of infection, skin coverage and soft tissue reconstruction should ideally be achieved within 1 week after the injury. In the case of a grade I or II open fracture for which the initial culture is negative, the wound may be allowed to close by granulation and secondary intention, or the patient may be returned to the OR in 5 to 7 days for delayed primary closure. For larger wounds, split-thickness skin grafts are often required. For grade III open fractures, some type of flap is often required for soft tissue coverage [see 27 Surface Reconstruction Procedures]. Local fasciocutaneous flaps are suitable for smaller defects with intact surrounding skin. Muscle flaps have the advantage of adding vitality to exposed bone and can cover substantial defects; they are frequently covered with a split skin graft. Large wounds and those for which a local flap is not suitable require a free flap that is anastomosed to the local vessels. The flap procedure should preferably be done early, 5 to 10 days after the injury; some authors have even reported good results with definitive soft tissue reconstruction completed during the initial operation (so-called fix and flap).[4,5,31]

A comparatively new method of wound coverage is negative-pressure wound therapy (NPWT) with a vacuum-assisted closure device (VAC Abdominal Dressing System; Kinetic Concepts, Inc., San Antonio, Texas).[32,33] The perceived advantages of this approach include provision of a moist wound healing environment, reduction of the wound volume, minimization of bacterial colonization, removal of excess fluid, and (most important) pro-

motion of granulation tissue. Sponges are available in different sizes and can be further trimmed to fit the size of the wound, filling all dead space. An airtight seal is created with an adhesive drape covering the wound and the sponge. Dressings are changed every 2 to 4 days until the desired goals are reached. NPWT has proved to be a viable adjunct for treatment of various soft tissue injuries, including open tibial fractures and pelvic injuries). It is also a useful means of securing skin grafts and is reported to lead to improved graft survival. Although NPWT has yielded promising results in several case series, it should still be regarded primarily as a method of providing temporary coverage of soft tissue defects, not as a replacement for surgical debridement. Surgeons using NPWT should take care not to delay definitive closure, even if such closure involves a complex free muscle transfer.

Rehabilitation should be started soon after the operation. It is facilitated by following an aggressive treatment algorithm consisting of adequate fracture stabilization and early soft tissue coverage to prevent prolonged immobilization of joints and soft tissues. Infection is the most common complication after an open fracture and can be the result of inadequate surgical technique, incomplete debridement, or delayed soft tissue coverage. Open fractures are also associated with a higher incidence of delayed union and nonunion, which often necessitate placement of a cancellous bone graft or, in the case of a large defect, a free fibular graft.

MANGLED EXTREMITY

One of the more difficult decisions for a trauma surgeon is whether to amputate a severely injured or mangled extremity [see 112 Injuries to the Peripheral Blood Vessels]. The Mangled Extremity Severity Score (MESS) is frequently used as an aid in making this decision,[4,5] with a score of 7 or higher generally considered an indication for amputation. The final decision whether to amputate or to attempt salvage, however, is based on the individual patient's overall condition, level of neurovascular function, and expected functional result.[34,35]

The decision between amputation and salvage does not necessarily have to be made immediately; often, it can wait until the involved specialists have discussed the matter in the hours or days following the initial operation. If a mangled extremity does not pose an acute threat to the patient during the initial resuscitation, it may be best treated with irrigation and debridement (as with open fractures), some form of external stabilization, and temporary soft tissue coverage. Amputation in the acute phase should be performed at a safe level by means of a guillotine technique, combined with open wound management.

The functional prognosis after limb salvage is based on the presence or absence of nerve injury and the surgeons' judgment of whether adequate vascularization, soft tissue coverage and long-term bony stabilization are likely to be achievable. Often, multiple operations must be performed over several months, and even then, the outcome may be uncertain. In patients with limbs at high risk for amputation, the 2-year outcomes after reconstruction typically are about the same as those after amputation.[36] Accordingly, some patients may be better served by early amputation as definitive treatment.

COMPARTMENT SYNDROME

Compartment syndrome is defined as high-pressure swelling within a fascial compartment [see 112 Injuries to the Peripheral Blood Vessels]. Many physicians still believe, incorrectly, that compartment syndrome cannot develop in conjunction with an open fracture, because the break in the skin provides decompression. This is a dangerous assumption: compartment syndrome occurs in a sig-

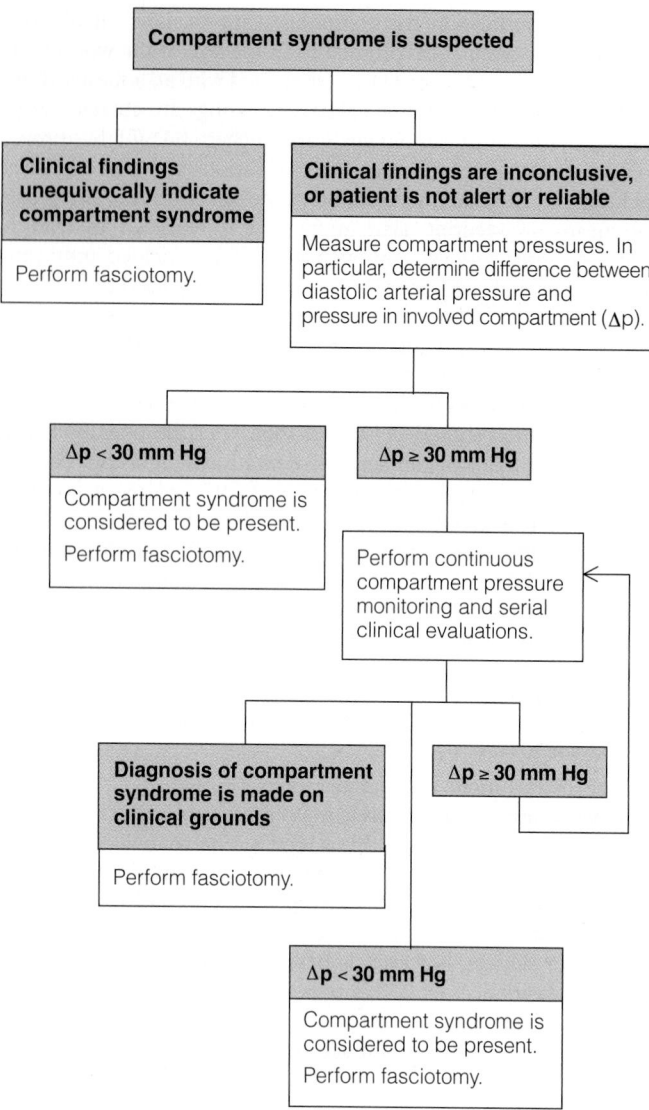

Figure 5 **Algorithm outlines diagnosis of suspected compart-ment syndrome.**

nificant number of patients with open fractures—for example, as many as 10% of patients with open tibial fractures. The most common cause of compartment syndrome is hemorrhage and edema in the damaged soft tissues seen with fractures. Other causes include a too-tight dressing or cast, disruption of the limb's venous drainage, advanced ischemia, and eschar from a circumferential burn. Multiply injured patients with hypovolemia and hypoxia are predisposed to compartment syndrome.[4,5,10]

The key to diagnosis of compartment syndrome [*see Figure 5*] is to maintain a high level of suspicion in any situation involving an extremity injury where there is a significant chance that this syndrome might develop (e.g., tibial fractures, forearm fractures, and all comminuted fractures associated with severe soft tissue injury). The diagnosis is primarily a clinical one, with the five Ps—*p*ain, *p*allor, *p*aresthesia, *p*aralysis, and *p*ulselessness—constituting the classic signs. The surgeon should not wait until all these signs are present; the prognosis is much better if they are not. Severe ischemic muscle pain occurs that is unrelieved by the expected amounts of analgesia. On palpation, the compartment is tense and swollen, and passive stretching of the digits of the extremity

increases the pain. Paresthesia occurs early and should be actively watched for; paralysis develops when ischemia has caused permanent damage. Pulselessness occurs late and is a relatively rare sign; it has been shown that irreversible damage can occur in a patient who still has palpable pulses.[4,5,10,37]

Measurement of compartment pressures is also employed in the diagnosis of compartment syndrome. Monitoring can be particularly helpful in patients who are not alert or are difficult to examine.[38] There is no agreement on what constitutes the critical pressure threshold for a definitive diagnosis. An absolute value of 30 to 35 mm Hg has frequently been adopted as a diagnostic indicator; however, the evidence suggests that the difference between the diastolic arterial pressure and the pressure in the involved compartment (delta pressure, or Δp) is more important than any particular absolute value. Currently, a diagnosis of compartment syndrome is usually made if Δp is less than 30 mm Hg, depending on the clinical signs and the level of suspicion.

If compartment syndrome is suspected, the first step is to remove all circumferential bandages to relieve any pressure. If a plaster cast is present, it should be split, spread, or removed; if necessary, maintenance of reduction should be sacrificed. If the clinical picture does not improve after these measures are taken, then a decompressive fasciotomy is indicated. Fasciotomy is described in greater detail elsewhere [*see 112 Injuries to the Peripheral Blood Vessels*].

PERIPHERAL VASCULAR INJURY

Vascular injuries can result from either blunt or penetrating trauma to the extremities, though the vascular injuries seen in urban trauma centers tend to be caused more often by penetrating trauma. Early diagnosis and prompt multidisciplinary treatment are crucial for successful management. The severity of the vascular injury and the length of the interval between injury and restoration of perfusion are the major determinants of outcome.[37,39-42] Diagnosis and management of such injuries are outlined in greater detail elsewhere [*see 112 Injuries to the Peripheral Blood Vessels*].

There has been considerable discussion regarding the optimal order of repair in cases of combined musculoskeletal and vascular trauma—that is, whether fracture stabilization should precede vascular repair or follow it.[43] Fracture stabilization facilitates the exposure needed for vascular repair and reduces the risk of subsequent disruption of a fresh arterial repair, but it inevitably takes time to perform. Rapid application of an external fixator is a good alternative for extensive fracture repairs. Insertion of a temporary intraluminal shunt can be valuable and limb-saving when DCS is performed in a patient with severe vascular extremity injury or when a patient has a grossly unstable fracture that must be stabilized before arterial repair is possible.[44] Endovascular repair plays a limited, albeit growing, role in the treatment of arterial injuries associated with extremity trauma.[45]

PERIPHERAL NERVE INJURY

Injury to a peripheral nerve can result in loss of motor function, sensory function, or both; it is the principal factor accounting for limb loss and permanent disability. Because the upper extremities have less muscle and bone mass and more neurologic structures than the lower extremities do, upper-extremity injuries are twice as likely to result in nerve damage as lower-extremity injuries are. Penetrating injuries from cuts or stab wounds that result in a clean laceration of a nerve are amenable to early intervention and repair; penetrating injuries from gunshot wounds are more difficult to assess and manage. Blunt injuries result primarily from compression or stretching.[4,5,46-48]

Nerve injuries are generally categorized according to the Seddon classification system, which divides them into three types: (1) neurapraxia, (2) axonotmesis, and (3) neurotmesis. Complete recovery from neurapraxia and axonotmesis can usually be achieved, but neurotmesis usually necessitates surgical intervention. How quickly and successfully nerves regenerate depends on several factors, including age, type of nerve (sensory or motor), level of injury, and duration of innervation.

Careful assessment of motor and sensory function is essential for diagnosis. Additional diagnostic information can be obtained by means of electromyography (EMG), MRI, and nerve conduction studies.

In the setting of blunt trauma, surgical treatment is recommended for closed injuries when the injured nerve shows no evidence of recovery either clinically or on electrodiagnostic studies done 3 months after the injury. It is also recommended for gunshot wounds without vascular or bony problems; such wounds have relatively good potential for neurologic recovery. For most open injuries (e.g., laceration with neurotmesis), surgical exploration at the earliest opportunity is recommended. If possible, the nerve is reapproximated primarily and the epineurium is sutured, or (sural) nerve grafts are employed.[4,5,46]

Physical therapy should be started soon after nerve injury to maintain passive range of motion in the affected joints and preserve muscle strength in the unaffected muscles. Splinting of affected joints may be necessary to prevent contractures and minimize deformities.

CRUSH SYNDROME

Crush syndrome (also referred to as traumatic rhabdomyolysis) is a clinical syndrome consisting of rhabdomyolysis, myoglobinuria, and subsequent renal failure. It is caused by prolonged compression of muscle tissue (frequently in the thigh or the calf) and is usually seen in victims of motor vehicle accidents who required a long extrication procedure or in earthquake victims who are rescued from beneath rubble after being trapped for several hours or days. Once released from entrapment, crush syndrome patients are likely to exhibit agitation, severe pain, muscle malfunction, swelling, and other systemic symptoms.[4,5,10,49,50]

The pathophysiologic process underlying this syndrome begins with muscle breakdown from direct pressure, impaired muscle perfusion leading to ischemia and necrosis, and the release of myoglobin. As long as the patient is entrapped, the ischemic muscle is isolated from the circulation, and this isolation affords some protection against the systemic effects of the released myoglobin and other toxic materials. Extrication and the resulting reperfusion of necrotic and ischemic muscle lead to the second insult, the reperfusion injury. This injury is caused by the formation of toxic reactive oxygen metabolites, which leads to failure of ion pumps and increasing permeability of cell membranes and microvasculature. When large amounts of muscle are involved, the resulting fluid changes can rapidly induce shock. The large quantities of potassium, lactic acid, and myoglobin that are released into the circulation can lead to renal failure, disseminated intravascular coagulation, and circulatory arrest.[49,50]

Treatment should begin at the time of extrication so as to anticipate the onset of the syndrome. The first step is initiation of I.V. fluid therapy, starting with a 2 L crystalloid bolus and continuing with crystalloid infusion at a level of 500 ml/hr (the dosage must be adjusted in pediatric and cardiac patients). Cardiac monitoring is essential (T waves indicate hyperkalemia). Intravascular fluid expansion and osmotic diuresis, by maintaining high tubular vol-

ume and urine flow, may prevent renal failure. Forced diuresis can be achieved by giving mannitol or other diuretics. Alkalization of the urine with sodium bicarbonate (1 mEq/kg I.V. to a total of 100 mEq) is a controversial measure but is recommended by some on the grounds that it should, in theory, reduce intratubular precipitation of myoglobin. If compartment syndrome is suspected, compartment pressures should be measured [see Compartment Syndrome, above].[49,50]

General Management of Fractures

FIXATION METHODS AND IMPLANT TYPES

Fracture fixation can be accomplished either nonoperatively (by means of external splinting) or surgically. Surgical fixation can be achieved with many different techniques, which yield varying degrees of stability. Screws, metal wires (e.g., Kirschner or cerclage wires), plates, nails, and external fixators have all been used for this purpose. Surgical fixation methods may be broadly divided into techniques of absolute stability and techniques of relative stability.[4]

Treatment of fractures with techniques of absolute stability was widely promoted by the ASIF. Anatomic reduction and achievement of absolute stability by means of interfragmentary compression plating were advised for treatment of articular, metaphyseal, and diaphyseal fractures. This method reduces strain at the fracture site and allows bone healing without visible callus formation (so-called direct bone healing). However, obtaining interfragmentary compression usually necessitates a fairly extensive surgical approach, which disturbs the local blood supply.

Unlike techniques of absolute stability, techniques of relative stability (e.g., intramedullary nailing, use of bridging plates across a comminuted fracture, and external fixation) allow small interfragmentary movements to occur when a load is applied across the fracture site. Such movements can stimulate callus formation and lead to union of the bone in four stages: (1) inflammation, (2) soft callus, (3) hard callus, and (4) remodeling. The various techniques of relative stability (also referred to as splinting or bridging techniques) yield varying degrees of stiffness.

Both biologic factors (fracture healing) and biomechanical factors (strength and stiffness) are important for recovery after a fracture. Over the past two decades, clinical experience and data from basic studies have led to a shift in focus away from the mechanical aspects of fracture treatment and toward the biological aspects. Today, a common practice is so-called biologic osteosynthesis, which means careful handling of the soft tissues to take advantage of the remaining biologic support, coupled with the use of techniques of relative stability to stimulate callus formation. Anatomic reduction is no longer considered a goal in itself, except in the case of intra-articular fractures.[4]

Conventional dynamic compression plates are applied tightly against the bone. Their application can compromise the blood supply and thereby induce partial necrosis of the underlying bone. The presence of avascular tissues may reduce the healing potential and lower the local resistance to infection. To overcome some of these disadvantages, plates with smaller contact areas were developed. This process has culminated in the introduction of locking compression plates (e.g., LCP; Synthes, West Chester, Pennsylvania), which can be regarded as noncontact plates. The LCP is a plate-and-screw system in which the screws are also locked in the plate by means of an extra thread in the head of the screw; thus, the plate is no longer tightly fixed to the bone and the periosteum. Locking compression plates (also referred to as locked internal fixators) are designed in such a way that both conventional dynamic compression techniques and bridging techniques can be used, depending on the fracture type. They may be applied via a less invasive approach using closed reduction techniques.[4,5]

Intramedullary nails are placed within the medullary canal and therefore have the same biomechanical properties in both the frontal and the sagittal plane. They differ from plates in that the latter are attached eccentrically to the bone. Intramedullary nails may be inserted in either an unreamed or a reamed fashion; both techniques have advantages and disadvantages. With unreamed nailing, the nails are inserted without widening the medullary canal. This approach causes somewhat less operative trauma than reamed nailing, but it places some limitations on the diameter and strength of the nail and the locking bolts. If larger-diameter nails (> 9 mm) are needed, the medullary canal must be reamed to accommodate them. Reaming takes time, leads to increased intramedullary pressure, and produces debris that may be embolized in the pulmonary circulation. The clinical consequences of reamed intramedullary nailing have not yet been fully clarified. Current evidence suggests, however, that reamed nailing is associated with significantly lower rates of nonunion and implant failure than unreamed nailing is.[4,5,51]

External fixators consist of metal pins (Schanz screws) that are placed in the bone proximal and distal to the fracture and connected outside the skin by one or more rods. Most external fixators are used only on one side of the limb, but in specific instances, multiplanar or circular devices may be used. The stability of the frame depends primarily on the stiffness of the rods, the distance between the rod or rods and the bone (the smaller the distance, the greater the rigidity), and the number, placement, and diameter of the fixator pins. As a general rule, two pins proximal and distal to the fracture are sufficient for fixation of long bone fractures. The main advantage of external fixators is that their use minimizes additional surgical trauma. The main disadvantages are the occurrence of pin-tract infections and the frequent lack of stability for definitive fracture treatment. Appropriate placement of fixator pins requires a detailed knowledge of the cross-sectional anatomy of the injured limb.[4,5]

BASIC PRINCIPLES OF TREATMENT

Although most fractures heal readily with casting, long periods of immobilization with restriction of muscle activity, joint motion, and weight bearing are known to lead to so-called fracture disease, characterized by muscle atrophy, joint stiffness, disuse osteoporosis, and persistent edema. Accordingly, the goals of fracture treatment should include not only the achievement of bony union but also the early restoration of muscle function, joint mobility, and weight bearing.[4,5]

Currently, there are seven main indications for operative treatment of fractures:

1. Preservation of life (e.g., decreasing morbidity and mortality through fixation of femoral shaft fractures);
2. Preservation of a limb (as with open fractures, fractures associated with vascular injury, and fractures complicated by compartment syndrome);
3. Articular incongruity;
4. Facilitation of early mobilization and rehabilitation;
5. Inability to maintain reduction with conservative treatment;
6. The presence of more than one fracture in the same limb (so-called floating joint); and
7. The presence of additional fractures in other limbs (e.g., bilateral humeral or tibial fractures).

Improved understanding of the biology of fracture repair and the importance of the soft tissues has led to substantial changes in the treatment of diaphyseal fractures. It is now widely recognized that anatomic reduction of each fracture fragment is not always a prerequisite for restoration of normal limb function (see above). For most long bone fractures, radial and ulnar fractures excepted, the most important goal is restoration of the mechanical axis of the limb without significant shortening, angulation, or rotational deformity. Good functional results may be expected even if fracture fragments lying between the proximal and distal main fragments are not anatomically reduced.[4,5]

In the upper extremity, both plates and intramedullary implants are frequently used for operative fixation of fractures. In the lower extremity, intramedullary nails are generally preferred because they allow early weight bearing, in contrast to plates and screws, which are more susceptible to failure. However, intramedullary nailing may not be suitable for shaft fractures that extend into the metaphysis or the adjacent joint. The treatment plan may also be influenced by the local condition of the soft tissues (e.g., the presence or absence of contusions or wounds), the quality of the bone (e.g., the presence or absence of osteoporosis), and the origin of the fracture (pathologic or nonpathologic).[4,5]

For intra-articular fractures, alignment alone is insufficient. Anatomic reduction of the articular surface is required to restore joint congruity, and rigid fixation is necessary to allow early motion and thereby prevent the joint stiffness resulting from prolonged immobilization. Impacted osteochondral fragments are elevated, and the resulting metaphyseal defect underneath is filled with cancellous bone or a bone substitute. Fracture fragments may be reduced either via direct exposure or via more limited approaches, with the assistance of an image intensifier an arthroscope, or both. Regardless of which approach is followed, care must be taken not to devascularize bone fragments. Fixation may be achieved with metal wires, screws, and plates. The reconstructed articular surface is connected to the diaphysis with plates or, alternatively, external fixators.[4,5]

Nonoperative treatment usually consists of application of plasters or (less frequently) traction and may be employed as either temporary or definitive therapy. It reduces the risk of infection and eliminates operative risk, but it also frequently results in a longer time to union, a higher risk of malunion, and a greater likelihood of stiffness of the involved joints. Accordingly, nonoperative management is mostly reserved for extra-articular and minimally displaced fractures.[4,5]

Autologous bone grafting remains the gold standard for improving and accelerating fracture healing. In recent years, however, various other methods have been developed and evaluated for this purpose. There is some evidence from randomized trials indicating that low-intensity pulsed ultrasonography may shorten the healing time for fractures treated nonoperatively.[52,53] Ultrasound treatment does not, however, appear to confer any additional benefit after intramedullary nailing with prior reaming. The discovery of specific bone growth factors (bone morphogenetic proteins [BMPs]) was an important step forward in the understanding of bone physiology and raised the possibility that these factors could be locally applied to enhance fracture healing. However, clinical trials have not yet determined the most appropriate indications for the use of BMPs in managing specific fractures or nonunions.[54]

The indications for implant removal are not well established. There are few definitive data to guide the decision as to whether an implant should be removed or left in place. In general, implants in most adult patients may be left in place; the same is true of implants in the upper extremity. When implants are removed for relief of pain and mitigation of presumed functional impairment alone, the results are unpredictable and depend on both the implant type and its anatomic location. Implant removal is often technically challenging and may lead to complications such as infection, neurovascular injury, or refracture. Current data do not support routine removal of implants to protect against allergy, carcinogenesis, or metal detection. The decision for or against implant removal is therefore based on individual patient and surgeon preferences, as well as on the clinical circumstances.[55,56]

Management of Upper-Extremity Injuries

SHOULDER

Fractures of the clavicle are common and are usually caused by falling on the shoulder. Approximately 80% of clavicular fractures occur in the middle third of the bone, 15% in the lateral third, and 5% in the medial third. Dislocation results from traction of the pectoral and sternocleidomastoid muscles. Neurovascular injury is uncommon, but the patient should always be evaluated for such injury nonetheless. Treatment is primarily conservative, employing a collar and cuff or a sling; union rates approach 95%. Operative fixation is indicated only when there is impending perforation of the overlying skin, an associated injury to the subclavian artery and brachial plexus, an ipsilateral scapular neck fracture (so-called floating shoulder), a dislocation greater than 2 cm (a relative rather than absolute indication), or painful nonunion. Fixation methods include plate osteosynthesis and intramedullary osteosynthesis.[57]

Scapular fractures result from high-energy trauma and are frequently accompanied by life-threatening injuries to the head, the chest, or the abdomen. CT scanning is usually required to determine the fracture pattern. Most scapular fractures can be treated conservatively. Severely (> 40°) dislocated scapular neck fractures and dislocated intra-articular glenoid fractures are treated with open reduction and internal screw or plate fixation.

HUMERUS

Proximal

Fractures of the proximal humerus are common, especially in elderly women. Correct positioning of the four main bony structures of the proximal humerus (the head, the greater tuberosity, the lesser tuberosity, and the shaft) and their muscle attachments is important for a good shoulder function. Consequently, fractures of this segment of the humerus may have significant functional consequences. Damage to the blood supply of the head may lead to avascular necrosis of this part of the bone. Conservative treatment with a sling is preferred for elderly patients with minimally displaced fractures, and early range-of-motion exercises are encouraged. Operative treatment is indicated for patients with dislocated two-, three-, or four-part fractures and fracture-dislocations. The optimal fixation method has not been established, but plate osteosynthesis is frequently employed; alternatives include intramedullary techniques and prosthetic replacement.[58,59] Rehabilitation usually takes several months, and continuing impairment of shoulder function is a common complaint.

Shoulder (glenohumeral joint) dislocations mostly occur in young persons participating in sports. The size difference between the large articular surface of the humeral head and the small surface of the glenoid renders the shoulder particularly vulnerable to dislocation. The majority (95%) of patients have anterior dislocations, resulting from abduction and exorotation. The relatively few posterior dislocations that occur tend to be difficult to diagnose and are frequently missed initially. A particularly rare and severe type of shoulder dislocation is luxatio erecta, characterized by inferior dislocation of the abducted arm. Injuries associated with shoulder dislocation include injury to the axillary nerve, injury to the labrum (Bankart lesion), and a depression in the humeral head (Hill-Sachs lesion); the last two predispose to recurrence. Radiographs should be obtained in AP, axillary, and Y-scapular views to determine the position of the humeral head and detect any fractures. Treatment consists of gentle and closed reduction. This can usually be done in the ED; if necessary, it can be done in the OR with the patient under general anesthesia. Reduction is followed by immobilization in a sling.[5]

Dislocations of the sternoclavicular joint are rare, but they are potentially life-threatening when they occur posteriorly (anterior dislocations are far less dangerous). Diagnosis of these injuries is difficult with conventional x-rays; accordingly, CT is recommended when sternoclavicular joint dislocation is suspected. Compression of the mediastinal vessels and trachea can sometimes lead to respiratory and circulatory failure. In such cases, urgent operative reduction, performed with an eye to potential vascular emergencies, is warranted.[5,10]

Dislocations of the acromioclavicular joint result from falling on the shoulder and are frequently classified according to the system formulated by Tossy. Tossy 1 dislocations (sprains) and Tossy 2 dislocations (subluxations) are treated conservatively with a collar and a cuff. For Tossy 3 dislocations (complete separations), operative treatment may be considered, though the optimal technique remains to be determined and the results of operative fixation are still uncertain.[5]

Shaft

Fractures of the humeral shaft typically result from direct trauma. Depending on the level of the fracture, dislocation mainly results from traction placed on the deltoid or pectoral muscles. Fractures of the middle and distal thirds of the humeral shaft can result in injury to the radial nerve, which is the most severe functional complication. Most closed AO-ASIF type A1 and A2 fractures can initially be treated conservatively with functional bracing techniques (rather than hanging casts); this approach yields good or excellent results in the majority of cases. Moderate angulation, rotation, and shortening are well tolerated. Generally accepted indications for operative treatment include open fractures, AO-ASIF type B and C fractures, associated vascular injury, multiple trauma, bilateral fractures, combined humeral shaft and forearm fractures (so-called floating elbow), pathologic fractures, secondary radial nerve palsy, and nonunion.[60] The standard technique is open reduction and plate fixation; the main alternative is locked intramedullary nailing, either antegrade (entering in the proximal humerus) or retrograde (entering in the distal humerus).[61,62] External fixation is employed in the presence of severe soft tissue injuries and in polytrauma patients as part of DCS.

Distal

Fractures of the distal humerus result from falling on the elbow with the forearm flexed. In elderly persons, many of whom are osteoporotic, a fall from a standing position is often sufficient to cause such a fracture, whereas in young patients, high-energy trauma is required. Extra-articular injuries usually have a good prognosis. Intra-articular fractures are more difficult to manage: limitation of flexion and extension and pain often occur, even after optimal treatment. In addition to AP and lateral x-rays, it may be advisable to obtain CT scans to help clarify the fracture pattern. For minimally displaced AO-ASIF type A fractures, conservative treatment is appropriate, but for all other fractures, open reduction and plate osteosynthesis are required, frequently in conjunction with an olecranon osteotomy to provide adequate exposure. In comminuted fractures, the articular surface can be difficult to reduce. In osteoporotic bone, finding good bone stock can be a serious problem.[4,5,63,64]

ELBOW

Olecranon fractures are the most common fractures in the area of the elbow and usually are caused by falling directly on the elbow. They frequently lead to impaired extension as a consequence of the discontinuity between the triceps and the proximal ulna. All dislocated olecranon fractures are treated operatively, with Kirschner wires and a tension band employed for simple fractures and plate osteosynthesis for comminuted fractures. Both methods allow early functional therapy postoperatively.

Fractures of the radial head are caused by falling on the outstretched arm and may occur either in isolation or in combination with an elbow dislocation, an ulnar shaft fracture (Monteggia fracture), a coronoid process fracture, or a medial collateral ligament rupture. In addition, the interosseous membrane between the ulna and the radius may be disrupted over its entire length, thereby disturbing the distal radioulnar joint at the wrist (Essex-Lopresti injury). Fractures with dislocations smaller than 2 mm can be treated conservatively with early range-of-motion exercises; external support is usually unnecessary. Dislocated fractures and fractures causing mechanical blockage (e.g., of pronation or supination) are mostly treated operatively, with plate or screw fixation. When the fracture is comminuted, adequate reduction and fixation may be impossible. If the elbow is otherwise stable, radial head excision may be performed; if not, a radial head prosthesis may be inserted to stabilize the joint. Active and passive range-of-motion exercises should be started soon after the operation.

Elbow dislocations are typically caused by falling on the outstretched hand. Posterior dislocations, characterized by dorsal displacement of the radius and the ulna, are more common than anterior dislocations. Associated injuries may include coronoid process fractures and collateral ligament injuries, as well as neurovascular injuries. Most elbow dislocations can be treated with closed reduction by applying traction with the forearm flexed 30°. After reduction, the stability of the elbow should be carefully evaluated. Plaster immobilization should not be continued beyond 3 weeks. Operative reduction is necessary only when the dislocation is associated with an open fracture, when interposing fragments preclude adequate closed reduction, or when neurovascular injury is present.[4,5]

FOREARM

The bones in the forearm have a complex relation with each other and with the elbow and the wrist, and this complex relation allows numerous different combinations of flexion, extension, pronation, and supination. The mechanism of a forearm injury is a frequently a vehicular accident or a fall; isolated fractures of the radius or the ulna are rare and usually result from a direct blow. The goal of treatment is to achieve anatomic restoration of length, axial alignment, and rotation with stable fixation in a manner that permits free movement (especially pronation and supination) of the elbow and the wrist postoperatively [see Figure 6]. Only nondisplaced fractures may be treated nonoperatively; all other forearm fractures must be treated operatively. The standard technique is open reduction with plate fixation; intramedullary fixation is an alternative. The radial nerve is at risk during plate fixation of the proximal radius.[65-67]

Approximately 10% of ulnar fractures are accompanied by a

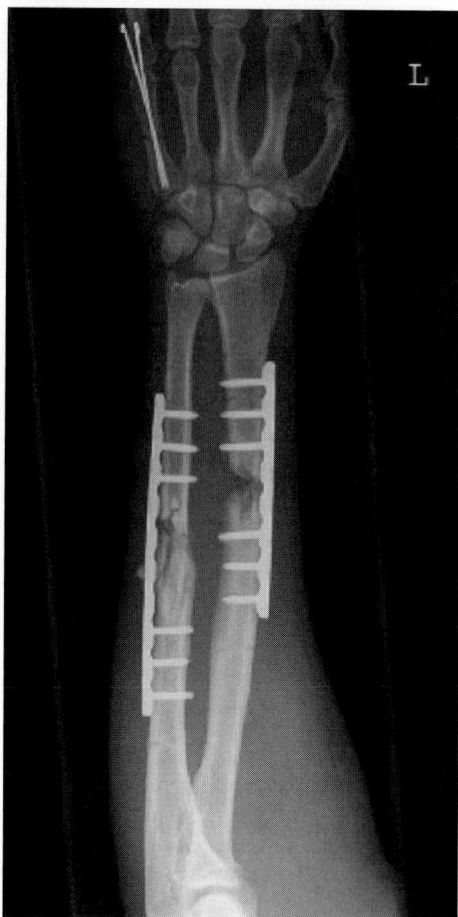

Figure 6 Shown is grade II open forearm fracture with segmental bone loss in the radius, intially stabilized with debridement and external fixation. Injury is treated with secondary plate osteosynthesis and Kirschner wire fixation of metacarpal fracture.

radial head dislocation (Monteggia fracture). Appropriate x-rays must be obtained to ensure that this injury is not missed. The radial head is reduced by closed or open methods during plate fixation of the ulna. Radial shaft fractures are sometimes associated with a dislocation of the ulna in the distal radioulnar joint (Galeazzi fracture). If the distal radioulnar joint remains unstable after plate fixation of the radius, temporary transfixation is necessary.[4,5]

WRIST

Distal radial fractures are among the most commonly encountered fractures. Like elbow dislocations, they are usually caused by falling on the outstretched hand. The incidence rises sharply with increasing age, especially in osteoporotic women. Associated injuries include ulnar styloid process fractures and ligamentous carpal injuries. Dislocations are classified as dorsal (Colles type) or volar (Smith type); the former are more common. Partial articular fractures (AO-ASIF type B) are also referred to as dorsal or volar Barton fractures. Diagnostic imaging plays an important role in assessment; the critical radiographic parameters are radial angle, radial length, and dorsal angulation. Radiologic signs of instability include initial dorsal angulation greater than 20°, greater than 5 mm reduction in radial length, intra-articular involvement, and metaphyseal comminution. An articular stepoff greater than 2 mm is associated with a poor prognosis.

Minimally displaced AO-ASIF type A distal radial fractures and stable impacted fractures may be treated conservatively in plaster for 4 to 6 weeks. If necessary, this can be done after closed reduction, though loss of reduction may occur after an initial satisfactory position has been achieved. For all other fractures, operative treatment is advised, depending on fracture type and patient status [see Figure 7]. AO-ASIF type B fractures are best treated with open reduction and screw or plate fixation; however, optimal treatment of AO-ASIF type C fractures remains to be determined. External fixation combined with Kirschner wires and plate osteosynthesis is frequently employed. In some cases, it may be necessary to fill a subchondral or metaphyseal defect with a cancellous bone graft or a bone substitute. Reflex sympathetic dystrophy develops in some patients [see Special Considerations, Complications, Reflex Sympathetic Dystrophy, below]. Treatment of this syndrome can be difficult, and complete functional loss is occasionally the final result.[4,5,68]

Fracture of the scaphoid typically is caused by falling on the outstretched or dorsally flexed hand. It tends to be difficult to diagnose and is easily missed. Signs such as pain, functional impairment, and tenderness at the anatomic snuff box are often absent initially, and standard AP and lateral x-rays of the wrist may be insufficient to identify the injury. If special scaphoid views do not confirm the presence of a fracture, the wrist is immobilized and x-rays are repeated after 7 to 10 days. Alternatively, CT, MRI, or bone scintigraphy may be performed to confirm the diagnosis.[3] Undisplaced fractures may be treated conservatively in plaster. Immobilization should be continued for 6 to 12 weeks to minimize the risk that disturbance of the delicate blood supply of the scaphoid might result in avascular necrosis or pseudarthrosis. Dislocated fractures (with dislocation greater than 2 mm or angulation greater than 25°) are treated with screw osteosynthesis.[4,5,69]

Perilunate dislocations result from high-energy trauma and include a spectrum of severe ligamentous wrist injuries, fractures, and dislocations characterized by dorsal dislocation of the distal carpal row, the scaphoid, and the triquetrum with respect to the lunate. Perilunate dislocations may be missed initially in multiply injured patients if the physical examination is incomplete or the x-rays of the wrist are inadequate or not carefully examined. Treatment consists of closed or open reduction; additional fixation may be performed as needed, depending on the degree of stability achieved after reduction. Associated fractures of the radius or the scaphoid are treated operatively.[5]

HAND

Fractures of the hand can result from direct blows, twisting injuries, crush injuries, and gunshot wounds. Neurovascular status, wounds (e.g., bites), and tendon function should all be carefully evaluated. Most fractures can be detected on posteroanterior, lateral, and oblique views.

Metacarpal neck fractures, most frequently of the fourth or fifth metacarpal (so-called boxer's fracture), can usually be treated conservatively with 3 to 4 weeks of immobilization and early range-of-motion exercises.[70] Fracture healing may result in cosmetic deformity but good function. Severely dislocated fractures are typically treated with Kirschner wires or plate fixation. Most fractures of the metacarpal shafts can be treated nonoperatively with immobilization in a cast or splint for 4 weeks. If the wrist is immobilized in plaster, it should be positioned in 20° of extension, with the the metacarpophalangeal joints in 70° to 90° of flexion and the interphalangeal joints in complete extension to prevent shortening of ligaments. Rotation (as indicated by nail position) should be checked frequently. Indications for operative treatment include angulation greater than 10° to 30°, shortening, malrotation (more

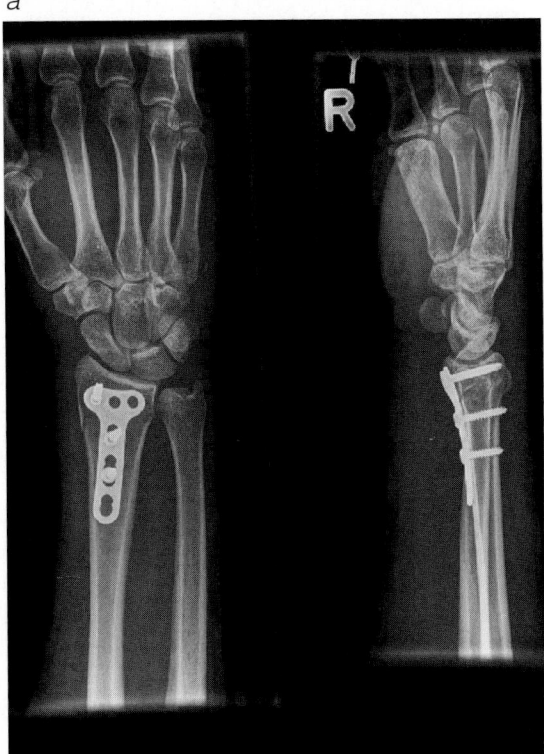

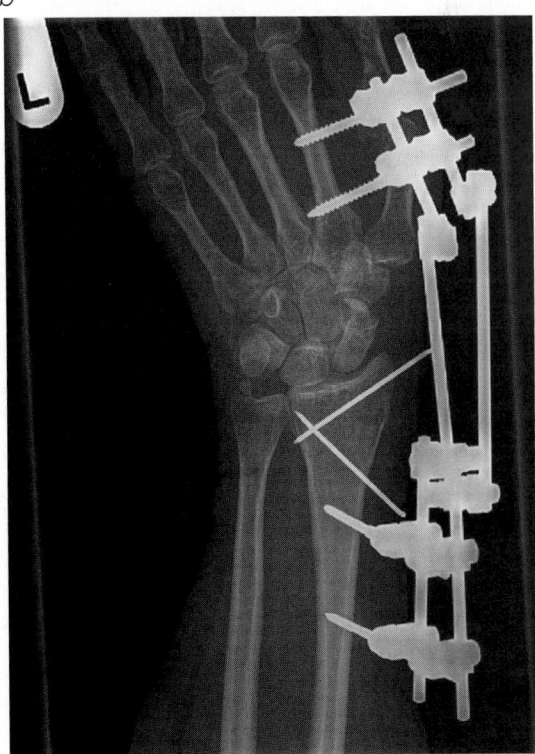

Figure 7 **Illustrated is treatment of distal radial fracture with (*a*) volar plate osteosynthesis and (*b*) external fixation.**

frequent in the second and fifth metacarpals), and multiple fractures. Bennet's fracture (an intra-articular fracture of the base of the first metacarpal with a small ulnar fragment that remains attached to the second metacarpal) should be treated with reduction or, if unstable, fixation with percutaneously placed Kirschner wires or screws. Other metacarpal base fractures are less frequent but may also be associated with carpometacarpal dislocations. Treatment focuses on reduction of the joint and restoration of alignment and the articular surface, if necessary by means of open reduction.[5,71,72]

Phalangeal fractures are common. In the distal phalanx, fractures often result from crush injury and may be associated with subungual hematoma (which should be drained) and soft tissue injury. The vitality of the fingertip may be compromised. Nondisplaced fractures may be treated with immobilization in plaster or a splint for 3 weeks, followed by active range-of-motion exercises. Dislocated fractures may be treated with closed or open reduction and fixation with Kirschner wires or small screws or plates.[71,72]

Dislocations of the interphalangeal joints usually are easily recognized by the obvious deformity they cause, but x-rays must still be obtained to exclude fractures. Dorsal dislocations are associated with injuries to the volar plate or collateral ligaments, which tend to increase instability. Treatment consists of closed or open reduction, followed by testing through the range of motion to check stability and x-rays to ensure adequate reduction. If reduction is unstable, transarticular Kirschner wire fixation may be necessary.[5]

So-called gamekeeper's thumb is an injury to the ulnar collateral ligament of thumb metacarpophalangeal joint that causes instability at that joint; the ulnar collateral ligament frequently becomes dislodged between the adductor pollicis aponeurosis and its normal position (Stener lesion). Partially unstable lesions (< 20° to 30° opening at stress examination in comparison with the uninjured side) may be treated in a plaster splint for 3 to 4 weeks. Completely unstable lesions are treated with surgical repair to prevent chronic instability.[5]

TENDONS

Injuries to the rotator cuff reduce the shoulder's strength and impair its function. Most ruptures occur in cuff muscles or tendons that are already affected by degenerative changes. Operative treatment is advised for young patients and for patients who have experienced substantial ruptures as a result of recent trauma.

Rupture of the distal biceps tendon occurs mainly in middle-aged men. The tendon is torn off the radial tuberosity during flexion against resistance. The muscle belly is visibly retracted proximally, and flexion and supination are reduced by 30% to 40%. In cases where the diagnosis is not clear, MRI or ultrasonography may be helpful. Treatment consists of reattaching the tendon to the radius with suture anchors or drill holes.

In the case of tendon injuries around the wrist and the hand, appropriate clinical testing and diagnosis depend on a solid knowledge of the exact anatomy and function of the various tendons. The extensor tendons are located just under the skin, directly on the bone, on the back of the hands and the fingers; their superficial location makes them easily injured even by a minor cut. The flexor tendons pass through fibrous rings called pulleys, which guide the tendons and keep them close to the bones; because of the more complex anatomy, flexor tendon injuries are usually more challenging than extensor tendon injuries. Partial injuries with intact function may be treated conservatively, but most injuries, especially sharp lacerations, are treated with surgical repair followed by

protected motion. Postoperative treatment and rehabilitation of tendon injuries are very important and require the services of a special hand therapist.

A commonly encountered extensor tendon injury is so-called mallet finger, which results from forcible flexion of the extended distal interphalangeal joint. The extensor tendon is torn off the distal phalanx, with or without an intra-articular fragment of its base. Clinically, the distal interphalangeal joint is in flexion, and active extension of the distal phalanx is impossible. Most lesions can be treated with a special splint that keeps the distal interphalangeal joint in extension for 4 to 6 weeks.[5]

Management of Pelvic and Acetabular Injuries

PELVIC RING

Pelvic fractures occur in about 3% of trauma patients. These injuries can have a devastating influence on the outcome of trauma care and therefore must be identified as early as possible. Internal retroperitoneal bleeding is the main concern in the early management of these patients because over 40% of the mortality from pelvic trauma is attributable to persistent bleeding. Accordingly, the initial physical examination and the AP pelvic x-ray (which is diagnostic in 90% of cases) during the primary survey are essential for placing the focus on the potential risk of internal bleeding. Additional inlet and outlet views (taken at a 45° angle from cephalad and caudal) may be useful for accurate classification and determination of dislocation.[4,5] CT scanning is performed in nearly all cases but not necessarily as an emergency evaluation. The CT scan facilitates fracture classification and provides additional information on active bleeding and associated injuries. Administration of I.V. contrast material during CT scanning helps in detecting active arterial bleeding, which suggests the need for early angiographic embolization. Angiographic embolization may be lifesaving in patients with pelvic arterial bleeding.

Pelvic injuries are frequently associated with other serious injuries. Fractures of the anterior pelvic ring, especially when seen in combination with blood from the urethral meatus, are an indication for retrograde urethrography before placement of a transurethral catheter to detect or exclude urethral and bladder injuries. Vaginal and rectal examinations are components of the standard workup for detecting or excluding fracture perforations and abnormalities of prostate position (indicative of urethral injury).

Posterior pelvic ring injuries may be accompanied by sacral plexus nerve injuries. Perineal and groin wounds often are in continuity with fracture components and pose a serious threat of further complications. With open pelvic injuries, early surgical debridement and fecal deviation must be considered.

The AO-Tile classification of pelvic ring and acetabular fractures is based on the degree of pelvic stability or instability. The pelvis is divided into an anterior section (comprising the symphysis pubis and the pubic rami) and a posterior section (comprising the ilium, the sacroiliac joint complex, and the sacrum).[4] Determination of whether and to what extent the posterior section is displaced is crucial for estimating the stability of the injury. Depending on the degree of posterior bony or ligamentous instability, pelvic ring injuries may be classified into three types as follows:

1. Type A: injuries where the mechanical stability of the pelvic ring is intact—the most common type, seen in 50% to 70% of pelvic fracture patients.
2. Type B: injuries characterized by partial posterior stability (i.e., injuries that are rotationally unstable but vertically stable)— seen in 20% to 30% of pelvic fracture patients.

3. Type C: injuries characterized by combined anterior and posterior instability (i.e., injuries that are both rotationally and vertically unstable)—seen in 10% to 20% of pelvic fracture patients.

Another system used to categorize pelvic fractures is the Young-Burgess classification, which is based on the force vectors causing the fracture. In this system, pelvic ring fractures are divided into the following four major groups: (1) lateral compression, (2) anteroposterior compression, (3) vertical shear, and (4) combined mechanical injury. The stability or instability of the fracture can be determined on the basis of knowledge of the ligamentous anatomy of the pelvis coupled with assessment of the fracture pattern and the direction of the injuring force.[4,5]

Provisional stabilization is advised after manual reduction of pelvic ring disruption, especially in open-book fractures with significant dislocation. External fixation is one means of achieving provisional stabilization; however, it is more time consuming than applying a sheet wrap or a similar device for temporary stabilization. For this reason, many institutions prefer the latter approach during initial management in the ED. The Pelvic C-Clamp (Synthes, West Chester, Pennsylvania) is also employed for external stabilization, primarily in hemodynamically unstable patients with unstable (i.e., type B or C) pelvic ring injuries. This device acts by exerting direct compression on the posterior part of the pelvic ring, thereby reducing the intrapelvic volume, compressing fracture parts, and providing stability. Application of this device should also be considered if operative retroperitoneal pelvic packing is necessary.

Definitive treatment of pelvic injuries depends on the type of injury, the classification (stability), the local soft tissue situation, and the general condition of the patient [see Figure 8]. Type A fractures are stable and usually need not be treated operatively. Functional treatment, with early ambulation and weight bearing as tolerated, usually suffices.

Type B1 (open-book) injuries with minimal dislocation of the symphysis may be treated conservatively. If symphyseal dislocation is less than 2.5 cm, anterior plate fixation of the symphysis is usually sufficient. If the patient cannot undergo formal internal fixation, an external fixator (which may have been applied initially for bleeding control) is a reasonable alternative for definitive treatment. However, the discomfort and the complications (e.g., infection) caused by external fixator pins motivate many surgeons to convert to internal plate fixation after the initial stabilization phase. In the setting of an emergency laparotomy, early anterior plate fixation may be considered during the same laparotomy, provided that patient is or has been rendered physiologically stable. Type B2 (lateral compression) injuries with minimal anterior dislocation often have good intrinsic stability and can frequently be treated conservatively.

For type C injuries, both anterior and posterior stabilization is required. Of the many techniques currently in use, plate fixation of the anterior pelvic ring combined with either percutaneous sacroiliac screws or plate fixation of the posterior pelvis provides the best mechanical stability. The main goals are to restore the anatomy and prevent any leg-length discrepancy while encouraging allowing early mobilization of the patient to prevent the complications of prolonged bed rest.[4,5,73-75]

Percutaneous placement of iliosacral screws under fluoroscopic guidance is already the preferred technique for stabilization of the majority of unstable sacroiliac injuries. The continuing development and growing availability of modern surgical tools (e.g., computer-assisted intraoperative navigation) are providing ever more opportunities for minimally invasive approaches to pelvic fracture fixation. Nevertheless, stabilization of the pelvis through open surgical reduction and internal fixation using standard plate and screw techniques are still proper alternatives and are the treatment of choice for many pelvic ring fractures.

ACETABULUM

Traumatic acetabular fractures may occur either in isolation or as part of a pelvic ring injury [see Figure 8a]. On occasion, they occur in combination with hip dislocation; in such cases, urgent

a

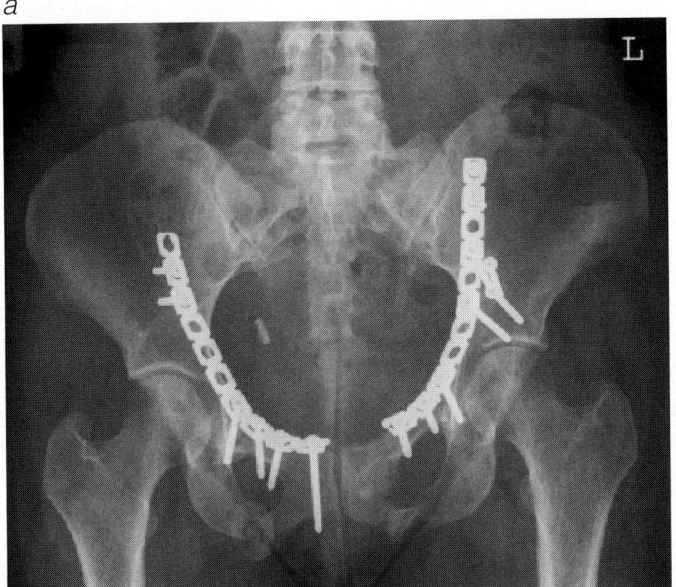

b

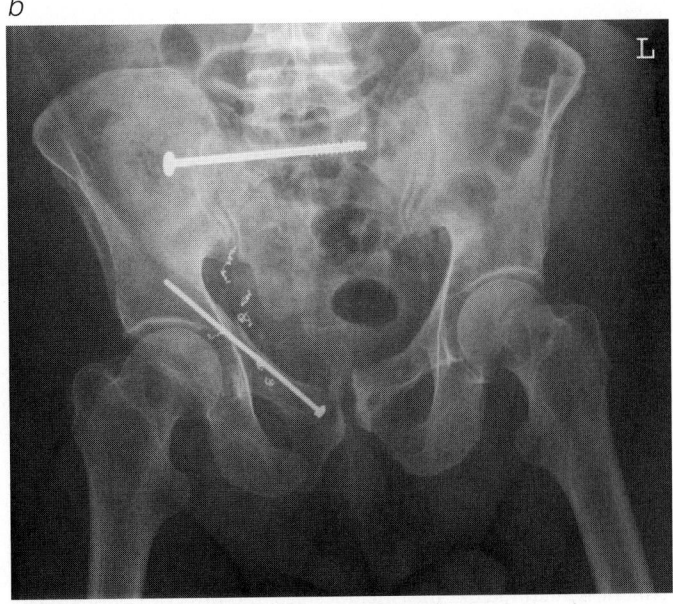

Figure 8 Shown are (*a*) plate osteosynthesis for combined pelvic ring injury and left-side acetabular fracture in a multiply injured patient and (*b*) treatment of type C unstable pelvic ring injury with initial angioembolization (coils visible) and external fixation, followed by secondary percutaneous placement of sacroiliac and pubic screws.

reduction of the dislocated hip is essential for restoring blood flow to the femoral head. For adequate fracture classification, x-rays must be obtained in Judet views (oblique views taken with the beam stationary and with the patient rolled 45° to both sides along the vertical axis). CT scanning with axial and three-dimensional reconstructions can greatly clarify the extent of the injury and help identify the number and size of fracture fragments. An accurate neurologic examination that includes assessment of the integrity of the sciatic nerve should also be part of the initial workup.

Until the 1960s, the vast majority of patients with acetabular fractures were treated conservatively. Thanks to the impressive efforts of Letournel and Judet (who also introduced the most frequently used classification system), operative treatment has become standard for dislocated acetabular fractures.[76,77] The most important goal of operative treatment is to restore the articular surface so that a congruent hip joint can be obtained. Achievement of this goal nearly always requires open reduction and internal fixation with plates or screws through anterior or posterior approaches. Extensive experience on the part of the operating team is necessary to ensure optimal long-term results. After the operation, the patient should be able to take part in non–weight-bearing exercises.

The majority of acetabular fractures can be treated in a delayed fashion between 3 and 14 days after the injury. Acute operative fracture treatment may be indicated if a dislocated hip cannot be reduced, if redislocation of the hip cannot be prevented, or if interposition of intra-articular fracture fragments occurs. In many instances, however, initial skeletal traction (if indicated after hip reduction) will be applied.

Adequate prophylaxis of deep vein thrombosis (DVT) is essential for both patients with pelvic fractures and those with acetabular fractures. Functional outcome after acetabular fracture surgery is determined by many factors, the most important of which are anatomic fracture reduction, the development of osteoarthritis, avascular necrosis, and heterotopic ossification.[4,5,77-79]

Management of Lower-Extremity Injuries

FEMUR

Proximal (Hip Fracture)

Fracture of the proximal femur (hip fracture) is one of the most common conditions seen by orthopedic and trauma surgeons. It is particularly common in the elderly. Substantial force is required to fracture a hip in a young person, whereas a minor trauma or fall may be sufficient to do so in an elderly osteoporotic woman. Almost 90% of patients with proximal femoral fractures are older than 65 years. Between 5% and 10% of these elderly patients die during hospital admission; 25% die within the first year after the accident.

Hip fractures are typically classified into four broad categories according to their anatomic site: (1) femoral head fractures, (2) intracapsular (femoral neck) fractures, (3) intertrochanteric fractures, and (4) subtrochanteric fractures. Within these broad categories, they may be further divided into subcategories according to various classification systems (see below). Such classifications can be helpful in guiding decision making with respect to treatment, which necessarily differs from one type of hip fracture to another.[4,5] In general, the choice of treatment is influenced by a range of patient-related factors that includes age, the presence and severity of comorbid medical conditions, previous mobility, cognitive status, fracture classification, and the status (i.e., preserved or disrupted) of the all-important blood supply to the femoral head. Failure of treatment frequently results from inappropriate choice of a

fixation method or misinterpretation of the fracture configuration.

Fractures of the femoral head are the most devastating of hip injuries and must be handled as surgical emergencies. They are generally classified according to Pipkin's system. Because substantial force is required to produce femoral head fractures, they are often seen in association with hip joint dislocations and acetabular fractures, most commonly in multiply injured patients who were involved in motor vehicle accidents. The diagnosis is made on the basis of pelvic and acetabular x-rays, supplemented by CT scans. Concomitant hip dislocations (most often posterior) should ideally be reduced with the patient under general anesthesia and with muscle relaxation achieved by upward traction with the hip in 90° of flexion.[80] If possible, this should be done in the ED to minimize delay in restoring blood flow to the femoral head. After reduction, the stability of the joint is tested clinically, and CT scanning is performed to assess impaction fractures, loose fragments in the hip joint, and the integrity of the acetabulum.

Most femoral head fractures are treated operatively if the patient's condition permits. For optimal results, this should be done within 24 to 48 hours after the injury, if possible. Closed treatment of dislocated fractures yields uniformly poor results. Internal fixation of these injuries is technically demanding and should allow early passive and active motion exercises postoperatively. Indomethacin is administered to prevent heterotopic ossification around the hip. Weight bearing is allowed after 10 to 12 weeks. In some patients, particularly physiologically older patients with major fractures, it may be best to insert a hip prosthesis primarily. Although operative treatment is usually necessary to provide the best chance of recovery, the magnitude of the initial trauma is generally such that good results can be obtained in only 50% to 70% of cases.[4,5,81]

A typical patient with an intracapsular (femoral neck) fracture presents with a shortened, externally rotated, and abducted lower extremity. These fractures are often classified according to Garden's system. Treatment is determined by the fracture type and associated patient factors. Especially in young patients, because of the risk of nonunion and avascular necrosis, dislocated femoral neck fractures should preferably be treated on an emergency basis within 12 hours after the injury.[82] In otherwise healthy and ambulatory patients, incomplete and impacted fractures (intact trabeculae of the inferior neck; Garden 1) may be managed with conservative treatment, consisting of early mobilization with crutches or a walker (to the extent permitted by the pain experienced) and supervised by a physical therapist. Secondary dislocation occurs in 10% to 50% of cases, leading to secondary operative treatment. Complete but undislocated fractures (Garden 2) are mostly treated operatively with cannulated screws or a sliding hip screw (e.g., Dynamic Hip Screw [DHS]; Synthes, West Chester, Pennsylvania). Sliding hip screws allow controlled compression of the fracture to be obtained during weight bearing as the lag screw slides into the plate. Complete fractures with partial (Garden 3) or complete displacement (Garden 4) are treated by means of early anatomic reduction with fixation to eliminate the risk of displacement and permit rapid mobilization. When the patient is physiologically older than 70 years, placement of a primary hip prosthesis is often indicated instead of internal fixation; however, this procedure is associated with higher perioperative morbidity and mortality.[4,5,81,83]

Trochanteric fractures are the most common fractures of the proximal femur. They do not threaten the blood supply to the femoral head, because they occur below the extracapsular ring of vessels. Trochanteric fractures are classified according to the AO-ASIF system. Almost all patients with such fractures are candidates for internal fixation. The main exceptions are elderly patients who

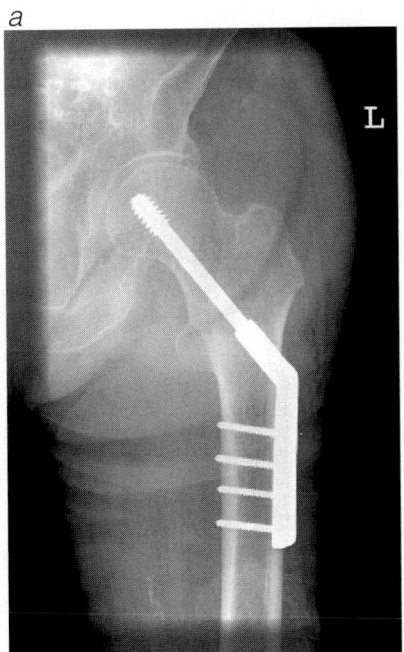
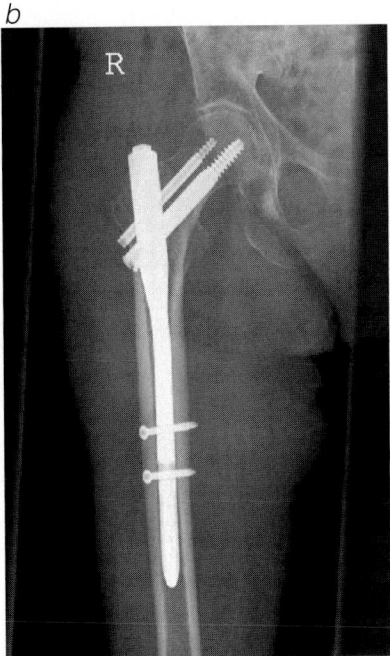

Figure 9   Shown are (*a*) fixation of AO-ASIF type A1 fracture with the Dynamic Hip Screw and (*b*) fixation of AO-ASIF type A2 fracture with the Proximal Femoral Nail.

had significant arthritis of the hip before sustaining the fracture; for these patients, placement of a hip prosthesis is an alternative.

The lesser trochanter provides crucial support for the medial femoral cortex; thus, assessment of its integrity is important for determining the stability of the fracture, which, in turn, helps determine treatment. The main treatment options are extramedullary and intramedullary implants. Extramedullary implants include sliding hip screws (see above), which are relatively easy to insert and also allow open reduction of the fracture if necessary. These implants are most suitable for stable (AO-ASIF type A1) fractures [*see Figure 9a*]. For unstable (AO-ASIF type A2 and A3) intertrochanteric fractures, intramedullary fixation is the treatment of choice because of the favorable position of the implants in the biomechanical loading axis of the femur. Examples include the Proximal Femoral Nail (PFN; Synthes, West Chester, Pennsylvania) [*see Figure 9b*], the Intramedullary Hip Screw (IMHS; Smith & Nephew, London, England), and the Gamma Nail (Stryker, Kalamazoo, Michigan). The operative technique for intramedullary fixation is more complex and unforgiving than that for extramedullary fixation, and various complications may arise, including malpositioning and femoral shaft fractures during insertion. Intramedullary implants are usually inserted percutaneously on a traction table with one or more screws in the femoral head and one or more distal locking screws. Internal fixation of trochanteric fractures should allow mobilization from postoperative day 1, preferably with full weight bearing or the use of a walker.[4,5,84]

Subtrochanteric (AO-ASIF type A3) fractures are inherently unstable. Operative treatment may be difficult because high bending forces in the region (resulting from the angular shape of the proximal femur) often lead to implant failure before union. The preferred management approach is intramedullary nailing; the use of angled blade plates is an alternative, especially in young patients who require anatomic reduction.[4,5]

Shaft

In most adults, considerable force is necessary to fracture the femoral shaft; a simple fall seldom results in this type of fracture unless the bone has been weakened by osteoporosis or other disease. A patient with a femoral shaft fracture should therefore be considered a victim of high-energy trauma and evaluated accordingly.

Most fractures of the femoral shaft are easily recognized clinically on the basis of pain and abnormal position or movement. Because of the shape of the thigh, more than 1 L of blood may be lost into this space with little or no external indication. Neurovascular injuries are relatively uncommon in this setting; however, when the fracture is in the distal third of the femoral shaft, injury to either the superficial femoral artery or the popliteal artery may ensue as a consequence of the tethering of these vessels against the shaft at the level of the adductor canal. Femoral shaft fractures are often associated with injuries to knee ligaments, which are difficult to assess in the presence of the femoral fracture. Thus, when the patient is under anesthesia for treatment of the fracture, the stability of the knee should be assessed as well. Imaging consists of AP and lateral x-rays, with the hip and knee joints included.

In the ED, a fractured femur is immobilized with a vacuum splint or a Thomas splint. This measure reduces blood loss and lessens patient discomfort, and the splints need not be removed for x-rays to be taken. Ideally, femoral shaft fractures should be treated within 12 to 24 hours after the injury; preoperative skeletal traction is therefore superfluous. The main goal is stable fixation that yields correct length, rotation, and alignment, with full weight bearing possible within a few days of the operation.

Femoral shaft fractures of AO-ASIF types A to C are best treated with locked intramedullary nailing [*see Figure 10*]. In isolated instances, a plate or an external fixator may be indicated. Nailing lowers the incidence of respiratory distress syndrome, blood loss, and tissue trauma and reduces the patient's need for narcotics. In the setting of DCS, femoral fractures are initially stabilized by means of external fixation. The external fixator can then be exchanged for an intramedullary nail 2 to 10 days later without a significant increase in complications.[12,13,85] Nailing can be performed with the patient supine on a fracture table or in a lateral

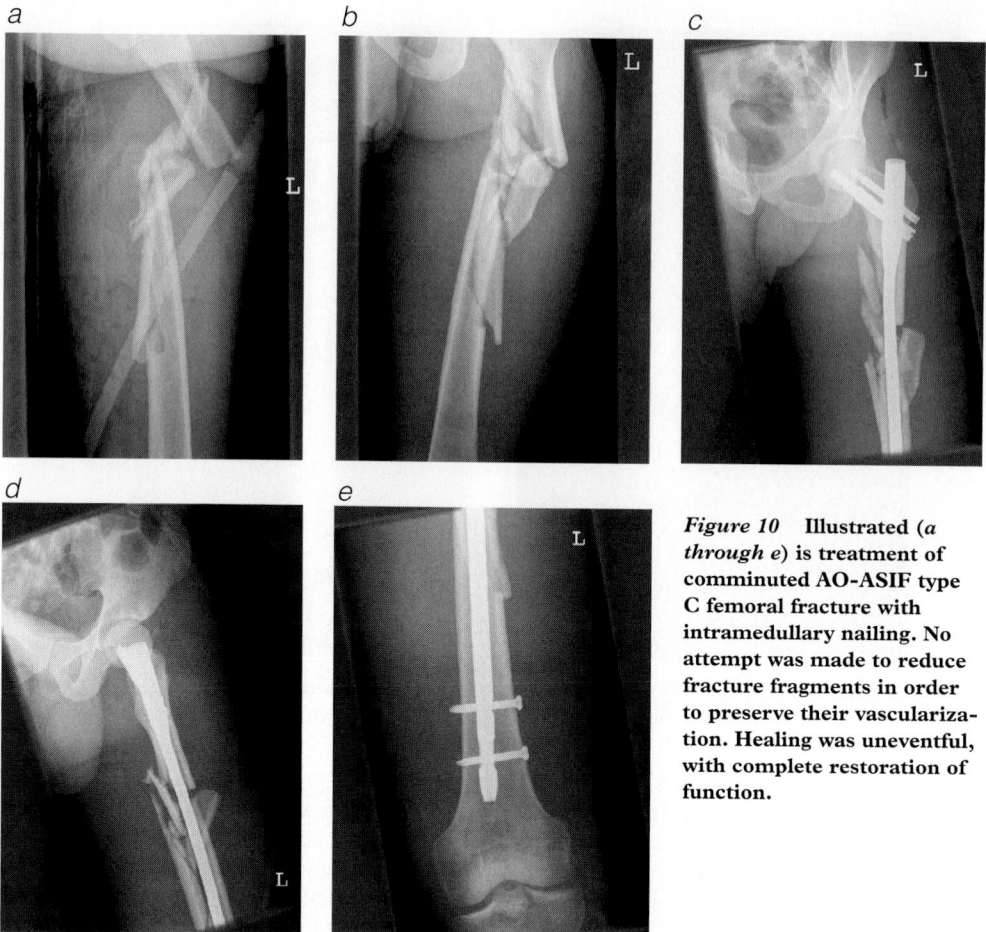

a

b

c

d

e

Figure 10 Illustrated (*a through e*) is treatment of comminuted AO-ASIF type C femoral fracture with intramedullary nailing. No attempt was made to reduce fracture fragments in order to preserve their vascularization. Healing was uneventful, with complete restoration of function.

decubitus position with closed reduction (or, if necessary, open reduction) of the fracture. Most nails are inserted in an antegrade manner through the greater trochanter or piriform fossa, though retrograde nailing through the intercondylar notch is becoming increasingly popular for distal shaft fractures. Reaming is generally advised because it reduces the rate of nonunion.[51]

Most complications with femoral shaft fractures are secondary to technical problems at the time of nailing and can therefore be prevented by paying close attention to technical details (in particular, the entry point of the nail and correct rotation). In rare instances, embolization of debris from reaming may lead to fat embolism syndrome (FES) [*see* Special Considerations, Complications, Fat Embolism Syndrome, *below*]. Infections occur mostly in open fractures and fractures where there is substantial soft tissue involvement. Compartment syndrome of the thigh may occur after femoral shaft fracture, albeit infrequently; it should be suspected if severe swelling is present.[4,5]

Distal

Supracondylar (AO-ASIF type A) and intercondylar (AO-ASIF type B and C) fractures of the distal femur typically occur in young patients who have sustained high-energy trauma or in elderly patients with osteoporotic bone. Careful assessment of neurovascular status is important. X-rays focused on the knee should be supplemented with x-rays of the femoral and tibial shafts. CT can provide additional information on the fracture pattern and help in preoperative planning. Standard treatment consists of operative reduction and internal fixation, followed by partial–weight-bearing or non–weight-bearing active or passive exercises.

Supracondylar fractures can be treated with retrograde

intramedullary nailing or plating, depending on the surgeon's preference. Open reduction with extensive techniques for applying angled blade plates, condylar plates, sliding hip screws, and similar devices is currently being replaced by less invasive plating techniques using screws that are locked into the plate. An example of the latter is the Less Invasive Stabilization System (LISS; Synthes, West Chester, Pennsylvania), which allows submuscular fixation and percutaneous placement of self-drilling unicortical fixed-angle screws. The focus with this system is more on correction of length and alignment and less on anatomic reduction.

Intercondylar fractures are treated with anatomic reduction and screw fixation of the articular surface to allow early motion and thereby facilitate cartilage healing. Either open methods or image intensifier-assisted closed methods may be employed. The reconstructed articular surface is then connected en bloc to the femoral shaft with one of the previously described techniques (usually plating).[4,5,86]

KNEE

Patellar Fracture

Knee injuries are common in multiply injured patients, in large part because of the vulnerability of this joint to dashboard injuries in automobile accidents and to direct trauma in motorcycle accidents. Patellar fractures usually result from a fall on the knee, a sudden forceful contraction of the quadriceps muscle with knee flexion, or a combination of the two. Other injuries (e.g., cruciate ligament failure and femoral fracture) may be present as well. The most important task in the examination is to confirm that the extensor mechanism is intact by asking the patient to raise the leg with the knee fully extended. X-rays should include AP, lateral, and (optionally) tangential views.

Transverse and stellate fractures with minimal (< 1 to 2 mm) displacement and an intact extensor mechanism may be treated conservatively by keeping the joint in a cast for 6 weeks, with weight bearing allowed. All other fractures are treated by open reduction with internal fixation, typically with Kirschner wires and tension bands or cerclage wires. Postoperatively, early active motion and partial weight bearing are allowed. Severely comminuted patellar fractures may be irreparable; in such instances, a partial or total patellectomy with reconstruction of the extensor apparatus may be required. Ligamentous patellar injuries (e.g., to the quadriceps tendon or the patellar tendon) are treated by means of operative repair and reinsertion to the patella.[4,5]

Dislocation

Knee dislocations, though potentially severe injuries, are generally rare, with only a few small series having been reported. They result primarily from motor vehicle and pedestrian accidents, falls, and sports activities, though they also occur spontaneously in morbidly obese persons. Their severity is determined by the complexity of the ligamentous injury and any associated trauma, including popliteal artery and vein injury (20% to 30% of cases) and peroneal nerve injury (25% to 35%). Failure to recognize vascular injury can lead to muscle necrosis and amputation. It is therefore essential that reduction of knee dislocations be carried out immediately, either before arrival at the hospital or in the ED, followed by vascular examination and x-rays. Anterior dislocation (30% to 40% of cases) is often caused by severe knee hyperextension, whereas posterior dislocation (25% to 30%) occurs with the application of force to the proximal tibia in an anterior-to-posterior direction, as in a dashboard-type injury or a high-energy fall on a flexed knee.

Physical examination reveals gross deformity around the knee with swelling and immobility. Occasionally, the knee will have relocated spontaneously before the patient arrives at the ED. Attention should be focused on the presence or absence of hard signs of vascular injury [see 112 Injures to the Peripheral Blood Vessels]; if preferred, the ankle-brachial index (ABI), duplex scanning, or both may be employed in addition.[5,37] Although many authors recommend mandatory arteriography or operative exploration for all knee dislocations, this recommendation is increasingly being questioned.[87-89] The current literature indicates that the absence of hard signs reliably excludes a significant arterial injury that necessitates operative repair. The presence of hard signs of vascular injury, however, is an indication for arteriography; because about 25% of patients with hard signs actually have no vascular injury, arteriography serves to prevent many unnecessary vascular explorations. Another potentially valid (and timesaving) approach may be to take those with hard signs directly to the OR and obtain an on-table angiogram. In some instances, noninvasive tests may be able to distinguish patients who have vascular injures requiring repair from those who do not.

Asymptomatic intimal injuries visualized by angiography do not call for surgical exploration, and the clinical value of interventional radiology techniques (e.g., stent placement) in this context is questionable. If there is a vascular injury that requires surgical repair, an external fixator that spans the knee joint should be quickly placed. Restoration of circulation has absolute priority in this situation; the amputation rate exceeds 80% when vascular repairs are done more than 8 hours after injury. Operative repair of nerve injuries is controversial. Optimal treatment of multiple ligament ruptures is also subject to debate. Many authors recommend early operative ligamentous repair followed by functional bracing and mobilization for optimal results, whereas others recommend primary immobilization followed, if necessary, by late reconstructions.[4,5,90]

Ligamentous Injury and Meniscal Tearing

Distortions of the knee are common injuries; most involve varus, valgus, or rotational deformities. The history should focus on the mechanism of injury, the type and location of pain, any associated symptoms, the amount of immediate dysfunction, the presence and onset of joint edema, and any history of past knee problems. The physical examination should include inspection, active motion, and stress testing to detect instability. Hemarthrosis is a sign of possible cruciate ligament injury. If pain and swelling preclude reliable examination, the examination should be repeated in 5 to 7 days. Collateral ligament injuries are graded on a scale of I to III. A grade I injury is a sprain (with stretching but no tearing of the ligament, local tenderness, minimal edema, and no gross instability on stress testing), a grade II injury is a partial ligament tear (with moderate local tenderness and mild instability on stress testing), and a grade III injury is a complete tear (with discomfort on manipulation, a variable amount of edema, and clear instability on stress testing).

X-rays of the knee are obtained to detect any fractures of the tibial plateau or the intercondylar eminence. The number of unnecessary x-rays may be substantially and safely reduced by applying the so-called Ottawa knee rule. This rule specifies the following indications for x-rays: age 55 years or older, tenderness at the head of the fibula, isolated tenderness of the patella, inability to flex the knee 90°, and inability to walk four weight-bearing steps immediately after the injury and in the ED. MRI is useful for detecting ligamentous, meniscal, and cartilage injuries but is rarely indicated on an emergency basis.

Treatment depends on the patient's age and activity level and should always include appropriate reeducation and strengthening of the relevant muscles (hamstrings and quadriceps). Grade I and II collateral ligament injuries (which are usually medial) may be treated conservatively with early active motion, with or without a knee brace. Grade III medial collateral ligament injuries may be treated in a knee brace for 6 weeks, but grade III lateral collateral ligament injuries must be treated surgically because conservative treatment frequently leads to chronic instability. Anterior cruciate ligament ruptures are increasingly being treated by operative means in serious athletes and other physically active persons. The ligament is arthroscopically reconstructed with a section of the patellar tendon or the semitendinous tendon. Isolated posterior cruciate ligament ruptures, which are considerably less common, are primarily treated nonoperatively.[4,5,91]

Meniscal tears occur mainly in physically active persons, though they may also result from simple distortions experienced during activities of daily living, especially if the meniscus has previously undergone some degeneration. Complaints include mild pain, swelling, grinding, locking, and "giving way." Clinical diagnosis is aided by provocative tests (e.g., the McMurray and Appley tests), but when symptoms persist, MRI is often performed. Mild meniscal tears may be treated conservatively, whereas symptomatic lesions usually call for surgical treatment. In general, meniscal repair is indicated when the tear is in the vascular outer one third of the meniscus, and partial excision is indicated when the injury is in the avascular inner two thirds.[5]

TIBIA

Proximal

Tibial plateau fractures are intra-articular fractures that mostly result from indirect varus or valgus trauma. The amount of displacement and comminution is determined by the magnitude and direction of the forces applied. High-energy fractures may be associated with severe soft tissue injuries, as well as ligamentous and meniscal tears. It is important to recognize that severe proximal tibial fractures can represent a reduced fracture dislocation of the knee, and thus, the neurologic and vascular concerns that accompany knee dislocations can apply to these fractures as well [see Knee, Dislocation, above].

Tibial plateau fractures are characterized by local pain, swelling from hemarthrosis, and, in some cases, instability of the knee joint. Aspiration of a tense hemarthrosis is sometimes required to decompress the joint and relieve pain. Only 6% of patients with knee trauma have a fracture. The need for x-rays is generally determined according to the Ottawa knee rule [see Knee, Ligamentous Injury and Meniscal Tearing, above].[92] If a fracture is confirmed, CT scanning with axial, coronal, and sagittal reconstructions is done to delineate the severity and orientation of the fracture lines. This measure also helps the physician decide whether operative or nonoperative treatment is indicated and, if the former, which operative approach should be taken. If the condition of the soft tissues precludes early definitive operative treatment, a plaster splint or temporary external fixation may be employed to allow the soft tissues time to heal or to give the surgeon time to plan an operative procedure for soft tissue coverage.

Proximal tibial fractures are classified according to the AO-ASIF system or the Schatzker system. Extra-articular AO-ASIF type A1 and A2 fractures and minimally (< 2 mm) displaced intra-articular fractures (AO-ASIF type B and C) may be treated conservatively; all others should be treated operatively. Operative treatment consists of anatomic reduction of the articular surface, either under direct vision (arthrotomy) or via a less invasive approach (with arthroscopic or fluoroscopic assistance). Reduction is held with screws, plates, or both, and often, the use of iliac bone grafts or bone substitutes (e.g., calcium phosphates) is required to maintain the elevation of the articular surface. The articular "block" is connected to the tibial shaft by means of plates and screws; if soft tissue injuries preclude plating, special external fixation devices (i.e., ring fixators with tensioned wires) may be employed instead. Fixed-angle plating systems that allow less invasive insertion methods are also gaining popularity for use in the proximal tibia. Early motion is appropriate after operation, with weight bearing allowed after 8 to 12 weeks. Disabling complications include infection, posttraumatic arthritis, and instability of the knee.[4,5]

Shaft

Fractures of the tibial shaft are among the most common serious fractures. The subcutaneous location of the tibia affords little protection from direct violence, and high-energy fractures are associated with longer healing times. Tibial fractures can be fraught with complications (e.g., compartment syndrome, nonunion, delayed union, malunion, and infection), and in their most severe manifestations, they can end in amputation. Tibial shaft fractures are easily diagnosed clinically in the ED. Examination includes palpation for signs of possible compartment syndrome and assessment of the neurovascular status. If the fracture is grossly angulated or malaligned, gentle restoration of axial alignment helps relieve vascular kinking and compromise. The extremity should be splinted, and appropriate x-rays should then be obtained to allow full assessment of the fracture.

Selected closed fractures without dislocation and minimally displaced AO-ASIF type A fractures may be treated conservatively with an above-the-knee cast for 2 to 4 weeks, followed by functional bracing for 10 to 16 weeks. Bracing relies on the intact soft tissues, primarily the interosseous membrane, to prevent shortening and dislocation.[93] Displaced and unstable AO-ASIF type A, B, and C fractures, as well as all open fractures, are treated operatively. The severity of any associated soft tissue injury is a crucial factor in deciding how to manage of tibial shaft fractures. The standard treatment for such fractures—closed reduction with reamed, interlocking intramedullary nailing—has a high success rate and a low complication rate [see Figure 11]. In those unusual circumstances in which the fracture pattern does not permit insertion of an intramedullary rod (e.g., certain fractures in the proximal or distal third of the shaft), plate fixation may be employed instead; unfortunately, this procedure is associated with a high rate of nonunion.[4,5,51]

For open fractures associated with complex wounds, the standard treatment has been external fixation, which permits stabilization of the fracture, affords ready access to large open wounds, and facilitates nursing care. Currently, however, nailing appears be superior to external fixation for grade 1 and 2 open fractures: the infection rate is no higher, the complication rate is lower, and the functional end results are better. Grade 3 open fractures are highly complex injuries, and an expert team that includes a plastic surgeon is required for optimal management. Aggressive irrigation and debridement are followed by either external fixation or intramedullary nailing, depending on the state of the surrounding soft tissue factors, the fracture pattern, time-related factors, and the surgeon's preference. If secondary soft tissue procedures involving a pedicle or a free flap are warranted, they should be planned at an early stage in treatment. In multiply injured patients who require DCS, tibial shaft fractures are initially stabilized with external fixation, with care taken to place the fixator pins strategically, in anticipation of subsequent soft tissue coverage procedures. Once the patient is physiologically stable, the fixator may be removed and intramedullary nailing performed. In these patients, a combination of retrograde femoral nailing and antegrade tibial nailing done through a single knee incision offers an elegant and less invasive means of stabilizing a floating knee.

One of the most severe complications that may develop after a tibial fracture is compartment syndrome [see 112 Injuries to the Peripheral Blood Vessels]. When the fracture is in the distal third of the shaft, delayed union or nonunion is a particular risk as a consequence of the limited vascularization provided by the predominantly posterior soft tissue envelope.[4,5]

Distal

Fractures of the distal tibia mostly result either from vertical loading that drives the talus into the tibia (as in a fall from a height or a motor vehicle accident) or from low-energy trauma with torsion (as in skiing). Intra-articular fractures in this region are called tibial plafond (ceiling) or pilon fractures. Pilon fractures are frequently accompanied by severe soft tissue swelling and comminution of the articular surface and the metaphysis; the fibula may or may not be fractured. Standard AP and lateral x-rays are obtained in conjunction with CT scans to define the fracture pattern and aid in preoperative planning. The goals of treatment are to restore ankle joint integrity, congruency, and stability; to achieve bony union; and to allow functional painless motion. In cases where there is substantial soft tissue involvement, staged surgery may be advisable. A safe option is to apply a bridging external fixator from the midtibia to the foot, leaving enough distance between the fixator pins to allow future incisions in the distal tibia; this may be done with or without primary percutaneous screw fixation of the joint

a

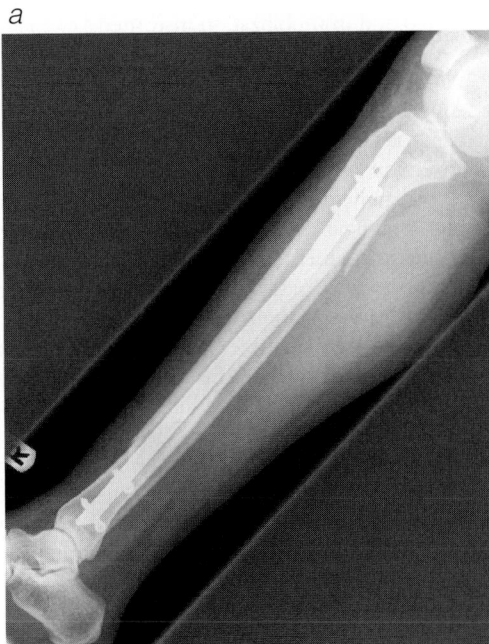

b

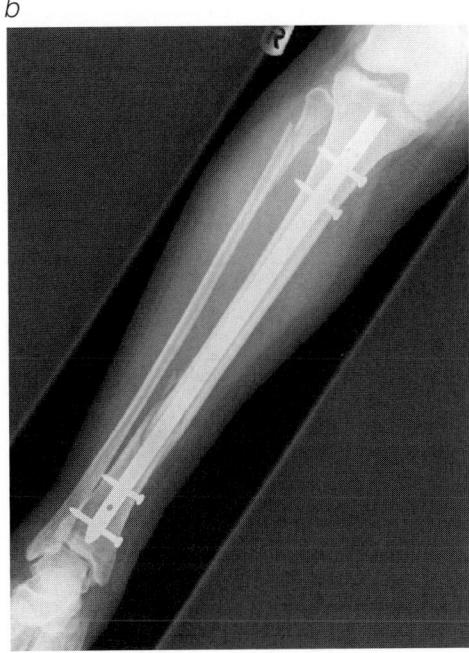

Figure 11   **Shown (*a, b*) is treatment of closed AO-ASIF type A1 tibial fracture with reamed intramedullary nailing.**

surface and with or without primary fixation of the fibula to restore the length of the ankle.

Fractures that are not accompanied by dislocation (mostly AO-ASIF type A1) may be treated conservatively in a cast for 8 weeks. All other distal tibial fractures generally require operative treatment, the basic principles of which resemble those appropriate for proximal tibial fractures. Because of the typical swelling and the frequent presence of fracture blisters, optimal timing of the procedure is critical. For extra-articular (AO-ASIF type A) fractures, a minimally invasive approach involving percutaneous insertion of a plate with locking screws (e.g., the LCP) may be feasible. For intra-articular (AO-ASIF type B and C) fractures, anatomic reduction of the articular surface and internal fixation are required, preferably performed by an experienced surgeon. As a rule, the fibula is fixed first through a lateral incision, and the tibia is then fixed via an anterior or medial approach. Dissection should be minimized to prevent further soft tissue injury. Any debris present in the joint is removed. After reconstruction of the articular surface, a connection with the tibial shaft is made, most frequently with a plate and screws or with a hybrid ring fixator. With most AO-ASIF type C distal tibial fractures, the use of a bone graft or bone substitute is required to support the articular surface. After the procedure, the patient is allowed to engage in active movement without weight bearing for 8 to 12 weeks. The outcome of treatment of pilon fractures depends primarily on the quality of the articular reduction and the recovery of the soft tissues. Such fractures frequently give rise to severe posttraumatic arthritic pain, and delayed ankle fusion may be required.[4,5]

FIBULA

Shaft

Generally, fibular shaft fractures may be ignored. Such fractures heal readily, sometimes so readily that they interfere with the union of associated tibial fractures. Isolated midshaft fibular fractures that do not involve the ankle joint may be treated symptomatically, often without a cast. In some instances, plating the fibular fracture

provides additional stabilization for an unstable distal tibial shaft fracture; however, rendering the fibula stable may diminish the cyclic compression that occurs with weight bearing at the site of the tibial fracture and thus may delay healing. For this reason, in most cases of combined tibial and fibular fracture, the fibula is not stabilized.[5]

ACHILLES TENDON

Achilles tendon ruptures are mainly caused either by sudden forceful dorsiflexion of the foot with the knee extended (placing the soleus and gastrocnemius muscles on maximal stretch) or by sudden takeoff during athletics. They are frequently seen in weekend athletes, as well as in more regular participants in active sports (e.g., football, volleyball, tennis, and squash). A common scenario is one in which the patient wrongly believes that someone has hit him or her on the heel; sometimes, the patient hears a snap as well. On physical examination, a visible or palpable dent is apparent in the tendon 2 to 6 cm above the calcaneus. The Thompson test is useful for confirming or ruling out an Achilles tendon rupture. For this test, the patient is placed in the prone position with both feet extending past the end of the examining table. If squeezing of the calf muscles on the affected side does not result in plantar flexion of the foot, the tendon is ruptured; if this maneuver does result in plantar flexion, the tendon is intact. If the patient does not present until several days after the injury, diagnosis may be more difficult. In such cases, ultrasonography or MRI may be helpful.

Treatment may be nonoperative (i.e., immobilization in plantar flexion) in certain patients, but it is operative in most. Operative treatment consists of surgical repair of the tendon either via full exposure of the tendon or via a minimally invasive approach (e.g., suture anchors); the latter may be preferable for minimizing wound healing problems. After the procedure, the injured area is kept in a soft cast for 6 weeks, during which period the patient is allowed active movement with weight bearing. Surgical treatment substantially reduces the incidence of recurrent ruptures; however, it is also associated with an increased risk of wound healing problems and surgical site infection.[5,94]

ANKLE

Fracture and Dislocation

Ankle fractures are usually caused by indirect trauma. They are generally categorized according to the AO-ASIF classification system, which also guides treatment decisions. The factors that determine the type of fracture present include age, bone density, the position of the foot at the time of injury (pronation or supination), and the direction of the forces that acted on the joint to produce the injury (adduction, abduction, exorotation, or axial loading). The history and physical examination reveal pain, swelling, functional impairment, and inability to bear weight. Conventional x-rays usually suffice for diagnosis. A true AP (mortise) view requires 20° of internal rotation for adequate assessment of the joint. If the fracture is particularly complex, CT scanning should be performed to obtain additional information. The two main factors to consider in the management of ankle fractures are the congruency of the ankle joint medially, laterally, and superiorly (i.e., with respect to the tibia, the fibula, and the talus) and the presence of soft tissue injury (because there is little muscle coverage in this area). Even small disturbances of ankle congruity (e.g., widening of the mortise) can lead to overloading of the cartilage and predispose to posttraumatic arthritis.

Type A fractures are transverse lateral malleolar fractures that occur distal to the syndesmosis, at or just below the level of the ankle joint. They may be treated either conservatively in a plaster cast or functionally in a soft cast for 4 to 6 weeks with full weight bearing allowed.

Type B fractures are oblique or spiral fractures of the lateral malleolus that occur at the level of the syndesmosis, with or without a fracture of the medial malleolus. Whereas nondislocated type B fractures may be treated conservatively, all other type B fractures are treated by means of open reduction and internal fixation with a plate or screws, followed by protected weight bearing. The best time for operative treatment is within the 8 hours following admission. After 24 hours, edema increases, and surgery is best postponed until 5 to 7 days later, when the condition of the soft tissue has improved. In the meantime, the fracture or dislocation is reduced, and a splint is applied.

Type C fractures occur above the syndesmosis. Sometimes, a fracture is located near the fibular head proximally. In such cases, the interosseous membrane and the syndesmosis are ruptured between the fibular fracture and the ankle joint (Maisonneuve fracture). This type of injury is easily missed if a careful examination is not performed and the appropriate proximal x-ray obtained. Type C fractures are generally treated surgically with plating or with one or two fibulotibial syndesmotic positioning screws, which allow the syndesmosis to heal with a correct length and position relative to the talus of the fibula.

Malleolar fractures are frequently associated with fractures of the posterior lip of the tibial plafond (trimalleolar fractures). Large fragments (> 20% of articular surface) should be reduced and fixed to prevent posterior dislocation of the talus. Early complications include inadequate reduction and fixation, wound problems, and infection. Long-term results are primarily determined by the presence and extent of cartilage damage and by the congruency of the ankle joint. Approximately 30% of patients experience persistent symptoms around the ankle.[4,5,95]

Isolated ankle dislocations without fractures are rare; 30% of these injuries are associated with an open wound extending into the joint. A dislocated ankle should immediately be reduced—before x-rays are taken if possible—to minimize further neurovascular compromise. After closed or open reduction, wound care is provided and immobilization instituted.[5]

Ligamentous Injury

Ankle ligament injuries are among the most common injuries seen in the ED. They often occur during sports activities as a result of inversion during plantar flexion of the ankle. Approximately 85% of ligamentous ankle injuries involve one or another of the three lateral ligaments: the anterior talofibular ligament, the calcaneofibular ligament, and the posterior talofibular ligament. Approximately 65% of ankle sprains resulting from inversion occur in the anterior talofibular ligament alone. Ankle sprains are commonly classified into three grades: grade I is a sprain with stretching of the ligament, grade II is a partial ligament tear, and grade III is a complete tear. This classification does not, however, guide treatment. Diagnosis is based on the history and the physical examination (including the anterior drawer test). X-rays are obtained if a fracture is suspected. The number of unnecessary x-rays can be markedly and safely reduced by applying the so-called Ottawa ankle rule [see Figure 12], which is analogous to the Ottawa knee rule described earlier [see Knee, Ligamentous Injury and Meniscal Tearing, above].[96]

The main treatment options for ankle ligament injuries are immobilization in plaster, functional treatment (early mobilization with the joint in tape or a soft cast), and surgical repair. Current evidence indicates that functional treatment is the recommended strategy for most patients.[97,98] Approximately 20% of patients experience varying levels of recurrent or chronic symptoms.

FOOT

The foot is a complex system consisting of numerous bones, ligaments, and tendons. Accordingly, many different types of foot injury are seen. The history plays an important role in identifying the mechanism of injury. Foot injuries do occur as isolated events, but they also frequently occur in conjunction with distant injuries and thus may easily be missed initially in cases of polytrauma. Physical examination includes assessment of the soft tissues of the foot and ankle, the degree of pain felt on compression, the stability of the injured area, and the neurovascular status of the foot. Conventional x-rays are often supplemented with CT scans; MRI and bone scintigraphy are also sometimes employed, though less frequently.[4,5] The pain, swelling, functional impairment, and deformity associated with foot injuries can markedly limit the patient's mobility. In recent years, it has become clear that function can be improved by restoring the normal anatomy and avoiding prolonged immobilization in plaster.

Talus

The talus plays an important role in the transmission of force to the rest of the foot, with 60% of its surface covered by cartilage. This cartilaginous covering, in combination with a delicate blood supply, makes talus fractures complex injuries. Fractures and dislocations of the talus typically result from high-energy trauma (as in motor vehicle accidents or falls). Most talus fractures are intra-articular; sometimes, the only damage consists of an osteochondral flake (e.g., from an ankle sprain).

Most talus fractures are treated operatively. Ideally, surgical treatment should be carried out as early as possible, especially if the fracture involves the talar neck. Screw fixation may be accomplished either via open reduction or percutaneously (if displacement is minimal). After the operation, active motion is allowed, and weight bearing is started after 8 to 12 weeks. The outcome of treatment is determined primarily by the presence or absence of open wounds, the fracture type, and the status of the remaining

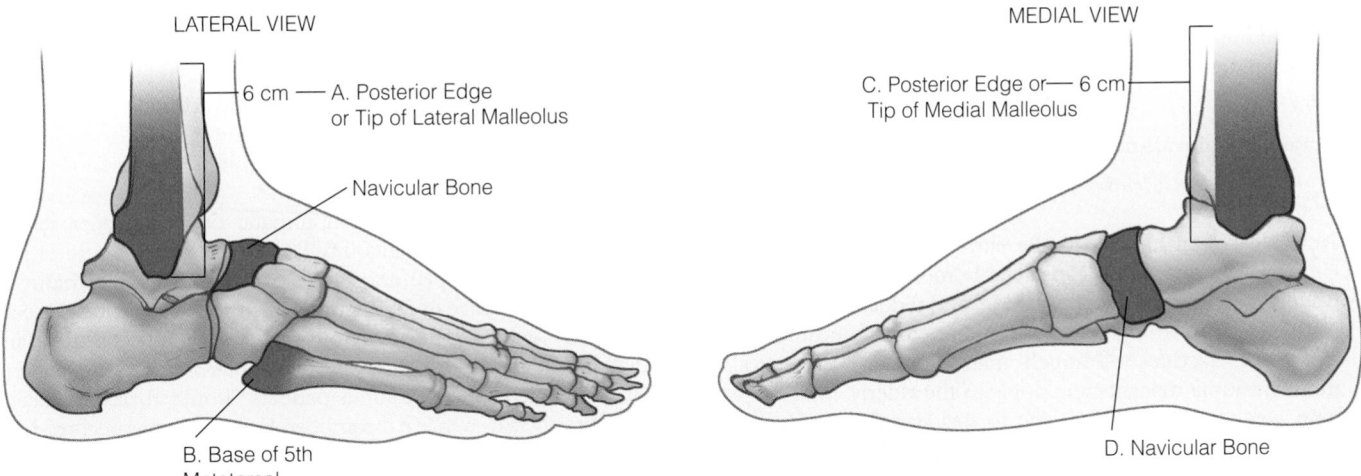

Figure 12 Illustrated is the Ottawa ankle rule. According to this rule, an ankle or foot x-ray series is required only if (1) palpation of the marked areas is painful or (2) the patient is completely unable to bear his or her own weight both immediately after the injury and for four steps in the ED.

blood supply. Avascular necrosis, infection, and posttraumatic arthritis can lead to severe disability.[4,5,99]

Calcaneus

The calcaneus is the most frequently fractured bone in the foot. Fractures of the calcaneus are primarily caused by falling or jumping from a height and thus are commonly seen in combination with other injuries (e.g., spine fractures). Examination typically reveals marked swelling of the foot, with or without deformity. Lateral x-rays of the foot show a reduction in Böhler's angle (the posterior angle formed by the intersection of a line from the posterior to the middle facet with a line from the anterior to the middle facet) from the normal range of 20° to 40°. Conventional x-rays are always supplemented with CT scans to delineate the extent of the fracture.

Most extra-articular and nondislocated intra-articular fractures can be treated conservatively with non–weight-bearing mobilization of the ankle and the foot over a period of 6 to 12 weeks; there is no need for a splint or a cast. Optimal treatment of intra-articular fractures—in particular, the role of surgery—remains subject to debate, however. Depending on the fracture configuration, reduction and internal fixation of the joint surfaces may be accomplished either via an open approach or percutaneously. The same measures recommended as conservative treatment are then carried out as postoperative treatment. Whether this strategy yields better functional results than conservative treatment is not clear. However, there is currently a trend toward operative treatment in situations where anatomic reconstruction of the subtalar and calcaneocuboidal joints can be achieved. Smoking, advanced age, diabetes, and noncompliance are relative contraindications to surgical management. A substantial percentage of patients heal with malunion or experience posttraumatic arthritis. These patients are candidates for arthrodesis of the subtalar joint.[4,5,100,101]

Midfoot

The midfoot contains the navicular bone, the cuboid bone, and the three cuneiform bones (medial, intermediate, and lateral). Proximally, the navicular and the cuboid articulate with the talus and the calcaneus (Chopart's joint); distally, the cuboid and the cuneiforms articulate with the metatarsals (Lisfranc's joint). Fractures and ligamentous injuries in these joints are easily missed

and can lead to prolonged deformity, pain, and functional impairment. Restoration of the anatomy both medially and laterally is important for a good outcome.

The majority of nondislocated fractures, extra-articular fractures, and ligament avulsion fractures of the midfoot can be treated nonoperatively in plaster or with functional therapy and early motion. Dislocated fractures are generally treated operatively with screw or plate fixation unless such treatment is precluded by severe comminution. Fractures in Lisfranc's joint mainly result from high-energy trauma and are often associated with dislocation of one or more metatarsal bones. Such fractures are treated by means of operative reduction and fixation with Kirschner wires or screws.[4,5,102,103]

Metatarsals and Toes

Most metatarsal fractures result from direct trauma (e.g., from a heavy object falling on the foot); however, they can also occur with chronic repetitive loading in the absence of obvious trauma (so-called stress or march fracture).

For the most part, fractures of the second through fourth metatarsals and nondislocated fractures of the first and fifth metatarsals can be treated nonoperatively by using a plaster cast or a heavy supportive shoe for 4 to 6 weeks. With the majority of displaced fractures, closed reduction can be achieved, but maintenance of the reduction requires internal fixation; malunion can disturb ambulation. Many fractures of the lesser metatarsals and subcapital fractures can be treated with percutaneous pinning. Fractures with joint involvement and multiple fragments frequently necessitate treatment with open reduction and plate fixation. Fractures of the base of the fifth metatarsal form a special group. The mechanism of injury is identical to that seen in ankle sprains. These fractures are generally divided into two types: avulsion fractures (involving the insertion of the peroneus brevis tendon) and transverse fractures of the base of the fifth metatarsal (Jones fracture). Both types may be treated nonoperatively if displacement is minimal, but delayed healing is common with Jones fractures. Operative treatment consists of tension-band wiring or screw or plate fixation.[4,5,104]

Fractures and dislocations of the toes result from direct trauma. Virtually all toe fractures can be treated conservatively by taping the injured toe to an adjacent, uninjured toe (so-called buddy tape). On rare occasions, reduction and Kirschner wire fixation of a dislocated toe fracture are indicated. Toe dislocations are reduced with traction and are treated in much the same way as toe fractures.[5]

Special Considerations

GERIATRIC TRAUMA

Musculoskeletal injuries in the elderly are a rapidly growing health problem and cause considerable morbidity and mortality. Advanced age, increased risk of falling, and reduced bone mineral density are the most important risk factors for the occurrence of osteoporotic fractures. Although many standard principles of extremity trauma management apply to the elderly, there are also certain concerns that are specific to this population. Hence, in evaluating an elderly person who has sustained an extremity injury, it is essential to assess the entire patient, not just the affected bone or joint.

One issue is that injured elderly persons often have one or more comorbid conditions, the presence of which increases perioperative risk. Advances in medical and anesthetic techniques have made it safe for many patients to undergo surgical procedures that previously would have been contraindicated; however, the timing of surgery can still pose problems. Ideally, sufficient time should be taken to ensure that patients receive optimal preoperative preparation, but such preparation should be provided with the understanding that delaying surgery unnecessarily will increase mortality. Inadequate nutrition is common in the elderly and should receive appropriate attention. The presence of osteoporosis can be confirmed by measuring bone mineral density (e.g., with dual-energy x-ray absorptiometry). Treatment of osteoporosis consists of a combination of physical exercise, dietary supplementation (with calcium and vitamin D), and administration of biphosponates (e.g., alendronate). Elderly patients have special needs with regard to rehabilitation, in that dependence or immobility may necessitate institutional care.[105-107]

REHABILITATION

The care of a patient with musculoskeletal injuries does not stop when the last operation is performed. Adequate rehabilitation is critical for ensuring the best possible functional outcome. Physical therapists, occupational therapists, speech trainers, dietitians, social workers, and psychologists may all play roles in this process. To ensure optimal continuity of treatment from the hospital to the rehabilitation center, rehabilitation experts should be involved early after the admission of a patients who has sustained severe pelvic or extremity trauma.[4,5]

COMPLICATIONS

Systemic complications of pelvic and extremity trauma include FES, ARDS, hemorrhagic complications, crush syndrome, and thromboembolism. Severe local complications include compartment syndrome, acute and chronic infection, infected nonunion, malunion, and posttraumatic reflex sympathetic dystrophy.

Fat Embolism Syndrome

FES is most commonly associated with fractures of long bones of the lower extremity. The classic clinical triad consists of respiratory distress, cerebral dysfunction, and petechial rash. The pathophysiology is not clear, but there is some evidence to suggest that extravasation of fat particles from long bone fractures may play an important part. Furthermore, early stabilization of long bone fractures has been shown to decrease the incidence of FES. Signs and symptoms of clinical FES usually begin within 24 to 48 hours after trauma. Treatment is primarily prophylactic and supportive, consisting of early fracture fixation, careful volume replacement, analgesia, and respiratory support. The role of corticosteroids in this setting is controversial.[4,5,108,109]

Thromboembolism

Both symptomatic and asymptomatic DVT can pose serious problems in trauma patients. DVT is an important cause of pulmonary embolism (PE) and often results in major morbidity or death. The incidence of DVT ranges from 4% in patients with conservatively treated lower-extremity injuries to between 20% and 35% in patients with pelvic and acetabular injuries and patients with hip fractures. All trauma patients should therefore receive DVT prophylaxis. Once a thromboembolic event has occurred, the patient should be immediately be treated with I.V. anticoagulants according to local protocols. Prevention and treatment of DVT and PE are discussed in greater detail elsewhere [see 85 Venous Thromboembolism].[4,5,10,110-113]

Infection

Infections that develop after osteosynthesis are nearly always caused by exogenous bacteria. Contamination may occur in the course of the injury (as with an open fracture), during surgical treatment, or postoperatively (as a result of disturbed wound healing). Most infections manifest themselves within the first 7 days after the operation. Some become apparent only after a longer period has elapsed; these are often preceded by an unnoticed low-grade infection. The infection types most frequently associated with osteosynthesis are implant-related infections (involving colonization of fixation materials), osteomyelitis (a bone infection), and infectious arthritis. Diagnosis is based primarily on clinical signs (e.g., redness, fever, and pain), laboratory studies (e.g., C-reactive protein level and leukocyte count), and bacteriologic tests. In patients with late-developing infections, x-rays, CT, and MRI can provide additional useful information. Treatment consists of surgical debridement, open or closed wound management, and supplemental local or systemic antibiotic coverage. For cases of chronic osteomyelitis, advanced soft-tissue coverage procedures are frequently required. Implant removal is generally unnecessary as long as the implant provides stable fixation.

Gas gangrene is the most serious infection seen in traumatic wounds; *Clostridium perfringens* is the classic causative pathogen. Other gas-forming organisms common seen include coliforms, anaerobic streptococci, and *Bacteroides*. Pain is the initial symptom of gas gangrene, followed by edema and exudation of a thin, dark fluid. The wound acquires a bronze discoloration and a musty smell, and crepitations develop in the muscles. Symptoms progress rapidly, and profound shock and MODS usually ensue. The diagnosis is made on clinical grounds, supported by Gram's staining. Successful treatment depends on early diagnosis, radical surgical debridement, fasciotomy, and I.V. antibiotic therapy.[4,5,114]

Delayed Union, Nonunion, and Malunion

At present, there is no consensus among surgeons on how best to assess fracture healing—and, therefore, no consensus on precisely what constitutes delayed union, nonunion, or malunion. In general, delayed union refers to a fracture that heals more slowly than the average. "Average" depends on the fracture's location and type, but 3 months is a frequently accepted time limit for delayed union.

Nonunion refers to a failure of bone healing that results from an arrested growth process; 6 months is the usual time limit. Nonunion has numerous potential causes, but the most important factors leading to nonunion are disturbance of the blood supply and insufficient fracture stability. The blood supply is disturbed both by the injury itself and by the surgical procedure performed to treat the injury. Instability results from inadequate fixation technique, a suboptimal implant choice, or implant failure. In some nonunions, a false joint with a fibrocartilaginous cavity lined with synovium is formed (a condition also referred to as pseudarthrosis). Treatment of hypertrophic nonunions focuses primarily on achieving adequate stability, whereas treatment of atrophic nonunions requires not only achieving stability but also reversing the atrophy to the extent possible. The gold standard for treatment of atrophic nonunions is placement of a cancellous autologous bone graft, which has the advantage of being osteogenic, osteoinductive, and osteoconductive. Unfortunately, the morbidity from cancellous bone harvesting can be considerable.

Malunion is a deformity characterized by abnormal length, rotation, or angulation. The degree of malunion that is acceptable with respect to function and cosmesis varies with the age of the patient and the location of the fracture.[4,5]

Reflex Sympathetic Dystrophy

Posttraumatic reflex sympathetic dystrophy (also referred to as complex regional pain syndrome) is a poorly understood complication that may develop in any of the extremities after an operation or even minor trauma. It is capable of causing severe disability.[4,5,115,116] Symptoms include unexplained diffuse pain, skin changes, edema, temperature changes, and functional impairment. The optimal treatment regimen has not been established; common therapeutic measures include free radical scavenger treatment (e.g., with systemic acetylcysteine and local dimethyl sulfoxide cream), administration of vitamin C, analgesia, vasodilatation, and careful physical therapy.

References

1. American College of Surgeons Committee on Trauma: Advanced Trauma Life Support Student Manual, 7th ed. American College of Surgeons, Chicago, 2004
2. Biffl WL, Harrington DT, Cioffi WG: Implementation of a tertiary trauma survey decreases missed injuries. J Trauma 54:38, 2003
3. Breitenseher MJ, Metz VM, Gilula LA, et al: Radiographically occult scaphoid fractures: value of MR imaging in detection. Radiology 203:245, 1997
4. AO Principles of Fracture Management. Rüedi TP, Murphy WM, Eds. Thieme, Stuttgart and New York, 2000
5. Skeletal Trauma, 3rd ed. Browner BD, Jupiter JB, Levine AM, et al, Eds. WB Saunders, Philadelphia, 2003
6. Hildebrand F, Giannoudis P, Kretteck C, et al: Damage control: extremities. Injury 35:678, 2004
7. Roberts CS, Pape HC, Jones AL, et al: Damage control orthopaedics: evolving concepts in the treatment of patients who have sustained orthopaedic trauma. Instr Course Lect. 54:447, 2005
8. Brundage SI, McGhan R, Jurkovich GJ, et al: Timing of femur fracture fixation: effect on outcome in patients with thoracic and head injuries. J Trauma 52:299, 2002
9. Dunham CM, Bosse MJ, Clancy TV, et al; EAST Practice Management Guidelines Work Group: Practice management guidelines for the optimal timing of long-bone fracture stabilization in polytrauma patients: the EAST Practice Management Guidelines Work Group. J Trauma 50:958, 2001
10. Trauma, 5th ed. Moore EE, Feliciano DV, Mattox KL, Eds. McGraw-Hill, New York, 2004
11. Goslings JC, Haverlag R, Ponsen KJ, et al: Facilitating damage control surgery with a dedicated DCS equipment trolley. Injury 37:466, 2006
12. Nowotarski PJ, Turen CH, Brumback RJ, et al: Conversion of external fixation to intramedullary nailing for fractures of the shaft of the femur in multiply injured patients. J Bone Joint Surg Am 82:781, 2000
13. Scalea TM, Boswell SA, Scott JD, et al: External fixation as a bridge to intramedullary nailing for patients with multiple injuries and with femur fractures: damage control orthopedics. J Trauma 48:613, 2000
14. Eastridge BJ, Starr A, Minei JP, et al: The importance of fracture pattern in guiding therapeutic decision-making in patients with hemorrhagic shock and pelvic ring disruptions. J Trauma 53:446, 2002
15. Heetveld MJ, Harris I, Schlaphoff G, et al: Hemodynamically unstable pelvic fractures: recent care and new guidelines. World J Surg 28:904, 2004
16. Blackmore CC, Jurkovich GJ, Linnau KF, et al: Assessment of volume of hemorrhage and outcome from pelvic fracture. Arch Surg 138:504, 2003
17. Starr AJ, Griffin DR, Reinert CM, et al: Pelvic ring disruptions: prediction of associated injuries, transfusion requirement, pelvic arteriography, complications, and mortality. J Orthop Trauma 16:553, 2002
18. Krieg JC, Mohr M, Ellis TJ, et al: Emergent stabilization of pelvic ring injuries by controlled circumferential compression: a clinical trial. J Trauma 59:659, 2005
19. Miller PR, Moore PS, Mansell E, et al: External fixation or arteriogram in bleeding pelvic fracture: initial therapy guided by markers of arterial hemorrhage. J Trauma 54:437, 2003
20. Pereira SJ, O'Brien DP, Luchette FA, et al: Dynamic helical computed tomography scan accurately detects hemorrhage in patients with pelvic fracture. Surgery 128:678, 2000
21. Agolini SF, Shah K, Jaffe J, et al: Arterial embolization is a rapid and effective technique for controlling pelvic hemorrhage. J Trauma 43:395, 1997
22. Velmahos GC, Toutouzas KG, Vassiliu P, et al: A prospective study on the safety and efficacy of angiographic embolization for pelvic and visceral injuries. J Trauma 53:303, 2002
23. Smith WR, Moore EE, Osborn P, et al: Retroperitoneal packing as a resuscitation technique for hemodynamically unstable patients with pelvic fractures: report of two representative cases and a description of technique. J Trauma 59:1510, 2005
24. Giannoudis PV, Pape HC: Damage control orthopaedics in unstable pelvic ring injuries. Injury 35:671, 2004
25. Dyer GS, Vrahas MS: Review of the pathophysiology and acute management of haemorrhage in pelvic fracture. Injury 37:602, 2006
26. Giannoudis PV, Papakostidis C, Roberts C: A review of the management of open fractures of the tibia and femur. J Bone Joint Surg Br 88:281, 2006
27. Boxma H, Broekhuizen T, Patka P, et al: Randomised controlled trial of single-dose antibiotic prophylaxis in surgical treatment of closed fractures: the Dutch Trauma Trial. Lancet 347:1133, 1996
28. Gillespie WJ, Walenkamp G: Antibiotic prophylaxis for surgery for proximal femoral and other closed long bone fractures. Cochrane Database Syst Rev (1):CD000244, 2001
29. Parrett BM, Matros E, Pribaz JJ, et al: Lower extremity trauma: trends in the management of soft-tissue reconstruction of open tibia-fibula fractures. Plast Reconstr Surg 117:1315, 2006
30. Egol KA, Tejwani NC, Capla EL, et al: Staged management of high-energy proximal tibia fractures (OTA types 41): the results of a prospective, standardized protocol. J Orthop Trauma 19:448, 2005
31. Gopal S, Majumder S, Batchelor AG, et al: Fix and flap: the radical orthopaedic and plastic treatment of severe open fractures of the tibia. J Bone Joint Surg Br 82:959, 2000
32. Herscovici D Jr, Sanders RW, Scaduto JM, et al: Vacuum-assisted wound closure (VAC therapy) for the management of patients with high-energy soft tissue injuries. J Orthop Trauma 17:683, 2003
33. Archdeacon MT, Messerschmitt P: Modern papineau technique with vacuum-assisted closure. J Orthop Trauma 20:134, 2006
34. Durham RM, Mistry BM, et al: Outcome and utility of scoring systems in the management of the mangled extremity. Am J Surg 172:569, 1996
35. Bosse MJ, MacKenzie EJ, Kellam JF, et al: A prospective evaluation of the clinical utility of the lower-extremity injury-severity scores. J Bone Joint Surg Am 83-A:3, 2001
36. Bosse MJ, MacKenzie EJ, Kellam JF, et al: An analysis of outcomes of reconstruction or amputation after leg-threatening injuries. N Engl J Med 347:1924, 2002
37. Vascular Trauma, 2nd ed. Rich NM, Mattox KL, Hirschberg A, Eds. Elsevier Saunders, Philadelphia, 2004
38. Harris IA, Kadir A, Donald G: Continuous compartment pressure monitoring for tibia fractures: does it influence outcome? J Trauma 60:1330, 2006
39. Lin CH, Wei FC, Levin LS, et al: The functional outcome of lower-extremity fractures with vascular injury. J Trauma 43:480, 1997
40. Rozycki GS, Tremblay LN, Feliciano DV, et al: Blunt vascular trauma in the extremity: diagnosis, management, and outcome. J Trauma 55:814, 2003
41. Hafez HM, Woolgar J, Robbs JV: Lower extremity

arterial injury: results of 550 cases and review of risk factors associated with limb loss. J Vasc Surg 33:1212, 2001

42. Dennis JW, Frykberg ER, Veldenz HC, et al: Validation of nonoperative management of occult vascular injuries and accuracy of physical examination alone in penetrating extremity trauma: 5- to 10-year follow-up. J Trauma 44:243, 1998

43. McHenry TP, Holcomb JB, Aoki N, et al: Fractures with major vascular injuries from gunshot wounds: implications of surgical sequence. J Trauma 53:717, 2002

44. Rasmussen TE, Clouse WD, Jenkins DH, et al: The use of temporary vascular shunts as a damage control adjunct in the management of wartime vascular injury. J Trauma 61:8, 2006

45. Lonn L, Delle M, Karlstrom L, et al: Should blunt arterial trauma to the extremities be treated with endovascular techniques? J Trauma 59:1224, 2005

46. Mohler LR, Hanel DP: Closed fractures complicated by peripheral nerve injury. J Am Acad Orthop Surg 14:32, 2006

47. DeFranco MJ, Lawton JN: Radial nerve injuries associated with humeral fractures. J Hand Surg [Am] 31:655, 2006

48. Shao YC, Harwood P, Grotz MR, et al: Radial nerve palsy associated with fractures of the shaft of the humerus: a systematic review. J Bone Joint Surg Br 87:1647, 2005

49. Smith J, Greaves I: Crush injury and crush syndrome: a review. J Trauma 54(5 suppl):S226, 2003

50. Gonzalez D: Crush syndrome. Crit Care Med 33(1 suppl):S34, 2005

51. Bhandari M, Guyatt GH, Tong D, et al: Reamed versus nonreamed intramedullary nailing of lower extremity long bone fractures: a systematic overview and meta-analysis. J Orthop Trauma 14:2, 2000

52. Busse JW, Bhandari M, Kulkarni AV, et al: The effect of low-intensity pulsed ultrasound therapy on time to fracture healing: a meta-analysis. CMAJ 166:437, 2002

53. Malizos KN, Hantes ME, Protopappas V, et al: Low-intensity pulsed ultrasound for bone healing: an overview. Injury 37(suppl 1):S56, 2006

54. Termaat MF, Den Boer FC, Bakker FC, et al: Bone morphogenetic proteins: development and clinical efficacy in the treatment of fractures and bone defects. J Bone Joint Surg Am 87:1367, 2005

55. Busam ML, Esther RJ, Obremskey WT: Hardware removal: indications and expectations. J Am Acad Orthop Surg 14:113, 2006

56. Brown OL, Dirschl DR, Obremskey WT: Incidence of hardware-related pain and its effect on functional outcomes after open reduction and internal fixation of ankle fractures. J Orthop Trauma 15:271, 2001

57. Zlowodzki M, Zelle BA, Cole PA, et al; Evidence-Based Orthopaedic Trauma Working Group: Treatment of acute midshaft clavicle fractures: systematic review of 2144 fractures: on behalf of the Evidence-Based Orthopaedic Trauma Working Group. J Orthop Trauma 19:504, 2005

58. Handoll HHG, Gibson JNA, Madhok R: Interventions for treating proximal humeral fractures in adults. Cochrane Database Syst Rev (4):CD000434, 2003

59. Helmy N, Hintermann B: New trends in the treatment of proximal humerus fractures. Clin Orthop Relat Res 442:100, 2006

60. Shao YC, Harwood P, Grotz MR, et al: Radial nerve palsy associated with fractures of the shaft of the humerus: a systematic review. J Bone Joint Surg Br 87:1647, 2005

61. Chapman JR, Henley MB, Agel J, et al: Randomized prospective study of humeral shaft fracture fixation: intramedullary nails versus plates. J Orthop Trauma 14:162, 2000

62. McCormack RG, Brien D, Buckley RE, et al: Fixation of fractures of the shaft of the humerus by dynamic compression plate or intramedullary nail. A prospective, randomised trial. J Bone Joint Surg Br 82:336, 2000

63. Boyer MI, Galatz LM, Borrelli J Jr, et al: Intraarticular fractures of the upper extremity: new concepts in surgical treatment. Instr Course Lect 52:591, 2003

64. O'Driscoll SW, Jupiter JB, Cohen MS, et al: Difficult elbow fractures: pearls and pitfalls. Instr Course Lect 52:113, 2003

65. Hertel R, Pisan M, Lambert S, et al: Plate osteosynthesis of diaphyseal fractures of the radius and ulna. Injury 27:545, 1996

66. Mackay D, Wood L, Rangan A: The treatment of isolated ulnar fractures in adults: a systematic review. Injury 31:565, 2000

67. Handoll HHG, Pearce PK: Interventions for isolated diaphyseal fractures of the ulna in adults. Cochrane Database Syst Rev (2):CD000523, 2004

68. Handoll HHG, Madhok R: Surgical interventions for treating distal radial fractures in adults. Cochrane Database Syst Rev (3):CD003209, 2003

69. Saeden B, Tornkvist H, Ponzer S, et al: Fracture of the carpal scaphoid: a prospective, randomised 12-year follow-up comparing operative and conservative treatment. J Bone Joint Surg Br 83:230, 2001

70. Poolman RW, Goslings JC, Lee JB, et al: Conservative treatment for closed fifth (small finger) metacarpal neck fractures. Cochrane Database Syst Rev (3):CD003210, 2005

71. Schaefer M, Siebert HR: Finger and metacarpal fractures: surgical and nonsurgical treatment procedures. Unfallchirurg 103:482, 2000

72. Freeland AE, Orbay JL: Extraarticular hand fractures in adults: a review of new developments. Clin Orthop Relat Res 445:133, 2006

73. Pohlemann T, Tscherne H, Baumgartel F, et al: Pelvic fractures: epidemiology, therapy and long-term outcome: overview of the multicenter study of the Pelvis Study Group. Unfallchirurg 99:160, 1996

74. Routt ML Jr, Simonian PT, Swiontkowski MF: Stabilization of pelvic ring disruptions. Orthop Clin North Am 28:369, 1997

75. Routt ML Jr, Nork SE, Mills WJ: Percutaneous fixation of pelvic ring disruptions. Clin Orthop Relat Res 375:15, 2000

76. Letournel E: Acetabulum fractures: classification and management. Clin Orthop Relat Res 151:81, 1980

77. Letournel E, Judet R: Fractures of the Acetabulum, 2nd ed. Springer Verlag, Berlin, 1993

78. Matta JM: Fractures of the acetabulum: accuracy of reduction and clinical results in patients managed operatively within three weeks after the injury. J Bone Joint Surg Am 78:1632, 1996

79. Giannoudis PV, Grotz MR, Papakostidis C, et al: Operative treatment of displaced fractures of the acetabulum: a meta-analysis. J Bone Joint Surg Br 87:2, 2005

80. Stannard JP, Harris HW, Volgas DA, et al: Functional outcome of patients with femoral head fractures associated with hip dislocations. Clin Orthop Relat Res 377:44, 2000

81. Parker MJ, Stockton G, Gurusamy K: Internal fixation implants for intracapsular proximal femoral fractures in adults. Cochrane Database Syst Rev (4):CD001467, 2001

82. Bottle A, Aylin P: Mortality associated with delay in operation after hip fracture: observational study. BMJ 332:947, 2006

83. Parker MJ, Gurusamy K: Internal fixation versus arthroplasty for intracapsular proximal femoral fractures in adults. Cochrane Database Syst Rev (4):CD001708, 2006

84. Parker MJ, Handoll HHG: Gamma and other cephalocondylic intramedullary nails versus extramedullary implants for extracapsular hip fractures in adults. Cochrane Database Syst Rev (4):CD000093, 2005

85. Bhandari M, Zlowodzki M, Tornetta P 3rd, et al: Intramedullary nailing following external fixation in femoral and tibial shaft fractures. J Orthop Trauma 19:140, 2005

86. Forster MC, Komarsamy B, Davison JN: Distal femoral fractures: a review of fixation methods. Injury 37:97, 2006

87. Barnes CJ, Pietrobon R, Higgins LD: Does the pulse examination in patients with traumatic knee dislocation predict a surgical arterial injury? A meta-analysis. J Trauma 53:1109, 2002

88. Miranda FE, Dennis JW, Veldenz HC, et al: Confirmation of the safety and accuracy of physical examination in the evaluation of knee dislocation for injury of the popliteal artery: a prospective study. J Trauma 52:247, 2002

89. Hollis JD, Daley BJ: 10-year review of knee dislocations: is arteriography always necessary? J Trauma 59:672, 2005

90. Robertson A, Nutton RW, Keating JF: Dislocation of the knee. J Bone Joint Surg Br 88:706, 2006

91. Azar FM, Aaron DG: Surgical treatment of anterior cruciate ligament-posterior cruciate ligament-medial side knee injuries. J Knee Surg 18:220, 2005

92. Stiell IG, Greenberg GH, Wells GA, et al: Derivation of a decision rule for the use of radiography in acute knee injuries. Ann Emerg Med 26:405, 1995

93. Sarmiento A, Latta LL: 450 closed fractures of the distal third of the tibia treated with a functional brace. Clin Orthop Relat Res 428:261, 2004

94. Khan RJ, Fick D, Keogh A, et al: Treatment of acute achilles tendon ruptures. A meta-analysis of randomized, controlled trials. J Bone Joint Surg Am 87:2202, 2005

95. Petrisor BA, Poolman R, Koval K, et al; on behalf of the Evidence-Based Orthopaedic Trauma Working Group: Management of displaced ankle fractures. J Orthop Trauma 20:515, 2006

96. Stiell IG, Greenberg GH, McKnight RD, et al: Decision rules for the use of radiography in acute ankle injuries: refinement and prospective validation. JAMA 269:1127, 1993

97. Kerkhoffs GMMJ, Handoll HHG, de Bie R, et al: Surgical versus conservative treatment for acute injuries of the lateral ligament complex of the ankle in adults. Cochrane Database Syst Rev (3):CD000380, 2002

98. Kerkhoffs GMMJ, Rowe BH, Assendelft WJJ, et al: Immobilisation and functional treatment for acute lateral ankle ligament injuries in adults. Cochrane Database Syst Rev (3):CD003762, 2002

99. Vallier HA, Nork SE, Benirschke SK, et al: Surgical treatment of talar body fractures. J Bone Joint Surg Am 86-A(suppl 1 pt 2):180, 2004

100. Bridgman SA, Dunn KM, McBride DJ, et al: Interventions for treating calcaneal fractures. Cochrane Database Syst Rev (2):CD001161, 2000

101. Rammelt S, Zwipp H: Calcaneus fractures: facts, controversies and recent developments. Injury 35:443, 2004

102. Rammelt S, Grass R, Schikore H, et al: Injuries of the Chopart joint. Unfallchirurg 105:371, 2002

103. Sands AK, Grose A: Lisfranc injuries. Injury 35(suppl 2):SB71, 2004

104. Rammelt S, Heineck J, Zwipp H: Metatarsal fractures. Injury 35(suppl 2):SB77, 2004

105. Gillespie LD, Gillespie WJ, Robertson MC, et al: Interventions for preventing falls in elderly people.

Cochrane Database Syst Rev (4):CD000340, 2003

106. Jacobs DG, Jacobs DO, Kudsk KA, et al; EAST Practice Management Guidelines Work Group: Practice management guidelines for nutritional support of the trauma patient. J Trauma 57:660, 2004

107. Jacobs DG, Plaisier BR, Barie PS, et al; EAST Practice Management Guidelines Work Group: Practice management guidelines for geriatric trauma: the EAST Practice Management Guidelines Work Group. J Trauma 54:391, 2003

108. Habashi NM, Andrews PL, Scalea TM: Therapeutic aspects of fat embolism syndrome. Injury 37(suppl 4):S68, 2006

109. White T, Petrisor BA, Bhandari M: Prevention of fat embolism syndrome. Injury 37(suppl 4):S59, 2006

110. Rogers FB, Cipolle MD, Velmahos G, et al: Practice management guidelines for the prevention of venous thromboembolism in trauma patients: the EAST practice management guidelines work group. J Trauma 53:142, 2002

111. Kock H, Schmit-Neuerburg KP, Hanke J, et al: Thromboprophylaxis with low-molecular-weight heparin in outpatients with plaster cast immobilisation of the leg. Lancet 346:459, 1995

112. Wille-Jørgensen P, Jorgensen LN, Crawford M: Asymptomatic postoperative deep vein thrombosis and the development of postthrombotic syndrome: a systemic review and meta-analysis. Thromb Haemost 93:236, 2005

113. Amaragiri SV, Lees TA: Elastic compression stockings for prevention of deep vein thrombosis. Cochrane Database Syst Rev (3):CD001484, 2000

114. Gross T, Kaim AH, Regazzoni P, et al: Current concepts in posttraumatic osteomyelitis: a diagnostic challenge with new imaging options. J Trauma 52:1210, 2002

115. Zollinger PE, Tuinebreijer WE, Kreis RW, et al: Effect of vitamin C on frequency of reflex sympathetic dystrophy in wrist fractures: a randomised trial. Lancet 354:2025, 1999

116. Stanton-Hicks M, Janig W, Hassenbusch S, et al: Reflex sympathetic dystrophy: changing concepts and taxonomy. Pain 63:127, 1995

Acknowledgments

Figures 1, 2, and 12   Thom Graves, CMI.

The authors would like to thank Gregory J. Jurkovich, M.D., F.A.C.S. (Harborview Medical Center, Seattle, Washington), and W.R. Smith, M.D. (Denver Health Medical Center, Denver, Colorado), for their reviewing of the manuscript.

112 INJURIES TO THE PERIPHERAL BLOOD VESSELS

Todd R. Vogel, M.D., M.P.H., and Gregory J. Jurkovich, M.D., F.A.C.S.

Before and during World War II, management of extremity vascular trauma consisted of vessel ligation, which resulted in amputation rates as high as 70%. As surgical techniques improved and primary arterial repair became standard, amputation rates declined to approximately 30%. By the time of the Vietnam War, the use of routine angiography and repair had reduced amputation rates to 15%.[1] On the modern battlefield, the incidence of extremity injury remains high, with 88% of vascular injuries occurring in the extremities.[2] Current management of extremity arterial trauma yields amputation rates ranging from 5% to 20%.[2-4]

In this chapter, we outline the current standard of care for vascular injuries in the extremities. Management of such injuries requires knowledge of mechanisms of injury, awareness of high-risk injury patterns, familiarity with modern diagnostic techniques and their indications, and comprehensive understanding of the assessment, triage, and management decisions that influence outcome in this setting.

Mechanisms and Sites of Extremity Vascular Injury

BLUNT VERSUS PENETRATING TRAUMA

Arterial trauma is typically classified according to the general mechanism of injury—that is, blunt or penetrating—because different mechanisms tend to produce different types of injuries. After blunt trauma, the vascular injury most commonly seen is avulsion, in which the artery is stretched. This stretching results in disruption either of the tunica intima alone or of both the tunica intima and the tunica media, leaving the highly thrombogenic tunica externa to maintain temporary vessel continuity [*see Figure 1*]. Complete occlusion typically occurs when significant intimal damage leads to thrombosis of the artery. Injuries that do not produce occlusion may give rise to an intimal flap, a pseudoaneurysm (secondary to partial arterial injury), or an arteriovenous (AV) fistula.

Penetrating trauma may transect the vessel completely and may be manifested as thrombosis resulting from vessel spasm or frank bleeding. If the vessel is only partially transected, it may contract and continue to bleed; even if it is initially controlled, it may rebleed as the patient is resuscitated and arterial pressure rises toward normal. In many cases of penetrating trauma, the location of a presumed vascular injury may be determined simply by following the path of the penetrating object. If there is evidence of ongoing bleeding from a penetrating vascular injury, prompt operative intervention, without further evaluation, is indicated. The risk of amputation varies: stab wounds are unlikely to lead to amputation, whereas high-velocity firearm injuries with concomitant blast effect and tissue loss are considerably more likely to do so.[5] In modern military contexts, blast injuries account for 50% to 70% of cases of vascular trauma.[2] Vascular trauma from blast wounds may present as thrombosis (related to intimal injury resulting from the application of kinetic force to the tissue) or as deep cavitary injuries with vessel disruption and even segmental arterial loss.

LOCATION OF INJURY AND RISK OF AMPUTATION

Extremity vascular trauma is commonly encountered by surgeons in both urban and rural practices. In urban settings, upper- and lower-extremity injuries account for 40% and 20% of all vascular injuries, respectively.[6] In rural settings, extremity injuries account for approximately 50% of all vascular injuries.[3]

Current military data indicate that the most frequently injured lower-extremity vessel in the setting of penetrating trauma is the superficial femoral artery (SFA), followed by the popliteal artery, the profunda femoris, the tibial arteries, and the common femoral artery (CFA); the most frequently injured upper-extremity vessel

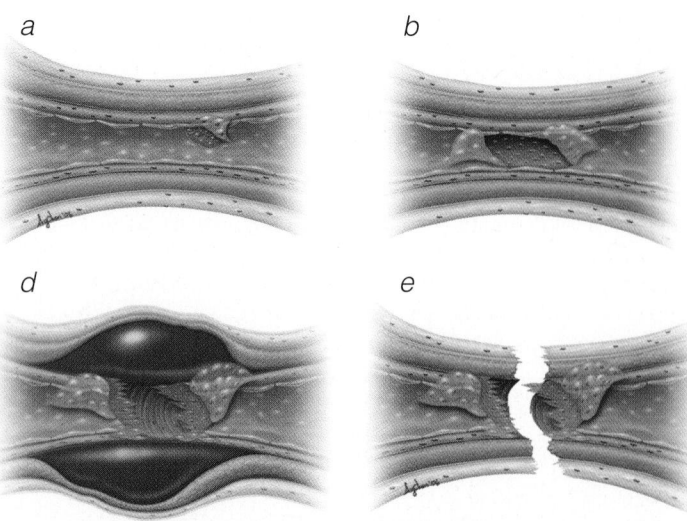

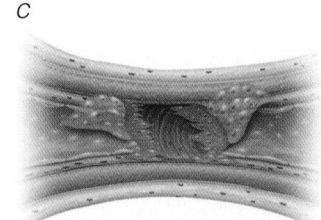

Figure 1 Shown is an avulsion injury, in which the artery is stretched, resulting either in partial (*a*) or complete (*b*) intimal disruption or in complete intimal or medial disruption (*c*), with or without pseudoaneurysm formation (*d*) and complete separation of all layers of the vessel wall (*e*).

is the brachial artery, followed by the radial artery and the ulnar artery.[2] In civilian settings, injuries leading to limb loss often include damage to bones and nerves.

Stepwise logistic regression analysis demonstrates that the following are independent risk factors for amputation: occluded grafts, combined above-the-knee and below-the-knee injury, tense compartments, arterial transections, and associated compound fractures.[5]

Initial Assessment

HISTORY

Assessment of an injured extremity starts with a history, which can be obtained in parallel with the physical examination. The information that should be collected includes the patient's bleeding history at the scene, the time of injury, and the mechanism of injury.

PHYSICAL EXAMINATION

The physical examination is the most important part of the assessment. A careful evaluation of the extremities can provide information on the location and severity of vascular injuries; identify the trajectory and the entrance and exit points of wounds; and suggest appropriate triage and management of vascular injuries.

The initial part of the examination should follow advanced trauma life support (ATLS) guidelines, with attention paid to the ABCs (*A*irway, *B*reathing, and *C*irculation). Areas of obvious hemorrhage should be addressed in the primary survey; more specific evaluation of the extremities for vascular injury can be carried out during the secondary survey. Blood pressure, temperature, and distal pulses are evaluated. Side-to-side symmetry is important; thus, injured extremities should be compared with their uninjured counterparts.

If pulses are absent and a joint dislocation or fracture-dislocation is present, then reduction should be done. Frequently, a pulseless extremity regains pulses once the fracture or dislocation is reduced. If pulses return after reduction, the assessment may move on to the next priority. If pulses do not return, vascular injury is assumed, and treatment of such injury becomes the immediate priority.

Once the initial part of the examination has been carried out, a neurologic examination should be done. Motor and sensory function should be assessed in a distal-to-proximal direction on each extremity. Any gross limb deformities should be reduced and splinted to yield a more anatomic alignment of the extremity and relieve any compromise of neural or vascular structures.

CLINICAL CATEGORIZATION OF VASCULAR INJURY

Traditionally, clinical evidence of vascular injury has been divided into hard and soft signs. Hard signs of extremity vascular injury include arterial bleeding, ongoing hemorrhage with shock, an expanding or pulsatile hematoma, a palpable thrill or audible bruit over the injured area, absent distal pulses, and limb ischemia. When a patient presents with hard signs of vascular injury, immediate surgical exploration and vascular repair are warranted. The exception to this rule is the case where the patient presents with multilevel trauma to an extremity and the level of arterial injury is in question. In this situation, arteriography is indicated—preferably intraoperative angiography to minimize delay in repairing the injury and to facilitate intraoperative decision making.

Soft signs of vascular injury include a history of severe hemorrhage at the scene; hypotension; a stable, small hematoma that is not expanding or pulsatile; diminished or unequal pulses; a neurologic deficit (primary nerve injury occurs immediately after injury, whereas the onset of ischemic neuropathy may be delayed for minutes to hours); and a wound that is in proximity to vascular structures.[7] Management of patients with soft signs of injury presents a more difficult diagnostic dilemma and is discussed in more detail elsewhere (see below).

It is important to keep in mind that palpation of a pulse is a subjective measure and is thus prone to wide interobserver variation. Furthermore, pulses may be palpable distal to major arterial lesions, including complete arterial disruptions.[7,8] These limitations notwithstanding, a precise and well-documented physical examination is an appropriate screening tool for vascular injuries.

NONINVASIVE EVALUATION IN CONJUNCTION WITH PHYSICAL EXAMINATION

In patients with soft signs of arterial injury, the ankle-brachial index (ABI)—also known as the arterial pressure index (API), the Doppler pressure index (DPI), or the ankle-arm index (AAI)—is a highly useful adjunct to the physical examination. The ABI is obtained by placing a blood pressure cuff on the supine patient proximal to the ankle or wrist of the injured limb. The systolic pressure is determined with a Doppler probe at the respective posterior tibial and dorsalis pedis arteries or at the ulnar and radial arteries. The ratio of the highest systolic pressure obtained in the affected extremity to the systolic pressure in an unaffected extremity (most often a brachial artery) is the ABI [*see Figure 2*].

A 1991 study assessed the sensitivity and specificity of Doppler-derived arterial pressure measurements in trauma patients undergoing evaluation for possible extremity vascular injury.[9] An ABI was obtained in 100 consecutive injured limbs, and all patients then underwent contrast arteriography. An ABI lower than 0.90 was 87% sensitive and 97% specific for arterial injury. The authors concluded that in the absence of hard signs of arterial injury, ABI is a reasonable substitute for screening arteriography, particularly if continued observation can be ensured.

The use of the ABI has been extended to the management of blunt extremity trauma associated with high-risk fractures and dislocations. In a controlled trial that included 75 consecutive patients with blunt high-risk orthopedic injuries, the negative predictive value of a Doppler-derived ABI higher than 0.9 was 100%. In the 70% of patients who had an ABI higher than 0.9, clinical follow-up revealed no major or minor arterial injuries. Of the 30% who had an ABI lower than 0.9, 70% had an injury that was diagnosed by arteriography, and 50% of these injuries necessitated operative repair.[10,11]

It is important to remember that there are several situations in which a vascular injury may not lead to an abnormal ABI. For example, an injury that is considered nonaxial (e.g., an injury to the profunda femoris in the thigh or the profunda brachii in the arm) may not lower the ABI and thus may be missed. In addition, a lesion that does not disrupt arterial flow (e.g., an intimal flap or a transected artery that is maintained in continuity by connective tissue) may yield a normal ABI. Finally, an AV fistula may be associated with a normal ABI.

Certain patient characteristics may affect the ABI as well. For example, noninvasive measurement of the ABI may fail to detect an injury if the patient is severely hypotensive or in shock and the clinical circumstances do not permit placement of a cuff around an injured site or extremity. Moreover, elderly patients may have abnormal preinjury ABIs as a consequence of atherosclerosis. In these situations, the concept of symmetry is crucial. It is also important to consider the possibility that the patient may have previously undergone peripheral vascular surgery, though this is rarely the case in the typical trauma population.

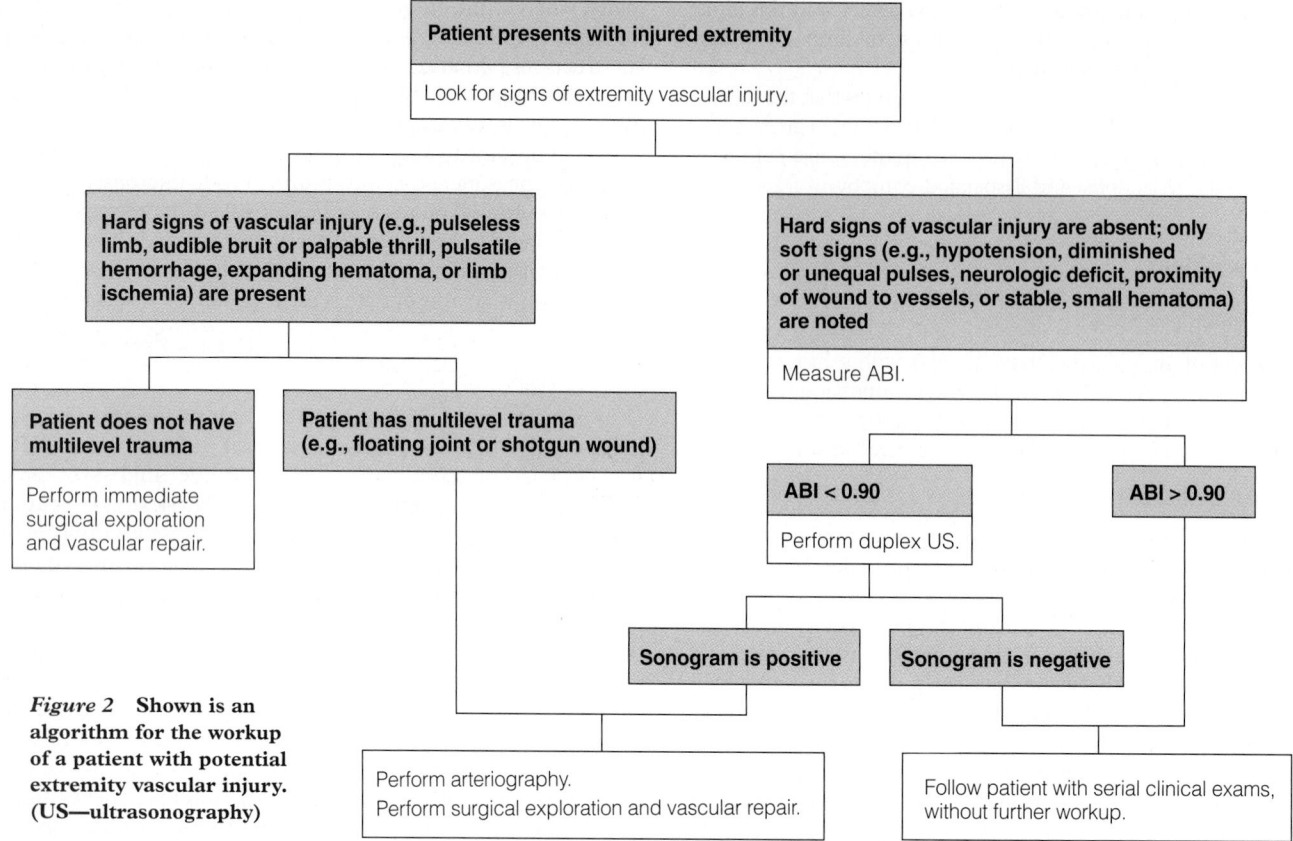

Figure 2 Shown is an algorithm for the workup of a patient with potential extremity vascular injury. (US—ultrasonography)

IMAGING

Diagnostic Angiography

Arteriography has a sensitivity of 95% to 100% and a specificity of 90% and 98% and is therefore considered the gold standard for evaluation or confirmation of arterial injury.[12,13] In the setting of extremity injury, however, nonselective angiography has not been found to be cost effective, and it is often overly sensitive, detecting minimal injuries that do not call for further management.[14-16] Furthermore, arteriography can be time consuming, can delay definitive treatment, and can give rise to complications of its own, including renal contrast toxicity and pseudoaneurysm formation.[16]

Angiography should be reserved for patients with soft signs of vascular injury and an abnormal ABI; there is little reason to perform angiography in a patient with hard signs of injury, unless an intraoperative angiogram is needed to delineate the anatomy. In no case should transport to the OR for definitive treatment be delayed so that arteriography can be performed. Several reviews have supported reserved use of arteriography in this setting. A 2002 report concluded that physical examination in conjunction with measurement of the DPI (i.e., the ABI) was an appropriate method of identifying significant vascular injuries caused by penetrating extremity trauma.[17] Patients with normal physical examinations and normal DPIs could safely be discharged; angiography was indicated only for asymptomatic patients with abnormal DPIs.[17]

Duplex Ultrasonography

Several studies have evaluated the efficacy and accuracy of duplex ultrasonography in the setting of extremity vascular trauma. The sensitivity of duplex ultrasonography is between 90% and 95%, the specificity is in the range of 99%, and the overall accuracy is between 96% and 98%. These figures approach those reported for arteriography in the evaluation of similar vascular trauma patients. Duplex ultrasonography has no inherent risks, and it may be more cost-effective for screening certain injuries than either arteriography or exploration. Duplex ultrasonography has been shown to be a reliable method of diagnosis in patients with potential peripheral vascular injuries.[18,19]

The advantages of duplex ultrasonography notwithstanding, it is important to remember that this imaging modality may not be equally appropriate in all scenarios. As an example, given that duplex ultrasonography is highly operator dependent, the results of duplex examination may not be reliable in situations where the examiner has not had sufficient access to the technology or experience with the technique. As another example, injuries in certain anatomic locations (e.g., injuries in regions where bone structures interpose themselves, injuries in areas with concomitant soft tissue injuries, injuries that dive into the pelvis or chest, and injuries in patients with a large body habitus) may not be well visualized by duplex ultrasonography. Such considerations are important in assessing patients with potential extremity vascular injuries; if either applies in a given case, angiography may be required.

Computed Tomographic Angiography

Ongoing radiologic advances have led some centers to consider using computed tomographic angiography (CTA) to evaluate arterial injury. To date, this approach has been formally evaluated in only a modest number of studies, though there is reason to believe that it will be more widely used in the future. A few small series found CTA to have a sensitivity and specificity of approximately 90% in the evaluation of large arteries; other studies suggested that this modality might be a reasonable alternative to conventional arteriography for diagnosis of traumatic arterial injuries. Before CTA can be considered equivalent to the gold standard, large randomized trials will have to be performed.[20,21]

MANAGEMENT ALGORITHMS

On the basis of the data available on noninvasive assessment and diagnostic imaging, an effective management algorithm can be created [*see Figure 2*].[22,23] If the ABI is higher than 0.9, the patient may be followed clinically without further workup. If the ABI is lower than 0.9, arteriography or duplex ultrasonography

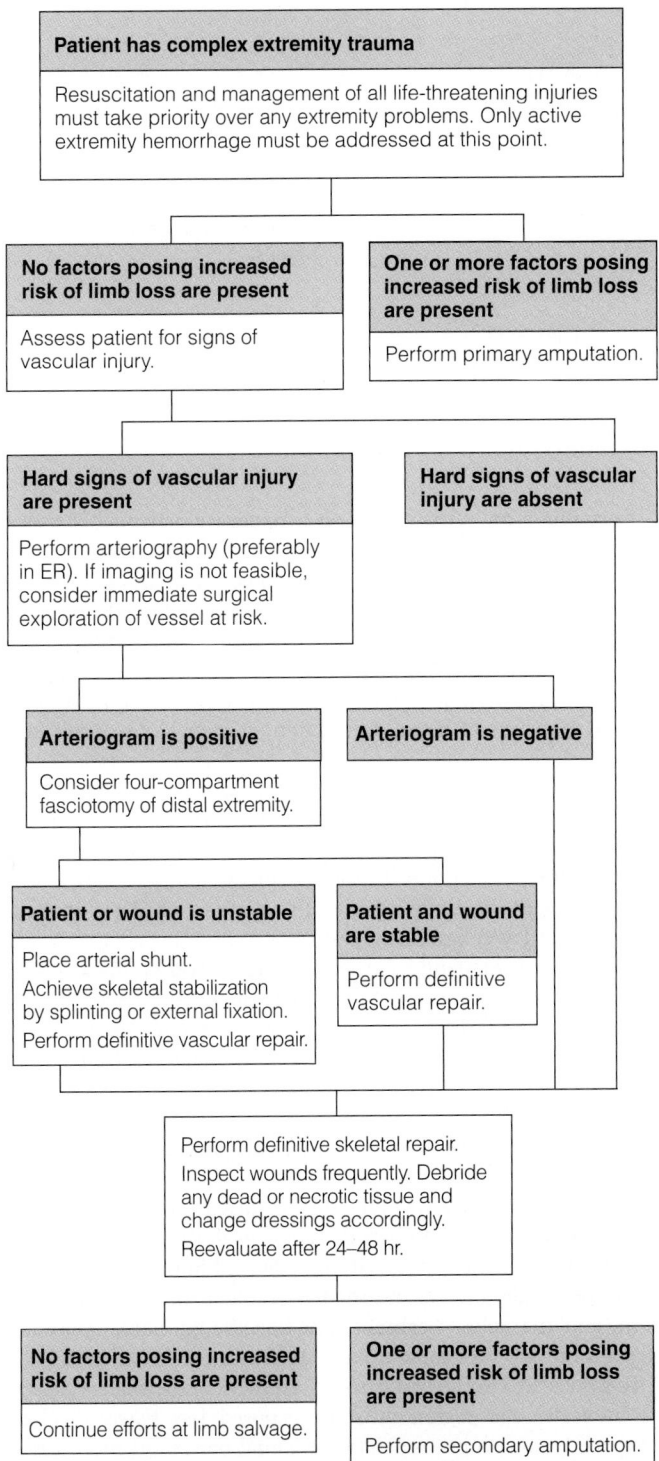

Figure 3 Shown is an algorithm for the management of complex extremity trauma, adapted from an algorithm developed by the ACS Committee on Trauma. The full annotated version of the ACS algorithm is available at the ACS Web site (http://www.facs.org/trauma/publications/mancomplextrauma.pdf).

should be performed, the results of which will dictate the final plan of action. It is impossible to define every single clinical scenario that could possibly give rise to arterial trauma. The ABI fulfills the requirements of a useful screening tool, in that it is sensitive, specific, reproducible, noninvasive, and inexpensive.

Management of complex extremity trauma involving soft tissue, nerve, and arterial injury must include consideration of primary amputation to increase patient survival. This issue is well addressed by an algorithm for complex extremity trauma created by the Committee on Trauma of the American College of Surgeons (ACS) [*see Figure 3*].[24] The algorithm incorporates the environment, the type of injury sustained, and the stability of the patient into the process of deciding whether to attempt limb salvage or perform amputation.

HIGH-RISK LOWER-EXTREMITY INJURIES

Certain lower-extremity injuries—such as knee dislocations, displaced medial tibial plateau fractures and other displaced bicondylar fractures around the knee, open or segmental distal femoral shaft fractures, floating joints, gunshot wounds in proximity to neurovascular structures, and mangled extremities—are associated with a particularly high incidence of vascular trauma.[25] The most commonly injured lower-extremity artery in the setting of blunt trauma is the popliteal artery, which starts below the adductor hiatus and ends at the soleus arch. Because the vessel's start and end points areas are relatively fixed, there is a potential for significant stretch injury at the knee joint. A purely ligamentous knee dislocation is associated with a high risk of arterial injury, despite the lack of sharp fracture fragments. The risk of popliteal injury may be as high as 40% in patients with knee dislocations. Although the arterial disruption may be only a minor intimal tear and examination may reveal no evidence of injury, such internal tears are thrombogenic and may result in delayed thrombosis. Because lower extremities are often splinted and covered during stabilization, delayed thrombosis may not be recognized in a timely fashion.

Workup of a patient with a posterior knee dislocation may or may not require angiography. Some authors maintain that angiography is unnecessary in routine evaluation of patients with blunt lower-extremity trauma who present with a normal neurovascular examination and that angiography or duplex ultrasonography should be used selectively for patients with diminished pulses who lack associated indications for mandatory operative exploration.[26] In addition, the use of the ABI has been validated in the setting of blunt lower extremity trauma. The ABI has proved to be a rapid, reliable, noninvasive tool for diagnosing vascular injury associated with knee dislocation. At present, the evidence suggests that routine arteriography for all patients with knee dislocation is not indicated but that a secondary study should be ordered when the ABI is low or the neurovascular examination yields abnormal results.[10,12,27] When managing a posterior knee dislocation, one should have a high index of suspicion for vascular injury and a low threshold for obtaining secondary studies.

Management

INITIAL TREATMENT CONSIDERATIONS

Time to Repair

A warm ischemia time of less than 6 hours is generally accepted as the standard interval within which arterial continuity must be restored to prevent permanent damage to the soft tissues.[28,29]

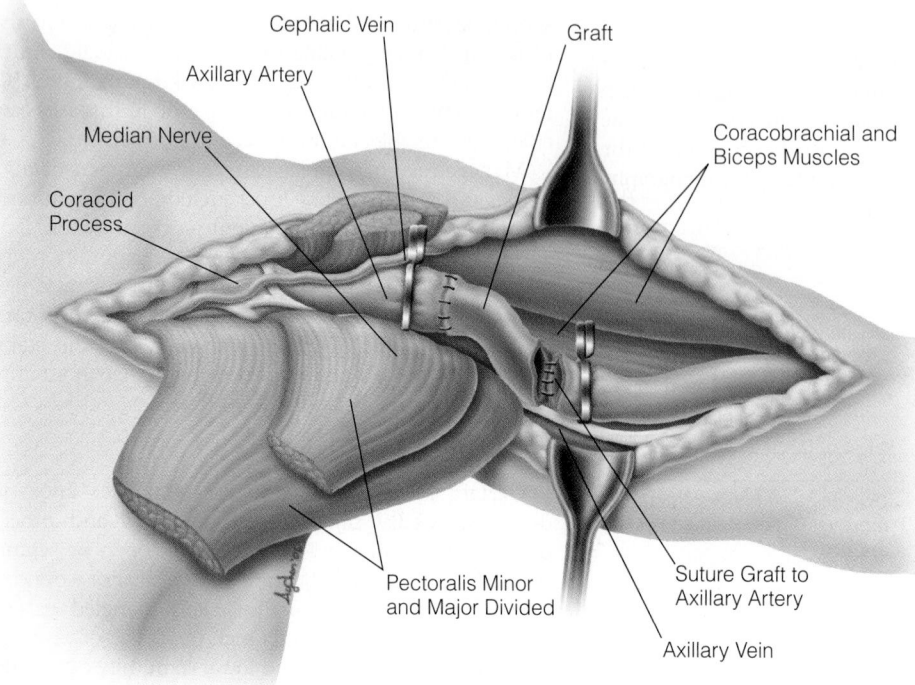

Figure 4 **Depicted is exposure of the axillary artery.**

This interval may vary depending on several factors, including the level of injury, previous vascular disease, the presence of collateral vessels, and previous extremity surgery.

Vascular Control

As has long been a dictum in vascular surgery, it is important to gain proximal control of the injured vessel—meaning control at a point one level higher than the injured area—before assessing the site of the injury. This maneuver reduces blood loss from the injury during repair and minimizes hematoma formation and subsequent loss of tissue planes. Entering an injured area without first obtaining proximal control can be dangerous, can cause additional injury to other neurovascular structures, and can result in belated attempts to gain proximal control in a hurried fashion, which may cause secondary injury to the vessel. In situations where proximal control has not yet been obtained or cannot be obtained, an intraluminal or intra-arterial balloon (e.g., a Fogarty catheter or even a Foley catheter, in larger arteries) may be used to achieve temporary control. This simple technique sometimes proves to be lifesaving.

Use of Tourniquets

Surgeons have long debated the use of tourniquets in the management of vascular trauma. Undoubtedly, the tourniquet can be a lifesaving addition to the surgeon's armamentarium if used correctly and appropriately. Proximal application of a tourniquet may facilitate examination, permit definitive control of a bleeding point, and help determine whether significant nerve, muscle, or tendon injury has occurred. Even if a tourniquet is kept in place for only a short period, it may be invaluable for the control of hemorrhage.

When a tourniquet is used, it must be applied correctly. Incorrectly applied tourniquets actually increase bleeding from an extremity wound and increase the risk of early exsanguination. This paradoxical effect results from occlusion of the lower-pressure venous outflow and inadequate occlusion of the higher-pressure arterial inflow. A properly applied tourniquet causes substantial pain, which should be managed with intravenous or intramuscular analgesics.[30]

Tourniquets are often placed on hypotensive patients before resuscitation, and these patients sometimes start bleeding through their tourniquets when resuscitation is initiated. Accordingly, tourniquets should be continuously monitored and tightened for maximal effectiveness during resuscitation. In the hospital setting, pneumatic tourniquets may be used as temporizing proximal clamps in patients with multiple injuries, as well as patients with blast injuries, massive soft-tissue destruction, or mangled extremities.[30]

EXPOSURE OF INJURY

Once the decision has been made to transport the patient to the operating room, the next step is to determine the operative approach that will optimize exposure of the injury. Often, exposures of upper-extremity arteries prove more challenging than exposures of lower-extremity vessels, primarily because they are performed less frequently. A thorough discussion of all extremity vascular exposures is beyond the scope of this chapter. Accordingly, in what follows, we discuss those exposures of the upper and lower extremities that are particularly useful in the trauma setting.

Upper Extremity

Operative exposure of potential vascular injuries in the upper extremity requires detailed knowledge of the anatomy of the axillary and brachial arteries. The axillary artery is surrounded by muscle on all sides, including the chest wall, the pectoral girdle, and the brachium. The vessel itself is divided into three segments by the pectoralis minor: the medial segment, the posterior segment, and the lateral segment. The specific operative approach depends on which of these three segments has been injured.

To gain access to the first (medial) segment of the axillary artery, the infraclavicular region must be exposed [*see Figure 4*]. This approach may also be useful for proximal control of more distal injuries, depending on the location and type of injury being treated. A horizontal incision is made 2 cm below the middle third of the clavicle, and dissection continues through the subcutaneous fascia, the pectoral fascia, the pectoralis fibers, and the clavipectoral fascia. At this level, the neurovascular bundle can be identified,

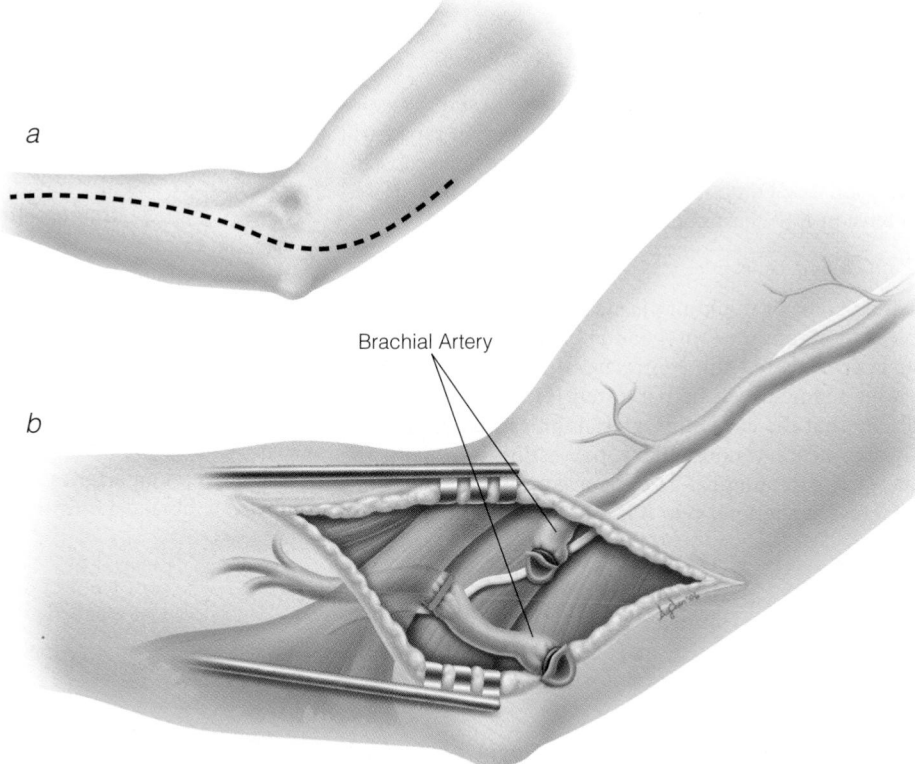

Figure 5 (*a*) Depicted is exposure of the brachial artery, with removal of an occluded segment to restore blood flow to the hand and forearm. (*b*) The incision is extended onto the forearm in an S shape to afford complete exposure.

with the artery lying superior and deep to the axillary vein. Exposure and control of the artery are obtained by means of sharp dissection. To gain access to the second (posterior) and third (lateral) portions of the axillary artery, an incision is made along the lateral border of the pectoralis major from the chest wall to the biceps. The coracobrachialis can then be identified; the neurovascular sheath is located at the posterior border of this muscle.[31]

As an alternative, the deltopectoral approach may be employed to gain access to any of the segments of the axillary artery. An incision is made from the midpoint of the clavicle along the anterior border of the deltoid muscle. The incision is deepened through subcutaneous tissue to reach the intramuscular groove. The cephalic vein is retracted, and the axillary artery may then be traced proximally and distally.

To expose the brachial artery, a longitudinal incision is made in the medial arm between the biceps and the triceps [*see Figure 5*], and dissection is carried out through the subcutaneous tissue. The basilic vein can then be identified. This vein is retracted inferiorly, and the neurovascular bundle is exposed by opening the deep fascia at the medial border of the biceps. To expose the brachial artery along with the arteries in the forearm, an S-shaped incision is made over the antecubital fossa. The superior portion of the incision follows the medial border of the biceps muscle and extends horizontally in the antecubital fossa; the inferior portion is made laterally on the volar forearm. Such an incision affords complete exposure of all of the target vessels. On subcutaneous dissection, multiple veins can be seen, including the median cubital vein, the cephalic vein, and the basilic vein. Exposure of the deep fascia and entrance into the bicipital aponeurosis allows exposure of the median nerve, the brachial artery, and two deep veins. The incision can be extended to track the radial and ulnar arteries.[31]

Lower Extremity

In addressing potential vascular injuries in the lower extremity, it is essential to be able to expose the CFA and the popliteal artery.

To gain access to the femoral artery, a vertical skin incision is made midway between the superior iliac spine and the pubic tubercle [*see Figure 6*]. This incision is opened to expose the superficial epigastric and superficial circumflex branches. The fascia lata is incised along the medial portion of the sartorius up to the inguinal ligament, and the femoral sheath is exposed and opened. (In an emergency situation where retroperitoneal or abdominal exposure is not warranted, the inguinal ligament can also be divided if necessary for more proximal control.) The CFA can then be identified lateral to the femoral vein and can be tracked downward to the point where it bifurcates into the profunda femoris and the SFA. Typically, the profunda femoris branches laterally off of the CFA 3 to 5 cm distal to the inguinal ligament; the SFA lies superior to the profunda femoris. The incision may be extended inferiorly as necessary to locate more distal vascular injuries.[31]

In the setting of trauma, exposure of the popliteal artery is best accomplished via a medial approach. To expose the proximal (supragenicular) popliteal artery, an incision is made in the distal portion of the thigh along the anterior border of the sartorius [*see Figure 7*]. The fascia can be incised, the muscle retracted posteriorly, and the popliteal vessels may be identified. It may be necessary to divide the adductor tendon or the semimembranous muscle for exposure. If necessary, this incision can be extended down the leg for exposure of the tibial vessels. To expose the distal (infragenicular) popliteal artery, an incision is made just behind the posteromedial surface of the tibia [*see Figure 8*]. The gastrocnemius is retracted posteriorly, and the semitendinous, gracilis, and sartorius muscles are retracted superiorly. (These muscles may also be divided if more exposure is needed.) The popliteal vein is the first and most superficial portion of the neurovascular bundle. The tibial nerve is posterior and medial to the popliteal artery and should always be identified and protected during the dissection. If necessary, this exposure can be extended inferiorly to the tibial peroneal trunk for control of the distal arteries.[31]

DEFINITIVE REPAIR OF INJURY

Primary Repair versus Grafting

Once the need for operation has been established and the exposure chosen, the next step to determine which type of repair will be performed. Primary repair is preferred when possible; substantial proximal and distal mobilization of the artery may be required to allow a tension-free anastomosis.

Choice of Conduit

Often, the extent of the injury is such that primary repair is impossible and a conduit (autogenous or prosthetic) must be placed. It is crucial that the contralateral leg be prepared, so that a venous segment can be harvested if needed. In view of the possibility that the extremity arterial injury may be accompanied by significant venous injury, harvesting vein from the ipsilateral leg is discouraged. The most commonly used conduit is the great saphenous vein (GSV), which can be cut and made to form a larger conduit by using a spiral technique or a panel graft technique.[32] The superficial femoral vein (SFV) may also be used as a conduit,[33] but the dissection required is tedious and time-consuming and may be associated with significant morbidity.

Autogenous conduits should be used in contaminated wounds when direct vascular repair is not feasible. Nonautogenous conduits (e.g., polytatrafuoroethylene [PTFE] or Dacron grafts) may also be employed, but as a rule, they should be reserved for extreme situations in which native vein is not available. For patients with severe peripheral vascular injuries but without adequate available vein, PTFE appears to be an acceptable choice for primary reconstruction; graft infection is rare if the graft is covered with healthy tissue.[34,35]

Management of Arteries in Distal Extremity

On occasion, arteries in the distal extremities (e.g., the radial, ulnar, or tibial arteries) may have to be repaired or ligated after

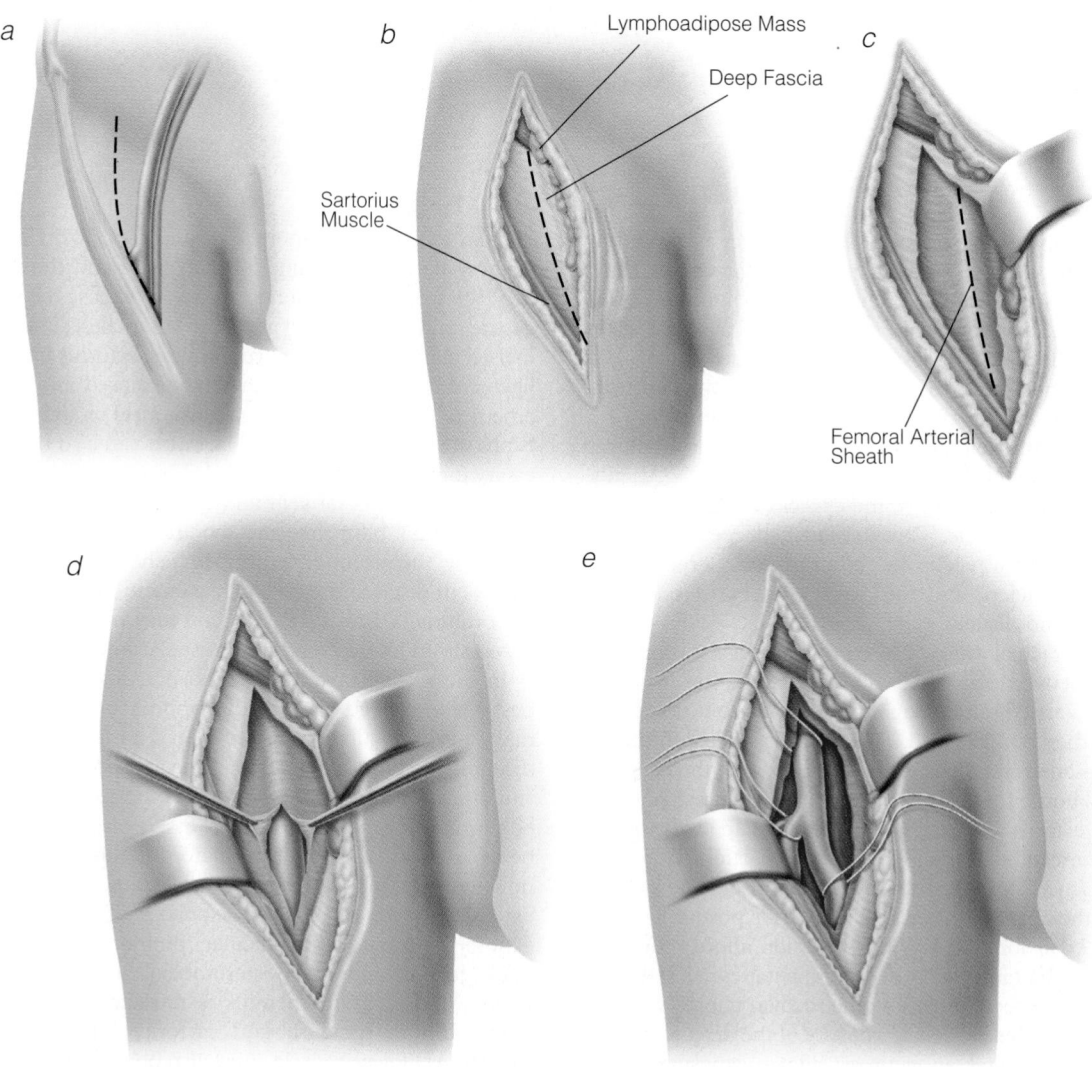

Figure 6 Depicted is exposure of the femoral artery. (*a*) A curved 10 to 12 cm. skin incision is made slightly lateral to the pulsation of the femoral artery. (*b*) Lymphoadipose tissue is retracted to expose the deep fascia overlying the course of the femoral artery. (*c*) The deep fascia is incised, exposing the femoral arterial sheath, which is then opened along its axis (*d*). (*e*) The common and superficial femoral arteries are mobilized and encircled with Silastic vessel loops.

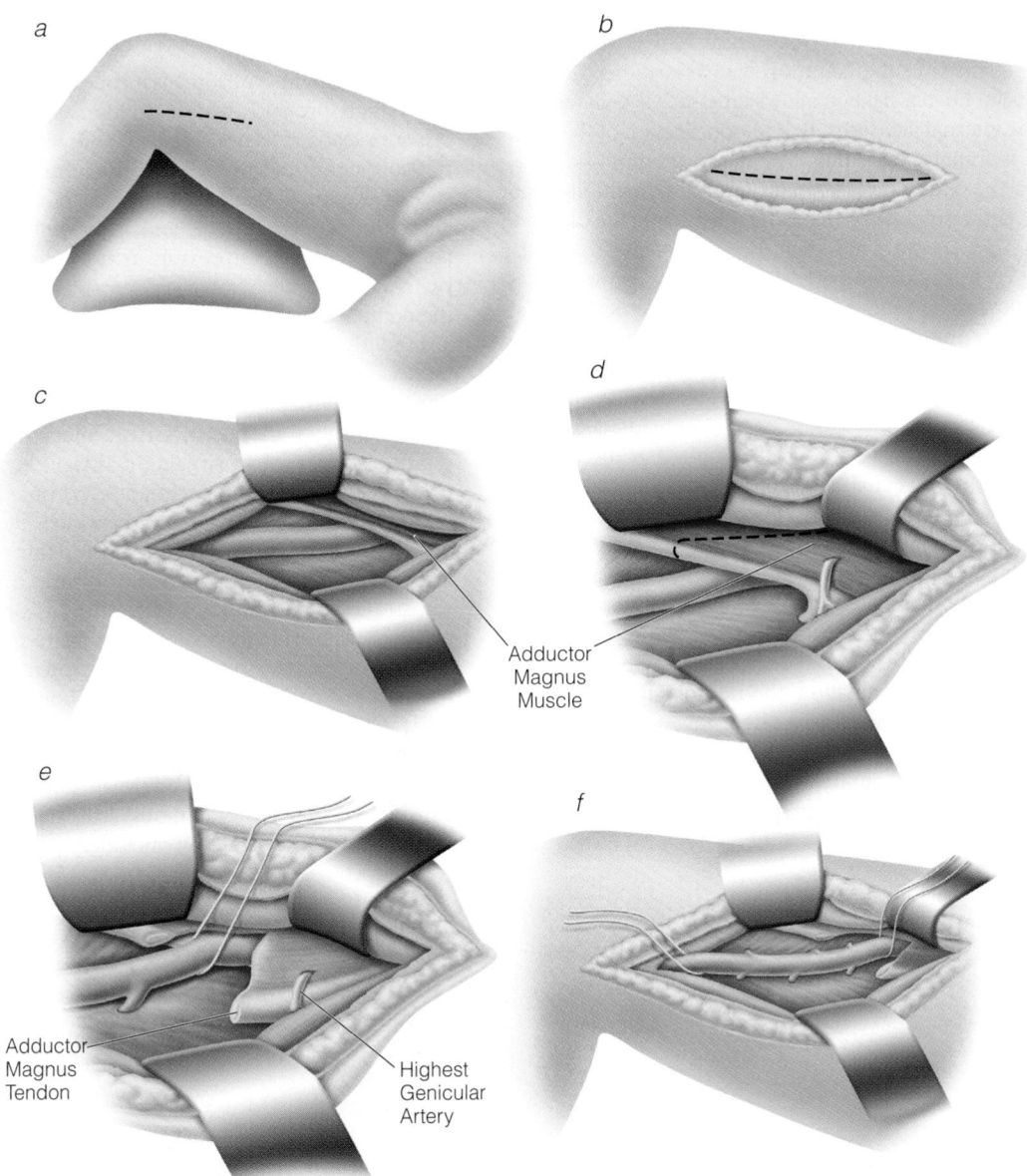

Figure 7 Depicted is medial exposure of the proximal popliteal artery. (*a*) An incision is made in the lower third of the thigh, anterior to the sartorius muscle. (*b*) The deep fascia is incised, and the sartorius muscle is retracted posteriorly, allowing the popliteal artery to be readily palpated. (*c*) The popliteal arterial sheath is opened, exposing the vessel and its surrounding venules. The adductor magnus tendon may be seen covering the proximal end of the artery (*d*), and it may have to be divided (*e*) to provide better exposure of the artery. (*f*) The popliteal artery, freed of the venous plexus, is mobilized between two vessel loops.

trauma. In most patients, there is little need for repair of these arteries, which can typically be ligated without deleterious effects. The safety of ligation is predicated on the presence of adequate arterial flow from the nonaffected arteries, as well as retrograde blood flow from an intact palmar or plantar arch.[36,37] Repair of injuries to these arteries is associated with the possibility of embolization or other surgical problems. In addition, the patency rate for grafts in the distal extremities tends to be low.[38]

Repair of Venous Injuries

In most regions of the extremities, repair of any concomitant venous injuries is recommended, on the grounds that it may help keep an arterial repair open and prevent postoperative edema. Primary repair involves closing the venotomy transversely; this may be facilitated by mobilizing the proximal and distal venous

structures. If primary repair is not possible, a patch is recommended. To augment venous flow and help maintain patency, an AV fistula may be created, then ligated at a later point. The administration of heparin and the use of a foot pump may also help maintain the patency of a venous repair, as well as reduce the hypercoagulability associated with Virchow's triad and venous occlusion.

If the vein cannot be repaired, it may have to be ligated. For injuries to the tibial vein and some injuries to the brachial vein or a more distal arm vein, ligation may be chosen over repair, with few deleterious consequences. For injuries to the popliteal vein or the SFV, repair is recommended when possible to optimize continued venous drainage of the extremity. As noted [*see* Choice of Conduit, *above*], if vein is harvested, it should come from the contralateral leg so as to permit continued outflow from the injured lower extremity.[39,40]

If proximal ligation of a lower-extremity vein is required, it should be performed on the common iliac vein rather than the external iliac vein. Higher ligation allows cross-pelvis collateral circulation via the internal iliac veins. In addition, ligation of the external iliac vein is fraught with difficulty. Every attempt should be made to repair the vein to prevent major morbidity, including poor venous return and resultant severe edema. Ligation of the common femoral vein (CFV) is also not ideal, because of the risk of leg edema; however, if ligation at the level of the CFV proves necessary, it does allow some venous return flow via the cruciate collateral vessels, the obturator vein (from the medial circumflex femoral vein), and the gluteal vein (from the lateral circumflex femoral vein).

Postoperative Care

After repair of a vascular injury, patients require 24 hours of monitoring in the intensive care unit for serial pulse and Doppler assessments, monitoring of hemodynamic status, and evaluation of the site of the repair. In addition, patients must be watched for the development of metabolic derangements (e.g., metabolic acidosis, hyperkalemia, myoglobinuria, and renal failure) after hemorrhagic shock and reperfusion of ischemic limbs. Changes in the findings from physical examination, the neurologic status of the extremity, or the ABI warrant immediate investigation, usually beginning with duplex ultrasonography. Typically, a duplex examination is also performed in the early postoperative period to establish a baseline for subsequent surveillance of the graft or repair.

MANAGEMENT OF COMPARTMENT SYNDROME

Compartment syndrome is a condition characterized by abnormally high pressure within a closed space. The elevated tissue pressure leads to venous obstruction within the space. When the pressure continues to increase, the intramuscular arteriolar pressure is eventually exceeded. At that point, blood can no longer enter the capillary space, and the result is shunting within the compartment. If the pressure is not released, muscle and nerve ischemia occurs, leading to irreversible damage to the contents of the compartment.[41]

Underlying pathologic processes that reduce the size or increase the contents of a compartment include hemorrhage, reperfusion edema, a tight cast, constrictive dressings, and pneumatic antishock garments. Crush injury may be associated with rapid development of swelling and rigid compartments. The key to the diagnosis of compartment syndrome is continuous assessment of any extremity injury in which elevated pressures may develop. It must always be remembered that the diagnosis is a clinical one; although compartment pressures may be measured, clinical suspicion and findings suggestive of compartment syndrome on physical examination should suffice to mandate therapy.

Current management of compartment syndrome is derived from a 1970 review by Patman and Thompson, in which fasciotomy was performed after arterial reconstruction in 164 patients with peripheral vascular disease.[42] The investigators concluded that fasciotomy could result in limb salvage and implied that it should be considered after restoration of arterial inflow to an extremity. Indications for fasciotomy included pain on palpation of the

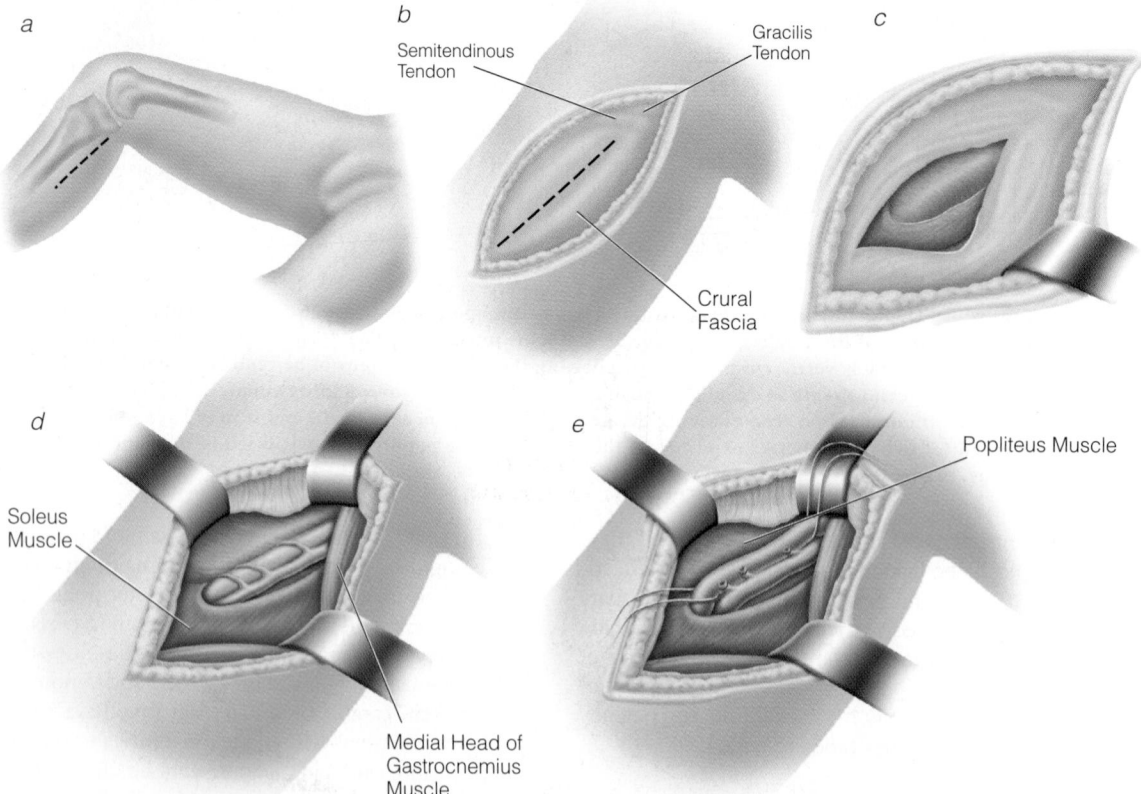

Figure 8 Depicted is medial exposure of the distal popliteal artery. (*a*) **An incision is made just behind the posteromedial surface of the tibia.** (*b*) **The crural fascia is exposed.** (*c*) **The fascia is incised, exposing the vascular bundle.** (*d*) **The medial head of the gastrocnemius muscle is retracted posteriorly, exposing the distal popliteal vessels and the arcade of the soleus muscle.** (*e*) **The distal popliteal artery is freed and mobilized between vessel loops.**

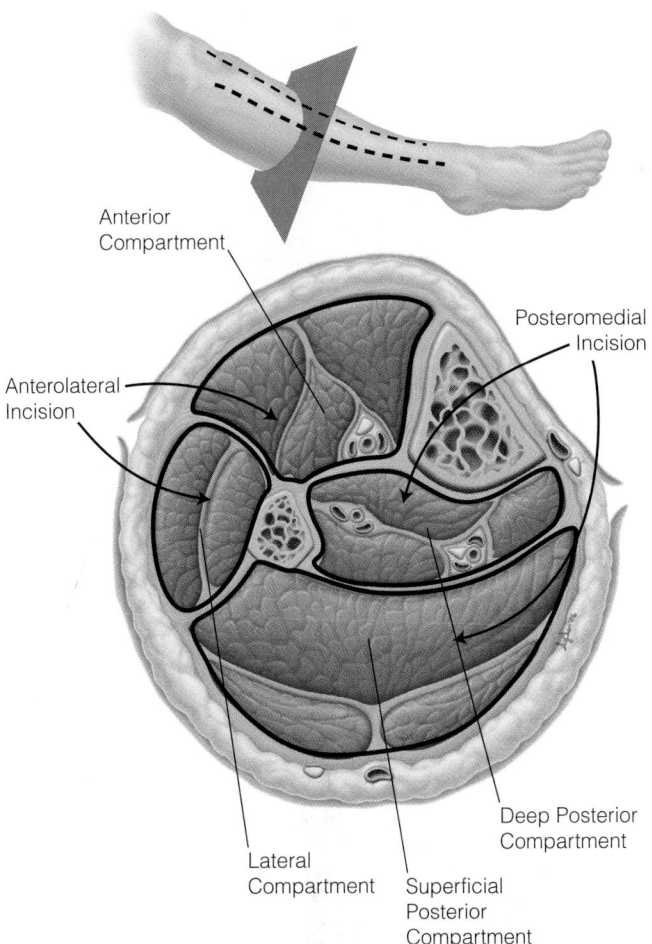

Figure 9 (*a*) Illustrated is the two-incision technique for lower leg decompression in compartment syndrome. Two vertical skin incisions are made from knee to ankle, separated by a skin bridge at least 8 cm wide. (*b*) Fasciotomies are then performed in all four compartments along the dashed lines.

swollen compartment, reproduction of symptoms with passive muscle stretch, a sensory deficit in the territory of a nerve traversing the compartment, muscle weakness, diminished pulses (a very late sign), and compartment pressure exceeding 30 to 35 mm Hg.

It has been noted that the difference between the diastolic pressure and the measured compartment pressure may be a more reliable clinical indicator of compartment syndrome than the compartment pressure by itself. A difference of less than 30 mm Hg between the two pressures is significant and may be the most reliable indicator of when fasciotomy is warranted.

There are a number of clinical situations in which fasciotomy should be considered: when there is a 4- to 6-hour delay before revascularization, when arterial injuries are present in conjunction with venous injuries, when crush injuries or high–kinetic energy injuries have been sustained, when vascular repair has already been performed (reperfusion), when an artery or vein has been ligated, when a patient is comatose or has a head injury and physical examination is impossible, and when a patient has tense compartments or elevated compartment pressures. In these scenarios, fasciotomy should be considered as a prophylactic maneuver.

Fasciotomy

The lower leg contains four osseofascial compartments: the anterior compartment, the lateral compartment, the superficial posterior compartment, and the deep posterior compartment. The thigh contains three osseofascial compartments: the quadriceps, the hamstrings, and the adductors. For fasciotomies of the lower leg, there are two techniques: perifibular fasciotomy and the double-incision technique. Perifibular fasciotomy affords access to all four compartments of the leg via a single lateral incision that extends from the head of the fibula to the ankle, following the general line of the fibula. The double-incision technique employs two vertical skin incisions that are separated by a bridge of skin at least 8 cm wide [*see Figure 9*]. The first incision extends from knee to ankle and is centered over the interval between the anterior and lateral compartments; the second also extends from knee to ankle and is centered 1 to 2 cm behind the posteromedial border of the tibia.[41] Although decompression in the lower extremity may be achieved via either of the two techniques, the double-incision technique is preferred in the setting of trauma because it readily ensures that all four compartments have been decompressed.

The forearm consists of three osseofascial compartments: the superficial flexor compartment, the deep flexor compartment, and the extensor compartment. To decompress the upper extremity, a volar fasciotomy, a dorsal fasciotomy, or both may be performed. A volar fasciotomy decompresses the superficial and deep flexor compartments of the forearm via a single skin incision.[41] This incision begins medial to the biceps tendon, crosses the elbow crease, proceeds toward the radial side of the forearm, and extends distally along the medial border of the brachioradialis, finally continuing across the palm along the thenar crease [*see Figure 10*]. After the superficial and deep flexor compartments of the forearm are decompressed, intraoperative pressure measurements may be obtained to help determine whether fasciotomy is necessary to decompress the extensor compartment. If the pressure continues to be elevated in the extensor compartment, a dorsal fasciotomy should be performed. With the arm pronated, a straight incision is made from the lateral epicondyle to the midline of the wrist.[41]

After fasciotomy, both the fascia and the skin are left widely open. The skin defects may be closed with skin grafts at the time of original operation, provided that this can be done without excessive tension or pressure. Alternatively, the patient may be returned to the OR after the swelling resolves for delayed skin closure (with the fascia left open) or split-thickness skin grafting, as indicated.

It is important to consider fasciotomy in patients with arterial injuries associated with crush injury and venous injury or occlusion. These secondary injuries may be associated with a higher risk of compartment syndrome than either isolated arterial injuries or ischemia-reperfusion alone.[43] In any setting, the most important concerns in performing a fasciotomy are that the procedure must be done in a timely manner and that all of the compartments must be completely decompressed.

Special Considerations

MANAGEMENT OF INTIMAL INJURIES

How best to manage small traumatic intimal injuries identified by means of angiography has been the subject of considerable debate. In general, patients who have injuries shorter than 2 mm and involving less than 50% of the vessel circumference, with no noted pulse deficits, may be placed on an antiplatelet regimen and followed clinically; evidence from animal studies supports this approach.[44] There is some clinical evidence to suggest that antiplatelet medication (e.g., acetylsalicylic acid) and observation alone may be adequate treatment in such patients; however, addi-

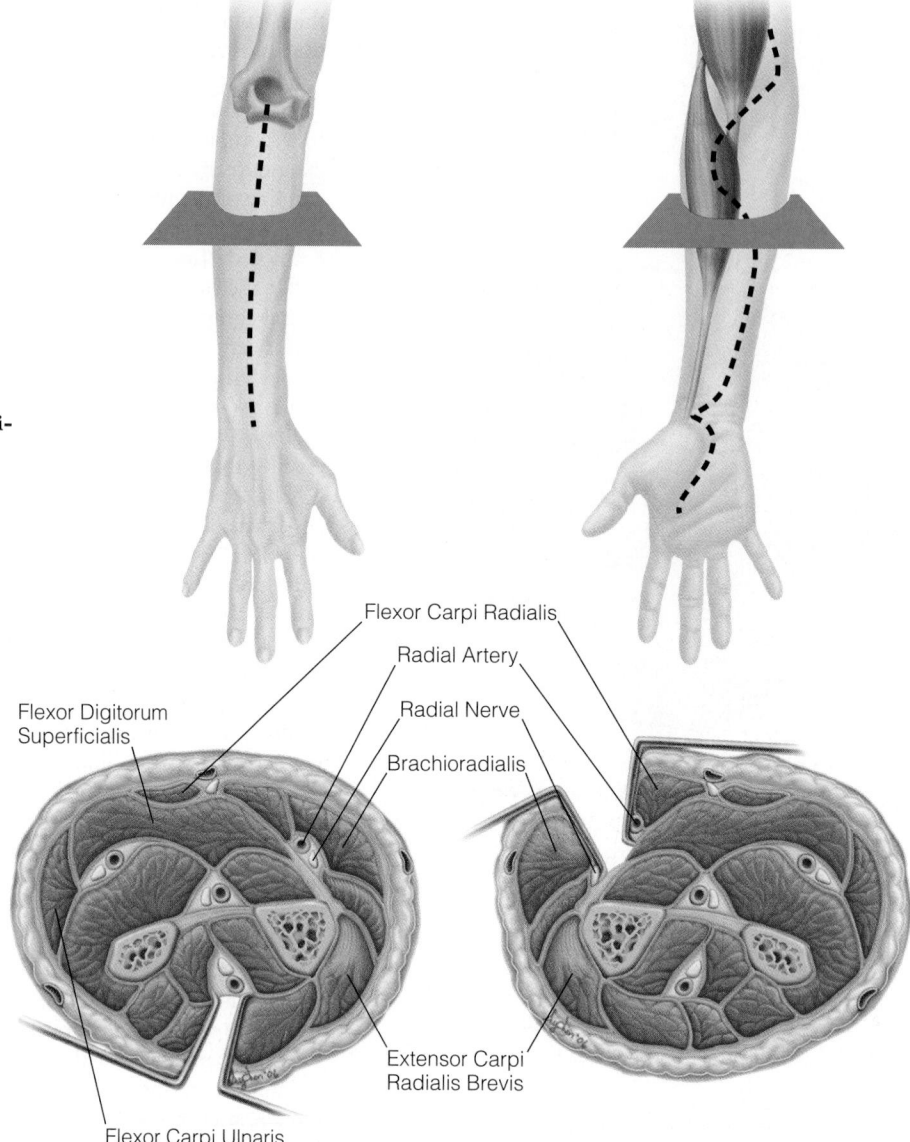

Figure 10 **Shown are incisions for forearm decompression in compartment syndrome.**

Flexor Carpi Radialis
Radial Artery
Flexor Digitorum Superficialis
Radial Nerve
Brachioradialis
Extensor Carpi Radialis Brevis
Flexor Carpi Ulnaris

tional follow-up studies are required before this recommendation can be confirmed.[45]

Even though some cases can be treated conservatively, it is important not to underestimate the potential importance of angiographically identified intimal injuries. Patients with such injuries are at risk for the development of a pseudoaneurysm, AV fistula, dissection, or even thrombosis.[44,46,47]

ANTICOAGULATION

Whether anticoagulation is indicated in patients with vascular trauma is also debatable. It has been suggested that early administration of systemic anticoagulant therapy (heparin, 100 U/kg) may reduce amputation rates by preventing microvascular thrombosis. There is some evidence that anticoagulation may improve limb salvage rates while posing only a minimal risk of bleeding complications.[48] Systemic anticoagulation may be contraindicated in certain situations, such as active hemorrhage, coagulopathy, and craniocerebral injury. If heparin cannot be given systemically, it may be administered locally during the operation, at the site of the arterial repair.

ENDOVASCULAR INTERVENTION

At present, although there are several potential uses for endovascular techniques in the trauma setting, there are no clear indications for such interventions in the management of extremity vascular injuries. The reality is that there are few long-term data on the use of stents in the peripheral arteries even in nontrauma settings. For example, the patency rate for endoluminal stents in the SFA is between 60% and 80% at 2 years, a range lower than that of primary repairs or interposition grafts.[49] In addition, many patients who sustain extremity trauma are younger than the average vascular stent patient and have poorer access to health care; consequently, close long-term follow-up after an endovascular intervention may be harder to carry out in this population.

Endovascular therapy may be considered in certain instances of extremity vascular trauma, such as when systemic conditions rule out operative repair and a temporizing measure is warranted. It should be kept in mind, however, that endovascular repair of peripheral vascular injuries is still a developing form of treatment and not the standard of care.[50,51]

TIMING OF ORTHOPEDIC REPAIR VIS-À-VIS VASCULAR REPAIR

Another issue that continues to evoke controversy is the timing of repair of concomitant vascular and orthopedic injuries—in particular, the order in which these injuries should be repaired. In general, vascular repair should take precedence over orthopedic reconstruction when possible. Vascular surgeons have long been concerned about the instability of knee dislocations and distal femoral or proximal tibial fractures, fearing that a fragile vascular reconstruction might be undone by subsequent orthopedic maneuvers; however, the data do not support this fear. There is some evidence that in patients with combined injuries, giving priority to revascularization over orthopedic fixation leads to shorter hospital stays and a trend toward lower fasciotomy rates. In a 2002 study, revascularization before fracture fixation was not found to result in iatrogenic disruption of the vascular repair.[43]

When an extremity has been substantially destabilized as a consequence of bony injury, short-term external fixation may be employed to facilitate vascular repair. A temporary intraluminal shunt is often used to maintain perfusion during initial orthopedic stabilization. One study demonstrated that routine use of intraluminal shunts in patients with complex extremity vascular injuries had the potential to reduce excessive morbidity (e.g., the need for fasciotomy and the resultant prolonged hospital stay) from prolonged arterial insufficiency.[52] In selected patients with combined skeletal and vascular injuries to the upper or lower limb, temporary vascular shunting may reduce complications resulting from prolonged ischemia and permit an unhurried and reasonable sequence of treatment.[53]

SALVAGE OF SEVERELY INJURED OR MANGLED EXTREMITIES

When an extremity is severely injured or mangled, a decision must be made whether to attempt salvage or perform amputation. Because of the need to take the patient's emotional and medical concerns into account, evaluation of an extremity for potential salvage is a difficult undertaking. Several scoring systems have been developed to help make this decision-making process somewhat easier. The most commonly used system is the Mangled Extremity Scoring System (MESS), which uses four objective criteria to predict the likelihood of amputation after lower-extremity trauma: skeletal/soft tissue injury, limb ischemia, shock, and patient age. A MESS score of 7 or higher predicts amputation with an accuracy approaching 100%. However, it is essential to remember that each patient must be carefully evaluated and that attempts at limb salvage must not be based solely on a high MESS score.[54,55]

The need for amputation may be best predicted by the occurrence of severe injuries to the sciatic or tibial nerves, the presence of associated fractures, and the failure of arterial repair.[5] Often, the decision to amputate is not made at the time of presentation or during the initial operation. If, after revascularization and skeletal stabilization, the extremity is clearly nonviable or remains insensate, then delayed amputation may be performed under more controlled circumstances.[56]

The optimal approach to evaluating a severely injured extremity involves a multispecialty group, including the trauma surgeon, the vascular surgeon, and the orthopedic surgeon. With full knowledge of the patient's condition, an attempt at limb salvage may be appropriate. In some cases, though, amputation may be preferable to preservation of an insensate, nonfunctional limb.

References

1. Rich NM: Vascular trauma in Vietnam. J Cardiovasc Surg (Torino) 11:368, 1970

2. Fox CJ, Gillespie DL, O'Donnell SD, et al: Contemporary management of wartime vascular trauma. J Vasc Surg 41:638, 2005

3. Oller DW, Rutledge R, Clancy T, et al: Vascular injuries in a rural state: a review of 978 patients from a state trauma registry. J Trauma 32:740, 1992

4. Clouse WD, Rasmussen TE, Perlstein J, et al: Upper extremity vascular injury: a current in-the-ater wartime report from Operation Iraqi Freedom. Ann Vasc Surg 20:429, 2006

5. Hafez HM, Woolgar J, Robbs JV: Lower extremity arterial injury: results of 550 cases and review of risk factors associated with limb loss. J Vasc Surg 33:1212, 2001

6. Bongard F, Dubrow T, Klein S: Vascular injuries in the urban battleground: experience at a metropolitan trauma center. Ann Vasc Surg 4:415, 1990

7. Snyder WH 3rd, Thal ER, Bridges RA, et al: The validity of normal arteriography in penetrating trauma. Arch Surg 113:424, 1978

8. Weaver FA, Yellin AE, Bauer M, et al: Is arterial proximity a valid indication for arteriography in penetrating extremity trauma? A prospective analysis. Arch Surg 125:1256, 1990

9. Lynch K, Johansen K: Can Doppler pressure measurement replace "exclusion" arteriography in the diagnosis of occult extremity arterial trauma? Ann Surg 214:737, 1991

10. Mills WJ, Barei DP, McNair P: The value of the ankle-brachial index for diagnosing arterial injury after knee dislocation: a prospective study. J Trauma 56:1261, 2004

11. Bunt TJ, Malone JM, Moody M, et al: Frequency of vascular injury with blunt trauma-induced extremity injury. Am J Surg 160:226, 1990

12. Kendall RW, Taylor DC, Salvian AJ, et al: The role of arteriography in assessing vascular injuries associated with dislocations of the knee. J Trauma 35:875, 1993

13. Anderson RJ, Hobson RW 2nd, Padberg FT Jr, et al: Penetrating extremity trauma: identification of patients at high-risk requiring arteriography. J Vasc Surg 11:544, 1990

14. Francis H 3rd, Thal ER, Weigelt JA, et al: Vascular proximity: is it a valid indication for arteriography in asymptomatic patients? J Trauma 31:512, 1991

15. Reid JD, Redman HC, Weigelt JA, et al: Wounds of the extremities in proximity to major arteries: value of angiography in the detection of arterial injury. AJR Am J Roentgenol 151:1035, 1988

16. Reid JD, Weigelt JA, Thal ER, et al: Assessment of proximity of a wound to major vascular structures as an indication for arteriography. Arch Surg 123:942, 1988

17. Conrad MF, Patton JH Jr, Parikshak M, et al: Evaluation of vascular injury in penetrating extremity trauma: angiographers stay home. Am Surg 68:269, 2002

18. Bynoe RP, Miles WS, Bell RM, et al: Noninvasive diagnosis of vascular trauma by duplex ultrasonography. J Vasc Surg 14:346, 1991

19. Kuzniec S, Kauffman P, Molnar LJ, et al: Diagnosis of limbs and neck arterial trauma using duplex ultrasonography. Cardiovasc Surg 6:358, 1998

20. Busquets AR, Acosta JA, Colon E, et al: Helical computed tomographic angiography for the diagnosis of traumatic arterial injuries of the extremities. J Trauma 56:625, 2004

21. Soto JA, Munera F, Cardoso N, et al: Diagnostic performance of helical CT angiography in trauma to large arteries of the extremities. J Comput Assist Tomogr 23:188, 1999

22. Graves M, Cole PA: Diagnosis of peripheral vascular injury in extremity trauma. Orthopedics 29:35, 2006

23. Levy BA, Zlowodzki MP, Graves M, et al: Screening for extermity arterial injury with the arterial pressure index. Am J Emerg Med 23:689, 2005

24. Pasquale MD Frykberg ER, Tinkoff GH, et al: Management of complex extremity trauma. Bull Am Coll Surg 91(6):36, 2006

25. Subasi M, Cakir O, Kesemenli C, et al: Popliteal artery injuries associated with fractures and dislocations about the knee. Acta Orthop Belg 67:259, 2001

26. Abou-Sayed H, Berger DL: Blunt lower-extremity trauma and popliteal artery injuries: revisiting the case for selective arteriography. Arch Surg 137:585, 2002

27. Rozycki GS, Tremblay LN, Feliciano DV, et al: Blunt vascular trauma in the extremity: diagnosis, management, and outcome. J Trauma 55:814, 2003

28. Menzoian JO, Doyle JE, LoGerfo FW, et al: Evaluation and management of vascular injuries of the extremities. Arch Surg 118:93, 1983

29. Green NE, Allen BL: Vascular injuries associated

with dislocation of the knee. J Bone Joint Surg Am 59:236, 1977

30. Starnes BW, Beekley AC, Sebesta JA, et al: Extremity vascular injuries on the battlefield: tips for surgeons deploying to war. J Trauma 60:432, 2006

31. Valentine RJ, Wind GG, Wind GG: Anatomic Exposures in Vascular Surgery, 2nd ed. Lippincott Williams & Wilkins, Philadelphia, 2003

32. Keen RR, Meyer JP, Durham JR, et al: Autogenous vein graft repair of injured extremity arteries: early and late results with 134 consecutive patients. J Vasc Surg 13:664, 1991

33. MacDonald S, Meneghetti AT, Lokanathan R, et al: Superficial femoral vein for arterial reconstruction in trauma. J Trauma 59:747, 2005

34. Shah DM, Leather RP, Corson JD, et al: Polytetra-fluoroethylene grafts in the rapid reconstruction of acute contaminated peripheral vascular injuries. Am J Surg 148:229, 1984

35. Feliciano DV, Mattox KL, Graham JM, et al: Five-year experience with PTFE grafts in vascular wounds. J Trauma 25:71, 1985

36. Aftabuddin M, Islam N, Jafar MA, et al: Management of isolated radial or ulnar arteries at the fore-arm. J Trauma 38:149, 1995

37. Sultanov DD, Usmanov NU, Baratov AK, et al: Traumatic injuries of the popliteal and tibial arter-ies: limb ischemia and problems of surgical man-agement. Angiol Sosud Khir 10:104, 2004

38. Johnson M, Ford M, Johansen K: Radial or ulnar artery laceration: repair or ligate? Arch Surg 128:971, 1993

39. Parry NG, Feliciano DV, Burke RM, et al: Management and short-term patency of lower extremity venous injuries with various repairs. Am J Surg 186:631, 2003

40. Pasch AR, Bishara RA, Schuler JJ, et al: Results of venous reconstruction after civilian vascular trau-ma. Arch Surg 121:607, 1986

41. Browner BD: Skeletal Trauma: Basic Science, Management, and Reconstruction, 3rd ed. WB Saunders Co, Philadelphia, 2003

42. Patman RD, Thompson JE: Fasciotomy in periph-eral vascular surgery: report of 164 patients. Arch Surg 101:663, 1970

43. McHenry TP, Holcomb JB, Aoki N, et al: Fractures with major vascular injuries from gun-shot wounds: implications of surgical sequence. J Trauma 53:717, 2002

44. Sawchuk AP, Eldrup-Jorgensen J, Tober C, et al: The natural history of intimal flaps in a canine model. Arch Surg 125:1614, 1990

45. Hernandez-Maldonado JJ, Padberg FT Jr, Teehan E, et al: Arterial intimal flaps: a comparison of pri-mary repair, aspirin, and endovascular excision in an experimental model. J Trauma 34:565, 1993

46. Tufaro A, Arnold T, Rummel M, et al: Adverse outcome of nonoperative management of intimal injuries caused by penetrating trauma. J Vasc Surg 20:656, 1994

47. Perry MO: Complications of missed arterial injuries. J Vasc Surg 17:399, 1993

48. Guerrero A, Gibson K, Kralovich KA, et al: Limb loss following lower extremity arterial trauma: what can be done proactively? Injury 33:765, 2002

49. Vogel TR, Shindelman LE, Nackman GB, et al: Efficacious use of nitinol stents in the femoral and popliteal arteries. J Vasc Surg 38:1178, 2003

50. Risberg B, Lonn L: Management of vascular injuries using endovascular techniques. Eur J Surg 166:196, 2000

51. Lonn L, Delle M, Karlstrom L, et al: Should blunt arterial trauma to the extremities be treated with endovascular techniques? J Trauma 59:1224, 2005

52. Johansen K, Bandyk D, Thiele B, et al: Temporary intraluminal shunts: resolution of a management dilemma in complex vascular injuries. J Trauma 22:395, 1982

53. Reber PU, Patel AG, Sapio NL, et al: Selective use of temporary intravascular shunts in coincident vascular and orthopedic upper and lower limb trauma. J Trauma 47:72, 1999

54. Johansen K, Daines M, Howey T, et al: Objective criteria accurately predict amputation following lower extremity trauma. J Trauma 30:568, 1990

55. Helfet DL, Howey T, Sanders R, et al: Limb sal-vage versus amputation: preliminary results of the Mangled Extremity Severity Score. Clin Orthop Relat Res (256):80, 1990

56. Poole GV, Agnew SG, Griswold JA, et al: The mangled lower extremity: can salvage be predict-ed? Am Surg 60:50, 1994

Acknowledgment

Figures 1, 4 through 10   Alice Y. Chen.

The authors thank Kimberly Riehle, M.D., University of Washington School of Medicine, for her help in the editing of the manuscript.

113 MANAGEMENT OF THE PATIENT WITH THERMAL INJURIES

Nicole S. Gibran, M.D., F.A.C.S., and David M. Heimbach, M.D., F.A.C.S.

Optimal care of the burn patient requires not only specialized equipment but also, more important, a team of dedicated surgeons, nurses, therapists, nutritionists, pharmacists, social workers, psychologists, and operating room staff. Burn care was one of the first specialties to adopt a multidisciplinary approach, and over the past 30 years, burn centers have decreased burn mortality by coordinating prehospital patient management, resuscitation methods, and surgical and critical care of patients with major burns. Detailed practice guidelines for burn patients, as well as lists of the resources needed in a burn center, have been developed.[1,2]

Where to Treat Burn Patients

Patients with critical burns, as defined by the American Burn Association [*see Table 1*], should be transferred to a specialized burn center as soon as possible after their initial assessment and resuscitation. A community general or plastic surgeon with an interest in burns could manage moderate burns that do not involve functionally significant body sites. However, even patients with small burns benefit from the expertise of a specialized burn care team. Furthermore, the burn center's focused approach facilitates patient and family education, reentry into society, long-term rehabilitation needs, and reconstructive surgical needs.

OUTPATIENT VERSUS INPATIENT MANAGEMENT

Outpatient management may be appropriate for small burns (1% to 5% of total body surface area [TBSA]) that do not involve joints or vital structures. However, successful outcomes in such cases require a well-organized plan and clear communication with the patient and family. Many outpatient management plans fail because insufficient teaching during a short visit to an emergency department leads to inadequate pain control, wound infection, and limited movement.

Three important reasons for hospitalizing a patient with a burn injury are wound care, physical therapy, and pain management. A short hospital stay immediately after the injury gives the burn team the opportunity to teach the patient how to properly clean and dress the burn; this is especially important for burns to the extremities. A therapist should assess patient movement and educate the patient about expected activity levels and exercise programs. Background pain (pain experienced with ordinary daily activities) and procedural pain (pain experienced during wound care) should be carefully assessed, and analgesic medications should be titrated to the individual patient's pain levels.

Complex burn wound management is discussed in detail elsewhere [*see 114 Management of the Burn Wound*]. For outpatient management, however, simplicity is the key to success. Patients and their families are unlikely to manage complicated dressing plans. For outpatient burn care, once-daily dressing changes are adequate. A common misconception is that these wounds must be cleaned with sterile saline. In fact, burns can be effectively washed during a daily shower or bath with regular tap water and nonperfumed soap. A second misconception is that the patient must scrub the wound to debride all the superficial exudates. Simply wiping the wound with a soapy washcloth to remove the topical ointment and wipe away the bacteria that have accumulated over the past day provides adequate care. Intact blisters can be left as a protective wound cover if they do not prevent movement of a joint. Dressings must allow full range of motion.

Physical therapy is an essential component of burn management. A common misconception is that burns over joints should be immobilized to promote healing. Actually, immobilization of extremities leads to swelling, which worsens burn wound pain and increases the risk of wound infection. Patients with hand burns must be taught exercises to maintain range of motion. Likewise, patients with foot burns must ambulate without assistive devices, so that normal muscle contraction can facilitate lymphatic drainage of the lower extremity. Patients must be taught to elevate burned extremities when they are not actively exercising.

Inadequate pain management is a frequent reason for return visits to the emergency department or readmission to the hospital. Often, inadequate pain control results from poor patient understanding of how to care for the burn (e.g., excessive scrubbing during wound care or inactivity and subsequent swelling). Although a healing partial-thickness burn may become more painful as the epithelial buds begin to emerge and healing progresses [*see 114 Management of the Burn Wound*], an acute increase in stinging pain may be the first sign of a superficial wound infection. This is an indication that the burn should be evaluated for signs of infection, including erythema and breakdown of a previously epithelized wound; cellulitis may or may not surround an infected burn. Systemic antibiotics and a change in the topical antimicrobial agent are indicated in this situation.

Socioeconomic issues can be important contraindications to

Table 1 American Burn Association Criteria for Burn Injuries That Warrant Referral to a Burn Unit

Partial-thickness burns of greater than 10% of total body surface area
Third-degree burns
Electrical burns, including lightning injury
Chemical burns
Inhalation injury
Burn injury in patients with preexisting medical disorders that could complicate management, prolong recovery, or increase mortality
Burns with concomitant trauma

Table 2 Criteria for Outpatient Management of Burn Patients

Outpatient Management Appropriate	Outpatient Management Inappropriate
Patients with small burns* who have demonstrated understanding of wound care, pain control, and therapy	Abused patients Demented patients Intoxicated patients Homeless patients Patients with comorbid conditions Patients with a language barrier

*1%–5% of total body surface area.

outpatient management of a burn wound [*see Table 2*]. Any suggestion of abuse—of a child or an adult—mandates admission for full evaluation of the home situation by the burn team; if the history and the burn distribution are consistent with a nonaccidental injury or potential neglect, the patient must be referred to protective services. Likewise, suggestion of a self-induced burn injury should trigger admission for psychological evaluation. For example, the presence of multiple small cigarette burns in various phases of healing is an absolute indication for admission to the hospital for psychological evaluation, even though the burns themselves may be easily cared for at home with small adhesive bandages. Although language barriers are not an absolute indication for hospital admission, there must be assurance that patients fully understand the treatment plan before they leave the emergency department. Underinsured and homeless patients may not have the resources to care for a wound outside the hospital and should be admitted for initial wound care and planning for transfer to a facility where they have access to a daily shower. Finally, the success of outpatient burn wound management depends on the ability to arrange a follow-up visit with an outpatient health care provider who can assess the outcome.

For patients with large burns, transition from inpatient to outpatient status is based on the same principles listed above. When burn pain can be controlled with oral medication and the patient and family can provide wound care, perform range-of-motion exercises, and manage splints and other assistive devices, outpatient management is appropriate. In some cases, daily or weekly outpatient therapy sessions to maintain range of motion may be included. If there are concerns about nonhealing wounds, weekly follow-up visits with the burn surgeon may be indicated initially. Because of possible long-term sequelae—scarring, contractures, and rehabilitation difficulties—the burn team should follow burn patients for 1 to 2 years after injury; longer follow-up may be necessary for patients with persistent contractures and scar formation. Prolonged follow-up is especially important with young children, who may encounter difficulties as they grow and may therefore require periodic monitoring until adulthood.

Fluid Management

In the late 1960s, Charles Baxter developed objective criteria for resuscitation of the thermally injured patient.[3,4] The Baxter formula (also known as the Parkland formula) calls for the infusion, over 24 hours, of 3 to 4 ml of crystalloid per percentage of TBSA burned. Half of this volume is delivered during the first 8 hours after injury, and the other half is delivered over the subsequent 16 hours. It is important to remember that this is an esti-

mate of need; individual patients may have higher or lower fluid requirements, depending on their overall condition and comorbidity. Continuous monitoring and reliance on objective clinical outcomes must dictate patient management.

The reliability of the Parkland formula directly depends on accurate assessment of burn depth and percentage of TBSA affected.[5] There are two formulas for quick estimation of burn size. One is the commonly used Rule of Nines: each arm is considered to be 9% of TBSA, each leg 18%, the anterior trunk 18%, the posterior trunk 18%, and the head 9% [*see Figure 1*]. Another easy method involves using the patient's full palm, including digits, to represent 1% of TBSA. First-degree burns [*see 114 Management of the Burn Wound*] should not be included in the calculation of burned areas.

Despite improvements in invasive monitoring techniques, the most reliable measures of adequate tissue perfusion for burn resuscitation continue to be mean arterial pressure (MAP) and adequate urine output (UOP). MAP should be maintained above 60 mm Hg to ensure adequate cerebral perfusion. For an otherwise healthy adult, a UOP of 30 ml/hr should be adequate; for a child, 1.0 to 1.5 ml/kg/hr should suffice. No evidence supports the use of pulmonary arterial (PA) catheter measurements for routine resuscitation; in fact, reliance on PA catheters may lead to over-resuscitation and contribute to the development of fluid-related complications (see below). Use of diuretics and inotropes should be restricted to patients with underlying comorbidity, especially preexisting cardiac disease. Use of inotropes will not stop the leak of plasma into the extravascular space but may lead to ischemia in the wound, resulting in conversion of a partial-thickness wound into a full-thickness wound. Use of mannitol may be appropriate for patients with myoglobinuria who require an osmotic diuretic to maintain a UOP of 100 ml/hr [*see 115 Miscellaneous Burns and Cold Injuries*].

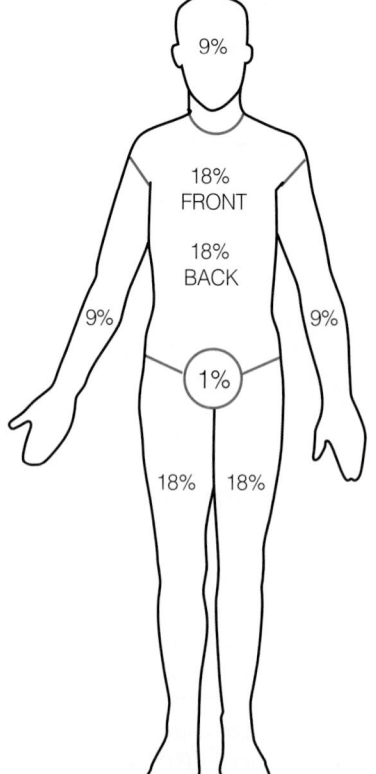

Figure 1 **The size of a burn can be estimated by means of the Rule of Nines, which assigns percentages of total body surface to the head, the extremities, and the front and back of the torso.**

Table 3 Acute Physiologic Changes during Burn Resuscitation

Measurement	Comment	Goal	Signs of Underresuscitation	Signs of Overresuscitation
Fluid volume	Fluid input generally exceeds output during the early post-burn period as edema develops	Urine output: adults, 30 ml/hr; children < 20 kg, 1.0–1.5 ml/kg/hr	Low urine output	Urine output > 30 ml/hr; hyper-osmolar diuresis from hyper-glycemia must be excluded
Body weight	An accurate dry weight is necessary for estimation of resuscitation fluid requirements	Weight will increase because of intravascular leak and resuscitation volume	Weight approaches dry weight	Massive weight gain from anasarca
Body temperature	Hyperthermia may indicate a hyperdynamic state	Normothermia	—	—
Electrocardiographic status	Dysrhythmias are uncommon in young patients but may complicate management of older patients	Normal sinus rhythm	Tachycardia may reflect intravascular contraction	Dysrhythmias may reflect poor oxygenation, electrolyte imbalance, or pH abnormality

Although the first 24 hours after a burn is usually considered the resuscitative phase of a burn injury, stabilization of the flux of mediators and closure of capillary leaks in fact take place on a continuum, occurring gradually from 12 to 48 hours after the burn injury. As capillary leakage resolves, the amount of fluids needed to maintain a MAP of 60 mm Hg and a UOP of 30 ml/hr should progressively decrease. A patient with both a large, deep burn and a profound inhalation injury or a patient in whom resuscitation has been delayed may require significantly more fluid than predicted by the Parkland formula to maintain blood pressure and UOP.

Colloid administration (albumin or fresh frozen plasma) after the capillary leak has closed (12 to 72 hours) may facilitate resuscitation in the patient with persistent low urine output and hypotension despite adequate crystalloid delivery. In such cases, the formula used is 5% albumin, 0.3 to 0.5 ml/kg/% TBSA burned over 24 hours. Alternatively, plasmapheresis may reduce intravenous fluid requirements in patients who are not responding to resuscitation.[6] Indications for plasmapheresis include a sustained MAP of less than 60 mm Hg and a UOP less than 30 ml/hr in a patient with ongoing fluid needs that exceed twice the estimated volume requirements. Early plasmapheresis (12 to 24 hours after injury) may decrease the incidence of complications from administration of excessive fluid (see below). Why plasmapheresis works is unknown, but theoretically, the process should remove inflammatory mediators that cause vasodilatation and capillary leak.

Once resuscitation is complete (24 to 48 hours after injury), insensible losses and hyperthermia associated with a hyperdynamic state may indicate the need for ongoing fluid administration. The route of administration can be intravenous or, preferably, enteral. Reliable daily weights can be extremely valuable for detection and measurement of insensible fluid loss or fluid retention.

Along with MAP and UOP, several laboratory variables can be used to ensure that patients are receiving appropriate amounts of resuscitation fluid [*see Tables 3 and 4*].

COMPLICATIONS OF FLUID ADMINISTRATION

Before the development of current resuscitation formulas, inadequate resuscitation was a common cause of death in burn patients, as a result of decreased tissue perfusion and subsequent multiorgan failure.[7] In addition, this ischemia caused conversion of the burn to a deeper injury, thereby increasing surgical requirements. However, there are also complications associated with overresuscitation, or so-called fluid creep.[8,9] Whereas Baxter sug-

gested that 12% of patients would require more than 4.3 ml/kg/%TBSA resuscitation fluid, subsequent reports suggest that more than 55% of patients receive this amount of fluid.[8] Excessive fluid resuscitation increases the risk of complications, including poor tissue perfusion, compartment syndrome involving the abdomen or extremities, pulmonary edema, and pleural effusion.

Abdominal compartment syndrome (ACS) is an increasingly well-recognized posttraumatic complication that occurs in patients who require extensive fluid resuscitation. Increased abdominal pressure decreases lung compliance and impedes lung expansion, resulting in elevated airway pressures and hypoventilation. The classic presentation includes high peak airway pressures, decreased venous return, oliguria, and intra-abdominal pressures exceeding 25 mm Hg.[10] Sustained intra-abdominal hypertension is often fatal. Bedside decompressive laparotomy can alleviate ACS and can be performed safely through burn wounds,[11] and its use should be considered in patients with hemodynamic instability, hypoventilation, and elevated abdominal pressures. Whether the patient survives, however, depends on the comorbid conditions that led to the requirement for large resuscitative volumes.

Airway Management

Abnormal pulmonary function commonly complicates the management of thermally injured patients. It may result from inhalation injury or from the systemic response to the burn. Understanding the management of pulmonary dysfunction in the thermally injured patient requires a working knowledge of pulmonary function measurements and of pulmonary pathophysiology [*see Tables 5 and 6*].

INHALATION INJURY

Inhalation injuries occur in approximately one third of all major burns, and mortality is more than double that of cutaneous burns.[12-14] Curiously, isolated inhalation injuries do not result in high mortality.[15] Presumably, the combination of inhalation injury and cutaneous thermal injury creates a double insult in which recurrent or persistent bacteremia aggravates the pulmonary injury.

Three distinct components of inhalation injury exist: carbon monoxide (CO) poisoning, upper airway thermal burns, and inhalation of products of combustion. Diagnosis of an inhalation injury requires a thorough history of the circumstances surrounding the injury and is often suggested by fire in a closed

Table 4 Acute Biochemical and Hematologic Changes during Burn Resuscitation

Measurement	Comment	Goal	Signs of Underresuscitation	Signs of Overresuscitation
Serum creatinine and blood urea nitrogen	Normal baseline values rule out preexisting renal disease, which reduces urine output reliability as an index of tissue perfusion	Normal values	Rising values may reflect underresuscitation or acute tubular necrosis	May be normal
Hematocrit and hemoglobin	Significant blood loss from incorrectly performed surgical interventions such as escharotomies or central venous line placement may lower values	Should approach normal	May be elevated with severe intravascular depletion; this is typical with delayed resuscitation	May be low in patients with excessive intravascular volumes
White blood cell count (WBC)	The initial WBC may vary, depending on the stress response and cell margination; the absolute value is not particularly useful during the early postburn period; once leukopoiesis increases, neutropenia resolves without treatment with stimulatory factors	Normal values	May increase	May decrease, but this generally represents margination of circulating neutrophils into the wound
Blood glucose	Increased release of catecholamines in burn patients may lead to hyperglycemia; diabetic patients may require insulin	Levels maintained at ≤ 120 mg/dl	Hyperglycemia, which may misleadingly increase urine output	Hypoglycemia, especially in infants (< 20 kg), who have decreased glycogen stores
Electrolytes	Electrolyte status depends on the type of crystalloid used for resuscitation; hypernatremia and hyponatremia can be avoided by resuscitation with lactated Ringer solution; use of normal saline should be avoided because it can lead to hyperchloremic acidosis	Normal electrolyte levels	—	—
Plasma protein and myoglobin levels	Patients with very deep burns or electrical burns may have elevated plasma myoglobin levels	Decreased albumin level within the first 8 hr after burn injury may be normal	Myoglobinemia may result from prolonged underresuscitation and tissue ischemia	Myoglobinemia may result if excessive resuscitation leads to compartment syndrome; escharotomy should be performed to minimize rhabdomyolysis
Prothrombin time, partial thromboplastin time, and platelet count	Initial values are useful to determine whether the patient has preexisting hepatic or hematologic disease	Normal	Prolonged shock and underresuscitation may lead to disseminated intravascular coagulation; coagulation factors and platelets may be needed in such cases	Unrecognized compartment syndrome and delayed escharotomy may cause tissue ischemia and disseminated intravascular coagulation; a dropping platelet count may indicate heparin-induced thrombocytopenia

space, carbonaceous sputum, and an elevated carboxyhemoglobin level (> 15%).

Carbon Monoxide Poisoning

CO injury is the most commonly recognized form of inhalation injury and the most common cause of death in inhalation injury. Clinical signs and symptoms of CO toxicity correlate with arterial carboxyhemoglobin levels, which can be used to quickly and precisely determine the degree of CO intoxication [*see Table 7*]. CO intoxication can be easily treated with 100% inhaled oxygen, which rapidly accelerates the dissociation of CO from hemoglobin [*see Table 8*]. Hyperbaric oxygen therapy has been touted as a superior treatment for quickly reducing carboxyhemoglobin levels,[16] but the data are controversial and the studies are generally poorly controlled.[17] Hyperbaric oxygen therapy may be appropriate in a patient with impaired neurologic status and a markedly elevated carboxyhemoglobin level (≥ 25%). However, the risks (including barotrauma) associated with isolation in a hyperbaric chamber may be too significant for a burn patient (≥ 10% TBSA) undergoing resuscitation. In one study of 10 patients with combined inhalation injury and burns treated acutely with hyperbaric oxygen, seven patients survived but the complications included aspiration (two cases), cardiac arrest (two cases), hypovolemia with metabolic acidosis (three cases), respiratory acidosis (four cases), cardiac dysrhythmia (three cases), and eustachian tube occlusion (two cases).[18] Consensus is growing that when cardiac arrest complicates inhalation injury, the result is uniformly fatal regardless of aggressive therapy, including hyperbaric oxygen therapy.[19]

Upper Airway Thermal Injury

Direct thermal damage tends to occur in the upper airway rather than in the lower airway because the oropharyngeal cavity has a substantial capacity to absorb heat. Upper airway thermal injury constitutes an important indication for intubation, because it is mandatory to control the airway before airway edema develops during resuscitation.

The diagnosis of upper airway thermal injury is achieved with direct laryngoscopic visualization of the oropharyngeal cavity. The decision whether to intubate should be based on visual evidence of pharyngeal burns or swelling or carbonaceous sputum coming from below the level of the vocal cords. If a patient is phonating without stridor, intubation can often be delayed. Singed facial and nasal hair does not constitute an adequate independent indication for intubation.

Treatment of upper airway injuries includes hospital admission for observation and provision of humidified oxygen, pulmonary toilet, bronchodilators as needed, and prophylactic endotracheal intubation as indicated. Upper airway thermal burns usually manifest within 48 hours after injury, and airway swelling can be expected to peak at 12 to 24 hours after injury. A patient with a true upper airway burn will likely require airway protection for 72 hours. A short course of steroids may facilitate earlier resolution of airway edema in a patient with small cutaneous burns, but a patient with a burn larger than 20% TBSA should not be treated with steroids because of the risk of infection and failure to heal. The decision whether to extubate can be based on pulmonary weaning criteria but also on the presence of an air leak around the endotracheal tube.

Lower Airway Burn Injury

Burn injury to the tracheobronchial tree and the lung parenchyma results from combustion products in smoke [*see Table 9*] and, under unique conditions, inhaled steam. Numerous irritants in smoke or the vaporized chemical reagents in steam can cause direct mucosal injury, leading to mucosal slough and bronchial edema, bronchoconstriction, and bronchial obstruction. Tracheo-bronchial mucosal damage also leads to neutrophil chemotaxis and release of inflammatory mediators into the lung parenchyma, accentuating the injury with exudate formation and microvascular permeability. Together, these may progress to pulmonary edema, pneumonia, and acute respiratory distress syndrome (ARDS). Reduced myocardial contractility secondary to smoke-toxin inhalation may also contribute to resus-

citation failures in burn victims with concomitant inhalation injury.

Inhalation injury can often be a clinical diagnosis.[14] Lower airway injury can be confirmed by bronchoscopy or xenon-133 ventilation-perfusion scan,[20] but these modalities do not change therapeutic choices or clinical outcome.[21]

ACUTE LUNG INJURY AND ACUTE RESPIRATORY DISTRESS SYNDROME

Understanding of the pathophysiology of ARDS has improved since its initial description in the late 1960s,[22] and ARDS-related deaths were lower in the period 1995 through 1998 than in the period 1990 through 1994; however, 40% to 70% of patients with ARDS still die of the disease.[23] ARDS is an independent risk factor for death in burn patients.[24] Mortality in burn patients with ARDS is attributable to overwhelming sepsis and

Table 5 Measures of Pulmonary Function

Measurement	Normal Values	Abnormal Values Indicating Need for Mechanical Ventilation
Tidal volume (V_T), ml/kg	5–8	< 5
Vital capacity (V_C), ml/kg	65–75	< 10; < 15*
Forced expiratory volume in 1 sec (FEV_1), ml/kg	50–60	< 10
Functional residual capacity (FRC), % of predicted value	80–100	< 50
Respiratory rate (f), breaths/min	12–20	> 35
Maximum inspiratory force (MIF), cm H_2O	80–100	< 20; < 25; < 30*
Minute ventilation (V_E), L/min	5–6	> 10
Maximum voluntary ventilation (MVV), L/min	120–180	< 20; < (2 × V_E)*
Dead space fraction (V_D/V_T), %	0.25–0.40	> 0.60
P_aCO_2, mm Hg	36–44	> 50; > 55*
P_aO_2, mm Hg	75–100 (breathing room air)	< 50 (room air); < 70 (mask O_2)*
Alveolar-to-arterial PO_2 gradient [$P(A-a)O_2$], mm Hg	25–65 (breathing 100% O_2)	> 350; > 450*
Arterial-alveolar PO_2 ratio (P_aO_2/P_AO_2)	0.75	< 0.15
Arterial PO_2–inspired O_2 (P_aO_2/F_IO_2), mm Hg	350–450	< 200
Intrapulmonary right-to-left shunt fraction (Qs/Qt), %	≤ 5%	> 20%; > 25%; > 30%*

*More than one value indicates lack of uniform agreement in the literature.

Table 6 Mechanisms of Pulmonary Dysfunction and Indications for Mechanical Ventilation

Mechanism	Best Indicator
Inadequate alveolar ventilation	P_aCO_2 and pH
Inadequate lung expansion	Tidal volume, respiratory rate, VC
Inadequate respiratory muscle strength	MIF; MVV; VC
Excessive work of breathing	V_E required to keep PCO_2 normal; V_D/V_T; respiratory rate
Unstable ventilatory drive	Breathing pattern, clinical setting
Severe hypoxemia	$P(A-a)O_2$; P_aO_2/P_AO_2; P_aO_2/F_IO_2; Qs/Qt

MIF—maximum inspiratory force   MVV—maximum voluntary ventilation $P(A-a)O_2$—alveolar-to-arterial PO_2 gradient P_aO_2/F_IO_2—ratio of arterial PO_2 to inspired O_2 Qs/Qt—intrapulmonary right-to-left shunt fraction   VC—vital capacity V_D/V_T—dead space fraction V_E—minute ventilation

Table 7 Clinical Manifestations of Carbon Monoxide Poisoning

Carboxyhemoglobin Level (%)	Clinical Manifestations
< 10	None
15–25	Nausea, headache
30–40	Confusion, stupor, weakness
40–60	Coma
> 60	Death

Table 8 Half-life of Carbon Monoxide–Hemoglobin Bonds with Inhalation Therapy

Carboxyhemoglobin Half-life	Treatment Modality
4 hr	Room air
45–60 min	100% oxygen
20 min	100% oxygen at 2 atm (hyperbaric oxygen)

Table 9 Clinical Findings Associated with Specific
Inhaled Products of Combustion

Source	Product of Combustion	Clinical Effect
Organic matter	Carbon monoxide Carbon dioxide	Poor tissue oxygen delivery Narcosis
Wood, paper, anhydrous ammonia	Nitrogen oxides (NO, NO₂)	Airway mucosal irritation, pulmonary edema, dizziness
Polyvinyl chloride (plastics)	Hydrogen chlorine	Airway mucosal irritation
Wool, silk, polyurethane (nylon)	Hydrogen cyanide	Respiratory failure, headache, coma
Petroleum products (gasoline, kerosene, propane, plastics)	Carbon monoxide, nitrogen oxide, benzene	Airway mucosal irritation, coma
Wood, cotton, paper	Aldehydes	Airway mucosal irritation, lung parenchyma damage
Polyurethane (nylon)	Ammonia	Airway mucosal irritation

multiple organ failure rather than to respiratory failure alone.[25]

Clinically, ARDS is characterized by pulmonary edema, refractory hypoxemia, diffuse pulmonary infiltrates, and altered lung compliance. Pathologically, it is distinguished by diffuse alveolar epithelial damage with microvascular permeability and subsequent inflammatory cell infiltration into the lung parenchyma, interstitial and alveolar edema, hyaline membrane formation, and, ultimately, fibrosis.

The development of ARDS is presaged by high fluid resuscitation requirements, reflecting increased microvascular permeability and leading to increased pulmonary edema. ARDS commonly develops within 7 days after injury. The likelihood of death is significantly increased in patients with a multiple organ dysfunction score of 8 or higher and a lung injury score of 2.76 or higher. In one review, burn patients with inhalation injury had a 73% incidence of respiratory failure (with hypoxemia, multiple pulmonary infections, or prolonged ventilator support) and a 20% incidence of ARDS, whereas patients without inhalation injury had a 5% incidence of respiratory failure and a 2% incidence of ARDS.[24] Advanced age is also an important risk factor for the development of ARDS—indeed, one small retrospective study has suggested that age is the only independent major predisposing factor for ARDS.[26] Curiously, acute lung injury rarely develops in patients with inhalation injury but without cutaneous burns.[27,28]

Inflammatory Mediators in ARDS with Burn Injuries

Local and systemic inflammatory mediators released in response to burn injury include platelet-activating factor, interleukins (IL-1, IL-2, IL-6, and IL-8), prostaglandin, thromboxane, leukotrienes, hematopoietic growth factors (granulocyte-macrophage colony-stimulating factor, macrophage colony-stimulating factor, and granulocyte colony-stimulating factor), cell adhesion molecules (intercellular cell adhesion molecule–1, endothelial-leukocyte adhesion molecule–1, and vascular cell adhesion molecule–1), and nitric oxide (NO).[29,30] Systemic levels of circulating tumor necrosis factor–α (TNF-α) and IL-1 correlate with ARDS severity. IL-2 promotes multisystem organ edema,

lung neutrophil sequestration, and platelet activation through alterations in microvascular permeability. Clinical studies have correlated infection—but not isolated inhalation injury—with increased IL-2 levels, which reemphasizes the potential significance of the double insult inflicted by the combination of a burn and an inhalation injury.[31] Some data suggest that relative imbalances in levels of inflammatory mediators may be more important than absolute values.

An important cell in the inflammatory cycle is the pulmonary alveolar macrophage, a phagocytic cell that produces reactive oxygen intermediates (ROIs) as a means of killing microorganisms. In animal models, addition of a burn injury to a smoke insult exaggerates lipid peroxidation and hypoproteinemia, implicating reactive oxygen species in the pathophysiology of ARDS. With systemic inflammation, unchecked ROI production may lead to local tissue injury. ROIs damage cells by direct oxidative injury to cellular proteins and nucleic acids, as well as by inducing lipid peroxidation, which leads to the destruction of the cell membrane. ROIs are generated under conditions of ischemia-reperfusion (as with failed resuscitations), which occurs when the flow of oxygenated blood is restored to ischemic tissue such as unexcised eschar. During ischemia, there is increased activity of xanthine oxidase and increased hypoxanthine production; when reperfusion reintroduces oxygen, the xanthine oxidase and hypoxanthine generate ROIs, which cause more tissue injury.

Management of ARDS

In spite of 30 years of advances in ARDS treatment, patients with ARDS still must depend on mechanical respiratory support—not treatment—as the primary therapeutic intervention while the alveolar epithelium repairs itself, the capillary permeability resolves, and the lung heals. Restricting fluids to prevent further edema formation has increased survival. The most encouraging strategy to prevent lung injury and increase survival has been low tidal volume mechanical ventilation, commonly called lung protective ventilation, with or without high levels of positive end-expiratory pressure.[32] Pharmacologic approaches to treating ARDS in burn patients parallel those used in other critically ill surgical patients and are addressed elsewhere [see *120 Pulmonary Insufficiency*].

For most patients with pulmonary complications from thermal injury, conventional ventilatory approaches will be adequate. However, the population at risk for development of ARDS may need more sophisticated management to reduce barotrauma and pulmonary infection in the minimally compliant lung with increased airway pressures. In the past, conventional ventilator management of inhalation injury and ARDS, which emphasizes normalization of blood gases, promoted high rates of barotrauma—that is, ventilator-induced lung injury that is physiologically and histopathologically indistinguishable from ARDS itself. Overdistention and cyclic inflation of injured lung exacerbates underlying lung injury and perpetuates systemic inflammation. These effects can be minimized by maintaining low tidal volumes and peak pressures and by applying positive end-expiratory pressure. Hence, the use of alternative modes of ventilation (e.g., volume-limited ventilation with or without inverse-ratio ventilation, prone positioning, and tracheal gas insufflation) has increased in patients at risk for ARDS. No single approach is likely to benefit all patients, and adjustment of ventilatory controls must be based on individual clinical responses.

Lung-protective ventilation Lung-protective ventilation utilizes low inspiratory volumes (4 to 6 ml/kg) to keep peak inspiratory pressures below 40 cm H_2O. This strategy is limited by the accumulation of carbon dioxide (so-called permissive hypercapnia), although respiratory acidosis with a pH as low as 7.20 is tolerated.

The ARDS Network Study found that ARDS patients ventilated with low tidal volumes had a 22% lower mortality than patients ventilated with conventional means.[32,33] The volume-preset, assist-control mode is recommended for tidal volume control, and the respiratory rate should be slowly increased as tidal volume is reduced to maintain minute ventilation and prevent acute hypercapnia. Tidal volume can be increased for severe acidosis (pH ≤ 7.15). Ventilator inspiratory flow should be optimized to minimize dyspnea. If dyspnea results in asynchronous breaths, sedation may be necessary or the tidal volume can be titrated to 7 to 8 ml/kg, provided that peak inspiratory pressures are below 40 cm H_2O. Pressure support levels between 5 and 20 cm H_2O can be titrated to keep the respiratory rate below 35 breaths/min and may be useful for weaning.

One study of children with burns found that low tidal volume ventilation was associated with low incidences of ventilator-induced lung injury and respiratory-related deaths,[34] which supports the use of this modality in thermally injured patients. In fact, in patients with large burns and inhalation injury, it may be warranted to use low tidal volume ventilation before ARDS develops. The early resuscitative phase may be the optimal time to initiate this approach.

Prone positioning Changing a patient's position from supine to prone is emerging as a simple and inexpensive strategy to improve gas exchange in acutely injured lungs. Studies report that despite concerns about airway protection, this is a safe intervention that may improve the ratio of arterial oxygen pressure to fraction of inspired oxygen (P_aO_2/F_1O_2) early in the course of ARDS.[35] Some data suggest that prone positioning in conjunction with NO administration may improve arterial oxygenation.[36] However, no clinical trials have examined the use of prone positioning in burn patients. If prone positioning has a significant effect, this positive result presumably would be evident during operative procedures when a patient with an acute lung injury is placed in this position (e.g., for excision of a posterior torso burn). Furthermore, prone positioning may be relatively contraindicated in a patient with a burned head who is at extreme risk for loss of control of the airway because of facial swelling and difficulty securing an endotracheal tube.

Extracorporeal membrane oxygenation Few centers have experience with extracorporeal membrane oxygenation (ECMO), and published information on its use for the treatment of ARDS in patients with inhalation injury and burns is mostly confined to anecdotal case reports.[37] Given its experimental nature and its high cost, ECMO is reserved for patients in whom other ventilatory modalities fail. Although ECMO has been shown to increase survival in some children with large burns and severe acute lung injury, patients with higher ventilator requirements before undergoing ECMO generally do not survive, suggesting that if ECMO is to be successful, it must be instituted early to prevent barotrauma and irreversible lung injury.[38] Early implementation of permissive hypercapnia may be equally effective.

High-frequency percussive ventilation High-frequency percussive ventilation (HFPV) is another strategy for maintaining low peak pulmonary pressure and preventing alveolar overdistention. HFPV has the added advantage of facilitating mucosal clearance of tracheobronchial casts that occlude the airway and predispose to pulmonary infection. Although HFPV is usually described as rescue therapy for patients in whom conventional therapy has failed, there is some evidence that it can reduce mortality and the incidence of pneumonia in patients with inhalation injury.[39,40] Improved oxygenation and pulmonary toilet has been reported in patients treated early with HFPV,[41] which suggests that a larger-scale prospective trial is warranted to determine whether the benefits of HFPV justify the added cost and effort of maintaining multiple types of ventilators and credentialing for respiratory therapists.

A similar method, high-frequency oscillatory ventilation, may have no impact on burn mortality. However, it may have a role in the supportive management of burn patients with severe oxygenation failure that is unresponsive to conventional ventilation.[42]

Nitric oxide inhalation Endogenously produced NO plays an important role in the changes in systemic and pulmonary microvascular permeability seen in an animal model of combined smoke inhalation and third-degree burn.[30] Clinically, inhaled NO may be useful in burn patients with severe acute lung injury in whom conventional ventilatory support is failing.[43] The safety of inhaled NO in these patients is indicated by low methemoglobin levels and absence of hypotension attributable to the NO. Strong, immediate, and sustained improvement in the P_aO_2/F_1O_2 and reduction in pulmonary arterial mean pressure in response to NO seem to correlate with survival. However, the use of inhaled NO has been reported in only small numbers of burn patients, and a prospective study is warranted.

Corticosteroids The use of corticosteroids in the treatment of burns is problematic because of the negative effect these agents have on wound healing. Nevertheless, there is some evidence that rescue treatment with corticosteroids in the late chronic fibroproliferative phase of ARDS may decrease mortality and lower the P_aO_2/F_1O_2.[44] Ongoing multicenter studies in patients with small burns and inhalation injury are under way.

TRACHEOSTOMY VERSUS ENDOTRACHEAL INTUBATION

Transmural airway inflammation from inhaled gases and heat necessitates endotracheal airway protection, yet the use of endotracheal tubes in such cases may be complicated by tracheal pressure necrosis. Hence, survivors of inhalation injury may develop laryngotracheal strictures. One report suggests that there is a 5.5% incidence of tracheal stenosis in patients with burns and inhalation injury.[45] The relative risks and benefits of tracheostomies and endotracheal intubation have been debated since the early 1970s. Each modality has its own advantages and complications. Nasotracheal intubation is the least advantageous form of airway protection because of its association with paranasal sinusitis,[46] as well as pressure necrosis of the alar rim of the burned nose, which is nearly impossible to reconstruct. Therefore, nasotracheal intubation should be avoided unless absolutely necessary.

Tracheostomies are also associated with complications, including tracheal malacia, tracheal stenosis, trachea–innominate artery fistulas, tracheoesophageal fistulas, and posttracheostomy dysphagia.[47] However, complications associated with tracheostomy may relate to previous long-term endotracheal intubation and to the underlying pathophysiology, suggesting that if tracheostomy is to be done, it should be done early on; furthermore, the tracheostomy tube should be removed at the earliest possible time. In a 1985 study of airway management, tracheal stenosis and tracheal scar granuloma formation were reported to be more frequent and more severe after tracheostomy than after translaryngeal intubation.[48] As expected, the duration of tube placement significantly affected the development of permanent damage, leading to the conclusion that initial respiratory support with translaryngeal tubes is preferable for up to 3 weeks. Burn patients who undergo tracheostomy before postburn day 10 may have a lower incidence of subglottic stenosis with no difference in pneumonia incidence, when compared with orally intubated patients.[49] Nevertheless, tracheostomy has been reported to provide no benefit for early extubation or overall outcome for burn patients.[50] One major consideration in deciding whether to perform a tracheostomy has been the presence of eschar at the insertion site, which complicates tracheostomy-site care and increases the risk of airway infection. Percutaneous dilatational tracheostomy may provide a reasonable, less invasive approach for patients who are likely to need prolonged ventilatory support.[51] This procedure can be safely performed at the bedside, at one quarter the cost of a conventional tracheostomy. Given ongoing controversies over the relative risks and benefits of endotracheal intubation and tracheostomy in burn patients and the rarity of complications from intubation in our own practice, we perform tracheostomies only when multiple attempts at extubation have failed; these failures usually occur because the patients cannot protect their airway.

Temperature Regulation

Because the burn patient has lost the barrier function of the skin, temperature regulation is an important goal of successful management. Keeping a patient warm and dry is a major goal during resuscitation, especially during the pre–burn center transport of patients. This includes maintaining a warm ambient temperature. Large evaporative losses[52] combined with administration of large volumes of intravenous fluids that are at room temperature or colder may accentuate the hypovolemia, which will complicate the patient's overall course and may lead to disseminated intravascular coagulopathy. Mild hyperthermia may occur in the first 24 hours as a result of pyrogen release or increased metabolic rate[53] and may cause tachycardia that misleadingly suggests hypovolemia. Because infection is unlikely early on, especially within the first 72 hours after injury, elevated temperatures should be treated with antipyrogens to control the energy expenditure associated with increased catabolism.[54] About 72 hours after injury, patients with thermal injuries commonly develop a hyperdynamic state, the systemic inflammatory response syndrome (SIRS), which is characterized by tachycardia, hypotension, and hyperthermia—classic signs of sepsis that in this case do not have an infectious source.

Although patients with burns are likely to have elevated temperatures and may even have elevated white blood cell counts, fevers in burn patients are not reliable indicators of infections.[55] At least one study has demonstrated that in pediatric burn patients, physical examination is the most reliable tool for evaluating the source of fever.[55]

Infection Control

Infection is a major potential problem for patients with large thermal injuries. In one review, up to 100% of such patients developed an infection from one or more sources during the hospital stay. It is important to apply sound epidemiologic practice to treating infections, both to limit development of opportunistic infections in individual patients and to achieve good infection control in the burn unit itself.

Tetanus prophylaxis has been standard for patients admitted for

---

Table 10 Formulas for Estimating Caloric Needs in Burn Patients

HARRIS-BENEDICT FORMULA

Basal energy expenditure (BEE)* × activity factor† = calories needed daily

CURRERI FORMULA

25 kcal / kg + 40 kcal / %TBSA burned = calories needed daily

---

*Women: BEE = 65.5 + 9.6(weight in kg) +1.8 (height in cm) – 4.7 (age in years).

Men: BEE = 66.5 + 13.8(weight in kg) + 5.0 (height in cm) – 6.8 (age in years).

†For burns, the activity factor is 2, which may overestimate caloric needs for patients with smaller burns.

TBSA—total body surface area

---

any type of trauma, primarily because the disease is so devastating and its prevention so simple. There are a few cases in modern medical literature of tetanus in patients who had received immunization during childhood.[56]

For many years, all patients admitted with burn injuries received antibiotic prophylaxis against gram-positive organisms. This practice often led to the development of gram-negative bacterial infections or, even worse, fungal infections. Studies have now verified that prophylactic antibiotics not only are unnecessary but may well be contraindicated in patients with burns.[57] Therefore, treatment of infections in patients with burns should be based on clinical judgment and supportive laboratory and radiologic findings.

The wound is a primary source of infection for patients with burns [see 114 Management of the Burn Wound]. The mainstay of both prevention and treatment is daily washing with soap and water and application of a topical broad-spectrum antimicrobial agent. As soon as it becomes evident that a burn wound will not heal, excision and grafting should be performed. Preferably, the decision to proceed with surgery should be made before postburn day 21. For patients who undergo surgery, perioperative antibiotics may reduce postoperative wound infection.[57]

Nutrition

In the early 1970s, Curreri and others recognized that patients with major thermal injury experience hypermetabolism, with an increased basal metabolic rate, increased oxygen consumption, negative nitrogen balance, and weight loss; hence, these patients have exaggerated caloric requirements.[58] Furthermore, inadequate caloric intake can be associated with delayed wound healing, decreased immune competence, and cellular dysfunction.

A patient with a large burn may lose as much as 30 g of nitrogen a day because of protein catabolism. Not only is urinary excretion of urea nitrogen increased, but large amounts of nitrogen are lost from the wound itself. Therefore, total urea nitrogen levels do not accurately reflect all nitrogen losses in burn patients.[59] A patient with a small burn (≤ 10% TBSA) may lose nitrogen at a rate of 0.02 g/kg/day. A moderate burn (11% to 29% TBSA) may be associated with nitrogen losses equaling 0.05 g/kg/day. A large burn (≥ 30% TBSA) may result in the loss of as much as 0.12 g/kg/day, which may be equivalent to daily losses of 190 g of protein or about 300 g of muscle.

Catabolism generally continues until wounds have healed. However, once a patient becomes anabolic, preburn muscle takes three times as long to regain as it took to lose.[60,61] Therefore, a patient in whom it takes 1 month for burn wounds and donor sites to heal may need 3 or more months to regain preburn weight and muscle mass. These statistics underscore the importance of accurately estimating each patient's caloric needs during hospitalization. Over the years, a number of equations have been developed to estimate calorie needs [see Table 10]. Probably the most widely used formula is the Harris-Benedict equation, which estimates basal energy expenditure according to gender, age, height, and weight. The basal energy expenditure is then multiplied by an activity factor that reflects the severity of injury or the degree of illness; for burns, this multiplier is 2, the maximal factor for this formula. The limitation of the Harris-Benedict equation is that it may overestimate caloric needs for patients with burns smaller than 40% TBSA. A formula specific for patients with burns is the Curreri formula,[62] which is based on patient weight and burn size; this formula may overestimate caloric needs for patients with large burns and therefore is best used for patients with burns less than 40% TBSA.[63,64]

Ongoing evaluation of metabolic status of the burn patient is necessary to take into account changes in wound size and clinical condition. Metabolic demands decrease with burn healing or grafting; on the other hand, donor sites create new wounds, which may increase catabolic rates. Development of infection or ARDS greatly increases catabolism and may alter caloric needs.[65] Simple assessment of nitrogen requirements can be determined by measuring 24-hour total urea nitrogen levels in the urine. However, this does not account for nitrogen lost from the wound itself. Serum albumin levels are notoriously unreliable markers of adequate nutrition because they lag behind clinical progress; they are especially known to be low in patients with burns larger than 20% TBSA.[66] Transthyretin (also known as prealbumin, although it is not related to albumin in structure or function) levels correlate more closely with catabolic status,[67] and a trend over several weeks may indicate whether the patient's caloric needs are being met.[68] C-reactive protein levels also provide an indication of the patient's general inflammatory state; high levels may correlate with increased catabolism.[67] For intubated patients, indirect calorimetry may be helpful in measuring caloric needs but may not be more exact than the Curreri formula.[69] The so-called metabolic cart is a portable gas analyzer that quantifies volumes of inspired O_2 and expired CO_2 and calculates nutritional requirements according to the following formula:

$$\text{kcal/day} = ([3.9 \times V_{O_2}] + [1.1 \times V_{CO_2}]) \times 1.44$$

This result can also be indirectly measured in patients with pulmonary artery catheters in place by using the Fick equation:

$$\text{kcal/day} = \text{cardiac output} \times (\text{arterial } P_{O_2} - \text{venous } P_{O_2}) \times 10 \times 6.96$$

ENTERAL NUTRITION

As early as 1976, the benefits of enteral nutrition over parenteral nutrition had already been identified for patients with functional gastrointestinal systems.[70] The problems of prolonged ileus and Curling stress ulcers in burn patients have been largely eliminated by early feeding.[71] Multiple studies have shown that patients with major thermal injury can receive adequate calories within 72 hours after injury.[72] At the University of Washington burn center, tube feeding is started a median of 5 hours after admission.

There is ongoing debate about the benefits of gastric feeding versus duodenal feeding. Although feeding distal to the pylorus should pose less aspiration risk, one study found evidence of enteral formula in pulmonary secretions of 7% of patients receiving gastric feeds compared with 13% of patients receiving transpyloric

feeding.[73] Hence, for burn patients with high caloric needs, the benefit of decreased aspiration with transpyloric feeds may only be theoretical and may be offset by the delay in feeding for confirmation of tube placement; such confirmation is necessary because these tubes can easily flip back into the stomach.

Continuation of tube feedings during surgery in intubated patients who require multiple operations is a safe way to maximize caloric intake and decrease wound infection. There is no need to stop feedings for anesthesia induction and endotracheal intubation[74]; however, intraoperative positioning, especially if the patient will be prone during surgery, may necessitate stopping feedings preoperatively. Mayes and colleagues have presented data that support continuation of tube feedings in critically ill burn patients undergoing decompressive laparotomy.[75]

GLUCOSE LEVELS

The adverse effects of hyperglycemia on wound healing and morbidity highlight the importance of maintaining blood glucose levels at 80 to 110 mg/dl.[76] In pediatric burn patients, poor glucose control has been associated with bacteremia, reduced skin-graft take, and higher mortality.[77]

ALBUMIN LEVELS

Burn patients characteristically have hypoalbuminemia that persists until wounds are healed and the rehabilitation phase of recovery has begun. In fact, patients with large burns have serum albumin levels that average 1.7 g/dl and never exceed 2.5 g/dl.[66] Management of hypoalbuminemia is controversial, but there is general agreement that once burn resuscitation is complete, infusion of exogenous albumin to serum levels above 1.5 g/dl does not affect burn patient length of stay, complication rate, or mortality.[78]

NUTRITIONAL SUPPLEMENTS

Specialized nutritional formulas with purported effects on metabolic rate and immunologic status have garnered a great deal of interest as adjuncts in the management of critically ill and injured patients.[79] Much of the information on nutritional requirements for critically ill patients was derived from an animal burn model,[80] however, and studies on the efficacy of specialized nutritional supplements in humans have generated contradictory data. A randomized trial of nutritional formulas that were intended to enhance immune status and that included essential amino acids and omega-3 fatty acids showed no clinical advantage in burn patients.[81] However, another study demonstrated that glutamine supplementation in adult burn patients resulted in significantly lower mortality and infection rates.[82] Other nutritional or metabolically active supplements that have demonstrated promise in promoting anabolism in burn patients include insulin, recombinant human growth factor, the anabolic steroid oxandrolone, and propranolol.[83] Oxandrolone in particular has produced marked improvements in weight gain, return to function, and length of hospital stay.[84] Early administration of antioxidant supplementation with α-tocopherol and ascorbic acid has been shown to reduce the incidence of organ failure and shorten ICU length of stay in critically ill surgical patients.[85] Whether this is true for burn patients remains to be demonstrated, but the relative low cost and the low risk of complications make this an attractive intervention for burn patients at risk for ARDS.

Anemia

Because acute blood loss is uncommon in a patient with an isolated burn injury, a rapidly decreasing hematocrit during resuscitation should prompt an evaluation for associated injuries. Procedures during resuscitation, such as central venous line placement or escharotomies, should not be associated with significant blood loss.

Anemia was a major problem in burn management before early excision and grafting became commonplace. As excision techniques have become more sophisticated [see 114 Management of the Burn Wound], operative blood loss has decreased, as has the need for transfusion.[86,87] Nevertheless, excision and grafting may be associated with large blood loss, and the operating team must be prepared for intraoperative blood transfusion.

Decisions about transfusion must be based on the patient's age, overall condition, and comorbidity. The risks of viral transmission and transfusion reactions, as well as the cost, must also be carefully considered. For an otherwise healthy patient who does not need surgery, a hematocrit as low as 20% may be tolerated. However, patients with inhalation injury or ARDS may benefit from the greater oxygen-carrying capacity afforded by a higher hematocrit. Patients with large burns and anticipated blood loss during hospitalization should probably receive iron supplements.

Given that the literature contains some indication that erythropoietin levels may be elevated in patients with large burns, the benefit of exogenous erythropoietin is debatable.[88] At least one prospective study suggests that administration of recombinant erythropoietin in acutely burned patients does not prevent anemia or decrease transfusion requirements.[89]

Pain Management

Pain management for patients with burn injuries can be challenging. The simplest approaches work best; polypharmacy is likely to confuse both patient and health care providers and should therefore be avoided. Burn patients experience several different classes of pain: background, breakthrough, and procedural. Each responds to a different approach.

Background pain is the discomfort that burn patients experience throughout the day and night. It is best treated with long-acting pain relievers. For a hospitalized patient with large burns, methadone or controlled-release morphine sulfate may be the most appropriate choice for background pain. In an outpatient with a small burn, a nonsteroidal anti-inflammatory drug (NSAID) may be optimal; if excision and grafting are planned, the NSAID should be stopped at least 7 days before surgery to permit recovery of platelet function.

Breakthrough pain results when activities of daily living exacerbate burn-wound discomfort. Short-acting narcotics or acetaminophen are used to alleviate breakthrough pain. Persistent breakthrough pain indicates that the dose of the long-acting medication should be increased.

Procedural pain is the discomfort that patients experience during wound care and dressing changes. This usually requires treatment with a short-acting narcotic. For inpatients with larger burns,

oral narcotics or transmucosal fentanyl citrate[90] work well for wound care; I.V. morphine or fentanyl is used for uncontrolled pain. For outpatients, oxycodone (5 to 15 mg) works well for daily wound care.

Anxiety related to wound care is an underdiagnosed and undertreated source of discomfort that is often construed as pain, especially in children. Therefore, patients with large burns requiring wound care once or twice a day should be evaluated to determine whether they would benefit from a short-acting anxiolytic agent for procedures.

Learning to accurately assess pain in burn patients can help prevent complications related to excessive narcotic use, such as prolonged sedation, delirium, and, more urgently, loss of airway control. This is especially true in young children and elderly patients, who may have decreased ability to tolerate narcotics.[91,92]

Nonpharmacologic approaches are also an important component of pain management in burn patients. Hypnosis—administered either by trained health care providers or, more efficiently, by patients themselves—has proved to be a useful tool for reducing narcotic use in patients with burns.[93] Another distraction modality that has shown promise and garnered significant publicity has been virtual reality. Although it is not a standard of care for all patients admitted with burn injuries, preliminary observations suggest that use of virtual reality can enhance patient comfort during wound care and intense therapy.

Discomfort in the healed wound may persist for months after injury. In general, narcotics do not control such symptoms; exercise and deep massage are more effective. Itching can be a pervasive long-term symptom for which there is no reliable topical or systemic therapy. Diphenhydramine, cyproheptadine, or cetirizine may relieve itching. There are also promising data on the use of doxepin ointment as a topical treatment for itching of healed wounds.[94] Keeping the wound moist with a topical salve may be as effective as other pharmacologic approaches.

Deep Vein Thrombosis Prophylaxis

The incidence of deep vein thrombosis (DVT) and, thus, the need for DVT prophylaxis in patients with thermal injury have never been clearly defined. Whereas some studies report DVT in as many as 25% of all hospitalized burn patients and advocate DVT prophylaxis,[95] others report that thromboembolism is responsible for only 0.14% of deaths in burn patients and does not warrant the potential complications of anticoagulation therapy.[96] At the University of Washington burn center, a quality-assurance review found that in patients with burns larger than 20% TBSA, clinically evident thromboembolic disease occurred in 9% of those who received prophylaxis with unfractionated heparin and in 18% of those who received low-molecular-weight heparin. On the basis of these data, patients with burns larger than 20% TBSA receive prophylaxis with subcutaneous unfractionated heparin, 5,000 U twice a day.

References

1. Practice Guidelines for Burn Care. J Burn Care Rehabil 22:1S, 2001

2. Guidelines for the operation of burn units. American Burn Association, 1999 http://www.ameriburn.org/pub/guidelinesops.pdf

3. Baxter CR, Shires T: Physiological response to crystalloid resuscitation of severe burns. Ann NY Acad Sci 150:874, 1968

4. Baxter CR: Fluid volume and electrolyte changes of the early postburn period. Clin Plast Surg 1:693, 1974

5. Neuwalder JM, Sampson C, Breuing KH, et al: A review of computer-aided body surface area determination: SAGE II and EPRI's 3D Burn Vision. J Burn Care Rehabil 23:55, 2002

6. Warden GD, Stratta RJ, Saffle JR, et al: Plasma exchange therapy in patients failing to resuscitate from burn shock. J Trauma 23:945, 1983

7. Engrav LH, Colescott PL, Kemalyan N, et al: A biopsy of the use of the Baxter formula to resuscitate burns or do we do it like Charlie did it? J Burn Care Rehabil 21:91, 2000

8. Sharar SR, Heimbach DM, Green M, et al: Effects of body surface thermal injury on apparent renal and cutaneous blood flow in goats. J Burn Care Rehabil 9:26, 1988

9. Pruitt BA Jr: Protection from excessive resuscitation: "pushing the pendulum back." J Trauma 49:567, 2000

10. Greenhalgh DG, Warden GD: The importance of intra-abdominal pressure measurements in burned children. J Trauma 36:685, 1994

11. Hobson KG, Young KM, Ciraulo A, et al: Release of abdominal compartment syndrome improves survival in patients with burn injury. J Trauma 53:1129, 2002

12. Rue LW 3rd, Cioffi WG, Mason AD, et al: Improved survival of burned patients with inhalation injury. Arch Surg 128:772, 2001

13. Muller MJ, Pegg SP, Rule MR: Determinants of death following burn injury. Br J Surg 88:583, 2001

14. Heimbach DM, Waeckerle JF: Inhalation injuries. Ann Emerg Med 17:1316, 1988

15. Hantson P, Butera R, Clemessy JL, et al: Early complications and value of initial clinical and paraclinical observations in victims of smoke inhalation without burns. Chest 111:671, 1997

16. Hampson NB, Mathieu D, Piantadosi CA, et al: Carbon monoxide poisoning: interpretation of randomized clinical trials and unresolved treatment issues. Undersea Hyperb Med 28:157, 2001

17. Juurlink DN, Stanbrook MB, McGuigan MA: Hyperbaric oxygen for carbon monoxide poisoning. Cochrane Database Syst Rev (2):CD002041, 2000

18. Grube BJ, Marvin JA, Heimbach DM: Therapeutic hyperbaric oxygen: help or hindrance in burn patients with carbon monoxide poisoning? J Burn Care Rehabil 9:249, 1988

19. Hampson NB, Zmaeff JL: Outcome of patients experiencing cardiac arrest with carbon monoxide poisoning treated with hyperbaric oxygen. Ann Emerg Med 38:36, 2001

20. Schall GL, McDonald HD, Carr LB, et al: Xenon ventilation-perfusion lung scans: the early diagnosis of inhalation injury. JAMA 240:2441, 1978

21. Bingham HG, Gallagher TJ, Powell MD: Early bronchoscopy as a predictor of ventilatory support for burned patients. J Trauma 27:1286, 1987

22. Ashbaugh DG, Bigelow DB, Petty TL, et al: Acute respiratory distress in adults. Lancet 2:319, 1967

23. Bulger EM, Jurkovich GJ, Gentilello LM, et al: Current clinical options for the treatment and management of acute respiratory distress syndrome. J Trauma 48:562, 2000

24. Darling GE, Keresteci MA, Ibanez D, et al: Pulmonary complications in inhalation injuries with associated cutaneous burn. J Trauma 40:83, 1996

25. Hollingsed TC, Saffle JR, Barton RG, et al: Etiology and consequences of respiratory failure in thermally injured patients. Am J Surg 166:592, 1993

26. Dancey DR, Hayes J, Gomez M, et al: ARDS in patients with thermal injury. Intensive Care Med 25:1231, 1999

27. Hantson P, Butera R, Clemessy JL, et al: Early complications and value of initial clinical and paraclinical observations in victims of smoke inhalation without burns. Chest 111:671, 1997

28. Tasaki O, Goodwin CW, Saitoh D, et al: Effects of burns on inhalation injury. J Trauma 43:603, 1997

29. Kowal-Vern A, Walenga JM, Sharp-Pucci M, et al: Postburn edema and related changes in interleukin-2, leukocytes, platelet activation, endothelin-1, and C1 esterase inhibitor. J Burn Care Rehabil 18:99, 1997

30. Soejima K, Traber LD, Schmalstieg FC, et al: Role of nitric oxide in vascular permeability after combined burns and smoke inhalation injury. Am J Respir Crit Care Med 163:745, 2001

31. Moss NM, Gough DB, Jordan AL, et al: Temporal correlation of impaired immune response after thermal injury with susceptibility to infection in a murine model. Surgery 104:882, 1988

32. Ventilation with lower tidal volumes as compared with traditional tidal volumes for acute lung injury and the acute respiratory distress syndrome. The Acute Respiratory Distress Syndrome Network. N Engl J Med 342:1301, 2000

33. Kallet RH, Corral W, Silverman HJ, et al: Implementation of a low tidal volume ventilation protocol for patients with acute lung injury or acute respiratory distress syndrome. Respir Care 46:1024, 2001

34. Sheridan RL, Kacmarek RM, McEttrick MM, et al: Permissive hypercapnia as a ventilatory strategy in burned children: effect on barotrauma, pneumonia, and mortality. J Trauma 39:854, 1995

35. Blanch L, Mancebo J, Perez M, et al: Short-term effects of prone position in critically ill patients with acute respiratory distress syndrome. Intensive Care Med 23:1033, 1997

36. Venet C, Guyomarc'h S, Migeot C, et al: The oxygenation variations related to prone positioning during mechanical ventilation: a clinical comparison between ARDS and non-ARDS hypoxemic patients. Intensive Care Med 27:1352, 2001

37. Patton ML, Simone MR, Kraut JD, et al: Successful utilization of ECMO to treat an adult burn patient with ARDS. Burns 24:566, 1998

38. Kane TD, Greenhalgh DG, Warden GD, et al: Pediatric burn patients with respiratory failure: predictors of outcome with the use of extracorporeal life support. J Burn Care Rehabil 20:145, 1999

39. Reper P, Van Bos R, Van Loey K, et al: High frequency percussive ventilation in burn patients: hemodynamics and gas exchange. Burns 29:603, 2003

40. Cioffi WG Jr, Rue LW 3rd, Graves TA, et al: Prophylactic use of high-frequency percussive ventilation in patients with inhalation injury. Ann Surg 213:575, 1991

41. Paulsen SM, Killyon GW, Barillo DJ: High-frequency percussive ventilation as a salvage modality in adult respiratory distress syndrome: a preliminary study. Am Surg 68:852, 2002

42. Cartotto R, Cooper AB, Esmond JR, et al: Early clinical experience with high-frequency oscillatory ventilation for ARDS in adult burn patients. J Burn Care Rehabil 22:325, 2001

43. Sheridan RL, Zapol WM, Ritz RH, et al: Low-dose inhaled nitric oxide in acutely burned children with profound respiratory failure. Surgery 126:856, 1999

44. Thompson BT: Glucocorticoids and acute lung injury. Crit Care Med 31:S253, 2003

45. Yang JY, Yang WG, Chang LY, et al: Symptomatic tracheal stenosis in burns. Burns 25:72, 1999

46. Bowers BL, Purdue GF, Hunt JL: Paranasal sinusitis in burn patients following nasotracheal intubation. Arch Surg 126:1411, 1991

47. Hunt JL, Purdue GF, Gunning T: Is tracheostomy warranted in the burn patient? Indications and complications. J Burn Care Rehabil 7:492, 1986

48. Lund T, Goodwin CW, McManus WF, et al: Upper airway sequelae in burn patients requiring endotracheal intubation or tracheostomy. Ann Surg 201:374, 1985

49. Barret JP, Desai MH, Herndon DN: Effects of tracheostomies on infection and airway complications in pediatric burn patients. Burns 26:190, 2000

50. Saffle JR, Morris SE, Edelman L: Early tracheostomy does not improve outcome in burn patients. J Burn Care Rehabil 23:431, 2002

51. Caruso DM, al-Kasspooles MF, Matthews MR, et al: Rationale for 'early' percutaneous dilatational tracheostomy in patients with burn injuries. J Burn Care Rehabil 18:424, 1997

52. Salisbury R, Carnes R, Enterline D: Biological dressings and evaporative water loss from burn wounds. Ann Plast Surg 5:270, 1980

53. Childs C, Little RA: Acute changes in oxygen consumption and body temperature after burn injury. Arch Dis Child 71:31, 1994

54. Gore DC, Chinkes D, Sanford A, et al: Influence of fever on the hypermetabolic response in burn-injured children. Arch Surg 138:169, 2003

55. Parish RA, Novack AH, Heimbach DM, et al: Fever as a predictor of infection in burned children. J Trauma 27:69, 1987

56. Karyoute SM, Badran IZ: Tetanus following a burn injury. Burns Incl Therm Inj 14:241, 1988

57. Durtschi MB, Orgain C, Counts GW, et al: A prospective study of prophylactic penicillin in acutely burned hospitalized patients. J Trauma 22:11, 1982

58. Curreri PW, Luterman A: Nutritional support of the burned patient. Surg Clin North Am 58:1151, 1978

59. Waxman K, Rebello T, Pinderski L, et al: Protein loss across burn wounds. J Trauma 27:136, 1987

60. Demling RH, Orgill DP: The anticatabolic and wound healing effects of the testosterone analog oxandrolone after severe burn injury. J Crit Care 15:12, 2000

61. Hart DW, Wolf SE, Mlcak R, et al: Persistence of muscle catabolism after severe burn. Surgery 128:312, 2000

62. Curreri PW, Richmond D, Marvin J, et al: Dietary requirements of patients with major burns. J Am Diet Assoc 65:415, 1974

63. Schane J, Goede M, Silverstein P: Comparison of energy expenditure measurement techniques in severely burned patients. J Burn Care Rehabil 8:366, 1987

64. Gore DC, Rutan RL, Hildreth M, et al: Comparison of resting energy expenditures and caloric intake in children with severe burns. J Burn Care

Rehabil 11:400, 1990

65. Khorram-Sefat R, Behrendt W, Heiden A, et al: Long-term measurements of energy expenditure in severe burn injury. World J Surg 23:115, 1999

66. Sheridan RL, Prelack K, Cunningham JJ: Physiologic hypoalbuminemia is well tolerated by severely burned children. J Trauma 43:448, 1997

67. Manelli JC, Badetti C, Botti G, et al: A reference standard for plasma proteins is required for nutritional assessment of adult burn patients. Burns 24:337, 1998

68. Rettmer RL, Williamson JC, Labbe RF, et al: Laboratory monitoring of nutritional status in burn patients. Clin Chem 38:334, 1992

69. Saffle JR, Larson CM, Sullivan J: A randomized trial of indirect calorimetry-based feedings in thermal injury. J Trauma 30:776, 1990

70. Blackburn GL, Bistrian BR: Nutritional care of the injured and/or septic patient. Surg Clin North Am 56:1195, 1976

71. Raff T, Germann G, Hartmann B: The value of early enteral nutrition in the prophylaxis of stress ulceration in the severely burned patient. Burns 23:313, 1997

72. Raff T, Hartmann B, Germann G: Early intragastric feeding of seriously burned and long-term ventilated patients: a review of 55 patients. Burns 23:19, 1997

73. Esparza J, Boivin MA, Hartshorne MF, et al: Equal aspiration rates in gastrically and transpylorically fed critically ill patients. Intensive Care Med 27:660, 2001

74. Jenkins ME, Gottschlich MM, Warden GD: Enteral feeding during operative procedures in thermal injuries. J Burn Care Rehabil 15:199, 1994

75. Mayes T, Gottschlich MM, Warden GD: Nutrition intervention in pediatric patients with thermal injuries who require laparotomy. J Burn Care

Rehabil 21:451, 2000

76. van den Berghe G, Wouters P, Weekers F, et al: Intensive insulin therapy in the critically ill patients. N Engl J Med 345:1359, 2001

77. Gore DC, Chinkes D, Heggers J, et al: Association of hyperglycemia with increased mortality after severe burn injury. J Trauma 51:540, 2001

78. Greenhalgh DG, Housinger TA, Kagan RJ, et al: Maintenance of serum albumin levels in pediatric burn patients: a prospective, randomized trial. J Trauma 39:67, 1995

79. Gottschlich MM, Jenkins M, Warden GD, et al: Differential effects of three enteral dietary regimens on selected outcome variables in burn patients. JPEN J Parenter Enteral Nutr 14:225, 1990

80. Saito H, Trocki O, Alexander JW, et al: The effect of route of nutrient administration on the nutritional state, catabolic hormone secretion, and gut mucosal integrity after burn injury. JPEN J Parenter Enteral Nutr 11:1, 1987

81. Saffle J, Wiebke G, Jennings K, et al: Randomized trial of immune-enhancing enteral nutrition in burn patients. J Trauma 42:793, 1997

82. Garrel D, Patenaude J, Nedelec B, et al: Decreased mortality and infectious morbidity in adult burn patients given enteral glutamine supplements: a prospective, controlled, randomized clinical trial. Crit Care Med 31:2444, 2003

83. Herndon DN: Nutritional and pharmacological support of the metabolic response to injury. Minerva Anestesiol 69:264, 2003

84. Demling RH, DeSanti L: Oxandrolone induced lean mass gain during recovery from severe burns is maintained after discontinuation of the anabolic steroid. Burns 29:793, 2003

85. Nathens AB, Neff MJ, Jurkovich GJ, et al: Randomized, prospective trial of antioxidant supplementation in critically ill surgical patients. Ann Surg

236:814, 2002

86. Mann R, Heimbach DM, Engrav LH, et al: Changes in transfusion practices in burn patients. J Trauma 37:220, 1994

87. Sheridan RL, Szyfelbein SK: Trends in blood conservation in burn care. Burns 27:272, 2001

88. Deitch EA, Sittig KM: A serial study of the erythropoietic response to thermal injury. Ann Surg 217:293, 1993

89. Still JM Jr, Belcher K, Law EJ, et al: A double-blinded prospective evaluation of recombinant human erythropoietin in acutely burned patients. J Trauma 38:233, 1995

90. Sharar SR, Carrougher GJ, Selzer K, et al: A comparison of oral transmucosal fentanyl citrate and oral oxycodone for pediatric outpatient wound care. J Burn Care Rehabil 23:27, 2002

91. Honari S, Patterson DR, Gibbons J, et al: Comparison of pain control medication in three age groups of elderly patients. J Burn Care Rehabil 18:500, 1997

92. Martin-Herz SP, Patterson DR, Honari S, et al: Pediatric pain control practices of North American burn centers. J Burn Care Rehabil 24:26, 2003

93. Ohrbach R, Patterson DR, Carrougher G, et al: Hypnosis after an adverse response to opioids in an ICU burn patient. Clin J Pain 14:167, 1998

94. Groene D, Martus P, Heyer G: Doxepin affects acetylcholine induced cutaneous reactions in atopic eczema. Exp Dermatol 10:110, 2001

95. Wahl WL, Brandt MM, Ahrns KS, et al: Venous thrombosis incidence in burn patients: preliminary results of a prospective study. J Burn Care Rehabil 23:97, 2002

96. Rue LW 3rd, Cioffi WG Jr, Rush R, et al: Thromboembolic complications in thermally injured patients. World J Surg 16:1151, 1992

114 MANAGEMENT OF THE BURN WOUND

Matthew B. Klein, M.D., David M. Heimbach, M.D., F.A.C.S., and Nicole S. Gibran, M.D., F.A.C.S.

Advances in resuscitation and critical care have significantly improved survival after thermal injury. Ultimately, survival remains contingent on effective wound management and complete wound closure. Current approaches to burn management are based on an understanding of the biology and physiology of human skin and the pathophysiology of the burn wound.

Anatomic and Physiologic Considerations

BIOLOGY OF SKIN

Skin consists of two distinct layers, the epidermis and the dermis; these layers are integrated by a structure known as the basement membrane zone (BMZ) [*see Figure 1*]. The epidermis is the outer layer and acts as the barrier between body tissues and the environment. This layer protects against infection, ultraviolet light, and evaporation of fluids and provides thermal regulation. The epidermis is derived from fetal ectoderm and thus, like other ectodermal derivatives, is capable of regeneration. Repair of epidermal wounds is achieved through regeneration of epidermal cells both from the perimeter of the wound and from the adnexal structures of the epidermis (i.e., hair follicles, sweat glands, and sebaceous glands). Accordingly, pure epidermal injuries heal without scarring.[1]

The principal cell of the epidermis is the keratinocyte. These cells are arranged into five progressively differentiated layers, or strata: the stratum basale, the stratum spinosum, the stratum granulosum, the stratum lucidum, and the stratum corneum. The outermost of these layers—the relatively impermeable stratum corneum—provides the barrier mechanism that protects the underlying tissues. Besides keratinocytes, the epidermis contains cells from other embryologic layers that carry out specific functions. Melanocytes, derived from fetal neuroectoderm, produce melanosomes, which become pigmented as a result of the formation of melanin through the action of the enzyme tyrosinase. Melanin provides the skin with its pigment and absorbs harmful ultraviolet radiation. Langerhans cells, derived from bone marrow cells, play a critical role in the immune function of the skin. These cells recognize, phagocytize, process, and present foreign antigens and, through their expression of class II antigens, initiate the rejection process in skin transplantation.[1]

In contrast to the epidermis, the dermis is a complex network comprising cellular and acellular components. This layer provides skin with its durability and elasticity. Structurally, the dermis consists of two sublayers, a superficial one (the papillary dermis) and a deeper one (the reticular dermis). Collagen is the major structural matrix molecule, constituting approximately 70% of the skin's dry weight. Elastic fibers account for approximately 2% of the skin's dry weight and play an important role in maintaining the integrity of the skin after mechanical perturbation.[1] Glycosaminoglycans (GAGs), the third major extracellular component of the dermis, regulate intracellular and intercellular events by binding to, releasing, and neutralizing cytokines and growth factors.[2,3]

The fibroblast is the principal cell of the dermis and is responsible for synthesis and degradation of fibrous and elastic dermal proteins. The dermis also contains various inflammatory cells (derived from bone marrow stem cells), mast cells, and cells associated with vascular, lymphatic, and nervous tissue.

The BMZ is a complex region of extracellular matrix connecting the basal cells of the epidermis with the papillary dermis. At the light-microscopic level, the dermal-epidermal junction consists of protrusions of dermal connective tissue known as dermal papillae, which interdigitate with epidermal projections known as rete ridges. The structure of the BMZ is best appreciated on electron microscopy, where it appears as a trilaminar zone consisting of a central electron-dense region (the lamina densa) flanked on both sides by regions of lower electron density [*see Figure 2*]. Within the basal cells of the epidermis are multiple sites of attachment to the basal lamina, which are known as hemidesmosomes. On the dermal side of the basal lamina are numerous anchoring fibrils, which reach from the lamina into the connective tissue of the dermis.[1] The BMZ plays a significant role in burn wound healing: epithelialized wounds undergo blis-

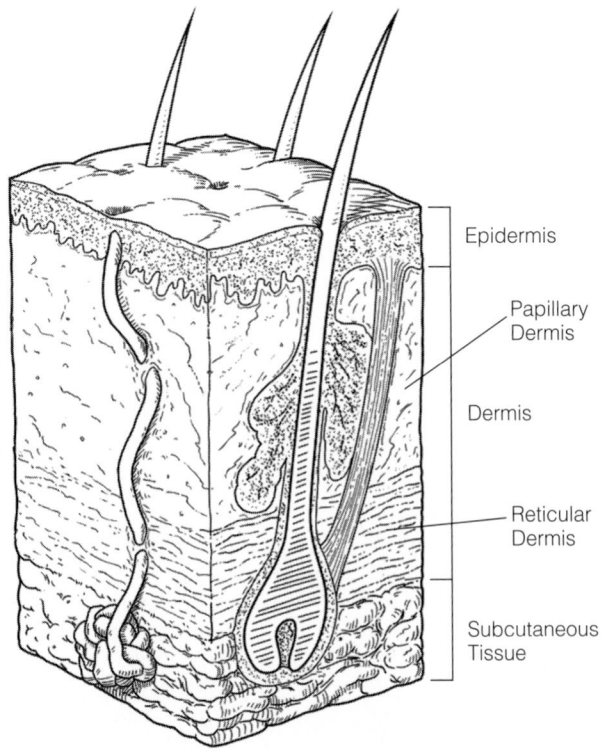

Figure 1 **Cross-sectional diagram shows the two distinct layers of the skin—the epidermis and the dermis (papillary and reticular)—and the underlying subcutaneous fat.**

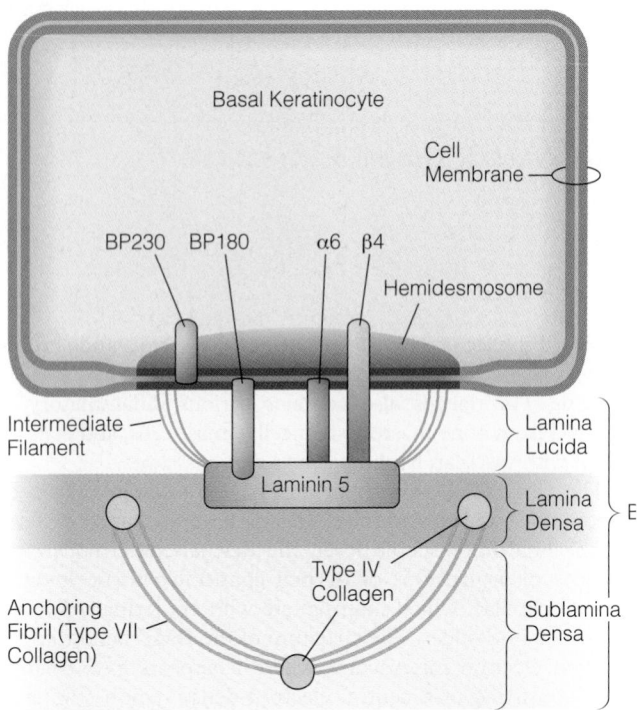

Figure 2 **The basement membrane zone (BMZ) integrates the epidermis with the underlying dermis. On electron microscopy, the BMZ has three layers: a central electron–dense region known as the lamina densa and two regions of lower electron density to either side of this central region.**

tering until the anchoring structures of the BMZ mature and provide protection from shearing.

PATHOPHYSIOLOGY OF THERMAL INJURY

Jackson's classification of burn wounds remains the foundation of our understanding of the pathophysiology of thermal injury to the skin.[4] In this classification, there are three zones of tissue injury resulting from a burn [see Figure 3]. The central, most severely damaged area is called the zone of coagulation because the cells in this area are coagulated or necrotic. Tissue in this zone must be debrid-

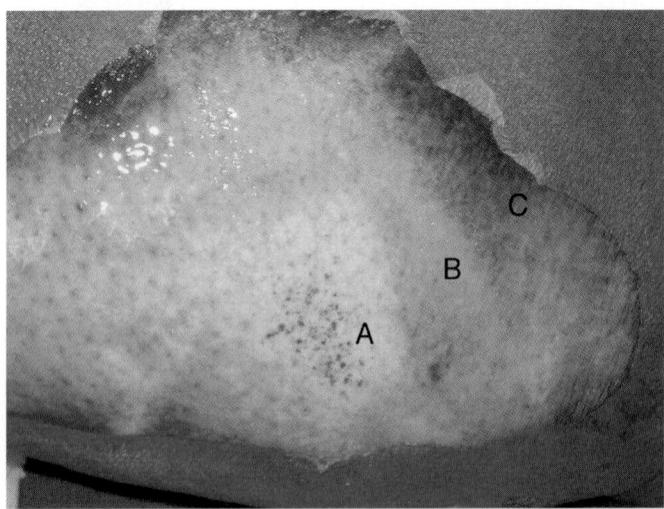

Figure 3 **A burn wound is characterized by three zones of injury: A represents the zone of coagulation, B the zone of stasis, and C the zone of hyperemia.**

Table 1 Overview of Burn Wound Management

Burn Wound Type	Clinical Features	Management
Superficial	Erythematous, painful	Soothing, moisturizing lotions (i.e., aloe)
Partial-thickness	Blistered, pink, moist, painful	Silver sulfadiazine; greasy gauze once epithelial buds are present
Deep partial-thickness	Dry, mottled pink-and-white, less painful	Silver sulfadiazine dressings daily; surgical excision and grafting if not going to heal within 3 wk
Full-thickness	Dry, leathery, black or white, painless	Silver sulfadiazine; early excision and skin grafting

ed. The zone of coagulation is surrounded by the zone of stasis, an area characterized by vasoconstriction and ischemia. Tissue in this zone is initially viable; however, it may convert to coagulation as a consequence of the development of edema, infection, and decreased perfusion.[4] With good wound perfusion, tissue in the zone of stasis generally remains viable. Surrounding the zone of stasis is the zone of hyperemia, an area characterized by vasodilation resulting from the release of inflammatory mediators from resident cutaneous cells. Tissue in this zone typically remains viable.

Clinical Evaluation and Initial Care of Burn Wound

After admission to the burn center, the burn wound is cleaned with soap and water, blisters and debris are removed, and the extent and depth of the wound are assessed. Management of tar burns warrants special mention. When tar that has been heated to maintain a liquid form comes into contact with skin, it can transfer sufficient energy to cause a significant burn injury. As the tar cools on the skin, it solidifies, thereby becoming difficult to remove. Solvents such as petrolatum, petrolatum-based ointments, lanolin, and Medi-Sol (Orange-Sol, Inc., Gilbert, Arizona) are useful for tar removal. For optimal effect, 10 to 15 minutes should be allowed after solvent application before removal of the tar is attempted. Repeat applications may be necessary for complete removal.

ASSESSMENT OF BURN DEPTH

Thermal injury can damage the epidermis alone, the epidermis along with a portion of the dermis, or the entire skin and can even extend into the underlying subcutaneous tissue. The depth of the injury affects the subsequent healing of the wound; thus, assessment of burn wound depth is important for selection of wound dressings and, ultimately, for determination of the need for surgery [see Table 1].

Superficial burns involve only the epidermis. They typically are erythematous and painful, much as a sunburn would be. Most such burns heal within 3 to 4 days, without scarring. The usual treatment is a soothing moisturizing lotion (e.g., one containing aloe vera), which both optimizes the rate of reepithelialization and provides comfort to the patient.

Partial-thickness burns extend through the epidermis and into the papillary dermis. Blistering is their hallmark [see Figure 4]. These burns can be further categorized as superficial or deep. Superficial partial-thickness burns are typically pink, moist, and

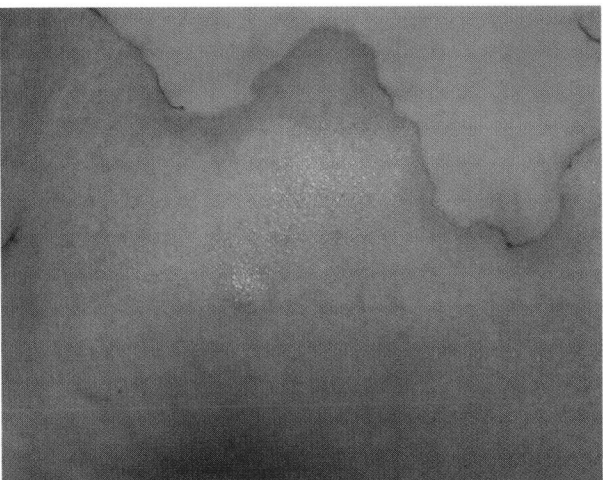
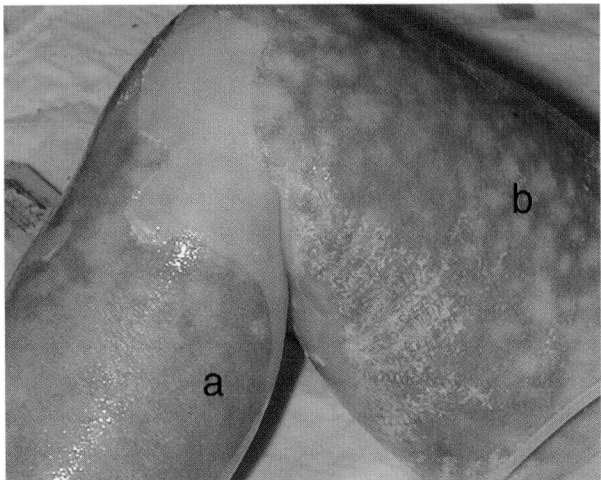

Figure 4 Shown at left is a shallow scald burn with the pink, moist appearance typical of a superficial partial-thickness burn wound. Such injuries typically heal without the need for excision and grafting. A superficial partial-thickness burn (right, *a*), which involves only the papillary dermis, is visually distinct from a deep partial-thickness burn (right, *b*), which is mottled in appearance, extends into the reticular dermis, and is more likely to require excision and grafting.

painful. They usually heal within 2 to 3 weeks, without scarring or functional impairment. Deep partial-thickness wounds extend into the reticular layer of the dermis. They are typically a mottled pink-and-white, dry, and variably painful. In some cases, they may be difficult to distinguish from full-thickness burns. Deep partial-thickness burn wounds, if they do not become infected, typically heal in 3 to 8 weeks, with severe scarring, contraction, and loss of function. Therefore, if a partial-thickness burn has not healed by 3 weeks, surgical excision and skin grafting may be required.

Full-thickness burn wounds extend through the entire dermis and into the subcutaneous tissue. These burns are typically white or black, dry, and painless [*see Figure 5*]. Some full-thickness burns appear red, but they can be distinguished from superficial burns because they are not moist and do not blanch with pressure. Because all skin appendages are burned away, full-thickness burns can heal only by contraction or migration of keratinocytes from the periphery of the wound. Accordingly, all full-thickness burns, unless they are quite small (e.g., the size of a quarter or smaller), must be treated with excision and grafting.

As a rule, both superficial and full-thickness burns are easily recognized, and treatment decisions are relatively straightforward. It is frequently difficult, however, to determine the ultimate fate of intermediate partial-thickness burns soon after injury. For this reason, these wounds are often referred to as indeterminate-thickness wounds. Over the course of the first several postburn days, it usually becomes easier to determine which indeterminate-thickness wounds are likely to heal in a timely manner, without the need for grafting.

Various techniques for accurately and readily assessing burn depth have been described, including the use of vital dyes, laser flowmetry, thermography, and magnetic resonance imaging, but none of these has ever been shown to yield a more precise determination of burn depth than clinical evaluation by an experienced burn care provider.[5]

DETERMINATION OF NEED FOR ESCHAROTOMY

Burn wound eschar consists of dead skin, has the consistency of leather, and may restrict limb perfusion by creating a nonelastic exoskeleton. A key issue in assessing burn wounds is whether

escharotomies are necessary. In general, escharotomies are required only for circumferential full-thickness extremity burns in which distal perfusion has been compromised or for chest burns in which eschar poses an external mechanical barrier to respiration. Escharotomies can be performed at the bedside with either a scalpel or an electrocautery. They should extend through the eschar only, not through the muscle fascia. Adequate release is signaled by separation of the eschar, improved distal perfusion, and, sometimes, a popping sound. Because an escharotomy is a superficial incision through dead tissue, only minimal doses of analgesics and anxiolytics are required.

DAILY BURN WOUND CARE

The use of hydrotherapy tanks, previously a standard component of burn unit wound care, has fallen from favor somewhat because of the risks of cross-contamination between one burn wound area and another. It is preferable to place the patient on a

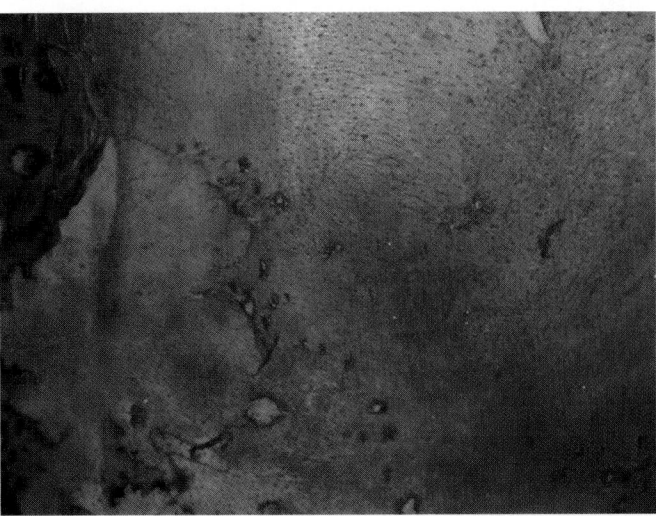

Figure 5 Shown is a full-thickness flame burn with a characteristic brown, leathery appearance. Such wounds require excision and subsequent skin grafting.

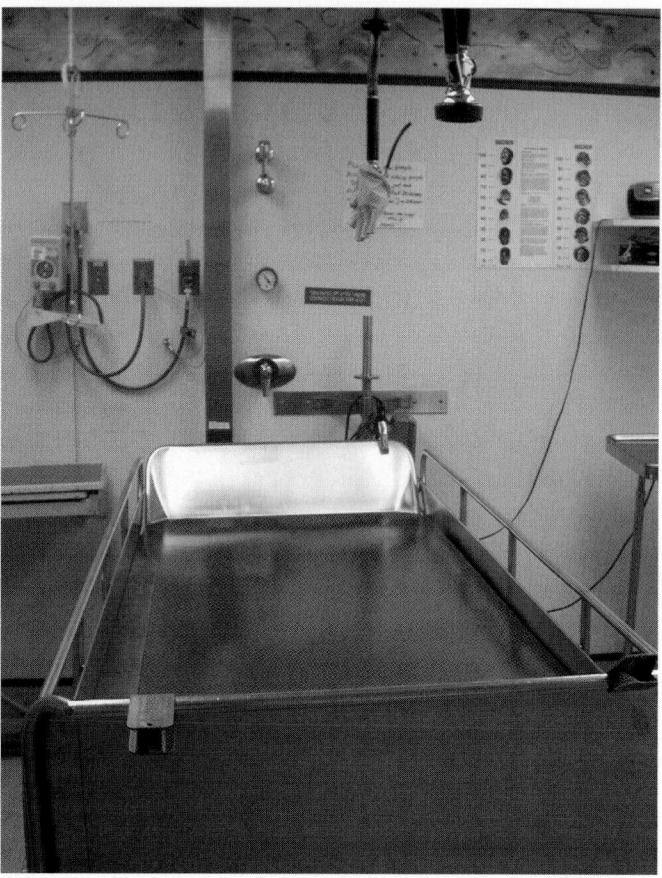

Figure 6 **Shower tables are generally preferred to Hubbard tanks for burn wound care. A clean plastic drape can be used to cover the shower table during patient care.**

shower table, which is inclined so that water runs off the wounds and into a drain [*see Figure 6*]. Smaller wounds can often be managed with bedside wound care after a shower. Washing with tap water and regular soap suffices for daily burn wound cleansing. It is important to be cognizant of the need to provide adequate sedation and analgesia while performing daily wound care—a particularly challenging task with infants and elderly patients.

Topical Burn Wound Treatment

GENERAL PRINCIPLES

Because thermal injury disrupts the protective barrier function of the skin, dressings are needed to protect the body against environmental flora. Burn dressings also protect against evaporative heat loss. The ideal burn dressing would be inexpensive and comfortable and would not require frequent changing. Daily dressing changes allow the burn care provider not only to apply clean dressings but also to clean the wounds and debride fragments of separated eschar and devitalized tissue.

Numerous topical agents and dressings are available for use in burn patients; we limit our discussion to the ones that are most commonly employed and have proved most effective. Selection of an appropriate dressing for a given wound is governed by the specific goals of management. With purely superficial wounds, the goal is to create a moist environment that will optimize reepithelialization. Typically, this is achieved by applying ointments or lotions. With partial-thickness and full-thickness wounds, however, it is necessary to include agents that protect against microbial colonization (see below). Once a partial-thickness burn demonstrates evidence of epithelialization, dressings should be changed to a regimen that facilitates healing (e.g., greasy gauze with ointment).

ANTIMICROBIAL AGENTS

It must be emphasized that systemic antibiotic prophylaxis plays no role in the management of acute burn wounds and provides no protection against microbial colonization of burn eschar[6]; in fact, use of prophylactic antibiotics in burn patients increases the risk that opportunistic infections will develop. Because eschar has no microcirculation, it is impossible for systemically administered antibiotics to reach the eschar surface, where colonization occurs. Therefore, topical preparations, which are capable of supplying high concentrations of antimicrobial agents at the wound surface, must be used. In the early postburn period, the dominant colonizing organisms are staphylococci and streptococci—typical skin flora. Over time, however, the burn wound becomes colonized with gram-negative organisms.[5] Thus, topical antimicrobial agents used in early burn care should have broad-spectrum coverage to minimize colonization of the wound, but they need not be able to penetrate the burn eschar deeply.

Of the antimicrobial agents used in this setting [*see Table 2*], sil-

Table 2 Topical Antimicrobial Agents Used in Burn Care

Agent	Antimicrobial Coverage	Advantages	Disadvantages/Precautions
Bacitracin	Gram-positive bacterial	Soothes and moisturizes; good for facial care and epithelializing wounds	Not appropriate for deeper wounds
Mafenide	Broad-spectrum antibacterial; anticlostridial	Penetrates eschar well; available as solution or cream	Painful on application; causes metabolic acidosis (via carbonic anhydrase inhibition)
Mupirocin	Anti-MRSA	Effective against MRSA	Narrow (poor gram-negative) antimicrobial coverage
Nystatin	Antifungal (*Candida*)	Provides fungal prophylaxis with swish-and-swallow solution	May interfere with activity of mafenide
Silver nitrate	Broad-spectrum antibacterial	Effective for both prophylaxis and treatment of wound infection	Penetrates eschar poorly; causes hyponatremia; stains linen and dressings; induces methemoglobinemia
Silver sulfadiazine	Broad-spectrum antibacterial; antipseudomonal	Soothes on application and causes no pain	Penetrates eschar poorly; causes leukopenia

ver sulfadiazine is the one most commonly employed for partial-thickness and full-thickness burns. Silver sulfadiazine is soothing on application and is active against a broad spectrum of microorganisms. Because it does not penetrate eschar, very little is systemically absorbed; therefore, it is ineffective against already established burn wound infections. Wounds treated with silver sulfadiazine may form a tenacious yellow-gray pseudoeschar, which can be mistaken for true eschar. This pseudoeschar develops when silver sulfadiazine combines with the wound exudates; it can be gently debrided during daily wound care. It has been suggested that silver sulfadiazine may be responsible for the leukopenia that sometimes develops during the first week after a major burn. This attribution may not be entirely accurate, however, given that this leukopenia may also develop in patients treated with silver nitrate. It is possible that the leukopenia results not from either agent but from the margination of neutrophils secondary to the pathophysiology of the burn injury itself. In any case, the leukopenia is typically self-limited and necessitates no change in therapy. Patients with a history of sulfa allergy typically do not have adverse reactions to silver sulfadiazine; however, if there is concern about a possible reaction, a test patch can be applied to a small area of the wound. If the patient is allergic, silver sulfadiazine will cause pain on application or, in some case, a rash.

Mafenide acetate is also commonly used in the management of burn wounds. It provides excellent coverage against gram-negative organisms, but it is not as active against staphylococci and has no antifungal activity. Unlike silver sulfadiazine, mafenide penetrates eschar very well, and this ability makes it effective in treating as well as preventing burn wound infections. Mafenide does, however, have some drawbacks. Because it is a potent carbonic anhydrase inhibitor, regular use and the consequent ongoing systemic absorption can lead to metabolic acidosis. In addition, because it is so well absorbed, twice-daily administration is necessary. Finally, topical application of mafenide, particularly to partial-thickness burns, is painful, which limits its utility in the routine management of burn wounds. Mafenide is frequently used on the ears and the nose because of its ability to penetrate eschar and protect against suppurative chondritis; however, silver sulfadiazine appears to be equally effective in this setting.[7] Mafenide is available both as a cream and as a solution. The solution is useful as a topical agent for skin grafts when the wound bed is considered likely to benefit from postoperative antimicrobial treatment.

Silver nitrate provides broad-spectrum antimicrobial coverage, including good activity against staphylococci and gram-negative organisms (e.g., Pseudomonas). It is relatively painless on administration and must be reapplied every 4 hours to keep the dressings moist. It does not readily penetrate eschar. Silver nitrate is used in the form of a 0.5% solution, which is bacteriostatic but is not toxic to epithelial cells. The hypotonic formulation (it is reconstituted in water) can cause osmolar dilution, resulting in hyponatremia and hypochloremia. Therefore, careful electrolyte monitoring and diligent replacement are necessary. In rare cases, use of silver nitrate solution can also lead to methemoglobinemia; if this condition is detected, administration of silver nitrate should be discontinued. A principal disadvantage of silver nitrate solution is that it stains everything it touches black.

Acticoat (Smith & Nephew, London, England), a relatively new antimicrobial dressing, consists of a polyethylene mesh impregnated with elemental silver. Silver has unique antimicrobial properties and works by disrupting bacterial cellular respiration. Acticoat has been successfully used for coverage of partial-thickness burns, as well as for coverage of donor sites and meshed skin grafts. With burn wounds, the Acticoat dressing is typically changed every 3 days. The reduced frequency of dressing changes simplifies burn care somewhat but can hinder evaluation of evolving partial-thickness burns. With donor sites, Acticoat can be left in place until the underlying partial-thickness wound heals. Typically, an adhesive tape such as Hypafix (Smith & Nephew) is used to secure the dressing to the donor site for 7 days. Once the tape has been removed, the Acticoat usually is sufficiently adherent to allow patients to shower daily and towel-dry the dressing until it eventually peels off the healed wound. The development of Acticoat has led to the introduction of several other silver-based dressings.

Bacitracin, neomycin, and polymyxin B have all been used for coverage of superficial wounds in conjunction with Xeroform or petrolatum gauze to accelerate epithelialization and minimize colonization. These ointments also are commonly administered several times daily in the care of superficial face burns. Mupirocin has proved effective in treating methicillin-resistant Staphylococcus aureus (MRSA) colonization; however, because of the potential for the development of bacterial resistance, it should be employed only in MRSA-positive wounds.

Surgical Burn Wound Management

As noted [see Clinical Evaluation and Initial Care of Burn Wound, Assessment of Burn Depth, above], superficial burns and superficial partial-thickness burns typically heal without any need for surgical excision and grafting. Dressing changes and daily wound care can remove necrotic debris and provide an environment conducive to healing in a timely fashion (2 to 3 weeks), with minimal scarring. For deep partial-thickness and full-thickness burns, however, operative debridement with subsequent skin graft coverage is necessary. Timely removal of eschar is critical for successful management. Surgical excision removes necrotic tissue that serves as a nidus for microbial proliferation and the development of burn wound sepsis.[8]

EARLY EXCISION AND GRAFTING

Surgical excision of burn wounds is a concept whose importance was not fully appreciated until the 1970s. Previously, the usual practice was to leave eschar intact over the wound surface, the idea being that proteolytic enzymes produced by migrating neutrophils and bacteria within the contaminated eschar would cause a natural separation of the eschar from the wound bed (sloughing) and that the resulting granulating wound would serve as the bed for grafting.[9] The rationale for delaying surgical management was that it would presumably allow the burn care provider time to determine which wounds would heal spontaneously and which would have to be covered with skin grafts. It has since become clear, however, that in cases of extensive burn injury, delayed management results in more extensive bacterial colonization, as well as an increased likelihood of burn wound sepsis, multiple organ failure, and, ultimately, death.[9]

Early excision and skin grafting of small burn wounds were first described by Lusgarten in 1891. After the Cocoanut Grove fire in 1942, Cope suggested that patients treated with early excision and grafting had better overall outcomes.[10] In 1960, Jackson and associates reported discouraging results with early burn wound excision,[11] and it was not until 10 years later, when Janzekovic reported good results with surgical burn wound excision,[12] that enthusiasm for early excision was rekindled. As clinical experience with early excision was accumulated, the benefits became clear.

Since Janzekovic's report, studies have repeatedly shown that early wound excision and closure improve survival, reduce the infection rate, and shorten hospital stay.[13-24] Other studies have demonstrated that early removal of dead and severely damaged tissue interrupts and attenuates the systemic inflammatory response syndrome (SIRS).[8,25] Early excision of deep burn wounds also appears to decrease hypertrophic scarring. Similarly, early excision and grafting have been shown to be beneficial for burns of indeterminate depth as well. In one study of patients with burns covering less than 20% of their total body surface area (TBSA), early excision and grafting reduced length of stay, cost of care, and time away from work in comparison with nonoperative treatment.[17]

Wound Excision

Early staged excision, beginning as early as postburn day 3 if feasible, is now conventional treatment for major burns. Operations are spaced 2 to 3 days apart until all eschar is removed and full wound coverage is achieved. Debrided wounds can be temporarily covered with biologic dressings or cadaveric allograft until autogenous donor sites are available.

Generally, the decision whether to perform operative wound excision is guided by whether spontaneous wound healing is likely to occur in a timely fashion (i.e., within 2 to 3 weeks after the burn). Burn wounds over joint surfaces, however, should undergo excision and grafting sooner so as to minimize healing by wound contraction, which can ultimately lead to disabling contractures. In patients with extensive burns, hemodynamic and pulmonary status must be considered in deciding on the timing of operation. Any critically ill burn patient will have some degree of respiratory dysfunction, but the patient should at least be capable of being safely transported from the ICU to the operating room and back. The risk of hypothermia and the need for blood transfusion must be anticipated before operation and clearly communicated to the anesthesiologist.

There are two main technical approaches to surgical excision of the burn wound: fascial excision and tangential excision. Fascial excision, as the name suggests, involves excising the burned tissue and the underlying subcutaneous tissue down to the muscle fascia [see Figure 7]. A major advantage of fascial excision is that it yields an easily defined plane that is well vascularized and therefore can readily accept a graft. In addition, bleeding is generally easier to control at the fascial level of dissection because the vessels are easier to identify and coagulate. Furthermore, the entire excision can be performed with the electrocautery, and blood loss is thereby minimized. The principal drawback of this approach is that the excision inevitably includes some healthy, viable subcutaneous tissue. Another disadvantage is that the removal of subcutaneous tissue may create an unaesthetic contour deformity.

Tangential excision, as the name suggests, involves sequentially excising the layers of eschar in a tangential fashion until a layer of viable bleeding tissue capable of supporting a skin graft is encountered [see Figure 8].[26,27] The goal is to remove only the nonviable tissue, particularly in the case of deep dermal wounds. Typically, tangential excision is performed with a handheld knife (a Watson knife or a Weck/Goulian blade). A back-and-forth carving motion is used, and very little force is applied. The guard on the knife can be used to control the depth of excision. The appearance of diffuse punctate bleeding signals that viable tissue has been reached. The main disadvantages of tangential excision are that (1) it may be difficult to control the diffuse bleeding from the wound bed, and (2) it may be difficult to assess the suitability of the underlying fat for accepting a graft.

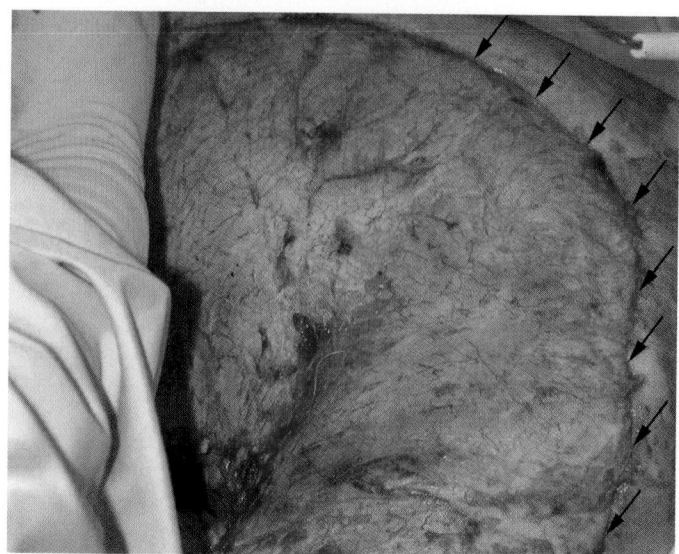

Figure 7 Fascial excision involves excision of the burned skin and the underlying subcutaneous tissue down to the level of the muscle fascia. It is typically performed with the electrocautery. As shown (arrows), the edges should be tacked down to minimize the ledge at the edge where normal tissue adjoins the exposed fascia.

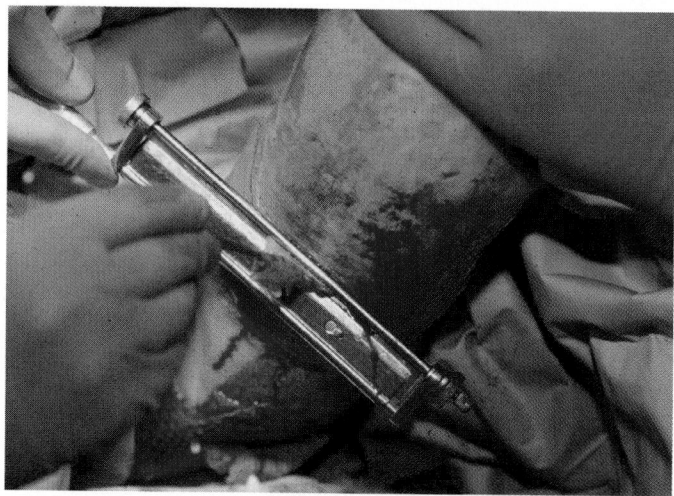

Figure 8 Tangential excision of the burn wound is carried out with a Watson knife (as shown here) or a Weck/Goulian blade. Eschar is tangentially excised until healthy, bleeding tissue that is suitable for skin grafting is reached.

Regardless of which excision technique is used, tourniquets can be placed on extremities to minimize blood loss, and the extremities can be suspended from OR ceiling hooks [see Figure 9] to provide access to their entire circumference.

A water jet–powered instrument (VersaJet Hydrosurgery System; HydroCision, Andover, Massachusetts) is available that can be used for tangential burn wound excision. This device offers an easy and relatively precise way of excising eschar and is particularly useful for excising nonviable tissue from the concave surfaces of the hands and feet, as well as the eyelids and ears.

To minimize hematoma formation and graft loss, it is critical that adequate hemostasis be achieved before the placement of skin grafts, cadaveric grafts, or skin substitutes. Telfa pads (Kendall, Mansfield, Massachusetts) soaked in an epinephrine solution (1:10,000) are a mainstay of hemostasis, combined with topical

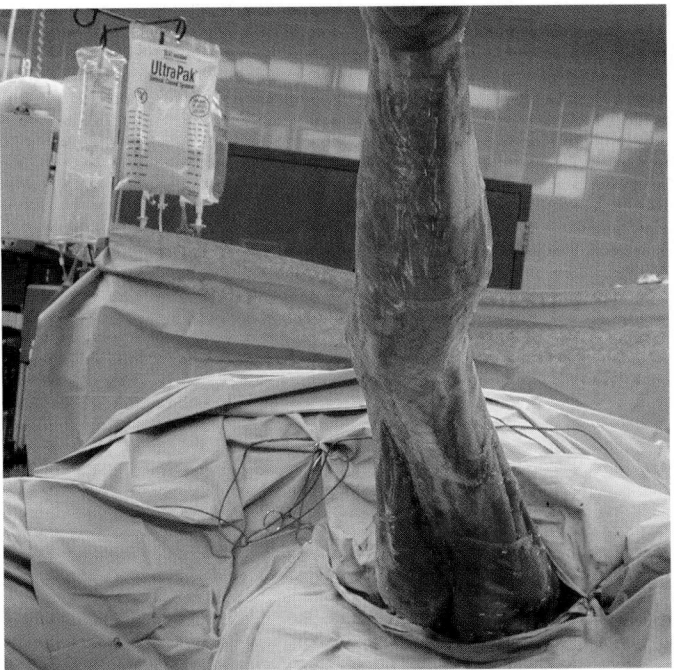

Figure 9 **Extremities can be suspended from OR ceiling hooks to facilitate exposure for burn excision and grafting.**

pressure and cauterization when necessary. A fibrinogen thrombin delivery system (Tisseel Fibrin Sealant; Baxter, Deerfield, Illinois) is commercially available that improves the ability to control bleeding after excision.

Skin Grafting

The best replacement for lost skin is clearly skin itself. The first known report of skin grafting comes from the *Sushruta Samhita*, an ancient Indian surgical treatise that may date back as far as the seventh century B.C. This text describes the use of both skin flaps and grafts for the repair of mutilations of the nose, the ears, and the lips. The Indian method of grafting was first introduced to Western medicine by English surgeons, who observed it during the late 18th century.[28]

It was not until 1804 that successful transplantation of free skin grafts was reported by Baronio of Milan, who successfully grafted large pieces of autogenous skin onto different sites on sheep.[28] In 1869, F. J. C. Guyon and Jacques Reverdin, in a report to the Societe Imperiale de Chirurgie, described the use of a small epidermal graft, which became known as the pinch graft. This technique did not, however, gain wide recognition until 1870, when successful experiments in skin grafting for the treatment of burn patients were performed by George David Pollock.[29] In 1872, Ollier described the use of both full-thickness and split-thickness skin grafts and realized the possibility of covering large areas with such grafts if a satisfactory method of cutting them could be devised.[28]

Currently, a 95% success rate is the standard of care for skin grafting. To achieve this level of success requires adequate wound bed preparation (see above), careful selection of suitable donor sites, and appropriate postoperative care.

Skin grafts are broadly classified as either full-thickness or split-thickness grafts, depending on whether they contain the full thickness of the dermis or a partial thickness [*see 27 Surface Reconstruction Procedures*]. Split-thickness grafts are further categorized as thin, intermediate, or thick, depending on the amount of dermis harvested with the graft. The thinner the skin graft, the greater the degree of contraction that occurs at the recipient site after engraftment. Although thicker grafts have the advantage of contracting less, they leave a greater dermal deficit at the donor site, which can lengthen the time needed for healing and increase the risk of hypertrophic scarring at that site.

Full-thickness skin grafts can be harvested either through use of a dermatome or through direct excision of skin from the flank, the groin crease, the hypothenar eminence, or the forearm and can be used for coverage of small defects of the hand or the face. Standard (intermediate) split-thickness grafts are typically harvested at a thickness of 0.010 to 0.012 in. Thin (0.006 in.) split-thickness skin grafts are generally used in conjunction with skin substitutes, whereas thick (0.018–0.025 in.) split-thickness grafts are typically used in grafting of the hand and the face. The thickness of the graft depends both on the dermatome setting and on the pressure the harvester applies to the dermatome during harvesting.[30]

Donor site selection for split-thickness skin grafts is based on the distribution of the burn. The anterolateral thigh, when available, is the donor site of choice for most adult patients: it can be harvested in the supine position, it can easily be left open to the air so the donor-site dressing can dry, and it can be covered by shorts if desired. When larger grafts are needed or the thighs are burned, the back, the buttocks, and the abdomen can serve as donor sites. Subcutaneous infiltration of a physiologic salt solution yields a smooth, firm surface that facilitates the harvesting of these areas. If this is done, the anesthesiologist should be informed that additional fluid is being administered. In children, the buttocks and the scalp are commonly employed as donor sites. Once healed, these sites are usually inconspicuous: the buttock donor site can be harvested in such a way that it can be covered by a bikini, and the scalp donor site is typically covered by regrown hair. It is important to reassure the patient's parents that if the graft is harvested appropriately, the donor site will not exhibit alopecia and the recipient site will not grow hair. Generally, however, these sites are sufficient only for the grafting of small wounds.

Skin grafts can be applied as sheet (or unmeshed) grafts, or they can be meshed at ratios ranging from 1:1 to 4:1 [*see 27 Surface Reconstruction Procedures*]. Meshing allows the egress of serum and blood from wounds, thereby minimizing the risk that hematomas or seromas will form that could compromise graft survival. In addition, meshed grafts can be expanded or stretched to cover larger surface areas. When grafts are meshed at ratios of 3:1 or higher, allograft skin or another biologic dressing can be applied over them to prevent the interstices from becoming desiccated before they close.[20] Because of the lack of dermis in the interstices, widely expanded mesh always scars, takes a long time to close, and results in permanent unattractive mesh marks. In our center, widely spread mesh is never used unless it is grafted onto a dermal template to minimize scarring (see below).

Sheet grafts should be used on the face, the neck, the hands [*see Figure 10*], and, whenever possible, on the forearms and the legs. In these exposed areas, the superior cosmetic and functional results obtainable with sheet grafts make such grafts preferable. Because sheet grafts have no interstices, they must be closely monitored and periodically rolled with a cotton-tipped applicator to drain any fluid collection. Any serous or bloody blebs that form beneath the graft should be incised with a No. 11 scalpel and drained expeditiously. A common practice known as pie-crusting, which involves making incisions in a sheet graft at the time of surgery, actually does not yield much improvement in graft survival, because blebs often form in areas without incisions. Use of fibrin sealant at the time of grafting may lower the incidence of blebs.

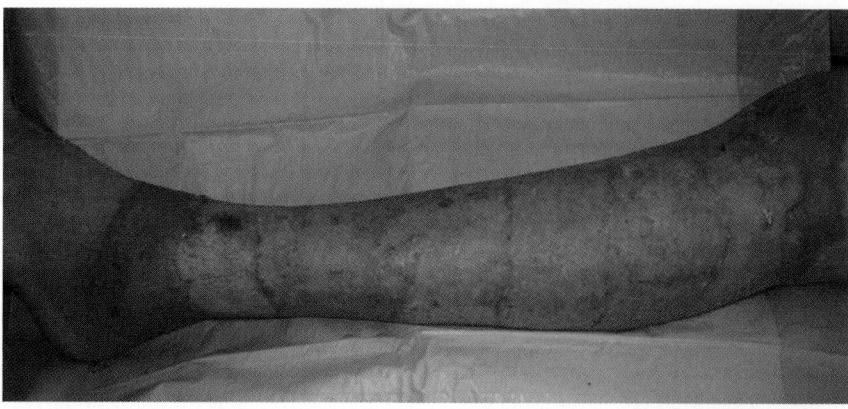

Figure 10 Sheet grafts are the gold standard for skin grafting of the face, the neck, and, whenever possible, the forearms and the legs. This 1-month follow-up demonstrates the aesthetic superiority of sheet grafts.

Graft and Donor Site Dressings

Once the graft is secured in place, a dressing may be applied to protect it from shearing, as well as to accelerate closure of meshed graft interstices. Numerous options for graft dressings exist, including wet dressings and greasy gauze. The use of a nonadherent dressing such as Conformant 2 (Smith & Nephew) along with an outer antimicrobial wet dressing allows the overlying dressings to be periodically removed without dislodging the graft from the wound bed. Bolsters consisting of cotton and greasy gauze are employed to help grafts conform to concave wound surfaces, and splinting of extremities may be necessary for safe graft immobilization, especially over joints. The Vacuum Assisted Closure system (Kinetic Concepts Inc., San Antonio, Texas) is another option for promoting graft healing. Alternatively, an Unna boot can be placed on both the upper and the lower extremity to immobilize the graft and provide vascular support, allowing mobilization of the extremity in the immediate postoperative period.[31]

Sheet grafts can be either left open to the air to allow continuous monitoring and rolling (depending on the patient) or wrapped with dry dressings, which can be removed if necessary to allow interval inspection and deblebbing.

There are also various options for donor-site dressings. The ideal donor-site dressing would not only minimize pain and infection but also be cost-effective. Greasy gauze and Acticoat are often employed for this purpose. Typically, these dressings are left in place until the donor site reepithelializes, at which time the dressing is easily separated from the healed wound. Op-Site, a transparent polyvinyl adherent film, is also commonly used. With Op-Site, the underlying wound is easily examined without removal of the dressing; however, intermittent drainage of the wound fluid that accumulates is necessary. Op-Site does not work well over joint surfaces and concave or convex areas (e.g., the back). Silver sulfadiazine in a diaper is an excellent covering for buttock donor sites in children; dressing changes can be done with each diaper change.

Postoperative Wound Care

Even with complete graft take and timely donor-site reepithelialization, several wound management issues may still arise in the early postoperative period. Physical therapy must be initiated in this period, and management of scarring must be addressed. Blisters are common on newly healed donor sites and ungrafted wounds. The new epithelial layer of these wounds lacks the connections to the underlying wound bed normally provided by the BMZ, which protect the epidermis from shearing. During the months it takes for these structures to reconstitute, their absence frequently leads to blistering. These blisters are usually best man-

aged by draining them with a clean pin, reapplying the epithelial layer to the wound surface, and covering the site with adhesive bandages. The bandages can be soaked off in the shower to ensure that the adhesive causes no additional injury.

Inclusion cysts may develop in healed grafts that were placed over excised wound beds that still contained a thin layer of dermis with adnexal structures. The secretions from the adnexal structures collect beneath the skin graft to form the cysts. Inclusion cysts are treated by unroofing the affected area with a needle.

A condition known as sponge deformity (so called because the skin looks like a bridge of coral sponge [*see Figure 11*]) may occur if a skin graft is placed over a wound that heals underneath the graft in multiple small areas, with or without sloughing of the overlying graft.[32] Where the graft does not slough, a bridge forms. This unsightly deformity can be treated by incising the bridges over the healed tissue with sharp scissors.

Healed donor sites, skin grafts, and ungrafted burns can also break down as a result of infection—a process referred to as melting. Such melting can occur quite rapidly: a graft or healed wound that demonstrates complete take one day may exhibit significant breakdown the next day. Wound cultures should be obtained from these areas, and the open sites should be treated with topical antibiotic ointment and, if the problem worsens, systemic antibiotics.

Malignant degeneration can occur in healed burn wounds decades after the initial injury. These tumors—known as Marjolin ulcers—are usually squamous cell carcinomas and are more aggressive than typical skin cancers.[33] Marjolin ulcers have a high metastatic potential and are associated with a high mortality. New or chronic ulcers in burn wounds should raise the suspicion of malignancy and be considered an indication for biopsy.

BIOLOGIC DRESSINGS AND SKIN SUBSTITUTES

As noted [*see* Early Excision and Grafting, *above*], conventional burn wound management dictates early, aggressive excision of burn wound eschar to minimize the chances of sepsis or progression of burn wound depth.[15,17,34-36] In some cases, the body surface area to be excised is larger than can be covered by autografts from the available donor sites. The solution is to strategically select areas for autograft coverage and then temporarily cover the remaining open areas with biologic dressings. Donor sites typically reepithelialize within about 2 weeks, after which time they can be reharvested, allowing temporary dressings to be serially removed and covered with new autograft.[37]

Biologic dressings perform several important functions. By adhering to the wound bed, they provide a physical covering that controls water vapor transmission, thus minimizing loss of water, electrolytes, and proteins and preventing desiccation and maceration of wounded tissue (which can lead to extension of the depth of injury). In addition, biologic dressings help prevent microbial invasion from the environment.[38]

Allograft and Xenograft Skin

Although the technique of skin grafting is thousands of years old, skin grafting between individuals was not reported until the late 19th century. In 1869, Reverdin published a report on the transplantation of small epidermal grafts from his own arm onto a patient's burn wound.[28] In 1881, Girdner described transplantation of skin grafts from a cadaver to a burn patient and reported a 75% immediate take rate. It was widely noted that these grafts initially performed well but survived for only 6 to 8 weeks.[28] The mechanisms underlying the rejection of these grafts were eventually elucidated by the efforts of Sir Peter Medawar, who received the Nobel Prize in 1960 for his seminal work on defining the basis of allograft rejection and tolerance induction.

The use of allograft was popularized by James Barrett Brown in the 1940s and 1950s,[39] and with the subsequent development of skin banking, allograft became the standard temporary graft for excised burn wounds when sufficient autograft is unavailable or autografting is not indicated.[40]

Ultimately, allograft skin is always rejected unless the donor and the recipient are immunologically identical. The rejection process usually begins within 10 days in an immunologically competent host, but allografts can be tolerated for up to 1 month in a host who is severely immunocompromised (e.g., as a result of extensive burn injury).[9,41] The use of immunosuppressive agents such as cyclosporine has led to the achievement of prolonged allograft tolerance,[14,42-44] but it also exposes the burn patient to the risks inherent in prolonged systemic immunosuppression.

In addition to providing temporary wound closure, allograft has been used as an overlay for meshed autograft with the aim of accelerating epithelialization of the interstices. Allograft has also been used to cover donor sites after autograft harvesting and to cover wounds after excision as a means of assessing the suitability of a bed for autograft placement.[15]

Recognition of the weaker immunogenicity of the dermal layer of cadaver allograft stimulated various attempts to employ allograft for permanent dermal replacement. Jackson was the first to report the use of alternating strips of autograft and allograft for

definitive closure of large burn wounds.[11] In 1985, Heck and associates constructed the first deliberate combination of allogeneic dermis with autologous epidermis.[36] This basic idea was subsequently expanded on by Cuono and colleagues, who used cryopreserved allogeneic dermis as a bed for autologous keratinocyte cultures.[45,46] These investigators demonstrated long-term survival and documented the reconstitution of a normal-appearing BMZ with anchoring fibrils.

Use of allograft skin as a temporary cover or as the permanent dermal replacement in the composite technique does have several drawbacks, including the limited availability of suitable skin, the variable quality of the skin obtained, the substantial cost of allograft procurement and preservation, and the significant potential for disease transmission.[47] In addition, the cryopreservation process significantly compromises the viability, and therefore the efficacy, of the allograft.[38]

Xenografts from a number of species have also been used as biologic dressings. Porcine xenograft has been used in the management of exfoliative skin disorders (e.g., toxic epidermal necrolysis) as well as for temporary wound coverage after excision and before definitive autografting.[48]

Since the 1980s, research efforts have focused on the development of skin replacements that could serve as either a temporary or a permanent substitute for human skin. Conceptually, any skin replacement must recapitulate the native skin biology—that is, it must include an epidermal component, a dermal component, and a BMZ equivalent linking the two.

Cultured Epidermal Autografts

Replacement of the epidermis alone was successfully accomplished in the 1970s with the development of cultured epidermal autografts (CEAs). In 1975, Rheinwald and Green reported the successful isolation and culture of epidermal keratinocytes,[49] and several years later, O'Connor and coworkers reported the first clinical use of CEAs to cover burn wounds.[9] In 1984, Gallico and associates described the use of CEAs to resurface the burn wounds of two children who had sustained injuries over 95% of their TBSA.[29] CEAs are grown in the laboratory from a biopsy of the patient's own skin. A current example is Epicel (Genzyme Biosurgery, Cambridge, Massachusetts), which is approved by the Food and Drug Administration for use in the United States.

CEAs are most commonly applied to the granulation tissue of chronic wound beds. As more clinical experience with CEAs was amassed, the drawbacks of using epidermal components alone to replace full-thickness skin loss became evident.[50-54] The lack of a dermal component made the CEAs extremely fragile and led to high rates of sloughing and infection. Even when CEA engraftment occurred, the BMZ structures critical to graft durability were poorly reconstructed.[54] Compton and coworkers compared the outcome of wounds covered with CEAs alone with the outcome of wounds covered first with allograft dermis and then with CEAs. They found that in wounds containing the allograft dermal component, there was greater initial take, better long-term durability, and accelerated formation of important BMZ structures.[55] It is now well recognized that CEAs are capable of replacing the epidermis but are not effective when used alone to resurface deep partial-thickness and full-thickness wounds.

In vitro development of an epidermal replacement was made possible by the simpler biology of the epidermis. Development of a dermal replacement has proved a more formidable challenge. Dermis consists mainly of extracellular matrix, and its complex structure is not amenable to growth in culture.

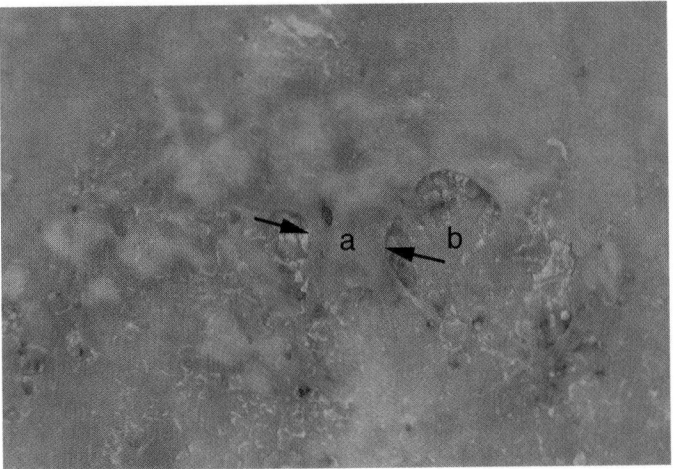

Figure 11 **Sponge deformity can occur if a skin graft is placed over a wound that heals beneath without sloughing of the overlying graft. Arrows depict the bridge of skin graft (*a*) that forms over healed skin (*b*).**

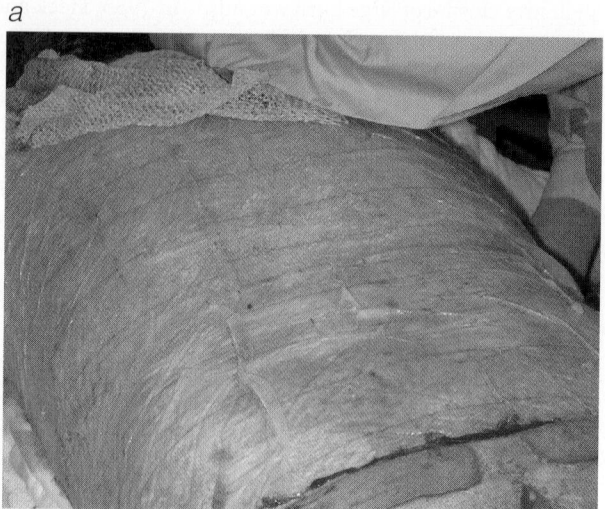
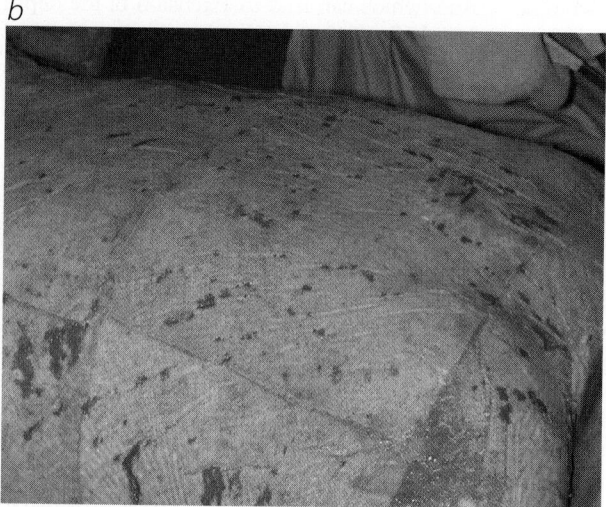

Figure 12 A bilaminar skin substitute is placed on the excised burn wound (*a*) and secured with staples. The skin substitute typically vascularizes in 2 weeks, at which point the Silastic outer layer is removed (*b*) and the neodermis can be autografted.

Skin Substitutes

The drawbacks of allograft and xenograft skin have further underscored the need for an off-the-shelf dermal replacement. A pioneering approach to the development of a skin replacement containing both an epidermal and a dermal component was described by Yannis and Burke in the early 1980s.[56-59] Recognizing the importance of the dermis in skin replacement, they developed a bilayer construct that is now commercially available under the name Integra (Integra LifeSciences Corporation, Plainsboro, New Jersey). The epidermal component of this construct consists of a layer of Silastic film, which acts as a protective barrier against infection and evaporation from the wound bed; the dermal layer consists of a porous matrix of fibers composed of cross-linked bovine collagen and a single type of GAG (chondroitin-6-sulfate). Integra can be placed on a completely excised, noninfected wound bed. Initial studies indicated that a neodermis forms, created by the ingrowth of fibroblasts and endothelial cells into the dermal matrix template provided by the Integra. Once this neodermis forms and the dermal scaffold is well incorporated into the wound (typically, after 14 days), the Silastic component is removed. A thin (0.006 in.) split-thickness autograft is then placed on the neodermis [*see Figure 12*].[56,60] Integra not only is a useful adjunct in the management of large burn wounds but also can play an important role in the management of hand and facial burns requiring excision and grafting.[61] It must be emphasized, however, that for Integra to vascularize completely, it must be applied to a viable, noninfected wound bed. In addition, meticulous surgical technique and appropriate postoperative care are critical for a successful outcome.[62]

Another product marketed for dermal replacement is Alloderm (LifeCell, Branchburg, New Jersey), which is an acellular dermal matrix produced from human cadaveric skin. The cadaveric skin is first stored in normal saline for 15 hours to remove the epidermal component. The cadaveric dermis is then incubated in sodium dodecyl sulfate to extract any remaining cellular components. The decellularized substrate is freeze-dried and reconstituted by soaking it in crystalloid solution before use.[44] Alloderm can be used for immediate wound coverage in combination with a thin split-thickness autograft. Data from multicenter trials indicate that Alloderm works best with thin (0.006–0.008 in.) autografts: the

thicker the autograft, the lower the take rates.[44,63] Alloderm has also been used for abdominal wall reconstruction and for soft tissue augmentation in the face.[64]

A product known as TransCyte (Smith & Nephew)—formerly Dermagraft-TC—is approved by the FDA as a temporary (as opposed to permanent) cover for full-thickness wounds after excision. TransCyte is produced by seeding neonatal fibroblasts isolated from foreskin onto Biobrane, a synthetic dressing consisting of Silastic attached to a nylon mesh, which is coated with porcine peptides prepared from type I collagen. The Silastic layer of Biobrane serves as a temporary impermeable barrier, whereas the fibroblast-impregnated nylon mesh serves as a dermal component.[65] TransCyte is placed on an excised wound bed; when clinically indicated, it is removed and replaced with split-thickness autograft. TransCyte has been found to be statistically equivalent to cryopreserved human allograft skin with respect to adherence to the wound bed, fluid accumulation, and ease of removal.[66] It has also been used as a dressing for partial-thickness wounds, including donor sites.[67,68]

Dermagraft (Smith & Nephew), in contrast, is employed as a permanent dermal replacement. Dermagraft consists of human neonatal fibroblasts seeded onto an absorbable polyglactin mesh scaffold, which is intended to mimic the native dermal architecture.[35,69] It is approved by the FDA for treatment of venous stasis ulcers, but it was developed for coverage of excised burn wounds in conjunction with a split-thickness autograft.

Although a permanent off-the-shelf skin replacement has yet to be developed, the available products have already significantly influenced the management of burn wounds. In addition, the shortcomings of each product and strategy have improved our understanding of skin biology and physiology and confirmed the importance of both the epidermis and the dermis in the structure and function of skin. One group has combined keratinocytes genetically modified to overproduce vascular endothelial growth factor with a fibroblast-collagen-GAG biopolymer matrix to accelerate the vascularization of these constructs and improve the overall healing of wounds covered with them.[70] This approach addresses the shortcomings of using CEAs alone and the absence of an epidermal component in the currently available dermal substitutes.

References

1. Cuono CB: Skin replacements in severe burn injury: biologic requirements and therapeutic approaches. Prespect Plast Surg 2:123, 1988

2. Antonelli A, D'Amore PA: Density-dependent expression of hyaluronic acid binding to vascular cells in vitro. Microvasc Res 41:239, 1991

3. Faham S, Hileman RE, Fromm JR, et al: Heparin structure and interactions with basic fibroblast growth factor. Science 271:1116, 1996

4. Jackson D: The diagnosis of the depth of burning. Br J Surg 40:588, 1953

5. Heimbach D, Mann R, Engrav L: Evaluation of the burn wound management decisions. Total Burn Care, 2nd ed. WB Saunders Co, New York, 2002

6. Durtschi MB, Orgain C, Counts GW, et al: A prospective study of prophylactic penicillin in acutely burned hospitalized patients. J Burn Care Rehabil 9:606, 1982

7. Engrav LH, Richey KJ, Walkinshaw MD, et al: Chondritis of the burned ear: a preventable complication if…" Ann Plast Surg 23:1, 1989

8. Drost A, Burleson D, Cioffi W, et al: Plasma cytokines following thermal injury and their relationship with patient mortality, burn size, and time postburn. J Trauma 35:335, 1993

9. O'Connor BE, Mulliken JB, Banks-Schlagel S, et al: Grafting of burns with cultured epithelium prepared from autologous epidermal grafts. Lancet 1:75, 1981

10. Cope O, Langohr J, Moore F, et al: Expeditious care of full-thickness burn wounds by surgical excision and grafting. Ann Surg 125:1, 1947

11. Jackson D, Topley E, Cason JS, et al: Primary excision and grafting of large burns. Ann Surg 152:167, 1960

12. Brcic A, Zdarvic F: Lessons learnt from 2409 burn patients operated by early excision. Scand J Plast Surg 13:107, 1979

13. Janzekovic Z: A new concept in the early excision and immediate grafting of burns. J Trauma 10:1103, 1970

14. Burke JF, Bondoc CC, Quinby WC: Primary burn excision and immediate grafting: a method of shortening illness. J Trauma 14:389, 1974

15. Chicarelli ZN, Cuono CB, Heinrich JJ, et al: Selective aggressive burn excision for high mortality subgroups. J Trauma 26:18, 1986

16. Deitch E, Clothier J: Burns in the elderly: an early surgical approach. J Trauma 23:891, 1983

17. Engrav L, Heimbach D, Reus J, et al: Early excision and grafting versus nonoperative treatment of burns of indeterminate depth: a randomized prospective study. J Trauma 23:1001, 1983

18. Heimbach D: Early burn excision and grafting. Surg Clin North Am 67:93, 1987

19. Heimbach DM: Burn care update: the results of early primary excision. J Burn Care Rehabil 2:272, 1981

20. Herndon D, Parks D: Comparison of serial debridement and autografting and early massive excision with cadaver skin overlay in the treatment of large burns in children. J Trauma 26:149, 1986

21. Thompson P, Herndon D, Abston S, et al: Effect of early excision on patients with major thermal injury. J Trauma 27:205, 1987

22. Tompkins RG, Burke JFF, Schenfield DA, et al: Prompt eschar excision: a treatment contributing to reduced burn mortality. Ann Surg 204:272, 1986

23. Tompkins RG, Remensnyder JP, Burke JF, et al: Significant reduction in mortality for children with burn injuries through the use of prompt eschar excision. Ann Surg 208:577, 1988

24. Yamamoto H, Siltharm S, deSerres S, et al: Immediate burn wound excision restores antibody synthesis to bacterial antigen. J Surg Res 63:157, 1996

25. Demling R, LaLonde C: Early burn excision attenuates the postburn lung and systemic response to endotoxin. Surgery 108:28, 1990

26. Monafo W: Tangential excision. Clin Plast Surg 1:591, 1974

27. Monafo W, Auelenbacher C, Papplardo C: Early tangential excision of the eschars of major burns. Arch Surg 104:503, 1972

28. Bollinger RR, Delford LS: Transplantation. Textbook of Surgery, 14th ed. Sabiston DC, Ed. WB Saunders Co, Philadelphia, 1991

29. Gallico, O'Connor BE, Compton C, et al: Permanent coverage of large burn wounds with autologous cultured human epithelium. N Engl J Med 331:448, 1984

30. Cole JK, Engrav LH, Heimbach DM, et al: Early excision and grafting of face and neck burns in patients over 20 years. Plast Reconstr Surg 109:1266, 2002

31. Nakamura DY, Gibran NS, Mann R, et al: The Unna's sleeve: an effective postoperative dressing for pediatric arm burns. J Burn Care Rehabil 19:349, 1998

32. Engrav LH, Gottlieb JR, Walkingshaw MD, et al: The "sponge deformity" after tangential excision and grafting of burns. Plast Reconstr Surg 83:468, 1989

33. Fleming MD, Hunt JL, Purdue GF, et al: Marjolin's ulcer: a review and reevaluation of a difficult problem. J Burn Care Rehabil 11:460, 1990

34. Freshwater MF, Krizek TJ: George David Pollock and the development of skin grafting. Ann Plast Surg 1:96, 1978

35. Hansbrough JF, Morgan JL, Greenleaf GE, et al: Composite grafts of human keratinocytes grown on a polyglactin mesh-cultured fibroblast dermal substitute function as a bilayer skin replacement in full-thickness wounds on athymic mice. J Burn Care Rehabil 14:485, 1993

36. Heck E, Bergstresser P, Baxter C: Composite skin graft: frozen dermal allografts support the engraftment and expansion of autologous epidermis. J Trauma 25:106, 1985

37. Pruitt BA, Levine NS: Characteristics and uses of biologic dressings and skin substitutes. Arch Surg 119:312, 1984

38. Hansbrough JF: Wound coverage with biologic dressings and cultured skin substitutes. RG Landes Co, Galveston, Texas, 1992

39. Brown RFR, Kemble JVH: Tetrazolium reductase as an index of the viability of stored skin. Burns 1:179, 1975

40. Bondoc CC, Burke JF: Clinical experience with viable frozen human skin and a frozen skin bank. Ann Surg 174:371, 1971

41. Ninneman JL, Fisher JC, Frank HA: Prolonged survival of human skin allografts following thermal injury. Transplantation 25:69, 1978

42. Burke, JF, Bondoc CC: A method of secondary closure of heavily contaminated wounds providing physiologic primary closure. J Trauma 8:228, 1968

43. Towpick E, Jupiec-Weglinski JW, Tyler DS, et al: Cyclosporine and experimental skin allografts: long-term survival in rats treated with low maintenance doses. Plast Reconstr Surg 77:268, 1986

44. Wainwright D, Madden M, Luterman A, et al: Clinical evaluation of an acellular allograft dermal matrix in full thickness burns. J Burn Care Rehabil 17:124, 1996

45. Cuono CB, Langdon R, Birchall N, et al: Composite autologous-allogeneic skin replacement: development and clinical application. Plast Reconstr Surg 80:626, 1987

46. Cuono CB, Langdon R, McGuire J: Use of cultured epidermal autografts and dermal allografts as skin replacement after burn injury. Lancet 1:1123, 1986

47. Monafo WW, Tandon SN, Bradley RE, et al: Bacterial contamination of skin used as a biologic dressing: a potential hazard. JAMA 235:1248, 1976

48. Heimbach DM, Engrav LH, Marvin J, et al: Toxic epidermal necrolysis: a step forward in treatment. JAMA 257:2171, 1987

49. Rheinwald JG, Green H: Serial cultivation of strains of human epidermal keratinocytes: the formation of keratinizing colonies from single cells. Cell 6:331, 1975

50. Herzog S, Meger A, Woodley D, et al: Wound coverage with autologous keratinocytes: use after burn wound excision, including biopsy follow-up. J Trauma 28:195, 1988

51. McAree KG, Klein RL, Boeckman CR: The use of cultured epithelial autografts in the wound care of severely burned patients. J Pediatr Surg 28:166, 1993

52. Rue LW, Cioffi WG, McManus WF, et al: Wound closure and outcome in extensively burned patients treated with cultured autologous keratinocytes. J Trauma 34:662, 1993

53. Williamson JS, Snelling CFT, Clugston P, et al: Cultured epithelial autografts: five years of clinical experience with twenty eight patients. J Trauma 39:309, 1995

54. Woodley DT, Peterson AD, Herzog SR, et al: Burn wounds resurfaced by cultured epidermal autografts show abnormal reconstitution of anchoring fibrils. JAMA 259:2566, 1988

55. Compton C, Hickerson W, Nadire K, et al: Acceleration of skin regeneration from cultured epithelial autografts by transplantation to human dermis. J Burn Care Rehabil 14:653, 1993

56. Burke JF, Yannas IV, Quinby WC, et al: Successful use of a physiologically acceptable artificial skin in the treatment of extensive burn wound injury. Ann Surg 194:413, 1981

57. Dagalakis N, Flink J, Stasikelis P, et al: Design of an artificial skin III: control of pore structure. J Biomed Mater Res 14:511, 1980

58. Yannas IV, Burke JF: Design of an artificial skin: I. Basic design and principles. J Biomed Mater Res 14:65, 1980

59. Yannas IV, Burke JF: Design of an artificial skin: II. Control of chemical composition. J Biomed Mater Res 14:107, 1980

60. Fang P, Engrav LH, Gibran NS, et al: Dermatome settings for autografts to cover INTEGRA. J Burn Care Rehabil 23:327, 2002

61. Heimbach D, Luterman A, Burke J, et al: Artificial dermis for major burns: a multi-center randomized clinical trial. Ann Surg 208:313, 1988

62. Holmes JH, Honari S, Gibran NS: Excision and grafting of the large burn wound. Problems in General Surgery. Lippincott Williams & Wilkins Philadelphia, 2003

63. Lattari B, Jones LM, Varcelotti JR, et al: The use of a permanent dermal allograft in full thickness burns of the hand and foot: a report of three cases. J Burn Care Rehabil 18:147, 1997

64. Terino EO: Alloderm acellular dermal graft: applications in aesthetic soft-tissue augmentation. Clin Plast Surg 28:83, 2001

65. Hansbrough JF, Morgan J, Greenleaf G, et al: Development of a temporary living skin replace-

ment composed of human fibroblast cultured in Biobrane, a synthetic dressing material. Surgery 115:633, 1995

66. Purdue GF, Hunt JL, Still JM, et al: A multicenter trial of a biosynthetic skin replacement, Dermagraft-TC, compared with cryopreserved human cadaver skin for temporary coverage. J Burn Care Rehabil 18:52, 1997

67. Hansbrough JF, Mozingo DW, Kealey P, et al: Clinical trials of a bio-synthetic temporary skin replacement, Dermagraft-Transitional Covering, compared with cryopreserved human cadaver skin for temporary coverage of excised burn wounds. J Burn Care Rehabil 18:43, 1997

68. Hansbrough J: Dermagraft-TC for partial thickness burns: a clinical evaluation. J Burn Care Rehabil 18:24S, 1997

69. Hansbrough JF, Dore C, Hansbrough W: Clinical trials of a living dermal tissue replacement placed beneath meshed, split-thickness skin grafts on excised burn wounds. J Burn Care Rehabil 13:519, 1992

70. Supp DM, Boyce ST: Overexpression of vascular endothelial growth factor accelerates early vascularization and improves healing of genetically modified cultured skin substitutes. J Burn Care Rehabil 23:10, 2002

Acknowledgments

Figure 1   Tom Moore.
Figure 2   Seward Hung.

115 MISCELLANEOUS BURNS AND COLD INJURIES

David M. Heimbach, M.D., F.A.C.S., and Nicole S. Gibran, M.D., F.A.C.S.

Electrical Injury

Three main forms of electrical injury exist: low-voltage burns (i.e., burns resulting from contact with circuits of less than 440 volts [V]), high-voltage burns (i.e., burns resulting from circuits of greater than 1,000 V), and super–high-voltage burns (caused by lightning). There is also a poorly defined "intermediate-voltage" category, which includes burns caused by contact with industrial circuits of 440 to 800 V; these burns have characteristics of both high-voltage and low-voltage burns, depending on the circumstances.

A common "electrical," though noncontact, injury is an intense flash burn resulting from the short-circuiting of an industrial circuit by an electrician with a metal tool. Such a short-circuiting causes the metal part of the tool to vaporize, as if it were an uncontrolled arc welder; this vaporization results in a very high temperature flash that causes deep burns to the hand holding the tool and less deep burns to the upper body and face. Clothing can catch fire, compounding the problem. These burns are not, however, associated with the problems of contact electrical burns, and they should be treated in much the same way as other thermal burns.

An electrical burn is managed in essentially the same way as any other burn except that a higher urinary output is necessary in the presence of myoglobinuria. In addition to the potentially devastating tissue destruction seen with high-voltage injury, electrical injuries can lead to chronic and debilitating nonsurgical conditions that must be addressed.

LOW-VOLTAGE INJURIES

The human body is three to four times as sensitive to alternating current as it is to direct current. Alternating current has generally replaced direct current for all commercial power applications because it is cheaper to transmit and can be more easily transformed to any required voltage. The amount of 60-cycle alternating current that can just be perceived in the hand is about 1.1 milliamperes (mA), which produces a tingling sensation. Skin resistance, however, varies according to the thickness of the epidermal keratin layer, as well as the cleanliness and dryness of the skin. The calloused hand may provide resistance of as much as 1,000,000 ohms/in² while dry; normal skin provides resistance of 5,000 ohms/in²; and wet skin provides resistance of only 1,000 ohms/in². With currents higher than 2 to 4 mA, the tingling gives way to muscle contractions, which get stronger as the current increases. The "let go" current is reached at approximately 15 mA, above which the victim cannot release his or her grasp of the conductor. Above 20 mA, there is sustained spasm of the respiratory muscles. If the passage of current lasts less than 4 minutes, respiration will resume; however, if it lasts longer than 4 minutes, asphyxiation may occur, and mouth-to-mouth resuscitation may be required. At levels above 30 to 40 mA, ventricular fibrillation (VF) may be induced. As the current is increased, the heart's susceptibility to fibrillation first increases and then decreases. At 1 to 5 A, the heart goes into sustained contraction, and the likelihood of VF becomes negligible. When the high current is terminated, the heart usually reverts back to sinus rhythm, just as happens in cardiac defibrillation, when such high currents are deliberately applied to the chest to depolarize the entire heart.

In the event that the victim of electric shock is unconscious, the initial responder should remove the source of the current (taking care not to become a victim of shock himself or herself) and then provide cardiopulmonary resuscitation (CPR); paramedics may then begin defibrillation. If a sinus rhythm has not been established on arrival at the emergency department (ED), the physician should treat the patient as he or she would any other dysrhythmia patient. If sinus rhythm has been established, the patient should be treated as a sudden death victim, with evaluation for anoxic damage and cardiac monitoring.

Many patients come to the ED after receiving an electric shock from household current. If the electrocardiogram and rhythm strip are normal, the patient should be reassured and discharged without hospital admission. Muscle soreness will resolve spontaneously in 24 to 48 hours and may be treated with analgesics, such as nonsteroidal anti-inflammatory drugs (NSAIDs).

Cutaneous burns with significant tissue necrosis rarely result from contact with low-voltage current. Usually, the area of contact is large enough to dissipate the heat of the current, and underlying tissue destruction is minimal.

Mouth Burns in Children

The exception to this rule is a child who may chew on the end of a live electric extension cord. The child's saliva completes the circuit between the positive and neutral leads; the resulting electrical short may cause significant tissue destruction of the lips, tongue, or both [see Figure 1]. These burns should be evaluated and treated by a plastic surgeon or a burn surgeon. The patient is often admitted to ensure he or she receives proper nourishment and that the parent is comfortable with pain management and wound cleansing. The parent should be forewarned that the eschar might separate in a few days, resulting in bleeding from the labial branch of the facial artery. In an emergency setting, this bleeding can be easily treated by pinching the lip between thumb and forefinger while the child is brought to the ED for suture ligation.

There are two plans for definitive care.[1-3] Long-term results appear to be about equal for nonoperative and operative acute management. If nonoperative management is chosen, splinting is usually recommended to keep the mouth stretched to prevent contracture, but patients and parents do not always comply fully with splint use. Immediate coverage with flaps hastens the healing but leaves a permanent scar and may result in the sacrifice of some normal tissue.

HIGH-VOLTAGE INJURIES

Current in wires containing 1,000 V or more may cause massive tissue destruction. The tissue destruction results from electrical energy being converted to heat as it meets resistance in the tissues.

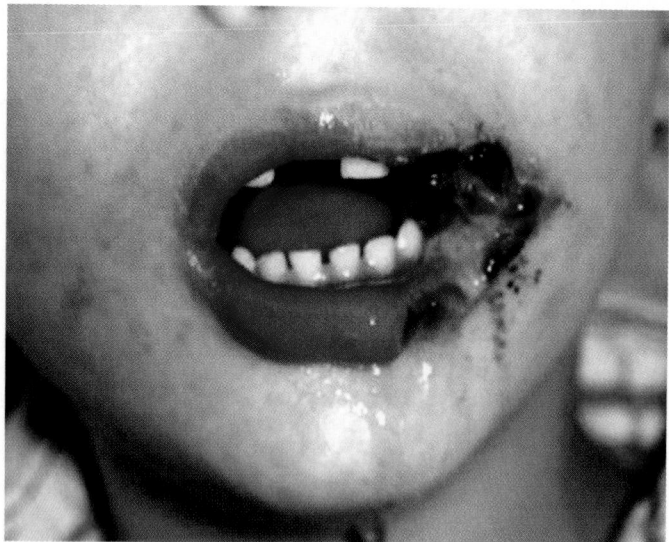

Figure 1 Shown is an electrical burn caused by a 110-volt household current. The injury resulted from the patient's sucking on an extension plug. The burn was treated conservatively with a mouth splint, which resulted in a nearly normal-appearing mouth with good function.

The smaller the size of the body part through which the electricity passes, the more intense the heat and the less the heat is dissipated. Fingers, hands, forearms, feet, and lower legs frequently are totally destroyed; areas of larger volume (e.g., the trunk) usually dissipate enough current to prevent extensive damage to viscera unless the contact wound is on the abdomen or the chest. As current passes through the body, arc burns, as well as the usual contact wounds, are common. These deep wounds, which may be as destructive as contact wounds, occur when current takes a direct path, often between joints in close apposition to one another at the time of injury. Burns of the volar aspect of the wrist, the antecubital fossa when the elbow is flexed at the time of injury, and the axilla are most common. Such injuries should always be seen immediately by a surgeon with a special interest in burns. The immediate evaluation of the patient with a major electrical burn is similar to that of any severely injured patient and includes evaluation of the ABCs (*A*irway, *B*reathing, and *C*irculation).

In addition to burns, which may be obvious, the patient may have other associated injuries resulting from falls or may have broken bones resulting from the tetanic spasms of major muscle groups. Common potential fractures include those of the lumbar spine and hip.

RESUSCITATION

Flash and flame burns without electrical contact injuries are treated in the same manner as all thermal burns are. For patients with electrical contact injuries, fluid requirements are considerably greater than are predicted by the various formulae used for thermal burn victims; the reason is that the cutaneous injury is usually only the "tip of the iceberg," and underlying deep tissue damage may be extensive. A good general starting point is to administer lactated Ringer solution at two to three times the quantity specified by the Baxter (Parkland) burn formula. This would initially require providing 8 to 10 ml/kg/% of total body surface area (TBSA) that is burned. Fluid administration should be adjusted, with the aims of correcting metabolic acidosis, normalizing vital signs, and attaining a urinary output of approximately 100 ml/hr

in adults, especially in the presence of myoglobinuria. With significant myonecrosis, rhabdomyolysis results in increased levels of circulating myoglobin and hemoglobin, as well as cell fragments, which can plug the renal tubules and cause acute tubular necrosis. Myoglobin precipitation is accentuated by acidic urine and decreased by alkaline urine. There has never been a report of a correlation between exact myoglobin levels in the urine or the blood and development of renal failure.[4,5] Because urinary myoglobin levels can be significantly elevated even when the urine is clear, the clinical relevance of quantifying such levels is unclear. However, gross myoglobin in the urine should be treated with aggressive fluid hydration. If the urine is red or reddish black, urinary flow of at least 1 ml/kg/hr is indicated until the pigment clears, and acidosis should be corrected. An osmotic diuretic such as mannitol (25 g bolus, followed by 12.5 g every 2 to 4 hours) may be necessary to maintain adequate urinary output. Use of sodium bicarbonate to maintain urinary pH above 7 without raising blood pH above 7.5 theoretically may minimize protein precipitation in the urine.

SURGICAL CONSIDERATIONS

There are two indications for early operation in a patient with a high-voltage electrical burn. If the burn is making the patient sick (e.g., myoglobin will not clear or acidosis will not resolve), the wound should be explored and all grossly necrotic tissue removed. If the burn is making an extremity sick (e.g., there are signs of a compartment syndrome), early escharotomy, fasciotomy, or both should be performed. Otherwise, delaying surgical exploration by a few days can often allow definitive debridement and wound closure through a single operation.[6,7]

Escharotomy and Fasciotomy

In general, an escharotomy is indicated for a circumferential deep burn when there is evidence of impaired distal perfusion. Fasciotomy is indicated for concomitant electrical injury to underlying muscle when there is evidence of increased compartment pressure, myoglobinuria, tense muscle compartments, or nerve or vessel compression. Careful monitoring, including measurement of compartment pressures, is mandatory, and escharotomies and fasciotomies should be performed at the slightest suggestion of progression. Routine compartment pressure measurements may be helpful, but any of the signs of impending compartment syndrome (i.e., increased pain, pallor, absence of pulse, decreased sensation, and tense swelling) mandate prompt compartment release in the operating theater.

One unique injury that must be considered in patients with electrical injuries to the hand is a carpal tunnel injury.[7] With the associated swelling, relatively small electrical injuries can lead to swelling in the carpal tunnel that manifests as increasing paresthesias and numbness in the distribution of the median nerve. If the injury is sufficiently devastating to create a mummified hand, carpal tunnel release probably has no role in the treatment plan.

CONTACT SITES

Because most electrical injuries result from alternating current, entrance and exit sites are better referred to as contact points. These are thermal burns resulting from heat generation, but unlike flame burns, they are often associated with significant injury to the deep tissues. The amount of heat generated depends on the resistance to current flow. A dry hand or foot in contact with high voltage may generate heat in excess of 1,000° C, leading to mummification at the contact site [*see Figure 2*].

With the passage of a large current, multiple contact sites may be seen along the route of the current, resulting in injuries that suggest the effects of an explosion. Sites of current arcing (see above) should be treated in the same manner as primary contact sites because the underlying damage can be just as severe.

WOUND MANAGEMENT

In general, if there are large amounts of necrotic muscle as a result of high-voltage electrical contact, aggressive surgical debridement to decrease myoglobinemia is indicated. This intervention may minimize subsequent organ dysfunction. If gross myoglobinuria does not resolve after several hours of aggressive hydration, diuresis, and compartment release, the presence of a large amount of dead muscle is a virtual certainty. Muscle of indeterminate viability should be spared, but if a limb is obviously unsalvageable, guillotine amputation may be appropriate and lifesaving. The goal of subsequent surgical procedures is to conserve viable tissue while removing neighboring dead tissue. The uneven nature of the injuries makes this approach difficult and time-consuming. If they are not exposed, small, scattered areas of injured muscle will be replaced by fibrous tissue. A high fever and tachycardia, however, may be physiologic evidence that remaining nonviable muscle has become infected. Because bone resists current and becomes very hot, there may be a substantial amount of nonviable necrotic muscle tissue along the bone that must be debrided. It is not uncommon for superficial forearm muscles to appear viable while necrotic muscle surrounds the radius and ulna. Use of vascular grafts to replace clotted arteries is sometimes an option. However, such grafts may actually increase morbidity and prolong recovery; amputation followed by use of one of the newer prostheses may result in better function than would be available in a hand or foot that has poor sensation and motor function.

In accordance with the principles used for thermal burns, devitalized tissue below the skin at the contact sites should be debrided within 7 days after injury [see Figure 3]. Sequential debridement of residual necrotic tissue may be necessary over the ensuing 3 to

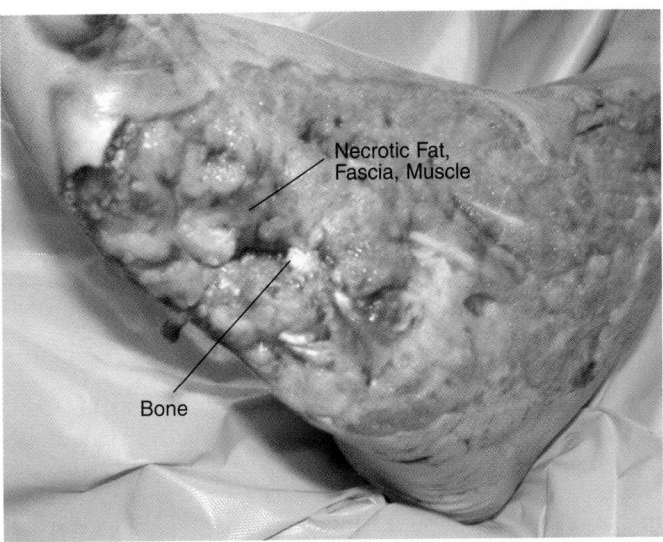

Figure 3 Shown is the same injury seen in Figure 2 just before a second debridement on day 7. Because this patient's right leg was amputated, every attempt was made to salvage as much of the left foot as possible. At initial debridement, it is difficult to tell precisely how much of the foot is possibly viable; note that there is still considerable nonviable soft tissue under the metatarsals and that the metatarsals are considerably exposed. After the second debridement, the foot was treated in a Wound Vac to stimulate vascularization.

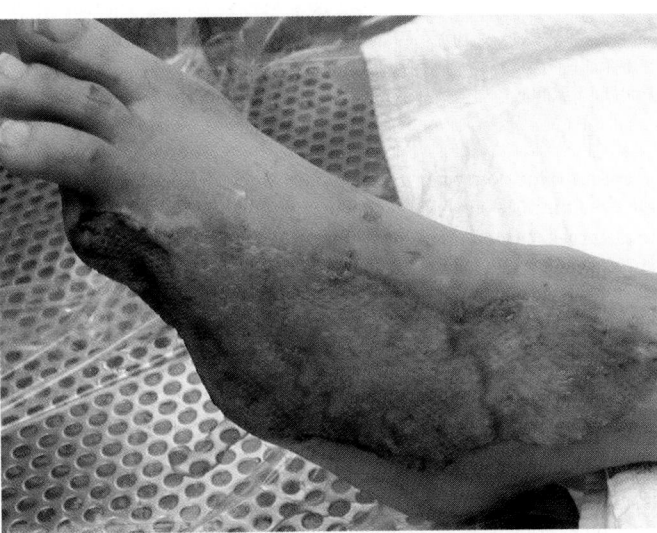

Figure 4 Shown is the same foot as in Figures 2 and 3 at the time of discharge (day 21 after injury). Two toes and the fifth metatarsal were removed, leaving a stable, sensate foot with satisfactory cover.

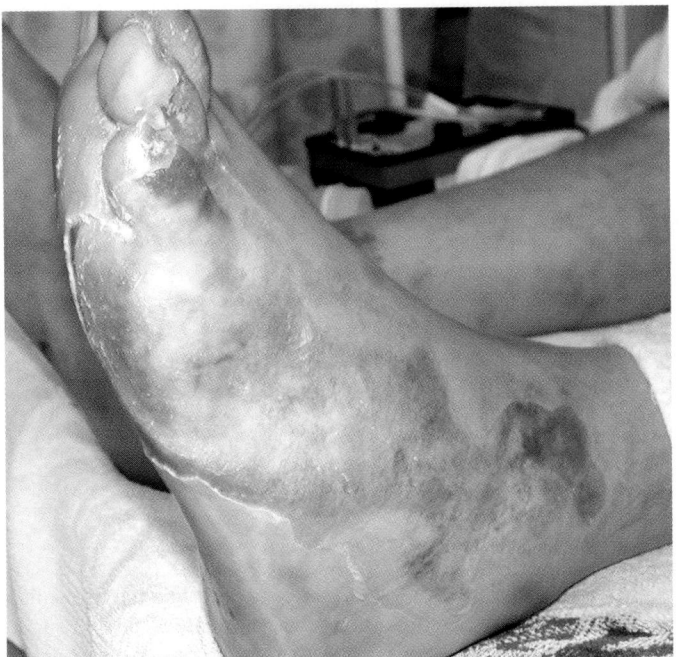

Figure 2 Shown is a contact-point injury caused by a 15,000-volt current, seen on day 1. Although the injury looks relatively simple, a similar injury to this patient's right foot led to a below-the-knee amputation. Careful monitoring for compartment syndrome in the leg is mandatory in such injuries.

5 days. Early aggressive debridement, followed immediately by reconstructive surgery with tissue transfer by rotation or free flaps to cover remaining viable tissue, nerves, vessels, and bone, may facilitate early recovery [see Figure 4].

To help determine the optimal timing and results of operation, one group reviewed the charts of 62 patients who underwent treatment for high-voltage electrical burns of the upper extremities.[6] A total of 100 upper extremities were treated. Of these, 22% underwent decompression within 24 hours because of progressive nerve dysfunction, clinical compartment syndrome, or failure of resuscitation. This subset required a mean of 4.2 operations; the amputation rate was 45%, which was similar to that reported in other series. For another 35% of the burned extremities, the first operative procedure was delayed until resuscitation was complete. This subset required a mean of 2.1 operations and no amputations. For the remaining 43% of the extremities, no operations were required to achieve healing. Overall results showed a 10% amputation rate and a mean hospital stay of 27 days; these results were better than the results reported by others.

NONSURGICAL PROBLEMS RELATED TO ELECTRICAL INJURY

Cardiac Injuries

Immediate cardiac arrest is the most common cause of death from electrical injury. Low-voltage exposure is likely to induce ventricular fibrillation, whereas high-voltage exposure is more likely to produce cardiac standstill. Cardiac standstill and respiratory arrest may revert spontaneously if CPR prevents anoxia; VF is more likely to necessitate defibrillation. Conventional wisdom states that patients who have sustained high-voltage injuries should be admitted for 24-hour telemetry monitoring and that cardiac isoenzyme levels should be followed. Studies have shown that if the ECG is normal on admission, subsequent cardiac dysrhythmias are rare and intensive monitoring is probably not necessary.[8,9] The transient interest in isoenzyme and troponin levels has now waned, and assessment of these variables has not proved useful in predicting cardiac damage.[8,10-13]

Myocardial infarction is uncommon, but it has been reported in a small percentage of cases in each series. In one patient at the University of Washington (UW) Burn Center, a papillary muscle ruptured within 24 hours; this led to immediate, fatal congestive heart failure.

Neurologic Complications

Neurologic complications are common sequelae of high-voltage electrical injuries and can affect the brain, spinal cord, and peripheral nerves. Immediate but frequently transient symptoms include varying levels of unconsciousness, respiratory paralysis, and motor paralysis. Permanent changes include cortical encephalopathy, caused by the electrical injury itself or resulting from hypoxia at the time of the accident. Spinal cord injuries are rare but may present as progressive muscular atrophy, amyotrophic lateral sclerosis, or transverse myelitis. These conditions may occur days to months after the injury and progress slowly.[14-16]

A study of 90 patients (82 male and 8 female) with electrical burns was conducted at the UW Burn Center to identify and evaluate neurologic consequences.[17] There were four deaths. Of the 86 remaining patients, 22 sustained low-voltage injury. Of these 22, 11 had immediate neurologic symptoms; these symptoms resolved in nine of the 11 patients. A total of 64 patients sustained high-voltage injury; of these, two thirds had immediate central or peripheral neurologic symptoms (or both). Loss of consciousness accounted for the largest percentage of central nervous system sequelae in the high-voltage group (45%). Of the 29 patients who lost consciousness, 23 (79%) regained consciousness before arrival at the hospital. Six patients remained comatose, three died, and three awoke but had neurologic sequelae. One third of the patients in the high-voltage group had one or more acute peripheral neuropathies; of these neuropathies, 64% resolved or improved. Five patients had transient initial paralysis, but there were no delayed spinal cord symptoms. Eleven patients experienced one or more delayed peripheral neuropathies; half of these delayed neuropathies resolved or improved.

Peripheral neuropathies are relatively common in burned extremities, resulting either from direct nerve injury or from fibrosis occurring around the nerves. Reflex sympathetic dystrophy is not uncommon. Many patients suffer aches, headaches, chronic pain, and various nonanatomic neurologic complaints for some months after injury.[18-20]

Cataracts

The incidence of premature cataract development may be as high as 5% to 10% after electrical injury.[21-23] Surprisingly, cataracts occur equally in patients who have obvious contact points on the face or head and in those who do not. The latent period may range from weeks to years, with the average being 6 months.[23] Therefore, complete ophthalmologic examination for cataracts at the time of hospitalization and, subsequently, with any subjective decrease in visual acuity is warranted. For workers' compensation claims, an eye examination shortly after the injury is indicated to document normal lens transparency in case cataracts occur as an injury-related disease and not from preexisting problems.

Psychological Effects

Posttraumatic stress syndrome is more common after electrical burns than after thermal burns.[24] However, general rehabilitation and self-assessed quality of life are comparable after thermal burns and after electrical burns.[25]

LIGHTNING INJURY

A lightning strike is an extraordinarily high-voltage discharge of brief duration. The current generated may reach 300,000 A and 100 million V. Fortunately, the current often flows around the surface of, rather than through, the body; this "flashover" permits an overall survival rate of 65% or higher.[26-28] The most common immediate potentially fatal complications are paralysis of the respiratory center and cardiac standstill. Cardiac activity will usually resume spontaneously, but apnea may be present for 15 minutes or longer—long enough to cause anoxic brain injury in the absence of pulmonary resuscitation. A rare but fascinating complication is keraunoparalysis, which is a transient paralysis associated with extreme vasoconstriction and sensory disturbances of one or more extremities. It usually lasts only an hour (in rare instances, as long as 24 hours); a lifeless appearance should not result in the patient's being treated as a victim of sudden death.[29] Cardiac and neurologic complications are frequent and are generally similar to those resulting from man-made high-voltage injuries.[30] Dendritic superficial skin burns, known as Lichtenberg's flowers or fractals,[31] are sometimes seen. These superficial burns heal rapidly without sequelae. Ruptured tympanic membranes and vertigo are common accompaniments.[32,33] Treatment of systemic effects is generally supportive; tissue injuries are treated in the same manner as other high-voltage injuries.

Chemical Burns

GENERAL EMERGENCY CARE

Immediate treatment of chemical burns involves the immediate removal of affected clothing; the burns should then be thoroughly flushed with copious amounts of water at the scene of the accident. The only exception to this is for chemical burns involving dry powder; for such burns, the powder should be brushed from clothing and skin. Chemicals will continue to burn until removed; washing for at least 15 minutes under a stream of running water may limit the overall severity of the burn. No thought should be given to searching for a specific neutralizing agent. Delay results in deepening of the burn, and neutralizing agents may cause burns themselves; they frequently generate heat while neutralizing the offending agent, adding a thermal burn to the already potentially serious chemical burn.

Chemical burns, usually caused by strong acids or alkalis, are most often the result of industrial accidents, assaults, or the improper use of harsh solvents and drain cleaners. In contrast to a thermal burn, chemical burns cause progressive damage until the chemicals are inactivated by reaction with the tissue or are diluted by being flushed with water. Individual circumstances vary, but acid burns may be more self-limiting than alkali burns. Acid tends to tan the skin, creating an impermeable barrier that limits further penetration of the acid. Alkalis combine with cutaneous lipids to create soap and thereby continue dissolving the skin until they are neutralized. A full-thickness chemical burn may appear deceptively superficial, seeming to cause only a mild brownish discoloration of the skin. The skin may appear to remain intact during the first few days after the burn and only then begin to slough spontaneously. Chemical burns should be considered deep dermal or full-thickness burns until proved otherwise. In general, definitive treatment of these burns is the same as for thermal injuries—shallow burns heal with infection prevention; deep burns are excised and grafted as soon as their depth is determined.

Some chemicals, such as phenol, cause severe systemic effects; others, such as hydrofluoric acid, may cause death from hypocalcemia even after moderate exposure. Unless the characteristics of the chemical are well known, the treating physician is advised to call the local poison control bureau for specifics on treatment.

ALKALIS

Lime (calcium oxide/hydroxide) and sodium or potassium hydroxide are examples of common alkalis used in industry and around the home.

Sodium or potassium hydroxide (drain cleaner) is ingested by children accidentally and by adults attempting suicide. Mouth burns are the tip of the iceberg. Emergency treatment should be directed to the oropharynx and the upper GI tract; description of such treatment is beyond the scope of this chapter. Sodium or potassium hydroxide is also used in assaults, especially in areas where people cannot afford handguns.[34] Teen hoodlums sometimes fill water pistols with sodium hydroxide and squirt sleeping homeless people. Contact of concentrated sodium hydroxide with the cornea results in prompt and permanent corneal destruction and blindness. Drain and oven cleaners are also favorite substances of patients who deliberately and repeatedly inflict injury on themselves (Munchausen syndrome).[35-37]

The unwitting homeowner or novice construction worker who does not protect the skin when working with concrete cement (calcium hydroxide) is often surprised at day's end with painful red contact areas on the hands, feet, knees, and forearms. By bedtime, these injuries have become excruciating and require emergency treatment and, frequently, excision and grafting.[38,39]

Strong alkali burns are invariably deep, though they may seem deceptively shallow at their onset.

ANHYDROUS AMMONIA

Anhydrous ammonia is a colorless, pungent gas that is stored and transported under pressure in liquid form. Ammonia injury is uncommon, but it is associated with high morbidity and mortality. Particularly devastating is severe acute respiratory distress syndrome (ARDS) and long-term restrictive disease with bronchiectasis. Most of the literature consists of case reports, but all emphasize the severity and long-term sequelae of the respiratory and ocular problems.[40-44]

ACIDS

As noted (see above), acid burns tend to denature (tan) the skin. Although they may be full-thickness burns, destruction of deeper tissues is often limited as a result of the formation of an impervious carapace of the dermis.

Hydrochloric and Nitric Acids

Hydrochloric and nitric acids are strong acids that denature proteins but usually do not result in systemic poisoning unless inhaled or ingested.

Chromic Acid

Some acids, such as chromic acid and dichromate, cause both systemic and cutaneous problems. Chromium poisoning is characterized by complete anuria, hepatic damage, and progressive anemia. It can occur from the cutaneous absorption of chromium from chromic acid burns that are as small as 1% of TBSA. Aggressive surgical excision and prompt hemodialysis may be lifesaving.[45-48]

Formic Acid

Similarly, formic acid causes metabolic acidosis, intravascular hemolysis, and hemoglobinuria when ingested or when concentrated solutions contact the skin.[49,50]

Carbolic Acid

Phenol (carbolic acid) is used as a hospital, industrial, and home disinfectant. Exposure may lead to rapid CNS depression, vomiting, coughing, stridor, and, in rare instances, seizures.[51] The cutaneous burns are usually first degree.

Hydrofluoric Acid

Hydrofluoric acid burns are unique in terms of their presentation and current treatment. Hydrofluoric acid is used in industrial cleaners and rust removers. It is used in concentrated form in the etching of circuit boards and in dilute form as a cleaner for glass and milk cans. Hydrofluoric acid is a very strong acid that coagulates skin and allows entry of fluoride ions, which then chelate calcium and magnesium in tissue and plasma. Local cell death results; with severe exposure, severe systemic hypocalcemia and hypomagnesemia can result in fatal cardiac dysrhythmias.[52-54] Fluoride, as the most electronegative element, tightly binds many cations essential to hemostasis, inhibiting normal blood coagulation. As a metabolic poison, it stimulates some enzymes (e.g., adenylate cyclase) and severely inhibits others (e.g., Na^+,K^+-ATPase and the enzymes of carbohydrate metabolism).[55] Treatment of severe poisoning requires careful monitoring in an ICU, replacement of magnesium and calcium, and consideration of dialysis.

More commonly, industrial exposure is limited to the hand.[56] Exposure to concentrated solution will cause immediate symptoms, but the more common dilute solutions may not cause symptoms for hours. Often, the worker will go home and experience increasingly severe pain, which will prevent sleep and lead to a nighttime visit to the ED. The worker will likely be unaware of the cause of the pain; the emergency physician should question the patient about solvents used that day.

Conventional treatment of burns to the hand and digits has consisted of local application of calcium liquids and gels. Direct injection of calcium gluconate into the injury site is somewhat effective but may cause pressure necrosis of fingers that are already swollen. A much better treatment that can yield almost magical results is direct intra-arterial infusion of a dilute calcium gluconate solution through the radial or brachial artery. The sooner the infusion is started after the onset of pain, the better the result. Pain is immediately mitigated if not cured, and tissue destruction is often minimal.[57,58] This measure has become the treatment of choice in the UW Burn Center and has yielded good results with no complications to date. However, therapy must be started within the first 24 hours; after this point, tissue damage is permanent. An alternative is intravenous infusion of calcium gluconate with the Bier block technique (i.e., a venous tourniquet applied proximal to the infusion site),[59-61] but this measure can increase swelling in the extremity.

War and Chemicals of Mass Destruction

NAPALM

Napalm is jellied gasoline that is generally ignited and sprayed on material and combatants in wartime. It causes devastating burns because the gasoline sticks to clothing and skin while it is burning. Injuries are usually fourth-degree thermal burns, which are treated in the same manner as other very deep thermal burns.

WHITE PHOSPHORUS

White phosphorus is used in many types of military munitions, as well as in fireworks and in industrial and agricultural products. In the presence of oxygen, it ignites spontaneously; when in contact with skin, it causes deep thermal injuries. It may also give rise to multiple organ dysfunction syndrome (MODS) because of its toxic effects on erythrocytes, the liver, the kidneys, and the heart. Treatment of the injured patient is difficult. The particles must be debrided to prevent continued burning and systemic poisoning. Conventional wisdom was to use a solution of copper sulfate to convert the elemental phosphorus into copper phosphate. However, this approach has fallen into disfavor because copper poisoning may result, the effects of which are often as bad as those of phosphorus poisoning.[62,63] During debridement in the operating theater, exposure of the particles to air can reignite the phosphorus and thereby endanger the patient and the operating team.

MUSTARD GAS, LEWISITE, AND PHOSGENE

Sulfur mustard is a vesicant that alkylates DNA. In liquid or gas form, its main targets are the skin, the eyes, and the lungs.[64-68] Its clinical effects are similar to those of burns, with loss of immunity, respiratory failure, and ophthalmic, gastrointestinal, and hematologic signs. In the Iraq-Iran war (1981–1989), extensive use of chemical weapons such as mustard gas caused injuries with high mortality and morbidity, as well as chronic side effects in vital organs, especially the respiratory tract. In a study that examined long-term effects of mustard gas exposure in 220 survivors, nearly all the victims complained of cough, dyspnea, and suffocation. Hemoptysis was found in six victims. Respiratory distress with use of accessory muscles was observed in four. Two thirds of the subjects had wheezing and coarse rales. Most had obstructive patterns on pulmonary function testing.[69] Cutaneous exposure is manifested by a delayed erythema of skin occurring after about 4 hours, followed by blistering in 12 to 48 hours. The blisters rupture, leaving shallow, painful ulcers. Other vesicants are more corrosive: lewisite (arsine) and phosgene are both more potent than mustard gas, and symptoms appear sooner with these agents.[70]

Rescuers should be protected with suitable clothing, respirators, gloves, and boots. The victim's clothing is removed, and extensive water lavage is provided, along with copious isotonic eye irrigation. Once decontamination has been completed, there is no danger to attendants; blister fluid does not contain chemicals.[71] Burns are usually of partial thickness and can be treated in the same manner as other partial-thickness burns.

Cold Injury

Cold injuries limited to digits, extremities, or exposed surfaces are the result of either direct tissue freezing (frostbite) or more chronic exposure to an environment just above freezing (chilblain or pernio; trench foot). Cold injury has been a major cause of morbidity during war, and it is described as being the single major injury sustained by British soldiers in the Falklands expedition. Cold injury resulted in over 7 million soldier fighting days lost by Allied forces in World War II.[72]

CHILBLAIN, PERNIO, AND TRENCH FOOT

Chilblain and pernio are descriptive terms for a form of local cold injury characterized by red-purple, pruritic skin lesions (papules, macules, plaques, or nodules) that are often associated with edema or blistering. These lesions are caused by a chronic vasculitis of the dermis, and their development appears to be provoked by repeated exposure to cold, though not freezing, temperatures. The injury typically occurs on the face, the anterior tibial surface, or the dorsum of the hands and feet—areas that are poorly protected or are subject to long-term exposure to the environment. With continued exposure, ulcerative or hemorrhagic lesions may appear and progress to scarring, fibrosis, and atrophy. Treatment consists of sheltering the patient, elevating the affected part on sheepskin, and allowing gradual rewarming at room temperature. Rubbing or massage is contraindicated, because further damage and secondary infection may result.[73-75]

Trench foot or cold immersion foot (or hand) describes a nonfreezing injury of the hands or feet, typically sustained by sailors, fishermen, or soldiers as a consequence of long-term exposure to wet conditions (e.g., water or mud) and temperatures just above freezing.[76-80] Alternating arterial vasospasm and vasodilatation appear to occur, with the affected tissue first cold and anesthetic and then becoming hyperemic after 24 to 48 hours of exposure. With the hyperemia comes an intense, painful burning and dysesthesia, as well as tissue damage characterized by edema, blistering, redness, ecchymosis, and ulceration. Complications consisting of local infection and cellulitis, lymphangitis, and gangrene may occur. After 2 to 6 weeks, a posthyperemic phase ensues, resulting in tissue cyanosis with increased sensitivity to cold. Treatment is best started during or before the reactive hyperemia state; it consists of immediate removal of the extremity from the cold, wet environment and exposure of the extremity to warm, dry air. The limb is elevated to minimize edema, pressure spots are protected, and local and systemic measures to combat infection are undertaken. Massage, soaking of the feet, and rapid rewarming are not indicated.

FROSTBITE

Frostbite is a common, severe form of cold injury that involves local freezing of tissues. Frostbite is classified into four grades of severity[81,82]:

1. First-degree injury involves the freezing of tissue with hyperemia and edema but without blistering.
2. Second-degree frostbite involves the freezing of tissue with hyperemia, edema, and characteristic large, clear blisters.

3. Third-degree frostbite involves the freezing of tissue with the death of subcutaneous tissues and skin, resulting in hemorrhagic vesicles that are generally smaller than those seen in second-degree frostbite.

4. Fourth-degree frostbite is notable for tissue necrosis, gangrene, and, eventually, full-thickness tissue loss.

The degree of severity of frostbite is often not apparent for several days. For all forms of frostbite, the initial presentation is pain or discomfort, as well as pruritus if the injury is mild. With more severe injury, there is a progressive decrease in range of motion, and edema becomes prominent. The injury progresses to numbness and eventual loss of all sensation in the affected tissue. The involved area appears white or blue-white and is firm or even hard (frozen) to the touch. The tissue is cold and insensate. Although the initial symptoms may be mild and may be overlooked by the patient, severe pain, burning, edema, and even necrosis and gangrene may appear with rewarming.

Weather conditions, altitude, degree of protective clothing, duration of exposure, and degree of tissue wetness are all contributing external factors to the development of frostbite. Acclimation to cold may be protective, whereas a previous history of frostbite probably does predispose an individual to another cold tissue injury. Smoking and a history of arterial disease also are contributing factors. In urban environments, more than 50% of frostbite injuries are alcohol related, and a significant percentage (16%) of patients have an underlying psychiatric illness.[83,84]

Current evidence suggests that frostbite injury may in fact have two components: (1) the initial freeze injury and (2) a reperfusion injury that occurs during rewarming.[85-87] The initial response to tissue cooling is vasoconstriction and arteriovenous shunting, relieved intermittently (every 5 to 7 minutes) by vasodilatation. With prolonged exposure, this response fails, and the temperature of the freezing tissue will approximate ambient temperature until a temperature of $-2°$ C is reached. At this point, extracellular ice crystals form; as these crystals enlarge, the osmotic pressure of the interstitium increases, resulting in the movement of intracellular water into the interstitium. Cells begin to shrink and become hyperosmolar, disrupting cellular enzyme function. If freezing is rapid (i.e., if the temperature falls by more than $10°$ C/min), intracellular ice crystal formation will occur, resulting in immediate cell death. Intravascularly, endothelial cell disruption and red cell sludging result in cessation of circulation.[88-91]

During rewarming, red cell, platelet, and leukocyte aggregation is known to occur; this results in patchy thrombosis of the microcirculation.[92] These accumulated blood elements are thought to release, among other products, the toxic oxygen free radicals and the arachidonic acid metabolites prostaglandin F_2 and thromboxane A_2, which further aggravate vasoconstriction and platelet and leukocyte aggregation. However, the exact mechanism of tissue destruction and death after freeze injury remains poorly defined. Animal studies suggest that vascular injury, in the form of endothelial cell damage and subsequent interstitial edema (but not vessel thrombosis) is the primary initial event in rewarming injury. It has been demonstrated that a marked amelioration of the frostbite injury can be achieved in a rabbit ear model by treating the animals (after cold injury and before rewarming) with a monoclonal antibody to the neutrophil CD18 glycoprotein complex.[93] The implication of this observation is that neutrophil adherence to the endothelium of frostbitten tissue during rewarming (reperfusion) is at least partially responsible for the subsequent tissue injury. Clinical application of these experimental observations remains untested.

TREATMENT

Prehospital or field care of a victim of cold injury should focus on removing the patient from the hostile environment and protecting the injured body part from further damage. Rubbing or exercising the affected tissue does not augment blood flow and risks further cold injury or mechanical trauma. Because repeated bouts of freezing and thawing worsen the injury, it is preferable for the patient with frostbite of the hands or feet to seek definitive shelter and care immediately rather than to rewarm the tissue in the field and risk refreezing. Once rewarming has begun, weight bearing should be avoided.

The ED treatment of a frostbite victim should first focus on the basic ABCs of trauma resuscitation [see 100 Initial Management of Life-Threatening Trauma] and on identifying and correcting systemic hypothermia. Frostbitten tissue should be immersed in a large water bath of $40°$ to $42°$ C ($104°$ to $108°$ F). The bath should be large enough to prevent rapid loss of heat, and the water temperature should be maintained. This method of rapid rewarming may significantly decrease tissue necrosis caused by full-thickness frostbite.[88,90,91] Dry heat is not advocated, because it is difficult to regulate and places the patient at risk for a burn injury. The rewarming process should take about 30 to 45 minutes for digits. The affected area appears flushed when rewarming is complete and good circulation has been reestablished. Narcotics are required, because the rewarming process may be quite painful.

The skin should be gently but meticulously cleansed and air-dried, and the affected area should be elevated to minimize edema. A tetanus toxoid booster should be administered as indicated by the immunization history. Sterile cotton should be placed between toes or fingers to prevent skin maceration, and extreme care should be taken to prevent infection and to avoid even the slightest abrasion. Prophylactic antibiotics and dermal blister debridement are both controversial; most clinicians debride blisters and reserve antibiotics for identified infections. A 2005 study reported a lower than expected digit amputation rate when rapid rewarming was followed by treatment with hepatin and tissue plasminogen activator (tPA), but to date, this finding has not been confirmed by other studies.[94]

After rewarming, the treatment goals are to prevent further injury while awaiting the demarcation of irreversible tissue destruction. All patients with second- and third-degree frostbite should be hospitalized. The affected tissue should be gently cleansed in a warm ($38°$ C) whirlpool bath once or twice a day; some clinicians add an antiseptic such as chlorhexidine or an iodophor to the bath. On the basis of findings of arachidonic acid metabolites in the blisters of frostbite victims, some authors advocate the use of topical aloe vera (a thromboxane inhibitor) and systemic ibuprofen or aspirin. After resolution of edema, digits should be exercised during the whirlpool bath, and physical therapy should begin. Tobacco, nicotine, and other vasoconstrictive agents must be withheld.

Numerous adjuvants have been suggested and tried in an effort to restore blood supply to frostbitten areas. Because of the intense vasoconstrictive effect of cold injury, attention has been focused for many years on increased sympathetic tone. Sympathetic blockade and even surgical sympathectomy have been advocated as early therapy, the theoretical rationale being that sympathetic blockade should release the vasospasm that may precipitate thrombosis in the affected tissue. Unfortunately, this method of treatment has produced inconsistent results in experimental studies and is difficult to evaluate clinically.[89,95] Experience with intra-arterial vasodilating drugs such as reserpine and tolazoline has also failed to verify this hypothesis. In a controlled clinical study, immediate (mean, 3 hours) ipsilateral intra-arterial reserpine infusion coupled with early (mean, 3 days) ipsilateral operative sympathectomy failed to alter the natural history of acute frostbite injury.[89] Sympathectomy may, however, mollify the chronic pain, hyperhidrosis, and vasospasm of cold injuries; some clinicians also suggest that it reduces the risk of subsequent cold injury. Heparin, low-molecular-weight dextran, thrombolytic agents, and hyperbaric oxygen have failed to demonstrate any substantial treatment benefit (despite the suggestive results of the 2005 study by Twomey and associates[94]).

The difficulty in determining the depth of tissue destruction in cold injury has led to a conservative approach to the care of frostbite injuries. As a general rule, amputation and surgical debridement are delayed for at least 1 month unless severe infection with sepsis occurs. The natural history of a full-thickness frostbite injury leads to the gradual demarcation of the injured area; dry gangrene or mummification clearly delineate nonviable tissue. Often, the permanent tissue loss is much less than originally suspected. In one review, only 39% of urban frostbite victims required debridement and skin grating or amputation.[84] Emergency surgery is unusual, but during the rewarming phase, vigilance should be maintained to detect the development of a compartment syndrome necessitating fasciotomy. Open amputations are indicated in patients with persistent infection and sepsis that is refractory to debridement and antibiotics.

Frostbitten tissues seldom recover completely. Some degree of cold insensitivity invariably remains. Hyperhidrosis (occurring in as many as 72% of patients), neuropathy, decreased nail and hair growth, and persistent Raynaud phenomenon in the affected part are frequent sequelae of cold injury.[96] The affected tissue remains at risk for reinjury and should be carefully protected during any cold exposure. Treatment with antiadrenergics (e.g., prazosin hydrochloride, 1 to 2 mg/day) or calcium channel blockers (e.g., nifedipine, 30 to 60 mg/day) and careful protection from further exposure are often helpful. However, there is little that appears to afford significant relief to the chronic symptoms that follow tissue freeze injury; sympathectomy, beta- and alpha-adrenergic blocking agents, calcium channel blockers, topical and systemic steroids, and a host of home remedies have all been tried, with only occasional individual success.[78]

Toxic Epidermal Necrolysis

Toxic epidermal necrolysis (TEN) is a devastating, though (fortunately) rare, exfoliative disease of the skin and mucous membranes that results in full-thickness epidermal necrosis. The first published report of adult TEN appeared in 1956, when Lyell, in Lyon, France, compared four cases to scald burns.[97] Some authors describe a similar skin sloughing but with lesser involvement, termed the Stevens-Johnson syndrome. In reality, the two diseases are exactly the same: Stevens and Johnson anticipated Lyell by 34 years when they described the same pathology in two children in South Africa.[98] Dermatologists have long known the disease as erythema multiforme majus exudativum. Thus, even though only one disease process is involved, various names continue to be used: Europeans refer to this condition as Lyell disease, pediatricians call it the Stevens-Johnson syndrome, dermatologists refer to it as erythema multiforme majus, and American surgeons and internists call it TEN.

TEN can be precipitated by the administration of medications, most commonly sulfonamides, antibiotics, and anticonvulsants. It can also be caused by events such as immunizations, systemic diseases, and viral illnesses. Some cases have no known precipitating cause.

The molecular etiology of TEN remains unclear. According to one theory, certain offending drugs that should be metabolized are instead deposited in the epidermis, leading to an immune response, which causes the body to reject the skin. In 1998, Viard pointed out that keratinocytes normally express the death receptor Fas (CD95); keratinocytes from TEN patients were found to express lytically active Fas ligand (FasL). Antibodies present in pooled human intravenous immunoglobulins (IVIg) blocked Fas-mediated keratinocyte death in vitro. In a pilot study, 10 consecutive individuals with clinically and histologically confirmed TEN were treated with IVIg; disease progression was rapidly reversed, and the outcome was favorable in all cases. The implication was that Fas-FasL interactions were directly involved in the epidermal necrolysis of TEN and that IVIg might be an effective treatment.[99] This report sparked numerous small clinical series, the results of which have been, at best, inconclusive.[100-104] A 2005 study of the effect of IVIg on ocular complications was unable to demonstrate any benefit.[105] There may be a role for γ-globulin, but current data indicate that it is no miracle cure. Because of the high cost of γ-globulin and its potential for inducing renal damage, we no longer use it to treat TEN at the UW Burn Center.

TEN should be distinguished from a somewhat similar disease, staphylococcal scalded skin syndrome (SSSS). This entity is caused by a bacterial exotoxin, which splits the epidermis above the dermal-epidermal junction. Although patients with SSSS experience severe erythema, the skin exfoliates rather than blisters. SSSS does not involve mucosa, and the patients are in a septic state from the underlying staphylococcal infection. SSSS usually affects newborns, becoming much less common as people get older. This unusual disease is treated with antibiotics directed against staphylococci.[106]

The TEN-induced areas of denudation are comparable to those affected by a very shallow second-degree burn. Oropharyngeal, esophageal, anal, urethral, and vaginal[107,108] mucosal sloughing are also characteristic of TEN. The disease attacks squamous epithelium, so the remainder of the GI tract is usually spared. There is only one case report of intestinal epithelial sloughing.[109] Complications such as infection, malnutrition, negative nitrogen balance, severe wound pain, and MODS are identical to those seen in patients with major burns. The most common causes of death in TEN patients are systemic infection and pneumonia. The potential mortality from TEN is high, but it is reduced by treatments and protocols common in burn centers (e.g., wound coverage with biologic dressings). There is good evidence that patients affected with TEN should be referred early for management in a burn center.[110-112] The role of the dermatologist is to define the diagnosis and determine the potential cause.

CLINICAL MANIFESTATIONS

A prodrome of TEN usually consists of fever, sore throat, and malaise; 1 to 2 days after these symptoms appear, the skin of the face and extremities usually becomes tender and erythematous. Lesions appear either as large areas of red skin or as target lesions that are about 2 cm in diameter and consist of concentric rings of erythema. At the same time, ulcerations in the lips and mouth appear, making oral intake painful.

In 24 to 96 hours, the involved skin begins to form both small blisters and bullae. Moderate traction of the erythematous skin results in separation of the epidermis from the dermis—a positive Nikolsky sign.[113] When the bullae rupture, large denuded areas of skin become apparent. Fingernails, toenails, and the skin of the palms and soles may also slough.

One hallmark of this disease is severe inflammation of the mouth. Blisters develop on the oral mucosa, leaving a very raw, red surface. The lips quickly become swollen and crusted with clotted blood. The oral lesions may be confined to the oral cavity or may extend to the larynx or even to the trachea and the esophagus. The patient is usually unable to eat. The eyelids swell as conjunctival inflammation develops. Conjunctival infection, usually caused by *Staphylococcus aureus,* may lead to scarring and permanent blindness.[114] The nasal and urethral mucosa may also become inflamed, and erosions can develop on the genital and perianal skin.

Renal failure can occur as a result of hypovolemia, the septic response, or membranous glomerulonephritis. In as many as 50% of cases, there are abnormalities in liver enzymes, including modest increases in aspartate aminotransferase (AST) and alanine aminotransferase (ALT). Bilirubin levels often show modest to severe increases.[115] The mechanism of these increases, which appear to be a part of the toxic component of TEN, is unknown.

TREATMENT

The initial focus of treatment is on restoration and maintenance of cardiopulmonary stability. Because TEN does not induce the intense cytokine reaction that is associated with similar-sized burns, massive anasarca is unusual; resuscitation need not proceed in the manner recommended for burns. Maintenance of normal vital signs and adequate urinary output (0.5 ml/kg) is satisfactory. Because of the high incidence of catheter infection in the absence of epidermis, use of Swan-Ganz catheters is usually avoided when possible.[116]

Treatment involves aggressive wound management, similar to that of a massive second-degree burn, in which the emphasis is on optimizing healing and controlling infection. A crucial feature of TEN is an intact and uninjured dermis, which, if protected, rapidly reepithelializes from sweat glands and hair follicles, which appear to remain intact. Treatment must, therefore, protect the dermis from desiccation and infection. Routine use of ointments and salves not only creates intense pain but also increases the risk of the formation of a "pseudo eschar" of crusts and devitalized dermis that impairs wound healing.

Biologic or manufactured covers have formed an important role in wound treatment.[111,117,118] Emergency operative wound cleansing and application of commercially available pigskin (porcine xenograft) has been the standard of care at the University of Washington Burn Center in more than 130 cases. The pigskin is stapled in place, the patient is treated for several days in a fluidized bed, and the pigskin is removed as the denuded areas heal. The pigskin is relatively inexpensive, adheres well, is nontoxic, and probably provides some growth factors to hasten healing. With this management plan and meticulous systemic care, mortality at the UW Burn Center has been below 20% for the past 15 years.[119] Alternative covers include Acticoat[120] (Smith & Nephew, London, United Kingdom) and Biobrane[121-124] (Mylan Laboratories, Canonsburg, Pennsylvania), which follow the same principle of dermal protection to permit uninfected healing.

In addition, associated physiologic and psychological care must be meticulous. Lung function is often impaired as a result of the aspiration of secretions from involved oral mucosa and a reduction in the clearance of secretions as a result of oral pain and overall weakness. Pain control and aggressive pulmonary toilet to assist the patient's cough are the first line of defense. Suctioning can lead to significant bleeding and should be used either sparingly or only after an endotracheal tube is in place. The patient should be intubated if lung function is progressively impaired. If the patient is intubated, partial ventilatory assistance is often required because chest wall pain, systemic toxicity, and weakness can severely impair spontaneous ventilatory efforts.

Cardiovascular function is initially impaired as a result of hypovolemia caused by plasma leaking from the blisters, increased skin evaporative losses, and decreased oral intake. Controlling the febrile response will also help decrease fluid losses, vasodilatation, and the resulting hyperadrenergic response. Careful use of NSAIDs is often necessary to keep the patient's temperature below 102° F (38.9° C). Adequate pain control is essential. Methadone is effective for long-acting pain control, and morphine is a good choice for procedural pain.

Aggressive oral care is critical because of the high risk of local mouth infection and consequent wound and lung infection. Early and continued assessment and aggressive management of corneal involvement are required. Administration of ophthalmic antibiotic ointments and gentle breaking of adhesions between conjunctiva and eyelids with a small glass rod are the standard treatment.[125]

OPTIMIZING NUTRITION

Nutrition is a major component of care, and it often cannot be delivered orally because of oral lesions. A small gastric feeding tube is preferred, as the GI tract between stomach and anus is usually intact and is normally functional.[126] In general, standard tube-feeding formulas for an individual under moderate stress are sufficient because the full ravages of postburn hypermetabolism are probably not present. When sepsis is avoided, it is very unusual for the gut to fail and for intravenous parenteral nutrition to be needed.

The role of corticosteroids in the treatment of TEN remains unclear. Although some patients who were receiving steroids before the development of TEN still get severe disease,[127] a number of dermatologists feel that the administration of steroids when the disease process is just beginning, before skin sloughing occurs, can attenuate the process and thereby reduce subsequent sloughing. However, once vesicles have formed and the separation has occurred, corticosteroids no longer effectively attenuate skin sloughing; in fact, the use of corticosteroids retards the rate of healing. In one study, the complication rate was found to be higher in patients who received steroids.[128] This study, however, did not take into account the patients whose disease might have been sufficiently limited by steroid use to make burn center treatment unnecessary.

FOLLOW-UP CARE

Fortunately, when treatment is successful, the disease usually resolves without hypertrophic scarring, though some mismatching of epidermal pigmentation may be evident. Nails may remain deformed, and eyes are usually dry, requiring periodic lubrication. Obviously, patients must not again contact the medication that caused the disease; for common medications, a Medic Alert bracelet is useful.

Ionizing Radiation Burns

The burn surgeon may encounter ionizing radiation injuries in three settings. Of these, by far the most common involves deliberate exposure to radiation (i.e., radiation used in treatment) or accidental radiation in a hospital, a laboratory, or an industrial complex. In such settings, a single individual is likely to be injured. The second scenario involves failure of a nuclear energy plant, such as occurred at Chernobyl; in this scenario, dozens to hundreds of exposures may occur. The third setting is that resulting from a nuclear explosion through military or terrorist action. In such a scenario, thousands of casualties will immediately overwhelm all resources.

LOCALIZED INJURY

A gray (Gy) is the current unit of radiation, defined as 1 joule (J) of energy deposited in 1 kg of tissue; 1 Gy is the equivalent of 100 rads.

Localized injury is produced by local irradiation of a small area; no systemic effects are produced. As with thermal burns, the degree of injury is dependent on the type of radiation encountered, the radiation dose delivered, and the susceptibility of the tissue. An initial erythema appears within minutes or hours of exposure and subsides over 2 to 3 days. Secondary erythema occurs 1 to 3 weeks after exposure and is associated with hair loss and desquamation of the epidermis. At about 3 weeks, blisters (after doses of about 20 Gy) or ulcerations (after doses in excess of 25 Gy) may occur. Ulceration may recur months to years after injury. Blood vessels become telangiectatic, and deeper vessels become occluded, leading to fibrosis, atrophy, and necrosis.[129]

Wounds are generally treated in a manner similar to the treatment of thermal burns, with the additional caveat that radiation sickness is accompanied by immunosuppression, and that endarteritis obliterans will markedly diminish the blood supply. Infection is common, and the optimal timing of excision and grafting of deep ulcers is not known.

WHOLE-BODY IRRADIATION AND RADIATION SICKNESS

A detailed description of whole-body radiation exposure and its treatment is beyond the scope of this chapter. Radiation sickness, also known as the acute radiation syndrome, may begin within hours of exposure. It is initially characterized by nausea, vomiting, diarrhea, and lethargy; this is followed by the hematopoietic syndrome (neutropenia and thrombocytopenia) and the gastrointestinal syndrome (severe diarrhea, bowel ischemia, bacterial translocation, and sepsis).[130] Treatment is mainly supportive.

A nuclear explosion is characterized by a supersonic blast, a fireball extending miles from the epicenter, and immense amounts of ionizing radiation. These three components interact, causing severe mechanical injury, flash and flame burns from the ignition of clothing, and, of course, severe radiation exposure.[131] The flash has been described as being so intense that the side of a victim facing the flash will be charred to bone while the opposite side is unburned. Doctors in Hiroshima after the atomic bombing there observed that for a time, thermal burns appeared to be healing, but in the second and third weeks, the wounds broke down and infection set in as the acute radiation syndrome became manifest.

References

1. Milano M: Oral electrical and thermal burns in children: review and report of case. ASDC J Dent Child 66:116, 1999

2. Canady JW, Thompson SA, Bardach J: Oral commissure burns in children. Plast Reconstr Surg 97:738, 1996

3. Thomas SS: Electrical burns of the mouth: still searching for an answer. Burns 22:137, 1996

4. Gupta KL, Kumar R, Sekhar MS, et al: Myoglobinuric acute renal failure following electrical injury. Ren Fail 13:23, 1991

5. Rosen CL, Adler JN, Rabban JT, et al: Early predictors of myoglobinuria and acute renal failure following electrical injury. J Emerg Med 17:783, 1999

6. Mann R, Gibran N, Engrav L, et al: Is immediate decompression of high voltage electrical injuries to the upper extremity always necessary? J Trauma 40:584, 1996

7. Engrav L, Gottlieb J, Walkinshaw M, et al: Outcome and treatment of electrical injury with immediate median and ulnar nerve palsy at the wrist: a retrospective review and a survey of members of the American Burn Association. Ann Plast Surg 25:166, 1990

8. Purdue GF, Hunt JL: Electrocardiographic monitoring after electrical injury: necessity or luxury. J Trauma 26:166, 1986

9. Bailey B, Gaudreault P, Thivierge RL: Experience with guidelines for cardiac monitoring after electrical injury in children. Am J Emerg Med 18:671, 2000

10. Hammond J, Ward CG: Myocardial damage and electrical injuries: significance of early elevation of CPK-MB isoenzymes. South Med J 79:414, 1986

11. Murphy JT, Horton JW, Purdue GF, Hunt JL: Evaluation of troponin-I as an indicator of cardiac dysfunction after thermal injury. J Trauma 45:700, 1998

12. Pereira C, Fram R, Herndon D: Serum creatinine kinase levels for diagnosing muscle damage in electrical burns. Burns 31:670, 2005

13. Kopp J, Loos B, Spilker G, et al: Correlation between serum creatinine kinase levels and extent of muscle damage in electrical burns. Burns 30:680, 2004

14. Ratnayake B, Emmanuel ER, Walker CC: Neurological sequelae following a high voltage electrical burn. Burns 22:578, 1996

15. Kanitkar S, Roberts AH: Paraplegia in an electrical burn: a case report. Burns Incl Therm Inj 14:49, 1988

16. Ko SH, Chun W, Kim HC: Delayed spinal cord injury following electrical burns: a 7-year experience. Burns 30:691, 2004

17. Grube B, Heimbach D, Engrav L, et al: Neurologic consequences of electrical burns. J Trauma 30:254, 1990

18. Selvaggi G, Monstrey S, Van Landuyt K, et al: Rehabilitation of burn injured patients following lightning and electrical trauma. NeuroRehabilitation 20:35, 2005

19. Tan SR, McDermott MR, Castillo CJ, et al: Pemphigus vulgaris induced by electrical injury. Cutis 77:161, 2006

20. Isao T, Masaki F, Riko N, et al: Delayed brain atrophy after electrical injury. J Burn Care Rehabil 26:456, 2005

21. Boozalis GT, Purdue GF, Hunt JL, et al: Ocular changes from electrical burn injuries: a literature review and report of cases. J Burn Care Rehabil 12:458, 1991

22. Reddy SC: Electric cataract: a case report and review of the literature. Eur J Ophthalmol 9:134, 1999

23. Saffle JR, Crandall A, Warden GD: Cataracts: a long-term complication of electrical injury. J Trauma 25:17, 1985

24. Mancusi-Ungaro HR Jr, Tarbox AR, Wainwright DJ: Posttraumatic stress disorder in electric burn patients. J Burn Care Rehabil 7:521, 1986

25. Cochran A, Edelman LS, Saffle JR, et al: Self-reported quality of life after electrical and thermal injury. J Burn Care Rehabil 25:61, 2004

26. Milzman DP, Moskowitz L, Hardel M: Lightning strikes at a mass gathering. South Med J 92:708, 1999

27. Graber J, Ummenhofer W, Herion H: Lightning accident with eight victims: case report and brief review of the literature. J Trauma 40:288, 1996

28. O'Keefe Gatewood M, Zane RD: Lightning injuries. Emerg Med Clin North Am 22:369, 2004

29. ten Duis HJ, Klasen HJ, Reenalda PE: Keraunoparalysis, a 'specific' lightning injury. Burns Incl Therm Inj 12:54, 1985

30. Muehlberger T, Vogt PM, Munster AM: The long-term consequences of lightning injuries. Burns 27:829, 2001

31. ten Duis HJ, Klasen HJ, Nijsten MW, et al: Superficial lightning injuries: their 'fractal' shape and origin. Burns Incl Therm Inj 13:141, 1987

32. Ogren FP, Edmunds AL: Neuro-otologic findings in the lightning-injured patient. Semin Neurol 15:256, 1995

33. Jones D, Ogren F, Roh L, et al: Lightning and its effects on the auditory system. Laryngoscope 101:830, 1991

34. Branday J, Arscott GD, Smoot EC, et al: Chemical burns as assault injuries in Jamaica. Burns 22:154, 1996

35. Barocas D, Difede J, Viederman M, et al: A case of chronic factitious disorder presenting as repeated, self-inflicted burns [letter]. Psychosomatics 3:79, 1998

36. Lutzow-Holm C: [Psycho-cutaneous disorders in practice: self-inflicted skin diseases of psychological origin.] Tidsskr Nor Laegeforen 117:3241, 1997

37. Wiechman SA, Ehde DM, Wilson BL, et al: The management of self-inflicted burn injuries and disruptive behavior for patients with borderline personality disorder. J Burn Care Rehabil 21:310, 2000

38. Buckley D: Skin burns due to wet cement. Contact Derm 8:407, 1982

39. Early S, Simpson R: Caustic burns from contact with wet cement. JAMA 254:528, 1985

40. George A, Bang RL, Lari AR, et al: Liquid ammonia injury. Burns 26:409, 2000

41. Close L, Catlin F, Cohn A: Acute and chronic effects of ammonia burns of the respiratory tract. Arch Otolaryngol 106:151, 1980

42. Leduc D, Gris P, Lheureux P, et al: Acute and long term respiratory damage following inhalation of ammonia. Thorax 47:755, 1992

43. Kerstein MD, Schaffzin DM, Hughes WB, et al: Acute management of exposure to liquid ammonia.

Mil Med 166:913, 2001

44. Flury K, Dines D, Rodarte J, et al: Airway obstruction due to inhalation of ammonia. Mayo Clin Proc 58:389, 1983

45. Laitung J, Earley M: The role of surgery in chromic acid burns: our experience with two patients. Burns Incl Therm Inj 10:378, 1984

46. Matey P, Allison KP, Sheehan TM, et al: Chromic acid burns: early aggressive excision is the best method to prevent systemic toxicity. J Burn Care Rehabil 21:241, 2000

47. Schiffl H, Weidmann P, Weiss M, et al: Dialysis treatment of acute chromium intoxication and comparative efficacy of peritoneal versus hemodialysis in chromium removal. Miner Electrolyte Metab 7:28, 1982

48. Terrill P, Gowar J: Chromic acid burns: beware, be aggressive, be watchful. Br J Plast Surg 43:699, 1990

49. Chan TC, Williams SR, Clark RF: Formic acid skin burns resulting in systemic toxicity. Ann Emerg Med 26:383, 1995

50. Sigurdsson J, Bjornsson A, Gudmundsson ST: Formic acid burn: local and systemic effects: report of a case. Burns Incl Therm Inj 9:358, 1983

51. Spiller HA, Quadrani KDA, Cleveland P: A five year evaluation of acute exposures to phenol disinfectant (26%). J Toxicol Clin Toxicol 31:307, 1993

52. Sanz-Gallen P, Nogue S, Munne P, et al: Hypocalcaemia and hypomagnesaemia due to hydrofluoric acid. Occup Med (Lond) 51:294, 2001

53. Mayer T, Gross P: Fatal systemic fluorosis due to hydrofluoric acid burns. Ann Emerg Med 14:149, 1985

54. Ohtani M, Nishida N, Chiba T, et al: Pathological demonstration of rapid involvement into the subcutaneous tissue in a case of fatal hydrofluoric acid burns. Forensic Sci Int, Jan 17, 2006 [Epub ahead of print]

55. McIvor M: Acute fluoride toxicity: pathophysiology and management. Drug Saf 5:79, 1990

56. Piraccini BM, Rech G, Pazzaglia M, et al: Peri- and subungual burns caused by hydrofluoric acid. Contact Dermatitis 52:230, 2005

57. Siegel DC, Heard JM: Intra-arterial calcium infusion for hydrofluoric acid burns. Aviat Space Environ Med 63:206, 1992

58. Lin TM, Tsai CC, Lin SD, et al: Continuous intra-arterial infusion therapy in hydrofluoric acid burns. J Occup Environ Med 42:892, 2000

59. Gupta R: Intravenous calcium gluconate in the treatment of hydrofluoric acid burns. Ann Emerg Med 37:734, 2001

60. Ryan JM, McCarthy GM, Plunkett PK: Regional intravenous calcium: an effective method of treating hydrofluoric acid burns to limb peripheries. J Accid Emerg Med 14:401, 1997

61. Graudins A, Burns MJ, Aaron CK: Regional intravenous infusion of calcium gluconate for hydrofluoric acid burns of the upper extremity. Ann Emerg Med 30:604, 1997

62. Eldad A, Wisoki M, Cohen H, et al: Phosphorous burns: evaluation of various methods for primary treatment. J Burn Care Rehabil 16:49, 1995

63. Eldad A, Simon GA: The phosphorous burn: a preliminary comparative experimental study of various forms of treatment. Burns 17:198, 1991

64. Etezad-Razavi M, Mahmoudi M, Hefazi M, et al: Delayed ocular complications of mustard gas poisoning and the relationship between respiratory and cutaneous complications. Clin Experiment Ophthalmol 34:342, 2006

65. Balali-Mood M, Hefazi M, Mahmoudi M, et al: Long-term complications of sulphur mustard poisoning in severely intoxicated Iranian veterans. Fundam Clin Pharmacol 19:713, 2005

66. Saladi RN, Smith E, Persaud AN: Mustard: a potential agent of chemical warfare and terrorism.

Clin Exp Dermatol 31:1, 2006

67. Ghanei M, Moqadam FA, Mohammad MM, et al: Tracheobronchomalacia and air trapping after mustard gas exposure. Am J Respir Crit Care Med 173:304, 2006

68. Hefazi M, Attaran D, Mahmoudi M, et al: Late respiratory complications of mustard gas poisoning in Iranian veterans. Inhal Toxicol 17:587, 2005

69. Bijani K, Moghadamnia AA: Long-term effects of chemical weapons on respiratory tract in Iraq-Iran war victims living in Babol (north of Iran). Ecotoxicol Environ Saf 53:422, 2002

70. Devereaux A, Amundson DE, Parrish JS, et al: Vesicants and nerve agents in chemical warfare: decontamination and treatment strategies for a changed world. Postgrad Med 112:90, 2002

71. Mellor SG, Rice P, Cooper GJ: Vesicant burns. Br J Plast Surg 44:434, 1991

72. DeGroot DW, Castellani JW, Williams JO, et al: Epidemiology of U.S. Army cold weather injuries, 1980–1999. Aviat Space Environ Med 74:564, 2003

73. White AD: Chilblains. Med J Aust 154:406, 1991

74. Goette DK: Chilblains (perniosis). J Am Acad Dermatol 23(2 pt 1):257, 1990

75. Cribier B, Djeridi N, Peltre B, et al: A histologic and immunohistochemical study of chilblains. J Am Acad Dermatol 45:924, 2001

76. Irwin MS, Sanders R, Green CJ, et al: Neuropathy in non-freezing cold injury (trench foot). J R Soc Med 90:433, 1997

77. Irwin MS: Nature and mechanism of peripheral nerve damage in an experimental model of non-freezing cold injury. Ann R Coll Surg Engl 78:372, 1996

78. Mills WJ Jr, Mills WJ 3rd: Peripheral non-freezing cold injury: immersion injury. Alaska Med 35:117, 1993

79. Wrenn K: Immersion foot: a problem of the homeless in the 1990s. Arch Intern Med 151:785, 1991

80. Kyosola K: Clinical experiences in the management of cold injuries: a study of 110 cases. J Trauma 14:32, 1974

81. Cauchy E, Chetaille E, Marchand V, et al: Retrospective study of 70 cases of severe frostbite lesions: a proposed new classification scheme. Wilderness Environ Med 12:248, 2001

82. Schedule for rating disabilities: cold injuries—VA. Final rule. Fed Regist 63:37778, 1998

83. Urschel JD, Urschel JW, Mackenzie WC: The role of alcohol in frostbite injury. Scand J Soc Med 18:273, 1990

84. Urschel JD: Frostbite: predisposing factors and predictors of poor outcome. J Trauma 30:340, 1990

85. Murphy JV, Banwell PE, Roberts AH, et al: Frostbite: pathogenesis and treatment. J Trauma 48:171, 2000

86. Zook N, Hussmann J, Brown R, et al: Microcirculatory studies of frostbite injury. Ann Plast Surg 40:246, 1998

87. Manson PN, Jesudass R, Marzella L, et al: Evidence for an early free radical-mediated reperfusion injury in frostbite. Free Radic Biol Med 10:7, 1991

88. Greenwald D, Cooper B, Gottlieb L: An algorithm for early aggressive treatment of frostbite with limb salvage directed by triple-phase scanning. Plast Reconstr Surg 102:1069, 1998

89. Bouwman DL, Morrison S, Lucas CE, et al: Early sympathetic blockade for frostbite: is it of value? J Trauma 20:744, 1980

90. Valnicek SM, Chasmar LR, Clapson JB: Frostbite in the prairies: a 12-year review. Plast Reconstr Surg 92:633, 1993

91. Reamy BV: Frostbite: review and current concepts. J Am Board Fam Pract 11:34, 1998

92. Marzella L, Jesudass RR, Manson PN, et al: Mor-

phologic characterization of acute injury to vascular endothelium of skin after frostbite. Plast Reconstr Surg 83:67, 1989

93. Mileski WJ, Raymond JF, Winn RK, et al: Inhibition of leukocyte adherence and aggregation for treatment of severe cold injury in rabbits. J Appl Physiol 74:1432, 1993

94. Twomey JA, Peltier GL, Zera RT: An open-label study to evaluate the safety and efficacy of tissue plasminogen activator in treatment of severe frostbite. J Trauma 59:1350, 2005

95. Porter JM, Wesche DH, Rosch J, et al: Intra-arterial sympathetic blockade in the treatment of clinical frostbite. Am J Surg 132:625, 1976

96. Purdue GF, Hunt JL: Cold injury: a collective review. J Burn Care Rehabil 7:331, 1986

97. Lyell A: Toxic epidermal necrolysis: an eruption resembling scalding of the skin. Br J Dermatol 68:355, 1956

98. Stevens A, Johnson F: A new eruptive fever associated with stomatitis and opthalmia. Am J Dis Child 24:526, 1922

99. Viard I, Wehrli P, Bullani R, et al: Inhibition of toxic epidermal necrolysis by blockade of CD95 with human intravenous immunoglobulin. Science 282:490, 1998

100. Abe R, Shimizu T, Shibaki A, et al: Toxic epidermal necrolysis and Stevens-Johnson syndrome are induced by soluble fas ligand. Am J Pathol 162:1515, 2003

101. French LE, Tschopp J: Protein-based therapeutic approaches targeting death receptors. Cell Death Differ 10:117, 2003

102. Bachot N, Revuz J, Roujeau JC: Intravenous immunoglobulin treatment for Stevens-Johnson syndrome and toxic epidermal necrolysis: a prospective noncomparative study showing no benefit on mortality or progression. Arch Dermatol 139:33, 2003

103. Stella M, Cassano P, Bollero D, et al: Toxic epidermal necrolysis treated with intravenous high-dose immunoglobulins: our experience. Dermatology 203:45, 2001 [PMID 11549799]

104. Paquet P, Jacob E, Damas P, et al: Treatment of drug-induced toxic epidermal necrolysis (Lyell's syndrome) with intravenous human immunoglobulins. Burns 27:652, 2001

105. Yip LW, Thong BY, Tan AW, et al: High-dose intravenous immunoglobulin in the treatment of toxic epidermal necrolysis: a study of ocular benefits. Eye 19:846, 2005

106. Patel GK, Finlay AY: Staphylococcal scalded skin syndrome: diagnosis and management. Am J Clin Dermatol 4:165, 2003

107. Meneux E, Paniel BJ, Pouget F, et al: Vulvovaginal sequelae in toxic epidermal necrolysis. J Reprod Med 42:153, 1997

108. Meneux E, Wolkenstein P, Haddad B, et al: Vulvovaginal involvement in toxic epidermal necrolysis: a retrospective study of 40 cases. Obstet Gynecol 91:283, 1998

109. Sugimoto Y, Mizutani H, Sato T, et al: Toxic epidermal necrolysis with severe gastrointestinal mucosal cell death: a patient who excreted long tubes of dead intestinal epithelium. J Dermatol 25:533, 1998

110. Kelemen JJ 3rd, Cioffi WG, McManus WF, et al: Burn center care for patients with toxic epidermal necrolysis. J Am Coll Surg 180:273, 1995

111. Heimbach DM, Engrav LH, Marvin JA, et al: Toxic epidermal necrolysis: a step forward in treatment. JAMA 257:2171, 1987

112. Honari S, Gibran NS, Heimbach DM, et al: Toxic epidermal necrolysis (TEN) in elderly patients. J Burn Care Rehabil 22:132, 2001

113. Salopek TG: Nikolsky's sign: is it 'dry' or is it 'wet'? Br J Dermatol 136:762, 1997

114. de Felice GP, Caroli R, Autelitano A: Long-term

complications of toxic epidermal necrolysis (Lyell's disease): clinical and histopathologic study. Ophthalmologica 195:1, 1987

115. Masia M, Gutierrez F, Jimeno A, et al: Fulminant hepatitis and fatal toxic epidermal necrolysis (Lyell disease) coincident with clarithromycin administration in an alcoholic patient receiving disulfiram therapy. Arch Intern Med 162:474, 2002

116. Heimbach DM, Engrav LH, Marvin JA, et al: Toxic epidermal necrolysis: a step forward in treatment [published erratum appears in JAMA 258:1894, 1987]. JAMA 257:2171, 1987

117. Sheridan RL, Weber JM, Schulz JT, et al: Management of severe toxic epidermal necrolysis in children. J Burn Care Rehabil 20:497, 1999

118. Yarbrough DR 3rd: Treatment of toxic epidermal necrolysis in a burn center. J S C Med Assoc 93:347, 1997

119. Imahara SD, Holmes JHt, Heimbach DM, et al: SCORTEN overestimates mortality in the setting of a standardized treatment protocol. J Burn Care Res 27:270, 2006

120. Clennett S, Hosking G: Management of toxic epidermal necrolysis in a 15-year-old girl. J Wound Care 12:151, 2003

121. Arevalo JM, Lorente JA: Skin coverage with Biobrane biomaterial for the treatment of patients with toxic epidermal necrolysis. J Burn Care Rehabil 20:406, 1999

122. Al-Qattan MM: Toxic epidermal necrolysis: a review and report of the successful use of Biobrane for early wound coverage. Ann Plast Surg 36:224, 1996

123. Bradley T, Brown RE, Kucan JO, et al: Toxic epidermal necrolysis: a review and report of the successful use of Biobrane for early wound coverage. Ann Plast Surg 35:124, 1995

124. Kucan JO: Use of Biobrane in the treatment of toxic epidermal necrolysis. J Burn Care Rehabil 16(3 pt 1):324, 1995

125. Power WJ, Ghoraishi M, Merayo-Lloves J, et al: Analysis of the acute ophthalmic manifestations of the erythema multiforme/Stevens-Johnson syndrome/toxic epidermal necrolysis disease spectrum. Ophthalmology 102:1669, 1995

126. Palmieri TL, Greenhalgh DG, Saffle JR, et al: A multicenter review of toxic epidermal necrolysis treated in U.S. burn centers at the end of the twentieth century. J Burn Care Rehabil 23:87, 2002

127. Rzany B, Schmitt H, Schopf E: Toxic epidermal necrolysis in patients receiving glucocorticosteroids. Acta Derm Venereol 71:171, 1991

128. Halebian PH, Corder VJ, Madden MR, et al: Improved burn center survival of patients with toxic epidermal necrolysis managed without corticosteroids. Ann Surg 204:503, 1986

129. Nenot JC: Medical and surgical management for localized radiation injuries. Int J Radiat Biol 57:783, 1990

130. Gus'kova AK, Baranov AE, Barabanova AV, et al: [The diagnosis, clinical picture and treatment of acute radiation sickness in the victims of the Chernobyl Atomic Electric Power Station. II. Non-bone marrow syndromes of radiation lesions and their treatment]. Ter Arkh 61:99, 1989

131. Iijima S: Pathology of atomic bomb casualties. Acta Pathol Jpn 32(suppl 2):237, 1982

116 CARDIAC RESUSCITATION

Terry J. Mengert, M.D.

Approach to Cardiovascular Resuscitation

Out-of-hospital sudden cardiac arrest claims the lives of more than 300,000 persons in the United States each year, making it the leading cause of death.[1-4] In fact, approximately 50% of all cardiac deaths are sudden deaths.[5] In hospitals, a minimum of 370,000 patients also suffer a cardiac arrest, followed by an attempted, but only sometimes successful, resuscitation.[6] Although most victims of sudden death have underlying coronary artery disease (70% to 80%), sudden death is the first manifestation of the disease in half of these persons.[2] Other causes and contributing factors include abnormalities of the myocardium (i.e., chronic heart failure or hypertrophy from any cause), electrophysiologic abnormalities, valvular heart disease, congenital heart disease, and miscellaneous inflammatory and infiltrative disease processes (e.g., myocarditis, sarcoidosis, and hemochromatosis).[7-9]

The pathophysiology that culminates in a sudden cardiac death is complex and poorly understood. It likely represents a mix of electrical abnormalities combined with acute functional triggers, such as myocardial ischemia, central and autonomic nervous system effects, electrolyte abnormalities, and even pharmacologic influences.[1] Classically, most sudden deaths that occur in adults in the community are thought to be secondary to ventricular tachycardia (VT) that quickly degenerates into ventricular fibrillation (VF). In a 10-year study in the Seattle area, the different arrhythmias found in prehospital cardiac arrest patients presumed to have underlying cardiovascular disease were VF (45%), asystole (31%), pulseless electrical activity (PEA; 10%), VT (1%), and other arrhythmias (14%).[3] Studies indicate that the out-of-hospital incidence of VF has decreased in recent years, probably because of the decrease in mortality from coronary artery disease.[10]

The Chain of Survival

The resuscitation of an adult victim of sudden cardiac arrest should follow an orderly sequence, no matter where the patient's collapse occurs. This sequence is called the chain of survival.[11] It comprises four elements, all of which must be instituted as rapidly as possible: activation of the emergency medical service network, cardiopulmonary resuscitation (CPR), early defibrillation, and provision of advanced care.

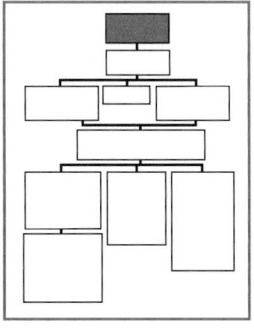

ACTIVATION OF EMERGENCY MEDICAL SERVICES

A person in cardiac arrest is unresponsive and pulseless, although agonal respirations may last for minutes. Confirm unresponsiveness by speaking loudly and gently shaking the patient. If the patient is truly unresponsive, immediately call for help by activating the emergency medical service in the community (in most locales, this means calling 911); or if the patient is already in the hospital, call a code (e.g., code blue, code 199). If an automated external defibrillator (AED) is available, have it brought to the resuscitation scene. AEDs are both easily used and lifesaving.[12-16]

INITIATION OF CPR

While awaiting the arrival of a defibrillator and advanced help, the rescuer assesses the patient's airway, breathing, and circulation [see The Primary Survey, *below*] and initiates CPR [see Table 1]. When CPR is started within 4 minutes of collapse, the likelihood of patient survival at least doubles.[17,18]

INITIATION OF DEFIBRILLATION

When the AED or monitor-defibrillator arrives, attach it appropriately to the patient and analyze the patient's rhythm; if the patient is in VF or pulseless VT, a defibrillatory shock should be rapidly applied [see Tables 2 and 3]. If required, two additional shocks may be administered sequentially. The importance of rapid access to defibrillation cannot be overemphasized. In a patient who is dying from a shockable rhythm, the chance of survival declines by 7% to 10% for every minute that defibrillation is delayed.[19]

INITIATION OF ADVANCED CARE

If the patient remains pulseless despite the steps described above, resume CPR; establish a definitive airway, confirm its correct placement, and then secure it; establish intravenous access; then administer appropriate medications as determined by the rhythm and the arrest circumstances. If the patient is in VF or pulseless VT, repeated attempts at defibrillation are interspersed with delivery of vasoactive and antiarrhythmic drugs [see Table 4].

RESUSCITATION OUTCOME

When every link in the chain of survival is quickly and sequentially available, the patient is provided an optimal opportunity for return of spontaneous circulation.[19-22] In the United States, individual communities report survival rates of 4% to 40% or more in cases of sudden cardiac death.[23-27] Prehospital victims of VF have had survival rates to hospital discharge of greater than 50% when an AED was expeditiously used.[28] Many other factors also influence patient survival, however; these include whether the patient's collapse was witnessed, the rapidity and effectiveness of bystander CPR, the rhythm associated with the cardiac arrest, and underlying comorbidities.[29,30] With inpatient cardiac arrest, for example, overall survival rates vary from 9% to 32%,[31-37] but in one study, survival to hospital discharge was 30% for patients with primary heart disease, 15% for patients with infectious diseases, and only 8% for patients with other end-stage diseases (e.g., cancer, lung disease, liver failure, or renal failure).[38]

Such statistics underline the importance of using cardiac resuscitation appropriately and with discrimination. Cardiac resuscitation provides rescuers with powerful tools that save the lives of thousands of people every year. These techniques are capable of returning patients who would otherwise die to productive and meaningful lives. However, cardiac resuscitation should not be employed to reverse timely and natural death. Under those circumstances, it has the potential to lengthen the dying process and to increase human suffering. All practitioners are well advised to remember that "death is not the opposite of life, death is the opposite of birth. Both are as-

Approach to Cardiovascular Resuscitation

Patient is in cardiac arrest

Confirm unresponsiveness.
If out of hospital, call EMS.
If in hospital, activate appropriate code.
Call for a defibrillator.

Primary survey

Assess ABCs.
Begin CPR; when defibrillator arrives, attach to patient and briefly withhold CPR.
Assess rhythm.

Pulseless VT or VF

Immediately administer shock, first at 200 J, then 200–300 J, then 360 J; if patient is already attached to a monitor-defibrillator, begin resuscitation with immediate defibrillation.
Resume CPR.

Pulseless electrical activity

Resume CPR.

Asystole

Resume CPR and confirm asystole.
Ensure that patient is appropriately attached to monitor-defibrillator, that ECG gain control on the defibrillator is at maximum, and that the rhythm is assessed in several leads.

Secondary survey

Endotracheally intubate, confirm tube placement, secure tube, establish I.V. access.
Concomitantly with preceding steps, identify and correct technical difficulties hampering resuscitation [see Table 6]; initiate emergency therapy for conditions contributing to cardiac arrest [see Table 7].

Pulseless VT or VF

Subsequent steps assume continuing VT or VF despite interventions; do not interrupt CPR except as required for rapid performance of lifesaving procedures.
Administer vasoactive drugs with ongoing CPR:
 Epinephrine, 1 mg I.V. push, repeated every 3–5 min throughout CPR
  or
 Vasopressin, 40 U I.V. push in a single dose; if no response after 10 min, administer epinephrine as described above.

Administer antiarrhythmic drugs with ongoing CPR:
 Amiodarone, 300 mg I.V. push; if a second dose is needed, 150 mg after 5 min
  or
 Lidocaine, 1.0–1.5 mg/kg I.V. push; if a second dose is needed, repeat initial dose in 3–5 min.
Hypomagnesemia or torsade de pointes is suspected:
 Magnesium sulfate, 1–2 g I.V. push
Intermittent or recurrent VT/VF after an initial response to shocks:
 Procainamide, 20–50 mg/min I.V. infusion to a total dose of 17 mg/kg.
Follow medication delivery with a 20 ml saline bolus; elevate extremity with I.V. line, and continue CPR for 30–60 sec to circulate medication; then administer shock (360 J for up to three shocks).

Pulseless electrical activity

Subsequent steps assume continuing PEA despite interventions; do not interrupt CPR except as required for rapid performance of lifesaving procedures.
Administer epinephrine, 1 mg I.V. push, with ongoing CPR; repeat every 3–5 min as long as CPR is required.
If heart rate as shown on monitor is slow, administer atropine, 1 mg I.V. push, with ongoing CPR; may repeat every 3–5 min to a total dose of 3 mg.
Follow medication delivery with a 20 ml saline bolus and elevation of the extremity containing the I.V. line.

Asystole

Subsequent steps assume continuing asystole despite interventions; do not interrupt CPR except as required for rapid performance of lifesaving procedures.
Attempt transcutaneous pacing, if available (may be initiated simultaneously with above steps).
Administer medications with ongoing CPR:
 Epinephrine, 1 mg I.V. push; repeat every 3–5 min for as long as patient requires CPR (vasopressin, 40 U I.V. one time, is a reasonable alternative)
  and
 Atropine, 1 mg I.V. push; repeat every 3–5 min to a total dose of 3 mg
Follow medication delivery with a 20 ml saline bolus and elevation of the extremity containing the I.V. line.
End resuscitation attempt if patient remains in confirmed asystole for > 10 min and there is no technical problem preventing resuscitation, no imminently treatable cause, and no extenuating circumstance.

Table 1   Initial Resuscitation Steps in the Unresponsive Patient

Confirm unresponsiveness
Activate the emergency medical system
  In most community locales, call 911
  In the hospital, activate the appropriate code response
Call for an automatic external defibrillator (AED)
Begin basic life support (CPR)
  Open airway
  Check breathing; if not breathing, deliver two initial breaths
  Check for a carotid pulse; if pulseless, do the following:
    Begin chest compressions at the rate of 100 compressions/min, depressing the sternum 4–5 cm per compression in patients older than 8 yr
    Intersperse ventilations with chest compressions: in nonintubated patients, deliver 15 compressions, pause for two breaths, then repeat; in intubated patients, deliver one breath every 5 sec, with no pause in compressions
Reassess for return of spontaneous circulation every 1–3 min
When defibrillator arrives, immediately analyze and treat arrhythmia
  Attach patient to AED [see Table 2] or the monitor-defibrillator [see Table 3]
  Analyze arrhythmia and treat as appropriate

pects of life."[39] It is untimely death that requires immediate intervention with cardiac resuscitation.

The Primary and Secondary Surveys of Cardiac Resuscitation

A cardiac resuscitation is a stressful event for everyone involved. Too often, clinic and inpatient cardiac arrests and their management are episodes of chaos in the busy lives of resident and attending physicians. Yet, it has been eloquently stated that a good resuscitation team should function like a fine symphony orchestra.[40] Such skill levels require dedicated individual and team practice and careful code-team organization. Mastery in cardiac resuscitation is in fact a lifelong pursuit that requires training and retraining in advanced cardiac life support (ACLS); regular practice and review; and leadership and team skill development. Its key elements include not only the resuscitation itself but the response to the announcement of a code, postresuscitation stabilization of the patient, notification of the family and primary care provider, and code critique and debriefing. To help practitioners learn and apply some of the most essential techniques used in cardiac resuscitation more easily and effectively, the American Heart Association (AHA) has developed the concepts of primary and secondary surveys of a patient in atraumatic cardiac arrest.[41]

THE PRIMARY SURVEY

The primary survey for the victim of sudden cardiac arrest consists of the appropriate assessment of the patient's airway (A), breathing (B), and circulation (C) and the simultaneous application of expert CPR until defibrillation (D) becomes possible (assuming the patient is in VF or pulseless VT). Thus, the primary survey includes the second and third links in the chain of survival (see above).

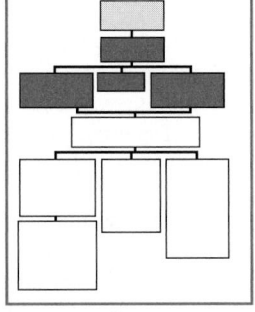

In 1958, Kouwenhoven noted that when his research fellow forcefully applied external defibrillating electrodes on a dog's chest

in the laboratory, an arterial pressure wave occurred.[42] Further study and refinements led to the technique of closed-chest CPR, the careful description of which was published in 1960.[43] The first report of the use of this technique in patients was in 1961.[44] Since those early days, the fundamentals of closed-chest CPR have remained relatively unchanged. Mouth-to-mouth, mouth-to-mask, or bag-valve-mask ventilation oxygenates the blood. Chest compressions produce forward blood flow. This flow appears to result from a combination of direct compression of the heart and intrathoracic pressure changes.[45,46]

CPR in isolation does not defibrillate the heart. Its main benefit is to extend patient viability until a defibrillator and advanced interventions become available and, one hopes, succeed in restoring spontaneous circulation in the patient. CPR is not nearly as effective as a contracting heart; systolic arterial pressure peaks of 60 to 80 mm Hg may be generated, but diastolic blood pressure remains low, and a cardiac output of only 25% to 30% of normal can be achieved even under optimal conditions.[47] Still, effective CPR is critical to keeping the patient alive. It is worth remembering that the most important rescuers at a cardiac resuscitation are those who are performing expert CPR, because it is only through their efforts that the patient's heart and brain are kept viable until defibrillation and other advanced interventions can restore spontaneous circulation.

After unresponsiveness is confirmed, the emergency medical system is activated and an AED is called for; the primary survey (A, B, C, and D) proceeds as described (see below) until the AED arrives.

Airway Optimization

Open the patient's mouth and optimize the airway in the nontrauma patient by use of the head-tilt and chin-lift maneuver. A jaw-thrust maneuver should be used instead of the head-tilt technique if cervical spine injury is suspected. In patients with suspected spine injury, proper spine alignment must be maintained throughout all phases of the resuscitation. In such circumstances, as

Table 2   Using an Automatic External Defibrillator in Patients Older than 8 Years

Automatic external defibrillator (AED) arrives (CPR is in progress)
  Place AED beside patient.
  Turn on the AED.
  Attach the electrodes to the AED (they may be preattached).
  Attach the electrode pads to the patient (as diagrammed on the pads).
AED analyzes patient's rhythm
  Stop CPR (and ensure no one is touching the patient).
  Press the Analyze button on the AED (some devices analyze the rhythm automatically as soon as the pads are placed on the patient).
AED instructs rescuers (via an audible voice prompt and/or on-screen instructions)
  Shock is indicated: clear the patient (ensure no one is touching the patient) and push the Shock button.
  After delivering shock, press the Analyze button again; the sequence of analysis followed by shock (if so indicated) may be performed a total of three times.
              or
  Shock not indicated: reassess the patient for signs of circulation; if present, assess the adequacy of breathing; if there are no signs of circulation, resume CPR for 1–2 min. After 1 min of CPR, assess the patient again for signs of circulation; if present, assess the adequacy of breathing. If the patient is still pulseless, repeat analysis, followed (if indicated) by shock steps.

Table 3 Using a Manual Defibrillator[52,89]

Defibrillator arrives (CPR is in progress)

Place defibrillator beside patient.

Turn defibrillator on (initial energy level setting is typically 200 J).*

Set Lead Select switch to Paddles. Alternatively, if patient is already attached to monitor leads, set Lead Select switch to lead I, II, or III; ensure all three leads are correctly attached to the patient and the defibrillator: white to right shoulder, black to left shoulder, red to ribs on left side.

Apply gel to paddles or place conductor pads on patient's chest. Some devices use disposable electrode patches that are prepasted with a conducting gel. In either case, the appropriate positions of the paddles with applied gel, conductor pads, or disposable paddles are as follows: sternal paddle is placed to the right of the sternum, just below the right clavicle; apex paddle is placed to the left of the left breast, centered in the left midaxillary line at the fifth intercostal space.

Analyze rhythm

Briefly withhold CPR

If using paddles to assess rhythm, apply paddles as described with firm pressure (25 lb of pressure to each paddle) and visually assess rhythm on monitor (if using leads, briefly withhold CPR and assess rhythm in leads I, II, or III). If rhythm is either pulseless VT or VF, proceed as follows:

Defibrillate, then reassess

Announce to resuscitation team, "Charging defibrillator, stand clear!" and press Charge button on either paddles or defibrillator (initial energy, 200 J, not synchronized).*

Warn resuscitation team that a defibrillatory shock is coming: "I am going to shock on three! ONE, I'm clear; TWO, you're clear, THREE, everybody's CLEAR!" Simultaneously with these statements, visually ensure that no resuscitation team member is in contact with patient.

Press the Discharge buttons on both paddles simultaneously to deliver a defibrillatory shock.

Reassess rhythm on monitor; if patient is still in VT or VF, recharge defibrillator (now 300 J)* and repeat process of loudly informing team members by giving the warning statements as above, and then apply defibrillatory shock.

Reassess rhythm on monitor; if patient is still in VT or VF, recharge defibrillator (now 360 J)* and repeat process of loudly informing team members by giving the warning statements as above, and then apply defibrillatory shock.

Reassess rhythm on monitor; if patient is still in VT or VF, resume CPR and continue with resuscitation sequence.

---

*Note: if using a biphasic defibrillator, a lower initial defibrillatory energy level (< 200 J) without energy escalation on subsequent shocks is acceptable.

VF—ventricular fibrillation   VT—ventricular tachycardia

---

equipment becomes available, the patient's spine requires immobilization with a padded backboard, hard cervical collar, appropriate bolstering around the patient's head to prevent movement, and strapping of the patient to the backboard.[48]

Breathing Assessment

To assess breathing, the rescuer places his or her cheek close to the patient's mouth and looks, listens, and feels for patient respirations. If the respirations are agonal or the patient is apneic, the rescuer then delivers two initial breaths. Each breath is delivered over 1.5 to 2.0 seconds. The patient's chest should rise with each delivered breath, and exhalation is allowed for between breaths. Breaths may be delivered using the mouth-to-mouth technique with appropriate barrier precautions (the patient's nose should be pinched if the mouth-to-mouth technique is used) or mouth-to-mask technique. The ideal device, if available, is a bag-valve-mask device attached to high-flow oxygen; this allows the delivery of a substantially higher oxygen concentration to the patient. If the patient cannot be ventilated, the rescuer repositions the airway and attempts the technique again. If the airway is still obstructed, up to five abdomi-

nal thrusts are then applied, followed by a finger sweep of the oropharynx to relieve suspected obstruction, and then ventilation attempts are repeated. Definitive intervention for an obstructed airway in the hospital setting may involve laryngoscopic visualization of the cause of obstruction and foreign-body removal. If an adequate airway cannot be established by less invasive means, cricothyrotomy may be required.

CPR Initiation

The health care rescuer next checks for a carotid pulse in the unresponsive patient but should allow no more than 10 seconds to do so. (The AHA no longer recommends pulse checks for rescuers who are not health care providers.[49] Instead, lay rescuers should initiate chest compressions if the patient is not breathing, coughing, or moving after the initial two breaths.) If the patient has no carotid pulse, begin chest compressions. The patient should be on a firm surface, and the heel of the rescuer's hand should be in the center of the inferior half of the patient's sternum (but cephalad to the xiphoid process). The rescuer's other hand is placed on top of the lower hand, with the fingers interlocked.

The rescuer's arms are held straight, with the force of each compression coming from the rescuer's trunk. In patients older than 8 years, the sternum is smoothly compressed by 1.5 to 2.0 inches, then released. The duration of the compression-release cycle is divided equally between compression and release. The rate of chest compression is 100 compressions/min in patients older than 8 years. The chest should be allowed to rebound to its precompression dimensions between compressions, but the resuscitator's palm closest to the patient should remain in contact with the sternum.

In nonintubated patients, chest compressions are regularly interrupted for the delivery of ventilations. The sequence is the same, regardless of whether one-rescuer or two-rescuer CPR is being performed: the rescuer delivers 15 compressions, pauses for two breaths (each given over 2 seconds), then resumes compressions. In endotracheally intubated patients, no pause for ventilation is necessary; every 5 seconds, one ventilation is delivered over a period of 1 to 2 seconds, while compressions continue.[18]

The optimal timing and ratio of ventilations to compressions in CPR is an ongoing area of research, which may lead to changes in the current recommendations. In the porcine model, for example, optimal neurologic outcome was achieved with the use of only compressions for the first 4 minutes, followed by a compression-ventilation ratio of 100:2.[50] In the prehospital setting, when rapid advanced care is available within minutes, bystander-initiated mouth-to-mouth ventilation combined with chest compressions offers no advantage over chest compressions alone.[51]

Good technique is critical throughout CPR delivery. The patient should have carotid pulses with chest compressions and should have appropriate breath sounds and chest movement with ventilations. Interestingly, femoral pulsations with CPR do not necessarily indicate effective CPR; these pulsations often are venous rather than arterial. Quantitative end-tidal carbon dioxide levels can be monitored, if practical. Higher levels correlate with more effective CPR and increased survival.[52] The patient should be reassessed for return of spontaneous circulation every 1 to 3 minutes [see Table 1].

Defibrillation

When the monitor-defibrillator or AED arrives, it is attached to the patient; the rhythm is analyzed, and if the patient is in VF or pulseless VT, defibrillation is provided [see Tables 2 and 3].

Defibrillation is thought to work by simultaneously depolarizing a sufficient mass of cardiac myocytes to make the cardiac tissue ahead of the VT or VF wavefronts refractory to electrical conduction. Subse-

Table 4   Drugs Useful in Cardiac Arrest[3,90]

Category	Drug and Doses Supplied	Indications in Cardiac Arrest	Adult Dosage	Comments
Vasopressors	Epinephrine, 1 mg in 10 ml emergency syringe; 1 mg/ml (1 ml and 30 ml vials)	Pulseless VT or VF unresponsive to initial defibrillatory shocks; PEA; asystole	1 mg I.V. push; may repeat every 3–5 min for as long as patient is pulseless; can also be given via the endotracheal route: 2–2.5 mg diluted with normal saline (NS) to 10 ml total volume	I.V. boluses of epinephrine (1 mg) are appropriate only in pulseless cardiac arrest patients; if continued epinephrine is required after resuscitation, a continuous infusion should be started (1–10 μg/min). High-dose epinephrine (up to 0.2 mg/kg I.V. per dose) does not improve survival to hospital discharge in cardiac arrest patients and is no longer recommended in adults.
	Vasopressin, 20 IU/ml (1 ml vial)	Pulseless VT or VF unresponsive to initial defibrillatory shocks	40 IU I.V. push, single dose only; can also be given via endotracheal tube: same dose, diluted with NS to 10 ml total volume	If no response after 10 min of continued resuscitation, administer epinephrine, as above.
Antiarrhythmics	Amiodarone, 50 mg/ml (3 ml vial)	Pulseless VT or VF unresponsive to initial defibrillatory shocks and epinephrine plus shock(s)	VT/VF: 300 mg diluted in 20–30 ml; NS or D5W rapid I.V. push; a repeat dose of 150 mg may be given if required in 5 min; maximum dose in 24 hr should not exceed 2,200 mg	Side effects may include hypotension and bradycardia in the postresuscitation phase.
	Lidocaine, 50 mg or 100 mg in 5 ml emergency syringes; premixed bag, 1 g/250 ml or 2 g/250 ml	Pulseless VT or VF unresponsive to initial defibrillatory shocks and epinephrine plus shock(s)	Initial dose: 1–1.5 mg/kg I.V.; for refractory VF or unstable VT, may repeat 1–1.5 mg/kg I.V. in 3–5 min; maximum dose, 3 mg/kg. May also be given endotracheally: 2–4 mg/kg diluted with NS to 10 ml total volume	If lidocaine is effective, initiate continuous I.V. infusion at 2–4 mg/min when patient has return of a perfusing rhythm (but do not use if this rhythm is an idioventricular rhythm or third-degree heart block with an idioventricular escape rhythm). Continuous infusion should begin at 1 mg/min in congestive heart failure or chronic liver disease or in elderly patients.
	Magnesium sulfate, 500 mg/ml (2 ml and 10 ml vials), or 10 ml emergency syringe	Pulseless VT or VF unresponsive to initial defibrillatory shocks and epinephrine plus shock(s) if suspected hypomagnesemic state	Administer 1–2 g diluted in 100 ml D5W I.V. over 1–2 min. Total body magnesium deficits should be replaced gradually after initial therapy has stabilized the emergency: administer 0.5–1 g/hr for 3–6 hr, then reassess continued need	Measured magnesium levels correlate only approximately with the actual level of deficiency. Patients with renal insufficiency are at risk for dangerous hypermagnesemia; use appropriate caution. Side effects may include bradycardia, hypotension, generalized weakness, and temporary loss of reflexes.
	Procainamide, 100 mg/ml (10 ml injection); 500 mg/ml (2 ml vial)	Recurrent or intermittent pulseless VT or VF	20–30 mg/min I.V. (up to 50 mg/min if situation is critical); maximum dose is 17 mg/kg over time (but maximum dose is reduced to 12 mg/kg in setting of cardiac or renal dysfunction). Maintenance infusion is 1–4 mg/min	Administer procainamide during a perfusing rhythm. Stop procainamide administration when arrhythmia is adequately suppressed, hypotension occurs, QRS widens to > 50% of original duration, or maximum dose is administered.
Anticholinergic	Atropine, 1 mg in 10 ml emergency syringe	Asystole or PEA (if rate of rhythm is slow)	For asystole or PEA: 1 mg I.V. every 3–5 min up to 3 mg. May be given via ET tube: 2–3 mg diluted with NS to 10 ml	Minimal adult dose is 0.5 mg. Avoid use in type II second-degree heart block or third-degree heart block.
Miscellaneous	Bicarbonate, 50 mEq in 50 ml emergency syringe	Significant hyperkalemia. Significant metabolic acidosis unresponsive to optimal CPR, oxygenation, and ventilation. Certain drug overdoses, including tricyclic antidepressants and aspirin	Hyperkalemia therapy: 50 mEq I.V. Metabolic acidosis: 1 mEq/kg slow I.V. push; may repeat half initial dose in 10 min; ideally, ABGs should help guide further therapy. Use in overdose: discuss with toxicologist	In non–dialysis-dependent hyperkalemic patients, bicarbonate is most useful if metabolic acidosis is also present; bicarbonate is less effective in dialysis-dependent renal failure patients. The use of bicarbonate in metabolic acidosis management in cardiac arrest patients is controversial. Side effects may include sodium overload, hypokalemia, and metabolic alkalosis.
	Calcium chloride, 100 mg/ml in 10 ml prefilled syringe	Significant hyperkalemia. Calcium channel blocker drug overdose. Profound hypocalcemia of other causes	In hyperkalemia: 5–10 ml slow I.V. push; may repeat if required. In calcium channel blocker overdose: discuss with toxicologist	Do not use if suspected cause of hyperkalemia is acute digoxin poisoning. Do not combine in same I.V. with sodium bicarbonate. Calcium chloride is not a routine medication in cardiac arrest.

Note: All medications used during cardiac arrest, when given via a peripheral venous site in an extremity, should be followed by a 20 ml I.V. saline bolus and elevation of the extremity for 10 to 20 sec.
ABG—arterial blood gases   D5W—5% dextrose in water   ET—endotracheal   PEA—pulseless electrical activity   VF—ventricular fibrillation   VT—ventricular tachycardia

quently, the sinus node or another appropriate pacemaker region of the heart with inherent automaticity can resume orderly depolarization-repolarization, with return of a perfusing rhythm.[15,53] The sooner defibrillation occurs, the higher the likelihood of resuscitation. When defibrillation is provided immediately after the onset of VF, its success rate is extremely high.[54] In a study of sudden cardiac arrest patients in Nevada gambling casinos, the survival rate to hospital dis-

charge was 74% for patients who received their first defibrillation no later than 3 minutes after a witnessed collapse.[28] In this study, defibrillation was delivered via an AED operated by casino security officers.

Early defibrillation is so critical that if a defibrillator is immediately available, its use traditionally takes precedence over CPR for patients in VF or pulseless VT of recent onset. If CPR is already in progress, it should of course be halted while defibrillation takes place. Newer defibrillators can compensate for thoracic impedance, ensuring that the selected energy level is in fact the energy that is delivered to the myocardial tissue. In addition, defibrillators that deliver biphasic defibrillation waveforms instead of the standard monophasic damped sinusoidal waveforms allow effective defibrillation at lower energy levels (< 200 joules) and without the need for energy-level escalation during subsequent shocks.[15,55-58] In the Optimized Response to Cardiac Arrest (ORCA) study, which involved 115 patients with prehospital VF, the 150-joule biphasic-shock AED was more effective than the traditional high-energy monophasic-shock AED in four respects: it was more successful in producing defibrillation with the first shock (96% versus 59%); it led to a higher rate of ultimate success with defibrillation (100% versus 84%); it had a better rate of return of spontaneous circulation (76% versus 54%); and its use was associated with a higher rate of good cerebral performance in the survivors (87% versus 53%).[59] There were no differences, however, in terms of survival to hospital admission or discharge, and replication of the ORCA findings is lacking at this time. Current AHA guidelines state that lower-energy biphasic waveform defibrillators are safe and have equivalent or higher efficacy for termination of VF, as compared with the standard monophasic waveform defibrillator.[15,49]

Ongoing research suggests that the duration of VF is a consideration in deciding whether to defibrillate immediately and as soon as a defibrillator is available or to perform CPR for a brief period first to "prime the pump" before proceeding to defibrillation. In the porcine model in the setting of prolonged VF (> 10 minutes), CPR before countershock provides several physiologic benefits.[60] Studies have found that patients with VF of longer than 5 minutes' duration had better return of spontaneous circulation, survival to hospital discharge, and 1-year survival if ambulance personnel provided 3 minutes of CPR before performing defibrillation than if ambulance personnel performed defibrillation immediately after arriving at the scene; however, some experts question the validity of these results, on the basis of study design.[61,62]

THE SECONDARY SURVEY

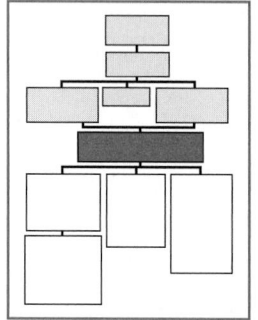

The secondary survey for a victim of persistent cardiac arrest takes place after completion of the primary survey. Like the primary survey, the secondary survey follows an ABCD format, which in this case consists of advanced airway interventions (A); optimized oxygenation and ventilation by confirmation of endotracheal (ET) tube placement and repeated reassessment of the adequacy of delivered breaths (B); intravenous access and appropriate medication delivery to the patient's circulation (C); and definitive therapy (D), based on a differential diagnosis that considers the specific disease processes thought to be responsible for, or contributing to, the cardiac arrest. The secondary survey includes the fourth link in the chain of survival, rapid advanced care (see above).

Placement of an Advanced Airway

Patients who remain in cardiac arrest after completion of the primary survey require placement of an advanced airway. Depending on the setting and the experience of the rescuers, this advanced airway may be a laryngeal mask airway, an esophageal-tracheal Combitube (a tracheal tube bonded side by side with an esophageal obturator), or an ET tube.[36,63,64] The laryngeal mask airway and the Combitube can be placed by personnel with less training than that required for endotracheal intubation, and they do not require additional special equipment or visualization of the vocal cords. Never-

---

Table 5 Confirmation of Endotracheal Tube Placement

Intubation process
  Vocal cords are visualized by intubator
  Tip of ET tube is seen passing between the cords
  Cuff of ET tube also passes cords by 1 cm
Postintubation checks
  Esophageal detector device or end-tidal CO_2 detector confirms ET tube placement in trachea
  Breath sounds are symmetrical (auscultate over lateral anterior chest and in midaxillary line bilaterally)
  No gurgling with auscultation over epigastrium
  Patient's chest rises and falls appropriately with ventilation
  ET tube depth is appropriate: 21 cm at the corner of the mouth in women, 23 cm in men
Secure the ET tube to prevent dislodgment
Reassess the adequacy of oxygenation and ventilation throughout the resuscitation (bedside patient assessment; also obtain ABGs when feasible)
After resuscitation, obtain a portable chest radiograph

ABG—arterial blood gas   ET—endotracheal

---

theless, oral endotracheal intubation is generally the preferred advanced airway technique for cardiac resuscitation, especially in the hospital setting, where experienced intubators are generally present; in the prehospital setting, the evidence supporting endotracheal intubation remains inconsistent. Endotracheal intubation isolates the airway, maintains airway patency, helps protect the trachea from the ever-present risk of aspiration, helps permit optimal oxygenation and ventilation of the patient, allows for tracheal suctioning, and even provides a route for delivery of some medications to the systemic circulation (via the pulmonary circulation) if intravenous access is unobtainable or lost.[63]

Optimization of Breathing and Ventilation

When a cardiac arrest patient undergoes endotracheal intubation, correct positioning of the ET tube must be immediately confirmed and regularly reconfirmed during and after the resuscitation [*see Table 5*]. Routine use of an esophageal detector device or end-tidal CO_2 detector is recommended, along with careful patient examination. Caution is necessary with qualitative colorimetric end-tidal CO_2 detectors because both false positive and false negative results have been documented during cardiac arrests.[65] Breath sounds should be present during auscultation over the anterior and lateral chest walls, and the patient's chest should rise and fall with delivered ventilations. No gurgling should be heard when the epigastrium is auscultated. The ET tube should be inserted to the appropriate depth marking: for average-sized adults, this is 21 cm at the corner of the mouth in a woman and 23 cm in a man. The patient's skin color should be reasonable (i.e., not dusky or cyanotic), provided that the patient's pigmentation allows such assessment.

Once correct positioning is confirmed, the ET tube is then appropriately secured to prevent its dislodgment. When feasible, an arterial blood gas (ABG) measurement will help further confirm the adequacy of oxygenation and ventilation as the resuscitation proceeds.

Establishment of Circulation Access

Access to the patient's venous circulation is mandatory; such access may be achieved by a code-team member or members simultaneously while other resuscitators pursue steps A and B of the secondary survey. Ideally, a large intravenous cannula is placed in a

Table 6 Technical Problems That May Prevent a Successful Resuscitation

Problem	Patients at Risk	Recommendations
Ineffective CPR	All cardiac arrest patients	Ensure technically perfect CPR. Confirm carotid pulses with CPR. If arterial line was in place before cardiac arrest, confirm adequate arterial waveform with CPR on arterial line monitor. Monitor end-tidal CO_2 if available (higher levels correlate with better CPR and improved patient survival). Confirm adequate oxygenation with an ABG when feasible.
Inadequate oxygenation and ventilation	All cardiac arrest patients	Ensure optimal airway positioning and control. Have suction immediately available to manage pharyngeal and airway secretions. Ensure use of properly fitting, tightly sealed face mask for bag-valve mask (BVM) ventilation until a definitive airway is established. Apply cricoid pressure to prevent gastric distention during BVM ventilation until a definitive airway is established. Ensure that supplemental oxygen is flowing to BVM at 15 L/min. Deliver an appropriate tidal volume per breath (6–7 ml/kg if oxygen is available) at the rate of 12–15 breaths/min. Confirm bilateral and equal breath sounds with ventilation. Confirm that patient's chest rises with each ventilation. Allow adequate time for exhalation between breaths. Confirm optimal oxygenation and ventilation with an ABG when feasible.
ET tube difficulties	All patients intubated with ET tube	Allow 20–30 sec/intubation attempt. Intubator should see tip of ET tube and cuff pass between vocal cords at time of intubation. After intubation, immediately confirm correct ET tube placement; regularly reconfirm ET tube placement throughout resuscitation. Confirm adequacy of oxygenation and ventilation with an ABG. After intubation, consider nasogastric tube placement to decompress stomach and optimize diaphragmatic excursions with ventilation.
Intravenous line difficulties	All cardiac arrest patients	Place one or more 18-gauge or larger I.V. cannulas in an antecubital or external jugular vein site. Check for I.V. infiltration regularly throughout the resuscitation. Follow all medications administered through a peripheral I.V. site with a 20 ml saline bolus and elevation of the extremity containing the I.V. for 10–15 sec (if possible). Consider central line placement if the resuscitation is prolonged. Be aware of all I.V. infusions the patient is receiving. Stop all nonessential medications that had been started before the cardiac arrest. During the resuscitation, the only infusions the patient should receive are normal saline, blood products (if clinically indicated), and pertinent medications necessary to assist with return of spontaneous circulation. Pulmonary artery catheters and central lines occasionally act as an arrhythmogenic focus within the right ventricle. If applicable, deflate all relevant balloons on the catheter and withdraw the catheter to a superior vena cava position.
Monitor defibrillator difficulties	All cardiac arrest patients	Make sure Synchronization Mode button is in the off position when defibrillating patients in pulseless VT or VF. Make sure electricity is not arcing over the patient's chest because of perspiration or smeared conducting gel; dry patient's chest with a towel except for areas directly beneath pads or paddles. Do not administer shock through nitroglycerin paste or patches. If the patient has an internal cardioverter-defibrillator (ICD) or a pacemaker, the patient may still be manually defibrillated, but do not shock directly over the internal device. Under these circumstances, place the pads or paddles at least 2.5 cm away from the patient's internal device. If the ICD is intermittently firing but not defibrillating the patient and if the ICD is thought to be compromising the resuscitation, turn the device off with a magnet so that manual defibrillation may take place without interference. Maximize the gain or electrocardiography "size" and check the rhythm in several leads (or change the axes of the paddles if reading the rhythm in Paddles mode) to confirm asystole when the initial rhythm appears to be asystole.

ABG—arterial blood gas   ET—endotracheal   VF—ventricular fibrillation   VT—ventricular tachycardia

prominent upper-extremity vein or the external jugular vein to optimize delivery of needed medications. If a peripheral line is not achievable, additional access possibilities include central line placement via the internal jugular, subclavian (via the supraclavicular approach), or, less ideally, femoral vein; even intraosseous access is possible (intraosseous access is a common emergency vascular access site in pediatric patients, but it is an unusual route of access in adults). It is useful to remember, as already noted, that some important resuscitation medications can be delivered via the ET tube in cases of failed intravenous access; such medications include naloxone, atropine, vasopressin, epinephrine, and lidocaine (mnemonic: NAVEL).

The commonly used medications in cardiac resuscitation may be grouped into the following general categories: vasopressors (epinephrine or vasopressin), antiarrhythmics (amiodarone, lidocaine, magnesium, and procainamide), anticholinergic agents (atropine, if

the arrest arrhythmia is asystole or PEA is slow), and miscellaneous drugs used to treat specific problems contributing to the arrest state, such as sodium bicarbonate (for severe metabolic acidosis, hyperkalemia, and certain drug overdoses), and calcium chloride (for hyperkalemia, calcium channel blocker drug overdose, or severe hypocalcemia) [*see Table 4*].

Persons in cardiac arrest (which can result from pulseless VT, VF, PEA, or asystole) require a vasopressor for as long as they remain pulseless. Typically, this consists of 1 mg of epinephrine intravenously every 3 to 5 minutes. Epinephrine stimulates adrenergic receptors, which leads to vasoconstriction and optimization of CPR-generated blood flow to the heart and brain. Vasopressin (40 units I.V. once only) is a reasonable alternative to epinephrine, at least initially. Vasopressin in the recommended dose is a potent vasoconstrictor. It also has the theoretical advantage over epinephrine of not increasing myocardial

Table 7 Potentially Treatable Conditions That May Cause or Contribute to Cardiac Arrest[3]

Condition	Clinical Setting	Diagnostic and Corrective Actions
Acidosis	Preexisting acidosis, diabetes, diarrhea, drugs, toxins, prolonged resuscitation, renal disease, shock	Obtain stat ABG. Reassess technical quality of CPR, oxygenation, and ventilation. Confirm correct endotracheal tube placement. Hyperventilate patient (P_aCO_2 of 30–35 mm Hg) to partially compensate for metabolic acidosis. If pH < 7.20 despite above interventions, consider I.V. sodium bicarbonate, 1 mEq/kg I.V. slow push.
Cardiac tamponade	Hemorrhagic diathesis, malignancy, pericarditis, post cardiac surgery, post myocardial infarction, trauma	Initiate large-volume I.V. crystalloid resuscitation. Confirm diagnosis with emergency bedside echocardiogram, if available. Perform pericardiocentesis. Immediate surgical intervention is appropriate if pericardiocentesis is unhelpful but cardiac tamponade is known or highly suspected clinically.
Hypoglycemia	Adrenal insufficiency, alcohol abuse, aspirin overdose, diabetes, drugs, toxins, liver disease, renal disease, sepsis, certain tumors	Consider clinical setting and obtain finger-stick glucose or stat blood glucose measurements (may be obtained on ABG specimen). If glucose < 60 mg/dl, treat: 50 ml = 25 g of D50W I.V. Follow glucose levels closely post treatment.*
Hypomagnesemia	Alcohol abuse, burns, diabetic ketoacidosis, severe diarrhea, diuretics, drugs (e.g., cisplatin, cyclosporine, pentamidine), malabsorption, poor intake, thyrotoxicosis	Obtain stat serum magnesium level. Treat: 1–2 g magnesium sulfate I.V. over 2 min. Follow magnesium levels over time, because blood levels correlate poorly with total body deficit.
Hypothermia	Alcohol abuse, burns, central nervous system disease, debilitated and elderly patients, drowning, drugs, toxins, endocrine disease, exposure history, homelessness, poverty, extensive skin disease, spinal cord disease, trauma	Obtain core body temperature. If severe hypothermia (< 30° C), limit initial shocks for pulseless VT/VF to three, initiate active internal rewarming and cardiopulmonary support, and hold further resuscitation medications or shocks until core temperature > 30° C†. If moderate hypothermia (30°–34° C), proceed with resuscitation (space medications at intervals greater than usual), passively rewarm, and actively rewarm truncal body areas.
Hypovolemia, hemorrhage, anemia	Major burns, diabetes, gastrointestinal losses, hemorrhage, hemorrhagic diathesis, malignancy, pregnancy, shock, trauma	Initiate large-volume I.V. crystalloid resuscitation. Obtain stat hemoglobin level on ABG specimen. Emergently transfuse packed red blood cells (O negative if type-specific blood not available) if hemorrhage or profound anemia is contributing to arrest. Emergently consult necessary specialty for definitive care. Emergency thoracotomy with open cardiac massage is a consideration if experienced providers are available for the patient with penetrating trauma and cardiac arrest.
Hypoxia	All cardiac arrest patients are at risk	Reassess technical quality of CPR, oxygenation, and ventilation. Confirm correct ET tube placement. Obtain stat ABG to confirm adequate oxygenation and ventilation.
Myocardial infarction	Consider in all cardiac arrest patients, especially those with risk factors for coronary artery disease, a history of ischemic heart disease, or prearrest picture consistent with an acute coronary syndrome	Review prearrest clinical presentation and ECG. Continue resuscitation algorithm; proceed with definitive care as appropriate for the immediate circumstances (e.g., thrombolytic therapy, cardiac catheterization/coronary artery reperfusion, circulatory assist device, emergency cardiopulmonary bypass).

(continued)

oxygen consumption or lactate production in the arrested heart.[66] Despite its potential advantages, however, in a study of 200 inpatient cardiac arrest patients, vasopressin did not provide a better survival rate than epinephrine.[67] Vasopressin was also found to be comparable to epinephrine in out-of-hospital cardiac arrests when the rhythm was VF or PEA but superior to epinephrine for patients in asystole.[68,69]

During resuscitation with ongoing CPR, medication delivery through an intravenous cannula needs to be followed by a 20 ml saline bolus; if the cannula is in a peripheral vein, the extremity containing the cannula should then be elevated for 10 to 15 seconds to augment delivery of the medication to the central circulation. This is especially important because of the low-flow circulatory state with closed-chest CPR.

Differential Diagnosis and Definitive Care

The most challenging part of the secondary survey, as well as cardiac resuscitation management in general, is the problem-solving required when spontaneous circulation does not return despite appropriate initial interventions. This situation poses a critical question to the resuscitators: Why is this patient dying right now? The intellectual challenge of that question, which the resuscitators must try to answer expeditiously and at the bedside, is compounded by the emotional intensity that pervades most cardiac resuscitations.

The solvable problems that may interfere with resuscitation can be grouped into three broad categories: technical [see Table 6], physiologic, and anatomic [see Table 7]. Technical problems consist of difficulties with the resuscitators' equipment or skills; such difficulties include ineffective CPR, inadequate oxygenation and ventilation, ET tube complications, intravenous access difficulties, and monitor-defibrillator malfunction or misuse. The physiologic and anatomic problems consist of life-threatening but potentially treatable conditions that may have led to the cardiac arrest in the first place. This differentiation between physiology and anatomy is admittedly artificial, given that physiology is always involved in a car-

Table 7   (continued)

Condition	Clinical Setting	Diagnostic and Corrective Actions
Poisoning	Alcohol abuse, bizarre or puzzling behavioral or metabolic presentation, classic toxic syndrome, occupational or industrial exposures, history of ingestion, polysubstance abuse, psychiatric disease	Consider clinical setting and presentation; provide meticulous supportive care. Emergently consult toxicologist (through regional poison center) for resuscitative and definitive care advice, including appropriate antidote use. Prolonged resuscitation efforts are appropriate. If available, immediate cardiopulmonary bypass should be considered.
Hyperkalemia	Metabolic acidosis, excessive administration, drugs and toxins, vigorous exercise, hemolysis, renal disease, rhabdomyolysis, tumor lysis syndrome, significant tissue injury	Obtain stat serum potassium level on ABG specimen. Treatment: calcium chloride 10% (5–10 ml I.V. slow push [do not use if hyperkalemia is secondary to digitalis poisoning]), followed by glucose and insulin (50 ml of D50W and 10 U regular insulin I.V.); sodium bicarbonate (50 mEq I.V.); albuterol (15–20 mg nebulized or 0.5 mg I.V. infusion).[‡]
Hypokalemia	Alcohol abuse, diabetes, diuretic use, drugs and toxins, profound gastrointestinal losses, hypomagnesemia, excess mineralocorticoid states, metabolic alkalosis	Obtain stat serum potassium level on ABG specimen. If profound hypokalemia ($K^+ < 2$–2.5 mEq/L) is contributing to cardiac arrest, initiate urgent I.V. replacement (2 mEq/min I.V. for 10–15 mEq) then reassess.[§]
Pulmonary embolism	Hospitalized patients, recent surgical procedure, peripartum, known risk factors for venous thromboembolism (VTE), history of VTE, prearrest presentation consistent with acute pulmonary embolism	Review prearrest clinical presentation; initiate appropriate volume resuscitation with I.V. crystalloid and augment with vasopressors as necessary. Attempt emergency confirmation of diagnosis, depending on availability and clinical circumstances; consider emergency cardiopulmonary bypass to maintain patient viability. Continue resuscitation algorithm; proceed with definitive care (thrombolytic therapy, embolectomy via interventional radiology, or surgical thrombectomy) as appropriate for immediate circumstances and availability.
Tension pneumothorax	Post central line placement, mechanical ventilation, pulmonary disease (including asthma, COPD, necrotizing pneumonia), post thoracentesis, trauma	Consider risks and clinical presentation (prearrest history, breath sounds, neck veins, tracheal deviation). Proceed with emergency needle decompression, followed by chest tube insertion.

*Unrecognized hypoglycemia can cause significant neurologic injury and can be life threatening, but caution with I.V. glucose is appropriate in the setting of cardiac arrest. Available evidence indicates that hyperglycemia may contribute to impaired neurologic recovery in cardiac arrest survivors.

†Active internal or core rewarming includes warm (42°–46° C) humidified oxygen delivered through the endotracheal tube; warm I.V. fluids; peritoneal lavage; esophageal rewarming tubes; bladder lavage; and extracorporeal rewarming if immediately available. Active external rewarming includes warming beds, hot-water bottles, heating pads, and radiant heat sources applied externally to the patient.

‡Glucose is not necessary initially if patient is already hyperglycemic, but glucose levels should be followed closely after administration of I.V. insulin because of the risk of hypoglycemia (especially in patients with renal failure, because of the long duration of action of I.V. insulin in such patients). Sodium bicarbonate is most helpful in patients with concomitant metabolic acidosis; it is less effective in lowering serum potassium in dialysis-dependent renal failure patients. High-dose nebulized albuterol should lower serum potassium by 0.5 to 1.5 mEq/L within 30 to 60 min, but administration during cardiac arrest may be difficult.

§In a non–cardiac arrest situation, usual I.V. potassium replacement guidelines for patients requiring parenteral therapy are generally 10 to 20 mEq/hr with continuous electrocardiographic monitoring. If profound hypokalemia is contributing to cardiac arrest, however, these usual replacement rates are not timely enough, given the critical nature of the situation. Under these circumstances, potassium chloride, 2 mEq/min I.V. for 10 to 15 mEq, is reasonable, but reassessment and careful attention to changing levels, redistribution, and ongoing clinical circumstances are essential to prevent life-threatening hyperkalemia from developing.

ABG—arterial blood gas   COPD—chronic obstructive pulmonary disease   D50W—50% dextrose in water   ET—endotracheal   VF—ventricular fibrillation   VT—ventricular tachycardia

diac arrest, but it has some usefulness as a teaching and problem-solving tool. Physiologic problems classically include hypoxia, acidosis, hyperkalemia, severe hypokalemia, hypothermia, hypoglycemia, and drug overdose. Anatomic problems are hypovolemia/hemorrhage, tension pneumothorax, cardiac tamponade, myocardial infarction, and pulmonary embolism.[41]

Whenever possible, the patient's medical and surgical history and the circumstances and symptoms immediately before the cardiac arrest should be sought from family members, bystanders, or hospital staff as the resuscitation proceeds. This information may contain important clues to the principal arrest problem and how it may be expeditiously treated. For example, a patient who presents to an emergency department with chest pain and then suffers a VF cardiac arrest is probably dying of a massive myocardial infarction, pulmonary embolism, or aortic dissection, with tension pneumothorax or cardiac tamponade also being possibilities.

Specific questions to consider include the following: Does the patient have risk factors for heart disease, pulmonary embolism, or aortic disease? What was the quality of the patient's pain and its radiation before the cardiac arrest? What were the prearrest vital signs and physical examination findings? What did the prearrest ECG show (if available)? Can any of this information be used now, at the bedside, to dictate the needed resuscitation interventions during the D phase of the secondary survey? For example, if the prearrest

ECG showed prominent ST segment elevation in leads V1 through V4 consistent with a large anterior myocardial infarction, if the patient's resuscitation is failing despite appropriate interventions, and if there appear to be no technical problems hampering the resuscitation, a working diagnosis of massive myocardial infarction can be made; intravenous thrombolytic therapy may then be a reasonable and needed step in such a resuscitation.[70]

Thoughtful consideration of the possible reasons why a resuscitation is failing will regularly push the code-team captain's and resuscitation team's expertise and clinical skills to the limits. Nevertheless, the failure to consider these formidable issues will deprive the patient of an optimal opportunity to survive the cardiac arrest.

Cardiac Resuscitation Based on Rhythm Findings

When a monitor-defibrillator arrives at the scene of a cardiac arrest, the patient's rhythm is immediately analyzed. This step constitutes the beginning part of the defibrillation stage, or step D, of the AHA's primary survey. There are four rhythm possibilities [see Figure 1]: (1) pulseless VT; (2) VF; (3) organized or semiorganized electrical activity despite the absence of a palpable carotid pulse, which defines PEA; and (4) asystole. The detailed management of these different cardiac resuscitation scenarios is based on the recommendations of the AHA[49] and the International Liaison Committee on Resuscitation.[71] In following these guidelines, the clinician should remember that, with the exception of early CPR and early defibrillation for VF and pulseless VT, many of the recommendations that form the foundation of modern resuscitation are evidence supported or consensus based (rather than evidence based, as would be ideal). Because of the nature of cardiac arrest and the multiple variables involved, it is exceptionally difficult to perform high-quality research in cardiac resuscitation.

PULSELESS VENTRICULAR TACHYCARDIA OR VENTRICULAR FIBRILLATION

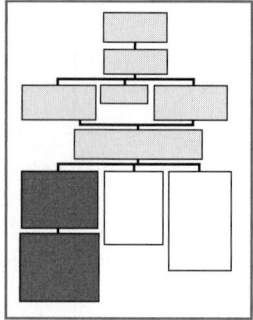

The appearance of either VF or pulseless VT on the rhythm monitor in a patient with ongoing CPR is a relatively favorable finding, because there is reasonable hope for a successful outcome with these rhythms. In addition, the interventions and medications sequentially used in the resuscitation are plainly delineated, and the initial course of action is clear. VF and pulseless VT are managed identically.

Initiation of Defibrillation

Defibrillation with 200 joules should be attempted immediately. However, if the time from onset of arrest to CPR to the availability of defibrillation is estimated to be longer than 5 minutes, it may be reasonable to continue CPR for another 3 minutes before initiating defibrillation [see Defibrillation, above]. If the VF or VT persists after the initial shock, subsequent attempts should be made with 200 to 300 joules and then 360 joules.

A lower, nonescalating equivalent biphasic energy level is acceptable, if the defibrillator offers this option. Manually checking the patient's carotid pulse between shocks is no longer recommended, but the displayed rhythm on the monitor must be carefully assessed after each defibrillation attempt. If there are any doubts concerning the rhythm or if there is suspicion of a dysfunctional lead or paddle cable, then a manual pulse check would be appropriate. If VF or pulseless VT persists, CPR is resumed, the patient endotracheally intubated, correct ET tube placement confirmed, and the tube secured. Simultaneously, intravenous access should be established.

Initiation of Drug Therapy

In patients with ongoing VF, drug therapy begins with the administration of a vasoconstrictor (either epinephrine or vasopressin) [see Table 4]. If there is no intravenous access, the drug can be given endotracheally. After each intravenous dose, drug delivery is followed by a 20 ml saline bolus and the extremity containing the I.V. line is elevated. Rescuers continue CPR for 30 to 60 seconds to allow the drug to reach the heart, then attempt defibrillation again with one to three shocks at 360 joules each. As long as the patient remains pulseless, epinephrine is administered every 3 to 5 minutes, with each dose followed by one to three attempts at defibrillation. When vasopressin is the chosen initial drug, only a single dose is given; if the resuscitation continues 10 minutes or longer after vasopressin is administered, epinephrine should be substituted for vasopressin for the remainder of the code. If VF or pulseless VT persists despite the initial administration of a vasoconstrictor and repeated defibrillation attempts, parenteral antiarrhythmic drug therapy is added; amiodarone or lidocaine is an appropriate agent [see Choice of Antiarrhythmic Drugs, below]. Throughout all of these steps, the code-team leader is also actively looking for and correcting any technical and physiologic or anatomic problems that may be preventing a successful resuscitation [see Tables 6 and 7].

Emergency Laboratory Tests

If spontaneous circulation does not return after the first round of antiarrhythmic drug therapy, the resuscitation team must also endeavor to identify and treat the clinically relevant conditions causing

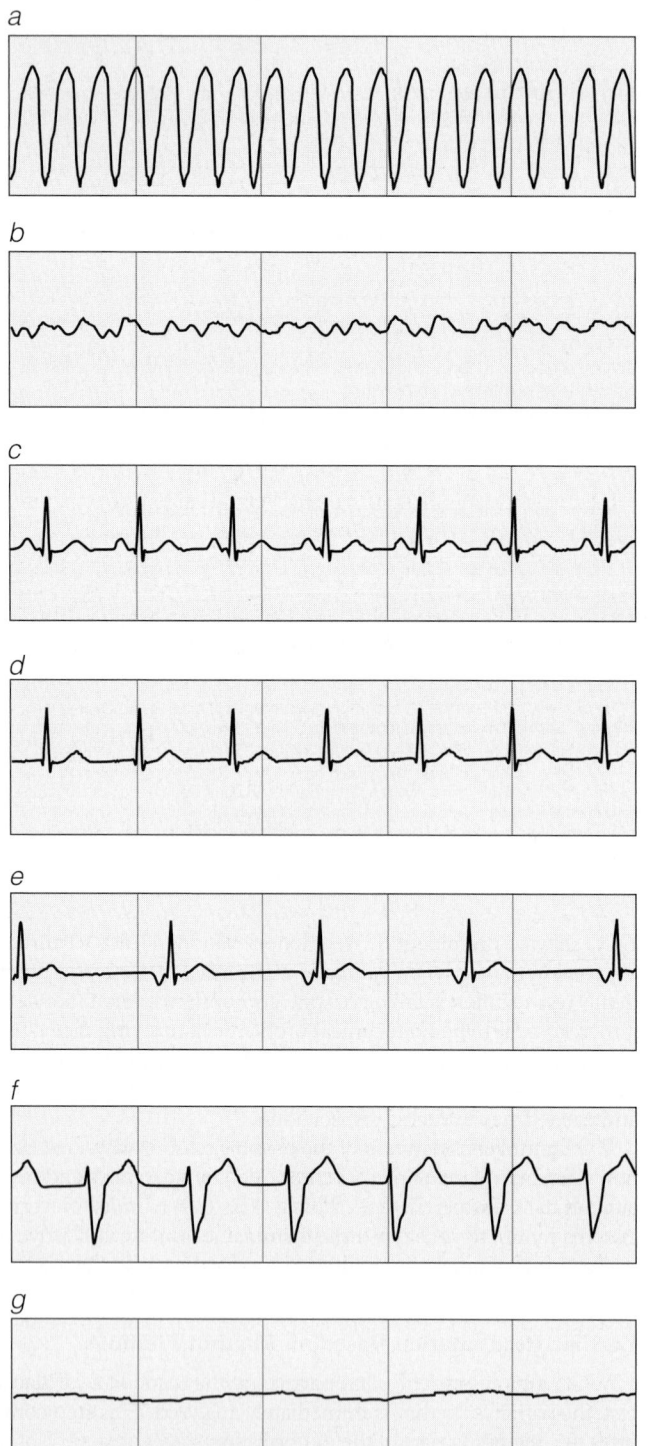

Figure 1   The sudden cardiac arrest arrhythmias. (*a*) Ventricular tachycardia. (*b*) Ventricular fibrillation. Pulseless electrical activity encompasses any of several forms of organized electrical activity in the pulseless patient; these include (*c*) normal sinus rhythm, (*d*) junctional rhythm, (*e*) bradycardic junctional rhythm, and (*f*) idioventricular rhythm. (*g*) Asystole.

or contributing to the cardiac arrest [*see Table 7*]. In theory, the interventions conducted to this point should have resulted in a perfusing rhythm. The code team must ask why this has not occurred and then attempt to answer this question as the resuscitation continues. Emergency laboratory studies that may prove helpful include a stat ABG measurement and measurements of hemoglobin, potassium, magnesium, and blood glucose levels (most of which can be obtained from the ABG specimen).

Choice of Antiarrhythmic Drugs

Four antiarrhythmic drugs are used in cardiac resuscitation: amiodarone, lidocaine, magnesium (if the patient is thought or proved to be hypomagnesemic), and procainamide (for intermittent or recurrent VT or VF that initially responds to defibrillation).[72] It is not known which one of these drugs or which combination of them will optimize the chances of patient survival to hospital discharge. Despite many years of routine use, there are no controlled studies demonstrating a survival benefit with lidocaine, versus placebo, in the management of VF or pulseless VT. Two studies in patients with shock-refractory prehospital VF showed that survival to hospital admission was better with amiodarone than with placebo (44% versus 34%; $P = 0.03$)[73] or with lidocaine (22.8% versus 12.0%; $P = 0.009$).[74] Neither of these studies demonstrated an improved survival to hospital discharge in the amiodarone groups, but neither study had the statistical power to demonstrate such a difference. Amiodarone is also considerably more expensive than lidocaine.

The optimal role and the exact benefit of antiarrhythmic medications in cardiac resuscitation are yet to be fully elucidated. According to AHA guidelines, either amiodarone or lidocaine is an acceptable initial antiarrhythmic drug for the treatment of patients with VF or pulseless VT that is unresponsive to initial shocks, CPR, airway management, and administration of epinephrine or vasopressin plus shocks. On the basis of available evidence, however, amiodarone may be the antiarrhythmic agent of first choice in the setting of prehospital refractory VF, allowing for optimal survival to hospital arrival.[72-74]

PULSELESS ELECTRICAL ACTIVITY

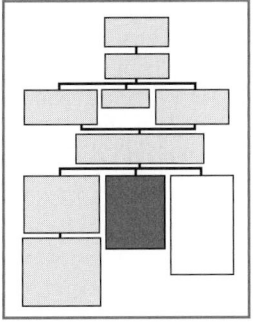

Community ACLS providers are encountering nonventricular arrhythmias (i.e., PEA and asystole) with increasing frequency. Classically, the prognosis for PEA has been poor, with outpatient survival rates generally reported as 0% to 7%.[75,76] The sequence of resuscitation steps in the management of PEA is as follows: activation of the emergency medical or code response, primary survey (CPR and rhythm evaluation), and secondary survey (intubation and confirmation of correct ET tube placement, optimal oxygenation and ventilation, establishment of I.V. access, epinephrine administration, and, finally, problem solving for technical difficulties and establishment of the cause of the cardiac arrest). The two core drugs for PEA management are epinephrine (repeated every 3 to 5 minutes for as long as the patient is pulseless) and atropine (up to 3 mg over time if the PEA rhythm on the monitor is inappropriately slow). Although not currently on the AHA PEA algorithm, vasopressin is probably a reasonable alternative to epinephrine. The best hope for a successful resuscitation is to find and treat the cause of PEA; therein lies the exceptionally challenging aspect of PEA resuscitation management [*see Tables 6 and 7*]. Because coronary artery thrombosis and pulmonary thromboembolism are common causes of cardiac arrest, a trial evaluated the efficacy of tissue plasminogen activator (t-PA) in the setting of PEA of unknown or presumed cardiovascular cause in 233 patients in prehospital and emergency department settings.[77] No benefit was found with thrombolytic therapy for PEA in this study; the proportion of patients with return of spontaneous circulation was 21.4% in the t-PA group and 23.3% in the placebo group.

ASYSTOLE

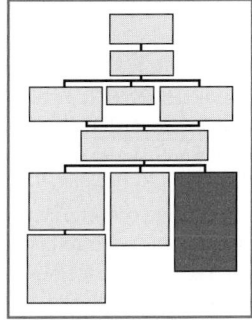

The prognosis for asystole is generally regarded as dismal unless the patient is hypothermic or there are other extenuating but treatable circumstances. The sequence of resuscitation steps in the management of asystole is as follows: activation of the emergency medical or code response, primary survey (CPR, rhythm evaluation, and asystole confirmation), and secondary survey (intubation and confirmation of correct ET tube placement, optimal oxygenation and ventilation, I.V. access with epinephrine and atropine administration, immediate transcutaneous pacing, if available, and problem solving for technical difficulties and establishment of the cause of cardiac arrest). The two core drugs for asystole management are epinephrine (repeated every 3 to 5 minutes for as long as the patient is pulseless) and atropine (up to 3 mg over time). As with PEA, vasopressin appears to be a reasonable and possibly beneficial substitute for epinephrine in asystole. A single dose of aminophylline (250 mg I.V.) may also be beneficial in atropine-resistant asystole.[78] Potentially treatable causes of asystole include hypoxia, acidosis, hypothermia, hypokalemia, hyperkalemia, and drug overdose. Resuscitation efforts should stop if asystole persists for longer than 10 minutes despite optimal CPR, oxygenation and ventilation, and epinephrine or atropine administration; if extenuating circumstances (e.g., hypothermia, cold-water submersion, or drug overdose) are not present; and if no other readily treatable condition is identified.

Immediate Postresuscitation Care

Even when the resuscitation is successful, the patient's situation remains tenuous and continued meticulous patient care is essential. When the cardiac monitor indicates what should be a perfusing rhythm, the rescuer should immediately confirm that the patient has a palpable pulse. If there is a pulse, the patient's blood pressure is then obtained. Simultaneously, resuscitation team members need to quickly reassess the adequacy of the patient's airway, the ET tube position, oxygenation and ventilation, and the patient's level of consciousness and comfort.

If the patient is hypotensive, appropriate blood pressure management depends on the presence or absence of fluid overload, as judged at the bedside. If the patient is clinically volume overloaded or in frank pulmonary edema and hypotensive, dopamine is started at inotropic doses (5 μg/kg/min I.V.) and titrated to a target systolic blood pressure of 90 to 100 mm Hg. If the patient's clinical status suggests normovolemia or hypovolemia, intravenous crystalloid boluses (in 250 to 500 ml increments) can be administered instead of dopamine to support adequate tissue perfusion. In patients who are regaining consciousness, their level of comfort mandates careful assessment and administration of analgesia and sedation, as appropriate.

If the arrest rhythm was either VT or VF, the parenteral antiarrhythmic drug used immediately before the return of spontaneous circulation is continued as a maintenance infusion (amiodarone, 1 mg/min for 6 hr, then 0.5 mg/min for 18 hr as blood pressure allows; or lidocaine, 2 to 4 mg/min). If an antiarrhythmic drug has not yet been administered, it is usually started at this point to prevent the recurrence of VF or pulseless VT. There are important exceptions to this guideline, however. If the perfusing postarrest arrhythmia is an idioventricular rhythm or third-degree heart block accompanied by an idioventricular escape rhythm, an antiarrhythmic medication should not be started at this time, because the antiarrhythmic agent could eliminate the ventricular perfusing focus and return the patient to a pulseless state.

Initial postresuscitation studies usually include an ECG; portable chest radiography; and measurement of ABGs, a serum electrolyte panel, fingerstick or blood glucose, serum magnesium and cardiac enzyme levels, and hemoglobin and hematocrit. The resuscitated patient requires urgent transfer to the optimal site for continued definitive care. Depending on the circumstances, this may be either the cardiac catheterization laboratory or the intensive care unit.

Ongoing research continues to look at optimal postresuscitation management strategies to improve neurologic outcome and survival to hospital discharge.[79] Hyperthermia and hyperglycemia compromise postresuscitation neurologic outcome, whereas mild to moderate induced hypothermia appears to improve neurologic outcome and decrease mortality.[80-83]

Ending a Resuscitation Attempt

Throughout the resuscitation, the team leader must speak with calmness and authority, and all resuscitations should be orchestrated with clarity and finesse. If possible, the code captain should make clinical decisions without directly performing specific procedures. Cardiac arrests are emotionally charged, but the leader must insist on a composed, orderly, and technically sound resuscitation. It is appropriate to invite suggestions from team members and to ensure that all members are comfortable with the decision to stop the resuscitation, should that time arrive.

The decision whether to stop a cardiac resuscitation is burdensome. Clearly, the circumstances of the event, patient comorbidities, the nature of the lethal arrhythmia, and the resuscitation team's ability to correctly identify and treat potential contributing causes of the arrest are all important considerations. Resuscitation efforts beyond 30 minutes without a return of spontaneous circulation are usually futile unless the cardiac arrest is confounded by intermittent or recurrent VF or pulseless VT, hypothermia, cold-water submersion, drug overdose, or other identified and readily treated contributing conditions.[84,85]

With nontraumatic cardiac arrest in the prehospital setting (assuming proper equipment and medications are available and no ex-

tenuating circumstances suggest otherwise), full resuscitation efforts take place at the scene of the arrest in preference to rapid transport to an emergency department. A prehospital resuscitation that has been appropriately conducted but has not resulted in at least temporary return of spontaneous circulation to the patient may be discontinued. It is important that certain criteria are adhered to, however, including the following: high-quality CPR provided, an adequate airway successfully placed, appropriate oxygenation and ventilation delivered, intravenous access established, appropriate medications specific to the arrest scenario administered, and resuscitation attempted for at least 10 minutes; in addition, the patient must not be in persistent VF, and there can be no extenuating circumstances that mandate in-hospital continuation of the resuscitation (e.g., hypothermia, drug overdose). The decision whether to cease resuscitation efforts in the field is bolstered by direct discussion with EMS physicians. It is also essential that social services be available to provide immediate assistance and support to the family and loved ones of the patient who has now died.

Discontinuing in-hospital resuscitations is advisable when three criteria are met: (1) the arrest was unwitnessed, (2) the initial rhythm was other than VF or VT, and (3) spontaneous circulation does not return after 10 minutes of ongoing resuscitation.[86] In a study of this three-component decision rule, only 1.1% of patients (three out of 269) who met these criteria survived to hospital discharge, and none of the three survivors were capable of independent living.[87] In a study of 445 prospectively recorded resuscitation attempts in hospitalized patients, no patient survived who suffered a cardiac arrest between 12 A.M. and 6 A.M. if the arrest was unwitnessed and if it occurred in an unmonitored bed.[38]

A resuscitation attempt in a persistently asystolic patient should not last longer than 10 minutes, assuming all of the following conditions apply: asystole is confirmed through proper rhythm monitoring and assessment; high-quality CPR is taking place; ET intubation is correctly performed and confirmed; adequate oxygenation and ventilation are provided; intravenous access is secured; appropriate medications (epinephrine or vasopressin and atropine) have been administered; and the patient is not the victim of hypothermia, cold-water submersion, drug overdose, or other readily identified and reversible cause.

After all resuscitation attempts, the code-team captain should debrief the team so that all may learn from the experience. Finally, marked empathy and skill are needed to carefully and compassionately inform family members about the outcome of the resuscitation.[88]

References

1. Callans DJ: Management of the patient who has been resuscitated from sudden cardiac death. Circulation 105:2704, 2002

2. Zipes DP, Wellens HJ: Sudden cardiac death. Circulation 98:2334, 1998

3. Eisenberg MS, Mengert TJ: Cardiac resuscitation. N Engl J Med 344:1304, 2001

4. 1999 Heart and Stroke Statistical Update. American Heart Association, Dallas, 1998

5. Huikuri HV, Castellanos A, Myerburg R: Sudden death due to cardiac arrhythmias. N Engl J Med 345:1473, 2001

6. Ballew KA, Philbrick JT: Causes of variation in reported in-hospital CPR survival: a critical review. Resuscitation 30:203, 1995

7. Myerburg RJ, Castellanos A: Cardiac arrest and sudden cardiac death. Heart Disease: A Textbook of Cardiovascular Medicine. Braunwald E, Ed. WB Saunders Co, Philadelphia, 1997, p 742

8. Osborn LA: Etiology of sudden death. Cardiac Arrest: The Science and Practice of Resuscitation

Medicine. Paradis NA, Halperin HR, Nowak RM, Eds. Williams & Wilkins, Philadelphia, 1996, p 243

9. Maron BJ: Sudden death in young athletes. N Engl J Med 349:1064, 2003

10. Cobb LA, Fahrenruch CD, Olsufka M, et al: Changing incidence of out-of-hospital ventricular fibrillation, 1980–2000. JAMA 288:3008, 2002

11. Cummins RO, Ornato JP, Thies W, et al: Improving survival from cardiac arrest: the chain of survival concept: a statement for health professionals from the Advanced Cardiac Life Support Subcommittee and the Emergency Cardiac Care Committee, American Heart Association. Circulation 83:1832, 1991

12. Capussi A, Aschieri D, Piepoli MF, et al: Tripling survival from sudden cardiac arrest via early defibrillation without traditional education in cardiopulmonary resuscitation. Circulation 106:1065, 2002

13. Callaham M, Madsen CD: Relationship of timeliness of paramedic advanced life support interventions to outcome in out-of-hospital cardiac arrest treated by first responders with defibrillators. Ann Emerg Med 27:638, 1996

14. Marenco JP, Wang PJ, Link MS, et al: Improving survival from sudden cardiac arrest: the role of the automated external defibrillator. JAMA 285:1193, 2001

15. Peberdy MA: Defibrillation. Cardiol Clin 20:13, 2002

16. Public-access defibrillation and survival after out-of-hospital cardiac arrest. The Public Access Defibrillation Trial Investigators. N Engl J Med 351:637, 2004

17. Cummins RO, Eisenberg MS: Prehospital cardiopulmonary resuscitation: is it effective? JAMA 253:2408, 1985

18. Stapleton ER: Basic life support cardiopulmonary resuscitation. Cardiol Clin 20:12, 2002

19. Valenzuela TD, Roe DJ, Cretin S, et al: Estimating effectiveness of cardiac arrest interventions: a logistic regression survival model. Circulation 96:3308, 1997

20. Eisenberg MS, Bergner L, Hallstrom A: Cardiac resuscitation in the community: the importance of

rapid delivery of care and implications for program planning. JAMA 241:1905, 1979

21. Weaver WD, Cobb LA, Hallstrom AP, et al: Considerations for improving survival from out-of-hospital cardiac arrest. Ann Emerg Med 15:1181, 1986

22. Larsen MP, Eisenberg MS, Cummins RO, et al: Predicting survival from out-of-hospital cardiac arrest: a graphic model. Ann Emerg Med 270:1211, 1993

23. Eisenberg MS, Horwood BT, Cummins RO, et al: Cardiac arrest and resuscitation: a tale of 29 cities. Ann Emerg Med 19:179, 1990

24. Lombardi G, Gallagher J, Gennis P: Outcome of out-of-hospital cardiac arrest in New York City: the Pre-Hospital Arrest Survival Evaluation (PHASE) study. JAMA 271:678, 1994

25. Becker LB, Ostrander MP, Barrett J, et al: Outcome of CPR in a large metropolitan area: where are the survivors? Ann Emerg Med 20:355, 1991

26. Killien SY, Geyman JP, Gossom JB, et al: Out-of-hospital cardiac arrest in a rural area: a 16-year experience with lessons learned and national comparisons. Ann Emerg Med 28:294, 1996

27. Bunch TJ, White RD, Gersh BJ, et al: Long-term outcomes of out-of-hospital cardiac arrest after successful early defibrillation. N Engl J Med 348:2626, 2003

28. Valenzuela TD, Roe DJ, Nichol G, et al: Outcomes of rapid defibrillation by security officers after cardiac arrest in casinos. N Engl J Med 343:1206, 2000

29. Eisenberg M, Bergner L, Hallstrom A: Sudden Cardiac Death in the Community. Praeger, Philadelphia, 1984

30. Becker L: The epidemiology of sudden death. Cardiac Arrest: The Science and Practice of Resuscitation Medicine. Paradis NA, Halperin HR, Nowak RM, Eds. Williams & Wilkins, Philadelphia, 1996, p 28

31. Jastremski MS: In-hospital cardiac arrest. Ann Emerg Med 22:113, 1993

32. Rosenberg M, Wang C, Hoffman-Wilde S, et al: Results of cardiopulmonary resuscitation failure to predict survival in two community hospitals. Arch Intern Med 153:1370, 1993

33. Ballew KA, Philbrick JT, Caven DE, et al: Predictors of survival following in-hospital cardiopulmonary resuscitation: a moving target. Arch Intern Med 154:2426, 1994

34. De Vos R, Koster RW, De Haan RJ, et al: In-hospital cardiopulmonary resuscitation: prearrest morbidity and outcome. Arch Intern Med 159:845, 1999

35. Goodlin SJ, Zhong Z, Lynn J, et al: Factors associated with use of cardiopulmonary resuscitation in seriously ill hospitalized adults. JAMA 282:2333, 1999

36. Van Walraven C, Forster AJ, Stiell IG: Derivation of a clinical decision rule for the discontinuation of in-hospital cardiac arrest resuscitations. Arch Intern Med 159:129, 1999

37. Zoch TW, Desbiens NA, DeStefano F, et al: Short- and long-term survival after in-hospital cardiopulmonary resuscitation. Arch Intern Med 160:1969, 2000

38. Dumot JA, Burval DJ, Sprung J, et al: Outcome of adult cardiopulmonary resuscitations at a tertiary referral center including results of "limited" resuscitations. Arch Intern Med 161:1751, 2001

39. Meade M: Men and the Water of Life. Harper, San Francisco, 1993, p 442

40. Burkle FM Jr, Rice MM: Code organization. Am J Emerg Med 5:235, 1987

41. ACLS Provider Manual. American Heart Association, Dallas, 2001

42. Safar P: On the history of modern resuscitation. Anesthesiol Clin North Am 13:751, 1995

43. Kouwenhoven WB, Jude JR, Knickerbocker GG: Closed-chest cardiac massage. JAMA 173:1064, 1960

44. Jude JR, Kouwenhoven WB, Knickerbocker GG: Cardiac arrest: report of application of external cardiac massage on 118 patients. JAMA 178:1063, 1961

45. Halperin HR: Mechanisms of forward flow during external chest compression. Cardiac Arrest: The

Science and Practice of Resuscitation Medicine. Paradis NA, Halperin HR, Nowak RM, Eds. Williams & Wilkins, Philadelphia, 1996, p 252

46. Ornato JP, Peberdy MA: Cardiopulmonary resuscitation. Textbook of Cardiovascular Medicine. Topol EJ, Ed. Lippincott-Raven, Philadelphia, 1998, p 1779

47. Paradis NA, Martin GB, Goetting MG, et al: Simultaneous aortic, jugular bulb, and right atrial pressures during cardiopulmonary resuscitation in humans: insights into mechanisms. Circulation 80:361, 1989

48. Daya MR, Mariani RJ: Out-of-hospital splinting. Clinical Procedures in Emergency Medicine, 3rd ed. Roberts JR, Hedges JR, Eds. WB Saunders Co, Philadelphia, 1998, p 1297

49. Guidelines 2000 for cardiopulmonary resuscitation and emergency cardiovascular care: international consensus on science. Circulation 102(suppl I):1, 2000

50. Sanders AB, Kern KB, Berg RA, et al: Survival and neurologic outcome after cardiopulmonary resuscitation with four different chest compression–ventilation ratios. Ann Emerg Med 40:553, 2002

51. Hallstrom A, Cobb L, Johnson E, et al: Cardiopulmonary resuscitation by chest compression alone or with mouth-to-mouth ventilation. N Engl J Med 342:1546, 2000

52. Levine RL, Wayne MA, Miller CC: End-tidal carbon dioxide and outcome of out-of-hospital cardiac arrest. N Engl J Med 337:301, 1997

53. Hedges JR, Greenberg MI: Defibrillation. Clinical Procedures in Emergency Medicine, 3rd ed. Roberts JR, Hedges JR, Eds. WB Saunders Co, Philadelphia, 1998, p 1297

54. Hossack KF, Hartwig R: Cardiac arrest associated with supervised cardiac rehabilitation. J Cardiac Rehab 2:402, 1982

55. Bardy GH, Marchlinski FE, Sharma AD, et al: Multicenter comparison of truncated biphasic shocks and standard damped sine wave monophasic shocks for transthoracic ventricular defibrillation. Circulation 94:2507, 1996

56. Gliner BE, White RD: Electrocardiographic evaluation of defibrillation shocks delivered to out-of-hospital sudden cardiac arrest patients. Resuscitation 41:129, 1999

57. Gliner BE, Jorgenson DB, Poole JE, et al: Treatment of out-of-hospital cardiac arrest with a low-energy impedance-compensating biphasic waveform automatic external defibrillator. Biomed Instrum Technol 32:631, 1998

58. Poole JE, White RD, Kanz KG, et al: Low-energy impedance-compensating biphasic waveforms terminate ventricular fibrillation at high rates in victims of out-of-hospital cardiac arrest. J Cardiovasc Electrophysiol 8:1373, 1997

59. Schneider T, Martens PR, Paschen H, et al: Multicenter, randominzed, controlled trial of 150-J biphasic shocks compared with 200- to 360-J monophasic shocks in the resuscitation of out-of-hospital cardiac arrest victims. Circulation 102:1780, 2000

60. Berg RA, Hilwig RW, Kern KB, et al: Precountershock cardiopulmonary resuscitation improves ventricular fibrillation median frequency and myocardial readiness for successful defibrillation from prolonged ventricular fibrillation: a randomized, controlled swine study. Ann Emerg Med 40:563, 2002

61. Wik L, Hansen TB, Fylling F, et al: Delaying defibrillation to give basic cardiopulmonary resuscitation to patients with out-of-hospital ventricular fibrillation. JAMA 289:1389, 2003

62. Weisfeldt ML, Becker LB: Resuscitation after cardiac arrest: a 3-phase time sensitive model. JAMA 288:3035, 2002

63. Aehlert B: ACLS: Quick Review Study Guide, 2nd ed. CV Mosby, St Louis, 2001

64. Rumball CJ, MacDonald D: The PTL, Combitube, laryngeal mask, and oral airway: a randomized prehospital comparative study of ventilatory device effectiveness and cost-effectiveness in 470 cases of cardiorespiratory arrest. Prehosp Emerg Care 1:1, 1997

65. Garnett AR, Ornato JP, Gonzales ER, et al: End-tidal carbon dioxide monitoring during cardiopulmonary resuscitation. JAMA 257:512, 1987

66. Paradis NA, Wenzel V, Southall J: Pressor drugs in the treatment of cardiac arrest. Cardiol Clin 20:61, 2002

67. Stiell IG, Hebert PC, Wells GA, et al: Vasopressin versus epinephrine for inhospital cardiac arrest: a randomized controlled trial. Lancet 358:105, 2001

68. Wenzel V, Krismer AC, Arntz HR, et al: A comparison of vasopressin and epinephrine for out-of-hospital cardiopulmonary resuscitation. N Engl J Med 350:105, 2004

69. McIntryre KM: Vasopressin in asystolic cardiac arrest. N Engl J Med 350:179, 2004

70. Tiffany PA, Schultz M, Stueven H: Bolus thrombolytic infusions during CPR for patients with refractory arrest rhythms: outcome of a case series. Ann Emerg Med 31:124, 1998

71. Cummins RO, Chamberlain DA: Advisory statements of the International Liaison Committee on Resuscitation. Circulation 95:2172, 1997

72. Kudenchuk PJ: Advanced cardiac life support antiarrhythmic drugs. Cardiol Clin 20:79, 2002

73. Kudenchuk PJ, Cobb LA, Copass MK, et al: Amiodarone for resuscitation after out-of-hospital cardiac arrest due to ventricular fibrillation. N Engl J Med 341:871, 1999

74. Dorian P, Cass D, Schwartz B, et al: Amiodarone as compared with lidocaine for shock-resistant ventricular fibrillation. N Engl J Med 346:884, 2002

75. Myerburg RJ, Conde CA, Sung RJ, et al: Clinical, electrophysiologic, and hemodynamic profile of patients resuscitated from prehospital cardiac arrest. Am J Med 68:568, 1980

76. Stratton SJ, Niemann JT: Outcome from out-of-hospital cardiac arrest caused by nonventricular arrhythmias: contribution of successful resuscitation to overall survivorship supports the current practice of initiating out-of-hospital ACLS. Ann Emerg Med 32:448, 1998

77. Abu-Laban RB, Christenson JM, Innes GD, et al: Tissue plasminogen activator in cardiac arrest with pulseless electrical activity. N Engl J Med 346:1522, 2002

78. Mader TJ, Smithline HA, Durkin L, et al: A randomized controlled trial of intravenous aminophylline for atropine-resistant out-of-hospital asystolic cardiac arrest. Acad Emerg Med 10:192, 2003

79. Angelos MG, Menegazzi JJ, Callaway CW: Bench to bedside: resuscitation from prolonged ventricular fibrillation. Acad Emerg Med 8:909, 2001

80. Zeiner A, Holzer M, Sterz F, et al: Hyperthermia after cardiac arrest is associated with an unfavorable neurological outcome. Arch Intern Med 161:2007, 2001

81. Moghissi E: Hospital management of diabetes: beyond the sliding scale. Cleve Clin J Med 71:801, 2004

82. Bernard SA, Gray TW, Buist MD, et al: Treatment of comatose survivors of out-of-hospital cardiac arrest with induced hypothermia. N Engl J Med 346:557, 2002

83. Mild therapeutic hypothermia to improve the neurologic outcome after cardiac arrest. The Hypothermia After Cardiac Arrest Study Group. N Engl J Med 346:549, 2002

84. Bonnin MJ, Pepe PE, Kimball KT, et al: Distinct criteria for termination of resuscitation in the out-of-hospital setting. JAMA 270:1457, 1993

85. Kellermann AL, Hackman BB, Somes G: Predicting the outcome of unsuccessful prehospital advanced cardiac life support. JAMA 270:1433, 1993

86. Van Walraven C, Forster AJ, Stiell IG: Derivation of a clinical decision rule for the discontinuation of in-hospital cardiac arrest resuscitations. Arch Intern Med 159:129, 1999

87. Van Walraven C, Forster AJ, Parish DC, et al: Validation of a clinical decision aid to discontinue in-hospital cardiac arrest resuscitations. JAMA 285:1602, 2001

88. Iserson K: Grave Words: Notifying Survivors about Sudden, Unexpected Deaths. Galen Press, Tucson, Arizona, 1999

89. Cummins RO, Field JM, Hazinski MF, et al: ACLS Provider Manual. American Heart Association, Dallas, 2001, p 36

90. Part 1: introduction to the international guidelines 2000 for CPR and ECC: a consensus on science. Circulation 102(8 suppl):I1, 2000

Caesar Ursic, M.D., F.A.C.S., and Alden H. Harken, M.D., F.A.C.S.

Management of Acute Dysrhythmias

After successful cardiopulmonary resuscitation (CPR) or any myocardial ischemic event, the most common source of hemodynamic instability is an abnormal heart rhythm. This chapter outlines the approach to a patient with an apparent acute cardiac dysrhythmia.

The purpose of the heart's electrical activity is to induce mechanical activity. Abnormal electrical activity that occurs in the absence of hemodynamic compromise should be examined but treated with forbearance because therapy itself poses some hazards: all antidysrhythmic agents, except oxygen, are negatively inotropic. In the evaluation of a patient who appears to exhibit an acute cardiac dysrhythmia, four questions should be asked:

1. Does the patient actually have a cardiac dysrhythmia?
2. Does the patient require any therapy (i.e., is the patient sufficiently stable that treatment is NOT indicated)?
3. How soon should therapy be started (i.e., how unstable is the patient)?
4. Which therapy is the safest and most effective?

Patient Is Hemodynamically Unstable

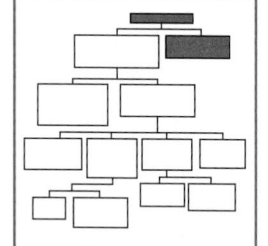

The choice of therapy is determined by the stability of the patient and the origin of the dysrhythmia. An electrocardiogram is helpful but not required. Patients with asystole require CPR [*see 116 Cardiac Resuscitation*]. All hemodynamically unstable patients who have a dysrhythmia other than asystole should be treated immediately by cardioversion. Actually, cardioversion of asystole will do no harm; it just will not help, because there is no underlying rhythm to reorganize. If in doubt, therefore, one should proceed with cardioversion.

The two primary goals in the management of an acute dysrhythmia are to control the ventricular rate and to maintain a normal sinus rhythm. It is important to note that hemodynamic instability in a patient who has a ventricular rate between 60 and 100 beats/min is almost certainly not the result of a cardiac rhythm disturbance. Furthermore, heart rates in excess of 100 beats/min do not necessarily require therapy. Most patients can remain hemodynamically stable—and, in fact, increase their cardiac output—while raising their heart rate to 220 beats/min minus their age. In addition, it is not critical to reestablish normal sinus rhythm in all cases.[1] In a young, healthy patient with a normal heart, the so-called atrial kick adds almost nothing to cardiac output.[2] If normal sinus rhythm is abolished and atrial fibrillation is electrically induced in a young healthy patient, the ventricles and the rest of the cardiovascular system compensate almost immediately to prevent a fall in cardiac output.[3] On the other hand, loss of synchronous atrial activity in patients with end-stage cardiac decompensation may decrease cardiac output by as much as 40%[4]; fortunately, such a degree of end-stage cardiac compromise is rare.

CARDIOVERSION

Cardioversion delivers sufficient electrical energy to the precordium (or directly to the heart) to depolarize cells, even those in a relatively refractory state. Cardioversion imposes electrical reorganization on the heart. In theory, after this massive depolarization, all the myocardial cells will repolarize simultaneously and then reinstitute a synchronous beat [*see Sidebar* The Intracardiac Cardioverter Defibrillator].

Certain precautions are necessary with cardioversion. The procedure is of no use in patients who are in asystole or who have fine ventricular fibrillation (VF), because these patients have no cardiac activity to organize—though, again, cardioversion does no harm in such cases (as it is said, "you cannot fall off the floor"). Supraventricular dysrhythmias such as atrial flutter can be converted with extremely low energy levels (e.g., ≤ 5 joules), but such low levels should not be employed in emergency situations. For a hemodynamically unstable patient, the initial cardioversion should be with 100 joules; if the dysrhythmia is not abolished, the voltage should be increased rapidly (to a maximum of 360 joules).

Patient Is Hemodynamically Stable

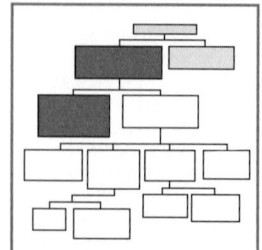

VENTRICULAR RATE IS SLOW

If the patient is bradycardic before or after cardioversion, atropine should be administered in a 0.5 mg I.V. push. This dose may be repeated at 2-minute intervals. Because the effects of atropine are transient, a temporary internal or external pacemaker should be used to maintain the heart rate. Insertion of an internal pacemaker consistently takes longer than predicted; an external pacemaker is a very effective temporizing maneuver [*see Sidebar* Troubleshooting a Pacemaker].

Management of Acute Dysrhythmias

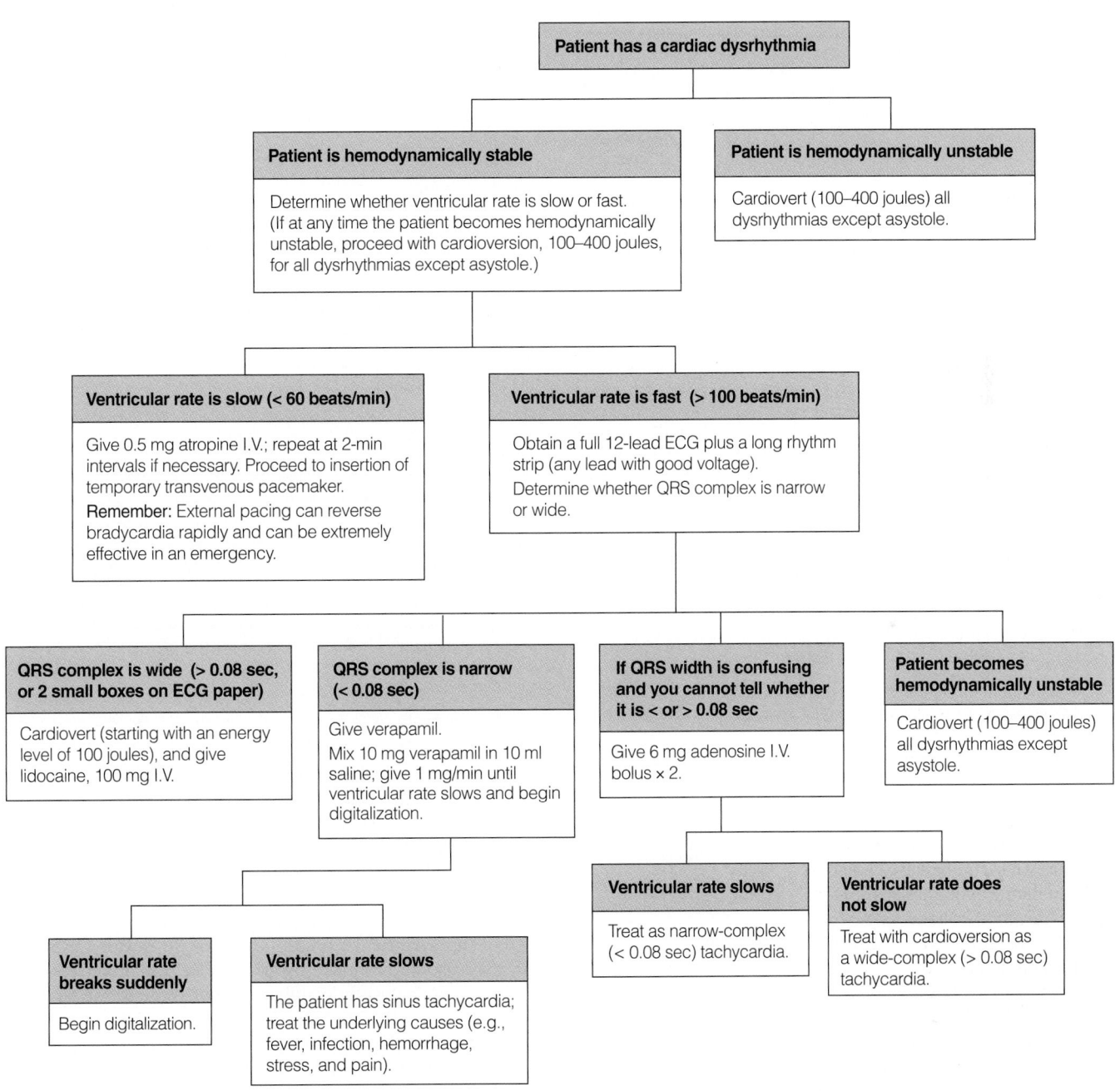

The Intracardiac Cardioverter Defibrillator

Over 30 years ago, Michel Mirowski developed the first automatic intracardiac cardioverter defibrillator (ICD), a device that detects dangerous tachyarrhythmias and delivers a cardioverting shock.[55] In the intervening time, it has become abundantly clear that some of the 400,000 Americans who die "suddenly" of tachyarrhythmias each year could have been identified as high risk, although they could not have been saved by pharmacologic or surgical treatment. For these patients, an ICD can be lifesaving.[56]

The ICD identifies dangerous rhythm patterns by means of two algorithms. The first of these algorithms analyzes the patient's heart rate. The patient's maximum attainable sinus rate must be determined by exercise testing before the device is implanted; the ICD is then programmed to detect heart rates above this value. (The ICD can be externally programmed to detect rates between 155 and 200 beats/min.[57])

Using rate criteria alone, however, the ICD cannot discriminate between sinus tachycardia and ventricular or supraventricular tachycardia. Inappropriate shocks are the Achilles heel of the ICD: almost one third of patients experience at least one inappropriate shock annually, when the device detects an episode of sinus tachycardia in which the rate exceeds the threshold programmed earlier. The ICD misinterprets the event as ventricular tachycardia and delivers a shock to the hemodynamically stable patient.[58] Patients liken this to being punched hard in the chest. Although rarely of electrophysiologic significance, an inappropriate shock can be psychologically crippling.[59]

Although computer circuitry is facile and rapid, an ICD recognizes patterns poorly. Fine (or even coarse) VF may not exhibit enough positive spikes to be recognized as a tachyarrhythmia by the ICD. A second algorithm (the probability density function algorithm) was developed to analyze electrophysiologic data and improve the specificity of the ICD's sensing circuitry. A unique feature of ventricular fibrillation is the virtual absence of isoelectric time. Conversely, during sinus tachycardia and supraventricular tachycardia, the ECG is at the isoelectric baseline much of the time. The probability density function algorithm enables the ICD to determine the proportion of time that the ECG is spending at the isoelectric baseline and thereby to detect ventricular fibrillation.

The ICD typically requires more than 5 seconds to appreciate ventricular tachycardia or fibrillation. It then charges its energy storage capacitors for 15 seconds and delivers a 30-joule cardioverting shock. If necessary, the device will deliver a second, third, fourth, and fifth countershock. If the rhythm disorder persists after the fifth countershock, the device will not recycle.

ICD systems are not complex. The device consists of a battery, which is heavy (though newer batteries are becoming lighter), and circuitry, which is light, with a total weight of less than 100 g. Most implanted defibrillators are currently placed without a thoracotomy. A sensing and defibrillating lead system (14 French) is inserted percutaneously via the subclavian vein into right ventricular–right atrial position. The distal electrode tip senses ventricular fibrillation and tachycardia. The cardioverting energy is then discharged between a coil electrode on the diaphragmatic surface of the right ventricle and another coil electrode positioned in the superior vena cava.

It is now clear that ICDs really do work and are capable of extending life. The most effective predictor of outcome in patients with ICDs is the severity of heart failure.[60] The ICD does not prevent malignant arrhythmias: it is, in essence, a safety net that cardioverts ventricular tachycardia or VF when it occurs. Therefore, it must still be used in conjunction with antidysrhythmic drugs.[61,62]

It is easy for a surgeon to become spooked by an ICD. The most effective strategy for managing a patient with an ICD is simply to ignore the ICD. If such a patient is being transported to the OR, however, the device should be inactivated before the electrocautery is used: the ICD will misinterpret the cautery current as VF and respond by delivering a shock to the patient.

The aura of mystery surrounding the ICD may be instantly eliminated by turning off the device (see below). Once the ICD is inactivated, the patient can be treated as any other patient would be. If external cardioversion is indicated, the ICD can be disregarded; external cardioversion will not harm or activate it.

How to Turn the ICD Off

1. If you can find the industry representative to program the device to remain off, do so. Then treat the patient exactly as you would if the ICD were not present.
2. If you cannot find the representative or the situation is urgent:
    a. Palpate the ICD generator, which is typically implanted in the left subcostal region.
    b. Place a heavy pacemaker (or, better yet, an ICD magnet) over the upper corner of the device, toward the patient's left shoulder. Older devices used to emit a soft beep (synchronous with the heartbeat) in response to a magnet when they were active. Unfortunately, that feature has since been engineered out, and newer ICDs are silent.
    c. Tape the magnet in place over the upper border of the device. As long as the magnet is in place, the ICD is off and the electrocautery can be used safely.

VENTRICULAR RATE IS FAST

If a patient is hemodynamically stable, a full 12-lead electrocardiogram is helpful; a long rhythm strip should be obtained as well. The best ECG lead to use for evaluating acute dysrhythmias is one that has good-voltage QRS complexes and maximal P waves, if the latter are present at all.

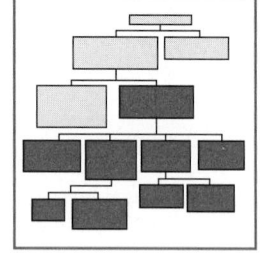

Electrocardiography

A cardiac impulse produces a positive, or upward, deflection on the monitor or oscilloscope as it approaches an ECG electrode and a negative, or downward, deflection as it moves away from the electrode. The important factor in dysrhythmia recognition, however, is not the direction of the impulse but its duration and location. Normal conduction velocity is fast: an impulse is transmitted by healthy Purkinje fibers at a rate of 2 to 3 m/sec.[3] Hence, when an impulse that arises in the atrium (supraventricular) is transmitted via the atrioventricular (AV) node to the high-velocity Purkinje system, the entire ventricle is electrically activated in 0.08 second (80 milliseconds; or two small boxes on ECG paper). An impulse that is generated at an ectopic ventricular site, however, cannot access the high-velocity Purkinje fibers as rapidly as a normal impulse, and ventricular activation is delayed. The QRS complex arising from an ectopic ventricular locus is therefore wider, signifying aberrant ventricular conduction [*see Figure 1*].

Because dysrhythmias of supraventricular origin typically display a narrow QRS complex, the width of the QRS can generally be used to distinguish dysrhythmias of ventricular origin from those of supraventricular origin [*see Figure 2*]. A wide QRS, however, may also be produced by an impulse that originates in the atrium and is aberrantly conducted to or through the ventricles (supraventricular rhythm with aberrancy). Such rhythms are relatively uncommon, constituting approximately 10% of all wide-complex tachycardias; more important, these patients will not suffer if their dysrhythmias are treated as though they were of ventricular origin.

When the ventricular rate is fast and the QRS is narrow, the 12-lead ECG should be searched for P waves, which indicate the presence of atrial activity. If P waves are absent and the QRS complexes occur at irregular intervals [*see Figure 3*], the patient probably has atrial fibrillation. It is not crucial to know this, however; the focus should be on the width of the QRS complex. A calcium channel blocker (verapamil or diltiazem) should be administered to control the ventricular rate. For verapamil, 10 mg is

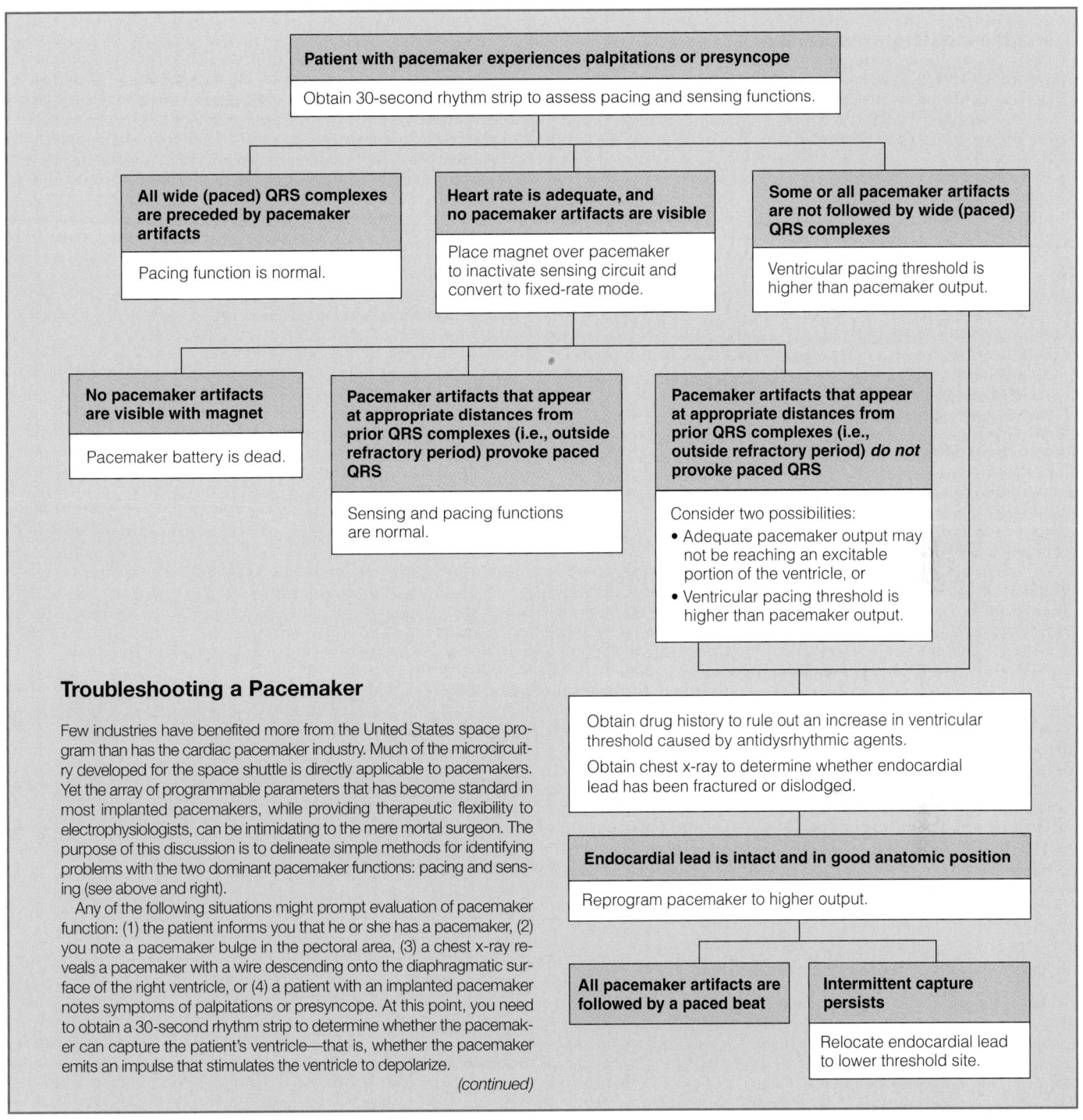

Patient with pacemaker experiences palpitations or presyncope

Obtain 30-second rhythm strip to assess pacing and sensing functions.

All wide (paced) QRS complexes are preceded by pacemaker artifacts

Pacing function is normal.

Heart rate is adequate, and no pacemaker artifacts are visible

Place magnet over pacemaker to inactivate sensing circuit and convert to fixed-rate mode.

Some or all pacemaker artifacts are not followed by wide (paced) QRS complexes

Ventricular pacing threshold is higher than pacemaker output.

No pacemaker artifacts are visible with magnet

Pacemaker battery is dead.

Pacemaker artifacts that appear at appropriate distances from prior QRS complexes (i.e., outside refractory period) provoke paced QRS

Sensing and pacing functions are normal.

Pacemaker artifacts that appear at appropriate distances from prior QRS complexes (i.e., outside refractory period) *do not* provoke paced QRS

Consider two possibilities:
• Adequate pacemaker output may not be reaching an excitable portion of the ventricle, or
• Ventricular pacing threshold is higher than pacemaker output.

Obtain drug history to rule out an increase in ventricular threshold caused by antidysrhythmic agents.

Obtain chest x-ray to determine whether endocardial lead has been fractured or dislodged.

Endocardial lead is intact and in good anatomic position

Reprogram pacemaker to higher output.

All pacemaker artifacts are followed by a paced beat

Intermittent capture persists

Relocate endocardial lead to lower threshold site.

Troubleshooting a Pacemaker

Few industries have benefited more from the United States space program than has the cardiac pacemaker industry. Much of the microcircuitry developed for the space shuttle is directly applicable to pacemakers. Yet the array of programmable parameters that has become standard in most implanted pacemakers, while providing therapeutic flexibility to electrophysiologists, can be intimidating to the mere mortal surgeon. The purpose of this discussion is to delineate simple methods for identifying problems with the two dominant pacemaker functions: pacing and sensing (see above and right).

Any of the following situations might prompt evaluation of pacemaker function: (1) the patient informs you that he or she has a pacemaker, (2) you note a pacemaker bulge in the pectoral area, (3) a chest x-ray reveals a pacemaker with a wire descending onto the diaphragmatic surface of the right ventricle, or (4) a patient with an implanted pacemaker notes symptoms of palpitations or presyncope. At this point, you need to obtain a 30-second rhythm strip to determine whether the pacemaker can capture the patient's ventricle—that is, whether the pacemaker emits an impulse that stimulates the ventricle to depolarize.

(continued)

mixed into 10 ml of saline, and 1 mg/min is given until the ventricular rate slows. For diltiazem, 0.25 mg/kg—15 to 20 mg is a reasonable dose for the average patient—is given over 2 minutes; the dose can be repeated in 15 minutes at 20 to 25 mg (0.35 mg/kg) over 2 minutes. A patient with a wide-complex tachycardia—or any patient who is hemodynamically unstable—is treated by cardioversion (see above), commonly followed by administration of lidocaine, 100 mg I.V., whereas a patient with a narrow-complex tachycardia should be treated with verapamil[3,5] or diltiazem to retard impulse conduction through the AV node. Therefore, it is not necessary to identify the specific type of dysrhythmia in order to treat it effectively.

Verapamil and diltiazem act by producing profound AV nodal blockade (see below); however, they are also peripheral vasodilators.[6] Moderate to profound systemic hypotension can be anticipated until the patient converts to sinus rhythm.

Much has been written about the risks of using calcium channel blockers in patients who are already receiving beta blockers. Abrupt and complete AV block rarely occurs, however, and in the vast majority of patients, persistent supraventricular tachycardia poses a greater risk than the possibility of third-degree heart block. Therefore, previous beta blockade should not be considered a contraindication to the use of a calcium channel blocker. Some clinicians may prefer to use adenosine.

Troubleshooting a Pacemaker (continued)

Ventricular Capture

a

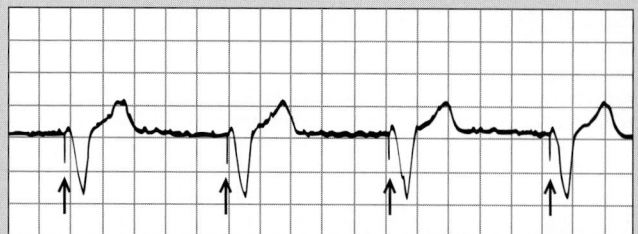

Note the pacemaker artifact (↑) that precedes each wide QRS complex in rhythm strip *a*, above. The QRS complex is wide because ventricular activation does not originate from the AV node, and ventricular conduction is therefore aberrant. At this point, you know that your patient is pacing, and you can determine the pacing rate. You do not, however, know the pacing threshold (i.e., the minimum voltage required for ventricular capture) or the safety margin between pacemaker output and pacing threshold. At this moment (and presumably yesterday and tomorrow), this pacemaker is appropriately discharging its most important function—pacing the heart and maintaining an adequate rate.

Ventricular Sensing

b

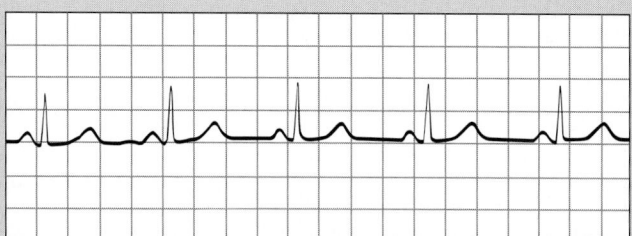

In rhythm strip *b*, above, normal P waves are followed by regular QRS complexes, and no pacemaker artifacts are evident. It is most likely that this patient's pacemaker has been programmed to fire at a paced rate that is slower than this patient's intrinsic heart rate, and the pacemaker is thus appropriately sensing each QRS complex. It is unlikely but possible, however, that the pacemaker is not sensing appropriately. Instead, one of the following problems may be occurring: (1) the pacemaker battery is dead, which is unlikely unless the battery was implanted more than 5 years ago, (2) the intracardiac electrode has been fractured, which is also unlikely, because current leads are remarkably durable, (3) the intracardiac electrode has been dislodged (this is an uncommon late problem that typically results in pacemaker artifacts unrelated to each QRS complex), or (4) the patient is taking an antidysrhythmic drug that has profoundly depressed ventricular excitability below threshold level for capture (this problem is very rare and can be excluded by taking a drug history). It is overwhelmingly likely, therefore, that rhythm strip *b* simply demonstrates that the pacemaker is sensing appropriately.

Assessing Ventricular Capture When the Spontaneous Heart Rate Is High

Typically, by the time you see the syncopal patient in the emergency department or recovery room, the patient is sufficiently excited that his or her

heart rate has recovered, and the rhythm strip will look like rhythm strip *b*. In a patient in whom heart rate is adequate and no pacemaker artifacts are visible, it is necessary to override the pacemaker's sensing circuit to determine whether the pacemaker is capable of emitting a pacing impulse that will capture the ventricle. The pacemaker's sensing circuit may be inactivated by placing a magnet over the pacemaker. Alternatively, the pacemaker may be reprogrammed to a paced rate that is faster than the patient's intrinsic heart rate. In this fashion, capture may easily be assessed. (Unfortunately, the programmers are expensive and are therefore often locked in some inaccessible closet. Programmers have great theoretical value but very little practical value to the surgeon.)

c

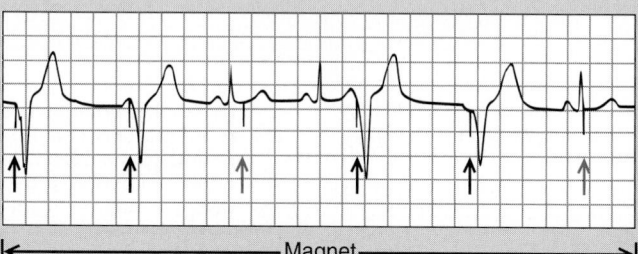

|← Magnet →|

In rhythm strip *c*, above, a magnet has converted the patient's pacemaker from the demand mode to the fixed-rate mode. The pacemaker artifacts that precede the wide (paced) QRS complexes in this rhythm strip (black arrows) show that the pacing function of this pacemaker is intact. Occasionally, a pacemaker artifact occurs during the electrical refractory period that immediately follows the QRS complex (red arrows). Pacing during the refractory period will not result in ventricular capture. Pacing during the refractory period should not result in ventricular capture and must not be interpreted as intermittent capture. In a patient whose pacemaker seems to be sensing appropriately (as in rhythm strip *b*), the magnet permits assessment of ventricular capture. Rhythm strip *c* demonstrates normal ventricular capture in the presence of a magnet.

Some or All Pacemaker Artifacts Are Not Followed by Wide QRS Complexes

If a pacemaker impulse that occurs outside the refractory period is not followed by a wide QRS complex, two possibilities should be considered. First, an adequate pacemaker impulse may not be reaching an excitable portion of the ventricle because of fracture or dislodgment of the endocardial lead. This problem can usually be identified by a chest x-ray. Second, if the chest x-ray shows that the lead is intact and in good anatomic position, the pacemaker output is not sufficient to reach the pacing threshold. Occasionally, this problem is caused by fibrosis at the endocardial electrode tip. If the pacemaker can be reprogrammed to a higher output, the capture problem should resolve. Otherwise, the lead must be repositioned to a site at which the pacing threshold is lower.

Occasional Pacemaker Artifacts Closely Follow a Spontaneous QRS Complex

If the patient's rhythm strip looks like rhythm strip *c*, *in the absence of a magnet*, the pacemaker is not sensing properly. In the demand mode, most pacemakers require at least a 2.5 mV signal to suppress output. Thus, if the pacemaker emits stimuli in spite of a normal spontaneous heart rate, an adequate QRS signal either is not being sensed (the lead tip may be lodged at the site of a prior myocardial infarction or scar) or is not being transmitted to the pacemaker (because of lead fracture or dislodgment).

Adenosine (see below) produces conduction delay in the AV node and deserves recognition as a second very good option (albeit only a transiently effective one) for treatment of paroxysmal narrow-complex tachycardia or for diagnosis of supraventricular tachycardia with aberrancy (including Wolff-Parkinson-White syndrome). Adenosine is given in a 6 mg I.V. push, followed 2 minutes later by a 12 mg I.V. push and then, after another 2 min-

utes, by a final 12 mg I.V. push over 2 seconds.[2,7]

Patients receiving adenosine complain of a frightening feeling of breathlessness and pressure that is not angina or dyspnea. This feeling typically resolves within 30 seconds. Facial flushing is also common. Unlike verapamil, adenosine is associated with hypotension in fewer than 1% of patients. Transient atrial or ventricular ectopy, with varying degrees of AV block, occurs in more

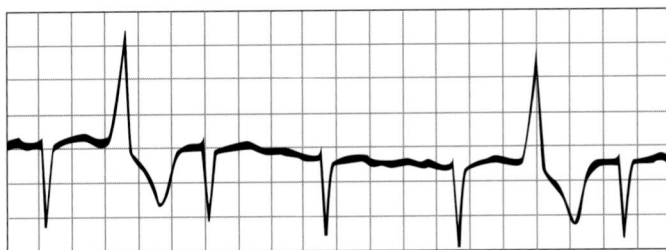

Figure 1 This tracing depicts frequent ventricular ectopic depolarizations interspersed among depolarizations from a supraventricular source. Note that the QRS depolarizations of supraventricular origin are narrow, whereas the QRS complexes of ectopic ventricular origin are wide.

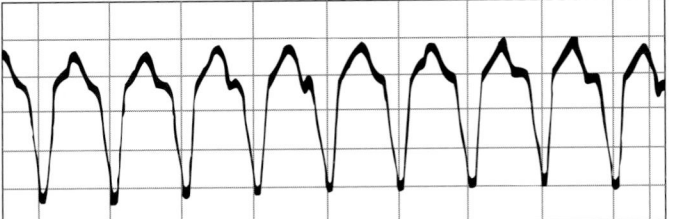

Figure 2 In a wide-complex tachycardia, each impulse is conducted aberrantly through the ventricles. The QRS complex is therefore prolonged to more than 0.08 second and occupies more than two small boxes on the ECG tracing.

than half of patients. None of the side effects of adenosine necessitate therapy.

Compared with calcium channel blockers, adenosine has certain advantages. Because of its rapid onset and short duration of action, and because its side effects are trivial and self-limited, adenosine can be used diagnostically. If, as is often the case, the QRS width is confusing and it is therefore uncertain whether the rhythm disorder is supraventricular (QRS < 0.08 second) or ventricular (QRS > 0.08 second), a 6 mg I.V. bolus of adenosine may be infused, and repeated if necessary. If the dysrhythmia slows or breaks, it was supraventricular. If it does not break, proceed to cardioversion (see above). On the other hand, even if a dysrhythmia responds to adenosine, the profound neuroendocrine and electrolyte perturbations that provoked the dysrhythmias in the first place—perturbations that are very common in the surgical intensive care unit—are likely to persist, and the dysrhythmia disorder typically recurs. Continuous (therapeutic) infusion of adenosine (150 to 300 μg/kg/min) is rational from a physiologic standpoint but is frighteningly expensive. Therefore, if adenosine works transiently, it is appropriate to follow with one of the longer-acting calcium channel blockers.

Calcium Channel Blockers

Both the sinoatrial (SA) node and the AV node are activated by the movement of calcium through the so-called slow calcium channels.[8] Calcium channel blockers are the most powerful agents currently available for blocking the transmission of impulses across the AV node. A supraventricular dysrhythmia produces an acceleration in the ventricular rate because impulses generated by an ectopic source above the AV node are transmitted too rapidly to the ventricle [see Figure 4]. Calcium channel blockers produce a pharmacologic blockade of the AV node, reducing the number of impulses reaching the ventricles and thereby controlling the ventricular rate (Remember, keeping the

ventricular rate between 60 and 100 beats/min is the ultimate goal of antidysrhythmia therapy).

Adenosine

Adenosine is an endogenous nucleoside that has differential antidysrhythmic effects in both supraventricular and ventricular tissue. The appeal of adenosine as a therapeutic and diagnostic tool is that it depresses automaticity and conduction within the SA and AV nodes.[9] Two clinically relevant types of adenosine receptors are present in cardiac tissue: (1) A_1 receptors, which are present on AV nodal tissue and cardiomyocytes and which thus mediate AV block and even bradycardia; and (2) A_2 receptors, which reside on vascular endothelial and smooth muscle cells and mediate coronary vasodilatation.[10] A_3 receptors are present in the myocardium, and selective activation of these has a cardioprotective (cardiac preconditioning) effect; however, these receptors are not relevant in antidysrhythmic therapy.[11]

Adenosine and acetylcholine exhibit identical cardiac effects and share similar receptor-effector coupling systems. Adenosine and acetylcholine provide an opposing balance to the sympathetic neurotransmitters norepinephrine and epinephrine. Thus, predictably, the adenosine antagonists caffeine, theophylline, and aminophylline provoke tachycardia and ectopy.

Because of the rapid intravascular metabolism of adenosine (half-life, 6 seconds), an intravenous bolus of adenosine (6 mg or 100 μg/kg) produces a negligible effect on systemic blood pressure, as confirmed by multiple clinical studies. Thus, adenosine is safe, but its effects are transient.

Adenosine is useful in blocking AV nodal conduction. Intracardiac recordings exhibit prolongation of the A-H interval with no alteration in conduction distal to the His bundle and on into the ventricular myocardium (the His-Purkinje system is unaffected).

In more than 90% of cases, adenosine is effective in terminating supraventricular tachycardia. Interestingly, adenosine has proved as effective at terminating atrioventricular reentry (85%) as at terminating atrioventricular node reentry (86%).[9] Because of adenosine's short half-life, however, the supraventricular dysrhythmia is likely to recur within minutes in up to one third of patients. For that reason, adenosine is often used diagnostically, to discriminate supraventricular from ventricular dysrhythmias (see above).

Several clinical studies have compared adenosine with verapamil for therapeutic AV nodal blockade, with predictable results. Both agents block the AV node and control the ventricular rate: cumulative efficacy with either agent is more than 90%. Postconversion dysrhythmias in the two groups were similar. Spontaneous reinitiation of supraventricular dysrhythmias occurs more frequently with adenosine, whereas systemic hypotension is more commonly associated with verapamil (at least until the dysrhythmia breaks). Thus, for help in seconds (approximately 20 seconds), use adenosine (6 mg I.V. bolus, may be repeated); for help in minutes (3 to 5 minutes), use verapamil (1 mg/min I.V. up

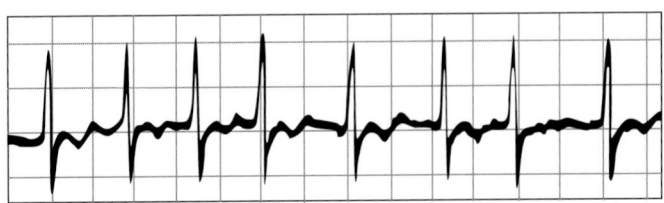

Figure 3 P waves are absent and the QRS complexes are narrow and irregular in this ECG tracing from a patient with atrial fibrillation.

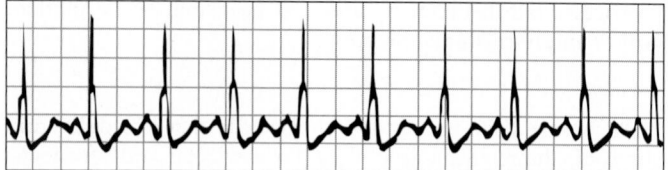

Figure 4 In a narrow-complex tachycardia, the entire ventricle is activated in less than 0.08 second. Presumably, the impulse originated at a supraventricular source and accessed the ventricle via the high-velocity Purkinje system.

to 10 mg); and for help in hours, infuse digoxin, 0.5 mg I.V. Although digitalis effectively blocks the AV node, it should be remembered that digitalis actually increases automaticity and excitability in both the atrium and the ventricle. The calcium channel blockers are superior to digoxin in controlling the ventricular rate.[8]

The adverse effects of adenosine, like the beneficial effects, are transient.[9] Facial flushing, chest pressure (adenosine has been implicated in the sensation of angina), and transient third-degree heart block are very common. Significant side effects are rare. Nebulized adenosine can cause bronchoconstriction, especially in asthmatic patients. Bronchoconstriction has not been reported after intravenous administration of adenosine.

Magnesium

Magnesium is the second most abundant cation in humans. It is involved in many enzymatic reactions that influence the production and utilization of cellular energy. Abnormalities in electrolyte homeostasis (potassium and calcium in particular) are associated with a robust increase in cardiac myocellular excitability and automaticity, especially when these abnormalities are concurrent with myocardial ischemia.[12] Multiple clinical studies confirm the efficacy of intravenous magnesium infusion even when the measured serum values are normal. The mechanism is unknown. When confronted with a patient exhibiting either supraventricular or ventricular ectopy, it is safe (and often effective) to administer magnesium chloride at a dosage of 7 g or 100 mg/kg I.V. over 1 to 3 hours. It is not necessary to measure the serum magnesium concentration first; the serum value will not influence therapy.

Amiodarone

Amiodarone is a class III antiarrhythmic drug that exerts its primary effect by prolongation of the myocardial action potential and refractory period and by delay of both SA node function and AV conduction. Amiodarone is also unique among these compounds by virtue of exhibiting, to varying degrees, the pharmacologic traits of all four classes of antiarrhythmic drugs [see Discussion, Antidysrhythmic Agents, *below*].[13] Among these is its ability to inhibit alpha- and beta-adrenergic stimulation without the classic side effects associated with beta receptor blockade. It also reduces transmural proarrhythmic heterogeneity (which predisposes to arrhythmias) in the human heart [see Discussion, Pathophysiology of Cardiac Dysrhythmias, Reentrant Dysrhythmias, *below*].[14]

Intravenous amiodarone was approved in the United States for use against malignant ventricular tachyarrhythmias in 1995. Rates of effective suppression for ventricular arrhythmias have been reported to be as high as 91% in uncontrolled trials.[15] Intravenous amiodarone has also proved effective against refractory ventricular tachycardia and VF. In one double-blind, randomized, placebo-controlled trial, amiodarone significantly improved survival in patients suffering out-of-hospital cardiac

arrest.[16] Amiodarone also proved superior to lidocaine (78% versus 27%) for termination of ventricular tachycardia in a randomized, prospective study of 29 patients with ventricular tachycardia refractory to external shock therapy.[17]

Another prospective, double-blind study comparing amiodarone with ibutilide (another class III antiarrhythmic agent) showed the drugs to be equally efficacious in the conversion of atrial fibrillation to sinus rhythm and in the subsequent maintenance of sinus rhythm.[18] Although two patients (10%) in the amiodarone group experienced hypotension during treatment, long-term maintenance therapy using the oral form of amiodarone may make it the drug of choice for this purpose, given ibutilide's lack of oral bioavailablity. Amiodarone was also found superior to both sotalol and propafenone in preventing the recurrence of atrial fibrillation in a randomized, prospective multicenter study of 403 patients with a mean follow-up period of 16 months.[19]

Although gratifyingly effective, amiodarone has significant side effects.[20] In trials of low-dose amiodarone (200 mg/day), thyroid, neurologic, cutaneous, ocular, bradycardic, and hypotensive problems were statistically more frequent; interestingly, pulmonary fibrosis was not.[21]

For the first 24 hours, the recommended dosages for adults are a loading dose of 150 mg I.V. over the first 10 minutes (15 mg/min) followed by 360 mg I.V. over the next 6 hours (1 mg/min); a maintenance infusion of 540 mg (0.5 mg/min) is given over the remaining 18 hours. The maintenance infusion may be continued for up to 3 weeks, at the rate of 0.5 mg/min, or the patient may be converted to oral dosing at 400 to 1,600 mg daily, depending on the duration of the preceding I.V. infusion.

Cardiac Dysrhythmias during Pregnancy

Fortunately, cardiac dysrhythmias are not frequent in young women of childbearing age. When rhythm problems do occur, they tend not to be hemodynamically destabilizing. The most commonly used obstetric drug with electrophysiologic side effects is magnesium sulfate.[22] When magnesium is infused intravenously into the mother, the fetus may exhibit a dose-dependent bradycardia and a progressive decrease in healthy heart rate variability.[23,24] Antidysrhythmic (indeed, any) drugs should be avoided during the first trimester of pregnancy, although most antidysrhythmic agents carry relatively little risk.[22] Quinidine, procainamide, lidocaine, digoxin, adenosine, and beta blockers all have a long record of safety during pregnancy. Flecainide has proved to be effective in treating fetal supraventricular tachycardia complicated by hydrops. Phenytoin and amiodarone have been associated with congenital abnormalities.[22]

The important point is that if the mother is hemodynamically unstable and exhibits a dysrhythmia, direct current cardioversion is safe and effective.

Proarrhythmia with Antidysrhythmic Drugs

Proarrhythmic manifestations of ostensibly antiarrhythmic drugs have been linked primarily to agents that prolong repolarization. Early afterdepolarizations associated with agents that retard repolarization or an increase in spatial and temporal dispersion of repolarization are the putative mechanisms of drug-induced or drug-enhanced arrhythmias.[25,26]

The class III antidysrhythmic agents have traditionally been the agents most likely to cause dysrhythmias.[26] The best way of preventing dysrhythmias, however, is to follow the general policy of not using drugs at all if they are not needed.[27]

Discussion

Antidysrhythmic Agents

Verapamil (or another calcium channel blocker), lidocaine, and adenosine are the only drugs essential for the acute treatment of cardiac dysrhythmias. Because patients may already be taking oral agents for chronic dysrhythmias, however, it is important to be aware of the actions and side effects of these drugs when treating an individual with an acute dysrhythmia. Antidysrhythmic drugs have been classified on the basis of their dominant electrophysiologic effect[28]; this classification has been reviewed and placed in a clinical context.[5] Adenosine has a unique receptor that modulates cyclic adenosine monophosphate (cAMP), resulting in cholinergic activity. It is not similar to other antidysrhythmic agents and is therefore unclassified.

CLASS I AGENTS (MEMBRANE ACTIVE)

Class I agents are fast sodium channel blockers. All class I agents—which include lidocaine, procainamide, quinidine, and disopyramide—are local anesthetics. These agents block the fast inward sodium current and thereby decrease both the amplitude of the action potential, or phase 0 depolarization (see below), and conduction velocity. These agents also depress the rate of spontaneous phase 4 depolarization, or automaticity, and thus are useful for abolishing premature ventricular contractions (PVCs); class I agents are sometimes termed PVC killers. Because these agents slow the conduction velocity, they can actually increase the likelihood of reentrant cardiac dysrhythmias in some patients.[25,27]

CLASS II AGENTS (BETA BLOCKERS)

Class II agents are beta blockers and include such drugs as propranolol. Sympathetic hyperactivity, marked by increased release of catecholamines, is one of the major causes of cardiac dysrhythmias that result from increased automaticity (hyperexcitability).[25,27,29] Beta-adrenergic blockade has produced a decrease in such automatic dysrhythmias under both clinical and experimental conditions.[29]

CLASS III AGENTS (TO PROLONG REPOLARIZATION)

Class III agents, such as bretylium, act directly on the myocardial cell membrane to delay phases 2 and 3 of repolarization and thereby prolong refractoriness. Bretylium is effective in terminating reentrant dysrhythmias because it prolongs the refractory period of the ectopic focus to beyond the point at which an impulse reenters the circuit.[1,2] Bretylium apparently has no effect on either automaticity or conduction velocity.[30]

CLASS IV AGENTS (CALCIUM CHANNEL BLOCKERS)

Class IV agents, of which verapamil and diltiazem are the most effective, block the movement of calcium across the slow calcium channels but have virtually no effect on the so-called fast sodium channels.[28] Because both the SA node and the AV node are composed of slow-response fibers that are activated by the movement of calcium ions across the slow channels, the class IV agents are particularly effective in preventing unwanted supraventricular impulses from reaching the ventricles. These agents decrease the conduction velocity through the AV node and increase the refractory period of the AV node.

CLASS V AGENTS (UNCLASSIFIED)

The vagus nerve innervates the SA node, the atria, and the AV node, but it has almost no influence over the His-Purkinje system or ventricular muscle. At therapeutic levels, digitalis has an antidysrhythmic action that is mediated almost exclusively via the vagus nerve. Toxic doses of digitalis, however, may produce an increased automaticity characterized by multifocal premature ventricular depolarizations [*see* Pathophysiology of Cardiac Dysrhythmias, *below*]. Caution must be observed in digitalizing a patient who is prone to atrial dysrhythmias, because digitalis increases atrial excitability and hence increases the risk of atrial ectopy. Because digitalis also induces AV nodal blockade mediated by the vagus nerve, however, any atrial dysrhythmias produced by digitalization will be less clinically significant.[31,32]

Cellular Electrophysiology

Electromechanical activity of all muscle, including the heart, is determined by the concentration and flow of ions, particularly calcium, potassium, and sodium. Knowledge of cardiac electrophysiology can serve as a conceptual framework on which to build a rational therapeutic program. Direct observation of cellular electrical activity using a glass microelectrode reveals that the cell membrane is semipermeable: it permits easy passage of cations such as sodium, potassium, and calcium but provides a barrier to anions and proteins. Negatively charged intracellular proteins that cannot cross the cell membrane create a transmembrane potential in which the interior of the cell is negatively charged relative to the exterior. The membrane potential of a cell, E_K, is proportional to the difference between the logarithms of the intracellular potassium concentration, $[K]_i$, and the extracellular potassium concentration, $[K]_o$:

$$E_K = c(\log [K]_i - \log [K]_o)$$

The proportionality constant, c, varies with temperature, but at 37° C it is –60 mV. Thus, under physiologic conditions,

$$E_K = -60 \text{ mV} \times \log [K]_i / [K]_o$$

This relation, termed the Nernst equation, can be used to calculate the myocardial cell membrane potential if the potassium concentrations are known. For example, if the potassium concentration is normal—that is, 150 mEq/L intracellularly and 3.8 mEq/L extracellularly—then the membrane potential is

$$E_K = -60 \text{ mV} \times \log 150 / 3.8$$
$$E_K = -90 \text{ mV}$$

If, however, the serum potassium concentration rises to 6.0 mEq/L, then the membrane potential also changes:

$$E_K = -60 \text{ mV} \times \log 150 / 6.0$$
$$E_K = -80 \text{ mV}$$

Thus, the resting membrane potential is determined primarily by the concentration gradient for potassium across the cell membrane. The transmembrane potential can be calculated if the transmembrane potassium concentrations are measured with a glass microelectrode. Under clinical conditions, however, only the serum potassium level can be measured. This value does not provide an adequate guide to the transmembrane electrical voltage, because many physiologic factors are capable of altering the intracellular potassium concentration.[13] Such factors include electrolyte and acid-base balance, the level of osmotic and metabolic activity, and the serum levels of glucose and insulin.

Any factor that causes osmotic movement of water into the cell

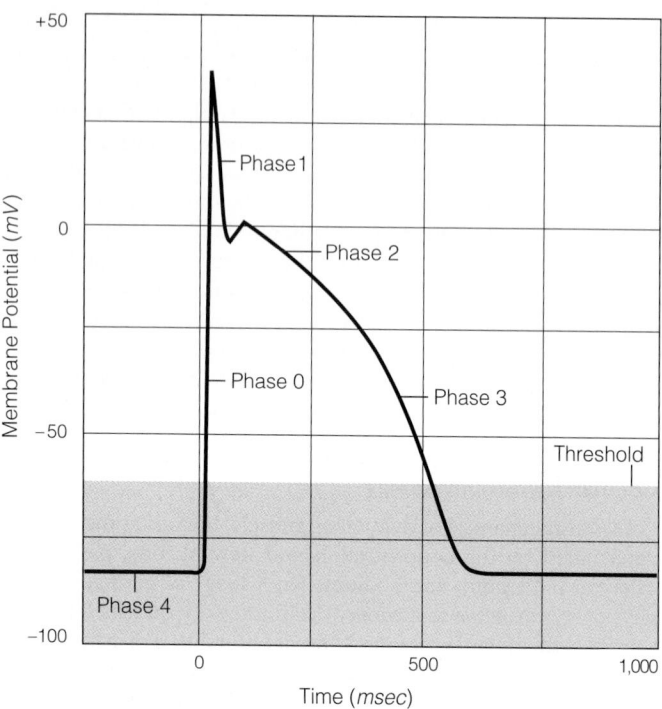

Figure 5 **The standard Purkinje (or ventricular muscle) action potential has five distinct phases: phase 0, rapid depolarization; phase 1, early repolarization; phase 2, plateau; phase 3, rapid repolarization; and phase 4, diastole.**

will dilute and thus decrease the intracellular potassium concentration. The transmembrane gradients of sodium and calcium are maintained by energy-requiring pumps in the cell membrane. When these pumps are inactivated, as during myocardial ischemia,[12] sodium and calcium can leak into the cell. If, as often occurs, sodium leaks into the cell faster than potassium leaks out, water will be drawn in, producing myocardial edema. Tissue acidosis can also alter the transmembrane potassium gradient. In acidosis, hydrogen ions can leak into the cell in exchange for potassium, thereby decreasing the intracellular potassium concentration and increasing the membrane potential. Variations in glucose transport can also affect the potassium gradient. Under the influence of insulin and epinephrine, glucose may move across the membrane into the myocardial cell, drawing in water by osmosis. The decline in intracellular potassium concentration stimulates the sodium pump to exchange extracellular potassium for intracellular sodium. Concurrent administration of glucose and insulin is the standard method for treating hyperkalemia because it shifts potassium from the extracellular fluid back into the cells.

ACTION POTENTIAL GENERATION

Stimulation of either cardiac muscle or skeletal muscle produces an action potential. Unlike a skeletal muscle action potential, which lasts only several milliseconds, a cardiac action potential may persist for as long as several hundred milliseconds.[33] The standard Purkinje, or ventricular muscle, action potential has five discernible phases [see Figure 5].

Phase 4

In phase 4, the resting membrane potential, or diastolic potential, of the cell is generated by active metabolic processes that produce substantial transmembrane potassium and sodium gradi-

ents. An energy-dependent (ATP-dependent) sodium-potassium pump counteracts a significant influx of sodium and efflux of potassium in the resting cell to maintain this resting membrane potential. As noted, when the extracellular potassium concentration rises from a typical value of 3.8 mEq/L to 6.0 mEq/L, the resting membrane potential increases from −90 mV to −80 mV. This effect would tend to increase automaticity, but it is superseded by the effect of hyperkalemia on the sodium current. A rise in the extracellular potassium level progressively impairs the flux of sodium through sodium-specific channels, leading to an overall decrease in myocardial excitability.[34]

Phase 0

During phase 0, an electrical stimulus causes the sodium-specific fast channels and the calcium-specific slow channels to open, usually for no longer than 1 msec. As positive ions rush in, depolarization occurs as the membrane potential rises to threshold, or −60 mV, and an action potential is generated [see Figure 5]. Under normal physiologic conditions, the stimulus that produces an action potential is electrical, but any stimulus—electrical, physical (such as a precordial thump), or chemical—that depolarizes a membrane up to threshold (again, −60 mV) can generate an action potential. There are various abnormalities that can cause the resting membrane potential to move toward threshold. For example, conditions that produce a decrease in energy supply (or, alternatively, an increase in energy demand) will have this effect because energy is required to maintain the potassium and sodium gradients across the resting membrane. Under such conditions, automaticity is enhanced because lesser stimuli can achieve the threshold potential, and the cardiac muscle is said to be hyperexcitable, or irritable.

Phases 1 and 2

Phase 1 is characterized by repolarization to the plateau phase, or phase 2. During phase 2, the slow calcium channels as well as the fast sodium channels are activated, and the membrane potential remains relatively constant for as long as 100 msec.[35] The long duration of this plateau phase is the most dramatic difference between an action potential in cardiac muscle and one in skeletal muscle. During this interval, termed the effective refractory period, the myocardium is relatively resistant to further excitation.

Phase 3

During phase 3, potassium channels reopen to promote efflux of potassium from the cell. Rapid repolarization ensues, and the resting membrane potential is reestablished at −90 mV.

Spontaneous Phase 4 Depolarization

Unlike ordinary atrial and ventricular muscle, the Purkinje fibers do not have a stable phase 4 diastolic potential [see Figure 6]. Instead, these fibers undergo continuous depolarization during diastole as a result of deactivation of the potassium efflux current.[35,36] If the Purkinje fibers reach the threshold voltage, they will fire an action potential. Under normal conditions, however, the SA and AV nodes exhibit faster diastolic depolarization and reach threshold sooner than the Purkinje fibers. Because the cells in the SA node normally reach threshold first—winning the race, so to speak—the SA node typically assumes the pacemaker function of the heart. Premature ventricular contractions develop when a hyperexcitable cell or fiber in ventricular myocardium undergoes rapid diastolic depolarization and reaches threshold before the cells in the SA node. This cell or fiber then assumes the pacemaker function of the heart for that beat. The PVCs (or,

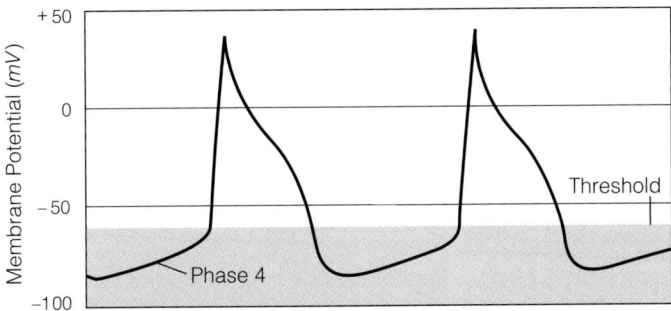

Figure 6 *In normal cardiac Purkinje fibers, the membrane potential does not remain flat during phase 4 but instead rises gradually. This spontaneous phase 4 depolarization is the result of a resting potassium current.*

more accurately, premature ventricular depolarizations) that result from such ventricular ectopy can be abolished by overdrive pacing. In this situation, a mechanical pacemaker is used to pace the heart at a rate faster than that of the PVC (i.e., the R–R interval is shorter). The artificial device thereby wins the race; it assumes the pacemaker function and regularizes the heart rate, producing a beneficial cosmetic effect on the ECG without altering the hyperexcitability of the diseased cell.

Pathophysiology of Cardiac Dysrhythmias

All dysrhythmias are caused by enhanced automaticity, reentry, or a combination of these two mechanisms.

AUTOMATIC DYSRHYTHMIAS

Any area of myocardial tissue that independently depolarizes, reaches threshold, and fires is termed automatic, and the electrical impulse that activates the adjacent myocardium generates an automatic rhythm. Acute dysrhythmias tend to be automatic; such automatic dysrhythmias are frequently seen in patients in emergency departments and coronary care units and in patients undergoing surgery. Five common clinical phenomena that tend to increase automaticity have been identified: local myocardial hypoxia, hypokalemia, hypercalcemia, increased catecholamine levels, and drugs (most commonly digitalis).

Local Myocardial Hypoxia

Energy-dependent cell membrane pumps maintain the resting membrane potential, and when oxygen supply to myocardial tissue is inadequate because of ischemia, the pumps fail to function properly. Consequently, the potassium gradient declines, and the membrane potential drifts closer toward threshold. Small membrane potential fluctuations or stimuli of less than normal magnitude are then sufficient to bump the membrane potential up to threshold and initiate an action potential. Ventricular muscle cells, not only those cells in specialized conduction tissue, can spontaneously generate electrical fluctuations, or oscillations, in membrane potential [see Slow Afterdepolarizations, below]. If the resting membrane potential is initially closer to normal because of local myocardial hypoxia, then these spontaneous oscillations are more likely to achieve threshold and fire an action potential.[37]

Hypokalemia

Extracellular hypokalemia increases the resting membrane potential, drawing it further away from threshold and producing hyperpolarization. This effect tends to decrease tissue excitability,

or automaticity.[37,38] Hypokalemia also increases the size of the sodium channels, however, thereby promoting more rapid influx of sodium during phase 0. Because the net result of hypokalemia is increased automaticity, the effect of hypokalemia on sodium influx appears to override its effect on membrane hyperpolarization. Hypokalemia is one of the most easily treated (and overtreated) forms of hyperexcitability.

Hypercalcemia

Calcium is a potent inotropic agent, mediating the interaction between actin and myosin that produces muscle contraction.[35] High extracellular calcium levels may cause myocardial work to exceed the energy supply and thus impair the function of the membrane pump. As a result, the resting membrane potential drifts up toward threshold, enhancing automaticity. Excess calcium also appears to promote spontaneous oscillations in membrane potential [*see* Slow Afterdepolarizations, *below*].[39] Because of calcium's inotropic effect, such oscillations are accompanied by muscle activity.

Elevated Catecholamine Levels

Increased catecholamine levels also appear to predispose to automaticity, as evidenced by an increase in the incidence of multiple PVCs reported in patients who have been infused with high doses of catecholamines, such as epinephrine or dopamine. Catecholamines increase both heart rate and contractility. As with hypercalcemia, elevated catecholamine levels may increase cardiac work beyond the limits of energy supply and cause the membrane potential to move closer to threshold. This effect on the energy-dependent membrane pumps has been observed in isolated preparations of Purkinje muscle fibers. The addition of catecholamines to preparations of Purkinje muscle fibers has decreased the outward potassium current to the point that the resting membrane potential was shifted as much as 25 mV toward depolarization, enhancing automaticity.[36,37] In addition to affecting the operation of the membrane pumps, catecholamines can produce large spontaneous oscillations in membrane voltage.[36,40] Catecholamines are elaborated endogenously; a patient who is in pain, for example, may be releasing large amounts of epinephrine into the circulation. In such cases, morphine can be used effectively as an antidysrhythmic agent.[40]

Drugs

Digitalis is the prototypical cardiac stimulant. Typically, any

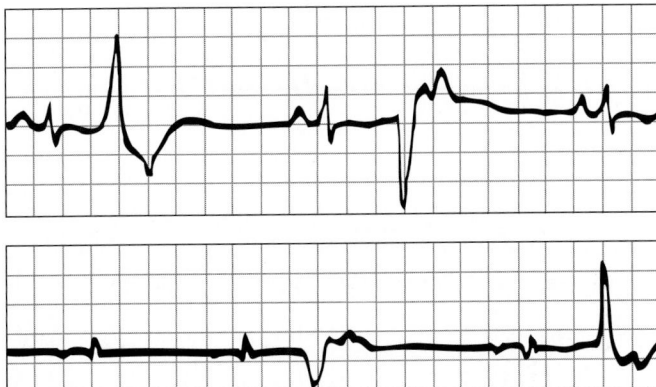

Figure 7 ECG demonstrates multifocal PVCs, indicating a diffuse hyperexcitability of the ventricles. Such hyperexcitability may arise from a metabolic abnormality such as hypokalemia or a pharmacologic cause such as digitalis toxicity.

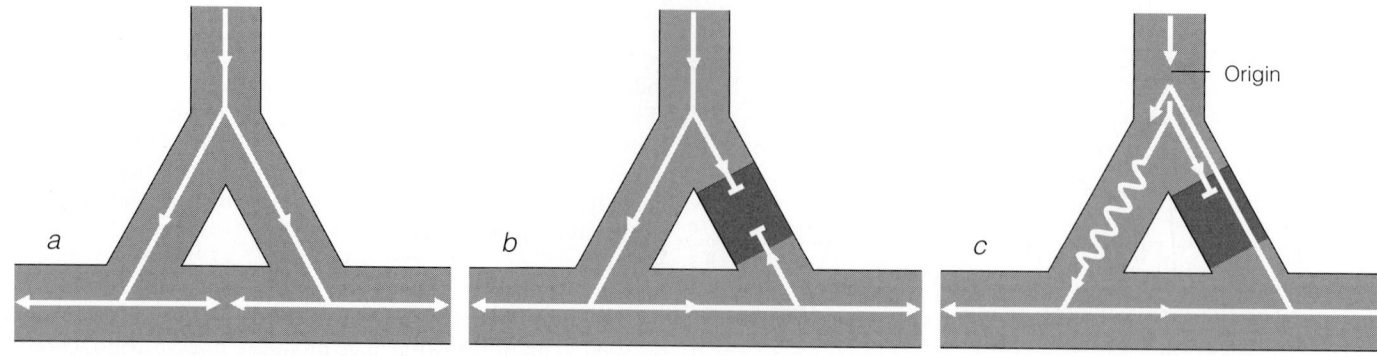

Figure 8 **Schematic diagram portrays a conceptual framework for understanding the generation of reentrant dysrhythmias. In normal conduction (*a*), as in sinus rhythm or ventricular pacing, an impulse is propagated along two different anatomic pathways and is extinguished at the bottom. In (*b*), one pathway has a region of slow conduction (red area), which results in a rate-dependent block. In (*c*), the impulse is also blocked in the right limb (red area), but it travels over the alternative pathway sufficiently slowly (zigzag line) for the origin to be able to repolarize before the initial impulse returns; the conducted impulse then depolarizes the origin and reenters the circuit.**

agent other than oxygen that causes the heart to pump harder and faster also increases cardiac excitability. Digitalis toxicity can produce diffuse myocardial hyperexcitability, manifested by so-called automatic ventricular ectopy. In this condition, the cardiac impulse originates from multiple sites in the ventricle. In patients with ventricular ectopy caused by digitalis intoxication, the whole myocardium becomes hyperexcitable and spontaneous depolarizations derive from multiple different sites. When the QRS complex originates at multiple loci, the ECG will exhibit multiple morphologies, and multifocal PVCs are apparent on the ECG—the classic multifocal ectopy of digitalis toxicity [*see Figure 7*].[41-43]

REENTRANT DYSRHYTHMIAS

In the normally functioning heart, the rich cell-cell conduction pathways promote uniform activation of the atria or ventricles in waves. Because activation occurs by means of large electrical wave fronts and because all cardiac tissue has a long refractory period, it is highly unlikely that any cells will remain excitable at the completion of each beat. However, disorders such as myocardial ischemia, fibrosis, and necrosis slow electrical conduction and also produce nonconductive areas that interrupt the normal electrical wavefront.[44] These conditions set up one of the requirements for reentry: areas of differential myocardial repolarization.[45]

A circuit whose length exceeds the duration of the reentrant impulse circuit is required for the initiation of reentry (i.e., in order to sustain continuous conduction); such a circuit may develop because of anatomic or physiologic heterogeneity in myocardial tissue.[44,45] Slow conduction, a shortened refractory period, and anatomic heterogeneity all favor reentry [*see Figure 8*]. The circuit wavelength of an impulse is the product of the conduction velocity and the duration of the longest refractory period in the circuit.[46] For example, for normal myocardium, the

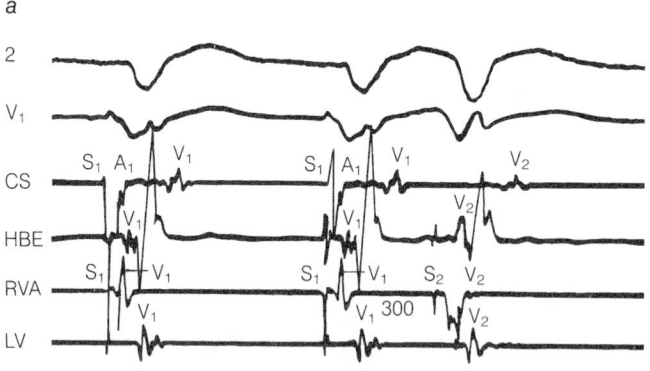

Figure 9 **In electrophysiologic testing, the electrical complexes are spread out to facilitate the recognition of ventricular electrical morphology. In (*a*), critically timed paced stimuli capture one ventricle, but when pacing is stopped, the rhythm reverts to sinus rhythm. In (*b*), critically timed paced stimuli achieve rate-dependent block in one arm of a reentrant circuit. When the activation wave front returns to the origin, this tissue is no longer refractory and undergoes depolarization. With reexcitation, the conditions for reentry are met, and the impulse continues after pacing stops.**

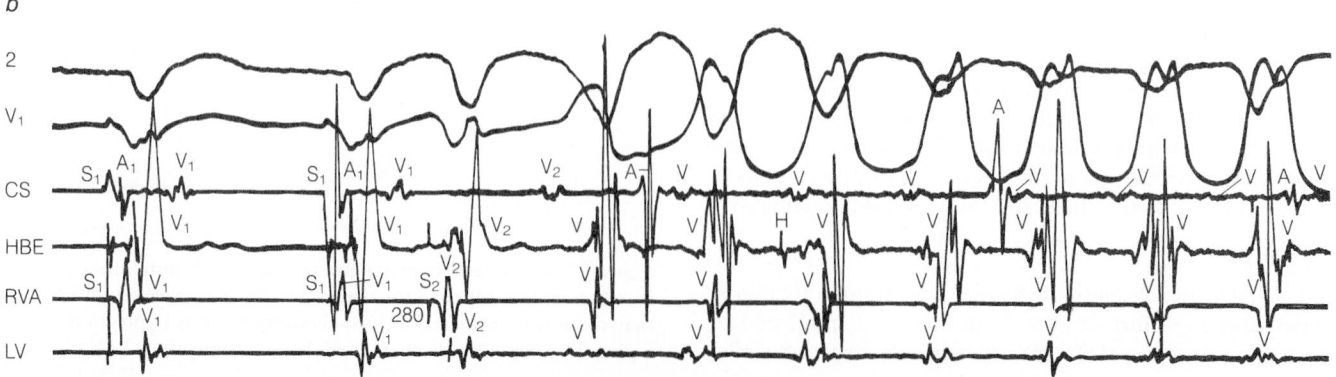

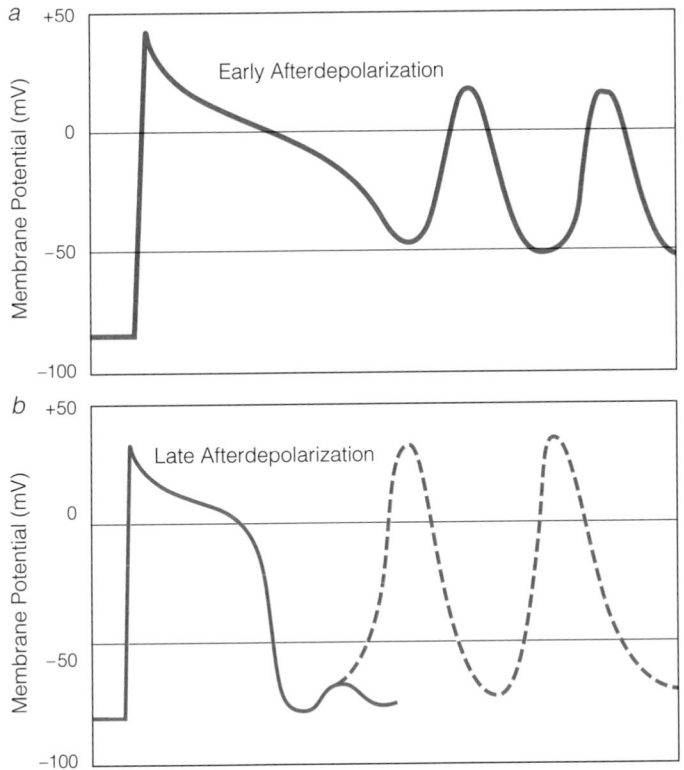

Figure 10 **Membrane oscillatory instability may be manifested by either (*a*) early afterdepolarizations or (*b*) late afterdepolarizations. If the late afterdepolarizations achieve the threshold voltage, they can fire an action potential (dotted lines).**

conduction velocity is 200 cm/sec and the refractory period is 0.4 second; therefore, the circuit length for a normally conducted myocardial impulse would have to be 80 cm. Because the reentrant circuit would have to be extraordinarily tortuous to encompass 80 cm, it would appear that concomitant slow conduction is essentially mandatory to shorten the circuit wavelength and permit initiation of a reentrant dysrhythmia. Regions such as the AV and SA nodes normally exhibit slow conduction, and therefore, any disturbance that produces minor additional slowing in these areas predisposes to reentry. It has also been suggested that extreme anatomic heterogeneity might permit microreentry.[45] For example, a tortuous path over stunned, slowly conducting ventricular muscle in an individual with heterogeneous myocardial infarction might achieve the prerequisites for reentry.

In vitro studies have investigated physiologic factors that might produce changes in conduction and excitability that predispose to reentrant dysrhythmias. For example, abnormal conduction has been observed in a Purkinje network subjected to local changes in potassium concentration.[33,40] The decrease in conduction velocity can vary in different areas of the Purkinje network, leading to functional conduction block.[37,38] In T- or X-shaped Purkinje preparations, the impulses either summate electrically or, conversely, inhibit each other when they arrive at the junction simultaneously. It is difficult to study the cardiac microenvironment in living animals or humans, but in these studies,[47] electrical instability results when the Purkinje network is subjected to potassium fluctuations (which certainly occur with induced cardioplegia during cardiac surgery, and probably occur in myocardial ischemia).

Electrophysiologic testing with programmed stimulation in a patient with a history of cardiac dysrhythmias can reveal whether latent substrates of reentry are present. Because organized ventricular reentry does not occur in normal myocardium, all reentrant dysrhythmias, whether they are induced or spontaneous, are pathologic. Rapidly paced stimuli may provoke a decrease in action potential duration and shorten refractoriness in myocardium in which the conduction velocity has already been reduced. Critically timed premature paced stimuli may then penetrate selective zones of myocardium, leading to a reentrant dysrhythmia [*see Figure 9*].[48] A ventricular tachydysrhythmia that can be induced by programmed stimulation carries an ominous prognosis unless it can be abolished by pharmacotherapy or surgery.[48]

SLOW AFTERDEPOLARIZATIONS

Damaged atrial and ventricular muscle exhibits resting membrane potential instability.[49] The oscillations in membrane potential may at times be large enough to raise the membrane voltage to threshold level and cause the cell to fire. The phenomenon of oscillatory instability, which was first recognized in the 1940s,[50] is now thought to play an important role in the genesis of cardiac dysrhythmias. Injury,[49] elevated calcium levels,[33] digitalis,[41,42] and catecholamines all promote membrane oscillatory instability, which may be manifested as either early or late afterdepolarizations. Both phenomena occur after an action potential; however, an early afterdepolarization occurs before repolarization of the cell, whereas a late afterdepolarization occurs after repolarization [*see Figure 10*]. Both early and late afterdepolarizations may be followed by extreme membrane oscillatory instability that leads to slow-response action potentials [*see Figure 11*]. If any of these slow potentials reach threshold, they may result in either organized electrical activity (premature ventricular depolarization) or disorganized electrical activity (fibrillation).

The recognition of slow potentials, depressed fast responses, and very slow conduction was originally based on in vitro studies of cardiac tissue.[51] For example, bathing superfused Purkinje fibers in a solution with a high potassium concentration inactivates the fast sodium channels and markedly alters normal phase 0 depolarization. Under such circumstances, slow potentials that are less than 80 mV in amplitude, that depolarize at a rate of 1 to

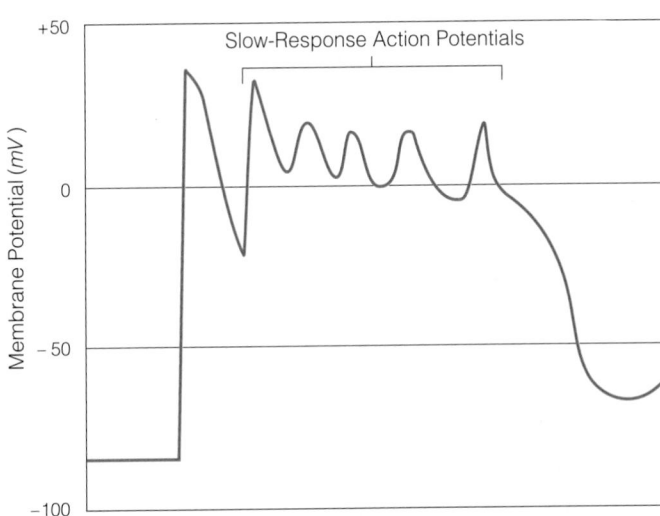

Figure 11 **Early afterdepolarizations may lead to slow-response action potentials. If any of these potentials reach threshold, they may lead to either organized electrical activity (premature ventricular depolarization) or disorganized electrical activity (fibrillation).**

2 V/sec, and that last for up to 1 second are frequently documented.[40,51] The amplitude and the overshoot of these slow potentials can be magnified by increasing the extracellular calcium concentration and can be abolished by adding manganese, an agent that blocks the slow calcium channels. These results suggest that the slow potentials are mediated by the slow calcium channels rather than by the fast sodium channels responsible for routine phase 0 depolarization. Although extraordinary nonphysiologic conditions are employed to induce such slow potentials in the laboratory, the myocardial microenvironment during the peri-infarction and postinfarction periods as well as after cardioplegia may well be similarly bizarre and equally nonphysiologic.

For example, even after extensive myocardial infarction, there are often healthy Purkinje fibers overlying areas of damaged, ischemic myocardium.[52] Slow conduction and slow potentials are characteristic of stunned myocardium.[53,54]

Slow potentials have been incriminated in the generation of reentrant dysrhythmias for three reasons: (1) because they are caused by an active calcium influx that produces 40 to 80 mV depolarizations, they may be conducted long distances; (2) because the conduction velocity may be 1,000 times slower than normal, the circuit wavelength is reduced accordingly; and (3) because slow potentials leave a long refractory wake, they set up zones of functional conduction block.[53,54]

References

1. Saxonhouse SJ, Curtis AB: Risks and Benefits of rate control versus maintenance of sinus rhythm. Am J Cardiol 91:27D, 2003

2. Reiffel JA: Selecting an antiarrhythmic agent for atrial fibrillation should be a patient-specific, data-driven decision. Am J Cardiol 82:72N, 1998

3. Naccarelli GV, Wolbrette DL, Khan M, et al: Old and new antiarrhythmic drugs for converting and maintaining sinus rhythm in atrial fibrillation: comparative efficacy and results of trials. Am J Cardiol 91:15D, 2003

4. Raichlen JS, Campbell FW, Edie RN, et al: Effect of the site of placement of temporary epicardial pacemakers on ventricular function in patients undergoing cardiac surgery. Circulation 70:I, 1984

5. Sarubbi B, Ducceschi V, D'Andrea A, et al: Atrial fibrillation: what are the effects of drug therapy on the effectiveness and complications of electrical cardioversion? Can J Cardiol 14:1267, 1998

6. Bertaglia E, D'Este D, Zerbo F, et al: Effects of verapamil and metoprolol on recovery from atrial electrical remodeling after cardioversion of long-lasting atrial fibrillation. Int J Cardiol 87:167, 2003

7. Bigger JT Jr: Epidemiological and mechanistic studies of atrial fibrillation as a basis for treatment strategies. Circulation 98:943, 1998

8. Botto GL, Bonini W, Broffoni T: Modulation of ventricular rate in permanent atrial fibrillation: randomized, crossover study of the effects of slow-release formulations of gallopamil, diltiazem, or verapamil. Clin Cardiol 11:837, 1998

9. Glatter KA, Cheng J, Dorostkar P, et al: Electrophysiologic effects of adenosine in patients with supraventricular tachycardia. Circulation 99:1034, 1999

10. Hayes A: Adenosine receptors and cardiovascular disease: the adenosine-1 Receptor (A(1)) and A(1) selective ligands. Cardiovasc Toxicol 3:71, 2003

11. Tracey WR, Magee W, Masamune H, et al: Selective activation of adenosine A3 receptors with N6-(3-chlorobenzyl)-5'-N-methylcarboxamidoadenosine (CB-MECA) provides cardioprotection via KATP channel activation. Cardiovasc Res 40:138, 1998

12. Zumino AP, Baiardi G, Schanne OF, et al: Differential electrophysiologic effects of global and regional ischemia and reperfusion in perfused rat hearts. Effects of Mg2+ concentration. Mol Cell Biochem 186:79, 1998

13. Letelier LM, Udol K, Ena J, et al: Effectiveness of amiodarone for conversion of atrial fibrillation to sinus rhythm: a meta-analysis. Arch Intern Med 163:777, 2003

14. Drouin E, Lande G, Charpentier F: Amiodarone reduces transmural heterogeneity of repolarization in the human heart. J Am Coll Cardiol 32:1063, 1998

15. Kowey PR, Marinchak RA, Rials SJ, et al: Intravenous amiodarone. J Am Coll Cardiol 29:1190, 1997

16. Kudenchuk PJ, Cobb LA, Copass MK, et al: Amiodarone for resuscitation after out-of-hospital cardiac arrest due to ventricular fibrillation. N Engl J Med 341:871, 1999

17. Somberg JC, Bailin SJ, Haffajee CI, et al: Intravenous lidocaine versus intravenous amiodarone (in a new aqueous formulation) for incessant ventricular tachycardia. Am J Cardiol 90:853, 2002

18. Bernard EO, Schmid ER, Schmidlin D, et al: Ibutilide versus amiodarone in atrial fibrillation: a double-blinded, randomized study. Crit Care Med 31:1031, 2003

19. Roy D, Talajic M, Dorian P, Connolly S, et al: Amiodarone to prevent recurrence of atrial fibrillation. N Engl J Med 342:913, 2000

20. Using oral amiodarone safely. Drug Therapy Bull 41:9, 2003

21. Vorperian VR, Havighurst TC, Miller S, et al: Adverse effects of low-dose amiodarone: a meta-analysis. J Am Coll Cardiol 30:791, 1997

22. Gowda RM, Khan IA, Mehta NJ, et al: Cardiac arrhythmias in pregnancy: clinical and therapeutic considerations. Int J Cardiol 88:129, 2003

23. Cardosi RJ, Chez RA: Magnesium sulfate, maternal hypothermia, and fetal bradycardia with loss of heart rate variability. Obstet Gynecol 92:691, 1998

24. Hamersley SL, Landy HJ, O'Sullivan MJ: Fetal bradycardia secondary to magnesium sulfate therapy for preterm labor: a case report. J Reprod Med 43:206, 1998

25. Hohnloser SH: Proarrhythmia with class III antiarrhythmic drugs: types, risks, and management. Am J Cardiol 80:82G, 1997

26. Wolbrette DL: Risk of proarrhythmia with class III antiarrhythmic agents: sex-based differences and other issues. Am J Cardiol 91:39D, 2003

27. Sager PT: New advances in class III antiarrhythmic drug therapy. Curr Opin Cardiol 14:15, 1999

28. The Sicilian gambit: a new approach to the classification of antiarrhythmic drugs based on their actions on arrhythmogenic mechanisms. Task Force of the Working Group on Arrhythmias of the European Society of Cardiology. Circulation 84:1831, 1991

29. Brodsky MA, Orlov MV, Allen BJ, et al: Clinical assessment of adrenergic tone and responsiveness to beta-blocker therapy in patients with symptomatic ventricular tachycardia and no apparent structural heart disease. Am Heart J 131:51, 1996

30. Kowey PR, Marinchak RA, Rials SJ, et al: Pharmacologic and pharmacokinetic profile of class III antiarrhythmic drugs. Am J Cardiol 80:16G, 1997

31. Stafford RS, Robson DC, Misra B, et al: Rate controls and sinus rhythm maintenance in atrial fibrillation: national trends in medication use, 1980-1996. Arch Intern Med 158:2144, 1998

32. Van Gelder IC, Brugemann J, Crijns HJ: Current treatment recommendations in antiarrhythmic therapy. Drugs 55:331, 1998

33. Uchida T, Yashima M, Gotoh M, et al: Mechanism of acceleration of functional reentry in the ventricle: effects of ATP-sensitive potassium channel opener. Circulation 99:704, 1999

34. Light PE, Wallace CH, Dyck JR: Constitutively active adenosine monophosphate-activated protein kinase regulates voltage-gated sodium channels in ventricular myocytes. Circulation 107:1962, 2003

35. Meldrum DR, Cleveland JC Jr, Rowland RT, et al: Cardiac surgical implications of calcium dyshomeostasis in the heart. Ann Thorac Surg 61:1273, 1996

36. Cleveland JC Jr, Meldrum DR, Rowland RT, et al: Optimal myocardial preservation: cooling, cardioplegia, and conditioning. Ann Thorac Surg 61:760, 1996

37. Janse MJ: Why does atrial fibrillation occur? Eur Heart J 18(suppl C):C12, 1997

38. Yue L, Feng J, Gaspo R, et al: Ionic remodeling underlying action potential changes in a canine model of atrial fibrillation. Circ Res 81:512, 1997

39. Priebe L, Beuckelmann DJ: Simulation study of cellular electric properties in heart failure. Circ Res 82:1206, 1998

40. Levi AJ, Dalton GR, Hancox JC, et al: Role of intracellular sodium overload in the genesis of cardiac arrhythmias. J Cardiovasc Electrophysiol 8:700, 1997

41. Riaz K, Forker AD: Digoxin use in congestive heart failure: current status. Drugs 55:747, 1998

42. Reddy S, Benatar D, Gheorghiade M: Update on digoxin and other oral positive inotropic agents for chronic heart failure. Curr Opin Cardiol 12:233, 1997

43. Umans VA, Cornel JH, Hic C: Digoxin in patients with heart failure. N Engl J Med 337:129, 1997

44. Patterson E, Kalcich M, Scherlag BJ: Phase 1B ventricular arrhythmia in the dog: localized reentry with the mid-myocardium. J Interv Card Electrophysiol 2:145, 1998

45. Boineau JP, Cox JL: Slow ventricular activation in acute myocardial infarction: source of reentrant premature ventricular contractions. Circulation 48:702, 1973

46. Swynghedaauw B: Molecular mechanisms of myocardial remodeling. Physiol Rev 79:215, 1999

47. Koning MMG, Gho BCG, Klaarwater EV, et al: Rapid ventricular pacing produces myocardial protection by nonischemic activation of K+-ATP channels. Circulation 93:178, 1996

48. Kastor JA, Horowitz LN, Harken AH, et al: Clinical electrophysiology of ventricular tachycardia. N Engl J Med 304:1004, 1981

49. Burashnikov A, Antzelevitch C: Reinduction of atrial fibrillation immediately after termination of the arrhythmia is mediated by late phase 3 early afterdepolarization-induced triggered activity. Circulation 107:2355, 2003

50. Bozler E: The initiation of the cardiac impulse. Am J Physiol 138:273, 1943

51. Carmeliet EE, Vereecke J: Adrenaline and the plateau phase of the cardiac action potential. Pflugers Arch 313:303, 1969

52. Friedman P, Stewarts J, Fenoglio J: Survival of subendocardial Purkinje fibers after extensive myocardial infarction in dogs. Circ Res 33:597, 1973

53. Masui A, Tamura K, Tarumi N, et al: Resolution of late potentials with improvement of left ventricular systolic pressure in patients with first myocardial infarction. Clin Cardiol 20:466, 1997

54. Ferrari R, Pepi P, Ferrari F, et al: Metabolic derangement in ischemic heart disease and its therapeutic control. Am J Cardiol 82:2K, 1998

55. Pires LA, Lehmann MH, Steinman RT, et al: Sudden death in implantable cardioverter-defibrillator recipients: clinical context, arrhythmic events and device responses. J Am Coll Cardiol 33:24, 1999

56. Yee R, Connolly SJ, Gillis AM: Appropriate use of the implantable cardioverter defibrillator: a Canadian perspective. Canadian Working Group on Cardiac Pacing. Pacing Clin Electrophysiol 22:1, 1999

57. Swygman CA, Homoud MK, Link MS, et al: Technologic advances in implantable cardioverter defibrillators. Curr Opin Cardiol 14:9, 1999

58. Grimm W, Menz V, Hoffmann J, et al: Complications of third generation implantable cardioverter defibrillator therapy. Pacing Clin Electrophysiol 22:201, 1999

59. Pauli P, Wiedemann G, Dengler W, et al: Anxiety in patients with an automatic implantable cardioverter defibrillator: what differentiates them from panic patients? Psychosom Med 61:69, 1999

60. Anvari A, Gottsauner-Wolf M, Turel Z, et al: Predictors of outcome in patients with implantable cardioverter defibrillators. Cardiology 90:180, 1998

61. Movsowitz C, Marchlinski FE: Interactions between implantable cardioverter-defibrillators and class III agents. Am J Cardiol 82:41I, 1998

62. Dorian P, Newman D, Greene M: Implantable defibrillators and/or amiodarone: alternatives or complementary therapies. Int J Clin Pract 52:425, 1998

118 SHOCK

James W. Holcroft, M.D., F.A.C.S., John T. Anderson, M.D., F.A.C.S., and Matthew J. Sena, M.D.

Approach to Management of Shock

Like a Carnot engine, the heart generates power (the product of pressure and flow), and under normal conditions, it does so in an extremely efficient manner. The generated power is used to deliver nutrients to and remove waste products from metabolizing tissues, to carry heat from these tissues to the surface of the skin (where the heat is dissipated into the environment to help keep body temperature under control), and to transport hormones from one part of the body to another. If a patient's heart becomes incapable of carrying out these functions, he or she is said to be in shock.

For the purposes of treatment, it is helpful to classify shock into six main types on the basis of the underlying processes responsible for the shock state. Most cases of shock fall readily into one of these six categories; however, some cases involve more than one underlying process and thus belong to more than one category.

Classification

HYPOVOLEMIC SHOCK

In hypovolemic shock, small ventricular end-diastolic volumes lead to inadequate cardiac generation of both pressure and flow (and thus of power). Causes include bleeding, protracted vomiting or diarrhea, fluid sequestration in obstructed gut or injured tissue, excessive use of diuretics, adrenal insufficiency, diabetes insipidus, and dehydration.

INFLAMMATORY SHOCK

Inflammatory shock arises from the release of inflammatory and coagulatory mediators. It can be caused by ischemia-reperfusion injury, trauma, or infection (in which case it is sometimes referred to as septic shock). Clinical conditions capable of causing inflammatory shock include pneumonia, peritonitis, cholangitis, pyelonephritis, soft tissue infection, meningitis, mediastinitis, crush injuries, major fractures, high-velocity penetrating wounds, major burns, retained necrotic tissue, pancreatitis, anaphylaxis, and wet gangrene.

For inflammatory shock to develop, the infected or traumatized or reperfused tissues must be in proximity to a robust drainage of blood from the tissues. An avascular infection (e.g., a contained abscess), in which the inflammatory mediators do not have access to the circulation, will not cause inflammatory shock, whereas an uncontained abscess (e.g., a ruptured appendiceal abscess or an acutely drained subphrenic abscess), which allows vascular dissemination of the mediators, can do so. Similarly, dry gangrene, because of its poor vascular supply, will not cause inflammatory shock, whereas wet gangrene can.

The hemodynamic problems in inflammatory shock are caused by two basic mechanisms. The first mechanism is disruption of the microvascular endothelium, both at the inflammatory site and distally. On the one hand, the increased permeability of the endothelium gives inflammatory mediators access to the injured or infected tissues and helps promote wound healing and control of infection; on the other, it also leads to leakage of plasma into the interstitium, which results in hypovolemia and inadequate ventricular end-diastolic volumes. The second mechanism, which arises from the need to offload heat generated by the inflammatory process, is a severalfold increase in blood flow to the skin. Blood pressure falls because of cutaneous arteriolar dilation and because of sequestration of blood in the cutaneous venules and small veins.

Other problems can arise from these two basic mechanisms. Myocardial contractility may decrease, either as a result of inadequate coronary perfusion or as a direct cardiodepressant effect of the inflammatory mediators. The afterload may fall even further, presumably in an effort to produce the residual cardiac power more efficiently. The heart rate may rise in an effort to increase the cardiac output; alternatively, it may remain largely unchanged in an effort to allow more time for ventricular filling and perfusion of the coronary vasculature during diastole.

If the predominant feature of the shock state is loss of plasma volume into the interstitium through a permeable microvasculature, the patient's skin will be cool and clammy (hence the terms cold septic shock and cold inflammatory shock). The mean blood pressure and the cardiac output will both be inadequate. If, however, the blood volume has been restored or the predominant feature of the shock state is cutaneous vasodilatation, the patient's skin will be flushed and warm (hence the term warm inflammatory shock). The mean blood pressure will be low, but the cardiac output may be high as a consequence of the cutaneous arteriolar dilatation and the reduced afterload.

COMPRESSIVE SHOCK

In compressive shock, external forces compress the thin-walled chambers of the heart (the atria and the right ventricle), the great veins (systemic or pulmonary), the great arteries (systemic or pulmonary), or any combination of these. Compression of any of these structures can drastically decrease ventricular production of both pressure and flow.

Clinical conditions capable of causing compressive shock include pericardial tamponade, tension pneumothoraces, positive pressure ventilation with large tidal volumes or high airway pressures (especially in a hypovolemic patient), an elevated diaphragm (as in pregnancy), displacement of abdominal viscera through a ruptured diaphragm, and the abdominal compartment syndrome (e.g., from ascites, abdominal distention, abdominal or retroperitoneal bleeding, or a stiff abdominal wall, as in a patient with deep burns to the torso).

INTRAVASCULAR OBSTRUCTIVE SHOCK

Intravascular obstructive shock results when intravascular obstruction, excessive stiffness of the arterial walls, or obstruction of the microvasculature imposes an undue burden on the heart. The obstruction to flow can be on either the right or the left side of the heart. Causes include pulmonary valvular stenosis, pulmonary embolism, air embolism, acute respiratory distress syndrome (ARDS), aortic stenosis, calcification of the systemic arteries, thickening or stiffening of the arterial walls as a result of the loss of elastin and its replacement with collagen (as occurs in old age), and obstruction of the systemic microcirculation as a result of chronic hypertension or the arteriolar disease of diabetes. The blood pressure in the pulmonary artery or the aorta will be high; the cardiac output will be low.

NEUROGENIC SHOCK

Neurogenic shock arises from the loss of autonomic innervation of the vasculature. The arterioles, the venules, and the small veins are the vessels most strongly affected by this denervation; the arteries may be affected as well, but not to the same extent. In some cases, the denervation also involves the heart. Causes include spinal cord injury, regional anesthesia, administration of drugs that block the adrenergic nervous system (including some systemically administered anesthetic agents), certain neurologic disorders, and fainting.

In some patients (e.g., those who have a spinal cord injury or have received a regional anesthetic), the denervation is localized, which means that only the vasculature in the denervated areas will be blocked. In other patients (e.g., those who have received a general anesthetic), the vasculature throughout the body will be blocked.

All patients in neurogenic shock have small ventricular end-diastolic volumes because of the pooling of blood in the denervated venules and small veins. If the blockade is generalized or at a high enough level, the denervation can also reduce myocardial contractility and lower the heart rate. All patients also have low blood pressures because of the arteriolar denervation and the depletion of the ventricular end-diastolic volumes. In cases of distal denervation, in which the heart is not involved, the cardiac output may be high, depending on the offsetting effects of the decreased afterload and the decreased end-diastolic volumes. In cases of generalized denervation, however, the cardiac output is low.

CARDIOGENIC SHOCK

In cardiogenic shock, the heart itself, because of an intrinsic abnormality, is incapable of delivering blood into the vasculature with adequate power. Sometimes, the problem is with the muscle; sometimes, it is with the rhythm. Causes include bradyarrhythmia, tachyarrhythmia, myocardial ischemia, myocardial infarction, cardiomyopathy, myocarditis, myocardial contusion (rare), cardiac valvular insufficiency, papillary muscle rupture, and septal defects. The mean arterial pressure (MAP) is usually low, depending on the degree of compensatory constriction of the systemic arterioles; the cardiac output is always low.

Characteristic Clinical Markers

The presence of a shock state is typically signaled by one or more characteristic clinical markers [see Table 1].

HYPOTENSION

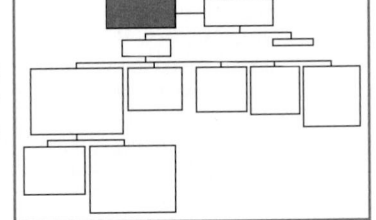

In the initial assessment and resuscitation of a patient in shock, it is usually necessary to rely on the brachial systolic pressure as measured by sphygmomanometry, with the manometer zeroed

Table 1 Clinical Markers of Possible Shock State

Clinical Marker	Value or Findings Indicative of Shock
Systolic blood pressure	
Adult	≤ 110 mm Hg
Schoolchild	≤ 100 mm Hg
Preschool child	≤ 90 mm Hg
Infant	≤ 80 mm Hg
Sinus tachycardia	
Adult	≥ 90 beats/min
Schoolchild	≥ 120 beats/min
Preschool child	≥ 140 beats/min
Infant	≥ 160 beats/min
Cutaneous vasoconstriction	Pale, cool, clammy skin with constricted subcutaneous veins
Respiratory rate	
Adult	≤ 7 or ≥ 29 breaths/min
Child	≤ 12 or ≥ 35 breaths/min
Infant	≤ 20 or ≥ 50 breaths/min
Mental changes	Anxiousness, agitation, indifference, lethargy, obtundation
Urine output	
Adult	$\leq 0.5 \ ml \cdot kg^{-1} \cdot hr^{-1}$
Child	$\leq 1.0 \ ml \cdot kg^{-1} \cdot hr^{-1}$
Infant	$\leq 2.0 \ ml \cdot kg^{-1} \cdot hr^{-1}$
Myocardial ischemia or failure	Chest pain, third heart sound, pulmonary edema, abnormal ECG
Metabolic acidemia	$[HCO_3^-] \leq 21$ mEq/L Base deficit ≥ 3 mEq/L
Hypoxemia (on room air)	
0–50 yr	≤ 90 mm Hg
51–70 yr	≤ 80 mm Hg
≥ 71 yr	≤ 70 mm Hg

at the midaxillary line and with the pressures referenced to the atmosphere (as all physiologic pressures are unless otherwise specified).

The brachial systolic pressure has several advantages in this context: it is easy to measure and understand, it can be measured in almost any setting, and its measurement does not require expensive, complicated, or difficult-to-calibrate equipment. Moreover, in the treatment of shock, it is the pressure with which most physicians feel most comfortable. Nonetheless, the brachial systolic pressure is not the most pertinent variable in the early stages of resuscitation. The mean aortic root pressure is more relevant [see Figure 1]. This pressure, however, usually is not available until a later stage of resuscitation, when it is possible to cannulate and directly monitor the intra-arterial pressures (see below).

A low brachial systolic pressure can serve as an indicator of shock, though what constitutes a significantly low value depends to an extent on the age of the patient [see Table 1]. In an adult, a low brachial systolic pressure (≤ 110 mm Hg) frequently indicates shock; a very low brachial peak-systolic pressure (≤ 89 mm Hg) almost always does, especially in a patient who is under stress. (Admittedly, many normal patients, especially young women, may have a systolic pressure of 89 mm Hg or lower when supine, but only when in an unstressed state.

Approach to Management of Shock

Patient appears to be in shock

Characteristic clinical markers:
- Hypotension
- Tachycardia or bradycardia
- Tachypnea
- Cutaneous hypoperfusion
- Mental abnormalities
- Oliguria
- Myocardial ischemia
- Metabolic acidemia
- Hypoxemia

Shock persists

Initiate specific therapy based on type of shock present.

Hypovolemic or inflammatory shock

Control bleeding; obtain vascular access; infuse crystalloid (e.g., normal saline) in initial boluses of 60 ml/kg body weight; give RBCs to maintain [Hb] ≥ 9 g/dl; treat pain, hypothermia, acidemia, and coagulopathy. *Goals:* resolution of clinical abnormalities and generation of adequate pressure to perfuse CNS and organs with obstructed arterial inflow.

If patient remains unstable, transfer to setting where MAP and CVP can be transduced. *Goal:* resolution of shock without excessive CVP. If necessary, give dobutamine (5–15 $\mu g \cdot kg^{-1} \cdot min^{-1}$) or milrinone (loading dose followed by infusion of 0.375–0.750 $\mu g \cdot kg^{-1} \cdot min^{-1}$).

Insert Swan-Ganz catheter if patient (1) requires excessive fluid, (2) requires inotropes for > 30 min, (3) might need vasoconstrictors, (4) may have nonviable myocardium, or (5) requires excessively high F_IO_2.

Decide on priority for subsequent resuscitation:

- To ensure tissue perfusion (even at the cost of possible edema formation and increased ventricular O_2 requirements), or

- To minimize edema and ventricular O_2 requirements (even at the cost of possible slow or incomplete resuscitation from shock).

Compressive shock

Compression of heart or great vessels, as immediately life-threatening condition (see above), should already have been treated. Nevertheless, reassess periodically (specifically, for adverse effects of mechanical ventilation and for abdominal compartment syndrome).

If compressive shock is a possibility, insert Swan-Ganz catheter. Treat as for hypovolemic or inflammatory shock (see left).

Priority is ensuring resuscitation; edema is not a major problem, and myocardium is not at risk

Infuse fluids. *Goal:* RVEDV and LVEDV ≥ normal (2.5 ml/kg).

Give inotropes. *Goal:* normal contractility in both right ventricle (0.4 mm Hg/ml) and left (2 mm Hg/ml).

If absolutely necessary, *and only as last resort,* give vasopressors, starting with vasopressin. If HR ≤ 89 beats/min, add dopamine (2–20 $\mu g \cdot kg^{-1} \cdot min^{-1}$). If HR ≥ 90 beats/min, use norepinephrine (2–12 μg/kg). Increase left ventricular afterload until it equals contractility; do not let it exceed contractility except in desperate cases.

Priority is minimizing edema formation and protecting heart; less than full resuscitation is acceptable

Give fluids or diuretics (e.g., furosemide, 10–40 mg) as needed. *Goal:* either RVEDV or LVEDV (whichever is smaller) normal, with neither volume below normal.

If contractility is subnormal on either side, increase with dobutamine or milrinone. If it is supranormal on both sides, give beta blocker, starting with esmolol (loading dose followed by infusion of 50 $\mu g \cdot kg^{-1} \cdot min^{-1}$, increased as needed) and switching to metoprolol (5–15 μg q. 6 hr). *Goal:* normal contractility on both right and left.

Adjust left ventricular afterload to equal 50% of contractility. If afterload ≤ 49% of contractility, give dopamine or dobutamine. Rarely (as last resort), use vasopressin and norepinephrine, but reassess frequently.

If afterload ≥ 51% of contractility, reduce arterial stiffness with diuretic, beta blocker, ACE inhibitor (e.g., enalaprilat, 1.25–5.0 mg q. 6 hr), and nitroglycerin (5–200 $\mu g \cdot kg^{-1} \cdot min^{-1}$).

If HR ≥ 90 beats/min, increase beta blockade until limited by hypotension or wheezing. If HR is still too fast, add calcium channel blocker (e.g., diltiazem, 5–15 mg/hr).

Identify and treat any immediately life-threatening conditions:
- Dysrhythmias
- Airway compromise, inadequate ventilation or compression of heart and great vessels (or both)
- Bleeding
- Medical emergencies

Shock resolves

Intravascular obstructive shock

Reduce RVESP and LVESP by decreasing arterial stiffness with diuretics, beta blockers, ACE inhibitors, and nitroglycerin.

If pressures remain too high, insert Swan-Ganz catheter. Treat as for hypovolemic or inflammatory shock (see left).

If pulmonary vasculature is obstructed, ventilator mode may have to be changed. If systemic vasculature is obstructed, aortic counterpulsating balloon pump may be needed.

Neurogenic shock

Place in Trendelenburg position.

Infuse fluids as necessary, and give vasoconstrictors (dopamine if HR $\leq$ 89 beats/min; norepinephrine if HR $\geq$ 90 beats/min).

Periodically reassess for possibility of hypovolemia or other cause of inadequate end-diastolic volume (e.g., cardiac compression). If such possibility is significant, insert Swan-Ganz catheter. Treat as for hypovolemic or inflammatory shock (see left).

Cardiogenic shock

If RVEDV and LVEDV seem too large, initiate diuresis.

Initiate beta blockade to keep HR $\leq$ 89 beats/min unless patient is hypotensive or wheezing.

Control LVESP. Reduce arterial stiffness with more aggressive diuresis, increased beta blockade, ACE inhibition, and nitroglycerin.

Goals: adequate MAP, adequate peripheral perfusion, and HR $\leq$ 89 beats/min, with no sign of myocardial ischemia.

If efforts are unsuccessful, insert Swan-Ganz catheter. Adjust left ventricular afterload to equal 50% of contractility. Balloon pump, coronary angioplasty, or cardiac surgery may be required. If problem is with right ventricle, adjustment of ventilator may help.

The pain or stress associated with an injury or acute illness will drive that normally low pressure to much higher levels, particularly in well-conditioned patients who are ideally suited to deal with threats to the cardiovascular system. A patient whose brachial systolic pressure is low in the presence of stress can be assumed to be in shock.) A sustained (> 30 seconds) systolic pressure drop greater than 10 mm Hg in a patient who has arisen from a supine to an upright position can also be an indicator of underlying shock.

The absence of hypotension does not, however, rule out shock. Adrenergic discharge and the release of circulating vasoconstrictors (e.g., vasopressin and angiotensin) and locally produced vasoconstrictors (e.g., endothelin) often sustain blood pressure during shock despite volume depletion or depressed myocardial contractility. As a result, visceral hypoperfusion may precede clinically evident changes in the supine blood pressure. In addition, some forms of shock can even be associated with hypertension (as in a hypertensive crisis). Finally, the definition of hypotension can vary, depending on the patient's usual blood pressure, which the physician may not know. For example, in a patient with severe preexisting hypertension, a brachial systolic pressure of 120 mm Hg might be an indicator of shock.

TACHYCARDIA OR BRADYCARDIA

The pulse rate—perhaps the most evident of all the physical findings in clinical medicine—can increase in shock, and the possibility of shock should be considered in any patient with a tachycardia. An abnormally high pulse rate—with "high" determined in relation to the patient's age [see Table 1]—can serve as an indicator of shock.

The absence of tachycardia should not, however, be taken as a sign that the patient is not in shock. A slow or normal heart rate may even indicate that decompensation is imminent. In severe shock, the pulse rate may have to slow down to allow more time both for ventricular filling and for coronary perfusion of the myocardium.

TACHYPNEA AND BRADYPNEA

Any patient with tachypnea must be promptly evaluated not only for possible pulmonary insufficiency but also for possible shock. The rapid respiratory rate may be a response to a metabolic acidemia; it may also be a means of compensating for inadequate filling of the ventricles, in that it will lower the mean intrathoracic pressure and facilitate the influx of blood into the heart from the capacitance venules and small veins in the periphery. In severe decompensated shock, the respiratory rate may fall to very low levels, perhaps because of ischemia in the muscles providing the ventilation.[1]

CUTANEOUS HYPOPERFUSION

Diminished skin perfusion is often the first sign of shock. In all types of shock other than warm inflammatory shock and neurogenic shock, blood flow to the skin is reduced because of adrenergic discharge and high circulating levels of vasopressin and angiotensin II. The result is the pale, cool, and clammy skin of a person exhibiting the fight-or-flight reaction. Cutaneous hypoper-

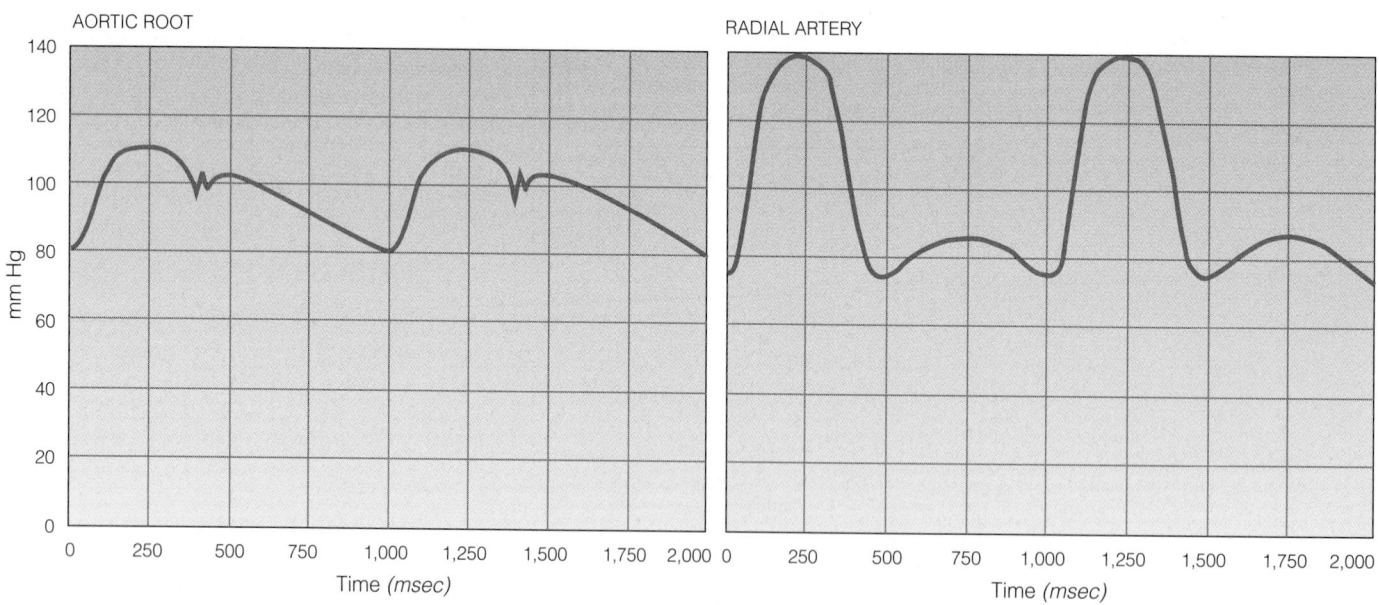

Figure 1 The mean pressure is defined as the area under a pressure tracing divided by the time needed to produce the tracing. A pressure wave in the ascending aorta with a blood pressure of 110/80 mm Hg will have the same mean pressure as a pressure wave in the radial artery of the same patient, even though the radial artery pressure might be 140/75 mm Hg. The systolic pressure in the radial artery is usually inscribed more rapidly. Therefore, even though the peak pressure in the radial artery is greater than that in the aorta, the areas under the tracings will be the same for the two vessels. Sometimes, the mean pressure can be approximated by taking one third of the difference between the systolic and diastolic pressures and adding that value to the diastolic pressure. Frequently, however, the formula does not work. In this example, the mean aortic pressure would be approximated at 90 mm Hg, whereas the mean radial artery pressure would be approximated at 97 mm Hg. Such results would be impossible: if the mean pressure in the radial artery were greater than the mean pressure in the aorta, blood would flow backward. This confusion is avoided by measuring the area under the curve and calculating the mean pressure exactly, which can be done with computer circuits that are available in all modern pressure-monitoring systems. It should also be noted that the systolic pressure in the radial artery is about 30 mm Hg higher than the systolic pressure in the aortic root. In extreme cases, it can be as much as 80 mm Hg higher.

fusion is not specific for shock—it can also be the result of hypothermia, for example—but it can be a warning that the patient may decompensate at any time.

MENTAL ABNORMALITIES

Patients in severe shock frequently exhibit mental abnormalities, which can range from anxiousness to agitation to indifference to obtundation. These findings are not sensitive—indeed, they develop only in the late stages of shock—nor are they specific. They are, however, a strong warning to the physician that something must be done quickly. The body protects the blood supply to the brain at all costs. Changes in mental status as a result of severe shock suggest impending circulatory collapse.

OLIGURIA

The stress imposed by all forms of shock—in the absence of diuretic use, high alcohol levels, or administration of radiographic contrast agents—stimulates the release of vasopressin (antidiuretic hormone) and aldosterone (through activation of the angiotensin system).[2,3] The result is oliguria, which is a sign of stress at the very least and a sign of decreased blood flow to the kidneys in extreme cases.

Whenever the diagnosis of shock is being entertained, a Foley catheter should be placed. Successful treatment should reduce the stress and decrease the plasma levels of vasopressin and aldosterone. It should also increase renal blood flow if the shock is indeed so severe that inadequate blood flow to the kidneys is compromising their viability. With successful treatment, the urine output should improve; if it does not, further therapeutic measures are probably necessary.

MYOCARDIAL ISCHEMIA

Electrocardiography is indicated whenever the suspicion of shock arises. The electrocardiogram may show signs of ischemia, which may be caused either by a primary myocardial problem or by a secondary extracardiac problem (e.g., hypotension resulting from hemorrhage). In either case, the presence of myocardial ischemia should prompt quick action.

METABOLIC ACIDEMIA

Metabolic acidemia, as a sign of shock, may be manifested by an increased respiratory rate. Serum chemistry may also demonstrate a decrease in the total concentration of carbon dioxide (bicarbonate plus dissolved CO_2), but analysis of blood gases is usually required for confirmation. The acidosis may take the form of either a low calculated bicarbonate level or a base deficit. Often, it does not become evident until after the shock has been recognized and treatment is under way. In severe, untreated shock, the anaerobic products of metabolism are confined to the periphery; they may not be washed into the central circulation until resuscitation has reestablished some flow to the ischemic tissues. The degree of acidosis after resuscitation can, however, provide information about the duration and severity of the initial insult.

HYPOXEMIA

Shock may be associated with significant arterial hypoxemia. Low flow results in marked desaturation of the blood leaving the metabolizing peripheral tissue, which eventually ends up in the pulmonary artery (yielding a low mixed venous oxygen saturation $[S_{mv}O_2]$). In patients with coexisting pulmonary dysfunction and an intrapulmonary shunt, the markedly desaturated pulmonary arterial blood is only partially saturated as it passes through the lungs, ultimately mixing with fully saturated blood. The increased

admixture of oxygen-poor blood results in a reduced oxygen saturation in the systemic arterial blood.

Identification and Treatment of Immediately Life-Threatening Conditions

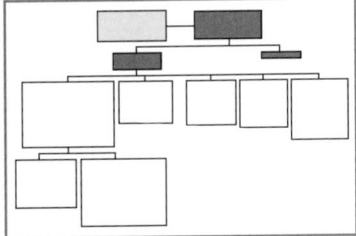

If the patient shows signs suggestive of shock, the next step is to search for and treat any conditions that could be immediately fatal, such as (1) dysrhythmias; (2) compromise of the airway, inadequate ventilation, compression of the heart, compression of the great vessels, or any combination of these conditions (they often go together); (3) acute intravascular obstruction of the great vessels; (4) bleeding; and (5) certain life-threatening medical conditions (e.g., anaphylaxis, severe electrolyte disturbances, and life-threatening endocrine abnormalities).

There are roughly 10 to 20 clinical entities (depending on how one categorizes them) that can kill a patient quickly. Identification and management of these conditions requires early and continuous patient assessment and depends heavily on pattern recognition. Although not all of these entities are immediately fatal, all are life-threatening. Delays in recognition will increase the duration of hypoperfusion and may result in significant late morbidity and mortality related to multiple organ failure.

DYSRHYTHMIAS

Given that an ECG should be obtained promptly in any case of suspected shock, any dysrhythmia present is usually recognized early in the course of resuscitation. If the patient is agonal, cardioversion should be performed. If the patient turns out to be in ventricular fibrillation, ventricular tachycardia, or atrial fibrillation, cardioversion may restore him or her to life with full neurologic function. Cardioversion takes precedence over all other resuscitative efforts, including gaining airway control and obtaining I.V. access (though if the team taking care of the patient can perform cardioversion, secure the airway, and gain I.V. access at the same time, it should do so). The goal is to get blood flowing again to the brain. Even if the initial reperfusion is with desaturated blood, it is better than no perfusion at all. If the agonal patient turns out to be in asystole, cardioversion will be of no value. It is likely, however, that no other treatment will restore an asystolic patient to life with full neurologic function either. In the case of asystole, it rarely makes any difference what mode of therapy is attempted—or, indeed, whether therapy is attempted at all.

A nonagonal patient should be treated in accordance with standard resuscitation routines [see 116 Cardiac Resuscitation and 117 Acute Cardiac Dysrhythmia].

COMPROMISE OF AIRWAY, INADEQUATE VENTILATION, AND COMPRESSION OF HEART OR GREAT VESSELS

If a patient can talk in a full voice without undue effort, the airway can be assumed to be intact. Supplemental oxygen should be given via a mask or nasal prongs; nothing else need be done.

If the patient cannot talk in a full voice, possible compromise of the airway and possible inadequate ventilation must be assumed. Causes range from loss of protective reflexes to mechanical obstruction to a host of other problems that can limit ventilation. Sometimes, a jaw thrust is all that is needed for diagnosis and treatment of the problem. In cases of profound shock, however,

Table 2 Selected Cardiopulmonary Variables in
Resting Subjects of Different Age-Adjusted Weights

Height (ft, in)	Lean Weight (kg)	Approximate Lean Weight (kg)	O_2 Consumption (ml/min)	Cardiac Output (L/min)	Tidal Volume (ml)
5'0"	48.9	50	175	5.0	350
5'6"	59.1	60	210	6.0	420
6'0"	70.4	70	245	7.0	490
6'6"	82.6	83	290	8.3	580

the patient should be intubated. Initially, the patient should be ventilated by using an Ambu bag with 100% oxygen; later, when the situation has stabilized sufficiently, the patient should be switched to mechanical ventilation.

In the mechanical ventilation of a patient in severe shock, the goal is to achieve ventilation and oxygenation without unduly compromising cardiac production of pressure and flow. The ventilator should be set so as to produce ventilation with a minimal mean airway pressure (mean pressure being defined as the integral of the pressure over time divided by the time over which the pressure is produced). A respiratory rate of 12 to 15 breaths/min and an initial tidal volume of approximately 7 to 8 ml/kg lean body weight should result in sufficient alveolar ventilation to normalize the carbon dioxide tension (mild hyperventilation is acceptable if the patient has a profound acidemia) [see Table 2 and Sidebar Expectations for Cardiopulmonary Values in Patients of Different Sizes and Ages]. Although a lung-protective ventilation strategy may ultimately be desirable in certain patients who have sustained lung injury, the initial ventilatory settings should be adjusted so that respiratory acidosis is avoided during the acute resuscitation phase.[4] The end-expiratory pressure should be set at 0 mm Hg. Oxygenation should be assured with a fractional concentration of inspired oxygen (F_1O_2) of 1.00.

When blood gas analysis becomes available, the ventilator should be adjusted to ensure adequate arterial oxygen saturation (S_aO_2) and adequate alveolar ventilation. Managing the ventilator during the acute resuscitation of a patient in severe shock is a dynamic process. Close attention to the tidal volume and the airway pressure is necessary to ensure adequate gas exchange and avoid unnecessary cardiovascular sequelae and potential lung injury [see 121 Mechanical Ventilation and 120 Pulmonary Insufficiency].

Even when intubation appears to have been successful and the ventilator seems to be functioning normally, there are still many things that can go wrong. Misplacement or displacement of the endotracheal tube and malfunction of the ventilator can be hard to detect. If the chest wall does not rise with inspiration, the patient should be removed from the ventilator, and the almost foolproof Ambu bag should again be used to ensure adequate airflow through the endotracheal tube. Malfunction is rare with modern ventilators, but it remains a potential problem that must be eliminated. The easiest way of dealing with ventilator malfunction is to change the ventilator.

If increasing abdominal distention is apparent, the possibility of esophageal intubation or displacement of the endotracheal tube into the hypopharynx should be considered. Whenever the placement of the tube is questionable, reintubation is mandatory. Reintubation is obviously hazardous in these circumstances, but it is clearly preferable to leaving a misplaced endotracheal tube in place. If breath sounds are absent on the left, right mainstem

bronchial intubation is a possibility. The tube should be withdrawn into the trachea (or what one believes to be the trachea).

If the endotracheal tube is obstructed by clotted blood or inspissated secretions, the obstruction can usually be cleared by suctioning. If this measure is unsuccessful, the patient should be reintubated.

Bleeding in the tracheobronchial tree (from injuries or from friable bronchial mucosa or tumor tissue) can eliminate ventilation from the lung segment supplied by the injured or obstructed bronchus and flood the initially uninjured lung with blood. If the bleeding is thought to be coming from the left lung, the endotracheal tube should be advanced into the right mainstem bronchus. Bleeding from the right lung is more problematic. Selective left mainstem intubation is usually impossible under emergency conditions. If selective mainstem intubation is not feasible or substantial bleeding continues on either side, definitive control of the bleeding will have to be obtained by means of either endobronchial techniques or open surgical intervention.

Bleeding into the pleural cavity can eliminate ventilation of the affected side and push the mediastinum into the nonbleeding side. This problem is treated with insertion of a chest tube and, if necessary, surgical intervention.

Pneumothoraces may arise from injuries to the lung, from attempts to place a central venous line, or from positive pressure ventilation. They are treated by inserting a chest tube.

Tension pneumothoraces sometimes develop in a patient who is breathing spontaneously; more often, however, they are created by superimposition of positive pressure ventilation on a previously existing pneumothorax. The tension pneumothorax not only eliminates ventilation on the side of the pneumothorax but also limits ventilation on the uninjured side and compresses the heart and great vessels. Characteristic signs include decreased or absent breath sounds on the involved side, a hyperresonant hemithorax, and, if the patient is normovolemic, distended neck veins. (A tracheal shift—a commonly described feature in patients with tension pneumothoraces—is hard to detect and, in our experience, rarely helpful in making the diagnosis.) A tension pneumothorax should be the first diagnosis considered in any patient who suddenly decompensates when placed on positive pressure ventilation. Treatment consists of needle decompression followed by tube thoracostomy.

Air leaks almost always mean loss of ventilation on the side of the leak. If they are large, they also mean loss of ventilation on the uninjured side, in that the administered air preferentially exits the airway through the chest wall defect or the chest tube on the injured side. A left-side leak can sometimes be treated by advancing the endotracheal tube into the right mainstem bronchus; a right-side leak usually necessitates surgical intervention, as does any large leak that does not close quickly.

Acute pericardial tamponade is usually manifested by muffled heart tones and occasionally by an exaggerated (> 10 mm Hg)

Expectations for Cardiopulmonary Values in Patients of Different Sizes and Ages

Some numerical descriptors of physiologic variables that can be altered in shock (e.g., blood pressure, body temperature, and arterial pH) are independent of the amount of metabolically active tissue the patient has; others (e.g., tidal volume, minute ventilation, ventricular end-diastolic volumes, stroke volume, cardiac output, oxygen consumption, carbon dioxide production, and caloric needs) are not.

The question of how to interpret, or index, these size-dependent variables dates back at least to the 1800s. It seemed logical at that time (and still seems so today) to index the variables to body surface area.[69] The body surface, as the site where the body dissipates its heat into the environment, plays a critical role in keeping the body from becoming overheated. The amount of heat produced by the body in a resting condition depends on the mass of the metabolizing tissue. (During exercise or illness, more heat is generated from the same mass of tissue. Presumably, humans evolved so as to be able to deal with both resting and stressful conditions. In either type of condition, however, some surface area through which heat can be dissipated is necessary.) The amount and activity of metabolically active tissue correlates with oxygen consumption. Thus, a patient's body surface area should correlate with the amount of heat generated by his or her metabolizing tissue, the mass and activity of the metabolizing tissue, and the oxygen consumption.

In the 1920s, when it became possible to measure cardiac output as part of metabolic studies, many investigators began to express cardiac output, as well as metabolic rate, in terms of body surface area, on the grounds that these two quantities should also be correlated. Although it was recognized that the relation was not necessarily a linear one, this approach to indexing worked, in the sense that it minimized some of the inherent variability observed in nonindexed values. By the end of the 1920s, body surface area had become the most commonly used parameter for indexing both metabolic rate and cardiac output to body size.[70,71]

In the 1930s, however, Max Kleiber made the empirical observation that the metabolic rates—and presumably the cardiac outputs and some of the ventilatory parameters—of members of one species of animals could best be compared with those of another species by indexing to body weight raised to the three-fourths power. Such indexing seemed to reduce variability even more effectively than indexing to body surface area did, though it was difficult to explain why.[72]

Over the ensuing six decades, more and more accumulated evidence came to support Kleiber's contention, but only in the past two decades have his observations been satisfactorily explained. It now seems established that the Kleiber hypothesis can be proved by using a mathematical model that takes into account not only the thermodynamic considerations just described but also the fractal geometry of the vasculature in metabolizing organs and the thermodynamic constraints placed on such systems.[73]

Thus, the problem of correlating size-dependent cardiopulmonary variables between species seems to be settled, and the different metabolic rates, cardiac outputs, and minute ventilations in different species appear to be well explained. However, the practice of using body weight raised to the three-fourths power does not solve the problem of how to make comparisons between members of the same species (e.g., between a large mouse and a small one or between a linebacker and a ballerina). In addressing this second problem, some clinicians, particularly those with a primary interest in the cardiovascular system, continue to index cardiopulmonary variables to body surface area. Others, particularly those with a primary interest in the respiratory system, favor indexing to body weight instead. A few prefer to use body weight raised to the three-fourths power. Still others choose not to index at all.

Not only is there no consensus on the preferred indexing method, but there also is no agreement on how and whether to adjust for obesity and aging. Body surface area is typically calculated on the basis of height and weight. Usually, the measured weight is used, which includes the weight of the fat. Thus, the calculation gives equal emphasis to metabolically active muscle and to metabolically inactive fat. Old age introduces a similar problem: for a given weight, older patients have less lean muscle mass and more fat than younger patients do. Some authors make an adjustment for age; others do not.

(continued)

---

decrease in systolic blood pressure on spontaneous breathing. If the patient is not hypovolemic, the neck veins are typically distended. Nowadays, the diagnosis is frequently confirmed by echocardiography (if that modality is immediately available). Treatment consists of needle decompression or surgical creation of a pericardial window. Chronic tamponade can also cause shock but may not give rise to the findings characteristic of acute tamponade. The diagnosis usually is made by means of echocardiography. Treatment is the same as for acute tamponade.

Diaphragmatic rupture and the ensuing intrusion of abdominal viscera into the chest can compress the venae cavae, the heart, the pulmonary arteries, the pulmonary microvasculature, the pulmonary veins, the left atrium, and the lungs. Treatment consists of operative reduction and repair.

The abdominal compartment syndrome can be caused by ascites, intestinal distention or edema, intra-abdominal or retroperitoneal bleeding, or noncompliance of the abdominal wall (as in patients with deep burns of the torso). The result is compression of the vasculature of the organs within the abdomen and intrusion of the diaphragm into the chest, which compromise ventilation and decrease ventricular end-diastolic volumes. If the patient is also hypovolemic, the hemodynamic consequences can be devastating. Infusion of fluid can restore ventricular end-diastolic volumes but can also worsen the underlying problem, either by increasing the central venous pressure (CVP) and encouraging the development of ascites or edema or by exacerbating bleeding.[5-7] The situation is made even worse because the increased venous pressures further reduce the perfusion pressures (calculated as MAP minus the venous pressure) in the organs at risk.

Initial treatment of ascites consists of paracentesis of just enough fluid to decrease the abdominal pressure, but no more. Treatment of intestinal edema may necessitate opening the abdomen. Bleeding may be controllable by operative or endovascular means; if such measures fail to control bleeding, the abdomen may have to be opened and left open. Treatment of the burned abdominal wall may involve escharotomies.

Pregnancy can elevate the diaphragm and complicate a shock state. If a woman in the late stages of pregnancy is thought to be in shock, she should be turned onto her left side to relieve compression of the right common iliac vein and the inferior vena cava. If shock persists, one may consider attempting to induce labor or perform a cesarean section.

INTRAVASCULAR OBSTRUCTION OF GREAT VESSELS

To treat pulmonary thromboembolism, aggressive anticoagulation with heparin, at the very least, is required; fibrinolytics, sometimes infused through a pulmonary arterial catheter, may also be necessary [*see 85 Venous Thromboembolism*].

Right-side air embolism can arise either from penetrating injuries to large veins in the upper part of the body or from percutaneous

Expectations for Cardiopulmonary Values in Patients of Different Sizes and Ages (*continued*)

Even though there is, at present, no unanimity on how best to deal with these issues, it is obvious that some form of indexing (or nonindexing) is necessary, both for the management of patients and for the creation of written reference sources. Our current practice is to start with the assumption that lean persons (e.g., those with a body mass index [BMI] of 21 or so) do not have very much body fat. Assuming a BMI of 21, we then use the patient's height to assign a weight, which we assume is mostly metabolically active tissue. This assigned weight is employed in interpreting the size-dependent variables. For patients 50 years of age or younger, we use the assigned weight as is. For patients 51 years of age or older, we calculate an age-adjusted lean weight based on the assumption that 1% of body weight has been lost each year after the age of 50.[74] (Although this loss is in fact exponential in nature, we have not found it necessary to reflect this fact in the calculation.) As an example, with an 83-year old patient, we subtract 33% from the lean weight that the patient would have had at 50 years of age. For older subjects who have kept themselves in particularly good condition, we assume that 0.5% of body weight has been lost each year after the age of 50. Finally, we make subjective adjustments if muscle mass appears to be either abnormally large (as in male patients who worked out extensively when young) or abnormally small (as in malnourished patients or patients with a preexisting prolonged critical illness).

This practice means that we do not use the patient's actual weight when setting up the ventilator or when managing the patient on the basis of other size-dependent variables. The weight at the time of measurement can be inflated by fluid resuscitation, the hardware used for fracture fixation, bedclothes, or obesity. It can also be difficult to measure accurately in critically ill patients, who often cannot easily be moved to a bedside scale. We also do not adjust for gender. For longevity and freedom from debilitating illnesses, a BMI of 21 is close to ideal for both men and women (though it appears that a slightly higher fat percentage may be appropriate for women). The value we use is also conveniently close to the predicted body weight that has been advocated for use in setting tidal volumes.[4,75]

We have found it useful to assign expected values for size-dependent cardiopulmonary variables in subjects of different age-adjusted lean weights who are resting, fasting, well conditioned, supine, spontaneously breathing, and in a thermoneutral environment [see Table 2]. We make three assumptions in assigning these values, using the age-adjusted lean weight for all of the calculations:

1. The normal resting oxygen consumption is 3.5 ml • kg^{-1} • min^{-1}.
2. The normal resting cardiac output is 100 ml • kg^{-1} • min^{-1}.
3. The normal resting tidal volume is 7 ml/kg.

In practice, we usually approximate the height to the nearest half-foot [see Table 2], then approximate the lean weight for that approximate height. Once this is done, the values for oxygen consumption, cardiac output, and tidal volume tend to come out in a pleasing, almost linear way. We then make any additional adjustments necessary—in particular, for age and cardiovascular variables.

An example will demonstrate how use of the age-adjusted lean weight can influence assessment and treatment. The hypothetical patient is an 83-year-old man with an admission weight of 80 kg and a height of 5 feet 6 inches. If a Swan-Ganz catheter were in place, one would expect a cardiac output of 8 L/min. The patient's age-adjusted lean weight, however, is 40 kg (60 kg was the lean weight at 50 years of age, minus 33% for the subsequent 33 years—on the assumption the patient did not work out much over the past few decades). One would expect a resting cardiac output of 4 L/min. (We would accept this value unless the patient had excessive metabolic needs.) This is not an unusual example; one could easily think of more extreme cases. The patient in this example has a BMI of 28, and there are many patients in the ICU today with indices that exceed this level.

puncture of a large central vein in the upper part of the body with a large-bore needle (if the needle is unintentionally left open to atmospheric pressure and air). In both situations, the air typically gains access to the venous system during spontaneous deep breathing. Patients are particularly vulnerable when upright. Right-side air embolism can also arise as a complication of insufflation of gas into the peritoneal cavity during laparoscopy.[8]

In all of these situations, the air that gains access to the veins can form an obstructing air bubble in the outflow tract of the right ventricle. Treatable sources of air should be searched for and eliminated, and 100% oxygen should be administered to wash out residual nitrogen in the trapped air. The patient should be placed in the Trendelenburg position with the left side down to induce translocation of air from the outlet of the right ventricle to the apex of the chamber. A long central venous catheter should then be advanced centrally to allow aspiration of any air that may be present.

Left-side air embolism can arise from right-side air embolism if the right-side air embolizes to the pulmonary microvasculature, backs up blood in the right side of the heart, increases pressures in the right atrium, and opens up a potentially patent foramen ovale. It can also be the consequence of a penetrating injury to the lung parenchyma (either from trauma or from a needle puncture) in a patient placed on positive pressure ventilation: the positive airway pressure can push air from an injured bronchus into an adjacent injured pulmonary vein. The air and its contained nitrogen can occlude the vasculature of the brain and heart, as well as that of other organs. The diagnosis is usually made when a patient with a penetrating thoracic injury suddenly and catastrophically decompensates after initiation of positive pressure ventilation. (The differential diagnosis in this case consists of tension pneumothorax and air embolism. Accordingly, the first therapeutic measure is to insert chest tubes on both the right and the left. If it turns out that the patient has not had a tension pneumothorax, the diagnosis of possible air embolism should be kept in mind as other conditions are ruled out.)

Treatment consists of surgical control. In the case of a penetrating injury, the chest should be opened through an anterolateral thoracotomy on the side with the suspected injury. The hilum of the injured lung should be cross-clamped. Then, if the right side was opened first, the incision should be extended into the left chest. The heart should be massaged while the descending thoracic aorta is compressed. Vasoconstrictors should be given to increase the aortic pressure and to drive the air bubbles through and out of the arterial circulation. If neither side of the chest is known to have had a penetrating injury, the left side should be opened first. The primary goal of treatment is to prevent further embolism. Thus, if the left chest is opened first and no injury to the lung is detected, yet the diagnosis is certain (based on the finding of bubbles of air in the coronary arteries), the incision should be carried into the right chest in an effort to find a treatable injury there.

BLEEDING

Bleeding should be controlled by any means necessary. In some cases (e.g., bleeding from an easily accessible site in an extremity), compression will suffice; in others, immobilization of a fracture may be enough; in still others, operative control (e.g., for a ruptured spleen), endoscopic control (e.g., for GI hemorrhage), or endovascular control (e.g., for arterial hemorrhage after a severe pelvic fracture) may be possible. In any case, control is paramount: it makes no sense to infuse fluid or blood or to persist with ancillary measures while controllable bleeding continues unabated.

MEDICAL EMERGENCIES

In the appropriate clinical circumstances, early consideration should be given to certain medical conditions that may cause shock. In diabetic patients, severe hypoglycemia should always be considered. Rapid assessment with a bedside glucose monitor or empirical I.V. dextrose therapy may prevent the neurologic consequences of prolonged hypoglycemia. Anaphylaxis can be addressed with I.V. or subcutaneous epinephrine and antihistamine therapy and may help prevent life-threatening airway and circulatory compromise. In patients with significant renal dysfunction, life-threatening electrolyte abnormalities should always be considered. Finally, whenever standard resuscitative measures are unsuccessful in reversing shock, severe endocrine abnormalities (e.g., addisonian crisis and myxedema), though often difficult to diagnose, should be considered.

Specific Treatment Based on Category of Shock

If shock persists after immediately life-threatening conditions have been treated, the next step is to categorize the shock state on the basis of the underlying physiologic abnormality and treat the patient accordingly.

As a rule, all that is needed to make this preliminary classification is the history, the physical examination, a chest x-ray, an ECG, and, in some cases, a complete blood count, electrolyte concentrations, a glucose level, and arterial blood gas analysis. The categorization is seldom neat: more than one cause of cardiovascular inadequacy is usually present, as when a patient with a myocardial infarction requires mechanical ventilation or when a patient with a ruptured abdominal aortic aneurysm has a distended and tight abdomen. Nevertheless, classification is useful, in that it focuses the physician's attention on the primary problem, which should be treated first.

Management of Hypovolemic or Inflammatory Shock

CONTROL OF BLEEDING AND ONGOING INFLAMMATION

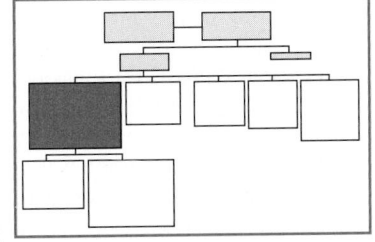

At first glance, it might seem obvious that treatment of the underlying causes of shock should have the highest priority. This is indeed the case with hypovolemic shock caused by hemorrhage; however, with inflammatory shock, a temporary delay in source control (e.g., abscess drainage or tissue debridement) may be warranted until the patient has been adequately resuscitated. This is a particularly important consideration when the process of source control is likely to result in further cardiovascular compromise. An obvious example is the patient who requires a laparotomy for a hollow viscus perforation. In this situation, briefly delaying administration of a vasodilating inhaled anesthetic while intra-

vascular volume is restored may prevent cardiovascular collapse during anesthetic induction.

At the risk of belaboring the obvious again, it must be emphasized that early resuscitation should be the goal. Delaying recognition and treatment by as little as several hours may result in increased mortality.[9] Once resuscitation has been initiated and the physiologic abnormalities addressed, source control becomes the priority. From a practical standpoint, these two processes are frequently performed in parallel—that is, resuscitation continues while the infectious or inflammatory source is being addressed.

VASCULAR ACCESS

On the assumptions that an airway has been established, that the patient is being ventilated, and that bleeding is being controlled, the next step is to obtain vascular access (this is frequently done simultaneously). If possible, superficial veins in the upper extremities should be percutaneously cannulated with two large-bore catheters. If this is impossible, venous access can be achieved by means of cutdown on veins in the extremities or percutaneous puncture of central veins; access to the bone marrow can be obtained by means of percutaneous insertion of a thick needle through cortical bone.

Cutdowns in the upper extremity cause little morbidity. They sometimes take time to perform, however, and the veins may be thrombosed from earlier use. The cephalic vein at the shoulder is less likely to be thrombosed, but it lies below the deep fascia and is sometimes difficult to isolate. The external jugular vein is deep to the platysma and can be difficult to identify when the lighting is poor. The saphenous vein at the ankle is readily exposed by cutdown and is large and easy to cannulate; however, it cannot be used if there is extensive trauma to the extremity, and if the cannula is left in place for more than 24 hours, superficial thrombophlebitis is likely to develop. The saphenous vein in the groin is large and easy to cannulate, but the end of the catheter will lie in the external iliac vein. Iliofemoral deep vein thrombosis (DVT) or even septic DVT is common; either can be a potentially fatal complication in a patient who becomes critically ill.

Percutaneous cannulation of the internal jugular vein or the subclavian vein not only affords access for infusion of fluids and drugs but also provides a port for central venous monitoring. Obtaining central venous access with percutaneous techniques, however, can be difficult and risky, particularly in a hypovolemic patient with collapsed central veins. The puncture can cause a pneumothorax. An artery adjacent to the vein may be punctured. At times, an arterial puncture may not be recognized, and the artery may even be dilated and cannulated. Once the vessel is cannulated, the problem may initially go undetected. Furthermore, blood drawn from a cannulated artery in a shock patient may be flowing in a nonpulsatile fashion, giving the impression that the targeted vein has been successfully accessed. In severe shock, the arterial blood may be blue, thereby supporting this mistaken impression. A damaged artery can also bleed into the pleural cavity, an untamponaded space. If this occurs in a patient who is already compromised, the patient will probably die.

Percutaneous puncture of the common femoral vein is among the easiest of all venous access techniques and avoids the problems of pneumothorax and bleeding into a pleural cavity. If this vein is cannulated, the access site should be changed to a vein in the upper body as soon as the patient is stable. The incidence of DVT and septic complications is relatively high with femoral venous cannulation, and long-term use of this site should be avoided if possible.[10-12]

If the adjacent femoral artery is unintentionally cannulated, it is sometimes best to use this vessel for vascular access. Intra-arterial infusion of fluids is as effective as I.V. infusion. Care must be taken, however, to ensure that no air enters the system. The catheter should be removed as soon as other access is gained.

In pediatric patients, intraosseous access (e.g., via the proximal tibia, the distal femur, the iliac crest, or the sternum) is a useful means of gaining vascular access under difficult conditions. On rare occasions, this approach may be used in adults when other sites are unavailable or in special situations.[13-16]

The first attempts at obtaining vascular access should be made in the upper extremities with a percutaneous technique. If these attempts fail, one should fall back on a technique with which one is comfortable. There is no single best approach.

INITIAL FLUID RESUSCITATION

Once vascular access is obtained, a 20 ml/kg bolus of normal saline should be infused. If the patient is in profound shock, the fluid bolus should be given within 5 minutes if possible, and the use of a rapid infusion device should be considered; if the situation is less urgent, the bolus may be given over a period of 15 minutes or so. If the shock does not resolve, two more boluses should be given.

We consider normal saline (NS) the fluid of choice for initial resuscitation in most shock patients. The sodium concentration of NS (154 mmol/L) is close to that of normal serum. Its chloride concentration (also 154 mmol/L) can induce hyperchloremic metabolic acidemia; however, this state is generally well tolerated and usually clears as renal perfusion is restored and bicarbonate is regenerated.

If the patient already has significant lactic acidosis or the chloride concentration exceeds 115 mmol/L, lactated or acetated Ringer solution is used. Some favor initial use of lactated Ringer solution to reduce the chance that a hyperchloremic acidosis will develop in the first place. Both lactate and acetate accept a proton to form an organic acid, which is converted in the liver to CO_2 and water. The CO_2 is excreted by the lungs; the water, by the kidneys. As long as hepatic function and pulmonary function are adequate, which is usually the case, the result of this process is buffering of the acidemia that can accompany the shock state. Both lactated and acetated versions of Ringer solution, however, are hyponatremic and hypoosmotic; the latter is a potential problem in patients at risk for increased intracranial pressure.

Solutions containing glucose should not be used in the initial stages of resuscitation unless the patient is known to be hypoglycemic. Most patients in shock, in fact, are hyperglycemic as a result of high plasma levels of epinephrine and cortisol. Excessively high plasma glucose concentrations can induce an inappropriate diuresis.

Colloid and Hypertonic Solutions

Although crystalloid solutions have been the primary resuscitation fluid in the United States for many years, the use of colloid solutions in the resuscitation of critically ill patients is still the subject of debate. Factors such as the type of colloid used (albumin or hydroxyethyl starch), the timing of administration (early versus delayed), and the environment of care (prehospital, battlefield, or hospital) continue to be explored in laboratory, bedside, and field settings. Colloid solutions have the advantage of producing a much greater intravascular volume expansion for a given volume of fluid infused than crystalloid solutions do, and this advantage may be significant in prehospital, mass-casualty, or battlefield environments. In addition, colloid solutions theoretically increase colloid osmotic pressure (in the absence of increased permeability) and may decrease interstitial and cellular edema.[17,18]

The colloid solution that has probably been the object of the greatest amount of interest is albumin. Until comparatively recently, no large, randomized trials of albumin had been done, and thus, there was an ongoing controversy as to whether albumin should be given to critically ill patients.[19,20] In 2004, however, the Saline versus Albumin Fluid Evaluation (SAFE) study, which randomly assigned nearly 7,000 critically ill patients to receive either 4% albumin or NS, found outcomes to be identical in the two groups.[21] In the light of these data, coupled with the relatively low availability and high cost of albumin, the use of albumin solution as a resuscitation fluid is probably not warranted unless logistical or environmental constraints limit the use of crystalloid solutions.

Hydroxyethyl starch solutions share the same theoretical advantages as albumin, but they are less expensive and are therefore a more attractive alternative. They may have additional properties affecting inflammation and coagulation, the clinical significance of which is unknown.[22-25] To date, no large, randomized trials have shown these solutions to have a significant beneficial effect on outcome when used in place of isotonic crystalloid. A 2004 meta-analysis (which, admittedly, included a relatively small number of patients) was unable to demonstrate any significant effect.[26] Accordingly, the role of hydroxyethyl starch solutions in the resuscitation of critically ill patients remains to be determined.

Hypertonic saline solutions containing up to 7.5% sodium chloride (compared with 0.9% for normal saline) show promise for resuscitating patients in situations where large-volume resuscitation with isotonic solutions is impossible (e.g., combat, events involving mass casualties, and prehospital trauma care).[27] Hypertonic solutions provide far more blood volume expansion than isotonic solutions and result in less cellular edema. In addition, they may have favorable effects on the inflammatory response to injury.[28-33] These solutions are approved for use and commercially available in Brazil (where the idea originated), Chile, Argentina, and Europe; they are not currently approved for use in the United States or Canada. Both hypertonic saline and hydroxyethyl starch have been recommended as first-line solutions for the resuscitation of U.S. combat casualties in the field.[34]

TRANSFUSION

Transfusion of red blood cells (RBCs) restores intravascular volume and increases hemoglobin concentration, both of which improve oxygen delivery. Accordingly, it is ideal for resuscitation of a patient in shock. Unfortunately, allogeneic blood falls far short of being the ideal resuscitation fluid. Factors such as the age of the blood, the presence of allogeneic leukocytes, and the presence of soluble factors have been implicated in the observed association between RBC transfusions and poor patient outcomes.[35-40] The data suggest that limiting RBC transfusions in critically ill patients may lead to better patient outcomes. When this more restrictive approach to transfusion was prospectively evaluated against a more liberal transfusion strategy in critically ill patients, it resulted in equivalent or better patient outcomes.[41]

These findings provide useful guidance as to what an appropriate transfusion strategy might be for the average critically ill patient who is euvolemic, but they may not be applicable to the patient who is in shock. With shock patients, the first priority is restoration of intravascular volume. Volume replenishment should be initiated with isotonic crystalloid; when clinical or laboratory findings suggest significant anemia (hemoglobin concentration < 10.0 g/dl), transfusion of packed RBCs should be considered. In general, packed RBCs, reconstituted with normal saline, should be given to ensure that the patient's hemoglobin concentration is at least 7 g/dl, if not substantially higher. Certain patients require higher concentrations.

The following guidelines provide a reasonable approach to patients in all classes of shock, with the key variables being (1) the possibility of a continued decrease in the hemoglobin concentration (from bleeding or hemolysis) and (2) the estimated or measured values for the relation between oxygen supply and oxygen demand (determined via mixed venous or central venous oximetry).

1. A hemoglobin concentration of 7 g/dl is adequate in a young patient whose coronary arteries are in good shape and whose bleeding is known to be under control.
2. A hemoglobin concentration of 8 g/dl is adequate in a young patient who may be at slight risk for further bleeding.
3. A hemoglobin concentration of 9 g/dl is required if the risk of bleeding is substantial.
4. A hemoglobin concentration of 10 g/dl should be the goal if overt ischemia is present or there is a significant risk of occult ischemic disease (e.g., in a patient with peripheral vascular disease), even in the absence of ongoing myocardial ischemia.

In an emergency, O-negative RBCs should be given. There is no need for typing or crossmatching, and in the case of the confusion that can attend the treatment of multiple casualties, there is no danger that a patient will receive the wrong type of blood. However, with multiple casualties, there is a danger that the blood bank will be rapidly depleted of O-negative cells. If the patient can wait a few more minutes and if there is minimal risk of giving the wrong type of blood, type-specific blood should be given so as to conserve the supply of O-negative blood.

Although whole blood can be administered more quickly than packed RBCs can, its use in the civilian setting has almost become a matter of purely historical interest. Use of packed RBCs has the advantage of conserving the blood bank's supply of fresh frozen plasma and platelets. Under austere conditions, however, whole-blood transfusions may be more practical.[42,43]

From a conceptual perspective, the use of blood substitutes for resuscitation is an attractive option. Multiple preparations of hemoglobin-based oxygen carriers (HBOCs) have been developed, several of which have been tested clinically. Although the results obtained with an early HBOC were disappointing, those obtained with newer, polymerized HBOCs have been encouraging. In the light of the potential risks and the limited availability of allogeneic blood, HBOCs appear to be a promising alternative to RBC transfusion that will play a growing role in the future.[44,45]

MANAGEMENT OF PAIN, HYPOTHERMIA, ACIDEMIA, AND COAGULOPATHY

Once blood volume has been at least partially replenished, pain should be treated with small I.V. doses of narcotics. On the one hand, pain relief can reduce the stress response associated with shock and perhaps mitigate the severity of its late sequelae.[46] On the other, narcotics can also decrease tone in the venules and small veins, thereby exacerbating the shock state. Accordingly, one should titrate the doses and be ready to reverse the effect with a narcotic antagonist if necessary. A drop in blood pressure after administration of a narcotic suggests that the patient may still be hypovolemic, in which case more aggressive resuscitation may be indicated.

If hypothermia is present initially, it should be corrected; if not, it should be kept from developing. Hypothermia slows metabolic processes. In some situations (e.g., cold-water drowning), this effect may be beneficial, but in most cases, it is better for the patient to have a normal body temperature, normal myocardial contractility, and intact coagulatory and immune function.

The patient must be unclothed during the initial evaluation but should be covered afterward, with particular attention paid to covering the head. The room should be kept warm, and any fluids administered should be prewarmed either in an oven or with heating devices.

If the arterial pH is low, it should be raised to 7.20 by means of either modest degrees of hyperventilation or administration of bicarbonate. (Although agents other than bicarbonate can be given to correct a metabolic acidemia, it is not clear that they have any more to offer than bicarbonate does.) No efforts should be made to raise the pH above 7.20. Moderate degrees of acidemia are well tolerated, and excessive administration of bicarbonate may worsen intracellular acidosis [see Initial Fluid Resuscitation, above].[47] Instead, efforts should continue to be directed toward managing the underlying cause of shock.

Coagulopathy should be treated with fresh frozen plasma and platelets [see 8 Bleeding and Transfusion]. The decision whether to use these components should be based on observation of bleeding and clotting in the patient, not on laboratory measurements of coagulation or platelet counts, which can be normal even during exsanguination.

MODULATION OF INFLAMMATORY RESPONSE

In the case of inflammatory shock, there has long been interest in therapeutic approaches aimed at blocking or counteracting inflammatory and coagulatory mediators released from the inflamed tissues. To date, almost all of these approaches have failed to show any benefit, and some have proved dangerous. A study published in 2001 yielded apparently more promising results, concluding that infusion of activated protein C seemed to improve survival in some patients with severe sepsis. Since that study was published, several other trials have been carried out in an attempt to define the role of activated protein C in the treatment of severe sepsis with more precision.[48-50] Taken as a whole, the current data suggest that in view of the side-effect profile and potential complications of activated protein C, its use should be considered only in patients who have severe sepsis and are at high risk for death.[51] We do not currently use this agent in the treatment of surgical patients with severe sepsis.

The use of corticosteroids in the treatment of sepsis has been studied extensively over the past several decades. Older regimens frequently involved administering these agents in high doses, and the bulk of the evidence suggested that such regimens were not beneficial and might actually have had an adverse effect.[52] Newer regimens have been developed that employ lower steroid doses, and the results have been encouraging. A multicenter study published in 2002 found that administration of modest doses of hydrocortisone and fludrocortisone to patients in septic shock with impaired adrenal function led to improvements in mortality.[53] Although these data are compelling, it remains the case that corticosteroids have well-established potential side effects in this setting. Further study will be required before the role of steroids in the management of critically ill patients can be fully defined.

ASSESSMENT OF AND GOALS FOR CARDIOVASCULAR VARIABLES

In most cases of shock, regardless of category, the initial approach just described is all that is needed. Some patients, however, will not respond. These patients should be transferred to a setting in which cardiovascular pressures can be transduced and monitored. A systemic artery, usually a radial artery, should be cannulated, and central venous access should be obtained. An attempt should be made to assess the cardiac output.

Mean Arterial Pressure

Arterial cannulation provides blood for analysis of blood gases and allows reliable measurement of the MAP [*see Figure 1*], which is more useful in managing shock than the peak systolic brachial pressure is. The MAP is the pressure that drives the perfusion of the noncardiac tissues. It is close to the mean diastolic aortic root pressure and is thus a good approximation for the pressure that perfuses the myocardium. Finally, it is the pressure that provides the energy required to drive the blood back to the right atrium and ventricle.

The mean pressure in the transducer used to monitor the arterial pressure is the same as the mean pressure in the monitored artery. Furthermore, the mean pressure in the monitored artery is the same as the mean pressure in the aortic root, unless there is arterial obstruction between the aortic root and the monitored artery or spasm of the proximal conducting arteries (as may be the case in severe shock). Thus, knowing the MAP is as close as one can get to knowing the pressure that is providing perfusion for the body. Accordingly, one should focus on the MAP, once it can be accurately determined by intra-arterial monitoring.

In treating a patient who is unresponsive to initial care, the goal is to generate an adequate MAP and an adequate cardiac output without producing an undue degree of peripheral edema (i.e., without driving the CVP to unnecessarily high levels). However, it can be difficult to determine what constitutes an adequate MAP. To begin with, the MAP must be high enough to perfuse the CNS. The brain and the spinal cord have high metabolic rates, and their vasculature is chronically dilated. (An injured CNS is capable of autoregulation, but only over a relatively narrow range of blood pressure.) A fall in the perfusion pressure can lead to a profound loss of flow.

In addition, the MAP must be high enough to perfuse organs supplied by arteries obstructed by preexisting disease. The microvasculature of the gut in a patient with an occluded superior mesenteric artery is maximally dilated, and thus, a fall in proximal pressure can shut off critical perfusion. The same is true in the case of a kidney with an obstructed renal artery, an extremity with obstructed proximal arteries, or a heart with obstructed coronary arteries. However, if these non-CNS organs have an unobstructed arterial supply, they are protected from hypotension, unless the hypotension is profound. All of the organs in the body, except for the brain and the spinal cord, have some degree of chronic resting arteriolar constriction. A fall in the perfusion pressure, in conjunction with the expected production of local ischemia and accumulation of waste products of metabolism, causes reflex dilation of the arterioles in the organ at risk. Unless the hypotension is extreme, this dilation permits compensatory flow. As noted, the CNS does not enjoy this luxury, but then, the cardiovascular system is designed to maintain a normal pressure for the brain: it is no accident that the primary baroreceptors are placed at the carotid bifurcations.

If a patient is alert and able to move all extremities, and if there is no reason to suspect that any of the major arteries are obstructed by preexisting disease, any MAP that is high enough to maintain full neurologic function is adequate. Determining the adequacy of the MAP in obtunded, sedated, or anesthetized patients, however, can be a challenge.

In certain cases, one might know that at some previous point, perhaps during the same hospitalization, the patient was alert and neurologically intact with a given MAP (e.g., 50 mm Hg). If so, it can be assumed that the same pressure would still be adequate now. If, however, one does not have this information, one must err on the side of giving more fluids to keep the blood pressure high. In the case of an obtunded patient with no indications of possible carotid disease or obstructed blood supply to the spinal cord, an arbitrary value can be assigned. A reasonable MAP might be 60 mm Hg for a younger patient (or somewhat higher for an older patient).

If it is possible that the arterial supply to an actively metabolizing organ is obstructed, some assessment of the organ must be made. For the heart, the absence or resolution of chest pain with resuscitation and the absence of ischemic changes on the ECG suggest that pressure and perfusion are adequate. For the gut, the absence of pain and the presence of bowel activity are reassuring. For the kidneys, adequate urine output and excretion of creatinine are generally indicative of acceptable pressure and perfusion. For the extremities, physical examination of the skin usually suffices.

Mean Central Venous Pressure

As a rule, the tip of the catheter used to measure the CVP ends up in either the superior vena cava or the right atrium. The pressures at these sites vary both with the cardiac cycle and with ventilation. These variations can be substantial, depending on atrial activity and on the pressures produced by the labored breathing of the critically ill patient or by the effects of mechanical ventilation.

With respect to prevention of unnecessary edema, the mean CVP is the most pertinent variable. In addition, we consider the mean CVP the most useful measurement for assessing the right ventricular end-diastolic volume (RVEDV) (i.e., for making an initial assessment of the adequacy of volume restoration). The mean CVP is close to the ventricular end-diastolic pressure averaged over the ventilatory cycle. It is also the simplest central pressure to obtain. Typically, the number is read directly off the digital readout on the monitor; if the transducer is calibrated and zeroed properly, interobserver variation should be nonexistent.

Care must be exercised, however, in extrapolating from the mean CVP (or the ventricular end-diastolic pressure) to the ventricular end-diastolic volume. All measurements of central or vascular pressures, whether mean or end-diastolic, are measured with respect to the atmosphere (i.e., to the outside of the body). It would be useful to know the transmural pressure—the pressure inside the ventricle minus the pressure immediately outside—because the end-diastolic transmural pressure correlates best with the end-diastolic volume. Unfortunately, it is not possible to determine the transmural pressure accurately in this setting, because the extramural pressure is not known.

Some assumptions can, however, be made about the extramural pressure. In a normal, supine, spontaneously breathing person, the mean pressure immediately outside the heart, measured with respect to the atmosphere, is usually on the order of -3 mm Hg. The intracavitary right ventricular end-diastolic pressure (RVEDP), measured with respect to the atmosphere, is approximately 5 mm Hg. Thus, the end-diastolic transmural pressure will be about 8 mm Hg. This level of transmural pressure is usually enough to generate an adequate RVEDV. In a normal patient who is undergoing mechanical ventilation, the mean pressure outside the heart is on the order of 4 mm Hg; an RVEDP of 12 mm Hg produces a transmural pressure of 8 mm Hg and usually suffices to produce an adequate RVEDV.

These values work for patients with essentially normal lungs. Unfortunately, most patients on mechanical ventilators do not have normal lungs. In such patients, the lungs can form a stiff compartment around the heart that does not give. The problem is compounded when the diaphragm is elevated, as it is in many surgical patients. The heart can be trapped between the inflated stiff lungs and the elevated stiff diaphragm, and the extramural pressures can be very high.

Furthermore, the stiffness of the ventricular wall during diastole must be taken into account. A ventricle with stiff musculature (or low compliance) during diastole needs a high intracavitary pressure to achieve an adequate end-diastolic volume. The conditions that can increase diastolic stiffness are manifold and include myocardial ischemia, tachycardia in a patient with preexisting coronary artery disease, edema, fibrosis, and hypertrophy.

Thus, to extrapolate from the intracavitary mean CVP to the RVEDV (and to an initial assessment of the adequacy of volume resuscitation), one must consider not only the measurement recorded but also the patient's clinical condition. In some patients, the intracavitary CVP may have to be as high as 20 mm Hg to achieve adequate filling of the ventricle.

Cardiac Output

In two clinical scenarios—warm inflammatory shock and neurogenic shock—the adequacy of cardiac output can be assessed by means of physical examination, as long as the MAP is adequate. Physical examination will determine whether the cutaneous arterioles are dilated. If they are, there will be a short circuit in the vasculature. Hindrance to ventricular contraction will be minimal; cardiac output will be robust. In other scenarios, however, one cannot be sure about the cardiac output without more sophisticated monitoring.

INDICATIONS FOR ADDITIONAL MEASURES

Fluids

If the patient is still in shock—that is, if it appears that the MAP, cardiac output, or both may be inadequate for tissue perfusion—additional fluids should be infused until, in one's best judgment, the RVEDV is probably normal.

Inotropes

If the patient is still in shock and further fluid administration is unlikely to be beneficial, an inotrope should be given. Dobutamine is a good first choice in this situation. The dosage should be 5 µg · kg^{-1} · min^{-1} initially, then be increased as needed, to an upper limit of 15 µg · kg^{-1} · min^{-1}. If necessary, milrinone may be added, administered in a 50 µg loading dose followed by infusion of 0.375 to 0.75 µg · kg^{-1} · min^{-1}. Neither agent has any vasoconstrictor effects, and both are safe, at least for a short time. The goal is to achieve an adequate MAP without producing signs of peripheral constriction (e.g., cutaneous hypoperfusion) or causing tachycardia (defined as a heart rate exceeding 110 beats/min in a young patient, exceeding

90 beats/min in an older patient, or exceeding 75 beats/min in a patient with coronary artery disease).

Swan-Ganz Catheter

In this setting, inotropes can usually be used safely for 30 minutes or so. If it appears that inotropes may be needed for a longer period, that more fluids will have to be given despite a high CVP, that the myocardium is at risk (as suggested by chest pain or signs of ischemia on ECG), that a vasoconstrictor may be needed, or that the patient requires an excessively high F$_I$O$_2$, then a decision must be made about what the goals of resuscitation will be from this point forward. There is no general agreement on precisely how this decision should be made, but we believe that the decision-making process frequently benefits from considering measurements obtained by means of a Swan-Ganz catheter.

Measurements and derived values obtained via Swan-Ganz catheter The Swan-Ganz catheter can provide an enormous amount of information about the cardiovascular system. Insertion of the catheter is described elsewhere [see 119 Cardiovascular Monitoring], as are details and caveats about the measurements that can be made with it.

The S$_{mv}$O$_2$ can be directly measured by an oximeter on the end of the catheter. An excessively low value (< 60%) is cause for concern. It can arise from an inadequate cardiac output, an excessively low hemoglobin concentration, marked desaturation of systemic arterial blood, or, in rare cases, from excessive and unnecessary consumption of oxygen (as in a patient who is shivering).

The cardiac output can be measured directly with thermodilution technology,[54] and the stroke volume can be calculated by dividing the cardiac output by the heart rate.

The intracavitary mean CVP can be measured through a port in the superior vena cava or the right atrium. It can be taken as a very close approximation of the mean pressure in the right ventricle and of RVEDP. The RVEDV can be measured directly with thermodilution technology.[55] The end-systolic pressure in the root of the pulmonary artery and the right ventricular end-systolic pressure (RVESP) can be approximated as 90% of the directly measured peak systolic pressure in the pulmonary artery, measured through the port on the end of the catheter (provided that the catheter monitoring system is properly set up [see 119 Cardiovascular Monitoring]). The mean pulmonary arterial pressure (MPAP) can be directly and accurately measured through the same port.

The LVEDP can be approximated from the pulmonary arterial wedge pressure (PAWP) [see 119 Cardiovascular Monitoring]. To smooth out variations introduced by both ventilation and the cardiac cycle, we use the mean value for the pressure, which is typically 1 or 2 mm Hg lower than the end-diastolic pressures aver-

Table 3 Influence of Body Size on Selected Cardiovascular Parameters*

Weight (kg)	End-Diastolic Volume (ml)	Stroke Volume (ml)	End-Systolic Volume (ml)	Contractility (mm Hg/ml)	Afterload (mm Hg/ml)
50	125	83	42	2.4	1.2
60	150	100	50	2.0	1.0
70	175	117	58	1.7	0.85
80	200	133	67	1.5	0.75

*On the assumptions that (1) ventricular end-diastolic volume is 2.5 ml/kg, (2) stroke volume is 1.67 ml/kg, and (3) ventricular end-systolic pressure is 100 mm Hg.

aged over several ventilatory cycles. The LVEDV can be estimated on the basis of the PAWP, in conjunction with all the available clinical information (including physical examination, chest x-ray, and ventilator settings). It must be kept in mind that the PAWP and the LVEDP are both intracavitary pressures. For extrapolation to the LVEDV, the pressure applied to the outside of the heart and the stiffness of the ventricular wall during diastole must be taken into account.

The information from the right ventricle can be used to estimate the pressure outside the left ventricle. If a reasonably low CVP generates a reasonably large directly measured RVEDV, it follows that the extracardiac pressures are not excessively high. The information from the right ventricle can also be (cautiously) used to estimate the stiffness of the left ventricular wall during diastole (i.e., ventricular diastolic compliance). If a low CVP generates a generous RVEDV, it follows that the right ventricular diastolic compliance is large. Often, one can tentatively assume that the values measured in the right ventricle reflect the status of the left ventricle as well. This is not always the case, however: many patients with ischemic heart disease have a stiff diastolic left ventricle and a normal right ventricle.

The estimates of end-diastolic volume can sometimes be confirmed by increasing the filling pressures of the heart with a fluid bolus and assessing the cardiovascular response. The fluid should be given rapidly, in an amount sufficient to effect changes in the filling pressures. Increases in stroke volume, especially if associated with increases in pulmonary and systemic arterial pressures, suggest that the initial end-diastolic volumes were small.

If increases in filling pressures have minimal effects on the stroke volume and pressures, there are two possibilities. The first is that the end-diastolic volumes were already generous. If so, a diuretic can be given; if stroke volumes and blood pressures do not decrease, further diuresis is indicated. The second possibility is that the volumes were small but the diastolic compliances were poor or the extramural pressures large. In either case, caution should be exercised in giving additional fluid (though there may be little choice). In the case of poor diastolic compliance, it may be possible to find and treat a potentially correctable cause of the stiffness (e.g., myocardial ischemia). In the case of high extramural pressures, it may be possible to find and treat the underlying causative condition. (Admittedly, neither problem is easy to deal with, but the effort should be made nonetheless.)

It cannot be assumed that the LVEDV is the same as the directly measured RVEDV. In fact, the two volumes are frequently different in critically ill patients. Studies comparing RVEDVs (measured with a fast thermistor) with LVEDVs (measured with transesophageal echocardiography) have shown that right ventricular values are often larger than left ventricular values in patients in inflammatory shock, sometimes by a factor of 3.[56] In patients with left-side congestive heart failure, however, left ventricular values can be substantially larger than right ventricular values. Thus, the volume of one chamber is not necessarily an accurate indicator of the volume of the other chamber, though the clinical scenario can provide some guidance in this regard.

The aortic root end-systolic pressure (or the left ventricular end-systolic pressure [LVESP]) is the most important pressure to consider in estimating left ventricular oxygen requirements and in assessing the left ventricular afterload. The LVESP can be roughly approximated as 90% of the estimated peak pressure in the aortic root.[57]

Estimating the peak aortic root pressure can be a difficult process. One approach is to measure the peak systolic pressures in the radial artery, then cautiously extrapolate back to the corresponding pressures in the root of the aorta. To this end, the equipment used to measure the radial artery pressure must be satisfactorily matched to the physical characteristics of the artery [see 119 Cardiovascular Monitoring]. Once the peak systolic pressure in the radial artery is known, several clinical scenarios may be considered.

If the arteries supplying the upper extremity are stiff or calcified (as they will be in many older patients or in diabetics), the peak systolic pressure in the radial artery will be as much as 80 mm Hg higher than that in the root of the aorta. If the arterioles in the hand are constricted (as they may be in hypovolemic, compressive, obstructive, or cardiogenic shock), the peak systolic pressure in the radial artery may be 40 mm Hg higher than that in the aortic root. If the arteries are in spasm, the difference may be greater; in severe spasm, all of the pressures in the radial artery are lower than the central pressures. If the microvasculature in the hand is dilated (as in warm inflammatory shock), the proximal and distal systolic pressures will be nearly the same.

The peak aortic root pressure can also be estimated by extrapolating from the MAP, which will always be less than the systolic pressure.[58] In young patients with compliant arteries and no abnormal arteriolar constriction, the peak systolic pressure in the aortic root is usually about 20 mm Hg higher than the MAP. In patients with stiff or calcified arteries, the central peak systolic pressure can be much higher than the MAP. In patients who are in warm inflammatory shock or neurogenic shock, the central systolic pressure may be only 10 mm Hg higher than the MAP.

Thus, although it is necessary to estimate the LVESP so that ventricular oxygen requirements and left ventricular afterload can be assessed, one must be wary in doing so, just as one must be careful in treating a patient on the basis of the estimated LVEDV.

The mean aortic root pressure is usually the same as the mean pressure in the radial artery. It can be misleading if the patient has an obstruction in a proximal artery. To rule out the possibility of a subclavian stenosis, the pressures in the two arms should be measured at the beginning of hospitalization. In severe shock, the arteries may go into spasm that is severe enough to narrow the lumina; if this occurs, the mean pressures in the extremities will be lower than those in the aortic root. Otherwise, however, the MAP in the extremities, as a surrogate for the mean aortic root pressure, is one of the most reliable measurements made in clinical medicine.

Right ventricular contractility, in the absence of congestive failure, can be approximated as the RVESP divided by the right ventricular end-systolic volume (RVESV), which is obtained by subtracting the stroke volume from the RVEDV. A normal value for a 60 kg person is 0.4 mm Hg/ml [see Table 3]. Contractility can rise to double that value with full adrenergic stimulation, and it can probably fall to levels as low as 50% of normal.

The right ventricular afterload can be approximated as the RVESP divided by the stroke volume. Because only a few conditions need be met to obtain these two measurements, the approximation is quite accurate. A normal value is 0.2 mm Hg/ml [see Table 3]. With severe respiratory failure, the right ventricular afterload can increase by a factor of 5.

Left ventricular contractility, in the absence of congestive failure, can be approximated as the LVESP divided by the left ventricular end-systolic volume (LVESV). A normal value for a 60 kg person is 2.0 mm Hg/ml. This value is approximately five times greater than the corresponding value for the right ventricle, which is to be expected, given that the wall of the left ventricle is approximately five times thicker [see Table 3]. Left ventricular contractility can double with adrenergic stimulation and can fall to levels as low as 50% of normal in severe congestive failure.

Frequently, the clinical scenario gives the physician some idea of the state of left ventricular contractility. In most cases of mild or moderate shock (except cardiogenic shock), it can be assumed that contractility is normal or slightly above normal. In cases of severe shock, however, this assumption cannot be made. Often, contractility is reduced as a consequence of poor perfusion of the coronary vasculature or downregulation of the beta receptors in the myocardium.

The calculated value for left ventricular contractility must always be considered in terms of the clinical context. It is not as reliable as the calculated value for right ventricular contractility, because the approximations for the LVESP and the LVESV are not highly accurate. Potential inaccuracies notwithstanding, the calculated left ventricular contractility can be useful for following upward or downward trends.

The left ventricular afterload can be approximated by dividing the LVESP by the stroke volume. A normal value is 1.0 mm Hg/ml [see Table 3]. With normal physiologic adjustments in intense isometric exercise, the left ventricular afterload can temporarily increase by a factor of 4. It can also rise by a similar factor in patients who have hypertensive disease or who have received excessive doses of vasoconstrictors. Under less extreme circumstances (e.g., aerobic exercise), it increases by no more than a factor of 2.

The power available for perfusing the lungs and filling the left atrium and ventricle during diastole is the MPAP multiplied by the product of the heart rate and the stroke volume (i.e., cardiac output). The power available for perfusing the systemic tissues, including the heart (on the assumption that the MAP is approximately equal to the mean diastolic pressure in the aortic root), and for filling the right atrium and ventricle during diastole is the MAP multiplied by the product of the heart rate and the stroke volume (i.e., cardiac output).

DETERMINATION OF PRIORITIES FOR SUBSEQUENT RESUSCITATION

Increases in heart rate, ventricular end-diastolic volume, contractility, and afterload all increase ventricular oxygen requirements. They also increase the power production of the ventricle, as long as afterload is not allowed to exceed contractility. If afterload is allowed to exceed contractility, the power production falls off. That is, increased ventricular power production almost always means increased myocardial oxygen requirements. There is no thermodynamic free lunch.

At this point, therefore, if the patient still has not responded to resuscitative measures, one must decide whether the priority for subsequent treatment should be (1) to increase ventricular power production, at the cost of possible edema and increased myocardial oxygen requirements, or (2) to minimize edema formation and myocardial oxygen requirements, at the cost of possible compromise of ventricular power production.

This fundamental decision must be made on clinical grounds. Occasionally, the decision is straightforward, as in a young trauma patient with extensive noncardiac injuries and a robust myocardium or in an older patient with an uncomplicated MI. More often, however, the choice is not so clearcut, because most initially nonresponding patients do not fall cleanly into either category. Nevertheless, it is necessary to choose one priority or the other.

Once a priority is decided on, the planned treatment should be adjusted to take into account the particular needs of individual patients.

Priority Is Ensuring Resuscitation: Edema Not a Major Problem and Myocardium Not at Risk

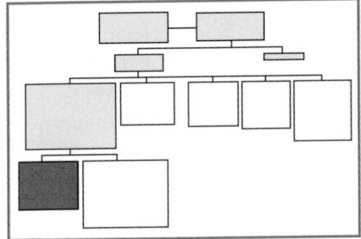

Fluid infusion If priority is given to the periphery, fluid administration is probably necessary. The initial goal should be to achieve a CVP in the low teens and a PAWP in the midteens (on the assumption that the patient is undergoing mechanical ventilation). As therapy progresses and more measurements are made, this goal may have to be modified. Ultimately, however, the goal is not to produce any specific filling pressures but, rather, to produce generous right and left ventricular end-diastolic volumes.

Administration of inotropes Inotropes (e.g., dobutamine and milrinone) can be safely used for a few days if necessary, provided that the patient is being monitored with a Swan-Ganz catheter. These agents increase myocardial oxygen requirements, but this is not a problem in a patient with a strong heart. The goal is to increase ventricular contractility to normal or slightly supranormal levels. Supranormal contractility leads to increased ventricular production of power, but the additional power is rarely needed. The dosages should be kept low enough that the heart rate does not exceed 110 beats/min in younger patients or 90 beats/min in older patients.

Administration of vasopressors: last resort There are only two indications for the administration of vasoconstrictors to patients in whom the primary concern is perfusion of the periphery: (1) a MAP that may be inadequate for perfusion of the CNS and (2) hypotension in a patient who has a critical stenosis in the cerebral, coronary, hepatic, mesenteric, or renal arteries or in the arteries supplying the spinal cord or an ischemic limb. If a vasoconstrictor is indicated, low-dose I.V. vasopressin should be given first. If the heart rate is 89 beats/min or slower, dopamine, 2 to 20 µg · kg⁻¹ · min⁻¹, should be added. The heart rate should not be driven above 110 beats/min, even in young patients. If the initial heart rate is 90 beats/min or higher, norepinephrine, 2 to 12 µg/kg, may be given.

In either ventricle, the afterload should not be allowed to exceed the contractility, except in desperate circumstances. Matching the afterload to the contractility produces the maximum attainable work on the aortic root for a given end-diastolic volume. Allowing the afterload to exceed the contractility causes a rise in the blood pressure but a sharp fall in the stroke volume. The afterload should be increased to this degree only if there appears to be no other way to perfuse the CNS or organs with an obstructed arterial supply. If this is the case, the vasoconstrictor should be given and the effect on the perfusion of the organ in question evaluated. If the increased pressure does not produce the desired effect, the vasoconstrictor dosage should be reduced. Again, the goal is to achieve adequate perfusion, not to reach an arbitrary numerical pressure value. The great fear in using vasoconstrictors is that they can lead to ischemia and even necrosis of the skin, the kidneys, the gut, and the liver. Accordingly, they should be used in this context only as a last resort.

Priority Is Minimizing Edema and Protecting Heart

Fluid administration versus diuresis Fluid management must be finely tuned in patients who have both inadequate peripheral perfusion and marginal myocardial reserve.

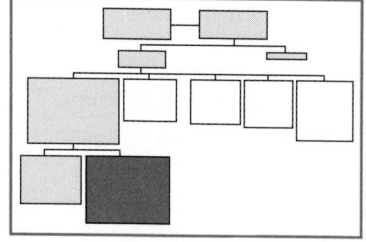

On the one hand, too-large end-diastolic volumes unnecessarily increase myocardial oxygen requirements and produce edema; on the other, too-small end-diastolic volumes make it impossible for the ventricles to produce adequate pressure and stroke volumes. In some patients, diuresis (e.g., with furosemide, 10 to 40 mg I.V.) is indicated; in others, fluids should be given. Sometimes, it is necessary to rely on trial and error.

Adjustment of contractility If pressures and stroke volumes are still inadequate after end-diastolic volumes have apparently been optimized, measures for adjusting contractility may be considered.

If contractility seems to be reduced on either side, inotropes such as dobutamine or milrinone should be tried (cautiously, in view of their effect on myocardial oxygen requirements). If, by chance, contractility seems to be excessively high in either ventricle (or both), a beta blocker should be given. Esmolol is a good first choice because it has a short duration of action. A 500 μg/kg loading dose is given, followed by a 50 μg · kg^{-1} · min^{-1} infusion, which is increased as necessary. Metoprolol, 5 to 15 mg every 6 hours, may be given later if it is clear that beta blockade was needed and still is. The goal is normal contractility on both the right side and the left.

Adjustment of afterload with respect to contractility Left ventricular afterload should be adjusted so that it is 50% of left ventricular contractility. This ratio does not produce the maximum transfer of energy to the aortic root, but it is efficient, in that it produces the greatest amount of work per milliliter of oxygen required by the ventricular musculature.

If left ventricular afterload is less than or equal to 49% of left ventricular contractility, vasopressin, dopamine, and norepinephrine should be given as necessary. The heart rate should not be driven above 90 beats/min. As with any patient receiving vasoconstrictors, frequent reassessment is essential. The goal is to wean the patient from the drugs as soon as possible. If left ventricular afterload is equal to or greater than 51% of left ventricular contractility, the stiffness of the arteries should be decreased by performing further diuresis, by increasing the beta blocker dosage, by adding an angiotensin-converting enzyme (ACE) inhibitor (e.g., enalaprilat, 1.25 to 5 mg every 6 hours), or by adding nitroglycerin, 5 to 200 μg · kg^{-1} · min^{-1}.

If the heart rate exceeds 90 beats/min after these adjustments, the beta-blocker dosage should be increased, and a calcium channel blocker (e.g., diltiazem, 5 to 15 mg/hr) should be added. Maintenance of a slow heart rate is the single most important factor for minimizing myocardial oxygen requirements, but as with the other interventions mentioned (see above), it usually can be achieved only at the cost of decreased pressures and stroke volumes.

Management of Compressive Shock

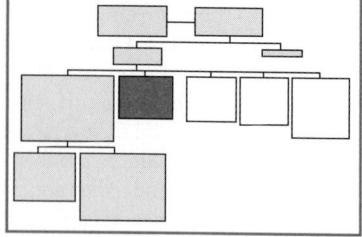

In many cases, extracardiac compressive and extracardiac obstructive shock, being conditions that can kill quickly, will already have been treated by this point in management. It is wise, however, to keep these two causes of shock in mind as workup proceeds: they often develop secondarily. Examples of problems that can arise as treatment progresses are a tension pneumothorax that develops in a mechanically ventilated patient who is being worked up or treated for some nonpulmonary problem and an abdominal compartment syndrome that develops in a patient who is being resuscitated after a major injury or burn. In patients with more complicated problems (e.g., possible abdominal compartment syndrome), a Swan-Ganz catheter should be inserted. When dealing with the conflicting demands made on the cardiovascular system in compressive shock, one needs all the information one can get.

Management of Intravascular Obstructive Shock

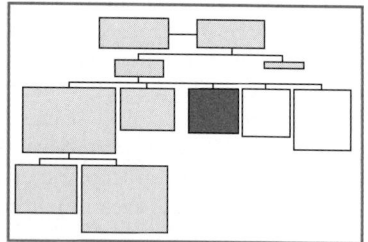

The immediately life-threatening problems caused by intravascular obstruction should already have been treated by this point. The pharmacologically treatable problems (e.g., systemic hypertension) should be treated with diuresis, beta blockade, ACE inhibition, and nitroglycerin, as described (see above). If hypertension persists and inadequate ventricular production of power is a possibility, a Swan-Ganz catheter should be inserted. The goal is to adjust the afterload for each ventricle so that it is approximately 50% of the contractility.

This goal can be particularly difficult to achieve for the right ventricle and the pulmonary vasculature. In patients with severe ARDS, there is some evidence to suggest that administration of prostacyclin or inhaled nitrous oxide may help reduce excessive right ventricular afterload,[59] though these interventions have not been particularly successful in our own experience. In any case, one should always attempt to address the underlying problem causing the ARDS. One can try to adjust the ventilator in an effort to relieve the potentially confounding problem of extravascular obstruction of the vasculature.

To achieve the desired goal in the systemic vasculature, it may be necessary to employ aortic balloon counterpulsation to deal with the reflected waves generated by the transmission of energy into these vessels. This measure can be extremely effective; however, it puts the perfusion of the limb with the cannulated artery at risk. Furthermore, it is only a short-term solution: the underlying problem will have to be dealt with eventually [*see* Management of Cardiogenic Shock, *below*].

Management of Neurogenic Shock

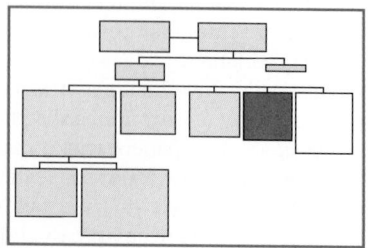

The initial management of neurogenic shock is much the same as that of hypovolemic and inflammatory shock, with two exceptions: the use of the Trendelenburg position and the use of vasoconstrictors.

TRENDELENBURG POSITION

Patients in neurogenic shock often benefit from being placed in the Trendelenburg position. Autonomic denervation of the systemic venules and small veins leads to pooling of blood in these capacitance vessels. The Trendelenburg position causes this blood to be translocated to the vascular structures in the chest, including the heart, thereby helping to restore ventricular end-diastolic volumes.

Patients with other forms of shock, however, derive no benefit from the Trendelenburg position.[60] In hypovolemic shock, for example, the systemic venules and small veins are already depleted of blood as a consequence of both volume loss and adrenergic constriction of the vessel walls. In cardiogenic shock, the end-diastolic volumes are already too large, and there is no point in trying to increase them.

ADMINISTRATION OF VASOCONSTRICTORS

As noted (see above), vasoconstrictors should play almost no role in the initial management of hypovolemic or inflammatory shock. For these forms of shock, fluid replenishment is the crucial initial measure, and these agents can shut off residual flow to organs already rendered ischemic by the shock state. For the initial management of neurogenic shock, however, vasoconstrictors are often beneficial. In neurogenic shock, the denervated arterioles are fully dilated, leading to substantial (and sometimes profound) drops in the central arterial pressure. Cerebral or myocardial infarction may occur. Constriction of the arterioles increases the pressure and offers protection. In addition, constriction of the denervated systemic venules and small veins causes translocation of blood back into the chest and helps restore depleted ventricular end-diastolic volumes.

If the heart rate is slow, as it may be if denervation extends high enough to block the sympathetic nerves going to the heart, dopamine may be given. If the heart rate is rapid, norepinephrine or phenylephrine (in an initial dosage of 100 to 180 μg/min, which is then decreased to 40 to 60 μg/min) may be used.

The danger in giving a vasoconstrictor to a patient in neurogenic shock is that the underlying condition that caused the shock state may also have caused occult bleeding. Thus, the vasoconstrictor may maintain the blood pressure, reassuring the physician while the patient bleeds to death. Vasoconstrictors should be employed to treat neurogenic shock only after it has been established that the shock state has no hypovolemic component. If there is a possibility that hypovolemia or another abnormality (e.g., cardiac compression) may be contributing to the shock state, a Swan-Ganz catheter should be inserted. Treatment should then be governed by the information gathered by means of the catheter.

Management of Cardiogenic Shock

If the priority is the heart and there is comparatively little reason for concern about noncardiac tissues, treatment is usually straightforward, though the results may be less

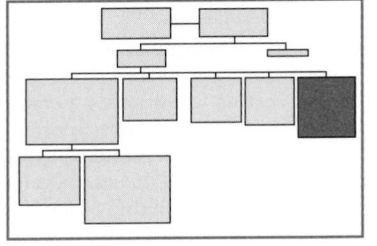

than might be hoped for. The approach to treatment of a patient in cardiogenic shock should be patterned on the approach to treatment of a patient in hypovolemic or inflammatory shock in whom there are grounds for concern about myocardial viability or formation of edema (see above).

If the ventricular end-diastolic volumes seem excessively large, either diuresis should be initiated or morphine sulfate, 1 to 4 mg/hr, should be given, both to relieve pain and stress and to allow pooling of blood in the systemic capacitance vessels.

If the heart rate is excessively rapid, beta blockade is indicated, accompanied, if necessary, by calcium channel blockade. If myocardial ischemia is a possibility, the heart rate should not be allowed to exceed 75 beats/min. If myocardial damage is unlikely, as in a patient with uncomplicated valvular problems, the heart rate should not be allowed to reach or exceed 90 beats/min.

If the ventricular end-systolic pressure seems excessively high, more aggressive attempts should be made to reduce arterial stiffness with diuresis and beta blockade. An ACE inhibitor and nitroglycerin should be added as needed. As a rule, hydralazine should not be used. Because its principal effects are on the arterioles, not the arteries, it lowers the MAP without reducing the stiffness of the arteries (which is more important for decreasing the ventricular oxygen requirements). Hydralazine can also increase the heart rate and thereby markedly increase myocardial oxygen requirements, thus defeating the very purpose for which it was originally given. The use of clonidine should also be avoided if possible. It, too, works mainly on the arterioles instead of the arteries, and it can cause nightmares and disorientation, side effects that can be a major problem in critically ill patients.

The goal of treatment is to achieve an acceptable LVESP, an adequate MAP, adequate peripheral perfusion, and an acceptable heart rate, with no sign of myocardial ischemia. If this goal cannot be achieved, the next step is to insert a Swan-Ganz catheter and manage the patient so that the left ventricular afterload is 50% of the attainable contractility. Some degree of compromise may prove necessary, but every effort should be made to keep the afterload from exceeding this value. A high afterload will indeed produce a higher blood pressure, but only at the cost of increased myocardial oxygen requirements, which are rarely desirable in a patient with a compromised myocardium.

In some patients with acute myocardial ischemia and shock, all of the aforementioned treatments will fail. Such patients should undergo emergency coronary angiography, as should any patient with an acute coronary syndrome that becomes unstable or that is associated with ST-T segment elevation. The purpose of the angiography is to find a correctable lesion that can be treated with coronary angioplasty, stenting, or surgical revascularization. If necessary, an intra-aortic balloon pump may be placed before or at the time of angiography, angioplasty, or stenting. This pump can be left in place while the underlying problem awaits possible surgical correction (if indicated).

Treatment of primary right-side cardiogenic shock is the same as that of primary left-side cardiogenic shock, except that in right-side failure, it may be possible to adjust the ventilator so as to reduce the right ventricular afterload.

The hemoglobin concentration should probably be maintained at a generous level (i.e., 10 to 11 g/dl) in patients with cardiogenic shock, especially if the higher levels obliterate symptoms of ischemia.

Discussion

Contractility

Defining a numerical descriptor for contractility has been a challenge since the beginning of the 20th century. Of the many descriptors that have been suggested since Starling's Linnacre lecture, the one we and many others have come to prefer is ventricular end-systolic stiffness, or elastance (the engineering term for this characteristic). The elastance of a chamber with a given volume and pressure is the slope of the line that is drawn tangentially to the pressure-volume relation in the chamber around that point. In terms of the calculus, it is the first derivative with respect to volume of the pressure-volume relation. If the pressure-volume relation in the chamber is a straight line, the elastance is equivalent to the difference between the pressures at any two points on the line divided by the difference between the volumes associated with those two pressures.

Elastance (or stiffness) is the inverse of compliance (or distensibility or elasticity). The term compliance and its synonyms refer to the first derivative of the volume of a chamber with respect to pressure. Thus, all of these terms are dealing with the same fundamental physical property of elastic materials: the tendency of the pressure inside a chamber to be related to the volume within the chamber. Usually, the relation is a direct one. In the case of the heart, however, the relation is not linear and varies with time.[61,62] The ventricle is much stiffer during systole than during diastole, and its stiffness varies during systole and diastole—hence the concept of systolic function as opposed to diastolic function.

Traditionally, in plotting the pressure-volume relation, physicists, engineers, and cardiovascular physiologists have preferred to assign volume to the x-axis as the independent variable and to assign pressure to the y-axis as the dependent variable. Pulmonary physiologists, however, have generally preferred to reverse this assignment. Neither way is right or wrong: the assignment of variables to axes is essentially arbitrary. Nevertheless, for the purposes of consistency and clarity, one must make a decision about how these concepts are to be represented. Accordingly, in the ensuing discussion, we will treat volume as the independent variable and, for the most part, will address stiffness or elastance rather than compliance, distensibility, or elasticity.

The pressure-volume relation in the left ventricle can be determined by simultaneous measurement of ventricular volume (with implanted microsonographic crystals, conductance catheter techniques, contrast ventriculography, or echocardiography) and intraventricular pressure. These measurements are then repeated while either the LVEDV or the afterload is altered, thereby yielding a "family" of pressure-volume relations. From this family, the elastances of the ventricle during an entire cardiac cycle can be calculated.[61,62]

How ventricular elastance varies during a single cardiac cycle can be illustrated by considering typical values for a normal 60 kg woman in a resting state [see Figure 2]. At the end of diastole (or the beginning of systole), the elastance is 0.2 mm Hg/ml. When systole begins, this value increases rapidly (within about 50 milliseconds) to 1.0 mm Hg/ml. At this point in the cardiac cycle, the pressure inside the ventricle is high enough to open the aortic valve. The elastance continues to increase as the ventricle pushes its blood into the aortic root, reaching its maximum at the end of systole. Typically, the end-systolic elastance is some 10 times greater than the end-diastolic elastance, or about 2.0 mm Hg/ml.

The elastance rapidly decreases during isovolumic relaxation until the beginning of diastolic filling of the ventricle; it then gradually and slightly increases until the end of diastole, returning to the initial value of 0.2 mm Hg/ml.

It is worthwhile to compare these variations in elastance with those seen in a person with maximal adrenergic stimulation of the heart and in a person with profound beta blockade [see Figure 2]. In the former, the end-systolic elastance is double the normal value, or 4.0 mm Hg/ml, and the ventricle reaches its maximal elastance more quickly. In the latter, the end-systolic elastance is half the normal value, or 1.0 mm Hg/ml, and the ventricle reaches its maximal elastance more slowly.

Thus, the end-systolic elastance can serve as a reasonably complete and simple measure of ventricular function. It provides a single-number quantitative description of the concept of contractility; it can be precisely measured, at least in the catheterization laboratory; it has been shown to be independent of end-diastolic volumes and afterload in experimental animals; and it is ideally suited for dealing with one of the fundamental problems in managing

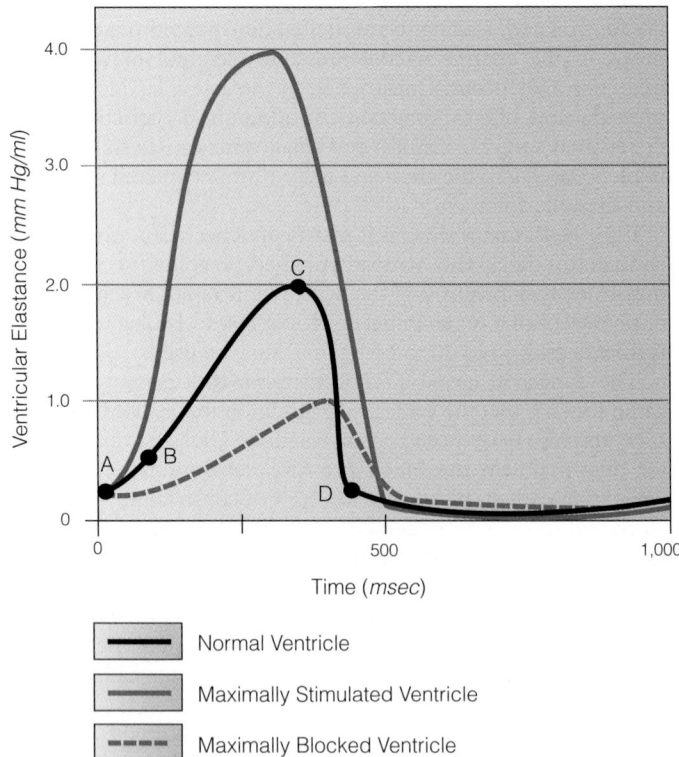

Normal Ventricle

Maximally Stimulated Ventricle

Maximally Blocked Ventricle

Figure 2 **Illustrated is the elastance (stiffness) of the left ventricle over a cardiac cycle in a 60 kg person, as seen in a normal person under resting conditions, a person with a maximally contractile ventricle, and a person with profound beta blockade or congestive heart failure. Point A is the beginning of systolic contraction; point B is the opening of the aortic valve; point C is end-systole; and point D is the beginning of diastolic filling. With maximal contractility, elastance rises more quickly than normal, and maximal stiffness, at end-systole, is twice the normal value. With congestive failure, elastance rises more slowly, and maximal stiffness is half the normal value. The elastance during diastole is lowest under conditions of maximal contractility, at least in this example.**

critically ill patients—namely, the problem of predicting how a ventricle with a given contractility will interact with a vasculature with a given afterload [*see* Ventricular-Arterial Coupling, *below*].

Afterload

As with contractility, defining a numerical descriptor for afterload has proved challenging since the early 1900s. In our view and that of many others, the impedance faced by the ventricle is a good choice for this purpose. We use the impedance as the descriptor for afterload for many of the same reasons that we use the ventricular end-systolic elastance as the descriptor for contractility. The impedance can be precisely defined by making precise measurements of flow and pressure in the aortic root in the cardiac catheterization laboratory; it can, with reservations, be expressed as a single number; it can, with reservations, be approximated with values obtained from measurements made with a Swan-Ganz catheter; and it is ideally suited for dealing with ventricular-arterial coupling.

The impedance (or hindrance) faced by the ventricle during emptying has three components. (We use the left ventricle as an example here, but the same concepts apply to the right ventricle.) The first component is the elastance (or stiffness) of the named arteries, including the aorta, which hinders the accommodation of blood in the arteries as the ventricle empties during systole. The second component is the resistance to steady-state flow offered by the arterioles throughout the body. The third component is the resistance to flow offered by the large veins as they enter the chest, coupled with the stiffness of the right atrium and ventricle as they accept blood returning from the body.

At first glance, the way in which these components relate to impedance appears simple. The stiffer the arteries, the higher the impedance; the greater the arteriolar constriction, the higher the impedance; and the greater the hindrance to the filling of the contralateral heart, the higher the impedance. The concept becomes more complex, however, when one tries to understand how these components interact with one another, as they do when connected to a pulsatile energy source (e.g., a contracting ventricle). One way of exploring this interaction is to consider the pressure wave that is propagated throughout the vasculature when the ventricle pumps blood into the aortic root.

When the left ventricle contracts, it pushes the blood it contains into a standing column of blood in the aortic root. Initially, this column of blood remains stagnant; however, the energy impulse imparted to it by the inrush of ventricular blood generates a pressure wave that propagates throughout the arteries until it reaches the arterioles, which are situated throughout the body at differing distances from the heart. Part of the propagated wave bounces off the arterioles, generating reflected waves that return to the aortic root and the heart.

The amplitude of the reflected waves depends on the degree to which the arterioles are constricted: the greater the constriction, the higher the amplitude. Some of the reflected waves return during systole, some during diastole. The timing, as one might expect, depends to a large extent on the spatial distribution of the arterioles: waves from nearby arterioles return sooner, and waves from distant arterioles return later. The timing also depends on the propagation velocity of the waves, which itself depends on the elastance of the walls of the arteries through which the waves pass. Finally, the timing depends to an extent on the viscoelastic properties of the conducting medium (i.e., the blood), but aside from limiting blood transfusions and keeping the patient warm, there is little that the physician can do to influence these properties. There is, however, a great deal that the physician can do to influence arterial elastance (see below).

The velocity of the propagating pressure wave can be measured quite simply in humans by means of Doppler technology. On average, it is about 4 m/sec in young children and 18 m/sec in octogenarians.[63,64] The increased velocity in older persons is caused by the replacement of elastin in the arterial walls with collagen as part of the aging process. The velocities in the upper part of the body are slower than those in the lower part because the arterial walls in the upper extremities are thinner and more compliant than those in the lower extremities. Arterial walls possess receptors for norepinephrine, vasopressin, and angiotensin II; activation of these receptors increases the stiffness of the walls and the velocity of the pressure wave. Stretching of the walls also increases their stiffness and the velocity of the pressure wave, as does arterial mural calcification (e.g., in patients with diabetes).

A key point is that the propagation velocities of the pressure waves are much faster than the velocities with which the blood moves through the arteries. Blood flow velocities, unlike pressure wave propagation velocities, are not affected by changes in arterial wall elastance. During a cardiac cycle, blood flow velocity ranges from 0 to 50 cm/sec, with a mean value of about 15 cm/sec. Thus, for a child, pressure wave propagation velocity (4 m/sec) is more than 25 times faster than mean blood flow velocity, whereas for an 80-year-old, pressure wave propagation velocity (18 m/sec) is more than 100 times faster. The differences between pressure wave propagation velocity and blood flow velocity indicate that although the blood is indeed moved by the energy waves generated by ventricular contraction, it has inertia. The blood does accelerate and gain speed as the pressure wave moves through it, but it cannot be expected to keep up with the wave.

As a general rule, a patient is better off with compliant arteries and slow propagation velocities. With high velocities, the waves return too rapidly to the aortic root, arriving even before the ven-

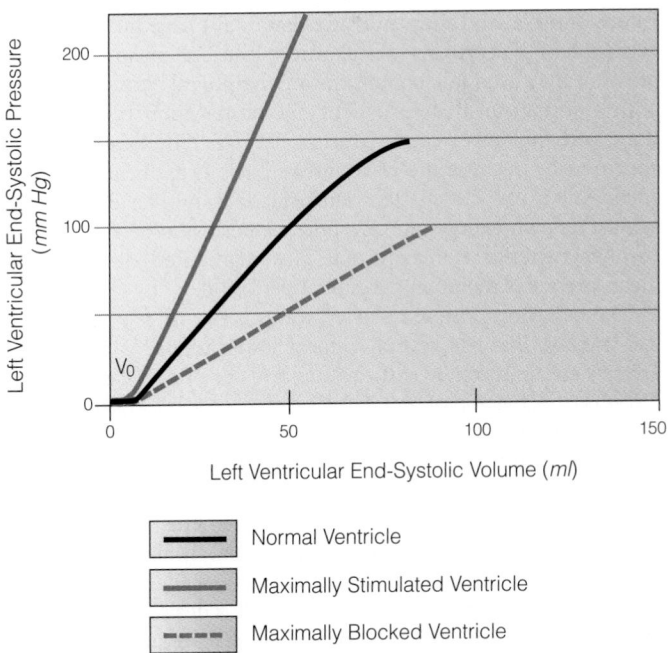

Figure 3 **Shown is LVESP plotted against LVESV at end-systole, as seen in a normal ventricle, a maximally stimulated ventricle, and a maximally blocked ventricle. Once the LVESV exceeds the unstressed volume (V_0), the LVESP increases in a fairly linear way. The contractilities of the three ventricles can be taken as the slopes of the relations: 2.0, 4.0, and 1.0 mm Hg/ml, respectively [*see Figure 1*].**

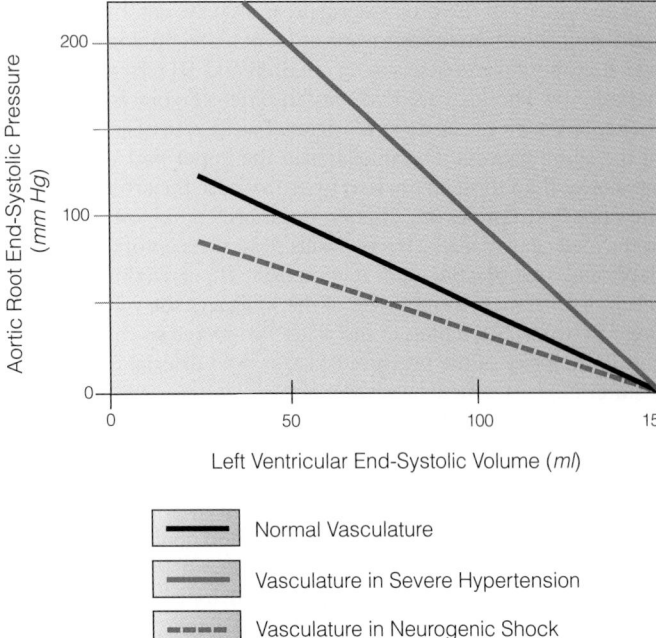

Figure 4 Shown is aortic root end-systolic pressure plotted against LVESV, as seen in a normal vasculature, the vasculature of a patient with severe hypertension, and the vasculature of a patient in neurogenic shock. The LVESV is assumed to be 150 ml. The magnitudes of the slopes of the relations for the three vasculatures (1.0, 2.0, and 0.75, respectively) can be taken to represent the afterloads.

tricle has finished contracting; as a result, the ventricle fights itself, pumping against the pressure wave that it generated. Another problem with high propagation velocities is that the waves die out before diastole, and thus, pressure that could have been used for perfusion of the coronary vasculature is lost. The mean aortic root pressure may even fall, compromising peripheral perfusion.

In a young, unstressed patient, the propagation velocities are slow, and the waves return during diastole. The heart benefits enormously. Because the waves arrive back at the heart after the aortic valve has closed, the ventricle does not have to pump against its own energy impulse, and the perfusion pressure of the coronary arteries is maximized. The augmented diastolic and mean pressures maintain peripheral perfusion.

The behavior of these reflected waves is not merely of theoretical interest but has several clinical implications. If a patient's arteries are abnormally stiff (e.g., as a result of age, calcification, distention, activation of vessel wall receptors, or external compression), the propagation velocity will be high, which means that the waves will return early, the systolic pressure at the aortic root will rise, and the diastolic pressure will fall. The elevated systolic pressure will increase ventricular oxygen requirements; the unaffected MAP will do nothing for tissue perfusion. If the propagation velocity can be reduced, the systolic pressure will come down and the MAP will stay the same. This is usually a desirable result for a shock patient, in that myocardial oxygen requirements will decrease while perfusion pressures are maintained. Accordingly, in the treatment of shock, there is often a real clinical benefit to be gained from interventions aimed at reducing arterial stiffness.

Several options are available for decreasing arterial stiffness, including diuresis or fluid restriction, beta blockade, ACE inhibition, and the use of agents that increase the production of nitric oxide near the arterial walls (and, admittedly, at the arteriolar and venular walls). The aortic counterpulsating balloon pump can be extremely effective in dealing with systemic arterial stiffness. (In fact, that is its only function.) Options for treating stiff arteries on the right side of the circulation are more limited, though the pharmacologic interventions just mentioned are sometimes helpful. One may also adjust the ventilator.

The impedance facing the ventricles can be determined with precision in the catheterization laboratory by using catheters that can precisely measure pressures and flows at the roots of the arteries. To describe this complex interplay of wave propagation and reflection with a single number, to quantify responses to interventions, and to do both of these things with numbers available in the intensive care unit, one can calculate the hindrance facing the left ventricle as the LVESP (or, equivalently, the aortic root end-systolic pressure) divided by the stroke volume. The resulting value—the effective aortic root elastance—will be high if a given stroke volume creates a high systolic pressure and low if the stroke volume creates a low pressure. (It is worth mentioning that although this value is an elastance and is expressed in the units used for elastance, it reflects not only the properties of the arteries but also the properties of the arterioles. After all, the amplitude of the reflected waves depends on the arterioles. The value for effective elastance takes into account all of the factors that may hinder ventricular emptying.)

Ventricular-Arterial Coupling

In addressing the problem of ventricular-arterial coupling, it is useful to start by considering the pressure-volume relations in the left ventricle and the aortic root. One could just as well start by considering the right side of the heart, which in some surgical patients is the critical side; however, there is far more information in the literature about the left side, and more options are available for intervention on that side. Regardless of which side of the heart is considered, the essential concepts are the same.

The left ventricle is stiffest at end-systole. If the intraventricular pressure is plotted as a function of the intraventricular volume at end-systole, a fairly straight line will be generated [see Figure 3]. The slope of this line is the end-systolic elastance (or stiffness), which, as noted [see Contractility, above], serves as a descriptor for contractility.[62]

It is noteworthy that the x-intercept of the relation is not 0 but a value slightly greater than 0. This is because a ventricle can contain a small amount of blood without generating any pressure at all; it is only when the volume exceeds a certain threshold—the so-called unstressed volume (V_0)—that the pressure starts to increase as the volume increases.[61,62] A typical value for the end-systolic unstressed volume in a 60 kg person is quite low, on the order of 0.1 ml/kg, or 6 ml. In patients with severe congestive heart failure, the unstressed volume can be as high as 60 ml, as a manifestation of a globally flabby heart, but in most patients, it can be assumed to be close to 0 ml.

The slope of the line can then be approximated as the LVESP divided by the LVESV. Other points on the line can also be used to make this calculation, but they will not be known unless one is in the catheterization laboratory and can make sophisticated measurements of both pressure and volume as end-diastolic volumes or afterloads are altered. Accordingly, the aforementioned approximation is the most clinically useful calculation. As with ventricular elastance, the plot will look quite different in a person with maximal beta-adrenergic stimulation or a person with maximal beta blockade [see Figure 3].

The pressure-volume relation for the aortic root can be plotted on a graph in a similar fashion [see Figure 4]. In this case, the LVESV is still plotted on the x-axis, whereas the end-systolic pressure in the aortic root is plotted on the y-axis. This relation depends on the LVEDV. For example, in a 60 kg person with an LVEDV of 150 ml, if the LVESV is 150 ml, the stroke volume will be 0 ml. If the stroke volume is 0 ml, the heart will generate no pressure for filling the aortic root, and the aortic root pressure will be 0 mm Hg. If, however, the LVESV is 50 ml (a normal value) and the LVEDV is held constant at 150 ml, the stroke volume will be 100 ml. A stroke volume of 100 ml will generate an LVESP of 100 mm Hg.

If points representing these two scenarios are plotted on the graph, a line can be drawn between them to represent the relation between the end-systolic pressure in the aortic root and the LVESV. The magnitude of the slope of this line is calculated by dividing the LVESP by the stroke volume. In this case, the calculation yields a value of 1.0 mm Hg/ml. This value can be taken as the effective elastance of the aortic root at end-systole, which, in turn, can be taken as a single-number representation of the hindrance facing the left ventricle (i.e., the impedance).[61,62] Different values will be obtained in a patient with severe hypertension or a patient in warm septic shock [see Figure 4], even when the LVEDV is the same.

To deal with the problem of ventricular-arterial coupling, one then plots the two pressure-volume relations (for the left ventricle and the aortic root) at end-systole on the same graph [see Figure 5]. The LVESP must equal the end-systolic pressure in the aortic root. (In fact, the pressures throughout most of systole, with the exception of isovolumic contraction, are about the same.) The only point on the graph where the two pressures are equal is the point where the two lines intersect. This point defines the specific end-systolic volume and pressure for a patient with a specific unstressed ventricular end-systolic volume, a specific contractility, a specific end-diastolic volume, and a specific afterload. That is, this graphic analysis allows one to predict how a particular ventricle with particular characteristics will interact with an arterial system with a particular afterload.

Pressure-Volume Loops and Thermodynamics of Ventricular Contraction

The next step is to draw a pressure-volume loop for the ventricle, working on the assumption that the unstressed end-systolic volume, the contractility, the end-diastolic volume, and the afterload are known. Typical values would be 6 ml, 2 mm Hg/ml, 150 ml, and 1 mm Hg/ml, respectively. From the analysis previously described (see above), it follows that the end-systolic volume will be 50 ml and the end-systolic pressure will be 100 mm Hg [see Figure 6].

At the beginning of systole (point A), the ventricle has a volume of 150 ml and an end-diastolic pressure of 8 mm Hg (if the patient is breathing spontaneously). The ventricle then contracts until the pressure in the chamber exceeds the pressure in the aortic root and the aortic valve opens (point B).

As the blood contained in the ventricle is pushed into the aortic root, ventricular volume decreases until end-systole (point C) is reached. It should be kept in mind that the pressure inside the ventricle at any point during ventricular emptying is determined by the balance between the volume and the stiffness of the chamber at that point. The pressure increases from the beginning of ventricular emptying to, roughly, the midportion of systole. That is, the effect of the rapidly increasing stiffness of the ventricle [see Figure 2] overcomes the effect of the decreasing volume as the ventricle empties. From the midportion of systole to end-systole, the effect of the decreasing volume starts to dominate as it overcomes the still-increasing stiffness, and the pressure gradually falls.

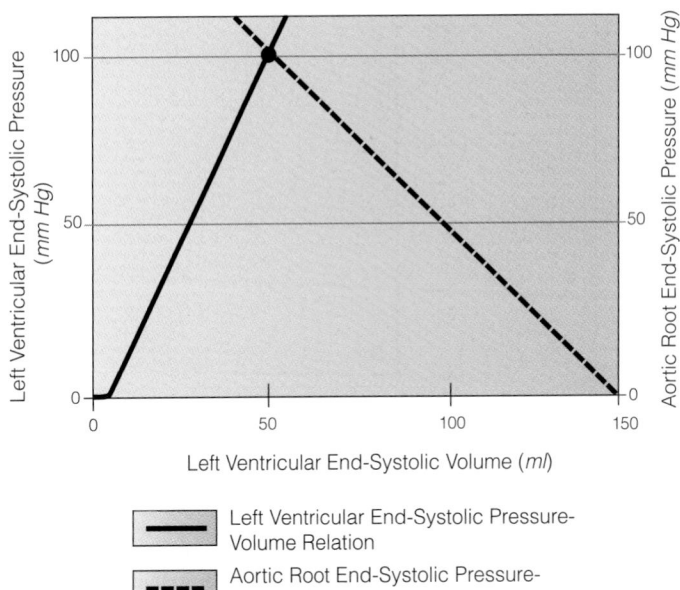

Figure 5   Illustrated is the superposition of the normal pressure-volume relation for the left ventricle at end-systole [see Figure 3] onto the normal pressure-volume relation for the aortic root at end-systole [see Figure 4]. The two pressures must be the same. Thus, in this case, the LVESV must be 50 ml, and both the LVESP and the aortic root end-systolic pressure must be 100 mm Hg (point C). That is, the end-systolic point is determined by the end-systolic unstressed volume, the contractility, the end-diastolic volume, and the afterload.

At end-systole (point C), the actin and myosin myofilaments suddenly disengage, and the ventricle switches from its maximally contracted state to an increasingly compliant one. The ventricle then goes through another isovolumic phase as its pressure drops to its lowest value during the cardiac cycle, at the beginning of diastolic filling (point D). Finally, the chamber fills again and returns to its initial state.

The work done on the ventricle during diastole is represented by the area under the diastolic pressure-volume curve and the x-axis, which is approximately equal to the mean diastolic pressure multiplied by the stroke volume.[61,62] The work done on the aortic root by the contraction of the ventricle is represented by the area contained within the curve, or the difference between the end-systolic and mean diastolic pressures multiplied by the stroke volume. The total work done on the aortic root with each cardiac cycle is represented by the entire area under the curve, down to the x-axis. It can be approximated as the end-systolic pressure multiplied by the stroke volume.

Also illustrated is the wasted energy associated with the loop (i.e., the heat dissipated in the ventricular wall during isovolumic relaxation). This variable is represented by the area contained within a triangle whose apices are the points V_0, D, and C (i.e., the unstressed volume, the beginning of diastolic filling, and end-systole). Under normal circumstances, this area can be ignored. It can become substantial, however, if the afterload comes to exceed the contractility (see below).

The total amount of energy transmitted into the aortic root per minute is the total work done on the root per heartbeat multiplied by the heart rate. The total amount of heat dissipated in the ventricular wall during isovolumic relaxation is the area of the aforementioned triangle multiplied by the heart rate. The left-side oxy-

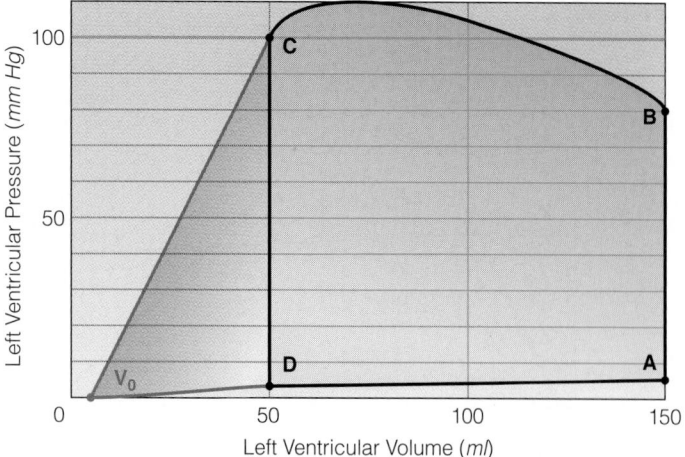

Figure 6 Illustrated is the pressure-volume relation for the left ventricle over an entire cardiac cycle. The work done on the left ventricle during diastole (or, equivalently, the energy added to the ventricle during systole) is the area under the curve DA. The energy added to the aortic root by virtue of ventricular contraction is the area contained within the loop ABCD. The total energy added to the aortic root during a single heartbeat is the sum of these two areas. The heat dissipated in the ventricular wall during isovolumic relaxation is equal to the area contained within the triangle CV_0D.

gen requirements for the myocardium are directly proportional to the sum of the total amount of power produced and the total amount of heat dissipated in the ventricular wall.

The goal of resuscitation in a patient in shock is to achieve adequate cardiac production of power while minimizing myo-

cardial oxygen requirements. If the effective arterial elastance is adjusted so that it equals the contractility, maximum work per heartbeat will be achieved, but a substantial amount of heat will be dissipated in the ventricular wall during isovolumic relaxation [*see Figure 7*]. If the afterload is adjusted so that it is approximately half the contractility, some work will be lost, but substantially less heat will be dissipated; thus, power will be produced much more efficiently. If the afterload is allowed to exceed the contractility, the work produced will fall off and the myocardial oxygen requirements will increase—a situation that is rarely good for the patient.

These conclusions can be demonstrated by graphing the pressure-volume relations for ventricles and aortic roots at end-systole under these different conditions. The predicted end-systolic values for the ventricular volumes and pressures can then be used to generate the different pressure-volume loops. The conclusions can also be proved by means of mathematical analysis.

Although there is no thermodynamic free lunch, there are certainly more expensive and less expensive lunches. To make the thermodynamic lunch as inexpensive as possible, one should avoid letting the afterload exceed the contractility, and one should try to minimize the systolic pressures while maintaining the mean pressures.

Goals for Cardiovascular Resuscitation in Treatment of Shock

Efforts have been made to avoid using any invasive cardiovascular measurements in resuscitation from severe shock (e.g., by using gastric mucosal pH as an end point for resuscitation), but to date, such efforts have not proved helpful outside carefully controlled research environments. There is wide agreement that invasive monitoring is still needed in the treatment of severe shock;

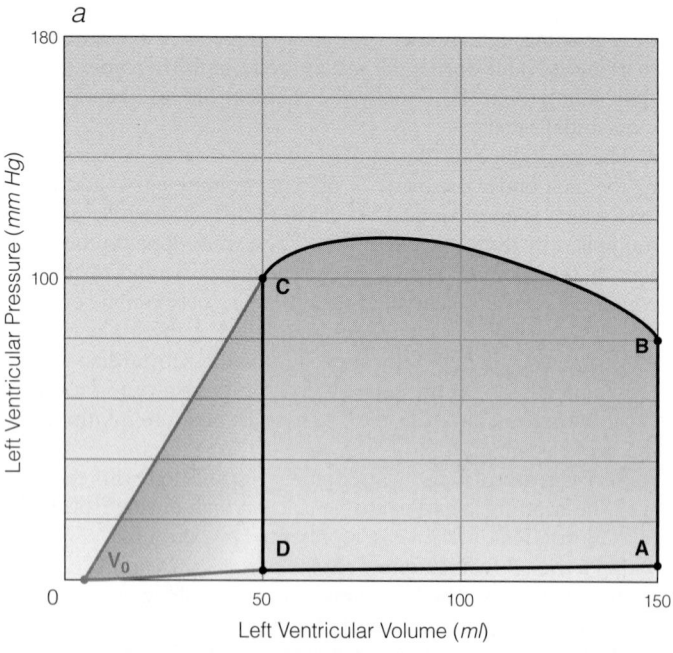

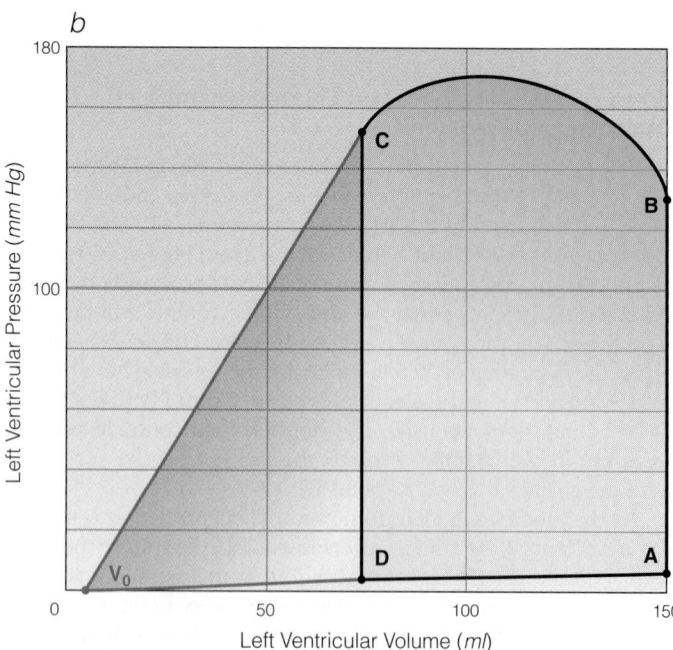

Figure 7 Shown are pressure-volume loops generated by different ratios of afterload to contractility. If the afterload is approximately half the contractility (*a*), as in a patient in septic shock who has reduced contractility and afterload, the ventricle will produce its work with optimal efficiency. If the afterload equals the contractility (*b*), as when the same patient is given a vasoconstrictor, the pressure will increase and the ventricle will produce slightly more work, but substantially more energy will be wasted in the form of heat dissipation during isovolumic relaxation. If the vasoconstrictor is given to produce a higher pressure, the work will begin to fall off, and the heat dissipated in the ventricular wall will continue to increase.

Table 4 Effects of Position and Strenuous Exercise on Cardiovascular
Volumes and Pressures in a Young, Well-Conditioned 60 kg Woman

Variables	Supine (Resting)	Upright (Resting)	Upright (Exercising)
Lower body venular volume (ml)	1,920	> 1,920	< 1,920
Lower body venular pressure (mm Hg)	20	> 20	< 20
Upper body venular volume (ml)	960	< 960	> 960
Upper body venular pressure (mm Hg)	10	< 10	> 10
Right ventricular end-diastolic volume (ml)	150	133	145
Right ventricular end-diastolic pressure (mm Hg)	5	5	5
Right ventricular and pulmonary arterial end-systolic pressure (mm Hg)	22.5	22.5	35
Mean pulmonary arterial pressure (mm Hg)	15	15	20
Left ventricular end-diastolic volume (ml)	150	133	145
Left ventricular end-diastolic pressure (mm Hg)	8	8	8
Left ventricular and aortic root end-systolic pressure (mm Hg)	100	100	145
Mean aortic pressure (mm Hg)	90	90	110

however, there is no consensus on what to do with the values obtained from monitoring.

One approach is to try to find a single parameter that can serve as the goal of resuscitation. The best candidate parameter is probably the $S_{mv}O_2$, measured with a pulmonary arterial catheter. This value can be quite helpful in minute-to-minute management during resuscitation from hemorrhagic shock. It is considerably less helpful, however, in patients in inflammatory shock, who often have quite high venous saturations, partly because of peripheral shunting through the cutaneous vasculature and partly because of functional shunting by cells that cannot metabolize the oxygen presented to them. In the setting of inflammatory shock, a high $S_{mv}O_2$ may even indicate a severe metabolic derangement rather than resolution of shock.

Another approach is to attempt to determine whether the patient's oxygen consumption (measured with a pulmonary arterial catheter and based in part on measurements of cardiac output) depends on oxygen delivery (the product of cardiac output, hemoglobin concentration, and S_aO_2). Unquestionably, at very low levels of oxygen delivery, oxygen consumption must decrease. At excessively high levels, however, oxygen consumption may continue to rise if oxygen delivery is increased by the administration of inotropes. These agents usually have beta-adrenergic effects and can increase peripheral oxygen metabolism; they also increase myocardial oxygen requirements. Thus, the act of increasing delivery can increase overall consumption.

Yet another approach is to maintain all patients at very high levels of oxygen delivery without making any attempt to ascertain whether there is a correlation between delivery and peripheral consumption. Two randomized trials evaluated this approach; neither found any evidence of benefit.[65,66]

Our approach is to start, as any clinician would, by attempting to resolve the clinical abnormalities observed without subjecting the patient to invasive monitoring. If this attempt is unsuccessful, we insert monitoring catheters and use the information obtained from them to try to achieve reasonable ventricular power production with acceptable efficiency while minimizing the formation of edema. This approach is supported by a compelling study that underscored the value of taking a thermodynamic approach to resuscitation and indicated that the goal for resuscitation of the typical shock patient need be little more than a reasonable blood pressure and a reasonable cardiac output.[67,68]

Different goals may, however, be appropriate in other patients. For example, cardiovascular conditioning increases the blood vol-

ume, increases the ventricular end-diastolic volumes, increases the stroke volume, and decreases the resting heart rate. In other words, it prepares the body for stress. Accordingly, we aim for a higher cardiac output if we know that a patient was in good car-

Table 5 Effects of Position and Exercise
on Organ Blood Flow and Oxygen Consumption
in a Young, Well-Conditioned 60 kg Woman

Variables	Supine (Resting)	Upright (Resting)	Upright (Exercising)
Whole body			
Blood flow (L/min)	6.0	5.0	22.0
Venous O_2 saturation	76%	71.6%	11%
O_2 consumption (ml/min)	210	210	3,180
Splanchnic viscera			
Blood flow (L/min) (% of total)	1.50 (25%)	1.25 (25%)	0.30 (1%)
Venous O_2 saturation	77%	73%	18%
O_2 consumption (ml/min)	50	50	40
Kidneys			
Blood flow (L/min) (% of total)	1.20 (20%)	1.00 (20%)	0.25 (1%)
Venous O_2 saturation	91%	90%	65%
O_2 consumption (ml/min)	12	12	12
Brain			
Blood flow (L/min) (% of total)	0.90 (15%)	0.75 (15%)	0.75 (3%)
Venous O_2 saturation	67%	60%	59%
O_2 consumption (ml/min)	45	45	45
Heart			
Blood flow (L/min) (% of total)	0.24 (4%)	0.20 (4%)	0.80 (4%)
Venous O_2 saturation	46%	35%	1%
O_2 consumption (ml/min)	20	20	130
Skeletal muscle			
Blood flow (L/min) (% of total)	1.20 (20%)	1.00 (20%)	19.5 (89%)
Venous O_2 saturation	61%	54%	8%
O_2 consumption (ml/min)	70	70	2,940
Skin			
Blood flow (L/min) (% of total)	0.30 (5%)	0.25 (5%)	0.30 (1%)
Venous O_2 saturation	93%	91%	88%
O_2 consumption (ml/min)	2	2	2
Other organs			
Blood flow (L/min) (% of total)	0.66 (11%)	0.55 (11%)	0.10 (0%)
Venous O_2 saturation	87%	85%	31%
O_2 consumption (ml/min)	11	11	11

diovascular condition before the acute problem developed.

We also aim for slightly higher (but not excessively high) values in patients with major injuries or overwhelming infections. Hyperthermia or systemic inflammation can raise oxygen consumption to values as high as twice those encountered in normothermic, uninjured, or uninfected persons. (To put these changes in perspective, oxygen consumption in a strenuously exercising young subject can increase by a factor of 15 to 20.) In addition, if the environment is cold enough to induce shivering, oxygen consumption can rise to levels several times higher than those observed in a thermoneutral environment. In these situations, a higher cardiac output is to be expected. (In contrast, hypothermia in the absence of shivering decreases oxygen consumption. In this situation, the cardiac output can fall to quite low levels with no detrimental effect on the patient's survival. Efforts to increase cardiac output in severely cold patients can even induce fatal ventricular arrhythmias.)

Sometimes, a goal for cardiac output can be arrived at by means of trial and error. For example, if a supranormal cardiac output causes an abnormality (e.g., metabolic acidosis) to resolve when a normal output did not, an effort should be made to keep the cardiac output high for a while.

We also consider values gleaned from the wealth of studies done on both normal and exercising subjects in cardiac catheterization and exercise physiology laboratories, keeping in mind that normal values can vary from subject to subject [see Tables 4 and 5]. Gaining a sense of what the heart and lungs can do in different circumstances can give the clinician a useful perspective on how a patient is likely to respond to shock and what to expect from resuscitation.

Studies have shown that the physiologic responses to standing up are similar to those that come into play in the early stages of shock (with the exception of neurogenic shock, in which there are very few responses) [see Tables 4 and 5]: activation of the adrenergic system, activation of the renin-angiotensin system, release of vasopressin from the hypothalamus, and release of aldosterone from the adrenal glands. These responses are also similar to those that develop when a patient is placed on mechanical ventilation, a therapeutic intervention that results in small ventricular end-diastolic volumes because of redistribution of blood into the systemic venules and small veins (just as standing up results in redistribution of blood from the ventricles to the dependent venules and small veins). The pressures are maintained with minor stresses, but the cardiac output drops, as does flow to the kidneys and the splanchnic organs.

In strenuous exercise, oxygen consumption can increase by a factor of 15 to 20, and cardiac output can increase by a factor of 3 to 4. Blood flow to the splanchnic viscera and the kidneys falls to levels as low as 20% of normal, with no long-term ill effects. (The organs survive by extracting a higher percentage of the oxygen delivered to them.) Blood flow to the skin during strenuous but not exhausting exercise in a warm environment can increase from a baseline of 300 ml/min to levels as high as 6 L/min in an effort to offload heat and keep body temperature within acceptable limits. (We are not aware of any studies that have measured blood flow to the skin of patients in inflammatory shock, but we suspect that the flow rate may be as high as 3 L/min for a 60 kg person.)

Shock patients cannot be expected to be capable of achieving these sorts of values, but the numbers do give the physician a feeling for what the body can do and thus some idea of what to expect. A patient in shock has an excellent chance of surviving with normal function of all organs if resuscitation can be achieved expeditiously.

References

1. Aubier M, Trippenbach T, Roussos C: Respiratory muscle fatigue during cardiogenic shock. J Appl Physiol 51:499, 1981

2. Davis JO, Freeman RH: Mechanisms regulating renin release. Physiol Rev 56:1, 1976

3. Share L: Role of vasopressin in cardiovascular regulation. Physiol Rev 68:1248, 1988

4. Ventilation with lower tidal volumes as compared with traditional tidal volumes for acute lung injury and the acute respiratory distress syndrome. The Acute Respiratory Distress Syndrome Network. N Engl J Med 342:1301, 2000

5. Mayberry JC, Welker KJ, Goldman RK, et al: Mechanism of acute ascites formation after trauma resuscitation. Arch Surg 138:773, 2003

6. Jones RM, Moulton CE, Hardy KJ: Central venous pressure and its effect on blood loss during liver resection. Br J Surg 85:1058, 1998

7. Balogh Z, McKinley BA, Cox CS Jr, et al: Supranormal trauma resuscitation causes more cases of abdominal compartment syndrome. Arch Surg 138:637, 2003

8. Derouin M, Couture P, Boudreault D, et al: Detection of gas embolism by transesophageal echocardiography during laparoscopic cholecystectomy. Anesth Analg 82:119, 1996

9. Rivers E, Nguyen B, Havstad S, et al: Early goal-directed therapy in the treatment of severe sepsis and septic shock. N Engl J Med 345:1368, 2001

10. Deshpande KS, Hatem C, Ulrich HL, et al: The incidence of infectious complications of central venous catheters at the subclavian, internal jugular, and femoral sites in an intensive care unit population. Crit Care Med 33:13, 2005

11. Goetz AM, Wagener MM, Miller JM, et al: Risk of infection due to central venous catheters: effect of site of placement and catheter type. Infect Control Hosp Epidemiol 19:842, 1998

12. Trottier SJ, Veremakis C, O'Brien J, et al: Femoral deep vein thrombosis associated with central venous catheterization: results from a prospective, randomized trial. Crit Care Med 23:52, 1995

13. Macnab A, Christenson J, Findlay J, et al: A new system for sternal intraosseous infusion in adults. Prehosp Emerg Care 4:173, 2000

14. Advanced Trauma Life Support for Doctors: Student Course Manual, 6th ed. American College of Surgeons Committee on Trauma, Chicago, 1997, p 289

15. PALS Provider Manual. American Heart Association, Dallas, 2002, p 155

16. Calkins MD, Fitzgerald G, Bentley TB, et al: Intraosseous infusion devices: a comparison for potential use in special operations. J Trauma 48:1068, 2000

17. Moon PF, Hollyfield-Gilbert MA, Myers TL, et al: Fluid compartments in hemorrhaged rats after hyperosmotic crystalloid and hyperoncotic colloid resuscitation. Am J Physiol 270(1 pt 2):F1, 1996

18. Morisaki H, Bloos F, Keys J, et al: Compared with crystalloid, colloid therapy slows progression of extrapulmonary tissue injury in septic sheep. J Appl Physiol 77:1507, 1994

19. Wilkes MM, Navickis RJ: Patient survival after human albumin administration: a meta-analysis of randomized, controlled trials. Ann Intern Med 135:149, 2001

20. Human albumin administration in critically ill patients: systematic review of randomised controlled trials. Cochrane Injuries Group Albumin Reviewers. BMJ 317:235, 1998

21. Finfer S, Bellomo R, Boyce N, et al: A comparison of albumin and saline for fluid resuscitation in the intensive care unit. N Engl J Med 350:2247, 2004

22. Collis RE, Collins PW, Gutteridge CN, et al: The effect of hydroxyethyl starch and other plasma volume substitutes on endothelial cell activation: an in vitro study. Intensive Care Med 20:37, 1994

23. Treib J, Haass A, Pindur G: Coagulation disorders caused by hydroxyethyl starch. Thromb Haemost 78:974, 1997

24. Boldt J, Ducke M, Kumle B, et al: Influence of different volume replacement strategies on inflammation and endothelial activation in the elderly undergoing major abdominal surgery. Intensive Care Med 30:416, 2004

25. Huttner I, Boldt J, Haisch G, et al: Influence of different colloids on molecular markers of haemostasis and platelet function in patients undergoing major abdominal surgery. Br J Anaesth 85:417, 2000

26. Roberts I, Alderson P, Bunn F, et al: Colloids versus crystalloids for fluid resuscitation in critically ill patients. Cochrane Database Syst Rev (4):CD000567, 2004

27. Vassar MJ, Fischer RP, O'Brien PE, et al: A multicenter trial for resuscitation of injured patients with 7.5% sodium chloride: the effect of added dextran

70. The Multicenter Group for the Study of Hypertonic Saline in Trauma Patients. Arch Surg 128: 1003, 1993

28. Rotstein OD: Novel strategies for immunomodulation after trauma: revisiting hypertonic saline as a resuscitation strategy for hemorrhagic shock. J Trauma 49:580, 2000

29. Horton JW, Maass DL, White DJ: Hypertonic saline dextran after burn injury decreases inflammatory cytokine responses to subsequent pneumonia-related sepsis. Am J Physiol Heart Circ Physiol Nov 18, 2005 [Epub ahead of print]

30. Rizoli SB, Rhind SG, Shek PN, et al: The immunomodulatory effects of hypertonic saline resuscitation in patients sustaining traumatic hemorrhagic shock: a randomized, controlled, double-blinded trial. Ann Surg 243:47, 2006

31. Deitch EA, Shi HP, Feketeova E, et al: Hypertonic saline resuscitation limits neutrophil activation after trauma-hemorrhagic shock. Shock 19:328, 2003

32. Mazzoni MC, Borgstrom P, Intaglietta M, et al: Capillary narrowing in hemorrhagic shock is rectified by hyperosmotic saline-dextran reinfusion. Circ Shock 31:407, 1990

33. Angle N, Hoyt DB, Coimbra R, et al: Hypertonic saline resuscitation diminishes lung injury by suppressing neutrophil activation after hemorrhagic shock. Shock 9:164, 1998

34. Alam HB, Koustova E, Rhee P: Combat casualty care research: from bench to the battlefield. World J Surg 29(suppl 1):S7, 2005

35. Raghavan M, Marik PE: Anemia, allogenic blood transfusion, and immunomodulation in the critically ill. Chest 127:295, 2005

36. Marik PE, Sibbald WJ: Effect of stored-blood transfusion on oxygen delivery in patients with sepsis. JAMA 269:3024, 1993

37. Zallen G, Offner PJ, Moore EE, et al: Age of transfused blood is an independent risk factor for postinjury multiple organ failure. Am J Surg 178:570, 1999

38. Agarwal N, Murphy JG, Cayten CG, et al: Blood transfusion increases the risk of infection after trauma. Arch Surg 128:171, 1993

39. Moore FA, Moore EE, Sauaia A: Blood transfusion: an independent risk factor for postinjury multiple organ failure. Arch Surg 132:620, 1997

40. Vincent JL, Baron JF, Reinhart K, et al: Anemia and blood transfusion in critically ill patients. JAMA 288:1499, 2002

41. Hebert PC, Wells G, Blajchman MA, et al: A multicenter, randomized, controlled clinical trial of transfusion requirements in critical care. Transfusion Requirements in Critical Care Investigators, Canadian Critical Care Trials Group. N Engl J Med 340:409, 1999

42. Peoples GE, Gerlinger T, Budinich C, et al: The most frequently requested precombat refresher training by the Special Forces medics during Operation Enduring Freedom. Mil Med 170:31, 2005

43. Holcomb JB: The 2004 Fitts Lecture: current perspective on combat casualty care. J Trauma 59:990, 2005

44. Sloan EP, Koenigsberg M, Gens D, et al: Diaspirin cross-linked hemoglobin (DCLHb) in the treatment of severe traumatic hemorrhagic shock: a randomized controlled efficacy trial. JAMA 282:1857, 1999

45. Moore EE: Blood substitutes: the future is now. J Am Coll Surg 196:1, 2003

46. Wilmore DW: Metabolic response to severe surgical illness: overview. World J Surg 24:705, 2000

47. Adrogue HJ, Madias NE: Management of life-threatening acid-base disorders. First of two parts. N Engl J Med 338:26, 1998

48. Bernard GR, Vincent JL, Laterre PF, et al: Efficacy and safety of recombinant human activated protein C for severe sepsis. N Engl J Med 344:699, 2001

49. Barie PS, Williams MD, McCollam JS, et al: Benefit/risk profile of drotrecogin alfa (activated) in surgical patients with severe sepsis. Am J Surg 188:212, 2004

50. Vincent JL, Bernard GR, Beale R, et al: Drotrecogin alfa (activated) treatment in severe sepsis from the global open-label trial ENHANCE: further evidence for survival and safety and implications for early treatment. Crit Care Med 33:2266, 2005

51. Dellinger RP: Recombinant activated protein C: decisions for administration. Crit Care Med 34:530, 2006

52. Cronin L, Cook DJ, Carlet J, et al: Corticosteroid treatment for sepsis: a critical appraisal and meta-analysis of the literature. Crit Care Med 23:1430, 1995

53. Annane D, Sebille V, Charpentier C, et al: Effect of treatment with low doses of hydrocortisone and fludrocortisone on mortality in patients with septic shock. JAMA 288:862, 2002

54. Swan HJ, Ganz W, Forrester J, et al: Catheterization of the heart in man with use of a flow-directed balloon-tipped catheter. N Engl J Med 283:447, 1970

55. Dhainaut JF, Brunet F, Monsallier JF, et al: Bedside evaluation of right ventricular performance using a rapid computerized thermodilution method. Crit Care Med 15:148, 1987

56. Kraut EJ, Owings JT, Anderson JT, et al: Right ventricular volumes overestimate left ventricular preload in critically ill patients. J Trauma 42:839, 1997

57. Kelly R, Fitchett D: Noninvasive determination of aortic input impedance and external left ventricular power output: a validation and repeatability study of a new technique. J Am Coll Cardiol 20:952, 1992

58. Kelly R, Hayward C, Avolio A, et al: Noninvasive determination of age-related changes in the human arterial pulse. Circulation 80:1652, 1989

59. Putensen C, Hormann C, Kleinsasser A, et al: Cardiopulmonary effects of aerosolized prostaglandin E1 and nitric oxide inhalation in patients with acute respiratory distress syndrome. Am J Respir Crit Care Med 157:1743, 1998

60. Sibbald WJ, Paterson NA, Holliday RL, et al: The Trendelenburg position: hemodynamic effects in hypotensive and normotensive patients. Crit Care Med 7:218, 1979

61. McDonald's Blood Flow in Arteries: Theoretical, Experimental and Clinical Principles, 4th ed. O'Rourke MF, Nichols WW, Eds. Arnold and Oxford University Press, London and New York, 1998

62. Suga H: Ventricular energetics. Physiol Rev 70:247, 1990

63. Avolio AP, Chen SG, Wang RP, et al: Effects of aging on changing arterial compliance and left ventricular load in a northern Chinese urban community. Circulation 68:50, 1983

64. Avolio AP, Deng FQ, Li WQ, et al: Effects of aging on arterial distensibility in populations with high and low prevalence of hypertension: comparison between urban and rural communities in China. Circulation 71:202, 1985

65. Gattinoni L, Brazzi L, Pelosi P, et al: A trial of goal-oriented hemodynamic therapy in critically ill patients. SvO2 Collaborative Group. N Engl J Med 333:1025, 1995

66. Hayes MA, Timmins AC, Yau EH, et al: Elevation of systemic oxygen delivery in the treatment of critically ill patients. N Engl J Med 330:1717, 1994

67. Chang MC, Meredith JW, Kincaid EH, et al: Maintaining survivors' values of left ventricular power output during shock resuscitation: a prospective pilot study. J Trauma 49:26, 2000

68. Chang MC, Mondy JS, Meredith JW, et al: Redefining cardiovascular performance during resuscitation: ventricular stroke work, power, and the pressure-volume diagram. J Trauma 45:470, 1998

69. Schimdt-Nielson K: Scaling: Why Is Animal Size So Important? Cambridge University Press, Cambridge, United Kingdom, 1994

70. Gephart F, Dubois A, Dubois E: Clinical calorimetry: the basal metabolism of normal adults with special reference to surface area. Arch Intern Med 17:902, 1916

71. Grollman A: Physiological variations in the cardiac output of man. Am J Physiol 90:210, 1929

72. Kleiber M: Body size and metabolic rate. Physiol Rev 27:511, 1947

73. West GB, Brown JH, Enquist BJ: The fourth dimension of life: fractal geometry and allometric scaling of organisms. Science 284:1677, 1999

74. Brandfonbrener M, Landowne M, Shock NW: Changes in cardiac output with age. Circulation 12:557, 1955

75. Willett WC, Dietz WH, Colditz GA: Guidelines for healthy weight. N Engl J Med 341:427, 1999

Acknowledgment

Figure 1 Albert Miller.

119 CARDIOVASCULAR MONITORING

James W. Holcroft, M.D., F.A.C.S., and John T. Anderson, M.D., F.A.C.S.

Making and interpreting measurements of cardiovascular function in critically ill patients can be a challenge. Invasive monitoring, which is still necessary for many of the measurements, can give rise to complications. Differences among the ICU personnel who make the measurements can raise concerns about accuracy. The measurements, as well as the descriptors of cardiovascular function derived from them, are often abstract and must be interpreted mathematically. Moreover, the measurements are frequently indirect, involving surrogate variables; extrapolating from these surrogate variables back to the primary parameters of interest can be an involved process. Finally, the patient care decisions that are based on these measurements often must be made quickly; thus, one must already have a clear understanding of what the measurements mean. When dealing with problems of metabolism, nutrition, and infection, one usually has time to reflect on how best to proceed, but when dealing with a cardiovascular catastrophe, one may not have this luxury.

Vascular Pressures

PERIPHERAL ARTERIAL PRESSURES AS SURROGATES FOR AORTIC ROOT PRESSURES

The pressures in the aortic root are critical for assessment of tissue perfusion and for estimating the load placed on the left ventricle. The mean aortic root pressure [*see 118 Shock*] is the pressure of consequence for the evaluation of perfusion of noncardiac tissues. (This pressure is also close to the pressure that perfuses the coronary arteries, though, admittedly, the mean aortic root diastolic pressure is the better descriptor. In most patients, the two pressures are not very different.) The ventricular end-systolic pressure, which is approximately 90% of the peak systolic pressure in the aortic root, is the most important pressure for estimating myocardial oxygen requirements. The aortic root end-systolic pressure is also the key pressure for assessing afterload [*see 118 Shock*].

Direct measurement of the aortic root pressures would be ideal; however, it is impractical. Instead, one must use peripheral arterial pressures—typically, the pressures in a brachial or radial artery—as surrogates for aortic root pressures. This is rarely a problem. Mean pressure decreases ever so slightly as one proceeds distally from the aortic root, unless the arteries between the aortic root and the measurement site in the extremity are in spasm or obstructed. In the absence of spasm or obstruction, the drop in pressure is minimal, and the mean pressure in an artery in an extremity closely approximates the mean pressure in the aortic root. One need only be concerned about the closeness of the approximation if the patient is in severe shock or has obvious obstructive disease—problems that usually are easy to recognize.

The diastolic pressure in the periphery is usually somewhat lower than that in the aortic root, but this too is rarely a problem.[1] The diastolic pressure in the periphery is usually close to the mean pressure distally, which is almost identical to the mean aortic root pressure. The mean aortic root pressure, in turn, is just slightly larger than the mean aortic root diastolic pressure. Thus, the distal and central diastolic pressures are close to being the same (though not as close to each other as the central and distal mean pressures are).

Using the systolic pressure in the periphery as a surrogate for the systolic pressure in the aorta can, however, be a major problem. The systolic pressure in a peripheral artery is almost always higher than its counterpart in the aortic root, sometimes substantially so. This difference can best be understood by considering that the heart is a pulsatile energy source and that the energy it generates travels to the periphery through a vascular network with complex physical characteristics.[1,2]

NONINVASIVE MEASUREMENT OF ARTERIAL PRESSURES

In the initial management of a patient with potential cardiovascular instability, arterial pressures must be measured noninvasively and in an extremity. Despite the problems associated with using the systolic pressure in an extremity as a surrogate for the aortic root systolic pressure, it remains true that a great deal of useful information can be obtained from such surrogate measurements. The goal, then, is to make these measurements with the greatest possible accuracy.

In the cuff technique, a blood pressure cuff is applied around the extremity and artery of interest, and a reference point is selected for the pressure measurement. Selection of this point is arbitrary, but most physicians use the right atrium. If the patient is supine, the reference point is placed at the level of the midaxillary line; if upright, the point is situated at the level of the fifth intercostal space in the midaxillary line.[3] The cuff is inflated to a pressure that is sufficient to eliminate flow in the underlying artery (e.g., as determined by obliteration of a distal palpable pulse), then gradually deflated while one listens with a stethoscope over the artery at the distal edge of the cuff. When cuff pressure falls below systolic pressure, blood begins to flow again through the artery. Because the artery is still partially compressed, arterial blood flow is turbulent and thus creates sound that is audible through the stethoscope. The pressure in the cuff at the point where this sound first becomes audible is taken to be the peak systolic pressure in the artery encompassed by the cuff.[4,5]

As deflation continues and the pressure in the cuff falls to levels between the peak systolic pressure and the nadir of the diastolic pressure, the artery becomes less compressed, but some compression remains. Thus, some turbulence and sound remain as well, though their characteristics change. When the pressure in the cuff falls below the nadir of the diastolic pressure in the artery, the vessel becomes widely patent, and turbulence and sound vanish. The pressure in the cuff at the point where sound disappears is taken to be the nadir of the diastolic pressure in the artery.[4]

A stethoscope is generally used to detect the sounds in the artery, but other techniques can also be used to detect distal flow. With all of these techniques, the pressure in the cuff at the point where flow begins to appear distally is taken to be the peak systolic pressure in the artery. A Doppler device may be used to pick up movement of individual red blood cells in a distal artery; the absence of such movement implies the absence of arterial flow. Arterial flow can also be detected by means of pulse oximetry and evaluated by means of photoplethysmography.[6] One can even measure volume changes in the distal portion of the extremity as the heart beats: the limb expands during systole as blood is forced into the arteries and veins, and it shrinks during diastole as blood runs out of the vessels. This concept can be used to measure arterial pressure waveforms in the finger. Pressure in a cuff around the finger is regulated to maintain a constant blood volume in the finger; the pressure waveform required to accomplish this reflects the finger arterial pressure waveform.[7]

Sphygmomanometry poses no risk to the patient, and systolic pressures are usually easy to obtain.[8] Measured pressures can be misleading, however, in that the technique relies on the assumption that the pressures in the cuff are the same as those in the encompassed artery. This condition is usually met, except in diabetic patients with calcified arteries and obese patients, in whom the pressure in the cuff is higher than the pressure in the artery. An additional problem arises when diastolic pressures are measured with a cuff and a stethoscope: the sounds are frequently quite soft, and in a noisy ICU, it is often hard to tell exactly when they vanish. Measurement of diastolic pressure is also difficult if the patient is in shock: flow through the brachial artery can be so minimal that very little turbulence is created and very little sound generated. Only a stethoscope can be used to measure diastolic pressure. Audible Doppler signals in a distal artery change little as a proximal artery goes from partial obstruction to full patency; changes are also minimal if oximetry is used. Finally, the mean pressure cannot be determined with standard sphygmomanometry. Although the mean pressure is commonly approximated as a value that is one third of the way from the diastolic pressure to the systolic pressure, this approximation can be substantially inaccurate [see 118 Shock].

The problem of how to determine the mean pressure accurately can be solved by using oscillometric techniques, which have the enormous advantage of being able to measure the mean pressure in an artery in an extremity. Devices that use these techniques sense pulsatility in the volume of the extremity enclosed by the cuff. The point where pulsation amplitudes are maximal corresponds to the mean arterial pressure; various algorithms are used to determine systolic and diastolic arterial pressures.[9-11] Unfortunately, oscillometric methods do not work well in the setting of hypovolemia, which is where they are most often needed, nor are they particularly accurate in determining systolic or diastolic pressures.

Thus, all of these noninvasive methods for measuring arterial pressures have limitations: the inability to measure any pressures accurately in patients who are obese or have calcified arteries, the uncertainty associated with diastolic pressure measurements in all patients, and the difficulty of making measurements in patients in shock.

INVASIVE MEASUREMENT OF ARTERIAL PRESSURES VIA INTRA-ARTERIAL CATHETERS

Except for the problem of using a peripheral systolic arterial pressure as a surrogate for the aortic root systolic pressure, all of the limitations of noninvasive measurement techniques can be overcome by using intra-arterial catheters. In addition, such catheters provide ready access to systemic arterial blood, though not without a degree of risk.[12,13] Catheter-related infection can occur, albeit infrequently [see 131 Nosocomial Infection].[14] Thrombosis associated with insertion and maintenance of indwelling arterial catheters can lead to ischemia and even necrosis distal to the insertion site. Catheters should be inserted in arteries with abundant collateral circulation. The radial artery is safer to use than the brachial artery, and the dorsalis pedis artery is safer than the femoral artery. To reduce the risk of thrombosis, we continuously infuse an isotonic solution through the catheter.[15,16] If the patient is at high risk for thrombosis, we use a dilute heparin solution for flushing, accepting a slight risk of heparin-induced thrombocytopenia; if not, we use normal saline. Flushing must be done carefully, either as a slow continuous infusion or with boluses no larger than 2 ml. Rapid infusion of large amounts of any solution can lead to retrograde flow. In the case of the radial artery, retrograde flushing can lead to embolization of platelet aggregates or air through the vertebral artery to the brain stem.

The decision whether to use intra-arterial monitoring rests on assessment of the potential risks and benefits. We insert arterial catheters if it appears that blood gases will have to be measured more often than three times daily. We also use them in patients who might bleed suddenly (e.g., those undergoing a major operation), patients whose blood pressure is labile (e.g., those who are in a septic state or require titration of vasoactive or cardiotonic drugs), and patients in whom management of one failing organ system might precipitate failure in another.

Once the decision is made to use intra-arterial monitoring, the artery is cannulated. A pressure transducer is calibrated, then opened to the atmosphere and zeroed at the level of the right atrium.[3] The transducer is connected to the cannula with tubing. The pressure waveform from the transducer is displayed on a monitor, along with digital readouts of the running averages (means) of the systolic, diastolic, and mean pressures. These running averages are calculated by computer circuitry in the transducer equipment. To calculate mean peak systolic pressure, for example, the computer might be programmed to sample 10 consecutive heartbeats. It would then detect the peak systolic pressure for each of the 10, add the values, and divide the sum by 10. For the next sampling, it might take the last five values, add these to the next five, and divide the sum by 10. A similar logic is followed for diastolic pressures. The mean pressure is calculated as the area under the tracing divided by the time over which the tracing is sampled (typically, about 10 beats), and a running average is obtained in the same manner as the running averages of systolic and diastolic pressures [see 118 Shock]. In all cases, the number of sampled beats is large enough that pressure variations introduced by ventilation are averaged out.

The pressures measured in the transducer are very accurate, and the computer's calculation of the running averages is very sophisticated. A problem remains, nevertheless: the displayed pressures represent the pressures in the transducer, not the pressures in the cannulated artery. This is not, however, a major concern with mean pressure. Because there is no net transfer of energy between the catheterized artery and the transducer, the mean pressure in the transducer is the same as that in the artery, as long as the catheter and the tubing are unobstructed. Nor, as a rule, is diastolic pressure a problem. In both the transducer and the artery, mean pressure largely determines diastolic pressure. Because the mean pressures are the same, the diastolic pressures are usually of approximately equal value.

The peak systolic pressure in the transducer, however, is sometimes substantially different from that in the cannulated artery.

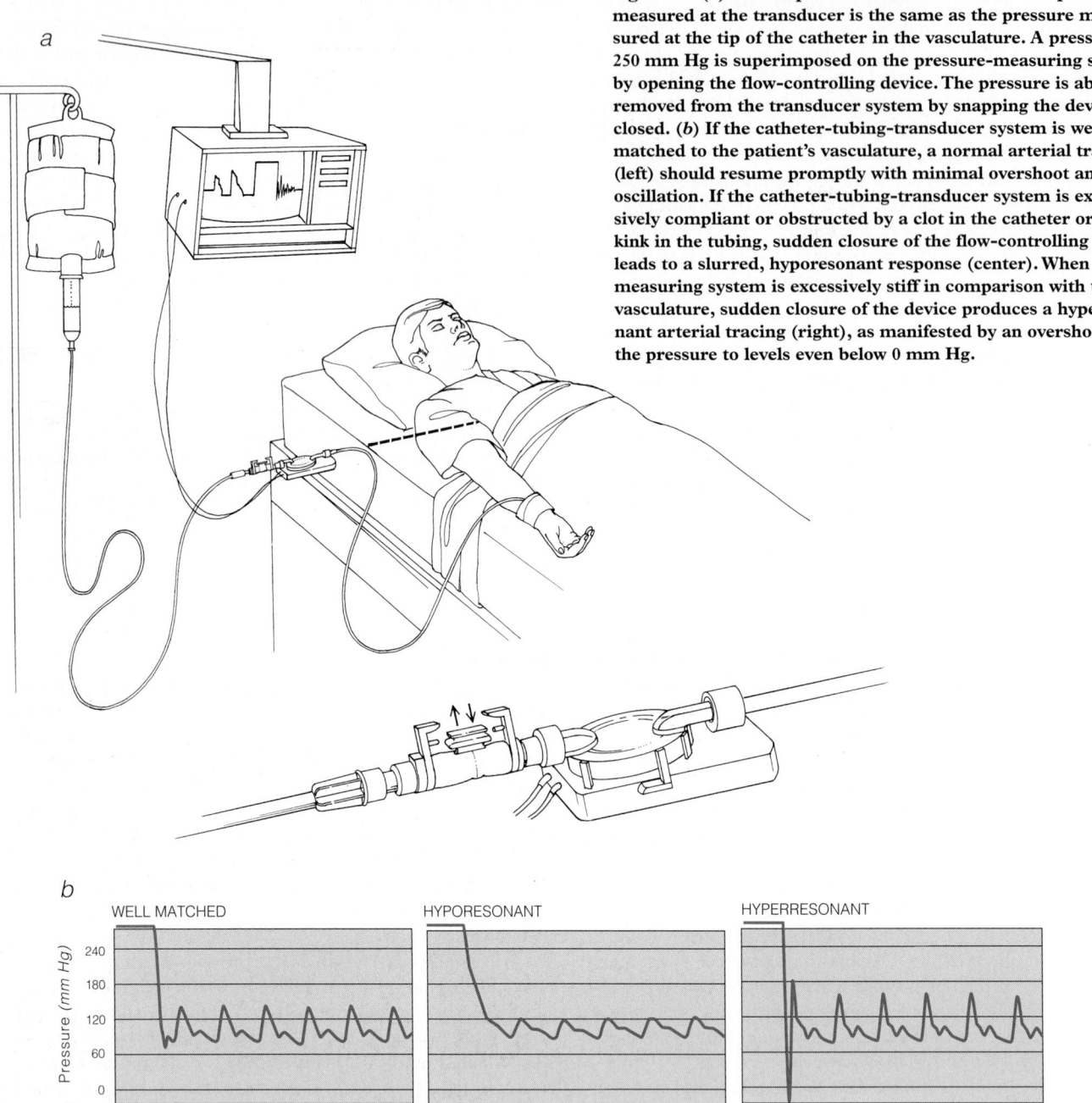

a

Figure 1 (*a*) The snap test will indicate whether the pressure measured at the transducer is the same as the pressure measured at the tip of the catheter in the vasculature. A pressure of 250 mm Hg is superimposed on the pressure-measuring system by opening the flow-controlling device. The pressure is abruptly removed from the transducer system by snapping the device closed. (*b*) If the catheter-tubing-transducer system is well matched to the patient's vasculature, a normal arterial tracing (left) should resume promptly with minimal overshoot and oscillation. If the catheter-tubing-transducer system is excessively compliant or obstructed by a clot in the catheter or by a kink in the tubing, sudden closure of the flow-controlling device leads to a slurred, hyporesonant response (center). When the measuring system is excessively stiff in comparison with the vasculature, sudden closure of the device produces a hyperresonant arterial tracing (right), as manifested by an overshoot of the pressure to levels even below 0 mm Hg.

b

WELL MATCHED   HYPORESONANT   HYPERRESONANT

Pressure (mm Hg)   240 180 120 60 0

This difference arises because of (1) mismatching between the physical characteristics of the measuring system and those of the artery[17,18] and (2) catheter whip (or fling).

If the catheter-tubing-transducer system is excessively stiff compared with the vasculature, systolic pressure will be much higher and diastolic pressure somewhat lower in the transducer than in the artery. Conversely, if the measuring system is more compliant than the vasculature, if the vascular catheter is obstructed by a blood clot, or if the tube is too narrow or too long or has a kink, damping at the transducer will be introduced. When such damping occurs, systolic pressure will be lower and diastolic pressure somewhat higher in the transducer than in the artery.

Maintenance of an arterial catheter's patency requires a continuous infusion of fluid, usually from a high-pressure reservoir. A valve inserted in the circuit between the reservoir and the artery limits the amount of fluid infused. One can take advantage of this arrangement by using the so-called snap test to determine whether the systolic and diastolic pressures in the transducer accurately reflect those in the artery [*see Figure 1*]. In this test, a square pressure wave is introduced into the catheter-tubing-transducer system by pulling on the tab that allows fluid to flow from the high-pressure bag into the transducer and the artery. The tab is then snapped shut, and the pressure in the system returns abruptly to baseline levels [*see Sidebar* Snap Test for Detection of Mismatch between Artery and Measuring System].[19] If the system is adequately matched to the vasculature, the pressures in the transducer will abruptly return to baseline with minimal oscillation. If the measuring system is too stiff, the snap test will result in hyperresonance, evidenced by prolonged and exaggerated oscillation. If the measuring system is too compliant or if the catheter or tubing is obstructed, the snap test will lead to a slow and slurred descent toward baseline.

To derive the most accurate representation of the arterial pressure from measurements of the pressures in the transducer, the catheter-tubing-transducer system should be set up with the stiffest available tubing, which should be kept as short as is consonant with patient care and should be kept free of compression or clogging. Care should be taken to remove any air bubbles in the tubing or the transducer. Furthermore, the system should be as simple as possible; extraneous connectors and three-way valves should be removed.

If the system ends up with good matching, all of the measured pressures in the transducer can be accepted as accurate reflections of the pressures in the cannulated artery. If the system is hyperresonant, one should make a note of it and keep in mind that systolic and, to a lesser extent, diastolic pressures are not to be trusted. Mean pressures will still be accurate, and in many patients, these are all that is needed. If there is a need to know the systolic and diastolic pressures, any of several commercially available damping devices can be inserted in the transducer-tubing system. If the system is or becomes hyporesonant, an attempt should be made to clear the catheter, both to make the measurements from the catheter more accurate and to prevent propagation of thrombus into the artery from the catheter. If the system continues to be severely damped, it should be replaced and a new catheter inserted, if practicable. None of the measurements from a severely damped system are of any value. In the extreme case of occlusion of the catheter or the tubing, even the mean pressure in the transducer will bear no relation to the mean pressure in the artery.

Another potential problem with using the pressure in the transducer as a surrogate for the pressure in the cannulated artery is catheter whip—that is, movement of the intravascular catheter in the vascular lumen as the heart beats [see Figure 2]—which, like mismatch between the artery and the measuring system, can render systolic (and, to a lesser extent, diastolic) pressures unreliable.[20] Catheter whip usually is not a problem in the radial artery, where the catheter cannot move around very much, but it can cause difficulties in the femoral artery or the pulmonary artery, where the catheter has ample room for free movement in the lumen. Catheter whip can introduce errors of 20 mm Hg or more in measurements of femoral and pulmonary arterial pressures. Often, distortion introduced by a hyperresonant measuring system looks very much like catheter whip, and the two cannot be distinguished. When this is the case, a device can be added to the catheter-tubing-transducer system to eliminate hyperresonance; any remaining distortion must be the result of catheter whip. Usually, however, it is sufficient just to make a note of possible catheter whip and then refrain from using the systolic or diastolic values in patient management; mean pressures will not be greatly affected and will remain usable.

CENTRAL VENOUS PRESSURE

Central venous pressure is very close to right atrial pressure, which is a critical determinant in the formation of peripheral edema. Right atrial pressure, in turn, is very close to right ventricular end-diastolic pressure (in the absence of tricuspid valvular disease), and end-diastolic pressure gives an idea of end-diastolic volume [see 118 Shock]. Right ventricular end-diastolic volume is a critical determinant of right ventricular stroke volume, end-systolic pressure, and stroke work, which, in turn, are critical determinants of right ventricular oxygen requirements.[21] Thus, central

---

Snap Test for Detection of Mismatch between Artery and Measuring System

Clinically, arterial pressures are measured with low-fidelity disposable fluid-filled catheter-tubing-transducer systems. The response of these systems can be characterized by two variables: a damped natural frequency and a damping coefficient.[17,18] The natural frequency reflects how rapidly the system oscillates in response to a pressure impulse; the damping coefficient reflects how rapidly the system comes to rest after a pressure impulse.

An arterial pressure waveform is made up of various individual harmonic components. The baseline component depends on the heart rate. For example, at a heart rate of 60 beats/min, the first harmonic component is at a frequency of 1 Hz. Adequate representation of an arterial pressure waveform can be obtained from the first several harmonic components. As the frequency of the arterial pressure waveform approaches the natural frequency of the catheter-tubing-transducer system, there will be resonance and amplification of the signal. The measured systolic pressure will be higher than the input arterial pressure, and the measured diastolic pressure will be lower. For an adequate representation of the arterial pressure waveform, the damped natural frequency of the system should be as large as possible—ideally, at least 7.5 to 8 Hz.

In addition, adequate characterization of the arterial pressure waveform requires a certain degree of damping (quantified by the damping coefficient). A completely undamped system will oscillate continuously in response to a pressure input. At the other extreme, an excessively damped system will respond sluggishly to changes in arterial pressures. Ideally, just enough damping should be present to allow minimal overshooting (i.e., a small amount of oscillatory motion).[17] This optimal damping represents a balance between responsiveness and instability.

Measurement of the damped natural frequency and the damping coefficient is readily accomplished by means of the snap test [see Figure 1].[17,19] This test results in transmission of a square wave impulse to the catheter-tubing-transducer system. Through trial and error, this impulse can be timed to a portion of the arterial waveform that is relatively flat, thereby facilitating evaluation. An arterial pressure waveform strip can generally be printed from a central monitor station. The damped natural frequency is calculated as the inverse of the period of one oscillation. As an approximation, at a standard rate of 25 mm/sec, one oscillatory period should be no longer than three small boxes (0.12 second, corresponding to a frequency of 8.3 Hz). The damping coefficient is reflected by the ratio between the amplitudes of successive oscillations. As the natural frequency of the catheter-tubing-transducer system increases, the range of acceptable damping coefficient values increases as well, while still allowing adequate representation of the arterial pressure waveform. A natural frequency requires a damping coefficient that results in a ratio of roughly 0.15 between successive oscillation amplitudes. Thus, a natural frequency of 10 Hz requires a ratio of 0.1 to 0.25. As the frequency increases to 20 Hz, a ratio ranging from 0.01 to 0.5 would be acceptable.[17]

---

venous pressure can give the clinician substantial insight into the functioning of the right side of the heart.

Quantitative measurement of central venous pressure requires insertion of either a central venous catheter or a pulmonary arterial catheter. Access is usually achieved through either a jugular or a subclavian approach. Certain risks are associated with puncture of these large central veins.[22] Penetration of the parietal pleura can produce a pneumothorax. Puncture of the subclavian artery can lead to exsanguination into the pleural cavity. Improper catheter placement can result in intrapleural infusion of fluids. Puncture of one of the major trunks or divisions of the brachial plexus lying near the large veins can permanently impair the extremity. Puncture of the trachea, the esophagus, or the lung can lead to subcutaneous emphysema and mediastinitis. Puncture of the internal

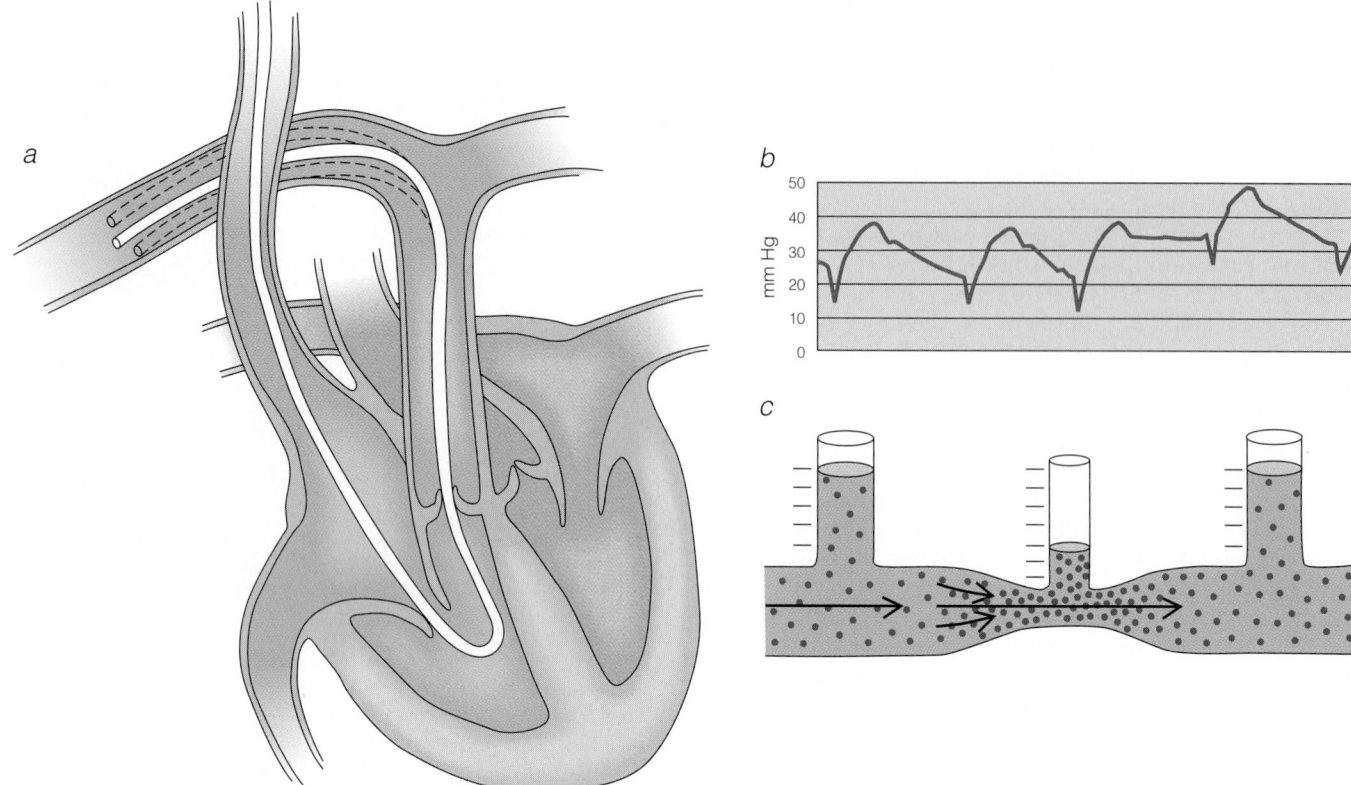

Figure 2 Catheter whip (or fling) results from movement of a catheter within the vasculature (*a*) that produces hydrostatic pressure changes at the tip of the catheter that are independent of any changes in hydrostatic pressure within the vessel itself. Pressure drops during diastole that are the result of catheter whip could be falsely interpreted as true vascular diastolic pressure. In the pressure tracing shown (*b*), the true diastolic pressure in the pulmonary artery is 24 mm Hg; catheter fling produces the lower pressure of 12 mm Hg at the tip of the catheter.

The total energy in a hydraulic system, such as the vasculature, is the sum of hydrostatic pressure and kinetic energy. The kinetic energy depends on the square of the velocity of the fluid. The narrower the system (*c*), the greater the velocity—and, thus, the greater the kinetic energy. The total energy measured at any point in the system is constant; therefore, the hydrostatic pressure must be less in the narrow portion of the tube, where the velocity of flow is higher.

If a femoral or pulmonary arterial catheter moves within the vasculature as the heart beats, the velocity of blood across its orifice will increase; as the velocity increases and the kinetic energy increases, the hydrostatic pressure as measured at the tip will fall. This transient decrease in hydrostatic pressure at the tip of the catheter (as seen in the tracing) does not reflect the true hydrostatic pressure in the artery.

The radial artery catheter is best for determining the total energy in the blood flow. The catheter will not whip, because the artery is small and the catheter has no room to move about, and there will be no kinetic energy component in the blood, because the radial artery catheter is end-on to (i.e., faces into) the direction of the flow; thus, the velocity of the blood as it runs into the end of the catheter is zero. Therefore, the hydrostatic pressure will represent the total energy of the blood at that point of the vasculature. A catheter placed in the ascending aorta will be buffeted by the rapidly accelerating blood in the aorta, and catheter whip will be introduced. A pulmonary arterial catheter potentially has both the problem of catheter whip and the problem that it measures pressure in the direction of flow rather than end-on.

jugular vein on the left side can damage the thoracic duct and lead to a chylothorax. Improper use of the introducing needle can result in shearing of the catheter and catheter emboli. No matter how experienced the person performing the procedure, these complications will occur occasionally; the goal is to keep their incidence to a minimum. The alternative to direct puncture of a central vein is to cannulate a peripheral vein and pass the catheter centrally. This technique, however, carries a very high risk of thrombophlebitis.[23] On balance, it is better to gain direct access to a central vein if this can be accomplished safely.

The central pressures obtained vary with the respiratory cycle. Intracardiac pressures fall during spontaneous inspiration as the lungs pull away from the great veins and cardiac chambers, and they rise during mechanical ventilation as insufflation of the lungs compresses the cardiac chambers. With pressure control or pres-

sure support ventilation, end-expiratory pressures will be close to those that would result from spontaneous breathing. Intermittent mandatory ventilation, however, can create a confusing picture, producing augmented vascular pressures when the ventilator gives a mechanical breath but lowered intracardiac pressures when the patient takes a spontaneous breath [*see Figure 3*].

Substantial pressures can be generated during inspiration with these different modes of ventilation. The intracardiac pressure variations induced by mechanical ventilation can exceed 20 mm Hg. To deal with this problem, some clinicians use end-expiratory values, which can be read from the pressure tracings on the monitor screen. The disadvantage of this approach is that even the most experienced physicians and nurses sometimes find end-expiratory pressure tracings difficult to read.[24,25] Another approach is to take the patient off the ventilator while making the measure-

SPONTANEOUS VENTILATION

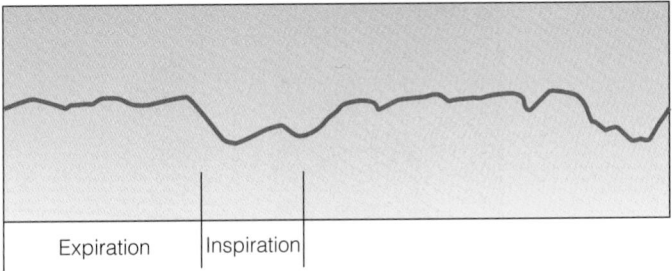

Expiration | Inspiration

MECHANICAL VENTILATION

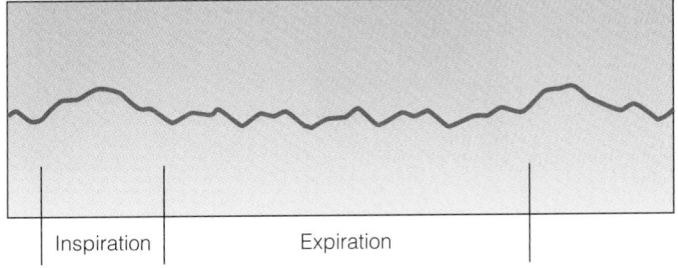

Inspiration | Expiration

INTERMITTENT MANDATORY VENTILATION

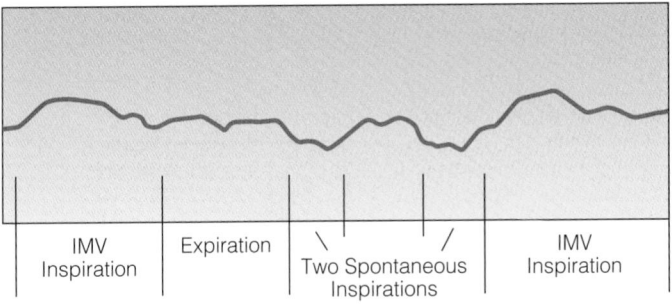

IMV Inspiration | Expiration | Two Spontaneous Inspirations | IMV Inspiration

Figure 3 **Ventilation can have marked effects on all of the pressures on the right side of the circulation. For example, in a patient breathing spontaneously (top), central venous pressure (or, equivalently, right atrial pressure) falls as the lungs pull away from the intrathoracic great veins and the right atrium. In these patients, the end-expiratory pressure is the highest pressure measured during the ventilatory cycle. During mechanical ventilation (middle), the lungs are pushed against the outside of the heart and the great veins; intracavitary and intravascular pressures are thereby increased during inspiration, and the end-expiratory pressure is the lowest pressure measured during the ventilatory cycle. If intermittent ventilation is used, the problem is made even more complicated (bottom). The machine-generated breaths produce increases in the atrial pressure and spontaneous breaths produce decreases; the end-expiratory pressure is the plateau pressure between the two extremes. The same considerations come into play with measurement of pulmonary arterial pressure and pulmonary arterial wedge pressure. One way to avoid these problems is to take the reading for all of these right-side pressures from the digital display of the monitoring equipment. These values are the running means of the various pressures, taken over a number of breaths.**

ments. This approach does make it easier to interpret the pressures. Its disadvantage is that the most significant pressures are the ones prevailing while the patient is being ventilated; removing the patient from the ventilator produces a condition that no longer represents his or her physiologic status.

Currently, most physicians rely on the mean pressure over the entire ventilatory cycle, which is calculated as the integral of the pressure over time divided by the time during which the area is measured. The computer circuits that govern modern pressure transducers make these calculations routinely and display them in digital form on the monitor screen, along with the pressure tracings. This approach has two advantages: (1) the readings are independent of the person making the measurement, and (2) the measurements reflect the actual conditions to which the patient is exposed. We also use the running means for pulmonary arterial pressure and pulmonary arterial wedge pressure (see below).

PULMONARY ARTERIAL PRESSURES

Monitoring of the pressures in the pulmonary artery of an ICU patient can only be accomplished by means of a Swan-Ganz catheter.[26] These pressures, along with other values obtainable from the modern catheter (e.g., cardiac output, right ventricular end-diastolic volume, and mixed venous oxygen levels) can give the clinician an enormous amount of information about a patient's cardiac status.

Pulmonary arterial peak systolic pressure is the same as right ventricular peak systolic pressure. Right ventricular end-systolic pressure can be approximated, as 90% of the peak systolic pressure. This value, along with right ventricular end-diastolic volume, is a critical determinant of right ventricular stroke volume, stroke work, and oxygen requirements.[21] It is also useful, along with stroke volume, for estimating the hindrance against which the ventricle contracts [see 8:3 Shock]. Mean pulmonary arterial pressure is the most important of the pressures for assessing the perfusion of the pulmonary microvasculature and for filling the left atrium and ventricle during diastole.

Pulmonary arterial wedge pressure can also be measured with a Swan-Ganz catheter. Because there are no valves between the pulmonary arteries and the left atrium, the pressure obtained with occlusion of proximal flow will be the same as the pressure in the left atrium [see Figure 4], provided that there is no significant bronchial blood flow.[27-29] In the absence of mitral valvular disease, left atrial pressure will be the same as left ventricular end-diastolic pressure.

Knowledge of the pulmonary arterial wedge pressure can help management in two ways. First, it alerts one to possible formation of pulmonary edema. The pulmonary microvascular pressure must lie between the mean pulmonary arterial pressure and the left atrial (or wedge) pressure. If the wedge pressure is high, the pulmonary microvascular pressure must be high as well. A high wedge pressure (≥ 25 mm Hg) is always associated with microvascular pressures that generate at least some interstitial pulmonary edema, even if the microvascular endothelium is intact.[30] If the endothelium is disrupted, as in sepsis, pulmonary edema can be produced even with wedge pressures in the midteens.

Second, knowledge of the wedge pressure can facilitate estimation of left ventricular end-diastolic volume, which is one of the prime factors determining left ventricular end-systolic pressure, stroke volume, stroke work, and myocardial oxygen consumption.[21] As noted (see above), pulmonary arterial wedge pressure, in the absence of mitral valvular disease, is essentially equal to ventricular end-diastolic pressure. End-diastolic pressure can then be extrapolated to derive end-diastolic volume.

A caveat is in order here, however. To make this extrapolation, one must take into account ventricular end-diastolic compliance, which can decrease in the face of myocardial ischemia or hypertrophy or scarring of the ventricular wall.[31] One must also consider the possibility of external forces that are compressing the heart. A high end-diastolic pressure in a compliant ventricle that is not compressed from the outside will be associated with a large end-dia-

a

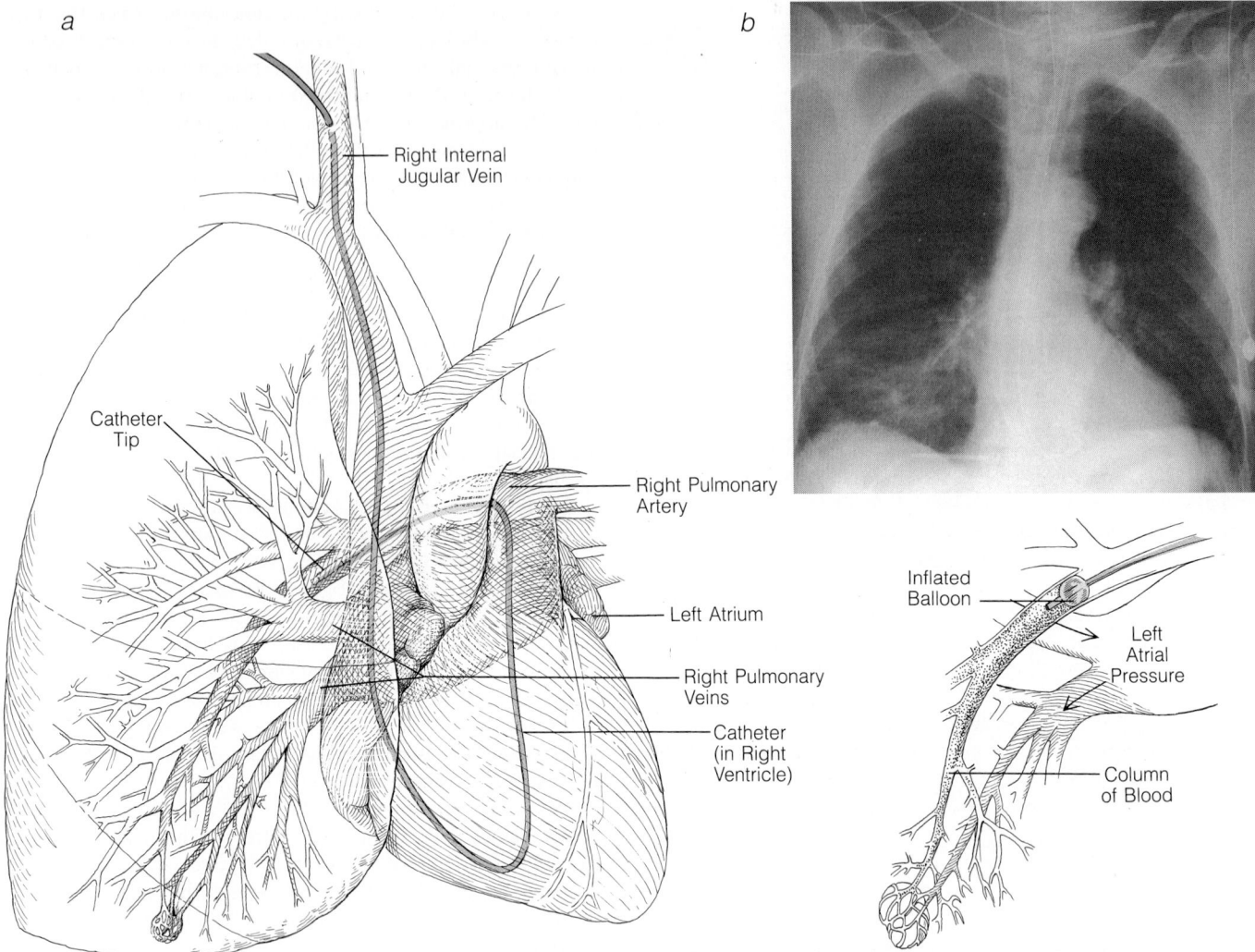

b

Figure 4 (*a*) The pulmonary arterial catheter measures pressure in the pulmonary artery when the balloon is deflated. Because flow in the vascular system generates a pressure drop as the blood passes through the microvasculature, the pressure gradually falls as blood flows from the pulmonary artery to the left atrium. When the balloon is inflated, flow in the vasculature distal to the tip is eliminated; therefore, there is no pressure drop. Because there is no pressure drop and because there are no valves between the left atrium and the pulmonary artery, the pressure in the pulmonary artery distal to the point of occlusion must equal the pressure in the left atrium, provided that there is an open column of blood between the end of the catheter and the left atrium. That is, pulmonary arterial wedge pressure will equal left atrial pressure as long as the catheter is in a dependent portion of the lung with a vasculature that remains open during ventilation. Because the catheter is flow directed, it usually will end up in such a dependent, well-perfused area. This is not a certainty, however. If inflated alveoli occlude the microvasculature, wedge pressure will equal alveolar pressure. This inaccuracy might not be easily detected. (*b*) Verification that the catheter is in the dependent portion of the lung requires a cross-table lateral chest x-ray. We do not routinely obtain these x-rays unless the wedge pressures are absolutely critical for treatment and unless the reliability of the wedge pressure tracing is suspect. Suspicion usually arises when excessively wide pressure swings are evident as the lungs are inflated and deflated.

stolic volume; a similarly high pressure in a ventricle that is stiff or compressed will be associated with a small volume [*see 118 Shock*].

There are other potential pitfalls in interpreting measurements from a Swan-Ganz catheter. As with intra-arterial monitoring of systemic arterial pressures, the pressure in the transducer must be extrapolated to the pressure in the artery. The mean pressures are the same, and the diastolic pressures are nearly the same; but again, the systolic pressures can be misleading because of mismatching and catheter whip. These concerns can be dealt with in the same way as in systemic arterial monitoring.

In contrast with measurement of peripheral systemic arterial pressures and extrapolation back to aortic root pressures, measurement of the pressures at the outflow of the ventricle with the Swan-Ganz catheter is not problematic. The lumen of the catheter used for measuring pulmonary arterial pressure is placed far enough proximally that it gives a direct measurement of the pressure to which the right ventricle is exposed.

Typical pulmonary arterial, left atrial, and left ventricular end-diastolic pressures have been determined [*see 118 Shock*]. Like typical systemic arterial pressures, these values are not necessarily either ideal or desirable: they merely give an idea of what the cardiovascular system can do when demands are placed on it.

Problems Associated with Swan-Ganz Catheters

In addition to the problems arising from interpretation of measurements made with a Swan-Ganz catheter, there are general problems associated with gaining access to a central vein [see Central Venous Pressure, *above*] and specific problems associated with passage and maintenance of a pulmonary arterial catheter.[32]

Ventricular dysrhythmias are common during passage of the catheter, particularly in patients who have suffered recent myocardial infarctions or who have an irritable myocardium (as indicated by a preexisting arrhythmia or conduction defect). For some of these patients, prophylactic administration of lidocaine is indicated. In rare instances, aggressive treatment of such dysrhythmias may be required. Usually, the dysrhythmia subsides when the end of the catheter finally passes through the ventricle and enters the pulmonary artery; sometimes, however, it can be eliminated only by complete removal of the catheter. The balloon on the end of the catheter should be kept inflated during passage to cushion the tip and minimize myocardial irritability.

Passing a Swan-Ganz catheter in a patient with left bundle branch block can be particularly hazardous. The catheter can eliminate conduction through the right ventricle, producing complete heart block. If this condition does not resolve upon prompt withdrawal of the catheter, insertion of a transvenous pacemaker or the use of external pacing may be necessary. The time required to establish a rhythm, however, can be so long that the patient may die first. Therefore, Swan-Ganz catheters should be placed in patients with left bundle branch block only when absolutely necessary.

Lodging of the catheter tip in the trabeculae of the right ventricle is a common problem during catheter passage. On rare occasions, the end of the catheter may puncture the right ventricular wall. The puncture site may not be immediately obvious and may in fact seal by itself; however, it is far more likely to lead to pericardial tamponade and, possibly, death. Measurements from the Swan-Ganz catheter will indicate pericardial tamponade, which mandates emergency operation.

Passage of the catheter through the tricuspid and pulmonic valves can damage them, especially if the device is roughly pulled back through the valves with the balloon inflated. In addition, if the catheter is left in place for more than a few days, valvular damage may result. Besides minimizing long-term use of the catheter, little can be done to prevent this problem.

A problem unique to the Swan-Ganz catheter is intracardiac knotting, which is most likely to develop during placement. The knot can occasionally be untied by manipulating the catheter under fluoroscopic guidance. Passage of a J-wire into the right side of the heart from the groin can also be effective. If these approaches do not work, the catheter must be withdrawn to the site of entry and then removed, usually under direct surgical control.

Swan-Ganz catheters left in place for more than a few days can migrate distally and cut off the blood supply to the pulmonary parenchyma, resulting in pulmonary infarction. This situation is best prevented by continuous monitoring of the pulmonary arterial waveform. Development of a permanently wedged wave pattern is an indication that the catheter should immediately be withdrawn far enough to reestablish a normal pulmonary arterial tracing.

On rare occasions, the catheter can perforate the pulmonary artery. This event typically presents with hemoptysis but may present with acute cardiopulmonary collapse during or immediately after measurement of wedge pressure. Risk factors include advanced age, pulmonary arterial hypertension, warfarin anticoagulation, clotting deficiencies, distal migration of the catheter into the pulmonary vasculature, and balloon overinflation. Patients with tumors surrounding the pulmonary artery are also at increased risk. The balloon itself may disrupt the pulmonary artery directly, or inflation of the balloon may force the tip of the catheter through the vessel wall. Prevention consists of continuous monitoring of pulmonary arterial pressure tracings. The catheter location should be confirmed by chest x-ray at least once daily. Wedge pressures should be measured only when needed. The degree of balloon inflation necessary to obtain a wedge tracing should be noted and overinflation avoided. The balloon inflation port should be identified so that infusions are not misdirected into the balloon. The catheter should never be left in the wedge position. Rupture associated with mild hemoptysis can be treated by removing the catheter; rupture associated with cardiovascular collapse calls for lobectomy or pneumonectomy, which occasionally permits patient salvage.

Given the limitations of interpreting measurements from the Swan-Ganz catheter and the risks associated with its use, some have asked whether the potential benefits (i.e., increased knowledge of the state of the cardiovascular system) are enough to justify its use, given the concerns that have been expressed about increased risks of morbidity[33,34] and mortality.[35] However, a 2005 meta-analysis of 13 randomized clinical trials that assessed the use of pulmonary arterial catheters in critically ill patients did not find this practice to be either beneficial or detrimental.[36] The authors of the meta-analysis pointed out several limitations of the studies evaluated. First, they noted that all of the trials excluded patients whom the treating physicians believed to require a Swan-Ganz catheter. Second, they emphasized that the Swan-Ganz catheter is a diagnostic tool and that any improvement in outcome would require a beneficial therapeutic intervention or change in management that was based on the results of the Swan-Ganz catheter measurements. Third, they observed that only five of the 13 studies evaluated had an outline protocol to achieve specified hemodynamic goals. Fourth, they suggested that the interventions chosen as a result of the Swan-Ganz catheter measurements might be responsible for differences in outcome. For example, they pointed out that vasodilators and inotropes were used more frequently in patients who had a Swan-Ganz catheter in place. In patients with advanced heart failure, some of these agents have been associated with increased morbidity and mortality.[37,38]

In our view, the question of whether and when to use a Swan-Ganz catheter remains unresolved. There is still a need for a study with a high enrollment rate of eligible patients and with inclusion and exclusion criteria that select a population with an expected mortality confirming severe preexisting illness. We believe that use of the Swan-Ganz catheter is still appropriate and beneficial in selected patients,[39-41] provided that the information obtained thereby is employed intelligently[42,43] and that the associated risks are kept to a minimum.[22]

For example, it would seem reasonable to use a Swan-Ganz catheter when myocardial function is severely compromised. The catheter can provide crucial information on the efficacy of pharmacologic support and can aid in the diagnosis of abnormalities such as pericardial tamponade and acute mitral regurgitation. Another reasonable indication would be hypovolemic shock that does not respond readily to volume administration. The catheter may reveal abnormalities of myocardial function or of the pulmonary or systemic vasculature that require specific interventions in addition to volume loading. Pulmonary arterial monitoring would also seem reasonable in patients with sepsis who have inadequate urine output or who are hypotensive. The catheter can provide valuable information about the adequacy of oxygen consumption and pharmacologic support. Pulmonary disorders, especially those that carry a high probability of associated myocardial dysfunction, might constitute another reasonable indication. Pulmonary arterial catheters might also be useful in patients with good cardiopulmonary function who are undergoing procedures associated with large volume requirements and fluid shifts, as well as in patients with severe preexisting myocardial or pulmonary disease who are undergoing elective procedures. Finally, pulmonary arterial catheterization might be indicated if the patient is experiencing failure of two organs with competing priorities.

Flows, Volumes, and Other Determinants of Cardiovascular Thermodynamics

CARDIAC OUTPUT

Modern pulmonary arterial catheters are equipped to obtain a number of other measurements besides pulmonary arterial pressures. Thermistor-tipped catheters can measure cardiac output by means of thermodilution.[44] Originally, these values were obtained by injecting a known quantity of a cool solution in the right atrium and analyzing the temperature drop in the pulmonary artery as the cooled blood flowed past the thermistor. Nowadays, a heater coil is used to heat the blood in the right ventricle, and the resulting rise in temperature in the pulmonary artery is used to calculate the output. The temperature pulses are generated randomly. The measured outputs are obtained over the entirety of the respiratory cycle. Commercially available computers make the calculations on the basis of indicator dilution theory.

Methods of measuring cardiac output have also been developed that do not involve placement of pulmonary arterial catheters. The direct Fick method is best used in awake, alert patients.[45] Transthoracic electrical impedance measurement requires placement of electrodes, which may interfere with surgical procedures.[46] Doppler ultrasonography probes have been placed at the suprasternal notch and the esophagus for measurement of blood flow velocity and calculation of continuous cardiac output in the ascending aorta, distal to the coronary ostia, and in the descending thoracic aorta, distal to the origin of the left subclavian artery.[47,48] Suprasternal notch probes require estimation of the diameter of the ascending aorta; esophageal probes require estimation of the diameter of the descending aorta. Expired gas analysis, with rebreathing techniques, has also been used to obtain cardiac output.[49-51] These methods are currently under clinical evaluation and have not been widely used in clinical settings.

Typical cardiac output values for a well-conditioned person vary under conditions of rest and strenuous exertion [see 118 Shock]. Once again, these typical values are to be used as indicators of what the heart can do, not as target values for every critically ill patient.

RIGHT VENTRICULAR END-DIASTOLIC VOLUME

The introduction of fast-response thermistors has allowed development of thermodilution pulmonary arterial catheters that can measure right ventricular end-diastolic volume directly.[52] The measurements are accurate as long as the patient has a regular rhythm and a heart rate lower than 140 beats/min.

Right ventricular end-diastolic volume varies with cardiovascular condition, total blood volume, positioning, exercise, ventricular

compliance during diastole, pressures applied to the outside of the ventricle, hindrances against which the ventricles contract, and other factors. The right ventricular end-diastolic volume in a resting, supine, well-conditioned 60 kg person is approximately 150 ml. With assumption of an erect position, some of the blood in the thoracic portions of the cardiovascular system pools in the capacitance vessels of the abdominal viscera and the lower extremities. Ventricular end-diastolic volume decreases by perhaps one eighth, to 133 ml. With exercise, muscular contraction in the lower extremities and the abdomen squeezes the capacitance vessels. Blood is redistributed back to the heart and the pulmonary vasculature, raising the end-diastolic volume to perhaps 145 ml. In most 60 kg patients on mechanical ventilation, an end-diastolic volume of 150 ml will be needed to sustain adequate stroke volumes and ventricular pressures.

LEFT VENTRICULAR END-DIASTOLIC VOLUME

Direct measurement of left ventricular end-diastolic volume requires transesophageal echocardiography. This modality is available in most ORs, but it requires the attendance of a physician, usually an anesthesiologist or a cardiologist. This level of physician involvement is not routinely available in most ICUs. Transthoracic imaging can be used for this purpose, but results are frequently misleading in critically ill surgical patients because of bandaging, chest wall edema, and movement of mediastinal structures with mechanical ventilation.

Left ventricular end-diastolic volume can be estimated by measuring the pulmonary arterial wedge pressure and taking into account the factors discussed in relation to pressures in the pulmonary artery [see Pulmonary Arterial Pressures, above, and 118 Shock]. A noninvasive and accurate means of determining left ventricular end-diastolic volume would be extremely useful in the management of critically ill patients. Unfortunately, the technology is not yet available.

In a supine, well-conditioned, spontaneously breathing, normal person weighing 60 kg, left ventricular end-diastolic volume is approximately 150 ml. With assumption of an upright position, it decreases by perhaps one eighth; with exercise, it returns to a value close to 150 ml [see 118 Shock]. A volume of 150 ml or greater is necessary if the patient is undergoing mechanical ventilation.

VENTRICULAR END-SYSTOLIC VOLUMES

End-systolic volumes can be obtained by subtracting stroke volume from end-diastolic volumes. In a 60 kg person with ventricular end-diastolic volumes of 150 ml and a stroke volume of 100 ml, end-systolic volumes are 50 ml.

Ventricular End-Systolic Unstressed Volumes

The term end-systolic unstressed volume refers to the volume that a ventricle would assume if all of its blood were removed with the ventricle in a fully contracted state. Unstressed volumes cannot be measured routinely in the ICU, but they can be measured during cardiac catheterization. In most patients, unstressed volumes are quite small (~ 6 ml). In those with severe congestive heart failure, however, they can be as large as 50 ml.

AFTERLOAD

The aortic root end-systolic pressure-volume relation can be calculated by dividing left ventricular end-systolic pressure by stroke volume; the pulmonary arterial end-systolic pressure-volume relation can be determined by dividing right ventricular end-systolic pressure by stroke volume. These relations give a good approximation of the total hindrances or input impedances or afterloads facing the ventricles when they inject their blood into their respective vasculatures [see 118 Shock].[53,54]

Part of the afterload is accounted for by vascular resistance, calculated as pressure divided by flow. To calculate systemic vascular resistance, the difference between mean aortic pressure and right atrial pressure is divided by cardiac output. To calculate pulmonary vascular resistance, the difference between mean pulmonary arterial pressure and pulmonary arterial wedge pressure is divided by cardiac output.[32]

Of the two resistances, pulmonary vascular resistance is more difficult to measure and more likely to change under different conditions. Because pulmonary vascular resistance depends on the difference between two relatively small pressures, a slight error in the measurement of either one can result in a large error in the calculation of resistance. For this reason, pulmonary vascular resistance is not, in our view, a reliable descriptor.

In contrast, systemic vascular resistance depends on the difference between a large pressure and a small one. Hence, a slight error in the measurement of either pressure has little effect on the calculation of resistance, and the calculation produces an accurate, reproducible number. In many situations, however, we do not bother to make the calculation, because the general level of resistance is frequently obvious on clinical grounds. A high cardiac output in the face of a low mean arterial pressure—a common finding in inflammatory shock or neurogenic shock—means that the systemic resistance must be low. A low cardiac output with a normal or high pressure—as in obstructive shock or, sometimes, cardiogenic shock—means that the resistance must be high. Furthermore, as noted, the systemic resistance makes up only part of the afterload facing the left ventricle. To assess the total hindrance to outflow from the ventricle, the afterload should be calculated as previously described—that is, as the approximated aortic root end-systolic pressure divided by the stroke volume. On occasion, we do calculate the systemic resistance and use it to direct therapy. If the afterload (or impedance) is high and the resistance is low (a common situation), we direct initial therapy toward reduction of arterial stiffness. If the afterload is high and the resistance is also high, we direct therapy toward both the arteries and the arterioles.

The units used to express vascular resistances vary from hospital to hospital. It is simplest, as well as perfectly acceptable scientifically, to use arbitrary units. We prefer mm Hg · L⁻¹ · min—that is, we use the number obtained through the simple calculation described without making any further corrections. A normal systemic arterial resistance is about 14 mm Hg · L⁻¹ · min in a supine, resting 60 kg person. Some multiply this raw number by 80 to convert the resistances to units in the centimeter-gram-second (CGS) system.

POWER

Power calculations are a useful way of quantifying the energy available for delivery of nutrients to tissues and delivery of energy to the contralateral heart. The total power delivered into the aorta can be calculated by multiplying left ventricular end-systolic pressure by cardiac output.[55] Steady-flow aortic power is mean arterial pressure multiplied by cardiac output. Oscillatory power is the difference between total power and steady-flow power. Most of the steady-flow power is dissipated as heat in the microvasculature; the amount of heat dissipated can be calculated by subtracting central venous pressure from mean arterial pressure and multiplying the difference by cardiac output. The remaining steady-flow power fills the right atrium and ventricle during diastole. This value can be calculated by multiplying central venous pressure by cardiac output. The power delivered by the right side of the heart into the pulmonary vasculature can be calculated similarly [see 118 Shock].

Summary Measures of Factors Affecting Cardiopulmonary Function

HEMOGLOBIN CONCENTRATION

Although hemoglobin concentration and hematocrit are commonly measured, there is no consensus regarding the values that are desirable in critically ill patients. Normal values vary substantially from person to person, depending on the altitude at which the person lives, physical conditioning, and gender. One might expect these variations to shed light on the question of what constitutes desirable values in the critically ill. There is no reason why humans should evolve to have hemoglobin or hematocrit levels that are not beneficial; on the contrary, there is every reason why humans should evolve to have values that are ideal for the conditions to which they might be exposed.

As an example of how hemoglobin and hematocrit levels in human beings adapt to changing conditions, living at high altitude, not surprisingly, results in high values.

As another example, good cardiovascular conditioning, especially in a warm environment, results in lower hemoglobin and hematocrit levels. Conditioning causes both plasma volume and red cell volume to expand, with the former expanding more than the latter. Consequently, the hematocrit falls, typically by several percentage points. Although it is not known why conditioning results in an anemia, the reason may have to do with the importance of efficient heat dissipation with exercise. Exercise, in some cases, is limited by the oxygen supply to exercising muscles, but it can also be limited by hyperthermia. (For example, in 30 seconds or so of intense running, a cheetah's core temperature can rise above 40° C. The duration of the animal's pursuit of its prey is limited by hyperthermia, not by exhaustion of oxygen supplies.) Heat dissipation is optimized by the lowest possible hematocrit (which decreases viscosity and eases the flow of heated water, either in plasma or red cells, to the skin, where the heat is dissipated to the environment). Oxygen supply is increased by higher hematocrits. We suspect that conditioning generates the hematocrit that best serves these two competing priorities.

As yet another example, hematocrits are lower in women. This difference, too, is probably explainable in terms of heat dissipation. The thicker layer of subcutaneous fat in women has the obvious advantage of improving survival or performance in cold conditions or in situations of limited food supply; however, this fat also makes it more difficult for women to offload heat. Lower hematocrits help alleviate this difficulty.

As a final example, hematocrits are lower in pregnant women. Pregnancy causes both plasma volume and red cell volume to increase, but as with physical conditioning, the former increases more than the latter, leading to a decrease in the hematocrit. This is probably not a surprising result, given the substantial degree of physical conditioning required to carry an increasingly heavy load for the greater part of the day over a period of months. In addition, the lower hematocrit should help the pregnant woman avoid hyperthermia, thereby protecting the fetus from excessively high intrauterine temperatures.

The desirable value for a hematocrit in a critically ill patient depends on many variables, as is discussed in more detail elsewhere [see 118 Shock]. We suggest that there can be an advantage in being anemic, especially in the face of an inflammatory process characterized by increased oxygen consumption and heat production. There are also obvious advantages in higher levels of hemoglobin (see below).

BLOOD LEVELS OF OXYGEN AND CARBON DIOXIDE

The term oxygen saturation (S_{O_2}) refers to the fraction of hemoglobin occupied by oxygen. Oxygen content (C_{O_2}), or concentration, is the amount of oxygen contained in a given volume of blood. In the United States, it is typically expressed as milliliters of oxygen dissolved in 100 ml (1 dl) of blood. The partial pressure (tension) of oxygen (P_{O_2}) or carbon dioxide (P_{CO_2}) in blood is the pressure that the dissolved gas exerts on the walls of the blood vessel. Systemic arterial oxygen saturation (S_aO_2) can be obtained by means of pulse oximetry. Measurement of blood gases, however, requires blood, usually obtained from indwelling catheters.

Pulse oximeters have proved extremely useful for monitoring S_aO_2 in the ICU, in that they are noninvasive and easy to use and require minimal calibration. The basic principle is that oxygenated hemoglobin and reduced hemoglobin have different absorption properties for light of known wavelengths. Pulse oximeters measure absorption of selected wavelengths of light from pulsatile (i.e., arterial) blood flow, typically in the nail bed on a finger or toe or in the earlobe. They can be used only in patients who have good perfusion: hypoperfusion and inadequate pulsation of blood in the arterioles make it impossible for the oximeter to distinguish between arteriolar and venular blood.

Oxygen saturations may not give enough information, however. For a more complete clinical assessment, it may be necessary to measure arterial oxygen tension (P_aO_2), arterial CO_2 tension (P_aCO_2), and pH. Saturation can be approximated from these three measurements, along with temperature. These calculations are typically made by computer in the blood gas laboratory, and the approximated saturation value is returned by the laboratory along with the measured P_aO_2, P_aCO_2, and pH. Oxygen saturation can also be measured directly on a blood specimen by means of a co-oximeter. This simple and inexpensive device gives a more accurate value because it measures saturation directly. It does require another several milliliters of blood, however, thereby adding to the amount of blood drawn from the patient.

The greatest significance of S_aO_2, whether obtained via pulse oximetry or via direct measurement, lies in its role in yielding values for arterial oxygen content (C_aO_2), which is the value that usually counts most. C_aO_2 is a measure of all the oxygen in the blood, including that attached to hemoglobin and that dissolved in plasma, and may be approximated as follows:

$$C_aO_2 = 1.39 \times [Hb] \times S_aO_2 + 0.0031 \times P_aO_2$$

where [Hb] is the hemoglobin concentration in blood and 0.0031 is the so-called Bunsen coefficient. [Hb] is expressed in g/dl; S_aO_2 is expressed as a percentage; and P_aO_2 is expressed in mm Hg.

The amount of oxygen dissolved in plasma is small compared with the amount bound to hemoglobin. As long as P_aO_2 is less than about 100 mm Hg, the contribution of the oxygen in the plasma to the total oxygen content need not be considered, provided that the hemoglobin concentration is at least 7 g/dl. If the oxygen dissolved in plasma is left out, calculation of C_aO_2 is even simpler:

$$C_aO_2 = 1.39 \times [Hb] \times S_aO_2$$

Thus, if the hemoglobin concentration is 11.4 g/dl and S_aO_2 is 97%, the oxygen content of the blood (excluding that dissolved in plasma) is 15.4 ml/dl. If the oxygen dissolved in plasma is added

back in, C_aO_2 is 15.7 ml/dl, assuming a P_aO_2 of 97 mm Hg. This is a normal value for a woman who is in good cardiovascular condition or in the late stages of pregnancy, with a hematocrit of 34%.

Although 1.39 is probably the most accurate figure for the purposes of this calculation, other values—some as low as 1.33—have also been reported. Accordingly, the calculation can be simplified yet further by using a value of 4/3 instead of 1.39.

The blood obtained for direct measurement of P_aO_2 and S_aO_2 can also be used for measurement of P_aCO_2 and pH. P_aCO_2 is a measure of the amount of CO_2 dissolved in the plasma. Arterial CO_2 content (C_aCO_2) can be calculated, but it seldom is, because within physiologic ranges of P_aCO_2, CO_2 content is almost linearly related to partial pressure. Hydrogen ion concentration is usually expressed as pH and is obtained by direct measurement with ion-sensitive electrodes. It can also be expressed in nmol/L.

Blood drawn for blood gas determinations should be placed on ice immediately to inhibit oxygen consumption by neutrophils. Before being measured in the blood gas apparatus, it is rewarmed to 37° C by a heating element in the cuvette, and P_aO_2, P_aCO_2, and pH are then determined with the blood at this temperature. The patient's blood, however, may be either warmer or colder than 37° C. If, for example, the patient's blood is 35° C when it is drawn, some of the oxygen and CO_2 will come out of solution when it is warmed to 37° C. Consequently, the partial pressures measured by the apparatus will be higher than the actual pressures in the blood when it was circulating in the patient.

The physician and nurse caring for the patient need not make this temperature correction themselves: the blood gas laboratory typically reports temperature-corrected values for the partial pressures and pH if the patient's temperature is supplied to the laboratory along with the specimen.[56] An increasing number of clinicians, however, no longer make temperature corrections for blood gases and manage hypothermic and hyperthermic patients with the so-called alpha-stat method.[57] Treatment based on this method is thought to induce fewer abnormalities in acid-base balance when the patient's temperature returns to normal.

There are several pitfalls in measuring oxygen levels in mixed venous blood. Mixed venous blood, by definition, represents a mixture of all blood returned from all organs. Venous blood from the heart is returned to the right atrium through the coronary sinus. This blood is markedly desaturated. Thus, blood in the right ventricle or in the pulmonary artery is truly mixed venous blood because it includes both the blood from the heart and that from the rest of the body. Blood from the superior vena cava, however, is not mixed venous blood, because it does not include the blood from the heart. Accordingly, blood gas measurements from vena caval blood may be falsely elevated. Measurements of gases in blood obtained from the right atrium may be falsely low if the catheter tip is placed near the coronary sinus.

Two errors in obtaining pulmonary arterial blood can lead to misleading measurements. The first, contamination of the specimen with residual fluid in the lumen of the catheter, is easily avoided by discarding the initial 3 ml of blood drawn through the catheter. The second error is harder to avoid. It arises if the blood sample is withdrawn too forcefully through the catheter. The pulmonary artery may collapse around the end of the catheter, causing the blood to be drawn in a retrograde manner past ventilated alveoli [see Figure 5]. This results in a specimen with very high oxygen levels, which does not accurately reflect desaturated pulmonary arterial blood. The possibility that blood was drawn in a retrograde fashion can be checked by measuring the P_{CO_2} in the specimen. CO_2 tension in true pulmonary arterial blood ($P_{mv}CO_2$) is typically

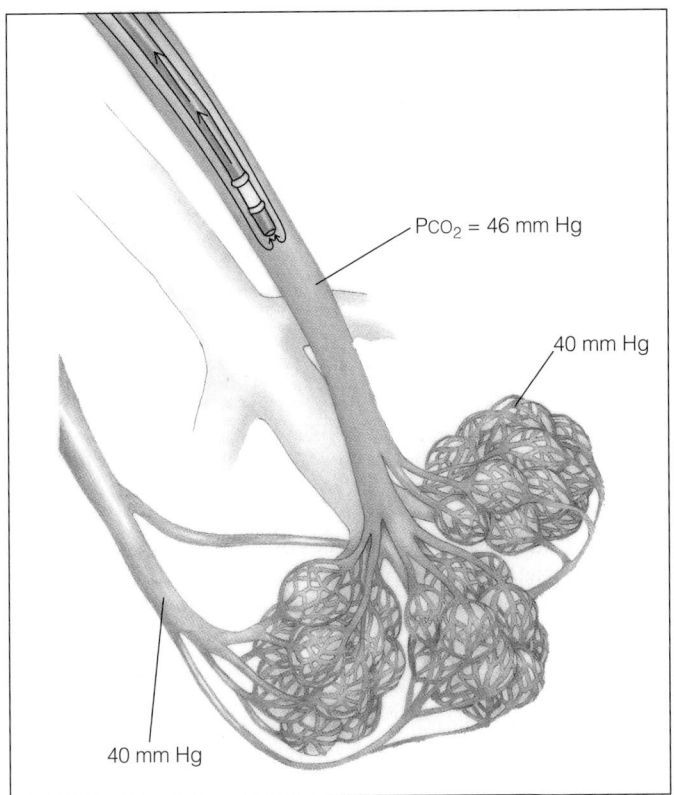 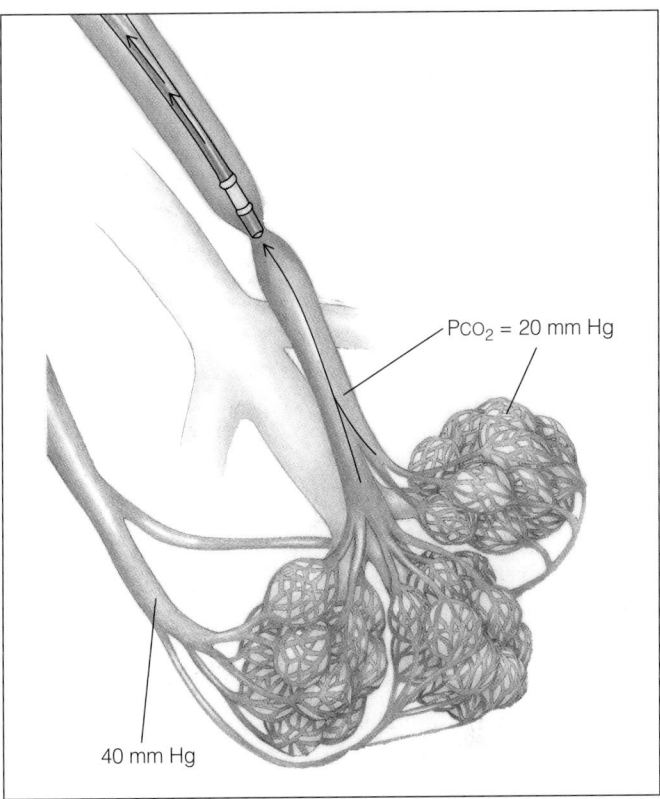

Figure 5 **The Swan-Ganz catheter allows collection of mixed venous blood for measurement of $S_{mv}O_2$ and $C_{mv}O_2$ (left). If blood from the pulmonary artery is withdrawn through the catheter too forcefully, however, arterial walls can collapse around the tip of the catheter (right). The sample will in that case consist of blood from the distal pulmonary vasculature that has been pulled back past ventilated alveoli. To determine whether this has happened, the P_{CO_2} in the sample should be checked. $P_{mv}O_2$ is typically about 5 mm Hg greater than P_aCO_2. If the arterial walls have collapsed around the catheter, the sample will consist of blood from which much of the CO_2 will already have been excreted into the ventilated alveoli, and the $P_{mv}CO_2$ in the recovered blood may be as much as 20 mm Hg lower than a simultaneously obtained P_aCO_2. Specimens of this sort should be discarded and new specimens obtained. Taking care in obtaining true mixed venous blood is equally important when using a catheter with an oximeter mounted on its tip. Calibration of the oximeter requires direct measurement of $S_{mv}O_2$ in a correctly obtained specimen.**

5 mm Hg higher than that in simultaneously drawn systemic arterial blood.[58] Blood drawn back past ventilated alveoli will have a very low $P_{mv}CO_2$. If the CO_2 tension in the specimen is equal to or less than that in systemic arterial blood, the specimen should be discarded and another specimen obtained by drawing back on the syringe more slowly. One should rely on the oxygen saturation of the specimen (measured by co-oximetry) rather than on the oxygen tension. Mixed venous partial pressure of oxygen ($P_{mv}O_2$) and oxygen saturation ($S_{mv}O_2$) lie on the steep portion of the oxyhemoglobin dissociation curve. A minor error in measurement of the former can result in a major error in calculation of the latter.

It is frequently worthwhile to monitor $S_{mv}O_2$ continuously with a specially equipped pulmonary arterial catheter that has an oximeter attached to the tip. Calibration of the oximeter requires occasional cross-checking with measurement of $S_{mv}O_2$ in a correctly obtained sample of pulmonary arterial blood. A fall in the $S_{mv}O_2$ can arise from a decline in the cardiac output, a decrease in the hemoglobin concentration, a fall in the S_aO_2, or an increase in oxygen consumption (including an increase in myocardial oxygen consumption).

It must be kept in mind, however, that even though a falling $S_{mv}O_2$ may be a warning signal, a normal or high value does not guarantee that cardiopulmonary status is satisfactory or that there is adequate oxygen for metabolic demands. In patients with low-output septic shock, for example, well-oxygenated blood is

returned to the heart because blood is functionally shunted away from the tissues. The high $S_{mv}O_2$ in these patients does not indicate that their metabolic needs are being met; rather, it is the result of deranged peripheral metabolic processes characterized by futile metabolic cycling. In patients with high-output septic shock, $S_{mv}O_2$ may be high because large amounts of blood are shunted to the skin so as to attenuate hyperthermia. Because the skin is metabolically inactive, the blood returning from it will have a high oxygen saturation. Similarly, in cirrhotic patients, who have functional arteriovenous shunts, a high $S_{mv}O_2$ is generated in the presence of inadequate metabolic activity.

Mixed venous oxygen content ($C_{mv}O_2$) is easily calculated in the same manner as C_aO_2. In normal persons, $S_{mv}O_2$ is about 76%. Therefore, if oxygen dissolved in plasma is excluded, $C_{mv}O_2$ is 1.39 × 11.4 × 76%, or 12.0 ml/dl. If the oxygen in the plasma is added back in, $C_{mv}O_2$ becomes 12.2 ml/dl, on the assumption that $P_{mv}O_2$ is 41 mm Hg.

OXYGEN TRANSPORT

Oxygen transport—the amount of oxygen delivered to the tissues—is calculated by multiplying cardiac output by C_aO_2. The calculation is simple, though care must be taken to obtain the correct units. Cardiac output is typically expressed in L/min, C_aO_2 in ml/dl. In multiplying the two, it is necessary to introduce a factor of 10 (to convert the liters of blood in cardiac output to the deciliters of blood in C_aO_2). Thus, in a patient with a normal cardiac output of 6 L/min, a normal hemoglobin concentration of 11.4 g/dl, a normal S_aO_2 of 97%, and a normal P_aO_2 of 97 mm Hg, normal oxygen transport is approximately 940 ml/min:

$$O_2 \text{ transport} = \text{cardiac output} \times C_aO_2$$
$$= 60 \text{ dl/min} \times 15.7 \text{ ml/dl}$$
$$= 940 \text{ ml/min}$$

A reduction in cardiac output, hemoglobin concentration, or S_aO_2 decreases oxygen transport.

OXYGEN RETURN

The amount of oxygen returned to the heart can be calculated by multiplying cardiac output by $C_{mv}O_2$. For a normal cardiac output of 6 L/min and a $C_{mv}O_2$ of 12.2 ml/dl, oxygen return is approximately 730 ml/min.

OXYGEN CONSUMPTION

Oxygen consumption is the difference between oxygen transport and oxygen return. It is therefore calculated by multiplying cardiac output by the difference in oxygen content between systemic arterial blood and mixed venous blood:

$$\text{Oxygen consumption} = \text{cardiac output} \times (C_aO_2 - C_{mv}O_2)$$

Normal oxygen consumption in a resting, supine, well-conditioned woman is 210 ml/min.

Oxygen consumption seems to have even more normal variability than the other parameters already discussed (see above), and it covers a range of values. It is probably easiest to memorize a single normal value, however, rather than a range. As long as the physician recognizes that, for example, an oxygen consumption of 180 ml/min in a 60 kg patient is close to the average of 210, no harm will be done. An oxygen consumption of 150 ml/min, however, would clearly be abnormally low and should prompt investigation to correct a low cardiac output, a low hemoglobin concentration, or a low S_aO_2.

NONINVASIVE SUMMARY MEASUREMENTS

Three main goals can be identified for cardiovascular monitoring as technology advances. The first is to make as many measurements as possible noninvasively so as to eliminate the risks now associated with monitoring. The second is to find a single measurement that summarizes overall patient status. If this parameter indicates that a patient is doing well, current therapy can be continued; if not, therapy can be reassessed. The third goal—which contradicts the second to some degree but is nonetheless desirable—is to know the status of the individual organs. If a patient is not doing well, one would like to know where to direct therapeutic efforts. Ideally, one could identify the organ at greatest risk, keeping in mind that treating one organ usually comes at the expense of another. If one could monitor the state of all organs at

once, this problem would be close to being solved. Having a feeling for the flows and metabolic activities of individual organ systems, in both baseline and stressful conditions, is a start toward these goals. This knowledge can provide a useful perspective on the measurements available now.

Skin temperature can be monitored on the toe or the thumb with noninvasive devices. It is directly correlated with cutaneous blood flow and can be a sensitive indicator of overall perfusion.[59] A gradient of less than 2° C between skin temperature and ambient temperature indicates critically low perfusion; a gradient exceeding 2° C suggests that the heart is capable of generating a fairly robust output. Accurate measurements, however, are difficult to obtain unless there is good control of ambient temperatures.

Oxygen tension in soft tissues, which can also be a good indicator of overall perfusion, can be determined by monitoring conjunctival or cutaneous tissues. Conjunctival oxygen tension is measured with a small oxygen sensor placed directly on the conjunctiva. The device is safe, and it does reflect changes in oxygen delivery to the tissue, but it is not commonly used, perhaps because of the potential for damage to the eye. Transcutaneous oxygen tension can be determined by placing a polarographic surface oxygen electrode directly on heated skin; tissue oxygen tension is measured beneath this surface electrode. This value correlates well with P_aO_2 if local tissue perfusion is good.

Urine output is a good indicator of overall status. It is determined primarily by plasma levels of antidiuretic hormone and aldosterone. Stress increases these levels and thereby reduces output. Blood flow to the kidneys is of secondary importance, but it too can contribute to oliguria. The kidneys, however, are rarely at risk solely because of decreased blood flow. In strenuous exercise, for example, blood flow drops to very low levels, but the kidneys fare well. Their metabolic needs are easily met by increased extraction of oxygen from renal arterial blood. Although a low urine output usually reflects stress and perhaps decreased blood flow to the kidneys, an adequate or even high urine output does not necessarily mean that stress is absent or blood flow is more than adequate. For unclear reasons, some patients in inflammatory and even hypovolemic shock continue to produce apparently adequate urine output. Thus, although oliguria can be a warning sign of patient distress, normal urine production is not a guarantee that all is well.

Blood flow to the gastric mucosa can be assessed by means of gastric tonometry.[60] Low values suggest shock; normal values suggest adequate cardiovascular function. At the same time, blood flow to the gut mucosa and mucosal oxygen consumption can be influenced by other factors, such as body temperature, nutrients in the gut lumen, levels of stress hormones, and underlying individual variations in gastrointestinal physiology. To date, gastric tonometry has been most useful in those ICUs that have a research interest in this measurement technique. Physicians in other ICUs have found it difficult to derive reproducible values from the measurements.

References

1. Nichols WW, O'Rourke MF, Hartley C, et al: McDonald's Blood Flow in Arteries: Theoretic, Experimental, and Clinical Principle, 4th ed. Edward Arnold, London, 1998

2. Karamanoglu M, O'Rourke MF, Avolio AP, et al: An analysis of the relationship between central aortic and peripheral upper limb pressure waves in man. Eur Heart J 14:160, 1993

3. Gardner RM, Hollingsworth KW: Optimizing the electrocardiogram and pressure monitoring. Crit Care Med 14:651, 1986

4. Arabidze GG, Petrov VV, Staessen JA: Blood pressure by Korotkoff's auscultatory method: end of an era or bright future? Blood Press Monit 1:321, 1996

5. Geddes LA: Handbook of blood pressure measurement. Humana Press, Clifton, New Jersey, 1991

6. Talke P, Nichols RJ Jr, Traber DL: Does measurement of systolic blood pressure with a pulse oximeter correlate with conventional methods? J Clin Monit 6:5, 1990

7. Penaz J: Photoelectric measurement of blood pressure, volume and flow in the finger. Digest of the 10th International Conference on Medical and Biological Engineering. Albert A, Vogt W, Heilbig W, Eds. International Federation for Medical and Biological Engineering, Dresden, 1973, p 104

8. Jones DW, Appel LJ, Sheps SG, et al: Measuring blood pressure accurately: new and persistent challenges. JAMA 289:1027, 2003

9. Brinton TJ, Walls ED, Chio SS: Validation of pulse dynamic blood pressure measurement by auscultation. Blood Press Monit 3:121, 1998

10. Bur A, Herkner H, Vlcek M, et al: Factors influencing the accuracy of oscillometric blood pressure measurement in critically ill patients. Crit Care Med 31:793, 2003

11. Geddes LA, Voelz M, Combs C, et al: Characterization of the oscillometric method for measuring indirect blood pressure. Ann Biomed Eng 10:271, 1982

12. Mandel MA, Dauchot PJ: Radial artery cannulation in 1,000 patients: precautions and complications. J Hand Surg [Am] 2:482, 1977

13. Slogoff S, Keats AS, Arlund C: On the safety of radial artery cannulation. Anesthesiology 59:42, 1983

14. Band JD, Maki DG: Infections caused by aterial catheters used for hemodynamic monitoring. Am J Med 67:735, 1979

15. Kulkarni M, Elsner C, Ouellet D, et al: Heparinized saline versus normal saline in maintaining patency of the radial artery catheter. Can J Surg 37:37, 1994

16. Randolph AG, Cook DJ, Gonzales CA, et al: Benefit of heparin in peripheral venous and arterial catheters: systematic review and meta-analysis of randomised controlled trials. BMJ 316:969, 1998

17. Gardner RM: Direct blood pressure measurement—dynamic response requirements. Anesthesiology 54:227, 1981

18. Kleinman B: Understanding natural frequency and damping and how they relate to the measurement of blood pressure. J Clin Monit 5:137, 1989

19. Kleinman B, Powell S, Gardner RM: Equivalence of fast flush and square wave testing of blood pressure monitoring systems. J Clin Monit 12:149, 1996

20. Kofke WA, Levy JH: Postoperative Critical Care Procedures of the Massachusetts General Hospital. Little, Brown & Co, Boston, 1986

21. Suga H: Ventricular energetics. Physiol Rev 70:247, 1990

22. McGee DC, Gould MK: Preventing complications of central venous catheterization. N Engl J Med 348:1123, 2003

23. Merrer J, De Jonghe B, Golliot F, et al: Complications of femoral and subclavian venous catheterization in critically ill patients: a randomized controlled trial. JAMA 286:700, 2001

24. Komadina KH, Schenk DA, LaVeau P, et al: Interobserver variability in the interpretation of pulmonary artery catheter pressure tracings. Chest 100:1647, 1991

25. Morris AH, Chapman RH, Gardner RM: Frequency of wedge pressure errors in the ICU. Crit Care Med 13:705, 1985

26. Swan HJ, Ganz W, Forrester J, et al: Catheterization of the heart in man with use of a flow-directed balloon-tipped catheter. N Engl J Med 283:447, 1970

27. Marini JJ: Obtaining meaningful data from the Swan-Ganz catheter. Respiratory Care 30:572, 1985

28. O'Quin R, Marini JJ: Pulmonary artery occlusion pressure: clinical physiology, measurement, and interpretation. Am Rev Respir Dis 128:319, 1983

29. Raper R, Sibbald WJ: Misled by the wedge? The Swan-Ganz catheter and left ventricular preload. Chest 89:427, 1986

30. Sibbald WJ, Driedger AA, Moffat JD, et al: Pulmonary microvascular clearance of radiotracers in human cardiac and noncardiac pulmonary edema. J Appl Physiol 50:1337, 1981

31. Grossman W: Diastolic dysfunction in congestive heart failure. N Engl J Med 325:1557, 1991

32. Civetta JM, Taylor RW, Kirby RR: Critical Care. Lippincott-Raven, Philadelphia, 1997

33. Polanczyk CA, Rohde LE, Goldman L, et al: Right heart catheterization and cardiac complications in patients undergoing noncardiac surgery: an observational study. JAMA 286:309, 2001

34. Sandham JD, Hull RD, Brant RF, et al: A randomized, controlled trial of the use of pulmonary-artery catheters in high-risk surgical patients. N Engl J Med 348:5, 2003

35. Connors AF Jr, Speroff T, Dawson NV, et al: The effectiveness of right heart catheterization in the initial care of critically ill patients. SUPPORT Investigators. JAMA 276:889, 1996

36. Shah MR, Hasselblad V, Stevenson LW, et al: Impact of the pulmonary artery catheter in critically ill patients: meta-analysis of randomized clinical trials. JAMA 294:1664, 2005

37. Sackner-Bernstein JD, Kowalski M, Fox M, et al: Short-term risk of death after treatment with nesiritide for decompensated heart failure: a pooled analysis of randomized controlled trials. JAMA 293:1900, 2005

38. Stevenson LW: Clinical use of inotropic therapy for heart failure: looking backward or forward? Part I: inotropic infusions during hospitalization. Circulation 108:367, 2003

39. Celoria G, Steingrub JS, Vickers-Lahti M, et al: Clinical assessment of hemodynamic values in two surgical intensive care units: effects on therapy. Arch Surg 125:1036, 1990

40. Eisenberg PR, Jaffe AS, Schuster DP: Clinical evaluation compared to pulmonary artery catheterization in the hemodynamic assessment of critically ill patients. Crit Care Med 12:549, 1984

41. Mimoz O, Rauss A, Rekik N, et al: Pulmonary artery catheterization in critically ill patients: a prospective analysis of outcome changes associated with catheter-prompted changes in therapy. Crit Care Med 22:573, 1994

42. Gnaegi A, Feihl F, Perret C: Intensive care physicians' insufficient knowledge of right-heart catheterization at the bedside: time to act? Crit Care Med 25:213, 1997

43. Iberti TJ, Fischer EP, Leibowitz AB, et al: A multicenter study of physicians' knowledge of the pulmonary artery catheter. Pulmonary Artery Catheter Study Group. JAMA 264:2928, 1990

44. Hosie KF: Thermal dilution technics. Circ Res 10:491, 1962

45. Selzer A, Sudrann RB: Reliability of the determination of cardiac output in man by means of the Fick principle. Circ Res 6:485, 1958

46. Porter JM, Swain ID: Measurement of cardiac output by electrical impedance plethysmography. J Biomed Eng 9:222, 1987

47. Huntsman LL, Stewart DK, Barnes SR, et al: Noninvasive Doppler determination of cardiac output in man. Clinical validation. Circulation 67:593, 1983

48. Singer M, Clarke J, Bennett ED: Continuous hemodynamic monitoring by esophageal Doppler. Crit Care Med 17:447, 1989

49. Homer LD, Denysyk B: Estimation of cardiac output by analysis of respiratory gas exchange. J Appl Physiol 39:159, 1975

50. Gedeon A, Forslund L, Hedenstierna G, et al: A new method for noninvasive bedside determination of pulmonary blood flow. Med Biol Eng Comput 18:411, 1980

51. Jaffe MB: Partial CO_2 rebreathing cardiac output—operating principles of the NICO system. J Clin Monit Comput 15:387, 1999

52. Dhainaut JF, Brunet F, Monsallier JF, et al: Bedside evaluation of right ventricular performance using a rapid computerized thermodilution method. Crit Care Med 15:148, 1987

53. Suga H: Total mechanical energy of a ventricle model and cardiac oxygen consumption. Am J Physiol 236:H498, 1979

54. Piene H: Pulmonary arterial impedance and right ventricular function. Physiol Rev 66:606, 1986

55. Asanoi H, Sasayama S, Kameyama T: Ventriculo-arterial coupling in normal and failing heart in humans. Circ Res 65:483, 1989

56. Andritsch RF, Muravchick S, Gold MI: Temperature correction of arterial blood-gas parameters: a comparative review of methodology. Anesthesiology 55:311, 1981

57. Swain JA: Hypothermia and blood pH: a review. Arch Intern Med 148:1643, 1988

58. Klocke RA: Carbon dioxide transport. Handbook of Physiology, sect 3, vol 4. American Physiological Society, Bethesda, Maryland, 1987, p 173

59. Kaplan LJ, McPartland K, Santora TA, et al: Start with a subjective assessment of skin temperature to identify hypoperfusion in intensive care unit patients. J Trauma 50:620, 2001

60. Ivatury RR, Simon RJ, Islam S, et al: A prospective randomized study of end points of resuscitation after major trauma: global oxygen transport indices versus organ-specific gastric mucosal pH. J Am Coll Surg 183:145, 1996

Acknowledgments

Figures 1a, 2a, 2c, and 5   Dana Burns-Pizer.
Figures 1b, 2b, and 3   Albert Miller.
Figure 4   Carol Donner.

Robert H. Bartlett, M.D., F.A.C.S., and Preston B. Rich, M.D., F.A.C.S.

Approach to Pulmonary Insufficiency

Pulmonary insufficiency is the most common complication after surgical procedures. It ranges in incidence from 5% to 50% and in severity from minor atelectasis to lethal acute respiratory distress syndrome (ARDS). The reason why the lung is so vulnerable in the postoperative period is that both of the essential components of lung function—ventilation (anatomy and physiology of breathing) and pulmonary circulation (anatomy and physiology of the pulmonary endothelium and interstitium)—are affected by all the events surrounding tissue injury, anesthesia, and tissue dissection.[1] Abnormal ventilation leads to alveolar collapse, decreased functional residual capacity (FRC), and atelectasis. Abnormal capillary homeostasis leads to lung edema. Bacterial pneumonitis can initiate these events or can be a secondary complication. The term ARDS refers to a combination of atelectasis and edema, with edema predominating; it will be used sparingly in this chapter, primarily to describe the occurrence of pulmonary edema caused by increased capillary permeability.

In what follows, we discuss the care of patients at risk for pulmonary complications, including clinical presentation, pathogenesis, recognition, prevention, and treatment of pulmonary insufficiency. Atelectasis and lung edema are considered as separate events, though it is obvious that both abnormalities can and do occur simultaneously after operation. The emphasis of this chapter is on disorders of the pulmonary parenchyma as opposed to pulmonary insufficiency secondary to cardiac disease, thromboembolism, CNS depression, and other conditions. The discussion is limited to mild to moderate pulmonary insufficiency because major insufficiency is discussed more fully elsewhere [*see 121 Mechanical Ventilation*]. Perioperative problems related to operations for primary pulmonary disease also are not addressed in this chapter.

Preoperative Pulmonary Function Testing

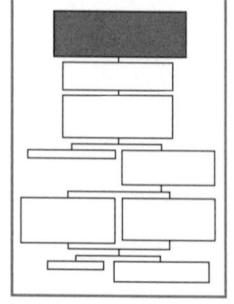

Given that identification of the high-risk patient can reduce the incidence of pulmonary complications, preoperative assessment of respiratory status is clearly important. The history is the most valuable step. Factors indicating a need for more detailed study of pulmonary function include exercise intolerance, dyspnea on exertion, wheezing, cigarette smoking, cough, and sputum production.

Physical examination should include auscultation and percussion of the lung bases during tidal breathing and maximal inspiration to detect hypoventilation in weak or debilitated patients and

hyperinflation in patients with chronic airway disease. Wheezing, rales, or rhonchi should trigger further examination. Cardiac insufficiency, obesity, clubbing, tobacco stains, and poor oral hygiene are all relative indications for more detailed pulmonary function testing. Chest x-ray should be considered part of the routine physical examination for any patient with an abnormality detected from the history or physical examination, any patient scheduled to undergo a thoracotomy, and any patient older than 40 years. As part of the physical examination, the patient should be instructed to inhale to the maximum, then to perform a vigorous forced expiration. By observing the patient's chest and the sound of forced expiration, one can make a good guess at the volume of inspiration (which should be at least 1 L/50 kg), forced expiratory volume (which should be at least 2 L/50 kg), and expiratory flow (most of the exhaled volume should come out in the first second without wheezing). Forced expiratory volume—or vital capacity (the two are different names for the same thing)—and maximum voluntary ventilation (MVV) can be directly measured with a handheld turbine spirometer.

The ability to climb one or two flights of stairs at a steady pace without dyspnea provides information about the patient that is not available in any other way short of treadmill or exercise testing. A patient who cannot do this simple exercise may have respiratory, cardiac, or joint disease or may be too obese, too weak, too sedentary, or too debilitated to manage mild exertion. Whatever the cause, an elective operation should be delayed if the patient cannot do the exercise.

Simple spirometry should be done whenever the history, the physical examination, or bedside tests yield findings indicating abnormal pulmonary function. Tidal volume, inspiratory capacity, vital capacity (total and timed intervals), and MVV are measured, and the results are compared with tables for normal persons of the same age, sex, and size and then reported as percentages of predicted normal values. Results between 80% and 120% of predicted values are considered normal. If these tests of lung volume and flow are within the normal range, the risk of pulmonary complications is small (though the tests do not address endurance). Abnormally high values are not important; however, abnormal values below 70% of predicted levels indicate small airway or obstructive lung disease (if the expiratory flow rate is low), loss of lung volume (if vital capacity is low), or localized or generalized muscle weakness. If expiratory flow is abnormally low, spirometry should be repeated after the administration of aerosolized bronchodilators. Low expiratory flow that improves after bronchodilation indicates bronchospasm, which will require special management during and after operation. The test result that correlates best with the incidence of postoperative pulmonary complications is an MVV value below 50% of the

Assess pulmonary function preoperatively

Review history; perform physical exam. Evaluate for wheezing, rales, and rhonchi; cough and sputum production; cardiac insufficiency; and obesity. Estimate volume of inspiration, forced expiration, and expiratory flow.
Obtain chest x-ray if abnormality is detected, thoracotomy is planned, or patient is > 40 years.
If pulmonary dysfunction is suspected:
- Measure tidal volume, inspiratory capacity, vital capacity, and maximum voluntary ventilation.
- Obtain baseline blood gas measurements.
- In special circumstances: Measure FRC. Assess for chronic fibrotic disease.
  Obtain ventilation-perfusion lung scan if pulmonary resection is contemplated.

Correct abnormalities, and prepare patient before operation

Teach breathing maneuvers, and exercise patient's respiratory muscles.
Reduce risk factors (e.g., smoking, LV failure).
Assess effects of bronchodilators in patients with bronchospasm.
Provide adequate nutrition.

Follow pulmonary prophylaxis regimen during and after operation

Inflate all alveoli regularly:
- Use breathing exercise with incentive spirometer. Use IPPB if necessary.
- Use mechanical ventilation in high-risk patients.
- Use bronchodilators for bronchospasm.
Maintain normal body fluid volume and composition:
- Give blood and fluids as needed, but not excessively.
- If fluid overload is unavoidable, diurese when stable.
Minimize the risk of venous thrombosis and pulmonary embolism.

Postoperative pulmonary insufficiency does not develop

Postoperative pulmonary insufficiency develops (e.g., dyspnea, tachypnea, tachycardia, confusion, cyanosis, abnormal x-ray)

Rule out mechanical limitation of breathing, bronchospasm, pulmonary embolism, congestive heart failure, and hypovolemia.
Evaluate for atelectasis or pulmonary edema.
General support: Give O_2 during preliminary investigations (10 L/min by cannula or mask).

Approach to Pulmonary Insufficiency

Treat atelectasis

Establish large-volume inflation via deep breathing exercises. If unsuccessful, try IPPB without intubation.
Initiate chest physiotherapy and postural drainage. Administer hydration, nebulized bronchodilators, and mucolytic drugs via airway. Perform bronchoscopy or tracheal suctioning as indicated.
If ventilation is still inadequate: Intubate and initiate mechanical ventilation. Provide nutritional support. Treat coexisting lung edema and lung infection. Maintain $F_IO_2 < 60\%$ and airway pressure < 40 cm H_2O.

Treat increased lung water

Decrease pulmonary hydrostatic pressure by improving LV function pharmacologically. (Monitor changes in cardiac output.)
Reduce total extracellular fluid volume by forced diuresis, dialysis, or hemofiltration.
Increase plasma oncotic pressure by administering colloids during diuresis.
Establish and maintain normal pulmonary microvascular integrity by treating any extrapulmonary site of infection or inflammation.

Pulmonary insufficiency resolves

Pulmonary insufficiency progresses to ARDS or pneumonia

Provide specific treatment for respiratory failure or postoperative pneumonia as indicated.

predicted level. MVV may be abnormally low for many reasons, both pulmonary and nonpulmonary.

Arterial blood gas values are obtained only if major pulmonary dysfunction is suspected, and they serve primarily as a baseline for postoperative comparison and for decisions about postoperative ventilation rather than as a screening test for adequacy of pulmonary function. Arterial carbon dioxide tension (P_aCO_2) greater than 45 mm Hg at rest indicates significant alveolar hypoventilation. If the cause is muscle weakness, bronchospasm, or chronic bronchitis, it should be treated before any elective operation is undertaken. If the arterial oxygen tension (P_aO_2) is greater than 70 mm Hg, the patient has significant right-to-left shunting, diffusion block, or ventilation-perfusion mismatch—usually the last, though two or all three of these may occur together. These three causes of hypoxemia can be further identified by the response to breathing 100% oxygen, but this evaluation requires special equipment (a face mask or nasal catheter is not satisfactory), and the information gained is generally not worth the effort for the purposes of preoperative pulmonary assessment.

More detailed tests of pulmonary function are needed only in special situations. The most useful of these is measurement of FRC, which is done in association with simple spirometry using helium dilution or nitrogen washout. FRC is the most difficult lung volume to measure but also the most important: following the FRC is the most specific way of determining when the patient is in optimal pulmonary condition. An abnormally high FRC indicates air trapping from small airway disease or bronchospasm, which should be treated before any elective operation. An abnormally low FRC indicates loss of lung volume that may result from atelectasis, pneumonia, pleural effusion, or congestive heart failure, all of which should be treated until the FRC is normal. Measurement of diffusing capacity by carbon monoxide inhalation is not helpful. Measurement of P_aO_2 during carefully monitored breathing of 100% oxygen is more useful when chronic fibrotic lung disease is suspected. Oxygen consumption, CO_2 production, and respiratory quotient are measures of systemic metabolism rather than of pulmonary function; accordingly, whereas they may be helpful in preoperative screening for the purposes of detecting sepsis or planning nutritional therapy, they generally are not useful guides to pulmonary functional status. Ventilation-perfusion scanning should be added to the regimen of routine preoperative testing in any patient with evidence of compromised pulmonary function in whom resection of pulmonary tissue is contemplated.

In summary, the history, the physical examination, and chest x-ray constitute sufficient preoperative pulmonary assessment in almost all cases. Patients at risk for pulmonary complications, as identified by history or examination, should undergo simple spirometry to identify abnormalities that can be corrected before elective operations. Arterial blood gases should be measured preoperatively in patients with major respiratory dysfunction to serve as a baseline for postoperative management.

Preoperative Measures to Prevent Pulmonary Insufficiency

PREVENTION OF ATELECTASIS AND EDEMA

Given an understanding of how pulmonary insufficiency arises and how patients at high risk for this complication can be detected, one can identify the appropriate steps in prevention. First, measures must be adopted to prevent atelecta-

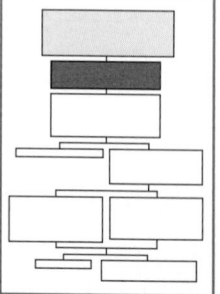

Table 1   Prevention of Atelectasis during and after Operation

Ensure frequent inflation to total lung capacity
   Deep breathing exercises facilitated by incentive spirometer
   Mechanical ventilation after major operations until alert and awake
   Positive pressure breathing for patients who cannot take deep breaths

Minimize respiratory depression
   Adequate, but not excessive, narcotic dosage
   Local and regional anesthesia

Minimize absorption atelectasis from increased F_IO_2
   Add nitrogen (lowest F_IO_2 to keep $S_aO_2 > 90\%$)
   Use PEEP if $F_IO_2 > 50\%$

Avoid pulmonary edema

Clear pleural space of air and fluid

Use abdominal viscera to increase lung volume
   Sitting or standing position
   Avoidance of supine position and high abdominal pressure

F_IO_2—fraction of inspired oxygen   PEEP—positive end-expiratory pressure
S_aO_2—arterial oxygen saturation

---

sis [*see Table 1*]. The most important of these is to maintain a normal pattern of breathing with regular maximal lung inflation. The patient can usually do this voluntarily and spontaneously, taking deep forced inspiratory breaths at least 10 times each hour. The incentive spirometer may be used to encourage the patient's efforts and to measure the volume of inspiration. If the patient cannot take deep breaths spontaneously, mechanical assistance should be employed—usually on an intermittent basis with a mechanical ventilator and mouthpiece (intermittent positive pressure breathing, or IPPB). In high-risk patients who have undergone major operations, postoperative prophylactic intubation and mechanical ventilation are appropriate preventive measures and should be continued until the patient can sustain a normal breathing pattern. Keeping the airway clear with humidification and postural drainage is important in patients with chronic bronchitis. Coughing is not useful for preventing postoperative pulmonary complications.

Second, measures must be adopted to prevent lung edema [*see Table 2*]. Advising the surgeon to avoid cardiac failure, endotoxemia, and shock is an oversimplified platitude, but it is important to remember that pulmonary insufficiency may be the presenting symptom of these conditions. If preoperative and intraoperative resuscitation has resulted in major fluid overload, diuresis should be instituted when the patient is hemodynamically stable to minimize the potential for symptomatic lung edema and to raise plasma oncotic pressure.

CORRECTION OF ABNORMALITIES

If a patient is scheduled for an elective operation, as much time as is necessary should be spent measuring lung function, correcting abnormalities where present, and changing conditions that may predispose to pulmonary complications. This is particularly true in patients with preexisting cardiopulmonary disease. Patients should be advised to train for a major operation as they would for an athletic event. The respiratory muscles should be exercised and specific breathing maneuvers learned.

Correction of factors that may decrease the efficiency of ventilation includes cessation of smoking, elective weight loss in gross-

Table 2 Prevention of Pulmonary Edema during and after Operation

Avoid extracellular fluid overload
  Routine intraoperative fluids limited to 3% of body weight
  Low threshold for blood or colloid during resuscitation or blood loss
Treat or prevent left ventricular failure
  Optimization of cardiac output with inotropes when filling pressures are elevated
Restore or maintain colloid osmotic pressure
  Diuresis to concentrate proteins
  Administration of 25% albumin or plasma if pulmonary edema is symptomatic
Minimize pulmonary capillary leakage
  Drainage of pus and excision of dead tissue

ly obese patients, and treatment of existing bacterial infection (chronic bronchitis) with culture-specific antibiotics where indicated. Patients with a known tendency for bronchospasm should become accustomed to undergoing bronchodilator treatment preoperatively, and the effect of bronchodilators on pulmonary mechanics should be directly measured, particularly in patients with known bronchospastic disorders (e.g., asthma).

Patients with preexisting lung disease require special consideration beyond the preparation related to bronchospasm or chronic bronchitis (see above). Patients with acute pulmonary insufficiency, increased lung water levels, and atelectasis secondary to an acute disorder such as pancreatitis or sepsis often show improvement during the operation and postoperative mechanical ventilation.

The condition of a patient with severe, chronic obstructive lung disease should be improved as much as possible by means of bronchodilators, treatment of chronic bronchitis (if present), nutritional support, and training in deep breathing. If the pulmonary disorder is very severe (i.e., if P_aO_2 is less than 50 mm Hg on room air or if CO_2 retention is evident), prolonged postoperative intubation and mechanical ventilation should be anticipated and the patient advised accordingly.

Intraoperative Measures to Prevent Pulmonary Complications

Intraoperatively, several factors may minimize the risk of postoperative pulmonary complications. The operation may directly improve pulmonary function (e.g., by repairing a mitral valve or a large abdominal wall hernia) or may mitigate or eliminate factors that of themselves are causing pulmonary insufficiency (e.g., by draining an empyema, removing a foreign body, or resecting dead tissue).

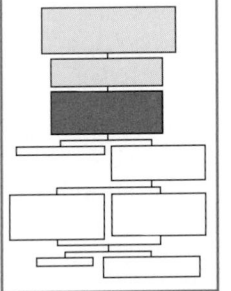

The operative procedure should be planned so as to simultaneously treat the patient and avoid any factors that may cause postoperative complications. With regard to the pulmonary system, planning includes various components, as follows.

Abdominal incisions should be planned to minimize postoperative pain and to maintain the strength of the abdominal wall for forced inspiration. Transverse incisions should be used whenever possible, particularly in patients with chronic heavy sputum production who will have to cough excessively after operation.

Gastrostomy should be considered to avoid prolonged nasogastric intubation. Bone fragments should be manipulated as gently as possible to prevent possible marrow embolism. Veins under negative pressure (e.g., those in the brain) must be managed carefully to prevent air embolism. If the patient has a history of pulmonary embolism or existing deep vein thrombosis (DVT) in the legs, prophylaxis for these conditions is particularly important.

Ventilation with 100% O_2 before intubation is standard practice, and a fraction of inspired oxygen (F_IO_2) higher than 90% is commonly used during operation. However, elimination of inert nitrogen in the alveoli leads to absorption atelectasis very rapidly. Accordingly, restoring normal alveolar nitrogen levels and volume through sustained inspiratory pressure with air before extubation is a valuable maneuver.[2] By the same token, however, maintaining a high F_IO_2 throughout the operation and during the early postoperative period significantly decreases the risk of a surgical site infection.[3]

Much of the intraoperative prevention of pulmonary complications is carried out by the anesthesiologist. Maintaining large tidal volume ventilation (10 to 15 ml/kg) at a low respiratory rate during operation helps maintain alveolar inflation. Particularly during long procedures, alveoli begin to collapse unless regularly hyperinflated at least every hour. The anesthesiologist contributes greatly toward preventing pulmonary complications by avoiding crystalloid fluid overload during operation. Blood and protein losses can be replaced intraoperatively with lactated Ringer solution. Generally, blood or plasma lost during operation should be replaced with blood or plasma. Moderate amounts of saline-type solutions are permissible, but caution should be observed.

Mechanical ventilation should be continued postoperatively until adequate spontaneous ventilation has been clearly established. The action of paralytic drugs should be reversed completely, and a voluntary vital capacity at least twice the tidal volume should be documented before extubation.

Postoperative Measures to Prevent Pulmonary Insufficiency

ROUTINE MEASURES

In the recovery room, the endotracheal tube should be maintained in place as long as is necessary. Patients with preexisting pulmonary dysfunction or those at high risk for pulmonary complications may need to remain intubated and be maintained on mechanical ventilation for hours or days after operation.

Abundant evidence suggests that well-ventilated alveoli are less susceptible to humoral capillary damage than atelectatic alveoli are. Elderly, debilitated patients, patients who have undergone major cardiac procedures, and patients with extensive injuries, multiple fractures, pancreatitis, dead tissue, or severe peritonitis are commonly left intubated and maintained on mechanical ventilation for 12 hours or longer after operation. When the patient is fully alert and awake, when perfusion and cardiac status are stable, and when blood and extracellular fluid volumes are demonstrated to be normal, then the patient is ready for spontaneous ventilation and extubation.

Deep breathing exercises, clearing of sputum and mucus, and avoidance of prolonged periods in the supine position must begin in the recovery room. Profound hypoventilation, ventilation-perfusion imbalance, and resultant hypoxemia are the rule in patients awakening from anesthesia. For this reason, it is common practice to administer moderate amounts (5 to 10 L/min) of supplemental oxygen to all patients in the recovery room. This is a wise precaution for the first hour or two after anesthesia, but it is really prophylactic only against hypoxic arrhythmias, and it may actually impair lung function by suppressing whatever deep breathing may result from moderate hypoxemia. Consequently, supplemental oxygen should not be administered for more than a few hours unless serial blood gas analyses so dictate.

Airway cleaning, suctioning, expectorant drugs, mist inhalation, and mucolytic agents are all useful in patients with preexisting chronic bronchitis or thick, tenacious tracheobronchial secretions. However, these maneuvers and agents may not be necessary in patients who can inflate their lungs adequately by means of inspiratory maneuvers. In the past, a compulsion to force patients to cough dominated much of the thinking on postoperative pulmonary care. Currently, it is generally recognized that coughing maneuvers are painful in thoracotomy or laparotomy patients and should not be necessary if the lung remains well ventilated.

Breathing maneuvers and devices designed to encourage those maneuvers are important adjuncts to postoperative care. Because shallow breathing, the lack of spontaneous deep breaths, and alveolar collapse are the steps that lead to postoperative pulmonary complications, respiratory maneuvers must emphasize maximal lung inflation. Emphasis on breathing out (i.e., with coughing, tracheal stimulation, or so-called blow bottles) does nothing to accomplish alveolar inflation, aside from the preparatory inspiration the patient may take beforehand. The greater the emphasis placed on inhaled volume and inspiratory pressure, the more effective the maneuver will be.

Routine IPPB is not particularly effective in preventing pulmonary complications.[4] This does not mean that IPPB is not a useful treatment method. On the contrary, it is quite useful for patients who are severely obtunded, those who are too weak to carry out spontaneous breathing maneuvers, and those with already established atelectasis. In such circumstances, however, the device should be used frequently (preferably each hour) and monitored by direct measurement of exhaled volumes, with maximum volume inflation attempted with each breath.

Deep inspiratory maneuvers can be done spontaneously or with the aid of a nurse or physical therapist but are better done with the aid of the incentive spirometer. This device allows the patient to see the inspired volume with each breath, thereby assuring the physician, the nurse, the respiratory therapist, and the patient that the maneuver is being done correctly and frequently enough to maintain alveolar inflation. Regular performance of deep breathing exercises using an incentive spirometer can decrease the incidence of pulmonary complications from about 30% to about 10%.[5]

Another method of preventing postoperative atelectasis is the application of continuous positive airway pressure (CPAP) or bilevel positive airway pressure (BiPAP) with a tight-fitting face mask. The potential complications of mask CPAP—gastric distention, vomiting and aspiration, and patient discomfort—are rare but remain a cause for concern. This technique, perhaps combined with mask IPPB, may prove useful in patients who are extubated but cannot or will not breathe deeply.

Whatever method is used to accomplish maximal inflation after operation must be carefully taught to the patient before the procedure: most patients cannot learn breathing exercises in a painful, narcotized, postoperative state.

For patients requiring care in an ICU, keeping the head of the bed elevated at least 30° significantly decreases the risk of developing ventilator-associated pneumonia.[6-8] Accordingly, unless there is a contraindication (e.g., spinal fracture), semirecumbent positioning should be employed routinely. Frequent change of position and early ambulation will minimize fluid collection in the dependent portions of the lung. Postoperative nutrition should be maintained [see 137 Nutritional Support]. If the patient must go without oral intake for more than 4 or 5 days, total parenteral nutrition is advisable for several reasons, not the least of which is to maintain the strength of the respiratory effort. Fluids must be managed carefully to avoid overloading the extracellular space and diluting the serum proteins.

Pulmonary thromboembolism from the deep veins of the leg or the pelvis is a constant threat after operation [see 85 Venous Thromboembolism]. Patients older than 40 years and patients with cancer are at particularly high risk. Several methods are used to prevent DVT, including anticoagulation, pharmacologic inhibition of platelet function, and application of pressure to the legs with plastic wraps or stockings. Regular muscle exercise is the easiest preventive maneuver, has the fewest complications, and is advised for all postoperative patients.

MEASURES IN PATIENTS WITH PREEXISTING LUNG DISEASE

Patients with chronic disease of the airways or the pulmonary parenchyma have less pulmonary reserve; consequently, in these patients, acute respiratory failure may develop after a minimal insult to the lung. The patient with emphysema or asthma presents an interesting problem. Because of the primary disease, residual volume and FRC are abnormally expanded. The patient is protected to some extent against alveolar collapse secondary to shallow breathing; however, the involved alveoli are difficult to ventilate, even with maximal effort. The dead space is abnormally large, so that the minute ventilation must be higher than normal just to achieve normal CO_2 excretion. In addition, alveolar destruction, fibrosis, or bullae may be present, decreasing oxygenation as well as CO_2 excretion. The effect of shallow breathing in such a patient will not be atelectasis, as would occur with a normal lung, but rather CO_2 retention and hypoxemia. Supplemental oxygen may reverse the hypoxemia, but CO_2 narcosis may result, particularly if the patient is also sedated with narcotics or anesthetics.

Chronic bronchitis (daily production of purulent sputum) narrows the small airways, increasing susceptibility to inadequate inflation and alveolar collapse. Heavy cigarette smoking has the same effect. In these conditions, treating the airways before elective operation (with antibiotics or cessation of smoking) is advisable. Severe restrictive disease from pulmonary fibrosis, pleural thickening, fibrosis, or chest wall deformities predisposes to atelectasis.

Patients with acute respiratory failure may require operation; in fact, the respiratory failure may exist because of the indication for operation (e.g., abscess, ischemic tissue, or long bone fractures). Such patients come to operation with a decreased FRC and increased pulmonary water, following the pathogenetic sequence of acute respiratory failure [see Discussion, Pathogenesis of Postoperative Pulmonary Insufficiency, below]. The pulmonary problem may be mitigated or eliminated by the operation itself (e.g., when pus is drained or a fracture immobilized), but even if pulmonary function does not improve, these patients cannot afford any worsening of alveolar collapse or pulmonary edema. In such patients, further deterioration of pulmonary function must be prevented by means of prolonged postoperative intubation and mechanical ventilation and fine-tuning of hydrostatic pressure and colloid osmotic pressure in relation to cardiac output and blood volume.

Clinical Presentation of Postoperative Pulmonary Insufficiency

At any time during the first week after a major operation, a patient may manifest dyspnea, tachypnea, tachycardia, confusion, and cyanosis—the syndrome of pulmonary insufficiency. Although the most likely causes of this syndrome are atelectasis and edema, the first step in evaluation is to rule out mechanical limitation of breathing, acute bronchospasm (asthma), pulmonary thromboembolism, congestive heart failure, and hypovolemia.

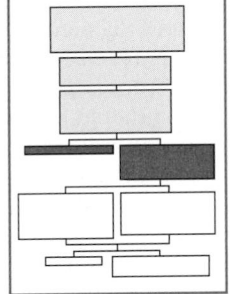

Mechanical limitation of breathing may be caused by gastric or intestinal distention, ascites, pneumothorax, hydrothorax, or splinting of the chest wall to treat pain or rib fractures. It is diagnosed by physical examination and chest x-ray and treated by removing the limitation.

Bronchospasm occurs in patients with a history of asthma. The diagnosis is made by finding wheezes on physical examination and hyperinflation on x-ray. Treatment consists of bronchodilators.

Pulmonary embolism is the first consideration when the onset of pulmonary insufficiency is sudden, but it is the least common cause. Small (lobar) pulmonary emboli rarely cause symptoms. A patient who is symptomatic from embolism has had a major embolus (or a series of minor emboli) occluding more than 50% of the pulmonary circulation. It is usually easy to differentiate pulmonary embolism from atelectasis on the basis of clinical examination and blood gas measurements [see Table 3].

Congestive heart failure in the postoperative period may be either an exacerbation of a chronic condition or acute cardiac failure secondary to myocardial infarction. In either case, the diagnosis is made by physical and x-ray examination of the chest. In the patient who is fluid overloaded, the use of a pulmonary arterial catheter may be required to differentiate cardiogenic from capillary-injury pulmonary edema. The initial steps in management are the same, however, for the acutely ill patient: diuresis, supplemen-

tal oxygen, review of body weight and fluid balance records, and transfer to the ICU for more invasive monitoring.

Hypovolemia is often first manifested by dyspnea associated with metabolic acidosis, and postoperative shortness of breath should always raise the possibility of occult bleeding or third-space sequestration. Clinical examination elicits findings typical of hypovolemia. The chest x-ray is usually clear, and blood gases demonstrate normal oxygenation and CO_2 clearance with metabolic acidosis.

In postoperative pulmonary insufficiency caused by atelectasis and edema, physical examination shows diminished breath sounds over one or both lung bases. Rales and rhonchi may be heard in the middle and lower lung fields. Although tidal volume is normal, vital capacity (judged or actually measured) is abnormally small. Chest x-ray demonstrates incomplete lung inflation, usually with overt collapse or consolidation apparent in the lower lobes. If lung edema is the predominant cause of pulmonary insufficiency, a diffuse increase in lung density is seen, which, when combined with irregular inflation, is often described as diffuse fluffy infiltrates. This radiographic finding will usually differentiate this state from cardiogenic pulmonary edema, which is typically more apparent in the lower and middle lung fields when the x-ray is taken with the patient sitting or standing. Measurement of arterial blood gas values while the patient is breathing air demonstrate hypoxemia, hypocarbia, and respiratory alkalosis.

Supplemental high-flow oxygen (10 L/min) supplied by nasal catheter or face mask supplies approximately 40% inspired oxygen (regardless of the settings on the equipment). Supplemental oxygen substantially mitigates the hypoxemia resulting from ventilation-perfusion mismatch, pulmonary embolism, or cardiogenic pulmonary edema, typically resulting in a P_aO_2 greater than 150 mm Hg. In contrast, supplemental oxygen has a minor effect on hypoxemia caused by atelectasis, yielding a P_aO_2 typically rising from the 40s to the 80s. Fever and mild leukocytosis often accompany atelectasis, and the differential diagnosis between atelectasis and pneumonia is based primarily on con-

Table 3 Differential Diagnosis of Postoperative Dyspnea

	Atelectasis/ Edema	Pulmonary Embolism	Bronchospasm	Congestive Heart Failure
Lung bases	Not aerated	Clear	Wheezes	Rales
Chest x-ray	Consolidation, general edema	Clear ↑ Diameter of main pulmonary artery	Hyperinflated	Hydrostatic edema ↑ Diameter of main pulmonary artery
Central venous pressure	Normal	Elevated	Normal	Elevated
Pulmonary arterial wedge pressure	Normal	Normal or low	Normal or high	High
Arterial P_{O_2} (breathing air) (mm Hg)	40–60	40–80	70–90	40–60
Arterial P_{O_2} (breathing O_2) (mm Hg)	50–100	100–300	200–300	100–300
Arterial P_{CO_2}	Low	Normal or low	High	Normal or high
Lung scan	Regional ischemia	Regional ischemia	± Normal	± Normal
Pulmonary angiogram	Normal	Diagnostic	Normal	Normal

tinuing signs of infection without another obvious source, combined with pathogenic organisms on sputum culture. Thickened or copious bronchial secretions may be present in any patient after operation, particularly if the patient underwent endotracheal intubation, general anesthesia, or both during the procedure. Bronchial secretions are neither the cause nor the result of atelectasis. However, sputum samples for a Gram stain and culture should be acquired from every patient with pulmonary complications.

Treatment of Postoperative Pulmonary Insufficiency Caused by Atelectasis or Edema

GENERAL SUPPORT

Beginning during the preliminary clinical and laboratory examinations and the differential diagnosis, supplemental oxygen should be supplied by nasal catheter or face mask at a rate of 10 L/min. If the patient has a history of severe pulmonary disease with hypoxemia and hypercarbia, preoperative supplemental oxygen may correct the hypoxemia but diminish the respiratory drive and result in CO_2 narcosis; accordingly, special precautions should be taken. The patient should be positioned so as to maximize diaphragmatic excursion—that is, sitting but not hunched forward, with care taken to ensure that the stomach and the abdomen are not distended.

TREATMENT OF ATELECTASIS

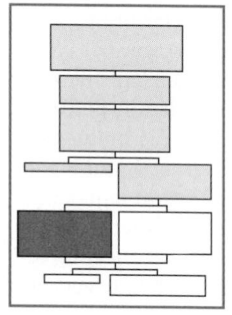

The cornerstone of treatment aimed at alveolar inflation [see Figure 1] is to establish large-volume inflation by instituting deep breathing exercises. The patient should be taught to carry out a sustained maximal inspiration (basically a yawn maneuver); as noted, an incentive spirometer will encourage and quantitate the patient's efforts. If adequate volumes cannot be generated in this manner, mechanical assistance is necessary—initially with IPPB with a mechanical ventilator, without intubation. This step must be done with direct measurement of exhaled volume, and it often requires high pressures (30 to 40 cm H_2O) with the IPPB device. All of the inflation techniques of mechanical ventilation (positive end-expiratory pressure [PEEP], sighs, inspiratory hold, CPAP) can be used in nonintubated patients. Again, coughing is not a treatment for pulmonary insufficiency: forced expiration collapses alveoli, does not clear small airways, and is painful and ineffective in the postoperative patient.

When an area of lung is not ventilated, mucus secreted in the bronchi draining from that lung segment may become thickened and impacted, hindering efforts at reexpansion. Chest physical therapy (percussion) and postural drainage should clear this mucus. Hydration and nebulized bronchodilator and mucolytic drugs may be used as well. Although coughing is not effective in preventing atelectasis, it is necessary for expelling mucus from airways that have been inflated distally. Coughing will not dislodge mucus from airways leading to nonventilated areas of lung. In this situation, mucus must be removed directly with tracheal suction or bronchoscopy, preferably the latter.

Tracheal suctioning exacerbates hypoxia if not done properly. The catheter is inserted through the nose, passed through the larynx (with passage confirmed by a change in voice), and connected to oxygen administered at 5 L/min. Then, 5 ml of saline

is injected, and the oxygen is reconnected for several coughing breaths. Suction is applied for no longer than 10 seconds, after which oxygen is resumed. This process is repeated until the suction return is clear (1 to 5 minutes). Electrocardiographic monitoring should be done during and after suctioning. Atropine is given for bradycardia. In adults, the primary value of this technique is the stimulation of deep breathing associated with the vigorous coughing that it induces. However, deep breathing can be easily accomplished by other means without the potential vagal complications associated with tracheal suctioning. Thus, routine tracheal suctioning has no rational place in the care of postoperative adult patients. In infants, who have much narrower airways, even a very small amount of mucus may suffice to cause major tracheal or bronchial occlusion. Infants breathe rapidly, with large ventilation of the dead space; thus, their tracheal secretions tend to dry out, and they may have difficulty coughing material from the lower trachea or from the bronchi. Consequently, endotracheal suctioning can be valuable for infants who have undergone operations on the thorax or the upper abdomen.

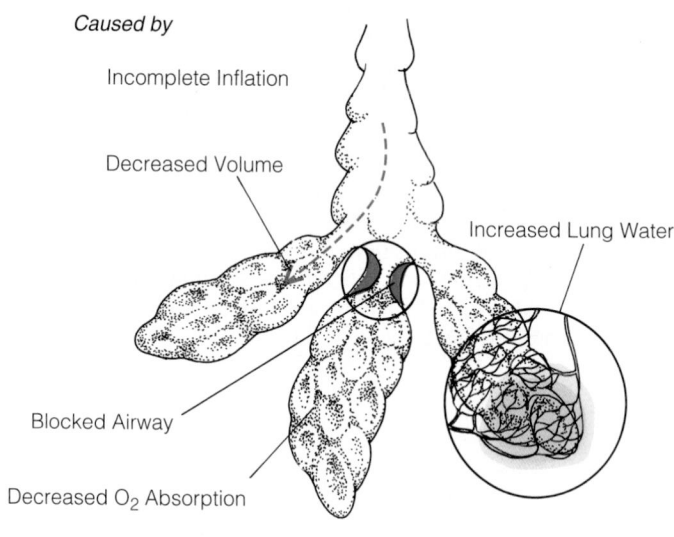

ALVEOLAR COLLAPSE

Caused by

Incomplete Inflation

Decreased Volume

Increased Lung Water

Blocked Airway

Decreased O_2 Absorption

Leads to   Ventilation-Perfusion Imbalance
              Hypoxemia
              Decreased FRC
              Decreased Compliance
              Increased Work

Treatment: Maximum Inflation
                  Yawn, Mechanical Ventilator, IPPB, CPAP
              Maintain Lowest Possible F_IO_2
              Decrease Lung Water
              Treat Infection
              Optimize Nutrition

Figure 1 Illustrated are causes and effects of alveolar collapse in postoperative pulmonary insufficiency.

Flexible fiberoptic bronchoscopy is preferable to blind tracheal suctioning in the management of atelectasis. Bronchoscopy is performed to examine the airways and clear mucus from the atelectatic area. Use of the endotracheal tube facilitates repeated removal and reinsertion of the bronchoscope, which may be necessary if mucus is too thick to be aspirated through the small suction lumen.

If adequate ventilation cannot be established with these methods, respiratory support is warranted. In many cases, endotracheal intubation can be avoided by using noninvasive mechanical ventilation.[9-11] Mechanical ventilation is indicated if the respiratory rate is consistently higher than 30 breaths/min or if the patient is severely hypoxemic (oxygen saturation < 92% despite supplemental oxygen via nasal cannula or face mask). If either of these indications cannot be reversed by the measures described, intubation and mechanical ventilation are carried out. Intubation with spontaneous breathing and CPAP (5 to 10 cm H_2O) without mechanical ventilation are standard therapy for the respiratory distress syndrome of the newborn and are commonly employed when that syndrome is complicated by a surgical procedure. CPAP may be useful in some adults with respiratory insufficiency associated with absence of surfactant. Generally, if the patient requires intubation, mechanical ventilation is also indicated.

If supplemental oxygen has been instituted as general support, the amount of oxygen should be kept as low as possible to avoid displacing nitrogen from alveoli and causing absorption atelectasis. Nutritional support should be instituted to achieve a positive nitrogen balance so as to maintain respiratory muscle strength and optimize host defenses. To prevent overfeeding, the amount of nutrients given should be based on measured energy expenditure. Overfeeding with carbohydrate causes an excess CO_2 load that may exacerbate pulmonary insufficiency.

TREATMENT OF EDEMA

The amount of lung water can be reduced by decreasing the entire extracellular fluid space, decreasing the hydrostatic pressure in the pulmonary capillary bed, and increasing plasma oncotic pressure without increasing oncotic pressure in the interstitial fluid of the lung [see Figure 2]. Mechanical positive pressure ventilation is not a means of decreasing lung water. In fact, positive pressure ventilation with 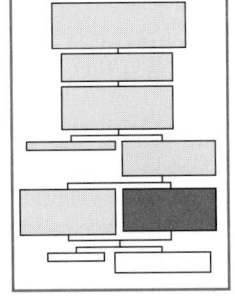 PEEP actually increases lung water slightly, probably by stretching the pulmonary tissue.[12] Mechanical ventilation improves gas exchange in patients with pulmonary edema by overcoming the ventilation-perfusion mismatch associated with bronchodilators or alveolar thickening, but it does not decrease lung water itself.

Patients with simple atelectasis need no treatment for increased lung water other than avoidance of fluid overload and cardiac failure. Increased lung water warrants treatment when diffuse interstitial fluid collection is evident from x-rays and the hospital course. For example, patients who have had an episode of severe systemic infection, disseminated intravascular coagulation, or fat embolism; those with peritonitis; those experiencing revascularization of ischemic tissue; and those who received 4 L of lactated Ringer solution during a 3-hour operation are likely to have increased lung water in association with other pulmonary problems.

Total extracellular fluid volume is reduced by forced diuresis (or, if the patient is in renal failure, by dialysis or hemofiltra-tion). Diuresis is induced with a potent agent such as furosemide. The course of diuresis is followed with careful daily measurement of body weight and hourly measurement of fluid intake and output. Usually, a patient with postoperative pulmonary insufficiency is 4 to 5 kg overloaded, primarily with extracellular fluid.

Adequate treatment of increased lung water must include removing excess extravascular fluid (i.e., returning the patient to baseline weight). Diuresis is continued until the patient is close to dry weight and is maintained in this condition. The major decrease in total extracellular fluid volume is accompanied by a minor decrease in pulmonary extracellular fluid volume, but this change is usually enough to improve pulmonary function greatly. Diuretic drugs remove water, sodium, and potassium at differing rates; thus, all of these must be monitored carefully and frequently. Usually, more water is removed than electrolytes, so that extreme forced diuresis leads to a hypernatremic, hyperosmotic state. Serum sodium concentrations should be monitored closely: when they are between 145 and 150 mEq/L, diuresis has reached its limit.

Diuresis concentrates serum proteins, increasing oncotic pressure. It should be combined with colloid loading to further increase plasma oncotic pressure transiently, thereby forcing

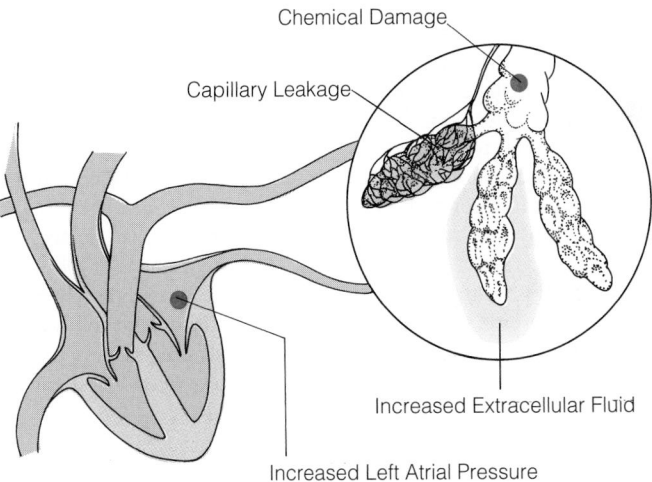

INCREASED LUNG WATER

Caused by

Chemical Damage

Capillary Leakage

Increased Extracellular Fluid

Increased Left Atrial Pressure

Leads to	Increased Pulmonary Vascular Resistance Decreased FRC Ventilation-Perfusion Imbalance Infection
Treatment:	Decrease Extracellular Fluid through Diuresis and Decreased Intake Increase Plasma Oncotic Pressure Treat Capillaries Decrease Hydrostatic Pressure

Figure 2 **Illustrated are causes and effects of increased lung water in postoperative pulmonary insufficiency.**

fluid to move from the extravascular to the intravascular space. Diuresis and colloid loading should be done concomitantly because most agents used for colloid loading (e.g., albumin) have a molecular weight between 50 and 100 kd and will gradually find their way into the extracellular space within 4 to 12 hours of infusion. The advantages of colloid loading come during the first hour or two after infusion and before the colloid load joins the lymphatic system and is metabolized. Although some studies suggest a deleterious effect from albumin loading in this setting, treatment of individuals with colloid loading (and diuresis) is usually highly successful.[13,14] The technique should be used when capillary integrity has been restored, as determined by response to small initial doses.

Decreasing pulmonary hydrostatic pressure by improving left ventricular function is accomplished pharmacologically; it can and should be done in all patients with major pulmonary insufficiency. A short-acting inotrope (e.g., dopamine) is preferred. The effectiveness of this treatment can be determined only through direct measurement of cardiac output and left atrial (or pulmonary capillary wedge) pressure, for which insertion of a pulmonary arterial catheter is required. Pulmonary arterial pressure monitoring and mixed venous blood sampling are as important as direct arterial blood gas sampling in managing patients with pulmonary insufficiency who have a major increase in lung water. The exact position of the catheter must be carefully determined and the pressure tracings properly interpreted; continuous display on an oscilloscope and careful selection of the end-expiratory point for pressure readings are required.

An effort should be made to establish and maintain normal pulmonary capillary permeability. The most common cause of pulmonary capillary leakage or ARDS is infection or inflammation at a site distant from the lungs. Any postoperative pulmonary insufficiency should trigger a search for wound infection, deep abscess, pancreatitis, and septic phlebitis. Drugs that inhibit the inflammatory response, block mediators of capillary injury, or prevent fibrosis have been investigated for the prevention or treatment of ARDS. Corticosteroids definitely diminish the inflammatory response and appear to be effective against some disorders (e.g., fat embolism), but they have not been confirmed as effective in randomized trials.[15] Drugs such as cyclooxygenase inhibitors, which block production of inflammatory mediators more specifically than steroids do, have been studied.[16] Drugs that inhibit the action of specific mediators—such as antihistamines, superoxide dismutase,[17] catalase, and ketoconazole[18]—have been investigated, but none have proved effective in clinical trials.

Progression to Pneumonia, Intubation, or ARDS

Bacterial infection often complicates atelectasis and edema, and it may occur as a primary event after operation. The progression from atelectasis to pneumonia can be difficult to identify because pulmonary infiltration and consolidation, fever, leukocytosis, and sputum production occur in both conditions. This differential diagnosis is one of the most difficult in postoperative

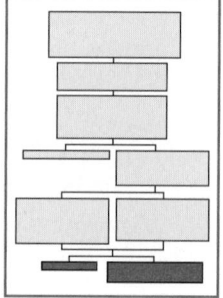

Table 4 Empirical Antibiotic Regimens for Postoperative Pneumonia

Patient Status	Likely Organisms	Empirical Antibiotics
Normal postoperative patients	Pharyngeal organisms; staphylococci; enterococci	Core combination (quinolone plus aminoglycoside)
Postoperative patients with aspirated gastric contents in association with operation	Pharyngeal organisms plus gram-negative organisms and *Candida*	Core combination plus fluconazole
Immunocompromised patients	Pharyngeal organisms plus *Candida* and methicillin-resistant staphylococci	Core combination plus vancomycin or fluconazole
Patients with chronic pulmonary infection	Gram-negative organisms (especially *Pseudomonas* and *Klebsiella*)	Aminoglycoside plus antipseudomonal agent

care; decisions must be based on repeated examination of the patient and the sputum or bronchoalveolar lavage fluid.

In patients with no preexisting lung disease, the organisms that most commonly cause early (first 3 days) postoperative bacterial pneumonia come from the pharynx during the operation: staphylococci, enterococci, or gram-negative bacteria. The same organisms invariably invade the lower airway in chronically intubated ICU patients. Rarely, streptococcal pneumonia occurs in the postoperative period if the pharynx was colonized at the time of the operation. *Candida* is commonly found in the pharynx but rarely causes pneumonia except in immunosuppressed hosts. Treatment for presumed early postoperative pneumonia includes vigorously treating the edema and atelectasis and giving empirical antibiotics. A Gram stain of the sputum will show the common pharyngeal flora but occasionally identifies one predominant organism, the presence of which guides selection of antibiotics while cultures are pending. Usually, however, the Gram stain is not definitive, and antibiotic treatment is therefore selected to cover the most common bacteria.

In patients with preexisting lung disease (emphysema) or lung infection (bronchitis, cystic fibrosis), pneumonia is usually caused by overgrowth of the bacteria already present in the lower airway. Gram-negative organisms predominate. In this circumstance, it is wise to culture a tracheal aspirate sample at the time of operation and to give culture-specific antibiotics if pneumonia occurs. Several choices for empirical antibiotic coverage for postoperative pneumonia are available [*see Table 4*].

The combination of atelectasis, edema, and pneumonia may necessitate intubation and mechanical ventilation. The subjective findings of dyspnea and confusion, combined with the objective findings of tachypnea and cyanosis, usually trigger ICU transfer, careful monitoring, and intubation. More precise indicators of the need for intubation and ventilation include (1) respiratory rate higher than 30/min; (2) arterial oxygen saturation (S_aO_2) lower than 92% on supplemental O_2; (3) P_aCO_2 higher than 45 mm Hg; (4) inspiratory force less than 20 cm H_2O; and (5) vital capacity less than twice tidal volume. Management of severe respiratory failure is discussed more fully elsewhere [*see 121 Mechanical Ventilation*].

Discussion

Normal Pulmonary Physiology

VENTILATION AND PULMONARY MECHANICS

The term pulmonary mechanics refers to the gas volumes in the chest and the gas flow rates during forced inspiration and exhalation. These values are depicted in a normal spirogram [*see Figure 3*]. As noted, FRC is approximately 2 L in a normal adult. During tidal breathing, the patient inhales about 500 ml, then exhales back to FRC. During a maximal inspiratory maneuver, the patient inhales to total lung capacity (typically twice the FRC). During pulmonary function testing to measure gas flow and volume, the patient inhales to total lung capacity, then breathes out as hard and fast as possible. The volume that the patient exhales is referred to as the forced expiratory volume or vital capacity. The rate at which the gas is exhaled is measured as the timed vital capacity, or the maximal midexpiratory flow rate. The volume of tidal breaths multiplied by the respiratory rate yields the minute ventilation (typically 8 L/min in a normal adult). Approximately one third of this ventilation passes through the conducting airways (dead space), and two thirds reaches the alveoli, where gas exchange takes place. Inspiration occurs when the diaphragm contracts, generating an intrapleural pressure that is negative relative to the atmosphere and resulting in the influx of air through the airway into the alveoli. Exhalation is largely a passive event, involving relaxation of the diaphragm and the accessory muscles of inspiration. Forced expiration requires the exertion of effort by the abdominal muscles.

The relation between gas volume and alveolar inflating pressure is referred to as pulmonary compliance [*see Figure 4*]. During diaphragmatic contraction, beginning at FRC, an intrapleural pressure of –10 cm H_2O is generated, which results in inspiration. During normal breathing, an inspiratory pressure of –5 to –10 cm H_2O results in inhalation of 500 to 1,000 ml. During forced inhalation against an open airway, intrathoracic pressures of –40 to –50 cm H_2O can be generated, resulting in inhalation to total lung capacity. Exhalation back to atmospheric pressure returns gas volume in the chest to FRC. An inspiratory pressure greater than –40 cm H_2O during spontaneous breathing (or greater than 40 cm

H_2O during mechanical ventilation) causes overdistention of alveoli, stretching of alveolar capillaries, interstitial and pulmonary edema, and potentially severe lung injury.

Compliance relationships obviously depend on the size of the patient [*see Figure 4*]. The actual volumes for FRC, tidal volume, and total lung capacity related to inflating pressure are low for infants, children, and small adults and relatively high for normal large adults. Patients with alveolar collapse, atelectasis, or interstitial pneumonia have an abnormally small FRC; consequently, their compliance characteristics tend to resemble those of a child. Under these circumstances, if a normal inflating tidal volume is used for such adult patients, high pressures are reached, overstretching occurs, and lung injury results.[19]

Minute ventilation (rate and depth of breathing) is controlled by the respiratory center in the brain stem to maintain P_aCO_2 at 40 mm Hg. By definition and in practice, hypoventilation results in a P_aCO_2 higher than 40 mm Hg and hyperventilation in a P_aCO_2 lower than 40 mm Hg. If a patient is hypermetabolic because of exercise or fever, excess CO_2 is produced, and minute ventilation increases proportionately to keep the P_aCO_2 at 40 mm Hg.

GAS EXCHANGE

Although O_2 exchange and CO_2 exchange occur simultaneously and at the same place in the lung, it is worthwhile to consider CO_2 clearance and O_2 uptake as if they were separate physiologic events. CO_2, being highly soluble in water and very diffusible, is readily eliminated from the pulmonary capillary blood to the alveolar gas space, even though the driving gradient is only about 45 mm Hg. The amount of CO_2 removed depends on the amount of alveolar ventilation [*see Figure 5*]. Minute ventilation (and hence alveolar ventilation) is regulated to remove all metabolically produced CO_2 each minute. Dissolved CO_2 combines with water to become carbonic acid (H_2CO_3), which is in equilibrium with the bicarbonate (HCO_3^-) in blood at a definite ratio. As long as this ratio is 1:20, the pH will be 7.4 (the Henderson-Hasselbalch equation). In postoperative patients, hypoventilation can be caused by respiratory-depressing drugs (e.g., narcotics and anesthetics), paralysis or

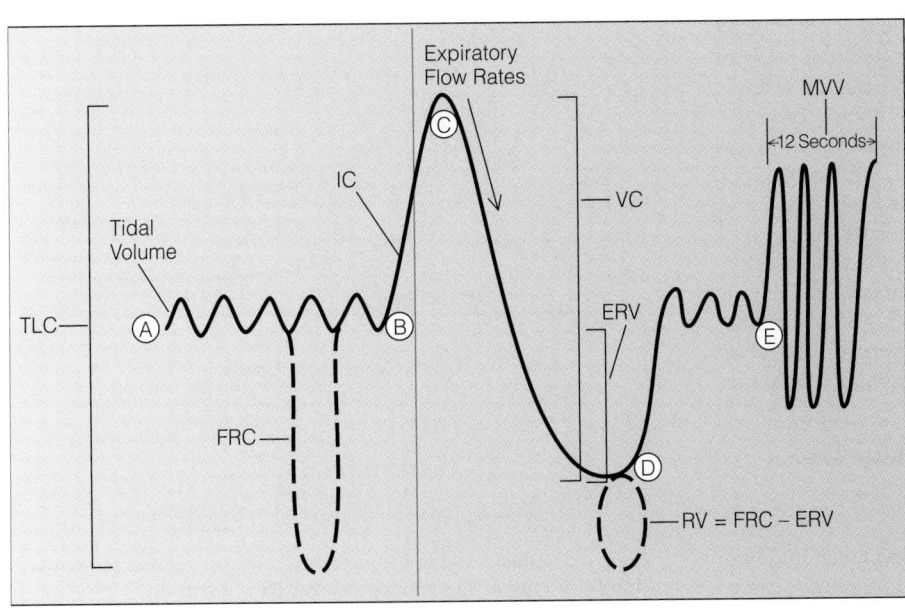

Figure 3 **Depicted are gas volume and flow as demonstrated by spirometry. The subject is instructed to (A) breathe normally, (B) inhale as much as possible, (C) blow out as hard and fast as possible, (D) breathe normally, and (E) breathe as hard and fast as possible for 12 seconds. FRC is measured by a separate test, and residual volume (RV) is determined by subtracting expiratory reserve volume (ERV) from FRC.[1] (TLC—total lung capacity; IC—inspiratory capacity; VC—vital capacity)**

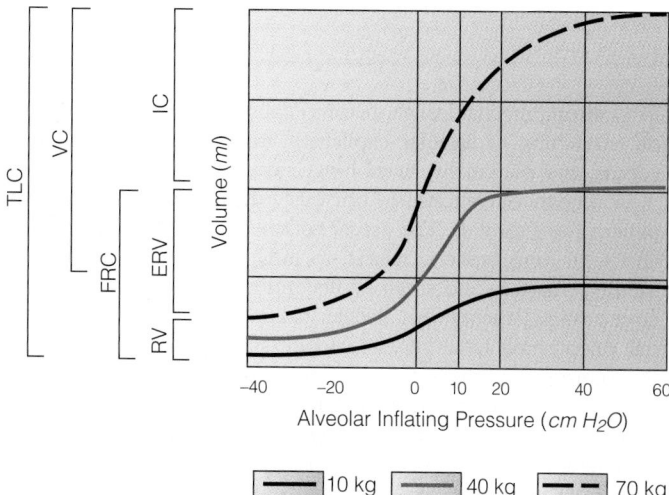

Figure 4 **Shown are volume-pressure curves for three subjects. Compliance is quantified as volume per inflating pressure normalized to body size (80 ml/cm H₂O/kg). Regardless of subject size, total lung capacity is reached at 40 cm H₂O.**[1]

weakness, obesity, and gastric distention, all of which result in CO_2 retention and respiratory acidosis.

Oxygenation of the blood depends more on matching of perfused alveoli to inflated alveoli than on minute ventilation. Under normal conditions, as long as inhaled alveolar gas contains at least 20% oxygen, red blood cells are fully oxygenated and exit the pulmonary capillaries at 100% saturation. During hypoventilation, the concentration of inspired oxygen in the alveoli does not reach 20% unless supplemental oxygen is given at the upper airway. In the recovery room, it is common practice to give supplemental oxygen; thus, a patient may be severely hypoventilated but remain fully oxygenated. The gradient for oxygen transfer from alveolar gas to red blood cells is much higher than that for CO_2 clearance. In a patient breathing room air, the oxygen tension (Po_2) in inhaled gas is approximately 150 mm Hg, and Po_2 in pulmonary capillary blood is approximately 40 mm Hg. Hence, the red cells are oxygenated during a single pass through the pulmonary capillary network. Oxygen in the blood is commonly measured in terms of either saturation (So_2) or Po_2, but the most useful measure is actually oxygen content (Co_2) because that is the major determinant of oxygen delivery at the tissue level. It is noteworthy that when Co_2 is plotted against So_2 and Po_2 at different levels of hemoglobin concentration [see *Figure 6*], blood that is severely hypoxic because of anemia still exhibits normal So_2 and Po_2.

Factors that impair oxygen delivery to blood include hypoventilation causing ventilation-perfusion mismatch, diffusion block caused by chronic lung disease with fibrosis in the interstitial space, and complete atelectasis resulting in transpulmonary shunting of blood from the pulmonary arterial circulation to the venous circulation without participating in gas exchange. The first two generic causes of hypoxemia can be completely corrected by supplemental oxygen breathing, but supplemental oxygen has very little effect on oxygenation when the problem is caused by a transpulmonary shunt.

Pathogenesis of Postoperative Pulmonary Insufficiency

CHANGES IN LUNG FUNCTION

After any major operation, changes occur in lung function. These changes occur in all patients but are not detected on routine exam-

ination. Aside from shallow tidal ventilation and some decreased breath sounds at the lung bases, the patient shows no signs of respiratory abnormality. On direct measurement, lung volumes are decreased (particularly residual volume, expiratory reserve volume, FRC, and vital capacity). Compliance is decreased because of the decrease in FRC. The work of breathing is increased for the same reason: more pressure is required to inhale a given volume into the decreased lung air space. Further evidence that alveoli are not being ventilated is absolute or relative arterial hypoxemia, which occurs with the patient breathing room air or 100% oxygen, indicating that nonventilated alveoli are being perfused (transpulmonary shunting).

These changes in lung function are present immediately after operation, progress slowly over 1 to 2 days, and then return to normal in most patients [see *Figure 7*]. The extent and duration of abnormality are related to the site of operation, the duration of operation and anesthesia, the quality of postoperative care, and preexisting pulmonary status.

The extent and duration of postoperative pulmonary abnormalities are greatest for operations on the thorax and upper abdomen and progressively decrease as the site of operation moves more distally and more superficially on the body structures. These changes may occur after only 1 to 2 hours of general anesthesia if careful attention is not paid to maximal lung inflation during anesthesia. They are superimposed on the patient's preexisting lung status. If, for example, the patient requires operation for complication of pancreatitis 2 weeks after the onset of disease, he or she may already have pleural effusions, increased pulmonary capillary permeability, and existing transpulmonary shunting and thus may be unable to tolerate any further deterioration of lung function. Likewise, if the patient has preexisting chronic obstructive lung disease with high airway resistance, maximal work of breathing, and minimal functional lung tissue before operation, CO_2 retention may develop if the work of breathing is even slightly increased after the procedure. Advanced age per se does not cause lung dysfunction, but elderly patients may have chronic lung disease or cardiac disease and thus be at higher risk for pulmonary failure. More important, elderly patients may be weak, and weak respiratory muscles predispose to alveolar collapse.

Several factors contribute to these changes in pulmonary function, but shallow breathing with incomplete alveolar inflation is the common denominator. If spontaneous deep breaths to maximal

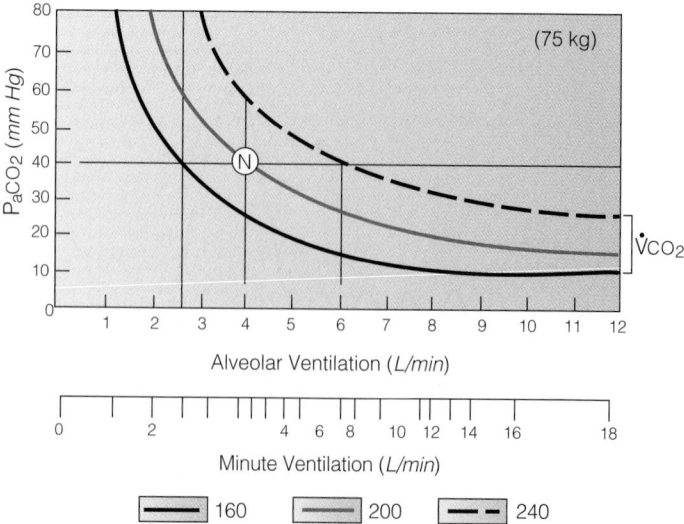

Figure 5 **Illustrated is CO_2 excretion ($\dot{V}CO_2$) related to ventilation for a typical 75 kg adult subject (N = normal).**[1]

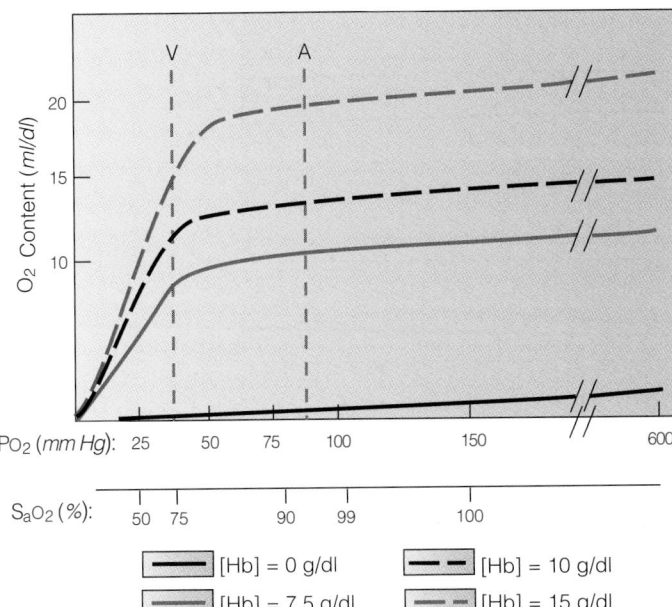

Figure 6 **Shown is measurement of oxygen content in blood at four levels of hemoglobin (Hb) concentration. Dotted lines show values for arterial (A) and venous (V) blood. There is much more oxygen in normal venous blood with a P_{O_2} of 40 mm Hg than there is in anemic arterial blood with a P_{O_2} of 150 mm Hg.**[1]

lung inflation are eliminated from the pattern of breathing, alveolar collapse begins within 1 hour and progresses rapidly to produce significant transpulmonary shunting. Several studies have shown that because of severe pain, anesthetics, or narcotic drugs, postoperative patients often lack the normal pattern of spontaneous deep breaths.[4,20] This finding is further supported by the observation that the postoperative changes in lung function can be returned toward normal by instituting maximal-inflation deep breathing exercises at regular intervals.[5] Excessive tracheobronchial secretions, aspiration of oral or gastric contents, and intraoperative fluid overload or blood transfusion may also contribute to postoperative changes in lung function.

The effects of an increased F_IO_2 and nitrogen washout are important to consider. The higher the concentration of oxygen in the alveoli, the lower the concentration of nitrogen. Nitrogen accounts for 80% of alveolar gas. Because nitrogen is inert, it merely occupies space, holding alveoli open as O_2 and CO_2 are rapidly exchanged during each breath. When nitrogen is washed out during O_2 breathing, alveoli tend to decrease in volume or collapse altogether with each breath. Major atelectasis can occur with just a few minutes of 100% O_2 breathing. In one study,[2] chest CT scans during O_2 breathing demonstrated major atelectasis occurring within minutes [*see Figure 8*]. Because a high F_IO_2 is commonly (and correctly) used during anesthesia with inhalational agents, it is important to minimize the risk of postoperative atelectasis through frequent recruitment of collapsed alveoli by inflation to total lung capacity and restoration of alveolar nitrogen at the end of the operation.

If the pattern of decreased lung volume and shunting is progressing rather than returning to normal, this development becomes clinically evident within 2 to 4 days after operation [*see Figure 7*]. Decreased lung volume is detectable as decreased breath sounds on physical examination, and atelectatic areas may be visible on chest x-ray. Shunt-produced hypoxemia leads to an increased ventilatory rate and the sensation of dyspnea.

Severe hypoxemia may cause cyanosis. Atelectasis causes fever and pooling of mucus secretions in nonventilated areas, leading to

an apparent increase in sputum production. Against the background of the changes that normally accompany major operations, a more complete picture of pulmonary pathophysiology in the surgical patient can be drawn.

As noted, abnormal ventilation leads to altered pulmonary function; the abnormal pattern of tidal breathing without spontaneous deep breaths after operation is a good example of this phenomenon. A patient supine in bed preferentially ventilates the anterior superior lobes while blood preferentially flows to the posterior dependent lobes. This ventilation-perfusion imbalance itself will result in hypoxemia. If it progresses over time, lower-lobe alveoli begin to collapse in the pathogenetic pathway described earlier. Alveolar collapse will occur in any patient who remains in one position for a prolonged period and in whom the pattern of breathing is that of shallow tidal ventilation. It should be emphasized that 600 ml breaths delivered with a mechanical ventilator will lead to alveolar collapse, just as shallow spontaneous breathing will, if regular maximal inflations are not carried out.

Obesity as a Risk Factor

Obesity is a common risk factor for postoperative pulmonary insufficiency. In the morbidly obese patient, the effort required to lift the chest wall and push the abdominal viscera and omentum aside during inspiration may be more than diaphragmatic contraction can handle. This condition is exacerbated after operation, when the patient may still be partially paralyzed, sedated from anesthetics or narcotics, and lying in the supine position (which allows the abdominal weight to push up on the diaphragm). In addition, obesity narrows the posterior pharyngeal space by the simple accumulation of fat in the submucosal tissues. This combination of factors makes hypoventilation a common problem in the obese patient [*see 49 Morbid Obesity*]. The hypoventilation can be profound but may be masked because the patients are receiving supplemental oxygen, so that P_aO_2 remains normal while P_aCO_2 may exceed 100 mm Hg. Moving the obese patient into a sitting position can minimize hypoventilation.

EDEMA AND THE PULMONARY INTERSTITIUM

Increased pulmonary hydrostatic pressure, decreased plasma oncotic pressure, and increased capillary permeability may all occur in the surgical patient. All of these states will cause increased pulmonary extravascular water and deterioration of lung function.

Fluid flux is a net function of the hydrostatic pressure that tends to force fluid out of the vascular space, on one hand, and the oncotic pressure that tends to pull fluid in, on the other hand. High hydrostatic pressure or low plasma oncotic pressure results in accumulation of fluid in the extravascular space. If the pulmonary endothelium is damaged, fluid may leak into the extracellular space at normal hydrostatic or oncotic pressures (as in ARDS) [*see Figure 2*]. Pulmonary vascular resistance increases because of periarteriolar cuffing. Ventilation-perfusion imbalance is created by peribronchiolar and alveolar compression. Shunting occurs if the alveoli become completely collapsed or filled with fluid. Finally, boggy atelectatic areas of lung are ideal breeding grounds for bacterial pulmonary infection.

Well-intentioned therapy in the normal course of treatment or resuscitation may cause increased lung water. An example is replacement of lost blood or plasma with crystalloid, which must equilibrate into the entire extracellular space, including that in the lung. Excess exogenous fluid combines with increased endogenous production of the water of metabolism during hypermetabolic states to yield increased total body extracellular fluid—the

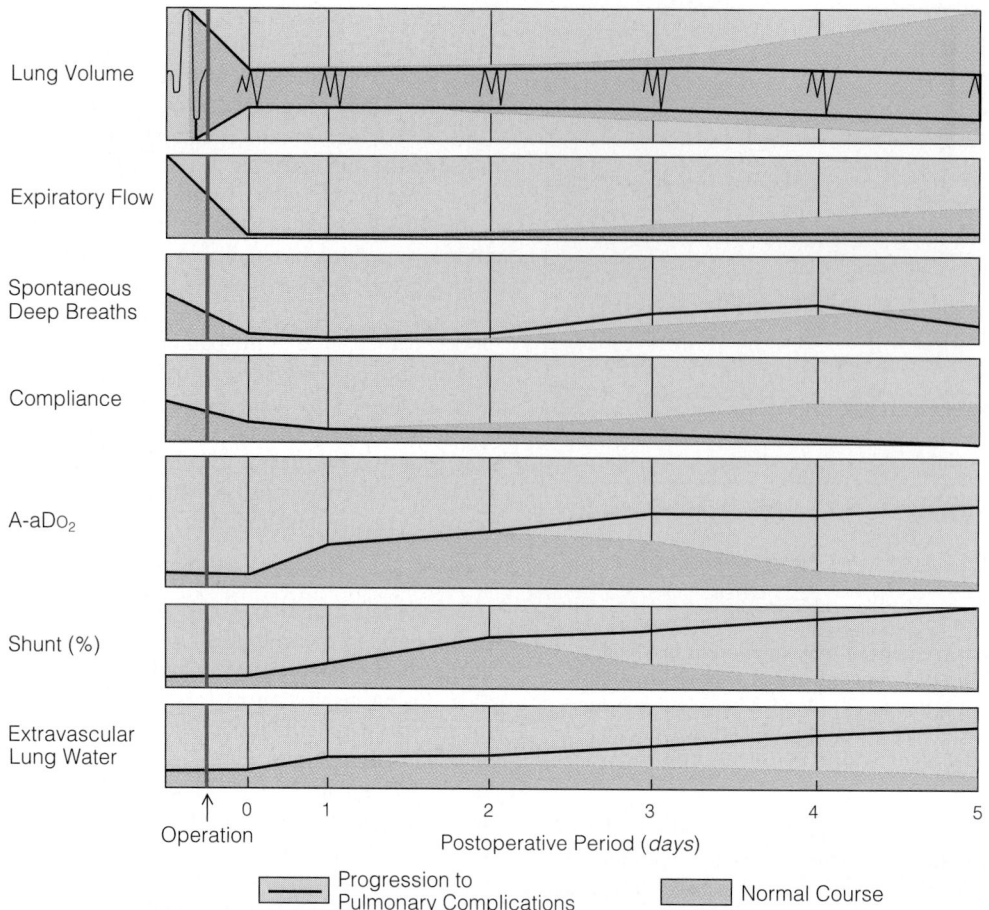

Lung Volume

Expiratory Flow

Spontaneous
Deep Breaths

Compliance

A-aDo₂

Shunt (%)

Extravascular
Lung Water

↑ 0   1   2   3   4   5
Operation   Postoperative Period (*days*)

Progression to
Pulmonary Complications   Normal Course

Figure 7   **Shaded areas represent normal changes in pulmonary function after an operation. Solid lines represent progression to pulmonary insufficiency. (A-aDo₂—alveolar-arterial difference in oxygen)**

major cause of pulmonary extravascular water collection. The effect is compounded by the decreased oncotic pressure that results when protein is lost or replaced with non–colloid-containing fluids. When plasma proteins are diluted in this way, lung interstitial proteins are also diluted; thus, the oncotic gradients stay unchanged, whereas the entire extracellular space expands.

The pulmonary capillary endothelium is the first major vascular bed to be exposed to any toxic substances arising from peripheral organ metabolism or perfusion of ischemic or infected tissue. The venous effluent from underperfused tissue (whether localized to a single organ, as in arterial embolism, or pervading the entire body, as in any type of shock) arrives directly at the lung, where pulmonary capillary damage occurs. Humoral substances (e.g., lysosomal enzymes and bacterial endotoxin) or particulate materials (e.g., microemboli, major thromboemboli, platelet aggregates, and fat particles) may lodge in the pulmonary capillary bed. As these materials are cleared, leaky pulmonary capillaries are left behind, with the resultant accumulation of extravascular water. If the material trapped in pulmonary capillaries includes large amounts of platelets, secondary effects caused by platelet breakdown products (notably serotonin and thromboxane) are also seen. In major thromboembolism, for example, hypoxemia occurs because of ventilation-perfusion imbalance owing to bronchial spasm, presumably secondary to serotonin released from platelets.

The pulmonary effects of materials released into the venous blood in shock entrain a particularly vicious circle.[21] Increased pulmonary vascular resistance and hypoxia resulting from the capillary damage lead to decreased cardiac output and peripheral oxygen delivery, exacerbating the shock state and perpetuating the pulmonary lesion.

Left ventricular failure with increased left atrial pressure results in pulmonary transcapillary transudation, which may be subtle or grossly obvious, as in congestive heart failure with overt pulmonary edema. Left ventricular pressures may waver at the point of high left atrial pressure for short periods—even minutes—resulting in a transient increase in lung water, then return to a balanced state. This situation in itself may not lead to severe pulmonary edema, but it probably makes the lung more vulnerable when minor capillary damage coexists.

The pulmonary interstitium is particularly vulnerable to the events surrounding an operation. Saltwater infusion usually greatly exceeds fluid losses and thus expands the extracellular space. Bleeding and compression of veins by retractors may cause hypotension and necessitate infusion of blood or fluid. Mediators from sterile tissue injury or bacterial invasion may injure pulmonary capillary endothelium. Transient myocardial depression may cause hydrostatic pulmonary edema. With all of these factors, it is remarkable that there is no primary change in lung water volume after uncomplicated operations, even operations including cardiopulmonary bypass. Nonetheless, it should be remembered that the patient usually leaves the OR overloaded with fluid and primed for the development of lung edema.

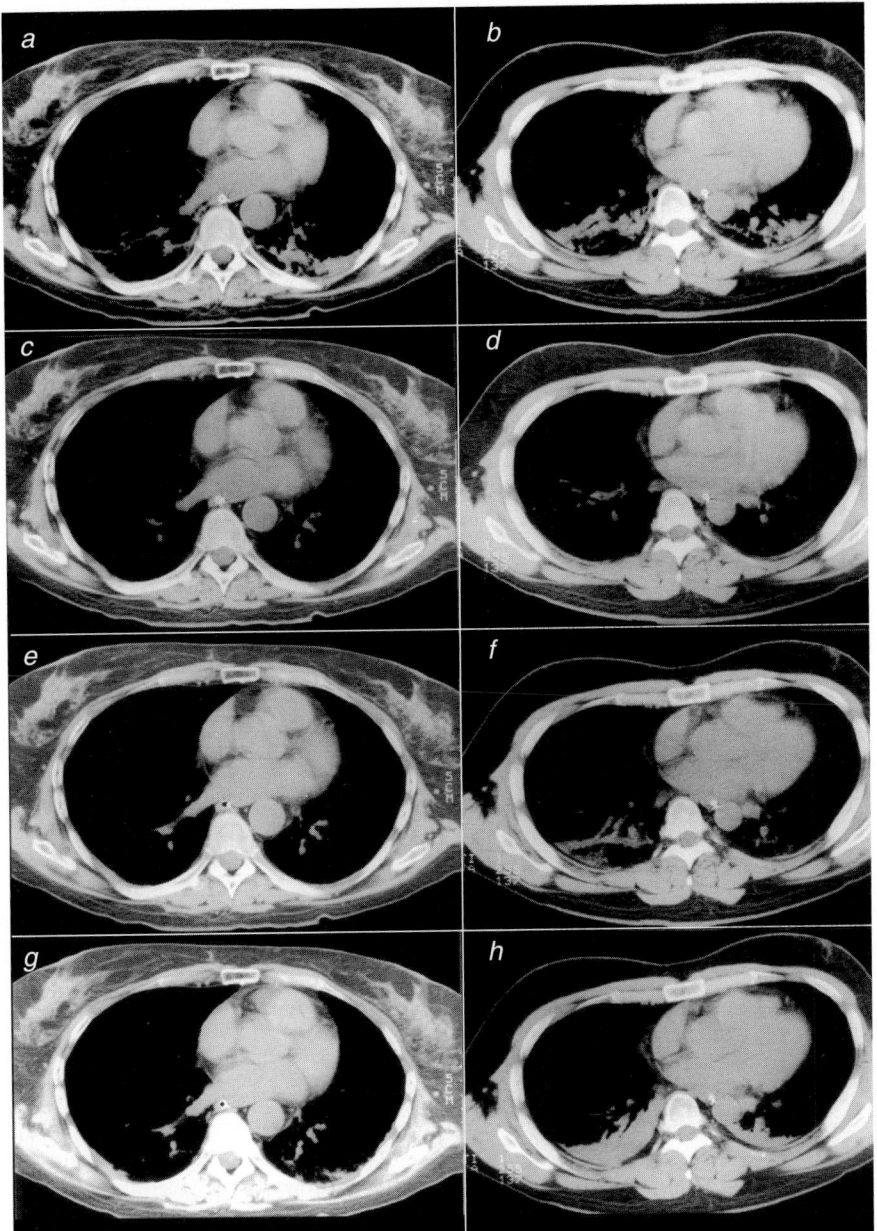

Figure 8 **The subject on the left (*a, c, e, g*) is ventilated with 40% O_2; the subject on the right (*b, d, f, h*), with 100% O_2. Atelectasis occurs (posteriorly, of course) after induction and several minutes of tidal breathing (*a, b*) and is completely reversed by inflation to total lung capacity (plateau pressure 40 cm H_2O; *c, d*). Inflation was sustained for 5 and 40 minutes while the patient was breathing 60% nitrogen (*e, g*), but atelectasis recurred by absorption while the patient was breathing 0% nitrogen (*f, h*). Used with permission.**[2]

CONDITIONS AND EVENTS ASSOCIATED WITH PULMONARY INSUFFICIENCY

Fat Embolism

In a small percentage of patients with extensive fractures, the clinical syndrome of fat embolism develops. This syndrome results from pulmonary embolization of neutral fat globules from the marrow cavity and is often associated with embolization of megakaryocytes and other marrow cells. Hypoxemia and bilateral patchy pulmonary infiltrates, beginning 12 to 36 hours after an injury or a bone operation, are typical of this lesion. Associated findings include a falling hematocrit, hemolysis, high fever, cerebral symp-

toms, petechiae (particularly in the anterior axillary folds, the sclerae, and the eyelids), and possibly fat globules in urine, blood, or sputum. Pulmonary capillary damage occurs, apparently as a consequence of sterile inflammation from fatty acids released as the triglyceride particles break down in the lung parenchyma. Steroids have been shown to reduce the inflammation and hence the mortality from the pulmonary lesion, though they must be given early and in large doses to be effective. Intubation and mechanical ventilation are indicated as soon as the syndrome has been diagnosed. Care must be taken to keep the patient's fluid balance as dry as possible because the pulmonary capillaries leak even at normal hydrostatic pressures. This is often difficult in patients with multiple injuries, who may have active bleeding or oliguria concomitantly with the developing pulmonary lesion.

Smoke Inhalation

Several investigators have demonstrated a generalized permeability increase in capillaries (including pulmonary capillaries) after a small burn; the more extensive the burn, the greater the capillary leakage.[22] The pulmonary capillary bed shows signs of increased capillary permeability first, in the form of increased lung water. This phenomenon has confused clinicians caring for patients with smoke inhalation syndrome for many years. However, it has now been clarified by work showing that smoke inhalation injury is a relatively mild pulmonary insult in itself but is a major insult when combined with a body surface burn, as is often the case in humans.[23]

Toxic components of smoke include carbon monoxide, heat, various aldehydes and other organic materials, and a wide range of vaporized compounds. Materials that are totally combustible (e.g., natural gas and gasoline) burn to yield CO_2 and water, producing few toxic organic compounds and causing minimal lung damage when inhaled in smoke. On the other hand, materials that burn incompletely (e.g., wood, paint, and upholstery), yield a number of toxic vapors in addition to the usual products of combustion, and these vapors damage the respiratory epithelium and the alveoli. The heat carried in smoke is a relatively minor cause of lung damage because air is such a poor heat conductor. Deep lung damage from heat is unusual unless the thermal injury is conveyed by hot steam.

Carbon monoxide is the major toxic material in smoke. It does not damage the lungs but renders the brain hypoxic by associating with hemoglobin, thereby inducing potentially lethal brain damage. Patients with smoke inhalation injury who do not have a body surface burn usually pass through a period of mild pulmonary insufficiency and recover completely unless they have suffered irreversible brain damage or metabolic acidosis as a result of carboxyhemoglobinemia. Patients with the same degree of smoke inhalation injury who also have a moderate body surface burn are subject to serious pulmonary insufficiency with combined atelectasis and increased lung water; intubation, mechanical ventilation, and efforts to reduce lung water usually prove necessary.

Chest Trauma

Direct injury to the chest may cause damage to the chest wall, the lung parenchyma, the diaphragm, the airway, and other intrathoracic structures (e.g., the heart and the great vessels) [see 104 Injuries to the Chest]. These injuries are usually associated with hemothorax or pneumothorax. Life-threatening hypoventilation may result from injuries to the chest wall or from alveolar collapse caused by fluid or blood in the pleural space. Emergency treatment includes placement of a large chest tube to empty the pleural space and reexpand the lung along with mechanical ventilation if spontaneous breathing is inadequate.

With blunt trauma, fracture of the ribs or sternum may create a segment of the chest wall that moves inward in response to the negative pressure created during spontaneous inspiration (so-called paradoxical motion); this floating segment is referred to as a flail segment, or flail chest. A small amount of paradoxical motion with no physiologic side effects does not warrant specific treatment. If flail chest is associated with hypoxemia or CO_2 retention, then lung contusion is probable and intubation and ventilation are indicated.

If air or fluid is detected in the pleural space, a large chest tube should be placed. If a patient with minor chest injuries requires immediate operation for other problems (e.g., ruptured spleen or head injury), prophylactic chest tubes should be replaced on both sides to eliminate the possibility of a tension pneumothorax or hemothorax developing during anesthesia. Mechanical ventilation is required for patients with major flail segments and lung contusion of chest injury complicating other serious injuries.

Penetrating trauma may result in a sucking chest injury, in which air is inhaled into the pleural space during inspiration, filling the pleural space, eliminating the pressure gradient that would normally cause the lung to inflate, and resulting in atelectasis. If the injury allows air to be inhaled into the pleural space but prevents it from exiting, a tension pneumothorax results, with hypoventilation and blockage of venous return; bleeding into the pleural space from the chest wall or the lung complicates this problem. Placing a chest tube to drain accumulated air and blood, along with appropriate replacement of lost blood, usually returns cardiac output and respiration to normal quite promptly. Because the lung vasculature is a low-pressure system, bleeding from the lung itself usually subsides relatively quickly. Air leaks from the lung usually seal within 1 or 2 days. Prolonged major air leaks suggest the presence of an injury to a large bronchus, the trachea, or the esophagus that requires operative repair.

Thoracotomy and Pulmonary Resection

On the whole, patients experiencing pulmonary problems after thoracic operations are managed in much the same way as those with pulmonary insufficiency from other causes. Special attention should, however, be given to patients who have undergone resection of part or all of a lung as treatment for infection, cancer, congenital abnormalities, or, rarely, trauma. If the remaining lung is normal, removal of lung tissue does not cause a major physiologic deficit. Nevertheless, pulmonary resection does give rise to certain unique concerns. In particular, the empty space formerly occupied by the lung tissue must be managed very carefully, or poor healing and infection may result. If pleural space infection, leakage from the closed bronchus, or pulmonary failure occurs after pulmonary resection, challenging ventilatory problems ensue.

References

1. Bartlett RH: Critical Care Physiology. JB Lippincott Co, Philadelphia, 1996
2. Routhen H, Sporre B, Engberg G, et al: Influence of gas composition on recurrence of atelectasis after a reexpansion maneuver during general anesthesia. Anesthesiology 82:832, 1995
3. Greif R, Akca O, Horn EP, et al: Supplemental perioperative oxygen to reduce the incidence of surgical-wound infection. Outcomes Research Group. N Engl J Med 342:161, 2000
4. Bartlett RH, Gazzaniga AB, Geraghty TR: Respiratory maneuvers to prevent postoperative pulmonary complications: a critical review. JAMA 224:1017, 1973
5. Bartlett RH: Respiratory therapy to prevent postoperative pulmonary complications. Respiratory Intensive Care. Pierson DJ, Ed. Daedalus Enterprises, Dallas, 1986, p 369
6. Drakulovic MB, Torres A, Bauer TT, et al: Supine body position as a risk factor for nosocomial pneumonia in mechanically ventilated patients: a randomised trial. Lancet 354:1851, 1999
7. Orozco-Levi M, Torres A, Ferrer M, et al: Semirecumbent position protects from pulmonary aspiration but not completely from gastroesophageal reflux in mechanically ventilated patients. Am J Respir Crit Care Med 152:1387, 1995

8. Torres A, Serra-Batlles J, Ros E, et al: Pulmonary aspiration of gastric contents in patients receiving mechanical ventilation: the effect of body position. Ann Intern Med 116:540, 1992

9. Antonelli M, Conti G, Rocco M, et al: A comparison of noninvasive positive-pressure ventilation and conventional mechanical ventilation in patients with acute respiratory failure: pressure support ventilation in COPD patients with postextubation hypercapnic respiratory insufficiency. N Engl J Med 339:429, 1998

10. Girou E, Schortgen F, Delclaux C, et al: Association of noninvasive ventilation with nosocomial infections and survival in critically ill patients. JAMA 284:2361, 2000

11. Brochard L, Mancebo J, Wysocki M, et al: Noninvasive ventilation for acute exacerbations of chronic obstructive pulmonary disease. N Engl J Med 333:817, 1995

12. Demling R, Staub N, Edmunds LH: Effect of end expiratory pressure on accumulation of extravascular lung water. J Appl Physiol 38:907, 1975

13. Hauser CJ, Shoemaker W, et al: Hemodynamic and oxygen transport responses to body shifts produced by colloids and crystalloids in critically ill patients. Surg Gynecol Obstet 150:811, 1980

14. Shoemaker W, Hauser CJ: Critique of crystalloid versus colloidal therapy in shock and shock lung. Crit Care Med 7:117, 1979

15. Bernard GR, Luce JM, Sprung CL, et al: High-dose corticosteroids in patients with the adult respiratory distress syndrome. N Engl J Med 317:1565, 1987

16. Johnson A, Malik AB: Pulmonary transvascular fluid and protein exchange after thrombin-induced microembolism: differential effects of cyclooxygenase inhibitors. Am Rev Respir Dis 132:70, 1985

17. Flick MR, Hoeffel JM, Staub NC: Superoxide dismutase with heparin prevents increased lung vascular permeability during air emboli in sheep. J Appl Physiol 55:1284, 1983

18. Yu M, Tomasa G: A double blind prospective randomized trial of ketoconazole, a thromboxane synthase inhibitor, in the prophylaxis of the adult respiratory distress syndrome. Crit Care Med 21:1635, 1993

19. Kolobow T, Moretti MP, Fumagalli R, et al: Severe impairment in lung function induced by high peak airway pressure during mechanical ventilation. Am Rev Respir Dis 135:312, 1987

20. Okinaka AJ: The pattern of breathing after operation. Surg Gynecol Obstet 125:785, 1967

21. Demling R: The pathogenesis of respiratory failure after trauma and sepsis. Surg Clin North Am 60:1373, 1980

22. Staub N: Pulmonary edema: physiologic approaches to management. Chest 74:559, 1978

23. Alpard SK, Zwischenberger JB, Tao W, et al: New clinically relevant sheep model of severe respiratory failure secondary to combined smoke inhalation/cutaneous flame burn injury. Crit Care Med 28:1469, 2000

121 MECHANICAL VENTILATION

Matthew J. Sena, M.D., and Avery B. Nathens, M.D., Ph.D., M.P.H., F.A.C.S.

Approach to the Use of the Mechanical Ventilator

Patients requiring mechanical ventilation account for a large percentage of admissions to medical and surgical intensive care units. The initial indications for mechanical ventilation can be divided into two main categories: (1) airway instability necessitating endotracheal intubation (as a consequence of operation, brain trauma, or intoxication) and (2) primary respiratory failure from any of several diverse causes, including the acute respiratory distress syndrome (ARDS), trauma, cardiogenic pulmonary edema, and exacerbation of chronic obstructive pulmonary disease (COPD).[1] In the first category, ventilator management is relatively straightforward, and support is temporary, maintained only until the patient's airway is stabilized. In the second category, a prolonged period of mechanical ventilation (> 2 to 3 days) is frequently required. The majority of ventilated ICU patients fall into this second group,[1] and it is these patients in whom specific attention should be paid to the cause of respiratory failure and the goals of therapy. The ventilator mode and settings can then be appropriately tailored to minimize lung injury and facilitate resolution of the underlying disease.

Proper use of a mechanical ventilator requires a solid understanding of normal and abnormal pulmonary mechanics, gas exchange, and the relation between systemic oxygen delivery and consumption. Mechanical ventilators, along with currently available noninvasive and invasive monitoring devices, allow support of critically ill patients while the acute physiologic derangements that led to respiratory failure resolve. In addition, specific ventilator strategies geared toward minimizing further lung injury and expediting the process of liberation from the ventilator not only yield improved support of patients with respiratory failure but also appear to have an impact on outcome.

Ventilator terminology has become increasingly complex as the technology has advanced, but the basic principles of management remain unchanged: to facilitate gas exchange for tissue oxygen delivery, to provide ventilation for removal of carbon dioxide, and to minimize the detrimental effects of both endotracheal intubation and mechanical ventilation. With these priorities in mind, the clinician can use an evidence-based approach to ventilator management as a component of multimodal therapy to improve patient outcome in the ICU. Such management includes use of a lung-protective strategy for patients with acute lung injury (ALI) or ARDS, performance of daily spontaneous breathing trials (SBTs) to identify patients who are ready for liberation from the ventilator, and, when possible, consideration of a nurse-driven or respiratory therapist–driven protocol to minimize delays in extubation. Newer therapies have been developed that offer attractive alternatives to conventional modes of ventilation. Most such therapies are of unproven efficacy, and must therefore be employed with caution in clinical settings. Nonetheless, they provide the clinician with more options for treating patients with advanced respiratory failure and should be considered in extreme cases.

Ventilation and Oxygenation

An essential concept in mechanical ventilation is the distinction between two key processes, ventilation and oxygenation. The primary purpose of ventilation is to excrete carbon dioxide. The minute ventilation ($\dot{V}_E$) is the total amount of gas exhaled per minute, computed as the product of the rate and the tidal volume (V_T). Minute ventilation has two components, alveolar ventilation ($\dot{V}_A$) and dead space ventilation ($\dot{V}_D$). Under normal conditions, approximately two thirds of $\dot{V}_E$ reaches the alveoli and takes part in gas exchange ($\dot{V}_A$); the remaining third moves in and out of the conducting airways and nonperfused alveoli ($\dot{V}_D$). Thus, the ratio of dead space to tidal volume (V_D/V_T) is normally 0.33. The amount of CO_2 excreted is directly related to the amount of alveolar ventilation and inversely proportional to the partial pressure of CO_2 in the alveoli (P_ACO_2). During spontaneous breathing, $\dot{V}_E$ is regulated by the brain stem respiratory center. The brain stem respiratory center responds primarily to changes in plasma pH and in the partial pressure of CO_2 in arterial blood (P_aCO_2). In the face of normal CO_2 production (~ 200 ml/min) and normal minute ventilation (6 L/min), alveolar ventilation amounts to approximately 4 L/min and corresponds to a P_aCO_2 of 40 mm Hg.

In a patient requiring mechanical ventilation, $\dot{V}_E$ is at least partially determined by the mode and settings of the ventilator. Respiratory rate and tidal volume can be set independently, and the mode of ventilation can be set to allow additional spontaneous breathing if necessary. In most cases, the primary goal is maintenance of a near-normal P_aCO_2. The physician must be cognizant of factors that might increase CO_2 production (e.g., fever, sepsis, injury, and overfeeding) or $\dot{V}_D$ (e.g., lung injury, ARDS, and massive pulmonary embolism), any of which would increase the $\dot{V}_E$ requirements in a ventilated patient.

Oxygenation refers to the equilibrium between oxygen in the pulmonary capillary blood and oxygen in inflated alveoli. The oxygen tension gradient between the alveoli and the capillaries favors the transfer of oxygen into the blood. Although the partial pressure of oxygen in arterial blood (P_aO_2) is partially dependent on ventilation, it depends less on adequate alveolar ventilation than on the appropriate matching of pulmonary blood flow to well-inflated alveoli, a process referred to as ventilation-perfusion ($\dot{V}/\dot{Q}$) matching. $\dot{V}/\dot{Q}$ matching can be affected by many factors, including patient position, airway pressure, pulmonary parenchymal disease, and small-airway disease. The efficiency of $\dot{V}/\dot{Q}$ matching, and thus of oxygenation, can be evaluated by measuring the P_aO_2 at a known value of the fraction (concentration) of inspired oxygen (F_IO_2). Under normal circumstances, oxygenation is very efficient, with P_aO_2 values approaching 90% of P_AO_2. Its efficiency can be assessed by calculating the alveolar-arterial oxygen gradient (i.e., $P_AO_2 - P_aO_2$).

Under normal conditions, P_aO_2 is approximately 90 mm Hg. To determine P_AO_2, the following formula is employed:

1532

$$P_{A O_2} = [F_I O_2 (\text{barometric pressure} - P_{H_2 O}) - P_a CO_2 / RQ]$$

where RQ represents the respiratory quotient and $P_{H_2 O}$ represents the partial pressure of water vapor at sea level. Normally, at sea level, barometric pressure is approximately 760 mm Hg, $F_I O_2$ is 0.21, $P_{H_2 O}$ is 47 mm Hg, $P_a CO_2$ is 40 mm Hg, and RQ is 0.8. Accordingly,

$$P_{A O_2} = [0.21(760 - 47) - 40/0.8]$$
$$P_{A O_2} \cong 150 - 50$$
$$P_{A O_2} \cong 100$$
$$P_{A O_2} - P_a O_2 \cong 100 - 90 \cong 10$$

Thus, the alveolar-arterial gradient under these conditions is approximately 10 mm Hg, which falls within the standard range of 8 to 12 mm Hg.

A shorthand method of quantifying the degree of hypoxemia is to calculate the $P_a O_2 / F_I O_2$ ratio (also referred to as the P/F ratio), which is simply an assessment of the efficiency of gas exchange. At sea level, with the patient breathing room air, P/F $\cong 100/0.21 \cong 500$.

Unlike regulation of $\dot{V}_E$, adjustment of the rate or V_T generally has little effect on $P_a O_2$, except at extremely low levels of ventilation. Greater effects on arterial oxygenation are achieved through adjustment of either $F_I O_2$ or mean airway pressure (P_{aw}), both of which can be readily manipulated with a mechanical ventilator.

Ventilator Modes

Current mechanical ventilators possess a wide, and potentially confusing, array of modes, settings, and capabilities. All of them, however, control three variables: trigger, limit, and cycle.

The trigger variable is the signal that serves to initiate the inspiratory phase. This signal occurs as a result of patient effort that leads to a change in either flow or pressure within the ventilator circuit. Flow-triggered ventilators deliver a continuous flow of gas across the inspiratory and expiratory limbs of the ventilator circuit and initiate the inspiratory phase when patient effort results in a change in this flow. The required change can be as little as 0.1 L/min; the sensitivity of the trigger is decreased by increasing the required flow change and therefore increasing the patient effort necessary to begin inspiration. Pressure-triggered ventilators initiate the inspiratory phase when a patient's spontaneous effort results in a change in pressure. At the most sensitive setting, a pressure change of approximately −1 cm H_2O is required; at the least sensitive setting, a change of −15 cm H_2O is required. Finally, a time trigger is used to start the inspiratory phase in mandatory ventilation modes, as well as in assisted modes.

The limit variable is the maximal set inspiratory pressure or flow. Pressure-controlled ventilation (PCV) and pressure-support ventilation (PSV) are both modes of pressure-limited ventilation. Because volume is the product of flow and time, volume-controlled ventilation is actually flow-limited ventilation during the inspiratory phase with the inspiratory time set independently.

The cycling variable is the factor that terminates the inspiratory cycle (i.e., time, flow, pressure, or volume). To add more confusion, each breath can be considered as a mandatory breath (which is time triggered), a spontaneous breath (which is patient initiated), or a combination of the two.

PRESSURE-LIMITED VERSUS VOLUME-LIMITED VENTILATION

Pressure-support ventilation is the simplest form of pressure-limited ventilation and, by definition, is a purely spontaneous mode of ventilatory support. In PSV, the patient triggers a breath

through an inspiratory effort, which leads to the delivery of a breath at a variable flow rate to meet a preset pressure. As the lung inflates, compliance decreases and flow decreases to maintain a constant inspiratory pressure. The result is a descending flow curve that is similar to air flow in unassisted breathing. Cycling in this mode occurs when flow declines to a specified percentage of the maximal flow rate (approximately 5% of the peak flow rate in some ventilator models) [see Figure 1]. When inspiratory flow ceases, the patient exhales passively.

Pressure-controlled ventilation is related to PSV in that flow descends in amplitude during the inspiratory cycle. It differs from PSV primarily in that the inspiratory time is set by the ventilator, not by the patient. PCV is generally used in the assist-control mode, which allows full support of patient-initiated breaths in addition to ventilator-initiated breaths (which are time triggered). It can also be used in conjunction with the intermittent mandatory ventilation (IMV) mode in newer ventilator models. The largest drawback of PCV is that V_T can change as lung compliance changes, necessitating frequent adjustments to ensure adequate $\dot{V}_E$. For example, as the lung becomes less compliant with increasing pulmonary edema, V_T will decrease, as will $\dot{V}_E$. This problem can be addressed by using another form of pressure-limited ventilation, known as pressure-regulated volume control (PRVC) [see Combined Modes of Ventilation, below].

Volume-controlled ventilation (VCV) is delivered at a set frequency (in the IMV or the assist-control mode) or may be patient initiated (in the assist-control mode). After the ventilator is triggered, a fixed flow of gas is generated for a specific time, thus providing a preset inspiratory volume (volume = flow × time). Volume-limited ventilation is generally easier to regulate than pressure-limited ventilation, but it may be less comfortable for awake patients, because the flow curve is a square wave, which is markedly different from the normal inspiratory flow pattern in nonventilated patients.

MANDATORY VERSUS SPONTANEOUS VENTILATION

There are several modes of ventilation that provide mandatory ventilator support with or without patient-triggered ventilation. For example, assist-control ventilation ensures delivery of a minimum (mandatory) set $\dot{V}_E$ but also allows additional patient-triggered (spontaneous) breaths. Each breath, regardless of the trigger, is completely supported, so that either a fixed volume (with VCV) or a fixed pressure (with PCV) is provided for a preset inspiratory time. Full support can be provided by increasing the mandatory rate. If the patient has respiratory drive, $\dot{V}_E$ might be increased by adding spontaneous breaths. The major drawback of this approach is that agitated patients may become hyperventilated and may manifest respiratory alkalosis if not sedated.

The IMV mode allows only the preset number of breaths to be supported. In most cases, breaths are synchronized with the patient's effort (so-called synchronized IMV [SIMV]) if spontaneous respiration is occurring. Patient efforts at inspiration above the preset frequency are not supported with gas flow from the ventilator unless pressure support is added. In the past, IMV was frequently used as a weaning mode: by gradually decreasing the set frequency, patients gradually assumed a greater role in their own respirations. Today, however, it is not frequently employed for this purpose and plays only a limited role in weaning patients from the ventilator.

INSPIRATORY TIME, FLOW, RESPIRATORY RATE, AND INSPIRATORY-EXPIRATORY RATIO

Inspiratory time, flow, respiratory rate, and inspiratory-expira-

Approach to Use of the Mechanical Ventilator

Mechanical ventilation is initiated

Initial ventilator settings are as follows (depending on clinical scenario): F_{IO_2} = 0.5; PEEP = 5 cm H_2O; respiratory rate = 12–15 breaths/min; V_T = 8–10 ml/kg predicted body weight. Measure S_aO_2.

$S_aO_2 < 90\%$

Increase F_{IO_2} in stepwise manner to keep $S_aO_2 \geq 90\%$.
Increase PEEP by 2–5 cm H_2O.
Continue increasing PEEP by 2–5 cm H_2O to maximum of 20 cm H_2O if $S_aO_2 < 90\%$ despite $F_{IO_2} \geq 0.8$.
Identify and treat cause of respiratory failure.
Look for evidence of acute lung injury.

Evidence of ALI is present

Utilize low–tidal volume (lung-protective) ventilation:
• Reduce V_T to 6 ml/kg.
• Increase RR to up to 35 breaths/min to achieve pH > 7.20 and $P_aCO_2 \cong$ 40–50 mm Hg.
(Traumatic brain injury is a relative contraindication to this approach. Patients without intracranial hemorrhage but with intracranial pressure monitors may be considered if P_aCO_2 is normal and $S_aO_2 > 95\%$.)
Attempt to determine best PEEP through clinical or invasive assessment of $\dot{D}O_2$.
Measure S_aO_2.

$S_aO_2 < 90\%$

Diagnose and treat associated conditions:
• Pneumothorax
• Hydrothorax/hemothorax
• Asynchrony (increase sedation; consider NMBA)
Consider adjunctive measures:
• Nitric oxide
• Prone positioning
• HFOV
• ECLS

$S_aO_2 \geq 90\%$

Measure P_{stat}.

$P_{stat} > 30$ cm H_2O

Reduce V_T in stepwise manner to 4 ml/kg to keep $P_{stat} \leq 30$ cm H_2O. (In patients with morbid obesity or ascites, P_{stat} may reflect transdiaphragmatic pressure rather than transpulmonary pressure. The lung-protective approach should be maintained, but consideration should be given to allowing a higher P_{stat} before lowering V_T significantly below 6 ml/kg.)
When lung compliance improves, begin increasing V_T to 6 ml/kg while maintaining $P_{stat} \leq 30$ cm H_2O.

$P_{stat} \leq 30$ cm H_2O

Continue lung-protective ventilation strategy until P_aO_2/F_{IO_2} ratio ≥ 300 or patient meets criteria for SBT.

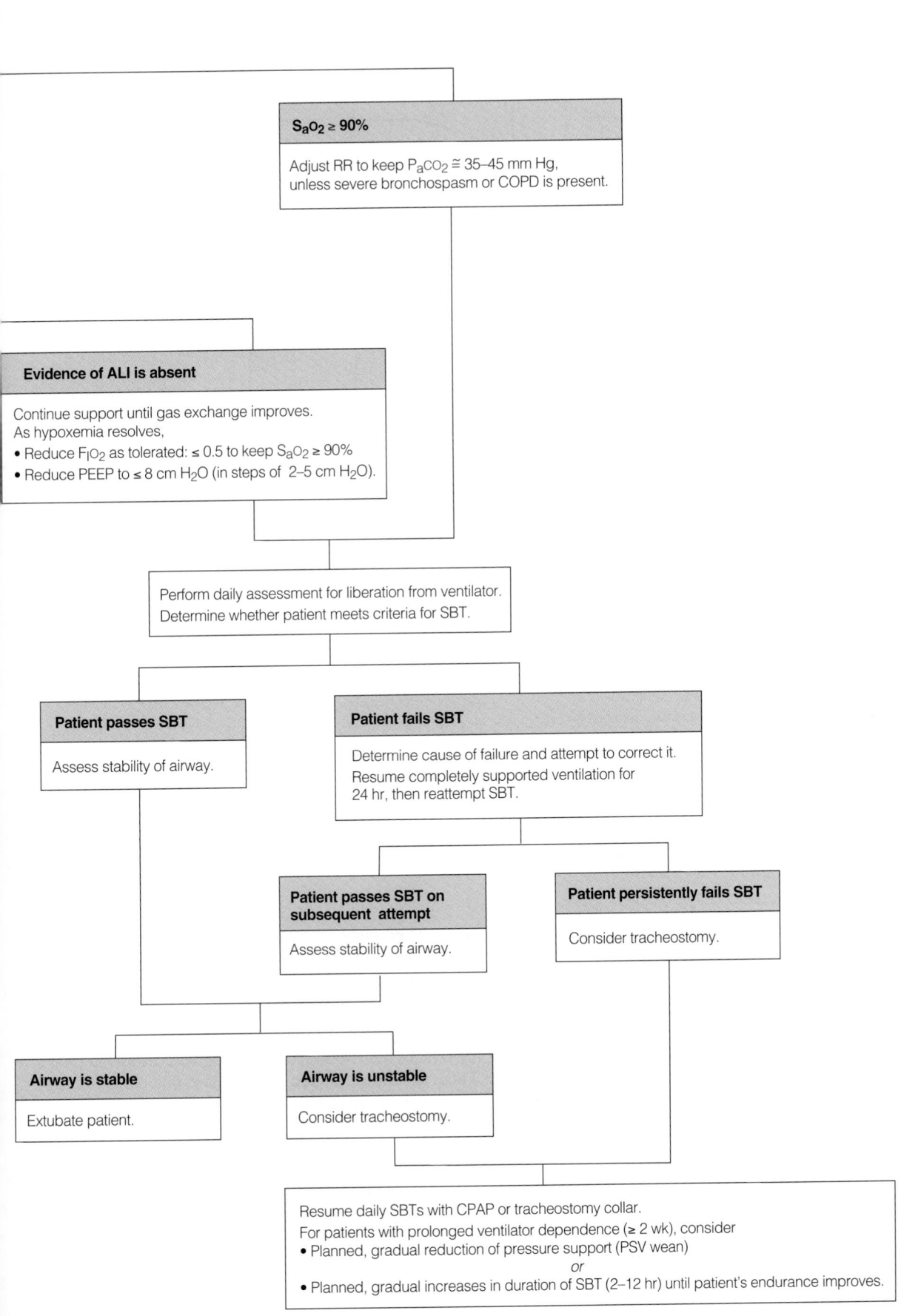

S_aO₂ ≥ 90%

$S_aO_2 \geq 90\%$

Adjust RR to keep $P_aCO_2 \cong$ 35–45 mm Hg,
unless severe bronchospasm or COPD is present.

Evidence of ALI is absent

Continue support until gas exchange improves.
As hypoxemia resolves,
• Reduce F_IO_2 as tolerated: ≤ 0.5 to keep $S_aO_2 \geq 90\%$
• Reduce PEEP to ≤ 8 cm H_2O (in steps of 2–5 cm H_2O).

Perform daily assessment for liberation from ventilator.
Determine whether patient meets criteria for SBT.

Patient passes SBT

Assess stability of airway.

Patient fails SBT

Determine cause of failure and attempt to correct it.
Resume completely supported ventilation for
24 hr, then reattempt SBT.

**Patient passes SBT on
subsequent attempt**

Assess stability of airway.

Patient persistently fails SBT

Consider tracheostomy.

Airway is stable

Extubate patient.

Airway is unstable

Consider tracheostomy.

Resume daily SBTs with CPAP or tracheostomy collar.
For patients with prolonged ventilator dependence (≥ 2 wk), consider
• Planned, gradual reduction of pressure support (PSV wean)
or
• Planned, gradual increases in duration of SBT (2–12 hr) until patient's endurance improves.

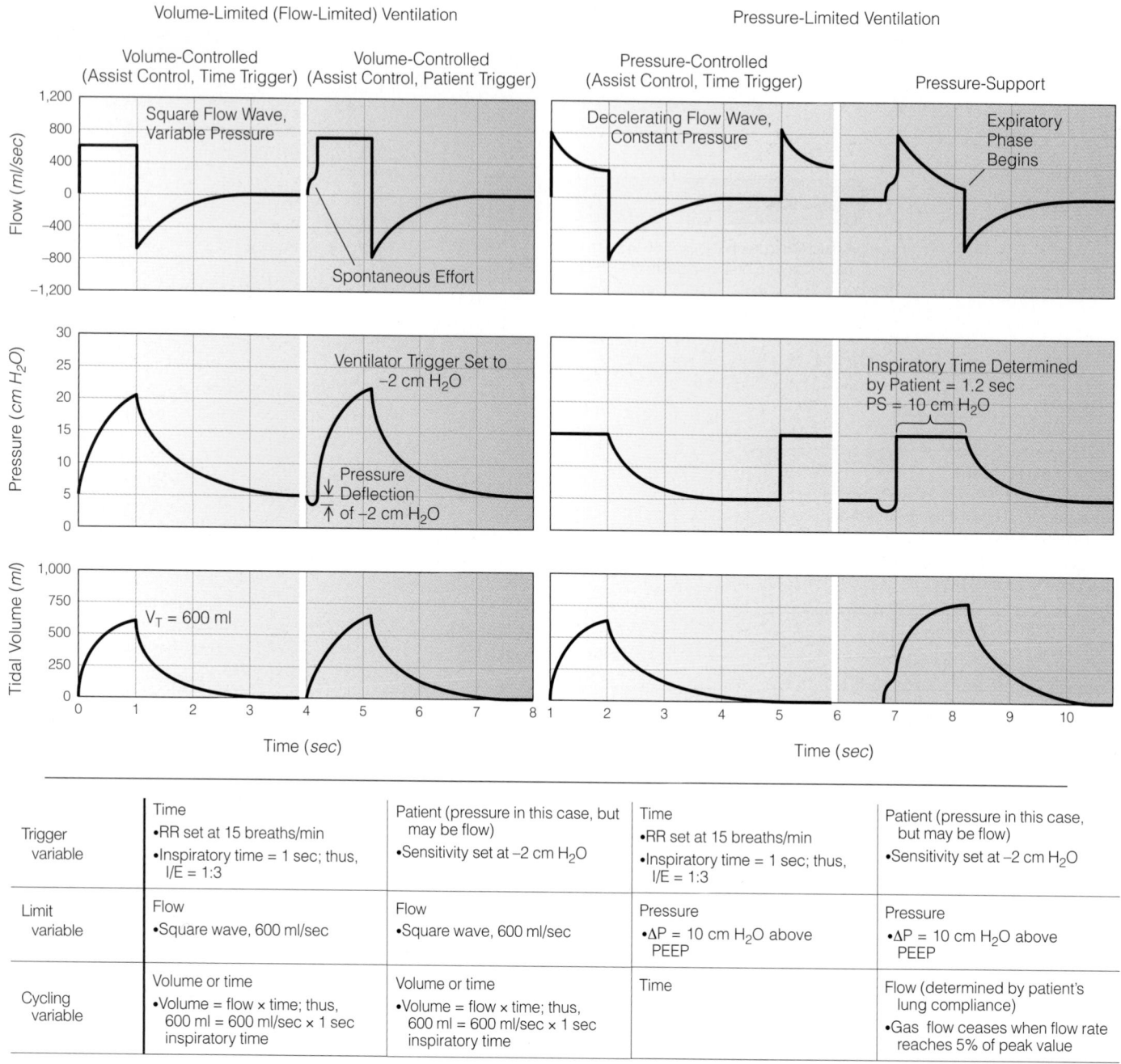

Figure 1 Shown are flow, pressure, and volume profiles in volume-limited and pressure-limited ventilation modes.

tory (I/E) ratio are all closely related. In most patients, they can be preset to mimic the normal respiratory cycle. The normal I/E ratio is approximately 1:3. With the respiratory rate set at 15 breaths/ min, the inspiratory time is 1 second, with 3 seconds of expiratory time. The flow rate can then be manipulated so as to achieve a desired tidal volume (in VCV) or can be adjusted automatically by the ventilator so as to achieve a certain pressure (in PCV). Manipulation of these variables can be useful in certain conditions, such as a high level of intrinsic positive end-expiratory pressure (PEEP) [see Discussion, Special Problems in Ventilator Management, Chronic Obstructive Pulmonary Disease, below]. In the past, manipulation of the I/E ratio has been used to treat severe hypoxemia [see Alternative Modes of Ventilation and Adjunctive Therapies, Inverse-Ratio Ventilation, below].

AIRWAY PRESSURES, LUNG INJURY, AND OXYGENATION

The flow of gas through the ventilator circuit produces pressure both at the level of the endotracheal tube and across the alveolar surface. These pressures, though related, have different implications for the assessment and treatment of pulmonary dysfunction [see Figure 2]. Peak inspiratory pressure (PIP) is the pressure measured in the ventilator circuit during maximal gas flow; it primarily represents the interaction between the inspiratory flow rate and airway resistance. Mean airway pressure is the area under the pressure-time curve divided by the time required for a complete respiratory cycle. Because the normal respiratory cycle is dominated by the expiratory phase, P_{aw} is determined primarily by PEEP. P_{aw} is important in that it has a direct effect on alveolar recruitment and gas exchange; it also is the major determinant of

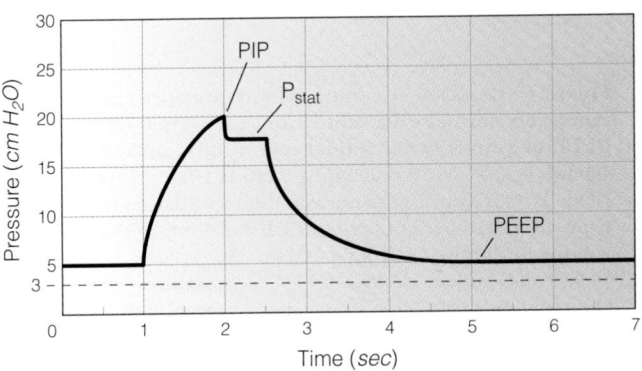

Figure 2 **Shown are measured ventilator pressures during a single machine-triggered volume breath during VCV. (PEEP—positive end-expiratory pressure; PIP—peak inspiratory pressure; (P$_{stat}$—static pressure measured during a 0.5 sec inspiratory pause)**

intrathoracic pressure and thus is the parameter to follow when there is concern about the cardiovascular sequelae of higher ventilatory pressures. Static pressure (P$_{stat}$) is measured in the ventilator circuit during a 1-second pause at the end of inspiration. P$_{stat}$ is generally considered to be the pressure distending the alveoli, on the assumption that intrathoracic pressure is equivalent to atmospheric pressure; this distending pressure is also referred to as transpulmonary pressure. Limitation of P$_{stat}$ plays an important role in minimizing ventilator-induced lung injury [*see* Discussion, Special Problems in Ventilator Management, Acute Lung Injury and Acute Respiratory Distress Syndrome, *below*].

COMBINED MODES OF VENTILATION

Many newer modes of ventilation are hybrids, incorporating combinations of pressure control and volume control and combinations of spontaneous and mandatory breathing. One such mode is pressure-regulated volume control. PRVC is a variant of PCV but has the ability to prevent significant changes in V$_T$ if lung compliance changes. The ventilator accomplishes this by continuously evaluating changes in delivered V$_T$ at a given pressure over several respiratory cycles and adjusting the pressure accordingly. The operator can preset the inspiratory pressure limit to prevent barotrauma.

Another hybrid mode is mandatory minute ventilation, which is a form of assisted VCV. In the assist mode, the patient may trigger a complete volume-cycled breath. The operator sets a specific V̇$_E$, rather than a specific rate and V$_T$. In this way, the operator can ensure adequate CO$_2$ removal in patients with variable respiratory drive.

In general, these combined modes are of limited utility in ventilator management. The overwhelming majority of patients can be managed with simple PCV or VCV or, if they have adequate respiratory drive, with PSV.

Use of the Mechanical Ventilator in Respiratory Failure

After endotracheal intubation, the initial ventilator settings should be determined by assessing the cause and severity of the patient's respiratory

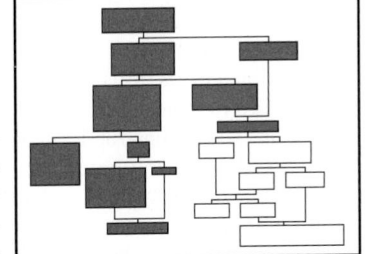

failure. After an initial stabilization period of approximately 30 minutes, blood gas values should be obtained and the ventilator

adjusted accordingly. Certain patients—specifically, those with profound hypoxemia—may require an immediate increase in F$_I$O$_2$, PEEP, or both; such increases should not be postponed to await blood gas results. F$_I$O$_2$ and PEEP can be manipulated on the basis of information from pulse oximetry, so that there is less need for frequent arterial blood gas assessment. Further treatment should be prioritized on the basis of the underlying problem of oxygenation or ventilation.

OXYGENATION

The purpose of ensuring adequate arterial oxygenation is ultimately to maintain adequate delivery of oxygen to the tissues. A P$_a$O$_2$ higher than 60 mm Hg generally results in an arterial hemoglobin saturation (S$_a$O$_2$) of 90% or greater and is sufficient for most patients, provided that the other components of oxygen delivery are normal or nearly so. An adequate P$_a$O$_2$ can be obtained by altering either F$_I$O$_2$ or P$_{aw}$. Increasing the F$_I$O$_2$ is the simplest maneuver, but it is not necessarily the correct adjustment in patients with pulmonary dysfunction. Nonetheless, it should be tried first, while other options are being considered. Generally, a moderate increase in F$_I$O$_2$ (to ≤ 0.6) has minimal adverse consequences. The desired and immediate effect is to increase the gradient for oxygen diffusion across the alveolar and pulmonary capillary membranes. In normal lungs, this increased gradient results in a proportional increase in P$_a$O$_2$. If an intrapulmonary shunt is present, however, increasing F$_I$O$_2$ has little effect on P$_a$O$_2$.

Often, an effort to increase F$_I$O$_2$ is combined with some measure aimed at increasing P$_{aw}$, the idea being that a smaller increase in F$_I$O$_2$ will then be required to produce the desired effect. Although a high F$_I$O$_2$ (> 0.6) has few negative consequences in the short term, prolonged maintenance of F$_I$O$_2$ at this level can

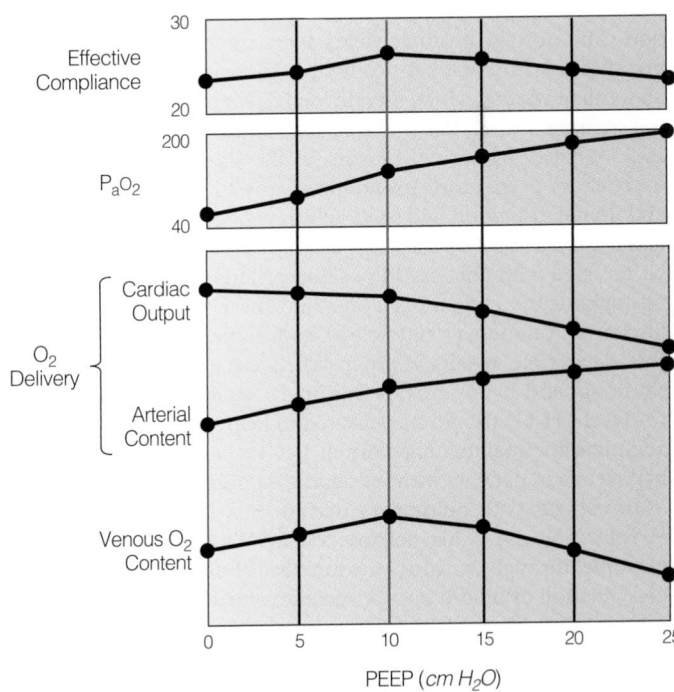

Figure 3 **Shown are measurements for determining the optimal PEEP. The objective is to maximize the ratio of oxygen delivery to oxygen consumption, which is determined by measuring mixed venous saturation. Here, the best PEEP is 10 cm H$_2$O, even though the P$_a$O$_2$ and the arterial oxygen content are higher at higher levels of PEEP.**

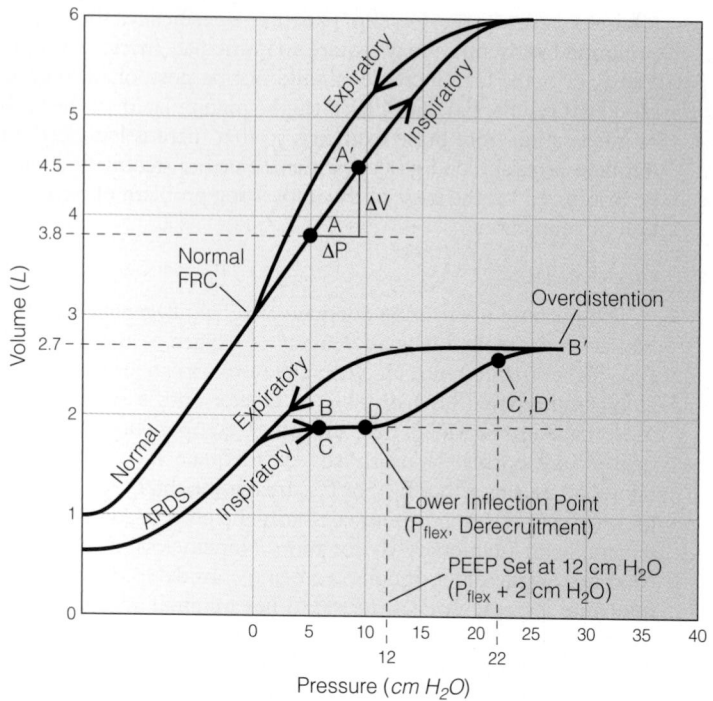

Figure 4 Depicted is a static volume-pressure curve. A → A′ represents normal tidal ventilation in a normal lung, with a PEEP of 5 cm H_2O and a tidal volume of 10 ml/kg × 70 kg = 700 ml. $C_{stat} = \Delta V/\Delta P = 700$ ml ÷ 5 cm H_2O/kg = 2 ml/cm H_2O ÷ 70 kg. B → B′ represents normal tidal ventilation in a lung from an ARDS patient, with a PEEP of 5 cm H_2O and a tidal volume of 10 ml/kg × 70 kg = 700 ml. $C_{stat} = 700 ÷ 22$ cm H_2O ÷ 70 kg = 0.45 ml/cm H_2O/kg. C → C′ represents a low–tidal volume, lung-protective ventilation strategy, with a PEEP of 5 cm H_2O and a tidal volume of 6 ml/kg × 70 kg = 420 ml. $C_{stat} = 420 ÷ 17$ cm H_2O ÷ 70 kg = 0.35 ml/cm H_2O/kg. D → D′ represents a low–tidal volume, lung-protective ventilation strategy, with a PEEP of 12 cm H_2O (best PEEP), which is above P_{flex}. The tidal volume is 6 ml/kg × 70 kg = 420 ml. $C_{stat} = 420 ÷ 10$ cm H_2O ÷ 70 kg = 0.60 ml/cm H_2O/kg. The low–tidal volume strategy prevents the overdistention that occurs at higher tidal volumes, whereas the higher PEEP level prevents the derecruitment that can occur at lower volumes. Although low–tidal volume ventilation strategies have been demonstrated to improve outcome in ARDS, higher PEEP levels, though theoretically attractive, have not been shown to be efficacious.

result in nitrogen washout, resorption atelectasis, and an increased pulmonary shunt fraction, with consequent exacerbation of hypoxemia.

The simplest way of increasing P_{aw} is to increase PEEP. The purpose of PEEP is to prevent loss of functional residual capacity (FRC), defined as the volume maintained in the lungs at the end of expiration. In normal persons, FRC is maintained by a balance between the negative intrapleural pressure and the elastic recoil of the lung. Negative intrapleural pressure is affected by patient position. The upright position yields a greater negative intrapleural pressure than the supine position, because of the weight of the abdominal viscera, which literally pull down on the diaphragm. In the supine position, this pull is absent, and FRC may be as much as 25% lower in normal persons in the supine position.[2,3] This decrease is even more pronounced in patients with ascites or abdominal distention and especially in patients with intra-abdominal hypertension.[4] In a normal alert patient, the loss of FRC can be reversed with changes in position or intermittent sigh breaths throughout the respiratory cycle, and there will be minimal net impact on pulmonary physiology. In a supine ventilated patient, the loss of FRC results in progressive atelectasis, intrapulmonary shunting, and hypoxemia. Accordingly, small amounts of PEEP (5–10 cm H_2O) should be delivered to help restore FRC to levels adequate for maintaining normal gas exchange and preventing hypoxemia in patients without significant pulmonary dysfunction.

In patients with pulmonary dysfunction, FRC is lost through alveolar collapse. This collapse occurs by several means—for example, through extrinsic pressure (see above) or through some combination of blood, pus, or secretions that results in occlusion of small airways. In these settings, increasing PEEP improves $\dot{V}/\dot{Q}$ matching by "recruiting" these collapsed alveoli and thereby bringing about improved gas exchange and P_aO_2. Unfortunately, the increased intrathoracic pressure that may develop when PEEP is increased can have detrimental effects on cardiac output. Because the overall goal is to improve tissue oxygen delivery (not just P_aO_2), assessment of the net effect of an increase in PEEP should take into consideration the effect on oxygen delivery ($\dot{D}o_2$). The amount of PEEP necessary to maximize $\dot{D}o_2$ in a given patient is

referred to as best PEEP and generally corresponds to the PEEP setting that results in maximal static lung compliance.[5] PEEP levels above this point may increase arterial oxygen content (C_aO_2) but typically impair cardiac output and result in decreased $\dot{D}o_2$ [see Figure 3].

The improvement in lung compliance achieved by increasing PEEP levels in patients with pulmonary dysfunction can be demonstrated by using a static or low-flow volume-pressure curve to determine the lower inflection point (P_{flex}) [see Figure 4]. P_{flex} corresponds to the point at which recruitable alveoli open and become available for tidal ventilation and gas exchange. Setting PEEP slightly higher (+2 cm H_2O) allows tidal ventilation over the range of maximal lung compliance and prevents the repetitive end-expiratory derecruitment that may be associated with ventilator-induced lung injury.[6] Although this approach is theoretically attractive, determining P_{flex} is technically cumbersome and may not be tolerated by the sickest patients.

In practice, F_IO_2 and PEEP are manipulated simultaneously, with the specifics depending on the cause of arterial hypoxemia and on an empirical determination of best PEEP. Best PEEP is determined by means of stepwise increases in PEEP coupled with serial assessments of arterial oxygenation and cardiovascular function. At high levels of PEEP (> 15 cm H_2O), consideration should be given to using a pulmonary arterial catheter for assessment of $\dot{D}o_2$ and mixed venous oxygen saturation (S_vO_2). If an increase in PEEP results in a drop in either S_vO_2 or $\dot{D}o_2$, then the increase was detrimental to the goal of improving tissue oxygenation. As a rule, the maximal PEEP level that may provide benefit rarely exceeds 20 cm H_2O.[7] Above this level, it is fairly common for detrimental effects on cardiovascular function to predominate and $\dot{D}o_2$ to decline.[8]

The initial settings for F_IO_2 and PEEP depend on the clinical scenario. Patients intubated for postoperative airway protection may require an F_IO_2 of 0.3 and a PEEP of 5 cm H_2O. In contrast, multiply injured patients who have been resuscitated may require an F_IO_2 of 1.0 and a PEEP of 15 cm H_2O. In either case, early evaluation of arterial blood gas concentrations can guide further manipulations. Alternatively, oxygen saturation and end-tidal CO_2

values may be followed noninvasively with pulse oximetry and capnography. Sudden decreases in P_aO_2 (or S_aO_2) should be treated by first increasing F_IO_2 and then increasing PEEP. These measures should be followed by attempts to ascertain the cause of the acute change. A first assessment—including suctioning, arterial blood gas measurements, and a chest radiograph—should be carried out immediately, with particular attention to rapidly reversible causes (e.g., mucous plugging, pneumothorax, a large hemothorax or hydrothorax, and cardiogenic pulmonary edema). A more detailed assessment should then follow to look for other possible causes (e.g., pulmonary embolism, worsening ARDS, aspiration pneumonitis, and pneumonia).

It must be kept in mind that in many cases, the etiology is multifactorial, and that in the treatment of profound hypoxemia, it is important to address any and all correctable abnormalities, even when the potential gain is small. For example, in a patient with no pulmonary reserve, drainage of a large hydrothorax may yield a significant improvement in oxygenation, whereas in a patient with near-normal pulmonary function, this measure would have little, if any, effect.

In a minority of cases, a mismatch between patient effort and ventilatory support can result in increased work of breathing, progressive respiratory muscle fatigue, and, on rare occasions, arterial desaturation. This situation, referred to as patient-ventilator asynchrony, occurs as a consequence of the ventilator's failure to match the patient's respiratory drive and pulmonary mechanics. It only occurs during spontaneous breathing modes and may be secondary to a problem in the inspiratory trigger (inspiratory asynchrony), the expiratory trigger (expiratory asynchrony), or the flow rate (flow asynchrony).[9] In these cases, direct patient observation often suffices to establish the diagnosis. Therapy is aimed at improving the patient-ventilator interaction and may involve changing the mode of ventilation (e.g., from VCV or PCV to PSV), the trigger setting (e.g., from pressure to flow), the inspiratory gas flow (either the rate or the waveform), or the cycling variable (time, flow, or pressure). Alternatively, in severe cases that result in hypoxemia, it may be necessary to increase sedation to the point where spontaneous respiratory efforts are eliminated. Neuromuscular blocking agents should only be considered if other measures have failed and hypoxemia is worsening. Generally, use of these agents should be avoided in critically ill patients when possible, because their administration has been associated with significant complications.[10]

VENTILATION

Adequate CO_2 elimination can be achieved with either PCV or VCV; the two methods can be used to achieve the same end points, and neither has any overwhelming advantage over the other. Accordingly, it is reasonable to choose between them on the basis of individual or institutional experience, simply for ease of management. The initial settings should include a V_T of 8 to 10 ml/kg predicted body weight[11] and a set respiratory rate of 12 to 15 breaths/min. In general, the assist mode is preferable, because it allows the patient to regulate P_aCO_2 while still receiving completely supported ventilation. If PCV is preferred, the inspiratory pressure can be adjusted at the bedside to achieve a V_T of 8 to 10 ml/kg. In either case, if the V_D/V_T ratio is nearly normal, the resultant alveolar ventilation should be sufficient to eliminate all of the metabolically produced CO_2 and maintain a P_aCO_2 of 40 mm Hg. After approximately 30 minutes, blood gases should be measured and the respiratory rate adjusted accordingly.

In a patient with adequate respiratory drive, PSV is a reasonable choice. In the past, it was largely considered a weaning mode.

Table 1   Criteria for Liberation from Mechanical Ventilation

Patient criteria for spontaneous breathing trial (SBT) to assess readiness for liberation from mechanical ventilator

Resolution or stabilization of underlying disease process
No evidence of residual pharmacologic neuromuscular blockade
Spontaneous respiratory efforts
Hemodynamic stability (no recent increase in pressor or inotrope requirements)
Ventilator settings as follows:
  F_IO_2 0.5
  PEEP   8 cm H_2O
  P_aO_2 > 75 mm Hg
  Minute ventilation < 15 L/min
  pH 7.30 – 7.50

Patient criteria to assess readiness for extubation

Suctioning required less often than every 4 hr
Good spontaneous cough
Endotracheal tube cuff leak*
No recent upper airway obstruction or stridor†
No recent reintubation for bronchial hygiene

Criteria for a failed SBT‡

Respiratory rate > 35 breaths/min for   5 min
S_aO_2 < 90% for   30 sec
HR > 140 beats/min, or 20% increase or decrease from baseline
Systolic BP > 180 mm Hg or < 90 mm Hg
Sustained evidence of increased work of breathing (e.g., retractions, accessory muscle use)
Cardiac instability or dysrhythmias
pH   7.32

---

*Absence of a cuff leak is not an absolute contraindication to extubation. Each patient's risk for postextubation upper airway obstruction should be assessed individually.

†If extubation has recently failed because of airway obstruction, patient should be assessed and the underlying cause addressed (if possible) before extubation is reattempted. Appropriate adjunctive measures (e.g., racemic epinephrine or helium-oxygen) should be available before patient is extubated.

‡If any of these criteria are met, SBT should be terminated and the patient placed back on previous ventilator settings for 24 hr.

Currently, however, it is considered to be best suited for patients in whom the acute physiologic derangements leading to respiratory failure are resolving but who are not ready to be liberated from the ventilator. The main difference from past applications of PSV is that in current practice, pressure support is not intentionally decreased over time [see Liberation from Mechanical Ventilation, below]; instead, the patient is completely supported while daily assessments of the patient's readiness for extubation are made. A potential advantage of PSV is enhanced patient comfort. This is a particularly important consideration when the patient's overall condition is improving and minimization of sedation may allow earlier extubation.

In the pressure-support mode, the patient determines the respiratory rate, inspiratory time, and $\dot{V}_E$. In a patient with normal lung compliance, pressure support of between 5 and 10 cm H_2O is usually sufficient and should result in a V_T of at least 600 ml. Pressure support may be increased as needed for patient comfort and should be titrated to keep the respiratory rate below 25 breaths/min. When pressures higher than 20 cm H_2O are required, most physicians elect to support the patient in the assist mode until pulmonary compliance improves.

If P_aCO_2 is elevated despite a $\dot{V}_E$ of 100 ml · kg^{-1} · min^{-1} (6–7 L/min), then the metabolic production of CO_2 is excessively high, alveolar ventilation is an inappropriately low percentage of V_T (increased V_D/V_T), or both. To increase ventilation, the first step should be to increase the respiratory rate in a stepwise fashion to 20 to 25 breaths/min. In addition, the use of low-compliance ventilator tubing should be considered to minimize dead space in the ventilator circuit. If the P_aCO_2 is still elevated, V_D and total CO_2 production can be measured directly by using a metabolic cart. If CO_2 production is higher than normal (130 ml • m^{-2} • min^{-1}), it can be decreased by reducing muscular activity or seizures, controlling hypermetabolic states (if possible), and minimizing the exogenous carbohydrate load.

If the P_aCO_2 is still elevated after all of these measures have been taken, the respiratory rate may be increased to 30 breaths/min or higher. It should be kept in mind, however, that the efficiency of ventilation decreases as the respiratory rate increases. This loss of efficiency occurs because the percentage of $\dot{V}_E$ used for gas exchange decreases as the respiratory rate increases because in the face of a fixed volume of dead space, there may be inadequate time for alveolar emptying during expiration. In addition, steps may be taken to increase V_T, though significant increases may worsen ventilator-induced lung injury through either barotrauma or volutrauma [see Discussion, Special Problems in Ventilator Management, Acute Lung Injury and Acute Respiratory Distress Syndrome, below].

The importance of maintaining a normal P_aCO_2 is often overstated. Allowing P_aCO_2 to climb above 40 mm Hg has no intrinsic detrimental effects in the absence of increased intracranial pressure, and it is not uncommon to permit the P_aCO_2 to rise to avert the adverse consequences of high tidal volumes and the ventilatory pressures required to generate these volumes. This approach, referred to as permissive hypercapnia, is safe as long as pH remains above 7.15. Over time, pH will increase with compensatory increases in renal bicarbonate preservation, provided that renal function is normal.

Liberation from Mechanical Ventilation

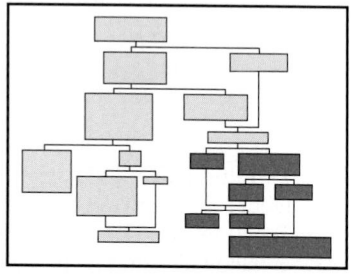

As the patient's condition improves, it is useful to distinguish between the need for continued endotracheal intubation and the ongoing requirement for mechanical ventilation. The need for endotracheal intubation requires an assessment of airway stability and is relatively straightforward (see below). Deciding when pulmonary function and respiratory muscle reserve are adequate for unassisted breathing is considerably more complex. The latter is what has traditionally been referred to as weaning from mechanical ventilation.

The term weaning implies a planned, gradual reduction in ventilator support whereby the patient assumes more and more of the work of breathing that had been performed by the ventilator. This is an inaccurate description of the actual process, which essentially involves assessment of a patient's ability to sustain independent ventilation and adequate gas exchange. Although the amount of support provided does decline as the patient improves, this decline is patient driven and is different from the physician-driven reduction of support historically used to wean the patient from the ventilator gradually.[12] Multiple indices have been devised for determining a patient's readiness for unassisted breathing, with variable degrees of success. Perhaps the optimal method might involve an

algorithm that incorporates clinical data, ventilator-derived data, and laboratory data to determine the timing and likelihood of successful liberation from the ventilator.

A randomized trial from 1995 compared four different weaning methods: (1) daily 2-hour SBTs, (2) twice-daily 2-hour SBTs, (3) gradual reduction of pressure support, and (4) gradual reduction of the IMV rate. The two SBT methods were superior in predicting successful extubation.[13] In a follow-up study, the investigators reported that a 30-minute SBT was as effective as a 2-hour SBT, and the shorter duration is now preferred for most patients.[14] Other traditional parameters used to predict the end of the need for mechanical ventilation are respiratory rate, rapid-shallow breathing index (RSBI; calculated as frequency divided by V_T), V_T, vital capacity, pressure-time product, and negative inspiratory force. These variables are useful adjuncts in the assessment of a patient's readiness to undergo an SBT, but they are not highly accurate in predicting the likelihood of successful extubation when used alone.[15]

It is not necessary for the acute process to have resolved completely before an SBT can be performed, provided that other predetermined criteria are met [see Table 1]. To await normalization of the P/F ratio or resolution of the chest x-ray abnormality would result in a needless delay in extubation should the patient successfully complete the SBT. Unnecessary prolongation of mechanical ventilation heightens the risk of ventilator-associated pneumonia [see 132 Postoperative and Ventilator-Associated Pneumonia], increases sedation requirements, postpones mobilization, and delays discharge from the ICU.[16]

SPONTANEOUS BREATHING TRIAL

SBTs should be performed on a daily basis once the acute respiratory process has resolved and the patient is hemodynamically normal [see Table 1]. PEEP should be set at 5 cm H_2O, with or without an additional 5 cm H_2O of pressure support (if the endotracheal tube is less than 7.0 mm in diameter). The F_IO_2 should be set to a value approximately 10% greater than required while the patient is fully supported, and the patient should be allowed to breathe spontaneously for 30 to 120 minutes. At the conclusion of the SBT, blood gas values should be obtained, and the patient should be placed back on the ventilator at the previous settings. At all times, the patient's vital signs should be monitored for evidence of increased work of breathing. Criteria for a failed SBT include (1) significant changes in the respiratory rate, (2) evidence of increased work of breathing, (3) significant dysrhythmia, and (4) hemodynamic instability [see Table 1]. In addition, the arterial blood gas values should be evaluated for evidence of worsening hypoxemia or hypercarbia, though it should be kept in mind that a normal P_aCO_2 is less important if the pH is within the normal range.

If the patient successfully completes the SBT, extubation should be attempted. There are few reasons to continue mechanical ventilation in this situation. If it is suggested that the patient remain intubated, one should ask whether a further delay in extubation would improve the chances of success, and if so, how. Among the reasons frequently cited for continuing intubation are altered mental status and inability to protect the airway, a potentially technically difficult reintubation, the presence of an unstable injury to the cervical spine, the likelihood of return trips to the operating room, and the need for frequent suctioning. Each of these reasons must be balanced against the inherent risks of continued intubation, and a clear plan should be developed outlining how postponing extubation will alter the situation for the better.

The patient with traumatic brain injury (TBI) presents a unique problem, for two reasons. First, the patient is often unable to maintain an adequate airway. Second, the patient is often unable to clear upper and lower airway secretions adequately and thus is at risk for continued aspiration and pneumonia. In patients whose mental status is altered but who are expected to recover quickly, the risk imposed by 1 or 2 additional days of intubation is relatively small, and delaying extubation to wait for mental status to clear can be justified. In TBI patients whose recovery is anticipated to take months (if it happens at all), the options are early tracheostomy [see Tracheostomy, below] and attempted extubation. Ultimately, the choice between these two options should be made on a case-by-case basis. Although tracheostomy is often preferred, these patients can frequently be extubated without significant sequelae.[17]

Failed SBT

When a patient fails an SBT, the first priority is to determine the reason for the failure. Initially, it is important to distinguish between patients who fail to meet the extubation criteria for unrelated reasons (e.g., agitation or cerebral storming in a TBI patient) and those who truly are not ready to be liberated from the ventilator. Direct observation of the patient during the SBT, if feasible, may provide insight into the failed attempt. The next step is to attempt to identify the specific cause of the failure. In these situations, a thorough knowledge of the patient's history is important, with special attention paid to age, comorbid conditions, reasons for and duration of mechanical ventilation, other indices of critical illness, and nutritional status [see Table 2]. Failure is frequently multifactorial, and actions to improve one or more of these factors should be undertaken to alter the outcome of the next SBT. After a failed attempt, it is best to provide a stable, nonfatiguing form of respiratory support (e.g., PSV) until the following day, thus allowing the patient a period of rest.

Patients who persistently fail SBTs are typically classified as exhibiting failure to wean. Comorbid conditions, including congestive heart failure, chronic lung disease, and renal or hepatic insufficiency, should be treated medically to the extent possible before further trials are attempted. The excess sodium and water frequently administered to critically ill patients can have negative effects on pulmonary mechanics, making liberation from the ventilator more difficult. Hydrostatic pulmonary edema, chest wall or visceral edema, and pleural effusions can have a greater impact on patients recovering from critical illness, who may be malnourished and deconditioned.

General measures to facilitate weaning include judicious use of diuretics, upright positioning, correction of electrolyte abnormalities (in particular, low serum potassium or phosphate levels), and, in some cases, drainage of hydrothoraces. In addition, attention should be given to providing appropriate nutritional support while avoiding excessive carbohydrate administration (which can increase CO_2 production). Physical therapy should begin as soon as possible to prevent further muscle atrophy. In addition to these general measures, consideration should be given to performing a tracheostomy. Although there is disagreement about the optimal timing and method of tracheostomy in this setting (see below), it is obvious that this measure can greatly facilitate attempts to discontinue mechanical ventilation by eliminating the risks associated with extubation. When the tracheostomy is in place and all general measures have been considered, SBTs should resume.

A very small percentage of patients are unable to tolerate the sudden reduction in support that occurs when they are treated with continuous positive airway pressure (CPAP) or a tracheostomy collar. These patients, who are often severely deconditioned after having been mechanically ventilated for several

Table 2 Causes of Failed Spontaneous Breathing Trials

Cause of Failure	Treatment
Anxiety/agitation	Judicious use of benzodiazepines ± haloperidol
Infection (pulmonary or extrapulmonary)	Diagnosis and treatment of causative infection
Electrolyte abnormalities (low K^+, low PO_4^-)	Correction of electrolyte concentrations
Pulmonary edema/cardiac ischemia	Administration of diuretics ± nitrates
Deconditioning/malnutrition	Aggressive nutritional support (via enteral route whenever possible) Physical therapy
Neuromuscular disease (critical illness polyneuropathy, myasthenia gravis)	Aggressive bronchopulmonary hygiene Specific treatment of myasthenia gravis (pyridostigmine, steroids, plasmapheresis) Early consideration of tracheostomy
Increased intra-abdominal pressure (obesity, abdominal distention)	Semirecumbent positioning Nasogastric decompression
Hypothyroidism	Thyroid replacement
Large hydrothoraces (rarely primary cause but may increase work of breathing in patients with marginal reserve)	Initiation of diuresis ± thoracentesis
Excessive auto-PEEP (COPD, asthma)	Bronchodilator therapy I.V. sedation to prevent agitation and air trapping
Excessive minute ventilation requirements: ↑ CO_2 production Metabolic acidosis	Reduction of carbohydrate intake Treatment of underlying cause (e.g., lactate production or renal failure) Consideration of HCO_3^- replacement if wasting is present (e.g., with renal tubular acidosis or pancreatic fistula)

weeks or longer, may benefit from a more gradual reduction in ventilatory support. In these cases, the term weaning is probably an accurate description of the process. A planned gradual reduction in support may be better tolerated with scheduled decreases in pressure support or, alternatively, with gradual increases in the duration of periods of unassisted breathing. In the setting of chronic ventilator dependence, neither method is necessarily superior to the other. What is important is that the patient should never be allowed to continue until exhaustion during the weaning process. Formulating a well-defined plan for weaning is more important than choosing a particular weaning method. One approach is to use a daily workout calendar similar to those used for athletic training, so that the details of the plan are clear and easily understandable by the patient, the family, the nursing staff, the respiratory staff, and the ICU team. Finally, both patients and families should be counseled to expect weaning to last a long time.

PROTOCOL-BASED VENTILATOR MANAGEMENT

Once respiratory failure has resolved, the patient's readiness for extubation is assessed. Traditionally, this assessment has been made by the physician. Unfortunately, both physician factors and patient factors can result in unnecessary delays that prolong the duration of mechanical ventilation. As a result, many institutions have developed respiratory therapist–driven and nurse-driven protocols that allow SBTs to occur without physician input. Implementation of these protocols has been shown to shorten ventilator time, reduce the incidence of ventilator-associated pneumonia, and lower costs.[18-20]

Although respiratory therapist–driven or nurse-driven protocols improve outcome when applied to a population of ventilated patients, individual patient characteristics should still be a consideration when deciding on extubation in a given case. Successful completion of an SBT simply implies that the patient has the ventilatory capacity to breathe spontaneously; it does not guarantee that the airway is stable or that the patient can adequately clear tracheobronchial secretions. The decision to end ventilatory support must rest on a careful assessment of the risks of continued intubation and mechanical ventilation against those of failed extubation.

AIRWAY ASSESSMENT

Once a patient has successfully completed an SBT, a second assessment should be made to determine the need for continued airway support with the endotracheal tube. In patients who were initially intubated for a condition necessitating airway protection (e.g., altered level of consciousness or angioedema), the condition should be resolved before extubation. Alternatively, patients who have been ventilated for long periods may have secondary airway edema related to fluid resuscitation or vocal cord damage secondary to the use of the translaryngeal tube.[21]

One way of determining whether the patient will have significant airway compromise is to perform the so-called cuff leak test. In this test, the patient is placed on VCV, and the volume of air lost during a single respiratory cycle when the cuff is deflated is measured. Although the cuff leak test was originally described as a qualitative test in children with croup, it has since proved to have some value as a quantitative test, affording a degree of improvement in the ability to predict which patients will have significant postextubation upper airway edema.[22-24] Leak values below 9% to 15% of the inspired volume have been associated with increased rates of postextubation stridor and the need for reintubation.[24-26] Unfortunately, the cuff leak test is an imperfect predictor. In one study, a cutoff value of 15% had a positive predictive value of only 25% for reintubation.[24] With this cutoff value, a patient would have a 75% chance of successful extubation in the absence of an air leak. Results such as these suggest that the cuff leak test is best used as a tool for assessing risk and that failure on this test should not be an absolute contraindication to extubation. Patients who fail the test may be candidates for postextubation adjunctive measures, such as racemic epinephrine (to enlarge the upper airway aperture, helium-oxygen mixtures (to decrease airflow resistance), or both. Although evidence supporting the use of such measures in adults is lacking, there are some data to support their use in children to treat upper airway obstruction and postextubation stridor.[27-30] Parenterally administered steroids have been employed to prevent postextubation stridor in children, with some success, but there is no evidence that they reduce the rate of reintubation in adults.[31] Finally, patients who require prolonged intubation because of airway instability should be considered for tracheostomy (see below).

TRACHEOSTOMY

The decision as to when a patient can be liberated from the mechanical ventilator is often complicated by concerns about the risks associated with failure and reintubation. Prolonged endotracheal intubation can injure the airway and result in airway edema, making reintubation difficult. In addition, the possibility that reintubation may be required at night or at other times when qualified personnel may not be readily available contributes to delays in extubation. The main theoretical advantage of tracheostomy in this context is that the issue of airway stability can be separated from the issue of readiness for extubation, and this separation may hasten the physician's decision to discontinue mechanical ventilation. Tracheostomy has other potential advantages as well, including decreased work of breathing, avoidance of continued vocal cord injury, improved bronchopulmonary hygiene, patient comfort, and improved patient communication.[32-34] On the other hand, it has several disadvantages, including the long-term risk of tracheal stenosis and the significant procedure-related complication rate (reported to be between 4% and 36%).[35-37] Despite the potential risks, it is generally believed that in properly selected patients, tracheostomy placement may assist in liberation from the mechanical ventilator, though the evidence supporting this belief is inconsistent.[38-41]

A relatively new technique that is rapidly gaining acceptance is the use of a percutaneous dilational approach to tracheostomy placement at the bedside. Several commercially available kits are available, and the long-term complication rate is similar to that seen with open tracheostomy.[36,37,42] Percutaneous access is obtained with a needle, followed by serial dilation of the tracheotomy over a guide wire. Many advocate doing this procedure under bronchoscopic guidance, which may be associated with a lower periprocedural complication rate.[43] The main advantage of the percutaneous dilational approach is that it avoids the delays associated with obtaining OR time and obviates the risks associated with patient transport.[44]

The main controversy surrounding tracheostomy in this setting is whether there is any benefit to performing the procedure early in the course of critical illness. To answer this question, several authors compared early tracheostomy (generally < 1 week) to prolonged translaryngeal intubation or, alternatively, to late tracheostomy (> 1 week).[38,40,41,45-47] Outcome measures included duration of mechanical ventilation, number of episodes of ventilator-associated pneumonia, length of ICU stay, and mortality. Unfortunately, many of these reports were limited by their observational design, their small sample size, or their inclusion of only certain specific patient subgroups (e.g., medical or neurosurgical patients). Furthermore, surgeons have traditionally held very strong biases with regard to the use and timing of tracheostomy, and these biases tend to impede the conduct of randomized, controlled trials. One group carried out a multicenter randomized trial evaluating the use of tracheostomy in trauma and nontrauma patients who were expected to need mechanical ventilation for more than 7 days. In this trial, early tracheostomy offered no overall benefit; however, these results may be of limited applicability, in that the authors reported experiencing significant difficulty in obtaining the participation of physicians and institutions, mostly because of strong physician bias.[40] As a result, no clear consensus has yet been reached regarding the optimal use, timing, and method of tracheostomy in the ICU setting.

Discussion

Special Problems in Ventilator Management

ACUTE LUNG INJURY AND ACUTE RESPIRATORY DISTRESS SYNDROME

ALI and ARDS are common problems in the ICU and carry a high mortality [see 120 Pulmonary Insufficiency].[48] Over the past decade, an improved understanding of the pathophysiology of ventilator-induced lung injury has resulted in significant changes in ventilator management in patients with ARDS. It is now clear that the volume and pressure associated with mechanical ventilation can induce and perpetuate lung injury and the systemic inflammatory response syndrome (SIRS). As a result, the primary goals of ventilator management in ALI and ARDS patients are (1) to avoid repetitive expansion and collapse of recruitable alveolar units and (2) to avoid overdistention of functioning alveoli (volutrauma).

Several prospective trials have employed a low-V_T ventilation strategy to prevent ventilator-induced lung injury.[49-53] The largest of these trials compared a lung-protective approach that used a V_T of 6 ml/kg of predicted body weight with a more traditional approach that used a V_T of 12 ml/kg. Mortality was reduced by 22% in the patients treated with lower tidal volumes, and both SIRS and the alveolar inflammatory response were attenuated. Accordingly, a low-V_T, lung-protective strategy is now standard for treatment of patients with ALI and ARDS.[49]

High versus Low PEEP in ARDS

ARDS is characterized by a heterogeneously distributed loss of functioning alveoli, with normally compliant, open alveoli mixing with collapsed, nonrecruited alveoli.[54] In the setting of inadequate PEEP, a lung-protective ventilation strategy may contribute to further alveolar collapse and may perpetuate lung injury secondary to repetitive opening and closing of alveolar units.[55] It follows that higher levels of PEEP may prevent the injury associated with this phenomenon and perhaps improve patient outcome. Additionally, a frequent point of controversy in managing the hypoxemic patient is whether it is preferable to employ higher levels of PEEP with lower levels of F_IO_2 or lower levels of PEEP with higher levels of F_IO_2. Many intensivists prefer to use higher levels of PEEP to keep F_IO_2 below 0.6, believing that higher oxygen levels may induce hyperoxic lung injury. However, a randomized, controlled trial that compared a high-PEEP strategy with a high-F_IO_2 strategy found the outcomes to be similar.[56] Thus, it is not currently possible to determine the optimal PEEP for ALI or ARDS patients with any certainty; the values chosen should be based on individual patient response.

CHRONIC OBSTRUCTIVE PULMONARY DISEASE

COPD is an uncommon indication for the initiation of mechanical ventilation in surgical patients; however, COPD may be present in varying degrees as a comorbid condition in ventilated patients and may thereby complicate ventilator management. Ventilated patients with COPD may be oxygen or steroid dependent and typically are in a tenuous state even in the absence of a surgical insult. The basic principles of management are (1) to treat the underlying cause of respiratory failure (e.g., sepsis or trauma), (2) to minimize airway hyperreactivity through generous use of bronchodilators and steroids when necessary, (3) to manage tracheobronchial secretions aggressively, and (4) to minimize the work of breathing.[57]

The expiratory flow limitation observed in patients with COPD can result in incomplete expiration, air trapping, and intrinsic positive end-expiratory pressure (PEEPi, also referred to as auto-PEEP). These results can further impair respiration by decreasing the effective contribution of diaphragmatic contraction. Although reducing PEEPi can be difficult, there are several maneuvers that should be attempted initially to decrease air trapping and the resulting PEEPi. The first is to maximize the expiratory time by increasing the inspiratory flow rate or decreasing the respiratory rate. A reduction in tidal volume is also effective, in that less time is required for complete expiration of a smaller volume. Another maneuver is to administer bronchodilators liberally so as to minimize airflow limitation. If this measure is ineffective, adjusting the ventilator's PEEP setting to match the PEEPi should be considered for patients who are using a spontaneous mode of ventilation. This will minimize the increased work necessary to trigger the ventilator [see Figure 5]. Extubation can generally be accomplished once the acute episode resolves; it should be kept in mind that blood gas parameters were unlikely to have been normal at baseline. It is also reasonable to attempt a short period of bilevel positive-pressure ventilation immediately after extubation in patients with severe COPD in an effort to avoid having to reintubate these patients.

BRONCHOPLEURAL FISTULAS

Bronchopleural (or parenchymal pleural) fistulas (BPFs) are an infrequent but severe complication of thoracic trauma or pulmonary resection. The incidence ranges from 2% to 12%, and the condition is associated with a high mortality.[58-60] Ventilator management of BPF patients is difficult because large air leaks through the fistula, which may represent the path of least resistance to airflow, limit adequate alveolar ventilation. Care is complicated by the need for a higher P_{aw} to maintain oxygenation, which may only increase flow through the fistula.

The determinants of flow through a BPF have important implications for ventilator management and have been investigated in animal models and in several small case series.[61-64] Transpulmonary pressure and fistula resistance are the main factors influencing the size of the air leak. Specifically, P_{aw} appears to have the greatest impact on flow through the fistula; there is little or no change when peak inspiratory pressure is varied.[62,65] Intrapleural pressure plays a role as well. Conventional chest tube management involves the use of –10 or –20 cm H_2O suction to evacuate the pleural space and promote pleural apposition. In the setting of a significant BPF, this measure increases the pressure gradient and may increase the size of the air leak.[62,64]

There is no clearly beneficial method of ventilator management in BPF patients, but most would agree that limitation of P_{aw} should be the first step and that early extubation is indicated whenever possible. Various techniques for managing respiratory failure associated with large BPFs have been described in single case reports or small case series.[65-75] High-frequency jet ventilation (HFJV) to support patients with BPF has been advocated on the basis of the low P_{aw} generated with this ventilatory mode. Several case reports have described a decrease in fistula airflow with subsequent closure of the BPF after the institution of HFJV.[66,69,74-76] Unfortunately, although this technique may be useful in cases of isolated BPF, most of the reports do not involve patients with simultaneous lung parenchymal disease. The elevated P_{aw} required to treat the profound hypoxemia associated with ALI and ARDS

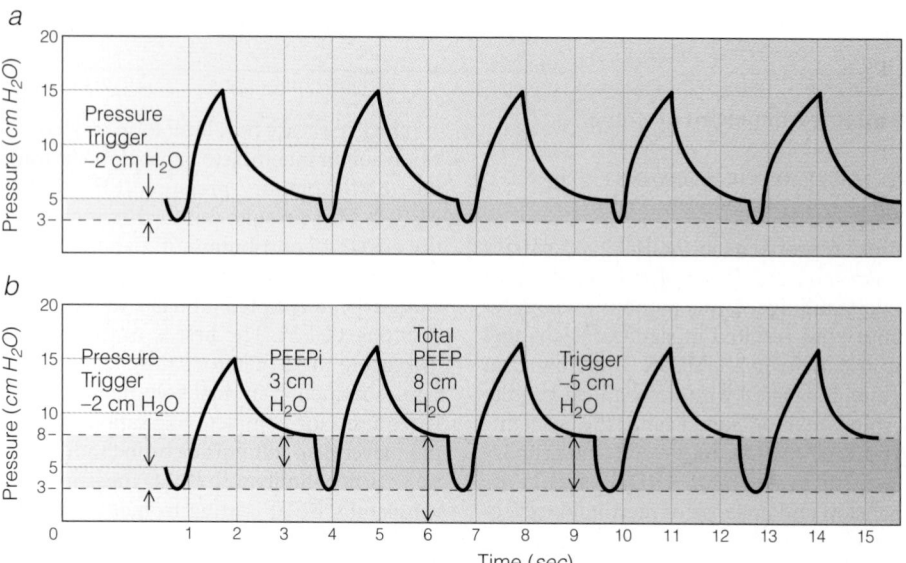

Figure 5 Illustrated is intrinsic PEEP during assisted spontaneous ventilation. In *a*, the patient is breathing spontaneously on VCV in the assist-control mode. The respiratory rate is 20 breaths/min, and the effective I/E ratio is 1:2 (inspiration, 1 sec; expiration, 2 sec). Expiratory time is adequate; therefore, no intrinsic PEEP (PEEPi) develops, and total PEEP is equal to the set PEEP (5 cm H_2O). In *b*, a patient who is breathing spontaneously on identical ventilator settings requires a longer expiratory phase to prevent air trapping and auto-PEEP. Incomplete expiration results in an auto-PEEP equivalent to 3 cm H_2O and a new total PEEP of 8 cm H_2O. This results in increased P_{aw}, but more important, the patient must now generate 5 cm H_2O of negative pressure during inspiration to trigger the ventilator.

may negate any potential benefit associated with HFJV.[61,63]

Besides HFJV, a number of other unconventional modes of ventilation have been used to manage BPF patients, including the use of a double-lumen tube with a variable flow resistor,[71] airway pressure-release ventilation (APRV),[72] high-frequency conventional ventilation,[70] and differential lung ventilation using any combination of these modalities.[66,70,75,77] Intermittent occlusion of the chest tube during inspiration in an effort to lower transpulmonary pressure has also been reported to assist ventilation in certain cases.[65] Bronchial blockade[78] and other newer therapies (e.g., bronchial stenting[79,80] and endobronchial application of fibrin or other tissue sealants[81,82]) may be useful in refractory cases. Ideally, large BPFs should undergo early operative revision if the injury and the patient's condition permit.

Alternative Modes of Ventilation and Adjunctive Therapies

INVERSE-RATIO VENTILATION

Inverse-ratio pressure control ventilation (PC-IRV) has been used to treat patients with ARDS and severe hypoxemia for several decades.[83,84] This mode makes use of a prolonged inspiratory time to deliver a pressure-limited breath that results in an inverted I/E ratio (e.g., 2:1, 3:1, or 4:1 rather than the normal 1:3). The rationale for PC-IRV is based on two principles. The first principle is that a prolonged inspiratory time results in better gas distribution with a lower peak inspiratory pressure; the second is that the elevated P_{aw} improves alveolar recruitment, resulting in improved oxygenation. The theoretical advantages notwithstanding, both animal models of ALI and several observation studies in humans that compared normal-ratio ventilation with PC-IRV have failed to find any significant advantages to the latter when patients are ventilated with appropriate levels of PEEP.[85-87] As

noted (see above), PEEP prevents derecruitment. This not only improves oxygenation but also has the theoretical advantage of preventing the repetitive collapse and reinflation of lung units associated with ventilator-induced lung injury. To date, there have been no randomized trials assessing outcome after PC-IRV, but the available data suggest that this mode is unlikely to improve patient outcomes in the setting of adequate PEEP.

PRONE VENTILATION

The finding of dependent atelectasis in patients with ARDS makes prone positioning an attractive therapeutic option.[54] Advocates cite several theoretical benefits, including recruitment of previously collapsed alveoli, relief of diaphragmatic pressure secondary to the abdominal viscera, and improved drainage of tracheobronchial secretions.[88] Several prospective randomized trials have evaluated the use of prone positioning in adults and children with ARDS.[89-91] Despite consistent improvements in oxygenation, no significant benefit in terms of mortality has yet been demonstrated.

In practice, prone positioning is performed intermittently throughout the day for periods ranging from 4 to 12 hours, with the remaining time spent in the supine position. The primary risk associated with prone positioning is accidental removal of the endotracheal tube, a chest tube, or an intravenous line. It is possible to place patients with an open abdomen prone in some cases; however, this remains technically challenging. Newer patient beds designed specifically for prone positioning (e.g., Rotoprone; KCI, San Antonio, Texas) facilitate prone ventilation, but they remain costly and are not universally available.

Multiply injured patients with increased intracranial pressure can pose a difficult challenge. Hypoxemia is associated with a worse neurologic outcome in this population, but because of the increased intracranial pressure that may occur, prone positioning is contraindicated. In this situation, limited axial rotation (i.e., continuous partial axial rotation to varying degrees, depending on patient tolerance) is an option that may yield similar improvements in oxygenation.[92]

Other injuries (e.g., unstable spinal fractures or pelvic or long-bone fractures that call for traction) can be significant problems and are relative contraindications to prone positioning. In patients with ARDS and profound hypoxemia, they are generally secondary concerns and should not prevent the use of prone positioning as an adjunctive therapy.

HIGH-FREQUENCY OSCILLATORY VENTILATION

For several decades, high-frequency oscillatory ventilation (HFOV) has been used to treat respiratory failure in premature infants.[93] More recently, it has been used in adults with ARDS, both as primary treatment and as rescue therapy for severe hypoxemia.[94-96] HFOV differs from HFJV in that it employs an oscillating piston or diaphragm that provides high-frequency, low-amplitude ventilation superimposed on an elevated P_{aw}. Its primary theoretical rationale is based on the so-called open lung approach to limiting ventilator-induced lung injury: it avoids the repetitive alveolar opening and closing that can occur at low airway pressures while also avoiding the overdistention that occurs at higher airway pressures.

P_{aw} is determined by the operator and is maintained by continuous gas flow from the ventilator through a resistance valve at the end of the circuit. The oscillating piston or diaphragm lies perpendicular to the gas flow. The oscillating frequency is set by the clinician and generally ranges from 3 to 6 Hz (180 to 360 breaths/min). As in conventional ventilation, oxygenation is achieved by adjusting P_{aw}, as well as F_IO_2. Ventilation is altered by changing both the frequency and the amplitude of the piston's oscillation. HFOV differs from conventional ventilation in that increases in ventilation are achieved by reducing the frequency of oscillation and increasing the amplitude, which allow more time for the expiratory phase of piston displacement. It also differs in that the expiratory phase is assisted by the backward piston movement.

The primary side effect of HFOV is potential hemodynamic compromise secondary to the elevated P_{aw}. Pneumothorax has also been associated with HFOV, but it may be a marker of the severity of lung injury rather than a consequence of the mode of ventilation.[94-96] In addition, most patients require neuromuscular blocking agents to prevent spontaneous respiratory effort while being maintained on the oscillating ventilator. The requirement for a specialized adult oscillating ventilator and the general lack of familiarity with HFOV has hindered broad application of this technique.

Despite these limitations, several studies have shown HFOV to be well tolerated by patients with severe ARDS. In addition, consistent improvements in oxygenation have been documented when patients are converted from conventional ventilation to HFOV.[95-98] As a result, HFOV is a potential option for patients with profound hypoxemia, either alone (as rescue therapy) or in combination with other adjunctive measures (e.g., nitric oxide [NO] inhalation and prone ventilation). Improved oxygenation, however, is not necessarily correlated with improved mortality. The role of HFOV in primary treatment of early ARDS remains to be determined.[99]

AIRWAY PRESSURE-RELEASE VENTILATION

APRV is a relatively new mode of ventilation that, like HFOV, is based on the open lung approach to limiting ventilator-induced lung injury. APRV employs a high CPAP, which is intermittently released for short periods to allow lung emptying.[100] The primary rationale is based on the idea that optimal alveolar recruitment depends both on differential alveolar opening pressures and on variations in regional alveolar time constants.[101] Elevation of transpulmonary pressure above the upper inflection point is avoided because the sustained P_{aw} is generally below the peak or plateau pressures observed in conventional PCV or VCV. Compared with modes that induce a high P_{aw} (e.g., HFOV and PC-IRV), APRV has the advantage of allowing spontaneous respiration, thereby eliminating the need for neuromuscular blocking agents.

APRV has been studied extensively in animal models of ALI,[101-104] but human data are limited to case series and a few observational studies that reported primarily on application and safety.[105-109] In practice, three variables are manipulated: the high continuous pressure (P_{high}), which ranges from 20 to 30 cm H_2O; the release period, which generally lasts no longer than 1 second; and the low release pressure (P_{low}), which is between 0 and 5 cm H_2O. The P_{high} and P_{low} settings can be manipulated along with the F_IO_2 to achieve adequate arterial oxygenation [see Figure 6]. The release phase can be changed with respect to both duration and frequency to ensure adequate ventilation. Spontaneous respirations occur and are superimposed on the high CPAP.

No significant complications have been associated with APRV. There is a theoretical potential for hemodynamic compromise; however, because of the high levels of PEEP and the high plateau pressures already observed in patients with severe ARDS, P_{aw} is generally lower with APRV, and as a result, cardiovascular function may actually improve.[108] The theoretical benefits of APRV make it an attractive alternative to conventional ventilation. Unfortunately, this mode of ventilation has not been directly compared with low–tidal volume, lung-protective ventilation. APRV probably will not be widely used until it is shown to have a beneficial effect on outcome.

NONINVASIVE POSITIVE-PRESSURE VENTILATION

Noninvasive positive-pressure ventilation (NPPV) is positive-pressure ventilation administered through either a nasal or a full-face mask in the form of either CPAP or bilevel positive airway pressure (BiPAP). PEEP is generally set at 5 to 10 cm H_2O (CPAP), with or without additional pressure support at levels ranging from 5 to 20 cm H_2O (BiPAP), and titrated to keep the respiratory rate under 25 breaths/min. In comparison with medical therapy alone, NPPV has been demonstrated to reduce both the need for intubation and mortality in patients with exacerbated COPD.[57] Patients in whom medical therapy fails—as signaled by worsening tachypnea, hypoxemia, and respiratory acidosis—are candidates for NPPV. This mode should be used in conjunction with other measures, such as inhaled bronchodilators, inhaled steroids, and oral or parenteral steroids and antibiotics when appropriate.[57]

NPPV has sometimes been used to treat respiratory failure associated with cardiogenic pulmonary edema.[110-113] In this setting, NPPV has certain theoretical benefits, including decreased work of breathing, decreased left ventricular afterload,[114] and, possibly, decreased preload as a result of the positive intrathoracic pressure. Nevertheless, the available data are inconclusive. One randomized trial was stopped early because a higher rate of myocardial ischemia was recorded in the BiPAP group than in the CPAP group.[110] Another study reported no significant cardiac events in either group.[111] Both modes of NPPV, however, were superior to standard oxygen therapy in preventing the need for intubation.[111] These studies are limited by their sample sizes, and as a result, it is difficult to draw definitive conclusions. It is possible that NPPV may have a beneficial effect on outcome in patients with cardiogenic pulmonary edema, but whether CPAP or BiPAP is therapeutically optimal has yet to be determined.

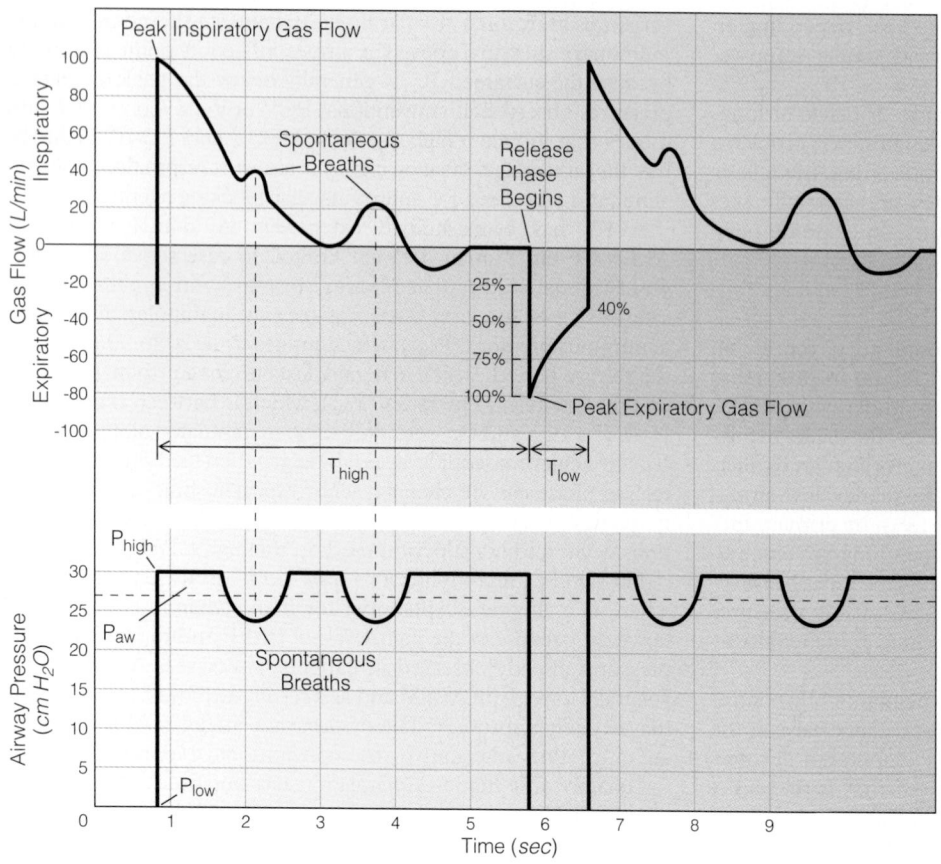

Figure 6 **Illustrated is airway pressure-release ventilation, a ventilation mode that maintains a high CPAP with intermittent release periods. The operator sets the high and low pressure settings (P_{high}, P_{low}) and the release time (T_{low}). The mode has several theoretical advantages over conventional ventilation, including lower alveolar distending pressures (in patients with ARDS), avoidance of alveolar derecruitment, and the ability for the patient to breathe spontaneously.**

The use of NPPV to treat hypoxemic respiratory failure that is not due to cardiogenic pulmonary edema (e.g., respiratory failure resulting from pneumonia, thoracic trauma, ALI, or ARDS) has also been addressed in several small randomized trials and a systematic review.[115] The results of the individual studies vary somewhat, but the overall indication is that there may be some benefit to be derived from reducing the need for mechanical ventilation, the duration of the ICU stay, and mortality in certain patient populations—particularly those in whom intubation portends a particularly poor prognosis (e.g., immunocompromised patients and recent lung transplant recipients).[115]

There are several relative contraindications to NPPV, including severe facial deformity or trauma (either of which can prevent sealing around the edges of the mask), a decreased level of consciousness that is not expected to improve with improved ventilation, hemodynamic instability, a need for endotracheal intubation for other reasons (e.g., airway protection or surgery), and a recent upper GI operation. In addition, NPPV should not be performed by physicians, therapists, or nurses unfamiliar with its use or in situations where patient monitoring is inadequate. Inappropriate performance of NPPV may lead to unrecognized patient intolerance, worsening respiratory status, and delays in endotracheal intubation.[116]

Complications of NPPV include skin breakdown over the mask pressure areas, gastric distention, ventilator asynchrony, and treatment failure (associated with worsening mental status, aspiration, and delayed endotracheal intubation). In addition, NPPV should generally be avoided as a method of preventing reintubation in the ICU, because it has been associated with a worse outcome.[117] Despite these limitations, NPPV is generally well tolerated and should be considered as a treatment option in certain patient populations with acute respiratory failure.

NITRIC OXIDE INHALATION

NO is a potent vasodilator that is administered as an inhaled gas. The delivery mode allows NO to exert its vasodilatory effect on pulmonary arterioles supplying ventilated (and only ventilated) alveoli, thereby improving $\dot{V}/\dot{Q}$ matching, reducing intrapulmonary shunting, and increasing oxygenation.[118,119] Because of its short half-life in the circulation (100 milliseconds), inhaled NO is not associated with systemic vasodilation and hypotension.[120]

NO is administered through a specialized delivery system in doses of 5 to 40 parts per million. Several randomized trials have shown it to yield modest improvements in oxygenation in adults and children with ARDS.[121-124] There are also numerous reports of NO administration in conjunction with prone positioning,[125] HFOV,[126,127] and HFJV,[76] as well as in patients with BPFs.[76] Unfortunately, the use of NO has not been demonstrated to improve mortality. On the other hand, there have been no reports of significant adverse effects. The high cost of NO administration has kept it from being routinely used in ARDS patients.

SURFACTANT REPLACEMENT

Surfactant production in adult patients with ARDS is both diminished and abnormal.[128,129] The loss of surfactant may contribute to the alveolar collapse, intrapulmonary shunting, and hypoxemia seen in ARDS. Theoretically, surfactant replacement would prevent derecruitment and improve lung compliance and oxygenation. In addition, prevention of alveolar collapse is important in limiting ventilator-induced lung injury. As a result, surfactant replacement is an attractive therapeutic option for patients with ARDS.

Several methods of surfactant replacement in adults have been assessed in randomized, multicenter placebo-controlled trials. In an early trial of aerosolized surfactant given to patients with sepsis-induced ARDS, no benefit was observed with respect to either oxygenation indices or mortality.[130] This trial was limited both by the particular surfactant formulation used and by the failure to employ a low–tidal volume, lung-protective ventilation strategy. A subsequent report, summarizing data from two large trials of a protein C–based surfactant formulation given for 24 hours, documented modest improvements in oxygenation during surfactant administration. Neither trial, however, demonstrated any significant impact on mortality.[131] In view of the lack of mortality benefit, it is probably best to limit the use of surfactant in adults with ARDS to the setting of clinical trials.

EXTRACORPOREAL LIFE SUPPORT

Extracorporeal life support (ECLS) is the use of a modified heart-lung machine to support gas exchange while allowing the diseased lung to rest. The theoretical advantage of this technique is that it should avoid the oxygen toxicity and the volutrauma or barotrauma that may accompany mechanical ventilation in patients experiencing severe respiratory failure. ECLS has become the standard treatment of severe respiratory failure in neonates[132] and has also been used in the pediatric population.[133] In adult patients with severe respiratory failure, it has been employed mainly in specialized centers, with reported survival rates of approximately 50%.[134,135] Vascular access may be obtained via either a venoarterial or a venovenous circuit. The latter is typically used in adult patients; the former is preferred in patients with marginal cardiovascular function.

In some centers, ECLS is employed when the risk of death with continuing conventional ventilation is more than 90% and the primary process is reversible. In 2004, one group reported on their use of ECLS to treat 255 patients with severe ARDS (defined as a P/F ratio lower than 100 when F_IO_2 was 1.0, an alveolar-arterial gradient higher than 600 mm Hg, or a transpulmonary shunt fraction greater than 30% despite maximal ventilatory support). More than half (53%) of the patients survived to hospital discharge.[136] Although these results are difficult to interpret in the absence of a control group, the mortality appears to be lower than would be expected with traditional ventilator management.

The main contraindications to the use of ECLS are advanced age, malignancy, severe neurologic injury, and mechanical ventilation lasting longer than 5 to 7 days. Complications include bleeding (heparinization is required), hemolysis, cerebral infarction, renal failure, infection, and venous thrombosis. In view of the risks, ECLS should be reserved for patients at specialized centers who have profound hypoxemia that is refractory to other, less invasive measures.

References

1. Esteban A, Anzueto A, Alia I, et al: How is mechanical ventilation employed in the intensive care unit? An international utilization review. Am J Respir Crit Care Med 161:1450, 2000
2. Linderholm H: Lung mechanics in sitting and horizontal postures studied by body plethysmographic methods. Am J Physiol 204:85, 1963
3. Navajas D, Farre R, Rotger MM, et al: Effect of body posture on respiratory impedance. J Appl Physiol 64:194, 1988
4. Mutoh T, Lamm WJ, Embree LJ, et al: Abdominal distension alters regional pleural pressures and chest wall mechanics in pigs in vivo. J Appl Physiol 70:2611, 1991
5. Suter PM, Fairley B, Isenberg MD: Optimum end-expiratory airway pressure in patients with acute pulmonary failure. N Engl J Med 292:284, 1975
6. Dreyfuss D, Saumon G: Ventilator-induced lung injury: lessons from experimental studies. Am J Respir Crit Care Med 157:294, 1998
7. Gattinoni L, D'Andrea L, Pelosi P, et al: Regional effects and mechanism of positive end-expiratory pressure in early adult respiratory distress syndrome. JAMA 269:2122, 1993
8. Bruhn A, Hernandez G, Bugedo G, et al: Effects of positive end-expiratory pressure on gastric mucosal perfusion in acute respiratory distress syndrome. Crit Care 8:R306, 2004
9. Sassoon CS, Foster GT: Patient-ventilator asynchrony. Curr Opin Crit Care 7:28, 2001
10. Murray MJ, Cowen J, DeBlock H, et al: Clinical practice guidelines for sustained neuromuscular blockade in the adult critically ill patient. Crit Care Med 30:142, 2002
11. Hamwi GJ: Therapy: changing dietary concepts. Diabetes Mellitus: Diagnosis and Treatment. American Diabetes Association, New York, 1964
12. Hall JB, Wood LD: Liberation of the patient from mechanical ventilation. JAMA 257:1621, 1987
13. Esteban A, Frutos F, Tobin MJ, et al: A comparison of four methods of weaning patients from mechanical ventilation. Spanish Lung Failure Collaborative Group. N Engl J Med 332:345, 1995
14. Esteban A, Alia I, Tobin MJ, et al: Effect of spontaneous breathing trial duration on outcome of attempts to discontinue mechanical ventilation. Spanish Lung Failure Collaborative Group. Am J Respir Crit Care Med 159:512, 1999
15. Meade M, Guyatt G, Cook D, et al: Predicting success in weaning from mechanical ventilation. Chest 120(6 suppl):400S, 2001
16. Girou E: Prevention of nosocomial infections in acute respiratory failure patients. Eur Respir J Suppl 42:72s, 2003
17. Coplin WM, Pierson DJ, Cooley KD, et al: Implications of extubation delay in brain-injured patients meeting standard weaning criteria. Am J Respir Crit Care Med 161:1530, 2000
18. Ely EW, Bennett PA, Bowton DL, et al: Large scale implementation of a respiratory therapist-driven protocol for ventilator weaning. Am J Respir Crit Care Med 159:439, 1999
19. Dries DJ, McGonigal MD, Malian MS, et al: Protocol-driven ventilator weaning reduces use of mechanical ventilation, rate of early reintubation, and ventilator-associated pneumonia. J Trauma 56:943, 2004
20. Marelich GP, Murin S, Battistella F, et al: Protocol weaning of mechanical ventilation in medical and surgical patients by respiratory care practitioners and nurses: effect on weaning time and incidence of ventilator-associated pneumonia. Chest 118:459, 2000
21. Darmon JY, Rauss A, Dreyfuss D, et al: Evaluation of risk factors for laryngeal edema after tracheal extubation in adults and its prevention by dexamethasone: a placebo-controlled, double-blind, multicenter study. Anesthesiology 77:245, 1992
22. Adderley RJ, Mullins GC: When to extubate the croup patient: the "leak" test. Can J Anaesth 34:304, 1987
23. Miller RL, Cole RP: Association between reduced cuff leak volume and postextubation stridor. Chest 110:1035, 1996
24. De Bast Y, De Backer D, Moraine JJ, et al: The cuff leak test to predict failure of tracheal extubation for laryngeal edema. Intensive Care Med 28:1267, 2002
25. Jaber S, Chanques G, Matecki S, et al: Post-extubation stridor in intensive care unit patients: risk factors evaluation and importance of the cuff leak test. Intensive Care Med 29:69, 2003
26. Sandhu RS, Pasquale MD, Miller K, et al: Measurement of endotracheal tube cuff leak to predict postextubation stridor and need for reintubation. J Am Coll Surg 190:682, 2000
27. Kemper KJ, Ritz RH, Benson MS, et al: Helium-oxygen mixture in the treatment of postextubation stridor in pediatric trauma patients. Crit Care Med 19:356, 1991
28. Rodeberg DA, Easter AJ, Washam MA, et al: Use of a helium-oxygen mixture in the treatment of post extubation stridor in pediatric patients with burns. J Burn Care Rehabil 16:476, 1995
29. Weber JE, Chudnofsky CR, Younger JG, et al: A randomized comparison of helium-oxygen mixture (Heliox) and racemic epinephrine for the treatment of moderate to severe croup. Pediatrics 107:E96, 2001
30. Hess D, Chatmongkolchart S: Techniques to avoid intubation: noninvasive positive pressure ventilation and Heliox therapy. Int Anesthesiol Clin 38:161, 2000
31. Meade MO, Guyatt GH, Cook DJ, et al: Trials of corticosteroids to prevent postextubation airway complications. Chest 120(6 suppl):464S, 2001
32. Astrachan DI, Kirchner JC, Goodwin WJ Jr: Prolonged intubation vs. tracheotomy: complications, practical and psychological considerations. Laryngoscope 98:1165, 1988
33. Diehl JL, El Atrous S, Touchard D, et al: Changes in the work of breathing induced by tracheotomy in ventilator-dependent patients. Am J Respir Crit Care Med 159:383, 1999
34. Davis K Jr, Campbell RS, Johannigman JA, et al: Changes in respiratory mechanics after tracheostomy. Arch Surg 134:59, 1999

35. Freeman BD, Isabella K, Lin N, et al: A meta-analysis of prospective trials comparing percutaneous and surgical tracheostomy in critically ill patients. Chest 118:1412, 2000

36. Melloni G, Muttini S, Gallioli G, et al: Surgical tracheostomy versus percutaneous dilatational tracheostomy: a prospective-randomized study with long-term follow-up. J Cardiovasc Surg (Torino) 43:113, 2002

37. Kearney PA, Griffen MM, Ochoa JB, et al: A single-center 8-year experience with percutaneous dilational tracheostomy. Ann Surg 231:701, 2000

38. Boynton JH, Hawkins K, Eastridge BJ, et al: Tracheostomy timing and the duration of weaning in patients with acute respiratory failure. Crit Care 8:R261, 2004

39. Maziak DE, Meade MO, Todd TR: The timing of tracheotomy: a systematic review. Chest 114:605, 1998

40. Sugerman HJ, Wolfe L, Pasquale MD, et al: Multicenter, randomized, prospective trial of early tracheostomy. J Trauma 43:741, 1997

41. Rumbak MJ, Newton M, Truncale T, et al: A prospective, randomized, study comparing early percutaneous dilational tracheotomy to prolonged translaryngeal intubation (delayed tracheotomy) in critically ill medical patients. Crit Care Med 32:1689, 2004

42. Freeman BD, Isabella K, Cobb JP, et al: A prospective, randomized study comparing percutaneous with surgical tracheostomy in critically ill patients. Crit Care Med 29:926, 2001

43. Dulguerov P, Gysin C, Perneger TV, et al: Percutaneous or surgical tracheostomy: a meta-analysis. Crit Care Med 27:1617, 1999

44. Waydhas C: Intrahospital transport of critically ill patients. Crit Care 3:R83, 1999

45. Arabi Y, Haddad S, Shirawi N, et al: Early tracheostomy in intensive care trauma patients improves resource utilization: a cohort study and literature review. Crit Care 8:R347, 2004

46. Bouderka MA, Fakhir B, Bouaggad A, et al: Early tracheostomy versus prolonged endotracheal intubation in severe head injury. J Trauma 57:251, 2004

47. Brook AD, Sherman G, Malen J, et al: Early versus late tracheostomy in patients who require prolonged mechanical ventilation. Am J Crit Care 9:352, 2000

48. Milberg JA, Davis DR, Steinberg KP, et al: Improved survival of patients with acute respiratory distress syndrome (ARDS): 1983–1993. JAMA 273:306, 1995

49. Ventilation with lower tidal volumes as compared with traditional tidal volumes for acute lung injury and the acute respiratory distress syndrome. The Acute Respiratory Distress Syndrome Network. N Engl J Med 342:1301, 2000

50. Amato MB, Barbas CS, Medeiros DM, et al: Effect of a protective-ventilation strategy on mortality in the acute respiratory distress syndrome. N Engl J Med 338:347, 1998

51. Brochard L, Roudot-Thoraval F, Roupie E, et al: Tidal volume reduction for prevention of ventilator-induced lung injury in acute respiratory distress syndrome. The Multicenter Trail Group on Tidal Volume Reduction in ARDS. Am J Respir Crit Care Med 158:1831, 1998

52. Brower RG, Shanholtz CB, Fessler HE, et al: Prospective, randomized, controlled clinical trial comparing traditional versus reduced tidal volume ventilation in acute respiratory distress syndrome patients. Crit Care Med 27:1492, 1999

53. Stewart TE, Meade MO, Cook DJ, et al: Evaluation of a ventilation strategy to prevent barotrauma in patients at high risk for acute respiratory distress syndrome. Pressure- and Volume-Limited Ventilation Strategy Group. N Engl J Med 338:355, 1998

54. Gattinoni L, Caironi P, Pelosi P, et al: What has computed tomography taught us about the acute respiratory distress syndrome? Am J Respir Crit Care Med 164:1701, 2001

55. Richard JC, Maggiore SM, Jonson B, et al: Influence of tidal volume on alveolar recruitment: respective role of PEEP and a recruitment maneuver. Am J Respir Crit Care Med 163:1609, 2001

56. Brower RG, Lanken PN, MacIntyre N, et al: Higher versus lower positive end-expiratory pressures in patients with the acute respiratory distress syndrome. N Engl J Med 351:327, 2004

57. Celli BR, MacNee W: Standards for the diagnosis and treatment of patients with COPD: a summary of the ATS/ERS position paper. Eur Respir J 23:932, 2004

58. Wright CD, Wain JC, Mathisen DJ, et al: Postpneumonectomy bronchopleural fistula after sutured bronchial closure: incidence, risk factors, and management. J Thorac Cardiovasc Surg 112:1367, 1996

59. Sonobe M, Nakagawa M, Ichinose M, et al: Analysis of risk factors in bronchopleural fistula after pulmonary resection for primary lung cancer. Eur J Cardiothorac Surg 18:519, 2000

60. de Perrot M, Licker M, Robert J, et al: Incidence, risk factors and management of bronchopleural fistulae after pneumonectomy. Scand Cardiovasc J 33:171, 1999

61. Bishop MJ, Benson MS, Sato P, et al: Comparison of high-frequency jet ventilation with conventional mechanical ventilation for bronchopleural fistula. Anesth Analg 66:833, 1987

62. Walsh MC, Carlo WA: Determinants of gas flow through a bronchopleural fistula. J Appl Physiol 67:1591, 1989

63. Spinale FG, Linker RW, Crawford FA, et al: Conventional versus high frequency jet ventilation with a bronchopleural fistula. J Surg Res 46:147, 1989

64. Tilles RB, Don HF: Complications of high pleural suction in bronchopleural fistulas. Anesthesiology 43:486, 1975

65. Powner DJ, Grenvik A: Ventilatory management of life-threatening bronchopleural fistulae: a summary. Crit Care Med 9:54, 1981

66. Mortimer AJ, Laurie PS, Garrett H, et al: Unilateral high frequency jet ventilation: reduction of leak in bronchopleural fistula. Intensive Care Med 10:39, 1984

67. Carlon GC, Ray C Jr, Klain M, et al: High-frequency positive-pressure ventilation in management of a patient with bronchopleural fistula. Anesthesiology 52:160, 1980

68. Litmanovitch M, Joynt GM, Cooper PJ, et al: Persistent bronchopleural fistula in a patient with adult respiratory distress syndrome: treatment with pressure-controlled ventilation. Chest 104:1901, 1993

69. McGuire GP: Lung ventilation and bronchopleural fistula. Can J Anaesth 43:1275, 1996

70. Feeley TW, Keating D, Nishimura T: Independent lung ventilation using high-frequency ventilation in the management of a bronchopleural fistula. Anesthesiology 69:420, 1988

71. Carvalho P, Thompson WH, Riggs R, et al: Management of bronchopleural fistula with a variable-resistance valve and a single ventilator. Chest 111:1452, 1997

72. Darwish RS, Gilbert TB, Fahy BG: Management of a bronchopleural fistula using differential lung airway pressure release ventilation. J Cardiothorac Vasc Anesth 17:744, 2003

73. Charan NB, Carvalho CG, Hawk P, et al: Independent lung ventilation with a single ventilator using a variable resistance valve. Chest 107:256, 1995

74. Turnbull AD, Carlon G, Howland WS, et al: High-frequency jet ventilation in major airway or pulmonary disruption. Ann Thorac Surg 32:468, 1981

75. Wippermann CF, Schranz D, Baum V, et al: Independent right lung high frequency and left lung conventional ventilation in the management of severe air leak during ARDS. Paediatr Anaesth 5:189, 1995

76. Campbell D, Steinmann M, Porayko L: Nitric oxide and high frequency jet ventilation in a patient with bilateral bronchopleural fistulae and ARDS. Can J Anaesth 47:53, 2000

77. Crimi G, Candiani A, Conti G, et al: Clinical applications of independent lung ventilation with unilateral high-frequency jet ventilation (ILV-UHFJV). Intensive Care Med 12:90, 1986

78. Otruba Z, Oxorn D: Lobar bronchial blockade in bronchopleural fistula. Can J Anaesth 39:176, 1992

79. Watanabe S, Shimokawa S, Yotsumoto G, et al: The use of a Dumon stent for the treatment of a bronchopleural fistula. Ann Thorac Surg 72:276, 2001

80. Tayama K, Eriguchi N, Futamata Y, et al: Modified Dumon stent for the treatment of a bronchopleural fistula after pneumonectomy. Ann Thorac Surg 75:290, 2003

81. Lin J, Iannettoni MD: Closure of bronchopleural fistulas using albumin-glutaraldehyde tissue adhesive. Ann Thorac Surg 77:326, 2004

82. Glover W, Chavis TV, Daniel TM, et al: Fibrin glue application through the flexible fiberoptic bronchoscope: closure of bronchopleural fistulas. J Thorac Cardiovasc Surg 93:470, 1987

83. Tharratt RS, Allen RP, Albertson TE: Pressure controlled inverse ratio ventilation in severe adult respiratory failure. Chest 94:755, 1988

84. Wang SH, Wei TS: The outcome of early pressure-controlled inverse ratio ventilation on patients with severe acute respiratory distress syndrome in surgical intensive care unit. Am J Surg 183:151, 2002

85. Neumann P, Berglund JE, Andersson LG, et al: Effects of inverse ratio ventilation and positive end-expiratory pressure in oleic acid-induced lung injury. Am J Respir Crit Care Med 161:1537, 2000

86. Ludwigs U, Philip A: Pulmonary epithelial permeability and gas exchange: a comparison of inverse ratio ventilation and conventional mechanical ventilation in oleic acid-induced lung injury in rabbits. Chest 113:459, 1998

87. Huang CC, Shih MJ, Tsai YH, et al: Effects of inverse ratio ventilation versus positive end-expiratory pressure on gas exchange and gastric intramucosal PCO_2 and pH under constant mean airway pressure in acute respiratory distress syndrome. Anesthesiology 95:1182, 2001

88. Pelosi P, Brazzi L, Gattinoni L: Prone position in acute respiratory distress syndrome. Eur Respir J 20:1017, 2002

89. Kornecki A, Frndova H, Coates AL, et al: A randomized trial of prolonged prone positioning in children with acute respiratory failure. Chest 119:211, 2001

90. Gattinoni L, Tognoni G, Pesenti A, et al: Effect of prone positioning on the survival of patients with acute respiratory failure. N Engl J Med 345:568, 2001

91. Guerin C, Gaillard S, Lemasson S, et al: Effects of systematic prone positioning in hypoxemic acute respiratory failure: a randomized controlled trial. JAMA 292:2379, 2004

92. Staudinger T, Kofler J, Mullner M, et al: Comparison of prone positioning and continuous rotation of patients with adult respiratory distress syndrome: results of a pilot study. Crit Care Med 29:51, 2001

93. Bhuta T, Henderson-Smart DJ: Elective high-frequency oscillatory ventilation versus conventional ventilation in preterm infants with pulmonary dysfunction: systematic review and meta-analyses. Pediatrics 100:E6, 1997

94. Mehta S, Granton J, MacDonald RJ, et al: High-frequency oscillatory ventilation in adults: the Toronto experience. Chest 126:518, 2004

95. Mehta S, Lapinsky SE, Hallett DC, et al: Prospective trial of high-frequency oscillation in adults with acute respiratory distress syndrome. Crit Care Med 29:1360, 2001

96. Derdak S, Mehta S, Stewart TE, et al: High-frequency oscillatory ventilation for acute respiratory distress syndrome in adults: a randomized, controlled trial. Am J Respir Crit Care Med 166:801, 2002

97. Cartotto R, Ellis S, Gomez M, et al: High frequency oscillatory ventilation in burn patients with the acute respiratory distress syndrome. Burns 30:453, 2004

98. Fort P, Farmer C, Westerman J, et al: High-frequency oscillatory ventilation for adult respiratory distress syndrome—a pilot study. Crit Care Med 25:937, 1997

99. Wunsch H, Mapstone J: High-frequency ventilation versus conventional ventilation for treatment of acute lung injury and acute respiratory distress syndrome. Cochrane Database Syst Rev (1): CD004085, 2004

100. Garner W, Downs JB, Stock MC, et al: Airway pressure release ventilation (APRV): a human trial. Chest 94:779, 1988

101. Stock MC, Downs JB, Frolicher DA: Airway pressure release ventilation. Crit Care Med 15:462, 1987

102. Neumann P, Hedenstierna G: Ventilatory support by continuous positive airway pressure breathing improves gas exchange as compared with partial ventilatory support with airway pressure release ventilation. Anesth Analg 92:950, 2001

103. Martin LD, Wetzel RC, Bilenki AL: Airway pressure release ventilation in a neonatal lamb model of acute lung injury. Crit Care Med 19:373, 1991

104. Smith RA, Smith DB; Does airway pressure release ventilation alter lung function after acute lung injury? Chest 107:805, 1995

105. Rasanen J, Cane RD, Downs JB, et al: Airway pressure release ventilation during acute lung injury: a prospective multicenter trial. Crit Care Med 19:1234, 1991

106. Sydow M, Burchardi H, Ephraim E, et al: Long-term effects of two different ventilatory modes on oxygenation in acute lung injury: comparison of airway pressure release ventilation and volume-controlled inverse ratio ventilation. Am J Respir Crit Care Med 149:1550, 1994

107. Davis K Jr, Johnson DJ, Branson RD, et al: Airway pressure release ventilation. Arch Surg 128:1348, 1993

108. Kaplan LJ, Bailey H, Formosa V: Airway pressure release ventilation increases cardiac performance in patients with acute lung injury/adult respiratory distress syndrome. Crit Care 5:221, 2001

109. Hering R, Peters D, Zinserling J, et al: Effects of spontaneous breathing during airway pressure release ventilation on renal perfusion and function in patients with acute lung injury. Intensive Care Med 28:1426, 2002

110. Mehta S, Jay GD, Woolard RH, et al: Randomized, prospective trial of bilevel versus continuous positive airway pressure in acute pulmonary edema. Crit Care Med 25:620, 1997

111. Park M, Sangean MC, Volpe MdeS, et al: Randomized, prospective trial of oxygen, continuous positive airway pressure, and bilevel positive airway pressure by face mask in acute cardiogenic pulmonary edema. Crit Care Med 32:2407, 2004

112. Delclaux C, L'Her E, Alberti C, et al: Treatment of acute hypoxemic nonhypercapnic respiratory insufficiency with continuous positive airway pressure delivered by a face mask: a randomized controlled trial. JAMA 284:2352, 2000

113. Masip J, Betbese AJ, Paez J, et al: Non-invasive pressure support ventilation versus conventional oxygen therapy in acute cardiogenic pulmonary oedema: a randomised trial. Lancet 356:2126, 2000

114. Lenique F, Habis M, Lofaso F, et al: Ventilatory and hemodynamic effects of continuous positive airway pressure in left heart failure. Am J Respir Crit Care Med 155:500, 1997

115. Keenan SP, Sinuff T, Cook DJ, et al: Does noninvasive positive pressure ventilation improve outcome in acute hypoxemic respiratory failure? A systematic review. Crit Care Med 32:2516, 2004

116. Wood KA, Lewis L, Von Harz B, et al: The use of noninvasive positive pressure ventilation in the emergency department: results of a randomized clinical trial. Chest 113:1339, 1998

117. Esteban A, Frutos-Vivar F, Ferguson ND, et al: Noninvasive positive-pressure ventilation for respiratory failure after extubation. N Engl J Med 350:2452, 2004

118. Rossaint R, Falke KJ, Lopez F, et al: Inhaled nitric oxide for the adult respiratory distress syndrome. N Engl J Med 328:399, 1993

119. Dellinger RP, Zimmerman JL, Taylor RW, et al: Effects of inhaled nitric oxide in patients with acute respiratory distress syndrome: results of a randomized phase II trial. Inhaled Nitric Oxide in ARDS Study Group. Crit Care Med 26:15, 1998

120. Moncada S, Palmer RM, Higgs EA: Nitric oxide: physiology, pathophysiology, and pharmacology. Pharmacol Rev 43:109, 1991

121. Taylor RW, Zimmerman JL, Dellinger RP, et al: Low-dose inhaled nitric oxide in patients with acute lung injury: a randomized controlled trial. JAMA 291:1603, 2004

122. Krafft P, Fridrich P, Fitzgerald RD, et al: Effectiveness of nitric oxide inhalation in septic ARDS. Chest 109:486, 1996

123. Sokol J, Jacobs SE, Bohn D: Inhaled nitric oxide for acute hypoxic respiratory failure in children and adults: a meta-analysis. Anesth Analg 97:989, 2003

124. Fioretto JR, de Moraes MA, Bonatto RC, et al: Acute and sustained effects of early administration of inhaled nitric oxide to children with acute respiratory distress syndrome. Pediatr Crit Care Med 5:469, 2004

125. Johannigman JA, Davis K Jr, Miller SL, et al: Prone positioning and inhaled nitric oxide: synergistic therapies for acute respiratory distress syndrome. J Trauma 50:589, 2001

126. Varkul MD, Stewart TE, Lapinsky SE, et al: Successful use of combined high-frequency oscillatory ventilation, inhaled nitric oxide, and prone positioning in the acute respiratory distress syndrome. Anesthesiology 95:797, 2001

127. Mehta S, MacDonald R, Hallett DC, et al: Acute oxygenation response to inhaled nitric oxide when combined with high-frequency oscillatory ventilation in adults with acute respiratory distress syndrome. Crit Care Med 31:383, 2003

128. Hallman M, Spragg R, Harrell JH, et al: Evidence of lung surfactant abnormality in respiratory failure: study of bronchoalveolar lavage phospholipids, surface activity, phospholipase activity, and plasma myoinositol. J Clin Invest 70:673, 1982

129. Gunther A, Ruppert C, Schmidt R, et al: Surfactant alteration and replacement in acute respiratory distress syndrome. Respir Res 2:353, 2001

130. Anzueto A, Baughman RP, Guntupalli KK, et al: Aerosolized surfactant in adults with sepsis-induced acute respiratory distress syndrome. Exosurf Acute Respiratory Distress Syndrome Sepsis Study Group. N Engl J Med 334:1417, 1996

131. Spragg RG, Lewis JF, Walmrath HD, et al: Effect of recombinant surfactant protein C-based surfactant on the acute respiratory distress syndrome. N Engl J Med 351:884, 2004

132. Stolar CJ, Snedecor SM, Bartlett RH: Extracorporeal membrane oxygenation and neonatal respiratory failure: experience from the extracorporeal life support organization. J Pediatr Surg 26:563, 1991

133. Swaniker F, Kolla S, Moler F, et al: Extracorporeal life support outcome for 128 pediatric patients with respiratory failure. J Pediatr Surg 35:197, 2000

134. Kolla S, Awad SS, Rich PB, et al: Extracorporeal life support for 100 adult patients with severe respiratory failure. Ann Surg 226:544, 1997

135. Michaels AJ, Schriener RJ, Kolla S, et al: Extracorporeal life support in pulmonary failure after trauma. J Trauma 46:638, 1999

136. Hemmila MR, Rowe SA, Boules TN, et al: Extracorporeal life support for severe acute respiratory distress syndrome in adults. Ann Surg 240:595, 2004

Acknowledgment

Figures 1, 2, 4, 5, and 6   Seward Hung.

Sean M. Bagshaw, M.D., M.Sc., F.R.C.P.C., and Rinaldo Bellomo, M.D., F.R.A.C.P., F.J.F.I.C.M.

Acute renal failure (ARF) remains one of the major therapeutic challenges facing the modern physician. The term describes a syndrome characterized by a rapid decrease (occurring within hours to days) in the kidney's ability to eliminate waste products, regulate extracellular volume, and maintain electrolyte and acid-base homeostasis. This loss of excretory function is manifested clinically by the accumulation of end products of nitrogen metabolism (e.g., urea and creatinine). Other typical clinical manifestations include decreased urine output (which is not always present), the accumulation of nonvolatile acids, and an increased serum potassium concentration.

In the literature, the incidence of ARF has been variable, depending on the criteria used to define the condition. ARF has been reported to occur in approximately 5% to 8% of hospitalized patients and 15% to 30% of patients admitted to an intensive care unit. Despite the advances that have been made in understanding the pathophysiology of ARF and developing extracorporeal therapies, the mortality associated with this condition continues to be alarmingly high. Moreover, there is evidence to suggest that the mortality is even higher in patients with ARF that is severe enough to warrant initiation of renal replacement therapy (RRT).

The term acute tubular necrosis (ATN) has frequently been used in the context of ARF, but current evidence suggests that this term has limited clinical relevance, in that it describes only the histopathology and is not reliably linked with differences in patient management. The concept of ATN comes from animal models that do not accurately reflect clinical situations and from old biopsy data. Even in cases where the term seems appropriate, the so-called necrosis is frequently patchy and mostly isolated to the thick ascending loop of Henle. Furthermore, cells found in the urinary tubular casts of such patients are viable on staining studies, a finding that partly invalidates the use of the term necrosis.

General Principles

DEFINITION OF ACUTE RENAL FAILURE

A logical approach to organ failure might reasonably begin by defining what a particular organ does. In the case of the kidney, the list of functions is long. Many of these functions, however, are either shared with other organs (e.g., acid-base control, which is shared with the lung) or require complex neurohormonal interactions that involve other organs (e.g., the renin-angiotensin-aldosterone axis). Other renal functions are not routinely measured (e.g., small peptide excretion, tubular metabolism, and hormonal production).

There are only two functions that are routinely and easily measured in patients and are unique to the kidney: (1) production of urine and (2) excretion of waste products of nitrogen metabolism. Accordingly, clinicians have focused on these two functions in their efforts to define the presence of so-called ARF.

The two waste products whose levels are routinely measured in patients are urea and creatinine. The urea level is the one that is affected more by extrarenal factors (e.g., gastrointestinal blood, changes in nitrogen intake, and changes in protein catabolic rate) and that varies more rapidly. The creatinine level is a more reliable marker of the glomerular filtration rate (GFR) and is commonly used to define the presence or absence of ARF; however, it does not change in direct proportion to the loss of nephron mass and is not a real-time descriptor of the GFR. Nonetheless, using urea and creatinine levels to define ARF seems a practical and reasonable approach to the biochemical definition of this condition. The problem, however, is that in current practice, there are too many essentially arbitrary biochemical cutoff values for the definition of ARF. This point was highlighted by a review of 28 studies of postoperative ARF, in which each study used a different definition of this condition.[1] The lack of agreement on the operative definition of ARF has significantly hindered research in this field, especially with regard to the design and execution of randomized, controlled trials. In 2004, however, the work of the Acute Dialysis Quality Initiative (ADQI) (http://www.ADQI.net) led to the development and publication of a consensus definition of ARF. It is hoped that acceptance and use of this definition will lead to more consistent, reproducible, and generalizable results from epidemiologic and interventional studies of ARF [see Figure 1].[2]

ASSESSMENT OF RENAL FUNCTION

Waste Product Levels

As noted (see above), to establish that ARF is present, one must be able to measure renal function and detect that it has been altered; however, the complexity of renal function can make this a difficult undertaking. Accordingly, in the clinical context, monitoring of renal function is limited to indirect assessment of the GFR through measurement of urea and creatinine levels in blood. These levels are relatively inaccurate markers of GFR and are heavily influenced by patient age, patient sex, nutritional status, steroid use, and the presence of GI bleeding or muscle injury. Furthermore, they generally only become abnormal once the GFR has fallen by 50% or more; they do not reflect real-time dynamic changes in the GFR and can be grossly modified by aggressive fluid resuscitation. Determining creatinine clearance by means of 2-hour or 4-hour collections or calculating clearance by means of formulas adjusted for body weight, sex, or age may increase the accuracy of the results, but it rarely, if ever, changes clinical management. Sophisticated radionuclide-based tests are available, but they are cumbersome and are useful only for research purposes.

Urine Output

Urine output is a commonly measured parameter of renal function and often is more sensitive to changes in renal hemodynamics than biochemical markers of solute clearance are. However, urine output is also of limited sensitivity and specificity; some patients have severe ARF, as indicated by a markedly elevated serum creatinine level, while maintaining normal urine output (so-called nonoliguric ARF). Because nonoliguric ARF has a lower

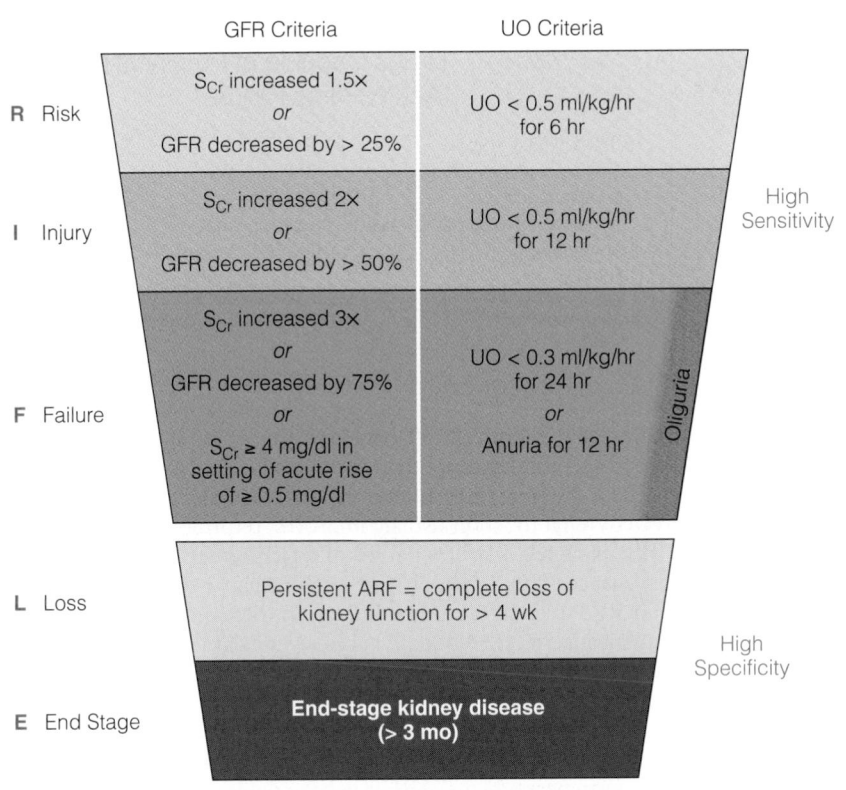

Figure 1 Depicted is the RIFLE (*R*isk, *I*njury, *F*ailure, *L*oss, *E*nd stage) classification scheme for ARF.[2] The classification system includes separate criteria for GFR and urine output (UO). Those criteria that lead to the worst possible classification of renal failure should be used. The designation RIFLE-F (for failure) is appropriate even if there is a less than threefold increase in the serum creatinine concentration (S_{Cr}), provided that the new S_{Cr} is higher than 4.0 mg/dl (350 µmol/L) in the setting of an acute increase of at least 0.5 mg/dl (44 µmol/L). In this case, the designation RIFLE-FC should be used to denote acute-on-chronic disease. Similarly, when the presence of renal failure (RIFLE-F) is determined on the basis of urine output criteria only, the designation RIFLE-FO should be used to denote oliguria. The shape of the figure illustrates the point that more patients are included in the mild category (top), including some who do not have renal failure (higher sensitivity, lower specificity). In the severe category (bottom), the criteria are strict and therefore specific, but some patients with renal dysfunction may be missed (higher specificity, lower sensitivity).

mortality than oliguric ARF, urine output is frequently used as a means of distinguishing varieties of ARF.[3] Classically, oliguria has been defined (approximately) as a urine output of less than 5 to 6 ml/kg/day or less than 0.5 ml/kg/hr. Often, changes in urine output can develop before biochemical changes in renal function become apparent.

Serum and Urine Biomarkers

Overall, it would be highly desirable to have markers of renal function that would enable physicians to diagnose true reductions in function associated with renal injury; the ability to diagnose such functional impairments would allow the identification of those patients in whom early intervention might be justified.

In the past few years, several serum and urine biomarkers have been developed for use in the detection of early renal dysfunction or injury. One such biomarker is cystatin C, a cysteine proteinase inhibitor of low molecular weight. This substance has many features that would make it an ideal tool for the assessment of renal function, especially its constant rate of production (which appears to be independent of any pathologic states), its exclusively renal excretion, and the good inverse correlation of its blood levels with radionuclide-derived measurements of the GFR.[4,5] Another biomarker is kidney injury molecule–1 (KIM-1), a transmembrane protein that is present in the proximal renal tubule and is markedly upregulated and excreted in the urine in response to injury.[6] Several other urinary biomarkers have been described that also appear to have potential for the detection of renal injury, including interleukin-18 (IL-18), Na^+/H^+ exchanger isoform 3 (NHE3), and neutrophil gelatinase-associated lipocalin (NGAL).[7-9]

These biomarkers are all promising; however, they are still relatively new, and thus, their roles in the diagnosis and management of ARF have not yet been assessed in large multicenter studies. At present, therefore, clinicians continue to rely on serum creatinine levels, plasma urea levels, and urine output as the three clinical pillars of the diagnosis of ARF. They accept and understand the inaccuracy of these tests because they recognize that in this setting, obtaining absolute values is less important than detecting change and identifying the direction of change.

CLASSIFICATION OF ACUTE RENAL FAILURE

The classification of ARF into clinically useful etiologic categories remains challenging and problematic, for several reasons. First, several of the test results that are time-honored and commonly cited classifiers of ARF—such as a relatively high fractional excretion of sodium (FE_{Na}), a high urinary sodium level, a low specific gravity, the presence of casts, and a relatively low urinary osmolality—have yet to be validated against a widely accepted definition of ARF or a gold-standard test. Second, these test results have not been characterized in blinded, controlled, or standardized studies. Third, classification of ARF on the basis of these test results has not been shown to alter either patient management or outcome. Nevertheless, despite their limitations, these test results are widely used in the literature to classify and define ARF.

Unfortunately, there is no easy solution to the problems associated with classification of ARF. Clearly, more research is necessary before our understanding of ARF reaches the point where more reliable and objective subdivisions can be created (as has been done with pneumonia). The comprehensive process initiated by the ADQI (see above) should facilitate such research.[2]

These classification difficulties notwithstanding, there does exist a practical and useful approach to stratifying patients presenting with ARF. Traditionally, ARF is classified according to the probable source of renal injury: prerenal, renal (parenchymal), or postrenal (obstructive) [*see Table 1*].

Prerenal

Prerenal ARF is by far the most common type of ARF. The term prerenal typically indicates that the kidney is malfunctioning predominantly as a result not of reasons intrinsic to the kidney but of systemic factors, which, through variable mechanisms, can alter renal blood flow (RBF) or intraglomerular hemodynamics and result in a decrease in GFR.

Clinicians frequently use terms such as prerenal azotemia or prerenal ARF to indicate not only that the cause or trigger of ARF is external to the renal parenchyma but also that a given patient has functional loss of GFR (i.e., loss of GFR without structural cell injury) as opposed to structural loss. In cases of suspected structural injury to the kidney, they typically use the term ATN instead. This clinical distinction probably does not reflect a true difference between two separate pathophysiologic states; more likely, these states simply represent two different points on a continuum of renal injury. Furthermore, no biopsy studies of ARF in patients treated in the ICU have been conducted to demonstrate that so-called ATN is the histopathologic basis of prolonged renal dysfunction.[10]

Common systemic causes of ARF include a low cardiac output state (e.g., myocardial infarction, tamponade, or valvular disease), cardiac surgery, major vascular surgery, trauma with hypovolemia, shock of any type (anaphylactic, hemorrhagic, or hypovolemic), hemodynamic instability associated with surgery, hepatic failure, increased intra-abdominal pressure, intra-abdominal hypertension, and rhabdomyolysis.[3,11] The mechanisms by which these events induce ARF vary according to the causative trigger and are poorly understood; however, they are likely to be complex and to involve multiple pathways of renal injury. By far the most significant systemic factors contributing to ARF in developed countries

Table 1   Differential Diagnosis of Acute Renal Failure

Probable Source of Renal Injury	Differential Diagnosis
Prerenal	States of low cardiac output (myocardial, valvular, pericardial, or arrhythmic disease; pulmonary hypertension; pulmonary embolism; mechanical ventilation) States of decreased intravascular volume (dehydration; hemorrhage; burns; GI losses from vomiting, diarrhea, or surgery; renal losses from diuretics, osmotic diuresis, or diabetes insipidus) States of low systemic vasodilation (sepsis or septic shock; anaphylaxis; drugs; HRS) States of altered renal hemodynamics (from antiprostaglandin agents, ACE inhibitors, or exogenous vasopressors)
Renal (parenchymal)	Glomerulonephritis or vasculitis Renovascular disease (renal artery or vein occlusion; malignant hypertension) Exposure to toxins, either endogenous (myoglobin; hemoglobin; uric acid) or exogenous (radiocontrast media; antimicrobials; chemotherapeutic agents; immunosuppressive agents; ethylene glycol) Interstitial nephritis (from antimicrobials, diuretics, malignancy, or infection) Tubular deposition or obstruction (from bilateral cortical necrosis, multiple myeloma, or amyloidosis) Renal allograft rejection Trauma
Postrenal (obstructive)	Obstruction of ureter (from compression or kinking of ureters or pelvicaliceal area, calculi, malignancy, or external compression [e.g., retroperitoneal fibrosis]) Obstruction of bladder (from prostatic hypertrophy, calculi, malignancy, blood clot, or neurogenic bladder) Obstruction of urethra (from stricture, phimosis, or trauma)

ACE—angiotensin-converting enzyme   HRS—hepatorenal syndrome

Table 2   Drugs Capable of Precipitating Acute Renal Failure

Radiocontrast media	ACE inhibitors
Aminoglycosides	Methotrexate
β-Lactam antibiotics	Cisplatin
Trimethoprim-sulfamethoxazole	Cyclosporine
Amphotericin	FK-506 (tacrolimus)
NSAIDs	

ACE—angiotensin-converting enzyme   NSAIDs—nonsteroidal anti-inflammatory drugs

(especially in critically ill patients) are sepsis and septic shock, which account for more than 50% of all cases of ARF.[12-14]

If the systemic cause of prerenal ARF is rapidly removed or corrected, renal function usually improves, returning to near-normal or baseline levels over a period of days. If intervention is delayed or unsuccessful, however, renal injury can become established, and RRT may have to be initiated. In these circumstances, if the patient survives, it frequently takes several days or weeks to achieve renal recovery with independence from RRT.[13,15-17]

Parenchymal

Parenchymal ARF is generally less common than prerenal ARF. The term parenchymal ARF is used to define a syndrome in which the principal source of damage is within the kidney and in which typical structural changes can be seen on microscopy. This syndrome can result from any of a number of disorders that affect the microvasculature, the glomerulus, the tubules, or the interstitium [see Table 1].

Nephrotoxic drugs are a particularly important cause of parenchymal ARF, especially in hospitalized patients.[3,11] Many patients with drug-induced ARF show rapid improvement once the offending agent is removed. The drugs most commonly implicated in the development of ARF are aminoglycosides, penicillin or penicillin derivatives, nonsteroidal anti-inflammatory drugs (NSAIDs), trimethoprim-sulfamethoxazole, amphotericin B, cyclosporine, chemotherapeutic agents, and angiotensin-converting enzyme (ACE) inhibitors [see Table 2].[11] Not uncommonly, patients may be receiving several potentially nephrotoxic drugs concurrently. Accordingly, in all patients with ARF, a thorough history of drug administration is mandatory.

Other conditions that can cause parenchymal ARF include glomerulonephritis, vasculitis, interstitial nephropathy, malignant hypertension, pelvicaliceal infection, bilateral cortical necrosis, amyloidosis, and trauma.

Postrenal

Obstruction to urine outflow gives rise to postrenal ARF, which is the most common cause of functional renal impairment in the community (i.e., in nonhospitalized patients) and is usually secondary to prostatic hypertrophy. Obstructive ARF is also seen in hospitalized patients, albeit less commonly; typical causes in this population include prostatic hypertrophy, pelvic tumors, retroperitoneal fibrosis, papillary necrosis, and large calculi [see Table 1].

The clinical presentation of obstruction may be acute or acute-on-chronic in patients with long-standing renal calculi; oliguria is not always present. If obstruction is suspected, ultrasonography can be easily performed at the bedside. However, in some cases of acute obstruction, the ultrasonogram is abnormal, and in many cases, the obstruction occurs in conjunction with other renal insults (e.g., staghorn calculi and severe sepsis of renal origin), so that the renal dysfunction is actually caused by a combination of factors.

Specific Syndromes

Hepatorenal syndrome Hepatorenal syndrome (HRS) is a form of ARF that typically occurs in the setting of advanced cirrhosis but can also occur in the setting of severe liver dysfunction caused by alcoholic hepatitis or in association with other forms of acute hepatic failure.[18]

The pathophysiologic hallmark of HRS is profound renal vasoconstriction in the setting of systemic and splanchnic vasodilation. The pathogenesis of HRS is incompletely understood; however, there are several mechanisms that may contribute to its development, including (1) activation of the renin-angiotensin system in response to systemic hypotension; (2) activation of the sympathetic nervous system in response to systemic hypotension and increased intrahepatic sinusoidal pressure; (3) increased release of arginine vasopressin in response to systemic hypotension; and (4) reduced hepatic clearance of various vascular mediators (e.g., endothelin, prostaglandins, and endotoxin).[18,19]

HRS can occur spontaneously in patients with advanced cirrhosis. Much more frequently, however, it is caused by other precipitating conditions, including sepsis (specifically, spontaneous bacterial peritonitis), paracentesis-induced hypovolemia, elevated intraabdominal pressure (from tense ascites), GI bleeding, diuretic-induced or lactulose-induced hypovolemia, and various combinations of these. Other contributing factors to ARF should be routinely sought, including cardiomyopathy related to alcoholism, nutritional deficiencies, viral infection, and exposure to nephrotoxins.

Typically, HRS patients have advanced cirrhosis and show evidence of portal hypertension with ascites in the absence of other apparent causes of ARF. They generally are oligoanuric, with progressive increases in serum creatinine or blood urea nitrogen levels and bland urinary sediment. These patients experience profound sodium and water retention, with significant hyponatremia, a urine osmolality higher than the plasma osmolality, and a very low urinary sodium concentration (< 10 mEq/L).

Rhabdomyolysis-associated ARF Rhabdomyolysis-induced ARF is estimated to occur in about 1% of hospitalized patients; however, it may account for close to 5% to 7% of cases of ARF in critically ill patients, depending on the setting.[11,14,20] The pathogenesis of this condition involves the interplay of prerenal, parenchymal, and postrenal factors, including concurrent hypovolemia, renal ischemia, direct tubular toxicity mediated by the heme pigment in myoglobin, and intratubular obstruction.[21,22]

The causes of muscle injury that can result in rhabdomyolysis include major trauma or compression, a drug overdose, vascular embolism, prolonged seizures, malignant hyperthermia, neuroleptic malignant syndrome, various infections (e.g., pyomyositis, necrotizing fasciitis, influenza, and HIV infection), severe exertion, alcoholism, and certain drug interactions (e.g., the combination of a macrolide antibiotic or cyclosporine with a statin).

Clinically, rhabdomyolysis is variably manifested by an elevated serum creatine kinase level, pigmented granular urinary casts, and a red-to-brown color in the urine. Various electrolyte disorders may also develop as a result of muscle breakdown, including hyperphosphatemia, hyperkalemia, hypocalcemia, and hyperuricemia.

Contrast-induced nephropathy Contrast-induced nephropathy (CIN) is currently the third most frequent cause of ARF in hospitalized patients, and its incidence is likely to increase further with the broader utilization of radiocontrast media for diagnostic and interventional procedures.[3,11] CIN results in prolonged hospitalization, higher mortality, excessive health care costs, and, possibly, long-term kidney impairment.[23-25] In addition, CIN (or concerns regarding the risk of CIN) may result in delay or cancellation of important diagnostic or therapeutic procedures.

Experimental studies suggest that the pathophysiologic basis of CIN is the interplay among direct tubular epithelial cell toxicity, alterations in renal hemodynamics with ensuing ischemia, and concomitant atheroembolic showers of the renovasculature after procedures involving exposure to radiocontrast media.

Several different definitions of CIN appear in the literature. Generally, however, CIN is defined as an acute decline in kidney function occurring after the administration of intravascular radiocontrast media in the absence of other precipitants of renal dysfunction. Although it may seem obvious that CIN is the cause of the renal dysfunction, other important possible causes (e.g., atheroembolic disease, renal ischemia, and other nephrotoxic agents) should be considered before the diagnosis is made.[26] For research purposes and for better generalizability of results and outcomes across clinical studies, CIN has traditionally been defined as a 25% or greater (or ≥ 0.5 mg/dl [44 μmol/L]) increase in the serum creatinine level from the baseline value.[27,28]

Patients with CIN typically present with an acute rise in the serum creatinine level within 24 to 48 hours after injection of a radiocontrast agent. Oliguria is usually absent, and FE_{Na} may be low initially.[29] Urine studies may reveal granular brown casts, tubular epithelial cells, and minimal proteinuria (< 300 mg/day). The presentation may vary, however. In some cases, there is no significant increase in the serum creatinine level, but urinalysis yields abnormal results or markers of renal tubular injury are present. In other cases, there is a clear increase in the serum creatinine level, but results of urinalysis are bland and nondiagnostic. As a rule, the serum creatinine level peaks within 3 to 5 days after radiocontrast injection and returns to baseline within 7 to 10 days. In some patients, however, kidney function does not return to baseline, and a degree of renal impairment persists.

Although transient declines in renal function have been reported after administration of radiocontrast media in almost all patients, clinically important declines are exceedingly uncommon in patients with normal baseline kidney function. In general, clinically important declines in renal function are associated with the presence of preexisting risk factors. In several epidemiologic studies, multivariate analyses suggested that the presence of preexisting chronic kidney disease (GFR < 60 ml/min/1.73 m²), a diagnosis of diabetes mellitus, the administration of a substantial quantity of radiocontrast media, the presence of hypotension or hypertension, increased age, anemia, a recent acute myocardial infarction, a history of congestive heart failure, the use of an intra-aortic balloon pump, and the presence of shock were independently associated with a risk of the development of CIN.[30-34]

Clinical Evaluation

In all patients presenting with renal failure, it is important to determine whether the reduction in kidney function is truly acute or whether chronic kidney disease was already present. In this context, it is worth noting that more than one third of patients in whom ARF develops have some degree of preexisting chronic kidney disease with chronic parenchymal changes (e.g., as a result of aging, long-standing hypertension, diabetes, or atheromatous disease of the renal vessels). Such patients may also have preexisting elevations of the serum creatinine concentration; however, this is

Table 3 Laboratory Tests Used to Help Diagnose Established Acute Renal Failure

Test	Result in Prerenal ARF	Result in Established ARF
Urine sediment	Normal	Epithelial casts
Specific gravity	> 1.020	< 1.020
U_{Na}	< 10 mEq/L	> 20 mEq/L
FE_{Na}	< 1%	> 1%
Urinary osmolality	> 500 mOsm/kg H_2O	< 300 mOsm/kg H_2O
U_{Cr}/P_{Cr} ratio	> 40	< 10
Plasma urea/ creatinine ratio	High	Normal

ARF—acute renal failure FE_{Na}—fractional excretion of sodium P_{Cr}—plasma creatinine concentration U_{Cr}—urinary creatinine concentration U_{Na}—urinary sodium concentration

not always the case. Often, an insult that would be considered relatively trivial and incapable of fully explaining the onset of ARF in a normal patient is in fact sufficient to unmask a lack of renal functional reserve in another patient.

In general, diagnosis and management of ARF should always be based on four principles: (1) confirmation of the probable cause, (2) elimination of potential contributing factors, (3) institution of disease-specific therapy if appropriate, and (4) prevention and management of the complications of ARF.

In most cases, important clues to the cause of ARF in a given patient and an accurate working diagnosis can be obtained from a careful review of the medical record (with particular attention to medications administered, exposure to potential nephrotoxins, and recent events in the hospital, including any operative or other procedures undergone), in conjunction with physical examination and selected radiologic and laboratory investigations [see Investigative Studies, *below*]. In these cases, one can proceed to a therapeutic trial without having to resort to renal biopsy.

An important caveat in the workup of a patient with ARF is that one should not assume that ARF can always be correctly or simply attributed to a single mechanism. As an example, patients with postrenal obstruction frequently have some degree of sepsis, often are hypotensive, and sometimes are hypovolemic and underresuscitated. As another example, patients with crescentic glomerulonephritis are often systemically unwell and may have pulmonary disease with hypoxemia or hypotension (from volume depletion caused by inadequate oral intake or from the vasodilatory effect of inflammation). The possibility that several mechanisms can contribute to ARF in a single patient underscores the importance of careful clinical assessment in the approach to the patient with ARF of recent onset.

ARF patients frequently are critically ill and require admission to an ICU. Such patients often have sustained a major systemic insult. Upon transfer and admission to the ICU, fluid resuscitation either is well under way or has already been completed. Despite such efforts, patients often are profoundly oliguric or anuric, with a rising serum creatinine level and developing metabolic acidosis. Potassium and phosphate levels may be rising as well. Concomitant multiple organ dysfunction (signaled by the need for mechanical ventilation and vasoactive drugs) is common in ARF patients. Fluid resuscitation is typically continued or reinstituted under the guidance of invasive hemodynamic monitoring. Vasoactive drugs

are often used to restore mean arterial pressure (MAP) to acceptable levels (typically, 70 to 75 mm Hg or higher). Improvement may be noted over time, and urine output may return, with or without the assistance of diuretic agents. If urine output does not return, however, early implementation of RRT should be considered. If the cause of ARF has been removed or resolved and the patient has become physiologically stable, renal recovery may occur slowly, over a period as short as 4 to 5 days or as long as 3 or 4 weeks. In some cases, even after renal recovery occurs, urine output continues to be higher than normal for several days. If the cause of ARF has not been adequately remedied, the patient remains gravely ill, the kidneys do not recover, and death from multiple organ dysfunction syndrome (MODS) commonly ensues.

Investigative Studies

As noted (see above), it is vital to identify the underlying condition or conditions responsible for ARF. The diagnosis may be obvious from the results of the clinical assessment; however, in many patients, it is best to consider all possibilities and to exclude common treatable causes by performing some simple investigative studies.

LABORATORY TESTS

A key study is microscopic examination of the urinary sediment. Urinalysis is an essential and simple noninvasive test that can yield important diagnostic information and highlight patterns suggestive of specific syndromes. For example, the finding of dysmorphic red blood cells (RBCs) or RBC casts is virtually diagnostic of active glomerulonephritis or vasculitis. Similarly, the finding of heavy proteinuria suggests some form of glomerular disease. The finding of white blood cell (WBC) casts can suggest either interstitial nephropathy or infection. A urinalysis that yields no abnormal findings can also provide important diagnostic information, suggesting that ARF is prerenal or obstructive. Finally, examination of the urine helps the clinician determine whether a urinary tract infection is present.

Several measures of urine and blood biochemistry have traditionally been used to help clinicians distinguish between prerenal ARF and so-called ATN or established ARF [see Table 3]. One such measure is the FE_{Na}.[35,36] In the setting of prerenal ARF, filtered sodium is avidly reabsorbed from glomerular filtrate in the renal tubules, resulting in an FE_{Na} lower than 1%, whereas in the setting of renal tubular injury in established ARF, the resulting FE_{Na} is higher than 1%. However, the diagnostic utility of FE_{Na} has been questioned, and several reports have concluded that FE_{Na} must be interpreted with caution.[37,38] For example, FE_{Na} is often higher than 1% in patients who have received diuretic therapy, regardless of the effective circulating volume (ECV).[39,40] Furthermore, FE_{Na} may be lower than 1% in patients with conditions associated with parenchymal ARF (e.g., sepsis, rhabdomyolysis, and exposure to radiocontrast media), perhaps reflecting nonhomogeneous injury to the renal parenchyma and preservation of tubular function in some regions.[41-43]

Overall, the clinical utility of these tests in hospitalized and critically ill patients who receive fluids in massive amounts, loop diuretics, or vasopressors is untested and questionable. Furthermore, it is important to keep in mind that, as noted [see Classification of Renal Failure, *above*], prerenal ARF and established ARF are part of a continuum of disease and that separating the two conditions, though conceptually valid, is of only limited clinical relevance. In general terms, therapy is the same for prerenal ARF as for established ARF: one treats the underlying cause while promptly resuscitating the patient, using hemodynamic monitoring to guide therapy.

In certain circumstances, other laboratory investigations may be necessary to establish the diagnosis. Marked anemia in the absence of blood loss may suggest acute hemolysis, thrombotic microangiopathy, or paraproteinemia related to malignancy. If thrombotic-thrombocytopenic purpura or another cause of microangiopathic hemolytic anemia is suspected, a peripheral blood smear should be obtained and examined for evidence of hemolysis or schistocytes, and levels of lactic dehydrogenase, haptoglobin, unconjugated bilirubin, and free hemoglobin should be measured. If paraproteinemia from multiple myeloma or lymphoma is suspected, serum and urine protein electrophoresis should be done and the serum calcium concentration measured. A history of cancer or chemotherapy should prompt measurement of uric acid to detect possible tumor lysis syndrome.

In patients with a potential mechanism of muscle injury, creatine kinase and free myoglobin levels should be determined. If an elevated–anion gap metabolic acidosis is present and there is evidence that a toxin may have been ingested, ethylene glycol or methanol levels should be measured.

Systemic eosinophilia suggests the possibility of systemic vasculitis, allergic interstitial nephritis, or atheroembolic disease. Measurements of levels of specific antibodies (e.g., anti–glomerular basement membrane [GBM] antibodies, antineutrophil cytoplasmic antibodies [ANCAs], antinuclear antibodies [ANAs], anti-DNA antibodies, or anti–smooth muscle antibodies) or cryoglobulins are extremely useful screening tests to support the diagnosis of vasculitis, certain types of collagen vascular diseases, or glomerulonephritis.

IMAGING

Renal ultrasonography is a rapid, noninvasive imaging modality that is designed primarily to look for evidence of obstruction, stones, cysts, masses, or overt renovascular disease. Doppler ultrasonography or magnetic resonance imaging can be useful in screening for renovascular occlusion. A chest x-ray may be indicated, either to assess possible pulmonary complications of ARF or to help confirm or rule out a diagnosis of systemic vasculitis.

BIOPSY

On rare occasions, percutaneous renal biopsy is necessary to confirm the diagnosis, determine the severity of renal injury, guide therapy, and estimate the potential for renal recovery.[44,45] Renal biopsy is indicated when a thorough noninvasive investigation has failed to yield the diagnosis, after prerenal and postrenal causes have been excluded, and before aggressive immunosuppressive therapy is initiated. The biopsy is generally performed under ultrasonographic guidance, using local anesthesia. As a rule, the risk associated with performing a renal biopsy in a critically ill patient undergoing mechanical ventilation is comparable to that associated with performing a biopsy under standard conditions.[46]

Prevention

GENERAL MEASURES

The fundamental principle of ARF prevention is to eliminate and treat precipitating causes of renal dysfunction. If prerenal factors are contributing to the problem, they must be identified, and hemodynamic resuscitation must be quickly instituted. Intravascular volume must be maintained or rapidly restored; this is often best done with the help of invasive hemodynamic monitoring. Oxygenation must be maintained. An adequate hemoglobin con-

centration (≥ 8 g/dl) must be maintained or immediately restored during the acute phase of resuscitation. Some patients remain hypotensive (MAP < 75 mm Hg) even after intravascular volume has been restored. In these patients, autoregulation of RBF may be impaired or lost. Restoration of MAP to near-normal levels is likely to improve RBF and increase GFR. Such restoration requires the administration of vasopressor drugs. In patients with hypertension or renovascular disease, a MAP of 75 to 80 mm Hg may still be inadequate.

Despite these measures, progressive ARF may still develop in patients whose cardiac output is inadequate. To improve cardiac output may require a variety of interventions, such as the addition of inotropic drugs or the application of ventricular assist devices. Whether additional fluid therapy in a patient with normal or increased cardiac output and adequate blood pressure provides any significant renal protection is questionable; such therapy may in fact contribute to excess accumulation of extravascular fluid, resulting in pulmonary edema.

Once hemodynamic resuscitation has been accomplished and nephrotoxins removed, it is unclear whether additional pharmacologic measures provide any further benefit to the kidneys. So-called renal-dose (or low-dose) dopamine therapy is still frequently used. There is little evidence that this regimen is effective in critically ill patients[47-49]; however, dopamine is a tubular diuretic that occasionally increases urine output,[50] and the increased output may be incorrectly interpreted as an increase in GFR.[51] A large phase III trial that examined the use of low-dose dopamine in critically ill patients showed it to be no better than placebo for prevention of renal dysfunction.[52] In patients with low cardiac output, however, higher-dose dopamine may increase cardiac output, RBF, and GFR (as might dobutamine or milrinone).

Fenoldopam is a selective D_1 dopamine receptor agonist with no affinity for adrenergic D_2, α, or β receptors. It has been shown to reduce systemic vascular resistance while increasing RBF through reversal of the vasoconstrictive effects of angiotensin II and endothelin.[53] Fenoldopam improves both renal cortical and renal medullary blood flow and decreases sodium reabsorption in the proximal tubule.[54] In a randomized, controlled trial of prophylactic continuous infusion of fenoldopam in critically ill patients with sepsis, this measure led to a reduction in the incidence of ARF; however, it had no impact on the need for RRT or on mortality.[55] At present, the clinical implications of this study are uncertain; a clearer understanding of the role of fenoldopam prophylaxis will have to await the results of a larger clinical trial.

There is a biologic rationale for the use of mannitol in this setting, as there is for the use of dopamine. Whereas animal experiments have yielded some encouraging findings, there are as yet no data from controlled human studies to support the clinical application of mannitol.[56] The value of mannitol as a renal-protective agent remains questionable.

Loop diuretics may protect the loop of Henle from ischemia by reducing its transport-related workload through inhibition of the $Na^+/K^+/2 Cl^-$ pump.[57] The results of animal studies have been encouraging, as have those of ex vivo experiments.[58] To date, however, no double-blind, randomized, controlled studies of suitable size have definitively shown that these agents reduce the incidence of ARF in humans.[59-62] A few studies, however, have suggested that loop diuretics can induce polyuria, which may translate into prevention or easier control of volume overload, metabolic acidosis, and hyperkalemia—the three major triggers of RRT.[59,60] When RRT can be avoided, treatment is simpler and less costly. Thus, loop diuretics may be useful for the purposes of prophylaxis, especially if given via continuous infusion.[63,64]

Other agents, such as adenosine antagonists (e.g., theophylline) and atrial natriuretic peptides (e.g., urodilatin and anaritide), have also been suggested for prevention of ARF.[65-68] In a randomized, controlled trial that included 504 critically ill patients with ARF, administration of atrial natriuretic peptide did not yield any overall improvement in dialysis-free survival.[66] Subgroup analysis suggested that this measure was of some benefit in patients with oliguric ARF; however, a follow-up study of 222 critically ill patients with oliguric ARF found no differences in dialysis-free survival or overall mortality between those who received atrial natriuretic peptide and those who received placebo.[67]

SPECIFIC SYNDROMES

Rhabdomyolysis-Associated ARF

The principles of prevention of rhabdomyolysis-associated ARF are based primarily on animal studies, retrospective data, small case series, and multivariate logistic regression analyses; to date, no randomized, controlled trials have been conducted. These principles include (1) identification and elimination of potential causative agents or correction of underlying compartment syndromes; (2) prompt and aggressive fluid resuscitation to restore vascular volume and maintenance of polyuria (> 300 ml/hr) to flush obstructing cellular casts (if present); and (3) alkalinization of the urine (to a pH > 6.5) to reduce renal toxicity from myoglobin-induced lipid peroxidation and improve the solubility of myoglobin.[22] Experimental studies suggest that mannitol may act as a scavenger of free radicals and thereby reduce cellular toxicity; however, the role of forced diuresis with mannitol remains controversial.

Contrast-Induced Nephropathy

Measures aimed at preventing CIN have been studied in several randomized trials; to date, however, few prophylactic or therapeutic interventions have conclusively been shown to reduce the incidence of CIN, and no therapeutic intervention has been found to be efficacious once CIN is established. The most prudent method of preventing CIN is to identify patients with risk factors before radiocontrast media are administered, then to consider either delaying the diagnostic or interventional procedure until kidney function can be optimized or switching to an alternative imaging modality. At the same time, every effort should be made to identify and correct underlying volume depletion and discontinue potential nephrotoxins. If the procedure is performed, the volume of radiocontrast media employed should be kept to a minimum.

The adoption of periprocedural hydration protocols and the use of nonionic iso-osmolar radiocontrast media (e.g., iodixanol) have reduced the incidence and severity of radiocontrast-associated renal injury.[69-72] In the first few years of the 21st century, randomized trials assessed the efficacy of *N*-acetylcysteine for the prevention of CIN, with highly variable results.[73-82] These results were further analyzed in several meta-analyses, which concluded that there appears to be a potential reduction in renal injury with *N*-acetylcysteine (though this conclusion remains controversial).[83-87] It is reasonable to use *N*-acetylcysteine for prevention of CIN in routine care, in view of its relative ease of use, its low cost, and its good safety profile, especially in patients at high risk for CIN. There is also some evidence to suggest that adenosine antagonists may confer some protection against CIN; however, further evidence is required to confirm that the benefit is real.[88,89]

Management

The fundamental principles of the management of ARF are (1) to identify, treat, and remove any precipitating factors and (2) to maintain physiologic homeostasis while renal recovery takes place.

PREVENTION OR TREATMENT OF COMPLICATIONS

Complications of ARF such as encephalopathy, pericarditis, severe electrolyte disturbances (e.g., hyperkalemia), serious metabolic disturbances (e.g., severe metabolic acidosis), myopathy, neuropathy, or major fluid derangements should never be permitted to occur in a modern hospital setting. Prevention of these complications may entail several different measures, which may vary in complexity from fluid restriction to the initiation of extracorporeal RRT.

Extracellular fluid expansion is a common complication in patients with ARF, particularly in those who have a diminished capacity for sodium and water excretion as a consequence of oliguria. Accumulation of extracellular fluid is manifested by weight gain, dependent interstitial edema, elevated central venous pressure, pleural effusion and ascites, and pulmonary interstitial and alveolar edema. Extracellular fluid overload can be further exacerbated in patients who require large volumes of parenteral medications or nutritional formulas. If a patient is nonoliguric, fluid overload can generally be prevented through judicious use of loop diuretics. If a patient is oliguric, however, the only way of averting dangerous fluid overload is to institute RRT at an early stage.

Marked azotemia (urea concentration > 112 mg/dl [40 mmol/L] or serum creatinine concentration > 4.5 mg/dl [400 μmol/L]) is undesirable and should probably be treated with RRT unless (1) recovery is imminent or already under way and (2) a return toward baseline or normal values is expected within 24 hours. It should be recognized, however, that to date, no randomized, controlled trials have defined the ideal time at which intervention with artificial renal support should be initiated.

Hyperkalemia (potassium concentration > 6 mEq/L) is another frequent complication of ARF. Obviously, patients with ARF and oliguria should never receive any potassium-containing solution, either orally or via continuous infusion. Spurious hyperkalemia secondary to hemolysis, thrombocytosis, and a very high WBC count may occur and must be excluded. Genuine hyperkalemia must be promptly treated to prevent the development of a life-threatening cardiac dysrhythmia. Patients should receive insulin with dextrose, bicarbonate (if acidosis is present), nebulized salbutamol, or all three together. If the serum potassium level exceeds 7 mEq/L or there are electrocardiographic signs of hyperkalemia, calcium gluconate (10 ml of a 10% solution I.V.) should also be immediately administered. These measures are temporizing actions only; urgent RRT should be arranged.

Metabolic acidosis is almost always present as a consequence of reduced excretion of nonvolatile acids produced through metabolism of dietary protein. In itself, the metabolic acidosis is rarely severe enough to necessitate treatment, but it can be greatly exacerbated by a host of concomitant processes when the kidney's capacity for generation of bicarbonate is diminished. Increased endogenous production of acid can occur in all types of shock, with elevated lactate production, severe sepsis, diabetic or starvation ketoacidosis, and liver disease. In addition, various exogenous sources can worsen metabolic acidosis, including toxins (e.g., ethylene glycol and salicylates) and solutions containing large amounts of chloride. When refractory severe metabolic acidosis (pH < 7.1) is present, early initiation of RRT should be considered.

ARF can also result in the development of anemia via any of several mechanisms, including bleeding, hemodilution, hemolysis, decreased RBC lifespan, and reduced erythropoiesis. One large randomized study suggested that a restrictive transfusion protocol for correction of hemoglobin levels higher than 7 g/dl in critically ill patients with anemia is adequate.[90] However, more liberal and aggressive transfusion may be necessary, depending on the results of individual patient assessments.

Nutritional support must be started early and must contain an adequate amount of calories (30 to 35 kcal/kg/day) in a mixture of carbohydrates and lipids. Sufficient protein (about 1 to 2 g/kg/day) must be administered. There is no evidence that specific renal nutritional solutions are useful. Vitamins and trace elements should be administered in amounts that at least match the recommended dietary allowance. The role of the newer immunonutritional solutions remains controversial. The enteral route is generally preferred to the parenteral route.

All drug regimens must be adjusted to take into account the effect of the decreased clearances associated with impaired renal function. Finally, assiduous attention should be paid to the prevention of infection.

MANAGEMENT OF HEPATORENAL SYNDROME

Management of HRS remains challenging. In general, it should include systematic identification and prompt treatment of any potentially reversible precipitating factors (especially infections and volume depletion). Prevention of hypovolemia by administering albumin to patients with spontaneous bacterial peritonitis has been shown to decrease the incidence of HRS and improve outcome.[91]

One small nonrandomized study found that treating HRS patients with a combination of midodrine and octreotide resulted in improved kidney function and outcome.[92] Another small uncontrolled study suggested that I.V. N-acetylcysteine might improve GFR in patients with HRS through reductions in splanchnic vasodilatation achieved by decreasing the formation of nitric oxide and oxygen free radicals.[93]

There is some evidence to suggest that vasopressin derivatives (ornipressin and terlipressin) may improve GFR in patients with HRS. In a small uncontrolled trial, administration of ornipressin, in conjunction with volume expansion, reduced plasma renin and norepinephrine levels and improved RBF, GFR, and urinary sodium excretion.[94] In other small studies, the combination of terlipressin and volume expansion led to similar improvements in systemic hemodynamics and kidney function, with a suggestion of improved short-term outcome.[95,96] At present, however, the precise role of these agents in the management of HRS remains unclear.

Transjugular intrahepatic portosystemic shunting (TIPS) [see 52 Portal Hypertension] has been associated with modest improvements in kidney function in HRS patients, may improve outcome, and thus may be an option for patients who are not candidates for transplantation or are awaiting transplantation.[97-99] In general, however, the ideal solution for reversal of ARF in HRS patients is to improve hepatic function by treating the underlying primary liver disease, to refer patients for orthotopic liver transplantation, or both.

RENAL REPLACEMENT THERAPY

When ARF is severe, resolution can take days to weeks. In these situations, extracorporeal techniques of blood purification often must be applied to prevent complications [see Prevention or Treatment of Complications, above]. Such techniques, collectively referred to as renal replacement therapy, include continuous renal replacement therapy (CRRT), intermittent hemo-

---

Table 4 Modern Criteria for Initiation of Renal Replacement Therapy*

Anuria (no urine output for ≥ 6 hr)
Oliguria (urine output < 200 ml/12 hr)
Serum urea concentration > 28 mmol/L or BUN > 80 mg/dl
Serum creatinine concentration > 3 mg/dl (265 μmol/L)
Serum potassium concentration ≥ 6.5 mEq/L or rapidly rising
Pulmonary edema unresponsive to diuretics
Uncompensated refractory metabolic acidosis (pH < 7.1)
Any uremic complication (encephalopathy, myopathy, neuropathy, or pericarditis)
Temperature ≥ 40° C (104° F)
Overdose with a dialyzable toxin (e.g., lithium or salicylates)

*If one criterion is met, RRT should be considered. If two criteria are met simultaneously, RRT is strongly recommended.
BUN—blood urea nitrogen

---

dialysis (IHD), and peritoneal dialysis (PD). The basis of all of these RRT techniques is the removal of unwanted solutes and water through a semipermeable membrane. Such a membrane may be either biologic (i.e., the peritoneum) or artificial (i.e., hemodialysis or hemofiltration membranes); each type has its advantages, disadvantages, and limitations.

In general, RRT for ARF should be initiated early, before complications develop. The commonly expressed concerns regarding early RRT stem from the adverse effects of conventional IHD with cuprophane membranes (in particular, hemodynamic instability) and from the risks and limitations associated with CRRT or PD. In the past few years, however, improved use of CRRT and the development of new hybrid techniques adapted from conventional IHD (e.g., sustained low-efficacy dialysis [SLED] and extended daily dialysis [EDD]) have reduced the incidence of these adverse effects.[100-102]

The criteria governing the initiation of RRT in patients with chronic renal failure may be inappropriate for patients with ARF, particularly if they are critically ill. Accordingly, a set of modern criteria for the initiation of RRT has been developed [see Table 4].

With either CRRT or IHD, the available data are insufficient to establish precisely what constitutes adequate intensity of dialysis; however, there is some evidence that a higher prescribed dose of RRT may improve survival.[103,104] At a minimum, RRT should be of sufficient intensity to maintain homeostasis at all levels. An appropriate target urea level is 42 to 70 mg/dl (15 to 25 mmol/L), with a protein intake of about 1.5 g/kg/day. This target level can easily be achieved by using CRRT at urea clearances of 30 to 40 L/day (depending on patient size and catabolic rate).[104] If IHD is employed, daily treatment and extended treatment become desirable.[103]

There remains considerable controversy regarding which modality of RRT is ideal for reducing mortality and enhancing renal recovery, in particular for patients who are hemodynamically unstable or critically ill. A major reason for the controversy is the difficulty of comparing the results of various small randomized, controlled trials that made use of different techniques.[13,105-107] Large trials of sufficient statistical power would be hard to conduct and may never be performed. In the absence of such trials, RRT techniques should be judged on the basis of the following criteria: (1) biocompatibility, (2) hemodynamic side effects, (3) uremic control, (4) ability to control fluid status, (5) ability to control acidosis, (6) ability to allow full nutritional support, (7) risk of infection, (8) absence of specific side effects, and (9) cost.

CRRT and SLED may offer many advantages over conventional IHD and PD; however, the necessary technology and expertise are not available everywhere, and practice preferences vary widely from one country to another.[108] Therefore, it will be worthwhile to review certain salient features of CRRT and IHD.

Continuous Renal Replacement Therapy

CRRT was initially performed as an arteriovenous procedure (i.e., continuous arteriovenous hemofiltration [CAVH]), in which blood flow through the hemofilter was driven by the patient's blood pressure. A drawback of this approach was that the cannulation of an artery was associated with a morbidity of 15% to 20%. Accordingly, CRRT is now more commonly performed as a venovenous procedure using double-lumen catheters and peristaltic blood pumps (continuous venovenous hemofiltration [CVVH]), with or without control of the ultrafiltration rate. In a venovenous system, dialysate can also be delivered against the direction of blood flow (a technique known as continuous venovenous hemodiafiltration [CVVHDF]) to achieve either almost pure diffusive clearance or a mixture of diffusive and convective clearance. No matter which CRRT technique is used, the following outcomes are predictable: (1) a high level of biocompatibility, (2) hemodynamic stability, (3) continuous control of fluid balance, (4) control of acid-base status, (5) control of electrolytes (including phosphate and calcium), (6) the ability to provide protein-rich nutrition while achieving uremic control, (7) a minimal risk of infection, and (8) prevention of dangerous swings in intracerebral water balance.

Generally, performance of CRRT is restricted to ICUs and requires that specifically trained nursing and medical staff members be available 24 hours a day. Many small ICUs cannot provide this level of support. If CRRT is only performed five to 10 times a year, the cost of training may not be economically justifiable, and expertise may be hard to maintain. Furthermore, depending on how patient care is organized at a particular institution, CRRT may be more expensive than IHD.[109] In addition, the need for continuous anticoagulation of the extracorporeal circuit during CRRT raises the issues of possible hemorrhage, immune thrombotic thrombocytopenia, and increased transfusion requirements.[110-112] In view of these concerns, it is essential to consider the risks and benefits of more or less intensive anticoagulation and of alternative strategies.

In the vast majority of patients, low-dose heparin (< 500 IU/hr) is sufficient to achieve an adequate filter lifespan, is relatively easy and cheap to administer, and has almost no effect on coagulation test results. In some patients, a higher dose is necessary. In others (e.g., those with pulmonary embolism or myocardial ischemia), full heparinization may be indicated. Regional citrate anticoagulation is highly effective but somewhat complex, in that it requires a special dialysate or replacement fluid.[113] Regional heparin or protamine anticoagulation is also somewhat complex, but it may be helpful if frequent filter clotting occurs and further anticoagulation of the patient is considered dangerous. Low-molecular-weight heparin (LMWH) is easy to administer but is more expensive than standard heparin.[114] The LMWH dose must be adjusted for the loss of renal function, which is difficult to monitor. Heparinoids and prostacyclin may be useful if the patient has heparin-induced thrombocytopenia and thrombosis.[115] Finally, in perhaps 10% to 20% of patients, anticoagulation is contraindicated because of endogenous coagulopathy or recent surgery. In such patients, mean filter lives longer than 24 hours can be achieved, provided that blood flow is kept at about 200 ml/min and reliable vascular access is maintained.[116]

Particular attention must be paid to the adequacy and ease of flow through the double-lumen catheter.[117] Smaller (11.5 French)

catheters in the subclavian position pose particular problems; larger (13.5 French) catheters in the femoral position appear to function more reliably.[118] The choice of membrane is a matter of some debate. There are several biosynthetic membranes on the market (e.g., those made of AN69, polyamide, polysulfone, or cellulose triacetate) that have excellent biocompatibility. To date, however, no controlled studies have shown any of them to possess a clinical advantage over any of the others.

Intermittent Hemodialysis

In IHD, as in CRRT, vascular access is typically obtained via a double-lumen catheter. Also as in CRRT, the circuit consists of venovenous blood flow driven by a peristaltic pump. As in CVVH, countercurrent dialysate flow is employed; however, standard IHD differs from CVVH in that it uses high dialysate flows (300 to 400 ml/min), generates dialysate by using purified water and concentrate, and is applied for short periods (3 to 4 hours). These differences have important implications. First, volume removal must be completed within a short time, and this process may be poorly tolerated by patients who are hemodynamically unstable or critically ill. There is a high incidence of hypotension in such patients, and repeated hypotensive episodes may contribute to delayed renal recovery.[119] Second, solute removal is episodic, resulting in inferior uremic and acid-base control, decreased therapeutic efficacy, and a lower delivered dose of RRT. Suboptimal fluid and uremic control imposes unnecessary limitations on nutritional support. Furthermore, rapid solute shifts increase brain water content and raise intracranial pressure.[120]

The issue of membrane bioincompatibility has given rise to a great deal of controversy. In comparison with high-flux synthetic membranes (also used for CVVH), standard low-flux dialyzing membranes made of cuprophane have been found to trigger the activation of several inflammatory pathways. It is possible that this proinflammatory effect contributes to further renal damage and delays recovery or even affects mortality. The controversy has not yet been resolved.

The limitations of conventional IHD in the setting of ARF led to the development of the new hybrid techniques SLED and EDD,[100,101] which adapt IHD to specific clinical circumstances so as to make it easier to tolerate and more effective. At present, PD is rarely used in the treatment of adult ARF in developed countries; however, it may be a reasonable option in developing countries or in the treatment of children when alternatives are unavailable or are considered too expensive or invasive.[108]

BLOOD PURIFICATION FOR INDICATIONS OTHER THAN ACUTE RENAL FAILURE

There is growing interest in the possibility that blood purification, by removing circulating mediators, may provide a clinically significant benefit for patients who are in a severe septic state.[121-123] Various techniques, including plasmapheresis, high-volume hemofiltration, very-high-volume hemofiltration, and coupled plasma filtration adsorption, are currently being assessed in animal studies and in phase I and II human studies.[124,125] Initial findings suggest that continued exploration of this therapeutic option is worthwhile[126]; however, randomized, controlled trials of sufficient statistical power have not yet been performed. Blood purification technology, in combination with the use of bioreactors containing either human or porcine liver cells, is also under active investigation as a form of artificial liver support for patients with fulminant or acute-on-chronic liver failure.[127] Some promising results have been reported.

Discussion

Pathogenesis of Acute Renal Failure

The pathogenesis of ARF varies, depending on the primary mechanism and contributing factors underlying the acute decline in kidney function.

For postrenal or obstructive ARF, the pathogenesis typically involves several humoral responses, as well as a host of mechanical factors. As a rule, a single functioning kidney has adequate capacity for clearance of daily nitrogenous waste and maintenance of water and acid-base homeostasis. Therefore, for postrenal ARF to develop, urinary flow must be obstructed in the urethra, in the bladder, or in both ureters (one ureter if the patient has only a single kidney). These mechanical factors can arise from within the genitourinary system (e.g., stones or strictures) or from extrinsic causes (e.g., ureteral compression or kinking) [*see Table 1*]. When urinary flow is obstructed, glomerular filtration initially continues, gradually elevating the intraluminal pressures proximal to the site of obstruction. Over time, the elevated pressures result in progressive distention and dilation of the proximal ureter, the renal pelvis, and the calyx and directly cause GFR to decline.

The pathogenesis of parenchymal ARF is typically immunologic. It is a complicated process that includes a wide variety of possible causative conditions (including glomerulonephritis, vasculitis, and interstitial nephropathy) and involves an extraordinary array of cell-mediated and humoral mechanisms, discussion of which exceeds the scope of this chapter.

The pathogenesis of prerenal ARF is of greater direct relevance to the surgeon. Traditionally, prerenal ARF is, by definition, the result of a reduction in ECV and a concomitant reduction in renal perfusion. A reduction in ECV is frequently accompanied by a reduction in MAP, which can stimulate several humoral and neural processes by activating arterial and cardiac baroreceptors. Increased activity in these baroreceptors stimulates the sympathetic nervous system and the renin-angiotensin-aldosterone system and triggers the release of arginine vasopressin from the posterior pituitary in an attempt to compensate for any reduction in GFR.

At the level of the kidney, there are several mechanisms that may play a major role in the development of prerenal injury, including (1) ischemia of the outer medulla, (2) activation of the tubuloglomerular feedback system (afferent arteriolar constriction), (3) tubular obstruction from cell casts, (4) interstitial edema secondary to back-diffusion of fluid, (5) inflammatory response to cell injury and local release of mediators, (6) disruption of normal cellular adhesion to the basement membrane, (7) oxygen free radical–induced apoptosis, and (8) phospholipase A_2–induced cell membrane injury. It must be kept in mind, however, that to date, most of these mechanisms have been demonstrated to be operative only in animal models. Because such models bear limited resemblance to the clinical scenarios in which ARF develops in humans, the relevance of these findings to human disease remains highly speculative. Even if these experimentally proven mechanisms are operative in humans, their hierarchy and their time sequence remain unknown, which makes the development of specific therapeutic targets for prevention and management a difficult task.

Epidemiology of Acute Renal Failure

As noted [*see* General Principles, Definition of Acute Renal Failure, *above*], defining ARF can be problematic. Even so, several useful observations can be made about the epidemiology of this condition.

First, some degree of acute renal injury (manifested by albuminuria; the loss of small tubular proteins; the inability to excrete a water, sodium, or amino acid load; or any combination of these) can be demonstrated in most ICU patients. The manifestations of renal injury may be seen in patients who are undergoing simple and successful cardiac surgery with cardiopulmonary bypass, as well as in patients who have severe sepsis but a normal serum creatinine concentration. Their significance is unclear, beyond the observation that some of them (e.g., albuminuria) have been associated with increased mortality.

Second, ARF is common in hospitalized patients, affecting between 5% and 8% (depending on the specific population being assessed and the criteria being used to define ARF).[3,11] In a report from the Madrid ARF Study Group, the overall annual incidence of ARF was 209 cases/million, with ARF defined as either (1) a sudden increase in the serum creatinine concentration to 2.0 mg/dl (177 μmol/L) or higher in a patient with normal premorbid renal function or (2) a 50% or greater increase in the serum creatinine concentration in a patient with chronic kidney disease.[128] In several other population-based epidemiologic studies, the annual incidence of ARF ranged from 20 to 187 cases/million (again, depending on the operative definition of ARF used).[15,129-131] If these general observations are applied to the more economically developed countries, which have a total population of approximately 1 billion people, it may be estimated that about 200,000 cases of ARF occur in this population each year. Unfortunately, little information is available on the incidence of ARF in the less developed countries.

Third, current trends suggest that the incidence of and mortality attributable to ARF may actually be increasing, particularly in critically ill patients, despite advances in the understanding of the pathophysiology of ARF and the development of new and improved methods for its treatment. One explanation for this increase may be that ARF as a manifestation of single-organ dysfunction is becoming less common, whereas MODS with associated ARF is becoming more common.[132] In a multinational, multicenter study carried out by the Beginning and Ending Supportive Therapy for the Kidney (BEST Kidney) Investigators, it was estimated that ARF associated with admission to an ICU develops in approximately 6% of critically ill patients worldwide.[12] ARF was severe enough to warrant initiation of RRT in approximately 70% of the patients studied.[12] In other studies, the annual incidence of ARF severe enough to necessitate RRT has been estimated to range from 40 to 130 cases/million.[12-14,132,133]

Fourth, large epidemiologic studies have identified a number of risk factors for the development of ARF, including greater age, male sex, preexisting illness, severe sepsis or septic shock, major surgery (in particular, cardiac surgery), cardiogenic shock, hypovolemia, and exposure to various nephrotoxic drugs.[12,13] Smaller cohort studies have shown that ARF is common in the setting of MODS, specifically when there is concomitant acute circulatory, pulmonary, and hepatic organ dysfunction.[134-137]

Fifth, although the studies cited above suggest that ARF may in part be an expression of overall illness severity, there is evidence that ARF, in and of itself, significantly and independently increases mortality.[138] The overall hospital mortality for patients with ARF is estimated to be about 20%; however, the hospital mortality for patients with more severe increasing renal injury (serum creatinine concentration ≥ 3.0 mg/dl [265 μmol/L]) ranges from 40% to 60%.[3,11] There is also evidence that the short- and long-term prognosis is worse for patients who are critically ill and patients who require RRT. In these patients, the hospital mortality is 45% to 60%, and the long-term mortality is 60% to 70%.[12-14,20,132,138-140]

Sixth, independence from RRT is associated with enhanced overall quality of life and improved functional status and probably has important health economic implications[133,141]; thus, renal recovery after ARF or an episode of critical illness is an important outcome to consider. Estimates of dependence on RRT at hospital discharge for survivors of ARF vary, ranging from 5% to 33%.[12-14,16,20,109,133] Several factors may be associated with a higher likelihood of renal recovery with independence from RRT, including male sex, little or no preexisting comorbid illness, no evidence of preexisting chronic kidney disease, the use of CRRT rather than IHD, and earlier initiation of RRT.[13] Despite the high overall mortality for survivors of ARF, there is evidence that the majority (70% to 80%) recover renal function and gain independence from RRT within 90 days to 1 year.[13]

References

1. Novis BK, Roizen MF, Aronson S, et al: Association of preoperative risk factors with postoperative acute renal failure. Anesth Analg 78:143, 1994

2. Bellomo R, Ronco C, Kellum JA, et al: Acute renal failure—definition, outcome measures, animal models, fluid therapy and information technology needs: the Second International Consensus Conference of the Acute Dialysis Quality Initiative (ADQI) Group. Crit Care 8:R204, 2004

3. Hou SH, Bushinsky DA, Wish JB, et al: Hospital-acquired renal insufficiency: a prospective study. Am J Med 74:243, 1983

4. Villa P, Jimenez M, Soriano MC, et al: Serum cystatin C concentration as a marker of acute renal dysfunction in critically ill patients. Crit Care 9:R139, 2005

5. Herget-Rosenthal S, Marggraf G, Husing J, et al: Early detection of acute renal failure by serum cystatin C. Kidney Int 66:1115, 2004

6. Han WK, Bailly V, Abichandani R, et al: Kidney Injury Molecule–1 (KIM-1): a novel biomarker for human renal proximal tubule injury. Kidney Int 62:237, 2002

7. du Cheyron D, Daubin C, Poggioli J, et al: Urinary measurement of Na$^+$/H$^+$ exchanger isoform 3 (NHE3) protein as new marker of tubule injury in critically ill patients with ARF. Am J Kidney Dis 42:497, 2003

8. Mishra J, Dent C, Tarabishi R, et al: Neutrophil gelatinase-associated lipocalin (NGAL) as a biomarker for acute renal injury after cardiac surgery. Lancet 365:1231, 2005

9. Parikh CR, Jani A, Melnikov VY, et al: Urinary interleukin-18 is a marker of human acute tubular necrosis. Am J Kidney Dis 43:405, 2004

10. Hotchkiss RS, Swanson PE, Freeman BD, et al: Apoptotic cell death in patients with sepsis, shock, and multiple organ dysfunction. Crit Care Med 27:1230, 1999

11. Nash K, Hafeez A, Hou S: Hospital-acquired renal insufficiency. Am J Kidney Dis 39:930, 2002

12. Uchino S, Kellum JA, Bellomo R, et al: Acute renal failure in critically ill patients: a multinational, multicenter study. JAMA 294:813, 2005

13. Bagshaw SM, Laupland KB, Doig CJ, et al: Prognosis for long-term survival and renal recovery in critically ill patients with severe acute renal failure: a population-based study. Crit Care 9:R700, 2005

14. Silvester W, Bellomo R, Cole L: Epidemiology, management, and outcome of severe acute renal failure of critical illness in Australia. Crit Care Med 29:1910, 2001

15. Robertson S, Newbigging K, Isles CG, et al: High incidence of renal failure requiring short-term dialysis: a prospective observational study. QJM 95:585, 2002

16. Spurney RF, Fulkerson WJ, Schwab SJ: Acute renal failure in critically ill patients: prognosis for recovery of kidney function after prolonged dialysis support. Crit Care Med 19:8, 1991

17. Bhandari S, Turney JH: Survivors of acute renal failure who do not recover renal function. QJM 89:415, 1996

18. Gines P, Guevara M, Arroyo V, et al: Hepatorenal syndrome. Lancet 362:1819, 2003

19. Arroyo V, Guevara M, Gines P: Hepatorenal syndrome in cirrhosis: pathogenesis and treatment. Gastroenterology 122:1658, 2002

20. Cole L, Bellomo R, Silvester W, et al: A prospective, multicenter study of the epidemiology, management, and outcome of severe acute renal failure in a "closed" ICU system. Am J Respir Crit Care Med 162:191, 2000

21. Holt S, Moore K: Pathogenesis of renal failure in rhabdomyolysis: the role of myoglobin. Exp Nephrol 8:72, 2000

22. Holt S, Moore K: Pathogenesis and treatment of renal dysfunction in rhabdomyolysis. Intensive Care Med 27:803, 2001

23. Gruberg L, Mintz GS, Mehran R, et al: The prognostic implications of further renal function deterioration within 48 h of interventional coronary procedures in patients with pre-existent chronic renal insufficiency. J Am Coll Cardiol 36:1542, 2000

24. Levy EM, Viscoli CM, Horwitz RI: The effect of acute renal failure on mortality: a cohort analysis. JAMA 275:1489, 1996

25. Powe NR, Moore RD, Steinberg EP: Adverse reactions to contrast media: factors that determine the cost of treatment. AJR Am J Roentgenol 161:1089, 1993

26. Saklayen MG, Gupta S, Suryaprasad A, et al: Incidence of atheroembolic renal failure after coronary angiography: a prospective study. Angiology 48:609, 1997

27. Barrett BJ: Contrast nephrotoxicity. J Am Soc Nephrol 5:125, 1994

28. Murphy SW, Barrett BJ, Parfrey PS: Contrast nephropathy. J Am Soc Nephrol 11:177, 2000

29. Fang LS, Sirota RA, Ebert TH, et al: Low fractional excretion of sodium with contrast media-induced acute renal failure. Arch Intern Med 140:531, 1980

30. Rihal CS, Textor SC, Grill DE, et al: Incidence and prognostic importance of acute renal failure after percutaneous coronary intervention. Circulation 105:2259, 2002

31. Rich MW, Crecelius CA: Incidence, risk factors, and clinical course of acute renal insufficiency after cardiac catheterization in patients 70 years of age or older: a prospective study. Arch Intern Med 150:1237, 1990

32. Guitterez NV, Diaz A, Timmis GC, et al: Determinants of serum creatinine trajectory in acute contrast nephropathy. J Interv Cardiol 15:349, 2002

33. Cigarroa RG, Lange RA, Williams RH, et al: Dosing of contrast material to prevent contrast nephropathy in patients with renal disease. Am J Med 86:649, 1989

34. Manske CL, Sprafka JM, Strony JT, et al: Contrast nephropathy in azotemic diabetic patients undergoing coronary angiography. Am J Med 89:615, 1990

35. Espinel CH: The FENa test. Use in the differential diagnosis of acute renal failure. JAMA 236:579, 1976

36. Miller TR, Anderson RJ, Linas SL, et al: Urinary diagnostic indices in acute renal failure: a prospective study. Ann Intern Med 89:47, 1978

37. Zarich S, Fang LS, Diamond JR: Fractional excretion of sodium: exceptions to its diagnostic value. Arch Intern Med 145:108, 1985

38. Pru C, Kjellstrand CM: The FENa test is of no prognostic value in acute renal failure. Nephron 36:20, 1984

39. Kaplan AA, Kohn OF: Fractional excretion of urea as a guide to renal dysfunction. Am J Nephrol 12:49, 1992

40. Carvounis CP, Nisar S, Guro-Razuman S: Significance of the fractional excretion of urea in the differential diagnosis of acute renal failure. Kidney Int 62:2223, 2002

41. Fang L, Sirota R, Ebert T, et al: Low fractional excretion of sodium with contrast media-induced acute renal failure. Arch Intern Med 140:531, 1980

42. Corwin HL, Schreiber MJ, Fang LS: Low fractional excretion of sodium: occurrence with hemoglobinuric- and myoglobinuric-induced acute renal failure. Arch Intern Med 144:981, 1984

43. Vaz AJ: Low fractional excretion of urine sodium in acute renal failure due to sepsis. Arch Intern Med 143:738, 1983

44. Korbet SM: Percutaneous renal biopsy. Semin Nephrol 22:254, 2002

45. Whittier WL, Korbet SM: Renal biopsy: update. Curr Opin Nephrol Hypertens 13:661, 2004

46. Conlon PJ, Kovalik E, Schwab SJ: Percutaneous renal biopsy of ventilated intensive care unit patients. Clin Nephrol 43:309, 1995

47. Jones D, Bellomo R: Renal-dose dopamine: from hypothesis to paradigm to dogma to myth and, finally, superstition? J Intensive Care Med 20:199, 2005

48. Kellum JA, M Decker J: Use of dopamine in acute renal failure: a meta-analysis. Crit Care Med 29:1526, 2001

49. Friedrich JO, Adhikari N, Herridge MS, et al: Meta-analysis: low-dose dopamine increases urine output but does not prevent renal dysfunction or death. Ann Intern Med 142:510, 2005

50. Bellomo R, Ronco C: The renal effects of nora-drenaline and dopamine. Contrib Nephrol:146, 2001

51. Bellomo R, Cole L, Ronco C: Hemodynamic support and the role of dopamine. Kidney Int Suppl 66:S71, 1998

52. Bellomo R, Chapman M, Finfer S, et al: Low-dose dopamine in patients with early renal dysfunction: a placebo-controlled randomised trial. Australian and New Zealand Intensive Care Society (ANZ-ICS) Clinical Trials Group. Lancet 356:2139, 2000

53. Nichols AJ, Ruffolo RR Jr, Brooks DP: The pharmacology of fenoldopam. Am J Hypertens 3:116S, 1990

54. Mathur VS, Swan SK, Lambrecht LJ, et al: The effects of fenoldopam, a selective dopamine receptor agonist, on systemic and renal hemodynamics in normotensive subjects. Crit Care Med 27:1832, 1999

55. Morelli A, Ricci Z, Bellomo R, et al: Prophylactic fenoldopam for renal protection in sepsis: a randomized, double-blind, placebo-controlled pilot trial. Crit Care Med 33:2451, 2005

56. Zager RA, Mahan J, Merola AJ: Effects of mannitol on the postischemic kidney: biochemical, functional, and morphologic assessments. Lab Invest 53:433, 1985

57. Brezis M, Agmon Y, Epstein FH: Determinants of intrarenal oxygenation. I. Effects of diuretics. Am J Physiol 267:F1059, 1994

58. Heyman SN, Rosen S, Epstein FH, et al: Loop diuretics reduce hypoxic damage to proximal tubules of the isolated perfused rat kidney. Kidney Int 45:981, 1994

59. Shilliday IR, Quinn KJ, Allison ME: Loop diuretics in the management of acute renal failure: a prospective, double-blind, placebo-controlled, randomized study. Nephrol Dial Transplant 12:2592, 1997

60. Cantarovich F, Rangoonwala B, Lorenz H, et al: High-dose furosemide for established ARF: a prospective, randomized, double-blind, placebo-controlled, multicenter trial. Am J Kidney Dis 44:402, 2004

61. Brown CB, Ogg CS, Cameron JS: High dose frusemide in acute renal failure: a controlled trial. Clin Nephrol 15:90, 1981

62. Kleinknecht D, Ganeval D, Gonzalez-Duque LA, et al: Furosemide in acute oliguric renal failure: a controlled trial. Nephron 17:51, 1976

63. Schetz M: Diuretics in acute renal failure? Contrib Nephrol 144:166, 2004

64. Martin SJ, Danziger LH: Continuous infusion of loop diuretics in the critically ill: a review of the literature. Crit Care Med 22:1323, 1994

65. Huber W, Jeschke B, Page M, et al: Reduced incidence of radiocontrast-induced nephropathy in ICU patients under theophylline prophylaxis: a prospective comparison to series of patients at similar risk. Intensive Care Med 27:1200, 2001

66. Allgren RL, Marbury TC, Rahman SN, et al: Anaritide in acute tubular necrosis. Auriculin Anaritide Acute Renal Failure Study Group. N Engl J Med 336:828, 1997

67. Lewis J, Salem MM, Chertow GM, et al: Atrial natriuretic factor in oliguric acute renal failure. Anaritide Acute Renal Failure Study Group. Am J Kidney Dis 36:767, 2000

68. Rahman SN, Kim GE, Mathew AS, et al: Effects of atrial natriuretic peptide in clinical acute renal failure. Kidney Int 45:1731, 1994

69. Merten GJ, Burgess WP, Gray LV, et al: Prevention of contrast-induced nephropathy with sodium bicarbonate: a randomized controlled trial. JAMA 291:2328, 2004

70. Mueller C, Buerkle G, Buettner HJ, et al: Prevention of contrast media-associated nephropathy: randomized comparison of 2 hydration regimens in 1620

71. Aspelin P, Aubry P, Fransson SG, et al: Nephrotoxic effects in high-risk patients undergoing angiography. N Engl J Med 348:491, 2003

72. Stevens MA, McCullough PA, Tobin KJ, et al: A prospective randomized trial of prevention measures in patients at high risk for contrast nephropathy: results of the P.R.I.N.C.E. Study. Prevention of Radiocontrast Induced Nephropathy Clinical Evaluation. J Am Coll Cardiol 33:403, 1999

73. Tepel M, van der Giet M, Schwarzfeld C, et al: Prevention of radiographic-contrast-agent-induced reductions in renal function by acetylcysteine. N Engl J Med 343:180, 2000

74. Webb JG, Pate GE, Humphries KH, et al: A randomized controlled trial of intravenous N-acetylcysteine for the prevention of contrast-induced nephropathy after cardiac catheterization: lack of effect. Am Heart J 148:422, 2004

75. Oldemeyer JB, Biddle WP, Wurdeman RL, et al: Acetylcysteine in the prevention of contrast-induced nephropathy after coronary angiography. Am Heart J 146:E23, 2003

76. Ochoa A, Pellizzon G, Addala S, et al: Abbreviated dosing of N-acetylcysteine prevents contrast-induced nephropathy after elective and urgent coronary angiography and intervention. J Interv Cardiol 17:159, 2004

77. Kay J, Chow WH, Chan TM, et al: Acetylcysteine for prevention of acute deterioration of renal function following elective coronary angiography and intervention: a randomized controlled trial. JAMA 289:553, 2003

78. Kefer JM, Hanet CE, Boitte S, et al: Acetylcysteine, coronary procedure and prevention of contrast-induced worsening of renal function: which benefit for which patient? Acta Cardiol 58:555, 2003

79. Fung JW, Szeto CC, Chan WW, et al: Effect of N-acetylcysteine for prevention of contrast nephropathy in patients with moderate to severe renal insufficiency: a randomized trial. Am J Kidney Dis 43:801, 2004

80. Diaz-Sandoval LJ, Kosowsky BD, et al: Acetycysteine to prevent angiography-related renal tissue injury (the APART trial). Am J Cardiol 89: 356, 2002

81. Briguori C, Manganelli F, Scarpato P, et al: Acetylcysteine and contrast agent-associated nephrotoxicity. J Am Coll Cardiol 40:298, 2002

82. Azmus AD, Gottschall C, Manica A, et al: Effectiveness of acetylcysteine in prevention of contrast nephropathy. J Invasive Cardiol 17:80, 2005

83. Bagshaw SM, Ghali WA: Acetylcysteine for prevention of contrast-induced nephropathy after intravascular angiography: a systematic review and meta-analysis. BMC Med 2:38, 2004

84. Birck R, Krzossok S, Markowetz F, et al: Acetylcysteine for prevention of contrast nephropathy: meta-analysis. Lancet 362:598, 2003

85. Isenbarger DW, Kent SM, O'Malley PG: Meta-analysis of randomized clinical trials on the usefulness of acetylcysteine for prevention of contrast nephropathy. Am J Cardiol 92:1454, 2003

86. Kshirsagar AV, Poole C, Mottl A, et al: N-acetylcysteine for the prevention of radiocontrast induced nephropathy: a meta-analysis of prospective controlled trials. J Am Soc Nephrol 15:761, 2004

87. Pannu N, Manns B, Lee H, et al: Systematic review of the impact of N-acetylcysteine on contrast nephropathy. Kidney Int 65:1366, 2004

88. Ix JH, McCulloch CE, Chertow GM: Theophylline for the prevention of radiocontrast nephropathy: a meta-analysis. Nephrol Dial Transplant 19:2747, 2004

89. Bagshaw SM, Ghali WA: Theophylline for prevention of contrast-induced nephropathy: a systematic review and meta-analysis. Arch Intern Med 165:1087, 2005

90. Hebert PC: Transfusion requirements in critical care (TRICC): a multicentre, randomized, controlled clinical study. Transfusion Requirements in Critical Care Investigators and the Canadian Critical Care Trials Group. Br J Anaesth 81(suppl 1):25, 1998

91. Sort P, Navasa M, Arroyo V, et al: Effect of intravenous albumin on renal impairment and mortality in patients with cirrhosis and spontaneous bacterial peritonitis. N Engl J Med 341:403, 1999

92. Angeli P, Volpin R, Gerunda G, et al: Reversal of type 1 hepatorenal syndrome with the administration of midodrine and octreotide. Hepatology 29:1690, 1999

93. Holt S, Goodier D, Marley R, et al: Improvement in renal function in hepatorenal syndrome with N-acetylcysteine. Lancet 353:294, 1999

94. Guevara M, Gines P, Fernandez-Esparrach G, et al: Reversibility of hepatorenal syndrome by prolonged administration of ornipressin and plasma volume expansion. Hepatology 27:35, 1998

95. Ortega R, Gines P, Uriz J, et al: Terlipressin therapy with and without albumin for patients with hepatorenal syndrome: results of a prospective, nonrandomized study. Hepatology 36:941, 2002

96. Solanki P, Chawla A, Garg R, et al: Beneficial effects of terlipressin in hepatorenal syndrome: a prospective, randomized placebo-controlled clinical trial. J Gastroenterol Hepatol 18:152, 2003

97. Guevara M, Gines P, Bandi JC, et al: Transjugular intrahepatic portosystemic shunt in hepatorenal syndrome: effects on renal function and vasoactive systems. Hepatology 28:416, 1998

98. Schroeder ET, Anderson GH Jr, Smulyan H: Effects of a portacaval or peritoneovenous shunt on renin in the hepatorenal syndrome. Kidney Int 15: 54, 1979

99. Brensing KA, Textor J, Perz J, et al: Long term outcome after transjugular intrahepatic portosystemic stent-shunt in non-transplant cirrhotics with hepatorenal syndrome: a phase II study. Gut 47:288, 2000

100. Marshall MR, Golper TA, Shaver MJ, et al: Hybrid renal replacement modalities for the critically ill. Contrib Nephrol 132:252, 2001

101. Kumar VA, Yeun JY, Depner TA, et al: Extended daily dialysis vs. continuous hemodialysis for ICU patients with acute renal failure: a two-year single center report. Int J Artif Organs 27:371, 2004

102. Kumar VA, Craig M, Depner TA, et al: Extended daily dialysis: a new approach to renal replacement for acute renal failure in the intensive care unit. Am J Kidney Dis 36:294, 2000

103. Schiffl H, Lang SM, Fischer R: Daily hemodialysis and the outcome of acute renal failure. N Engl J Med 346:305, 2002

104. Ronco C, Bellomo R, Homel P, et al: Effects of different doses in continuous veno-venous haemofiltration on outcomes of acute renal failure: a prospective randomised trial. Lancet 356:26, 2000

105. Augustine JJ, Sandy D, Seifert TH, et al: A randomized controlled trial comparing intermittent with continuous dialysis in patients with ARF. Am J Kidney Dis 44:1000, 2004

106. Gasparovic V, Filipovic-Grcic I, Merkler M, et al: Continuous renal replacement therapy (CRRT) or intermittent hemodialysis (IHD)—what is the procedure of choice in critically ill patients? Ren Fail 25:855, 2003

107. Mehta RL, McDonald B, Gabbai FB, et al: A randomized clinical trial of continuous versus intermittent dialysis for acute renal failure. Kidney Int 60:1154, 2001

108. Phu NH, Hien TT, Mai NT, et al: Hemofiltration and peritoneal dialysis in infection-associated acute renal failure in Vietnam. N Engl J Med 347:895, 2002

109. Manns B, Doig CJ, Lee H, et al: Cost of acute renal failure requiring dialysis in the intensive care unit:

clinical and resource implications of renal recovery. Crit Care Med 31:449, 2003

110. van de Wetering J, Westendorp RG, van der Hoeven JG, et al: Heparin use in continuous renal replacement procedures: the struggle between filter coagulation and patient hemorrhage. J Am Soc Nephrol 7:145, 1996

111. Samuelsson O, Amiral J, Attman PO, et al: Heparin-induced thrombocytopenia during continuous haemofiltration. Nephrol Dial Transplant 10:1768, 1995

112. Cutts MW, Thomas AN, Kishen R: Transfusion requirements during continuous veno-venous haemofiltration: the importance of filter life. Intensive Care Med 26:1694, 2000

113. Bagshaw SM, Laupland KB, Boiteau PJ, et al: Is regional citrate superior to systemic heparin anticoagulation for continuous renal replacement therapy? A prospective observational study in an adult regional critical care system. J Crit Care 20:155, 2005

114. Reeves JH, Cumming AR, Gallagher L, et al: A controlled trial of low-molecular-weight heparin (dalteparin) versus unfractionated heparin as anticoagulant during continuous venovenous hemodialysis with filtration. Crit Care Med 27:2224, 1999

115. Fiaccadori E, Maggiore U, Rotelli C, et al: Continuous haemofiltration in acute renal failure with prostacyclin as the sole anti-haemostatic agent. Intensive Care Med 28:586, 2002

116. Uchino S, Fealy N, Baldwin I, et al: Continuous venovenous hemofiltration without anticoagulation. ASAIO J 50:76, 2004

117. Baldwin I, Bellomo R, Koch B: Blood flow reductions during continuous renal replacement therapy and circuit life. Intensive Care Med 30:2074, 2004

118. Baldwin I, Bellomo R: Relationship between blood flow, access catheter and circuit failure during CRRT: a practical review. Contrib Nephrol 144:203, 2004

119. Palevsky PM, Baldwin I, Davenport A, et al: Renal replacement therapy and the kidney: minimizing the impact of renal replacement therapy on recovery of acute renal failure. Curr Opin Crit Care 11:548, 2005

120. Bagshaw SM, Peets AD, Hameed M, et al: Dialysis disequilibrium syndrome: brain death following hemodialysis for metabolic acidosis and acute renal failure—a case report. BMC Nephrol 5:9, 2004

121. Bellomo R: Continuous hemofiltration as blood purification in sepsis. New Horiz 3:732, 1995

122. Bellomo R, Ronco C: Blood purification in the intensive care unit: evolving concepts. World J Surg 25:677, 2001

123. Uchino S, Bellomo R, Goldsmith D, et al: Super high flux hemofiltration: a new technique for cytokine removal. Intensive Care Med 28:651, 2002

124. Bellomo R, Baldwin I, Ronco C: High-volume hemofiltration. Contrib Nephrol 132:367, 2001

125. Bellomo R, Honore PM, Matson J, et al: Extra-corporeal blood treatment (EBT) methods in SIRS/sepsis. Int J Artif Organs 28:450, 2005

126. Cole L, Bellomo R, Journois D, et al: High-volume haemofiltration in human septic shock. Intensive Care Med 27:978, 2001

127. Strain AJ, Neuberger JM: A bioartificial liver—state of the art. Science 295:1005, 2002

128. Liano F, Pascual J: Epidemiology of acute renal failure: a prospective, multicenter, community-based study. Madrid Acute Renal Failure Study Group. Kidney Int 50:811, 1996

129. Abraham G, Gupta RK, Senthilselvan A, et al: Cause and prognosis of acute renal failure in Kuwait: a 2-year prospective study. J Trop Med Hyg 92:325, 1989

130. Feest T, Round A, Hamad S: Incidence of severe acute renal failure in adults: results of a community based study. BMJ 306:481, 1993

131. Metcalfe W, Simpson M, Khan IH, et al: Acute renal failure requiring renal replacement therapy: incidence and outcome. QJM 95:579, 2002

132. Liano F, Junco E, Pascual J, et al: The spectrum of acute renal failure in the intensive care unit compared with that seen in other settings. The Madrid Acute Renal Failure Study Group. Kidney Int Suppl 66:S16, 1998

133. Korkeila M, Ruokonen E, Takala J: Costs of care, long-term prognosis and quality of life in patients requiring renal replacement therapy during intensive care. Intensive Care Med 26:1824, 2000

134. Tran D, Cuesta M, Oe P: Acute renal failure in patients with severe civilian trauma. Nephrol Dial Transplant 9:121, 1994

135. McCarthy J: Prognosis of patients with acute renal failure in the intensive care unit: a tale of two eras. Mayo Clin Proc 71:117, 1996

136. Groeneveld A, Tran D, van der Meulen J, et al: Acute renal failure in the medical intensive care unit: predisposing, complicating factors and outcome. Nephron 59:602, 1991

137. de Mendonca A, Vincent JL, Suter PM, et al: Acute renal failure in the ICU: risk factors and outcome evaluated by the SOFA score. Intensive Care Med 26:915, 2000

138. Ympa YP, Sakr Y, Reinhart K, et al: Has mortality from acute renal failure decreased? A systematic review of the literature. Am J Med 118:827, 2005

139. Chertow GM, Christiansen CL, Cleary PD, et al: Prognostic stratification in critically ill patients with acute renal failure requiring dialysis. Arch Intern Med 155:1505, 1995

140. Mehta RL, Pascual MT, Soroko S, et al: Spectrum of acute renal failure in the intensive care unit: the PICARD experience. Kidney Int 66:1613, 2004

141. Hamel MB, Phillips RS, Davis RB, et al: Outcomes and cost-effectiveness of initiating dialysis and continuing aggressive care in seriously ill hospitalized adults. SUPPORT Investigators. Study to Understand Prognoses and Preferences for Outcomes and Risks of Treatments. Ann Intern Med 127:195, 1997

Acknowledgment

Figure 1 Seward Hung.

123 ACID-BASE DISORDERS

John A. Kellum, M.D., and Juan Carlos Puyana, M.D., F.A.C.S.

Anticipation and early identification of conditions that alter the body's ability to compensate for acid-base disorders are vital in the management of surgical and critically ill patients. A clear understanding of metabolic-respiratory interactions and a systematic approach aimed at identifying the separate components of acid-base disorders not only serves as a diagnostic tool but also helps in formulating therapeutic interventions. For example, abnormal acid-base balance may be harmful in part because of the patient's response to the abnormality, as when a spontaneously breathing patient with metabolic acidosis attempts to compensate by increasing minute ventilation. Such a response may lead to respiratory muscle fatigue with respiratory failure or diversion of blood flow from vital organs to the respiratory muscles, eventually resulting in organ injury. The increased catecholamine levels associated with acidemia may provoke cardiac dysrhythmias in critically ill patients or increase myocardial oxygen demand in patients with myocardial ischemia. In such cases, it may be prudent not only to treat the underlying disorder but also to provide symptomatic treatment for the acid-base disorder itself. Accordingly, it is important to understand both the causes of acid-base disorders and the limitations of various treatment strategies.

To treat acid-base disorders, it is not sufficient simply to return one or two laboratory parameters to normal values; one must understand the overall course of the disorder, as well as the specific forces involved at any particular time. For example, in a patient with acute lung injury and moderate hypercapnia, allowing mild acidemia may be preferable to forcing the lung to achieve a normal carbon dioxide tension (P_{CO_2}). Similarly, prescribing bicarbonate therapy without anticipating the effects on the body's own compensatory efforts may induce an unwanted rebound alkalemia. A comprehensive understanding of the pathophysiology and a practical approach to bedside evaluation are complementary components of care and are equally necessary in the management of an acid-base disorder.

General Principles

DESCRIPTION AND CLASSIFICATION OF ACID-BASE DISORDERS

There are three widely accepted methods of describing and classifying acid-base abnormalities. Essentially, they differ from one another only with respect to assessment of the metabolic component of the abnormality; all three treat P_{CO_2} as an independent variable. The first method quantifies the metabolic component by using the bicarbonate ion (HCO_3^-) concentration (in the context of P_{CO_2}); the second, by using the standard base excess (SBE); and the third, by using the strong ion difference (SID). In practice, these three methods yield virtually identical results when employed to quantify the acid-base status of a given blood sample.[1-4] Thus, the only significant distinctions between the methods are conceptual ones, related to how each one approaches the understanding of the mechanism of the disorder.[5-7] In this chapter, we emphasize the physicochemical determinants of pH in the blood and the tissues; however, it is a simple matter to convert from one approach to the other if desired.

There are three mathematically independent determinants of blood pH: (1) the SID, defined as the difference in concentration between strong cations (e.g., sodium [Na^+] and potassium [K^+]) and strong anions (e.g., chloride [Cl^-] and lactate); (2) the total concentration of weak acids (A_{tot}), mainly consisting of albumin and phosphate; and (3) P_{CO_2}. These three variables, and only these three, can independently affect plasma pH. The H^+ and HCO_3^- concentrations are dependent variables whose values in plasma are determined by the SID, A_{tot}, and P_{CO_2}. Changes in the plasma H^+ concentration occur as a result of changes in the dissociation of water and A_{tot}, brought about by the electrochemical forces generated by changes in the SID and P_{CO_2}. The SBE is mathematically equivalent to the difference between the current SID and the SID required to restore the pH to 7.4, given a P_{CO_2} of 40 mm Hg and the prevailing A_{tot}. Thus, an SBE of –10 mEq/L means that the SID is 10 mEq less than the value required to achieve a pH of 7.4.

The essential element of this physicochemical approach is the emphasis on independent and dependent variables. Only changes in the independent variables can bring about changes in the dependent variables. That is, movement of H^+ or HCO_3^- cannot affect plasma H^+ or HCO_3^- concentrations unless changes in the SID, A_{tot}, or P_{CO_2} also occur. Several reviews of this approach are available in the literature.[3-9] In what follows, we discuss the clinical application of this approach to the diagnosis and treatment of individual acid-base disorders.

ASSESSMENT OF ACID-BASE BALANCE

Acid-base homeostasis is defined by the plasma pH and by the conditions of the acid-base pairs that determine it. Normally, arterial plasma pH is maintained between 7.35 and 7.45. Because blood plasma is an aqueous solution containing both volatile acids (e.g., CO_2) and fixed acids, its pH is determined by the net effects of all these components on the dissociation of water. The determinants of blood pH can be grouped into two broad categories, respiratory and metabolic. Respiratory acid-base disorders are disorders of P_{CO_2}; metabolic acid-base disorders comprise all other conditions affecting pH, including disorders of both weak acids (often referred to as buffers, though the term is imprecise) and strong acids (organic and inorganic) and bases. Any of the following indicators serves to identify an acid-base disorder:

1. An abnormal arterial blood pH (pH < 7.35 signifies acidemia; pH > 7.45 signifies alkalemia).
2. An arterial P_{CO_2} (P_aCO_2) that is outside the normal range (35 to 45 mm Hg).
3. A plasma HCO_3^- concentration that is outside the normal range (22 to 26 mEq/L).
4. An arterial SBE that is either abnormally high (≥ 3 mEq/L) or abnormally low (≤ -3 mEq/L).

Once identified, an acid-base disorder can be classified according to a simple set of rules [see Table 1]. A disorder that does not fit well into the broad categories established by these rules can be considered a mixed (or complex) disorder. Some of the basic categories can be further divided into various subcategories (see

Table 1 Differentiation of Acid-Base Disorders[6]

Disorder	Physicochemical Parameter		
	HCO_3^- Concentration (mEq/L)	Pco_2 (mm Hg)	SBE (mEq/L)
Metabolic acidosis	< 22	$= (1.5 \times HCO_3^-) + 8$ $= 40 + SBE$	< -5
Metabolic alkalosis	> 26	$= (0.7 \times HCO_3^-) + 21$ $= 40 + (0.6 \times SBE)$	$> +5$
Acute respiratory acidosis	$= [(Pco_2 - 40)/10] + 24$	> 45	$= 0$
Chronic respiratory acidosis	$= [(Pco_2 - 40)/3] + 24$	> 45	$= 0.4 \times (Pco_2 - 40)$
Acute respiratory alkalosis	$= 24 - [(40 - Pco_2)/5]$	< 35	$= 0$
Chronic respiratory alkalosis	$= 24 - [(40 - Pco_2)/2]$	< 35	$= 0.4 \times (Pco_2 - 40)$

SBE—standard base excess

below), but before the issue of classification is addressed in detail, three general caveats must be considered.

First, interpretation of arterial blood gas values and blood chemistries depends on the reliability of the data. Advances in clinical chemistry have improved the sensitivity of instruments used to measure electrolyte concentrations (e.g. ion-specific electrodes) and have greatly enhanced the speed and ease of analysis. Inevitably, however, prolonged exposure to the atmosphere results in a lowering of the Pco_2, and over time, there may be ongoing cellular metabolism. Accordingly, prompt measurement is always advisable. Even with prompt measurement, laboratory errors may occur, and information may be incorrectly reported. Samples drawn from indwelling lines may be diluted by fluid or drug infusions (a notorious source of error). When the situation is confusing, it is usually best to repeat the measurement.

Second, interpretation of arterial blood gas values may be problematic in patients with severe hypothermia (e.g., trauma patients undergoing damage-control interventions, who often are severely hypothermic and sometimes experience severe acidosis), in that the findings may not reflect the actual blood gas values present. Because blood samples are "normalized" to a temperature of 37° C before undergoing analysis, the results obtained in samples from a patient whose body temperature is significantly lower than 37° C may not be sufficiently accurate. To obviate this potential problem, the results may have to be adjusted to take the patient's actual temperature into account. At present, however, such temperature correction is not routinely done, and there has been some controversy regarding whether it has real clinical value.[10,11]

Third, whereas the aforementioned four indicators are useful for identifying an acid-base disorder, the absence of all four does not suffice to exclude a mixed acid-base disorder (i.e., alkalosis plus acidosis) in which the two components are completely matched. Fortunately, such conditions are rare. In addition, apart from distinguishing a respiratory acid-base disorder from a metabolic acid-base disorder, the four indicators and the rules previously mentioned [*see Table 1*] provide no information on the mechanism of an acid-base disorder.

Metabolic Acid-Base Disorders

Metabolic acid-base derangements are produced by a significantly greater number of underlying disorders than respiratory disorders are, and they are almost always more difficult to treat. Traditionally, metabolic acidoses and alkaloses are categorized

according to the ions that are responsible (e.g., lactic acidosis and chloride-responsive alkalosis).

It is important to recognize that metabolic acidosis is caused by a decrease in the SID, which produces an electrochemical force that acts to increase the free H^+ concentration. A decrease in the SID may be brought about by the generation of organic anions (e.g., lactate and ketones), by the loss of cations (as with diarrhea), by the mishandling of ions (as with renal tubular acidosis), or by the addition of exogenous anions (as with iatrogenic acidosis or poisoning). By contrast, metabolic alkalosis is caused by an inappropriately large SID (though it may be possible for the SID to be inappropriately large without exceeding the normal range of 40 to 42 mEq/L). An increase in the SID may be brought about by the loss of more strong anions than strong cations (as with vomiting or diuretic therapy) or, in rare instances, by the administration of more strong cations than strong anions (as with transfusion of large volumes of banked blood containing sodium citrate).

Because metabolic acid-base disorders are caused by changes in the SID, their treatment necessarily involves normalization of the SID. Metabolic acidoses are corrected by increasing the plasma Na^+ concentration more than the plasma Cl^- concentration (e.g., by administering $NaHCO_3$), and metabolic alkaloses are corrected by replacing lost Cl^- (e.g., by giving sodium chloride [NaCl], potassium chloride [KCl], or even hydrochloric acid [HCl]). So-called chloride-resistant metabolic alkaloses [*see Metabolic Alkalosis, Chloride-Resistant Alkalosis, below*] are resistant to chloride administration only because of ongoing renal Cl^- loss that increases in response to increased Cl^- replacement (as with hyperaldosteronism).

PATHOPHYSIOLOGY

Disorders of metabolic acid-base balance occur in one of three ways: (1) as a result of dysfunction of the primary regulating organs, (2) as a result of exogenous administration of drugs or fluids that alter the body's ability to maintain normal acid-base balance, or (3) as a result of abnormal metabolism that overwhelms the normal defense mechanisms. The organ systems responsible for regulating the SID in both health and disease are the renal system and, to a lesser extent, the gastrointestinal tract.

Renal System

Plasma flows to the kidneys at a rate of approximately 600 ml/min. The glomeruli filter the plasma, producing filtrate at a rate of 120 ml/min. The filtrate, in turn, is processed by reabsorption and secretion mechanisms in the tubular cells along which it passes on its way to the ureters. Normally, more than 99% of the filtrate is reabsorbed and returned to the plasma. Thus, the kidney can excrete only a very small amount of strong ion into the urine each minute, which means that several minutes to hours are required to make a significant impact on the SID.

The handling of strong ions by the kidney is extremely important because every chloride ion that is filtered but not reabsorbed reduces the SID. Most of the human diet contains similar ratios of strong cations to strong anions, and thus, there is usually sufficient Cl^- available for renal Cl^- handling to be the primary regulating mechanism. Given that renal Na^+ and K^+ handling is influenced by other priorities (e.g., intravascular volume and plasma K^+ homeostasis), it is logical that so-called acid handling by the kidney is generally mediated through management of the Cl^- balance.

Traditional approaches to the question of renal acid handling have focused on H^+ excretion, emphasizing the importance of ammonia (NH_3) and its add-on cation, ammonium (NH_4^+). However, H^+ excretion per se is irrelevant, in that water provides an essentially infinite source of free H^+. Indeed, the kidney does not excrete H^+ to any greater degree in the form of NH_4^+ than in the form of H_2O. The purpose of renal ammoniagenesis is to allow the excretion of Cl^- without Na^+ or K^+. This purpose is achieved by supplying a weak cation (NH_4^+) that is "coexcreted" with Cl^-. The mechanisms of renal tubular acidosis are currently being reinterpreted by some authors in the light of a growing body of evidence showing that abnormal chloride conductance, rather than H^+ or HCO_3 handling per se, is responsible for these disorders.[3]

Kidney-Liver Interaction

The importance of NH_4^+ to systemic acid-base balance, then, rests not on its carriage of H^+ or its direct action in the plasma (normal plasma NH_4^+ concentration < 0.01 mEq/L) but on its coexcretion with Cl^-. Of course, production of NH_4^+ is not restricted to the kidney. Hepatic ammoniagenesis (as well as glutaminogenesis) is also important for systemic acid-base balance, and as expected, it is tightly controlled by mechanisms sensitive to plasma pH.[12] Indeed, this reinterpretation of the role of NH_4^+ in acid-base balance is supported by the evidence that hepatic glutaminogenesis is stimulated by acidosis.[13] Metabolism of nitrogen by the liver can yield urea, glutamine, or NH_4^+. Normally, the liver releases only a very small amount of NH_4^+, incorporating most of its nitrogen into either urea or glutamine. Hepatocytes have enzymes to enable them to produce either of these end products, and both allow regulation of plasma NH_4^+ at suitably low levels. At the level of the kidneys, however, the production of urea or glutamine has significantly different effects, in that the kidneys use glutamine to generate NH_4^+ and facilitate the excretion of Cl^-. Thus, production of glutamine by the liver can be seen as having an alkalinizing effect on plasma pH because of the way in which the kidneys use this substance.

Further support for this scenario comes from the discovery that hepatocytes are anatomically organized according to their enzymatic content.[14] Hepatocytes with a propensity to produce urea are positioned closer to the portal venule; those with a propensity to produce glutamine are positioned farther downstream. The upstream (urea-producing) hepatocytes have the first chance at the NH_4^+ delivered. However, acidosis inhibits ureagenesis, thereby leaving more NH_4^+ available for the downstream (glutamine-producing) hepatocytes. The leftover NH_4^+ is thus, in a sense, packaged as glutamine for export to the kidney, where it is used to facilitate Cl^- excretion.

Gastrointestinal Tract

The GI tract is an underappreciated component of acid-base balance. In different regions along its length, the GI tract handles strong ions quite differently. In the stomach, Cl^- is pumped out of the plasma and into the lumen, thereby reducing the SID of the gastric juice and thus the pH as well. On the plasma side, the SID is increased by the loss of Cl^-, and the pH rises, producing the so-called alkaline tide that occurs at the beginning of a meal, when gastric acid secretion is maximal.[15]

In the duodenum, Cl^- is reabsorbed and the plasma pH restored. Normally, only slight changes in plasma pH are evident because Cl^- is returned to the circulation almost as soon as it is removed. If, however, gastric secretions are removed from the patient, whether by catheter suctioning or vomiting, Cl^- will be progressively lost and the SID will steadily increase. It is important to remember that it is the loss of Cl^-, not of H^+, that determines the plasma pH. Although H^+ is lost as HCl, it is also lost with every molecule of water removed from the body. When Cl^-, a strong anion, is lost without the corresponding loss of a strong cation, the SID is increased, and therefore, the plasma H^+ concentration is decreased. When H^+ is lost as water rather than as HCl, the SID does not change, and thus, the plasma H^+ concentration does not change either.

The pancreas secretes fluid into the small intestine that possesses an SID much higher than the plasma SID and is very low in Cl^-. Thus, the plasma perfusing the pancreas has its SID decreased, a phenomenon that peaks about 1 hour after a meal and helps counteract the alkaline tide. If large amounts of pancreatic fluid are lost (e.g., as a consequence of surgical drainage), the resulting decrease in the plasma SID will lead to acidosis.

In the large intestine, the fluid also has a high SID, because most of the Cl^- was removed in the small intestine and the remaining electrolytes consist mostly of Na^+ and K^+. Normally, the body reabsorbs much of the water and electrolytes from this fluid, but when severe diarrhea occurs, large amounts of cations may be lost. If this cation loss persists, the plasma SID will decrease and acidosis will result.

In addition to the acid-base effects of abnormal loss of strong ions from the GI lumen, the small intestine, in particular, may contribute strong ions to the plasma. This contribution is most apparent when mesenteric blood flow is compromised and lactate is produced, sometimes in large quantities. Although global hypoperfusion may compromise the mesentery, the intestine does not appear to be a source of lactic acid in patients resuscitated from a septic state [see Metabolic Acidosis, Positive–Anion Gap Acidosis, Lactic Acidosis, below].[16] Moreover, whether the GI tract is capable of regulating strong ion uptake in a compensatory fashion has not been well studied. There is some evidence that the gut may modulate systemic acidosis in experimental endotoxemia by removing anions from the plasma[17]; however, the full capacity of the gut to affect acid-base balance remains to be determined.

METABOLIC ACIDOSIS

Traditionally, metabolic acidoses are categorized according to the presence or absence of unmeasured anions. These unmeasured anions are routinely detected by examining the plasma electrolytes and calculating the anion gap (AG) (see below). The differential diagnosis for a positive-AG acidosis includes various common and rare causes [see Table 2]. Generally speaking, non-AG acidoses can be divided into three types: renal, gastrointestinal, and iatrogenic [see Table 3]. In the ICU, the most common types of metabolic acidosis are lactic acidosis, ketoacidosis, iatrogenic acidosis, and acidosis secondary to toxins.

Table 2 Causes of Positive–Anion Gap Acidosis

Common causes	Renal failure Elevated ketone levels (ketoacidosis) Elevated lactate levels (lactic acidosis) Toxins (methanol, ethylene glycol, salicylate, paraldehyde, toluene) Sepsis
Rare causes	Dehydration Alkalemia Decreased concentrations of unmeasured cations (Mg^{2+}, K^+, Ca^{2+}) Sodium salts (lactate, citrate, acetate, penicillin, carbenicillin) Rhabdomyolysis

Even extreme acidosis appears to be well tolerated by healthy persons, particularly when the duration of the acidosis is short. For example, healthy individuals may achieve an arterial pH lower than 7.15 and a lactate concentration higher than 20 mEq/L during maximal exercise, with no lasting effects.[18] Over the long term, however, even mild acidemia (pH < 7.35) may lead to metabolic bone disease and protein catabolism. Furthermore, critically ill patients may not be able to tolerate even brief episodes of acidemia.[19] There do appear to be significant differences between metabolic and respiratory acidosis with respect to patient outcome, and these differences suggest that the underlying disorder may be more important than the absolute degree of acidemia.[20]

If prudence dictates that symptomatic therapy is to be provided, the likely duration of the disorder should be taken into account. When the disorder is expected to be a short-lived one (e.g., diabetic ketoacidosis), maximizing respiratory compensation is usually the safest approach. Once the disorder resolves, ventilation can be quickly reduced to normal levels, and there will be no lingering effects from therapy. If the SID is increased (e.g., by administering $NaHCO_3$), there is a risk of alkalosis when the underlying disorder resolves. When the disorder is likely to be a more chronic one (e.g., renal failure), therapy aimed at restoring the SID to normal is indicated. In all cases, the therapeutic target can be accurately determined from the SBE. As noted (see above), the SBE corresponds to the amount by which the current SID differs from the SID necessary to restore the pH to 7.4, given a P_{CO_2} of 40 mm Hg. Thus, if the SID is 30 mEq/L and the SBE is –10 mEq/L, the target SID is 40 mEq/L. Accordingly, the plasma Na^+ concentration would have to increase by 10 mEq/L for $NaHCO_3$ administration to correct the acidosis completely.

It should be noted that the target SID is the SID at the equilibrium point between the SID, P_{CO_2}, and A_{tot} and that it may not be equal to 40 mEq/L, as in the example given. By convention, P_{CO_2}

Table 3 Differential Diagnosis for Normal–Anion Gap Metabolic Acidosis

Urine SID > 0 mEq/L	Renal tubular acidosis
Urine SID < 0 mEq/L	GI condition Diarrhea Pancreatic or small bowel drainage Iatrogenesis Parenteral nutrition Saline

SID—strong ion difference

is set at 40 mm Hg, but the SBE is not corrected for abnormalities in A_{tot}. In many hypoalbuminemic patients, A_{tot} is lower than normal, and thus, the SID at the equilibrium point will be less than 40 mEq/L. Also, it is rare that the choice would be made to correct the acid-base abnormality completely. Therefore, the target SID should be used as a reference value, but in most cases, partial correction is all that is required.

If increasing the plasma Na^+ concentration is inadvisable for other reasons (e.g., hypernatremia), $NaHCO_3$ administration is inadvisable. It is noteworthy that $NaHCO_3$ administration has not been shown to improve outcome in patients with lactic acidosis.[21] In addition, $NaHCO_3$ administration is associated with certain disadvantages. Large (hypertonic) doses, if given rapidly, may actually reduce blood pressure[22] and may cause sudden, severe increases in P_{aCO_2}.[23] Accordingly, it is important to assess the patient's ventilatory status before $NaHCO_3$ is administered, particularly if the patient is not on a ventilator. $NaHCO_3$ infusion also affects serum K^+ and Ca^{2+} concentrations, which must be monitored closely.

To avoid some of the disadvantages of $NaHCO_3$ therapy, alternative therapies for metabolic acidosis have been developed. Carbicarb is an equimolar mixture of sodium carbonate (Na_2CO_3) and $NaHCO_3$.[24] Like $NaHCO_3$, carbicarb works by increasing the plasma Na^+ concentration, except that it does not raise the P_{CO_2}. Results with carbicarb in animal studies have been mixed,[25] and experience in humans is extremely limited.

THAM (tris-hydroxymethyl aminomethane) is a synthetic buffer that consumes CO_2 and readily penetrates cells.[26] It is a weak base (pK = 7.9) and, as such, is unlike other plasma constituents. The major advantage of THAM is that it does not alter the SID, which means that there is no need to be concerned about having to increase the plasma Na^+ concentration to achieve a therapeutic effect. Accordingly, THAM is often used in situations where $NaHCO_3$ cannot be used because of hypernatremia. Although THAM has been available since the 1960s, there is surprisingly little information available regarding its efficacy in humans with acid-base disorders. In small uncontrolled studies, THAM appears to be capable of reversing metabolic acidosis secondary to ketoacidosis or renal failure without causing obvious toxicity[27]; however, adverse reactions have been reported, including hypoglycemia, respiratory depression, and even fatal hepatic necrosis, when concentrations exceeding 0.3 mol/L are used. In Europe, a mixture of THAM, acetate, $NaHCO_3$, and disodium phosphate is available. This mixture, known as tribonate (Tribonat; Pharmacia & Upjohn, Solna, Sweden), seems to have fewer side effects than THAM alone does, but as with THAM, experience with its use in humans is still quite limited.

Anion Gap

Determination of anion gap The AG has been used by clinicians for more than 30 years and has evolved into a major tool for evaluating acid-base disorders.[28] It is calculated—or, rather, estimated—from the difference between the routinely measured concentrations of serum cations (Na^+ and K^+) and the routinely measured concentrations of anions (Cl^- and HCO_3^-). Normally, albumin accounts for the bulk of this difference, with phosphate playing a lesser role. Sulfate and lactate also contribute a small amount to the gap (normally, < 2 mEq/L); however, there are also unmeasured cations (e.g., Ca^{2+} and Mg^{2+}), which tend to offset the effects of sulfate and lactate except when the concentration of either one is abnormally increased. Plasma proteins other than albumin can be either positively or negatively charged, but in the aggregate, they tend to be electrically neutral,[29] except in rare cases of abnormal paraproteins (as in multiple myeloma). In practice, the AG is calculated as follows:

$$AG = (Na^+ + K^+) - (Cl^- + HCO_3^-)$$

Because of its low extracellular concentration, K^+ is often omitted from the calculation. In most laboratories, normal values fall into the range of 12 ± 4 mEq/L (if K^+ is considered) or 8 ± 4 mEq/L (if K^+ is not considered). In the past few years, the introduction of more accurate methods of measuring Cl^- concentration has led to a general lowering of the normal AG range.[30,31] Because of the various measurement techniques employed at various institutions, however, each institution is expected to report its own normal AG values.

Clinical utility of anion gap The primary value of the AG is that it quickly and easily limits the differential diagnosis in a patient with metabolic acidosis. When the AG is increased, the explanation is almost invariably one of the following five disorders: ketosis, lactic acidosis, poisoning, renal failure, and sepsis.[32]

In addition to these disorders, however, there are several conditions that can alter the accuracy of AG estimation and are particularly frequent in critical illness.[33,34] Dehydration increases the concentrations of all of the ions. Severe hypoalbuminemia lowers the AG, with each 1 g/dl decline in the serum albumin reducing the apparent AG by 2.5 to 3 mEq/L; accordingly, some recommend adjusting the AG for the prevailing albumin concentration.[35] Alkalosis (respiratory or metabolic) is associated with an increase of as much as 3 to 10 mEq/L in the apparent AG as a consequence of enhanced lactate production (from stimulated phosphofructokinase enzymatic activity), reduction in the concentration of ionized weak acids (A^-)(as opposed to A_{tot}, the total concentration of weak acids), and, possibly, the additional effect of dehydration (which, as noted, has its own impact on AG calculation). A low Mg^{2+} concentration with associated low K^+ and Ca^{2+} concentrations is a known cause of an increased AG, as is the administration of sodium salts of poorly reabsorbable anions (e.g., β-lactam antibiotics).[36] Certain parenteral nutrition formulations (e.g., those containing acetate) may increase the AG. In rare cases, citrate may have the same effect in the setting of multiple blood transfusions, particularly if massive doses of banked blood are used (as during liver transplantation).[37] None of these rare causes, however, will increase the AG significantly,[38] and they usually are easily identified.

In the past few years, some additional causes of an increased AG have been reported. The nonketotic hyperosmolar state of diabetes has been associated with an increased AG that remains unexplained.[39] Unmeasured anions have been reported in the blood of patients with sepsis,[40,41] patients with liver disease,[42,43] and experimental animals that received endotoxin.[44] These anions may be the source of much of the unexplained acidosis seen in patients with critical illness.[45]

The accepted clinical utility of the AG notwithstanding, doubt has been cast on its diagnostic value in certain situations.[33,41] Some investigators have found routine reliance on the AG to be "fraught with numerous pitfalls."[33] The primary problem with the AG is its reliance on the use of a supposedly normal range produced by albumin and, to a lesser extent, phosphate. Concentrations of albumin and phosphate may be grossly abnormal in patients with critical illness, and these abnormalities may change the normal AG range in this setting. Moreover, because these anions are not strong anions, their charge is altered by changes in

pH. These concerns have led some authors to advocate adjusting the normal AG range on the basis of the patient's albumin[35] or even phosphate[6] concentration. Each 1 g/dl of albumin carries a charge of 2.8 mEq/L at a pH of 7.4 (2.3 mEq/L, pH = 7.0; 3.0 mEq/L, pH = 7.6), and each 1 mg/dl of phosphate carries a charge of 0.59 mEq/L at a pH of 7.4 (0.55 mEq/L, pH = 7.0; 0.61 mEq/L, pH = 7.6). Thus, the normal AG for a given patient can be conveniently estimated as follows[6]:

$$Normal\ AG = 2(albumin\ [g/dl]) + 0.5(phosphate\ [mg/dl])$$

or, in international units,

$$Normal\ AG = 0.2(albumin\ [g/L]) + 1.5(phosphate\ [mmol/L])$$

In one study, when this formula for calculating a patient-specific normal AG range was used to determine the presence of unmeasured anions in the blood of critically ill patients, its accuracy was 96%, compared with an accuracy of 33% with the routine AG (normal range = 12 mEq/L).[6] This technique should be employed only when the pH is less than 7.35; even in this situation, it is only accurate within 5 mEq/L. When more accuracy is needed, a slightly more complicated method of estimating unmeasured anions is required.[42,46]

Strong anion gap Another alternative to relying on the traditional AG is to use a parameter derived from the SID. By definition, the SID must be equal and opposite to the sum of the negative charges contributed by A^- and total CO_2. This latter value (A^- + total CO_2) has been termed the effective SID (SIDe).[29] The apparent SID (SIDa) is obtained by measuring concentrations of each individual ion. The SIDa and the SIDe should both equal the true SID. If the SIDa differs from the SIDe, unmeasured ions must be present. If the SIDa is greater than the SIDe, these unmeasured ions are anions; if the SIDa is less than the SIDe, they are cations. The difference between the SIDa and the SIDe has been termed the strong ion gap (SIG) to distinguish it from the AG.[42] Unlike the AG, the SIG is normally 0 and is not affected by changes in the pH or the albumin concentration.

Positive–Anion Gap Acidosis

Lactic acidosis In many forms of critical illness, lactate is the most important cause of metabolic acidosis.[47] Lactate concentrations have been shown to correlate with outcomes in patients with hemorrhagic[48] and septic shock.[49] Traditionally, lactic acid has been viewed as the predominant source of the metabolic acidosis that occurs in sepsis.[50] In this view, lactic acid is released primarily from the musculature and the gut as a consequence of tissue hypoxia, and the amount of lactate produced is believed to correlate with the total oxygen debt, the magnitude of hypoperfusion, and the severity of shock.[47] This view has been challenged by the observation that during sepsis, even in profound shock, resting muscle does not produce lactate. Indeed, various studies have shown that the musculature may actually consume lactate during endotoxemia.[16,51,52]

The data on lactate release by the gut are less clear. There is little question that the gut can release lactate if it is underperfused. It appears, however, that if the gut is adequately perfused, it does not release lactate during sepsis. Under such conditions, the mesentery either is neutral with respect to lactate release or takes up lactate.[16,51] Perfusion is likely to be a major determinant of mesenteric lactate metabolism. In a canine model of sepsis induced by infusion of endotoxin, production of lactate by the gut could not be demonstrated when flow was maintained with dopexamine.[52]

Both animal studies and human studies have shown that the lung may be a prominent source of lactate in the setting of acute lung injury.[16,53,54] These studies do not address the underlying pathophysiologic mechanisms of hyperlactatemia in sepsis, but they do suggest that the conventional wisdom regarding lactate as evidence of tissue dysoxia is, at best, an oversimplification. Indeed, many investigators have begun to offer alternative explanations for the development of hyperlactatemia in this setting [see Table 4].[54-58] One proposed mechanism is metabolic dysfunction from mitochondrial enzymatic derangements, which can and do lead to lactic acidosis. In particular, pyruvate dehydrogenase (PDH), the enzyme responsible for moving pyruvate into the Krebs cycle, is inhibited by endotoxin.[59] Current data, however, suggest that increased aerobic metabolism may be more important than metabolic defects or anaerobic metabolism. In a 1996 study, production of glucose and pyruvate and oxidation were increased in patients with sepsis.[60] Furthermore, when PDH was stimulated by dichloroacetate, there was an additional increase in oxygen consumption but a decrease in glucose and pyruvate production. These results suggest that hyperlactatemia in sepsis occurs as a consequence of increased aerobic metabolism rather than of tissue hypoxia or PDH inhibition.

Such findings are consistent with the known metabolic effects of lactate production on cellular bioenergetics.[61] Lactate production alters cytosolic, and hence mitochondrial, redox states, so that the increased ratio of reduced nicotinamide adenine dinucleotide to nicotinamide adenine dinucleotide (NADH/NAD) supports oxidative phosphorylation as the dominant source of ATP production. Finally, the use of catecholamines, especially epinephrine, also results in lactic acidosis, presumably by stimulating cellular metabolism (e.g., increasing hepatic glycolysis), and may be a common source of lactic acidosis in the ICU.[62,63] It is noteworthy that this phenomenon does not appear to occur with either dobutamine or norepinephrine[64] and does not appear to be related to decreased tissue perfusion.

Although the source and interpretation of lactic acidosis in critically ill patients remain controversial, there is no question about the ability of lactate accumulation to produce acidemia. Lactate is a strong ion because at a pH within the physiologic range, it is almost completely dissociated. (The pK of lactate is 3.9; at a pH of 7.4, 3,162 ions are dissociated for every one ion that is not.) Because lactate is rapidly produced and disposed of by the body, it functions as one of the most dynamic components of the SID. Therefore, a rise in the concentration of lactic acid can produce significant acidemia. Just as often, however, critically ill patients have a degree of hyperlactatemia that far exceeds the degree of acidosis observed. In fact, hyperlactatemia may exist without any metabolic acidosis at all. This is not because acid generation is separate from lactate production (e.g., through "unreversed ATP hydrolysis"), as some have suggested.[64] Phosphate is a weak acid and does not contribute substantially to metabolic acidosis, even under extreme circumstances. Furthermore, the H^+ concentration is determined not by how much H^+ is produced or removed from the plasma but by changes in the dissociation of water and weak acids. Virtually anywhere in the body, the pH is higher than 6.0, and lactate behaves as a strong ion. Generation of lactate reduces the SID and results in an increased H^+ concentration; however, the plasma lactate concentration may also be increased without an accompanying increase in the H^+ concentration.

Table 4 Mechanisms Associated with Increased Serum Lactate Concentration

Tissue hypoxia	Hypodynamic shock Organ ischemia
Hypermetabolism	Increased aerobic glycolysis Increased protein catabolism Hematologic malignancies
Decreased clearance of lactate	Hepatic failure Shock
Inhibition of pyruvate dehydrogenase	Thiamine deficiency ?Endotoxin
?Activation of inflammatory cells	

There are two possible explanations for these observations. First, if lactate is added to the plasma, not as lactic acid but rather as the salt of a strong acid (e.g., sodium lactate), the SID will not change significantly, because a strong cation (Na^+) is being added along with a strong anion. Indeed, as lactate is metabolized and removed, the remaining Na^+ will increase the SID, resulting in metabolic alkalosis. Hence, it would be possible to give enough lactate to increase the plasma lactate concentration without increasing the H^+ concentration. However, given that normal metabolism results in the turnover of approximately 1,500 to 4,500 mmol of lactic acid each day, rapid infusion of a very large amount of lactate would be required to bring about an appreciable increase in the plasma lactate concentration. For example, the use of lactate-based hemofiltration fluid may result in hyperlactatemia with an increased plasma HCO_3^- concentration and an elevated pH.

A more important mechanism whereby hyperlactatemia can exist without acidemia (or with less acidemia than expected) involves correction of the SID by the elimination of another strong anion from the plasma. In a study of sustained lactic acidosis induced by lactic acid infusion, Cl^- was found to move out of the plasma space, thereby normalizing the pH.[65] Under these conditions, hyperlactatemia may persist, but compensatory mechanisms may normalize the base excess and thus restore the SID.

Traditionally, lactic acidosis has been subdivided into type A, in which the mechanism is tissue hypoxia, and type B, in which there is no hypoxia.[66] This distinction may, however, be an artificial one. Disorders such as sepsis may be associated with lactic acidosis through a variety of mechanisms [see Table 4], some conventionally labeled type A and others type B. A potentially useful method of distinguishing between anaerobically produced lactate and lactate from other sources is to measure the serum pyruvate concentration. The normal lactate-to-pyruvate ratio is 10:1,[67] with ratios greater than 25:1 considered to be evidence of anaerobic metabolism.[58] This approach makes biochemical sense because pyruvate is shunted into lactate during anaerobic metabolism, dramatically increasing the lactate-to-pyruvate ratio. However, the precise test characteristics, including normal ranges and sensitivity and specificity data, have not yet been defined for patients. Accordingly, this method remains investigational.

Treatment of lactic acidosis continues to be subject to debate. At present, the only noncontroversial approach is to treat the underlying cause; however, this approach assumes that the underlying cause can be identified with a significant degree of certainty, which is not always the case. The assumption that hypoperfusion is always the most likely cause has been seriously challenged, especially in well-resuscitated patients (see above). Thus, therapy aimed at increasing oxygen delivery may not be effective. Indeed, if epinephrine is used, lactic acidosis may worsen.

Administration of $NaHCO_3$ to treat lactic acidosis remains unproven.[21] In perhaps the most widely quoted study on this topic, hypoxic lactic acidosis was induced in anesthetized dogs by ventilating them with gas containing very little oxygen.[68] These animals were then assigned to treatment with $NaHCO_3$ or place-bo, and surprisingly, the group receiving $NaHCO_3$ actually had higher plasma concentrations of both lactate and H^+ than the con-trol group did. Furthermore, the $NaHCO_3$-treated animals exhib-ited decreases in cardiac output and blood pressure that were not seen in the control group. One possible explanation for these find-ings is that the HCO_3^- was converted to CO_2, and this conversion raised the PCO_2 not only in the blood but also inside the cells of these animals with a fixed minute ventilation; the resulting intra-cellular acidosis might have been detrimental to myocardial func-tion. This hypothesis has not, however, been supported by subse-quent experimental studies, which have not documented para-doxical intracellular acidosis or even detrimental hemodynamic effects after $NaHCO_3$ treatment of hypoxic lactic acidosis.[69] Furthermore, it is not clear how this type of hypoxic lactic acido-sis, induced in well-perfused animals, relates to the clinical condi-tions in which lactic acidosis occurs. The results of clinical studies have been mixed, but overall, they do not support the use of $NaHCO_3$ therapy for lactic acidosis.[21]

Ketoacidosis Another common cause of a metabolic acido-sis with a positive AG is excessive production of ketone bodies, including acetone, acetoacetate, and β-hydroxybutyrate. Both ace-toacetate and β-hydroxybutyrate are strong anions (pK 3.8 and 4.8, respectively).[70] Thus, their presence, like the presence of lac-tate, decreases the SID and increases the H^+ concentration.

Ketones are formed through beta oxidation of fatty acids, a process that is inhibited by insulin. In insulin-deficient states (e.g., diabetes), ketone formation may quickly get out of control. The reason is that severely elevated blood glucose concentrations pro-duce an osmotic diuresis that may lead to volume contraction. This state is associated with elevated cortisol and catecholamine secretion, which further stimulates free fatty acid production.[71] In addition, an increased glucagon level relative to the insulin level leads to a decreased malonyl coenzyme A level and an increased carnitine palmityl acyl transferase level—a combination that increases ketogenesis.

Ketoacidosis may be classified as either diabetic ketoacidosis (DKA) or alcoholic ketoacidosis (AKA). The diagnosis is estab-lished by measuring serum ketone levels. It must be kept in mind, however, that the nitroprusside reaction measures only acetone and acetoacetate, not β-hydroxybutyrate. Thus, the measured ketosis is dependent on the ratio of acetoacetate to β-hydroxybu-tyrate. This ratio is low when lactic acidosis coexists with ketoaci-dosis because the reduced redox state characteristic of lactic aci-dosis favors production of β-hydroxybutyrate.[72] In such circum-stances, therefore, the apparent degree of ketosis is small relative to the degree of acidosis and the elevation of the AG. There is also a risk of confusion during treatment of ketoacidosis, in that ketone levels, as measured by the nitroprusside reaction, sometimes rise even though the acidosis is resolving. This occurs because the nitroprusside reaction does not detect β-hydroxybutyrate, and as β-hydroxybutyrate is cleared, ketosis persists despite improvement in acid-base balance. Furthermore, conversion of β-hydroxybu-tyrate to acetoacetate may cause an apparent increase in ketone levels—again, because the nitroprusside reaction detects the rising levels of acetoacetate but misses the falling levels of β-hydroxybu-

tyrate. Hence, it is better to monitor the success of therapy by measuring the pH and the AG than by assaying serum ketones.

Treatment of DKA includes administration of insulin and large amounts of fluid (0.9% saline is usually recommended); potassium replacement is often required as well. Fluid resuscitation reverses the hormonal stimuli for ketone body formation, and insulin allows the metabolism of ketones and glucose. Administration of $NaHCO_3$ may produce a more rapid rise in the pH by increasing the SID, but there is little evidence that this result is desirable. Furthermore, to the extent that the SID is increased by increasing the plasma Na^+ concentration, the SID will be too high once the ketosis is cleared, thus resulting in a so-called overshoot alkalosis. In any case, such measures are rarely necessary and should proba-bly be avoided except in extreme cases.[73]

A more common problem in the treatment of DKA is the per-sistence of acidemia after the ketosis has resolved. This hyper-chloremic metabolic acidosis occurs as Cl^- replaces ketoacids, thus maintaining a decreased SID and pH. There appear to be two reasons for this phenomenon. First, exogenous Cl^- is often provided in the form of 0.9% saline, which, if given in large enough quantities, will result in a so-called dilutional acidosis (see below). Second, some degree of increased Cl^- reabsorption appar-ently occurs as ketones are excreted in the urine. It has also been suggested that the increased tubular Na^+ load produces electrical-chemical forces that favor Cl^- reabsorption.[74]

AKA is usually less severe than DKA. Treatment consists of administration of fluids and (in contrast to treatment of DKA) glucose rather than insulin.[75] Insulin is contraindicated in AKA patients because it may cause precipitous hypoglycemia.[76] Thiamine must also be given to keep from precipitating Wernicke encephalopathy.

Acidosis secondary to renal failure Although renal failure may produce a hyperchloremic metabolic acidosis, especially when it is chronic, the buildup of sulfates and other acids frequently increases the AG; however, the increase usually is not large.[77] Similarly, uncomplicated renal failure rarely produces severe aci-dosis, except when it is accompanied by high rates of acid genera-tion (e.g., from hypermetabolism).[78] In all cases, the SID is decreased and is expected to remain so unless some therapy is pro-vided. Hemodialysis permits the removal of sulfate and other ions and allows the restoration of normal Na^+ and Cl^- balance, thus returning the SID to a normal (or near-normal) value. However, those patients who do not yet require dialysis and those who are between treatments often require some other therapy aimed at increasing the SID. $NaHCO_3$ may be used for this purpose, pro-vided that the plasma Na^+ concentration is not already elevated.

Acidosis secondary to toxin ingestion Metabolic acidosis with an increased AG is a major feature of various types of intox-ication [see Table 2]. Generally, it is more important to recognize these conditions and provide specific therapy for them than it is to treat the acid-base imbalances that they produce.

Acidosis secondary to rhabdomyolysis The extensive muscle tissue breakdown associated with myonecrosis may also be a source of positive-AG metabolic acidosis. In this situation, the acidosis results from accumulation of organic acids. The myoglo-binuria associated with the disorder may also induce renal failure. In most cases, the diagnosis is a clinical one and can be facilitated by measuring creatinine kinase or aldolase levels. Early identifica-tion and aggressive resuscitation may prevent the onset of renal failure and improve the prognosis.[79]

Acidosis of unknown origin   Several causes of an increased AG have been reported that have yet to be elucidated. An unexplained AG in the nonketotic hyperosmolar state of diabetes has been reported.[39] In addition, even when very careful measurement techniques have been employed, unmeasured anions have been reported in the blood of patients with sepsis,[40,41] patients with liver disease,[42] and animals to which endotoxin had been administered.[43] Furthermore, unknown cations also appear in the blood of some critically ill patients.[41] The significance of these findings remains to be determined.

Prognostic significance of positive-AG metabolic acidosis
Several studies have examined whether the presence of unmeasured anions in the blood is associated with particular outcomes in critically ill patients. Two such studies focused on trauma patients. In one, the investigators examined 2,152 sets of laboratory data from 427 trauma patients and found that the SIG altered the acid-base disorder diagnosis in 28% of the datasets.[80] Simultaneous measurements of blood gas, serum electrolyte, albumin, and lactate values were used to calculate the base deficit, the AG, and the SIG. Unmeasured anions (defined by the presence of an elevated SIG) were present in 92% of patients (mean SIG, 5.9 ± 3.3); hyperlactatemia and hyperchloremia occurred in only 18% and 21% of patients, respectively. The arterial SBE at ICU admission was poorly predictive of hospital survival, and its predictive ability was only slightly improved by controlling for unmeasured ions. In this dataset, survivors could not be differentiated from nonsurvivors in the group as a whole on the basis of the SIG. However, in the subgroup of patients whose lactate level was normal at admission, there was a significant difference in the SIG between survivors and nonsurvivors, though no such differences were noted in the conventional measures (i.e., SBE and AG).

The poor predictive ability of the SBE, the AG, and even the SIG has been confirmed by studies of general ICU patients. In one study, analysis of data from 300 adult ICU patients demonstrated statistically significant but weak correlations between these measures and hospital mortality.[81] In another study, however, pretreatment SIG was found to be a very strong predictor of outcome in 282 patients who had sustained major vascular injury.[82] All but one of the nonsurvivors had an initial emergency department (ED) pH of 7.26 or lower, an SBE of –7.3 mEq/L or lower, a lactate concentration of 5 mmol/L or higher, and an SIG of 5 mEq/L or higher. All of the acid-base descriptors were strongly associated with outcome, but the SIG was the one that discriminated most strongly. The investigators concluded that initial ED acid-base variables, especially SIG, could distinguish survivors of major vascular injury from nonsurvivors.

Even though the uncorrected AG and the SBE correlate poorly with the arterial lactate concentration in trauma patients,[83] several investigators have proposed that these parameters be used as surrogate measures of the severity of shock or lack of resuscitation. Various studies have shown that the SBE is a poor predictor of lactic acidosis and mortality both in medical patients and in surgical or trauma patients and that it cannot be substituted for direct measurement of the serum lactate concentration.[33,84,85] Some investigators, however, have found that the SBE can be used as a marker of injury severity and mortality and as a predictor of transfusion requirements.[86-88] Unfortunately, the SBE can determine only the degree of acid-base derangement, never the cause. In many critically injured patients, abnormalities in body water content, electrolyte levels, and albumin concentration limit any potential correlation between SBE and lactate concentration, even when other sources of acid are absent.

Several reports in the trauma literature have focused on the prognostic value of persistently elevated lactic acid levels during the first 24 to 48 hours after injury. In one study, involving 76 patients with multiple injuries who were admitted directly to the ICU from the operating room or the ED, serum lactate levels and oxygen transport were measured at ICU admission and at 8, 16, 24, 36, and 48 hours.[89] In those patients whose lactate levels returned to normal within 24 hours, the survival rate was 100%, and in those whose lactate levels returned to normal between 24 and 48 hours, the survival rate was 75%. However, in those whose lactate levels did not return to normal by 48 hours, the survival rate was only 14%. Thus, the rate of normalization of the serum lactate level is an important prognostic factor for survival in a severely injured patient.

Non–Anion Gap (Hyperchloremic) Acidoses

Hyperchloremic metabolic acidosis occurs as a result of either an increase in the level of Cl^- relative to the levels of strong cations (especially Na^+) or a loss of cations with retention of Cl^-. The various causes of such an acidosis [see Table 3] can be distinguished on the basis of the history and the measured Cl^- concentration in the urine. When acidosis occurs, the kidney normally responds by increasing Cl^- excretion; the absence of this response identifies the kidney as the source of the problem. Extrarenal hyperchloremic acidoses occur because of exogenous Cl^- loads (iatrogenic acidosis) or because of loss of cations from the lower GI tract without proportional loss of Cl^- (gastrointestinal acidosis).

Renal tubular acidosis   Most cases of renal tubular acidosis (RTA) can be correctly diagnosed by determining urine and plasma electrolyte levels and pH and calculating the SIDa in the urine [see Table 3].[90] However, caution must be exercised when the plasma pH is greater than 7.35, because urine Cl^- excretion may be turned off. In such circumstances, it may be necessary to infuse sodium sulfate or furosemide. These agents stimulate excretion of Cl^- and K^+ and may be used to unmask the defect and to probe K^+ secretory capacity.

Establishing the mechanisms of RTA has proved difficult. It is likely that much of the difficulty results from the attempt to understand the physiology from the perspective of regulation of H^+ and HCO_3^- concentrations. As noted, however (see above), this approach is simply inconsistent with the principles of physical chemistry. The kidney does not excrete H^+ to any greater extent as NH_4^+ than it does as H_2O. The purpose of renal ammoniagenesis is to allow the excretion of Cl^-, which balances the charge of NH_4^+. In all types of RTA, the defect is the inability to excrete Cl^- in proportion to excretion of Na^+, though the precise reasons for this inability vary by RTA type. Treatment is largely dependent on whether the kidney will respond to mineralocorticoid replacement or whether there is Na^+ loss that can be counteracted by administering $NaHCO_3$.

Classic distal (type I) RTA responds to $NaHCO_3$ replacement; generally, the required dosage is in the range of 50 to 100 mEq/day. K^+ defects are also common in this type of RTA, and thus, K^+ replacement is also required. A variant of the classic distal RTA is a hyperkalemic form, which is actually more common than the classic type. The central defect in this variant form appears to be impaired Na^+ transport in the cortical collecting duct. Patients with this condition also respond to $NaHCO_3$ replacement.

Proximal (type II) RTA is characterized by defects in the reabsorption of both Na^+ and K^+. It is an uncommon disorder and usually occurs as part of Fanconi syndrome, in which reabsorption of glucose, phosphate, urate, and amino acids is also impaired. Treatment of type II RTA with NaHCO$_3$ is ineffective; increased ion delivery merely results in increased excretion. Thiazide diuretics have been used to treat this disorder, with varying degrees of success.

Type IV RTA is caused by aldosterone deficiency or resistance. It is diagnosed on the basis of the high serum K$^+$ and the low urine pH (< 5.5). The most effective treatment usually involves removal of the cause (most commonly a drug, such as a nonsteroidal anti-inflammatory agent, heparin, or a potassium-sparing diuretic). Occasionally, mineralocorticoid replacement is required.

Gastrointestinal acidosis Fluid secreted into the gut lumen contains more Na$^+$ than Cl$^-$; the proportions are similar to those seen in plasma. Massive loss of this fluid, particularly if lost volume is replaced with fluid containing equal amounts of Na$^+$ and Cl$^-$, will result in a decreased plasma Na$^+$ concentration relative to the Cl$^-$ concentration and a reduced SID. Such a scenario can be prevented by using solutions such as lactated Ringer solution (LRS) instead of water or saline. LRS has a more physiologic SID than water or saline and therefore does not produce acidosis except in rare circumstances [see Positive–Anion Gap Acidosis, Lactic Acidosis, above].

Iatrogenic acidosis Two of the most common causes of a hyperchloremic metabolic acidosis are iatrogenic, and both involve administration of Cl$^-$. One of these potential causes is parenteral nutrition. Modern parenteral nutrition formulas contain weak anions (e.g., acetate) in addition to Cl$^-$, and the proportions of these anions can be adjusted according to the acid-base status of the patient. If sufficient amounts of weak anions are not provided, the plasma Cl$^-$ concentration will increase, reducing the SID and causing acidosis.

The other potential cause is fluid resuscitation with saline, which can give rise to a so-called dilutional acidosis (a problem first described more than 40 years ago).[91,92] Some authors have argued that dilutional acidosis is, at most, a minor issue.[93] This argument is based on studies showing that in healthy animals, large doses of NaCl produce only a minor hyperchloremic acidosis.[94] These studies have been interpreted as indicating that dilutional acidosis occurs only in extreme cases and even then is mild. However, this line of reasoning cannot be applied to critically ill patients, for two reasons. First, it is common for patients with sepsis or trauma to require large-volume resuscitation; sometimes, such patients receive crystalloid infusions equivalent to 5 to 10 times their plasma volumes in a single day. Second, critically ill patients frequently are not in a state of normal acid-base balance to begin with. Often, they have lactic acidosis or renal insufficiency. Furthermore, critically ill patients may not be able to compensate for acid-base imbalance normally (e.g., by increasing ventilation), and they may have abnormal buffer capacity as a result of hypoalbuminemia. In ICU and surgical patients,[95-97] as well as in animals with experimentally induced sepsis,[98] saline-induced acidosis does occur and can produce significant acidemia.

The reason why administration of saline causes acidosis is that solutions containing equal amounts of Na$^+$ and Cl$^-$ affect plasma concentrations of Na$^+$ and Cl$^-$ differently. The normal Na$^+$ concentration is 35 to 45 mEq/L higher than the normal Cl$^-$ concentration. Thus, adding (for example) 154 mEq/L of each ion in 0.9% saline will result in a greater relative increase in the Cl$^-$ concentration than in the Na$^+$ concentration. So much is clear; what may be less clear is why critically ill patients are more susceptible to this disorder than healthy persons are.

It appears that many critically ill patients have a significantly lower SID than healthy persons do, even when these patients have no evidence of a metabolic acid-base derangement.[99] This finding is not surprising, in that the positive charge of the SID is balanced by the negative charges of A$^-$ and total CO$_2$. Because many critically ill patients are hypoalbuminemic, A$^-$ tends to be reduced. Because the body maintains Pco$_2$ for other reasons, a reduction in A$^-$ leads to a reduction in SID so that a normal pH can be maintained. Thus, a typical ICU patient may have an SID of 30 mEq/L, rather than 40 to 42 mEq/L. If a metabolic acidosis (e.g., lactic acidosis) then develops in this patient, the SID will decrease further. If this patient is subsequently resuscitated with large volumes of 0.9% saline, a significant metabolic acidosis will result.

The clinical implication for management of ICU patients is that if large volumes of fluid are to be given for resuscitation, fluids that are more physiologic than saline should be used. One alternative is LRS, which has a more physiologic ratio of Na$^+$ content to Cl$^-$ content and thus has an SID that is closer to normal (roughly 28 mEq/L, compared with an SID of 0 mEq/L for saline). Of course, the assumption here is that the lactate in LRS is metabolized, which, as noted (see above), is almost always the case. Volume resuscitation also reduces the weak acid concentration, thereby moderating the acidosis. One ex vivo study concluded that administration of a solution with an SID of approximately 24 mEq/L will have a neutral effect on the pH as blood is progressively diluted.[100]

Unexplained hyperchloremic acidosis Critically ill patients sometimes manifest hyperchloremic metabolic acidosis for reasons that cannot be determined. Often, other coexisting types of metabolic acidosis are present, making the precise diagnosis difficult. For example, some patients with lactic acidosis have a greater degree of acidosis than can be explained by the increase in the lactate concentration,[40] and some patients with sepsis and acidosis have normal lactate levels.[101] In many instances, the presence of unexplained anions is the cause,[40-42] but in other cases, there is a hyperchloremic acidosis. Saline resuscitation may be responsible for much of this acidosis (see above), but experimental evidence from endotoxemic animals suggests that as much as a third of the acidosis cannot be explained in terms of current knowledge.[98]

One potential explanation for unexplained hyperchloremic acidosis is partial loss of the Donnan equilibrium between plasma and interstitial fluid. The severe capillary leakage that accompanies this loss of equilibrium results in loss of albumin from the vascular space, which means that another ion must move into this space to maintain the charge balance between the two compartments. If Cl$^-$ moves into the plasma space to restore the charge balance, a strong anion is replacing a weak anion, and a hyperchloremic metabolic acidosis results. This hypothesis appears reasonable but, at present, remains unproven.

METABOLIC ALKALOSIS

Metabolic alkalosis occurs as a result of an increased SID or a decreased A$_{tot}$, secondary either to loss of anions (e.g., Cl$^-$ from the stomach and albumin from the plasma) or increases in cations (rare). Metabolic alkaloses can be divided into those in which Cl$^-$ losses are temporary and can be effectively replaced (chloride-responsive alkaloses) and those in which hormonal mechanisms produce ongoing losses that, at best, can be only temporarily offset by Cl$^-$ administration (chloride-resistant alkaloses) [see Table 5]. Like hyperchloremic acidosis, metabolic alkalosis can be confirmed by measuring the urine Cl$^-$ concentration.

Table 5 Differential Diagnosis for Metabolic Alkalosis

Chloride loss (Cl⁻ < Na⁺)	Chloride-responsive alkalosis (urine Cl⁻ concentration < 10 mmol/L)
	  GI loss
	    Vomiting
	    Gastric drainage
	    Chloride-wasting diarrhea (villous adenoma)
	  Diuretic use
	  Hypercapnia
	Chloride-resistant alkalosis (urine Cl⁻ concentration > 20 mmol/L)
	  Mineralocorticoid excess
	    Primary hyperaldosteronism (Conn syndrome)
	    Secondary hyperaldosteronism
	    Cushing syndrome
	    Liddle syndrome
	    Bartter syndrome
	    Exogenous corticoids
	    Excessive licorice intake
	  Ongoing diuretic use

Exogenous sodium load (Na⁺ > Cl⁻)	Sodium salt administration (acetate, citrate)
	  Massive blood transfusions
	  Parenteral nutrition
	  Plasma volume expanders
	  Sodium lactate (Ringer solution)

Other	Severe deficiency of intracellular cations (Mg^{2+}, K^+)

Chloride-Responsive Alkalosis

Chloride-responsive metabolic alkalosis usually occurs as a result of loss of Cl⁻ from the stomach (e.g., through vomiting or gastric drainage). Treatment consists of replacing the lost Cl⁻, either slowly (with NaCl) or relatively rapidly (with KCl or even HCl). Because chloride-responsive alkalosis is usually accompanied by volume depletion, the most common therapeutic choice is to give saline along with KCl. Dehydration stimulates aldosterone secretion, which results in reabsorption of Na⁺ and loss of K⁺. Saline is effective even though it contains Na⁺ because the administration of equal amounts of Na⁺ and Cl⁻ yields a larger relative increase in the Cl⁻ concentration than in the Na⁺ concentration (see above). In rare circumstances, when neither K⁺ loss nor volume depletion is a problem, it may be desirable to replace Cl⁻ by giving HCl.

Diuresis and other forms of volume contraction cause metabolic alkalosis mainly by stimulating aldosterone secretion; however, diuretics also directly stimulate excretion of K⁺ and Cl⁻, further complicating the problem and inducing metabolic alkalosis more rapidly.

Chloride-Resistant Alkalosis

Chloride-resistant alkalosis [see Table 5] is characterized by an increased urine Cl⁻ concentration (> 20 mmol/L) and ongoing Cl⁻ loss that cannot be abolished by Cl⁻ replacement. Most commonly, the proximate cause is increased mineralocorticoid activity. Treatment involves identification and correction of the underlying disorder.

Alkalosis from Other Causes

In rare situations, an increased SID—and therefore metabolic alkalosis—occurs secondary to cation administration rather than to anion depletion. Examples include milk-alkali syndrome and intravenous administration of strong cations without strong anions. The latter occurs with massive blood transfusion because Na⁺ is given with citrate (a weak anion) rather than with Cl⁻. Similar results ensue when parenteral nutrition formulations contain too much acetate and not enough Cl⁻ to balance the Na⁺ load.

Respiratory Acid-Base Disorders

Respiratory disorders are far easier to diagnose and treat than metabolic disorders are because the mechanism is always the same, even though the underlying disease process may vary. CO_2 is produced by cellular metabolism or by the titration of HCO_3^- by metabolic acids. Normally, alveolar ventilation is adjusted to maintain the P_aCO_2 between 35 and 45 mm Hg. When alveolar ventilation is increased or decreased out of proportion to the P_aCO_2, a respiratory acid-base disorder exists.

PATHOPHYSIOLOGY

CO_2 is produced by the body at a rate of 220 ml/min, which equates to production of 15 mol/L of carbonic acid each day.[102] By way of comparison, total daily production of all the nonrespiratory acids managed by the kidney and the gut amounts to less than 500 mmol/L. Pulmonary ventilation is adjusted by the respiratory center in response to P_aCO_2, pH, and PO_2, as well as in response to exercise, anxiety, wakefulness, and other signals. Normal P_aCO_2 (40 mm Hg) is attained by precisely matching alveolar ventilation to metabolic CO_2 production. P_aCO_2 changes in predictable ways as a compensatory ventilatory response to the altered arterial pH produced by metabolic acidosis or alkalosis [see Table 1].

RESPIRATORY ACIDOSIS

Mechanism

When the rate of CO_2 elimination is inadequate relative to the rate of tissue CO_2 production, the P_aCO_2 rises to a new steady state, determined by the new relation between alveolar ventilation and CO_2 production. In the short term, this rise in the P_aCO_2 increases the concentrations of both H⁺ and HCO_3^- according to the carbonic acid equilibrium equation. Thus, the change in the HCO_3^- concentration is mediated not by any systemic adaptation but by chemical equilibrium. The higher HCO_3^- concentration does not buffer the H⁺ concentration. The SID does not change, nor does the SBE. Tissue acidosis always occurs in respiratory acidosis because CO_2 inevitably builds up in the tissue.

If the P_aCO_2 remains elevated, a compensatory response will occur, and the SID will increase to return the H⁺ concentration to the normal range. The increase in the SID is accomplished primarily by removing Cl⁻ from the plasma space. If Cl⁻ moves into tissues or red blood cells, it will result in intracellular acidosis (complicated by the elevated tissue PCO_2); thus, to exert a lasting effect on the SID, Cl⁻ must be removed from the body. The kidney is designed to do this, whereas the GI tract is not (though the adaptive capacity of the GI tract as a route of Cl⁻ elimination has not been fully explored). Accordingly, patients with renal disease have a very difficult time adapting to chronic respiratory acidosis.

Patients whose renal function is intact can eliminate Cl⁻ in the urine; after a few days, the SID rises to the level required to restore the pH to a value of 7.35. It is unclear whether this amount of time is necessary because of the physiologic constraints of the system or because the body benefits from not being overly sensitive to transient changes in alveolar ventilation. In any case, this response yields an increased pH for any degree of hypercapnia. According to the Henderson-Hasselbalch equation, the increased pH results in an increased HCO_3^- concentration for a given PCO_2. Thus, the "adaptive" increase in the HCO_3^- concentration is actually the consequence, not the cause, of the increased pH. Although the HCO_3^- concentration is a convenient and reliable marker of metabolic compensation, it is not the mechanism of the compensatory response. This point is not merely a semantic one: as noted (see above), only changes in the independent variables of acid-base balance (PCO_2, A_{tot}, and SID) can affect the plasma H^+ concentration, and HCO_3^- concentration is not an independent variable.

Management

Treatment of underlying ventilatory impairment As with virtually all acid-base disorders, treatment begins by addressing the underlying disorder. Acute respiratory acidosis may be caused by CNS suppression; neuromuscular diseases or conditions that impair neuromuscular functions (e.g., myasthenia gravis, hypophosphatemia, and hypokalemia); or diseases affecting the airway or the lung parenchyma (e.g., asthma and acute respiratory dysfunction syndrome [ARDS]). The last category of conditions produces not only alveolar hypoventilation but also primary hypoxia. The two can be distinguished by means of the alveolar gas equation:

$$P_{A}O_2 = P_IO_2 - P_aCO_2/R$$

where R is the respiratory exchange coefficient (generally taken to be 0.8), and P_IO_2 is the inspired oxygen tension (approximately 150 mm Hg in room air). Thus, as the P_aCO_2 increases, the $P_{A}O_2$ should also decrease in a predictable fashion. If the $P_{A}O_2$ falls by more than the predicted amount, there is a defect in gas exchange.

In most cases, chronic respiratory acidosis is caused by either chronic lung disease (e.g., chronic obstructive pulmonary disease [COPD]) or chest wall disease (e.g., kyphoscoliosis). In rare cases, it is caused by central hypoventilation or chronic neuromuscular disease.

Control of hypoxemia Another aspect of respiratory acidosis that is illustrated by the alveolar gas equation is that the primary threat to life comes not from acidosis but from hypoxemia. In patients breathing room air, the P_aCO_2 cannot exceed 80 mm Hg before life-threatening hypoxemia results. Accordingly, supplemental oxygen is required in the treatment of these patients. Unfortunately, oxygen administration is almost never sufficient treatment by itself, and it generally proves necessary to address the ventilatory defect. When the underlying cause can be addressed quickly (as when the effects of narcotics are reversed with naloxone), endotracheal intubation may be avoidable. In the majority of patients, however, this is not the case, and mechanical ventilation must be initiated. Mechanical support is indicated for patients who are unstable or at risk for instability and patients whose CNS function is deteriorating. Furthermore, in patients who exhibit signs of respiratory muscle fatigue, mechanical ventilation should be instituted before respiratory failure occurs. Thus, it is not the absolute P_aCO_2 value that is the most important consideration in this situation but, rather, the clinical condition of the patient.

Chronic hypercapnia must be treated if the patient's clinical condition is deteriorating acutely. In this setting, it is important not to try to restore the P_aCO_2 to the normal range of 35 to 45 mm Hg. Instead, the patient's baseline P_aCO_2, if known, should be the therapeutic target; if the baseline P_aCO_2 is not known, a target P_aCO_2 of 60 mm Hg is perhaps a reasonable choice. Overventilation can have two undesirable consequences. First, if the P_aCO_2 is rapidly normalized in a patient with chronic respiratory acidosis and an appropriately large SID, life-threatening alkalemia may ensue. Second, even if the P_aCO_2 is corrected slowly, the plasma SID may decrease over time, making it impossible to wean the patient from mechanical ventilation.

One option for treatment of hypercapnia is noninvasive ventilation with a bilevel positive airway pressure (BiPAP) system. This technique may be useful in the management of some patients, particularly those whose sensorium is not impaired.[103] Rapid infusion of $NaHCO_3$ in patients with respiratory acidosis may induce acute respiratory failure if alveolar ventilation is not increased to account for the increased CO_2. Thus, if $NaHCO_3$ is to be given, it must be administered slowly, with alveolar ventilation adjusted appropriately. Furthermore, it must be remembered that $NaHCO_3$ works by increasing the plasma Na^+ concentration; if this effect is not possible or not desirable, $NaHCO_3$ should not be given.

Occasionally, it is useful to reduce CO_2 production. This can be accomplished by reducing the amount of carbohydrates supplied in feedings (in patients requiring nutritional support), controlling body temperature (in febrile patients), or providing sedation (in anxious or combative patients). In addition, treatment of shivering in the postoperative period can reduce CO_2 production. Rarely, however, can hypercapnia be controlled with these CO_2-reducing techniques alone.

Permissive hypercapnia. In the past few years, there has been considerable interest in ventilator-associated lung injury. Overdistention of alveoli can result in tissue injury and microvascular permeability, which lead to interstitial and alveolar edema. In animal studies, prolonged use of elevated airway pressures and increased lung volumes resulted in increased pathologic pulmonary changes and decreased survival when compared with ventilatory strategies employing lower pressures and volumes.[104,105] In a large multicenter clinical trial, simply lowering the tidal volume on the ventilator from 12 ml/kg to 6 ml/kg in patients with acute lung injury resulted in a 9% absolute reduction in mortality risk.[106] Although the protocol followed in this trial did not advocate a reduced minute ventilation and hence an elevated P_aCO_2, this approach, often referred to as permissive hypercapnia or controlled hypoventilation, has become increasingly popular. Uncontrolled studies suggest that permissive hypercapnia may reduce mortality in patients with severe ARDS.[20] This strategy is not, however, without risks. Sedation is mandatory, and neuromuscular blocking agents are frequently required. Intracranial pressure rises, as does transpulmonary pressure; consequently, this technique is unusable in patients with brain injury or right ventricular dysfunction. There is controversy regarding how low the pH can be allowed to fall. Some authors have reported good results with pH values of 7.0 or even lower,[20] but most have advocated more modest pH reductions (i.e., ≥ 7.25).

RESPIRATORY ALKALOSIS

Respiratory alkalosis may be the most frequently encountered acid-base disorder. It occurs in residents of high-altitude locales and in persons with any of a wide range of pathologic conditions, the most important of which are salicylate intoxication, early sepsis, hepatic failure, and hypoxic respiratory disorders. Respiratory alkalosis also occurs in association with pregnancy and with pain or anxiety. Hypocapnia appears to be a particularly strong negative prognostic indicator in patients with critical illness.[107] Like acute respiratory acidosis, acute respiratory alkalosis results in a small change in the HCO_3^- concentration, as dictated by the Henderson-Hasselbalch equation. If hypocapnia persists, the SID begins to decrease as a consequence of renal Cl⁻ reabsorption. After 2 to 3 days, the SID assumes a new and lower steady state.[108]

Severe alkalemia is unusual in respiratory alkalosis. Management therefore is typically directed toward the underlying cause. In general, these mild acid-base changes are clinically important more for what they can alert the clinician to, in terms of underlying disease, than for any direct threat they pose to the patient. In rare cases, respiratory depression with narcotics is necessary.

Pseudorespiratory Alkalosis

The presence of arterial hypocapnia in patients experiencing profound circulatory shock has been termed pseudorespiratory alkalosis.[109] This condition occurs when alveolar ventilation is supported but the circulation is grossly inadequate. In such circumstances, the mixed venous P_{CO_2} is significantly elevated, but the P_aCO_2 is normal or even decreased as a consequence of reduced CO_2 delivery to the lung and increased pulmonary transit time. Overall CO_2 clearance is therefore markedly decreased, and profound tissue acidosis—usually both metabolic and respiratory—ensues. The metabolic component of the acidosis comes from tissue hypoperfusion and hyperlactatemia. Arterial oxygen saturation may also appear adequate despite tissue hypoxemia. Pseudorespiratory alkalemia is rapidly fatal unless the patient's systemic hemodynamic status can be normalized.

References

1. Kellum JA, Bellomo R, Kramer DJ, et al: Splanchnic buffering of metabolic acid during early endotoxemia. J Crit Care 12:7, 1997

2. Schlichtig R, Grogono AW, Severinghaus JW: Human PaCO₂ and standard base excess compensation for acid-base imbalance. Crit Care Med 26:1173, 1998

3. Corey HE: Stewart and beyond: new models of acid-base balance. Kidney Int 64:777, 2003

4. Wooten EW: Calculation of physiological acid-base parameters in multicompartment systems with application to human blood. J Appl Physiol 95:2333, 2003

5. Stewart P: Modern quantitative acid-base chemistry. Can J Physiol Pharmacol 61:1444, 1983

6. Kellum JA: Determinants of blood pH in health and disease. Crit Care 4:6, 2000

7. Sirker AA, Rhodes A, Grounds RM, et al: Acid-base physiology: the 'traditional' and the 'modern' approaches. Anaesthesia 57:348, 2002

8. Leblanc M, Kellum JA: Biochemical and biophysical principles of hydrogen ion regulation. Critical Care Nephrology. Ronco C, Bellomo R, Eds. Kluwer Academic Publishers, Dordrecht, The Netherlands, 1998, p 261

9. Jones NL: A quantitative physicochemical approach to acid-base physiology. Clin Biochem 23:189, 1990

10. Hansen JE, Sue DY: Should blood gas measurement be corrected for the patient's temperature? N Engl J Med 303:341, 1980

11. Delaney KA, Howland MA, Vassallo S, et al: Assessment of acid-base disturbances in hypothermia and their physiologic consequences. Ann Emerg Med 18:72, 1989

12. Bourke E, Haussinger D: pH homeostasis: the conceptual change. Contrib Nephrol 100:58, 1992

13. Oliver J, Bourke E: Adaptations in urea and ammonium excretion in metabolic acidosis in the rat: a reinterpretation. Clin Sci Mol Med 48:515, 1975

14. Atkinson DE, Bourke E: pH Homeostasis in terrestrial vertebrates; ammonium ion as a proton source. Comparative and Environmental Physiology. Mechanisms of Systemic Regulation, Acid-Base Regulation, Ion Transfer and Metabolism. Heisler N, Ed. Springer, Berlin, 1995, p 1

15. Moore EW: The alkaline tide. Gastroenterology 52:1052, 1967

16. Bellomo R, Kellum JA, Pinsky MR: Visceral lactate fluxes during early endotoxemia in the dog. Chest 110:198, 1996

17. Kellum JA, Bellomo R, Kramer DJ, et al: Splanchnic buffering of metabolic acid during early endotoxemia. J Crit Care 12:7, 1997

18. Lindinger MI, Heigenhauser GJF, McKelvie RS, et al: Blood ion regulation during repeated maximal exercise and recovery in humans. Am J Physiol 262:R126, 1992

19. Forrest DM, Walley KR, Russel JA: Impact of acid-base disorders on individual organ systems. Critical Care Nephrology. Ronco C, Bellomo R, Eds. Kluwer Academic Publishers, Dordrecht, The Netherlands, 1998, p 297

20. Hickling KG, Walsh J, Henderson S, et al: Low mortality rate in adult respiratory distress syndrome using low-volume, pressure-limited ventilation with permissive hypercapnia: a prospective study. Crit Care Med 22:1568, 1994

21. Forsythe SM, Schmidt GA: Sodium bicarbonate for the treatment of lactic acidosis. Chest 117: 260, 2000

22. Kette F, Weil MH, Gazmuri RJ: Buffer solutions may compromise cardiac resuscitation by reducing coronary perfusion pressure. JAMA 266: 2121, 1991

23. Hindman BJ: Sodium bicarbonate in the treatment of subtypes of lactic acidosis: physiologic considerations. Anesthesiology 72:1064, 1990

24. Bersin RM, Arieff AI: Improved hemodynamic function during hypoxia with carbicarb, a new agent for the management of acidosis. Circulation 77:227, 1998

25. Spital A, Garella S: Correction of acid-base derangments. Critical Care Nephrology. Ronco C, Bellomo R, Eds. Kluwer Academic Publishers, Dordrecht, The Netherlands, 1998, p 311

26. Bleich HL, Swartz WB: Tris buffer (THAM): an appraisal of its physiologic effects and clinical usefulness. N Engl J Med 274:782, 1966

27. Arieff AI: Bicarbonate therapy in the treatment of metabolic acidosis. The Pharmacologic Approach to the Critically Ill Patient. Chernow B, Ed. Williams & Wilkins, Baltimore, 1994, p 973

28. Narins RG, Emmett M: Simple and mixed acid-base disorders: a practical approach. Medicine 59:161, 1980

29. Figge J, Mydosh T, Fencl V: Serum proteins and acid-base equilibria: a follow-up. J Lab Clin Med 120:713, 1992

30. Sadjadi SA: A new range for the anion gap. Ann Intern Med 123:807, 1995

31. Winter SD, Pearson R, Gabow PG, et al: The fall of the serum anion gap. Arch Intern Med 150: 311, 1990

32. Levinsky NG: Acidosis and alkalosis. Harrison's Principles of Internal Medicine, 11th ed. Braunwald E, Isselbacher KJ, Petersdorf RG, et al, Eds. McGraw-Hill Press, New York, 1987

33. Salem MM, Mujais SK: Gaps in the anion gap. Arch Intern Med 152:1625, 1992

34. Oster JR, Perez GO, Materson BJ: Use of the anion gap in clinical medicine. South Med J 81:229, 1988

35. Gabow PA: Disorders associated with an altered anion gap. Kidney Int 27:472, 1985

36. Whelton A, Carter GG, Garth M, et al: Carbenicillin-induced acidosis and seizures. JAMA 218:1942, 1971

37. Kang Y, Aggarwal S, Virji M, et al: Clinical evaluation of autotransfusion during liver transplantation. Anesthesia & Analgesia 72:94, 1991

38. Narins RG, Jones ER, Townsend R, et al: Metabolic acid-base disorders: pathophysiology, classification and treatment. Fluid Electrolyte and Acid-Base Disorders. Arieff AI, DeFronzo RA, (Eds). Churchill Livingston Press, New York, 1985, p 269

39. Arieff AI, Carroll HJ: Nonketotic hyperosmolar coma with hyperglycemia: clinical features, pathophysiology, renal function, acid-base balance, plasma-cerebrospinal fluid equilibria and effects of therapy in 37 cases. Medicine 51:73, 1972

40. Mecher C, Rackow EC, Astiz ME, et al: Unaccounted for anion in metabolic acidosis during severe sepsis in humans. Crit Care Med 19:705, 1991

41. Gilfix BM, Bique M, Magder S: A physical chemical approach to the analysis of acid-base balance in the clinical setting. J Crit Care 8:187, 1993

42. Kellum JA, Kramer DJ, Pinsky MR: Strong ion gap: a methodology for exploring unexplained anions. J Crit Care 110:51, 1995

43. Kirschbaum B: Increased anion gap after liver transplantation. Am J Med Sci 313:107, 1997

44. Kellum JA, Bellomo R, Kramer DJ, et al: Hepatic anion flux during acute endotoxemia. J Appl Physiol 78:2212, 1995

45. Mehta K, Kruse JA, Carlson RW: The relationship between anion gap and elevated lactate. Crit Care Med 14:405, 1986

46. Schlichtig R: [Base excess] vs [strong ion difference]: which is more helpful? Adv Exp Med Biol 411:91, 1997

47. Mizock BA, Falk JL: Lactic acidosis in critical illness. Crit Care Med 20:80, 1992

48. Weil MH, Afifi AA: Experimental and clinical studies on lactate and pyruvate as indicators of the severity of acute circulatory failure (shock). Circulation 41:989, 1970

49. Blair E: Acid-base balance in bacteremic shock. Arch Intern Med 127:731, 1971

50. Madias NE: Lactic acidosis. Kidney Int 29:752, 1986

51. van Lambalgen AA, Runge HC, van den Bos GC, et al: Regional lactate production in early canine endotoxin shock. Am J Physiol 254:E45, 1988

52. Cain SM, Curtis SE: Systemic and regional oxygen uptake and delivery and lactate flux in endotoxic dogs infused with dopexamine. Crit Care Med 19:1552, 1991

53. Brown S, Gutierrez G, Clark C, et al: The lung as a source of lactate in sepsis and ARDS. J Crit Care 11:2, 1996

54. Kellum JA, Kramer DJ, Lee KH, et al: Release of lactate by the lung in acute lung injury. Chest 111:1301, 1997

55. De Backer D, Creteur J, Zhang H, et al: Lactate production by the lungs in acute lung injury. Am J Respir Crit Care Med 156:1099, 1997

56. Stacpoole PW: Lactic acidosis and other mitochondrial disorders. Metab Clin Exper 46:306, 1997

57. Fink MP: Does tissue acidosis in sepsis indicate tissue hypoperfusion? Intensive Care Med 22:1144, 1996

58. Gutierrez G, Wolf ME: Lactic acidosis in sepsis: A commentary. Intensive Care Med 22:6, 1996

59. Kilpatrick-Smith L, Dean J, Erecinska M, et al: Cellular effects of endotoxin in vitro. II. Reversibility of endotoxic damage. Circ Shock 11:101, 1983

60. Gore DC, Jahoor F, Hibbert JM, et al: Lactic acidosis during sepsis is related to increased pyruvate production, not deficits in tissue oxygen availability. Ann Surgery 224:97, 1996

61. Connett RJ, Honig CR, Gyeski TEJ, et al: Defining hypoxia: a systems view of VO$_2$, glycolysis, energetics, and intracellular PO$_2$. J Appl Physiol 68:833, 1990

62. Bearn AG, Billing B, Sherlock S: The effect of adrenaline and noradrenaline on hepatic blood flow and splanchnic carbohydrate metabolism in man. J Physiol 115:430, 1951

63. Levy B, Bollaert P-E, Charpentier C, et al: Comparison of norepinephrine and dobutamine to epinephrine for hemodynamics, lactate metabolism, and gastric tonometric variables in septic shock: a prospective randomized study. Intensive Care Med 23:282, 1997

64. Zilva JF: The origin of acidosis in hyperlactatemia. Ann Clin Biochem 15:40, 1978

65. Madias NE, Homer SM, Johns CA, et al: Hypochloremia as a consequence of anion gap metabolic acidosis. J Lab Clin Med 104:15, 1984

66. Cohen RD, Woods HF: Lactic acidsosis revisited. Diabetes 32:181, 1983

67. Kreisberg RA: Lactate homeostasis and lactic acidosis. Ann Intern Med 92:227, 1980

68. Graf H, Leach W, Arieff AI: Evidence for a detrimental effect of bicarbonate therapy in hypoxic lactic acidosis. Science 227:754, 1985

69. Rhee KH, Toro LO, McDonald GG, et al: Carbicarb, sodium bicarbonate, and sodium chloride in hypoxic lactic acidosis. Chest 104:913, 1993

70. Magder S: Pathophysiology of metabolic acid-base disturbances in patients with critical illness. Critical Care Nephrology. Ronco C, Bellomo R, Eds. Kluwer Academic Publishers, Dordrecht, The Netherlands, 1998, p 279

71. Alberti KG: Diabetic emergencies. Br Med Bull 45:242, 1989

72. Bakerman S, Bakerman P, Strausbauch P: Bakerman's ABC's of Interpretive Laboratory Data, 4th ed. Interpretive Laboratory Data, Inc, Scottsdale, Arizona, 2002

73. Androque HJ, Tannen RL: Ketoacidosis, hyperosmolar states, and lactic acidosis. Fluids and Electrolytes. Kokko JP, Tannen RL, Eds. WB Saunders Co, Philadelphia, 1996, p 643

74. Good DG: Regulation of bicarbonate and ammonium absorption in the thick ascending limb of the rat. Kidney Int 40:S36, 1991

75. Fulop M: Alcoholic ketoacidosis. Endocrinol Metabol Clin North Am 22:209, 1993

76. Wrenn KD, Slovis CM, Minion GE, et al: The syndrome of alcoholic ketoacidosis. Am J Med 91:119, 1991

77. Widmer B, Gerhardt RE, Harrington JT, et al: Serum electrolyte and acid base composition: the influence of graded degrees of chronic renal failure. Arch Intern Med 139:1099, 1979

78. Harrington JT, Cohen JJ: Metabolic acidosis. Acid-Base. Cohen JJ, Kassirer JP, Eds. Little, Brown and Co, Boston, 1982, p 121

79. Abassi ZA, Hoffman A, Better OS: Acute renal failure complicating muscle crush injury. Semin Nephrol 18:558, 1998

80. Martin M, Murray J, Berne T, et al: Diagnosis of acid-base derangements and mortality prediction in the trauma intensive care unit: the physiochemical approach. J Trauma 58:238, 2005

81. Rocktaschel J, Morimatsu H, Uchino S, et al: Unmeasured anions in critically ill patients: can they predict mortality? Crit Care Med 31:2131, 2003

82. Kaplan L, Kellum JA: Initial pH, base deficit, lactate, anion gap, strong ion difference, and strong ion gap predict outcome from major vascular injury. Crit Care Med 32:1120, 2004

83. Mikulaschek A, Henry SM, Donovan R, et al: Serum lactate is not predicted by anion gap or base excess after trauma resuscitation. J Trauma 40:218, 1996

84. Iberti TJ, Leibowitz AB, Papadakos PJ, et al: Low sensitivity of the anion gap as a screen to detect hyperlactatemia in critically ill patients. Crit Care Med 18:275, 1990

85. Husain FA, Martin MJ, Mullenix PS, et al: Serum lactate and base deficit as predictors of mortality and morbidity. Am J Surg 185:485, 2003

86. Rutherford EJ, Morris JA Jr, Reed GW, et al: Base deficit stratifies mortality and determines therapy. J Trauma 33:417, 1992

87. Davis JW, Kaups KL, Parks SN: Base deficit is superior to pH in evaluating clearance of acidosis after traumatic shock. J Trauma 44:114, 1998

88. Davis JW, Kaups KL: Base deficit in the elderly: a marker of severe injury and death. J Trauma 45:873, 1998

89. Abramson D, Scalea TM, Hitchcock R, et al: Lactate clearance and survival following injury. J Trauma 35:584, 1993

90. Batlle DC, Hizon M, Cohen E, et al: The use of the urine anion gap in the diagnosis of hyperchloremic metabolic acidosis. N Engl J Med 318:594, 1988

91. Cheek DB: Changes in total chloride and acid-base balance in gastroenteritis following treatment with large and small loads of sodium chloride. Pediatrics 17:839, 1956

92. Shires GT, Tolman J: Dilutional acidosis. Ann Intern Med 28:557, 1948

93. Garella S, Chang BS, Kahn SI: Dilution acidosis and contraction alkalosis: review of a concept. Kidney Int 8:279, 1975

94. Garella S, Tzamaloukas AH, Chazan JA: Effect of isotonic volume expansion on extracellular bicarbonate stores in normal dogs. Am J Physiol 225:628, 1973

95. Waters JH, Bernstein CA: Dilutional acidosis following hetastarch or albumin in healthy volunteers. Anesthesiology 93:1184, 2000

96. Waters JH, Miller LR, Clack S, et al: Cause of metabolic acidosis in prolonged surgery. Crit Care Med 27:2142, 1999

97. Wilkes NJ, Woolf R, Mutch M, et al: The effects of balanced versus saline-based hetastarch and crystalloid solutions on acid-base and electrolyte status and gastric mucosal perfusion in elderly surgical patients. Anesth Analg 93:811, 2001

98. Kellum JA, Bellomo R, Kramer DJ, et al: Etiology of metabolic acidosis during saline resuscitation in endotoxemia. Shock 9:364, 1998

99. Kellum JA: Recent advances in acid-base physiology applied to critical care. Yearbook of Intensive Care and Emergency Medicine. Vincent JL, Ed. Springer-Verlag, Heidelberg, 1998, p 577

100. Morgan TJ, Venkatesh B, Hall J: Crystalloid strong ion difference determines metabolic acid-base change during in vitro hemodilution. Crit Care Med 30:157, 2002

101. Gilbert EM, Haupt MT, Mandanas RY, et al: The effect of fluid loading, blood transfusion, and catecholamine infusion on oxygen delivery and consumption in patients with sepsis. Am Rev Respir Dis 134:873, 1986

102. Gattinoni L, Lissoni A: Respiratory acid-base disturbances in patients with critical illness. Critical Care Nephrology. Ronco C, Bellomo R, Eds. Kluwer Academic Publishers, Dordrecht, The Netherlands, 1998, p 297

103. Brochard L, Mancebo J, Wysocki M, et al: Noninvasive ventilation for acute exacerbations of chronic obstructive pulmonary disease. N Engl J Med 333:817, 1995

104. Tsuno K, Miura K, Takeya M, et al: Histopathologic pulmonary changes from mechanical ventilation at high peak airway pressures. Am Rev Respir Dis 143:1115, 1991

105. Sugiura M, McCulloch PR, Wren S, et al: Ventilator pattern influences neutrophil influx and activation in atelectasis-prone rabbit lung. J Appl Physiol 77:1355, 1994

106. Ventilation with lower tidal volumes as compared with traditional tidal volumes for acute lung injury and the acute respiratory distress syndrome. The Acute Respiratory Distress Syndrome Network. N Engl J Med 342:1301, 2000

107. Gennari FJ, Kassirer JP: Respiratory alkalosis. Acid-Base. Cohen JJ, Kassirer JP, Eds. Little, Brown and Co, Boston, 1982, p 349

108. Cohen JJ, Madias NE, Wolf CJ, et al: Regulation of acid-base equilibrium in chronic hypocapnia: evidence that the response of the kidney is not geared to the defense of extracellular [H$^+$]. J Clin Invest 57:1483, 1976

109. Adrogue HJ, Madias NE: Management of life-threatening acid-base disorders: part II. N Engl J Med 338:107, 1998

124 HEPATIC FAILURE

Juan R. Sanabria, M.D., M.Sc., F.A.C.S., and Achilles A. Demetriou, M.D., Ph.D., F.A.C.S.

Approach to the Patient with Liver Failure

Hepatic failure continues to be a frequent and major cause of morbidity and mortality in critically ill patients. In the past decade, new approaches to hepatic failure have been developed. Advances in critical care, the increasing use of sophisticated diagnostic modalities, and the adoption of a team approach to patient care (with active collaboration among intensivists, hepatologists, anesthesiologists, transplant surgeons, and other specialists) have resulted in improved overall outcomes.

Hepatic failure may be encountered as an instance of primary organ failure caused by a liver-specific disease process or as part of the multiple organ dysfunction syndrome (MODS). Typically, patients with secondary liver failure have no preexisting liver disease: their liver dysfunction is simply a reflection of their overall critical condition, and management usually involves treatment of underlying nonhepatic disorders. In what follows, we outline general management guidelines for primary hepatic failure and its complications.

Clinical Evaluation and Investigative Studies

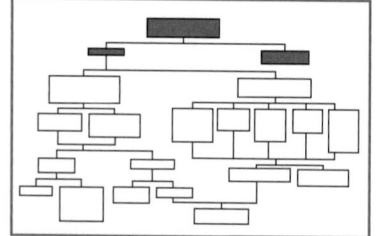

Evaluation of patients with suspected liver disease is often complex and typically requires extensive patient workup—including a detailed history and physical examination, as well as various diagnostic studies—to establish the diagnosis and confirm the underlying cause of the disease. Common risk factors include a history of alcohol or I.V. drug abuse, previous transfusion of blood or blood products,[1] the use of certain medications, tattoos, sexual promiscuity, and incarceration. Less common risk factors include a family history of liver disease and exposure to various toxins and chemicals.

CHARACTERISTIC FINDINGS

Liver disease gives rise to several easily recognizable manifestations. Jaundice and encephalopathy are common symptoms. In the early stages of liver disease, increasing fatigue, changes in sleep patterns, loss of short-term memory, inability to concentrate, and reduced libido may be noted. In the later stages, portal hypertension (PHT) is signaled by the development of ascites and upper or lower gastrointestinal bleeding. In addition, hypersplenism and abdominal wall collateral vessels may be detected on physical examination. Changes that occur primarily as a consequence of altered liver metabolism include palmar erythema, spider angiomata, gynecomastia, testicular atrophy, and encephalopathy. Many patients exhibit a degree of protein-calorie malnutrition, with muscle wasting and reduced physical activity.

Initial laboratory evaluation should include a complete blood count, a platelet count, liver function tests, a coagulation profile, and assessment of renal function. In addition, a toxicology screen should be ordered and a sepsis workup initiated. Detection of one or more drugs in the urine or blood may help establish the diagnosis and direct treatment. Specific tests to detect other conditions (e.g., metabolic or autoimmune disorders) are ordered as needed. Blood and urine cultures are done to look for a concomitant or causative infectious agent; if ascites is present, analysis of the ascitic fluid (including a cell count with differential, Gram staining, and culture) is recommended. Serologic testing for hepatitis viruses and other viruses (e.g., herpesvirus, cytomegalovirus [CMV], and Epstein-Barr virus [EBV]) is indicated. In addition, a chest x-ray must be obtained, and additional imaging studies should be performed as indicated. At times, a liver biopsy is required to establish or confirm the diagnosis of liver disease.

Most patients with primary hepatic failure have a history of preexisting liver disease and possibly of cirrhosis, generally presenting with one or more complications of chronic liver disease (e.g., GI bleeding, hepatic encephalopathy, spontaneous bacterial peritonitis [SBP], or renal failure). In one subgroup of patients, hepatic failure occurs as a result of an acute exacerbation of preexisting liver disease (e.g., acute reactivation of hepatitis B, acute decompensated Wilson disease, or autoimmune hepatitis). In another subgroup, primary hepatic failure develops acutely in the absence of any preexisting liver disease or known risk factors; this condition is known as fulminant hepatic failure (FHF). These patients present with massive liver necrosis, jaundice, and profound coagulopathy and often go on to experience deep coma and cerebral edema, which may lead to irreversible brain damage and death.

The distinction between an acute liver process and a chronic one is important. Acute liver failure (ALF) may be associated with severe multisystem organ involvement, as in the acute respiratory distress syndrome (ARDS) or MODS. The etiology of ALF includes the use of medications (in particular, acetaminophen), infection (specifically, viral hepatitis), miscellaneous conditions, and indeterminate causes. ALF may also develop after liver transplantation secondary to primary graft nonfunction (PNF) or hepatic artery thrombosis (HAT). It is manifested mainly by encephalopathy, progressive coagulopathy, poor urinary output, and elevated liver enzyme levels. Cerebral edema is uncommon in patients with PNF.

PROGNOSTIC FACTORS

A thorough initial physical examination is important for establishing a baseline for comparison, so that trends toward improvement or deterioration can be detected during clinical evaluations subsequently conducted at 4- to 6-hour intervals. Worsening encephalopathy with rapidly deteriorating mental status is an indication for early endotracheal intubation. Reduced urine output in a euvolemic patient is a sign of impending renal failure. Elevated liver enzyme concentrations and an elevated international normalized ratio (INR) suggest that spontaneous liver recovery is unlikely. The development of hypoglycemia is a sign that only a limited amount of functional liver tissue remains. Metabolic acidosis may also reflect lack of functional liver reserve in a euvolemic patient setting. In addition, factor V levels and the degree of hepatocyte necrosis observed at liver biopsy may help guide further therapy. Increasing levels of α-fetoprotein (AFP) have been associated with liver regeneration and liver recovery. Finally, the patient's overall medical status (e.g., the presence of severe coronary artery disease or a history of recent myocardial infarction) may determine the final outcome.

Initial Management

Initial management of a patient with hepatic failure includes the following components:

1. Airway protection. Airway management and maintenance should be established early in the course of the disease to prevent hypoxia with worsening brain edema or bronchial aspiration with pneumonitis, decreased gas exchange, and sepsis. Patients with cerebral edema require hyperventilation to lower the carbon dioxide tension (Pco_2) and reduce cerebral vasodilatation; however, the effect on Pco_2 is transient.
2. Monitoring of serum glucose levels. In patients who have experienced an acute loss of functional liver tissue, the lack of gluconeogenic pathways leads to decreased metabolism of lactic acid. The result is a high–anion gap metabolic acidosis with hypoglycemia, a state that is exaggerated in cases of sepsis with poor tissue perfusion.
3. Monitoring of cerebral perfusion pressure (CPP). The mental status of a patient with ALF should be followed by means of serial neurologic examinations, serial computed tomograms of the brain as indicated, and monitoring of intracranial pressure (ICP) and CPP. The signs detected by physical examination are not reliable, and changes in cerebral CT scans may develop late after the establishment of cerebral edema. Measuring CPP is the most reliable means of monitoring the degree of cerebral edema and can help guide early therapy.
4. Hemodynamic monitoring. Continuous assessment of central venous pressure is desirable in ALF patients to optimize fluid administration. Every effort should be made to establish adequate perfusion pressure without significantly increasing right-side cardiac pressures, diminishing venous return from the brain, and subsequently aggravating cerebral edema. Placement of a pulmonary artery catheter may be indicated in severely ill patients who may be hemodynamically unstable.
5. Correction of coagulopathy. The platelet count and the INR are the main variables monitored for assessment of coagulation. Because ALF patients typically are subjected to multiple interventions, invasive monitoring, and other procedures, fresh frozen plasma (FFP) and platelets are frequently administered.
6. Diagnostic workup. A rapid diagnostic workup is undertaken to allow appropriate disease management. Specific treatment should be instituted promptly to enhance liver recovery (e.g., administration of N-acetylcysteine to treat acetaminophen toxicity). It is of particular importance to identify any conditions that may rule out liver transplantation as a therapeutic option; such conditions include active infection, cancer, irreversible brain damage, and MODS. Evaluation of the patient for potential liver transplantation should begin early. To this end, it is important that the liver transplant team take part in the initial assessment and management of ALF patients.

Management of Acute Liver Failure

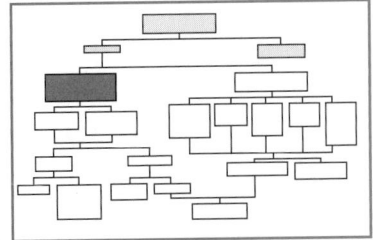

In the United States, ALF affects 2,300 to 2,800 patients each year.[2] How liver failure is defined depends largely on the temporal relation between the onset of illness and the appearance of jaundice, encephalopathy, and coagulopathy. For example, some define FHF as ALF in which the interval between disease onset and the appearance of major symptoms is 8 weeks or less.[3] In most cases, however, it is difficult to establish the precise time of onset of the disease process and thus hard to determine precisely how much time elapsed before hepatic failure developed. Recognizing that clinical findings and prognosis vary depending on the interval between the onset of jaundice and the appearance of encephalopathy, some authorities distinguish between FHF and subfulminant hepatic failure (SHF). Bernuau and coworkers defined FHF as an episode of ALF that was complicated by encephalopathy developing within 2 weeks of the onset of jaundice and defined SHF as ALF that was complicated by encephalopathy developing 2 to 12 weeks after the onset of jaundice.[4] We use the term ALF for cases in which there is no evidence of chronic liver disease and in which liver disease develops within 8 weeks after the initial onset of illness.

CLASSIFICATION

ALF may be classified into three major categories on the basis of the underlying cause of the disease: infectious, substance-induced, and miscellaneous. In two multicenter studies, acetaminophen-induced toxicity was found to be the most common cause (20% and 39%) of ALF, followed by cryptogenic or indeterminate causes (15%).[5,6]

Infectious (Viral Hepatitis)

Infectious ALF can be caused by several different viruses. Most cases are attributable to hepatitis viruses (types A through G), though herpesviruses (e.g., herpes simplex virus, varicella-zoster virus, CMV, and EBV), coxsackieviruses, echoviruses, adenoviruses, and parvovirus B19 are also capable of causing ALF.

Hepatitis A   The incidence of FHF and SHF in patients with hepatitis A virus (HAV) infection is very low (< 0.01%).[4] The virus is transmitted orally. HAV infection usually occurs in children and typically gives rise to minimal manifestations that resolve uneventfully, resulting in detectable levels of antibodies. About 10% of patients experience a relapse, usually within 2 to 3 months after an initial clinical improvement. Relapse is signaled by increased serum transaminase and bilirubin levels and the reappearance of the virus in the stool. If encephalopathy develops during this period, the prognosis is poor.[7] The clinical course of the disease tends to be more severe in older patients. Immunoglobulin therapy may reduce infection rates among young family members and HAV-naive health care workers.

Hepatitis B   ALF related to hepatitis B virus (HBV) occurs in fewer than 1% of HBV infections but is the most common form of virus-induced FHF.[4,5,8] Like HAV infection, HBV infection leads to FHF more often than to SHF. HBV is transmitted by contact with blood or body fluids and by intercourse. Detection of hepatitis B surface antigen (HBsAg) and a quantitative polymerase chain reaction (PCR) for HBV DNA establish the diagnosis. In

Approach to the Patient with Liver Failure

Patient has signs of liver disease or known risk factors

Perform extensive workup: history, physical examination, laboratory tests, and imaging studies as needed. Liver biopsy is occasionally required.

Distinguish primary from secondary hepatic failure.

Primary hepatic failure

Acute liver failure

Determine etiology—infectious (viral), substance-induced, or other—and treat accordingly.

Begin medical management of complications.

Concurrently, assess prognosis by means of King's College criteria.

Cerebral edema

Initiate invasive ICP monitoring.
Manage elevated ICP.

Extrahepatic complications

Treat fluid, electrolyte, and nutritional abnormalities; renal failure; hemodynamic and pulmonary complications; infectious complications; and coagulopathy and bleeding.

Good prognosis with medical management

Continue medical therapy.

Poor prognosis with medical management

Medical management succeeds

Medical management fails

Consider emergency OLT if not contraindicated.

Treat toxic liver syndrome with total hepatectomy and end-to-side portacaval shunt, followed by OLT.

Consider use of BAL support system.

Transplantation is contraindicated

Manage medically.

No contraindications to transplantation are present

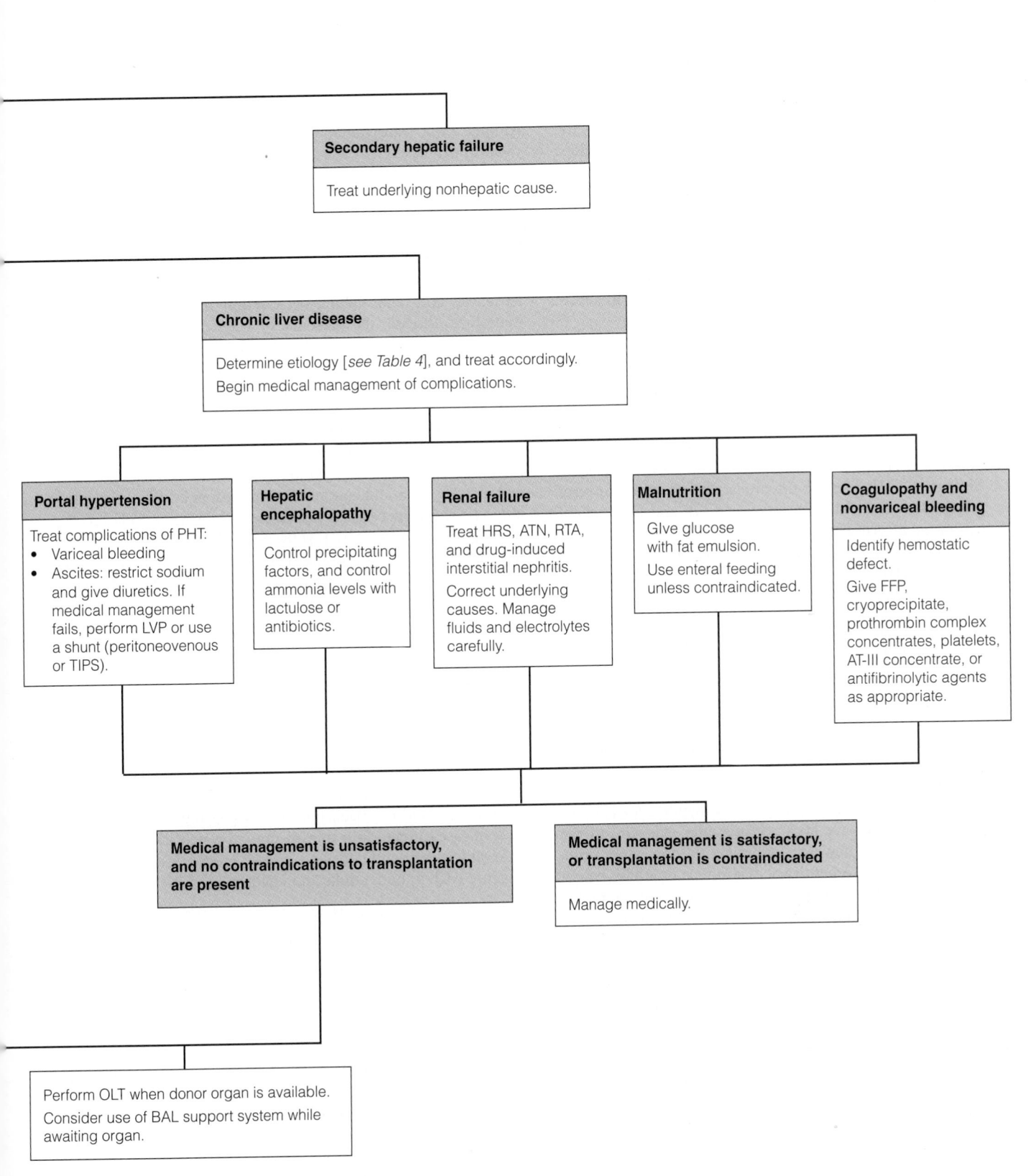

Secondary hepatic failure

Treat underlying nonhepatic cause.

Chronic liver disease

Determine etiology [*see Table 4*], and treat accordingly.
Begin medical management of complications.

Portal hypertension

Treat complications of PHT:
- Variceal bleeding
- Ascites: restrict sodium and give diuretics. If medical management fails, perform LVP or use a shunt (peritoneovenous or TIPS).

Hepatic encephalopathy

Control precipitating factors, and control ammonia levels with lactulose or antibiotics.

Renal failure

Treat HRS, ATN, RTA, and drug-induced interstitial nephritis.
Correct underlying causes. Manage fluids and electrolytes carefully.

Malnutrition

GIve glucose with fat emulsion.
Use enteral feeding unless contraindicated.

Coagulopathy and nonvariceal bleeding

Identify hemostatic defect.
Give FFP, cryoprecipitate, prothrombin complex concentrates, platelets, AT-III concentrate, or antifibrinolytic agents as appropriate.

Medical management is unsatisfactory, and no contraindications to transplantation are present

Medical management is satisfactory, or transplantation is contraindicated

Manage medically.

Perform OLT when donor organ is available.
Consider use of BAL support system while awaiting organ.

some cases of FHF secondary to HBV infection, however, these markers may be absent,[9] which indicates that in certain FHF patients, an enhanced immune response prevents further HBV replication and results in more rapid clearance of HBsAg. The survival rate is much lower for patients who are HBsAg-positive on presentation (17%) than for patients who are HBsAg-negative (47%).[4] Clearance of HBsAg and HBV DNA results in better survival, as well as lower recurrence rates after emergency liver transplantation.[10] Protocols based on antiviral therapy with lamividine and anti-HBV immunoglobulin yield low rates of HBV recurrence after successful liver transplantation.

Hepatitis D   Hepatitis D virus (HDV, also referred to as the delta agent) is a defective virus that uses HBsAg as its envelope protein. HDV RNA is detected in only 10% of patients with fulminant hepatitis D.[11] HDV infection can be either a coinfection (in conjunction with HBV infection) or a superinfection (in patients with previous HBV infection).[12] In FHF patients, HDV coinfection is more common than HDV superinfection; however, the latter is associated with a higher mortality than the former (72% versus 52%), as well as a stronger predisposition to subsequent chronic liver disease (54% versus 31%).[13]

Hepatitis C and indeterminate hepatitis   Previously, FHF of indeterminate etiology was attributed to non-A, non-B viral hepatitis. It is now clear that some such cases are caused by hepatitis C virus (HCV) infection, though the precise extent to which HCV infection contributes to this indeterminate group is unclear. Unlike HAV and HBV infection, HCV infection is more likely to cause SHF than FHF. Despite the availability of advanced serologic testing, there are still many cases of FHF and SHF whose cause cannot be determined.[14,15] These cases may be attributable to other, more recently described types of hepatitis viruses (e.g., hepatitis E virus [HEV], hepatitis F virus [HFV], and hepatitis G virus [HGV]). ALF caused by HEV infection, though rare in Western countries, is the most common form of FHF in India.[16]

Substance-Induced

Drugs   Drug toxicity accounts for 35% of all cases of FHF and SHF and usually runs a subfulminant course.[5] Drug ingestion causes hepatic injury in fewer than 1% of patients, about 20% of whom manifest FHF or SHF. In most cases of drug-induced hepatoxicity, the degree of the toxicity correlates with the dose ingested and the serum drug level, but in others (e.g., certain cases of valproic acid–induced toxicity), patients manifest an idiosyncratic reaction with massive liver necrosis after exposure to the drug. As a general rule, however, increasing the total drug dose, simultaneously ingesting other drugs that induce or inhibit hepatic enzymes (synergistic toxicity), and continuing drug administration after the onset of liver disease all increase the risk of hepatic failure.[4]

Acetaminophen toxicity is the most common cause of drug-induced hepatic failure. The prognosis for patients with FHF caused by acetaminophen is usually better than that for patients with FHF caused by other drugs (e.g., isoniazid, psychotropic drugs, antihistamines, and nonsteroidal anti-inflammatory drugs).[17] Halothane-induced FHF occurs within 2 weeks after general anesthesia and carries a high mortality.[18]

Toxins   Most cases of toxin-induced FHF involve mushroom poisoning or exposure to industrial hydrocarbons. In mushroom poisoning, the active agents are heat-stable and are not destroyed by cooking.[19] Liver damage from mushroom toxins is delayed and is usually preceded by several days of vomiting and diarrhea. Mortality is high: up to 22% in one series. Emergency liver transplantation is sometimes successful.[20] Industrial hydrocarbons (e.g., carbon tetrachloride, trichloroethylene) are rare causes of FHF. In developing nations, aflatoxin and herbal medicines have been implicated as causes of FHF.

Acute, severe ethanol intoxication may result in the development of acute alcoholic hepatitis (AAH), a condition associated with high mortality. Treatment with steroids improves survival in AAH patients; other measures are instituted to treat complications and associated conditions (e.g., withdrawal syndrome and malnutrition). Liver transplantation has not been advocated for treatment of acute AAH.

Miscellaneous

ALF may be caused by any of a number of miscellaneous processes, including metabolic, vascular, and autoimmune conditions. The most frequent metabolic cause of ALF is Wilson disease, which may present as FHF or SHF with intravascular hemolysis and renal failure.[21,22] A family history of hepatic and neurologic disease, the presence of Kayser-Fleischer rings, and low serum ceruloplasmin levels help establish the diagnosis. Acute decompensated Wilson disease carries a high mortality and is an indication for emergency liver transplantation.[23]

Acute fatty liver of pregnancy is a rare cause of FHF associated with high mortality for both mother and infant. Delivery of the fetus results in regression of the microvesicular steatosis and improvement in liver function for the mother. The risk of FHF is increased with misdiagnosis and continuation of pregnancy. Liver transplantation has been successfully performed to treat this condition.[24]

An unusual cause of ALF is the Budd-Chiari syndrome (acute hepatic vein thrombosis). The typical patient is a young woman who presents with right upper quadrant pain of acute onset, hepatomegaly, and ascites. The clinical course is usually benign, and liver enzyme levels normalize promptly. Occasionally, however, the syndrome progresses to FHF. Portal decompression sometimes treats this type of ALF successfully if done before massive hepatic necrosis occurs; once FHF develops, liver transplantation is the only option.

Acute autoimmune hepatitis can cause FHF. It is typically seen in female patients and may occur either with or without known autoimmune disorders. A panel of reactive antibodies confirms the diagnosis. High-dose steroid therapy usually arrests the process, resulting in rapid normalization of liver enzyme levels. In 10% to 20% of cases, urgent liver transplantation is necessary.

Several other conditions and disease processes are also known to cause ALF in both adults and children [see Table 1].

ASSESSMENT OF PROGNOSIS

Several prognostic criteria and indicators have been developed for predicting outcome after optimal medical management of FHF. The two main factors determining likelihood of survival are (1) the extent of liver necrosis and (2) the potential for hepatocyte regeneration. In a 1989 study, investigators at King's College Hospital in London compiled a set of indicators for predicting a poor outcome after medical therapy and hence the need for emergency liver transplantation.[25] The underlying cause of FHF was the single most important predictive variable. Accordingly, patients were divided into two groups, one comprising all cases of acetaminophen-induced FHF and the other all cases of FHF from other causes. Age, degree of encephalopathy, serum pH, prothrombin time (PT),

Table 1 Etiology of Acute Liver Failure

Infectious

Viral: hepatitis A, B, C, D, E, F, and G and hepatitis of indeterminate etiology; infection by herpes simplex virus, cytomegalovirus, Epstein-Barr virus, or adenovirus

Bacterial: Q fever

Parasitic: amebiasis

Drugs

Toxins

Mushrooms: *Amanita phalloides, verna,* and *virosa; Lepiota* species

Bacillus cereus

Hydrocarbons: carbon tetrachloride, trichloroethylene, 2-nitropropane, chloroform

Copper

Aflatoxin

Yellow phosphorus

Miscellaneous conditions

Wilson disease

Acute fatty liver of pregnancy

Reye syndrome

Hypoxic liver cell necrosis

Hypothermia or hyperthermia

Budd-Chiari syndrome

Veno-occlusive disease of the liver

Autoimmune hepatitis

Massive malignant infiltration of the liver

Partial hepatectomy

Liver transplantation

Postjejunoileal bypass

Galactosemia

Hereditary fructose intolerance

Tyrosinemia

Erythropoietic protoporphyria

Irradiation

α_1-Antitrypsin deficiency

Niemann-Pick disease

Neonatal hemochromatosis

Cardiac tamponade

Right ventricular failure

Circulatory shock

Tuberculosis

---

time of onset of encephalopathy, and admission serum creatinine and bilirubin levels also proved to be significant variables [*see Table 2*]. Patients who met the criteria in either group had a 95% chance of dying with medical therapy alone and were identified as candidates for emergency liver transplantation. The major strength of the King's College study is that it based patient assessment on parameters that are easily obtained within a few hours of admission to the emergency department. This approach to assessment facilitates early transfer of patients with a poor prognosis to a specialized liver unit for evaluation for transplantation.

In another study, plasma factor V level and age were found to be independent predictors of survival.[26] The criteria for liver transplantation were the presence of hepatic encephalopathy (stage III or IV) and a factor V level either less than 20% of normal in patients younger than 30 years or less than 30% of normal in patients older than 30 years.

Other predictive models have been developed. A study of 59 patients with non–acetaminophen-induced FHF showed that plasma levels of albumin, lactate, valine, and pyruvate were predic-

tive of survival when measured within 6 hours after admission.[27] Assessment of the residual functional reserve of the liver has been studied as an indicator of prognosis. The ratio of acetoacetate to β-hydroxybutyrate in an arterial blood sample (also known as the arterial ketone body ratio [AKBR]) is thought to reflect hepatic energy status.[28] Galactose clearance reflects both residual liver mass and hepatic blood flow.[29] This test has long been considered a standard test of hepatic functional reserve, and newer tests are routinely compared to it. At present, functional assessment tools are not widely used.

At our center, we apply the King's College criteria on admission to predict the likely outcome with medical therapy. Once the initial assessment is completed, the decision to proceed with emergency evaluation for liver transplantation is made. Evaluation, if indicated, is usually completed within 12 to 24 hours. The evaluation is similar to that of patients with chronic liver disease [*see Chronic Liver Disease, below*], with a few exceptions. Patients with FHF usually do not have preexisting liver disease; thus, it is vital that the evaluation [*see Table 3*] reveal the probable cause of liver failure. Unlike chronic liver disease, FHF is associated with cerebral edema and elevated ICP, which is the leading cause of death in these patients. Therefore, an extensive neurologic evaluation should be completed before a patient is listed for transplantation. Serial neurologic assessment is necessary to rule out irreversible brain damage and brain-stem herniation; use of short-acting sedatives make this evaluation less difficult.

TREATMENT OF
COMPLICATIONS

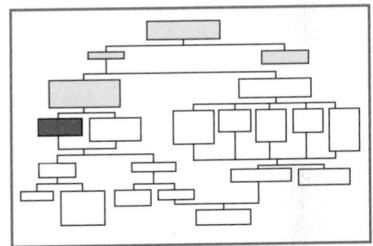

Cerebral Edema

Cerebral edema develops in most patients with FHF, and its presence significantly influences management and outcome. Autopsy studies indicate that cerebral edema is present in 80% of patients who die of FHF.[30,31] It occurs in advanced stages of FHF and can be recognized by clinical, radiologic, or invasive means. Clinical findings include decerebrate posturing, myoclonus, spastic rigidity, seizure activity, systemic hypertension, bradycardia, hyperventilation, and mydriasis with diminished pupillary response. These findings initially are paroxysmal but later become persistent. Papilledema is a late finding and often does not occur at all, even in advanced stages of the disease.[32] Noninvasive diagnostic modalities (e.g., CT scanning, electroencephalographic monitoring, and transcranial Doppler flow measurement) have not proved helpful for early detection and management of cerebral edema.[33,34] CT scanning of the brain is not a sensitive test for detecting early cerebral edema: 25% to 30% of patients with elevated ICP exhibit no radiographic changes.[35] It is, however, useful for ruling out intracranial bleeding.

Currently, ICP monitoring is the best means of monitoring intracranial hypertension and is recommended for guiding treatment in patients with stage III or IV encephalopathy. ICP can be measured by using epidural, subdural, or intraventricular catheters. Although epidural catheters are slightly less sensitive to ICP changes, they have the lowest complication rate (3.8%) and the lowest rate of fatal hemorrhage (1%).[36] Despite a slightly higher complication rate, we prefer subdural catheters: in our view, they offer more reliable ICP monitoring. Institution of ICP monitoring is followed by aggressive treatment of any concomitant coagulopathy. FFP infusions are given to bring the PT below 25 seconds, and platelet transfusions are given if the patient has severe thrombocytopenia (platelet count < 50,000/mm³). Once ICP monitoring is established, bolus administration of FFP is repeated as needed to keep the INR below 5 so as to reduce the risk of intracranial bleeding. To minimize the need for ICP monitoring, it has been suggested that patient selection should be based on reverse jugular oxygen saturation; saturations lower than 65% or higher than 80% are associated with a high likelihood of elevated ICP.[37]

The goal of invasive monitoring is to keep the ICP below 15 mm Hg while keeping CPP, which is a better predictor of outcome, above 50 mm Hg. CPP is calculated by subtracting the ICP from the mean arterial pressure (MAP). ICP monitoring allows early detection of cerebral edema and hence earlier introduction of aggressive management. To date, no randomized, controlled trials have addressed the effect of high ICP and low CPP on outcome after liver transplantation; however, it appears that persistence of either an ICP higher than 25 mm Hg or a CPP lower than 40 mm Hg for more than 2 hours is associated with an increased risk of irreversible brain damage and a poor outcome.[38,39]

Management of elevated ICP involves hyperventilation, minimization of external stimuli, deep sedation, elevation of the head, maintenance of hemodynamic stability, and infusion of mannitol. Patients are usually sedated with a short-acting agent (e.g., propofol) in small boluses before a procedure, nasotracheal suction, venipuncture, or line placement. Mechanical hyperventilation reduces ICP by lowering arterial carbon dioxide tension (P_aCO_2) to 25 to 30 mm Hg, thereby maximizing cerebral vascular constriction and reducing blood flow. This vascular effect diminishes progressively after 6 hours of therapy, though a clinical response is apparent for days. As many as 80% of patients without renal failure respond to mannitol infusions.[40] Serum osmolality should be measured frequently and maintained at 300 to 320 mOsm/L. Mannitol should be withheld if osmolality reaches or exceeds 320 mOsm/L, if renal failure occurs, or if oliguria and rising serum osmolality develop simultaneously. Repeated administration of mannitol may reverse the osmotic gradient. Mannitol should be discontinued if the ICP does not respond after the first few boluses.

Table 2 King's College Hospital Prognostic Criteria Predicting Poor Outcome for Patients with FHF

Acetaminophen-induced FHF	pH < 7.30 (irrespective of grade of encephalopathy) *or* All of the following: PT > 100 sec (INR > 6.5) Serum creatinine > 3.4 g/dl Stage III or IV hepatic encephalopathy
Non–acetaminophen-induced FHF	PT > 100 sec (INR > 6.5) (irrespective of grade of encephalopathy) *or* Any three of the following (irrespective of grade of encephalopathy): Age < 10 or > 40 yr Etiology: non-A, non-B hepatitis, halothane hepatitis, drug toxicity Duration of jaundice to encephalopathy > 7 days PT 50 sec (INR > 3.5) Serum bilirubin > 17.5 g/dl

FHF—fulminant hepatic failure   INR—international normalized ratio
PT—prothrombin time

Table 3 Liver Transplant Evaluation and Workup for FHF Patients

Laboratory workup
  CBC and differential count
  Chemistry panel
  Coagulation profile
  24-hr creatinine clearance
  Urinalysis
  Arterial blood gases
  ANA, AMA, ceruloplasmin, urinary copper, α_1-antitrypsin
  AFP
  RPR
  Thyroid function tests
  Alcohol and drug toxicology screen
Viral serologies
  Hepatitis A virus (IgM, IgG)
  Hepatitis B virus (HBsAg, HBcAb, HBeAg, HBV DNA)
  Hepatitis C virus (HCV antibody, HCV RNA-PCR)
  Cytomegalovirus
  Epstein-Barr virus
  HIV
Cultures
  Bacterial, fungal, and viral cultures
  Blood
  Sputum
  Urine
  Ascites
12-lead ECG
Chest x-ray
Pulmonary function tests
Abdominal Doppler ultrasonography
CT scans of head

AFP—α-fetoprotein   AMA—antimitochondrial antibody   ANA—antinuclear antibody   RPR—rapid plasma reagent

Acute renal failure is a frequent complication. Fluid management is very difficult in this setting. Continuous hemofiltration or continuous venovenous hemodialysis (CVVHD) can be beneficial. Continuous hemofiltration is less deleterious than intermittent therapy in the management of patients with brain edema and renal dysfunction,[16] probably because it does not cause the large fluid shifts that can occur with the intermittent technique.

Patients who do not respond to conventional therapy may be placed in a barbiturate coma. Thiopental infusion decreases cerebral metabolic activity, lowers CNS oxygen demand, and protects the brain from ischemic injury secondary to decreased cerebral blood flow. In a retrospective, nonrandomized study, it lowered ICP and reduced mortality from FHF.[41] In our experience, however, the effect of thiopental infusion on ICP is transient and unpredictable. Subclinical seizure activity has been detected in as many as 24% of ALF patients, but in a 2004 study, administration of phenytoin with control of the abnormal electrical activity did not affect overall outcome in ALF patients with seizures.[42] In a study of 30 patients with ALF, the use of hypertonic saline led to significantly decreased ICP levels.[43] Administration of indomethacin or dexamethasone has led to modest reductions of ICP.

Studies evaluating the use of mild hypothermia (32° to 33° C [89.6° to 91.4° F]) in managing ALF reported significant decreases in ICP in all patients, some of whom were cooled for as long as 5 days.[44,45] Bleeding and other coagulation disorders were not observed; however, upon rewarming, a rebound effect was noted with an increase in ICP. In view of these findings, the authors suggested caution and recommended gradual, gentle rewarming. In addition, they found that liver implantation could be successfully performed under hypothermic conditions. Moderate hypothermia appears to be a promising experimental technique in ALF patients, but its utility in clinical practice remains to be determined.

Other Complications

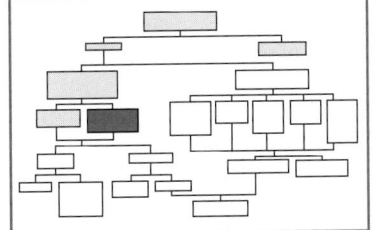

In addition to cerebral edema and increased ICP, MODS and a variety of life-threatening complications are associated with FHF. Most of these complications are similar to those seen in chronic liver disease [*see* Chronic Liver Disease, Treatment of Complications, *below*]; however, the following complications are seen with particular frequency in FHF.

Fluid, electrolyte, and nutritional abnormalities Euvolemia must be maintained to prevent fluid overload, pulmonary edema, and dehydration; extreme fluid shifts should be avoided. The presence of cerebral edema and intracranial hypertension calls for careful fluid administration so as not to expand the intravascular space or exacerbate the edema. Electrolyte and acid-base imbalances are frequent in FHF patients and should be managed appropriately. Hyperkalemia may be multifactorial; usually it is secondary to liver necrosis, massive transfusion, acid-base imbalance, and renal failure. Acidosis results from increased lactic acid production and decreased handling of lactate by the failing liver. Compensatory respiratory alkalosis develops initially, but if encephalopathy progresses, respiratory acidosis may result. Sodium or potassium bicarbonate infusions should be administered in cases of severe acidosis. Acetate provides twice the bicarbonate load and is metabolized outside the liver; thus, if sodium and potassium intake is severely restricted, continuous infusion of acetate salts may be useful.

Initially, amino acids should be withheld to prevent excessive nitrogen loading; later, limited nitrogen supplementation (70 to 80 g protein/day) may be provided. Most patients present with severe hypoglycemia that can be fatal and warrants aggressive therapy. Hypoglycemia should be corrected rapidly by infusion of 50% dextrose, followed by continuous infusion of a more dilute solution at a rate of 4 mg/kg/min. A 10% solution is usually adequate; however, higher concentrations should be considered in patients whose hypoglycemia persists or whose fluid intake is restricted. Caloric supplementation has not been extensively studied in FHF.

Renal failure Renal failure occurs in as many as 55% of FHF patients. Functional renal failure is a common cause of renal failure in this population. However, acute tubular necrosis (ATN) is more common in these patients than in those with chronic liver disease and cirrhosis.[46] This is especially true in patients who have not been resuscitated adequately, who have experienced prolonged hypotension, or who have ingested hepatotoxins that are also nephrotoxic (e.g., acetaminophen).

Adequate urine volume can be maintained by judicious volume expansion, administration of loop diuretics, or both, along with infusion of low doses of dopamine. Depleted intravascular volume may be managed by giving blood products, volume expanders, or both. Because plasma albumin levels are invariably low, salt-poor

albumin solutions may be preferable to carbohydrate-based volume expanders. If oliguria is present, especially if mannitol is administered to treat ICP, hemodialysis or hemofiltration may be needed to maintain optimal fluid volume.

Hemodynamic and pulmonary complications Circulatory disturbances tend to occur at an early stage of ALF and to worsen over the course of the illness; they are characterized by generalized vasodilatation, resulting in increased cardiac output and reduced systemic vascular resistance and MAP.[47-49] The mechanisms of these hemodynamic disturbances are unclear, but increased levels of nitric oxide and cyclic guanosine monophosphate (cGMP) have been demonstrated during the later stages of the disease.[50] Fluids are managed so as to achieve euvolemia (see above). A particular problem in managing hypotension related to ALF is that autoregulation of cerebral blood flow is typically lost.[51] Terlipressin (a vasopressin analogue) is widely used in patients with end-stage liver disease (ESLD) and hepatorenal syndrome (HRS). This agent acts through both V1 receptors, which are distributed in the systemic circulation and mediate vasoconstriction, and V2 receptors, which are distributed in the cerebral vasculature and mediate cerebral vasodilatation. The role of terlipressin in the hemodynamic management of patients with ALF remains unclear.

Pulmonary complications, especially pulmonary edema, aspiration pneumonia, and ARDS, are common in FHF patients.[52] Pulmonary edema is seen in as many as 40% of patients. Supplemental oxygen and mechanical ventilation are indicated. Sedative and paralytic agents may be required to ensure tolerance of ventilation; however, they should be used sparingly because they may hinder neurologic evaluation. Aspiration pneumonia is a potential contraindication to transplantation and should therefore be treated aggressively.

Infectious complications Infection poses a serious threat to FHF patients both by placing them at risk for sepsis and by being a contraindication to liver transplantation. Immunologic defects observed in this setting include impaired opsonization, impaired chemotaxis, impaired neutrophil and Kupffer cell function, and complement deficiency.[53,54] Bacterial translocation through a failed mucosal barrier has been implicated as one of the factors responsible for a high incidence of septic episodes in this population. Gram-negative organisms and the lipopolysacharide derived from their cell walls promote a systemic inflammatory response that aggravates the patient's overall condition.[55] To lower the risk of infectious complications, some groups advocate selective gut decontamination. This practice appears to have no significant advantages over systemic antibiotic prophylaxis alone.[56]

Bacterial infection, usually originating from the respiratory or the urinary tract or from a central venous catheter, occurs in more than 80% of cases. In one study, bacteremia was documented in 25% of patients, with staphylococci, streptococci, and gram-negative rods the most common pathogens.[57] Because most FHF patients have percutaneous lines and indwelling catheters in place, iatrogenic sources must always be considered. Fungal infection is less common than bacterial infection in this setting; however, one series found a significant incidence of fungal infections, with *Candida albicans* cultured in 33% of the patients studied.[58] The majority of the patients had renal failure and had been treated with antibiotics for longer than 5 days.

The high prevalence of infection notwithstanding, we do not advocate antibiotic prophylaxis in this population unless either there is strong suspicion of active infection or an ICP monitor is in place. However, our decision threshold for initiating antibiotic therapy is low, given that the usual clinical presentation (fever and leukocytosis) may be absent in as many as 30% of FHF patients.[57] Surveillance cultures for bacteria and fungi must be obtained at frequent intervals from blood (peripheral and central lines), urine, sputum, and open wounds. If ascites is present, the ascitic fluid should be cultured. In addition, chest radiographs should be obtained to identify developing infiltrates. Administration of broad-spectrum antibiotics should be initiated at the first sign of infection; as soon as an organism is identified, specific treatment may be focused more narrowly. Initiation of antifungal therapy with either fluconazole or another agent should be considered if a fungal culture is positive and if fever persists beyond 5 days while the patient is on antibiotics, especially if renal failure is present. The duration of antimicrobial therapy should be individualized for each patient. Follow-up cultures are recommended if a specific organism is isolated.

Coagulopathy and bleeding Bleeding is a frequent complication of FHF, typically resulting from massive liver necrosis, impaired hepatic synthesis of clotting factors, and platelet dysfunction. All clotting factors synthesized by the liver (i.e., factors II, V, VII, IX, and X) exhibit depressed plasma activity in FHF. Factor II, with a half-life of 2 hours, is the first to be depleted with hepatocellular dysfunction and also the first to be repleted during hepatocellular recovery. PT is invariably prolonged, reflecting a generalized clotting factor deficiency; it is used as one of the criteria for determining the likelihood of spontaneous recovery. At some centers, FFP transfusion is withheld and PT is followed carefully to determine upward or downward trends in the course of the disease and hence the likelihood of either spontaneous recovery or need for transplantation (unless the PT is greater than 25 seconds or the INR is greater than 5, especially if an ICP monitor is in place). Intracranial bleeding is the most devastating complication of coagulopathy in FHF patients with ICP monitors in place. In a 2003 study, administration of recombinant factor VIIa showed promising results in a group of patients with refractory coagulopathy.[59]

Thrombocytopenia and abnormalities of platelet function are also common in FHF. Acute splenomegaly, consumptive coagulopathy, and bone marrow suppression all contribute to the development of thrombocytopenia. Conversely, clearance of older platelets from the blood by the reticuloendothelial system is hindered, resulting in an older, less effective platelet pool. In one study, a mean platelet count of 50,000/mm³ was associated with a higher incidence of GI hemorrhage.[60] Our current practice is to give platelets to patients who either are thrombocytopenic (platelet count < 50,000/mm³) or are actively bleeding.

MULTIDISCIPLINARY MEDICAL THERAPY AND INDICATIONS FOR LIVER TRANSPLANTATION

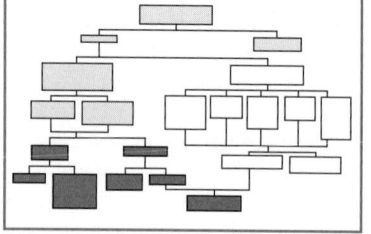

Because of the complexity of the underlying disease, medical management of FHF requires a multidisciplinary approach. Hemodynamic and respiratory support and prevention and treatment of cerebral edema are major goals. Complications of hepatic failure must be treated aggressively to prevent sepsis, ARDS, and MODS, which is the second most common cause of death in these patients if they survive the first few days. As noted [see Assessment of Prognosis, above], liver transplant evaluation must be carried out simultaneously with aggressive ICU care, and the patient's chances of spon-

taneous recovery must be assessed. In addition to determining the King's College prognostic score on admission, we follow the general trend in clinical course with respect to the development of encephalopathy, ICP elevation, coagulopathy, metabolic acidosis, and renal failure. The decision whether to continue with medical therapy or to perform liver transplantation must be made whenever a donor liver becomes available. In general, patients who appear to be deteriorating rapidly and who have no contraindications to liver transplantation should undergo emergency liver transplantation. Similarly, patients whose synthetic function does not improve within the first 48 to 72 hours should be considered for liver transplantation: the risk of complications and death from MODS if transplantation is not performed outweighs the risk of the procedure.

Toxic Liver Syndrome

Even with a multidisciplinary, comprehensive approach to therapy, a few patients with FHF go on to manifest the so-called toxic liver syndrome, characterized by severe intracranial hypertension, profound lactic acidosis, hemodynamic instability, and MODS. It has been suggested that removal of the necrotic liver may improve the hemodynamic status of these patients and lower their ICP. In such extreme cases, a two-stage procedure has been performed: total hepatectomy with an end-to-side portacaval shunt, followed by liver transplantation when an allograft becomes available. In one large series,[61,62] 32 adult patients with toxic liver syndrome underwent total hepatectomy with a portacaval shunt. The patients were anhepatic for 6.5 to 41.4 hours. Whereas 13 patients showed no signs of improvement after hepatectomy and soon died of MODS, 19 became more stable and underwent the full procedure. Only seven patients were alive at 46 months.

In the early 1990s, we used this approach to treat an 18-year-old female patient with uncontrollable cerebral edema secondary to FHF; she underwent total hepatectomy with a portacaval shunt, followed by orthotopic liver transplantation (OLT) 14 hours later.[63] During the anhepatic period, she was supported with the help of a bioartificial liver (BAL) [see Discussion, Bioartificial Liver Support System, below]. With artificial liver support, the severe neurologic dysfunction was reversed, ICP was normalized, and the serum ammonia level was reduced. The patient recovered completely, with no neurologic deficits. We subsequently used the same approach with another FHF patient, also successfully (unpublished data). It appears that for highly selected patients exhibiting severe toxic metabolic derangement and uncontrollable intracranial hypertension, total hepatectomy with a portacaval shunt—preferably accompanied by some form of artificial liver support—followed by OLT may be considered as a desperate salvage measure.

LIVER TRANSPLANTATION

With the introduction of orthotopic OLT as a treatment modality for FHF patients, overall patient survival improved from less than 20% to greater than 60%.[64,65] As more experience was gained with OLT, it became apparent that optimal patient selection is essential for a successful outcome. FHF patients must be considered for OLT before irreversible brain injury, MODS, and sepsis develop. Patient selection should be based on a clear understanding of the natural history of the disease, the underlying cause, and the likelihood of spontaneous recovery without transplantation.

One of the most difficult aspects of managing FHF patients is the lack of reliable prognostic criteria predicting outcome. In our experience, the King's College criteria are less sensitive and specific in determining prognosis for patients with acetaminophen-induced FHF than for patients with FHF from other causes. As a result, a small number of patients who either might have recovered spontaneously or might have sustained irreversible brain damage undergo unnecessary or unwarranted liver transplantation. Given the severe shortage of organ donors, as well as the cost and morbidity of liver transplantation and a commitment to lifelong immunosuppression, this is a significant problem.

Two interacting factors tend to influence the outcome of transplantation in the setting of ALF: (1) the severity of the illness before transplantation and (2) the condition of the graft used. The importance of the second factor was illustrated by the early experience with liver transplantation in France. Initially, French surgeons used the first available graft for ALF patients, regardless of its size, quality, or blood group compatibility. Subsequently, a study of 116 patients demonstrated that outcomes were significantly worse when adverse graft conditions (i.e., marginal quality, reduced size, and ABO incompatibility) were present.[66]

Some centers have successfully performed living donor liver transplantation in ALF patients.[67] This approach has been more commonly employed in pediatric patients.[68] Wider application has been limited by the risks this procedure poses to the donor in a setting where, because of the rapid progression of the disease, there is rarely enough time to evaluate potential donors appropriately and to eliminate the elements of pressure and coercion.[69] The potential for not just one but possibly two tragic outcomes must be emphasized.

Management of Chronic Liver Disease

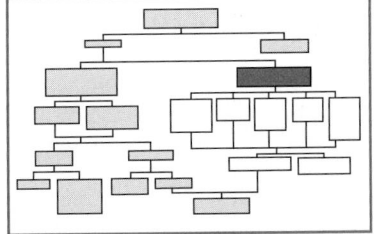

Chronic liver disease usually develops as a result of long-standing, ongoing liver injury. The repeated injury and the ensuing repair usually result in deposition of an excessive amount of extracellular matrix (ECM), with or without accompanying inflammation. As the disease process progresses, excess ECM forms connective tissue bridges linking portal and central areas (so-called bridging fibrosis), eventually leading to cirrhosis. Cirrhosis is an irreversible state that gives rise to significant physiologic impairment, including poor exchange of nutrients and metabolites between sinusoidal blood and hepatocytes. Eventually, the lobular architecture becomes distorted and blood flow altered, leading to PHT and its numerous complications. In addition to PHT, repeated parenchymal injury results in the loss of a large number of functioning hepatocytes and subsequently leads to hepatic failure.

CLASSIFICATION

Like ALF, chronic liver disease is usually classified on the basis of the underlying cause [see Table 4]. According to the United Network for Organ Sharing (UNOS), the most common indication for liver transplantation in North America is chronic liver disease resulting from HCV infection. Other common indications are alcohol-induced liver disease, cholestatic liver disease (primary sclerosing cholangitis, primary biliary cirrhosis, autoimmune liver disease), and cryptogenic cirrhosis. The occurrence of the metabolic syndrome (obesity, diabetes, and hypertension) is the most important risk factor for the development of nonalcoholic steatohepatitis (NASH), which is the most common cause of cryptogenic cirrhosis.

TREATMENT OF COMPLICATIONS

Chronic liver disease may be associated with a variety of complications, depending on the nature and extent of hepatocyte injury and regeneration. Most patients with chronic liver disease and possible cirrhosis are well compensated, maintain a relatively normal functional status, and remain essentially undiagnosed; however, a small percentage of patients become symptomatic. Hepatic failure secondary to cirrhosis is not an all-or-none process: patients may lose one or more specific liver functions while retaining the remainder. In addition to hepatic effects, cirrhosis and hepatic failure can exert a wide range of extrahepatic effects that involve virtually every organ system, leading to MODS and death in most cases if appropriate therapy is not instituted promptly. Consequently, treatment of cirrhosis and chronic hepatic failure must focus on treating both the underlying primary disease and all of its extrahepatic manifestations and complications.

Portal Hypertension

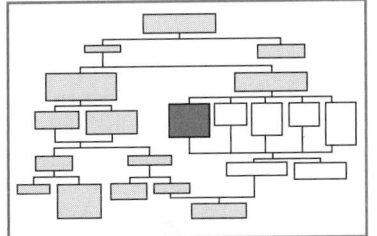

In most patients with chronic liver disease and cirrhosis, PHT develops as a result of increased resistance to portal venous blood flow within the liver. PHT is defined as a portal venous pressure higher than 12 mm Hg or a hepatic wedge venous pressure that exceeds the inferior vena cava pressure by more than 5 mm Hg. It is classified as prehepatic, hepatic, or posthepatic according to the anatomic site of increased portal venous resistance. Hepatic PHT is further classified according to the functional relationship to the hepatic sinusoids [see 52 Portal Hypertension]. Sinusoidal obstruction is more frequently seen with postnecrotic cirrhosis (e.g., cirrhosis resulting from HCV and HBV infection), whereas postsinusoidal obstruction is more common with alcoholic cirrhosis. Prehepatic and posthepatic causes of PHT are less often encountered in

---

Table 4 Etiology of Chronic Liver Disease

Alcoholic liver disease (exclude acute alcoholic hepatitis)
Viral hepatitis
   Hepatitis B virus
   Hepatitis C virus
Biliary cirrhosis
   Primary biliary cirrhosis
   Primary sclerosing cholangitis
   Secondary sclerosing cholangitis
   Biliary atresia
Autoimmune hepatitis
Metabolic abnormalities
   Wilson disease
   α_1-Antitrypsin deficiency
   Hemochromatosis
   Inborn errors of metabolism
Cryptogenic cirrhosis
Miscellaneous
   Vascular anomalies (Budd-Chiari syndrome)
   Toxin- or drug-induced
   Inborn errors of metabolism
   Other

patients with cirrhosis; however, efforts should always be made to rule out such causes, because these conditions all require different therapeutic approaches.

PHT is associated with numerous complications, most of which are life-threatening if not diagnosed and treated promptly. The most dramatic and catastrophic complication of PHT is bleeding from esophageal and gastric varices. Prompt diagnosis and management are vital. Since the early 1990s, management of variceal bleeding has evolved significantly, thanks to the advent of novel endoscopic therapies and nonoperative portosystemic shunt procedures. Although the esophagus and the stomach are the most common sites of bleeding varices, other sites within the GI tract may be involved as well, including the duodenum, the jejunum, the rectum, and ileostomy and colostomy sites.

One of the principal clinical manifestations of cirrhosis and PHT is ascites (i.e., leakage of lymph fluid into the peritoneal cavity). The appearance of ascites is indicative of advanced liver disease and is associated with a poor prognosis.[70] It is believed that increased hepatic sinusoidal pressure results in increased formation of lymph and causes hepatic lymph to weep from Glisson's capsule into the peritoneal cavity. As ascitic fluid accumulates, patients exhibit increasing abdominal distention, which in turn causes abdominal pain, decreased appetite, dyspnea, and, occasionally, pleural effusion (so-called hepatic hydrothorax).

An elevated WBC count in the ascitic fluid provides immediate information about possible bacterial infection. Cell counts higher than 500/mm³ suggest bacterial peritonitis, especially when the absolute neutrophil count exceeds 250/mm³.[71] More than 20% of cirrhotic patients with ascites eventually manifest SBP. Patients with a low total protein level in their ascitic fluid (< 1.5 g/dl) appear to be at highest risk as a result of the reduced complement level and opsonic activity in the fluid. The diagnosis of SBP should be considered in any cirrhotic patient with fever, abdominal pain, worsening encephalopathy, or deteriorating renal function. Ascitic fluid analysis [see Table 5] distinguishes SBP from secondary bacterial peritonitis that develops as a consequence of an intra-abdominal abscess or a perforated viscus. Like ascites, SBP carries a grave prognosis: the estimated 1-year survival is less than 50% without liver transplantation.[72,73]

Evaluation and management of PHT and its associated complications are addressed further elsewhere [see 52 Portal Hypertension].

Hepatic Encephalopathy

Hepatic encephalopathy is a complex neuropsychiatric syndrome that is seen in patients with severe hepatic insufficiency and cirrhosis. It is characterized by progressive alteration of cognitive function and coordination and depression of consciousness, leading to deep coma. Hepatic encephalopathy takes two main forms: (1) acute encephalopathy associated with FHF and (2) portosystemic encephalopathy (PSE) associated with cirrhosis and portosystemic shunts. It is classified into four stages according to the severity and extent of CNS impairment [see Table 6].

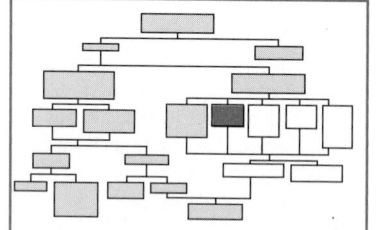

For accurate diagnosis of hepatic encephalopathy, it is necessary to recognize and correct all other disorders that affect cerebral function, including fluid and electrolyte abnormalities, hypoglycemia, azotemia, metabolic acidosis or alkalosis, hypoxia, and plasma hyperosmolality. Sedatives and paralytic agents should be avoided during the initial assessment period if possible; if sedation or paralysis is required, the combination of poor hepatic function with the shunting of blood away from the liver may greatly lengthen drug elimination, thereby complicating patient assessment. Frequently, patients with PSE carry out normal activities while the disorder goes unrecognized, and PSE is diagnosed only when its presentation is exaggerated by infection or GI bleeding. PSE is also exacerbated by constipation, the onset of portal vein thrombosis, and the development of a liver malignancy.

Management of PSE begins with treatment of all potential precipitating factors: sedatives and other drugs with CNS effects should be discontinued, fluid and electrolyte abnormalities should be corrected, GI bleeding should be controlled, and underlying infections (especially SBP) should be treated. Early endotracheal intubation for airway protection may be needed in patients with stage III or IV encephalopathy because of the high risk of aspiration and subsequent pneumonia.

The therapeutic objectives in the management of hepatic encephalopathy are (1) to minimize ammonia formation and (2) to augment ammonia elimination [see Discussion, Mechanism of Hepatic Encephalopathy, below]. Lactulose and certain antibiotics are commonly employed to achieve these ends. Lactulose is a synthetic disaccharide cathartic that can be delivered orally, through a nasogastric tube, or via a high enema and can be administered early in the course of the disease. The dosage should begin at 25 g/day and then be titrated to a level at which the patient can produce three or four loose bowel movements daily. Lactulose is nei-

Table 5 Differentiation of Spontaneous Bacterial Peritonitis from Secondary Bacterial Peritonitis through Analysis of Ascitic Fluid

Fluid Assay	Spontaneous Bacterial Peritonitis	Secondary Bacterial Peritonitis
WBC (cells/mm³)	> 500	> 500
Total protein (g/dl)	< 1.0	> 1.0
Glucose (mg/dl)	> 50	< 50
Lactic dehydrogenase (U/L)	< 225	> 225
Gram stain	Monomicrobial	Polymicrobial

Table 6 Grading of Hepatic Encephalopathy

Encephalopathy Stage	Neurologic Changes
Stage I	Mild confusion, euphoria or depression, decreased attention span, slowing of ability to perform mental tasks, irritability, disorder of sleep pattern
Stage II	Drowsiness, lethargy, gross deficit in ability to perform mental tasks, obvious personality changes, inappropriate behavior, intermittent and short-lived disorientation
Stage III	Somnolent but arousable, unable to perform mental tasks, disorientation with respect to time or place, marked confusion, amnesia, occasional fits of rage, speech present but incomprehensible
Stage IV	Coma

ther absorbed nor metabolized in the upper GI tract. When it reaches the colon, the ensuing bacterial degradation acidifies the luminal contents and causes an intraluminal osmotic shift. The more acidic environment inhibits coliform bacterial growth, thereby reducing ammonia production. Additionally, the low intraluminal gut pH causes ammonia to be converted to ammonium ions, which do not enter the bloodstream easily. Finally, the cathartic action of lactulose clears ammonium ions from the bowel. Aggressive lactulose therapy may induce volume depletion and electrolyte imbalance; metabolic acidosis is a rare occurrence.

Neomycin, an agent commonly used for bowel preparation, alters gut flora, especially *Escherichia coli* and other urease-producing organisms, and reduces the production of ammonia. About 1% of neomycin is absorbed systemically; because of possible ototoxicity and nephrotoxicity, special care should be taken if it is administered on a continuous basis.[74] Other oral antibiotics used to treat hepatic encephalopathy are polymyxin B, metronidazole, and vancomycin, which affect gut flora in much the same fashion as neomycin.

Aromatic amino acids (AAAs) are known neurotransmitter precursors. It has been suggested that their products interfere with the activity of true neurotransmitters. It has also been shown that the ratio of branched-chain amino acids (BCAAs) to AAAs in plasma decreases steeply with worsening encephalopathy. Because AAAs and BCAAs compete for the same blood-brain barrier carrier transport sites, the relative paucity of BCAAs leads to increased cerebral uptake of AAAs, which in turn promotes synthesis of false neurotransmitters that then compete with the endogenous transmitters dopamine and norepinephrine.[75] Parenteral administration of BCAA-enriched formulas to patients with hepatic encephalopathy has been advocated, but it has not proved beneficial when compared with administration of conventional amino acid solutions.[76]

Renal Failure

Liver disease and cirrhosis are commonly associated with functional renal failure—that is, impaired renal function in the absence of significant underlying renal pathology. The most common functional renal abnor-

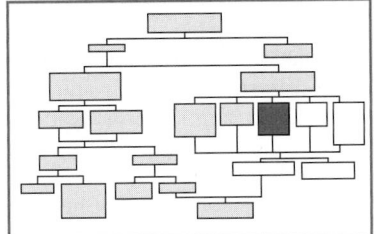

mality in cirrhotic patients is HRS, which is defined as a reversible state of renal failure characterized by azotemia, oliguria (< 10 mEq/L), and an increased urine-plasma osmolality ratio (U/P > 1.0) in the absence of urinary sedimentation. HRS occurs in 18% to 55% of cirrhotic patients with ascites and is typified by intense renal vasoconstriction, a decreased glomerular filtration rate (GFR), preserved tubular function, and normal renal histology.[46,77] Although the exact cause of HRS is not known, current evidence suggests that it is multifactorial, involving systemic vasodilatation and reduced effective plasma volume, along with increased activity of the renin-angiotensin-aldosterone system, which causes further reduction of the GFR. HRS is classified as either type 1 or type 2. In type 1 HRS, renal failure is rapidly progressive, as defined by a doubling of the initial serum creatinine level to a value higher than 2.5 mg/dl or a 50% reduction in the initial creatinine clearance to a value lower than 20 ml/min in less than 2 weeks. In type 2 HRS, renal failure takes a slower, more gradual course.

The prognosis for patients with HRS is poor: to date, all therapeutic approaches have proved unsuccessful. Pharmacologic therapy has consisted of correcting effective volume status and attempt-

ing to reverse renal vasoconstriction through I.V. administration of vasodilators (e.g., dopamine, misoprostol, and aminophylline) or drugs that inhibit the synthesis or the effects of endogenous vasoconstrictors (e.g., captopril and thromboxane inhibitors). These approaches have not yielded effective and reproducible improvements in renal hemodynamics and renal function. Several investigators have reported improved renal function after OLT.[46,77]

An approach to the management of HRS has been introduced that is aimed at correcting the primary underlying defect (i.e., systemic vasodilatation) instead of the secondary renal vasoconstriction. Two classes of drugs have been investigated: (1) agents that inhibit the effects of endogenous systemic vasodilators (e.g., prostacyclin, nitric oxide, and glucagon) and (2) agents that cause systemic vasoconstriction (e.g., ornipressin and terlipressin). In one small series of patients with type 1 HRS, a combination of an oral beta-adrenergic drug with midodrine and octreotide led to improved renal function and better long-term outcome.[78]

Besides functional renal failure, various types of nonfunctional (i.e., organic) renal failure may occur in patients with cirrhosis (e.g., ATN, renal tubular acidosis [RTA], and drug-induced interstitial nephritis). ATN is especially common in patients with chronic liver disease or FHF and is usually seen in patients who are poorly resuscitated, have experienced prolonged hypotension, have undergone severe septic episodes, or have ingested hepatotoxins that are also nephrotoxic (e.g., acetaminophen). ATN is characterized by an abrupt rise in blood urea nitrogen (BUN) and serum creatinine levels, accompanied by oliguria or anuria. Unlike HRS, ATN leads to impairment of the concentrating ability of the tubular system and to excessive urinary sodium excretion; accordingly, a urine sodium concentration greater than 10 mEq/L is considered diagnostic for ATN in cirrhotic patients [*see Table 7*]. RTA is commonly seen in patients with primary biliary cirrhosis, autoimmune liver disease, and alcoholic cirrhosis. It is characterized by the inability of the renal tubules to acidify the urine in the presence of a normal GFR.

Table 7 Differentiation of Hepatorenal Syndrome from Acute Tubular Necrosis

Criteria	Hepatorenal Syndrome	Acute Tubular Necrosis
Underlying liver disease	Advanced liver damage with jaundice and impaired synthetic function	Mild or severe liver disease
Precipitant	GI bleeding, diuretics, paracentesis, sepsis, or none	Shock, nephrotoxins, sepsis
Onset	Days to weeks	Hours to days
Urinalysis	Renal epithelial cells with or without pigmented granular cells	Pigmented granular casts with or without RBCs, WBCs
Urinary sodium concentration	< 10 mEq/L	> 10 mEq/L
Urinary osmolarity	> Serum osmolarity	Isotonic
Urinary volume	Oliguric	Variable
Course	Progressive, unremitting	Deterioration followed by improved renal function

Management of renal failure is usually aimed at correcting the underlying precipitating causes. In patients with ascites, who experience ongoing loss of fluid and protein into the peritoneum, it is important to maintain an adequate intravascular volume. If intravascular volume is depleted, blood components, volume expanders, or both should be given. Given that the plasma albumin level is invariably low in these patients, salt-poor albumin solutions may be preferable to carbohydrate-based volume expanders. Albumin replacement has been effectively used for volume expansion after LVP.[79]

Because of the complex physiologic liver-kidney interaction, fluid and electrolyte management often proves challenging. It is difficult to estimate the actual intravascular volume, which is depleted in most cirrhotic patients even though total body fluid volume is greater than normal. Sodium retention and free water retention are the two most common abnormalities of renal function that lead to ascites and dilutional hyponatremia. Typically, sodium retention is an early manifestation, whereas water retention and renal failure are late findings. Nephrotoxic drugs and I.V. contrast agents should be avoided, and dosages of antibiotics and other medications should be adjusted appropriately.

Hypernatremia and metabolic acidosis can develop secondary to excessive lactulose therapy and dehydration and result in renal function deterioration. Hypokalemia is also common; it develops secondary to increased serum aldosterone concentration, which leads to excessive excretion of potassium in exchange for sodium. Once renal failure develops, hyperkalemia, hypercalcemia, and hyperphosphatemia become significant problems, often necessitating dialysis.

Malnutrition

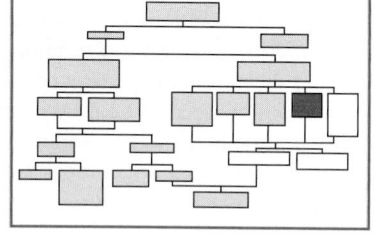

Most cirrhotic patients present with depleted glycogen stores, severe protein-calorie malnutrition, and wasting. Impaired hepatic synthetic activity, causing a deficiency of both visceral and structural proteins, is one of the hallmarks of advanced liver disease. In addition, poor appetite, tense ascites, abdominal pain, and excessive loss of protein through repeated LVP and overall increased energy expenditure tend to exacerbate malnutrition.

Excessive protein administration can induce hepatic encephalopathy; accordingly, protein intake should be limited to 1 to 1.2 g/kg/day. Glucose is the main energy source given to malnourished cirrhotic patients; however, its use is not without complications, in that these patients typically exhibit glucose intolerance. Lipid emulsion can be safely administered to most patients with hepatic failure and should be withheld only from patients with overt coma.[80] It is generally agreed that the ideal energy source should consist of a mixture of glucose and fat emulsion. Approximately 30% to 40% of all nonprotein calories can be provided in the form of fat. The total energy requirement should be 25 to 35 kcal/kg/day.

As noted [see Hepatic Encephalopathy, above], although AAAs have been implicated in the pathogenesis of hepatic encephalopathy, administration of BCAA solutions has not proved helpful, and current evidence does not support their routine use.[76,81]

In general, the potential risks and complications associated with total parenteral nutrition (TPN) outweigh the benefits in patients with a functioning GI tract. When properly administered, enteral nutrition is safer, more physiologically appropriate, and significantly more cost-effective than TPN. It should therefore be considered the first choice for nutritional support in most patients with chronic liver disease unless a contraindication to enteral feeding is present.

Coagulopathy and Nonvariceal Bleeding

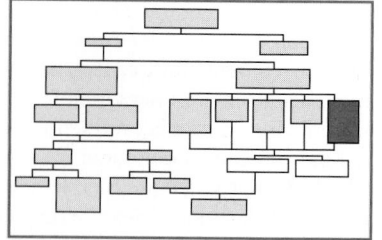

The spectrum of coagulation disorders in patients with liver disease ranges from minor localized bleeding to massive life-threatening hemorrhage. Abnormal bleeding may be spontaneous in some patients, but it is more often the result of a hemostatic challenge (e.g., surgical wounds or procedures, gastritis, portal hypertensive gastropathy, gastric or duodenal ulcers, or ruptured varices). The underlying anatomic lesion is believed to be as responsible for bleeding as the hemostatic defect; accordingly, therapy should be directed at correcting both. In addition, general physiologic monitoring is maintained. A physiologic pH and a normal core temperature optimize coagulation factors and platelet function. Poor nutrition and cholestatic diseases are associated with depleted levels of vitamin K. I.V. administration of vitamin K_1 can be accomplished with minor complications.

Although most bleeding episodes are secondary to decreased synthesis of clotting factors, other causes of bleeding (e.g., defective or dysfunctional factor synthesis and increased consumption of clotting components) must be ruled out. In most patients, the decreased levels of clotting factors parallel the progressive loss of parenchymal cell function. Usually, the levels of the vitamin K–dependent factors (i.e., prothrombin, factor VII, factor IX, factor X, protein S, and protein C) fall first, followed by the levels of other factors as cirrhosis progresses. Factor V is synthesized independently of vitamin K availability, and its concentration is of special interest because the plasma factor V level seems to be a predictor of the extent of liver cell damage. Impaired synthesis of coagulation proteins also has an impact on antithrombin III (AT-III), protein C inhibitor, plasminogen, and α_2-antiplasmin, as well as on several other inhibitors and activators of both the extrinsic coagulation pathway and the intrinsic pathway. The combination of decreased factor levels and impaired synthesis of coagulation proteins explains the prolongation of the PT, the activated partial thromboplastin time (aPTT), and the thrombin clotting time (TCT) in these patients.[82,83]

Given the complexity of hemostasis in cirrhotic patients, accurate diagnosis of a bleeding disorder is often hard to achieve. Several disorders and abnormalities may be present simultaneously, and one or more parameters of hemostasis and coagulation may be impaired. Therefore, any effective treatment approach should be broad-based and aimed at correcting several deficiencies or abnormalities at once. FFP contains all of the components of the clotting and fibrinolytic systems but lacks platelets. In most cases, transfusion of 6 to 8 units of FFP corrects severe clotting factor defects; however, the excess volume may not be well tolerated. Cryoprecipitate, the precipitate formed when FFP is thawed at 4° C, is rich in factor VIII, von Willebrand factor, and fibrinogen but lacks the vitamin K–dependent factors. Therefore, it should be given only when the fibrinogen level is lower than 100 mg/dl. Prothrombin complex concentrates contain only the vitamin K–dependent factors and proteins, and their use can provoke serious thromboembolic complications, including DIC. Therefore, their potential utility must be weighed carefully against the risk that thrombotic events may develop.[84]

Other major disorders of hemostasis in patients with chronic liver disease and cirrhosis involve platelets and are manifested as thrombocytopenia, abnormal platelet function (thrombocytopathy), or both. In most cases, thrombocytopenia is related to sple-

Table 8 Contraindications to Liver Transplantation

Absolute contraindications	Severe, irreversible brain damage HIV infection Extrahepatic malignancy Uncontrolled sepsis Severe pulmonary hypertension and advanced cardiopulmonary disease Active substance abuse or major psychosocial problems Extrahepatic portal vein thrombosis in patients with hepatocellular carcinoma
Relative contraindications	Elevated ICP or reduced CPP (in patients with FHF) Multiple organ dysfunction syndrome Hemodynamic instability Advanced age Portal vein thrombosis (except when secondary to hepatocellular carcinoma)

CPP—cerebral perfusion pressure   ICP—intracranial pressure

nomegaly and hypersplenism (a common feature of PHT). Abnormal platelet function is attributed to many causes, including intrinsic platelet defects and abnormal interaction among platelets, endothelial surfaces, and clotting factors. It is manifested by a prolonged bleeding time, impaired platelet aggregation, and reduced adhesiveness. Some authorities attribute the inhibition of platelet aggregation to fibrin degradation products (FDPs); however, the FDP levels noted in the plasma of cirrhotic patients are not sufficient to impair platelet aggregation, nor do they correlate with the observed reductions in platelet aggregation.[85]

Platelets should be transfused whenever a patient with either a quantitative or a qualitative defect experiences active bleeding. A normal response is a rise of 10,000/mm^3 with each unit transfused; however, in cases of hypersplenism and accelerated consumption, such a response is rare. Transfusion should be continued until all serious bleeding has ceased, with the therapeutic goal being the maintenance of a platelet count near 50,000/mm^3. Platelet transfusion is also indicated before any surgical or invasive procedure (e.g., paracentesis or liver biopsy). Indications for prophylactic platelet transfusion are less clear, and any potential gains must be balanced against potential side effects and development of antibodies. Most patients with advanced cirrhosis and liver failure have platelet counts lower than 100,000/mm^3; however, prophylactic platelet transfusion is usually not recommended until the count falls below 15,000 to 20,000/mm^3, at which point the risk of spontaneous bleeding is considerably increased.

Another feature of severe liver disease is increased fibrinolytic activity, which may be either primary or secondary to DIC.[86] The precise causes of primary fibrinolysis and DIC remain unclear. Primary fibrinolysis appears to be a result of increased activity of tissue plasminogen activator and decreased levels of α_2-antiplasmin.[87] DIC is believed to be triggered by the release of thromboplastic substances into the circulation as a consequence of liver cell damage or necrosis and by poor clearance of circulating activated tissue and clotting factors and FDPs by a defective reticuloendothelial system. Accelerated fibrinolysis is manifested by reductions in the whole blood clot lysis time and the euglobulin clot lysis time, as well as by elevated levels of fibrinolysis products (e.g., FDPs and D-dimer). Although enhanced fibrinolysis is relatively common in patients with cirrhosis, most of the characteristic abnormalities can occur after many types of physiologic stress and are not necessarily accompanied by a bleeding tendency.

At present, no satisfactory method of managing DIC is available. An extensive workup must be completed to rule out underlying causes (e.g., sepsis, ARDS, and MODS). FFP, platelet concentrates, and low-dose heparin (200 to 800 U/hr) may be given. AT-III concentrate has been used in an attempt to inhibit the action of thrombin, thereby decreasing procoagulant consumption, restoring normal levels of factors, and improving hemostasis. Clinical experience with AT-III therapy in this setting has been limited; however, there is evidence suggesting that AT-III may reduce hemostatic abnormalities and help control bleeding.[88]

Antifibrinolytic agents (e.g., ε-aminocaproic acid and tranexamic acid) impede fibrinolysis and may be useful in treating bleeding in patients who have liver disease and show evidence of fibrinolysis.[89] In patients with DIC, administration of antifibrinolytic agents is contraindicated because of the potential for thrombotic complications. D-dimer levels should be determined to rule out DIC before use of these medications is considered. Because it is difficult to rule out DIC in patients with liver disease, the use of antifibrinolytic agents in liver disease is limited. Other antifibrinolytic compounds have been tested for use in liver transplantation. Of these, apronitin has been shown to reduce the number of packed red blood cells given during liver implantation in selected patients.

LIVER TRANSPLANTATION

In 2005, 6,444 liver transplants were performed in the United States. The 1-year survival rates for patients and grafts have improved to greater than 90% and 85%, respectively. At present, the main limiting factor for the continued growth of liver transplantation is the scarcity of donors. Living related donor liver transplants account for approximately 5% of the total number of transplants.

End-Stage Liver Disease

Liver transplantation is an accepted therapy for ESLD. The standard indications for liver transplantation are well documented[90]; they include PHT, poor hepatic synthetic function, hepatic encephalopathy, progressing jaundice, severe malnutrition, and excessive fatigue. PHT is manifested by variceal bleeding, hypersplenism, thrombocytopenia, ascites, hepatic hydrothorax, and SBP. Poor synthetic function is usually manifested by an elevated INR and low serum albumin and cholesterol levels. In general,

Table 9 Child-Turcotte-Pugh Scoring System

Points	1	2	3
Encephalopathy	None	Stage I or II	Stage III or IV
Ascites	Absent	Slight (or controlled by diuretics)	Moderate despite diuretic treatment
Bilirubin (mg/dl) Patients with PBC or PSC	< 2 < 4	2–3 4–6	> 3 > 6
Albumin (g/L)	> 3.5	2.8–3.5	< 2.8
PT (prolonged sec) INR	< 4 < 1.7	4–6 1.7–2.3	> 6 > 2.3

PBC—primary biliary cirrhosis   PSC—primary sclerosing cholangitis any concurrent medical or psychosocial condition that prohibits a major surgical procedure or subsequent immunosuppression constitutes a contraindication to liver transplantation [see Table 8].

UNOS currently regulates organ allocation to transplant candidates. In January 1988, minimal listing criteria for liver transplantation were implemented.[91] These criteria were based on the Child-Turcotte-Pugh (CTP) scoring system [see Table 9], which includes five parameters: serum albumin and bilirubin levels, PT, ascites, and hepatic encephalopathy. Graft allocation had a subjective component, taking into account the time spent on the waiting list. The criteria currently used were implemented in February 2002 and are based on the Modeling for End-Stage Liver Disease (MELD) scoring system, which predicts patient survival without a liver transplant at 90 days.[92,93] This scoring system was developed to predict survival in patients with cirrhosis after TIPS, and it has been shown also to predict patient survival after liver trans-

plantation.[94] The MELD score is calculated from three laboratory values that feed into a logistic regression formula: INR, serum creatinine level, and total bilirubin concentration. Modifications have been implemented to improve allocation, and exception policies are evolving. A similar scoring system, the Pediatric End-Stage Liver Disease (PELD) system, has been developed for pediatric patients, incorporating information on serum albumin levels and growth failure. A patient who has FHF is listed as status 1, and no MELD score is assigned.

Liver Cancer

Hepatocellular carcinoma (HCC) [see 51 Tumors of the Pancreas, Biliary Tract, and Liver] is 30 times more common in cirrhotic patients than in noncirrhotic patients. Its high growth rate and high mortality have prompted the development of exception points that favor HCC patients for rapid graft allocation.

Discussion

Mechanism of Hepatic Encephalopathy

The association between liver disease and altered mental status and consciousness has been recognized for centuries, but the exact underlying mechanism remains unknown. It appears that this syndrome has a multifactorial etiology and is associated with a number of complex changes, which are manifested collectively as hepatic encephalopathy. It is generally believed that hepatocerebral dysfunction is caused by an accumulation of cerebral toxins as a result of low hepatic clearance.[95]

Of all the physiologic factors thought to contribute to the development of encephalopathy, the best known is ammonia. Arterial ammonia levels are frequently elevated in patients with hepatic encephalopathy; however, the clinical severity of hepatic encephalopathy correlates poorly with the ammonia level.[96] The precise contribution of ammonia to hepatic encephalopathy remains unclear; however, ammonia is known to inhibit the uptake of glutamate into astrocytes, thereby causing a rise in the extracellular glutamate level that appears to downregulate the postsynaptic glutamate receptors, resulting in decreased neuronal excitation.[97]

Endogenous or exogenously ingested benzodiazepines may also play a role in the etiology of acute and chronic hepatic encephalopathy by interacting with the high-affinity γ-aminobutyric acid (GABA)–benzodiazepine receptor complexes. These substances are known to enhance inhibitory GABA-ergic tone. Animal studies suggest that gut flora may contribute benzodiazepine ligand activity,[98] as well as increased benzodiazepine receptor agonist activity.[99] Studies of FHF patients show increased benzodiazepine receptor ligands with enhanced GABA-ergic tone in all stages of encephalopathy.[100] Ammonia-induced activation of peripheral-type benzodiazepine receptors on astrocytes may cause the release of neurosteroids that enhance GABA-ergic neurotransmission. Hence, neurosteroids may potentiate the inhibitory actions of GABA at the receptor level, as well as lengthen the period during which the GABA ligand remains in the synaptic cleft. Ammonia also acts directly to potentiate GABA-ergic tone by enhancing the affinity of GABA for GABA-A receptors.[101]

These findings notwithstanding, there is no apparent correlation between benzodiazepine ligand activity and clinical stage of encephalopathy, nor is ligand elevation a consistent finding in all

patients. Furthermore, clinical and animal studies in which a benzodiazepine receptor antagonist has been administered have not shown consistent effects. The anecdotal success of flumazenil, the principal benzodiazepine antagonist, has been ascribed to the antagonism of benzodiazepines ingested by patients. Support for the concept of so-called endogenous benzodiazepines arising from the intestine can be found in a number of sources, including studies of dogs with congenital portacaval shunts, which document ligand activity in stool samples.[102] Whether there is a causal relation to hepatic encephalopathy or whether this is merely a case of associated phenomena remains to be determined. Whatever the contribution of benzodiazepines to the pathophysiology of acute hepatic encephalopathy and cerebral edema, it appears likely that other mechanisms are involved.

Bioartificial Liver Support System

Despite the best management efforts, the morbidity and mortality associated with ALF remain exceptionally high. For most severe cases, liver transplantation is still the only effective therapeutic modality. Unfortunately, because of the severe organ donor shortage, the waiting period for transplantation is long, and patients consequently are at risk for the development of irreversible complications or contraindications to liver transplantation while awaiting a donor. In an effort to mitigate this problem, investigators have studied various artificial liver support systems designed to provide full metabolic, hemodynamic, and physiologic support until either the native liver regenerates or a liver becomes available for transplantation. From the 1970s to the 1990s, most therapeutic attempts focused primarily on detoxifying plasma. All such attempts either failed or had no significant impact on survival.[103]

The ongoing severe organ shortage led several investigators to develop and test xenogeneic-based liver support systems employing whole-organ perfusion or isolated hepatocytes. We developed and tested a hybrid bioartificial liver (BAL) support system employing isolated porcine hepatocytes in an extracorporeal perfusion circuit. We subsequently initiated a clinical trial addressing the use of this system in patients with severe ALF as a bridge to either transplantation or spontaneous recovery.[104-107]

In 1997, the BAL our group developed (HepatAssist; Circe Biomedical, Inc., Lexington, Massachusetts) was tested in a phase I clinical trial.[101] Patients were admitted to a dedicated liver support unit. Invasive hemodynamic monitoring (via peripheral arterial catheter and pulmonary artery catheter) was instituted after blood product administration for partial correction of coagulopathy. All patients received standard medical care, along with one to five BAL treatments (each lasting 6 to 7 hours). If signs of intracranial hypertension were observed, an ICP monitor was placed at the bedside for ICP and CPP monitoring. Patients were intubated endotracheally when in stage 4 encephalopathy and were placed on ventilatory support. The BAL treatments were well tolerated, and no technical problems were identified during BAL therapy. A total of 32 patients were treated with the BAL (29 patients with FHF and three with PNF after transplantation), of whom 84% survived with or without transplantation (unpublished data). Patients experienced remarkable neurologic improvement, with reversal of the decerebrate state after BAL treatments. Posturing, anisocoria, and sluggish pupil reactivity were reduced, and patients became more responsive to external stimuli. Brainstem function improved, and there was a significant reduction in ICP, with a concomitant increase in CPP. Other effects of BAL treatment included a decrease in ammonia, transaminase, and bilirubin levels and a significant increase in the BCAA-AAA ratio.

Subsequently, the safety and efficacy of the BAL were evaluated in a prospective, randomized, controlled, multicenter trial that included 171 patients with severe ALF (86 in the control group and 85 in the BAL group).[107] Both patients with FHF or SHF and patients with PNF after liver transplantation were enrolled in this trial. Data were analyzed with and without consideration of the following confounding factors: liver transplantation, time to transplant, disease etiology, disease severity, and treatment site. In the study population as a whole, 30-day survival was 71% for the BAL group and 62% for the control group. In the FHF/SHF subpopulation (with PNF patients excluded), 30-day survival was 73% for the BAL group and 59% for the control group. When survival was analyzed so as to take into account the aforementioned confounding factors, there was no difference in survival between the BAL group and the control group in the study population as whole, but in the FHF/SHF subpopulation, survival was significantly higher in the BAL group than in the control group. This was the first prospective, randomized, controlled trial of an extracorporeal liver support system to demonstrate a significant survival advantage in patients treated with such a system.

References

1. Kotwal GJ, Baroudy BM, Kuramoto IK: Detection of acute hepatitis C virus infection by ELISA using a synthetic peptide comprising a structural epitope. Proc Natl Acad Sci USA 89:4486, 1992

2. Hoofnagle JH, Carithers RL Jr, Shapiro C: Hepatic failure: summary of a workshop. Hepatology 21:240, 1995

3. Trey C, Davidson CS: The management of fulminant hepatic failure. Prog Liver Dis 3:202, 1970

4. Bernuau J, Rueff B, Benhamou J: Fulminant and subfulminant liver failure: definitions and causes. Semin Liver Dis 6:97, 1986

5. Schiodt FV, Atillasoy E, Shakil AO, et al: Etiology and outcomes for 295 patients with acute liver failure in the United States. Liver Transpl Surg 5:29, 1999

6. Ostapowicz G, Fontana RJ, Schiodt FV, et al: Results of a prospective study of acute liver failure at 17 tertiary care centers in the United States. Ann Intern Med 137:947, 2002

7. Ritt DJ, Whelan G, Werner DJ, et al: Acute hepatic necrosis with stupor or coma: an analysis of thirty-one patients. Medicine (Baltimore) 48:151, 1969

8. Lettau LA, McCarthy JG, Smith MH, et al: Outbreak of severe hepatitis due to delta and hepatitis B viruses in parenteral drug abusers and their contacts. N Engl J Med 317:1256, 1987

9. Gimson AE, Tedder RS, White YS, et al: Serological markers in fulminant hepatitis B. Gut 24:615, 1983

10. Samuel D, Bismuth A, Mathieu D, et al: Passive immunoprophylaxis after liver transplantation in HBsAg-positive patients. Lancet 337:813, 1991

11. Govindarajan S, Chin KP, Redeker AG, et al: Fulminant B virus hepatitis: role of delta agent. Gastroenterology 86:1417, 1984

12. Smedile A, Farci P, Verme G, et al: Influence of delta infection on severity of hepatitis B. Lancet 2:945, 1982

13. Lichtenstein D, Makadon H, Chopra S: Fulminant hepatitis B and delta virus coinfection in AIDS. Am J Gastroenterol 97:1643, 1992

14. Castells A, Salmeron JM, Navasa M, et al: Liver transplantation for acute liver failure: analysis of applicability. Gastroenterology 105:532, 1993

15. Rakela J, Lange SM, Ludwig J, et al: Fulminant hepatitis: Mayo Clinic experience with 34 cases. Mayo Clin Proc 60:289, 1985

16. Acharya SK, Dasarathy S, Kumer TL, et al: Fulminant hepatitis in a tropical population: clinical course, cause, and early prediction of outcome. Hepatology 23:1448, 1996

17. Zimmerman H: Update of hepatoxicity due to classes of drugs in common clinical use: non-steroidal drugs, antiinflammatory drugs, antibiotics, antihypertensives, and cardiac and psychotropic agents. Semin Liver Dis 10:322, 1990

18. Carney F, Van Dyke R: Halothane hepatitis: a critical review. Anesth Analg 51:135, 1972

19. Floersheim G: Treatment of human amatoxin mushroom poisoning: myths and advances in therapy. Med Toxicol 2:1, 1987

20. Klein AS, Hart J, Brems JJ, et al: Amanita poisoning: treatment and the role of transplantation. Am J Med 86:187, 1989

21. McCullough AJ, Fleming CR, Thistle JL, et al: Diagnosis of Wilson's disease presenting as fulminant hepatic failure. Gastroenterology 84:161, 1983

22. Rector WG Jr, Uchida T, Kanel GC, et al: Fulminant hepatic and renal failure complicating Wilson's disease. Liver 4:341, 1984

23. Stremmel W, Meyerrose KW, Niederau C, et al: Wilson disease: clinical presentation, treatment, and survival. Ann Intern Med 115:720, 1991

24. Amon E, Allen SR, Petrie RH, et al: Acute fatty liver of pregnancy associated with pre-eclampsia: management of hepatic failure with postpartum liver transplantation. Am J Perinatol 8:278, 1991

25. O'Grady JG, Alexander GJ, Hayllar KM, et al: Early indicators of prognosis in fulminant hepatic failure. Gastroenterology 97:439, 1989

26. Bernuau J, Goudeau A, Poynard T, et al: Multivariate analysis of prognostic factors in fulminant hepatitis B. Hepatology 6:648, 1986

27. Dabos KJ, Newsome PN, Parkinson JA, et al: Biochemical prognostic markers of outcome in non-paracetamol-induced fulminant hepatic failure. Transplantation 77:200, 2004

28. Saibara T, Onishi S, Sone J, et al: Arterial ketone body ratio as a possible indicator for liver transplantation in fulminant hepatic failure. Transplantation 51:782, 1991

29. Ranek L, Andreasen PB, Tygstrup N: Galactose elimination capacity as a prognostic index in patients with fulminant liver failure. Gut 17:959, 1976

30. Ware A, D'Agostino A, Combes B: Cerebral edema: a major complication of massive hepatic necrosis. Gastroenterology 61:877, 1971

31. Silk DB, Trewby PN, Chase RA, et al: Treatment of fulminant hepatic failure by polyacrylonitrile-membrane hemodialysis. Lancet 2:1, 1977

32. Lidofsky S: Fulminant hepatic failure. Crit Care Clin 11:415, 1995

33. Sidi A, Mahla M: Noninvasive monitoring of cerebral perfusion by transcranial Doppler during fulminant hepatic failure and liver transplantation. Anesth Analg 80:194, 1995

34. Wijdicks EF, Plevak DJ, Rakela J, et al: Clinical and radiological features of cerebral edema in fulminant hepatic failure. Mayo Clin Proc 70:119, 1995

35. Munoz SJ, Robinson M, Northrup B, et al: Elevated intracranial pressure and computed tomography of the brain in fulminant hepatocellular failure. Hepatology 13:209, 1991

36. Blei AT, Olafsson S, Webster S, et al: Complications of intracranial pressure monitoring in fulminant hepatic failure. Lancet 341:157, 1993

37. Jalan R: Intracranial hypertension in acute liver failure: pathophysiological basis of rational management. Semin Liver Dis 23:271, 2003

38. Davies MH, Mutimer D, Lowes J, et al: Recovery despite impaired cerebral perfusion in fulminant hepatic failure. Lancet 343:1329, 1994

39. Aldersley MA, O'Grady JG: Hepatic disorders: features and appropriate management. Drugs 49:83, 1995

40. Canalese J, Gimson AE, Davis C, et al: Controlled trial of dexamethasone and mannitol for the cerebral oedema of fulminant hepatic failure. Gut 23:625, 1982

41. Forbes A, Alexander GJ, O'Grady JG, et al: Thiopental infusion in the treatment of intracranial hypertension complicating fulminant hepatic failure. Hepatology 10:306, 1989

42. Bhatia V, Batra Y, Acharya S: Porphylactic phenytoin does not improve cerebral edema or survival in acute liver failure: a controlled clinical trial. J Hepatol 41:89, 2004

43. Murphy N, Auzinger G, Bernel W, et al: The effect of hypertonic sodium chloride on intracranial pressure in patients with acute liver failure. Hepatology 39:464, 2004

44. Jalan R, Olde Damink SW, et al: Moderate hypothermia prevents cerebral hyperemia and increase in intracranial pressure in patients undergoing liver transplantation for acute liver failure. Transplantation 75:2034, 2003

45. Jalan R, Damink SW, Deutz NE, et al: Moderate hypothermia for uncontrolled intracranial hypertension in acute liver failure. Lancet 354:1164, 1999

46. Ring-Larsen H, Palazzo U: Renal failure in fulminant hepatic failure and terminal cirrhosis: a comparison between incidence, types and prognosis. Gut 22:585, 1981

47. Shawcross DL, Davies NA, Mookerjee RP, et al: Worsening of cerebral hyperemia by the administration of terlipressin in acute liver failure with severe encephalopathy. Hepatology 39:471, 2004

48. Jalan R: Pathophysiological basis of therapy of raised intracranial pressure in acute liver failure. Neurochem Int 47:78, 2005

49. Jalan R: Acute liver failure: current management and future prospects. J Hepatol 42:115, 2005

50. Schneider F, Lutun P, Boudjema K, et al: In vivo evidence of enhanced guanylyl cyclase activation during the hyperdynamic circulation of acute liver failure. Hepatology 19:38, 1994

51. Larsen F: Cerebral circulation in liver failure; Ohm's law in force. Semin Liver Dis 16:281, 1996

52. Trewby PN, Warren R, Contini S, et al: Incidence and pathophysiology of pulmonary edema in fulminant hepatic failure. Gastroenterology 74:589, 1978

53. Bailey RJ, Woolf IL, Cullens H, et al: Metabolic inhibition of polymorphonuclear leucocytes in fulminant hepatic failure. Lancet 1:1162, 1976

54. Imawari M, Hughes RD, Gove CD, et al: Fibronectin and Kupffer cell function in fulminant hepatic failure. Dig Dis Sci 30:1028, 1985

55. Rolando N, Philpott-Howard J, Williams R: Bacterial and fungal infection in acute liver failure. Semin Liver Dis 16:389, 1996

56. Rolando N, Wade JJ, Stangou A, et al: Prospective study comparing the efficacy of prophylactic parenteral antimicrobials, with or without enteral decontamination, in patients with acute liver failure. Liver Transpl Surg 2:8, 1996

57. Rolando N, Harvey F, Brahm J, et al: Prospective study of bacterial infection in acute liver failure: an analysis of fifty patients. Hepatology 11:49, 1990

58. Rolando N, Harvey F, Brahm J, et al: Fungal infection: a common, unrecognized complicition of acute liver failure. J Hepatol 12:1, 1991

59. Shami VM, Caldwell SH, Hespenheide EE, et al: Recombinant activated factor VII for coagulopathy in fulminant hepatic failure compared with conventional therapy. Liver Transpl 9:138, 2003

60. O'Grady JG, Langley PG, Isola LM, et al: Coagulopathy of fulminant hepatic failure. Semin Liver Dis 6:159, 1986

61. Ringe B, Pichlmayr R, Lubbe N, et al: Total hepatectomy as temporary approach to acute hepatic or primary graft failure. Transplant Proc 20:552, 1988

62. Ringe B, Lubbe N, Kuse E, et al: Management of emergencies before and after liver transplantation by early total hepatectomy. Transplant Proc 25:1090, 1993

63. Rozga J, Podesta L, LePage E, et al: Control of cerebral oedema by total hepatectomy and extracorporeal live support in fulminant hepatic failure. Lancet 342:898, 1993

64. Emond JC, Aran PP, Whitington PF, et al: Liver transplantation in the management of fulminant hepatic failure. Gastroenterology 96:1583, 1989

65. Ascher NL, Lake JR, Emond JC, et al: Liver transplantation for fulminant hepatic failure. Arch Surg 128:677, 1993

66. Bismuth H, Samuel D, Castaing D, et al: Orthotopic liver transplantation in fulminant and subfulminant hepatitis. Ann Surg 23:1507, 1995

67. Marcos A, Ham JM, Fisher RA, et al: Emergency adult to adult living donor liver transplantation for fulminant hepatic failure. Transplantation 69:2202, 2000

68. Liu CL, Fan ST, Lo CM, et al: Live donor liver transplantation for fulminant hepatic failure in children. Liver Transpl 9:1185, 2003

69. Surman O: The ethics of partial liver donation. N Engl J Med 346:1038, 2002

70. Powell W, Klatskin G: Duration of survival in patients with Laennec's cirrhosis influence of alcohol withdrawal, and possible effects of recent changes in general management of the disease. Am J Med 44:406, 1968

71. Akriviadis E, Runyon B: Utility of an algorithm in differentiating spontaneous from secondary bacterial peritonitis. Gastroenterology 98:127, 1990

72. Hoefs JC, Canawati HN, Sapico FL, et al: Spontaneous bacterial peritonitis. Hepatology 2:399, 1982

73. Mihas AA, Toussaint J, Hsu HS, et al: Spontaneous bacterial peritonitis in cirrhosis: clinical and laboratory features, survival and prognostic indicators. Hepatogastroenterology 39:520, 1992

74. Berk D, Chalmers T: Deafness complicating antibiotic therapy of hepatic encephalopathy. Ann Intern Med 73:393, 1970

75. Soeters P, Fischer J: Insulin, glucagon, aminoacid imbalance, and heaptic encephalopathy. Lancet 2:880, 1976

76. DerSimonian R: Parenteral nutrition with branched-chain aminoacids in hepatic encephalopathy: meta analysis. Hepatology 11:1083, 1990

77. Gonwa TA, Goldstein M, Holman M, et al: Orthotopic liver transplantation and renal function: outcome of hepatorenal syndrome and trial of verapamil for renal protection in nonhepatorenal syndrome. Transplant Proc 25:1891, 1993

78. Angeli P, Volpin R, Gerunda G, et al: Reversal of type 1 hepatorenal syndrome with the administration of midodrine and octreotide. Hepatology 29:1690, 1999

79. Gines P, Tito L, Arroyo V, et al: Randomized comparative study of therapeutic paracentesis with and without intravenous albumin in cirrhosis. Gastroenterology 94:1493, 1988

80. Nagayama M, Takai T, Okuno M, et al: Fat emulsion in surgical patients with liver disorders. J Surg Res 47:59, 1989

81. Gluud C: Branched-chain amino acids for hepatic encephalopathy. Hepatology 13:812, 1991

82. Mammen E: Coagulopathies of liver disease. Clin Lab Med 14:769, 1994

83. Mammen E: Coagulation defects in liver disease. Med Clin North Am 78:545, 1994

84. Mannucci P, Franchi F, Dioguardi N: Correction of abnormal coagulation in chronic liver disease by combined use of fresh-frozen plasma and prothrombin complex concentrates. Lancet 2:542, 1976

85. Ballard H, Marcus A: Platelet aggregation in portal cirrhosis. Arch Intern Med 136:316, 1976

86. Brophy M, Fiore L, Deyken D: Hemostasis. Hepatology: A Textbook of Liver Disease, 3rd ed, vol 1. Zakim D, Boyer TD, Eds. WB Saunders Co, Philadelphia, 1996, p 691

87. Hersh S, Kunelis T, Francis RJ: The pathogenesis of accelerated fibrinolysis in liver cirrhosis: a critical role for tissue plasminogen activator inhibitor. Blood 69:1315, 1987

88. Riewald M, Riess H: Treatment options for clinically recognized disseminated intravascular coagulation. Semin Thromb Hemost 24:53, 1998

89. Bismuth H, Samuel D, Castaing D, et al: Liver transplantation in Europe for patients with acute liver failure. Semin Liver Dis 16:415, 1996

90. Rosen H, Shackleton C, Martin P: Indications for and timing of liver transplantation. Med Clin North Am 80:1069, 1996

91. Lucey MR, Brown KA, Everson GT, et al: Minimal criteria for placement of adults on the liver transplant waiting list: a report of a national conference organized by the American Society of Transplant Physicians and the American Association for the Study of Liver Diseases. Liver Transpl Surg 3:628, 1997

92. Freeman RB Jr, Wiesner RH, Harper A, et al: The new liver allocation system: moving toward evidence-based transplantation policy. Liver Transpl 8:851, 2002

93. Wiesner R, Edwards E, Freeman R, et al: Model for end-stage liver disease (MELD) and allocation of donor livers. Gastroenterology 124:91, 2003

94. Saab S, Wang V, Ibrahim AB, et al: MELD score predicts 1-year patient survival post-orthotopic liver transplantation. Liver Transpl 9:473, 2003

95. Butterworth R: The neurobiology of hepatic encephalopathy. Semin Liver Dis 16:235, 1996

96. Ferenci P, Puspok A, Steindi P: Current concepts in the pathophysiology of hepatic encephalopathy. Eur J Clin Invest 22:573, 1992

97. Maddison JE, Watson WE, Dodd PR, et al: Alterations in cortical [3H]kainate and alpha-[3H]amino-3-hydroxy-5-methyl-4-isoxazolepropionic acid binding in a spontaneous canine model of chronic hepatic encephalopathy. J Neurochem 56:1881, 1991

98. Yurdaydin C, Walsh TJ, Engler HD, et al: Gut bacteria provide precursors of benzodiazepine receptor ligands in a rat model of hepatic encephalopathy. Brain Res 679:42, 1995

99. Jones EA, Basile AS, Skolnick P: Hepatic encephalopathy, GABA-ergic neurotransmission and benzodiazepine receptor ligands. Adv Exp Med Biol 272:121, 1990

100. Basile AS, Harrison PM, Hughes RD, et al: Relationship between plasma benzodiazepine receptor ligand concentrations and severity of hepatic encephalopathy. Hepatology 19:112, 1994

101. Takahashi K, Kameda H, Kataoka M, et al: Ammonia potentiates GABA response in dissociated rat cortical neurons. Neurosci Lett 151:51, 1993

102. Aronson LR, Gacad RC, Kaminsky-Russ K, et al: Endogenous benzodiazepine activity in the peripheral and portal blood of dogs with congenital portosystemic shunts. Vet Surg 26:189, 1997

103. Demetriou A, Watanabe F: Support of the Acutely Failing Liver, 2nd ed. RG Landes Co, Austin, Texas, 2000

104. Rozga J, Holzman MD, Ro MS, et al: Development of a hybrid bioartificial liver. Ann Surg 217:502, 1993

105. Watanabe FD, Mullon CJ, Hewitt WR, et al: Clinical experience with a bioartificial liver in the treatment of severe liver failure: a phase I clinical trial. Ann Surg 225:484, 1997

106. Watanabe FD, Arnaout WS, Ting P, et al: Artificial liver. Transplant Proc 31:373, 1999

107. Demetriou AA, Brown RS Jr, Busuttil RW, et al: Prospective, randomized, multicenter, controlled trial of a bioartificial liver in treating acute liver failure. Ann Surg 239:660, 2004

125 ENDOCRINE PROBLEMS

Robert H. Bartlett, M.D., F.A.C.S., and Preston B. Rich, M.D., F.A.C.S.

Patients scheduled for operation may be receiving treatment with insulin, oral hypoglycemics, corticosteroids, thyroid hormone, or estrogen. The presence of any state calling for such treatment must be taken into consideration in planning operative management and perioperative care. In addition, glucose intolerance may develop in otherwise normal patients after operation, and this possibility must be taken into account as well. In what follows, we describe an approach to preventing and managing common endocrine conditions that occur as complicating factors in the perioperative period. We do not, however, address perioperative problems related to operations for primary endocrine disease.

Diabetes Mellitus

Diabetics have a 50% chance of undergoing a surgical procedure during their lifetime.[1] In the past, operation in these patients was associated with a mortality of 4% to 13%,[2] usually attributed to cardiovascular complications—clearly a significant operative risk. Any subsequent improvement in diabetes-related operative mortality has probably been offset by the increasing age of patients with diabetes and the larger variety of procedures they undergo.

Perioperative management of diabetic patients [see Figure 1] is complicated both by the metabolic abnormalities of the disease and by the effects of any diabetic complications that may be present. There is also an increased risk of postoperative surgical site infection (SSI).

EVALUATION OF THE DIABETIC PATIENT

History and Physical Examination

In taking a preoperative history from a diabetic patient, attention should be directed to any recent fluctuation in blood glucose level as well as to the type of therapy used to control the condition. The timing and dosage of medication should be considered, especially if the patient is taking long-acting insulin or an oral hypoglycemic. The extent to which diabetes is controlled in the perioperative period, which has a significant impact on postoperative recovery, may be affected by certain medications (e.g., antihypertensive agents). The presence of diabetic complications (e.g., atherosclerotic disease, diabetic nephropathy, and autonomic neuropathy) should be documented because these conditions may have serious effects during and after operation.

Medications used to control diabetes include the various forms of insulin as well as oral hypoglycemic agents. The most commonly used oral hypoglycemics are sulfonylurea, which acts by stimulating insulin secretion, and metformin, which acts by decreasing intestinal absorption. Patients should stop taking oral hypoglycemics before major operations, and their blood glucose should be controlled with insulin if necessary. Because sudden discontinuance of sulfonylurea can lead to hypoglycemia, blood

glucose levels should be carefully monitored in patients taking this medication who have experienced injury or undergone operation.

Laboratory Studies

The degree of control of diabetes can be assessed by recording blood glucose measurements at frequent intervals during fasting and at other times during the day and by determining what percentage of total hemoglobin is combined with carbohydrate (i.e., glycosylated). Normally, glycosylated hemoglobin (commonly called HbA_{1c}) accounts for 4% to 7% of total hemoglobin. HbA_{1c} levels increase when hyperglycemia occurs, and the increases are cumulative over time. The value of measuring HbA_{1c} in a preoperative patient known to be diabetic is that it gives the attending physicians some idea of how well hyperglycemic episodes are being controlled by insulin or oral hypoglycemics. Monthly measurements yield a good picture of the adequacy of glucose control over extended periods. HbA_{1c} percentages higher than 10% to 20% indicate that the hyperglycemic aspect of diabetes has been poorly controlled. Chronic diabetic complications are reduced when good control of blood glucose is maintained; diabetic patients are advised to measure their blood glucose levels frequently, which should result in normal HbA_{1c} levels. HbA_{1c} percentages higher than 15% suggest that the diabetes is quite brittle and that more frequent monitoring of blood glucose levels and closer control of insulin administration are indicated during and after operation. As long as the patient is carefully monitored, there is no evidence that high levels of HbA_{1c} are associated with any increased risk of impaired glucose control or complications after operation.

The other important laboratory study in diabetic patients is measurement of serum creatinine levels (or, perhaps, creatinine clearance) as an indicator of renal function. Renal insufficiency is a common complication of diabetes that may not be recognized during normal preoperative testing.

PREOPERATIVE MANAGEMENT

Metabolic Monitoring and Medications

All diabetic patients who are candidates for elective surgical procedures should undergo careful preoperative assessment, including metabolic monitoring. Ideally, glycemic control is achieved before a diabetic patient is admitted to the hospital. More realistically, however, admission may have to be scheduled for the day before the operation to allow time for optimizing metabolic control in all insulin-dependent patients as well as in non–insulin-dependent patients who have inadequate metabolic control. As a rule, target blood glucose levels before operation should be less than 125 mg/dl (6.9 mmol/L) during fasting and less than 180 mg/dl (10.0 mmol/L) postprandially. If emergency operation is required in patients with severe metabolic derangements (e.g., diabetic ketoacidosis or hyperosmolar nonketotic states), 6 to 8 hours of intensive treatment with insulin infusion

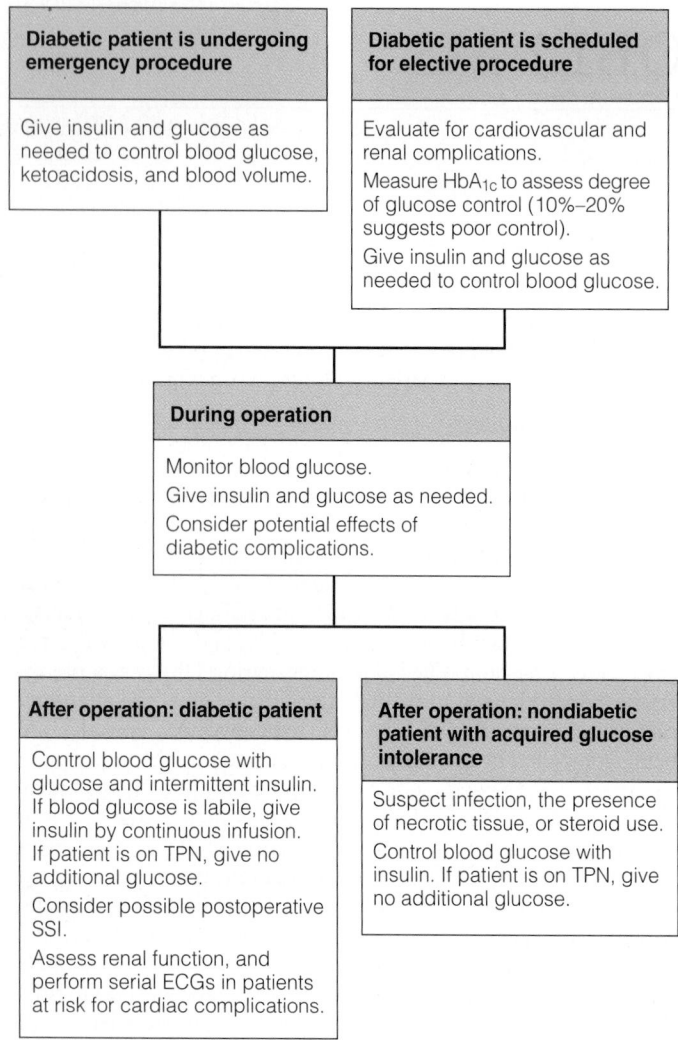

Diabetic patient is undergoing emergency procedure

Give insulin and glucose as needed to control blood glucose, ketoacidosis, and blood volume.

Diabetic patient is scheduled for elective procedure

Evaluate for cardiovascular and renal complications.
Measure HbA₁c to assess degree of glucose control (10%–20% suggests poor control).
Give insulin and glucose as needed to control blood glucose.

During operation

Monitor blood glucose.
Give insulin and glucose as needed.
Consider potential effects of diabetic complications.

After operation: diabetic patient

Control blood glucose with glucose and intermittent insulin. If blood glucose is labile, give insulin by continuous infusion. If patient is on TPN, give no additional glucose.
Consider possible postoperative SSI.
Assess renal function, and perform serial ECGs in patients at risk for cardiac complications.

After operation: nondiabetic patient with acquired glucose intolerance

Suspect infection, the presence of necrotic tissue, or steroid use.
Control blood glucose with insulin. If patient is on TPN, give no additional glucose.

Figure 1 Shown is an algorithm outlining preoperative and postoperative management of the diabetic surgical patient.

and volume restoration usually improves their general condition. This brief period permits clarification of the diagnosis in patients with acute abdominal pain, which may be the consequence of diabetic ketoacidosis rather than a so-called surgical abdomen.

In preparing diabetic patients for operation, all long-acting insulins (i.e., Ultralente preparations) should be replaced with intermediate-acting insulins (i.e., neutral protamine Hagedorn [NPH] or Lente preparations). If the patient has type 2 (non-insulin-dependent) diabetes mellitus, use of long-acting sulfonylureas (e.g., chlorpropamide and glyburide) should be stopped because of the risk of hypoglycemia; a short-acting preparation should be substituted. Use of metformin should be stopped because of the risk of lactic acidosis when renal function is impaired, as it may be during any procedure requiring anesthesia. Chronically hyperglycemic patients are frequently dehydrated, and this condition should be corrected before operation.

INTRAOPERATIVE MANAGEMENT

Metabolic Effects of Operation and Anesthesia

During anesthesia and operation, endogenous insulin secretion is suppressed, but the plasma levels of counterregulatory hormones (glucagon, epinephrine, cortisol, and growth hor-

mone) increase in nondiabetic as well as diabetic patients. Increased secretion of these hormones in the setting of low insulin levels stimulates hepatic production of glucose. In nondiabetic persons, major procedures are frequently associated with blood glucose levels of 150 to 200 mg/dl (8.3 to 11.1 mmol/L). In diabetic persons, the metabolic abnormality varies according to the extent and duration of the surgical procedure and the degree to which insulin secretion is impaired.

A study in patients with stable type 1 (insulin-dependent) diabetes mellitus showed that blood glucose levels rose from about 180 mg/dl (10.0 mmol/L) to about 270 mg/dl (15.0 mmol/L) postoperatively.[3] Ketone body levels increased by about 100%, as compared with levels in nondiabetic control subjects. Similar metabolic findings were reported even in patients with type 2 diabetes mellitus who underwent minor procedures that generated relatively little stress: blood glucose levels rose to 180 mg/dl (10.0 mmol/L), with higher than normal levels of ketone bodies and free fatty acids.[4]

Autonomic neuropathy can cause severe hypotension during induction of anesthesia. Diabetic nephropathy complicates fluid management and usually results in electrolyte abnormalities. All diabetic patients are at high risk for postoperative myocardial infarction, which is often asymptomatic. Poor nutrition and impaired phagocytosis make diabetic patients more susceptible to infection and slower to heal.

Insulin and Glucose Administration

Emergency procedures Diabetic patients may be more likely than nondiabetic patients to undergo emergency operation, which can cause rapid metabolic decompensation with dehydration, hyperglycemia, and ketoacidosis. In addition, a surgical emergency can precipitate uncontrolled diabetes in patients with no history of diabetes. Appropriate management depends, to a large extent, on the patient's metabolic condition. When one is faced with a so-called surgical abdomen, it is crucial to determine whether there is a metabolic abnormality that may be causing the condition. Given this possibility, it is sensible to manage the patient conservatively at first, with an emphasis on metabolic correction. If the underlying problem is in fact metabolic, it should resolve or improve in 3 to 4 hours; if the problem is surgical, it should remain the same or worsen over this period.

Elective major procedures In a patient undergoing general anesthesia, regardless of the duration of the operation, infusion of insulin and glucose is recommended if the patient is taking insulin for diabetes or is using drugs or diet therapy (or both) without achieving satisfactory control of type 2 diabetes mellitus.

Several methods of insulin administration may be used during the perioperative period. Most of the protocols include I.V. administration of short-acting insulin and 5% to 10% glucose. In some, glucose and insulin are administered together in a single infusion. The advantage of this approach is that if the glucose infusion is accidentally disconnected or obstructed, the insulin infusion is disconnected or obstructed as well, so that the risk of hypoglycemia is eliminated. The disadvantage of this method is that it is impossible to change the delivery rate of one agent without changing the delivery rate of the other. Administration of insulin and glucose in separate bags allows either infusion rate to be adjusted without the other being affected. The insulin infusion rate is progressively increased and the glucose infusion rate progressively decreased in accordance with the capillary blood glucose levels, measured hourly [*see Table 1*]. With this protocol,

Table 1 Representative Protocol for Insulin-Glucose Infusion during the Perioperative Period

1. Infuse 5% dextrose in water (D5W) I.V. via pump.

2. Make insulin solution with 0.5 U/ml of short-acting insulin (i.e., 250 U of regular insulin in 500 ml of normal saline). Administer in piggyback fashion via infusion pump into D5W infusion or through a separate I.V. site.

3. After initiating glucose-insulin infusion, stop all subcutaneous insulin therapy.

4. Measure capillary blood glucose levels every hour.

5. On the basis of hourly blood glucose levels, adjust each infusion according to the following schedule:

Blood Glucose (mg/dl)	Insulin Infusion		D5W Infusion (ml/hr)
	(ml/hr)	(U/hr)	
< 70*	1.0	0.5	150
71–100	2.0	1.0	125
101–150	3.0	1.5	100
151–200	4.0	2.0	100
201–250	6.0	3.0	100
251–300	8.0	4.0	75
> 300	12.0	6.0	50

*Give 10 ml D5W I.V. and repeat blood glucose measurement 15 min later.

a blood glucose level in the range of 125 to 200 mg/dl (6.9 to 11.1 mmol/L) can easily be maintained throughout the perioperative period. Close observation of blood glucose levels and prompt adjustment of insulin and glucose delivery are mandatory for achieving a stable blood glucose level. Electrolyte supplementation is administered via a separate infusion.

Minor procedures Diabetic patients who fast before minor operations (e.g., endoscopic procedures and operations performed with the patient under local anesthesia) should omit the morning dose of insulin or oral hypoglycemic agent, and their capillary blood glucose level should be measured every 2 to 4 hours. Supplemental subcutaneous short-acting insulin can be administered according to a variable insulin schedule, and the usual insulin or oral agent can be taken after the procedure [see Table 2]. This method of administration, which is associated with unpredictable absorption and variable plasma insulin levels, is restricted to surgical patients undergoing minor procedures and should not be used in those undergoing major operations.

POSTOPERATIVE MANAGEMENT

Insulin and Glucose Administration

After minor procedures, diabetic patients should receive I.V. glucose and insulin until their metabolic condition is stable and oral feeding can be tolerated. To prevent ketosis, the insulin and glucose infusions should be continued for at least 1 hour after the administration of subcutaneous short-acting insulin. After major procedures, patients should receive I.V. glucose and insulin until they are able to take solid food without difficulty. A regimen consisting of multiple subcutaneous injections of short-acting insulin before meals and intermediate-acting insulin twice

daily is recommended during the first 24 to 48 hours after cessation of the insulin and glucose infusions and before resumption of the patient's usual insulin regimen.

Total parenteral nutrition (TPN) [see 137 Nutritional Support], often required during the postoperative period, can cause serious metabolic derangements in diabetic patients. For a diabetic patient receiving TPN, a variable insulin infusion schedule [see Table 2] is recommended, with hourly determinations of blood glucose; however, additional glucose is not needed, because it is included in the TPN solution. Initially, the insulin should be given as a continuous infusion separate from the TPN solution. Once a stable dose of insulin is reached (usually within 24 to 48 hours), the total amount of insulin required over a 24-hour period can be added to the TPN bag. This amount may be high—often more than 100 units. At this point, capillary blood glucose levels can be measured every 2 to 4 hours.

Hypoglycemia can be difficult to detect in critically ill patients, in whom blood glucose levels are often elevated for any of a number of reasons. Accordingly, it has been common practice to accept blood glucose levels ranging from 150 to 200 mg/dl in these patients. This practice, however, was called into question by a 2001 randomized study of 1,548 ICU patients in which liberal glucose control (blood glucose level, 180 to 200 mg/dl) was compared with tight control (blood glucose level, 80 to 110 mg/dl).[5] ICU survival was significantly better in the tight control group (95.4%) than in the liberal control group (92%). In addition, the tight control group had a lower incidence of systemic infection, had less need of antibiotic therapy, required fewer transfusions, and were less subject to hypobilirubinemia. These findings support the view that tight regulation of glucose and insulin to maintain normal blood glucose levels is desirable in critically ill patients.

Cardiovascular and Renal Assessment

Serial postoperative electrocardiograms are recommended for older diabetic patients, those with long-standing type 1 diabetes mellitus, and those with known heart disease. Postoperative myocardial infarction, which may be silent, is associated with a high mortality. Careful monitoring of blood urea nitrogen and serum creatinine levels facilitates the detection of acute renal fail-

Table 2 Management of Diabetes in Patients Undergoing Minor Surgical Procedures[30]

If patient fasted

1. Withhold morning dose of insulin or oral agent.

2. Measure capillary blood glucose level before procedure and every 2–4 hr thereafter.

3. Give short-acting insulin every 2–4 hr, as follows:

Blood Glucose (mg/dl)	Short-Acting Insulin (U)
< 150	0
151–200	2
201–250	3
251–300	5
> 300	6

4. After procedure, give usual dose of insulin or oral agent.

ure [*see 122 Acute Renal Failure*]. If a contrast agent is used, the patient should be well hydrated before and after the procedure.

Infection

SSI is common in diabetic patients with poor metabolic control. Impaired granulocyte function resulting from hyperglycemia may predispose to bacterial infections. Autonomic neuropathy, if present, may lead to difficulty in postoperative voiding, which increases the risk of urinary tract infection. Poor circulation as a result of macroangiopathy or microangiopathy can also contribute to the likelihood of postoperative infection.

Tight metabolic control during the perioperative period can decrease the risk of postoperative infection. When SSIs do occur in the diabetic population, they are usually caused by mixed flora, including aerobic and anaerobic organisms such as *Escherichia coli*, Enterobacteriaceae, various streptococci, *Staphylococcus aureus*, and *Bacteroides fragilis*. Necrotizing infections (e.g., fasciitis, gangrene, and Fournier gangrene) are more common and spread more readily in diabetic patients.

Surgical debridement and drainage, if needed, should be performed early. Cultures should be obtained during drainage procedures. Ideally, antibiotic therapy awaits and is based on culture results; however, in practice, it is often preferable to initiate empirical therapy for the most likely organisms before the results are available. Swarming of *Proteus* organisms may obscure other pathogens on culture plates. Unless the patient is clearly manifesting a septic response, aminoglycosides should be avoided because of their nephrotoxicity and the likelihood that diabetic patients may have underlying renal disease. If severe infections do not respond to antibiotic therapy, the presence of *Candida* or other fungal species should be suspected.

Many factors play a role in the increased susceptibility of diabetics to infection, including macroangiopathy, microangiopathy, neuropathy, impaired neutrophil and lymphocyte function, increased capillary permeability, and impaired granulation and healing.[6] An obvious example of this interaction of multiple contributing factors is a chronically infected nonhealing ulcer on a neuropathic foot. A less obvious but more serious example is the failure of host defenses against peritonitis, soft tissue infection, and bacteremia that develops in diabetic patients. Chemotaxis, adherence, phagocytosis,[7] bacterial killing, and production of cytokines and complement are all impaired in patients with type 1 diabetes mellitus. The greater prominence of such abnormalities in patients with type 1 diabetes mellitus suggests that the most likely cause is related to chronic and irreversible glycosylation of many proteins, which limits the function of intracellular and intercellular messengers. The implication of this theory is that tight short- and long-term control of blood glucose should allow better control of infection.[5]

The impaired wound healing seen in diabetic patients clearly is related in part to increased susceptibility to infection; however, it is also observed with sterile wounds. Many animal studies have corroborated the clinical observation that skin, fascia, and bone all heal more slowly and with less strength in diabetic patients. Such studies have generally found that this impaired healing is partially mitigated by insulin control, which suggests that glycosylation of proteins is an important factor. A 1999 study indicated that the impaired healing is significantly mediated by endogenous corticosteroids.[8] Local application of inflammatory substances or growth factors (e.g., platelet-derived growth factor, tissue growth factor, bacterial by-products, growth hormone, and hyperosmotic sugar) has been shown to stimulate healing in diabetic animals.[6,9]

Adrenal Insufficiency

The anti-inflammatory properties of the glucocorticoid steroids [*see Table 3*] are commonly exploited to treat disease. Patients are often treated for long periods with large pharmacologic doses of steroids (commonly, prednisone by mouth) for inflammatory or autoimmune diseases such as arthritis, systemic lupus erythematosus, inflammatory bowel disease, and bronchial asthma. Primary failure of the hypothalamic-pituitary-adrenal (HPA) axis (as in Addison disease, Sheehan syndrome, and panhypopituitarism) is rare, but when it does occur, it must be treated with long-term administration of physiologic doses of corticosteroids. It is not uncommon for patients who are receiving such corticosteroid therapy to require operations, and this surgical population presents a unique perioperative management challenge [*see Figure 2*]. It is axiomatic that any patient treated with exogenous steroids may eventually manifest adrenal atrophy as a result of suppressed endogenous production of adrenocorticotropic hormone (ACTH). Actual or relative adrenal insufficiency may occur during or after a major operation, resulting in a syndrome whose manifestations can range from nausea, vomiting, fever, abdominal pain, and electrolyte abnormalities to complete circulatory collapse.

The adrenal cortex is central to the maintenance of homeostasis both at rest and during stress.[10] Cortisol, the predominant glucocorticoid hormone, is produced by the fascicular and reticular zones of the adrenal cortex. It is under the strict regulatory control of both the hypothalamus (via corticotropin-releasing hormone) and the anterior pituitary gland (via ACTH). Cortisol itself participates in its own regulation, imparting a potent negative feedback signal to both the hypothalamus and the ACTH-producing basophilic cells within the adenohypophysis of the pituitary. Together, these components, which constitute the HPA axis, form a finely regulated feedback loop for cortisol secretion.

Under unstressed physiologic conditions, the adrenal cortex constitutively produces approximately 20 to 25 mg of cortisol daily.[11] Cortisol secretion normally occurs in diurnal surges; consequently, simple measurements of serum cortisol levels in isolation generally do not suffice for accurate evaluation of the status of the HPA axis. Much of the daily variability in cortisol secretion can be tracked with 24-hour urinary measurements of the hydroxysteroid metabolites; however, there can be significant

Table 3 Selected Corticosteroid Preparations

Preparation	Equivalent Doses (mg)	Glucocorticoid Activity*	Mineralocorticoid Activity*
Short-acting (8–12 hr)			
Hydrocortisone	20	1	1
Cortisone	25	0.80	0.80
Intermediate-acting (12–36 hr)			
Prednisone	5	4	0.80
Prednisolone	5	4	0.80
Methylprednisolone	4	5	0
Triamcinolone	4	5	0
Long-acting (36–54 hr)			
Betamethasone	0.60	25	0
Dexamethasone	0.75	30	0
Mineralocorticoid			
Fludrocortisone	—	10	125

*Ranked on a scale rating hydrocortisone as 1.

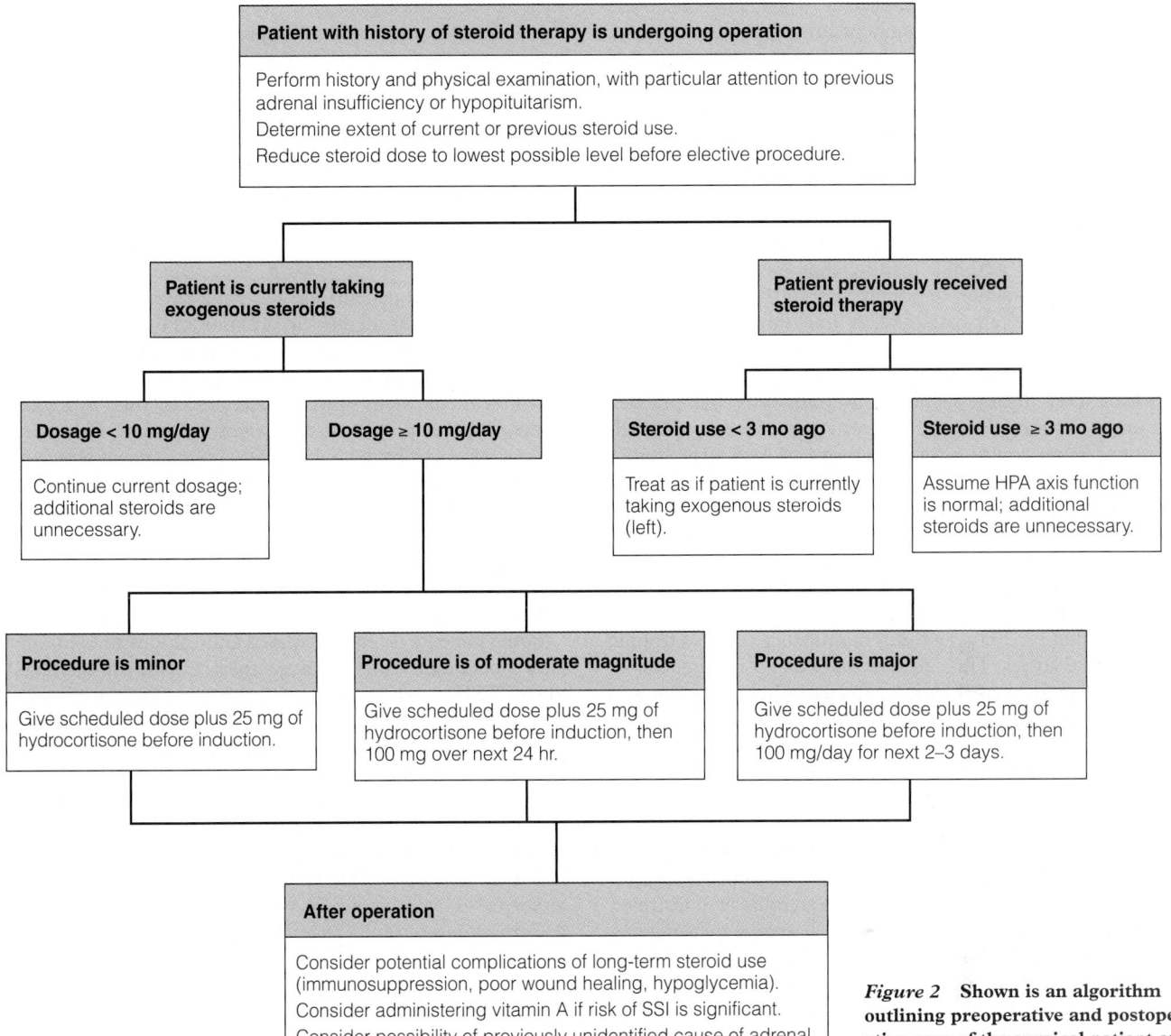

Patient with history of steroid therapy is undergoing operation

Perform history and physical examination, with particular attention to previous adrenal insufficiency or hypopituitarism.
Determine extent of current or previous steroid use.
Reduce steroid dose to lowest possible level before elective procedure.

Patient is currently taking exogenous steroids

Patient previously received steroid therapy

Dosage < 10 mg/day

Continue current dosage; additional steroids are unnecessary.

Dosage ≥ 10 mg/day

Steroid use < 3 mo ago

Treat as if patient is currently taking exogenous steroids (left).

Steroid use ≥ 3 mo ago

Assume HPA axis function is normal; additional steroids are unnecessary.

Procedure is minor

Give scheduled dose plus 25 mg of hydrocortisone before induction.

Procedure is of moderate magnitude

Give scheduled dose plus 25 mg of hydrocortisone before induction, then 100 mg over next 24 hr.

Procedure is major

Give scheduled dose plus 25 mg of hydrocortisone before induction, then 100 mg/day for next 2–3 days.

After operation

Consider potential complications of long-term steroid use (immunosuppression, poor wound healing, hypoglycemia).
Consider administering vitamin A if risk of SSI is significant.
Consider possibility of previously unidentified cause of adrenal insufficiency in ICU (e.g., emergency operation, trauma).

Figure 2 **Shown is an algorithm outlining preoperative and postoperative care of the surgical patient at risk for adrenal insufficiency.**

overlap between normal patients and those with clinical adrenal insufficiency.[12] Provocative testing of the HPA axis is based on the normal physiologic response of the adrenal gland to release cortisol in a receptor-mediated G-protein–coupled response to circulating ACTH.

Although there is some controversy regarding which laboratory evaluation is the best predictor of adequate adrenal response to a surgical stress, it is clear that ACTH stimulatory testing is more sensitive and specific than unprovoked steroid measurement alone. Hypoglycemia-induced release of ACTH in response to exogenous insulin infusion (the insulin tolerance test, or ITT) has long been considered the gold standard for determination of relative adrenal insufficiency, but various complications, including discomfort, seizures, and even death, limit its clinical usefulness as a routinely applied test.[13] In several studies, strong correlations have been observed between the ITT and adrenal stimulation with a synthetic corticotropin construct.[14,15] In this test, the plasma cortisol response is measured 0, 30, and 60 minutes after infusion of 250 μg of the ACTH analogue. Although there is no unanimously accepted cutoff value for stim-

ulated cortisol levels above which the HPA axis can be assumed to be intact, it has been suggested that a value higher than 600 mol/L at 30 minutes should be a sufficiently sensitive confirmation of an intact HPA axis.

Adrenal glucocorticoids are important modulators of the stress response: they play a complex role in the metabolic pathways for carbohydrates, fats, and proteins; modulate gluconeogenesis and lipolysis; mediate insulin resistance; and exert a host of well-documented effects on inflammation and wound healing. It is clear that physiologic stresses (e.g., burns, trauma, and iatrogenic tissue damage occurring during operations) result in an ACTH-induced surge in the adrenal steroid response.[16,17] Serum measurements reveal that this response can produce cortisol elevations several times greater than those produced under basal conditions. It is becoming apparent that although this exaggerated adrenal stress response may have conferred a certain evolutionary benefit, prolonged exposure to high doses of steroids may nonetheless have deleterious consequences. The potential complications of long-term or high-dose administration of glucocorticoids are well described: they include hypertension, cataracts, myopathy (especially when glucocorticoids are used in conjunction with nondepolarizing paralytic drugs), osteonecrosis (particularly on the femoral head), impaired wound healing, and immunosuppression.[18]

It was the observed (and presumably physiologic) magnitude of the cortisol response to stress that led to the long-held—albeit never corroborated—assumption that supraphysiologic levels of steroids were required to maintain homeostasis in the stressed environment. In the 1950s, two case reports were published that described perioperative deaths thought to result from untreated and unrecognized adrenal insufficiency.[19,20] Thereafter, it became common practice to supply supraphysiologic doses of exogenous steroids (i.e., doses two to three times that expected under basal conditions) to patients believed to be at risk for adrenal suppression and therefore unable to mount the expected cortisol surge during operation. Subsequently, this practice came under scrutiny. Primary studies suggested that although HPA suppression could occur as a result of long-term steroid use, normal physiologic replacement doses were sufficient to maintain perioperative homeostasis; supraphysiologic doses were unnecessary.[21] The concept that significantly lower doses of steroids are required to maintain homeostasis and normotension in the perioperative period than was once believed has been supported by prospective clinical studies in humans.[22]

It is clear that ACTH is not only stimulatory but also trophic for the adrenal cortex. There is evidence that if the adrenal cortex is not exposed to ACTH, it is subject to hyposecretion and anatomic atrophy. It was once thought that exposure to even low doses of steroids (< 10 mg of prednisone equivalent) was sufficient to suppress the endogenous release of ACTH and thus to result in a state of adrenal insufficiency. This belief led to the common practice of administering so-called stress-dose steroids to surgical patients who had received exogenous steroids even in small doses or as long ago as 1 year before operation. Provocative studies on patients previously exposed to steroids demonstrated that the HPA axis usually remains intact despite either ongoing exposure to small doses of exogenous steroids (< 10 mg of prednisone equivalent daily) or earlier steroid use (if the time since discontinuance was longer than 2 to 3 months).[23-26]

In summary, the glucocorticoids are essential components of human homeostasis both at rest and under stressful conditions

such as occur during surgery. Complete or even relative adrenal insufficiency is preventable; when it does occur, it can have disastrous consequences if not recognized and appropriately treated. Exogenous administration of steroids in sufficient doses is generally adequate to prevent the syndrome of adrenal insufficiency. The decision to administer supplemental perioperative steroids should be based on the specific details of the history of steroid use as well as on the magnitude of the proposed operation.

Hormone Replacement

Many surgical patients are receiving thyroid or ovarian hormone replacement therapy. In addition, the use of growth hormone, growth hormone precursors, and anabolic steroids has become more common in general practice. The effects of these hormone medications must be taken into account in any patient undergoing an elective or emergency operation. Because all of these substances have long half-lives, replacement is not necessary for the first 2 weeks after operation; however, if the illness or the operation itself prevents oral intake for more than 2 weeks, the possibility of hypothyroidism or estrogen depletion should be considered. Postoperative weakness, lack of energy, depression, and sleeping disorders can all be caused by the lack of long-term hormone supplements.

Some patients exhibit decreased endogenous thyroid function after operation, either because their thyroid-stimulating hormone (TSH) levels are depressed as a consequence of long-term thyroid medication or because they experience complications and become critically ill. Critical illness typically leads to reduced blood levels of triiodothyronine (T_3) and thyroxine (T_4). In addition, glucocorticoids, radiopaque dyes, propranolol, and amiodarone all lower plasma T_4 levels,[27] and dopamine decreases TSH secretion directly.[28] Most critically ill patients, however, do not exhibit metabolic or hemodynamic changes indicative of hypothyroidism. Measurement of TSH is helpful for determining the significance of thyroid function in critically ill patients. If the serum TSH level is lower than 5 µU/ml and the patient is not on high-dose dopamine therapy, thyroid function is considered adequate regardless of other plasma markers. If the TSH level is higher than 20 µU/ml, replacement with thyroxine is indicated.[29]

References

1. Root HF: Preoperative medical care of the diabetic patient. Postgrad Med 40:439, 1966

2. Galloway JA, Shuman CR: Diabetes and surgery: a study of 667 cases. Am J Med 34:177, 1963

3. Walts LF, Miller J, Davidson MB, et al: Perioperative management of diabetes mellitus. Anesthesiology 55:104, 1981

4. Thompson J, Husband DJ, Thai AC, et al: Metabolic changes in the non-insulin-dependent diabetic undergoing minor surgery: effect of glucose-insulin-potassium infusion. Br J Surg 73:301, 1986

5. van den Berghe G, Wouters P, Weekers F, et al: Intensive insulin therapy in critically ill patients. N Engl J Med 345:1359, 2001

6. Kamal K, Powell RJ, Sumpio BE: The pathobiology of diabetes mellitus: implications for surgeons. J Am Coll Surg 183:271, 1996

7. Davidson NJ, Snowden JM, Fletcher J: Defective phagocytosis in insulin controlled diabetics: evidence for a reaction between glucose and opsonizing proteins. J Clin Pathol 37:783, 1984

8. Bitar MS, Farook T, Wahid S, et al: Glucocorticoid dependent impairment of wound healing in experimental diabetes: amelioration by adrenalectomy and RU486. J Surg Res 82:234, 1999

9. Qiu JG, Chang TH, Steinberg JJ, et al: Single local installation of Staphylococcus aureus peptidoglycan prevents diabetes impaired wound healing. Wound Repair Regen 6:449, 1998

10. Orth DN, Kovacs WJ: The adrenal cortex. Williams Textbook of Endocrinology, 9th ed. Wilson JD, Foster DW, Kronenberg HM, et al, Eds. WB Saunders Co, Philadelphia, 1998, p 517

11. White PC, Pescovitz OH, Cutler GB: Synthesis and metabolism of corticosteroids. Principles and Practice of Endocrinology and Metabolism, 2nd ed. Becker KL, Ed. JB Lippincott Co, Philadelphia, 1995, p 647

12. Moore A, Aitken R, Burke C, et al: Cortisol assays: guidelines for the provision of clinical biochemistry service. Ann Clin Biochem 22:435, 1985

13. Jacobs HS, Nabarro JDN: Tests of hypothalamic-pituitary-adrenal function in man. Q J Med 38:475, 1969

14. Kehlet H, Binder C: Value of an ACTH test in assessing hypothalamic-pituitary-adrenocortical function in glucocorticoid-treated patients. BMJ 2:147, 1973

15. Clayton RN: Short Synacthen test versus insulin stress test for assessment of the hypothalamo-pituitary-adrenal axis: controversy revisited. Clin Endocrinol 44:147, 1996

16. Chernow B, Alexander R, Smallridge RC, et al: Hormonal responses to graded surgical stress. Arch Intern Med 147:1273, 1987

17. Hume DM, Bell CC, Bartter F: Direct measurement of adrenal secretion during operative trauma and convalescence. Surgery 52:174, 1962

18. Dujovne CA, Azarnoff DL: Clinical complica-

tions of corticosteroid therapy: a selected review. Med Clin North Am 57:1331, 1973

19. Fraser CG, Preuss FS, Bigford WD: Adrenal atrophy and irreversible shock associated with cortisone therapy. JAMA 149:1542, 1952

20. Lewis L, Robinson RF, Yee J, et al: Fatal adrenal cortical insufficiency precipitated by surgery during prolonged continuous cortisone treatment. Ann Intern Med 39:116, 1953

21. Udelsman R, Ramp J, Gallucci WT, et al: Adaptation during surgical stress: a re-evaluation of the role of glucocorticoids. J Clin Invest 77:1377, 1986

22. Symreng T, Karlberg BE, Kagedal B, et al: Physiological cortisol substitution of long-term steroid-treated patients undergoing major surgery. Br J Anesth 53:949, 1981

23. Bromberg JS, Baliga P, Cofer JB, et al: Stress steroids are not required for patients receiving a renal allograft and undergoing operation. J Am Coll Surg 180:532, 1995

24. Bromberg JS, Alfrey EJ, Barker CF, et al: Adrenal suppression and steroid supplementation in renal transplant recipients. Transplantation 51:385, 1991

25. Livanou T, Ferriman D, James VHT: Recovery of hypothalamo-pituitary adrenal function after corticosteroid therapy. Lancet 2:856, 1967

26. LaRochelle G, LaRochelle AG, Ratner RE, et al: Recovery of the hypothalamic-pituitary-adrenal (HPA) axis in patients with rheumatic diseases receiving low-dose prednisone. Am J Med 95:258, 1993

27. Wartofsky L, Burman KD: Alterations in thyroid function in patients with systemic illness: "the euthyroid sick syndrome." Endocr Rev 3:164, 1982

28. Kaptein EM, Spencer CA, Kamiel MD, et al: Prolonged dopamine administration and thyroid hormone economy in normal and critically ill subjects. J Clin Endocrinol Metab 51:387, 1980

29. Burman KD: Thyroid hormones. Pharmacologic Approach to the Critically Ill Patient. Chernow B, Ed. Williams & Wilkins, Baltimore, 1983, chap 30

30. Surgery: practical guidelines for diabetes management. Clin Diabetes 5:49, 1987

Maxim D. Hammer, M.D.

Coma is the neurologist's favorite consultation: the history is usually straightforward, the neurologic examination is focused, and the differential diagnosis is limited. A good neurologic examination, in combination with a thoughtful battery of tests, will invariably achieve the correct diagnosis. It is vital for the intensivist to become equally comfortable with the rapid assessment of coma. Once initial stabilization of the patient has been achieved, management of coma is determined by the specific causative condition or conditions present. Rapid recognition of potentially reversible causes of coma (e.g., basilar artery occlusion [BAO], nonconvulsive status epilepticus, and herniation), followed by the appropriate emergency consultations, can often prevent or reduce morbidity and mortality.

This chapter is intended as a practical, rational, and efficient approach to the diagnosis and management of coma. To that end, an algorithmic approach to diagnosis is formulated, general treatment measures for comatose patients are outlined, specific causes of coma are reviewed, and prognostic issues are considered. Detailed discussions of neuroanatomy and cranial nerve pathways, which are readily available elsewhere,[1] are intentionally omitted, as are detailed descriptions of specific treatment of individual causes of coma (other than BAO, status epilepticus, cardiac arrest, increased intracranial pressure [IICP], and certain metabolic derangements).

Classification of Levels of Consciousness

AWAKENESS, ALERTNESS, AND AWARENESS

A patient's level of consciousness can usefully be described in terms of the three As of consciousness: awake, alert, and aware. To be awake means to be fully roused and thus not asleep. To be alert means to be able to pay attention to one's environment or to an examiner. Finally, to be aware means to have an understanding of oneself and one's environment. Being oriented is a manifestation of being aware of one's environment [*see Figure 1*].

A person who is awake, alert, and aware may be said to be fully conscious. One who is awake and alert but has lost awareness is severely demented. Someone who is merely awake and not alert or aware is delirious. A delirious patient's level of wakefulness may wax and wane. A person who is not awake, alert, or aware either is asleep (in which case he or she can be rendered awake—i.e., is arousable) or is somewhere along the so-called spectrum of coma (see below).

Admittedly, describing patients simply in terms of awakeness, alertness, and awareness omits many important nuances; nevertheless, it is an excellent and easily reproducible way of assessing level of consciousness.

UNRESPONSIVE PATIENT

The term unresponsive is used frequently, but often in a vague manner that does not yield a clear meaning. Fortunately, in the setting of coma management, there are only three possible meanings that need be considered [*see Figure 2*].

First, the term unresponsive may be applied to a patient who is actually fully conscious but is unable or unwilling to respond verbally. For example, a patient with aphasia (a common manifestation of stroke) may be awake, alert, and aware, yet unable to speak. As another example, a patient who is in a locked-in state (either from a brain stem injury or from generalized muscle paralysis) is fully conscious but cannot speak and cannot communicate except through subtle eye movements. Finally, patients with a psychiatric disorder may present with a so-called functional coma while remaining fully conscious; simple examination techniques quickly reveal that they are completely awake.

Second, the term unresponsive may be applied to a patient who has a waxing-and-waning level of wakefulness. This fluctuation between wakefulness and coma is what defines delirium, and it is invariably caused by infection, metabolic disturbances, or alcohol withdrawal.

Third, the term unresponsive may be applied to a patient who truly is not even awake. In this sense, the term could of course be applied to a person who is simply asleep, but for the purposes of this chapter, it should be understood as referring to a patient who is comatose.

SPECTRUM OF COMA

Patients who are not aware, alert, or even awake (except for those who are simply asleep) fall somewhere along the spectrum of coma. This spectrum reflects varying levels of impairment of

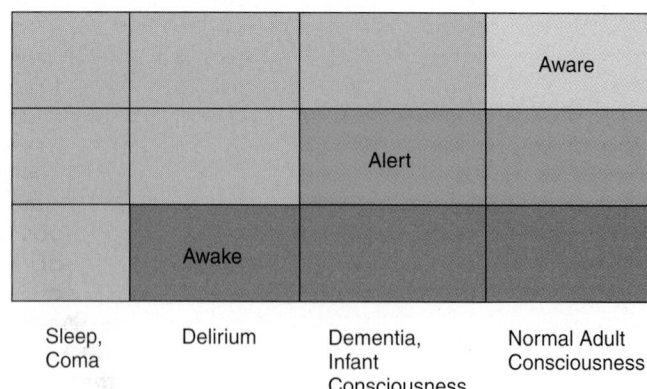

Figure 1 **Awareness depends on alertness, which in turn depends on arousal (i.e., how awake one is). Normally cognizant adults are aware of themselves and their environment. Persons who have lost awareness but retain alertness and wakefulness may be characterized as severely demented. Persons who have lost alertness are delirious by definition, though their level of wakefulness may wax and wane. Finally, persons who are not aware, alert, or awake may be either asleep or in a coma.**

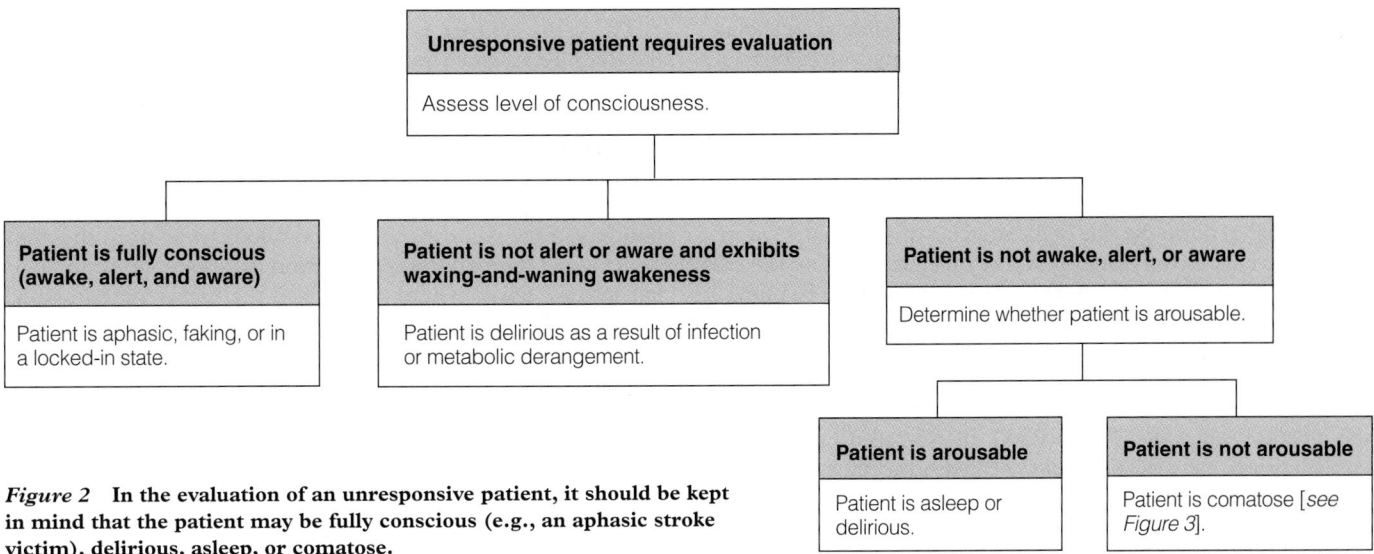

Figure 2 **In the evaluation of an unresponsive patient, it should be kept in mind that the patient may be fully conscious (e.g., an aphasic stroke victim), delirious, asleep, or comatose.**

the response to stimuli. On the high end of the spectrum, for example, is the patient who can be aroused (albeit perhaps only temporarily) by the sound of a voice. Somewhat farther down is the patient who can be temporarily aroused by a painful stimulus. Farther down still is the patient who cannot be aroused by a painful stimulus but at least exhibits some motor response to it. On the low end of the spectrum is the patient who has no motor response to a painful stimulus; this is the generally accepted definition of coma.

The terms lethargy, stupor, and obtundation, though widely used, have come to signify different things to different people. Accordingly, to ensure precise communication, it is perhaps advisable to employ clear clinical patient descriptions rather than rely on these particular terms.

Initial Stabilization

The first step in dealing with coma is to stabilize the patient by addressing the ABCs of resuscitation (*A*irway, *B*reathing, and *C*irculation). The patient's airway must be cleared of all foreign material, and the patency of the airway must be verified. The spontaneous rate and rhythm of respiration should be noted. Endotracheal intubation is indicated in patients who are dyspneic, hypoventilating, or vomiting uncontrollably. If a patient is to be intubated, however, it is extremely helpful first to obtain a focused neurologic examination (which can be done in 60 seconds) because the information that can be gained from this examination will be lost when the patient is paralyzed for the intubation. Hyperventilation with a bag and mask and 100% oxygen should be performed before intubation to ensure adequate oxygenation during the procedure. If there is any possibility of cervical spine injury, intubation should be delayed, if possible, until fracture can be ruled out radiographically.

Circulation must be vigorously supported, especially in the setting of brain injury or hypoxia. This is accomplished by inserting a large-bore I.V. or central venous catheter and infusing isotonic fluids or volume expanders. The use of solutions containing free water (e.g., 5% dextrose in water) should be avoided, especially in the setting of brain injury or stroke, because such solutions have the potential to increase cerebral edema.

Clinical Evaluation

As the patient is being stabilized, evaluation should be initiated. A witness or someone else capable of providing a history should be sought. The differential diagnosis of coma is wide but limited [*see Table 1*]. Clues from the history, the focused neurologic examination, and the general physical examination are often helpful and sometimes diagnostic [*see Figure 3*].

History

The ideal historian is a person who knows the patient well. Optimally, if the coma was of sudden onset, a witness was present who can describe what occurred. A history of trauma, drug use, medications, recent febrile illness, heart disease, organ failure, or seizures often rapidly leads to the correct diagnosis [*see Table 2*]. Typically, the most challenging cases are those patients who are "found down"; such cases necessitate a clear diagnostic approach that begins with the physical and neurologic examinations.

Focused Neurologic Examination

There are two good reasons for performing a neurologic examination on a coma patient. First, such an examination allows the physician to assign the patient a Glasgow Coma Scale (GCS) score [*see Table 3*], which may be used in making decisions about the necessity for intubation and which provides an objective means of following (at least superficially) the patient's neurologic status. Second, the neurologic examination may quickly yield important diagnostic information.

A complete and exhaustive neurologic examination is totally unnecessary. For the purposes of evaluating coma, a focused neurologic examination is preferable, being both valuable and rapid (~ 60 seconds). If intubation is indicated, the coma examination should be performed quickly before sedative and paralytic agents are given. This examination addresses a number of key findings [*see Table 4*], but in general, it may be thought of as assessing four neurologic variables: (1) spontaneous movements (~ 15 seconds), (2) pupillary response (~ 15 seconds), (3) ocular motility (~ 15 seconds), and (4) motor response (~ 15 seconds). A reflex hammer is not needed.

Spontaneous movements should be observed over a period of 10 to 20 seconds. Generalized seizures may present as tonic or tonic-clonic movements of one or both sides. Tonic seizures are characterized by sustained contractions with upper-extremity flexion and lower-extremity extension. Tonic-clonic seizures are characterized by tonic contractures alternating with periods of muscle atonia, resulting in rhythmic contractions. Myoclonus consists of motor jerks that are sudden, brief, shocklike, and randomly distributed; it may be seen in patients with hypoxic-ischemic encephalopathy (e.g., after cardiac arrest) or other metabolic disturbances. Other findings (e.g., a flaccid arm that hangs down the side of the stretcher or a leg that is extorted) may be indicative of hemiparesis. The motor response to pain can be tested and assigned a GCS score. Asymmetry should be noted.

Pupillary responses are important in that their presence or absence distinguishes structural from metabolic coma (because the pupils are generally resistant to metabolic insult); they also indicate the integrity of the brain stem [see Table 5]. The origin of the reticular activating system (RAS), the so-called on switch of consciousness, may be physically located adjacent to the brain stem nuclei that control pupillary response.

The pathways that control ocular motility also lie adjacent to the RAS. Roving eye movements usually indicate that the brain stem is intact and that a metabolic problem is affecting the brain. Minimal or absent eye movement in conjunction with reactive pupils also typically signifies a metabolic process. Gaze deviation may indicate a stroke: a cortical stroke will cause the eyes to look toward the damaged side of the brain, whereas a pontine stroke will cause the eyes to look away from the damaged side of the pons. Gaze deviation may also signify an ongoing seizure: the eyes look away from the hemisphere in which the seizure is occurring or, after the seizure is over, toward the postictal hemisphere. Vertical disconjugation of the eyes (skew deviation) is indicative of brain stem disease and frequently occurs during basilar artery thrombosis. Ocular bobbing (rapid downward movements with a slow drift back to the original position) is occasionally seen in the setting of extensive pontine damage.

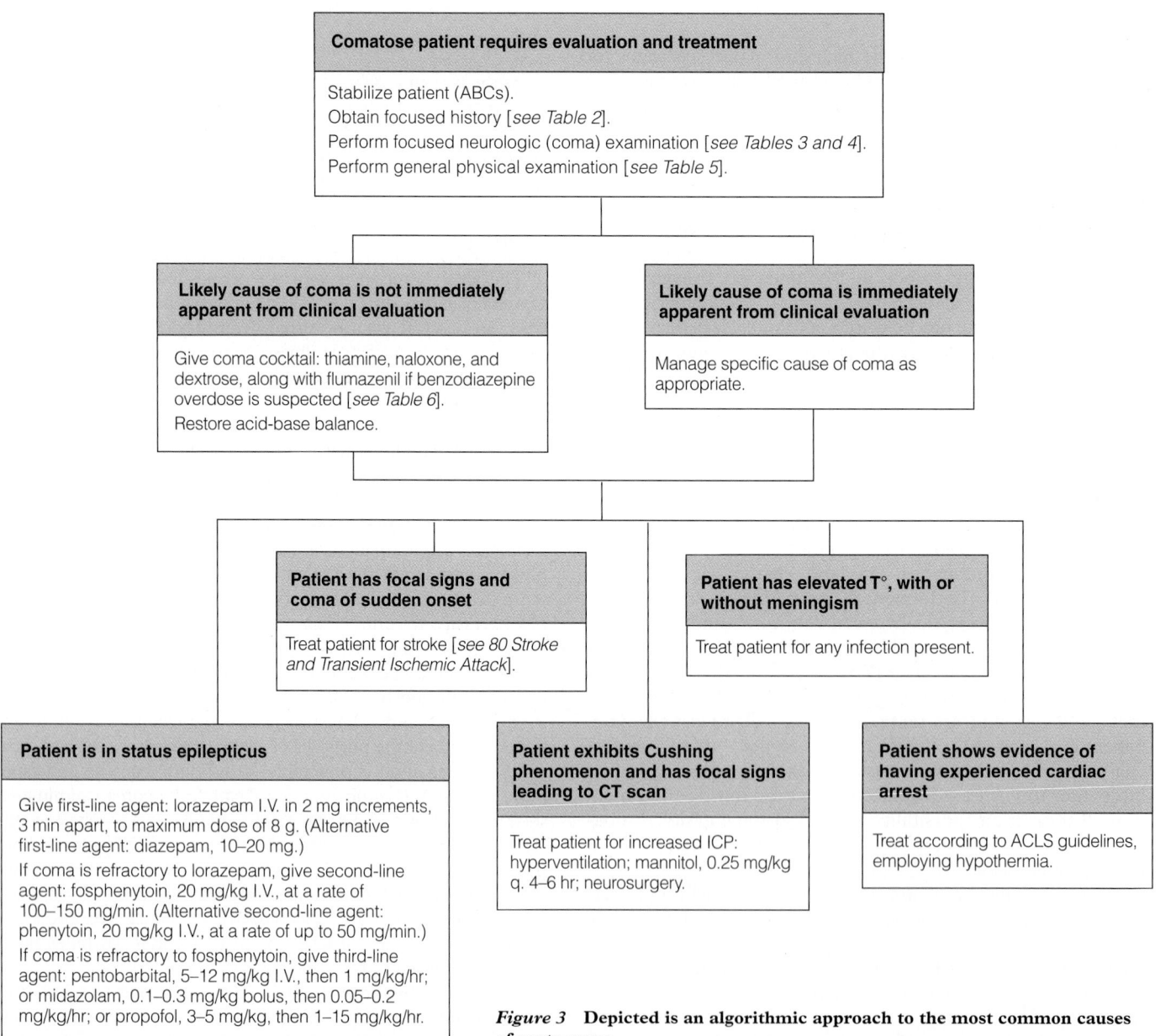

Figure 3 **Depicted is an algorithmic approach to the most common causes of acute coma.**

General Physical Examination

Blood pressure, heart rate, and cardiac rhythm are key to the diagnosis of the various cardiovascular and hemodynamic causes of coma [*see Table 1*]. Hypothermia is noted in cases of exposure,

Table 1 Differential Diagnosis of Coma

Potential Cause of Coma	Differential Diagnosis
Cerebrovascular	Large brain stem stroke (with or without basilar artery occlusion) Massive stroke or hemorrhage with mass effect Subarachnoid hemorrhage Subdural or epidural hematoma Hypoxic-ischemic encephalopathy after cardiac arrest Hypertensive encephalopathy
Cardiovascular	Cardiac arrest Cardiac arrhythmia Congestive heart failure Hypotension Myocardial infarction
Infectious	Bacteremia or sepsis Meningitis Encephalitis (e.g., herpesvirus, arbovirus)
Traumatic	Multiple severe concussions (diffuse axonal injury, second-hit syndrome) Subdural or epidural hematoma Multiple contusions Penetrating head injury

Toxic	Alcohol intoxication/withdrawal
	Opiate intoxication
	Anesthesia
	Overdose
	  Antianxiety agents or antidepressants
	  Anticholinergics
	  Anticonvulsants
	  Antihistamines
	  Insulin
	  Lithium
	  Neuroleptics
	  Opiates
	  Salicylates
	  Sedatives

Metabolic	Hyperglycemia or hypoglycemia
	  Diabetic ketoacidosis
	  Hyperosmolar nonketotic coma
	Hypernatremia or hyponatremia
	  Osmotic demyelination syndrome: central pontine myelinolysis
	Hepatic failure
	Renal failure
	Hypoxia or hypercarbia
	Hypothermia

Epileptic	Grand mal status epilepticus Nonconvulsive status epilepticus Postictal state
Mass	Massive stroke or hemorrhage with mass effect Tumor or abscess with mass effect
Hematologic	Thrombotic thrombocytopenic purpura
Psychiatric	Conversion Malingering

Table 2 Coma History

Questions to Be Asked	Possible Causes to Be Considered
Is there a witness?	[*If no, see Table 4.*]
Was it sudden?	Stroke If stepwise deterioration, consider BAO Seizure Cardiac arrest
Was there trauma?	Traumatic brain injury Subarachnoid hemorrhage Subdural or epidural hematoma with mass effect and herniation

Has there been drug use? If so, which drugs?	Recreational drug overdose
	  Opioids, alcohol
	Prescription drug overdose
	  Opioids, benzodiazepines, barbiturates, anticholinergics

Was there a recent febrile illness?	Meningitis or encephalitis Bacteremia or sepsis
Is there a history of heart disease?	Cardiac arrest Myocardial infarction Congestive heart failure Cardiac arrhythmia Hypotension
Is there a history of organ failure?	Renal failure Hepatic failure
Is there a history of seizures?	Postictal from single seizure Convulsive status epilepticus Nonconvulsive status epilepticus

BAO—basilar artery occlusion

drowning, methanol poisoning, and septic shock. Hyperthermia is obviously suggestive of an ongoing infectious process. A stiff neck is often caused by meningeal irritability resulting from infection or inflammation; it may be indicative of meningitis, but it also may be the only physical sign of subarachnoid hemorrhage. Various other physical findings may be observed in comatose patients as well [*see Table 5*].

A rise in intracranial pressure (ICP) occurs with any space-occupying lesion in the calvaria. Signs of rising ICP include increasing blood pressure, decreasing heart rate, and slowing or periodic respiration (Cushing phenomenon). Papilledema caused by increased ICP usually takes weeks to develop and is seldom a presenting sign.

Management

GENERAL MEASURES, TRIAGE, AND TEST BATTERY

As emergency management is being provided, laboratory studies should be obtained, including serum electrolyte, calcium, magnesium, phosphorus, blood urea nitrogen (BUN), and creatinine levels, as well as liver function tests. A complete blood count (CBC), a urinalysis, and a urine toxicity screen should also be obtained. A lumbar puncture should be performed only if meningitis is suspected on the basis of clinical examination.

The so-called coma cocktail—consisting of dextrose, naloxone, and thiamine—is administered if the cause of coma is not immediately apparent from the brief history and physical examination; the addition of flumazenil is considered if benzodiazepine over-

Table 3 Glasgow Coma Scale

Test	Response	Score
Eye opening (E)	Spontaneous	4
	To verbal command	3
	To pain	2
	None	1
Best motor response (arm) (M)	Obedience to verbal command	6
	Localization of painful stimulus	5
	Flexion withdrawal response to pain	4
	Abnormal flexion response to pain (decorticate rigidity)	3
	Extension response to pain (decerebrate rigidity)	2
	None	1
Best verbal response (V)	Oriented conversation	5
	Disoriented conversation	4
	Inappropriate words	3
	Incomprehensible sounds	2
	None	1
	Total (E + M + V)	3–15

dose is suspected [*see Table 6*].[2,3] It should be kept in mind that administering dextrose to a thiamine-depleted patient (especially one who is malnourished or alcoholic) may precipitate the Wernicke-Korsakoff syndrome. As a rule, therefore, thiamine should always be given before dextrose.

Any comatose patient with focal signs on the coma examination should undergo head CT scanning. Any patient with signs of meningitis on the physical examination should receive emergency antibiotic therapy. When drug overdose or toxin ingestion is suspected, activated charcoal, 50 to 100 mg (with or without gastric lavage), should be given to prevent systemic absorption. As noted, flumazenil may be given for suspected benzodiazepine overdose and may produce dramatic arousal; however, this agent is contraindicated in patients taking tricyclic antidepressants because of an increased risk of seizures.

Once the recommended general treatment measures have been carried out, the next step is to look for and address specific causes of coma.

MANAGEMENT OF SPECIFIC CAUSES OF COMA

Basilar Artery Occlusion

BAO is an uncommon cause of stroke but also an underrecognized one. Morbidity and mortality are high, with only about 15% to 45% of victims surviving.[4] BAO may be caused by embolism (most often from the heart but sometimes from the vertebral arteries), by intrinsic atherothrombosis, or by vertebral dissection. It frequently presents with a stepwise accumulation of neurologic deficits that culminates in a coma.

A typical case scenario for BAO, occasionally heard by stroke neurologists, is as follows. A patient presents with double vision, followed hours later by ataxia. This may prompt an emergency department (ED) visit. The patient is admitted to the hospital but, on the nursing unit, becomes suddenly unresponsive and needs intubation for airway protection. In another typical scenario, a patient who has just undergone cardiac catheterization becomes suddenly unresponsive on the angiography table but is hemodynamically stable.

Table 4 Focused Neurologic Examination (Coma Examination)

Neurologic Variable Assessed	Findings	Likely Cause of Coma
Spontaneous movement (15 sec)	Rhythmic movements	Seizure
	Random jerks (myoclonus)	Hypoxic-ischemic encephalopathy
Pupillary response (15 sec)	Unilateral fixed and dilated pupil	Brain herniation (mass) Posterior communicating artery aneurysm
	Midposition unreactive pupils	Midbrain lesion
	Pinpoint unreactive pupils	Pontine lesion
	Small and sluggishly reactive pupils	Drug intoxication
	Large and unreactive pupils	Atropine
	Unreactive pupils	Barbiturates, paralytics, lidocaine, phenothiazines, methanol, aminoglycoside antibiotics, hypothermia
Ocular motility (15 sec)	Roving eye movements	Metabolic insult to brain; brain stem is intact
	Gaze deviation	Stroke (eyes look toward damaged side of brain) Seizure (eyes look away from side of brain producing seizure)
	Skew deviation	BAO
	Ocular bobbing	Extensive damage to pons
	Unilateral weakness	Structural injury (e.g., stroke)
Motor response (15 sec)	Posturing (flexor or extensor)	Herniation (mass) Extensive cortical injury

Table 5 General Physical Examination

Physical Variable Assessed	Finding and Possible Causative Condition

Skin	Signs of trauma around head/neck
	Jaundice
	  Hepatic failure
	Exanthema
	  Viral infection
	Petechial rash
	  Meningococcal infection

Head and neck	Brudzinski or Kernig sign Meningitis, meningoencephalitis Subarachnoid hemorrhage

Temperature	Fever
	  Infection (meningitis, encephalitis, bacteremia, sepsis)
	Hypothermia
	  Exposure
	  Intoxication (alcohol, benzodiazepine, barbiturate)
	  Myxedema coma
	  Sepsis

Breath	Alcohol intoxication
	Fetor hepaticus
	  Hepatic failure
	Uriniferous smell
	  Uremia
	Ketoacidosis

Blood pressure	Hypotension
	  Shock
	  Sepsis
	  Intoxication
	  Myocardial infarction
	  Addison disease
	Hypertension
	  Hypertensive encephalopathy

Cardiac conduction and rhythm (ECG)	Arrhythmia Acute myocardial infarction
Abdomen	Hepatomegaly Splenomegaly

A comatose patient with BAO usually manifests obvious clinical signs of brain stem injury, such as quadriparesis, skew deviation, and diminished gag reflex (many physicians report that intubation is unexpectedly easy). On occasion, CT scanning may reveal an apparently hyperdense basilar artery [*see Figure 4*]; imaging of the posterior circulation invariably reveals the problem. Management of BAO should be aimed at immediate recanalization of the occluded artery. Thrombolysis, either intravenous (with tissue plasminogen activator) or intra-arterial (with urokinase or mechanical clot disruption), may be lifesaving.

As noted, patients with extensive brain stem injury resulting from BAO often die. Some enter what is known as the locked-in state, in which they remain conscious but are unable to move, breathe, or swallow. Occasionally, patients retain the capacity for subtle eye movements or eye blinking and thus are able to communicate through yes/no responses to questions. Most stroke neurologists consider the locked-in state a fate worse than death.

Seizures

A seizure disorder can cause coma in two different ways. First, the coma may be the initial manifestation of the immediate postictal state after a generalized seizure. In such cases, the coma resolves rapidly, and further management is unnecessary. The duration of the postictal coma may be directly correlated with patient age and inversely correlated with baseline functional status. Second, coma may develop when multiple generalized seizures occur in succession and there is not enough time between seizures to allow patients to recover. The resulting state is status epilepticus.

Generalized convulsive status epilepticus (GCSE) may be defined either as (1) continuous seizure activity lasting longer than 5 minutes or as (2) two or more discrete generalized seizures between which there is incomplete recovery of consciousness. GCSE is most frequently the result of noncompliance with an antiepileptic drug regimen, alcohol use or withdrawal, or drug toxicity. Less common causes include CNS infection, a cerebral tumor, trauma, refractory epilepsy, stroke, metabolic disorders, and cardiac arrest. If untreated, GCSE leads to cerebral edema, herniation, and death.

A tonic-clonic seizure begins with a tonic contraction that lasts as long as 30 seconds, followed by several minutes of repeated muscle contractions, loss of pupillary response to light, sweating, tachycardia, excessive bronchial secretion, and marked hypertension. Repeated seizures cause lactic and respiratory acidosis, rhabdomyolysis and myoglobinuria, aspiration and pulmonary edema, shoulder dislocations, rib fractures, and cardiac arrhythmias. The neuronal damage induces an inflammatory response, and if seizures continue, cerebral edema ensues.

In the treatment of GCSE, the aim is not to stop the body from convulsing but to stop the abnormal cerebral electrical activity immediately. The longer GCSE continues, the more refractory it will be to treatment. Paralytics mask (but do not prevent) the seizures; therefore, intubation and paralysis should be avoided if possible.

Like all other coma victims, patients with GCSE should first be stabilized [*see* Initial Stabilization, *above*]. I.V. access should then be obtained. Glucose should be given empirically, along with thiamine, and blood should be drawn and sent for laboratory tests (including anticonvulsant levels).

Anticonvulsant management of status epilepticus is discussed in detail elsewhere[5,6] and so need only be summarized here. The first-line treatment for GCSE consists of administration of lorazepam [*see Figure 3*]. Although there is no significant difference between the benzodiazepines with respect to rapidity of seizure control, lorazepam is thought to bind more tightly to brain receptors and thus is believed to have a longer duration of action. Lorazepam is given in 2 mg increments 3 minutes apart to a maximum dose of 8 mg before another agent is tried [*see Table 7*]. Diazepam may be employed as an alternative. The second-line agent is fosphenytoin, 20 mg/kg at up to 150 mg/min I.V.; phenytoin may be given as an alternative. If the patient does not respond to either lorazepam or fosphenytoin, a third-line agent—pentobarbital, midazolam, or propofol—should be given in a continuous infusion. Of the three third-line choices, midazolam may be the most effective, and it certainly has the lowest side effect profile.

The goal of therapy is to achieve a burst-suppression pattern on electroencephalography for 12 to 24 hours before any attempt is made to taper medications.

Increased Intracranial Pressure

If IICP is suspected on the basis of clinical examination and herniation is identified, treatment must be initiated immediate-

Table 6 Coma Cocktail

Drug	Indications	Dosing (Adults)	Potential Adverse Effects
Thiamine	Wernicke-Korsakoff syndrome Ethylene glycol ingestion	100 mg I.V. over 5 min	Anaphylactoid reaction Hypotension Angioedema
Dextrose	Symptomatic hypoglycemia Altered mental status without ability to rapidly obtain serum glucose level	50–100 ml of 50% dextrose I.V. Alternatively, 250 ml of 10% dextrose (to prevent the phlebitis that frequently occurs with administration of 50% dextrose)	Phlebitis Cellulitis
Naloxone	Reversal of CNS depression and respiratory depression caused by overdose of opioid medication	0.1 mg I.V. initially (I.V. route is more effective than subcutaneous or endotracheal), aimed at producing subtle improvement in ventilation Repeat doses given in 2–3 min intervals, increased very slowly each time If no response after total dose of 10 mg, opioid toxicity ruled out	Hypersensitivity reaction Precipitation of sudden narcotic withdrawal syndrome (If heroin has been tainted with scopolamine, withdrawal of opioid can precipitate anticholinergic crisis) Lung injury, hypertension, and cardiac arrhythmias (rarely reported)
Flumazenil	Benzodiazepine overdose	0.2 mg I.V. over 30 sec If no response, 0.3 mg I.V. over 30 sec If still no response, 0.5 mg I.V. every 30 sec to maximum dose of 3 mg	Contraindicated in patient experiencing seizure Benzodiazepine withdrawal, which may cause seizures and autonomic dysfunction

ly.[7] Medical management of IICP is a temporizing measure, aimed at slowing the process of herniation until the problem can be corrected neurosurgically.

The head of the patient's bed should be elevated to an angle of 30° to 45° to facilitate venous return from the head. If the patient is intubated, hyperventilation to bring the patient's carbon dioxide tension below 25 mm Hg will rapidly, but only transiently, lower

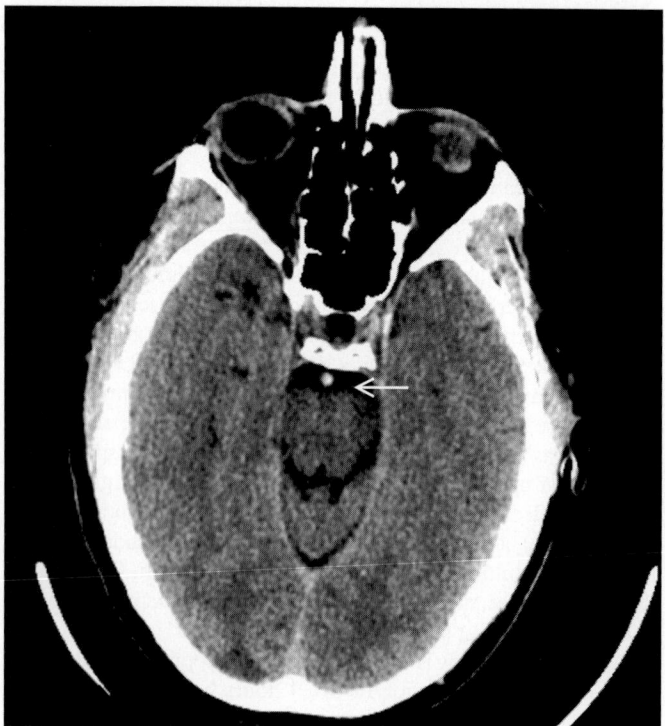

Figure 4 **In this noncontrast head CT scan, the basilar artery, which runs ventral to the pons and the lower midbrain, appears hyperdense. In the setting of acute coma, this finding suggests BAO.**

the ICP. Mannitol, 0.25 mg/kg every 4 to 6 hours, will also control IICP temporarily. Steroids may be used in the setting of tumors or abscesses of the brain. In most cases of IICP, the eventual treatment is neurosurgical decompression.

Cardiac Arrest

Cardiac arrest, if ongoing, is treated according to advanced cardiac life support (ACLS) guidelines. Several preliminary studies on the use of hypothermia for brain resuscitation after ventricular fibrillation (VF) cardiac arrest led to the publication of two randomized, controlled clinical trials in back-to-back issues of the *New England Journal of Medicine* in 2002.[8,9] Both trials clearly demonstrated that hypothermia significantly improved survival and neurologic outcomes. As a result, the Advanced Life Support Task Force of the International Liaison Committee on Resuscitation issued a guideline statement containing the following recommendation: "Unconscious adult patients with spontaneous circulation after out-of-hospital cardiac arrest should be cooled to 32°C to 34°C for 12 to 24 hours when the initial rhythm was VF. Such cooling may also be beneficial for other rhythms or in-hospital cardiac arrest."[10] This recommendation has spurred the implementation of hypothermia for resuscitation of cardiac arrest victims in many hospital centers.

Metabolic Derangements

Intoxication Many comatose patients who are seen in the ED are suffering from an overdose of alcohol, narcotics, sedatives, or some combination thereof. Most of these drugs induce depression of respiration and cardiovascular function, which is a major cause of mortality in comatose patients. Anticipation and early treatment of these complications may alleviate their effects. Early intubation, respiratory support, and maintenance of normal blood pressure are essential. Gastric lavage is effective when ingestion of a drug is discovered no more than 4 hours after the event (except in the case of salicylates, which may be removed in substantial amounts as long as 10 hours after ingestion). Accordingly, in most cases of drug overdose, little is gained by performing gastric lavage more than 4 hours after ingestion, unless the patient has been in shock and consequently manifests delayed gastric emptying and slowed absorption. When

Table 7 Drugs Used to Treat Status Epilepticus

Drug	Priority of Use	Dosing	Potential Adverse Effect
Lorazepam	First-line agent	2 mg increments I.V. 3 min apart to maximum of 8 mg	Respiratory depression Hypotension
Diazepam	Alternative first-line agent	10 mg I.V., 1 or 2 doses	Respiratory depression Hypotension
Fosphenytoin	Second-line agent	20 mg/kg, 150 mg/min	Arrhythmia Hypotension
Phenytoin	Alternative second-line agent	20 mg/kg, 50 mg/min	Arrhythmia Hypotension (Risk is lower than with fosphenytoin)
Pentobarbital	Third-line agent	5–12 mg/kg, 1–10 mg/kg/hr	Poor WBC chemotaxis Paralysis of respiratory cilia Poikilothermia
Midazolam	Third-line agent	0.1–0.3 mg/kg, 0.05–2.0 mg/kg/hr	Tachyphylaxis Death (mortality lower than with propofol)
Propofol	Third-line agent	3–5 mg/kg, 1–15 mg/kg/hr	Recurrent seizures after abrupt discontinuance Hypotension Hypertriglyceridemia Anemia Death (mortality higher than with midazolam)

WBC—white blood cell

a patient is comatose or uncooperative, however, the examiner is rarely able to determine the exact time of ingestion; thus, gastric lavage is almost always indicated in this situation.

Patients are intubated with a cuffed endotracheal tube (to protect the airway from aspirated gastric contents) and placed in the left lateral decubitus position (to allow pooling of the gastric contents) with the head down. Lavage is then performed with copious amounts of fluid until the returned fluid is clear. After evacuation, a slurry containing 10 g of activated charcoal in 30 to 50 ml is instilled into the stomach via a nasogastric tube. After lavage, cathartic agents may be used to shorten the transit time through the GI tract and thus to decrease absorption of the ingested material. Diuresis (saline, ionized, or osmotic), dialysis, and charcoal hemoperfusion all facilitate excretion of toxins. Specific antidotes exist for several common intoxicants; however, discussion of these antidotes is beyond the scope of this chapter.

Hypoglycemic coma Symptomatic hypoglycemia may occur when plasma glucose levels fall below 45 mg/dl. Symptoms may range from jitteriness with palpitations and diaphoresis to focal neurologic symptoms mimicking ischemic stroke to frank coma. The most common predisposing cause is diabetes; other common causes include alcoholism, hepatic failure, and renal failure.

If hypoglycemic coma is prolonged, it may result in permanent brain damage. Therefore, initial management involves urgent restoration of the patient to a euglycemic state. This may be accomplished through I.V. injection of glucose. Traditionally, injection of an ampule (50 ml) of a 50% solution is prescribed; however, this measure frequently results in loss of the peripheral I.V. site used. Alternatively, 250 ml of a 10% dextrose solution is rapidly injected; this measure provides the same amount of dextrose without causing any loss of venous access. If necessary, infusion of a 5% dextrose solution may be continued subsequently. As noted [*see* General Measures, Triage, and Test Battery, *above*], if the patient is thiamine depleted, 100 mg of thiamine should be given before dextrose so as not to precipitate Wernicke-Korsakoff syndrome.

Further treatment consists of prevention, in the form of educating patients in the use of insulin and encouraging them to carry glucose tablets or sweets with them at all times. A supply of glucagon (1 g I.M.) that can be administered by relatives may also be stored at home.

Diabetic ketotic coma Because patients who are comatose as a result of diabetic ketoacidosis often present in a profoundly dehydrated state, treatment must be initiated as soon as possible. The following are the key components of the management of diabetic ketoacidosis.

1. Replacement of fluid losses (the average fluid loss is approximately 7 L).
2. Normalization of electrolyte levels and careful monitoring of serum potassium.
3. Restoration of acid-base balance (bicarbonate infusion is reserved for severe cases).
4. Correction of insulin deficiency (4 to 6 U/hr).
5. Replenishment of energy stores (e.g., through dextrose infusion with insulin coverage until the patient can resume oral feeding).
6. Investigation to identify an underlying cause (infection is common).

Hyperglycemic hyperosmolar nonketotic coma Management of hyperosmolar nonketotic coma is essentially the same as that of diabetic ketotic coma. It is particularly important, however, that meticulous rehydration be performed, given that many patients with this condition are elderly.

Vegetative State

Approximately 10% to 12% of comatose patients eventually lapse into a vegetative state (VS). Whereas comatose patients have closed eyes and do not respond to pain, VS patients have spontaneous eye opening according to sleep-wake cycles and may have minimal, purposeless movement. Specifically, the diagnosis of VS can be made if there is intermittent wakefulness (sleep-wake cycles); no evidence of awareness of self or environment or ability to interact with others; no evidence of sustained, reproducible, purposeful, or voluntary behavioral responses to external stimuli; no evidence of language comprehension or expression; and sufficiently preserved hypothalamic and brain stem autonomic function to permit survival with medical and nursing care. VS that persists for more than 1 month is referred to as a persistent vegetative state (PVS); PVS that lasts for 1 year or longer is considered permanent VS.[11,12]

Prognosis

At least 50% of patients who are in traumatic VS will recover consciousness within 1 year, compared with only 15% of patients in nontraumatic VS. In one series, 69% of nontraumatic VS patients died, 20% survived with severe disability, and 8% survived without severe disability. Indicators of poor prognosis in nontraumatic VS patients include the absence of pupillary reflexes for 24 hours after the event; no withdrawal from painful stimuli after 72 hours; the absence of roving eye movements after 7 days; and the absence of motor response to noxious stimuli after 72 hours.[13-15]

References

1. Plum F, Posner JB: The pathologic physiology of signs and symptoms of coma. The Diagnosis of Stupor and Coma, 3rd ed. FA Davis Co, Philadelphia, 1982, p 1
2. Doyon S, Roberts JR: Reappraisal of the "coma cocktail": dextrose, flumazenil, naloxone, and thiamine. Emerg Med Clin North Am 12:301, 1994
3. Bartlett D: The coma cocktail: indications, contraindications, adverse effects, proper dose, and proper route. J Emerg Nurs 30:572, 2004
4. Devuyst G, Bogousslavsky J, Meuli R, et al: Stroke or transient ischemic attacks with basilar artery stenosis or occlusion. Arch Neurol 59:567, 2002
5. Wheless J: Acute management of seizures in the syndromes of idiopathic generalized epilepies. Epilepsia 44(suppl 2):22, 2003
6. Bassin S, Smith TL, Bleck TP: Status epilepticus.
Crit Care 6:137, 2002
7. Pickard JD, Czosnyka M: Management of raised intracranial pressure. J Neurol Neurosurg Psychiatry 56:845, 1993
8. The Hypothermia After Cardiac Arrest Study Group. Mild therapeutic hypothermia to improve the neurologic outcome after cardiac arrest. N Engl J Med 346:549, 2002
9. Bernard SA, Gray TW, Buist MD, et al: Treatment of comatose survivors of out-of-hospital cardiac arrest with induced hypothermia. N Engl J Med 346:557, 2002
10. International Liaison Committee on Resuscitation: Therapeutic hypothermia after cardiac arrest: an advisory statement by the advanced life support task force of the International Liaison Committee on Resuscitation. Circulation 108:118, 2003
11. Mercer WN, Childs NL: Coma, vegetative state, and the minimally conscious state: diagnosis and management. Neurologist 5:186, 1999
12. Laureys S, Owen AM, Schiff ND: Brain function in coma, vegetative state, and related disorders. Lancet Neurology 3:537, 2004
13. Overell J, Bone I, Fuller GN: An aid to predicting prognosis in patients with non-traumatic coma at one day. J Neurol Neurosurg Psychiatry 71(suppl I):i24, 2001
14. Booth CM, Boone RH, Tomlinson G, et al: Is this patient dead, vegetative, or severely neurologically impaired? Assessing outcome for comatose survivors of cardiac arrest. JAMA 291:870, 2004
15. Levy D, Caronna JJ, Singer BH, et al: Predicting outcome from hypoxic-ischemic coma. JAMA 253:1420, 1985

David Crippen, M.D., F.C.C.M.

He seems to be completely unreceptive
The tests I gave him show no sense at all
His eyes react to light; the dials detect it
He hears but cannot answer to your call
    "Go to the Mirror Boy" (from *Tommy*, The Who, 1969)

Brain Failure

BRAIN FAILURE AND IMPAIRMENT OF CONSCIOUSNESS

As a type of organ system failure, brain failure invariably affects consciousness. Consciousness is structurally produced in the cerebral hemispheres, including the pons and the medulla.[1] These structures are all interconnected by the reticular formation, which begins in the medulla and extends to the midbrain, where it forms the reticular activating system. This pathway modulates the perception of events and controls integrated responses.[2]

Clinical evaluation of consciousness states is heavily dependent on the findings from physical examination. When the physical examination yields visual and palpable clues to the integrity of consciousness, impairment thereof may be classified into one of the following categories[3]:

1. Cloudy consciousness. This state is defined as a mild deficit in the speed of information processing by the brain, resulting from disruption of cell-to-cell connectivity at the histologic level. Cloudy consciousness may be noted after mild to moderate head trauma and may persist for several months. Memory of recent events is often diminished, but long-term memory typically remains intact.
2. Lethargy. This state is defined as a decrease in alertness, resulting in impaired ability to perform tasks that are normally accomplished without effort. Patients rouse briefly in response to stimuli, then settle back into inactivity when left alone. They retain awareness of their immediate environment.
3. Obtundation. This state is defined as a decrease in awareness and alertness, in which patients rouse briefly in response to stimuli and follow simple commands but are unaware of their immediate surroundings. When stimulation ceases, they settle back into inactivity.
4. Stupor. In this state, patients cannot communicate clearly but can be aroused by continued painful stimulation. Arousal may be manifested only as withdrawal from painful stimuli. As soon as stimuli are removed, patients settle back into inactivity.
5. Coma. In this state, patients do not respond to even the most vigorous stimuli.
6. Brain death. This state is equivalent to functional decapitation and is characterized by irreversible cessation of whole brain function and function of the hemispheres and the brain stem.

It should be kept in mind that the efficacy of the physical examination in the evaluation of consciousness diminishes when visual clues disappear (e.g., during heavy sedation or therapeutic musculoskeletal paralysis). In such situations, monitoring of cerebral function is helpful in assessing the effect of therapy on neuronal function.

RELATION OF CARDIAC ARREST TO BRAIN FAILURE

In a substantial proportion of unconscious patients admitted to the intensive care unit, the brain failure resulted from metabolic and hemodynamic deteriorations that followed cardiac arrest.[4] There is a great difference between surviving cardiopulmonary resuscitation (CPR) and walking out of the hospital unaided after such an event. It is relatively easy to restart the heart with traditional CPR; it is considerably harder to restart the brain.[5] After several minutes of cardiac arrest, CPR will occasionally restore cardiac activity, but it will not necessarily restore useful brain function. Brain metabolism requires a constant high flow of oxygenated blood and nutrients. During cardiac resuscitation, cerebral perfusion decreases sufficiently to promote hypoxia and tissue edema. A number of mechanisms have been shown to underlie deteriorating and failed reflow. Hyperviscosity from hemoconcentration of plasma proteins and formed elements contributes to initial poor reperfusion at the capillary level. Endothelial cell swelling and edema of the pericapillary astrocytes also greatly inhibit reperfusion by reducing capillary diameter to less than 5 μm.

During reperfusion, abnormally high amounts of superoxide convert almost all available nitric oxide to peroxynitrite, which is regarded as the agent that causes most of the damage to brain capillary endothelial cells.[6] As noted (see above), damage to the endothelium not only increases edema (tissue swelling resulting from leakiness) but also causes endothelial protrusions (blebs) that can block capillaries. Calcium-mediated vasospasm also plays a role. L-type calcium channel blockers, given before the insult, have been shown to prevent the no-reflow phenomenon in dogs and to result in an 80% survival rate (compared with an 86% mortality in the control group).[7]

During CPR, cerebral perfusion tends to decrease dramatically over time if adequate flow is not quickly reestablished.[8] Maintaining a small amount of blood flow to the brain with CPR is not necessarily beneficial. Incomplete brain ischemia, which is created when only a small amount of blood is allowed into the brain after an anoxic insult (as in CPR), appears to result in more detrimental alterations in brain metabolism than does the complete anoxia resulting from the absence of any flow.[9] When a small amount of blood is allowed to flow into an actively distorted and stressed metabolic system, the resulting cellular activity generates more toxic products of metabolism than complete anoxia would have produced.[10] In other words, more brain damage seems to occur with prolonged CPR states than with no-flow states[11]— especially if there is an increased level of glucose in the small quantities of blood supplied by CPR.[12] To date, this phenomenon has not been completely explained. Acidosis, in and of itself, is unlikely to be the only damaging factor, because severe respiratory acidosis does not damage the brain.[13]

PATHOPHYSIOLOGY OF BRAIN FAILURE

In vitro, central nervous system neurons can tolerate between 20 and 60 minutes of complete ischemic anoxia without irreversible injury.[14] In vivo, however, injury occurs after a much shorter time and is much more severe. Immediately after the cessation of circulation to the brain, the cerebral vessels dilate in response to the local environmental factors and to increased arterial carbon dioxide tension (P_aCO_2). Because the brain has no stores of glucose, cellular metabolism quickly ceases. Absence of nutrients and hypoxia cause the most sensitive structures to lose their cellular integrity. This loss results in capillary leakage, edema, and cellular disruption and leads to the release of proteases and other damaging compounds into the surrounding tissues.[15]

These events, in turn, result in clogged microcirculation, stasis, and a vicious circle of worsening damage that backs up into the macrocirculation. If this process is allowed to continue for a substantial period and blood flow is then reestablished, the increased pressure gradient in the damaged area tends to disrupt the fragile architecture, much as the sudden bursting of a dam might do to downstream communities. The result is a progressive postresuscitative hypoperfusion state in which blood flow falls to less than 20% of normal within 90 minutes after reperfusion and remains at this low level for as long as 18 hours.[16,17]

Two explanations for these phenomena have been proposed. The first is that massive overloading of the cells with calcium ions (Ca^{2+}) may be the initial stage of irreversible damage.[18] Normally, the extracellular level of Ca^{2+} is high and the intracellular level is low. The damage to the cell membrane caused by hypoxia and loss of nutrient flow alters the gradient and allows Ca^{2+} to enter the cell, causing interference with enzymes, DNA, RNA, mitochondria, and energy production cycles. Infusion of high levels of Ca^{2+} into precapillary arterioles causes vasospasm and a vicious circle characterized by decreased flow and further depletion of oxygen and nutrients. The second theory is that during ischemia, abnormal metabolism may result in the creation of reactive oxygen metabolites, which attack DNA, RNA, and mitochondria, causing irreversible damage.[19]

Brain Death

DIAGNOSIS OF BRAIN DEATH

Brain death protocols have evolved to become highly specific and sensitive.[20] Brain death is a diagnosis of what is, not what might be. Initially, for an accurate diagnosis of brain death, there must be clear evidence of an acute, catastrophic, irreversible brain injury, and any reversible conditions that may obfuscate the clinical assessment (e.g., drug intoxication, hypothermia, and metabolic abnormalities) must be excluded.[21] Subsequently, the physical examination must show coma, absent motor responses, absent brain stem reflexes, and apnea. Some protocols call for a second examination, performed after a variable interval.[22] Further confirmatory studies (e.g., electroencephalography [EEG] or cerebral blood flow studies) may be ordered if there is any ambiguity in the clinical evaluation.[23]

A typical brain death protocol may be summarized as follows:

1. Confirm that the patient is in a coma.
2. Evaluate the patient for seizure activity and decerebrate or decorticate movements.
3. Test for motor response to painful stimulation.
4. Test for pupillary response to light.
5. Test for the corneal reflex.
6. Test for the oculocephalogyric reflex (the doll's head reflex).
7. Test for the vestibulo-ocular reflex (the caloric test).
8. Test for upper and lower airway stimulation (e.g., pharyngeal and endotracheal suction).
9. Test for the gag reflex.
10. Perform the apnea test. This test should be the last test and should be conducted after two clinical examinations (separated by the mandatory observation period) have confirmed the absence of brain stem functions. The patient is disconnected from the ventilator while oxygenation of the lungs is continued passively. On the basis of calculation (whereby P_aCO_2 is assumed to rise 4 mm Hg in the first minute and 3 mm Hg every minute thereafter), the patient is allowed to build up to a P_aCO_2 of 60 mm Hg or more without becoming hypoxic. If there is no respiratory effort, the apnea test is considered confirmatory.[24]
11. Consider ordering an EEG. The EEG should show electrocerebral silence for at least 30 minutes and must conform to established criteria for brain death.[25]
12. If the cause of death cannot be determined with absolute accuracy, consider cerebral angiography. The absence of intracranial arterial circulation, as demonstrated by four-vessel angiography, confirms brain death.[26]

DEFINITION OF DEATH

In earlier times, it could be said that a person was dead when the heart and lungs ceased functioning. Today, however, this view no longer suffices, because with the advent of critical care techniques such as mechanical ventilation, selected organ systems can be artificially supported.[27,28] In this era of critical care, death is more a process than an event. Lack of blood flow to the brain leads to loss of consciousness within seconds, but other functions of the brain may persist for much longer.[29] Other somatic organs may take hours to stop functioning, and connective tissues can take days to die.[30]

The evolution of life support systems capable of prolonging death indefinitely necessitated a more eclectic definition of death, which arrived in 1968 with the formulation of the Harvard criteria.[31] In essence, these criteria considered the irreversible loss of certain organ functions, rather than whole body metabolic cessation, to be indicative of death. When the Harvard criteria were met, death was inevitable, even with continuing treatment. A 1970 study found that a population of patients meeting the Harvard criteria all eventually died while undergoing continued medical treatment.[32] The Harvard criteria objectified the progression of disease, thereby making it possible for clinicians to predict death.

These early studies only predicted with a reasonable certainty that patients meeting particular criteria would eventually die. A prognosis of death, however, cannot serve as a diagnosis. In 1981, the President's Commission broke with the past and established brain death as a criterion for determining death, not simply for predicting the inevitability of death.[33] The Uniform Determination of Death Act (UDDA) made brain death and cardiopulmonary collapse criteria for death in 44 states[34]:

> An individual who has sustained either: (1) irreversible cessation of circulatory and respiratory functions, or (2) irreversible cessation of all functions of the entire brain, including the brain stem, is dead.

Under the UDDA, death is pronounced at the time the criteria are met, and families may not demand continuing mechanical ventilation or other forms of ICU life support (except in the states of New York and New Jersey, both of which have conscience clauses).[35]

Is Brain Death Equivalent to Death?

Physicians and ethicists continue to disagree on the question of whether whole brain death (WBD) is equivalent to death.[36] It is generally asserted that there is only one real definition of death—irreversible cessation of the integrated functioning of the organism as a whole—but as noted (see above), the determination of death can have either a cardiovascular or a neurologic basis. The connections between cardiovascular and neurologic criteria are tenuous, and the criteria mean different things to different people at different times. For example, the criterion of irreversible cessation of all circulatory and respiratory function does not imply the cessation of brain function.[37] Conversely, the criterion of irreversible cessation of all brain function does not imply the cessation of circulation and respiration.[38] It appears, then, that the definition of death does not require the permanent cessation of the functioning of the organism as a whole but, rather, cessation of only certain functions.[39]

Ethicists maintain that the criteria used to fulfill the definition of death should be both necessary and sufficient.[30] This is not an easy standard to meet. For example, loss of consciousness is necessary for death, but it is not sufficient. Although the UDDA endorses two criteria for death—cardiac death and WBD—only WBD is both a necessary and a sufficient criterion, because a declaration of death can be made without the heart having stopped beating. Therefore, the UDDA does not ensure that each of the two criteria is an instantiation of the other.[40] Loss of heartbeat and breathing is sufficient for death, but it is not necessary if WBD is present. Moreover, the UDDA does not require that every brain cell be dead for brain death to be declared—only those cells that contribute to the integration of the organism as a whole.[41] Accordingly, the UDDA suggests that death occurs when "critical" parts of the brain responsible for integrated functioning of the rest of the body cease functioning, in that, according to this argument, it is the brain that integrates the entire organism.

It is commonly postulated that when the brain dies, the body must die with it. However, there is a problem with the idea of the brain as the fundamental orchestrator of all body functions. It has been pointed out that many organ functions are, for variable periods, not obligately linked to the brain as an integrating controller.[30] In fact, the rest of the body can be viably sustained for some time in the absence of brain function simply by maintaining protection, ventilation, circulation, and nutrition. Some WBD patients actual-ly require less support than other patients who are clearly alive but gravely ill.[42] It can easily be shown that the brain will continue to function for a time after cessation of cardiopulmonary function.

Brain Death and Artificial Organ Support

Acceptance of WBD as essentially defining death involves the assumption that artificially maintained respiration and circulation are irrelevant because they are controlled by mechanical intervention rather than by the brain.[43] This assumption is based on the further assumption that because body functions are being manipulated externally, they cannot be functioning in any integrated manner. However, death cannot be predicated on the use of life-sustaining treatment, for two reasons. First, the availability of life-sustaining treatment ought not to determine who is alive and who is dead. Second, if the definition of death were to be contingent on the need for an artificial intervention, patients who require life-sustaining treatment to recover from an illness would have to be considered resurrected from the dead.[44] Furthermore, the definition of death does not require irreversible cessation of "spontaneous" organism functions, because spontaneous function is not necessary for life, as evidenced by the many patients who require life-sustaining treatment but who are very much alive.[45]

IMPLICATIONS FOR FUTURE DEFINITIONS OF DEATH

There are disturbing differences between a corpse in a morgue and a brain-dead patient. If the WBD patient is a corpse, he or she is certainly a corpse with some unusual properties—one that breathes, circulates blood, digests food, filters wastes, and is capable of carrying a pregnancy to term.[46] These considerations raise the issue of whether there is a practical or ethical difference between being dead, being almost dead, or being in the process of dying, and they show that the precise moment when death occurs cannot be accurately pinpointed. It is clear that a WBD patient can be maintained on life-sustaining treatment for much longer than was once thought and still retain definite characteristics of a living being. The organism as a whole, though disabled, is not yet dead and should not be represented as such—a fact that may have important consequences for our future conceptions of death and of life in death.

References

1. Crippen D: Agitation in the ICU: part one. Anatomical and physiologic basis for the agitated state. Crit Care 3:R35, 1999

2. Pinault D: The thalamic reticular nucleus: structure, function and concept. Brain Res Brain Res Rev 46:1, 2004

3. Crippen D: Neurologic monitoring in the intensive care unit. New Horiz 2:107, 1994

4. Berger R, Kelley M: Survival after in-hospital cardiopulmonary arrest of noncritically ill patients: a prospective study. Chest 106:872, 1994

5. Brindley PG, Markland DM, Mayers I, et al: Predictors of survival following in-hospital adult cardiopulmonary resuscitation. CMAJ 167:343, 2002

6. Wu S, Tamaki N, Nagashima T, et al: Reactive oxygen species in reoxygenation injury of rat brain capillary endothelial cells. Neurosurgery 43:577, 1998

7. Pharmacology of Cerebral Ischemia 1988. Krieglstein J, Ed. Wissenschaftliche Verlagsgesellschaft, Stuttgart, 1989, p 65

8. Nozari A, Rubertsson S, Gedeborg R, et al: Maximisation of cerebral blood flow during experimen-tal cardiopulmonary resuscitation does not ameliorate post-resuscitation hypoperfusion. Resuscitation 40:27, 1999

9. Asiedu-Gyekye IJ, Vaktorovich A: The "no-reflow" phenomenon in cerebral circulation. Med Sci Monit 9(11):BR394, 2003

10. Wolfson S, et al: Dynamic heterogeneity of cerebral hypoperfusion after prolonged cardiac arrest in dogs measured by the stable xenon/CT technique: a preliminary study. Resuscitation 23:1, 1992

11. del Zoppo GJ, Mabuchi T: Cerebral microvessel responses to focal ischemia. J Cereb Blood Flow Metab 23:879, 2003

12. Zygun DA, Steiner LA, Johnston AJ, et al: Hyperglycemia and brain tissue pH after traumatic brain injury. Neurosurgery 55:877, 2004

13. Bender TM, Johnston JA, Manepalli AN, et al: Association between brain tissue pH and brain injury during asphyxia in piglets. Resuscitation 59:243, 2003

14. Safar P, Bircher N: Cardiopulmonary Cerebral Resuscitation, 3rd ed. WB Saunders Co, Philadelphia, 1988

15. Steen PA, Milde JH, Michenfelder JD: No barbiturate protection in a dog model of complete cerebral ischemia. Ann Neurol 5:343, 1979

16. Nozari A, Rubertsson S, Wiklund L: Improved cerebral blood supply and oxygenation by aortic balloon occlusion combined with intra-aortic vasopressin administration during experimental cardiopulmonary resuscitation. Acta Anaesthesiol Scand 44:1209, 2000

17. Shaffner DH, Eleff SM, Koehler RC, et al: Effect of the no-flow interval and hypothermia on cerebral blood flow and metabolism during cardiopulmonary resuscitation in dogs. Stroke 29:2607, 1998

18. Bowersox SS, Singh T, Luther RR: Selective blockade of N-type voltage-sensitive calcium channels protects against brain injury after transient focal cerebral ischemia in rats. Brain Res 747:343, 1997

19. Maragos WF, Korde AS: Mitochondrial uncoupling as a potential therapeutic target in acute central nervous system injury. J Neurochem 91:257, 2004

20. Kaste M, Palo J: Criteria of brain death and

removal of cadaveric organs. Ann Clin Res 13:313, 1981

21. Jastremski M, Powner D, Snyder J, et al: Problems in brain death determination. Forensic Sci 11(3):201, 1978

22. Searle J, Collins C: A brain-death protocol. Lancet 1:641, 1980

23. Izac SM: Quality assurance in determinations of brain death. Am J Electroneurodiagnostic Technol 44(3):159, 2004

24. Benzel EC, Mashburn JP, Conrad S, et al: Apnea testing for the determination of brain death: a modified protocol. Technical note. J Neurosurg 76:1029, 1992

25. Vivien B, Paqueron X, Le Cosquer P, et al: Detection of brain death onset using the bispectral index in severely comatose patients. Intensive Care Med 28:419, 2002

26. Paolin A, Manuali A, Di Paola F, et al: Reliability in diagnosis of brain death. Intensive Care Med 21:657, 1995

27. Youngner SJ, Arnold RM: Philosophical debates about the definition of death: who cares? J Med Philos 26:529, 2001

28. Evans M: A plea for the heart. Bioethics 4:230, 1990

29. Crippen D: Terminally weaning awake patients from life sustaining mechanical ventilation: the critical

care physician's role in comfort measured during the dying process. Clin Intensive Care 2:260, 1991

30. Bernat JL: A defense of the whole-brain concept of death. Hastings Cent Rep 28(2):14, 1998

31. Morenski JD, Oro JJ, Tobias JD, et al: Determination of death by neurological criteria. J Intensive Care Med 18:211, 2003

32. Becker DP, Robert CM Jr, Nelson JR, et al: An evaluation of the definition of cerebral death. Neurology 20:459, 1970

33. Guidelines for the determination of death. Report of the medical consultants on the diagnosis of death to the President's Commission for the Study of Ethical Problems in Medicine and Biomedical and Behavioral Research. JAMA 246:2184, 1981

34. Determination of death (Uniform Determination of Death Act of 1981); natural death (Natural Death Act of 1981). Lexis DC Code DC. 1982; Sect. 6.2401 6.2421 to 6.2430 amended Feb 1982

35. Olick RS: Brain death, religious freedom, and public policy: New Jersey's landmark legislative initiative. Kennedy Inst Ethics J 1:275, 1991

36. Wijdicks EF: Brain death worldwide: accepted fact but no global consensus in diagnostic criteria. Neurology 58:20, 2002

37. Byrne P, O'Reilly S, Quay PM, et al: Brain Death: The Patient, the Physician, and Society. Kluwer

Academic Publishers, 2000, p 61

38. DeVita MA, Snyder JV, Arnold RM, et al: Observations of withdrawal of life-sustaining treatment from patients who became non-heart-beating organ donors. Crit Care Med 28:1709, 2000

39. Hayden MR: A philosophical critique of the brain death movement. Linacre Q 49:245, 1982

40. McMahan J: The metaphysics of brain death. Bioethics 9:94, 1995

41. Bernat JL: The biophilosophical basis of whole-brain death. Soc Philos Public Policy 19:337, 2002

42. Kamm FM: Brain death and spontaneous breathing. Philos Public Aff 30:297, 2001

43. Settergren G: Brain death: an important paradigm shift in the 20th century. Acta Anaesthesiol Scand 47:1053, 2003

44. Whetstine L: When is "dead" dead: an examination of the medical and philosophical literature on the determination of death. Dissertation, Duquesne University, 2004

45. Potts M: A Requiem for whole brain death: a response to D. Alan Shewmon's "The Brain and Somatic Integration." J Med Philos 26:483

46. Powner DJ, Bernstein IM: Extended somatic support for pregnant women after brain death. Crit Care Med 31:1241, 2003

128 MULTIPLE ORGAN DYSFUNCTION SYNDROME

John C. Marshall, M.D., F.A.C.S., F.R.C.S.C.

Approach to Multiple Organ Dysfunction Syndrome

The multiple organ dysfunction syndrome (MODS)—also known as progressive systems failure,[1] multiple organ failure,[2] and multiple system organ failure[3]—is characterized by progressive but potentially reversible physiologic dysfunction of two or more organ systems that arises after resuscitation from an acute life-threatening event. The term MODS was introduced by a 1991 consensus conference of the American College of Chest Physicians (ACCP) and the Society of Critical Care Medicine (SCCM).[4] The designation of MODS as a syndrome emphasizes that dynamic alterations in physiologic function in critically ill patients may have common pathophysiologic underpinnings. However, MODS is as much a paradigm as a syndrome—that is, it represents an approach to the care of the critically ill patient that emphasizes intensive monitoring and support of organ system function over specific therapies for isolated disease processes and that focuses on preventing or minimizing iatrogenic injury resulting from ICU interventions.

MODS evolves in the wake of a profound disruption of systemic homeostasis.[5,6] It was originally described in patients with overwhelming infection, multiple injuries, or tissue ischemia; however, it has many overlapping risk factors [see Table 1]. Preexisting illness—in particular, chronic alcohol abuse[7]—predisposes to the development of organ dysfunction in patients exposed to these risk factors.

Clinical Definitions of Organ Dysfunction

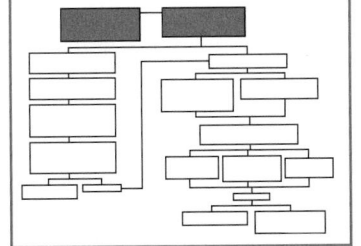

Although MODS is readily recognized by experienced clinicians, there is still no clear consensus on its description with respect to either the systems whose function is deranged, the descriptors that best measure that derangement, or the degree of derangement that constitutes organ dysfunction or failure.

A systematic review of 30 published clinical studies evaluated the organ systems and variables used to describe MODS.[8] Seven organ systems—the respiratory system (all 30 reports), the renal system (29 reports), the hepatic system (27 reports), the cardiovascular system (25 reports), the hematologic system (23 reports), the GI system (22 reports), and the CNS (18 reports)—were included in at least half of the studies. Scoring systems from both North America[9,10] and Europe[11,12] define MODS using six of these seven organ systems, eliminating the GI system because of the declining prevalence of stress-related upper GI bleeding and the lack of satisfactory measures of GI dysfunction. These scoring systems have many similarities [see Table 2].

In general terms, the dysfunction of a given organ system can be described in one of three ways:

1. As a physiologic derangement (e.g., an altered ratio of arterial oxygen tension [P_aO_2] to fractional inspiration of oxygen [F_IO_2] or an altered platelet count).
2. As the clinical intervention used to correct that derangement (e.g., mechanical ventilation or blood component replacement therapy).
3. As a discrete clinical syndrome incorporating several descriptive variables (e.g., acute respiratory distress syndrome [ARDS] or disseminated intravascular coagulation [DIC]).

Whichever of these three perspectives is adopted, common pathogenetic mechanisms underlie MODS, and common principles direct its prevention and management.

RESPIRATORY DYSFUNCTION

ARDS, initially described in the early 1960s,[13,14] is the prototypical expression of respiratory dysfunction in MODS.[15] In its

Table 1 Risk Factors for MODS

Infection	Peritonitis and intra-abdominal infections
	Pneumonia
	Necrotizing soft tissue infections
Inflammation	Pancreatitis
Injury	Multiple trauma
	Burn injury
Ischemia	Ruptured aneurysm
	Hypovolemic shock
	Mesenteric ischemia
Immune reactions	Autoimmune disease
	Transplant rejection
	Graft versus host disease
Iatrogenic factors	Delayed or missed injury
	Blood transfusion
	Injurious mechanical ventilation
	Total parenteral nutrition
Intoxication	Drug reactions
	Arsenic intoxication
	Drug overdose
Idiopathic factors	Thrombotic thrombocytopenic purpura
	Hypoadrenalism
	Pheochromocytoma

Approach to Multiple Organ Dysfunction Syndrome

Recognize susceptible patient

Patients at high risk for multiple organ dysfunction syndrome (MODS) are those who have experienced a disruption of systemic homeostasis resulting from one or more of the following:

- Infection
- Inflammation
- Injury
- Ischemia
- Immune system activation
- Intoxication
- Iatrogenic factors

Minimal organ dysfunction

Prevent progression to MODS by optimizing support of hemodynamic, metabolic, and immunologic function, taking care to minimize iatrogenic injury during the provision of physiologic support.

Hemodynamic support

Maximize O_2 delivery to tissues by the following measures:

- Fluid replacement therapy
- Inotropic agents
- Vasoactive agents
- Mechanical ventilation

Metabolic support

Reverse catabolic state with definitive intervention, including the following:

- Debridement of devitalized tissue
- Burn wound excision and grafting
- Fixation of long bone fractures

Provide early nutritional support by the enteral route. If gut function is inadequate, parenteral nutrition should be employed.

Immunologic support

Prevent nosocomial infection, treat documented infection, and minimize the consequences of injurious host defense responses by such measures as the following:

- Timely and appropriate surgical intervention
- Limiting breaches of mucosal defenses
- Selective, targeted use of antibiotics

Organ function is preserved or restored

Patient survives. Discharge patient from ICU.

Organ function deteriorates

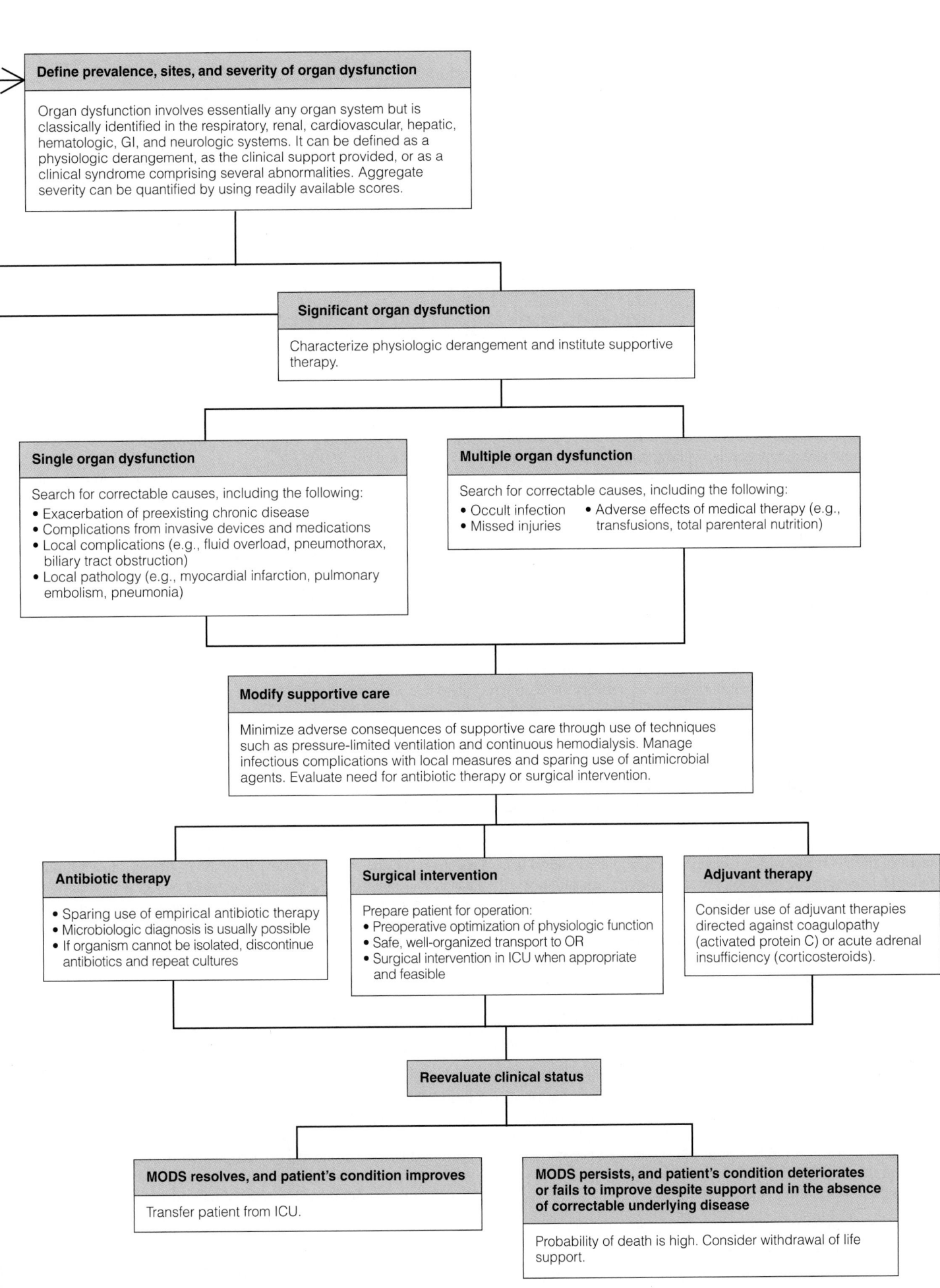

Define prevalence, sites, and severity of organ dysfunction

Organ dysfunction involves essentially any organ system but is classically identified in the respiratory, renal, cardiovascular, hepatic, hematologic, GI, and neurologic systems. It can be defined as a physiologic derangement, as the clinical support provided, or as a clinical syndrome comprising several abnormalities. Aggregate severity can be quantified by using readily available scores.

Significant organ dysfunction

Characterize physiologic derangement and institute supportive therapy.

Single organ dysfunction

Search for correctable causes, including the following:
• Exacerbation of preexisting chronic disease
• Complications from invasive devices and medications
• Local complications (e.g., fluid overload, pneumothorax, biliary tract obstruction)
• Local pathology (e.g., myocardial infarction, pulmonary embolism, pneumonia)

Multiple organ dysfunction

Search for correctable causes, including the following:
• Occult infection   • Adverse effects of medical therapy (e.g.,
• Missed injuries   transfusions, total parenteral nutrition)

Modify supportive care

Minimize adverse consequences of supportive care through use of techniques such as pressure-limited ventilation and continuous hemodialysis. Manage infectious complications with local measures and sparing use of antimicrobial agents. Evaluate need for antibiotic therapy or surgical intervention.

Antibiotic therapy

• Sparing use of empirical antibiotic therapy
• Microbiologic diagnosis is usually possible
• If organism cannot be isolated, discontinue antibiotics and repeat cultures

Surgical intervention

Prepare patient for operation:
• Preoperative optimization of physiologic function
• Safe, well-organized transport to OR
• Surgical intervention in ICU when appropriate and feasible

Adjuvant therapy

Consider use of adjuvant therapies directed against coagulopathy (activated protein C) or acute adrenal insufficiency (corticosteroids).

Reevaluate clinical status

MODS resolves, and patient's condition improves

Transfer patient from ICU.

MODS persists, and patient's condition deteriorates or fails to improve despite support and in the absence of correctable underlying disease

Probability of death is high. Consider withdrawal of life support.

Table 2 Multiple Organ Dysfunction (MOD) Score[9]

Organ System	Indicator of Dysfunction	Degree of Dysfunction				
		None (0)	Minimal (1)	Mild (2)	Moderate (3)	Severe (4)
Respiratory	P_aO_2/F_IO_2 ratio	> 300	226–300	151–225	76–150	75
Renal	Serum creatinine level	100 μmol/L	101–200 μmol/L	201–350 μmol/L	351–500 μmol/L	> 500 μmol/L
Hepatic	Serum bilirubin level	20 μmol/L	21–60 μmol/L	61–120 μmol/L	121–240 μmol/L	> 240 μmol/L
Cardiovascular	Pressure-adjusted HR*	< 10.0	10.1–15.0	15.1–20.0	20.1–30.0	> 30.0
Hematologic	Platelet count	> 120,000/mm³	81,000–120,000/mm³	51,000–80,000/mm³	21,000–50,000/mm³	20,000/mm³
Neurologic	Glasgow Coma Scale score	15	13–14	10–12	7–9	6

*Calculated as the product of HR and central venous pressure (CVP), divided by mean arterial pressure (MAP): (HR · CVP)/MAP.

mildest form, respiratory dysfunction is characterized by tachypnea, hypocapnia, and hypoxemia. As lung injury evolves, a combination of worsening hypoxemia and increased work of breathing necessitates mechanical ventilatory support [see *121 Mechanical Ventilation*].

Increased capillary permeability and neutrophil influx are the earliest pathologic events in ARDS. As the acute inflammatory process resolves, further lung injury results both from the process of repair, which involves fibrosis and the deposition of hyaline material, and from further lung trauma, resulting from positive pressure mechanical ventilation.[16]

Lung involvement in ARDS is inhomogeneous, with areas of functional and aerated alveoli interspersed with areas of non-functional alveoli.[17] The distribution of injury reflects the sequelae of care in the intensive care unit: consolidation occurs in the posterior dependent regions of the lung, and cystic changes develop from overdistention by the ventilator in the antidependent regions.[18]

Impaired lung function is reflected in a reduced P_aO_2. To ensure adequate oxygen delivery to the tissues, mechanical ventilation must be instituted and F_IO_2 increased. The ratio of P_aO_2 to F_IO_2, therefore, provides a sensitive and objective measurement of the degree to which oxygenation is impaired and so is a reliable measure of physiologic respiratory dysfunction.[19] Mechanical ventilation reflects the clinical intervention triggered by impaired oxygenation, and the additional criteria for ARDS—bilateral lung infiltrates and a normal pulmonary capillary wedge pressure—serve to exclude such primary causes of acute hypoxemia as pulmonary embolism, atelectasis, and congestive heart failure. By consensus, ARDS is defined as a P_aO_2/F_IO_2 ratio lower than 200 mm Hg in association with bilateral fluffy pulmonary infiltrates and a pulmonary capillary wedge pressure lower than 18 mm Hg.[20]

ARDS is a robust model for the complex interactions that result in MODS. Lung injury in ARDS is the outcome of an interaction between an insult, a susceptible host, and the clinical therapeutic response, and its severity reflects not only the degree of the initial insult but also various poorly defined genetic influences in the host[21] and the inadvertent adverse consequences of the mode of respiratory support employed.[22]

RENAL DYSFUNCTION

Acute renal failure (ARF) [see *122 Acute Renal Failure*] was first described as a significant clinical problem during World War II,[23] but supportive care, in the form of dialysis, did not become available until the 1950s.

Clinical or subclinical renal dysfunction is common in MODS. Early-onset renal dysfunction typically results from hypotension and decreased renal blood flow. The etiology of late-onset renal failure is multifactorial and includes both prerenal factors (e.g., decreased cardiac output and hypovolemia) and the cumulative renal effects of nephrotoxic agents (e.g., medications and radiocontrast material).[24] Intrarenal vasoconstriction results in a reduction in the glomerular filtration rate, hypoxic or oxidative injury to tubular epithelial cells, and desquamation of injured cells into the tubules, causing leakage of filtrate back into the renal interstitium and evoking neutrophil-mediated inflammation that causes further local tissue injury.[25] Intrarenal shunting of blood flow, coupled with occlusion of the renal microvasculature by thrombi or aggregated blood cells, further contributes to ischemia and physiologic dysfunction. The situation may be further aggravated by renal circulatory changes resulting from vasoactive agents administered to treat shock and by increased intra-abdominal pressure consequent to massive fluid resuscitation. Histologic studies show acute tubular necrosis with disruption of the basement membrane, patchy necrosis of the renal tubules, interstitial edema, and tubular casts; these microscopic changes correlate poorly with functional impairment.[26] Activated neutrophils have also been implicated in the pathogenesis of ARF,[27,28] as has the induction of apoptosis in renal epithelial cells.[29]

Renal dysfunction in MODS is reflected physiologically in a decreased urine output, biochemically in a rising serum creatinine level, and therapeutically as the introduction of exogenous renal replacement therapy or dialysis.

HEPATIC DYSFUNCTION

Hepatic dysfunction after trauma, like ARF, was first described during World War II [see *124 Hepatic Failure*].[30] Two clinical syndromes have been described. The first, ischemic hepatitis, or shock liver, characteristically follows an episode of profound hypotension with splanchnic hypoperfusion. Early elevations of aminotransferase levels are striking and may be associated with an increased international normalized ratio and hypoglycemia; centrilobular necrosis is evident histologically. Successful resuscitation of the shock state results in rapid normalization of the biochemical abnormalities.[31] The second syndrome, ICU jaundice, is much more common than ischemic hepatitis and typically evolves many days after the inciting physiologic insult. Conjugated hyperbilirubinemia is a prominent feature, whereas elevation of aminotransferase levels and alterations of hepatic synthetic function are less pronounced.[32] Histologic features include intrahepatic cholestasis, steatosis, and Kupffer cell hyperplasia. The pathogenesis is multifactorial and includes ongoing hepatic ischemia, total parenteral nutrition (TPN)–induced cholestasis, and drug toxicity.

An increased serum bilirubin level is the most commonly recognized feature of the hepatic dysfunction of MODS. Although extracorporeal support devices have been used for patients with end-stage liver disease, the hepatic dysfunction of critical illness is not considered to be life-threatening in itself, and no specific supportive therapy is indicated.

CARDIOVASCULAR DYSFUNCTION

Both peripheral vascular and myocardial function are altered in MODS. Characteristic changes in the peripheral vasculature include a reduction in vascular resistance and an increase in microvascular permeability, resulting in a hyperdynamic circulatory profile and peripheral edema. Both alterations jeopardize tissue oxygenation—reduced vascular resistance by facilitating shunting in the microvasculature and edema by increasing the distance across which oxygen carried in the blood must diffuse to reach the cell. Shunting also occurs as a result of occlusion of the microvasculature by thrombi and aggregates of nondeformable red cells[33]; it is signaled by a reduction in arteriovenous oxygen extraction and an increase in mixed venous oxygen saturation ($S_{mv}O_2$). Biventricular dilatation with a reduction in the right and left ventricular ejection fractions has been described.[34] Right ventricular dysfunction is particularly prominent, perhaps as a consequence of increased pulmonary vascular resistance secondary to concomitant lung injury.[35] Finally, a loss of normal heart rate variability characterizes advanced cardiovascular dysfunction.[36]

The cardiovascular dysfunction of MODS is apparent clinically as increased peripheral edema with hypotension that is refractory to volume challenge and therapeutically in the use of vasoactive agents to support the circulation. Nitric oxide (NO) has been implicated in both the peripheral vasodilatation[37] and the myocardial depression[38] associated with critical illness.

NEUROLOGIC DYSFUNCTION

Abnormalities of both central and peripheral nervous system function are common in critical illness. CNS dysfunction occurs in as many as 70% of critically ill patients, typically presenting as a reduced level of consciousness without localizing signs. Its pathophysiology is incompletely understood. Postulated mechanisms include the direct effects of proinflammatory mediators on cerebral function, the development of vasogenic cerebral edema, areas of cerebral infarction related to hypotension, and alterations in the blood-brain barrier resulting in changes in the composition of the interstitial fluid.[39] Electroencephalography typically shows one of four patterns indicating increasingly abnormal activity: diffuse theta wave rhythms, intermittent rhythmic delta waves, triphasic delta waves, and suppression or burst-suppression patterns.[39]

Peripheral nervous system dysfunction, also known as critical illness polyneuropathy, is also common in MODS, though its clinical presentation tends to be more subtle than that of CNS dysfunction.[40-42] Peripheral nervous system dysfunction may present as failure of weaning from mechanical ventilation[43] or as limb weakness with relative sparing of the cranial nerves. Endoneural edema and axonal hypoxia[44] contribute to its pathogenesis, as do the iatrogenic sequelae of neuromuscular blockade.[45]

HEMATOLOGIC DYSFUNCTION

The most common hematologic abnormality of critical illness is thrombocytopenia, which occurs in approximately 20% of all ICU admissions.[46,47] Causes include increased consumption, intravascular sequestration, and impaired thrombopoiesis secondary to suppression of bone marrow function. In addition, heparin-induced thrombocytopenia resulting from antibodies to complexes of heparin and platelet factor 4 develops in as many as 10% of patients receiving heparin.[48] The most fulminant expression of hematologic dysfunction in MODS is DIC, which is characterized by derangements in platelet numbers and clotting times and the presence of fibrin degradation products in plasma.[49] The coagulopathy of critical illness is complex, involving multiple alterations in the biochemical mediators of coagulation and resulting in a shift to a procoagulant state.[50]

Mild anemia is common in critical illness, though the nature of abnormalities in red cell production and removal are less well characterized in this setting.[51] Transient leukopenia may develop in response to an overwhelming inflammatory stimulus, but neutrophilia is much more commonly encountered; total lymphocyte counts are reduced. Abnormalities in white cell populations reflect, at least in part, altered expression of apoptosis, which is inhibited in the neutrophil[52] but accelerated in lymphoid cells.[53]

GASTROINTESTINAL DYSFUNCTION

Upper GI hemorrhage after burn injury was first described by Curling in 1842.[54] Stress bleeding was once a relatively common complication, but improved techniques of resuscitation and hemodynamic support, earlier diagnosis of infection, and the widespread use of stress ulcer prophylaxis have reduced the frequency of this event, to the point where it now is seen in fewer than 4% of ICU admissions.[55] Other manifestations of GI dysfunction in MODS include ileus and intolerance of enteral feeding,[56,57] pancreatitis,[58] and acalculous cholecystitis.[59]

OTHER ORGAN SYSTEM DYSFUNCTION

MODS is associated with functional abnormalities of virtually every organ system. Endocrine abnormalities include impaired glucose regulation with hyperglycemia and insulin resistance[60] and hypercortisolemia with impaired responsiveness to adrenocorticotropic hormone (ACTH) stimulation.[61,62] The sick euthyroid syndrome, characterized by reductions in serum T_3, with or without an increase in reverse T_3 levels and a normal T_4 level, is another manifestation of the endocrine dysfunction of MODS.[63]

Numerous derangements of immune function have been described in MODS patients. Cell-mediated immunity is impaired, as reflected by anergy to delayed hypersensitivity recall skin testing[64] and impaired in vitro lymphocyte proliferative responses.[65] The development of ICU-acquired infections caused by organisms of low intrinsic virulence can also be considered a manifestation of impaired immunity in MODS.[66]

Abnormal wound healing also occurs in MODS. Common manifestations of impaired wound healing are the failure of an open wound to develop satisfactory granulation tissue and the development of decubitus ulcers.[67]

Quantification of Organ Dysfunction

Physiologic instability is the major indication for ICU admission, and support of failing organ function is the ICU's raison d'être. The degree of physiologic derangement present at the time of ICU admission is a potent determinant of ICU survival,[68,69] and irreversible organ dysfunction is the preeminent

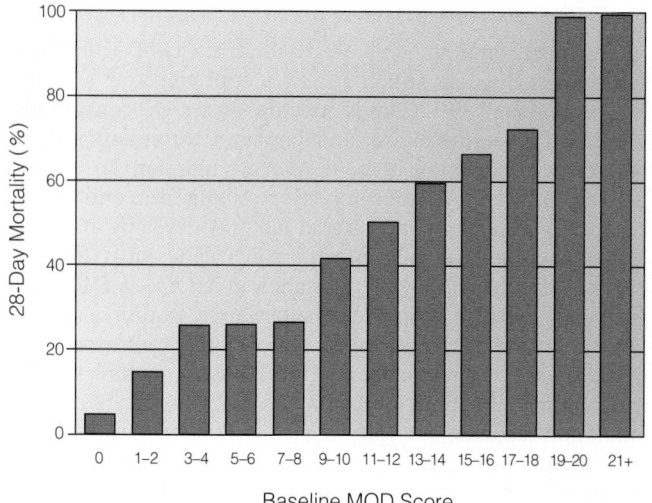

Figure 1 **Increasing severity of organ dysfunction is directly correlated with increasing ICU mortality.**

mode of ICU death.[6,70] Formal quantification of the severity of physiologic derangement or of the evolution of organ dysfunction over time is not generally incorporated into individual patient care in the ICU. However, validated scoring systems have proved invaluable in describing patient populations, stratifying patients for entry into clinical trials, and assessing ICU morbidity in patient groups.

There are a number of published systems for quantifying the severity of organ dysfunction in the critically ill.[9,10,12.66,71-74] These systems are all structurally similar, evaluating dysfunction in each of six or seven organ systems on a numerical scale in which more points are assigned for greater degrees of physiologic severity; they vary primarily with respect to the variables used to describe dysfunction. A representative example of such a scoring system is the Multiple Organ Dysfunction (MOD) score [see Table 2].[9]

The numerical scores can be obtained and applied in a variety of ways.[75] Scores can be calculated on the day of ICU admission or at the start of the institution of a novel therapy during the ICU stay; such scores provide a measure of baseline illness severity and correlate in a graded manner with the risk of ICU mortality [see Figure 1]. Scores can also be calculated daily, allowing the clinician to track net clinical improvement or deterioration over time[76] and to assess the progression or resolution of organ dysfunction (expressed as the area under the curve for the daily

scores).[77] Alternatively, the aggregate severity of organ dysfunction over time can be quantified by summing the worst values over time in each of the component systems. Such an approach permits quantitation of attributable ICU morbidity as the difference between the aggregate score and the score at baseline—thus identifying that component of ICU morbidity that can be prevented by an effective ICU intervention. Finally, morbidity and mortality can be combined into a single value by using a mortality-adjusted score that assigns a maximum number of points plus 1 to any patient who dies [see Table 3].

Prevention of Organ Dysfunction in Critically Ill Patients

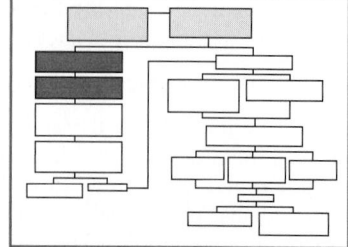

Acute organ dysfunction is the most common indication for admission to an ICU, and any patient with significant physiologic instability is at risk for MODS. A number of risk factors for the development of organ dysfunction have been identified [see Table 1]: these reflect a common pathogenesis for the syndrome through the activation of an innate immune response to tissue injury.

The first priority for optimal ICU care is to halt the progression of existing organ dysfunction while preventing the development of new organ dysfunction. Prevention of organ dysfunction is perhaps best approached from the perspective of optimization of hemodynamic, metabolic, and immune homeostasis. There are a number of interventions for which level 1 evidence of efficacy in reducing mortality or preventing organ dysfunction exists [see Table 4].

OPTIMIZING HEMODYNAMIC HOMEOSTASIS

The ability of the heart to pump blood is determined by (1) the preload delivered to the right atrium, (2) the intrinsic contractility of the myocardium, and (3) the afterload against which the heart must work—all of which may be deranged in critical illness. First, reduction of intravascular volume as a consequence of hemorrhage, third-space loss, and increased microvascular permeability reduces preload. Second, circulating mediators and NO depress myocardial contractility and thus impair the heart's intrinsic pumping ability. Third, reduced vascular tone, mediated by NO, reduces afterload. The first two abnormalities reduce cardiac output; the third increases it but may, by altering resistance gradients

Table 3 Approaches to Measuring Severity of MODS[75]

Objective	Approach	Uses
To quantify baseline severity of organ dysfunction	Calculate organ dysfunction score on day of admission (admission MODS)	To establish baseline severity (e.g., for entry criteria for a clinical trial) or to ensure comparability of study groups
To quantify severity of organ dysfunction at point in time	Calculate score on particular ICU day (daily MODS)	To determine intensity of resource utilization or evolution or resolution of organ dysfunction at discrete point in time
To measure aggregate severity of organ dysfunction over ICU stay	Sum individual worst scores for each organ system over defined time interval (aggregate MODS)	To determine severity of physiologic derangement over defined time interval (e.g., ICU stay)
To quantify new organ dysfunction arising after ICU admission	Calculate difference between aggregate and admission scores (delta MODS)	To measure organ dysfunction attributable to events occurring after ICU admission
To provide combined measure of morbidity and mortality	Adjust aggregate score so that all patients dying receive maximal number of points (mortality-adjusted MODS)	To create single measure that integrates impact of morbidity in survivors and mortality for nonsurvivors

Table 4   ICU Interventions That Reduce Mortality or Attenuate Organ Dysfunction

Objective	Intervention
Resuscitation	Early goal-directed resuscitation[243]
Prophylaxis	Selective digestive tract decontamination[90]
ICU support	Restrictive transfusion strategy[107] Low tidal volume ventilation[22] Daily wakening[144] Tight glucose control[60] Enteral feeding[86]
Mediator-targeted therapy	Activated protein C[146] Corticosteroids[148] Antibody to TNF[244]

in the microvasculature, alter nutrient flow to the tissues.

The first priority in supporting cardiovascular homeostasis, therefore, is to restore intravascular volume by administering fluids. There is no convincing evidence that any particular resuscitation fluid is superior in all patients, though crystalloid is associated with a lower mortality in trauma patients.[78] Either normal saline or lactated Ringer solution is an appropriate choice. The volume of fluid needed to restore optimal preload may be significant, reflecting not only acute losses but also the effective expansion of the vascular compartment because of vasodilatation and the loss of fluids into the extravascular compartment because of increased capillary permeability. Blood loss should be corrected by transfusing red cells, preferably in fresh, leukocyte-depleted blood. When hypotension is refractory to fluid administration, vasoactive agents, including vasopressors (e.g., dopamine and norepinephrine) and inotropes (e.g., dobutamine, epinephrine, and amrinone) may help increase blood flow to the tissues.[79]

Given that the goal of hemodynamic stabilization is to support organ function rather than to restore physiologic or biochemical normalcy, the best measures of the success of resuscitation are those that reflect either return of function (in particular, urine output) or adequate blood flow to the tissues (e.g., $S_{mv}O_2$ or lactate concentration). Each of these measures, however, has shortcomings of which the clinician must be aware. Urine output may be decreased because of intrinsic renal damage even in the face of adequate renal flow. $S_{mv}O_2$ may be artefactually high because of shunting and abnormalities of oxygen uptake in the microvasculature. Lactate concentration is relatively insensitive to mild degrees of inadequate oxygen delivery and may be elevated in patients with liver disease.

Gastric production of CO_2 as measured with a gastric tonometer has been proposed as a means of evaluating splanchnic blood flow, but the benefits of tonometry in improving outcome are unproven.[80] Microvascular flow can also be directly visualized in the tongue or another exposed mucosal surface by using orthogonal polarization spectral imaging.[81] Neither of these approaches has been widely used to guide resuscitation.

Blood pressure is widely used as an index of the initial adequacy of resuscitation, but pressure measurements may not reliably reflect flow in the microvasculature, particularly when systemic vascular resistance is low. Measurement of central venous or pulmonary capillary wedge pressures provides an estimate of the preload to the heart, though factors such as positive pressure ventilation, the extent of capillary leakage in the lungs, and

intrinsic myocardial dysfunction can all alter the pressure at which optimal preload is obtained.

In practice, resuscitation should be titrated to optimize the balance between several parameters rather than targeting any one parameter. It is sobering to recognize that current sophisticated approaches to resuscitation using the pulmonary arterial catheter have not been shown to yield net clinical benefit and may, in fact, cause harm.[82]

Hemodynamic resuscitation is most effective when it is early and rapid. A randomized trial of goal-directed therapy for sepsis, which employed a protocol comprising fluid administration, transfusion, and vasoactive support titrated to $S_{mv}O_2$ as measured from the superior vena cava through a central venous catheter, found that mortality was reduced from 46.5% to 30.5% when patients were resuscitated according to protocol in the emergency department within hours of their initial presentation. On the other hand, studies of goal-directed therapy initiated in the ICU have generally failed to demonstrate any evidence of benefit.[83,84]

Optimization of oxygen delivery presupposes the ability to oxygenate blood adequately in the lungs. Increased pulmonary capillary permeability, atelectasis, altered consciousness, and intrinsic lung disease can all reduce oxygen uptake in acutely ill patients. Support can be provided through the administration of oxygen to the spontaneously breathing patient, through the use of positive pressure ventilation by mask, or through endotracheal intubation and mechanical ventilation. Positive pressure ventilation can cause further lung injury, however, particularly when the lung has been rendered vulnerable by early acute lung injury. Limiting tidal volume during mechanical ventilation to 6 ml/kg has been shown to improve survival in patients with early ARDS.[22]

OPTIMIZING METABOLIC HOMEOSTASIS

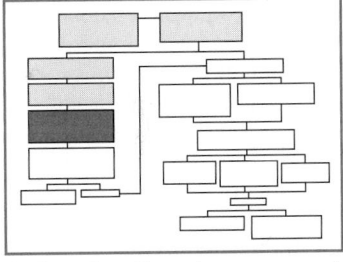

The acute response to stress and injury is a complex, coordinated process characterized by increases in levels of catecholamines, glucocorticoids, antidiuretic hormone, and hormones that regulate intermediary metabolism, including insulin, glucagon, and growth hormone.[6] The activation of this response results in a predictable series of metabolic alterations, including retention of salt and water, increased production of glucose, enhanced lipolysis, increased protein catabolism, and an altered pattern of hepatic protein synthesis known as the acute-phase response, characterized by increased synthesis of C-reactive protein, alpha$_1$-antitrypsin, and fibrinogen and reduced synthesis of albumin.

Metabolic prophylaxis of MODS is directed toward reversal of the stimuli responsible for the catabolic hormonal milieu and toward the provision of adequate biochemical substrate at a time of increased metabolic demand. Early definitive surgical therapy in the form of debridement of devitalized tissue, burn wound excision and grafting, and rigid fixation of long bone fractures can attenuate the postinjury hypermetabolic state and minimize the subsequent development of MODS, though the benefits of early definitive therapy must be weighed against the additional stress of blood loss and hemodynamic instability. In the face of overwhelming injury, a policy of damage control to permit stabilization of the patient in the ICU is associated with an improved clinical outcome.[85]

Nutritional support should be provided by the enteral route if possible [*see 137 Nutritional Support*]. Enteral nutrition is feasible in most patients, particularly if feedings are initiated early. The administration of even small quantities of enteral nutrition is considered advisable, even if it must be supplemented by some degree of parenteral nutrition. There is increasing evidence that immunologically enhanced enteral formulas can yield better clinical outcomes than standard enteral formulas.[86]

Close regulation of glucose levels in accordance with an intensive policy of monitoring and insulin administration has been shown to improve clinical outcome.[60] On the other hand, there is no evidence that administration of growth hormone offers any significant benefit.[87]

OPTIMIZING IMMUNOLOGIC HOMEOSTASIS

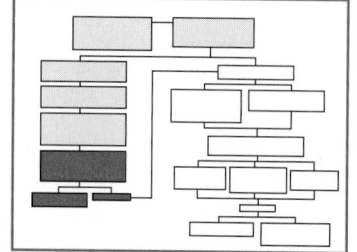

Infection is an important risk factor for MODS, but the converse is equally true: patients with MODS are at significantly increased risk for infection. This risk arises as a consequence both of impairment of normal host defense mechanisms and of colonization with potentially infectious nosocomial pathogens [*see 131 Nosocomial Infection*].

Of the numerous derangements of normal immune function with which critical illness is associated, impairment of mucosal defenses is probably the most important (and certainly the most preventable). Mucosal defenses are breached by surgical incisions and by invasive devices, including intravascular catheters, urinary catheters, and endotracheal and nasogastric tubes. Limiting the number of such devices in use and paying rigorous attention to their insertion and maintenance are important for minimizing nosocomial infection rates.[88] Gastric acid plays a primary role in maintaining the relative sterility of the stomach. Antacids ablate this defense and are a recognized risk factor for nosocomial pneumonia; they should not be used for stress ulcer prophylaxis. The declining incidence of clinically significant stress bleeding in the contemporary ICU suggests that prophylaxis should be limited to patients who are at increased risk for stress ulceration.[55] Cytoprotective agents (e.g., sucralfate) appear to have no significant advantages over H_2 receptor antagonists in reducing the risk of ventilator-associated pneumonia and are less efficacious in preventing bleeding[89]; accordingly, H_2 receptor antagonists appear to be the prophylactic agents of choice.

An alternative strategy for preventing pathologic gut colonization and nosocomial infection involves prophylactic administration of a combination of systemic antibiotics (e.g., cefotaxime) and topical nonabsorbed antibiotics (e.g., tobramycin, polymyxin, and amphotericin B). This approach, known as selective decontamination of the digestive tract (SDD), has proved effective in reducing nosocomial infection rates and even ICU mortality[90]; the effect is particularly evident in surgical patients who receive both systemic and topical therapy.[91]

Enteral feeding is beneficial in preventing nosocomial infection. Systemic antibiotics suppress the indigenous flora of mucosal surfaces, promoting pathologic colonization with resistant organisms.[92] Therefore, use of antimicrobial agents in critically ill patients must be selective and targeted, and the use of broad-spectrum empirical therapy should be minimized by regular reviews of culture and sensitivity results and restrictions on antibiotic prescription practices.

Although nosocomial infections in critically ill patients usually arise from endogenous reservoirs, pathogens may also spread from patient to patient and from environment to patient. Certain organisms—in particular, *Acinetobacter*, *Xanthomonas*, and *Legionella*—are transmitted through aqueous sources in the ICU, and the isolation of these organisms from a critically ill patient is evidence of a potential problem in environmental infection control. Hand washing is an important but underutilized mode of infection prevention in the ICU [*see 5 Prevention of Postoperative Infection*]. There is no clear evidence that protective isolation of critically ill patients warrants the increased costs and increased demands on nursing staff.

The role of immunomodulation in the prophylaxis of MODS remains undefined. At present, there is no defined role for chemoprophylaxis of MODS beyond the specific effects of drugs such as heparin (prevention of deep vein thrombosis [DVT]) and H_2 receptor antagonists (prevention of upper GI bleeding).

Evaluation of the Patient with Organ Dysfunction

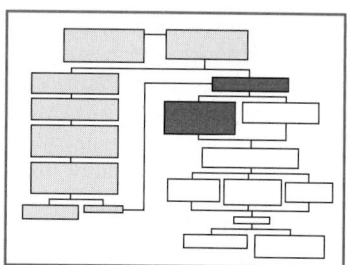

SINGLE ORGAN DYSFUNCTION

Single organ dysfunction suggests local disease and should trigger a search for potentially correctable causes in the organ system involved. Isolated organ dysfunction may reflect preexisting chronic disease or a local problem such as fluid overload, atelectasis, biliary tract obstruction, or elevated intracranial pressure. Complications related to invasive devices or the adverse effects of medications are common causes of single organ dysfunction; the diagnosis is often presumptive, established on the basis of clinical improvement after discontinuance of the agent or removal of the device. Finally, single organ dysfunction may indicate acute disease in the involved organ, such as myocardial infarction, pulmonary embolism, or bone marrow suppression.

Acute respiratory dysfunction, for example, may be caused by pneumonia, atelectasis, pleural effusion, pneumothorax, or pulmonary embolism. Central venous and pulmonary arterial catheters may induce tachyarrhythmias as a result of mechanical irritation of the conducting system. Isolated renal dysfunction may be a consequence of abdominal compartment syndrome or of the nephrotoxic effects of medications (e.g., acute tubular necrosis caused by aminoglycosides and interstitial nephritis caused by penicillins and cephalosporins). Occasionally, renal dysfunction arises from a postrenal cause, such as blockage of a Foley catheter.

Medications are important causes of liver dysfunction in the critically ill patient. Erythromycin, ketoconazole, and haloperidol, for example, can induce cholestatic liver injury. Thrombocytopenia is an important adverse effect of a number of medications, including heparin flushes to maintain the patency of arterial lines. A decreased level of consciousness is usually the result of the poorly characterized metabolic encephalopathy of critical illness; however, it is necessary to rule out local causes such as meningitis, encephalitis, brain abscess, and subdural hematoma. Excessive or prolonged use of narcotics or sedative-hypnotics may lead to sustained alterations in level of consciousness, particularly when hepatic or renal function is impaired. Nondepolarizing muscle relaxants (e.g., vecuronium) may cause prolonged neuromuscular blockade and peripheral neuropathy.[45]

MULTIPLE ORGAN DYSFUNCTION

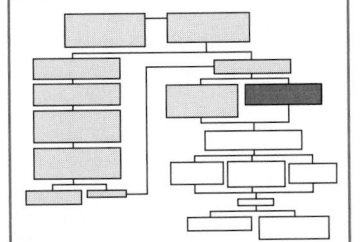

Although it has been suggested that there is a characteristic temporal sequence in the development of MODS [*see Table 5*],[3,9] the clinical course tends to be variable and depends in part on the criteria used to define organ system dysfunction (see above). The specific pattern of dysfunction is much less important than the course of the evolving syndrome. Resolution of dysfunction suggests an appropriate response to specific and supportive therapy. Worsening of dysfunction, on the other hand, should prompt a search for potentially correctable causes and a reevaluation of the methods of supportive care in use. Not infrequently, a treatable cause of evolving MODS is found; often, however, no cause is evident. When no specific cause of the deterioration can be identified, therapy should focus on optimizing supportive measures to limit iatrogenic injury either until the patient recovers or, alternatively, until a considered decision is made that continuing active care is futile.

Search for Correctable Causes

Occult infection Uncontrolled infection, particularly infection arising within the abdomen, is an important risk factor for MODS.[2,3,93] The development of otherwise unexplained organ dysfunction should trigger a careful radiologic search for an occult intra-abdominal focus.[94] However, MODS also develops in patients with pneumonia[58] and other life-threatening infections, and it sometimes evolves in patients in whom no infectious focus can be identified.[66,95]

When MODS develops in the postoperative period, a careful search for infection must be undertaken, concentrating in particular on the operative site and on any invasive devices used. With appropriate attention to the clinical possibilities, aided by ultrasonography and CT scanning, the presence or absence of significant intra-abdominal pathology can usually be established. Local wound exploration may suggest the possibility of occult intra-abdominal infection through the demonstration of impaired wound healing or fascial dehiscence or through the isolation of typical intestinal microflora from a wound infection. The diagnosis of pneumonia in intubated ICU patients is notoriously difficult; however, the use of quantitative techniques (e.g., protected specimen brush bronchoscopy and bronchoalveolar lavage) can aid in establishing or excluding the diagnosis.[96,97]

MODS is rarely caused by urinary tract infections or device-related bacteremias, though these conditions are common in patients with significant organ dysfunction. *Clostridium difficile* colitis or disseminated fungal infection may also present as deteriorating organ function in critically ill patients.[98]

Iatrogenic factors MODS can be considered the quintessential iatrogenic disorder, reflecting both the successes and the failures of contemporary ICU practice. On one hand, the syndrome arose only because the supportive care available today permits the prolonged survival of critically ill patients who, in an earlier era, would have died rapidly; on the other hand, potentially avoidable iatrogenic factors contribute prominently to the evolution of MODS.

Technical or judgmental errors often set the stage for MODS.[99-101] Whenever a patient manifests unexplained organ failure in the postoperative period, the surgeon must consider the possibility of an iatrogenic complication—for example, a missed intestinal perforation in a trauma victim, a leak from a tenuous anastomosis, or left colon ischemia after aneurysmectomy.

Many of the therapeutic interventions that are the mainstay of ICU care have the potential to cause local and remote organ injury. In the experimental setting, mechanical ventilation with high tidal volumes and low levels of positive end-expiratory pressure (PEEP) can induce both pulmonary injury and remote organ injury.[102,103] In a multicenter, randomized, controlled trial, it was confirmed that mechanical ventilation of patients with acute lung injury in accordance with a lung-protective strategy (i.e., a tidal volume of 6 ml/kg) significantly improves survival[22] and attenuates the local and systemic release of proinflammatory mediators [*see 121 Mechanical Ventilation*].[16] Oxygen in high concentrations can produce pulmonary damage, probably as a result of the generation of toxic oxygen intermediates.[104]

Blood transfusion has been implicated in the development of organ dysfunction, an effect that occurs independent of the effects of shock, blood loss, and fluid resuscitation.[105,106] A multicenter, randomized, controlled trial demonstrated a significant reduction in the severity of new organ dysfunction in a heterogeneous population of critically ill patients when transfusion was withheld unless the hemoglobin concentration was less than 70 g/L (7 g/dl).[107] The age of the blood administered may be an underappreciated factor in defining optimal transfusion strategies. The effects of blood transfusion on splanchnic blood flow as measured with a gastric tonometer are significantly dependent on the age of the transfused blood. Transfusion of blood that is more than 12 days old can have an adverse impact on oxygen delivery.[108]

TPN can also contribute to the de novo development of organ dysfunction. TPN-associated alterations in hepatic function with intrahepatic cholestasis and fatty infiltration are relatively common and are manifested by elevated aminotransferase and alkaline phosphatase levels.[109] TPN may also give rise to glucose intolerance and can aggravate ventilatory impairment through increased CO_2 production. In patients with borderline pulmonary function, this additional CO_2 production may prevent weaning from ventilatory support.[110] Parenteral nutrition is also associated with higher rates of postoperative and nosocomial infections after multiple trauma.[111]

Medications—in particular, analgesics, sedatives, and antibiotics—have also been associated with evolving organ dysfunction.

Table 5 Temporal Evolution of MODS[3,9]

System	Time from ICU Admission to Onset of Significant Dysfunction (days)
Respiratory	1–2
Hematologic	3
Central nervous	4
Cardiovascular	4
Hepatic	5–6
Renal	4–11
Gastrointestinal	10–14

Support of Patients with Established Organ Dysfunction

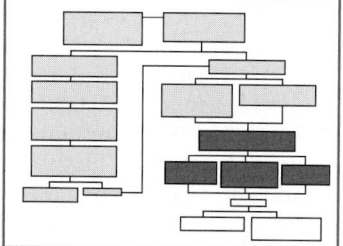

The fundamental challenge in providing intensive supportive care to patients with established organ dysfunction is how to support physiologic function while minimizing new iatrogenic organ dysfunction. As more is understood about the consequences of various treatment strategies, it is increasingly apparent that optimizing function is not synonymous with maximizing function and that the clinician must be acutely aware of the potential for causing more harm than good.

VENTILATORY SUPPORT

Although ventilatory support is generally provided by endotracheal intubation and mechanical ventilation, noninvasive positive pressure ventilation may be appropriate for patients with milder degrees of respiratory failure. A small randomized trial of patients with cardiogenic pulmonary edema found that when compared with conventional administration of oxygen by mask, noninvasive positive pressure ventilation shortened the time to resolution of respiratory failure and reduced the need for subsequent endotracheal intubation.[112] Whether this approach is useful in patients with early ARDS is less clear, however; it may be associated with a higher risk of complications.[113]

Endotracheal intubation and positive pressure ventilation constitute the mainstay of support for critically ill patients with respiratory failure. In unstable patients, it is best to use a controlled ventilatory mode (e.g., pressure control ventilation) rather than a spontaneous breathing mode (e.g., pressure support ventilation). Oxygenation can be optimized through the use of PEEP, a maneuver that may also decrease the accumulation of interstitial fluid and minimize ventilator-associated lung injury.[114] Ventilation with large tidal volumes and high peak inspiratory pressures contributes to lung injury, and it has been shown that the survival of ARDS patients can be improved by using low tidal volumes (~ 6 ml/kg).[22] Pressure-controlled ventilatory techniques limit peak airway pressures to a maximum predetermined level, optimizing gas exchange by inverting the inspiration-to-expiration ratio (I/E) from its normal value of 1:2 to 1:1 or higher and by changing the shape of the inspiratory flow curve (normally square) to one in which flow initially is rapid, then decelerates [*see 121 Mechanical Ventilation*].[115] Although oxygenation can be maintained with low tidal volumes, ventilation is jeopardized, with the result that CO_2 levels rise (so-called permissive hypercapnia).[116] Hypercapnia per se does not appear to be deleterious[117]; indeed, animal studies suggest that increased levels of CO_2 may be independently beneficial to critically ill patients.[118] For patients with refractory hypoxemia, high-frequency oscillation appears to be a promising ventilatory mode.[119,120]

Inhaled NO is selectively delivered to ventilated lung segments and may effect early improvement of oxygenation in ARDS patients[121]; whether this early physiologic effect translates into an improved clinical outcome is unknown. Extracorporeal lung support by means of extracorporeal membrane oxygenation or extracorporeal CO_2 removal can be lifesaving in patients with isolated severe respiratory failure that is refractory to other forms of respiratory support.[122,123] These techniques are resource intensive, however, and have not been convincingly shown to yield better outcomes than conventional mechanical ventilation.[124] If the patient remains hypoxemic despite optimization of ventilatory support, it may be necessary to accept an arterial oxygen saturation (S_aO_2) as low as 80%.

CARDIOVASCULAR SUPPORT

Tissue oxygen delivery ($\dot{D}O_2$) is a function of three variables—cardiac output, hemoglobin concentration, and S_aO_2 (oxygen dissolved in the plasma makes only a negligible contribution). Tissue oxygen consumption ($\dot{V}O_2$) is a function of cardiac output and oxygen extraction (defined as the difference between arterial and venous oxygen content). In practice, multiple factors can impair oxygen delivery and consumption, and it is important that the clinician recognize these.

Oxygen uptake in the tissues is an entirely passive process, resulting from the diffusion of oxygen toward the relatively hypoxic extravascular space along an oxygen saturation gradient that is highest in the microvasculature and lowest at the cell. This passive diffusion can be reduced if there is interstitial edema, which makes the concentration gradient less steep, or if blood flow through the microvasculature is rapid. Alternatively, a reduction in the resistance of small arterioles may impede the diversion of blood into the microvasculature. Moreover, nutrient vessels in the microcirculation may be occluded by aggregates of neutrophils, platelets, and aged (and thus less deformable) red blood cells. The net result of these abnormalities is the shunting of oxygenated blood from the arterial side of the circulation to the venous side. This phenomenon is readily detected through measurement of $S_{mv}O_2$, which is about 70% in normal persons but typically is much higher in patients with sepsis and organ dysfunction.

Paradoxically, each of the interventions commonly used to increase tissue oxygen delivery can also decrease it. Fluid resuscitation can increase cardiac output by increasing preload, but in patients with altered capillary permeability, it can create edema, thereby lengthening the distance across which oxygen must diffuse. Vasopressors can raise cardiac output by increasing peripheral vascular resistance, but at the cost of reducing flow through nutrient vessels in the microcirculation. Inotropes, on the other hand, directly increase cardiac output, albeit at the cost of increased myocardial oxygen consumption, but agents such as dobutamine may lead to further shunting by decreasing peripheral vascular resistance.

Currently, intensive invasive monitoring of critically ill patients with organ dysfunction is employed less frequently than it once was. The benefits of such monitoring remain somewhat uncertain. For example, a 1996 study suggested that the use of a pulmonary arterial catheter was associated with a 24% increase in mortality—not, presumably, because of complications of the catheter itself but rather because the decisions made on the basis of the data provided led to greater harm than benefit.[125] Although this estimate of harm may be exaggerated, there is little countervailing evidence of benefit to justify routine use of pulmonary arterial catheters. A 2003 study of 1,994 high-risk patients undergoing major elective surgery found that Swan-Ganz catheterization and preoperative optimization did not reduce mortality but was associated with a significant increase in the risk of pulmonary embolism.[84]

RENAL SUPPORT

Renal replacement therapy in critically ill patients with MODS serves three functions:

1. Regulation of fluid and electrolytes in patients in whom normal renal function is compromised and altered capillary permeability has led to total body fluid overload with edema.

2. Removal of products of metabolism, medications, and other toxins that the failing kidneys are unable to clear.
3. Removal of circulating mediators of inflammation.

The first two are classic indications for dialysis, though the therapeutic objectives may differ; the third lies more in the realm of promising experimental therapy.

Fluid overload is a common consequence of hemodynamic resuscitation during the early stages of acute illness. It results from increased capillary permeability, peripheral vasodilatation with expansion of the intravascular compartment, and impaired renal function. The use of continuous renal replacement therapies to titrate fluid balance and reduce uremia is conceptually appealing, but the benefits remain unproven. Both individual randomized trials[126,127] and a systematic review[128] failed to show that early and aggressive continuous renal replacement improved clinical outcome. On the other hand, a multicenter randomized trial of more than 400 ICU patients with ARF showed that high-flow ultrafiltration (at a rate of 35 ml/kg/hr or higher) increased survival,[129] and a prospective study demonstrated that daily (as opposed to alternate-day) intermittent hemodialysis improved survival and hastened the resolution of ARF.[130] Another systematic review suggested that imbalances between study groups might have masked a potential benefit of therapy associated with early continuous hemodialysis.[131]

Whether it significantly improves outcome or not, early continuous renal replacement therapy does facilitate early management of the patient with MODS by permitting the removal of fluid, and it is generally better tolerated by hemodynamically unstable patients than is intermittent hemodialysis. Evidence that dialytic therapy can accelerate the clearance of circulating mediators of sepsis is scant.[132]

SUPPORT OF OTHER ORGANS

Enteral nutritional support has been shown to reduce the rate of infectious complications in patients with multiple trauma[111,133] and in those with pancreatitis.[134] A systematic review of 15 randomized trials found that early enteral feeding reduced the infectious complication rate and shortened the ICU stay without affecting mortality.[135] The use of immunologically enhanced enteral formulas appears to be associated with a further reduction in infectious complications, ventilator days, and length of hospital stay.[136] Paralytic ileus makes the provision of enteral feeding more difficult. Erythromycin, which is a motilin secretagogue, can facilitate bedside placement of enteral feeding tubes[137] and accelerate gastric emptying.[138]

Techniques for extracorporeal support of the failing liver have been described, but their use is generally limited to a few centers with a particular interest in liver failure and organ transplantation.[139,140] Unlike primary liver failure, the hepatic dysfunction of MODS does not lead to life-threatening organ system insufficiency and rarely calls for specific support. Hypoalbuminemia is common in MODS, occurring as a consequence of increased vascular permeability, loss through the GI tract, and reduced hepatic synthesis from the activation of an acute-phase response. Although hypoalbuminemia is associated with increased ICU morbidity and mortality, there is no convincing evidence that albumin supplementation improves clinical outcome.[141]

A randomized trial of transfusion strategies in the ICU demonstrated that organ function was improved by a restrictive transfusion policy that withheld transfusion unless the hemoglobin level dropped below 70 g/L,[107] a conclusion supported by a large European multicenter observational study.[142] Benefit is also seen in patients with underlying cardiovascular disease.[143] Thrombocytopenia is corrected by transfusion of platelet concentrates, but this generally is done only if the platelet count drops below 20,000/mm^3. Coagulation factors can be replaced by giving fresh frozen plasma or cryoprecipitate.

Adequate analgesia and sedation are essential components of the care of MODS patients; however, the natural desire to alleviate pain and discomfort can lead to oversedation. A policy of daily awakening can reduce morbidity and shorten the ICU stay.[144]

PHARMACOLOGIC THERAPY TARGETING HOST RESPONSE

Experimental studies implicate an activated inflammatory response in the pathogenesis of MODS. Despite extensive evaluation of a variety of novel strategies to target the host response in sepsis, to date, only two approaches have demonstrated an ability to improve survival.

Activated protein C is an endogenous anticoagulant molecule that inhibits factors V and VIII; in addition to its anticoagulant activities, it exerts significant anti-inflammatory activity.[145] Activated protein C has been produced as a recombinant protein (drotrecogin alfa activated) and has been evaluated in a multicenter randomized trial involving 1,690 patients with severe sepsis. In this trial, treatment resulted in a 6.1% improvement in 28-day survival[146] and a more rapid resolution of cardiovascular, respiratory, and hematologic dysfunction.[147] The benefit appears to be greatest in patients who have more severe illness (reflected in an elevated APACHE II [Acute Physiology and Chronic Health Evaluation II] score or a greater number of dysfunctional organs), community-acquired infection, or coagulopathy.

Critical illness is associated with multiple abnormalities of endocrine function, including reduced responsiveness to endogenous glucocorticoids,[62] a state that predicts an increased risk of ICU mortality.[61] In a 2002 study, administration of pharmacologic doses of corticosteroids (50 mg of hydrocortisone every 6 hours and 50 μg of fludrocortisone) to patients with refractory septic shock and an impaired response to a short-course ACTH stimulation test reduced mortality by 10%.[148] In contrast, earlier studies of high-dose corticosteroids in more heterogeneous groups of patients with sepsis found no evidence of benefit.[149]

Systematic reviews have suggested that neutralization of tumor necrosis factor (TNF) or interleukin-1 (IL-1) can improve outcome in sepsis,[150] but neither of these approaches is clinically available at present. Other anticoagulant or anti-inflammatory strategies have been suggested but remain unproven.

MODS AND ICU-ACQUIRED INFECTION

Infection is a risk factor for organ dysfunction, but the converse is equally true: organ dysfunction is a risk factor for nosocomial infection, with the risk increasing as the severity of organ dysfunction increases.[66] The typical isolates are microbes of low intrinsic pathogenicity, including coagulase-negative *Staphylococcus*, *Enterococcus*, and *Candida* species and gram-negative organisms such as *Pseudomonas* and *Enterobacter*.[151] These organisms commonly colonize the upper GI tract of the critically ill patient,[152] they emerge under antibiotic pressures, and they form colonies on invasive devices—all of which may explain why they emerge as predominant infecting species in this setting. Studies of SDD have demonstrated that preventing such infections reduces ICU morbidity and mortality,[90,153] but there is scant evidence that aggressive antimicrobial therapy to treat suspected nosocomial infection improves outcome. In fact, two reports from 2000 suggested that a more restrictive approach to the prescription of antimicrobial agents reduced mortality and morbidity.[97,154] Worsening organ dysfunction should prompt a careful search for untreated foci of infection, but empirical therapy should be used cautiously; if such therapy is started, it should be discontinued promptly as culture data are obtained. Often, mere removal of a colonized device (e.g., a central line or a urinary catheter) amounts to definitive therapy for these infections.

The association of organ dysfunction with occult intra-abdominal infection[3,94] stimulated a period of enthusiasm for the practice of so-called blind laparotomy—that is, laparotomy undertaken to identify and treat an intra-abdominal infectious focus without radiographic evidence that infection is present.[155,156] The uniformly disappointing results of such intervention,[157] coupled with improvements in diagnostic imaging techniques, led to abandonment of this approach except in certain unusual circumstances (e.g., clinically compelling evidence of a surgically correctable problem, suspicion of visceral ischemia, or the absence of the appropriate imaging facilities). It goes without saying that the classic physical findings of peritonitis—particularly when no abdominal operation has been done—may be the sole indication for surgical exploration. Moreover, in a complicated postoperative patient transferred from another institution because of worsening organ dysfunction, repeat laparotomy may legitimately be considered a component of the admission physical examination.

Outcome

PROGNOSTIC INDICATORS

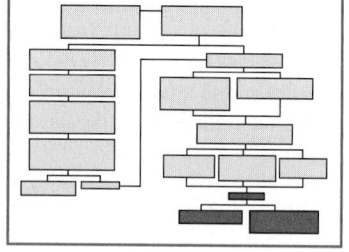

The prognosis of MODS is directly related to the severity of the underlying organ dysfunction, which can be expressed in terms of either the number of failing systems[3,73,158] [see Table 6] or the global severity of dysfunction as determined by an organ dysfunction score [see Figure 1]. It must be emphasized, however, that prognostic indicators reflect the expected outcome of a group of patients and are of limited use in making decisions about the care of an individual patient. Moreover, the prognostic weight of these scales reflects standards of care prevalent at a particular time and in a particular clinical setting. For example, at the time when Ranson's criteria were developed,[159] patients with pancreatitis and six or more

Table 6 Prognosis in MODS

Number of Failing Systems	Mortality (%)
0	3
1	15–30
2	50–60
3	60–100
4	70–100
5	100

positive indicators according to those criteria had a mortality of close to 100%; today, a majority of such patients survive.[93]

Organ dysfunction is potentially recoverable when the factors responsible for the persistence or progression of MODS can be reversed. Identifying these factors, treating them appropriately, and providing optimal physiologic support can prove a daunting challenge, and it is often advisable to consider seeking independent advice or transporting the patient to a center with the clinical expertise and facilities to manage the multidisciplinary problems faced by MODS patients. Given that MODS often evolves as a consequence of medical misadventure, early consultation or referral may be a sound approach from a medicolegal perspective as well. On the other hand, it is a common contemporary ICU scenario that MODS evolves and worsens despite optimal care, necessitating a decision whether to continue or discontinue active care.

WITHDRAWAL OF LIFE SUPPORT

The most common mode of death for a patient with advanced MODS is limitation or withdrawal of life support in the face of a persistent failure to respond to full, aggressive ICU care.[160] The decision to withdraw or withhold life support is a complex one, and there are considerable differences of professional opinion and practice regarding how best to make it.[161] Factors that must be taken into consideration include the nature of the underlying disease, the patient's premorbid health status, the wishes of the patient and the family regarding long-term ICU care, the patient's ultimate prospects for an independent existence, and the presence of active problems amenable to medical therapy. Although end-of-life deliberations may be difficult for medical staff and family alike, careful and realistic consideration of the expectations of all involved can facilitate a decision to discontinue active therapy in a manner that is dignified and humane rather than adversarial.

Discussion

MODS: Evolution of a Syndrome

The first ICU was established in Baltimore in the late 1950s.[162] Its development marked much more than a simple advance in medical technology. The improvements in fluid resuscitation achieved during World War II, followed by the development of techniques of positive pressure mechanical ventilation, hemodialysis, and central venous catheterization over the subsequent decade, had set the stage for an entirely new disease paradigm—that of a disease that arose only in patients who would have died in the absence of resuscitation and exogenous support. The need for that support to sustain life became the metaphor that described this new disorder, originally described as sequential systems failure[163] and now generally known as

MODS.[4] MODS is perhaps the classic instance of the new disease paradigm, in that it develops only in patients who would have died without medical intervention and evolves because of the inadvertent consequences of that intervention.

Earlier reports had described the physiologic failure of discrete organ systems after trauma or acute illness. Stress-related upper GI bleeding was described in 1842[54] and trauma-related renal[23] and hepatic[30] dysfunction during World War II. Description of respiratory failure awaited the widespread use of mechanical ventilators, but a process termed high-output respiratory failure was described in patients with peritonitis in 1963,[13] anticipating the classic description of ARDS 4 years later.[14] In each of these reports, however, the physiologic organ abnormality was viewed as an isolated problem of a single organ, albeit one that could have broader secondary consequences. The suggestion by Baue[1] in 1975 that each organ abnormality was simply the local manifestation of a systemic process set the stage for attempts to identify common systemic pathologic processes and hence to develop therapies that were not merely supportive but also targeted fundamental mechanisms in the pathogenesis of MODS. The search for such therapies is, admittedly, still in its infancy. Not only is the disease process complex, but our ability to describe and characterize it is limited as well.

MODS is invariably preceded by evidence of systemic activation of an adaptive host stress response to infection or tissue injury. This response, which includes changes in cardiorespiratory function, increased microvascular permeability, evidence of activation of innate immune mechanisms, and alterations in intermediary metabolism, is termed sepsis when caused by infection and the systemic inflammatory response syndrome (SIRS) when considered independent of cause.[4,164] SIRS is mediated through the release of a complicated network of host-derived mediator molecules (see below). The name notwithstanding, designation of SIRS as a syndrome may be somewhat presumptuous. There is no discrete or invariant pattern of clinical manifestations that identifies patients with activation of this complex response, nor is there convincing evidence that the response is common to all patients who meet the clinical criteria for SIRS.

It has been suggested that it is also possible to define a compensatory anti-inflammatory response syndrome (CARS) or a mixed acute response syndrome (MARS)[165]; however, these "syndromes" are more conceptual entities than they are diseases that can be diagnosed and treated.[166]

Theories of Pathogenesis

Organ dysfunction must ultimately be the consequence of the malfunctioning or death of cells in that organ. Although cellular derangements are readily documented under experimental conditions, it remains largely unknown how these derangements translate into the physiologic changes that define the clinical syndrome. Cellular dysfunction may reflect altered patterns of synthetic function, either because of activation of alternate patterns of gene expression or because of relative cellular oxygen deficiency from defective cellular respiration (so-called cytopathic hypoxia).[167] Mechanisms of fibrosis and repair may alter the normal cellular anatomic relationships and thereby impair function. Finally, cell death may result from mechanical or biochemical injury of sufficient severity to prevent oxidative metabolism and produce anatomic disruption of the cell or necrosis, but it may also occur through the activation of apoptosis (programmed cell death). Each of these abnormalities has been described in patients with sepsis, and each has multiple overlapping causes.

INFECTION AND HOST SEPTIC RESPONSE

The earliest descriptions of MODS emphasized its association with occult infection,[58,94] prompting the hypothesis that organ dysfunction arises through the direct effects of one or more microbial toxins. However, the observations that MODS could also develop in patients with no identifiable focus of infection[95] and that treatment of infection did not necessarily reverse the syndrome[168] suggested that infection may be a cause of organ dysfunction in critical illness but is not necessarily the fundamental mechanism.

Microbial products, independent of bacterial viability, can evoke the clinical features of sepsis. Injection of endotoxin, or lipopolysaccharide (LPS), derived from the cell wall of gram-negative bacteria reproduces the physiologic features of sepsis in human volunteers,[169] with larger doses producing life-threatening organ dysfunction.[170] Moreover, endotoxin can be detected in the circulation of patients at risk for MODS—not only patients with sepsis,[171,172] but also those who have experienced traumatic[173] or thermal injury[174] and those who are undergoing cardiopulmonary bypass or repair of an abdominal aortic aneurysm.[175]

Animal studies, however, have shown that the sequelae of endotoxemia are an indirect consequence of the activation of host innate immunity rather than a direct cytopathic effect of the endotoxin molecule. The C3h HeJ strain of mice arose through a spontaneous mutation of the parental C3h HeN strain, involving an alteration in a single gene product. This defect, later recognized as a point mutation in the gene encoding Toll-like receptor 4 (TLR4),[176] conferred complete resistance to endotoxin lethality in C3h HeJ mice. Studies involving bone marrow irradiation and crossover transplants of bone marrow cells between C3h HeN and C3h HeJ mice showed that endotoxin sensitivity was transferred with bone marrow cells[177] and confirmed that the sequelae of endotoxin challenge arose indirectly, through the activity of marrow-derived cells from the host. Microarray studies have demonstrated that literally hundreds of genes are expressed in macrophages, endothelial cells, and neutrophils after stimulation by LPS.[178,179] The importance of this enormously complex response is underlined by the observation that the lethality of murine endotoxemia can be prevented by neutralizing any one of several dozen of these gene expressions before endotoxin challenge.[145]

Endotoxin interacts with cells of the host innate immune system through TLR4. TLR4 is one of a family of 10 TLRs that have evolved to recognize danger signals in the extracellular environment and to activate cells to mount an appropriate response to a threat.[180] TLRs recognize not only microbial products (e.g., endotoxin) and components of the wall of gram-positive bacteria (e.g., lipoteichoic acid and peptidoglycan) (TLR2) but also bacterial DNA (TLR9) and even heat-shock proteins and structural components of damaged cells (TLR2) [see Table 7]. Thus, the response evoked appears not to be specific for the stimulus that elicited it, just as the clinical syndrome of systemic inflammation and organ dysfunction is not unique to patients with infection but can also be seen in association with other causes of tissue injury.[164,181]

The binding of endotoxin to TLR4 triggers a cascade of intracellular signaling pathways leading to the expression of hundreds of genes whose products mediate innate immunity [see Figure 2]. The resulting alterations in normal patterns of cellular protein synthesis are profound: not only does the initial stimulus trigger a complex response, but the newly synthesized protein products of this response also, in turn, are capable of acting on the cell to induce a further cascade of mediator molecules. Any attempt to classify the mediators involved is inevitably arbitrary and simplistic. It is useful, however, to consider the response as involving (1) early inflammatory mediators (e.g., TNF and IL-1), (2) late inflammatory mediators (e.g., macrophage inhibitory factor and high-mobility group box [HMGB]-1), (3) counterinflammatory and tissue repair mediators (e.g., IL-10 and transforming growth factor [TGF]–β), (4) enzymes involved in the regulation of nonprotein inflammatory mediators (e.g., inducible NO synthase, phospholipase A_2, and platelet-activating factor acetylhydrolase), (5) acute-phase reactants, and (6) cell surface adhesion or signaling molecules (e.g., intercellular adhesion molecule [ICAM]–1 and tissue factor).

Table 7 Toll-like Receptors and Their Ligands

Toll-like Receptor	Ligand(s)
TLR1	*Mycobacterium leprae* lipopeptide, *Borrelia* outer surface protein
TLR2	Peptidoglycan, lipoteichoic acid, bacterial lipoprotein, *Mycoplasma* lipopeptide, zymosan, CMV, *M. leprae* lipopeptide, lipoarabinomannans, injured cells
TLR3	Double-stranded RNA
TLR4	Endotoxin, HSP60, β-glucan, neutrophil elastase
TLR5	Flagellin
TLR6	*Mycoplasma* lipopeptide
TLR7	Imidazoquinolones, guanine ribonucleosides
TLR8	Unknown
TLR9	Bacterial CpG DNA
TLR10	Unknown

Blockade of any of these molecules prevents lethality in mice that are subsequently challenged with endotoxin. None of these mediators, however, is directly cytotoxic. This suggests that the role that these mediators play is to activate effector mechanisms of injury further downstream. The identity of those downstream mechanisms of cellular dysfunction or death is still a matter of speculation, though a number of attractive possibilities have been proposed.

GENETIC FACTORS IN HOST RESPONSE

A Scandinavian population-based study of causes of premature mortality in adoptees revealed that genetic factors play a significant role in the outcome of infection. When one of an adoptee's biologic parents died before the age of 50, the adoptee faced a six-fold increase in the risk of infectious mortality; this increased risk was substantially greater than that associated with premature death from cardiovascular disease or cancer.[182] It is now known that polymorphisms in genes for TLRs and cytokines are common in the general population[183] and are associated with both altered expression of the gene product and enhanced susceptibility to sepsis and organ dysfunction. A mutation in the gene for TLR4 has been associated with a significantly increased risk of gram-negative infection in ICU patients.[184,185] Polymorphisms in the genes for CD14,[186] TNF,[187,188] heat shock protein 70,[189] IL-10,[190] and IL-1 receptor antagonist[191] all have been associated with greater degrees of organ dysfunction and a worse clinical outcome in critical illness.

TISSUE INJURY MEDIATED BY PHAGOCYTIC CELLS OF INNATE IMMUNE SYSTEM

Polymorphonuclear neutrophils and monocytes form the first line of innate host defenses against invading microorganisms and injured tissue. Neutrophils are recruited to the site of tissue invasion or injury by locally released chemokines (e.g., IL-8). They adhere to the endothelium of the microvasculature through the interaction of the neutrophil adhesion molecule CD11b with ICAM-1 on the endothelial cell. Adherent neutrophils are then

able to extravasate by degrading the tight junctions between endothelial cells, probably through the action of the neutrophil enzyme elastase; this process can cause injury to the cell as the neutrophil transits.[192] Once localized to the site of challenge, the neutrophil releases a variety of molecules (e.g., proteases and reactive oxygen intermediates) that directly injure microorganisms and host tissue alike. Opsonization of bacteria by immunoglobulin or complement enables the neutrophil to phagocytose and kill invading pathogens. Activated neutrophils have been implicated in the pathogenesis of pulmonary,[193,194] hepatic,[195] GI,[196] and renal[28] injury in experimental models of inflammation. Similarly, though ablation of fixed tissue macrophages increased the number of bacteria isolated from an animal model of peritonitis, it nonetheless reduced the severity of septic symptoms and improved survival.[197]

Other studies have implicated natural killer (NK) cells[198,199] and CD8-positive T cells[200] in the lethality of experimental sepsis, though it is unclear whether lethality is a consequence of direct cellular cytotoxicity or of the activation of other biologic processes by secreted products of these cells.[201]

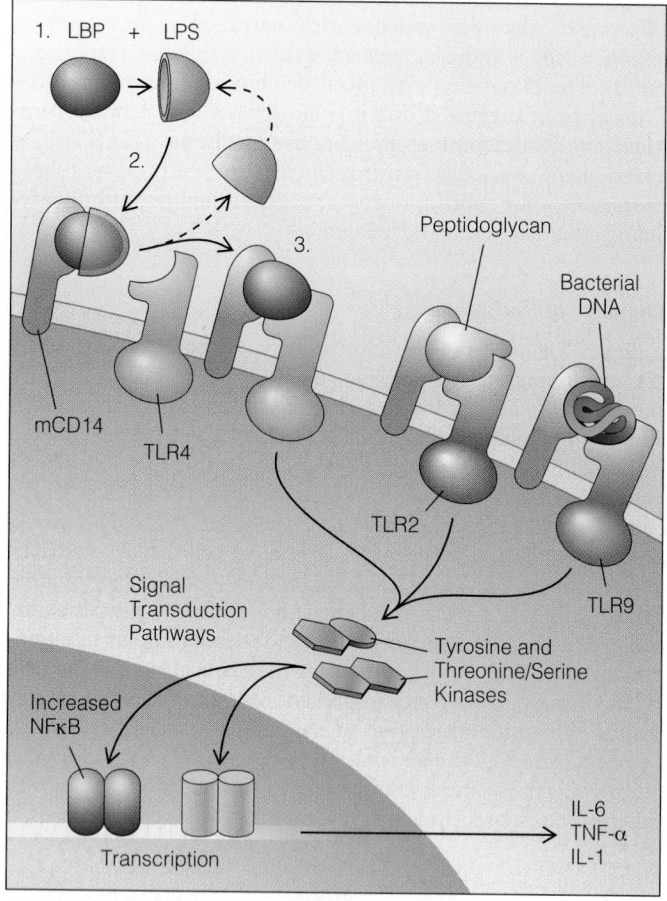

Figure 2 **During lipopolysaccharide (LPS) signaling, (1) LPS binds to LPS-binding protein (LPB). (2) This complex is delivered to membrane-bound CD14 (mCD14). (3) The CD14-LPS complex interacts with Toll-like receptor 4 (TLR4), which initiates the intracellular signal transduction pathway. The signal transduction pathway leads to NFκB translocation into the nucleus, with increased transcription of proinflammatory cytokines. TLR2 is known to signal membrane compounds of gram-positive bacteria such as peptidoglycan. TLR9 recognizes bacterial DNA. (IL—interleukin; NFκB—nuclear factor κB; TNF-α—tumor necrosis factor-α)**

ENDOTHELIAL INJURY

The network of endothelial cells lining the large and small vessels of the vascular tree is enormous, encompassing an area 600 times larger than that of the skin.[202] Far from being a passive conduit for blood cells and plasma, the endothelium contributes actively to the initiation, localization, and resolution of inflammation.[203] Circulating inflammatory mediators evoke an endothelial cell response characterized by upregulation of adhesion molecules such as ICAM-1 and vascular cell adhesion molecule (VCAM), expression of TLR2 and tissue factor, and shedding of endothelial cell thrombomodulin.[203,204] These changes result in neutrophil localization and local activation of coagulation with secondary tissue injury. In addition, healthy endothelial cells appear to play a role in limiting host injury during inflammation, as indicated by the observation that mice with a genetic deletion of syndecan-4 (a proteoglycan involved in endothelial cell adhesion and signaling) exhibit increased mortality and exaggerated release of IL-1 after endotoxin challenge.[205]

Postmortem studies of patients with ARDS show that ICAM-1 is upregulated throughout the lung, whereas VCAM is expressed in larger vessels,[206] and that circulating markers of endothelial activation are present in critically ill patients with organ failure.[207] Moreover, diffuse endothelial injury is suggested by the presence of circulating endothelial cells in the blood of patients in septic shock.[208] Therapeutic strategies that target the adhesive interactions of lymphocytes and endothelial cells have shown promise against inflammatory conditions such as psoriasis and Crohn disease; studies of agents targeting the interaction of neutrophils with endothelial cells have so far yielded disappointing results.[209]

INTRAVASCULAR COAGULATION

Although plasma contains all the factors necessary to induce coagulation and formation of a fibrin clot, intravascular coagulation is limited in healthy persons by the absence of a trigger and the presence of endogenous anticoagulant mechanisms. This balance is disrupted in persons experiencing systemic inflammation, resulting in microvascular coagulation and obstructing oxygen delivery to the cell. Injury and inflammation can upregulate endothelial cell tissue factor expression and activate the coagulation cascade by catalyzing the conversion of factor VII to factor VIIa. Sequential activation of circulating coagulation factors results in the conversion of prothrombin to thrombin and, in turn, the conversion of fibrinogen to fibrin. The activation of coagulation is inhibited by three important endogenous anticoagulant pathways: the protein C pathway, the antithrombin pathway, and the tissue factor pathway inhibitor (TFPI) pathway. Each of these is impaired in critical illness, leading to a net procoagulant state.

Protein C is synthesized in the liver and circulates as an inactive precursor. It is activated in the vascular tree through its interaction with thrombomodulin on the endothelial cell; activated protein C blocks thrombin generation through its inhibitory interactions with factors V and VIII.[210] Hepatic production of protein C is impaired in sepsis. Moreover, shedding of endothelial cell thrombomodulin results in a reduction in the activation of available protein C, whereas acute-phase reactants such as α_1-antitrypsin accelerate its degradation. The importance of this anticoagulant mechanism is underlined by a 2001 study of recombinant activated protein C in patients with severe sepsis, in which treated patients experienced a significant improvement in 28-day survival and those with the greatest degrees of organ dysfunction benefited most.[147]

Antithrombin is a serine protease inhibitor that binds to and inactivates thrombin and inhibits factors IXa, XIa, and XIIa. Levels of circulating antithrombin are reduced in sepsis. Administration of recombinant antithrombin failed to improve survival in a large multicenter study of patients with severe sepsis, though interaction with heparin may have masked a therapeutic effect.[211]

TFPI is synthesized by endothelial cells in response to cytokines and shear stress. It too is a serine protease inhibitor whose target is the complex of tissue factor, factor VIIa, and factor Xa that initiates the coagulation cascade. Recombinant TFPI has been evaluated as a therapy for sepsis; however, a large multicenter trial failed to show any survival benefit from such therapy.[212]

The interactions between coagulation and inflammation are complex. Protein C binds to a receptor expressed on endothelial cells and neutrophils, and prevention of this interaction results in a disseminated inflammatory process.[146] Binding of activated protein C to its receptor in brain endothelium inhibits endothelial cell apoptosis and is neuroprotective during cerebral ischemia.[213]

APOPTOSIS

Apoptosis, or programmed cell death, is a process through which cellular structural elements and DNA are degraded and residual cellular constituents are converted into membrane-bound vesicles (apoptotic bodies) that are cleared by macrophages. Phagocytosis of apoptotic bodies prevents the uncontrolled release of cellular constituents and so prevents an inflammatory response to the injured cell.[214] Apoptosis is also an intrinsically anti-inflammatory process, however, in that phagocytosis of an apoptotic cell by the macrophage evokes the expression of anti-inflammatory genes such as those for TGF-β and IL-10.[215,216] Apoptosis, like cell replication, is a physiologic process that is essential for normal growth and development; either excessive or inadequate apoptosis can produce disease.

Increased rates of apoptosis of colonic epithelial cells and splenic lymphocytes are seen in autopsy specimens from patients dying as a consequence of sepsis or multiple trauma.[217] Conversely, whereas circulating neutrophils survive less than a day in vivo in healthy persons, neutrophils isolated from the blood of patients with sepsis show both phenotypic features of activation and prolonged survival (a consequence of the inhibition of a constitutively expressed apoptotic program).[52] Animal studies have shown that inhibition of lymphoid cell apoptosis improves survival after septic challenge.[218] Conversely, induction of neutrophil apoptosis improved survival in a rodent model of intestinal ischemia-reperfusion injury.[219] The potential role of apoptosis in the pathogenesis of MODS is further suggested by animal studies of ventilator-induced lung injury, which demonstrated that injurious mechanical ventilation strategies can induce renal epithelial cell apoptosis and biochemical evidence of renal dysfunction.[220]

GASTROINTESTINAL DYSHOMEOSTASIS

Because MODS not infrequently evolves despite apparently adequate control of infection or other inciting triggers, it has been suggested that the GI tract may serve as the unseen motor of the pathologic state,[221-224] both as a reservoir of microorganisms and their products and as a mechanism for the evolution of inflammation.

The GI tract of a healthy human being harbors upward of 600 different microbial species, and bacteria outnumber human cells 10 to 1.[225] The composition of the GI flora is stable over a person's lifetime, but intercurrent disease can produce profound changes in bacterial numbers and patterns of colonization. In critically ill surgical patients, the normally sterile proximal GI tract becomes heavily colonized with the same organisms that predominate in nosocomial ICU-acquired infection—*Staphylococcus epidermidis*, *Pseudomonas*, *Candida*, and *Enterococcus*. Colonization is significantly associated with the development of nosocomial infection with the same organism.[152] Extensive studies in animal models have shown that acute insults (e.g., endotoxemia, peritonitis, pneumonia, trauma, burns, biliary tract obstruction, malnutrition, and lack of enteral feeding) can induce bacterial overgrowth in the gut and translocation of enteric bacteria to regional lymph nodes of the peritoneal cavity.[226] Similar stimuli result in translocation in humans,[227,228] and prevention of colonization with topical nonabsorbed antibiotics reduces the incidence of nosocomial infections, including bacteremias.[153] Detection of circulating endotoxin after burns[174] or major vascular surgery[175] suggests that endotoxin is also absorbed from the gut under conditions of altered gut barrier function.

The role of the gut in MODS is not limited to that of a microbial reservoir. The GI tract and adjacent structures constitute the largest aggregation of immune cells in the body. Normal interactions between the indigenous flora and the gut immune system serve to prevent the generation of immune responses to luminal antigens. Loss of these tonic inhibitory interactions may, in turn, contribute to a state of systemically activated inflammation. Accordingly, hemorrhagic shock results in significantly elevated levels of TNF and IL-6 in portal venous blood,[229] and portal endotoxemia replicates systemic features of MODS, such as hypermetabolism,[230] impairment of cell-mediated immunity,[231] and activation of coagulation.[232] Ablation of the hepatic Kupffer cell population has improved survival in animal models of peritonitis.[197] Mesenteric lymph has been shown to contain factors that can evoke inflammatory changes in organs remote from the gut.[233] Thus, dysfunction of normal microbiologic and immunologic homeostasis in the GI tract and the liver results in the gut serving as a secondary source of the stimuli that induce and perpetuate MODS.

A clinically relevant role for the gut in the pathogenesis of MODS is supported by the results of randomized trials of SDD.[153]

Table 8 Characteristics of Linear and Complex Systems[241]

Assumptions of Linear Systems	Assumptions of Complex Systems
Mediators have unique, consistent biologic effects	Mediators have redundant, variable, and context-dependent effects
Antagonism of effect is mediated by specific inhibitor	Antagonism of effect is not attributable to single mediator or process
Biologic processes occur sequentially	Biologic processes occur concurrently
Biologic response is reliably predicted by measurement of responsible mediator	Biologic response is not consistently predicted by measure of single mediator
Modulation of biologic process occurs in dose-dependent fashion; small intervention has small effect	Modulation of process is not predictably dose-dependent; small perturbation may have large effect
Normal behavior of system results in physiologic stability	Normal integrated behavior of system results in physiologic variability or oscillations over time

TWO-HIT HYPOTHESIS

A complementary hypothesis of MODS pathogenesis suggests that an acute insult, such as infection or trauma, primes the host so that a subsequent, relatively trivial, insult produces a markedly exaggerated host response.[234] Such a model would account for the severity of MODS developing late after multiple trauma[181] as well as the substantial morbidity associated with nosocomial infection in the ICU.[151] Studies in animal models have revealed that previous hemorrhagic shock leads to an exaggerated response to subsequent endotoxin challenge.[235]

MODS and Complexity Theory

None of the various theories of pathogenesis described so far is adequate to explain the evolution of the clinical syndrome of MODS. These models are not mutually exclusive; rather, they reflect differing perspectives on a profoundly deranged state of systemic homeostasis—one that has evolved only because the health care team has intervened to subvert an otherwise lethal process. The enormously complicated interactions among multiple predisposing patient factors, a series of physiologic insults, and an endogenous response effected via multiple cell types and many hundreds of biochemical mediators is best modeled by means of complexity theory.[236,237]

According to the precepts of complexity theory, a complex system cannot be understood through isolated analysis of its component parts: it can be understood only through an appreciation of the various interactions of those parts. The result of these multiple interactions is neither a state of anarchy nor a limitless series of unpredictable outcomes but, rather, a series of stable responses known as an emergent order. This stable order is dependent on the interactions of all its parts but is much more than their simple sum. It is characterized both by a resilience to potentially disruptive external influences and by a degree of intrinsic variability. Loss of intrinsic variability is a marker of a failing or diseased system. The healthy human heart exhibits normal variability in rate and rhythm, which is lost in patients with significant congestive heart failure.[238] Loss of intrinsic heart rate and blood pressure variability is also evident in patients with septic shock.[239,240]

The idea that concepts inherent in complex nonlinear systems can be applied to the understanding of MODS is compelling.[241] Clinicians are most familiar with linear models of disease, and the assumptions on which these models are based generally lead to effective clinical responses. For example, diabetes results from the deficiency of a single protein and is treated effectively by replacing that protein; cholangitis is the consequence of obstruction of the bile duct and is treated by relieving that obstruction. For linear diseases such as these, a single abnormality produces the clinical phenotype, and definitive therapy involves correcting that abnormality. Disorders of biologic pathways such as the coagulation cascade represent a somewhat more elaborate variation on the same theme. For example, pathologic coagulation resulting in DVT can be treated by means of a variety of different strategies aimed at disrupting the clotting cascade. Similarly, hypertension can be managed by means of various pharmacologic strategies that modify different aspects of the regulation of vasomotor tone.

Complex disorders such as MODS, however, are not so predictable, and the therapeutic modulation required is much more difficult [*see Table 8*]. The consequences of manipulating a particular mediator may be highly context dependent, varying with the nature of the insult, the predisposition of the host, and the timing of administration.[145] Moreover, intervention carries the potential cost of inadvertent iatrogenic harm. A sobering consequence of high-quality clinical trials performed in the ICU over the past decade has been the realization that making a normal or supranormal physiologic state the therapeutic target in a critically ill patient whose homeostasis is profoundly disrupted may, on occasion, be detrimental rather than beneficial.[22,107,242]

References

1. Baue AE: Multiple, progressive, or sequential systems failure: a syndrome of the 1970s. Arch Surg 110:779, 1975

2. Eiseman B, Beart R, Norton L: Multiple organ failure. Surg Gynecol Obstet 144:323, 1977

3. Fry DE, Pearlstein L, Fulton RL, et al: Multiple system organ failure: the role of uncontrolled infection. Arch Surg 115:136, 1980

4. Bone RC, Balk RA, Cerra FB, et al: ACCP/SCCM Consensus Conference. Definitions for sepsis and organ failure and guidelines for the use of innovative therapies in sepsis. Chest 101:1644, 1992

5. Deitch EA: Multiple organ failure: pathophysiology and potential future therapy. Ann Surg 216:117, 1992

6. Beal AL, Cerra FB: Multiple organ failure syndrome in the 1990's: systemic inflammatory response and organ dysfunction. JAMA 271:226, 1994

7. Moss M, Parsons PE, Steinberg KP, et al: Chronic alcohol abuse is associated with an increased incidence of acute respiratory distress syndrome and severity of multiple organ dysfunction in patients with septic shock. Crit Care Med 31:869, 2003

8. Marshall JC: Multiple organ dysfunction syndrome (MODS). Clinical Trials for the Treatment of Sepsis. Sibbald WJ, Vincent J-L, Eds. Springer-Verlag, Berlin, 1995, p 122

9. Marshall JC, Cook DJ, Christou NV, et al: Multiple organ dysfunction score: a reliable descriptor of a complex clinical outcome. Crit Care Med 23:1638, 1995

10. Bernard G: The Brussels score. Sepsis 1:43, 1997

11. Vincent JL: The sepsis-related organ failure assessment (SOFA) score. Intens Care Med 1996

12. Le Gall JR, Klar J, Lemeshow S, et al: The logistic organ dysfunction system—A new way to assess organ dysfunction in the intensive care unit. JAMA 276:802, 1996

13. Burke JF, Pontoppidan H, Welch CE: High output respiratory failure: an important cause of death ascribed to peritonitis or ileus. Ann Surg 158:581, 1963

14. Ashbaugh DG, Bigelow DB, Petty TL, et al: Acute respiratory distress in adults. Lancet 2:319, 1967

15. Kollef MH, Schuster DP: Medical progress: the acute respiratory distress syndrome. N Engl J Med 332:27, 1995

16. Ranieri VM, Suter PM, Tortorella C, et al: Effect of mechanical ventilation on inflammatory mediators in patients with acute respiratory distress syndrome: a randomized controlled trial. JAMA 282:54, 1999

17. Gattinoni L, Pesenti A, Bombino M: Relationships between lung computed tomographic density, gas exchange, and PEEP in acute respiratory failure. Anesthesiology 69:824, 1988

18. Pinhu L, Whitehead T, Evans T, et al: Ventilator-associated lung injury. Lancet 361:332, 2003

19. Murray JF, Matthay MA, Luce JM, et al: An expanded definition of the adult respiratory distress syndrome. Am Rev Respir Dis 138:720, 1988

20. Bernard GR, Artigas A, Brigham KL, et al: The American-European consensus conference on ARDS. Definitions, mechanisms, relevant outcomes, and clinical trial coordination. Am J Respir Crit Care Med 149:818, 1994

21. Marshall RP, Webb S, Bellingan GJ, et al: Angiotensin converting enzyme insertion/deletion polymorphism is associated with susceptibility and outcome in acute respiratory distress syndrome. Am J Respir Crit Care Med 166:646, 2002

22. Brower RG, Matthay MA, Morris A, et al: Ventilation with lower tidal volumes as compared with traditional tidal volumes for acute lung injury and the acute respiratory distress syndrome. N Engl J Med 342:1301, 2000

23. Bywaters EGL, Beall O: Crush injuries with impairment of renal function. Br Med J 1:427, 1941

24. Morris JA Jr, Mucha P Jr, Ross SE, et al: Acute posttraumatic renal failure: a multicenter perspective. J Trauma 31:1584, 1991

25. Lameire N, Vanholder R: Pathophysiologic features and prevention of human and experimental acute tubular necrosis. J Am Soc Nephrol 12:S20, 2001

26. Tilney NL, Lazarus JM. Acute renal failure in surgical patients: causes, clinical patterns and care. Surg Clin North Am 63:357, 1983

27. Lauriat S, Linas SL: The role of neutrophils in acute renal failure. Semin Nephrol 18:498, 1998

28. Heinzelmann M, Mercer-Jones MA, Passmore JC: Neutrophils and renal failure. Am J Kidney Dis 34:384, 1999

29. Faraco PR, Ledgerwood EC, Smith KGC: Apoptosis and renal disease. Sepsis 2:31, 1998

30. Bywaters EGL: Anatomical changes in the liver after trauma. Clin Sci 6:19, 1946

31. Hawker F. Liver dysfunction in critical illness. Anaesth Intens Care 19:165, 1991

32. Schwartz DB, Bone RC, Balk RA, et al: Hepatic dysfunction in the adult respiratory distress syndrome. Chest 95:871, 1989

33. Langenfeld JE, Machiedo GW, Lyons M, et al: Correlation between red blood cell deformability and changes in hemodynamic function. Surgery 116:859, 1994

34. Parrillo JE, Parker MM, Natanson C, et al: Septic shock in humans. Advances in the understanding of pathogenesis, cardiovascular dysfunction, and therapy. Ann Intern Med 113:227, 1990

35. Vincent JL, Gris P, Coffernils M, et al: Myocardial depression characterizes the fatal course of septic shock. Surgery 111:660, 1992

36. Yien HW, Hseu SS, Lee LC, et al: Spectral analysis of systemic arterial pressure and heart rate signals as a prognostic tool for the prediction of patient outcome in the intensive care unit. Crit Care Med 25:258, 1997

37. Lorente JA, Landin L, Renes E, et al: Role of nitric oxide in the hemodynamic changes of sepsis. Crit Care Med 21:759, 1993

38. Finkel MS, Oddis CV, Jacob TD, et al: Negative inotropic effects of cytokines on the heart mediated by nitric oxide. Science 257:387, 1992

39. Bolton CF, Young GB, Zochodne DW: The neurological complications of sepsis. Ann Neurol 33:94, 1993

40. Bolton CF: Sepsis and the systemic inflammatory response syndrome: Neuromuscular manifestations. Crit Care Med 24:1408, 1996

41. Hund E: Neurological complications of sepsis: critical illness polyneuropathy and myopathy. J Neurol 248:929, 2001

42. de Letter MA, Schmitz PI, Viseer LH, et al: Risk factors for the development of polyneuropathy and myopathy in critically ill patients. Crit Care Med 29:2281, 2001

43. Coronel B, Mercatello A, Couturier JC, et al: Polyneuropathy: potential cause of difficult weaning. Crit Care Med 18:486, 1990

44. Bolton CF: Neuromuscular complications of sepsis. Intensive Care Med 19(suppl 2):S58, 1993

45. Segredo V, Caldwell JE, Matthay MA, et al: Persistent paralysis in critically ill patients after long-term administration of vecuronium. N Engl J Med 327:524, 1992

46. Baughmann RP, Lower EE, Flessa HC, et al: Thrombocytopenia in the intensive care unit. Chest 104:1243, 1993

47. Gando S, Nanzaki S, Kemmotsu O: Disseminated intravascular coagulation and sustained systemic inflammatory response syndrome predict organ dysfunctions after trauma: application of clinical decision analysis. Ann Surg 229:121, 1999

48. Aster RH: Heparin-induced thrombocytopenia and thrombosis. N Engl J Med 332:1374, 1995

49. van der Poll T, de Jonge E, Levi M, et al: Pathogenesis of DIC in sepsis. Sepsis 3:103, 1999

50. Marshall JC: Inflammation, coagulopathy, and the pathogenesis of the multiple organ dysfunction syndrome. Crit Care Med 29(suppl):S106, 2001

51. Todd JC III, Mollitt DL: Effect of sepsis on erythrocyte intracellular calcium homeostasis. Crit Care Med 23:459, 1995

52. Jimenez MF, Watson RWG, Parodo J, et al: Dysregulated expression of neutrophil apoptosis in the systemic inflammatory response syndrome (SIRS). Arch Surg 132:1263, 1997

53. Hotchkiss RS, Tinsley KW, Swanson PE, et al: Sepsis-induced apoptosis causes progressive profound depletion of B and CD4+ T lymphocytes in humans. J Immunol 166:6952, 2001

54. Curling TB: On acute ulceration of the duodenum in cases of burns. Med-Chir Tr London 25:260, 1842

55. Cook DJ, Fuller H, Guyatt GH, et al: Risk factors for gastrointestinal bleeding in critically ill patients. N Engl J Med 330:377, 1994

56. Chang RWS, Jacobs S, Lee B: Gastrointestinal dysfunction among intensive care unit patients. Crit Care Med 15:909, 1987

57. van der Spoel JI, Oudemans-van Straaten HM, Stoutenbeek CP, et al: Neostigmine resolves critical illness-related colonic ileus in intensive care patients with multiple organ failure—a prospective, double-blind, placebo-controlled trial. Intensive Care Med 27:822, 2001

58. Bell RC, Coalson JJ, Smith JD, et al: Multiple organ system failure and infection in adult respiratory distress syndrome. Ann Intern Med 99:293, 1983

59. Glenn F, Becker CG: Acute acalculous cholecystitis: an increasing entity. Ann Surg 195:131, 1982

60. Van den Berghe G, Wouters P, Weekers F, et al: Intensive insulin therapy in the surgical intensive

care unit. N Engl J Med 345:1359, 2001

61. Annane D, Sebille V, Troche G, et al: A 3-level prognostic classification in septic shock based on cortisol levels and cortisol response to corticotropin. JAMA 2834:1038, 2000

62. Cooper MS, Stewart PM: Corticosteroid insufficiency in acutely ill patients. N Engl J Med 348:727, 2003

63. Vasa FR, Molitch ME: Endocrine problems in the chronically critically ill patient. Clin Chest Med 22:193, 2003

64. Christou NV, Meakins JL, Gordon J, et al: The delayed hypersensitivity response and host resistance in surgical patients—20 years later. Ann Surg 222:534, 1995

65. Grbic JT, Mannick JA, Gough DB, et al: The role of prostaglandin E_2 in immune suppression following injury. Ann Surg 214:253, 1991

66. Marshall JC, Christou NV, Horn R, et al: The microbiology of multiple organ failure. The proximal GI tract as an occult reservoir of pathogens. Arch Surg 123:309, 1988

67. Eachempati SR, Hydo LJ, Barie PS: Factors influencing the development of decubitus ulcers in critically ill surgical patients. Crit Care Med 29:1678, 2001

68. Knaus WA, Wagner DP, Lynn J: Short-term mortality predictions for critically ill hospitalized adults: science and ethics. Science 254:389, 1991

69. Lemeshow S, Le Gall JR: Modeling the severity of illness of ICU patients: a systems update. JAMA 272:1049, 1994

70. Vincent JL, De Mendonca A, Cantraine F, et al: Use of the SOFA score to assess the incidence of organ dysfunction/failure in intensive care units: results of a multicenter, prospective study. Crit Care Med 26:1793, 1998

71. Goris RJA, te Boekhorst TPA, Nuytinck JKS, et al: Multiple organ failure. Generalized autodestructive inflammation? Arch Surg 120:1109, 1985

72. Moore FA, Moore EE, Poggetti R, et al: Gut bacterial translocation via the portal vein: a clinical perspective with major torso trauma. J Trauma 31:629, 1991

73. Hebert PC, Drummond AJ, Singer J, et al: A simple multiple system organ failure scoring system predicts mortality of patients who have sepsis syndrome. Chest 104:230, 1993

74. Vincent J-L, Moreno R, Takala J, et al: The SOFA (sepsis-related organ failure assessment) score to describe organ dysfunnction/failure. Intensive Care Med 22:707, 1996

75. Marshall JC: Charting the course of critical illness: prognostication and outcome description in the intensive care unit. Crit Care Med 27:676, 1999

76. Cook RJ, Cook DJ, Tilley J, et al: Multiple organ dysfunction: baseline and serial component scores. Crit Care Med 29:2046, 2001

77. Ferreira FL, Bota DP, Bross A, et al: Serial evaluation of the SOFA score to predict outcome in critically ill patients. JAMA 286:1754, 2001

78. Choi PT, Yip G, Quinonez LG, et al: Crystalloids vs. colloids in fluid resuscitation: a systematic review. Crit Care Med 27:200, 1999

79. Dellinger EP: Cardiovascular management of septic shock. Crit Care Med 31:946, 2003

80. Gomersall CD, Joynt GM, Freebairn RC, et al: Resuscitation of critically ill patients based on the results of gastric tonometry: a prospective, randomized, controlled trial. Crit Care Med 28:607, 2000

81. De Backer D, Creteur J, Preiser JC, et al: Microvascular blood flow is altered in patients with sepsis. Am J Respir Crit Care Med 166:98, 2002

82. Connors AF Jr, Speroff T, Dawson NV, et al: The effectiveness of right heart catheterization in the initial care of critically ill patients. JAMA 276:889, 1996

83. Gattinoni L, Brazzi L, Pelosi P, et al: A trial of goal-oriented hemodynamic therapy in critically ill patients. N Engl J Med 333:1025, 1995

84. Sandham JD, Hull RD, Brant RF, et al: A randomized, controlled trial of the use of pulmonary-artery catheters in high-risk surgical patients. N Engl J Med 348:5, 2003

85. Pape HC, Giannoudis P, Krettek C: The timing of fracture treatment in polytrauma patients: relevance of damage control orthopedic surgery. Am J Surg 183:622, 2002

86. Heyland DK, Novak F, Drover JW, et al: Should immunonutrition become routine in critically ill patients? A systematic review of the evidence. JAMA 286:944, 2001

87. Takala J, Ruokonen E, Webster NR, et al: Increased mortality associated with growth hormone treatment in critically ill adults. N Engl J Med 341:785, 1999

88. Maki DG: Risk factors for nosocomial infection in intensive care: devices vs nature and goals for the next decade. Arch Intern Med 149:30, 1989

89. Cook DJ, Guyatt GH, Marshall JC, et al: A randomized trial of sucralfate versus ranitidine for stress ulcer prophylaxis in critically ill patients. N Engl J Med 338:791, 1998

90. D'Amico R, Pifferi S, Leonetti C, et al: Effectiveness of antibiotic prophylaxis in critically ill adult patients: systematic review of randomized controlled trials. Br Med J 316:1275, 1998

91. Nathens AB, Marshall JC: Selective decontamination of the digestive tract in surgical patients. Arch Surg 134:170, 1999

92. Van Der Waaij D: The ecology of the human intestine and its consequences for overgrowth by pathogens such as *Clostridium difficile*. Annu Rev Microbiol 43:69, 1989

93. Le Mee F, Paye F, Sauvanet A, et al: Incidence and reversibility of organ failure in the course of sterile or infected necrotizing pancreatitis. Arch Surg 136:1386, 2001

94. Polk HC, Shields CL: Remote organ failure: a valid sign of occult intraabdominal infection. Surgery 81:310, 1977

95. Meakins JL, Wicklund B, Forse RA, et al: The surgical intensive care unit: current concepts in infection. Surg Clin North Am 60:117, 1980

96. Heyland DK, Cook DJ, Marshall JC, et al: The clinical utility of invasive diagnostic techniques in the setting of ventilator-associated pneumonia. Chest 115:1076, 1999

97. Fagon J-Y, Chastre J, Wolff M, et al: Invasive and noninvasive strategies for management of suspected ventilator-associated pneumonia: a randomized trial. Ann Intern Med 132:621, 2000

98. Nieto-Rodriguez JA, Kusne S, Mañez R, et al: Factors associated with the development of candidemia and candidemia-related death among liver transplant recipients. Ann Surg 223:70, 1996

99. Henao FJ, Daes JE, Dennis RJ: Risk factors for multiorgan failure: a case control study. J Trauma 31:74, 1991

100. Muckart DJ, Thomson SR: Undetected injuries: a preventable cause of increased morbidity and mortality. Am J Surg 162:457, 1991

101. Davis JW, Hoyt DB, McArdle MS, et al: The significance of critical care errors in causing preventable death in trauma patients in a trauma system. J Trauma 31:813, 1991

102. Muscedere JG, Mullen JBM, Gan K, et al: Tidal ventilation at low airway pressures can augment lung injury. Am J Respir Crit Care Med 149:1327, 1994

103. Slutsky AS, Tremblay LN: Multiple system organ failure. Is mechanical ventilation a contributing factor? Am J Respir Crit Care Med 157(6 pt 1):1721, 1998

104. Deneke SM, Fanburg BL: Normobaric oxygen toxicity of the lung. N Engl J Med 303:76, 1980

105. Maetani S, Nishikawa T, Tobe T, et al: Role of blood transfusion in organ system failure following major abdominal surgery. Ann Surg 203:275, 1986

106. Sauaia A, Moore FA, Moore EE, et al: Early risk factors for postinjury multiple organ failure. World J Surg 20:392, 1996

107. Hebert PC, Wells G, Blajchman MA, et al: A multicentre randomized controlled clinical trial of transfusion requirements in critical care. N Engl J Med 340:409, 1999

108. Marik PE, Sibbald WJ: Effect of stored blood transfusion on oxygen delivery in patients with sepsis. JAMA 269:3024, 1993

109. Grant JP, Cox CE, Kleinman LM, et al: Serum hepatic enzyme and bilirubin elevations during parenteral nutrition. Surg Gynecol Obstet 145:2398, 1977

110. Askanazi J, Rosenbaum SH, Hyman AI, et al: Respiratory changes induced by the large glucose loads of total parenteral nutrition. JAMA 243:1444, 1980

111. Moore FA, Feliciano DV, Andrassy RJ, et al: Early enteral feeding, compared with parenteral, reduces postoperative septic complications: the results of a meta-analysis. Ann Surg 216:172, 1992

112. Masip J, Betbese AJ, Paez J, et al: Non-invasive pressure support ventilation versus conventional oxygen therapy in acute cardiogenic pulmonary oedema: a randomised trial. Lancet 356:2126, 2000

113. Delclaux C, L'Her E, Alberti C, et al: Treatment of acute hypoxemic nonhypercapnic respiratory insufficiency with continuous positive airway pressure delivered by a face mask: a randomized controlled trial. JAMA 284:2352, 2000

114. Parker JC, Hernandez LA, Peevy KJ: Mechanisms of ventilator induced lung injury. Crit Care Med 21:131, 1993

115. Munoz J, Guerrero JE, Escalante JL, et al: Pressure-controlled ventilation versus controlled mechanical ventilation with decelerating inspiratory flow. Crit Care Med 21:1143, 1993

116. Hickling KG, Henderson SJ, Jackson R: Low mortality associated with low volume pressure limited ventilation with permissive hypercapnia in severe adult respiratory distress syndrome. Intensive Care Med 16:372, 1990

117. Hickling KG, Walsh J, Henderson S, et al: Low mortality rate in adult respiratory distress syndrome using low-volume, pressure-limited ventilation with permissive hypercapnia: a prospective study. Crit Care Med 22:1568, 1994

118. Laffey JG, Tanaka M, Engelberts D, et al: Therapeutic hypercapnia reduces pulmonary and systemic injury following in vivo lung reperfusion. Am J Respir Crit Care Med 162:2287, 2000

119. Derdak S, Mehta S, Stewart TE, et al: High-frequency oscillatory ventilation for acute respiratory distress syndrome in adults: a randomized, controlled trial. Am J Respir Crit Care Med 166:801, 2002

120. Ferguson ND, Stewart TE: The use of high-frequency oscillatory ventilation in adults with acute lung injury. Respir Care Clin North Am 7:647, 2001

121. Dellinger RP, Zimmerman JL, Taylor RW, et al: Effects of inhaled nitric oxide in patients with acute respiratory distress syndrome: results of a randomized phase II trial. Crit Care Med 26:15, 1998

122. Lewandowski K: Extracorporeal membrane oxygenation for severe acute respiratory failure. Crit Care 4:156, 2000

123. Mols G, Loop T, Geiger K, et al: Extracorporeal membrane oxygenation: a ten-year experience. Am J Surg 180:144, 2000

124. Morris AH, Wallace CJ, Menlovet RL, et al: Randomized clinical trial of pressure-controlled inverse ratio ventilation and extracorporeal CO_2 removal for adult respiratory distress syndrome. Am J Respir Crit Care Med 149:295, 1994

125. Connors AF Jr, Speroff T, Dawson NV, et al: The effectiveness of right heart catheterization in the initial care of critically ill patients. JAMA 276:889, 1996

126. Mehta RL, McDonald B, Gabbai FB, et al: A randomized clinical trial of continuous versus intermittent dialysis for acute renal failure. Kidney Int 60:1154, 2001

127. Bouman CS, Oudemans-van Straaten HM, Tijssen JG, et al: Effects of early high-volume continuous venovenous hemofiltration on survival and recovery of renal function in intensive care patients with acute renal failure: a prospective, randomized trial. Crit Care Med 30:2205, 2002

128. Tonelli M, Manns B, Feller-Kopman D: Acute renal failure in the intensive care unit: a systematic review of the impact of dialytic modality on mortality and renal recovery. Am J Kidney Dis 40:875, 2002

129. Ronco C, Bellomo R, Homel P, et al: Effects of different doses in continuous veno-venous haemofiltration on outcomes of acute renal failure: a prospective randomised trial. Lancet 356:26, 2000

130. Schiffl H, Lang SM, Fischer R: Daily hemodialysis and the outcome of acute renal failure. N Engl J Med 346:362, 2002

131. Kellum JA, Angus DC, Johnson JP, et al: Continuous versus intermittent renal replacement therapy: a meta-analysis. Intensive Care Med 28:29, 2002

132. Cole L, Bellomo R, Hart G, et al: A phase II randomized, controlled trial of continuous hemofiltration in sepsis. Crit Care Med 30:100, 2002

133. Kudsk KA, Croce MA, Fabian TC, et al: Enteral *versus* parenteral feeding: effects on septic morbidity after blunt and penetrating abdominal trauma. Ann Surg 215:503, 1992

134. McGregor CS, Marshall JC: Enteral feeding in acute pancreatitis: just do it. Curr Opin Crit Care 7:89, 2001

135. Marik PE, Zaloga GP: Early enteral nutrition in acutely ill patients: a systematic review. Crit Care Med 29:2264, 2003

136. Beale RJ, Bryg DJ, Bihari DJ: Immunonutrition in the critically ill: a systematic review of clinical outcome. Crit Care Med 27:2799, 1999

137. Griffith DP, McNally AT, Battey CH, et al: Intravenous erythromycin facilitates bedside placement of postpyloric feeding tubes in critically ill adults: a double-blind, randomized, placebo-controlled study. Crit Care Med 31:39, 2003

138. Berne JD, Norwood SH, McAuley CE, et al: Erythromycin reduces delayed gastric emptying in critically ill trauma patients: a randomized, controlled trial. J Trauma 53:422, 2002

139. Rozga J, Podesta L, LePage EA, et al: A bioartificial liver to treat severe acute liver failure. Ann Surg 219:538, 1994

140. Mitzner SR, Stange J, Klammt S, et al: Extracorporeal detoxification using the molecular adsorbent recirculating system for critically ill patients with liver failure. J Am Soc Nephrol 12(17 suppl):S75, 2001

141. Alderson P, Bunn F, Lefebvre C, et al: Human albumin solution for resuscitation and volume expansion in critically ill patients. Cochrane Database Syst Rev (1):CD001208, 2002

142. Vincent JL, Baron JF, Reinhart K, et al: Anemia and blood transfusion in critically ill patients. JAMA 288:1499, 2002

143. Hebert PC, Yetisir E, Martin C, et al: Is a low transfusion threshhold safe in patients with cardiovascular diseases? Crit Care Med 29:227, 2001

144. Kress JP, Pohlman AS, O'Connor MF, et al: Daily interruption of sedative infusions in critically ill patients undergoing mechanical ventilation. N Engl J Med 342:1471, 2000

145. Taylor FB Jr, Stearns-Kurosawa DJ, Kurosawa S, et al: The endothelial cell protein C receptor aids in host defense against *Escherichia coli* sepsis. Blood 95:1680, 2000

146. Bernard GR, Vincent J-L, Laterre PF, et al: Efficacy and safety of recombinant human activated protein C for severe sepsis. N Engl J Med 344:699, 2001

147. Vincent J-L, Angus DC, Artigas A, et al: Effects of drotrecogin alfa (activated) on organ dysfunction in the PROWESS trial. Crit Care Med 31:834, 2003

148. Annane D, Sebille V, Charpentier C, et al: Effect of treatment with low doses of hydrocortisone and fludrocortisone on mortality in patients with septic shock. JAMA 288:862, 2002

149. Cronin L, Cook DJ, Carlet J, et al: Corticosteroid treatment for sepsis: a critical appraisal and meta-analysis of the literature. Crit Care Med 23:1430, 1995

150. Marshall JC: Such stuff as dreams are made on: mediator-targeted therapy in sepsis. Nat Rev Drug Discov 2:391, 2003

151. Vincent JL, Bihari DJ, Suter PM, et al: The prevalence of nosocomial infection in intensive care units in Europe: results of the European Prevalence of Infection in Intensive Care (EPIC) Study. JAMA 274:639, 1995

152. Marshall JC, Christou NV, Meakins JL: The gastrointestinal tract: the "undrained abscess" of multiple organ failure. Ann Surg 218:111, 1993

153. Nathens AB, Marshall JC: Selective decontamination of the digestive tract (SDD) in surgical patients. Arch Surg 134:170, 1999

154. Singh N, Rogers P, Atwood CW, et al: Short-course empiric antibiotic therapy for patients with pulmonary infiltrates in the intensive care unit: a proposed solution for indiscriminate antibiotic prescription. Am J Respir Crit Care Med 162(2 pt 1):505, 2000

155. Ferraris VA: Exploratory laparotomy for potential abdominal sepsis in patients with multiple-organ failure. Arch Surg 118:1130, 1983

156. Hinsdale JG, Jaffe BM: Re-operation for intra-abdominal sepsis. Indications and results in modern critical care setting. Ann Surg 199:31, 1984

157. Bunt TJ: Non-directed relaparotomy for intraabdominal sepsis: a futile procedure. Am Surg 52:294, 1986

158. Knaus WA, Draper EA, Wagner DP, et al: Prognosis in acute organ system failure. Ann Surg 202:685, 1985

159. Ranson JHC, Rifkind KM, Turner JW: Prognostic signs and nonoperative peritoneal lavage in acute pancreatitis. Surg Gynecol Obstet 143:209, 1976

160. Prendergast TJ, Claessens MT, Luce JM: A national survey of end-of-life care for critically ill patients. Am J Respir Crit Care Med 158:1163, 1998

161. Cook DJ, Guyatt GH, Jaeschke R, et al: Determinants in Canadian health care workers of the decision to withdraw life support from the critically ill. JAMA 273:703, 1995

162. Safar P, DeKornfeld T, Pearson J, et al: Intensive care unit. Anesthesia 16:275, 1961

163. Tilney NL, Bailey GL, Morgan AP: Sequential system failure after rupture of abdominal aortic aneurysms: an unsolved problem in postoperative care. Ann Surg 178:117, 1973

164. Muckart DJJ, Bhagwanjee S: The ACCP/SCCM consensus conference definitions of the systemic inflammatory response syndrome (SIRS) and allied disorders in relation to critically injured patients. Crit Care Med 25:1789, 1997

165. Bone RC: Sir Isaac Newton, sepsis, SIRS, and CARS. Crit Care Med 24:1125, 1996

166. Marshall JC: Rethinking sepsis: from concepts to syndromes to diseases. Sepsis 3:5, 1999

167. Fink MP: Cytopathic hypoxia. Crit Care 6:491, 2002

168. Norton LW: Does drainage of intraabdominal pus reverse multiple organ failure? Am J Surg 149:347, 1985

169. Suffredini AF, Fromm RE, Parker MM, et al: The cardiovascular response of normal humans to the administration of endotoxin. N Engl J Med 321:280, 1989

170. Taveira Da Silva AM, Kaulach HC, Chuidian FS, et al: Brief report: shock and multiple organ dysfunction after self administration of salmonella endotoxin. N Engl J Med 328:1457, 1993

171. Danner RL, Elin RJ, Hosseini JM, et al: Endotoxemia in human septic shock. Chest 99:169, 1991

172. Bates DW, Parsonnet J, Ketchum PA, et al: Limulus amebocyte lysate assay for detection of endotoxin in patients with sepsis sydrome. Clin Infect Dis 27:582, 1998

173. Hoch RC, Rodriguez R, Manning T, et al: Effects of accidental trauma on cytokine and endotoxin production. Crit Care Med 21:839, 1993

174. Winchurch RA, Thupari JN, Munster AM: Endotoxemia in burn patients: Levels of circulating endotoxins are related to burn size. Surgery 102:808, 1987

175. Roumen RMH, Frieling JTM, van Tits HWHJ, et al: Endotoxemia after major vascular operations. J Vasc Surg 18:853, 1993

176. Poltorak A, He X, Smirnova I, et al: Defective LPS signaling in C3H/HeJ and C57BL/10ScCr mice: mutations in the *Tlr4* gene. Science 282:2085, 1998

177. Michalek SM, Moore RN, McGhee JR, et al: The primary role of lymphoreticular cells in the mediation of host responses to bacterial endotoxin. J Infect Dis 141:55, 1980

178. Zhao B, Bowden RAS, Stavchansky SA, et al: Human endothelial cell response to gram-negative lipopolysaccharide assessed with cDNA microarrays. Am J Physiol Cell Physiol 281:C1587, 2001

179. Fessler MB, Malcolm KC, Duncan MW, et al: A genomic and proteomic analysis of activation of the human neutrophil by lipopolysaccharide and its mediation by p38 mitogen-activated protein kinase. J Biol Chem 277:31291, 2002

180. Aderem A, Ulevitch RJ: Toll-like receptors in the induction of the innate immune response. Nature 406:782, 2000

181. Faist E, Baue AE, Dittmer H, et al: Multiple organ failure in polytrauma patients. J Trauma 23:775, 1983

182. Sorenson TI, Nielsen GG, Andersen PK, et al: Genetic and environmental influences on premature death in adult adoptees. N Engl J Med 318:727, 1988

183. Lazarus R, Vercelli D, Palmer LJ, et al: Single nucleotide polymorphisms in innate immunity genes: abundant variation and potential role in complex human disease. Immunol Rev 190:9, 2002

184. Agnese DM, Calvano JE, Hahm SJ, et al: Human toll-like receptor 4 mutations but not CD14 polymorphisms are associated with an increased risk of gram-negative infections. J Infect Dis 186:1522, 2002

185. Lorenz E, Mira J-P, Frees KL, et al: Relevance of mutations in the TLR4 receptor in patients with

gram-negative septic shock. Arch Intern Med 162:1028, 2002

186. Gibot S, Cariou A, Drouet L, et al: Association between a genomic polymorphism within the CD14 locus and septic shock susceptibility and mortality rate. Crit Care Med 30:969, 2002

187. Mira J-P, Cariou A, Grall F, et al: Association of TNF2, a TNF-a promoter polymorphism, with septic shock susceptibility and mortality. JAMA 282:561, 1999

188. Appoloni O, Dupont E, Vandercruys M, et al: Association of tumor necrosis factor-2 allele with plasma tumor necrosis factor-α levels and mortality from septic shock. Am J Med 110:486, 2001

189. Schroder O, Schulte KM, Ostermann P, et al: Heat shock protein 70 genotypes HSPA1B and HSPA1L influence cytokine concentrations and interfere with outcome after major injury. Crit Care Med 31:73, 2003

190. Reid CL, Perrey C, Pravica V, et al: Genetic variation in proinflammatory and anti-inflammatory cytokine production in multiple organ dysfunction syndrome. Crit Care Med 30:2216, 2003

191. Ma P, Chen D, Pan J, et al: Genomic polymorphism within interleukin-1 family cytokines influences the outcome of septic patients. Crit Care Med 30:1046, 2002

192. Ginzberg HH, Cherapanov V, Dong Q, et al: Neutrophil-mediated epithelial injury during transmigration: role of elastase. Am J Physiol Gastrointest Liver Physiol 281:G705, 2001

193. Yum HK, Arcaroli J, Kupfner J, et al: Involvement of phosphoinositide 3-kinases in neutrophil activation and the development of acute lung injury. J Immunol 167:6601, 2001

194. Lee WL, Downey GP: Leukocyte elastase. Physiological functions and role in acute lung injury. Am J Respir Crit Care Med 164:896, 2001

195. Jaeschke H, Smith CW. Mechanisms of neutrophil-induced parenchymal cell injury. J Leukoc Biol 61:647, 1997

196. Kubes P, Hunter J, Granger DN: Ischemia/reperfusion induced feline intestinal dysfunction: importance of granulocyte recruitment. Gastroenterology 103:807, 1992

197. Nieuwenhuijzen GAP, Haskel Y, Lu Q, et al: Macrophage elimination increases bacterial translocation and gut origin septicemia but attenuates symptoms and mortality rate in a model of systemic inflammation. Ann Surg 218:791, 1993

198. Carson WE, Yu H, Dierksheide J, et al: A fatal cytokine-induced systemic inflammatory response reveals a critical role for NK cells. J Immunol 162:4943, 1999

199. Badgwell B, Parihar R, Magro C, et al: Natural killer cells contribute to the lethality of a murine model of Escherichia coli infection. Surgery 132:205, 2002

200. Sherwood ER, Lin CY, Tao W, et al: Beta2 microglobulin knockout mice are resistant to lethal intraabdominal sepsis. Am J Respir Crit Care Med 167:1641, 2003

201. Sempowski GD, Lee DM, Scearce RM, et al: Resistance of CD7-deficient mice to lipopolysaccharide-induced shock syndromes. J Exp Med 189:1011, 1999

202. Henneke P, Golenbock DT: Innate immune recognition of lipopolysaccharide by endothelial cells. Crit Care Med 30(5 suppl):S207, 2002

203. Aird WC: The role of the endothelium in severe sepsis and multiple organ dysfunction syndrome. Blood 101:3765, 2003

204. Faure E, Thomas L, Xu H, et al: Bacterial lipopolysaccharide and IFN-gamma induce Toll-like receptor 2 and Toll-like receptor 4 expression in human endothelial cells: role of NF-kappa B activation. J Immunol 166:2018, 2001

205. Ishiguro K, Kadomatsu K, Kojima TY, et al: Syndecan-4 deficiency leads to high mortality of lipopolysaccharide-injected mice. J Biol Chem 276:47483, 2001

206. Muller AM, Cronen C, Muller KM, et al: Heterogeneous expression of cell adhesion molecules by endothelial cells in ARDS. J Pathol 198:170, 2002

207. Ueno H, Hirasawa H, Oda S, et al: Coagulation/fibrinolysis abnormality and vascular endothelial damage in the pathogenesis of thrombocytopenic multiple organ failure. Crit Care Med 30:2242, 2002

208. Mutunga M, Fulton B, Bullock R, et al: Circulating endothelial cells in patients with septic shock. Am J Respir Crit Care Med 163:195, 2001

209. Harlan JM, Winn RK: Leukocyte-endothelial interactions: clinical trials of anti-adhesion therapy. Crit Care Med 30(suppl):S214, 2002

210. Esmon C: The protein C pathway. Crit Care Med 28(suppl):S44, 2000

211. Warren BL, Eid A, Singer P, et al: High-dose antithrombin III in severe sepsis: a randomized, controlled trial. JAMA 286:1869, 2001

212. Abraham E, Reinhart K, Opal S, et al: Efficacy and safety of tifacogin (recombinant tissue factor pathway inhibitor) in severe sepsis. JAMA 290:283, 2003

213. Cheng T, Liu D, Griffin JH, et al: Activated protein C blocks p53-mediated apoptosis in ischemic human brain endothelium and is neuroprotective. Nature Med 9:338, 2003

214. Thompson CB: Apoptosis in the pathogenesis and treatment of disease. Science 267:1456, 1995

215. Fadok VA, Bratton DL, Konowal A, et al: Macrophages that have ingested apoptotic cells in vitro inhibit proinflammatory cytokine production through autocrine/paracrine mechanisms involving TGFb, PGE2, and PAF. J Clin Invest 101:890, 1998

216. Byrne A, Reen DJ: Lipopolysaccharide induces rapid production of IL-10 by monocytes in the presence of apoptotic neutrophils. J Immunol 168:1968, 2002

217. Hotchkiss RS, Schmieg RE Jr, Swanson PE, et al: Rapid onset of intestinal epithelial and lymphocyte apoptotic cell death in patients with trauma and shock. Crit Care Med 28:3207, 2000

218. Hotchkiss RS, Tinsley KW, Swanson PE, et al: Prevention of lymphocyte cell death in sepsis improves survival in mice. Proc Natl Acad Sci USA 96:14541, 1999

219. Sookhai S, Wang JH, McCourt M, et al: A novel mechanism for attenuating neutrophil-mediated lung injury in vivo. Surg Forum 50:205, 1999

220. Imai Y, Parodo J, Kajikawa O, et al: Injurious mechanical ventilation and end-organ epithelial cell apoptosis and organ dysfunction in an experimental model of acute respiratory distress syndrome. JAMA 289:2104, 2003

221. Carrico CJ, Meakins JL, Marshall JC, et al: Multiple organ failure syndrome. The gastrointestinal tract: the 'motor' of MOF. Arch Surg 121:196, 1986

222. Marshall JC, Nathens AB: The gut in critical illness: evidence from human studies. Shock 6:S10, 1996

223. Deitch EA. The role of intestinal barrier failure and bacterial translocation in the development of systemic infection and multiple organ failure. Arch Surg 125:403, 1990

224. Fink MP: Gastrointestinal mucosal injury in experimental models of shock, trauma, and sepsis. Crit Care Med 19:627, 1991

225. Savage DC: Microbial ecology of the gastrointestinal tract. Annu Rev Med 31:107, 1977

226. Wells CL, Maddaus MA, Simmons RL: Proposed mechanisms for the translocation of intestinal bacteria. Rev Infect Dis 10:958, 1988

227. O'Boyle CJ, MacFie J, Mitchell CJ, et al: Microbiology of bacterial translocation in humans. Gut 42:29, 1998

228. MacFie J, O'Boyle C, Mitchell CJ, et al: Gut origin of sepsis: a prospective study investigating associations between bacterial translocation, gastric microflora, and septic morbidity. Gut 45:223, 1999

229. Deitch EA, Xu D, Franko L, et al: Evidence favoring the role of the gut as a cytokine generating organ in rats subjected to hemorrhagic shock. Shock 1:141, 1994

230. Arita H, Ogle CK, Alexander JW, et al: Induction of hypermetabolism in guinea pigs by endotoxin infused through the portal vein. Arch Surg 123:1420, 1988

231. Marshall JC, Ribeiro MB, Chu PTY, et al: Portal endotoxemia stimulates the release of an immunosuppressive factor from alveolar and splenic macrophages. J Surg Res 55:14, 1993

232. Sullivan BJ, Swallow CJ, Girotti MJ, et al: Bacterial translocation induces procoagulant activity in tissue macrophages: a potential mechanism for end-organ dysfunction. Arch Surg 126:586, 1991

233. Gonzalez RJ, Moore EE, Ciesla DJ, et al: Posthemorrhagic shock mesenteric lymph activates human pulmonary microvascular endothelium for in vitro neutrophil-mediated injury: the role of intercellular adhesion molecule-1. J Trauma 54:219, 2003

234. Moore FA, Moore EE: Evolving concepts in the pathogenesis of postinjury multiple organ failure. Surg Clin North Am 75:257, 1995

235. Fan J, Marshall JC, Jimenez M, et al: Hemorrhagic shock primes for increased expression of cytokine-induced neutrophil chemoattractant in the lung: role in pulmonary inflammation following lipopolysaccharide. J Immunol 161:440, 1998

236. Godin PJ, Buchman TG: Uncoupling of biological oscillators: a complementary hypothesis concerning the pathogenesis of multiple organ dysfunction syndrome. Crit Care Med 24:1107, 1996

237. Seely AJE, Christou NV: Multiple organ dysfunction syndrome: exploring the paradigm of complex non-linear systems. Crit Care Med 28:2193, 2000

238. Ivanov PC, Nunes Amaral LA, Goldberger AL, et al: Multifractality in human heartbeat dynamics. Nature 399:461, 1999

239. Korach M, Sharshar T, Jarrin I, et al: Cardiac variability in critically ill adults: influence of sepsis. Crit Care Med 29:1380, 2001

240. Annane D, Trabold F, Sharshar T, et al: Inappropriate sympathetic activation at onset of septic shock: a spectral analysis approach. Am J Respir Crit Care Med 160:458, 1999

241. Marshall JC: Complexity, chaos, and incomprehensibility: parsing the biology of critical illness. Crit Care Med 28:2646, 2000

242. Hayes MA, Timmins AC, Yau EHS, et al: Elevation of systemic oxygen delivery in the treatment of critically ill patients. N Engl J Med 330:1717, 1994

243. Rivers E, Nguyen B, Havstad S, et al: Early goal-directed therapy in the treatment of severe sepsis and septic shock. N Engl J Med 345:1368, 2001

244. Panacek EA, Marshall JC, Fischkoff S, et al: Neutralization of TNF by a monoclonal antibody improves survival and reduces organ dysfunction in human sepsis: results of the MONARCS trial. Chest 118:88S, 2000

129 CLINICAL AND LABORATORY DIAGNOSIS OF INFECTION

David C. Evans, M.D., F.A.C.S., and Jonathan L. Meakins, M.D., D.Sc., F.A.C.S.

Approach to Diagnosis of Surgical Infection

Surgical infection is a term that, though frequently used, is not clearly defined. In the strictest sense, it implies infection amenable to operative management through surgical source control, as in the case of complicated diverticulitis or necrotizing soft tissue infection. More generally, however, the term can refer to any infection commonly seen in surgical patients (e.g., central line infection or postoperative pneumonia). Both definitions are pertinent, in that the same diagnostic principles apply in each situation.

The presence of surgical infectious disease is usually determined clinically and confirmed microbiologically. Identification of an infection is rarely incidental: most often it is sought in response to a clinical signal. This signal is frequently fever but may be one or more of a number of other symptoms and signs.

Most surgical infections are outpatient conditions that are easily diagnosed and treated. Infections in hospitalized patients, whether related to the primary surgical disease or resulting from surgical therapy, are less easily managed. The greatest challenges in diagnosis and treatment of surgical infections arise in the perioperative and postoperative periods.

Terminology

Traditionally, the terms infection, sepsis, septicemia, bacteremia, endotoxemia, and septic shock have borne similar connotations; this imprecision of terminology has led to considerable confusion about the specific role of microbial infection as a cause of the common clinical presentation of fever, tachycardia, and occasional hypotension. The traditional tendency to conflate these distinct concepts in this simplistic and unrefined manner has had major implications for how antibiotics are used—or, more to the point, misused—in surgical patients.

The human body's physiologic response to systemic infection is well characterized and is often referred to as sepsis. However, infection and sepsis are distinct entities. The normal septic response to infection may, in fact, be completely absent in immunosuppressed patients. Most surgeons, for example, have encountered a patient receiving high doses of steroids who has a perforated intra-abdominal viscus and fecal peritonitis but whose leukocyte count, temperature, and blood pressure are all normal. Conversely, a systemic inflammatory response mimicking sepsis may be present in noninfected patients.[1,2] For example, patients with acute pancreatitis, tissue necrosis, or fractures may manifest physiologic and metabolic changes that are indistinguishable from those associated with bacteremia, even in the absence of infection. Animal studies have confirmed that a sepsislike syndrome can occur without microbial invasion of host tissues.[3]

Accordingly, several clinicians have used the term sepsis syndrome to refer to the group of signs, symptoms, and physiologic changes that result from a variety of sterile inflammatory processes as well as from systemic infection.[2,4] The problem with using the term in this way, however, is that it derives from a Greek word (*sepsis,* "decay") that implies infection with microorganisms. It is therefore not surprising that application of the term sepsis syndrome to noninfectious settings has led to some confusion.[5,6]

To clarify the relevant terminology and provide a common vernacular with which to discuss surgical infection, the American College of Chest Physicians and the Society of Critical Care Medicine held a joint consensus conference in 1991 that led to the publication in 1992 of the currently used terminology and definitions [*see Sidebar Definitions of Key Concepts*].[7] A key outcome was the definition of the nonspecific clinical picture of temperature, heart rate, respiratory rate, and white blood cell (WBC) count abnormalities as the systemic inflammatory response syndrome (SIRS). SIRS may or may not be due to infection; when it is, it is referred to as sepsis. When sepsis results in organ dysfunction, the ensuing state is referred to as severe sepsis; when it results in persistent cardiovascular decompensation, the ensuing state is referred to as septic shock.

Definitions of Key Concepts

- *Systemic inflammatory response syndrome (SIRS):* This response is manifested by the occurrence of two or more of the following conditions as a result of infection: (a) temperature higher than 38° C (100.4° F) or lower than 36° C (96.8° F), (b) heart rate greater than 90 beats/min, (c) respiratory rate greater than 20 breaths/min or arterial carbon dioxide tension less than 32 mm Hg, and (d) white blood cell count greater than 12,000/mm³ or less than 4,000/mm³, or immature (band) forms accounting for more than 10% of the neutrophils present.
- *Sepsis:* SIRS when specifically caused by infection.
- *Severe sepsis:* Sepsis associated with organ dysfunction, hypoperfusion, or hypotension. Hypoperfusion and perfusion abnormalities may include, but are not limited to, lactic acidosis, oliguria, or acute alteration of mental status.
- *Septic shock:* Sepsis with hypotension despite adequate fluid resuscitation, with persistent perfusion abnormalities that may include, but are not limited to, lactic acidosis, oliguria, or acute alteration of mental status. Patients receiving inotropes or vasopressors may not be hypotensive at the time perfusion abnormalities are measured.
- *Multiple organ dysfunction syndrome (MODS):* MODS is the presence of altered organ function in an acutely ill patient such that homeostasis cannot be maintained without intervention.

Approach to Diagnosis of Surgical Infection

Clinical signal of possible infection is noted

Assess patient characteristics and circumstances of presentation:
• Health of host   • Intensity of physiologic response
• Nature of pathogen

Host status is assessed: normal vs. compromised/complex

Response to infection in compromised or complex patients differs from that in normally responsive patients.

Patient is normally responsive

Cardinal signs of inflammation are
• Redness   • Heat   • Pain   • Swelling   • Loss of function
Other signals include
• New or persistent postoperative fever
• Tachypnea/tachycardia   • Confusion   • Ileus

Patient is compromised or complex

Risk factors include
• Advanced age   • Major trauma   • End-organ failure
• Thermal injury   • Chemotherapy   • ≥ 1 chronic disease
Cardinal signs may be present, but more often, infection is occult. Clinical manifestations may include
• Confusion   • Ileus   • Gastric bleeding
• Intermittent hypotension and septic shock   • Water retention
• Delayed wound healing
Laboratory signs of occult infection include
• Renal, hepatic, or respiratory failure   • Thrombocytosis or
  thrombocytopenia   • Hyperglycemia and insulin resistance
• Immune failure

Patient is evaluated for presence of infection

Begin with history and physical examination.

Perform laboratory assessment:
• Obtain Gram stain and cultures of wound tissue, sputum, urine, and drainage effluent
• Consider percutaneous aspiration and microbiologic examination of potentially infected fluid
• Obtain WBC and blood chemistry measurements
• Obtain chest x-ray; consider imaging of operative site

Therapy is initiated

Treatment is governed by health of host, nature of response to infection (local vs. SIRS; mild sepsis vs. septic shock/MODS), and nature of pathogen (suspected or proven).

Patient has SIRS or uncomplicated sepsis

Withhold antibiotics until definitive diagnosis is made, unless patient is compromised or situation is urgent.
Restore homeostasis (give fluids).
Identify and control source of infection.
Identify pathogen and give suitable antibiotics.

Patient has severe sepsis or is in septic shock

Simultaneously resuscitate, identify infectious focus, give empirical broad-sprectrum antibiotics, and undertake source control if able.
Antibiotic choice should reflect (1) likely source of infection, (2) hospital- vs. community-acquired, (3) previous antibiotic therapy.

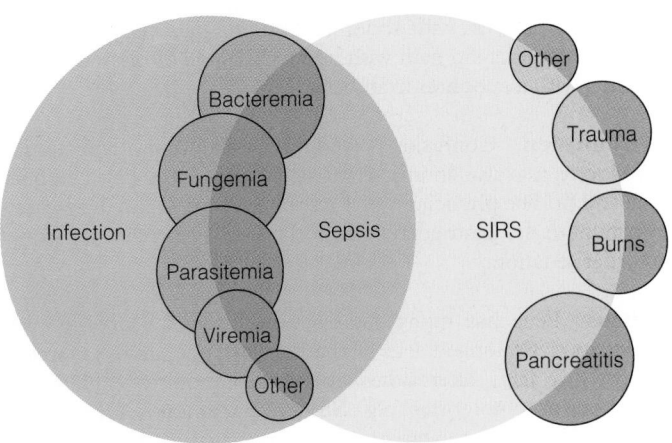

Figure 1 **Depicted are the interrelationships among infection, sepsis, and the systemic inflammatory response syndrome (SIRS).**

Clearly, SIRS includes all the signs, symptoms, and physiologic changes characteristic of the sepsis syndrome; however, use of the term SIRS avoids the idea that such manifestations are necessarily the product of infection. Sepsis may be thought of as a special case of SIRS—SIRS associated with infection [*see Figure 1*]. The term sepsis syndrome, although very useful in guiding clinical thinking, is insufficiently precise for our current needs and probably should no longer be used. The term septicemia should not be used either.

The crucial point is that infection and sepsis are conceptually distinct: infection is a process, and sepsis is the response to that process. The response provides the clinical signals that lead to diagnosis of the initiating process. As a rule, infection, once diagnosed, is easily treated with antibiotics and drainage. It is the management of sepsis that is difficult [*see 128 Multiple Organ Dysfunction Syndrome*].

General Approach to Diagnosis of Infection

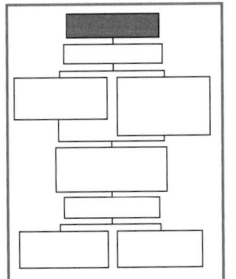

The search for an infection is prompted by a clinical signal indicating a problem in need of resolution [*see Table 1*]. The signal denotes the response of a patient to an infectious stimulus and is a function of the patient's physiologic ability to react to the endogenous and exogenous mediators liberated through the infectious process. A thorough history and physical examination are imperative and should be followed by selected laboratory tests. Normally responsive patients tend to show the classic signals, whereas compromised or complex patients often show more subtle signs that may only be noted as abnormalities on routine bloodwork.

The diagnostic approach to suspected infection must be modified according to patient characteristics and the circumstances of presentation; for example, the specific differential diagnosis for infection appearing on postoperative day 1 will clearly be different from that for infection appearing after 1 week in the ICU. There are three important elements at play when a surgical patient experiences an infection: (1) the health of the host, (2) the intensity of the physiologic response to infection, and (3) the nature of the pathogen. All three factors must be considered carefully in the diagnosis of surgical infection.

Host Status: Normally Responsive versus Compromised or Complex

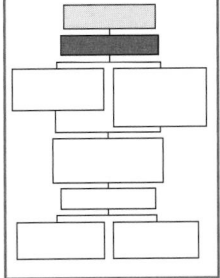

That signs and symptoms of infection in compromised or complex patients differ from those in normally responsive hosts has important diagnostic implications. Normally responsive patients, for whom the physician can obtain a history and perform a physical examination, respond to infection in the classic manner—typically, with fever, tachycardia, leukocytosis, malaise, and other appropriate symptoms. For many reasons—even simply if the infection is severe—normally responsive patients may become compromised. Compromised or complex patients are unable to meet inflammatory or infectious challenges in the normal manner. Hence, the clinical signals of infection in such patients differ from those in normally responsive patients, often being absent or developing at a later stage of infection. Indeed, a multitude of clinical conditions or physiologic states define compromised or complex patients. These include the extremes of age, immunosuppression as a result of either disease (e.g., HIV infection or lymphoma) or medication (e.g., chemotherapy), thermal injury, major trauma, acute end-organ failure in the ICU, and the presence of more than one chronic disease. The prevalence of such patients in modern hospital surgical practice is increasing steadily.

It must be kept in mind, however, that the normally responsive patient and the compromised or complex patient are merely extreme points on the clinical spectrum rather than categorically distinct populations.

Physiologic Response to Infection

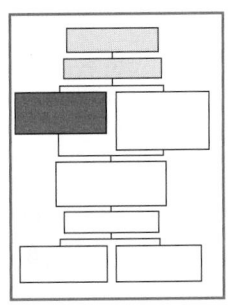

NORMALLY RESPONSIVE PATIENTS

Cardinal Signs of Inflammation

Rubor, calor, dolor, tumor, and functio laesa—that is, redness, heat, pain, swelling, and loss of function—have been considered the cardinal signs of localized inflammation since the times of Hippocrates and Galen. They remain the primary signals leading to medical consultation for outpatient surgical infections and for many of the infectious complications of operation. They are emblematic of the host's effort to contain infection locally, and they may signal the presence of infection even in cases where the primary site of infection is a deeply situated organ or tissue. Infections amenable to surgical intervention may present in this way; however, nosocomial infections complicating the course of surgical patients are generally signaled in more subtle ways.

Fever

Fever is perhaps the most common signal that an infectious process is present. Postoperative fever is a normal part of the recovery process; understanding the typical febrile course is important in differentiating normal from pathologic fever. It is unusual for a sudden, very high fever to be the first signal of an infection. Infection usually begins to manifest itself with a prodrome, recognition of which speeds diagnosis and therapy. Investigation should be started when the patient's temperature reaches 38° C (100.4° F) rather than 40° C (104° F). Although this point may seem obvious, many of the crisis intervention measures required

---

Table 1 Fundamental Approach to Diagnosis of Infection

Recognize clinical signal and observe its characteristics:
  Nature
  Intensity
  Rapidity of development

Make best guess as to source and likely pathogen on the basis of
  History of surgical disease
  Physical examination
  Microbiologic examination of stained specimens
  Radiologic findings

Confirm presence of infection by means of
  Laboratory results
  Observation of clinical course
  Invasive procedures (e.g., paracentesis, thoracentesis, interventional radiology, operation)

---

in managing fevers could be avoided if the significance of more modest temperature elevations were recognized more often.

A fever that appears after the normal postoperative temperature elevation has resolved must not be ignored. To simply wait for such a fever to dissipate is to court disaster. In the absence of a clear diagnosis, a thorough physical examination of the patient, directed by laboratory tests and followed by reexamination as necessary, is required to identify occult infection.

Miscellaneous Signals

It is common wisdom that the signals communicating underlying infection in the compromised or complex host may be subtle. The astute clinician will be in tune with these and, with experience, will recognize when to undertake a diligent search for infection.

Altered heart rate A heart rate that is either too high or too low may signal an infection. On rare occasions, a change in rhythm in the elderly (e.g., paroxysmal atrial tachycardia, flutter, or atrial fibrillation) indicates an infectious process. Gram-negative sepsis may produce a so-called relative bradycardia, meaning that the resulting tachycardia is not as pronounced as one might expect. An unexplained sustained increase in heart rate should not be ignored.

Tachypnea Whereas tachypnea occurs commonly after operation in response to pain or poor pulmonary toilet, it may also signal either the prodrome of infection or the onset of SIRS. Because tachypnea may herald not only infection but also other important diagnoses (e.g., pulmonary embolism), it must be thoughtfully and methodically evaluated.

Pain Pain that persists or is out of proportion to the expected response deserves attention. Whenever a surgical wound that was healing favorably for the first 5 to 7 days becomes more painful, a deep surgical site infection (SSI) must be suspected and ruled out, even if other signs are absent. Unexplained muscular pain is often the first harbinger of deadly necrotizing soft tissue infection caused by gram-positive bacteria (e.g., group A streptococci), the early recognition of which may be lifesaving and limb-preserving [*see 22 Soft Tissue Infection*]. Sometimes pain is referred, and the painful area appears normal on examination. Pneu-

monia that presents with abdominal findings is a classic example, as is the shoulder-tip pain with a normal range of motion seen in patients with a subphrenic abscess.

Confusion Confusion is a common symptom of infection in the elderly; it is also an important signal in patients who had been well and fit. The physician's first response to confusion in an elderly patient in the postoperative period must be to seek a cause, not to order sedation.

Ileus Ileus has many causes, some of which are not well understood. Prolonged ileus after abdominal operation—as well as almost any ileus after other operations—requires explanation. Infections at remote sites (e.g., SSI and pneumonia) can produce ileus, as if the bowel were a target organ such as the kidney, the liver, or the lung.

COMPROMISED OR COMPLEX PATIENTS

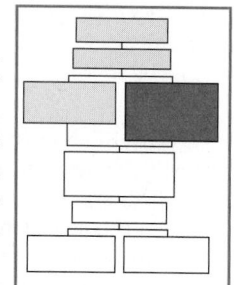

The presence of fever remains a common signal of infection in the compromised or complex patient; however, it may be absent, or the patient's temperature may already be elevated as a result of other causes. Cardinal signs of infection may be present. More often, however, the infection is occult, and classic signals are unrelated to the infectious focus. In some very ill immunocompromised patients, findings that usually signal an infection may already be present. Slight changes in clinical status (e.g., minor temperature elevations, increased fluid requirements, confusion, and ileus) or changes in laboratory findings (e.g., an elevated WBC count, glucosuria, and hyperglycemia) should trigger investigation.

Patients in whom the first signal of an infectious process is organ dysfunction or failure, rather than fever and tachycardia, are likely to be physiologically compromised and seriously ill; perhaps more important, however, is that they are a group whose diagnosis and management require expert clinical skills. Because the classic septic response may not be present, it is essential to be alert to the signs and symptoms of occult infection (see below). In these patients, the laboratory and the radiology suite become increasingly important in diagnosing and documenting the evolution of the infection.

Clinical Signs and Symptoms of Occult Infection

Subtle changes in temperature, mental status, pulse rate, or respiratory rate may signal occult infection, as may the development of pain or ileus.

Intermittent hypotension and septic shock Septic shock, an important manifestation of an unrecognized focus of infection, is the original expression of multisystem failure. Fortunately, it rarely occurs without warning. The prodrome often includes fever and sometimes other signals. Recurring hypotension is the most characteristic signal; it usually is not catastrophic and responds quickly to fluid resuscitation. Oliguria may accompany the hypotension. If this clinical state is allowed to progress, the hypotension will lead to renal failure (see below), with substantial water retention. Septic shock will result if the infection is not identified and treated with appropriate antibiotics and source control as necessary.

Both clinical assessment and laboratory studies are necessary to confirm the presence of septic shock, although florid septic shock is easily recognized on clinical examination alone [*see 118*

Shock]. Any or all of the following findings may be present in varying degrees: tachycardia; tachypnea; hypotension; warm, dry extremities; generalized flushing; and other signs suggesting a hyperdynamic, hypermetabolic state. Swan-Ganz catheter measurements confirm high cardiac output and low peripheral vascular resistance.

Gastric hemorrhage Gastric hemorrhage may be the presenting symptom of serious infection even if prophylactic measures against such hemorrhage have been taken. It is particularly suggestive of perigastric abscess resulting from anastomotic leakage after upper abdominal surgery. Gastric hyperacidity and bleeding generally respond to drainage of an abscess. Hemorrhagic gastritis must always be considered a signal of occult infection, which demands prompt diagnosis and treatment.

Delayed wound healing The absence of wound healing can indicate the presence of a significant infection. Typically in such a case, wounds left for delayed primary closure or secondary closure do not exhibit the appropriate granulation tissue and appear pale, dry, and unhealthy. The development of good granulation tissue is a sign that infection is controlled.

Laboratory Signs of Occult Infection

Renal failure Renal failure [*see 122 Renal Failure*] is identified by elevations in serum creatinine and blood urea nitrogen (BUN) levels, which can be highly sensitive signals of developing infection. A still more sensitive indicator is an alteration in creatinine clearance, a laboratory test underutilized in the ICU. Such alterations are generally evident before changes in serum levels. Creatinine clearance should be measured at an early stage in high-risk patients. In the presence of shock, renal failure can develop suddenly. Otherwise, loss of renal function is insidious, but it can usually be identified if sought before oliguria or anuria develops. Resolution of infection is associated with return of function.

Hepatic and respiratory failure Hepatic failure [*see 124 Hepatic Failure*], primarily manifested as jaundice, and respiratory failure [*see 120 Pulmonary Insufficiency*], initially presenting as a falling arterial oxygen tension and subsequently marked by a need for mechanical ventilation [*see 121 Mechanical Ventilation*] or by a change in the fraction of inspired oxygen (F_IO_2) requirement, can behave in the same way as renal failure (i.e., with drainage and control of infection leading to restoration of function).

Abnormal platelet count Thrombocytosis is often seen in association with infection, particularly with compromised hosts, in whom the infection may be occult. Thrombocytopenia may also indicate serious infection, though it is not a common signal. When this occurs in the context of sepsis, it is either because disseminated intravascular coagulation (DIC) has developed or because there is a diminution of all blood lines indicating marrow dysfunction. The cause of any abnormal platelet count should be identified promptly if possible.

Hyperglycemia and insulin resistance Hyperglycemia and insulin resistance are often reliable signals of the presence of infection in diabetic patients as well as in nondiabetic patients. The degree of insulin resistance can reflect the severity of the infection as well as the effectiveness of infection control.

Immune failure Severe infection is immunosuppressive.

The most clinically applicable measure of immune failure at present is probably delayed wound healing.

Evaluation for Presence of Infection

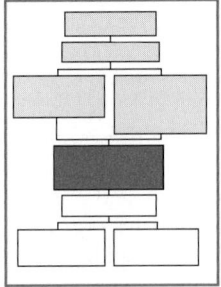

Once the surgeon has evaluated in which ways the patient may be compromised or susceptible to infection and to which degree the physiologic response is inappropriate or harmful (i.e., provokes multiple organ dysfunction or shock), then it is important to consider which microorganisms might be responsible for the presenting clinical picture. This obviously varies with the clinical situation and requires knowledge of specific condition-associated pathogens, as well as the prevalence of certain pathogens in a particular hospital or ICU.

The prevalence of resistant bacterial strains should be monitored in clinical settings in order to guide empirical therapy. Methicillin-resistant *Staphylococcus aureus* (MRSA), once an occasional finding, has become so common in some ICUs and chronic wards that surveillance and isolation programs are no longer employed. It is now the rule for extensive invasive monitoring and access devices to be used in the care of critically ill patients, who thereby become particularly predisposed to gram-positive infection; accordingly, it is important to appreciate the likelihood that MRSA will be encountered. The same is true of *Pseudomonas aeruginosa*, a ubiquitous commensal and a common gram-negative pathogen in hospitals. In compromised patients exposed to multiple antibiotics, *P. aeruginosa* readily acquires antibiotic resistance that usually necessitates the use of double-agent or broad-spectrum coverage for effective management.

Recognizing the virulence of certain pathogens is as important as appreciating their antibiotic susceptibilities. Enteroinvasive *Escherichia coli* 0157-H7, for example, may cause a rapidly progressive hemorrhagic enteritis and provoke a fatal septic syndrome marked by acute renal failure, bleeding, and coma. Necrotizing soft tissue infections, particularly when caused by gram-positive organisms, may be precipitously fatal. Early Gram stain microscopy to identify the specific pathogen is a critical step in the management of this condition.

Essentially the same clinical and laboratory assessments are used to evaluate normally responsive and compromised or complex patients for the presence of infection. There is, however, a significant difference in emphasis. In normally responsive patients, the diagnosis of infection is usually made on clinical grounds with laboratory support, whereas in compromised or complex patients, the diagnosis is usually made on the basis of laboratory findings with clinical support.

The ICU patient presents a particular conundrum. Nosocomial infection is identified in an estimated 20% of such patients.[8] Despite the frequency with which it is suspected and reported, it is difficult to prove unequivocally. The perceived prevalence of nosocomial infection has created a strong predisposition toward instituting empirical antibiotic therapy in ICU patients; however, the global value of this action in terms of both patient outcome and the impact on the ecology of the ICU is unconfirmed and requires validation. The enormous inconsistencies in how infections are diagnosed have a tremendous effect on our ability to assess the efficacy of therapy for infection. The current approach to diagnosing infection in surgical patients, particularly those who are critically ill or compromised, is still in great need of clarification and standardization.[9] Until these issues are resolved, the clinician must be familiar with the strengths and limitations of a variety of current diagnostic methodologies and then exercise thoughtfulness and disciplined diligence. The likelihood that a particular patient is infected (i.e., the pretest probability) is as important in the decision to treat as the fulfillment of any particular constellation of diagnostic criteria.

HISTORY AND PHYSICAL EXAMINATION

The history should include all comorbid conditions (e.g., diabetes, lung disease, cirrhosis, hepatitis, kidney disease necessitating dialysis, and previous important infections) as well as a hospitalization history that covers health status, surgical diagnosis and therapy, additional therapeutic interventions (including interventional radiology, monitoring devices, drains, and drugs), and other related variables.

In the early postoperative period (3 to 6 days after operation), the traditional causes of the signals of infection have their origin in the wound, intravascular lines, the urinary tract, and the lungs. Deep thrombophlebitis, with or without pulmonary embolism, may also initiate a systemic inflammatory response that mimics sepsis. The general physical examination is often unrewarding, but a number of specific examinations should be carefully performed, with emphasis given to (1) all wounds and surgical sites, (2) all invasive monitoring or therapeutic devices and surrounding areas (notably central and peripheral I.V. lines), (3) all drainage systems and surrounding tissue, with particular attention paid to the nature of the drainage and whether it has recently changed in character or volume (particularly if it has stopped), (4) the rectal examination (for pelvic or prostatic infection), (5) areas of potential decubitus ulcers, (6) the neck (for CNS infection), (7) intravascular lines, surrounding tissue, and proximal vessels, (8) the lungs, and (9) the legs. The physical examination is important as a guide for selecting specimens for microbiologic analysis, particularly when there have recently been significant changes in wounds or drainage. The decision to seek radiologic consultation may depend on the findings on physical examination.

DIAGNOSTIC TESTS

Hematologic and Biochemical Tests

After physical assessment, laboratory blood tests are routinely relied on to orient the surgeon toward or away from a clinical diagnosis of infection. Leukocytosis, particularly with an increase in band forms, is a usual but inconsistent marker for infection. The WBC count is widely used to follow the response of infection to therapy and thus has been adopted as a surrogate indicator of the success or failure of therapy. Surprisingly, however, the documentation supporting this ubiquitous practice is sparse.[10,11] Not only is the daily series of complete blood counts often ordered in conjunction with the initiation of antibiotic therapy wasteful and unpleasant for the patient, but it also typically tells the clinician little about the clinical course that cannot be gleaned at the bedside.

In more complex surgical patients, other biochemical cues are used to varying degrees as means of assessing the likelihood of infection. In addition to thrombocytosis, thrombocytopenia, hyperglycemia, and metabolic acidosis, which commonly reflect the stress of severe infection, changes in the erythrocyte sedimentation rate (ESR) and in blood levels of C-reactive protein (CRP), procalcitonin (PCT), interleukin-6 (IL-6), and tumor necrosis factor (TNF) have a significant association with the presence of clinical infection. Plasma CRP concentration, which has been extensively used in some

European countries to monitor the evolution of infection, has been found to be significantly elevated in patients with pulmonary aspiration that has induced bacterial infection, compared with patients with sterile pneumonitis.[12] Some investigators have suggested that because CRP concentration appears to be particularly responsive to bacterial infection, it may be useful as a monitor of the efficacy of antibiotic use, thereby guiding discontinuance of treatment.[13] A host of cytokines, cellular adhesion molecules, oxidants, and other biomolecules known to participate in systemic inflammation from numerous causes are being extensively investigated to establish both diagnostic and therapeutic functions. As yet, however, no single mediator of systemic inflammation has been validated as a reliable clinical tool for surveillance of the progression of infection or the response of infection to treatment.

Case Study: Clinical Picture of Sepsis without Infection

Infection is a process; sepsis is the response.

The difficulty of managing the patient who manifests the septic response in the absence of infection is illustrated by the following case.

A 55-year-old insulin-dependent man with peripheral vascular disease presented with evidence of infection in both feet. Hydration and antibiotic therapy did not prevent progression of the infection, and within 18 hours, it was apparent that amputation would be required for source control. In the course of the operation, gas gangrene, more extensive than had been clinically suspected, was discovered. The initial below-the-knee amputations were eventually followed by a hip disarticulation on one side and a high above-the-knee amputation on the other. Over the 36-hour period during which the infectious process was being controlled, classic septic shock, renal failure, coma, and respiratory failure developed. There was no change in the patient's hyperdynamic and hypermetabolic state after the amputations. During the next 3 weeks, he required ventilator support and daily hemodialysis or hemofiltration; became jaundiced and more deeply comatose; received fluids in amounts significantly in excess of output to maintain blood volume; was hyperglycemic despite receiving regular insulin in dosages of 3 to 5 U/hr; and remained in a hyperdynamic state. Shortly after the last operation, an ileus developed, accompanied by gross fluid retention, which further increased the patient's girth. This state of overt sepsis with hypermetabolism persisted while the wounds healed by primary closure, but no focus of infection could be found.

Antibiotic therapy was stopped for 10 days after operation; the patient's clinical status did not change. Frequent searches were made to ensure that no infection had been overlooked. Suggestions—seriously put forward—to explore the patient's abdomen because "there must be something there" were not heeded. At the end of the third week, for no obvious reason, the patient started to urinate, his ileus resolved, and he was gradually weaned from the ventilator. His level of consciousness improved, the massive edema cleared, and the high cardiac output and low peripheral resistance resolved over a period of 72 hours. He was discharged from the surgical ICU 1 day later and from the hospital in 3 weeks. Some noninfectious process that had maintained this patient's persistent septic response had disappeared or had been turned off, and the result was rapid resolution of the septic state and recovery of health.

As noted, initial control of infection, though difficult, was achieved relatively early. Subsequent therapeutic efforts involved providing hemodynamic, metabolic, and physiologic support of the patient's failing organs and organ systems while waiting for the septic response to resolve. The real problem in this case was not the infection but the patient's unremitting septic response, which was initiated by the infection but maintained in its absence.

Microbiologic Studies

As a rule, Gram stains and cultures of wound tissue, sputum, urine, and drainage effluent are useful studies. In some cases, a battery of cultures of potential sites of infection may be the only feasible approach. Culture techniques are discussed more thoroughly elsewhere [*see 131 Nosocomial Infection*].

The use of polymerase chain reaction (PCR) technology to detect bacterial DNA is emerging as a useful alternative to microbiologic culture for determining the presence of infection. PCR identifies and amplifies a specific bacterial DNA sequence by means of a chemical proliferation process that may take no longer than a few hours. Unfortunately, the sensitivity and specificity of this powerful technique is highly variable. Although investigations have shown PCR to be a sensitive method of confirming the presence of bacteria in the blood of clinically septic ICU patients,[14] comparison of PCR results with blood culture results is problematic in that nonviable bacteria or bacterial debris are likely to create false positive results, leaving the clinician uncertain as to whether treatment is indicated. The accuracy of PCR thus remains to be established, but the rapidity with which it yields results makes it highly promising as a potential guide to therapeutic intervention.

Radiology

A chest x-ray is mandatory. Ultrasonographic examination of the operative site may be useful to evaluate the possibility of a deep abscess. Computed tomography of the operative site is often more useful than ultrasonography because the presence of wounds, dressings, and drainage tubes may obscure ultrasonographic findings. The possibility of acalculous cholecystitis must be kept in mind, though this is probably an overdiagnosed entity of unvalidated clinical significance [*see 133 Intra-abdominal Infection*]. In compromised or complex patients who have not recently undergone an operation, the medical and surgical history combined with the radiologic examination may be the only guide to the potential infectious focus (e.g., ulcer, diverticulitis, cholecystitis or cholangitis, or obstructed ureter). Percutaneous aspiration of potentially infected fluid should be considered, and this fluid should be microbiologically examined if possible.

Institution of Therapy

As noted, the response to infection occupies a continuum ranging from virtually no clinical expression in the immunosuppressed patient to full-blown septic shock. Sepsis, in its basic form, represents a mild to moderate response to infection that occurs in normally responsive patients as well as in many compromised or complex patients. On the basis of the results of clinical or laboratory tests, the clinician can 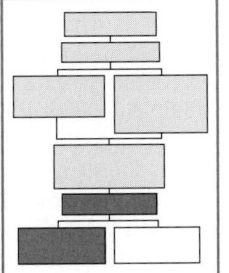 evaluate the magnitude of the septic response and thus its clinical gravity.

It is therefore the magnitude of the host response, in combination with the health of the patient and the nature of the likely infecting organism, that directs the clinician's approach to therapy. The greater the degree of sepsis, the greater the clinical urgency of solving the two fundamental problems involved: resolution of the initiating process (i.e., treatment of the infection) and modulation of the response to that process (i.e., management of sepsis) [*see 128 Multiple Organ Dysfunction Syndrome*]. The therapeutic approach to a given patient is based on the need for speed.

SIRS

As mentioned, SIRS was specifically defined in such a way as to emphasize that this common clinical syndrome frequently occurs without infection and does not routinely necessitate treatment, especially with empirical antibiotic therapy. As an illustration, simply climbing a set of stairs is often enough to enable a healthy individual to fulfill the diagnostic criteria for SIRS—albeit briefly.

The point that SIRS is not invariably associated with microbial invasion is especially relevant to critically ill and traumatized ICU patients, in whom it is not uncommon for clinical signs and symptoms indistinguishable from those of severe sepsis to arise or persist in the absence of any infection [*see Sidebar* Case Study: Clinical Picture of Sepsis without Infection]. Burn injury and pancreatitis are classic examples of conditions that can provoke such a response: both can give rise to a hyperdynamic, hypermetabolic clinical picture identical to that of sepsis or severe sepsis, even when no infection is present. Surgeons have learned not to give antibiotics unless there is evidence of infection. The instinctive reflex to do something must be held in check: "masterful inactivity" is the appropriate response until a specific source that can be controlled is identified.

UNCOMPLICATED SEPSIS

The approach to treatment of infection in both normally responsive and compromised patients with mild to moderate sepsis includes five steps: (1) resuscitation and reestablishment of homeostasis and organ function, if necessary; (2) identification of the focus of infection by clinical or radiologic examination; (3) source control, which implies removal, containment or control of the infectious focus (e.g., open drainage of an infected wound; resection of compromised bowel, as for appendicitis or advanced diverticulitis; or percutaneous drainage, as for pancreatic abscess); (4) microbiologic characterization of the offending pathogen by means of culture, Gram stain, or both; and (5) empirical or targeted treatment with antibiotics, depending on the clinical urgency.

In compromised patients, empirical antibiotic therapy is often started before diagnosis, and its efficacy gauged by the patient's subsequent clinical course [*see Discussion, below*]. In normal hosts with uncomplicated sepsis, many would consider it appropriate to withhold empirical therapy until source control has been effected and the pathogen or pathogens characterized. Adequate source control, when possible, is often all that is required for successful management of sepsis, particularly in healthy hosts. In such cases, antibiotic use for prophylaxis against complications such as SSIs is of proven benefit; however, there actually is little evidence to indicate that antibiotics are necessary to treat sepsis if mechanical source control has been definitively achieved.

Antibiotic Treatment

In the absence of convincing culture data, antibiotic treatment must be directed against a likely cause, as determined by recent history (particularly procedures), past history, and physical examination. Examples of likely causes are (1) urinary manipulation, which necessitates coverage against enterococci and gram-negative bacteria with ampicillin and an aminoglycoside; (2) colonic flora, which mandates wide coverage against anaerobes and aerobes; (3) infected vascular lines, which warrant coverage against gram-positive organisms; (4) cholangitis, which calls for coverage against aerobic gram-negative bacteria with ceftriaxone or an aminoglycoside; and (5) pneumonia, which necessitates coverage against gram-positive and gram-negative aerobes.

Drainage

The search for the focus of infection is important because drainage may resolve the entire problem. The clinical state can be changed dramatically by technical or mechanical management of pus behind an obstruction (e.g., in the biliary tree, the urinary tract, or the tracheobronchial tree) or pus under pressure (e.g., an abscess), by manipulation of a drain, or by removal of a foreign body (e.g., an intravascular line). Prompt elimination of all foci of infection that can be drained or are operable is critical. Needle aspiration of peritoneal or pleural fluid may be very helpful. Wounds must be reevaluated constantly and the presence of pressure sores ruled out. Drainage can often be performed either percutaneously (e.g., for pyelonephritis from ureteral obstruction or for subphrenic abscess) or endoscopically (e.g., for cholangitis). Antibiotics alone may suffice to treat small collections not accessible by means of percutaneous techniques.

SEVERE SEPSIS AND SEPTIC SHOCK

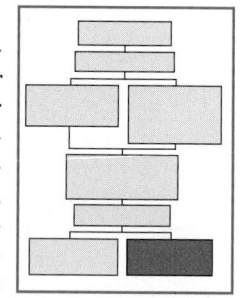

For assessment and management of severe sepsis and septic shock [*see Sidebar Definitions of Key Concepts*], the four steps in treatment—resuscitation, diagnosis of the infectious focus, antibiotic therapy, and drainage—must be performed concurrently. Specifically, I.V. administration of empirical antibiotics must be initiated promptly, before the diagnostic process is completed, and any potentially drainable focus must be identified via physical examination or radiologic imaging. The choice of antibiotic depends on (1) what the likely source of infection is (e.g., a lung, a perforated viscus, or the biliary tract), (2) whether the infection is hospital acquired (in which case antibiotic resistance must be considered), and (3) whether the patient has previously received antibiotic therapy.

Discussion

Approaches to Specific Infections in Complex Surgical Patients

The following infections may occur in all surgical patients. They are, however, much more difficult to identify in complex surgical patients, such as those admitted to the ICU. Because the signals of infection are less specific and extremely difficult to interpret after injury or operation, the approach to diagnosing and treating infection must be cautious and disciplined.

SURGICAL SITE INFECTION

SSIs include all infections occurring within the operative field, from the skin to the actual area of surgery [*see 5 Prevention of Postoperative Infection*].[15] The patient history should address previous diseases as well as issues concerning the operation itself, such as wound risk classification, duration, difficulty, urgency, use of drains, other details of the procedure, time elapsed since the operation, and whether the patient was immunosuppressed, experienced trauma, or received chemotherapy. Physical examination should focus on the cardinal signs of infection and the absence or presence of a healing ridge.

Deeper infections tend to become apparent later in the postoperative course, often after a period in which the patient appears to be recovering, and are associated with a variety of signals, some of which can appear suddenly. The physical examination is often useless or misleading because of discomfort associated with the operation. Surgical site pain that increases or fails to resolve in the 7 to 10 days following surgery is an important yet subtle marker for occult infection that calls for investigation. Rectal examination is important because it may detect abscess formation or bleeding. Return of ileus after an abdominal operation is a significant clue to the presence of abdominal infection.

Culture is essential because use of the correct antibiotics is particularly vital in treatment of compromised or complex patients. Knowledge of the organism and its sensitivities is the key to identifying epidemic or multiresistant strains.

URINARY TRACT INFECTION

Nearly all patients admitted to the ICU have a urinary catheter in place; of these, it is estimated that about 20% progress to urinary tract infection (UTI).[8] Bacteria adhere to urinary catheter surfaces, where they promote growth of a so-called biofilm composed of microorganisms, bacterial glycocalices, Tamm-Horsfall protein, and urinary salts. Eradication of this infectious nidus is essentially impossible without catheter removal.[16] The standard criterion for the diagnosis of UTI (10^5 bacteria/ml) is difficult to apply in catheterized patients because antibiotic therapy without removal of the catheter and the source of bacteriuria would be ineffective. Furthermore, it is well established that urine cultures demonstrating as few as 10^1 or 10^2 bacteria/ml increase 1,000-fold within 1 to 2 days[17]; effectively, therefore, any bacterial growth on a urine culture from a catheterized patient signals heavy colonization, if not infection.

More important than quantifying the degree of bacteriuria is determining whether there is any evidence of tissue invasion by urinary bacteria, which would present as pyelonephritis, cystitis, prostatitis, epididymitis, bacteremia, or sepsis. The patient history should determine whether a Foley catheter was used and for how long; how, when, and why it was inserted; instrumentation (e.g., a so-called in-and-out catheter, cystoscopy, or transurethral resection of the prostate); and whether the patient has had any previous UTIs. The physical examination should ascertain whether there is any costovertebral angle tenderness or evidence of prostatic or epididymal tenderness.

Laboratory tests should include gross and microscopic urinalysis, urine culture, and sensitivity tests. Blood culture is important because it may substantiate the diagnosis, identify the bacteria present, and determine the degree of invasiveness of the infectious process.

VASCULAR CATHETER INFECTION

The most frequent sites of infection postoperatively are I.V. catheters, particularly peripheral ones. Diagnosis of peripheral catheter infection is simple and is made on clinical grounds. Diagnosis of central venous catheter (CVC) infection is more difficult. Because hospitalized patients are increasingly being managed with monitoring or therapeutic modalities that depend on vascular access (e.g., total parenteral nutrition and dialysis), line infections have become more common, with an incidence ranging from two to 30 infections per 1,000 CVC days.[18] The combined pressures imposed by (1) the need to maintain vascular access in sicker and more complex patients and (2) the increasing predominance of gram-positive CVC infections observed since the late 1970s have led clinicians in many centers to administer empirical therapy without line removal to complex patients as a matter of course; some even advocate 10 to 21 days of vancomycin-based therapy. The problems associated with the latter approach—emerging vancomycin resistance, nephrotoxicity, and rash—are serious and relate specifically to the diagnostic strategy used to manage potential CVC infections. Distinguishing between contamination, colonization, and true infection is problematic; as a result, a number of diagnostic strategies have been advocated that are predicated more on practicality and cost-effectiveness than on microbiologic reality.

It is believed that CVC infection most commonly arises from invasion by skin microorganisms (*S. aureus* or *S. epidermidis* in about 80% of cases), which may manifest itself as exit-site purulence with or without local cellulitis, as a tunnel infection that may be clinically difficult to detect, or as catheter-related bloodstream infection (CR-BSI). Of these, CR-BSI, which complicates as many as 5% of line placements, is the most clinically important entity. It is strictly diagnosed by identification of the same microorganism (identical species and antibiogram) grown from both the catheter and a peripheral blood culture.

The catheter may be cultured in one of several ways, the most common of which is the roll-plate method [see 131 Nosocomial Infection]. Because it is theoretically possible that this technique may fail to detect bacteria harbored within the catheter lumen, some authorities advocate the more sensitive sonication method, in which the catheter segment is immersed and agitated in a medium to produce a broth that contains bacteria from both the internal and the external surfaces of the line. This technique is both more costly and more time consuming, in that it requires quantitative cultures that are deemed positive only when more than 10^3 colony-forming units are detected. More often, blood drawn through the CVC or cultured from an exit-site exudate is compared with peripheral cultures, and thus there is no need to remove the line. If quantitative cultures are done, a line blood culture showing five to 10 times more growth than the peripheral sample strongly suggests that the catheter is the source of the bacteremia. A less costly method that renders quantitative cultures unnecessary relies on the speed of bacterial growth: if growth in catheter-drawn blood is faster than that in peripherally drawn blood, a primary line infection is likely. On its own, a line blood culture is not sensitive or specific enough to be diagnostically useful.

PULMONARY INFECTION

Diagnosis and management of nosocomial pneumonia in surgical patients is addressed elsewhere [see 132 Postoperative and Ventilator-Associated Pneumonia]. The central issue is that there is no universal agreement as to how pneumonia—particularly ventilator-associated pneumonia—should be diagnosed. Of the innumerable diagnostic options, none can rely on demonstration of tissue invasion by microorganisms, as would be ideal: all are to some degree nonspecific, and any may be invoked to justify initiation of antibiotic therapy.[19] Randomized trials linking mode of diagnosis to therapeutic strategy and then to outcome are yet to resolve this issue.[20]

SINUSITIS

All patients undergoing prolonged nasogastric intubation are predisposed to sinus infection. Previous facial trauma and a history of sinusitis are potential contributing factors as well. (Otitis and pharyngitis, which are not often considered, occur in much the same group of patients.) Because maxillary or frontal area tenderness is nonspecific in very ill surgical patients, the diagnosis is usually based on CT demonstration of sinus opacification or air-fluid levels. As a first step, sinus drainage should be reestablished by removal of an unnecessary nasogastric tube. Some authorities advocate sinus aspiration for culture before empirical antibiotic therapy is begun in urgent cases.

PAROTITIS

Parotitis is an increasingly common clinical diagnosis in elderly patients. It is usually caused by *S. aureus* and diagnosed on the basis of the presence of the classic local signs of inflammation. Culture of Stensen's duct and blood culture are useful.

PROSTATITIS

Prostatitis (diagnosed by rectal examination) and epididymitis are clinical expressions of Foley catheter–related infection. The aid of prostatic massage is important in obtaining specimens for culture. It should be remembered that a blocked Foley catheter is the most common cause of hospital anuria. This obstruction can lead to devastating purulent cystitis and upper UTI.

PSEUDOMEMBRANOUS ENTEROCOLITIS

Antibiotic-associated pseudomembranous enterocolitis is diagnosed by obtaining specimens for serology and culture and performing proctosigmoidoscopy. *Clostridium difficile* is frequently identified as the causative pathogen. Although pseudomembranous colitis is rarely clinically impressive and is easy to overlook, it can be rapidly fatal. Initial appropriate antibiotic therapy is not always successful; therefore, reevaluation at the end of the treatment course is required.

Problems with Empirical Treatment of Infection

The frequent presence of SIRS in complex or critically ill surgical patients usually prompts a reflexive response to "pan-culture" the patient if no credible source of infection is apparent. When permissive or loose diagnostic criteria for infection are invoked, the inevitable result is the commencement of empirical antibiotic therapy for suspected infection, which is often, by default, continued for days, if not weeks, pending definitive culture results or clinical improvement. This strategy may seem reasonable and is understandably difficult to resist, but it is potentially deleterious in many ways, and there are many sound objections to its reflexive use.[21]

Empirical antibiotic therapy can obfuscate future cultures, predispose to the emergence of resistant organisms (which are associated with increased attributable mortality), promote derepression of homeostasis-maintaining endogenous flora, cause toxic reactions and secondary effects, alter the ecology of the unit in which it is used (as shown by the rising prevalence of MRSA and vancomycin-resistant enterococci in both European and North American centers), and raise the cost of patient care. This widely used strategy is largely unvalidated.[10,11] It must be emphasized that the paramount principle of therapy for infection is treatment focused on appropriate microbiologic cultures in the context of strict diagnostic criteria for infection.

Many authorities espouse streamlining of empirically begun broad-spectrum antibiotic therapy in response to microbiologic data once culture results are available; however, it is frequently difficult to discontinue antibiotics once they have been started. When strict diagnostic criteria for infection are not met or, more important, when antibiotic therapy based on nonmicrobiologic evidence of infection yields negligible results, strong consideration should be given to stopping the antibiotics, and an exhaustive effort should be made to identify and control any occult persistent cause of the inflammatory state. Of course, this is easier said than done. Moreover, positive cultures do not automatically confirm infection, and great discretion must be exercised in determining how the microbiologic information obtained should be used. For example, tracheal aspirates from intubated patients routinely reveal gram-negative flora, but this finding in no way confirms pneumonia. A single blood culture growing *S. epidermidis* is similarly difficult to interpret.

Despite ubiquitous use in surgical patients, there is not a great deal of evidence in the clinical literature to substantiate the effectiveness of either empirical or streamlined antibiotic therapy. Further efforts must be made to find such evidence because this practice could theoretically exact a substantial cost from both the patient and the environment in which the patient is cared for. In the meantime, clinicians must approach the development of SIRS or other nonspecific signs of infection in their patients by predicating antimicrobial use on carefully formulated diagnostic criteria for the presence of infection; CDC consensus definitions of infection are a good starting point.

Source Control for Management of SIRS

In the past, because the term sepsis was loosely used to describe any general systemic inflammatory state and because such states often arose as a result of infection, it was assumed that antimicrobial therapy was generally appropriate in the management of "septic" patients. Now that sepsis has been redefined exclusively as SIRS in a patient in whom a causative source of infection has been identified, it is clear that the use of antibiotics in "septic" (i.e., SIRS) patients should be more discriminating.

In the same vein, so-called source control was developed as a strategy for managing "septic" patients. Like the term sepsis, the term source control traditionally connotes management of infection rather than, more generally, management of a cause of inflammation. Classically, source control consists of a three-pronged approach employing measures to (1) eradicate a focus of infection, (2) eliminate ongoing microbial contamination, and (3) render the local environment inhospitable to microbial growth and tissue invasion. Diligent source control has long been considered pivotal to successful management of sepsis. Although this traditional approach addresses the infectious causes of local or systemic inflammation very well in a great variety of clinical situations, good judgment must not yield to dogmatism in deciding which processes are required to control infection and inflammation. Challenging convention, a surprising number of investigators have successfully managed many supposedly surgical conditions (e.g., appendicitis[22] and intra-abdominal abscess[23]) without intervention or by using only prolonged antibiotic therapy. Seasoned general surgeons are well aware that if acute cholecystitis is not operated on urgently, it may certainly harm the patient or cause recurring discomfort, but

it may also resolve completely on its own. What actually constitutes adequate source control and how this can be measured are critical questions and remain the subject of debate. These questions become particularly problematic with respect to ICU patients, in whom SIRS is highly nonspecific.

It would seem rational to take our current understanding of SIRS as encompassing both infectious and noninfectious pathology and extrapolate it to the concept of source control. Indeed, as regards more complex surgical patients, it may be appropriate to broaden the definition of source control to include control of all causes of SIRS, not merely infectious ones. For example, debriding devitalized injured tissue, removing a rejected allograft, and resolving postoperative atelectasis are all important for successfully abating a systemic inflammatory state that might easily be mistaken for a manifestation of infection. Deemphasizing infection as the predominant cause of SIRS and withholding antibiotic therapy until stricter, more focused diagnostic criteria for infection are met should make treatment paradigms for managing difficult surgical patients, if not altogether more effective, at least more evaluable.

If one assumes that source control is in fact a therapeutic response to the presence of SIRS, one may then think of it as being either assisted or unassisted. The therapeutic response is initiated by the host, with either complete or partial success. Only in the latter instance should one assist the host's efforts at source control by providing antibiotics or taking surgical measures. This is by no means to suggest that one should not search diligently for a correctable cause of infection or inflammation but rather to suggest that when such an effort yields negligible results, one should consider the possibility that SIRS may be not only appropriate but desirable and may represent the patient's own adequate management of the underlying physiologic insult. Thus, in certain situations, source control may be best regarded as an endogenous or unassisted event. For instance, when fever, tachycardia, and leukocytosis are observed in a surgical patient who is coping well, antibiotics should not necessarily be given automatically. Indeed, such "default therapy" should be actively discouraged. One should also keep in mind that some forms of injury or insult (e.g., some viral infections) not only are very well managed without intervention but may not even prompt clinically evident SIRS.

The notion that no intervention may be required is understandably difficult for many surgeons to embrace at the bedside. Nonetheless, extensive ongoing research elucidating the complex dynamic of circulating proinflammatory and counterinflammatory mediators (e.g., TNF, the interleukins, and a host of other cytokines) suggests that a poorly understood but highly sophisticated biologic apparatus exists for responding to injury and insult. Indeed, it is widely hypothesized (though yet unproved) that this systemic response can be manipulated to restore health in stressed or deteriorating surgical patients. The prospect of untangling the complex biology of systemic inflammation through advances in this field is truly engaging.

References

1. Marshall J, Sweeny D: Microbial infection and the septic response in critical surgical illness. Arch Surg 125:17, 1990

2. Meakins JL, Marshall JC: The gut as the motor of multiple system organ failure. Splanchnic Ischemia and Multiple Organ Failure. Marston A, Ed. Edward Arnold, London, 1989, p 339

3. Goris RJA, Boekhorst TAP, Nuytinck JKS, et al: Multiple organ failure: generalized autodestructive inflammation? Arch Surg 120:1109, 1985

4. Bone RC, Fisher CJ Jr, Clemmer TP, et al: Sepsis syndrome: a valid clinical entity. Crit Care Med 17: 389, 1989

5. Bone RC: Let's agree on terminology: definitions

of sepsis. Crit Care Med 19:973, 1991

6. Sibbald WJ, Marshall J, Christou N, et al: "Sepsis"—clarity of existing terminology . . . or more confusion? Crit Care Med 19:996, 1991

7. American College of Chest Physicians/Society of Critical Care Medicine Consensus Conference: Definitions for sepsis and organ failure and guide-

lines for the use of innovative therapies in sepsis. Crit Care Med 20:864, 1992

8. Vincent J, Bihari DJ, Suter PM, et al: The prevalence of nosocomial infection in intensive care units in Europe: results of the European Prevalence of Infection in Intensive Care (EPIC) Study. JAMA 274:639, 1995

9. Casadevall A: Crisis in infectious diseases: time for a new paradigm? Clin Infect Dis 32:790, 1996

10. Lennard ES, Mineshew BH, Dellinger EP, et al: Leukocytosis at termination of antibiotherapy: its importance for intra-abdominal sepsis. Arch Surg 115:918, 1980

11. Stone HH, Bourneuf AA, Stinson LD: Reliability of criteria for predicting recurrent sepsis. Arch Surg 120:17, 1985

12. Adnet F, Borron SW, Vicault E, et al: Value of C-reactive protein in the detection of bacterial contamination at the time of presentation in drug-induced aspiration pneumonia. Chest 112:466, 1997

13. Young B, Gleeson M, Cripps AW: C-reactive protein: a critical review. Pathology 23:118, 1991

14. Cursons RTM, Jeyerajah E, Sleigh JW: The use of polymerase chain reaction to detect septicemia in critically ill patients. Crit Care Med 27:937, 1999

15. The Society for Hospital Epidemiology of America, the Association for Practitioners in Infection Control, the Centers for Disease Control, the Surgical Infection Society: Consensus paper on the surveillance of surgical wound infections. Infect Control Hosp Epidemiol 13:599, 1992

16. Stamm WE, Hooton TM: Management of urinary tract infection in adults. N Engl J Med 329:1328, 1993

17. Stark RP, Maki DG: Bacteriuria in the catheterized patient: what quantitative level of bacteriuria is relevant? N Engl J Med 311:560, 1984

18. Bullard KM, Dunn DL: Diagnosis and treatment of bacteremia and intravascular catheter infections. Am J Surg 172(suppl 6A):13S, 1996

19. American Thoracic Society: Hospital-acquired pneumonia in adults: diagnosis, assessment of severity, initial antimicrobial therapy, and preventive strategies: a consensus statement. Am J Respir Crit Care Med 153:1711, 1995

20. Sterling TR, Ho EJ, Brehm WT, et al: Diagnosis and treatment of ventilator-associated pneumonia-impact on survival. Chest 110:1025, 1996

21. Timsit M, Misset B, Renaud B, et al: Effect of previous antimicrobial therapy on the accuracy of the main procedures used to diagnose nosocomial pneumonia in patients who are using mechanical ventilation. Chest 108:1036, 1997

22. Eriksson S, Granstrom L: Randomized controlled trial of appendectomy versus antibiotic therapy for acute appendicitis. Br J Surg 82:166, 1995

23. Montgomery RS, Wilson SE: Intraabdominal abscess: image-guided diagnosis and therapy. Clin Infect Dis 23:28, 1996

130 ANTIBIOTICS

Nicolas V. Christou, M.D., Ph.D., F.A.C.S.

Several important advances in antimicrobial therapy have been made since the early 1980s. Among these advances are (1) improved understanding of the microbiologic spectrum of so-called optimal therapy, (2) better application of pharmacokinetic principles to drug administration, (3) the development of several new classes of antibiotics, and (4) greater insight into the interplay among host resistance factors, microorganisms, and chemotherapy.

General Principles of Antimicrobial Therapy

EMPIRICAL THERAPY

Even with the most rapid bacteriologic tests currently available, it may not be possible to identify a pathogen in less than 24 hours, and antimicrobial sensitivities can rarely be obtained in less than 48 to 72 hours. In seriously ill patients, treatment cannot be delayed for 2 to 3 days until these data become available. If therapy is to be successful, it must be started as soon as a life-threatening infection is diagnosed or, in some patients, as soon as such an infection is suspected. Which antimicrobial agents are to be used depends on the suspected site of infection and on the organisms that are commonly pathogenic at this site. Therapy is initiated with an agent or combination of agents whose action is broad enough to cover all the suspected microbial pathogens. The application of such broad-spectrum antibiotic therapy in the absence of microbiologic confirmation is termed empirical therapy.

To make a rational decision regarding empirical therapy, the surgeon must be familiar with the organisms that are likely to be encountered when a particular infection (e.g., an intra-abdominal abscess) is suspected. Selection of the agent or agents is based on the history, the physical examination, where the infection was likely to have been acquired, the host defense status, the overall clinical severity of the infection, and the response of the host. Definitive therapy is initiated after the host response to the infection and to the empirical treatment has been monitored and the results from the microbiology laboratory—specifically, identification of the isolated organisms and the minimal inhibitory concentrations (MICs) of various antimicrobial agents—have been assessed.

LABORATORY TESTS

Many laboratory tests, if used in the proper context, can guide selection of optimal antimicrobial therapy.

In vitro susceptibility tests are indicated when the susceptibility of an organism is not completely predictable or when certain other specific problems arise, such as the necessity of determining whether resistance has developed during the course of therapy. An organism is generally considered susceptible if the concentration of antimicrobial agent necessary to inhibit its growth is lower than that usually attainable in body fluids, particularly blood, cerebrospinal fluid, or urine.

The disk diffusion method has been standardized by the

National Committee for Clinical Laboratory Standards (NCCLS)[1] for in vitro susceptibility testing. Commercially available paper disks containing specific amounts of antimicrobial agents are placed on Mueller-Hinton agar plates that contain a standard bacterial inoculum. A zone of inhibition of bacterial growth develops around each active antibiotic after overnight incubation. The size of the zone determines the organism's susceptibility or resistance; prior studies have correlated zone sizes with MICs obtained through dilution tests. Arbitrary zone-size break points for susceptibility have been established by clinical and laboratory investigators on the basis of such additional factors as achievable serum levels, degree of protein binding, and toxicity.

The broth dilution method exposes an inoculum of bacteria to various concentrations of an antimicrobial agent during incubation. The MIC of an agent that inhibits growth can be determined, and this value can be correlated with blood, urine, or other body fluid levels of the antimicrobial agent. Moreover, those tubes that show inhibition of growth can be subcultured to an antimicrobial-free medium, and the minimal bactericidal concentration (MBC) can be determined. Unfortunately, this test is not well standardized at present, and its reproducibility is poor when it is subjected to intralaboratory and interlaboratory comparisons.[2]

The agar dilution method works in much the same way as the broth dilution method, except that the former employs agar plates that contain various dilutions of antimicrobial agents, and as many as 36 organisms can be efficiently inoculated on each plate by means of a replicator device. The MIC is determined by reading inhibition of colony growth on the agar surface. Agar dilution has the advantage of producing MIC data efficiently in a laboratory that performs large numbers of tests daily.

In the serum bactericidal test (SBT), samples of the serum of the treated patient are obtained and incubated with the infecting organism in doubling dilutions with broth to determine the highest dilution that is bactericidal. (Not all antimicrobial agents exhibit bactericidal activity; some exhibit only bacteriostatic activity [see Table 1].) The drawing of serum specimens can be timed to coincide with anticipated peak and trough antimicrobial levels. In effect, this test indirectly assesses both the susceptibility of the organism and the serum concentration of the antimicrobial agent, as well as the interactions between serum and organism and serum and drug. The NCCLS has developed proposed guidelines for the SBT.[3] A comprehensive review of the technical and clinical considerations associated with the SBT has been published.[4]

Factors Influencing Application of Antimicrobial Therapy

ROUTE OF ADMINISTRATION

Many antibiotics are absorbed sufficiently well via the oral route to provide effective blood levels in patients with normal GI function.[5] The enteral absorption of some antimicrobials is impeded by food and some medications (e.g., antacids). Many antibiotics cannot be given intramuscularly because of local pain or necrosis at the injection site. Intravenous administration must be used in the treatment of major and life-threatening infections such as suppurative diffuse peritonitis. In many cases, patients are clinically stable during intravenous treatment, and it is often possible to discharge them and to administer parenteral antibiotics on an outpatient basis. Supervision by special teams of physicians, nurses, and pharmacists is required[6]; antibiotics can be administered either in the hospital outpatient department or at home if competent family members are available. New antibiotics with long half-lives can be used with improved intravenous catheters and delivery devices in simplified regimens; this leads to substantial economic benefits, enhanced patient comfort, and good therapeutic results with few complications.[7]

HOST FACTORS

Hypersensitivity to Antibiotics

Because of widespread exposure to antimicrobial agents, many patients develop allergies to them.[8] A careful history of hypersensitivity should thus be obtained [see Hypersensitivity Reactions, below].

Concurrent Illnesses

Patients with immunosuppressive illnesses are vulnerable to opportunistic pathogens. These patients may require broader antimicrobial coverage as well as intense therapy for ordinary pathogens. The same is true to a lesser extent for patients with a chronic debilitating illness. Patients with renal insufficiency or liver disease may be unusually susceptible to direct drug toxicity.

Pregnancy

The administration of antimicrobial agents during pregnancy and in the postpartum period poses several problems. Foremost is the question of safety, both for the mother and the fetus or neonate. Although most antibiotics cross the placenta and enter maternal milk, the concentrations to which the fetus or neonate is exposed vary widely. Because the immature liver may lack the enzymes required to metabolize certain drugs, pharmacokinetics and toxicities in the fetus are often very different from those in older children and adults. Teratogenicity is a major concern when any drug is administered during pregnancy. Finally, it may be necessary to alter the dosage schedules of drugs that appear to be safe to use during pregnancy; increases in maternal blood volume, glomerular filtration rule (GFR), and hepatic metabolic activity often reduce the maternal serum levels of antimicrobials by 10% to 50%, especially late in pregnancy and in the early postpartum period. In some women, delayed gastric emptying may reduce the absorption of antibiotics that have been administered orally during pregnancy.

Even though 25% to 40% of women receive antibiotics during pregnancy, data regarding safety and efficacy in this setting are often scarce. Some general recommendations have been proposed, but they are intended only as a guide [see Table 2]; in all cases, therapy must be individualized, and both the indications for antibiotics and the possible risks to mother and fetus must be considered. Individual decisions are also required for lactating mothers; although most antimicrobials appear safe for breast-fed infants, chloramphenicol and the tetracyclines should be avoided.[9]

Advanced Age

Physiologic changes that occur with age can alter the pharmacokinetics of antimicrobial agents. For example, decreased gastric acidity and intestinal motility can impair drug absorption; increased body fat and decreased serum albumin levels can alter drug distribution; and decreased hepatic blood flow and enzymatic action can delay drug metabolism. Although these factors have not consistently affected antibiotic levels in the elderly, the decrease in GFR that occurs with age can lead to the accumulation of drugs excreted by the kidney. The high therapeutic index of the penicillins and cephalosporins obviates major changes in dosage schedules in elderly patients who have normal serum creatinine levels. However, in the case of aminoglycosides and vancomycin, decreased dosage schedules are often required; ideally, drug levels should be measured and renal function should be monitored when these agents are given. The dosage of amantadine and rimantadine should also be reduced in elderly patients.

Antibiotic Selection for Infections in Surgical Patients

The term surgical infection is difficult to define, but for the purposes of this chapter, it means infections that are related to surgical procedures or that require, in addition to antibiotic therapy, surgical debridement or control of the source of the infection. Such infections include infections of the soft tissues of the integument; muscles; bones; and body cavities (e.g., empyema, intra-abdominal infections, pyelonephritis, and infections of the retroperitoneum).

A framework for antibiotic selection for intra-abdominal infections is presented [see Table 3]; this framework can be modified for the selection of antibiotic for other types of surgical infection. A therapeutic regimen for the treatment of intra-abdominal infection should include agents that are active against *Staphylococcus aureus*, enteric gram-negative bacilli, and anaerobes, including *Bacteroides fragilis*. The regimen that has been regarded as the gold standard consists of an aminoglycoside, to cover the enteric gram-negative organisms, and clindamycin or metronidazole, to cover the anaerobes; other approaches, however, look promising.

A well-designed, controlled, prospective, randomized trial that compared imipenem therapy with acceptable aminoglycoside-based regimens supports the use of imipenem as monotherapy for intra-abdominal infections in which an enteric mixed flora is anticipated.[10] When the analysis was restricted to the residual effect of treatment assignment, a significant improvement in outcome was found in the patients receiving imipenem ($P = 0.043$).

Table 1 Bactericidal and Bacteriostatic Agents[155]

Bactericidal Agents	Bacteriostatic Agents
Aminoglycosides*	Chloramphenicol
Aztreonam	Clindamycin
Bacitracin	Erythromycin
Cephalosporins	Sulfonamides
Imipenem	Tetracyclines
Penicillins	Trimethoprim
Polymyxins†	
Quinolones‡	
Vancomycin	

*Including streptomycin, neomycin, kanamycin, gentamicin, tobramycin, amikacin, and netilmicin.
†Including polymyxin B and colistimethate.
‡Including norfloxacin and ciprofloxacin.

Table 2 Antibiotics in Pregnancy[155]

Drug	Major Toxic Potential		Pharmacology	
	Maternal	Fetal	Maternal Serum Levels	Excreted in Mother's Milk
Considered safe				
Cephalosporins	Allergies	None known	Decreased	Trace
Erythromycin base	Allergies, GI intolerance	None known	Decreased	Yes
Penicillins	Allergies	None known	Decreased	Trace
Spectinomycin	?	None known	?	?
Use with caution				
Aminoglycosides	Ototoxicity, nephrotoxicity	Ototoxicity	Decreased	Yes
Clindamycin	Allergies, colitis	None known	Unchanged	Trace
Ethambutol	Optic neuritis	Probably safe	?	?
Isoniazid	Allergies, hepatotoxicity	Neuropathy, seizures	Unchanged	Yes
Rifampin	Hypersensitivity, hepatotoxicity	Probably safe	Unchanged	Yes
Sulfonamides (contraindicated at term)	Allergies, crystalluria	Kernicterus (at term), hemolysis (G6PD deficiency)	Unchanged	Yes
Avoid if possible				
Metronidazole	Hypersensitivity, alcohol intolerance, neuropathy	None known (teratogenic in animals)	Probably unchanged	Yes
Contraindicated				
Chloramphenicol	Blood dyscrasias	Gray syndrome	Unchanged	Yes
Erythromycin estolate	Hepatotoxicity	None known	Decreased	Yes
Nalidixic acid	GI intolerance	Increased intracranial pressure	?	?
Nitrofurantoin	Allergies, neuropathy, GI intolerance	Hemolysis (G6PD deficiency)	Decreased	Trace
Norfloxacin, ciprofloxacin, ofloxacin, lomefloxacin	GI intolerance	Arthropathies in immature animals	?	?
Tetracyclines	Hepatotoxicity, renal failure	Tooth discoloration and dysplasia, impaired bone growth	Probably unchanged	Yes
Trimethoprim	Hypersensitivity	Teratogenicity	Unchanged	Yes

Meropenem was found to be as effective as imipenem for the treatment of moderately severe intra-abdominal infections.[11]

Ertapenem has a pharmacokinetic profile and an antimicrobial spectrum that support its use as a once-daily agent for the treatment of common mixed aerobic and anaerobic infections. A prospective, randomized, controlled, double-blind trial compared ertapenem with piperacillin-tazobactam as therapy following adequate surgical management of complicated intra-abdominal infections. The modified intent-to-treat population consisted of 633 patients, of whom 396 met all criteria for the evaluable population. Patients with a wide range of infections were enrolled. A prospective expert-panel review was conducted to assess the adequacy of surgical source control in patients in whom therapeutic failure was a component of evaluability. For the modified intent-to-treat groups, 245 of 311 patients treated with ertapenem (78.8%) were cured; 232 of 304 patients (76.3%) treated with piperacillin-tazobactam were cured. Of 203 microbiologically evaluable patients treated with ertapenem, 176 (86.7%) were cured; 157 of the 193 patients (81.3%) treated with piperacillin-tazobactam were cured. In this study, ertapenem, 1 g once a day, was equivalent to piperacillin-tazobactam, 3.375 g every 6 hours, in the treatment of a range of intra-abdominal infections. Ertapenem may be a useful option that could eliminate the need for combination therapy, multidose antibiotic regimens, or both for the empirical treatment of intra-abdominal infections.[12]

Appropriate surgical control of the source of the intra-abdominal infection is of utmost importance in determining outcome; antibiotics play a necessary but secondary role.[13,14] The controversies regarding the pathogenicity of enterococci have been addressed by guidelines published by members of the Surgical Infection Society.[15] The third-generation cephalosporins have been proposed as candidates for single-agent therapy for infection in the abdominal cavity because their spectra of activity encompass both the aerobic gram-negative bacilli and some of the anaerobic isolates that cause infection in this region. No cephalosporin, of any generation, has been shown to have a clear advantage over an aminoglycoside-clindamycin combination in the treatment of intra-abdominal infections.

Interpretation of overall results in intra-abdominal infections is difficult because of the numerous variables involved, including the diversity of the possible infectious processes, the variable quality of the surgical technique employed, the variety of the patient characteristics observed, the possibility of one or more underlying diseases, and the differing doses of antibiotics used in individual studies.[16] Most third-generation cephalosporins do not cover anaerobes well and should be used in conjunction with an antianaerobic agent, such as clindamycin or metronidazole, for empirical therapy for serious intra-abdominal infections. In a recent prospective, randomized, double-blind study, cefoxitin was found to be comparable to imipenem with regard to outcome (defined as survival); failure to cure infections was attributed to resistant organisms at the primary site in the cefoxitin arm of the trial.[17]

Adverse Reactions to Antimicrobial Agents

There are three general types of adverse reactions to antimicrobial agents: hypersensitivity reactions (which are not dose related), direct drug toxicity (which usually is dose related and

Table 3 Antibiotic Selection for Infections in Surgical Patients

Type of Infection	Expected Pathogen	First Choice I.V. Rx	Second Choice I.V. Rx	Switch to P.O. Choice
Brain infection (abscess, subdural empyema, intracranial suppurative thrombophlebitis)				
Traumatic brain injury	*Staphylococcus aureus,* Enterobacteriaceae, *Pseudomonas aeruginosa*	Cefepime, 2 g I.V. q. 8 hr	Meropenem, 1 g I.V. q. 8 hr	Not recommended
Postneurosurgical procedure	*S. aureus, S. epidermidis*	Nafcillin, 2 g I.V. q. 4 hr *or* Cefepime, 2 g I.V. q. 8 hr *or* If methicillin resistant: Linezolide, 600 mg I.V. q. 12 hr	Meropenem, 1 g I.V. q. 8 hr	Linezolid, 600 mg p.o., q. 12 hr
Vascular graft infection				
Arteriovenous graft/shunt	*S. aureus*, Enterobacteriaceae, enterococci	Vancomycin, 1 g I.V. *plus* Gentamicin, 240 mg I.V. and remove graft	Meropenem, 1 g I.V. q. 8 hr and remove graft	Moxifloxacin, 400 mg p.o. and remove graft
Aortic graft (treat with antibiotics until graft is replaced)	*S. aureus, S. epidermidis,* Enterobacteriaceae	Cefepime, 2 g I.V. q. 12 hr *or* Imipenem, 1 g I.V. q. 8 hr *or* Meropenem, 1 g I.V. q. 8 hr	Ceftizoxime, 2 g I.V. q. 8 hr *or* Cefotaxime, 2 g I.V. q. 6 hr	Levofloxacin, 500 mg p.o., q. 24 hr *or* Moxifloxacin, 400 mg p.o., q. 24 hr
Intra-abdominal infection (peritonitis, abscess)				
Gastric perforation (peptic ulcer disease)	*Candida,* oral anaerobes, *S. aureus*	Cefazolin, 1 g I.V. q. 8 hr	Ceftizoxime, 2 g I.V. q. 8 hr *or* Cefotaxime, 2 g I.V. q. 6 hr	Levofloxacin, 500 mg p.o., q. 24 hr *or* Moxifloxacin, 400 mg p.o., q. 24 hr
Gastric perforation (malignancy)	*S. aureus, S. epidermidis,* Enterobacteriaceae, *Candida*	Cefepime, 2 g I.V. q. 12 hr *or* Imipenem, 1 g I.V. q. 8 hr *or* Meropenem, 1 g I.V. q. 8 hr	Ceftizoxime, 2 g I.V. q. 8 hr *or* Cefotaxime, 2 g I.V. q. 6 hr	Levofloxacin, 500 mg p.o., q. 24 hr *or* Moxifloxacin, 400 mg p.o., q. 24 hr
Cholecystitis with gangrene/perforation	*Escherichia coli, Klebsiella,* enterococci	Piperacillin-tazobactam, 4.5 g I.V. q. 8 hr	Cefotaxime, 2 g I.V. q. 6 hr	Levofloxacin, 500 mg p.o., q. 24 hr *or* Moxifloxacin, 400 mg p.o., q. 24 hr
Emphysematous cholecystitis	*Clostridium perfringens*	Piperacillin-tazobactam, 4.5 g I.V. q. 8 hr	Ertapenem, 1 g I.V. q. 24 hr	Clindamycin, 300 mg p.o., q. 8 hr
Ascending cholangitis	*E. coli, Klebsiella,* enterococci	Imipenem, 1 g I.V. q. 8 hr *or* Meropenem, 1 g I.V. q. 8 hr	Cefoperazone, 2 g I.V. q. 12 hr	Levofloxacin, 500 mg p.o., q. 24 hr *or* Moxifloxacin, 400 mg p.o., q. 24 hr
Infected hemorrhagic/ necrotizing pancreatitis	Enterobacteriaceae, *Bacteroides fragilis*	Imipenem, 1 g I.V. q. 8 hr *or* Meropenem, 1 g I.V. q. 8 hr *or* Ertapenem, 1 g I.V. q. 24 hr	Piperacillin-tazobactam, 4.5 g I.V. q. 8 hr *or* Ampicillin-sulbactam, 3 g I.V. q. 6 hr	Clindamycin, 300 mg p.o., q. 8 hr *plus* Levofloxacin, 500 mg p.o., q. 24 hr *or* Moxifloxacin, 400 mg p.o., q. 24 hr
Liver abscess (bacterial)	Enterobacteriaceae, *B. fragilis*	Imipenem, 1 g I.V. q. 8 hr *or* Meropenem, 1 g I.V. q. 8 hr *or* Ertapenem, 1 g I.V. q. 24 hr	Metronidazole, 1 g I.V. q. 24 hr *plus* Levofloxacin, 500 mg I.V. q. 24 hr *or* Moxifloxacin, 400 mg I.V. q. 24 hr	Metronidazole, 500 mg p.o., q. 12 hr *plus* Levofloxacin, 500 mg p.o., q. 24 hr *or* Moxifloxacin, 400 mg p.o., q. 24 hr
Liver abscess (amebiasis)	*Entamoeba histolytica*	Metronidazole, 750 mg p.o., q. 8 hr	Tinidazole, 2 g/day p.o. in three divided doses	Not applicable

(continued)

Table 3 (continued)

Type of Infection	Expected Pathogen	First Choice I.V. Rx	Second Choice I.V. Rx	Switch to P.O. Choice
Intra-abdominal Infection (peritonitis, abscess) (continued)				
Distal small bowel, appendix, colon, rectum perforation in nonhospitalized patient (mild to moderate infection)	Enterobacteriaceae, enterococci, B. fragilis	Piperacillin-tazobactam, 4.5 g I.V. q. 8 hr *or* Ertapenem, 1 g I.V. q. 24 hr	Cefoxitin, 2 g I.V. q. 6 hr *or* Ampicillin-sulbactam, 3 g I.V. q. 6 hr	Ciprofloxacin, 250–750 mg p.o., q. 12 hr *plus* Metronidazole, 500 mg p.o., q. 12 hr
Distal small bowel, appendix, colon, rectum perforation in hospitalized patient (severe infection requiring ICU support)	Enterobacteriaceae, enterococci, B. fragilis, P. aeruginosa, Acinetobacter	Imipenem, 1 g I.V. q. 8 hr *or* Meropenem, 1 g I.V. q. 8 hr	Tobramycin, 5 mg/kg loading dose, then 3 mg/kg I.V. q. 8 hr *plus* Clindamycin, 900 mg I.V. q. 8 hr	Moxifloxacin, 400 mg p.o., q. 24 hr
Spontaneous bacterial peritonitis	Enterobacteriaceae	Ciprofloxacin, 400 mg I.V. q. 12 hr	Cefepime, 2 g I.V. q. 12 hr	Ciprofloxacin, 250–750 mg p.o., q. 12 hr *plus* Metronidazole, 500 mg p.o., q. 12 hr
Pelvic inflammatory disease (tubo-ovarian abscess, salpingitis, endometritis, infected abortion)				
Mild to moderate infection (outpatients)	Enterobacteriaceae, B. fragilis, Neisseria gonorrhoeae, Chlamydia trachomatis	Moxifloxacin, 400 mg p.o., q. 24 hr	None	Ciprofloxacin, 250–750 mg p.o., q. 12 hr *plus* Doxycycline, 100 mg p.o., q. 12 hr
Severe infection (hospitalized patient)	Enterobacteriaceae, B. fragilis, N. gonorrhoeae, C. trachomatis	Doxycycline, 200 mg I.V. q. 12 hr *plus* Clindamycin, 600 mg I.V. q. 8 hr	Levofloxacin, 500 mg p.o., q. 24 hr *plus* Metronidazole, 1 g I.V. q. 24 hr	Moxifloxacin, 400 mg p.o., q. 24 hr

manifests in a single organ or, occasionally, in several organs), and microbial superinfection.

HYPERSENSITIVITY REACTIONS

A history of allergies should be taken before antimicrobial therapy is initiated in any patient. More information is available regarding allergies to the penicillins than allergies to other agents, but skin eruptions, drug fever, and even anaphylaxis may be produced by many antibiotics. Allergic reactions occur in 1% to 10% of patients who receive penicillin. Fatal anaphylactic reactions are much less frequent.

DIRECT DRUG TOXICITY

Although antimicrobials can produce damage to virtually all human organ systems, the potential for toxicity varies widely from drug to drug.[18] The principal antibiotics that are directly toxic to the kidney are aminoglycosides, polymyxins, and amphotericin B; azotemia and renal tubular damage may be caused by any of these drugs. Patients with preexisting renal insufficiency are at increased risk for toxic reactions to various antibiotics, including nephrotoxicity, coagulopathies and other hematologic toxicities, seizures, and ototoxicity and other neurotoxicities.

Penicillins, cephalosporins, tetracyclines, and rifampin can cause hemolytic anemia, thrombocytopenia, and leukopenia that involve an immune mechanism, but these reactions are uncommon. Macrolides and trimethoprim-sulfamethoxazole have been associated with agranulocytosis. Trimethoprim can produce anemia, leukopenia, and thrombocytopenia from folate deficiency; the effect is reversible with folinic acid. Amphotericin B commonly produces a reversible normocytic normochromic anemia,

probably secondary to injury to the red cell membrane. Flucytosine causes bone marrow suppression (leukopenia or pancytopenia) when its excretion is reduced by renal failure. Linezolid can also produce myelosuppression; although experience is limited, bone marrow function usually recovers when the drug is discontinued. Neutropenia can occur during therapy with penicillins, cephalosporins, or vancomycin. It may be severe, but it is self-limited; recovery occurs 1 to 7 days after the antibiotic is withdrawn. Penicillins inhibit platelet aggregation by adenosine diphosphate, which may account for the bleeding that occurs in some patients receiving these antibiotics in high doses. Various cephalosporins may produce coagulopathies by prolonging the prothrombin time; the methylthiotetrazole side chain present in cephalosporins such as cefotetan appears to be responsible.

Antibiotics may produce a wide range of toxic effects on the central and peripheral nervous systems. Ototoxicity, either vestibular or auditory, can be produced by any of the aminoglycosides; neuromuscular blockade is much less common. Minocycline has occasionally been reported to produce significant vestibular reactions. Vancomycin can cause auditory neurotoxicity. Intravenous administration of large doses of penicillin and other β-lactams may produce seizures, especially when administered in very high doses or when given to azotemic patients or to patients with underlying epilepsy.

Metronidazole can sometimes cause ataxia, encephalopathy, seizures, or peripheral neuropathies. Ofloxacin has been reported to cause seizures; mania has been attributed to clarithromycin. Optic neuritis, usually manifested by decreased visual acuity and decreased perception of the color green, may occur as a side effect of ethambutol.

Table 4 Antimicrobial Drugs of Choice for Various Infections in Adults[18]

	Causative Organism	Drug of Choice	Alternative Drugs

Gram-Positive Cocci	*Staphylococcus aureus*
	  Methicillin-sensitive
	  Methicillin-resistant[1]
		Vancomycin,[2] with or without rifampin or gentamicin
		Penicillinase-resistant penicillin[5]
			Linezolid; quinupristin-dalfopristin
			Trimethoprim-sulfamethoxazole (TMP-SMX),[2] with or without rifampin[2]; a fluoroquinolone[3]; a tetracycline[4]
			A cephalosporin,[6] clindamycin, vancomycin,[7] meropenem or imipenem,[8] ticarcillin–clavulanic acid, ampicillin-sulbactam, amoxicillin–clavulanic acid, piperacillin-tazobactam, a fluoroquinolone[3]

	Coagulase-negative staphylococci[9]	Vancomycin,[7] with or without rifampin[2] or gentamicin	Linezolid, quinupristin-dalfopristin, a cephalosporin, a penicillinase-resistant penicillin, meropenem or imipenem,[8] a fluoroquinolone[3]
	Anaerobic streptococcus (*Peptostreptococcus*)	Penicillin G[10]	Clindamycin, a cephalosporin,[6] vancomycin[7]
	Streptococcus bovis	Penicillin G[10,11]	A cephalosporin,[6] vancomycin[7]
	Groups A, G, and C streptococci	Penicillin G[10,12] or penicillin V	A cephalosporin,[6] vancomycin,[7] an erythromycin,[13] clindamycin, clarithromycin, azithromycin
	Group B streptococcus	Penicillin G[10,12] or ampicillin	A cephalosporin,[6] vancomycin,[7] an erythromycin
	S. pneumoniae (pneumococcus) Penicillin sensitive	Penicillin G[10,12] or penicillin V, amoxicillin	An erythromycin,[12,13] a cephalosporin,[6] meropenem or imipenem,[8] vancomycin,[7,12] azithromycin, clarithromycin, a fluoroquinolone; a tetracycline[4]
	Non–penicillin sensitive	Vancomycin; ceftriaxone or cefotaxime[6]; levofloxacin, moxifloxacin, or gatifloxacin[3]; linezolid; quinupristin-dalfopristin; imipenem or meropenem	—
	Viridans streptococcus	Penicillin G,[10,11] with or without gentamicin	A cephalosporin,[6] vancomycin[7]
	Enterococcus Endocarditis or other serious infection	Penicillin or ampicillin, plus gentamicin[14] or streptomycin	Vancomycin,[7] with gentamicin or streptomycin; linezolid; quinupristin-dalfopristin
	Uncomplicated urinary tract infection	Ampicillin or amoxicillin	A fluoroquinolone,[3] nitrofurantoin,[15] fosfomycin
Gram-Positive Bacilli	*Bacillus cereus, B. subtilis*	Vancomycin	Meropenem or imipenem,[8] clindamycin
	Bacillus anthracis	Penicillin G	Ciprofloxacin,[3] a tetracycline,[4] an erythromycin[2]
	Clostridium difficile	Metronidazole[16]	Vancomycin[16]
	C. perfringens	Penicillin G; clindamycin	Metronidazole, meropenem or imipenem,[8] chloramphenicol[7]
	C. tetani	Metronidazole	Penicillin G, a tetracycline[4]
	Corynebacterium diphtheriae	An erythromycin	Penicillin G
	Corynebacterium, JK group	Vancomycin	Penicillin G, with gentamicin; an erythromycin
	Listeria monocytogenes	Ampicillin, with or without gentamicin	TMP-SMX
	Propionibacterium	Penicillin G	Clindamycin, an erythromycin
Gram-Negative Cocci	*Moraxella* (formerly *Branhamella*) *catarrhalis*	Cefuroxime,[6] a fluoroquinolone[3]	TMP-SMX, amoxicillin–clavulanic acid, an erythromycin, a tetracycline, third-generation cephalosporins, clarithromycin, azithromycin
	Neisseria gonorrhoeae[17]	Ceftriaxone or cefixime,[6] ciprofloxacin, ofloxacin, or gatifloxacin[3]	Cefotaxime,[10] penicillin or ampicillin
	N. meningitidis Meningitis, bacteremia	Penicillin G	A third-generation cephalosporin,[6] TMP-SMX, a fluoroquinolone,[3] chloramphenicol[7]
	Carrier state	Rifampin	Minocycline, ciprofloxacin
Enteric Gram-Negative Bacilli	*Bacteroides* GI tract strains (*B. fragilis*)	Metronidazole or clindamycin	Cefoxitin, cefotetan, ceftizoxime, or cefmetazole; chloramphenicol[18]; imipenem or meropenem[8]; ticarcillin–clavulanic acid; ampicillin-sulbactam, piperacillin-tazobactam
	Respiratory tract strains	Penicillin G or clindamycin	Metronidazole, cefoxitin,[6] cefotetan, ceftizoxime, cefmetazole, chloramphenicol[7]
	Campylobacter fetus	Imipenem or meropenem[8]	Gentamicin
	C. jejuni	Azithromycin or an erythromycin	A fluoroquinolone,[3] a tetracycline,[4] gentamicin[7]
	Citrobacter	Imipenem or meropenem[8]	A fluoroquinolone,[3] amikacin; TMP-SMX; a tetracycline[4]; a third-generation cephalosporin[6]
	Enterobacter	Imipenem or meropenem[8]	A third-generation cephalosporin[6]; for serious infections, use with a fluoroquinolone[3] or gentamicin; gentamicin, tobramycin, amikacin, a fluoroquinolone,[3] a carboxypenicillin or acylaminopenicillin,[19] aztreonam[20]
	Escherichia coli	Ampicillin, a cephalosporin,[6] a fluoroquinolone,[3] TMP-SMX[22]	Gentamicin,[21] tobramycin, amikacin, imipenem or meropenem,[8] aztreonam[20]

Note: all superscript numbers refer to footnotes that follow table.

(continued)

Table 4 (*continued*)

	Causative Organism	Drug of Choice	Alternative Drugs
Enteric Gram-Negative Bacilli (continued)	*Helicobacter pylori*	Tetracycline with metronidazole and bismuth subsalicylate or omeprazole with amoxicillin and clarithromycin	Amoxicillin with metronidazole and bismuth subsalicylate; tetracycline with clarithromycin and bismuth subsalicylate; clarithromycin with omeprazole; amoxicillin with clarithromycin
	Klebsiella	A cephalosporin[6]	Imipenem or meropenem,[9] gentamicin,[23] tobramycin, amikacin, TMP-SMX,[21] a carboxypenicillin or acylaminopenicillin,[21] amoxicillin–clavulanic acid, ampicillin-sulbactam, ticarcillin–clavulanic acid, piperacillin-tazobactam, aztreonam,[20] a fluoroquinolone[3]
	Proteus		
	mirabilis	Ampicillin	A cephalosporin, gentamicin or tobramycin, chloramphenicol,[7] a carboxypenicillin or acylaminopenicillin,[19] imipenem or meropenem,[8] TMP-SMX, aztreonam,[20] a fluoroquinolone[3]
	non-*mirabilis*, including *P. vulgaris, Morganella morganii,* and *Providencia rettgeri*	A third-generation cephalosporin[6]	Gentamicin, tobramycin, amikacin, a carboxypenicillin or acylaminopenicillin,[19] imipenem or meropenem,[8] aztreonam,[20] ampicillin-sulbactam, ticarcillin–clavulanic acid, piperacillin-tazobactam, amoxicillin–clavulanic acid, a fluoroquinolone[3]
	Providencia stuartii	A third-generation cephalosporin[6]	An aminoglycoside, TMP-SMX,[21] imipenem or meropenem,[8] aztreonam,[20] a carboxypenicillin or acylaminopenicillin,[19] a fluoroquinolone[3]
	Salmonella typhi	Ceftriaxone or a fluoroquinolone[3]	Chloramphenicol or ampicillin,[22] TMP-SMX
	Other *Salmonella* species	Ceftriaxone or cefotaxime or a fluoroquinolone[3]	Ampicillin or amoxicillin, TMP-SMX, chloramphenicol[7]
	Serratia	Imipenem or meropenem	A third-generation cephalosporin,[6] gentamicin or amikacin, a carboxypenicillin or acylaminopenicillin,[19] chloramphenicol,[7] aztreonam, a fluoroquinolone[3]
	Shigella	A fluoroquinolone[3]	TMP-SMX, ampicillin, ceftriaxone, azithromycin
Other Gram-Negative Bacilli	*Acinetobacter (Herellea)*	Imipenem or meropenem[8]	Tobramycin, gentamicin, amikacin, doxycycline, minocycline, a carboxypenicillin or acylaminopenicillin,[19] TMP-SMX, a fluoroquinolone,[3] ceftazidime
	Aeromonas hydrophilia	TMP-SMX[2]	A fluoroquinolone,[3] gentamicin, tobramycin, imipenem or meropenem[8]
	Bartonella henselae (cat-scratch disease)	Azithromycin	Ciprofloxacin,[3] TMP-SMX, gentamicin; rifampin, erythromycin
	Bartonella henselae (bacillary angiomatosis)	Erythromycin	Doxycycline, azithromycin
	Bordetella pertussis (whooping cough)	Erythromycin	TMP-SMX; azithromycin or clarithromycin
	Brucella	A tetracycline, with rifampin	A tetracycline with gentamicin or streptomycin; chloramphenicol,[7] with or without streptomycin; TMP-SMX[2] with or without gentamicin; ciprofloxacin[3] with rifampin
	Eikenella corrodens	Ampicillin	An erythromycin, a tetracycline,[4] amoxicillin–clavulanic acid, ampicillin-sulbactam, ceftriaxone
	Francisella tularensis (tularemia)	Streptomycin	Gentamicin, a tetracycline,[4] chloramphenicol,[7] ciprofloxacin[3]
	Fusobacterium	Penicillin	Clindamycin, metronidazole, chloramphenicol[7]; cefoxitin
	Gardnerella (formerly *Haemophilus*) *vaginalis*	Metronidazole[2] (oral)	Intravaginal metronidazole, intravaginal or oral clindamycin
	Haemophilus influenzae Bronchitis, otitis media	TMP-SMX	Ampicillin or amoxicillin; a tetracycline[4]; amoxicillin–clavulanic acid, cefuroxime axetil, ceftizoxime, clarithromycin, azithromycin, a fluoroquinolone[3]
	Meningitis, epiglottitis, life-threatening infections	Cefotaxime or ceftriaxone	Chloramphenicol,[24] meropenem[9]
	Legionella species	Azithromycin or a fluoroquinolone[3]	Erythromycin, rifampin,[25] TMP-SMX,[2] doxycycline[4]
	Pasteurella multocida	Penicillin G	A tetracycline,[4] a cephalosporin,[6] amoxicillin–clavulanic acid, ampicillin-sulbactam
	Calymmatobacterium granulomatis (granuloma inguinale)	TMP-SMX	A tetracycline[4]; ciprofloxacin with or without rifampin
	H. ducreyi (chancroid)	Ceftriaxone or azithromycin	A fluoroquinolone[3]
	Pseudomonas aeruginosa Urinary tract infections	Ciprofloxacin[3]	Levofloxacin; gentamicin or tobramycin; amikacin; ceftazidime,[6] with or without gentamicin or tobramycin; imipenem or meropenem[8]; aztreonam,[20] a carboxypenicillin or acylaminopenicillin[19]
	Other infections	Gentamicin or tobramycin, with or without a carboxypenicillin or acylaminopenicillin[19]; ceftazidime or cefipime; imipenem or meropenem[8]; aztreonam,[20] alone or with gentamicin or tobramycin	Amikacin, with or without a carboxypenicillin or acylaminopenicillin[19]; ciprofloxacin[7]
	P. cepacia	TMP-SMX	Chloramphenicol,[7] ceftazidime,[2] imipenem[2,8] or meropenem[8]
	Streptobacillus moniliformis (rat-bite fever)	Penicillin G	A tetracycline,[4] streptomycin

Note: all superscript numbers refer to footnotes that follow table.

(continued)

Table 4 (*continued*)

	Causative Organism	Drug of Choice	Alternative Drugs
Other Gram-Negative Bacilli (continued)	*Vibrio cholerae*	A tetracycline[4]	TMP-SMX, a fluoroquinolone[3]
	V. vulnificus	A tetracycline[4]	Cefotaxime
	Agents of Vincent stomatitis (trench mouth)	Penicillin G	A tetracycline,[4] an erythromycin
	Stenotrophomonas (formerly *Xanthomonas*) *maltophilia*	TMP-SMX	Minocycline, ceftazidime,[6] a fluoroquinolone[3]
	Yersinia enterocolitica	TMP-SMX[2]	A fluoroquinolone, gentamicin,[2] tobramycin,[2] amikacin, cefotaxime[2,6] or ceftizoxime[2,6]
	Y. pestis (plague)	Streptomycin with or without a tetracycline	A tetracycline,[4] chloramphenicol,[7] gentamicin,[2] TMP-SMX
Acid-Fast Bacilli	*Mycobacterium avium* complex	Clarithromycin or azithromycin plus one or more of the following: ethambutol, rifabutin, ciprofloxacin	Rifampin, amikacin
	M. fortuitum	Amikacin[2] with clarithromycin	Rifampin,[2] cefoxitin, a sulfonamide, doxycycline, ethambutol, linezolid
	M. kansasii	Isoniazid with rifampin, with or without ethambutol or streptomycin	Cycloserine, ethionamide, clarithromycin
	M. leprae	Dapsone[7] with rifampin, with or without clofazimine	Minocycline,[4] ofloxacin or sparfloxacin,[3] clarithromycin
	M. marinum (*balnei*)[26]	Minocycline	TMP-SMX, rifampin, clarithromycin, doxycycline
	M. tuberculosis[27]	Isoniazid with rifampin, and pyrazinamide with or without ethambutol or streptomycin	Ciprofloxacin or ofloxacin; third-line agent
Actino-mycetes	*Actinomyces israelii*	Penicillin G	A tetracycline[4]; an erythromycin; clindamycin
	Nocardia	TMP-SMX	Minocycline, sulfisoxazole, imipenem or meropenem,[8] amikacin,[2] cycloserine, linezolid
Chlamydia	*Chlamydia psittaci* (psittacosis)	A tetracycline[4]	Chloramphenicol[7]
	C. trachomatis		
	Inclusion conjunctivitis	An erythromycin (oral or I.V.)	A sulfonamide (topical plus oral)
	Lymphogranuloma venereum	A tetracycline[4]	An erythromycin
	Pneumonia	An erythromycin	A sulfonamide
	Trachoma	Azithromycin	A tetracycline[4] (topical plus oral), a sulfonamide (topical plus oral)
	Urethritis or pelvic inflammatory disease	Doxycycline or azithromycin	Erythromycin, ofloxacin, amoxicillin
	C. pneumoniae	An erythromycin or clarithromycin or azithromycin; a fluoroquinolone	A tetracycline
Myco-plasma	*Mycoplasma pneumoniae*	An erythromycin, clarithromycin or azithromycin; a fluoroquinolone,[3] doxycycline[4]	—
	Ureaplasma urealyticum	An erythromycin	A tetracycline,[4] clarithromycin, or azithromycin; ofloxacin[3]
Rickettsia	Various rickettsial organisms Rocky Mountain spotted fever, epidemic and endemic (murine) typhus, rickettsial pox, Q fever, scrub typhus	Doxycycline[4]	Chloramphenicol,[7] a fluoroquinolone,[3] rifampin
Spirochetes	*Borrelia burgdorferi* (Lyme disease)	Doxycycline or amoxicillin or ceftriaxone	Penicillin, an erythromycin, clarithromycin, azithromycin, cefuroxime
	B. recurrentis (relapsing fever)	A tetracycline[4]	Penicillin G
	Leptospira	Penicillin G	A tetracycline,[4] an erythromycin
	Treponema pallidum	Penicillin G	A tetracycline,[4] an erythromycin, ceftriaxone

1. Some strains of *S. aureus* and most strains of coagulase-negative staphylococci are resistant to penicillinase-resistant penicillins; these strains are also resistant to cephalosporins.

2. Not approved for this indication by the FDA.

3. None of these drugs is recommended for children. In 1999, the FDA limited trovafloxacin to inpatient use for limb- or life-threatening infections.

4. Doxycycline is the safest tetracycline for treatment of extrarenal infections in renal insufficiency. Tetracyclines should be avoided in pregnant women and in children younger than 8 yr.

5. For severe infections, I.V. nafcillin or oxacillin should be used. For mild infections, oral cloxacillin, dicloxacillin, or oxacillin may be employed. Between 1% and 2% of *S. aureus* strains are resistant to penicillinase-resistant penicillins (and usually to cephalosporins) but are susceptible to vancomycin. High doses of penicillin G, ampicillin, amoxicillin, carbenicillin, or ticarcillin do not overcome the clinical resistance of penicillinase-producing staphylococci to these drugs.

6. Cephalosporins are sometimes used as alternatives to penicillin in patients with suspected penicillin allergy but not in patients with serious hypersensitivity (especially immediate anaphylactic or accelerated urticarial reactions). Patients allergic to penicillin may be hypersensitive to cephalosporins. Only third-generation cephalosporins are effective in bacterial meningitis.

7. In view of the occurrence of adverse reactions, this drug should be used only for serious infections and when less toxic drugs are ineffective.

8. Imipenem and meropenem are β-lactam antibiotics that should be used with caution in patients who are allergic to penicillins and cephalosporins.

9. In vitro sensitivity testing with cephalosporins or penicillins may be misleading because of heteroresistance and because these antibiotics may be bacteriostatic only. For serious infections, vancomycin is preferred (see text).

10. Crystalline penicillin G is administered parenterally for serious infections. For less severe infections caused by pneumococci, group A streptococci, gonococci, or *T. pallidum,* procaine penicillin is administered I.M. once or twice daily. For mild infections caused by streptococci and pneumococci, oral penicillin V is preferable to oral penicillin G. Benzathine penicillin G is given I.M. (once monthly for the prophylaxis of rheumatic fever,

(continued)

Table 4 (continued)

10. ... a single injection for the treatment of group A streptococcal pharyngitis) when patients' compliance for oral medication is questionable and for treatment of syphilis, in one to three doses at weekly intervals, depending on the stage of the disease.

11. The combination of penicillin G with streptomycin for the first 2 wk of treatment of endocarditis caused by viridans streptococci is preferred by some.

12. In patients with major allergy to penicillin, erythromycin is the alternative for respiratory tract infections; chloramphenicol is the preferred alternative for meningitis. Occasional strains of pneumococci have high-level resistance to penicillin and to most other antibiotics except vancomycin.

13. Some strains of pneumococci and group A streptococci are erythromycin resistant.

14. Various aminoglycosides have been used in synergistic combination with penicillin or vancomycin. Because of the appearance of enterococcal strains resistant to the synergistic action with streptomycin (but not gentamicin), gentamicin is preferred for use in the combination.

15. Contraindicated in pregnancy or in the presence of renal insufficiency.

16. Antibiotics may be administered orally for antibiotic-associated pseudomembranous enterocolitis. Vancomycin and metronidazole are equally effective but metronidazole is much less expensive.

17. Large doses of penicillin G or ampicillin (or amoxicillin) may be required because some strains are resistant to these drugs. Penicillinase-producing gonococci, which are more resistant to penicillin, have appeared in the United States; spectinomycin is the treatment of choice for infections with such strains.

18. In CNS infection, metronidazole or chloramphenicol should be used.

19. The carboxypenicillins are carbenicillin and ticarcillin; the acylaminopenicillins are mezlocillin, azlocillin, and piperacillin. When one of these drugs is used for a severe infection, an aminoglycoside is often recommended as well.

20. Aztreonam is a β-lactam antibiotic; cross-sensitivity has not occurred, but use with caution in patients allergic to penicillins, cephalosporins, or imipenem.

21. Principally in treatment of uncomplicated urinary tract infections.

22. Ampicillin or amoxicillin may be effective in milder cases.

23. In severely ill patients, an aminoglycoside is combined with a cephalosporin.

24. Some encapsulated *H. influenzae* (type b) strains and some unencapsulated strains are resistant to ampicillin, and rare strains are resistant to chloramphenicol. Chloramphenicol plus ampicillin (or chloramphenicol alone) should be used for initial treatment of meningitis or epiglottitis in children until the organism is identified and its susceptibility is determined. For adults with meningitis of unknown etiology and an indeterminate Gram stain and in whom *H. influenzae* is suspected, chloramphenicol is added to ampicillin (or penicillin G) for the first 24 hr until the results of culture are available. Ampicillin is preferred when the infecting strain of *H. influenzae* is susceptible.

25. Not an FDA-approved use. Evidence for possible efficacy comes only from in vitro susceptibility testing and from treatment of infections in experimental animals. In both cases, *L. pneumophila* is highly susceptible to rifampin.

26. Most infections are self-limited without therapy.

27. Various combination treatments are available.

Trovafloxacin was restricted for use in seriously ill patients because of hepatotoxicity, but other fluoroquinolones have not been implicated. The tetracyclines can occasionally cause fatty liver; hepatotoxicity is most likely to occur in patients receiving 2 g or more daily by the intravenous route. Patients receiving high-dose β-lactam antibiotics may develop hepatitis or cholestasis, presumably as a result of hypersensitivity reactions. Nitrofurantoin may cause chronic active hepatitis in some patients. Erythromycins and sulfonamides have been associated with acute hepatitis, and a case of fatal hepatic necrosis has been attributed to fluconazole.

GI reactions to antibiotics result either from direct irritation by the drug, the occurrence of which is usually dose related, or from bacterial overgrowth.[19] Irritative GI side effects are usually produced when antibiotics are administered orally rather than parenterally. The predominant site of irritation varies from drug to drug; for example, erythromycin more commonly produces gastric irritation with epigastric distress and nausea, whereas tetracyclines may produce diarrhea as well as upper GI symptoms. Some qualitative and quantitative changes in the intestinal flora occur after antibiotic administration; they may contribute to flatulence and other lower GI symptoms, which are quite common when broad-spectrum antibiotics are administered orally. Selective overgrowth of *Clostridium difficile* can result in antibiotic-induced pseudomembranous enterocolitis.[20]

Antibiotics may cause various other toxicities. Erythromycin and other macrolides can cause prolongation of the QT interval and polymorphic ventricular tachycardia; in rare instances, this toxicity occurs in the absence of predisposing factors, but it is more likely to occur in patients with significant heart disease and in patients taking terfenadine, astemizole, or cisapride. Several fluoroquinolones, such as moxifloxacin, gatifloxacin, and sparfloxacin, can have similar effects on cardiac conduction.[21,22] All fluoroquinolones can cause tendinitis. Trimethoprim-sulfamethoxazole can cause hyperkalemia, particularly in azotemic patients. Sulfonamides, fluoroquinolones, and tetracyclines can produce photosensitivity.[23]

MICROBIAL SUPERINFECTION

Antimicrobial therapy reduces susceptible organisms from the normal flora of the skin, oral and genitourinary mucosae, and GI tract and exerts selective pressures that favor survival of drug-resistant organisms. Such resistant organisms can occasionally establish a superinfection, either at the site of the original infection or at remote sites.

Public Health Considerations

ANTIMICROBIAL RESISTANCE

The extensive use of antimicrobial agents, especially in ICUs[24] and other health care facilities, strongly favors the selection of resistant microbial species, particularly bacterial strains harboring plasmids that confer transmissible resistance.[25,26] Although antibiotics have played a major role in the treatment of such infections, the pathogens have responded to the antibiotic challenge, developing resistance to all available antimicrobial agents to a greater or lesser degree. Specific mechanisms of resistance are evident in the reduced permeability of cell wall membranes, changes in the target sites of antimicrobial agents, enzymatic inactivation of antibiotics, and the development of pathways bypassing antimicrobial targets.[27]

The widespread use of antibiotics for animals compounds the problem; about 50% of the 25,000 tons of antibiotics that are sold annually in the United States are used in agriculture and aquiculture.[28] Infections from highly resistant strains of *Enterococcus, Pneumococcus, Staphylococcus aureus, Gonococcus, Salmonella, Serratia, Klebsiella, Acinetobacter, Enterobacter,* and *Mycobacterium* have become important problems. Infections from resistant strains can spread rapidly, first within an institution, then throughout a community, and eventually even globally.[29] Although antibiotic resistance is a worldwide problem, control depends on local measures, beginning with the judicious prescription of antibiotics by individual practitioners[30] and with formulary restrictions that reinforce prudence.[31] Patients harboring resistant strains should be identified rapidly, treated appropriately, and isolated as needed to prevent the spread of infection.

The incidence of suprainfection with cephalosporin therapy is actually quite low (< 5%); however, the organisms encountered are often more virulent and difficult to eradicate than the original infecting pathogen.[32] Commonly seen suprainfecting pathogens include *Enterobacter* species, *Pseudomonas aeruginosa, S. aureus, Acinetobacter* species, enterococci, and *Candida* species. Because these organisms are generally multiresistant, therapy with antibiotic combinations, including aminoglycosides, is usually necessary. There appear to be no significant differences among the cephalosporins with respect to the incidence of suprainfection or the types of suprainfecting pathogens found.

The most worrisome resistance is that of vancomycin-resistant enterococci (VRE). Risk factors for bloodstream infection with VRE are an increasing APACHE II (Acute Physiology and

Table 5 Antimicrobial Drug Dosages for Treatment of Bacterial Infections in Adults with Normal Renal Function[155]

Class of Agent	Specific Agent	Trade Names	Modest Infections*			
			Oral		Intramuscular	
			Daily Dose	Interval	Daily Dose	Interval
Penicillinase-susceptible penicillins	Penicillin G	Pentids, Crystifor, Pfizerpen, etc.	0.8–3.2 million units	6 hr	1.2 million units	8 hr
	Penicillin G benzathine	Bicillin	—	—	1.2–2.4 million units	See fn. 1
	Penicillin G procaine	Crysticillin, Duracillin, etc.	—	—	0.6–4.8 million units	6–24 hr
	Penicillin V	Pen-Vee K, V-Cillin K, etc.	0.8–3.2 million units (0.5–2.0 g)	6 hr	—	—
Penicillinase-susceptible penicillins with activity against gram-negative bacilli	Amoxicillin	Amoxil, Larotid, etc.	750–1,500 mg	8 hr	—	—
	Ampicillin	Omnipen, Polycillin, etc.	1–4 g	6 hr	1–2 g	6 hr
	Azlocillin	Azlin	—	—	—	—
	Carbenicillin indanyl sodium	Geocillin	—	—	—	—
	Mezlocillin	Mezlin	—	—	—	—
	Piperacillin	Pipracil	—	—	See fn. 3	See fn. 3
	Ticarcillin	Ticar	—	—	See fn. 4	See fn.4
Penicillinase-resistant penicillins	Cloxacillin	Tegopen	1–3 g	6 hr	—	—
	Dicloxacillin	Dynapen, Pathocil	1–2 g	6 hr	—	—
	Nafcillin	Nafcil, Unipen	2–4 g[5]	6 hr	2–3 g	4–6 hr
	Oxacillin	Bactocill, Prostaphlin	2–4 g	6 hr	1–2 g	6 hr
Penicillins with β-lactamase inhibitors	Amoxicillin-clavulanate	Augmentin	750 mg–1.5 g (amoxicillin)	8 hr	—	—
	Ampicillin-sulbactam	Unasyn	—	—	1 g (ampicillin)	6 hr
	Piperacillin-tazobactam	Zosyn	—	—	—	—
	Ticarcillin-clavulanate	Timentin	—	—	—	—
Cephalosporins	Cefaclor	Ceclor	750 mg–1.5 g	8 hr	—	—
	Cefadroxil	Duricef, Ultracef	500 mg–2g	12–24 hr	—	—
	Cefamandole	Mandol	—	—	2–4 g	6 hr
	Cefazolin	Ancef, Kefzol	—	—	750 mg–1.5 g	8 hr
	Cefdinir	Omnicef	600 mg	24 hr	—	—
	Cefditoren pivoxil	Spectracef	200–400 mg	12 hr	—	—
	Cefepime	Maxipime	—	—	—	—
	Cefixime	Suprax	400 mg	24 hr	—	—
	Cefmetazole	Zefazone	—	—	—	—
	Cefonicid	Monocid	—	—	See fn. 7,8	See fn. 7,8
	Cefoperazone	Cefobid	—	—	See fn. 7,8	See fn. 7,8
	Ceforanide	Precef	—	—	See fn. 7,8	See fn. 7,8
	Cefotaxime	Claforan	—	—	See fn. 7,8	See fn. 7,8
	Cefotetan	Cefotan	—	—	See fn. 7,8	See fn. 7,8
	Cefoxitin	Mefoxin	—	—	2–4 g	6 hr
	Cefpodoxime	Vantin	200–800 mg	12 hr	—	—
	Cefprozil	Cefzil	500 mg–1 g	12–24 hr	—	—
	Ceftazidime	Fortaz, Tazidime	—	—	See fn. 7,8	See fn. 7,8
	Ceftibutin	Cedax	400 mg	—	—	—
	Ceftizoxime	Cefizox	—	—	See fn. 7,8	See fn. 7,8
	Ceftriaxone	Rocephin	—	24 hr	See fn. 7,8	See fn. 7,8
	Cefuroxime	Zinacef, Ceftin (p.o.)	250–500 mg	12 hr	See fn. 7,8	See fn. 7,8
	Cephalexin	Keflex	1–4 g	6 hr	—	—
	Cephapirin	Cefadyl	—	—	2–3 g	6 hr
	Cephradine	Anspor, Velosef	1–4 g	6 hr	2 g	6 hr
	Loracarbef	Lorabid	400–800 mg	12 hr	—	—
Carbapenems	Imipenem-cilastatin	Primaxin	—	—	—	—
	Meropenem	Merrem	—	—	—	—
	Ertapenem	Ivanz	—	—	—	—

Note: all superscript numbers refer to footnotes following table.
*Infections of the upper respiratory tract, soft tissues, etc.

(continued)

Table 5 (*continued*)

Uncomplicated Urinary Tract Infections		Major and Systemic Infections[†]			
Oral		Intramuscular		Intravenous	
Daily Dose	Interval	Daily Dose	Interval	Daily Dose	Interval
—	—	—	—	4–24 million units	2–4 hr
—	—	—	—	—	—
—	—	—	—	—	—
—	—	—	—	—	—
750–1,500 mg	8 hr	—	—	—	—
2–4 g	6 hr	—	—	4-12 g	2–4 hr
—	—	—	—	12–18 g	4 hr
4–8 tablets[2]	6 hr	—	—	—	—
—	—	—	—	12–18 g	4 hr
—	—	See fn. 3	See fn. 3	12–18 g	4 hr
—	—	—	—	16–24 g	3–6 hr
—	—	—	—	—	—
—	—	—	—	4–12 g	4–6 hr
—	—	—	—	4–12 g	4–6 hr
750 mg (amoxicillin)	8 hr	—	—	—	—
—	—	1–2 g (ampicillin)	6 hr	1–2 g (ampicillin)	6 hr
—	—	—	—	12 g (piperacillin)	6 hr
—	—	—	—	12–18 g (ticarcillin)	4–6 hr
750 mg–1.5 g	8 hr	—	—	—	—
500 mg–2 g	12–24 hr	—	—	—	—
—	—	—	—	4–12 g	2–4 hr
See fn. 6	See fn. 6	2–3 g	6–8 hr	2–6 g	6–8 hr
—	—	—	—	—	—
—	—	—	—	2–6 g	8–12 hr
400 mg	24 hr	—	—	—	—
—	—	—	—	2–4 g	12 hr
—	—	—	—	4–8 g	6–12 hr
—	—	—	—	0.5–2.0 g	12–24 hr
—	—	—	—	2–12 g	6–8 hr
—	—	—	—	1–2 g	12 hr
—	—	—	—	2–12 g	4–6 hr
—	—	—	—	2–6 g	12 hr
—	—	—	—	4–12 g	4 hr
200 mg	12 hr	—	—	—	—
—	—	—	—	—	—
—	—	—	—	2–6 g	8–12 hr
400 mg	24 hr	—	—	—	—
—	—	—	—	2–6 g	8–12 hr
—	—	—	—	1–4 g	12–24 hr
—	—	—	—	3–6 g	6 hr
1–4 g	6 hr	—	—	—	—
—	—	—	—	4–12 g	2–4 hr
2 g	6 hr	—	—	3–8 g	4–6 hr
400 mg	12 hr	—	—	—	—
—	—	—	—	1–4 g	6–8 hr
—	—	—	—	3 g	8 hr
—	12 hr	—	—	1 g	24 hr

[†]Osteomyelitis, peritonitis, bacteremia, meningitis, endocarditis, etc.

(continued)

Table 5 (*continued*)

Class of Agent	Specific Agent	Trade Names	Modest Infections*			
			Oral		Intramuscular	
			Daily Dose	Interval	Daily Dose	Interval
Monobactams	Aztreonam	Azactam	—	—	1–2 g	8–12 hr
Aminoglycosides	Amikacin	Amikin	—	—	—	—
	Gentamicin	Garamycin	—	—	3–5 mg/kg[11]	8 hr
	Kanamycin	Kantrex	—	—	—	—
	Neomycin	—	See fn. 15	See fn. 15	—	—
	Netilmicin	Netromycin	—	—	4–6 mg/kg[11,12]	8 hr
	Streptomycin	—	—	—	1–2 g	12 hr
	Tobramycin	Nebcin	—	—	3–5 mg/kg[11]	8 hr
Tetracyclines	Demeclocycline	Declomycin	600 mg	6 hr	—	—
	Doxycycline	Vibramycin, etc.	100–200 mg[17]	12 hr	—	—
	Minocycline	Minocin	200 mg[19]	12 hr	—	—
	Oxytetracycline	Terramycin	1–2 g	6 hr	See fn. 21	See fn. 21
	Tetracycline	Achromycin, Panmycin, Sumycin, Tetracyn, etc.	1–2 g	6 hr	See fn. 21	See fn. 21
Macrolides	Azithromycin	Zithromax	500 mg day 1 250 mg days 2–5	24 hr	—	—
	Clarithromycin	Biaxin	500 mg–1 g	12 hr	—	—
	Dirithromycin	Dynabac	500 mg	24 hr	—	—
	Erythromycin	E-Mycin, Erythrocin, Ilotycin	1–2 g	6 hr	See fn. 21	See fn. 21
	Erythromycin estolate[23]	Ilosone	1–2 g	6 hr	—	—
Sulfonamides	Sulfadiazine	—	2–4 g[24]	6 hr	—	—
	Sulfisoxazole	Gantrisin	2–6 g[24]	6 hr	—	—
	Trimethoprim-sulfamethoxazole	Bactrim, Septra	4 tablets[25]	12 hr	—	—
Miscellaneous antibacterial agents	Clindamycin	Cleocin	600 mg–1.8 g	6 hr	600 mg–1.2 g	6–8 hr
	Chloramphenicol	Chloromycetin	1.5–3.0 g	6 hr	See fn. 26	See fn. 26
	Metronidazole	Flagyl	250 mg	8 hr	—	—
	Spectinomycin	Trobicin	—	—	2 g[28]	Single injection
	Trimethoprim	Proloprim, Trimpex	200 mg	12 hr	—	—
	Vancomycin	Vancocin	2 g[29]	6 hr	—	—
Urinary tract disinfectants	Fosfomycin	Monurol	—	—	—	—
	Methenamine mandelate	Mandelamine	—	—	—	—
	Methenamine hippurate	Hiprex	—	—	—	—
	Nalidixic acid	NegGram	—	—	—	—
	Nitrofurantoin	Furadantin, Macrodantin	—	—	—	—
Antifungal drugs	Amphotericin B	Fungizone	—	—	—	—
	Fluconazole[31]	Diflucan	100–200 mg[32]	24 hr	—	—
	Flucytosine	Ancobon	50–150 mg/kg[33]	6 hr	—	—
	Itraconazole	Sporanox	100–400 mg	12 or 24 hr	—	—
	Ketoconazole	Nizorol	200 mg[33]	24 hr	—	—
	Miconazole	Monistat	—	—	—	—
	Nystatin	Mycostatin	1.5–3.0 million units[35]	8 hr	—	—
Fluoroquinolones[36]	Alatrofloxacin[36]	Trovan I.V.	—	—	—	—
	Ciprofloxacin	Cipro	500 mg	12 hr	—	—
	Levofloxacin	Levaquin	500 mg	24 hr	—	—
	Lomefloxacin	Maxaquin	400 mg	24 hr	—	—
	Norfloxacin	Noroxin	—	—	—	—
	Ofloxacin	Floxin	400–800 mg	12 hr	—	—
	Sparfloxacin	Zagam	400 mg first day, then 200 mg	24 hr	—	—
	Trovafloxacin[36]	Trovan	See fn. 36	See fn. 36	—	—
	Gatifloxacin	Tequin	400 mg	24 hr	—	—
	Moxifloxacin	Avelox	400 mg	—	—	—

Table 5   (continued)

| Uncomplicated Urinary Tract Infections | | Major and Systemic Infections[†] | | | |
| Oral | | Intramuscular | | Intravenous | |
Daily Dose	Interval	Daily Dose	Interval	Daily Dose	Interval
—	—	—	—	3–8 g	6–8 hr
—	—	15 mg/kg[9]	8–12 hr	15 mg/kg[10]	8 hr
—	—	3–5 mg/kg	8 hr	3–5 mg/kg[12]	8 hr
—	—	15 mg/kg[13]	8–12 hr	15 mg/kg[14]	8 hr
—	—	—	—	—	—
—	—	4–6 mg/kg	8 hr	4–6 mg/kg[16]	8 hr
—	—	1–2 g	12 hr	—	—
—	—	3–5 mg/kg	8 hr	3–5 mg/kg[16]	8 hr
600 mg	6 hr	—	—	—	—
100–200 mg[17]	12 hr	—	—	100–200 mg[18]	12 hr
200 mg[19]	12 hr	—	—	200 mg[20]	12 hr
1–2 g	6 hr	—	—	—	—
1–2 g	6 hr	See fn. 21	See fn. 21	750 mg–1.0 g[22]	6–12 hr
—	—	—	—	—	—
—	—	—	—	—	—
—	—	—	—	—	—
—	—	See fn. 21	See fn. 21	2–4 g	6 hr
—	—	—	—	—	—
2–4 g[24]	6 hr	—	—	—	—
2–6 g[24]	6 hr	—	—	100 mg/kg[24]	4–6 hr
4 tablets[25]	12 hr	—	—	8–12 mg/kg[25] (trimethoprim)	6 hr[25]
—	—	1.2–2.4 g	6–8 hr	1.8–3.0 g	6–8 hr
1.5–2.0 g[27]	6 hr	See fn. 26	See fn. 26	2–4 g	6 hr
—	—	—	—	30 mg/kg	6 hr
—	—	—	—	—	—
200 mg	12 hr	—	—	—	—
—	—	—	—	1–2 g	6–12 hr
3 g	1 dose	—	—	—	—
4 g	6 hr	—	—	—	—
2 g	12 hr	—	—	—	—
2–4g	6 hr	—	—	—	—
200–400 g	6 hr	—	—	Not recommended	—
—	—	—	—	0.25–1.0 mg/kg[30]	24 hr
—	—	—	—	200 mg[31]	24 hr
—	—	—	—	—	—
—	—	See fn. 32	See fn. 32	See fn. 32	See fn. 32
—	—	—	—	600 mg–3.6 g[34]	8 hr
—	—	—	—	—	—
—	—	—	—	200 mg	24 hr
200–500 mg	12 hr	—	—	400 mg	12 hr
500 mg	24hr	—	—	500 mg	24 hr
400 mg	24 hr	—	—	—	—
800 mg	12 hr	—	—	—	—
400 mg	12 hr	—	—	800 mg	12 hr
—	—	—	—	—	—
—	—	—	—	—	—
400 mg	24 hr	—	—	400 mg	24 hr
400 mg	24 hr	—	—	—	—

(continued)

Table 5 (*continued*)

Class of Agent	Specific Agent	Trade Names	Modest Infections*			
			Oral		Intramuscular	
			Daily Dose	Interval	Daily Dose	Interval
Streptogramins	Quinupristin-dalfopristin	Synercid	—	—	—	—
Oxazolidinones	Linezolid	Zyvox	400 mg	12 hr	—	—

Note: all superscript numbers refer to footnotes following table.
*Infections of the upper respiratory tract, soft tissues, etc.
†Osteomyelitis, peritonitis, bacteremia, meningitis, endocarditis, etc.

1. Benzathine penicillin G is used primarily in three circumstances. (1) Treatment of streptococcal pharyngitis in cases in which patient compliance is questionable (a single dose of 1.2 million units I.M.). (2) Prophylaxis of rheumatic fever recurrences (1.2–2.4 million units I.M. once monthly). (3) Treatment of syphilis: for primary, secondary, or early (< 1 yr) latent syphilis, a single dose of 2.4 million units I.M.; for late syphilis (late latent, cardiovascular, neurosyphilis, etc.), 2.4 million units I.M. weekly for three doses has been recommended, but many authorities now treat neurosyphilis with high-dose I.V. penicillin.

2. Each tablet of carbenicillin indanyl sodium is equivalent to 382 mg of carbenicillin (usual dosage is one to two tablets p.o., q.i.d.).

3. Piperacillin is most often used in the treatment of serious infections caused by susceptible *Pseudomonas, Klebsiella, Enterobacter,* and non-*mirabilis Proteus* strains; the agent is given in maximal dosage (12–18 g I.V. daily). It is commonly used in synergistic combination with tobramycin or gentamicin for treatment of *Pseudomonas* infections. Occasionally, it is given in smaller dosages (1.0–1.5 g I.M. or I.V. q. 6 hr) to treat an uncomplicated urinary tract infection caused by the same organisms.

4. Ticarcillin, piperacillin, mezlocillin, and azlocillin are usually used in the treatment of serious infections caused by susceptible *Pseudomonas, Enterobacter,* and non-*mirabilis Proteus* strains and are given in maximal dosage (12–24 g I.V. daily). One of these agents is commonly used in synergistic combination with tobramycin or gentamicin for treatment of *Pseudomonas* infections. Occasionally, they are given in smaller dosages (1 g I.M. or I.V. q. 6 hr) to treat an uncomplicated urinary tract infection caused by the same organisms.

5. Nafcillin is not reliably absorbed by the oral route.

6. Cefazolin may be used in the treatment of acute uncomplicated urinary tract infections caused by susceptible gram-negative bacilli (*E. coli, P. mirabilis,* and *Klebsiella*). It is administered I.M. in a dosage of 2 g daily (given as aliquots q. 8 hr).

7. Although the second- and third-generation cephalosporins can be used for milder infections at the lower end of their recommended dosage range, these potent but expensive agents should generally be reserved for treatment of serious infections or for the treatment of resistant organisms when the alternative is a more toxic antimicrobial drug.

8. The I.M. route is acceptable for milder illnesses, but the I.V. route is recommended for serious infections, including bacteremias and meningitis. The range for the I.M. dosage is the same as that for the I.V. dosage.

9. Dosage must be reduced in the presence of renal insufficiency. The daily parenteral dose should not exceed 15 mg/kg, and the total daily amount administered should not exceed 1.5 g, regardless of the patient's weight.

10. The I.V. dose should be infused during a period of 30–60 min q. 8 hr.

11. For urinary tract infections caused by resistant organisms.

12. Dosage must be reduced in the presence of renal insufficiency. The I.V. dose should be administered for a period of 30–60 min q. 8 hr. In patients with meningitis caused by susceptible gram-negative bacilli, intrathecal gentamicin (5 mg for adults, 1–2 mg for infants) is often administered once daily along with parenteral gentamicin until CSF cultures are negative.

13. Dosage must be reduced in the presence of renal insufficiency. The daily parenteral dose should not exceed 15 mg/kg (daily dose should not exceed 1.5 g, regardless of the patient's weight); the total quantity administered in a therapeutic course should not exceed 15 g.

14. The I.V. route should be employed only when I.M. administration is not possible. The I.V.

dose should be administered during a period of at least 60 min q. 8 hr.

15. There are no clinical indications for the parenteral administration of neomycin in view of its marked toxicity and the availability of safer alternative drugs. The drug is given p.o. or by nasogastric tube (4–6 g daily in 4 divided doses) to reduce the number of ammonia-forming bacteria in the intestine in the short-term treatment of acute hepatic coma. It is also given in a total daily dose of 2–3 g in long-term therapy for chronic hepatic encephalopathy or episodic hepatic coma. Nephrotoxicity and ototoxicity have followed prolonged high-dose therapy in hepatic coma, particularly in patients with some renal impairment. Neomycin is also used along with vigorous mechanical cleansing of the large bowel as preoperative prophylaxis for bowel surgery. In this situation, it is administered for 1–3 days preoperatively (40 mg/ kg p.o. daily in 6 divided doses).

16. Dosage must be reduced in the presence of renal insufficiency. The I.V. dose should be administered during a period of 30–60 min q. 8 hr.

17. Usually administered as 100 mg p.o. q. 12 hr on the first day of treatment, followed by 50 mg q. 12 hr. For more difficult infections, the dosage may be continued at 100 mg q. 12 hr.

18. Usually administered as 100 mg I.V. q. 12 hr on the first day of treatment. Thereafter, it may be given as 50–100 mg I.V. q. 12 hr. Each I.V. dose should be given during a period of 1–4 hr.

19. Usually administered initially as 200 mg p.o., followed by 100 mg q. 12 hr.

20. Usually given initially as 200 mg I.V., followed by 100 mg q. 12 hr. Maximum dose in any 24-hr period is 400 mg.

21. I.M. administration is generally unsatisfactory because of poor absorption and local irritation.

22. In special circumstances, it may be given in higher doses but not in excess of 500 mg q. 6 hr.

23. Cholestatic hepatitis may develop as a hypersensitivity response to erythromycin estolate but not to the other erythromycin preparations. For this reason, erythromycin base or erythromycin stearate is preferable.

24. A loading dose of one half the daily dose is given initially. In severe infections, the dosage of sulfonamide is adjusted to provide a blood level of 10–15 mg/dl. Sulfonamides must be used with caution in patients with renal insufficiency. Sulfisoxazole is the preferred sulfonamide.

25. Each tablet contains 80 mg trimethoprim and 400 mg sulfamethoxazole. Double-strength tablets are also available (usual dosage is 1 tablet q. 12 hr). Pediatric suspensions contain 40 mg trimethoprim and 200 mg sulfamethoxazole/5 ml. Trimethoprim-sulfamethoxazole has also been used in the treatment of typhoid fever in the same dosage as recommended for urinary tract infections. It has been used in a dosage of 4–8 standard tablets daily in the treatment of brucellosis. For pneumonia caused by *Pneumocystis carinii*, the oral dosage is 20 mg/kg trimethoprim and 100 mg/kg sulfamethoxazole/24 hr (equally divided doses q. 6 hr). The I.V. dosage of trimethoprim-sulfamethoxazole ranges from 8 mg/kg trimethoprim and 40 mg/kg sulfamethoxazole/24 hr to 20 mg/kg trimethoprim and 100 mg/kg sulfamethoxazole/24 hr. The lower dosage range is used in the treatment of urinary tract infections that require parenteral antimicrobial therapy and in the treatment of shigellosis; the larger dosage is employed in the treatment of *P. carinii* pneumonia.

26. Chloramphenicol sodium succinate, the parenteral preparation, should only be used I.V. It is ineffective when administered I.M.

27. Chloramphenicol should not be used in the treatment of a urinary tract infection that could

(continued)

Chronic Health Evaluation II) score, treatment with vancomycin, and a diagnosis of hematologic malignancy. Thus, severe illness, underlying disease, and the use of vancomycin are major risk factors for infection of the bloodstream with VRE.[33] Fueling the excessive use of broad-spectrum antimicrobial drugs is the lack of reliable tests that would permit physicians to discern when antimicrobial drugs are not needed. When antimicrobial therapy is needed, improved diagnostic tests would permit better targeting and thereby reduce the widespread administration of broad-spectrum drugs. Selective pressure exerted by widespread antimicrobial use is the driving force in the development of antibiotic resistance. The association between increased rates of antimicro-

bial use and resistance has been documented for nosocomial infections[34] and community-acquired infections in studies associating resistance patterns with rates of drug use on a regional or national basis.[35]

Resistance to antimicrobial drugs is a global problem. Multidrug-resistant pathogens travel not only locally but globally. Because of increased international travel and increased foreign trade in fresh-food products, the threat of global spread of antibiotic resistance is greater than ever. There is no national or global surveillance system for the monitoring of antibiotic resistance in animals or humans. New classes of antimicrobials are being developed to deal with drug resistance.

Table 5 (continued)

| Uncomplicated Urinary Tract Infections | | Major and Systemic Infections[†] | | | |
| Oral | | Intramuscular | | Intravenous | |
Daily Dose	Interval	Daily Dose	Interval	Daily Dose	Interval
—	—	—	—	7.5 mg/kg	8 hr
—	—	—	—	600 mg (I.V. or p.o.)	12 hr

[†]Osteomyelitis, peritonitis, bacteremia, meningitis, endocarditis, etc.

be managed with another, safer, effective antimicrobial.

28. The only approved indication for the use of spectinomycin is in the treatment of anogenital and urethral gonorrhea in a penicillin-allergic patient or when the infecting organism is highly penicillin resistant. In geographic areas where antibiotic-resistant gonococci are prevalent, treatment with 4 g of spectinomycin (2 g in each gluteal region) may be indicated.

29. Vancomycin is not absorbed through the GI tract. Its use orally is for treatment of staphylococcal enterocolitis or antibiotic-associated enterocolitis.

30. The dry powder is reconstituted by addition of Sterile Water for Injection, USP, without a bacteriostatic agent. The solution is then added to a bottle of 5% Dextrose Injection, USP. The pH of the dextrose solution should first be checked to verify that it is above 4.2. If it is not, a buffer solution (as described in package insert) should be added. Amphotericin B solutions should be administered promptly after preparation and should be protected from light during administration. It is given once a day over 6 hr. (Later in the course of administration, double the daily dose is sometimes given on an alternate-day schedule.) Dosage is 1 mg on the first day and then increased in 5 mg increments each day until maintenance dosage is reached. The daily dose is determined by the susceptibility of the organism and the occurrence of toxic side effects. In some instances (e.g., cryptococcal meningitis), combination therapy with flucytosine p.o. may allow employment of smaller daily doses (0.3–0.4 mg/kg) of amphotericin B. In fungal meningitis, intrathecal administration may be necessary (0.1 mg initially, increased gradually to 0.5 mg q. 48–72 hr), depending on the evaluation of the patient's condition.

31. Fluconazole is very useful for the treatment of oropharyngeal, esophageal, and disseminated infections caused by Candida and for control of cryptococcus, especially chronic suppression of cryptococcal meningitis in patients with AIDS. To initiate therapy, a loading dose of twice the usual daily dose should be used. A daily dose of 400 mg can be used for cryptococcal meningitis, depending on the patient's response to therapy. The dose should be reduced in patients who have renal insufficiency.

32. Used in the treatment of urinary tract infections and visceral infections caused by Candida. Also used in cryptococcal infections in which amphotericin B is not tolerated. Resistance to flucytosine may develop during treatment of candidal and cryptococcal infections. Sometimes

used in combination with amphotericin B to treat systemic fungal infections.

33. Ketoconazole is indicated in the treatment of patients with susceptible fungal infections that have failed to respond to amphotericin B or in the treatment of patients unable to tolerate the toxic effects of amphotericin B. In either role, it is generally preferred to therapy with miconazole when the patients can take oral medications. It is also the drug of choice in the long-term treatment of chronic mucocutaneous candidiasis. It has been useful in the treatment of histoplasmosis, coccidioidomycosis, chromomycosis, and paracoccidioidomycosis. In view of its poor penetration of the CSF, it should not be used in the treatment of coccidioidal or cryptococcal meningitis. Ketoconazole requires gastric acidity for dissolution and absorption. Antacids and cimetidine, if needed, should be given at least 2 hr after a dose of ketoconazole. The most frequent side effects have been nausea and vomiting. Several cases of liver injury of varying severity, possibly the result of idiosyncratic reactions, have occurred during ketoconazole therapy. Liver function tests, therefore, should be evaluated before and periodically during treatment, especially in patients who are on prolonged therapy or who have preexisting hepatic disease. Ketoconazole, in daily dosages of 200–1,800 mg p.o., is used in major and systemic fungal infections for which the mycotic agent is susceptible and amphotericin B cannot be employed.

34. Miconazole is available for parenteral therapy for systemic mycoses. Experience is relatively limited, and it should probably be reserved for patients who cannot tolerate or who do not respond to amphotericin B and flucytosine. Miconazole is metabolized by extrarenal mechanisms, and patients with fungal bladder infections require supplementary bladder irrigation with the drug. Side effects of miconazole include phlebitis, fever, rash, nausea and vomiting, anemia, thrombocytopenia, and transient hyperlipidemia caused by the diluent used.

35. Not absorbed from the GI tract. Use only in treatment of intestinal tract colonization by Candida species and not for any systemic mycotic infection. Nystatin suspension (400,000–600,000 units q.i.d.) is used as a mouthwash in treatment of oral thrush. The suspension can also be swallowed for use in the treatment of candidal esophagitis.

36. None of these drugs is recommended for children. In 1999, the FDA limited trovafloxacin to inpatient use for limb- or life-threatening infections.

Discussion

The antimicrobial agents of choice for various infections (e.g., community-acquired pneumonia[7-9]) in adults are well established [see Table 4], as are their dosages in patients with normal renal function [see Table 5]. Excellent reviews and practice guidelines have been published.[18,19]

Penicillins

Although the original penicillins are still useful against specific bacteria, there are some infections in which both they and the penicillinase-resistant semisynthetic penicillins are ineffective because of the emergence of penicillinase-producing staphylococci and methicillin-resistant staphylococci. The penicillins can be classified by structure, β-lactamase susceptibility, and spectrum of action [see Figure 1].

The action of the penicillins depends on the presence of a bacterial cell wall containing peptidoglycans that are accessible to the agent. In actively growing bacteria, interference with biosynthesis of the peptidoglycan structure—specifically, of the cross-linkages between the peptide chains—prevents the bacterium from developing its normal structural firmness, and this lack of firmness leads to lysis.

NATURAL PENICILLINS

Aqueous Crystalline Penicillin G

Aqueous crystalline penicillin G is used when a high serum concentration of the agent is required.[36] Its half-life is normally 30 minutes but may be as long as 10 hours in patients with anuria. Approximately 50% of penicillin G is bound to plasma proteins.

Generic Name	Side-Chain Substituent (R)	Penicillin Structure
Penicillin G	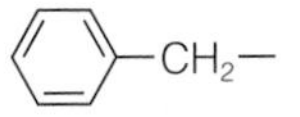	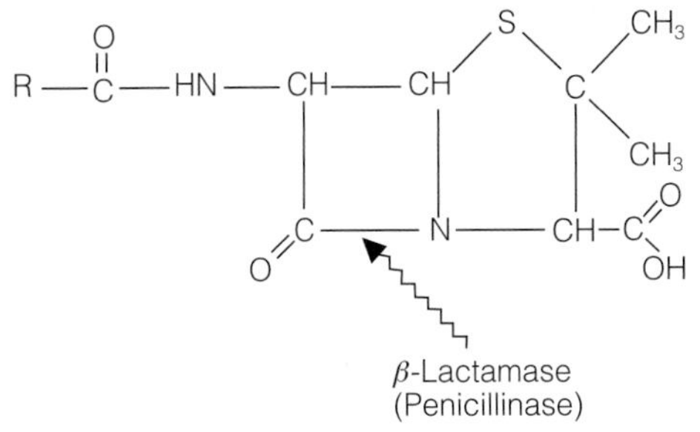
Oxacillin	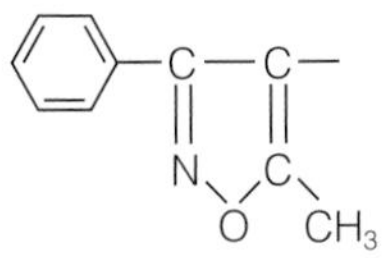	
Nafcillin	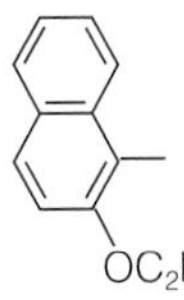	
Ampicillin	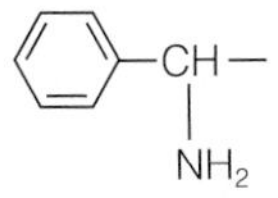	
Carbenicillin	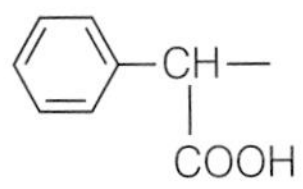	

Figure 1 Various semisynthetic penicillins have been produced by modifying the structure of the side chain (R) attached to the penicillin nucleus (right). In this way, penicillins have been developed that lack some of the drawbacks of penicillin G, such as poor gastrointestinal absorption, limited spectrum of antibacterial activity, and inactivation by penicillinase-producing microorganisms; for example, oxacillin and nafcillin are resistant to inactivation by penicillinase. This bacterial enzyme (also termed β-lactamase) cleaves the β-lactam ring of penicillin to form an inactive product; the site of action of penicillinase is shown at right.

Penicillin G sodium contains approximately 2 mEq of sodium per one million units. Therefore, the potassium salt of penicillin G should be used except in patients with renal insufficiency, who may not be able to tolerate the 1.7 mEq of potassium contained in each one million units. This agent is destroyed by gastric acid when given orally.

Penicillin G Benzathine

Penicillin G benzathine, 1.2 to 2.4 million units I.M., is used in the definitive management of certain infections, such as streptococcal sore throat, and as prophylaxis for several conditions, such as rheumatic fever, in which reinfection by β-hemolytic streptococci is a constant threat.

Penicillin G Procaine

Penicillin G procaine is used intramuscularly when a long-acting preparation is preferred and high blood levels are not required. It is indicated for the treatment of pneumococcal pneumonia, uncomplicated cases of which are adequately treated by administration of one or two daily doses of 300,000 units, and for treatment of acute genitourinary gonorrhea, for which a dose of 4.8 million units is divided and injected at two sites and 1 g of probenecid is given orally before the injection.

Penicillin V

Phenoxymethyl penicillin, or penicillin V, is resistant to gastric acid and therefore reaches higher serum concentrations, when given orally, than penicillin G does at similar doses. Penicillin V should not be substituted for parenterally administered penicillin G when such therapy is needed, but it can be given orally to treat mild infections of the throat, the respiratory tract, or soft tissue in doses of 125 to 500 mg given four to six times daily.

PENICILLINASE-RESISTANT PENICILLINS

Methicillin

Methicillin is the least protein-bound of this group (39%); nafcillin (90%), oxacillin (94%), cloxacillin (95%), and dicloxacillin (98%) all have higher rates of protein binding. Methicillin was the first of the semisynthetic penicillinase-resistant penicillins.[37] It must be administered parenterally and is usually given every 4 to 6 hours in a total daily dose of 100 to 300 mg/kg body weight.

Oxacillin and Nafcillin

Oxacillin seems to be as effective as methicillin against staphylococcal infections, and it causes interstitial nephritis less often. For parenteral use, oxacillin or nafcillin can be given in dosages of 100 to 300 mg/kg/day for children and up to 4 to 12 g/day for adults.

Cloxacillin and Dicloxacillin

If penicillinase-producing organisms are identified or suspected and oral therapy is desired, cloxacillin or dicloxacillin, 1 to 2 g/day, can be given.

AMINOPENICILLINS

Ampicillin

Ampicillin is active against a variety of bacteria, including many strains of *Escherichia coli, Proteus mirabilis, Salmonella, Shigella,*

Listeria, and *Haemophilus influenzae*. Most strains of *Klebsiella* and all strains of *P. aeruginosa* are resistant.

Because it is stable in gastric juices, ampicillin is suitable for oral as well as parenteral use. When it is given orally, peak serum levels are reached in about 2 hours, but they seldom exceed 0.3 μg/ml. When it is given intramuscularly, peak serum levels are achieved in 1 hour, and they are both higher and more prolonged than the peak levels achieved after oral administration. About 10% of ampicillin is bound to plasma proteins. The recommended daily dose is 1 to 4 g; parenteral administration of up to 12 g/day is recommended for major systemic infections.

Amoxicillin

Amoxicillin is closely related to ampicillin, both in chemical structure and in spectrum of antibacterial activity.[38] Amoxicillin, however, is more completely absorbed than ampicillin: approximately 70% of a dose of amoxicillin is absorbed, compared with approximately 50% of a dose of ampicillin. Consequently, the blood levels attainable with a given dose of amoxicillin are usually about twice those attainable with a comparable dose of ampicillin. Amoxicillin is at least as effective as ampicillin in the treatment of respiratory disorders that are caused by susceptible bacteria, including otitis media, sinusitis, and bronchitis.

CARBOXYPENICILLINS

Carbenicillin

Carbenicillin has an antibacterial range similar to that of ampicillin, with the added benefit of activity against certain strains of *P. aeruginosa*,[39] indole-positive *Proteus* species, and *Enterobacter* species.[40] Because carbenicillin is inactivated by penicillinase, penicillinase-producing *S. aureus* is resistant to it. *Klebsiella* species are resistant to carbenicillin, as are many *Serratia* organisms. Carbenicillin is bactericidal and is recoverable from blood, urine, lymph, CSF, and most body tissues. About 50% of the drug is bound to serum proteins.[41]

Ticarcillin

The antibacterial spectrum of ticarcillin is similar to that of carbenicillin; however, it is two to four times more active against *P. aeruginosa*. It is frequently preferred to carbenicillin in the treatment of serious gram-negative infections because of its greater potency and the lower incidence of adverse effects.[42] The primary use of ticarcillin is in the treatment of proven or suspected *Pseudomonas* infections. The recommended dosage is 16 to 24 g/day.

UREIDOPENICILLINS

Mezlocillin, Azlocillin, and Piperacillin

Mezlocillin, azlocillin, and piperacillin are semisynthetic penicillins derived from the ampicillin molecule with side-chain adaptations. The ureidopenicillins are generally bactericidal and act primarily by inhibiting cell wall synthesis in dividing bacteria. In comparison with the carboxypenicillins carbenicillin and ticarcillin, the ureidopenicillins exhibit less pronounced plasma protein binding, a shorter serum half-life, and a greater volume of distribution.[43-45] They are minimally metabolized (10%) and are primarily excreted in an active form by glomerular filtration and tubular secretion. Unlike carbenicillin and ticarcillin, the ureidopenicillins achieve high concentrations in bile because of increased biliary excretion.

In vitro, the ureidopenicillins are active against streptococci, enterococci, most Enterobacteriaceae, *Pseudomonas*, β-lactamase–negative staphylococci, *Neisseria*, and *Haemophilus*.[46-48] β-Lactamase–producing staphylococci and *H. influenzae* are resistant. The major advantage the ureidopenicillins have over other penicillins in clinical use is their increased activity against *P. aeruginosa* and *Klebsiella*.

The recommended dosages of the ureidopenicillins are 6 to 16 g/day for mild to moderate infections and 18 to 24 g/day for severe to life-threatening infections. Small doses may be given intramuscularly, but large doses must be given intravenously. The dosing interval is usually 4 to 6 hours.

Cephalosporins

Cephalosporium acremonium was discovered in 1948. This fungus was found to produce cephalosporin C, from which cephalothin, the first cephalosporin to be introduced, was in turn derived. The basic cephalosporin structure consists of a dihydrothiazine ring fused to a β-lactam ring.

Substitutions at the acyl side chain have led to differences in antibacterial spectrum and β-lactamase stability. The side chains substituted at this position interfere with proper stereotactic binding of the molecule to the β-lactamase active site, thus preventing degradation of the cephalosporin. Some of the side effects involving platelet aggregation that have been observed with the use of moxalactam can be traced to substitutions at this position.

For convenience, cephalosporins are divided into four generations or groups according to the nature and extent of their antibacterial spectra. More specifically, the division into generations is based on the number of gram-negative bacterial species against which each cephalosporin demonstrates clinical activity. It must be remembered, however, that although the members of each generation are sufficiently similar to be grouped together, they also are different from one another in a number of ways [*see* Table 6].

FIRST-GENERATION CEPHALOSPORINS

First-generation cephalosporins have good activity against aerobic gram-positive cocci such as *S. aureus*, group B streptococci, and *Streptococcus pneumoniae*. In addition, they are effective against three aerobic gram-negative bacilli—*E. coli*, *K. pneumoniae*, and *P. mirabilis*—although even among these three, resistance is common, occurring in as many as 30% of cases. First-generation cephalosporins are also active against most anaerobic cocci and bacilli (other than *B. fragilis*). They have little or no activity against *Enterobacter*, *Serratia*, *Acinetobacter*, *Pseudomonas*, methicillin-resistant *S. aureus*, *S. epidermidis*, and enterococci. They are also inactive against *B. fragilis*, *Citrobacter*, *Listeria monocytogenes*, *Proteus* (except for *P. mirabilis*), and *Providencia*.

First-generation cephalosporins are used for infections caused by gram-positive cocci, such as skin infections and osteomyelitis, although penicillins are the agents of choice for all streptococcal infections and for infections proven by culture to be caused by susceptible staphylococci. The best use for first-generation cephalosporins is in surgical prophylaxis. For this application, cefazolin sodium is the preferred agent.

SECOND-GENERATION CEPHALOSPORINS

Second-generation cephalosporins possess the same spectrum of activity as the first-generation cephalosporins, with the addition of broader coverage of gram-negative organisms, including *H. influenzae*, *E. aerogenes*, and some *Neisseria* species. Fewer than

Table 6 Properties of Cephalosporins[155]

	Specific Agent	Trade Names	Comment*
First Generation	**Oral**		
	Cefadroxil	Duricef, Ultracef	Longer half-life
	Cephalexin	Keflex	Most experience with this agent
	Cephradine	Anspor, Velosef	Properties are similar to those of cephalexin
	Parenteral		
	Cefazolin	Ancef, Kefzol	Longer half-life; well tolerated when given I.M.
	Cephapirin	Cefadyl	Properties are similar to those of other first-generation cephalosporins
	Cephradine	Anspor, Velosef	Properties are similar to those of other first-generation cephalosporins
Second Generation	**Oral**		
	Cefaclor	Ceclor	Moderately active against *Haemophilus influenzae*
	Cefprozil	Cefzil	Active against *H. influenzae*
	Cefuroxime axetil	Ceftin	Active against *H. influenzae*
	Loracarbef	Lorabid	A carbacephem with properties and spectrum similar to those of cefuroxime
	Parenteral		
	Cefamandole	Mandol	Active against *H. influenzae*; may cause bleeding
	Cefmetazole	Zefazone	Spectrum and half-life similar to cefoxitin; may cause bleeding
	Cefonicid	Monocid	Spectrum similar to that of cefamandole
	Ceforanide	Precef	Spectrum similar to that of cefamandole
	Cefotetan	Cefotan	Spectrum similar to that of cefoxitin; longer half-life than cefoxitin; may cause bleeding
	Cefoxitin	Mefoxin	Active against *Bacteroides fragilis, Serratia, Neisseria gonorrhoeae*
	Cefuroxime	Zinacef, Kefurox	Active against *H. influenzae*; only second-generation drug approved for meningitis (selected pathogens)
Third Generation	**Oral**		
	Cefixime	Suprax	More active against gram-negative bacilli, gonococci, *Moraxella catarrhalis*, and *H. influenzae* than other oral cephalosporins but much less active against *Staphylococcus aureus*; not active against *Pseudomonas*
	Cefpodoxime	Vantin	Similar to cefixime but more active against *S. aureus*
	Ceftibuten	Cedax	Similar to cefixime but has poor activity against pneumococci and staphylococci
	Parenteral		
	Cefepime	Maxipime	Active against most gram-positive cocci (except enterococci and methicillin-resistant staphylococci), *Neisseria, Haemophilus*, enteric gram-negative bacilli, and *Pseudomonas*
	Cefoperazone	Cefobid	Increased activity against *Pseudomonas aeruginosa* but less against Enterobacteriaceae; may cause bleeding
	Cefotaxime	Claforan	More active against gram-positive cocci
	Ceftazidime	Fortaz, Tazidime, Tazicef	Most active against *Pseudomonas*
	Ceftizoxime	Cefizox	Properties are similar to those of cefotaxime
	Ceftriaxone	Rocephin	Longer half-life; less active against *Pseudomonas, B. fragilis*

Note: detailed information about the various cephalosporins is covered in the text.
*Agents are being compared with other members of the same generation of cephalosporins.

5% of *E. coli* and *Proteus* strains are resistant to second-generation cephalosporins. The activity of second-generation agents against *S. pyogenes* and *S. pneumoniae* is equal to that of the first-generation agents, but their activity against staphylococci is variable: the MIC ranges from 0.20 to 25 µg/ml. Of the second-generation agents, the most active against staphylococci is cefamandole, which has an MIC of 0.6 µg/ml for *S. aureus*. Cefotetan and cefoxitin have significant activity against *B. fragilis*. Cefoxitin is less active against *H. influenzae* and *E. aerogenes* than other second-generation cephalosporins, but it is more active against *Serratia* species. Cefoxitin by itself is effective in patients with community-acquired peritonitis who are unlikely to be infected with *Enterobacter* or *P. aeruginosa*.[49] Cefuroxime and cefamandole have been used with some success in empirical therapy for community-acquired pneumonia.[50] Cefotetan, a cephamycin introduced in 1986, has a spectrum of activity very similar to that of cefoxitin.[51] It is as active as cefoxitin against *B. fragilis* but is less active against other strains in the *B. fragilis* group. Unlike cefoxitin, cefotetan is active against *H. influenzae*. Cefotetan has proved effective and safe in a variety of clinical situations, including gynecologic infections and surgical prophylaxis.[52]

Cefprozil is an oral agent whose spectrum of activity includes gram-positive and gram-negative pathogens. It has achieved good results in patients with pharyngitis or tonsillitis.[53]

Loracarbef is an oral agent of the carbacephem class that is active in vitro against the common pathogens associated with skin infections, otitis media, sinusitis, bronchopulmonary infections, and urinary tract infections.[54]

THIRD-GENERATION CEPHALOSPORINS

In the third-generation cephalosporins, activity against gram-positive cocci is replaced by broader gram-negative coverage. This development is illustrated by susceptibility testing done on *S. aureus*: the MIC of first-generation cephalosporins is 1 µg/ml, that of second-generation cephalosporins is 2 µg/ml, and that of third-generation cephalosporins is 3 µg/ml. Third-generation cephalosporins are more active against the enteric gram-negative bacilli covered by first- and second-generation cephalosporins. Their spectrum of activity includes *Serratia* and *Citrobacter*. They are also highly active against *H. influenzae* and *N. gonorrhoeae* and moderately active against *P. aeruginosa* and some anaerobes. At first, the third-generation cephalosporins seemed capable of providing the same spectrum of activity as the aminoglycosides but without their inherent toxicity; however, they have failed to gain wide popularity in the treatment of high-risk patients or patients with extensive infections. The reasons for this failure include their incomplete spectra of activity against the range of organisms likely to be encountered in polymicrobial infections, their unexpected agent-specific toxicity, their suboptimal pharmacokinetic properties, and their high propensity for inducing resistance.

Cefixime, an orally absorbed iminomethoxyaminothiazolyl cephalosporin, inhibits 90% of *S. pneumoniae*, *H. influenzae*, and *H. parainfluenzae* strains, whether they produce β-lactamase or not, at concentrations of less than 0.25 mg/L. It inhibits 90% of *Moraxella catarrhalis* strains at concentrations of less than 1 mg/L.

Ceftibuten is an orally active third-generation cephalosporin that possesses increased potency against members of the Enterobacteriaceae.[55] Generally, it is about 16 times more active than cefuroxime, cefaclor, cephalexin, or amoxicillin-clavulanate; its activity is comparable to that of cefixime. Ceftibuten is ineffective against staphylococci and only partially effective against *S. pneumoniae*. *H. influenzae* and *Neisseria* species, however, are highly susceptible to this agent.

Pharmacokinetics

After I.V. administration, third-generation cephalosporins conform to an open, two-compartment model, characterized by an initial rapid distribution phase followed by a slower terminal elimination phase. The relatively long elimination half-lives of many of the newer β-lactam antibiotics make less frequent dosing possible. Most third-generation cephalosporins are primarily eliminated renally, with two exceptions: cefoperazone and ceftriaxone. Cefoperazone is primarily eliminated unchanged in the bile, and only about 25% of an administered dose is recovered in the urine after 24 hours.[56] Peak biliary concentrations of cefoperazone approach or exceed 2,000 µg/ml after a 2 g I.V. dose.[57] Fifty percent of an administered dose of ceftriaxone is eliminated in the bile; the rest is eliminated renally. Ceftriaxone elimination is decreased to a small extent in end-stage renal disease; however, because the drug is normally given every 12 to 24 hours, there is little accumulation and therefore no need to adjust the dose. In general, third-generation cephalosporins penetrate most tissue and fluid compartments in amounts that, though variable, usually exceed the MIC for most susceptible pathogens. Sputum concentrations in the range of 0.3 to 6.0 µg/ml are attained with all the agents, and higher concentrations are found in purulent sputum. Ascitic fluid concentrations ranging from 2.4 µg/ml with ceftizoxime to greater than 60 µg/ml with cefoperazone are seen in patients with peritonitis.[58]

Concentrations in excess of the MIC for susceptible aerobic and anaerobic organisms (except for *B. fragilis*) are achieved in female genital tissue with all these agents.[59] These compounds also appear to penetrate the prostate, the testes, the ureters, and renal tissue in significant amounts.[60]

With each of these agents, therapeutic concentrations can be obtained in the gallbladder wall; these concentrations may be as high as 60 µg/g with cefoperazone. Bone-penetration studies reveal penetration with each of these agents.[61]

Clinical Utility

Many studies have compared third-generation cephalosporins in an effort to establish a superior drug or drug combination for life-threatening infections; most have found no statistically significant differences. It is important to remember that even if there is a difference in efficacy between two or more antibiotics, that difference may not be apparent if the study group is not large enough. For example, if one agent fails in 10% of patients and another in only 5%, a study group of 250 to 500 patients would be required to show a statistical difference.[62,63] Most comparative antibiotic trials, however, have reported on fewer than 60 patients and thus have not been able to pinpoint small differences in efficacy between antibiotics.[64] Many studies that find no difference between two regimens are in fact subject to this type of error.

FOURTH-GENERATION CEPHALOSPORINS

Cefepime is an extended-spectrum parenteral cephalosporin that provides coverage against both gram-positive and gram-negative organisms, including *S. aureus* and *P. aeruginosa*. Cefepime, which is a zwitterion, has a net neutral charge that allows it to penetrate the outer membrane of gram-negative bacteria faster than third-generation cephalosporins. It is more stable against β-lactamases because of the lower affinity of the enzymes for cefepime when compared with third-generation cephalosporins. In comparison with third-generation cephalosporins, cefepime appears to be less likely to induce resistance, because of a lower rate of hydrolysis by β-lactamases, a low affinity for these enzymes, and more rapid permeation into the cell. It has been used to treat patients with pneumonia, with results comparable to those obtained with ceftazidime.[65] Because of its antibacterial coverage and proven tissue penetration in acute pancreatitis, cefepime should be studied in patients with severe acute pancreatitis.[66] However, it offers poor coverage against *Bacteroides* and must be combined with metronidazole or clindamycin. The combination of cefepime and metronidazole was found to be equivalent to imipenem in a prospective, randomized study of intra-abdominal infections.[67]

ADVERSE EFFECTS

Cephalosporins are associated with a number of adverse side effects. The adverse reactions associated with their use are similar to those associated with use of other β-lactam compounds, such as local pain and irritation, hypersensitivity reactions, positive Coombs reaction, leukopenia, thrombocytopenia, transient abnormalities in liver function enzyme levels, and GI disturbances.[68,69] These reactions are usually mild and reversible, except in those rare patients who manifest life-threatening hypersensitivity reactions. Cephalosporins may be administered to most patients who are allergic to penicillin, because only 5% to 15% of penicillin-allergic patients react adversely to cephalosporins.[70] An excellent review of cephalosporin allergy and its treatment has been published.[71]

Aminoglycosides

Aminoglycosides are composed of two or more amino sugars bound by glycosidic linkage to a central hexose (aminocyclitol) nucleus. Their highly polar, polycationic structure contributes to their poor GI absorption and their meager ability to penetrate the blood-brain barrier. They bind irreversibly to the 30S bacterial ribosome and interfere with protein synthesis. Aminoglycosides also disturb calcium homeostasis and induce cell death as a result of efflux of potassium, sodium, and other essential bacterial constituents. Unlike most other antimicrobial agents that inhibit protein synthesis, aminoglycosides are bactericidal.

All aminoglycosides share certain pharmacokinetic properties. Because they are poorly absorbed when given orally, adequate serum concentrations can be obtained only through parenteral administration. Protein binding is negligible,[72] and the volume of distribution approximates the volume of the extracellular space.[73] In adults with normal renal function, the aminoglycosides have a half-life of about 2 hours, but there is considerable variation between individual patients.[74] In patients with deteriorating renal function, the half-life of an aminoglycosides increases, often exceeding 24 hours in patients with end-stage renal disease.[75]

The prolonged half-lives of aminoglycosides are substantially shortened during hemodialysis[76]; these agents are much less efficiently removed by peritoneal dialysis.[77] The aminoglycosides do not penetrate the blood-brain barrier well, even in patients with meningeal inflammation.[78,79] Drug levels in pulmonary secretions are typically 20% to 40% of serum levels. Low concentrations of aminoglycosides in purulent fluids are probably related to local inactivation caused by DNA released from leukocytes[80] and by the low regional pH.

The aminoglycosides are rapidly excreted, primarily by glomerular filtration. Urine concentrations may be 100 times the serum level in patients with normal renal function. The aminoglycosides accumulate in the renal cortex; sensitive assay techniques can detect them in urine and serum for up to 10 days after cessation of therapy.

STREPTOMYCIN

Widespread resistance among Enterobacteriaceae has limited the usefulness of streptomycin. At present, streptomycin is almost always employed in combination with other antimicrobial agents. With penicillin or vancomycin, streptomycin is used to treat infective endocarditis caused by viridans streptococci or susceptible enterococcal streptococci. It may also be given in conjunction with other antituberculous drugs to treat mycobacterial diseases and in conjunction with tetracycline to treat brucellosis. Streptomycin is used alone in the treatment of tularemia and plague.

KANAMYCIN

Because of widespread resistance among Enterobacteriaceae and *P. aeruginosa*, kanamycin is rarely used today. It is occasionally used as a second-line agent in combination with other antibiotics in the treatment of tuberculosis.

GENTAMICIN

Gentamicin is used for serious hospital-acquired infections caused by Enterobacteriaceae and most strains of *P. aeruginosa* in institutions in which there is minimal background resistance to this agent (other *Pseudomonas* species are predictably resistant to aminoglycosides). Gentamicin is given with penicillin to treat enterococcal endocarditis and with vancomycin plus rifampin to treat prosthetic valve endocarditis caused by *S. epidermidis*.

TOBRAMYCIN

Tobramycin closely resembles gentamicin with respect to antimicrobial spectrum and pharmacokinetics. Tobramycin is more active against some strains of *A. calcoaceticus* but less active against *S. marcescens*. Although tobramycin has slightly greater intrinsic activity against *P. aeruginosa*, most gentamicin-resistant strains of this organism are also resistant to tobramycin. The difference in nephrotoxicity between gentamicin and tobramycin is clinically insignificant.[81-83]

AMIKACIN

Amikacin is a semisynthetic derivative of kanamycin. Its major advantage is its resistance to aminoglycoside-modifying enzymes, the production of which is the principal mechanism of bacterial resistance to aminoglycosides. Amikacin may therefore be used against gentamicin-resistant organisms, and it is clearly the aminoglycoside of choice where gentamicin resistance is prevalent. Fortunately, no substantial increase in amikacin resistance has been noted, even in medical centers where it has been used extensively.[84]

NETILMICIN AND SISOMICIN

Netilmicin, a semisynthetic derivative of sisomicin, is not metabolized by most of the aminoglycoside-modifying enzymes and therefore is active against some strains of Enterobacteriaceae that are resistant to gentamicin and tobramycin; however, it is less active against *P. aeruginosa*. Animal studies suggest that netilmicin may be less nephrotoxic than other aminoglycosides,[82,85] and human studies suggest that it is somewhat less likely to exert toxic effects on cranial nerve VIII.[82] Sisomicin is more active than gentamicin against Enterobacteriaceae and *P. aeruginosa*, but the nephrotoxicity it has exhibited in animal studies exceeds that of other aminoglycosides.[86]

ADVERSE EFFECTS

Unlike β-lactam antibiotics, aminoglycosides, have a narrow range between therapeutic and toxic levels and are thus more likely to cause side effects. Their ototoxicity is potentially more significant than their nephrotoxicity because it is often irreversible. Cochlear toxicity has been reported in 8% to 10% of patients and has been clinically evident in as many as 4% of patients treated with aminoglycosides for various infections.[87] Vestibular toxicity, as manifested by electronystagmographic changes, has been found in 5% to 10% of patients and has been clinically significant in 1% to 5%.[82] Vestibular toxicity is more frequently associated with streptomycin, gentamicin, and tobramycin, whereas auditory toxicity is more typical of kanamycin and amikacin. Ototoxicity and vestibular toxicity are difficult to monitor, particularly in hospitalized patients for whom formal audiometry and caloric testing may be cumbersome or uncomfortable. Because aminoglycoside-associated auditory toxicity generally affects the higher frequencies, early bedside detection is difficult. Toxic effects on cranial nerve VIII seem to be related to advanced age, previous aminoglycoside treatment, and excessive serum levels.

AMINOGLYCOSIDE PHARMACOKINETICS

Peak aminoglycoside concentrations higher than 5 μg/ml are associated with improved survival in patients with gram-negative infections.[88,89] With gram-negative pulmonary infections, peak concentrations of 8 to 10 μg/ml are necessary because of poor penetration of aminoglycosides into the lungs.[90,91] It has been shown that a loading dose of gentamicin or tobramycin of 2 mg/kg of lean body weight cannot guarantee adequate peak concentrations in acutely ill patients. The most likely explanation for the usually low peak serum concentrations of aminoglycosides in acutely ill patients is an expanded volume of distribution.[92-96] Dosage adjustments based on blood levels should be made as soon as possible after the beginning of therapy and after the steady state has been reached.

Once-Daily Dosing of Aminoglycosides

Efforts to improve the toxic-to-therapeutic ratio of aminoglycosides include once-daily dosing schedules and reevaluations of the recommended therapeutic ranges. In conventional administration of aminoglycosides to patients with normal renal function, divided doses are administered at 8- to 12-hour intervals. In an effort to improve efficacy and decrease toxicity and cost, once-daily regimens have been compared with conventional regimens. In most protocols, the total doses were equivalent in the single and divided-dose regimens. Two meta-analyses of such trials have concluded that once-daily dosing is as effective as divided dosing and has a lower risk of toxicity in patients with normal renal function.[97,98] Although most trials evaluated immunocompetent adults, similar trends were noted for children and for patients with febrile neutropenia. In elderly patients, however, the high peak serum concentrations that occur with once-daily dosing may increase the risk of nephrotoxicity,[99] probably because of diminished renal clearance. There are several excellent reviews of the subject in the literature.[100,101]

Tetracyclines

The tetracyclines act against microorganisms by inhibiting protein synthesis; their site of action is the bacterial ribosome. Resistance to the tetracyclines appears slowly and in a stepwise fashion and is mediated by plasmids. Plasmids impart resistance by coding for proteins that interfere with active transport of tetracycline through the cytoplasmic membrane. Microorganisms that acquire resistance to one tetracycline are usually resistant to the other tetracyclines as well.

At appropriate dosages, peak serum concentrations 1 hour after intravenous administration of tetracycline, doxycycline, or minocycline are typically 10 to 20 μg/ml. The newer semisynthetic tetracyclines—doxycycline, methacycline, and minocycline—have considerably longer serum half-lives than the older agents.

Tetracyclines are metabolized by the liver and concentrated in the bile. Biliary concentrations of these agents are, on average, five to 10 times higher than concurrent plasma concentrations. The tetracyclines penetrate body tissues well and are capable of entering the CSF even in the absence of inflammation of the meninges. They readily cross the placental barrier, and relatively high concentrations are found in human milk.

Tetracyclines are useful in the treatment of sexually transmitted diseases. Tetracyclines are also effective for the treatment of other chlamydial infections, such as lymphogranuloma venereum, psittacosis, inclusion conjunctivitis, and trachoma. A tetracycline may also be used in the treatment of gonococcal infections in patients who are unable to tolerate penicillin G. Other sexually transmitted diseases that may be treated with tetracyclines are chancroid and granuloma inguinale.

A tetracycline or erythromycin is the agent of choice for the treatment of *Mycoplasma pneumoniae* infection. Tetracyclines are also effective against rickettsial infections, tularemia, and cholera; in patients unable to tolerate penicillin, they may be used to treat actinomycosis. Doxycycline is useful as prophylaxis against traveler's diarrhea caused by toxicogenic strains of *E. coli*. Unfortunately, the widespread use of tetracyclines as additives to livestock feed has resulted in increasing bacterial resistance to these agents.

Macrolides

ERYTHROMYCIN

Erythromycin is a macrolide that contains a many-membered lactone ring to which one or more deoxy sugars are attached. Erythromycin and other macrolide antibiotics inhibit protein synthesis through reversible binding to the 50S ribosomal subunits of susceptible microorganisms.

Erythromycin is well absorbed from the GI tract. The presence of food in the stomach reduces absorption of the drug, except when it is in the estolate form.[102] Erythromycin is excreted primarily in the bile; only 2% to 5% of a given dose is excreted in the urine. Concentrations in the bile may be more than 10 times those in plasma. Erythromycin diffuses readily into most tissues, except for the brain and the CSF.

Erythromycin is the agent of choice for the treatment of *M. pneumoniae* and *Legionella* infections. It is also effective against infections caused by group A β-hemolytic streptococci or *S. pneumoniae*. Accordingly, it is the agent of choice for the treatment of community-acquired pneumonia in nonimmunosuppressed patients who do not require hospitalization and who are allergic to penicillin.[103] In addition, erythromycin may be used to treat gonorrhea and syphilis in patients who are unable to tolerate penicillin G or tetracycline. The incidence of serious erythromycin-related adverse effects is low.

CLARITHROMYCIN AND AZITHROMYCIN

Clarithromycin and azithromycin are new semisynthetic macrolides that are structurally related to erythromycin. They inhibit protein synthesis in susceptible organisms by binding to the 50S ribosomal subunit. Clarithromycin and azithromycin are well absorbed and widely distributed, with excellent cellular and tissue penetration. Both agents have a broader spectrum of activity than erythromycin does; in addition, they have fewer GI side effects (a major obstacle to compliance with erythromycin therapy).

Clarithromycin is several times more active against gram-positive organisms in vitro than erythromycin, whereas azithromycin is two to four times less potent than erythromycin. Azithromycin has excellent in vitro activity against *H. influenzae*; clarithromycin, although less active against *H. influenzae* according to standard in vitro testing, is metabolized into an active compound with twice the in vitro activity of the parent drug. Azithromycin and clarithromycin also are active against some unexpected pathogens (e.g., *Borrelia burgdorferi*, *Toxoplasma gondii*, *M. avium* complex, and *M. leprae*). At present, clarithromycin appears to be the more active of the two against atypical mycobacteria, giving new hope to surgeons faced with what has become a difficult group of infections to treat.

Superior pharmacodynamic properties distinguish these new macrolides from the prototypical macrolide, erythromycin. Azithromycin has a large volume of distribution, and although serum concentrations remain low, it concentrates readily within tissues, demonstrating a tissue half-life of approximately 3 days; a 5-day course of therapy will provide therapeutic tissue concentrations for at least 10 days. These properties allow novel dosing schemes. For instance, azithromycin can be given once daily for 5 days to treat respiratory tract and soft tissue infections, and administration of a single 1 g dose of azithromycin can effectively treat *Chlamydia trachomatis* genital infections; these more convenient dosing schedules improve patient compliance.

DIRITHROMYCIN

Dirithromycin is an oral macrolide antibiotic with an antibacterial spectrum similar to that of erythromycin; it can be administered once daily but has no other advantages over erythromycin. The drugs produce similar GI side effects, and dirithromycin is substantially more expensive.

Clindamycin

Clindamycin is a 7-deoxy-7-chloro derivative of lincomycin that consists of an amino acid attached to a sulfur-containing octose. Clindamycin binds exclusively to the 50S subunit of bacterial ribosomes and suppresses the synthesis of protein. Clindamycin, erythromycin, and chloramphenicol all act at the same site, and the binding of one of these antibiotics to the ribosome may inhibit the binding of the others. Plasmid-mediated resistance to clindamycin has been reported in *B. fragilis*; this may be caused by methylation of bacterial RNA found in the 50S ribosomal subunit.[104] Peak serum concentrations 1 hour after intravenous administration of a 600 mg dose are approximately 10 to 12 μg/ml. Clindamycin is metabolized by the liver and excreted in an inactive form in the urine. It readily penetrates most body tissues but not the CSF.[105]

Clindamycin is active against *B. fragilis* and other anaerobic microorganisms and is useful in the treatment of patients with intra-abdominal, pelvic, and pulmonary infections. It is associated with a modest number of adverse effects.

Chloramphenicol

Chloramphenicol is unique among antibiotics in that it contains a nitrobenzene moiety and is a derivative of dichloroacetic acid. Like clindamycin, it inhibits bacterial protein synthesis by binding reversibly to the 50S ribosomal subunit, thus keeping the amino acid–containing end of aminoacyl–transfer RNA (tRNA) from binding to the ribosome. Chloramphenicol is rapidly and completely absorbed from the GI tract, and absorption is not impaired by concomitant ingestion of food or administration of antacids. It is inactivated in the liver by glucuronyl transferase. Chloramphenicol and its metabolites are excreted rapidly in the urine. About 80% to 90% of a dose is excreted in this way, about 5% to 10% of which is in the biologically active form. The drug penetrates well into all tissues, including the brain; it also penetrates well into the CSF and the aqueous humor.

Because of the risk of serious or fatal bone marrow toxicity, chloramphenicol should be used only against those infections for which the benefits of its use outweigh the risks of its potential toxicity. It still plays a major role in the treatment of typhoid fever, although plasmid-mediated resistance of *S. typhi* to chloramphenicol has been reported. Chloramphenicol is effective therapy for bacterial meningitis and brain abscesses caused by susceptible microorganisms; in conjunction with penicillin, it is effective empirical therapy for brain abscesses.

Vancomycin

Vancomycin is a narrow-spectrum antibiotic derived from *Nocardia orientalis*. Vancomycin exerts its bactericidal effect by inhibiting the biosynthesis of the major structural cell wall polymer, peptidoglycan.[106] Vancomycin is about 55% protein bound. Its activity is not significantly affected by pH values between 6.5 and 8.0. It is poorly absorbed from the GI tract. Because patients invariably experience pain after intramuscular injections, parenteral administration is limited to the intravenous route. Vancomycin is primarily excreted by the kidneys; about 80% to 90% of the dose is eliminated in a 24-hour period. Its half-life is approximately 6 hours in patients with normal renal function. In anuric patients, the half-life may be prolonged to approximately 7 days.[107] Vancomycin is not removed by hemodialysis or peritoneal dialysis.

Vancomycin is mainly effective against gram-positive organisms. No cross-resistance has been demonstrated between vancomycin and other antibiotics, and resistance is uncommon. Vancomycin, given alone, is the agent of choice in the treatment of methicillin-resistant *S. aureus* infections.[108,109] Some strains of methicillin-resistant *S. aureus*, however, are resistant to vancomycin. If vancomycin therapy is ineffective against severe infections caused by such strains, the addition of either an aminoglycoside or rifampin, or both, should be considered. Several reports

have indicated that vancomycin is not bactericidal for enterococci.[110] Vancomycin is indicated for other serious infections caused by organisms with multiple antibiotic resistance, such as CSF shunt infections and prosthetic valve infection caused by *S. epidermidis* or *Corynebacterium diphtheriae*.[111] It is the agent of choice for infections caused by penicillin-resistant group JK corynebacteria[112] and is uniformly active against rare, multiply resistant strains of *S. pneumoniae*.[113] Given orally, vancomycin is also the agent of choice for *C. difficile*–associated enterocolitis,[114] although less expensive agents, such as bacitracin[115] and metronidazole,[116] may be as effective.

Anaphylactoid reactions to vancomycin have been reported since the earliest clinical trials. Such reactions can occur with the first dose; signs and symptoms range from mild pruritus to dramatic hypotension and cardiovascular arrest. The rapid intravenous infusion of vancomycin can cause a peculiar reaction consisting of pruritus; an erythematous or maculopapular rash involving the face, neck, and upper torso; and possible hypotension.

Metronidazole

Metronidazole acts by disrupting bacterial DNA and inhibiting nucleic acid synthesis[117;] it is bactericidal against almost all anaerobic gram-negative bacilli, including *B. fragilis*, and against most *Clostridium* species. Although true anaerobic streptococci are generally susceptible to it, microaerophilic streptococci as well as *Actinomyces* and *Propionibacterium* species are often resistant.

Metronidazole is excellent for anaerobic infections of the abdomen and pelvis. For serious anaerobic infections, the drug is administered intravenously; a loading dose of 15 mg/kg is given, followed by 7.5 mg/kg every 6 hours until the patient is well enough to take an oral dosage of 7.5 mg/kg every 6 hours. The dosage need not be reduced in azotemic patients, but it should be reduced in patients with hepatic insufficiency. Because of its bactericidal action and excellent tissue penetration, intravenous metronidazole may be the treatment of choice for *B. fragilis* endocarditis and central nervous system infections, both of which are uncommon. When metronidazole is administered orally, it is well absorbed and is widely distributed in body tissues, including those of the CNS.

Side effects of metronidazole include dry mouth (associated with a metallic taste) and nausea. Concurrent use of alcohol may cause a reaction similar to that produced when alcohol is ingested after taking disulfiram. Neurologic symptoms, including peripheral neuropathy and encephalopathic reactions, and neutropenia are uncommon. Pancreatitis has been reported,[118] but alternative drugs are available.

Carbapenems

Imipenem and meropenem were the first carbapenems available for clinical use in the United States; the third, ertapenem, was released in 2002. Like other β-lactam antibiotics, they are bactericidal and act by inhibiting bacterial cell wall synthesis.[119] Three properties account for the extraordinarily broad antibacterial spectrum of the carbapenems: there is no permeability barrier excluding the drugs from bacteria; they have high affinity for penicillin-binding protein 2, which is a crucial component of cell wall structure; and they are extremely resistant to hydrolysis by β-lactamases.

Carbapenems are extraordinarily active against gram-negative bacteria. Whereas imipenem tends to be more active against gram-positive cocci, meropenem appears to be more active against gram-negative bacilli. Virtually all Enterobacteriaceae are susceptible. *Haemophilus* and *Neisseria* species are also susceptible to carbapenems but at concentrations somewhat higher than those of third-generation cephalosporins. Acinetobacter, which is resistant to most other β-lactam antibiotics, is susceptible to imipenem and meropenem, as are *Serratia, Salmonella, Citrobacter, Yersinia,* and *Brucella* species. Gram-negative anaerobes, including *B. fragilis,* are susceptible. *P. aeruginosa* is also susceptible, but some resistant strains have emerged during therapy; as a result, imipenem or meropenem should probably be combined with a second antipseudomonal drug when they are used to treat serious pseudomonal infections. Certain nosocomial pathogens, such as *Stenotrophomonas maltophilia* and *P. cepacia,* are resistant, as are *Flavobacterium* species.

Imipenem is extensively degraded in the renal tubule, which results in low urinary levels of the drug. This drawback can be prevented by using cilastatin, an inhibitor of the brush-border enzyme dehydropeptidase-1. Cilastatin also appears to prevent the tubular damage that is occasionally observed in animals given imipenem alone in high doses. For clinical use, imipenem and cilastatin are administered simultaneously in equal doses.

Meropenem is pharmacologically similar to imipenem except that it is not susceptible to degradation by dehydropeptidase; as a result, it can be administered without cilastatin. About 70% of both meropenem and imipenem is excreted in the urine; the dosage should be reduced in azotemic patients. Like imipenem, meropenem is active against most clinically active gram-positive and gram-negative bacteria, including anaerobes; however, neither drug is active against methicillin-resistant staphylococci or *E. faecium.* Resistant strains of *P. aeruginosa* have emerged during therapy with each drug.

The clinical efficacy and toxicity of meropenem are similar to those of imipenem, except that meropenem appears more likely to be effective in meningitis and less likely to cause seizures.

Because the newest carbapenem, ertapenem, has a longer half-life than the other members of the group, it can be administered in a single daily intravenous dose.[120] Like the other carbapenems, ertapenem is excreted in the urine, and the dosage should be reduced in azotemic patients. The antibacterial spectrum of ertapenem is similar to that of meropenem, except that *Pseudomonas* and *Acinetobacter* strains are less susceptible, and *E. faecalis* is resistant.[121] Ertapenem appears effective against community-acquired pneumonias, intra-abdominal infections, complicated skin and soft tissue infections, and complicated urinary tract infections, but experience is limited.

The carbapenems have broader antibacterial spectrums than any other β-lactam antibiotics. They are active against most gram-positive bacteria—both aerobes and anaerobes. Exceptions include some enterococci; many *E. faecalis* strains are sensitive to imipenem and meropenem but not ertapenem, and most *E. faecium* strains are resistant to all three drugs. Some diphtheroids are resistant. Although most *S. aureus* strains are very sensitive, the susceptibility of methicillin-resistant *S. aureus* and coagulase-negative staphylococci is highly variable. Methicillin-resistant *S. aureus* and *Listeria* exhibit carbapenem tolerance. Finally, some strains of *C. difficile* are resistant.

Ertapenem has a spectrum of activity similar to that of meropenem, except that *Pseudomonas* and *Acinetobacter* strains are much less susceptible, and *E. faecalis* is resistant.

The safety of carbapenems seems comparable to that of other β-lactam antibiotics. Nausea and vomiting, local pain at injection sites, and hypersensitivity are the most common reactions. Seizures, although unusual, are a potential concern with imipen-

em; they have been observed in 0.9% of patients who have received the drug; risk factors for seizure include excessive dosages of the drugs, preexisting CNS lesions, epilepsy, and renal insufficiency. Meropenem is less likely to provoke seizures.[119] Transient elevations of liver enzymes and leukopenia can occur in patients who are given carbapenems. Antibiotic-associated pseudomembranous colitis has occurred.

Because the structure of the carbapenems resembles that of the penicillins and cephalosporins, there is potential for cross-reactivity in patients allergic to other β-lactam antibiotics. Clinical experience in this situation is limited, but it appears prudent to avoid carbapenems in patients with anaphylactic sensitivity to β-lactam drugs and to use them with caution in patients with milder allergies to penicillins or cephalosporins.[122]

Carbapenems have been used successfully in patients with pneumonia, intra-abdominal infections, urinary tract infections, endocarditis, bacteremia, osteomyelitis, cellulitis, and febrile neutropenia. The broad spectrum and apparent low toxicity of carbapenems is impressive, but they should be used selectively and with restraint.

Monobactams

The monobactams are monocyclic β-lactam antibiotics that lack the thiazolidine ring found in penicillins and the dihydrothiazine ring found in cephalosporins. Although there are several monobactams under investigation, only aztreonam has been approved for clinical use in the United States. It has been evaluated in open and comparative studies against a number of agents currently used to treat infections.[123,124] It inhibits only aerobic gram-negative species. It can be administered two or three times daily. It is a poor hapten and has been successfully administered to small numbers of patients with proven allergy to penicillins and cephalosporins.[125]

Aztreonam has been shown to be effective against bacteremia caused by *E. coli, K. pneumoniae, P. mirabilis, S. marcescens, P. aeruginosa, Enterobacter* species, *Proteus* species, and *Providencia* species.[126,127] It has also been used, alone or in combination with clindamycin, to treat gram-negative aspiration pneumonia, with results comparable or superior to those obtained with an aminoglycoside-clindamycin combination.[128,129]

Aztreonam has been advocated as directed therapy to obviate more toxic drugs. It seems possible that aztreonam could replace aminoglycosides in many situations in which they are combined with other agents.

β-Lactamase Inhibitors

A novel approach to antibacterial chemotherapy is the use of β-lactamase inhibitors with β-lactam agents. Clavulanate has been combined with both amoxicillin and ticarcillin. Because neither clavulanate nor sulbactam inhibits the β-lactamases that function primarily as cephalosporinases in *Enterobacter, Serratia,* and *P. aeruginosa* infections, the addition of clavulanate or sulbactam does not enhance ticarcillin's activity against *Pseudomonas.* The principal use of amoxicillin-clavulanate has been in the treatment of upper respiratory tract infections caused by β-lactamase–producing *H. influenzae* or *M. catarrhalis.* Ticarcillin-clavulanate has been used to treat pneumonia caused by *P. aeruginosa* and mixed β-lactamase–producing flora as well as intra-abdominal infections and gynecologic infections in which the infecting organisms often possess β-lactamases. In febrile neutropenic patients, its efficacy is comparable to that of other agents, but superinfections may be a problem.[130,131] Because some strains of *K. pneumoniae* are not adequately inhibited by ticarcillin-clavulanate, addition of an aminoglycoside would be appropriate in neutropenic patients. Sulbactam has also been combined with ampicillin.

Clavulanate, sulbactam, and tazobactam have all been combined with piperacillin in an attempt to enhance the agent's activity against β-lactamase–producing bacteria.[132,133] Tazobactam enhances the spectrum of action and potency of piperacillin to a greater extent than sulbactam does. Although piperacillin-clavulanate is more potent than piperacillin-tazobactam, the two combinations are effective against virtually the same spectrum of resistant β-lactamase–producing gram-negative organisms. Piperacillin-tazobactam is more potent than ticarcillin-clavulanate and is effective against a wider range of gram-negative enteric organisms. Combinations of piperacillin with tazobactam or clavulanate have a broader spectrum of activity than combinations of piperacillin with sulbactam against bacteria that produce characterized plasmid-mediated enzymes of clinical significance. In particular, piperacillin-tazobactam and piperacillin-clavulanate inhibit TEM-1, TEM-2, and SHV-1 β-lactamases, but piperacillin-sulbactam does not. In mice infected with β-lactamase–producing *E. coli, K. pneumoniae, P. mirabilis,* and *S. aureus,* both tazobactam and clavulanate have provided greater enhancement of the therapeutic efficacy of piperacillin than sulbactam has. Reviews of the TEM-type β-lactamases[134] and the piperacillin-tazobactam combinations[135] have been published.

Quinolones

The addition of a fluorine group and a piperazine substituent to the first quinolones has greatly improved the antibacterial spectrum of this class of drugs; the addition of a methyl group on the piperazine ring appears to further enhance the bioavailability of these compounds.

The fluoroquinolones are bactericidal compounds that act by inhibiting DNA gyrase, the bacterial enzyme responsible for maintaining the supertwisted helical structure of DNA; DNA topoisomerase IV is a secondary target.[136] The fluoroquinolones rapidly kill bacteria, probably by impairing DNA synthesis and possibly by mechanisms involving the cleaving of bacterial chromosomal DNA. Bacterial resistance to the fluoroquinolones depends on a change in their DNA gyrase. Bacterial strains that are resistant to one fluoroquinolone tend to be cross-resistant to related compounds; such resistance is usually mediated by chromosomes, but plasmid-mediated resistance raises the possibility of transferable resistance.

The fluoroquinolones are broad-spectrum antimicrobials. Most enteric gram-negative bacilli, including *E. coli, Proteus, Klebsiella,* and *Enterobacter,* are highly susceptible; common GI pathogens, such as *Salmonella, Shigella,* and *Campylobacter* species, are also very sensitive. Other gram-negative organisms that are killed by low concentrations of the fluoroquinolones are *N. gonorrhoeae* and *N. meningitidis, H. influenzae, P. multocida, M. catarrhalis,* and *Y. enterocolitica. Acinetobacter* and *Serratia* are somewhat less susceptible. *P. aeruginosa* is susceptible to ciprofloxacin and trovafloxacin; ofloxacin and levofloxacin are moderately active, but the other quinolones are not effective. *P. cepacia* and *S. maltophilia* are quinolone-resistant. Ciprofloxacin is the drug of choice for *Bacillus anthracis;* ofloxacin and levofloxacin are also active in vitro.[137] Among gram-positive cocci, methicillin-sensitive strains of *S. aureus* and coagulase-negative staphylococci are usually susceptible to quinolones, but methicillin-resistant *S. aureus* and enterococci are not. Lomefloxacin is not active against pneumococci and

other streptococci; ciprofloxacin and ofloxacin are moderately active; and levofloxacin, sparfloxacin, gatifloxacin, moxifloxacin, and trovafloxacin are highly effective, even against non–penicillin-sensitive pneumococci. Even fastidious intracellular pathogens can be inhibited by the quinolones; *Chlamydia, Mycoplasma, Listeria, Legionella,* and *M. tuberculosis* are in this category. Only trovafloxacin is highly active against anaerobes. Levofloxacin, gatifloxacin, moxifloxacin, and sparfloxacin demonstrate some activity against anaerobes, but the other quinolones do not. *C. difficile* is resistant to quinolones.

The fluoroquinolones are rapidly absorbed from the GI tract. Penetration into body fluids and tissues is generally excellent; therapeutic concentrations are readily achieved in blister fluid, bile, urine, saliva and sputum, bone, and muscle. Excellent concentrations of these drugs are achieved in the prostate, and stool levels are extraordinarily high. The fluoroquinolones appear to penetrate the CSF in the presence of meningeal inflammation,[138] but experience in treating meningitis is scant.

Although serum protein binding is modest, the fluoroquinolones have long serum half-lives, which range from 3 to 4 hours for ciprofloxacin to 12 hours for moxifloxacin. Most fluoroquinolones are eliminated by glomerular filtration and tubular secretion, and their dosages should be reduced in the presence of moderately severe renal failure. Trovafloxacin and moxifloxacin, however, are excreted chiefly by the liver.

The fluoroquinolones appear to be very well tolerated, with mild GI side effects (nausea, vomiting, or anorexia), CNS side effects (light-headedness, dizziness, somnolence, or insomnia), or rash occurring in fewer than 10% of treated patients. Lomefloxacin and sparfloxacin can cause phototoxicity. Less common side effects include allergic intestinal nephritis, pseudomembranous colitis, and neutropenia. Sparfloxacin and moxifloxacin may cause QT interval prolongation and should not be used by patients who have conditions or are using drugs known to prolong the QT interval or predispose to arrhythmias.[139] Tendinitis has been reported; in severe cases, it has resulted in rupture of the tendons of the shoulder and hand and the Achilles tendon. Crystalluria has been reported after the use of very large doses. Because fluoroquinolones have caused arthropathy in young animals, these drugs should be avoided in children and in women who are pregnant or nursing. Ciprofloxacin is safe in long-term use; there is less long-term experience with the other fluoroquinolones.

The fluoroquinolones have been useful clinically in a variety of infections, including urinary tract, genital, prostatic, GI, respiratory tract, soft tissue, and bone infections. Because of its excellent activity against anaerobes, trovafloxacin was considered useful in intra-abdominal and pelvic infections, but concerns about serious hepatotoxicity have restricted its use to infections deemed life- or limb-threatening and for patients in whom the benefit of trovafloxacin outweighs its potential risks. If it must be used, liver function must be monitored carefully.

The fluoroquinolones, administered in various regimens ranging from a single dose to 5 days of therapy, are effective in preventing and treating traveler's diarrhea and shigellosis. They have been highly effective in the treatment of typhoid fever. However, prolongation of the carrier state limits their role in nontyphoidal *Salmonella* enteritis, and the development of resistance limits their role in *Campylobacter* enteritis. The fluoroquinolones may be useful in the empirical treatment of severe community-acquired gastroenteritis, particularly if treatment is started early.

Because of their extraordinarily broad antimicrobial activity, their favorable pharmacokinetics, and their low toxicity,[140] the fluoroquinolones are extremely valuable new drugs. Like all antimicrobials, however, fluoroquinolones should be used judiciously, especially in view of new concerns about resistance[141,142] and toxicity and practical considerations about expense.

ADVERSE EFFECTS

Adverse reactions to the quinolones are estimated to occur in 4% to 8% of cases.[143] Most such reactions are not severe: cessation of therapy has been necessary in only about 1% to 2% of patients, and in all cases, the reactions have been reversible. The most common adverse effects are gastrointestinal—namely, nausea, vomiting, and diarrhea. The next most common are CNS effects, which include dizziness, headache, insomnia, hallucinations, agitation, and seizures. (The last three have been attributed to coadministration of enoxacin and theophylline.) Other effects include skin rash, pruritus, photosensitivity (with ofloxacin and pefloxacin), and mild alterations in hematologic and biochemical laboratory values.

Streptogramins

Quinupristin and dalfopristin are two structurally distinct streptogramins that bind to separate sites on the bacterial 50S ribosomal subunit; they thus act synergistically to inhibit protein synthesis. The drugs are marketed together in a 30:70 ratio as Synercid.[144]

Although quinupristin-dalfopristin is active against a variety of bacteria, its major use is in the treatment of serious infections caused by vancomycin-resistant strains of E. faecium. The drugs may also be useful in occasional vancomycin-intolerant patients with severe infections caused by methicillin-resistant S. aureus or coagulase-negative staphylococci. Resistance to quinupristin-dalfopristin is emerging.[145]

Quinupristin-dalfopristin is administered intravenously; because of a high incidence of phlebitis, a central line should be used. Other adverse effects include arthralgias and myalgias, which may be severe, and elevated bilirubin levels. The antibiotic may elevate levels of drugs that are metabolized by the hepatic enzyme CYP3A4; nifedipine and cyclosporine are examples.

The usual dose of quinupristin-dalfopristin is 7.5 mg/kg given intravenously over 1 hour every 8 hours. The drug is metabolized by the liver, so no dose reduction is required in azotemic patients. Quinupristin-dalfopristin is extremely expensive.

Oxazolidinones

In 2000, linezolid became the first member of the oxazolidinone class to be approved for clinical use in the United States.[146] Linezolid is a synthetic antibiotic that inhibits protein synthesis by binding to a site on the bacterial 23S ribosomal RNA of the 50S subunit, thus preventing function of the initiation complex that is required for ribosomal function.[147] Because no other antibiotic acts in this way, bacteria that have developed resistance to other ribosomally active antimicrobials do not display cross-resistance to linezolid.

Linezolid is active against nearly all aerobic gram-positive cocci at concentrations of 4 mg/ml or less,[148] including penicillin-resistant pneumococci, methicillin-resistant staphylococci, and vancomycin-resistant enterococci; however, resistant strains have been isolated.[149] The drug is bacteriostatic against staphylococci and enterococci, but it is bactericidal against most streptococcal strains. Linezolid is also active against L. monocytogenes, M. catarrhalis, H. influenzae, N. gonorrhoeae, Bordetella pertussis, Pasteurella multocida, and Nocardia species. C. difficile, C. perfringens, and Bacteroides species are susceptible, but enteric gram-negative bacilli and Pseudomonas species are not.[150]

Intravenous and oral preparations of linezolid are available; the oral form is absorbed rapidly and completely with 100% bioavailability that is not affected by meals. Linezolid is widely distributed in well-perfused tissues. Nonrenal mechanisms account for 65% of the drug's clearance. Patients with mild to moderate renal or hepatic insufficiency do not appear to require reduced doses; linezolid is removed by hemodialysis.

Linezolid is well tolerated. Adverse effects have been reported in about 2.8% of all patients[150]; nausea, vomiting, and headaches are the most common side effects, but reversible marrow suppression, including thrombocytopenia, leukopenia, and anemia, can also occur. Because linezolid is a reversible inhibitor of monoamine oxidase, patients taking linezolid may experience an exaggerated hypertensive response to sympathomimetic agents. In addition to avoiding decongestants, patients taking linezolid should avoid foods or beverages with a high tyramine content; aged cheeses, air-dried meats, tap beer, red wine, soy sauce, and sauerkraut are examples. Monoamine oxidase inhibitors and other antidepressants should not be administered during linezolid therapy.

Linezolid has been used successfully in the therapy of multidrug-resistant gram-positive bacterial infections.[146,147,151] The drug is approved for vancomycin-resistant enterococcal infections and for pneumonias and skin and soft tissue infections. The usual dosage is 600 mg every 12 hours (p.o. or I.V.); uncomplicated skin and soft tissue infections may be treated with 400 mg every 12 hours.

Linezolid is a very promising new antimicrobial agent, but clinical experience is still limited. Although resistance is uncommon, it can develop during therapy. As a result, it may be wise to reserve this unique antibiotic for serious infections in hospitalized patients; in particular, linezolid should be useful for infections caused by methicillin-resistant S. aureus or coagulase-negative staphylococci that do not respond to vancomycin, for penicillin-resistant pneumococcal infections that do not respond to other agents, and for vancomycin-resistant enterococcal infection. An excellent general review of the use of linezolid in serious gram-positive infections has been published.[152]

Fosfomycin

Fosfomycin is a broad-spectrum antibiotic that inhibits cell wall synthesis in infections caused by E. coli, S. saprophyticus, and many other common urinary tract pathogens.[153] Although it has been used parenterally in Europe for many years, the drug is approved in the United States only for the single-dose treatment of uncomplicated urinary tract infections in women. A 3 g dose is generally effective and well tolerated; diarrhea is the most common side effect. Because of its activity against vancomycin-resistant enterococci (VRE), fosfomycin may be a useful alternative to linezolid and quinupristin-dalfopristin in the treatment of VRE infections in certain clinical situations (e.g., uncomplicated urinary tract infections). In addition, the use of fosfomycin could limit the use of newer agents, thus reducing the chance of development of further resistance in the enterococci.[154]

Concerns for the Future

Despite a century of often-successful prevention and control efforts, infectious diseases remain an important global problem in public health, causing over 13 million deaths each year. Changes in society, technology, and the microorganisms themselves are contributing to the emergence of new diseases, the reemergence of diseases once controlled, and the development of antimicrobial resistance. Two areas of special concern in the 21st century are food-borne disease and antimicrobial resistance. The effective control of infectious diseases in the new millennium will require effective public health infrastructures that will rapidly recognize and respond to outbreaks and will prevent emerging problems.

Over the past 40 years, the search for new antibiotics has been largely restricted to well-known classes of compounds that are active against a standard set of drug targets. Although many effective compounds have been discovered, insufficient chemical variability has been generated to prevent a serious escalation in clinical resistance. Recent advances in genomics have provided an opportunity to expand the range of potential drug targets and have facilitated a fundamental shift from direct antimicrobial screening programs toward rational target-based strategies. The application of genome-based technologies such as expression profiling and proteomics will lead to further changes in the drug discovery paradigm by combining the strengths and advantages of both screening strategies in a single program.

References

1. Jones RN: NCCLS regulatory guidelines. Antimicrobic Newsletter 1:5, 1984

2. Murray PR, Jorgensen JH: Quantitative susceptibility test methods in major United States medical centers. Antimicrob Agents Chemother 20:66, 1981

3. Reller LB: The serum bactericidal test. Rev Infect Dis 8:803, 1986

4. Weinstein MP, Stratton CW, Ackley A, et al: Multicenter collaborative evaluation of a standardized serum bactericidal test as a prognostic indicator in infective endocarditis. Am J Med 78:262, 1985

5. Sensakovic JW, Smith LG: Oral antibiotic treatment of infectious diseases. Med Clin North Am 85:115, 2001

6. Hoffman-Terry ML, Fraimow HS, Fox TR, et al: Adverse effects of outpatient parenteral antibiotic therapy. Am J Med 106:44, 1999

7. Gilbert DN, Dworkin RJ, Raber SR, et al: Outpatient parenteral antimicrobial-drug therapy. N Engl J Med 337:829, 1997

8. Lee CE, Zembower TR, Fotis MA, et al: The incidence of antimicrobial allergies in hospitalized patients: implications regarding prescribing patterns and emerging bacterial resistance. Arch Intern Med 160:2819, 2000

9. Ito S: Drug therapy for breast-feeding women. N Engl J Med 343:118, 2000

10. Solomkin JS, Dellinger EP, Christou NV, et al: Results of a multicenter trial comparing imipenem/cilastatin to tobramycin/clindamycin for intra-abdominal infections. Ann Surg 212:581, 1990

11. Zanetti G, Harbarth JS, Trampuz A, et al: Meropenem (1.5 g/day) is as effective as imipenem/cilastatin (2 g/day) for the treatment of moderately severe intra-abdominal infections. Int J Antimicrob Agents 11:107, 1999

12. Solomkin JS, Yellin AE, Rotstein OD, et al: Ertapenem versus piperacillin/tazobactam in the treatment of complicated intraabdominal infections: results of a double-blind, randomized comparative phase III trial. Ann Surg 237:235, 2003

13. Nichols RL: Empiric antibiotic therapy for intraabdominal infections. Rev Infect Dis 5:S90, 1983

14. Lea AS, Feliciano DV, Gentry LO: Intra-abdominal infections: an update. J Antimicrob Chemother 9(suppl A):107, 1982

15. Barie PS, Christou NV, Dellinger EP, et al: Pathogenicity of the enterococcus in surgical infections. Ann Surg 212:155, 1990

16. Solomkin JS, Dellinger EP, Christou NV, et al: Design and conduct of antibiotic trials: a report of the Scientific Studies Committee of the Surgical Infection Society. Arch Surg 122:158, 1987

17. Christou NV, Turgeon P, Wassef R, et al: Management of intra-abdominal infections: the case for intra-operative cultures and comprehensive broad spectrum antibiotic coverage. Arch Surg 131:1193, 1996

18. Cunha BA: Antibiotic side effects. Med Clin North Am 85:149, 2001

19. Hogenauer C, Hammer HF, Krejs GJ, et al: Mechanisms and management of antibiotic-associated diarrhea. Clin Infect Dis 27:702, 1998

20. Barlett JG: Antibiotic-associated diarrhea. N Engl J Med 346:334, 2002

21. Gatifloxacin and moxifloxacin: two new fluoroquinolones. Med Lett Drugs Ther 42:1, 2000

22. Bertino JS Jr, Owens RC Jr, Carnes TD, et al: Gatifloxacin-associated corrected QT interval prolongation, torsades de pointes, and ventricular fibrillation in patients with known risk factors. Clin Infect Dis 34:861, 2002

23. Vassileva SG, Mateev G, Parish LC: Antimicrobial photosensitive reactions. Arch Intern Med 158:1993, 1998

24. Kollef MH, Fraser VJ: Antibiotic resistance in the intensive care unit. Ann Intern Med 134:298, 2001

25. Virk A, Steckelberg JM: Clinical aspects of antimicrobial resistance. Mayo Clin Proc 75:200, 2000

26. Moellering RC Jr: Antibiotic resistance: lessons for the future. Clin Infect Dis 27(suppl 1):S135, 1998

27. Jenkins SG: Mechanisms of bacterial antibiotic resistance. New Horizons 4:321, 1996

28. Tenover FC: Development and spread of bacterial resistance to antimicrobial agents: an overview. Clin Infect Dis 33(suppl 3):S108, 2001

29. Williams RJ: Globalization of antimicrobial resistance: epidemiological challenges. Clin Infect Dis 33(suppl 3):S116, 2001

30. de Man P, Verhoeven BAN, Verbrugh HA, et al: An antibiotic policy to prevent emergence of resistant bacilli. Lancet 355:973, 2000

31. Cunha BA: Effective antibiotic-resistance control strategies. Lancet 357:1307, 2001

32. Moellering RC Jr: Enterococcal infections in patients treated with moxalactam. Rev Infect Dis 4(suppl):S708, 1982

33. Shay DK, Maloney SA, Montecalvo M, et al: Epidemiology and mortality risk of vancomycin-resistant enterococcal bloodstream infections. J Infect Dis 172:993, 1995

34. McGowen JE: Antimicrobial resistance in hospital organisms and its relation to antibiotic use. Rev Infect Dis 5:1033, 1983

35. Baquero F, Martinez-Beltran J, Loza E: 1991: A review of antibiotic resistance patterns of *Streptococcus pneumoniae* in Europe. J Antimicrob Chemother 28(suppl C):31, 1991

36. Wormer DC, Martin WJ, Nichold DR, et al: Concentrations in serum of procaine and crystalline penicillin G administered orally or parenterally. Antibiotics in Medicine 1:589, 1955

37. Gilbert DN, Sanford JP: Methicillin: critical appraisal after a decade of experience. Med Clin North Am 54:1113, 1970

38. Amoxicillin. Med Lett Drugs Ther 16:49, 1974

39. Bodey GP, Whitecar JP Jr, Middleman E, et al: Carbenicillin therapy for *Pseudomonas* infections. JAMA 218:62, 1971

40. Hoffman TA, Bullock WE: Carbenicillin therapy of *Pseudomonas* and other gram-negative bacillary infections. Ann Intern Med 73:165, 1970

41. Butler K, English AR, Ray VA, et al: Carbenicillin: chemistry and mode of action. J Infect Dis 122(suppl):S1, 1970

42. Ticarcillin. Med Lett Drugs Ther 19:17, 1977

43. Tjandramaga TB, Mullie A, Verbesselt R, et al: Piperacillin: human pharmacokinetics after intravenous and intramuscular administration. Antimicrob Agents Chemother 14:829, 1978

44. Bergan T: Pharmacokinetics of mezlocillin in healthy volunteers. Antimicrob Agents Chemother 14:801, 1978

45. Bergan T, Brodwall EK, Wiik-Larsen E: Mezlocillin pharmacokinetics in patients with normal and impaired renal functions. Antimicrob Agents Chemother 16:651, 1979

46. Gentry LO, Jemsek JG, Natelson EA: Effects of sodium piperacillin on platelet function in normal volunteers. Antimicrob Agents Chemother 19:532, 1981

47. Fu KP, Neu HC: Azlocillin and mezlocillin: new ureido penicillins. Antimicrob Agents Chemother 13:930, 1978

48. Bodey GP, Le Blanc B: Piperacillin: in vitro evaluation. Antimicrob Agents Chemother 14:78, 1978

49. Tally FP, McGowan K, Kellum JM, et al: A randomized comparison of cefoxitin with or without amikacin and clindamycin plus amikacin in surgical sepsis. Ann Surg 193:318, 1981

50. Donowitz GR, Mandell GL: Empiric therapy for pneumonia. Rev Infect Dis 5(suppl):S40, 1983

51. Cefotetan disodium (Cefotan). Med Lett Drugs Ther 28:70, 1986

52. Orr JW Jr, Varner RE, Kilgore LC, et al: Cefotetan versus cefoxitin as prophylaxis in hysterectomy. Am J Obstet Gynecol 154:960, 1986

53. McCarty JM, Renteria A: Treatment of pharyngitis and tonsillitis with cefprozil: review of three multicenter trials. Clin Infect Dis 14(suppl 2):S224, 1992

54. Doern G: In vitro activity of loracarbef and effects of susceptibility test methods. Am J Med 92:7S, 1992

55. Wise R, Andrews JM, Ashby JP, et al: Ceftibuten: a new orally absorbed cephalosporin: in vitro activity against strains from the United Kingdom. Diagn Microbiol Infect Dis 14:45, 1991

56. Boscia JA, Korzeniowski OM, Snepar R, et al: Cefoperazone pharmacokinetics in normal subjects and patients with cirrhosis. Antimicrob Agents Chemother 23:385, 1983

57. Kemmerich B, Lode H, Borner K, et al: Biliary excretion and pharmacokinetics of cefoperazone in humans. J Antimicrob Chemother 12:27, 1983

58. Wittmann DH, Schassan HH: Distribution of moxalactam in serum, bone, tissue fluid, and peritoneal fluid. Rev Infect Dis 4(suppl):S610, 1982

59. Saito Y, Kushima T, Seimori T, et al: Absorption and excretion of cefotaxime and its levels in uterine arterial blood, female internal genital organ tissue and pelvic cavity fluid. Jpn J Antibiot 34:481, 1981

60. Grabe M, Andersson KE, Forsgren A, et al: Concentrations of cefotaxime in serum, urine, and tissues of urological patients. Infection 9:154, 1981

61. Kosmidis J, Stathakis C, Mantopoulos K, et al: Clinical pharmacology of cefotaxime including penetration into bile, sputum, bone and cerebrospinal fluid. J Antimicrob Chemother 6(suppl A):147, 1980

62. Watts JM, McDonald PJ, Woods PJ: Clinical trials of antimicrobials in surgery. World J Surg 6:321, 1982

63. Solomkin JS, Meakins JL Jr, Allo MD, et al: Antibiotic trials in intra-abdominal infections: a critical evaluation of study design and outcome reporting. Ann Surg 200:29, 1984

64. Feinstein AR: Clinical Biostatistics. CV Mosby Co, St Louis, 1977

65. Edelstein H, Chirurgi V, Oster S, et al: A randomized trial of cefepime (BMY-28142) and ceftazidime for the treatment of pneumonia. J Antimicrob Chemother 28:569, 1991

66. Gloor B, Worni M, Strobel O, et al: Cefepime tissue penetration in experimental acute pancreatitis. Pancreas 26:117, 2003

67. Barie PS, Vogel SB, Dellinger EP, et al: A randomized, double-blind clinical trial comparing cefepime plus metronidazole with imipenem-cilastatin in the treatment of complicated intra-abdominal infections. Cefepime Intra-abdominal Infection Study Group. Arch Surg 132:1294, 1997

68. Smith CR: Cefotaxime and cephalosporins: adverse reactions in perspective. Rev Infect Dis 4(suppl):S481, 1982

69. Parks D, Layne P, Uri J, et al: Ceftizoxime: clinical evaluation of efficacy and safety in the U.S.A. J Antimicrob Chemother 10(suppl C): 327, 1982

70. Petz LD: Immunologic cross-reactivity between penicillins and cephalosporins: a review. J Infect Dis 137:S74, 1978

71. Kelkar PS, Li JT-C: Cephalosporin allergry. N Engl J Med 345:804, 2001

72. Gordon RC, Regamey C, Kirby WMM: Serum protein binding of the aminoglycoside antibiotics. Antimicrob Agents Chemother 2:214, 1972

73. Siber GR, Echeverria P, Smith AL, et al: Pharmacokinetics of gentamicin in children and adults. J Infect Dis 132:637, 1975

74. Walker JM, Wise R: The pharmacokinetics of amikacin and gentamicin in volunteers: a comparison of individual differences. J Antimicrob Chemother 5:95, 1979

75. Lockwood WR, Bower JD: Tobramycin and gentamicin concentrations in the serum of normal and anephric patients. Antimicrob Agents Chemother 3:125, 1973

76. McHenry MC, Wagner JG, Hall PM, et al: Pharmacokinetics of amikacin in patients with impaired renal function. J Infect Dis 134(suppl):S343, 1976

77. Regeur L, Colding H, Jensen H, et al: Pharmacokinetics of amikacin during hemodialysis and peritoneal dialysis. Antimicrob Agents Chemother 11:214, 1977

78. Goitein K, Michel J, Sacks T: Penetration of parenterally administered gentamicin into the cerebrospinal fluid in experimental meningitis. Chemotherapy 21:181, 1975

79. Briedis DJ, Robson HG: Cerebrospinal fluid penetration of amikacin. Antimicrob Agents Chemother 13:1042, 1978

80. Vaudaux P, Waldvogel FA: Gentamicin inactivation in purulent exudates: role of cell lysis. J Infect Dis 142:586, 1980

81. Smith CR, Lipsky JJ, Laskin OL, et al: Double-blind comparison of the nephrotoxicity and auditory toxicity of gentamicin and tobramycin. N Engl J Med 302:1106, 1980

82. Kahlmeter G, Dahlager JI: Aminoglycoside toxicity: a review of clinical studies published between 1975 and 1982. J Antimicrob Chemother 13(suppl A):9, 1984

83. Kumin GD: Clinical nephrotoxicity of tobramycin and gentamicin: a prospective study. JAMA 244:1808, 1980

84. Betts RF, Valenti WM, Chapman SW, et al: Five-year surveillance of aminoglycoside usage in a university hospital. Ann Intern Med 100:219, 1984

85. Luft FC, Yum MN, Kleit SA: Comparative nephrotoxicities of netilmicin and gentamicin in rats. Antimicrob Agents Chemother 10:845, 1976

86. Robbins G, Tettenborn D: Toxicity of sisomicin in animals. Infection 4(suppl 4):S349, 1976

87. Fee WE Jr: Gentamicin and tobramycin: comparison of ototoxicity. Rev Infect Dis 5(suppl 2):S304, 1983

88. Moore RD, Smith CR, Lietman PS: The association of aminoglycoside plasma levels with mortality in patients with gram-negative bacteremia. J Infect Dis 149:443, 1984

89. Noone P, Parsons TMC, Pattison JR, et al: Experience in monitoring gentamicin therapy during treatment of serious gram-negative sepsis. Br Med J 1:477, 1974

90. Alexander MR, Schoell J, Hicklin G, et al: Bronchial secretion concentrations of tobramycin. Am Rev Respir Dis 125:208, 1982

91. Moore RD, Smith CR, Lietman PS: Association of aminoglycoside plasma levels with therapeutic outcome in gram-negative pneumonia. Am J Med 77:657, 1984

92. Zaske DE, Cipolle RJ, Strate RJ: Gentamicin dosage requirements: wide interpatient variations in 242 surgery patients with normal renal function. Surgery 87:164, 1980

93. Kaye D, Levison ME, Labovitz ED: The unpredictability of serum concentrations of gentamicin: pharmacokinetics of gentamicin in patients with normal and abnormal renal function. J Infect Dis 130:150, 1974

94. Zaske DE, Cipolle RJ, Strate RG: Increased gentamicin dosage requirements: rapid elimination in 249 gynecology patients. Am J Obstet Gynecol 139:896, 1981

95. Dasta JF, Armstrong DK: Variability in aminoglycoside pharmacokinetics in critically ill surgical patients (abstr). Crit Care Med 14:393, 1986

96. Hassan E, Ober J: Predicted and measured aminoglycoside pharmacokinetic parameters in critically ill patients (abstr). Crit Care Med 14:394, 1986

97. Hatala R, Dinh T, Cook DJ: Once-daily aminoglycoside dosing in immunocompetent adults: a meta-analysis. Ann Intern Med 124:717, 1996

98. Barza M, Loannidis JPA, Cappelleri JC, et al: Single or multiple daily doses of aminoglycosides: a meta-analysis. BMJ 321:338, 1996

99. Koo J, Tight R, Rajkumar V, et al: Comparison of once-daily versus pharmacokinetic dosing of aminoglycosides in elderly patients. Am J Med 101:177, 1996

100. Schumock GT, Raber SR, Crawford SY, et al: National survey of once-daily dosing of aminoglycoside antibiotics. Pharmacotherapy 15:201, 1995

101. Preston SL, Briceland LL: Single daily dosing of aminoglycosides. Pharmacotherapy 15:297, 1995

102. Griffith RS, Black HR: Comparison of the blood levels obtained after single and multiple doses of erythromycin estolate and erythromycin stearate. Am J Med Sci 247:69, 1964

103. Washington JA II, Wilson WR: Erythromycin: a microbial and clinical perspective after 30 years of clinical use (pt 2). Mayo Clin Proc 60:271, 1985

104. Steigbigel NH: Erythromycin, lincomycin, and clindamycin. Principles and Practice of Infectious Diseases, 2nd ed. Mandell GL, Douglas RG Jr, Bennett JE, Eds. John Wiley & Sons, New York, 1985, p 224

105. Panzer JD, Brown DC, Epstein WL, et al: Clindamycin levels in various body tissues and fluids. J Clin Pharmacol 12:259, 1972

106. Sande MA, Mandell GL: Antimicrobial agents: tetracyclines, chloramphenicol, erythromycin, and miscellaneous antibacterial agents. Goodman and Gilman's The Pharmacological Basis of Therapeutics, 7th ed. Gilman AG, Goodman LS, Rall TW, et al, Eds. Macmillan Publishing Co, New York, 1985, p 1170

107. Moellering RC Jr: Pharmacokinetics of vancomycin. J Antimicrob Chemother 14(suppl D):43, 1984

108. Myers JP, Linnemann CC Jr: Bacteremia due to methicillin-resistant Staphylococcus aureus. J Infect Dis 145:532, 1982

109. Watanakunakorn C: Treatment of infections due to methicillin-resistant Staphylococcus aureus. Ann Intern Med 97:376, 1982

110. Harwick HJ, Kalmanson GM, Guze LB: In vitro activity of ampicillin or vancomycin combined with gentamicin or streptomycin against enterococci. Antimicrob Agents Chemother 4:383, 1973

111. Van Scoy RE, Cohen SN, Geraci JE, et al: Coryneform bacterial endocarditis: difficulties in diagnosis and treatment, presentation of three cases, and review of literature. Mayo Clin Proc 52:216, 1977

112. Riley PS, Hollis DG, Utter GB, et al: Characterization and identification of 95 diphtheroid (group JK) cultures isolated from clinical specimens. J Clin Microbiol 9:418, 1979

113. Liñares J, Perez JL, Garau J, et al: Comparative susceptibilities of penicillin-resistant pneumococci to co-trimoxazole, vancomycin, rifampicin and fourteen β-lactam antibiotics. J Antimicrob Chemother 13:353, 1984

114. Fekety R, Silva J, Armstrong J, et al: Treatment of antibiotic-associated enterocolitis with vancomycin. Rev Infect Dis 3(suppl):S237, 1981

115. Dudley MN, McLaughlin JC, Carrington G, et al: Oral bacitracin vs vancomycin therapy for Clostridium difficile–induced diarrhea: a randomized double-blind trial. Arch Intern Med 146:1101, 1986

116. Teasley DG, Gerding DN, Olson M, et al: Pro-

spective randomised trial of metronidazole versus vancomycin for *Clostridium difficile*–associated diarrhoea and colitis. Lancet 2:1043, 1983

117. Koch-Wesser J, Goldman P: Drug therapy: metronidazole. N Engl J Med 303:1212, 1980

118. Corey WA, Doebbeling BN, Dejong KJ, et al: Metronidazole-induced acute pancreatitis (note). Rev Infect Dis 13:1213, 1990

119. Hellinger WC, Brewer NS: Carbapenems and monobactams: imipenem, meropenem, and aztreonam. Mayo Clin Proc 74:420, 1999

120. Odenholt I: Ertapenem: a new carbapenem. Expert Opin Investig Drugs 10:1157, 2001

121. Livermore DM, Carter MW, Bagel S, et al: In vitro activities of ertapenem (MK-0826) against recent clinical bacteria collected in Europe and Australia. Antimicrob Agents Chemother 45:1860, 2001

122. McConnell SA, Penzak SR, Warmack TS, et al: Incidence of imipenem hypersensitivity reactions in febrile neutropenic bone marrow transplant patients with a history of penicillin allergy. Clin Infect Dis 31:1512, 2000

123. Barry AL, Thornsberry C, Jones RN, et al: Aztreonam: antibacterial activity, β-lactamase stability, and interpretive standards and quality control guidelines for disk-diffusion susceptibility tests. Rev Infect Dis 7(suppl 4):S594, 1985

124. Swabb EA: Clinical pharmacology of aztreonam in healthy recipients and patients: a review. Rev Infect Dis 7(suppl 4):S605, 1985

125. Adkinson NF Jr, Saxon A, Spence MR, et al: Cross-allergenicity and immunogenicity of aztreonam. Rev Infect Dis 7(suppl 4):S613, 1985

126. Scully BE, Henry SA: Clinical experience with aztreonam in the treatment of gram-negative bacteremia. Rev Infect Dis 7(suppl 4):S789, 1985

127. Pierard D, Boelaert J, Van Landuyt HW, et al: Aztreonam treatment of gram-negative septicemia. Antimicrob Agents Chemother 29:359, 1986

128. Rodriguez JR, Ramirez-Ronda CH, Nevárez M: Efficacy and safety of aztreonam-clindamycin versus tobramycin-clindamycin in the treatment of lower respiratory tract infections caused by aerobic gram-negative bacilli. Antimicrob Agents Chemother 27:246, 1985

129. Scully BE, Neu HC: Use of aztreonam in the treatment of serious infections due to multiresistant gram-negative organisms, including *Pseudomonas aeruginosa*. Am J Med 78:251, 1985

130. Meylan PR, Calandra T, Casey PA, et al: Clinical experience with Timentin in severe hospital infections. J Antimicrob Chemother 17(suppl C):127, 1986

131. Meunier F, Snoeck R, Lagast H, et al: Empirical antimicrobial therapy with Timentin plus amikacin in febrile granulocytopenic cancer patients. J Antimicrob Chemother 17(suppl C):195, 1986

132. Kuck NA, Jacobus NV, Petersen PJ, et al: Comparative in vitro and in vivo activities of piperacillin combined with the beta-lactamase inhibitors tazobactam, clavulanic acid, and sulbactam. Antimicrob Agents Chemother 33:1964, 1989

133. Fass RJ, Prior RB: Comparative in vitro activities of piperacillin-tazobactam and ticarcillin-clavulanate. Antimicrob Agents Chemother 33:1268, 1989

134. Knox J: Extended spectrum and inhibitor-resistant TEM-type β-lactamases: mutations, specificity, and three-dimensional structure. Antimicrob Agents Chemother 39:2593, 1995

135. Sanders E, Sanders C: Piperacillin/tazobactam: a critical review of the evolving clinical literature. Clin Infect Dis 22:107, 1996

136. Hooper DC: Mechanisms of action of antimicrobials: focus on fluoroquinolones. Clin Infect Dis 32(supp 1):S9, 2001

137. Swartz MN: Recognition and management of anthrax: an update. N Engl J Med 345:1621, 2001

138. Lipman J, Allworth A, Wallis SC: Cerebrospinal fluid penetration of high doses of intravenous ciprofloxacin in meningitis. Clin Infect Dis 31:1131, 2000

139. Gatifloxacin and moxifloxacin: two new fluoroquinolones. Med Lett Drugs Ther 42:15, 2000

140. Mandell LA, Ball P, Tillotson G: Antimicrobial safety and tolerability: differences and dilemmas. Clin Infect Dis 32(suppl 1):S72, 2001

141. Chen DK, McGeer A, de Azavedo JC, et al: Decreased susceptibility of *Streptococcus pneumoniae* to fluoroquinolones in Canada. N Engl J Med 341:233, 1999

142. Thomson CJ: The global epidemiology of resistance to ciprofloxacin and the changing nature of antibiotic resistance: a 10 year perspective. J Antimicrob Chemother 43:31, 1999

143. Halkin H: Adverse effects of the fluoroquinolones. Rev Infect Dis 10(suppl 1):S258, 1988

144. Quinupristin/dalfopristin. Med Lett Drugs Ther 41:109, 1999

145. Johnson AP, Livermore DM: Quinupristin/dalfopristin, a new addition to the antimicrobial arsenal. Lancet 354:2012, 1999

146. Linezolid (Zyvox). Med Lett Drugs Ther 42:1, 2000

147. Diekema DJ, Jones RN: Oxazolidinone antibiotics. Lancet 358:77, 2001

148. Cercenado E, García-Garrote F, Bouza E: In vitro activity of linezolid against multiply resistant gram-positive clinical isolates. J Antimicrob Chemother 47:77, 2001

149. Tsiodras S, Gold HS, Sakoulas G, et al: Linezolid resistance in a clinical isolate of *Staphylococcus aureus*. Lancet 358:207, 2001

150. Clemett D, Markham A: Linezolid. Drugs 59:815, 2000

151. Chien JW, Kucia ML, Salata RA: Use of linezolid, an oxazolidinone, in the treatment of multidrug-resistant gram-positive bacterial infections. Clin Infect Dis 30:146, 2000

152. Perry CD, Jarvis B: Linezolid: A review of its use in the management of serious gram-positive infections. Drugs 61:525, 2001

153. Fosfomycin for urinary tract infections. Med Lett Drugs Ther 39:66, 1997

154. Shrestha NK, Chua JD, Tuohy MH, et al: Antimicrobial susceptibility of vancomycin-resistant *Enterococcus faecium*: potential utility of fosfomycin. Scand J Infect Dis 35:12, 2003

155. Simon HB: XIV Antimicrobial chemotherapy. 7 Infectious Disease. WebMD Scientific American® Medicine. Dale DC, Federman DD, Eds. WebMD Inc. New York, 2003. http://www.samed.com. June 2003

E. Patchen Dellinger, M.D., F.A.C.S.

Approach to Postoperative Symptoms of Infection

Nosocomial infections are a potential threat to all hospitalized patients. They increase morbidity and mortality, prolong hospital stay, increase patient care costs,[1-5] and occur in almost every body site.

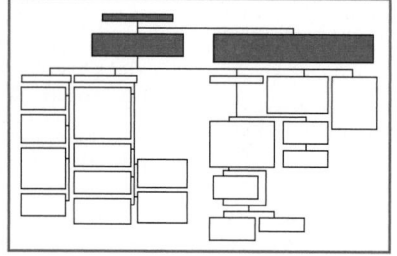

At any time during hospitalization, but especially postoperatively, the onset of fever or an elevated white blood cell count may signal an infectious process. Fever that begins or persists after postoperative day 4 is more likely to represent true infection. Although an infection will not develop in many febrile postoperative patients [*see* Discussion, *below*], a careful, directed examination of the patient, guided by history and operative procedure, should be undertaken, including inspection of the ears and the pharynx. Laboratory tests and x-rays are complementary. The use of empirical antibiotics or the prolonged administration of perioperative prophylactic antibiotics in the absence of a specific diagnosis is rarely efficacious. In fact, either may confuse the clinical picture and may lead to separate toxic or allergic complications. Antibiotics alone rarely constitute an adequate response to infectious complications, especially in the early postoperative period.

Respiratory infections are the most common early infection, with most wound infections presenting between postoperative days 4 and 7 and urinary tract infections (UTIs) occurring throughout hospitalization. However, if a high fever (temperature > 38.9° C [102° F]) develops in a patient within 48 hours of an operation, three diagnoses are most likely: atelectasis [*see 120 Pulmonary Insufficiency*], peritonitis caused by a leaking viscus after intra-abdominal operation [*see 133 Intra-abdominal Infection*], and invasive wound infection. Of these, atelectasis is most often diagnosed. It is not serious if recognized and treated. Atelectasis can be diagnosed on the basis of decreased breath sounds, rales, or both on physical examination and on the basis of platelike densities or volume loss on chest x-ray. Atelectasis may be accompanied by hypoxemia and usually responds to standard physical measures. However, many patients with x-ray evidence of atelectasis are not febrile, and more than one third of patients with fever and no other apparent cause have no evidence of atelectasis.[6,7]

Clues to the diagnosis of peritonitis caused by a leaking viscus are knowledge of problems in the conduct of the operation, evidence of the hemodynamic and fluid balance changes that usually accompany a leaking viscus, and suggestive findings on abdominal examination. Technical difficulties with anastomoses, excessive operative blood loss, and multiple bowel injuries can all increase the risk of leakage. Diffuse abdominal tenderness away from the incision, excessive fluid requirements in the early postoperative interval, and tachycardia all suggest iatrogenic peritonitis. Treatment always involves operation and antibiotics. The least common cause of early high postoperative fever is an invasive wound infection, either with β-hemolytic streptococci or with clostridia. Diagnosis is made by local inspection of the wound and by a Gram stain of the wound's contents; treatment requires operative intervention in addition to antibiotics [*see* Infection Related to Operative Site or Injury, *below*].

Respiratory Infection

Pneumonia is the third most common nosocomial infection on surgical services and is the one most commonly associated with death [*see 132 Postoperative and Ventilator-Associated Pneumonia*].[8]

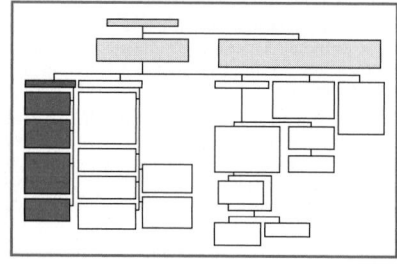

Diagnosis is not usually difficult in a patient without respiratory failure who is breathing spontaneously. In a patient with acute respiratory distress syndrome (ARDS) who is intubated and being ventilated, however, the diagnosis may be extremely difficult.[9] This is because ARDS is associated with markedly abnormal chest x-ray findings and gas exchange abnormalities and may also include an elevated temperature without infection. A number of techniques for diagnosis, including bronchoalveolar lavage both with and without a bronchoscope and protected specimen brush cultures, have been reported to increase the sensitivity and specificity of diagnosis of pneumonia in this setting but have not been widely adopted.[10,11]

The prevention of pneumonia in ventilated patients would be the best alternative, but there is not widespread agreement about the best means of prevention. Recommendations include standard infection control measures, elevation of the head of the bed, and possibly the use of endotracheal tubes that permit the aspiration of subglottic secretions.[10,12-14]

The diagnosis of pneumonitis or atelectasis (see above) is frequently entertained during the workup of postoperative fever. It is important to remember that a common cause of basilar atelectasis and pleural effusion in the postlaparotomy patient is an inflammatory process below the diaphragm. Tracheitis or bronchitis, as indicated by purulent sputum in the absence of pulmonary infiltrate, is often seen in modern ICUs, most commonly in association with an endotracheal or tracheostomy tube. Pneumonia may or may not follow. There is often a febrile response, in which case antibiotics may be appropriate on the basis of culture and sensitivity information. Sorting out the cause of purulent secretions in intubated patients is not easy but is important. Other causes of fever should be sought and an overall judgment rendered regarding the probable cause. If tracheitis or bronchitis is suspected, it can be treated with a brief course of antibiotics. A 2000 report described empirical treatment of patients for suspected pneumonia, followed by reevaluation at 3 days.[15] By stopping antibiotic treatment at 3 days for patients without a confirmed diagnosis, the investigators were able to reduce antibiotic use threefold in that group, lower costs by more than half, and decrease the frequency with which resistant bacteria were isolated by more than half.

Paranasal sinusitis is a potentially lethal nosocomial infection, especially in ICU patients with nasogastric or nasotracheal tubes in place.[16-18] In one report, it accounted for 5% of all nosocomial infections.[16] The diagnosis of paranasal sinusitis should be considered in any febrile postoperative patient with nasal tubes or with facial fractures. Purulent nasal drainage is an important clue but may not be present. Plain films can be diagnostic but are often difficult to interpret in these patients because of superimposition of tubes, preexisting injuries, and suboptimal portable films. Fluid, air-fluid levels, and mucosal thickening are more easily detected by computed tomography. Diagnosis ultimately requires demonstration of white blood cells and bacteria on a Gram stain of sinus aspirate as well as culture for identification and sensitivity testing.

In one study of 67 patients with craniofacial injuries who underwent prospective otoscopy three times a week, 11 patients experienced either serous or purulent otitis media and were all found to have purulent paranasal sinusitis.[19] Eleven of 12 patients who were ultimately diagnosed as having purulent paranasal sinusitis had coexistent otitis media.

The spectrum of causative bacteria of paranasal sinusitis is similar to that of nosocomial pneumonia. Treatment includes removal of all nasal tubes and administration of decongestants and antibiotics. Occasionally, sinus irrigation, drainage, or both may be required. If empirical therapy must be initiated before specific culture results are known, the agents chosen should be effective against bacteria known to be present in sputum. The best method of prevention is to limit the number and the duration of use of nasal tubes.

Inflammation and infection of the nasopharyngeal mucosa can be significant in an ICU patient, though it is not often identified. Eustachian tube blockage, either from tubes or from inflammation, can be associated with either serous or infective otitis media. Prudent use of tubes is the most effective preventive measure. If clinical infection is recognized, tube removal and decongestants will usually provide adequate treatment.

Infection Related to Operative Site or Injury

SURGICAL SITE INFECTION

An infection of a surgical wound—that is, an incisional surgical site

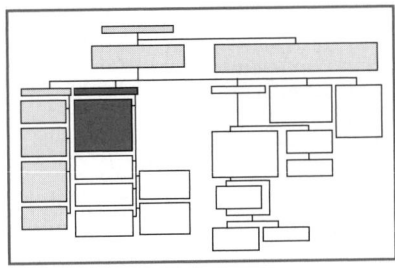

infection (SSI)—traditionally reflects on a surgeon's care and skill and is the classic surgical nosocomial infection [see 5 Prevention of Postoperative Infection] Such infections are diagnosed primarily on the basis of local findings. Erythema, swelling, and drainage, as well as increasing local pain and tenderness in a site at which pain should be decreasing, all suggest infection. Fever and an elevated white blood cell count may or may not be present. An incisional SSI develops most commonly in the subcutaneous layer, though animal studies fail to explain this observation.[20] In an obese patient, however, a thick, overlying layer of uninfected tissue may obscure evidence of infection and thus delay diagnosis. Presentation may also be delayed if the infection begins in anatomic layers below fascial and muscular barriers, as may be the case after a thoracotomy or an operation on the femur.

Whether an infection will occur in a wound is probably determined within the first few hours of wounding[21,22]; efforts to prevent wound infection are probably ineffective after this period.[23-27] The incidence of SSI is reduced with appropriate use of perioperative antibiotics.[28,29] However, there is no advantage to continuing prophylactic antibiotics beyond the perioperative period in response to fever or local wound erythema in the hope of preventing an overt SSI.[30-32]

The risk that an SSI will develop in an individual patient is best described by an index defined by the Centers for Disease Control and Prevention (CDC) in its National Nosocomial Infections Surveillance (NNIS) System. The index awards one point each for an American Society of Anesthesiologists (ASA) preoperative assessment score of III, IV, or V; an operation classified as either contaminated or dirty-infected; and an operation duration exceeding the 75th percentile for that procedure.[33,34] Examination of the NNIS data demonstrates that in patients undergoing procedures commonly performed laparoscopically, SSI rates are decreased to levels comparable to those reported in patients with a one point lower risk index who undergo equivalent open procedures.[35] The CDC definitions for SSI were agreed to by a consensus panel representing the CDC, the Society for Hospital Epidemiology of America, the Association for Practitioners in Infection Control, and the Surgical Infection Society.[34,36] In addition to appropriate use of prophylactic antibiotics, proper management of intraoperative temperature, oxygen concentrations, and blood glucose levels exerts a powerful influence on the risk of SSI and of other nosocomial infections.[37-41]

Primary treatment of an SSI consists of opening the wound. When an SSI is suspected, the patient should not be given antibiotics without the wound having been opened. In most cases, the infection is confined to the incision. If the infection is of a superficial wound and if no major systemic manifestations are present, antibiotic therapy is unnecessary. If the local reaction around an infected wound is severe or extensive, administration of antibiotics is advisable until the reaction subsides (which usually takes no more than 3 days). In clean wounds that are away from the perineum and that are not associated with an operation that entered the bowel, the likely pathogens are Staphylococcus aureus, streptococci, or both. In such cases, treatment with cefazolin, 1 g I.V. every 8 hours, or oxacillin, 1 g I.V. every 6 hours, is satisfactory. By contrast, SSIs in the perineum and those that occur after bowel operations often involve mixed aerobic and anaerobic bacterial flora. If the infection is not very serious, it can be treated with cefoxitin, 1 g I.V. every 6 hours, or with cefotetan, 1 g I.V. every 12 hours. For more aggressive infections accompanied by evidence of tissue invasion or necrosis beyond the immediate

Approach to Postoperative Symptoms of Infection

Fever or an elevated WBC develops postoperatively

Fever begins or persists after 4th postoperative day

Identify source of infection:
- Perform physical examination guided by history and prior operations.
- Inspect all intravascular devices and urinary catheters.
- Order appropriate x-rays and laboratory tests.

Respiratory infection

Pneumonia, as suggested by ↑ WBC, ↑ temperature, purulent sputum, and lung infiltrate

Give appropriate antibiotics; provide supportive care.

Tracheitis or bronchitis, as suggested by purulent sputum, normal x-ray findings, and endotracheal or tracheostomy intubation

Give appropriate antibiotics if patient is febrile.

Paranasal sinusitis, as suggested by purulent nasal drainage, otitis media, and/or CT findings of fluid, air-fluid levels, and mucosal thickening

Identify pathogen via Gram stain and culture of sinus aspirate. Remove all nasal tubes; administer decongestants and appropriate antibiotics. Perform sinus irrigation or drainage for unresponsive cases.

Otitis media (associated with eustachian tube blockage from nasal tubes or inflammation)

Remove nasal tube, and give decongestants.

Infection related to operative site or injury

Wound infection (incisional SSI), as suggested by erythema, swelling, drainage, and increasing local pain and tenderness

Incise and drain. For minimal local soft tissue and systemic response, treat with dressing changes and no antibiotics. If antibiotics are required, give as follows. **Clean wounds:** Give cefazolin, 1 g I.V. q. 8 hr, or oxacillin, 1 g I.V. q. 6 hr. **Other wounds:** If infection is aggressive, give a third-generation cephalosporin or a quinolone plus clindamycin or metronidazole; or aztreonam plus clindamycin; or imipenem-cilastatin, meropenem, or piperacillin-tazobactam alone. If infection is less serious, give cefotetan, 1 g I.V. q. 12 hr, or cefoxitin, 1 g I.V. q. 6 hr. Invasive and necrotizing infection requires aggressive debridement. Stop antibiotics as soon as local inflammation and systemic signs of infection have resolved.

Intra-abdominal infection (organ/space SSI), as suggested by fever and abdominal tenderness

Confirm diagnosis by CT or ultrasonography. Perform appropriate operative or percutaneous procedure; give antibiotics.

Sternal and mediastinal infection, as suggested by sternal instability

Debride the sternum and affected mediastinal tissues. Consider transposition of viable soft tissue for wound closure.

Osteomyelitis (suggested by nonunion of a fracture, loosening of a prosthesis, or prolonged wound drainage)

Repeated operative debridement, prolonged use of antibiotics, and fracture stabilization may be required.

Empyema, as suggested by systemic signs and pleural effusion

Examine and culture pleural fluid. Drain pleural space. Give appropriate antibiotics. If empyema fails to resolve, consider thoracoscopy, thoracotomy, and decortication.

Posttraumatic meningitis (anticipate if there is a history of CSF rhinorrhea or otorrhea)

Perform lumbar puncture for examination and culture of CSF if unexplained fever, headache, spinal pain or stiffness, or changes in mental status develop. Give appropriate antibiotics.

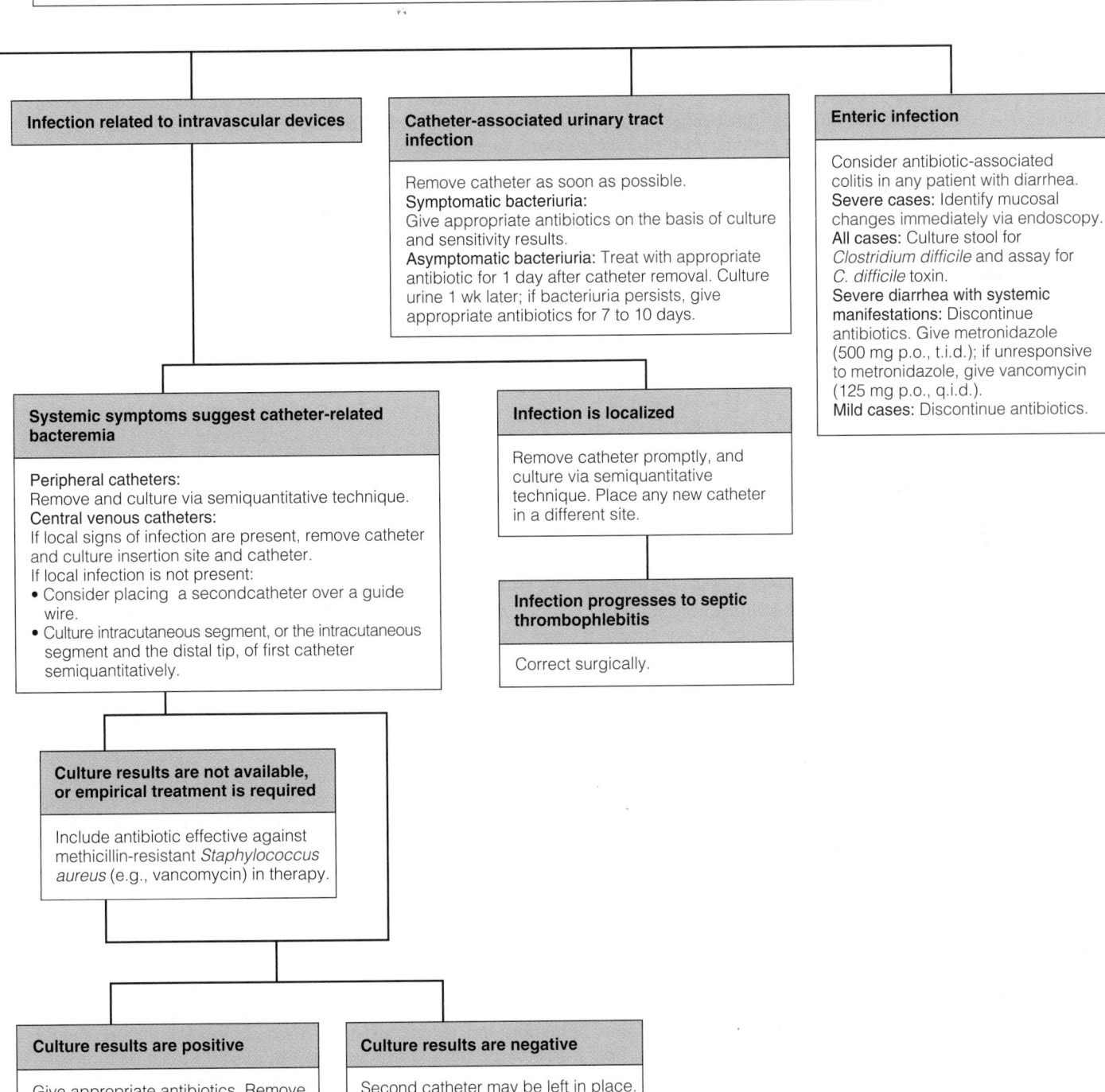

High fever (> 38.9° C [102° F]) develops within 48 hr of operation

Consider:
- Atelectasis (suggested by decreased breath sounds or rales, or both, and by platelike densities or volume loss on x-ray): Manage via standard physical measures.
- Peritonitis from a leaking viscus (suggested by hemodynamic changes, diffuse abdominal tenderness, excessive early fluid requirements, and tachycardia): Treat with operative intervention and antibiotics.
- Invasive wound infection: Inspect wound and obtain Gram stain of wound contents; treat with operative intervention and antibiotics.

Infection related to intravascular devices

Catheter-associated urinary tract infection

Remove catheter as soon as possible.
Symptomatic bacteriuria:
Give appropriate antibiotics on the basis of culture and sensitivity results.
Asymptomatic bacteriuria: Treat with appropriate antibiotic for 1 day after catheter removal. Culture urine 1 wk later; if bacteriuria persists, give appropriate antibiotics for 7 to 10 days.

Enteric infection

Consider antibiotic-associated colitis in any patient with diarrhea.
Severe cases: Identify mucosal changes immediately via endoscopy.
All cases: Culture stool for *Clostridium difficile* and assay for *C. difficile* toxin.
Severe diarrhea with systemic manifestations: Discontinue antibiotics. Give metronidazole (500 mg p.o., t.i.d.); if unresponsive to metronidazole, give vancomycin (125 mg p.o., q.i.d.).
Mild cases: Discontinue antibiotics.

Systemic symptoms suggest catheter-related bacteremia

Peripheral catheters:
Remove and culture via semiquantitative technique.
Central venous catheters:
If local signs of infection are present, remove catheter and culture insertion site and catheter.
If local infection is not present:
- Consider placing a secondcatheter over a guide wire.
- Culture intracutaneous segment, or the intracutaneous segment and the distal tip, of first catheter semiquantitatively.

Infection is localized

Remove catheter promptly, and culture via semiquantitative technique. Place any new catheter in a different site.

Infection progresses to septic thrombophlebitis

Correct surgically.

Culture results are not available, or empirical treatment is required

Include antibiotic effective against methicillin-resistant *Staphylococcus aureus* (e.g., vancomycin) in therapy.

Culture results are positive

Give appropriate antibiotics. Remove any second catheter placed by guide wire; place any new catheter in a different site.

Culture results are negative

Second catheter may be left in place.

wound or by a severe systemic reaction, more comprehensive antibiotic treatment is indicated—that is, a third-generation cephalosporin or a quinolone combined with clindamycin or metronidazole; aztreonam combined with clindamycin; or imipenem-cilastatin, meropenem, or piperacillin-tazobactam alone. Infection of an abdominal incision may be a superficial manifestation of an underlying intra-abdominal abscess or of peritonitis.

Occasionally, infection is invasive and necrotizing. In surgical wounds, such an infection is most common after a GI procedure in which the wound was exposed to colonic microflora and in which wound closure was difficult. Necrotizing infection is also more likely in a patient who is seriously ill or who has evidence of multiple organ failure. Such infection should be suspected if there is undermining of the wound edges, extensive fascial necrosis, distant signs of infection, or a marked systemic response. It requires aggressive operative debridement and administration of antibiotics [see 22 Soft Tissue Infection].

Clostridium species, which can cause life-threatening postoperative necrotizing SSI, can also cause routine postoperative incisional infection limited to the wound and without myonecrosis.[42] Such infection is marked by the absence of the systemic symptoms associated with clostridial myonecrosis and by the presence of intact white blood cells on a Gram stain of the wound contents. (Clostridial myonecrosis, on the other hand, is characterized by a Gram stain that shows gram-positive rods but few or no white blood cells [see 22 Soft Tissue Infection].)

INTRA-ABDOMINAL INFECTION

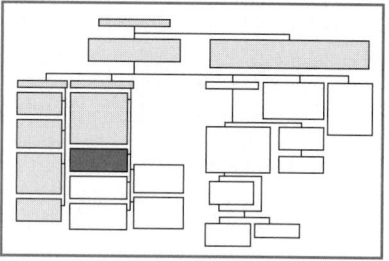

Intra-abdominal infections—that is, organ/space SSIs—are a major cause of postoperative morbidity and mortality, particularly when diagnosis is delayed.[43,44] Suspected intra-abdominal organ/space SSI in a patient with fever or abdominal tenderness, or both, after an abdominal procedure or injury should not be treated with antibiotics alone; after a specific diagnosis is made, the appropriate operative or percutaneous procedure must be performed [see 133 Intra-abdominal Infection].

EMPYEMA

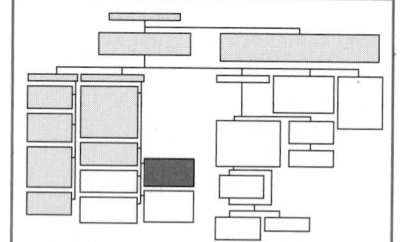

Empyema, which may follow thoracotomy or chest trauma necessitating tube thoracostomy, is a significant cause of posttraumatic infection.[45] Less commonly, empyema develops as a complication of pneumonia. Empyema should be suspected in any patient with systemic signs of infection, a pleural effusion, and no other obvious source of infection. Diagnosis requires thoracentesis of pleural fluid for a Gram stain and culture. The most common pathogen is *S. aureus,* though many other pathogens may be found as well. Initial treatment is by drainage with a chest tube and by administration of appropriate antibiotics based on the results of the Gram stain and culture. Because treatment is invasive, it should not be instituted until the diagnosis is confirmed.

Cases that do not resolve promptly and completely may ultimately require thoracoscopy or thoracotomy and decortication. Empyema after pulmonary resection or esophageal operation raises the possibility of a leaking bronchial closure or esophageal anastomosis. A leak is almost certain if an air-fluid level is present on chest x-ray. An esophageal leak is treated with repair or diversion.

STERNAL AND MEDIASTINAL INFECTION

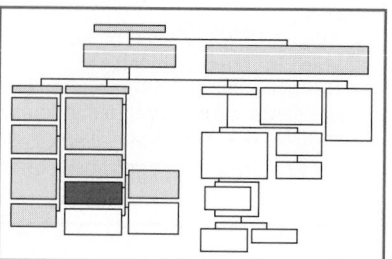

Sternal and mediastinal infections are the most serious infectious complications of operations that involve a median sternotomy.[46] The risk that a superficial infection will spread to involve the sternum and mediastinum is high because there is little soft tissue between the skin and the sternum. Infection may also start deep to the sternum without early superficial evidence. Sternal instability is an important indication of sternal infection. Computed tomography of the chest is sensitive and specific for the diagnosis of sternal osteomyelitis and mediastinitis.[47] All such infections require operative debridement of the sternum and of affected mediastinal tissues. Some wounds can then be closed. Many wounds require closure of the mediastinal space by transposition of viable soft tissue. Pectoralis or rectus muscle flaps, omental flaps, or both are commonly used.[48]

POSTTRAUMATIC MENINGITIS

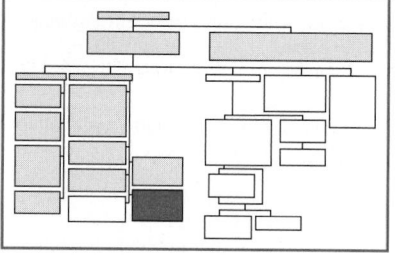

A basilar skull fracture with a cerebrospinal leak increases the risk of posttraumatic meningitis.[49] The most common pathogens are *Streptococcus pneumoniae, S. aureus,* other streptococcal species, and *Haemophilus influenzae,* but any oropharyngeal organism can be responsible.[50] Since the association between trauma and meningitis was first reported in 1970,[49] the appropriate use of antibiotics in these patients has been debated. Some researchers advocate prophylactic administration of antibiotics until any CSF leakage ceases,[51] whereas others advocate them for an arbitrary period after injury (usually 5 days); however, controlled studies have failed to support a specific protocol.[50] Furthermore, experience in other clinical settings suggests that prophylactic antibiotics would be as likely to promote the development of resistant oropharyngeal flora and subsequent meningitis as they are to prevent it.[52,53]

The ideal approach to patients with CSF rhinorrhea or otorrhea is to maintain a high index of suspicion for the development of meningitis. Fever not clearly attributable to another source or not immediately responsive to specific treatment for its presumed cause should prompt a lumbar puncture for examination and culture of spinal fluid. Lumbar puncture should also be performed to investigate headache, spinal pain or stiffness, or unexplained changes in mental status. Such an approach should result in a prompt diagnosis and permit early specific treatment of the responsible pathogen if meningitis is diagnosed.

OSTEOMYELITIS

Osteomyelitis is a relatively rare complication after elective orthopedic procedures. Its diagnosis and management are similar to those of infections involving other operative sites, but because the

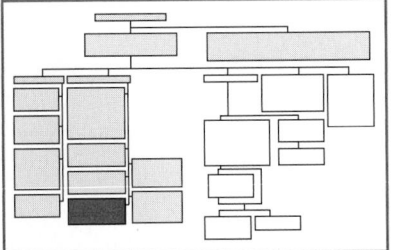

infection is deep and covered by muscular and fascial planes, diagnosis may be delayed. Nonunion of a fracture or loosening of a prosthesis may be the first sign of infection. Infection after open fractures is common; rates range from 5% to 50%.[54-56] The primary determinants of infection after open fracture are the degree of soft tissue damage surrounding the fracture and the surgeon's ability to stabilize the fracture fragments.[55] Other important factors include the patient's age and overall condition, the severity of other injuries, the interval between injury and definitive management, and the use of prophylactic antibiotics. A brief course of perioperative antibiotics may prevent subsequent infection as effectively as a more prolonged course.[30,57]

Treatment of osteomyelitis may require repeated operative debridement, prolonged use of specific antibiotics, and fracture stabilization. Pathogens include *S. aureus* for all grades of open fracture and, increasingly, gram-negative bacteria (e.g., *Pseudomonas aeruginosa* and *Klebsiella* and *Enterobacter* species) for grade III fractures.[57]

Infection Associated with Intravascular Devices

Every type and location of intravascular device has been associated with clinically significant nosocomial bloodstream infection. The inci-

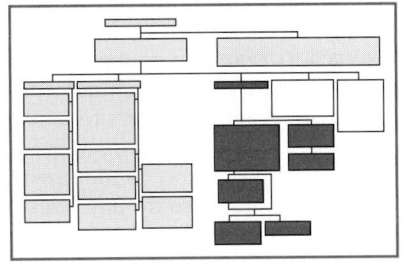

dence of infection is highest with central venous catheters used for monitoring purposes.[58,59]

It is important to specify the different definitions of catheter infection and catheter-related bloodstream infection (CRBSI). Infection at the catheter site is commonly defined as the presence of lymphangitis, purulence, or at least two of the following: erythema, tenderness, increased warmth, and a palpable thrombosed vein. However, many cases of phlebitis with no evidence of bacterial infection present with erythema and with tenderness, a palpable thrombosed vein, or both.[60] Few or no premonitory signs occur before phlebitis is obvious, and the first evidence of as many as 45% of phlebitis cases appears more than 24 hours after catheter removal. If a functional catheter remains in place for 12 hours after the onset of phlebitis symptoms, the duration and severity of symptoms increase markedly.[61]

CRBSI is characterized by (1) isolation of the same organism from the catheter and the blood, (2) clinical (or autopsy) and microbiologic data disclosing no other source of the bloodstream infection, and (3) clinical features of bloodstream infection (e.g., fever and leukocytosis).[62] For indwelling, long-term central venous catheters (e.g., Hickman, Broviac, and Groshong), infections have been classified as exit-site and tunnel infections. Infections at the exit site are defined as the presence of erythema, tenderness, induration, or purulence within 2 cm of the skin around the exit site. They are presumably confined to the portion

of the catheter external to the subcutaneous Dacron cuff. Tunnel infections are defined as the presence of the same signs along the subcutaneous tract, at a distance more than 2 cm from the tract.[63,64] The importance of this distinction is that many infections at the exit site are successfully treated with antibiotic therapy and local wound care, whereas tunnel infections usually necessitate removal of the catheter.[63,64]

A semiquantitative technique for culturing intravascular catheters has been shown to distinguish between infection and contamination of the catheter and is more specific in the diagnosis of CRBSI than is broth culture of the catheter.[62] The catheter is removed from the patient after antiseptic cleansing of the insertion site to prevent contamination from surrounding skin. A 5 to 6 cm segment of the catheter is aseptically removed; transported to the laboratory in a dry, sterile tube; placed on the surface of an agar culture plate; and rolled at least four times across the surface of the plate [see Figure 1]. If the plate grows at least 15 colonies, the culture is positive. Most catheters associated with bloodstream infection actually grow more than 1,000 colonies [see Figure 1]. For peripheral catheters, the entire catheter is cultured. For central catheters that are longer than 6 cm, either the distal tip or both the intracutaneous segment and the distal tip should be cultured [see Figure 2].

The most common source of bacteria involved in catheter infection is the skin around the insertion site.[65,66] Patients who have a skin colonization at the insertion site of greater than 10^3 colony-forming units/25 cm^2 are 10 times more likely to have a catheter infection than those whose skin colonization is less. Of catheters that test positive with the semiquantitative culture technique, 16% to 44% appear to be primary sources of septicemia.[62,67-69]

The catheter hub and lumen are recognized as important routes of infection. Colonization at these sites is detected not by roll-plate cultures but by sonication culture of catheter segments or by simultaneous cultures of blood drawn through the suspect catheter and from a distant site. Either sonication cultures recovering more than 10^2 colonies or catheter cultures more than five times the number recovered from distant sites are sensitive and specific indicators of catheter infection.[70,71]

For catheters that are only locally infected and not responsible for CRBSI, removal is adequate treatment; the same is true for most catheters that cause bloodstream infection. If the patient's temperature and white blood cell (WBC) count return to normal within 24 hours after removal of the catheter and if local signs of inflammation at the catheter insertion site resolve within that period, antibiotics are not necessary. However, if the patient continues to show clinical signs of infection or has a documented bacteremia, a brief course of specific antibiotic therapy is indicated. Specific antibiotic therapy is also indicated if semiquantitative catheter culture reveals a large number of *S. aureus* organisms in conjunction with systemic signs of infection. If empirical therapy for CRBSI is undertaken before culture and sensitivity results are available, the antibiotic regimen should include vancomycin or another antibiotic known to be effective against methicillin-resistant *S. aureus* (MRSA): coagulase-negative staphylococci are the most commonly implicated pathogens,[58,70,72] and there is a high rate of methicillin resistance among these organisms. In candidemic patients with I.V. catheters in place, candidemia resolves an average of 3 days earlier if the catheters are removed at the time of diagnosis and initiation of antifungal therapy.[73]

For patients with documented catheter-associated bacteremia, treatment depends on the organism or organisms present. The available data on the necessary duration of treatment for coagulase-negative staphylococci are inconclusive. Often, good results

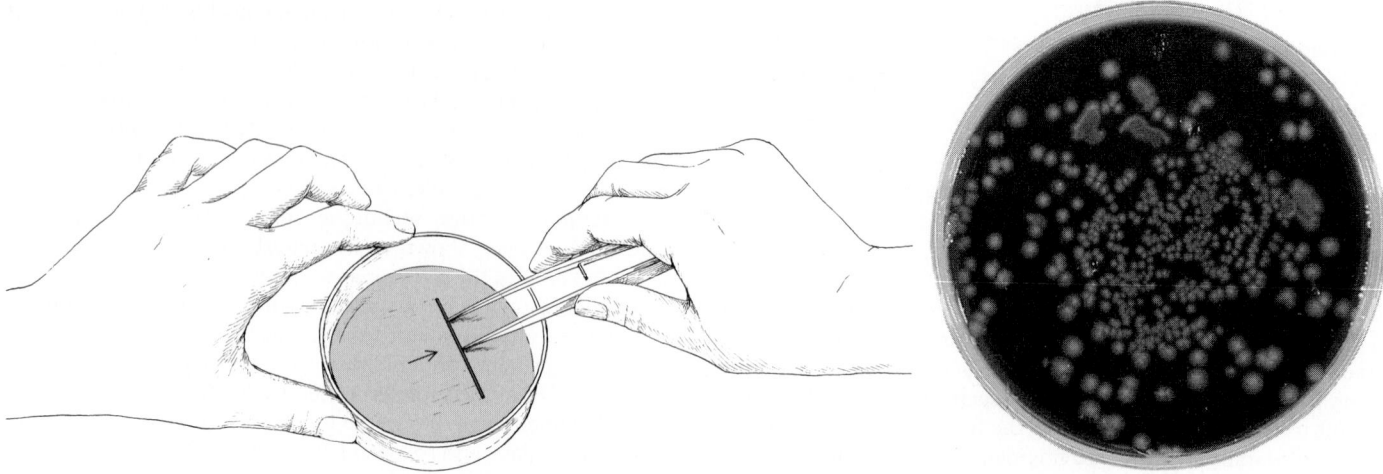

Figure 1 In a semiquantitative technique used to distinguish between infection and contamination of intravascular catheters, a 5 to 6 cm segment of the catheter is rolled at least four times across the surface of an agar culture plate (left). Typically, a positive culture grows far more than 15 colonies (right).

are achieved with catheter removal and either no antibiotics or a short course (1 to 3 days) of antibiotics; some experts recommend a 5- to 7-day course, but there is no compelling evidence that this is necessary. For *S. aureus* bacteremia, a 10- to 14-day antibiotic course is recommended if the infection is uncomplicated and a 4- to 6-week course if the infection is complicated. The relevant data on CRBSI caused by gram-negative bacilli or *Candida* are even sparser. Current recommendations call for antibiotic treatment lasting 10 to 14 days for gram-negative pathogens and 14 days or longer for *Candida*.[74]

In a small proportion of patients, local catheter-related infection may progress to a life-threatening condition characterized by the formation of microabscesses within the cannulated vein and by persistent bacteremia after catheter removal. Septic thrombophlebitis can occur in a broad range of hospitalized patients and should be suspected when clinical signs of systemic sepsis, local signs of inflammation, and positive blood cultures persist after removal of the catheter. A surgical approach to the affected vein is required. When possible, the vein should be excised over the affected area and the wound left open. The presence of gross pus within the vein wall is not necessary for the diagnosis. The wall of the affected vein may simply appear thickened, with inflammation surrounding it and an edematous, pale thrombus enclosed within it. Fungal peripheral thrombophlebitis may be especially difficult to diagnose because the local site often does not appear infected. In the presence of continued candidemia without an obvious source, any palpably thrombosed vein near a site of present or previous catheterization must be suspected. Gram staining and hematoxylin-eosin staining of the vein contents or the vein wall are significantly less sensitive than silver staining and culture.[59]

Even more rare is catheter-related septic central venous thrombosis. The diagnosis is made by the occurrence of (1)

thrombosis of the internal jugular, subclavian, or brachiocephalic vein proved by venography or duplex Doppler examination; (2) central venous catheter infection with positive catheter tip culture and positive peripheral blood cultures; and (3) persistent bacteremia or candidemia after catheter removal.[75,76] Initial therapy consists of catheter removal, systemic antibiotics based on sensitivity testing and administered in a quantity and duration appropriate to treatment of endocarditis, and systemic anticoagulation during the same period. Surgical excision or drainage is reserved for failure of nonoperative measures.

At one time, it was common practice for both central and peripheral venous catheters to be either completely changed or exchanged over a guide wire at fixed intervals to reduce the risk of infection. Data from randomized, controlled, prospective trials did not demonstrate any advantage to this policy.[60,70,77,78] These trials demonstrated that the risk of infection is linear, increasing with the duration of I.V. catheterization, whether one or multiple catheters are used.

Current practice is to change catheters when infection is suspected when the catheters are not working or not needed.[60,70,77,79,80] Clearly, any catheter that is a cause of bloodstream infection must be removed, as should infected catheters that may not yet have caused such infection. The practical problem is that not all infected catheters show external evidence of infection. In addition, catheter culture and the subsequent clinical course confirm infection in only a small proportion of patients with central venous catheters or pulmonary artery catheters in place who are suspected on clinical grounds of having CRBSI.[81] Changing central venous catheters over a guide wire circumvents most of the mechanical complications associated with central venous catheterization, saves time, and is more comfortable for the patient.[82] However, if a culture of the first catheter is positive, the second catheter should be removed immediately, and any new

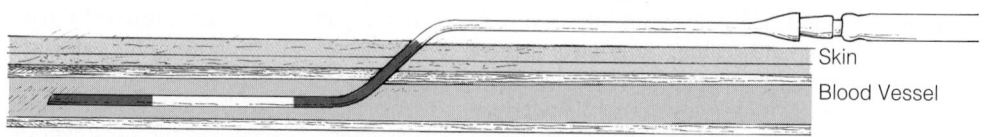

Figure 2 When a catheter is longer than 6 cm, either 5 to 6 cm of the catheter tip or both this segment and a 5 to 6 cm intracutaneous segment (red) can be cultured.

catheter should be placed in a different location.[60,70,77,79-81]

Recommendations for changing central venous and pulmonary artery catheters are as follows:

1. Signs of inflammation, skin irritation, or purulence at the insertion site should prompt immediate removal of the catheter. Any new catheter should be inserted in a different site. In a patient with systemic signs of infection (fever, leukocytosis, malaise), culture of the insertion site or of the catheter, or both, is indicated to identify potential pathogens and to direct therapy. In a patient without systemic signs of infection, culture is not necessary.

2. If a patient with a catheter experiences systemic signs and symptoms of infection without a readily apparent source, the catheter should be removed even in the absence of inflammation at the insertion site. In this setting, however, approximately 75% of catheters are not infected, and a new catheter can be inserted at the same site over a guide wire placed through the first catheter.[81,83-85] However, a catheter exchange places the new catheter in the old subcutaneous tunnel, which would be the most likely origin of catheter infection. The first catheter should be cultured semiquantitatively. If the culture is negative (i.e., < 15 colonies), the second catheter can be left in place. If the culture is positive (i.e., ≥ 15 colonies), the second catheter should be removed immediately, and any new catheter should be placed at a different site.

Sterile technique is always required for catheter insertion. However, most authorities advocate a surgical approach to preparation of the insertion site, with the operator wearing gown, gloves, mask, and hat for the procedure, if any of the following risk factors is present[70,86]: (1) the location is central, (2) catheterization will probably be long term, (3) the patient is seriously ill, or (4) parenteral nutrition is to be employed. Educational efforts to reinforce these guidelines in the hospital setting can reduce the incidence of catheter-related infections.[87]

Traditionally, central venous catheters have been inserted most commonly via either the subclavian or the internal jugular route. There is a well-demonstrated increase in infection risk when catheters are inserted by the jugular route instead of the subclavian.[69,80,88] The infection rate for the femoral route of insertion appears to be higher than that for the subclavian route and possibly higher than that for the internal jugular route[89]; however, it can be reduced by tunneling.[90] The femoral route can be used if other access routes are not available, but at the cost of a higher rate of thrombotic complications.[91]

A promising approach to prevention of catheter infection is antibiotic bonding of the entire catheter surface. Two trials reported fewer catheter and bloodstream infections in patients with antimicrobial-bonded catheters than in patients with unbonded catheters,[92,93] and one trial reported a lower infection rate with a catheter coated on both internal and external surfaces with minocycline and rifampin than with a catheter coated only on the external surface with chlorhexidine and silver sulfadiazine.[94]

The ideal method of caring for intravascular catheters after insertion is not firmly established. Sterile dressings of gauze and tape, as well as a variety of commercially available transparent dressings, have been advocated. The transparent dressings appear to save nursing time and permit the insertion site to be inspected without changing the dressing, but they promote bacterial growth on the underlying skin, as compared with gauze and tape dressings.[95] Transparent dressings have also been associated with an increased number of cases of catheter infection and CRBSI in patients with central venous catheters.[96] Thus, use of transparent dressings is not recommended, at least for central lines.

In addition, there is no firm evidence that the use of polyantibiotic ointments or iodophor ointments at the insertion site prevents infection, though such ointments have not been associated with an increase in infections with resistant organisms. Catheter teams are recommended to care for vascular catheters. Regular inspection of insertion sites and adherence to a specific protocol for catheter care can result in acceptably low infection rates.[70]

Catheters with two or three internal lumina have become widely available and are often sold in kits that include equipment for guide-wire insertion. These catheters are more convenient when a patient requires multiple lines for monitoring and for delivery of intravenous medications and parenteral nutrition. However, these multiple-lumen lines may be associated with a higher incidence of catheter-associated bloodstream infection than are single-lumen catheters[97,98]; the data are inconclusive.[85,99] In one small study, the insertion of two single-lumen catheters did not result in a lower complication rate than the insertion of one double-lumen catheter.[100] A catheter with multiple infusion ports is likely to be manipulated more often than a single-lumen catheter, but it is unclear whether the extra manipulation results in a higher infection rate. In situations in which one lumen would suffice, the temptation to insert a multiple-lumen line in case additional lumina are needed later should be resisted. One study showed that 53% of all triple-lumen lines observed had only one lumen in use, indicating that multiple-lumen lines are often used unnecessarily.[97]

When long-term use of catheters is required, insertion of a Silastic catheter with a subcutaneous Dacron cuff (e.g., Broviac, Hickman, or Groshong) is associated with the lowest rate of catheter-associated infection and the longest useful catheter life.[63] In the largest reported study of these catheters, the incidence of infection was only 0.14 infection per 100 catheter-days (range, 0.0 to 0.8).[63] The study also showed that double-lumen catheters did not have a higher rate of infection than single-lumen catheters, but the rate of catheter infections was increased 10-fold in patients who had catheter-related thrombosis. The mean catheter life span in this report was greater than 120 days.

Very low infection rates and long catheter life are also reported with nontunneled Silastic catheters and with peripherally inserted central catheters (PICC).[70,101] The lowest infection rates are associated with totally implantable devices with subcutaneous reservoirs.[102]

Use of warfarin to prevent thrombosis may result in a reduced rate of catheter infection. A prospective trial found a clinically and statistically significant reduction in the incidence of catheter-associated thrombosis (from 38% to 10%) over 90 days with the administration of 1 mg of warfarin daily, beginning 3 days before catheter insertion.[103] Measured prothrombin times did not increase, and no bleeding complications occurred.

Urinary Tract Infection

The traditional definition of urinary tract infection in patients without urinary catheters specifies the presence of at least 10^5 organisms/ml, but this criterion is probably not appropriate for catheterized patients. Research has

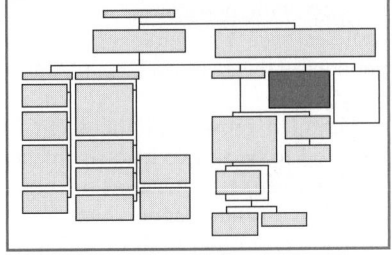

shown that of catheterized patients who have any detectable organisms in their urine (even < 10²/ml), whose catheters remain in place, and who receive no specific antimicrobial therapy, 96% have organism counts higher than 10⁵/ml within 3 days.[104] (By comparison, 27% of patients with sterile urine subsequently have colony counts higher than 10⁵/ml before catheter removal.)

Although a catheter-associated UTI is a significant nosocomial infection with measurable morbidity and mortality [see Discussion, below], not all cases of bacteriuria should be treated with antibiotics. If a patient with bacteriuria is symptomatic, treatment should be initiated according to culture results and sensitivity testing. Although bacteriuria can sometimes be cleared without removal of the catheter, the risk of a new episode continues while the catheter is in place.[105] Ideally, the catheter should be removed as soon as possible. In one study, only 36% of untreated women with asymptomatic bacteriuria had sterile urine within 2 weeks after catheter removal, and 17% progressed to symptomatic bacteriuria; however, 81% of patients treated with a single dose of trimethoprim-sulfamethoxazole had sterile urine within 2 weeks after catheter removal.[106] Thus, it is prudent to obtain a culture at the time of catheter removal and to treat any bacteriuria detected.

A condom catheter is often used in male patients in place of a urethral catheter when neurologic injury or incontinence mandates long-term drainage. The available data are not sufficient to establish the ideal care of these devices and the true infection rate associated with their use. UTI rates as low as 0% in 79 patients managed with condom catheter drainage[107] and as high as 53%[105] to 63%[108] have been reported. Severe noninfectious local complications (e.g., ulceration and maceration of the penis) also can occur.[107,108]

Because indwelling urinary catheters are a major source of nosocomial infection, they should be employed only when necessary and removed as soon as practicable. The most effective method of reducing infections among patients with urinary catheters is to use completely closed urinary drainage systems and to limit breaks in the closed system.[109] The incidence of new infections doubles on any day in which a closed urinary drainage system is opened.[110] Urine samples for culture should be aspirated with a needle and syringe from the catheter lumen after antiseptic cleansing of the catheter sampling port. The catheter junction should not be disconnected to obtain a specimen. The use of a preconnected and sealed catheter and drainage bag system has been shown to result in a 2.7-fold reduction in the rate of catheter-associated UTIs and an adjusted risk ratio for death of 0.29.[111]

Antibiotic irrigation systems do not reduce infections, but they do increase the incidence of resistant organisms.[110] Systemic antibiotics reduce infections to a modest degree in the first 4 days of catheterization but at the expense of an increase in resistant organisms. The infection rate is higher in females than in males, in older patients than in younger ones, and in patients with critical illness than in those without critical illness.[109] Patients with nosocomial diarrhea and an indwelling bladder catheter have a ninefold higher risk of subsequent UTI than patients with an indwelling bladder catheter who do not have diarrhea.[112]

Although most UTIs acquired by hospitalized patients are assumed to be simple bladder infections, there is no strong correlation between location of infection and clinical symptoms.[113,114] Many patients with upper UTIs do not have flank pain, fever, or other signs of systemic infection, and patients with a bladder infection may not have dysuria or suprapubic tender-

ness. Many patients with upper UTIs are treated without the diagnosis ever being made. Systemic infection and associated bacteremia or complications such as intrarenal or perinephric abscesses occur more commonly in immunocompromised patients (e.g., those with urinary tract obstruction or diabetes).[115] In patients with a neurogenic bladder or indwelling bladder catheters, urinary sepsis may develop without symptoms referable to the urinary tract. However, symptoms of localized flank or low back pain, along with systemic signs, such as fever, rigors, sweats, and nausea, are relatively specific indicators of renal infection.[116]

If a patient has fever and bacteriuria during the postoperative period, the surgeon should perform a careful evaluation to determine whether he or she has pyelonephritis or a postoperative intra-abdominal infectious complication. Pyelonephritis can be treated solely with antimicrobial therapy in most cases, whereas all postoperative intra-abdominal infectious complications call for surgical intervention as well as antimicrobial therapy. No simple methods are available to distinguish between these diagnoses. The operating surgeon should carefully evaluate all of the patient's clinical signs and symptoms. A hospitalized patient with pyelonephritis should usually receive antimicrobial therapy for at least 14 days. An agent demonstrated to be effective against the causative organism by in vitro sensitivity testing should be used. In any patient who has severe signs of systemic infection or does not respond promptly to treatment, ultrasonography, renal scanning, or I.V. pyelography should be done to rule out obstruction. If obstruction is found, it must be corrected. If the patient has an indwelling bladder catheter, the catheter should be removed, appropriate therapy started, and a new, clean catheter inserted.[116]

Enteric Infection

Any organism that can cause food-borne enteric infection in the community can do so in the hospital,[117] but cultures for routine enteric pathogens are not useful for patients

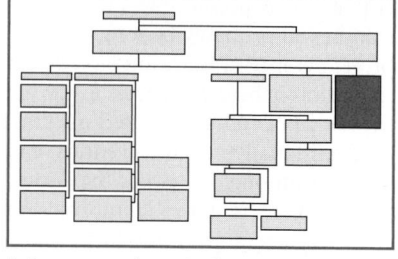

who have been hospitalized for more than 3 days.[118] The most important nosocomial enteric disease to confront most surgeons is antibiotic-associated diarrhea, which can range from trivial, self-limited episodes of diarrhea to fulminant disease with systemic signs of sepsis, collapse, and death.

The first step in diagnosis is to consider antibiotic-associated colitis in any hospitalized patient with diarrhea. Mild cases may not be associated with any systemic signs or pathologic findings in the colon, and in the majority of mild episodes, there are no identifiable pathogens. More severe cases are marked by one or more of the following signs: nonspecific hyperemia, edema, granularity, or ulceration of colonic mucosa. The most severe cases are marked by pseudomembrane formation.

The single most efficient measure for detecting C. difficile–associated diarrhea is to send a stool sample for cytotoxin determination, a procedure that has a sensitivity of 70% to 100%. By sending a sample is sent for stool culture as well, one can increase sensitivity slightly (to 96%); however, if C. difficile is grown on the culture, the organism must still be tested for cytotoxin production, and this takes another day.[118,119] Rectal swab cultures transported in anaerobic containers are at least as sensitive as conventional stool cultures,[120] but they are not adequate for detection of cytotoxin.[119] Although it is possible that poly-

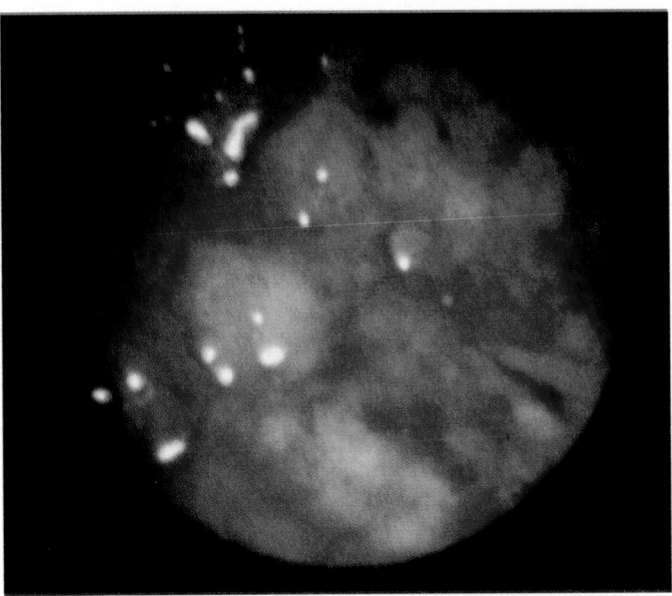

Figure 3 **An endoscopic view of pseudomembrane formation is shown.**

merase chain reaction assays for the cytotoxin gene in stool can eventually be developed, such assays are not available at present. Stool smears for detection of WBCs are not helpful.[118,119] Endoscopy to detect pseudomembranes is indicated if the patient is seriously ill and a prompt diagnosis and initiation of specific treatment are desired. Administration of empirical therapy until a specific pathogen is identified is appropriate in this circumstance.[119]

Severe and persistent cases of antibiotic-associated diarrhea are most commonly associated with the recovery of *C. difficile* by culture and of *C. difficile* toxin by tissue culture assay.[121] In more than 90% of patients who have pseudomembranous colitis, *C. difficile* toxin will be present on tissue culture assay. In antibiotic-associated diarrhea without pseudomembrane formation, positive toxin titers may be found in 70% of patients with signs of colitis and in 11% to 27% of patients without colitis.[122-124]

Pseudomembranes, present in about half of patients with *C. difficile*–associated diarrhea,[119] are elevated, whitish plaques that vary in size from a few millimeters to 1 to 2 cm and may coalesce and slough. Histologically, the plaques show epithelial debris, polymorphonuclear infiltrate, chronic inflammatory cells, and fibrin deposition.[121] The diagnosis of pseudomembrane formation is made by endoscopy [*see Figure 3*]. Most cases involve the rectum and the left colon, but as many as 25% may be missed by rigid sigmoidoscopy; by comparison, the false negative rate with flexible endoscopy is only 10%.[125] Although the great majority of cases involve only the colon, two fatal cases that primarily involved the ileum and the jejunum have been recorded.[126,127] The clinical picture of pseudomembranous colitis includes watery diarrhea in 90% to 95% of cases, with bloody diarrhea in the remaining cases. Abdominal cramps, leukocytosis, and elevated temperature are present in approximately 80% of cases.[121]

All commonly employed antibiotics have been implicated in cases of antibiotic-associated pseudomembranous colitis, including vancomycin[128-130] and antibiotics used for perioperative antibiotic prophylaxis, even in a single dose.[131] Treatment should include cessation of the offending antimicrobial agent, if possible. In mild cases, this step may be all that is necessary: in 23% of

such cases, resolution occurs within 2 to 3 days of discontinuance of antibiotic therapy.[119]

A patient with systemic symptoms should also receive one of the agents with proven efficacy against the disease. The agent with which there has been the most recorded experience is vancomycin, but it is more expensive than the alternatives. The usual dosage is 500 mg/day orally in four divided doses. Metronidazole, 500 mg three or four times daily for at least 10 days, is an effective alternative.[132] Bacitracin, 20,000 to 25,000 units four times daily, is also effective but should be considered the third choice.[119,132] The current recommendation is to begin therapy with metronidazole to reduce the risk of inducing vancomycin-resistant enterococci [*see* Pathogens, *below*].[119,133]

Relapses after treatment for *C. difficile* colitis are common, occurring in 5% to 30% of cases, perhaps because of persistence of the organism in spore form; 92% of these cases respond to a second course of treatment without relapse.[119,132] Cases that do recur involve both persistent infection and new reinfection.[132]

A profound ileus is sometimes associated with the severe form of the disease and may prevent the delivery of oral antibiotics to the site of infection. Limited experience suggests that parenteral metronidazole may be effective in these cases. However, there have been several cases of unsuccessful treatment of *C. difficile*–associated colitis with I.V. metronidazole and of the development of *C. difficile* colitis in patients receiving I.V. metronidazole alone or together with other antibiotics.[132,134] In the most severe cases, the clinical evolution resembles that of toxic colitis associated with inflammatory bowel disease, and the patient may require a colectomy if the disease is unresponsive to nonoperative management. If operative treatment proves necessary, subtotal colectomy is preferred to hemicolectomy.[132] In as many as 5% of cases, colitis may present as acute abdominal pain and tenderness and leukocytosis without diarrhea.[135,136] Any patient with acute abdominal symptoms who has received antibiotics within the past 2 months should be considered for the diagnosis of *C. difficile*–associated colitis.[132] If colitis is suspected because of previous antibiotic administration, sigmoidoscopy may facilitate the correct diagnosis and avert unnecessary abdominal exploration. CT may show thickening of the bowel wall, but operative exploration often does not yield significant findings.[136] Extraintestinal infections have also been reported.[137]

Transfusion-Associated Infection

The transfusion of blood would seem to be an excellent method for transmitting blood-borne diseases; however, transmission of disease by blood transfusion is rare.[138,139] Transfusion-associated malaria is occasionally reported in North America but occurs quite infrequently. The primary method for preventing malaria transmission is careful screening of donors by history. A handful of cases of babesiosis, Chagas disease, trypanosomiasis, toxoplasmosis, and infections with various herpesviruses, parvovirus, or West Nile virus have been reported over many years, but these are rare as well.[138-141]

In the early years of blood collection and transfusion, cases of syphilis related to blood transfusion were reported infrequently. The practice of refrigerating blood, which kills circulating spirochetes within 1 to 2 days, is probably responsible for the absence of transfusion-associated syphilis today. Unfortunately, refrigerating blood does not kill all potential pathogens. Bacterial pathogens that can survive blood storage and cause subsequent symptomatic infection include *Yersinia enterocolitica, Pseudomonas fluorescens, P. putida, Campylobacter jejuni, Escherichia coli, Serratia* species, *Salmonella* species, *Enterobacter* species, *Providencia* species, *S. aureus,* and streptococci. When transfusion-associated bacteremia or endotoxemia is suspected, the residual blood product in the bag should be examined by means of a hematologic stain, and the blood in the bag and samples of the recipient's blood should be cultured.

Bacterial contamination of transfused blood components accounted for 11% of all fatal transfusion reactions reported to the FDA between 1985 and 1999. In 2001, CDC investigators published a prospective survey of bacterial infections resulting from blood component transfusion in the United States between January 1998 and December 2000.[142] This survey covered approximately 60% to 70% of all transfusions recorded in the United States during that period. The investigators identified 34 confirmed cases of bacterial infection from transfused blood components, nine (27%) of which were responsible for deaths. The estimated rates of transfusion-transmitted bacteremia were one per 100,000 single or pooled units of platelets and one per 5 million units of red blood cells. The estimated fatality rates were one per 500,000 units of platelets and one per 8 million units of red blood cells.

Until recently, the most severe and most common disease transmitted by blood transfusion in North America was viral hepatitis [*see 135 Viral Infection*]. With the development of specific and sensitive tests for detecting hepatitis B surface antigen (HBsAg), the incidence of posttransfusion hepatitis B dropped from 25% to 30% of all cases of transfusion-associated hepatitis to 5% to 10%. However, the advent of serologic tests for hepatitis B did not result in an overall decrease in posttransfusion hepatitis (PTH), because 80% to 90% of cases of PTH were caused by hepatitis C virus (HCV). Since the development of sensitive antibody tests for HCV, the incidence of PTH has dropped dramatically, and since the introduction in 1999 of nucleic acid amplification technology (NAT) (e.g., PCR and transcription-mediated amplification), it has fallen even further, to the point where the current estimated risk is one per 1.9 million transfused units.[143]

The spread of AIDS [*see 136 Acquired Immunodeficiency Syndrome*] brought a new risk of transfusion-associated viral disease. The risk of acquiring transfusion-associated HIV infection is extremely low compared with posttransfusion hepatitis; transfusion-associated HIV infection is vastly less likely to occur and

has accounted for fewer deaths. Nevertheless, transfusion-associated AIDS is much more frightening to most patients and physicians than PTH because of its usually fatal prognosis. Prevention of HIV transmission during transfusion is accomplished by screening potential donors to eliminate those at high risk for infection and by testing all donated units for HIV with both antibody tests and NAT.[143-145] It has been estimated that predonation screening is 98% effective in eliminating donation of positive units and that postdonation antibody testing is more than 95% effective, for a combined effectiveness of approximately 99.9%.[144] Overall, posttransfusion HIV infections were reduced by 76% between 1985 and 1988, a time during which the overall prevalence of the condition was increasing.[144]

The continued concern about possible HIV transmission during transfusion arises from the so-called window of seronegativity between the time at which a potential donor becomes infected and the time at which the donor's antibody test becomes positive. A 1989 analysis of available data from most United States blood banks concluded that the risk of receiving a unit of blood that contained HIV but was negative for anti-HIV antibody in 1987 was approximately one per 153,000 transfusions on the basis of an average window period of 8 weeks.[144] A 2002 report, making use of data obtained since the introduction of NAT, established the current risk at one per 2.1 million transfusions.[143] In comparison, the risk of experiencing a fatal hemolytic transfusion reaction is one per 100,000 transfusions.[145] Thus, a transfusion recipient is much more likely to die of a hemolytic reaction than of infection.

Analysis of transfusion practices in the United States between 1982 and 1988 reveals a decrease in the number of blood, platelet, and plasma transfusions after 1986; before 1986, the number of these transfusions increased each year. In addition, between 1982 and 1987, the number of autologous units donated increased from 30,000 to 397,000 a year. In 1987, autologous units accounted for 3% of all blood transfused.[146] Since 1987, refinements of operative techniques have reduced the need for transfusion in many procedures, and research has demonstrated that in many cases, transfusion can safely be withheld until hemoglobin levels lower than 7 g/dl are reached [*see 8 Bleeding and Transfusion*].[147] In addition to the overall decline in transfusions since the late 1980s, the number of autologous units of blood transfused yearly has declined.[148]

Discussion

Postoperative Fever

Many patients experience fever in the postoperative period without infection. In a prospective study of 871 general surgery patients, 213 (24%) had a documented infection or an unexplained fever in the postoperative period.[149] The most common occurrence was unexplained fever in 81 cases (38%), followed by wound infection in 55 (26%), UTI in 44 (21%), respiratory tract infection in 27 (13%), and other infections in 6 (3%). Of all unexplained fevers, 72% occurred in the first 2 days, and of all occurrences in the first 3 days, 67 (71%) of 95 were unexplained, with only 18 (27%) representing true infection. In another study, 73 (45%) of 162 patients experienced unexplained fever after general surgical or orthopedic procedures; 25% of the unexplained fevers were at least 38.3° C (101° F).[150]

At Harborview Medical Center, 316 (98%) of 322 patients who underwent laparotomy for penetrating trauma had a temperature of at least 37.5° C (99.5° F) orally during the first 5 days after operation. Of these, however, only 67 (21%) actually acquired any infection during a 30-day follow-up. Even for the 80 patients whose temperatures were as high as 39° C (102.2° F) orally, only 48% actually acquired an infection before discharge. Fever that persisted or began after postoperative day 4 was more likely to represent true infection. Similarly, an elevated WBC count was nonspecific during the first 5 postoperative days: 89% of all patients had a WBC count greater than 10,000/mm³.[151,152] A high fever should prompt examination of the patient, but in the absence of systemic signs of sepsis, an extensive laboratory or radiologic workup during the first 4 to 5 days is usually unhelpful.[153]

Magnitude and Significance of Nosocomial Infection

An understanding of the prevalence of nosocomial infections and of the factors predisposing to their occurrence will help in prevention, diagnosis, and treatment. Since 1970, the NNIS system has collected and analyzed data on the frequency of nosocomial infections in a voluntary sample of hospitals (currently numbering 280) in the United States.[154] Although it has been suggested that the NNIS system underestimates the true incidence of nosocomial infections by 30% to 40%,[3,155,156] the large number of cases studied during consecutive years provides a useful description of the most frequently encountered infections, their relative incidences, and the responsible pathogens.

INCIDENCE

In the 1986 NNIS report, the overall incidence of nosocomial infection was 33.5 per 1,000 discharges; the range extended from 13.3 per 1,000 pediatric discharges to 46.7 per 1,000 surgical discharges. Generally, the rate of infection is highest in large teaching hospitals and lowest in nonteaching hospitals. The higher incidence of infection among surgical patients is largely attributable to SSI. SSIs are the most frequent adverse events reported for hospitalized surgical patients and account for 38% of all nosocomial infections in surgical patients.[157] Two thirds of SSIs are incisional infections, and one third are organ/space infections.[35,158] Some 38% of all SSIs result in readmission to the hospital.[35]

Across all services, UTIs are the most common infections, accounting for 38.5% of all nosocomial infections, followed by lower respiratory tract infections (17.8%), surgical wound infections (16.6%), primary bacteremias (7.5%), and cutaneous infections (5.8%). All other categories combined account for 13.8% of nosocomial infections. The total incidence of nosocomial infection from all sites on surgical services ranges from 30.8 to 59.3 per 1,000 discharges. The risk that a surgical patient will acquire any infection varies according to the type of procedure performed as well as to the patient's underlying risk.[159]

In the 1993 NNIS report, the most common nosocomial infections for surgical patients after an SSI were UTIs (27%), pneumonias (15%), primary bloodstream infections (7%), and all other sites combined (15%).[159] Of the infected surgical patients, 17% had more than one nosocomial infection, and 9% of surgical patients with nosocomial infections subsequently died; nosocomial infections were reported to have caused or contributed to 60% of the deaths. Of infections related to death, 38% were pneumonias, 21% occurred at the surgical site, and 20% were primary bloodstream infections. The likelihood that a specific infection will be related to death varies with the type of infection [see Table 1].

Urinary Tract Infection

With so many cases of bacteriuria occurring in catheterized patients, it would be easy to become complacent about the problem. Urinary tract catheterization is performed seven to eight million times a year in acute care hospitals in the United States.[160] Approximately 5% to 8% of catheterized, uninfected patients will acquire a urinary tract infection for each day of catheterization, leading to a cumulative infection rate of 40% to 50% after 10 days.[109] However, the great majority of catheterized patients with bacteriuria are asymptomatic.[109,161] It has been estimated that only 0.7% of catheterized patients will acquire a symptomatic infection and that 8% to 10% of patients will have bacteriuria after the catheter has been removed.[109]

In many of these patients, the bacteriuria resolves without specific therapy after the catheter has been removed. However, a

Table 1 Contribution of Nosocomial Infection to Death in Infected Surgical Patients Who Died[159]

Type of Nosocomial Infection	Probability That Infection Was Related to Death (%)
Organ/space surgical site infection	89
Primary bloodstream infection	79
Pneumonia	77
Other	48
Incisional surgical site infection	46
Urinary tract infection	22

careful study of more than 1,458 patients clearly demonstrated that mortality is higher in catheterized patients who acquire bacteriuria than in those who do not.[160] In this study, 9% of all catheterized patients acquired catheter-related UTIs; these infections were associated with a threefold increase in deaths occurring during hospitalization, even after correction for other factors (e.g., age, severity of illness, hospital service, duration of catheterization, and renal function). In surgical patients between 50 and 70 years of age with normal renal function and without a fatal underlying disease, a 3% increase in the death rate per patient per hospitalization was associated with the occurrence of a UTI. Of all deaths occurring in catheterized patients, 14% were associated with a UTI.[160] By extrapolation, this mortality suggests that as many as 56,000 deaths a year in the United States may be related to catheter-acquired UTI.

Although the risk of bacteremia is small for any individual patient with bacteriuria, the large number of hospitalized patients with bacteriuria means that many bacteremic episodes are seen in this population. UTI is the most commonly diagnosed source of gram-negative sepsis, and the rate of bacteremia secondary to urinary catheters is estimated to be between 0.7% and 2%.[109] In a case-matched study from 1978, a postoperative UTI was associated with a 2.4-day prolongation of hospital stay and an excess cost of more than $500.[162] A subsequent study revealed that 2.3% of postoperative patients with UTIs were subsequently diagnosed as having a wound infection caused by the same organism responsible for the UTI.[163] This finding accounted for 3.4% of the wound infections occurring during the study.

Infection Associated with Intravascular Devices

Nosocomial infection associated with intravascular devices, which are placed for either monitoring or therapeutic purposes, assumed increasing importance during the 1970s and 1980s. In the United States, central venous catheters are in place for approximately 15 million patient-catheter-days per year, resulting in approximately 250,000 catheter-associated bloodstream infections.[70] Of all cases of nosocomial bacteremia occurring in NNIS hospitals between September 1984 and July 1986, 82% were associated with intravascular devices[164]: 27% were associated with parenteral nutrition catheters and 55% with other vascular access devices. Reports from as early as 1963 called attention to the risk of serious systemic infections arising from peripheral I.V. catheters.[165] For ICU patients with bloodstream infections associated with central venous catheters, the attributable mortality is 25% to 35%, and the excess cost for survivors is $34,000 to $56,000 per patient, for a total annual cost of $296 million to $2.3 billion.[70]

In terms of infection risk, pulmonary arterial catheters are no different from central venous catheters, except for their potential to cause right-side heart lesions that could predispose to right-side endocarditis.[166] Pulmonary arterial catheters can be responsible for bloodstream infection, and they require as much attention during insertion and subsequent care as central venous catheters do.[68,167]

The arterial catheters used for monitoring purposes in the ICU have been thought to be less frequently associated with infection than central venous catheters are, but it is clear that life-threatening infections can originate with peripheral arterial lines.[168,169] In early studies of radial artery catheters in which nonquantitative culture techniques were employed, catheter contamination rates of 4% to 39% were recorded, but there were no cases of CRBSI or clinical infection in 605 catheterizations.[170] In these studies, the majority of catheters were removed from patients within 3 days.

Prospective studies of arterial catheters demonstrated that 18% to 35% of the lines were locally infected, as reflected in semiquantitative cultures of at least 15 colonies.[171] In one study, five cases of CRBSI occurred, representing an overall incidence of 4% and an incidence of 23% among locally infected catheters.[171] The incidence of CRBSI was increased in catheters that were inserted by cutdown rather than by percutaneous puncture and in catheters with signs of local inflammation. In another, the clinical features of bloodstream infection arising from an arterial catheter were indistinguishable from the clinical features of episodes arising from a central venous line, and 12%

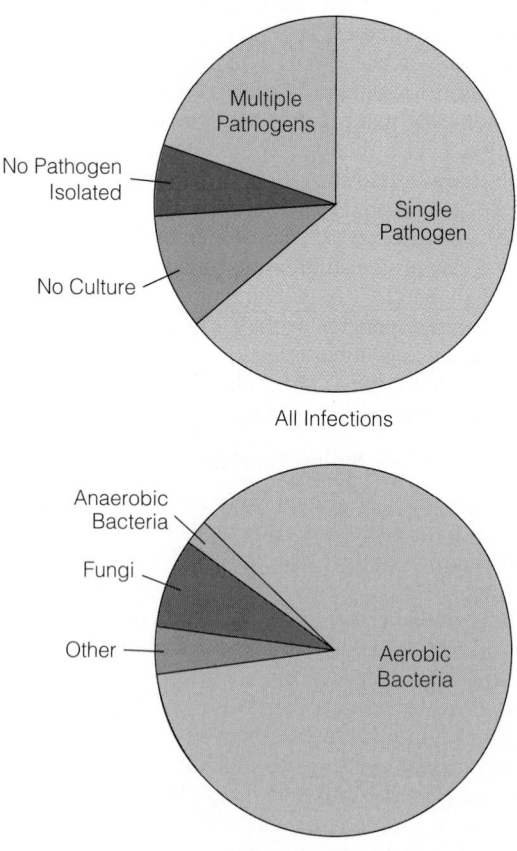

All Infections

Infections of Known Etiology

Figure 4 **Illustrated is a breakdown of the etiology of 26,965 nosocomial infections from the National Nosocomial Infections Surveillance System.**[173]

Table 2 Five Most Common Pathogens Isolated from Surgical Patients and Percentage of Total within Each Site[173]

Infection Site	Organism	Isolates at That Site (%)
Urinary tract infection	*Escherichia coli*	29
	Pseudomonas aeruginosa	16
	Enterococci	13
	Proteus species	7
	Klebsiella species	7
Surgical wound infection	*Staphylococcus aureus*	19
	Enterococci	12
	E. coli	12
	P. aeruginosa	10
	Coagulase-negative staphylococci	8
Lower respiratory infection	*P. aeruginosa*	17
	S. aureus	12
	Enterobacter species	11
	Klebsiella species	11
	Serratia species	7
Bacteremia	Coagulase-negative staphylococci	14
	S. aureus	10
	Enterobacter species	9
	Enterococci	9
	Klebsiella species	8
Cutaneous infections	*S. aureus*	19
	P. aeruginosa	13
	Enterococci	11
	Coagulase-negative staphylococci	10
	E. coli	8

of all nosocomial bacteremias in the ICU originated from an arterial catheter.[171] Clearly, arterial lines as well as venous lines must be considered in the examination of a patient for the source of fever or bloodstream infection in the ICU.[68,169,171,172] Twelve cases of radial artery rupture after arterial line infection have been reported. All but one were associated with *S. aureus* infection, and nearly all demonstrated systemic signs of infection for 2 days or longer after catheter removal.[169] Although there is no published experience with the use of guide wires to change and culture arterial lines in relation to possible catheter-related infection, the technique can be applied with the same rationale used for central venous catheters.

PATHOGENS

In 1984, the NNIS reported on 26,965 infections. Of these cases, 64% were caused by single pathogens, 20% were caused by multiple pathogens, 6% had no pathogen identified on culture, and 10% were not cultured [*see Figure 4*].[173] Of the 84% in which a pathogen was identified, 86% were caused by aerobic bacteria, 2% by anaerobes, and 8% by fungi [*see Figure 4 and Table 2*]. Overall on the surgical services, the most common pathogen isolated was *E. coli*, followed by *P. aeruginosa*, enterococci, *S. aureus*, *Enterobacter* species, *Klebsiella* species, coagulase-negative staphylococci, *Proteus* species, *Candida* species, and *Serratia* species. These 10 types of pathogens accounted for 84% of all isolates. Gram-negative rods were most common in UTIs and lower respiratory tract infections, though *S. aureus* was the second most common pathogen isolated in lower respiratory tract infections. *S. aureus* was the most common isolate from surgical wound infections, whereas coagulase-negative staphylococci, followed closely by *S. aureus*, were the pathogens most often responsible for primary bacteremias.

As a consequence of changing hospital practices, hospitalized patients today tend to be more severely ill than was once the case. Large amounts of antibiotics are being used in hospitals, and antibiotic-resistant pathogens have become increasingly problematic. Current NNIS data indicate that the frequency with which antibiotics are administered to hospitalized patients who are not in an ICU is approximately 468 defined daily doses (DDD) per 1,000 patient-days.[174] For hospitalized ICU patients, the frequency is between 800 and 1,031 DDD per 1,000 patient-days. MRSA accounts for 51% of total *S. aureus* isolates in ICU patients, 40% in non-ICU patients, and 24% in outpatients with nosocomial infections; the corresponding figures for quinolone-resistant *P. aeruginosa* in relation to total *P. aeruginosa* isolates are 37%, 27%, and 27%.[174] In 2002, the second clinical isolate of vancomycin-resistant *S. aureus* in the United States was reported.[175]

Nosocomial infections with resistant enterococci have become a serious problem. Enterococci were the third most common nosocomial bloodstream isolate reported by NNIS hospitals between 1990 and 1992.[176] The incidence of vancomycin-resistant enterococci (VRE) increased 26-fold between 1989 and 1993, from 0.3% to 7.9%, with a 34-fold rise in ICUs,[177] and the rate has continued to increase. The 2001 NNIS report stated that 13% of enterococci were resistant to vancomycin in ICU patients, 12% in non-ICU patients, and 5% in outpatients.[174] These strains arise from the patient's endogenous flora, but nosocomial spread within the hospital environment is also an important source.[177,178] The environment around infected patients is heavily contaminated with VRE, and gown and glove isolation techniques are required to stop transmission.[178] Strict application of hand hygiene is also important for reducing the spread of VRE and other nosocomial pathogens. According to the available data and current CDC recommendations, the use of alcohol-based hand-rub solutions is superior to washing with soap and water: it can be performed more rapidly and is less damaging to the skin.[179]

VRE are also highly resistant to other available antibiotics. Acquisition of VRE is significantly associated with prior hospitalization and with use of third-generation cephalosporins, vancomycin, or multiple antibiotics.[180,181] In one study, 16% of stool specimens submitted for testing for *C. difficile* toxin were colonized with VRE, and all surgical patients in that study had the same strain.[182]

High mortality can be associated with VRE infections. In a study comparing the outcome of patients having VRE bacteremia with the outcome of patients having bacteremia caused by vancomycin-sensitive enterococci (VSE), mortality was 2.3 times higher in those with VRE bacteremia, and 89% of patients with VRE bacteremia were colonized or infected with VRE at another site.[183] Prior treatment with third-generation cephalosporins is another risk factor for increased mortality.[176] Liver transplant patients with VRE bacteremia had a 92% higher mortality than comparable patients with VSE bacteremia, and those with VRE bacteremia also had a higher recurrence rate and greater need for invasive procedures.[184]

Current recommendations include decreased—and possibly restricted—use of vancomycin, as well as aggressive infection control measures whenever VRE are isolated in a hospitalized patient.[177] In particular, vancomycin should not be used as primary treatment for *C. difficile*–associated diarrhea and should be avoided for surgical prophylaxis unless the hospital has a specific problem with MRSA or the patient cannot receive other appropriate antibiotics.

ENTERIC INFECTION

C. difficile is often found in patients with severe antibiotic-associated enteric infections. In one report, 691 (2%) of 32,757 consecutive postoperative patients experienced watery diarrhea significant enough to stimulate a request for *C. difficile* toxin assay.[185] Of this number, 75 (11% of patients with diarrhea) had a positive toxin assay. All cases were associated with antibiotic administration. Approximately 94% of the patients had received a cephalosporin either alone or in combination with other antibiotics; 29% of these responded to cessation of antibiotics and supportive measures, and the remainder were treated with vancomycin, metronidazole, or bacitracin. Six (14%) of the patients who required specific therapy relapsed after initial response to treatment and were subsequently cured with one or more additional courses of treatment. Two patients died, and the overall hospital stay for the remaining patients was prolonged by an average of 50%.

Most patients with mild cases of antibiotic-associated diarrhea do not have either positive cultures for *C. difficile* or positive toxin assays, and the etiologic role of *C. difficile* is unclear. Many hospitalized patients without diarrhea also have *C. difficile* in the stool, with or without toxin production,[123,186] and the likelihood of isolating this pathogen increases with patients' increasing length of stay.[118] A nonpathogenic yeast, *Saccharomyces boulardii*, when administered by mouth to hospitalized patients receiving antibiotics, significantly reduced the occurrence of antibiotic-associated diarrhea without affecting the rate of acquisition of *C. difficile*.[123]

Some 3% of asymptomatic adults carry *C. difficile* in their stools, but 30% to 40% of healthy neonates may carry the organism. The rate of carriage declines after the age of 1 to 2 years. *C. difficile* can be spread in the hospital and has been isolated from 10% of inanimate objects in the environment of patients with *C. difficile* colonization, compared with 3% in hospital areas with no known cases.[187] In one report,[187] this organism was recovered from the hands of 13% of medical personnel working in a ward with affected patients; in another,[188] it was recovered from 60% of personnel immediately after they had cared for an affected patient. Soap-and-water washing was ineffective in preventing acquisition, but the combination of glove use and chlorhexidine washing was effective. In another medical center,[189] clusters of new nosocomial *C. difficile* diarrhea were prevented by screening all patients with diarrhea by active surveillance (using culture to identify *C. difficile* infection) and by instituting isolation precautions and daily disinfection of infected patients' rooms.

The prevalence of *C. difficile* in the environment is increased when a patient has diarrhea.[187,188] In one prospectively studied cohort, 21% of patients without *C. difficile* in their stools on admission acquired the organism during hospitalization, and 37% of these patients experienced diarrhea; no cases of colitis occurred.[187] Diarrhea was more common in patients who received antibiotics. The rate of acquisition of *C. difficile* was 73% higher if a patient had a roommate colonized with *C. difficile*.

COST

The cost of nosocomial infections, both in dollars and in morbidity, is high. According to one estimate, 8.7 million extra hospital days and $4.5 billion in hospital charges were attributable to nosocomial infections in United States hospitals in 1976.[190]

Estimates of the number of deaths caused by nosocomial infections run as high as 58,000 a year; 9,700 of these deaths and 36% of all costs attributed to nosocomial infections are due to wound infections.[190] The actual numbers may be even higher. Another study found that 63 of 200 consecutive patients dying in the hospital had nosocomial infections; 18 (29%) of the 63 were judged causal and 26 (41%) contributory.[8] Most of the causal and contributory infections were of the lower respiratory tract, and deaths were significantly associated with invasive devices (e.g., intra-arterial and central venous pressure monitoring devices and nasogastric tubes). Of the 57 deaths occurring on the surgical service, 27 (47%) were associated with nosocomial infections.

RISK

The risk of acquiring a nosocomial infection is clearly related to the reason for hospitalization as well as to the underlying disease.[8,191] Patients admitted to the hospital with a fatal underlying disease have a nosocomial infection rate of 24%, compared with 10% in patients with ultimately fatal disease and 2% in those with nonfatal disease. Among 100 consecutive trauma patients admitted to the ICU at Harborview Medical Center in 1986, 42 acquired 64 nosocomial infections, including 23 lower respiratory tract infections, 17 urinary tract infections, and 6 wound infections.[152] These 100 ICU admissions and 101 consecutive trauma admissions to the general ward were examined together. Of 153 patients admitted with injury severity scores of 25 or less, nosocomial infection occurred in 32 (21%). Of 48 patients with injury severity scores higher than 25, nosocomial infection occurred in 26 (54%).[152] A statewide survey of hospitals in Virginia from 1978 to 1982 found that infections in ICU patients accounted for 25% of all cases of nosocomial infections, although fewer than 10% of the beds were in ICUs.[192]

References

1. Haley RW, Schaberg DR, Crossley KB, et al: Extra charges and prolongation of stay attributable to nosocomial infections: a prospective interhospital comparison. Am J Med 70:51, 1981

2. Haley RW, Schaberg DR, Von Allmen SD, et al: Estimating the extra charges and prolongation of hospitalization due to nosocomial infections: a comparison of methods. J Infect Dis 141:248, 1980

3. Haley RW, Culver DH, White JW, et al: The nationwide nosocomial infection rate: a new need for vital statistics. Am J Epidemiol 121:159, 1985

4. Haley RW, White JW, Culver DH, et al: The financial incentive for hospitals to prevent nosocomial infections under the prospective payment system: an empirical determination from a nationally representative sample. JAMA 257:1611, 1987

5. Haley RW, Culver DH, Morgan WM, et al: Increased recognition of infectious diseases in US hospitals through increased use of diagnostic tests, 1970 to 1976. Am J Epidemiol 121:182, 1985

6. Roberts J, Barnes W, Pennock M, et al: Diagnostic accuracy of fever as a measure of postoperative pulmonary complications. Heart Lung 17:166, 1988

7. Engoren M: Lack of association between atelectasis and fever. Chest 107:81, 1995

8. Gross PA, Neu HC, Aswapokee P, et al: Deaths from nosocomial infections: experience in a university hospital and a community hospital. Am J Med 68:219, 1980

9. Andrews CP, Coalson JJ, Smith JD, et al: Diagnosis of nosocomial bacterial pneumonia in acute, diffuse lung injury. Chest 80:254, 1981

10. Craven DE, Steger KA: Ventilator-associated bacterial pneumonia: challenges in diagnosis, treatment, and prevention. New Horizons 6:S30, 1998

11. Croce MA, Fabian TC, Schurr MJ, et al: Using bronchoalveolar lavage to distinguish nosocomial pneumonia from systemic inflammatory response syndrome: a prospective analysis. J Trauma 39:1134, 1995

12. Valles J, Artigas A, Rello J, et al: Continuous aspiration of subglottic secretions in preventing ventilator-associated pneumonia. Ann Intern Med 122:179, 1995

13. Fernandez-Crehuet R, Diaz-Molina C, de Irala J, et al: Nosocomial infection in an intensive-care unit: identification of risk factors. Infect Control Hosp Epidemiol 18:825, 1997

14. Guidelines for prevention of nosocomial pneumonia. Centers for Disease Control and Prevention. Respir Care 39:1191, 1994

15. Singh N, Rogers P, Atwood CW, et al: Short-course empiric antibiotic therapy for patients with pulmonary infiltrates in the intensive care unit: a proposed solution for indiscriminate antibiotic prescription. Am J Respir Crit Care Med 162:505, 2000

16. Caplan ES, Hoyt NJ: Nosocomial sinusitis. JAMA 247:639, 1982

17. Deutschman CS, Wilton P, Sinow J, et al: Paranasal sinusitis associated with nasotracheal intubation: a frequently unrecognized and treatable source of sepsis. Crit Care Med 14:111, 1986

18. Grindlinger GA, Niehoff J, Hughes SL, et al: Acute paranasal sinusitis related to nasotracheal intubation of head-injured patients. Crit Care Med 15:214, 1987

19. Christensen L, Schaffer S, Ross SE: Otitis media in adult trauma patients: incidence and clinical significance. J Trauma 31:1543, 1991

20. Roettinger W, Edgerton MT, Kurtz LD, et al: Role of inoculation site as a determinant of infections in soft tissue wounds. Am J Surg 126:354, 1973

21. Miles AA, Milles EM, Burke J: The value and duration of defence reactions of the skin to the primary lodgement of bacteria. Br J Exp Pathol 38:79, 1957

22. Burke JF, Miles AA: The sequence of vascular events in early infective inflammation. J Pathol Bacteriol 76:1, 1958

23. Burke JF: The effective period of preventive antibiotic action in experimental incisions and dermal lesions. Surgery 50:161, 1961

24. Alexander JW, Altemeier WA: Penicillin prophylaxis of experimental staphylococcal wound infections. Surg Gynecol Obstet 120:243, 1965

25. Edlich RF, Smith QT, Edgerton MT: Resistance of the surgical wound to antimicrobial prophylaxis and its mechanisms of development. Am J Surg 126:583, 1973

26. McKittrick LS, Wheelock FC: The routine use of antibiotics in elective abdominal surgery. Surg Gynecol Obstet 99:376, 1954

27. Barnes J, Pace WG, Trump DS, et al: Prophylactic postoperative antibiotics: a controlled study of 1007 cases. AMA Arch Surg 79:190, 1959

28. Dellinger EP, Gross PA, Barrett TL, et al: Quality standard for antimicrobial prophylaxis in surgical procedures. Clin Infect Dis 18:422, 1994

29. Page CP, Bohnen JMA, Fletcher JR, et al: Antimicrobial prophylaxis for surgical wounds: guidelines for clinical care. Arch Surg 128:79, 1993

30. Dellinger EP: Antibiotic prophylaxis in trauma: penetrating abdominal injuries and open fractures. Rev Infect Dis 13(suppl 10):S847, 1991

31. Fabian TC, Croce MA, Payne LW, et al: Duration of antibiotic therapy for penetrating abdominal trauma: a prospective trial. Surgery 112:788, 1992

32. McDonald M, Grabsch E, Marshall C, et al: Single- versus multiple-dose antimicrobial prophylaxis for major surgery: a systematic review. Aust N Z J Surg 68:388, 1988

33. Culver DH, Horan TC, Gaynes RP, et al: Surgical wound infection rates by wound class, operative procedure, and patient risk index: National Nosocomial Infections Surveillance System. Am J Med 91:152S, 1991

34. Consensus paper on the surveillance of surgical wound infections. The Society for Hospital Epidemiology of America, The Association for Practitioners in Infection Control, The Centers for Disease Control, The Surgical Infection Society. Infect Control Hosp Epidemiol 13:599, 1992

35. Gaynes RP, Culver DH, Horan TC, et al: Surgical site infection (SSI) rates in the United States, 1992-1998: the National Nosocomial Infections Surveillance System basic SSI risk index. Clin Infect Dis 33(suppl 2): S69, 2001

36. Horan TC, Gaynes RP, Martone WJ, et al: CDC definitions of nosocomial surgical site infections, 1992: a modification of CDC definitions of surgical wound infections. Am J Infect Control 20:271, 1992

37. Kurz A, Sessler DI, Lenhardt R: Perioperative normothermia to reduce the incidence of surgical-wound infection and shorten hospitalization. Study of Wound Infection and Temperature Group. N Engl J Med 334:1209, 1996

38. Greif R, Akca O, Horn EP, et al: Supplemental perioperative oxygen to reduce the incidence of surgical-wound infection. Outcomes Research Group. N Engl J Med 342:161, 2000

39. Furnary AP, Zerr KJ, Grunkemeier GL, et al: Continuous intravenous insulin infusion reduces the incidence of deep sternal wound infection in diabetic patients after cardiac surgical procedures. Ann Thorac Surg 67:352, 1999

40. Latham R, Lancaster AD, Covington JF, et al: The association of diabetes and glucose control with surgical-site infections among cardiothoracic surgery patients. Infect Control Hosp Epidemiol 22:607, 2001

41. van den Berghe G, Wouters P, Weekers F, et al:

Intensive insulin therapy in the surgical intensive care unit. N Engl J Med 345:1359, 2001

42. MacLennan JD: The histotoxic clostridial infections of man. Bacteriologic Reviews 26:177, 1962

43. Pitcher WD, Musher DM: Critical importance of early diagnosis and treatment of intra-abdominal infection. Arch Surg 117:328, 1982

44. Bohnen J, Boulanger M, Meakins JL, et al: Prognosis in generalized peritonitis: relation to cause and risk factors. Arch Surg 118:285, 1983

45. Caplan ES, Hoyt NJ, Rodriguez A, et al: Empyema occurring in the multiply traumatized patient. J Trauma 24:785, 1984

46. Milano CA, Kesler K, Archibald N, et al: Mediastinitis after coronary artery bypass graft surgery: risk factors and long-term survival. Circulation 92:2245, 1995

47. Gur E, Stern D, Weiss J, et al: Clinical-radiological evaluation of poststernotomy wound infection. Plast Reconstruct Surg 101:348, 1998

48. Pairolero PC, Arnold PG, Harris JB: Long-term results of pectoralis major muscle transposition for infected sternotomy wounds. Ann Surg 213:583, 1991

49. Hand WL, Sanford JP: Posttraumatic bacterial meningitis. Ann Intern Med 72:869, 1970

50. MacGee EE, Cauthen JC, Brackett CE: Meningitis following acute traumatic cerebrospinal fluid fistula. J Neurosurg 33:312, 1970

51. Leech PJ, Paterson A: Conservative and operative management for cerebrospinal-fluid leakage after closed head injury. Lancet 1:1013, 1973

52. Davis CH: Traumatic CSF fistula: investigation and treatment. Current Controversies in Neurosurgery. Morley TP, Ed. WB Saunders Co, Philadelphia, 1976, p 572

53. Petersdorf RG, Curtin JA, Hoeprich PD, et al: A study of antibiotic prophylaxis in unconscious patients. N Engl J Med 257:1001, 1957

54. Chapman MW, Mahoney M: The role of early internal fixation in the management of open fractures. Clin Orthop 138:120, 1979

55. Gustilo RB, Mendoza RM, Williams DN: Problems in the management of type III (severe) open fractures: a new classification of type III open fractures. J Trauma 24:742, 1984

56. Rittmann WW, Schibli M, Matter P, et al: Open fractures: long-term results in 200 consecutive cases. Clin Orthop 138:132, 1979

57. Dellinger EP, Miller SD, Wertz MJ, et al: Risk of infection after open fracture of the arm or leg. Arch Surg 123:1320, 1988

58. Sattler FR, Foderaro JB, Aber RC: Staphylococcus epidermidis bacteremia associated with vascular catheters: an important cause of febrile morbidity in hospitalized patients. Infect Control 5:279, 1984

59. Maki DG, Mermel LA: Infections due to infusion therapy. Hospital Infections, 4th ed. Bennett JV, Brachman PS, Eds. Lippincott-Raven Publishers, Philadelphia, 1998, p 689

60. Bregenzer T, Conen D, Sakmann P, et al: Is routine replacement of peripheral intravenous catheters necessary? Arch Intern Med 158:151, 1998

61. Hershey CO, Tomford JW, McLaren CE, et al: The natural history of intravenous catheter-associated phlebitis. Arch Intern Med 144:1373, 1984

62. Maki DG, Weise CE, Sarafin HW: A semiquantitative culture method for identifying intravenous-catheter-related infection. N Engl J Med 296:1305, 1977

63. Press OW, Ramsey PG, Larson EB, et al: Hickman catheter infections in patients with malignancies. Medicine (Baltimore) 63:189, 1984

64. Clarke DE, Raffin TA: Infectious complications of indwelling long-term central venous catheters. Chest 97:966, 1990

65. Maki DG, Cobb L, Garman JK, et al: An attachable silver-impregnated cuff for prevention of infection with central venous catheters: a prospective randomized multicenter trial. Am J Med 85:307, 1988

66. Conly JM, Grieves K, Peters B: A prospective, randomized study comparing transparent and dry gauze dressings for central venous catheters. J Infect Dis 159:310, 1989

67. Myers ML, Austin TW, Sibbald WJ: Pulmonary artery catheter infections: a prospective study. Ann Surg 201:237, 1985

68. Cooper GL, Hopkins CC: Rapid diagnosis of intravascular catheter-associated infection by direct Gram staining of catheter segments. N Engl J Med 312: 1142, 1985

69. Charalambos C, Swoboda SM, Dick J, et al: Risk factors and clinical impact of central line infections in the surgical intensive care unit. Arch Surg 133:1241, 1998

70. O'Grady NP, Alexander M, Dellinger EP, et al: Guidelines for the prevention of intravascular catheter-related infections. MMWR Recomm Rep 51:1, 2002

71. Sherertz RJ, Heard SO, Raad II: Diagnosis of triple-lumen catheter infection: comparison of roll plate, sonication, and flushing methodologies. J Clin Microbiol 35:641, 1997

72. Ponce de Leon S, Wenzel RP: Hospital-acquired bloodstream infections with Staphylococcus epidermidis. Am J Med 77:639, 1984

73. Rex JH, Bennett JE, Sugar AM, et al: Intravascular catheter exchange and duration of candidemia: NIAID Mycoses Study Group and the Candidemia Study Group. Clin Infect Dis 21:994, 1995

74. Mermel LA, Farr BM, Sherertz RJ, et al: Guidelines for the management of intravascular catheter-related infections. Clin Infect Dis 32:1249, 2001

75. Kaufman J, Demas C, Stark K, et al: Catheter-related septic central venous thrombosis: current therapeutic options. West J Med 145:200, 1986

76. Strinden WD, Helgerson RB, Maki DG: Candida septic thrombosis of the great central veins associated with central catheters: clinical features and management. Ann Surg 202:653, 1985

77. Cobb DK, High KP, Sawyer RG, et al: A controlled trial of scheduled replacement of central venous and pulmonary-artery catheters. N Engl J Med 327: 1062, 1992

78. Mermel LA: Prevention of intravascular catheter-related infections. Ann Intern Med 132:391, 2000

79. Cook D, Randolph A, Kernerman P, et al: Central venous catheter replacement strategies: a systematic review of the literature. Crit Care Med 25:1417, 1997

80. Reed CR, Sessler CN, Glauser FL, et al: Central venous catheter infections: concepts and controversies. Intens Care Med 21:177, 1995

81. Pettigrew RA, Lang SD, Haydock DA, et al: Catheter-related sepsis in patients on intravenous nutrition: a prospective study of quantitative catheter cultures and guidewire changes for suspected sepsis. Br J Surg 72:52, 1985

82. Newsome HH, Armstrong CW, Mayhall GC, et al: Mechanical complications from insertion of subclavian venous feeding catheters: comparison of de novo percutaneous venipuncture to change of catheter over guidewire. J Parenter Enteral Nutr 8:560, 1984

83. Sitzmann JV, Townsend TR, Siler MC, et al: Septic and technical complications of central venous catheterization: a prospective study of 200 consecutive patients. Ann Surg 202:766, 1985

84. Bozzetti F, Terno G, Bonfanti G, et al: Prevention and treatment of central venous catheter sepsis by exchange via a guidewire: a prospective controlled trial. Ann Surg 198:48, 1983

85. Norwood S, Ruby A, Civetta J, et al: Catheter-related infections and associated septicemia. Chest 99:968, 1991

86. Raad II, Hohn DC, Gilbreath BJ, et al: Prevention of central venous catheter-related infections by using maximal sterile barrier precautions during insertion. Infect Control Hosp Epidemiol 15:231, 1994

87. Sherertz RJ, Ely EW, Westbrook DM, et al: Education of physicians-in-training can decrease the risk for vascular catheter infection. Ann Intern Med 132:641, 2000

88. Richet H, Hubert B, Nitemberg G, et al: Prospective multicenter study of vascular-catheter-related complications and risk factors for positive central-catheter cultures in intensive care unit patients. J Clin Microbiol 28:2520, 1990

89. Goetz AM, Wagener MM, Miller JM, et al: Risk of infection due to central venous catheters: effect of site of placement and catheter type. Infect Control Hosp Epidemiol 19:842, 1998

90. Timsit JF, Bruneel F, Cheval C, et al: Use of tunneled femoral catheters to prevent catheter-related infection: a randomized, controlled trial. Ann Intern Med 130:729, 1999

91. Merrer J, De Jonghe B, Golliot F, et al: Complications of femoral and subclavian venous catheterization in critically ill patients: a randomized controlled trial. JAMA 286:700, 2001

92. Central venous catheters coated with minocycline and rifampin for prevention of catheter-related colonization and bloodstream infections: a randomized, double-blind trial. The Texas Medical Center Catheter Study Group. Ann Intern Med 127:267, 1997

93. Maki DG, Stolz SM, Wheeler S, et al: Prevention of central venous catheter-related bloodstream infection by use of an antiseptic-impregnated catheter: a randomized, controlled trial. Ann Intern Med 127:257, 1997

94. Darouiche RO, Raad II, Heard SO, et al: A comparison of two antimicrobial-impregnated central venous catheters. N Engl J Med 340:1, 1999

95. Maki DG, Band JD: A comparative study of polyantibiotic and iodophor ointments in prevention of vascular catheter-related infection. Am J Med 70:739, 1981

96. Hoffman KK, Weber DJ, Samsa GP, et al: Transparent polyurethane film as an intravenous catheter dressing: a meta-analysis of the infection risks. JAMA 267:2072, 1992

97. Hilton E, Haslett TM, Borenstein MT, et al: Central catheter infections: single- versus triple-lumen catheters: influence of guidewires on infection rates when used for replacement of catheters. Am J Med 84:667, 1988

98. Pemberton LB, Lyman B, Lander V, et al: Sepsis from triple- vs single-lumen catheters during total parenteral nutrition in surgical or critically ill patients. Arch Surg 121:591, 1986

99. Miller JJ, Venus B, Mathru M: Comparison of the sterility of long-term central venous catheterization using single lumen, triple lumen, and pulmonary artery catheters. Crit Care Med 12:634, 1984

100. Powell C, Fabri PJ, Kudsk KA: Risk of infection accompanying the use of single-lumen vs. double-lumen subclavian catheters: a prospective randomized study. J Parenter Enteral Nutr 12:127, 1988

101. Raad I, Davis S, Becker M, et al: Low infection rate and long durability of nontunneled Silastic catheters: a safe and cost-effective alternative for long-term venous access. Arch Intern Med 153:1791, 1993

102. Groeger JS, Lucas AB, Thaler HT, et al: Infectious morbidity associated with long-term use of venous access devices in patients with cancer. Ann Intern

Med 119:1168, 1993

103. Bern MM, Lokich JJ, Wallach SR, et al: Very low doses of warfarin can prevent thrombosis in central venous catheters: a prospective randomized trial. Ann Intern Med 112:423, 1990

104. Stark RP, Maki DG: Bacteriuria in the catheterized patient: what quantitative level of bacteriuria is relevant? N Engl J Med 311:560, 1984

105. Kunin CM: Genitourinary infections in the patient at risk: extrinsic risk factors. Am J Med 76:131, 1984

106. Harding GK, Nicolle LE, Ronald AR, et al: How long should catheter-acquired urinary tract infection in women be treated? A randomized controlled study. Ann Intern Med 114:713, 1991

107. Hirsh DD, Fainstein V, Musher DM: Do condom catheter collecting systems cause urinary tract infection? JAMA 242:340, 1979

108. Johnson ET: The condom catheter: urinary tract infection and other complications. South Med J 76: 579, 1983

109. Stamm WE: Urinary tract infections. Hospital Infections, 4th ed. Bennett JV, Brachman PS, Eds. Lippincott-Raven Publishers, Philadelphia, 1998, p 477

110. Warren JW, Platt R, Thomas RJ, et al: Antibiotic irrigation and catheter-associated urinary tract infections. N Engl J Med 299:570, 1978

111. Platt R, Polk BF, Murdock B, et al: Reduction of mortality associated with nosocomial urinary tract infection. Lancet 1:893, 1983

112. Lima NL, Guerrant RL, Kaiser DL, et al: A retrospective cohort study of nosocomial diarrhea as a risk factor for nosocomial infection. J Infect Dis 161:948, 1990

113. Jones SR, Smith JW, Sanford JP: Localization of urinary-tract infections by detection of antibody-coated bacteria in urine sediment. N Engl J Med 290:591, 1974

114. Latham RH, Stamm WE: Role of fimbriated Escherichia coli in urinary tract infections in adult women: correlation with localization studies. J Infect Dis 149:835, 1984

115. Anderson RU: Urinary tract infections in compromised hosts. Urol Clin North Am 13:727, 1986

116. Stamm WE, Stapleton AE: Approach to the patient with urinary tract infection. Infectious Disease, 2nd ed. Gorbach SL, Bartlett JG, Blacklow NR, Eds. WB Saunders Co, Philadelphia, 1998, p 943

117. DuPont HL, Ribner BS: Infectious gastroenteritis. Hospital Infections, 4th ed. Bennett JV, Brachman PS, Eds. Lippincott-Raven Publishers, Philadel-phia, 1998, p 537

118. Hines J, Nachamkin I: Effective use of the clinical microbiology laboratory for diagnosing diarrheal diseases. Clin Infect Dis 23:1292, 1996

119. Gerding DN, Johnson S, Peterson LR, et al: Clostridium difficile–associated diarrhea and colitis. Infect Control Hosp Epidemiol 16:459, 1995

120. McFarland LV, Coyle MB, Kremer WH, et al: Rectal swab cultures for Clostridium difficile surveillance studies. J Clin Microbiol 25:2241, 1987

121. George WL: Antimicrobial agent-associated colitis and diarrhea: historical background and clinical aspects. Rev Infect Dis 6:S208, 1984

122. Grube BJ, Heimbach DM, Marvin JA: Clostridium difficile diarrhea in critically ill burned patients. Arch Surg 122:655, 1987

123. Surawicz CM, Elmer GW, Speelman P, et al: Prevention of antibiotic-associated diarrhea by Saccha-romyces boulardii: a prospective study. Gastroente-rology 96:981, 1989

124. McFarland LV, Surawicz CM, Stamm WE: Risk factors for Clostridium difficile carriage and C. difficile–associated diarrhea in a cohort of hospitalized patients. J Infect Dis 162:678, 1990

125. Tedesco FJ, Corless JK, Brownstein RE: Rectal sparing in antibiotic-associated pseudomembranous colitis: a prospective study. Gastroenterology 83:1259, 1982

126. Dane TE, King EG: Fatal pseudomembranous enterocolitis following clindamycin therapy. Br J Surg 63:305, 1976

127. Cheung A, Tank RE, Dellinger EP: Antibiotic-associated enterocolitis involving the small bowel. Surgical Rounds 14:821,1991

128. Hecht JR, Olinger EJ: Clostridium difficile colitis secondary to intravenous vancomycin. Dig Dis Sci 34:148, 1989

129. Miller SN, Ringler RP: Vancomycin-induced pseudomembranous colitis (letter). J Clin Gastroenterol 9:114, 1987

130. Oliva SL, Guglielmo BJ, Jacobs R, et al: Failure of intravenous vancomycin and intravenous metronidazole to prevent or treat antibiotic-associated pseudomembranous colitis (letter). J Infect Dis 159:1154, 1989

131. Freiman JP, Graham DJ, Green L: Pseudomembranous colitis associated with single-dose cephalosporin prophylaxis (letter). JAMA 262:902, 1989

132. Gerding DN: Treatment of Clostridium difficile–associated diarrhea and colitis. Curr Top Microbiol Immunol 250:127, 2000

133. Recommendations for preventing the spread of vancomycin resistance. Hospital Infection Control Practices Advisory Committee. MMWR Morb Mortal Wkly Rep 44:1, 1995

134. Gerding DN, Olson MM, Johnson S, et al: Clostridium difficile diarrhea and colonization after treatment with abdominal infection regimens containing clindamycin or metronidazole. Am J Surg 159:212, 1990

135. Drapkin MS, Worthington MG, Chang TW, et al: Clostridium difficile colitis mimicking acute peritonitis. Arch Surg 120:1321, 1985

136. Chatila W, Manthous CA: Clostridium difficile causing sepsis and an acute abdomen in critically ill patients. Crit Care Med 23:1146, 1995

137. Byl B, Jacobs F, Struelens MJ, et al: Extraintestinal Clostridium difficile infections. Clin Infect Dis 22: 712, 1996

138. Infectious risks of blood transfusions. Transfusion Medicine Bulletin 4:1, 2001

139. Kahn RA, Barrios SDP: Diseases transmitted by blood transfusion. Transfusion Therapy: Principles and Procedures. Rutman RC, Miller WV, Eds. Aspen Publishers, Rockville, Maryland, 1985, p 311

140. Herwaldt BL, Kjemtrup AM, Conrad PA, et al: Transfusion-transmitted babesiosis in Washington State: first reported case caused by a WA1-type parasite. J Infect Dis 175:1259, 1997

141. Update: investigations of West Nile virus infections in recipients of organ transplantation and blood transfusion—Michigan, 2002. MMWR Morb Mortal Wkly Rep 51:879, 2002

142. Kuehnert MJ, Roth VR, Haley NR, et al: Transfusion-transmitted bacterial infection in the United States, 1998 through 2000. Transfusion 41:1493, 2001

143. Dodd RY, Notari EP, Stramer SL: Current prevalence and incidence of infectious disease markers and estimated window-period risk in the American Red Cross blood donor population. Transfusion 42:975, 2002

144. Cumming PD, Wallace EL, Schorr JB, et al: Exposure of patients to human immunodeficiency virus through the transfusion of blood components that test antibody-negative. N Engl J Med 321:941, 1989

145. Menitove JE: Current risk of transfusion-associated human immunodeficiency virus infection. Arch Pathol Lab Med 114:330, 1990

146. Surgenor DMacN, Wallace EL, Hao SH: Collection and transfusion of blood in the United States, 1982– 1988. N Engl J Med 322:1646, 1990

147. Hebert PC, Wells G, Blajchman MA, et al: A multicenter, randomized, controlled clinical trial of transfusion requirements in critical care. Transfusion requirements in critical care investigators, Canadian Critical Care Trials Group. N Engl J Med 340:409, 1999

148. Goldman M, Savard R, Long A, et al: Declining value of preoperative autologous donation. Transfusion 42:819, 2002

149. Garibaldi RA, Brodine S, Matsumiya S, et al: Evidence for the non-infectious etiology of early postoperative fever. Infect Control 6:273, 1985

150. Dykes MH: Unexplained postoperative fever: its value as a sign of halothane sensitization. JAMA 216: 641, 1971

151. Dellinger EP, Wertz MJ, Oreskovich MR, et al: Specificity of fever and leukocytosis after laparotomy for penetrating abdominal trauma (abstr.) J Trauma 23:633, 1983

152. Dellinger EP: Prevention and management of infections. Trauma, 2nd ed. Moore EE, Mattox KL, Feliciano DV, Eds. Appleton & Lange, Norwalk, 1988, p 231

153. Dellinger EP: Approach to the patient with postoperative fever. Infectious Diseases, 3rd ed. Gorbach S, Bartlett J, Blacklow N, Eds. WB Saunders Co, Philadelphia (in press)

154. Richards C, Emori TG, Edwards J, et al: Characteristics of hospitals and infection control professionals participating in the National Nosocomial Infections Surveillance System 1999. Am J Infect Control 29:400, 2001

155. Haley RW, Culver DH, White JW, et al: The efficacy of infection surveillance and control programs in preventing nosocomial infections in US hospitals. Am J Epidemiol 121:182, 1985

156. Haley RW, Hooton TM, Culver DH, et al: Nosocomial infections in US hospitals, 1975 to 1976: estimated frequency by selected characteristics of patients. Am J Med 70:947, 1981

157. Brennan TA, Leape LL, Laird NM, et al: Incidence of adverse events and negligence in hospitalized patients: results of the Harvard Medical Practice Study I. N Engl J Med 324:370, 1991

158. Mangram AJ, Horan TC, Pearson ML, et al: Guideline for prevention of surgical site infection, 1999. Hospital Infection Control Practices Advisory Committee. Infect Control Hosp Epidemiol 20:250, 1999

159. Horan TC, Culver DH, Gaynes RP, et al: Nosocomial infections in surgical patients in the United States, January 1986–June 1992: National Nosocomial Infections Surveillance (NNIS) System. Infect Control Hosp Epidemiol 14:73, 1993

160. Platt R, Polk BF, Murdock B, et al: Mortality associated with nosocomial urinary tract infection. N Engl J Med 307:637, 1982

161. Tambyah PA, Knasinski V, Maki DG: The direct costs of nosocomial catheter-associated urinary tract infection in the era of managed care. Infect Control Hosp Epidemiol 23:27, 2002

162. Givens CD, Wenzel RP: Catheter-associated urinary tract infections in surgical patients: a controlled study on the excess morbidity and costs. J Urol 124:646, 1980

163. Krieger JN, Kaiser DL, Wenzel RP: Nosocomial urinary tract infections cause wound infections postoperatively in surgical patients. Surg Gynecol Obstet 156:313, 1983

164. Dickinson GM, Bisno AL: Infections associated with indwelling devices: concepts of pathogenesis; infections associated with intravascular devices. Antimicrob Agents Chemother 33:597, 1989

165. Druskin MS, Siegel PD: Bacterial contamination

of indwelling intravenous polyethylene catheters. JAMA 185:966, 1963

166. Rowley KM, Clubb KS, Walker Smith GJ, et al: Right-sided infective endocarditis as a consequence of flow-directed pulmonary-artery catheterization: a clinicopathological study of 55 autopsied patients. N Engl J Med 311:1152, 1984

167. Hudson-Civetta JA, Civetta JM, Martinez OV, et al: Risk and detection of pulmonary artery catheter-related infection in septic surgical patients. Crit Care Med 15:29, 1987

168. Meakins JL: Infection associated with radial artery catheters (editorial). Can Med Assoc J 121:1564, 1979

169. Arnow PM, Costas CO: Delayed rupture of the radial artery caused by catheter-related sepsis. Rev Infect Dis 10:1035, 1988

170. Gardner RM, Schwartz R, Wong HC, et al: Percutaneous indwelling radial-artery catheters for monitoring cardiovascular function: prospective study of the risk of thrombosis and infection. N Engl J Med 290:1227, 1974

171. Band JD, Maki DG: Infections caused by arterial catheters used for hemodynamic monitoring. Am J Med 67:735, 1979

172. Kaye W, Wheaton M, Potter-Bynoe G: Radial and pulmonary artery catheter-related sepsis (abstr). Crit Care Med 11:249, 1983

173. Horan TC, White JW, Jarvis WR, et al: Nosocomial infection surveillance, 1984. CDC Surveillance Summaries. MMWR Morb Mortal Wkly Rep 35:17SS, 1986

174. National Nosocomial Infections Surveillance (NNIS) System Report, Data Summary from January 1992–June 2001, issued August 2001. Am J Infect Control 29:404, 2001

175. Vancomycin-resistant *Staphylococcus aureus*—Pennsylvania, 2002. MMWR Morb Mortal Wkly Rep 51:902, 2002

176. Stroud L, Edwards J, Danzing L, et al: Risk factors for mortality associated with enterococcal blood-stream infections. Infect Control Hosp Epidemiol 17:576, 1996

177. Recommendations for preventing the spread of vancomycin resistance: recommendations of the Hospital Infection Control Practices Advisory Committee (HICPAC). Centers for Disease Control and Prevention. MMWR Morb Mortal Wkly Rep 44(RR-12):1, 1995

178. Murray BE: What can we do about vancomycin-resistant enterococci? Clin Infect Dis 20:1134, 1995

179. Boyce JM, Pittet D: Guideline for hand hygiene in health-care settings. Recommendations of the Healthcare Infection Control Practices Advisory Committee and the HICPAC/SHEA/APIC/IDSA Hand Hygiene Task Force. Society for Healthcare Epidemiology of America/Association for Professionals in Infection Control/Infectious Diseases Society of America. MMWR Recomm Rep 51:1, 2002

180. Weinstein JW, Roe M, Towns M, et al: Resistant enterococci: a prospective study of prevalence, incidence, and factors associated with colonization in a university hospital. Infect Control Hosp Epidemiol 17:36, 1996

181. Tornieporth NG, Roberts RB, John J, et al: Risk factors associated with vancomycin-resistant *Enterococcus faecium* infection or colonization in 145 matched case patients and control patients. Clin Infect Dis 23:767, 1996

182. Rafferty ME, McCormick MI, Bopp LH, et al: Vancomycin-resistant enterococci in stool specimens submitted for *Clostridium difficile* cytotoxin assay. Infect Control Hosp Epidemiol 18:342, 1997

183. Edmond MB, Ober JF, Dawson JD, et al: Vancomycin-resistant enterococcal bacteremia: natural history and attributable mortality. Clin Infect Dis 23:1234, 1996

184. Linden PK, Pasculle AW, Manez R, et al: Differences in outcomes for patients with bacteremia due to vancomycin-resistant *Enterococcus faecium* or vancomycin-susceptible *E. faecium*. Clin Infect Dis 22:663, 1996

185. Rosenberg JM, Walker M, Welch JP, et al: *Clostridium difficile* colitis in surgical patients. Am J Surg 147:486, 1984

186. McFarland LV, Elmer GW, Stamm WE, et al: Correlation of immunoblot type, enterotoxin production, and cytotoxin production with clinical manifestations of *Clostridium difficile* infection in a cohort of hospitalized patients. Infect Immun 59:2456, 1991

187. Fekety R, Kim KH, Brown D, et al: Epidemiology of antibiotic-associated colitis: isolation of *Clostridium difficile* from the hospital environment. Am J Med 70: 906, 1981

188. McFarland LV, Mulligan ME, Kwok RY, et al: Nosocomial acquisition of *Clostridium difficile* infection. N Engl J Med 320:204, 1989

189. Struelens MJ, Maas A, Nonhoff C, et al: Control of nosocomial transmission of *Clostridium difficile* based on sporadic case surveillance. Am J Med 91(suppl 3B):138S, 1991

190. Martone WJ, Jarvis WR, Edwards JR, et al: Incidence and nature of endemic and epidemic nosocomial infections. Hospital Infections, 4th ed. Bennett JV, Brachman PS, Eds. Lippincott-Raven, Philadelphia, 1998, p 461

191. Britt MR, Schleupner CJ, Matsumiya S: Severity of underlying disease as a predictor of nosocomial infection: utility in the control of nosocomial infection. JAMA 239:1047, 1978

192. Wenzel RP, Thompson RL, Landry SM, et al: Hospital-acquired infections in intensive care unit patients: an overview with emphasis on epidemics. Infect Control 4:371, 1983

Acknowledgments

Figures 1 and 2   Carol Donner.
Figure 4   Albert Miller.

132 POSTOPERATIVE AND VENTILATOR-ASSOCIATED PNEUMONIA

Craig M. Coopersmith, M.D., F.A.C.S., and Marin H. Kollef, M.D.

Pulmonary complications are common after surgical procedures, accounting for nearly one of every four deaths that occur in the first postoperative week.[1] Overall, pneumonia is the third most common postoperative infection, after urinary tract infection and surgical site infection.[2] In critically ill patients, however, the respiratory tract is the most common site of nosocomial infection[3]: in the intensive care unit, pneumonia accounts for 28% to 47% of all nosocomial infections.[4,5]

In discussing pneumonia occurring in surgical patients after operation, it is useful to distinguish between postoperative pneumonia and ventilator-associated pneumonia (VAP). Throughout this chapter, we make this distinction where appropriate [*see* Incidence and Risk Factors *and* Diagnosis, *below*].

Pathogenesis

Under basal conditions, the lower respiratory tract is sterile. Thus, for pneumonia to develop, bacteria must be introduced into the lungs, typically by being aspirated from either the upper respiratory tract or the gastrointestinal tract. This introduction of bacteria is generally associated with impairment of host defenses, both locally and systemically.

A leading hypothesis regarding the pathogenesis of VAP is that the oropharynx is overgrown by microbes, which subsequently are aspirated into the lungs and colonize the airway.[6] This hypothesis is supported by the observation that whereas enteric gram-negative bacteria are absent from the oropharynx under basal conditions, they can be detected in the oropharynx in nearly 75% of critically ill patients.[7] Upper airway colonization by enteric bacteria occurs in 45% to 100% of intubated patients. Besides being colonized by aspirated endogenous flora, the airways may be colonized by exogenous flora as a result of cross-contamination from other ICU patients (through inadvertent transmission by health care workers).

A complementary hypothesis is that the upper GI tract plays a critical role in the pathogenesis of VAP. According to this view, the stomach is a primary site of colonization that may subsequently infect the lung through retrograde movement of bacterial overgrowth, followed by aspiration of organisms from the oropharynx. The small decrease in mortality seen in certain ICU patient populations who undergo selective decontamination of the digestive tract (SDD) supports the possibility that endogenous gut flora plays a role in the pathogenesis of VAP, though this possibility remains controversial.[8] Chronic infection of biofilms in an endotracheal tube may also play a role in the pathogenesis of VAP.[9] Either suctioning or performing bronchoscopy in a patient with a biofilm may result in distal embolization of bacteria. The importance of biofilms in this setting, however, remains to be fully determined.

Incidence and Risk Factors

For an accurate assessment of the incidence of and risk factors for pneumonia in postoperative patients, it is helpful to consider postoperative pneumonia separately from VAP. Postoperative VAP, by definition, occurs in a patient who has undergone a surgical procedure and is on mechanical ventilation for longer than 48 to 72 hours; however, not every patient who acquires pneumonia after an operation is on a ventilator or in the ICU. The severity of an episode of pneumonia and its ultimate outcome are at least partially related to the comorbid conditions present; therefore, a surgical ICU patient with multiple organ dysfunction typically has a worse prognosis than a patient who acquires pneumonia while recovering from an operation on the surgical ward.

POSTOPERATIVE PNEUMONIA

A wide-ranging assessment of pneumonia in the postoperative setting was provided by a retrospective review of 160,805 patients who underwent major noncardiac surgical procedures at 100 Veterans Affairs Medical Centers between 1997 and 1999.[2] Pneumonia was diagnosed in a total of 2,466 (1.5%) of the 160,805 patients. The 30-day mortality was 21% in patients who experienced postoperative pneumonia and 2% in those who did not. Multivariate analysis identified several risk factors that led to an increased risk of postoperative pneumonia, including type of surgery, age, functional status, recent weight loss, chronic obstructive pulmonary disease (COPD), type of anesthesia, impaired sensorium, history of a cerebrovascular accident, blood urea nitrogen (BUN) level, substantial transfusion, emergency surgical intervention, long-term steroid use, recent smoking, and significant recent alcohol use [*see Table 1*]. This review represents by far the most substantial effort yet made to quantify the incidence and risk factors of postoperative infections. However, it has two major limitations: (1) it was retrospective rather than prospective, and (2) more than 95% of the patients involved in the study were male.

VENTILATOR-ASSOCIATED PNEUMONIA

In contrast to postoperative pneumonia, VAP has been the subject of a good deal of epidemiologic study, though to date, surgical patients have made up only a subset of the patients studied. The reported overall incidence of VAP in ICU patients varies widely among published studies, ranging from 1 to more than 20 cases per 1,000 ventilator days[4,10]; the average incidence across the various studies is approximately 7 cases per 1,000 ventilator days.[6] Although VAP can occur in any patient undergoing mechanical ventilation, it is substantially more common in surgical ICU patients than in medical ICU patients, reaching its highest prevalences in trauma, neurosurgical, surgical, and burn ICUs. As an example of how VAP disproportionately affects surgical patients, ventilator usage in trauma ICUs is nearly identical to that in respiratory ICUs (0.58 versus 0.57 ventila-

Table 1 Preoperative Predictors of
Postoperative Pneumonia[2]

Predictor	Odds Ratio (95% CI)
Type of surgical procedure	
AAA repair	4.29 (3.34–5.50)
Thoracic	3.92 (3.36–4.57)
Upper abdominal	2.68 (2.38–3.03)
Neck	2.30 (1.73–3.05)
Neurologic	2.14 (1.66–2.75)
Vascular	1.29 (1.10–1.52)
Other	1.00 (referent)
Age	
80 yr	5.63 (4.62–6.84)
70–79 yr	3.58 (2.97–4.33)
60–69 yr	2.38 (1.98–2.87)
50–59 yr	1.49 (1.23–1.81)
< 50 yr	1.00 (referent)
Functional status	
Totally dependent	2.83 (2.33–3.43)
Partially dependent	1.83 (1.63–2.06)
Independent	1.00 (referent)
Weight loss > 10% in past 6 mo	1.92 (1.68–2.18)
History of COPD	1.72 (1.55–1.91)
Type of anesthesia	
General	1.56 (1.36–1.80)
Spinal, monitored, or other	1.00 (referent)
Impaired sensorium	1.51 (1.26–1.82)
History of cerebrovascular accident	1.47 (1.28–1.68)
BUN level	
< 2.86 mmol/L (< 8 mg/dl)	1.47 (1.26–1.72)
2.86–7.50 mmol/L (8–21 mg/dl)	1.00 (referent)
7.85–10.70 mmol/L (22–30 mg/dl)	1.24 (1.11–1.39)
10.70 mmol/L (30 mg/dl)	1.41 (1.22–1.64)
Transfusion > 4 units	1.35 (1.07–1.72)
Emergency operative intervention	1.33 (1.16–1.54)
Use of steroids for chronic condition	1.33 (1.12–1.58)
Current smoker within 1 yr	1.28 (1.17–1.42)
Alcohol intake > 2 drinks/day in past 2 wk	1.24 (1.08–1.42)

tor days/patient days), but VAP develops nearly four times as often in the former as in the latter (15.1 versus 4.2 cases per 1,000 ventilator days).[11] It should be remembered, however, that patients in respiratory ICUs may have already had an episode of pneumonia while in the hospital, which may make diagnosis of secondary VAP more difficult in this population.

The single greatest risk factor for VAP is related to the duration of mechanical ventilation. The risk peaks at day 5 on the ventilator, plateaus after day 15, and then declines significantly, with the result that VAP is uncommon in patients on long-term mechanical ventilation.[6,12] Other risk factors associated with the development of VAP are trauma, thermal injury, male gender, increased age, acute lung injury, and greater severity of illness.[12,13]

The absolute mortality in VAP patients ranges from 12% to more than 50%, with a substantially lower crude mortality in surgical patients than in medical patients.[14,15] The attributable mor-

tality associated with VAP has not been determined with certainty: estimates range from no increased risk of death to a relative risk increase of 3.6.[6,13,15] Attributable mortality is especially difficult to establish in patients with ARDS, though one study of 11 predominantly medical ICUs in France found that mortality in ARDS patients was not appreciably affected by whether they had VAP.[16]

Studies that demonstrate an increased relative risk of death with VAP frequently also demonstrate an increased prevalence of resistant organisms (e.g., *Pseudomonas aeruginosa* and *Acinetobacter baumanii*).[17] VAP patients as a group remain in the ICU approximately 6 days longer than comparable patients without VAP and incur more than $40,000 in additional charges.[13,15] When the subgroup of surgical patients is considered on its own, however, the increase in length of stay in the ICU is closer to 1 day,[13] and the increase in hospital charges is almost certainly smaller (though still substantial).

Diagnosis

Pneumonia is commonly defined as distal air-space inflammation caused by microorganisms or products of microorganisms.[6] Although this definition is simple, diagnosis of pneumonia is often complex, for two reasons. First, it is frequently difficult to isolate microorganisms from the lower respiratory tract, even if the patient has an active infection. Second, in the unlikely circumstance that a patient undergoes an open lung biopsy that demonstrates inflammation, this finding does not indicate that pneumonia is present, because there are a number of noninfectious insults that can result in both local and systemic inflammation.

DIAGNOSTIC CRITERIA

Postoperative Pneumonia

Most postoperative fevers are of noninfectious origin, and even when an elevated temperature and an increased white blood cell (WBC) count result from an infection, pneumonia still is not the most likely diagnosis. It is therefore critical to establish objective criteria for diagnosing pneumonia after a surgical procedure. Of the several different diagnostic approaches that have been formulated, one of the more popular uses a combination of clinical and radiographic criteria to diagnose pneumonia in nonventilated postoperative patients [*see Table 2*].[2,18] Typically, in a surgical ward patient, the diagnosis requires either new onset of purulent sputum or a change in the character of the sputum in combination with a worsening chest x-ray that demonstrates either new or progressive infiltrate or consolidation.

Ventilator-Associated Pneumonia

Diagnosing VAP is more complicated than diagnosing postoperative pneumonia in a patient on the surgical ward, though with invasive quantitative cultures, it may be possible to make the diagnosis more accurately in a ventilated patient. In ICU patients, as in surgical ward patients, fever and leukocytosis are very common and are frequently of noninfectious origin. Unlike surgical ward patients, however, ICU patients often have chronically purulent secretions and abnormal chest x-rays that are not representative of pneumonia.[19] There is no absolute gold standard for diagnosing VAP, and attempts to define VAP objectively for surveillance purposes have so far failed to reach any resolution.[6] In addition to fever, leukocytosis, increased or changed sputum production, and an abnormal chest x-ray, indicators used to diagnose VAP may include sputum culture, the clinical pulmonary infection score (CPIS), and (less commonly) pleural fluid culture or open lung biopsy.[20,21]

Table 2 Criteria* for Definition of Postoperative Pneumonia[2]

Rales or dullness to percussion on physical examination of chest AND any of the following:

  New onset of purulent sputum or change in character of sputum

  Isolation of organism from blood culture

  Isolation of pathogen from specimen obtained by transtracheal aspiration, bronchial brushing, or biopsy

Chest radiography showing new or progressive infiltrate, consolidation, cavitation, or pleural effusion AND any of the following:

  New onset of purulent sputum or change in character of sputum

  Isolation of organism from blood culture

  Isolation of pathogen from specimen obtained by transtracheal aspiration, bronchial brushing, or biopsy

  Isolation of virus or detection of viral antigen in respiratory secretions

  Diagnostic single antibody titer (IgM) or fourfold increase in paired serum samples (IgG) for pathogen

  Histopathologic evidence of pneumonia

---

*Only one criterion need be fulfilled to establish the diagnosis.

INVASIVE AND NONINVASIVE CULTURES

Samples for sputum culture may be obtained either noninvasively, via tracheal aspiration, or invasively, via bronchoscopy with either bronchoalveolar lavage (BAL) or a protected specimen brush (PSB). Tracheal cultures, though commonly employed, overestimate the rate of VAP and fail to diagnose some occurrences of pneumonia documented by postmortem pathologic study of the lung[20,22]; these failings persist even when quantitative cultures are used. Moreover, the threshold used for documenting VAP with tracheal cultures changes both the sensitivity and the specificity of the test. In one study, reducing this threshold from 10^6 to 10^5 colony-forming units (cfu)/ml increased sensitivity from 55% to 63% while decreasing specificity from 85% to 75%, as determined by comparison with postmortem specimens in a sample of 28 patients who died within 3 days after culture.[23]

Invasive sampling is significantly more accurate than tracheal aspiration in diagnosing VAP. Both BAL and PSB have sensitivities and specificities higher than 80% [see Table 3].[23,24] A study involving 22 patients with suspected VAP who had five samples taken from the same site during the same bronchoscopy procedure found that the two techniques yielded similar results.[25] In this study, PSB isolated the same organisms each time, but quantitation with BAL varied within one log 59% of the time, leading to a change in diagnosis (from presence to absence of pneumonia or vice versa) in 13% of cases.

It must be noted that simply placing a bronchoscope through an endotracheal tube or a tracheostomy and obtaining a sample is still essentially tracheal aspiration, not BAL. As noted (see above), pneumonia is defined as the presence of microorganisms in the distal airways; thus, obtaining a sample from the proximal airways (even if access is obtained with a bronchoscope), though it can provide information about the microbial content of the proximal airways, suffers from the same limitations that obtaining a culture with a catheter placed down the endotracheal tube does.

Techniques for performing BAL vary somewhat among institutions. Generally, however, the bronchoscope is wedged in the most distal airway in the lobe of interest before cultures are obtained, and a 20 or 50 ml aliquot of normal saline is lavaged, returned, and discarded. Another aliquot of normal saline is then lavaged, and the returned fluid is sent off for quantitative culture.

Using invasive sampling techniques to obtain a diagnosis is especially important in trauma patients, who often have fever, leukocytosis, purulent sputum, and radiographic abnormalities as a consequence of the systemic inflammatory response syndrome (SIRS). A study of 43 trauma patients exhibiting all these symptoms and signs who underwent BAL found that 20 had culture results consistent with VAP, whereas 23 had bacterial growth amounting to fewer than 10^5 cfu/ml.[26] Antibiotics were stopped after culture results in all patients with low or no bacterial growth (average, 3.3 days); 65% of patients showed improvement after discontinuance of antibiotics, and there was no difference in mortality between the SIRS group and the VAP group. These findings highlight the need to obtain invasive cultures in the trauma setting, in that a high percentage of the patients in this study would have been incorrectly diagnosed as having pneumonia on clinical grounds alone.

Several nonbronchoscopic quantitative sampling techniques are now available, including mini-BAL and blind sampling PSB.[27,28] These techniques involve blind passage of a catheter or telescoping catheters to a wedged position in the lung.[20] Both mini-BAL and blind sampling PSB are slightly less accurate than their bronchoscopic counterparts, with sensitivities ranging from 58% to 100% and specificities ranging from 66% to 100%.[6] In addition, these techniques may miss unilateral left-side pneumonia, presumably because blind insertion is more likely to result in wedging of the catheter in the right lung.

Regardless of the culture technique used, previous antibiotic therapy can reduce the chances of obtaining a positive culture. The determining factor appears to be the duration of such therapy. Initiation of antibiotic therapy within the preceding 24 hours decreases the chances of obtaining a positive culture and reduces the number of microorganisms recovered, though these effects are less pronounced with BAL than with other diagnostic techniques[6]; however, in patients who have been receiving antibiotics for more than 72 hours, the sensitivity and specificity of BAL and PSB for the diagnosis of pneumonia are largely unaffected.[29,30] These findings have clear implications for treating pneumonia in postoperative patients. Specifically, cultures should be accurate in a patient who is in the middle of a 1-week antibiotic course for complicated intra-abdomi-

---

Table 3 Diagnostic Techniques Used in Diagnosis of VAP[20]

Diagnostic Technique	Sensitivity (%)	Specificity (%)	Positive Predictive Value (%)	Negative Predictive Value (%)
PSB cultures (10^3 cfu/ml)	82	89	90	89
BAL cultures (10^4 cfu/ml)	91	78	83	87
Microscopic examination of BAL fluid (5% intracellular organisms)	91	89	91	89

nal infection, but starting antibiotic therapy immediately before obtaining a culture for suspected VAP will adversely affect the ability of the surgeon to diagnose this condition.

CLINICAL PULMONARY INFECTION SCORE

The CPIS quantifies a number of clinical findings suggestive of pneumonia—temperature, WBC count, tracheal secretions, tracheal cultures, oxygenation, chest x-rays, and the presence of and progression of infiltrates on x-rays—in an attempt to diagnose pneumonia noninvasively [see Table 4].[21] A CPIS higher than 6 is associated with a high likelihood of pneumonia, and there is a clear correlation between a high CPIS and a high concentration of bacteria found with invasive culture techniques.[31] The main use of the CPIS is as a method of defining the probability of pneumonia in a given patient that is more objective than clinical judgment alone. A patient with a low CPIS probably need not be treated for pneumonia, whereas one with a high CPIS is likely to benefit from invasive culturing, followed by rapid institution of broad-spectrum antibiotic therapy. The main drawbacks of the CPIS are (1) that all of its elements are weighted equally (for example, the presence of an infiltrate is given the same weight as a WBC count of 11,000/mm³, even though it is substantially more suggestive of pneumonia) and (2) that assessment of chest x-rays and sputum production is necessarily subjective, meaning that an equivocal CPIS could lead to an inappropriate treatment decision.

OTHER MODALITIES FOR DIAGNOSING VAP

Although the use of invasive culture methods in conjunction with clinical judgment is the most common approach to diagnosing VAP, there are rare circumstances in which other diagnostic modalities may be useful.[20] The most likely surgical situation in which pneumonia might be diagnosed without invasive cultures involves a patient with empyema in whom a positive purulent fluid culture is obtained at the time of either chest tube placement or thoracocentesis. Histopathologic examination of tissue obtained at open lung biopsy that demonstrates the presence of both bacteria and inflammation is diagnostic of VAP. Rapid cavitation of a pulmonary infiltrate in a patient who has a negative workup for both cancer and tuberculosis, though extremely uncommon after operation, is likely to represent pneumonia when it does occur in this setting.

Management

IDENTIFICATION OF PATHOGENS

For effective treatment of pneumonia in the postoperative patient, it is critical to know which organism or organisms are causing the disease. Overall, pneumonia in ICU patients is more frequently caused by gram-negative bacteria than by gram-positive bacteria [see Table 5]. The most commonly isolated gram-negative pathogen is P. aeruginosa, and the most commonly isolated gram-positive pathogen is Staphylococcus aureus.[13,32]

It is important to note that the microbes isolated in the first 3 to 4 days of an ICU stay are dramatically different from those isolated later.[6] The pathogens found early (e.g., S. aureus, Haemophilus influenzae, and Streptococcus pneumoniae) are typically sensitive to many classes of antibiotics, whereas the pathogens identified later (e.g., P. aeruginosa, A. baumanii, methicillin-resistant S. aureus [MRSA], and Stenotrophomonas maltophilia) are more likely to be resistant. In a large United States database, S. aureus was the most commonly isolated organism in patients whose VAP was identified during the first 4 days of mechanical ventilation, P. aeruginosa in patients whose VAP was identified after the first 4 days of ventilation (23.7% and 19.7%,

Table 4 Calculation of Clinical Pulmonary Infection Score[6]

Variable	Finding	Points
Temperature (°C)	36.5 and ≤ 38.4	0
	38.5 and ≤ 38.9	1
	39 or ≤ 36	2
Blood leukocytes (No./mm³)	4,000 and ≤ 11,000	0
	< 4,000 or > 11,000	1
	Plus band forms 50%	Add 1
Tracheal secretions	Absent	0
	Nonpurulent secretions present	1
	Purulent secretions present	2
Oxygenation (P$_a$O$_2$/F$_I$O$_2$)	> 240 or ARDS*	0
	≤ 240 and no ARDS	2
Pulmonary radiography	No infiltrate	0
	Diffuse (or patchy) infiltrate	1
	Localized infiltrate	2
Progression of pulmonary infiltrate	No radiographic progression	0
	Radiographic progression (after CHF and ARDS excluded)	2
Culture of tracheal aspirate	Pathogenic bacteria cultured in very low to low quantity or not at all	0
	Pathogenic bacteria cultured in moderate or high quantity	1
	Same pathogenic bacteria seen on Gram stain	Add 1

*Defined as P$_a$O$_2$/F$_I$O$_2$ 200 and PAWP ≤ 18 mm Hg, with acute bilateral infiltrates. ARDS—acute respiratory distress syndrome CHF—congestive heart failure F$_I$O$_2$—fraction of inspired oxygen P$_a$O$_2$—arterial oxygen tension PAWP—pulmonary arterial wedge pressure

respectively).[13] In more than 50% of VAP cases, more than one organism is isolated.[24] Isolation of an organism, in itself, does not establish the diagnosis of pneumonia, and colonization can occur at any time during the course of mechanical ventilation. It is crucial to distinguish infection from colonization: the former calls for aggressive antimicrobial therapy, and the latter need not be treated at all—in fact, inappropriate use of antibiotics to treat colonization may adversely affect outcome. A study of 26 patients undergoing mechanical ventilation demonstrated that 22 were colonized by at least a single bacterial strain during their ICU stay, with 16 being colonized within 5 days after intubation.[33] Of these 22 patients, 21 were colonized by aerobes and 15 by anaerobes, and five went on to acquire VAP (three with aerobic pathogens, two with anaerobic pathogens).

The role of anaerobes in VAP is controversial[33,34]: although they may represent as many as 23% of the isolated strains in patients with VAP (typically in early-onset cases in which aspiration was witnessed), their presence is not associated with an increase in mortality,[35] and there is no evidence that antianaerobic therapy changes outcomes in patients with VAP.

The role played by so-called commensal bacteria in the normally sterile lower respiratory tract is also unclear. Approximately 50% of isolates from ventilated patients are from bacterial species that are believed to be nonpathogenic except in immunocompromised patients; however, the significance of commensal bacteria in the airways of immunocompetent patients is unknown. The possible importance of commensal bacteria in the lower respiratory tract was highlighted by a study of 369 patients with VAP, a group comprising all patients diagnosed with the disease over a 10-year period in a mixed medical/surgical ICU.[36] The investigators identified 23 cases of VAP (through a combination of PSB and clinical signs) as resulting from a monomicrobial infection involving an organism typically considered to be commensal (most commonly, non–β-hemolytic *Streptococcus*, *Neisseria* species, and coagulase-negative *S. aureus*). Because the idea that commensal bacteria could cause VAP was, and is, controversial, the diagnosis was reported only if agreed on by three independent experts. Mortality in these patients was not different from that in patients without VAP. At present, the importance of commensal bacteria in the pathogenesis of VAP remains undetermined.

ANTIMICROBIAL THERAPY

Importance of Rapid Initial Treatment

The cornerstone of therapy for hospital-acquired pneumonia is rapid institution of an appropriate broad-spectrum antibiotic regimen. Appropriate initial antimicrobial treatment is typically defined as an antibiotic regimen that is known to possess in vitro activity against the identified bacterial species.

The importance of rapid institution of appropriate antibiotic therapy has been highlighted in a number of trials involving postoperative patients. In one such trial, a group of 65 patients in a medical/surgical ICU who had positive BAL cultures and were diagnosed with VAP were retrospectively subdivided into a group that received adequate antibiotic therapy at the time of bronchoscopy and a group that received inadequate therapy.[37] Mortality in the adequate-therapy group was 38%, but that in the inadequate-therapy group was 91%. Similar results, albeit with substantially lower mortalities, were obtained in a study from a different medical/surgical ICU involving 113 patients with VAP diagnosed by means of either PSB or BAL.[38] Patients receiving inadequate initial antimicrobial therapy had a mortality of 37%, whereas those receiving adequate therapy had a mortality of only 15%.

A link between adequate initial antimicrobial therapy and mortality was also documented in a study of 2,000 consecutive ICU patients, including 793 surgical ICU patients.[39] In more than 60% of the 655 patients with documented infections, the respiratory tract was the source of the infection. Of the 655 infected patients, 210 had previously been operated on. Infection-related mortality was 42% in infected patients who initially received inadequate antimicrobial therapy, compared with 18% in those who received adequate therapy. Using a logistic regression model, the investigators found inadequate institution of antibiotic therapy to be the single most important independent determinant of hospital mortality.

At present, there are no data from surgical populations on the impact of delayed initiation of appropriate antimicrobial therapy; however, the findings of one study from a medical ICU suggest that this is not an effective strategy for preventing mortality caused by initial selection of inadequate antibiotics.[40] In this study, 107 consecutive ICU patients with VAP, all of whom were treated with appropriate antimicrobial therapy, were followed prospectively. Of these patients, 31% experienced delays longer than 24 hours in receiving antimicrobial therapy, almost always because of delays in order writing. The mean time to initiation of antibiotic therapy was 28.6 hours in this group, compared with 12.5 hours in the control group (in whom antimicrobial therapy was initiated in a timely manner). Even though all of the patients in this study received appropriate antimicrobial treatment, mortality differed dramatically between the delayed-initiation group and the control group. VAP-attributable mortality was 39.4% in the former group, compared with 10.8% in the latter. Logistic regression analysis identified delayed initiation of antibiotics as a major independent risk factor for hospital mortality.

Choice of Appropriate Antibiotic

When pneumonia is suspected on the basis of clinical and radiographic signs, there is no way of knowing precisely which bacteria are causing the disease, and culture results usually are not available until 2 to 3 days after a specimen is obtained. In the current era of increasing antibiotic resistance, it is critical to provide broad initial coverage of both sensitive and resistant microorganisms. Because resistance patterns vary among countries, among institutions, and even among ICUs within a single hospital, what constitutes adequate initial antibiotic therapy may be country specific, institution specific, or even ICU specific.

The makeup of the flora causing nosocomial infection tends to evolve as a patient's hospitalization proceeds, with bacterial resistance increasing in the later stages, and this evolution must be taken into account in prescribing the initial antibiotic regimen. Several other factors must be considered as well: (1) the hospital-specific (or, if available, ICU-specific) antibiogram documenting antibiotic resistance, (2) key patient-specific characteristics (for example, an immunosuppressed liver transplant patient may be susceptible to microorganisms that a previously healthy trauma patient would not be), and (3) the efficacy, toxicity, and lung penetration of the antibiotics. If an antibiotic has poor lung penetration (as is the case with vancomycin and the aminoglycosides), a higher dosage may be needed for treatment of VAP than for treatment of other conditions. In addi-

Table 5 **Most Common Pathogens Isolated from Pneumonia Patients in Different Types of ICUs**[32]

Pathogen	Type of ICU					
	Burn [No. (%)]	Cardiothoracic [No. (%)]	Medical/Surgical [No. (%)]	Neurosurgical [No. (%)]	General Surgical [No. (%)]	Trauma [No. (%)]
Enterobacter species	51 (8.0)	375 (13.1)	1,022 (10.6)	257 (10.5)	1,557 (12.8)	281 (13.4)
Escherichia coli	21 (3.4)	139 (4.8)	402 (4.1)	112 (4.6)	593 (4.9)	93 (4.4)
Klebsiella pneumoniae	34 (5.3)	169 (5.9)	720 (7.4)	182 (7.5)	878 (7.2)	146 (7.0)
Haemophilus influenzae	42 (6.6)	165 (5.8)	340 (3.5)	181 (7.4)	532 (4.4)	155 (7.4)
Pseudomonas aeruginosa	137 (21.5)	375 (13.1)	1,507 (15.5)	294 (12.1)	2,087 (17.2)	360 (17.1)
Staphylococcus aureus	157 (24.7)	326 (11.3)	1,750 (18.0)	527 (21.6)	2,065 (17.0)	379 (18.1)
Enterococcus species	12 (1.9)	66 (2.3)	177 (1.8)	32 (1.3)	215 (1.8)	24 (1.1)
Candida albicans	18 (2.8)	180 (6.3)	592 (6.1)	104 (4.3)	468 (3.9)	32 (1.5)
All others	164 (25.8)	1,073 (37.4)	3,197 (33.0)	749 (30.7)	3,759 (30.9)	626 (29.9)

Table 6 Initial Empirical Therapy for Hospital-Acquired Pneumonia, VAP, and Health Care–Associated Pneumonia in Patients with Late-Onset Disease or Risk Factors for Multidrug-Resistant Pathogens[41]

Potential Pathogens	Combination Antibiotic Regimen	Initial Dosage*

Streptococcus pneumoniae
Haemophilus influenzae
Methicillin-sensitive *Staphylococcus aureus*
Antibiotic-sensitive enteric gram-negative bacilli
  Escherichia coli
  Klebsiella pneumoniae
  Enterobacter species
  Proteus species
  Serratia marcescens
Multidrug-resistant pathogens
  Pseudomonas aeruginosa
  K. pneumoniae (ESBL+)†
  Acinetobacter species†
	Antipseudomonal cephalosporin
	
	or
	
	Antipseudomonal carbapenem
	
	or
	
	β-Lactam/β-lactamase inhibitor
	
	plus
	Antipseudomonal fluoroquinolone
	
	or
	
	Aminoglycoside
		Cefepime, 1–2 g q. 8–12 hr
		Ceftazidime, 2 g q. 8 hr
		
		Imipenem, 500 mg q. 6 hr *or* 1 g q. 8 hr
		Meropenem, 1 g q. 8 hr
		
		Piperacillin-tazobactam, 4.5 g q. 6 hr
		
		Levofloxacin, 750 mg/day
		Ciprofloxacin, 400 mg q. 8 hr
		
		Gentamicin, 7 mg/kg/day¶
		Tobramycin, 7 mg/kg/day¶
		Amikacin, 20 mg/kg/day‖

MRSA *Legionella pneumophila*‡	*plus* Vancomycin or linezolid§	Vancomycin, 15 mg/kg q. 12 hr** Linezolid, 600 mg q. 12 hr

* Dosage recommendations assume normal renal and hepatic function. Initial dosages should be adjusted or streamlined in accordance with microbiologic data and clinical response to therapy.
†If an ESBL+ strain or *Acinetobacter* is suspected, a carbapenem is recommended.
‡If *Legionella* is suspected, a macrolide or a fluoroquinolone is preferable to an aminoglycoside.
§Indicated if there are risk factors for MRSA or local incidence of MRSA is high.
¶Trough levels should be < 1 μg/ml.
‖Trough levels should be < 4–5 μg/ml.
**Trough levels should be 15–20 μg/ml.
ESBL—extended-spectrum β-lactamase   MRSA—methicillin-resistant *S. aureus*

tion, when different classes of drugs possess similar efficacy, those with higher side-effect profiles (e.g., aminoglycosides) should not be used as primary monotherapy.

As a rule, initial antibiotic treatment decisions must be tailored to local antibiograms. In 2005, however, the American Thoracic Society and the Infectious Diseases Society of America published consensus recommendations that outlined an evidence-based strategy for initiating antimicrobial therapy in patients with suspected VAP.[41] Patients with early-onset postoperative pneumonia or VAP who have no risk factors for multidrug-resistant pathogens may be treated with ceftriaxone, a quinolone (ciprofloxacin, levofloxacin, or moxifloxacin), ampicillin-sulbactam, or ertapenem. In contrast, patients with late-onset postoperative pneumonia or VAP and those with risk factors for multidrug-resistant organisms must be treated more aggressively. They should be started on combination therapy for gram-negative infections and should receive agents that provide broad coverage of gram-positive infections [*see Table 6*].

Gram-positive infections The optimal initial antibiotic regimen for gram-positive infections has not been established. A number of antibiotics can effectively treat infections caused by sensitive gram-positive organisms, but the options for treating infections caused by MRSA are limited. Historically, MRSA infection has been treated with vancomycin because no other commonly used antibiotic has been effective. Unfortunately, vancomycin has relatively poor lung penetration. For this reason, linezolid has been proposed as an alternative therapy for nosocomial pneumonia. Two prospective, randomized, multicenter trials comparing vancomycin with linezolid for the treatment of nosocomial pneumonia found the two agents to have similar clinical cure rates and microbiologic success rates in all of the patients studied, suggesting that these agents will be equally effective in the typical patient with gram-positive nosocomial pneumonia.[42,43]

Two retrospective analyses pooled patients from the two trials just mentioned (see above), comparing vancomycin to linezolid in a subset of patients with MRSA nosocomial pneumonia[44] and in a smaller subset comprising patients with VAP from MRSA.[45] Both analyses demonstrated significantly improved survival and clinical cure rates in patients treated with linezolid. In the 160 patients with MRSA nosocomial pneumonia, treatment with linezolid was associated with an increase in the Kaplan-Meier survival rate from 63.5% to 80.0% and an increase in the clinical cure rate from 35.5% to 59.0%.[44] In the 91 patients with VAP from MRSA, logistic regression analysis showed that treatment with linezolid was an independent predictor of survival (odds ratio, 4.6) and clinical cure (odds ratio, 20.0). In contrast, a study comparing vancomycin with quinupristin-dalfopristin found the two drugs to have similar cure rates both in nosocomial pneumonia patients as a whole and in a subset of patients with MRSA pneumonia.[46] Although the favorable linezolid results are obviously limited by the fact that they derive from retrospective analyses of data pooled from two studies, they do raise the question of whether linezolid should be the antibiotic of choice in patients with MRSA pneumonia. If vancomycin is used to treat MRSA, it should be given in an initial dose of 15 mg/kg, and trough levels should be maintained between 15 and 20 μg/ml.[41]

Gram-negative infections The optimal initial antibiotic regimen for gram-negative infection involves starting the patient on combination therapy until culture results can be obtained. Options commonly employed include an antipseudomonal penicillin with a β-lactamase inhibitor, an antipseudomonal cephalosporin, or an antipseudomonal carbapenem combined with either an antipseudomonal fluoroquinolone or an aminoglycoside. If the patient has recently received antimicrobial therapy, the initial antibiotic regimen for VAP should employ a different class of antibiotic so as to avoid the risk of microbial resistance induced by previous antibiotic use.

A prospective study of 156 patients with VAP in two medical/surgical ICUs showed that treatment with antipseudomonal penicillin with β-lactamase inhibitors yielded better outcomes than treatment with cephalosporins, fluoroquinolones, or aminoglycosides (carbapenems were not given as first-line therapy).[47] The concept that even within the bounds of what constitutes appropriate initial antibiotic therapy there may be a single "most appropriate" antibiotic is intriguing and worthy of further study. At present, however, no single antibiotic class can be recommended over the others as optimal treatment of gram-negative infections.

Rotation of Antibiotics

VAP developing later in a patient's ICU stay is more likely to be caused by resistant organisms. An increase in resistant organisms is associated with an increased relative risk of death in patients with VAP.[17] Furthermore, patients who are isolated for infection control purposes because of MRSA experience more preventable adverse events and receive less documented care.[48] Accordingly, scheduled rotation of antibiotics on a protocol basis has been proposed as a technique for hindering the emergence of resistant organisms by manipulating prevailing antibiotic pressures in the hospital environment.[49,50]

Antibiotic rotation has been studied in both surgical ICUs and surgical wards. A study of 1,456 patients in a surgical ICU compared infection-related mortality during a 1-year period without

an antibiotic protocol with infection-related mortality during a 1-year period in which antibiotics were rotated on a quarterly basis.[49] Antibiotic rotation reduced infection-related mortality from 9.6 to 2.9 deaths per 100 admissions; in addition, it reduced the rates of resistant gram-positive coccus infection (from 14.6 to 7.8 infections per 100 admissions) and resistant gram-negative bacillus infection (from 7.7 to 2.5 infections per 100 admissions).

A follow-up study examined 2,088 patients both in a surgical ICU and in the ward they were transferred to, using a study design in which ICU patients (but not floor patients) were treated for 1 year without an antibiotic rotation protocol and for 1 year with such a protocol.[50] In the first quarter of the year, patients received ciprofloxacin with or without clindamycin for pneumonia; in the second, piperacillin-tazobactam; in the third, carbapenem; and in the fourth, cefepime with or without clindamycin. The study demonstrated that the overall number of hospital-acquired infections was decreased on the surgical ward in the year that antibiotic rotation was instituted in the ICU [see Table 7]. Similarly, the incidence of resistant gram-positive and resistant gram-negative infections was reduced on the surgical ward when antibiotic rotation was practiced in the ICU. Perhaps surprisingly, the decrease in resistance came from patients who were not transferred from the ICU.

Although antibiotic cycling has not been definitively proved to be useful in postoperative patients, antibiotic cycling for VAP in the surgical ICU appears to be a strategy that is relatively easy to implement and that may not only decrease the incidence of resistant infection but also, possibly, decrease the overall incidence of infection.

Deescalation of Antibiotic Therapy

Although early initiation of adequate antimicrobial therapy has been demonstrated to reduce mortality in patients with pneumo-

Table 7 Differences in Infection-Related Outcomes for Non–ICU Ward Patients with and without ICU Antibiotic Rotation[50]

Outcome	Nonrotation	ICU Rotation	P
Infections	407	213	—
Infected patients	333	161	—
Infections/infected patient	1.3 ± 0.04	1.2 ± 0.05	0.1
Infections/100 admissions	19.7	9.8	< 0.0001
Infected patients/100 admissions	15.9	7.4	< 0.0001
Infections by service [No. (%)]			
Transplantation	95 (23)	39 (18)	0.2
General surgery	292 (72)	155 (73)	0.8
Trauma	21 (5)	19 (9)	0.1
rGPC infections	52	34	—
rGPC infections/100 admissions	2.5	1.6	0.04
rGNR infections	20	8	—
rGNR infections/100 admissions	1.0	0.4	0.03
Time from intervention to discharge (days)	11.3 ± 0.8	13.5 ± 1.0	0.1
Total utilization of antibiotics (days)	11.2 ± 0.9	8.7 ± 0.5	0.02
Length of stay (days)	18.8 ± 1.3	26.4 ± 1.7	0.0004
Deaths	28	23	—
Deaths/100 admissions	1.3	1.1	0.5
rGPC deaths	6	5	—
rGPC deaths/100 admissions	0.3	0.2	0.9
rGNR deaths	4	3	—
rGNR deaths/100 admissions	0.2	0.1	1.0

rGNR—resistant gram-negative rod   rGPC—resistant gram-positive coccus

Table 8 Effect of Duration of Antibiotic Therapy for VAP
on Outcomes 28 Days after Bronchoscopy[54]

Outcome	8-Day Regimen (N = 197) [No./Total (%)]	15-Day Regimen (N = 204) [No./Total (%)]	Risk Difference between Groups (90% CI) (%)
Death from all causes			
All patients	37/197 (18.8)	35/204 (17.2)	1.6 (–3.7 to 6.9)
Nonfermenting GNB	15/64 (23.4)	19/63 (30.2)	–6.7 (–17.5 to 4.1)
MRSA	6/21 (28.6)	5/21 (23.8)	4.8 (–13.9 to 23.4)
Other bacteria	16/112 (14.3)	11/120 (9.2)	5.1 (–0.7 to 10.9)
Recurrence of pulmonary infection			
All patients	57/197 (28.9)	53/204 (26.0)	2.9 (–3.2 to 9.1)
Superinfection	39/197 (19.8)	38/204 (18.6)	1.2 (–4.3 to 6.6)
Relapse	33/197 (16.8)	23/204 (11.3)	5.5 (0.7 to 10.3)
Nonfermenting GNB	26/64 (40.6)	16/63 (25.4)	15.2 (3.9 to 26.6)
Superinfection	13/64 (20.3)	8/63 (12.7)	7.6 (1.1 to 14.2)
Relapse	21/64 (32.8)	12/63 (19.0)	13.8 (7.8 to 19.7)
MRSA	7/21 (33.3)	9/21 (42.9)	–9.5 (–30.1 to 11.1)
Superinfection	6/21 (28.6)	5/21 (23.8)	4.8 (–8.8 to 18.3)
Relapse	3/21 (14.3)	4/21 (19.0)	–4.8 (–9.9 to 0.4)
Other bacteria	24/112 (21.4)	28/120 (23.3)	–1.9 (–9.5 to 5.6)
Superinfection	20/112 (17.9)	25/120 (20.8)	–3.0 (–8.2 to 2.2)
Relapse	9/112 (8.0)	7/120 (5.8)	2.2 (–1.3 to 5.7)
	Mean No. (SD)		Mean Difference (95% CI) (%)
Antibiotic-free days			
All patients	13.1 (7.4)	8.7 (5.2)	4.4 (3.1 to 5.6)
Nonfermenting GNB	12.0 (7.4)	7.5 (5.4)	4.5 (2.2 to 6.7)
MRSA	12.9 (7.0)	4.9 (5.7)	8.0 (4.6 to 12.1)
Other bacteria	13.7 (7.5)	10.0 (4.6)	3.7 (2.1 to 5.3)

GNB—gram-negative bacillus

nia, it is inappropriate to continue broad-spectrum agents for the entire treatment period. Instead, antibiotic therapy should be reassessed 2 to 3 days after initiation, when culture results become available, and specifically tailored in accordance with these results. If a single pathogen is identified in a culture, all antibiotics may be stopped except for a single agent to which the microbe is sensitive. The exception to this rule is *P. aeruginosa* infection, which many experts recommend treating with two synergistic agents.[41] Although there is little evidence that dual-agent therapy changes outcome, except in cases where VAP is accompanied by bacteremia,[51] the recommendation is made because resistance frequently develops if a patient is treated with a single agent. There is no evidence that maintaining broad-spectrum antibiotic therapy after a positive culture has been obtained improves outcome; however, there is abundant evidence that inappropriate antibiotic use breeds resistant organisms, which are a potential threat not only to the infected patient but also to nearby patients, who may become infected secondarily.

Unfortunately, even invasive quantitative cultures do not identify all pneumonia-causing organisms. How best to tailor antibiotic therapy in a patient with suspected VAP whose cultures are negative remains somewhat controversial. A common approach divides such patients into two broad groups: (1) those whose condition is improving with broad-spectrum therapy and (2) those whose condition is staying the same or becoming worse. In the first group, antibiotic therapy should be tailored to cover gram-negative (and, possibly, sensitive gram-positive) bacteria.

MRSA is fairly easy to culture; thus, if invasive cultures are negative for this organism, vancomycin or linezolid that was started for coverage of resistant gram-positive organisms can be stopped. If there is good evidence of VAP (i.e., CPIS > 6 with both radiographic and sputum evidence of pneumonia), it is reasonable to continue gram-negative coverage for an appropriate period (see below). In the second group, treatment must be individualized. Repeat cultures should be obtained, and a search for nonpulmonary sources of infection, particularly those related to the patient's surgical procedure or to an indwelling central venous catheter, should be initiated. Depending on the clinical situation, all antibiotics may be discontinued, the current antimicrobial regimen may be continued, or a switch to a different class of antibiotic may be made.

Optimal Duration of Antibiotic Therapy

The length of the treatment period for VAP has long been a matter of controversy, thanks largely to the paucity of data on the subject. Historically, 7 to 10 days of treatment has been recommended for sensitive organisms and 14 to 21 days for multiresistant organisms that may be difficult to eradicate from the respiratory tract.[52,53] Expert opinion also has suggested treating either multilobar or cavitary pneumonia for 14 to 21 days.[52] To date, few recommendations have been published regarding postoperative pneumonia in surgical patients who are not in an ICU. Given that these patients are healthier than critically ill patients, the duration of antibiotic therapy in this population should be similar to or shorter than that in patients with

VAP, though many surgeons treat any pneumonia for 10 to 14 days, regardless of the initiating organism.

In an attempt to resolve this issue, a prospective, randomized trial was undertaken that assessed mortality in 401 patients (including surgical patients) treated for VAP with antibiotics in 51 different ICUs.[54] All patients received adequate antimicrobial therapy within 24 hours of the diagnosis of VAP. Antibiotics were withdrawn after either 8 or 15 days, regardless of the patient's clinical condition, except in the case of a documented pneumonia recurrence that occurred before the conclusion of the study. At 28 days, mortality in patients treated with antibiotics for 8 days (18.8%) was comparable to that in patients treated for 15 days (17.2%) [see Table 8]. In addition, the two groups were comparable with respect to the overall recurrent infection rate (28.9% and 26.0%, respectively). The only exception to this latter finding arose in patients with infections caused by nonfermenting gram-negative bacilli (e.g., P. aeruginosa), in whom 8-day therapy was associated with a recurrence rate of 40.6%, compared with 25.4% for 15-day therapy; this increase in recurrence was not associated with excess mortality. Overall number of mechanical ventilation–free days and organ failure–free days, length of stay, and 60-day mortality were also similar in the two groups. Not surprisingly, patients receiving 8-day therapy had significantly more antibiotic-free days (13.1) than those receiving 15-day therapy (8.7). This increase was associated with a decrease in resistant organisms in patients who acquired recurrent infections: recurrence was associated with a 42.1% incidence of multiresistant pathogens in the 8-day group but a 62.0% incidence in the 15-day group. Such results are consistent with other observational studies documenting an increase in resistant organisms that is directly related to the duration of antimicrobial therapy.[55,56]

In another study, 102 consecutive patients with VAP were prospectively evaluated before and after the implementation of a clinical guideline restricting the total duration of antibiotics to 7 days in selected patients who became afebrile under therapy and were neither bacteremic nor neutropenic.[57] Implementation of the guideline reduced the average duration of antibiotic therapy from 14.8 days to 8.6 days. As in the study mentioned earlier (see above),[54] no differences in either hospital mortality or length of stay were noted. However, VAP recurrence rates were actually lower in patients restricted to 7 days of antibiotics than in patients receiving physician-directed therapy.

On the basis of the evidence currently available in the literature, it is possible to formulate a treatment approach that is generally appropriate for the treatment of postoperative pneumonia and VAP [see Figure 1].

TREATMENT FAILURE

A 2004 study of 71 patients with ICU-acquired pneumonia in five medical and surgical ICUs found that 62% of patients did not respond 3 days after therapy was initiated.[58] No cause of treatment failure could be identified in one third of the cases; in the remaining two thirds, the most common causes were inappropriate treatment (23%); concomitant infection (27%); misdiagnosis of infection, with the pulmonary disease being of noninfectious origin (16%); and superinfection (14%). When treatment fails, the patient should be reevaluated to look for a nonpulmonary source of fever, a noninfectious causative condition, or a pneumonia caused by organisms that are resistant to the empirical antibiotic regimen. Aerosolized antibiotics may have a role to play as adjunctive therapy in patients with multidrug-resistant pneumonia who do not respond to I.V. antibiotics.

Discussion

Prevention of Pneumonia after Operation

Before undergoing elective surgical procedures, patients should be instructed about taking deep breaths and ambulating postoperatively (unless there is a medical contraindication to doing so).[59] Such instruction is especially important in patients who are at high risk for pneumonia after operation. This group includes patients scheduled for abdominal aortic aneurysm repair or thoracic procedures, those older than 60 years, those undergoing general anesthesia, those whose functional status is poor, those with greater than 10% weight loss, those on long-term steroid therapy, those with COPD, smokers, those with abnormally low or high BUN levels, and those receiving more than 4 units of blood preoperatively.[2,60] Patients who are also at high risk but are not candidates for preoperative respiratory instruction include those undergoing emergency surgical intervention, those with impaired sensoria, and those with a history of cerebrovascular accident with residual neurologic deficit (though, depending on the type of deficit, this patient population may benefit from preoperative teaching as well).

Incentive spirometry is valuable for preventing pneumonia after operation and is a cost-effective adjunct to early ambulation. It benefits a wide range of patients but is especially effective in moderate-risk and high-risk patients, who should receive extra attention in ensuring compliance with this simple intervention.[61] Although chest physiotherapy has been proposed as a means of potentially decreasing postoperative pneumonia, a meta-analysis of 14 published studies assessing the usefulness of this modality after upper abdominal procedures did not support its routine use.[62]

Like many other infections in critically ill patients, VAP is often preventable.[63] Well-designed studies have found numerous interventions to be effective in lowering the incidence of VAP. Some of these interventions are as simple as positioning the patient appropriately or educating health care workers about risk factors for VAP.

HAND HYGIENE

Appropriate hand hygiene is a simple but underutilized method of preventing nosocomial infection [see 5 Prevention of Postoperative Infection]. Lack of attention to hand hygiene has been a persistent problem worldwide for decades, and physicians often have the poorest compliance.[64] The alcohol foams and gels currently available are more effective than handwashing in killing the bacteria present on the hands and take substantially less time to use, improving compliance with hand hygiene in the ICU.[65] Such preparations now represent the hand hygiene method of choice in most cases and should be readily available throughout the ICU. Hands that are visibly dirty or are soiled with blood or body fluids should still be washed with antimicrobial soap and water, however.[59] Appropriate hand hygiene practices should be followed both before and after contact with a patient who has an endotracheal tube or tracheostomy in place,

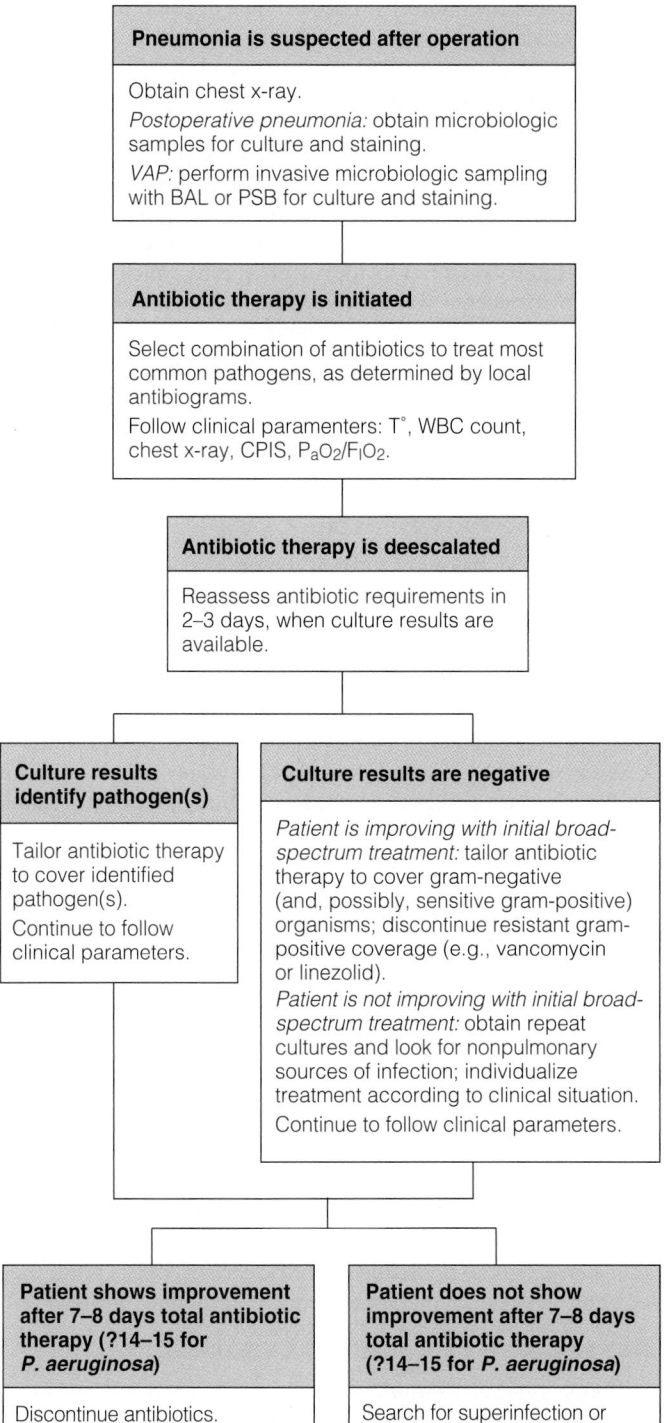

Figure 1 Algorithm outlines recommended approach to antibiotic treatment of suspected pneumonia after operation.[40]

regardless of whether gloves are worn. In addition, hand decontamination is required before and after contact with any respiratory device that is used on a mechanically ventilated patient.[66]

Gloves should be worn for handling respiratory secretions or objects contaminated with such secretions.[66] They should be changed between contacts with different patients, after handling respiratory secretions. In addition, gloves should be changed between contacts with a contaminated body site and the respira-

tory tract or any portion of the ventilator circuit on the same patient.[59] Gowns are also recommended when soiling with respiratory secretions is anticipated; they should be removed after the soiling occurs and before any contact with other ICU patients.[66]

PATIENT POSITIONING

Aspiration of upper airway secretions occurs in healthy adults as well as in ill ones. It is, however, a matter of much greater concern in critically ill patients with decreased host defenses, who are at increased risk for VAP. Maneuvers to reduce aspiration of gastric contents therefore have the potential to decrease the incidence of VAP. Because the supine position is associated with an increased risk of aspiration (especially if the patient is receiving tube feedings via a nasoenteric tube), placing the patient in a semirecumbent position—via the simple expedient of raising the head of the bed to an angle of 30° to 45° or greater—is recommended as a means of possibly preventing VAP (if not medically contraindicated).

A prospective, randomized trial involving 86 patients in two ICUs (neither of them surgical) was stopped at the first interim analysis because of the significant difference in the incidence of VAP between semirecumbent patients and supine patients.[67] The incidence of both clinically suspected VAP and microbiologically proven VAP was drastically reduced in patients positioned with the head of the bed at a 45° angle (from 34% to 8% and from 23% to 5%, respectively). Enteral feeding was also independently associated with the risk of VAP: supine patients receiving enteral feedings had a 50% chance of acquiring VAP.

The supine position has been identified as an independent risk factor for VAP in other observational studies of ICU patients as well.[68] In addition, patients who require transport from the ICU are at substantially higher risk for VAP than those who do not (24.2% versus 4.4%).[69] It is possible that the VAP rate is increased because patients requiring transport are sicker at baseline, but it is also possible that the rate is higher in this group partly because patients are supine for much or all of their transport time.

Because static bed rest is known to increase the risk of pulmonary (and nonpulmonary) complications, it has been theorized that postural oscillation and rotation may prevent VAP. Specialized kinetic beds are available that provide continuous movement and are capable of reducing pulmonary complications in surgical patients. A study of 106 blunt trauma patients in a surgical ICU demonstrated a significant decrease in VAP in patients randomly selected to undergo continuous postural oscillation.[70] A study of 65 surgical patients immobilized because of head injury or traction showed a nonstatistical trend toward a decreased risk of pneumonia in patients treated with kinetic beds.[71] Finally, a study of 69 liver transplant patients randomly assigned to either continuous lateral rotation or a conventional bed found that the incidence of lower respiratory tract infections was decreased in the study group, as was length of time to development of infection; however, duration of mechanical ventilation and length of stay were unchanged.[72]

Overall, there appears to be a trend toward decreased VAP in surgical patients treated with kinetic beds. In addition, there are various accompanying nonpulmonary complications that can also be prevented by this treatment (e.g., decubitus ulcers). Accordingly, kinetic beds should be used in surgical patients who are expected to have a prolonged ICU course.

CHOICE OF FEEDING ROUTE

Although elevation of the head of the bed reduces aspiration, it does not prevent gastroesophageal reflux.[73] Because gastric overdistention is also associated with an increased risk of aspiration, there has been considerable interest in identifying a route of feeding that is associated with a decreased incidence of VAP. This issue is directly relevant to the postoperative setting, in which many patients, as a consequence of the surgical procedure, experience ileus, which is often exacerbated by narcotics given for pain relief. The generally appropriate reluctance to feed a patient with a large gastric residuum in the ICU setting should be balanced against the desire to provide adequate nutrition as soon as is practicable after an operation, as well as against the multiple advantages of enteral feeding over parenteral feeding. Accordingly, the timing for initiating feedings postoperatively must be individualized on the basis of each patient's situation and condition. In addition, whereas feeding a supine patient greatly increases the risk of VAP,[67] there is no documented benefit to postpyloric feeding or to using smaller nasogastric tubes,[74,75] and no clear recommendations can be made regarding how best to feed a postoperative patient enterally.

MINIMIZATION OF ENDOTRACHEAL INTUBATION

Extended mechanical ventilation is a major risk factor for VAP; it follows, then, that decreasing or eliminating the need for an endotracheal tube has the potential to lower the incidence of VAP. There are two major strategies by which this goal can be accomplished: (1) earlier extubation (i.e., removing an endotracheal tube when it is no longer needed) and (2) noninvasive ventilation (i.e., continuing ventilatory support without the presence of an endotracheal tube). In addition, the route of intubation (oral versus nasal) can influence the development of pneumonia.[76]

Although the optimal mode of weaning has not been definitively determined, it is clear that many patients are kept intubated even when they no longer require mechanical ventilation. The use of a weaning protocol, a sedation protocol, or both has been shown to reduce the duration of mechanical ventilation.[69] In addition, daily interruption of sedation until a patient is awake has been demonstrated to decrease the number of ventilator days in a medical ICU population[77]; however, this approach has not been studied in the surgical ICU, where the issue is complicated by the greater need for postoperative narcotics. Regardless of the technique or protocol employed, patients should be assessed daily to determine whether ventilatory support is still necessary. Extubated patients have a substantially lower incidence of postoperative pneumonia than patients with an endotracheal tube in place.

The presence of an endotracheal tube in itself, independent of the need for mechanical ventilation, also appears to be a risk factor for VAP. The tube hinders both airway reflexes and coughing, allowing secretions that accumulate above the tube to enter the airways over time and serve as a nidus of infection. This problem is eliminated in patients who are ventilated noninvasively with bilevel positive airway pressure (BiPAP). Multiple studies have found noninvasive ventilation to be associated with lower pneumonia rates and mortalities than conventional ventilation.[78,79] However, these studies were done in medical ICUs, predominantly on patients with COPD exacerbations, and it is unclear whether similar results are achievable in patients with postoperative respiratory failure.

Reintubation is also an independent risk factor for the development of VAP.[80] However, fear of the potential adverse consequences of reintubation should not prevent an awake patient who passes a spontaneous breathing trial from being extubated. Many postoperative patients who are extubated and have unexpected ventilatory problems can be managed without reintubation on BiPAP. In addition, although it is unclear what the correct percentage of extubation attempts that require reintubation would be,

it is clear that the number is not zero. The decision to extubate is, in a way, comparable to the decision to perform an appendectomy. If every patient on whom an appendectomy is done has appendicitis, it is likely that too few operations are being done and that some patients are being allowed to experience a ruptured appendix needlessly. Similarly, if every patient who is extubated postoperatively does well, it is likely that too few extubations are being done and that some patients are being kept intubated inappropriately and thus experiencing preventable morbidity.

Nasal intubation increases the risk of sinusitis, which, even though only 10% of patients with opacified sinuses have recoverable bacteria, is associated with an increased incidence of VAP.[81] It is not clear whether sinusitis causes VAP or merely represents a marker of patients who are at higher risk for pneumonia. In either case, given the association between nasotracheal intubation and increased infection rate and mortality, nasotracheal intubation should not be considered a first-line method of obtaining airway control.

MANAGEMENT OF VENTILATOR

Although in theory, ventilator tubing, suction catheters, and humidification systems could all play a role in the development of pneumonia, none of them have been convincingly shown to have an impact on VAP rates. Condensate in the ventilator tubing can become contaminated, but multiple randomized trials have demonstrated that routinely changing ventilator circuits in patients with respiratory failure does not lower the VAP rate.[82-84] Circuits should be changed when they are visibly soiled with vomit or blood or are malfunctioning. In addition, condensate should periodically be drained and discarded.

Heat moisture exchangers (HMEs) are frequently used instead of heated water humidification systems, because HMEs are relatively inexpensive and require neither electricity nor active heating elements. HMEs minimize the formation of condensate within ventilator circuits, thereby, in theory, potentially decreasing VAP rates. One study found HMEs to yield lower infection rates than humidification systems,[85] but at present, there is no clear consensus in favor of either type of device.[8,59]

Either an open single-use catheter system or a closed multiuse catheter system may be used for suctioning. Although open systems are associated with increased environmental contamination, current evidence suggests that the incidence of VAP is not significantly affected by the type of suctioning system used.[14,86] In addition, when closed systems are used, routine changing of inline suction catheters does not reduce the incidence of VAP,[87] nor is there convincing evidence that more frequent suctioning prevents VAP.

PREVENTION OF OROPHARYNGEAL COLONIZATION

Oropharyngeal colonization can be decreased by means of either antiseptic therapy or a comprehensive oral hygiene program. Oral chlorhexidine gluconate (0.12%), given before and after cardiac procedures, has proved effective in preventing postoperative pneumonia.[88] In a prospective, randomized, blinded trial, patients receiving a chlorhexidine rinse, which has documented activity against both aerobes and anaerobes, experienced a 69% decrease in the incidence of postoperative pneumonia. This decrease was not associated with a change in antibiotic resistance patterns after operation and was accompanied by a reduction in postoperative antibiotic use. The effect of a chlorhexidine rinse on the development of postoperative pneumonia in a general surgical population, however, has not yet been adequately studied.

A comprehensive oral hygiene program includes daily oral assessment, frequent tooth brushing, readily available dental care, mouth swabs, and, possibly, a chlorhexidine rinse. These measures have proved effective in preventing pneumonia in nursing-home patients.[89] One retrospective study examining the application of a comprehensive oral care protocol in medical/surgical ICU patients demonstrated a decrease in the VAP rate after the initiation of such a program.[90]

DRAINAGE OF SUBGLOTTIC SECRETIONS

Secretions that pool above an inflated endotracheal cuff may be a source of aspirated material that results in VAP. Specially designed endotracheal tubes are available that have a separate opening above the cuff of the tube to allow either continuous suctioning or intermittent irrigation and drainage of secretions that accumulate in the subglottic space.

Three prospective, randomized trials have evaluated the role of subglottic secretion drainage. A study of 190 patients in a medical/surgical ICU demonstrated a decrease in the VAP rate from 39.6 to 19.9 episodes per 1,000 ventilator days.[91] VAP developed later in the subglottic-drainage group (12.0 versus 5.9 days). A study of 150 patients in a general ICU reported similar results, with the VAP rate decreasing from 16% in the control group to 4% in patients receiving intermittent subglottic drainage.[92] However, continuous aspiration of subglottic secretions does not appear to reduce the VAP rate significantly in cardiac surgical patients. A prospective, randomized trial of 343 cardiac surgical patients demonstrated that pneumonia developed in 5.0% of patients who received subglottic suctioning, compared with 8.2% of control patients.[93] As in other studies of subglottic drainage, pneumonia developed later in patients who received the intervention (5.6 days) than in those who did not (2.9 days).

At present, utilization of subglottic secretion drainage is hindered by logistical difficulties. Not only must these specialized tubes and the expertise required to care for them be readily available in the ICU, but the decision to place the tubes must also be made preoperatively and communicated to the anesthesiologist before the patient is intubated.

PHARMACOLOGIC APPROACHES

Widely varying study results and significant infection control concerns have made SDD an extremely controversial practice. The term selective decontamination of the digestive tract is actually a misnomer, in that successful SDD protocols employ a combination of systemic antibiotics and nonabsorbable antibiotics given both orally and via a nasogastric tube. This is an important point: meta-analyses of SDD studies show that SDD is not effective if systemic antibiotics are not included.[94,95]

A prospective, randomized, unblinded trial of 934 patients in a mixed medical/surgical ICU who received either 4 days of SDD or standard treatment reported that hospital mortality decreased from 31% to 24% in SDD patients.[8] The treatment protocol consisted of intravenous cefotaxime and oral and enteral polymyxin E, tobramycin, and amphotericin B. The results mirrored those of two meta-analyses that documented decreases in both VAP rate and mortality in patients given SDD,[94,95] with surgical patients deriving greater benefit than medical patients.[94]

Nearly all of the studies supporting the value of SDD were performed in ICUs with low baseline levels of resistant organisms. The effectiveness of SDD in ICUs where basal antimicrobial resistance is moderate or high is unknown. For instance, a 6-year study of 360 trauma patients receiving SDD reported a moderate increase in the development of resistant organisms.[96] Owing to infection control concerns, SDD is not widely accepted in the United States. It is noteworthy that routine use of SDD to prevent VAP is not recommended either by the CDC guidelines for preventing health care–associ-

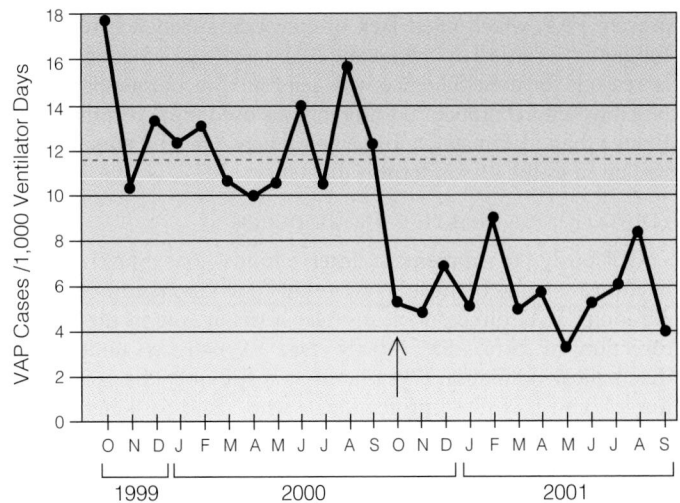

Figure 2 **Illustrated is the influence of an education program for health care workers on the monthly rate of VAP per 1,000 ventilator days between October 1999 and 2001.[100] (Dotted line represents the VAP rate cited by the National Nosocomial Infection Surveillance system for ICUs in the United States; arrow represents the point at which the education program was initiated.**

ated pneumonia[59] or by the Fourth International Consensus Conference in Critical Care on ICU-Acquired Pneumonia.[6]

Another pharmacologic approach that has been proposed as a means of preventing VAP is avoidance of drugs that raise stomach pH, on the assumption that these agents may lead to bacterial overgrowth and eventually to VAP. The available data, however, indicate that this assumption is incorrect. A prospective, randomized trial involving 1,200 patients in 16 ICUs that compared the H_2 receptor antagonist ranitidine with sucralfate found no difference in VAP rate between the ranitidine group and the sucralfate group.[97] Notably, the rate of clinically important GI bleeding was higher in the sucralfate group. On the basis of this definitive study, drugs that raise stomach pH should not be avoided for infection control reasons.

COMPLIANCE WITH EVIDENCE-BASED GUIDELINES FOR PREVENTION

Pneumonia in the postoperative setting cannot be eliminated, but its incidence can be substantially decreased by following evidence-based prevention guidelines. Unfortunately, compliance with such guidelines is far from uniform.

In an attempt to understand why guidelines for preventing VAP are not more widely implemented, a study was performed in which a questionnaire was sent to 110 opinion leaders from 22 countries to ascertain whether 33 practices with the potential to prevent VAP[63] were instituted in their ICUs.[98] If respondents did not follow these practices, they were asked to indicate why not. The overall nonadherence rate among the 62 physicians who returned the survey was 37.0%. For strategies clearly recommended for clinical use, the nonadherence rate was 25.2%; for less effective strategies, the rate rose to 45.6%. Self-reported compliance ranged from 11.7% for continuous subglottic suctioning to 100% for removal of endotracheal tubes as soon as clinically feasible and avoidance of unnecessary reintubation. The most common reasons for nonadherence were disagreement with the interpretation of the clinical trials (35%), unavailability of the necessary resources (31.3%), and high cost (16.9%).

The findings of this study complement those of a separate survey of 103 ICU directors in France and Canada on strategies to prevent VAP, which cited lack of convincing evidence (e.g., for subglottic secretion drainage) and high cost (e.g., of kinetic beds) as reasons for nonadherence with published recommendations.[99] Notably, semirecumbent positioning was used more commonly in France than in Canada, and the convenience for the nursing staff was given as the reason for this difference.

EDUCATION OF HEALTH CARE WORKERS

Obviously, to implement interventions that prevent VAP, health care workers must be aware that such interventions exist. Although ICU directors clearly play a major role in the overall direction of care, direct daily care of patients undergoing mechanical ventilation is provided by respiratory therapists and nurses, and it is these professionals who stand to benefit most from educational efforts.

To test the effect of education in reducing VAP rates, a program was initiated that was directed toward respiratory care practitioners and nurses in five ICUs at a single academic center.[100] Initially, 114 respiratory therapists and 146 nurses took a 20-question pretest to determine their level of knowledge about methods of preventing VAP. They then received a 10-page self-study module that provided information about VAP and outlined prevention strategies. Both immediately after the intervention and 6 months later, participants took a posttest that was identical to the original test. Test scores improved at both time points, demonstrating that the information taught was both learned and retained.

In the 12 months before implementation of the education program, 191 episodes of VAP were identified (12.6 per 1,000 ventilator days). In the 12 months following completion of the program, however, only 81 episodes of VAP (5.7 per 1,000 ventilator days) were identified [see Figure 2]. The greatest success in VAP prevention was achieved in the surgical/trauma/burn ICU, where VAP rates decreased from 18.1 to 6.6 per 1,000 ventilator days. These results highlight the importance of disseminating information on VAP prevention to the health care workers who are providing the day-to-day care for patients at risk for VAP.

References

1. Brooks-Brunn JA: Postoperative atelectasis and pneumonia. Heart Lung 24:94, 1995

2. Arozullah AM, Khuri SF, Henderson WG, et al: Development and validation of a multifactorial risk index for predicting postoperative pneumonia after major noncardiac surgery. Ann Intern Med 135:847, 2001

3. Vincent JL: Nosocomial infections in adult intensive-care units. Ann Intern Med 361:2068, 2003

4. Richards MJ, Edwards JR, Culver DH, et al: Nosocomial infections in combined medical-surgical intensive care units in the United States. Infect Control Hosp Epidemiol 21:510, 2000

5. Papia G, McLellan BA, El Helou P, et al: Infection in hospitalized trauma patients: incidence, risk factors, and complications. J Trauma 47:923, 1999

6. Hubmayr RD, Burchardi H, Elliot M, et al: Statement of the 4th International Consensus Conference in Critical Care on ICU-Acquired Pneumonia—Chicago, Illinois, May 2002. Intensive Care Med 28:1521, 2002

7. Johanson WG, Pierce AK, Sanford JP: Changing pharyngeal bacterial flora of hospitalized patients: emergence of gram-negative bacilli. N Engl J Med 281:1137, 1969

8. de Jonge E, Schultz MJ, Spanjaard L, et al: Effects of selective decontamination of digestive tract on mortality and acquisition of resistant bacteria in intensive care: a randomized controlled trial. Ann Intern Med 362:1011, 2003

9. Adair CG, Gorman SP, Feron BM, et al: Implications of endotracheal tube biofilm for ventilator-associated pneumonia. Intensive Care Med 25:1072, 1999

10. Fagon JY, Chastre J, Domart Y, et al: Nosocomial pneumonia in patients receiving continuous mechanical ventilation: prospective analysis of 52 episodes with use of a protected specimen brush and quantitative culture techniques. Am Rev Respir Dis 139:877, 1989

11. National Nosocomial Infections Surveillance (NNIS) System Report, data summary from January 1992 through June 2003, issued August 2003. Am J Infect Control 31:481, 2003

12. Cook DJ, Walter SD, Cook RJ, et al: Incidence of and risk factors for ventilator-associated pneumonia in critically ill patients. Ann Intern Med 129:433, 1998

13. Rello J, Ollendorf DA, Oster G, et al: Epidemiology and outcomes of ventilator-associated pneumonia in a large US database. Chest 122:2115, 2002

14. Cook D, De Jonghe B, Brochard L, et al: Influence of airway management on ventilator-associated pneumonia: evidence from randomized trials. JAMA 279:781, 1998

15. Heyland DK, Cook DJ, Griffith L, et al: The attributable morbidity and mortality of ventilator-associated pneumonia in the critically ill patient. The Canadian Critical Trials Group. Am J Respir Crit Care Med 159:1249, 1999

16. Markowicz P, Wolff M, Djedaini K, et al: Multicenter prospective study of ventilator-associated pneumonia during acute respiratory distress syndrome: incidence, prognosis, and risk factors. ARDS Study Group. Am J Respir Crit Care Med 161:1942, 2000

17. Fagon JY, Chastre J, Domart Y, et al: Mortality due to ventilator-associated pneumonia or colonization with Pseudomonas or Acinetobacter species: assessment by quantitative culture of samples obtained by a protected specimen brush. Clin Infect Dis 23:538, 1996

18. Garner JS, Jarvis WR, Emori TG, et al: CDC definitions for nosocomial infections, 1988. Am J Infect Control 16:128, 1988

19. Torres A, el Ebiary M, Padro L, et al: Validation of different techniques for the diagnosis of ventilator-associated pneumonia: comparison with immediate postmortem pulmonary biopsy. Am J Respir Crit Care Med 149:324, 1994

20. Mayhall CG: Ventilator-associated pneumonia or not? Contemporary diagnosis. Emerg Infect Dis 7:200, 2001

21. Pugin J, Auckenthaler R, Mili N, et al: Diagnosis of ventilator-associated pneumonia by bacteriologic analysis of bronchoscopic and nonbronchoscopic "blind" bronchoalveolar lavage fluid. Am Rev Respir Dis 143:1121, 1991

22. Jourdain B, Novara A, Joly-Guillou ML, et al: Role of quantitative cultures of endotracheal aspirates in the diagnosis of nosocomial pneumonia. Am J Respir Crit Care Med 152:241, 1995

23. Marquette CH, Copin MC, Wallet F, et al: Diagnostic tests for pneumonia in ventilated patients: prospective evaluation of diagnostic accuracy using histology as a diagnostic gold standard. Am J Respir Crit Care Med 151:1878, 1995

24. Chastre J, Fagon JY, Bornet-Lecso M, et al: Evaluation of bronchoscopic techniques for the diagnosis of nosocomial pneumonia. Am J Respir Crit Care Med 152:231, 1995

25. Marquette CH, Herengt F, Mathieu D, et al: Diagnosis of pneumonia in mechanically ventilated patients: repeatability of the protected specimen brush. Am Rev Respir Dis 147:211, 1993

26. Croce MA, Fabian TC, Schurr MJ, et al: Using bronchoalveolar lavage to distinguish nosocomial pneumonia from systemic inflammatory response syndrome: a prospective analysis. J Trauma 39:1134, 1995

27. Kollef MH, Bock KR, Richards RD, et al: The safety and diagnostic accuracy of minibronchoalveolar lavage in patients with suspected ventilator-associated pneumonia. Ann Intern Med 122:743, 1995

28. Pham LH, Brun-Buisson C, Legrand P, et al: Diagnosis of nosocomial pneumonia in mechanically ventilated patients: comparison of a plugged telescoping catheter with the protected specimen brush. Am Rev Respir Dis 143:1055, 1991

29. Timsit JF, Misset B, Renaud B, et al: Effect of previous antimicrobial therapy on the accuracy of the main procedures used to diagnose nosocomial pneumonia in patients who are using ventilation. Chest 108:1036, 1995

30. Souweine B, Veber B, Bedos JP, et al: Diagnostic accuracy of protected specimen brush and bronchoalveolar lavage in nosocomial pneumonia: impact of previous antimicrobial treatments. Crit Care Med 26:236, 1998

31. Flanagan PG, Findlay GP, Magee JT, et al: The diagnosis of ventilator-associated pneumonia using non-bronchoscopic, non-directed lung lavages. Intensive Care Med 26:20, 2000

32. National Nosocomial Infections Surveillance (NNIS) System Report, data summary from January 1990–May 1999, issued June 1999. Am J Infect Control 27:520, 1999

33. Robert R, Grollier G, Frat JP, et al: Colonization of lower respiratory tract with anaerobic bacteria in mechanically ventilated patients. Intensive Care Med 29:1062, 2003

34. Marik PE, Careau P: The role of anaerobes in patients with ventilator-associated pneumonia and aspiration pneumonia: a prospective study. Chest 115:178, 1999

35. Dore P, Robert R, Grollier G, et al: Incidence of anaerobes in ventilator-associated pneumonia with use of a protected specimen brush. Am J Respir Crit Care Med 153:1292, 1996

36. Lambotte O, Timsit JF, Garrouste-Orgeas M, et al: The significance of distal bronchial samples with commensals in ventilator-associated pneumonia: colonizer or pathogen? Chest 122:1389, 2002

37. Luna CM, Vujacich P, Niederman MS, et al: Impact of BAL data on the therapy and outcome of ventilator-associated pneumonia. Chest 111:676, 1997

38. Rello J, Gallego M, Mariscal D, et al: The value of routine microbial investigation in ventilator-associated pneumonia. Am J Respir Crit Care Med 156:196, 1997

39. Kollef MH, Sherman G, Ward S, et al: Inadequate antimicrobial treatment of infections: a risk factor for hospital mortality among critically ill patients. Chest 115:462, 1999

40. Iregui M, Ward S, Sherman G, et al: Clinical importance of delays in the initiation of appropriate antibiotic treatment for ventilator-associated pneumonia. Chest 122:262, 2002

41. Guidelines for the management of adults with hospital-acquired, ventilator-associated, and healthcare-associated pneumonia. Am J Respir Crit Care Med 171:388, 2005

42. Rubinstein E, Cammarata S, Oliphant T, et al: Linezolid (PNU-100766) versus vancomycin in the treatment of hospitalized patients with nosocomial pneumonia: a randomized, double-blind, multicenter study. Clin Infect Dis 32:402, 2001

43. Wunderink RG, Cammarata SK, Oliphant TH, et al: Continuation of a randomized, double-blind, multicenter study of linezolid versus vancomycin in the treatment of patients with nosocomial pneumonia. Clin Ther 25:980, 2003

44. Wunderink RG, Rello J, Cammarata SK, et al: Linezolid vs vancomycin: analysis of two double-blind studies of patients with methicillin-resistant Staphylococcus aureus nosocomial pneumonia. Chest 124:1789, 2003

45. Kollef MH, Rello J, Cammarata SK, et al: Clinical cure and survival in gram-positive ventilator-associated pneumonia: retrospective analysis of two double-blind studies comparing linezolid with vancomycin. Intensive Care Med 30:388, 2004

46. Fagon J, Patrick H, Haas DW, et al: Treatment of gram-positive nosocomial pneumonia: prospective randomized comparison of quinupristin/dalfopristin versus vancomycin. Nosocomial Pneumonia Group. Am J Respir Crit Care Med 161:753, 2000

47. Fowler RA, Flavin KE, Barr J, et al: Variability in antibiotic prescribing patterns and outcomes in patients with clinically suspected ventilator-associated pneumonia. Chest 123:835, 2003

48. Stelfox HT, Bates DW, Redelmeier DA: Safety of patients isolated for infection control. JAMA 290:1899, 2003

49. Raymond DP, Pelletier SJ, Crabtree TD, et al: Impact of a rotating empiric antibiotic schedule on infectious mortality in an intensive care unit. Crit Care Med 29:1101, 2001

50. Hughes MG, Evans HL, Chong TW, et al: Effect of an intensive care unit rotating empiric antibiotic schedule on the development of hospital-acquired infections on the non-intensive care unit ward. Crit Care Med 32:53, 2004

51. Hilf M, Yu VL, Sharp J, et al: Antibiotic therapy for Pseudomonas aeruginosa bacteremia: outcome correlations in a prospective study of 200 patients. Am J Med 87:540, 1989

52. Hospital-acquired pneumonia in adults: diagnosis, assessment of severity, initial antimicrobial therapy, and preventive strategies: a consensus statement, American Thoracic Society, November 1995. Am J Respir Crit Care Med 153:1711, 1996

53. Rello J, Mariscal D, March F, et al: Recurrent Pseudomonas aeruginosa pneumonia in ventilated patients: relapse or reinfection? Am J Respir Crit Care Med 157:912, 1998

54. Chastre J, Wolff M, Fagon JY, et al: Comparison of 8 vs 15 days of antibiotic therapy for ventilator-associated pneumonia in adults: a randomized trial. JAMA 290:2588, 2003

55. Neuhauser MM, Weinstein RA, Rydman R, et al: Antibiotic resistance among gram-negative bacilli in US intensive care units: implications for fluoroquinolone use. JAMA 289:885, 2003

56. Kollef MH, Fraser VJ: Antibiotic resistance in the intensive care unit. Ann Intern Med 134:298, 2001

57. Ibrahim EH, Ward S, Sherman G, et al: Experience with a clinical guideline for the treatment of ventilator-associated pneumonia. Crit Care Med 29:1109, 2001

58. Ioanas M, Ferrer M, Cavalcanti M, et al: Causes and predictors of nonresponse to treatment of intensive care unit-acquired pneumonia. Crit Care Med 32:938, 2004

59. Tablan OC, Anderson LJ, Besser R, et al: Guidelines for preventing health-care–associated pneumonia, 2003: recommendations of CDC and the Healthcare Infection Control Practices Advisory Committee. MMWR Recomm Rep 53(RR-3):1, 2004

60. Brooks-Brunn JA: Predictors of postoperative pulmonary complications following abdominal surgery. Chest 111:564, 1997

61. Chumillas S, Ponce JL, Delgado F, et al: Prevention of postoperative pulmonary complications through respiratory rehabilitation: a controlled clinical study. Arch Phys Med Rehabil 79:5, 1998

62. Thomas JA, McIntosh JM: Are incentive spirometry, intermittent positive pressure breathing, and deep breathing exercises effective in the prevention of postoperative pulmonary complications after upper abdominal surgery? A systematic overview and meta-analysis. Phys Ther 74:3, 1994

63. Kollef MH: The prevention of ventilator-associated pneumonia. N Engl J Med 340:627, 1999

64. Pittet D, Mourouga P, Perneger TV: Compliance with handwashing in a teaching hospital: infection control program. Ann Intern Med 130:126, 1999

65. Maury E, Alzieu M, Baudel JL, et al: Availability of an alcohol solution can improve hand disinfection compliance in an intensive care unit. Am J Respir Crit Care Med 162:324, 2000

66. Garner JS: Guideline for isolation precautions in hospitals. The Hospital Infection Control Practices Advisory Committee. Infect Control Hosp Epidemiol 17:53, 1996

67. Drakulovic MB, Torres A, Bauer TT, et al: Supine body position as a risk factor for nosocomial pneumonia in mechanically ventilated patients: a randomised trial. Ann Intern Med 354:1851, 1999

68. Fernandez-Crehuet R, Diaz-Molina C, de Irala J, et al: Nosocomial infection in an intensive-care unit: identification of risk factors. Infect Control Hosp Epidemiol 18:825, 1997

69. Kollef MH, Von Harz B, Prentice D, et al: Patient transport from intensive care increases the risk of developing ventilator-associated pneumonia. Chest 112:765, 1997

70. Fink MP, Helsmoortel CM, Stein KL, et al: The efficacy of an oscillating bed in the prevention of lower respiratory tract infection in critically ill victims of blunt trauma: a prospective study. Chest 97:132, 1990

71. Gentilello L, Thompson DA, Tonnesen AS, et al: Effect of a rotating bed on the incidence of pulmonary complications in critically ill patients. Crit Care Med 16:783, 1988

72. Whiteman K, Nachtmann L, Kramer D, et al: Effects of continuous lateral rotation therapy on pulmonary complications in liver transplant patients. Am J Crit Care 4:133, 1995

73. Orozco-Levi M, Torres A, Ferrer M, et al: Semirecumbent position protects from pulmonary aspiration but not completely from gastroesophageal reflux in mechanically ventilated patients. Am J Respir Crit Care Med 152:1387, 1995

74. Kearns PJ, Chin D, Mueller L, et al: The incidence of ventilator-associated pneumonia and success in nutrient delivery with gastric versus small intestinal feeding: a randomized clinical trial. Crit Care Med 28:1742, 2000

75. Ferrer M, Bauer TT, Torres A, et al: Effect of nasogastric tube size on gastroesophageal reflux and microaspiration in intubated patients. Ann Intern Med 130:991, 1999

76. Holzapfel L, Chastang C, Demingeon G, et al: A randomized study assessing the systematic search for maxillary sinusitis in nasotracheally mechanically ventilated patients: influence of nosocomial maxillary sinusitis on the occurrence of ventilator-associated pneumonia. Am J Respir Crit Care Med 159:695, 1999

77. Kress JP, Pohlman AS, O'Connor MF, et al: Daily interruption of sedative infusions in critically ill patients undergoing mechanical ventilation. N Engl J Med 342:1471, 2000

78. Nava S, Ambrosino N, Clini E, et al: Noninvasive mechanical ventilation in the weaning of patients with respiratory failure due to chronic obstructive pulmonary disease: a randomized, controlled trial. Ann Intern Med 128:721, 1998

79. Girou E, Schortgen F, Delclaux C, et al: Association of noninvasive ventilation with nosocomial infections and survival in critically ill patients. JAMA 284:2361, 2000

80. Torres A, Gatell JM, Aznar E, et al: Re-intubation increases the risk of nosocomial pneumonia in patients needing mechanical ventilation. Am J Respir Crit Care Med 152:137, 1995

81. George DL, Falk PS, Umberto Meduri G, et al: Nosocomial sinusitis in patients in the medical intensive care unit: a prospective epidemiological study. Clin Infect Dis 27:463, 1998

82. Long MN, Wickstrom G, Grimes A, et al: Prospective, randomized study of ventilator-associated pneumonia in patients with one versus three ventilator circuit changes per week. Infect Control Hosp Epidemiol 17:14, 1996

83. Dreyfuss D, Djedaini K, Weber P, et al: Prospective study of nosocomial pneumonia and of patient and circuit colonization during mechanical ventilation with circuit changes every 48 hours versus no change. Am Rev Respir Dis 143:738, 1991

84. Kollef MH, Shapiro SD, Fraser VJ, et al: Mechanical ventilation with or without 7-day circuit changes: a randomized controlled trial. Ann Intern Med 123:168, 1995

85. Kirton OC, DeHaven B, Morgan J, et al: A prospective, randomized comparison of an in-line heat moisture exchange filter and heated wire humidifiers: rates of ventilator-associated early-onset (community-acquired) or late-onset (hospital-acquired) pneumonia and incidence of endotracheal tube occlusion. Chest 112:1055, 1997

86. Combes P, Fauvage B, Oleyer C: Nosocomial pneumonia in mechanically ventilated patients, a prospective randomised evaluation of the Stericath closed suctioning system. Intensive Care Med 26:878, 2000

87. Kollef MH, Prentice D, Shapiro SD, et al: Mechanical ventilation with or without daily changes of in-line suction catheters. Am J Respir Crit Care Med 156:466, 1997

88. DeRiso AJ, Ladowski JS, Dillon TA, et al: Chlorhexidine gluconate 0.12% oral rinse reduces the incidence of total nosocomial respiratory infection and nonprophylactic systemic antibiotic use in patients undergoing heart surgery. Chest 109:1556, 1996

89. Yoneyama T, Yoshida M, Ohrui T, et al: Oral care reduces pneumonia in older patients in nursing homes. J Am Geriatr Soc 50:430, 2002

90. Schleder B, Stott K, Lloyd RC: The effect of a comprehensive oral care protocol on patients at risk for ventilator-associated pneumonia. Journal of Advocate Health Care 4:27, 2002

91. Valles J, Artigas A, Rello J, et al: Continuous aspiration

of subglottic secretions in preventing ventilator-associated pneumonia. Ann Intern Med 122:179, 1995

92. Smulders K, van der Hoeven H, Weers-Pothoff I, et al: A randomized clinical trial of intermittent subglottic secretion drainage in patients receiving mechanical ventilation. Chest 121:858, 2002

93. Kollef MH, Skubas NJ, Sundt TM: A randomized clinical trial of continuous aspiration of subglottic secretions in cardiac surgery patients. Chest 116:1339, 1999

94. Nathens AB, Marshall JC: Selective decontamination of the digestive tract in surgical patients: a systematic review of the evidence. Arch Surg 134:170, 1999

95. D'Amico R, Pifferi S, Leonetti C, et al: Effectiveness of antibiotic prophylaxis in critically ill adult patients: systematic review of randomised controlled trials. BMJ 316:1275, 1998

96. Leone M, Albanese J, Antonini F, et al: Long-term (6-year) effect of selective digestive decontamination on antimicrobial resistance in intensive care, multiple-trauma patients. Crit Care Med 31:2090, 2003

97. Cook D, Guyatt G, Marshall J, et al: A comparison of sucralfate and ranitidine for the prevention of upper gastrointestinal bleeding in patients requiring mechanical ventilation. Canadian Critical Care Trials Group. N Engl J Med 338:791, 1998

98. Rello J, Lorente C, Bodi M, et al: Why do physicians not follow evidence-based guidelines for preventing ventilator-associated pneumonia? A survey based on the opinions of an international panel of intensivists. Chest 122:656, 2002

99. Cook D, Ricard JD, Reeve B, et al: Ventilator circuit and secretion management strategies: a Franco-Canadian survey. Crit Care Med 28:3547, 2000

100. Zack JE, Garrison T, Trovillion E, et al: Effect of an education program aimed at reducing the occurrence of ventilator-associated pneumonia. Crit Care Med 30:2407, 2002

133 INTRA-ABDOMINAL INFECTION

Robert G. Sawyer, M.D., F.A.C.S., Jeffrey S. Barkun, M.D., F.A.C.S., Robert Smith, M.D., Tae Chong, M.D., and George Tzimas, M.D.

Recognition and Management of Intra-abdominal Infection

The basic principles of rapid diagnosis, timely physiologic support, and definitive intervention for intra-abdominal infections have remained unchanged over the past century. Specific management of these conditions, however, has been transformed of late as a result of numerous advances in technology. Improved radiologic and laboratory techniques have led to more precise preoperative diagnoses, and newer procedures have led to treatment algorithms that cause less morbidity and permit faster recovery. Whereas the pathophysiology of these infections remains largely unchanged, their management is now marked by an ever-growing complexity. It is no longer true that the diagnosis of intra-abdominal infection, even in association with a perforated viscus, necessitates urgent exploration, but it remains the case that decisions regarding the ultimate course of action for any individual patient are solely the responsibility of the surgeon.

Clinical Evaluation

HISTORY

The general approach to a patient suspected of having an intra-abdominal infection is much like that to a patient with any other acute surgical condition. Specific approaches to various intra-abdominal infections are addressed in more detail elsewhere [see Infections of the Upper Abdomen *and* Infections of the Lower Abdomen, *below*].

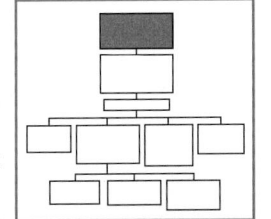

The first step is an accurate history. To begin with, cases of peritonitis are broadly classified as primary, secondary, or tertiary; this classification provides a useful framework for suggesting general approaches to treatment. Primary peritonitis arises spontaneously, without a demonstrable source of contamination, and is generally treated with antibiotics alone; an example is spontaneous bacterial peritonitis in the setting of ascites. Secondary peritonitis is caused by a breach in the GI tract that leads to contamination of a normally sterile space. Control of the source of infection via drainage, resection, diversion, or some combination thereof is imperative for optimizing outcome. Tertiary peritonitis is a poorly defined entity associated with recurrence of intra-abdominal infection after the treatment of secondary peritonitis. It frequently features a diffuse infection in a critically ill patient and may be caused by any of a long list of nosocomial pathogens (e.g., *Pseudomonas aeruginosa, Staphylococcus aureus,* and *Candida albicans*). Management of tertiary peritonitis is complex and must be individualized for each patient.

The acuteness and severity of the presenting symptoms may help localize the origin of the infection. More important, however, they allow appropriate triage of these patients, who are frequently seen in a crowded emergency department. For example, a patient with sudden onset of severe abdominal pain and physiologic derangement must take precedence over almost all other patients, whereas a stable patient presenting with a chronic complaint can be evaluated in a more deliberate fashion. The specifics of the presenting episode (e.g., the onset, location, and nature of the pain and any changes in bowel habits) are undeniably crucial, but the patient's medical and surgical histories, as well as any previous similar illnesses, are equally critical. Many medical problems and therapies are associated with abdominal pain or discomfort, and an accurate accounting of previous surgical manipulation of the abdomen is vital for refining the differential diagnosis, as well as for prioritizing further tests. The question of whether a patient has presented with similar symptoms before (particularly if those symptoms led to a diagnosis) may be important for determining the timing of any intervention, as well as for putting the current complaint in the context of an ongoing condition. In fact, many patients arrive for medical treatment with a strong (and frequently correct) concept of the nature of their disease.

PHYSICAL EXAMINATION

Once the history has been obtained, a thorough physical assessment is performed, with the emphasis on the abdomen, the pelvis (including the vagina), and the rectum. The usual sequence—inspection, auscultation, percussion, and palpation—should be followed as traditionally taught. This sequence need not be extensively reviewed here; however, certain points should be emphasized. With the advent of laparoscopy, inspection must include a careful search for scars indicating previous operations, given that any laparoscopic procedure can be undertaken by way of a variety of trocar sites. Auscultation, though occasionally helpful, is also probably the least specific form of examination. Percussion is valuable for assessing tenderness, as well as for differentiating abdominal distention caused by intraluminal gas or free air (signaled by tympany) from that caused by fluid in the peritoneum, such as ascitic fluid or blood (signaled by dullness).

Proper and humane assessment of the abdomen for tenderness via palpation can be learned only through extensive experience. Gaining the patient's trust is fundamental: an anxious or distressed examinee may respond in a hypersensitive manner, thereby hindering the acquisition of information. An individualized approach is essential as well. Palpation should not be performed in a uniform manner from patient to patient; rather, the amount of tenderness present ought to be judged by the degree of pressure or indentation required to cause a given patient significant discomfort. In the setting of severe abdominal pain, elicitation of rebound tenderness by means of deep palpation followed by rapid release of pressure usually does not improve diagnostic accuracy or alter subsequent evaluation and should therefore be discouraged. Finally, administration of small doses of narcotics to patients with abdominal pain is unlikely to alter an experienced examiner's diagnostic ability for the worse.

Occasionally, a young patient whose history and physical examination (including vital signs) fit the classic clinical picture of appendicitis may be taken to the OR without further assessment.

Recognition and Management of Intra-abdominal Infection

Patient has suspected intra-abdominal infection

Obtain history, including previous surgical manipulation of abdomen.

Perform physical examination, focusing on abdomen, pelvis and vagina, and rectum (inspection, auscultation, percussion, palpation).

Order blood tests as appropriate.
- General tests of systemic response to infection
- Specific tests to localize source or focus of infection

On occasion, a young patient with classic presentation of appendicitis may be taken to OR without blood tests or imaging.

Order diagnostic imaging as appropriate.

Patient has "certain" appendicitis

Resuscitate, give antibiotics, and take to OR.

History and physical exam warrant exploration of abdomen for peritonitis, but confirmation (free air) is needed first; or index of suspicion for peritonitis is very low

Obtain plain abdominal films, including upright chest film.

Patient has upper abdominal pain, elevated bilirubin level or liver function test results, or history of biliary tract disease

Order upper abdominal US. Treat specific infection as appropriate [*see Figure 1*].

All other patients

Order abdominal and pelvic CT scans.

Treat specific infection as appropriate [*see Figure 9*].

Free peritoneal air is present

Resuscitate, give antibiotics, and take to OR.

No free peritoneal air is present, and index of suspicion for peritonitis is low

Discharge from surgical care.

No free peritoneal air is present, but index of suspicion for peritonitis is high

Order abdominal and pelvic CT scans (see above, right).

Practically speaking, however, almost all patients with significant intra-abdominal infections undergo blood tests, and most also undergo some sort of radiologic evaluation.

Investigative Studies

LABORATORY TESTS

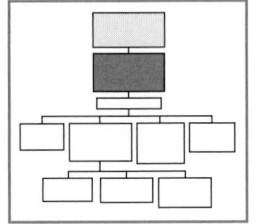

Blood work can be divided into two categories: (1) general tests designed to assess the systemic response to infection and (2) specific tests designed to localize the source or site of infection. The former category includes serum chemistries and hematology studies. The latter category commonly includes amylase and lipase concentrations (in patients suspected of having pancreatitis), bilirubin levels and liver function tests (to evaluate hepatic or biliary tract disease), and lactate levels (when an ischemic bowel is suspected). These tests are discussed further elsewhere, in connection with specific infections (see below). Urinalysis, of course, is necessary whenever urinary tract infection or urolithiasis is a possibility.

DIAGNOSTIC IMAGING

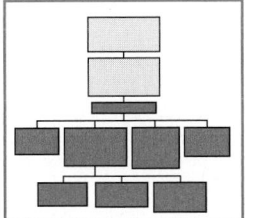

The use of various radiologic studies in the diagnosis of intra-abdominal infection continues to evolve rapidly. Outside the setting of trauma, it is now very rare for patients to undergo operations or other major interventions without first undergoing imaging. At one time, plain films of the abdomen (including an upright chest film) were routinely obtained whenever a significant intra-abdominal infection was suspected, principally to detect free peritoneal air, bowel obstruction, or fecaliths. Abdominal plain films proved to lack sensitivity, specificity, and anatomic definition in this setting and consequently have, in many cases, been supplanted by abdominal and pelvic computed tomographic scanning. There are, however, two circumstances in which plain films of the abdomen remain a reasonable first study for a patient with suspected peritonitis: (1) when the surgeon has almost decided, on the basis of the history and physical examination, to explore the patient yet needs confirming evidence of perforation (i.e., free air), and (2) when the index of suspicion for peritonitis is so low that the plain film studies are intended to rule out an unexpected positive finding and will not be followed by an abdominal CT scan if negative.

Ultrasonography for intra-abdominal infection is useful only for focused examination of specific organ systems; it is inferior to CT scanning for generalized surveillance of the abdomen because of the inability of sound waves to penetrate gas in the bowel. By far the best-delineated use of ultrasonography is in the diagnosis of liver and biliary tract disease, for which its ability to demonstrate cholelithiasis makes it superior to CT and for which it should almost always be the first radiologic test in the appropriate circumstances (e.g., a classic history of biliary colic or an elevated serum bilirubin level). Ultrasonography also visualizes the spleen, the kidneys, and the gynecologic pelvic organs well and has the additional benefit of using no ionizing radiation.

The abdominal and pelvic CT scan, appropriately, has become the key diagnostic test for evaluating patients with suspected peritonitis. This modality is widely available throughout much of the world, and newer scanners yield significantly higher resolution than older ones, with reduced scanning times and radiation exposure. CT is highly sensitive for free air, fluid collections, bowel wall abnormalities, and inflammatory changes. Now that significant intra-abdominal infections—perhaps even in the setting of a perforated viscus—are no longer automatically considered to mandate operative intervention, the ability of CT scanning to identify the source and assess the chronicity of an infection is critical to effective modern management. Multiple common conditions have now been defined for which an adequate CT scan allows nonoperative management either as definitive therapy (e.g., expectant treatment of a simple perforated duodenal ulcer) or as a means of temporizing (e.g., percutaneous drainage of a periappendiceal or peridiverticular abscess). In addition, in experienced hands, a negative CT scan of the abdomen and the pelvis virtually excludes any significant acute surgical illness.

It must be noted, however, that a CT scan is not necessary in all patients with abdominal pain, and the decision whether to obtain one should be made on the basis of predefined guidelines or with the input of a general surgeon. When the need for operative intervention has already been determined, as in a classic case of appendicitis, imaging is unnecessary. In addition, some patients with an intra-abdominal infection amenable to nonoperative management (e.g., simple, mild diverticular disease that can be treated with oral antibiotics on an outpatient basis) do not necessarily benefit from CT scanning.

In selected cases, other forms of imaging may be used. Magnetic resonance imaging, though usually more difficult to obtain in an emergency and logistically more complicated than CT scanning, yields excellent tomographic images and has the added benefit of imaging vascular structures and the pancreaticobiliary tree more precisely. Nonetheless, MRI has no significant role in the evaluation of acute peritonitis. Nuclear medicine scans and fluoroscopic studies, though occasionally useful adjuncts for evaluating biliary tract and upper GI disorders, also play no role in the assessment of acute peritonitis.

Options for Intervention

Once an intra-abdominal infection is diagnosed, there are multiple options for intervention. Not infrequently, an approach combining several modalities is warranted. Occasionally, administration of systemic antibiotics is all that is necessary (or practical), as in cases of spontaneous primary bacterial peritonitis or of multiple infected fluid collections that are small but too numerous to drain. Single abscesses, particularly those without thick or particulate contents, can be adequately treated with simple aspiration and a short course of antibiotics. For discrete infected fluid collections in almost any setting, placement of a percutaneous indwelling drain (most commonly under radiologic guidance) is currently the treatment of choice. Operative management, either open or laparoscopic, is employed for resection of damaged or inflamed and unsalvageable organs, diversion of enteric contents, or drainage of collections that are too thick or numerous for percutaneous drainage. Beyond these general guidelines, therapy for specific intra-abdominal infections must be individualized (see below).

Infections of the Upper Abdomen

Biliary tract and pancreatic infections present as a systemic septic response or as infections localized in the upper abdomen [see Figure 1]. Typical findings include abdominal pain, a tender upper abdominal mass, fever and leukocytosis, and jaundice. Various combinations of these symptoms may occur, but it is convenient to consider three common clinical presentations. In each of the presentations, one or two symptoms dominate: (1) upper abdom-

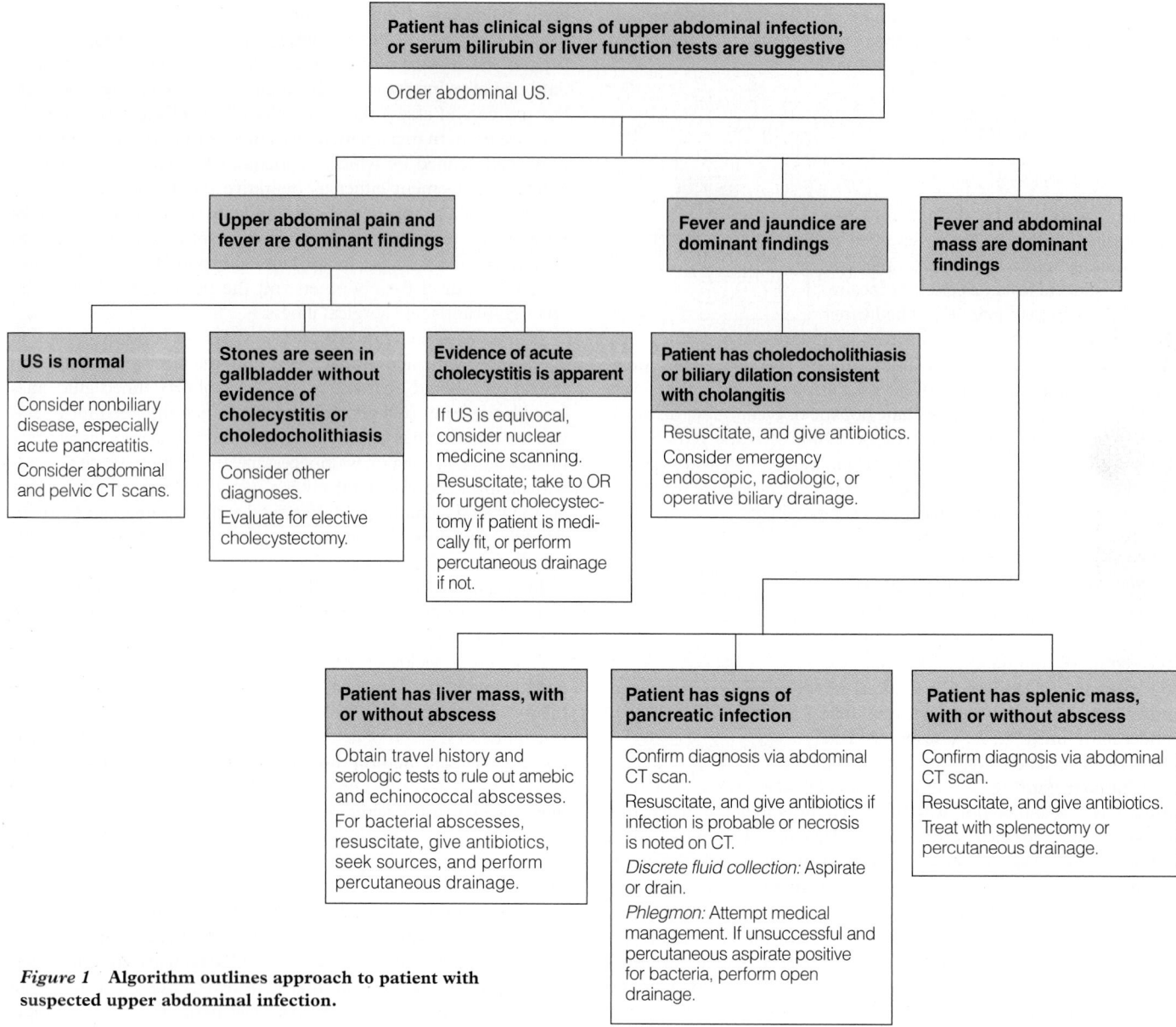

Patient has clinical signs of upper abdominal infection, or serum bilirubin or liver function tests are suggestive

Order abdominal US.

Upper abdominal pain and fever are dominant findings

Fever and jaundice are dominant findings

Fever and abdominal mass are dominant findings

US is normal

Consider nonbiliary disease, especially acute pancreatitis.
Consider abdominal and pelvic CT scans.

Stones are seen in gallbladder without evidence of cholecystitis or choledocholithiasis

Consider other diagnoses.
Evaluate for elective cholecystectomy.

Evidence of acute cholecystitis is apparent

If US is equivocal, consider nuclear medicine scanning.
Resuscitate; take to OR for urgent cholecystectomy if patient is medically fit, or perform percutaneous drainage if not.

Patient has choledocholithiasis or biliary dilation consistent with cholangitis

Resuscitate, and give antibiotics.
Consider emergency endoscopic, radiologic, or operative biliary drainage.

Patient has liver mass, with or without abscess

Obtain travel history and serologic tests to rule out amebic and echinococcal abscesses.
For bacterial abscesses, resuscitate, give antibiotics, seek sources, and perform percutaneous drainage.

Patient has signs of pancreatic infection

Confirm diagnosis via abdominal CT scan.
Resuscitate, and give antibiotics if infection is probable or necrosis is noted on CT.
Discrete fluid collection: Aspirate or drain.
Phlegmon: Attempt medical management. If unsuccessful and percutaneous aspirate positive for bacteria, perform open drainage.

Patient has splenic mass, with or without abscess

Confirm diagnosis via abdominal CT scan.
Resuscitate, and give antibiotics.
Treat with splenectomy or percutaneous drainage.

Figure 1 **Algorithm outlines approach to patient with suspected upper abdominal infection.**

inal pain and fever, (2) fever and jaundice, and (3) an upper abdominal mass and fever. These clinical findings signal the need for a battery of screening tests, including a complete blood count (CBC); routine blood tests of liver function; determination of serum amylase level, prothrombin time (PT), and partial thromboplastin time (PTT); blood culture; chest and abdominal x-rays; and abdominal ultrasonography. When considered together, the clinical findings and the test results allow early differentiation of the three most common disease entities: acute cholecystitis, acute cholangitis, and acute pancreatitis.

UPPER ABDOMINAL PAIN AND FEVER

Patients with upper abdominal sepsis may present with epigastric or right upper quadrant pain and fever. Only two thirds of these patients admitted with a working diagnosis of acute cholecystitis have acute biliary inflammation.[1] In some patients, non-surgical conditions (e.g., pneumonia, acute hepatitis, familial Mediterranean fever, herpes zoster of the intercostal nerves, and gastroenteritis) can be distinguished clinically from biliary disease. The most important screening test for acute biliary infection is the

abdominal ultrasound examination: an abnormal image of the gallbladder or bile ducts supports a biliary etiology [*see Figure 2*].

The differential diagnosis should include acute cholecystitis, biliary colic, acute pancreatitis, and acute cholangitis, each of which requires specific management [*see Table 1*]. For example, initial management of biliary colic and mild acute pancreatitis is usually nonoperative, whereas severe acute cholangitis and acute cholecystitis are treated by means of surgical, endoscopic, or radiologic intervention (see below). Clinical features and blood test results, though helpful, may be inconclusive. The abdominal ultrasonogram may provide specific clues. Stones appear in biliary colic [*see Figure 2*]; stones and thickening of the gallbladder wall, in acute cholecystitis; gallstones and dilatation of the common bile duct (CBD), in acute cholangitis; and pancreatic enlargement and sonolucency, in pancreatitis.

Pancreatitis

Diagnosis Differentiating acute pancreatitis from acute cholecystitis may be difficult. The serum amylase level lacks specificity, but if the clinical findings suggest acute pancreatitis, an ele-

Table 2 Ranson's Early Objective Signs
of Severity of Acute Pancreatitis[2]

On Admission	After Initial 48 Hours
Age > 55 yr Glucose > 200 mg/dl WBC > 16,000/mm³ LDH > 350 IU/L AST > 250 Sigma Frankel U/dl	Serum Ca²⁺ < 8 mg/dl Arterial PO₂ < 60 mm Hg Base deficit > 4 mEq/L BUN increase > 5 mg/dl Hematocrit fall > 10% Fluid sequestration > 6,000 ml

Note: < 3 signs = mild pancreatitis;   3 signs = severe pancreatitis.
AST—aspartate aminotransferase   BUN—blood urea nitrogen   PO₂—oxygen tension
WBC—white blood cell

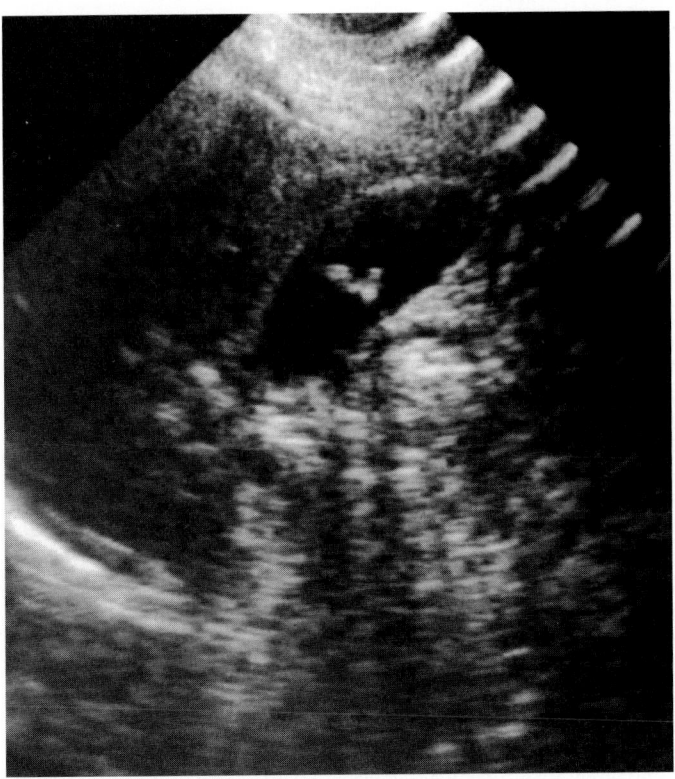

Figure 2 **Abnormal abdominal ultrasound examination shows calculi in gallbladder casting shadows on underlying liver tissue.**

vated level of serum amylase clinches the diagnosis. In one study, the initial laboratory results in 100 patients with acute pancreatitis were compared with those in 100 patients with acute abdominal pain caused by acute cholecystitis, perforated peptic ulcer, or acute appendicitis.[2] The serum amylase concentrations were elevated in 95% of patients with acute pancreatitis but were normal in 95% of patients with acute abdominal pain from other causes. These concentrations peak within the first 48 hours and are almost always elevated in biliary pancreatitis[3]; in fact, a serum amylase concentration above 1,000 U/L strongly suggests a biliary origin of the pancreatitis.[4] In addition, determination of serum lipase levels has been shown to be more specific than and at least as sensitive as determination of amylase levels for the detection of

acute pancreatitis.[5,6] Unless clinical findings and the results of biochemical tests and ultrasonography are unequivocal, a contrast-enhanced spiral abdominal CT scan is usually performed to establish the diagnosis and stage acute pancreatitis. It has been suggested, however, that CT scanning should be reserved for patients with clinically suspected severe acute gallstone pancreatitis, on the grounds that the results would not change the recommended course of action in other patients.[7] Occasionally, a very mild pancreatitis may give rise to no findings on a CT scan, and a normal technetium-99m (⁹⁹ᵐTc)–labeled HIDA (lidofenin) scan may help differentiate this condition from acute cholecystitis.

Treatment Given that pancreatitis encompasses a wide range of diseases with varying degrees of severity, treatment must be individualized for each patient. Possible therapeutic strategies range from outpatient management with temporary dietary modification (for very mild cases) to open debridement and complex intensive care (for severe cases). It is therefore useful to base possible treatment approaches in particular cases on the cause and severity of the pancreatitis.

Gallstone pancreatitis. Standard therapy for gallstone pancreatitis includes I.V. fluids and narcotic analgesics. Nasogastric suction is useful in patients with significant ileus but need not be used routinely.[8] The use of systemic antibiotics is controversial; they are of benefit in the 10% to 34% of patients who have concomitant cholangitis.[9] Other treatments suggested previously—including total parenteral nutrition (TPN) and various pharmacologic agents (e.g., cimetidine, somatostatin, glucagon, and insulin)—have not proved useful in all cases of gallstone pancreatitis.[10] Continuous intraduodenal infusion of an elemental diet has reduced exocrine pancreatic secretions in animal experiments.[11] Furthermore, enteral feeding has been shown to be beneficial and to decrease disease severity in patients with acute pancreatitis.[12-14]

In clinical practice, the need for further treatment depends on the severity of the acute pancreatitis. Severity determines both the risk of sepsis, which governs outcome, and the risk associated with early cholecystectomy [*see 63 Cholecystectomy and Common Bile Duct Exploration*]. The most commonly used clinical prognostic index in North America was developed by Ranson and reliably defines the severity of pancreatitis [*see Table 2*].[2] In mild pancreatitis, one or two Ranson signs are present; in more severe pancreatitis, three to five signs are present; and in very severe pancreatitis, more than five signs are present. This distinction serves to stratify further treatment. Other clinical prognostic scores, such as the APACHE-II (Acute Physiology and Chronic Health Evaluation II) and APACHE-III scores and the Balthazar score, have been shown to possess discriminatory value in identifying patients at high risk for complications.[15,16]

Table 1 Diagnostic Indicators of
Upper Abdominal Pain and Fever

	Biliary Colic	Acute Cholecystitis	Acute Pancreatitis
Duration	Short: 40% < 1 hr	Persistent	Persistent
Pathogenesis	Visceral	Somatic	Retroperitoneal
Signs	Tender	Guarding and spasm	Guarding and spasm
Laboratory tests Liver function tests	Occasionally abnormal	Abnormal	Abnormal
Serum amylase	Normal	Normal or slightly increased	Increased
Leukocyte counts	Often normal	Increased	Increased

Mild pancreatitis usually subsides within 1 week of onset. Most surgeons defer cholecystectomy until then; urgent operation should be reserved for cases complicated by biliary sepsis, and it may reveal acute cholecystitis in as many as 31% of patients.[17]

An attack of acute gallstone pancreatitis is initiated by obstruction at the confluence of the lower end of the CBD and the pancreatic duct by a stone or by edema at the ampulla of Vater resulting from stone migration. These stones may be found and removed in 63% to 78% of patients who undergo operation within 72 hours of admission[17-19] [see 64 Procedures for Benign and Malignant Biliary Tract Disease], but they are present in only 3% to 33% of patients explored after the first week.[18-22] A randomized trial exploring the optimal timing of surgery for gallstone pancreatitis showed that early surgery (≤ 48 hours after admission) was not associated with significantly increased morbidity or mortality in patients with mild pancreatitis but did not change prognosis.[23]

Endoscopic retrograde cholangiopancreatography (ERCP). Early ERCP and sphincterotomy [see 60 Gastrointestinal Endoscopy] has been suggested as an alternative to surgery of the CBD in patients with mild pancreatitis. However, randomized trials comparing endoscopic treatment with conservative treatment within the first 72 hours in patients with mild pancreatitis did not find that urgent endoscopic sphincterotomy improved outcome in this group of patients.[24,25] Other studies showed that delaying surgery beyond 6 weeks may lead to a 32% to 57% risk of recurrent pancreatitis.[26,27] Therefore, cholecystectomy and cholangiography should be delayed only until just before patients are discharged from the hospital, 5 to 15 days after the onset of symptoms. Laparoscopic

cholecystectomy has facilitated this approach safely without prolonging hospital stay.

Severe pancreatitis. Patients with three or more Ranson signs are at particular risk for pancreatic sepsis.[28] Repeated clinical and radiologic evaluation is required in these patients to ensure early detection of complications, because the outcome of an episode of pancreatitis depends on whether sepsis supervenes. When infection occurs, operative debridement and drainage are required [see Fever and Abdominal Mass, below]. Some surgeons have attempted to alter the course of severe disease by early operation; however, urgent operation is associated with a high mortality in patients with more than three Ranson signs.[19,21,23,29] To avoid the mortality associated with early operative intervention, some clinicians advocate early diagnosis by ERCP [see Figure 3], followed by biliary decompression by means of endoscopic sphincterotomy and stone extraction. In a randomized trial comparing early ERCP and sphincterotomy with conservative therapy in patients with severe acute pancreatitis, ERCP and sphincterotomy decreased morbidity from 61% to 24% and lowered mortality from 18% to 4%.[24] The results of this trial, however, have been the subject of debate, and the success of this approach has been attributed by some authors to the treatment of a concomitant cholangitis rather than of the actual pancreatitis.[25] A well-conducted trial that excluded patients with concomitant cholangitis was published in 1997; unfortunately, this trial was unable to answer the question definitively, because too few patients with severe pancreatitis had been recruited.[30] It appears that ERCP is warranted mainly in cases of acute pancreatitis complicated by cholangitis and biliary sepsis.[31,32]

Use of peritoneal lavage in early severe pancreatitis was advocated in one study to decrease morbidity and mortality.[33] Use of standard lavage over a 2-day period did not improve patient outcome, but use of peritoneal lavage for 7 days (long peritoneal lavage) yielded some improvement in outcome.[34] Early use of antibiotics and selective decontamination have been proposed as a means of reducing septic complications, but neither has convincingly or reproducibly been shown to improve prognosis.[35,36] Although prophylactic antibiotics have been shown to decrease the rate of infectious complications in severe acute pancreatitis, they have not clearly been shown to reduce overall disease mortality.[35,37-40] Attempts have been made to modulate the initial systemic inflammatory response seen in early severe acute pancreatitis to reduce the risk of subsequent infection and improve overall prognosis; somatostatin has exhibited limited success in this regard.[41,42] Another drug in this category, the platelet-aggregating factor (PAF) inhibitor lexipafant, initially yielded promising results in animal models[43,44] and in phase II trials[45]; however, a 2001 trial using the same drug did not find it efficacious for treating severe acute pancreatitis.[46]

Acute Cholecystitis

Diagnosis Acute cholecystitis is the most common diagnosis in patients presenting with upper abdominal pain and fever and is characterized by the clinical finding of a midinspiratory arrest on palpation of the right upper quadrant (Murphy's sign). As noted (see above), with the widespread availability of ultrasonography, acute cholecystitis can usually be diagnosed rapidly on the basis of the findings of gallbladder wall thickening, pericholecystic fluid, and stones. Occasionally, more complex cases must be evaluated with nuclear medicine scanning to look for cystic duct obstruction. Concurrent acute obstructive cholangitis must also be considered in all patients with acute cholecystitis. Supportive laboratory data include a high serum bilirubin level and an increased

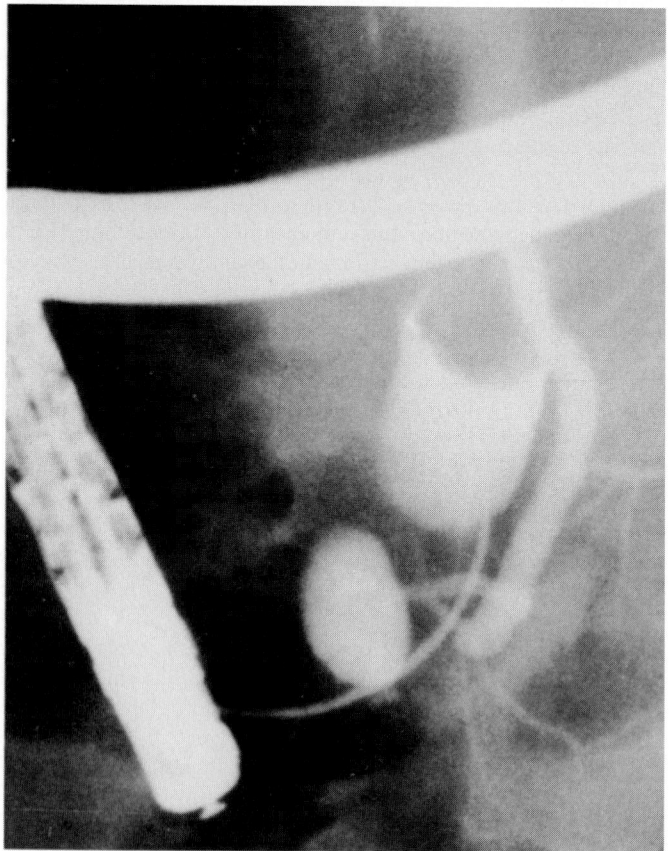

Figure 3 **Endoscopic retrograde cholangiopancreatography shows distal CBD stone in acute pancreatitis. Papillotome has been placed through sphincter of Oddi in preparation for endoscopic sphincterotomy.**

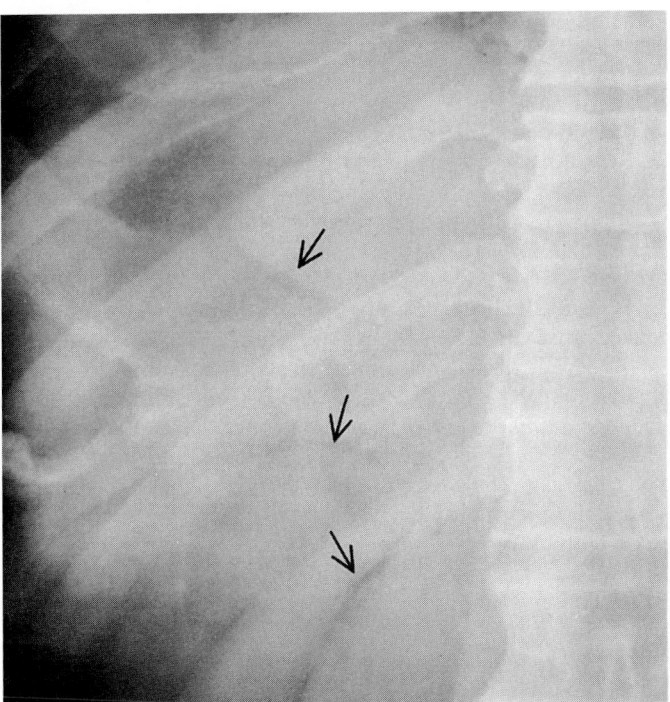

Figure 4 **Air outlines gallbladder and bile ducts in emphysematous cholecystitis.**

Table 3 Comparison of Acute Cholecystitis and Emphysematous Cholecystitis

	Emphysematous Cholecystitis	Acute Cholecystitis
Gender	70% male	70% female
Stones	70%	90%
Bile culture positive	95%	66%
Clostridia found	46%	1.2%
Gangrenous gallbladder	75%	2.5%
Perforation of gallbladder	20%	4%
Mortality at age < 60 yr	15%	1.5%
Pathogenesis	Ischemia, obstruction	Obstruction

alkaline phosphatase level. Positive blood cultures and dilated biliary ducts on abdominal ultrasonography usually confirm the diagnosis.

Emphysematous cholecystitis. An uncommon and insidious variant of acute cholecystitis, emphysematous cholecystitis is characterized by gas in the gallbladder lumen or wall or in the pericholecystic soft tissue and biliary ducts secondary to gas-forming bacteria. The key to the diagnosis is the presence of air on abdominal x-ray [*see Figure 4*] or ultrasound examination. Three stages of emphysematous cholecystitis have been defined: (1) gas is seen only in the lumen of the gallbladder, (2) a ring of gas is identified in the wall of the gallbladder, and (3) gas is seen in the tissues adjacent to the wall. Compared with ordinary acute cholecystitis, emphysematous cholecystitis is associated with a fivefold increase in the risk of gallbladder perforation, as well as a 10-fold increase in mortality in patients younger than 60 years [*see Table 3*].[47]

Studies from the 1960s noted an increased risk of gangrene and perforation of the acutely inflamed gallbladder in patients with diabetes mellitus.[48,49] The mortality for acute cholecystitis was also shown to be five to 10 times higher in patients with diabetes than in other patients. Later studies, however, did not show an increased mortality in patients with both diabetes and acute cholecystitis.[50,51] Nevertheless, one third of patients with emphysematous cholecystitis also have diabetes. This factor, coupled with the current tendency to perform cholecystectomy early in most patients with acute cholecystitis, may account for the disparity between previous studies and later reports.

Acute acalculous cholecystitis. Another variant of acute cholecystitis is acalculous cholecystitis; though still rare, it became more common from the 1950s through the 1990s. This disease was originally described as occurring after surgical treatment of unrelated disease but was subsequently identified in patients with multiple trauma, prolonged critical illness, and sepsis. Predisposing factors include gallbladder ischemia (in patients with shock or trauma) and biliary stasis (in prolonged fasting, hyperalimentation, and

sustained narcotics therapy). In addition, focal inflammation may cause biliary colonization or may activate coagulation factor XII, thereby causing severe injury to the blood vessels in the gallbladder muscularis and serosa. A high index of suspicion is necessary. Acute acalculous cholecystitis should be considered in any postoperative or acutely ill patient with upper abdominal pain and fever or with unexplained fever and leukocytosis. It is particularly common 2 to 4 weeks after injury. The diagnosis is confirmed by findings on abdominal ultrasound examination [*see Figure 5*] and ⁹⁹ᵐTc-labeled HIDA scanning coupled with infusion of cholecystokinin and morphine.[52-54]

Treatment Standard treatment of acute cholecystitis consists of I.V. fluids, analgesics, and cholecystectomy. Although the timing of operation is controversial in ordinary acute cholecystitis, cholecystectomy should be performed at the earliest opportunity [*see 63 Cholecystectomy and Common Bile Duct Exploration*]. This approach has been confirmed by at least one randomized trial comparing early with late laparoscopic cholecystectomy.[55] The delayed-surgery group had a greater need for conversion to open cholecystectomy (23% versus 11%), as well as a longer average total

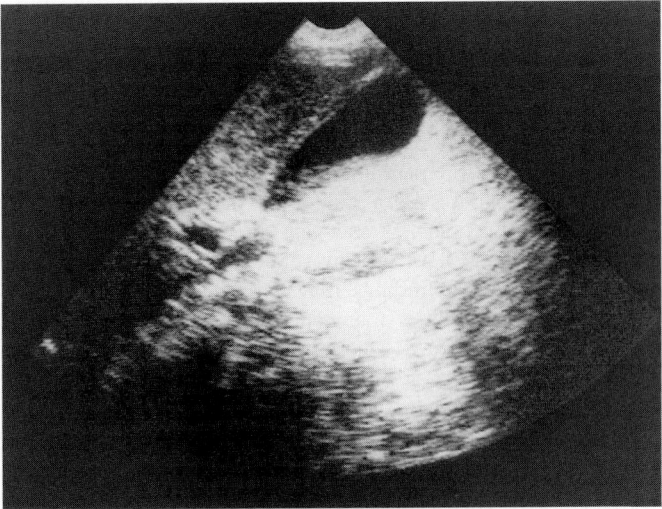

Figure 5 **Abnormal abdominal ultrasound examination confirms diagnosis of acute acalculous cholecystitis. When image is compared with that in Figure 2, thickening of gallbladder wall and intraluminal debris are obvious.**

hospital stay and convalescence. Systemic antibiotics are not required; however, single-dose antibiotic prophylaxis (e.g., cefazolin, 2 g I.V.) can be given at the start of the operation [see 5 Prevention of Postoperative Infection].[56-58]

Some patients with acute cholecystitis are at high risk for gangrene and perforation of the gallbladder. It is crucial to identify these patients and perform cholecystectomy promptly because delay increases morbidity and mortality. Clinically, gangrene and perforation of the gallbladder in this high-risk population are suggested by marked systemic toxicity or by the radiologic demonstration of either emphysematous cholecystitis or acute acalculous cholecystitis.

With ordinary acute cholecystitis, body temperature is slightly increased in most patients—averaging 37.8° C (100.04° F)—but is normal in 20% of patients. By comparison, the risk of gangrene and perforation is reportedly higher in patients with marked systemic toxicity, manifested by a pulse rate greater than 120 beats/min, a body temperature higher than 39° C (102.2° F), and a left shift in the differential white blood cell count, showing more than 90% polymorphonuclear leukocytes. Unfortunately, findings of systemic toxicity are frequently absent in elderly patients.

Patients with acute cholecystitis who have signs of systemic toxicity, emphysematous cholecystitis, or acalculous cholecystitis are at high risk for gallbladder gangrene and perforation and therefore require prompt and aggressive treatment. I.V. antibiotic therapy with a single agent (e.g., ceftriaxone, piperacillin, or a quinolone such as ciprofloxacin or ofloxacin) can be given.[59,60] Early cholecystectomy is the treatment of choice. Unfortunately, mortality may be as high as 20% to 30% with the traditional surgical approach.[61] If perforation and gangrene are not suspected but medical illness poses a high risk of mortality from operation, nonoperative supportive therapy may suffice. If this fails, another treatment option is cholecystostomy.

Percutaneous transhepatic cholecystostomy has been recommended for these high-risk patients,[62] particularly where there is a low risk for perforation of the gallbladder.[63] To determine the risk of gallbladder perforation, a risk score can be assigned to each of seven findings that may be present on the preoperative abdominal ultrasound examination: pericholecystic fluid, 7 points; distention of the gallbladder, 4 points; intraluminal membrane, 4 points; intraluminal debris, 3 points; round gallbladder, 3 points; sonolucent zone in the gallbladder wall, 2 points; and a thick gallbladder wall (> 3.5 mm), 1 point.[63] A patient with a total risk score of 12 or more points requires urgent cholecystectomy; one with a lower score who does not respond to conservative treatment may be treated with percutaneous transhepatic cholecystostomy.

A 1997 review of 59 patients exhibiting the septic response who underwent successful percutaneous radiologic cholecystostomy defined predictors of a successful clinical outcome: localized right upper quadrant tenderness and gallstones, as well as gallstones and pericholecystic fluid on ultrasound examination.[64] Patients with more equivocal findings may derive greater benefit from more invasive techniques that can simultaneously be used for diagnostic purposes (e.g., laparoscopy, which can even be performed at the ICU bedside[65]).

A few patients with acute cholecystitis will have concurrent acute cholangitis. Cholecystostomy is contraindicated in these patients because of its high mortality; adequate drainage of the CBD is required in such cases [see Fever and Jaundice, below].

FEVER AND JAUNDICE

An alternative presentation of upper abdominal infection includes patients whose predominant symptoms are fever and jaundice, with pain a less marked component. Jaundice is almost always associated with obstruction of the biliary tree, either intrahepatic or extrahepatic. The combination of fever with jaundice always suggests acute cholangitis, a condition that can have a fulminant and fatal course if not treated promptly.

Acute Cholangitis

Diagnosis If a patient presents with a temperature higher than 38.5° C (101.3° F) in conjunction with jaundice [see 45 Jaundice], the possibility of acute cholangitis should always be investigated. If cholangitis is present, laboratory studies will reveal leukocytosis, and blood cultures will often be positive. A finding of gallstones and dilated biliary ducts on abdominal ultrasound examination supports the diagnosis. Reynolds' pentad is present in the full-blown syndrome.[66] This syndrome includes upper abdominal pain, fever and chills, jaundice, hypotension, and mental status changes. Acute cholangitis is usually related to choledocholithiasis, recent biliary manipulation, or biliary stenting performed for chronic obstruction.

Gallbladder infections. Gallbladder empyema can duplicate most of the findings associated with acute cholangitis. In this condition, acute cholecystitis is complicated by suppuration within the gallbladder, which then becomes the focus of generalized sepsis. The distended gallbladder may be palpable and tender. When jaundice is associated with empyema of the gallbladder, it is less likely to be obstructive than when it is associated with acute cholecystitis. True empyema of the gallbladder is rare. Treatment includes administration of I.V. fluids, systemic antibiotic therapy, analgesics, and early cholecystectomy.

In some patients with jaundice and inflammation, a stone impacted in the cystic duct or in Hartmann's pouch may suggest choledocholithiasis, but preoperative ERCP shows an extrinsic compression of the duct known as Mirizzi syndrome. Two types of Mirizzi syndrome exist. In type I, a stone impacted in the cystic duct or Hartmann's pouch compresses the common hepatic duct and causes inflammation, leading to jaundice. Treatment consists of obliteration of the cystic duct and careful partial cholecystectomy, with the neck of the gallbladder left in place. In type II, protrusion of the stone into the hepatic duct erodes the septum between the cystic duct and the hepatic duct and causes a cholecystocholedochal fistula. Treatment involves internal biliary drainage to the wall of the cholecystocholedochal defect, usually with a choledochojejunostomy [see 64 Procedures for Benign and Malignant Biliary Tract Disease], in addition to cholecystectomy.[67]

Primary sclerosing cholangitis. Patients with primary sclerosing cholangitis, especially those who have undergone internal or external biliary drainage, are at high risk for recurrent bouts of ascending cholangitis. Primary sclerosing cholangitis predominantly affects young males, particularly those with chronic ulcerative colitis. The diagnosis is suggested by the dominant cholestatic biochemical profile—that is, elevation of the serum bilirubin concentration, the serum alkaline phosphatase level, and aspartate aminotransferase activity. Because of the concomitant hepatic scarring, ultrasonography may not reveal the presence of dilated intrahepatic ducts. Definitive diagnosis requires visualization of the beaded appearance of the biliary tree by means of cholangiography. Cholangiocarcinoma and secondary sclerosing cholangitis in patients with Caroli disease or choledochal cysts may mimic these clinical, biochemical, and radiologic features, but this is an unusual occurrence and can be distinguished by careful follow-up of patients.

Currently, magnetic resonance cholangiopancreatography (MRCP) is the imaging modality of choice for elective management of patients with primary sclerosing cholangitis, in that it yields results comparable to those of ERCP without being invasive.[68-71]

Other causes of cholangitis. An uncommon cause of recurrent cholangitis in North America is Oriental cholangiohepatitis, which is characterized by intrahepatic duct scarring, biliary strictures, and hepatolithiasis, as demonstrated by cholangiography. Irreversible intrahepatic and extrahepatic liver damage may result because of the overwhelming propensity of these patients to form calcium bilirubinate stones.

A few patients with cholangiocarcinoma causing bile duct obstruction or liver metastases causing intrahepatic bile duct obstruction may also present with a clinical picture suggestive of cholangitis. CT followed by MRCP can delineate the diagnosis in most such cases. Treatment consists of I.V. antibiotics and biliary drainage by radiographic or surgical means.

Treatment Once acute cholangitis is diagnosed, resuscitation is started with I.V. fluids and antibiotics, such as fluoroquinolones, mezlocillin, cefoperazone, or piperacillin,[59,72-75] particularly in patients with marked hyperbilirubinemia, in whom treatment with aminoglycosides may contribute to renal toxicity in up to 33% of cases [see *122 Acute Renal Failure*].[76] These antibiotics are required to deal with the various aerobic bacteria, of which *Escherichia coli*, *Klebsiella* species, and enterococci are the most frequently encountered in this setting. Anaerobes may be isolated in 15% to 30% of patients and are particularly likely to be present in diabetics, the elderly, and patients who have previously undergone biliary manipulation. In patients with indwelling catheters, *Enterobacter*, *Pseudomonas*, and *Candida* organisms are being isolated with increasing frequency. Indications of high risk include a serum bilirubin concentration higher than 3 mg/dl.

Approximately 75% of patients with acute cholangitis respond to conservative measures,[77] and supportive treatment is continued. Subsequent investigations usually include CT followed by MRCP.[78,79] Because of their invasive nature, ERCP and needle percutaneous transhepatic cholangiography (PTC) are reserved for cases in which a drainage procedure is anticipated or the information from the MRCP is deemed inadequate.

For the 25% of patients who do not respond to conservative treatment, early recognition may improve their prognosis. In one study, patients who did not respond immediately to antibiotics had a mortality of 62%, compared with a mortality of 1.5% in those who improved.[80] In another study, indicators of high risk were an arterial blood pH less than 7.4, a serum bilirubin concentration above 9 mmol/L, a blood platelet count below 150,000/mm³, and a serum albumin concentration lower than 3 g/dl.[102] These high-risk patients often have systemic hypotension, mental confusion, a temperature higher than 39° C (102.2° F), or hypothermia. Occasionally, acute cholangitis is complicated by disseminated intravascular coagulation (DIC), which manifests itself as a tendency to bruise and bleed or merely as prolongation of the PT and the PTT, together with a fall in the blood platelet count [see *8 Bleeding and Transfusion*]. If DIC is suspected, the diagnosis should be confirmed and treatment started before biliary decompression.

Patients with refractory cholangitis who do not improve within 24 hours require urgent biliary decompression. Urgent biliary decompression had traditionally been accomplished via surgical exploration of the CBD and T-tube drainage [see *64 Procedures for Benign and Malignant Biliary Tract Disease*]. Cholecystostomy is an inadequate and often fatal option in this context. Rarely, T-tube insertion alone may be lifesaving in a desperately ill patient; generally, however, definitive internal decompression is preferable.

Unfortunately, any surgical decompression in these critically ill patients can result in a mortality of 30% to 40%.[82-85] Furthermore, reoperation is required in one third of survivors because important diagnostic information is not available at the initial laparotomy. As a result, nonoperative methods of biliary decompression, including percutaneous transhepatic biliary drainage (PTBD) and endoscopic sphincterotomy at ERCP, have gained favor. PTBD was originally developed for preoperative management of biliary obstruction without cholangitis but has not been found to be beneficial in that setting. At present, it is mainly used for the management of proximal bile duct strictures or for the treatment of cases not amenable to ERCP; its complication rate is less than 10%.[86]

Although PTBD can reduce the mortality associated with initial biliary decompression, many patients still require a definitive operation. Consequently, endoscopic sphincterotomy [see *60 Gastrointestinal Endoscopy*] has been proposed for decompression of the biliary tree in patients with acute cholangitis from choledocholithiasis [see *Figure 6*]. In a study of 82 patients with acute cholangitis caused by CBD calculi, early operation was employed in 28 patients, endoscopic sphincterotomy in 43, and antibiotic therapy alone in 11.[87] Surgical mortality was 21% and morbidity 57%; by comparison, mortality for endoscopic sphincterotomy was 5% and morbidity 28%. Others confirmed these findings.[81] In patients whose gallbladder is still in place, endoscopic sphincterotomy alone, without cholecystectomy, may even be a reasonable long-term option. Of 23 patients whose gallbladders were left in situ,[87] only two required cholecystectomy in the 1- to 7-year follow-up period: one for empyema of the gallbladder and one for recurrent cholangitis.

An increasingly recognized cause of cholangitis is biliary sepsis after manipulation of the biliary tree with ERCP or PTBD. Treatment includes I.V. fluids and antibiotics. To prevent this complication, prophylactic antibiotics should be administered before every biliary manipulation.[88]

FEVER AND ABDOMINAL MASS

A third group of patients with upper abdominal infection present with fever and an upper abdominal mass identified either by clinical signs or through diagnostic imaging. Even if the mass is only vaguely palpable, the mass effect is demonstrable on ultrasound examination of the abdomen. If the abdominal ultrasound examination is technically unsatisfactory because of intestinal gas, contrast-enhanced CT of the abdomen will facilitate the diagnosis.

The differential diagnosis is aided by the location of the mass. A mass in the right upper quadrant usually indicates acute cholecystitis, though the possibility of a liver abscess must also be considered. A mass in the epigastrium or in the left upper quadrant usually signals a pancreatic infection; in rare instances, a solitary splenic abscess is found. Patients with an intra-abdominal abscess in the subphrenic space or an interloop abscess may also present in this manner.

Liver Abscess

Diagnosis In the setting of acute upper abdominal sepsis, a tender mass in the right upper quadrant is most likely an enlarged, inflamed gallbladder, possibly wrapped with omentum [see Upper Abdominal Pain and Fever, Acute Cholecystitis, *above*]. The next most common cause of fever and abdominal mass in the right upper quadrant, however, is liver abscess.

Pyogenic abscess. Today, pyogenic liver abscess is most commonly related to biliary tract obstruction from gallstones or malignant disorders (35% of cases), and the ultrasound examination may

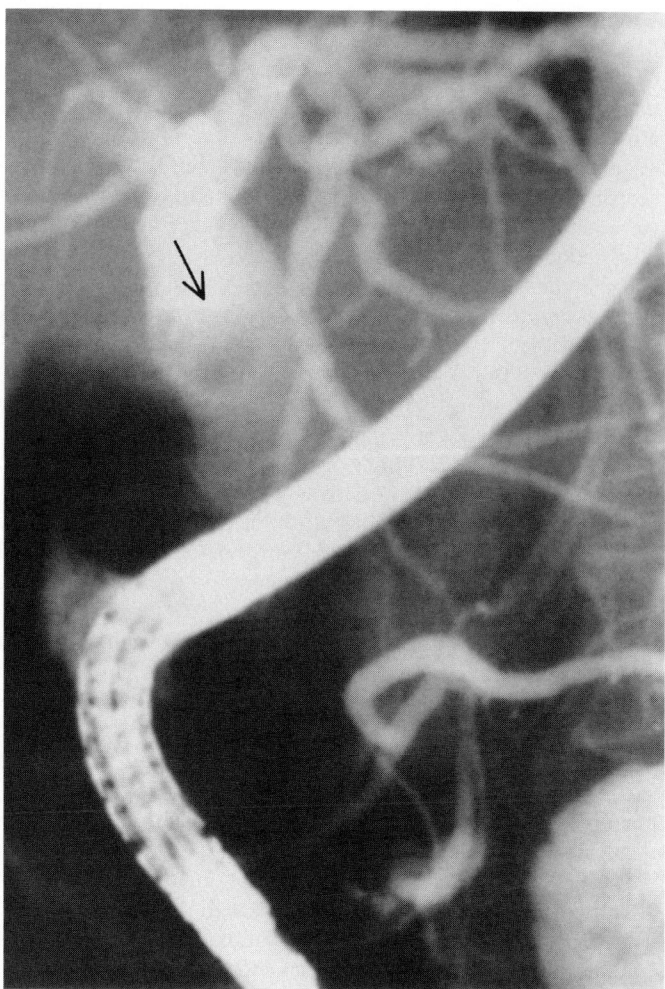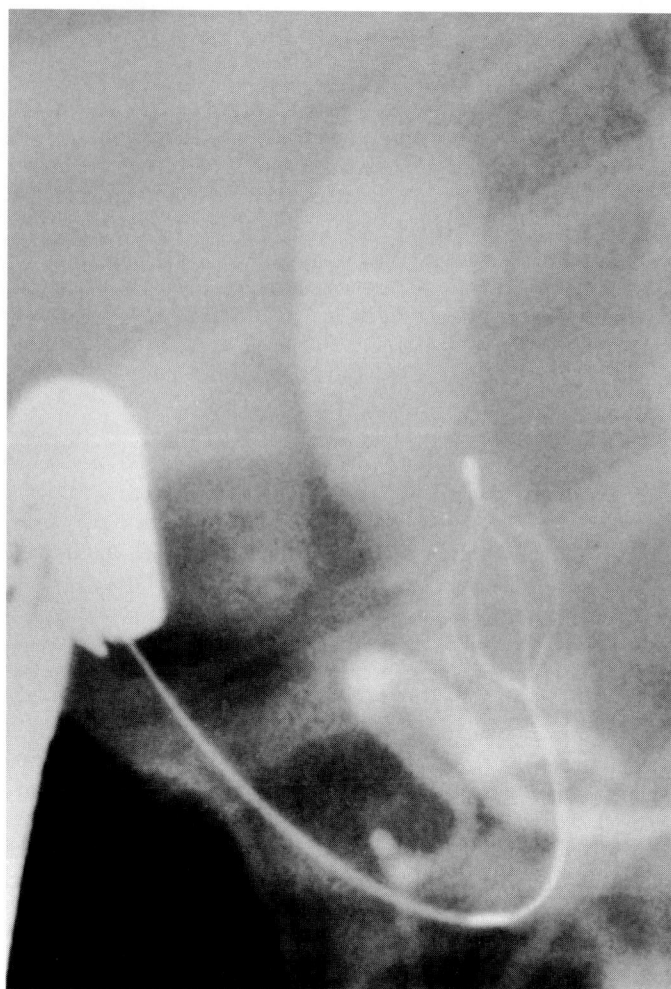

Figure 6 Endoscopic sphincterotomy for acute biliary decompression in acute obstructive cholangitis is shown. At left, stone is visible in common hepatic duct, and papillotome has been passed through sphincter of Oddi. At right, stone is held within a Dormia basket before extraction.

reveal both the abscess and the dilated biliary ducts. Previously, portal pyemia from diverticulitis, inflammatory bowel disease (IBD), or perforated appendicitis had been the most common cause; it now accounts for 20% of cases. Even less common is hematogenous spread via the hepatic artery. Approximately 20% of hepatic abscesses are cryptogenic. Ultrasonographic imaging of the liver may demonstrate lesions as small as 2 cm in the liver substance. CT scanning, however, is superior to ultrasonography for evaluating the presence of air and abscesses as small as 0.5 cm in diameter, especially near the hemidiaphragms.[89] Abdominal CT is also the diagnostic modality of choice in the postoperative patient.[90] ERCP and PTC are indicated only when gallstone disease or a biliary malignancy is the potential source of the abscess. Most liver abscesses occur in the right lobe: 40% are 1.5 to 5 cm in diameter, 40% are 5 to 8 cm in diameter, and 20% are greater than 8 cm in diameter.

Amebic abscess. Although pyogenic abscesses are commonly multiple, no imaging technique can reliably differentiate them from amebic abscesses. The best indication of a parasitic infection is a history of travel to an endemic area (e.g., Mexico, Central America, or Southeast Asia). However, when a hepatic abscess is detected by an imaging technique, serologic tests should be performed to rule out active amebiasis or echinococcal infection. Examination of stool for amebae is insensitive; consequently,

isoenzyme analysis, *Entamoeba histolytica*–specific antigen detection, or even polymerase chain reaction (PCR) is preferred to confirm the diagnosis of amebiasis.[91]

Echinococcal abscess. The diagnosis of echinococcal liver abscess can be confirmed by means of elevated indirect hemagglutination (IHA) titers (> 250). In the late 1980s, a combination of tests that included IHA for *Echinococcus granulosus* and enzyme-linked immunosorbent assay (ELISA) using *E. multilocularis* antigen yielded an 89% species-specific diagnosis of echinococcal disease.[92] Later work indicated that IgG ELISA and IHA were the best tests for follow-up after resection of the abscess. In patients with a favorable clinical outcome, the specific IgG level decreased toward the end of the first year, though in some cases, a positive serologic result persisted beyond 6 years.[93] Diagnostic aspiration is indicated when a diagnosis of pyogenic or amebic abscess is in doubt, but not in echinococcal disease. Aspiration may also be beneficial in patients with left-side abscesses and abscesses greater than 10 cm in diameter. The chest x-ray is abnormal in as many as 50% of cases of amebic abscess, and the plain abdominal x-ray may show calcification of an echinococcal cyst with secondary pyogenic infection.

It is essential to differentiate infected echinococcal cysts from pyogenic abscess: special precautions are required for drainage of echinococcal cysts because of the risk of spillage and anaphylaxis.

Blood cultures are positive in as many as 50% of patients with pyogenic abscess, particularly in those with multiple abscesses; in fact, the presence of *Streptococcus milleri* in the blood suggests a visceral abscess.

Treatment *Pyogenic abscess.* The preferred treatment of pyogenic abscess is closed continuous percutaneous drainage guided by CT or ultrasonography, provided that it is technically feasible and no other indication for laparotomy exists.[94] More than one catheter may be required for complete drainage. An alternative treatment is repeated percutaneous needle aspiration, the results of which are comparable to those of continuous drainage.[95] One advantage to repeated needle aspiration is the elimination of cumbersome, painful drainage tubes, which are prone to dislodgment. Although initial studies showed a good response rate with repeated needle aspiration,[96] the results were not duplicated in a subsequent randomized trial.[97]

The abscess cavity dimensions are followed by serial imaging until the cavity collapses, and the catheter can usually be removed 2 to 3 weeks later. Continuous percutaneous drainage has been associated with a complication rate of 4% and a failure rate of 15%.[98] However, operative drainage is the treatment of choice in patients with an identified intra-abdominal focus of infection and in patients in whom percutaneous drainage is not feasible or has failed.[99] Operative drainage, especially via a laparoscopic approach, is a highly effective treatment option that is associated with low mortality and morbidity.[100] In some patients, a limited hepatic resection [*see 65 Hepatic Resection*] may be required to eliminate multiple abscesses, particularly when an underlying intrahepatic stricture is the source.[101]

Treatment of pyogenic liver abscess should include systemic antibiotic therapy. Approximately 70% of pyogenic liver abscesses yield polymicrobial isolates,[102] and 25% to 45% of the organisms are anaerobic.[103] Multiple anaerobic isolates suggest the colon as a source, whereas a single isolate of *E. coli* suggests a nidus in the biliary tree. Antibiotic treatment should include initial coverage of both aerobes and anaerobes with either a single agent or multiple agents. The need to cover enterococci has been debated, but these organisms clearly are increasingly important nosocomial pathogens. An acceptable initial treatment regimen consists of a single broad-spectrum agent (e.g., ticarcillin-clavulanate or meropenem). It should be noted that significant changes have occurred in the etiology, bacteriology, and treatment of liver abscesses. There is a trend toward a higher incidence of pseudomonal and streptococcal infections, and the frequency of fungal infection is increasing as well.[104] The mortality from this disease remains high, and appropriate antibiotic coverage with drainage is of paramount importance.

The duration of antibiotic therapy is controversial[105]; according to one set of guidelines, antibiotics should be continued for 3 to 4 weeks when the abscess has been excised, 4 to 8 weeks when a solitary abscess has been drained, and 6 to 8 weeks when multiple macroscopic abscesses have been drained.[106] Multiple microscopic abscesses usually require that a biliary source also be treated.[85] The overall prognosis for multiple small hepatic abscesses is not as good as that for solitary abscesses, and the development of a pyogenic abscess in a patient with an underlying hepatobiliary or pancreatic malignancy has been identified as a preterminal event associated with a hospital mortality of 28% and survival of less than 6 months.[107]

Amebic abscess. Medical treatment is now the standard approach to management of amebic liver abscesses. Metronidazole, 750 mg orally three times a day for 10 days, is a highly effective regimen.[108] A favorable response to treatment occurs within 4 to 5 days, and a decrease in the size of the abscess is apparent within 1 week on ultrasonographic examination, though a small residual cavity may persist for as long as 2 years. If the patient's condition does not improve, needle aspiration and culture are indicated. Secondary infection is treated as a pyogenic abscess. Otherwise, oral emetine, 65 mg/day, is added for up to 10 days.

Echinococcal abscess. Symptomatic or secondarily infected echinococcal cysts are best treated by means of surgical excision or marsupialization. The use of oral anthelmintics (e.g., albendazole and mebendazole) has met with limited success. Nevertheless, preoperative treatment with albendazole or mebendazole for 1 month, combined with postoperative treatment, is indicated to reduce the risk of intraoperative seeding or postoperative recurrence.[109,110]

Pancreatic Infection

Diagnosis When the mass is located in the epigastrium or the left upper quadrant, a pancreatic source is most likely. Prompt and accurate diagnosis is crucial because severe pancreatic infection is fatal if left untreated. The key to successful treatment is early diagnosis of infected pancreatic necrosis, infected pseudocyst, and pancreatic abscess. A high index of suspicion is required to diagnose these three infectious processes and to differentiate them from a pancreatic inflammatory mass or phlegmon,[28] in which pancreatic edema and inflammation are present without necrosis or infection.

Correct diagnosis and treatment of infected pancreatic necrosis, infected pseudocyst, and pancreatic abscess require an understanding of their pathophysiology. It is generally assumed that infected pancreatic necrosis develops as a transmural, transductal, lymphatic, or hematogenous infection of a necrotic region of the pancreas. Infection develops in 40% of cases of pancreatic necrosis, usually in week 2 or 3 after development of the acute pancreatitis.[111] Surgical debridement is required in these cases to prevent death. Pancreatic abscesses form by liquefaction of infected necrosis. They usually occur after week 5 of pancreatitis, when the acute phase of the disease has subsided.[112] Pancreatic abscesses are associated with a lower mortality than infected pancreatic necrosis. Like pancreatic abscesses, infected pancreatic collections and pseudocysts present late in the course of pancreatitis. They are associated with a lower mortality than pancreatic abscesses. Caused by infection in 13% of localized collections resulting from ductal blowout, infected pancreatic collections and pseudocysts may occur in the pancreas itself, in contiguous peripancreatic tissue, or in remote (extrapancreatic) tissue.

Clinical evaluation alone is generally insufficient to diagnose pancreatic infection. A clearly defined upper abdominal mass is palpable in only 50% to 75% of cases.[28] In most patients, the screening battery of tests reveals leukocytosis with leukocyte counts greater than 15,000/mm³. Blood cultures are positive in 50% of cases. CT-guided percutaneous aspiration with Gram stain and culture provides the best method of diagnosing pancreatic infection. In one study of 75 patients with clinical toxicity suggestive of pancreatic sepsis, infection was confirmed in only 40%.[113] In another study of 21 patients with pancreatic infection, only five had specific signs on abdominal CT scan.[114] CT-guided diagnostic needle aspiration leads to a correct diagnosis within 72 hours in two thirds of patients, and the mortality associated with operative intervention is 19%; however, CT-guided needle aspiration is beneficial only if pancreatic infection is suspected and if the technique is used early in the course of disease.

Several laboratory markers of pancreatic necrosis have been investigated, such as serum methemalbumin, serum ribonuclease, and C-reactive protein. Most of these markers are too insensitive for routine clinical practice. However, serum levels of C-reactive protein above 10 mg/dl have been reported to be 95% accurate in predicting necrosis.[115]

Currently, the best indicators of infected pancreatic necrosis or abscess are a combination of Ranson's objective prognostic signs [see Table 2] and dynamic abdominal CT scan findings. In Ranson's series, the pancreatic findings on CT were graded in five categories [see Figure 7][116]: (a) normal, (b) pancreatic enlargement alone, (c) inflammation of the pancreas and peripancreatic fat, (d) one peripancreatic fluid collection, and (e) two or more peripancreatic fluid collections. Only category e was associated with a high (61%) incidence of pancreatic abscess. The number of objective prognostic signs present also predicted the subsequent development of an abscess: fewer than three signs, 12.5%; three to five signs, 31.8%; and more than five signs, 80%. However, the value of this method was limited because only five of the 83 patients evaluated had more than five prognostic signs. By combining the objective prognostic signs with positive abdominal CT findings, the investigators identified 30 patients who had three or more objective signs and were graded as category c, d, or e on abdominal CT scan; in these patients, the incidence of pancreatic abscess was 56.7%. By contrast, no patient with fewer than three prognostic signs and graded as category a or b on abdominal CT scan had a pancreatic abscess.

Treatment   Once pancreatic infection is diagnosed, supportive measures are initiated, including nasogastric suction, withholding of oral feedings, meticulous attention to respiratory care and fluid and electrolyte balance, systemic antibiotic therapy, and nutritional support. The key to successful treatment, however, is surgical, radiologic, or endoscopic drainage.

Pancreatic necrosis. Sterile pancreatic necrosis alone is not an indication for surgical debridement. In one prospective study, 11 patients with sterile pancreatic necrosis were all followed successfully with conservative treatment.[117] However, once infected pancreatic necrosis is confirmed by Gram stain or culture, surgical debridement is required to remove the characteristically thick necrotic material; radiologic or endoscopic methods alone are not as effective for this purpose.

The choice of drainage technique is nevertheless controversial. Many clinicians prefer operative debridement and sump drainage. The mortality associated with extensive operative debridement (so-called necrosectomy) and sump drainage may range from 30% to 40%,[118] and this technique may be associated with a 30% to 40% reoperation rate because of sepsis or GI complications.[28,119]

Open drainage. To reduce the frequency of reoperation and to lower mortality, some clinicians opt for open drainage or marsupialization of the infected pancreas. One modification involves the use of a prosthetic mesh and a zipper to facilitate reexploration in patients with severe intra-abdominal abscess.[120] A 1991 meta-analysis of published surgical studies on infected pancreatic necrosis found statistically better results with debridement and lavage or debridement and open packing than with extensive debridement and sump drainage.[121] However, surgical treatment should be customized for each patient. In one study, open packing was used for massive necrosis (more than 100 g removed by debridement at operation or CT evidence of at least 50% pancreatic necrosis) or for extrapancreatic necrosis, whereas conventional debridement and sump drainage were used in other cases; the overall mortality in this study was only 14%.[122]

Pancreatic abscess. Pancreatic abscess resulting from liquefaction of necrosis is also best treated by surgical drainage because residual necrosis may cause failure of treatment by percutaneous methods.[123] On the other hand, infected pancreatic fluid collections and pseudocysts can usually be treated nonoperatively. In one prospective study, percutaneous and surgical drainage were equally successful in treating infected pancreatic fluid collections and pseudocysts.[124] Clinical signs of progress rather than CT findings are the best indicators of the need for intervention, and nonoperative methods should be attempted before open surgery is planned.

Adjunctive procedures. In the past, debridement and sump drainage were accompanied by the so-called triple ostomy technique, which involved cholecystostomy, gastrostomy, and jejunostomy. The role of these ancillary procedures, however, is controversial at best, and currently, cholecystostomy is employed only if gallstones are detected.

Other operative procedures may be required to manage gastric or colonic complications. Gastric bleeding, gastric outlet obstruction, and gastric fistula necessitating reoperation are relatively infrequent in this setting. By contrast, colonic necrosis and fistula formation are relatively common and occur either spontaneously or as complications of treatment. The usual site of involvement is the splenic flexure or upper descending colon. Treatment consists of colonic resection or a diverting colostomy.

Antibiotic therapy. The role of systemic antibiotic therapy in the prophylaxis of pancreatic abscess is controversial. Experimental evidence suggests that antibiotics may sometimes decrease the severity of pancreatitis,[125] and endoscopic cannulation of the pancreatic duct has yielded bacteria in pancreatic secretions of patients with acute pancreatitis.[126] In patients with pancreatic abscess, bacteriologic cultures are usually polymicrobial, the most common organisms being *E. coli*, enterococci, *Klebsiella pneumoniae*, *P. aeruginosa*, *S. aureus*, *Bacteroides fragilis*, and *Clostridium perfringens*. There is a growing trend toward early use of prophylactic antibiotics in cases of pancreatic necrosis, even though there are no data that convincingly demonstrate a clinical benefit. This trend may be partly responsible for the increasing prevalence of *Candida* species in pancreatitis-related sepsis; a 1996 report stated that *Candida* infection was detected in 21% of patients.[127]

Nutrition. Nutritional support of patients with pancreatic abscesses usually consists of TPN, though small bowel feeding may be attempted occasionally. These patients have high metabolic demands and may experience glucose intolerance or hyperlipidemia. Nevertheless, they generally tolerate I.V. feeding well. A 10-fold increase in mortality (from 2.5% to 21%) was reported in patients in whom a positive nitrogen balance could not be achieved.[128]

Splenic Abscess

Diagnosis   A splenic abscess should be considered in patients who present with fever and a left upper quadrant mass, though it remains a rare cause of these symptoms. Most splenic abscesses encountered in clinical practice are solitary; multiple abscesses are usually covert and are typically found at autopsy in patients with disseminated malignancy, collagen vascular disease, or chronic debility.

Because splenic abscess is rare, correct diagnosis requires a high index of suspicion. The main clue is the clinical setting: both bacteremia and local splenic disease are required to produce splenic abscess. In the preantibiotic period, this combination was seen most frequently in patients with bacterial endocarditis and typhoid. Even today, more than three quarters of splenic abscesses occur in patients who already have an infection elsewhere in the body; splenic abscesses can also occur in patients with splenic infarcts, splenic hematomas, or local splenic disease caused by hemoglobinopathies.

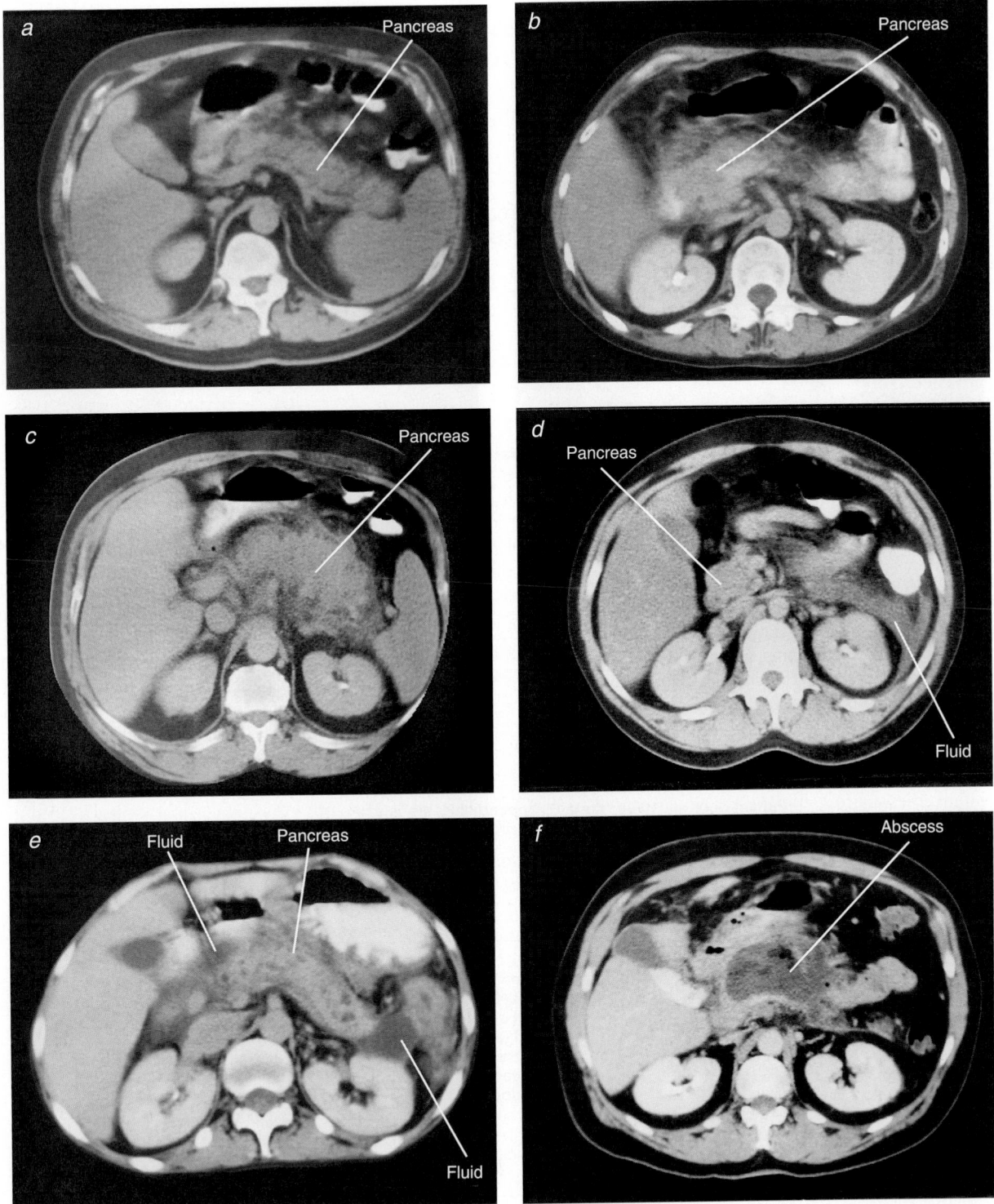

Figure 7 **Pancreatic findings on CT scan have been graded by Ranson into five categories: grade A—normal pancreas (a); grade B—diffuse enlargement of pancreas and nonhomogeneous density of gland (b); grade C—diffuse enlargement of pancreas associated with peripancreatic inflammation (c); grade D—high-density fluid collection in left anterior pararenal space (only head of pancreas is visualized at this level) (d); and grade E—diffuse enlargement of pancreas with several intrapancreatic small fluid collections and poorly defined fluid collections adjacent to tail and head of pancreas (e). In final CT scan (f), pancreatic abscess is demonstrated; partially encapsulated fluid collection containing bubbles of air represents large abscess.**

The diagnosis of splenic abscess may be supported by indirect radiologic signs, such as an elevated left hemidiaphragm or the finding of a left upper quadrant air-fluid level (mimicking the stomach). To clinch the diagnosis, an abdominal ultrasound examina-tion or abdominal CT scan is required. The abdominal CT scan, enhanced with I.V. or oral contrast material, is preferred [*see Figure 8*].[129] This technique provides a direct image of the spleen, on which abscesses appear as low-density areas that may contain gas.

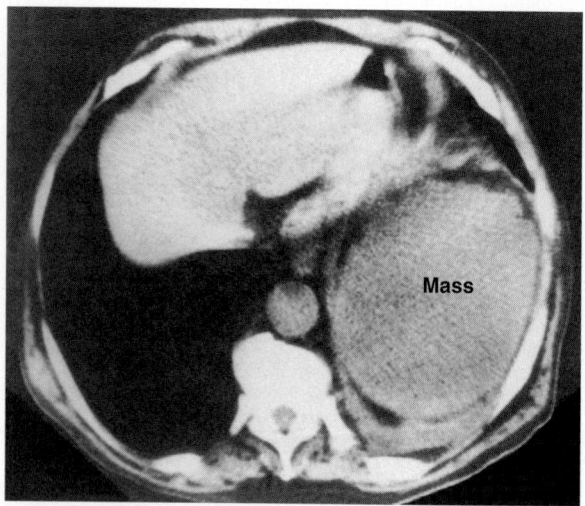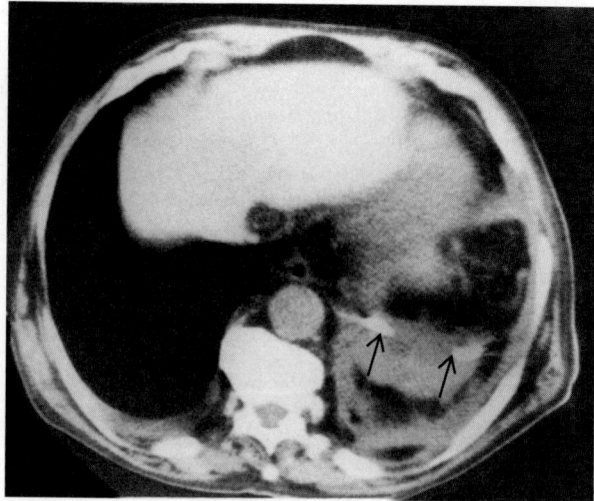

Figure 8 Abdominal CT scan, enhanced by contrast material, confirms diagnosis of splenic abscess.

Treatment Treatment of splenic abscess includes I.V. administration of antibiotics and splenectomy [*see 67 Splenectomy*]. The usual pathogenic organisms found are staphylococci and streptococci, though gram-negative bacilli and anaerobes may also be present. When splenic abscesses are not drained, mortality approaches 100%. At one time, splenotomy was the preferred operative treatment, but splenectomy is currently the preferred approach. Percutaneous catheter drainage is being performed with increasing frequency and appears to be as effective as operative drainage.[8,130,131]

Infections of the Lower Abdomen

Although enteric perforations, like pancreatitis and cholecystitis, present most commonly with pain and fever, their diagnosis differs from that of upper abdominal infections of the solid organs. The pain associated with enteric perforation frequently is not well localized; consequently, CT scanning is used more frequently than ultrasonography because it is superior for evaluating the entire abdomen [*see Figure 9*]. Moreover, a perforated viscus may present more acutely than other forms of infection do, and it is a common indication for emergency exploration. Thus, in the setting of a possible lower

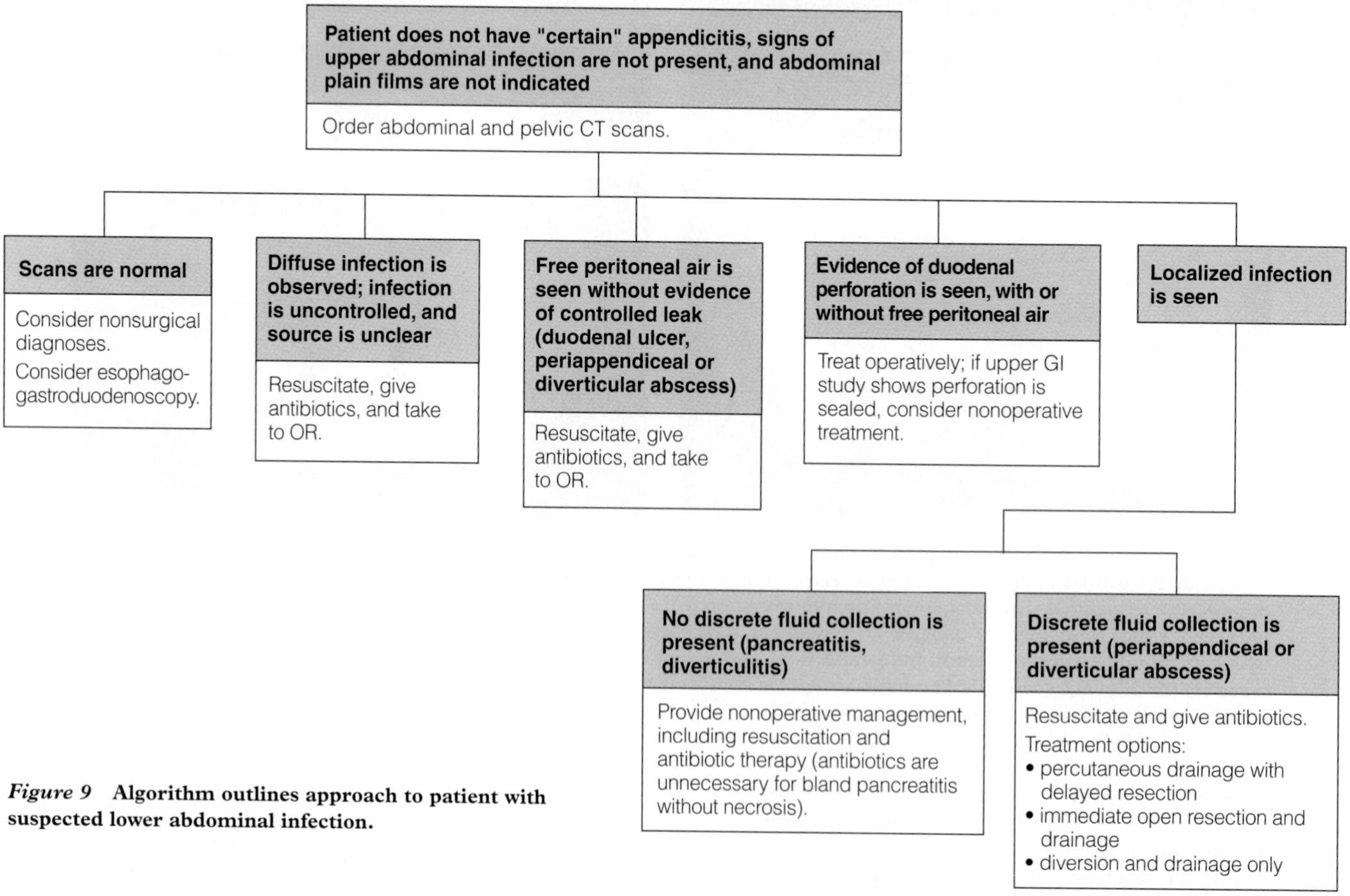

Patient does not have "certain" appendicitis, signs of upper abdominal infection are not present, and abdominal plain films are not indicated

Order abdominal and pelvic CT scans.

Scans are normal

Consider nonsurgical diagnoses.
Consider esophago-gastroduodenoscopy.

Diffuse infection is observed; infection is uncontrolled, and source is unclear

Resuscitate, give antibiotics, and take to OR.

Free peritoneal air is seen without evidence of controlled leak (duodenal ulcer, periappendiceal or diverticular abscess)

Resuscitate, give antibiotics, and take to OR.

Evidence of duodenal perforation is seen, with or without free peritoneal air

Treat operatively; if upper GI study shows perforation is sealed, consider nonoperative treatment.

Localized infection is seen

No discrete fluid collection is present (pancreatitis, diverticulitis)

Provide nonoperative management, including resuscitation and antibiotic therapy (antibiotics are unnecessary for bland pancreatitis without necrosis).

Discrete fluid collection is present (periappendiceal or diverticular abscess)

Resuscitate and give antibiotics.
Treatment options:
• percutaneous drainage with delayed resection
• immediate open resection and drainage
• diversion and drainage only

Figure 9 Algorithm outlines approach to patient with suspected lower abdominal infection.

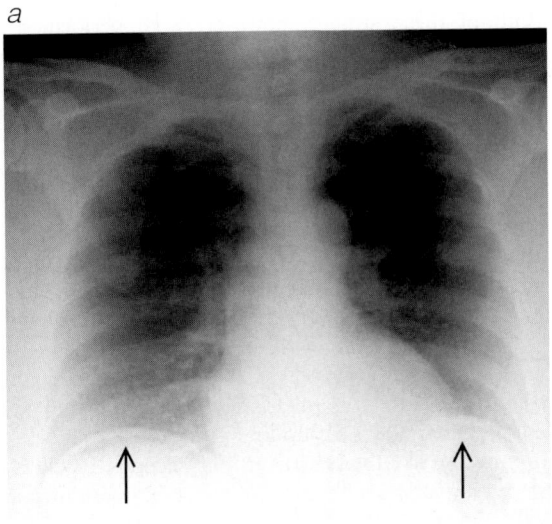

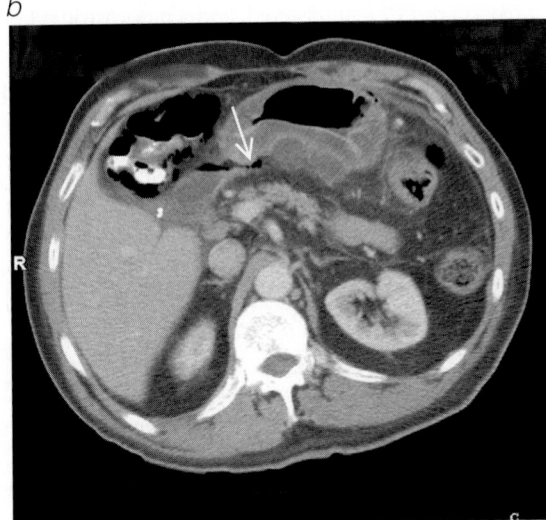

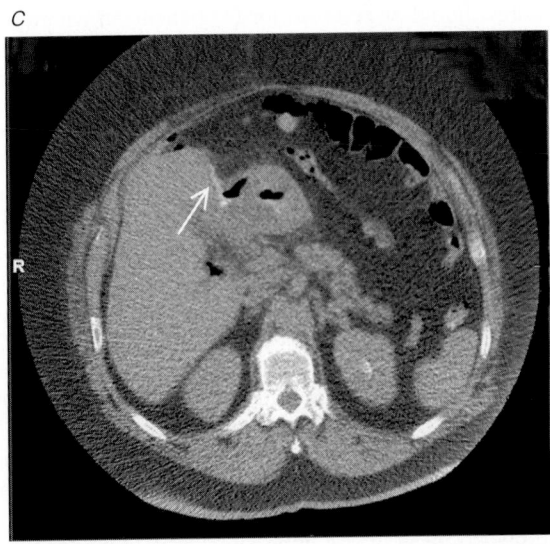

Figure 10 (*a*) Upright chest x-ray of patient with sudden onset of diffuse abdominal pain demonstrates free peritoneal air underneath both diaphragms (black arrows). Emergency exploration was carried out without further studies, and perforated gastric ulcer was excised. (*b*) Abdominal CT scan of patient with history of ulcer disease and 1-week history of increasing abdominal pain shows retrogastric fluid collection with air that appears to be in communication with duodenum (white arrow). Patient underwent laparotomy, and perforated duodenal ulcer was repaired. (*c*) Abdominal CT scan of patient with 2- to 3-day history of worsening abdominal pain demonstrates extravasation of oral contrast from anterolateral aspect of duodenum (white arrow). Patient underwent laparoscopic omental patch closure.

abdominal infection, the diagnostic emphasis is on confirming or ruling out the presence of an acute condition necessitating operation, rather than on fine localization of a more chronic illness.

PEPTIC ULCER PERFORATION

The incidence of peptic ulcer perforation has decreased significantly as a consequence of the changes in disease progression and incidence of intractable ulcers brought about by the advent of H_2 receptor antagonists and proton pump inhibitors (PPIs). Still, a significant percentage of all hospital admissions are secondary to perforated peptic ulcers, and the patient population is becoming older and more evenly balanced between men and women, presumably because of increased use of nonsteroidal anti-inflammatory drugs and cigarettes.[132]

Several studies found a high (80% to 92%) incidence of *Helicobacter pylori* infection in patients with perforated peptic ulcers.[133,134] Although the prevalence of *H. pylori* infection in this population is well established, the causal role that such infection plays in peptic ulcer perforations has been questioned.[135] In a 1999 study involving 50 patients with juxtapyloric perforations related to crack cocaine use who were successfully managed with simple omental patch closure, the investigators found that approximately 80% of the patients who underwent antral mucosal biopsy at the time of closure had a positive urease test, a finding that suggested

a role for *H. pylori* infection in the pathogenesis of these perforations as well.[136]

Diagnosis

A patient with a perforated peptic ulcer will complain of the sudden onset of intense abdominal pain and will often be able to pinpoint the exact time when the symptoms began. If the perforation has not spontaneously sealed or been managed with operative closure, the clinical picture can progress to florid sepsis and shock. Evidence of free air on plain upright and left lateral decubitus radiographs will be seen in as many as 70% of cases [*see Figure 10a*].[137] Endoscopy should be avoided, but equivocal cases or spontaneously sealed perforations can be evaluated with water-soluble contrast studies. CT scanning can be used to localize an infection to the duodenum, particularly if communication of air or fluid with the duodenum is established [*see Figure 10b*] or if extravasation of contrast is seen [*see Figure 10c*].

Treatment

Surgical management centers on control of the site of perforation (via surgical closure or spontaneous sealing), with or without an acid-reducing procedure [*see 62 Procedures for Benign and Malignant Gastric Disease*]. Before this is done, I.V. fluids should be given, metabolic derangements corrected, appropriate antibiotics and an H_2 receptor blocker or PPI administered, and a nasogastric tube placed for decompression.

Operative versus conservative management Several studies have shown nonoperative management to be safe and effective for perforations that have sealed spontaneously. A 1989 study evaluated 35 patients with acute duodenal perforations—excluding those with a history of chronic ulcer disease who ultimately went on to primary repair and acid-reducing surgery—who were managed nonoperatively after evidence of a sealed perforation was noted on a water-soluble upper GI study. The investigators reported one death, in a patient with a history of metastatic breast cancer, and one intra-abdominal abscess.[138] In a 1989 prospective trial of 83 patients with perforated peptic ulcers randomly assigned to either conservative or operative management, the two groups experienced similar morbidity and mortality (~5%), and 73% of the patients in the conservatively managed group experienced full resolution of their symptoms.[139] The only significant difference between the groups was in the length of hospital stay. It has been suggested that patients with evidence of a sealed perforation confirmed by a Gastrografin upper GI study can be managed conservatively with a low incidence of reperforation and intra-abdominal abscess formation.[140] These patients must undergo repeated clinical examination and receive supportive therapy until clinical symptoms resolve.

Laparoscopic versus open repair A prospective, randomized trial of perforated peptic ulcers to either open or laparoscopic suture omental patch repair concluded that for perforations smaller than 10 mm, laparoscopic repair was associated with reduced operating times, less need for analgesics, fewer postoperative chest infections, earlier return to normal activities, and shorter hospitalizations.[141] An earlier study also demonstrated reduced analgesic times and earlier return to normal activities but reported longer operating times.[142] These studies confirm that small perforations can be adequately managed laparoscopically without exacerbation of bacterial sepsis. It must be emphasized, however, that biopsy of perforated gastric ulcers is critical for ruling out malignancies, and laparoscopic repair of the perforation may preclude biopsy.

Simple repair with medical management versus repair with acid-reducing procedure Definitive surgical management of ulcer disease during repair of a perforated peptic ulcer is contraindicated in patients who are hemodynamically unstable, have diffuse peritonitis, have an abscess, or have multiple underlying comorbid conditions.[143] The significant side effects associated with definitive surgery (dumping and diarrhea) and the success of medical management (PPIs, H_2 receptor blockers, and *H. pylori* eradication) have further contributed to the reduced popularity of proximal vagotomy at the time of repair. Now that fewer acid-reducing operations are being performed, there is some justifiable concern that younger surgeons will not be able to obtain the degree of training they would need to perform a definitive operation (highly selective vagotomy) in an urgent or emergency scenario.

A 1987 study found that simple closure with a Graham patch, without a concurrent operation to reduce ulcer recurrence, resulted in a higher recurrence rate than closure with proximal gastric vagotomy did (52% versus 16%; median follow-up, 54 months).[144] In a subsequent study of patients with acute perforations who were randomly assigned to undergo either simple closure or simple closure with proximal vagotomy, ulcer recurrence rates in the two groups after 2 years were 36.6% and 10.6%, respectively.[145]

Both of these studies, however, were performed before PPIs became routinely available.

Some 40% of patients with duodenal perforation treated with simple closure may experience recurrent duodenal ulcer. A 1995 series associated such recurrence with *H. pylori* infection.[146] To further study the role of *H. pylori* eradication in ulcer recurrence after peptic ulcer perforation, a randomized study was done in which patients with perforated duodenal ulcers and *H. pylori* infection after simple closure received either quadruple anti–*H. pylori* therapy (1 week of bismuth, tetracycline, and metronidazole with 4 weeks of omeprazole) or omeprazole alone.[133] After 1 year, 38.1% of patients managed with PPIs alone experienced ulcer recurrence, compared with 4.8% of patients managed with PPIs and *H. pylori* eradication. A similar study followed patients with perforated duodenal ulcers for up to 2 years after simple closure and randomization to either short-term H_2 receptor blockers or H_2 blockers with quadruple therapy; ongoing *H. pylori* infection correlated with recurrent ulcers for up to 2 years.[147]

On the basis of these findings, definitive acid-reducing procedures should be reserved for (1) patients in whom medical management of peptic ulcers and *H. pylori* fails, (2) patients whose ulcer symptoms have persisted for longer than 3 months, and (3) patients with otherwise complicated ulcers (e.g., lesions that are bleeding or causing obstruction).[148]

Antibiotic therapy In fasting persons, gastric juice contains as many as 10^3 organisms/ml. These organisms are typically facultative gram-positive salivary bacteria (e.g., lactobacilli and streptococci) and fungi (e.g., *Candida* species). In induced states of achlorhydria (e.g., from treatment with H_2 receptor blockers or PPIs), there is an increase in the total number of organisms, including enterococci and nitrate-reducing organisms. This phenomenon suggests a proliferation of salivary and enteric organisms, but its clinical relevance is unknown.[149]

Eradication of *H. pylori* in patients with uncomplicated ulcers and bleeding ulcers is now the standard of care.[150,151] Infection with this organism is associated with a 1% per year risk of peptic ulcer disease, a level of risk approximately 10 times that seen in uninfected patients. Eradication of *H. pylori* with medical management typically results in resolution of the ulcer, and recurrence is rare. Consequently, acid-reducing procedures are not often required.[152]

SMALL INTESTINAL PERFORATION

Diagnosis

Small intestinal perforation is a very difficult entity to diagnose, in large part because of its relative rarity. There are certain clinical scenarios (e.g., strangulated hernia and Crohn disease) in which the likelihood of this condition is heightened, but in the setting of blunt small intestinal injury, the low incidental occurrence of perforation (~1%[153]) and the complexity of the presentation frequently lead to a delay in diagnosis. Such delay is associated with increases in the morbidity and mortality directly attributable to the injury.[154] The radiographic modality most useful in diagnosis is CT scanning.[155]

Treatment

The basics of treatment are the same for small bowel perforation as for all perforations: isolation and control of the source of contamination. In the acute setting, this is accomplished through laparotomy and excision of the disease segment, whether the perforation is the result of ischemic necrosis, of blunt injury, or of IBD. Primary reanastomosis is generally accepted in these patients [see 71 Intestinal Anastomosis]. For patients with Crohn disease, perforation (usually presenting as a fistula) is a risk factor for postoperative disease recurrence[156]; accordingly, close postoperative follow-up is indicated.

There are two additional issues regarding small bowel perforations that warrant special mention. The first has to do with small bowel perforation secondary to obstruction. When this event occurs, it is important not only that the perforated segment be resected but also that the cause of obstruction be identified to prevent recurrence. The second issue has to do with anastomotic leakage. Not all leaks call for surgical intervention. If the leak is a late complication, it is likely to have walled itself off into an abscess, in which case CT-guided drainage of the abscess is the treatment of choice. Efforts at reducing the luminal transport are also made to improve healing.

Nutritional support plays a major supportive role in the treatment of patients with small bowel perforation. Many of these patients, either because of their underlying pathology (e.g., Crohn disease) or because of their hypermetabolic state (e.g., from trauma), lose some of their innate ability to heal and prevent anastomotic breakdown. The presence of a knowledgeable nutrition staff can dramatically enhance patient recovery in this setting.

Antibiotic therapy   The small bowel flora is typically sparse (10^3 to 10^4/ml), with salivary organisms predominating. In conditions of stasis, obstruction, or impaired motility, however, colonic flora can proliferate, with *E. coli*, enterococci, and obligate anaerobes the dominant organisms. In the distal ileum, there are typically about 10^6 colony-forming units/ml, with an increasing proportion of enteric organisms and anaerobic bacteria, presumably as a result of backwash through the ileocecal valve.[157] Although there are generally far fewer bacteria in the small intestine than in the colon (which contains about 10^{12} organisms/ml), the standard antimicrobial therapy remains broad-spectrum coverage (e.g., fluoroquinolone plus an antianaerobic agent for 5 days).[158]

APPENDICITIS

Obstruction of the appendiceal lumen by a fecalith, a hyperplastic lymph node, or a foreign body is typically the inciting event in the pathogenesis of appendicitis. Luminal obstruction with continued secretion results in progressive distention, proliferation of luminal microorganisms, ischemia, gangrene, and subsequent perforation. The clinical history during this evolution is marked by diffuse epigastric pain with anorexia, nausea, and vomiting. The pain typically progresses first to the periumbilical region and then to the right lower quadrant (at McBurney's point). Patients have a low-grade fever and exhibit direct tenderness at McBurney's point but may also manifest rebound tenderness, guarding, rigidity, and marked temperature elevation if the appendix perforates and results in diffuse peritonitis. As the viscera and the omentum localize and sequester the perforation, the symptoms may subside to a degree, with localized pain and a palpable abdominal mass the primary manifestations remaining.

Diagnosis

Classically, the diagnosis of appendicitis has been made primarily through clinical examination, with laboratory tests consistent with inflammation (i.e., an elevated leukocyte count with a left shift and an elevated C-reactive protein level) serving as confirmation. In as many as 20% of patients with appendicitis, however, the incorrect diagnosis is made, and the incidence of removal of a normal appendix can approach 40%.[159-161] Early diagnosis of appendicitis can decrease the risk of postoperative complications

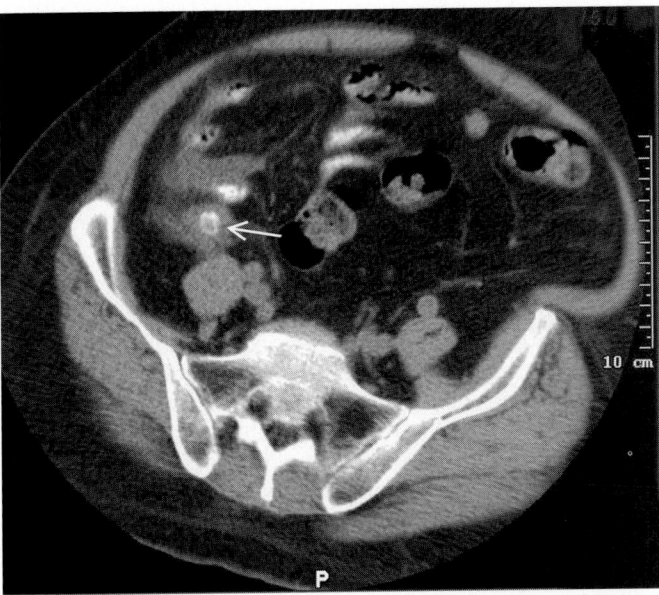

Figure 11   **Pelvic CT scan of patient with distant history of right lower quadrant abdominal pain with recurrent acute attack demonstrates inflamed and thickened appendix with surrounding fat stranding (white arrow). Gangrenous appendix was removed laparoscopically.**

from 39% to 8%, and one retrospective study found that the use of diagnostic CT lowered the rate of misdiagnosis to 7%.[162] CT scanning is reported to be 93% to 98% in diagnosing appendicitis, with significantly improved accuracy achieved by using an appendicitis protocol after retrograde water-soluble contrast administration.[163] CT findings suggestive of appendicitis [see Figure 11] include enlargement and dilation of the appendix (to > 6 mm), nonfilling of the appendix, and periappendiceal inflammation (fat stranding, abscess, phlegmon, and dependent fluid collections); these findings do not differ significantly between acute appendicitis and chronic, recurrent appendicitis.[164,165]

Current evidence supports the role of CT scanning in the diagnostic evaluation of patients with suspected appendicitis. Studies have demonstrated decreases both in the incidence of normal appendectomies and in the incidence of prolonged, unnecessary observations.[166,167] Furthermore, alterations in patient management attributable to diagnostic CT have been shown to decrease overall hospital and patient costs. Nevertheless, the utility of CT in young men whose history, physical examination, and laboratory test results fit the classic picture of appendicitis remains unproven; this subset of patients may be managed without confirmatory CT.[166] On the other hand, CT scanning appears to be quite useful for diagnosing appendicitis in women, in which setting it decreases the incidence of normal appendectomies and facilitates diagnosis of other causes of the symptoms.[168,169] Preoperative CT scanning assists in planning an operation, identifying a periappendiceal abscess that may delay immediate appendectomy, and recognizing other sources of intra-abdominal pathology.

Treatment

Initial management consists of fluid resuscitation, appropriate prophylactic antibiotics, and preparation for surgery. Currently, acute nonperforated appendicitis, gangrenous appendicitis, and perforated appendicitis without an associated abscess are managed with urgent appendectomy [see 73 Appendectomy]. The main dilemmas in management center on the appropriate use of laparoscopic appendectomy and the role of conservative management for periappendiceal masses with interval appendectomy.

Laparoscopic versus open appendectomy In several prospective, randomized clinical trials that compared laparoscopic with open appendectomy, the consensus was that the former was associated with a lower incidence of wound infection, decreased utilization of pain medication, earlier return to normal activities, and reduced cost of hospitalization (though the data were conflicting on this last point).[170-173] On the other hand, the trials found the laparoscopic approach to be associated with significantly longer operating time, equivalent duration of hospitalization, and a possible increased risk of abscess formation. A retrospective review published in 2000, however, found that when a dedicated laparoscopic service was established for patients with appendicitis, the rates of intra-abdominal abscess formation after laparoscopic appendectomy decreased to levels equivalent to those reported after open appendectomy.[174]

Although laparoscopic appendectomy is associated with a higher incidence of intra-abdominal abscess formation in the setting of perforated appendicitis, it is not associated with a higher incidence of wound infection or abscess in patients with gangrenous or nonperforated appendicitis.[175] Furthermore, a prospective, randomized trial found that laparoscopic appendectomy was associated with reduced overall cost of hospitalization, decreased use of pain medication, and earlier return to functional status in patients with uncomplicated appendicitis.[170]

Two groups of patients clearly benefit from laparoscopic appendectomy: women and obese patients. In women, laparoscopy aids in the diagnosis of other pelvic pathologic conditions and lowers the incidence of negative appendectomies; in obese patients, it results in less postoperative pain and a shorter recovery time, even though it does not significantly reduce the postoperative complication rate.[176,177] Patients who present with evidence of perforated or complicated appendicitis may be better managed with the traditional open approach to minimize the risk of postoperative abscess formation.[178] Improvements in laparoscopic techniques, however, may eventually reduce the incidence of this complication to a level comparable to that seen with open management.

Periappendiceal abscess and interval appendectomy The mainstays of conservative management have been parenteral antibiotics, supportive fluid resuscitation, and percutaneous drainage of radiographically amenable fluid collections. In a 2001 review of 155 patients with periappendiceal abscesses, the complication rate was 36% for patients managed with surgical incision and drainage and appendectomy, compared with 17% for patients managed nonoperatively.[179] The recurrence rate was 8% in the conservatively managed patients, and nonoperative management failed in five patients. Patients with perforated appendicitis and abscess or phlegmon diagnosed by CT scanning but without a palpable mass were safely managed with conservative therapy. In a 2002 study, immediate appendectomy was associated with a higher postoperative complication rate and an increased incidence of more extensive initial operations (e.g., ileocecal resection, right hemicolectomy, and temporary ileostomy).[180]

The recurrence rate after conservative management ranges from 10% to 20%. In one study of patients managed with interval appendectomy for periappendiceal mass, histologic evaluation revealed that a significant majority of samples had a patent appendiceal lumen and were at risk for recurrent appendicitis.[181] In a 2002 report, 45.8% of interval appendectomy pathologic samples showed evidence of chronic active inflammation.[182] The risk of re-

currence and progression to chronic appendicitis supports the use of interval appendectomy in young patients, but in adults, the decision algorithm must also consider the incidental diagnosis of tumor.

Interval appendectomy is typically performed between 6 weeks and 3 months after percutaneous intervention and clinical resolution [see Figure 12]. The risk of recurrence is greatest after the 6-month point in the clinical progression of acute appendicitis managed conservatively.[183] In several retrospective analyses, interval appendectomy proved to be a safe management plan, but to date, there have been no randomized, prospective trials evaluating its role in management.[184,185]

Antibiotic therapy The pathogenic organisms recovered in peritoneal cultures derive from the colon and consist of aerobic or facultative bacteria and anaerobes. The most frequently isolated organisms are *E. coli*, enterococci, viridans streptococci, *B. fragilis*, *Lactobacillus* species, *Prevotella melaninogenica*, and *Bilophila wadsworthia*.[186,187] It is noteworthy that the use of intraoperative peritoneal cultures has not been shown to affect the incidence of wound infection, abscess formation, or small bowel obstruction if patients are presumptively managed with antibiotics that cover gram-negative bacteria and enteric anaerobes.[188]

Appropriate coverage can be obtained with any of the following: ampicillin-sulbactam, piperacillin-tazobactam, ticarcillin-clavulanate, cefoxitin, cefotetan, and ciprofloxacin plus metronidazole.[189-192] In a trial involving children with perforated appendicitis, conversion to oral therapy after parenteral therapy was equivalent to parenteral therapy alone.[193] In a study of patients with acute nonperforated appendicitis, preoperative administration of cefoxitin was superior to placebo in reducing the incidence of wound infection.[190] In a study of children with acute nonperforated appendicitis, prolonged antibiotic administration (5 days) had no advantage over a single preoperative dose with respect to the incidence of wound infection or subsequent abscess formation.[194] The duration and timing of antibiotic administration in patients with nonperforated gangrenous appendicitis have not been shown to correlate with the wound infection rate.[195]

COLONIC PERFORATION

Diagnosis

Diagnostic strategies for identifying colon lesions associated with intra-abdominal infection follow the general approach outlined earlier [see Clinical Evaluation *and* Investigative Studies, *above*]. For unstable patients with generalized peritonitis, there is no need to delay operative intervention to wait for radiologic confirmation: the pathologic condition will be identified in the course of the operation. However, for patients who have localized peritonitis or those who are stable and whose physical examination is not conclusive for peritonitis, radiologic evaluation is pivotal in planning treatment.

Although plain films may reveal free air in the abdomen and prompt surgical intervention, CT scanning may be a more valuable first study because of its ability to delineate the bowel wall and surrounding soft tissues with remarkable accuracy. In a 2002 study comparing abdominal radiography with CT for the evaluation of acute nontraumatic abdominal pain in the ED, the former was not nearly as diagnostically sensitive as the latter (a nonspecific diagnosis in 68%, compared with a specific diagnosis in 80%).[196] The investigators concluded that CT was the initial radiographic modality of choice for patients with acute abdominal pain in the ED. Another study found that CT scans frequently changed physicians' initial diagnoses, increased diagnostic certain-

a
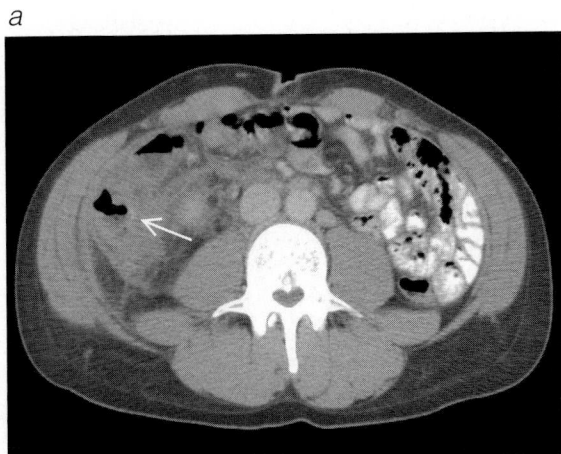

b
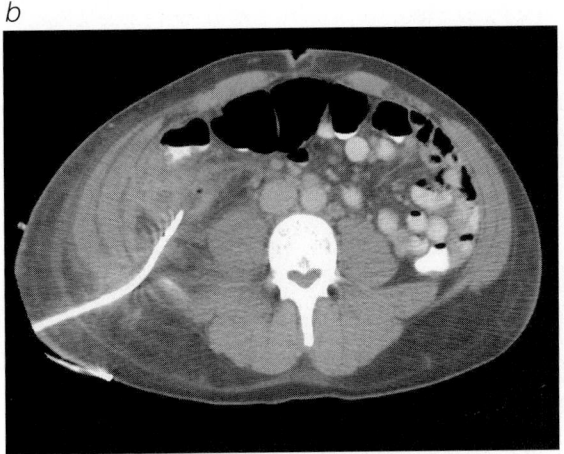

Figure 12 (*a*) **Pelvic CT scan of young patient with a 5-day history of right lower quadrant abdominal pain shows fluid collection containing air adjacent to appendix and consistent with appendiceal perforation and abscess formation (white arrow). (*b*) Pelvic CT scan of same patient after percutaneous ultrasound-guided placement of drainage catheter shows evacuation of air and much fluid. Patient underwent uneventful interval appendectomy 6 weeks later.**

ty, and led to more appropriate treatment in patients with acute abdominal pain in the ED.[197]

In view of the relatively high cost of CT scanning, the concomitant radiation exposure, and the use of I.V. contrast agents to enhance the scans, some have suggested using ultrasonography to make diagnoses. However, the well-documented dependency of this modality on the skill of the individual technician makes it less attractive to the broader health care community, where full-time sonographers are not always available. Finally, it should be noted that there is no role for MRI in the acute setting. Although it is both sensitive and specific, the logistic hindrances associated with its use greatly limit its applicability.

Treatment

Diverticulitis Diverticular disease ranges in severity from minor to serious. The focus of our discussion will be on management of complicated (perforated) diverticular disease, for which resection should be considered after only one attack.

In the past, treatment of perforated diverticular disease involved a multistage surgical approach whereby the patient underwent three separate procedures: one for fecal diversion and drainage of the infection, a second for resection of the diseased segment, and a third for closure of the colostomy. This three-stage approach proved to be associated with high morbidities, high cumulative mortalities, and prolonged hospitalizations.[198-200] Since then, CT-guided percutaneous drainage, primary resection of the diseased segment, and improved patient selection for resection and primary anastomosis have improved patient outcomes dramatically. Few adequately powered multicenter, prospective, randomized trials evaluating treatment of complicated diverticular disease have been done; accordingly, many of the current treatment standards have been derived by consensus on the basis of thorough review of the literature.

Therapy for perforated diverticular disease depends greatly on the patient's condition at the time of presentation and on the stage of the disease. The Hinchey staging system[201] [*see Table 4*] classifies perforated diverticular disease according to the associated inflammatory process and is used to guide and compare treatment options.[202-204]

In stage I disease, a small pericolic abscess [*see Figure 13a*] in a stable and otherwise healthy patient may resolve with conservative management, including broad-spectrum antibiotics and bowel rest. The patient can be evaluated for definitive surgical treatment later, after the episode resolves and the patient is in better condition for surgery. For larger abscesses or stage II disease [*see Figure 13b*], the standard of care is CT-guided percutaneous abscess drainage, if feasible. After drainage, resuscitation, and bowel preparation, a one-stage colectomy can be done (resection of the diseased segment with primary anastomosis) so as to avoid the potential increased morbidity of a two-stage procedure.[205]

For patients who have abscesses that are inaccessible to percutaneous drainage or who experience persistent symptoms despite drainage, operative correction is required. If adequate bowel preparation can be carried out, primary anastomosis at the time of surgery should be considered. If adequate bowel preparation is not possible, a two-stage approach, including a Hartmann procedure and subsequent stoma reversal, should be considered. Alternatively, depending on the patient's condition, resection with primary anastomosis may be attempted. There is some evidence that employing intraoperative colonic lavage to reduce the fecal column and thus allow primary anastomosis may reduce morbidity, especially in patients with stage I or II disease.[206-208] However, the studies supporting this view are not conclusive enough for such a regimen to be considered standard; further investigation is warranted before it is generally accepted. Finally, whether to add a covering stoma to a primary anastomosis is a case-by-case decision that is usually guided by the presence of risk factors such as poor nutritional status, inadequate bowel preparation, blood loss, or intraoperative hypotension.[209]

Table 4 Hinchey System for Classification of Perforated Diverticulitis[201]

Stage	Description
Stage I	Pericolic or mesenteric abscess
Stage II	Pelvic or retroperitoneal abscess that is walled off
Stage III	Purulent peritonitis
Stage IV	Feculent peritonitis

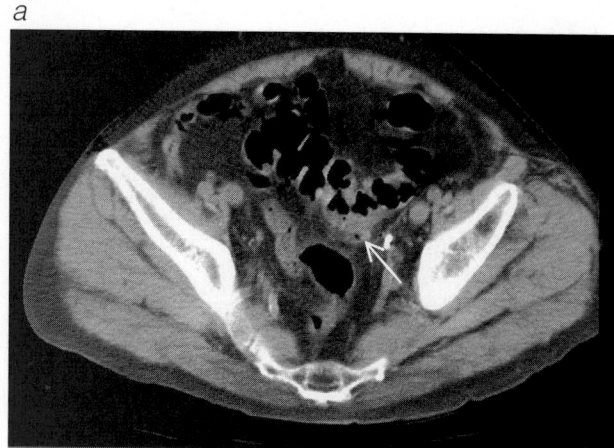
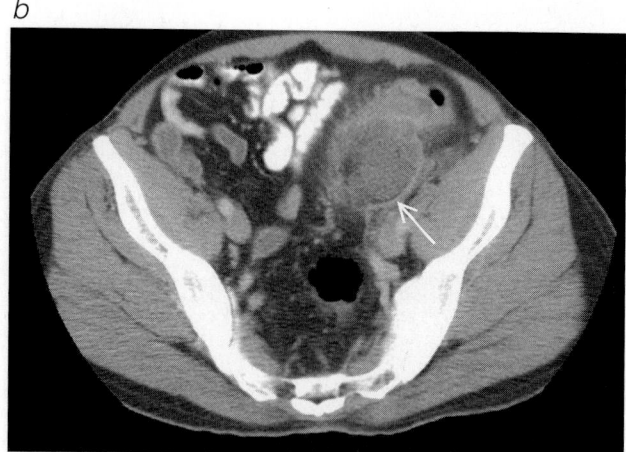

a

b

Figure 13 (*a*) **Pelvic CT scan of elderly patient with left lower quadrant abdominal pain of 2 days' duration shows diverticulitis with small amount of extraluminal air (white arrow). Patient was treated acutely with resuscitation and antibiotics alone and was discharged home without complications. (*b*) Pelvic CT scan of middle-aged patient with 1-week history of constipation and moderate pelvic pain shows left lower quadrant fluid collection consistent with peridiverticular abscess (white arrow). Proximal bowel is seen anterior to abscess, distal bowel posterior. Percutaneous drain was placed, and elective colectomy with primary reanastomosis was performed 12 days later.**

Stage III or IV diverticulitis is a surgical emergency that calls for prompt resuscitation and administration of broad-spectrum antibiotics, followed rapidly by surgical treatment. The Hartmann procedure is the most widely accepted operation for this presentation.[210-212] It is associated with a substantially lower mortality than drainage followed by colostomy as a separate, delayed procedure (12% versus 28%).[213] In certain circumstances, with appropriate patient selection and low feculent contamination, primary anastomosis, with or without a covering stoma, may be feasible.[214-216]

The goals of resection are to remove the focus of infection and to prevent recurrent attacks. Recurrent diverticulitis after resection is the result of incomplete removal of the diseased segment, especially at the rectosigmoid junction. Therefore, when the diseased segment is resected, the entire sigmoid must be removed, and the distal resection margin must extend below the confluence of the taeniae coli and onto pliable rectum.[217] Proximally, the colon is mobilized until a margin of uninflamed bowel is identified. It is not, however, necessary to remove the entire colon affected by diverticuli.

Laparoscopy. Laparoscopic treatment of diverticular disease is becoming more common but remains controversial. Many feel that there is no place for laparoscopic-assisted colectomy in the treatment of stage III or IV disease,[202] but there is growing acceptance of this approach in the treatment of stage I and II disease. A review of several small studies concluded that laparoscopic colectomy had a high potential for reducing hospitalization time and operative morbidity; however, the cost analysis data were conflicting, and some of the trials reported very high conversion rates.[218]

Right-side disease. Particular mention should be made of right-side diverticulitis. In the past, this condition was often misdiagnosed as appendicitis before exploration, but today, with the increased use of CT scanning, this error is less frequently made. Given that diagnosis is difficult and the disease is surgically curable, some authors suggest that it should be treated with aggressive resection, ranging from simple diverticulectomy to right hemicolectomy.[219,220] Others argue that the disease is relatively benign in the absence of perforation and suggest leaving the diseased bowel in situ, performing an incidental appendectomy, and then treating the patient conservatively.[221,222] There is no standard therapy for cecal diverticulitis, mainly because of the small number of patients

it affects annually, which translates into small series reported in the literature. In the course of follow-up, it is important that these patients undergo thorough evaluation for colon cancer.

Antibiotic therapy. Appropriate antibiotic administration is an integral part of standard therapy for diverticular disease and is started at diagnosis. The most frequently isolated organisms are anaerobes, including *Bacteroides, Peptostreptococcus, Clostridium,* and *Fusobacterium* species. Gram-negative aerobes (predominantly *E. coli*) and facultative gram-positive bacteria (predominantly streptococci) are also associated with these infections.[223] Parenterally administered broad-spectrum antibiotics are standard. A particularly common regimen is ciprofloxacin plus metronidazole, but there are other regimens that are equally efficacious for treatment. According to a 2002 report from the Surgical Infection Society, the duration of therapy for complicated intra-abdominal infections should be no longer than 5 to 7 days.[158] If ongoing infection is suspected at termination of treatment, investigation into a potential source of infection is warranted.

Other colon lesions associated with perforation and peritonitis A number of colonic conditions besides diverticular disease may be manifested by colonic perforation and secondary peritonitis. Whatever the specific cause, the general goals of therapy remain the same: (1) to identify and control the source of bacterial contamination, (2) to reduce the level of peritoneal contamination, and (3) to prevent recurrent infections.

Colon cancer. After diverticular disease, colon cancer is the next leading cause of colonic perforation in uninjured patients. In general, perforated colon cancer carries a high mortality,[224,225] and the operative technique of choice is controversial. Perforation typically occurs at the site of the lesion but can also occur proximally (e.g., at the cecum) as a result of luminal obstruction.

Generally, perforations at the site of cancer in the ascending and transverse colon are treated with primary resection and anastomosis, with or without a diverting stoma, regardless of whether localized or diffuse peritonitis is present. When perforations occur at the site of cancer in the descending and sigmoid colon, however, there is some debate over the appropriate surgical approach, with some advocating primary resection and others staged proce-

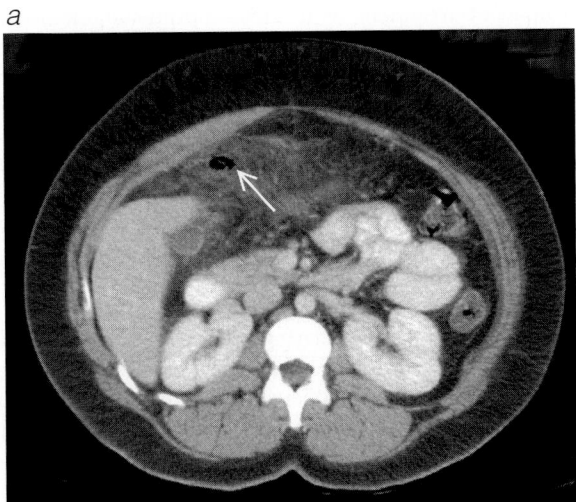
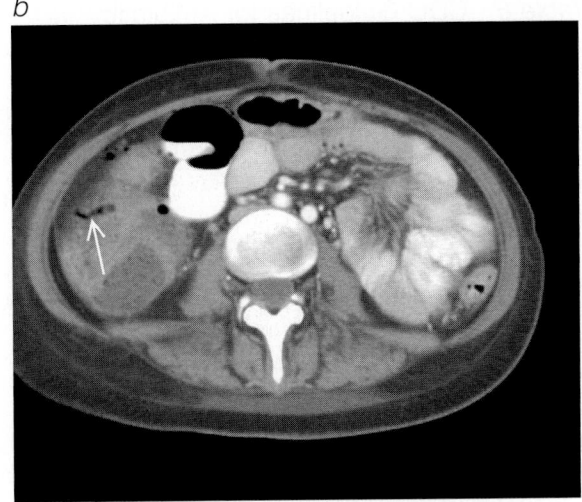

Figure 14 (*a*) **Abdominal CT scan of elderly patient with history of vascular disease and worsening abdominal pain over a 3-day period shows diffuse inflammation and right upper quadrant extraluminal air (white arrow). Patient underwent emergency exploration, and ischemic perforation of cecum was found. Right hemicolectomy and temporary diverting ileostomy were performed. (*b*) Abdominal CT scan of patient with history of Crohn disease and worsening abdominal pain demonstrates thickening of colonic wall with both intramural and extramural air (white arrow). Patient was treated with emergency total abdominal colectomy for pancolitis with creation of temporary diverting ileostomy.**

dures. Two studies from the early 1990s suggested improved long-term mortality after primary resection.[226,227] A subsequent study, however, suggested that the improved mortality associated with primary resection was secondary to preselection and therefore could not be considered conclusive proof of the superiority of this approach. The authors of this latter study concluded that primary resection was appropriate for a select patient population with minimal comorbidity and that staged resection was beneficial for patients with a high degree of acute illness and comorbidity (e.g., elderly patients).[228]

Less common causes of colonic perforation. Other diagnoses associated with colonic perforation and peritonitis (localized or diffuse) are ischemic necrosis as a result of vasculopathology [*see Figure 14a*] or volvulus, missed traumatic injury, and IBD [*see Figure 14b*]. Except for IBD, the standard therapy is excision of the affected segment and reanastomosis, with or without a covering stoma. For patients with numerous comorbidities, a high degree of feculent contamination, or very severe illness necessitating an extremely abbreviated operating time, a Hartmann procedure with a mucous fistula or an oversewn distal segment is the primary treatment. Because perforation associated with IBD is typically a self-limited disease, treatment is directed at the underlying pathophysiology and excision of the diseased segment is not always indicated.[229]

Other Abdominal Infections

PELVIC INFLAMMATORY DISEASE

Because of the diverse clinical presentations of pelvic inflammatory disease (PID) and the significant sequelae associated with delayed diagnosis, women with this condition can pose a major diagnostic dilemma in the ED. In 2002, the Centers for Disease Control and Prevention (CDC) updated their established diagnostic guidelines for initiating therapy in patients with suspected PID.[230] According to these guidelines, empirical treatment should be started if a young sexually active woman or any woman at risk for sexually transmitted diseases presents with minimal symptoms

[*see Table 5*] that cannot be attributed to another cause. To reduce undue treatment-associated morbidity, additional criteria are supplied to aid in specifying precisely who should receive treatment.

Treatment of PID, according to the CDC, includes broad-spectrum antibiotics directed toward *Neisseria gonorrhoeae, Chlamydia trachomatis,* anaerobes, gram-negative facultative bacteria, and streptococci [*see Table 6*]. Hospitalization is suggested when surgical emergencies (e.g., appendicitis) cannot be excluded or when the patient is pregnant; does not respond clinically to oral antimicrobial therapy; cannot follow or tolerate an outpatient oral regimen; has severe illness, nausea and vomiting, or high fever; or has a tubo-ovarian abscess. Surgical intervention for PID is generally limited to patients with symptomatic pelvic masses, ruptured

---

Table 5 CDC Guidelines for Diagnosis of Pelvic Inflammatory Disease[230]

Minimal symptoms
Uterine/adnexal tenderness
Cervical motion tenderness

Additional supportive criteria (enhance specificity of minimal symptoms)
Oral temperature >101° F (> 38.3° C)
Abnormal cervical or vaginal mucopurulent discharge
Presence of white blood cells on saline microscopy of vaginal secretions
Elevated erythrocyte sedimentation rate
Elevated C-reactive protein
Laboratory documentation of cervical infection with *Neisseria gonorrhoeae* or *Chlamydia trachomatis*

Most specific criteria
Endometrial biopsy with histopathologic evidence of endometritis
Transvaginal sonography or magnetic resonance imaging techniques showing thickened, fluid-filled tubes with or without free pelvic fluid or tubo-ovarian complex
Laparoscopic abnormalities consistent with PID

Table 6 CDC Guidelines for Antibiotic Treatment of PID[230]

Parenteral Regimens

A	Cefotetan, 2 g I.V. q. 12 hr *or* Cefoxitin, 2 g I.V. q. 6 hr *plus* Doxycycline, 100 mg p.o. or I.V. q. 12 hr
B	Clindamycin, 900 mg I.V. q. 8 hr *plus* Gentamicin, loading dose I.V. or I.M. (2 mg/kg body weight) followed by maintenance dose (1.5 mg/kg) q. 8 hr; single daily dosing may be substituted
Alternative	Ofloxacin, 400 mg I.V. q. 12 hr *or* Levofloxacin, 500 mg I.V. s.i.d. *with or without* Metronidazole, 500 mg I.V. q. 8 hr *or* Ampicillin-sulbactam, 3 g I.V. q. 6 hr *plus* Doxycycline, 100 mg p.o. or I.V. q. 12 hr

Enteral Regimens

A	Ofloxacin, 400 mg p.o., b.i.d., for 14 days *or* Levofloxacin, 500 mg p.o., s.i.d., for 14 days *with or without* Metronidazole, 500 mg p.o., b.i.d., for 14 days
B	Ceftriaxone, 250 mg I.M. in single dose *or* Cefoxitin, 2 g I.M. in single dose, and probenecid, 1 g p.o. administered concurrently in a single dose *or* Other parenteral third-generation cephalosporin (e.g., ceftizoxime or cefotaxime) *plus* Doxycycline, 100 mg p.o., b.i.d., for 14 days *with or without* Metronidazole, 500 mg p.o., b.i.d., for 14 days

tubo-ovarian abscesses, or draining abscesses that do not respond to antibiotic therapy. Aspiration has also been considered as a treatment modality; it may limit morbidity and preserve fertility.[231]

PYELONEPHRITIS

Pyelonephritis is a complication of urinary tract infection; consequently, it affects women more often than men. The diagnosis is typically made on the basis of systemic symptoms in the setting of a known, bacteriologically confirmed urinary tract infection. Pyelonephritis may be classified as either complicated or uncomplicated, depending on patient factors (e.g., previous transplantation or an anatomic abnormality) and infectious characteristics (e.g., sepsis).

The typical pathogen in uncomplicated disease is *E. coli*, and outpatient treatment with trimethoprim-sulfamethoxazole or a fluoroquinolone usually suffices.[232] Complicated pyelonephritis, however, often is caused by microbes other than *E. coli*, including *Pseudomonas* species and enterococci. Hospitalization is required, and treatment usually involves parenteral administration of ceftriaxone and gentamicin[233] or piperacillin-tazobactam[234]; vancomycin is indicated if the patient is allergic to penicillin. More aggressive therapies, including percutaneous nephrostomy or abscess drainage, may be considered on a case-by-case basis.

SPONTANEOUS BACTERIAL PERITONITIS

In adult patients, primary peritonitis usually accompanies cirrhosis and ascites[235]; however, the presentation can be highly variable. To diagnose spontaneous bacterial peritonitis, paracentesis is performed and the fluid sent for Gram stain and culture; pH determination; measurement of glucose, protein, lactate, and lactic dehydrogenase levels; and a cell count with differential. According to a consensus statement from the International Ascites Club, diagnostic paracentesis is recommended for every cirrhotic patient with ascites upon admission to the hospital.[236] Empirical therapy is started if the neutrophil count is higher than 250/mm³, the pH is lower than 7.35, and the lactate concentration is greater than 32 ng/ml. If the results of other studies suggest peritonitis, radiographic evaluation is indicated to rule out potential causes of secondary peritonitis.

Treatment consists of cefotaxime at a minimum dosage of 2 g every 12 hours for 5 days, with follow-up paracentesis scheduled for 48 hours after the start of treatment.[237,238] If the neutrophil count does not decrease significantly (to < 25% of the pretreatment value), treatment may be assumed to have failed. Surgical intervention is undertaken if the patient is refractory to medical management, the ascitic fluid grows mixed aerobes and anaerobes, or radiographic studies suggest bowel perforation.

PERITONEAL DIALYSIS CATHETER–RELATED INFECTIONS

Peritonitis is a major cause of failure of peritoneal dialysis in long-term studies.[239] Peritonitis is especially difficult to diagnose in dialysis patients because the presentation is usually vague. Accordingly, it is critical to maintain a low threshold for testing. The definition of peritonitis in this population includes satisfaction of two of the following three criteria: (1) a Gram stain demonstrating microorganisms or a positive culture of the dialysis effluent, (2) a dialysate white blood cell count higher than 100/mm³, with at least 50% neutrophils, and (3) peritoneal signs or symptoms.[240] The microbes most commonly identified are *S. epidermidis* and *S. aureus* (~60% of isolates), followed by gram-negative bacteria (~30% of isolates); the remaining isolates are largely accounted for by fungi, anaerobes, and mycobacteria.

Treatment usually includes cefazolin and an aminoglycoside, with or without vancomycin (depending on local *S. aureus* resistance patterns). Antibiotics are administered via the catheter and allowed to dwell intraperitoneally. When treatment is complete, the antibiotic effluent is drained via the catheter. If infection continues despite antibiotic treatment, a recurrent infection with the same microbe is likely. If fecal contamination occurs, the catheter must be removed.

Discussion

Controversies and Special Cases

The controversies surrounding the management of intra-abdominal infections are numerous and ongoing, in large part because of the relative lack of well-organized, unbiased clinical evidence. There are several reasons for this information deficit.

First, although in the aggregate, peritonitis is a common problem seen by general surgeons, any given practitioner sees most of the life-threatening forms of the disease (e.g., free perforation from colon cancer) infrequently. Second, advances in nonsurgical medicine and technology (e.g., laparoscopy) have made new forms of treatment available and have improved outcomes from older techniques. As a result, conclusions drawn from older data may no longer be accurate. Third, many forms of intra-abdominal infection routinely present in such a complex and ill patient population (e.g., elderly patients with multiple comorbidities) that randomized studies with multiple exclusion criteria can rarely capture a high percentage of what is a highly heterogeneous group. Fourth, patients presenting with common causes of intra-abdominal infection that occur in relatively healthy and homogeneous populations (e.g., acute appendicitis and cholecystitis) tend to do well no matter what reasonable therapy is applied. Consequently, it is frequently difficult to detect any significant differences between therapeutic modalities. For example, despite multiple randomized trials, it is still unclear whether a laparoscopic approach has any long-term superiority over an open approach in patients with right lower quadrant pain and suspected appendicitis: outcomes are excellent with either method. Finally, for almost any given argument, sufficient supporting data, whether in the form of randomized trials or—equally valuable—of large observational studies performed with statistical rigor, simply do not exist at present. Even simple questions, such as the optimum duration of antibiotic treatment for a patient with a single well-drained liver abscess, lack good answers.

In the end, most controversies in this area are not so much a matter of precisely determining the right or the wrong intervention for a disease as they are a matter of making a judgment about which of many possible interventions is likely to result in the lowest morbidity and mortality. For example, the decision to perform a primary colon reanastomosis in a patient with a perforated colon cancer cannot be considered either universally correct or universally incorrect; rather, it is subject to the surgeon's opinion about the specific patient involved. In what follows, we focus on several controversial decision points and discuss important factors that ought to be considered in attempting to optimize patient care.

NEW CONCEPTS IN PATHOPHYSIOLOGY OF ACUTE BACTERIAL CHOLANGITIS

Longmire's widely accepted classification of acute bacterial cholangitis consists of five categories: acute nonobstructive, acute nonsuppurative, acute suppurative, acute obstructive suppurative, and acute suppurative with intrahepatic abscess. It implies that the severity of disease parallels the degree of obstruction of biliary ducts.[241] This suggestion is well founded. In acute nonobstructive cholangitis associated with acute cholecystitis, infection ascends along the intrahepatic and extrahepatic lymphatics. In obstructive cholangitis, the bile duct contains bacteria under pressure. When the pressure is at or above the normal secretion pressure (i.e., 200 mm Hg), bacteria pass into the lymphatic system. At a pressure greater than 250 mm Hg, bacteria may pass directly from the bile ductules through the spaces of Mall and Disse and into the hepatic sinusoids via cholangiovenous reflux.[242] One study confirmed the clinical significance of increasing ductal pressure by demonstrating a higher ductal pressure and a higher incidence of bacteremia in patients with proximal ductal obstruction, compared with those with distal malignant biliary obstruction.[243] However, no correlation exists between the degree of suppuration in the duct and the clinical or pathologic severity of obstructive cholangitis.[82] Therefore, the terms acute nonsuppurative cholangitis and acute suppurative cholangitis are purely descriptive and do not imply differing degrees of severity.

The source of bacteria in acute cholangitis is most often the duodenum. The ease with which organisms reflux from the duodenum depends on the degree of obstruction. Thus, in patients with malignant biliary obstruction, in whom obstruction is usually complete, bile culture is positive in only 10% to 15% of patients[244]; acute cholangitis is seldom spontaneous in this setting but often follows radiologic intervention.[245] By comparison, in patients with ductal stones or benign strictures, in whom biliary obstruction is often incomplete, bile cultures obtained on ERCP are positive in 64% to 87% of cases; in these patients, acute cholangitis occurs frequently, both spontaneously and after ductal manipulation.[246]

An alternative source of organisms in acute bacterial cholangitis is portal venous blood. In patients who have recurrent pyogenic cholangitis, which occurs frequently in the Far East, a 40% incidence of positive portal blood culture has been reported.[247] In studies of rats with ligated bile ducts, bacteria were shown to be effectively transmitted to the bile ducts and the liver through portal blood.[248] Finally, in nonobstructive cholangitis and acute cholecystitis, as well as in the early stages of obstructive cholangitis, infection ascends to the liver through the lymphatic system.

CHANGING BACTERIOLOGY OF ACUTE BILIARY INFECTION

Most biliary infections are polymicrobial. The organisms most frequently cultured are *E. coli*, *Klebsiella* species, *Enterobacter* species, and enterococci. Anaerobic bacteria are infrequently implicated in biliary infections. Peptostreptococci and clostridia are found occasionally; clostridia are especially common in patients with emphysematous cholecystitis.[47] Gram-negative anaerobic bacilli are rarely present in patients with biliary infection. In one study, only two of 28 patients with acute cholangitis had anaerobic bacteria in the bile; another investigator found anaerobic bacteria in 3% to 4% of cultures in similar patients.[83] However, a higher incidence of anaerobic bacteria has been reported in patients who have acute cholangitis and acute cholecystitis than in patients who have chronic cholecystitis and cholelithiasis.[249]

One investigator noted an increased incidence of anaerobic bacteria in biliary infection and suggested that *B. fragilis* may play a more important role in the polymicrobial flora of biliary tract infection than was previously appreciated.[250] These findings remain controversial. *Bacteroides* species are generally considered to be of limited importance in biliary tract infections, except in selected groups of patients. These groups include diabetics, the elderly,[251] and those with acute cholangitis who have previously undergone biliary operation[252,253]; in particular, malfunctioning biliary-intestinal anastomoses increase the risk of *Bacteroides* infection.[254]

NECESSITY OF DIVERSION AFTER EMERGENCY COLONIC PROCEDURES

The goal of safely repairing or resecting the colon in an emergency setting without leaving a patient with a temporary or permanent stoma for diversion has been pursued for decades. Through much of the 20th century, largely on the basis of wartime experience, diversion was routinely performed. Today, however, it is apparent that this approach is not always necessary either for trauma or for intrinsic colon disease. Thus, the question is no longer whether primary repair or reanastomosis can be achieved safely but, rather, in which individual patient a given treatment is prudent.

Traditionally, clinical studies have attempted to define patient characteristics associated with complications after attempted primary repair or reanastomosis. Not surprisingly, hypotension, blood loss, delay before treatment, and extensive contamination have all been associated with postoperative complications after primary repair; however, these risk factors are associated with complications after diversion as well. The nature of the colon injury is clearly an important consideration: multiple studies now support a one-step approach to traumatic colon injury in all except the most ill patients, but primary resection and reanastomosis for other causes of perforation (e.g., diverticulosis and cancer) remain controversial. Many nonrandomized studies have demonstrated that for nontraumatic causes of perforation, on-table lavage and primary resection yield outcomes equivalent to those of the Hartmann procedure, which suggests that both approaches are safe and that surgeons are capable of identifying the patients best suited to each one.

Perhaps more important than determining how likely a patient is to experience a complication after a given operation, however, is assessing how well the patient is likely to tolerate that complication in the early postoperative period. Thus, elderly patients with multiple comorbidities might be better off undergoing diversion and thus avoiding the potential significant physiologic stress posed by an anastomotic leak in the early postoperative period, even though they will face the additional risk associated with reoperation if they subsequently choose to have a stoma reversed.

ROLE OF LAPAROSCOPY IN MANAGEMENT OF PERITONITIS

Laparoscopy has altered the surgical landscape by offering a minimally invasive approach that reduces the morbidity associated with a large incision, generally decreasing convalescence time and hastening return to normal activity. Nonetheless, laparoscopic management of intra-abdominal infection is still hindered somewhat by the difficulty of inspecting the entire bowel, the decreased tactile sensation, and the significantly greater expertise required for laparoscopic resection and reanastomosis of the bowel. These obstacles notwithstanding, almost every intra-abdominal procedure used to treat infection has been performed laparoscopically with acceptable results.

The single most important factor in the decision whether to take a laparoscopic approach is the skill and experience of the surgeon. From a theoretical point of view, it is almost always possible to treat a patient with peritonitis laparoscopically; the real question is whether the attending surgeon can perform the procedure most safely and efficiently via an open or a minimally invasive approach. The answer to this question will rely to a large extent on preoperative imaging studies. In addition, even if the surgeon does not plan to complete the operation laparoscopically, initial placement of the scope may aid in planning the most appropriate open incision and procedure by localizing the lesion of interest.

MANAGEMENT OF ANASTOMOTIC LEAKS

Dehiscence of a gastrointestinal anastomosis is a common and too frequently fatal complication of modern GI surgery. Again, there is little debate regarding which therapeutic options are available to surgeons managing this problem. The options include the following: supporting the patient with medical care only, in the case of a tiny radiographically evident but clinically insignificant leak seen on fluoroscopic study; reoperating and performing primary repair and drainage, in the case of a small early leak from an enteroenterostomy with minimal soilage; performing percutaneous drainage, in the case of a moderately symptomatic leak presenting in a delayed manner with an abscess; and reexploring and performing a diverting procedure, in the case of complete disruption of an anastomosis with widespread fecal contamination. The only controversy has to do with which course (or combination of courses) to take in an individual patient.

Some general guidelines for the management of anastomotic dehiscence may be recommended, with the caveat that they have not yet been rigorously tested. Leaks diagnosed in the immediate postoperative period are easily approached because the relevant tissue planes have been dissected free. After 1 to 2 weeks, however, early adhesion formation makes reoperation more difficult, especially if the initial operation was for an infectious or inflammatory process, and increases the risk of complications, particularly inadvertent enterotomy and enterocutaneous fistula formation. Small, contained leaks, if accessible, frequently respond to percutaneous drainage and antibiotics alone, with the small fistula resolving spontaneously. Medical management in such cases generally includes TPN, though enteral nutrition is occasionally feasible if it is shown to have no effect on drain output. Larger leaks, on the other hand, are more likely to call for direct operative repair, resection and reanastomosis, or diversion. Once it is decided that surgical treatment is warranted and is not precluded by the state of the abdomen, definitive management should not be delayed. Exactly which operation is to be performed depends on the health of the bowel, the severity of abdominal contamination, and the level of overall physiologic dysfunction.

MANAGEMENT OF ENDOSCOPIC BOWEL PERFORATION

Large rents in a peritoneal portion of the bowel generally call for operative repair (most commonly to the colon), though it should be noted that simple repair or resection without diversion is almost always all that is required. Extraperitoneal or retroperitoneal perforations, however, can be managed nonoperatively with antibiotics and I.V. fluids if the patient is stable. This situation occurs most frequently after ERCP or with low rectal perforations. Typically, CT scanning demonstrates retroperitoneal air with minimal free peritoneal air. In these circumstances, patients can be safely observed as long as their condition does not deteriorate; oral intake can be restarted after 5 to 7 days. Endoscopic perforations of a normal distal esophagus can also be managed nonoperatively, though a perforation proximal to a tumor or stricture is unlikely to heal and almost always must be treated operatively.

NONOPERATIVE MANAGEMENT OF INFECTED FLUID COLLECTIONS

It is axiomatic that abscesses are best treated with drainage rather than with antibiotics, but there are certain circumstances in which drainage may not be possible. Pyogenic liver abscesses may not be amenable to either percutaneous or open drainage if they are multiple and involve both lobes. In such circumstances, aspiration or drainage of the largest abscess, followed by a long course of antibiotics, is generally successful. It has been argued that this approach works because of the liver's luxurious dual blood supply.

On the other hand, multiple peritoneal fluid collections (without a natural blood supply) are not infrequently seen even after successful management of diffuse or fecal peritonitis yet can occasionally be managed without drainage. Even if these collections are subsequently proved to be infected, they may be too numerous to approach percutaneously, and ongoing inflammation of the bowel may render an operative approach unsafe. Again, drainage of the largest accessible collection to establish a diagnosis and guide antibiotic management, followed by long-term antibiotic therapy, is the most feasible course. In this case, sampling is imperative because a hospital-acquired intra-abdominal infection is more likely to involve less common but more resistant pathogens, including fungi. Regardless of the situation, though, the optimal duration of antibiotic therapy for small undrained abscesses remains to be established.

ADJUNCTIVE MEDICAL THERAPIES

Until recently, it could be said that advances in surgical therapy for intra-abdominal infection were outpacing other aspects of patient management. Too often, operations were technically successful, yet patients died afterward as a result of their systemic response to the original insult. Such deaths are still attributed to overwhelming sepsis, to multiple organ dysfunction syndrome, or to any number of other terms used to describe an irreversible sequence of organ failure and death [see 128 Multiple Organ Dysfunction Syndrome].

Multiple attempts over the years to alter this downward trajectory by using novel therapies to target this generalized inflammatory response proved unsuccessful. In the past few years, however, both recombinant human activated protein C and corticosteroid replacement therapy (for those with sepsis-associated adrenal insufficiency) were shown to improve survival in randomized, placebo-controlled trials involving mixed populations of patients with sepsis. Although the number of patients with intra-abdominal infection was relatively small in each study, there was no indication that these agents would not be similarly effective in this specific subgroup. The overall benefit of each of these treatments appears to be small, but the results of these trials are highly encouraging in that they suggest that related agents might be able to achieve further decreases in mortality. These possibilities, combined with significant improvements in general critical care, portend a future in which significant reductions in mortality may be realized even in the most severely infected patients.

References

1. Schofield PF, Hulton NR, Baildam AD: Is it acute cholecystitis? Ann R Coll Surg Engl 68:14, 1986

2. Ranson JH: Acute pancreatitis. Curr Probl Surg 16:1, 1979

3. Winslet M, Hall C, London NJ, et al: Relation of diagnostic serum amylase levels to aetiology and severity of acute pancreatitis. Gut 33:982, 1992

4. Patti M, Pellegrini CA, Way LW: Serum amylase is useful in the differential diagnosis of acute abdominal pain. Gastroenterology 90:1580, 1986

5. Yadav D, Agarwal N, Pitchumoni CS: A critical evaluation of laboratory tests in acute pancreatitis. Am J Gastroenterol 97:1309, 2002

6. Smotkin J, Tenner S: Laboratory diagnostic tests in acute pancreatitis. J Clin Gastroenterol 34:459, 2002

7. Toosie K, Chang L, Renslo R, et al: Early computed tomography is rarely necessary in gallstone pancreatitis. Am Surg 63:904, 1997

8. Sarr MG, Sanfey H, Cameron JL: Prospective, randomized trial of nasogastric suction in patients with acute pancreatitis. Surgery 100:500, 1986

9. Bradley EL 3rd: Antibiotics in acute pancreatitis: current status and future directions. Am J Surg 158:472, 1989

10. Steinberg WM, Schlesselman SE: Treatment of acute pancreatitis: comparison of animal and human studies. Gastroenterology 93:1420, 1987

11. McArdle AH, Rosenberg M, Fried GM, et al: Pancreatic exocrine secretion in response to continuous and bolus feeding (abstract), 19th Annual Meeting, Association for Academic Surgery, Cincinnati, Ohio, 1985

12. Erstad BL: Enteral nutrition support in acute pancreatitis. Ann Pharmacother 34:514, 2000

13. Scolapio JS, Malhi-Chowla N, Ukleja A: Nutrition supplementation in patients with acute and chronic pancreatitis. Gastroenterol Clin North Am 28:695, 1999

14. Windsor AC, Kanwar S, Li AG, et al: Compared with parenteral nutrition, enteral feeding attenuates the acute phase response and improves disease severity in acute pancreatitis. Gut 42:431, 1998

15. Chatzicostas C, Roussomoustakaki M, Vardas E, et al: Balthazar computed tomography severity index is superior to Ranson criteria and APACHE II and III scoring systems in predicting acute pancreatitis outcome. J Clin Gastroenterol 36:253, 2003

16. Liu TH, Kwong KL, Tamm EP, et al: Acute pancreatitis in intensive care unit patients: value of clinical and radiologic prognosticators at predicting clinical course and outcome. Crit Care Med 31:1026, 2003

17. Stone HH, Fabian TC, Dunlop WE: Gallstone pancreatitis: biliary tract pathology in relation to time of operation. Ann Surg 194:305, 1981

18. Acosta JM, Rossi R, Galli OM, et al: Early surgery for acute gallstone pancreatitis: evaluation of a systematic approach. Surgery 83:367, 1978

19. Kelly TR: Gallstone pancreatitis: the timing of surgery. Surgery 88:345, 1980

20. Dixon JA, Hillam JD: Surgical treatment of biliary tract disease associated with acute pancreatitis. Am J Surg 120:371, 1970

21. Ranson JH: The timing of biliary surgery in acute pancreatitis. Ann Surg 189:654, 1979

22. Paloyan D, Simonowitz D, Skinner DB: The timing of biliary tract operations in patients with pancreatitis associated with gallstones. Surg Gynecol Obstet 141:737, 1975

23. Kelly TR, Wagner DS: Gallstone pancreatitis: a prospective randomized trial of the timing of surgery. Surgery 104:600, 1988

24. Neoptolemos JP, Carr-Locke DL, London NJ, et al: Controlled trial of urgent endoscopic retrograde cholangiopancreatography and endoscopic sphincterotomy versus conservative treatment for acute pancreatitis due to gallstones. Lancet 2:979, 1988

25. Fan ST, Lai EC, Mok FP, et al: Early treatment of acute biliary pancreatitis by endoscopic papillotomy. N Engl J Med 328:228, 1993

26. Williamson RC: Early assessment of severity in acute pancreatitis. Gut 25:1331, 1984

27. Srinathan SK, Barkun JS, Mehta SN, et al: The management of gallstone pancreatitis in the laparoscopic era. J Gastrointest Surg (in press)

28. Ranson JH, Spencer FC: Prevention, diagnosis, and treatment of pancreatic abscess. Surgery 82:99, 1977

29. Osborne DH, Imrie CW, Carter DC: Biliary surgery in the same admission for gallstone-associated acute pancreatitis. Br J Surg 68:758, 1981

30. Folsch UR, Nitsche R, Ludtke R, et al: Early ERCP and papillotomy compared with conservative treatment for acute biliary pancreatitis. The German Study Group on Acute Biliary Pancreatitis. N Engl J Med 336:237, 1997

31. Chang L, Lo S, Stabile BE, et al: Preoperative versus postoperative endoscopic retrograde cholangiopancreatography in mild to moderate gallstone pancreatitis: a prospective randomized trial. Ann Surg 231:82, 2000

32. Nitsche R, Folsch UR, Ludtke R, et al: Urgent ERCP in all cases of acute biliary pancreatitis? A prospective randomized multicenter study. Eur J Med Res 1:127, 1995

33. Kozarek RA, Patterson DJ, Ball TJ, et al: Endoscopic placement of pancreatic stents and drains in the management of pancreatitis. Ann Surg 209:261, 1989

34. Ranson JH, Berman RS: Long peritoneal lavage decreases pancreatic sepsis in acute pancreatitis. Ann Surg 211:708, 1990

35. Pederzoli P, Bassi C, Vesentini S, et al: A randomized multicenter clinical trial of antibiotic prophylaxis of septic complications in acute necrotizing pancreatitis with imipenem. Surg Gynecol Obstet 176:480, 1993

36. Luiten EJ, Hop WC, Lange JF, et al: Controlled clinical trial of selective decontamination for the

treatment of severe acute pancreatitis. Ann Surg 222:57, 1995

37. Sharma VK, Howden CW: Prophylactic antibiotic administration reduces sepsis and mortality in acute necrotizing pancreatitis: a meta-analysis. Pancreas 22:28, 2001

38. Golub R, Siddiqi F, Pohl D: Role of antibiotics in acute pancreatitis: a meta-analysis. J Gastrointest Surg 2:496, 1998

39. Uhl W, Warshaw A, Imrie C, et al: IAP Guidelines for the Surgical Management of Acute Pancreatitis. Pancreatology 2:565, 2002

40. Howard TJ, Temple MB: Prophylactic antibiotics alter the bacteriology of infected necrosis in severe acute pancreatitis. J Am Coll Surg 195:759, 2002

41. Fiedler F, Jauernig G, Keim V, et al: Octreotide treatment in patients with necrotizing pancreatitis and pulmonary failure. Intensive Care Med 22:909, 1996

42. Paran H, Neufeld D, Mayo A, et al: Preliminary report of a prospective randomized study of octreotide in the treatment of severe acute pancreatitis. J Am Coll Surg 181:121, 1995

43. de Souza LJ, Sampietre SN, Assis RS, et al: Effect of platelet-activating factor antagonists (BN-52021, WEB-2170, and BB-882) on bacterial translocation in acute pancreatitis. J Gastrointest Surg 5:364, 2001

44. Lane JS, Todd KE, Gloor B, et al: Platelet activating factor antagonism reduces the systemic inflammatory response in a murine model of acute pancreatitis. J Surg Res 99:365, 2001

45. Kingsnorth AN, Galloway SW, Formela LJ: Randomized, double-blind phase II trial of lexipafant, a platelet-activating factor antagonist, in human acute pancreatitis. Br J Surg 82:1414, 1995

46. Johnson CD, Kingsnorth AN, Imrie CW, et al: Double blind, randomised, placebo controlled study of a platelet activating factor antagonist, lexipafant, in the treatment and prevention of organ failure in predicted severe acute pancreatitis. Gut 48:62, 2001

47. Mentzer RM Jr, Golden GT, Chandler JG, et al: A comparative appraisal of emphysematous cholecystitis. Am J Surg 129:10, 1975

48. Turner RJ 3rd, Becker WF, Coleman WO, et al: Acute cholecystitis in the diabetic. South Med J 62:228, 1969

49. Turrill RL: Gallstones and diabetes: an ominous association. Am J Surg 102:184, 1961

50. Walsh DB, Eckhauser FE, Ramsburgh SR, et al: Risk associated with diabetes mellitus in patients undergoing gallbladder surgery. Surgery 91:254, 1982

51. Pickleman J: Controversies in biliary tract surgery. Can J Surg 29:429, 1986

52. Weissmann HS, Berkowitz D, Fox MS, et al: The role of technetium-99m iminodiacetic acid (IDA) cholescintigraphy in acute acalculous cholecystitis. Radiology 146:177, 1983

53. Chen CC, Holder LE, Maunoury C, et al: Morphine augmentation increases gallbladder visualization in patients pretreated with cholecystokinin. J Nucl Med 38:644, 1997

54. Cabana MD, Alavi A, Berlin JA, et al: Morphine-augmented hepatobiliary scintigraphy: a meta-analysis. Nucl Med Commun 16:1068, 1995

55. Lo CM, Liu CL, Fan ST, et al: Prospective randomized study of early versus delayed laparoscopic cholecystectomy for acute cholecystitis. Ann Surg 227:461, 1998

56. Koc M, Zulfikaroglu B, Kece C, et al: A prospective randomized study of prophylactic antibiotics in elective laparoscopic cholecystectomy. Surg Endosc, June 17, 2003, Epub

57. Higgins A, London J, Charland S, et al:

Prophylactic antibiotics for elective laparoscopic cholecystectomy: are they necessary? Arch Surg 134:611, 1999

58. Illig KA, Schmidt E, Cavanaugh J, et al: Are prophylactic antibiotics required for elective laparoscopic cholecystectomy? J Am Coll Surg 184:353, 1997

59. Karachalios GN, Nasiopoulou DD, Bourlinou PK, et al: Treatment of acute biliary tract infections with ofloxacin: a randomized, controlled clinical trial. Int J Clin Pharmacol Ther 34:555, 1996

60. Krajden S, Yaman M, Fuksa M, et al: Piperacillin versus cefazolin given perioperatively to high-risk patients who undergo open cholecystectomy: a double-blind, randomized trial. Can J Surg 36:245, 1993

61. Skillings JC, Kumai C, Hinshaw JR: Cholecystostomy: a place in modern biliary surgery? Am J Surg 139:865, 1980

62. Klimberg S, Hawkins I, Vogel SB: Percutaneous cholecystostomy for acute cholecystitis in high-risk patients. Am J Surg 153:125, 1987

63. Miyazaki K, Uchiyama A, Nakayama F: New approach to the timing of operative intervention for acute cholecystitis: use of ultrasound risk score (abstr). 32nd World Conference of Surgery, Sydney, Australia, September 20–26, 1987

64. England RE, McDermott VG, Smith TP, et al: Percutaneous cholecystostomy: who responds? AJR Am J Roentgenol 168:1247, 1997

65. Orlando R 3rd, Crowell KL: Laparoscopy in the critically ill. Surg Endosc 11:1072, 1997

66. Reynolds BM, Dargan EL: Acute obstructive cholangitis: a distinct clinical syndrome. Ann Surg 150:299, 1959

67. Baer HU, Matthews JB, Schweizer WP, et al: Management of the Mirizzi syndrome and the surgical implications of cholecystcholedochal fistula. Br J Surg 77:743, 1990

68. Textor HJ, Flacke S, Pauleit D, et al: Three-dimensional magnetic resonance cholangiopancreatography with respiratory triggering in the diagnosis of primary sclerosing cholangitis: comparison with endoscopic retrograde cholangiography. Endoscopy 34:984, 2002

69. Ferrara C, Valeri G, Salvolini L, et al: Magnetic resonance cholangiopancreatography in primary sclerosing cholangitis in children. Pediatr Radiol 32:413, 2002

70. Chen JH, Chai JW, Chu WC, et al: Free breathing magnetic resonance cholangiopancreatography (MRCP) at end expiration: a new technique to expand clinical application. Hepatogastroenterology 49:593, 2002

71. Matos C, Nicaise N, Deviere J, et al: Choledochal cysts: comparison of findings at MR cholangiopancreatography and endoscopic retrograde cholangiopancreatography in eight patients. Radiology 209:443, 1998

72. Gerecht WB, Henry NK, Hoffman WW, et al: Prospective randomized comparison of mezlocillin therapy alone with combined ampicillin and gentamicin therapy for patients with cholangitis. Arch Intern Med 149:1279, 1989

73. Thompson JN, Edwards WH, Winearls CG, et al: Renal impairment following biliary tract surgery. Br J Surg 74:843, 1987

74. Thompson JE Jr, Pitt HA, Doty JE, et al: Broad spectrum penicillin as an adequate therapy for acute cholangitis. Surg Gynecol Obstet 171:275, 1990

75. Muller EL, Pitt HA, Thompson JE Jr, et al: Antibiotics in infections of the biliary tract. Surg Gynecol Obstet 165:285, 1987

76. Pitt HA, Postier RG, Cameron JL: Consequences of preoperative cholangitis and its treatment on the outcome of operation for choledocholithiasis. Surgery 94:447, 1983

77. Leung JW, Chung SC, Sung JJ, et al: Urgent endoscopic drainage for acute suppurative cholangitis. Lancet 1:1307, 1989

78. Lomanto D, Pavone P, Laghi A, et al: Magnetic resonance-cholangiopancreatography in the diagnosis of biliopancreatic diseases. Am J Surg 174:33, 1997

79. Becker CD, Grossholz M, Mentha G, et al: MR cholangiopancreatography: technique, potential indications, and diagnostic features of benign, postoperative, and malignant conditions. Eur Radiol 7:865, 1997

80. Gigot JF, Leese T, Dereme T, et al: Acute cholangitis: multivariate analysis of risk factors. Ann Surg 209:435, 1989

81. Lai EC, Tam PC, Paterson IA, et al: Emergency surgery for severe acute cholangitis: the high-risk patients. Ann Surg 211:55, 1990

82. O'Connor MJ, Schwartz ML, McQuarrie DG, et al: Acute bacterial cholangitis: an analysis of clinical manifestation. Arch Surg 117:437, 1982

83. Thompson JE Jr, Tompkins RK, Longmire WP Jr: Factors in management of acute cholangitis. Ann Surg 195:137, 1982

84. Bismuth H, Kuntziger H, Corlette MB: Cholangitis with acute renal failure: priorities in therapeutics. Ann Surg 181:881, 1975

85. Cho SR, Turner MA: Hepatic abscesses due to suppurative cholangitis. South Med J 75:488, 1982

86. Gould RJ, Vogelzang RL, Neiman HL, et al: Percutaneous biliary drainage as an initial therapy in sepsis of the biliary tract. Surg Gynecol Obstet 160:523, 1985

87. Leese T, Neoptolemos JP, Baker AR, et al: Management of acute cholangitis and the impact of endoscopic sphincterotomy. Br J Surg 73:988, 1986

88. Davis AJ, Kolios G, Alveyn CG, et al: Antibiotic prophylaxis for ERCP: a comparison of oral ciprofloxacin with intravenous cephazolin in the prophylaxis of high-risk patients. Aliment Pharmacol Ther 12:207, 1998

89. Saini S: Imaging of the hepatobiliary tract. N Engl J Med 336:1889, 1997

90. Bearcroft PW, Miles KA: Leucocyte scintigraphy or computed tomography for the febrile postoperative patient? Eur J Radiol 23:126, 1996

91. Haque R, Ali IK, Akther S, et al: Comparison of PCR, isoenzyme analysis, and antigen detection for diagnosis of *Entamoeba histolytica* infection. J Clin Microbiol 36:449, 1998

92. Auer H, Picher O, Aspock H: Combined application of enzyme-linked immunosorbent assay (ELISA) and indirect haemagglutination test (IHA) as a useful tool for the diagnosis and postoperative surveillance of human alveolar and cystic echinococcosis. Zentralbl Bakteriol Mikrobiol Hyg [A] 270:313, 1988

93. Force L, Torres JM, Carrillo A, et al: Evaluation of eight serological tests in the diagnosis of human echinococcosis and follow-up. Clin Infect Dis 15:473, 1992

94. Aeder MI, Wellman JL, Haaga JR, et al: Role of surgical and percutaneous drainage in the treatment of abdominal abscesses. Arch Surg 118:273, 1983

95. Ch Yu S, Hg Lo R, Kan PS, et al: Pyogenic liver abscess: treatment with needle aspiration. Clin Radiol 52:912, 1997

96. Giorgio A, Tarantino L, Mariniello N, et al: Pyogenic liver abscesses: 13 years of experience in percutaneous needle aspiration with US guidance. Radiology 195:122, 1995

97. Rajak CL, Gupta S, Jain S, et al: Percutaneous treatment of liver abscesses: needle aspiration versus catheter drainage. AJR Am J Roentgenol 170:1035, 1998

98. Gerzof SG, Johnson WC, Robbins AH, et al: Intrahepatic pyogenic abscesses: treatment by percutaneous drainage. Am J Surg 149:487, 1985

99. Seeto RK, Rockey DC: Pyogenic liver abscess: changes in etiology, management, and outcome. Medicine (Baltimore) 75:99, 1996

100. Herman P, Pugliese V, Montagnini AL, et al: Pyogenic liver abscess: the role of surgical treatment. Int Surg 82:98, 1997

101. Klatchko BA, Schwartz SI: Diagnostic and therapeutic approaches to pyogenic abscess of the liver. Surg Gynecol Obstet 168:332, 1989

102. Gyorffy EJ, Frey CF, Silva J Jr, et al: Pyogenic liver abscess: diagnostic and therapeutic strategies. Ann Surg 206:699, 1987

103. Sabbaj J, Sutter VL, Finegold SM: Anaerobic pyogenic liver abscess. Ann Intern Med 77:627, 1972

104. Huang CJ, Pitt HA, Lipsett PA, et al: Pyogenic hepatic abscess: changing trends over 42 years. Ann Surg 223:600, 1996

105. Schein M, Wittmann DH, Lorenz W: Duration of antibiotic treatment in surgical infections of the abdomen. Forum statement: a plea for selective and controlled postoperative antibiotic administration. Eur J Surg Suppl (576):66, 1996

106. Rubin RH, Swartz MN, Malt R: Hepatic abscess: changes in clinical, bacteriologic and therapeutic aspects. Am J Med 57:601, 1974

107. Yeh TS, Jan YY, Jeng LB, et al: Pyogenic liver abscesses in patients with malignant disease: a report of 52 cases treated at a single institution. Arch Surg 133:242, 1998

108. Cohen HG, Reynolds TB: Comparison of metronidazole and chloroquine for the treatment of amoebic liver abscess: a controlled trial. Gastroenterology 69:35, 1975

109. Turkcapar AG, Ersoz S, Gungor C, et al: Surgical treatment of hepatic hydatidosis combined with perioperative treatment with albendazole. Eur J Surg 163:923, 1997

110. Saimot AG: Medical treatment of liver hydatidosis. World J Surg 25:15, 2001

111. Stiles GM, Berne TV, Thommen VD, et al: Fine needle aspiration of pancreatic fluid collections. Am Surg 56:764, 1990

112. Bittner R, Block S, Buchler M, et al: Pancreatic abscess and infected pancreatic necrosis. Different local septic complications in acute pancreatitis. Dig Dis Sci 32:1082, 1987

113. Banks PA, Gerzof SG, Chong FK, et al: Bacteriologic status of necrotic tissue in necrotizing pancreatitis. Pancreas 5:330, 1990

114. Crass RA, Meyer AA, Jeffrey RB, et al: Pancreatic abscess: impact of computerized tomography on early diagnosis and surgery. Am J Surg 150:127, 1985

115. Buchler M, Malfertheiner P, Schoetensack C, et al: Sensitivity of antiproteases, complement factors and C-reactive protein in detecting pancreatic necrosis: results of a prospective clinical study. Int J Pancreatol 1:227, 1986

116. Ranson JH, Balthazar E, Caccavale R, et al: Computed tomography and the prediction of pancreatic abscess in acute pancreatitis. Ann Surg 201:656, 1985

117. Bradley EL 3rd, Allen K: A prospective longitudinal study of observation versus surgical intervention in the management of necrotizing pancreatitis. Am J Surg 161:19, 1991

118. Warshaw AL: Pancreatic abscesses. N Engl J Med 287:1234, 1972

119. Frey CF, Lindenauer SM, Miller TA: Pancreatic abscess. Surg Gynecol Obstet 149:722, 1979

120. Hedderich GS, Wexler MJ, McLean AP, et al: The septic abdomen: open management with Marlex mesh with a zipper. Surgery 99:399, 1986

121. D'Egidio A, Schein M: Surgical strategies in the treatment of pancreatic necrosis and infection. Br J Surg 78:133, 1991

122. Stanten R, Frey CF: Comprehensive management of acute necrotizing pancreatitis and pancreatic abscess. Arch Surg 125:1269, 1990

123. Rotman N, Mathieu D, Anglade MC, et al: Failure of percutaneous drainage of pancreatic abscesses complicating severe acute pancreatitis. Surg Gynecol Obstet 174:141, 1992

124. Lang EK, Paolini RM, Pottmeyer A: The efficacy of palliative and definitive percutaneous versus surgical drainage of pancreatic abscesses and pseudocysts: a prospective study of 85 patients. South Med J 84:55, 1991

125. Williams LF Jr, Byrne JJ: The role of bacteria in hemorrhagic pancreatitis. Surgery 64:967, 1968

126. Gregg JA: Detection of bacterial infection of the pancreatic ducts in patients with pancreatitis and pancreatic cancer during endoscopic cannulation of the pancreatic duct. Gastroenterology 73:1005, 1977

127. Farkas G, Marton J, Mandi Y, et al: Surgical strategy and management of infected pancreatic necrosis. Br J Surg 83:930, 1996

128. Grant JP, James S, Grabowski V, et al: Total parenteral nutrition in pancreatic disease. Ann Surg 200:627, 1984

129. Johnson JD, Raff MJ, Drasin GF, et al: Radiology in the diagnosis of splenic abscess. Rev Infect Dis 7:10, 1985

130. Sones PJ: Percutaneous drainage of abdominal abscesses. AJR Am J Roentgenol 142:35, 1984

131. Berkman WA, Harris SA Jr, Bernardino ME: Nonsurgical drainage of splenic abscess. AJR Am J Roentgenol 141:395, 1983

132. Espinoza R, Rodriguez A: Traumatic and nontraumatic perforation of hollow viscera. Surg Clin North Am 77:1291, 1997

133. Ng EK, Lam YH, Sung JJ, et al: Eradication of Helicobacter pylori prevents recurrence of ulcer after simple closure of duodenal ulcer perforation: randomized controlled trial. Ann Surg 231:153, 2000

134. Tokunaga Y, Hata K, Ryo J, et al: Density of Helicobacter pylori infection in patients with peptic ulcer perforation. J Am Coll Surg 186:659, 1998

135. Matsukura N, Onda M, Tokunaga A, et al: Role of Helicobacter pylori infection in perforation of peptic ulcer: an age- and gender-matched case-control study. J Clin Gastroenterol 25(suppl 1):S235, 1997

136. Feliciano DV, Ojukwu JC, Rozycki GS, et al: The epidemic of cocaine-related juxtapyloric perforations: with a comment on the importance of testing for Helicobacter pylori. Ann Surg 229:801, 1999

137. Cho KC, Baker SR: Extraluminal air: diagnosis and significance. Radiol Clin North Am 32:829, 1994

138. Berne TV, Donovan AJ: Nonoperative treatment of perforated duodenal ulcer. Arch Surg 124:830, 1989

139. Crofts TJ, Park KG, Steele RJ, et al: A randomized trial of nonoperative treatment for perforated peptic ulcer. N Engl J Med 320:970, 1989

140. Donovan AJ, Berne TV, Donovan JA: Perforated duodenal ulcer: an alternative therapeutic plan. Arch Surg 133:1166, 1998

141. Siu WT, Leong HT, Law BK, et al: Laparoscopic repair for perforated peptic ulcer: a randomized controlled trial. Ann Surg 235:313, 2002

142. Lau WY, Leung KL, Kwong KH, et al: A randomized study comparing laparoscopic versus open repair of perforated peptic ulcer using suture or sutureless technique. Ann Surg 224:131, 1996

143. Feliciano DV: Do perforated duodenal ulcers need an acid-decreasing surgical procedure now that omeprazole is available? Surg Clin North Am 72:369, 1992

144. Christiansen J, Andersen OB, Bonnesen T, et al: Perforated duodenal ulcer managed by simple closure versus closure and proximal gastric vagotomy. Br J Surg 74:286, 1987

145. Boey J, Branicki FJ, Alagaratnam TT, et al: Proximal gastric vagotomy: the preferred operation for perforations in acute duodenal ulcer. Ann Surg 208:169, 1988

146. Sebastian M, Chandran VP, Elashaal YI, et al: Helicobacter pylori infection in perforated peptic ulcer disease. Br J Surg 82:360, 1995

147. Kate V, Ananthakrishnan N, Badrinath S: Effect of Helicobacter pylori eradication on the ulcer recurrence rate after simple closure of perforated duodenal ulcer: retrospective and prospective randomized controlled studies. Br J Surg 88:1054, 2001

148. Kauffman GL Jr: Duodenal ulcer disease: treatment by surgery, antibiotics, or both. Adv Surg 34:121, 2000

149. Ruddell WS, Axon AT, Findlay JM, et al: Effect of cimetidine on the gastric bacterial flora. Lancet 1:672, 1980

150. Hosking SW, Ling TK, Chung SC, et al: Duodenal ulcer healing by eradication of Helicobacter pylori without anti-acid treatment: randomised controlled trial. Lancet 343:508, 1994

151. Sung JJ, Leung WK, Suen R, et al: One-week antibiotics versus maintenance acid suppression therapy for Helicobacter pylori–associated peptic ulcer bleeding. Dig Dis Sci 42:2524, 1997

152. Sung JJ, Chung SC, Ling TK, et al: Antibacterial treatment of gastric ulcers associated with Helicobacter pylori. N Engl J Med 332:139, 1995

153. Wisner DH, Chun Y, Blaisdell FW: Blunt intestinal injury: keys to diagnosis and management. Arch Surg 125:1319, 1990

154. Fakhry SM, Watts DD, Luchette FA: Current diagnostic approaches lack sensitivity in the diagnosis of perforated blunt small bowel injury: analysis from 275,557 trauma admissions from the EAST multi-institutional HVI trial. J Trauma 54:295, 2003

155. Malhotra AK, Fabian TC, Katsis SB, et al: Blunt bowel and mesenteric injuries: the role of screening computed tomography. J Trauma 48:991, 2000

156. Lautenbach E, Berlin JA, Lichtenstein GR: Risk factors for early postoperative recurrence of Crohn's disease. Gastroenterology 115:259, 1998

157. Walker AP, Krepel CJ, Gohr CM, et al: Microflora of abdominal sepsis by locus of infection. J Clin Microbiol 32:557, 1994

158. Mazuski JE, Sawyer RG, Nathens AB, et al: The Surgical Infection Society guidelines on antimicrobial therapy for intra-abdominal infections: an executive summary. Surg Infect (Larchmt) 3:161, 2002

159. Reynolds SL: Missed appendicitis in a pediatric emergency department. Pediatr Emerg Care 9:1, 1993

160. Rothrock SG, Green SM, Dobson M, et al: Misdiagnosis of appendicitis in nonpregnant women of childbearing age. J Emerg Med 13:1, 1995

161. Izbicki JR, Knoefel WT, Wilker DK, et al: Accurate diagnosis of acute appendicitis: a retrospective and prospective analysis of 686 patients. Eur J Surg 158:227, 1992

162. Rao PM, Rhea JT, Rattner DW, et al: Intro-

duction of appendiceal CT: impact on negative appendectomy and appendiceal perforation rates. Ann Surg 229:344, 1999

163. Rao PM, Boland GW: Imaging of acute right lower abdominal quadrant pain. Clin Radiol 53:639, 1998

164. Rao PM, Rhea JT, Novelline RA, et al: The computed tomography appearance of recurrent and chronic appendicitis. Am J Emerg Med 16:26, 1998

165. Rao PM, Rhea JT, Novelline RA: Sensitivity and specificity of the individual CT signs of appendicitis: experience with 200 helical appendiceal CT examinations. J Comput Assist Tomogr 21:686, 1997

166. Rao PM, Rhea JT, Novelline RA, et al: Effect of computed tomography of the appendix on treatment of patients and use of hospital resources. N Engl J Med 338:141, 1998

167. Walker S, Haun W, Clark J, et al: The value of limited computed tomography with rectal contrast in the diagnosis of acute appendicitis. Am J Surg 180:450, 2000

168. Rao PM, Feltmate CM, Rhea JT, et al: Helical computed tomography in differentiating appendicitis and acute gynecologic conditions. Obstet Gynecol 93:417, 1999

169. Wilson EB, Cole JC, Nipper ML, et al: Computed tomography and ultrasonography in the diagnosis of appendicitis: when are they indicated? Arch Surg 136:670, 2001

170. Long KH, Bannon MP, Zietlow SP, et al: A prospective randomized comparison of laparoscopic appendectomy with open appendectomy: clinical and economic analyses. Surgery 129:390, 2001

171. Pedersen AG, Petersen OB, Wara P, et al: Randomized clinical trial of laparoscopic versus open appendectomy. Br J Surg 88:200, 2001

172. Ortega AE, Hunter JG, Peters JH, et al: A prospective, randomized comparison of laparoscopic appendectomy with open appendectomy. Laparoscopic Appendectomy Study Group. Am J Surg 169:208, 1995

173. Frazee RC, Roberts JW, Symmonds RE, et al: A prospective randomized trial comparing open versus laparoscopic appendectomy. Ann Surg 219:725, 1994

174. Katkhouda N, Friedlander MH, Grant SW, et al: Intraabdominal abscess rate after laparoscopic appendectomy. Am J Surg 180:456, 2000

175. Krisher SL, Browne A, Dibbins A, et al: Intraabdominal abscess after laparoscopic appendectomy for perforated appendicitis. Arch Surg 136:438, 2001

176. Larsson PG, Henriksson G, Olsson M, et al: Laparoscopy reduces unnecessary appendicectomies and improves diagnosis in fertile women: a randomized study. Surg Endosc 15:200, 2001

177. Enochsson L, Hellberg A, Rudberg C, et al: Laparoscopic vs open appendectomy in overweight patients. Surg Endosc 15:387, 2001

178. Horwitz JR, Custer MD, May BH, et al: Should laparoscopic appendectomy be avoided for complicated appendicitis in children? J Pediatr Surg 32:1601, 1997

179. Oliak D, Yamini D, Udani VM, et al: Initial nonoperative management for periappendiceal abscess. Dis Colon Rectum 44:936, 2001

180. Tingstedt B, Bexe-Lindskog E, Ekelund M, et al: Management of appendiceal masses. Eur J Surg 168:579, 2002

181. Mazziotti MV, Marley EF, Winthrop AL, et al: Histopathologic analysis of interval appendectomy specimens: support for the role of interval appendectomy. J Pediatr Surg 32:806, 1997

182. Hoffmann J, Lindhard A, Jensen HE: Appendix mass: conservative management without interval appendectomy. Am J Surg 148:379, 1984

183. Samuel M, Hosie G, Holmes K: Prospective evaluation of nonsurgical versus surgical management of appendiceal mass. J Pediatr Surg 37:882, 2002

184. Lasson A, Lundagards J, Loren I, et al: Appendiceal abscesses: primary percutaneous drainage and selective interval appendicectomy. Eur J Surg 168:264, 2002

185. Lidar Z, Kuriansky J, Rosin D, et al: Laparoscopic interval appendectomy for periappendicular abscess. Surg Endosc 14:764, 2000

186. Bennion RS, Baron EJ, Thompson JE Jr, et al: The bacteriology of gangrenous and perforated appendicitis—revisited. Ann Surg 211:165, 1990

187. Bennion RS, Thompson JE, Baron EJ, et al: Gangrenous and perforated appendicitis with peritonitis: treatment and bacteriology. Clin Ther 12(suppl C):31, 1990

188. Bilik R, Burnweit C, Shandling B: Is abdominal cavity culture of any value in appendicitis? Am J Surg 175:267, 1998

189. Ferzoco LB, Raptopoulos V, Silen W: Acute diverticulitis. N Engl J Med 338:1521, 1998

190. Bauer T, Vennits B, Holm B, et al: Antibiotic prophylaxis in acute nonperforated appendicitis. The Danish Multicenter Study Group III. Ann Surg 209:307, 1989

191. Liberman MA, Greason KL, Frame S, et al: Single-dose cefotetan or cefoxitin versus multiple-dose cefoxitin as prophylaxis in patients undergoing appendectomy for acute nonperforated appendicitis. J Am Coll Surg 180:77, 1995

192. Salam IM, Abu Galala KH, el Ashaal YI, et al: A randomized prospective study of cefoxitin versus piperacillin in appendicectomy. J Hosp Infect 26:133, 1994

193. Rice HE, Brown RL, Gollin G, et al: Results of a pilot trial comparing prolonged intravenous antibiotics with sequential intravenous/oral antibiotics for children with perforated appendicitis. Arch Surg 136:1391, 2001

194. Gorecki WJ, Grochowski JA: Are antibiotics necessary in nonperforated appendicitis in children? A double blind randomized controlled trial. Med Sci Monit 7:289, 2001

195. Almqvist P, Leandoer L, Tornqvist A: Timing of antibiotic treatment in non-perforated gangrenous appendicitis. Eur J Surg 161:431, 1995

196. Ahn SH, Mayo-Smith WW, Murphy BL, et al: Acute nontraumatic abdominal pain in adult patients: abdominal radiography compared with CT evaluation. Radiology 225:159, 2002

197. Tsushima Y, Yamada S, Aoki J, et al: Effect of contrast-enhanced computed tomography on diagnosis and management of acute abdomen in adults. Clin Radiol 57:507, 2002

198. Rodkey GV, Welch CE: Surgical management of colonic diverticulitis with free perforation or abscess formation. Am J Surg 117:265, 1969

199. Byrne JJ, Garick EI: Surgical treatment of diverticulitis. Am J Surg 121:379, 1971

200. Graves HA Jr, Franklin RM, Robbins LB 2nd, et al: Surgical management of perforated diverticulitis of the colon. Am Surg 39:142, 1973

201. Hinchey EJ, Schaal PG, Richards GK: Treatment of perforated diverticular disease of the colon. Adv Surg 12:85, 1978

202. Kohler L, Sauerland S, Neugebauer E: Diagnosis and treatment of diverticular disease: results of a consensus development conference. The Scientific Committee of the European Association for Endoscopic Surgery. Surg Endosc 13:430, 1999

203. Farthmann EH, Ruckauer KD, Haring RU: Evidence-based surgery: diverticulitis—a surgical disease? Langenbecks Arch Surg 385:143, 2000

204. Wong WD, Wexner SD, Lowry A, et al: Practice parameters for the treatment of sigmoid diverticulitis—supporting documentation. The Standards Task Force. The American Society of Colon and Rectal Surgeons. Dis Colon Rectum 43:290, 2000

205. Ambrosetti P, Robert J, Witzig JA, et al: Incidence, outcome, and proposed management of isolated abscesses complicating acute left-sided colonic diverticulitis: a prospective study of 140 patients. Dis Colon Rectum 35:1072, 1992

206. Koruth NM, Krukowski ZH, Youngson GG, et al: Intra-operative colonic irrigation in the management of left-sided large bowel emergencies. Br J Surg 72:708, 1985

207. Lee EC, Murray JJ, Coller JA, et al: Intraoperative colonic lavage in nonelective surgery for diverticular disease. Dis Colon Rectum 40:669 1997

208. Murray JJ, Schoetz DJ Jr, Coller JA, et al: Intraoperative colonic lavage and primary anastomosis in nonelective colon resection. Dis Colon Rectum 34:527, 1991

209. Belmonte C, Klas JV, Perez JJ, et al: The Hartmann procedure: first choice or last resort in diverticular disease? Arch Surg 131:612, 1996

210. Nagorney DM, Adson MA, Pemberton JH: Sigmoid diverticulitis with perforation and generalized peritonitis. Dis Colon Rectum 28:71, 1985

211. Illert B, Engemann R, Thiede A: Success in treatment of complicated diverticular disease is stage related. Int J Colorectal Dis 16:276, 2001

212. Tucci G, Torquati A, Grande M, et al: Major acute inflammatory complications of diverticular disease of the colon: planning of surgical management. Hepatogastroenterology 43:839, 1996

213. Krukowski ZH, Matheson NA: Emergency surgery for diverticular disease complicated by generalized and faecal peritonitis: a review. Br J Surg 71:921, 1984

214. Gooszen AW, Gooszen HG, Veerman W, et al: Operative treatment of acute complications of diverticular disease: primary or secondary anastomosis after sigmoid resection. Eur J Surg 167:35, 2001

215. Maggard MA, Chandler CF, Schmit PJ, et al: Surgical diverticulitis: treatment options. Am Surg 67:1185, 2001

216. Wedell J, Banzhaf G, Chaoui R, et al: Surgical management of complicated colonic diverticulitis. Br J Surg 84:380, 1997

217. Benn PL, Wolff BG, Ilstrup DM: Level of anastomosis and recurrent colonic diverticulitis. Am J Surg 151:269, 1986

218. Wexner SD, Moscovitz ID: Laparoscopic colectomy in diverticular and Crohn's disease. Surg Clin North Am 80:1299, 2000

219. Fang JF, Chen RJ, Lin BC, et al: Aggressive resection is indicated for cecal diverticulitis. Am J Surg 185:135, 2003

220. Lane JS, Sarkar R, Schmit PJ, et al: Surgical approach to cecal diverticulitis. J Am Coll Surg 188:629, 1999

221. Oudenhoven LF, Koumans RK, Puylaert JB: Right colonic diverticulitis: US and CT findings—new insights about frequency and natural history. Radiology 208:611, 1998

222. Graham SM, Ballantyne GH: Cecal diverticulitis: a review of the American experience. Dis Colon Rectum 30:821, 1987

223. Brook I, Frazier EH: Aerobic and anaerobic microbiology in intra-abdominal infections associated with diverticulitis. J Med Microbiol 49:827, 2000

224. Runkel NS, Schlag P, Schwarz V, et al: Outcome after emergency surgery for cancer of the large intestine. Br J Surg 78:183, 1991

225. Welch JP, Donaldson GA: Perforative carcinoma of colon and rectum. Ann Surg 180:734, 1974

226. Nespoli A, Ravizzini C, Trivella M, et al: The choice of surgical procedure for peritonitis due to colonic perforation. Arch Surg 128:814, 1993

227. Anderson JH, Hole D, McArdle CS: Elective versus emergency surgery for patients with colorectal cancer. Br J Surg 79:706, 1992

228. Koperna T, Kisser M, Schulz F: Emergency surgery for colon cancer in the aged. Arch Surg 132:1032, 1997

229. Nathens AB, Rotstein OD: Therapeutic options in peritonitis. Surg Clin North Am 74:677, 1994

230. Sexually transmitted diseases treatment guidelines 2002. Centers for Disease Control and Prevention. MMWR Recomm Rep 51:1, 2002

231. Cohn DE, Rader JS: Gynecology. Surgery: Basic Science and Clinical Evidence. Surgery: Basic Science and Clinical Evidence. Norton JA, Bollinger RR, Chang AE, et al, Eds. Springer, New York, 2001, p 1923

232. Nickel JC: The management of acute pyelonephritis in adults. Can J Urol 8(suppl 1):29, 2001

233. Roberts JA: Management of pyelonephritis and upper urinary tract infections. Urol Clin North Am 26:753, 1999

234. Naber KG, Savov O, Salmen HC: Piperacillin 2 g/tazobactam 0.5 g is as effective as imipenem 0.5 g/cilastatin 0.5 g for the treatment of acute uncomplicated pyelonephritis and complicated urinary tract infections. Int J Antimicrob Agents 19:95, 2002

235. Conn HO: Spontaneous bacterial peritonitis: variant syndromes. South Med J 80:1343, 1987

236. Rimola A, Garcia-Tsao G, Navasa M, et al: Diagnosis, treatment and prophylaxis of spontaneous bacterial peritonitis: a consensus document. International Ascites Club. J Hepatol 32:142, 2000

237. Runyon BA, Antillon MR: Ascitic fluid pH and lactate: insensitive and nonspecific tests in detecting ascitic fluid infection. Hepatology 13:929, 1991

238. Felisart J, Rimola A, Arroyo V, et al: Cefotaxime is more effective than is ampicillin-tobramycin in cirrhotics with severe infections. Hepatology 5:457, 1985

239. Kawaguchi Y: Peritoneal dialysis as long-term treatment: comparison of technique survival between Asian and Western populations. Perit Dial Int 19(suppl 2):S327, 1999

240. Vas SI: Infections of continuous ambulatory peritoneal dialysis catheters. Infect Dis Clin North Am 3:301, 1989

241. Longmire WP: Suppurative cholangitis. Critical Surgical Illness. Hardy JD, Ed. WB Saunders Co, Philadelphia, 1971, p 400

242. Stewart L, Pellegrini CA, Way LW: Cholangiovenous reflux pathways as defined by corrosion casting and scanning electron microscopy. Am J Surg 155:23, 1988

243. Lygidakis NJ, Brummelkamp WH: Bacteremia in relation to intrabiliary pressure in proximal v. distal malignant biliary obstruction. Acta Chir Scand 152:305, 1986

244. Flemma RJ, Flint LM, Osterhout S, et al: Bacteriologic studies of biliary tract infection. Ann Surg 166:563, 1967

245. Weissglas IS, Brown RA: Acute suppurative cholangitis secondary to malignant obstruction. Can J Surg 24:468, 1981

246. Elson CO, Hattori K, Blackstone MO: Polymicrobial sepsis following endoscopic retrograde cholangiopancreatography. Gastroenterology 69:507, 1975

247. Ong GB: A study of recurrent pyogenic cholangitis. Arch Surg 84:199, 1962

248. Jackaman FR, Triggs CM, Thomas V, et al: Experimental bacterial infection of the biliary tract. Br J Exp Pathol 61:369, 1980

249. Lewis RT, Goodall RG, Marien B, et al: Biliary bacteria, antibiotic use, and wound infection in surgery of the gallbladder and common bile duct. Arch Surg 122:44, 1987

250. Finegold SM: Anaerobes in biliary tract infection. Arch Intern Med 139:1338, 1979

251. Shimada K, Inamatsu T, Yamashiro M: Anaerobic bacteria in biliary disease in elderly patients. J Infect Dis 135:850, 1977

252. Shimada K, Noro T, Inamatsu T, et al: Bacteriology of acute obstructive suppurative cholangitis of the aged. J Clin Microbiol 14:522, 1981

253. Lee WJ, Chang KJ, Lee CS, et al: Surgery in cholangitis: bacteriology and choice of antibiotic. Hepatogastroenterology 39:347, 1992

254. Bourgault AM, England DM, Rosenblatt JE, et al: Clinical characteristics of anaerobic bactibilia. Arch Intern Med 139:1346, 1979

Acknowledgments

Figures 2 through 5   Dr. L. Stein, Montreal, Quebec.

Figure 6   From "Computed Tomography and the Prediction of Pancreatic Abscess in Acute Pancreatitis," by J. H. C. Ranson, E. Balthazar, R. Caccavale, et al, in *Annals of Surgery* 201:656, 1985. Used by permission.

Figure 7   From "Nonsurgical Drainage of Splenic Abscess," by W. A. Berkman, S. A. Harris Jr., and M. E. Bernardino, in *American Journal of Roentgenology* 141:395, 1983. Used by permission.

134 FUNGAL INFECTION

Elias J. Anaissie, M.D., Albair B. Bishara, M.D., and Joseph S. Solomkin, M.D., F.A.C.S.

Approach to the Surgical Patient at Risk for Candidiasis

The infectious diseases that are most commonly encountered by surgeons are acute events in which fever, leukocytosis, and localized signs of inflammation develop in a reasonably healthy host. In this clinical situation, the presence of microorganisms in such normally sterile foci as blood and intra-abdominal sites indicates an infection and the need for antimicrobial chemotherapy.

The clinical setting in which *Candida* species are isolated from various body sites is generally much different. Patients harboring *Candida* infections frequently have had antecedent infections that were treated with antibacterial agents, have received therapy that suppressed their immunologic responses,[1] or have undergone extensive surgery or several operations, especially on the gastrointestinal tract. Such patients are generally long-term residents in acute care hospitals. Previous operative intervention may have left surgical wounds or drainage tracts. These circumstances favor colonization by various opportunistic pathogens, with the resultant risk of overgrowth or invasion by normal enteric microorganisms such as *Candida* species. In this setting, the elements that characterize most infectious processes (i.e., an acute change from wellness to illness and isolation of microorganisms from ordinarily sterile sites) no longer have great diagnostic value.

The problem of defining indications for administration of antifungal therapy in surgical patients is compounded by the limited data available, the difficulty of establishing a diagnosis, and the small number of effective antifungal agents. Although amphotericin B is currently the standard antifungal agent, fluconazole, a newer triazole antifungal that is generally well tolerated, appears to be effective in the treatment of serious *Candida* infections in surgical patients.

Noncandidal fungal infections, although still rare in surgical patients, may cause morbidity and mortality. Because infections such as aspergillosis and mucormycosis may be refractory to standard antifungal therapy, there is an urgent need to define the role of novel antifungal agents in surgical patients.

This chapter summarizes the current understanding of fungal infections, particularly candidiasis, in nonneutropenic surgical patients and provides recommendations for prophylaxis and therapy.

Magnitude of the Problem in the Surgical Patient

Whereas the high mortality associated with bacterial infections in surgical patients has been reduced by the early administration of antibacterial therapy, the incidence of fungal infections, particularly with *Candida* species, has dramatically increased.[2] In a 1984 nationwide survey of medical and surgical patients, *Candida* species were the eighth most common cause of nosocomial bloodstream infection.[3] In a similar survey conducted between October 1986 and December 1990, *Candida* species became the fourth leading cause of nosocomial bloodstream infection, preceded only by coagulase-negative-staphylococci, *Staphylococcus aureus*, and enterococci.[3] According to the National Nosocomial Infections Surveillance (NNIS) system, the percentage of nosocomial infections caused by *C. albicans* increased from 2% in 1980 to an average of 5% over the 4-year period from 1986 through 1989.[4] Data from NNIS hospitals also show that between 1980 and 1989, the incidence of primary bloodstream infections attributable to *Candida* species increased by 487% in large teaching hospitals and by 219% in small (< 200 bed) hospitals.[5] In addition, the NNIS system reported that the rate of nosocomial fungal infection increased from 2.0 to 3.8 infections per 1,000 patients discharged between 1980 and 1990.[6] Current data from the SCOPE (Surveillance and Control of Pathogens of Epidemiologic Importance) system confirm that *Candida* species were the fourth leading cause of bloodstream infection.[7] These data are supported by the Surveillance Network–USA, which compiles information from more than 100 laboratories in the United States. Fungi including *Candida* species were isolated from 17% of 10,038 patients included in a European study of the prevalence of infection in patients in intensive care units.[8]

The most marked increase in candidiasis occurred in surgical patients, particularly in burn and trauma patients followed by cardiac surgery patients and general surgery patients. *Candida* species now account for 78% of all nosocomial fungal infections.[6]

Nosocomial bloodstream infections caused by *Candida* species are an independent predictor of risk of mortality (38% mortality directly attributable to candidiasis) and prolonged hospital stay (30 additional days in comparison with controls).[1] In a more recent prospective study, *Candida* species were the only microorganisms that independently influenced the outcome of nosocomial primary infections of the bloodstream (odds ratio for mortality, 1.84; 95% confidence interval [CI]) and were associated with the highest mortalities (35% at 28 days and 69% at discharge).[9] In properly conducted multivariate analyses, the most important prognostic factors in patients with hematogenous candidiasis include older age, poor performance status (on Acute Physiology and Chronic Health Evaluation [APACHE] or other measures), the presence and persistence of neutropenia, and dissemination of the infection to noncontiguous organs. Central venous catheter retention appears to play a minimal role.[8,10]

Definitions of Hematogenous *Candida* Infection Syndromes

In this chapter, the general term hematogenous candidiasis is used to identify all infections involving the bloodstream. Hence, hematogenous candidiasis refers to candidemia, disseminated candidiasis, or both.

CANDIDEMIA

Candidemia is defined as the isolation of any pathogenic species of *Candida* from at least one blood culture specimen. The recovery of *Candida* species from the bloodstream can be a significant observation in the absence of clinical signs and symptoms, especially if the patient is debilitated or uremic or is receiving adrenal corticosteroid therapy.

CATHETER-ASSOCIATED CANDIDEMIA

Catheter-associated candidemia is candidemia that occurs in a patient with an intravascular catheter and no other obvious origin of infection after careful clinical and laboratory evaluation. Several procedures have been developed to aid in the diagnosis of catheter-associated candidemia. If the catheter is removed, a quantitative culture of the tip should recover at least 15 colony-forming units (CFU) of the same *Candida* species as that found in blood culture by the roll-plate technique (or at least 100 CFU of the same *Candida* species as that found in blood culture by the sonication technique). If the catheter is not removed, a quantitative blood culture collected through a central catheter should contain at least a 10-fold greater concentration of *Candida* species than a simultaneously collected quantitative peripheral blood culture. Routine catheter tip cultures appear to be of no value.

ACUTE DISSEMINATED CANDIDIASIS

Patients who have several noncontiguous organs infected by *Candida* species have a disseminated infection acquired through hematogenous spread. For diagnosis, the organism must be identified by histologic analysis, culture of tissue samples obtained from at least one internal organ, or both; the patient should have radiographic, pathologic, or cultural evidence of infection in at least one other organ. Candidemia associated with *Candida* skin lesions or endophthalmitis consistent with a diagnosis of *Candida* infection also indicates a diagnosis of disseminated candidiasis.[11]

CHRONIC DISSEMINATED CANDIDIASIS

Chronic disseminated candidiasis, a chronic form of disseminated infection that is also known as hepatosplenic candidiasis, occurs in cancer patients who have been afflicted with protracted neutropenia.[12] This form of hematogenous candidiasis has not yet been described in the nonneutropenic surgical patient.

Characteristics of Surgical Patients at Risk for Candidiasis

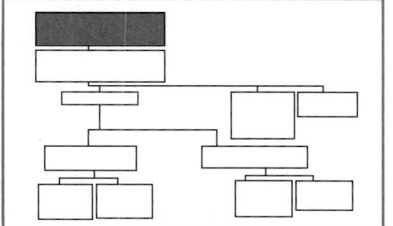

Fungal translocation that leads to hematogenous candidiasis is believed to be promoted by (1) colonization of the GI tract by *Candida* species, (2) physical disruption of the intestinal mucosal barrier, and (3) immunosuppression of the host leading to dissemination of the infection in the bloodstream and other organs [*see* Discussion, *below*].

Other important risk factors for hematogenous candidiasis include malignancies,[13] neutropenia and immunosuppressive therapy,[14] use of urinary catheters and diarrhea, prematurity,[15] heroin addiction,[16] abdominal surgery,[17] organ transplantation,[18] and extensive burns.[19]

The reported frequency of hematogenous candidiasis in burn patients ranges from 2% to 14%, depending on the reporting center and the study period.[19-21] Colonization by *Candida* species, hematogenous dissemination, and mortality caused by *Candida* infections have been found to correlate with the amount of body surface area burned and with the extent of full-thickness burn.

The pathogenesis, the incidence, and the microbial etiology of fungal infection vary in different groups of transplant recipients, depending on the organ transplanted, the donor source, the type of surgical procedure performed, and the recipient's age and general condition at the time of the procedure; other influential factors are the conditioning regimen, the type and duration of immunosuppressive therapy, and the presence or absence of organ rejection and graft versus host disease. In heart transplant recipients, for example, *Aspergillus* infection is a major problem, whereas in other organ transplant recipients, most fungal infections are attributable to *Candida*.[22] The infection is usually located at the site of the operation (e.g., an intra-abdominal abscess in liver[18] or pancreas[23] transplantation, the mediastinum or the lungs in heart[24] or heart-lung[25] transplantation, and the urinary tract in kidney[26] transplantation); however, dissemination from the primary site is common.

The central venous catheter has been reported as a risk factor in some studies but not in others,[10] particularly with *Candida parapsilosis*. This species, which may become part of the biofilm of intravascular catheters, may not respond to antifungal agents. Alternatively, *Candida* colonization of the catheter may result from gut-derived hematogenous seeding.[27,28]

Laboratory and Clinical Assessment of Candidiasis

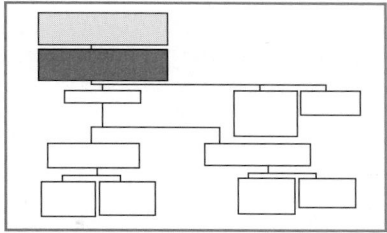

CULTURES

The workup of the surgical patient suspected of having hematogenous candidiasis begins with a complete set of cultures of sputum, oropharynx, stool, urine, all drain sites, and blood [*see Table 1*]. Candidiasis rarely develops in patients whose cultures show no evidence of *Candida* at some site. Obtaining more than six sets of blood cultures has little value, and there is no evidence to support arterial cultures.

The incidence of positive antemortem blood cultures in patients found to have candidiasis at autopsy is about 30% to 50%, possibly as a result of concomitant bacteremia, which may decrease the recovery of *Candida* species from the bloodstream. Because *Candida* species grow poorly under anaerobic conditions, venting the blood culture bottles is thought to improve the yield. The use of biphasic media also improves recovery of *Candida* species from the blood. Improved sensitivity and time to positivity of fungal blood cultures has been achieved with the development of new media, including biphasic media, automated radiometric and nonradiometric systems, and the lysis-centrifugation technique, a system that allows estimation of the number of *Candida* CFU/ml blood).[29] Commercial applications of these techniques include the BACTEC high-blood-volume fungal media system and the BacT/Alert system, both having comparable sensitivity to lysis-centrifugation. There is little evidence, however, that use of these newer methods provides a clinical advantage in the management of patients with hematogenous candidiasis. In a study by Berenguer and colleagues, the sensitivity of the lysis-centrifugation method increased with increasing numbers of involved organs but was still only 58% overall.[30]

Identify patient at risk for *Candida* infection

Major risk factors include
- Previous bacterial infection and therapy with multiple antibiotics.
- Isolation of *Candida* from ≥ 2 sites.
- Disruption of the intestinal mucosal barrier (total parenteral nutrition, severe diarrhea, colitis, major operation, trauma, or extensive burns).
- Immunosuppression (neutropenia, cancer, organ transplantation, hemodialysis, or extensive burns).

Other risk factors include
- Tunneled central venous catheters • Urinary catheters • Prematurity • Heroin addiction.

Initiate studies to diagnose candidiasis

Obtain cultures of sputum, oropharynx, stool, urine, drain sites, and blood.

Obtain 2 sets of blood cultures daily for 2 days (or longer if the patient remains febrile).

Consider serologic tests and histologic analyses (see text).

Look for findings that may signal hematogenous candidiasis:
- Endophthalmitis • Suppurative thrombophlebitis • High-grade candiduria without instrumentation of the bladder or the renal pelvis.

Exclude other possible causes of persistent fever.

Blood cultures are positive for *Candida*, or clinical or laboratory signal of potential hematogenous candidiasis is present

Patient is hemodynamically stable, does not have high-grade candidemia, and does not appear to have organ infection

Remove all venous catheters.
or
Leave venous catheter in place initially, and consider removal if clinical condition deteriorates or does not improve after 2 days of therapy.

Patient is infected or colonized by *C. albicans*, *C. tropicalis*, *C. parapsilosis*, or other germ tube–positive candidal organism

Give fluconazole, 600–800 mg/day I.V. for 2–3 days, then, if possible, lower dosage to 400 mg/day p.o.

Treat for 7–10 days (patient should be free of signs and symptoms of infection for 5 days before treatment is ended).

Patient is infected or colonized by *C. krusei*, *C. glabrata*, or *C. lusitaniae*

Give amphotericin B, 0.5–0.7mg/kg/day. (Consider adding flucytosine, 25 mg/kg/day p.o. in 2 divided doses, for *C. glabrata* and *C. lusitaniae*.)

Treat for 5–7 days (patient should be free of signs and symptoms of infection for 5 days before treatment is ended).

Approach to the Surgical Patient at Risk for Candidiasis

Blood cultures are negative for *Candida*, and no clinical or laboratory signal of potential hematogenous candidiasis is present, but *Candida* is isolated from ≥ 2 remote sites (≥ 1 site for *C. tropicalis*)

Give fluconazole, 400 mg/day I.V. for 2–3 days, then 400 mg/day p.o. If patient is colonized by *C. krusei, C. glabrata,* or *C. lusitaniae,* give amphotericin B, 0.5 mg/kg/day. (Consider adding flucytosine, 25 mg/kg/day p.o. in 2 divided doses, for *C. glabrata* and *C. lusitaniae.*)

Treat for 7–10 days (patient should be free of signs and symptoms of infection for 5 days before treatment is ended).

Blood cultures are negative for *Candida*, no clinical or laboratory signal of potential hematogenous candidiasis is found, and *Candida* is isolated from ≤ 1 remote site (0 sites for *C. tropicalis*)

Continue surveillance cultures weekly.

Patient is hemodynamically unstable, has high-grade candidemia, or shows evidence of organ infection

Remove all venous catheters.

Treat any associated syndromes of hematogenous candidiasis (e.g., endophthalmitis, pericarditis, suppurative thrombophlebitis, endocarditis).

Patient is infected or colonized by *C. albicans, C. tropicalis, C. parapsilosis,* or other germ tube–positive candidal organism

Give fluconazole, 800 mg/day I.V. (Consider adding flucytosine, 25 mg/kg/day p.o. in 2 divided doses. Also consider adding G-CSF, 300 g/day.)

Treat for 10–14 days after disappearance of all signs and symptoms of infection.

Patient is infected or colonized by *C. krusei, C. glabrata,* or *C. lusitaniae*

Give amphotericin B, 0.7–1.0 mg/kg/day I.V. (Consider adding flucytosine, 25 mg/kg/day p.o. in 2 divided doses. Also consider adding G-CSF, 300 g/day).

Treat for 10–14 days after disappearance of all signs and symptoms of infection.

1737

Table 1 Clinical Presentation and Diagnostic Methods for Common Fungal Infections[139]

Host Fungus	Major Clinical Presentations	Diagnostic Methods
Normal host		
Aspergillus	Allergic bronchopulmonary	Serum IgE, precipitins
Blastomyces	Acute pneumonitis: chronic lung or skin	Culture, tissue
Candida	Vaginitis, thrush, candidemia, I.V. catheter	Culture/smear
Coccidioides	Acute pneumonitis, chronic cavitary, pulmonary nodule	Precipitins, complement fixation, culture
Cryptococcus	Pulmonary, meningitis	Culture, latex agglutination
Histoplasma	Acute pulmonary, progressive dissemination in infants and elderly, chronic cavitary in chronic airway obstruction	Culture, antigen detection
Compromised host		
Diabetes mellitus		
Candida	Disseminated, pyelonephritis, vaginitis	Culture/smear
Torulopsis	Pyelonephritis	Culture
Zygomycetes	Rhinocerebral, paranasal, pulmonary, gastrointestinal, cutaneous	Culture, tissue
Malignancy or corticosteroids		
Aspergillus	Invasive/lung, sinuses, disseminated	Culture, tissue
Candida	Fungemia, acute and chronic disseminated candidiasis	Culture, tissue
Coccidioides	Disseminated	Culture, precipitins, complement fixation
Cryptococcus	Pulmonary, meningeal, disseminated	Culture, latex agglutination, India ink preparation
Dematiaceous fungi	Lung, sinuses, brain, disseminated	Culture, tissue
Fusarium	Lung, sinuses, cellulitis at site of onychomycosis, disseminated	Culture, tissue
Histoplasma	Progressive disseminated	Culture, antigen detection
Torulopsis	Disseminated	Culture, tissue
Trichosporon	Disseminated	Culture, tissue
Zygomycetes	Rhinocerebral, paranasal, pulmonary, gastrointestinal, cutaneous, disseminated	Culture, tissue
Extensive surgery and previous antibiotic therapy		
Candida	Vaginitis, thrush, esophagitis, disseminated	Culture, tissue
Torulopsis	Disseminated	Culture

A rapid and inexpensive test is the germ tube test that can distinguish *C. albicans* (positive test) from other *Candida* species. More than 90% of *C. albicans* isolates produce germ tubes when incubated in serum for 2 to 3 hours at 37° C.

Several newer culture media allow the rapid identification of *C. albicans*. These include Albicans ID (bioMerieux, France), CandiSelect (Sanofi Diagnostics Pasteur, France), CHROMagar *Candida* (Becton Dickinson, USA), Fluoroplate *Candida* (Merck, Germany), Fongiscreen 4H (Sanofi Diagnostics Pasteur), and Murex *Candida albicans* (Murex Diagnostics, USA). CHROMagar and Fongiscreen 4H are also used for detection of other *Candida* species, including *C. glabrata*, *C. tropicalis*, and *C. krusei*. A recent study of 485 isolates (350 of *C. albicans* and 135 of other candidal species) evaluated the presumptive identification of *C. albicans* by comparing results of the germ-tube test to results of these six commercial tests. For *C. albicans*, the sensitivity and specificity of all six tests were greater than 97%. The sensitivity and specificity of the two tests that allow presumptive identification of other candidal species (CHROMagar *Candida* and Fongiscreen 4H) were lower, especially for *C. glabrata* and *C. tropicalis*.

Positive cultures from nonsterile sites (sputum, urine, and wound drainage) need to be interpreted with caution because of the frequent occurrence of *Candida* as a normal commensal of humans. Such cultures are useful mainly as an indication of colonization and, consequently, of the risk of infection in the appropriate setting.

ANTIBODY DETECTION

Previous studies have reported the use of incompletely characterized antigenic extracts of *C. albicans* to detect anticandidal antibod-

ies in human sera. Difficulties with consistent production of uniform materials[31] have limited the usefulness of these tests. A variety of detection technologies (enzyme-linked immunosorbent assay [ELISA], immunodiffusion, and latex agglutination) have been used in attempts to detect antibodies directed toward defined purified antigen, but the sensitivity and specificity of these methods are low.[32] Methods using newly described antigens appear more promising.[33]

ANTIGEN DETECTION AND POLYMERASE CHAIN REACTION

Mannan, a polysaccharide component of the *Candida* cell wall, has the disadvantages of a short serum half-life and binding by antimannan antibody.[34] Although mannan can be detected by several methods,[35] complicated techniques are required to dissociate the mannan-antibody complex.[36] The sensitivity of mannan detection is approximately 70%.

A simple test available commercially (CAND-TEC *Candida* detection system, manufactured by Ramco Laboratories, USA) relies on the detection of a heat-labile antigen; however, its low sensitivity (as low as 19%) and specificity have limited its clinical use.[37] An antigen studied more recently is an immunodominant 48 kd cytoplasmic protein, *Candida* enolase. Because it is thought that cytoplasmic antigens are released during invasive infection, detection of this antigen may be able to distinguish between colonization and invasive infection.[33] A sensitivity of 54% was demonstrated in a study of 24 patients with invasive candidiasis,[38] but the sensitivity increases to 75% with the use of multiple samples. A sensitivity of 65% and a specificity of 97% were shown in a study assessing multiple samples.[39] Unfortunately, this test is not commercially available.

A commercial kit (Bichro-latex albicans) using monoclonal antibodies against cell wall extracts of *C. albicans* mannoprotein appears to have high sensitivity and specificity for *C. albicans*.[40]

Another antigen studied is (1-3)-β-D-glucan, an important cell wall constituent of fungi that is not shared with bacteria. Studies of this assay, which indicates the presence of fungi but does not identify the genus causing infection, have been promising in patients with fungal colonization. In these patients, its concentration remains lower than 20 pg/ml.

Amplification of the DNA of *Candida* species appears to be a quick and specific diagnostic tool. Although multiple approaches have been pursued,[41-43] several limitations need to be overcome before this method can be used routinely.[44]

METABOLITES

Systems based on the detection of D-arabinitol and mannose release by the fungus have been proposed,[45] but only those detecting D-arabinitol have been extensively developed. D-Arabinitol, a pentose produced by all of the major *Candida* species except *C. krusei* and *C. glabrata,* is excreted by the kidneys in the same rate as creatinine, and the ratio of D-arabinitol to creatinine must be used to interpret any observed concentration of D-arabinitol. Gas-liquid chromatographic as well as enzymatic methods are available for the detection of D-arabinitol, but gas-liquid chromatography is both technically demanding and expensive; it has been replaced by the recently developed enzymatic assay system. The sensitivity of the serum D-arabinitol–creatinine ratio for the diagnosis of invasive candidiasis, reported in the range of 40% to 83%, rises with repeated sampling.[46] Sensitivity is highest in patients with fungemia (74% to 83%) and lowest in patients with tissue-invasive *Candida* infections (40% to 44%). The magnitude of the D-arabinitol–creatinine ratio is strongly related to the degree of tissue invasion.[28,46] Although this assay may produce false positive results in some patients, it offers the promise of earlier detection of invasive candidiasis.[46]

Mannose, the other metabolite of *Candida* species that has been studied, can be detected only by a complicated gas-liquid chromatographic system. Initial estimates of its sensitivity (39%) have limited interest in this technique.[45]

HISTOLOGIC ANALYSES

Fungal smears are relatively insensitive methods of diagnosing candidiasis in otherwise sterile sites (e.g., joint fluid, peritoneal fluid, vitreous humor, or cerebrospinal fluid). Centrifugation of these fluids and examination of the sediment may improve the diagnostic yield. Conventional fungal stains, such as hematoxylin-eosin, periodic acid–Schiff (PAS), and Gomori methenamine-silver (GMS), are useful. The most sensitive stain is calcofluor white, but unfortunately, it requires fluorescent microscopy. Deep tissue biopsy provides a definitive diagnosis of candidiasis.

CLINICAL DIAGNOSIS

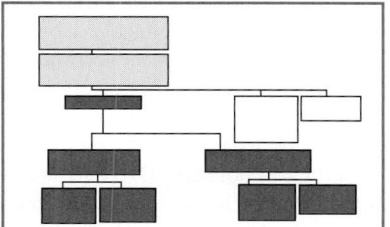

Hematogenous candidiasis has no characteristic clinical picture. Three clinical findings that may lead to an early diagnosis of hematogenous candidiasis in the surgical patient are candidal endophthalmitis, suppurative phlebitis, and candiduria in the absence of bladder instrumentation. A careful eye examination to identify the presence of candidal infection should be performed while the results of cultures of various sites are being awaited, and a repeat exam-

ination should be performed after therapy for proven candidemia. Candidal endophthalmitis may remain asymptomatic until late in the course of infection.

The presence of peripheral suppurative phlebitis that fails to yield bacteria or does not respond to antibacterial agents may be an early clue to the presence of hematogenous candidiasis. Gentle squeezing of the venous catheter exit site may express pus that yields *Candida* species on a smear or culture. Surgical excision of the infected vein usually reveals *Candida* infection in its lumen.

The presence of high-grade candiduria in surgical patients who have not had instrumentation of the renal pelvis or the bladder suggests hematogenous candidiasis and should prompt a workup for this infection. In this setting, candiduria may result from seeding of or filtering through the kidney.

Fever may be the only sign of infection but may be absent in patients who are receiving corticosteroids. Occasionally, a patient with hematogenous candidiasis presents with the systemic inflammatory response syndrome (SIRS) or septic shock. The diagnosis should be seriously considered in high-risk patients who are persistently febrile. Because of the high mortality associated with this infection, empirical antifungal therapy is recommended for early treatment of a clinical occult fungal infection or for the prevention of new fungal infections.

Management of Hematogenous Candidiasis

CANDIDEMIA AND ACUTE DISSEMINATED CANDIDIASIS

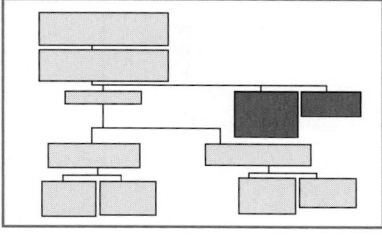

During the 1960s and the 1970s, the standard approach to managing candidemia was to classify patients according to degree of risk of disseminated candidiasis and to withhold antifungal treatment from those in whom dissemination appeared to be unlikely. This approach was based on unawareness of the magnitude of the problem in surgical patients and on acute awareness of the toxicities of amphotericin B, which was the only systemic antifungal agent available at the time; eventually, this type of management was found to be associated with a substantial mortality and a high incidence of long-term sequelae (e.g., deep-seated candidiasis presenting with endophthalmitis or other organ infection).[1] Consequently, it is now common practice to treat all candidemic patients except those who are afebrile, asymptomatic, or at low risk for disseminated candidiasis [see Table 2].

Candidates for empirical antifungal therapy are at high risk for candidiasis, colonized by *Candida* species (at one or more sites for *C. tropicalis* or at two or more for other candidal species), and unresponsive to broad-spectrum antibiotics in the absence of any other cause for their fever. Unresponsive patients may be characterized by rapid clinical deterioration, particularly if there is evidence of physical disruption of the intestinal mucosal barrier or immunosuppression.

The role of amphotericin B in the treatment of hematogenous candidiasis in surgical patients has been difficult to determine—first, because most of the studies that evaluated amphotericin B were retrospective trials with small sample sizes, and second, because few of the studies defined hematogenous candidiasis in the same way. In one study, treatment with amphotericin B had no effect on overall outcome in a mixed population of patients; however, the timing of therapy and the dose administered were not clearly stated.[47] In general, mortality was lower in patients who re-

Table 2 Antimicrobial Agents of Choice for Candidal Infections*

Infection	Agent of Choice	Alternative Agents	Comments
Hematogenous			
Candidemia and acute disseminated candidiasis	Fluconazole, or amphotericin B ± flucytosine	Lipid formulations of amphotericin B	Fluconazole should be given for *C. albicans*, amphotericin for all other *Candida* species; a 2-drug regimen should be given to hemodynamically unstable patients with persistent high-grade fungemia
Candida endophthalmitis	Fluconazole	Amphotericin B + flucytosine	Patients with vitral involvement require vitrectomy in addition to antifungal therapy
Suppurative phlebitis	Fluconazole + flucytosine	Amphotericin B + flucytosine	The central venous catheter should be removed and the infected vein excised
Endocarditis	Amphotericin B + flucytosine	—	Surgical replacement or repair of valves is essential to prevent death from embolization or cardiac failure; oral fluconazole should be given after successful completion of a prolonged course of amphotericin B therapy
Pericarditis	Amphotericin B	Fluconazole	
Prosthetic device–related infection	Fluconazole or amphotericin B	—	Removal of device is required for successful therapy
Arthritis	Fluconazole	—	—
Osteomyelitis	Amphotericin B	Fluconazole	Surgical drainage of pus is required
Meningitis	Amphotericin B + flucytosine	Fluconazole + flucytosine	—
Nonhematogenous			
Oropharyngeal			
Otherwise normal host	Nystatin	Ketoconazole, fluconazole, clotrimazole troches	—
Patients at risk for hematogenous infection (e.g., cancer patients, surgical patients)	Fluconazole	Ketoconazole	—
Deep candidiasis			
Esophagitis and GI candidiasis	Fluconazole	Amphotericin B	Amphotericin B should be reserved for cases of fluconazole failure without endoscopic evidence of other causes of disease
Peritonitis and intra-abdominal	Fluconazole	Amphotericin B	—
Wound	Fluconazole	Amphotericin B	Antifungal therapy should be given to patients who do not respond to antibacterial therapy
Urinary tract			
Cystitis	Fluconazole	Amphotericin B	Fluconazole is preferable because of its high drug concentration in urine and because it is better tolerated
Pyelitis			
Without papillitis	Fluconazole	—	—
With papillitis	Fluconazole + flucytosine	Amphotericin B	—
Pyelonephritis	Fluconazole + flucytosine	Amphotericin B	—

'Therapy is individualized on the basis of the patient's clinical condition and the infecting species.

ceived amphotericin B than in those who did not.[48] Significant amphotericin B–related nephrotoxicity may occur.

The discovery of the azole antifungal agents has changed the management of *Candida* infections. The first two azoles, clotrimazole and miconazole, were not, however, suitable for systemic use. As for ketoconazole, the lack of a parenteral formulation and the erratic bioavailability of the drug in patients receiving H_2 receptor blockers or antacids have limited its use in the treatment of hematogenous candidiasis in surgical patients.

Fluconazole is a well-tolerated triazole with good activity in hematogenous candidiasis. Data available from several clinical trials suggest that the drug is as effective as and better tolerated than amphotericin B. Overall, four comparative studies have been completed in various patient populations. Two were randomized,[49,50] one was prospective observational,[51] and one used matched cohorts.[50] Fluconazole dosages ranged from 200 to 800 mg/day, given orally or intravenously, while intravenous amphotericin B was given at doses of 0.3 to 1.2 mg/kg.

The first prospective, randomized study of fluconazole included 40 surgical patients with hematogenous candidiasis, of whom 20 received 300 mg/day of fluconazole and 20 received 0.5 mg/kg/day of amphotericin B plus flucytosine.[52] There were no significant differences in outcome between the two study groups.

A matched-pair study compared the outcomes of 45 candidemic cancer patients who were treated with fluconazole with the outcomes of 45 candidemic cancer patients who were treated with amphotericin B[53]; in several of the 90 patients, hematogenous candidiasis had developed after operation. This study demonstrated that fluconazole was as effective as and better tolerated than amphotericin B. In one prospective, randomized multicenter study, 164 patients with documented or presumed invasive candidiasis received either amphotericin B, 0.7 mg/kg/day, or fluconazole, 400 mg/day.[50] The response rate for fluconazole (62%) was virtually identical to that for amphotericin B (63%), and fluconazole was better tolerated. In another prospective, randomized multicenter study, 206 nonimmunocompromised candidemic patients received either amphotericin B or fluconazole.[49] Once again, the two drugs were comparable in their efficacy, and fluconazole had a better safety profile.

Newer therapeutic options have now become available with the advent of the lipid-associated formulations of amphotericin B, which are less nephrotoxic than the parent compound.[54] Thus far, three lipid products of amphotericin B have been marketed in Europe or the United States: Abelcet (amphotericin B lipid complex), Amphocil (amphotericin B colloidal dispersion), and AmBisome (liposomal amphotericin B). A prospective, randomized trial has shown that Abelcet is as efficacious as conventional amphotericin B in hematogenous candidiasis.[55]

All patients with candidemia should receive antifungal therapy. We recommend the administration of fluconazole, 600 to 800 mg/day I.V. for 3 days, particularly if the infecting organism is known to be or is likely to be *C. albicans*. If the patient responds rapidly to this regimen, the dosage may be decreased to 400 mg/day and administered orally. For patients with hematogenous candidiasis who are known to be colonized by *C. glabrata*, *C. krusei*, or *C. lusitaniae*, amphotericin B, 0.5 to 0.7 mg/kg/day, should remain the treatment of choice. For patients who are hemodynamically unstable and for those who have high-grade persistent fungemia, we recommend a two-drug antifungal regimen: the combination of fluconazole and flucytosine or the combination of amphotericin B and flucytosine, depending on the infecting strain.

Clinical data on the effect of itraconazole in hematogenous candidiasis are scant. Given that itraconazole has limited bioavailability in the presence of antacids and H_2 receptor blockers, it should not be used to treat hematogenous candidiasis in the critically ill. However, an I.V. formulation of itraconazole is now available, and it is possible that this formulation may prove effective in patients with hematogenous candidiasis.

Liposomal formulations of amphotericin B offer new therapeutic alternatives. Their substantial cost limits their routine use, but they are appropriate if the patient has renal failure and is infected with an azole-resistant strain. Of the three available formulations, AmBisome is the best tolerated and yields the highest blood levels of amphotericin B.

The duration of therapy depends on the extent and severity of the infection. Therapy can be limited to 7 to 10 days for patients with low-grade fungemia and no evidence of organ involvement or hemodynamic instability. Patients with high-grade fungemia and evidence of organ involvement or hemodynamic instability need to receive antifungal therapy for 10 to 14 days after resolution of all signs and symptoms of infection.

Catheter Management

Controversy remains concerning the role of central venous lines in patients' outcome in hematogenous candidiasis. According to Nguyen and colleagues,[51] patients with catheter-related candidemia had a more favorable prognosis than patients with candidemia from other sources, but the prognosis was worse in patients whose catheters were retained. In contrast, studies by Carroll and colleagues, Nucci and coworkers,[56] and Anaissie and associates[10] failed to show a major role for retention of central venous catheters in the outcome of hematogenous candidiasis. The study by Anaissie and associates[10] examined the impact of catheter management on outcome in 416 cancer patients with candidemia who had an indwelling catheter at the time of candidal infection. Catheter exchange within 0, 2, or 4 days of the first positive blood culture had no significant effect on outcome. A second analysis, performed in a subset of 363 patients who had a central venous catheter in place and received antifungal therapy, revealed that catheter exchange was associated with improved outcome (80% versus 54%; $P < 0.001$). However, the subset in which the catheter was not exchanged had higher APACHE III scores and were more likely to be neutropenic. By multivariate analysis, catheter retention was not found to significantly affect outcome.

In one study in noncancer patients, Rex and colleagues[57] showed that replacement of all vascular catheters shortened the duration of candidemia from 5.6 days to 2.6 days. This finding suggests that catheters may play a role in perpetuating infection in nonneutropenic patients. In neutropenic patients, however, the primary source of candidemia is usually the GI tract, not the intravenous catheter, and other factors (e.g., the severity of disease, visceral dissemination, and neutrophil recovery) appear to have more impact on the outcome of neutropenic patients with candidemia.

Given the available data, we recommend that physicians consider the removal of all intravascular catheters in inpatients who have candidemia with persistent fever, persistent or high-grade fungemia, or *C. parapsilosis* (which is more likely to be catheter related than infection with other *Candida* species).

Cytokine Therapy for Opportunistic Infections

Polymorphonuclear leukocytes and macrophages are the predominant host defense against candidal infections. Candidal antigens induce lymphocyte proliferation and cytokine synthesis (interferon gamma and tumor necrosis factor); tumor necrosis factor enhances the candidacidal activity of phagocytes,[58] probably through increased production of reactive oxygen radicals. Another mechanism by which interferon gamma may augment host defenses against candidal infections is modulation of endothelial cell phagocytosis of *C. albicans*.[59] Granulocyte colony-stimulating factor (G-CSF) and granulocyte-macrophage colony-stimulating factor (GM-CSF) activate phagocytic cells to restrict the growth of *C. albicans*.[60]

Recently, a multicenter, double-blind, randomized phase II trial examined the activity of G-CSF in combination with fluconazole for treatment of hematogenous candidiasis in nonneutropenic patients. Preliminary analysis (Kullberg BJ and associates, unpublished report, 2000) indicated that an increase in the number of circulating neutrophils strongly correlates with accelerated clearance of bloodstream infection and reduced mortality. Additional data are needed to confirm these findings.

Antifungal Prophylaxis

Prophylaxis may be considered in surgical patients at high risk for invasive candidiasis. To date, there have been few trials of antifungal prophylaxis, whether as part of selective bowel decontamination[61] or in the form of low-dose amphotericin B[62] or liposomal formulations of amphotericin B in surgical transplant recipients.[63]

Fluconazole prophylaxis has been shown to reduce the rate of superficial and systemic fungal infections in cancer patients undergoing chemotherapy (with or without bone marrow transplantation)[64,65] and oropharyngeal and esophageal candidiasis in patients infected with HIV.[66] A recent double-blind randomized trial showed that intravenous fluconazole prophylaxis was effective in preventing candidal colonization and invasive intra-abdominal candidal infections in high-risk surgical patients.[67]

A retrospective study in burn patients reported that topical nystatin in the wound dressing was associated with a significant decrease in yeast acquisitions in burn wounds and fungemia but with an increase in colonization and fungemia caused by nystatin-resistant, amphotericin B–susceptible *C. rugosa*.[68]

Invasive fungal infection is one of the most important causes of mortality in organ transplant recipients.[69] Antifungal prophylaxis has been recommended in organ transplant recipients undergoing immunosuppressive therapy, but there is controversy about which drug is most effective and least toxic. Some physicians use fluconazole prophylactically in organ transplant recipients, but others recommend itraconazole or liposomal amphotericin B.[1,70,71]

ORGAN INFECTIONS

Candida *Endophthalmitis*

The diagnosis of candidal endophthalmitis usually implies hematogenous spread to multiple organs and the need for systemic antifungal therapy. Patients with chorioretinitis alone respond better to drug therapy alone than do those with vitreal involvement. Because antifungal drugs do not penetrate the vitreous body as well as the other ocular compartments,[72] patients with vitreal involvement require early vitrectomy in addition to antifungal therapy. Fluconazole is currently the drug of choice because of its proven efficacy and its higher concentration (20% to 70% of the corresponding plasma level) in ocular tissue, including the vitreous body.[73] Thus, we recommend 800 mg/day of fluconazole until a major response is observed, at which time it may be possible to reduce the dose to 400 mg/day. Although endophthalmitis due to *C. albicans* is commonly seen, recent series have reported on the importance of endophthalmitis caused by other candidal species. If the infecting organism (especially *C. krusei*) is potentially resistant to fluconazole, the recommended therapy is amphotericin B, 0.7 to 1.0 mg/kg/day I.V., preferably in conjunction with flucytosine.[74] Intravitreal injection of amphotericin B is recommended for vitreal infections.

The optimal duration of therapy for endogenous endophthalmitis is unknown, but we recommend that treatment be continued for at least 10 to 14 days after complete resolution of all signs and symptoms of infection. Ophthalmologic consultation is critical in establishing the diagnosis, assessing the patient's response to therapy, detecting complications, and determining whether early vitrectomy is indicated to prevent loss of sight.[75]

Suppurative Thrombophlebitis

A rare but serious consequence of hematogenous candidemia is suppurative thrombophlebitis, which results from infection of a vessel traumatized by prolonged catheterization. Endothelial disruption exposes the basement membrane and leads to thrombus formation and propagation. Suppurative thrombophlebitis is particularly serious because intravascular infection results in a persistent high-density fungemia. Management of this disease consists of high-dose antifungal therapy, removal of the central venous catheter, and excision of the infected vein, when possible.[76] Typically, blood cultures remain positive for several days; sometimes, they remain positive for as long as 3 to 4 weeks despite appropriate antifungal therapy, if the infected vein is not excised.

Endocarditis

Hematogenous candidiasis may also lead to the establishment of endocarditis, particularly in patients with a prosthetic heart valve or with a previously damaged native valve. Intravenous drug abuse and central intravenous catheterization appear to be predisposing factors. Candidal endocarditis after permanent pacemaker implantation has also been reported. The clinical picture is similar in many respects to that of bacterial endocarditis, although embolic phenomena have been more commonly associated with fungal endocarditis. Transesophageal echocardiography is more sensitive than transthoracic echocardiography in detecting candidal vegetation. Mortality due to *Candida* prosthetic valve endocarditis (PVE) is high, especially when complicated by congestive heart failure and persistent fungemia. For uncomplicated PVE, the mortality for patients receiving antifungal therapy alone (40%) is no worse than that for patients receiving combined medical and surgical therapy (33%).

Candidal endocarditis is very difficult to treat. Surgical replacement or repair of valves is essential to prevent death from embolization or cardiac failure in patients with complicated PVE. Amphotericin B, with or without flucytosine, has been the therapy of choice; however, neither the optimal dosage nor the optimal duration of therapy has been determined. There is anecdotal information on the successful use of fluconazole in this setting, primarily as long-term suppressive therapy after the initial administration of amphotericin B.[73,77] Because of the high risk of late relapse, long-term maintenance therapy with oral fluconazole should be begun after successful completion of a prolonged course of amphotericin B.

Pericarditis

Candidal pericarditis is a very rare complication of hematogenous candidiasis. The surgical patients at risk for purulent pericarditis caused by *Candida* species are those who have undergone a cardiac operation, those who have a malignancy and whose host defenses are impaired, and those who have a debilitating chronic disease.[78] High-dose amphotericin B therapy, with or without surgical drainage, is recommended in these cases.

Arthritis

Joint infections with *Candida* species have resulted from hematogenous spread from inadvertent direct inoculation during joint procedures or intra-articular injection of corticosteroids. These infections typically involve a single joint, most frequently the knee, and tend to occur in patients with rheumatoid arthritis or prosthetic joint devices.[79] Local symptoms of pain on weight bearing or on full extension may be present. Diagnosis is best achieved by visualizing or growing the organisms from the joint fluid. Early diagnosis and systemic antifungal therapy are important to prevent destruction of the cartilage or loosening of the prosthesis. Successful treatment with fluconazole has been reported in several patients with fungal arthritis.[80] We recommend a dose of 400 to 800 mg/day for 6 months. Fluconazole can be used in acute therapy, alone or in combination with surgery, as well as in long-term suppressive therapy in patients at risk for recurrence or those who cannot undergo surgical debridement.

Osteomyelitis

Except for sternal infections complicating median sternotomy, most cases of candidal osteomyelitis have followed hematogenous spread. Vertebral body involvement is common. Back pain and fever may be followed by radiculopathy. Surgical drainage of pus is essential for a good response; however, surgical debridement of bony lesions may not be needed. Although amphotericin B has been the standard drug of choice, fluconazole offers an alternative in the treatment of these cases.[81]

Meningitis

Candidal meningitis may follow hematogenous spread or be a complication of neurosurgery or the implantation of ventriculoperitoneal shunts.[82] The infection is insidious and may remain undiagnosed. Most patients have recently received antibacterial agents, and half have had antecedent bacterial meningitis. The overall mortality is around 10%. The standard therapy is amphotericin B with flucytosine. The combination of high-dose fluconazole (800 mg/day) and flucytosine (50 mg/kg/day) is a particularly attractive approach because of the high CSF concentrations achieved with both agents. Removal of the infected shunts is recommended when possible.[51,82] The duration of treatment should be based on clinical response and culture results.

Nonhematogenous Candidiasis

SUPERFICIAL INFECTION

Oral candidiasis (thrush) appears as a whitish, patchy pseudomembrane covering an inflamed oropharynx and commonly involves the tongue, the hard and soft palates, and the tonsillar pillars. Controlled trials have documented the efficacy of nystatin suspension, clotrimazole troches, oral ketoconazole, fluconazole, or itraconazole in eradicating the clinical symptoms of oral candidiasis.[83,84]

Nystatin should be given as a 10 to 30 ml suspension five times daily, and the patient should be instructed to swish it around the mouth before swallowing; alternatively, the patient may take one or two troches five times daily. Clotrimazole troches are given five times daily as a 10 mg troche that should be held in the mouth until dissolved. In surgical patients at risk for hematogenous infection, systemic therapy with ketoconazole (200 to 400 mg once daily), itraconazole (100 to 200 mg/day), or fluconazole (100 mg once daily) is preferred.[85] Antifungal therapy should be administered for 1 week, except for fluconazole therapy, which is likely to be effective when given for 2 or 3 days.

DEEP CANDIDIASIS

Esophagitis and Gastrointestinal Candidiasis

Superficial candidiasis involving only mucosal surfaces used to be a common finding at autopsy in surgical patients who had a protracted hospital stay characterized by recurrent sepsis. Such lesions may arise at any site in the GI tract but appear most commonly in the esophagus and the small bowel and may progress to hematogenous infection [see Figure 1].

In a minority of patients, the pathology of infection of the lower GI tract by Candida species may change from diarrhea without demonstrable tissue invasion to direct penetration into the submucosa, which eventually leads to pseudomembranous enterocolitis. Direct vascular invasion through the bowel wall has been reported only in patients receiving immunosuppressive chemotherapy.[86] These patients may have extensive involvement of the GI tract from mouth to anus. Nonneutropenic surgical patients exhibit more localized involvement.

The preferred therapy for esophageal candidiasis is fluconazole or itraconazole, 200 mg daily. In patients who remain symptomatic after 5 days of therapy, endoscopy is needed to rule out other causes of esophagitis. If endoscopy proves that esophagitis is caused by candidal infection, low-dose amphotericin B (0.4 mg/kg/day) should be administered. Therapy for esophageal candidiasis should be continued for at least 4 days after symptoms resolve; immunosuppressed patients generally require more extended therapy to prevent relapse.

Because stool cultures do not differentiate between colonization and infection, candidiasis in the lower gastrointestinal tract is usually a postmortem diagnosis; hence, there are no reliable criteria governing when and how to treat this condition. It has been reported, however, that patients who have diarrhea that can only be caused by heavy colonization with Candida species may respond dramatically to 2 to 4 days of nystatin therapy.[87]

Peritonitis and Intra-abdominal Abscess

Perhaps the most controversial aspect of Candida infectious syndromes in surgical patients is whether specific systemic therapy is required to eradicate the infection within intra-abdominal abscesses, peritoneal fluid, or fistula drainage. Candida is frequently cultured from intra-abdominal infectious foci but should be considered a serious threat only in high-risk patients. Four risk factors for intra-abdominal candidiasis are gastrointestinal perforations, anastomotic leakage, surgery for acute pancreatitis, and splenectomy.[88]

Patients with peritonitis and intra-abdominal abscesses should receive systemic antifungal therapy, usually in combination with antibacterial therapy, given that these infections are almost always polymicrobial in origin. The risk of dissemination is increased by

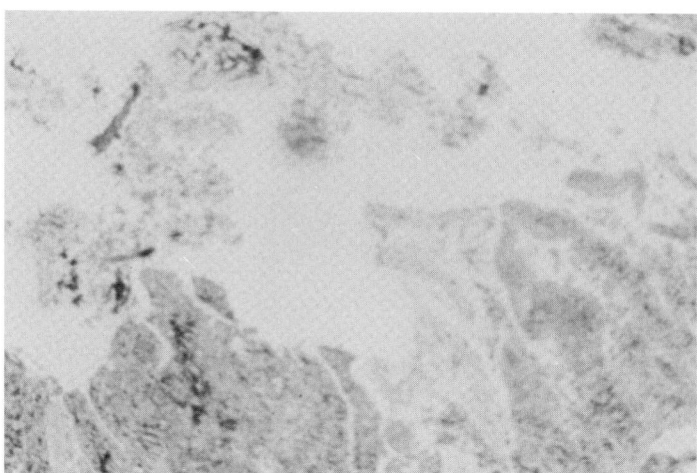

Figure 1 Superficial candidiasis may be found at all levels of the GI tract. Here, the esophagus of a patient found at autopsy to have disseminated candidiasis shows disrupted epithelium, submucosal inflammation, and the presence of yeast in the submucosa.

both the recurrence of intra-abdominal infections and the presence of extensive areas of communication between the abdominal cavity and the external environment via either fistulas or drain tracts.

On rare occasions, candidal peritonitis occurs after long-term ambulatory peritoneal dialysis. In such cases, the infection tends to remain localized and to manifest with low-grade fever and abdominal pain and tenderness. The peritoneal dialysate is usually cloudy and contains more than 100 neutrophils/mm³. Therapy consists of systemic antifungal therapy and removal of the peritoneal catheter. The abdominal pain caused by the addition of amphotericin B to the dialysate has raised concern that chemical peritonitis might give rise to adhesions and thus impair the efficacy of dialysis.

Because fluconazole is very safe and is capable of reaching high concentrations in peritoneal fluid, it is likely to be useful in the management of candidal peritonitis.[89] Fluconazole should be given at a dosage of 100 to 200 mg/day orally for 2 to 6 weeks. Immediate removal of the peritoneal catheter has been recommended. In one study, however, seven of nine patients treated with oral flucytosine responded to therapy without catheter removal.[90]

A prospective, randomized study in patients on continuous ambulatory dialysis found that successful prophylaxis for Candida peritonitis was achieved with oral nystatin (tablets containing 500,000 units given four times a day).[91]

Occasionally, Candida species may cause cholangitis, biliary tract disease, pancreatic abscess, or liver abscess. This problem is increasingly found in patients with percutaneously placed drainage catheters for malignancy. Such patients must be given systemic therapy for clinical evidence of infection, including candidemia, and the drainage catheter must be changed. Diverticulitis complicated by candidal pylephlebitis has also been reported.

Wound Infections

The diagnosis and treatment of candidal wound infections are problematic. Recovering Candida species from drains and wounds does not necessarily mean that this organism is causing tissue infection. Colonization of wounds by Candida species should not compel physicians to use systemic antifungal therapy. However, such therapy should be administered to those patients whose wound infections do not respond to appropriate antibacterial therapy, particularly if one Candida species is repeatedly isolated from the site and the patient is at high risk for hematogenous infection. Antifungal therapy should be administered to prevent the establishment of *Candida* osteomyelitis when sternal wound cultures obtained after coronary artery bypass surgery yield *Candida* species.

Urinary Tract and Genital Candidiasis

The recovery of *Candida* species from the urinary tract most commonly results from contamination from the perirectal or the genital area or from colonization of the bladder, which is usually seen in patients who have undergone prolonged catheterization or who have diabetes mellitus or another disease that leads to incomplete bladder emptying. In addition, *Candida* species usually colonize ileal conduits. Persistent candiduria in the surgical intensive care unit may, however, be an early marker of disseminated infection in critically ill high-risk patients.[92] In a study of 91 pediatric ICU patients who were clinically suspected of having disseminated candidiasis, the isolation of candidal species other than *C. albicans* from the urine was a better indicator of candidemia than was isolation of *C. albicans*; 60% of the patients whose urine contained candidal species other than *C. albicans* had candidemia, versus 33.3% of the patients whose urine contained *C. albicans*.[93]

Alkalization of the urine with oral potassium-sodium hydrogen citrate is a simple and effective method of treating candiduria in patients with an indwelling catheter.[94] Replacing or removing the bladder catheter is preferable. If *Candida* colonization persists, particularly if the patient has a risk factor for cystitis (e.g., diabetes mellitus or a disease that leads to incomplete bladder emptying) or for hematogenous dissemination (e.g., immunosuppression or manipulation of the genitourinary system), antifungal therapy should be considered. Amphotericin B bladder irrigation provides only temporary clearance of funguria, and systemic agents (a single I.V. dose of amphotericin B or a 5-day course of oral fluconazole) are usually needed.

The spectrum of urinary tract infection by *Candida* species includes cystitis, pyelitis (i.e., infection of the renal pelvis), fungus ball of the ureter, and renal abscesses. The diagnosis of cystitis is based on the presence of symptoms of cystitis, diffuse erythema or fungal plaques on cystoscopy, candiduria, and pyuria. *Candida* cystitis warrants therapy. If a triple-lumen catheter is in place, bladder irrigation with amphotericin B, 50 mg/L/day for 2 days, may be tried. Fluconazole, 200 mg once daily, is a more attractive approach because of the convenience, lower cost, and very high drug concentrations achieved in the urine.[95] Flucytosine is excreted in the urine in high concentrations and may be particularly useful against *C. glabrata* infection.

The management of pyelitis depends on whether the renal papillae are invaded or the ureter is obstructed with a fungus ball. Patients with no papillitis and an open ureter usually respond to irrigation with amphotericin B through a ureteral or percutaneous catheter. If papillitis is present, systemic antifungal therapy with fluconazole, 400 mg daily, is recommended. If fungus balls are present, surgical removal should be considered in addition to treatment with antifungal agents.

Hematogenous infections of the kidneys leading to multiple renal abscesses are treated as instances of hematogenous candidiasis. However, because both fluconazole and flucytosine are well tolerated, have good tissue diffusion, and are excreted in the urine in high concentrations, it is reasonable to assume that the combination of these two agents represents the therapy of choice for candidiasis that involves renal parenchyma.

Surgical patients are also at risk for vulvovaginal candidiasis. The diagnosis is based on the clinical findings and on the presence of pseudohyphae on a fungal smear. Various antifungal agents, including oral azoles and topical medications (suppositories, creams, and vaginal tablets) are effective in more than 80% of uncomplicated infections. Oral agents include fluconazole (150 mg in a single dose), ketoconazole (400 mg daily for 5 days), and itraconazole (200 mg in a single dose). However, women with four or more episodes of vulvovaginal candidiasis during a 12-month period and women with acute severe attacks of candidal vaginitis are less likely to respond to conventional therapy. Preventive measures include control of host factors such as diabetes mellitus, antifungal prophylaxis during the use of antibiotics and under other high-risk conditions, and the avoidance of systematic corticosteroids, oral contraceptives, and antibiotics if possible. Therapy with oral fluconazole, itraconazole, or ketoconazole is recommended for approximately 14 days to ensure clinical remission and negative fungal culture, followed by a maintenance regimen of fluconazole (150 mg once weekly for 6 months). Recurrence of vulvovaginal candidiasis is common, occurring in 30% to 40% of patients after cessation of the maintenance regime.[96]

Other Fungal Infections

ASPERGILLOSIS

Aspergillosis, a rare infection in the surgical patient, usually occurs in those who are markedly immunosuppressed after undergoing chemotherapy with cytotoxic agents or adrenal corticosteroids. Most cases of nosocomial aspergillosis are acquired via airborne transmission.[13,97] Colonization of the respiratory tract is followed by invasive disease if these predisposing factors are present. Sources of airborne fungi in microepidemics frequently are associated with construction within the hospital or at adjacent sites. Other modes of transmission of aspergillosis have been reported, including infections associated with foreign bodies, catheters, and bandages.

Acute invasive pulmonary aspergillosis is the most common form of *Aspergillus* infection in immunocompromised surgical patients. The organisms tend to invade blood vessels and cause thrombosis and infarction of the surrounding tissues. The infection may manifest itself in the form of acute vascular events such as pulmonary embolus or, more rarely, myocardial infarction, cerebral hemorrhage, or Budd-Chiari syndrome. Pulmonary *Aspergillus* infections include necrotizing bronchopneumonia and hemorrhagic pulmonary infarction, each accounting for about one third of these infections. Pulmonary aspergillosis may extend to contiguous organs or be disseminated. The rhinocerebral form of aspergillosis occurs less often than pulmonary infection. It originates in the sinuses and progresses through soft tissues, cartilage, and bone, causing lesions in the palate and the nose. Occasionally, the infection progresses through the base of the skull and involves the brain.

Diagnosis of *Aspergillus* infection is difficult and relies on identifying the organism in culture or histopathologic specimens.[13] The recovery of *Aspergillus* species from the respiratory tract culture of a surgical patient should be considered to represent contamination or colonization unless the patient is symptomatic and severely immunosuppressed. The standard therapy is high-dose amphotericin B (1 mg/kg/day) for a minimum of 2 g.[98] The addition of flucytosine may be useful. Liposomal formulations of amphotericin B and itraconazole offer additional treatment alternatives; at present, however, clinical experience with these new antifungal agents in patients with aspergillosis is limited.

ZYGOMYCOSIS (MUCORMYCOSIS)

Agents of zygomycosis have caused nosocomial infections in the surgical patient. The reservoir, the mode of transmission, the pathogenesis, and the clinical presentations are similar to those of *Aspergillus* species. In the surgical patient, the major risk factors include diabetic ketoacidosis, immunosuppression after cytotoxic chemotherapy, adrenocorticosteroid therapy, organ transplantation, skin damage (e.g., from adhesive tape, an arm board, or severe burns), and a prolonged postoperative stay.[99] Zygomycotic infections include rhinocerebral, paranasal, pulmonary, gastrointestinal, cutaneous, and, very rarely, disseminated disease.

Appropriate management of zygomycosis consists of extensive surgical debridement of infected areas, rapid correction of the underlying disease, and high-dose amphotericin B therapy up to a total dose of 2 to 3 g.

EMERGING PATHOGENS

Fungi such as *Fusarium* species, *Curvularia* species, *Alternaria* species, and *Trichosporon beigelii* were once thought to represent contamination or harmless colonization when isolated from tissue specimens. These and other newly recognized fungi have since been clearly shown to be potentially serious pathogens in immunosuppressed surgical patients.[100] In such patients, the recovery of any fungus from any site should prompt an evaluation by an infectious disease specialist to determine the clinical significance of the isolate.

Systemic Antifungal Agents

AMPHOTERICIN B

Amphotericin B is structurally similar to membrane sterols, and its major mechanism of action is believed to be through interaction with membrane sterols and creation of pores in the fungal outer membrane. The clinical usefulness of amphotericin B is believed to be attributable to the greater affinity of amphotericin B for ergosterol (found in fungal cell membranes) than for cholesterol (the principal sterol found in mammalian cell membranes). Oxidation-dependent amphotericin B-induced stimulation of macrophages is another proposed mechanism of action.[101] Most species of fungi that cause human infections are susceptible to amphotericin B.

Amphotericin B is supplied as a sterile lyophilized powder in vials containing 50 mg of amphotericin B, deoxycholate, and buffer. The contents are then diluted in 5% dextrose in water at a concentration of 10 mg/dl. Less precipitation occurs in saline solutions. The agent is stable at room temperature for 24 hours and is not sensitive to light. An acute infusion-related reaction, consisting of fever, hypotension, and tachycardia, occurs in about 20% of patients.[90] Premedication with acetaminophen may blunt this response. If this approach is unsuccessful, premedication with meperidine (25 to 50 mg I.V.) or hydrocortisone (25 to 50 mg I.V.) is recommended. Hypotension, hypertension, hypothermia, and bradycardia are other reported infusion-related toxic effects of amphotericin B deoxycholate. Ventricular arrhythmias have been associated with rapid infusion of amphotericin B deoxycholate and with administration of the agent to patients with severe hypokalemia or renal failure. Through inhibition of erythropoietic production secondary to nephrotoxicity, amphotericin B suppresses the production of red blood cells, causing a normocytic, normochromic anemia.

Common practice is to give a 1 mg test dose and observe the patient for 1 hour in the hope of identifying patients at risk for severe acute reactions. The full dose of the drug (0.6 to 1 mg/kg/day) is then infused over a period of 4 to 6 hours, although there is evidence to suggest that much shorter infusion times (e.g., 1 hour in patients with adequate cardiopulmonary and renal function) may be acceptable. The total dose depends on the extent of the infec-

tion and the patient's condition. Patients must be monitored carefully during the first day of therapy. The infusion should be discontinued if the patient becomes hemodynamically unstable.

If acute reactions limit the amount of drug that can be infused, patients are premedicated with hydrocortisone, 25 to 50 mg I.V., either alone or in combination with meperidine, 25 to 50 mg I.V., 30 minutes before amphotericin B infusion is begun.

The distribution of the drug after I.V. infusion does not directly correlate with the daily dose. This finding is consistent with the unusual pharmacokinetics of amphotericin B. The initial serum half-life of the drug is about 24 hours, and the terminal half-life is about 15 days.

Renal toxicity and hypokalemia are the primary toxicities of amphotericin B [*see Table 3*]. Amphotericin B-induced nephrotoxicity may be glomerular, characterized by a decrease in glomerular filtration rate and renal blood flow, or tubular, with urinary casts, hypokalemia, hypomagnesemia, renal tubular acidosis, and nephrocalcinosis.[102] All of these abnormalities occur to varying degrees in almost all patients receiving the drug. In most patients, renal dysfunction gradually resolves after discontinuance of therapy. Amphotericin B nephrotoxicity may be minimized by avoiding other agents with synergistic nephrotoxicity (e.g., aminoglycosides, vancomycin, cisplatin, and cyclosporine) and by the administration of sodium supplementation. The latter approach consists of I.V. infusion of 500 ml of 0.9% saline solution 30 minutes before the administration of amphotericin B and a second infusion of the same amount of saline after the amphotericin B infusion is completed.

If the serum creatinine level exceeds 3.5 mg/dl, amphotericin B should be discontinued and the serum creatinine level monitored twice weekly. Administration of amphotericin B may be resumed at 50% to 75% of the original dosage when the serum creatinine level falls below 3 mg/dl.

The combined use of amphotericin B deoxycholate and other nephrotoxic agents, such as cyclosporine, aminoglycosides, and foscarnet, may result in synergistic nephrotoxicity.[103] Less nephrotoxic lipid formulations of amphotericin B include amphotericin B lipid complex (Abelcet), amphotericin B colloidal dispersion (Amphotec), and liposomal amphotericin B (AmBisome). These preparations differ in the amount of amphotericin B and the type of lipid used as well as in the physical form, pharmacokinetics, and toxicities. Of the three formulations, AmBisome is the one that is best tolerated.

FLUCYTOSINE

Flucytosine can be useful for the treatment of hematogenous candidiasis; however, a high failure rate and secondary emergence of resistance have been reported when flucytosine was used alone, and serious concerns exist regarding its myelosuppressive potential. A review of the literature on the activity of flucytosine in acute disseminated candidiasis and candidemia indicates a good response rate.

The standard dosage for flucytosine is 37.5 mg/kg every 6 hours. On the basis of the pharmacokinetics of flucytosine and the in vitro susceptibility of *Candida* species to the drug, much lower dosages of flucytosine (e.g., 12.5 mg/kg every 12 hours) would probably maintain serum and tissue levels significantly above the minimal inhibitory concentration (MIC) needed for most susceptible strains throughout therapy. For example, giving 25 mg/kg/day at 12-hour intervals would result in peak and trough serum levels of about 25 and 5 μg/ml, respectively, given a steady state and normal kidney function in a 70 kg patient. Because the MIC of flucytosine for most susceptible *Candida* species is usually 1 μg/ml or less, such a dosage schedule will constitute

Table 3   Antifungal Chemotherapy[140]

Drug	Indications	Route of Administration	Major Side Effects
Amphotericin B	Hematogenous and deep-seated candidiasis; aspergillosis; blastomycosis; coccidioidomycosis; histoplasmosis; cryptococcosis	Intravenous, intrathecal	Anemia, headache, chills, fever, nausea, renal dysfunction, hypotension, tachypnea, hypokalemia, phlebitis
Clotrimazole	Oropharyngeal candidiasis	Oral	—
Flucytosine	Candidiasis (septicemia, endocarditis, and urinary tract infections); cryptococcosis	Oral	Leukopenia, thrombocytopenia, liver dysfunction, diarrhea
Fluconazole	Oropharyngeal and esophageal candidiasis; hematogenous candidal infection; other candidal infections (e.g., urinary tract infections, peritonitis); meningeal coccidioidomycosis; cryptococcosis	Oral, intravenous	Nausea and vomiting, skin rash, liver dysfunction
Itraconazole	Histoplasmosis; blastomycosis; aspergillosis	Oral	Nausea, vomiting, liver dysfunction
Ketoconazole	Candidiasis (chronic mucocutaneous candidiasis or oropharyngeal candidiasis); candiduria; blastomycosis; coccidioidomycosis; histoplasmosis; chromomycosis; paracoccidioidomycosis	Oral	Hepatotoxicity, nausea or vomiting, occasional suppression of adrenal function

appropriate therapy, given that the drug is used in combination with other antifungals. This approach may decrease the myelosuppressive potential that the drug usually exhibits at levels of 100 μg/ml, and it may lead to the drug's wider use.

Peak serum concentrations should be monitored and the dosage adjusted so as to maintain a peak level of about 25 μg/ml. Flucytosine is removed by hemodialysis and peritoneal dialysis. Patients undergoing hemodialysis should receive a 37.5 mg/kg dose of flucytosine after each dialysis session unless their initial peak serum concentration is higher than 25 μg/ml or their postdialysis concentration is higher than 10 μg/ml. Patients undergoing peritoneal dialysis should receive a single 37.5 mg/kg dose daily.

FLUCONAZOLE

The mechanism of action of fluconazole is preferential inhibition of cytochrome P-450 enzymes in fungal organisms. Fluconazole is active against several *Candida* species, including *C. tropicalis. C. krusei*, however, is highly resistant to this agent.[90] Fluconazole also does not appear to have good clinical activity against *Aspergillus* species. Fluconazole is available in either an oral form or an I.V. form, both of which are rapidly and almost completely absorbed from the GI tract. The serum concentrations after oral administration are almost identical to those achieved when the drug is administered intravenously. A major advantage of fluconazole over ketoconazole is its high degree of GI absorption, which is not affected by gastric acidity or the presence of food. Steady-state serum concentrations of fluconazole are obtained within 5 to 10 days. An initial loading dose that is twice the usual daily dose is recommended. Fluconazole is distributed evenly in body tissues, penetrates into the vitreous humor and the aqueous humor of the eye, and crosses the blood-brain barrier. The drug is excreted largely unchanged in the urine, with only minimal liver metabolism. Consequently, dosage schedules must be adjusted in patients with renal impairment. Hemodialysis significantly reduces the serum concentrations, and the drug appears also to be removed by peritoneal dialysis. A standard dose should be given after each course of dialysis.

The toxicities of fluconazole are similar to those of other azoles and include nausea and vomiting in about 2% of patients, as well as headache, fatigue, abdominal pain, and diarrhea[104]; exfoliative dermatitis also occurs, but very rarely. Transient abnormalities of liver function have been observed in 3% of patients receiving fluconazole. In addition, fatal hepatic necrosis developed in two patients who were receiving fluconazole, but it was unclear whether the agent played a causal role in this event. No significant hormonal abnormalities have been reported after administration of fluconazole.

Because fluconazole interacts with warfarin, phenytoin, and cyclosporine when given in a daily dose of 200 mg or more,[104] serum concentrations of these agents should be monitored.

ITRACONAZOLE

Itraconazole is the only available azole that has substantial activity against *Aspergillus* species. It exists in an oral capsule formulation, the bioavailability of which is approximately 55%. Absorption is enhanced by the presence of food in the stomach but is significantly reduced by the presence of antacids or H_2 receptor blockers. A new solution, which has significantly higher bioavailability, may not be well tolerated by patients. When erratic absorption is of concern, use of the I.V. formulation is recommended. The serum elimination half-life, 15 to 25 hours, increases to 34 to 42 hours after weeks of administration and with increasing itraconazole doses.

Metabolized by the liver, itraconazole is excreted as metabolites primarily in the feces (54%) and urine (35%). A hepatic metabolite, hydroxyitraconazole, has an antifungal spectrum similar to that of the parent compound. Because itraconazole is metabolized to a large degree in the liver, the dosage must be adjusted in patients with hepatic failure; however, its pharmacokinetics are not affected by renal impairment or hemodialysis. Serum concentrations of digoxin may increase when this agent is given with itraconazole,[105] and the metabolism of itraconazole may be accelerated when drugs that induce hepatic enzymes are given simultaneously.[106] Serum concentrations of itraconazole should therefore be measured in patients with invasive infections.

Itraconazole is generally well tolerated in dosages of up to 400 mg/day. The most common side effects are nausea, vomiting, diarrhea, and abdominal discomfort. Headaches, rash, pruritus, and dizziness occasionally occur. At higher doses, a mineralocorticoid excess syndrome (hypokalemia, hypertension, and edema) has been described, and hypokalemia develops in as many as 6% of patients who take 400 mg/day for several months.[107]

Itraconazole is available in 100 mg capsules and oral suspension (10 mg/ml). Because itraconazole may be teratogenic, it should be avoided in pregnant patients. A large number of drug interactions occur with itraconazole, many related to inhibition of the cytochrome P-450 enzyme system. Care should be taken in prescribing itraconazole with these agents. Itraconazole is currently approved for the treatment of blastomycosis, histoplasmosis, and aspergillosis but is also effective for the treatment of candidiasis and cryptococcosis.

KETOCONAZOLE

Ketoconazole is effective against yeast infections of the skin and the mucous membranes; however, it should not be used to treat hemato-

Table 4 Characteristics of Currently Available Azoles*[139]

	Ketoconazole	Fluconazole	Itraconazole
Spectrum	Narrow	Expanded	Expanded
Route(s) of administration	Oral	Oral, intravenous	Oral
Bioavailability	Erratic, requires gastric acidity	Excellent	Erratic, requires gastric acidity
Plasma half-life (hr)	6–9	30	20–40
Hepatotoxicity	Occasional	Occasional	Occasional
Gastrointestinal intolerance	Frequent	Occasional	Occasional
CSF penetration	No	Yes	No
Renal excretion	No	Yes	No
Interaction with other drugs	Frequent	Occasional	Frequent

*Intravenous miconazole is also available but offers no advantage over the currently available azoles.

genous candidiasis. Ketoconazole is not available in an intravenous form, and the serum levels it is capable of reaching depend largely on gastric acidity [*see Table 4*]. The same adverse events and drug-drug interactions observed with itraconazole occur with ketoconazole.

SPECIAL CONSIDERATIONS IN ORGAN TRANSPLANT RECIPIENTS

Intravenous amphotericin B (0.4 to 0.8 mg/kg/day) has been the mainstay of treatment in organ transplant recipients, but concerns have been expressed about increased nephrotoxicity, particularly in patients receiving cyclosporine or tacrolimus. The lipid formulations of amphotericin B (1 to 3 mg/kg/day) are less nephrotoxic, particularly liposomal amphotericin B (AmBisome). Fluconazole has a minimal effect on hepatic microsomal enzymes in comparison with ketoconazole and itraconazole and therefore is the drug of choice in organ transplant recipients who have candidiasis caused by fluconazole-susceptible strains.

Conclusion

Continued progress in supportive care, including the development of antibiotics with increasingly broad spectra of activity, has resulted in an increased incidence of fungal infections, particularly candidiasis. Because of the inadequacy of the available knowledge base, we do not fully understand the pathophysiology of these infections in surgical patients, nor can we be certain precisely when prophylaxis and therapy should be administered.

Despite these limitations, there is now sufficient information available to justify an aggressive therapeutic approach to suspected *Candida* infections. Now that less toxic agents are available (the newer triazoles, particularly fluconazole, and the lipid formulations of amphotericin B), the clinical approach to presumed fungal infections in surgical patients has been made far simpler.

Discussion

Microbiologic Characteristics of Pathogenic *Candida* Species

Candida species multiply by producing buds from ovoid yeast cells. They are differentiated from other yeasts (e.g., *Saccharomyces* species) by their ability to produce pseudohyphae on certain media and, in the case of *C. albicans*, true hyphae in serum [*see Figure 2*].

VIRULENCE FACTORS

Four virulence factors have been demonstrated for *Candida* species: adherence to mucosal epithelial cells; secretion of proteinases, which degrade connective tissue proteins, thereby allowing yeast to enter beyond connective tissue barriers; ambient pH[108]; and resistance to oxidative killing by neutrophils.

For *Candida* species to disseminate, the organisms must be able to adhere to the vascular system (i.e., endothelium, the basement membrane, or both), an ability that is probably receptor mediated.[109] In vitro, however, *Candida* adheres more avidly to the subendothelial extracellular matrix than to endothelial cells. This finding

may explain the increased risk of hematogenous candidiasis in patients receiving cytotoxic chemotherapy. Such therapy causes denudation of endothelium and consequent exposure of the basement membrane, to which *Candida* then readily adheres.

Genetic studies have evaluated the role of various virulence factors for *Candida* species, including ambient pH,[108] adherence mechanisms, and enzyme production. Mechanisms by which *Candida* species lose virulence include the following: gene dysregulation, stopping the switch from budding yeast to filamentous form; disruption of a gene that results in decreased hyphal growth, adherence, and virulence[110]; deficiency of *C. albicans* in mannosyl transferase, resulting in decreased adherence and virulence; and deletion of the gene that encodes the production of phospholipase leading to decreased cell wall penetration.

CHANGING MICROBIOLOGIC SPECTRUM OF *CANDIDA*

Although there are more than 100 described species of *Candida*, only four are commonly associated with infection: *C. albicans, C. tropi-*

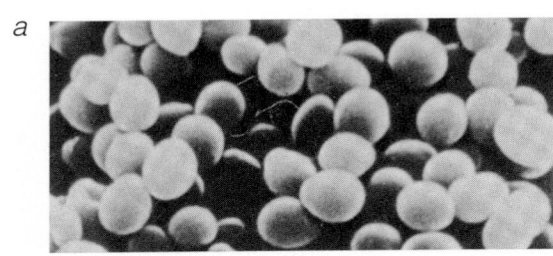

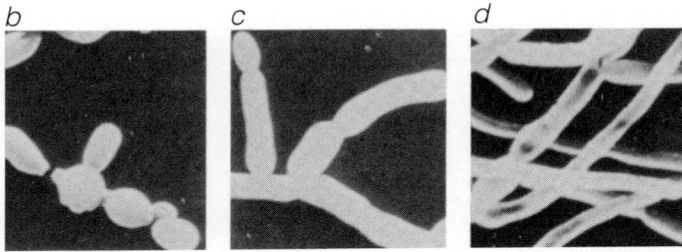

Figure 2 Candida **takes several forms as it grows. A blastospore is a unicellular form (*a*). Blastospores divide by budding, a process in which new cellular material grows from a site on the blastospore (*b*). Nuclear division then occurs, and a septum forms between the two new cells. A hypha is a long tube of several cells divided by septa (*c*). A mycelium is a cellular aggregate that includes a hypha and its branches (*d*). A pseudohypha differs from a true hypha in that it is composed of morphologically distinct, elongated blastospores.**

calis, C. parapsilosis, and *C. glabrata.*[10] Of these, *C. albicans* has been isolated from more than 60% of candidal infections; the other three major species are seen at rates varying from 5% to 20%. Mucosal colonization by *C. tropicalis,* a virulent organism, frequently leads to invasive infection. *C. glabrata* and *C. parapsilosis* appear to be relatively less virulent,[111] and the latter typically causes infection in association with prosthetic materials (e.g., catheters) or glucose-rich intravenous solutions.[10] Finally, *C. krusei* and *C. lusitaniae* rarely cause disease, being isolated from fewer than 1% of cultures.[10] The epidemiology of candidiasis has changed, with reduced rates of *C. albicans* in favor of other candidal species—in particular, *C. glabrata* and *C. krusei.*[112] This change is important because *C. krusei* and several strains of *C. glabrata* are highly resistant to the triazoles such as fluconazole and itraconazole.[10,112]

A study by the NNIS group evaluated 1,579 bloodstream isolates of *Candida* species obtained from more than 50 hospitals in the United States over a 7-year period (1992–1998) to detect trends in species distribution and susceptibility to fluconazole. *C. albicans* accounted for 52% of isolates, followed by *C. glabrata* (18%), *C. parapsilosis* (15%), *C. tropicalis* (11%), and *C. krusei* (2%). Since 1995, *C. glabrata* has been more prevalent than *C. parapsilosis.* The susceptibility of all *Candida* species to fluconazole has remained stable.[113]

Pathogenesis of Candidiasis in the Surgical Patient

COLONIZATION OF THE GUT BY *CANDIDA* SPECIES

That colonization is a necessary prelude to infection is supported by studies demonstrating (1) that 95% of neutropenic patients and 84% of nonneutropenic patients were infected with the same strains that had previously colonized them and (2) that infection was significantly less likely to develop in patients who were not colonized.[114,115] In a study investigating the sequence of colonization and candidemia in nonneutropenic patients, Voss and colleagues[114] found that the strains recovered from the initial colonized or infected site and from

the bloodstream were identical in patients with disseminated candidiasis; furthermore, nearly every patient was infected with a distinct or unique *Candida* strain. In another study, positive surveillance cultures were found to be highly predictive of systemic infection, whereas negative surveillance cultures correlated with a low risk of candidal dissemination.[116] Clinical studies of antifungal prophylaxis in neutropenic cancer patients have also suggested that antifungal regimens effectively prevent hematogenous infection when they can eliminate or reduce colonization by *Candida.*[117]

The density of colonization appears to be predictive of the risk of hematogenous candidiasis. In two large series of neutropenic cancer patients, hematogenous candidiasis almost never developed in noncolonized patients, compared with an infection rate of more than 30% in patients with multiple colonized sites.[115,118] In a study of patients with acute lymphocytic leukemia, a relatively high concentration of *Candida* organisms in the stools was found to be a significant risk factor for hematogenous candidiasis.[119] In 40 infants of very low birth weight, a value of 8×10^6 *Candida* CFU/g stool was established as a threshold, beyond which GI symptoms (attributed to *Candida*) developed in 50% of the infants and a systemic septic response in 28.5% during 1 to 3 weeks of heavy colonization.[120] In a prospective study of patients admitted to surgical and neonatal intensive care units, Pittet and coworkers demonstrated that the intensity of *Candida* colonization (as determined by a *Candida* colonization index) was significantly higher in patients who subsequently became infected than in those who did not.[121] Other case-control studies have demonstrated that colonization by *Candida* species at various body sites and exposure to several antibiotics were independent risk factors for candidemia.[122]

The normal endogenous intestinal flora inhibits GI colonization and overgrowth by potentially pathogenic bacteria and fungi by forming what may be thought of as living wallpaper in the large intestine. Suppression of endogenous microflora as a consequence of antimicrobial administration[123] may permit overgrowth of pathogenic strains in the GI tract and selection of resistant strains, which may result in enterocolitis, systemic infection, or the septic response.

PHYSICAL DISRUPTION OF THE INTESTINAL MUCOSAL BARRIER

In humans, as well as in animals, the GI tract is considered to be the most important portal of entry for microorganisms, including yeasts, into the bloodstream. The passage of endogenous fungi from the GI tract to extraintestinal sites can be referred to as fungal translocation (by analogy with bacterial translocation).

Although yeast cells have no intrinsic motility, they are able to translocate from the intestinal lumen within a few hours of ingestion. In a study conducted in the 1960s, two nonpathogenic yeasts were surgically instilled into the rat duodenum and were recovered from the cisterna chyli within 4 hours.[124] Even in the absence of disease, any marked increase in the intestinal population of *Candida* can lead to fungal translocation and subsequent hematogenous infection. That candidal species can translocate from the gut to the bloodstream was demonstrated in a study in which signs and symptoms of sepsis developed in a healthy volunteer 2 hours after ingestion of a suspension containing 10^{12} *C. albicans* organisms, and blood cultures taken 3 and 6 hours after ingestion were positive for *Candida.*[125] In addition, autopsy studies conducted in patients with hematogenous candidiasis found involvement of the GI tract and submucosal invasion in almost all patients.[86]

Microbial translocation has been demonstrated in several animal models and has been shown to be enhanced by several factors, including fasting, which induces complex changes in host defenses, and protein deficiency, which results in intestinal microbial overgrowth, increased intestinal absorption of intact proteins, and decreased intracellular killing of bacteria and fungi. In one study involving *C. albicans,* volatile fatty acids and secondary bile salts

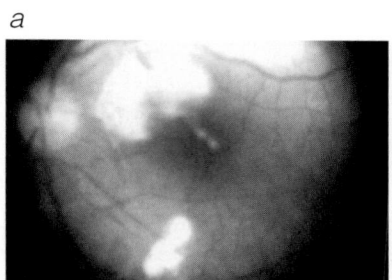
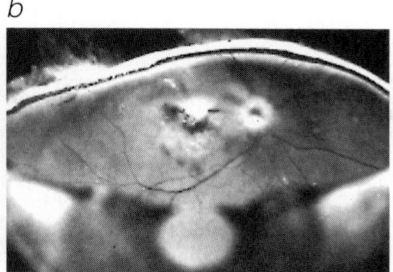
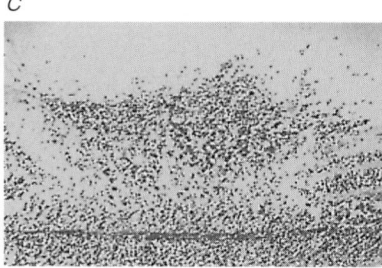

Figure 3 *Candida* endophthalmitis is common in patients with persistent fungemia. On funduscopy, a characteristic white, cotton-wool–like exudate can be seen (*a*). Cut section of an eye shows *Candida* retinitis (*b*). A microscopic view of *Candida* chorioretinitis is also provided (*c*).[138]

reduced fungal adhesion to the mucosa, colonization, and dissemination in mice by causing the formation of a dense layer of bacteria in the mucus gel; these bacteria successfully competed with the yeast cells for the same adhesion sites and produced various substances that inhibited fungal growth.[126] In another animal model, bile duct ligation resulted in bacterial translocation.[127] In yet another, splanchnic ischemia in guinea pigs increased fungal translocation.[128] Similar results were obtained in guinea pigs and rats that had burns covering 50% of their total body surface area. After the yeast cells penetrated the lamina propria, the cells were found either free in the lymphatic vessels and in the blood vessels or engulfed by macrophages.[129]

Microbial translocation has been shown to be clinically relevant in humans. Surveillance cultures from patients with leukemia have demonstrated an association between the bacterial biotype or serotype that was most prevalent in the patient's feces and the bacterial biotype or serotype that subsequently caused septicemia. Significant microbial translocation has been demonstrated in patients who underwent operation for colorectal carcinoma, intestinal obstruction, or Crohn disease. In addition, translocation is thought to occur as a result of flattening of the intestinal villi that results from the administration of total parenteral nutrition.[130]

Immunosuppression Leading to Dissemination of Candidiasis

Host defenses against *Candida* infections include T cell immunity, to prevent colonization and superficial invasion, and phagocytic immunity, to prevent deeper tissue invasion and hematogenous dissemination. Any condition that suppresses any of these arms of the immune system puts the patient at increased risk for candidiasis. Phagocytes ingest intestinal microbes. In a patient whose immune system has been compromised, these phagocytes transport microbes out of the intestine, fail to kill them, and finally liberate them in extraintestinal sites. Examples of immunosuppression include hematologic malignancy, bone marrow or organ transplantation, and immunosuppressive therapy such as cancer chemotherapy and corticosteroid therapy. Total parenteral nutrition (TPN) may result in immunosuppression. Transient hyperglycemia in patients receiving TPN causes an acceleration in the nonenzymatic glycosylation of immunoglobulin G, leading to its inactivation and impairment of complement fixation.[131] In a randomized, prospective study,[132] long-chain triglycerides in TPN significantly decreased the ratio of helper B cells to suppressor T cells. There is evidence that fat emulsions may impair polymorphonuclear and macrophage function.[133] In animal models, TPN induced macrophage suppression with decreased peritoneal macrophage superoxide production and *Candida* phagocytosis, associated with bacterial translocation to mesenteric lymph nodes.[134]

Pathology of *Candida* Colonization and Infectious Syndromes

The evolution of *Candida* microabscesses after hematogenous distribution has been studied in animal models. After intravenous infusion in nonneutropenic animals, the liver, the kidneys, the heart, the eyes, the brain, and the skin show a pattern of intracapillary fungi (yeasts and pseudohyphae) with an accumulation of neutrophils. In time, focal areas of necrosis occur, resulting in organ dysfunction that ultimately leads to death.

In nonneutropenic patients who are dying of candidiasis, a similar histologic picture and a similar pattern of organ involvement are seen. The organs most frequently involved are the brain, the heart, the kidneys, and the eyes. *Candida* produces microabscesses and, frequently, noncaseating granulomas. The histologic picture suggests that blood-borne fungi are lodged in the microvasculature, resulting in vasculitis. This multifocal microscopic disease explains the absence of localizing findings despite the progressive cerebral, renal, and cardiac dysfunction seen in infected persons.

The high incidence of cerebral involvement has been underscored by findings in an autopsy study of 41 nonneutropenic patients with tissue-verified deep candidiasis, of whom 26 (63%) had undergone major operations.[135] Nineteen (46%) were found to have cerebral candidal infections; all 19 individuals had antecedent proven or suspected gram-negative sepsis and had been treated with appropriate antibiotic therapy. In every patient studied, *Candida* organisms were identified at sites outside the brain, including the kidneys (90%) and the heart (80%). Candidiasis produced intracerebral microabscesses and noncaseating granulomas without diffuse leptomeningitis.

In a nearly identical autopsy series, 18 patients with disseminated candidiasis were found to have myocardial involvement.[136] This mycosis was characterized by myocardial microabscesses with yeasts and pseudohyphal elements. Noncaseating granulomas were seen in only one patient. Eight patients had recognized conduction disturbances, including alterations in both heart rate and heart rhythm.

As in the animal models, ocular involvement is a common finding in patients with disseminated candidiasis and by itself is an indication for systemic therapy. The eye pathology is a chorioretinitis with microabscess formation. Funduscopic examination, mandatory in patients suspected of having systemic *Candida* infection, reveals patchy, wool-like tufts [*see Figure 3*].

Despite the frequent finding of *Candida* in sputum cultures, primary *Candida* pneumonitis is extremely uncommon[137]; when it occurs, it usually follows aspiration of oropharyngeal contents. However, pulmonary involvement resulting from hematogenous seeding is common.

References

1. Wey SB, Mori M, Pfaller MA, et al: Hospital-acquired candidemia: the attributable mortality and excess length of stay. Arch Intern Med 148:2642, 1988

2. Pfaller M, Wenzel R: Impact of the changing epidemiology of fungal infections in the 1990s. Eur J Clin Microbiol Infect Dis 11:287, 1992

3. Jarvis WR, Martone WJ: Predominant pathogens in hospital infections. J Antimicrob Chemother 29:19, 1992

4. Schaberg DR, Culver DH, Gaynes RP: Major trends in the microbial etiology of nosocomial infection. Am J Med 91:72S, 1991

5. Banerjee SN, Emori TG, Culver DH, et al: Secular trends in nosocomial primary bloodstream infections in the United States, 1980-1989. National Nosocomial Infections Surveillance System. Am J Med 91(3B):86S, 1991

6. Beck-Sagué C, Jarvis WR: Secular trends in the epidemiology of nosocomial fungal infections in the United States, 1980-1990. National Nosocomial Infections Surveillance System. J Infect Dis 167:1247, 1993

7. Pfaller MA, Jones RN, Messer SA, et al: National surveillance of nosocomial blood stream infection due to Candida albicans: frequency of occurrence and antifungal susceptibility in the SCOPE Program. Diagn Microbiol Infect Dis 31:327, 1998

8. Vincent JL, Anaissie E, Bruining H, et al: Epidemiology, diagnosis and treatment of systemic Candida infection in surgical patients under intensive care. Intens Care Med 24:206, 1998

9. Pittet D, Li N, Woolson RF, et al: Microbiological factors influencing the outcome of nosocomial bloodstream infections: a 6-year validated, population-based model. Clin Infect Dis 24:1068, 1997

10. Anaissie EJ, Rex JH, Uzun O, et al: Predictors of adverse outcome in cancer patients with candidemia. Am J Med 104:238, 1998

11. Bodey GP, Luna M: Skin lesions associated with disseminated candidiasis. JAMA 229:1466, 1974

12. Anaissie E, Bodey GP, Kantarjian H, et al: Fluconazole therapy for chronic disseminated candidiasis in patients with leukemia and prior amphotericin B therapy. Am J Med 91:142, 1991

13. Anaissie E: Opportunistic mycoses in the immunocompromised host: experience at a cancer center and review. Clin Infect Dis 14:S43, 1992

14. Meunier F, Aoun M, Bitar N: Candidemia in immunocompromised patients. Clin Infect Dis 14:S120, 1992

15. Baley JE, Annable WL, Klegman RM: Candida endophthalmitis in the premature infant. J Pediatr 98:458, 1981

16. Dupont B, Drouhet E: Cutaneous, ocular, and osteoarticular candidiasis in heroin addicts: new clinical and therapeutic aspects in 38 patients. J Infect Dis 152:577, 1985

17. Eubanks PJ, de Virgilio C, Klein S, et al: Candida sepsis in surgical patients. Am J Surg 166:617, 1993

18. Castaldo P, Stratta RJ, Wood RP, et al: Clinical spectrum of fungal infections after orthotopic liver transplantation. Arch Surg 126:149, 1991

19. Prasad JK, Feller I, Thomson PD: A ten-year review of Candida sepsis and mortality in burn patients. Surgery 101:213, 1987

20. Desai MH, Rutan RL, Heggers JP, et al: Candida infection with and without nystatin prophylaxis: an 11-year experience with patients with burn injury. Arch Surg 127:159, 1992

21. Desai MH, Herndon DN: Eradication of Candida burn wound septicemia in massively burned patients. J Trauma 28:140, 1988

22. Paya CV: Fungal infections in solid-organ transplantation. Clin Infect Dis 16:677, 1993

23. Hesse UJ, Sutherland DE, Simmons RL, et al: Intra-abdominal infections in pancreas transplant recipients. Ann Surg 203:153, 1986

24. Hofflin JM, Potasman I, Baldwin JC, et al: Infectious complications in heart transplant recipients receiving cyclosporine and corticosteroids. Ann Intern Med 106:209, 1987

25. Brooks RG, Hofflin JM, Jamieson SW, et al: Infectious complications in heart-lung transplant recipients. Am J Med 79:412, 1985

26. Ramsey DE, Finch WT, Birtch AG: Urinary tract infections in kidney transplant recipients. Arch Surg 114:1022, 1979

27. Anaissie E, Samonis G, Kontoyiannis D, et al: Role of catheter colonization and infrequent hematogenous seeding in catheter-related infections. Eur J Clin Microbiol Infect Dis 14:134, 1995

28. Walsh TJ, Lee JW, Sien T, et al: Serum D-arabinitol measured by automated quantitative enzymatic assay for detection and therapeutic monitoring of experimental disseminated candidiasis: correlation with tissue concentrations of Candida albicans. J Med Vet Mycol 32:205, 1994

29. Brannon P, Kiehn TE: Large-scale clinical comparison of the lysis-centrifugation and radiometric systems for blood culture. J Clin Microbiol 22:951, 1985

30. Berenguer J, Buck M, Witebski F, et al: Lysis-centrifugation blood cultures in the detection of tissue-proven invasive candidiasis: disseminated versus single-organ infection. Diagn Microbiol Infect Dis 17:103, 1993

31. Ho YM, Ng MH, Teoh-Chan CH, et al: Indirect immunofluorescence assay for antibody to germ tube of Candida albicans—a new diagnostic test. J Clin Pathol 29:1007, 1976

32. Greenfield RA, Stephens JL, Bussey MJ, et al: Quantitation of antibody to Candida mannan by enzyme-linked immunosorbent assay. J Lab Clin Med 101:758, 1983

33. van Deventer AJM, van Vlient HJA, Hop WCJ, et al: Diagnostic value of anti-Candida enolase antibodies. J Clin Microbiol 32:17, 1994

34. Jones JM: Quantitation of antibody against cell wall mannan and a major cytoplasmic antigen of Candida in rabbits, mice, and humans. Infect Immun 30:78, 1980

35. Weiner MH, Coats-Stephen M: Immunodiagnosis of systemic candidiasis: mannan antigenemia detected by radioimmunoassay in experimental and human infections. J Infect Dis 140:989, 1979

36. Bailey JW, Sada E, Brass C, et al: Diagnosis of systemic candidiasis by latex agglutination for serum antigen. J Clin Microbiol 21:749, 1985

37. Fung JC, Donta ST, Tilton RC: Candida detection system (CAND-TEC) to differentiate between Candida albicans colonizations and disease. J Clin Microbiol 24:542, 1986

38. Walsh TJ, Hathorn JW, Sobel JD, et al: Detection of circulating Candida enolase by immunoassay in patients with cancer and invasive candidiasis. N Engl J Med 324:1026, 1991

39. Gutiérrez J, Maroto C, Piédrorla G, et al: Circulating Candida antigens and antibodies: useful markers of candidemia. J Clin Microbiol 31:2550, 1993

40. Freydiere AM, Buchaille L, Guinet R, et al: Evaluation of latex reagents for rapid identification of Candida albicans and C. krusei colonies. J Clin Microbiol 35:877, 1997

41. Fujita S-I, Lasker BA, Lott TJ, et al: Microtitration plate enzyme immunoassay to detect PCR-amplified DNA from Candida species in blood. J Clin Microbiol 33:962, 1995

42. Sandhu GS, Kline BC, Stockman L, et al: Molecular probes for diagnosis of fungal infections. J Clin Microbiol 33:2913, 1995

43. Walsh TJ, Francesconi A, Kasai M, et al: PCR and single-strand conformational polymorphism for recognition of medically important opportunistic fungi. J Clin Microbiol 33:3216, 1995

44. Reiss E, Morrison CJ: Nonculture methods for diagnosis of disseminated candidiasis. Clin Microbiol Rev 6:311, 1993

45. de Repentigny L, Marr LD, Keller JW, et al: Comparison of enzyme immunoassay and gas-liquid chromatography for the rapid diagnosis of invasive candidiasis in cancer patients. J Clin Microbiol 21:972, 1985

46. Walsh TJ, Merz WG, Lee JW, et al: Diagnosis and therapeutic monitoring of invasive candidiasis by rapid enzymatic detection of serum D-arabinitol. Am J Med 99:164, 1995

47. Dyess DL, Garrison N, Fry DE: Candida sepsis: implications of polymicrobial blood-borne infection. Arch Surg 120:345, 1985

48. Rantala A, Niinikoski J, Lehtonen OP: Yeasts in blood cultures: impact of early therapy. Scand J Infect Dis 21:557, 1989

49. Rex JH, Bennett JE, Sugar AM, et al: A randomized trial comparing fluconazole with amphotericin B for the treatment of candidemia in patients without neutropenia. Candidemia Study Group and the National Institute. N Engl J Med 331:1325, 1994

50. Anaissie EJ, Vartivarian SE, Abi-Said D, et al: Fluconazole versus amphotericin B in the treatment of hematogenous candidiasis: a matched cohort study. Am J Med 101:170, 1996

51. Nguyen MH, Peacock JE Jr, Tanner DC, et al: Therapeutic approaches in patients with candidemia: evaluation in a multicenter, prospective, observational study. Arch Intern Med 155:2429, 1995

52. Kujath P, Lerch K, Kochendorfer P, et al: Comparative study of the efficacy of fluconazole versus amphotericin B/flucytosine in surgical patients with systemic mycoses. Infection 21:376, 1993

53. Van't Wout JW, Mattie H, van Furth R: A prospective study of the efficacy of fluconazole (UK-49,858) against deep-seated fungal infections. J Antimicrob Chemother 21:665, 1988

54. de Marie S, Janknegt R, Bakker-Woudenberg IA: Clinical use of liposomal and lipid-complexed amphotericin B. J Antimicrob Chemother 33:907, 1994

55. Walsh TJ, Hiemenz JW, Seibel NL, et al: Amphotericin B lipid complex for invasive fungal infections: analysis of safety and efficacy in 556 cases. Clin Infect Dis 26:1383, 1998

56. Nucci M, Colombo AL, Silveira F, et al: Risk factors for death in patients with candidemia. Infect Control Hosp Epidemiol 19:846, 1998

57. Rex JH, Bennett JE, Sugar AM, et al: Intravascular catheter exchange and duration of candidemia: NIAID Mycoses Study Group and the Candidemia Study Group. Clin Infect Dis 21:994, 1995

58. Stevenhagen A, van Furth R: Interferon-gamma activates the oxidative killing of Candida albicans by human granulocytes. Clin Exp Immunol 91:170, 1993

59. Fratti RA, Ghannoum MA, Edwards JE Jr, et al: Gamma interferon protects endothelial cells from damage by Candida albicans by inhibiting endothelial cell phagocytosis. Infect Immun 64:4714, 1996

60. Gaviria JM, van Burik JA, Dale DC, et al: Comparison of interferon-gamma, granulocyte colony-stimulating factor, and granulocyte-macrophage colony-stimulating factor for priming leukocyte-mediated hyphal damage of opportunistic fungal pathogens. J Infect Dis 179:1038, 1999

61. Gorensek MJ, Carey WD, Washington JA 2nd, et al: Selective bowel decontamination with quinolones and nystatin reduces gram-negative and fungal infections in orthotopic liver transplant recipients. Cleve Clin J Med 60:139, 1993

62. Mora NP, Cofer JB, Solomon H, et al: Analysis of severe infections (INF) after 180 consecutive liver transplants: the impact of amphotericin B prophylaxis for reducing the incidence and severity of fungal infections. Transplant Proc 23:1528, 1991

63. Tollemar J, Ringden O, Andersson S, et al: Randomized double-blind study of liposomal amphotericin B (AmBisome) prophylaxis of invasive fungal infections in bone marrow transplant recipients. Bone Marrow Transplant 12:577, 1993

64. Slavin MA, Osborne B, Adams R, et al: Efficacy and safety of fluconazole prophylaxis for fungal infections after bone marrow transplantation—a prospective, randomized, double-blind study. J Infect Dis 171:1545, 1995

65. Rotstein C, Bow EJ, Laverdiere M, et al: Randomized placebo-controlled trial of fluconazole prophylaxis for neutropenic cancer patients: benefit based on purpose and intensity of cytotoxic therapy. The Canadian Fluconazole Prophylaxis Study Group. Clin Infect Dis 28:331, 1999

66. Powderly WG, Finkelstein D, Feinberg J, et al: A randomized trial comparing fluconazole with clotrimazole troches for the prevention of fungal infections in patients with advanced human immunodeficiency virus infection. NIAID AIDS Clinical Trials Group. N Engl J Med 332:700, 1995

67. Eggimann P, Francioli P, Bille J, et al: Fluconazole prophylaxis prevents intra-abdominal candidiasis in high-risk surgical patients. Crit Care Med 27:1066, 1999

68. Dube MP, Heseltine PN, Rinaldi MG, et al: Fungemia and colonization with nystatin-resistant Candida rugosa in a burn unit. Clin Infect Dis 18:77, 1994

69. Torbenson M, Wang J, Nichols L, et al: Causes of death in autopsied liver transplantation patients. Mod Pathol 11:37, 1998

70. Lumbreras C, Cuervas-Mons V, Jara P, et al: Randomized trial of fluconazole versus nystatin for the prophylaxis of Candida infection following liver transplantation. J Infect Dis 174:583, 1996

71. Lorf T, Braun F, Ruchel R, et al: Systemic mycoses during prophylactical use of liposomal amphotericin B (AmBisome) after liver transplantation. Mycoses 42:47, 1999

72. Savani DV, Perfect JR, Cobo LM, et al: Penetration of new azole compounds into the eye and efficacy in experimental Candida endophthalmitis. Antimicrob Agents Chemother 31:6, 1987

73. Venditti M, De Bernardis F, Micozzi A, et al: Fluconazole treatment of catheter-related right-sided endocarditis caused by Candida albicans and associated with endophthalmitis and folliculitis. Clin Infect Dis 14:422, 1992

74. Moyer DV, Edwards JE Jr: Candida endophthalmitis and central nervous system infection. Candidiasis: Pathogenesis, Diagnosis, and Treatment. Bodey GP, Ed. Raven Press, New York, 1993, p 331

75. Martinez-Vazquez C, Fernandez-Ulloa J, Bordon J, et al: Candida albicans endophthalmitis in brown heroin addicts: response to early vitrectomy preceded and followed by antifungal therapy. Clin Infect Dis 27:1130, 1998

76. Yackee JM, Topiel MS, Simon GL: Septic phlebitis caused by Candida albicans and diagnosed by needle aspiration. South Med J 78:1262, 1985

77. Czwerwiec FS, Bilsker MS, Kamerman ML, et al: Long-term survival after fluconazole therapy of candidal prosthetic valve endocarditis. Am J Med 94:545, 1993

78. Kraus WE, Valenstein PN, Corey GR: Purulent pericarditis caused by Candida: report of three cases and identification of high-risk populations as an aid to early diagnosis. Rev Infect Dis 10:34, 1988

79. Cuende E, Barbadillo C, E-Mazzucchelli R, et al: Candida arthritis in adult patients who are not intravenous drug addicts: report of three cases and review of the literature. Semin Arthritis Rheum 22:224, 1993

80. Penk A, Pittrow L: [Status of fluconazole in the therapy of endogenous Candida endophthalmitis]. Mycoses 41(suppl 2):41, 1998

81. Tang C: Successful treatment of Candida albicans osteomyelitis with fluconazole. J Infect 26:89, 1993

82. Shapiro S, Javed T, Mealey J Jr: Candida albicans shunt infection. Pediatr Neurosci 15:125, 1989

83. Mascarenas CA, Hardin TC, Pennick GJ, et al: Treatment of thrush with itraconazole solution: evidence for topical effect. Clin Infect Dis 26:1242, 1998

84. Crutchfield CE 3rd, Lewis EJ: The successful treatment of oral candidiasis (thrush) in a pediatric patient using itraconazole (letter). Pediatr Dermatol 14:246, 1997

85. Tunkel AR, Thomas CY, Wispelwey B: Candida prosthetic arthritis: report of a case treated with fluconazole and review of the literature. Am J Med 94:100, 1993

86. Walsh TJ, Merz WG: Pathologic features in the human alimentary tract associated with invasiveness of Candida tropicalis. Am J Clin Pathol 85:498, 1986

87. Gupta TP, Ehrinpreis MN: Candida-associated diarrhea in hospitalized patients. Gastroenterology 98:780, 1990

88. Calandra T, Bille J, Schneider R, et al: Clinical significance of Candida isolated from peritoneum in surgical patients. Lancet 2:1437, 1989

89. Corbella X, Sirvent JM, Carratala J: Fluconazole treatment without catheter removal in Candida albicans peritonitis complicating peritoneal dialysis. Am J Med 90:277, 1991

90. Eisenberg ES, Leviton I, Soeiro R: Fungal peritonitis in patients receiving peritoneal dialysis: experience with 11 patients and review of the literature [published erratum appears in Rev Infect Dis 8:839, 1986]. Rev Infect Dis 8:309, 1986

91. Lo WK, Chan CY, Cheng SW, et al: A prospective randomized control study of oral nystatin prophylaxis for Candida peritonitis complicating continuous ambulatory peritoneal dialysis. Am J Kidney Dis 28:549, 1996

92. Huang CT, Leu HS: Candiduria as an early marker of disseminated infection in critically ill surgical patients (letter; comment). J Trauma 39:616, 1995

93. Chakrabarti A, Reddy TC, Singhi S: Does candiduria predict candidaemia? Ind J Med Res 106:513, 1997

94. Strassner C, Friesen A: [Therapy of candiduria by alkalinization of urine: oral treatment with potassium-sodium-hydrogen citrate]. Fortschr Med 113:359, 1995

95. Tacker JR: Successful use of fluconazole for treatment of urinary tract fungal infections. J Urol 148:1917, 1992

96. Sobel JD: Recurrent vulvovaginal candidiasis: a prospective study of the efficacy of maintenance ketoconazole therapy. N Engl J Med 315:1455, 1986

97. Walsh TJ, Dixon DM: Nosocomial aspergillosis, environmental microbiology, hospital epidemiology, diagnosis and treatment. Eur J Epidemiol 5:131, 1989

98. Denning DW, Stevens DA: Antifungal and surgical treatment of invasive aspergillosis: review of 2,121 published cases [published erratum appears in Rev Infect Dis 13:345, 1991]. Rev Infect Dis 12:1147, 1990

99. Anaissie E, Bodey GP: Nosocomial fungal infections: old problems and new challenges. Infect Dis Clin North Am 3:867, 1989

100. Anaissie E, Bodey GP, Kantarjian H, et al: New spectrum of fungal infections in patients with cancer. Rev Infect Dis 11:369, 1989

101. Sokol-Anderson ML, Brajtburg J, Medoff G: Amphotericin B-induced oxidative damage and killing of Candida albicans. J Infect Dis 154:76, 1986

102. Burgess JL, Birchall R: Nephrotoxicity of amphotericin B, with emphasis on changes in tubular function. Am J Med 53:77, 1972

103. Kennedy MS, Deeg HJ, Siegel M, et al: Acute renal toxicity with combined use of amphotericin B and cyclosporine after marrow transplantation. Transplantation 35:211, 1983

104. Zervos M, Meunier F: Fluconazole (Diflucan): a review. Int J Antimicrob Agents 3:147, 1993

105. McClean KL, Sheehan GJ: Interaction between itraconazole and digoxin (letter; comment). Clin Infect Dis 18:259, 1994

106. Drayton J, Dickinson G, Rinaldi MG: Coadministration of rifampin and itraconazole leads to undetectable levels of serum itraconazole (letter). Clin Infect Dis 18:266, 1994

107. Tucker RM, Haq Y, Denning DW, et al: Adverse events associated with itraconazole in 189 patients on chronic therapy. J Antimicrob Chemother 26:561, 1990

108. De Bernardis F, Muhlschlegel FA, Cassone A, et al: The pH of the host niche controls gene expression in and virulence of Candida albicans. Infect Immun 66:3317, 1998

109. Klotz SA: Fungal adherence to the vascular compartment: a critical step in the pathogenesis of disseminated candidiasis. Clin Infect Dis 14:340, 1992

110. Gale CA, Bendel CM, McClellan M, et al: Linkage of adhesion, filamentous growth, and virulence in Candida albicans to a single gene, INT1. Science 279:1355, 1998

111. Lecciones JA, Lee JW, Navarro EE, et al: Vascular catheter-associated fungemia in patients with cancer: analysis of 155 episodes. Clin Infect Dis 14:875, 1992

112. Abi-Said D, Anaissie E, Uzun O, et al: The epidemiology of hematogenous candidiasis caused by different Candida species [published erratum appears in Clin Infect Dis 25:352, 1997]. Clin Infect Dis 24:1122, 1997

113. Pfaller MA, Messer SA, Hollis RJ, et al: Trends in species distribution and susceptibility to fluconazole among blood stream isolates of Candida species in the United States. Diagn Microbiol Infect Dis 33:217, 1999

114. Voss A, Hollis RJ, Pfaller MA, et al: Investigation of the sequence of colonization and candidemia in nonneutropenic patients. J Clin Microbiol 32:975, 1994

115. Martino P, Girmenia C, Venditti M, et al: Candida colonization and systemic infection in neutropenic patients: a retrospective study. Cancer 64:2030, 1989

116. Pfaller M, Cabezudo I, Koontz F, et al: Predictive value of surveillance cultures for systemic infection due to Candida species. Eur J Clin Microbiol Infect Dis 6:628, 1987

117. Uzun O, Anaissie EJ: Antifungal prophylaxis in patients with hematologic malignancies: a reappraisal. Blood 86:2063, 1995

118. Martino P, Girmenia C, Micozzi A, et al: Fungemia in patients with leukemia. Am J Med Sci 306:225, 1993

119. Richet HM, Andremont A, Tancrede C, et al: Risk factors for candidemia in patients with acute lymphocytic leukemia. Rev Infect Dis 13:211, 1991

120. Pappu-Katikaneni LD, Rao KP, Banister E: Gastrointestinal colonization with yeast species and Candida septicemia in very low birth weight infants.

Mycoses 33:20, 1990

121. Pittet D, Monod M, Suter PM, et al: Candida colonization and subsequent infections in critically ill surgical patients. Ann Surg 220:751, 1994

122. Wey SB, Mori M, Pfaller MA, et al: Risk factors for hospital-acquired candidemia: a matched case-control study. Arch Intern Med 149:2349, 1989

123. Giuliano M, Barza M, Jacobus NV, et al: Effect of broad-spectrum parenteral antibiotics on composition of intestinal microflora of humans. Antimicrob Agents Chemother 31:202, 1987

124. Wolochow H, Hildebrand GJ, Lamanna C: Translocation of microorganisms across the intestinal wall of the rat: effect of microbial size and concentration. J Infect Dis 116:523, 1966

125. Krause W, Matheis H, Wulf K: Fungaemia and funguria after oral administration of Candida albicans. Lancet 1:598, 1969

126. Kennedy MJ, Volz PA: Ecology of Candida albicans gut colonization: inhibition of Candida adhesion, colonization, and dissemination from the gastrointestinal tract by bacterial antagonism. Infect Immun

49:654, 1985

127. Deitch EA, Sittig K, Li M, et al: Obstructive jaundice promotes bacterial translocation from the gut. Am J Surg 159:79, 1990

128. Gianotti L, Alexander JW, Fukushima R, et al: Translocation of Candida albicans is related to the blood flow of individual intestinal villi. Circ Shock 40:250, 1993

129. Alexander JW, Boyce ST, Babcock JF, et al: The process of microbial translocation. Ann Surg 212:496, 1990

130. Pappo I, Polacheck I, Zmora O, et al: Altered gut barrier function to Candida during parenteral nutrition. Nutrition 10:151, 1994

131. Hennessey PJ, Black CT, Andrassy RJ: Nonenzymatic glycosylation of immunoglobulin G impairs complement fixation. JPEN J Parenter Enteral Nutr 15:60, 1991

132. Gogos CA, Kalfarentzos FE, Zoumbos NC: Effect of different types of total parenteral nutrition on T-lymphocyte subpopulations and NK cells. Am J Clin Nutr 51:119, 1990

133. Gogos CA, Kalfarentzos F: Total parenteral nutrition and immune system activity: a review. Nutrition 11:339, 1995

134. Shou J, Lappin J, Minnard EA, et al: Total parenteral nutrition, bacterial translocation, and host immune function. Am J Surg 167:145, 1994

135. Parker JC Jr, McCloskey JJ, Lee RS: Human cerebral candidosis—a postmortem evaluation of 19 patients. Hum Pathol 12:23, 1981

136. Parker JC Jr: The potentially lethal problem of cardiac candidosis. Am J Clin Pathol 73:356, 1980

137. Haron E, Vartivarian S, Anaissie E, et al: Primary Candida pneumonia: experience at a large cancer center and review of the literature. Medicine (Baltimore) 72:137, 1993

138. Gaines JD, Remington JS: Disseminated candidiasis in the surgical patient. Surgery 72:730, 1972

139. Greenburg SB: Fungal and viral infections. Critical Care, 2nd ed. Civetta JM, Taylor RW, Kirby RR, Eds. JB Lippincott Co, Philadelphia, 1993, p 1055

140. Medoff G, Kobayashi GS: Systemic fungal infections: an overview. Hosp Pract 26(2):41, 1991

135 VIRAL INFECTION

Jennifer W. Janelle, M.D., and Richard J. Howard, M.D., Ph.D., F.A.C.S.

Approach to Viral Exposure

Compared with primary care physicians, such as internists, family physicians, and pediatricians, surgeons are seldom called on to treat viral infections. Viral infections nonetheless deserve the attention of surgeons because these infections can cause illness in patients after operation, albeit infrequently, and can spread to the hospital staff. Some viral infections (e.g., infections with the hepatitis viruses, HIV, and cytomegalovirus [CMV]) can result from administration of blood or blood products or can be transmitted to hospital personnel through needle-stick injury. Viral infections can also result from organ transplantation or trauma (e.g., rabies, which is transmitted by the bite of an infected animal). Some viruses, especially the herpesviruses, frequently infect immunosuppressed patients, in whom the viruses can cause severe illness and even death. In many surgical practices, there are increasing numbers of immunosuppressed patients, including organ transplant recipients; patients with cancer; patients receiving cancer chemotherapy, steroids, and other immunosuppressive drugs; the elderly; and the malnourished. Some viral infections can cause neoplastic disease for which operation may become necessary. Examples are hepatitis B virus (HBV) and hepatitis C virus (HCV), which are implicated in the etiology of hepatocellular carcinoma; Epstein-Barr virus (EBV), which can cause a lethal lymphoproliferative disorder in immunosuppressed patients; and human T cell lymphotropic virus type I (HTLV-I), which can induce a T cell leukemia. Viral infections very likely can cause other neoplasms as well.

Prevention of Transmission of HIV, Hepatitis B Virus, and Hepatitis C Virus

TRANSMISSION FROM PATIENTS TO HEALTH CARE WORKERS

The Centers for Disease Control and Prevention (CDC) has published extensive recommendations for preventing transmission of HIV, the etiologic agent of AIDS.[1-5] Applicable to clinical and laboratory staffs,[3,4] to workers in health care settings [see Table 1][1] and in other occupational settings,[1] and to health care workers performing invasive procedures,[1-5] these precautions are appropriate for preventing transmission not only of HIV but also of other blood-borne viruses, including HBV and HCV. The recommendations share the objective of minimizing exposure of personnel to blood and body secretions from infected patients, whether through needle-stick injury or through contamination of mucous membranes or open cuts.

Despite the apparently low risk of such exposure, the CDC recommends enforcement of these as well as other standard infection control precautions, regardless of whether health care workers or patients are known to be infected with HIV or HBV. The CDC has taken the position that blood and body fluid precautions should be used consistently for all patients because medical history and physical examination cannot reliably identify all patients infected with HIV or other blood-borne pathogens and because in emergencies there may be no time for serologic testing. If these universal precautions are implemented, as the CDC recommends,[1-5] no additional precautions should be necessary for patients known to be infected with HIV.

The CDC does not recommend routine HIV serologic testing for all patients.[1-5] HIV serologic testing of patients is recommended for management of health care workers who sustain parenteral or mucous membrane exposure to blood or other body fluids, for patient diagnosis and treatment, and for counseling associated with efforts to prevent and control HIV transmission in the community.[1-5]

Nevertheless, some hospitals and physicians are likely to perform serologic testing of patients if it is possible that health care workers will be exposed to the patients' blood or other body fluids, as would be the case with patients undergoing major operative procedures or receiving treatment in intensive care units. Those who favor routine preoperative testing of patients undergoing invasive procedures maintain that precautions are more likely to be followed and additional steps taken to lower the likelihood of virus transmission from patients to health care workers when it is known which patients are HIV positive.[6,7] If such policies are adopted, the CDC advocates certain principles: (1) obtain consent for testing, (2) inform patients of results and provide counseling to seropositive patients, (3) ensure confidentiality, (4) ensure that seropositive patients will not receive compromised care, and (5) prospectively evaluate the efficacy of the program in reducing the incidence of exposure of health care workers to blood or body fluids of patients who are infected with HIV.

Although possible acquisition of HIV infection is the major concern for any health care worker who is exposed to blood products in the workplace, acquisition of viral hepatitis is actually much more likely. From a single needle-stick exposure, the estimated average risk of HIV transmission is 0.3%, whereas that of HCV transmission ranges from 0% to 10%.[8] The risk that HBV will be transmitted from a single needle-stick exposure varies according to the hepatitis B e antigen (HBeAg) status of the source patient, ranging from 1% to 6% for HBeAg-negative patients to 22% to 40% for HBeAg-positive patients.[9-11] That health care workers are at increased risk for hepatitis B is indicated by the seroprevalence of HBV in this population, which is two to four times that in the general United States population (6% to 15% versus < 5%).[9,12] This seroprevalence is expected to decrease with the availability of the hepatitis B vaccine and the mandate from the Occupational Safety

Human immunodeficiency virus (HIV)

Health care worker is exposed to any patient's blood or body secretions by a needle stick or by a splash in the eye or mouth

The health care worker should be counseled about the risk of HIV infection and should follow U.S. Public Health Service recommendations for preventing HIV transmission.

Patient is judged on clinical and epidemiologic grounds to be a likely source of HIV infection

Ask the patient to consent to serologic testing for HIV.

Patient refuses to be tested

Follow state and local laws regarding testing for a nonconsenting patient's HIV source status.

Patient is seropositive

Evaluate the health care worker for clinical or serologic evidence of HIV infection as soon as possible after the exposure. Consider prophylaxis:
Low to moderate risk: AZT plus 3TC.
High risk: AZT plus 3TC plus indinavir.

Health care worker is seronegative

Repeat serologic testing 6 wk and 3, 6, 12 mo after exposure.

Patient is seronegative and has no other evidence of HIV infection

No further follow-up of the health care worker is necessary.

Patient is seronegative but has engaged in high-risk behavoirs

Perform baseline HIV testing of the health care worker. Repeat test 3 months and 6 months after exposure.

Rabies

All bites and wounds should be immediately and thoroughly cleansed with soap and water.

Bite of domestic animal (dog or cat)

Animal is healthy at time of attack

Observe the animal for 10 days. If the animal shows signs of rabies, proceed with treatment.

Animal shows signs of rabies

Animal escapes

Consult with public health officials to determine need for treatment.

Bite of wild animal (skunk, bat, fox, coyote, raccoon, bobcat, or other carnivore)

Regard as rabid unless proved negative by laboratory tests.

Bite of another animal (e.g., livestock)

Consult with public health officials to determine need for treatment.

Give the exposed person RIG (20 IU/kg). If anatomically feasible, infiltrate the full dose around the wounds. Infiltrate any remaining RIG I.M. at a site distant from that of vaccine administration. Also, administer 1.0 ml of HDCV into the deltoid muscle or, in children, the upper thigh on days 0, 3, 7, 14, and 28. If the animal is available, kill it and immediately examine its brain tissue for the presence of rabies by using fluorescent antibody tests. If the tests are negative, discontinue HDCV.

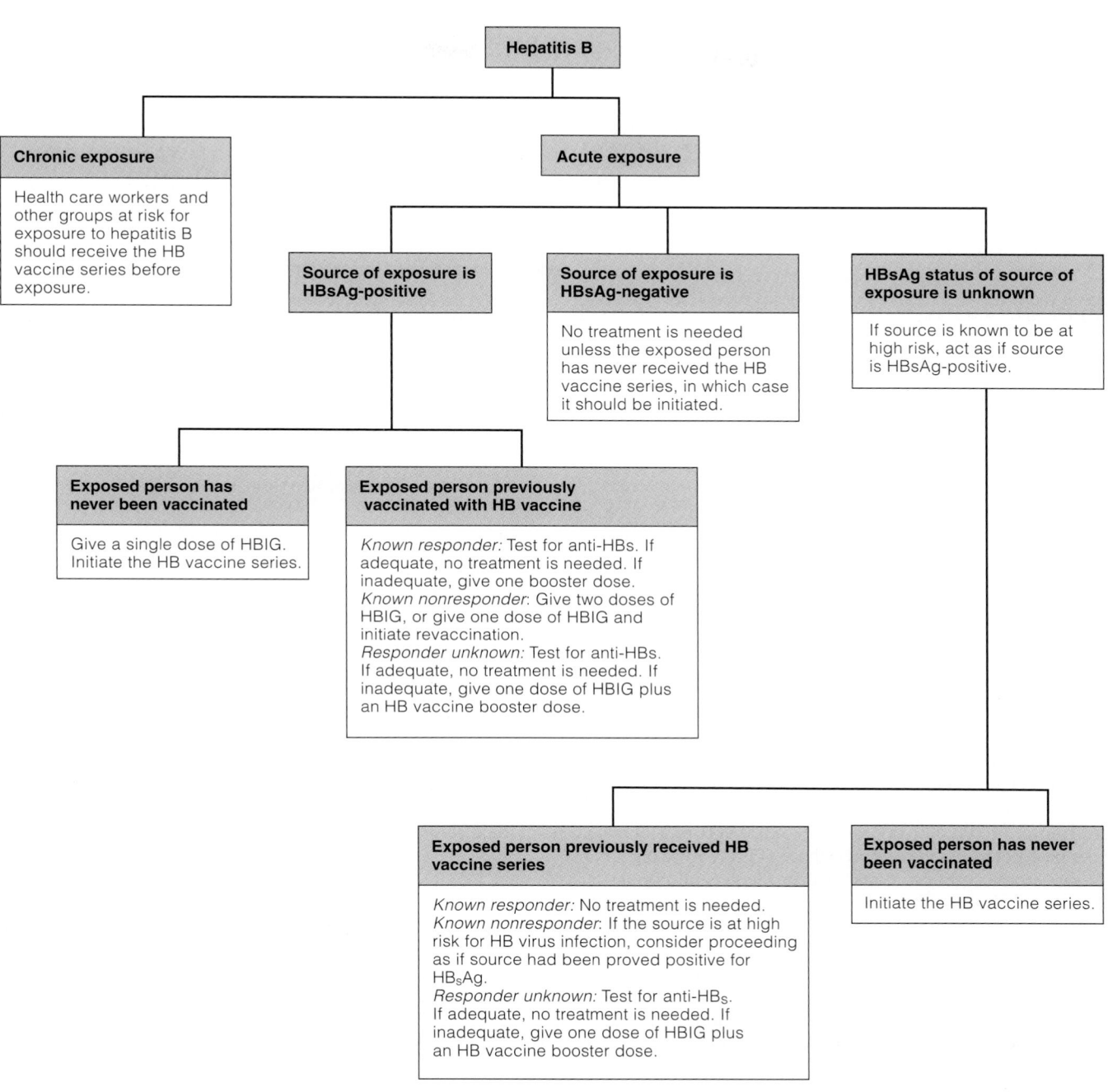

Hepatitis B

Chronic exposure

Health care workers and other groups at risk for exposure to hepatitis B should receive the HB vaccine series before exposure.

Acute exposure

Source of exposure is HBsAg-positive

Source of exposure is HBsAg-negative

No treatment is needed unless the exposed person has never received the HB vaccine series, in which case it should be initiated.

HBsAg status of source of exposure is unknown

If source is known to be at high risk, act as if source is HBsAg-positive.

Exposed person has never been vaccinated

Give a single dose of HBIG. Initiate the HB vaccine series.

Exposed person previously vaccinated with HB vaccine

Known responder: Test for anti-HBs. If adequate, no treatment is needed. If inadequate, give one booster dose.
Known nonresponder: Give two doses of HBIG, or give one dose of HBIG and initiate revaccination.
Responder unknown: Test for anti-HBs. If adequate, no treatment is needed. If inadequate, give one dose of HBIG plus an HB vaccine booster dose.

Exposed person previously received HB vaccine series

Known responder: No treatment is needed.
Known nonresponder: If the source is at high risk for HB virus infection, consider proceeding as if source had been proved positive for HBsAg.
Responder unknown: Test for anti-HBs. If adequate, no treatment is needed. If inadequate, give one dose of HBIG plus an HB vaccine booster dose.

Exposed person has never been vaccinated

Initiate the HB vaccine series.

Approach to Viral Exposure

Hepatitis C

Perform serologic testing for ALT and HCV antibody at time of exposure and again at 6 months. If anti-HCV is detected, confirmatory testing with recombinant immunoblot is indicated. HCV immunoglobulin is no longer recommended.

Table 1 Precautions to Prevent Transmission of HIV[1]

Universal Precautions

1. All health care workers should use appropriate barrier precautions routinely to prevent skin and mucous membrane exposure when contact with blood or other body fluids of any patient is anticipated. Gloves should be worn for touching blood and body fluids, mucous membranes, or nonintact skin of all patients; for handling items or surfaces soiled with blood or body fluids; and for performing venipuncture and other vascular-access procedures. Gloves should be changed after contact with each patient. During procedures that are likely to generate aerosolized droplets of blood or other body fluids, masks and protective eyewear or face shields should be worn to prevent exposure of mucous membranes of the mouth, nose, and eyes. Gowns or aprons should be worn during procedures that are likely to generate splashes of blood or other body fluids.

2. Hands and other skin surfaces should be washed immediately and thoroughly if contaminated with blood or other body fluids. Hands should be washed immediately after gloves are removed.

3. All health care workers should take precautions to prevent injuries caused by needles, scalpels, and other sharp instruments or devices during procedures; when cleaning used instruments; during disposal of used needles; and when handling sharp instruments after procedures. To prevent needle-stick injuries, needles should not be recapped, purposely bent or broken by hand, removed from disposable syringes, or otherwise manipulated by hand. After they are used, disposable syringes and needles, scalpel blades, and other sharp items should be placed in puncture-resistant containers for disposal; the puncture-resistant containers should be located as close as practical to the area of use. Large-bore reusable needles should be placed in a puncture-resistant container for transport to the reprocessing area.

4. Although saliva has not been implicated in HIV transmission, to minimize the need for emergency mouth-to-mouth resuscitation, mouthpieces, resuscitation bags, or other ventilation devices should be available for use in areas in which the need for resuscitation is predictable.

5. Health care workers who have exudative lesions or weeping dermatitis should refrain from all direct patient care and from handling patient care equipment until the condition resolves.

6. Pregnant health care workers are not known to be at greater risk for contracting HIV infection than health care workers who are not pregnant; however, if a health care worker acquires HIV infection during pregnancy, the infant is at risk for infection resulting from perinatal transmission. Because of this risk, pregnant health care workers should be especially familiar with and strictly adhere to precautions to minimize the risk of HIV transmission.

Additional Precautions for Invasive Procedures

1. All health care workers who participate in invasive procedures must use appropriate barrier precautions routinely to prevent skin and mucous membrane contact with blood and other body fluids of all patients. Gloves and surgical masks must be worn for all invasive procedures. Protective eyewear or face shields should be worn for procedures that commonly result in the generation of aerosolized droplets, splashing of blood or other body fluids, or the generation of bone chips. Gowns or aprons made of materials that provide an effective barrier should be worn during invasive procedures that are likely to result in the splashing of blood or other body fluids. All health care workers who perform or assist in vaginal or cesarean deliveries should wear gloves and gowns when handling the placenta or the infant until blood and amniotic fluid have been removed from the infant's skin and should wear gloves during postdelivery care of the umbilical cord.

2. If a glove is torn or a needle-stick or other injury occurs, the glove should be removed and a new glove used as promptly as patient safety permits; the needle or instrument involved in the incident should also be removed from the sterile field. In the event of an injury, postexposure evaluation should be sought as soon as possible.

& Health Administration (OSHA) directing that all health care workers potentially exposed to blood or other potentially infectious material either be offered hepatitis B vaccine free of charge, demonstrate immunity to hepatitis B, or formally decline vaccination.[13] That vaccination has been effective in decreasing the incidence of hepatitis B in health care workers is shown by the decrease in infection rates from 174/100,000 in 1982 to 17/100,000 in 1995.[14] Most series have not found the seroprevalence of HCV to be higher in health care worker groups at risk than in the general population.[14] That hepatitis B and hepatitis C are much more common than HIV in health care workers is a strong argument for using universal precautions in all patients.

One reason why hepatitis B is so much more transmissible than HIV is the greater number of virus particles in the blood of hepatitis B carriers. These persons have blood concentrations of 10^8 to 10^9 virus particles/ml, compared with 10^2 to 10^4/ml for persons with HIV infection and 10^6/ml for persons with HCV infection.

The extensive guidelines that have been established by the CDC for the care of patients with HBV infection[4,15-17] also apply to patients with HIV infection. Patients known to have hepatitis B, hepatitis C, or AIDS need not be put in a private room unless they are fecally incontinent or are shedding virus in body fluids. Health care workers should wear gloves and gowns when they have contact with or may have contact with a patient's blood, feces, or other body fluids. Needles used for drawing blood should be disposed of with special care: they must not be reused, recapped, or removed from the syringe. Hands must be washed before and after direct contact with the patient or with items that have been in contact with the patient's blood, feces, or body fluids.

Published recommendations also provide guidelines for health care workers who are not directly involved in patient care (e.g., housekeeping personnel, kitchen staff, and laundry workers).[1-7]

No additional precautions are necessary for these individuals because their risk of acquiring HIV, HCV, or HBV is so low; in fact, transmission to them has not been documented. However, staff should be educated about appropriate procedures. Workers should wear gloves when handling blood and body fluids of all patients and should wear masks in areas where blood may spatter (e.g., the dialysis unit or the obstetrics unit).

TRANSMISSION FROM HEALTH CARE WORKERS TO PATIENTS

To date, there have been only two reports of HIV transmission from infected health care workers to patients. In one report, DNA sequence analysis linked a Florida dentist with AIDS to HIV infection in six of his patients.[18] In the other, an orthopedic surgeon in France may have transmitted HIV to one of his patients in the course of an operation.[19] Despite extensive investigation, no break in infection control precautions was documented in either case, nor was any clear-cut means of transmission identified.

HBV transmission from health care workers to patients is known to occur. Nineteen case reports have documented physician-to-patient transmission.[20-32] Eighteen of the 19 physicians were surgeons; seven of the surgeons were gynecologists, three were cardiac surgeons, and one was an orthopedic surgeon. All of the physicians were positive for HBeAg. Three of the gynecologists made a practice of handling needle tips. Of the 135 patients studied, 121 had clinical hepatitis B, and 14 had only serologic evidence of infection. Forty-one of the 135 patients were accounted for by the only nonsurgeon, a family practitioner from rural Switzerland. There are many additional cases of HBV having been transmitted by dentists and oral surgeons. In addition, three patients' relatives, two members of a surgeon's family, and one laboratory technician became infected.

In five studies, patients of 16 health care workers (including two surgeons) who were positive for hepatitis B surface antigen (HBsAg) were prospectively followed for evidence of hepatitis.[33-37] A total of 784 patients were followed and were compared with 656 patients cared for by health care workers who were HBsAg negative. None of the patients acquired overt hepatitis or became seropositive for HBsAg. Eight (1.02%) of the 784 patients cared for by HBsAg-positive health care workers developed antibody to HBsAg (anti-HBs), but so did six (0.91%) of the 656 patients cared for by health care workers who were negative for HBsAg. These reports suggest that the likelihood of infected surgeons' or other health care workers' transmitting HIV or HBV to their patients is extremely low. Chronic carriers of HBsAg who are seronegative for HBeAg are much less likely to transmit HBV than persons who are HBeAg positive.

Before the cases of transmission of HIV from the dentist to six of his patients were reported, the CDC had not taken a position on whether HBV- or HIV-infected surgeons should be allowed to continue practicing medicine. After these cases were reported, the CDC held meetings of health care professionals and other interested parties and published its recommendations on July 12, 1991.[38] These recommendations called for physicians not to perform "exposure-prone invasive procedures" unless they sought counsel from an expert review panel and were advised under what circumstances, if any, they might be allowed to continue to perform these procedures. Physicians would have to notify prospective patients of their seropositivity. These recommendations were strongly resisted by the medical community because at that time, only one health care worker, the dentist, had been implicated in transmitting HIV to his patients, no mechanism of transmission had been elucidated, no other patients had HIV transmitted by a health care worker, and invasive procedures that were "exposure prone" (exposing the patient to blood of the health care worker) were impossible to define. After subsequent meetings, the CDC abandoned its attempts to define exposure-prone procedures but did not alter its recommendations. Rather, it left it up to the states to define exposure-prone procedures. Subsequently, the President's Commission on AIDS recommended that HIV-infected health care workers should not have to curtail their practices or inform their patients of their infection.

Transmission of HCV from health care workers to patients has been reported. In one such case, a cardiac surgeon transmitted HCV to at least five patients during valve replacement surgery.[39] In another, an anesthesiologist in Spain may have infected more than 217 patients by first injecting himself with narcotics, then giving the remainder of the drugs to his patients.[40] At present, no recommendations exist for restricting the professional activities of health care workers with HCV infection.

Management of Viral Exposure

HIV

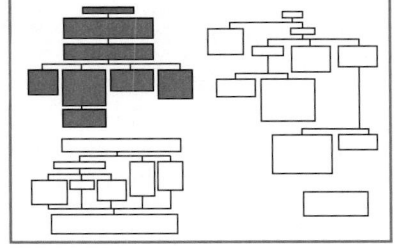

The CDC has issued recommendations for the management of potential exposure of health care workers to HIV.[1,4,41] If a health care worker is exposed by a needle stick or by a splash in the eye or mouth to any patient's blood or other body fluids, and the HIV serostatus of the patient is unknown, the patient should be informed of the incident and, if consent is obtained, tested for serologic evidence of HIV infection. If consent cannot be obtained, procedures for testing the patient should be followed in accordance with state and local laws. Testing of needles or other sharp instruments associated with exposure to HIV is not recommended, because it is unclear whether the test results would be reliable and how they should be interpreted.[41]

Health care workers exposed to HIV should be evaluated for susceptibility to blood-borne infection with baseline testing, including testing for HIV antibody. If the patient who is the source of exposure is seronegative and exhibits no clinical evidence of AIDS or symptoms of HIV infection, further follow-up of the health care worker is usually unnecessary.[41] If the source patient is seropositive or is seronegative but has engaged in high-risk behaviors, baseline and follow-up HIV-antibody testing of the health care worker at 6 weeks, 3 months, and 6 months after exposure should be considered.[41] Seroconversion usually occurs within 6 to 12 weeks of exposure; infrequently, it occurs considerably later. Three cases of delayed HIV seroconversion among health care workers have been reported.[42-44] In all three patients, an HIV antibody test yielded negative results at 6 months but positive results at some point during the following 1 to 7 months. In two cases, coinfection with HCV had occurred and took an unusually severe course. At present, it is unclear whether coinfection with these two viruses directly influences the timing or severity of either infection, but most experts recommend close monitoring for up to 1 year for health care workers exposed to both viruses in whom serologic evidence of HCV infection develops.

Treatment of the exposed health care worker should begin with careful washing of the exposure site with soap and water. Mucous membranes should be flushed with water. There is no evidence that either expressing fluid by squeezing the wound or applying antiseptics is beneficial, though antiseptics are not contraindicated. The use of caustic agents (e.g., bleach) is not recommended.

Any health care worker concerned about exposure to HIV should receive follow-up counseling regarding the risk of HIV transmission, postexposure testing, and medical evaluation, regardless of whether postexposure prophylaxis is given. HIV antibody testing should be performed at specified intervals for at least 6 months after the exposure (e.g., at 6 weeks, 3 months, and 6 months). The risk of HIV transmission is believed to depend on several factors: how much blood is involved in the exposure, whether the blood came from a source patient with terminal AIDS (thought to be attributable to the presence of large quantities of HIV), whether any host factors are present that might affect transmissibility (e.g., abnormal CD4 receptors for HIV), and whether the source patient carries any aggressive HIV viral mutants (e.g., syncytia-inducing strains). Factors indicating exposure to a large quantity of the source patient's blood (and thus a high risk of HIV transmission) include a device visibly contaminated with the patient's blood, a procedure that involved a needle placed directly in a vein or artery, and a deep injury.[45]

During the follow-up period, especially the first 6 to 12 weeks, exposed health care workers should follow the U.S. Public Health Service recommendations for preventing further transmission of HIV.[1-4] These recommendations include refraining from blood, semen, or organ donation and either abstaining from sexual intercourse or using measures to prevent HIV transmission during intercourse.[46]

The circumstances of the exposure should be recorded in the worker's confidential medical record and should include the following:

Table 2 Recommendations for Hepatitis B Prophylaxis after Percutaneous or Permucosal Exposure[15]

Hepatitis B Vaccination Status of Exposed Person	HBsAg Status of Source of Exposure		
	HBsAg-Positive	HBsAg-Negative	Untested or Unknown
Unvaccinated	Give single dose of HBIG Initiate HB vaccine series	Initiate HB vaccine series	Initiate HB vaccine series
Previously vaccinated Known responder	Test exposed person for anti-HBs If anti-HBs levels are adequate,* no treatment is needed; if they are inadequate, give an HB vaccine booster dose	No treatment is needed	No treatment is needed
Known nonresponder	*No response to three-dose vaccine series:* give two doses of HBIG or one dose of HBIG plus revaccination *No response to three-dose vaccine series plus revaccination:* give one dose of HBIG as soon as possible and a second dose 1 mo later	No treatment is needed	If source is at high risk for hepatitis B infection, consider proceeding as if source had been demonstrated to be HBsAg-positive
Response unknown	Test exposed person for anti-HBs If anti-HBs levels are adequate,* no treatment is needed; if they are inadequate, give one dose of·HBIG plus an HB vaccine booster dose	No treatment is needed	Test exposed person for anti-HBs If anti-HBs levels are adequate,* no treatment is needed; if they are inadequate, initiate revaccination

*An adequate anti-HBs level is ≥ 10 mIU/ml, which is approximately equivalent to 10 sample ratio units (SRU) on radioimmunoassay or a positive result on enzyme immunoassay.

1. The date and time of the exposure.
2. Details of the exposure, including (a) where and how the exposure occurred, (b) the type and amount of fluid or other material involved, and (c) the severity of the exposure (for a percutaneous exposure, this would include the depth of injury and whether fluid was injected; for a skin or mucous membrane exposure, it would include the extent and duration of contact and the condition of the skin—chapped, abraded, or intact).
3. A description of the source of the exposure, including (if known) whether the source material contained HIV or other blood-borne pathogens, whether the source was HIV positive, the stages of any diseases present, whether the patient had previously received antiretroviral therapy, and the viral load.
4. Details about counseling, postexposure management, and follow-up.[41]

The data currently available on primary HIV infection indicate that systemic infection does not occur immediately. There may be a brief window of opportunity during which postexposure antiretroviral therapy may modify viral replication. Findings from animal and human studies provide indirect evidence of the efficacy of antiretroviral drugs in postexposure prophylaxis. The majority of these studies included zidovudine (AZT); consequently, all postexposure prophylaxis regimens now in use include AZT. Combination treatment regimens using nucleoside reverse transcriptase inhibitors and protease inhibitors have proved effective. Accordingly, most experts now recommend dual therapy with two nucleosides (zidovudine and lamivudine) for low- to moderate-risk exposures. For high-risk exposures, most experts would add a protease inhibitor (usually either indinavir or nelfinavir) to the two nucleoside reverse transcriptase inhibitors. These medications should be started as soon as possible after the exposure (within hours rather than days) and should be continued for 4 weeks.

An important component of postexposure care is encouraging and facilitating compliance with the lengthy course of medication. Therefore, careful consideration must be given to the toxicity profiles of the antiretroviral agents chosen. All of these agents have been associated with side effects, include GI (e.g., nausea or diarrhea), hematologic, endocrine (e.g., diabetes), and urologic effects (e.g., nephrolithiasis with indinavir). According to some early data, 50% to 90% of health care workers receiving combination regimens for postexposure prophylaxis (e.g., zidovudine plus 3TC, with or without a protease inhibitor) reported one or more subjective side effects that were substantial enough to cause 24% to 36% of the workers to discontinue postexposure prophylaxis.[47-49]

Whether antiretroviral agents should be chosen for postexposure prophylaxis on the basis of the resistance patterns of the source patient's HIV remains unclear. Transmission of resistant strains has been reported[50-52]; however, in the perinatal clinical trial that studied vertical transmission of HIV, zidovudine prevented perinatal transmission despite genotypic resistance of HIV to zidovudine in the mother.[53] Further study of the significance of genotypic resistance is necessary before definitive recommendations can be made.

HEPATITIS B

Both passive immunization with hepatitis B immune globulin (HBIG) and active immunization with hepatitis B vaccine (HB vaccine) are currently available for prophylaxis against hepatitis B [*see* Table 2].

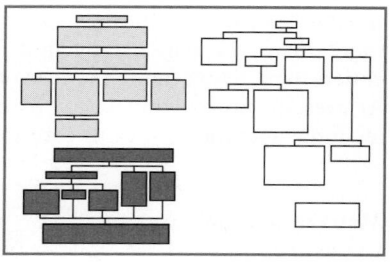

Passive Immunoprophylaxis

HBIG is prepared by Cohn ethanol fractionation from plasma selected to contain a high titer of anti-HBs; this process inactivates and eliminates HIV from the final product. In the United States, HBIG has an anti-HBs titer of at least 1:100,000 by radioimmunoassay.[54] HBIG provides temporary, passive protection. It is indicated after low-volume percutaneous or mucous membrane exposure to HBV; it is not effective for high-

Table 3 Candidates for Hepatitis B Vaccine[15]

Preexposure vaccination	Persons with occupational risk (e.g., health care workers, public safety workers)
	Clients and staffs of institutions for the developmentally disabled
	Hemodialysis patients
	Sexually active homosexual men
	Users of illicit injectable drugs
	Recipients of certain blood products (e.g., patients with clotting disorders who receive clotting factor concentrates)
	Household and sexual contacts of HBV carriers
	Adoptees from countries of high HBV endemicity
	Other contacts of HBV carriers (vaccination is usually not required unless there are special circumstances, such as biting or scratching, or medical conditions, such as severe skin disease, that facilitate transmission)
	Populations with high endemicity of HBV infection (e.g., Alaskan natives, Pacific islanders, and refugees from HBV-endemic areas)
	Inmates of long-term correctional facilities
	Sexually active heterosexual persons with multiple sexual partners
	International travelers who spend more than 6 mo in HBV-endemic areas and have close contact with the local population
	All infants born in the United States
	Adolescents 11 to 12 years old who have not previously been vaccinated
Postexposure vaccination	Perinatal exposure (infants born to HBsAg-positive mothers)
	Acute exposure to blood that contains (or might contain) HBsAg
	Sexual partners of persons with acute HBV infections
	Household contacts of persons with acute HBV infections (infants and older persons who have had identifiable blood exposure to the index patient)

volume exposure (e.g., blood transfusion). The recommended dose of HBIG for adults is 0.06 ml/kg I.M. Passive prophylaxis with HBIG should begin as soon as possible after exposure—ideally, within 24 hours.[54]

Active Immunoprophylaxis

Two types of HB vaccine are currently licensed in the United States, plasma-derived vaccine (Heptavax-B) and recombinant vaccine (Recombivax HB and Engerix-B). Heptavax-B contains alum-adsorbed 22 nm HBsAg particles purified from human plasma and processed to inactivate the infectivity of HBV and other viruses. Plasma-derived vaccine is no longer being produced in the United States, but similar vaccines are produced and used in China and other countries. In the United States, use of Heptavax-B is limited to persons allergic to yeast. Recombivax HB and Engerix-B are prepared by recombinant DNA technology in common baker's (or brewer's) yeast, *Saccharomyces cerevisiae*.

For primary vaccination, three I.M. injections (into the deltoid muscle in adults and children and into the anterolateral thigh muscle in infants and neonates) are given, with the second and third doses 1 and 6 months after the first dose.[54] The dose for Heptavax-B and Engerix-B is 20 μg (volume, 1.0 ml) for persons older than 11 years, and that for Recombivax HB is 10 μg (1.0 ml) for persons older than 19 years and 5 μg (0.5 ml) for persons 11 to 18 years of age. For immunologically impaired patients, including hemodialysis patients, the dose is 40 μg for all three vaccines. For postexposure prophylaxis with Engerix-B, a regimen of four doses given soon after exposure and 1, 2, and 12 months afterward has been approved.

HB vaccine is more than 90% effective at preventing infection or clinical hepatitis in susceptible persons. Protection is virtually complete in persons who develop adequate antibody. Routine testing for immunity after vaccination is not recommended, but testing should be considered for persons at occupational risk who require postexposure prophylaxis for needle-stick exposure.

Between 30% and 50% of persons who have been vaccinated will cease to have detectable antibody levels within 7 years, but protection against infection and clinical disease appears to persist.[54,55] The need for booster doses has not been established. Revaccination of individuals who do not respond to the primary series will produce adequate antibody in 15% to 25% of cases after one additional dose and in 30% to 50% after three additional doses.[56]

Although effective HB vaccines have been available since 1982, the incidence of hepatitis B in the United States continued to increase in the first decade of HB vaccine use. In 1991, the Advisory Committee for Immunization Practices (ACIP), citing the safety of the vaccine and the evidence of continuing spread of HBV, recommended universal vaccination of all infants born in the United States.[57]

Recommendations for Exposure to Blood That Contains (or May Contain) HBsAg

Acute exposure The U.S. Public Health Service has provided recommendations for hepatitis B prophylaxis after accidental percutaneous, mucous membrane, or ocular exposure to blood that contains (or may contain) HBsAg [*see Table 2*].[43] These recommendations are based on consideration of several factors: (1) whether the source of the blood is available, (2) the HBsAg status of the source, and (3) the hepatitis B vaccination and vaccination-response status of the exposed person. After exposure, a blood sample should be obtained from the person who was the source of the exposure and should be tested for HBsAg. The hepatitis B vaccination status and the anti-HBs response status (if known) of the exposed person should be reviewed. Because passive administration of antibody with HBIG does not inhibit the active antibody response to HB vaccine, the two can be given simultaneously.

Chronic exposure The U.S. Public Health Service recommends that persons who are at risk for exposure to HBV receive the HB vaccine series [*see Table 3*].[54] Health care workers who are at increased risk for acquiring hepatitis B include all physicians (especially surgeons), dentists, and laboratory and support personnel, such as nurses and technicians who work in the operating room or who have contact with infected patients, blood or blood products, or excreta. Because of their frequent exposure to blood and their high risk of hepatitis B, all surgeons should receive HB vaccine. As of 1994, however, only 50% of surgeons had been vaccinated, despite the proven efficacy and safety of the vaccine and surgeons' increased risk of exposure.[58] Hospital personnel who do not have frequent contact with blood or blood products (e.g., the janitorial, laundry, and kitchen staffs) need not be vaccinated.

Screening of personnel and patients for anti-HBs before vaccination is indicated only for individuals in high-risk groups; it has not been found to be cost-effective outside these groups.

HEPATITIS C

The only tests currently approved by the U.S. Food and Drug Administration for diagnosis of hepatitis C are those that measure antibody to HCV. These tests detect anti-HCV in at least 97% of infected patients, 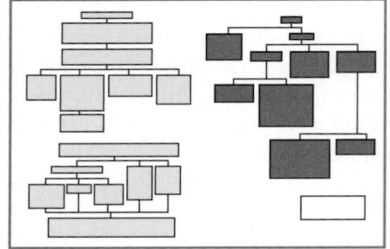 but they cannot distinguish between acute, chronic, and resolved infection.[59] The positive predictive value of enzyme immunoassay (EIA) for anti-HCV varies depending on the prevalence of the infection in the population. Therefore, supplemental testing of a specimen with a positive EIA result with a more specific assay (e.g., the recombinant immunoblot assay [RIBA]) may detect false positives, especially when asymptomatic persons are being tested. Qualitative polymerase chain reaction (PCR) testing for HCV RNA can also be used to identify HCV. This test can detect HCV at concentrations as low as 100 to 1,000 viral genome copies/ml, and it can detect HCV RNA in serum or plasma within 1 to 2 weeks after viral exposure and weeks before alanine aminotransferase (ALT) levels rise or anti-HCV appears.[59] Under optimal conditions, the reverse transcriptase PCR assay for HCV can identify 75% to 85% of persons who are anti-HCV–positive and more than 95% of persons with acute or chronic hepatitis C.[59] Quantitative assays for measuring HCV RNA are also available but are less sensitive and should not be used as primary tests for confirming or excluding the diagnosis of HCV infection or monitoring the end point of treatment.[59] The data currently available on prevention of HCV infection with immune globulin (IG) indicate that this approach is not effective as postexposure prophylaxis for HCV infection.[59] Interferon may have a role in the treatment of acute hepatitis C: several studies have shown that interferon may delay or prevent the onset of chronic hepatitis C in patients treated early in the course of acute HCV infection.[60-62]

RABIES

The CDC has made recommendations for the prevention of rabies in people bitten by animals [see Table 4].[63] Bite wounds should always be thoroughly scrubbed with soap and water. Postexposure anti- 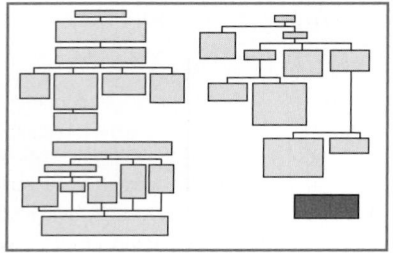 rabies treatment includes both rabies immune globulin (RIG) and human diploid cell (rabies) vaccine (HDCV). The decision to administer such treatment should be based on the following considerations.

Species and Availability of Biting Animal

In the United States, rabies is most commonly transmitted by skunks, raccoons, foxes, and bats. Livestock occasionally transmit the virus, but rodents and lagomorphs (i.e., rabbits and hares) are rarely infected.[64] In different parts of the country, different animals predominate in the transmission of the virus. The likelihood that domestic cats or dogs in the United States will be infected varies from region to region. The chances of rabies transmission by a domestic animal that has been properly immunized are minimal.

Whether an animal is available for observation after biting someone also influences the need for antirabies prophylaxis. In certain cases, an animal that bites a person must be killed and tissue from its brain checked for the presence of rabies by fluorescent antibody tests as soon as possible [see Table 4].

Type of Exposure

Infected animals transmit rabies primarily by biting, although licking may introduce the virus into open cuts in skin or mucous membranes. Transmission occasionally occurs as a result of aerosol exposure: the virus may be excreted in the urine and feces of infected bats, aerosolized during urination and defecation, and then inhaled, for example, by spelunkers exploring caves.

Table 4 Rabies Postexposure Prophylaxis[63]

	Animal Species	Condition of Animal at Time of Attack	Treatment of Exposed Person*
Domestic	Dog, cat	Healthy and available for 10 days of observation	None, unless animal develops rabies†
		Rabid or suspected rabid	RIG (20 IU/kg)‡ and HDCV§ (five 1.0 ml doses intramuscularly, on days 0, 3, 7, 14, and 28)
		Unknown (escaped)	Consult public health officials. If treatment is indicated, give RIG‡ and HDCV
Wild	Skunk, bat, fox, coyote, bobcat, raccoon, other carnivores	Regard as rabid unless proved negative by laboratory tests‖	RIG (20 IU/kg)‡ and HDCV (five 1.0 ml doses intramuscularly, on days 0, 3, 7, 14, and 28)
Other	Livestock, rodents, lagomorphs (rabbits and hares)	Consider individually. Local and state public health officials should be consulted on questions about the need for rabies prophylaxis. Bites of squirrels, hamsters, guinea pigs, chipmunks, gerbils, rats, mice, other rodents, and lagomorphs almost never call for antirabies prophylaxis.	

*All bites and wounds should immediately be thoroughly cleansed with soap and water. If antirabies treatment is indicated, both rabies immune globulin (RIG) and human diploid cell rabies vaccine (HDCV) should be given as soon as possible, regardless of the interval from exposure. (The administration of RIG is the more urgent procedure. If HDCV is not immediately available, start RIG and give HDCV as soon as it is obtained.) Local reactions to vaccines are common and do not contraindicate continuing treatment. Discontinue vaccine if fluorescent antibody tests of the animal are negative.

†During the usual holding period of 10 days, begin treatment with RIG and HDCV at first sign of rabies in a dog or cat that has bitten someone. The symptomatic animal should be killed immediately and tested.

‡The full dose should be infiltrated around the wounds; any remaining RIG should be given I.M. at a site distant from that of vaccine administration. If RIG is not available, use antirabies serum, equine (ARS). Do not use more than the recommended dosage of RIG or ARS.

§HDCV should be administered into the deltoid (not the gluteus) muscle in adults and adolescents. In children, it may be administered into the upper thigh.

‖The animal should be killed and tested as soon as possible. Holding for observation is not recommended.

Circumstances of the Bite

An unprovoked attack is more indicative of a rabid animal than is a provoked attack.

If the animal shows signs of rabies or the patient has been bitten by a wild animal that is not captured, the patient should be treated as soon as possible with both RIG and HDCV. The recommended dose of RIG for postexposure prophylaxis is 20 IU/kg.[63] If anatomically feasible, the entire dose of RIG should be infiltrated into the area around the wound.[65,66] Postexposure HDCV should be given I.M. in five 1.0 ml doses on days 0, 3, 7, 14, and 28.[63] Those with adequate preexposure immunization should receive two 1.0 ml doses of HDCV I.M. on days 0 and 3 but should receive no RIG. For adults, the vaccine should be administered in the deltoid area. For children, the anterolateral aspect of the thigh is also acceptable. The gluteal area should never be used for HDCV injections, because administration in this area results in lower neutralizing antibody titers.[63] HDCV must not be given in the same region as RIG.

The CDC recommends that preexposure immunization be considered for high-risk groups, such as animal handlers, certain laboratory workers and field personnel, and persons planning to stay for more than 1 month in areas where canine rabies is highly prevalent and access to appropriate medical care is limited. The recommended preexposure regimen is 0.1 ml of HDCV on days 0, 7, and 21 or 28.[67] Testing for adequate antibody response is not necessary for persons at low risk for exposure, but administration of booster doses every 2 to 3 years is recommended for those at high risk for exposure. Postexposure treatment for persons who have received preexposure immunization consists of 1 ml HDCV on days 0 and 3 only, without RIG.[68]

Although only a few cases of clinical rabies occur each year in the United States, approximately 30,000 persons a year are given postexposure prophylaxis. In 1992, 49 states, the District of Columbia, and Puerto Rico collectively reported 8,644 cases of animal rabies and one case of human rabies to the CDC.[69] The total expense associated with one rabid dog in California was $105,790, even though no human contracted rabies.[70] This amount represents the costs of human antirabies treatment, vaccination of other animals, and animal-containment programs.

Discussion

Size and Structure of Viruses

Viruses are among the smallest and simplest of microorganisms. Human viruses can be as small as 18 to 26 nm in diameter (parvoviruses) or as long as 300 nm (vaccinia virus), slightly longer than *Chlamydia* (a bacterium). Viruses do not have the complex enzyme systems required for synthesis of nucleic acid precursors, they lack ribosomes for protein synthesis, and they have no energy-generating mechanism. Consequently, they cannot replicate outside cells.

The core of a virus is made of either RNA or DNA, but never both. The nucleic acid can be either single stranded or double stranded. This nucleic acid core is surrounded by the capsid, which is a protein coat made up of capsomers, repetitive subunits consisting of one protein or at most a few. Because the viral nucleic acid must code for coat proteins, a limitation in the number of capsid proteins conserves viral nucleic acid. The capsid protects the nucleic acid from nucleases in the environment, serves as its vehicle of transmission from one host to another, and plays a role in the attachment of the virus to the receptor sites on susceptible cells. The complete nucleic acid–protein coat complex is termed the nucleocapsid. For many viruses, the nucleocapsid is the complete virus particle, the virion. Other viruses, such as herpesviruses, may acquire an envelope, an additional lipid-containing membrane coat around the nucleocapsid, by budding through a membrane of the host cell [*see Figure 1*]. Some viruses may also have an enzyme associated with their core that replicates the nucleic acid. Examples are the DNA polymerase of the HBV and the reverse transcriptase of retroviruses.

Classification of Viruses

Viruses, like other organisms, are classified into families, genera, and species, but most viral species do not have formal names and in practice are referred to by common names (e.g., cytomegalovirus, coxsackievirus, Norwalk virus, and varicella-zoster virus). Viruses can also be classified by chemical characteristics and by structural characteristics determined from electron microscopy (e.g., dimensions and site of assembly). Viruses are categorized into two broad groups depending on whether their nucleic acid is RNA or DNA. These two groups can be subdivided first according to whether the nucleic acid is single stranded or double stranded and then according to the presence or absence of an envelope. Single-stranded RNA viruses that replicate by means of a DNA step (i.e., retroviruses) are grouped separately from those that do not.

Identification of Viruses

Viruses can be identified by means of (1) serologic tests, (2) isolation of virus, (3) histologic examination, (4) detection of viral antigens, (5) detection of viral nucleic acid, and (6) electron microscopy. One or more of these techniques may be applicable to a given viral infection.

Specimens must be handled properly to maximize the likelihood of identifying the virus. If isolation of the virus is desired, blood and tissue samples should be taken promptly to the virology laboratory and inoculated onto the appropriate cell line. Samples obtained at night or on weekends can be placed in a balanced salt solution or tissue culture medium and kept in a refrigerator until taken to the laboratory. If microscopic identification of the virus is planned, specimens must be preserved appropriately. Routine preservation in formalin, for example, permits visualization of viral inclusions by routine staining and light microscopy. For identification of viral antigens by immunofluorescence techniques, the tissue specimen should be immediately frozen, preferably in liquid nitrogen. Specimens to be examined by electron microscopy must be placed in glutaraldehyde or another appropriate fixative.

SEROLOGIC TESTS

The antibody response to viral antigens can be detected in the serum of patients with viral infections. An IgM response usually indicates recent exposure to the virus, whereas the presence of IgG reflects past exposure.

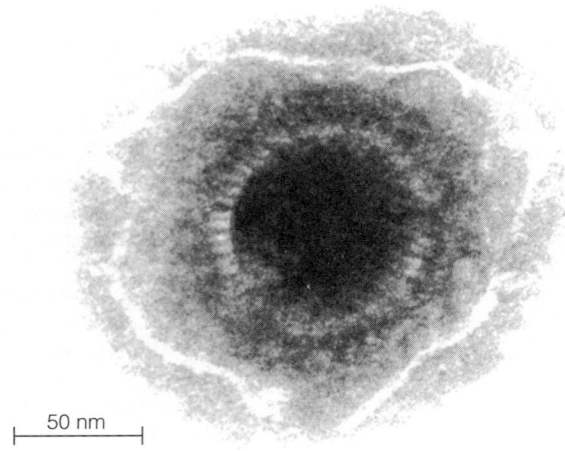

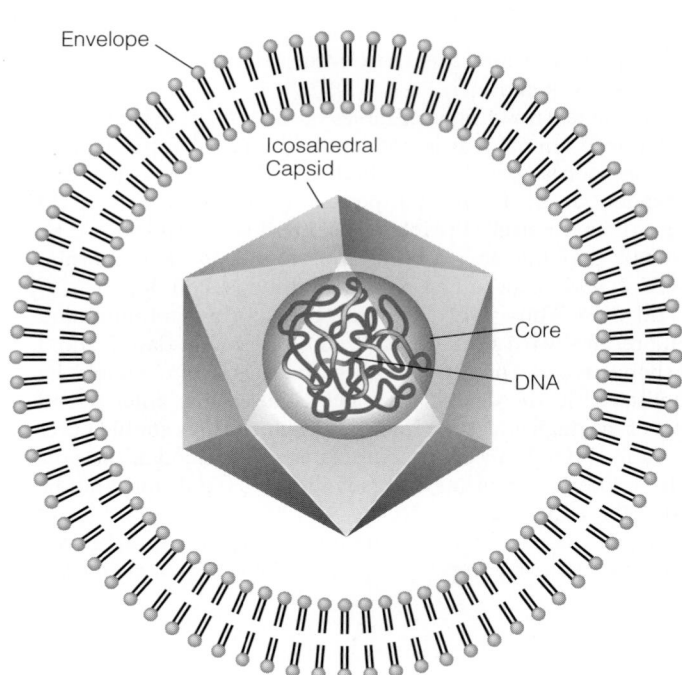

Figure 1 **The capsomers and the irregularly shaped surrounding envelope of a cytomegalovirus are highlighted by negative staining with uranyl acetate (above). A typical herpesvirus (right) consists of a central core containing DNA; an icosahedral capsid, a surrounding layer of protein made up of 162 individual capsomers; and an envelope, a membrane coat acquired when the virus buds from the nuclear membrane of the host cell.**

For most acute primary infections, serum obtained during late recovery or after recovery (convalescent serum) has an increased antibody titer, compared with serum obtained early in the course of the disease (acute serum). Most tests are performed on an initial serum dilution of 1:2 or 1:10 and on serial twofold dilutions thereafter. A fourfold increase in titer (indicated by reactivity of a two-tube dilution) usually represents a significant increase in antibody response and is considered to constitute seroconversion. An immunocompromised host may occasionally fail to mount an antibody response.

Some viruses are so common that patients may already have antibody titers when the disease is first suspected. Herpesviruses are ubiquitous and are present in many healthy people in latent form. At the onset of herpesvirus infections, patients may already have the corresponding antibody. Nevertheless, their antibody titer will almost always increase significantly after recovery.

A variety of serologic tests are available in the clinical laboratory: complement fixation, radioimmunoassay, enzyme-linked immunosorbent assay (ELISA), immunofluorescence, immune precipitation, immune blotting, latex agglutination, virus neutralization, indirect hemagglutination, immune adherence hemagglutination, and hemagglutination inhibition. None of these serologic tests is appropriate for identification of all viruses.

ISOLATION OF VIRUS

The isolation of virus requires appropriate specimen collection and inoculation into animals or onto appropriate cell lines. Blood sent for virus isolation should be unclotted because some viruses, such as herpesviruses, are found primarily in lymphocytes. If cell-associated viruses are suspected, lymphocytes should be inoculated directly onto target cells. Several types of cells are available for growing viruses, and no single cell line is appropriate for all of them. Therefore, it is helpful to the laboratory to know which virus the clinician suspects.

Viruses that grow in cell monolayers in tissue culture have cytopathic effects that can be recognized under the microscope (e.g., rounding, transformation, or death) [*see Figure 2*]. Some viruses, such as rubella, produce no direct cytopathic effects but can be

detected because they inhibit the cytopathic effects of a second test virus. This phenomenon is called viral interference. Other viruses (e.g., myxoviruses) cause changes in the cell membrane so that red blood cells adhere to the cell surface (hemadsorption). The identity of isolated viruses can be confirmed by use of specific antisera that are known to inhibit viral growth.

Tissue suspected of containing an encephalitis or other neurotropic virus can be minced and the extract injected intracerebrally into an infant mouse. If the mouse dies and bacteria cannot be cultured from the brain, the injected material presumably contained such a virus. If antiserum of known specificity neutralizes the virus, the specificity of the antiserum indicates the specific identity of the virus. The criterion for neutralization is that inoculation of neutralized virus will not kill the mouse.

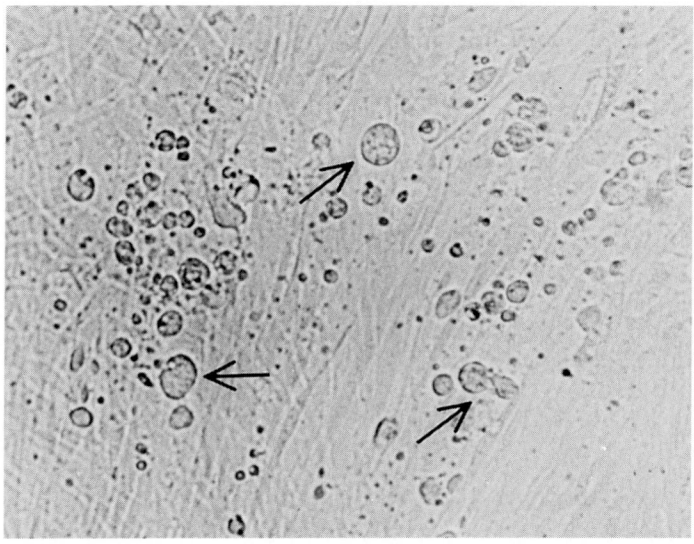

Figure 2 **Cells infected with cytomegalovirus become large and round (arrows). Note the uniform appearance of adjacent uninfected cells.**

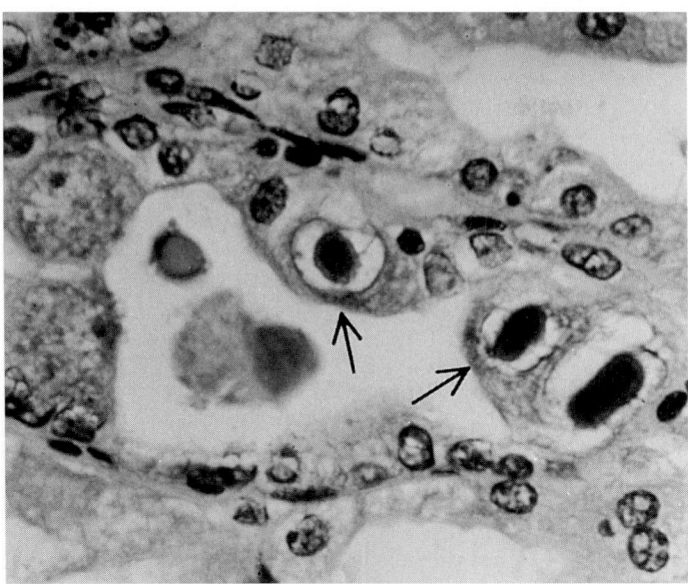

Figure 3 **Kidney biopsy shows cytomegalovirus-infected tubular epithelial cells (arrows). In such cells, a dark intranuclear inclusion is surrounded by a clear halo. Inclusions usually indicate sites of previous or current viral replication.**

HISTOLOGIC EXAMINATION

Histologic examination of biopsy and autopsy tissues may demonstrate changes that are typical of certain viruses. Members of the herpesvirus group can be characterized by intranuclear inclusions surrounded by a clear halo [*see Figure 3*]. RNA viruses usually produce inclusions in the cytoplasm; for instance, dark-staining intracytoplasmic inclusions in the brain tissue of animals or patients are diagnostic of rabies infection and are called Negri bodies. Inclusion bodies are either masses of closely packed virus particles or remnants of prior virus replication.

DETECTION OF VIRAL ANTIGENS

Viral antigens can be detected in tissues by techniques employing their corresponding antibodies. If virus is present, these antigens may be visible microscopically under ultraviolet light either by direct immunofluorescence (i.e., in tissue sections stained with fluorescein-labeled antiviral antibody) or by indirect immunofluorescence (i.e., in tissue sections exposed first to antiviral antibody and then to fluorescein-labeled anti–γ-globulin antibody). Fluorescence microscopy requires specimens that are fresh frozen (preferably in liquid nitrogen). Immunofluorescence staining of cells in tissue culture can detect viral antigens before cytopathic effects are evident. Viral antigens in formalin-fixed tissue can be identified by immunohistochemical microscopy (e.g., using peroxidase-labeled antibodies).

DETECTION OF VIRAL NUCLEIC ACID

Viral nucleic acids can be detected in body fluids and tissues at virus concentrations too low to be detected by other means. The PCR permits amplification of even a small number of copies of viral nucleic acid. In theory, even a single copy of a specific DNA can be detected by PCR. Before PCR is performed, DNA can be synthesized from viral RNA by means of reverse transcriptase. The PCR product can be detected by gel electrophoresis and compared with known viral DNA. This test is currently being used to diagnose CMV infection and is more sensitive than current serologic testing for HCV. Nucleic acid hybridization can detect viral nucleic acid in tissue specimens. Epstein-Barr virus genomes can be detected in this way in EBV-related cancers and lymphoproliferative disorders.

ELECTRON MICROSCOPY

Although seldom used routinely, electron microscopy allows rapid identification (in a matter of hours) of viruses in body fluids, tissues, and tissue extracts. Identification of viruses in body fluids and tissue extracts by this method is easier if the samples are first concentrated by ultracentrifugation, evaporation, or ultrafiltration. HBV has been observed in specimens from hepatitis patients only after ultracentrifugation.

Epidemiology of Viral Infections of Interest to Surgeons

Viral infections are spread to humans via several patterns of transmission: (1) direct transmission from humans with symptomatic infection (e.g., HBV, HCV herpesviruses, and HIV), (2) transmission from asymptomatic human carriers (e.g., HBV, HCV, HIV, and varicella-zoster virus), (3) transmission from arthropods (e.g., encephalitis and dengue viruses), and (4) transmission from other animals (e.g., rabies virus).

Viral infections are common in immunosuppressed patients in general and especially in recipients of organ transplants, who must take immunosuppressive drugs to prevent rejection. The overwhelming majority of these infections are caused by members of the herpesvirus family (e.g., CMV, herpes simplex viruses, varicella-zoster virus, and EBV); infections with HBV and with papovaviruses (e.g., human papillomavirus, which causes warts, and BK virus) are also frequent.

Because surgical patients are frequently given transfusions of blood or blood products and because hospital staff often incur accidental needle-stick injury, viruses that can be transmitted by these routes are of prime interest to surgeons and their patients. Examples of such viruses are HBV, hepatitis D, HCV, HIV, HTLV-I, and the herpesviruses, including EBV and CMV. These viruses can also be transmitted by organ transplantation either from the cells of the organ itself (e.g., HBV in liver cells or CMV in kidney cells) or from blood that has not been completely removed from the organ. Changes in donor acceptance and screening policies over time have increased the safety of the blood supply and should continue to do so in the future [*see Table 5*].[71]

HIV

Two serotypes of HIV, HIV-1 and HIV-2, have been identified. Both can cause AIDS. HIV-1 accounts for virtually all cases of AIDS in the United States and equatorial Africa. HIV-2 is found almost exclusively in West Africa; only a few cases of HIV-2 infection have occurred in the United States.

Because AIDS patients are immunodepressed, they are susceptible to opportunistic infections and neoplasms, especially non-Hodgkin lymphoma, *Pneumocystis carinii* pneumonia, and Kaposi sarcoma. AIDS is most prevalent in the United States among male homosexuals, abusers of I.V. drugs, and hemophiliacs. Since the implementation of testing for blood-borne HIV and the near-elimination of HIV from blood products, the incidence of HIV infection in the hemophiliac population has diminished markedly; however, in recent years, the incidence in the heterosexual population has been increasing rapidly.

HIV can be transmitted by transfusion of whole blood, packed red cells, plasma, factor VIII concentrates, factor IX concentrates, and platelets. The likelihood that a person will become infected with HIV after receiving a single-donor blood product that tests

Table 5 Changes in Donor Acceptance and Screening Policies Instituted to Reduce the Risk of Transmitting Infectious Diseases[71]

Policy	Implementation Date
Screening for HBsAg	July 1972
Voluntary exclusion of persons at high risk for AIDS	March 1983
Redefinition of high-risk behavior to include men who have had sex with more than one man since 1979	December 1984
Testing for antibody to HIV-1	Spring 1985
Redefinition of high-risk behavior to include any man who has had sex with another man since 1977	September 1985
Implementation of a mechanism to allow donors to indicate confidentially that their donations should not be used for transfusion	October 1986
Testing for alanine aminotransferase (ALT, formerly SGPT)	Winter 1986–1987
Testing for anti-HBc	Spring 1987
Testing for antibody to HTLV-1	January 1990
Testing for antibody to HCV	May 1990
Testing for antibody to HIV-2	April 1992
Testing for HIV-1 antigen	March 1996

positive for HIV approaches 100%.[72-73] Before the advent of serologic testing for HIV in 1985, 0.04% of 1,200,000 blood donations in the United States were estimated to be HIV positive.[74] AIDS has developed in more than 8,500 recipients of blood transfusions, blood components, or transplanted organs or tissue.

Federal regulations now require that all prospective blood and plasma donors be screened for antibody to HIV by ELISA. Because this test yields a low rate of false positive results, assay by the more sensitive Western blot electrophoresis is always used to confirm positive ELISA results. Routine testing of blood donors has greatly reduced HIV transmission via blood transfusions, but infection can still occur if the donor has been infected with HIV but has not yet developed antibody.[75] The risk of HIV transmission via transfusion of screened blood that is negative for HIV is estimated to be one in 200,000 to one in 2,000,000 per unit transfused in the United States.[76] Antibody to HIV usually develops within 4 weeks to 6 months of HIV infection.[77] From the time of infection until the appearance of antibody, infected individuals will test negative by ELISA or Western blot, and their blood might still be used for transfusion.

HIV and AIDS can also be transmitted by organ transplantation.[78] So far, only a small number of patients have been found to be infected in this way, but more will undoubtedly be reported. These patients received transplants before HIV testing of potential donors became possible. All prospective organ and tissue donors now should be tested for HIV infection and other blood-borne viral infections.

HIV infection is also a potential problem in health care workers, who are exposed to a large and growing population of AIDS patients. In the United States, an estimated 1.0 to 1.5 million people are infected with HIV but as yet have no symptoms. HIV transmission from blood, tissue, or other body fluids can occur in the health care setting as a result of percutaneous injury (e.g., from needles or other sharp objects), contamination of mucous membranes or nonintact skin (e.g., skin that is chapped, abraded, or affected by dermatitis), prolonged contact with intact skin, or contamination involving an extensive area.[79] HIV infection may be contracted through a variety of sources including blood, semen, vaginal secretions, visibly bloody fluids, and a number of other fluids for which the precise risk of transmission is undetermined (e.g., cerebrospinal, synovial, pleural, peritoneal, pericardial, and amniotic fluid). Infection may also be contracted from concentrated HIV used in research settings.[79] The results of multiple prospective studies quantifying transmission risk associated with a discrete occupational HIV exposure indicate that the average risk of HIV transmission associated with needle punctures or similar percutaneous injuries is approximately 0.3%. The estimated risk of transmission from mucocutaneous exposure to HIV-contaminated material is 0.03%. As of December 1999, the CDC had received reports of 56 U.S. health care workers in whom documented HIV seroconversion was temporally related to occupational HIV exposure. Of these 56, 48 had percutaneous exposures, five mucocutaneous exposures, two both percutaneous and mucous membrane exposures, and one an unknown route of exposure.[80] Another 138 possible cases of occupational HIV transmission—six involving surgeons—have been reported in persons with no risk factors for HIV transmission other than workplace exposure; however, seroconversion after a specific exposure was not documented. There may be other health care workers who also have acquired HIV infection from needle-stick or mucous membrane exposure but have not been reported, either because they and their patients have not been tested or because they have other risk factors for HIV infection

The concentration of virus in the blood or serum of antigen-positive individuals is several orders of magnitude less for HIV than for HBV. The number of needle-stick exposures to HIV that have actually led to a positive test result for HIV has been extremely small, whereas hepatitis B occurs in as many as 40% of health care workers exposed to the virus by needle-stick injury. Despite this relatively low infectiousness, AIDS is much more feared than hepatitis B because AIDS is often fatal. Although hepatitis B is usually not fatal and is often of short duration, several health care workers die of hospital-acquired hepatitis B and hepatitis C each year.

Hepatitis

Several viruses can cause hepatitis. Hepatitis A virus (HAV) and HBV cause what were formerly known as infectious hepatitis and serum hepatitis, respectively. HCV is the major cause of parenterally transmitted non-A, non-B hepatitis. Hepatitis E virus is a common cause of epidemic non-A, non-B hepatitis, which is chiefly found in developing countries in Africa and Asia. Hepatitis D virus (HDV, formerly called the delta agent) is defective or incomplete and is pathogenic only in the presence of HBV. The hepatitis viruses are the most common infectious agents to which hospital personnel may be exposed. Herpesviruses can also cause serious and sometimes fatal hepatitis, especially in severely immunocompromised patients, such as recipients of organ or bone marrow transplants and patients receiving intensive chemotherapy for cancer.

HEPATITIS A

HAV is a small (27 nm), single-stranded RNA virus belonging to the enterovirus subgroup of picornaviruses. Its almost exclusive transmission by the fecal-oral route is enhanced by poor personal hygiene, poor sanitary conditions, and crowding. Transmission can be contained by careful hand washing and the isolation of excretions. Unlike other types of viral hepatitis, hepatitis A is rarely transmitted by blood, blood products, or needle sticks and is rarely transmitted among hemodialysis patients, health care workers, and I.V. drug abusers. The infrequent parenteral transmission of HAV is attributed in part to its lack of an asymptomatic carrier state. Hepatitis A can be transmitted percutaneously only during a brief period of viremia before the onset of symptoms and jaundice. The chance that an infected person will donate blood during this short period is small; also, patients are usually outside the hospital during this period.

HEPATITIS B

HBV is a member of the Hepadnaviridae family of DNA viruses. It is most prevalent in the Far East, the Middle East, Africa, and parts of South America, where as many as 15% of the general population are chronic carriers. Worldwide, the most common mode of transmission is from mother to child during the perinatal period. In the United States, however, sexual or parenteral transmission has been implicated in most infections. The high-risk groups for chronic HBV infection in the United States include I.V. drug users, men who have sex with men, other individuals with multiple sexual partners, household contacts and sexual partners of HBV carriers, health care workers, patients on long-term hemodialysis, and organ transplant recipients.[81]

Clinical Course

The clinical course of hepatitis B is extremely variable: infection ranges from the completely asymptomatic to the rapidly fatal. The incubation period averages 75 days but can last from 40 to 180 days. Exposure to HBV has five potential outcomes: (1) no infection occurs; (2) acute hepatitis develops, followed by clearance of infection; (3) acute fulminant infection develops, leading to hepatic necrosis and death; (4) acute hepatitis develops without clearance of infection, and a chronic carrier state ensues; and (5) no acute illness develops, but a chronic carrier state ensues.

Approximately 55% of adults infected with HBV have no symptoms despite serologic documentation of infection (see below), which explains why blood donors who seem to be in good health are capable of transmitting the virus. Other individuals infected with HBV may have such mild symptoms (e.g., slight malaise, fatigability, and loss of appetite) that they do not seek medical attention.

Approximately 45% of people infected with HBV experience typical acute, icteric hepatitis, which is characterized by fatigue, anorexia, nausea, vomiting, and hepatomegaly. In approximately 1% of adults infected with HBV, acute fulminant hepatitis develops. This condition is characterized by progressive hepatocellular destruction, encephalopathy, and deepening coma. Fulminant hepatitis causes death in approximately 80% of affected adults and 30% of affected children.

In approximately 5% to 10% of hepatitis B cases, the infection becomes chronic. Patients with chronic hepatitis may be asymptomatic or may have clinical and histologic evidence of the disease, as well as persistently elevated levels of serum aminotransferases [see Figure 4]. With time, many patients pass to an asymptomatic carrier state, and serum aminotransferase levels fall. The duration of the asymptomatic carrier state appears to be indefinite. Chronic HBV infection can result in hepatocellular carcinoma, which is especially common in China, Southeast Asia, and sub-Saharan Africa.

Because most patients remain asymptomatic until the development of end-stage liver disease, there are no specific clinical findings that are indicative of chronic HBV infection. There are, however, several clinical syndromes linked to HBV infection that may provide a clue to the presence of chronic HBV infection. These syndromes include polyarteritis nodosa, membranous or membranoproliferative glomerulonephritis, leukocytoclastic vasculitis, erythema nodosum, arthritis, and serum sickness.

Antigens

HBV has a diameter of 42 nm and contains circular, double-stranded DNA. The protein coat on its outer surface is termed hepatitis B surface antigen. HBsAg is made in quantities greatly exceeding the amount required to coat the nucleic acid. The excess surface antigen appears in the serum as spheres 22 nm in diameter or tubules of the same diameter and of varying length. These spheres and tubules contain no nucleic acid and hence are not infectious. They may persist in the serum for prolonged periods, even for life, and in great quantities, up to 10^{12} to 10^{14} surface antigen particles (500 μg protein) per milliliter.[82]

The hepatitis B virus also has a nucleocapsid core, the outside of which contains the hepatitis B core antigen (HBcAg). HBcAg is not detected in hepatitis B during acute infection, because its antigenic determinants are hidden by the outer surface antigen of the intact virion.

Inside the hepatitis B nucleocapsid is a DNA-dependent DNA polymerase and the hepatitis B e antigen, which is thought to be either an internal component or a degradation product of the core antigen. HBeAg is found only in the serum of individuals whose serum also contains HBsAg, and it appears in the serum of virtually all patients early in the course of HBV infection. The presence of HBeAg in serum is indicative of the presence of large numbers of circulating intact virions: serum containing HBeAg is estimated to be one million times more infectious than serum containing HBsAg but not HBeAg.

Serology

HBsAg can be detected in the serum within a few weeks of viral exposure [see Figure 5]. It usually persists throughout the symptomatic period and does not disappear until after recovery. Anti-HBs appears shortly after the disappearance of HBsAg [see Table 6]. During this window period, neither HBsAg nor anti-HBs is detectable [see Table 7]. Anti-HBs persists for years and is associated with immunity to reinfection. HBV can be differentiated into eight serotypes on the basis of determinants of the surface antigen.

Hepatitis B core antigen (HBcAg) is not found free in the serum, but antibody to HBcAg (anti-HBc) becomes detectable at an early stage in the course of acute infections, 1 to 2 weeks after the appearance of HBsAg. Titers of anti-HBc fall after the disappearance of HBsAg but persist for life. In patients with chronic hepatitis B, HBsAg remains detectable indefinitely, and titers of anti-HBc remain high. Years after infection, titers of anti-HBs may have fallen to undetectable levels, and anti-HBc may be the only marker of previous infection. HBeAg is detectable immediately after the appearance of HBsAg. Antibody to HBeAg (anti-HBe) appears just after HBeAg becomes undetectable (usually before the disappearance of HBsAg) and persists for 1 to 2 years [see Figure 5].

HEPATITIS D

HDV is a defective, 35 to 37 nm RNA virus that can infect only persons who are also infected with HBV, because it uses HBsAg for its structural protein shell. HDV is found worldwide and is especially prevalent in the Amazon basin, central Africa, southern Italy, and the Middle East.[83] HDV infection is less common in the United States and Western Europe, where it is generally associat-

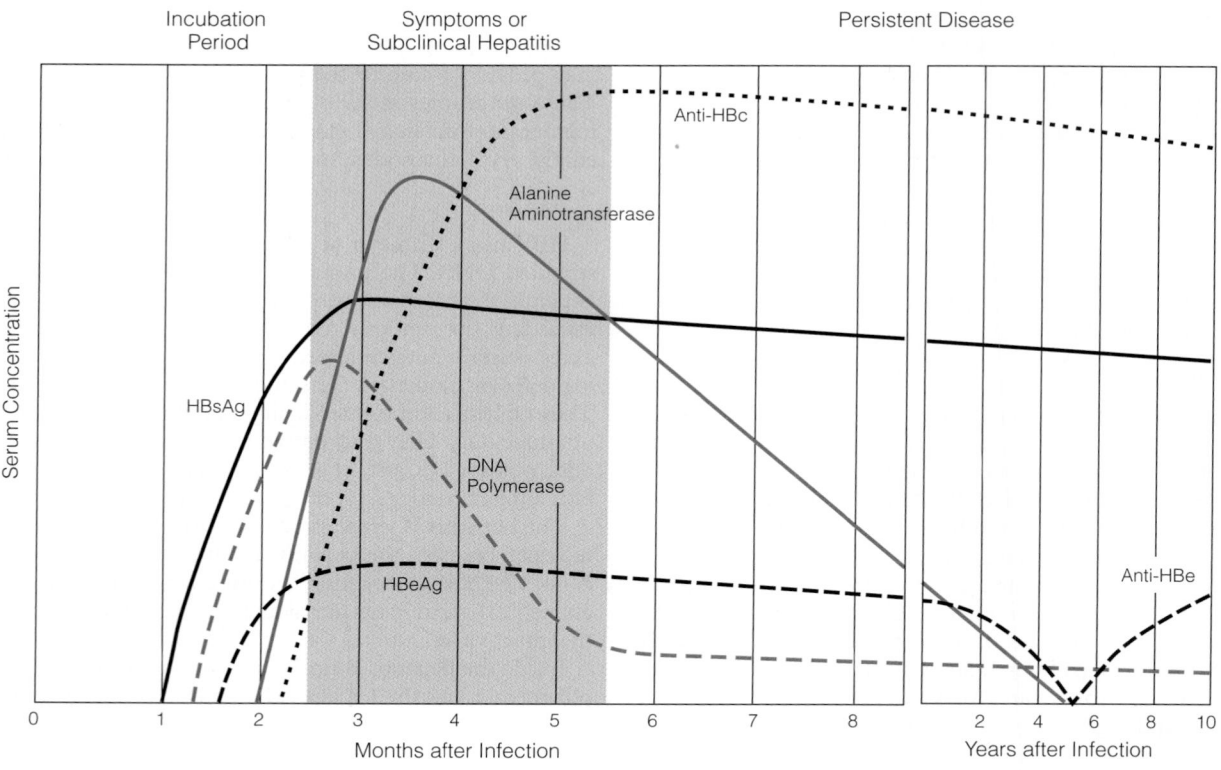

Figure 4   Schematic shows virologic, clinical, and serologic events of a hepatitis B infection that becomes persistent.

ed with parenteral blood exposure, typically in the setting of I.V. drug abuse or multiple transfusions.

Clinically, hepatitis D is found only in association with acute or chronic hepatitis B, and it cannot last longer than hepatitis B does. Depending on the state of the HBV infection, HDV infection appears either as a coinfection or a superinfection. Coinfection occurs when acute HDV infection and acute HBV infection are present simultaneously; superinfection occurs when acute HDV infection is superimposed on chronic HBV infection. Coinfection with HDV is associated with fulminant hepatitis and a mortality of 2% to 20%.[84] Fewer than 5% of cases of coinfection progress to chronic hepatitis D. In contrast, superinfection with HDV results in chronic HDV hepatitis, often with cirrhosis, in more than 70% of cases. The clinical and biochemical features of HDV infection resemble those of HBV infection alone. Chronic active hepatitis B progresses faster when hepatitis D is also present. Chronic HDV infection is more likely to result in severe morbidity and mortality than chronic HBV or HCV infection alone.

Diagnosis of acute HDV infection may be difficult: HDAg appears in the circulation only briefly and often goes undetected. Antibody to HDAg (anti-HD) of the IgM class subsequently appears in serum in low titers. Because no anti-HD IgG response occurs, no serologic marker of previous HDV infection may remain after recovery. Chronic HDV infection is easier to diagnose: high titers of anti-HD in the serum indicate ongoing HDV infection, and HDV antigen is detectable in the liver by means of immunohistochemical techniques. Moreover, IgM anti-HD remains detectable in serum.[83]

NON-A, NON-B HEPATITIS: HEPATITIS E AND HEPATITIS C

Non-A, non-B hepatitis is divided into two varieties, an epidemic form (hepatitis E) and a parenterally transmitted form (hepatitis C).[85] Hepatitis E is an acute, self-limited disease whose clinical features are similar to those of other types of hepatitis. Hepatitis E virus (HEV) is prevalent in the developing world, where it is spread by the fecal-oral route and has been associated with large outbreaks as well as sporadic cases. Outbreaks have been linked to contaminated water supplies. No cases of HEV infection acquired in the United States have been reported to date, but HEV acquisition has been reported in international travelers.

Hepatitis C is the most common cause of nonalcoholic liver disease in the United States. HCV is an RNA virus of the flavivirus family. It can be transmitted through parenteral exposure (usually in the setting of I.V. drug abuse), sexual contact, or the sharing of a household with an HCV-infected person; however, some persons with HCV infection have none of these risk factors, and there may be other means of transmission that have yet to be elucidated. Before the advent of antibody testing, HCV infection accounted for the majority (75% to 95%) of cases of posttransfusion hepatitis.[83] Since the spring of 1990, when a serologic test for HCV became available, all transfused blood has been screened for HCV, and the incidence of transfusion-associated hepatitis C has fallen precipitously. At present, however, I.V. drug use still accounts for a large proportion (60%) of HCV transmission in the United States.[59]

The presence of anti-HCV IgG appears not to be protective: blood donors with anti-HCV antibody can transmit hepatitis.[62] Surveys of HCV seropositivity indicate that 0.2% to 0.6% of volunteer blood donors carry anti-HCV IgG,[83] and the prevalence may be much higher among high-risk populations (e.g., residents of large inner-city communities). The prevalence of anti-HCV IgG is high among I.V. drug users, hemodialysis patients, and hemophiliacs.

Clinical Manifestations

The incubation period of hepatitis C averages 7 to 8 weeks in length but may be as short as 2 weeks or as long as 15. The clini-

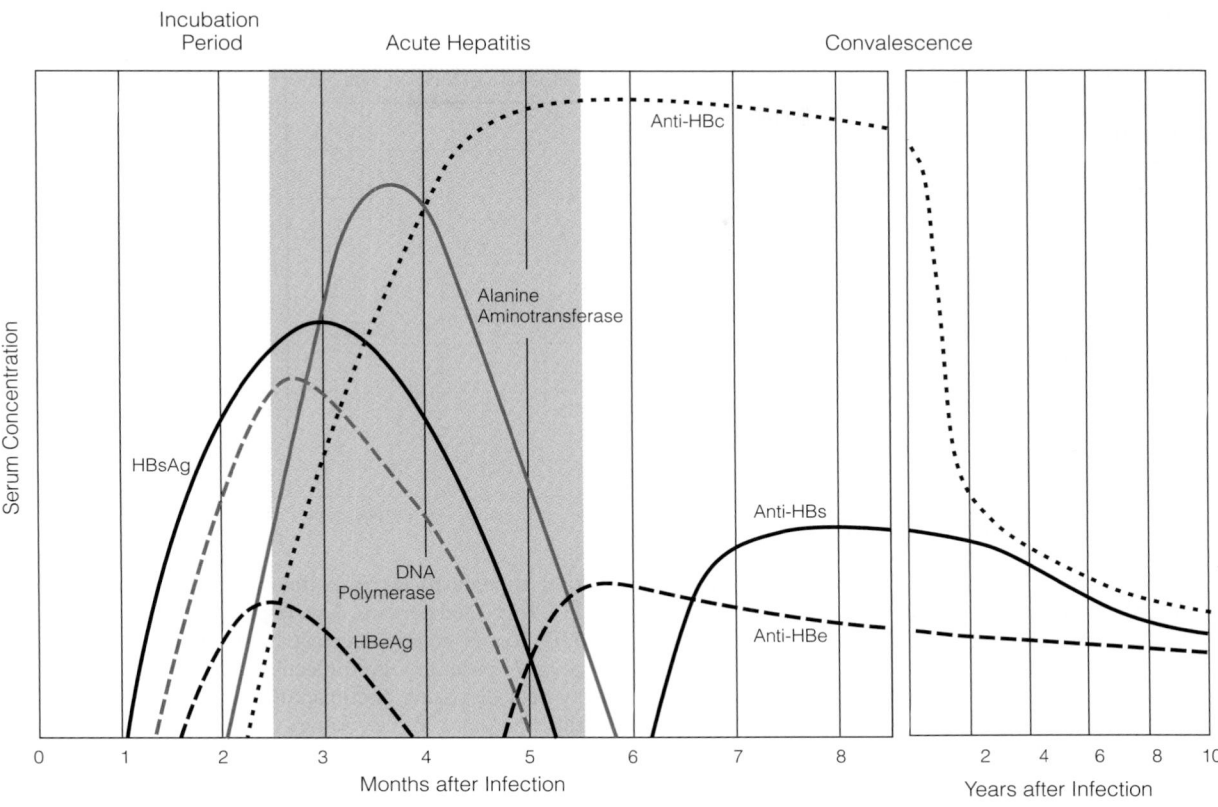

Incubation Period   **Acute Hepatitis**   **Convalescence**

Figure 5 **Schematic shows virologic, clinical, and serologic events during acute hepatitis B infection.**

cal manifestations and biochemical alterations associated with acute hepatitis C are similar to but milder than those associated with hepatitis B. Serum aminotransferase levels can fluctuate widely; the peak levels are lower than those seen in hepatitis B (10 to 20 times normal as opposed to 20 to 50 times normal). Only about 25% of cases of acute HCV infection are icteric, and the mortality for acute infection is about 1%. Most patients have no acute illness suggestive of HCV infection. Antibody is not always present early in infection, and there are no clinically available assays for detecting IgM antibody to HCV. Thanks to improvements in the immunodetection of HCV, however, the interval before anti-HCV can be detected has decreased from the 6 to 12 months required with the first-generation tests to 8 to 12 weeks with the second-generation assays.[83]

The most striking feature of HCV infection is its tendency to become chronic in as many as 50% to 75% of cases. One study found that even among the 1% to 10% of individuals with HCV whose bloodstreams had been cleared of HCV according to RT-PCR assay, as many as 90% still had HCV in the liver.[86] It is estimated that in the United States, nearly four million people are seropositive for HCV, and more than 30% of liver transplantations are performed to treat end-stage liver disease related to chronic HCV infection. The presence of anti-HCV IgG does not distinguish acute from chronic hepatitis. Within 10 years, cirrhosis may develop in as many as 20% to 25% of patients with active hepatitis[87]; accordingly, these patients must be followed up carefully.

Chronic active hepatitis is characterized by elevated serum aminotransferase levels; however, other test results remain normal, and the patient is usually asymptomatic until end-stage liver disease develops. Liver biopsy shows inflammation around the portal triads. Recombinant interferons have been used to treat

chronic HCV infection, with mixed results: frequently, there is little response to treatment, or viremia returns after treatment. The combination of interferon with ribavirin has shown promise, however. Interferon treatment is generally reserved for patients who have chronic HCV infection and show evidence of active necroinflammatory liver disease with persistent ALT elevations.

HEPATITIS IN HOSPITAL PERSONNEL

Patients with hepatitis can infect hospital personnel with the

Table 6   Serologic Markers of Hepatitis B Infection

HBsAg	Present in acute and chronic infection Indicator that person is infectious
Anti-HBs	Appears 2 to 16 wk after HBsAg disappears from the serum Persists for years Confers immunity
HBcAg	Not present in the serum Found in the hepatocyte
Anti-HBc	Appears in serum with or shortly after HBsAg Persists for years May be only indicator of hepatitis B infection
HBeAg	Appears in the early acute phase Indicates serum is highly infectious Persistence beyond 10 wk suggests progression to chronic carrier state
Anti-HBe	Good prognosis for resolution of infection

virus via needle-stick injuries and other forms of accidental exposure. Conversely, physicians who are chronic carriers of HBV or HCV can infect their patients. According to a nationwide seroepidemiologic survey reported in 1978, approximately 19% of physicians have anti-HBs, compared with 3.5% of healthy volunteer blood donors [see Table 8].[88] Anti-HBs was found in 28% of surgeons, the highest prevalence in any medical specialty. For physicians, the likelihood of being positive for anti-HBs correlates with age and the number of years in practice. The risk of hepatitis is greatest among medical staff members in renal dialysis units, oncology units, and the clinical laboratory. Since 1978, when these data were reported, HBV vaccination has made it impossible to perform similar, more recent studies, because vaccination rather than previous infection would be responsible for the presence of antibodies.

Physicians and other staff members who care for hemodialysis patients with end-stage renal disease are at greater risk for acquiring HBV because of the high prevalence of hepatitis in such patients [see Table 9].[89,90] Transmission of HBV decreases in dialysis centers when close attention is paid to hygienic technique. Isolation of patients who are carriers of HBsAg also reduces the incidence of HBV in hemodialysis patients and staff.[91]

From 0.28% to 9.3% of health care workers have antibody to HCV.[92-94] In one study from Connecticut, five (12.5%) of 40 surgeons had antibody to HCV.[92] In another study, from New York City, eight (1.75%) of 456 dentists had anti-HCV antibody.[93] The highest prevalence among dentists was found to occur in oral surgeons (9.3%). As use of vaccines for HBV becomes more widespread [see Management of Viral Exposure, Hepatitis B, above], HCV may come to predominate over HBV as the cause of the rare cases of hepatitis transmitted from hospital personnel to patients.

EPIDEMIOLOGY OF POSTTRANSFUSION HEPATITIS

Both HBV and HCV can be transmitted by percutaneous and other routes.[89] Rare cases of hepatitis have been attributed to the infusion of immune globulin, although its preparation by ethanol fractionation normally destroys hepatitis virus (as well as HIV). Albumin is pasteurized by heating at 60° C for 10 hours, which destroys hepatitis virus.

Because of the current criteria for acceptable blood donors, elimination of payment for blood donation, and serologic testing for HBV and HCV, the risk of contracting hepatitis B from a blood transfusion is now much lower than it once was. In the United States, it is now rare for either HBV or HCV to be transmitted via blood transfusion. According to the latest estimates available, the risk of HCV transmission via this route is approximately 1/103,000 (95% CI, 28,000 to 288,000), and that of HBV transmission is 1/63,000 (95% CI, 31,000 to 147,000).[95]

HDV can also be passed by transfusion. In a study of 262 patients who had posttransfusion hepatitis and whose serum was positive for HBsAg, anti-HD was found in nine patients.[96] HDV can be detected in 24% of HBsAg-positive drug abusers and in approximately 50% of HBsAg-positive hemophiliacs.

LONG-TERM EFFECTS OF CHRONIC HEPATITIS

Chronic hepatitis can lead to problems requiring surgical intervention. It can cause cirrhosis, which in turn can cause portal hypertension and bleeding varices that necessitate portal systemic shunting. In addition, HBV and HCV predispose to hepatocellular carcinoma, the most prevalent visceral cancer in the world. The condition is especially prevalent in China, Southeast Asia, and sub-Saharan Africa. It is estimated that 25% of chronically infected persons die of cirrhosis or hepatocellular carcinoma.[97] HBV coinfec-

Table 7 Serologic Patterns of Hepatitis B Infection

HBsAg	Anti-HBs	Anti-HBe	Interpretation
+	–	–	Early acute hepatitis B
+	–	+	Late acute hepatitis B
–	–	+	Window period between disappearance of HBsAg and appearance of anti-HBs *or* Chronic carrier with low HBsAg level *or* Infection in the remote past
–	+	+	Past hepatitis B infection
–	+	–	Infection in the remote past *or* Immunization with hepatitis B vaccine *or* HBIG received within the past 1 to 2 mo

+ = detectable   – = not detectable

tion appears to increase the risk of hepatocellular carcinoma in HCV-infected persons. A widespread program of vaccination against HBV could greatly decrease the incidence of hepatocellular carcinoma. Epidemiology, molecular biology, and comparative pathology provide strong circumstantial evidence that hepatitis B is a significant factor in the etiology of hepatocellular carcinoma. The risk of primary hepatocellular carcinoma is more than 250 times greater in carriers of HBV than in noncarriers. HBV markers can be found in 80% to 90% of patients with hepatocellular carcinoma. Perhaps the best epidemiologic data indicating that hepatitis B precedes hepatocellular carcinoma were obtained in Taiwan from male civil servants between 40 and 60 years of age.[98] Approximately 3,500 HBsAg carriers were matched by age and place of birth (either mainland China or Taiwan) to 3,000 HBsAg-negative men, who served as control subjects. An additional group of 16,000 HBsAg-negative men between 40 and 60 years of age served as unmatched control subjects. After subjects were followed for 2 to 4 years, 50 cases of hepatocellular carcinoma were found, all but one of which occurred in chronic HBsAg carriers.

HCV is also associated with chronic infection in a high percentage (approximately 50%) of cases. In many countries, chronic HBV infection remains the leading factor in the development of hepatocellular carcinoma, whereas in Japan, Korea, and southern Europe, 50% to 75% of cases of hepatocellular carcinoma are

Table 8 Frequency of Antibody to Hepatitis B Surface Antigen (Anti-HBs) by Physician Specialty[88]

Specialty	Number of Patients Tested	Positive Results (%)
Surgery	176	50 (28)
Pathology	37	10 (27)
Pediatrics	63	13 (21)
Internal medicine	259	46 (18)
Anesthesiology	59	10 (17)
Obstetrics-gynecology	63	10 (16)
Family practice	341	54 (16)
Nonpatient care	25	1 (4)
All others combined	169	26 (15)
Total	1,192	220 (18.5)

Table 9 Prevalence of Hepatitis B Virus (HBV)
Serologic Markers in Various Populations[90]

Population		Prevalence of Serologic Markers of HBV Infection (%)	
		HBsAg	All Markers
High risk	Immigrants or refugees from areas where HBV is highly endemic	13	70–85
	Clients in institutions for the mentally retarded	10–20	35–80
	Users of illicit parenteral drugs	7	60–80
	Homosexually active men	6	35–80
	Household contacts of HBV carriers	3–6	30–60
	Hemodialysis patients	3–10	20–80
Intermediate risk	Health care workers with frequent blood contact	1–2	15–30
	Prisoners (male)	1–8	10–80
	Staffs of institutions for the mentally retarded	1	10–25
Low risk	Health care workers with no or infrequent blood contact	0.3	3–10
	Healthy adults (first-time volunteer blood donors)	0.3	3–5

associated with chronic HCV infection.[99] In Japan, mortality from hepatocellular carcinoma increased approximately twofold in the 1980s, a change that may be attributable to a higher incidence of HCV-associated liver cancer.[100]

Herpesviruses

CYTOMEGALOVIRUS

CMV is a member of the B herpesvirus family and is the largest virus known to infect humans. In some U.S. cities, the seroprevalence of CMV is 60% to 70%. Like other members of the herpesvirus family, CMV is capable of remaining within its host in a latent state, probably by down-regulating cell surface markers (e.g., HLA-1) and thus avoiding immune destruction. Latent CMV has been found in circulating mononuclear cells, polymorphonuclear cells, vascular endothelium, renal epithelial tissue, and pulmonary secretions. The virus may become reactivated in the setting of immunodeficiency, such as may arise with HIV infection, transplantation, or significant stress from operations or injuries. In nonimmunocompromised patients, CMV typically causes a self-limited mononucleosis-like syndrome characterized by fever and mild hepatic transaminase abnormalities. In immunocompromised patients, however, CMV infection can be much more severe and even potentially life threatening, causing myelosuppression, pneumonitis, colitis, and retinopathy.

Posttransfusion Cytomegalovirus Infection (Posttransfusion or Postperfusion Syndrome)

The transmission of CMV by extracorporeal perfusion is responsible for the occasional development of a syndrome similar to mononucleosis in patients who have undergone open-heart operation. The syndrome characteristically appears 3 to 5 weeks after operation; its features are splenomegaly, fever, atypical lymphocytosis, and, occasionally, hepatomegaly, erythematous rash, and eosinophilia.[89] CMV can be isolated from the blood of virtually all patients with the typical posttransfusion syndrome and from the urine of half of these patients.[89] The condition is nonfatal and self-limited, but it may result in prolonged hospitalization and a long, expensive search for the source of fever. Although uncommon in adults 30 years of age and older, the syndrome can occur in as many as 10% of susceptible children and adults younger than 30 years.

This syndrome can also occur in patients who receive transfusions but who do not undergo open-heart operation. Occasional cases that develop postoperatively in patients who did not receive transfusions are thought to be the result of reactivation of latent infection. EBV can sometimes cause the syndrome.

The incidence of posttransfusion CMV infection is related to the kind of blood or blood product transfused. CMV is highly cell associated and is transmitted with leukocytes, which may be present in transfusions of packed red blood cells, platelets, or white blood cells; transmission from transfusion of fresh frozen plasma or cryoprecipitate has not been documented.[14] Therefore, efforts to decrease the number of white blood cells in the transfused blood would be expected to decrease the rate of transfusion-associated CMV infection. Approximately 50% of patients who receive whole blood seroconvert to CMV, whereas only 10% of those who receive washed packed red blood cells seroconvert. The risk of seroconversion to CMV is between 12% and 100% when whole blood, either fresh or stored, is transfused.[101] In one study, transfusion of frozen deglycerolized red blood cells resulted in seroconversion in only 3% of patients,[89] whereas in another, seroconversion occurred in 58% of 36 leukemic patients transfused with lymphocytes.[102]

The risk of posttransfusion CMV infection is also related to the volume of blood received. In one study, 7% of patients receiving a single unit of whole blood seroconverted, whereas anti-CMV antibody titers rose in 21% of patients receiving more than one unit.[103] The risk of infection per unit of blood transfused is estimated to range between 2.7% and 12%.[104]

Preexisting antibody to CMV does not protect transfusion recipients against reinfection. After transfusion of whole blood, titers of antibody to CMV will increase in 10% of recipients (an indication of reinfection) and in 19% of patients who did not have antibody to CMV before transfusion (an indication of infection). Whereas a seronegative recipient of CMV-positive blood has a 21% chance of seroconversion, the risk of seroconversion from the receipt of one unit of CMV-negative blood is only 2%.[89] However, the sensitivity of the serologic test for CMV is such that even when blood that tests seronegative is used, there is still a residual 0% to 6% risk of CMV transmission.[105]

Because so many patients receive blood transfusions during operation, it is understandable that evidence of posttransfusion CMV infection has been found in many patients postoperatively (e.g., after gynecologic surgery, cholecystectomy, appendectomy, lumbosacral fusion, splenectomy, and transplantation). It has also been found in surgical patients who are victims of trauma or burns.

However, it is surprising that infection with CMV, a ubiquitous virus, does not occur more frequently after transfusion. Between 30% and 54% of the adult population in the United States have antibody to CMV, an indication of previous infection.[89] Because infection with the virus is probably lifelong, a significant proportion of blood donors harbor the virus. The prevalence of antibody to CMV is 25% in units of blood from donors between 18 and 23 years of age and increases to 89% in blood from donors older than 60 years. The overall prevalence of seropositive blood donors is between 30% and 70%.

Cytomegalovirus in Transplant Recipients

CMV infection occurs not only in patients who have received blood transfusions but also in those who have suffered trauma, those receiving immunosuppressive therapy, and those with neoplastic disease. The groups at highest risk for CMV infection are probably recipients of organ transplants and of bone marrow transplants.[106-108] Numerous studies have documented the high incidence of CMV infection after organ transplantation: the rates range from 26% to 100%.[89,109,110] Primary CMV infection occurs in patients who do not have antibody to CMV before receiving transplants. Infections are considered to be reactivated if they occur in patients who did have antibody to CMV before receiving transplants. Rates of infection in patients receiving cardiac or bone marrow transplants are similar to those in patients receiving kidney transplants.

The high incidence of CMV infections after transplantation was recognized in the early days of such procedures. At autopsy of patients who died after renal transplantation, the intranuclear inclusions typical of CMV were found in tissue from the lungs, the parotid glands, the lymph nodes, the liver, the pancreas, the parathyroid, and the brain. CMV has been cultured repeatedly from the urine of transplant recipients, and the frequency of seroconversion among them has been high.

Likely sources of the virus are blood, because fresh blood can transmit CMV, and the organ transplant itself, because CMV can grow in renal tubular epithelial cells and can be transmitted as a latent virus. In several studies, recipients of kidney transplants had a much higher incidence of CMV infection when the donors had antibody to CMV than when the donors did not. In one study, 57% of recipients of kidneys from seropositive donors acquired CMV infection after transplantation, compared with 8% of recipients of kidneys from seronegative donors.[111] Even patients who have antibody to CMV can acquire new CMV infections as a result of transfusion or transplantation because there is more than one antigenic variety of the virus. Also, CMV that is latent in many patients who have antibody before transplantation may be reactivated after transplantation by host versus graft reactions, corticosteroids, or other immunosuppressive drugs. Hospital personnel, family members, and the environment play very small roles in transmission of CMV to transplant recipients.

Several systematic studies have demonstrated that CMV causes clinical illness in renal transplant recipients. In four studies, clinical illness developed in 83% of 76 patients with primary infection, compared with 44% of 268 patients with reactivation of a previous infection.[89,109,110]

Recipients of renal transplants in whom CMV causes clinical illness most commonly present with fever. Fever occurs in 95% of patients with CMV infection and may be prolonged. Patients with CMV infection also frequently present with anorexia, arthralgias, and leukopenia. Other clinical features of the disease are diffuse pulmonary infiltrates, pancreatitis, transplant malfunction, and systemic bacterial and fungal superinfections. Invasion of the GI tract by CMV may cause gastritis and ulcers in both the duodenum and the colon, which in turn may lead to hemorrhage and perforation. Biopsies demonstrate CMV inclusions at the base of the ulcers. The virus appears to invade the vascular endothelium, and bleeding is possibly a result of vascular occlusion and ischemic necrosis of the overlying tissue.

Lethal CMV disease is characterized by the presence of most of the features listed above. Liver dysfunction is found in 100% of patients with lethal disease but in only 50% to 75% of patients with mild or moderate infection, and CMV viremia occurs in 46% to 48% of patients with severe CMV infection but in only 26% to 28% of patients with mild to moderate infection. Leukopenia and the presence of atypical leukocytes also correlate with the severity of the disease. CMV infection after renal transplantation is also associated with pneumonia, hepatitis, encephalitis, and retinitis.

Whether or not CMV infection causes or leads to graft rejection is uncertain. Both the highest incidence of CMV infection (> 80%)[89,109,110] and the highest incidence of graft rejection occur within the first 3 months after transplantation. In several studies, young patients and recipients of second kidney transplants were at higher risk for graft loss if they had CMV than if they did not.[89,109,110] In most studies, however, it is extremely difficult to demonstrate a relation between CMV infection and graft rejection.

Of the multiple factors affecting the risk of CMV infection in transplant recipients, the most important are (1) the familial relation and HLA matching between the kidney donor and the recipient and (2) the CMV serology of both the donor and the recipient. The presence of antibody in transplant recipients before transplantation seems to offer a small amount of protection against fever caused by CMV but does not protect against more serious consequences of the infection, such as leukopenia, graft failure, and death.

CMV infection is also a major problem in liver, heart, and bone marrow transplant recipients.[106,108] In liver transplant recipients, CMV is a cause of hepatitis and liver dysfunction that can be confused with rejection or other causes of liver malfunction,[106] and it can lead to lethal infection. CMV pneumonitis in bone marrow transplant recipients is the most common life-threatening infectious complication after transplantation. The severity of infection in bone marrow transplant recipients may be attributable to the higher incidence of host versus graft disease in patients with CMV pneumonitis (82%) than in those without CMV pneumonitis (27%).[112]

Prevention and Treatment of Cytomegalovirus Infection

Several methods have been proposed to reduce the incidence of CMV infection after transfusion or transplantation. One method is to eliminate as many white blood cells as possible from transfused blood because CMV is almost certainly transmitted solely through these cells. From 90% to 100% of viable leukocytes in blood have been removed from frozen deglycerolized erythrocytes. In one study, transfusion of 24 hemodialyzed patients with leukocyte-free red blood cells from frozen deglycerolized blood prevented subsequent CMV infection.[104]

Another approach is to transfuse blood only from CMV-negative donors. Because the majority of posttransfusion CMV infections are asymptomatic, however, the increased cost of performing serologic tests on all donated units might be difficult to justify.

Storage of blood to reduce infectiousness of CMV is another approach, but storage from 48 to 72 hours does not significantly reduce transmission of CMV infection. Irradiating the blood to render the CMV noninfectious is unacceptable because it causes cell transformation in vitro. Furthermore, in one study, administration of leukocytes previously exposed to 1,500 cGy (1,500 rads) of gamma radiation resulted in an increased incidence of CMV infection among recipients of these cells.[102]

Because the incidence of CMV infection is higher in patients who receive kidney transplants from seropositive donors, some centers do not transplant kidneys from seropositive donors into seronegative recipients. However, no published reports indicate that this practice leads to a significant alteration in the outcome of renal transplantation with respect to graft rejection. Moreover, excluding kidneys from seropositive donors makes it more difficult to find kidneys for seronegative recipients.

Many attempts have been made to develop a CMV vaccine for administration before viral exposure by multiple passages of the virus in tissue culture. Two such vaccines have been used in clinical trials, one prepared from the AD169 strain and the other from the Towne 125 strain of the virus. Immunization with these vaccines can elicit both serum antibody and cell-mediated immunity. In one trial, the vaccine prepared from the Towne 125 strain lowered the incidence of clinical disease but not of infection, and the disease tended to be less severe in vaccinated patients than in control subjects who received placebo.[113]

Human IG has been administered after transfusion or transplantation in attempts to prevent associated CMV infection. In one study, it reduced life-threatening infection to a less severe form in most patients, but in other studies, not surprisingly, it provided no consistent benefit.[114-117] In patients who are already seropositive, the virus is latent inside their cells, where it is probably not accessible to serum antibody. Patients with primary infections may not benefit from antibody treatment, because herpesviruses seem to transfer from cell to cell without ever existing free in serum. Even CMV hyperimmune globulin has no clear benefit in patients with clinical CMV infection.[118] It may, however, help control severe infections, such as those seen in bone marrow transplant recipients.

Several antiviral agents have been used in attempts to reduce the incidence or lessen the effect of CMV infection. Among these agents are interferon, transfer factor, immune globulin, and nucleoside derivatives, such as cytarabine, vidarabine, and acyclovir (see below). Immune globulins, acyclovir, and ganciclovir are effective at preventing CMV infection in transplant recipients.[109,110,114,119,120] Ganciclovir and foscarnet are active against CMV in vitro. Ganciclovir is currently being used to treat CMV and is the most effective agent in organ transplant recipients (see below).[109,110,119-121]

EPSTEIN-BARR VIRUS

EBV is the herpesvirus responsible for infectious mononucleosis. It can be found in B cells in peripheral blood of infected patients and in tumor cells of patients with Burkitt lymphoma and nasopharyngeal carcinoma. It remains in a latent form in an infected host for years, probably for life. Most posttransfusion EBV infections are asymptomatic. Seroconversion to EBV will develop in approximately 8% of recipients transfused with between two and 14 units of blood. In as many as 5% of patients with preexisting antibody to EBV, significant elevations of antibody titers may develop, beginning 2 weeks after transfusion. These elevations indicate either reinfection or reactivation of a latent infection.[89] Because EBV is associated with cells and does not exist free in serum to any great extent, antibody to EBV in either donors or recipients is unlikely to provide substantial protection against infection resulting from blood transfusions or organ transplants. Among transfused patients who do not have preexisting antibody to EBV, the prevalence of EBV infection can reach 33% to 46%. In these patients, the absence of preexisting antibody presumably rules out reactivation of latent EBV infection as the source of infection.

EBV occurs worldwide. In the United States, nearly all adults and as many as 65% of persons of all ages have antibody to EBV. Infection is thought to occur in infancy, and as many as 17% of infants have antibody to EBV. By 5 years of age, 72% of children have antibody to EBV, and the prevalence in adults is similar.[122] Thus, the majority of blood donors in the United States have been previously infected with EBV and probably have latent virus in their leukocytes. Although it is clear that EBV can be transmitted by blood when the transfusion occurs within 3 days of donation, it is not known whether blood stored for longer periods can transmit the virus. Because EBV is predominantly intracellular, plasma and its derivatives do not transmit the virus.

The diagnosis of EBV infection is made serologically. Tests both for IgM antibody to capsid antigens and for IgG antibody to the early antigens of EBV or tests of serial samples for IgG antibody to capsid antigens must be used. The heterophil antibody test (the Paul-Bunnell test) and a rapid slide test that is equivalent (the monospot test) are also used in most clinical studies to screen for EBV infection before more specific diagnostic tests are performed.

In cases of posttransfusion infection, IgG antibody to EBV can be detected at least 10 days before the onset of symptoms, and EBV can be cultured from circulating lymphocytes 11 days before the onset of symptoms. In patients with acute infection, EBV is found in approximately three of every 10^4 peripheral blood lymphocytes.[123] In contrast, all recovered persons with antibodies to EBV are thought to have the virus in one of every 10^7 circulating lymphocytes.

EBV is strongly implicated in the etiology of a posttransplantation lymphoproliferative disorder (PTLD).[89,124,125] EBV has been isolated from the tissues of most cases of PTLD, but not all.[126,127] Non–EBV-related cases of PTLD typically occur later after transplantation, and their etiology has not been elucidated.

PTLD comprises three general clinical presentations: (1) a mononucleosis-like syndrome involving the tonsils and the peripheral lymph nodes, (2) a diffuse polymorphous B-cell infiltration in many visceral organs, and (3) localized extranodal tumors in the GI tract, the neck, the thorax, or other parts of the body. Patients whose disease is limited to a single organ or to lymph nodes often respond to a reduction in immunosuppression or antiviral therapy; however, once the infection becomes widespread, the disease progresses rapidly and is fatal in more than 75% of cases.[128] In solid organ transplant recipients, PTLD may be limited to the allograft. There is some evidence to suggest that PTLD may have organ-specific features that promote lymphoproliferation: allograft involvement has been reported in 17% of renal transplant recipients, 8.6% of liver transplant recipients, and as many as 60% to 80% of lung or intestinal transplant recipients.[128]

The persons at highest risk for PTLD are EBV-seronegative persons receiving EBV-positive organs or bone marrow. Most infections occur within the first 4 months after transplantation.[129] Several specific risk factors for the development of PTLD have been identified: a seropositive graft in a seronegative recipient, certain types of organ allografts (with intestinal transplants carrying the highest risk), any type of immunosuppression that blunts cellular immunity to EBV (with risk increasing as immunosuppression becomes more pronounced), and the presence of other infections (CMV in particular).

The optimal treatment of lymphoproliferative disorders remains unclear. Some early EBV-associated lymphoproliferative disorders in solid organ transplant recipients have regressed completely after reduction of immunosuppression.[130,131] Early PTLD may respond to antiviral therapy with acyclovir or ganciclovir, which may prevent infection of resting B cells, but such therapy is less likely to be effective in the face of high concentrations of latently infected circulating or tissue-invasive B cells. Some investigators also report resolution of PTLD after treatment with interferon alfa.[132,133]

Transmission of EBV can occur simultaneously with transmission of CMV or hepatitis virus. Although hepatitis accompanies EBV infections in sporadic cases, EBV alone has not been documented as a cause of posttransfusion hepatitis.

HERPES SIMPLEX VIRUS

Infection or reactivation of infection with herpes simplex virus type 1 (HSV-1) follows renal transplantation in 50% to 75% of patients, most often within 30 days after transplantation. Reactivation of infection is more common than primary infection: only 14% of patients who are seronegative before transplantation become infected, but infection is reactivated in 64% of patients who were already seropositive before transplantation.

Most cases of HSV-1 infection after transplantation are clinically inapparent and are indicated only by a significant rise in titer of antibody to the virus. The most prevalent clinical manifestation is herpes labialis, that is, fever blisters affecting not only the lips but also the mucous membranes of the oral cavity and the skin of the head and neck. Although these lesions are painful and may make eating, drinking, and taking oral medications difficult, they are usually self-limited and heal without treatment or reduction of immunosuppression. However, HSV-1 infection can take a much more malignant course, disseminating to cause pneumonitis, fulminant hepatitis, upper GI hemorrhage, encephalitis, aseptic meningitis, and death.

VARICELLA-ZOSTER VIRUS

Varicella-zoster virus (VZV), another herpesvirus, is the etiologic agent of herpes zoster and chicken pox. This virus resides in the dorsal root ganglia of adults who had primary varicella infection in childhood. Herpes zoster is more common in organ transplant recipients, in patients with cancer (especially those who have leukemia or lymphomas), in burn patients, and in patients receiving immunosuppressive drugs. Serologic evidence of VZV infection occurs in 8% to 16% of renal transplant recipients. The lesions of herpes zoster become evident 12 to 511 days after organ transplantation.

In children or adults who have not already had chicken pox and occasionally even in children who have, VZV can cause disseminated chicken pox in many organs, which may be fatal.

AGENTS EFFECTIVE AGAINST HERPESVIRUSES

Because the essential synthetic activities of viruses depend on the metabolic machinery of their host, it has been difficult to devise specific antiviral agents that interfere with viral replication but are not harmful to host cells.[134,135] Many antiviral agents are too toxic to be used clinically. In contrast, antibacterial agents that are both toxic to bacteria and safe for human cells are easier to design because the structure and metabolic machinery of bacteria are distinct from those of host cells.

Although intracellular processes unique to viral replication have

been identified and specifically targeted for chemotherapeutic attack, very few agents have been effective against human viruses. Among these is amantadine, which is used for both prophylaxis and treatment of influenza A. Agents that were found to be effective for prophylaxis against smallpox, such as methisazone, now have no use, because the disease has been eradicated.

There are few effective chemotherapeutic agents for hepatitis or most of the other major viral diseases that concern surgeons, but several agents have been used for the treatment of herpesvirus infections, especially in immunosuppressed patients [*see Table 10*]. These agents, derivatives of purines and pyrimidines, interfere with viral nucleic acid synthesis.

Acyclovir and Valacyclovir

Acyclovir (acycloguanosine) is a nucleoside derivative that is used to treat herpesvirus infections, especially herpes simplex and varicella-zoster infections in immunocompromised hosts. Valacyclovir is the L-valyl ester prodrug of acyclovir. In cases of mucocutaneous herpes simplex and herpes zoster, acyclovir can shorten the period of virus shedding, decrease pain, and promote more rapid scabbing and healing of lesions. Acyclovir is also the drug of choice for encephalitis caused by herpes simplex, but it is not effective in patients with established neurologic damage resulting from herpes simplex or varicella-zoster infections or in patients infected with CMV. Acyclovir inhibits the replication of EBV in actively replicating cells but does not affect latent or persistent infection.

The total daily dose of acyclovir is 10 to 25 mg/kg, given by I.V. infusion lasting 60 minutes. The recommended length of parenteral acyclovir therapy ranges from 5 to 10 days, depending on the indication. A major side effect of such therapy is phlebitis at the injection site; rash, leukopenia, and neurotoxicity may also occur. Acyclovir applied topically as a 5% ointment is effective in immunocompromised patients for the treatment of limited cutaneous herpes infections and in patients with normal immunity for the treatment of initial episodes (but not recurrent episodes) of genital herpes simplex infection. Oral acyclovir seems to be effective as prophylaxis against reactivated herpes simplex infection in recipients of bone marrow transplants and in patients immunosuppressed as a result of HIV infection.

Penciclovir and Famciclovir

Penciclovir is a nucleoside analogue that is similar to acyclovir with respect to spectrum of activity and potency against herpesviruses. Famciclovir is the diacetyl ester of penciclovir. Penciclovir requires thymidine kinase (TK) for phosphorylation and thus is inactive against thymidine kinase–deficient strains of HSV or VZV; however, it may be active against some TK-altered or polymerase mutants that are resistant to acyclovir as well as against some foscarnet-resistant HSV isolates. In experimental settings, topical, parenteral, and oral penciclovir and oral famciclovir have been effective against HSV infection.

Vidarabine

Vidarabine (ara-A) is effective against herpes simplex and varicella-zoster viruses as well as poxviruses, oncornaviruses, and rhabdoviruses. It is used mostly to combat herpesvirus infections in immunosuppressed patients. In these patients, vidarabine accelerates healing of cutaneous herpes zoster, decreases its rates of cutaneous dissemination and of visceral complications, and shortens the duration of postherpetic neuralgia. For systemic use, a daily dose of 10 to 15 mg/kg of vidarabine is administered I.V. over a period of 12 hours. The duration of therapy for herpes zoster is

Table 10 Antiviral Therapy of Clinical Benefit

Virus	Condition	Regimen
Herpes simplex virus	Keratitis	3% Acyclovir ointment *or* 1% Trifluridine solution *or* 3% Vidarabine ointment *or* 0.5% IDU ointment or 0.1% IDU drops
	Herpes labialis	Treatment usually not indicated; may use 1% penciclovir cream or topical acyclovir q. 2 hr while patient is awake for 4 days
	Genital herpes Primary	Acyclovir, 200 mg p.o. 5 times daily or 400 mg p.o., t.i.d., for 10 days, *or* Valacyclovir, 500 mg–1 g p.o., b.i.d., for 10–14 days, *or* Famciclovir, 250 mg p.o., t.i.d., for 10 days*
	Recurrent	Acyclovir, 200 mg p.o. 5 times daily or 400 mg p.o., t.i.d., for 5 days, *or* Valacyclovir, 500 mg p.o., b.i.d., for 5 days, *or* Famciclovir, 125 mg p.o., b.i.d., for 5 days
	Prophylaxis	Acyclovir, 400 mg p.o., b.i.d., *or* Valacyclovir, 500 mg–1 g p.o., q.d., *or* Famciclovir, 250 mg p.o., b.i.d.
	Encephalitis	Acyclovir,10 mg/kg t.i.d. I.V. for 14–21 days
	Neonatal HSV	Acyclovir, 10 mg/kg I.V. q. 8 hr for 10–21 days (20 mg/kg I.V. q. 8 hr if neonate is premature)
	Immunocompromised host	Acyclovir, 5 mg/kg I.V. q. 8 hr for 7 days or 400 mg p.o. 5 times daily for 14–21 days, *or* Famciclovir, 500 mg p.o., b.i.d., for 7 days,* *or* Valacyclovir, 1 g p.o., t.i.d., for 7 days*
Varicella-zoster virus	Immunocompetent host Eye infections Shingles	3% Acyclovir ointment Acyclovir, 800 mg p.o. 5 times daily for 7–10 days, *or* Valacyclovir, 1 g p.o., t.i.d., for 7–10 days, *or* Famciclovir, 500 mg p.o., t.i.d., for 7–10 days
	Immunocompromised host	Acyclovir, 10–12 mg/kg I.V. q. 8 hr for 7 days (500 mg/m²)
Cytomegalovirus	Immunocompromised host Retinitis	Ganciclovir, 5 mg/kg I.V. q. 12 hr for 14–21 days,† *or* Foscarnet, 90 mg/kg (adjusted for renal function) I.V. q. 12 hr for 14–21 days, *or* Cidofovir, 5 mg/kg I.V. weekly for 2 weeks, then every other week
	CMV pneumonia	Ganciclovir, 2.5 mg/kg I.V. q.d. for 20 days

*Not approved by the FDA for this indication.
†An intraocular insert is also available.

5 days. Side effects include anorexia, weight loss, nausea, vomiting, weakness, anemia, leukopenia, thrombocytopenia, tremors, and thrombophlebitis at the site of administration.

Idoxuridine

Idoxuridine (5-iodo-2'-deoxyuridine) (IUdR, IDU) was the first clinically effective antiviral nucleoside. It is a halogenated pyrimidine that resembles thymidine in structure. Topical application of either a 0.1% solution or a 0.5% ointment of idoxuridine is effective treatment of herpes simplex keratitis but not of recurrent herpes labialis or localized zoster. In the United States, IDU is approved only for topical treatment of HSV keratitis. When combined with dimethyl sulfoxide (DMSO), IDU is active against herpes zoster and recurrent or primary genital HSV infection. In Europe, IDU is available in combination with DMSO for the treatment of herpes labialis, herpes genitalis, and herpes zoster.

Ganciclovir

Ganciclovir (DHPG, 2'-NDG, or BIOLF-62) is an acyclic nucleoside structurally related to acyclovir but with greater activity against CMV in vitro and in vivo. It is effective in treating CMV disease in transplant recipients and AIDS patients. The usual total daily dose of ganciclovir is 7.5 to 10 mg/kg, given in two or three divided doses. The dosage should be adjusted if the patient has decreased renal function. Myelosuppression is the principal dose-limiting toxic side effect.

Foscarnet

Foscarnet (trisodium phosphonoformate) is a pyrophosphate derivative that inhibits herpesvirus DNA polymerases and retroviral reverse transcriptases.[134-136] In the United States, it has been used for the prevention and treatment of CMV retinitis in patients with AIDS. For patients who have received renal or bone marrow transplants, foscarnet is given in a bolus injection of 9 mg/kg followed by infusion of 0.015 to 0.090 mg/kg/min I.V. for 7 days. Foscarnet is also used to treat acyclovir-resistant HSV infection. The major toxicity associated with foscarnet is nephrotoxicity; CNS side effects (e.g., headache, tremor, irritability, and seizures) can also occur.

Viral Infections from Animal and Human Bites

Surgeons are frequently called on to treat patients who have been bitten by either an animal or another person. Such bites can transmit several viruses and other infections. Certainly, rabies is the most feared viral infection transmitted in this way. Viruses that are found in saliva, such as HBV, herpesviruses, and possibly HIV, can be transmitted by a human bite, although such cases are most likely rare.

From zero to five cases of human rabies occur each year in the United States. Animal rabies is widespread and is found in every state except Hawaii. In 1992, more than 8,600 cases of animal rabies were reported to the CDC by 49 states, the District of Columbia, and Puerto Rico. The great majority of cases occur in wild animals.[69] Before 1950, more than 8,000 cases of rabies in dogs were reported each year in the United States; the number is now fewer than 150 a year.

Rabies proceeds from a prodrome of fever, malaise, and headache, to hyperactivity and diffuse cerebral dysfunction, and then to coma and death. From 5% to 20% of patients may also show progressive paralysis. Occasionally, there is no history of an animal bite. Diagnosis can be confirmed by culture of saliva, cerebrospinal fluid, or brain tissue; demonstration of rabies antigen in the cornea or skin; or measurement of serum antibody to rabies virus. At postmortem examination, typical intracytoplasmic inclusions (Negri bodies) can be seen in the brain cells.

Although the number of cases of human rabies is small, the disease is an important problem because of the large number of animal bites that occur each year. Surgeons may have to consider rabies prophylaxis in patients whom they treat for bite injuries [*see* Management of Viral Exposure, Rabies, *above, and 11 Acute Wound Care*]. Also, two fatal cases of rabies have occurred in recipients of corneal transplants from a patient whose cause of death was later found to be rabies.[137]

References

1. Recommendations for prevention of HIV transmission in health-care settings. MMWR Morb Mortal Wkly Rep 36(suppl 2):1S, 1987

2. Recommendations for preventing transmission of infection with human T-lymphocyte type III/lymphadenopathy-associated virus in the workplace. MMWR Morb Mortal Wkly Rep 34:681, 1985

3. Update: universal precautions for prevention of transmission of human immunodeficiency virus, hepatitis B virus, and other blood-borne pathogens in health-care settings. MMWR Morb Mortal Wkly Rep 37:377, 1988

4. Guidelines for prevention of transmission of human immunodeficiency virus and hepatitis B virus to health-care and public-safety workers. MMWR Morb Mortal Wkly Rep 38(suppl 6):1, 1989

5. Recommendations for HIV testing services for inpatients and outpatients in acute-care hospital settings and technical guidance on HIV counseling. MMWR Morb Mortal Wkly Rep 42(RR-2):1, 1993

6. Rhame F, Maki D: The case for wider use of testing for HIV infection. N Engl J Med 320:1248, 1989

7. Telford GL, Quebbeman EJ, Condon RE: A protocol to reduce risk of contracting AIDS and other blood-borne disease in the OR. Surg Rounds 10:30, 1987

8. Recommendations for follow up of health care workers after occupational exposure to hepatitis C. MMWR Morb Mortal Wkly Rep 46:603, 1997

9. Mast EE, Alter MJ: Prevention of hepatitis B virus infection among health-care workers. Hepatitis B Vaccines in Clinical Practice. Ellis RW, Ed. Marcel Dekker, New York, 1993, p 295

10. Werner BG, Grady GF: Accidental hepatitis B-surface-antigen-positive inoculations: use of e antigen to estimate infectivity. Ann Intern Med 97:367, 1982

11. Gerberding JL: Management of occupational exposures to blood-borne viruses. N Engl J Med 125:917, 1996

12. Sepkowitz KA: Occupationally acquired infections in health care workers (part II). Ann Intern Med 125:917, 1996

13. Department of Labor, OSHA: Occupational exposure to blood-borne pathogens. Final rule. Fed Regist 56:64175, 1991

14. Sepkowitz KA: Nosocomial hepatitis and other infections transmitted by blood and blood products. Principles and Practice of Infectious Disease, 5th ed. Mandell GL, Bennet JE, Dolin R, Eds. Churchill Livingstone, Philadelphia, 2000, p 3039

15. Protection against viral hepatitis: recommendations of the Immunization Practices Advisory Committee (ACIP). MMWR Morb Mortal Wkly Rep 39 (RR-2):1, 1990

16. Syndman DR, Bryan JA, Dixon RE: Prevention of nosocomial viral hepatitis, type B (hepatitis B). Ann Intern Med 83:838, 1975

17. Favero MS, Maynard JE, Leger RT, et al: Guidelines for the care of patients hospitalized with viral hepatitis. Ann Intern Med 91:872, 1979

18. Ciesielski C, Marianos D, Ou C-Y, et al: Transmission of human immunodeficiency virus in a dental practice. Ann Intern Med 116:798, 1992

19. Lot F, Seguier J, Fegeux S, et al: Probable transmission of HIV from an orthopedic surgeon to a patient in France. Ann Intern Med 130:1, 1999

20. Welch J, Webster M, Tilzey A, et al: Hepatitis B infections after gynecological surgery. Lancet 1:205, 1989

21. Lettau LA, Smith JD, Williams D, et al: Transmission of hepatitis B with resultant restriction of surgical practice. JAMA 255:934, 1986

22. Communicable Disease Surveillance Centre: Acute hepatitis B associated with gynaecological surgery. Lancet 1:1, 1980

23. Carl M, Frances DP, Blakey DL, et al: Interruption of hepatitis B transmission by modification of a gynaecologist's surgical technique. Lancet 1:731, 1982

24. Coutinho RA, Albrecht-van Lent P, Stoutjesdijk L, et al: Hepatitis B from doctors (letter). Lancet 1:345, 1982

25. Grob PJ, Bischof B, Naeff F: Cluster of hepatitis B transmitted by a physician. Lancet 2:1218, 1981

26. Meyers JD, Stamm WE, Kerr MM, et al: Lack of transmission of hepatitis B after surgical exposure. JAMA 240:1725, 1978

27. Haerem JW, Siebke JC, Ulstrup J, et al: HBsAg transmission from a cardiac surgeon incubating hepatitis B resulting in chronic antigenemia in four patients. Acta Med Scand 210:389, 1981

28. Acute hepatitis B following gynecological surgery. J Hosp Infect 9:34, 1987

29. Polakoff S: Acute hepatitis B in patients in Britain related to previous operations and dental treatment. Br J Med 293:33, 1986

30. Heptonstall J: Outbreaks of hepatitis B virus infection associated with infected surgical staff. Communicable Disease Report 1:R81, 1991

31. Surgeons who are hepatitis B carriers. BMJ 303:184, 1991

32. Jones D: Hepatitis leaves Halifax surgeon an operating room outcast. Can Med Assoc J 145:1345, 1991

33. Alter HJ, Chalmers TC, Freeman BM, et al: Health-care workers positive for hepatitis B surface antigen: are their contacts at risk? N Engl J Med 292:454, 1975

34. Williams SV, Pattison CP, Berquist KR: Dental infection with hepatitis B. JAMA 232:1231, 1975

35. Gerber MA, Lewin EB, Gerety RJ, et al: The lack of nurse-infant transmission of type B hepatitis in a special care nursery. J Pediatr 91:120, 1977

36. LaBrecque DR, Dhand AK: The risk of hepatitis B transmission from staff to patients in hemodialysis units—an overrated problem? Hepatology 1:398, 1981

37. LaBrecque DR, Muhs JM, Lutwick LI, et al: The risk of hepatitis B transmission from health care workers to patients in a hospital setting—a prospective study. Hepatology 6:205, 1986

38. Recommendations for preventing transmission of human immunodeficiency virus and hepatitis B virus to patients during exposure-prone invasive procedures. MMWR Morb Mortal Wkly Rep 40(RR-8), 1991

39. Esteban JI, Gomez J, Martell M, et al: Transmission of hepatitis C by a cardiac surgeon. N Engl J Med 334:555, 1996

40. Bosch H: Hepatitis C outbreak astounds Spain. Lancet 352:1415, 1998

41. Public Health Service guidelines for the management of health-care worker exposures to HIV and recommendations for post-exposure prophylaxis. MMWR Morb Mortal Wkly Rep 47:1, 1998

42. Chiarello LA, Gerberding JL: Human immunodeficiency virus in health care settings. Principles and Practice of Infectious Disease, 5th ed. Mandell GL, Bennett JE, Dolin R, Eds. Churchill Livingstone, Philadelphia, 2000, p 3052

43. Ciesielski CA, Metler RP: Duration of time between exposure and seroconversion in healthcare workers

with occupationally acquired infection with human immunodeficiency virus. Am J Med 102(suppl 5B): S115, 1997

44. Busch MP, Satten GA: Time course of viremia and antibody seroconversion following human immunodeficiency virus exposure. Am J Med 102(suppl 5B):S117, 1997

45. Cardo DM, Culver DH, Ciesielski CA, et al: A case-control study of HIV seroconversion in healthcare workers after percutaneous exposure. N Engl J Med 337:1485, 1997

46. Public Health Service Statement on management of occupational exposure to human immunodeficiency virus, including considerations regarding zidovudine postexposure use. MMWR Morb Mortal Wkly Rep 39 (RR-1):1, 1990

47. Wang SA, the HIV PEP Registry Group: Human immunodeficiency virus (HIV) postexposure prophylaxis (PEP) following occupational HIV exposure: findings from the HIV PEP Registry (abstract 482). Program and abstracts of the 35th Annual Meeting of the Infectious Diseases Society of America, Alexandria, Virginia, Sept 13–16, 1997, p 161

48. Steger KA, Swotinsky R, Snyder S, et al: Recent experience with post-exposure prophylaxis (PEP) with combination antiretrovirals for occupational exposure (OE) to HIV (abstract 480). Program and abstracts of the 35th Annual Meeting of the Infectious Diseases Society of America, Alexandria, Virginia, Sept 13–16, 1997, p 161

49. Beekmann R, Fahrner R, Nelson L, et al: Combination post-exposure prophylaxis (PEP): a prospective study of HIV-exposed health care workers (HCW) (abstract 481). Program and abstracts of the 35th Annual Meeting of the Infectious Diseases Society of America, Alexandria, Virginia, Sept 13–16, 1997, p 161

50. Imrie A, Beveridge A, Genn W, et al: Transmission of human immunodeficiency virus type 1 resistant to nevirapine and zidovudine. J Infect Dis 175:1502, 1997

51. Veenstra J, Schuurman R, Cornelissen M, et al: Transmission of zidovudine-resistant human immunodeficiency virus type 1 variants following deliberate injection of blood from a patient with AIDS: characteristics and natural history of the virus. Clin Infect Dis 21:556-60, 1995

52. Fitzgibbon JE, Gaur S, Frenkel LD, et al: Transmission from one child to another of human immunodeficiency virus type 1 with a zidovudine-resistance mutation. N Engl J Med 329:1835, 1993

53. Coombs RW, Shapiro DE, Eastman PS, et al: Maternal viral genotypic zidovudine (ZDV) resistance and infrequent failure of ZDV therapy to prevent perinatal transmission (abstract 17). Program and abstracts of the 35th Annual Meeting of the Infectious Diseases Society of America, Alexandria, Virginia, Sept 13–16, 1997, p 74

54. Protection against viral hepatitis. Recommendations of the Immunization Practices Advisory Committee (ACIP). MMWR Morb Mortal Wkly Rep 39(RR-2):1, 1990

55. Hadler SC: Are booster doses of hepatitis B vaccine necessary? Ann Intern Med 108:457, 1988

56. Hadler SC, Francis DP, Maynard JE, et al: Long-term immunogenicity and efficacy of hepatitis B vaccine in homosexual men. N Engl J Med 315:209, 1986

57. Hepatitis B virus: A comprehensive strategy for eliminating transmission in the United States through universal childhood vaccination. Advisory Committee for Immunization Practices. MMWR Morb Mortal Wkly Rep 40:PR-13, 1991

58. Barie PS, Dellinger EP, Dougherty SH, et al: Assessment of hepatitis B virus immunization status among North American surgeons. Arch Surg 129:27, 1994

59. Recommendations for prevention and control of hepatitis C virus (HCV) infection and HCV-related chronic disease. MMWR Morb Mortal Wkly Rep 47(RR-19):1, 1998

60. Noguchi S, Sata M, Suzuki H, et al: Early therapy with interferon for acute hepatitis C acquired through the needlestick. Clin Infect Dis 24:992, 1997

61. Vogen W, Graziadei I, Umlauft F, et al: High-dose interferon-α_{2b} treatment prevents chronicity in acute hepatitis C: a pilot study. Dig Dis Sci 41(suppl 12):81S, 1996

62. Ohnishi K, Nomura F, Nakano M: Interferon therapy for acute posttransfusion non-A, non-B hepatitis: response with respect to anti-hepatitis C virus antibody status. Am J Gastroenterol 86:1041, 1991

63. Rabies prevention—United States, 1991: recommendations of the Immunization Practices Advisory Committee (ACIP). MMWR Morb Mortal Wkly Rep 40:1, 1991

64. Fishbein DB, Robinson LE: Rabies. N Engl J Med 329:1632, 1993

65. Rabies prevention—United States, 1999: recommendations of the Immunization Practices Advisory Committee (ACIP). MMWR Morb Mortal Wkly Rep 48(RR-1):1, 1999

66. WHO Recommendations on Rabies Post-exposure Treatment and the Correct Technique of Intradermal Immunization against Rabies. World Health Organization, Geneva, 1997

67. Rabies prevention: supplementary statement on the preexposure use of human diploid cell rabies vaccine by the intradermal route. MMWR Morb Mortal Wkly Rep 35:767, 1986

68. Bleck TP, Rupprecht CE: Rabies virus. Principles and Practice of Infectious Disease, 5th ed. Mandell GL, Bennett JE, Dolin R, Eds. Churchill Livingstone, Philadelphia, 2000, p 1811

69. Krebs JW, Strine TW, Childs JF: Rabies surveillance in the United States during 1992. J Am Vet Med Assoc 203:1718, 1993

70. The cost of one rabid dog—California. MMWR Morb Mortal Wkly Rep 30:527, 1981

71. Bove JR: Transfusion-associated hepatitis and AIDS: what is the risk? N Engl J Med 317:242, 1987

72. Donegan E, Stuart M, Niland JC, et al: Infection with the human immunodeficiency virus type 1 (HIV1) among recipients of antibody-positive blood donations. Ann Intern Med 113:733, 1990

73. Ward JW, Deppe DA, Samson S, et al: Risk of human immunodeficiency virus infection from blood donors who later developed the acquired immunodeficiency syndrome. Ann Intern Med 106:61, 1987

74. Ward JW, Grindon AJ, Feorino PM, et al: Laboratory and epidemiologic evaluation of an enzyme immunoassay for antibodies to HTLV-III. JAMA 256:357, 1986

75. Ward JW, Holmberg AD, Allen JR, et al: Transmission of human immunodeficiency virus (HIV) by blood transfusions screened as negative for HIV antibody. N Engl J Med 318:473, 1988

76. Schreiber GB, Bush MP, Kleinman SH, et al: The risk of transfusion-transmitted viral infections: the retrovirus epidemiology donor study. N Engl J Med 334:1685, 1996

77. Horsburgh BR Jr, Ou C-Y, Jason J, et al: Duration of human immunodeficiency virus infection before detection of antibody. Lancet 2:637, 1989

78. Erice A, Rhame FS, Heussner RC, et al: Human immunodeficiency virus infection in patients with solid-organ transplants: report of five cases and review. Rev Infect Dis 13:537, 1991

79. Public Health Service guidelines for the management of health-care worker exposures to HIV and recommendations for post-exposure prophylaxis. MMWR Morb Mortal Wkly Rep 47:1, 1998

80. Guidelines for national human immunodeficiency virus case surveillance, including monitoring for human immunodeficiency virus infection and acquired immunodeficiency syndrome. MMWR Morb Mortal Wkly Rep 48(RR-13):1, 1999

81. Alter M, Mast E: The epidemiology of hepatitis in the United States. Gastroenterol Clin North Am 23:437, 1994

82. Kim CY, Tilles JG: Purification and biophysical characterization of the hepatitis B antigen. J Clin Invest 52:1176, 1973

83. Kawai H, Feinstone SM: Acute viral hepatitis. Principles and Practice of Infectious Diseases, 5th ed. Mandell GL, Bennett JE, Dolin R, Eds. Churchill Livingstone, Philadelphia, 2000, p 1279

84. Omata M: Treatment of chronic hepatitis B infection. N Engl J Med 339:114, 1998

85. Kuo G, Choo Q-L, Alter HJ, et al: An assay for circulating antibodies to a major etiologic virus of non-A, non-B hepatitis. Science 244:362, 1989

86. Hayden GH, Jarvis LM, Blair CS, et al: Clinical significance of intrahepatic hepatitis C virus levels in patients with chronic HCV infection. Gut 42:570, 1998

87. Koretz RL, Stone O, Gitnick GL: The long-term course of non-A, non-B post-transfusion hepatitis. Gastroenterology 79:893, 1980

88. Denes AE, Smith JL, Maynard JE, et al: Hepatitis B infections in physicians: results of a nationwide seroepidemiologic survey. JAMA 239:210, 1978

89. Howard RJ: Viral infections in surgery. Problems in General Surgery 1:522, 1984

90. Recommendations for protection against viral hepatitis. MMWR Morb Mortal Wkly Rep 34:313, 1985

91. Valent WM, Wehrle PP: Selected viruses of nosocomial importance. Hospital Infections, 2nd ed. Bennett JV, Brachman PS, Eds. Little, Brown & Company, Boston, 1986, p 531

92. Cooper BW, Krusell A, Tilton RC, et al: Seroprevalence of antibodies to hepatitis C virus in high-risk hospital personnel. Infect Control Hosp Epidemiol 13:82, 1992

93. Klein RS, Freeman K, Taylor PE, et al: Occupational risk for hepatitis C virus infection among New York City dentists. Lancet 338:1539, 1991

94. Zuckerman J, Clewley G, Griffiths P, et al: Prevalence of hepatitis C antibodies in clinical health-care workers. Lancet 343:1618, 1994

95. Schreiber GB, Busch MP, Kleinman SH, et al: The risk of transfusion-transmitted viral infections. N Engl J Med 334:1685, 1996

96. Rosina F, Saracco G, Rizzetto M: Risk of posttransfusion infection with hepatitis delta virus: a multicenter study. N Engl J Med 312:1488, 1985

97. Friedman LS, Dienstag JL: Recent developments in viral hepatitis. Dis Mon 32:320, 1986

98. Beasley PR, Lin CC: Hepatoma risk among HBsAg carriers. Am J Epidemiol 108:247, 1978

99. Edamoto Y, Tani M, Durata T, et al: Hepatitis C and B virus infections in hepatocellular carcinoma—analysis of direct detection of viral genome in paraffin embedded tissues. Cancer 77:1787, 1996

100. Kiyosawa K, Furuta S: Hepatitis C virus and hepatocellular carcinoma. Curr Stud Hematol Blood Transfus 61:98, 1994

101. Rook AH, Quinnan GV Jr: Cytomegalovirus infections following blood transfusions. Infectious Complications of Blood Transfusion. Tabor E, Ed. Academic Press, San Diego, 1982, p 45

102. Winston DJ, Ho WG, Howell CL, et al: Cytomegalovirus infections associated with leukocyte transfusions. Ann Intern Med 93:671, 1980

103. Prince AM, Szmuness W, Millins SJ, et al: A serological study of cytomegalovirus infections associated with blood transfusions. N Engl J Med 284:1125, 1971

104. Tolkoff-Rubin NE, Rubin RH, Keller EE, et al: Cytomegalovirus infection in dialysis patients and personnel. Ann Intern Med 89:625, 1978

105. Bowden RA: Transfusion-transmitted cytomegalovirus infection. Hematol Oncol Clin North Am 9:155, 1995

106. Paya CV, Hermans PE, Wiesner RH, et al: Cytomegalovirus hepatitis in liver transplantation: prospective analysis of 93 consecutive orthotopic liver transplantations. J Infect Dis 160:752, 1988

107. Barkholt LM, Ericzon BG, Ehrnst A, et al: Cytomegalovirus infections in liver transplant patients: incidence and outcome. Transplant Proc 22:235, 1990

108. Englehard D, Or R, Strauss N, et al: Cytomegalovirus infection and disease after T cell depleted allogeneic bone marrow transplantation for malignant hematologic disease. Transplant Proc 21:3101, 1989

109. Griffiths PD: Current management of cytomegalovirus disease. J Med Virol (suppl 1):106, 1993

110. Farrusia E, Schwab TR: Management and prevention of cytomegalovirus infection after renal transplantation. Mayo Clin Proc 67:879, 1992

111. Ho M, Suwansirikul S, Dowling JN, et al: The transplanted kidney as a source of cytomegalovirus infection. N Engl J Med 293:1109, 1975

112. Myers JD, Fluornoy N, Thomas ED: Risk factors for cytomegalovirus infection after human marrow transplantation. J Infect Dis 153:478, 1986

113. Balfour HH Jr, Sachs GW, Welo P, et al: Cytomegalovirus vaccine in renal transplant candidates: progress report of a randomized, placebo-controlled, double-blind trial. Birth Defects 20:289, 1984

114. Snydman DR, Werner BG, Heinze-Lacey B, et al: Use of cytomegalovirus immune globulin to prevent cytomegalovirus disease in renal-transplant recipients. N Engl J Med 317:1049, 1987

115. Martin M: Antiviral prophylaxis for CMV infection in liver transplantation. Transplant Proc 25(suppl 4):10, 1993

116. Steinmuller DR, Novick AC, Streem SB, et al: Intravenous immunoglobulin infusions for the prophylaxis of secondary cytomegalovirus infection. Transplant 49:68, 1990

117. Kasiske BL, Heim-Duthoy KL, Tortorice KL: Polyvalent immune globulin and cytomegalovirus infection after renal transplantation. Arch Intern Med 149:2733, 1989

118. Lautenschlager I, Ahonen J, Eklund B, et al: Hyperimmune globulin therapy of clinical cytomegalovirus infection in renal allograft recipients. Scand J Infect Dis 21:139, 1989

119. Balfour HH Jr: Prevention of cytomegalovirus disease in renal allograft recipients. Scand J Infect Dis Suppl 80:88, 1991

120. Snydman DR, Rubin RH, Werner BG: New developments in cytomegalovirus prevention and management. Am J Kidney Dis 21:217, 1993

121. Emanuel D: Treatment of cytomegalovirus disease. Semin Hematol 27(suppl 1):22, 1990

122. Tabor E: Epstein-Barr virus and blood transfusion. Infectious Complications of Blood Transfusion. Tabor E, Ed. Academic Press, San Diego, 1982, p 65

123. Rocchi G, de Felici A, Ragona G, et al: Quantitative evaluation of Epstein-Barr-virus-infected mononuclear peripheral blood leukocytes in infectious mononucleosis. N Engl J Med 296:132, 1977

124. Armitage JM, Kormos RL, Stuart RS, et al: Posttransplant lymphoproliferative disease in thoracic organ transplant patients: ten years of cyclosporine-based immunosuppression. J Heart Lung Transplant 10:877, 1991

125. Lager DJ, Burgart LJ, Slagel DD: Epstein-Barr virus detection in sequential biopsies from patients with a posttransplant lymphoproliferative disorder. Mod Pathol 6:42, 1993

126. Dotti G, Fiocchi R, Motta T, et al: Epstein-Barr virus-negative lymphoproliferative disorders in long-term survivors after heart, kidney, and liver transplant. Transplantation 69:827, 2000

127. Leblond V, Davi F, Charlotte F, et al: Posttransplant lymphoproliferative disorders not associated with Epstein-Barr virus: a distinct entity? J Clin Oncol 16:2052, 1998

128. Preiksaitis JK, Cockfield AM: Epstein-Barr virus and lymphoproliferative disorders after transplantation. Transplant Infections. Bowden RA, Ljungman P, Paya CV, Eds. Lippincott-Raven Publishers, Philadelphia, 1998, p 245

129. Breinig MK, Zitelli B, Ho M: Epstein-Barr virus, cytomegalovirus and other viral infections in children after liver transplantation. J Infect Dis 156:273, 1987

130. Starzl TE, Porter KA, Iwatsuki SK, et al: Reversibility of lymphomas and lymphoproliferative lesions developing under cyclosporine-steroid therapy. Lancet 1:583, 1984

131. Hanto DW, Frizzera G, Gajl-Peczalska KJ, et al: Epstein-Barr virus, immunodeficiency, and B cell lymphoproliferation. Transplantation 39:461, 1985

132. Shapiro RS, McClain K, Frizzera G, et al: Epstein-Barr virus associated B cell lymphoproliferative disorders following bone marrow transplantation. Blood 71:1234, 1988

133. Benkerru M, Durandy A, Fischer A: Therapy for transplant-related lymphoproliferative diseases. Hematol Oncol Clin North Am 7:467, 1993

134. Keating MR: Antiviral agents. Mayo Clin Proc 67:160, 1992

135. de Clercq E: Antivirals for the treatment of herpesvirus infections. J Antimicrob Chemother 32(suppl A):121, 1993

136. Oberg B: Antiviral effects of phosphonoformate (PFA, foscarnet sodium). Pharmacol Ther 40:213, 1989

137. Houff SA, Burton RC, Wilson RW, et al: Human-to-human transmission of rabies virus by corneal transplant. N Engl J Med 300:603, 1979

Acknowledgments

Figure 1 Micrograph courtesy of F. K. Lee, A. J. Nahmias, and S. Stagno, Emory University. Drawing by George V. Kelvin.

Figures 4 and 5 Albert Miller.

136 ACQUIRED IMMUNODEFICIENCY SYNDROME

Kathleen Casey, M.D., and John Mihran Davis, M.D., F.A.C.S.

Approach to Human Immunodeficiency Virus Infection

In June 1981, the Centers for Disease Control and Prevention (CDC) published a report of *Pneumocystis carinii* pneumonia (PCP) in five previously healthy homosexual men living in Los Angeles.[1] At that time, the CDC was the sole distributor of pentamidine, the only treatment for this rare pulmonary infection. This outbreak represented a unique cohort for PCP, which until then had been seen only in severely immunosuppressed patients who were receiving chemotherapy for disseminated cancer. Even in this select group, PCP was rare, and *P. carinii* was not considered pathogenic in otherwise healthy adults. The sudden increase in demand for pentamidine in one geographic area raised the prospect of a new disease process. In July 1981, the CDC reported a group of young homosexual men with Kaposi sarcoma.[2] Like PCP, Kaposi sarcoma was a rare lesion not commonly seen in young adults. Many of these Kaposi sarcoma patients also had severe infections caused by organisms associated with immunodeficiency, including PCP, toxoplasmosis, candidiasis, cryptococcosis, and cytomegalovirus (CMV) infections.

These two accounts represented the first recognition of AIDS. The cause of the severe immunodepression in these patients, who were not otherwise at risk for opportunistic infection, was controversial until late 1983 and early 1984, when the human immunodeficiency virus (HIV) was isolated in AIDS patients.[3] This retrovirus—formerly known as human T cell lymphotropic virus (HTLV) type III and lymphadenopathy-associated virus (LAV)—is now recognized as the agent that causes AIDS. Presumably, the patients in the 1981 reports had become infected with HIV at least 3 to 4 years earlier.

In September 1987, the definition of AIDS was expanded to include symptomatic HIV-infected patients suspected of having an opportunistic infection. This new definition precipitated a potentially misleading sudden increase in new cases.[4] Since 1986, the percentage of homosexual or bisexual AIDS patients has steadily declined, and the percentage of AIDS patients who are I.V. drug abusers or are heterosexual has increased.

June 1, 2001, marked the 20th anniversary of the AIDS epidemic. Over those 2 decades, more than 20 million people died of AIDS, leaving an estimated 36 million people infected.[5] No immediate end to the epidemic is in sight, but current therapies have significantly altered the course of the illness. Until the advent of highly active antiretroviral agents (HAART), it was believed that everyone with an opportunistic infection or tumor associated with AIDS (e.g., Kaposi sarcoma or non-Hodgkin lymphoma) would die as a direct result of severe immunosuppression; that is no longer the case.[6] HIV-infected persons are living longer, are less likely to die of opportunistic infections, and are more likely to present with relatively well-preserved immune function.[7] With this increase in the prevalence of HIV infection, it is all the more important that surgeons have a basic under-standing of HIV disease and its treatment and be familiar with prophylaxis after occupational exposure.

Recognition of HIV Infection

PATHOGENESIS

HIV is an oncovirus belonging to the retrovirus family. The potential of retroviruses to cause neoplasia was first recognized in 1911 by the American pathologist Rous, who associated them with certain malignant disorders in animals.[8] For example, HTLV-I, a retrovirus related to HIV, has been identified as a cause of leukemia in humans.[9]

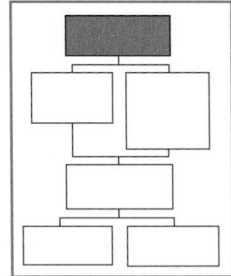

One of the characteristic features of retroviruses is the presence of an enzyme called reverse transcriptase. This enzyme allows the virus to transcribe viral RNA to DNA. The virus can synthesize double-stranded DNA from single-stranded DNA that has been liberated from the RNA-DNA hybrid. This double-stranded DNA inserts itself into the nucleus of the host cell and serves as a template for viral replication. Thus, whenever the infected host cell divides, new HIV particles are also reproduced. HIV has been isolated in many cell types, but it is thought that helper T cells (CD4+ cells) are most frequently infected. It is believed that when an HIV-infected CD4+ cell is activated by a secondary infection, the virus is replicated, resulting in the dissemination of mature virions and the death of the cell.

The latency period between acquisition of HIV infection and onset of AIDS has been estimated to be about 5 years. This estimate is probably misleading because it is based on experience with patients in high-risk groups, who are frequently exposed to other infectious challenges. Exposure to these other pathogens activates the T cells that harbor HIV, which promotes dissemination of the virus throughout the host and significant impairment in cellular immunity. Because the incidence of concomitant infections is lower in the general population than in high-risk groups, the latency period of HIV infection is probably longer in the general population.

DIAGNOSTIC TESTS

The enzyme-linked immunosorbent assay (ELISA) and the Western blot assay are designed to detect the presence of HIV antibody in serum. ELISA is considered very sensitive (93% to 100%; i.e., its false negative rate is low). The specificity of a repeatedly reactive ELISA approaches 99%. The weakness of the ELISA is that some persons have antibodies that react with HIV antigens but are not specific for HIV.

The Western blot assay is more specific than ELISA but is cumbersome and less sensitive. It is therefore not a good screen-

Approach to Human Immunodeficiency Virus Infection

Potential HIV infection in surgical setting

Infection is diagnosed by ELISA or Western blot assay. SUDS ELISA results must be confirmed by Western blot.

Categorize patients according to CDC classification. Patients receiving HAART may not behave in accordance with CDC class.

Surgical issues in infected patients

General clinical problems:
- Immunosuppression
- Renal failure
- Cardiac dysfunction

Other problems include
- Splenomegaly or thrombocytopenia
- Central venous catheter infections
- GI disease
- Lymphadenopathy

Risk of HIV transmission to patient or medical personnel

Risk to patient comes from transfusion, transplantation, or, theoretically, transmission from surgical personnel (HBV transmission is a far more significant possibility).

Risk to health care workers (HCWs) comes from infected patients. All HCWs should take precautions to prevent HIV transmission with *all* patients, not only those with known or suspected HIV infection. Again, transmission of hepatitis is much more common.

Postexposure prophylaxis

Need for prophylaxis and choice of drugs are based on (1) risk assessment of exposure, (2) size of inoculum, (3) arterial vs. venous exposure, (4) intact or nonintact skin or mucous membrane exposure.

Consider possible HCV coinfection.

Source is HIV positive with low viral load; source is of unknown HIV status but high risk; or worker has minor skin or mucous membrane exposure

Initiate two-drug therapy (zidovudine and lamivudine) within 24 hr of exposure.

Source is HIV positive with high viral load, or worker has extensive skin or mucous membrane exposure

Initiate three-drug therapy (zidovudine, lamivudine, and indinavir or nelfinavir) within 24 hr of exposure.

ing test; it is used most effectively for confirming ELISA results. However, most blood banks will not use blood that has demonstrated a positive ELISA reaction, even if HIV antibody was not detected by Western blot testing.[10]

The Single-Use Diagnostic System (SUDS; Murex Diagnostics, Norcross, Georgia) provides a rapid ELISA technology that can yield a reliable result in 15 minutes. A positive SUDS result must still be confirmed by Western blot assay. SUDS is especially useful in occupational-injury investigation.

There is a window period of 25 days between infection with HIV and seroconversion detectable by ELISA. It has been estimated that since 1985, when all banked blood began to be tested for HIV, 35 persons in the United States have contracted HIV infection from transfusions containing blood collected from an HIV-infected individual during this window period.[11,12] For that reason, on August 8, 1995, the Food and Drug Administration recommended that all blood donated for transfusion be screened for the p24 antigen (the core structural protein of HIV).[13] Additional laboratory tests that may help in the diagnosis of patients believed to have HIV infection in whom HIV antibody screening yields negative results include DNA polymerase chain reaction (PCR), antigen testing after immune complex disruption, and RNA reverse transcriptase PCR.[14]

In February 2002, the FDA approved a nucleic acid test system that detects ribonucleic acid from HIV and hepatitis C virus (HCV) in whole blood and blood component donors, thus permitting earlier results than tests based on detection of antibodies or antigens (http://www.fda/gov/cber/approvltr/hivhcvgen022702L.htm). Like ELISA, the nucleic acid test has a window period during which the virus can be present but escape detection; however, this window period is substantially shorter than that associated with antibody-based tests (12 versus 22 days, on average, for HIV; 25 versus 82 days, on average, for HCV).

CDC Classification of HIV Infection

In 1993, the CDC revised the classification of the HIV-infected adult and adolescent [*see Table 1*]. In this classification, a CD4$^+$ count below 200 cells/μl is considered an indicator of AIDS, regardless of the patient's symptoms. Once classified into a given group, a patient is not reclassified to a more favorable category, even if symptoms resolve or the CD4$^+$ cell count rises. However, if the disease progresses or the CD4$^+$ count falls, the patient is reclassified into the next less-favorable group. This system allows uniformity in patient classification for research trials and scientific communication and, of particular importance, facilitates formulation of health care policy and strategy.

Unfortunately, the system does not take into account the immune reconstitution that occurs with HAART. After successful treatment with HAART, patients originally classified as having AIDS (on the basis of their CD4$^+$ count or level of immunocompromise) often will no longer have signs and symptoms in accordance with their original CDC classification. A number of studies have now shown that secondary prophylaxis for PCP, CMV retinitis, *Toxoplasma* encephalitis, and cryptococcal meningitis may be safely discontinued in patients whose CD4$^+$ counts have risen and remained above 200 cells/μl because of HAART.[15] Similarly, recent studies of gynecologic procedures in HIV-infected patients have found that postoperative infection rates correlate only with the current CD4$^+$ count. In these studies, a CD4$^+$ level below 200 cells/μl at the time of the procedure was an independent risk factor for surgical complications, whereas the previous nadir had no influence on outcome.[14]

Surgical Issues

GENERAL

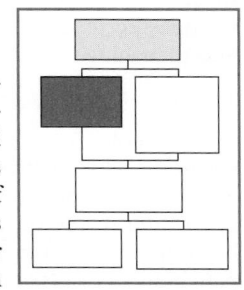

As a group, HIV-infected patients present the surgeon with three notable clinical problems: immunosuppression, renal failure, and cardiac dysfunction. Surgeons need to be aware of the immune status of their HIV-infected patients, because this has the greatest bearing on outcome. For example, in HIV-infected patients with normal CD4$^+$ counts, the risk of infectious complications after surgery for a perforated appendix is comparable to the risk in patients without HIV infection. In patients with AIDS (< 200 CD4$^+$ cells/μl), the risk of infection is higher, though it is from opportunistic organisms associated with severe immunosuppression rather than common pathogens.[16-20]

Renal failure in HIV-infected patients can be the result of specific HIV-related nephropathy, which occurs in up to 10% of this population.[21] Another possible cause is drug toxicity from antiviral and antimicrobial medications: pentamidine, foscarnet, and aminoglycosides cause acute tubular necrosis; acyclovir, indinavir, and sulfadiazine cause intratubular obstruction.

Until recently, the risk of cardiac disease in HIV-infected patients had not been as well documented as that of renal failure. With HIV-infected patients living longer, the problems of acquired heart disease have been increasingly appreciated.[22-24]

In addition, malignancy has been increasingly recognized over the past 2 decades as a consequence of HIV infection. Initially, the occurrence of AIDS-defining tumors, such as B cell lym-

Table 1 1993 Revised Classification for HIV Infection and Expanded AIDS Surveillance Case Definition for Adolescents and Adults[81]

CD4$^+$ T Cell Categories	Clinical Categories		
	A	B	C
	Asymptomatic, Acute (Primary) HIV, or PGL	Symptomatic, Not A or C Conditions	AIDS Indicator Conditions
500/μl	A1	B1	C1
200–499/μl	A2	B2	C2
< 200/μl AIDS-indicator T cell count	A3	B3	C3

PGL—persistent generalized lymphadenopathy

phoma and Kaposi sarcoma, was thought to relate to the immunosuppression of the host. Other tumors have now been associated with HIV infection, including squamous cell cancers of the cervix and anus and lung cancer. It is believed that at some point after infection with HIV, activation of oncogenes and loss of tumor suppressor genes give rise to microsatellite alterations. These are highly pleomorphic segments of DNA associated with the AIDS-defining malignancies.[25-27]

Treatment of patients with AIDS involves multimodal therapy and consultation with oncology and infectious disease specialists. It is beyond the scope of this discussion to describe the specific therapeutic approaches to the complications of HIV infections; however, three principal problems must be addressed. First, any opportunistic infection or secondary malignant disorder must be treated; second, the underlying immunodeficiency must be corrected; and finally, the cause—HIV infection—must be controlled. The role of the surgeon in the management of these chronically ill, and sometimes critically ill, patients includes performing diagnostic biopsies, giving supportive care, and managing complications of malignancy of infection.

SPLEEN

The role of splenectomy in patients with marked splenomegaly or with thrombocytopenia must be individualized. Some experts believe that coinfections such as HCV infection contribute to the development of HIV-related immune thrombocytopenic purpura (ITP). Thrombocytopenia occurs in AIDS patients as a result of the deposition of circulating immune complexes on platelets rather than as a result of a specific antiplatelet antibody.[28,29] Splenectomy has been extremely effective in the management of AIDS-related ITP, with a success rate of over 90%. Occasionally, patients who have debilitating fevers associated with significantly enlarged spleens experience dramatic palliation after splenectomy. Some data indicate that splenectomy favors a slower progression of HIV dissemination and progression to AIDS.[30,31] In patients with massive splenomegaly and fever, simple splenomegaly is sometimes difficult to distinguish from abscess or parenchymal necrosis, and splenectomy may be indicated to resolve the uncertainty. In addition, splenectomy may be indicated in instances in which there is merely a likelihood of injury and in those in which a large spleen compresses the stomach, thereby contributing to malnutrition.

IMPLANTABLE VENOUS ACCESS DEVICES

Placement of an indwelling central venous catheter is a request frequently directed to the general surgeon from the primary care physician, infectious disease consultant, or hematologist caring for an AIDS patient. Long-term venous access for treating fungal infections or, occasionally, for providing nutritional support in patients with debilitating diarrheal syndromes can enhance the care of these patients. However, lines are often placed when the patient is febrile, as a result of either the underlying infection or treatment with amphotericin B. Therefore, a close watch should be kept postoperatively to ensure that fevers are not related to a catheter infection. Although catheter-related infection develops in as many as 30% of AIDS patients with implanted lines, these infections do not increase mortality.[32] The high rate of infection relates in part to the high incidence of *Staphylococcus* colonization in these patients.

GASTROINTESTINAL DISEASES

Cryptosporidiosis and CMV infection of the biliary tree have been reported to cause both acute cholecystitis and acute cholan-

gitis, necessitating emergency surgical interventions.[12] Choledochoenteric bypass is thought to provide the best palliation in these patients. It is not known whether the biliary tree is ever cleared of the pathogens. *Candida* infection and Kaposi sarcoma have also caused cholangitis, necessitating bypass surgery.[17] The gallbladder is infected with unusual pathogens in over 50% of HIV-infected patients with cholangitis; therefore, the gallbladder wall should be sent for culture, and the pathologist should be alerted so that the tissue may be processed with special stains.[33-36]

Acute perforations of the GI tract from CMV infection, cryptosporidiosis, and candidiasis, as well as from necrotic lymphoma, have been reported in HIV-infected patients.[18,37,38] Obstruction of the GI tract by Kaposi sarcoma or lymphoma may also be an indication for resection, bypass, or colostomy. One study of AIDS patients requiring a laparotomy identified four distinct clinical syndromes that called for surgical intervention: (1) peritonitis secondary to CMV enterocolitis and perforation; (2) non-Hodgkin lymphoma of the GI tract (usually the terminal ileum), presenting as obstruction or bleeding; (3) Kaposi sarcoma of the GI tract; and (4) mycobacterial infection of the retroperitoneum or the spleen.[39]

Another GI lesion that has been increasingly associated with homosexual men who are infected with HIV is squamous cell carcinoma of the anus (SCCA). It is estimated that the risk of developing SCCA is nearly 25 times greater in HIV-infected homosexual men than in the general population. The underlying relationship is not well understood, because the development of SCCA is not related to the duration of the HIV infection. Some experts believe that human papillomavirus 16 (HPV-16) and HPV-18 are important cofactors in the evolution of SCCA.[40,41]

LYMPHADENOPATHY

Another group of HIV-infected patients defined by the CDC comprises those with persistent generalized lymphadenopathy—that is, palpable lymphadenopathy with nodes measuring greater than 1 cm in diameter in at least two extrainguinal sites and persisting for longer than 3 months. Before the introduction of HIV antibody testing, the relationship of such lymphadenopathy to systemic manifestations of immunosuppression (systemic symptoms, neurologic symptoms, secondary infections, or cancers) was not known. It is now clear that lymphadenopathy is part of the general clinical spectrum associated with HIV infection, and that opportunistic infection, Kaposi sarcoma, or large cell lymphoma will develop in some, if not all, patients with lymphadenopathy. The precise reason that lymphadenopathy occurs in some, but not all, patients with HIV infection is not known.

Lymph node biopsy in these patients is only of academic interest because of the development of serologic tests for HIV infection.[37] The histologic appearance of a clinically enlarged lymph node has prognostic value (see below); however, when the decision as to whether to perform a lymph node biopsy is being made, the value of the biopsy findings must be weighed against the value of the information that can be obtained by means of clinical staging with the ratio of helper T cells to suppressor T cells and the total lymphocyte count. The total number of helper T cells in the circulation has been correlated with the risk of AIDS in patients with generalized lymphadenopathy[20,42-44]; the Walter Reed classification provides the most detailed clinical staging system.[43,45] Should the clinical condition warrant, a lymph node biopsy may help in the diagnosis of an opportunistic infection. Performing a gallium scan to locate the most suspicious node can enhance the yield of the biopsy.

Four basic histologic patterns have been described in persistent generalized lymphadenopathy and have been correlated

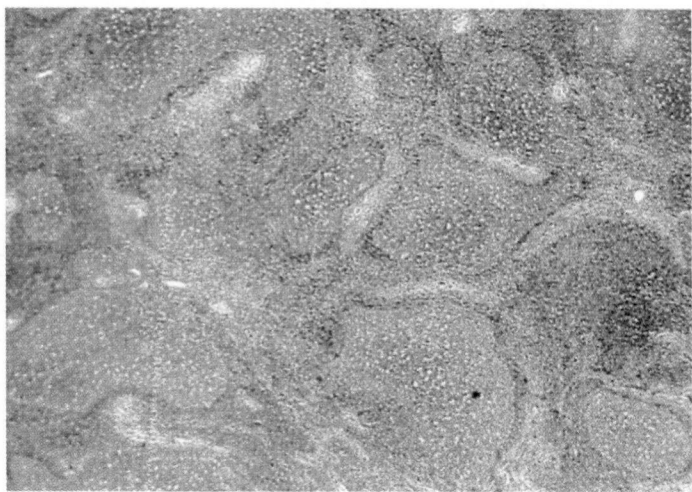

Figure 1 **Lymph node viewed under low power exhibits explosive follicular hyperplasia.**

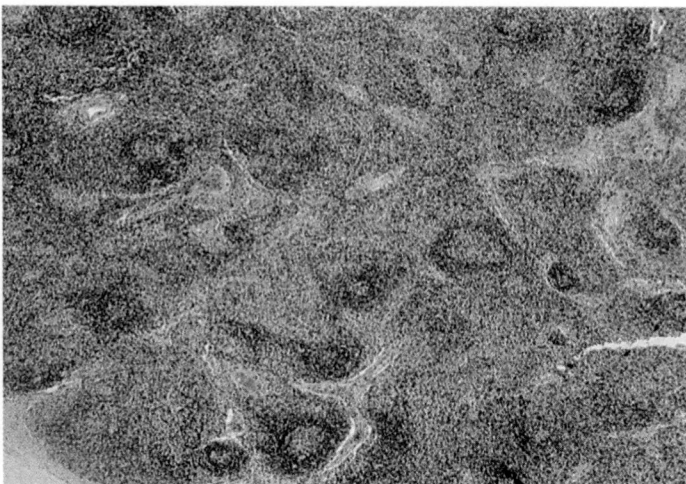

Figure 2 **Lymph node viewed under low power exhibits follicular involution.**

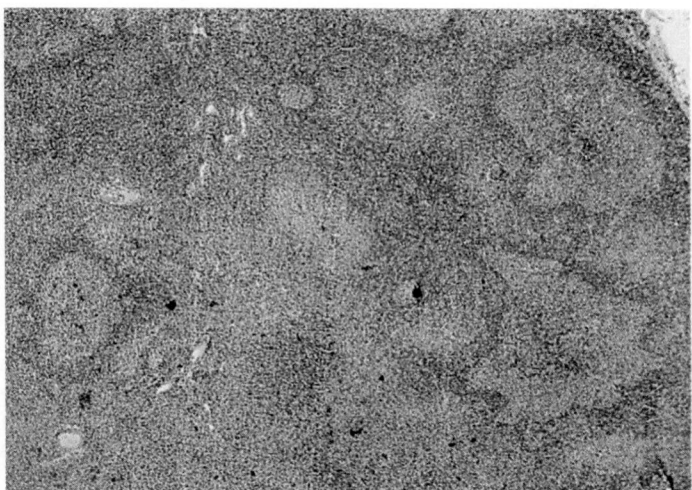

Figure 3 **Lymph node viewed under low power exhibits a mixed pattern of both explosive follicular hyperplasia and follicular involution.**

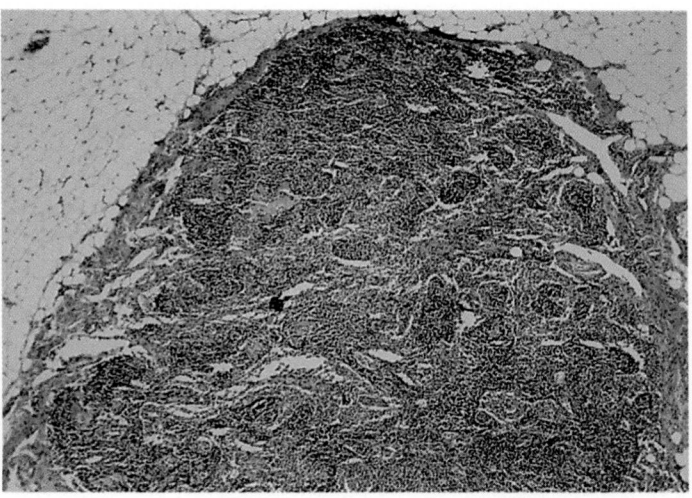

Figure 4 **Lymph node viewed under low power exhibits a pattern of lymphocyte depletion.**

with prognosis: explosive follicular hyperplasia, follicular involution, a mixed pattern, and a lymphocyte-depleted pattern. Explosive follicular hyperplasia describes a pattern of enlarged confluent follicles with disruption of the medullary zone of the lymph node [*see Figure 1*]. Follicular involution is associated with a hypocellular, frequently hyalinized follicle and with hyperplasia of the paracortical areas [*see Figure 2*]. The mixed pattern contains explosive follicular hyperplasia and follicular involution in the same lymph node [*see Figure 3*]. Finally, the lymphocyte-depleted pattern is characterized by the total absence of follicular and paracortical areas. The loss of lymphocytes in the lymph node is associated with the predominance of histiocytes and plasma cells [*see Figure 4*].

The presence of enlarged follicles is associated with a good immunologic response and slower progression of disease, whereas the presence of involuted, hyalinized follicles is more frequently associated with opportunistic infections, Kaposi sarcoma, and lymphoma. Evidence suggests that patients with either explosive follicular hyperplasia or the mixed pattern of explosive follicular hyperplasia and follicular involution have rather pro-

longed survival, even if they have Kaposi sarcoma. The presence of follicular involution in a lymph node is associated with a survival time of less than 1 year. Lymphocyte depletion was seen as a terminal finding in several autopsy cases, suggesting that the pattern represents the end stage of the hyperplastic process.[25] The pathologic findings reflect a progressive loss of the CD4+-bearing area of the lymph node.

After a lymph node is removed from an HIV-infected patient and before the tissue is removed from the operative field, representative specimens should be placed in sterile containers for routine bacterial culture, culture and smear for tuberculosis, fungal culture, and viral culture. Tissue from the same lymph node should then be delivered to the pathologist as quickly as possible. It is important that culture material from the same lymph node be examined microscopically, because granulomas or actual organisms may be detected before the culture results are available. Data from the pathologist may aid the microbiology laboratory staff in its handling of the cultures.

The pathologist needs to receive the fresh, gently handled specimen, in saline, as soon after the biopsy as possible, for two important reasons. First, because the tissue is not in formalin, it will rapidly autolyze if not processed immediately. Second, if the diagnosis is lymphoma, the pathologist must have the tissue when it is fresh to perform lymphocyte marker studies. Because different lymphomas respond to different chemotherapeutic regimens, the cell type of the lymphoma is critical. Most surgical pathology laboratories are equipped to perform membrane marker studies on lymph node tissue.

Prevention of Disease Transmission

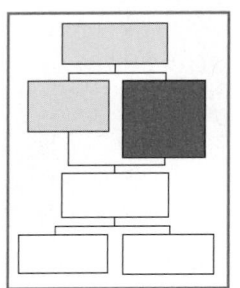

GENERAL

A key question for surgeons, operating room committees, infection control committees, and clinicians involved with endoscopy is how to effectively clean instruments, equipment, or other inanimate objects to be used with AIDS patients. Those agents that are effective against mycobacteria, the most resistant group of organisms encountered in this population, are also the agents considered most effective against other bacterial and viral pathogens.[46] A complete list of agents and their efficacies can be obtained from the Disinfectants Branch of the Office of Pesticides, United States Environmental Protection Agency, 401 M Street, S.W., Washington, DC 20460.

Agents are classified according to whether they are to be used for sterilization, disinfection, or antisepsis.[47] Agents that sterilize inanimate objects kill all microbial organisms as well as bacterial endospores. Disinfectants are not quite as effective, in that they are not capable of killing bacterial spores. In many cases, an agent may serve as a disinfectant when placed in contact for a short time with the object requiring cleansing and may be capable of sterilizing surgical instruments that are exposed to it for longer periods. Disinfectants are subclassified as having high-level, intermediate-level, or low-level germicidal activity. High-level agents are effective against bacterial spores. Intermediate-level disinfectants are less effective against spores but are mycobactericidal. Low-level disinfectants do not kill *Mycobacteria* and some fungi. Antiseptic agents are used on tissue and therefore must be less toxic than sterilants or disinfectants.

According to current CDC recommendations, agents classified by the United States Environmental Protection Agency as sterilants can be used for sterilization or high-level disinfection, depending on contact time. All instruments entering the bloodstream or other sterile tissues should be sterilized before use. Instruments that contact mucosal surfaces, such as endoscopes, should receive high-level disinfection, which can be achieved with solutions of glutaraldehyde (2%), hydrogen peroxide (3% to 6%), or formaldehyde (1% to 8%).

RISKS TO PATIENTS

Transfusions

Fresh whole blood, packed red blood cells, platelets, plasma, cryoprecipitate, and leukocytes can all carry HIV. In addition, clotting factor concentrates that are not generated by recombinant methods may also carry the virus. Some preparations of γ-globulin can temporarily cause a false positive ELISA result for HIV, but they do not contain the virus or transmit it to recipients. Albumin and plasma extracts (Plasmanate), although prepared from whole blood, do not carry HIV, hepatitis B virus (HBV), or

HCV, because the process by which they are purified inactivates the virus particles. Since adequate antibody testing became available in May 1985, the incidence of undetected HIV in transfused blood has been extremely low, and only anecdotal cases involving contaminated blood have been reported to the CDC. It is currently estimated that the risk of receiving a unit of blood that is contaminated with HIV is one in 150,000 (< 0.0007%).[48]

To minimize the risk of HIV being transmitted by transfusion, patients have increasingly requested the use of predeposited autologous blood donations (PAD) or blood donated by family members or friends (directed donations). This approach has been increasingly discouraged by blood bank and hospital administrators.[49] Both directed donations and PAD are very expensive methods of preserving homeostasis during surgery. Half of the PAD units of blood are discarded. In addition, the risk of an ABO mismatch error is as great as the risk of HIV transmission in standard bank blood. The use of intraoperative blood salvage and acute normovolemic hemodilution in combination with intravenous iron and erythropoietin provides a reasonable alternative to blood transfusion.[50]

Transplantation

Because it has been shown that HIV can be present in semen, blood, urine, tears, breast milk, cerebrospinal fluid, and saliva and because it is suspected that HIV can be present in all secretions and excretions, as well as all body tissues,[51] potential donors of tissue for transplantation must be tested for serum antibodies to HIV to prevent inadvertent transfer of the virus. Parenthetically, transmission of HIV by artificial insemination has also been documented, so this risk should be considered whenever artificial insemination is planned.[52]

Transmission from Surgical Personnel

An HIV-infected surgeon could theoretically transmit the virus to his or her patients. Although this concern has been well publicized,[53] there have been no documented reports of transmission from surgeon to patient. Furthermore, the CDC has not recommended restricting HIV-positive surgeons from operating.[54]

Unlike surgeon-to-patient transmission of HIV, HBV transmission from surgeon to patient is a significant concern. In a well-documented report involving a nonimmunized cardiac surgeon who acquired HBV infection in the workplace, transmission of the virus occurred in 19 of 122 patients (16%) on whom the surgeon operated over a 12-month period.[55] The surgeon's blood was positive for hepatitis B e antigen (HBeAg), and sweat from inside his glove was found to contain both HBV antigen and HBV DNA. No deficiencies were found in the surgeon's infection control practice by the CDC, which suggested that the virus might have spread through microperforations in his gloves. This case did not receive the same publicity that cases of HIV transmission have received in the lay press. However, its significance is clear: contact between health care workers who are HBV (HBeAg) positive and patients should be restricted.

RISKS TO HEALTH CARE WORKERS

The CDC now recommends that precautions to prevent HIV transmission be taken with all patients, not only those known to be infected with HIV or at high risk for such infection [see 135 *Viral Infection*].[18,20,38,39] It is important that any hospital personnel who come in contact with patients, their patients' tissues, or their blood, body fluids, or excreta know of the potential risk in

Table 2 Preventable Exposures to HIV among Health Care Workers*[49]

Circumstances of Preventable Exposure	Number of Health Care Workers (% of 938 Exposed Health Care Workers)
Recapping of needle	152 (16%)
Injury from improper disposal of needle or sharp object	119 (13%)
Contamination of open wound	93 (10%)
Use of needle-cutting device	9 (1%)
Total preventable exposures	373 (40%)

*The total sample under surveillance consisted of 938 health care workers exposed to blood or other body fluids of a patient with AIDS or an AIDS-related illness.

handling materials from these patients and take appropriate precautions. Patients in high-risk groups should be placed on enteric precautions to protect health care workers not only from HIV infection but also from HBV infection (up to 80% of such patients are HBV carriers). As part of any operative procedure on HIV-infected patients, all operating room, nursing, and anesthesia personnel, as well as employees of surgical pathology laboratories and any other laboratories, should employ universal precautions. Employees in ancillary areas, such as housekeeping and dietary services and the venipuncture team, need to be trained in the use of universal precautions.

Exposure to the virus in the workplace is considered to be preventable in many cases.[56] Most injuries result from carelessness in handling sharp objects, such as needles [*see Table 2*]. Self-inflicted puncture incurred in the course of recapping used needles is the most common cause of inadvertent exposure to HIV. Consequently, the most important rule to follow when handling used needles is to discard them uncapped in a container that is large enough to accommodate the attached syringe. Tissue specimens, wastes, soiled linen, blood samples, and sharp objects (e.g., surgical instruments, needles, and glassware) must be handled with extreme care. Dressings and other disposable materials should be discarded in specially marked containers and not with the regular hospital refuse.

The use of double gloves has been shown to minimize the possibility of contact with patient blood through small defects in the gloves, and it reduces the likelihood of blood contact with skin when a glove puncture occurs.[57,58] The following are additional precautions health care workers should take when handling any potentially infectious materials:

1. Wear gloves when handling body fluids.
2. Wear a gown to prevent contamination of clothing.
3. Wash hands after contact with body fluids.
4. Place fluid from a potentially contaminated host in two impervious containers.
5. Clean spills with either a 1:10 dilution of 5.25% sodium hypochlorite in water or with some other type of sterilant.
6. Wear masks and protective eyeglasses when there is a possibility of aerosolization of material.

Even health care workers who do not have exfoliative dermatitis or an open wound should wear gloves during patient care. Evidence suggests that the affinity of HIV for Langerhans cells may permit the virus to invade a host through intact skin or mucous membranes.[59]

RISKS TO SURGEONS

HIV Transmission

The risk that a surgeon will acquire an HIV infection while treating a patient who has undetected AIDS is quite low.[54,56] The CDC has prospectively evaluated nearly 1,500 health care workers who cared for AIDS patients. Serum samples were taken from these workers when they first began to work with AIDS patients and were stored in anticipation of a test for HIV. Of these workers, 666 were exposed to HIV through needlesticks or through cuts from sharp instruments. When tests were performed on these exposed individuals, none were found to have undergone seroconversion after their exposure to HIV. However, two health care workers for whom no baseline blood sample had been drawn did test positive for antibody to HIV after an injury. Because they did not belong to a known risk group for AIDS, they were believed to have generated antibody to HIV as a result of exposure in the workplace. On the basis of this study, the risk to a health care worker of acquiring HIV infection after an accidental needle-stick exposure was concluded to be 2 divided by 666, or 0.3%. A follow-up study found the rate of infection to be 0.5%.[60] Subsequent surveillance of health care workers identified 151 individuals who acquired HIV infection in the workplace [*see Table 3*]; 49 had proven seroconversion, and 102 were HIV positive but had no HIV-negative baseline serum sample.

The CDC conducted a serosurvey of 770 surgeons practicing in two inner-city areas where more than 3,000 cases of AIDS have been reported.[61] Accompanying the assay for HIV, HBV, and HCV was a questionnaire designed to elucidate the practice patterns of the surgeons tested. Of the 770 surgeons, 1 (0.13%) was HIV positive; he had practiced for more than 25 years and had performed more than 300 operations in the past year. The study did not specify how the surgeon acquired HIV, and it was noted that he did not participate in high-risk behavior. To date,

Table 3 Health Care Workers with Documented or Suspected HIV Infection[9]

Health Care Workers	No. of Workers	
	With Documented HIV (%)*	With Suspected HIV (%)†
Dental	0	7 (7%)
Mortician	0	3 (3%)
Emergency medical team/paramedic	0	9 (9%)
Health aide	1 (2%)	12 (12%)
Housekeeper	1 (2%)	7 (7%)
Laboratory technician	18 (37%)	15 (15%)
Nurse	19 (39%)	24 (24%)
Physician		
Surgeon	9	4 (4%)
Nonsurgeon	6 (12%)	10 (10%)
Respiratory therapist	1 (2%)	2 (2%)
Surgical technician	2 (4%)	1 (1%)
Other	1 (2%)	8 (8%)
Total	49	102

*Evidence of seroconversion after occupational exposure to HIV.
†HIV seropositivity in health care workers with occupational exposure to HIV who do not have behavioral or transfusion risks for HIV infection.

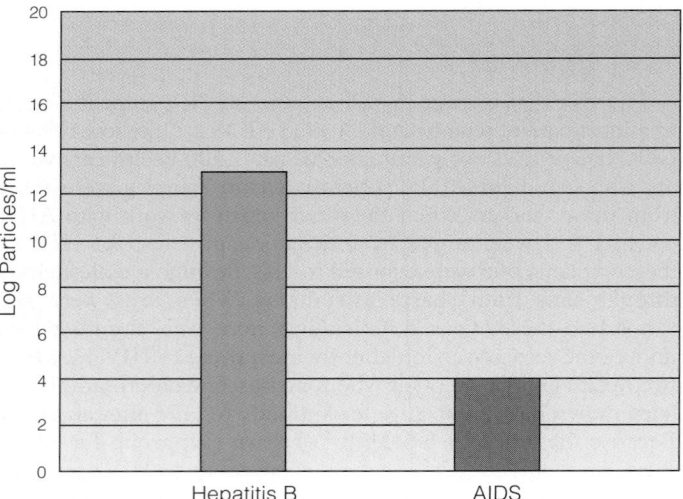

Figure 5   **The numbers of infectious viral particles per milliliter of blood in patients with active hepatitis B infections and in AIDS patients are compared.**[67]

there has been no documented seroconversion in operating room personnel after a solid-bore needle injury in the OR.

Transmission via skin contact with body fluids was documented in the case of a woman whose infant had received a transfusion from an HIV-infected donor at 3 months of age. The mother was closely involved in the baby's care and took no precautions against contact with the child's blood and body fluids. Seventeen months after the child received the contaminated blood, the mother tested positive on ELISA for HIV. No other risk factors accounted for the change in the mother's HIV antibody titer.[62]

Exposure to blood in the OR has been of great concern to all operating room personnel since the AIDS epidemic began. The average practicing surgeon has 30 parenteral exposures to blood a year.[63] The fact that hollow-bore needles carry more blood than solid-bore needles may be the reason that transmission in the operating room has not yet occurred. Four studies from the early 1990s established a blood-skin exposure rate of approximately 20% and a parenteral exposure rate of approximately 4% during surgical procedures.[46,64-66] Long operative procedures requiring transfusions are most likely to be associated with blood exposure. Types of procedures that pose a high risk of exposure to blood are cardiac surgery; obstetrics, especially cesarean sections; trauma surgery; and emergency surgery. Special care must be taken to minimize exposure in these procedures; eye protection and use of double gloves are barrier precaution measures that can reduce the likelihood of contact with the patient's blood.

Transmission of HIV to hospital workers is uncommon when compared with transmission of HBV because of the relatively low concentration of HIV in the blood of AIDS patients [*see Figure 5*]. The concentration of virus particles is estimated to be 10^4 particles/ml in an AIDS patient, whereas it is 10^{13} particles/ml in a patient who has an active HBV infection.[67]

Although HIV transmission is uncommon in the hospital environment, the risk to surgeons is very real. This is evidenced by the fact that even the lower reported rate of transmission by needle stick, 0.3%, is comparable to the 0.4% (1 in 250) rate of transmission by unprotected anal intercourse, which is considered high-risk behavior.[68,69] Three independent factors are important in determining a surgeon's risk of acquiring HIV infection: (1) the number of needle sticks or punctures contaminated with the patient's body fluids, (2) the percentage of HIV-infected patients in the surgeon's patient population, and (3) the number of years a surgeon is at risk for acquiring an HIV infection. If the risk of HIV transmission by a contaminated needle is 0.3% to 0.5%, if the HIV-infected population is 10%, if the number of needle sticks averages 30 a year, and if the surgeon has 40 years of exposure, then the lifetime risk of acquiring HIV infection can be as high as 60%.[70]

HEPATITIS TRANSMISSION

The primary health risk to surgeons caring for patients with HIV infection or AIDS is that of acquiring hepatitis B or hepatitis C. The hepatitis D virus (HDV) has been identified as posing an additional risk of death in patients with acute hepatitis; persons who are infected with both HBV and HDV have a higher mortality.[71]

The epidemiology of hepatitis B has been well studied because there are numerous antigen and antibody markers of the virus in the blood of chronic carriers. On the basis of data from assays of these markers, it is estimated that more than 200,000 persons in the United States acquire new HBV infections each year.[72] Of these 200,000, 25% will have symptoms of hepatitis, 5% will require hospitalization for their acute illness, and 1% to 2% of these hospitalized patients will develop fatal fulminant hepatitis [*see Figure 6*].

Between 5% and 10% of patients infected with HBV become chronic carriers—that is, they do not effectively clear the antigen from their systems, and they have a subclinical hepatic infection for prolonged periods. This group of patients is at risk for cirrhosis, with subsequent hepatic failure or hepatoma. Many chronic hepatitis carriers are unable to clear the infection because of immunosuppression as a result of another disease process, such as advanced HIV infection. AIDS patients are very likely to have had an HBV infection and to be chronic carriers. HIV-infected patients are also less likely to manifest an inflammatory response to hepatic infections. The CDC has estimated that as many as 80% of homosexual men, intravenous drug users, mentally retarded persons, and hemodialysis patients have serologic markers indicating a previous HBV infection.[73] Household contact or sexual relations with these high-risk individuals also involves a significant risk of acquiring HBV infection. It is estimated that up to 60% of such contacts have positive serology for HBV.

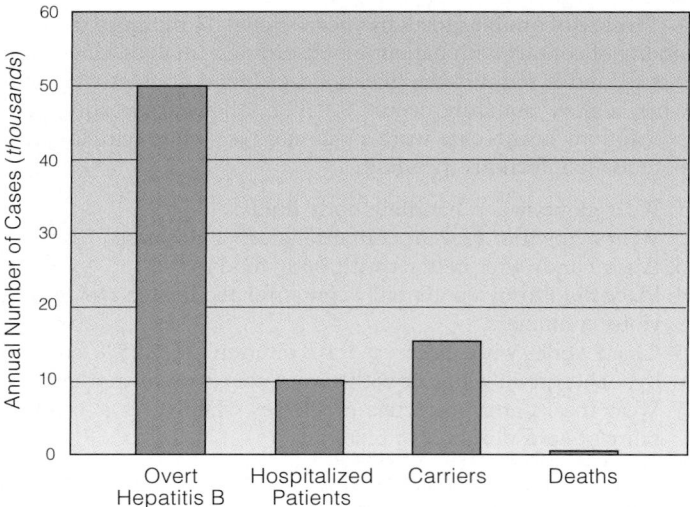

Figure 6   **The annual incidence of hepatitis B infection in the United States is 200,000 cases. Various subgroups of hepatitis B patients are shown.**[72]

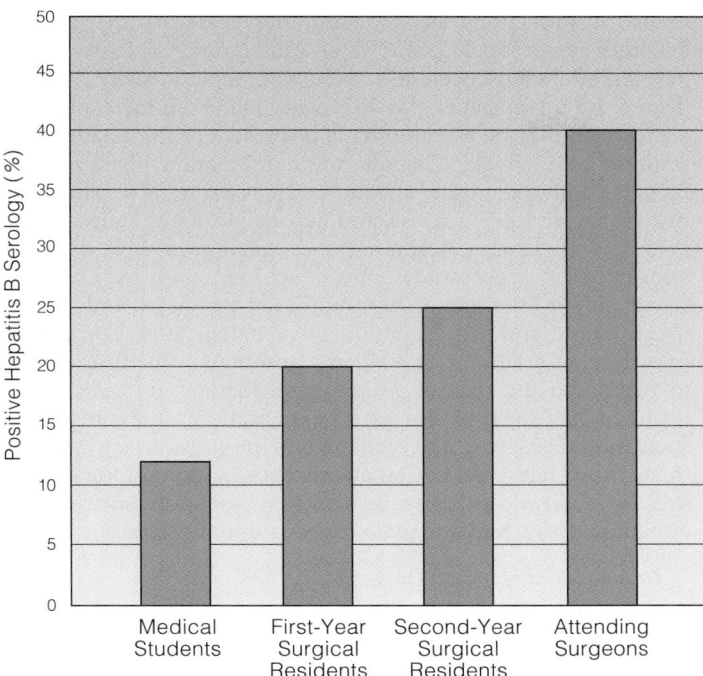

Figure 7 **The prevalence of positive serology for hepatitis B increases among individuals in successive stages of a surgical career.**[72]

Exposure to hepatitis carriers is a risk for health care workers, particularly for those who work with blood products [*see 135 Viral Infection*]. Physicians involved with direct patient care are at especially high risk.[74] Those in administrative situations who do not have clinical contact with patients have a relatively low risk of acquiring hepatitis, whereas surgeons, particularly cardiac surgeons and transplant surgeons, are at especially high risk. The risk of hepatitis infection also increases with age.[71,75] The incidence of positive hepatitis B serology is between 12% and 13% in students in their last year of medical school, nearly 20% in surgical residents at the end of their first year, and about 25% in surgical residents after the second year. During the course of an unimmunized senior surgeon's career, the risk of having hepatitis B approaches 50% [*see Figure 7*]. These risks are exceedingly high and emphasize the importance of widespread use of the hepatitis B vaccine [*see 135 Viral Infection*].

At least two studies have shown that there are numerous unimmunized practicing surgeons who finished medical school, training, or both before the hepatitis B vaccine first became available.[61,76] These surgeons are at substantial risk for HBV infection and consequently need to be immunized. Surgeons who were immunized 5 or more years ago should have their titers checked; if titers are low, a booster is advisable.

Postexposure Prophylaxis

MANAGEMENT AFTER EXPOSURE TO HIV

If a health care worker is injured by a sharp object that was contaminated by exposure to fluid or tissue from an HIV-positive patient, a series of blood samples should be drawn at the time of injury and again at 6 weeks and 3, 6, and 12 months after the injury to determine whether HIV

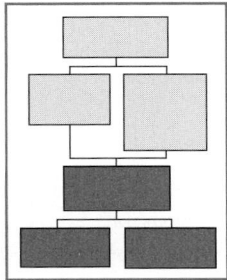

infection has occurred. Although administration of antiretroviral therapy is recommended,[77] to date, no prospective trials have been performed to confirm its effectiveness in humans. A retrospective case-control study published in 1996 supported the postexposure use of zidovudine.[78] The current recommendations for prophylaxis after a needle-stick injury are based on the likelihood of transmission from the incident.[79] In lower-risk situations, the risk of drug toxicity must be carefully weighed against the benefits of protection against HIV transmission.

The average risk of acquiring HIV after a percutaneous exposure is estimated to be 0.3%,[80] and the risk of acquiring HIV through mucocutaneous exposure approaches approximately 0.09%. It has been shown that the more blood transferred by a hollow-bore needle, the greater the likelihood of transmission. Clearly, patient factors such as viral burden and the presence of syncytia-inducing strains of virus will also influence the likelihood of seroconversion. Host factors such as cytotoxic T cell responses and perhaps T cell C3a/C5a receptors may also influence the outcome. With all this in mind, the CDC has formulated specific recommendations for postexposure prophylaxis (PEP).[81]

Because systemic infection after HIV exposure is thought not to occur immediately in primates, prompt initiation of antiretroviral therapy may sufficiently inhibit the initial replication to keep the inoculum of virus low and allow for effective immune clearance. Animal models are imperfect but have suggested that greatest efficacy of PEP was achieved when therapy was instituted within 24 hours of exposure. Overall efficacy of PEP is impossible to ascertain, because the incidence is fortunately low enough not to allow for a prospective study with sufficient statistical power to determine efficacy.

The current recommendations are based partly on the combination of simian studies, the experience with ziduvodine in a retrospective case-control study of health care workers, and collective experience with the prevention of vertical transmission through the use of antiviral prophylaxis. It is also recognized that as HIV-infected patients are increasingly likely to have been treated with a variety of retroviral agents, their likelihood of having multidrug-resistant strains of HIV increases correspondingly. Arbitrary selection of PEP agents may not be optimal; it is possible that knowledge of the patient's antiretroviral history and the results of genotypic antiretroviral resistance studies may need to be taken into account for optimal PEP selection. Whenever possible, physicians familiar with the source patient and local resistance patterns should be consulted on the choice of PEP regimens. However, institution of PEP should never be delayed for consultation, because the regimen can always be altered later if further information is obtained.

The choice of agents is largely empirical, but the need for PEP and the number of drugs to be used should be predicated on (1) the risk assessment of the injury, taking into account the source's HIV status (and, if the patient is HIV positive, the patient's clinical status and viral load); (2) solid-bore versus hollow-bore needle injury (large or small inoculum); (3) whether the source needle was used for arterial or venous puncture; and (4) whether the injury involved intact or nonintact skin or mucous membrane exposure.

A two-drug PEP regimen is probably adequate for situations in which the source is known to be HIV positive but thought to have a relatively low viral load, in which the source's HIV status is unknown but he or she is known to participate in high-risk activity, or in which the worker sustains either a minor percutaneous or mucous membrane exposure. A three-drug regimen would be advised with more severe percutaneous exposure, with

Table 4 Nucleoside Reverse Transcriptase Inhibitors

Agent	Toxicity
Zidovudine	Marrow suppression, myopathy, nausea
Stavudine	Peripheral neuropathy, pancreatitis, increased liver function tests
Lamivadine	Nausea, possible lipoatrophy, especially with concurrent stavudine
Didanosine	Pancreatitis, peripheral neuropathy, diarrhea
Abacavir	Life-threatening hypersensitivity reaction in approximately 5%

extensive exposure of intact skin or mucous membranes, or when the source is thought to have a high viral load. Because all the drugs used for PEP can have significant side effects, even in the short term, the potential risks of two-drug or three-drug therapy should be weighed against the likelihood of acquiring an HIV infection. With cases in which the source patient can be identified but the HIV status is unknown, a rapid HIV test such as the SUDS should be employed. If the results of such testing is negative, PEP should not be given. If rapid testing is not available, PEP can be offered until the source patient is proved to be HIV negative by conventional tests.

For the choice of agents, the 1998 CDC guidelines suggest zidovudine and lamivudine (3TC) for two-agent therapy, with the addition of indanivir or nelfinavir for three-drug therapy. Zidovudine and 3TC are now available in a combination pill that is taken twice a day, which makes it a more convenient alternative; however, the increasing prevalence of the 184 mutation that confers 3TC resistance makes this less likely to be effective in situations involving patients who have been treated with 3TC. Newer drugs such as efavirenz may offer more tolerable alternatives to adding a protease inhibitor, as was recommended in the past. The 2001 guidelines leave the choice more open to local expertise.

No discussion of occupational exposure is complete without mention of HCV coinfection. Approximately 40% of all HIV-infected patients are coinfected with HCV; in intravenous drug users, the incidence of HCV coinfection can be as high as 90%. Medical personnel exposed to HCV via occupational injury should undergo baseline testing for HCV antibodies and a baseline alanine transaminase (ALT) determination, with repeat testing in 4 to 6 months. There is no prophylactic regimen available, but some authorities recommend early intervention with HCV therapy (interferon alfa and ribavirin) if HCV remains detectable—a finding that would indicate persistence of infection.

TOXICITIES OF HIGHLY ACTIVE ANTIVIRAL THERAPY

Nucleoside Reverse Transcriptase Inhibitors

Long-term exposure to antiretroviral agents has not only improved survival but also introduced a variety of significant toxicities that physicians evaluating an HIV-infected patient must take into account. Nucleoside toxicities became apparent with the introduction of the first nucleoside reverse transcriptase inhibitor, zidovudine, 15 years ago, but a multitude of side effects are now known to be associated with all agents in this class. These agents appear to be toxic primarily through their ability to inhibit mitochondrial DNA synthesis. When critical

levels of mitochondrial depletion are reached, the patient becomes symptomatic [*see Table 4*]. All the nucleoside transcriptase inhibitors have been associated with hepatotoxicity to some degree. All these agents may also cause increased levels of lactic acid, which may be asymptomatic or present as fulminant lactic acidosis and shock. Patients on combination therapy that includes both didanosine and stavudine seem to be at particular risk for severe lactic acidosis and hepatic steatosis. Patients may present with nausea, vomiting, abdominal pain, and diarrhea and become progressively more acidotic and hypotensive. Lactate levels in excess of 10 mmol/L are associated with multi-organ failure and a mortality of greater than 80%. Symptoms may develop gradually or suddenly and may occur from weeks to years after the start of antiretroviral therapy. Routine monitoring of lactic acid levels is of no benefit, because the results of such monitoring are not predictive of progression to symptomatic lactic acidemia. Once patients become asymptomatic, the keys to survival are early recognition, discontinuance of the offending drugs, and adequate oxygenation of tissues.

Nonnucleoside Reverse Transcriptase Inhibitors

The nonnucleoside reverse transcriptase inhibitors [*see Table 5*] are increasingly used in triple-drug regimens. They are known to cause rashes and have also been associated with hepatitis. Nevirapine has been implicated in fulminant hepatic failure in the setting of postexposure prophylaxis and in South African women. There is some concern that it may be more hepatotoxic in patients with hepatitis C infection.

Protease Inhibitors

The protease inhibitors [*see Table 6*] have been more frequently associated with metabolic syndromes involving alterations in fat metabolism, blood glucose, and lipids than with hepatitis or lactic acidemia. Hypercholesterolemia and hypertriglyceridemia have been associated with HAART, especially in regimens that include protease inhibitors. It is well recognized that there is a

Table 5 Nonnucleoside Reverse Transcriptase Inhibitors

Agent	Toxicity
Nevirapine	Rash, fever, hepatitis
Delavirdine	Rash, fever, hepatitis
Efavirenz	Rash, somnolence, insomnia, nightmares

Table 6 Protease Inhibitors

Agent	Toxicity
Indinavir	Nephrolithiasis, elevated bilirubin, fat redistribution, hyperglycemia, dry mouth
Nelfinavir	Diarrhea, abdominal pain
Ritonavir	Femoral numbness, diarrhea, hyperlipidemia
Saquinavir	Diarrhea, liver function abnormalities
Amprenavir	Diarrhea, nausea
Lopinavir/ritonavir	Diarrhea, hyperlipidemia

higher incidence of cardiac disease in HIV-infected patients receiving HAART than in age-matched control patients and that the presence of other traditional risk factors such as smoking and hypertension magnifies the risk. This has led most HIV practitioners to aggressively attempt to correct lipid abnormalities through the use of lipid-lowering agents. The increased risk of premature cardiac disease has also led physicians to consider

tests to attempt to identify occult coronary disease. Patients on protease inhibitors have been found to have insulin resistance even in the absence of overt diabetes, which also contributes to increased risk of coronary artery disease. For that reason, when HIV-infected patients with blood lipid abnormalities are being evaluated for elective surgical procedures, it is prudent to include a cardiac assessment.

References

1. Pneumocystis pneumonia—Los Angeles. MMWR Morb Mortal Wkly Rep 30:250, 1981

2. Kaposi's sarcoma and *Pneumocystis* pneumonia among homosexual men: New York City and California. MMWR Morb Mortal Wkly Rep 30:305, 1981

3. Barre-Sinoussi F, Chermann JC, Rey F, et al: Isolation of a T-lymphotropic retrovirus from a patient at risk for acquired immune deficiency syndrome (AIDS). Science 220:868, 1983

4. Current trends update: acquired immunodeficiency syndrome—United States, 1981–1988. MMWR Morb Mortal Wkly Rep 38:229, 1989

5. The global HIV and AIDS epidemic, 2001. MMWR Morb Mortal Wkly Rep 50:434, 2001

6. Institute of Medicine and the National Academy of Sciences: Mobilizing against AIDS: The Unfinished Story of a Virus. Harvard University Press, Cambridge, Massachusetts, 1986

7. Valdez H, Chowdhry TK, Asaad R, et al: Changing spectrum of mortality due to human immunodeficiency virus: analysis of 260 deaths during 1995–1999. Clin Infect Dis 32:1487, 2001

8. Rous T: Transmission of a malignant growth by means of a cell-free filtrate. JAMA 56:198, 1911

9. Robert-Guroff M, Nakao Y, Notake K, et al: Natural antibodies to human retrovirus HTLV in a cluster of Japanese patients with adult T-cell leukemia. Science 215:975, 1982

10. Barnes D: Keeping the AIDS virus out of blood supply. Science 233:514, 1986

11. U.S. Public Health Service guidelines for testing and counseling blood and plasma donors for human immunodeficiency virus type 1 antigen. MMWR Recomm Rep 45(RR-2):1, 1996

12 Persistent lack of detectable HIV-1 antibody in a person with HIV infections—Utah. MMWR Morb Mortal Wkly Rep 45:182, 1996

13. Recommendations for donor screening with a licensed test for HIV-1 antigen. US Department of Health and Human Services, Public Health Service, Food and Drug Administration, Center for Biologics Evaluation and Research, Rockville, Maryland, 1995

14. Grubert TA, Reindell D, Kastner R, et al: Rates of postoperative complications among human immunodeficiency virus–infected women who have undergone obstetric and gynecologic surgical procedures. Clin Infect Dis 34:822, 2002

15. Kirk O, Reiss P, Uberti-Foppa C, et al: Safe interruption of maintenance therapy against previous infection with four common HIV-associated opportunistic pathogens during potent antiretroviral therapy. Ann Intern Med 137:285, 2002

16. Margulis SJ, Honig CL, Soave R, et al: Biliary tract obstruction in the acquired immunodeficiency syndrome. Ann Intern Med 105:207, 1986

17. Robinson G, Wilson SE, Williams RA: Surgery in patients with acquired immunodeficiency syn-drome. Arch Surg 122:170, 1987

18. Barone JE, Gingold BS, Arvanitis ML, et al: Abdominal pain in patients with acquired immunodeficiency syndrome. Ann Surg 204:619, 1986

19. Davis JM, Mouradian J, Fernandez RD, et al: Acquired immune deficiency syndrome: a surgical perspective. Arch Surg 119:90, 1984

20. Spach DH: HIV and AIDS. WebMD Scientific American Medicine, Section 7, Subsection XXIII. Dale DC, Federman DD, Eds. WebMD Inc, New York, 2001

21. Rao TK: Acute renal failure syndromes in human immunodeficiency virus infections. Semin Nephrology 18:370, 1998

22. Dube MP, Sprecher D, Henry WK, et al: Preliminary guidelines for the evaluation and management of dyslipidemia in adults infected with human immunodeficiency virus and receiving antiretroviral therapy: recommendations of the Adult AIDS Clinical Trial Group Cardiovascular Disease Focus Group. Clin Infect Dis 31:1216, 2000

23. Duong M, Cottin Y, Piroth L, et al: Exercise stress testing for detection of silent myocardial ischemia in human immunodeficieny virus–infected patients receiving antiretroviral therapy. Clin Infect Dis 34:523, 2002

24. Yunis NA, Stone VE: Cardiac manifestations of HIV/AIDS: a review of disease spectrum and clinical management. J Acquir Immune Defic Syndr Hum Retrovirol 18:145, 1998

25. Bedi GC, Westra WH, Farzadegan H, et al: Microsatellite instability in primary neoplasms from HIV + patients. Nat Med 1:65, 1995

26. Koblin BA, Hessol NA, Zauber AG, et al: Increased incidence of cancer among homosexual men, New York City and San Francisco, 1978–1990. Am J Epidemiol 144:916, 1996

27. Wistuba II, Behrens C, Milchgrub S, et al: Comparison of molecular changes in lung cancers in HIV-positive and HIV-indeterminate subjects. JAMA 279:1554, 1998

28. Morris L, Distenfeld A, Amorosi E, et al: Autoimmune thrombocytopenic purpura in homosexual men. Ann Intern Med 96:714, 1982

29. Walsh CM, Nardi MA, Karpatkin S: On the mechanism of thrombocytopenic purpura in sexually active homosexual men. N Engl J Med 311:635, 1984

30. Tsoukas CM, Bernard NF, Abrahamowicz M, et al: Effect of splenectomy on slowing human immunodeficiency virus disease progression. Arch Surg 133:25, 1998

31. Lord RV, Coleman MJ, Milliken ST: Splenectomy for HIV-related immune thrombocytopenia: comparison with results of splenectomy for non-HIV immune thrombocytopenic purpura. Arch Surg 133:205, 1998

32. Dega H, Eliaszewicz M, Gisselbrecht M, et al: Infections associated with totally implantable venous access devices (TIVAD) in human

immunodeficiency virus–infected patients. J Acquir Immune Defic Syndr Hum Retrovirol 13:146, 1996

33. French AL, Beaudet LM, Benator DA, et al: Cholecystectomy in patients with AIDS: clinicopathological correlations in 107 cases. Clin Infect Dis 21:852, 1995

34. Kavin H, Jonas RB, Chowdhury L, et al: Acalculous cholecystitis and cytomegalovirus infection in the acquired immunodeficiency syndrome. Ann Intern Med 104:53, 1986

35. Benator DA, French AL, Beaudet LM, et al: *Isospora belli* infection associated with acalculous cholecystitis in a patient with AIDS. Ann Intern Med 121:663, 1994

36. Pol S, Romana CA, Richard S, et al: *Microsporidia* infection in patients with the human immunodeficiency virus and unexplained cholangitis. N Engl J Med 328:95, 1993

37. Nugent P, O'Connell TX: The surgeon's role in treating acquired immunodeficiency syndrome. Arch Surg 121:1117, 1986

38. Potter DA, Danforth DN Jr, Macher AM, et al: Evaluation of abdominal pain in the AIDS patient. Ann Surg 199:332, 1984

39. Wilson SE, Robinson G, Williams RA, et al: Acquired immune deficiency syndrome (AIDS): indications for abdominal surgery, pathology, and outcome. Ann Surg 210:428, 1989

40. Schecter WP: Human immunodeficiency virus and malignancy: thoughts on viral oncogenesis. Arch Surg 136:1419, 2001

41. Whiteford MH, Stevens KR Jr, Oh S, et al: The evolving treatment of anal cancer: how are we doing? Arch Surg 136:886, 2001

42. Fernandez R, Mouradian J, Metroka C, et al: The prognostic value of histopathology in persistent generalized lymphadenopathy in homosexual men. N Engl J Med 309:185, 1983

43. Redfield RR, Wright DC, Tramont EC: The Walter Reed staging classification for HTLV-III/LAV infection. N Engl J Med 314:131, 1986

44. Davis JM, Chadburn A, Mouradian JA: Lymph node biopsy in patients with human immunodeficiency virus infections. Arch Surg 123:1349, 1988

45. Redfield RR, Burke DS: HIV infection: the clinical picture. Sci Am 259:90, 1988

46. Farero MS: Disinfection, sterilization, and decontamination procedures. Occup Med 4(suppl):35, 1989

47. Jawetz E, Melnick JL, Adelberg EA: Antimicrobial chemotherapy. Review of Medical Microbiology, 15th ed. Adelberg EA, Melnick JL, Jawetz E, Eds. Lange Medical Publications, Los Altos, California, 1982, p 117

48. McCray E: Occupational risk of the acquired immunodeficiency syndrome among health care workers. N Engl J Med 314:1127, 1986

49. Gerberding JL, Littell C, Tarkington A, et al: Risk of exposure of surgical personnel to patients'

blood during surgery at San Francisco General Hospital. N Engl J Med 322:1788, 1990

50. Quebbeman EJ, Telford GL, Wadsworth K, et al: Double gloving: protecting surgeons from blood contamination in the operating room. Arch Surg 127:213, 1992

51. Braathen LR, Ramirez G, Kunze RO, et al: Langerhans cells as primary target cells for HIV infection (letter). Lancet 2:1094, 1987

52. Cumming PD, Wallace EL, Schorr JB, et al: Exposure of patients to human immunodeficiency virus through the transfusion of blood components that test antibody-negative. N Engl J Med 321:941, 1989

53. Moore SB: AIDS, blood transfusions, and directed donations. N Engl J Med 314:1454, 1986

54. Monk TG, Goodnough LT, Brecher ME, et al: A prospective randomized comparison of three blood conservation strategies for radical prostatectomy. Anesthesiology 91:24, 1999

55. Ho DD, Byington RE, Schooley RT, et al: Infrequency of isolation of HTLV-III virus from saliva in AIDS. N Engl J Med 313:1606, 1985

56. Morgan J, Nolan J: Risks of AIDS with artificial insemination. N Engl J Med 314:386, 1986

57. Gerbert B, Maguire BT, Hulley SB, et al: Physicians and acquired immunodeficiency syndrome: what patients think about human immunodeficiency virus in medical practice. JAMA 262:1969, 1989

58. Summary: recommendations for preventing transmission of infection with human T-lymphotropic virus type III/lymphadenopathy-associated virus in the workplace. MMRW Morb Mortal Wkly Rep 34:681, 1985

59. Harpaz R, Von Seidlein L, Averhoff FM, et al: Transmission of hepatitis B virus to multiple patients from a surgeon without evidence of inadequate infection control. N Engl J Med 334:549, 1996

60. Marcus R: Surveillance of health care workers exposed to blood from patients infected with the human immunodeficiency virus. N Engl J Med 319:1118, 1988

61. Serosurvey of human immunodeficiency virus, hepatitis B virus, and hepatitis C virus infection among hospital-based surgeons. Serosurvey Study Group. J Am Coll Surg 180:16, 1995

62. Apparent transmission of human T-lymphotropic virus type III/lymphadenopathy-associated virus from a child to a mother providing health care. MMWR Morb Mortal Wkly Rep 35:76, 1996

63. Howard RJ: Human immunodeficiency virus testing and the risk to the surgeon of acquiring HIV. Surg Gynecol Obstet 171:22, 1990

64. Popejoy SL, Fry DE: Blood contact and exposure in the operating room. Surg Gynecol Obstet 172:480, 1991

65. Panlilio AL, Foy DR, Edwards JR, et al: Blood contacts during surgical procedures. JAMA 265:1533, 1991

66. Tokars JI, Bell DM, Culver DH, et al: Percutaneous injuries during surgical procedures. JAMA 267:2899, 1992

67. Levy JA, Kaminsky LS, Morrow WJ, et al: Infection by the retrovirus associated with the acquired immunodeficiency syndrome: clinical, biological, and molecular features. Ann Intern Med 103:694, 1985

68. Lorian V: AIDS, anal sex, and heterosexuals. Lancet 1:1111, 1988

69. Update: acquired immunodeficiency syndrome and human immunodeficiency virus infection among health-care workers. MMWR Morb Mortal Wkly Rep 37:229, 1988

70. Hagen MD, Meyer KB, Kopelman RI, et al: Human immunodeficiency virus infection in health care workers: a method for estimating individual occupational risk. Arch Intern Med 149:1541, 1989

71. Parry MF, Brown AE, Dobbs LG, et al: The epidemiology of hepatitis B infection in housestaff. Infection 6:204, 1978

72. Alter HJ: The evolution, implications, and applications of the hepatitis B vaccine (editorial). JAMA 247:2272, 1982

73. Recommendation of the Immunization Practices Advisory Committee (ACIP). MMWR Morb Mortal Wkly Rep 34:313, 1985

74. Denes AE, Smith JL, Maynard JE, et al: Hepatitis B infection in physicians: results of a nationwide seroepidemiologic survey. JAMA 239:210, 1978

75. Lenimer JH: Hepatitis B as an occupational disease of surgeons. Surg Gynecol Obstet 159:91, 1984

76. Barie PS, Dellinger EP, Dougherty SH, et al: Assessment of HBV immunization status among North American surgeons. Arch Surg 129:27, 1994

77. Henderson DK, Gerberding JL: Prophylactic zidovudine after occupational exposure to the human immunodeficiency virus: an interim analysis. J Infect Dis 160:321, 1989

78. Case-control study of HIV seroconversion in healthcare workers after percutaneous exposure to HIV infected blood—France, United Kingdom and United States. MMWR Morb Mortal Wkly Rep 44:929, 1996

79. Update: provisional Public Health Service recommendations for chemoprophylaxis after occupational exposure to HIV. MMWR Morb Mortal Wkly Rep 45:468, 1996

80. 1993 Revised classification system for HIV infection and expanded surveillance case definition for AIDS among adolescents and adults. MMWR Morb Mortal Wkly Rep 41(RR-17):1, 1992

81. Updated U.S. Public Health Service guidelines for the management of occupational exposures to HBV, HCV, and HIV and recommendations for postexposure prophylaxis. MMWR Recomm Rep 50(RR-11):1, 2001

137 NUTRITIONAL SUPPORT

Rolando H. Rolandelli, M.D., F.A.C.S., Dipin Gupta, M.D., and Douglas W. Wilmore, M.D., F.A.C.S.

Nutritional Management of Hospitalized Patients

Evaluation of the Need for Nutritional Support

INDICATIONS FOR NUTRITIONAL INTERVENTION

Nutritional support is required in patients who fall into one of the following general categories:

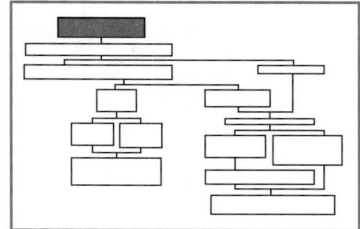

1. The patient has been without nutrition for 10 days. In a well-nourished individual, body stores are generally adequate to provide nutrients during shorter periods of stress without compromising physiologic functions, altering resistance to infection, or impairing wound healing. Provision of nutrients becomes more important as body stores become eroded because of inadequate food intake and accelerated catabolism. In general, deficits occur in surgical patients after 7 to 10 days of partial starvation; nutritional intervention should be initiated before this time.
2. The duration of illness is anticipated to be longer than 10 days. In this context, nutritional support should be considered essential care. Thus, individuals with severe peritonitis or pancreatitis, major injury (injury severity score > 15), or extensive burns (> 20% total body surface area) are candidates for nutritional support because of the known duration of their ill-

ness. (The duration of illness in chronically malnourished patients also would be expected to exceed 10 days.)
3. The patient is malnourished (loss of > 10% of usual body weight over 3 months). In general, weight loss can be used as an index of nutritional deficiency, and recovery may be compromised in patients who lack adequate body nutrient stores because of an existing nutritional deficit [*see Figure 1*]. The patient should receive nutritional support when weight loss approaches or exceeds 15% of usual body weight:

$$\% \text{ Weight loss} = \frac{\text{Usual weight} - \text{present weight}}{\text{Usual weight}} \times 100$$

Patients who do not meet one of these three general indications should be reassessed after 7 days to identify individuals in whom complications develop after hospital admission and who require nutritional support. Serum proteins with a short half-life, such as prealbumin, transferrin, or retinol-binding protein, are useful markers for assessing response to therapy.

PRIORITY OF CARDIOPULMONARY FUNCTION

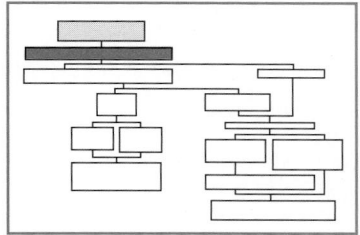

Intensive care unit patients are frequently candidates for nutritional support but often have complex medical and surgical problems that may take precedence. In decreasing order of importance, the priorities are to maintain airway patency, breathing, circulation, tissue oxygenation, acid-base neutrality, normal electrolyte concentrations, and adequate nutrition. The six functions that take priority over nutrition are usually impaired by acute and potentially life-threatening disorders that are often correctable over the short term. To optimize nutrient metabolism, circulation and tissue oxygenation must be adequate. In addition, hydrogen ion and electrolyte concentrations should be near normal in the extracellular fluid compartment, as reflected by blood or serum measurements.

If cardiopulmonary function is abnormal, nutrient administration may create additional problems. For example, in a patient with respiratory insufficiency, infusion of moderate quantities of carbohydrate could increase carbon dioxide tension (PCO_2) and lower serum potassium concentration, thereby potentially initiating a life-threatening cardiac arrhythmia. The need for nutritional support in the ICU patient should always be evaluated with respect to other care problems; acute disorders of cardiorespiratory function, disturbed acid-base status, and altered electrolyte

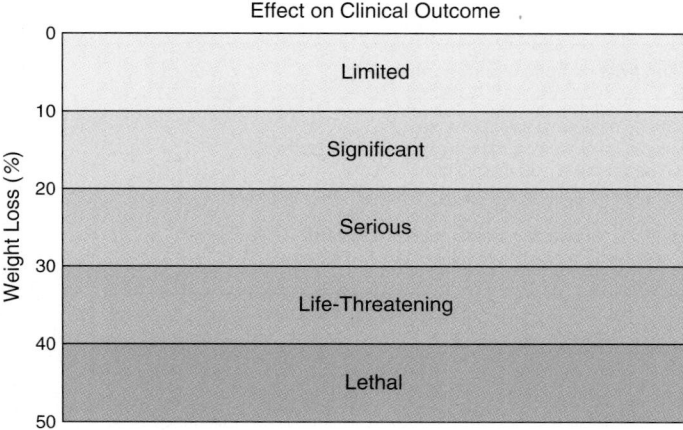

Figure 1 **The magnitude of weight loss is a rough predictor of its effect on clinical outcome.**

Give nutritional support if any of the following conditions is present:
- **Patient has been without nutrition for 7–10 days**
- **Expected duration of illness > 10 days**
- **Patient is malnourished (weight loss > 15% of usual weight)**

If nutritional intervention is not indicated initially, reassess patient after 5 days.

Initiate nutritional support only if tissue perfusion is adequate and PO$_2$, PCO$_2$, electrolyte concentrations, and acid-base balance are near normal

Estimate requirements for fluid, calories, protein, minerals, trace elements, and vitamins according to BMR, disease state, and activity level.

Abdominal distention, diarrhea, massive GI hemorrhage, obstruction, and hemodynamic instability are absent

Use existing nasogastric tube for enteral nutrition. Verify location of NG tube by aspiration of GI contents or by x-ray. Select balanced or disease-specific diet; deliver 30 ml/hr continuously at isotonicity for 24 hr. Elevate head during and after feeding to prevent regurgitation. Assess feeding tolerance.

Enteral feeding is tolerated

Assess risk for aspiration. Risk factors include depressed sensorium, gastroesophageal reflux, and history of aspiration or regurgitation.

Risk for aspiration is low

Give continuous gastric feedings of an isotonic formula at 30 ml/hr. Increase rate daily by 30 ml/hr. Increase tonicity after increasing volume.

Risk for aspiration is high

Pass feeding tube into jejunum; verify tube location by x-ray. Give formulas of 300 mOsm/kg at an initial rate of 30 ml/hr. Increase rate daily by 30 ml/hr. Increase tonicity after volume is fully increased.

Monitor patient; prevent and treat complications as necessary

Irrigate tube routinely with 20–25 ml normal saline or water.
If tube is blocked, clear by injection of a small volume of carbonated beverage.
For persistent diarrhea, give kaolin-pectin, 30 ml q. 3 hr.
To prevent peptic ulcers and bleeding, titrate gastric pH to 4.5–6.5 with antacids if necessary.
If nasoenteric tube dislodgment is recurrent, consider tube enterostomy.
If enterostomy tube leaks persistently, replace with tube of larger diameter.

Nutritional Management of Hospitalized Patients

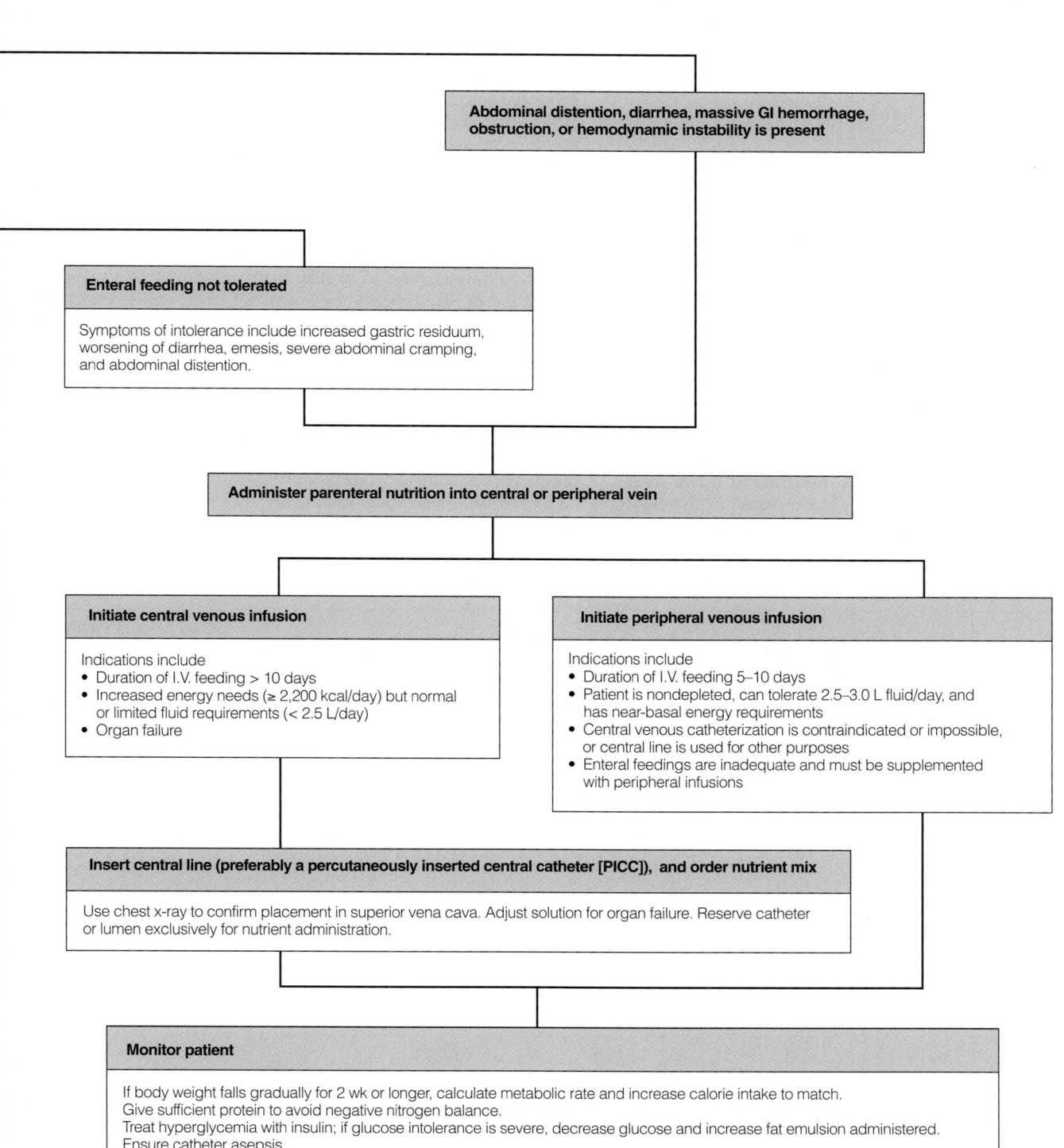

Abdominal distention, diarrhea, massive GI hemorrhage, obstruction, or hemodynamic instability is present

Enteral feeding not tolerated

Symptoms of intolerance include increased gastric residuum, worsening of diarrhea, emesis, severe abdominal cramping, and abdominal distention.

Administer parenteral nutrition into central or peripheral vein

Initiate central venous infusion

Indications include
- Duration of I.V. feeding > 10 days
- Increased energy needs (≥ 2,200 kcal/day) but normal or limited fluid requirements (< 2.5 L/day)
- Organ failure

Initiate peripheral venous infusion

Indications include
- Duration of I.V. feeding 5–10 days
- Patient is nondepleted, can tolerate 2.5–3.0 L fluid/day, and has near-basal energy requirements
- Central venous catheterization is contraindicated or impossible, or central line is used for other purposes
- Enteral feedings are inadequate and must be supplemented with peripheral infusions

Insert central line (preferably a percutaneously inserted central catheter [PICC]), and order nutrient mix

Use chest x-ray to confirm placement in superior vena cava. Adjust solution for organ failure. Reserve catheter or lumen exclusively for nutrient administration.

Monitor patient

If body weight falls gradually for 2 wk or longer, calculate metabolic rate and increase calorie intake to match.
Give sufficient protein to avoid negative nitrogen balance.
Treat hyperglycemia with insulin; if glucose intolerance is severe, decrease glucose and increase fat emulsion administered.
Ensure catheter asepsis.

Table 1 Alterations in Metabolic Rate

Patient Condition	Basal Metabolic Rate
No postoperative complications Fistula without infection	Normal
Mild peritonitis Long-bone fracture or mild to moderate injury	25% above normal
Severe injury or infection in ICU patient Multiorgan failure	50% above normal
Burn of 40%–100% of TBS	

concentrations should generally be corrected before nutritional support is initiated.

NUTRIENT REQUIREMENTS

Individual energy requirements are primarily related to body size, age, sex, and energy expenditure of activity (muscular work). In hospitalized patients who are generally inactive, the basal metabolic rate (BMR) accounts for the greatest amount of energy expenditure. The BMR in normal individuals is about 25 kcal/kg/day but can be calculated more precisely according to the Harris-Benedict formulas:

$$\text{Males: BMR (kcal/day)} = 66 + (13.7 \times \text{weight [kg]})$$
$$+ (5 \times \text{height [cm]}) - (6.8 \times \text{age [yr]})$$

$$\text{Females: BMR (kcal/day)} = 665 + (9.6 \times \text{weight [kg]})$$
$$+ (1.7 \times \text{height [cm]}) - (4.7 \times \text{age [yr]})$$

The BMR is influenced by the disease process. Hypermetabolism occurs in surgical patients with moderate to severe infection or injury, and the magnitude of the increase in the BMR depends on the extent of injury or infection. Patients generally fall into one of four categories according to their metabolic requirements [*see Table 1*].

Estimates that are based on normal basal metabolic requirements and adjusted only for disease state reflect the energy needs of patients requiring mechanical ventilation or those at bed rest. Further adjustments, however, are necessary for individuals who are out of bed and physically active. To meet the energy needs of such patients, who are in a nonbasal state, calculated requirements should be increased by an additional 15% to 20%. The metabolic response to stress and critical illness is complex and is mediated by interactions between the neuroendocrine system and circulating cytokines. This interaction produces a metabolic milieu in which the body cannot utilize supranormal amounts of nutritional substrates (i.e., hyperalimentation). In fact, administering excessive nutrients in an attempt at acute correction of nutrient deficits is often harmful, leading to an abnormal accumulation of hepatic glycogen, enhancing total energy expenditure, and causing increased urea production and elevation of the blood urea nitrogen (BUN).

Weight gain usually should not be a priority for ICU patients. Complications of nutrient delivery are minimized and nutrient metabolism generally optimized if only the energy necessary for weight maintenance is given. For most general surgical patients admitted to the ICU for non–trauma-related care, this amount is typically no more than 35 kcal/kg body weight/day. With resolution of the disease process, the hormonal environment is altered to favor anabolism. In addition, increases in spontaneous activity and in planned exercise stimulate rebuilding of lean body mass.

Protein

After energy requirements are determined, protein needs are calculated. For most patients, the protein requirement is 0.8 g/kg body weight/day (about 60 to 70 g/day). Critically ill patients, however, may need 1.5 to 2.0 g/kg/day (about 100 to 150 g/day). Most standard enteral and parenteral feeding mixtures provide this increased quantity of protein if enough formula is delivered to meet patients'

Table 2 Vitamin Requirements

Vitamin	Units	Recommended Dietary Allowance (RDA) for Daily Oral Intake	Daily Requirement of the Moderately Injured	Daily Requirement of the Severely Injured	Amount Provided by One Vitamin Pill	Daily Amount Provided by Standard Intravenous Preparations
Vitamin A (retinol)	IU	1,760 (females)–3,300 (males)	5,000	5,000	10,000	3,300 (retinal)
Vitamin D (ergocalciferol)	IU	200	400	400	400	200
Vitamin E (tocopherol)	mg TE	8–10	unknown	unknown	15	10 IU*
Vitamin K (phylloquinone)	µg	20–40†	20	20	0	0‡
Vitamin C (ascorbic acid)	mg	60	75	300	100	100
Thiamine (vitamin B₁)	mg	1.0–1.5	2	10	10	3.0
Riboflavin (vitamin B₂)	mg	1.2–1.7	2	10	10	3.6
Niacin	mg	13–19	20	100	100	40
Pyridoxine (vitamin B₆)	mg	2.0–2.2	2	40	5	4.0
Pantothenic acid	mg	4–7 (adults)†	18	40	20	15
Folic acid	mg	0.4	1.5	2.5	0	0.4
Vitamin B₁₂	µg	3.0	2	4	5	5
Biotin	µg	100–200†	unknown	unknown	0	60

*Equivalent to RDA.   †Estimated to be safe and adequate dietary intakes.   ‡Must be supplemented in peripheral venous solutions.

Table 3 Trace Mineral Requirements

Mineral	Recommended Dietary Allowance (RDA) for Daily Oral Intake (mg)	Suggested Daily Intravenous Intake (mg)	Daily Amount Provided by a Commercially Available Mixture (mg)
Zinc	15	2.5–5.0*	5.0
Copper	2–3†	0.5–1.5	1.0
Manganese	2.5–5.0†	0.15–0.8	0.5
Chromium	0.05–0.2†	0.01–0.015	0.1
Iron	10 (males)–18 (females)	3	—

increased caloric requirements. The nitrogen-to-calorie ratio for most feeding formulas prepared for surgical patients is 1:150 (i.e., 1 g of nitrogen for every 150 kcal).

The contraindications to this increased quantity of protein are renal failure before dialysis (BUN > 40 mg/dl) and hepatic encephalopathy. Patients with systemic inflammatory response syndrome (SIRS) often require increased quantities of dietary protein [*see 128 Multiple Organ Dysfunction Syndrome*]. Nutritional support reduces net nitrogen losses in such patients, but positive or even neutral nitrogen balance is generally not achieved because of the disturbance in metabolism and reduced intake of dietary protein.

Vitamins and Minerals

The requirements for vitamins, minerals, and trace elements are usually met when adequate volumes of balanced nutrient formulas are provided [*see Tables 2 and 3*]. The requirements for most of the major minerals (sodium, potassium, chloride, phosphorus, magnesium, and zinc) are satisfied by monitoring serum concentrations of these elements and adjusting intake to maintain levels within the normal range. Some minerals and electrolytes are restricted in patients with renal failure. Although serum concentrations may not directly reflect total body deficits, sufficient quantities of these nutrients are available to support normal cellular functions if adequate blood concentrations are maintained. Most premixed enteral formulas provide adequate quantities of these substances if caloric needs are met. Vitamins and trace elements must be added to parenteral solutions.

Pharmacologic recommendations for stress in surgical patients The doses of vitamins given are often not the recommended dietary allowance (RDA) but rather some multiple thereof; for example, stressed patients usually receive three to 10 times the normal RDA.

The prescription of vitamins and minerals for therapeutic use should be based on the patient's nutritional history as well as on estimated requirements for the current disease state. These considerations are particularly important for fat-soluble vitamins, which are stored in body fat and thus may become toxic at high levels. Current recommendations stipulate that therapeutic dosages of vitamins should not exceed 10 times the RDA[1]; however, it has been suggested that some vitamins may be safe if given at dosages 50 to 100 times the RDA [*see Table 4*].[2] Vitamins and minerals are sometimes given in large dosages to exert antioxidant effects. Vitamins A, C, and E and the minerals zinc and selenium can attenuate the tissue-damaging effects of free radicals. One randomized, prospective trial, primarily involving trauma patients, demonstrated a significant reduction in organ failure with the administration of vitamins C (1,000 mg) and E (1,000 IU).[3] Many physicians are giving these vitamins and minerals as supplements to injured and infected patients[4]; supplementation with glutamine should also be considered [*see Discussion, below*].

Electronic Ordering to Optimize Nutritional Support

In hospital settings, nutritional care is often standardized to optimize formula composition and delivery. A useful electronic approach to nutritional prescription is available on the Internet (http://epen.kumc.edu).

Enteral Nutrition

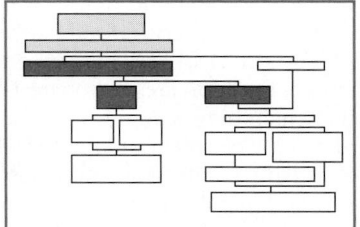

Enteral nutrition is the provision of liquid-formula diets by mouth or tube into the GI tract. It is the preferred method of feeding critically ill patients; however, it cannot be used safely in patients who are hemodynamically unstable or who have abdominal distention, intestinal obstruction, or massive GI bleeding [*see Table 5*]. For those who are able to receive enteral nutrition, either a balanced or a modified diet is selected on the basis of diagnosis and nutritional requirements. An isotonic (approximately 300 mOsm/kg) diet is given continuously for a trial period of 24 hours. If the patient tolerates this regimen but is at increased risk for aspiration, feeding is delivered into the jejunum rather than into the stomach. A standard protocol is helpful in reducing complications.

SAFE USE OF THE GI TRACT FOR FEEDING

Enteral nutrition should be prescribed only if safety and a low complication rate can be ensured. To determine whether enteral

Table 4 Safety Levels of Vitamins[2]

Safety Level	Vitamin
At least 50 to 100 times RDA	Vitamin B₁ Vitamin B₂ Niacin Vitamin C Vitamin E Biotin Folic acid Pantothenic acid
10 times RDA	Vitamin A Vitamin B₆ Vitamin D Vitamin K

Table 5 Indications for Enteral Nutrition
(Partial Listing)

Considered Routine Care in the Following:
Protein-calorie malnutrition with inadequate oral intake of nutrients for
  the previous 5–7 days
Normal nutritional status but < 50% of required oral intake of nutrients
  for the previous 7–10 days
Severe dysphagia
Major full-thickness burns
Low-output enterocutaneous fistulas
Major trauma

Usually Helpful in the Following:
Radiation therapy
Mild chemotherapy
Liver failure and severe renal dysfunction
Massive small bowel resection (> 50%) in combination with adminis-
  tration of total parenteral nutrition

Of Limited or Undetermined Value in the Following:
Intensive chemotherapy
Immediate postoperative period or poststress period
Acute enteritis
> 90% resection of small bowel

Contraindicated in the Following:
Complete mechanical intestinal obstruction
Abdominal distention
Ileus or intestinal hypomotility
Severe diarrhea
Severe GI bleeding
High-output external fistulas
Severe, acute pancreatitis
Shock
Case of aggressive nutritional support not desired by the patient or
  legal guardian and respect of such wish being in accordance with
  hospital policy and existing law
Prognosis not warranting aggressive nutritional support

---

nutrition is feasible, a clinical assessment of intestinal function is performed. If GI output—defined as the volume of effluent from a nasogastric tube, an ostomy, or a rectal tube—is less than 600 ml/24 hr, enteral nutrition is likely to be well tolerated. Examples of conditions in critically ill patients that produce excessively high (> 600 ml/24 hr) GI outputs and therefore preclude the use of enteral nutrition are gastroparesis, intestinal obstruction, paralytic ileus, high-output enteric fistulas, antibiotic-induced colitis, severe idiopathic diarrhea, and the initial phase of short bowel syndrome. Selected patients with enteric losses exceeding 600 ml/24 hr may receive enteral nutrition, however, if carefully monitored by an experienced team.

Massive GI bleeding may also cause increased GI output. Conditions that produce bleeding of this magnitude include peptic ulcer disease, esophageal varices, diverticulosis, and angiodysplasia of the colon. Mild bleeding (e.g., that produced by stress gastritis) may actually resolve with the delivery of enteral nutrition into the stomach because the liquid diet buffers gastric acid.[5] Enteral nutrition does not exacerbate mild lower intestinal bleeding.

Although commonly used at the bedside as indicators of intestinal function, bowel sounds and passage of flatus are nonspecific and are unrelated to the eventual tolerance of enteral nutrition.

In the absence of excessively high GI output, abdominal distention, and massive GI bleeding, a trial of enteral nutrition is warranted to determine if the GI tract can be used safely for feeding.

SELECTION OF DIET

Before delivery of enteral nutrition, the appropriate diet must be selected on the basis of the patient's nutrient requirements [see Indications for Nutritional Intervention, above]. Most liquid-formula diets consist of either a balanced or a modified formula.

Balanced diets contain carbohydrates, proteins, and fats in complex (polymeric) forms in proportions similar to those of a regular Western diet. Frequently, however, the fat content is reduced to 10% to 15% of total calories, and the carbohydrate content is increased. Carbohydrates are present as oligosaccharides, polysaccharides, or maltodextrins; fats consist of medium-chain triglycerides (MCTs) or long-chain triglycerides (LCTs). The nitrogen source is a natural protein, which may be either intact or partially hydrolyzed. In general, balanced diets are isotonic, lactose free, and available in ready-to-use, liquid form. Flavored balanced diets can be used for oral supplementation as well as for enteral tube feeding.

Selection of a balanced diet is based on nutrient and fluid requirements. The caloric density of balanced diets can be 1.0, 1.5, or 2.0 kcal/ml; the largest number of commercially available diets provide 1.0 kcal/ml. Nonprotein caloric content is derived from either carbohydrates or lipids. Balanced diets formulated with carbohydrates as the main caloric source have higher osmolarity than isocaloric diets containing lipids. These carbohydrate-based diets are well tolerated when administered directly into the stomach and may be helpful for patients with steatorrhea. Fat-based balanced diets may be more appropriate for patients with diarrhea caused by diet hyperosmolarity, especially when feedings are infused directly into the small intestine. However, fat malabsorption is common in critically ill patients when the fat content of the diet exceeds 30% of total calories.

In modified formulas (also known as elemental or chemically defined diets), the proportions and types of nutrients differ from those of a regular Western diet. Such diets may be characterized according to the conditions for which they are formulated: stress, immunomodulation, and hepatic, renal, respiratory, or GI dysfunction [see Table 6]. Modified diets contain crystalline amino acids or short peptides in compositions that differ from the reference composition of proteins of high biologic value (e.g., egg albumin). The fat-to-carbohydrate ratio of modified diets varies depending on the purpose of the modification. The source of carbohydrate is either dextrose or oligosaccharides; fats are usually in the form of MCTs, essential fatty acids, or both. Because they are not palatable, modified diets are rarely used as oral supplements.

Diets for patients with GI dysfunction have modified nitrogen and fat composition. Transport of dietary nitrogen across the intestinal mucosa is enhanced when nitrogen is provided in the form of short peptides rather than free amino acids. It is also well documented that small bowel mucosa utilizes glutamine as the preferred fuel [see Discussion, below]. Consequently, some modified diets contain nitrogen in the form of short peptides, whereas others contain extra glutamine. MCTs are more easily absorbed and metabolized than LCTs are; accordingly, diets modified for improved absorption contain a higher proportion of MCT oil. These diets may be efficacious when used during the transition phase after a period of prolonged bowel rest or when the intestine is inflamed. Controlled trials are necessary to verify their clinical efficacy. Stress formulas are indicated for hypercatabolic patients whose nitrogen balance continues to be negative despite increased intake of a balanced diet; these diets usually contain more nitrogen and frequently have an altered amino acid composition. Little evidence supports the use of diets that provide branched-chain amino acids (BCAAs) in concentrations higher than 20% to 25% of total amino acid content for stressed patients.

The fat sources used for enteral diets are primarily omega-6 fatty acids. Supplementation with omega-3 fatty acids results in the synthesis of eicosanoids that enhance the immune response. Enteral diets may also include other substances believed to have immunomodulatory effects [see Discussion, below].

ASSESSMENT OF FEEDING TOLERANCE

The selected formula is started at isotonicity and delivered continuously at 30 ml/hr for 24 hours. During this initial trial, the formula is delivered via a previously inserted Salem sump or rubber nasogastric (Levin) tube. If a nasogastric tube is not already in place, a soft tube made of either silicone rubber or polyurethane is inserted (see below).

Feeding tolerance is assessed for the first 24 hours. Poor tolerance is indicated by vomiting and severe abdominal cramps, a gastric residuum greater than 50% of the volume administered during the previous 4-hour feeding period, increased abdominal distention (particularly in patients who are comatose or undergoing mechanical ventilation), and worsening diarrhea. If any of these conditions is present, parenteral nutrition is recommended. If there is no evidence of feeding intolerance, the patient is assessed for the aspiration risk.

ASSESSMENT OF RISK OF ASPIRATION

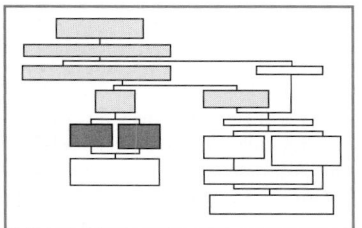

Aspiration is a major complication in patients receiving enteral nutrition. The propensity to aspirate enteral feedings is often related to the patient's primary disease and neurologic status as well as to the site of GI access and the method of delivery.

Important factors in assessing risk of aspiration include depressed sensorium, increased gastroesophageal reflux, and history of previously documented episodes of aspiration. Depressed sensorium in the critical care setting is secondary to organic lesions of the central nervous system, metabolic encephalopathies, or medications. Head trauma, hypoxemia, hepatic and septic encephalopathies, and the use of H_2 receptor blockers are common causes of depressed sensorium in critically ill patients. Increased gastroesophageal reflux may be present in individuals with reduced lower esophageal sphincter (LES) pressure and increased intragastric pressure. Many medications used in the ICU, such as theophylline, anticholinergics, calcium channel blocking agents, beta-adrenergic agonists, and alpha-adrenergic antagonists, cause a reduction in LES pressure. Finally, a history of aspiration places the patient at increased risk for recurrent episodes.

For most enterally fed patients, safety demands that the head be elevated at feeding time and for some period thereafter to prevent regurgitation. If this is not possible, an alternative nutrient delivery site should be considered. Nasogastric intubation, in particular, requires elevation of the head because the tube may render the upper and lower esophageal sphincters incompetent and liable to reflux. Even the presence of a tracheostomy or endotracheal tube does not ensure that regurgitated gastric contents will not be aspirated. Aspiration of liquid formulas can be verified if a bit of food coloring or methylene blue is included in the feeding mixture and subsequently detected in pharyngeal and tracheal secretions.[6]

ACCESS FOR FEEDING

In most general and thoracic surgical patients, access for feeding is most commonly obtained via the stomach or the jejunum. Methods of access for intragastric feedings include nasogastric tubes and feeding gastrostomies placed through a laparotomy or percutaneously with the aid of endoscopy, fluoroscopy, or laparoscopy.

Nasogastric tubes are the most commonly used access method for gastric feeding. Polyurethane or silicone rubber tubes are preferred because they are soft, nonreactive, and generally well tolerated; they are also less corrosive to the nasopharynx than rubber or polyvinyl chloride tubes. This very softness, however, often makes them hard to insert into critically ill patients and precludes checking of gastric residuum. Difficulties of tube passage into the stomach are increased when thin, floppy tubes are inserted into obtunded patients. Useful aids include stylets, judicious use of gravity and positioning, and designation of especially experienced and certified nursing personnel to assist in this task [see Table 7].

Passage of a tube through the pylorus into the jejunum may be necessary if the patient is at increased risk for aspiration (see above). Our practice is to place the tube into the stomach, to position the patient on the right side for several hours once or twice in the next 24 hours, and then to obtain an abdominal roentgenogram. If the tube has not passed, metoclopramide, 10 mg I.V., is given while the patient is still in the radiology department, and the roentgenogram is repeated. If the location of the feeding tube is not evident, a small amount of contrast material can be administered through the tube to verify its position. If the tube still has not passed through the pylorus, the aid of the fluoroscopist is enlisted. Finally, if all else has failed and no alternative route is appropriate, the endoscopist can capture the

Table 6 Composition of Modified Diets

Formula	Protein (g/L)	Carbohydrate (g/L)	Fat (g/L)	Ratio of Nitrogen (g) to Nonprotein Calories (kcal)	Caloric Density (kcal/ml)	Product* (Manufacturer)
Elemental	50	127	34	1:100	1.0	Subdue (Mead Johnson Nutritionals)
	40	127	39	1:131	1.0	Peptamen (Nestlé Clinical Nutrition)
Stress	56	130	28	1:71	1.0	Impact (Novartis)
	66	177	37	1:97	1.3	Perative (Ross Laboratories)
Hepatic	44	168	36	1:148	1.2	Hepatic Aid II (B. Braun Medical Inc.)
Renal	19	365	46	1:800	2.0	Amin-Aid (R&D Laboratories)

*Partial listing.

Table 7 Procedure for Inserting Nasoenteric Tubes

Provide privacy.

Explain procedure and its purpose.

Place patient in sitting position with neck flexed slightly and head of bed elevated to 45°.

Lubricate stylet and insert into feeding tube.

Inspect nares and determine optimal patency by having the patient breathe through one nostril while the other is temporarily occluded.

Estimate the length of tubing required to reach into the stomach by measuring the distance from the tip of the nose to the earlobe and then from the earlobe to the xiphoid process. Add 25 cm to this length for nasoduodenal intubation.

If the patient seems uncooperative, instill generous amounts of lidocaine jelly into the nares and nasopharynx before tube insertion. Lubricate the end of the tube and pass it posteriorly. Ask a cooperative patient to swallow water to facilitate passage of the tube.

Once the tube is beyond the nasopharynx, allow the patient to rest.

Have the patient continue neck flexion and swallowing while the tube is advanced.

If the patient begins to cough, withdraw the tube into the nasopharynx and then reattempt passage.

Confirm passage into the stomach by obtaining an abdominal x-ray.

Remove stylet.

Secure tube to bridge of nose or upper lip with nonallergenic tape and prevent undue pressure on external nares.

tube tip in the stomach with the biopsy forceps of the flexible endoscope (aided by a suture through the tube end) and guide the tube through the pylorus.

When any type of nasoenteric tube is placed for enteral nutrition, its location must be confirmed before feedings are started. The simplest means of accomplishing this is to aspirate gastric contents, the source of which can be determined by measuring the pH of the aspirate. Because small-bore, soft tubes tend to collapse under high negative pressure, a small syringe should be used to aspirate gastric contents. If gastric contents cannot be aspirated, radiographic confirmation of tube location is mandatory. Because feeding tubes are often radiopaque, a simple plain film of the abdomen may be adequate. If the exact location of the tube is still in doubt, a small amount of contrast material can be injected through the tube. Placement of the distal tip of the tube in the duodenum is usually confirmed by abdominal roentgenogram before transpyloric feedings are started. The tube should be inserted to a length sufficient to permit migration into the proximal jejunum.

Simple insufflation of air into the tube is not sufficient to verify its position. Auscultation over the stomach can detect sound transmitted through a tube that has been inadvertently passed into the bronchial tree. Many of these tubes are small enough to pass through the glottis and the trachea without markedly interfering with phonation or respiration. Enteral formulas delivered into the bronchial tree through a misplaced tube can cause severe pneumonitis and death.

The development of percutaneous techniques for the placement of gastrostomies has been a major contribution to enteral nutrition. Percutaneous endoscopic gastrostomy (PEG) [see 60 Gastrointestinal Endoscopy] and Witzel techniques for these procedures are well documented.

Concurrent decompression of the stomach and feeding into the small intestine have been used to reduce the risk of aspiration in critically ill patients. This combination of procedures requires either insertion of a multilumen nasojejunal tube, surgical placement of combined gastrojejunal tubes, modification of PEG, or insertion of a nasogastric tube in conjunction with a surgical jejunostomy. Such access to the GI tract also provides a route for

the delivery of crushed medications and the option to provide cyclic nocturnal enteral nutrition with gastric decompression (i.e., the patient receives nutrients by mouth during the day).

FEEDING REGIMENS

If the patient tolerates the initial trial of enteral nutrition, then the delivery site for future feeding is chosen according to the risk of aspiration, and the feeding regimen is gradually intensified. If the risk of aspiration is minimal, intragastric feedings are preferred: they are better tolerated physiologically, easier to administer, and less restrictive for the patient than continuous feeding into the small intestine. Patients fed into the stomach receive an isotonic formula delivered continuously at a rate of 30 ml/hr; the delivery rate is increased daily by 30 ml/hr [see Table 8]. If the risk of aspiration is increased, feedings are delivered via nasoduodenal or nasojejunal tubes. Patients fed into either the duodenum or the jejunum receive formulas of 300 mOsm/kg delivered at an initial rate of 30 ml/hr with the aid of a peristaltic pump; the rate is increased daily by 30 ml/hr [see Table 8]. Only isotonic feedings should be administered into the small bowel: hypertonic formulations have been associated with small bowel injury and necrosis.

MONITORING AND PREVENTION OF COMPLICATIONS

Patients receiving enteral nutrition require careful monitoring similar to that required by patients receiving parenteral nutrition. Particular attention is directed to metabolic

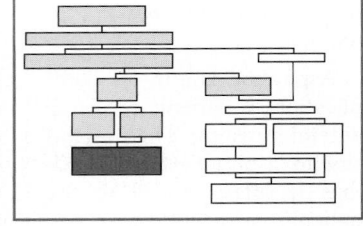

status and fluid and electrolyte balance. A protocol should be established and followed to ensure that nutritional goals are met and complications minimized. A standard checklist is helpful and prevents omission of important details [see Table 9].

Four types of complications are related to enteral nutrition: GI, mechanical, metabolic, and infectious. The first two are the most common.

The most frequent GI complication is diarrhea, which may occur in as many as 75% of critically ill patients receiving enteral nutrition. Diarrhea is best defined as stool weight greater than 300 g/24 hr or volume greater than 300 ml/24 hr. Given that such measurements are impractical and difficult to obtain, a more practical definition is more than three loose bowel movements during a 24-hour period. There are many causes of diarrhea in critically ill patients receiving enteral nutrition; the most frequent association is with antibiotic therapy [see Figure 2]. The desired therapeutic approach is to adjust the enteral nutrition regimen as necessary

Table 8 Suggested Starter and Advancement Regimens for Intragastric and Intrajejunal Feeding

Feeding Regimen	Days			
	1	2	3	4
Intragastric mOsm/kg ml/hr	300 30	300 60	300 90	480 90
Intrajejunal mOsm/kg ml/hr	300	300 60	300 90	300

Table 9 Standard Orders for Enteral Nutrition

Obtain abdominal x-ray to confirm tube location before feeding.

Elevate head of bed 45° when feeding into the stomach.

Record type and strength of diet and rate of infusion.

Check gastric residuum every 4 hr in patients receiving gastric feedings. Withhold feedings for 4 hr if residuum is 50% greater than ordered volume. Notify physician if two consecutive measurements detect excessive residuum.

Check for abdominal distention. Check frequency, consistency, and volume of stool output.

Weigh patient on Monday, Wednesday, and Friday. Record weight on graph.

Record intake and output daily. For every shift, chart volume of formula administered separately from water or other oral intake.

Change administration tubing and cleanse feeding bag daily.

Irrigate feeding tube with 20 ml of water at the completion of each intermittent feeding, when tube is disconnected, after the delivery of crushed medications, of if feeding is stopped for any reason.

When patient is ingesting oral nutrients, ask the dietitian to provide calorie counts daily for 5 days, then weekly thereafter.

On a weekly basis, obtain complete blood count with red blood cell indices, SMA-12, serum iron, and serum magnesium.

Obtain SMA-6 every Monday and Thursday.

Once a week, collect urine for 24 hours, starting at 8:00 A.M., and analyze for urea nitrogen.

The most common mechanical complications related to enteral nutrition are tube dislodgment, clogging of the tube, and leakage of enteric contents around the tube's exit site. Tube dislodgment occurs more frequently in agitated patients and hypoxic patients. Inadvertent tube removal can usually be prevented by adequate taping or, in agitated patients, by suturing the tube or using a Velcro abdominal wall binder.

Clogging or plugging of the tube often results from failure to use saline irrigation after intermittent feedings or inadvertent delivery of crushed medications through a small-bore tube. The incidence of this complication is reduced by routine irrigations of 20 to 25 ml of normal saline or water after each intermittent feeding. Liquid medications may also help prevent this complication, though such medications are frequently hyperosmolar and may produce discomfort

rather than to discontinue it completely. Only one variable of the feeding regimen (i.e., osmolality, volume, rate, or type of diet) should be altered at a time. In our experience, critically ill patients tolerate continuous feeding better than intermittent feeding. If the patient still has diarrhea when receiving 150 to 300 mOsm/kg at 30 ml/hr, antidiarrheal treatment is indicated.

In many instances, antidiarrheal medication is given without a definite diagnosis; therefore, it is essential to select medications with both a wide therapeutic range and a low incidence of side effects. For these reasons, we prefer kaolin-pectin over opiates such as paregoric. Every 3 hours, 30 ml of kaolin-pectin solution is given through the feeding tube, followed by 25 ml of normal saline for irrigation. If this regimen is unsuccessful after 48 hours and opiates are not contraindicated, paregoric is added at a dose of 1 ml/100 ml formula [see Figure 2]. Opiates act by slowing intestinal motility. Because the normal motility pattern is a defense against bacterial growth in the small bowel, administering opiates to patients with a contaminated small bowel can lead to bacterial overgrowth and worsen diarrhea. In addition, opiates are respiratory depressants and are contraindicated in patients with infectious diarrhea.

Several diagnostic methods may help identify the cause of diarrhea associated with enteral nutrition, including the assaying of stool for *Clostridium difficile* enterotoxin, analysis of stool for fat malabsorption, the D-xylose test for carbohydrate malabsorption, and breath H_2 analysis for bacterial overgrowth. The D-xylose test and breath H_2 analysis are more commonly used in non–critically ill patients.

To prevent peptic ulcers and bleeding, gastric acidity is controlled with H_2 receptor blockers in critically ill patients. Although these drugs help control hyperacidity, which is a cause of diarrhea, they also lead to bacterial overgrowth in the intestine.[7] Therefore, they should not be used in patients who receive intragastric feedings, because the liquid formula in the stomach already provides a physiologic means of buffering acid. If necessary, antacids rather than H_2 receptor blockers should be used to titrate gastric pH to 4.5 to 6.5. Glutamine is also used to prevent or treat ulceration of the upper GI tract.

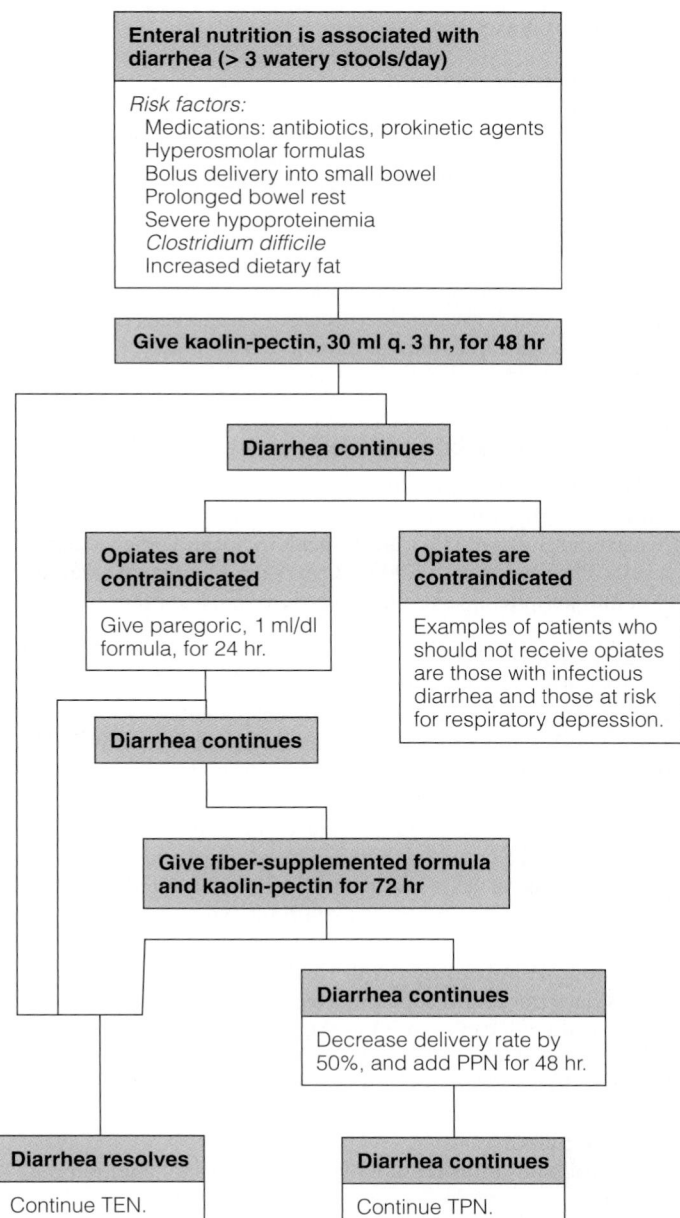

Figure 2 Shown is the decision-making approach for pharmacologic and dietary treatment of diarrhea associated with enteral nutrition.

and diarrhea when delivered rapidly into the jejunum. The injection of a small volume of a carbonated beverage into a plugged tube often clears the blockage. Occasionally, a guide wire and the help of the interventional radiologist will be needed.

Leakage of enteric contents onto the skin around the exit site is often uncomfortable for the patient and may produce a moderate amount of skin irritation. One cause of such leakage is inadequate approximation of the end of the tube to the gastric wall. Leakage around a tube is prevented by proper fixation of the end of the tube with a retention disk or bumper at the skin level. The aid of an enterostomal therapist is often useful, as are products such as karaya gum, zinc oxide, Stomahesive, and locally applied antacid. Also problematic is the inappropriate use of urinary catheters for enteral access; these devices were not designed to function as gastrostomy or enterostomy tubes.

Parenteral Nutrition

CENTRAL VENOUS VERSUS PERIPHERAL VENOUS INFUSIONS

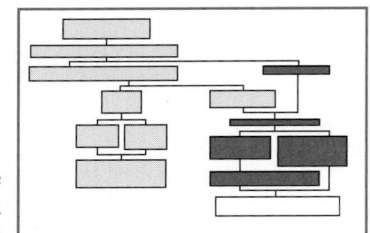

Central venous infusions are indicated in most critically ill patients who receive parenteral nutrition, because (1) patients in the ICU often require increased quantities of energy and cannot tolerate large fluid volumes and (2) solutions of much greater caloric density and tonicity can be infused into central veins than into peripheral veins. Nonetheless, peripheral venous infusions [see Peripheral Venous Nutrient Infusion, below] may be indicated in certain situations [see Table 10].

CENTRAL VENOUS NUTRIENT INFUSION

Hypertonic nutrient solutions are infused into the superior vena cava, where they are rapidly diluted. Usually, such solutions contain hypertonic glucose (25%), amino acids (5%), and other essential nutrients. Their tonicity (> 1,900 mOsm/kg) is so great that administration into peripheral veins would cause severe thrombophlebitis and venous sclerosis. These solutions contain at least 1 kcal/ml, and thus, infusion of 2.0 to 2.5 L/day provides 2,000 to 2,500 kcal and all essential nutrients. This calorie load is sufficient to meet energy requirements in more than 90% of surgical patients.

Once positioned, the catheter should be used exclusively for administering the hypertonic nutrient solution: drawing blood, monitoring central venous pressure, and administering medication through this dedicated lumen are to be avoided. If a multiple-lumen central venous catheter is used, as is the case in most patients today, at least one port should be devoted solely to the infusion of hypertonic nutrient solutions. Some reports have suggested that the incidence of catheter-related infection is higher with multiple-lumen than with single-lumen feeding catheters[8,9]; others have not found such differences.[10] It appears that multiple-lumen catheters can be used in the ICU for central venous nutrient infusions if strict protocols are maintained to ensure that one lumen is dedicated to nutrient infusion, that other lumens are handled safely, and that catheters are removed when they are no longer required.

Occasionally, infusion of a hypertonic nutrient solution may be required in a situation where percutaneous puncture of central veins is impossible or contraindicated. In such cases, catheterization of an antecubital vein and insertion of a peripherally inserted central catheter (PICC) with the tip positioned in the superior vena cava should be considered. These catheters are readily insert-

ed by the interventional radiologist, and they eliminate the complications associated with subclavian and internal jugular vein insertions. The PICC line has become the primary route of central venous access in many institutions.

Silastic catheters have been safely kept in place for extended periods and provide an additional option for central venous access. Catheterization of the femoral vein may provide a route for central venous access in some situations. Because of the high density of skin pathogens in the groin area, these catheters should be replaced every 2 to 3 days. If the catheter tip is positioned in the iliac vein or the inferior vena cava, the concentration of solution infused through the catheter should not exceed 15%. Strict care of the entrance site should be maintained because of the high complication rate associated with lines placed in the groin.

Central Venous Solutions

Central venous solutions are formulated in the hospital pharmacy. They are commonly combinations of 500 ml of 50% dextrose and 500 ml of a 10% amino acid mixture [see Table 11] to which electrolytes, vitamins, and trace elements are added (see below). Each day, 2 L of the solution can be infused. Administration of fat emulsion (500 ml, 20%) 1 day each week meets essential fatty acid requirements. Alternatively, the three major nutrients may be mixed together in a 3 L bag (triple mix or three-in-one) and the entire contents of the single bag infused over the 24-hour period [see Table 11]. In addition, an automated mixing device may be used to compound various proportions of 70% glucose, 10% amino acids, and 20% fat emulsions into 3 L bags. Such devices allow the hospital pharmacy to manufacture a variety of nutrient combinations with minimal effort. More concentrated solutions can be made, and the computer will generate a label for the bag that allows nurses to verify the order.

Electrolytes and minerals are added to the base formula as required [see Table 12]. Sodium and potassium salts are added as chloride or acetate, depending on the acid-base status of the patient. The solution should usually consist of approximately equal quantities of chloride and acetate; if chloride losses from the body are increased, as in a patient requiring nasogastric decompression, the solution should contain proportionately more chloride. Sodium bicarbonate is incompatible with the nutrient solutions; if additional base is re-

---

Table 10 Indications for Central Venous or Peripheral Venous Infusions

Central Venous Infusions

 To provide adequate intravenous nutritional support for 10 days or more

 To satisfy nutrient requirements in patients with increased energy needs and normal or decreased fluid requirements

 To support the patient with single- or multiple-organ failure by infusing modified nutrient solutions in a limited fluid volume

Peripheral Venous Infusions

 To provide initial feeding (< 5 days) before catheter insertion in a patient who will require central venous feedings

 To infuse less concentrated solutions via a multiuse central catheter (i.e., a line for blood drawing, medication, and nutrients) into an individual in whom other venous access cannot be easily or safely obtained

 To supplement enteral feedings that are inadequate because of gastrointestinal dysfunction

 To satisfy energy requirements that are near basal (1,500–1,800 kcal/day) in a nondepleted patient who can tolerate 2.5–3.0 L I.V. solution each day

Table 11 Composition of Central Venous Solutions

	Standard Solution	Triple-Mix Solution
Volume		
Amino acids 10% (ml)	500	1,000
Dextrose 50% (ml)	500	1,000
Fat emulsion 20% (ml)	—	250
Total (ml)	1,000	2,250
Contents		
Amino acids (g)	50	100
Dextrose (g)	250 (25%)	500
Total nitrogen (g)	8.4	16.8
Total calories (kcal)	1,050	2,600
Ratio of nitrogen to calories	1:125	1:154
Caloric density (kcal/ml)	1.0	1.15
Osmolarity (mOsm/kg)	1,970	1,900

quired, acetate, which generates bicarbonate when metabolized, is given. Phosphate is usually given as the potassium salt; if potassium phosphate is contraindicated, sodium phosphate is given. Phosphate is also present in fat emulsions.

Commercially available preparations of vitamins, minerals, and trace elements are also added to the nutrient mix for daily administration unless they are contraindicated. A solution containing both fat- and water-soluble vitamins should be added. Vitamin K_1 (phytonadione), 10 mg, is given once a week but is contraindicated in patients receiving warfarin.

Trace elements are given daily. Usual requirements are satisfied by adding commercially available mixtures either to 1 L of standard solution or to the triple-mix bag each day. Trace elements are indicated for all patients receiving central venous nutrient solutions, except those with chronic renal failure or severe liver disease. At especially high risk for zinc deficiency are alcoholics and patients with pancreatic insufficiency with malabsorption, massive small bowel resection, renal failure with dialysis, or nephrotic syn-

Table 12 Electrolytes Added to Central Venous Solutions

	Usual Electrolyte Concentration	Usual Range of Electrolyte Concentration
Sodium (mEq/L)	30	0–150
Potassium (mEq/L)	30	0–80
Phosphate (mmol/L)	15	0–20
Magnesium (mEq/L)	5	0–15
Calcium* (mEq/L)	4.7	0–10
Chloride (mEq/L)	50	0–150
Acetate (mEq/L)	70	70–220

drome; at high risk for copper deficiency are patients with short-bowel syndrome, jejunoileal bypass, malabsorptive conditions with severe diarrhea, or nephrotic syndrome. Copper and manganese are excreted primarily via the biliary tract. Therefore, in patients with biliary tract obstruction, excess retention of these elements should be prevented by decreasing intake of these ions, monitoring blood levels, or both. Although the main excretory route for zinc and chromium is via the feces, renal excretion minimizes dangers from modest excesses of these elements. In patients with renal insufficiency, however, daily zinc and chromium administration may be contraindicated. ICU patients usually do not require iron. Iron supports bacterial growth and thus is contraindicated in patients with systemic infection. It may be required to treat iron deficiency anemia, particularly during convalescence from this condition, but rarely does the anemia associated with chronic disease and inflammation respond to iron therapy during its active stages.

Like other invasive therapies, total parenteral nutrition (TPN) is associated with potential complications deriving from either central venous access or the composition of the formula. Most such complications are preventable with appropriate attention to detail [*see Table 13*].

PERIPHERAL VENOUS NUTRIENT INFUSION

Slightly hypertonic nutrient solutions (approximately 600 to 900 mOsm/kg) can be prepared for peripheral venous infusion from commercially available amino acid mixtures (5%), dextrose solutions (10%), and fat emulsions (20%). These nutrient mixtures have a low caloric density (approximately 0.3 to 0.6 kcal/ml) and thus provide only 1,200 to 2,300 kcal in 2,000 to 3,500 ml of solution. Such solutions are particularly useful in patients whose tube feedings are insufficient and who need additional nutrients.

These dilute nutrient mixtures can be infused through plastic cannulas placed in large-bore peripheral veins. The catheter insertion site and the surrounding tissue should be inspected periodically for signs of phlebitis or infiltration, and the infusion site should be rotated every 48 to 72 hours to prevent thrombophlebitis. Only fat emulsion can be administered simultaneously through the same I.V. site as a peripheral venous solution. The nutrient solution should be temporarily stopped if the catheter is used for administration of antibiotics, chemotherapeutic agents, blood, or blood products. The infusion line should then be flushed with saline and nutrient infusion resumed.

If the fat emulsion is infused in a piggyback manner, administration should take place over a period of 8 to 12 hours and be concluded in the early morning hours (e.g., 3:00 A.M.) to allow clearance of the emulsion from the bloodstream. Blood sampling should be avoided during short-term fat infusion because the associated hypertriglyceridemia will interfere with many of the serum measurements. In patients who are receiving peripheral venous solutions by triple mix, hypertriglyceridemia is rare because the rate of infusion is reduced and infusion extended over a 24-hour period.

Patients receiving peripheral venous feedings should be monitored in much the same fashion as those receiving central venous feedings (see below). Mechanical and infectious complications are uncommon. Fluid imbalances and alterations in serum electrolyte concentrations are similar to those seen with standard I.V. support, and corrections are made by altering the volume of the infusion or adding or omitting electrolytes. Hyperglycemia and glycosuria are rarely observed unless the patient is diabetic.

Table 13 Diagnosis, Treatment, and Prevention of Potential Mechanical and Metabolic Complications Associated with Total Parenteral Nutrition

	Complications	Diagnosis	Treatment	Prevention
Mechanical	Pneumothorax	Dyspnea, chest x-ray	Tube thoracostomy Observation	Avoid emergency procedures Trendelenburg's position
	Hemothorax	Dyspnea, chest x-ray	Remove catheter Observation	Insert catheter using appropriate technique
	Venous thrombosis	Inability to cannulate	Remove catheter Heparin therapy	Use silicone catheters Add heparin to solution
	Air embolism	Dyspnea, cyanosis, hypotension, tachycardia, precordial murmur	Trendelenburg's position Left lateral decubitus position	Trendelenburg's position Valsalva maneuver Tape intravenous connections
	Catheter embolism	Sheared catheter	Fluoroscopic retrieval	Never withdraw catheter through needle
	Arrhythmias	Catheter tip in right atrium	Withdraw catheter to superior vena cava	Estimate distance to SVC before insertion; confirm position with x-ray
	Subclavian artery injury	Pulsatile red blood	Remove needle Apply pressure Chest x-ray	Review anatomy
	Catheter tip misplacement	Chest x-ray	Redirect with a guide wire	Direct bevel of needle caudally
Metabolic	Hyperglycemic, hyperosmolar, nonketotic coma	Dehydration with osmotic diuresis, disorientation, lethargy, stupor, convulsions, coma, glucose 1,000 mg/dl, osmolarity 350 mOsm/kg	Discontinue TPN; infuse D5 in 0.45% S at 250 ml/hr Insulin 10–20 U/hr Bicarbonate Monitor glucose, potassium, pH	Monitor glucose
	Hypoglycemia	Headache, sweating, thirst, convulsions, disorientation, paresthesias	D50W I.V.	Taper TPN by $1/2$ for 12 hr; then 12 hr of D5W at 100 ml/hr
	CO_2 retention	Ventilator dependence, high respiratory quotient	Taper glucose	Provide 30%–40% of calories with fat
	Azotemia	Dehydration, elevated BUN	Increase nonprotein calories	Monitor fluid balance
	Hyperammonemia	Lethargy, malaise, coma, seizures	Discontinue amino acid infusions Infuse arginine	Avoid casein or fibrin hydrolysate
	Essential fatty acid deficiency	Xerosis, hepatomegaly, impaired healing, bone changes	Fat administration	Provide 25–200 mg/kg/day of essential fatty acids
	Hypophosphatemia	Lethargy, anorexia, weakness	Supplemental phosphate	Treat causative factors: alkalosis, gram-negative sepsis, vomiting, malabsorption Provide 20 mEq/kcal
	Abnormal liver enzymes	Fatty infiltrate in liver	Evaluate for other causes	Provide balanced TPN solution
	Hypomagnesemia	Weakness, nausea, vomiting, tremors, depression, hyporeflexia	Infuse 10% $MgSO_4$	Supply 0.35–0.45 mEq/kg/day
	Hypermagnesemia	Drowsiness, nausea, vomiting, coma, arrhythmia	Dialysis Infuse calcium gluconate	Monitor serum levels

PATIENT MONITORING: OPTIMIZING NUTRITIONAL SUPPORT, PREVENTING COMPLICATIONS, AND RESOLVING COMMON PROBLEMS

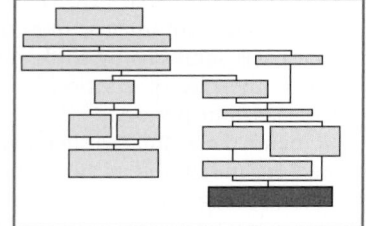

General Measures

Patients receiving central venous feedings should be weighed daily, and accurate intake and output records should be maintained. Blood glucose should be monitored daily. If levels are persistently elevated, a more stringent schedule of monitoring blood glucose should be instituted and specific therapy initiated.

The quantity of energy administered to most ICU patients should minimize the loss of lean body mass and adipose tissues. Thus, variations in body weight usually reflect alterations in fluid balance. If sustained weight loss occurs (as characterized by a gradual fall in body weight over a period of 2 weeks or more), caloric intake may be inadequate. Additional calories (500 to 1,000 kcal/day) should be administered to maintain weight. Alternatively, the metabolic rate can be calculated from oxygen consumption ($\dot{V}O_2$) and calorie intake, then matched to equal energy expenditure:

$$\text{Metabolic rate (kcal/hr)} = \dot{V}O_2 \text{ (ml/min)} \times 60 \text{ min/hr} \times 1 \text{ L/1,000 ml} \times 4.83 \text{ kcal/L}$$

This calculation is required in only 5% of our patients.

Sample Calculation of Nitrogen Balance

A 65-year-old man with an infected aortic graft and ileus is receiving 2.2 L triple-mix solution containing 16.8 g nitrogen each day. His UUN is 500 mg/dl, and his urine output is 2,000 ml/day. Is he receiving adequate nitrogen?

24-hour UUN = 500 mg/dl × 2,000 ml/day × 1 g/1,000 mg
     × 1 dl/100 ml
   = 10 g/day

Nitrogen output
   = 24-hr UUN + (0.20 × 24-hr UUN) + 2 g/day
   = 10 g/day + (0.20 × 10 g/day) + 2 g/day
   = 14 g/day

Nitrogen balance
   = 16.8 g/day (N intake) – 14 g/day (N output)
   = 2.8 g/day

The patient is in positive nitrogen balance, retaining approximately 2 to 3 g nitrogen/day. If positive nitrogen balance had not been achieved, his protein and caloric intake would have had to be increased and the nitrogen balance recalculated.

In non–ventilator-dependent patients, oxygen consumption and, in turn, the metabolic rate can be derived from measurements of respiratory gas exchange. In patients with a Swan-Ganz catheter in place, oxygen consumption can be calculated from cardiac output, mixed venous oxygen content ($C_{mv}O_2$), and arterial oxygen content (C_aO_2):

$$\dot{V}O_2 \text{ (ml/min)} = \text{cardiac output (L/min)} \times (C_aO_2 \text{ [ml/dl]} - C_{mv}O_2 \text{ [ml/dl]}) \times 1 \text{ L/10 dl}$$

Another objective of nutritional support in the ICU patient is the maintenance of lean body mass, reflected by nitrogen balance equilibration or positive nitrogen balance. Although complete nitrogen balance determination is a complex and sophisticated study, nitrogen equilibration can be estimated by simply subtracting total nitrogen loss (or output) from total nitrogen intake [*see Sidebar* Sample Calculation of Nitrogen Balance]. Calculation of total nitrogen loss requires several steps. The urine urea nitrogen (UUN) concentration is multiplied by the total urine output during a given day to yield the 24-hour UUN (i.e., the total amount of urea excreted during that period). Because urea accounts for only approximately 80% of the nitrogen excreted in the urine, the value for the 24-hour UUN is then increased by an additional 20%. This quantity and an additional 2 g/day are added to the value for the 24-hour UUN to account for nonurea nitrogen, stool, and integumentary losses:

$$24\text{-hour UUN (g/day)} = \text{UUN (mg/dl)} \times \text{urine output (ml/day)} \times 1 \text{ g/1,000 mg} \times 1 \text{ dl/100 ml}$$

$$\text{Total nitrogen loss (g/day)} = 24\text{-hour UUN (g/day)} + (0.20 \times 24\text{-hour UUN [g/day]}) + 2 \text{ g/day}$$

Metabolic Monitoring

A wide variety of metabolic complications may occur during parenteral feeding [*see Table 14*]. They are minimized by frequent monitoring [*see Table 15*] and appropriate adjustment of nutrients in the infusion.

The most common metabolic problems in ICU patients are hyperglycemia and glucosuria. The combination of excessive counterregulatory hormone release and overproduction of tumor necrosis factor (TNF)–α, interleukin (IL)-1, and IL-6 character-istic of critical illness is a major cause of stress-induced hyperglycemia in nondiabetic hosts.[11] Hypergylcemia has been associated with infectious complications,[12,13] worsened outcome after head injury and stroke,[14] and increased proteolysis.[15] Moreover, prevention of hyperglycemia by means of aggressive insulin treatment has been associated with reduced mortality in ICU patients.[16] Initially, elevated blood glucose levels should be treated by administering insulin (5.0 U s.c. every 4 to 6 hours for glucose 200 to 250 mg/dl; 7.5 U for 250 to 300 mg/dl; 10.0 U for 300 to 350 mg/dl). When the nutritional solution is ordered for the next 24-hour period, half of the quantity of insulin administered subcutaneously is added to the mixture. The initial insulin dose should be least 10 U of regular insulin/L of solution, and in some cases, as much as 40 U/L may be required. If larger doses of insulin are needed (> 100 U/day), a separate insulin infusion or drip should be employed.

In most patients with severe glucose intolerance, the rate of glucose administration should not exceed 5 mg/kg/min (~ 500 g/day). Additional calories should be administered as fat emulsion. The commercially available fat emulsions are all generally well tolerated by critically ill patients. Triglyceride levels should be monitored, and the emulsion should be administered at a reduced rate or temporarily discontinued if levels exceed 500 mg/dl. Fat emulsion should be used with caution in patients with known hypertriglyceridemia or in those with gram-negative bloodstream infection that is associated with hyperlipidemia.

Infusion of excess glucose or lipid may alter pulmonary function and in some patients prevent weaning from a mechanical ventilator. Excessive carbohydrate loads (usually > 500 g/day) increase CO_2 production. If more CO_2 is produced than the lungs can excrete, hypercapnia results. Fat emulsion may also interfere with diffusion of gas across the alveolar membranes. This interference is generally related to the concentration of the emulsion in the bloodstream; hence, it can be minimized by monitoring triglyceride levels and preventing hypertriglyceridemia.

Catheter Care and Catheter Infection

The most serious problem associated with central venous feedings is catheter infection [*see 131 Nosocomial Infection*]. Primary catheter infection is defined as the signs and symptoms of infection (usually a febrile episode), with the indwelling catheter being the only anatomic infectious focus; after removal of the catheter, the symptoms usually attenuate. Cultures of the catheter tip with semiquantitative techniques yield at least 10^3 organisms,[17] and the organisms are the same as those recovered in blood drawn from a peripheral vein during initial evaluation of the infection. Secondary catheter infection is associated with a primary infectious focus that causes bacteremia and thus seeds or contaminates the catheter; the infection clears after specific treatment of the primary infection. The microorganisms cultured from the catheter tip are similar to those cultured from the primary source.

Primary catheter infection is prevented or at least greatly reduced by following strict protocols governing use and manipulation of the central venous feeding catheter and by employing a systematic method of care and surveillance of the catheter entrance site. Usually, catheter care and its supervision and certification are performed by a nurse with expertise in maintenance of long-term I.V. access. Every 48 to 72 hours, the dressing covering the entrance site of the catheter is removed, the site inspected, the area around the entrance site cleaned, a topical antibiotic or antiseptic ointment applied, and the site redressed with a new sterile dressing. This procedure is documented in the clinical

Table 14 Metabolic Complications of Total Parenteral Nutrition

Problems	Possible Causes	Solutions
Glucose		
Hyperglycemia, glycosuria, osmotic diuresis, hyperosmolar nonketotic dehydration and coma	Excessive total dose or rate of infusion of glucose; inadequate endogenous insulin; increased glucocorticoids; sepsis	Reduce amount of glucose infused; increase insulin; administer a portion of calories as fat emulsion
Ketoacidosis in diabetes mellitus	Inadequate endogenous insulin response; inadequate exogenous insulin therapy	Give insulin; reduce glucose input
Postinfusion (rebound) hypoglycemia	Persistence of endogenous insulin production secondary to prolonged stimulation of islet cells by high-carbohydrate infusion	Administer 5%–10% glucose before infusate is discontinued
Fat		
Pyrogenic reaction	Fat emulsion, other solutions	Exclude other causes of fever
Altered coagulation	Hyperlipidemia	Restudy after fat has cleared bloodstream
Hypertriglyceridemia	Rapid infusion, decreased clearance	Decrease rate of infusion; allow clearance before blood tests
Impaired liver function	May be caused by fat emulsion or by an underlying disease process	Exclude other causes of hepatic dysfunction
Cyanosis	Altered pulmonary diffusion capacity	Discontinue fat infusion
Essential fatty acid deficiency	Inadequate essential fatty acid administration	Administer essential fatty acids in the form of one 500 ml bottle of fat emulsion every 2–3 days
Amino Acids		
Hyperchloremic metabolic acidosis	Excessive chloride and monohydrochloride content of crystalline amino acid solutions	Administer Na^+ and K^+ as acetate salts
Serum amino acid imbalance	Unphysiologic amino acid profile of the nutrient solution; differential amino acid utilization with various disorders	Use experimental solutions if indicated
Hyperammonemia	Excessive ammonia in protein hydrolysate solutions; deficiency of arginine, ornithine, aspartic acid, or glutamic acid, or a combination of these deficiencies in amino acid solutions; primary hepatic disorder	Reduce amino acid intake
Prerenal azotemia	Excessive amino acid infusion with inadequate calorie administration; inadequate free water intake, dehydration	Reduce amino acid intake; increase glucose calories; increase intake of free water
Calcium and Phosphorus		
Hypophosphatemia	Inadequate phosphorus administration; redistribution of serum phosphorus into cells or bones, or both	Administer phosphorous (20 mEq potassium dihydrogen phosphate/1,000 I.V. calories); evaluate antacid or calcium administration, or both
Hypocalcemia	Inadequate calcium administration; reciprocal response to phosphorus repletion without simultaneous calcium infusion; hypoalbuminemia	Administer calcium
Hypercalcemia	Excessive calcium administration with or without high doses of albumin; excessive vitamin D administration	Decrease calcium or vitamin D
Vitamin D deficiency; hypervitaminosis D	Inadequate or excessive vitamin D	Alter vitamin D administration
Miscellaneous		
Hypokalemia	Potassium intake inadequate relative to increased requirements for protein anabolism; diuresis	Alter nutrient administration
Hyperkalemia	Excessive potassium administration, especially in metabolic acidosis; renal failure	Alter nutrient administration
Hypomagnesemia	Inadequate magnesium administration relative to increased requirements for protein anabolism and glucose metabolism; diuresis; cisplatin administration	Alter nutrient administration
Hypermagnesemia	Excessive magnesium administration; renal failure	Alter nutrient administration
Anemia	Iron deficiency; folic acid deficiency; vitamin B_{12} deficiency; copper deficiency; other deficiencies	Alter nutrient administration
Bleeding	Vitamin K deficiency	Alter nutrient administration
Hypervitaminosis A	Excessive vitamin A administration	Alter nutrient administration
Elevations in AST (formerly SGOT), ALT (formerly SGPT), and serum alkaline phosphatase	Enzyme induction secondary to amino acid imbalance or to excessive deposition of glycogen or fat, or both, in the liver	Reevaluate status of patient

record; if drainage or crusting appears at the entrance site, appropriate cultures are taken. In addition, the dressing is changed if it becomes wet or soiled or no longer remains intact. In patients who have either draining wounds in close proximity to the catheter entrance site or tracheostomies, the entire dressing may be covered with a transparent barrier drape to minimize contamination.

If signs and symptoms of infection develop in a recipient of central venous parenteral nutrition, a history should be taken and a physical examination performed [see Figure 3]. Appropriate tests (e.g., complete blood count and urinalysis) and diagnostic studies (including roentgenogram) should also be performed. If blood cultures are needed, samples should be drawn from a peripheral vein. If trained nurses have maintained the catheter and there is no evidence of infection at the exit site, the dressing should not be removed, and the catheter should not be manipulated. Blood cultures should never be taken through the catheter—except, possibly, when the initial presentation of infection is characterized by marked hyperpyrexia or hypotension, in which case, contamination of the catheter is immaterial because the catheter will be removed. If no other infectious focus is identified, the physician may elect to remove all indwelling lines, including the feeding catheter. In addition, either drainage around the catheter or a previous positive culture from the catheter exit site may

Table 15 Variables to Be Monitored during Intravenous Alimentation and Suggested Frequency of Monitoring

Variables	Suggested Monitoring Frequency	
	First Week	Later
Energy Balance		
Weight	Daily	Daily
Metabolic Variables		
Blood measurements		
Plasma electrolytes (Na+, K+, Cl−)	Daily	3 × weekly
Blood urea nitrogen	3 × weekly	2 × weekly
Plasma osmolarity*	Daily	3 × weekly
Plasma total calcium and inorganic phosphorus	3 × weekly	2 × weekly
Blood glucose	Daily	3 × weekly
Plasma transaminases	3 × weekly	2 × weekly
Plasma total protein and fractions	2 × weekly	Weekly
Blood acid-base status	As indicated	As indicated
Hemoglobin	Weekly	Weekly
Ammonia	As indicated	As indicated
Magnesium	2 × weekly	Weekly
Triglycerides	Weekly	Weekly
Urine measurements		
Glucose	Daily	Daily
Specific gravity or osmolarity	Daily	Daily
General measurements		
Volume of infusate	Daily	Daily
Oral intake (if any)	Daily	Daily
Urinary output	Daily	Daily
Prevention and Detection of Infection		
Clinical observations (activity, temperature, symptoms)	Daily	Daily
WBC and differential counts	As indicated	As indicated
Cultures	As indicated	As indicated

also indicate immediate removal. If another primary source of infection is diagnosed, specific therapy should be instituted and parenteral nutrition continued. If no source of infection is identified, the catheter should be removed and the catheter tip cultured [*see 131 Nosocomial Infection*].

A dilemma arises if another source of infection is identified and if signs and symptoms of infection persist despite what appears to be appropriate therapy. If blood cultures are positive, we favor removal of the catheter to avoid the complications associated with a contaminated indwelling catheter. If, however, peripheral blood cultures are negative, the catheter can be changed over a guide wire and the catheter tip cultured; central venous feeding can be continued during this interval. If the cultured catheter tip is positive ($\geq 10^5$ organisms), the catheter should be removed.

Changing the central venous catheter over a guide wire can aid in the diagnosis of primary catheter infection.[18] Because most ICU patients have multiple potential sources for infection, this technique allows culture of the catheter tip but minimizes the risks associated with reinsertion of a new central catheter. With strict care of catheters, the incidence of catheter infection should be less than 6%.[19] Catheter-related bloodstream infection (CRBSI) is most commonly caused by growth and invasion of organisms along the catheter tract. Occasionally, bacteria are infused through the catheter because of a breach in sterility during care of the infusion

apparatus. The most common bacterial organisms causing catheter sepsis are *Staphylococcus epidermidis*, *S. aureus*, *Klebsiella pneumoniae*, and *Candida albicans*. In some rare cases, the I.V. solutions may be contaminated. Moreover, most patients requiring central venous alimentation are immunocompromised hosts; their resistance is lowered further by disease, severe malnutrition, or treatment or by some combination of these factors. Coexisting conditions such as urinary tract infection, abscess, pneumonia, or mucositis secondary to chemotherapy predispose to bacteremia, which may contaminate the central venous catheter.

Immunosuppressed critically ill patients receiving multiple broad-spectrum antibiotics are also at risk for *Candida* CRBSI. Blood cultures positive for *C. albicans* in an ICU patient are an indication for catheter removal and treatment with fluconazole. An ophthalmologist should examine the eyegrounds of patients with proven candidemia to exclude the possibility of metastatic *Candida* ophthalmitis [*see 134 Fungal Infection*].

Home Nutritional Support

HOME PARENTERAL NUTRITION

Home parenteral nutrition is indicated for patients who are unable to eat and absorb enough nutrients for maintenance. Most of the adult surgical patients who require home parenteral nutrition suffer from short-bowel syndrome caused by (1) extensive Crohn disease, (2) mesenteric infarction, or (3) severe abdominal trauma. Pseudo-obstruction, radiation enteritis, carcinomatosis, necrotizing enterocolitis, and intestinal fistulas are other indications for home parenteral nutrition. Patients with these conditions cannot receive adequate nutrition enterally, though sometimes compensatory mucosal growth occurs that may reduce or eventually eliminate the need for continued home parenteral nutrition.

Patients must receive extensive evaluation, teaching, and training during hospitalization if home parenteral nutrition is to prove successful. These services should be provided by a team consisting of a physician, a nurse, a dietitian, a pharmacist, and a social worker. The team's instructions should cover the basic principles of parenteral nutrition as well as provide mechanical guidelines for catheter care, asepsis, and use of infusion pumps. Patients should be objectively evaluated before discharge to ensure that they adequately understand the principles of I.V. nutrition and can carry out home parenteral nutrition properly.

Once a patient is judged to be a suitable candidate for home TPN, a Silastic catheter is placed that is designed for more permanent use than the central venous catheter employed during hospitalization. Typically, the catheter is 90 cm long, with a thin 55 cm intravascular segment that is inserted either by venous cutdown into the internal or external jugular vein or the cephalic vein or by venipuncture directly into the subclavian vein. Its intravascular portion is cut so that the tip will lie at the junction of the superior vena cava and the right atrium.

Catheter placement is done in the OR with the patient under local anesthesia (1% lidocaine) and adequate sedation. The catheter is tunneled subcutaneously from a small incision lateral to the sternum to the site of venous insertion. The exit site is chosen on the basis of the patient's sex, physique, and hand dominance. In women, lower paraxiphoid or upper abdominal exit sites permit a more natural appearance. If coagulation status is abnormal, the cephalic vein is isolated in the deltopectoral groove and tied distally, and the catheter is inserted proximally by means of venotomy; otherwise, it is inserted into the subclavian vein percutaneously. Proper position-

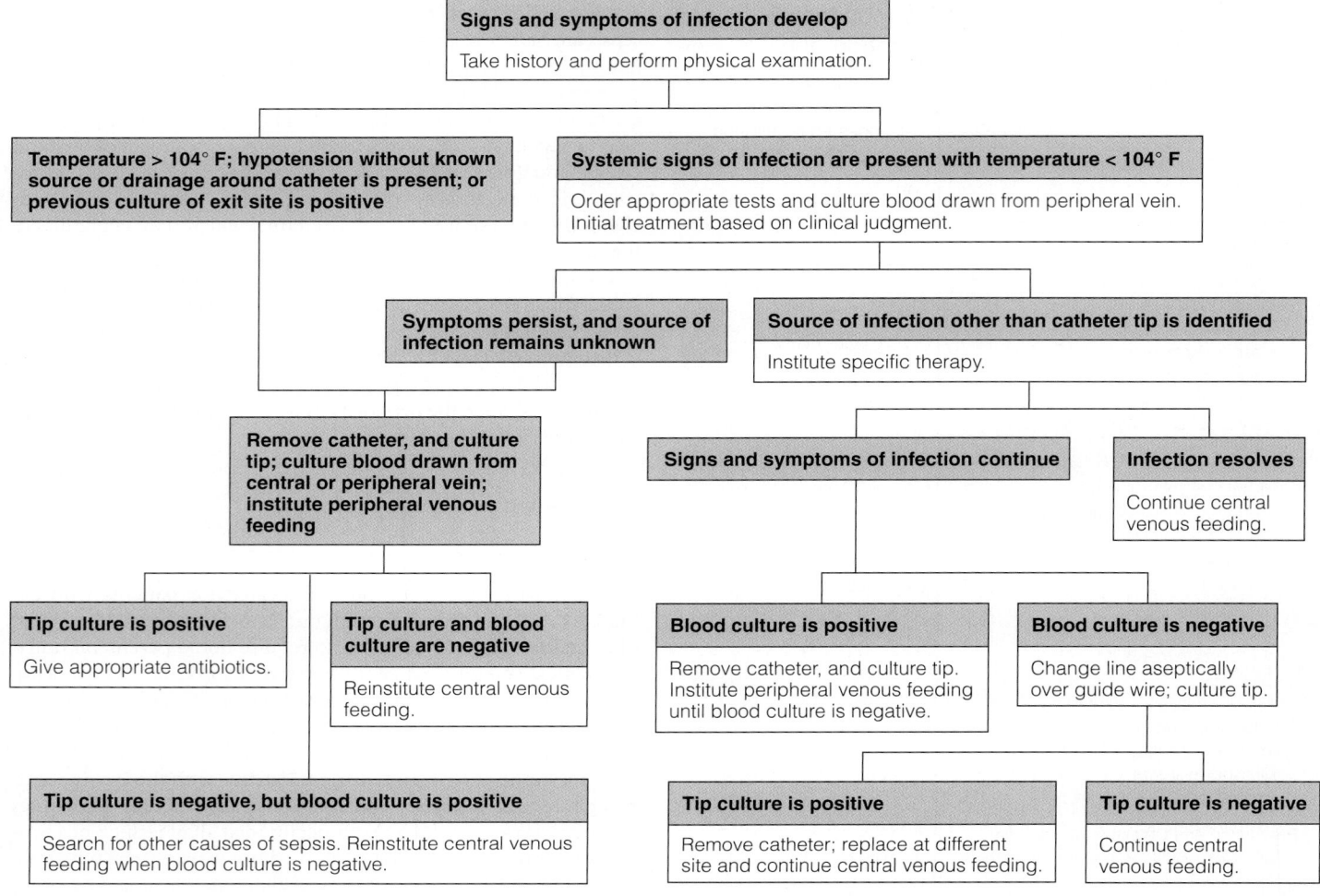

Figure 3 Shown is an algorithm for evaluating a febrile patient receiving central venous parenteral nutrition.

ing of the catheter is confirmed by fluoroscopy, and the incisions are closed with absorbable sutures. The catheter is sutured to the exit site, and the sutures are left attached for at least 2 weeks while tissue ingrowth into the cuff takes place. After the sutures are placed, sterile dressings are applied.

Calorie, protein, and fluid needs are carefully estimated for each patient, and the administration schedule is arranged so that the total volume may be infused nocturnally over 10 to 12 hours. Electrolytes, micronutrients, and trace minerals are added as indicated. Fat emulsions may be given either separately or admixed with glucose and protein and are used to reduce the requirement for dextrose calories and to prevent essential fatty acid deficiency.

The complications of home TPN are much the same as those of in-hospital TPN and may be divided into four categories: mechanical, infectious, metabolic, and psychosocial. Mechanical complications, which are generally easy to remedy, include catheter occlusion and dislodgment and damage to the external portion of the catheter. Infectious complications superficial to the cuff usually respond well to antibiotics. Catheter infections may necessitate removal of the device after the diagnosis is confirmed by blood cultures, but the usual therapeutic approach is to initiate a trial of parenteral antibiotics. Metabolic complications related to individual nutrient deficiencies may be corrected by adding the appropriate substance to the solution. The role of serum levels of trace minerals

and micronutrients in delineating nutrient deficiency states is unclear. In patients receiving insulin, hyperinsulinemia after infusion may be prevented by reducing the rate of administration gradually over the last hour of infusion. Psychosocial complications may vary from slight depression to suicidal tendencies, which must be treated with appropriate counseling.

The costs of a home TPN program may also be divided into four categories: patient training, equipment, supplies, and follow-up. It has been estimated that the average annual cost of home TPN is 70% less than that of in-hospital TPN. The growth of private companies that deliver equipment and supplies to the home, maintain inventory, bill patients, and help with health insurance reimbursement has considerably facilitated home care.

HOME ENTERAL NUTRITION

Home enteral nutrition is frequently used as either the sole source or a partial source of nutritional support. It is the preferred method when GI tract function is adequate. In patients undergoing surgery of the aerodigestive tract for cancer, jejunostomy feedings can supplement oral feedings, especially during adjuvant chemotherapy and radiation treatment. Patients are taught to cycle feedings over 12-hour periods, using an enteral pump system to provide 20 to 30 kcal/kg/day. Use of an appropriate feeding tube and immediate flushing of the tube after use reduce the incidence of clogging at home. If blockage occurs, proteases or carbonated beverages can be introduced into the tube in an attempt to open it. Jejunostomy feedings reduce the risk of aspiration and help maintain nutritional status during periods of inadequate oral intake. Use of inexpensive nutritionally complete commercial formulas is encouraged. For patients with more permanent disabilities that prevent adequate oral intake, a gastrostomy (or PEG [see 60 Gastrointestinal Endoscopy]) may be preferable; this reduces the GI complications of feeding by making use of the reservoir and admixing functions of the stomach.

Discussion

Evidence-Based Nutritional Support

EARLY ORAL FEEDINGS AFTER ELECTIVE OPERATIONS

Anesthetics, prolonged bed rest, and fluid shifts make the intestine susceptible to ileus after most operations, particularly abdominal ones. In the past, patients commonly underwent gastric decompression with a nasogastric tube until they showed obvious signs of bowel function. Over the past 10 years, however, several authors have questioned the necessity of postoperative nasogastric decompression.[20,21] Others have suggested not only that nasogastric decompression is unnecessary but also that perhaps patients should be fed earlier than is usually done.[22-24]

The traditional approach to postoperative feeding has been to start with a clear liquid or full liquid diet, continue this until the appearance of consistent flatus or bowel movements, and then switch to a regular diet. There is, however, no evidence that such a stepwise progression is necessary or leads to better outcomes. In fact, a 2002 study found no significant differences in time to diet tolerance, complications, or hospital stay between this approach and one in which postoperative feeding started with a regular diet.[25]

Use of opioids can have significant deleterious effects on nutrition. Opioid-induced constipation can lead to lower abdominal discomfort, fecal impaction, diarrhea, nausea, and inadequate absorption of oral drugs. The ensuing bowel dysfunction is a consequence both of CNS-mediated alteration of autonomic flow to the gut[26] and of a direct local opioid effect on the bowel.[27] Opioid receptor antagonists (e.g., naloxone and naltrexone) can reverse these changes, but at the cost of some reduction in analgesia. Newer agents (e.g., methylnaltrexone) are poorly lipid soluble and unable to penetrate the CNS and thus do not antagonize the central effects of opioids.[28] A 1996 study suggested, however, that I.V. methylnaltrexone could prevent opioid-induced delay in bowel motility without affecting analgesia.[29] Such drugs may be particularly useful as adjuncts, minimizing the side effects of opioids when these agents must be given.

Finally, early feeding has been combined with other therapies to enhance recovery. Patients who undergo epidural anesthesia, receive early oral feedings, and take part in an active exercise program experience much shorter convalescent recovery periods and require less hospitalization.[30]

DATA ON NUTRITIONAL SUPPORT IN SPECIFIC SETTINGS

Preoperative TPN

A number of studies have been conducted to evaluate the effect of preoperative TPN; most have involved patients with GI cancer who were considered at least moderately malnourished. A pooled analysis of the data showed that in patients who received preoperative TPN, the complication rate dropped from approximately 40% to 30%; in five studies, the differences reached statistical sig-

nificance.[31] The pooled analysis found no significant difference in mortality between the TPN groups and the control groups.

Intraoperative TPN

Although not yet tested in clinical trials, intraoperative TPN should be avoided. The stress associated with surgery and anesthesia results in hyperglycemia even without the infusion of dextrose. When infused during surgery the dextrose in the TPN solution can increase blood glucose levels severalfold, and these extreme increases have been associated with impaired immune function. Furthermore, it appears that hypotension or cardiac arrest during concentrated dextrose infusion can result in more irreversible damage to the CNS.

Postoperative TPN

TPN in the immediate postoperative period without preoperative TPN has been evaluated in multiple trials—again, mostly involving GI cancer patients who were considered at least moderately malnourished.[31] In contrast to the pooled analysis of the preoperative data, a pooled analysis of the postoperative data showed that in patients who received TPN after operation, the complication rate rose from approximately 30% to 40%.

Perioperative Enteral Nutrition

Two studies compared preoperative enteral nutrition with an ad libitum oral diet,[32,33] and in one,[32] postoperative complications were significantly lower in patients who received enteral tube feeding. Other studies compared early postoperative jejunal tube feeding with a standard oral diet that was advanced as tolerated and found no consistent differences in postoperative morbidity or mortality.[34-37] Yet another evaluated the use of postoperative jejunostomy tube feeding with a special formula enriched with arginine, ribonucleic acids, and omega-3 fatty acids after operation for upper GI tract cancer.[38] When only successfully fed patients were evaluated, those who received the enriched formula had fewer complications and a shorter hospital stay than those who received the standard formula.

Nutrition in Cancer Patients

Trials addressing perioperative nutritional support have been conducted in patients undergoing surgery for pancreatic, hepatocellular, and upper GI malignancies. In one, patients undergoing major pancreatic resection were randomly assigned either to a group that received TPN on postoperative day 1 or to a non-TPN group.[39] Patients in the TPN group derived no demonstrable benefit and experienced more complications (primarily infectious). It was concluded that routine postoperative TPN could not be recommended for patients undergoing major pancreatic resection for malignancy.

Another trial examined the effects of cyclic versus continuous enteral nutrition on postoperative gastric function after pylorus-preserving pancreaticoduodenectomy.[40] Patients were evaluated with respect to gastric emptying, resumption of normal diet, and length of hospital stay. Cyclic nutrition was associated with shorter periods of nasogastric intubation, earlier resumption of normal diet, and reduced hospital stay. It was concluded that cyclic enteral nutrition was clinically efficacious in this selected group of patients.

Nutritional support has been shown to reduce the catabolic response, improve protein synthesis, and enhance liver regeneration. In a 1994 study, 124 patients undergoing hepatectomy for hepatocellular carcinoma were randomly assigned either to a control group or to a group receiving perioperative I.V. nutritional support in addition to their oral diet.[41] The overall postoperative morbidity rate was reduced in the perioperative nutrition group (34% versus 55%), mainly because the rate of infection-related complications was lower (17% versus 37%). These benefits were mainly seen in patients with underlying cirrhosis who underwent major hepatectomy. It was concluded that perioperative nutritional support can reduce complications after major hepatectomy in such patients.

Early Postoperative Enteral Nutrition

In a nonrandomized, uncontrolled study of 38 patients who underwent colorectal surgery over a 3-month period,[42] the 31 patients who were able to tolerate an early feeding regimen had shorter postoperative stays (5.7 versus 10.6 days); the seven who were not had longer operative procedures and lost more blood intraoperatively (possibly as a result of a more difficult operation, which itself might lead to prolonged recovery and decreased tolerance of early enteral feeding). The investigators concluded (1) that early postoperative feeding is safe and is tolerated by the majority of patients and (2) that if early feeding is tolerated, it shortens hospital stay and may decrease health care costs.

In another study, 28 patients undergoing esophagectomy or pancreaticoduodenectomy received either immediate postoperative enteral feeding via jejunostomy or no feedings during the first 6 days after operation.[43] Postoperative vital capacity and forced expiratory volume in 1 second (FEV_1) were consistently lower in the fed group than in the unfed group, but there were no significant differences in grip strength and maximal inspiratory pressure between the two groups. Patients in the fed group were less mobile after operation and tended to recover less rapidly; however, there were no significant differences in fatigue or vigor between the two groups. The investigators concluded that immediate postoperative jejunal feeding is associated with impaired respiratory mechanics and postoperative mobility and does not influence the loss of muscle strength or the increase in fatigue occurring after major surgery; they further concluded that immediate postoperative enteral feeding should not be routine in well-nourished patients who are at low risk for nutrition-related complications.

Another trial evaluated early enteral feeding after resection of upper GI malignancies with the aim of determining whether early postoperative enteral feeding with an immune-enhancing formula supplemented with arginine, RNA, and omega-3 fatty acids could decrease morbidity, mortality, and length of hospital stay.[44] A total of 195 patients with upper GI cancer were randomly selected to receive either the immune-enhancing formula via jejunostomy or standard I.V. crystalloid solutions. There were no significant differences between the two groups with respect to number of minor, major, or infectious wound complications; length of hospital stay; or mortality.

In yet another trial, 43 patients with nontraumatic intestinal perforation and peritonitis were randomly assigned after laparotomy either to a control group or to a study group that received a feeding jejunostomy, with enteral feeding started 12 hours after operation.[45] Mortality was high in both the control group and the study group

(18% versus 19%).[45] The control group had more infectious complications (22 versus 8).

Nutrition in ICU Patients

A meta-analysis of 26 relevant randomized clinical trials involving 2,211 patients cared for in ICUs demonstrated that parenteral nutrition did not reduce morbidity or mortality, though the data did suggest that the most malnourished groups of patients might derive some benefit.[46] Therefore, use of this expensive therapy in the ICU should be carefully limited to patients who have specific nutritional needs and cannot accept enteral feedings.

Conclusions

Parenteral and enteral nutritional support is a valuable adjunctive—and sometimes lifesaving—therapy in selected surgical patients. It is generally agreed that patients who cannot ingest adequate nutrients for a prolonged period require nutritional therapy. It is not entirely clear, however, precisely how "adequate" and "prolonged" should be defined. In practice, definitions are likely to vary from patient to patient, depending on the amount of body energy stores and lean body mass, the presence or absence of preexisting medical illnesses, the number and severity of postoperative complications, and the nature of the surgical procedure.

Summation of data from numerous trials suggests that giving nutritional support for 7 days before operation decreases postoperative complications. Severely malnourished patients (defined on the basis of percentage of body weight lost or nutritional risk index score) may derive greater clinical benefit from preoperative nutritional support, but support for this view comes largely from retrospective analysis of prospective data. In addition, certain subsets of patients may derive particular benefit from nutritional support (e.g., patients undergoing hepatic resection for hepatocellular carcinoma and elderly patients with hip fractures). The increased complication rates in patients receiving postoperative TPN and the case reports of small bowel necrosis in patients receiving early postoperative enteral nutrition are evidence that nutritional support has risks and should not be given indiscriminately.

Nutritional Pharmacology and Immunonutrition

The role of nutrient administration to surgical patients has evolved from maintenance of a positive energy and nitrogen balance to modulation of tissue metabolism and organ system function. This new role is referred to as nutrition pharmacotherapy. Like other forms of adjuvant therapy, nutrition pharmacotherapy is usually a multitargeted therapeutic modality. For instance, one form of nutrition pharmacotherapy, immunonutrition, makes use of combinations of specific amino acids, fatty acids, and, in some enteral formulas, nucleotides. Another form, so-called bowel rehabilitation, uses an amino acid (glutamine) in combination with growth hormone and a modified diet. Inclusion of a specific nutrient as part of a plan of nutrition pharmacotherapy is based either on clinical studies or, more often, on extrapolations from experimental observations. In what follows, we discuss each of the nutrients used, or proposed for use, in nutrition pharmacotherapy, with emphasis on chemical characteristics, physiologic effects, available forms for exogenous administration, and, if available, clinical data supporting its use for this purpose.

GLUTAMINE

Glutamine is the most abundant amino acid in the body and appears to be the most versatile. Most free glutamine is synthesized and stored in skeletal muscle.[47] Skeletal muscle releases net glutamine for transport to the gut, immune cells, and the kidneys. The cells of the gut and the immune system proliferate rapidly, and glutamine acts as their main fuel source and as a biosynthetic precursor. One of the compounds derived from glutamine is glutathione, a tripeptide with potent antioxidant effects. Finally, glutamine participates in acid-base regulation via release of ammonia, which combines with H^+ to form NH_4^+ and is lost in urine.

Catabolism induced by major injury, surgery, sepsis, or burns results in increased release of glutamine from skeletal muscle.[48] This output of glutamine into the circulation is associated with increased uptake and consumption by the gut, the immune system, the liver, and the kidneys. The net effect is a profound fall in intracellular muscle stores of glutamine. This deficit exceeds all other amino acid deficits and persists even when stores of all other amino acids have already been replenished.[49]

Standard amino acid formulations have always included all of the essential amino acids and most of the nonessential ones. For a long time, glutamine was excluded from parenteral formulations because of its instability in aqueous solutions. However, the pharmaceutical industry has now begun to develop ways of keeping glutamine stable in an aqueous solution. For instance, Glamin (Pharmacia & Upjohn, Sweden), an amino acid formulation that is commercially available in Europe, includes the dipeptide glycyl-L-glutamine, which is readily hydrolyzed to free glutamine in plasma and tissues. These dipeptide formulations are not yet approved for use in the United States.

Several clinical studies of supplementation of parenteral formulas with glutamine have been published. Striking results have been reported in patients undergoing bone marrow transplantation. A randomized, double-blind, controlled study from 1992 investigated the effects of glutamine on metabolic parameters and clinical outcome in 45 adult patients undergoing bone marrow transplantation for hematologic malignancies.[50] Patients were randomly selected to receive either a formula supplemented with L-glutamine or a standard glutamine-free isonitrogenous formula for an average of 4 weeks after operation. The patients who received the glutamine-supplemented formula had a better nitrogen balance than the control group; more important, they also had a lower incidence of microbial colonization and clinical infection and a shorter hospital stay. These findings were subsequently confirmed by a study performed by a different group of investigators.[51]

Equally striking results have been reported in patients with the short-bowel syndrome that develops after massive small bowel resection. Although the advent of parenteral nutrition has improved survival for many patients with this syndrome, it has also created a dependency on such therapy, which in the long term can have life-threatening complications. For this reason, many surgical scientists have searched for ways of augmenting these patients' intestinal absorption capacity so as to reduce or eliminate the need for parenteral nutrition. A growing understanding of the roles of glutamine, dietary fiber, short-chain fatty acids, and growth factors in the process of intestinal adaptation led to clinical trials aimed at evaluating the effects of supplementation of these substances on patients with this syndrome.

In a randomized, double-blind, prospective multicenter trial, 41 patients with short-bowel syndrome were given an optimal diet and then randomly selected to receive oral glutamine, 30 g/day, plus placebo growth hormone; placebo glutamine plus growth hormone (GH), 0.1 mg/kg/day; or the two active agents together.[52] Patients were weaned from TPN according to standard criteria. At the end of 4 weeks, all subjects had decreased I.V. nutrient requirements, with the glutamine-GH group showing a greater reduction than the GH group, which in turn showed a greater reduction than the glutamine-placebo group.

The studies just cited were all conducted according to research protocols that used L-glutamine, which is not practical for I.V. administration, rather than the dipeptide form now commercially available (in Europe), which is stable in an aqueous solution. A meta-analysis of all the appropriate studies involving I.V. glutamine showed a significant reduction in postoperative infection associated with a decreased length of stay.[53] Reduced long-term (6 month) mortality was noted in critically ill patients—a finding that has not been recently associated with the administration of other specific nutrients.

ARGININE

Arginine is a nitrogen-dense amino acid that is considered semiessential because it is required for growth.[54] Its effect on growth seems to be mediated by its role in polyamine and nucleic acid synthesis. In addition, it is a potent secretagogue of growth hormone, insulin, glucagon, prolactin, and somatostatin[55-57]; when this effect is abolished by hypophysectomy, the stimulatory effect on wound healing is lost.[58] Supplemental dietary arginine has thymotrophic effects and enhances the responsiveness of thymic lymphocytes to mitogens in rats.[59] A similar response occurs in peripheral blood mononuclear cells of healthy human volunteers[60] and postoperative patients,[61] as evidenced by an enhanced response to concanavalin A and phytohemagglutinin.

Arginine enhances cellular immunity, as demonstrated by an increased delayed hypersensitivity response in animals with burns.[62] Dietary supplementation with arginine improves the response to dinitrofluorobenzene (DNFB) and enhances the survival of guinea pigs with 30% body surface burns. However, in a model of acute peritonitis in guinea pigs, supplemental arginine did not improve DNFB response or survival.[63]

Studies of arginine in humans have not been conclusive, because this substance is often administered with other active substances (e.g., RNA and omega-3 fatty acids). However, oral arginine supplementation has enhanced markers of wound healing in human volunteers,[64] and both enteral and parenteral arginine administration have improved immunologic measures.[65] Although arginine has antitumor properties in animals, the only relevant study done to date in humans found that arginine supplementation stimulated growth of breast cancer.[66] Because there is now controversy over increased mortality in critically ill patients receiving arginine [see Enteral Formulations to Counteract Immunosuppression, below], careful patient selection and full informed consent are necessary with this agent.

NUCLEOTIDES

Purines and pyrimidines are precursors of DNA and RNA, which are essential for cell proliferation. Purines and pyrimidines are synthesized by the liver de novo from amino acids and reutilized by salvage pathways. Reduction of dietary nucleotides results in suppression of cellular immune responses and prolongation of allograft survival.[67] The mechanism of this immunosuppression seems to be an inability of T cells to undergo blastogenesis. Dietary supplements containing RNA or uracil (but not adenine) maintain resistance to infection by C. albicans or S. aureus in rodents.[68,69] However, they do not enhance the immune response in comparison with a standard control diet.

On the basis of the immunosuppressive effect of dietary nucleotide restriction, it has been postulated that nucleotide supplementation could provide an immunostimulant effect. This postulate has been tested in studies of the RNA–fish oil–arginine formula now available [see Enteral Formulations to Counteract Immunosuppression, below].

FATTY ACIDS

Fatty acids in the systemic circulation can be used in two forms: as fuels to be stored and oxidized as needed by the organism and as precursors for other essential compounds, such as eicosanoids (prostaglandins, leukotrienes, and thromboxanes). Fatty acids may be classified in several different ways. One classification is based on chain length: short (two to five carbons), medium (six to 11 carbons), and long (12 to 26 carbons). Another classification is based on the presence of double bonds in the carbon chain: those with double bonds are called unsaturated and are further subclassified as either monounsaturated fatty acids or polyunsaturated fatty acids (PUFAs), depending on the number of double bonds. Another classification is the omega classification, which indicates where the first double bond is located when carbons are counted from the noncarboxyl end of the chain (e.g., omega-3, omega-6).

Humans can synthesize only fatty acids with double bonds at position 7 (counting from the noncarboxyl end toward the carboxyl end). Therefore, omega-6 or omega-3 fatty acids must be supplied exogenously. Because linoleic acid and α-linolenic acid can be elongated and desaturated to produce the remaining omega-6 and omega-3 PUFAs, these are considered the essential fatty acids. Requirements for omega-6 PUFAs exceed those for omega-3 PUFAs by a ratio of approximately 5:1. Omega-6 PUFAs are abundant in vegetable oils, whereas omega-3 PUFAs are abundant in fish oils and seed oils.

The availability of 20-carbon PUFAs—arachidonic acid in the omega-6 series and eicosapentaenoic acid in the omega-3 series—is the determining factor for the synthesis of eicosanoids. Cells obtain arachidonic acid and eicosapentaenoic acid from degradation of phospholipids by phospholipase A_2 and phospholipase C or by elongation and desaturation of linoleic acid and α-linolenic acid. Because mature immune cells (e.g., monocytes, macrophages, lymphocytes, and polymorphonuclear cells) lack an enzyme needed for transformation of 18-carbon PUFAs into 20-carbon PUFAs,[70] availability of precursors for eicosanoid synthesis in such cells is largely dependent on their lipid composition. The lipid composition of immune cells, in turn, is influenced by lipid intake, and thus, the type of PUFAs ingested can affect the immune response.[71,72]

Eicosanoids, especially prostaglandin E_2 (PGE_2), leukotriene B_4 (LTB_4), 5-hydroxyeicosatetraenoic acid (5-HETE), and 15-hydroxyeicosatetraenoic acid (15-HETE), are immunomodulatory; when produced in excess (as in posttraumatic states), they are generally immunosuppressive.[73] Dietary supplementation with omega-3 PUFAs has improved survival of endotoxic shock in guinea pigs.[74] Reduced intake of omega-6 PUFAs seems to be as important as increased intake of omega-3 PUFAs. When animals are made deficient in linoleic acid, mortality after endotoxin challenge is only 24%; however, when arachidonic acid is given 2 days before endotoxin challenge, mortality reaches 100%.[75] Similar results were reported in guinea pigs recovering from flame burns covering 30% of body surface area.[76] Compared with animals fed dietary safflower oil (74% linoleic acid) or linoleic acid alone, animals fed fish oil had less weight loss, better skeletal muscle mass, lower resting metabolic expenditure, better cell-mediated immune responses, better opsonic indices, higher splenic weight, lower adrenal weight, higher serum transferrin levels, and lower serum C3 levels.

The fat emulsions currently available for I.V. use in the United States are made with LCTs derived either from soybean oil alone or from soybean oil and safflower oil. All of the fatty acids in LCTs are in the form of PUFAs. Intravenously administered LCT emulsions are cleared in part through the reticuloendothelial system (RES).[77] When such emulsions are used as a calorie source, they may impair the ability of the RES to clear bacteria if given too rapidly or in excessively large amounts. Moreover, the PUFAs in LCT emulsions require carnitine-mediated transport to cross the mitochondrial membrane for oxidation. During sepsis, urinary excretion of free carnitine rises significantly, and the plasma acylcarnitine level falls.[78] One way of circumventing these problems is to use emulsions that contain MCTs.

MCT-containing emulsions possess an absorptive advantage over LCT-containing emulsions: whereas LCTs are absorbed via lacteals and the lymphatic system, MCTs are absorbed via the portal system. MCTs are obtained from coconut oil and contain saturated fatty acids (with octanoic acids predominating). Because MCTs are smaller than LCTs, they are more water soluble; they are also poorly bound to albumin and diffuse more easily across body compartments. Several reports on the use of I.V. administered MCT fat emulsions have been published. One study evaluated the effect of a 75% MCT/25% LCT emulsion on RES function as demonstrated by ^{99m}Tc-sulfur colloid (Tc-SC) clearance. Tc-SC clearance was significantly higher after 3 days of MCT/LCT administration than after 3 days of LCT administration.[79] Another study investigated the metabolic effects of MCT-containing emulsions on surgical patients.[80] Its main finding was the appearance of β-hydroxybutyrate in association with MCT infusion, which was indicative of a ketogenic effect. A tendency toward improved nitrogen balance was also observed but was not statistically significant.

In summary, specific fatty acids have significant potential for use in nutrition pharmacotherapy. Omega-6 fatty acids are potential immunosuppressants, whereas omega-3 fatty acids are potential immunostimulants. A reduction in the intake of omega-6 PUFAs appears prudent in patients who are immunocompromised or in posttraumatic states. Formulas for nutritional support should include omega-3 PUFAs, though the exact amount of omega-3 PUFAs and the precise ratio of omega-6 to omega-3 remain to be determined.

In the United States, the only emulsions commercially available for I.V. use at present are made of LCTs containing omega-6 PUFAs. MCTs offer some metabolic advantages over LCTs and obviate the side effects resulting from an excess of omega-6 PUFAs. Enteral diets containing omega-3 PUFAs appear to benefit stressed surgical patients, particularly those who are immunosuppressed as a result of therapy for cancer.

ENTERAL FORMULATIONS TO COUNTERACT IMMUNOSUPPRESSION

Impact (Sandoz Nutrition, Minneapolis, MN), a commercially available enteral formula enriched with omega-3 PUFAs, arginine, and RNA, was shown to reduce infectious complications in postoperative patients[81,82] and in some critically ill patients.[83] It was also shown to reduce hospital stay in selected patient groups.[84] However, concern was raised by the publication of data from a large meta-analysis of studies using this formula, which suggested that its use led to increased mortality.[85] The investigators suggested that the immunomodulation associated with this diet might be beneficial in some patients (generally the less seriously ill) but harmful in others (generally the more critically ill patients who require nutritional support).[86] Until this issue is resolved, patient selection is extremely important if this diet is to be administered to surgical patients.

Nutritional Support Guidelines

In 2002, the American Society for Parenteral and Enteral Nutrition (ASPEN) published an updated version of guidelines for use of nutritional support.[87] These guidelines are also available on the Internet (http://www.nutritioncare.org/publications/2002guidelines.pdf).

References

1. Vitamin preparations as dietary supplements and as therapeutic agents. Council on Scientific Affairs. JAMA 257:1929, 1987

2. Marks J: The safety of vitamins: an overview. Int J Vitam Nutr Res 30(suppl):12, 1989

3. Nathens AB, Neff MJ, Jurkovich GJ, et al: Randomized, prospective trial of antioxidant supplementation in critically ill surgical patients. Ann Surg 236:814, 2002

4. Demling R, LaLonde C, Saldinger P, et al: Multiple-organ dysfunction in the surgical patient: pathophysiology, prevention, and treatment. Curr Probl Surg 30:345, 1993

5. Pingleton SK, Hadzima SK: Enteral alimentation and gastrointestinal bleeding in mechanically ventilated patients. Crit Care Med 11:13, 1983

6. Treolar DM, Stechmiller J: Pulmonary aspiration in tube-fed patients with artificial airways. Heart Lung 13:667, 1984

7. Du Moulin GC, Paterson DJ, Hedley-White J, et al: Aspiration of gastric bacteria in antacid-treated patients: a frequent cause of postoperative colonization of the airway. Lancet 1:242, 1982

8. Pemberton LB, Lyman B, Lander V, et al: Sepsis from triple- vs single-lumen catheters during total parenteral nutrition in surgical or critically ill patients. Arch Surg 121:591, 1986

9. Miller JJ, Venus B, Mathru M: Comparison of the sterility of long-term central venous catheterization using single lumen, triple lumen, and pulmonary artery catheters. Crit Care Med 12:634, 1984.

10. Belliveau K: Catheter infection rate using multiple lumen catheters. Read before the National Intravenous Therapy Association, New Orleans, April 1986

11. McCowen KC, Malhotra A, Bistrian BR, et al: Endocrine and metabolic dysfunction syndromes in the critically ill—stress-induced hyperglycemia. Crit Care Clin 17:107, 2001

12. Fietsam R Jr, Bassett J, Glover JL: Complications of coronary artery surgery in diabetic patients. Am Surg 57:551, 1991

13. Schloerb PR: TPN or intravenous food poisoning? Nutrition 17:680, 2001

14. O'Neill PA, Davies I, Fullerton KJ, et al: Stress hormone and blood glucose response following acute stroke in the elderly. Stroke 22:842, 1991

15. Flakoll PJ, Hill JO, Abumrad NN: Acute hyperglycemia enhances proteolysis in normal man. Am J Physiol 265:E715, 1993

16. Van der Berghe G, Wouters P, Weekers F, et al: Intensive insulin therapy in critically ill patients. N Engl J Med 345:1359, 2001

17. Maki DG, Weise CE, Sarafin HW: A semiquantitative culture method for identifying intravenous-catheter-related infection. N Engl J Med 296:1305, 1977

18. Pettigrew RA, Lang SDR, Haydock DA, et al: Catheter-related sepsis in patients on intravenous nutrition: a prospective study of quantitative catheter cultures and guidewire changes for suspected sepsis. Br J Surg 72:52, 1985

19. Williams WW: Infection control during parenteral nutrition therapy. JPEN J Parenter Enteral Nutr 9:735, 1985

20. Pearl ML: A randomized controlled trial of postoperative nasogastric tube decompression in gynecologic oncology patients undergoing intraabdominal surgery. Obst Gynecol 88:399, 1996

21. Friedman SG: A prospective randomized study of abdominal aortic surgery without post-operative nasogastric decompression. Cardiovasc Surg 4:492, 1996

22. Reissman PR, Teoh TA, Cohen SM, et al: Is early oral feeding safe after elective colorectal surgery? A prospective randomized trial. Ann Surg 222:73, 1995

23. Behrns KE, Kircher AP, Galanko JA, et al: Prospective randomized trial of early initiation and hospital discharge on a liquid diet following elective intestinal surgery. J Gastrointest Surg 4:217, 2001

24. Pearl ML, Valea FA, Fischer M, et al: A randomized controlled trial of early post-operative feedings in gynecologic oncology patients undergoing intra-abdominal surgery. Obstet Gynecol 92:94, 1998

25. Pearl ML: A randomized controlled trial of a regular diet as the first meal in gynecologic oncology patients undergoing intraabdominal surgery. Obstet Gynecol 100:230, 2002

26. Shook JE, Pelton JT, Hruby VJ, et al: Peptide opioid antagonist separates peripheral and central opioid anti-transit effects. J Pharm Exp Ther 243:492, 1987

27. Manara L, Bianchi G, Ferretti P, et al: Inhibition of gastrointestinal transit by morphine in rats results primarily from direct action on gut opioid sites. J Pharm Exp Ther 237:945, 1986

28. Foss JF: A review of the potential role of methylnaltrexone in opioid bowel dysfunction. Am J Surg 182(5A suppl):19S, 2001

29. Yuan FS, Foss JF, O'Connor M, et al: Methylnaltrexone prevents morphine-induced delay in oral-cecal transit time without affecting analgesia: a double-blind randomized placebo-controlled trial. Clin Pharm Ther 59:469, 1996

30. Kehlet H, Wilmore DW: Multimodal strategies to improve surgical outcome. Am J Surg 183:630, 2002

31. Klein S, Kinney J, Jeejeebhoy K, et al: Nutrition support in clinical practice: review of published data and recommendations for further research directions. JPEN J Parenter Enteral Nutr 21:133, 1997

32. von Meyenfeldt MF, Meijrink WJHJ, Rouflart MMJ, et al: Perioperative nutritional support: a randomized clinical trial. Clin Nutr 11:180, 1992

33. Shukla HS, Rao RR, Banu N, et al: Enteral hyperalimentation in malnourished surgical patients. Ind J Med Res 80:339, 1984

34. Sagar S, Harland P, Shields R: Early postoperative feeding with elemental diet. Br Med J 1:293, 1979

35. Ryan JA, Page CP, Babcock L: Early postoperative jejunal feeding of elemental diet in gastrointestinal surgery. Am Surg 47:393, 1981

36. Smith RC, Hartemink RJ, Holinshead JW, et al: Fine bore jejunostomy feeding following major abdominal trauma: a controlled randomized clinical trial. Br J Surg 72:458, 1985

37. Tovinelli G, Marsili I, Varrassi G: Nutrition support after total laryngectomy. JPEN J Parenter Enteral Nutr 17:445, 1993

38. Daly JM, Lieberman MD, Goldfine J, et al: Enteral nutrition with supplemental arginine, RNA and omega-3 fatty acids in patients after operation: immunologic, metabolic and clinical outcome. Surgery 112:56, 1992

39. Brennan MF, Pisters PW, Posner M, et al: A prospective randomized trial of total parenteral nutrition after major pancreatic resection for malignancy. Am Surg 220:436, 1994

40. Van Berge Henegowen M, Akkermans L, van Gulik T, et al: Prospective, randomized trial on the effect of cyclic versus continuous enteral nutrition on postoperative gastric function after pylorus-preserving pancreatoduodenectomy. Ann Surg 226:677, 1997

41. Fan ST, Lo CM, Lai E, et al: Perioperative nutritional support in patients undergoing hepatectomy for hepatocellular carcinoma. N Engl J Med 331:1547, 1994

42. Bufo A, Feldman S, Daniels G, et al: Early postoperative feeding. Dis Colon Rectum 37:1260, 1994

43. Watters JM, Kirkpatrick SM, Norris SB, et al: Immediate postoperative enteral feeding results in impaired respiratory mechanics and decreased mobility. Ann Surg 226:369, 1997

44. Heslin MJ, Latkany L, Leung D, et al: A prospective, randomized trial of early enteral feeding after resection of upper gastrointestinal malignancy. Ann Surg 226:567, 1997

45. Singh G, Ram RP, Khanna SK: Early postoperative enteral feeding in patients with non-traumatic intestinal perforation and peritonitis. J Am Coll Surg 187:142, 1998

46. Heyland DK, MacDonald S, Keefe L, et al: Total parenteral nutrition in the critically ill patient: a meta-analysis. JAMA 280:2013, 1998

47. Souba WW, Herskowitz K, Augstgen TR, et al: Glutamine nutrition: theoretical considerations and therapeutic impact. JPEN J Parenter Enteral Nutr 14: 237S, 1990

48. Furst P, Albers S, Stehle P: Stress-induced intracellular glutamine depletion. Contr Infusion Ther Clin Nutr 17:117, 1987

49. Lacey JM, Wilmore DW: Is glutamine a conditionally essential amino acid? Nutr Rev 48:297, 1990

50. Ziegler TR, Young LS, Benfell K, et al: Clinical and metabolic efficacy of glutamine-supplemented parenteral nutrition after bone marrow transplantation. Ann Intern Med 116:821, 1992

51. Schloerb PR, Amare M: Total parenteral nutrition with glutamine in bone marrow transplantation and other clinical applications. JPEN J Parenter Enteral Nutr 17:407, 1993

52. Byrne TA, Morrissey T, Naltakom T, et al: Growth hormone, glutamine and a modified diet enhance nutrient absorption in patients with severe short bowel syndrome. JPEN J Parenter Enteral Nutr 19:296, 1995

53. Novak F, Heyland DK, Avenell A, et al: Glutamine supplementation in serious illness: a systematic review of the evidence. Crit Care Med 30:2022, 2002

54. Barbul A: Arginine and immune function. Nutrition 6:53, 1990

55. Rakoff JS, Siler TM, Sinha YN, et al: Prolactin and growth hormone release in response to sequential stimulation by arginine and synthetic TRF. J Clin Endocrinol Metab 37:641, 1973

56. Palmer JP, Walter RM, Ensinck JW: Arginine-stimulated acute phase of insulin and glucagon secretion: I. In normal man. Diabetes 24:735, 1975

57. Utsumi M, Makimura H, Ishihara K, et al: Determination of immunoreactive somatostatin in rat plasma and responses to arginine, glucose and glucagon infusion. Diabetologia 17:319, 1979

58. Barbul A, Rettura G, Levenson SM, et al: Wound healing and thymotropic effects of arginine: a pituitary mechanism of action. Am J Clin Nutr 37:786, 1983

59. Barbul A, Wasserkrug HL, Seifter E, et al: Immunostimulatory effects of arginine in normal and injured rats. J Surg Res 29:228, 1980

60. Barbul A, Sisto DA, Wasserkrug HL, et al: Arginine stimulates lymphocyte immune res-

ponse in healthy human beings. Surgery 90:244, 1981

61. Daly JM, Reynolds J, Thom A, et al: Immune and metabolic effects of arginine in the surgical patient. Ann Surg 208:512, 1988

62. Saito H, Trocki O, Alexander JW, et al: The effect of route of nutrient administration on the nutritional state, catabolic hormone secretion, and gut mucosal integrity after burn injury. JPEN J Parenter Enteral Nutr 11:1, 1987

63. Gonce SJ, Peck MD, Alexander JW, et al: Arginine supplementation and its effect on established peritonitis in guinea pigs. JPEN J Parenter Enteral Nutr 14:237, 1990

64. Kirk SJ, Hurson M, Regan MC, et al: Arginine stimulates wound healing and immune function in elderly human beings. Surgery 114:155, 1993

65. Daly JM, Reynolds J, Sigal RK, et al: Effect of dietary protein and amino acids on immune function. Crit Care Med 18:S86, 1990

66. Park KGM, Heys SD, Blessing K, et al: Stimulation of human breast cancers by dietary L-arginine. Clin Sci 82:413, 1992

67. Van Buren CT, Kim E, Kulkarni AD, et al: Nucleotide-free diet and suppression of immune response. Transplant Proc 19:57, 1987

68. Fanslow WC, Kulkarni AD, Van Buren CT, et al: Effect of nucleotide restriction and supplementation on resistance to experimental murine candidiasis. JPEN J Parenter Enteral Nutr 12:49, 1988

69. Kulkarni AD, Fanslow WC, Drath DB, et al: Influence of dietary nucleotide restriction on bacterial sepsis and phagocytic cell function in mice. Arch Surg 121:169, 1986

70. Chapkin RS, Somers SD, Erickson KL: Inability of murine peritoneal macrophages to convert linoleic acid into arachidonic acid. J Immunol 140:2350, 1988

71. Johnston DV, Marshall LA: Dietary fat, prostaglandins and the immune response. Prog Food Nutr Sci 8:3, 1984

72. Meade CJ, Mertin J: Fatty acids and immunity. Adv Lip Res 16:127, 1978

73. Kinsella JE, Lokesh B: Dietary lipids, eicosanoids, and the immune system. Crit Care Med 18(suppl):S94, 1990

74. Mascioli E, Leader L, Flores E, et al: Enhanced survival to endotoxin in guinea pigs fed IV fish oil emulsions. Lipids 23:623, 1988

75. Cook JA, Wise WC, Knapp DR, et al: Essential fatty acid deficient rats: a new model for evaluating arachidonate metabolism in shock. Adv Shock Res 6:93, 1981

76. Alexander JW, Saito H, Trocki O, et al: The importance of lipid type in the diet after burn injury. Ann Surg 204:1, 1986

77. Seidner DL, Mascioli EA, Istfan NW, et al: Effects of long-chain triglyceride emulsions on reticuloendothelial system function in humans. JPEN J Parenter Enteral Nutr 13:614, 1989

78. Nanni C, Pittiruti M, Giovannini I, et al: Plasma carnitine levels and urinary carnitine excretion during sepsis. JPEN J Parenter Enteral Nutr 9:483, 1985

79. Jonsen GL, Mascioli EA, Seidner DL, et al: Parenteral infusion of long- and medium-chain triglycerides and reticuloendothelial system function in man. JPEN J Parenter Enteral Nutr 14:467, 1990

80. Jiang Z, Zhang S, Wang X, et al: A comparison of medium-chain and long-chain triglycerides in surgical patients. Ann Surg 217:175, 1993

81. Daly J, Weintraub F, Shou J, et al: Enteral nutrition during multimodality therapy in upper gastrointestinal cancer patients. Ann Surg 221:127, 1995

82. Daly J, Lieberman M, Goldfine J, et al: Enteral nutrition with supplemental arginine, RNA, and omega-3 fatty acids in patients after operation: immunologic, metabolic, and clinical outcome. Surgery 112:56, 1992

83. Bower R, Lavin P, LiCari J, et al: A modified enteral formula reduces hospital length of stay (LOS) in patients in intensive care units (ICU). Crit Care Med 21(supp 4):S275, 1993

84. Galban C, Montejo JC, Mesejo A: An immune-enhancing enteral diet reduces mortality rate and episodes of bacteremia in septic intensive care unit patients. Crit Care Med 28:643, 2000

85. Heyland DK, Novak F, Drover JW, et al: Should immunonutrition become routine in critically ill patients? A systematic review of the evidence. JAMA 286:944, 2001

86. Suchner U, Heyland DK, Peter K: Immune-modulatory actions of arginine in the critically ill. Br J Nutr 87:S121, 2002

87. ASPEN Board of Directors and the Clinical Guidelines Task Force: Guidelines for the use of parenteral and enteral nutrition in adult and pediatric patients. JPEN J Parenter Enteral Nutr 26:62SA, 2002

Acknowledgments

Figure 2   Talar Agasyan.
Figure 4   Carol Donner.

138 CLINICAL PHARMACOLOGY

Jennifer J. Bonner, Pharm.D., Robert R. Bies, Pharm.D., Ph.D., Robert Weber, M.S., F.A.S.H.P., and Samuel A. Tisherman, M.D., F.A.C.S., F.C.C.M.

Modern surgical care is dependent on the use of drugs, many of which can be harmful as well as beneficial. Polypharmacy is the norm, and as a result, there is a high potential for adverse interactions between agents. In addition, surgical patients often exhibit abnormalities in drug metabolism, for various reasons. Overall, the incidence of drug-related adverse events in hospitalized patients is difficult to determine precisely because the causality is often unclear. In one review,[1] adverse drug events (defined as injuries caused by the use or nonuse of drugs) or adverse drug reactions (defined as nonpreventable drug reactions resultling from the appropriate use of drugs) occurred in approximately 2% to 6% of hospital admissions. These adverse occurrences increased the duration of hospitalization by 1.2 to 3.8 days and increased hospital costs by $2,284 to $5,640. A better understanding of pharmacokinetics and pharmacodynamics can help surgeons minimize the potential for harm associated with the use of pharmacologic agents.

Definitions of Key Terms

Pharmacokinetics may be defined in several ways. The word itself is a combination of the element *pharmaco-,* meaning "related to drugs" (from the Greek word *pharmakon* "drug or poison"), and the word *kinetics,* meaning "the change in one or more variables as a function of time," as Wagner succinctly put it.[2] In the discipline of pharmacokinetics, the variables in question relate to the time course and character of the body's absorption, distribution, metabolism, and excretion of drugs.[3] (These four processes are often collectively referred to by the abbreviation ADME.) Pharmacokinetics, then, can be thought of as the study of the actions of the body on a drug administered to it. The body's pharmacokinetic handling of a drug depends on many factors, including the chemical characteristics of the drug, the dosage, the route of administration, the pharmaceutical formulation, and the physiologic characteristics and disease status of the patient.

Pharmacodynamics can be thought of as the study of the actions of a drug on the body. The variables in question relate to the time course and character of a drug's effect at its site of action (i.e., at a receptor or another binding site). To ensure adequate patient response and prevent complications during the perioperative period, surgeons should possess a thorough understanding of both pharmacokinetics and pharmacodynamics.

Basic Pharmacokinetic Principles

ABSORPTION

Absorption is defined as the extent to which a substance moves into the systemic circulation from its site of administration. The pharmacokinetic parameter that is generally used to quantify drug absorption is bioavailability—that is, the fraction of an administered dose that becomes systemically available (often abbreviated as F). The bioavailability of a given drug in a given patient depends in large part on its route of administration. Inadequate bioavailability is a not uncommon cause of therapeutic failure.

The absorption of a drug across any membrane or barrier is determined by blood flow to the area of absorption, the molecular size of the drug, and the degree to which the drug is ionized. In critically ill patients, regional blood flow may be abnormal, and diffusion across tissues may be limited by the presence of edema. As molecular weight increases, diffusion decreases exponentially. The ionization of a drug can be estimated by means of the Henderson-Hasselbalch equation:

$$pH = pK_a + \log(\text{base form/acid form})$$

where pH represents the hydrogen ion concentration and pK_a represents the negative logarithm of the acid ionization constant. The ionized form of the drug is not lipid soluble and therefore does not cross cell membranes by diffusion; in some cases, it may be actively transported.

Routes of Drug Delivery

Intravenous Many drugs can be administered directly into the systemic circulation. Intravenous (I.V.) administration, by definition, yields a bioavailability of 100%, thereby rendering the issue of absorption irrelevant. Systemic availability is most rapidly achieved when the drug is administered by I.V. bolus (also referred to as I.V. push). This mode of administration involves injecting small, concentrated volumes of the drug directly into the vein, generally over a period of 1 to 5 minutes (though slower rates are sometimes called for and often preferred). Not surprisingly, there are many drugs that cannot be administered by I.V. bolus, because of the potential for vein irritation and toxicity. With a few exceptions (e.g., propofol, which is given in lipid emulsions), drugs are dissolved in aqueous solutions when administered I.V.

Many drugs that cannot be given in an I.V. bolus can be administered via I.V. infusion. Infusion may be either intermittent or continuous, depending on the drug's half-life or pharmacologic duration of action. For example, many antibiotics are administered via intermittent I.V. infusion, whereas drugs such as propofol, fentanyl, and dobutamine are typically administered via continuous infusion. Volumes as high as 1 L may be delivered via I.V. infusion; for most drugs, flow rates tend to be in the range of 2 to 3 ml/min. Use of precision infusion pumps is preferred to manual control of the infusion.

Oral Bioavailability is a critical consideration when a drug is being administered orally because the rate and extent of absorption from the gastrointestinal tract will have to be taken into account. The bioavailability of a drug after oral administration depends on three major variables: the fraction of the dose absorbed across the apical cell membrane (i.e., the portion of the membrane bordering the intestinal lumen) into the cellular space of the enterocyte (f_a), the intestinal first-pass extraction of the drug (E_G), and the hepatic first-pass extraction of the drug (E_H). The relations among these factors may be described by the following equation[4]:

$$F = f_a \times (1 - E_G) \times (1 - E_H)$$

Most drug absorption after oral administration occurs in the small intestine. The value of f_a depends on several factors, including the dissolution rate of the drug formulation (for drugs given in a solid form, such as a tablet or capsule), gastric motility and emptying rate, and the solubility of the drug in GI fluids. Enteral feeding can also affect drug absorption. For example, tube feedings can impair absorption of phenytoin.[5] Drugs and surgery can affect intestinal motility.

Once a drug molecule is absorbed through the intestinal cell membrane, it may be subject to intestinal first-pass metabolism by enzymes within the cells, as well as by efflux pumps embedded within the apical side of the cell membrane. Both cytochrome P-450 (CYP) and UDP-glucoronosyltransferase (UGT) enzymes are found in the small intestine. These enzymes contribute to the metabolism of certain orally administered drugs before they reach the systemic circulation. Drugs whose oral absorption is significantly affected by the intestinal enzyme CYP3A4 include the immunosuppressive agents cyclosporine, tacrolimus, and sirolimus; the calcium channel blockers; and some HIV protease inhibitors.

P-glycoprotein (P-gp) is a large protein that is the product of the multidrug resistance–1 (*MDR1*) gene. It is found on the apical membrane of enterocytes and acts as an efflux pump to remove exogenous substances.[6] P-gp is found in many organs, including the kidneys, the brain, the lungs, the liver, and the GI tract.[7] Many clinically used drugs are P-gp substrates, including tacrolimus, sirolimus, cyclosporine, verapamil, diltiazem, digoxin, dexamethasone, and methylprednisolone; most P-gp substrates are also substrates for CYP3A4.[8,9] The presence of the P-gp efflux pump keeps these drugs from undergoing enzymatic metabolism within the enterocytes. Some drugs are inhibitors or inducers of P-gp.

After a drug is absorbed into the intestine, it is transported to the liver via the portal vein. At this point, the drug may be subject to hepatic first-pass metabolism by enzymes within the liver. After passage through the liver, the drug, its metabolites, or both pass into the systemic circulation. Drugs that are substrates of CYP2D6 and CYP3A4 are especially vulnerable to hepatic first-pass metabolism.[5]

Intramuscular Drug absorption after I.M. injection is highly variable and depends on the properties of the drug molecule, the formulation, and the injection site. Because muscle is highly vascularized, drugs in aqueous solutions often are absorbed quite rapidly after I.M. administration (albeit more slowly than they are after I.V. administration). Any condition that reduces blood flow to the muscle at the site of injection will decrease the rate and extent of drug absorption after I.M. administration. Drugs in aqueous vehicles are absorbed more rapidly than those in lipid vehicles. In some cases, the slower absorption associated with lipid emulsions constitutes a practical advantage. For example, with certain medications (e.g., penicillin G benzathine, risperidone, and haloperidol), long-acting I.M. formulations are made by suspending the drug in a lipid vehicle specifically for the purpose of extending the duration of the therapeutic effect to as long as 4 weeks.

Subcutaneous In a subcutaneous injection, the drug is injected into the connective tissue that lies underneath the dermal layer of the skin. This tissue is not as well vascularized as muscle. Consequently, a drug typically is absorbed more slowly after subcutaneous administration than after I.M. administration. Drugs commonly given via subcutaneous injection include insulin, heparin (which, unlike most drugs, is rapidly absorbed via this route), and

low-molecular-weight heparins (LMWHs). Generally, no more than 0.5 to 1 ml of a drug may be administered subcutaneously. Peripheral edema or hypoperfusion may limit systemic absorption after subcutaneous injection.

Transdermal Although most topically administered drugs are meant to exert only local effects, some are meant to reach the systemic circulation. To be systemically distributed after topical application, drug molecules must pass through the stratum corneum and the epidermis to reach the blood vessels of the dermis. To traverse these outer layers of the skin, the molecules must be lipophilic, of a low molecular weight, and nonionized. Drugs that are administered transdermally bypass both hepatic and intestinal first-pass metabolism and are absorbed continuously for as long as any available drug remains in the skin. Most transdermal patches are designed so that the rate of drug release is significantly slower than the rate of absorption through the skin, thereby permitting gradual and continuous absorption into the systemic circulation. Sometimes, a loading dose is contained in the adhesive layer (as with the scopolamine patch for motion sickness), allowing more rapid attainment of therapeutic blood levels. Examples of common transdermal formulations include the fentanyl patch, which releases the drug over a 72-hour period, and the clonidine patch, which releases the drug continuously for 7 days.

The main advantage of the transdermal method of administration is that it allows blood levels of a drug to be maintained at a desired level for a relatively long period without I.V. administration. One disadvantage is that after removal of the patch or other formulation, a residual amount of the drug may be left in the skin layer, and this residuum may continue to be absorbed into the systemic circulation even after therapy has been discontinued.

Sublingual and transmucosal Some drugs (in particular, those that are in a nonionized form and that exhibit high lipid solubility) are well enough absorbed via the oral mucosa that they may be given sublingually or simply dissolved in the mouth. This route of administration is especially advantageous for drugs that undergo significant hepatic first-pass metabolism when administered orally (e.g., nitroglycerin) because when a drug is absorbed through the oral mucosa, it passes directly into the systemic circulation. Drugs that are sometimes administered in this manner include buprenorphine and fentanyl.

Rectal Rectal administration of a drug may be convenient in clinical situations where (1) nausea and vomiting is present or oral intake is restricted (e.g., before an operation), (2) I.V. administration is not desirable, and (3) the drug of interest is available in a suppository form. Unfortunately, drug absorption from the rectum is hard to predict and often incomplete. The rectum is drained by both the systemic circulation and the portal circulation. From a pharmacokinetic standpoint, this means that approximately 50% of a rectally administered drug dose will bypass the liver and reach the systemic circulation without undergoing hepatic first-pass metabolism.[10] Drugs available in rectal suppository form that are absorbed systemically include acetaminophen, aspirin, and the antiemetics promethazine and prochlorperazine. In addition, various drugs may be administered rectally with the intention of producing a local or colonic effect (e.g., anesthetic suppositories in patients with hemorrhoids and sucralose or neomycin retention enemas in patients with hepatic failure).

Vaginal Vaginal administration of drugs is usually intended to produce local effects, except in the case of hormonal treatments (e.g., the vaginal contraceptive ring, the estradiol ring, and estradiol or progesterone creams), which are intended to have at least some degree of systemic absorption. An important consideration prescribing topical vaginal products (e.g., antifungal agents) is the age of the patient. The pH of the vagina ranges from 3.5 to 4.2 in women of reproductive age, but it is either neutral or slightly basic in postmenopausal women and girls who have not yet reached puberty. These pH changes can alter the ionization state of antifungals such as ketoconazole. At an acidic pH, ketoconazole is protonated, but at a neutral or basic pH, it is nonionized and therefore able to cross the membranes of the vagina, undergoing unwanted systemic absorption and exerting undesired side effects.

Nasal Most drugs that are administered nasally are topical agents employed to produce local effects. However, the nasal mucosa has much the same capacity for systemic absorption that the oral mucosa does: the area is highly vascularized, allowing rapid absorption of lipophilic and nonionized drugs. Currently, only desmopressin acetate (1-deamino-8-D arginine vasopressin, or DDAVP) and calcitonin are administered nasally for systemic therapy, though intranasal formulations of other drugs (e.g., insulin) are now in development. The mucosal membranes of the nose contain a number of drug-metabolizing enzymes, including CYPs, which may result in first-pass metabolism of certain drugs.

Inhalational The large surface area of the lung, the high permeability of the alveolar surfaces, and the highly vascular nature of lung tissue allow rapid systemic absorption of drugs,[11] especially those in gaseous form (e.g., inhaled general anesthetics). In terms of the onset of therapeutic effect, however, the partial pressure of these agents in blood and tissue is more important than the actual concentration.[12] Inhalational general anesthetics aside, most inhaled prescription drugs (e.g., beta$_2$ agonists and corticosteroids for treatment of asthma and amphotericin B and tobramycin for treatment of lung infections) are designed to exert local effects on lung tissue. Systemic absorption does occur, but it is minimal and is partly attributable to swallowing of the drug during inhalation.

At present, the only inhaled drug formulation on the market that is designed for systemic delivery via the lungs is inhaled insulin (Exubera; Pfizer, New York, New York), which was approved by the United States Food and Drug Administration in January 2006. An advantage of this inhaled insulin formulation is that its absorption into the systemic circulation is independent of body mass index (BMI)—in contrast with subcutaneously administered regular insulin, which is absorbed more slowly in obese patients.[13]

The pulmonary route of administration is also particularly effective at ensuring a high spike in drug concentration in the central nervous system. Currently, this property is taken advantage of by cigarette smokers and users of freebase cocaine, crack cocaine, and crystal methamphetamine; in the future, it may be taken advantage of by developers of therapeutic drugs.

Nervous system In some situations, it is desirable to obtain particular drug levels in the cerebrospinal fluid. However, under normal circumstances (i.e., in the absence of conditions such as inflammation and trauma), many drugs, especially those that are water-soluble or ionized, have difficulty penetrating the blood-brain barrier. Even when a drug does cross this barrier and reach the brain, the choroid plexus may secrete it back into the blood, making it difficult to reach the desired drug levels in the CSF. To overcome this difficulty, certain drugs (typically local anesthetics or analgesics) may be injected in or near the spinal canal in the vicinity of the nerve fibers that are to be blocked. Examples of this type of injection include epidural blocks, paravertebral nerve blocks, and spinal nerve blocks. Systemic absorption occurs, but it should be kept to a minimum: it is not necessary

for the therapeutic effect, and it may cause toxicity.[14] The vasoconstrictor epinephrine is often administered along with a local anesthetic during a spinal block because it decreases blood flow around the injection area, thereby reducing systemic absorption and potentiating the effects of the anesthetic. Epinephrine also acts on alpha$_2$ adrenoceptors on the nerve terminals to enhance the anesthetic effect by inhibiting the release of substance P and reducing nerve firing.

DISTRIBUTION

While a drug is being absorbed into the systemic circulation, it may simultaneously be distributed into other physiologic fluids and tissues, depending on the physiology of the patient and the physiochemical properties of the drug. Patient variables that may affect distribution include body size, fluid distribution within the body, amount of adipose tissue, cardiac output, tissue blood flow, and amount of functional plasma proteins. Drug variables that affect distribution include lipophilicity, molecular weight, and affinity for plasma proteins and tissues. The distribution of a drug beyond the systemic circulation is typically described in terms of volume of distribution (V_d).

Volume of Distribution

V_d is a pharmacokinetic parameter that relates the amount of a given drug in the body to the concentration of the drug in the area from which it was sampled (usually the bloodstream). It is not an actual physical volume; rather, it is estimated by means of pharmacokinetic techniques. There are several types of V_d parameters, the calculation of which depends on the route of administration of the drug and the pharmacokinetic model used to describe its disposition. V_d is usually expressed in liters and may range from a value approximately equivalent to blood volume (5 to 7 L), in the case of a drug such as warfarin, to values as high as 200 L, in the case of digoxin (which is extensively distributed to and readily binds to tissues outside the vasculature). In a clinical setting, V_d may be used to estimate the quantity of drug (A) needed to achieve a desired plasma concentration (C), as follows:

$$A = V_d \times C$$

Plasma Protein Binding

A number of commonly used drugs exhibit significant plasma protein binding [see Table 1]. Of the more than 60 different proteins that are found in plasma,[15] three types are responsible for most instances of drug binding: albumin, α_1-acid glycoprotein (AAG), and lipoprotein.

Albumin is a 66.3 kd protein that comprises approximately 580 amino acid residues. It is made by the liver and broken down by the liver, the kidneys, the spleen, and the lymph nodes. Its half-life is approximately 19 days, and at any given point, 40% of the body's supply of albumin is circulating in plasma, with the remaining 60% located in interstitial fluid. The albumin molecule possesses two main drug-binding sites. The first site is called the warfarin-binding area, but it also binds other drugs, such as valproic acid, phenytoin, and sulfonamides. The second binding site is called the indole-benzodiazepine–binding area; it binds drugs such as certain penicillins and medium-chain fatty acids. Some drugs, such as the nonsteroidal anti-inflammatory drugs (NSAIDs), bind to both sites. In addition to the main binding sites, separate binding sites for bilirubin, digitoxin, and tamoxifen have been discovered. Albumin binds mainly with weakly acidic (anionic) drugs, though it also binds with certain basic drugs (e.g., benzodiazepines) and some neutral drugs (e.g., dexamethasone).

There are a few rare genetic polymorphisms that are known to affect albumin levels or function. Certain disease states may induce alterations in the concentration or binding ability of albumin, thereby potentially resulting in a higher free fraction of the drug (and thus an

Table 1 Commonly Used Drugs That Are Highly Bound to Plasma Proteins

Bound to Albumin	Bound to AAG	Bound to Albumin and AAG	Bound to Albumin and Lipoproteins	Bound to Albumin, AAG, and Lipoproteins
Ceftriaxone	Diisopyramide	Alfentanil	Amiodarone	Amphotericin B
Citalopram	Promethazine	Amprenavir	Cyclosporine	Bupivicaine
Clofibrate		Carbamazepine		Chlorpromazine
Dexamethasone		Clindamycin		Diltiazem
Diazepam		Erythromycin		Felodipine
Fluoxetine		Fosphenytoin		Propranolol
Fluvoxamine		Lidocaine		Quinidine
Ibuprofen		Lopinavir		
Indomethacin		Meperidine		
Itraconazole		Methadone		
Ketoconazole		Nelfinavir		
Ketorolac		Olanzapine		
Losartan		Ritonavir		
Mycophenolate		Saquinavir		
Nafcillin		Verapamil		
Naproxen				
Paroxetine				
Phenytoin				
Prednisolone				
Sertraline				
Thiopental				
Tiagabine				
Valproic acid				
Warfarin				

AAG—α_1-acid glycoprotein

increased amount of drug available to exert pharmacologic effects) and, often, lower total drug concentrations. In addition, drug displacement interactions may occur when a previously administered drug that is already bound to albumin is followed by a drug that has a higher affinity to albumin. Salicylate and the sulfonamides are examples of drugs with high albumin-binding affinities that are capable of displacing other drugs from albumin binding sites, thereby causing the unbound fraction of the displaced drug to increase. Nevertheless, the majority of displacements from binding sites on the albumin molecule result in the same free concentrations of the drug, though the total concentrations may decrease precipitously. In this situation, if the total concentrations are followed and the dosage increased to achieve a specific total concentration, the increase in the unbound fraction that results from the drug interaction (or from a decreased albumin concentration caused by a disease state) may lead to toxicity. Because albumin levels are frequently low in surgical patients, measurement of free drug levels is recommended if available.

AAG is an acute-phase protein that is both produced and metabolized by the liver. It is somewhat smaller than albumin (38 to 48 kd) and has a half-life of 5 days. Approximately 60% of the body's supply of AAG circulates in plasma, with the remaining 40% in interstitial fluid. AAG tends to bind basic drugs, but it also binds some that are neutral or acidic. There are three known genetic variants of AAG, but it is unclear whether this variation is of any clinical significance. Elevated AAG levels may lead to a decrease in the unbound fraction of a drug and thus to a reduction in the amount of drug available for pharmacologic activity.

The lipoproteins are a diverse group of proteins that vary significantly with respect to molecular weight, lipid content, and drug binding affinity. Structurally, they comprise a lipid core made up of cholesterol and triglycerides, which is surrounded by an outer layer made up of phospholipids, cholesterol, and apolipoproteins. They are produced by the liver and the intestinal mucosa and are metabolized by the liver, the kidneys, and the intestine. Lipoproteins are classified into four groups: very low-density lipoproteins (VLDLs), low-density lipoproteins (LDLs), intermediate-density lipoproteins (IDLs), and high-density lipoproteins (HDLs). Of these, VLDLs, LDLs, and HDLs account for the bulk of lipoprotein drug binding. The most common mechanism by which drugs attach to lipoproteins is believed to be a nonsaturable partitioning into the lipid core[15,16]; drugs that appear to exemplify this mechanism include cyclosporine,[17] propranolol, digoxin, and tetracycline.[15] Some drugs, however, such as propranolol and certain tricyclic antidepressants, are believed to bind to specific sites in a saturable manner.[15,16] Lipoproteins may bind additional drug when albumin binding sites become saturated.[18]

The amount of free (unbound) drug in the plasma has pharmacologic implications. Tissue and plasma protein binding influence the apparent volume of distribution of a drug according to the following equation:

$$V_d = V_B + (f_B/f_T)V_T$$

where V_B is blood volume (0.07 L/kg), V_T is tissue volume, f_B is the unbound fraction of drug in the blood, and f_T is the unbound fraction of drug in tissue. For lipophilic drugs, tissue volume is calculated as total body water minus plasma volume (approximately 0.6 L/kg). For hydrophilic drugs, tissue volume is calculated as extracellular fluid minus plasma volume (approximately 0.13 L/kg). The degree of a drug's affinity for plasma proteins as opposed to tissue components is the main determinant of its volume of distribution. Changes in f_B, however, lead to changes in V_d only when a drug has a V_d of at least 30 L (i.e., when blood volume constitutes no more than a small fraction the drug's total volume of distribution).[19]

Uremia, cirrhosis, nephrotic syndrome, epilepsy, hepatitis, and various other disease staes have been shown to decrease protein binding of drugs. Plasma protein binding is also reduced in pregnant women, neonates, and persons who have sustained severe burns. Accordingly, clinicians often assume that pregnant patients, newborns, or burn patients who are taking a highly protein-bound drug are automatically at risk for alterations in the unbound fraction of the drug; however, this assumption is not always valid.[19] As noted (see above), V_d depends on several factors, including f_B, f_T, V_B, and V_T.

Increased binding of drugs to plasma proteins decreases the amount of drug available for diffusion into tissues, thereby limiting V_d. In contrast, increased binding of drugs to tissue proteins increases the apparent V_d. Increased protein binding also limits drug elimination because for the most part, only unbound drug can be eliminated.

METABOLISM

Hepatic Metabolism

With a few exceptions, drug metabolism (also known as biotransformation) consists of converting a lipophilic drug to a more hydrophilic metabolite, which is then more easily excreted by the kidneys. (The only agents excreted by the pulmonary route are the volatile anesthetic agents.) Metabolic reactions are generally divided into two phases: phase I reactions, which include oxidation, reduction, and hydrolysis; and phase II reactions, which include glucuronidation, sulfation, methylation, acetylation, and amino acid and glutathione conjugation.

From a clinical standpoint, the most important drug-metabolizing enzymes are the CYP enzymes. They are part of the microsomal mixed-function oxidase system and work in combination with CYP reductase, molecular oxygen, and nicotinamide adenine dinucleotide phosphate (NADPH) to perform many of the phase I metabolic reactions. The CYP enzymes also help synthesize and metabolize endogenous substrates (including hormones) and break down nondrug xenobiotics (e.g., environmental pollutants). The liver, as the main metabolic organ of the body, contains more CYP enzymes than any other organ, but CYPs are also found in significant quantities in the small intestine, the colon, the kidneys, the brain, the lungs, the heart, the skin, the nasal mucosa, the heart, and the eyes.

To date, 18 families of CYP enzymes and 42 subfamilies have been identified. These enzymes exhibit many genetic polymorphisms, some of which do not affect function, some of which restrict function, and some of which encode nonfunctional proteins. Particular polymorphisms may alter a person's ability to metabolize drugs. In addition, some persons have gene duplications that give rise to increased enzyme activity. Thus, there is a great deal of interindividual variability with respect to CYP-related metabolic capacity.

A number of common drugs are known to induce, inhibit, or serve as substrates for CYP [see Table 2]. Some of these drugs have multiple effects.

ELIMINATION

Half-life

Half-life ($t_{1/2}$) is a pharmacokinetic parameter that represents the amount of time necessary for the amount or concentration of drug in the body to decrease by 50%. As a general rule, almost all (97%) of a drug will have been eliminated after five half-lives. For a first-order process, half-life is described by the following equation:

$$t_{1/2} = 0.693/k_e$$

where k_e is the elimination rate constant in inverse time units. It is important to remember that half-life should not be used as a measure of hepatic clearance or liver function, because it changes proportionately with clearance only when V_d remains constant.

Clearance of the drug [see Clearance, below] in volume units per unit of time (CL) and V_d are independent (albeit correlated) parameters that are related via k_e, as shown in the following equation:

$$CL = k_e \times V_d$$

Thus, k_e is equivalent to CL/V_d, which means that the equation for half-life (see above) can also be written as follows:

$$t_{1/2} = (0.693 \times V_d)/CL$$

Clearance

Clearance is an independent pharmacokinetic parameter that is defined as the volume of plasma, serum, or blood that is cleared of the drug per unit of time. The liver is the organ primarily responsible for drug clearance. Clearance may be considered the most important of the pharmacokinetic parameters because it determines what the maintenance dose (MD) of a drug should be to achieve a desired steady-state plasma concentration (C_{pss}):

$$MD = C_{pss} \times CL$$

Renal Clearance

Renal clearance of drugs is the result of three processes: tubular secretion, tubular reabsorption, and glomerular filtration. The glomerular filtration rate (GFR) is generally considered the best overall indicator of kidney function. It may be determined through I.V. administration of a substance (e.g., inulin or iothalamate) that is freely filtered at the glomerulus but is not subject to reabsorption or secretion by the tubules. In a routine clinical setting, however, estimation of renal function by direct measurement of the GFR is impractical. A common alternative is to measure creatinine clearance (CrCL), which is generally accepted as a reasonably accurate estimate of the GFR and therefore of renal function. This is done by collecting the patient's urine over a 24-hour period and determining the concentrations of creatinine in serum and urine. CrCL is then calculated according to the following equation:

Table 2 Common Substrates, Inducers, and Inhibitors of Cytochrome P-450

Substrates	Inducers	Inhibitors
Acetaminophen	Carbamazepine	Amiodarone
Caffeine	Cigarette smoke	Cimetidine
Cyclosporine A	Dexamethasone	Ciprofloxacin
Diazepam	Ethanol (in chronic setting)	Diltiazem
Diltiazem	Isoniazid	Ethanol (in acute setting)
Fentanyl	Omeprazole	
Fluoxetine	Phenobarbital	Fluconazole
Haloperidol	Phenytoin	Fluoxetine
Midazolam	Rifampin	Metronidazole
Morphine		Omeprazole
Phenobarbital		Propofol
Phenytoin		
Tacrolimus		
Warfarin		

CrCL (ml/min) = rate of urinary creatinine excretion/serum creatinine concentration

$$CrCL \text{ (ml/min)} = (U_{Cr}V \times 100)/(S_{Cr} \times 1{,}440)$$

where U_{Cr} is the urinary creatinine concentration (mg/ml), V is the volume of urine produced over a 24-hour period (ml), and S_{Cr} is the serum creatinine concentration (mg/dl) measured at the 12th hour (i.e., the midpoint) of the urine collection period.

For practical purposes, CrCL is usually estimated by applying any of a number of commonly accepted equations. The equation most frequently employed to estimate CrCL in patients with stable renal function is that of Cockcroft and Gault, which derives CrCL from the patient's age, ideal body weight (IBW), and S_{Cr}:

$$CrCL = [(140 - age) \times IBW]/(72 \times S_{Cr})$$

Because women have less muscle mass in relation to their body weight than men do, the value for CrCL in female patients is calculated by multiplying this equation by 0.85. The Cockcroft-Gault equation uses IBW rather than actual body weight because adipose tissue contains little if any muscle and therefore is believed to contribute little to the serum creatinine level; if actual body weight were used, CrCL might be overestimated.

It should be kept in mind that the various methods of estimating CrCL are necessarily imperfect, in that S_{Cr} may be abnormally high or abnormally low for reasons that have nothing to do with kidney function. For example, S_{Cr} may be decreased in elderly, bedridden, or wheelchair-bound patients (because of the loss of muscle mass), and it may be elevated in patients with increased muscle mass, those who have recently undergone strenuous exercise, trauma patients, and even persons who consume high quantities of red meat. Liver dysfunction can affect the accuracy of CrCL estimates by decreasing the conversion of creatine to creatinine.

Unbound drugs of low molecular weight are readily filtered by the glomeruli. The ionized fraction is then excreted. The nonionized fraction, however, is reabsorbed by the tubules and is typically metabolized by the liver to the ionized form. With some drugs, reabsorption is dependent on pH; consequently, when these drugs cause toxicity, manipulation of urinary pH to increase their elimination can be a useful therapeutic measure. Secretion of drugs into the renal tubules is an active process that is not particularly specific.

Thus, drugs may compete with each other or with endogenous substrates, and toxicities may result.

Metrics Reflecting Magnitude of Drug Exposure

AREA UNDER THE CURVE

Area under the curve (AUC) is a pharmacokinetic parameter that reflects the extent of a drug's bioavailability—that is, it reflects the total amount of active drug that reaches the systemic circulation after administration. The AUC is usually calculated from the actual area under a curve generated by plotting plasma concentrations of an administered drug over a period of time (whether from time 0 to infinity or from one dose to the next). For drugs exhibiting linear (i.e., first-order) kinetics, the AUC is proportional to the dose administered. With some drugs, however, this may not be the case at higher dosages, because drug elimination pathways may become saturated.

PEAK PLASMA CONCENTRATION

Peak plasma concentration (C_{max}) is a pharmacokinetic parameter that quantifies the highest level reached in the plasma after administration of a drug. Knowledge of C_{max} may be advantageous in certain situations. For example, some antibiotics (e.g., aminoglycosides) depend on a high C_{max} rather than on sustained drug levels for their bactericidal effects. Other drugs may cause toxicity if C_{max} reaches inappropriately high levels. C_{max} is expressed in units of concentration (e.g., μg/ml or mg/L). It may be calculated in several ways; which equation is used depends on the route of administration of the drug and the model used to describe its disposition.

TIME OF PEAK PLASMA CONCENTRATION

Time of peak plasma concentration (T_{max}) is simply the time at which the maximum plasma concentration is reached after extravascular drug administration. As such, it is also an indication of the time of peak drug absorption, at which absorption and elimination (expressed in mass units per time unit) are equal. Comparison of T_{max} between two extravascular dosage forms allows determination of relative absorption rates. T_{max} decreases as the absorption rate increases.

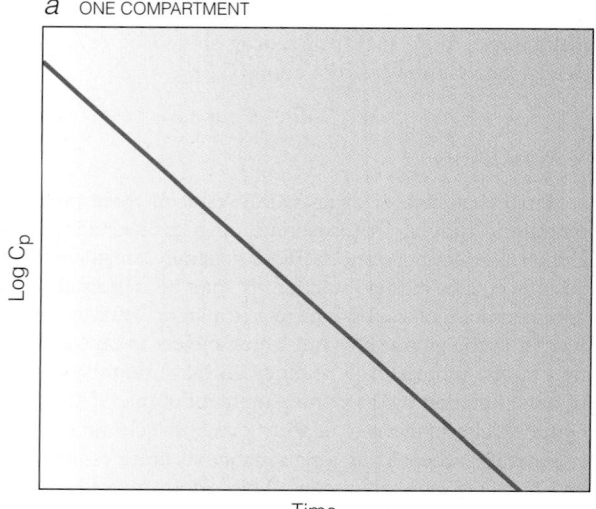

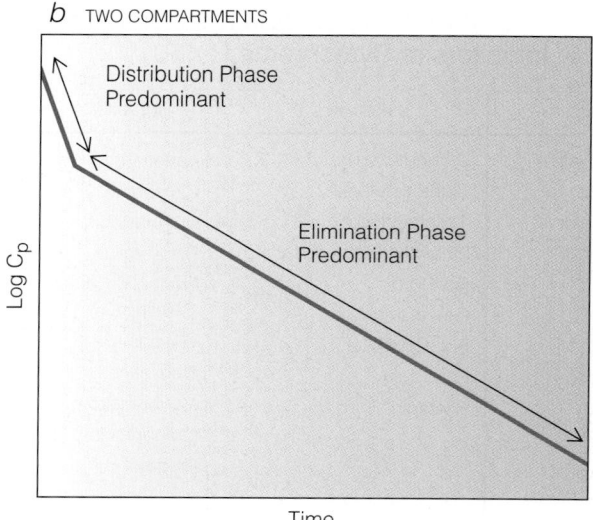

Figure 1 Depicted are (*a*) one-compartment and (*b*) two-compartment pharmacokinetic models. (C_p—plasma concentration)

Fundamental Pharmacokinetic Concepts

COMPARTMENTAL PHARMACOKINETIC MODELING

As the study of pharmacokinetics has progressed, various models for the disposition of drugs in the body have been proposed. Many of these models portray the body as a collection of spaces with volumes and elimination rates (clearance rates). These spaces, commonly referred to as compartments, are not actual anatomic realities, though they may have characteristics that are very similar to those of true anatomic spaces. They represent conceptual adaptations of monoexponential or multiexponential concentration-versus-time curves, in which the curves are converted to virtual spaces that have specific finite volumes and elimination rates.

The simplest compartmental model is the one-compartment model. This model assumes that the body is a single homogeneous unit in terms of a particular drug's pharmacokinetic profile. It therefore also assumes that the drug is instantaneously distributed throughout the compartment after administration. Obviously, this assumption is purely theoretical and, from a practical standpoint, impossible. Nevertheless, the one-compartment model adequately describes the disposition of many drugs that are rapidly distributed in the body. A concentration time profile that has a monoexponential character in the decline (see below) is often characterized as a one-compartment model. It is important to remember that the signal characteristic of the one-compartment model is not that the actual drug concentrations are the same in all body tissues as in blood or plasma (which is not necessarily the case) but that the rate at which drug or metabolite levels change is constant throughout the entire body.

Elimination from a compartment may be assumed to be a first-order or linear process. In a static first-order process, a constant proportion of the drug is eliminated over a given unit of time. The first-order elimination rate constant k (or k_e) is a proportionality constant that relates clearance to V_d. It is expressed in reciprocal time units (i.e., hr^{-1} or min^{-1}) because it is derived by dividing a rate (the volume from which all material is removed per unit of time, expressed in L/hr) by a volume (V_d, expressed in liters). The overall clearance of a drug is the sum of the clearances attributable to all of the routes by which the drug may be eliminated (e.g., $CL = CL_{renal} + CL_{hepatic} + CL_{biliary}$ ....); the precise value depends on the particular elimination pathways that are open to the drug. If a drug has nonlinear elimination characteristics, clearance will constantly change in conjunction with concentration.

As noted (see above), in a one-compartment model, whereas the rate of change in the drug concentration may be the same in all body tissues, the actual drug concentrations in particular tissues may be different from each other and from those in blood or plasma. The usual assumption, however, is that the ratios between tissue concentrations and plasma concentrations are constant. This assumption then leads to the further assumption that the relation between plasma concentration and the total amount of drug in the body is also constant. The relation between these two factors is represented by the volume of distribution term V_d.

For many drugs, distribution can be more accurately described by employing a multicompartment model, which incorporates both a central compartment (as in the one-compartment model) and one or two (or, in rare cases, more than two) peripheral compartments. These peripheral compartments may represent more poorly perfused tissues of the body that have a different affinity for the drug. Peripheral compartments are hypothetical constructs, in that the actual drug concentrations in tissues are not known, but their presence is often assumed on the basis of plasma concentrations measured over time after an I.V. bolus. When a concentration-time curve is plotted on a semilogarithmic graph after injection of an I.V. bolus, a drug that follows a one-compartment model shows a linear decline [see Figure 1a],

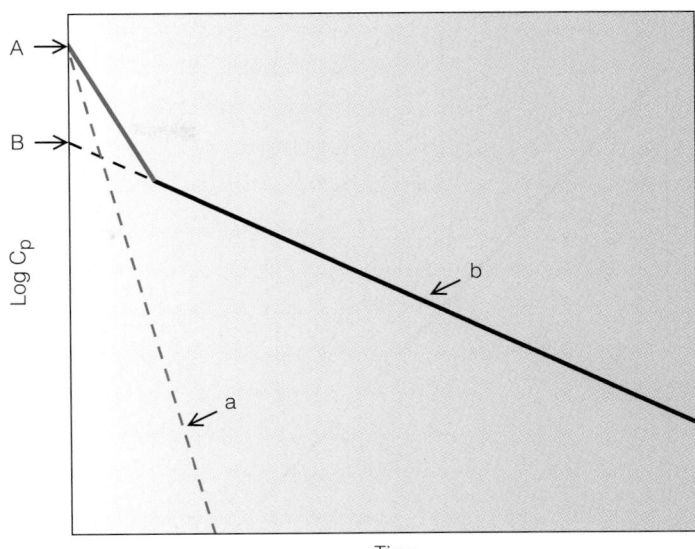

Figure 2 **In a two-compartment model of pharmacokinetics, plasma concentration can be estimated by using intercepts A and B and microconstants a and b.**

whereas a drug that follows a two-compartment model shows two distinct phases, a distribution phase and an elimination phase [*see Figure 1b*]. The drug does not switch from one phase to the other in an on-and-off fashion; rather, the two phases predominate at different stages of drug disposition after administration.

The first phase of the two-compartment concentration-time curve, the distribution phase, primarily reflects the distribution of the drug from the rapidly perfused tissues of the central compartment into the more poorly perfused tissues of the peripheral compartment. During this phase, the drug concentration in the peripheral compartment gradually increases until it reaches a maximum. At this maximum peripheral tissue concentration, the rate of drug input into the tissue is equal to the rate of drug output from the tissue, and the portion of drug in the central compartment is in equilibrium with the portion of drug in the peripheral compartment. This point in time is termed distribution equilibrium. After this point, the drug amounts in the central and peripheral compartments decline at similar rates, and the kinetics of the drug begin to resemble those of a one-compartment model.

The second portion of the concentration-time curve, the elimination phase, reflects the passage of the drug from the body. It is usually assumed that drug elimination occurs via the central compartment. This assumption is based on the observation that most drugs are eliminated mainly via the liver or the kidneys, both of which are highly perfused organs that are usually included in the central compartment.

The rate constants describing the rate of transfer between compartments in a two-compartment model are often referred to as microconstants because they cannot be determined by direct measurement; however, they can be estimated from a logarithmic graph of plasma concentration versus time after an I.V. bolus [*see Figure 2*]. Plasma (or central compartment) drug concentration ($C_{central}$) may be related to time by means of the following equation:

$$C_{central} = A_e{}^{-at} + B_e{}^{-bt}$$

where e is the base of the natural system of logarithms, and A and B are intercepts on the y axis for each segment of the concentration-time curve. The hybrid constants A and B have no real physiologic significance, but they are useful for solving this equation as a sum of exponentials. The terms a and b represent the first-order rate constants for

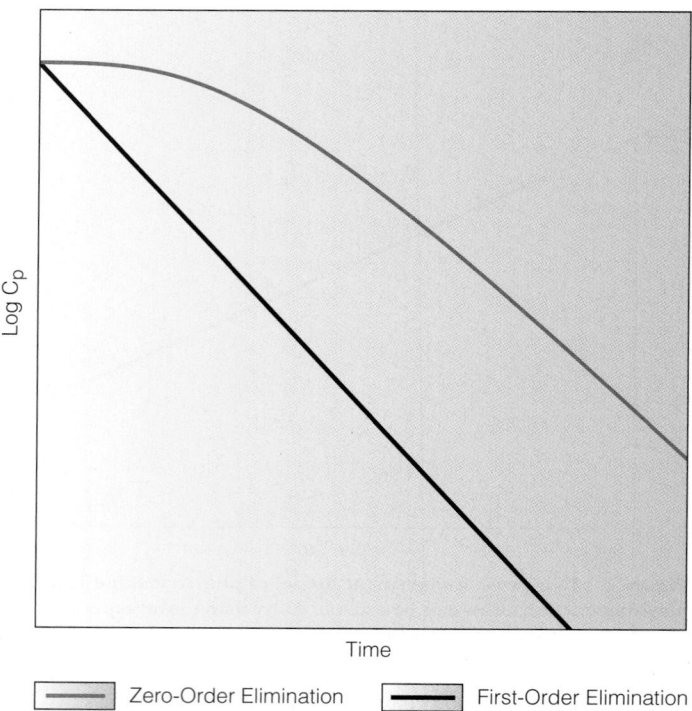

Y-axis: Log C_p
X-axis: Time

Legend: —— Zero-Order Elimination   —— First-Order Elimination

Figure 3 **Plotting of plasma concentration against time illustrates the difference between zero-order (saturable) drug elimination and first-order elimination.**

the distribution phase and the elimination phase, respectively. As may be seen from the concentration-time curve [*see Figure 2*], the decline in drug concentration is steeper in the initial (distribution) phase than in the second (elimination) phase.

Many agents are eliminated in a nonlinear manner (so-called zero-order elimination), and their elimination half-life lengthens as the dosage increases [*see Figure 3*]. This phenomenon is usually attributable to saturation of the enzyme systems responsible for metabolizing the drug. Such saturation can cause changes in the metabolite profile. When there is saturation of elimination, the area under the concentration-time curve ceases to be proportional to drug exposure, and the AUC does not increase linearly with increasing doses (as it does with first-order kinetic processes).

Saturable GI absorption may occur with drugs such as gabapentin, baclofen, and riboflavin, and saturation of intestinal metabolism may occur with propranolol. In addition, saturable plasma protein binding may occur with drugs such as lidocaine, ceftriaxone, warfarin, disopyramide, and phenytoin. Saturable tissue transport may occur with drugs such as methotrexate.[18] The most clinically relevant zero-order processes, however, are those related to hepatic metabolism. Two drugs with narrow therapeutic indices whose metabolism follows zero-order kinetics are the antiepileptic medications phenytoin and valproic acid.

A drug with saturable elimination will, at a large enough dose, demonstrate a disproportionately large increase in AUC with a dose increase once the saturation point of the elimination system is reached. The term Michaelis-Menten kinetics is used to describe elimination of drugs by saturable enzymatic processes. The standard Michaelis-Menten equation for estimating the elimination rate (V) is as follows:

$$V = V_{max}C_p/(K_m + C_p) = dC_p/dt$$

where V_{max} is the maximum metabolic rate of the enzymes, C_p is the plasma concentration, and dC_p/dt is the rate at which C_p changes over

time. When V_{max} is reached, a constant amount of drug is eliminated per unit of time, and elimination is truly a zero-order process. K_m, the so-called Michaelis constant, is a reflection of the metabolizing capacity of the enzyme system. It is equal to the drug concentration in the body when V is one half of V_{max}. This equation is appropriate at a wide range of drug concentrations because if C_p is much larger than K_m, the enzymatic processes become saturated, K_m can be considered negligible and drops out of the equation, and V is approximately equal to V_{max}.

PHYSIOLOGICALLY BASED PHARMACOKINETICS

A very useful pharmacokinetic modeling approach that is sometimes employed as an alternative to compartmental modeling is physiologically based pharmacokinetics (PBPK). PBPK is similar to compartmental modeling in that spaces are represented as instantaneously mixing compartments. However, it differs from classical compartmental modeling in that the compartments in a PBPK model are constrained to the actual space occupied by a particular tissue or organ. In addition, tissues are connected not by first-order rate constants or clearances but directly by blood flows originating in the arterial circulation and emptying into the venous system (with the exception of the lungs) [*see Figure 4*]. Drugs introduced into the vascular system circulate and are delivered to various tissues. Within tissues, any sort of transfer may be specified, from instantaneous transfer with a partition coefficient to linear or nonlinear transfer to or from a tissue space or within tissue subspaces. A great advantage of PBPK is that it permits modeling of tissue-specific concentrations and time courses of concentration changes. This advantage is especially important if the desired drug action depends on exposure within a particular space.

Pharmacodynamics

The discipline of pharmacodynamics aims to define the relation between pharmacokinetics and response to the drug. PBPK modeling is very useful for capturing effect-site concentrations that can be linked to a particular drug effect. Effect-site concentrations are not directly measurable in clinical situations, but estimating such concentrations can help distinguish distributional effects that cause a dissociation between observed plasma concentration and physiologic response from tolerance-type or sensitization-type responses that occur at the site of action. With sensitization, a plasma concentration observed early in the exposure profile evokes a lesser response than the same concentration observed later (i.e., the patient becomes more sensitive to the drug). This development is often seen as a counterclockwise hysteresis when the drug's concentration is plotted against its effect over time. With tolerance, a concentration observed early in the exposure profile evokes a greater response than the same concentration observed later (i.e., the patient becomes tolerant to the drug). This development is seen as a clockwise hysteresis when concentration is plotted against effect over time.

BASIC PHARMACODYNAMIC MODELS

The linear-response pharmacodynamic model, as its name suggests, describes the relation between drug concentration (whether in plasma, in a particular compartment, or at the biophase) and physiologic response as a linear one [*see Figure 5*]. The general form of this model is as follows:

Response = baseline + (concentration × response factor)

The maximum-response model determines the relation between concentration and response on the basis of the maximum response (E_{max}), the concentration at which 50% of E_{max} is observed (EC_{50}), and, optionally, other factors (e.g., exponents applied to both E_{max} and

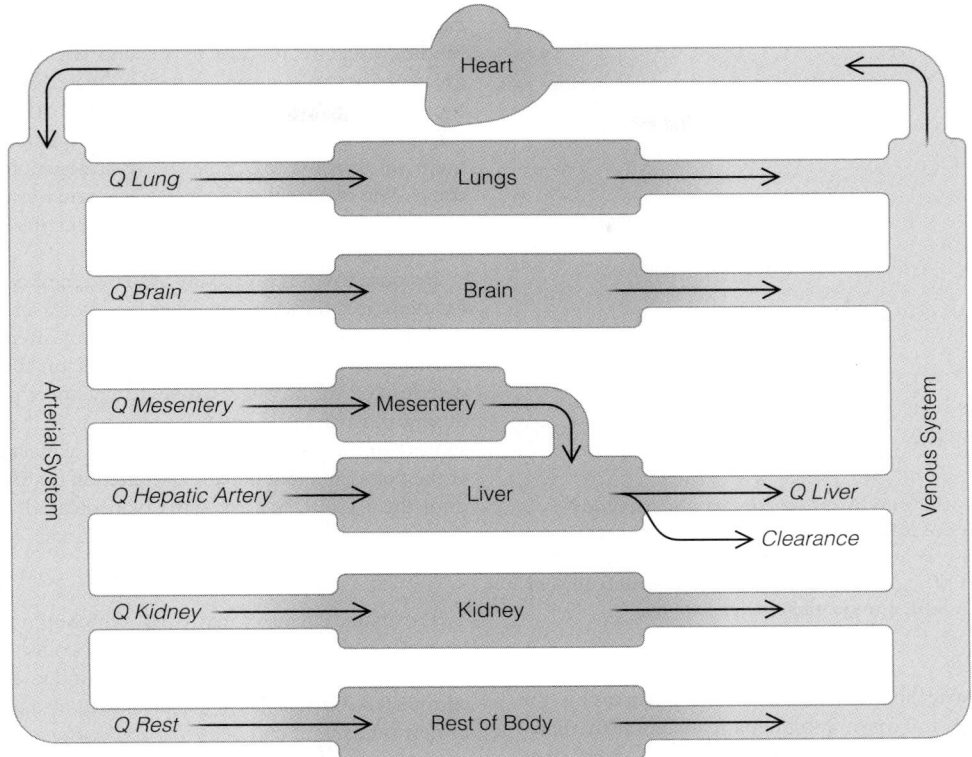

Figure 4 **Shown is a schematic structural depiction of physiologically based pharmacokinetics (PBPK). In PBPK, unlike standard one- or two-compartment modeling, the compartments are restricted to the actual spaces occupied by particular tissues or organs. In this example, elimination occurs as clearance from the liver. (Q—blood flow)**

EC_{50} that modify the steepness of the response). This model may also be modified to take into account the baseline response [*see Figure 6*]. The general form of the maximum-response model is as follows:

$$\text{Response} = (E_{max} \times \text{concentration})/(EC_{50} + \text{concentration})$$

Indirect-response models may be used to describe systems in which there is either constant production or constant elimination of the drug effect. In addition, however, the drug concentrations observed will have an impact on the elimination or production of the drug effect.

Physiologic Factors That Alter Pharmacokinetics and Pharmocodynamics

For the most part, the pharmocokinetic and pharmacodynamic modeling methods used to determine dosing regimens are based on study data from normal subjects. For this reason, they may not be applicable to surgical patients without some modification. Such patients often have significant physiologic derangements that alter drug metabolism. If these physiologic derangements are not taken into account, patients may be at risk not only for drug toxicity and adverse events but also for inadequate drug administration.

ORGAN SYSTEM DYSFUNCTION

Renal

Renal insufficiency, whether acute or chronic, can have pronounced effects on drug disposition, not only because of impaired excretion of drugs and metabolites eliminated by the kidneys but also because of other disease-induced physiologic alterations. The degree of impairment is proportional to the decrease in the GFR. If the patient becomes oliguric, the GFR is probably less than 10 ml/min. In critically ill patients, renal function may deteriorate rapidly. Because actual measurement of the GFR is usually impractical, estimation of the GFR, based on creatinine level and urine output, should be considered. Besides lowering the GFR, renal failure reduces tubular excretion. The transport systems in the renal tubules may become saturated, further decreasing drug elimination.

Other aspects of renal failure can affect pharmacokinetics. Renal

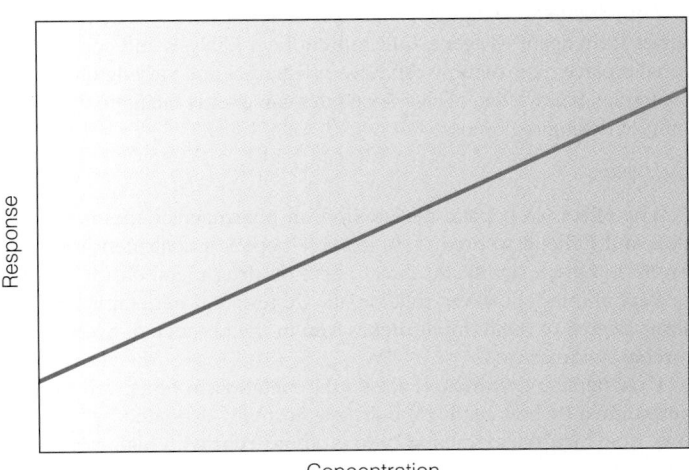

Figure 5 **Illustrated is the linear-response pharmacodynamic model, in which the relation between drug concentration and physiologic response is a linear one.**

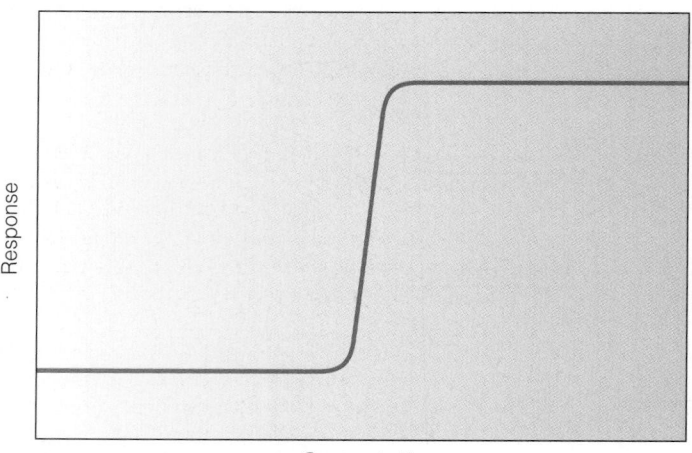

Figure 6 **Illustrated is the maximum-response pharmacodynamic model, in which the relation between drug concentration and physiologic response is a nonlinear one that is determined by the maximum response (E_{max}), the concentration at which 50% of E_{max} is observed (EC_{50}), and, sometimes, other factors.**

failure may reduce gastric acid secretion, thereby decreasing the absorption of some drugs, and may inhibit hepatic metabolism, thereby decreasing the first-pass effect and increasing systemic drug absorption.

Edema formation and decreased plasma protein levels may have complex effects on V_d and $t_{1/2}$. Although V_d tends to be increased, decreased plasma protein binding may raise unbound drug levels and increase potential toxicity. The higher unbound drug concentrations may actually increase drug excretion, thereby reducing $t_{1/2}$.

Great care should be taken in administering drugs that are mainly excreted by the kidneys and that have significant toxicity or a narrow therapeutic range. Typically, the initial loading dose is appropriate, but subsequent dosing should be based on estimates of the GFR. If possible, drug levels should be monitored. The timing of monitoring depends on the expected $t_{1/2}$. Trough drug levels are often used. Particular caution should be exercised with drugs whose levels or physiologic effects cannot be reliably monitored in a clinical setting (e.g., LMWHs). These drugs should be avoided in patients with significant renal impairment.

For patients who require renal replacement therapy, drug clearance varies from agent to agent. Intermittent hemodialysis and continuous renal replacement therapy can have substantial and varying effects on clearance. Knowledge of clearance rates can greatly facilitate the planning of dosing regimens.

Hepatic

The effects of hepatic dysfunction on pharmacokinetics are complex and difficult to predict. In general, hepatic impairment must be severe to have a significant direct effect on drug metabolism. It must be kept in mind, however, that hepatic dysfunction frequently leads to some degree of renal impairment, even in the absence of overt hepatorenal syndrome.

How hepatic dysfunction affects the metabolism of a given drug is determined by how readily the drug is normally extracted by the liver (i.e., how high the extraction ratio is). For drugs with high extraction ratios (e.g., morphine and labetalol), hepatic removal becomes dependent on hepatic blood flow. If blood flow is limited by end-stage liver disease or portosystemic shunting, bioavailability increases and elimination decreases, leading to a prolonged $t_{1/2}$. For drugs with lower extraction ratios (e.g., diazepam and warfarin), decreased protein binding and metabolism by hepatic enzymes such as CYP have a greater effect on pharmacokinetics. Decreased protein binding is common in surgical patients, whether from decreases in total proteins (especially albumin), production of abnormal proteins, or displacement of drugs from proteins by endogenous substances or other drugs. The end result of decreased protein binding is an increase in the level of active drug, which leads to an increased potential for toxicity or prolonged effects.

Because there is no readily available method for measuring hepatic function, it is difficult to predict the impact of hepatic dysfunction on the pharmacokinetics of a given drug. Any attempt at such a prediction must begin with a high index of suspicion that hepatic function has deteriorated to the point where it may affect pharmacokinetics. Drug dosing must then be carefully planned on the basis of the estimated severity of the dysfunction. In practice, clinicians often do not consider the possibility that hepatic dysfunction is affecting pharmacokinetics until the patient exhibits signs of decreased drug metabolism (e.g., slow awakening from anesthesia or benzodiazepine infusion).

Cardiac

The major effects of cardiac dysfunction on pharmacokinetics can be attributed to hypoperfusion, venous congestion, or both. Reduced gut perfusion and congestion can hinder absorption of enterally administered drugs. Hypoperfusion can also affect absorption via the intramuscular, subcutaneous, or transcutaneous route; accordingly, to ensure appropriate systemic drug levels, the I.V. route is preferred. With many hydrophilic drugs, congestion and increased total body water can lead to an increase in V_d. With lipophilic drugs, however, V_d may be unaffected or even reduced.

The effects of cardiac dysfunction on renal and hepatic blood flow may result in diminished elimination of drugs. Hepatic congestion may worsen the situation. Congestive heart failure tends to have more severe adverse effects on hepatic function than it does on renal function. It is important to keep this difference in mind when administering drugs that are mainly metabolized by the liver. Hemodynamically active medications (e.g., inotropes, afterload reducers, and vasopressors) or diuretics can have a significant impact on renal and hepatic blood flow and function.

Respiratory

Chronic pulmonary disease with pulmonary hypertension can lead to hepatic congestion. Less commonly, respiratory failure with secondary right heart failure can lead to hypoperfusion of the kidneys and liver. Mechanical ventilation can exacerbate the effects on congestion and hypoperfusion, especially if very high intrathoracic pressures are employed. The resulting hepatic or renal dysfunction can affect drug metabolism.

Systemic inflammatory responses can alter organ blood flow and thereby affect drug metabolism. In addition, if changes in arterial carbon dioxide tension (P_aCO_2) lead to changes in arterial pH, protein binding and drug ionization status can be affected.

AGE

Renal function (specifically, the GFR) varies significantly with age. In neonates, the normal value for the GFR is only 2 to 4 ml/min, compared to a normal adult value of more than 100 ml/min. Over the 6 months following birth, however, the GFR increases to a level approximately twice the normal adult level, then slowly decreases. Consequently, many drugs may have a shorter $t_{1/2}$ in children than in adults. Hepatic function, particularly with regard to drug metabolism, follows a similar pattern in the first few months of life: an increase to supra-adult levels followed by a slow decline.

Gastric emptying is slower in neonates than in adults, and gastric acidity is lower as well; both of these differences may affect absorption of oral medications. In addition, neonates have lower plasma protein levels, which may alter V_d. Common medications whose pharmacokinetics may be different in the pediatric population include antibiotics, narcotics, benzodiazepines, and anticonvulsants.

Increasing age leads to substantial changes in drug pharmacokinetics. Elderly persons have 10% to 15% less total body water than younger persons do, as well as a higher proportion of body fat; they also have 20% to 30% less lean body mass. These changes in body composition can affect V_d. Renal function decreases with age, resulting in decreased clearance of many drugs. Intrinsic hepatic function is usually well preserved, though blood flow to the liver may diminish.

NUTRITIONAL STATUS

Severe malnutrition leads to a relative increase in total body water as fat stores are depleted, as well as to a decrease in plasma protein levels. V_d increases, and the GFR decreases. Hepatic clearance of drugs is reduced, particularly in cases of protein malnutrition. Consequently, $t_{1/2}$ increases, thereby increasing the risk of drug toxicity. These abnormalities resolve with adequate nutritional support.

Obesity also can have significant effects on pharmacokinetics. To assess the potential implications, it is useful to compare total body weight (TBW) to IBW. IBW is calculated as follows:

Men: 50 kg + 2.3 kg for each 1 in. of height over 5 ft

Women: 45.5 kg + 2.3 kg for each 1 in. of height over 5 ft

For persons shorter than 5 ft, 2.3 kg is subtracted for each 1 in. below this height.

Because of the greatly increased amount of body fat in obese patients, lipophilic drugs can be distributed into and sequestered in adipose tissue. This effect becomes more pronounced with increasing lipid solubility. Deposition of drugs in fat increases V_d but also increases $t_{1/2}$. For highly lipophilic drugs (e.g., halothane, enflurane, sufentanil, and various benzodiazepines), the doses required to achieve the desired effect may be quite high. For hydrophilic medications, dosing adjustments generally are not necessary. Some agents, however, are relatively hydrophilic but are still distributed into fat stores to some extent. Ciprofloxacin is an example of such a drug; its partial absorption into fat has led many to recommend that the dose be based on 45% of TBW in addition to IBW. The initial dose of gentamicin should be increased by as much as 40% because of the risk of an increased V_d.

FLUID RESUSCITATION

Aggressive fluid resuscitation, such as is performed after trauma or a major surgical procedure, increases interstitial and intracellular volume, as well as plasma volume, and reduces plasma protein levels. Consequently, V_d is significantly increased for many drugs.[20] The concentration of a drug can be estimated on the basis of the relative quantity of fluid sequestration and the size of the reduction in the serum albumin concentration. Underdosing of medications is common in patients who have undergone aggressive fluid resuscitation.

Drug Dosing

INITIAL DOSING

In deciding on the initial dosing of a drug, particularly in the acute care setting, it is essential to strike a balance between the risk of causing toxicity, on one hand, and the risk of failing to achieve therapeutic efficacy because of underdosing, on the other. For example, there is ample evidence that inadequate dosing of antibiotics in patients with

pneumonia can lead to therapeutic failure.[21] The relative risks for any particular drug can be determined by considering the therapeutic index for that agent. The therapeutic index is approximated as follows:

$$\text{Therapeutic index} = LD_{50}/ED_{50}$$

where LD_{50} is the dose that would cause death in 50% of cases and ED_{50} is the dose that would be effective in 50% of cases. If there is any overlap between the range of effective doses and the lowest lethal dose for a given drug (i.e., if the risk of death is substantial even in the drug's therapeutic range), it is worthwhile to consider the drug's standard margin of safety. This parameter is defined as follows:

$$\text{Standard margin of safety} = LD_1/ED_{99}$$

where LD_1 is the dose that would cause death in 1% of cases and ED_{99} is the dose that would be effective in 99% of cases. For drugs with a narrow margin of safety, it is critical to monitor their levels whenever possible [see Drug Level Monitoring, below]. These metrics (i.e., standard margin of safety and therapeutic index) are confounded if the slopes of the concentration effect and concentration toxicity relationships are different.

A common way of achieving therapeutic drug levels is to administer a loading dose. The size of the loading dose can be calculated on the basis of volume of distribution, desired plasma concentration, and bioavailability:

$$\text{Loading dose} = (V_d \times C)/F$$

As noted (see above), F (i.e., bioavailability) equals 1 if the drug is administered I.V. If there is concern about potential toxicity, the drug dose may be given over a prolonged period (e.g., a phenytoin load over 1 hour) or divided into smaller doses and given over an even longer period (e.g., a digoxin load over 24 hours). The optimal dosing interval for the maintenance doses is often close to the drug's expected $t_{1/2}$.

The goal of maintenance dosing is to achieve a steady-state plasma concentration that is within the therapeutic range. Generally, this goal is reached after five half-lives of the drug. From this point on, the amount of drug administered with each dose is equal to the amount of drug eliminated between doses. The steady-state plasma concentration may be approximately calculated from the drug's bioavailability, the maintenance dose (MD), the clearance rate, and the dosing interval (τ):

$$C_{pss} = (F \times MD)/(CL \times \tau)$$

C_{pss} may be too low if the MD is too small, if F is too low, if CL is too high, or if τ is too long. Should it prove necessary to adjust the dosing regimen, changes in one or more of these parameters will be indicated. For example, if a higher peak drug level is desired, the maintenance dose can simply be increased. However, if a lower trough level is desired to alleviate concern about toxicity, the dosing interval can be extended, or (depending on the peak level) the maintenance dose can be decreased.

In addition to monitoring drug levels when possible [see Drug Level Monitoring, below], it is crucial to monitor the clinical effect of a drug regimen. At times, this effect may be immediate, as when a vasopressor is administered to a patient in septic shock. At other times, the effect may be delayed, as when a course of antibiotics is administered to for a patient with pneumonia. Monitoring the clinical efficacy of a treatment regimen is essential for determining the appropriate timing of discontinuance.

DRUG LEVEL MONITORING

Monitoring of the plasma concentration is most commonly employed with drugs that have a low therapeutic index—that is, drugs for which there is a narrow margin between the level that is therapeutic and the level that causes toxicity. It should be kept in mind, however, that these therapeutic and toxic levels are not absolute indicators of safety or efficacy: they only represent values at which certain percentages of patients are treated effectively or certain percentages experience suffer adverse events. Accordingly, such levels are not infallible guides for drug dosing. As an example, there are circumstances in which a clinician, knowing the drug levels and weighing the various risks and benefits, might elect to push the drug levels toward, or even into, the toxic range; for instance, in a patient with recalcitrant seizures, the plasma phenytoin level might be pushed to 25 µg/ml, which is above the standard therapeutic range. As another example, there are circumstances in which normal therapeutic drug levels are maintained, but the patient still experiences toxicity.

The timing of drug monitoring is important if the results are to be accurately interpreted. The sample for the peak level should be drawn 30 to 60 minutes after a dose is administered; the sample for the trough level should be drawn just before the next dose is to be administered. If there is significant concern about a potentially toxic trough level, the next dose may be held until the level can be determined. The timing of these blood draws should be noted as precisely as possible. Ideally, samples should not be drawn until the drug has been administered for five half-lives. When a patient is critically ill, however, five half-lives may be too long to wait. If so, samples may be drawn before and after the third dose (for trough and peak levels, respectively). In such cases, the levels obtained must be interpreted carefully, first, because a true steady-state may not have been achieved, and second, because these trough and peak levels are not from the same dose.

It should be kept in mind that standard drug level monitoring measures both the bound fraction and the unbound fraction of the drug. In certain circumstances (e.g., a patient with low plasma protein levels), the drug level can be misleading. Phenytoin is an example of a drug that is highly protein bound. If plasma protein levels are low, unbound drug levels can rise significantly even when total drug levels do not. In addition, a number of drugs are metabolized to an active metabolite that may contribute to toxicity. Some such metabolites, (e.g., the procainamide metabolite N-acetylprocainamide) can be measured.

Desired peak and trough ranges vary from one drug to another according to the desired effect and the risk of toxicity. With aminoglycosides, for example, toxicity is related to both the peak level (ototoxicity) and the trough level (renal toxicity), whereas efficacy is mostly based on the peak level (concentration-dependent bacterial killing). Once-daily administration of a large dose to achieve a high plasma concentration seems to be advantageous in terms of maximizing the efficacy of aminoglycosides and minimizing their toxicity. (This approach differs from the once-daily dosing that may be necessary in a patient with renal insufficiency.) In contrast, with vancomycin, efficacy depends on maintaining an adequate plasma level for as long as possible. Thus, the trough level is used to determine adequacy of dosing, particularly in situations where higher than normal levels may be

needed for adequate tissue penetration (as, for example, in patients with pneumonia).

Monitoring of the drug's effect is also important. For example, the prothrombin time may be measured in a patient receiving warfarin, or the activated partial thromboplastin time may be measured in a patient receiving heparin.

Drug Interactions

The more drugs a patient is given, the greater the potential for adverse drug interactions. This is particularly true for critically ill patients. Not only do such patients receive multiple medications, but they also are frequently experiencing organ system dysfunction that can affect drug metabolism, and they often have multiple medical issues that may mask the adverse drug effects. Interaction between drugs may lead directly to toxic effects, or it may be indirectly harmful by decreasing the efficacy of one or both agents.

Drug interactions may affect any or all of the four primary pharmacokinetic parameters (i.e., ADME). Absorption effects are mainly limited to simultaneous administration of enteral medications. Incompatibilities may also arise with I.V. medications, but usually, the only practical consequence is that the two incompatible agents cannot be administered through the same I.V. tubing at the same time. Distributional effects are usually secondary to competition for binding sites on proteins. Once the sites are saturated, the amount of free drug can increase if the metabolism and elimination pathways are intact and unsaturated. Clinically, drugs that compete with warfarin for protein binding sites may significantly increase the level of unbound warfarin, thus increasing the risk of bleeding. Metabolic effects primarily involve induction or inhibition of CYP enzymes [see Table 2]. Elimination effects primarily involve impairment of renal function or competition for tubular secretion pathways.

Pharmacodynamic interactions can either enhance or decrease the efficacy of a drug. For example, two antihypertensive medications from different classes may have additive effects when used together. In contrast, two β-lactam antibiotics may be antagonistic when used together if one induces production of a β-lactamase that subsequently metabolizes the other.

Adverse Effects of Drugs

As noted (see above), critically ill and postoperative patients tend to be experiencing multiple medical issues and to be taking multiple pharmacologic agents, both of which make it difficult to determine what the adverse effects of any single drug may be. Accordingly, a high index of suspicion is critical in these patients. Drugs can cause nephrotoxicity via acute tubular necrosis, interstitial nephritis, or glomerulonephritis. For example, aminoglycosides and amphotericin B can cause acute tubular necrosis, whereas penicillins tend to cause interstitial nephritis through immune responses. Hepatic dysfunction can be caused by direct hepatocellular effects or by cholestasis.

References

1. Rodriguez-Monguio R, Otero MJ, Rovira J: Assessing the economic impact of adverse drug effects. Pharmacoeconomics 21:623, 2003

2. Wagner JG: History of pharmacokinetics. Pharmacol Ther 12:537, 1981

3. Gibaldi M, Perrier D: Pharmacokinetics, 2nd ed. Drugs and the Pharmaceutical Sciences, vol 15. Swarbrick J, Ed. Marcel Dekker, Inc, New York, 1982, p 494

4. Lennernas H, Abrahamsson B: The use of biopharmaceutic classification of drugs in drug discovery and development: current status and future extension. J Pharm Pharmacol 57:273, 2005

5. Bauer LA: Applied clinical pharmacokinetics. McGraw-Hill, New York, 2001, p 759

6. Paine MF, Leung LY, Watkins PB: New insights into drug absorption: studies with sirolimus. Ther Drug Monit 26:463, 2004

7. Takano M, Yumoto R, Murakami T: Expression and function of efflux drug transporters in the intestine. Pharmacol Ther 109:137, 2006

8. Kivisto KT, Niemi M, Fromm MF: Functional interaction of intestinal CYP3A4 and p-glycoprotein. Fundam Clin Pharmacol 18:621, 2004

9. Cummins CL, Jacobsen W, Benet LZ: Unmasking the dynamic interplay between intestinal p-glycoprotein and CYP3A4. J Pharmacol Exp Ther 300:1036, 2002

10. Wilkinson GR: Pharmacokinetics: the dynamics of drug absorption, distribution, and elimination. Goodman & Gilman's The Pharmacological Basis of Therapeutics, 10th ed. Hardman JG, Limbird LE, Goodman Gilman A, Eds. McGraw-Hill, New York, 2001, p 3

11. Patton JS, Bukar JG, Eldon MA: Clinical pharmacokinetics and pharmacodynamics of inhaled insulin. Clin Pharmacokinet 43:781, 2004.

12. Buxton ILO: Pharmacokinetics and pharmacodynamics: the dynamics of drug absorption, distribution, action, and elimination. Goodman & Gilman's The Pharmacological Basis of Therapeutics, 11th ed. Brunron L, Lazo JS, Parker KL, Eds. McGraw-Hill, New York, 2005

13. Exubera package insert. Pfizer Labs, New York, 2006

14. Miller RD, Katzung BG: Local anesthetics. Basic and Clinical Pharmacology. Katzung BG, Ed. Lange Medical Books/McGraw-Hill, New York, 2001, p 436

15. MacKichan JJ: Influence of protein binding and use of unbound (free) drug concentrations. Applied Pharmacokinetics and Pharmacodynamics: Principles of Therapeutic Drug Monitoring, 4th ed. Burton ME, Shaw LM, Schentag JJ, et al, Eds. Lippincott Williams & Wilkins, Philadelphia, 2005, p 82

16. Wasan KM, Cassidy SM: Role of plasma lipoproteins in modifying the biological activity of hydrophobic drugs. J Pharm Sci 87:411, 1998

17. Lemaire M, Tillement JP: Role of lipoproteins and erythrocytes in the in vitro binding and distribution of cyclosporin A in the blood. J Pharm Pharmacol 34:715, 1982

18. Shargel L, Yu ABC: Applied Biopharmaceutics and Pharmacokinetics, 4th ed. Appleton & Lange, Stamford, Connecticut, 1999, p 768

19. Benet LZ, Hoener B-A: Changes in plasma protein binding have little clinical relevance. Clin Pharmacol Ther 71:115, 2002

20. McKindley DS, Boucher BA, Hess MM, et al: Pharmacokinetics of aztreonam and imipenem in critically ill patients with pneumonia. Pharmacotherapy 16:924, 1996

21. Moise PA, Forrest A, Bhavnani SM, et al: Area under the inhibitory curve and a pneumonia scoring system for predicting outcomes of vancomycin therapy for respiratory infections by *Staphylococcus aureus*. Am J Health Syst Pharm 57 (suppl 2):S4, 2000

James M. Watters, M.D., F.A.C.S., Jacqueline C. McClaran, M.D., and Malcolm G. Man-Son-Hing, M.D., F.R.C.P.C.

Principles of Care

Management of surgical illness in geriatric patients is different from that in younger patients and typically more complex. Assessment of the surgical problems and physiologic status of elderly persons must take into account (1) the marked variability of the changes associated with advancing age, both among individuals and among different organ systems in an individual; (2) changes in the incidence, prevalence, and natural history of certain disease processes; and (3) the increased likelihood of multiple medical diagnoses and polypharmacy.

These factors and others may alter the presentation of surgical illness. Symptoms may be diminished in intensity, nonspecific, indirect, or atypical and therefore may be inappropriately ignored or attributed to advanced age. Patients may postpone seeking medical attention, or physicians may fail to recognize the gravity of an acute surgical condition if pain, fever, and acute-phase responses are blunted [see Alterations in Clinical Presentation, *below*]. Furthermore, it may be difficult to obtain the details of the history if the patient is cognitively impaired (demented or delirious) or suffers from hearing loss. Unfortunately, as a result of this complexity and the increased likelihood of emergency presentation, hospitalized elderly patients are at significantly higher risk for preventable adverse events and their consequences.[1]

Both the potential benefits and the risks of surgical treatment are more difficult to assess in older persons. Assumptions about physiologic status and primary treatment goals that are reasonable in younger patients may not be appropriate in older patients. Often, the major concern of elderly patients is whether they will be able to enjoy an independent life after surgery, to at least the extent they did before. Consequently, such patients may find a radical procedure that offers potential cure less desirable than a more conservative procedure (or endoscopic, percutaneous, or nonoperative treatment) that relieves pain or other symptoms, largely restores function, and allows a return to normal surroundings. On the other hand, an early aggressive approach may obviate later procedures and prevent associated morbidity. A thorough knowledge of treatment alternatives and their risks, a close familiarity with the natural history of the disease in relation to life expectancy, and a clear understanding of the patient's goals are paramount in surgical decision making in older persons.

The risks associated with surgical treatment depend on the nature of the proposed procedure and on the patient's physiologic and medical status [see Preoperative Management, Risk Assessment, *below*]. Whereas minor elective procedures done with the patient under local anesthesia can be performed safely regardless of age, emergency thoracotomy and laparotomy are associated with significant mortality in elderly persons. Mortality from emergency procedures is markedly higher than mortality from elective procedures. Elective surgery may therefore be indicated when it can be predicted that complications will develop and emergency

intervention will be necessary. Cardiovascular and pulmonary complications remain important causes of postoperative mortality in elderly patients, much more so than in younger patients.

The elderly population is very heterogeneous. Some elderly persons are wholly independent, have maintained significant levels of physical activity, have preserved lean body mass and cardiopulmonary function, and have physiologic responses similar to those of younger individuals; in these patients, the risks associated with surgical illness and treatment are relatively low. At the opposite extreme, some elderly persons have multiple illnesses, are capable of only limited activity and independence, and suffer from cardiovascular and pulmonary disease; in these patients, surgery-associated risks are substantial. Physiologic status is a more fundamental determinant of risk than age is. As one surgeon put it as long ago as 1907, "In deciding for or [against] operation we depend upon the condition of the heart, the arteries, the lungs, and kidneys, rather more than the number of years the patient has lived."[2]

No matter how fit, active, and free of comorbidity the elderly individual appears, there is a gradual loss of physiologic reserve in various organ systems associated with aging [see Table 1]. This is most obvious in the oldest old but occurs to some extent even in younger old patients. In general, maximal physiologic functions decline, with the result that the ability to increase functions as needed is more and more limited. In addition, sensitivity to deviations from physiologic norms is decreased and mechanisms for reestablishing such norms are less efficient, with the result that homeostatic perturbations tend to be exaggerated.[3] These phenomena may be of little consequence in healthy daily life but can be critical to the elderly patient facing the stress of a major operation or acute illness. As a rule, the elderly surgical patient is less able to maintain homeostasis, is at increased risk for complications [see Figure 1], and tolerates complications poorly. All aspects of perioperative care must be focused on minimizing the stress of surgery and avoiding the added stresses of complications. The surgical procedure must be carefully chosen and conducted with meticulous technique. Careful attention must be given to drug and fluid and electrolyte therapy. Pain, tubes, and other restraining factors must be kept to a minimum so as to allow prompt resumption of physical activity and minimize the adverse effects of immobility. The potential for delirium (acutely impaired cognitive function) must also be recognized.

Five factors are critical for obtaining the best outcomes from the surgical treatment of elderly patients: (1) careful preoperative preparation of the patient and optimization of medical and physiologic status; (2) minimization of perioperative starvation and inactivity and the stresses of hypothermia, hypoxemia, and pain; (3) meticulous perioperative care, to avoid clinical complications from perturbations of fluid and electrolyte balance, impaired cardiovascular and respiratory function, and inappropriate pharmacotherapy; (4) careful surgical judgment and technique to achieve the desired goals and avoid technical complications; and (5) optimization of physical and cognitive function. Accomplishing such care requires thorough preoperative assessment and planning and the involvement of a multidisciplinary clinical team knowledgeable about and interested in the management of the elderly surgical patient.[4] With a comprehensive approach, major operations can be completed with low risk, a short hospital stay, and a rapid return to full function.[5]

Goals of Therapy

An elderly person with a surgical problem may not place the same emphasis on the various goals of therapy that a younger patient would [see Table 2]. Treatment goals must be carefully elicited and addressed in the treatment plan. Definitive cure of the presenting problem and maximization of longevity may be very reasonable and achievable goals, regardless of age. As the risks of surgical therapy increase in patients with significant comorbid conditions, however, priorities may shift. The major concern of an

Table 1 Physiologic Changes Associated with Aging

	Age-Related Changes	Clinical Consequences	Implications for Care
Respiratory System	Decreased strength and endurance of respiratory muscles Increased stiffness of the chest wall and increased reliance on diaphragm function Decreased vital capacity, FEV$_1$, maximal inspiratory and expiratory pressures, maximum midexpiratory flow rate, and maximum voluntary ventilation Diminished elastic lung recoil and increased closing volume Increased alveolar-arterial oxygen gradient Decreased arterial oxygen tension Decreased airway sensitivity and efficiency of mucociliary clearance mechanism Decreased compensatory responses to hypoxia or hypercarbia Increased sensitivity to narcotic respiratory depression	Less effective cough Predisposition to aspiration Increased closure of small airways during tidal respiration, especially postoperatively and when supine, leading to increased atelectasis and shunting Predisposition to hypoxemia Tachypnea and increased tidal volume may be less apparent as respiratory failure develops	Encourage early mobilization, assumption of upright rather than supine position Provide effective pain relief to allow mobilization, deep breathing Routinely supply supplemental oxygen in the immediate postoperative period, and then as needed Use nasogastric tubes sparingly Recognize decreased ventilatory responses to hypoxia and hypercarbia
Cardiovascular System	Decreased maximal heart rate, cardiac output, ejection fraction Reliance on increased end-diastolic volume to increase cardiac output Slowed ventricular filling, increased reliance on atrial contribution Decreased inotropic and chronotropic responses to beta-adrenergic stimuli Decreased baroreceptor sensitivity Increased prevalence of coronary artery disease, clinically apparent or occult; may influence cardiac function during acute stress	Greater reliance on ventricular filling and increases in stroke volume (rather than ejection fraction) to achieve increases in cardiac output Intolerance of hypovolemia Intolerance of tachycardia; dysrhythmias, including atrial fibrillation	Employ vigorous fluid resuscitation to achieve optimal ventricular filling Nonvasoconstricting inotropes and afterload reduction may be more effective if pharmacologic support is required Avoid tachycardia; correct significant arrhythmias Recognize potential for preexisting cardiac disease
Renal Function and Fluid-Electrolyte Homeostasis	Decreased sensitivity to fluid and electrolyte perturbations Decreased thirst response Decreased ability to concentrate urine and conserve water and solute Decreased efficiency of solute and water excretion Decreased renal mass, renal blood flow, and glomerular filtration rate Increased renal glucose threshold	Predisposition to hypovolemia Predisposition to extracellular fluid volume expansion, electrolyte disorders (e.g., hyponatremia) Predisposition to hyperglycemia Predisposition to hyperosmolar states	Pay meticulous attention to fluid and electrolyte management Recognize that a "normal" serum creatinine value reflects a decreased creatinine clearance, because muscle mass (i.e., creatinine excretion) is decreased concurrently: estimate creatinine clearance using age-adjusted formulas or measure Select drugs carefully: avoid agents that may be nephrotoxic (e.g., aminoglycosides) or adversely affect renal blood flow (e.g., NSAIDs) Adjust drug dosages as appropriate for altered pharmacokinetics
Body Composition	Significantly decreased muscle mass, accounting for much of the age-related decrease in lean tissue mass Increased fat mass	Erosion of muscle mass during acute illness may result in strength rapidly falling below important clinical threshold (e.g., impaired coughing, decreased mobility, increased risk of venous thrombosis) Altered volumes of drug distribution	Maintain physical function through effective pain relief; avoid tubes, drains, and other "restraints"; encourage early mobilization; and provide assistance with mobilization Minimize fasting, provide early nutritional supplementation or support (both protein-calorie and micronutrient) Adjust drug dosages for volume of distribution
Thermoregulation	Diminished sensitivity to ambient temperature and less efficient mechanisms of heat conservation, production, and dissipation Febrile responses to infection may be blunted in frail or malnourished elderly and those who are extremely old	Predisposition to hypothermia (e.g., decline in body temperature during surgery is more marked unless preventive measures are undertaken) If hypothermic, shivering may result, associated with marked increases in oxygen consumption and cardiopulmonary demands Fever may be absent despite serious infections, especially in frail elderly	Use active measures to maintain normothermia during surgical procedures and to rewarm after trauma: warmed I.V. fluids, humidified gases, warm air Maintaining intraoperative normothermia reduces wound infections, adverse cardiac events, and length of stay

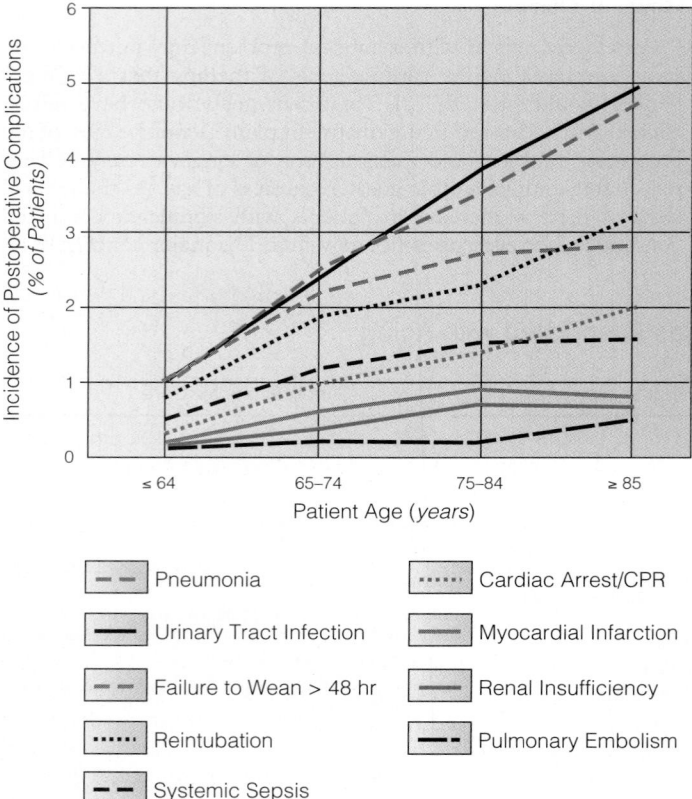

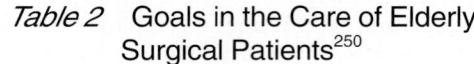

Figure 1 **Shown are the incidences of selected postoperative complications in different age groups after major operative procedures.**[1]

Table 2 Goals in the Care of Elderly Surgical Patients[250]

Cure presenting surgical problem	Relieve pain and other symptoms
Maximize potential life span	Maintain dignity, autonomy, and self-esteem
Maximize independent function	

elderly patient may be less willing than a younger patient to accept the risks of major surgical interventions, even if such measures are potentially curative, and more likely to pursue alternatives with less immediate risk and more limited goals. It is, of course, essential to recognize those situations in which timely elective intervention carries an acceptable risk and is likely to prevent discomfort, impairment, and the greater risks associated with emergency intervention in the future.

Major surgical procedures to maximize longevity may be entirely appropriate in an elderly patient who is fit from physiologic, functional, and cognitive perspectives. Current average expectations for 70-year-old men and women are an additional 12.5 and 15.3 years of life, respectively; for 85-year-old men and women, an additional 5.3 and 6.3 years, respectively; and for 100-year-old persons, 2 years.[6] Thus, the absolute gain in life expectancy resulting from even completely effective interventions declines as the age of the patient increases. Patients and clinicians probably recognize this principle intuitively but may find it difficult to quantify. It is based on an understanding of the effects of competing risks—that is, risks to survival from sources other than the condition of interest—and is reflected in the observation that life expectancy curves for normal individuals and for those with various medical conditions typically grow closer together as age increases [*see Figure 2*]. Competing risks increase progressively with age, decrease the impact of a new condition on life expectancy, and decrease the potential life expectancy gain from therapy.[7] For example, cancer-specific survival after resection of a colorectal tumor does not vary with age, whereas overall survival declines progressively as age rises.[8] The implications of competing risks are (1) that interventions carrying minimal risk are reasonable,

elderly patient may be whether he or she will be able to enjoy the same level of function and independence as before the onset of the problem. Relief of symptoms and maintaining quality of life may be more important than long-term survival. Maintaining reasonable function in the short term may be of special importance, for example, during the last stages of a spouse's illness or in advance of a landmark event in the family. In some circumstances, the

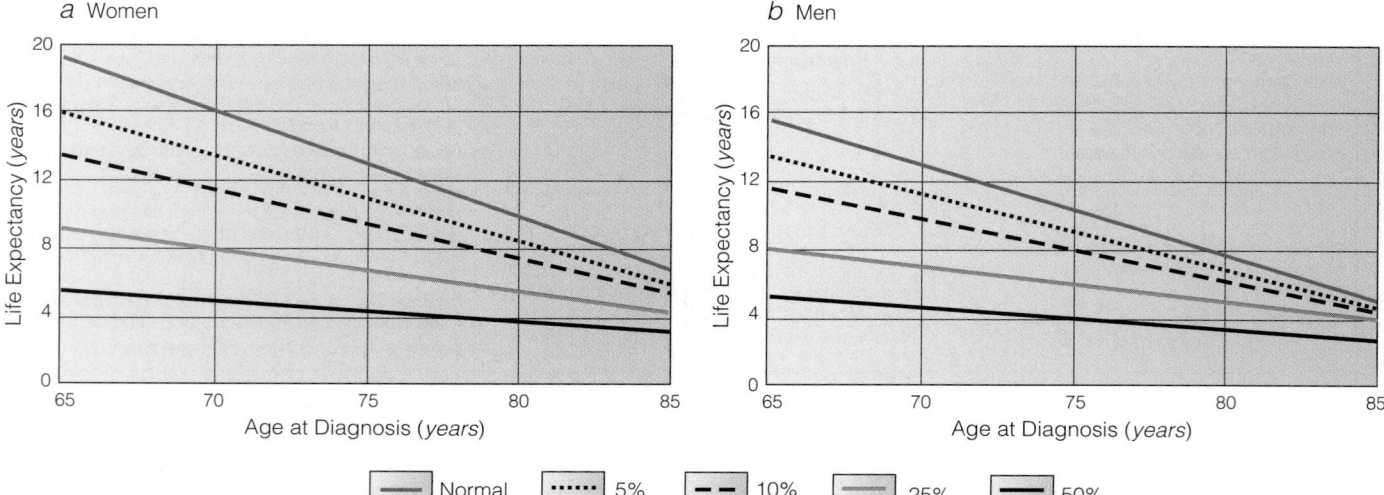

Figure 2 **Illustrated is the effect of disease-related mortality (5%, 10%, 25%, and 50%) on remaining life expectancy for women (*a*) and men (*b*).**[7] **As remaining life expectancy gradually declines with advancing age, the absolute impact of disease on life expectancy diminishes and the curves become closer together.**

regardless of age, and (2) that very elderly patients should select interventions that are clearly effective and are associated with a low complication rate when maximizing longevity is their goal. In the oldest old and those with greater than average competing risks (e.g., major comorbid conditions), net gains in longevity can be very modest indeed.

Discussion of the elderly patient's wishes regarding medical care in the event of serious postoperative complications should be encouraged before a major elective procedure, with family members or other possible substitute decision-makers involved as appropriate. Expectations about rehabilitation and convalescence should be discussed, with temporary placement after discharge, home care, and other discharge planning arranged as needed [see Planning of Rehabilitation and Convalescence, below]. Patients generally welcome the opportunity to discuss their wishes, and surgeons should not hesitate to raise these issues.

Some elderly patients may be unable to articulate goals and make treatment decisions on their own behalf. In some instances, they have previously expressed their wishes about medical care, perhaps in the form of an advance directive or "living will." (An example of the latter is available from the University of Toronto Joint Centre for Bioethics [http://www.utoronto.ca/jcb/outreach/living_wills.htm].) Discussions that patients may have had with their families, their caregivers, or both may be particularly helpful if they were held recently or were relevant to the specific situation at hand. When wishes have not been previously expressed, substitute decision-makers must consider what they know about the patient's values and arrive at a judgment about what the patient would have wished in this situation. Advance directives may provide a context in which to make decisions about limits to treatment, even though they usually apply to conditions that are irreversible or nearly so. In the absence of such information, a decision must be made in the best interests of the patient, taking into account the advantages and disadvantages of the treatment options, likely effects on quality of life, and similar concerns. It should be recognized that individuals may rate their quality of life highly despite significant health impairment and functional problems and that the assessments of physicians and family members may be quite different from those of patients.[9] In general, the literature suggests that clinicians do not adequately address issues related to the areas of planning, communicating, and implementing advance care preferences.[10]

Preserving patients' dignity and autonomy and minimizing distress are important health care goals that often are not met in the treatment of elderly persons.[11] Dignity (self-respect and being valued by others) is readily undermined in the health care setting by disrespect for patients' privacy and insensitivity to their needs and desires. Such disrespect and insensitivity may reflect stereotyped, negative attitudes toward older patients on the part of caregivers. Autonomy is inevitably diminished when sufficient information and opportunity to make informed choices about care are not provided.

Alterations in Clinical Presentation

The manifestations of surgical illness in the elderly patients may be considerably different from those in young or middle-aged individuals. Multiple medical disorders are often present, and the symptoms of acute surgical illness may be masked. The central nervous system is particularly sensitive to the effects of drugs and disease, and the presentation of surgical and medical illness may be nonspecific (e.g., lethargy, delirium, or agitation) or indirect (e.g., an unexplained fall). The clinical presentation will tend to reflect the most vulnerable organ system (often the CNS) in the earliest stages, not necessarily the organ system that is diseased.[12] Relative inactivity may limit the manifestations of important cardiac, pulmonary, or peripheral vascular disease. The patient, the family, or the surgeon may inappropriately attribute symptoms to the supposedly inevitable changes of advancing age. Cognitive or hearing impairment may make it difficult to obtain a reliable history. To ensure effective communication, the surgeon may have to make an extra effort when taking the history and reviewing the medical records.

Elderly patients may have a higher pain threshold than younger individuals. Older patients presenting with acute abdominal pain are more likely than younger individuals to require surgical intervention.[13] The localization of abdominal pain in patients with peritonitis may not be as reliable; elderly patients with appendicitis are less likely than younger patients to have pain localized to the right lower quadrant.[14] Abdominal pain is a less frequent presentation of colorectal carcinoma in geriatric patients than in younger patients.[15] These observations suggest that pain is a particularly important symptom in elderly patients and that its degree is not necessarily an adequate indication of the gravity of the underlying problem.[16]

Although febrile responses are generally intact, fever may be less marked in elderly individuals with infectious or inflammatory processes, particularly those older than 80 years. Hypothermia is more common in elderly patients who are seriously ill than in younger patients [see Discussion, Patterns of Change in Body Composition, Organ System Function, and Integrated Responses, below].

The prevalence and natural history of some pathologic processes, as well as their clinical manifestations, may be altered in the geriatric population. For example, elderly patients presenting with appendicitis are more likely to have gangrenous or perforated appendicitis than younger patients are, and elderly patients with perforated diverticulitis are more likely to have generalized peritonitis.[17] It is not clear whether these observations reflect a change in the onset of symptoms, a difference in the evolution of the pathologic process, or a delay in seeking medical attention. Similarly, elderly patients with symptomatic gallstones are more likely than younger patients to present with perforation, empyema, or gangrene of the gallbladder, acute cholecystitis, or cholangitis, and these patients are more likely to require urgent operative treatment.[18]

Preoperative Management

Preoperative assessment and optimization of cardiovascular, respiratory, nutritional, cognitive, and functional status in the elderly patient are addressed in some detail (see below). Smoking should be stopped as far in advance of surgery as possible, active respiratory infection resolved, airflow obstruction minimized, and exercise tolerance optimized. Strategies for preventing cardiovascular complications continue to evolve. Beta-adrenergic blockade is well tolerated and should be considered in patients undergoing major elective noncardiac procedures who are at increased risk for perioperative ischemic cardiac complications.[19]

The importance of micronutrients and compounds with antioxidant properties is being increasingly appreciated. Whether or not preexisting deficits are suspected, preoperative multivitamin supplementation should be considered in elderly patients. The preoperative period is also the optimal time to address protein-calorie deficiencies, using oral supplements in most malnourished patients, enteral feeding when necessary, and parenteral feeding when it is the only option. The diminished muscle mass, strength, and functional status that tend to accompany aging [*see* Nutritional Assessment, *below*] and the demonstrated effects of physical training in elderly nursing home residents raise the possibility that similar programs might minimize the development of muscle weakness and functional impairments after major operations.[20] In one randomized trial, patients awaiting coronary bypass grafting who participated in a supervised twice-weekly exercise training plus a broadly based educational program had shorter intensive care unit and hospital stays than control subjects did.[21] In an observational study, a home-based strength and aerobic training program was associated with increases in 6-minute walking distance, quality of life, strength, and peak oxygen consumption in patients preparing for lung volume reduction procedures.[22]

RISK ASSESSMENT

Assessment of risk in elderly patients must consider patient factors, the surgical problem, and the treatment options. Assessment of the elderly patient is typically more challenging and time-consuming, and it more often involves family members, the primary care physician, anesthetists, and other physicians and health care disciplines. Coexisting medical conditions are common and may markedly increase the risks associated with surgical intervention. The physical status scale developed by the American Society of Anesthesiologists (ASA) reflects functional status and comorbidity and is a strong predictor of postoperative and late mortality [*see* Figure 3].[23]

Surgical outcomes depend not only on physical or physiologic fitness but also on cognitive and social factors: a careful assessment must go beyond simply establishing a specific diagnosis and must include all of these elements.[24] A rational approach to risk assessment should take into account those specific factors that predict important adverse clinical outcomes, allowing risks and treatment goals to be weighed and preparation for surgery and perioperative care to be planned optimally. Given that aging is a very heterogeneous process, great caution should be exercised in applying generalizations about the elderly population to specific elderly persons. Decisions about surgical care must rest on criteria that are more specific and strongly predictive than chronologic age is.

Approaches to preoperative testing continue to evolve, but there is now considerable evidence that many tests ordered on a routine basis (i.e., without relation to history or clinical findings) do not contribute to preoperative assessment and are sometimes misleading. The value of routine preoperative electrocardiography and blood work was examined in a large randomized trial involving patients undergoing cataract surgery, most of whom were older.[25] The addition of routine testing to a careful clinical assessment did not improve the safety of this relatively minor procedure. A systematic review concluded that although the yield of abnormal chest x-rays increases with age, resulting changes in management are infrequent and the effect of such findings on clinical outcomes is unknown.[26] Similar conclusions were reached with respect to routine preoperative ECG (in patients undergoing noncardiac procedures), hematology, and biochemistry. Preoperative hypokalemia, however, has been associated with a higher incidence of perioperative arrhythmia and a greater need for cardiopulmonary resuscitation in patients undergoing elective coronary artery bypass grafting.[27] Possibly, older persons represent a population at increased risk for medical problems that are clinically subtle but potentially important after more major operations and that could usefully be identified by means of routine preoperative testing. Additional well-designed studies are needed to

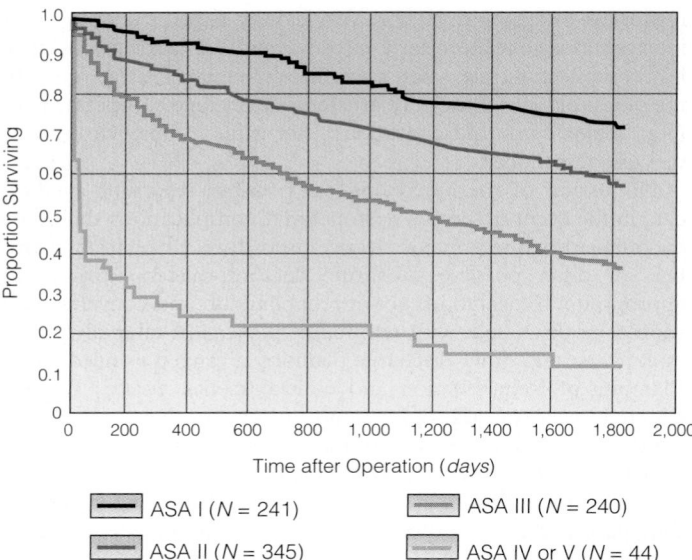

Figure 3 **Depicted is correlation between ASA grade and postoperative survival.**[23]

ASA I (*N* = 241)   ASA III (*N* = 240)
ASA II (*N* = 345)   ASA IV or V (*N* = 44)

evaluate routine testing in populations that are at increased risk for postoperative cardiopulmonary and other complications.

RESPIRATORY ASSESSMENT

Respiratory complications are among the most common complications after major surgical procedures and are more frequent in elderly patients [*see* Figure 1].[28,29] Postoperative pulmonary complications are considerably more common than cardiac complications and are equally likely to cause postoperative death after abdominal procedures. In a large prospective study of predominantly male patients undergoing major noncardiac procedures, the incidence of postoperative pneumonia was 1.5%, compared with 0.7% for cardiac arrest and 0.4% for myocardial infarction.[29] The 30-day mortality was 21% for patients in whom pneumonia developed and 2% for those in whom it did not. The risk of pneumonia was five times greater in patients aged 80 years or older than in those younger than 50 years. In another study, the combination of age 60 years or greater and ASA risk category II or higher identified nearly 90% of patients who experienced respiratory complications after abdominal operations.[28] In a systematic review of patients undergoing surgical treatment of colorectal cancer, the incidence of respiratory complications was 5% in patients younger than 65 years, 10% in those 65 to 74 years of age, 12% in those 75 to 84 years of age, and 15% in those 85 years of age or older.[8] Age-related changes in respiratory function [*see* Table 1] interact with the changes that occur after operation and during acute surgical illness, to the detriment of the elderly patient [*see* Postoperative Management, Respiratory Care, *below*].

Much of the unadjusted risk associated with advanced age is attributable to the presence of comorbid conditions. Significant patient-related risk factors for postoperative pulmonary complications include smoking, poor exercise capacity, chronic obstructive pulmonary disease (COPD), active pulmonary infection, and cognitive impairment.[30] Smoking should be stopped as far in advance of operation as possible: cessation of smoking 6 to 8 weeks beforehand significantly reduces cardiopulmonary and wound-related (as well as overall) postoperative complications.[31] Active respiratory infection should be resolved, even if this means delaying the operation. Airflow obstruction should be treated in patients with COPD and asthma. The aim should be to optimize respiratory status, as determined by exercise capacity, physical findings, and perhaps spirometry.[30] Bronchodilators, inhaled glucocorticoids, and chest physiotherapy may be helpful.

Procedure-related risk factors are also of some relevance. The risk of pulmonary complications is greatest after upper abdominal and thoracic procedures and is lower with laparoscopic procedures than with open procedures. On rare occasions, the risk of respiratory complications is considered so great that the choice of surgical procedure is based on the desire to avoid an abdominal (especially an upper abdominal) or thoracic procedure or general anesthesia. Lengthy surgical procedures (> 3 hours) are also accompanied by increased risk.

A careful history and a thorough physical examination directed at the risk factors discussed are the most important elements of preoperative assessment and should be completed in elderly patients undergoing abdominal and thoracic procedures. Whether routine preoperative chest roentgenography is warranted in healthy elderly patients at low risk for postoperative pulmonary complications is unknown.[26,32] The value of routine preoperative pulmonary function testing for procedures other than pulmonary resection is not supported by published reports, many of which have methodologic shortcomings.[30,32,33] Abnormal spirometry results should not be used in isolation to decide against a surgical procedure,[30] though they may be helpful in determining whether the status of a patient with known COPD has been optimized. The principles of risk assessment and preoperative optimization of respiratory function are essentially the same, regardless of age [see 120 Pulmonary Insufficiency].

CARDIOVASCULAR ASSESSMENT

The presence of coronary artery disease increases with age: significant coronary artery disease is present at autopsy in more than 50% of individuals older than 70 years [see Figure 4]. In unselected patients older than 40 years, the risk of perioperative myocardial infarction or cardiac death has been reported to range from 2.0% to 3.7%, with a pooled average of 2.5%.[34] Considerable disparity results from the use of inconsistent diagnostic criteria (e.g., biochemical, electrocardiographic, clinical) in the numerous studies examining this problem.[34] In a study of 323 patients 50 years of age or older who had ischemic heart disease and were undergoing noncardiac operations, perioperative myocardial infarction was defined by a predefined combination of criteria.[35] Myocardial infarction was identified in 5.6% of patients; it typically occurred early (nearly 80% on the day of surgery or postoperative day 1), was not usually accompanied by chest pain (17%), and was sometimes fatal (17%).

The risk of adverse cardiac events is strongly influenced by the nature of the surgical procedure.[36] The risk is very low in low-risk patients undergoing minor surgical procedures.[37] For example, in a study of more than 18,000 patients 50 years of age or older who underwent elective cataract surgery, perioperative death and unplanned hospitalization were rare.[25] The incidence of myocardial infarction, myocardial ischemia, or congestive heart failure was 1.2 per 1,000 patients. This incidence was not altered by the addition of routine testing (e.g., ECG) to a careful history and physical examination.

By contrast, the risk of major cardiac complications (e.g., myocardial infarction, pulmonary edema, and ventricular fibrillation) is relatively high after abdominal, noncardiac thoracic, and suprainguinal vascular procedures in individuals 50 years of age or older.[38] In a systematic review of surgical treatment of colorectal cancer, the overall rate of cardiac complications was 2%, with

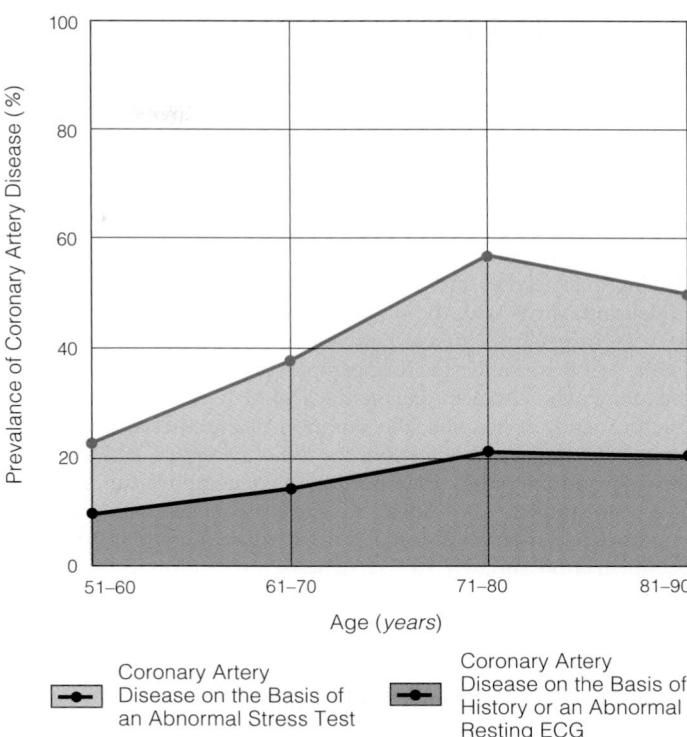

Figure 4 **Shown is an estimate of the prevalence of coronary artery disease in men between 51 and 90 years of age.**[245]

a linear relationship between increasing age and the frequency of such complications.[8] In another report, the rate of perioperative myocardial infarction or cardiac death was 6.2% in vascular surgical patients (range, 2.2% to 19.0%).[34]

Even major vascular procedures are accompanied by very low risk when cardiac functional status is good, coronary artery disease is absent, and the multifactorial risk index score is low.[39] It is noteworthy that advanced age (i.e., 70 years or older) did not correlate with cardiac complications in the 1999 revision of a widely cited cardiac risk index.[38] Presumably, this absence of correlation results, in part, from the inclusion in the index of specific factors (e.g., ischemic heart disease) that are associated with age but are stronger predictors of outcome. It is also noteworthy that cerebrovascular disease, renal insufficiency, and type 1 (insulin-dependent) diabetes are significant predictors of cardiac complications.

The concepts and practical approaches involved in assessing perioperative cardiac risk before major noncardiac procedures are discussed in detail elsewhere.

COGNITIVE ASSESSMENT

Preexisting impairment of cognitive function from dementia, delirium, or depression is associated with an increased risk of postoperative complications and worse early and 6-month survival.[40-42] For example, the risk of postoperative pulmonary complications after abdominal procedures is increased nearly sixfold in patients with preoperative cognitive dysfunction.[43] Patients with end-stage dementia have been reported to have a fourfold higher 6-month mortality (55%) than patients who were cognitively intact (13%).[42] Such patients were fully dependent in activities of daily living (ADLs) and unable to remember the names of family members. This poor short-term prognosis, which may even be an overestimate, appeared not to have been generally recognized by caregivers and families and was not reflected in differences in care, palliative measures, or decisions to forgo burdensome interventions or life-sustaining measures. Dementia, delirium, and depression are each associated with increased mortality after hip fracture.[44] The potential for diagnostic delays in cognitively impaired patients, leading to adverse outcomes, has been identified in patients with general surgical problems.[40]

Advanced age is associated with delirium (acute cognitive impairment) after major operations.[45-47] Postoperative delirium is, in turn, a predictor of prolonged hospital stay and functional decline that persists after hospital discharge.[45,46,48] The incidence of delirium varies with the surgical procedure and may be as high as 15% in general surgical patients and 60% in orthopedic patients.[49] Other risk factors for postoperative delirium are preexisting dementia, visual impairment, alcohol use, the diagnosis of fracture, and, in hospital, the duration of anesthesia, the occurrence of postoperative infection, the use of narcotics, and the need for a second operation. Late postoperative cognitive function has also been studied.[47,50,51] Advanced age is associated with cognitive impairment 3 months after major noncardiac operations; this state occurs in approximately 10% of patients but resolves in the major-

ity of patients 1 to 2 years after operation. Complaints about changes in cognitive function do not necessarily correlate well with measured performance. Early cognitive dysfunction after cardiac surgery with cardiopulmonary bypass is well recognized, and the likelihood of long-term dysfunction is considerable.[52]

The Mini-Mental State Examination (MMSE) is a valid and reliable preoperative screening instrument for cognitive impairment [see Table 3].[53] The MMSE requires approximately 10 minutes to complete and is suitable for repeated assessments. A modified "telephone" version requires only verbal responses and yields comparable results.[54] Alternative instruments are available.[55] An assessment of cognitive function should be completed as a routine in patients older than 75 years for whom major elective surgery is planned and in patients with existing cognitive impairments or other risk factors for postoperative delirium. A baseline assessment is valuable for assessing risk, implementing preventive strategies, and permitting reliable identification of postoperative cognitive deterioration; such deterioration may be the initial manifestation of a serious postoperative complication.

NUTRITIONAL ASSESSMENT

Elderly persons are at risk for malnutrition for several reasons, even in the absence of acute illness. The dietary range of older persons may be limited by physical and cognitive disabilities, social isolation, lack of awareness of the importance of a balanced diet, poverty, poor dentition, and the effects of medication on appetite, taste, nutrient absorption, and metabolism. The prevalence of overt protein-calorie malnutrition among the community-dwelling older persons is modest, but intakes of specific minerals and vitamins may be inadequate, especially to meet the increased demands of acute illness. Micronutrient (vitamin and trace element) supplementation has been shown to improve immune function and lower the incidence of clinical infections in both healthy community-dwelling and institutionalized elderly persons.[56,57] Oral protein-calorie and micronutrient supplements should be prescribed before major elective procedures if there is any question about the adequacy of nutrient intake. Malnutrition is more common in elderly residents of nursing homes and other long-term care facilities than in community-dwelling elderly persons. Reported rates vary considerably, ranging from 37% to 85%.[58-60] Malnutrition is quite common in hospitalized elderly patients but frequently goes unrecognized.[61,62] It is consistently associated with adverse outcomes, which intervention studies suggest can be improved by nutritional therapy.[63,64] Assessment of nutritional status should be routine in elderly patients for whom a major elective procedure is planned or who are admitted to hospital with an acute illness.

There is no single accepted standard for assessment of nutritional status. This is unsurprising, given the range of micronutrients and macronutrients to be considered and the myriad possible structural and functional consequences of what is perceived as malnutrition. Nonetheless, elderly surgical patients should routinely be screened for malnutrition through thoughtful clinical assessment.

Numerous anatomic, biochemical, and functional measures of nutritional status have been used, in some instances combined by means of multivariate statistical techniques.[65-68] A structured clinical assessment can be completed rapidly, is reliable, and is among the most useful tools for nutritional assessment in elderly surgical patients. Subjective global assessment (SGA) is one such approach that incorporates relevant features of history and physical examination.[69] The Mini Nutritional Assessment (http://www.mna-elderly.com/index.htm) incorporates brief questions and simple anthropometric measurements in an instrument designed for

---

Table 3 **Mini-Mental State Examination for Cognitive Function[53]**

Maximum Score	Score	Item
		Orientation
5	( )	"What is the date?" Give 1 point each for year, season, date, day, month.
5	( )	"Where are we?" Give 1 point each for state, county, town, building, floor or room.
		Registration
3	( )	Name three objects. Take 1 second to say each, then ask patient to name all three.
		Give 1 point for each correct answer. Repeat until patient learns all three (for later testing).
		Attention and Calculation
5		Ask patient to subtract serial sevens, starting at 100. Give 1 point for each correct answer.
		Stop after five answers. (Alternatively, ask patient to spell "world" backward.)
		Recall
3	( )	Ask patient to name the three objects mentioned previously. Give 1 point for each correct answer.
		Language
9	( )	Point to a pencil and a watch and ask patient to name them. Give 1 point for each correct answer.
		Ask patient to repeat the following: "No ifs, ands, or buts." Give 1 point if successful.
		Give patient a three-stage command: "Take a paper in your right hand, fold it in half, and put it on the floor." Give 1 point for each correct action.
		Ask patient to read and obey the following: "Close your eyes." Give 1 point if patient closes eyes.
		Ask patient to write a sentence. Give 1 point if sentence has a subject and a verb and makes sense.
		Ask patient to copy a simple design. Give 1 point if drawing is correct.
30	( )	Total Score*

*A score of 24 or more is considered normal.

rapid screening of nutrition status in elderly persons in outpatient, nursing home, and hospital settings.[70]

Decreased muscle mass in older persons is accompanied by decreased strength. Maximal voluntary handgrip strength can be evaluated rapidly and has been reported to be a useful predictor of postoperative complications and length of hospital stay after elective surgery and hip fracture.[71,72]

ASSESSMENT OF FUNCTION

Assessment of functional level is important at every stage of care of the elderly surgical patient [see Table 4]. Functional assessment is necessary for appropriate surgical decision making, governs perioperative care, and helps set realistic goals for postoperative functional level and quality of life. Tools for functional assessment (e.g., the FIM instrument, available from the Uniform Data System for Medical Rehabilitation, http://www.udsmr.org) should address basic ADLs, cognition, mood [see Table 5], health-related quality of life, and instrumental ADLs. Functional level is a rich field for surgical outcomes research.[24-29,43,73]

PROCEDURE-RELATED FACTORS

The site of the operation and the magnitude of tissue injury and physiologic perturbation are risk factors for postoperative complications. The increased risks of cardiac and pulmonary complications associated with major abdominal or thoracic procedures have been discussed (see above). The risk of perioperative complications is very low after relatively minor procedures, such as cataract surgery and hernia repair under local anesthesia.[25,74] Laparoscopic procedures appear to be well tolerated by elderly patients and yield the benefits seen in younger patients.[75] Morbidity and mortality are invariably greater for emergency

---

Table 4 Functional Level Assessment for Elderly Surgical Candidates

Why
To individualize and adapt therapy
To assign patients to particular treatment protocols, clinical guidelines, or critical pathways
To follow individual patients to determine outcome measures
To follow groups of patients
To conduct patient and institutional outcome research
To identify gaps in service

When
Preoperative planning period
Preoperative asssessment—immediate for baseline measures for elective patients
By history for nonelective cases
"Reflective" history for elective patients with functional compromise related to the condition that will receive surgical intervention (e.g., patient waiting for hip replacement—how long has gait been impaired?)

What
General function level (e.g., FIM)
Cognition (e.g., Mini-Mental State Examination) [see Table 3]
Depression (e.g., Geriatric Depression Scale) [see Table 5]
Quality of life (e.g., SF-36 or SF-12 v2)
Capacity for self-care (e.g., CSHA–modified OARS)

FIM—Functional Independence Measure SF-26—Short Form–S6 Health Survey SF-12 v2—Short Form–12, version 2 Health Survey CSHA—Canadian Study of Health and Aging OARS—Older Americans Research Survey

---

Table 5 Geriatric Depression Scale (Mood Scale) (Short Form)

Patient Name:
Date:

Choose the best answer for how you have felt over the past week:	Give 1 point if answer is:
1. Are you basically satisfied with your life?	No
2. Have you dropped many of your activities and interests?	Yes
3. Do you feel that your life is empty?	Yes
4. Do you often get bored?	Yes
5. Are you in good spirits most of the time?	No
6. Are you afraid that something bad is going to happen to you?	Yes
7. Do you feel happy most of the time?	No
8. Do you often feel helpless?	Yes
9. Do you prefer to stay at home, rather than going out and doing new things?	Yes
10. Do you feel you have more problems with memory than most?	Yes
11. Do you think it is wonderful to be alive now?	No
12. Do you feel pretty worthless the way you are now?	Yes
13. Do you feel full of energy?	No
14. Do you feel that your situation is hopeless?	Yes
15. Do you think that most people are better off than you are?	Yes
Total:	———

For clinical purposes, a score > 5 points is suggestive of depression and should warrant a follow-up interview. Scores > 10 almost always indicate depression.

---

operations than for elective ones, presumably because of the greater physiologic disturbance caused by the condition requiring urgent treatment and the limited opportunity to assess and optimize the patient's general medical condition [see Figure 5].[23,76,77] Mortality for emergency GI procedures, for example, has been reported to be as much as three times higher than that for elective procedures. Elderly surgical patients are less likely than young ones to tolerate the prolonged starvation, pain, immobility, and possible infection that accompany delayed operation and should therefore have a high priority for access to the OR for emergency procedures.[4] Overall operative mortality in older persons appears to have declined gradually over many years. This decline may be attributable to better preoperative preparation of patients, as well as to improvements in anesthetic and perioperative care and surgical technique.

PSYCHOLOGICAL PREPARATION

Psychological factors are of considerable importance in preparing the elderly patient for elective operation [see Sidebar Establishing Rapport with the Elderly Patient]. Preoperative patient education has been shown to enhance patient confidence and to hasten the resumption of ADLs after operation.[78] Acute mental stress has been associated with myocardial ischemia in patients with coronary artery disease. Preoperative reassurance and patient education reduce anxiety and the postoperative need for narcotic analgesics. Preoperative teaching probably also improves patient compliance with and the effectiveness of postoperative chest physiotherapy and other respiratory maneuvers.[79] Postoperative psychological adjustment is enhanced by the physician's caring attitudes, as displayed, for example, in preoperative diagnostic interviews with breast cancer patients, who perceived the actual information given in the interviews as the less important component.[80]

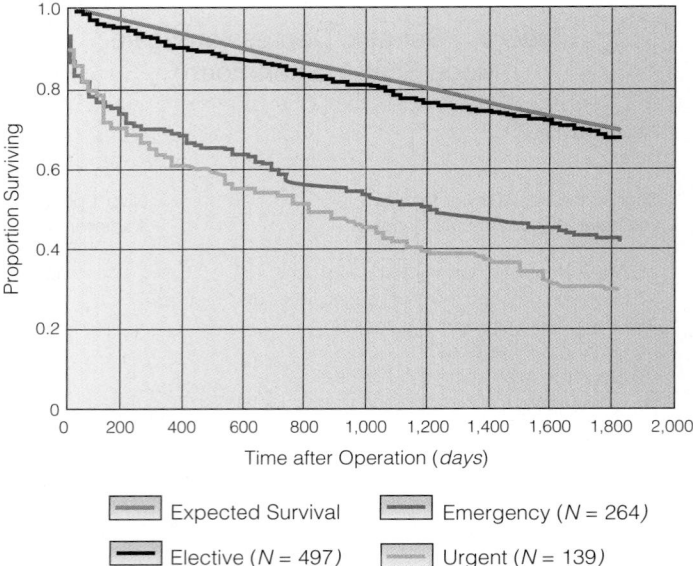

Expected Survival   Emergency (N = 264)
Elective (N = 497)   Urgent (N = 139)

Figure 5 **Depicted is the correlation between mode of admission and postoperative survival.**[23]

PLANNING OF REHABILITATION AND CONVALESCENCE

Rehabilitation and convalescence should be planned before operation, with full consideration given to both the potential impact of the planned procedure on function and the possible duration of functional impairment. Systematic reviews of programs of rehabilitative care after hip fracture and of supported discharge home for geriatric patients suggest that there is value to such interventions (e.g., in terms of hospital stay and the likelihood of returning to independent living) but that considerable uncertainty remains about the populations most likely to benefit and about optimal program design.[81-83]

The absence of any immediate family contributes not only to long hospital stays for elderly patients but also to the requirement for nursing home placement at discharge. These trends hold true regardless of surgical procedure, surgical service of admission, diagnosis, age, and gender. The adjusted odds ratio for very long hospital stays is 1.85 in patients with no adult child. The adjusted odds ratios for requirement of nursing home placement at discharge are 2.59 in patients with no spouse, 3.27 in patients with no adult child, and 8.47 in patients with neither.[84]

The caretaker is typically a daughter 50 to 70 years of age or an elderly spouse. The caretaker often has a wide range of concerns in addition to the elderly parent or spouse who is the surgical candidate. Such concerns might include holding down a job, supporting her adult children through school, minding her grandchildren, maintaining the traditional homemaker's role, and planning financially for her own retirement. Accordingly, she should plan to do one or more of the following: (1) hire a full-time housekeeper for her parent, (2) miss some work, or (3) arrange for convalescent care for a few weeks after the operation.

If family members are reluctant to participate in planning convalescence or arranging for live-in help or community support, they should be warned that they may eventually need to take as much as 8 weeks off from work to compensate for temporary and minor functional difficulties on the part of the patient. During convalescence, which may go on for weeks after discharge, family members should save their energy for those personal support activities in which they are irreplaceable (e.g., visits and telephone

conversations). They should not spend disproportionate amounts of time and effort on activities that another person could be paid to perform (e.g., washing sheets or delivering provisions). In this way, the family may avoid burnout or family stress, either of which may lead to neglect of the elderly member or to early placement.

The elderly patient should be advised to cultivate healthy habits preoperatively, such as exercising and having regular, balanced meals. Finally, the patient should come to the hospital prepared for an active postoperative period, bringing his or her clothes, jog-

---

Establishing Rapport with the Elderly Patient

The surgeon's personal rapport with the patient remains an important element of healing. The patient tends to interpret every aspect of preoperative, intraoperative, and postoperative care—including physiotherapy, nursing, and the ward routine as well as the surgical skills and knowledge displayed—as part of the surgeon's treatment. Older patients are often more in awe of physicians than are younger patients and thus may attribute almost shamanic powers to the surgeon. Such beliefs may be a valuable therapeutic aid.

The elderly generations comprise more disparate styles, cultures, vocabularies, and individual differences than any other generational group. It is therefore especially important that the surgeon attempt to understand and empathize with each patient's attitudes, beliefs, concerns, and modes of communication, some of which have been retained from an earlier time. The result will be a more confident patient, and confident elderly patients have been shown to experience fewer complications. Enhanced feelings of control and autonomy on the part of the patient correlate with a shorter hospital stay. These feelings can be promoted by specific behaviors on the part of the surgeon:

- Never call the patient by his or her first name, even if the patient calls you by yours. Never use "dear," "granny," or any other diminutive or familiar name.
- Address the patient, not the accompanying family member.
- When you speak to the patient, keep your expression calm, smile, bring your face close, and do not turn away. Speak slowly and distinctly, but do not raise your voice.
- Pause from time to time to permit the patient to speak. Do not allow the accompanying family member to fill all the pauses.
- To interrupt or to bring the patient back to the subject you want to discuss, touch him or her slowly on the hand or arm and repeat the question.
- Ask the patient if he or she understands what you have said.
- Ask the patient how he or she feels about what you have said, and address any concerns raised.

It is essential to avoid the appearance of haste or carelessness. If the surgeon is calm and supportive, the patient is likely to be calm and confident. Such nonverbal messages are more important to elderly persons than to younger adults and may be perceived as more valuable than the actual information given.

Confused, demented, or depressed elderly patients are not the only ones who benefit from reassuring nonverbal messages. This style of interaction may be used, for instance, with an active 70-year-old CEO who has sandwiched an appointment with the surgeon between a board meeting and a golf game, even if it seems somewhat exaggerated under the circumstances. Later, when the patient feels confused and cold, cannot see, hear, or smile normally, and has just suffered the indignity of a catheter, he or she will remember the respectful healing behaviors, and the surgeon-patient rapport will be enhanced.

Finally, it should be remembered that aged persons are subject to psychological, physical, and financial abuse. The surgeon should ask the patient directly about these potential problems and should, if necessary, request social and psychiatric assessment and legal intervention.

ging suit, shoes, walker or cane, hearing aid, glasses, pictures of loved ones, radio, and calendar.

INFORMED CONSENT AND ASSESSMENT OF COMPETENCE

Inherent in the idea of informed consent is that each patient has both the right to be informed about the therapeutic options available and the right to consent to—or refuse—intervention. Obtaining informed consent can be more complicated with elderly patients than with younger ones for several reasons. First, older patients may be psychologically or physically dependent on someone else; second, they may be overly deferential to (or suspicious of) the surgeon; third, they may be mildly demented but nonetheless competent to accept or reject a surgical choice. Occasionally, an elderly patient is capable in all the usual areas of function but acts incompetently when asked to accept or forgo a surgical intervention. When told that complications are rare, an older patient may believe the risk to be higher than a younger person would.[85] Older patients may be less interested in obtaining information about complications than younger patients are[86,87]; however, giving detailed information does not appear to raise their anxiety level.[88]

The term competence, as we use it here, is defined simply as the capacity to understand and appreciate the available options and their consequences and the ability to choose freely among these options.[89,90] Competence may refer to either clinical status or legal status. It should be remembered that guidelines allowing a parent or guardian to speak for a child or for a mentally challenged person cannot be generalized to apply to an elderly individual whom the surgeon may consider clinically incompetent but who has not yet been determined to be legally incompetent.

To maximize the possibilities for informed consent, the surgeon should arrange to spend some time with the patient, even if the patient seems severely demented. The patient should be asked the following questions:

1. Do you feel comfortable with the idea of surgery?
2. Do you understand what is planned?
3. Do you have any questions for me?

Only after these questions have been answered satisfactorily should the patient be reassured that surgical treatment is in his or her best interests. If the patient is unaccompanied, the surgeon should ask permission to speak with the spouse, a child, or anyone who may be assisting the patient either before or after the surgical procedure. The surgical plan is reviewed with family members and repeated to the patient in the presence of the family. Included in the review should be expectations for the patient's capacity to function in the immediate postoperative period as well as the amount of family support that will be required. Finally, the surgeon should make it very clear to both the patient and the family that although family members can help the patient to understand the available choices, they do not have the right to make the final decision, even if the patient is completely dependent and has dementia, unless there has been a valid formal delegation of responsibility for health care. Definitions and terminology vary among jurisdictions.

When the patient's competence is uncertain, assessment by a psychogeriatrician may be helpful, as may assessments by a geriatrician, a social worker, and the patient's family physician. Some variation of opinion is to be expected because the issue of competence is not a simple one. For example, a patient may be incompetent to manage money but competent to accept operation. Alternatively, a patient may have a borderline status and experience diurnal fluctuations in cognition. In a 1994 study, surgeons performed almost as well as psychiatrists on theoretical issues of competence but surpassed their psychiatric colleagues in the practical application of competence assessment.[91] The authors concluded that "the common clinical practice of relying on expert medical opinion may introduce bias and produce inaccurate results that undermine patient autonomy." Practical solutions and common sense must prevail. The patient's values, both cultural and personal, must be taken into account.

When the patient is deemed incompetent, the next step is to establish legal incompetence. Most provinces, states, and hospitals require two psychiatric opinions to declare incompetence and to place the patient under legal guardianship. The efforts of a social worker are usually vital to this process, which can be accomplished immediately in urgent situations, usually through the director of professional services. Once declared incompetent, the patient comes under the protection of the state, which may delegate the role of legal representative to the private sector in the form of family guardianship or the so-called committee of the person. These private-sector guardians are then overseen by the state.

It is vital to consult with, to educate, to reassure, and to work with the family when surgical decisions must be made about an elderly patient with dementia. Questions to the family should focus on gathering relevant information, such as what the patient's wishes would probably be if he or she could express them and what the patient's functional and biologic status was before the current surgical problem. The family must understand that such questions constitute a request not for permission but rather for information that will help the surgeon in the management of the patient with dementia.

If the family is the legal representative for health care and refuses operation but the surgeon feels strongly that surgical intervention is in the patient's best interest, legal review should be requested. This request may place the surgeon in a difficult position. In fact, it may relieve some of the burden of decision making carried by the most responsible family member, who may blame himself or herself or be blamed by siblings for everything that goes wrong with the aging parent in the remaining years of life, regardless of whether the problem is related to the surgical intervention.

Rarely, it may happen that even when the patient has been declared legally incompetent, the legal representative for health care has signed the consent form, hospital administrators and the psychogeriatric consultant are supportive of the decision to operate, the family is supportive of the patient, and the patient seems to accept surgical treatment, the patient will adamantly refuse to go to the operating room on the morning of the operation. In such cases, although the surgeon could choose to proceed with the operation, it is probably best to cancel it and reschedule it for the next day. The presence of someone the patient trusts (e.g., an old friend or a minister) through the perioperative period may allow the elderly patient with dementia to tolerate the procedure and the surgical milieu.

Finally, when surgical intervention is considered neither urgent nor life threatening, the surgeon may be frustrated waiting for the courts to appoint a legal representative for health care. If so, the help of other knowledgeable and action-oriented professionals (e.g., the family physician, a psychogeriatrician, or a social worker) may be valuable. Newer, more flexible mechanisms are being explored in various jurisdictions for management of the well-being of the patient who has lost some autonomy. These newer mechanisms include durable power of attorney, health care proxy, living wills, and judicial advisers. The surgeon's consultants should be able to assist in selecting the most appropriate mechanism, depending on the patient's medical status, prognosis, and family support and on local laws.

Intraoperative Management

POSITIONING

Because elderly patients commonly have diminished range of joint motion, particular attention must be paid to how they are positioned for operation. The use of regional or general anesthesia may allow positioning that would be uncomfortable and beyond the usual range of motion were the patient not anesthetized. Postoperative back pain is a well-recognized complication of the lithotomy position in elderly patients. The remarkable prevalence of osteoporosis and the high incidence of related fractures in the geriatric population emphasize the fragility of these patients' bone and the importance of gentleness and care in turning and positioning them, particularly when discomfort and protective musculoskeletal reflexes have been suppressed by anesthesia. In addition, the skin of elderly individuals is easily injured by tape, adhesive electrodes, cautery pads, and warming blankets. Injury to the skin can occur easily by shearing when elderly patients are lifted and moved or when sheets are pulled from underneath them. Careful padding is necessary to prevent localized pressure, which may result in nerve compression and skin injuries, and to maintain appropriate positioning throughout anesthesia. The head and neck should be kept in a position that is comfortable and limits hyperextension so that cerebral blood flow is not compromised.

MAINTENANCE OF CORE TEMPERATURE

Unless effective preventive measures are taken, a fall in core temperature is common in patients undergoing major operative procedures, whether general or neuraxial anesthesia is used.[92] Elderly patients are less well able to maintain normothermia, and in older studies, the extent and duration of postoperative hypothermia were found to be greater and shivering to be more common in elderly patients.[93] Shivering can result in a severalfold increase in oxygen consumption, which imposes a substantial burden on the cardiac and pulmonary systems in the immediate postoperative period.[94] If the oxygen transport system is unable to meet the increased oxygen demand, myocardial ischemia may result. Maintaining normothermia results in a marked reduction in morbid postoperative cardiac events in patients with cardiac risk factors who have undergone major noncardiac procedures.[95] The incidence of surgical site infection (SSI) is increased by even mild hypothermia, probably in part because of reduced cutaneous blood flow and tissue oxygen delivery.[96] Impaired platelet function and decreased activation of the coagulation cascade are believed to contribute to the increased blood loss and the greater need for blood transfusion associated with hypothermia during elective hip arthroplasty.[97]

Hypothermia should be minimized or prevented in the OR by controlling room temperature, minimizing exposure of body surfaces, warming I.V. fluids and ventilator gases, and using active warming devices (e.g., a warming blanket) as needed. The opportunity to restore an appropriate core temperature without excessive metabolic stress and cardiac work is a reason to consider a brief period of mechanical ventilation when hypothermia has developed.

PREVENTION OF SURGICAL SITE INFECTION AND DEEP VEIN THROMBOSIS

Advanced age is well recognized as associated with the development of postoperative deep vein thrombosis (DVT). Prophylaxis of DVT should be considered in elderly surgical patients [see 85 Venous Thromboembolism]. Advanced age has also been demonstrated to be associated with an increased incidence of postoperative SSI.[98] In one report, however, the likelihood of SSI (incision or organ/space) after elective resection of the colon and rectum was not influenced by patient age but was influenced by ASA class, male sex, the presence of a stoma, and other factors.[99]

Postoperative Management

RESPIRATORY CARE

Postoperative respiratory complications, respiratory failure, and inadequate oxygen transport remain important causes of death in the elderly population. Resting arterial oxygen tension and content decrease progressively with advancing age, and the further decrease associated with operation is more marked in elderly patients. In addition, the ventilatory responses to both hypoxia and hypercapnia are blunted in older persons. Postoperative hypothermia is more prominent in older patients, and oxygen demand is markedly increased by postoperative shivering. Abdominal procedures with general anesthesia induce decreases in vital capacity and forced expiratory volume in 1 second (FEV_1) that last as long as 2 weeks after operation[100]; similar declines in lung volume accompany aging. The combined result is increased closure of small airways, ventilation-perfusion mismatch, and an increased alveolar-arterial oxygen gradient. Impairment of diaphragmatic function after upper abdominal procedures results in a shift in ventilation away from dependent portions of the lung.[101] Because of stiff chest walls and diminished elastic lung recoil, elderly patients are more reliant on diaphragmatic function than younger patients are.[102] Protective airway reflexes are less sensitive in elderly persons, mucociliary transport is less efficient, and coughing is less effective because strength, elastic recoil of the lungs, vital capacity, and maximum expiratory flow rate are all diminished. The use of parenteral narcotics for postoperative analgesia has been associated with striking episodic falls in oxygen tension; the increased sensitivity of older persons to narcotics may further predispose them to such hypoxemia. The presence of coronary artery disease in many older persons underscores the importance of maintaining adequate oxygen delivery and avoiding excessive myocardial oxygen demand in the perioperative period.

Effective regional analgesia is associated with less marked postoperative decreases in vital capacity and functional residual capacity (FRC) and appears to be superior to parenteral narcotic analgesia in this regard.[100] The supine position is accompanied by the closure of small airways in dependent areas of the lung, ventilation-perfusion mismatch, an increased alveolar-arterial oxygen gradient, and hypoxemia. Small airway closure occurs at higher lung volumes in older persons, with the result that these adverse effects are more prominent. Simply changing from the supine position to the sitting position increases FRC and improves gas exchange in patients who have undergone abdominal procedures [see Figure 6].[103] For this reason, early resumption of physical activity must be encouraged, with appropriate assistance and analgesia provided.

Incentive spirometers, breathing exercises, and intermittent positive-pressure breathing are of some benefit in reducing pulmonary complications after upper abdominal operations and may help shorten the hospital stay.[104,105] These aids are probably most valuable when used on a regular and frequent basis by patients who are at high risk for pulmonary complications. Supplemental oxygen should be routinely provided to elderly patients who have undergone abdominal or thoracic procedures for a period of several days or until physical mobility is restored—that is, until FRC

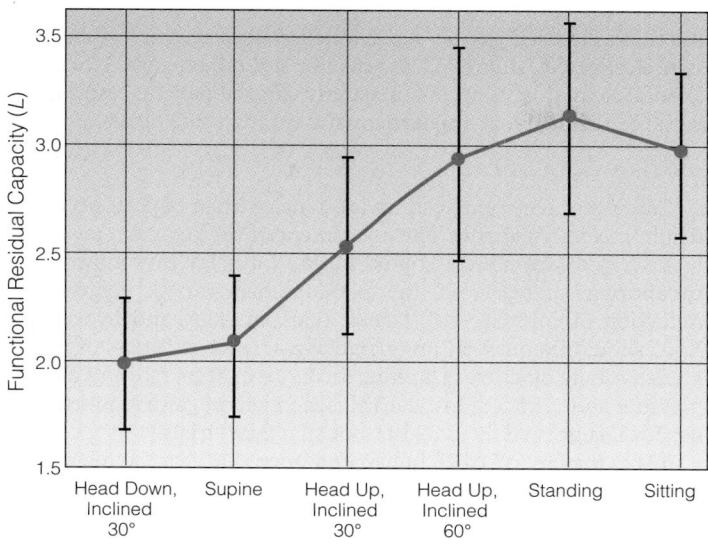

Figure 6 **Shown is the functional reserve capacity (FRC) in selected body positions.**[103] **Significant improvements in FRC are noted as the patient approaches the upright position.**

is close to preoperative values, ventilation and perfusion are better matched, and oxygen delivery is more reliable. Studies in which patients undergoing major elective procedures received an inspired oxygen fraction of either 80% or 30% during operation and for 2 hours afterward found that both the incidence of postoperative nausea and vomiting and that of SSI were lower in those receiving the higher fraction.[106,107]

RENAL FUNCTION AND FLUID AND ELECTROLYTE MANAGEMENT

A 1999 analysis of postoperative deaths in elderly patients in the United Kingdom identified poor fluid and electrolyte management as an important contributor.[4] Inadequate monitoring and documentation were common, and the predisposition of elderly patients to fluid and electrolyte imbalances and their clinical importance was not well recognized. Elderly patients are less able to restore and maintain acid-base, fluid, and electrolyte homeostasis during surgical illness. Compensatory mechanisms that can be relied on in younger patients function less rapidly in older ones. Renal handling of salt and water is less efficient, the physiology of aldosterone and vasopressin is altered, and renal and other mechanisms of acid-base regulation are more limited. As a result, elderly patients are less able to maintain the integrity of the extracellular space and other fluid compartments when challenged. Careful management, based on an understanding of physiologic mechanisms, is necessary if extreme abnormalities of fluid, electrolyte, and acid-base status are to be avoided.

The minimum requirement for water is increased in older patients as a result of increased insensible losses through thinned skin and impairment of the concentrating ability of the kidneys. Thirst is an important response to fluid deprivation, but it is known to be diminished in older persons.[108] In one study, thirst after a 24-hour period of water deprivation was less in healthy elderly men (67 to 75 years of age) than in younger patients (20 to 31 years of age) despite higher circulating vasopressin levels and higher plasma osmolality; urine osmolality was lower in the first group as well.[109] Hypothalamic responsiveness to osmotic signals appears to increase with age, as manifested by increased release of

vasopressin from the posterior pituitary.[110] Unlike the response to osmotic signals, however, the vasopressin response to volume-pressure changes is blunted in elderly persons. Renin responses to sodium restriction and postural changes are diminished in older patients, and circulating aldosterone levels are decreased as a result of diminished adrenal sensitivity to both renin-angiotensin and local sodium-potassium signals.[111]

Renal blood flow decreases progressively with advancing age, and the glomerular filtration rate (GFR) falls after the fifth or sixth decade. The ability of older persons to conserve or excrete water or solute is further reduced by the diminished efficiency of tubular processes, which is a result of decreased osmotic stratification in the medulla and decreased responsiveness to vasopressin.[112] One study found that in response to 12 hours of water deprivation, healthy young patients demonstrated a marked decrease in urine flow and a moderate increase in urine osmolality, whereas healthy elderly patients exhibited no decrease in urine flow or urine osmolality.[113] Sodium conservation is similarly impaired: the half-time to the achievement of sodium equilibrium in the face of sodium restriction is significantly longer in healthy individuals older than 60 years than in younger individuals.[114] Thus, inefficient renal conservation of salt and water exacerbates hypovolemic states in the elderly patient, and the onset of oliguria may be delayed.

A fall in the GFR also accounts for the decreased ability of the kidneys in elderly persons to excrete an acute load of salt or water, predisposing to extracellular fluid volume expansion.[115] Hyponatremia coupled with water intoxication is a serious disorder in older persons, presenting as anorexia, weakness, lethargy, delirium, and, if severe, seizures or coma. Elderly persons are prone to excessive secretion of antidiuretic hormone (ADH), particularly during the stress of surgical illness; this excessive ADH secretion is accompanied by extracellular fluid expansion, hyponatremia, and inappropriately concentrated (i.e., less than maximally dilute) urine despite normal renal function.[115]

Although the pH of body fluids is normally only slightly affected by age, the efficiency of acid-base homeostasis is decreased in elderly persons.[112] For example, persons 72 to 93 years of age take twice as long to eliminate an acid load as persons 17 to 35 years of age do.[116] Maintenance of normal pH depends on chemical buffer systems in body fluids, alterations in ventilation and elimination of carbon dioxide, and renal excretion of excess acid or base. The slight decreases in extracellular volume and in bicarbonate concentration that occur with advancing age may limit the capacity of rapid chemical buffering systems. Similarly, decreased plasma volume and lean body mass and bone demineralization decrease the availability of slower buffers (e.g., plasma and intracellular proteins and hydroxyapatite).[112] Bicarbonate buffering depends on the rapid elimination of carbon dioxide by the lungs. Neither arterial carbon dioxide tension (P_aCO_2) nor minute ventilation changes with age: increased physiologic dead space is compensated for by decreases in metabolic rate and carbon dioxide production. Ventilatory responses to hypercapnia are significantly diminished in healthy elderly persons[117]; however, because ventilation is increased and eucapnia maintained during exercise in older persons,[118] physiologic pH buffering by respiratory mechanisms probably is not limited during acute illness except perhaps in the face of a very large acid load.

The progressive decline in renal function that occurs with advancing age has been well described[119] and appears to be more consistent than changes in other organ systems [*see Table 1*]. Because of predictable decreases in skeletal muscle mass—and therefore in creatinine production—the serum creatinine concentration is likely to remain within the laboratory normal range despite the substantial concurrent decreases in GFR [see Figure 7]. Increased serum creatinine concentrations reflect a marked impairment of renal function. Creatinine clearance can be estimated from the assumptions that it is 100 ml/min at age 40 years and declines by 1 ml/min each subsequent year. Another approach to estimating this value is based on age, gender, and serum creatinine level: for males, creatinine clearance in ml/min = [(140 − age in years) × weight in kg] ÷ (72 × serum creatinine in mg/dl); for females, the result is multiplied by 0.85.[120] Creatinine clearance is most reliably assessed by determining creatinine clearance from 24-hour urine creatinine and serum creatinine concentration.

Nonsteroidal anti-inflammatory drugs (NSAIDs) have a number of potentially detrimental effects on the kidneys of older patients.[121] Inhibition of cyclooxygenase (COX)-catalyzed prostaglandin production by NSAIDs may allow unopposed vasoconstriction and marked decreases in renal blood flow and GFR in hypovolemic states, which may result in acute renal failure. In addition, NSAIDs potentiate hyponatremia and hyperkalemia through their effects on the renin-angiotensin-aldosterone system and may cause acute interstitial nephritis. Selective inhibition of the COX-2 isoform is associated with the therapeutic effects of NSAIDs. However, COX-2 is present in the kidney, and selective COX-2 inhibitors have effects on renal function that resemble those of nonselective NSAIDs.[122] Both selective and nonselective NSAIDs should be used with caution in elderly surgical patients, especially with preexisting renal impairment and during acute illness.

CARDIOVASCULAR CARE

Cardiovascular complications are a major cause of postoperative death in elderly patients. The assessment of cardiac risk previously described (see above) should be the basis for preventive and monitoring strategies in the perioperative period. Aggressive reduction of coronary risk factors (e.g., smoking and hypertension) should be pursued preoperatively. The effectiveness of perioperative beta blockers in limiting increases in heart rate and blood pressure and reducing myocardial ischemia and cardiac mortality has been suggested in some but not all clinical trials.[19,123]

It is in the first 48 to 96 hours after operation that the most significant shifts in fluid between body compartments occur, the onset of congestive heart failure is most frequent, and the hemodynamic abnormalities contributing to myocardial ischemia are most readily identified and treated. When invasive hemodynamic monitoring has been initiated in the OR, consideration should be given to continuing it during this period. In studies of patients of varying ages, myocardial infarction and reinfarction have tended to occur in the early postoperative period, often painlessly. Continuous ECG monitoring in the postoperative period may be a sensitive method for detecting myocardial ischemia and determining whether intensive therapy is needed. Many studies suggest the need for frequent clinical assessment and continuous ECG monitoring in elderly patients who are at high risk for cardiac complications (with respect to patient-, diagnosis-, and procedure-related factors) for at least 3 days postoperatively and possibly longer.

MANAGEMENT OF PAIN

Effective analgesia plays a critical role in allowing early resumption of physical activity, increasing lung volumes, and improving respiratory gas exchange after operation. In addition, postoperative pain is itself a stimulus to the elaboration of stress hormones and stress responses. Activation of the sympathoadrenal axis and other mediators results in increases in overall metabolic demand and in myocardial work. These effects serve no beneficial purpose in the postoperative patient and are detrimental from a physiologic perspective, quite apart from the fundamental clinical goal of preventing or relieving suffering.

Alternatives in the management of postoperative pain are discussed in detail elsewhere [see 10 Postoperative Pain]. Developments in anesthetic techniques, minimally invasive surgery, and perioperative care allow major procedures to be carried out with a very limited postoperative stress response, minimal pain, decreased organ dysfunction and morbidity, very brief periods of starvation and immobility, and early recovery.[124] Continuous blockade of neural signals from the operative site for 24 to 48 hours, often with epidural anesthesia, minimizes the stress response to surgery, reducing morbidity substantially and all-cause mortality by one third.[125] When such techniques are not available or applicable, patient-controlled analgesia may be appropriate for elderly patients who understand and are able to self-administer analgesic medication (usually intravenously).

Of note in elderly patients is the reported CNS stimulation induced by multiple doses of meperidine, which is attributed to accumulation of the metabolite normeperidine; meperidine should therefore be used with caution in these patients. The volume of distribution of morphine is smaller in the elderly patient, plasma and tissue drug levels are greater for a fixed dose, and the

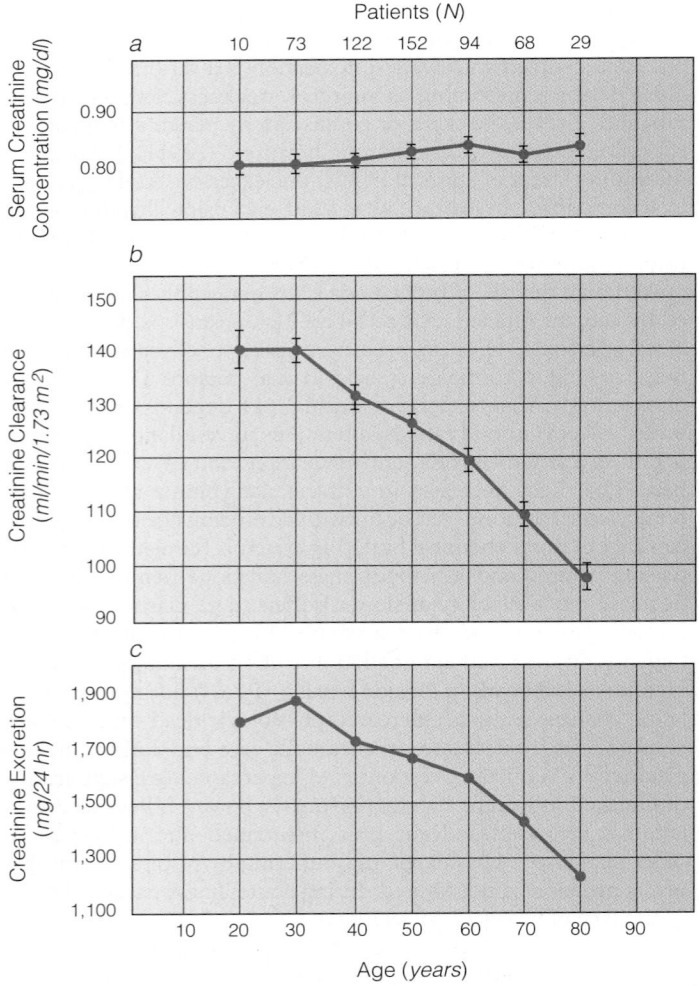

Figure 7 **Illustrated are cross-sectional differences in serum creatinine concentration, creatinine clearance, and creatinine excretion.**[246]

Table 6 Stratification of Modified Older Americans Research Survey ADLs and IADLs in Canadian Study of Health and Aging [251]

Basic Self-Care (Scale 1)	Intermediate Self-Care (Scale 2)	Complex Self-Management (Scale 3)
Toileting (ADL) Dressing (ADL) Eating (ADL) Transferring (ADL) Grooming (ADL)	Bathing (ADL) Walking (ADL) Housework (IADL) Meal preparation (IADL) Shopping (IADL) Walking outside (IADL)	Handling money (IADL) Phone use (IADL) Self-medicating (IADL)

ADL—activity of daily living IADL—instrumental ADL
Each item is scored as follows: 2—task performed without help; 1—task performed with some help; 0—task not performed. Valid for "self-report" and family or proxy report.

drug disappears more slowly from CSF; these differences would account for the more marked respiratory depression and other CNS effects observed in older patients. Plasma morphine concentration and morphine clearance also depend on renal function.

Age-related changes in pharmacokinetics and pharmacodynamics are relevant also to the use of fentanyl, sufentanil, and alfentanil.[126] Elderly patients reportedly obtain greater relief of pain from constant narcotic doses and show more marked CNS depression at given blood levels of benzodiazepines than younger patients do. Parenteral administration of narcotics can be associated with profound arterial oxygen desaturation, particularly in older patients and particularly during sleep, and may not provide optimal relief of pain.[127,128]

NSAIDs have been used in combination with narcotics and other analgesics in the management of postoperative pain. Such agents should be used with caution in elderly surgical patients.

MAINTENANCE OF FUNCTION

The goal of postoperative care is maximum function. Achievement of optimal functional level depends on three principal areas—mobility, continence, and cognition—and on how these areas are integrated with the six basic ADLs during hospitalization [*see Table 6 and Sidebar* Achievement of Optimal Functional Level].

Each patient should have a program designed to enhance independence in performing ADLs at every stage of recovery. Occasionally, postoperative ADL function may exceed preoperative ADL function, either because the operation has direct effects on function or because the patient had been unnecessarily limited (by self, family, or caregivers) preoperatively. All stages of step-down care must be individually tailored and modified when medical conditions are present that might inhibit progress.

Achievement of Optimal Functional Level

Optimal functional level is the goal of all diagnostics, therapeutics, and management in the elderly patient. According to a 1988 statement by the American College of Physicians, "maintenance of the patient's functional well-being is a fundamental goal of medical practice. Assessment of the impact of illness on physical, mental, and psychosocial functioning is an essential element of clinical diagnosis, a major determinant of therapeutic choices, a measure of their efficacy, and a guide in the planning of long-term care for the dependent elderly."[235]

Functional level assessment is intrinsic to geriatric care and should be practiced throughout the perioperative period to predict rehabilitation potential, to estimate biologic reserve, to follow progress, to signal complications, to identify appropriate social supports at discharge, and to ensure discharge. Functional level assessment is known to improve diagnostic and therapeutic outcomes.[236] Recognition of functional impairment leads to identification of previously undiagnosed conditions that may be treatable preoperatively or managed perioperatively. Another justification for functional level assessment is that disease states do not correlate as well with severity of impairment in elderly patients as they do in younger adults, even when clinical judgment has provided a reliable estimate of degree of aging and all disease states are known.[237,238]

The surgical literature reflects a growing awareness of functional outcomes—both specific outcomes related to pathology and surgery and general outcomes related to the patient's day-to-day activities and quality of life.[239-244]

For assessment of functional level, surgeons need fast, simple tools suitable for all stages of management (preoperative, perioperative, and postoperative) that correlate well with measures of cardiovascular, pulmonary, and renal function and that identify patients who will achieve maximum postoperative function and who need rehabilitation or other community supports at discharge. Unfortunately, no such tool exists; surgeons will probably have to develop one themselves. In the meantime, the ASA scale and other biologic assessments can be complemented with functional assessments borrowed from the medical, psychiatric, and social science literatures.

There are actually hundreds of functional assessment tools, some of which have been validated for use in the geriatric population and some of which were specifically developed for elderly patients. These tools have various goals, ranging from predicting social supports to monitoring deterioration. Most of them address one or more of the following areas: mobility, falls and balance, continence, cognition, emotional and affective status, nutrition, homeostasis, basic ADLs, instrumental ADLs, environment, and social supports. The various functional level scales cover items ranging from disability, handicap, and incapacity to independence and ranging from ability to self-development and self-realization.

In selecting functional measures, preoperative, perioperative, and postoperative surgical teams may focus on the following domains: basic ADLs (e.g., toilet and nutrition); instrumental ADL (e.g., banking, shopping for and preparing meals, and using public transportation); cognitive function (including memory and language); mood (primarily to validate data available in other domains); and quality of life from the patient's viewpoint [*see Table 4*].

It is worth remembering that assessments of basic and instrumental ADLs and cognition do not explain why a particular function is impaired but simply describe how well a patient is functioning at a given time. Any functional impairment is a signal that further assessment to identify correctable pathologic conditions is indicated. When areas of compromised function have been identified before an elective procedure, it may be wise to request a period of rehabilitation to maximize functional level before admission. For example, continence training may be provided by a community health nurse, and gait and mobility training may be provided by a geriatric physiotherapist. Complementary assessments by the family physician, a psychiatrist, or a geriatrician may help identify ways of achieving maximal function preoperatively.

In general, it is not expected that a preoperative functional impairment will be improved postoperatively unless the surgical intervention was specifically designed to address the impairment. For example, if mobility is compromised by an inguinal hernia, it is reasonable to expect the patient to resume his or her own banking after herniorrhaphy.

The nursing team should be made aware of the patient's functional deficits in the OR, in recovery, and in the ward afterward. To some degree, they may be able to compensate for disability in the surgical environment and may even prevent additional disability. For example, a patient who is encouraged to wear glasses and a hearing aid in recovery is more cooperative and better oriented and is ready to step down to the ward. Nurses who compensate for patient deafness by ensuring that the patient sees their lips when they speak and by speaking slowly and clearly can report patient level of consciousness more reliably.[78]

Physical Function and Early Mobility

Mobility and appropriate sensory stimulation should be maximized before and after operation. Even healthy elderly patients have lost a good deal of their muscle strength. The continued loss of strength that accompanies immobility may have marked functional consequences. Elderly patients are at increased risk for pulmonary complications after operation, and early mobilization helps minimize their incidence [see Table 7]. Cardiovascular deconditioning occurs regardless of age: the decrease in cardiac output on standing may be considerable after a period of prolonged bed rest and may be accompanied by orthostatic hypotension and tachycardia. Maximum oxygen consumption, cardiac output, and stroke volume at maximum exercise are all lower after prolonged immobilization. Bed rest results in a significant decrease in tissue sensitivity to insulin, exaggerating age-related glucose intolerance. Bed rest is also associated with an increased incidence of DVT. Constipation and fecal impaction are frequent in immobilized patients as a result of alterations in GI motility (related to inactivity and medications), lack of privacy, and the use of bedpans. Pressure ulcers are well-recognized complications of immobility to which elderly patients are predisposed because of diminished subcutaneous fat and decreased skin elasticity.

Expectations about postoperative mobilization, its importance, and the assistance that will be provided should be communicated preoperatively to patients and their families. Postoperatively, effective pain management is essential. Beginning in the immediate postoperative period, full passive range-of-motion exercises of all joints should be undertaken daily, even after the patient is able to sit up in a chair and walk a short distance in the corridor. These interventions not only conserve the patient's capacity for mobility but also help prevent pressure ulcers. The involvement of a phys-

iotherapist is almost invariably required. In addition to passive range-of-motion exercises, active resistance exercises appear feasible for many acutely ill, hospitalized, older patients.[129]

Once awake, the patient who requires glasses or a hearing aid should wear them at all times. As soon as the patient is able to sit in a chair, he or she should wear shoes, preferably solid, comfortable jogging shoes with Velcro closures. The patient should wear regular clothes, preferably a jogging suit, as soon as possible. A walker, a cane, or a wheelchair should be kept at the bedside and used as the physiotherapist advises. The patient should be encouraged to walk 100 m each day. Every effort should be made to minimize I.V. lines, drains, catheters, and other forms of physical restraint. If such devices must be employed, they should not be allowed to prevent planned activities, though they may necessitate accompaniment and assistance. Periods of activity should be systematically alternated with rest periods. The primary nurse is the caregiver best equipped to ensure that this routine is implemented.

These rehabilitation and maintenance efforts must be carried out in the surgical ward. There is no point to sending an elderly person to the physiotherapy/occupational therapy department: the patient will not learn to integrate the new skills into a daily routine. Older persons must work like athletes in the postoperative period. A training effect can be noted in skeletal muscle and in the cardiovascular and pulmonary systems. Accordingly, elderly patients deserve continual encouragement.

Aggressive rehabilitation instituted early will certainly lead to better function at discharge. However, a general surgical ward that properly serves elderly patients may also show a higher incidence of hip fracture and minor injuries. These risks must be accepted by staff, patients, and family.

Cognitive Function

In a dark, soundless, weightless chamber without aural, visual, sensory, or vestibular cues, young, fit adults are known to have a high incidence of transitory psychosis, presumably caused by the intense isolation and lack of stimulation. The elderly hospitalized patient who is medicated, deprived of glasses or a hearing aid, and restrained in a dimly lit room may exhibit a similar response, provoked by isolation and lack of cueing. The sensory deprivation characteristic of even brief confinement in a typical hospital setting may be accompanied by changes in affect, delirium, and perceptual distortions in the elderly patient. All staff members who have contact with older patients, including housekeeping personnel and technicians, should continually provide them with orienting cues, such as the weather, the season, the day of the week, the name of the hospital, and their own name and function. Many of the interventions described in the discussions of physical function, continence, and ADLs have the added advantage of increasing the amount of appropriate sensory stimulation provided to the patient, thereby reducing the incidence of delirium and contributing to improved cognition.

As discussed [see Risk Assessment and Cognitive Assessment, above], early postoperative delirium is relatively common in elderly patients and is best identified by means of an instrument such as the MMSE [see Table 3], especially if a preoperative baseline assessment is available. Postoperative delirium is characterized by an acute onset of fluctuating level of consciousness, shortened attention span, disorientation, cognitive impairment, visual hallucinations, disturbances in the sleep-wake cycle, and psychomotor changes, which may include agitation, retardation, or both. Delirium is much more common in those who have underlying dementia or undergo prolonged procedures. The diagnosis implies an underlying organic cause that must be actively sought and

Table 7 Potential Complications of Immobility[252]

Skin	Pressure Sores
Musculoskeletal	Muscular deconditioning and atrophy Contractures Bone loss (osteoporosis)
Cardiovascular	Deconditioning Decreased plasma volume Orthostatic hypotension Venous thrombosis, embolism
Pulmonary	Decreased ventilation Atelectasis Aspiration pneumonia
Gastrointestinal	Anorexia Constipation Fecal impaction, incontinence
Genitourinary	Urinary infection Urinary retention Bladder calculi Incontinence
Metabolic	Negative nitrogen balance Impaired glucose tolerance Altered drug pharmacokinetics
Psychological	Sensory deprivation Dementia, delirium Depression

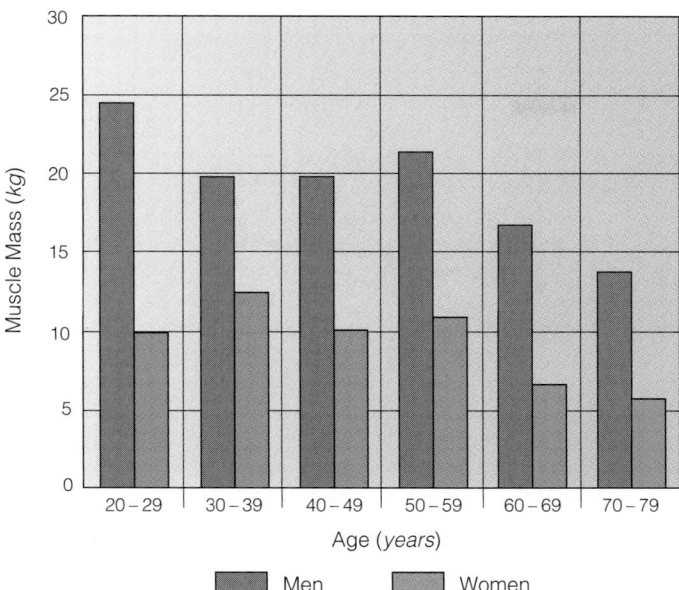

Figure 8 **A substantial portion of the muscle mass present in young adulthood is lost by 70 years of age. Age-related declines in muscle strength have been documented as well.**[150]

corrected. Delirium may be the first manifestation of a postoperative complication such as infection (e.g., pneumonia, SSI, or urinary tract infection) or hypoxemia (e.g., that resulting from congestive heart failure or pulmonary embolism). Medications must be reviewed, especially sedatives, narcotics, and agents with anticholinergic properties. Electrolyte disturbances (especially hyponatremia) are common contributors to delirium. Physical examination should look for potential sources of infection, signs of cardiorespiratory or other organ dysfunction, and focal neurologic deficits. Hematologic tests, blood chemistry, and oxygen saturation or blood gas analysis should be routinely ordered. Chest x-ray, other imaging, ECG, and other investigations should be undertaken as indicated.

Delirious patients require close supervision to ensure that they do not harm themselves. Reassurance and reorientation provided by someone familiar, especially a family member, in a calm, well-lit environment is often the most powerful intervention. If this is not fully effective and the patient is compromising his or her medical care, then judicious use of risperidone or other medications may be necessary. In a 1999 study of elderly general medical patients, a multicomponent intervention strategy was shown to be effective in reducing the incidence of delirium.[130] The strategy targeted the risk factors of cognitive impairment (orientation), sleep deprivation, immobility, hearing impairment, and dehydration.

Delirium, dementia, and other cognitive deficits are not normal consequences of aging. Their presence is an indication for diagnostic and therapeutic intervention.

Continence

Efforts to help the older patient achieve and maintain continence should begin preoperatively and should be reestablished postoperatively as soon as possible. Systematic toileting (i.e., every 2 hours) should be initiated by the primary nurse. Catheters should be removed as soon as possible: they are sources of infection, impair mobility, and should not be relied on for monitoring of input and output. Nurses should respond promptly to patient requests for toileting. In the postoperative period, narcotics and

immobility often contribute to urinary retention. If urinary incontinence recurs or persists, the postvoid residual volume should be assessed. If the volume is less than 100 ml, the toileting interval should be shortened until continence is achieved, then lengthened. If the volume is 100 ml or greater, potential causes of an acontractile bladder or obstruction should be sought. Stool incontinence (with or without diarrhea) should be considered the result of impaction until proved otherwise, even if there is no fecalith palpable on digital examination. A step-down program for encopresis should be started aggressively with osmotic agents (e.g., lactulose) and bulking agents, followed by enemas and stool softeners, with suppositories as needed; toileting should be performed 1 hour after each meal, as well as in response to urge. A behavioral program should be developed with the patient, who should participate in maintaining the toileting schedule and recording performance.

It is worth remembering that incontinence is never a normal consequence of aging. In every case, it should be explained by a specific diagnosis, managed, and treated.

Activities of Daily Living

Patients should take on the task of grooming and dressing themselves entirely (including putting on aids and prostheses) as soon as they are able. Self-medication should be introduced gradually, starting as soon as possible after recovery, and should be reviewed twice daily by the nursing staff. Dosette boxes and calendars are useful. Unit-dose pharmacy management has no place in geriatric care because it systematically teaches dependence.

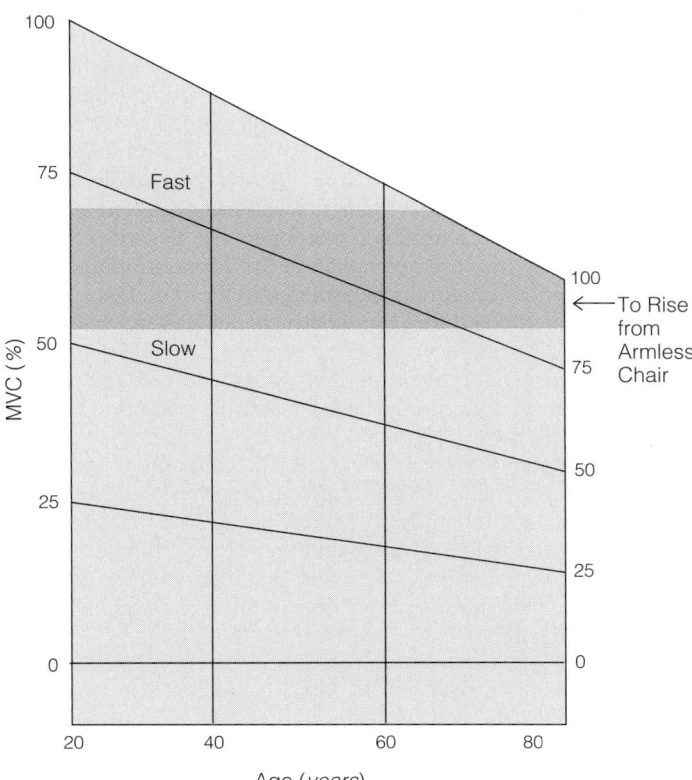

Figure 9 **Depicted is the effect of age on muscle strength in relation to the strength required to rise from a low, armless chair.**[132] **An elderly person may well be close to the strength threshold even before the onset of an acute illness. (MVC— maximal voluntary contraction)**

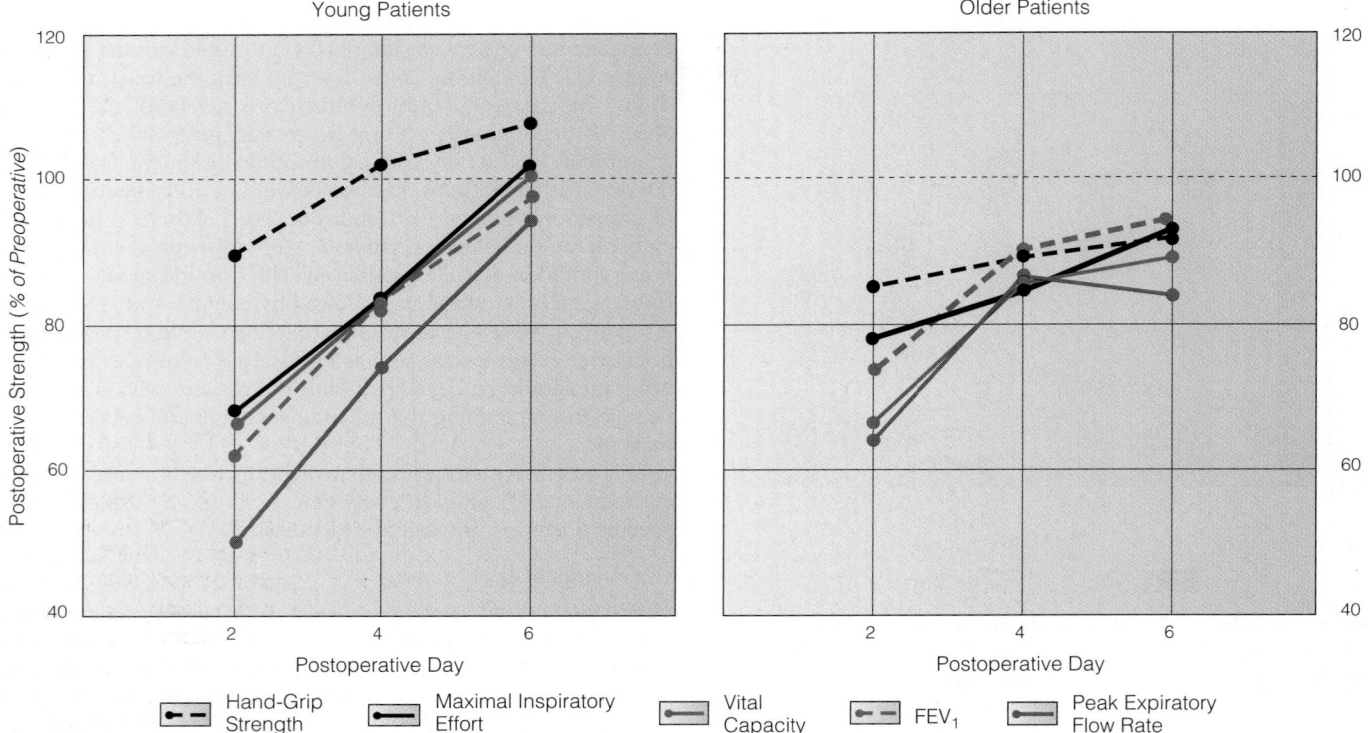

Figure 10 **Illustrated is the recovery of postoperative strength (assessed with respect to five variables) in younger and older patients.**[133]

The independence of the hospitalized elderly patient is continually undermined. To begin with, insisting on patient independence takes extra nursing time: it is quicker and easier to do things for patients than it is to instruct them. In addition, patients themselves may sabotage nurses' efforts to foster independence, arguing that because they are old and sick they should not be expected to do much for themselves. Consequently, nurses who encourage self-care sometimes have patients who feel neglected and who may even become resentful and uncooperative; in some cases, an unhappy family may even complain to the administration.

Families are not naturally helpful in mobilization. Instead, they often insist on doing things for geriatric patients even while scolding them for not doing more for themselves. Families must be taught by nurses and physiotherapists exactly how elderly persons are to get out of a chair and how far and how often they are to walk.

Persistent stepwise encouragement to regain autonomy is perhaps the most beneficial service nurses can offer elderly surgical patients in the postoperative period. A word from the surgeon to the patient and the family may gain the nurse and physiotherapist the patient's cooperation. If behavioral problems persist, a behaviorist, a psychiatrist, a geriatrician, or the patient's family physician should be consulted.

Summary

The surgeon should not make the mistake of assuming that paying attention to the patient's functional level in basic ADLs is the responsibility solely of the rehabilitation or convalescent unit. Orientation, mobility, and ADLs all are significantly and systematically compromised in the traditional surgical ward in just a few days. Once function is lost, even long-term rehabilitation cannot ensure that it will be recaptured. Immobility, inadequate nutrition, and sensory deprivation and other features of the usual acute

care hospital environment will contribute to a "cascade to dependency" in vulnerable elderly patients unless actively addressed by a multidisciplinary clinical team.[131]

Other patient skills to be demonstrated before discharge should match the environment to which the patient is going. Occupational and physical therapists should routinely follow geriatric surgical patients and integrate their management strategies with those of the nursing staff. Elderly patients are less likely than younger patients to integrate the skills demonstrated during rehabilitation in a traditional occupational/physical therapy work area or gymnasium into the performance of ADLs on the ward and, later, at home. Home visits by the occupational and physical therapists are often useful components of assessment and rehabilitation.

NUTRITIONAL CARE

Preexisting malnutrition is relatively common in elderly persons (see above) and is exacerbated in hospital by the periods of fasting that are commonplace and by the rapid erosion of skeletal muscle that accompanies the stress of major surgery and acute surgical illness. Such losses of muscle protein may be uniquely detrimental in elderly patients. Lean body mass and body cell mass both decrease considerably with normal aging, largely because of declining muscle mass: a loss of 40% of muscle mass or more is typical between young adulthood and the age of 80 years and is accompanied by a comparable decrease in strength [*see Figure 8*]. For example, the average 80-year-old woman is at the threshold of quadriceps strength necessary to rise from a low, armless chair [*see Figure 9*].[132] Thus, during prolonged or severe illness, the rapid erosion of muscle mass may reduce an elderly patient's muscle strength below that required for moving about in bed, sitting, and coughing effectively. Moreover, recovery of strength is impaired in older surgical patients compared with younger patients [*see Figure 10*].[133]

The typical diets followed by older persons may provide ade-

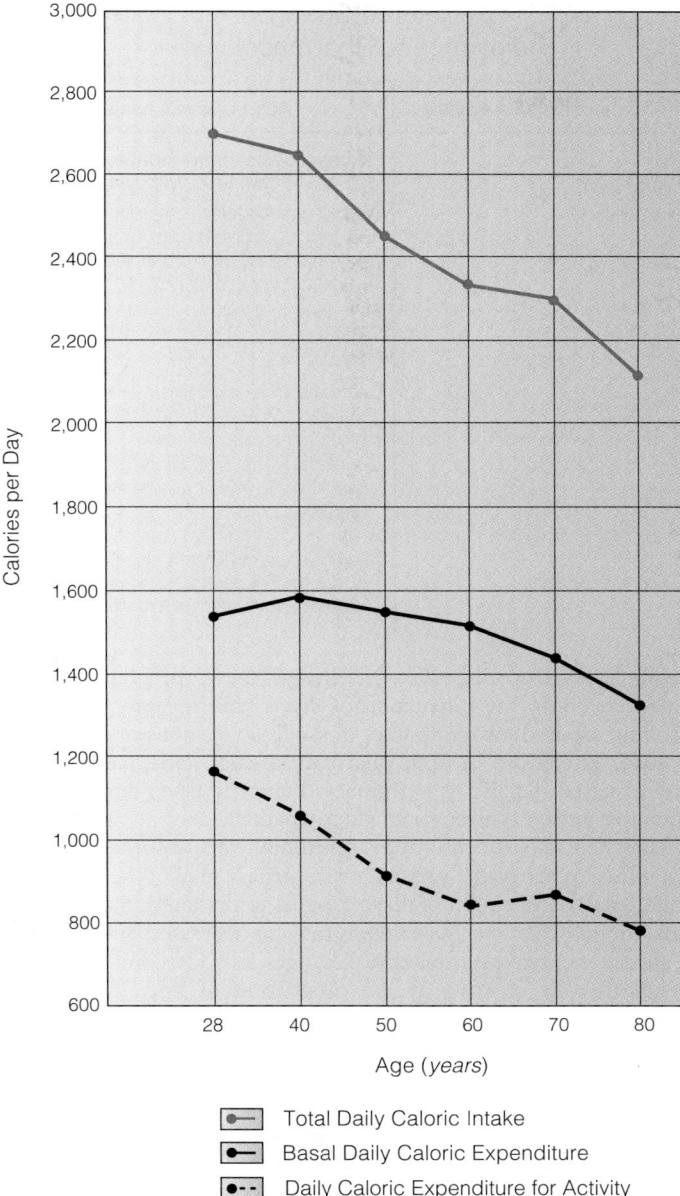

Total Daily Caloric Intake
Basal Daily Caloric Expenditure
Daily Caloric Expenditure for Activity

Figure 11 **Depicted are the daily intake and expenditure of calories in normal males of various age groups.**[139]

quate vitamins and trace minerals in the absence of stress, though it is worth remembering that there is a general lack of information about specific requirements in older persons. Body stores may be limited, however, and deficiencies may arise during illness. For example, plasma zinc concentration decreases after injury and other stresses, partly as a result of increased urinary losses. Zinc deficiency has been associated with impaired wound healing and depressed immune function. Skeletal muscle holds the largest store of zinc. The decrease in muscle bulk in the elderly persons, coupled with the inadequate zinc intake and impaired absorption reported in this age group, suggests that zinc supplementation may play an important role in the nutritional support of these patients. Decreased serum levels of a number of vitamins have been observed after burn injury, and increased requirements for several vitamins and minerals that may affect immune function, wound healing, and antioxidant defenses have been demonstrat-

ed during acute stress states.[134] Daily supplementation of the diets of healthy elderly persons with physiologic amounts of various vitamins and trace elements has been shown to enhance immune function and reduce the rate of clinical infection.[56] Early vitamin and trace element supplementation (i.e., within the first 24 to 48 hours) should be considered in all elderly patients, particularly in nonelective settings.

Volitional food intake is often inadequate in hospitalized elderly patients. Fortified meals and between-meal snacks have been shown to improve elderly patients' energy and protein intake.[135] Early provision of nutritional supplements or enteral or parenteral support should be considered in elderly patients who are not consuming sufficient nutrients in the form of a regular diet. Some, but not all, studies have suggested that protein-calorie supplementation has a beneficial effect on clinical outcomes after hip fracture.[136-138] Improvements in hospital stay, complications, and rehabilitation appear to be most apparent in malnourished patients, though methodologic limitations in published trials preclude definitive conclusions. Oral supplements are usually well tolerated and do not necessarily lead to a decrease in volitional intake.

Enteral feeding should be initiated promptly in any elderly patient whose voluntary intake is not adequate. Parenteral feeding can be used alone or as an adjunct when enteral feeding is being established or when prescribed nutrients cannot be fully administered via the enteral route. In healthy persons, energy intake and expenditure tend to decrease with advancing age as a result of diminished metabolic body size (i.e., body cell mass) and reduced activity [*see Figure 11*].[139] These changes must be considered in estimating the number of calories to be provided to elderly surgical patients. Protein intake should normally be 1 to 2 g/kg/day, depending on the severity of the primary illness and the nature of the associated disease states. Provision of nutritional support via enteral and parenteral routes is discussed in detail elsewhere [*see 137 Nutritional Support*].

Whereas the need for nutritional support appears to be greater in elderly patients, such support may be less efficacious and less well tolerated because of the combined influences of aging and acute illness on intermediary metabolism. Glucose tolerance decreases with normal aging, and enteral or parenteral feeding may result in marked hyperglycemia, particularly when coupled with the insulin resistance that accompanies trauma and critical illness.[140] Additionally, insulin responses to glucose loads are markedly diminished in older persons after injury [*see Figure 12*]. Decreased serum growth hormone and insulinlike growth factor–1 (IGF-1) responses to feeding have also been described in older trauma patients.[141,142] Renal clearance of glucose is normally an important defense against hyperglycemia; however, a reduced GFR and an increased renal threshold for glucose make elderly patients even more prone to hyperglycemia. Uncontrolled hyperglycemia resulting from either an enteral or a parenteral glucose load may give rise to hyperosmolar nonketotic coma, in which serum osmolarity and glucose are markedly elevated in association with a solute diuresis, dehydration, coma, and inappropriately low insulin and ketone levels. This condition is corrected by rehydration and insulin administration. In a trial involving patients admitted to a surgical ICU and given parenteral nutrition, intensive insulin therapy and control of blood glucose levels resulted in less frequent sepsis and organ dysfunction and improved survival.[143]

Even when insulin is used, hyperglycemia may limit the administration of calories in the form of glucose to the elderly patient. Fat emulsion may be used as an alternative energy source in parenteral feeding, but plasma triglyceride levels should be monitored because they tend to increase with age and because lipid clearance may be altered. Because of age-related decreases in GFR, protein loads that might be well tolerated in young patients can lead to uremia in elderly patients. Blood urea values should be monitored.

Nutritional support of the elderly patient should begin early, should take into account age-related changes in body composition, should include appropriate micronutrients, and should anticipate diminished tolerance of substrate and fluid loads.

CLINICAL PHARMACOLOGY

Use of both prescription and nonprescription drugs is heavy in the geriatric population, and a careful history of drug use must be obtained, if necessary by contacting family and pharmacist and examining the drug containers themselves. Noncompliance with drug prescriptions occurs but is probably no more frequent in elderly patients than in younger ones. Most instances of noncompliance may actually be underadherence, which can be an appropriate response to adverse drug effects. A knowledge of how aging affects clinical pharmacology is important because drugs and doses that would not normally cause toxicity in younger patients can do so in older ones.[12] Consequently, the incidence of adverse drug reactions increases substantially with age, and drug reactions are an important cause of hospital admission, morbidity, and mortality.[144-146] This increase may reflect the greater use of drugs by older patients (particularly drugs with a low therapeutic index, such as digoxin), polypharmacy and resultant interactions, the presence of multiple and more severe comorbidities in elderly patients, and aging-associated alterations in pharmacokinetics and pharmacodynamics [see Table 8].

The term pharmacokinetics refers to the absorption, distribution, protein binding, metabolism, and excretion of drugs and their

Table 8 Age-Related Changes with Potential Relevance to Pharmacology[253]

Pharmacologic Parameter	Age-Related Changes
Absorption	Decreased absorptive surface, splanchnic blood flow, and gastric acidity Altered gastrointestinal motility
Distribution	Decreased total body water, lean body mass, and serum albumin Increased body fat Altered protein binding
Metabolism	Decreased liver blood flow, enzyme activity, and enzyme inducibility
Excretion	Decreased renal blood flow, glomerular filtration rate, and tubular secretory function
Tissue sensitivity	Altered receptor number, receptor affinity, second-messenger function, and cellular and nuclear responses

metabolites (drug disposition), whereas the term pharmacodynamics refers to the interaction of drugs with receptors and the resulting desired or undesired physiologic responses (drug response). Alterations in both pharmacokinetics and pharmacodynamics are predictable to a degree and must be taken into account whenever a drug is given to an elderly patient.

Most clinically relevant drugs given orally are absorbed by passive diffusion across the very extensive surface area of the proximal small bowel. Absorption of these drugs is unimpaired in older persons, though gastric acid secretion may be decreased and the rate of gastric emptying diminished. Changes in body composition—specifically, an increase in the proportion of body fat and a decrease in the proportion of lean tissue [see Discussion, Patterns of Change in Body Composition, Organ System Function, and Integrated Responses, below]—may influence the distribution of drugs: the volume of distribution of relatively water-soluble drugs tends to decrease, and that of more fat-soluble drugs tends to increase. Altered distribution influences the elimination half-life of drugs, but it does not affect steady-state blood levels with multiple dosing if hepatic and renal drug clearances are unchanged.

Clearance of drugs primarily excreted by the kidneys declines predictably with advancing age and the concomitant decrease in GFR. Creatinine clearance is a much more reliable marker of the GFR than serum creatinine concentration, which depends on muscle mass. Drugs for which the dosage may require adjustment according to the patient's level of renal function include aminoglycosides, vancomycin, penicillins, cephalosporins, imipenem-cilastatin, metronidazole, digoxin, low-molecular-weight heparins, bisphosphonates, and procainamide. Age-related differences in the pharmacokinetics of renally excreted drugs, including the aminoglycosides, are unlikely when the creatinine clearance is greater than 80 ml/min/1.73 m². Drug levels should be monitored, particularly when drugs with a low therapeutic index are used.

Clearance of drugs by the liver depends on the delivery of the drug (i.e., on hepatic blood flow) and on the activity of biotransforming enzymes. Clearance of drugs that are metabolized relatively slowly is dependent on the function of hepatic enzymes; given that hepatic mass decreases with age, clearance of such drugs tends to be reduced.[147] Hepatic blood flow also decreases

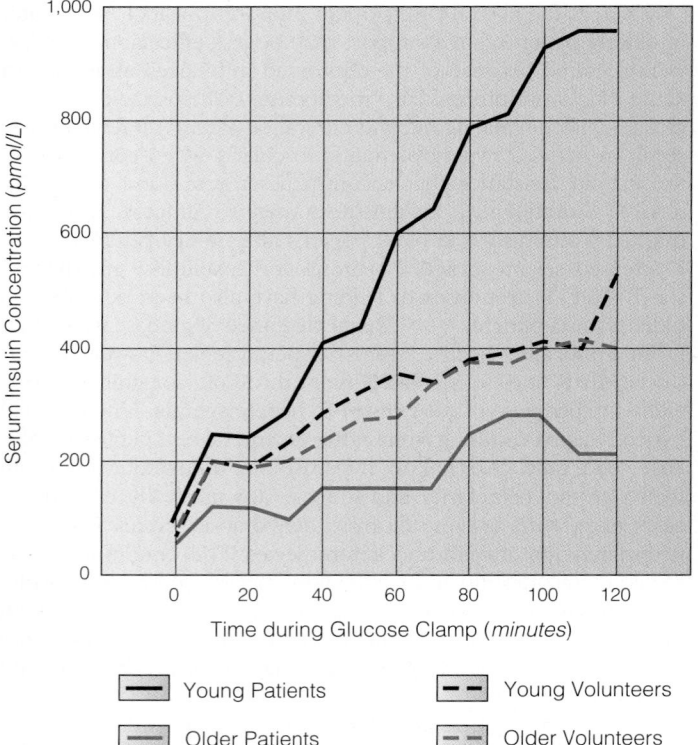

Figure 12 **Shown are serum insulin responses to glucose loading (during glucose clamp).**[247]

Legend for Figure 12:
- Young Patients
- Older Patients
- Young Volunteers
- Older Volunteers

Axis labels: Serum Insulin Concentration (*pmol/L*) vs Time during Glucose Clamp (*minutes*)

with age: it is 40% to 45% less in elderly persons than in young adults, and this decrease results in diminished flow-dependent clearance.[147] Age-related reductions in the clearance of diazepam, chlordiazepoxide, theophylline, and propranolol have been suggested on the basis of decreased hepatic biotransformation (whether dependent on blood flow or on enzyme function). Such reductions may be more pronounced in men. Plasma levels of drugs cleared in a flow-dependent fashion may be higher when hepatic blood flow is further decreased, as it is in conditions such as congestive heart failure or chronic liver disease.

The effects of age on the actions of drugs at target sites have not been extensively studied. A reduction in the sensitivity of beta-adrenergic receptors may contribute to the diminished effectiveness of sympathetic agonists in older persons. Synthesis of vitamin K–dependent clotting factors may be more strongly inhibited in older patients at a given plasma warfarin concentration.[148] Elderly persons also exhibit more marked CNS depression at given blood levels of benzodiazepines.[149]

Discussion

Patterns of Change in Body Composition, Organ System Function, and Integrated Responses

BODY COMPOSITION

Specific changes in body composition are characteristic of advancing age, though they are not inevitable. Whereas weight remains more or less stable, fat mass tends to increase and lean body mass tends to decrease.[150] The increase in total fat mass may be obscured by a reduction in subcutaneous fat and a concurrent increase in intra-abdominal fat.[151] Lean body mass comprises body cell mass—defined as the "component of body composition containing the oxygen-consuming, potassium-rich, glucose-oxidizing, work-performing tissue"[152]—and extracellular mass. Body cell mass decreases by an average of 23% in men and 25% in women from the third to the eighth decade.[150] Besides decreasing in absolute terms, body cell mass declines as a proportion of lean body mass; this decline is largely accounted for by diminished skeletal muscle mass [see Figure 8]. On average, about 40% to 45% of the muscle mass present in young adulthood is lost by the time a person reaches 70 years of age.[150] At the same time, muscle strength and function are lost as well.[153,154] Reductions in FEV_1 and maximal midexpiratory flow rate occur with advancing age; these reductions are partially attributable to a decrease in the strength of the respiratory musculature.[155] Together with decreased physical activity, changes in body composition contribute to decreased resting energy expenditure and therefore to decreased requirements for calories. Food intake decreases with aging in relation to alterations in GI physiology, endocrine function, and cytokine elaboration.[156]

The changes in body composition and muscle function appear to be at least partially determined by the level of habitual physical activity. For example, body weight and proportion of fat were constant in a cross-sectional study of lumberjacks 20 to 70 years of age, in contrast to the gradual increase in weight and body fat seen in men with sedentary occupations.[157] Another study found that the body composition of male endurance athletes 50 to 75 years of age was very similar to that of younger athletes, whereas both untrained individuals and visually matched lean older individuals had significantly higher levels of body fat.[158] One group of investigators demonstrated increased muscle strength and a modest but significant decrease in body fat in elderly men who underwent 6 weeks of training; significant increases in minute ventilation during exercise and vital capacity were also observed.[159] Another group experienced a 10% increase in lean tissue, a 17% decrease in skinfold thickness, a 4% to 5% increase in body potassium, and an apparent halting of age-related decreases in bone calcium during a 1-year physical-training program in individuals in their seventh decade.[160] Another investigator, who studied age-related muscle fiber atrophy in men 25 to 65 years of age, found that muscle fiber size and strength increased after twice-weekly exercise for 15 weeks, particularly in the older subjects.[161]

ORGAN SYSTEM FUNCTION

Aging is associated with a variety of predictable morphologic, functional, and pathologic changes in major organ systems. Such changes have been best described for cardiovascular, respiratory, and renal systems, which are also the systems most relevant to perioperative care [see Table 1].

INTEGRATED RESPONSES AND FUNCTIONS

Oxygen Transport

The earliest physiologic responses to tissue injury are directed at restoring and maintaining the perfusion of vital organs. These responses rely on rapid activation of the sympathoadrenal axis by signals from the site of injury and from baroreceptors and chemoreceptors. Blood flow to the skin and skeletal muscle is decreased by peripheral vasoconstriction, and cardiac output is redistributed to vital tissues. With advancing age, however, the efficiency of many of these critical responses is diminished, even in healthy individuals. Baroreflex sensitivity is decreased in older persons, presumably as a result of reduced arterial distensibility.[162] Vasoconstrictor responses are also reduced, probably because of alterations in autonomic neural pathways.[163] In addition, an age-associated decline in the inotropic and chronotropic effects of beta-adrenergic stimulation has been well described.[164] Thus, diminished arterial compliance, impaired vasoconstriction, altered autonomic function and sensitivity to catecholamines, and decreased baroreflex sensitivity all may limit the maintenance of cardiovascular homeostasis.

Delivery of oxygen to the tissues may be impaired in older persons at every step of the oxygen transport pathway and may be inadequate when oxygen demands are increased.[112,165] Ventilatory responses to both hypoxia and hypercapnia are diminished. The alveolar-arterial oxygen gradient increases, and arterial oxygen tension (P_aO_2) progressively declines. There is substantial variation in most cardiac variables among older individuals, reflecting aging, atherosclerosis and other diseases, and various lifestyle factors that interact and influence cardiovascular function in ways that are often difficult to disentangle.[164] In unselected individuals, cardiac output declines approximately 1% each year, beginning in the fourth decade.[112] Progressive decreases in resting stroke volume and cardiac output with increasing age have been observed in individuals without clinical evidence of cardiovascular disease, both at rest and during exercise[166,167]; in addition, older persons have had larger arteriovenous oxygen differences and increased arterial lactate concentrations. However, the older individuals in such studies may well have had clinically occult cardiovascular disease or deconditioning

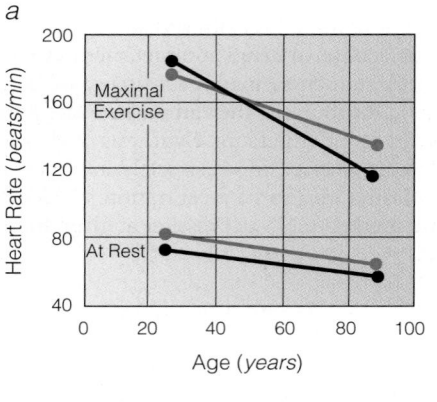
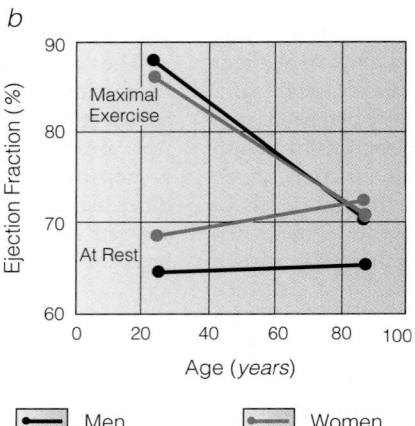
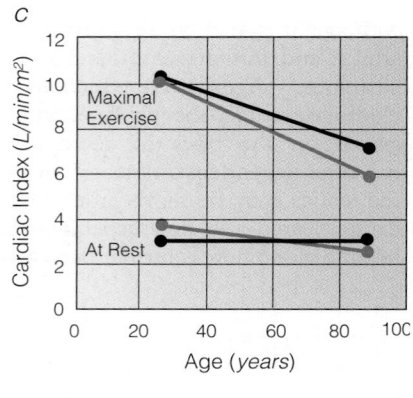

Figure 13 **Shown are linear regressions on age of (*a*) heart rate, (*b*) ejection fraction, and (*c*) cardiac index at rest and during maximal cycle ergometry in healthy, sedentary male and female volunteers who had been screened to exclude clinical hypertension and occult coronary artery disease.**[248]

resulting from long-standing limitations of physical activity (e.g., from time spent in nursing homes), and the use of invasive measurement techniques may have influenced observations.

Later studies of nonsedentary individuals who were screened with resting and stress ECG and dipyridamole-thallium scanning have demonstrated that older individuals, assessed noninvasively, maintain resting cardiac output, heart rate, stroke volume, and ejection fraction [*see Figure 13*].[164] Stiffening of the aorta and of more peripheral vessels tends to be associated with increased peripheral vascular resistance. A normal modest increase in left ventricular wall thickness with aging is exaggerated in persons with hypertension and coronary artery disease. Myocardial relaxation is typically prolonged, and early diastolic filling is slowed and delayed with advancing age.[164,168] Left ventricular end-diastolic volume at rest tends to be increased, with more rapid filling later in diastole; this tendency is associated with left atrial enlargement and an enhanced contribution to filling from atrial contraction.[169] Resting pulmonary arterial pressure and pulmonary vascular resistance increase moderately.[170]

Cardiovascular responses to exercise have been studied in detail and provide insight into the responses associated with acute surgical illness. The maximal heart rate achieved during exercise diminishes consistently with age, and maximum cardiac index tends to decline.[164] Older persons who are free of cardiovascular disease rely more on increases in stroke volume to achieve increases in their cardiac index during exercise than younger persons do.[171] Thus, end-diastolic volume index tends to increase in older persons; decreases in end-systolic volume index and increases in ejection fraction are less prominent than in young individuals [*see Figure 14*].[164,172] In one study of generally healthy persons who were not extensively screened, the likelihood of ventricular wall motion abnormalities during exercise rose consistently with age.[172] In an older study of persons with varying levels of habitual activity, the incidence of ECG abnormalities during and after maximal exercise rose with age and was much higher than the incidence at rest.[166]

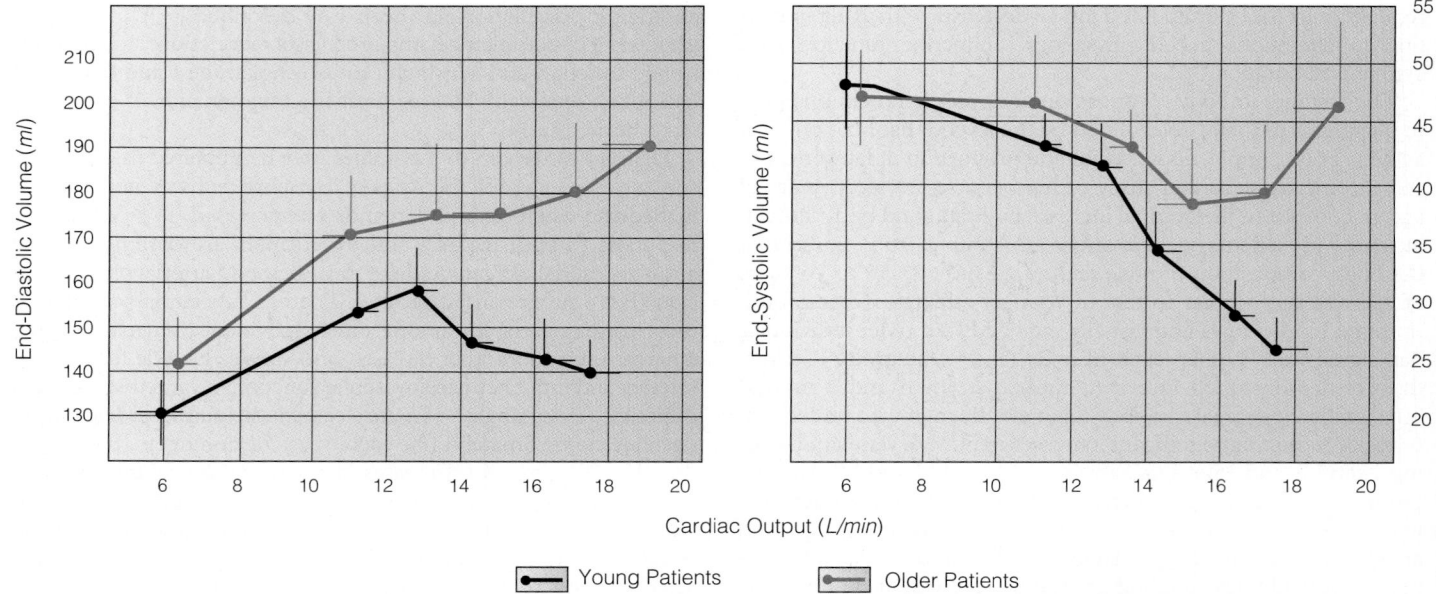

Figure 14 **Depicted are relations between end-diastolic volume, end-systolic volume, and cardiac output in young and older patients at rest and during graded upright bicycle exercise.**[249]

The response of healthy older individuals to an increase in cardiac afterload differs from that of young persons: significant left ventricular dilatation occurs, and contraction begins from a greater preload, presumably as a reflection of a diminished contractile reserve in the older persons.[173] Diminution of the inotropic, chronotropic, and arterial vasodilating effects of beta-adrenergic stimulation with advancing age may contribute to many age-related changes in cardiovascular function.[164] Isoproterenol infusion results in lesser increases in heart rate, left ventricular ejection fraction, and cardiac index in older persons than in younger ones.[174] Dobutamine augments cardiac output and stroke volume to a much lesser extent in elderly patients with decompensated congestive heart failure than in younger patients and provides no additional hemodynamic benefit at infusion rates higher than 5 mg/kg/min.[175]

Thus, older patients are predisposed to hemodynamic compromise related to tachyarrhythmias, atrial fibrillation, increased afterload, and coronary artery disease. Increased end-diastolic volume and stroke volume are compensatory mechanisms that maintain cardiac output in the face of other limitations, and appropriate filling volumes must be achieved. Inotropic drugs may be less beneficial in elderly patients, and agents that are non-vasoconstricting (e.g., dobutamine) or have nonadrenergic mechanisms of action (e.g., amrinone) may be useful. Agents that reduce afterload (e.g., angiotensin-converting enzyme inhibitors) may also play a greater role in older patients. Elderly patients are less able to increase oxygen delivery in the face of increased demand and, with a high prevalence of coronary artery disease, are at risk for myocardial ischemia if demands are excessive. It is probably not appropriate to arbitrarily set supranormal goals for cardiac index and oxygen delivery in elderly patients. In addition, every effort must be made to minimize unnecessary stresses that increase metabolic demands, such as hypothermia, shivering, exposure to a cool ambient environment, hypovolemia, acidosis, pain, and inappropriate weaning from ventilatory support. The principles of physiologic and invasive hemodynamic monitoring are the same in elderly patients as in the young; however, such monitoring is perhaps even more important in older persons when the direction of therapy is unclear because of the limitations in cardiopulmonary function and homeostatic mechanisms.

Age-associated changes in blood flow to (and, to a lesser extent, oxygen consumption in) specific organs have been investigated. The kidneys receive a diminishing proportion of cardiac output in elderly persons: renal plasma flow decreases by about 10% each decade after 40 years of age and decreases in relation to renal mass. Liver volume decreases by more than one third, apparent liver blood flow by one half, and liver perfusion by one fifth from age 24 to age 91.[147] Cerebral blood flow, blood volume, and oxygen consumption decrease by about 0.5% a year in pure gray- and white-matter regions, whereas the oxygen extraction ratio does not change or changes only to a minor degree.[176] Skeletal muscle blood flow at rest appears to be unaffected by age, but maximal blood flow after exercise is diminished in older subjects.[173,177] Average skin blood flow decreases by 30% to 40% from age 20 to age 70.[178]

Thermoregulation

The endogenous temperature set point is typically elevated after operation or injury and during sepsis, and ambient temperature is often kept inappropriately low in hospitals. Alterations in vasomotor activity are normally relied on in the range of temperatures between those that elicit shivering and those that cause sweating. When the core temperature is lower than the thermoregulatory set point and heat conservation is inadequate, shivering is initiated to generate heat. Shivering may be accompanied by a severalfold increase in oxygen consumption, which would constitute a substantial metabolic load. When the core temperature falls below 34° C (93.2° F), thermoregulation becomes impaired, metabolic activity slows, and further decreases in temperature are more rapid. The hypothermic myocardium is prone to intractable arrhythmias that may be triggered by minimal stimulation. Conditions that are associated with secondary hypothermia, such as hypothyroidism and diabetes mellitus, may be more frequent (or more frequently undiagnosed) in elderly persons.

Elderly persons, particularly those older than 80 years, are less sensitive to alterations in environmental temperature and less able to maintain thermal homeostasis.[179] These limitations result in a higher incidence of hypothermia and heatstroke, a lower maximum body temperature during febrile illness, and more marked and prolonged falls in body temperature with surgery.[93,94,179]

Mechanisms of heat conservation, production, and offloading are less efficient in elderly persons. Sensitivity to changes in ambient temperature is less precise, and behavioral responses are delayed. Vasoconstrictor responses to a cold stimulus are depressed in some elderly individuals, and shivering is delayed.[180] Moreover, the capacity for metabolic heat production by shivering is limited by the reduced muscle mass characteristic of the aged. With decreased blood flow in the skin, reduced sweat gland density, and delayed and diminished sweating responses, older patients are less able to offload heat and reduce body temperature than younger individuals are.[112]

Malnutrition may predispose to hypothermia and accidental injury. In a study of 744 elderly women with fractures of the neck of the femur, most of those who were very thin had a core temperature lower than 35° C (95.0° F) on admission, whereas most of those who were well nourished had a temperature higher than 36° C (96.8° F).[181] The increase in the incidence of fractures in cold weather was greatest among the very thin; the finding that most injuries occurred indoors suggested that impaired thermoregulation in the malnourished individuals resulted in hypothermia, lack of coordination, and subsequent injury. In a study of elderly patients exposed to a range of ambient temperatures after femur fracture, vasoconstrictor responses were generally maintained; however, whereas patients who were well nourished could increase metabolic heat production appropriately, those who were undernourished (by anthropometric measurements) could not.[182]

Wound Healing

Advanced age is cited as a risk factor for impaired wound healing, though not consistently. Any association is probably attributable primarily to a higher prevalence of specific risk factors in elderly persons, such as malnutrition, malignancy, uremia, diabetes mellitus, and atherosclerosis. Studies of healthy, well-nourished volunteers have shown minor delays in the epithelialization of split-thickness skin wounds in older persons; collagen synthesis in subcutaneous implants was similar in young persons and older ones, whereas accumulation of noncollagenous protein was decreased in the latter.[183] In a 2000 study of surgical patients, collagen deposition in subcutaneous implants decreased as a function of age in men but not in women.[184] Anastomotic leak rates after resection of colorectal cancer are not greater in elderly patients.[8] Outcome after abdominal wound dehiscence may be worse in elderly patients.[185]

Immune Function

There is abundant evidence that changes in immune function occur with advancing age and that these changes may predispose to infectious, neoplastic, and perhaps vascular disease.[186] However, there is considerable variability among studies in the age definition of elderly persons, consideration of comorbidity, and the immune functions examined [*see* Studies of Aging and Aged Populations, *below*]. A 2000 report suggests that many immune functions are relatively well preserved in healthy, independent-living, elderly persons.[187]

The delayed-type hypersensitivity (DTH) response to intradermal challenge with common antigens can be used as a global measure of immune function. For a normal response (i.e., erythema and induration), intact antigen processing and stimulation of lymphocytes, release of soluble mediators, and migration of macrophages to the injection site are necessary. The likelihood of diminished or absent DTH responses to common antigens increases after the eighth decade of life, and the probability of achieving primary sensitization to an antigen to which the individual had not previously been exposed is diminished after 70 years of age.[188,189] Aging-associated changes in cell-mediated and humoral immune responses have been well reviewed elsewhere.[186,187] Overall, responses to foreign antigens are diminished and responses to autologous antigens may be increased. The limited information available on phagocytic responses suggests that polymorphonuclear leukocyte function may decrease with age.

Specific Clinical Concerns

Much of the material we have presented to this point is relevant to the care of elderly surgical patients in general and of elderly patients undergoing major elective procedures specifically. In what follows, we discuss the clinical considerations that arise for elderly patients who have specific surgical problems or who have significant comorbidities and functional limitations.

TRAUMA

The management of trauma is typically more complex and challenging in elderly patients than in younger ones. The prevalence of preexisting medical conditions increases with age, and such conditions are associated with longer hospital stays and higher mortality after injury.[190,191] Mechanisms of injury change in relative frequency with age, as do the types of injuries that result from a given physical insult and the outcomes that follow a given injury. In the Major Trauma Outcome Study (MTOS), for example, falls were the predominant mechanism of injury in patients 65 years of age or older, but they were relatively infrequent in younger patients.[192]

Motor vehicle crashes are the most common mechanism of injury in younger patients and remain the second most common in older patients. Once involved in a crash, older persons are more likely to die than younger persons. The circumstances and nature of motor vehicle crashes tend to differ in elderly persons. Crashes involving older drivers occur mainly in daytime and close to home and result more often from errors of judgment or perception than from high speed, aggressive driving, loss of vehcle control, or the use of alcohol.[193] Older drivers are more likely to be in crashes involving right-of-way conflicts, improper turning or starting, and failure to recognize or obey traffic signals.[194] Older drivers are also more likely to be involved in multivehicle side-impact collisions.[193,195]

The direction of impact influences both the pattern of injuries sustained and mortality.[193] In one study, injuries to the face and the lower extremities were significantly more common in drivers involved in frontal collisions, whereas injuries to the chest, the abdomen, and the pelvis were more frequent in left lateral impacts.[193] Mortality was nearly doubled in left lateral impacts; this increase was independent of both Injury Severity Score and driver age.

The pattern of injuries resulting from a given physical insult also seems to differ to some extent in elderly persons: older drivers have a higher incidence of chest injuries, specifically rib and sternal fractures.[196] Greater chest wall stiffness and osteoporotic changes may predispose older persons to rib fractures after relatively minor trauma. Rib fractures or even flail chest may sometimes occur in elderly persons without the significant underlying pulmonary contusion that would be anticipated in a younger patient.[197,198] Striking age-related increases in fractures of the vertebrae, the hip, and the distal forearm have been documented, and the pivotal role of osteoporosis in such fractures is well recognized.[199] Patients who have major injuries despite an apparently insignificant mechanism of injury (e.g., a low-level fall) are more likely to be older than 55 years.[200] Burn injuries are more common in older persons, and these injuries tend to be more severe in terms of both surface area and depth; moreover, inhalation injury is more likely.[201] As a consequence, mortality is higher and hospital stay longer. The increased risk of burn injury in elderly patients may be attributable to a diminished sense of smell, impaired hearing or vision, or reduced mobility and reaction time. The tendency to more severe thermal injury may be attributable to age-related changes in skin morphology.

Elderly persons are, in general, less sensitive to deviations from physiologic norms and less able to maintain homeostasis.[202] They are less able to maintain adequate perfusion of vital organs after injury than younger patients are,[203] and they are more likely to arrive in the emergency department hypotensive, cold, and in shock after a given injury. Presumably, reduced homeostatic capacity contributes to the overrepresentation of older persons with regard to immediate and early trauma deaths, as well as late deaths related to infection and multiple organ dysfunction syndrome (MODS). Resuscitative measures, though identical in principle to those taken in younger patients, must be carried out with an eye to their physiologic limitations, particularly the need for volume loading to achieve increases in cardiac output. Preexisting medical conditions must be identified rapidly via history-taking, physical examination, and investigative studies as needed, and information about previous medication use should be obtained. Because thermoregulatory mechanisms are less efficient in elderly patients, measures should be taken to minimize ongoing heat loss from exposure and administration of cool fluids and to prevent the adverse effects of hypothermia.

Unfortunately, even an apparently good physiologic status in the ED (at least as reflected in the Trauma Score [TS] or the Revised Trauma Score [RTS]) does not guarantee survival for the elderly trauma patient: mortality in elderly patients with high TS or RTS is many times higher than that in younger patients with comparable scores.[192,204,205] MTOS data demonstrate that case-fatality rates are uniformly higher in patients 65 years of age or older than in younger patients for every injury mechanism for which sufficient data were available.[206] Mortality was consistently higher for each range of Injury Severity Scores and for each injury severity–body region combination. Patients 65 years of age or older accounted for 30% of the deaths that were unexpected according to Trauma and Injury Severity Score (TRISS) projections despite representing only 8% of the MTOS study population. Complications (pulmonary, cardiovascular, and infectious) were also more common in the older patients[192,206]; the difference was most striking in patients with mild to moderate injury. Others have noted the high incidence in elderly patients of respiratory complications (including pneumonia), as well as cardiac complications that are relatively uncommon in younger patients.[207,208]

Elderly patients are less likely to survive their injuries and be discharged from hospital than younger patients, but several reports indicate that many older survivors return to a satisfactory level of function and independence.[197,207-211] In subsequent studies, however, prolonged and profound functional limitations have been identified after major trauma when sophisticated assessments of long-term functional, psychological, and quality-of-life outcomes have been undertaken.[212] Variations in functional recovery and placement status result from a number of factors besides the specific mechanism and nature of the injury. For example, family and social support systems have been shown to be important for achieving discharge-to-home and optimal functional recovery in patients with isolated hip fracture, and some authors have reached similar conclusions with reference to trauma in older persons in general.[213] Very advanced age, preinjury placement, preinjury functional status, and preexisting medical conditions are also likely to influence postinjury rehabilitation. Injury-causing falls may, in some instances, be a reflection of important underlying problems, such as dementia or a poor physical state. The adverse impact of serious head injury on early and delayed mortality has been reported in a number of studies.[205,207,209-211] Admission to an ICU, even if the stay is longer than 2 weeks and even if mechanical ventilation is necessary, does not preclude a very good functional recovery in survivors.[197,207-209]

CANCER

The incidence of most cancers increases with age. One half of new cases of lung and colorectal cancer now occur in persons 70 years of age or older, as do nearly two thirds of new cases of prostate cancer and one third of new cases of breast cancer.[214] The importance of cancer as a cause of surgical illness in older persons is further indicated by the high proportion of surgical procedures related to malignancy and its frequency as a cause of death in surgical patients.[215]

The principles of cancer care are similar in elderly patients, and surgeons play a central role in determining the application of those principles. There is evidence, however, that in practice, the use of diagnostic modalities, the choice of surgical treatment, and other forms of cancer care differ in elderly patients.[8,216-220] This difference may be an appropriate response to the increased prevalence of comorbidity or to age-related differences in treatment goals, or it may reflect an inappropriate bias. Older cancer patients may assign greater importance to outcomes other than the traditional ones (survival, response rates, and disease-free intervals) than younger patients do.[218,221] They also appear more concerned about the effects of treatment and may be less willing to trade current health-related quality of life for potential survival advantage.[216,222]

Comorbidity in the elderly population may limit potential gains in life expectancy, alter treatment goals, and reduce the ability to tolerate major surgical procedures and other forms of therapy. Yet adjustments for measured comorbidity do not fully account for age-related differences in care.[223,224] The elderly population is very diverse and includes individuals who are physiologically very fit, as well as ones who are not. There is evidence that nondefinitive care is associated with poorer clinical outcomes.[225] Thus, it is inappropriate to generalize cancer care simply on the basis of chronologic age.

Older persons have been underrepresented in cancer clinical trials, with the result that our perceptions of the efficacy and safety of many therapies in this population must be based on inference rather than knowledge and may therefore be inaccurate.[226] The development of multidimensional assessment tools for the geriatric cancer patient should allow appropriate enrollment and stratification in clinical trials and permit identification of patients who can expect the most benefit from aggressive therapy.[227,228] There is considerable uncertainty about cancer screening in older populations, for the reasons discussed. A framework for making decisions about screening has been proposed, incorporating quantitative estimates of risks and benefits in relation to individual preferences and values.[229] When life expectancy is less than 5 years, cancer screening is unlikely to provide any survival benefit.

SIGNIFICANT COMORBIDITY AND FUNCTIONAL LIMITATION

Most elderly individuals live independently and function well. Nonetheless, elderly persons in nursing homes or similar facilities often have significant comorbid conditions and functional limitations and usually have a limited life expectancy. They experience a range of orthopedic, general surgical, vascular, and other surgical problems that may be relatively advanced and that commonly present as emergencies or in atypical or nonspecific ways.[41] Dementia and other cognitive impairments predict increased mortality [see Cognitive Assessment, above], presumably because of delays in presentation and diagnosis and the comorbidities that are frequently present. Many elderly patients manifest the limited mobility, weakness, relative inactivity, weight loss, and diminished physiologic reserves suggested by the term frail and thus are highly vulnerable to the stresses of acute surgical illness and hospitalization.[230] The term frail, however, has a number of distinct connotations within and among different health care disciplines and should therefore be used with due caution.

For elderly persons with significant comorbid conditions and functional limitations, the goals of surgical therapy are usually modest: to correct immediately life-threatening conditions or to address problems related to quality of life. Comfort, function, and dignity—rather than major gains in survival—are more often the primary goals. How well we achieve these goals with current surgical care is uncertain. Precise diagnosis is usually the most satisfactory basis for relieving suffering and achieving the other goals of importance to the elderly patient. However, it must be kept in mind that precise diagnosis is just one means to that end and that pathologic states of various kinds can almost always be identified in such individuals, whether relevant or not.[231]

Advance decisions to limit the use of specific therapies have been made and documented by some elderly individuals. Surgical care should not be precluded for patients for whom a do-not-resuscitate (DNR) order has been established. Outcomes in such patients are not necessarily worse than in other older patients. Agreement to rescind the DNR order temporarily in the immediate perioperative period should be sought because the causes of cardiopulmonary arrest during that period may be rapidly and readily correctible.

Surgical problems in nursing home patients should be addressed actively because they can often be managed more easily and safely when elective than when they have evolved into more difficult, high-risk, emergency conditions. The elective setting also provides more opportunity for informed decision-making and treatment planning and the development of consensus among those involved. The care of such patients is especially challenging and should be undertaken by surgeons who are interested in and knowledgeable about the problems that arise, who are prepared to deal with the complexities of comorbidity and cognitive and functional impairment, and who will educate their colleagues, patients, and families about the full range of therapies available for surgical conditions.[41]

THE OLDER ORTHOPEDIC PATIENT

The high prevalence of osteoporosis, combined with an increased predisposition to falls, leads to a high incidence of fractures (especially of the hips, the vertebrae, and the wrists) in older persons. The surgeon's role in the management of these patients should include a careful search for the cause of the fall. Loss of consciousness during the fall may signal that seizures, cardiac disease (e.g., dysrhythmias and aortic stenosis) or postural hypotension are contributors. Medications, including sedatives, narcotics, and anticholinergic agents, may also be implicated. Evidence of neurologic conditions (e.g., Parkinson disease and peripheral neuropathy) should be sought. Surgeons should also consider the need for medications to reduce bone fragility (e.g., calcium, vitamin D, and bisphosphonates). Involving a geriatrician often facilitates management of osteoporosis and falls.

For elderly hip fracture patients, the choice of type of surgical procedure performed must consider the need to avoid prolonged immobility and its resultant complications [see Table 7]. Fully 25% of patients with hip fractures die within 1 year as a consequence of complications of immobility. Therefore, the choice of procedure should allow full weight bearing as soon as possible postoperatively. Appropriate selection of procedures gives elderly patients the best chance of returning to their premorbid functional status.

Studies of Aging and Aged Populations

Age is often associated with adverse clinical outcomes. However, two related concepts must be considered in reviewing studies that are concerned with elderly patients and aged populations or in which age may be a significant variable. First, although age has obvious chronologic meaning, it is a surrogate for a range of biologic, clinical, social, and other variables. Some of the variables that we often recognize as changing in association with age are maximal organ system function (physiologic reserve), the prevalence of comorbidity, functional status, patterns of illness (e.g., a preponderance of perforated appendicitis in older persons), and disease incidence (e.g., cancer). A knowledge of age-related variables in the population being reported on is important in that it can help determine the extent to which findings can be generalized to one's own patients. Age-related variables must be excluded as fully as possible when basic disease mechanisms or causal relationships are being examined.

Second, the method by which elderly research subjects are selected greatly influences the findings of clinical studies. Aging is a highly variable process, both among individual and among different organ systems within an individual. Studies of institutionalized elderly persons who have multiple comorbidities and functional impairments will give very different results from studies of active, healthy, community-dwelling individuals. Again, such age-associated variables must be addressed to allow proper interpretation of study findings. It must also be remembered that aging is a continuous process. For example, a 65-year-old person and an 85-year-old person, each in good health, could well be very different with respect to physiologic and functional status, even though they would often be grouped together into a single "elderly" category.

Two basic study designs are employed in clinical studies of elderly and aged populations: cross-sectional and longitudinal. In cross-sectional studies, subjects of various ages are assembled, and observations are made at one point in time. Such studies are easier and less expensive to conduct than longitudinal studies, but they are subject to bias and confounding variables. For example, elderly patients, when younger, may have been very different from the young patients with whom they are being compared; that is, changes may occur in the population as a whole over time. In addition, elderly individuals (particularly those older than 75 years) make up what may be thought of as a biologically superior group in that they have been selected by the very fact of their survival from a larger group, many of whose members have died. Cross-sectional studies thus may demonstrate differences between current age groups rather than changes that occur with aging. Bias may also arise in relation to referral for surgical care or to particular institutions or from a wide range of other potential sources. A clear description of the source of the data and the basis on which the subjects came to be studied allows others to make judgments about bias and the generalizability of research findings.

In longitudinal studies, a cohort is assembled and followed prospectively, with observations made at planned intervals. Longitudinal studies require a stable, dedicated population observed over a prolonged period and are particularly sensitive to subtle alterations in methods. Among the most comprehensive and widely cited longitudinal studies is the Baltimore Longitudinal Study of Aging, conducted using carefully screened, community-residing, independent adults.[232]

Because research subjects cannot be randomized to an age group, prospective clinical studies of aging and of aged populations are necessarily observational in design. As a result, study groups that differ in age, by design, also unavoidably differ in terms of other variables (covariates), such as those already described. For this reason, although observational studies are very useful for descriptive and prognostic purposes, they are less satisfactory for examining causal relationships. Several strategies for study design and analysis are useful for minimizing or adjusting for imbalances in covariates between groups.[233]

Advanced age has, in the past, been a common exclusion criterion for research studies, with the result that there is a paucity of information pertaining specifically to older persons in certain important clinical areas.[226] Inferences about age effects on diseases and responses to therapy must then be made, exposing elderly patients to the risks of inaccuracy. In addition, outcomes that are likely to be of particular interest to elderly persons (e.g., quality of life) may not be well addressed when studies are designed with a focus on younger patients.[234] The unique problems and questions of the elderly population must be addressed in surgical research. Concerns about vulnerability and exploitation may sometimes arise, but they do not negate the obligation to conduct research in these individuals; to continue to exclude elderly patients would be to deny the potential benefits of research to a population that has great need of them.

References

1. Rothschild JM, Bates DW, Leape LL: Preventable medical injuries in older patients. Arch Intern Med 160:2717, 2000

2. Smith OC: Advanced age as a contraindication to operation. Med Rec (New York) 72:642, 1907

3. Kenney RA: Physiology of Aging: A Synopsis, 2nd ed. Year Book, Chicago, 1989, p 111

4. Callum K, Gray A, Hoile R, et al: Extremes of Age. The 1999 Report of the National Confidential Enquiry into Perioperative Deaths. National Confidential Enquiry into Perioperative Deaths, London, 1999

5. Bardram L, Funch-Jensen P, Kehlet H: Rapid rehabilitation in elderly patients after laparoscopic colonic resection. Br J Surg 87:1540, 2000

6. Ventura SJ, Peters KD, Martin JA, et al: Births and deaths: United States, 1996. Mon Vital Stat Rep 46(1 suppl 2):1, 1997

7. Welch HG, Albertsen PC, Nease RF, et al: Estimating treatment benefits for the elderly: the effect of competing risks. Ann Intern Med 124:577, 1996

8. Colorectal Cancer Collaborative Group: Surgery for colorectal cancer in elderly patients: a systematic review. Lancet 356:968, 2000

9. Carr AJ, Higginson IJ: Measuring quality of life: are quality of life measures patient centred? BMJ 322:1357, 2001

10. Making Health Care Safer: A Critical Analysis of Patient Safety Practices, Evidence Report/Technology Assessment No. 43. Agency for Healthcare Research and Quality, Rockville, Maryland, 2001 http://www.ahrq.gov/clinic/ptsafety

11. Lothian K, Philp I: Maintaining the dignity and autonomy of older people in the healthcare setting. BMJ 322:668, 2001

12. Resnick NM, Marcantonio ER: How should clinical care of the aged differ? Lancet 350:1157, 1997

13. Brewer RJ, Golden GT, Hitch DC, et al: Abdominal pain: an analysis of 1,000 consecutive cases in a university hospital emergency room. Am J Surg 131:219, 1976

14. Albano WA, Zielinski CM, Organ CH: Is appendicitis in the aged really different? Geriatrics 30:81, 1975

15. Rowe JW, Minaker KL: Geriatric medicine. Handbook of the Biology of Aging, 2nd ed. Finch CE, Schneider EL, Eds. Van Nostrand Reinhold, New York, 1985, p 932

16. Fenyö G: Acute abdominal disease in the elderly: experience from two series in Stockholm. Am J Surg 143:751, 1982

17. Watters J, Blakslee J, March R, et al: The influence of age on the severity of peritonitis. Can J Surg 39:142, 1996

18. Irvin TT, Arnstein PM: Management of symptomatic gallstones in the elderly. Br J Surg 75:1163, 1988

19. Auerbach AD, Goldman L: Beta-blockers and reduction of cardiac events in noncardiac surgery: clinical applications. JAMA 287:1445, 2002

20. Fiatarone MA, Oneill EF, Ryan ND, et al: Exercise training and nutritional supplementation for physical frailty in very elderly people. N Engl J Med 330:1769, 1994

21. Arthur HM, Daniels C, McKelvie R, et al: Effect of a preoperative intervention on preoperative and postoperative outcomes in low-risk patients awaiting elective coronary bypass graft surgery. Ann Intern Med 133:253, 2000

22. Debigare R, Maltais F, Whittom F, et al: Feasibility and efficacy of home exercise training before lung volume reduction. J Cardiopulm Rehabil 19:235, 1999

23. Edwards AE, Seymour DG, McCarthy JM, et al: A 5-year study of general surgical patients aged 65 years and over. Anaesthesia 51:3, 1996

24. Carpenter G, Bernabei R, Hirdes J, et al: Building evidence on chronic disease in old age: standardised assessments and databases offer one way of building the evidence. BMJ 320:528, 2000

25. Schein OD, Katz J, Bass EB, et al, for the Study of Medical Testing for Cataract Surgery: The value of routine preoperative medical testing before cataract surgery. N Engl J Med 342:168, 2000

26. Munro J, Booth A, Nicholl J: Routine preoperative testing: a systematic review of the evidence. Health Technology Assessment 1(12), 1997 http://www.hta.nhsweb.nhs.uk/

27. Wahr JA, Parks R, Boisvert D, et al, for the Multicenter Study of Perioperative Ischemia Research Group: Preoperative serum potassium levels and perioperative outcomes in cardiac surgery patients. JAMA 281:2203, 1999

28. Hall JC, Tarala RA, Hall JL, et al: A multivariate analysis of the risk of pulmonary complications after laparotomy. Chest 99:923, 1991

29. Arozullah AM, Khuri SF, Henderson WG, et al, for the Participants in the National Veterans Affairs Surgical Quality Improvement Program: Development and validation of a multifactorial risk index for predicting postoperative pneumonia after major noncardiac surgery. Ann Intern Med 135:847, 2001

30. Smetana GW: Preoperative pulmonary evaluation. N Engl J Med 340:937, 1999

31. Moller AM, Villebro N, Pedersen T, et al: Effect of preoperative smoking intervention on postoperative complications: a randomised clinical trial. Lancet 359:114, 2002

32. Lawrence VA, Dhanda R, Hilsenbeck SG, et al: Risk of pulmonary complications after elective abdominal surgery. Chest 110:744, 1996

33. De Nino L, Lawrence VA, Averyt EC, et al: Preoperative spirometry and laparotomy: blowing away dollars. Chest 111:1536, 1997

34. Mangano DT: Adverse outcomes after surgery in the year 2001—a continuing odyssey. Anesthesiology 88:561, 1998

35. Badner NH, Knill RL, Brown JE, et al: Myocardial infarction after noncardiac surgery. Anesthesiology 88:572, 1998

36. Eagle K, Rihal C, Mickel M, et al: Cardiac risk of noncardiac surgery: influence of coronary disease and type of surgery in 3368 operations. CASS Investigators and University of Michigan Heart Care Program. Coronary Artery Surgery Study. Circulation 96:1882, 1997

37. Mangano DT, Goldman L: Preoperative assessment of patients with known or suspected coronary disease. N Engl J Med 333:1750, 1995

38. Lee TH, Marcantonio ER, Mangione CM, et al: Derivation and prospective validation of a simple index for prediction of cardiac risk of major noncardiac surgery. Circulation 100:1043, 1999

39. Golden M, Whittemore A, Donaldson M, et al: Selective evaluation and management of coronary artery disease in patients undergoing repair of abdominal aortic aneurysms: a 16-year experience. Ann Surg 212:415, 1990

40. Bernstein GM, Offenbartl SK: Adverse surgical outcomes among patients with cognitive impairments. Amer Surgeon 57:682, 1991

41. Zenilman ME, Bender JS, Magnuson TH, et al: General surgical care in the nursing home patient: results of a dedicated geriatric surgery consult service. J Am Coll Surg 183:361, 1996

42. Morrison RS, Siu AL: Survival in end-stage dementia following acute illness. JAMA 284:47, 2000

43. Brooks-Brunn JA: Predictors of postoperative pulmonary complications following abdominal surgery. Chest 111:564, 1997

44. Nightingale S, Holmes J, Mason J, et al: Psychiatric illness and mortality after hip fracture. Lancet 357:1264, 2001

45. Gustafson Y, Brannstrom B, Berggren D, et al: A geriatric-anesthesiologic program to reduce acute confusional states in elderly patients treated for femoral neck fractures. J Am Geriatr Soc 39:655, 1991

46. Marcantonio ER, Goldman L, Mangione CM, et al: A clinical prediction rule for delirium after elective noncardiac surgery. JAMA 271:134, 1994

47. Moller JT, Cluitmans P, Rasmussen LS, et al, for the ISPOCD Investigators: Long-term postoperative cognitive dysfunction in the elderly: ISPOCD1 study. Lancet 351:857, 1998

48. Murray A, Levkoff S, Wetle T, et al: Acute delirium and functional decline in the hospitalized elderly patient. J Gerontol 48:M181, 1993

49. Parikh SS, Chung F: Postoperative delirium in the elderly. Anesth Analg 80:1223, 1995

50. Dijkstra J, Houx P, Jolles J: Cognition after major surgery in the elderly: test performance and complaints. Br J Anaesth 82:867, 1999

51. Abildstrom H, Rasmussen L, Rentowl P, et al: Cognitive dysfunction 1–2 years after non-cardiac surgery in the elderly ISPOCD group. International Study of Post-Operative Cognitive Dysfunction. Acta Anaesthesiol Scand 44:1246, 2000

52. Newman MF, Kirchner JL, Phillips-Bute B, et al, for the Neurological Outcome Research Group and the Cardiothoracic Anesthesiology Research Endeavors Investigators: Longitudinal assessment of neurocognitive function after coronary-artery bypass surgery. N Engl J Med 344:395, 2001

53. Folstein MF, Folstein SE, McHugh PR: "Mini-Mental State": a practical method for grading the cognitive state of patients for the clinician. J Psychiatr Res 12:189, 1975

54. Roccaforte W, Burke W, Bayer B, et al: Validation of a telephone version of the Mini-Mental State examination. J Am Geriatr Soc 40:697, 1992

55. Ritchie K: The screening of cognitive impairment in the elderly: a critical review of current methods. J Clin Epidemiol 41:635, 1988

56. Chandra RK: Effect of vitamin and trace-element supplementation on immune responses and infection in elderly subjects. Lancet 340:1124, 1992

57. Girodon F, Lombard M, Galan P, et al: Effect of micronutrient supplementation on infection in institutionalized elderly subjects: a controlled trial. Ann Nutr Metab 41(2): 98, 1997

58. Shaver HJ, Loper JA, Lutes RA: Nutritional status of nursing home patients. JPEN J Parenter Enteral Nutr 4:367, 1980

59. Pinchcofsky-Devin GD, Kaminski MV: Incidence of protein-calorie malnutrition in the nursing home patient. J Am Coll Nutr 6:109, 1987

60. Rudman D, Feller AG, Nagruj HS, et al: Relation of serum albumin concentration to death rate in nursing home men. JPEN J Parenter Enteral Nutr 11:360, 1987

61. Allison SP: Outcomes from nutritional support in the elderly. Nutrition 14:479, 1988

62. Sullivan DH, Sun S, Walls RC: Protein-energy undernutrition among elderly hospitalized patients: a prospective study. JAMA 281:2013, 1999

63. Bastow MD, Rawlings J, Allison SP: Benefits of supplementary tube feeding after fractured neck of femur: a randomised controlled trial. BMJ 287:1589, 1983

64. Potter J, Langhorne P, Roberts M: Routine protein energy supplementation in adults: systematic review. BMJ 317:495, 1998

65. Klein S, Kinney J, Jeejeebhoy K, et al: Nutrition support in clinical practice: review of published data and recommendations for future research directions. JPEN J Parenter Enteral Nutr 21:133, 1997

66. Omran M, Morley J: Assessment of protein energy malnutrition in older persons, part I: History, examination, body composition, and screening tools. Nutrition 16:50, 2000

67. Apovian CM: Nutritional assessment in the elderly: facing up to the challenges of developing new tools for clinical assessment. Nutrition 17:62, 2001

68. Corish CA: Pre-operative nutritional assessment in the elderly. J Nutr Health Aging 5:49, 2001

69. Detsky AS, McLaughlin JR, Baker JP, et al: What is subjective global assessment of nutritional status? JPEN J Parenter Enteral Nutr 11:8, 1987

70. Vellas B, Guigoz Y, Garry PJ, et al: The Mini Nutritional Assessment (MNA) and its use in grading the nutritional state of elderly patients. Nutrition 15:116, 1999

71. Klidjian AM, Foster KJ, Kammerling RM, et al: Relation of anthropometric and dynamometric variables to serious postoperative complications. BMJ 281:899, 1980

72. Twiston Davies CW, Moody Jones D, Shearer JR: Hand grip—a simple test for morbidity after fracture of the neck of femur. J Royal Soc Med 77:833, 1984

73. Hall JC, Hall JL: ASA status and age predict adverse events after abdominal surgery. J Qual Clin Pract 16:103, 1996

74. Nehme AE: Groin hernias in the elderly: management and prognosis. Am J Surg 146:257, 1983

75. Weber DM: Laparoscopic surgery: an excellent approach in elderly patients. Arch Surg 138:1083, 2003

76. Greenburg AG, Saik RP, Coyle JJ, et al: Mortality and gastrointestinal surgery in the aged: elective versus emergency procedures. Arch Surg 116:788, 1981

77. Seymour DG, Pringle R: A new method of auditing surgical mortality rates: application to a group of elderly general surgical patients. BMJ 284:1539, 1982

78. Gilliss CL, Gortner SR, Hauck WW, et al: A randomized clinical trial of nursing care for recovery from cardiac surgery. Heart & Lung 22:125, 1993

79. Milledge JS, Nunn JF: Criteria of fitness for anaesthesia in patients with chronic obstructive lung disease. Br Med J 3:670, 1975

80. Roberts CS, Cox CE, Reintgen DS, et al: Influence of physician communication on newly diagnosed breast patients' psychological adjustment and decision-making. Cancer 74(1 suppl):336, 1994

81. Huusko TM, Karppi P, Avikainen V, et al: Randomised, clinically controlled trial of intensive geriatric rehabilitation in patients with hip fracture: subgroup analysis of patients with dementia. BMJ 321:1107, 2000

82. Cameron I, Crotty M, Currie C, et al: Geriatric rehabilitation following fractures in older people: a systematic review. Health Technol Assess 4(2), 2000 http://www.hta.nhsweb.nhs.uk

83. Hyde CJ, Robert IE, Sinclair AJ: The effects of supporting discharge from hospital to home in older people. Age Ageing 29:271, 2000

84. McClaran J, Berglas R, Franco E: Long hospital stays and need for alternate level of care at discharge: does family make a difference for elderly patients? Can Fam Physician 42:449, 1996

85. Mazur DJ, Merz JF: How age, outcome severity, and scale influence general medicine clinic

86. Farnill D, Inglis S: Patients' desire for information about anaesthesia: Australian attitudes. Anaesthesia 49:162, 1994

87. Lonsdale M, Hutchison GL: Patients' desire for information about anaesthesia: Scottish and Canadian attitudes. Anaesthesia 46:410, 1991

88. Inglis S, Farnill D: The effect of providing preoperative statistical anaesthetic-risk information. Anaesth Intens Care 21:799, 1993

89. Lella J, Kaye M: Ethics and surgical practice with the elderly. Surgical Care of the Elderly. Meakins JL, McClaran JC, Eds. Year Book Medical Publishers, Chicago, 1988, p 50

90. Langslow A: Nursing and the law: who has the capacity to consent to surgery? Austr Nurs J 2:31, 1995

91. Markson LJ, Kern DC, Annas GJ, et al: Physician assessment of patient competence. J Am Geriatr Soc 42:1074, 1994

92. Sessler DI: Mild perioperative hypothermia. N Engl J Med 336:1730, 1997

93. Vaughan MS, Vaughan RW, Cork RC: Postoperative hypothermia in adults: relationship of age, anesthesia, and shivering to rewarming. Anesth Analg 60:746, 1981

94. Roe CF, Goldberg MJ, Blair CS, et al: The influence of body temperature on early postoperative oxygen consumption. Surgery 60:85, 1966

95. Frank SM, Fleisher LA, Breslow MJ: Perioperative maintenance of normothermia reduces the incidence of morbid cardiac events: a randomized clinical trial. JAMA 227:1127, 1997

96. Kurz A, Sessler DI, Lenhardt R: Perioperative normothermia to reduce the incidence of surgical-wound infection and shorten hospitalization. N Engl J Med 334:1209, 1996

97. Schmied H, Kurz A, Sessler D, et al: Mild hypothermia increases blood loss and transfusion requirements during total hip arthroplasty. Lancet 347:289, 1986

98. Cruse PJE, Foord R: The epidemiology of wound infection: a 10-year prospective study of 62,939 wounds. Surg Clin North Am 60:27, 1980

99. Tang R, Chen H, Wang Y, et al: Risk factors for surgical site infection after elective resection of the colon and rectum: a single-center prospective study of 2,809 consecutive patients. Ann Surg 234:181, 2001

100. Craig DB: Postoperative recovery of pulmonary function. Anesth Analg 60:46, 1981

101. Simonneau G, Vivien A, Sartene R, et al: Diaphragm dysfunction induced by upper abdominal surgery: role of postoperative pain. Am Rev Respir Dis 128:899, 1983

102. Rizzato G, Marrazini L: Thoracoabdominal mechanics in elderly men. J Appl Physiol 28:457, 1970

103. Vaughan RW, Wise L: Postoperative arterial blood gas measurement in obese patients: effect of position on gas exchange. Ann Surg 182:705, 1975

104. Celli BR, Rodriguez KS, Snider GL: A controlled trial of intermittent positive pressure breathing, incentive spirometry, and deep breathing exercises in preventing pulmonary complications after abdominal surgery. Am Rev Respir Dis 130:12, 1984

105. Ford GT, Guenter CA: Toward prevention of postoperative pulmonary complications. Am Rev Respir Dis 130:4, 1984

106. Greif R, Laciny S, Rapf B, et al: Supplemental oxygen reduces the incidence of postoperative nausea and vomiting. Anesthesiology 91:1246, 1999

107. Greif R, Akca O, Horn EP, et al, for the Outcomes Research Group: Supplemental perioperative oxygen to reduce the incidence of surgical-wound infection. N Engl J Med 342:161, 2000

108. Miller PD, Krebs RA, Neal BJ, et al: Hypodipsia in geriatric patients. Am J Med 73:354, 1982

109. Phillips PA, Rolls BJ, Ledingham JG, et al: Reduced thirst after water deprivation in healthy elderly men. N Engl J Med 311:753, 1984

110. Helderman JH, Vestal RE, Rowe JW, et al: The response of arginine vasopressin to intravenous ethanol and hypertonic saline in man: the impact of aging. J Gerontol 33:39, 1978

111. Saruta T, Suzuki A, Hayashi M, et al: Mechanism of age-related changes in renin and adrenocortical steroids. J Am Geriatr Soc 28:210, 1980

112. Kenney RA: Physiology of aging. Clin Geriatr Med 1:37, 1985

113. Rowe JW, Shock NW, DeFronzo RA: The influence of age on the renal response to water deprivation in man. Nephron 17:270, 1976

114. Epstein M, Hollenberg NK: Age as a determinant of renal sodium conservation in normal man. J Lab Clin Med 87:411, 1976

115. Rowe JW: Aging and renal function. Ann Rev Gerontol Geriatr 1:161, 1980

116. Adler S, Lindeman RD, Yiengst MJ, et al: Effect of acute acid loading on urinary acid excretion by the aging human kidney. J Lab Clin Med 72:278, 1968

117. Kronenberg RS, Drage CW: Attenuation of the ventilatory and heart rate responses to hypoxia and hypercapnia with aging in normal men. J Clin Invest 52:1812, 1973

118. Brischetto MJ, Millman RP, Peterson DD, et al: Effect of aging on ventilatory response to exercise and CO₂. J Appl Physiol 56:1143, 1984

119. Rowe JW, Andres R, Tobin JD, et al: The effect of age on creatinine clearance in men: a cross-sectional and longitudinal study. J Gerontol 31:155, 1976

120. Cockcroft DW, Gault MH: Prediction of creatinine clearance from serum creatinine. Nephron 16:31, 1976

121. Garella S, Matarese RA: Renal effects of prostaglandins and clinical adverse effects of non-steroidal anti-inflammatory agents. Medicine (Baltimore) 63:165, 1984

122. Brater D, Harris C, Redfern J, et al: Renal effects of COX-2-selective inhibitors. Am J Nephrol 21:1, 2001

123. Yang H, Raymer K, Butler R, et al: Metoprolol after vascular surgery (MaVS). Can J Anesth 51:A7, 2004

124. Wilmore DW, Kehlet H: Management of patients in fast-track surgery. BMJ 322:473, 2001

125. Rodgers A, Walker N, Schug S, et al: Reduction of postoperative mortality and morbidity with epidural or spinal anaesthesia: results from overview of randomised trials. BMJ 321:1, 2000

126. Jones AG, Hunter JM: Anaesthesia in the elderly: special considerations. Drugs & Aging 9:319, 1996

127. Catley DM, Thornton C, Jordan C, et al: Pronounced, episodic oxygen desaturation in the postoperative period: its association with ventilatory pattern and analgesic regimen. Anesthesiology 63:20, 1985

128. Wheatley RG, Somerville ID, Sapsford DJ, et al: Postoperative hypoxaemia: comparison of extradural, I.M., and patient-controlled opioid analgesia. Br J Anaesth 64:267, 1990

129. Mallery LH, MacDonald EA, Hubley-Kozey CL, et al: The feasibility of performing resistance exercise with acutely ill hospitalized older patients. BMC Geriatr 3:3, 2003, http://www.biomedcentral.com/1471-2318/3/3

130. Inouye SK, Bogardius ST, Jr, Charpentier PA, et al: A multi-component intervention to prevent delirium in hospitalized older patients. N Engl J Med 340:669, 1999

131. Creditor MC: Hazards of hospitalization of the

elderly. Ann Intern Med 118:219, 1993

132. Young A: Exercise physiology in geriatric practice. Acta Med Scand 711(suppl):227, 1986

133. Watters JM, Clancey SM, Moulton SB, et al: Impaired recovery of strength in older patients after major abdominal surgery. Ann Surg 218:380, 1993

134. DeBiasse MA, Wilmore DW: What is optimal nutritional support? New Horizons 2:122, 1994

135. Gall MJ, Grimble GK, Reeve NJ, et al: Effect of providing fortified meals and between-meal snacks on energy and protein intake of hospital patients. Clin Nutr 17:259, 1999

136. Bastow MD, Rawlings J, Allison SP: Benefits of supplementary tube feeding after fractured neck of femur: a randomised controlled trial. BMJ 287:1589, 1983

137. Delmi M, Rapin C-H, Bengoa J-M, et al: Dietary supplementation in elderly patients with fractured neck of the femur. Lancet 335:1013, 1990

138. Espaulella J, Guyer H, Diaz-Escriu F, et al: Nutritional supplementation of elderly hip fracture patients: a randomized, double-blind, placebo-controlled trial. Age Ageing 29:425, 2000

139. Shock NW: Energy metabolism, caloric intake and physical activity in the aging. Symposium on Nutrition in Old Age. 10th Symposium of the Swedish Nutrition Foundation. Carlson LA, Ed. Almqvist and Wiksell, Uppsala, Sweden, 1972, p 12

140. Watters JM, Moulton SB, Clancey SM, et al: Aging exaggerates glucose intolerance following injury. J Trauma 37:786, 1994

141. Jeevanandam M, Holaday NJ, Shamos RF, et al: Acute IGF-1 deficiency in multiple trauma victims. Clin Nutr 11:352, 1992

142. Jeevanandam M, Ramias L, Shamos RF, et al: Decreased growth hormone levels in the catabolic phase of severe injury. Surgery 111:495, 1992

143. Van den Berghe G, Wouters P, Weekers F, et al: Intensive insulin therapy in critically ill patients. N Engl J Med 345:1359, 2001

144. Lazarou J, Pomeranz B, Corey P: Incidence of adverse drug reactions in hospitalized patients: a meta-analysis of prospective studies. JAMA 279:1200, 1998

145. Pouyanne P, Haramburu F, Imbs J, et al: Admissions to hospital caused by adverse drug reactions: cross sectional incidence study. BMJ 320:1036, 2000

146. Thomas EJ, Brennan TA: Incidence and types of preventable adverse events in elderly patients: population based review of medical records. BMJ 320:741, 2000

147. Wynne HA, Cope LH, Mutch E, et al: The effect of age upon liver volume and apparent liver blood flow in healthy men. Hepatology 9:297, 1989

148. Shepherd AM, Hewick DS, Moreland TA, et al: Age as a determinant of sensitivity to warfarin. Br J Clin Pharmacol 4:315, 1977

149. Reidenberg MM, Levy M, Warner H, et al: Relationship between diazepam dose, plasma level, age, and central nervous system depression. Clin Pharmacol Ther 23:371, 1978

150. Cohn SH, Vartsky D, Yasumura S, et al: Compartmental body composition based on total-body nitrogen, potassium, and calcium. Am J Physiol 239:E524, 1980

151. Hughes VA, Roubenoff R, Wood M, et al: Anthropometric assessment of 10-y changes in body composition in the elderly. Am J Clin Nutr 80:475, 2004

152. Moore FD, Olesen KH, McMurrey JD, et al: The Body Cell Mass and Its Supporting Environment: Body Composition in Health and Disease. W B Saunders Co, Philadelphia, 1963

153. Skelton DA, Grieg CA, Davies JM, et al: Strength, power and related functional ability of healthy peo-

ple aged 65-89 years. Age Ageing 23:371, 1994

154. Metter EJ, Conwit R, Tobin J, et al: Age-associated loss of power and strength in the upper extremities in women and men. J Gerontol Biol Sci 52A:B267, 1997

155. Wahba WM: Influence of aging on lung function: clinical significance of changes from age twenty. Anesth Analg 62:764, 1983

156. Morley J: Anorexia, sarcopenia, and aging. Nutrition 17:660, 2001

157. Skrobak-Kaczynski J, Andersen KL: The effect of a high level of habitual physical activity in the regulation of fatness during aging. Int Arch Occup Environ Health 36:41, 1975

158. Heath GW, Hagberg JM, Ehsani AA, et al: A physiological comparison of young and older endurance athletes. J Appl Physiol 51:634, 1981

159. DeVries HA: Physiological effects of an exercise training regimen upon men aged 52 to 88. J Gerontol 25:325, 1970

160. Sidney KH, Shephard RJ, Harrison JE: Endurance training and body composition of the elderly. Am J Clin Nutr 30:326, 1977

161. Larsson L: Physical training effects on muscle morphology in sedentary males at different ages. Med Sci Sports Exerc 14:203, 1982

162. Gribbin B, Pickering TG, Sleight P, et al: Effect of age and high blood pressure on baroreflex sensitivity in man. Circ Res 29:424, 1971

163. Collins KJ, Exton-Smith AN, James MH, et al: Functional changes in autonomic nervous responses with ageing. Age Ageing 9:17, 1980

164. Lakatta EG: Cardiovascular regulatory mechanisms in advanced age. Physiol Rev 73:413, 1993

165. Davies CT: The oxygen-transporting system in relation to age. Clin Sci 42:1, 1972

166. Strandell T: Circulatory studies on healthy old men: with special reference to the limitation of the maximal physical working capacity. Acta Med Scand 175:1, 1964

167. Brandfonbrener M, Landowne M, Shock NW: Changes in cardiac output with age. Circulation 12:557, 1955

168. Gerstenblith G, Fleg JL, Becker LC, et al: Maximum left ventricular filling rate in healthy individuals measured by gated blood pool scans. Circulation 68(III):101, 1983

169. Miyatake K, Okamoto M, Kinoshita N, et al: Augmentation of atrial contribution to left ventricular inflow with aging as assessed by intracardiac doppler flowmetry. Am J Cardiol 53:586, 1984

170. Davidson WR Jr, Fee EC: Influence of aging on pulmonary hemodynamics in a population free of coronary artery disease. Am J Cardiol 65:1454, 1990

171. Rodeheffer RJ, Gerstenblith G, Becker LC, et al: Exercise cardiac output is maintained with advancing age in healthy human subjects: cardiac dilatation and increased stroke volume compensate for a diminished heart rate. Circulation 69:203, 1984

172. Port S, Cobb FR, Coleman RE, et al: Effect of age on the response of the left ventricular ejection fraction to exercise. N Engl J Med 303:1133, 1980

173. Yin FCP, Raizes GS, Guarnieri T, et al: Age-associated decrease in ventricular response to haemodynamic stress during beta-adrenergic blockade. Br Heart J 40:1349, 1978

174. Stratton JR, Cerqueira MD, Schwartz RS, et al: Differences in cardiovascular responses to isoproterenol in relation to age and exercise training in healthy men. Circulation 86:504, 1992

175. Rich MW, Imburgia M: Inotropic response to dobutamine in elderly patients with decompensated congestive heart failure. Am J Cardiol 65:519, 1990

176. Leenders KL, Perani D, Lammertsma AA, et al: Cerebral blood flow, blood volume, and oxygen

utilization. Brain 113:27, 1990

177. Lindbjerg IF: Diagnostic application of the ^{133}xenon method in peripheral arterial disease. Scand J Clin Lab Invest 17:589, 1965

178. Tsuchida Y: Age-related changes in skin blood flow at four anatomic sites of the body in males studied by xenon-133. Plast Reconstr Surg 85:556, 1990

179. Collins KJ, Exton-Smith AN: Thermal homeostasis in old age. 1983 Henderson Award Lecture. J Am Geriatr Soc 31:519, 1983

180. Wagner JA, Robinson S, Marino RP: Age and temperature regulation of humans in neutral and cold environments. J Appl Physiol 37:562, 1974

181. Bastow MD, Rawlings J, Allison SP: Undernutrition, hypothermia, and injury in elderly women with fractured femur: an injury response to altered metabolism? Lancet 1:143, 1983

182. Allison SP: Some metabolic aspects of injury. The Scientific Basis for the Care of the Critically Ill. Little RA, Frayn KN, Eds. Manchester University Press, Manchester, 1986, p 169

183. Holt DR, Kirk SJ, Regan MC, et al: Effect of age on wound healing in healthy human beings. Surgery 112:293, 1992

184. Lenhardt R, Hopf HW, Marker E, et al: Perioperative collagen deposition in elderly and young men and women. Arch Surg 135:71, 2000

185. White H, Cook J, Ward M: Abdominal wound dehiscence. Ann Royal Coll Surg Engl 59:337, 1977

186. Miller RA: Aging and the Immune Response. Handbook of The Biology of Aging, 3rd ed. Schneider EL, Rowe J, Eds. Academic Press, San Diego, 1996, p 355

187. Carson P, Nichol K, O'Brien J, et al: Immune function and vaccine responses in healthy advanced elderly patients. Arch Intern Med 160:2017, 2000

188. Waldorf DS, Willkens RF, Decker JL: Impaired delayed hypersensitivity in an aging population. JAMA 203:831, 1968

189. Pietsch JB, Meakins JL, MacLean LD: The delayed hypersensitivity response: application in clinical surgery. Surgery 82:349, 1977

190. Sacco WJ, Copes WS, Bain LWJ, et al: Effect of preinjury illness on trauma patient survival outcome. J Trauma 35:538, 1993

191. Morris JA Jr, MacKenzie EJ, Edelstein SL: The effect of preexisting conditions on mortality in trauma patients. JAMA 263:1942, 1990

192. Finelli FC, Jonsson J, Champion HR, et al: A case control study for major trauma in geriatric patients. J Trauma 29:541, 1989

193. Dischinger PC, Cushing BM, Kerns TJ: Injury patterns associated with direction of impact: drivers admitted to trauma centers. J Trauma 35:454, 1993

194. Fatality facts: elderly. Insurance Institute for Highway Safety, Highway Loss Data Institute. Arlington, Virginia, 2002. http://www.hwysafety.org/safety%5Ffacts/fatality%5Ffacts/elderly.htm

195. Viano DC, Culver CC, Evans L, et al: Involvement of older drivers in multivehicle side-impact crashes. Accid Anal & Prev 22:177, 1990

196. McCoy GF, Johnstone RA, Duthie RB: Injury to the elderly in road traffic accidents. J Trauma 29:494, 1989

197. Allen JE, Schwab CW: Blunt chest trauma in the elderly. Am Surgeon 51:697, 1985

198. Richardson JD, Adams L, Flint LM: Selective management of flail chest and pulmonary contusion. Ann Surg 196:481, 1982

199. Riggs BL, Melton LJ: Involutional osteoporosis. N Engl J Med 314:1676, 1986

200. Velmahos GC, Jindal A, Chan LS, et al: "Insignificant" mechanism of injury: not to be taken lightly.

J Am Coll Surg 192:147, 2001

201. Linn BS: Age differences in the severity and outcome of burns. J Am Geriatr Soc 28:118, 1980

202. Frankenfield D, Cooney RN, Smith JS, et al: Age-related differences in the metabolic response to injury. J Trauma 48:49, 2000

203. McKinley BA, Marvin RG, Cocanour CS, et al: Blunt trauma resuscitation: the old can respond. Arch Surg 135:688, 2000

204. Pellicane JV, Byrne K, DeMaria EJ: Preventable complications and death from multiple organ failure among geriatric trauma victims. J Trauma 33:440, 1992

205. Knudson MM, Lieberman J, Morris JA, et al: Mortality factors in geriatric blunt trauma patients. Arch Surg 129:448, 1994

206. Champion HR, Copes WS, Buyer D, et al: Major trauma in geriatric patients. Am J Public Health 79:1278, 1989

207. DeMaria EJ, Kenney PR, Merriam MA, et al: Aggressive trauma care benefits the elderly. J Trauma 27:1200, 1987

208. Carrillo EH, Richardson JD, Malias MA, et al: Long term outcome of blunt trauma care in the elderly. Surg Gynecol Obstet 176:559, 1993

209. Day RJ, Vinen J, Hewitt-Falls E: Major trauma outcomes in the elderly. Med J Australia 160:675, 1994

210. van Aalst JA, Morris JA Jr, Yates HK, et al: Severely injured geriatric patients return to independent living: a study of factors influencing function and independence. J Trauma 31:1096, 1991

211. Oreskovich MR, Howard JD, Copass MK, et al: Geriatric trauma: injury patterns and outcome. J Trauma 24:565, 1984

212. Holbrook TL, Anderson JP, Sieber WJ, et al: Outcome after major trauma:12-month and 18-month follow-up from the Trauma Recovery Project. J Trauma 46:765, 1999

213. Koval KJ, Zuckerman JD: Functional recovery after fracture of the hip. J Bone Joint Surg 76A: 751, 1994

214. Canadian cancer statistics. Canadian Cancer Society, Toronto, Ontario, Canada, 2001 http://www.cancer.ca/english/RS_CanCanStats.asp

215. Feldman AR, Kessler L, Myers MH, et al: The prevalence of cancer: estimates based on the Connecticut Tumor Registry. N Engl J Med 315:1394, 1986

216. Newcomb PA, Carbone PP: Cancer treatment and age: patient perspectives. J Natl Cancer Inst 85: 1580, 1993

217. Elsaleh H, Joseph D, Grieu F, et al: Association of tumour site and sex with survival benefit from adjuvant chemotherapy in colorectal cancer. Lancet 355:1745, 2000

218. Mahoney T, Kuo Y-H, Topilow A, et al: Stage III colon cancers: why adjuvant chemotherapy is not offered to elderly patients. Arch Surg 135:182, 2000

219. Hodgson DC, Fuchs CS, Ayanian JZ: Impact of patient and provider characteristics on the treatment and outcomes of colorectal cancer. J Nat Canc Inst 93:501, 2001

220. Yancik R, Wesley MN, Ries LAG, et al: Effect of age and comorbidity in postmenopausal breast cancer patients aged 55 years and older. JAMA 285:885, 2001a

221. Desch CE, Smith TJ: Defining treatment aims and end-points in older patients with cancer. Drugs & Aging 6:351, 1995

222. Yellen SB, Cella DF, Leslie WT. Age and clinical decision making in oncology patients. J Natl Cancer Inst 86:1766, 1994

223. Greenfield S, Blanco DM, Elashoff RM, et al: Patterns of care related to age of breast cancer patients. JAMA 257:2766, 1987

224. Silliman RA: Breast cancer care in old age: where do we go from here? J Natl Cancer Inst 88:701, 1996

225. Goodwin JS, Samet JM, Hunt WC: Determinants of survival in older cancer patients. J Natl Cancer Inst 88:1031, 1996

226. Hutchins LF, Unger JM, Crowley JJ, et al: Underrepresentation of patients 65 years of age or older in cancer-treatment trials. N Engl J Med 341:2061, 1999

227. Bernabei R, Venturiero V, Tarsitani P, et al: The comprehensive geriatric assessment: when, where, and how. Crit Rev Oncol Hematol 33:45, 2000

228. Yancik R, Ganz PA, Varriccchio CG, et al: Perspectives on comorbidity and cancer in older patients: approaches to expand the knowledge base. J Clin Oncol 19:1147, 2001

229. Walter LC, Covinsky KE: Cancer screening in elderly patients: a framework for individualized decision making. JAMA 285:2750, 2001

230. Fried LP, Ferrucci L, Darer J, et al: Untangling the concepts of disability, frailty, and comorbidity: implications for improved targeting and care. J Gerontol Med Sci 59:255, 2004

231. Goodwin JS: Geriatrics and the limits of modern medicine. N Engl J Med 340:1283, 1999

232. Normal Human Aging: The Baltimore Longitudinal Study of Aging. Shock NW, Greulich RC, Andres R, et al, Eds. NIH Publication No. 84-2450. US Government Printing Office, Washington, DC, 1984

233. Watters JM, O'Rourke K: Effects of age and gender. Surgical Research. Wilmore DW, Souba WW, Eds. Academic Press, San Diego, 2001

234. MacDonald P, Johnstone D, Rockwood K: Coronary artery bypass surgery for elderly patients: is our practice based on evidence or faith? CMAJ 162:1005, 2000

235. Comprehensive functional assessment for elderly patients. Health and Public Policy Committee, American College of Physicians. Ann Intern Med 109:70, 1988

236. McClaran JC: Preoperative assessment: the geriatrician's viewpoint. Surgical Care of the Elderly. Meakins JL, McClaran JC, Eds. Year Book Medi-cal Publishers, 1988, p 217

237. Katz S: The science of quality of life (editorial). J Chron Dis 40:459, 1987

238. Katz S: Assessing self-maintenance: activities of daily living, mobility, and instrumental activities of daily living. J Am Geriatr Soc 31:721, 1983

239. Haab F, Boccon-Gibod L, Delmas V, et al: Perineal versus retropubic radical prostatectomy for T1, T2 prostate cancer. Br J Urol 74:626, 1994

240. Oxman TE, Freeman DH Jr, Manheimer ED: Lack of social participation or religious strength and comfort as risk factors for death after cardiac surgery in the elderly. Psychosom Med 57:5, 1995

241. Bombardier C, Melfi CA, Paul J, et al: Comparison of a generic and a disease-specific measure of pain and physical function after knee replacement surgery. Med Care 33(4 suppl):AS131, 1995

242. Jaeger AA, Hlatky MA, Paul SM, et al: Functional capacity after cardiac surgery in elderly patients. J Am Coll Cardiol 24:104, 1994

243. Weller SJ, Rossitch E Jr: Unilateral posterolateral decompression without stabilization for neurological palliation of symptomatic spinal metastasis in debilitated patients. J Neurosurg 82:739, 1995

244. Munin MC, Kwoh CK, Glynn N, et al: Predicting discharge outcome after elective hip and knee arthroplasty. Am J Phys Med Rehabil 74:294, 1995

245. Lakatta EG: Heart and circulation. Handbook of the Biology of Aging, 2nd ed. Finch CE, Schneider EL, Adelman RC, et al, Eds. Van Nostrand Reinhold Co, New York, 1985, p 413

246. Seely JF: Renal function in the elderly. Surgical Care of the Elderly. Meakins JL, McClaran JC, Eds. Year Book Medical Publishers, Chicago, 1988

247. Watters JM, Moulton SB, Clancey SM, et al: Aging exaggerates glucose intolerance following injury. J Trauma 37:786, 1994

248. Lakatta EG: Cardiovascular reserve capacity in healthy older humans. Aging Clin Exp Res 6:213, 1994

249. Lakatta EG: Heart and circulation. Handbook of the Biology of Aging, 3rd ed. Schneider EL, Rowe JW, Eds. Academic Press, San Diego, 1990, p 181

250. Watters JM, Meakins JL: Surgical management in the elderly. Surgery. Williamson RCN, Corson JD, Eds. CV Mosby, London, 2001

251. Thomas VS, Rockwood K, McDowell K: Multi-dimensionality in instrumental and basic activities of daily living. J Clin Epidemiol 51:315, 1998

252. Kane RL, Ouslander JG, Abrass IB: Essentials of Clinical Geriatrics, 2nd ed. McGraw-Hill Information Services Co, New York, 1989, p 213

253. Kane RL, Ouslander JG, Abrass IB: Essentials of Clinical Geriatrics, 2nd ed. McGraw-Hill Information Services Co, New York, 1989, p 341

Acknowledgment

Figures 2, 4, and 8   Marcia Kammerer.

140 THE PEDIATRIC SURGICAL PATIENT

Andreas H. Meier, M.D., Robert E. Cilley, M.D., F.A.C.S., Peter W. Dillon, M.D., F.A.C.S., and Arnold G. Coran, M.D., F.A.C.S.

Surgical care of neonates, infants, and children differs in many respects from that of adults.[1] Accordingly, it is essential that surgeons caring for preadult patients be capable of recognizing and managing certain clinical problems that occur frequently in this population. To this end, we begin this chapter by discussing several basic considerations related to pediatric physiology, which is markedly different from adult physiology. With this general discussion as a background, we then provide an overview of specific surgical problems commonly encountered in pediatric patients.

Physiologic Considerations

HOMEOSTASIS

Fluids and Electrolytes

Management of fluids and electrolytes in neonates and infants requires a thorough understanding of the changes in body fluid compartments that occur during development [*see Figure 1*].[2-7] At birth, total body water accounts for roughly 75% of total body weight (TBW), but this percentage decreases rapidly in the first few days, falling slowly toward 60% over the first year. Similarly, extracellular fluid volume accounts for 45% of TBW at birth but only 20% by the end of the first year. Newborns have lower glomerular filtration rates and reduced renal concentrating ability[8,9]; consequently, they tolerate dehydration poorly and cannot excrete a water load as effectively as older persons with mature kidneys can. For this reason, adequate fluid management is especially challenging in these patients.

Measurement of urine output is a useful guide to fluid management, provided that accurate urine collections can be obtained. In critically ill infants and children, a urinary catheter should be inserted to ensure accurate urine collections. Catheterization of male neonates and infants carries a significant risk of trauma to the small urethra; in these patients, the use of properly secured collection bags may allow accurate measurement of urine output without the need for catheter insertion. An appropriate urine output is 1 to 2 ml/kg/hr.

Insensible water loss results from continuous evaporative loss of water through the respiratory tract and the skin.[10] In premature infants, a large proportion of insensible water loss occurs transcutaneously. Insensible water loss from the skin can be minimized by using incubators in the neonatal intensive care unit (NICU) and extremity coverings in the operating room. Insensible water loss from the lungs can be decreased by humidifying the inspired gases.

In general, the maintenance fluid requirement of a neonate is considered to be 70 ml/kg/24 hr initially; this figure rises to 100 ml/kg/24 hr after a few days of life. Neonates with surgical problems may require dramatically increased amounts of fluid.

The sodium requirement of a full-term infant is, on average, 2 mEq/kg/24 hr. Conditions such as intestinal obstruction [*see Com-

mon Surgical Problems in Newborns, Obstruction of the Gastrointestinal Tract, below*] and peritonitis increase sodium loss and therefore increase sodium requirements. Although full-term infants can retain sodium as well as adults do in the face of a sodium deficit, they are unable to excrete excess sodium as effectively. As a result, excessive infusion of sodium can rapidly result in hypernatremia.

The generally accepted potassium requirement is 2 mEq/kg/24 hr after the first 2 to 3 days of life. However, the need for potassium replacement can be significant in the first few days of life as well, especially after a major surgical intervention. Thus, potassium should be administered in the first 1 or 2 days of life after an operation once urine output has been established.

In view of the various fluid and electrolyte requirements of neonates and infants, the initial fluid used in surgical management of these patients, both preoperatively and postoperatively, should be 5% or 10% dextrose in 0.2% saline at a dosage of 100 to 150 ml/kg/24 hr [*see Table 1*].

Acid-Base Status

Metabolic alkalosis caused by loss of electrolytes (specifically, chloride) may occur with prolonged gastric suction or vomiting; usually, it is easily corrected by replacing the lost electrolytes (e.g., by administering potassium chloride). Metabolic acidosis, on the other hand, is usually the result of poor tissue perfusion and lactic acidosis; it is best corrected by treating the underlying cause of the

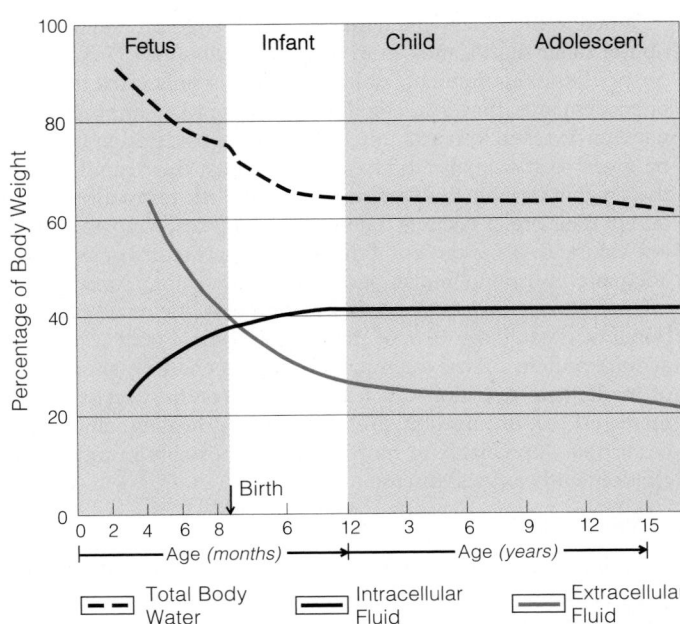

Figure 1 **Total body water (TBW) and extracellular fluid (ECF) decrease between fetal life and adulthood, and intracellular fluid (ICF) increases.**

Table 1 Daily Fluid Requirements for Neonates and Infants

Weight	Fluid Requirements*
Premature < 1.5 kg	150 ml/kg
Neonates and infants 1.5–10 kg	100 ml/kg
Infants and children 10–20 kg	1,000 ml + 50 ml/kg over 10 kg
Children > 20 kg	1,500 ml + 20 ml/kg over 20 kg

*Maintenance Na+ and K+ requirements range from 2 to 4 mEq/kg; solution can generally be given as 0.2% saline, with 5% or 10% dextrose and K+ added.

poor perfusion and by temporarily administering buffers (e.g., sodium bicarbonate). It should be noted that standard sodium bicarbonate solutions are extremely hypertonic and should be diluted before administration, especially when they are being given to neonates.

Temperature

In neonates, strict regulation of the environmental temperature is critical for preventing hypothermia. Compared with older children and adults, infants have a higher ratio of body surface area to weight, less subcutaneous fat (and therefore poorer thermal insulation), and less lean body mass (which is required for generating and retaining heat).

Maintaining the body temperature of neonates and young infants is critical both in the NICU and in the OR. In the NICU, the infant may be placed in an incubator (which is designed to reduce airflow across the skin and provide a tightly regulated, thermally neutral environment) or on a bed with an overhead radiant heater. In the OR, the ambient room temperature may be raised, overhead radiant warmers may be used, circulatory warm air blankets may be applied, and the head and extremities may be wrapped in plastic. Ventilatory gases are warmed and humidified, and warm intravenous and irrigation fluids are used.

NUTRITION

Whereas the nutritional requirements of children and teenagers do not differ significantly from those of adults [see 137 Nutritional Support], the requirements of infants do. Not only must the metabolic demands that a major illness or operation imposes on all patients be taken into account, but special consideration must also be given to the smaller body size of infants, their rapid growth, their highly variable fluid requirements, and the immaturity of certain of their organ systems. These characteristics, coupled with the low caloric reserves present if the infant is premature or sick, make adequate nutritional intake particularly important. Consequently, infants whose nutritional needs are not met as the result of a functional or organic disorder of the gastrointestinal tract can rapidly acquire protein-calorie malnutrition. Even a relatively short period of inadequate nutrition can lead to impaired host resistance, an increased risk of infection, and poor wound healing, all of which contribute appreciably to morbidity and mortality in infants and children with surgical disease.

Nutritional Requirements

Infants have higher weight-adjusted caloric requirements than older children and adults do [see Table 2], and these requirements are further increased by periods of active growth and extreme physical activity.[11,12] Major illness or surgical trauma may raise caloric requirements even further. However, measured energy expenditures do not appear to be elevated in neonatal surgical patients and critically ill premature infants.[13-15] In general, calories should be provided in the proportions found in a well-balanced diet: 50% carbohydrate, 35% fat, and 15% protein.

The protein needs of infants are based on the combined requirements for maintenance and growth. Most of the increase in body protein occurs during the first year of life, which explains why protein requirements are highest in infancy and decrease with age. Of the 20 amino acids from which proteins are synthesized, eight are essential in adults, but it is believed that in addition, histidine is essential in infants and cysteine and tyrosine in premature infants.

In general, infants require more vitamins and minerals than adults do. Increased amounts of calcium and phosphorus are particularly important because of the rapid growth rate of the infant's skeleton.

Nutritional Assessment

In many cases, a sick infant's history and overall appearance provide sufficient grounds for initiating nutritional support. For example, a preterm infant with respiratory distress who is small for his or her gestational age clearly requires parenteral nutrition, as does a newborn with gastroschisis. Physical variables that should be considered in nutritional assessment include weight, length, head circumference, chest circumference, and triceps skinfold thickness. No blood test reflects changes in the patient's nutritional status with ideal accuracy, but serum albumin, prealbumin, and transferrin levels are frequently used as markers.

Enteral Nutrition

The type of nutritional support to be employed depends on the disease affecting the patient and on the patient's overall health status. From a physiologic standpoint, enteral nutrition is preferable and is the first choice for patients whose GI tract is functioning adequately.[16] For infants younger than 1 year, breast milk or a standard infant formula is delivered orally or via a tube.[17] For older children who are unable or unwilling to eat, a liquid diet consisting of either blenderized food or liquid formula may be employed. A number of nutritionally complete liquid formulas are commercially available. Specialized formulas are available for use in patients who have lactose intolerance or protein sensitivity or who are experiencing renal or hepatic failure.

The use of predigested or elemental diets may allow patients with injured intestine or inadequate intestinal length to absorb enteral feedings. In children who cannot manage oral feedings, nasogastric and nasojejunal tubes are used. If the child's condition necessitates long-term tube feeding, a gastrostomy may be necessary.

Table 2 Daily Kilocalorie and Protein Requirements for Infants and Children

Age (yr)	Kilocalorie Requirements* (kcal/kg)	Protein Requirements (g/kg)
0–1	90–120	2.0–3.5
1–7	75–90	2.0–2.5
7–12	60–75	2.0
12–18	30–60	1.5
18+	25–30	1.0

*These numbers represent volume administered when 1 kcal/ml solutions are used. Growth can be maintained with 10% to 20% fewer calories if parenteral nutrition is employed.

Table 3 Normal Values for Vital Signs in Children[142]

Age (yr)	Pulse Rate (beats/min)	Systolic BP (mm Hg)	Respirations (breaths/min)	Urinary Output (ml/kg/hr)
0–1	< 160	> 60	< 60	2.0
1–3	< 150	> 70	< 40	1.5
3–5	< 140	> 75	< 35	1.0
6–12	< 120	> 80	< 30	1.0
> 12	< 100	> 90	< 30	0.5

Postoperative Feeding

Infants have more difficulty in feeding during the early months of life. This is especially true of premature infants, in whom the complex physiology of sucking and swallowing is not yet fully developed. In addition, the work of feeding accounts for most of an infant's caloric expenditure in the early months, and a stressed infant tires easily. For this reason, gavage or gastrostomy tube feedings are generally employed for the early stages of postoperative feeding in infants. Feeding is begun after the resolution of postoperative ileus has been demonstrated by the passage of meconium or stool. Further evidence that the bowel is beginning to function is the disappearance of the bilious green color of the gastric aspirate and the decrease in the volume of the aspirate from the nasogastric or gastrostomy tube. Initially, small volumes of rehydration fluid are given orally or via a gastrostomy tube. If these are tolerated, the feedings are increased incrementally until the nutritional goals for the patient have been reached.

Infants tolerate increases in volume more readily than increases in osmolarity. Accordingly, it is often best to start with diluted formulas (three-quarter–strength, half-strength, or quarter-strength), then, as nutritional requirements grow, increase the volume first and subsequently increase the concentration as necessary to supply the required amount of calories.

Elemental or chemically defined diets require a minimum of digestive work and are free of residual bulk. They may be accepted by infants if given orally; however, they are unpalatable and thus are usually given by tube. Because of the high osmolality of these diets, constant infusion with a pump may be necessary to prevent the development of dumping syndrome. The ease of GI absorption and the minimal residue make elemental diets useful as an intermediate step between parenteral nutrition and regular feedings. In infants, whenever possible, oral feedings or oral stimulation should accompany tube feedings.

Parenteral Nutrition

The concept of total parenteral nutrition (TPN) had been entertained for decades for its initial development, but it was not until the 1960s that the major breakthrough occurred, when Dudrick and associates successfully administered a hypertonic glucose solution into a central vein.[18,19] In the early years after the group's initial success, this approach to TPN began to be widely used in newborns with GI anomalies.[20,21] Since then, the technique has been applied to the care of patients of all age groups, with dramatic results [see 137 Nutritional Support]. Less concentrated solutions are available for administration into peripheral veins.

Generally, TPN is reserved for infants and children who are threatened by catabolic or nutritional deficits because feeding via the GI tract is hazardous, inadequate, or impossible. Conditions that may necessitate TPN include intestinal obstruction from congenital disorders, prolonged postoperative ileus, peritonitis, intestinal fistulas, chronic nonspecific diarrhea, necrotizing enterocolitis, short-bowel syndrome, extensive burns, and abdominal neoplasms treated with surgery, chemotherapy, and radiation. Besides being used for nutritional repletion of malnourished children, TPN may also be employed prophylactically when prolonged starvation is expected, as in cases of gastroschisis. In infants, TPN is indicated if nutrition is inadequate for longer than 3 days; however, in older children and adults, a longer period of inadequate nutrition may be tolerated, depending on patients' nutritional status before operation or at the onset of illness. The benefits of improved nutrition in terms of reducing mortality and morbidity must be weighed against the risks of serious complications, especially sepsis. TPN should not be employed when enteral nutrition is feasible. Every effort should be made to use the enteral route for feeding, including the use of transpyloric feeding tubes.

Infants receiving TPN must be carefully monitored. Essential clinical measurements include weight, length, and intake and output volumes. Blood tests must be employed judiciously and sparingly in infants and children because of their small total blood volume. At the start of therapy and once a week thereafter, a complete blood count should be done, blood urea nitrogen should be measured, and serum levels of electrolytes, glucose, calcium, phosphorus, magnesium, and albumin should be assessed. Serum levels of liver enzymes, bilirubin, and creatinine should be measured at the start of therapy and every 2 weeks thereafter.

On average, neonates gain 15 to 25 g/day with TPN, and older children gain 0.5% of TBW/day. Greater weight gains may signal excessive administration of fluids or intake of calories.

The main complications of parenteral nutrition include catheter-based problems (e.g., sepsis, malfunction, and venous thrombosis), electrolyte abnormalities, and (especially in infants receiving long-term TPN) hepatic cholestasis, which ultimately can result in cirrhosis and hepatic failure. Strategies to minimize liver damage include early and aggressive treatment of infection, avoidance of excessive caloric intake, limitation of protein intake, and supplemental trophic enteral nutrition.

HEMODYNAMIC IMBALANCE AND SHOCK

For proper assessment of shock in infants and children, it is necessary to be familiar with the normal vital signs in these age groups [see Table 3]. The two types of shock most frequently seen are hypovolemic shock and septic shock; in infants and children, septic shock is the most common form.[22] The response of newborns and infants to hypovolemic or septic shock is significantly different from the response of older children and adults. For example, neonates affected by profound shock tend to become bradycardic, whereas adults are more likely to become tachycardic. Moreover, neonates, especially premature neonates, normally have a low blood pressure; consequently, shock often does not evoke any further significant reduction of blood pressure. The hypovolemia caused by the shock results in decreased venous return, which lowers cardiac output; the reduced cardiac output leads to poor tissue perfusion and the development of lactic acidosis.

Gram-negative bacteria are the organisms most often responsible for septic shock. Peritonitis resulting from intestinal perforation is a common cause of septic shock in neonates and infants; other causes are urinary tract infections, respiratory tract infections, and contaminated intravascular catheters. The pathophysiology of septic shock differs substantially from that of hypovolemic shock; however, in both states, stasis and pooling of blood in the capillary bed lead to reduction of the circulating blood volume.[23]

Treatment

The mainstay of therapy for hypovolemic shock is administration of fluid and blood. In neonates, the hematocrit should be maintained at 45% to ensure adequate oxygen delivery. In many infants, hypovolemic shock is caused not by hemorrhage but by dehydration (e.g., from severe gastroenteritis). This dehydration is usually hypertonic because of the significant loss of hypotonic fluid. As a rule, neonates and infants in hypovolemic shock lose much more water than electrolytes, and as a result, serum sodium levels may exceed 150 mEq/L. Emergency treatment involves infusion of isotonic solutions of sodium chloride with careful monitoring of serum electrolyte concentrations.

Because septic shock, like hypovolemic shock, is characterized by reduced circulating blood volume, initial therapy involves infusion of large volumes of colloid solutions. Most of the experimental and clinical data suggest that colloid solutions are preferable to crystalloid solutions in this setting, both for children and for adults. In addition, broad-spectrum antibiotics should always be administered.

If fluid infusion has been maximally effective (as evidenced by a normal to elevated central venous pressure) but hypotension persists, pharmacologic agents must be given to improve myocardial contractility. The most commonly used agents are the alpha and beta agonists dopamine and dobutamine, which primarily have inotropic and mild vasodilatory effects at lower doses. Infants and children in shock require continuous monitoring and close clinical observation and should therefore be managed in the ICU.

Common Surgical Problems of Newborns

Neonatal surgical problems often present as emergencies and necessitate rapid stabilization and transfer of the patient to a pediatric surgical center. Proper initial management is crucial and may have a pronounced effect on overall outcome. The organ systems most commonly affected are the respiratory tract and the GI tract.

EMERGENCY SURGICAL PROBLEMS

In many communities, the general surgeon is frequently called on to assist in the diagnosis and initial care of a neonate with an apparent surgical problem. After stabilization measures have been carried out and preliminary tests have been performed to establish a diagnosis, the baby may be transported to a pediatric center that is specially equipped and staffed to manage the specific surgical problem present.

The steps in the stabilization of a critically ill neonate before transport are similar to the ABCs of initial care in an adult (*A*irway, *B*reathing, *C*irculation). By the time the surgeon is consulted, the neonatologist or pediatrician may have accomplished initial stabilization and begun to prepare the baby for transfer. The surgeon's immediate responsibility may be to establish vascular

access. In some cases, a peripheral venous cannula may be appropriate; more often, a central catheter is inserted via an umbilical vein or artery. In babies with omphalocele or gastroschisis, the I.V. line ideally should be placed in the upper extremities or the neck. Appropriate fluids should be infused to prevent dehydration and to correct any fluid or electrolyte deficits. When required, a nasogastric or esophageal pouch suction tube should be placed and decompression initiated. This maneuver is extremely important if transport by air is considered: trapped gases change in volume with alterations in barometric pressure, and such changes may have particularly deleterious effects on infants who have intestinal gas, pneumothorax, or pneumomediastinum.

Vitamin K should be given in the form of phytonadione, 1 mg (0.5 mg for babies who weigh less than 1,500 g). Appropriate antibiotics should also be administered. Finally, the infant should be wrapped and placed in an incubator or a radiant warmer to stabilize body temperature and maintain it at normal levels.

The use of sophisticated transport teams with appropriate equipment and supplies is the safest method of moving these babies between hospitals. Early stabilization and close communication between the referring physician, the accepting physician, and the transport team are essential for minimizing the potential risks and morbidity associated with patient transfer.

The following seven emergency surgical problems are commonly encountered in neonates. Each involves special considerations in the preparation of the patient for interhospital transfer.

1. Congenital diaphragmatic hernia (CDH): insert a nasogastric or orogastric tube. Ventilation by face mask is contraindicated; if ventilation is required, intubate.
2. Esophageal atresia: insert a tube to aspirate secretions from pouch (use a Replogle tube, if available). If possible, avoid mechanical ventilation; if intubation is required, use high-frequency, low-pressure ventilation to prevent distention and possible perforation of the stomach.
3. Congenital lobar emphysema: support normal oxygenation. Minimize mean airway pressure.
4. Intestinal obstruction: use nasogastric or orogastric suction. Confirm placement and function of I.V. lines.
5. Omphalocele or gastroschisis: use nasogastric or orogastric suction. Cover the sac with nonadherent gauze, and take care not to rupture the membrane (if present); cover the intestine with saline-soaked gauze and a see-through bowel bag. Place the I.V. line in the upper extremity or the neck, if possible. Maintain hydration by increasing fluid administration to replace fluid lost from the exposed bowel. Support the bowel with dressings. Maintain body temperature.
6. Exstrophy of the bladder: cover the exposed bladder with a nonadherent dressing.
7. Meningomyelocele: cover the sac with a nonadherent dressing.

RESPIRATORY PROBLEMS

Cystic Disease of the Lung

Cystic lung disease, especially congenital cystic adenomatoid malformation (CCAM) of the left lower lobe, can mimic diaphragmatic hernia both clinically and radiographically [*see Figure 2a*].[24,25] Unlike a newborn with diaphragmatic hernia, however, a newborn with CCAM will have an abdomen with the normal degree of protuberance. If an infant with CCAM experiences marked respiratory distress that necessitates intubation and mechanical ventilation, it is better to perform an emergency lobectomy than to subject the baby to a period of mechanical ventilation, with its

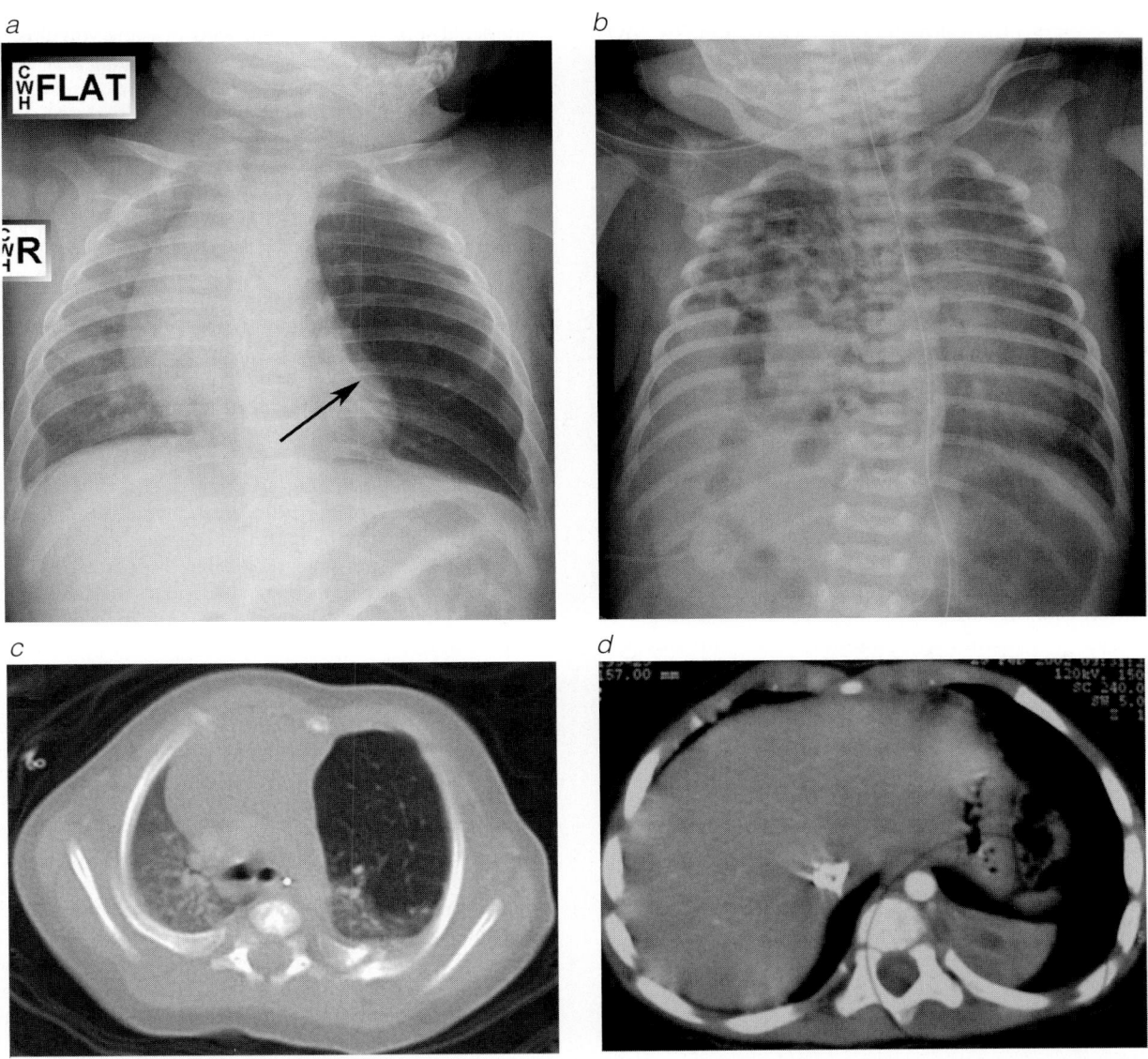

Figure 2 Shown are common neonatal chest abnormalities: (*a*) congenital cystic adenomatoid malformation (CCAM) with a large cyst in the left lung (arrow) and mediastinal shift; (*b*) congenital diaphragmatic hernia (CDH) on the right side, with the liver and intestines within the chest cavity; (*c*) hyperinflated left lung with mediastinal shift caused by lobar emphysema; and (*d*) pulmonary sequestration with consolidation caused by pneumonia.

attendant risks (i.e., barotrauma and oxygen toxicity). If the lesion is asymptomatic, it can be resected later in infancy to prevent infectious complications and possible (albeit rare) transformation into a malignancy.

Diaphragmatic Hernia

Infants with CDH may be quite ill at birth, often suffering from acute respiratory distress and hemodynamic instability. Because the intestines are located in the chest, an infant with CDH appears to have a scaphoid abdomen [*see Figure 2b*]. The entire stomach may be in the chest, and as a result, it may be difficult to pass a nasogastric tube into the stomach. A plain x-ray usually establishes the diagnosis.

CDH is an embryopathy that results from abnormal development of the diaphragm and the lungs. The defect in the diaphragm allows herniation of abdominal contents. On the affected side, as well

as on the contralateral side, the lung shows hypoplasia, which varies in severity. The small vessels (arterioles) are excessively muscularized and can easily constrict.[26] The main pathophysiologic consequence of CDH is not the presence of the hernia but, rather, severe pulmonary hypertension.[27] Accordingly, initial treatment is aimed at preventing or, if prevention is not possible, mitigating pulmonary hypertension and its sequelae.

Babies with CDH require immediate resuscitation, correction of acidosis, and, in most cases, endotracheal intubation. Placement of an orogastric tube can help decompress the GI tract. Once the baby is relatively stable, surgical intervention should be delayed to allow time for the pulmonary hypertension to decrease or disappear. There is evidence to suggest that gentle ventilation with permissive hypercapnia may decrease secondary barotrauma and long-term morbidity.[28] If the baby cannot be stabilized with conventional, jet, high-frequency, or oscillation ventilation and inhaled nitrous oxide,[29] extracorporeal membrane oxygenation (ECMO) may be indicated; the hernia should be addressed after the ECMO run is completed.[30-32] During the procedure, the intestines are reduced into the abdominal cavity, and the diaphragmatic defect is repaired, either in the OR or in the NICU.[33] However, the operative procedure usually does not significantly alter the underlying pathophysiologic condition. In many cases, the newborn's condition improves at first after the operation but then begins to deteriorate. This response is seen less frequently with delayed surgical repair. If conventional treatment fails to control the pulmonary hypertension, ECMO may be instituted postoperatively. The precise impact of ECMO on overall outcome for CDH is still a matter of debate, though most pediatric surgeons agree that this technique has a role as a lifesaving measure if all other interventions fail.[34-36]

Lobar Emphysema

The term lobar emphysema refers to overexpansion of a segment of lung, which can compromise ventilation in a newborn if significant compression of a healthy lung or a mediastinal shift occurs [see Figure 2c].[37] If the patient is exhibiting symptoms, urgent resection is usually required, though emergency bronchoscopic decompression has also been employed in this setting.[38] If the patient shows no significant symptoms, follow-up directed toward the affected areas of the lung is appropriate; occasionally, the condition resolves spontaneously.

Pulmonary Sequestration

The term pulmonary sequestration denotes a condition in which lung tissue is supplied with blood by the systemic circulation. Often, this condition is diagnosed prenatally by means of fetal ultrasonography.[39] Patients with pulmonary sequestration are often asymptomatic at birth, but if respiratory distress develops, urgent surgical intervention is required.[40] If the lesions remain asymptomatic, removal later in life is recommended so that they do not become a nidus for infection [see Figure 2d].

INTESTINAL OBSTRUCTION

Not uncommonly, surgeons are asked to evaluate newborns for possible obstruction of the GI tract. These patients usually present with choking or vomiting. The list of possible causative conditions is fairly extensive, and most of these conditions must ultimately be managed by a pediatric surgeon. Nevertheless, it may be helpful in the initial stages to employ an algorithmic approach, which often serves to narrow the range of possible causes [see Figure 3].[41]

The color of the emesis helps to establish the level of the obstruction. If the emesis is nonbilious, the obstruction is proximal to the ampulla of Vater. If an orogastric tube cannot be placed, the diagnosis is esophageal atresia, which can be confirmed by a chest x-ray that demonstrates a curled-up tube in the upper esophageal pouch. If the x-ray shows air below the diaphragm, the diagnosis is a distal tracheoesophageal fistula. If there is no mechanical obstruction of the esophagus, the diagnosis may simply be gastroesophageal reflux (GER). Other surgical causes of nonbilious emesis are preampullary duodenal atresia or web, neonatal pyloric stenosis (uncommon), and pyloric atresia (extremely rare).

Bilious emesis in a newborn is a potentially more serious problem. Except for medical ileus, the main causes are all related to underlying surgical problems. If the baby's abdomen is not distended, he or she may have a proximal obstruction. If an abdominal x-ray series shows a double-bubble sign without distal air, duodenal atresia is likely. If distal air is seen, the diagnosis is either

a duodenal web or malrotation with possible volvulus. The latter represents a much more worrisome situation and constitutes a true surgical emergency, which must be diagnosed quickly by means of an upper GI study. In a newborn with volvulus, prompt exploration is required to prevent extensive necrosis of the midgut.

If the abdomen is distended, the obstruction is more distal. Physical examination is warranted to rule out an incarcerated inguinal hernia. Inspection of the perineum is necessary to look for possible anorectal malformation. Stippled calcifications on an abdominal film are pathognomonic of meconium peritonitis, which usually necessitates surgical exploration. If the anus is patent, a contrast enema study helps establish a diagnosis. A microcolon represents an unused lower GI tract, which may be seen with jejunoileal atresia or meconium ileus. The latter condition is usually characterized by the presence of large amounts of meconium in the terminal ileum and can often be treated successfully by administering water-soluble contrast enemas. There are other meconium-related functional obstructions that occur without microcolon, such as meconium plug syndrome and small left colon syndrome, both of which usually respond to treatment with enemas. If the lower GI study shows a normal or slightly dilated colon with a narrowed or spastic-appearing rectosigmoid, the likely diagnosis is Hirschsprung disease, which can be confirmed by suction biopsy of the rectum.

ABDOMINAL WALL DEFECTS

The overall incidence of neonatal abdominal wall defects is approximately one in every 2,000 births; however, the incidence of gastroschisis appears to be rising slowly.[42-44] Omphalocele represents an arrest in development, which may explain the increased frequency of chromosomal abnormalities and other structural birth defects in children with this condition.[45] The exact cause of gastroschisis is unclear, but it does not represent a normal stage of development; it appears to be more common with younger mothers, and environmental factors seem to play a role.[43,46] The extra-abdominal intestine is prone to vascular compromise, which explains the higher incidence of bowel atresia in these patients.[47] Although debate continues, most authors believe that babies with gastroschisis can safely be delivered vaginally.[48-52]

Although omphalocele is associated with a higher overall mortality than gastroschisis is, the latter is more challenging to manage in the immediate postnatal period. The exposure of bowel results in greater insensible loss of fluid and heat. Kinking of the intestinal blood supply may lead to venous congestion and ischemia. It is crucial to place children with gastroschisis in a warm environment and to protect the bowel (which is easily accomplished with the help of a plastic bowel bag). Intravenous access should be established immediately, and resuscitation should be initiated, guided by the infant's heart rate. Transfer to a pediatric surgical center is mandatory. The surgical options are (1) primary repair of the defect, if the abdominal cavity accommodates the exposed organs easily, and (2) gradual reduction of the intestines by means of a silo technique.[53]

Emergency surgical intervention is rarely required for management of omphalocele. Such defects may be either closed primarily or repaired with any of several staged approaches, depending on their size. Giant omphaloceles are best treated observantly, with the overlying membrane used as a temporary silo and definitive repair delayed until a reasonable intra-abdominal domain has developed.

CIRCUMCISION

Circumcision remains one of the most commonly performed procedures in male newborns. Approximately 1.2 million circum-

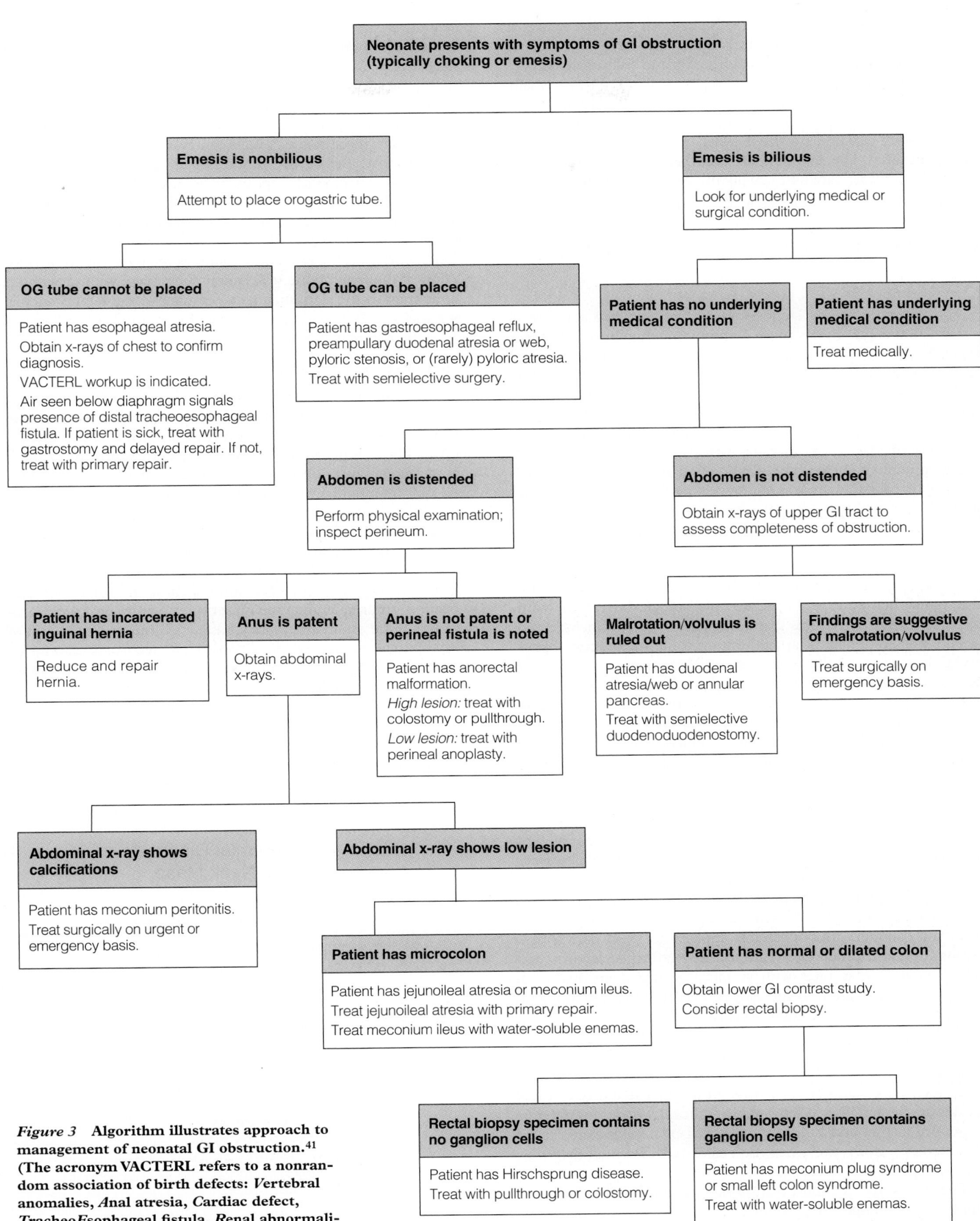

Figure 3 Algorithm illustrates approach to management of neonatal GI obstruction.[41] (The acronym VACTERL refers to a nonrandom association of birth defects: *V*ertebral anomalies, *A*nal atresia, *C*ardiac defect, *T*racheo*E*sophageal fistula, *R*enal abnormalities, and *L*imb abnormalities.)

cisions are performed in the United States each year, at a total cost of at least $150 million.[54] There continues to be a great deal of controversy regarding the medical benefits and risks of this procedure. Some authors argue that urinary tract infections, sexually transmitted diseases, and genital cancer occur less frequently in circumcised males; however, others dispute these findings.[55-57] Circumcision can be performed either in an outpatient setting or in the nursery. The use of local anesthesia is recommended.[54] Complications are rare and usually minor, but mutilating injuries to the penis have been reported.[58,59]

Common Surgical Problems in Infants and Children

PYLORIC STENOSIS

Hypertrophic pyloric stenosis affects between two and five of every 1,000 children; it is more common in white boys.[60] Patients typically present with progressive, projectile, nonbilious emesis 2 to 6 weeks after birth. They may show signs of severe dehydration with a hypochloremic, hypokalemic metabolic alkalosis (though the literature suggests that the incidence of this finding may be decreasing).[61] Medical approaches to managing this problem have been described,[62,63] but surgical correction after resuscitation is the treatment of choice. The classic open pyloromyotomy developed by Fredet-Ramstedt is still widely performed, and advances in minimally invasive techniques have made it possible to perform laparoscopic pyloromyotomy with safety and efficacy.[64,65]

GASTROESOPHAGEAL REFLUX

For appropriate treatment of GER in infants, it is important to distinguish between uncomplicated physiologic GER and symptomatic GER.[66] Symptoms that necessitate treatment include poor weight gain, esophagitis, apnea, apparent life-threatening events, and pulmonary complications. Upper GI contrast studies and 24-hour continuous pH monitoring are the gold standards for assessment. Endoscopy and esophageal biopsy may be useful for diagnosis and the evaluation of treatment. If GER does not resolve with simple feeding and positioning adjustments, acid suppressants, prokinetic therapy, or surface agents may prove effective. If GER is associated with anatomic abnormalities (e.g., hiatal hernia), apparent life-threatening events, or symptoms that persist despite optimal medical therapy, surgical intervention is usually indicated. In infants and younger children who require a feeding gastrostomy, a protective fundoplication is usually necessary if reflux is demonstrated on the upper GI study.

In the United States, the procedure most commonly performed to treat GER is a 360° Nissen fundoplication,[67] though partial posterior (Toupet) fundoplication appears to yield comparable results.[68,69] Both procedures can also be performed laparoscopically. Initial success rates with surgical treatment are high, but long-term complications (especially recurrent reflux) are frequent, resulting in redo rates ranging from 7% to 26%.[70]

NECK AND SOFT TISSUE MASSES

A neck mass [see 14 Neck Mass] is a common reason for a child to be seen by a surgeon. Even though the vast majority of these masses are benign, they often cause significant worries for parents. A detailed history and a thorough physical examination are crucial for narrowing down the otherwise extensive differential diagnosis [see Table 4].

The masses that are most commonly encountered in infants and children are enlarged lymph nodes caused by reactive postinfectious hyperplasia. Such masses feel soft, are often slightly tender on palpation, are mobile, and tend to shrink over time. A higher degree of concern is appropriate with neck masses that are located supraclavicularly, grow rapidly, develop at multiple sites, are fixed to surrounding tissues, or feel hard. Swift diagnosis of the underlying process is crucial in this situation. Fine-needle aspiration (FNA) biopsy may render an initial diagnosis,[71,72] but most treatment protocols require more tissue, which can be obtained through open surgical biopsy. Before the procedure, a chest x-ray should be obtained to determine whether the mass involves the mediastinum.

A mass in the anterior midline may be a remnant of the thyroglossal duct. Such masses should be excised at diagnosis to prevent any subsequent infectious complications. To minimize the risk of recurrence, the procedure includes the removal of the midportion of the hyoid bone.[73] A lateral neck mass, with or without a sinus tract to the skin, may be a remnant of the fetal branchial apparatus. Such masses should also be completely excised to reduce the risk of complications.

ABDOMINAL WALL HERNIA

Inguinal and umbilical hernia repairs are among the most commonly performed procedures in pediatric surgery. Umbilical hernias are commonly diagnosed at birth but tend to close spontaneously. The complication rate is very low, and thus, most pediatric surgeons postpone surgical repair until the patient is 2 to 4 years old. Inguinal hernias, on the other hand, pose a substantial risk of incarceration, especially during infancy, and should therefore be repaired as soon as they are diagnosed. High ligation of the sac is the treatment of choice. This operation is usually straightforward, but it can be challenging at times, particularly in premature infants with large hernias. Complications are rare; they tend to occur more frequently if the infant is premature or if the procedure was done on an emergency basis.[74] To minimize the risk of injury to the spermatic cord, a "no touch" technique should be employed. Whether the contralateral side should be explored remains controversial; some surgeons now use laparoscopy to assess the processus vaginalis of the opposite side.[75]

UNDESCENDED TESTICLES

Approximately 4% of male neonates have an undescended testis at birth, but only about 1% still have this condition at the age of

Table 4 Differential Diagnosis of Pediatric Neck Mass

Location	Conditions to Be Considered
Anterior midline	Epidermoid inclusion (sebaceous) cyst Thyroglossal duct cyst Benign reactive hyperplasia of lymph node Thyroid nodule Ectopic thymus Thymic cyst Ectopic thyroid tissue Lipoma Dermoid
Lateral	Branchial cleft remnant Lymphangioma/hemangioma Benign reactive hyperplasia of lymph node Neoplasms (lymphoma, rhabdomyosarcoma, neuroblastoma) Lipoma Torticollis

1 year.[76] Accordingly, most pediatric surgeons recommend that neonates with an undescended testis be observed during the first year of life. If the testicle has not descended by the end of this period, inguinal orchiopexy may be performed; the success rate with this option is higher than 80%.[77] It is not unusual to find a structurally abnormal testicle during exploration. Potential complications include testicular atrophy and recurrent ascent of the gonad. Hormonal treatment (with human chorionic gonadotropin or luteinizing hormone–releasing hormone) is widely employed in Europe but has a success rate of only about 50%. Laparoscopy is a useful and cost-effective option for the evaluation of nonpalpable testes.[78,79]

ABDOMINAL PAIN

Abdominal pain is a common finding in children and may arise from any of a wide variety of causes. Among surgical diseases, acute appendicitis is the most common cause of abdominal pain. In addition, however, the differential diagnosis must include perforated duodenal ulcer, Meckel's diverticulum, ulcerative colitis, Crohn disease, ruptured ovarian cyst, pelvic inflammatory disease, and, in younger children, intussusception. It is important to remember that medical problems (e.g., constipation, gastroenteritis, pancreatitis, and pneumonia) can also give rise to substantial abdominal discomfort.

Appendicitis

The diagnosis of appendicitis is based on the presence of localizing physical findings in the right lower quadrant of the abdomen. Even if the history and laboratory data are not typical, the presence of such findings should allow the surgeon to make the diagnosis and proceed with appropriate management.

If perforation of the appendix is suspected preoperatively, administration of broad-spectrum antibiotics should be started, and crystalloid should be infused. Intraoperative management of acutely perforated appendicitis varies widely among pediatric surgeons in the United States.[80] The evidence published to date on the benefits of intraoperative drain placement, peritoneal cultures, and laparoscopic techniques remains controversial.[74,81-85]

In most cases of perforated appendicitis, the wound can be closed primarily.[86] Although there is some debate regarding the utility of imaging studies in patients with the classic findings of acute appendicitis, it appears that CT can be quite helpful in patients with delayed presentations or atypical symptoms.[87-89] If perforated appendicitis with an abscess is identified, a safe and cost-effective treatment approach is to give antibiotics (first I.V., then oral), drain the collection percutaneously, and perform an interval appendectomy 6 weeks later.[90-94]

Crohn Disease

Occasionally, a teenager who exhibits the classic signs and symptoms of appendicitis turns out to have Crohn disease of the terminal ileum. This condition will be obvious at operation, when the mesenteric fat is seen to be creeping up along the sides of the inflamed ileum. If the base of the appendix is free of disease, appendectomy should be performed at the time of exploration.[95] When the child has fully recovered from the operation, a definitive workup, including a small bowel series and a colonoscopy with biopsy, should be performed to ascertain the extent of the Crohn disease. If an enterocutaneous fistula develops, TPN will be required for a prolonged period. If an intestinal stricture develops (typically, in the terminal ileum), resection may be required. Associated perianal Crohn disease can be very challenging to treat. Medical therapy and surgical therapy should be carried out conjointly. Conservative surgical options (e.g., local drainage, fistulotomy, and setons) are preferred; if sepsis does not resolve or if severe incontinence persists, a stoma may be required.[96]

Intussusception

Idiopathic intussusception usually develops between the ages of 6 months and 2 years. The invagination of small bowel into the cecum results in severe, crampy, intermittent abdominal pain, often associated with obstructive symptoms and bloody stools. Marked lethargy is also a frequent symptom. Air enemas and ultrasound-guided hydrostatic reduction have both been employed to treat this condition, with great success.[97-99] Surgical exploration should be reserved for patients in whom reduction is unsuccessful and patients in whom there is reason to suspect an anatomic lead point that is causing the intussusception.

Meckel's Diverticulum and Lower GI Hemorrhage

Meckel's diverticulum represents a remnant of the omphalomesenteric duct. It occurs in approximately 2% of the pediatric population. If symptomatic, it can be associated with acute and substantial lower GI bleeding, obstruction, or diverticulitis.[100] The differential diagnosis of lower GI bleeding in children also includes GI infections, colonic polyps, duplication cysts, and inflammatory bowel disease. Meckel diverticulitis presents with symptoms very similar to those of acute appendicitis and should always be ruled out if the appendix appears normal on exploration. Management of an asymptomatic diverticulum discovered during an abdominal operation remains controversial, even though resection has been shown to carry a low risk of complications.[101,102]

VENOUS ACCESS

To obtain venous access in an infant, a venous cutdown is performed, and a pediatric silicone (Broviac) catheter is passed through the common facial, external jugular, or internal jugular vein to the superior vena cava. This procedure is carried out in an OR or, if necessary, in the NICU. Adequate exposure must be obtained, proper instruments and fluoroscopy devices should be available, and strict aseptic conditions must be maintained. The venous catheter is tunneled from the point of entry into the vein to a skin exit site 5 to 10 cm away, with the aim of minimizing the likelihood of bloodstream contamination from dressing changes at the skin exit site. The catheter is brought out on the chest wall, where it is easily accessible and unlikely to be disrupted by an active patient. When no vein sites are available in the neck, the catheter may be advanced into the central venous circulation via a cutdown on the greater saphenous vein and tunneled to an exit site on the abdominal wall or the leg.[103] In older children and adults, percutaneous puncture of the subclavian vein is often performed in place of venous cutdown; this technique can also be used in infants.[104,105] Regardless of the technique employed, manipulation of the catheters must be done with close attention to asepsis and antisepsis to minimize the risk of bacterial and fungal infection.

Pediatric Trauma

Whereas accidents are the third most common cause of death in the United States population as a whole, they are the single most common cause of death in children between the ages of 1 and 15 years.[106] Every year, about 20 million injuries occur in children, resulting in approximately 15,000 deaths and 100,000 cases of permanent disability. The first approach to be considered in managing pediatric trauma is clearly prevention. In fact, preventive efforts have been gaining momentum, thanks in part to support from federal funds and from dedicated individual advocates. These efforts have included greater emphasis on the use of pediatric restraint devices in automobiles, improvements in the design of motor vehicles, the wearing of helmets by bicycle and motorcycle riders, improvements in the design of space heaters, the use of fire-retardant material for children's clothes (as dictated by the Flammable Fabrics Act), proper packing and labeling of poisons and medications, and the installation of appropriate fencing around swimming pools.

GENERAL PRINCIPLES

Although the general principles of trauma care are essentially the same for children as for adults, there are several significant differences that must be taken into account in the care of pediatric accident victims.[107] For example, children do not react to trauma in the same way as adults do. They often have difficulty in expressing pain and in articulating their complaints. They are often extremely frightened after an accident, and this fear may cause them to give misleading signals (e.g., by exhibiting signs of an acute abdomen even though no intra-abdominal injury has occurred). Children who experience stress often undergo developmental regression, typically accompanied by severe depression. All these psychological factors must be considered in the treatment of a pediatric accident victim.

Another key difference between children and adults is that children are still growing. Postoperative metabolic management after any form of stress, whether from a surgical procedure, from trauma, or from some other event, must take this difference into account. Children can compensate for hypovolemia effectively and keep their vital signs in the normal range, even in the presence of shock. However, a small blood loss that would be insignificant in an adult can result in marked hemodynamic changes in a small child. Moreover, water and heat loss can be far more extensive in small children than in older children and adults because smaller children have a greater surface area in relation to their weight and have a relative lack of insulating subcutaneous fat. Hypothermia aggravates acidosis and makes hemodynamic resuscitation much more difficult. Gastric dilatation, which can result in vomiting and pulmonary aspiration, is very common in young children after all forms of trauma. Finally, the nutritional requirements of injured children are greater than those of injured adults because children, as growing organisms, naturally have a high metabolic rate. Consequently, TPN often must be started earlier in the treatment of a child than it would be in the treatment of an adult in a comparable condition.

Not only are there significant physiologic and psychological differences between children and adults after trauma but there also are differences in accident patterns. Most childhood injuries result from blunt trauma. Head trauma is far more common in children than in adults: in fact, it accounts for most of the morbidity and mortality in the pediatric population. After motor vehicle accidents, which are the major cause of trauma in both children and adults, the next most frequent causes of trauma in children are events that are less important causes in adults: falls, bicycle accidents, drowning, poisoning, and burns from fires. Child abuse [see Child Abuse, below] is a unique and important cause of trauma in children.

Pediatric accident victims must be treated in centers that have experience in the care of traumatized children.[108,109] Such centers must have an emergency department with a section that is specifically set aside for the care of children and is staffed by nurses and physicians who are familiar with the management of pediatric trauma. They must have a hospital with a pediatric ICU that is also

Table 5 Pediatric Trauma Score

Variable	Coded Value
Size	
> 20 kg	+2
10–20 kg	+1
< 10 kg	−1
Airway status	
Normal	+2
Maintainable	+1
Not maintainable	−1
Systolic BP	
> 90 mm Hg	+2
50–90 mm Hg	+1
< 50 mm Hg	−1
In the absence of proper size BP cuff, assess BP by assigning these values:	
Pulse palpable at wrist	+2
Pulse palpable at groin	+1
Pulse not palpable	−1
CNS status	
Awake	+2
Partially conscious or unconscious	+1
Comatose or decerebrate	−1
Open wounds	
None	+2
Minor	+1
Major	−1
Skeletal injury	
None	+2
Closed fracture	+1
Open/multiple fractures	−1
Range of possible scores	−6 to +12
Scoring triage criterion for direct transport of patient to trauma center	< 9

staffed by experienced medical and paramedical personnel. Finally, they must have a transportation system that is capable of rapidly transporting critically ill pediatric trauma victims both by air and by land or water. The Pediatric Trauma Score [see Table 5] has been successfully used not only as a tool for grading severity of injury but also as a means of comparing trauma care across institutions.

AIRWAY MANAGEMENT, PAIN RELIEF, AND SEDATION

Establishing and maintaining a secure airway is of the utmost importance in treating any injured child. Most pediatric trauma programs have mechanisms in place that delegate this responsibility to the attending emergency physician or anesthesiologist so that the surgical team can continue assessing the patient. The airway team can also provide conscious sedation or elective intubation if a painful procedure (e.g., reduction of fractures or suturing of lacerations) proves necessary.

MANAGEMENT OF HEAD INJURY

Closed head injuries (CHIs) are the most common cause of death in children and account for close to 7,000 fatalities in the United States each year.[110] Any child who had a witnessed loss of consciousness, is mentally altered, or has an abnormal Glasgow Coma Scale (GCS) score should undergo urgent CT scanning of the head. If the GCS score is lower than 8, intubation is necessary to protect the airway. The main focus of therapy for severe CHI is on minimizing secondary insult to the brain by optimizing oxygen delivery. Management involves close monitoring of cerebral perfusion pressure and judicious use of sedatives, anticonvulsants, pressors, intraventricular drainage, or even surgical decompression to optimize cerebral perfusion. Evidence-based practice guidelines for the management of pediatric CHI patients are now available.[111]

Because children with even minor structural injuries to the brain are at risk for hyponatremia, close monitoring of sodium levels is required.[112,113] Patients who have postconcussive symptoms (e.g., vomiting, seizures, or headache) should be admitted, even if the head CT reveals no structural injury. It is our practice to follow these patients for 3 weeks after the injury to determine whether postconcussive symptoms are persisting. If these symptoms have not resolved, patients undergo a more detailed cognitive evaluation.

CERVICAL SPINE CLEARANCE

Cervical spine injuries in children are very rare but can have catastrophic consequences if missed. As with adult trauma patients, it is crucial to follow established protocols for systematically clearing the cervical spine. Early immobilization, clinical examination, plain x-rays, and advanced imaging studies can all be useful. Because of the anatomic differences between children and adults, certain modifications to adult protocols are necessary.[114,115]

BLUNT SOLID-ORGAN INJURY

Abdominal trauma in children is usually blunt. Penetrating injuries occur in only about 20% of children who sustain trauma and are managed in essentially the same way as they are in adults [*see Section 7 Trauma and Thermal Injury*].

Children who sustain major trauma often have intra-abdominal injuries. Because gastric dilatation and reflex ileus are far more common in children than in adults after a major injury, the initial clinical evaluation of the child's abdomen may be highly misleading. Early insertion of a nasogastric tube decompresses the stomach and allows more accurate physical examination of the abdomen; in addition, it reduces the risk of aspiration pneumonitis. Once the child is stable with respect to hemodynamic and respi-

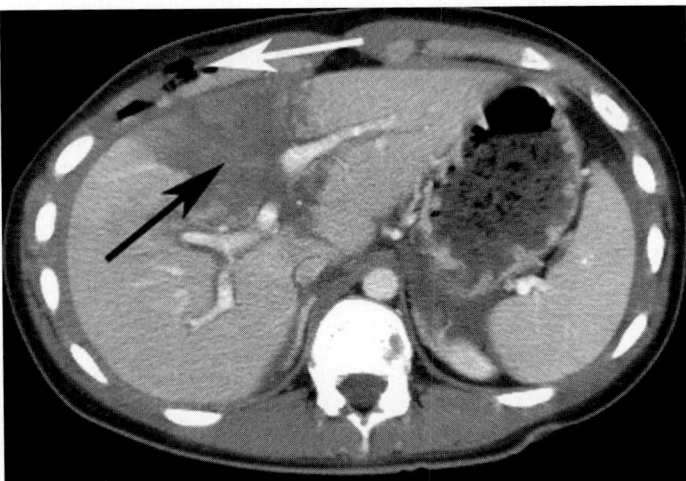

Figure 4 Shown is an abdominal CT scan from a patient who sustained multiple blunt injuries after being hit by an object through the windshield while driving. A deep central liver laceration is visible (black arrow), as is soft tissue emphysema (white arrow). The hepatic injury did not necessitate operative intervention.

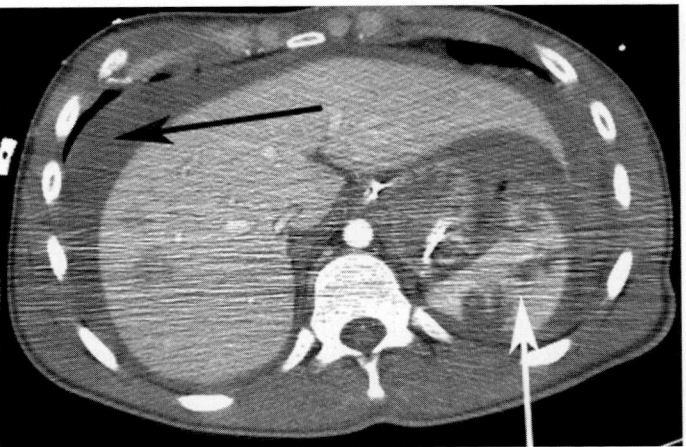

Figure 5 Shown is an abdominal CT scan from a child who sustained blunt trauma. Several large cracks in the spleen are apparent (white arrow). A significant amount of intraperitoneal blood can be seen over the liver (black arrow).

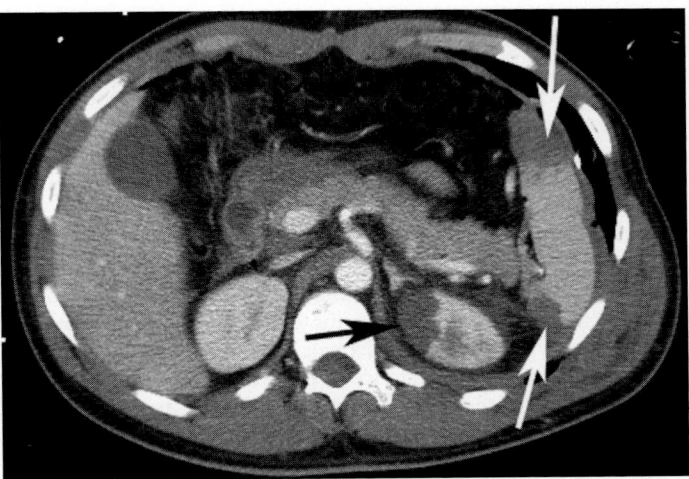

Figure 6 Blunt abdominal trauma can result in injury to multiple solid organs. Abdominal CT scan shows partial devascularization of the left kidney (black arrow) and multiple splenic contusions (white arrows).

ratory status, the abdomen should be carefully examined for external evidence of trauma (e.g., ecchymoses, abrasions, and tiretracks). The abdomen should then be carefully and gently palpated, with the awareness that a frightened child often tightens his or her rectus muscles in a way that gives a false impression of intra-abdominal injury. Serial abdominal examinations are essential.

CT has become the gold standard for evaluation of blunt abdominal injury in stable trauma patients.[116] This modality is extremely accurate in evaluating solid-organ injuries and determining the amount of blood in the peritoneal cavity [*see Figures 4 through 6*]. It is also useful for detecting pneumoperitoneum resulting from intestinal perforation.[117] To minimize exposure to radiation, the scan should be performed at the lowest radiation level feasible, and repeat scans should be avoided if possible.[118] The usefulness of the focused assessment for the sonographic examination of the trauma patient (FAST) in children remains controversial at present.[119-121]

Because hollow viscus injury is uncommon in children who sustain blunt abdominal trauma, nonoperative treatment is the accepted method of management for most hepatic and splenic injuries. Associated fractures of the lower ribs are rare in children with injuries to the liver or the spleen, though they are fairly common in adults with such injuries.[122]

The initial plain film of the abdomen often demonstrates medial and inferior displacement of the gastric bubble caused by accumulation of blood under the left diaphragm. A CT scan will then accurately confirm the diagnosis of a splenic injury. A major reason why nonoperative treatment is recommended for pediatric splenic injuries is that the risk of overwhelming postsplenectomy infection (OPSI) is far higher in children than in adults; the younger the child, the higher the risk of OPSI. OPSI develops in 3.3% of pediatric patients who have undergone splenectomy and carries a mortality of 50%.[123]

Once a hepatic or splenic injury has been diagnosed, management should follow the established guidelines for treatment of blunt solid-organ injuries in children.[124-126]

Ongoing hemodynamic instability despite aggressive resuscitation is the main indication for operative intervention; fortunately, it is a rare occurrence. The likelihood of successful nonoperative management of hepatic and splenic injuries continues to be higher in designated pediatric trauma centers.[127]

The finding of intraperitoneal fluid on a CT scan without evidence of solid-organ injury remains a challenging clinical problem. Management of patients with this finding should be individualized; treatment options include observation with serial examinations, laparoscopy, and surgical exploration.[117,128]

Among the less common injuries to intra-abdominal organs that occur in children are perforation of the stomach when an accident occurs shortly after eating (while the stomach is distended), perforation of the small intestine and large intestine at a point of fixation (e.g., the ligament of Treitz or the cecum), rupture of the left diaphragm, and damage to the duodenum or pancreas. The likelihood of visceral injury increases dramatically if bruising from a lap belt or a chance fracture is present.[129-131] Retroperitoneal perforation is suggested by the presence of air around the right kidney on a plain abdominal x-ray. Traumatic pancreatic injury is suggested by an elevation in serum amylase and lipase levels and by the presence of pancreatic edema on ultrasonography or CT. Obviously, perforations of the stomach, the intestine, or the duodenum call for exploratory laparotomy; in most cases, simple suture repair of the laceration is sufficient. Injury to the pancreas, on the other hand, can usually be managed nonoperatively with nasogastric decompression and I.V. fluids. Fracture of the pancreatic duct is quite rare in children and is usually secondary to compression of the pancreas against the vertebral column. In the past, this injury was usually treated with exploratory laparotomy and distal pancreatectomy, but current experience indicates that it can often be successfully treated by nonoperative means, though there is a risk that pseudocysts will subsequently develop.[132-134] Intramural duodenal hematoma is relatively uncommon in children

and is usually well managed by providing nasogastric decompression for about 10 days and instituting TPN.[135]

In any child who has sustained abdominal trauma, the diagnosis of a pelvic fracture should be seriously considered. Pelvic fractures can result in significant bleeding into the retroperitoneum, as well as injuries to the bladder and the urethra. The diagnosis can be confirmed by x-ray studies of the pelvis. In most cases, the fracture can be treated with bed rest, immobilization, and the replacement of lost blood.[136]

Children with blunt multisystem trauma seldom die if they are alive when brought to an emergency department, unless they have sustained head injuries. Care of these patients requires aggressive, coordinated efforts on the part of a multispecialty team that is under the direction of a pediatric surgeon. The establishment of specifically designated pediatric trauma centers around the country was one of the most important developments in the care of children to occur in the 1980s; since then, multiple studies have demonstrated that this measure has substantially improved outcomes for injured children.[137]

CHILD ABUSE

One of the unique varieties of pediatric trauma is child abuse, or the battered-child syndrome. It is a sad fact that intentional trauma is the most common cause of fatal injury in children younger than 1 year. The exact incidence of child abuse is not known, but it is believed that in the United States, about 160,000 children are seriously injured by deliberate abuse each year.[138] Risk factors include a low socioeconomic background, a single-parent family, low birth weight, and multiple siblings.[139,140] The victims tend to be younger than 2 years, except when sexual abuse is involved, in which case the average age is about 10 years. The abuse can take many different forms, such as physical or mental injury, nutritional or hygienic neglect, delayed or inadequate treatment of disease, sexual abuse, and verbal abuse. Salient clues to the diagnosis include an unreasonable delay in seeking medical help for the child, inconsistencies between the trauma observed and the injury mechanism described, poor hygiene, and marked depression or lack of emotion in the child. The injuries most commonly seen are soft tissue injuries, burns, fractures, and head trauma. X-ray evidence of healing fractures of different ages (a finding described as long ago as 1946) and of rib fractures is highly correlated with abuse.[122,141] Visceral injuries (e.g., hepatic fractures, splenic fractures, duodenal hematomas, and pancreatic fractures) are also associated with abuse, though less frequently.

Once a physician suspects child abuse, he or she is both legally and ethically obligated to report the situation to the appropriate hospital team and to the social services agency of the local jurisdiction. The typical hospital team usually includes a physician, a social worker, and a nurse. Prompt and full reporting often improves the chances that the parents will receive positive counseling, which may well reduce their subsequent abuse of the child.

References

1. Coran AG: Perioperative care of the pediatric patient. Surg Annu 23(pt 1):31, 1991

2. Friis-Hansen B: Changes in body water compartments during growth. Helv Paediatr Acta 10:12, 1955

3. Friis-Hansen BJ, Holiday M, Stapleton T, et al: Total body water in children. Pediatrics 7:321, 1951

4. Friis-Hansen B: Body water compartments in children: changes during growth and related changes in body composition. Pediatrics 28:169, 1961

5. Friis-Hansen B: Body composition during growth: in vivo measurements and biochemical data correlated to differential anatomical growth. Pediatrics 47(suppl 2):264, 1971

6. Friis-Hansen B: Water distribution in the foetus and newborn infant. Acta Paediatr Scand Suppl 305:7, 1983

7. Friis-Hansen B: The extracellular fluid volume in infants and children. Acta Paediatr 43:444, 1954

8. Aperia A, Broberger O, Thodenius K, et al: Renal control of sodium and fluid balance in newborn infants during intravenous maintenance therapy. Acta Paediatr Scand 64:725, 1975

9. Aperia A, Broberger O, Herin P, et al: Postnatal control of water and electrolyte homeostasis in pre-term and full-term infants. Acta Paediatr Scand 305(suppl):61, 1983

10. Doyle LW, Sinclair JC: Insensible water loss in newborn infants. Clin Perinatol 9:453, 1982

11. Dechert R, Wesley J, Schafer L, et al: Comparison of oxygen consumption, carbon dioxide production, and resting energy expenditure in premature and full-term infants. J Pediatr Surg 20:792, 1985

12. Dechert RE, Wesley JR, Schafer LE, et al: A water-sealed indirect calorimeter for measurement of oxygen consumption (VO_2), carbon dioxide production (VCO_2), and energy expenditure in infants. JPEN J Parenter Enteral Nutr 12:256, 1988

13. Jaksic T, Shew SB, Keshen TH, et al: Do critically ill surgical neonates have increased energy expenditure? J Pediatr Surg 36:63, 2001

14. Garza JJ, Shew SB, Keshen TH, et al: Energy expenditure in ill premature neonates. J Pediatr Surg 37:289, 2002

15. Agus MS, Jaksic T: Nutritional support of the critically ill child. Curr Opin Pediatr 14:470, 2002

16. Heymsfield SB, Bethel RA, Ansley JD, et al: Enteral hyperalimentation: an alternative to central venous hyperalimentation. Ann Intern Med 90:63, 1979

17. Johnson LR, Copeland EM, Dudrick SJ, et al: Structural and hormonal alterations in the gastrointestinal tract of parenterally fed rats. Gastroenterology 68:1177, 1975

18. Dudrick SJ, Wilmore DW, Vars HM, et al: Long-term total parenteral nutrition with growth, development, and positive nitrogen balance. Surgery 64:134, 1968

19. Dudrick SJ, Wilmore DW, Vars HM, et al: Can intravenous feeding as the sole means of nutrition support growth in the child and restore weight loss in an adult? An affirmative answer. Ann Surg 169:974, 1969

20. Heird WC, Winters RW: Total parenteral nutrition: the state of the art. J Pediatr 86:2, 1975

21. Filler RM, Eraklis AJ, Rubin VG, et al: Long-term total parenteral nutrition in infants. N Engl J Med 281:589, 1969

22. Wesley J, Coran A: Infants and children. Treatment of Shock: Principles and Practice. Barrett J, Nyhus LM, Eds. Lea & Febiger, Philadelphia, 1986, p 211

23. Holcroft JW, Trunkey DD, Carpenter MA: Extravasation of albumin in tissues of normal and septic baboons and sheep. J Surg Res 26:341, 1979

24. Wesley JR, Heidelberger KP, DiPietro MA, et al: Diagnosis and management of congenital cystic disease of the lung in children. J Pediatr Surg 21:202, 1986

25. Coran AG, Drongowski R: Congenital cystic disease of the tracheobronchial tree in infants and children: experience with 44 consecutive cases. Arch Surg 129:521, 1994

26. Stolar CJH, Dillon PW: Congenital diaphragmatic hernia and eventration. Pediatric Surgery. O'Neill JA, Rowe MI, Grosfeld JL, et al, Eds. CV Mosby, St Louis, 1998, p 819

27. Nobuhara KK, Wilson JM: Pathophysiology of congenital diaphragmatic hernia. Semin Pediatr Surg 5:234, 1996

28. Bagolan P, Casaccia G, Crescenzi F, et al: Impact of a current treatment protocol on outcome of high-risk congenital diaphragmatic hernia. J Pediatr Surg 39:313, 2004

29. Okuyama H, Kubota A, Oue T, et al: Inhaled nitric oxide with early surgery improves the outcome of antenatally diagnosed congenital diaphragmatic hernia. J Pediatr Surg 37:1188, 2002

30. Bartlett RH, Andrews AF, Toomasian JM, et al: Extracorporeal membrane oxygenation for newborn respiratory failure: forty-five cases. Surgery 92:425, 1982

31. Reickert CA, Hirschl RB, Schumacher R, et al: Effect of very delayed repair of congenital diaphragmatic hernia on survival and extracorporeal life support use. Surgery 120:766, 1996

32. Steimle CN, Meric F, Hirschl RB, et al: Effect of extracorporeal life support on survival when applied to all patients with congenital diaphragmatic hernia. J Pediatr Surg 29:997, 1994

33. Lago P, Meneghini L, Chiandetti L, et al: Congenital diaphragmatic hernia: intensive care unit or operating room? Am J Perinatol 22:189, 2005

34. Wilson JM, Lund DP, Lillehei CW, et al: Congenital diaphragmatic hernia—a tale of two cities: the Boston experience. J Pediatr Surg 32:401, 1997

35. Dillon PW, Cilley RE, Mauger D, et al: The relationship of pulmonary artery pressure and survival in congenital diaphragmatic hernia. J Pediatr Surg 39:307, 2004

36. Stege G, Fenton A, Jaffray B: Nihilism in the 1990s: The true mortality of congenital diaphragmatic hernia. Pediatrics 112:532, 2003

37. de Lorimier AA: Respiratory problems related to the airway and lung. Pediatric Surgery. O'Neill JA, Rowe MI, Grosfeld JL, et al, Eds. CV Mosby, St Louis, 1998, p 873

38. Phillipos EZ, Libsekal K: Flexible bronchoscopy in the management of congenital lobar emphysema in the neonate. Can Respir J 5:219, 1998

39. Shanmugam G, MacArthur K, Pollock JC: congenital lung malformations—antenatal and postnatal evaluation and management. Eur J Cardiothorac Surg 27:45, 2005

40. Bratu I, Flageole H, Chen MF, et al: The multiple facets of pulmonary sequestration. J Pediatr Surg 36:784, 2001

41. Ricketts RR: Workup of neonatal intestinal obstruction. Am Surg 50:517, 1984

42. Goldkrand JW, Causey TN, Hull EE: The changing face of gastroschisis and omphalocele in southeast Georgia. J Matern Fetal Neonatal Med 15:331, 2004

43. Kazaura MR, Lie RT, Irgens LM, et al: Increasing risk of gastroschisis in Norway: an age-period-cohort analysis. Am J Epidemiol 159:358, 2004

44. Salihu HM, Pierre-Louis BJ, Druschel CM, et al: Omphalocele and gastroschisis in the state of New York, 1992–1999. Birth Defects Res A Clin Mol Teratol 67:630, 2003

45. Stoll C, Alembik Y, Dott B, et al: Risk factors in congenital abdominal wall defects (omphalocele and gastroschisis): a study in a series of 265,858 consecutive births. Ann Genet 44:201, 2001

46. Drongowski RA, Smith RK Jr, Coran AG, et al: Contribution of demographic and environmental factors to the etiology of gastroschisis: a hypothesis. Fetal Diagn Ther 6:14, 1991

47. Snyder CL, Miller KA, Sharp RJ, et al: Management of intestinal atresia in patients with gastroschisis. J Pediatr Surg 36:1542, 2001

48. Moir CR, Ramsey PS, Ogburn PL, et al: A prospective trial of elective preterm delivery for fetal gastroschisis. Am J Perinatol 21:289, 2004

49. Hagberg S, Hokegard KH, Rubenson A, et al: Prenatally diagnosed gastroschisis—a preliminary report advocating the use of elective caesarean section. Z Kinderchir 43:419, 1988

50. How HY, Harris BJ, Pietrantoni M, et al: Is vaginal delivery preferable to elective cesarean delivery in fetuses with a known ventral wall defect? Am J Obstet Gynecol 182:1527, 2000

51. Lewis DF, Towers CV, Garite TJ, et al: Fetal gastroschisis and omphalocele: is cesarean section the best mode of delivery? Am J Obstet Gynecol 163:773, 1990

52. Langer JC: Abdominal wall defects. World J Surg 27:117, 2003

53. Komuro H, Imaizumi S, Hirata A, et al: Staged silo repair of gastroschisis with preservation of the umbilical cord. J Pediatr Surg 33:485, 1998

54. Circumcision Policy Statement. American Academy of Pediatrics. Task Force on Circumcision. Pediatrics 103:686, 1999

55. Agot KE, Ndinya-Achola JO, Kreiss JK, et al: Risk of HIV-1 in rural Kenya: a comparison of circumcised and uncircumcised men. Epidemiology 15:157, 2004

56. Schoen EJ: Benefits of newborn circumcision: is Europe ignoring medical evidence? Arch Dis Child 77:258, 1997

57. Hellsten SK: Rationalising circumcision: from tradition to fashion, from public health to individual freedom—critical notes on cultural persistence of the practice of genital mutilation. J Med Ethics 30:248, 2004

58. Williams N, Kapila L: Complications of circumcision. Br J Surg 80:1231, 1993

59. Sylla C, Diao B, Diallo AB, et al: [Complications of circumcision: report of 63 cases]. Prog Urol 13:266, 2003

60. Hernanz-Schulman M: Infantile hypertrophic pyloric stenosis. Radiology 227:319, 2003

61. Papadakis K, Chen EA, Luks FI, et al: The changing presentation of pyloric stenosis. Am J Emerg Med 17:67, 1999

62. Huang YC, Su BH: Medical treatment with atropine sulfate for hypertrophic pyloric stenosis. Acta Paediatr Taiwan 45:136, 2004

63. Yamataka A, Tsukada K, Yokoyama-Laws Y, et al: Pyloromyotomy versus atropine sulfate for infantile hypertrophic pyloric stenosis. J Pediatr Surg 35:338, 2000

64. van der Bilt JD, Kramer WL, van der Zee DC, et al: Laparoscopic pyloromyotomy for hypertrophic pyloric stenosis: impact of experience on the results in 182 cases. Surg Endosc 18:907, 2004

65. Yagmurlu A, Barnhart DC, Vernon A, et al: Comparison of the incidence of complications in open and laparoscopic pyloromyotomy: a concurrent single institution series. J Pediatr Surg 39:292, 2004

66. Rudolph CD, Mazur LJ, Liptak GS, et al: Guidelines for evaluation and treatment of gastroesophageal reflux in infants and children: recommendations of the North American Society for Pediatric Gastroenterology and Nutrition. J Pediatr Gastroenterol Nutr 32(suppl 2):S1, 2001

67. Fonkalsrud EW, Ashcraft KW, Coran AG, et al: Surgical treatment of gastroesophageal reflux in children: a combined hospital study of 7467 patients. Pediatrics 101:419, 1998

68. Bensoussan AL, Yazbeck S, Carceller-Blanchard A: Results and complications of Toupet partial posterior wrap: 10 years' experience. J Pediatr Surg 29:1215, 1994

69. Weber TR: Toupet fundoplication for gastroesophageal reflux in childhood. Arch Surg 134:717, 1999

70. Pacilli M, Chowdhury MM, Pierro A: The surgical treatment of gastro-esophageal reflux in neonates and infants. Semin Pediatr Surg 14:34, 2005

71. Tunkel DE, Baroody FM, Sherman ME: Fine-needle aspiration biopsy of cervicofacial masses in children. Arch Otolaryngol Head Neck Surg 121:533, 1995

72. Liu ES, Bernstein JM, Sculerati N, et al: Fine needle aspiration biopsy of pediatric head and neck masses. Int J Pediatr Otorhinolaryngol 60:135, 2001

73. Sistrunk W: The surgical treatment of cysts of the thyroglossal tract. Ann Surg 71:121, 1920

74. Meier DE, Guzzetta PC, Barber RG, et al: Perforated appendicitis in children: is there a best treatment? J Pediatr Surg 38:1520, 2003

75. Bhatia AM, Gow KW, Heiss KF, et al: Is the use of laparoscopy to determine presence of contralateral patent processus vaginalis justified in children greater than 2 years of age? J Pediatr Surg 39:778, 2004

76. Scorer CG: The descent of the testis. Arch Dis Child 39:605, 1964

77. Docimo SG: The results of surgical therapy for cryptorchidism: a literature review and analysis. J Urol 154:1148, 1995

78. Lorenzo AJ, Samuelson ML, Docimo SG, et al: Cost analysis of laparoscopic versus open orchiopexy in the management of unilateral nonpalpable testicles. J Urol 172:712, 2004

79. Leung AK, Robson WL: Current status of cryptorchidism. Adv Pediatr 51:351, 2004

80. Chen C, Botelho C, Cooper A, et al: Current practice patterns in the treatment of perforated appendicitis in children. J Am Coll Surg 196:212, 2003

81. Tirabassi MV, Tashjian DB, Moriarty KP, et al: Perforated appendicitis: is laparoscopy safe? JSLS 8:147, 2004

82. Tander B, Pektas O, Bulut M: The utility of peritoneal drains in children with uncomplicated perforated appendicitis. Pediatr Surg Int 19:548, 2003

83. Celik A, Ergun O, Ozcan C, et al: Is it justified to obtain routine peritoneal fluid cultures during appendectomy in children? Pediatr Surg Int 19:632, 2003

84. Krisher SL, Browne A, Dibbins A, et al: Intra-abdominal abscess after laparoscopic appendectomy for perforated appendicitis. Arch Surg 136:438, 2001

85. Perovic Z: [Drainage of the abdominal cavity and complications in perforating appendicitis in children]. Med Pregl 53:193, 2000

86. Burnweit C, Bilik R, Shandling B: Primary closure of contaminated wounds in perforated appendicitis. J Pediatr Surg 26:1362, 1991

87. Wilcox RT, Traverso LW: Have the evaluation and treatment of acute appendicitis changed with new technology? Surg Clin North Am 77:1355, 1997

88. Garcia Pena BM, Cook EF, Mandl KD: Selective imaging strategies for the diagnosis of appendicitis in children. Pediatrics 113:24, 2004

89. Pena BM, Taylor GA, Fishman SJ, et al: Costs and effectiveness of ultrasonography and limited computed tomography for diagnosing appendicitis in children. Pediatrics 106:672, 2000

90. Bufo AJ, Shah RS, Li MH, et al: Interval appendectomy for perforated appendicitis in children. J Laparoendosc Adv Surg Tech A 8:209, 1998

91. Ho CM, Chen Y, Lai HS, et al: Comparison of critical conservative treatment versus emergency operation in children with ruptured appendicitis with tumor formation. J Formos Med Assoc 103:359, 2004

92. Weber TR, Keller MA, Bower RJ, et al: Is delayed operative treatment worth the trouble with perforated appendicitis in children? Am J Surg 186:685, 2003

93. Hogan MJ: Appendiceal abscess drainage. Tech Vasc Interv Radiol 6:205, 2003

94. Jamieson DH, Chait PG, Filler R: Interventional drainage of appendiceal abscesses in children. AJR Am J Roentgenol 169:1619, 1997

95. Dagradi V, Delaini GG, Carolo F, et al: [Appendectomy and Crohn disease]. Chir Ital 36:986, 1984

96. Whiteford MH, Kilkenny J 3rd, Hyman N, et al: Practice parameters for the treatment of perianal abscess and fistula-in-ano (revised). Dis Colon Rectum 48:1337, 2005

97. Crystal P, Hertzanu Y, Farber B, et al: Sonographically guided hydrostatic reduction of intussusception in children. J Clin Ultrasound 30:343, 2002

98. Navarro OM, Daneman A, Chae A: Intussusception: the use of delayed, repeated reduction attempts and the management of intussusceptions due to pathologic lead points in pediatric patients. AJR Am J Roentgenol 182:1169, 2004

99. Rubi I, Vera R, Rubi SC, et al: Air reduction of intussusception. Eur J Pediatr Surg 12:387, 2002

100. St-Vil D, Brandt ML, Panic S, et al: Meckel's diverticulum in children: a 20-year review. J Pediatr Surg 26:1289, 1991

101. Fa-Si-Oen PR, Roumen RM, Croiset van Uchelen FA: Complications and management of Meckel's diverticulum—a review. Eur J Surg 165:674, 1999

102. Grimaldi L, Zingaro N, Trecca A: [Surgical management of incidental Meckel's diverticulum: the necessity to obtain the informed consent]. Minerva Chir 60:71, 2005

103. Fonkalsrud EW, Berquist W, Burke M, et al: Long-term hyperalimentation in children through saphenous central venous catheterization. Am J Surg 143:209, 1982

104. Venkataraman ST, Orr RA, Thompson AE: Percutaneous infraclavicular subclavian vein catheterization in critically ill infants and children. J Pediatr 113:480, 1988

105. Bonventre EV, Lally KP, Chwals WJ, et al: Percutaneous insertion of subclavian venous catheters in infants and children. Surg Gynecol Obstet 169:203, 1989

106. Dowd MD, Keenan HT, Bratton SL: Epidemiology and prevention of childhood injuries. Crit Care Med 30:S385, 2002

107. Kapklein MJ, Mahadeo R: Pediatric trauma. Mt Sinai J Med 64:302, 1997

108. Osler TM, Vane DW, Tepas JJ, et al: Do pediatric trauma centers have better survival rates than adult trauma centers? An examination of the National Pediatric Trauma Registry. J Trauma 50:96, 2001

109. Sanchez JL, Lucas J, Feustel PJ: Outcome of adolescent trauma admitted to an adult surgical intensive care unit versus a pediatric intensive care unit. J Trauma 51:478, 2001

110. Khoshyomn S, Tranmer BI: Diagnosis and management of pediatric closed head injury. Semin Pediatr Surg 13:80, 2004

111. Adelson PD, Bratton SL, Carney NA, et al: Guidelines for the acute medical management of severe traumatic brain injury in infants, children, and adolescents. Chapter 17. Critical pathway for the treatment of established intracranial hypertension in pediatric traumatic brain injury. Pediatr Crit Care Med 4:S65, 2003

112. Donati-Genet PC, Dubuis JM, Girardin E, et al: Acute symptomatic hyponatremia and cerebral salt wasting after head injury: an important clinical entity. J Pediatr Surg 36:1094, 2001

113. Berkenbosch JW, Lentz CW, Jimenez DF, et al: Cerebral salt wasting syndrome following brain injury in three pediatric patients: suggestions for rapid diagnosis and therapy. Pediatr Neurosurg 36:75, 2002

114. Buhs C, Cullen M, Klein M, et al: The pediatric trauma C-spine: is the 'odontoid' view necessary? J Pediatr Surg 35:994, 2000

115. Browne GJ, Lam LT, Barker RA: The usefulness of a modified adult protocol for the clearance of paediatric cervical spine injury in the emergency department. Emerg Med (Fremantle) 15:133, 2003

116. Lindner T, Bail HJ, Manegold S, et al: [Initial diagnosis after blunt abdominal trauma: a review of the literature]. Unfallchirurg 107:892, 2004

117. Albanese CT, Meza MP, Gardner MJ, et al: Is computed tomography a useful adjunct to the clinical examination for the diagnosis of pediatric gastrointestinal perforation from blunt abdominal trauma in children? J Trauma 40:417, 1996

118. Fenton SJ, Hansen KW, Meyers RL, et al: CT scan and the pediatric trauma patient—are we overdoing it? J Pediatr Surg 39:1877, 2004

119. Coley BD, Mutabagani KH, Martin LC, et al: Focused abdominal sonography for trauma (FAST) in children with blunt abdominal trauma. J Trauma 48:902, 2000

120. Miller MT, Pasquale MD, Bromberg WJ, et al: Not so FAST. J Trauma 54:52, 2003

121. Suthers SE, Albrecht R, Foley D, et al: Surgeon-directed ultrasound for trauma is a predictor of intra-abdominal injury in children. Am Surg 70:164, 2004

122. Garcia VF, Gotschall CS, Eichelberger MR, et al: Rib fractures in children: a marker of severe trauma. J Trauma 30:695, 1990

123. Bisharat N, Omari H, Lavi I, et al: Risk of infection and death among post-splenectomy patients. J Infect 43:182, 2001

124. Stylianos S: Evidence-based guidelines for resource utilization in children with isolated spleen or liver injury. The APSA Trauma Committee. J Pediatr Surg 35:164, 2000

125. Leinwand MJ, Atkinson CC, Mooney DP: Ap-

plication of the APSA evidence-based guidelines for isolated liver or spleen injuries: a single institution experience. J Pediatr Surg 39:487, 2004

126. Stylianos S: Compliance with evidence-based guidelines in children with isolated spleen or liver injury: a prospective study. J Pediatr Surg 37:453, 2002

127. Cochran A, Mann NC, Dean JM, et al: Resource utilization and its management in splenic trauma. Am J Surg 187:713, 2004

128. Beierle EA, Chen MK, Whalen TV, et al: Free fluid on abdominal computed tomography scan after blunt trauma does not mandate exploratory laparotomy in children. J Pediatr Surg 35:990, 2000

129. Griffet J, Bastiani-Griffet F, El-Hayek T, et al: Management of seat-belt syndrome in children: gravity of 2-point seat-belt. Eur J Pediatr Surg 12:63, 2002

130. Beaunoyer M, St-Vil D, Lallier M, et al: Abdominal injuries associated with thoraco-lumbar fractures after motor vehicle collision. J Pediatr Surg 36:760, 2001

131. Rogers LF: The roentgenographic appearance of transverse or chance fractures of the spine: the seat belt fracture. Am J Roentgenol Radium Ther Nucl Med 111:844, 1971

132. Canty TG Sr, Weinman D: Management of major pancreatic duct injuries in children. J Trauma 50:1001, 2001

133. Jobst MA, Canty TG Sr, Lynch FP: Management of pancreatic injury in pediatric blunt abdominal trauma. J Pediatr Surg 34:818, 1999

134. Keller MS, Stafford PW, Vane DW: Conservative management of pancreatic trauma in children. J Trauma 42:1097, 1997

135. Desai KM, Dorward IG, Minkes RK, et al: Blunt duodenal injuries in children. J Trauma 54:640, 2003

136. Chia JP, Holland AJ, Little D, et al: Pelvic fractures and associated injuries in children. J Trauma 56:83, 2004

137. Hall JR, Reyes HM, Meller JL, et al: The outcome for children with blunt trauma is best at a pediatric trauma center. J Pediatr Surg 31:72, 1996

138. Harris BH, Stylianos S: Special considerations in trauma: child abuse and birth injuries. Pediatric Surgery. O'Neill JA, Rowe MI, Grosfeld JL, et al, Eds. CV Mosby, St Louis, 1998, p 359

139. Wu SS, Ma CX, Carter RL, et al: Risk factors for infant maltreatment: a population-based study. Child Abuse Negl 28:1253, 2004

140. Palazzi S, de Girolamo G, Liverani T: Observational study of suspected maltreatment in Italian paediatric emergency departments. Arch Dis Child 90:406, 2005

141. Caffey J: Multiple fractures in the long bones of infants suffering from chronic subdural hematoma. Am J Radiol 56:163, 1946

142. American College of Surgeons Committee on Trauma: ATLS Student Course Manual. American College of Surgeons, Chicago, 2004, p 251

141 THE PREGNANT SURGICAL PATIENT

David C. Brooks, M.D., and Cherie P. Parungo, M.D.

Approach to Abdominal Pain in Pregnant Patients

Since the early 1990s, the number of live births in the United States has ranged from 3.88 to 4.12 million per year.[1] Complications related to nonobstetric surgery are relatively uncommon, occurring in only 1% to 2% of pregnancies.[2] Management of the pregnant patient differs from that of other patients in several ways. First, pregnancy induces a variety of mechanical, hormonal, and chemical alterations that may confuse and mislead even the most experienced surgeon [*see* Discussion, Physiologic Changes in Pregnant Patients, *below*]. Second, a surgeon's natural inclination, when faced with a pregnant patient experiencing abdominal pain, is to temporize. This tendency, which generally arises from the misconception that surgical intervention may injure the fetus, is responsible for delays in diagnosis and ultimately for the unfavorable outcomes often associated with acute abdominal pathology in pregnant patients. Third, pregnant patients require a multidisciplinary approach to care that involves the surgeon, the obstetrician, the radiologist, and the anesthesiologist. Finally, and most important, a surgeon treating a pregnant woman is actually caring for two patients and has the same responsibility to both.

In what follows, we first review urgent surgical problems in the pregnant patient, then discuss the physiologic changes of pregnancy and how these changes help shape general surgical principles in this population. Finally, we address certain nonurgent surgical problems associated with pregnancy.

Initial Management

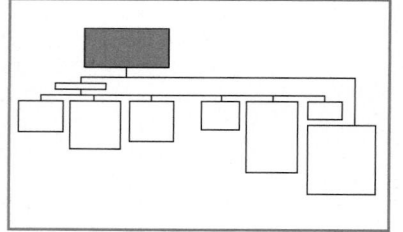

Initial management of any pregnant patient presenting with an acute abdomen or an acute surgical problem should include a thorough history and physical examination [*see 43 Acute Abdominal Pain*], with particular consideration given to historical aspects of the pregnancy, the expected date of delivery, and the presence of any pregnancy-related complications. Whenever possible, an obstetrician should be consulted and included in the decision-making process. Initial maneuvers should include administration of supplemental oxygen, placement of an I.V. line with the capacity to deliver ample amounts of fluid or blood, insertion of a nasogastric tube if significant vomiting is present, and performance of routine laboratory evaluations, such as a complete blood count, assessment of serum electrolyte levels, and urinalysis. If the pregnancy has passed the 26th week, a fetal monitor should be employed. Radiographic investigations should be kept to a minimum, although abdominal and pelvic ultrasonography may be especially useful not only in assessing the maternal pathology but also in evaluating the fetus.

Acute abdominal surgical problems must be dealt with immediately. Management of less acute problems, however, must take into account the stage of the pregnancy. The risk of spontaneous abortion at operation is highest during the first trimester. The optimal time for elective surgery is during the second trimester because the uterus is smaller at that time than it is in the third trimester and because the fetus can be maintained in a relatively stable condition during the administration of general anesthesia.

Urgent Surgical Problems

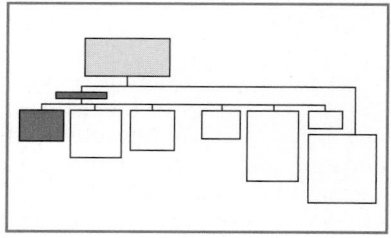

TRAUMA

Trauma is estimated to occur in approximately 6% to 7% of gestations.[3] It remains the leading cause of maternal death, accounting for 46.3% of deaths during pregnancy.[4] Homicide is the most common cause of traumatic maternal death, followed by motor vehicle accidents, accidental injury, and suicide.[5] Motor vehicle accidents account for 55% to 66% of all trauma during pregnancy, falls account for 22%, and domestic abuse and assaults account for 21%. The more severe the injury to the mother, the greater the risk of injury to the fetus. When the mother survives, fetal death is most commonly related to abruptio placentae. Major trauma causes placental abruption in 40% to 66% of cases; minor trauma causes placental abruption in 5% of cases.[6] Fetal death may also result from complications of premature delivery or from direct penetrating injury to the fetus.

Blunt Injury

In the mother, blunt trauma (as in motor vehicle accidents) may cause multiple life-threatening injuries, including head trauma, intra-abdominal hemorrhage, pelvic fracture, and uteroplacental vascular injury. Pelvic fractures are a particular concern: because of the extensive vascular supply in this area, there is a significant risk of substantial hidden blood loss. Uterine blood flow at term is approximately 500 ml/min; thus, pregnant women are at significant risk for massive hemorrhage if the uterus is injured. Uterine expansion displaces the bladder into the abdomen, thereby increasing the risk of traumatic bladder injury. The upper urinary tract is generally spared from injury, however, because the gravid uterus shields the retroperitoneum from direct injury. It should be kept in mind that mild hydroureter is physiologic in pregnancy. Hepatic, splenic, and

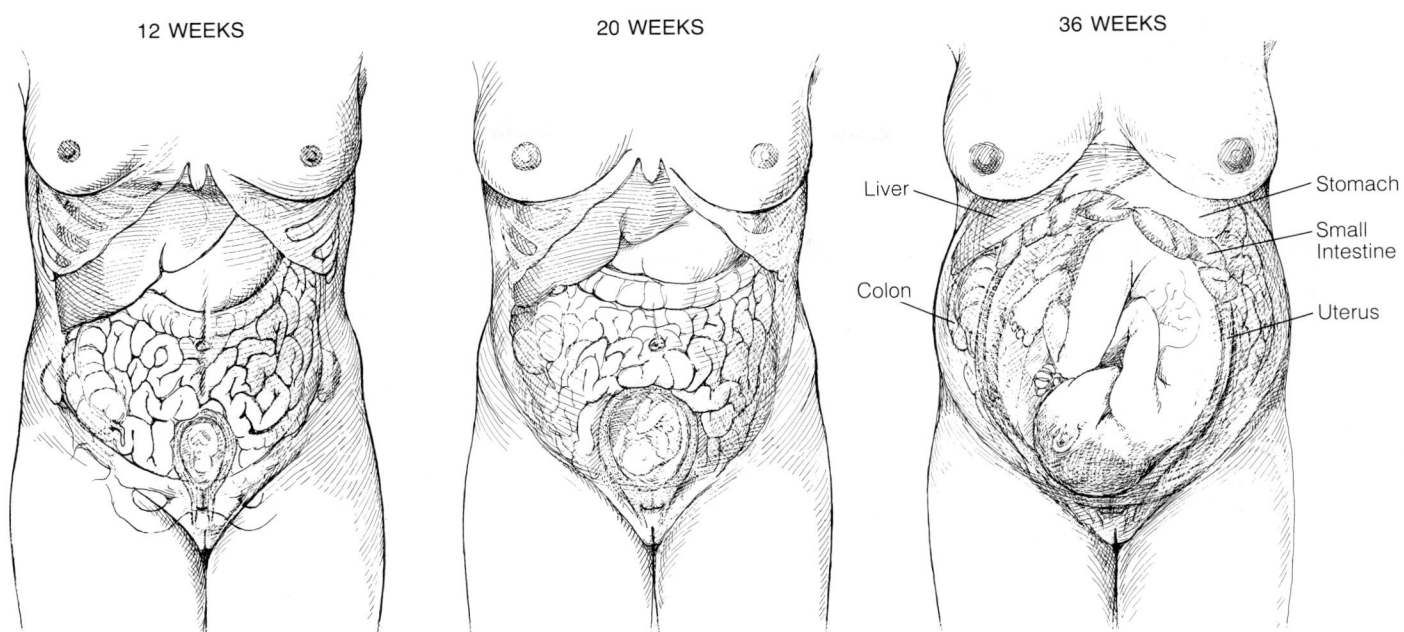

12 WEEKS   20 WEEKS   36 WEEKS

Liver —
Stomach
Small Intestine
Colon —
Uterus

Figure 1 **Enlargement of the uterus to accommodate the developing fetus shifts intra-abdominal contents superiorly and compresses retroperitoneal structures. These effects are particularly important during the second and third trimesters.**

uterine injuries are common in high-speed motor vehicle accidents, but injuries to the GI tract, surprisingly, appear to be uncommon, largely because of the protective effects of the gravid uterus.[7] Direct injury to the fetus as a result of blunt trauma is unusual because of the protection afforded by the maternal abdominal wall and the uterus. Blunt trauma may result in fetal skull fractures, fetal intracranial hemorrhage, or abruptio placentae; nevertheless, fetal demise is rare in this setting and usually is secondary to maternal demise.

Many women refrain from using seat belts during pregnancy because of discomfort or out of concern that the seat belt might injure the fetus; however, this practice has no effect on fetal death rates in automobile accidents. When unbelted women are ejected from an automobile, maternal mortality is 33% and fetal mortality is 47%.[8] Three-point restraint is the safest choice for pregnant women in motor vehicles.

Penetrating Injury

Penetrating injury is usually more damaging to the fetus than to the mother. Mortality is actually lower for pregnant women with penetrating injuries than for nonpregnant women with similar injuries, presumably because of the shielding effect of the uterus and the fetus.[9]

Penetrating trauma, however, often results in direct fetal injury. Fetal mortality in this setting ranges from 40% to 70%, whereas maternal mortality ranges from 5% to 10%.[10] In the first trimester, trauma generally poses little direct threat to fetal viability because the uterus is protected within the pelvis. In the second and third trimesters, however, when the uterus is located within the abdomen, penetrating trauma may result in direct fetal injury or rupture of the membranes. With penetrating abdominal trauma, the prognosis depends on which and how many organs are injured.

General principles of trauma management are applied when the need for laparotomy is under consideration. Visceral injury occurs 95% of the time if the peritoneum has been penetrat-

ed.[11] For this reason, many authorities advocate exploratory laparotomy for all high-velocity penetrating injury to the abdomen. How best to manage low-velocity penetrating injury remains somewhat controversial. Low-velocity injuries above the fundus of the uterus are almost always associated with visceral injury and thus call for exploratory laparotomy. Injuries below the fundus and anteriorly are seldom associated with visceral injury[7] and thus can generally be managed nonoperatively. Subsequent laparotomy is indicated for worsening maternal symptoms. Subsequent cesarean section is indicated for a viable fetus in distress.

Domestic or partner violence during pregnancy occurs in 7% to 23% of all pregnancies.[12] If the patient is in an abusive relationship, the severity and frequency of assault typically increase during pregnancy.[13] In addition, 20% of abused pregnant women attempt suicide[14] or abuse alcohol or drugs. Abuse has many far-reaching consequences for the mother and the fetus that cannot be accurately measured. Unfortunately, partner violence often goes undiagnosed and hence untreated: as few as 12% of abused women are correctly identified in emergency room settings.[15] Typical presentations of partner abuse include multiple injuries in various states of healing, inconsistent explanations of the injuries, minimization of the injuries, and delay in seeking medical attention.[16] The face and the abdomen are struck more frequently during pregnancy. If a suspicion of partner violence arises, the physician should ask direct questions about threats and should provide appropriate contacts and support. A well-documented evaluation, unedited quotes, and careful drawings or pictures are also necessary in case the patient wishes to take legal action immediately or in the future. In all 50 states, domestic violence is a crime, and in some, failure to report suspected violence is a crime as well.

Management

Trauma is managed in essentially the same way in pregnant patients as in nonpregnant patients [see *100 Initial Management*

Approach to Abdominal Pain in Pregnant Patients

Pregnant woman presents with acute abdomen

Obtain history, and perform physical examination.

Place I.V. line, and administer fluids as needed.

Insert nasogastric tube if significant vomiting is present.

Perform routine laboratory evaluations (e.g., CBC, serum electrolyte levels, urinalysis). Take into account normal changes in pregnancy.

Use fetal monitor after 26th week.

Use x-rays sparingly (only after first month); avoid radionuclide studies; employ abdominal and pelvic ultrasonography.

Identify conditions that require immediate operation.

Condition requires immediate operation

Trauma

Management: proceed essentially as for nonpregnant patients. *Mother is first priority.* Stabilization of mother improves fetal survival. Determine gestational age, and perform external fetal monitoring as indicated. In the event of acute maternal decompensation, consider cesarean section.

Acute appendicitis

Signs and symptoms: nausea and vomiting (differentiate from morning sickness); pain higher and more lateral in pregnancy; fever not a prominent finding; leukocytosis shifted to left. Pain that lessens when patient is turned to left is most likely of adnexal or ovarian origin. Use graded, real-time ultrasonography.

Management: perform laparotomy; use transverse incision when diagnosis is certain; use low midline incision, right paramedian incision, or exploratory laparoscopy if diagnosis indoubt (to permit examination of peritoneum).

Intestinal obstruction

Signs and symptoms: nausea and vomiting; history of abdominal operation or adhesions. Rule out pseudo-obstruction.

Management: pass nasogastric tube; initiate fluid resuscitation and total parenteral nutrition, if needed. Begin operation as soon as possible. For large-bowel obstruction, perform sigmoidoscopy, resection of threatened bowel, and cecopexy.

Perforated duodenal ulcer

Management: plication of the perforation. Definitive ulcer operation should not be attempted. If patient is close to term, avoid cesarean section because of risk of uterine contamination.

Spontaneous visceral rupture

General signs and symptoms: intra-abdominal hemorrhage, shock, acute abdomen.

- Hepatic rupture: severe right upper quadrant pain; complication ofpreeclampsia
- Renal rupture: probably secondary tohydronephrosis
- Splenic rupture: occurs in conjunction with splenic artery aneurysm or capsular rupture, usually secondary tohypervolemia and splenomegaly
- Esophageal rupture: may be associated with excessive vomiting duringpregnancy (hyperemesis gravidarum)
- Ruptured ectopic pregnancy

Note: in operation for hepatic rupture, cesarean section should be performed simultaneously.

Other conditions requiring urgent operation

Ectopic pregnancy.
Ovarian torsion.

Condition requires operation only if disease does not respond to medical management

Acute cholecystitis: presents with epigastric or upper right quadrant pain, nausea and vomiting, occasional radiation of pain to right scapula; use ultrasonography to visualize. Do not use HIDA scan. Manage nonoperatively during first and third trimesters (fluid resuscitation and antibiotics); during second trimester, perform cholecystectomy. Use intraoperative cholangiography.

Pancreatitis: presents with unremitting visceral pain that may radiate to the back and with raised amylase levels (2,000–3,000 IU). Operative intervention (preferably during second trimester) indicated by evidence of biliary obstruction but no evidence of stone passage or by failure of medical management.

Peptic ulcer disease: treatment is based on symptomatic relief. Prompt operative intervention is indicated in the event of perforated duodenal ulcer.

Inflammatory bowel disease: operative intervention is last resort if medical therapy ineffective. Indications for operation include abscess, fistula, or bowel obstruction (Crohn disease) or toxic megacolon (ulcerative colitis).

of Life-Threatening Trauma and Section 7 Trauma and Thermal Injury]. The mother is the first priority: stabilization of the mother improves both maternal and fetal survival. Initial measures include efforts to support the airway, breathing, and circulation (the ABCs). The physiologic alterations characteristic of pregnancy affect maternal responses to injury [*see* Discussion, Physiologic Changes in Pregnancy, *below*].

The increased blood volume and enhanced cardiac output mask hypovolemia. Tachycardia and hypotension may not be accurate indicators of hypovolemia: as much as 2 L, or 30% of maternal blood volume, may be lost before hemodynamic instability is detected.[17] The expansion of intravascular fluid volume that occurs in pregnancy affects the amount of replacement fluid needed. In the third trimester, patients should receive 1.5 times the amount of fluid that would ordinarily be given to compensate for this effect. Use of military antishock trousers (MAST) may decrease maternal venous return by compressing the uterus on the inferior vena cava; accordingly, their use is not recommended. Vasoconstrictive agents should never be used for hemodynamic stabilization until hypovolemia has first been treated. Epinephrine and norepinephrine lead to uteroplacental vasoconstriction and fetal compromise; ephedrine and phenylephrine may be used during pregnancy.

An important concern with advancing gestation is the possibility that the expansion of the gravid uterus [*see Figure 1*] can produce aortocaval compression, leading to supine hypotension. Left lateral displacement of the uterus is necessary to improve blood flow to both the mother and the fetus after the 20th week.

There are very few diagnostic procedures for which pregnancy is a contraindication. Radiographic investigation should be performed whenever necessary if the results are expected to affect management. It is usually possible to keep the total absorbed radiation dose below the level that is thought to increase teratogenic risk (i.e., 50 to 100 milliGrays [mGy]) [*see Table 1*].[18] Plain films of the cervical spine provide useful information on head and neck injuries; computed tomographic scanning of the abdomen with contrast may offer the greatest amount of information on injuries to the retroperitoneum, the peritoneum, and the pelvis. Ultrasonography is now being used for acute trauma assessment in both pregnant and nonpregnant patients; the results to date have been good. Peritoneal lavage done in an open fashion through a supraumbilical incision may facilitate rapid assessment of intra-abdominal hemorrhage in cases of blunt trauma.[19] A Kleihauer-Betke test for fetal red blood cells in the maternal circulation will reveal any fetomaternal hemorrhage present. (Fetomaternal hemorrhage is the passage of fetal blood into the maternal vascular system; it occurs more frequently in pregnant women who have suffered traumatic injury than in those who have not, and it can lead to fetal anemia, arrhythmias, and fetal exsanguination.[20]) Rh_O (D) immune globulin and tetanus toxoid should be administered when indicated.

Early determination of gestational age by means of ultrasonography is a critical guide to further management decisions. Ultrasonography can also be used to monitor fetal heart tones, fetal activity, and amniotic volume. After the 20th week of gestation, cardiotocographic monitoring is an important adjunct for determining fetal status after trauma. Such monitoring should also be employed in the event of preterm contractions. As many as 40% of women experience preterm contractions, but only 3% progress to premature delivery.[6] Preterm contractions in a pregnant trauma patient should initiate an evaluation for abruptio placentae, uterine hemorrhage, and intra-abdominal hemorrhage. Given that placental abruption occurs in 66% of cases of major trauma and 5% of cases of minor trauma, the patient should be evaluated for ruptured membranes. Placental abruption usually occurs within 4 hours of injury. Ultrasonography is not sensitive enough to detect this condition[21]; therefore, cardiotocographic monitoring should be continued for 4 to 6 hours after stabilization and longer if any irregularity in the mother or fetus is noted.[22] If the fetus has not yet reached the gestational age of 23 weeks or is not viable, the mother should receive supportive care. In these circumstances, cesarean section is reserved for cases of disseminated intravascular coagulation (DIC). If the fetus is viable and the mother stable, cesarean section can be carried out safely; if the fetus is viable and the mother unstable as a result of trauma, cesarean section should be carried out with the exploratory laparotomy.[6] When the need for concurrent hysterotomy is under consideration, however, each case must be assessed individually. Patients undergoing an emergency cesarean section should receive a broad-spectrum antibiotic preoperatively.

In the event of acute maternal decompensation that does not respond to standard resuscitative measures, a cesarean section may be appropriate. In cases of particularly severe trauma, emergency operative resuscitation should be considered. If the patient is in cardiac arrest, thoracotomy and open chest massage, with concurrent cesarean section if the fetus is viable, have been recommended.[5] Cesarean section may increase maternal circulating volume. Occasionally, cardiopulmonary resuscitation (CPR) is more effective after the gravid uterus is emptied. There is also less risk of supine hypotension after cesarean section, although the associated surgical blood loss may exacerbate maternal instability. Timing is critical: if anoxia is limited to 4 to 6 minutes, the fetus generally will not be harmed. Therefore, any attempt to deliver the fetus should begin within 4 to 6 minutes after maternal cardiac arrest. If the fetus appears to be still viable after this period has passed, cesarean section should be performed; isolated cases of fetal salvage after prolonged maternal anoxia have been reported. Fetal survival after delivery is dependent on its having reached a gestational age greater than 28 weeks. CPR of the mother

Table 1 Radiation Dose Absorbed by Unshielded Gravid Uterus from Radiographic Studies Often Performed in Trauma Patients

Radiographic Study	Unshielded Uterine Dose (mGy)
Cervical spine	No detectable contribution
Chest (AP)	0.003–0.043
Pelvis (AP)	1.42–4.86
Abdomen (AP)	1.33–4.51
IVP	2.02–8.15
Full spine (AP)	1.54–5.27
Femur (AP)	0.016–0.12
Humerus (AP)	< 0.00001
Cystography	1.35–4.41
CT scan	
Head	< 0.5
Thorax	< 10
Upper abdomen	< 30
Cumulative dose (without CT scan)	7.68–27.36
Cumulative dose (with CT scan)	> 7.68–67.86

AP—anteroposterior IVP—intravenous pyelography

should be continued during and after the delivery because it may improve maternal status and survival.

Two caveats should be kept in mind: (1) cesarean section should not be performed in an unstable patient because of an anticipated cardiac arrest, and (2) if CPR is successful before surgical delivery is attempted, cesarean section should not be performed, because in utero resuscitation is likely.[23]

APPENDICITIS

Appendicitis is the most common surgical problem in pregnancy, occurring in 0.05% to 0.1% of pregnancies, but it occurs no more often in pregnant women than in nonpregnant women.[24,25] The incidence is approximately the same in all three trimesters. The low maternal mortality—0.5% in 1977 and 0% in recent studies[26]—notwithstanding, of all surgical problems during pregnancy, appendicitis causes the most fetal loss.[27] The particular dangers of appendicitis in pregnancy lie in the varied presentation of symptoms, the higher chance of delayed diagnosis, and the significant risk that surgery presents to the fetus.

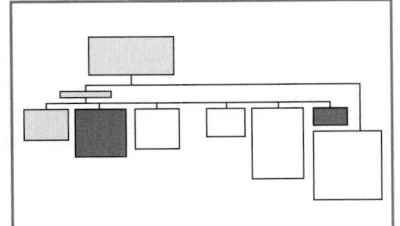

The symptoms of appendicitis mimic symptoms of normal pregnancy—namely, anorexia, nausea, vomiting, and abdominal discomfort. The most reliable symptom of appendicitis during pregnancy is periumbilical or diffuse abdominal pain that later localizes to the right lower quadrant.[28] Although as the gravid uterus grows, it pushes the appendix cephalad and posteriorly, right lower quadrant pain remains the most consistent symptom of appendicitis in any trimester.[28]

On physical examination, appendicitis presents with tenderness in the right lower quadrant. It can be differentiated from adnexal or uterine pain with the help of the Adler sign: if the point of maximal tenderness shifts medially with repositioning on the left lateral side, the etiology is generally adnexal or uterine. Abdominal guarding, rebound tenderness, or referred tenderness is present in 60% to 70% of patients with appendicitis; however, these findings are less common during the third trimester because of the laxity of the abdominal wall muscles.[29] Elevated body temperature is not a consistent finding in pregnant patients with appendicitis.[26,28]

Laboratory values can be misleading, in that pregnancy can cause a leukocytosis as high as 15,000 leukocytes/mm^3 in the absence of any source of infection.[30] The white cell differential is more useful than the absolute count; increased levels of band cells or immature forms suggest that the leukocytosis may be secondary to an infectious process. A urinalysis is necessary to rule out a urinary tract infection, which occurs in 10% to 20% of pregnant women.

Diagnostic radiology should be employed deliberately and judiciously. Ultrasonography of the lower abdomen or transvaginal ultrasonography can often visualize an inflamed appendix without risk to the fetus. It can also distinguish other causes of abdominal pain, such as an ovarian cyst. The clinical presentation and an ultrasonogram are often sufficient to establish the diagnosis of appendicitis.[31,32]

In very rare cases, a CT study of the pelvis should be done as well to elucidate a complicated presentation. A pelvic CT yields a total radiation dose of 25 mGy, and a directed helical, or spiral, CT study yields a total exposure of 30 mGy. Directed spiral CT has a sensitivity and specificity of 98%.[33] For both

pelvic CT and directed spiral CT, the total radiation doses are well below the threshold of safety established by the International Commission on Radiological Protection (ICRP), which is 100 mGy.[34] With plain films, the chance of obtaining valuable information is seldom worth the risk associated with the radiation. In certain cases, magnetic resonance imaging may be helpful for further delineation of the source of pain without the risk posed by ionizing radiation.

Differential Diagnosis

The condition most often confused with appendicitis is pyelonephritis, which occurs in 1% to 2% of pregnant women. The two diseases may present remarkably similar clinical pictures, especially when pyelonephritis occurs on the right side. Because of the mechanical effects of the gravid uterus on the ureter, pyelonephritis is more common in pregnant women than in nonpregnant ones. Furthermore, urinalysis yields abnormal results—either pyuria or hematuria—in as many as 20% of patients with appendicitis as a result of extraluminal irritation of the ureter by the inflamed appendix.[35] Nephrolithiasis can also be mistaken for appendicitis; it should be seriously considered whenever acute abdominal pain is present on the right side. Management of ureteral stones in pregnant patients presents a substantial challenge to both the surgeon and the urologist. Newer techniques, such as stents[36] and percutaneous nephrostomy tubes,[37] have been successful in obviating surgical intervention.

Right lower quadrant pain during early pregnancy may also be a presentation of ectopic implantation. Typically, a patient misses a period and then experiences some degree of vaginal bleeding or spotting. Abdominal or pelvic pain as well as cervical motion tenderness is present, and a mass is often appreciated on pelvic examination. When ectopic pregnancy is suspected, a serum human chorionic gonadotropin (hCG) assay should be performed along with transvaginal ultrasonography. If the serum hCG level is higher than 2,000 IU/L and an intrauterine gestational sac is not visualized by transvaginal ultrasonography, laparotomy or laparoscopy is indicated.

Torsion of an ovary or an ovarian cyst is also difficult to distinguish from appendicitis.[38] Although rare in pregnant patients, torsion of an ovarian cyst may occur in the early stages of the pregnancy. The physical examination is notable for pain in the right or left adnexa and the occasional presence of a tender mass. Transvaginal ultrasonography will frequently detect the cyst. Treatment requires laparotomy. The differential diagnosis of acute abdominal pain in pregnancy should also include ovarian cysts, mesenteric adenitis, degenerating fibroid tumors, salpingitis, inflammatory bowel disease, cholecystitis, ovarian vein thrombosis, ruptured corpus luteum, rectus hematoma, round ligament pain, abruptio placentae, chorioamnionitis, and adhesions.

Management

When there is evidence of appendicitis and no alternative diagnosis seems likely, operative intervention is warranted no matter what stage the pregnancy has reached.[39] The risk of the procedure to mother and child is minimal in comparison to the risks posed by delayed diagnosis, perforation, and abscess formation. Appendectomy in a pregnant patient does not increase the incidence of congenital malformation or stillbirth.[25] With routine surgical management, maternal mortality is negligible and fetal mortality is 2% to 8%.[26,40] For a ruptured appendix, maternal mortality is 1% and fetal mortality is as high as 35%.[38,41] Negative laparotomy rates of 15% or lower are considered acceptable in the nonpregnant population, but negative laparotomy rates as high as 35% are considered acceptable in pregnant patients in the light of the grave consequences of delayed diagnosis.[41]

For appendectomy in the pregnant patient, a right lower quadrant muscle-splitting approach should be employed over the point of maximal tenderness. With late trimester pregnancies, this point of maximal tenderness may be higher than the traditional McBurney's point [see 73 Appendectomy]. The patient should also be turned 30° to the left to reduce pressure on the inferior vena cava and to facilitate exposure of the cecum. If there is doubt about the diagnosis, a low midline incision or a right paramedian incision should be made, especially if the patient has diffuse peritonitis. If appendicitis is found at the time of laparotomy, no further investigation for other intra-abdominal processes should be performed; such investigation may disseminate the infectious process and lead to late pelvic or abdominal abscesses. If, however, appendicitis is not found, the surgeon should thoroughly examine the peritoneal contents on the right side of the abdomen, taking care to avoid exerting traction on the uterus, which might lead to preterm labor. Appendectomy is advisable to avoid later confusion. If perforation occurs, the abdomen should be irrigated and drained. Skin closure should be avoided if abscess, advanced perforation, or gangrene is encountered.

Laparoscopic appendectomy, like all laparoscopic procedures, is controversial in the setting of pregnancy [see Discussion, Laparoscopic Surgery in Pregnancy, below]. When the diagnosis of appendicitis is uncertain, a laparoscopic approach can help rule out salpingitis, adnexal mass, or ectopic pregnancy.[29] When diffuse peritonitis is present, however, laparoscopy is associated with higher complication rates than laparotomy is.[29]

For a laparoscopic appendectomy in a pregnant patient, the first trocar (i.e., that for the camera) is placed in the subxiphoid area under direct vision via an open technique; this step allows visualization of all pelvic structures and the appendix. Once the appendix has been visualized, the right upper quadrant and right lower quadrant trocars should be placed under direct vision. If the size and position of the uterus make laparoscopic appendectomy difficult or impractical, the camera can be used to help locate the best available spot for an open incision.[42]

Antibiotics should be given preoperatively. Postoperative wound infection can be minimized if adequate attention is paid to aseptic technique and handling of tissues. If perforation, peritonitis, or abscess formation is noted, I.V. antibiotics should be administered.

The premature delivery rate for pregnant women undergoing appendectomy ranges from 13% to 22%; this increased rate may contribute to the lower birth weights reported after maternal appendectomy.[24,28] The risk of premature delivery is especially high during the first week after appendectomy. Given that tocolytics have never been shown to improve outcome in this setting, beta$_2$ receptor agonists are a better choice[29]; they are indicated when advanced appendicitis is suspected or when active contractions have been documented.

INTESTINAL OBSTRUCTION

The incidence of bowel obstruction [see 46 Intestinal Obstruction] in pregnant patients ranges from one in 1,500 to one in 66,000.[43] The most

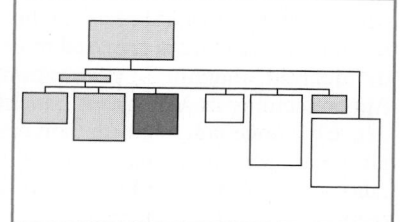

common cause of small-bowel obstruction during pregnancy is adhesions, which account for 55% of cases; volvulus accounts for 25% of cases, with hernia, cancer, and intussusception accounting for the remainder.[44,45] As the incidence of operative procedures and the average age of the mother at gestation have risen, the likelihood of adhesive obstruction has risen as well. This problem may be further exacerbated by the hypomotility or dysmotility known to occur during pregnancy.[46] The need for laparotomy and lysis of adhesive bands during pregnancy is extremely low; however, when surgical management is necessary, fetal mortality is 26% and maternal mortality 5%. With intestinal obstruction, the main concern is to ensure that diagnosis is not delayed. Accordingly, any pregnant patient presenting with nausea, vomiting, and a history of abdominal surgery should be presumed to have a small-bowel obstruction until it is proved otherwise.

Large-bowel obstruction is less common than small-bowel obstruction but can be seen more often as pregnancy progresses. The most common cause of large-bowel obstruction is cecal or sigmoid volvulus. Volvulus during pregnancy is associated with a 21% to 43% mortality.[47] Colonic pseudo-obstruction, or Ogilvie syndrome, has also been reported late in pregnancy or in the early puerperium.[48] Striking colonic dilatation without anatomic obstruction is apparent, with gas filling the entire length of the colon from cecum to rectum. The danger of cecal perforation is high when the maximum diameter of the cecum exceeds 12 cm.

Management

Any sign of bowel ischemia or perforation in a pregnant patient with intestinal obstruction should prompt immediate operation. For small-bowel obstruction, a nasogastric tube should be inserted, fluid resuscitation should be initiated, a Foley catheter should be placed, and a full battery of blood tests should be performed, including assessment of blood gas levels and electrolyte levels and a complete blood count. Because of the leukocytosis known to occur in pregnancy, close attention should be paid to the differential blood count. Any sign of increasing acute-phase activity may suggest ischemia or perforation. Evaluation of acid-base status may also be useful in assessing bowel viability. A flat-plate and an upright abdominal film can confirm the diagnosis of small-bowel obstruction and rule out free air. The risk of radiation exposure to the fetus must be weighed against the potential morbidity and mortality of a missed diagnosis.

Once ischemia and perforation are ruled out, small-bowel obstruction should be treated with aggressive fluid resuscitation to ensure euvolemia and correction of electrolyte abnormalities. If long-term bowel rest is anticipated, total parenteral nutrition should be considered [see 137 Nutritional Support]. If conservative management does not lead to resolution, prompt operative intervention maximizes the chances of an excellent outcome for both fetus and mother.[29] A vertical incision allows the best exposure. The entire bowel must be examined for points of obstruction and assessed for viability. Segments of necrotic bowel should be resected, and an ostomy should be fashioned if necessary.

Large bowel obstruction is usually caused by volvulus. Sigmoid volvulus can usually be reduced by rigid or flexible sigmoidoscopy. If sigmoidoscopy fails, operative intervention with bowel resection and possible colostomy is indicated.[29] Treatment of a recognized cecal volvulus involves prompt operative intervention, resection of any threatened bowel, and cecopexy to prevent recurrence.

Pseudo-obstruction should be managed initially with bowel rest, electrolyte replacement, and the placement of a rectal tube. If these conservative measures fail to reestablish normal peristaltic activity, colonoscopy and intraluminal aspiration of the gas-filled colon should be tried. This approach is effective in as many as 85% of cases; however, it should be undertaken only by a skilled endoscopist because the potential for iatrogenic perforation of the bowel is extremely high. If there is no change in the size of the colon after 72 hours, a cecostomy is indicated.

PERFORATED DUODENAL ULCER

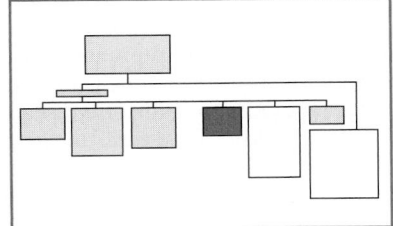

Although rare, perforated duodenal ulcer has been reported. When it occurs, it poses an extremely serious threat to both mother and fetus. There is no place for expectant, nonoperative therapy: prompt operative intervention is crucial. Surgical therapy should be directed at plication of the perforation, and no attempt should be made to perform a definitive ulcer operation. If the woman is close to term, the child should be delivered vaginally rather than by cesarean section because of the prohibitive risk of uterine contamination.

SPONTANEOUS VISCERAL RUPTURE

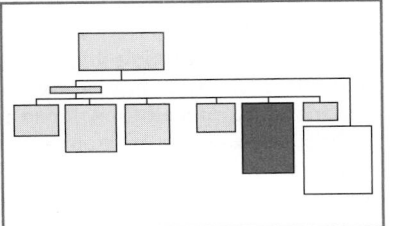

Spontaneous rupture during pregnancy can involve the liver, the kidney, the spleen, or the esophagus. Spontaneous hepatic rupture during pregnancy is extremely uncommon, occurring no more frequently than one in 50,000 pregnancies and perhaps as infrequently as one in 250,000 pregnancies.[49] It is thought to be an advanced development in preeclampsia or eclampsia. Abdominal trauma and events that increase intra-abdominal pressure (e.g., sudden coughing, sneezing, or unusually strong contractions) have also been implicated as causes of spontaneous rupture. Rupture may occur during the second or third trimester, during delivery, or even in the early postpartum period. Typically, it develops in older, multiparous women in the third trimester.[50] Patients present with several days of severe right upper quadrant or substernal pain radiating to the back. The pain may precede the actual rupture by as much as a few days. Nausea, vomiting, hypertension, coagulopathy, and thrombocytopenia are frequently present. In some cases of rupture, the patient presents with hypovolemic shock. A right upper quadrant ultrasonogram often visualizes the rupture or the preceding subcapsular hematoma.[29]

A limited number of renal ruptures have been described in conjunction with hydronephrotic kidneys; they are thought to be secondary to the physiologic hydronephrosis seen in pregnancy. Ultrasonography is the best imaging technique for diagnosis of renal rupture.[51] Splenic rupture is the most common nonobstetric cause of intra-abdominal hemorrhage during gestation. It usually occurs in conjunction with splenic artery aneurysms or spontaneous capsular rupture. In most cases, it is probably secondary to the increased blood volume and splenic enlargement seen toward the later part of pregnancy.

Esophageal rupture has also been described, generally in association with heavy vomiting. Patients report sudden epigastric pain on vomiting that may radiate to the back and the chest. X-rays may reveal air in the mediastinum. An upper GI series with water-soluble contrast material will demonstrate the site of the rupture. Although esophageal rupture is not more common in pregnancy, it may be associated with the frequent nausea and vomiting seen with hyperemesis gravidarum. Ultrasonography, radionuclide scanning, and, ultimately, angiography may be helpful in diagnosing rupture of the liver, the kidney, or the spleen.

Management

Prompt institution of volume support is essential, followed by emergency surgery and correction of any coagulopathy. Conservative management is reserved for stable patients with nonexpanding subcapsular hematomas. Serial ultrasonography is indicated. If adequate assessment of the hematoma, expanding hematoma, or rupture proves difficult or impossible, the patient should be taken to the OR for surgical treatment.[52]

Operative management of hepatic rupture or expanding hematoma involves debridement of nonviable liver, hemostasis with electrocoagulation or packing, and adequate drainage. Cesarean section should be performed simultaneously, depending on the gestational age and the likelihood of fetal survival. This maneuver, when indicated, is curative. Maternal mortality as high as 50% to 75% has been reported, even with prompt surgical intervention. Fetal mortality can be even higher, reaching nearly 80% in some series.[53] Renal rupture necessitates urgent operative exploration. Every effort should be made to salvage the ruptured kidney. Suspected splenic rupture necessitates immediate laparotomy and splenectomy. Esophageal rupture is treated with immediate repair through the left chest, if the injury is to the lower portion of the esophagus, or through the right chest, if the injury is to the upper portion.

Conditions for Which Medical Management Should Be Attempted

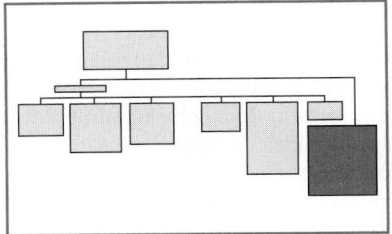

BILIARY TRACT DISEASE

Acute cholecystitis is the second most common nonobstetric emergency in pregnant women. Symptomatic gallstone disease is far more common in women than in men because of the differential effects of the sex steroids on bile lipid composition and cholesterol saturation.[54] The difference in incidence begins at menarche, increases during the childbearing years, and decreases at menopause. By the age of 75 years, at least 35% of women and 20% of men have gallstones.[55]

Gallstone disease is a result of cholesterol supersaturation and biliary stasis, both of which are promoted by pregnancy.[56] The elevated estrogen levels during pregnancy increase cholesterol secretion by the liver. Estrogen increases hepatic cholesterol uptake, increases cholesterol synthesis, and inhibits catabolism of cholesterol to bile acids. High concentrations of cholesterol in the bile overwhelm the solubilizing ability of bile salts, with the result that cholesterol stones form.[57] Elevated progesterone levels lead to bile stasis and decreased gallbladder contraction. Progesterone also causes incomplete emptying of the gallbladder after stimulation by cholecystokinin (CCK).[58] The mechanisms are not understood, but it is thought that progesterone may decrease gallbladder reactivity to CCK.[59] The decrease in small-bowel motility that occurs secondary to progesterone elevation may alter enterohepatic circulation and decrease bile acid return to the liver.[60] The balance of bile salts and cholesterol is further altered in such a way as to favor cholesterol supersaturation and stone formation. Pregnancy also alters the pool of bile acids. The decreased percentage of chenodeoxycholic acid and the increased percentage of cholic acid during pregnancy also promote stone formation.

The incidence of gallstone disease in pregnant women ranges from 3.3% to 12.2%[61] and increases with gestational age; however, only 30% to 40% of patients with gallstones are symptomatic.[62] The relative infrequency of symptomatic biliary disease is a function of the natural history of gallstones and of the time required to precipitate sufficient stones to generate symptoms.[63] Management of biliary colic consists of conservative therapy—namely, hydration, bowel rest if necessary, analgesia, and fetal monitoring. In pregnant patients, elective cholecystectomy for symptomatic gallstone disease should be delayed until after delivery. Fewer than 11% of symptomatic patients progress a more serious complication (e.g., cholecystitis, choledocholithiasis, or pancreatitis). Cholecystectomy during pregnancy is reserved for recurrent biliary colic or the aforementioned complications. It follows that cholecystectomy is rarely necessary in pregnant patients: it is undertaken once in every 10,000 live births.[64]

Gallstone disease causes acute cholecystitis in only 0.05% to 0.08% of births.[64] The clinical symptoms of cholecystitis consist of epigastric or right upper quadrant pain, fever, nausea, vomiting, and occasional radiation of the pain into the right scapula. Physical findings include tenderness in the right upper quadrant and, occasionally, the Murphy sign. Elevated liver function test results indicate that complicated biliary tract disease or choledocholithiasis is likely; however, elevated alkaline phosphatase levels are seen in normal pregnancies and thus are diagnostically unhelpful.

Ultrasonography can diagnose gallstones and biliary ductal dilatation with an accuracy of 97%.[56] It can also detect pericholecystic fluid, reveal gallbladder wall thickening, and elicit a sonographic Murphy sign, all of which are characteristic of cholecystitis.[65] Radionuclide scans introduce the risk of fetal exposure to radiation. This risk almost always outweighs the potential value of any information to be gained from such a scan.

Differential Diagnosis

The differential diagnosis of cholecystitis includes appendicitis (see above), pyelonephritis, nephrolithiasis, acute pancreatitis (see below), myocardial infarction, gastroesophageal reflux disease, peptic ulcer disease (see below), hepatitis, and hepatic liver abscess. Significant hepatic syndromes can occur during pregnancy, such as intrahepatic cholestasis of pregnancy, acute fatty liver of pregnancy, infectious hepatitis, the hemolysis–elevated liver enzymes–low platelet count (HELLP) syndrome, and eclampsia.[66-68] These syndromes should be considered if the clinical signs and symptoms in a pregnant patient do not conform to the typical picture of gallstone disease.

Management

Initial management of cholecystitis is conservative, comprising I.V. hydration, bowel rest, administration of meperidine and antibiotics, fetal monitoring, and, if necessary, nasogastric

decompression. This regimen is successful in 84% of patients.[69] Operative intervention is indicated in the presence of any of the following: failure of conservative management, recurrent disease, intractable nausea, maternal weight loss, fetal growth retardation, obstructive jaundice, gallstone pancreatitis, or peritonitis. Thus, serial monitoring of liver function test results and amylase levels is essential during conservative therapy. If cholecystectomy during pregnancy is necessary but not urgent, it is best to perform the operation in the second trimester: fetal mortality from a first-trimester cholecystectomy can be as high as 12%.[70] The rate of fetal loss decreases through gestation; however, beginning in the third trimester, the risk of preterm labor increases. Symptomatic gallstone disease is also a reasonable indication for surgical management.[64,71] Half of patients with symptomatic gallstone disease require repeat hospitalizations; in addition, several investigators have found the incidence of spontaneous abortion, preterm labor, or premature delivery to be higher in patients treated nonoperatively than in those undergoing cholecystectomy.[72] If cholecystectomy is performed in the second or third trimester, fetal mortality is lower than 5%.[73] There remains a degree of controversy regarding the relative merits of conservative management and aggressive surgical intervention for patients with symptomatic gallbladder disease.

Surgical treatment during pregnancy consists of either open cholecystectomy or laparoscopic cholecystectomy [see 63 Cholecystectomy and Common Bile Duct Exploration]. The advantages of laparoscopic over open cholecystectomy include earlier recovery, earlier mobility, reduced use of narcotics, smaller incisions, and fewer surgical site infections.[72] When carried out with standard precautions, laparoscopic cholecystectomy does not increase the rate of fetal loss (5%) or of spontaneous abortion, nor does it have a greater adverse effect on birth weight, Apgar scores, or the rate of preterm delivery than open cholecystectomy does.[74] Laparoscopic cholecystectomy can be performed safely and effectively throughout pregnancy.[74,75] Routine indications for conversion to open cholecystectomy apply, including uncontrolled bleeding and unclear anatomy. Additionally, conversion during pregnancy is indicated if the gravid uterus has expanded to the point where safe dissection of the gallbladder by laparoscopic means is impossible.[75-79] If the fetus shows signs of distress, deflation of the pneumoperitoneum and conversion to an open cholecystectomy may be necessary. Laparoscopic cholecystectomy is contraindicated in pregnant patients with gallstone pancreatitis.

In patients with choledocholithiasis, intervention should be performed without delay. The common bile duct (CBD) should be explored by means of endoscopic retrograde cholangiopancreatography (ERCP) [see 60 Gastrointestinal Endoscopy], with fluoroscopy used economically and lead aprons worn to shield the fetus.[29] ERCP with sphincterotomy successfully addresses choledocholithiasis without increasing fetal mortality or the rate of preterm delivery.[80] Surgical management of choledocholithiasis with open or laparoscopic cholecystectomy and CBD exploration should be reserved for patients in whom ERCP fails. Choledocholithiasis with right upper quadrant tenderness, fever, and jaundice (Charcot's triad) suggests cholangitis. The only treatment options for cholangitis when ERCP fails are open cholecystectomy and percutaneous intubation of bile ducts.[81] Intraoperative cholangiography can be used without problems after the second trimester,[82] provided that the fetus is shielded with lead during imaging to limit radiation exposure. Duct imaging should be reserved for patients who have risk factors for CBD stones (e.g., pancreatitis, a history of jaundice, or choledochal dilatation).[29]

PANCREATITIS

Pancreatitis is rare during pregnancy, occurring in every 1,000 to 10,000 pregnancies.[64] Its incidence, like that of gallstone disease, increases with gestational age. Associated gallstone disease is present in 70% to 90% of pregnant women presenting with pancreatitis.[64,80,83] Gallstone pancreatitis is associated with a maternal mortality of less than 37% and a fetal mortality of 10% to 60%.[82] In the nonpregnant population, pancreatitis is associated with biliary tract disease in only 40% of cases, with alcohol-induced pancreatitis accounting for another 40%. In pregnant patients, pancreatitis can be secondary to hypertriglyceridemia[84] as well as to thiazide administration and hyperparathyroidism.[85] At present, there is little evidence to suggest that pregnancy itself is an etiologic mechanism in the development of pancreatitis.[86,87]

The signs and symptoms of pancreatitis in pregnant women are indistinguishable from those seen in the general population. Patients report an unremitting, deep visceral pain that is usually midabdominal but may radiate into the back; nausea, vomiting, and anorexia are also typical symptoms. Findings in severe cases include hypotension, hypovolemia, and a rapid, thready pulse. Jaundice occurs in patients with CBD stones. The hallmark of the condition is diffuse abdominal pain combined with hyperamylasemia[88]; amylase levels may approach 2,000 to 3,000 U/L and may be accompanied by lipase elevations.[89] Albumin, calcium, and bilirubin levels should be measured and liver function tests performed. The results should be interpreted with caution in the light of the alkaline phosphatase elevation known to occur in normal pregnancies. Ultrasonography should be undertaken with the aim of searching for evidence of cholelithiasis and choledocholithiasis. Visualization of the inflamed pancreatic head may be informative; however, this structure is often difficult to locate.

Management

Treatment should be aimed at correction of the hypovolemia that invariably accompanies pancreatitis.[90] Restriction of oral intake is necessary. A nasogastric tube should be placed in cases of intractable nausea. Intramuscular administration of meperidine at a dosage of 50 to 75 mg every 3 to 4 hours provides adequate analgesia. Antibiotics should be reserved for treatment of a specific infectious complication. Calcium levels should be kept within the normal range. Arterial blood gases should be monitored as indicated. Prolonged pancreatitis may necessitate lengthy periods of bowel rest. During extended periods without oral feeding, pregnant women should be maintained on total I.V. hyperalimentation.[91]

In patients with pancreatitis caused by extrahepatic biliary obstruction, endoscopic management has achieved excellent results. ERCP and sphincterotomy [see 60 Gastrointestinal Endoscopy] can both be performed safely during pregnancy. Definitive treatment with cholecystectomy and intraoperative cholangiography can safely be delayed until after delivery. Operative intervention should be reserved for patients with biliary obstruction in whom there is no evidence of stone passage. Efforts aimed at postponing operative intervention have been somewhat successful, though the recurrence rate approaches 50%. Early operative intervention has not been shown to improve fetal survival.[83] During the first trimester, loss of the fetus is common[92]; however, in the second trimester, operative

intervention has a good chance of yielding excellent results for both mother and fetus.[93] Although unusual, pseudocyst formation has been reported in pregnant women. It is managed conservatively, without operative intervention. Laparotomy, debridement, drainage, and cholecystectomy are indicated for severe cases with pancreatic necrosis.

PEPTIC ULCER DISEASE

During pregnancy, symptoms of upper abdominal pain, nausea, and vomiting are not uncommon. Peptic ulcer disease usually begins with these same symptoms. Women with peptic ulcer disease usually experience symptomatic improvement during pregnancy. Elevated estrogen levels are believed to decrease gastric acidity during early pregnancy. Maternal gastrin production does not change during pregnancy, but histamine-stimulated acid output is lower. During the third trimester, however, maternal serum gastrin levels rise as a result of placental contribution, and symptomatic peptic ulcer disease may become more likely. During the late third trimester and the early postpartum period, basal and stimulated acid production returns to normal.

The diagnosis is made in much the same way in pregnant patients as in nonpregnant ones, except that physicians treating pregnant women should rely more on clinical information and less on radiologic intervention. Intractable pain that is not relieved by the usual therapeutic interventions should prompt endoscopic evaluation with a tissue biopsy for *Helicobacter pylori* culture.

Management

Safe symptomatic relief can be achieved with direct-acting agents (bismuth salicylate, sucralfate, aluminum hydroxide, and magnesium hydroxide). H_2 blockers and proton pump inhibitors are reserved for symptoms refractory to direct-acting agents. Most gastritis and ulcer disease is caused by infection by *H. pylori*. Treatment with the usual array of antibiotics (clarithromycin, amoxicillin, and metronidazole—but not tetracycline), direct-acting oral agents, and H_2 blockers is also safe in pregnancy.[94] Limitation of intake of nonsteroidal anti-inflammatory drugs (NSAIDs), tobacco, and caffeine also helps mitigate symptoms.

A perforated duodenal ulcer must be treated surgically [see Urgent Surgical Problems, Perforated Duodenal Ulcer, above]. Surgery is also indicated if significant hemorrhage—necessitating transfusion of more than six units over a 24-hour period—is observed. In this setting, maternal mortality is 14% after operation; however, it is 44% if surgical treatment is not provided.[95]

INFLAMMATORY BOWEL DISEASE

Pregnancy does not affect either ulcerative colitis or Crohn disease to any great degree, nor do these diseases affect the welfare of the fetus appreciably.[96-98] Active disease flare-ups are most common during the first trimester and during the early postpartum period.[99] In a review of pregnancies in patients with Crohn disease, the outcome of the pregnancy was not adversely affected by the disease. Although patients with active disease generally had poorer outcomes, neither pregnancy nor therapy affected the course of the disease.[100]

In addition to these frank forms of inflammatory bowel disease (IBD), ulcerative or granular proctitis may also occur in pregnancy. This poorly understood disorder is confined entirely to the distal 10 cm of the rectum. Endoscopically, the mucosa manifests multiple diffuse superficial ulcerations and friability. Above the distal 12 to 15 cm of the rectum, the mucosa assumes a normal appearance. Bleeding is observed, ranging from spotting with defecation to measurable loss. The disease is self-limited, almost never progressing to true IBD.

Management

Treatment of ulcerative colitis or Crohn disease involves administration of sulfadiazine, steroids, or both.[101] Treatment with both of these agents is often recommended.[102] Both steroids and sulfadiazine have been reported to cause congenital malformations in animal studies; however, because of the increased risk of fetal and maternal mortality in untreated cases of IBD, it is recommended that steroids and sulfadiazine be administered together as necessary to minimize the active effects of the disease.[103] If the disease does not respond to medical management, operative intervention may be undertaken, but only as a last resort. In patients with ulcerative colitis, the most common indication for operation is toxic megacolon, which, if left untreated, can cause significant infant and maternal mortality. In patients with Crohn disease, the uncommon problems of abscess, fistula formation, and bowel obstruction may force operation; these conditions should be treated in the usual fashion. Greater reliance should be placed on fecal diversion in pregnant patients because of the increased risk of anastomotic dysfunction. Active Crohn disease may necessitate complete bowel rest and maintenance of nutrition by central I.V. feedings.[104,105]

Patients with ulcerative or granular proctitis should not receive systemic treatment with steroids or sulfadiazine because of the potential toxicity to the fetus. Steroid enemas or enemas concocted from an elixir preparation of sulfasalazine may be administered. Low-residue diets may help control particularly bothersome symptoms.

Discussion

Physiologic Changes of Pregnancy

A variety of physiologic alterations occur during pregnancy. These include mechanical, hormonal, chemical, and hematologic changes [see Table 2] that are essential for maintenance of the pregnancy during the 40 weeks of gestation but that may also complicate the evaluation of abdominal problems in the pregnant patient.

RESPIRATORY CHANGES

The respiratory system undergoes several measurable changes as a result of the hormonal and physiologic influences of pregnancy. Elevated progesterone and estrogen levels cause blood volume and cardiac output to increase; as a result, pulmonary blood flow increases. With the added component of decreased blood albumin concentration and thus decreased oncotic pressure, mild lung edema may ensue.[106] Progesterone also acts as a direct respiratory stimulant, increasing the chemosensitivity of the respiratory center to CO_2.

In pregnant patients, both O_2 consumption and CO_2 production increase as gestation progresses. As the progesterone level rises, chemosensitivity to CO_2 and CO_2 production increase, and minute ventilation progressively rises by up to 30%.[107] Progesterone and increased CO_2 production are the main forces behind the condition known as hyperpnea of pregnancy. This condition results in a reduction in P_aCO_2 from 40 mm Hg to 34 mm Hg and an increase in arterial oxygen tension (P_aO_2) from 60 mm Hg to 100 mm Hg. This exaggerated gradient between the mother and the fetus facilitates efficient exchange of gases. With the decreased P_aCO_2, the pregnant patient also experiences respiratory alkalosis in relation to the fetus. The oxyhemoglobin dissociation curve is thus shifted to the right, again facilitating delivery of oxygen to the fetus. To prevent harmful pH increases, the kidneys respond appropriately by excreting bicarbonate.

As pregnancy progresses, tidal volume rises as a result of increases in chest circumference (usually about 5 cm). Although the growing uterus forces the diaphragm upward by as much as 4 cm, tidal volume is maintained, thanks to increased use of accessory muscles. Functional reserve capacity (FRC) decreases by 10% to 25% by week 12 of gestation because of decreased chest wall compliance. Relaxin, the hormone responsible for ligamentous relaxation of the pelvis, may also be responsible for laxity of the chest wall ligaments. As a consequence of this laxity, the subcostal angle increases from 68° to 103°.[108]

As many as 75% of pregnant women are affected by dyspnea. Dyspnea of pregnancy comprises mild pulmonary edema, increased breathing load, increased drive, and greater use of accessory muscles.[106] It can complicate the assessment of any pregnant patient with an underlying surgical issue. In addition,

Table 2 Chemical and Hematologic Alterations in Pregnant Patients[163]

Laboratory Test	Normal Values	
	Nonpregnant	Pregnant
Urinary acetone	Negative	Faint positive
Serum total protein (g/dl)	6.5–8.5	6.8
Serum albumin (g/dl)	3.5–5.0	2.5–4.5
Blood urea nitrogen (mg/dl)	10–25	5–15
Fasting blood glucose (mg/dl)	70–110	65–100
Two-hour postprandial blood glucose (mg/dl)	< 110	< 120 (plasma)
Serum calcium (mEq/L)	4.6–5.5	4.2–5.2
Serum phosphate (mg/dl)	2.5–4.8	2.3–4.6
Alkaline phosphatase (IU/L)	35–48	35–150
Cholesterol (mg/dl)	120–290	177–345
Triglycerides (mg/dl)	33–166	130–400
Serum folic acid (ng/ml)	5–21	4–14
Vitamin B_{12} (pg/ml)	430–1,025	Decreased
Hemoglobin (g/dl)	12	> 11
Hematocrit (%)	36	33
Serum iron (µg/dl)	> 50	> 60
TIBC (µg/dl)	250–400	300–600
% TIBC saturation	30	> 20
Serum zinc (µg/dl)	65–115	55–80
Urinary zinc (µg/dl)	200–450	200–450

TIBC—total iron-binding capacity

pregnant women typically have decreased oxygen reserve and thus are subject to rapid development of hypoxia and hypercapnia with hypoventilation or apnea. This vulnerability becomes especially important when such patients undergo intubation and anesthesia.

CARDIOVASCULAR CHANGES

During pregnancy, cardiac output rises by 30% to 50% [see Table 3]. This rise is attributable to an increased heart rate and, to a lesser extent, an increased stroke volume.[109] The HR increase may begin as early as 6 weeks after conception[110]; by the third trimester, HR is 15 to 20 beats/min faster than the baseline rate. The increase in the plasma volume may be as great as 50%. Despite the increases in cardiac output and blood volume, BP actually decreases because of the overwhelming effect of reduced systemic vascular resistance. BP reaches a nadir in the second trimester and returns to baseline levels by the time of delivery.[111]

The gravid uterus may press on the inferior vena cava, decreasing venous return and causing cardiac output to decrease by as much as 30%. Pregnant women may even experience dizziness or syncope. To optimize cardiac output, the pregnant patient should be placed in the left lateral decubitus position.[107]

Cardiovascular evaluation of the pregnant patient must take into account the altered cardiac output, blood volume, HR, and BP. Hypovolemia may not manifest itself as tachycardia or hypotension, as would normally be predicted; alternatively, tachycardia of pregnancy may be mistaken for hemorrhage. Careful analysis of the data is necessary whenever hypovolemia is under consideration. Additionally, pregnancy-associated signs and symptoms may complicate any evaluation of concurrent heart disease [see Cardiovascular Conditions during Pregnancy, below].[112]

GASTROINTESTINAL CHANGES

Appetite can vary greatly from one pregnant woman to another. The average increase in daily intake is 200 kcal/day during the first trimester. The recommended dietary allowance (RDA) is 300 kcal/day during pregnancy—more if the pregnant patient is an adolescent or especially physically active.[113] As many as 70% of pregnant patients experience nausea and vomiting. Nausea of pregnancy, or morning sickness, frequently occurs between weeks 4 and 16 of gestation. Most patients respond to conservative treatment, including selective eating and avoidance of dehydration. Persistent nausea and vomiting, termed hyperemesis gravidarum, can lead to dehydration, electrolyte imbalance, and organ failure. It is important to exclude other possible causes of nausea before attributing symptoms to nausea of pregnancy. This condition can complicate the diagnosis of appendicitis, gallbladder disease, pancreatitis, or bowel obstruction.

From 40% to 80% of pregnant women experience gastroesophageal reflux disease (GERD).[94] Esophagogastric junction tone decreases as intra-abdominal pressure increases, with reflux the result. In addition, under the influence of estrogen and progesterone, the stomach has decreased motility and an increased emptying time. Transit through the small bowel and the colon is also slowed.

Estrogens and progesterone are thought to influence cholestasis of pregnancy as well. The net effect of the two hormones is to increase the cholesterol concentration in bile. Estrogen also decreases bile flow. Progesterone promotes smooth muscle relaxation and stasis throughout the biliary system.[114] In the evaluation of cholestasis or any liver disease, it is important to remember that placental alkaline phosphatase can increase measured alkaline phosphatase levels by a factor of three or four.

URINARY CHANGES

As cardiac output increases, the glomerular filtration rate increases by 30% to 50%. This increase reaches a peak at the end of the first trimester. Accordingly, creatinine clearance and blood urea nitrogen (BUN) levels fall by 25% over the first trimester. The kidneys themselves increase in size by 1.5 cm as a result of increased vascularity.[115] The ureters become dilated as a consequence of the relaxing effects of progesterone on smooth muscle.[116] Dextrorotation of the uterus causes further dilatation of the right ureter.

HEMATOLOGIC CHANGES

Normal pregnancy causes numerous changes in coagulation and fibrinolysis. Platelets become more reactive, and destruction is enhanced; to compensate, the pregnant patient increases production of platelets. Normal pregnancy increases hepatic and endothelial cell synthesis of many procoagulant factors. Pregnant women have normal anticoagulant factor levels except for a sharp decrease in protein S antigen and activity. In general, fibrinolytic activity is impaired during pregnancy; however, bleeding time and clotting time are unchanged. Overall, pregnancy is a hypercoagulable state.[117] The risk of thromboembolism doubles during pregnancy.[118] Accordingly, compression stockings should be used whenever surgical management is embarked on.

Leukocytosis is normally seen in pregnancy. What the net effect of a decrease in CD4+ cells, an increase in CD8+ cells, and

Table 3 Hemodynamic Values in Healthy Nonpregnant, Pregnant, and Postpartum Subjects[109,164]

Parameter	Nonpregnant	36–38 Weeks' Gestation*	Postpartum
Heart rate (beats/min)	60–100	83 ± 10	71 ± 10
Central venous pressure (mm Hg)	5–10	3.6 ± 2.5	3.7 ± 2.6
Mean pulmonary arterial pressure (mm Hg)	15–20	—	—
Pulmonary arterial wedge pressure (mm Hg)	6–12	7.5 ± 1.8	6.3 ± 2.1
Mean arterial pressure (mm Hg)	90–110	90.3 ± 5.8	86.4 ± 7.5
Cardiac output (L/min)	4.3–6.0	6.2 ± 1.0	4.3 ± 0.9
Stroke volume (ml/beat)	57–71	74.7	60.6
Systemic vascular resistance (dyne · cm · sec⁻⁵)	900–1,400	1,210 ± 266	1,530 ± 520
Pulmonary vascular resistance (dyne · cm · sec⁻⁵)	< 250	78 ± 22	119 ± 47

*Values in pregnant patients were determined with patient in left lateral decubitus position.

an unchanged number of B cells may be is the subject of some controversy at present.[119] More important than the higher total number of cells is the altered activity exhibited by all leukocytes, a complicated picture that is still not fully understood.

Although pregnancy may appear to be an anemic state, it is not: blood volume actually increases (see above), and red cell mass rises by 30% [see Table 2].

General Perioperative Considerations in Pregnant Patients

The use of anesthesia in the course of an operation does not pose a teratogenic risk to the fetus.[120] Surgical treatment can be acceptably safe if appropriate attention is given to certain key perioperative considerations—namely, fetal monitoring, radiologic investigation, anesthesia, and the timing of the operation.

FETAL MONITORING

Monitoring consists of measuring uterine contractions with a tocometer, fetal HR with a Doppler transducer, and fetal movement and tone with ultrasonography. Together, these measurements yield a good indication of fetal health. Preoperative ultrasonography can also approximate gestational age when an accurate history cannot be obtained. Gestational age plays a pivotal role in all surgical decision making for a pregnant patient.

The fetal HR is routinely measured both preoperatively and postoperatively.[121] Though the fetal HR can be heard 14 weeks after conception, it serves as an indicator of fetal oxygenation only after week 26. Specific fetal HR abnormalities—absence of variability, late or variable decelerations, and bradycardia—are predictive of impending fetal hypoxia, physical damage, or death. In the absence of these extreme (and hence obvious) fetal HR patterns, interpretation of fetal tracings can be complex.[122] There are no conclusive data to suggest that any single monitoring technique reflects fetal outcome.[121] Optimization of maternal physiologic status is more important than any mode of fetal monitoring.

RADIOLOGIC INVESTIGATION

X-rays and CT scans must be employed judiciously, given the risk that radiation poses to the pregnant patient. Depending on the exposure time and the total dose, radiation may cause failure to implant, malformation, growth retardation, CNS abnormalities, or fetal loss.

The standard units of measure for radiation are the Gray (Gy) and the rad; 1 Gy is equivalent to 100 rad, and 1 rad thus is equivalent to 1 cGy or 10 mGy. The ICRP has stated that radiation doses lower than 100 mGy do not increase the risk of fetal death, malformation, or developmental delay.[34] Doses between 200 to 500 mGy during weeks 8 to 15 of gestation, however, result in measurable IQ reductions, and doses higher than 600 mGy result in growth retardation and CNS damage. Most diagnostic procedures fall within the accepted safe range. The average radiation dose from an abdominal x-ray is 1.4 mGy, that from an abdominal CT scan is 8.0 mGy, that from a pelvic CT scan is 25 mGy, and that from a selective spiral CT scan of the abdomen and the pelvis is 30 mGy.

In many instances, alternate diagnostic modalities that do not employ ionizing radiation, such as ultrasonography and MRI, are sufficient to determine the proper treatment. If, however, diagnostic radiation does prove necessary, the fetus should be shielded, radiation exposure should be minimized, and radiation doses should be carefully documented.[123] Careful cooperation with the radiologist will help limit radiation exposure. It is of particular importance that the patient be informed of the risks associated with radiation in comparison with the expected benefits of diagnostic radiation in her case.

ANESTHESIA

The physiologic changes associated with pregnancy have implications for anesthetic management. As noted (see above), oxygen reserve decreases with pregnancy. Upon intubation, hypoxia and hypercapnia with hypoventilation or apnea may develop rapidly. In one clinical study of obstetric anesthesia, airway difficulties occurred in 7.9% of intubated patients, compared with 2.5% of nonintubated patients[124]; it is noteworthy that the primary reasons for difficult intubation were airway anatomy and technique, just as would be the case in nonpregnant patients. During intubation, pregnant women are also at increased risk for gastric aspiration owing to the decreased gastroesophageal sphincter tone. Because of this increased risk of aspiration, nasogastric suction should be freely employed. The stomach should be emptied before emergency procedures and continually decompressed throughout the operation and the early postoperative period.

Anesthesia can suppress the normal physiologic compensation for aortocaval compression, in which event hypotension can ensue. Positioning of the patient in a leftward tilt or the left lateral decubitus position can minimize hypotension.[121] Liberal use of indwelling urinary catheters allows gross estimation of the adequacy of blood volume and splanchnic perfusion during general operative procedures. If intra-abdominal operation is necessary after weeks 12 to 16, the bladder must be decompressed to allow adequate exposure in the pelvis and the lower abdomen.

According to retrospective studies, all anesthetic, opioid, sedative-hypnotic, and anxiolytic agents pose some degree of risk to the fetus; none of them appears to be significantly more teratogenic or safer than any other.[121] If vasopressors are necessary, ephedrine is the drug of choice, in that it causes less uterine vasoconstriction than epinephrine or norepinephrine does. Small doses of phenylephrine are also safe for use in pregnant women who are hypotensive [see Table 4].

TIMING OF SURGERY

If a surgical problem arises during pregnancy, the urgency of surgical treatment must be balanced against the risk such treatment poses to the mother and the fetus. Urgent procedures, such as appendectomy, should be carried out in the usual timely fashion [see Urgent Surgical Problems, above]: in such cases, the risks to both mother and fetus outweigh the risks of miscarriage and preterm labor. Semielective procedures are best done during the second trimester.[72] In the first trimester, when organogenesis is ongoing, concerns arise about the teratogenic risks of medications and surgical interventions. During the first trimester, surgical procedures are associated with a miscarriage rate of 12%; during the second trimester, this rate falls to 0% to 5.6%. The incidence of preterm labor with surgical procedures is 5% in the second trimester but rises to 30% to 40% in the third trimester.[125] Elective procedures should be delayed until 6 weeks after delivery.

TOCOLYTICS

Even though surgical procedures have been associated with a higher incidence of preterm labor, especially in the third trimester, routine prophylactic use of tocolytics is not recom-

Table 4   Safety of Various Drugs Used during Pregnancy[165,166]

Drug (FDA Pregnancy Category)	Toxicity	Comments
Analgesics/tranquilizers		
Ibuprofen (B)	Risk of postpartum hemorrhage; premature patent ductus arteriosus closure; no teratogenic effects	Use with caution toward end of pregnancy
Meperidine (B)	Decreased neonatal respiration; CNS depression	Greatest risk near term
Morphine (C)	Small size for gestational age; respiratory depression; fetal death	Greatest risk near term
Codeine (C)	Possible congenital anomalies	Avoid in first trimester
Acetaminophen (B)	None known	Analgesic of choice
Aspirin (C)	Anticoagulation effect; fetal bleeding; possible prolongation of pregnancy; no teratogenesis known	Use with caution, especially toward end of pregnan not recommended for routine analgesia
Barbiturates (C)	Fetal addiction; neonatal bleeding; ?teratogenesis	Long-term administration not recommended
Diazepam (D)	?Cleft palate; ?heart defects; hypotonia; hypothermia; withdrawal symptoms	Long-term administration not recommended
Anesthetics		
Bupivacaine (C)	Bradycardia	Use with caution in late pregnancy
Lidocaine (B)	Bradycardia; CNS depression	Use with caution in late pregnancy
Halothane (C)	Uterine relaxation	Can cause abortion in early pregnancy
Nitrous oxide	?Teratogenesis in early pregnancy	Can be used in late pregnancy
Muscle relaxants (C)	Fetal curarization	Relatively safe; incidence of problems extremely lc
Antibiotics		
Ampicillin (B)	None known	Safe
Aztreonam (B)	Not teratogenic in rodents	Safety in pregnancy unclear
Cephalosporins (B)	No embryocidal reports	Safe
Clindamycin (B)	None known	Safety in pregnancy unclear
Erythromycin, azithromycin (B)	Risk of cholestatic hepatitis; no reported congenital defects	Avoid in pregnancy
Fluoroquinolones (C)	Irreversible arthropathy in immature animals	Avoid in pregnancy
Gentamicin (C)	Possible 8th nerve toxicity; no reported congenital defects, neonatal ototoxicity, or nephrotoxicity	Avoid in pregnancy
Imipenem (C)	None known	Safety in pregnancy unclear
Metronidazole (B)	Carcinogenic in rodents; possibly teratogenic	Contraindicated in first trimester; use with caution thereafter
Nitrofurantoin (C)	Hemolytic anemia in newborns; no known teratogenic effects	Contraindicated at term
Penicillin G (B)	None known	Safe
Streptomycin (D)	8th cranial nerve abnormality	Contraindicated
Tetracycline (D)	Adverse effects on fetal teeth and bones; maternal hepatotoxicity; congenital defects	Contraindicated
Trimethoprim-sulfamethoxazole (C)	Hemolysis in G6PD-deficient patients; risk of kernicterus	Contraindicated at term
Vancomycin (C)	Potential fetal ototoxicity, nephrotoxicity	Avoid in pregnancy

mended. Tocolytics have a several side effects and have not been shown to improve outcome when used prophylactically. Tocolytics are best employed to treat active uterine irritability. Uterine irritability can also be reduced by controlling maternal pain and anxiety.[126]

Laparoscopic Surgery in Pregnant Patients

The role of laparoscopic surgery in the management of pregnant patients remains to be established. Most current recommendations are based on retrospective and animal studies. Laparoscopy would appear to offer some significant benefits. For example, it leads to rapid postoperative recovery and mobilization and thus reduces the risk of thromboembolism associated with pregnancy. Hospital stays are shorter and hospital costs lower.[127] Often, less narcotic analgesia is required during recovery, and fetal depression from narcotic exposure is thereby minimized. Because laparoscopic surgery makes use of smaller incisions, incisional hernias are less common, and there is less incision-related discomfort as a result of the growing uterus and increasing intra-abdominal pressure.[125] Moreover, laparoscopic surgery involves less manipulation of the uterus and so may be less likely to induce uterine irritability, preterm

labor, premature delivery, or spontaneous abortion.[42] Finally, when the diagnosis is uncertain, the surgeon can often use laparoscopy to identify appendicitis, ovarian masses, ovarian torsion, and ectopic pregnancy.

Pregnancy adds a level of risk to any laparoscopic procedure. Insufflation with CO_2 and increased intra-abdominal pressure lead to decreased uterine blood flow, decreased maternal vena cava return, and decreased maternal functional residual capacity.[75,126] The combination of CO_2 pneumoperitoneum, the reverse Trendelenburg position, general anesthesia, and aortocaval compression by the gravid uterus can decrease maternal cardiac output by 50%.[127] Animal studies suggest that CO_2 pneumoperitoneum may also cause an increase in maternal arterial CO_2 tension (P_aCO_2), resulting in maternal and fetal acidosis[128]; however, there is active controversy as to whether these intraoperative alterations caused by CO_2 pneumoperitoneum actually affect fetal health.[129] Finally, when laparoscopic surgery is performed in a pregnant patient, the uterus is susceptible to direct damage, irritation, or penetration by a Veress needle or trocar.[130]

Certain precautions can be taken to limit the risks associated with laparoscopic surgery during pregnancy.[125] Using the Trendelenburg position (or minimizing use of the reverse

Trendelenburg position) and left uterine displacement enhance venous return. Keeping intra-abdominal pressure below 15 mm Hg can minimize the decreases in uterine blood flow, maternal inferior vena cava return, and maternal functional residual capacity. Limiting the duration of insufflation minimizes the risks associated with CO_2 pneumoperitoneum. During laparoscopy, a transvaginal Doppler transducer should be used for fetal monitoring when possible; any signs of distress can be combated by decreasing intra-abdominal pressure and hyperventilating the mother. Standard noninvasive monitoring methods (e.g., capnography) are sufficient guides to P_aCO_2 values in routine cases.[131] Ventilation should be adjusted in accordance with maternal P_aCO_2 levels. Finally, penetrating injury to the uterus can be minimized by entering the abdomen under direct vision and applying upward countertraction of the abdominal wall while placing a Hasson trocar.[42]

Currently, the general tendency is to limit laparoscopic surgery in pregnant women to the first 28 weeks of gestation. Later in pregnancy, when the uterus is no longer confined within the pelvis and the lower abdomen, laparoscopic surgery becomes substantially more difficult. Although laparoscopic surgery, like laparotomy, increases the likelihood of preterm labor, tocolytics should be administered only in the event of documented or perceived contractions; given the side effects of tocolytics, their prophylactic use is more worrisome than the potential risk of preterm contractions.[74]

When appropriate precautions are employed, laparoscopy poses no more risk to either the mother or the fetus than laparotomy does.[72,130,132] Again, there are no significant differences between the two approaches with respect to preterm delivery rate, birth weight, Apgar score, growth restriction, infant mortality, or risk of fetal malformation.[74,126]

Cardiovascular Conditions during Pregnancy

CARDIAC DISEASE

The incidence of heart disease during pregnancy is 1.5%, with rheumatic heart disease accounting for 60% to 75% of cases.[133] The current trend in the United States, however, is that fewer pregnant women are presenting with rheumatic heart disease and more are presenting with congenital heart disease.[112] Heart disease becomes an active issue during pregnancy because gestation places great stress on the cardiovascular system: cardiac output increases by 30% to 50%, HR by 15 to 20 beats/min, and plasma volume by 50%. Delivery places added stress on the heart as a result of physical exertion, pain, and drastic fluid shifts. There is some blood loss with delivery, but there is also an increase in venous return resulting from the release of the pressure imposed by the gravid uterus on the inferior vena cava. In addition, excess extracellular fluid is drawn into the vasculature after delivery. If the diseased heart has little reserve, pregnancy can push the patient into florid heart failure. Recognition of heart failure may be delayed because normal pregnant patients typically present with peripheral edema, dyspnea, and poor exercise tolerance.

The most common indication for cardiac surgery during pregnancy is native valve disease (36%),[134] of which mitral stenosis is the variety most commonly encountered. Progressive failure from mitral stenosis can cause arrhythmias that exacerbate symptoms. Pregnant women with aortic stenosis or hypertrophic cardiomyopathy may experience angina and syncope in addition to heart failure, and they tolerate arrhythmias

poorly. Aortic disease is the second most common indication for cardiac surgery during pregnancy (31%). Aortic dissection and aneurysm are associated with hypertension, atherosclerosis, and connective tissue disorders (e.g., Marfan syndrome and Ehlers-Danlos syndrome). Approximately 50% of all aortic dissections in women younger than 40 years occur during pregnancy. Other indications for cardiac surgery during pregnancy are prosthetic valve dysfunction (14%), congenital anomalies (e.g., atrial and ventricular septal defects) (7%), pulmonary embolism (6%), cardiac tumors (4%), and coronary artery disease (2%). Overall, cardiac surgery is associated with a maternal mortality of 0% to 3% and a fetal mortality of 12% to 20%.[133,135] The outcome of a cardiovascular operation performed in a pregnant patient is affected by the indication for surgery, the condition of the mother, and the timing of the procedure in relation to the gestational age.[136]

Management

Ideally, women of childbearing age who have heart disease should receive counseling before planned conception. Such counseling should address the risks of pregnancy, the issues related to anticoagulation, and the fetal mortality and morbidity associated with specific clinical situations. Any significant congenital heart condition should be corrected before pregnancy if possible. Vigilance for symptoms of heart failure should be an adjunct to routine prenatal care[137]; if signs of failure develop, the patient should be hospitalized for treatment of volume overload, tachycardia, and possible arrhythmias.[138] If aortic dissection is noted, hypertension should be controlled.

The question of the optimal timing of cardiac surgery during pregnancy introduces a potential maternal-fetal conflict of interest. On one hand, maternal mortality from cardiac surgery is lowest in the first trimester; delaying operative treatment increases maternal mortality substantially.[134] On the other hand, fetal mortality and morbidity from cardiac surgery are highest in the first trimester and decrease as gestation progresses. Hence, the issue of how to time surgical management so as to safeguard both mother and fetus as well as possible is still the subject of some debate. In general, operative intervention should be delayed until the fetus is deliverable, at which time cesarean section can be performed, followed by cardiac surgery or aortic surgery.[133,139] If it is necessary to perform a cardiac operation during the first or second trimester, precautions should be taken to minimize the effects of bypass on the fetus. High-flow, high-pressure bypass is favored by most surgeons, the rationale being that high rates are necessary during pregnancy to ensure perfusion to the fetus, especially in the context of a contracting uterus. Cardiotocographic monitoring should be instituted to measure the level of fetal stress during bypass. Bypass causes uterine contractions through dilution of progesterone, a natural inhibitor of uterine contractions. Patients with documented contractions should receive tocolytics.

Finally, any pregnant woman undergoing cardiac surgery should receive antibiotics as prophylaxis against endocarditis, the most lethal complication of such procedures.[134]

SPLENIC ARTERY ANEURYSMS

Splenic artery aneurysms are rare, with an incidence of less than 1%. They are, however, four times more common in women than in men, and 25% of all splenic artery ruptures in women occur during pregnancy. Several factors contribute to the relatively high incidence of such rupture in pregnant women. Splenic arterial pressure is unusually high during pregnancy as a result of the increased cardiac output, the increased blood volume, and the pressure placed on the abdominal aorta and the iliac arteries by the gravid uterus. Pregnancy is also believed to break down the connective tissue component of the arterial wall. Multiparous women in the third trimester are at highest risk for a ruptured splenic artery aneurysm. In the non-pregnant population, splenic artery rupture is associated with a 25% mortality; however, in pregnant women, it is associated with maternal and fetal mortalities ranging from 75% to 95%,[140] mainly as a consequence of erroneous diagnosis. Upon diagnosis of rupture, immediate operative repair is necessary. If a splenic artery aneurysm larger than 2 cm is found in a woman of childbearing age, elective resection is indicated.[141]

RENAL ARTERY ANEURYSMS

Renal artery aneurysms are uncommon, appearing in 0.09% of the population; most are diagnosed incidentally in the course of CT scanning done for other indications. Renal artery aneurysms not only are associated with brittle hypertension but also carry a high mortality when they rupture. Because of the connective tissue laxity that develops during pregnancy, the risk of rupture is higher in pregnant than in nonpregnant women. When renal artery rupture occurs, immediate operative repair of the aneurysm is necessary. The most important indication for surgery in this situation is hypertension and female gender; the size of the aneurysm is a secondary concern.[142]

Malignancies during Pregnancy

Cancer during pregnancy occurs in 0.07% to 0.1% of births.[143] The types most commonly encountered in this setting are breast cancer (19%), thyroid cancer (17%), cervical cancer (11%), Hodgkin disease (7%), and ovarian cancer (6%).[144] All cancers except for melanoma and hematologic tumors metastasize to the placenta but not to the fetus.[145,146] The major risk factor for malignancy during pregnancy is age greater than 40 years. Pregnant women with malignancies are more likely to experience complicated hospitalizations, as are their babies. Malignancy during pregnancy also increases the chances of low birth weight and premature labor.[144]

The measures commonly employed to treat cancer—surgery, irradiation, and chemotherapy—all pose significant risks to the fetus, especially in the first trimester. The degree of risk associated with operation depends not only on the gestational age but also on the disease, the stage of the cancer, and the nature of the procedure. Chemotherapy during the first trimester can cause fetal malformations, premature delivery, and restricted fetal growth in as many as 25% of cases; however, chemotherapy during the second and third trimester generally has a favorable long-term outcome.[147] Finally, any radiation therapy administered is likely to exceed the safety threshold for fetal radiation exposure.

Thus, treatment of cancer in a pregnant woman should involve close coordination between the oncology team, the obstetrician, and possibly a neonatologist. The patient must be well informed regarding the overall risks of treatment, the specific risks to herself if some components of therapy are delayed, and the specific risks to the fetus associated with each type of therapy.

BREAST CANCER

Pregnancy-associated breast cancer is defined as cancer diagnosed during pregnancy or up to 1 year after delivery. Pregnancy-associated breast cancer is associated with a worse outcome than other types of breast cancer are. The poorer prognosis may be attributable to aggressive tumor growth in response to hormones of pregnancy. In addition, diagnosis of pregnancy-associated breast cancer is often delayed because of the normal hypertrophic thickening of the breast during pregnancy, the inability of mammography and ultrasonography to differentiate between normal breasts and breasts with malignancies in pregnant women, or the reluctance of surgeons to perform biopsies during pregnancy.[148]

Management

Any suspicious breast mass should be aspirated to rule out the possibility that it is a cyst. If the mass disappears after aspiration, follow-up via physical examination is appropriate; mammography is not advisable, because it may damage the fetus. If the mass does not resolve, a core-needle biopsy or an open biopsy with local anesthesia should be performed [see 25 Breast Procedures], regardless of the stage of pregnancy. Strict attention to hemostasis and to ligature of obvious ductules is necessary to prevent postoperative hematoma or leakage of milk. Another common presentation is nipple discharge [see 21 Breast Complaints], which may signal a papilloma or duct ectasia and thus calls for biopsy. Inflammatory changes in breast skin are generally caused by staphylococcal or streptococcal infections; they occur most frequently in the postpartum period but also are occasionally seen during pregnancy. If inflammation does not resolve rapidly after antibiotics are administered, drainage is indicated and biopsy should be considered.

Management of breast cancer in pregnant patients does not vary greatly from that in nonpregnant patients.[149] Once the diagnosis of breast cancer is made, modified radical mastectomy [see 25 Breast Procedures] should be done expeditiously; it should not be delayed because of the pregnancy.[148] Given the high doses required, radiation therapy is contraindicated during pregnancy. Accordingly, lumpectomy with radiation therapy is an option only if radiation therapy can commence after delivery. As noted, chemotherapy is relatively safe during the second and third trimesters. For patients with stage III or IV breast cancer, termination of pregnancy may be considered to allow unrestricted treatment with chemotherapy and radiation. For all patients, treatment plans should be formulated on an individual basis, taking into account the risks facing both the fetus and the mother.

Burns during Pregnancy

Burns occurring during pregnancy should be evaluated in the same manner as burns occurring in the nonpregnant population [see Section 7 Trauma and Thermal Injury]. The total body surface (TBS) burned should be measured and documented (ideally with photographs). Adjustments must be made for the increased abdominal surface area seen in the later stages of gestation. Fetal outcome is dependent on the mother's condition: fetal mortality is 89% when the mother has burns over more than 50% of her TBS but falls to 21% when the mother has burns over less than 50% of her TBS.[150]

Management

Generally, burns are treated in much the same way in pregnant patients as in nonpregnant patients; however, special attention should be paid to securing the airway and ensuring adequate breathing. Pregnant patients have a lower FRC and are less able to compensate for hypoxia. Moreover, exposure to burns often puts the mother at risk for carbon monoxide inhalation. The fetus is especially susceptible to carbon monoxide poisoning because fetal hemoglobin has a higher affinity for carbon monoxide than maternal hemoglobin does; thus, carbon monoxide can easily lead to fetal hypoxia.[151] Silver sulfadiazine cream should not be used near term because of its association with kernicterus in the infant. Finally, if the fetus is older than 24 weeks and the mother sustains burns over 50% or more of her TBS, cesarean section is indicated.

Electrical accidents are associated with a fetal mortality of 50%. Any woman who has experienced electric shock should undergo serial ultrasonography until delivery. Maternal mortality with such injuries is minimal.

Minor Surgical Problems of Pregnancy

HEARTBURN

Heartburn is a common complaint of pregnancy that results in part from decreased lower esophageal sphincter pressure and regurgitation of stomach contents.[152] An alkaline reflux gastritis may in part be responsible because gastric acidity is decreased in pregnancy. Toward the later part of the pregnancy, 10% to 15% of pregnant women will also manifest severe reflux that is caused by a frank diaphragmatic hiatus hernia.

Management

Antacids containing aluminum hydroxide or magnesium hydroxide, such as Gelusil and Amphojel, should be taken 30 minutes to 1 hour after meals.[103] Positional changes, such as elevation of the head of the bed and maintenance of an upright posture for several hours after meals, should be encouraged. Chewing gum or sucking on hard candies tends to increase esophageal motility and decrease reflux. In severe cases, sucralfate may be given to soothe and possibly to heal active gastritis and esophagitis. Metoclopramide has also been found to be efficacious in cases of heartburn that is refractory to oral antacids.

CONSTIPATION

Increased levels of sex steroid hormones during pregnancy are thought to produce decreases in smooth muscle motility and subsequent functional decreases in bowel motility. Moreover, the pressure exerted on the bowel by the expanded and displaced uterus is thought to interfere with normal peristaltic activity.

Management

Stressing good bowel care and bowel training is helpful. Nonpharmacologic methods of increasing bowel activity, such as increasing the fiber and roughage in the diet to maximize stool bulk, are also useful. Foods with laxative properties, such as prunes, figs, apples, and citrus fruits, may facilitate stool passage. The patient should take at least eight to 10 extra glasses of fluid a day; water is preferable, but non–caffeine-containing liquids are also acceptable. Increased exercise may help in the passage of stool. A bulk laxative, such as Metamucil, or a stool softener, such as Colace, should be prescribed, regardless of whether the natural roughage foods are effective. Mild laxatives may be given when all other measures are inadequate. Small doses of milk of magnesia and similar osmotic reactive laxatives

are useful. Small amounts of mineral oil may be cautiously administered; prolonged use of mineral oil can cause liver degeneration and interferes with the absorption of fat-soluble vitamins.

HEMORRHOIDS

Nearly 10% of obstetric patients have hemorrhoids at some point during their pregnancy.[153] The development of hemorrhoids during pregnancy results from the decreased motility and the tendency toward constipation that occur in all pregnancies. These changes lead to straining at stool, during which the shearing force generated in the rectal canal can exacerbate and intensify preexisting hemorrhoid disease. Furthermore, the weight and pressure of the uterus itself tends to decrease venous return and increase the amount of pooling in vascular structures in the lower pelvis.[154] Hemorrhoids can present with itching, bleeding, or severe pain if the hemorrhoids thrombose.

Management

The best method of preventing hemorrhoids is to maintain adequate bowel function; when that is not feasible, the following general measures should be taken:

1. Warm sitz baths
2. A local astringent, such as a Tucks pad or witch hazel
3. Supine positioning with the legs elevated whenever that is possible
4. Manual replacement of the hemorrhoids after each bowel movement, regardless of the pain incurred
5. Astringent suppositories or creams, such as Anusol or Anusol HC
6. Minimization of constipation (see above)

Acutely thrombosed hemorrhoids should be incised with the patient under local anesthesia; the clot should be evacuated, astringent ointments applied, and bowel care resumed. Injection with sclerosing agents is not advisable. The potential for submucosal abscess formation and pelvic sepsis, though small, makes the procedure extremely dangerous.

Surgery is seldom indicated. In a study of 12,455 pregnant women, only 25 required surgical excision of the symptomatic tissue, which was done under local anesthesia. There were no maternal or fetal problems as a result of the procedure.[155] On rare occasions, hemorrhoid banding [see 79 Anal Procedures for Benign Disease] may be indicated for excessive bleeding. It should be performed very carefully because of the potential for necrosis and infection.

VARICOSE VEINS

Varicosities become a problem with successive pregnancies. They are generally a minor nuisance in the primipara but become more bothersome the more children a woman has. Thrombophlebitis is not uncommon, but embolism is a rare complication. Varicose veins develop in women who are predisposed to this problem as a result of weakness in the valvular structures in the veins. The increased stasis and venous pressure created by the expansion of the uterus leads to progressive enlargement and engorgement of the veins. Besides cosmetic problems, varicosities can cause muscle aching, swelling, and, in severe cases, ulceration.

Management

Increased exercise that includes regular walking and activity is suggested. Elevation of the legs at rest is advised; prolonged sitting is not. Support stockings and, in poor weather, support panty hose should be used. The stockings should be placed on the legs in the early morning, before substantial pooling has occurred. Injection therapy is contraindicated during pregnancy. Ligation of veins causing ulceration or phlebitis is recommended only in extreme cases. Administration of aspirin or other NSAIDs is also contraindicated. If anticoagulation is necessary, heparin should be given because it does not cause fetal damage and is fairly easily controlled.

DEEP VEIN THROMBOSIS

Pregnant women are more prone to deep vein thrombosis (DVT) [see 85 Venous Thromboembolism] during the later stages of pregnancy and the early postpartum period, largely because of alterations in the normal blood coagulation system, such as increased levels of clotting factors and decreased fibrinolytic activity. These intrinsic factors may be exacerbated by the venous stasis and increased blood viscosity that occur during pregnancy. Compression of the iliac veins by the growing uterus also predisposes pregnant women to thrombosis. Although venous thrombosis affects only 4.1% of women during pregnancy,[156] recognition and management of the disorder are important to prevent the potentially life-threatening sequelae of pulmonary embolism.

Leg swelling and prominent superficial veins are common in pregnancy and may delay the diagnosis of DVT. Phlebography is the most accurate, operator-independent study available for confirmation of DVT. Because the iliofemoral system is the most common site of DVT, it is crucial that it be well visualized; however, this may not be possible with the fetus shielded. Serial impedance plethysmography may be effective in diagnosing DVT while eliminating exposure of the fetus to radiation.[157] Doppler ultrasonography is relatively ineffective in predicting isolated pelvic thrombosis but may be attempted. Real-time B-mode ultrasonography is an extremely sensitive examination that is useful in detecting DVT. This technique achieves good visualization of venous thrombi within vessels; however, although it can readily visualize clots in leg veins, it is less specific above the inguinal ligament. Noninvasive screening is not useful during pregnancy because of the high false positive and false negative rates; it is not uncommon for DVT to occur immediately after a screening examination. Any signs or symptoms of DVT or pulmonary embolism are an indication for aggressive testing.[156] Radioactive fibrinogen should not be used near term, because of the potential hazard to the fetal thyroid.

Management

When the diagnosis is made, therapy with a low-molecular-weight heparin (LMWH) should be instituted for the duration of pregnancy, with postpartum antiocoagulation, in the form of an LMWH or warfarin, continued for 6 weeks. LMWH doses should be adjusted according to weight and thus may increase throughout pregnancy and decrease after delivery. Unfractionated heparin can also be used during pregnancy. Current experience with LMWHs suggests that they are as efficacious and safe as unfractionated heparin.[158,159] In addition, LMWHs have certain advantages over unfractionated heparin: once-daily or twice-daily subcutaneous administration, a predictable dose response, reduced passage across the placenta, and lower incidences of heparin-induced thrombocytopenia and heparin-induced osteoporosis. Warfarin should not ordinarily be given for maintenance anticoagulation: it has teratogenic potential during the first trimester and may induce bleeding during the later part of pregnancy.[160]

Prophylaxis of DVT is recommended for subsequent pregnancies. For most women, 4 to 6 weeks of postpartum anticoagulation with an LMWH followed by warfarin is sufficient.[161,162] For patients who are at high risk for DVT because of inherited thrombophilia, DVT outside of pregnancy, multiple episodes of DVT, morbid obesity, or prolonged bed rest, prophylactic anticoagulation may be necessary both ante partum and post partum. When surgery is planned during pregnancy, patients should be fitted with graded compression boots beforehand and should continue to wear them until they are ambulating regularly. Ambulation should commence on the night of the operation whenever possible.

ROUND LIGAMENT PAIN

The general surgeon is occasionally asked to evaluate the pregnant woman in the late stages of her pregnancy with a possible inguinal hernia. Groin hernia in the pregnant patient is extremely uncommon because the expanded uterus acts as a shield against the abdominal wall, preventing incarceration or strangulation of bowel contents. Groin pain is generally caused by excessive traction on the round ligament, usually on the left, during the later part of pregnancy. As the uterus rotates and the patient's position changes, this pain can become quite severe.

Treatment

Local heat and abdominal support are the mainstays of treatment. Positional changes are necessary, and the patient should rest in the supine position.

References

1. National Vital Statistics Report, vol 49, no 1, April 17, 2001

2. Barron WM: The pregnant surgical patient: medical evaluation and management. Ann Intern Med 101:683, 1984

3. Hoff WS, D'Amelio LF, Tinkoff GH, et al: Maternal predictors of fetal demise in trauma during pregnancy. Surg Gynecol Obstet 172:175, 1991

4. Fildes J, Reed L, Jones N, et al: Trauma: the leading cause of maternal death. J Trauma 32:643, 1992

5. Pearlman MD, Tintinalli JE, Lorenz RP: Blunt trauma during pregnancy. N Engl J Med 323:1609, 1990

6. Hanlon D, Duriseti RS: Current concepts in the management of the pregnant trauma patient. Trauma Rep 2:3, 2001

7. Awwad JT, Azar GB, Seoud MA, et al: High-velocity penetrating wounds of the gravid uterus: review of 16 years of civil war. Obstet Gynecol 83:259, 1994

8. Crosby WM, Costiloe JP: Safety of the lap-restraint for pregnant victims of automobile collisions. N Engl J Med 24:78, 1971

9. Kuhlmann RS, Cruikshank DP: Maternal trauma during pregnancy. Clin Obstet Gynecol 37:274, 1994

10. Hill DA, Lense JJ: Abdominal trauma in the pregnant patient. Am Fam Physician 53:1269, 1996

11. Edwards RK, Bennett BB, Ripley DL, et al: Surgery in the pregnant patient. Curr Probl Surg 38:4, 2001

12. Hamberger LK, Ambuel B: Maternity care: spousal abuse in pregnancy. Clin Fam Pract 3:2, 2001

13. Campbell JC: Women's responses to sexual abuse in intimate relationships. Health Care Women Int 10:335, 1989

14. Hilliard PJA: Physical abuse in pregnancy. Obstet Gynecol 66:185, 1985

15. Abbott J: Domestic violence against women: incidence and prevalence in an emergency department population. JAMA 273:1763, 1995

16. Helton AS, Snodgrass FG: Battering during pregnancy: intervention strategies. Birth 14:3, 1987

17. Baker RN: Hemorrhage in obstetrics. Obstet Gynecol Annu 6:295, 1977

18. Drost TF, Rosemurgy AS, Sherman HF, et al: Major trauma in pregnant women: maternal/fetal outcome. J Trauma 30:574, 1990

19. Sorensen VJ, Bivins BA, Obeid FN, et al: Management of general surgical emergencies in pregnancy. Am Surg 56:245, 1990

20. Goodwin TM, Breen MT: Pregnancy outcome and fetomaternal hemorrhage after noncatastrophic trauma. Am J Obstet Gynecol 162:665, 1990

21. Stone IK: Trauma in the obstetric patient. Obstet Gynecol Clin 26:3, 1999

22. Pearlman MD, Tintinalli JE, Lorenz RP: A prospective controlled study of outcome after trauma during pregnancy. Am J Obstet Gynecol 162:1502, 1990

23. Gonik B: Intensive care monitoring of the critically ill pregnant patient. Maternal-Fetal Medicine. Creasy RK, Resnik R, Eds. WB Saunders Co, Philadelphia, 1989, p 867

24. Mazze A, Kalln B: Appendectomy during pregnancy: a Swedish registry study of 778 cases. Obstet Gynecol 77:835, 1991

25. Al-Mulhim AA: Acute appendicitis in pregnancy: a review of 52 cases. Int Surg 81:295, 1996

26. Andersen B, Nielsen T: Appendicitis in pregnancy: diagnosis, management and complications. Acta Obstet Gynecol Scand 78:758, 1999

27. Squires RA: Surgical considerations in pregnancy. Audio Dig Gen Surg 45, 1998

28. Mourad J, Elliot JP, Erickson L, et al: Appendicitis in pregnancy: new information that contradicts long-held clinical beliefs. Am J Obstet Gynecol 182:5, 2000

29. Firstenberg MS, Malangoni MA: Pregnancy and gastrointestinal disorders: gastrointestinal surgery during pregnancy. Gastroenterol Clin 21:1, 1998

30. Lavin JP Jr, Polsky SS: Abdominal trauma during pregnancy. Clin Perinatol 10:423, 1983

31. Adams DH, Fine C, Brooks DC: High-resolution real-time ultrasonography: a new tool in the diagnosis of acute appendicitis. Am J Surg 155:93, 1988

32. Anderson JM, Lee TG, Nagel N: Ultrasound diagnosis of nonobstetric disease during pregnancy. Obstet Gynecol 48:359, 1976

33. Castro MA, Shipp TD, Castro EE, et al: The use of helical computed tomography in pregnancy for the diagnosis of acute appendicitis. Am J Obstet Gynecol 184:5, 2001

34. Pregnancy and medical radiation. Ann ICRP 30:1, 2000

35. Tamir IL, Bongard FS, Klein SR: Acute appendicitis in the pregnant patient. Am J Surg 160:571, 1990

36. Loughlin KR, Bailey RB Jr: Internal ureteral stents for conservative management of ureteral calculi during pregnancy. N Engl J Med 315:1647, 1986

37. Kavoussi LR, Albala DM, Basler JW, et al: Percutaneous management of urolithiasis during pregnancy (pt 2). J Urol 148:1069, 1992

38. Horowitz MD, Gomez GA, Santiesteban R, et al: Acute appendicitis during pregnancy: diagnosis and management. Arch Surg 120:1362, 1985

39. McComb P, Laimon H: Appendicitis complicating pregnancy. Can J Surg 23:92, 1980

40. Hee P, Viktrup L: The diagnosis of appendicitis during pregnancy and maternal and fetal outcome after appendectomy. Int J Gynaecol Obstet 65:129, 1999

41. Masters K, Levine BA, Gaskill HV, et al: Diagnosing appendicitis during pregnancy. Am J Surg 148:768, 1984

42. Curet MJ, Allen D, Josloff RK, et al: Laparoscopy during pregnancy. Arch Surg 131:546, 1996

43. Connolly MM, Unti JA, Nora PF: Bowel obstruction in pregnancy. Surg Clin North Am 75:101, 1995

44. de Paul M, Tew WL, Holiday RL: Perforated peptic ulcer in pregnancy with survival of mother and child: case report and review of the literature. Can J Surg 19:427, 1976

45. Perdue PW, Johnson HW, Stafford PW: Intestinal obstruction complicating pregnancy. Am J Surg 164:384, 1992

46. Milne B, Johnstone MS: Intestinal obstruction in pregnancy. Scott Med J 24:80, 1979

47. Ballantyne GH: Review of surgical volvulus: clinical patterns and pathogenesis. Dis Colon Rectum 25:494, 1985

48. Shaxted EJ, Jukes R: Pseudo-obstruction of the bowel in pregnancy: case reports. Br J Obstet Gynaecol 86:411, 1979

49. Ibrahim N, Payne E, Owen A: Spontaneous rupture of the liver in association with pregnancy. Br J Obstet Gynaecol 92:539, 1985

50. Hunter SK, Martin M, Benda JA, et al: Liver transplant after massive spontaneous hepatic rupture in pregnancy complicated by preeclampsia. Obstet Gynecol 85:819, 1995

51. Hwang SS, Park YH, Jung YJ: Spontaneous rupture of hydronephrotic kidney during pregnancy: value of serial sonography. J Clin Ultrasound 28:7, 2000

52. Barton JR, Sibai BM: HELLP and the liver diseases of preeclampsia. Clin Liver Dis 3:1, 1999

53. Henny CP, Lim AE, Brummelkamp WH, et al: A review of the importance of acute multidisciplinary treatment following spontaneous rupture of the liver capsule during pregnancy. Surg Gynecol Obstet 156:593, 1983

54. Braverman DZ, Johnson ML, Kern F Jr: Effects of pregnancy and contraceptive steroids on gallbladder function. N Engl J Med 302:362, 1980

55. Wilkinson EJ: Acute pancreatitis in pregnancy: a review of 98 cases and a report of 8 new cases. Obstet Gynecol Surv 28:281, 1973

56. Yates MR, Baron TH: Biliary tract disease in pregnancy. Clin Liver Dis 3:1, 1999

57. Everson GT, McKinley C, Kern F: Mechanisms of gallstone formation in women: effects of exogenous estrogen (Premarin) and dietary cholesterol on hepatic lipid metabolism. J Clin Invest 87:237, 1991

58. Tierney S, Nakeeb A: Progesterone alters biliary flow dynamics. Ann Surg 229:2, 1999

59. Ryan JP: Effect of pregnancy on gallbladder contractility in guinea pig. Gastroenterology 87:674, 1984

60. Kern F Jr, Everson GT, DeMark B, et al: Biliary lipids, bile acids, and gallbladder function in the human female: effects of pregnancy and the ovulatory cycle. J Clin Invest 68:1229, 1981

61. Valdivieso V, Covarrubias C, Siegel F, et al: Pregnancy and cholelithiasis: pathogenesis and natural course of gallstones diagnosed in early puerperium. Hepatology 17:1, 1993

62. Basso L, McCollum PT, Darling MRN, et al: A study of cholelithiasis during pregnancy and its relationship with age, parity, menarche, breast-feeding, dysmenorrhea, oral contraception and a maternal history of cholelithiasis. Surg Gynecol Obstet 175:41, 1992

63. Glenn F, McSherry CK: Gallstones and pregnancy among 300 young women treated by cholecystectomy. Surg Gynecol Obstet 127:1067, 1968

64. Ramin KD, Ramsey PS. Medical complications of pregnancy: disease of the gall bladder and pancreas in pregnacy. Obstet Gynecol Clin 28:3, 2001

65. Woodhouse DR, Haylen B: Gall bladder disease complicating pregnancy. Aust NZ J Obstet Gynaecol 25:233, 1985

66. Bynum TE: Hepatic and gastrointestinal disorders in pregnancy. Med Clin North Am 61:129, 1977

67. Cheng YS: Pregnancy in liver cirrhosis and/or portal hypertension. Am J Obstet Gynecol 128:812, 1977

68. Seymour CA, Chadwick VS: Liver and gastrointestinal function in pregnancy. Postgrad Med J 55:343, 1979

69. Landerd D, Carmona R, Cromblehome W: Acute cholecystitis in pregnancy. Obstet Gynecol 69:131, 1987

70. McKellar DP, Anderson CT, Boynton CJ: Cholecystectomy during pregnancy without fetal loss. Surg Obstet Gynecol 174:465, 1992

71. Dixon NP, Faddis DM, Silberman H: Aggressive management of cholecystitis during pregnancy.

Am J Surg 154:292, 1987

72. Curet MJ: Special problems in laparoscopic surgery: previous abdominal surgery, obesity and pregnancy. Surg Clin North Am 80:4, 2000

73. Printen KJ, Ott RA: Cholecystectomy during pregnancy. Am Surg 44:432, 1978

74. Affleck DG, Handrahan DL, Egger MJ, et al: The laparoscopic management of appendicitis and cholelithiasis during pregnancy. Am J Surg 178:6, 1999

75. Gouldman JW, Sticca RP, Rippon MB, et al: Laparoscopic cholecystectomy in pregnancy. Am Surg 64:93, 1998

76. Lanzafame RJ: Laparoscopic cholecystectomy during pregnancy. Surgery 118:627, 1995

77. Morrell DG, Mullins JR, Harrison PB: Laparoscopic cholecystectomy during pregnancy in symptomatic patients. Surgery 112:856, 1992

78. Soper NJ, Hunter JG, Petrie RH: Laparoscopic cholecystectomy during pregnancy. Surg Endosc 6:115, 1992

79. Weber AM, Bloom GP, Allen TR, et al: Laparoscopic cholecystectomy during pregnancy. Obstet Gynecol 78: 958, 1991

80. Baillie J, et al: Endoscopic management of choledocholithiasis during pregnancy. Surg Gynecol Obstet 171:1, 1990

81. Strasberg SM: Laparoscopic biliary surgery. Gastroenterol Clin 28:1, 1999

82. Hunt CM, Sharara AI: Liver disease in pregnancy. Am Fam Phys 59:4, 1999

83. McKay AJ, O'Neill J, Imrie CW: Pancreatitis, pregnancy and gallstones. Br J Obstet Gynaecol 87:47, 1980

84. Glueck CJ, Christopher C, Mishkel MA, et al: Pancreatitis, familial hypertriglyceridemia, and pregnancy. Am J Obstet Gynecol 136:755, 1980

85. Thomason JL, Sampson MB, Farb HF, et al: Pregnancy complicated by concurrent primary hyperparathyroidism and pancreatitis. Obstet Gynecol 57(suppl 6):34S, 1981

86. Young KR: Acute pancreatitis in pregnancy: two case reports. Obstet Gynecol 60:653, 1982

87. Hasselgren PO: Acute pancreatitis in pregnancy: report of two cases. Acta Chir Scand 146:297, 1980

88. Jouppila P, Mokka R, Larmi TK: Acute pancreatitis in pregnancy. Surg Gynecol Obstet 139:879, 1974

89. Strickland DM, Hauth JC, Widish J, et al: Amylase and isoamylase activities in serum of pregnant women. Obstet Gynecol 63:389, 1984

90. Dreiling DA, Bordalo O, Rosenberg V, et al: Pregnancy and pancreatitis. Am J Gastroenterol 64:23, 1975

91. Gineston JL, Capron JP, Delcenserie R, et al: Prolonged total parenteral nutrition in a pregnant woman with acute pancreatitis. J Clin Gastroenterol 6:249, 1984

92. Hiatt JR, Hiatt JC, Williams RA, et al: Biliary disease in pregnancy: strategy for surgical management. Am J Surg 151:263, 1986

93. Vonherzen J, Noe J, Goodlin R: Pancreatitis pseudocyst complicating pregnancy. Obstet Gynecol 45:588, 1975

94. Winbery SL, Blaho KE. Dyspepsia in pregnancy. Obstet Gynecol Clin 28:2, 2001

95. Cappell MS, Garcia A: Gastric and duodenal ulcers during pregnancy. Gastroenterol Clin North Am 27:169, 1998

96. Mogadam M, Korelitz BI, Ahmed SW, et al: The course of inflammatory bowel disease during pregnancy and postpartum. Am J Gastroenterol 75:265, 1981

97. Nielsen OH, Andreasson B, Bondesen S, et al: Pregnancy in Crohn's disease. Scand J

Gastroenterol 19:724, 1984

98. Vender RJ, Spiro HM: Inflammatory bowel disease and pregnancy. J Clin Gastroenterol 4:231, 1982

99. Baiocco PJ, Korelitz BI: The influence of inflammatory bowel disease and its treatment on pregnancy and fetal outcome. J Clin Gastroenterol 6:211, 1984

100. Woolfson K, Cohen Z, McLeod RS: Crohn's disease and pregnancy. Dis Colon Rectum 33:869, 1990

101. Warsof SL: Medical and surgical treatment of inflammatory bowel disease in pregnancy. Clin Obstet Gynecol 26:822, 1983

102. Mogadam M, Dobbins WO III, Korelitz BI, et al: Pregnancy in inflammatory bowel disease: effect of sulfasalazine and corticosteroids on fetal outcome. Gastroenterology 80:72, 1981

103. Witter FR, King TM, Blake DA: The effects of chronic gastrointestinal medication on the fetus and neonate. Obstet Gynecol 58(suppl 5):79S, 1981

104. Jacobson LB, Clapp DH: Total parenteral nutrition in pregnancy complicated by Crohn's disease. JPEN J Parent Enteral Nutr 11:93, 1987

105. Rivera-Alsina ME, Saldana LR, Stringer CA: Fetal growth sustained by parenteral nutrition in pregnancy. Obstet Gynecol 64:138, 1984

106. Wise RA, Polito AJ: Asthma and allergy during pregnancy, respiratory physiology changes in pregnancy. Immunol Allergy Clin North Am 20:4, 2000

107. Edwards RK, Bennett BB, Ripley DL, et al: Surgery in the pregnant patient. Curr Probl Surg 38:4, 2001

108. Sherwood OD, Downing SJ, Guico-Lamm ML, et al: The physiological effects of relaxin during pregnancy: studies in rats and pigs. Oxf Rev Reprod Biol 15:143, 1993

109. Clark SL, Cotton DB, Lee W, et al: Central hemodynamic assessment of normal term pregnancy. Am J Obstet Gynecol 161:1439, 1989

110. Stein PK, Hagley MT, Cole PL, et al: Changes in 24-hour heart rate variability during normal pregnancy. Am J Obstet Gynecol 180:4, 1999

111. Katz R, Karliner J, Resnik R: Effects of a natural volume overload state (pregnancy) on left ventricular performance in normal human subjects. Circulation 48:434, 1978

112. Thilen U, Olsson SB: Pregnancy and heart disease: a review. Obstet Gynecol 75:43, 1997

113. Obstetrics: Normal and Problem Pregnancies, 3rd ed. Gabbe SG, Niebyl JR, Simpson JL, Eds. London, Churchill Livingstone, 1996, p 92

114. Fagan EA: Cholestasis: intrahepatic cholestasis of pregnancy. Clin Liver Dis 3:3, 1999

115. Sanders CL, Lucas MJ: Medical complications of pregnancy: renal disease in pregnancy. Obstet Gynecol Clin 28:3, 2001

116. Fried A, Woodring JH, Thompson TJ: Hydronephrosis of pregnancy. J Ultrasound Med 2:225, 1983

117. Deitcher SR, Gardner JF: Pregnancy and liver disease: physiologic changes in coagulation and fibrinolysis during normal pregnancy. Clin Liver Dis 3:1, 1999

118. Martin C, Varner MW: Physiologic changes in pregnancy: surgical implications. Clin Obstet Gynecol 37:241, 1994

119. Heinly TL, Leiberman P: Asthma and allergy during pregnancy: anaphylaxis in pregnancy. Immunol Allergy Clin North Am 20:4, 2000

120. Czeizel AE, Pataki T, Rockenbauer M: Reproductive outcome after exposure to surgery under anesthesia during pregnancy. Arch Gynecol Obstet 261:193, 1998

121. Rosen MA, Weiskopf RB: Management of anes-

thesia for the pregnant surgical patient. Anesthesiology 91:4, 1999

122. Parer JT, King T: Fetal heart rate monitoring: is it salvageable? Am J Obstet Gynecol 182:982, 2000

123. Timins JK: Radiation during pregnancy. NJ Med 98:29, 2001

124. Ezri T, Szmuk P, Evron S, et al: Difficult airway in obstetric anesthesia: a review. Obstet Gynecol Surv 56:631, 2001

125. Fatum M, Rojansky N: Laparoscopic surgery during pregnancy. Obstet Gynecol Surv 56:50, 2001

126. Shay DC, Bhavani-Shankar K, Datta S: Laparoscopic surgery during pregnancy. Anesthesiol Clin North Am 19:57, 2001

127. Steinbrook RA, Brooks DC, Datta S: Laparoscopic cholecystectomy during pregnancy: review of anesthetic management, surgical considerations. Surg Endosc 10:511, 1996

128. Hunter J, Swanstrom L, Thornburgh K: Carbon dioxide pneumoperitoneum induces fetal acidosis in a preganat ewe model. Surg Endosc 9:272, 1995

129. Curet MJ, Vogt DM, Schob O, et al: Effects of CO_2 pneumoperitoneum in pregnant ewes. J Surg Res 63:1, 1996

130. Reedy MB, Galan HL, Richards WE, et al: Laparoscopy during pregnancy: a survey of laparoendoscopic surgeons. J Reprod Med 42:33, 1997

131. Bhavani-Shankar K, Steinbrook RA, Brooks DC, et al: Arterial to end-tidal carbon dioxide pressure difference during laparoscopic surgery in pregnancy. Anesthesiology 93:370, 2000

132. Sharp HT: Gastrointestinal surgical conditions during pregnancy. Clin Obstet Gynecol 37:306, 1994

133. Parry AJ, Westaby S: Cardiopulmonary bypass during pregnancy. Ann Thorac Surg 61:1865, 1996

134. Weiss BM, von Segesser LK, Alon E, et al: Outcome of cardiovascular surgery and pregnancy: a systematic review of the period 1984-1996. Am J Obstet Gynecol 179:6, 1998

135. Pomini F, Mercogliano D, Cavalletti C, et al: Cardiopulmonary bypass in pregnancy. Ann Thorac Surg 61:259, 1996

136. Gei AF, Hankins GDV: Medical complications of pregnancy: cardiac disease and pregnancy. Obstet Gynecol Clin 28:3, 2001

137. Vaska PL: Cardiac surgery in special populations, part 2: women, pregnant patients, and Jehovah's Witnesses. AACN Clinical Issues 8:1, 1997

138. Birincioglu CL, Kucuker SA, Yapar EG, et al: Perinatal mitral valve interventions: a report of 10 cases. Ann Thorac Surg 67:1312, 1999

139. Zeebregts CJ, Schepens MA, Hameeterman TM, et al: Acute aortic dissection complicating pregnancy. 64:1345, 1997

140. Hillemanns P, Knitza R, Muller-Hocker J: Rupture of splenic artery aneurysm in a pregnant patient with portal hypertension. Am J Obstet Gynecol 174:1665, 1996

141. Merbeck M, Horbach T, Putzenlachner C: Ruptured splenic artery aneurysm during pregnancy: a rare case with both maternal and fetal survival. Am J Obstet Gynecol 181:3, 1999

142. Henke PK, Cardneau JD, Welling TH, et al: Renal artery aneurysms. Ann Surg 234:4, 2001

143. Resnik R: Cancer during pregnancy. N Engl J Med 341:120, 1999

144. Smith LH, Dalrymple JL, Leiserowitz GS, et al: Obstetrical deliveries with maternal malignancy in California, 1992 through 1997. Am J Obstet Gynecol 184:7, 2001

145. Catlin EA, Roberts JD Jr, Erana R, et al:

Transplacental transmission of natural-killer-cell lymphoma. N Engl J Med 341:85, 1999

146. Dildy GA III, Moise KJ Jr, Carpenter RJ Jr, et al: Maternal malignancy metastatic to the products of conception: a review. Obstet Gynecol Surv 44:535, 1989

147. Ebert U, Loffler H, Kirch W: Cytotoxic therapy and pregnancy. Pharmacol Ther 74:207, 1997

148. Gemignani ML, Petrek JA, Borgen PI. Breast cancer and pregnancy. Surg Clin North Am 79:5, 1999

149. Barnavon Y, Wallack MK: Management of the pregnancy patient with carcinoma of the breast. Surg Gynecol Obstet 171:347, 1990

150. Rode H, Millar AJ, Cywes S, et al: Thermal injury in pregnancy: the neglected tragedy. S Afr Med J 77:346, 1990

151. Prentice-Bjerkeseth R: Perioperative anesthetic management of trauma in pregnancy. Anesthesiol Clin North Am 17:1, 1999

152. Hey VM, Cowley DJ, Ganguli PC, et al: Gastrooesophageal reflux in late pregnancy. Anaesthesia 32:372, 1977

153. Medich DS, Fazio VW: Hemorrhoids, anal fissure and carcinoma of the colon rectum and anus during pregnancy. Surg Clin North Am 75:77, 1995

154. Hulme-Moir M, Bartolo DC: Hemorrhoids. Gastroenterol Clin 30:1, 2001

155. Saleeby RG Jr, Rosen L, Stasik JJ, et al: Hemorrhoidectomy during pregnancy: risk or relief? Dis Colon Rectum 34:260, 1991

156. Ginsberg JS, Greer I, Hirsh J: Use of antithrombotic agents during pregnancy: sixth ACCP Consensus conference on antithrombotic therapy. Chest 169:122S, 2001

157. Hull RD, Raskob GE, Carter CJ: Serial impedance plethysmography in pregnant patients with clinically suspected deep-vein thrombosis. Ann Intern Med 112:663, 1990

158. Ginsberg JS, Hirsh J, Turner CD, et al: Risks to the fetus of anticoagulant therapy during pregnancy. Thromb Haemost 61:197, 1989

159. Sanson BJ, Lensing AWA, Prins MH, et al: Safety of low-molecular-weight heparin in pregnancy: a systematic review. Thromb Haemost 81:668, 1999

160. Ginsberg JS, Hirsh J: Anticoagulants during pregnancy. Annu Rev Med 40:79, 1989

161. Bolan JC: Thromboembolic complications of pregnancy. Clin Obstet Gynecol 26:913, 1983

162. Brill-Edwards P, Ginsberg JS: Safety of withholding antepartum heparin in women with a previous episode of venous thromboembolism. The Recurrence Of Clot In This Pregnancy (ROCIT) Study Group. N Engl J Med 343:20, 2000

163. MacBurney MM, Wilmore DW: Parenteral nutrition in pregnancy. Parenteral Nutrition. Rombeau JL, Caldwell M, Eds. WB Saunders Co, Philadelphia, 1986

164. Rosenthal MH: Intrapartum intensive care management of the cardiac patient. Clin Obstet Gynecol 24:789, 1981

165. Dashe JS, Gilstrap LC: Antibiotic use in pregnancy. Obstet Gynecol Clin North Am 24:617, 1997

166. Murray L, Seger D: Drug therapy during pregnancy and lactation. Emerg Med Clin North Am 12:129, 1994

Acknowledgment

Figure 1 Carol Donner.

142 UROLOGIC CONSIDERATIONS FOR THE GENERAL SURGEON

Ronald Rubenstein, M.D., and Robert B. Nadler, M.D., F.A.C.S.

An understanding of the urogenital system is a necessary component of general surgical education. Specifically, surgeons must be aware of the anatomic, physiologic, and pathologic features of urologic processes. Accordingly, in this chapter, we review the key features of genitourinary anatomy and discuss urologic problems that are commonly encountered by the general surgeon, including urologic trauma, iatrogenic injuries to the urogenital system, urologic malignancies, and benign prostatic hyperplasia (BPH).

Anatomic Considerations

KIDNEY AND URETER

The kidneys are obliquely placed on either side of the spine, deep within the retroperitoneum,[1] with the upper poles slightly more medial than the lower poles. On top of each kidney sits an adrenal gland, and these two structures are jointly surrounded by a perinephric fascial layer known as Gerota's fascia (an important anatomic structure that can act as a barrier to contain renal pathologic processes). The anterior and posterior leaves of Gerota's fascia, which extend anterior and posterior to the kidney, become fused around the kidney on three sides: laterally, medially, and superiorly. Inferiorly, however, Gerota's fascia remains an open potential space, containing the ureter and the gonadal vessels on either side. Gerota's fascia is surrounded by retroperitoneal fat.

A clear understanding of the position of the kidneys in the retroperitoneum is vital for surgical exploration. Generally, the right kidney is situated slightly lower than the left kidney, as a consequence of the mass effect of the liver; however, the positions of the kidneys vary somewhat with respiration. Posteriorly, the right kidney and the left have similar relations with adjacent structures. The diaphragm and the pleural reflections cover the upper posterior aspect of each kidney, and the 12th rib crosses the upper pole. On the left side, the 11th rib is directly posterior to the upper aspect of the kidney. The quadratus lumborum and the transversus abdominis aponeurosis cover the posterior surface, and the renal hilum lies against the psoas muscle. Anteriorly, the left kidney is in contact with the adrenal, the spleen, the stomach, the pancreas, the jejunum, and the splenic flexure of the colon [*see Figure 1*]. The anterior surface of the right kidney is covered to a large extent by the liver. The inferior portion of the right kidney is covered by the hepatic flexure, and the hilum is covered by the duodenum. It is important to recognize the planes between Gerota's fascia, the peritoneum, and the retroperitoneal organs.

Each kidney is supplied by a renal artery and drained by a renal vein. The renal arteries typically branch off the aorta just below the superior mesenteric artery at the level of the second lumbar vertebra, and the renal veins meet the vena cava at the same level. The left renal vein passes in front of the aorta and lies most anteriorly in the renal hilum. Behind the vein lies the renal artery, and the renal pelvis lies most posteriorly. Although, in general, there is one renal artery and one renal vein for each kidney, anatomic variations are common. The most common variation (occurring in 23% to 49% of persons) is the presence of supernumerary renal arteries arising from the lateral portion of the aorta.[2-7] Whereas there is extensive collateral circulation for the renal veins, the renal arteries are end arteries. Consequently, injury to the main renal artery or an accessory artery typically results in the loss of renal parenchyma. On the right side, the adrenal and gonadal vein drain directly into the vena cava; on the left side, these vessels drain into the renal vein [*see Figure 2*].

The renal collecting system includes the minor calices, the major calices, the renal pelvis, and the ureter. The ureter connects the renal pelvis to the bladder, and its role is to propel urine toward the bladder by means of peristalsis. The normal adult ureter is 22 to 30 cm long, and it exhibits three distinct narrowings as it travels through the abdomen and the pelvis: one at the ureteropelvic junction, one at the pelvic brim as it crosses over the iliac vessels, and one at the ureterovesical junction. For the purposes of surgical or radiographic description, the ureter is commonly divided into discrete segments. In surgical terms, the portion of the ureter that runs from the renal pelvis to the iliac vessels is the abdominal ureter, and the portion that runs from the iliac vessels down to the bladder is the pelvic ureter. In radiographic terms, the portion of the ureter that runs from the renal pelvis down to the upper border of the sacrum is the proximal ureter, the portion that runs from the upper border of the sacrum to the lower border is the medial ureter, and the portion that runs from the lower border of the sacrum down to the bladder is the distal ureter.

The ureter receives its blood supply from multiple branching vessels along its course. The proximal ureter is supplied medially by branches from the renal artery, the medial ureter is supplied medially by branches from the gonadal artery and the aorta, and the distal ureter is supplied laterally by branches from the common and internal iliac arteries. The arterial vessels then course longitudinally within the periureteral adventitia in an anastomosing plexus that can be extensively mobilized so long as it remains intact.

Posteriorly, the ureter runs along the psoas muscle to the point where the muscle crosses over the iliac vessels near the bifurcation of the common iliac arteries. Anteriorly, the right ureter is in contact with the ascending colon, the cecum, the appendix, the terminal ileum, and the corresponding mesenteries. The left ureter is in contact with the descending colon, the sigmoid colon, and the corresponding mesenteries. It is important to recognize that when these anterior structures are reflected during operation, the ureter tends to adhere to them rather than remain adherent to the psoas muscle. In women, specific attention must be paid to the status of the ureter at the pelvic brim, where it may be in contact with the fallopian tube and the ovary. Attention should also be paid to the uterine arteries, which cross anterior to the ureters near the cervix.

BLADDER

The bladder is a hollow organ that stores and expels urine. The normal adult bladder has a capacity of 400 to 500 ml. When empty, the bladder rests in the pelvis behind the pubic symphysis. As it fills, the bladder rises above the pubic bone, and if it is quite distended, it may be palpated in the lower abdomen.

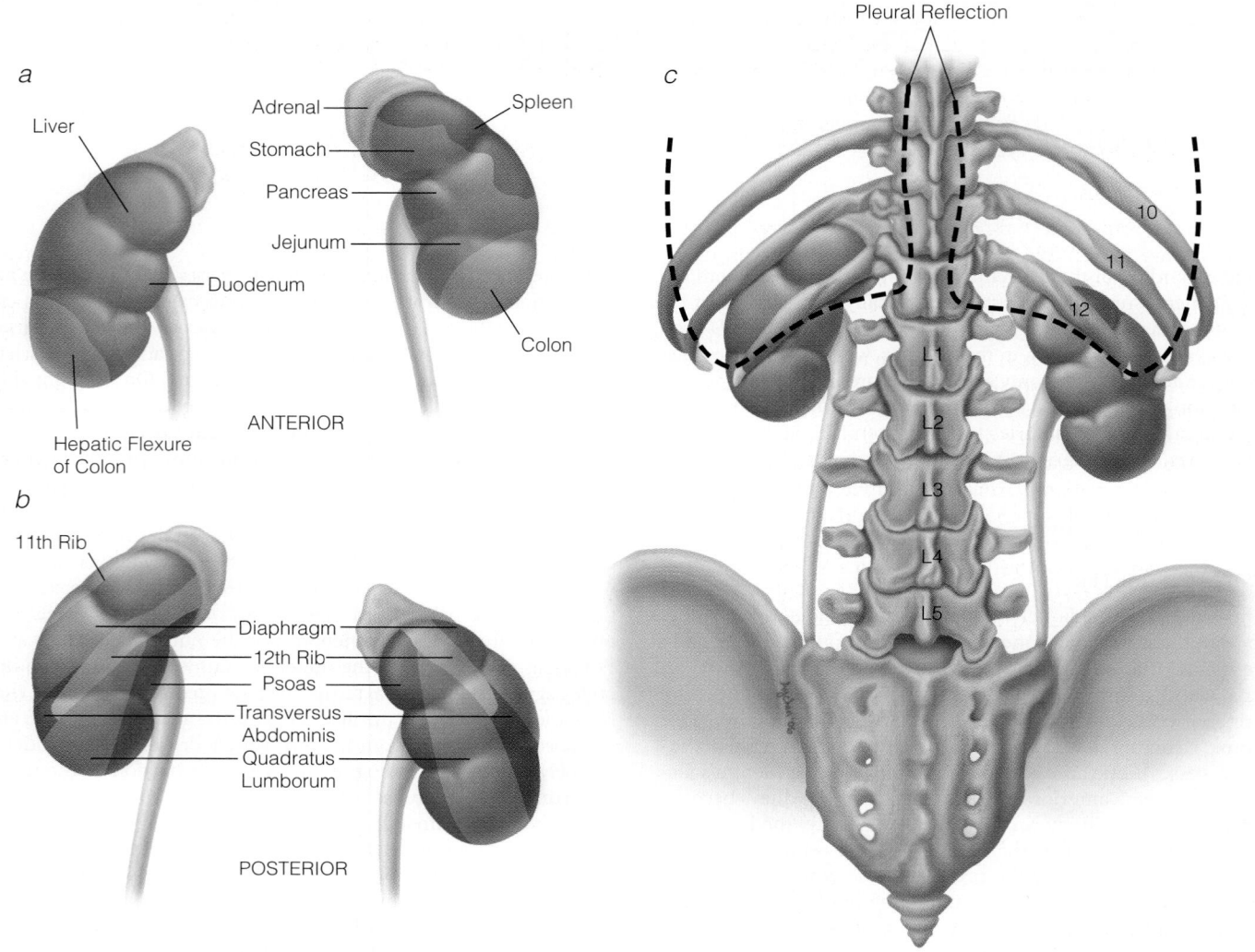

Figure 1 Shown are the anatomic relations of the kidneys (*a*) to the abdominal organs anteriorly, (*b*) to the body wall muscles and the ribs posteriorly, and (*c*) to the pleural reflections and the skeleton posteriorly.

The bladder is anatomically related to many other anatomic structures. Anteriorly, the bladder is tethered to the abdominal wall by the median umbilical ligament (i.e., the obliterated urachus). In rare cases, adenocarcinoma may develop in the urachal remnant; in other cases, the connection may remain patent and predispose to infection or drainage from the umbilicus. The superior aspect of the bladder is covered by a peritoneal layer that sweeps down from the anterior abdominal wall to meet the peritoneum covering either the anterior rectum (in males) or the uterus (in females). Laterally, the bladder is separated from the pelvic side walls by loose connective tissue and both retropubic and perivesical fat. In males, the base of the bladder is adjacent to the seminal vesicles, the ampullae of the vasa deferentia, the distal ureters, and the rectum. In females, the uterus and the vagina are interposed between the bladder and the rectum.

The bladder is very well vascularized and thus may be mobilized or partially resected without compromise of the blood supply. Most of the bladder's blood supply comes from the superior, middle, and inferior vesical arteries, which branch off from the anterior trunk of the internal iliac artery. In females, the bladder is further supplied by branches of the vaginal and uterine arteries.

The veins of the bladder come together to form several plexuses that drain into the internal iliac veins.

PROSTATE AND SEMINAL VESICLES

The prostate and the seminal vesicles produce constituents of the ejaculate. The normal prostate weighs between 18 and 20 g and is composed of glandular elements and fibromuscular stroma. Toward the apex, the prostate is tethered to the pubic bone by the puboprostatic ligaments. Laterally, the prostate is in direct contact with the pubococcygeal portion of the levator ani and is related to its overlying endopelvic fascia. Posteriorly, the prostate is separated from the rectum by the two layers of Denonvilliers' fascia. The prostate can be divided into transitional, central, and peripheral zones, and there is an anterior fibromuscular stroma that extends from the bladder neck to the striated urethral sphincter. The transitional zone is the area that gives rise to BPH, which can cause increased urinary resistance and voiding symptoms. The peripheral zone makes up the bulk of the prostate tissue and is the area where the majority of prostate cancers arise.

The seminal vesicles are about 6 cm long and lie in contact with the base of the bladder. Each seminal vesicle joins the ipsilateral vas deferens to form the ejaculatory ducts, which exit the prostate at the verumontanum (i.e., the colliculus seminalis).

The prostate and seminal vesicles are supplied by the inferior vesical, internal pudendal, and middle rectal arteries; the seminal vesicles are also supplied by the vesiculodeferential artery, a branch of the superior vesical artery.

PENIS AND URETHRA

The penis is composed of three bodies: the two corpora cavernosa, which are responsible for erectile function, and the corpus spongiosum, which contains the urethra and is contiguous with the glans. Individually, these bodies are covered by a dense fascial layer known as the tunica albuginea; together, they are covered by a thick layer of Buck's fascia. If one or more of the penile bodies is torn, the bleeding will be contained in Buck's fascia, and ecchymosis will be limited to the penile shaft.

The penis is supplied by the common penile artery, which is the terminal branch of the internal pudendal artery. This vessel travels through Alcock's canal and terminates in three branches: the bulbourethral artery, which supplies the urethra, the corpus spongiosum, and the glans; the deep artery, which travels within the corpus cavernosum and supplies the cavernous sinuses; and the dorsal artery, which runs in the neurovascular bundle beneath Buck's fascia and supplies the corpus spongiosum and the urethra.

The male urethra is approximately 20 cm long and can be divided into four anatomic sections: the prostatic urethra, the membranous urethra, the bulbous urethra, and the penile urethra. The sphincteric mechanism is located in the membranous urethra. The female urethra is approximately 4 cm long and travels from the bladder neck below the pubic symphysis to open anterior to the vagina.

TESTES

The testes have two important functions: spermatogenesis and production of testosterone. Each testis is approximately 20 ml in size and is surrounded by tunica albuginea, which projects inward to form the mediastinum testis.

The testis is supplied by the gonadal or testicular artery, the vasal artery, and the cremasteric artery. The gonadal artery arises from the aorta, just below the renal artery, and courses through the spermatic cord to the testis; the vasal artery is a branch of the superior vesical artery; and the cremasteric artery branches off from the inferior epigastric artery. At the level of the internal ring, these three arteries are in close proximity, and particular care must be taken to keep from injuring them. Venous outflow is provided by the gonadal vein. The right gonadal vein empties into the inferior vena cava below the renal vein, and the left gonadal vein empties directly into the left renal vein.

Urologic Injuries

UROGENITAL TRAUMA IN PATIENTS WITH MULTIPLE INJURIES

Urologic injuries are common when multiple organ systems are damaged, occurring in about 10% of cases of major trauma.

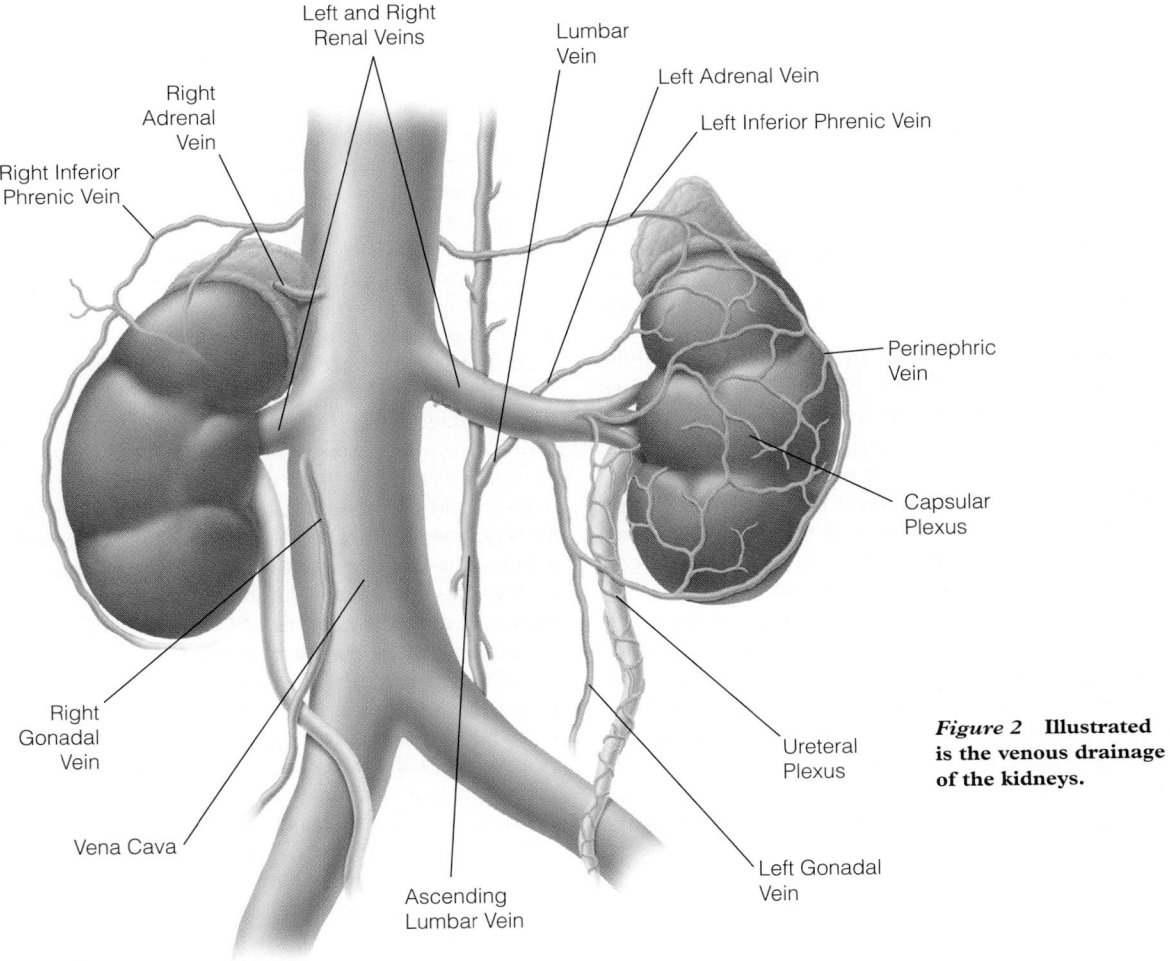

Figure 2 **Illustrated is the venous drainage of the kidneys.**

Although the majority of injuries to the urogenital tract are not life-threatening, they can result in substantial morbidity if they are not promptly diagnosed and treated. Accordingly, a surgical team treating a patient with multiple injuries must always keep in mind the possibility of concomitant urogenital trauma so that any urologic injuries found can be addressed in a timely manner.

Initial evaluation and resuscitation are generally carried out by an emergency department physician and a trauma surgeon; however, it is important that a urologist be involved as well. Assessment should proceed as outlined by advanced trauma life support (ATLS) protocol. The presence of gross hematuria, flank ecchymosis, rib fractures, pelvic fractures, or blood at the urethral meatus should raise the level of concern for urologic injury and serve as an indication for an expeditious urologic consultation.

Management of urologic trauma is addressed in more detail elsewhere [see 110 Injuries to the Urogenital Tract].

IATROGENIC INJURY TO UROGENITAL TRACT

Ureter

The majority of injuries to the ureter are iatrogenic. Iatrogenic ureteral injuries may be sustained during any open or laparoscopic procedure in the abdomen or the pelvis and may result from transection, ligation, laceration, resection, crushing, or ischemia. Such injuries are most likely to occur during gynecologic procedures; they also occur during general surgical and urologic procedures and, rarely, during orthopedic[8] and vascular procedures.[9] The ureter is most vulnerable to iatrogenic injury at several anatomic locations: at the pelvic brim, where gonadal and ovarian vessels cross; lateral to the uterus, where the ureter crosses under the uterine artery; over the iliac vessels, near the apex of the obturator fossa; and at the insertion of the trigone.

Although most ureteral injuries occur during routine, uncomplicated surgical procedures in which the pelvic anatomy appears normal,[10] the likelihood of such injuries is increased by the presence of conditions that disrupt the architecture of the ureter, such as a large mass, a malignancy, inflammatory disease, endometriosis, a previous operation, irradiation, and congenital abnormalities. Increased blood loss, longer operating times, increased transfusion requirements, and longer hospitalizations are all associated with ureteral injury.[11,12]

The best way of preventing iatrogenic ureteral injury is to clearly identify the ureter in the surgical field and in those regions where it is most susceptible to injury. Every attempt should be made to limit bleeding and to avoid placing sutures or using the electrocautery in areas where exposure is poor.

Placement of ureteral stents at the beginning of the procedure may facilitate identification of the course of the ureter. A 5-year review of prophylactic ureteral catheterization in patients undergoing colon surgery concluded that whereas stents did not prevent ureteral injuries, they could help surgeons recognize such injuries more quickly.[13] Accordingly, the authors recommended stenting in patients at high risk for ureteral injury. A subsequent study from another group also recommended the use of stents in doubtful cases, on the grounds that prevention is better than treatment.[14] Other authors, however, have argued that prophylactic ureteral stents are not without risk and have not affected the rate of ureteral injury.[15] Prophylactic ureteral stenting continues to be a controversial practice.

Bladder

The bladder is the genitourinary organ that is most frequently injured during an operation.[16] Fortunately, the bladder is very for-

giving of incidental injuries, and most such injuries are recognized intraoperatively, when they can easily be repaired with a two-layer closure using absorbable sutures. Bladder injury should be suspected when, during an operation, the Foley catheter is exposed, a laceration is noticed, urinary extravasation is present, urine in the Foley catheter becomes bloody, or (in the case of a laparoscopic procedure) gas begins to escape through the Foley catheter. Most patients have an identifiable predisposing factor that complicates the operation. Typically, this factor is previous surgery or inflammation, though bladder injuries resulting from surgery performed vaginally or laparoscopically do not seem to have a predisposing cause. The incidence of laparoscopic bladder injuries reportedly ranges from 0.02% to 0.3%.[17] Foley catheter drainage is maintained for 1 to 2 weeks after repair, and the resulting success rates are quite high.

Urologic Malignancies

RENAL CELL CARCINOMA

It is currently estimated that deaths attributable to cancer of the kidney and the renal pelvis account for approximately 3% of all cancer deaths in the United States, and the annual incidence of renal cell carcinoma (RCC) continues to rise.[18] Moreover, in 22% of patients, despite improvements in imaging and detection, the cancer will have already metastasized at the time of diagnosis.[18] Approximately 85% of kidney cancers originate in the parenchyma; the remaining 15% are transitional cell carcinomas and develop in the collecting system.

In most instances, RCC is diagnosed incidentally during an imaging procedure that is performed to address some other problem. The classic triad of flank pain, hematuria, and a palpable abdominal mass is present in as many as 10% of cases.[19] Because the range of possible presentations is quite wide, RCC is frequently referred to as the "internist's tumor." Patients may present with symptoms related to paraneoplastic manifestations, such as cachexia and fever (caused by cytokines), renin-mediated hypertension, nephropathy from immunoglobulin formation, hypercalcemia, cytokine-induced myelosuppression, polycythemia related to erythropoietin production, amyloidosis, or Stauffer syndrome (nonmetastatic hepatic dysfunction). Paraneoplastic symptoms tend to disappear once localized disease is treated.

All patients with hematuria or a renal mass should undergo further evaluation. The presence of gross or microscopic hematuria should prompt contrast evaluation of the kidneys and the ureters, as well as cystoscopy with urine cytology. The presence of a renal mass should prompt evaluation with either triple-phase computed tomography or magnetic resonance imaging with or without gadolinium (if the patient has a contrast allergy or renal insufficiency). No further assessment is required for simple cysts. Renal masses evaluated by means of CT are classified according to the Bosniak system, which correlates the appearance of the mass with the risk of malignancy [see Table 1].[20] Bosniak classes I, II, III, and IV roughly correspond to cancer risks of less than 2%, less than 12%, 52%, and greater than 90%, respectively.[21-27] The evaluation of a patient with a renal mass also includes a complete history, a careful physical examination, liver function tests, a comprehensive metabolic panel, and a chest x-ray.

If imaging identifies invasion into the renal vein or a tumor thrombus, further assessment (by means of venography, magnetic resonance angiography or venography, or CT reconstruction) aimed at determining the extent of vena cava involvement is necessary for successful removal of the mass. Renal masses that are

Table 1 Bosniak System for Classification of Renal Cysts[20]

Category	Cyst Characteristics
I	Benign simple cyst with hairline-thin wall that has no septa, calcifications, or solid components; cyst has density of water and does not enhance
II	Benign cyst that may contain a few hairline-thin septa in which perceived (but not measurable) enhancement may be present; wall or septa may contain fine calcification or short segment of slightly thickened calcification; category includes uniformly high-attenuation lesions < 3 cm ("high-density cysts") that are well marginated and do not enhance; no further evaluation required
IIF*	Cyst that may contain multiple hairline-thin septa or minimal smooth thickening of wall or septa; wall or septa may show perceived enhancement; calcification may be present in wall or septa that may be thick and nodular, but without measurable enhancement; lesions are generally well marginated; category includes intrarenal nonenhancing high-attenuation lesions > 3 cm; follow-up studies required to confirm benign status
III	Indeterminate cystic mass with thickened irregular or smooth walls or septa that show measurable enhancement; surgical management required, though some lesions will prove benign (e.g., hemorrhagic cysts, chronically infected cysts, multiloculated cystic nephromas) and others malignant (e.g., cystic and multiloculated cystic RCCs)
IV	Clearly malignant cystic mass that can have all criteria of category III but also contain enhancing soft tissue components adjacent to (but independent of) wall or septa; category includes cystic carcinomas; surgical removal required

*F signifies follow-up.

suspected of harboring cancer on the basis of diagnostic imaging should not routinely undergo biopsy except (1) in cases where there is a possibility of metastasis from another primary cancer or (2) in accordance with the protocol for minimally invasive treatment alternatives (e.g., cryoablation and radiofrequency ablation). Routine biopsies of kidney masses have high false negative rates and tend to yield nondiagnostic results.

Staging is a well-established predictor of prognosis. The TNM staging system developed by the American Joint Committee on Cancer (AJCC) has been widely used for prognostic purposes in RCC patients. In a European study, the 5-year and 10-year disease-specific survival probabilities were 95.3% and 91.4% for TNM stage pT1a RCC, 91.4% and 93.4% for stage pT1b disease, and 81.6% and 75.2% for stage pT2 disease.[28] In another study, the 5-year disease-specific survival probabilities were found to be significantly worse for more advanced RCC: 67% for TNM stage III disease and 32% for stage IV disease.[29] In the past few years, various other prognostic factors have been validated that are not included in the TNM staging system, including tumor grade, histologic subtype, sarcomatoid features, histologic tumor necrosis, collecting system invasion, and performance status.[30] Accordingly, many institutions are now using a more comprehensive staging system for RCC.

For localized RCC, the standard treatment is radical nephrectomy, either open or laparoscopic (hand assisted, retroperitoneal, or transperitoneal). This procedure involves removal of the entire kidney and the fat within Gerota's fascia, which is accomplished with early identification and ligation of the renal artery and the renal vein. To preserve adrenocortical function, it is best to avoid performing unconditional ipsilateral adrenalectomy with radical nephrectomy for RCC: the benefit of routine adrenalectomy in this setting is extremely limited, especially in patients with small lesions and low-stage disease.[31] If the tumor is small (generally, < 4 cm) and occupies an anatomically favorable position, it may be removed by means of partial nephrectomy—again, either open or laparoscopic. To prevent bleeding and leakage of urine, care must be taken to ensure that vessels are controlled and the collecting system is closed.

Metastatic RCC responds poorly to standard chemotherapy and radiation therapy. In patients whose disease burden is suitable, whose performance status and general health are adequate, and who are about to undergo immunotherapy with interferon or interleukin-2 (or other trial regimens, as appropriate), cytoreductive nephrectomy should be considered. In selected patients with solitary or limited metastases (confirmed by careful staging investigations), aggressive surgical resection of all disease may prolong survival and should be considered, possibly in conjunction with immunotherapy.[32]

BLADDER CANCER

Like RCC, cancer of the urinary bladder currently accounts for approximately 3% of cancer deaths in the United States. The median age at which bladder cancer is diagnosed is 73 years.[18] In the United States, approximately 90% of bladder cancers are transitional cell carcinomas, about 5% are squamous cell carcinomas, and some 2% are adenocarcinomas. Cigarette smoking is the primary environmental risk factor, associated with 50% to 66% of bladder tumors in men and 25% in women.[33] Another risk factor is exposure to carcinogenic aromatic amines, especially benzidine and β-naphthylamine.[34] Bladder cancer has been linked to occupational exposure in aromatic amine manufacturing, dyestuff manufacturing, rubber manufacturing, painting, the leather industry, the aluminum industry, and truck driving.[35] In Africa and the Middle East, squamous cell carcinoma, associated with *Schistosoma haematobium* infection, is the most common form of bladder cancer.

In 80% to 90% of patients, bladder cancer presents as gross or microscopic hematuria, which commonly is painless and sporadic.[36] In some patients, the presenting complaint is a change in voiding habits, such as urgency, increased frequency, painful urination, or difficulty in voiding. Decreased bladder capacity (as a result of a mass effect) and ureteral obstruction are less common presenting symptoms and are suggestive of more advanced disease. Systemic complaints are suggestive of metastatic disease.

The presence of hematuria should prompt a full evaluation consisting of upper urinary tract contrast imaging, cystoscopy, and urine cytology. Cystoscopy is the current standard for detecting bladder masses. Urine cytology has a specificity that approaches 100% and is useful in helping to identify small lesions, lesions that are atypical in appearance, and lesions that are located in the upper urinary tract.[37] All suspicious bladder lesions should be resected and sent for pathologic diagnosis. Biopsy specimens should be obtained from the muscle layer to determine whether the tumor has invaded the muscle.

The stage and grade of the tumor are important for determining treatment and are independently correlated with prognosis. As with RCC, the AJCC's TNM system is commonly employed for staging. Bladder tumors that involve the mucosa (Ta) and the lamina propria (T1) are referred to as superficial disease, whereas tumors that extend beyond the lamina propria and invade muscle (T2a) are referred to as invasive disease. Three categories are used for grading, corresponding to well-differentiated disease (grade 1), moderately well differentiated disease (grade 2), and poorly differentiated disease (grade 3). As the stage and grade of the tumor increase, the prognosis worsens. Carcinoma in situ is a separate disease entity whose presence is associated with a high risk of recurrence and a greater likelihood of disease progression.

Approximately 70% of bladder cancers initially present as superficial disease. Treatment consists of resection and cauterization. If pathologic examination confirms superficial disease, no further metastatic workup is necessary. Surveillance is mandatory, however, because of the high risk of recurrence and progression. Low-grade Ta lesions recur in 50% to 70% of cases and progress in approximately 5% of patients, whereas high-grade T1 lesions recur in more than 80% of cases and progress in 50% of patients within 3 years.[38] Patients with high-risk superficial disease—defined as carcinoma in situ; stage T1 lesions; or large, high-grade, recurrent, or multifocal Ta lesions—should receive further treatment with intravesical bacillus Calmette-Guérin (BCG).[39]

Approximately 25% of bladder cancers are invasive at the time of initial diagnosis. The standard treatment for organ-confined invasive bladder cancer is radical cystectomy with extended lymph node dissection; urine is diverted into a conduit or neobladder created from the large or the small bowel. Disease that extends through the muscle into the fat (T3), node-positive disease, or metastatic disease requires further treatment with chemotherapy after the postoperative period. In older series, if bladder cancer was left untreated, fewer than 15% of patients would survive 2 years.[40] In a 2001 study of 1,054 patients treated at the University of Southern California, the 5-year survival was 60% to 75% for pT2 tumors, 36% to 58% for pT3 tumors, and 4% to 35% for pT4 or node-positive tumors.[41]

PROSTATE CANCER

Cancer of the prostate accounts for approximately 10% of cancer deaths in the United States. It is estimated that prostate cancer will be diagnosed in one of every six men,[18] usually relatively late in life; between 1998 and 2002, the median age at which prostate cancer was diagnosed was 69 years. Over the past 2 decades, the incidence of prostate cancer has risen, partly because of the widespread use of the prostate-specific antigen (PSA) screening test. This rise, however, has not been uniform. Between 1989 and 1992, the incidence of prostate cancer increased by an average of 18% per year, but between 1992 and 1995, it declined by 14% per year; it may now have reached a plateau.[42]

In the early stages, prostate cancer is generally asymptomatic. Currently, most cases of prostate cancer are detected by an abnormal digital rectal examination or an abnormal PSA test result that prompts prostate biopsy. Routine screening with a PSA test and a digital rectal examination should begin at the age of 40 in men whose life expectancy is greater than 10 years. African-American men and men who have a first-degree relative with prostate cancer are at higher risk for prostate cancer. The generally accepted threshold value for an abnormal PSA level has been 4.0 ng/ml; however, some investigators now question this value, on the grounds that a significant number of men have been found to have cancer with PSA values between 2.6 and 4.0 ng/ml.[43-45] In addition, the rate at which the serum PSA level increases (i.e., PSA velocity) has become a very important factor in the diagnosis of prostate cancer.[46] For proper interpretation of PSA values, it is important to recognize that the serum PSA level can be influenced by multiple factors besides prostate cancer (including urinary retention, BPH, and prostatitis).

The stage and grade of the tumor play important roles in determining treatment and prognosis. As with RCC and bladder cancer, the most widely accepted staging system is the AJCC's TNM system. The most widely accepted grading system for prostate can-

cer is based on the Gleason score. In this system, the biopsy specimen is examined under low-power magnification, and the most prominent glandular pattern seen is graded on a scale of 1 to 5, with 1 representing the highest degree of differentiation and 5 the lowest. The next most prominent glandular pattern seen is then graded in the same fashion. The two grades are added to yield the Gleason score, which can range from a minimum of 2 (1 + 1) to a maximum of 10 (5 + 5). Cancers with scores of 6 (3 + 3) or lower are considered well differentiated; those with scores of 7 (3 + 4 or 4 + 3) are considered intermediate; and those with scores of 8 (4 + 4) or higher are considered poorly differentiated. The more poorly differentiated the cancer is, the more aggressive it will be and the worse the prognosis will be. In addition to the Gleason score, the clinical stage and the PSA level have important implications for treatment.

There are many options for treating prostate cancer, and there remains some controversy regarding what constitutes the most effective therapy. Typically, treatment is based on the stage and grade of the tumor, the PSA level, and patient characteristics such as general health status, comorbid conditions, age, body habitus, and personal bias. Clinically localized prostate cancer may be treated with curative intent by means of surgery or irradiation (i.e., external-beam radiation therapy or brachytherapy). When the disease is more advanced or the patient is unwilling to undergo operative treatment or radiation therapy, antiandrogen therapies or watchful waiting may be considered.

TESTICULAR CANCER

Testicular cancer accounts for only about 1% to 2% of all malignancies in men; however, it is the most common cancer in males between 15 and 34 years of age.[47] Moreover, since the middle of the 20th century, the incidence of testicular cancer has been increasing in the United States.[48] The exact cause of testicular cancer remains unknown. It has been hypothesized that testicular atrophy is a common pathway by which several etiologic factors may be involved in tumor development in the testis.[49,50] Familial tendency, white race, and a history of cryptorchidism are established risk factors.[51-53]

The classic presentation of testicular cancer is painless swelling or enlargement of the testis. A 1987 study of 5,172 patients with testicular cancer, however, found that the initial presenting complaints for this condition included a swollen or enlarged testis (58%), a mass in the testis (27%), a painful testis (33%), tender breasts (3%), and a history of trauma (4%).[54] Acute trauma is not a proven cause of testicular cancer, but it may lead to the awareness of a mass. Examination generally reveals an enlarged testis or a nodule on the testis; it may prove more difficult in a patient with a tender testis or a large hydrocele. Ultrasonography, which has been shown to be highly reliable in differentiating between intratesticular and extratesticular lesions, may be performed to supplement the evaluation.[55,56] In rare cases, testicular cancer may present with manifestations of systemic disease (e.g., pulmonary complaints or an abdominal mass).

Measurement of serum levels of tumor markers (i.e., human chorionic gonadotropin [hCG], α-fetoprotein [AFP], and lactic dehydrogenase [LDH]) is a well-established component of the management of testicular germ cell tumors and facilitates diagnosis, prognosis, monitoring of treatment, and prediction of relapse. Elevated serum concentrations of these markers are strongly suggestive of cancer, but the absence of such elevated concentrations in a patient with a testicular mass does not rule out cancer. hCG is secreted by the syncytiotrophoblasts present in certain germ cell tumors (i.e., embryonal tumors, teratomas, choriocarcinomas, and fewer than 20% of seminomas). Its serum half-life is 16 to 24 hours. AFP is synthesized by yolk sac components of germ cell tumors. Its presence is diagnostic of nonseminomatous disease; it is never produced by pure seminomas or choriocarcinomas. AFP concentrations peak between gestational weeks 12 and 14 and start to decline after week 16, falling to undetectable levels after the first year of life. The serum half-life of AFP is 4.5 days. LDH, though not a highly sensitive tumor marker, has proved to be an independent prognostic variable in several large multivariate analyses of testicular germ cell tumors. Serum tumor marker concentrations are followed after radical orchiectomy and should fall in proportion to their respective half-lives.

Treatment is determined by the pathology and stage of the tumor. Most testicular tumors are of germ cell origin and are classified as either seminomatous or nonseminomatous. Nonmetastatic disease can often be treated surgically by means of radical orchiectomy, which is completed through an inguinal incision after vascular control of the spermatic cord has been achieved. Follow-up with diagnostic imaging and measurement of serum tumor marker levels is carried out to look for possible metastatic disease.

Seminomas account for nearly 48% of germ cell tumors and usually present during the fourth and fifth decades.[57] Initial metastasis is typically to either the periaortic lymph nodes near the renal hilum (for left-side lesions) or the precaval lymph nodes between the aortic bifurcation and the renal pedicle (for right-side lesions). Crossover to the periaortic nodes is common with right-side lesions. Seminomas may also spread hematogenously to the lungs, the liver, the brain, bone, the kidneys, the adrenal glands, the gastrointestinal tract, or the spleen. These lesions are highly radiosensitive, and thus, irradiation is a key part of early-stage treatment. Low-stage disease is treated with radical orchiectomy and radiation therapy, whereas advanced or bulky disease is treated with chemotherapy. Close follow-up is the rule.

Nonseminomatous germ cell tumors tend to be more locally aggressive than seminomas, and they have a high metastatic potential. Overall, the patterns of lymphatic and hematogenous spread are similar to those of seminomatous germ cell tumors; however, choriocarcinoma demonstrates a particularly aggressive natural history, with early hematogenous spread. Nonseminomatous germ cell tumors are treated with surgery, with platinum-based chemotherapy, or with both, depending on the disease stage. Low-stage disease is treated with radical orchiectomy, followed by chemotherapy if tumor marker concentrations do not normalize. If the tumor marker concentrations normalize, subsequent options include surveillance and nerve-sparing retroperitoneal lymph node dissection (RPLND); without additional treatment, 30% of patients will experience relapses. The presence of lymphatic, vascular, scrotal, or spermatic cord invasion increases the likelihood of retroperitoneal lymph node involvement, and RPLND may therefore be preferred in these circumstances.[58] Disease with minor nodal involvement is treated with radical orchiectomy and RPLND, followed by chemotherapy if RPLND demonstrates the presence of cancer. Disease with more extensive nodal involvement and metastatic disease are treated with chemotherapy. Close follow-up is the rule.

Benign Prostatic Hyperplasia

BPH becomes increasingly common in men as they age: histologic evidence from autopsy studies suggests that the incidence of BPH exceeds 50% in men older than 50 years and exceeds 75% in men older than 70 years.[59] The prostate is composed of stromal and epithelial components, and either stroma or epithelium (or both) can give rise to hyperplastic nodules. Typically, nodules occur in the transition zone of the prostate. The etiology of BPH is multifactorial and is not yet completely understood. It is clear, however, that the endocrine system plays an important role and that the levels of testosterone and other hormones are significant factors. A positive family history and early onset of symptoms are associated with an increased risk of progression to more severe BPH. There may be an autosomal dominant or codominant pattern of inheritance.[60]

Patients with BPH may present with obstructive or irritative symptoms, which are collectively referred to as lower urinary tract symptoms. Obstructive symptoms include incomplete emptying, intermittency, a weak stream, and straining; irritative symptoms include urgency, frequency, and nocturia. Although most patients present with one or more of these complaints, some patients may present with urinary tract infections, acute urinary retention, or renal failure. Because lower urinary tract symptoms are not disease specific, one must consider other urologic and medical conditions besides BPH, such as urinary tract infection, stones, prostatitis, strictures, cancer, and neurologic disease.

Patients should be evaluated with a careful history and a thorough physical examination. Symptoms should be quantified by using the International Prostate Symptom Score (I-PSS) questionnaire. This questionnaire consists of seven questions, the answers to which are scored on a scale of 0 to 5 to yield a total score ranging from 0 to 35. A total score of 0 to 7 indicates mild symptoms, a total score of 8 to 19 indicates moderate symptoms, and a total score of 20 to 35 indicates severe symptoms. I-PSS scores can be used to help determine treatment and assess its effectiveness, and their utility in this setting has been reliably validated. A complete urologic examination and a limited neurologic examination should be carried out. Routine PSA screening (for healthy persons of suitable age) and urinalysis should be performed. Whether further examination and testing are required is determined by the initial findings and the course of treatment. Additional evaluation may include measurement of serum creatinine concentrations, cultures, assessment of PSA levels, cystoscopy, biopsy, or urodynamic testing.

Treatment of BPH may involve observation, medical therapy, or surgical management. Symptoms tend to wax and wane, and many patients tolerate their symptoms reasonably well and prefer to avoid therapeutic interventions. Watchful waiting is a viable option for patients who have minimal symptoms and no evidence of renal or bladder dysfunction. Medical therapy focuses on relaxing the bladder neck and shrinking the prostate to facilitate more complete emptying of the bladder. Two classes of medications are used: alpha blockers and 5α-reductase inhibitors. Alpha blockers are considered first-line treatment for all BPH patients. These medications act on the alpha-adrenergic receptors of the bladder neck and the prostate to help relax and open the channel. Their main side effects are related to their blood pressure–lowering effect. In 2003, the Medical Therapy of Prostatic Symptoms (MTOPS) Research Group published a study advocating combination therapy with an alpha blocker and a 5α-reductase inhibitor to reduce the risk of overall clinical progression of BPH and the long-term risk of acute urinary retention and need for invasive therapy.[61] Surgical intervention is generally reserved for patients who exhibit acute urinary retention and those who continue to experience significant symptoms despite medical treatment. Currently, surgical treatment is most often performed endoscopically. Prostatic tissue is resected with an electrocautery in the standard fashion, removed via transurethral resection of the prostate, or ablated with a laser. If the prostate is extremely large (> 80 g), an open or laparoscopic[62,63] simple prostatectomy may be performed.

Postoperative urinary retention, which occurs in 3.8% to 9% of cases,[64,65] is a particularly troubling development. It has been associated with preexisting voiding issues, immobility, analgesics, administration of high fluid volumes during operation, and impaired mental status. Treatment is based on eliminating as many of these predisposing factors as possible. After an unsuccessful first voiding attempt, a single catheterization is successful in resolving postoperative urinary retention in 39% of cases.[64] Generally, patients are given an alpha blocker first, and a voiding trial is administered once they have become ambulatory and are using less pain medication. Patients with a history of lower urinary tract symptoms should be started on an alpha blocker preoperatively, and administration of the medication should resume as soon as they are capable of tolerating liquids.

References

1. Kabalin JM: Surgical Anatomy of the Retroperitoneum, Kidneys and Ureters, 8th ed. WB Saunders Co, Philadelphia, 2002, p 1

2. Kapoor A, Kapoor A, Mahajan G, et al: Multispiral computed tomographic angiography of renal arteries of live potential renal donors: a review of 118 cases. Transplantation 77:1535, 2004

3. Kim JK, Park SY, Kim HJ, et al: Living donor kidneys: usefulness of multi-detector row CT for comprehensive evaluation. Radiology 229:869, 2003

4. Kawamoto S, Montgomery RA, Lawler LP, et al: Multidetector CT angiography for preoperative evaluation of living laparoscopic kidney donors. AJR Am J Roentgenol 180:1633, 2003

5. Halpern EJ, Mitchell DG, Wechsler RJ, et al: Preoperative evaluation of living renal donors: comparison of CT angiography and MR angiography. Radiology 216:434, 2000

6. Corral DA, Varma DG, Jackson EF, et al: Magnetic resonance imaging and magnetic resonance angiography before postchemotherapy retroperitoneal lymph node dissection. Urology 55:262, 2000

7. Del Pizzo JJ, Sklar GN, You-Cheong JW, et al: Helical computerized tomography arteriography for evaluation of live renal donors undergoing laparoscopic nephrectomy. J Urol 162:31, 1999

8. Khastgir J, Arya M, Patel HR, et al: Ureteral injury during radical orthopedic cancer surgery. J Urol 165:900, 2001

9. Arroyo A, Rodriguez J, Porto J, et al: Management and course of hydronephrosis secondary to inflammatory aneurysms of the abdominal aorta. Ann Vasc Surg 17:481, 2003

10. Brandes S, Coburn M, Armenakas N, et al: Diagnosis and management of ureteric injury: an evidence-based analysis. BJU Int 94:277, 2004

11. Carley ME, McIntire D, Carley JM, et al: Incidence, risk factors and morbidity of unintended bladder or ureter injury during hysterectomy. Int Urogynecol J Pelvic Floor Dysfunct 13:18, 2002

12. Neuman M, Eidelman A, Langer R, et al: Iatrogenic injuries to the ureter during gynecologic and obstetric operations. Surg Gynecol Obstet 173:268, 1991

13. Bothwell WN, Bleicher RJ, Dent TL: Prophylactic ureteral catheterization in colon surgery: a five-year review. Dis Colon Rectum 37:330, 1994

14. Dobrowolski Z, Kusionowicz J, Drewniak T, et al: Renal and ureteric trauma: diagnosis and management in Poland. BJU Int 89:748, 2002

15. Kuno K, Menzin A, Kauder HH, et al: Prophylactic ureteral catheterization in gynecologic surgery. Urology 52:1004, 1998

16. Armenakas NA, Pareek G, Fracchia JA: Iatrogenic bladder perforations: longterm followup of 65 patients. J Am Coll Surg 198:78, 2004

17. Ostrzenski A, Ostrzenska KM: Bladder injury during laparoscopic surgery. Obstet Gynecol Surv 53:175, 1998

18. SEER Cancer Statistics Review, 1975–2002. Ries LAG, Eisner MP, Kosary CL, et al, Eds. National Cancer Institute, Bethesda, Maryland, 2005

http://seer.cancer.gov/csr/1975_2002

19. Jayson M, Sanders H: Increased incidence of serendipitously discovered renal cell carcinoma. Urology 51:203, 1998

20. Israel GM, Bosniak MA: An update of the Bosniak renal cyst classification system. Urology 66:484, 2005

21. Siegel CL, McFarland EG, Brink JA, et al: CT of cystic renal masses: analysis of diagnostic performance and interobserver variation. AJR Am J Roentgenol 169:813, 1997

22. Aronson S, Frazier H, Baluch JD, et al: Cystic renal masses: usefulness of the Bosniak classification. Urol Radiol 13:83, 1991

23. Cloix P, Martin X, Pangaud C, et al: Surgical management of complex renal cysts: a series of 32 cases. J Urol 156:28, 1996

24. Curry NS, Cochran ST, Bissada NK: Cystic renal masses: accurate Bosniak classification requires adequate renal CT. AJR Am J Roentgenol 175:339, 2000

25. Limb J, Santiago L, Kaswick J, et al: Laparoscopic evaluation of indeterminate renal cysts: long term follow-up. J Endourol 16:79, 2002

26. Harisinghani MG, Maher MM, Gervais DA, et al: Incidence of malignancy in complex cystic renal masses (Bosniak category III): should imaging-guided biopsy precede surgery? AJR Am J Roentgenol 180:755, 2003

27. Koga S, Nishikido M, Inuzuka S, et al: An evaluation of Bosniak's radiological classification of cystic renal masses. BJU Int 86:607, 2000

28. Ficarra V, Schips L, Guille F, et al: Multiinstitutional European validation of the 2002 TNM staging system in conventional and papillary localized renal cell carcinoma. Cancer 104:968, 2005

29. Tsui KH, Shvarts O, Smith RB, et al: Prognostic indicators for renal cell carcinoma: a multivariate analysis of 643 patients using the revised 1997 TNM staging criteria. J Urol 163:1090, 2000

30. Lam JS, Shvarts O, Leppert JT, et al: Renal cell carcinoma 2005: new frontiers in staging, prognostication and targeted molecular therapy. J Urol 173:1853, 2005

31. Yokoyama H, Tanaka M: Incidence of adrenal involvement and assessing adrenal function in patients with renal cell carcinoma: is ipsilateral adrenalectomy indispensable during radical nephrectomy? BJU Int 95:526, 2005

32. Sengupta S, Leibovich BC, Blute ML, et al: Surgery for metastatic renal cell cancer. World J Urol 23:155, 2005

33. Marcus PM, Hayes RB, Vineis P, et al: Cigarette smoking, N-acetyltransferase 2 acetylation status, and bladder cancer risk: a case-series meta-analysis of a gene-environment interaction. Cancer Epidemiol Biomarkers Prev 9:461, 2000

34. Golka K, Wiese A, Assennato G, et al: Occupational exposure and urological cancer. World J Urol 21:382, 2004

35. Negri E, La Vecchia C: Epidemiology and prevention of bladder cancer. Eur J Cancer Prev 10:7, 2001

36. Pashos CL, Botteman MF, Laskin BL, et al: Bladder cancer: epidemiology, diagnosis, and management. Cancer Pract 10:311, 2002

37. Borden LS Jr, Clark PE, Hall MC: Bladder cancer. Curr Opin Oncol 17:275, 2005

38. Malkowicz S: Management of superficial bladder cancer. Campbell's Urology, 8th ed. Walsh PC, Retik AB, Vaughan ED, et al, Eds. WB Saunders Co, Philadelphia, 2002, p 2785

39. Nadler RB, Catalona WJ, Hudson MA, et al: Durability of the tumor-free response for intravesical bacillus Calmette-Guerin therapy. J Urol 152:367, 1994

40. Prout GR, Marshall VF: The prognosis with untreated bladder tumors. Cancer 9:551, 1956

41. Stein JP, Lieskovsky G, Cote R, et al: Radical cystectomy in the treatment of invasive bladder cancer: long-term results in 1,054 patients. J Clin Oncol 19:666, 2001

42. Routh JC, Leibovich BC: Adenocarcinoma of the prostate: epidemiological trends, screening, diagnosis, and surgical management of localized disease. Mayo Clin Proc 80:899, 2005

43. Babaian RJ, Johnston DA, Naccarato W, et al: The incidence of prostate cancer in a screening population with a serum prostate specific antigen between 2.5 and 4.0 ng/ml: relation to biopsy strategy. J Urol 165:757, 2001

44. Catalona WJ, Smith DS, Ornstein DK: Prostate cancer detection in men with serum PSA concentrations of 2.6 to 4.0 ng/mL and benign prostate examination: enhancement of specificity with free PSA measurements. JAMA 277:1452, 1997

45. Zhu H, Roehl KA, Antenor JA, et al: Biopsy of men with PSA level of 2.6 to 4.0 ng/mL associated with favorable pathologic features and PSA progression rate: a preliminary analysis. Urology 66:547, 2005

46. Berger AP, Deibl M, Steiner H, et al: Longitudinal PSA changes in men with and without prostate cancer: assessment of prostate cancer risk. Prostate 64:240, 2005

47. Devesa SS, Blot WJ, Stone BJ, et al: Recent cancer trends in the United States. J Natl Cancer Inst 87:175, 1995

48. Zheng T, Holford TR, Ma Z, et al: Continuing increase in incidence of germ-cell testis cancer in young adults: experience from Connecticut, USA, 1935–1992. Int J Cancer 65:723, 1996

49. Oliver RT: Atrophy, hormones, genes and viruses in aetiology of germ cell tumours. Cancer Surv 9:263, 1990

50. Oliver RT, Oliver JC: Endocrine hypothesis for declining sperm count and rising incidence of cancer. Lancet 347:339, 1996

51. Garner MJ, Turner MC, Ghadirian P, et al: Epidemiology of testicular cancer: an overview. Int J Cancer 116:331, 2005

52. Bosl GJ, Motzer RJ: Testicular germ-cell cancer. N Engl J Med 337:242, 1997

53. Richie JP: Detection and treatment of testicular cancer. CA Cancer J Clin 43:151, 1993

54. Kennedy BJ, Schmidt JD, Winchester DP, et al: National survey of patterns of care for testis cancer. Cancer 60:1921, 1987

55. Aragona F, Pescatori E, Talenti E, et al: Painless scrotal masses in the pediatric population: prevalence and age distribution of different pathological conditions—a 10 year retrospective multicenter study. J Urol 155:1424, 1996

56. Langer JE: Ultrasound of the scrotum. Semin Roentgenol 28:5, 1993

57. Smith R: Management of testicular seminoma. Genitourinary Cancer. Skinner DG, deKernion JB, Eds. WB Saunders Co, Philadelphia, 1978, p 460

58. Javadpour N, Canning DA, O'Connell KJ, et al: Predictors of recurrent clinical stage I nonseminomatous testicular cancer: a prospective clinicopatho-logic study. Urology 27:508, 1986

59. Grayhack J, McVary KT, Kozlowski JM: Benign prostatic hyperplasia. Adult and Pediatric Urology 4th ed, vol 2. Gillenwater J, Grayhack JT, Howard SS, et al, Eds. Lippincott Williams & Wilkins, Philadelphia, 2002, p 1401

60. Pearson JD, Lei HH, Beaty TH, et al: Familial aggregation of bothersome benign prostatic hyperplasia symptoms. Urology 61:781, 2003

61. McConnell JD, Roehrborn CG, Bautista OM, et al: The long-term effect of doxazosin, finasteride, and combination therapy on the clinical progression of benign prostatic hyperplasia. N Engl J Med 349: 2387, 2003

62. Sotelo R, Spaliviero M, Garcia-Segui A, et al: Laparoscopic retropubic simple prostatectomy. J Urol 173:757, 2005

63. Nadler RB, Blunt LW Jr, User HM, et al: Preperitoneal laparoscopic simple prostatectomy. Urology 63:778, 2004

64. Tammela T, Kontturi M, Lukkarinen O: Postoperative urinary retention: II. Micturition problems after the first catheterization. Scand J Urol Nephrol 20:257, 1986

65. Werner MU, Soholm L, Rotboll-Nielsen P, et al: Does an acute pain service improve postoperative outcome? Anesth Analg 95:1361, 2002

Acknowledgment

Figures 1 and 2   Alice Y. Chen.

143 GYNECOLOGIC CONSIDERATIONS FOR THE GENERAL SURGEON

Edward S. Podczaski, M.D., F.A.C.S., and Paul R. Kramer, Jr., M.D.

For many general surgeons, gynecologic surgery is not a major component of practice. In a report published in 1995, surgical residents who graduated that year had handled, on average, only 1.6 gynecologic cases.[1] Nevertheless, it is clear that some surgeons devote a significant portion of their practice to treating gynecologic disorders. In a prospective registry of consecutive cases reported by seven rural general surgeons, 20% of the procedures were classified as gynecologic.[2] Furthermore, in a National Survey of Ovarian Carcinoma published in 1993, 21% of the primary surgical procedures for ovarian cancer were actually performed by general surgeons.[3] At present, more than half of the general surgery residency programs in the United States offer no formal rotation in gynecology; accordingly, both residents and practicing surgeons may benefit from a discussion of basic gynecologic problems and their surgical management. In what follows, we consider the gynecologic conditions that are most commonly encountered by general surgeons. These conditions may be broadly classified as gynecologic emergencies, outpatient gynecologic problems (e.g., pelvic masses and abnormal uterine bleeding), or squamous dysplasias and gynecologic malignancies.

Gynecologic Emergencies

BLEEDING FROM OVARIAN CYSTS

Each month, the ovary of a premenopausal woman undergoes a cycle of hormonally driven changes characterized by follicular development, the emergence of a dominant follicle, ovulation, and the formation of a corpus luteum. Cystic enlargement of one of these physiologic structures is relatively common and is considered functional rather than neoplastic. Approximately 7% of asymptomatic women between the ages of 25 and 40 years have ovarian cysts larger than 2.5 cm.[4] Functional ovarian cysts should not cause pain unless accompanied by bleeding, rupture, or torsion.

Follicular cysts are fluid-filled structures that arise from a normal follicle that fails to ovulate or does not undergo atresia. Rupture of follicular cysts may result in acute pain, which is usually of brief duration. Corpus luteum cysts arise from a mature, well-vascularized corpus luteum and may be associated with prolonged secretion of progesterone. They tend to be larger than follicular cysts and are more likely to cause clinical symptoms. Corpus luteum cysts range in severity from masses that cause no symptoms to ruptured cysts that cause catastrophic bleeding. Dull, unilateral lower abdominal and pelvic pain is the typical presenting complaint. Pelvic examination may show an enlarged, tender ovary. Unruptured corpus luteum cysts are followed conservatively. However, events such as coitus, exercise, or trauma may rupture the cyst, resulting in slight to significant intraperitoneal bleeding, in which case the patient usually experiences the sudden onset of severe lower abdominal or pelvic pain. The acute pain of a bleeding corpus luteum cyst is indistinguishable from that of a ruptured ectopic pregnancy.

A negative serum β–human chorionic gonadotropin (β-hCG) determination rules out an ectopic pregnancy. In hemodynamically stable patients, pelvic ultrasonography may establish a diagnosis and permit expectant management even if some intraperitoneal bleeding has occurred. The appearance of hemorrhagic cysts on computed tomography depends on the age of the clot: blood from an acute hemorrhage has a high attenuation value, whereas blood from a previous hemorrhage has an attenuation value approaching that of water. In an acute setting, CT typically demonstrates a cystic adnexal mass with areas of high attenuation at intramural and intracystic sites. A hemoperitoneum may also be present, with high-attenuation clot and blood accumulating in the dependent pelvis. Laparoscopy may be useful when the diagnosis is uncertain or when a stable patient has a moderate hemoperitoneum. In hemodynamically unstable patients, adequate volume and blood replacement are initiated and emergency laparotomy is performed. Once it is confirmed that the bleeding is from a ruptured cyst, conservative therapy, consisting of removing the cyst and achieving hemostasis, is initiated.

ADNEXAL TORSION

Abnormal enlargement of the adnexa, either by neoplasms or by cysts, may predispose to torsion of the tube and the ovary around the infundibulopelvic ligament, resulting in vascular compromise. Adnexal torsion is a gynecologic emergency: if untreated, it will result in infarction of the adnexa with eventual peritonitis. Although torsion can occur in postmenopausal women, it is most common in patients of reproductive age.

The presenting complaint is severe pelvic pain of abrupt onset, often accompanied by nausea and vomiting of sudden onset. The pain may be colicky or knifelike and is usually related to the degree of vascular compromise. There may be a history of waxing and waning pelvic pain corresponding to previous episodes of partial twisting and detorsion. Physical examination often demonstrates an acute abdomen with lower abdominal tenderness and guarding. Pelvic examination usually demonstrates a mass that may be difficult to assess because of tenderness. Low-grade temperature elevations may be noted, but significant fevers are unlikely. In most series, the accuracy with which adnexal torsion is diagnosed is approximately 70%.[5] Ultrasonography demonstrates a mass in nearly all affected patients. However, the presence of arterial flow on Doppler ultrasonography does not exclude ovarian torsion: early in the development of ovarian torsion, lymphatic and venous flow may be obstructed while arterial perfusion is preserved.[6] CT may demonstrate ovarian enlargement, smooth-wall thickening of the mass or tube, and uterine deviation towards the affected adnexa. On occasion, a twisted vascular pedicle (torsion knot or whirling sign) or lack of contrast enhancement within the twisted ovarian mass may be observed. Prompt surgical intervention is necessary to prevent adnexal infarction.

In the past, adnexal torsion was commonly treated aggressively, with salpingo-oophorectomy. This approach continues to be warranted in perimenopausal and postmenopausal patients; however, a more conservative approach is now considered preferable for the treatment of women of reproductive age who desire future fertility. The traditional approach was based on two assumptions: first, that the twisted adnexum with vascular compromise was nonviable, and second, that detorsion was potentially dangerous because it might cause thrombus to be released from the clotted veins in the infundibulopelvic ligament. These assumptions proved to be unfounded. Accordingly, current management begins with untwisting the adnexum and assessing its viability. Once the torsion is unwound, the adnexum may demonstrate reperfusion or infarction without vascular recovery. Only a gangrenous adnexum must be completely removed.

Patients may be managed by means of either laparoscopy or laparotomy, depending on the clinical circumstances. In a series that included 40 young women with adnexal torsion, all of the patients were successfully managed conservatively, with unwinding of the torsion; laparotomy was performed in 26 of the 40 and operative laparoscopy in 14.[7] Ideally, cystectomy, along with removal of the cause of the torsion, should be done at the time of detorsion. However, cystectomy on an edematous and fragile ovary may be technically difficult and may cause a further vascular insult to the remaining tissue. In such cases, it is advisable to evaluate the patient 6 to 8 weeks after the acute episode. If an ovarian mass is still found at that time, ovarian cystectomy may be performed via operative laparoscopy.

PELVIC INFLAMMATORY DISEASE

Pelvic inflammatory disease (PID) is an acute infection of the upper female genital tract that involves the uterus, the fallopian tubes, and the ovaries. It is a community-acquired disease and is initiated by a sexually transmitted agent that results in the ascent of vaginal flora into the upper genital tract. The resulting polymicrobial infection (caused by a mixture of anaerobes, facultative anaerobes, and aerobic organisms) can lead to a wide spectrum of disorders, including endometritis, salpingitis, tubo-ovarian abscess, and pelvic peritonitis.

Lower abdominal pain is the most frequent complaint. The pain usually is bilateral, rarely is of more than 2 weeks' duration, and often begins with or follows menses. Approximately half of the patients are febrile. Abdominal palpation demonstrates diffuse tenderness that is more pronounced in the two lower quadrants. Rebound tenderness and diminished bowel sounds are common. Pelvic examination reveals a purulent endocervical discharge with cervical motion and adnexal tenderness.

Empiric treatment of PID should be initiated in sexually active young women or women at risk in the clinical setting of lower abdominal tenderness, adnexal tenderness, and cervical motion tenderness. Additional criteria supporting the diagnosis include fever (oral temperature > 101° F), abnormal cervical or vaginal mucopurulent discharge, the presence of abundant white cells on saline microscopy of vaginal secretions, an elevated sedimentation rate, an elevated C-reactive protein level, and documentation of cervical infection with *Neisseria gonorrhoeae* or *Chlamydia trachomatis*.[8] The differential diagnosis includes adnexal torsion, appendicitis, ectopic pregnancy, endometriosis, a hemorrhagic ovarian cyst, and urinary tract infection. Pertinent lab studies include determination of the serum β-hCG level (to rule out an ectopic pregnancy), microscopic examination of the vaginal discharge, a complete blood count, endocervical nucleic acid amplification tests for *N. gonorrhoeae* and *C. trachomatis*, sedimentation rate, and urinalysis. Clinical diagnosis of acute PID remains imprecise. Compared with laparoscopy (the gold standard for

Table 1 Recommended Outpatient and Inpatient Therapies for Pelvic Inflammatory Disease[8]

Type of Therapy	Regimen	Agents and Dosages
Outpatient	A	Ofloxacin, 400 mg p.o., once daily, for 14 days* *or* Levofloxacin, 500 mg p.o., once daily, for 14 days* *with or without* Metronidazole, 500 mg p.o., b.i.d., for 14 days
	B	Ceftriaxone, 250 mg I.M. in single dose *or* Cefoxitin, 2 g I.M. in single dose, and probenecid, 1 g p.o., administered concurrently *or* Another parenteral third-generation cephalosporin (e.g., cefotaxime or ceftizoxime) *plus* Doxycycline, 100 mg p.o., b.i.d., for 14 days *with or without* Metronidazole, 500 mg p.o., b.i.d., for 14 days
Inpatient	A	Cefotetan, 2 g I.V. q. 12 hr *or* Cefoxitin, 2 g I.V. q. 6 hr *plus* Doxycycline, 100 mg p.o. or I.V. q. 12 hr
	B	Clindamycin, 900 mg I.V. q. 8 hr *plus* Gentamicin, 2 mg/kg I.V. or I.M. loading dose, followed by maintenance dosage of 1.5 mg/kg q. 8 hr; once daily dosage may be substituted

*Should not be used in patients at increased risk for infection with quinolone-resistant *N. gonorrhoeae*.

diagnosis of PID), a presumptive diagnosis of PID has a positive predictive value of 65% to 90%.[8] Unfortunately, many episodes of PID go unrecognized and subsequently give rise to infertility, ectopic pregnancy, chronic pelvic pain, or tubo-ovarian abscesses.

PID treatment regimens are designed to provide broad-spectrum empiric therapy of likely pathogens, including *N. gonorrhoeae*, *C. trachomatis*, anaerobes, and gram-negative facultative bacteria. Quinolone-resistant *N. gonorrhoeae*, prevalent in parts of Asia and the Pacific, is becoming increasingly common in California and Hawaii; this and other geographic variables associated with PID may affect the choice of antimicrobial agents. The Centers for Disease Control (CDC) has made specific recommendations for outpatient and inpatient (parenteral) antibiotic therapy [*see Table 1*].[8] Criteria for inpatient therapy include inability to rule out a surgical emergency (e.g., appendicitis), severe symptoms, high fevers, failure to respond to oral antibiotics, and the presence of a tubo-ovarian abscess. Patients who are initially treated with parenteral antibiotics are usually switched to oral therapy within 24 hours after clinical improvement.

Tubo-ovarian abscess is the most serious manifestation of PID. There are no standardized diagnostic criteria for this condition, and a clinical diagnosis presents the same difficulties as a clinical diagnosis of PID itself. Most women with a tubo-ovarian abscess are young and desire future fertility. Fevers and pelvic pain are typical presenting complaints. Pelvic examination usually demonstrates a mass or extreme adnexal tenderness. Many unruptured tubo-ovarian abscesses, unlike unruptured abscesses elsewhere in the body, can be successfully managed with antibiotics alone. Ultrasonography is useful for diagnosis and follow-up of cases that are managed conservatively. Medical management of an unruptured abscess consists of administration of appropriate antibiotics, close monitoring, and, possibly, drainage via colpotomy. Indications for surgical intervention include a questionable diagnosis, rupture of the tubo-ovarian abscess (a true surgical emergency), and failure of medical (i.e., antibiotic) therapy.

ECTOPIC PREGNANCY

Pelvic pain and vaginal bleeding in the first trimester are the complaints most commonly associated with ectopic pregnancy. Although hypotension, tachycardia, and guarding may be noted and alert the clinician to impending tubal rupture, most patients present with less alarming findings. Patients with a suspected ectopic pregnancy are initially assessed by means of transvaginal ultrasonography [see Figure 1]. Given the risk that an ectopic preganancy may be coexisting with an intrauterine one (estimated to be between 1/4,000 and 1/15,000), the first task in the diagnostic evaluation is to exclude an intrauterine pregnancy.

Critical to the diagnosis of a suspected ectopic pregnancy is the concept of the so-called discriminatory cutoff,[9] which is defined as the serum β-hCG level at which a normal intrauterine pregnancy can be ultrasonographically identified in nearly all patients. With a transvaginal approach, the discriminatory cutoff is usually between 1,500 and 2,500 mIU/ml; however, this value can be affected by the equipment used and by the experience (or inexperience) of the sonographers. If the transvaginal ultrasonogram is nondiagnostic, a serum β-hCG test is performed to establish the serum level relative to the discriminatory cutoff. If an intrauterine pregnancy is not visualized above the discriminatory cutoff, the contents of the uterus are evacuated to distinguish an abnormal intrauterine gestation from an ectopic pregnancy. If the initial β-hCG is below the discriminatory cutoff, serial β-hCG measurements are required to document a viable or nonviable gestation. With a viable gestation, the β-hCG level should rise by at least 53% in 2 days.[9] A precipitous decline in the β-hCG level suggests a spontaneous abortion; however, if the β-hCG level does not decline by at least 21% to 35% in 2 days (depending on the initial value), an ectopic pregnancy should be suspected [see Figure 1].[9]

The clinical scenario of hypovolemic shock, an acute abdomen, and a positive pregnancy test usually establishes the diagnosis of a ruptured ectopic pregnancy. The rupture of the ectopic gestation through the tube is followed by the abrupt onset of pelvic pain lateralized to the affected adnexa. The clinical manifestations of hemoperitoneum ensue, including abdominal pain, diaphragmatic irritation and syncope. If the site of tubal rupture is small or tamponades itself, the physical findings may be more subtle. The predominant symptom is pain, usually described as dull or cramping. A history of menstrual irregularity is usually present and may be accompanied by subjective symptoms of pregnancy. Current rapid urine β-hCG assays have a sensitivity of 20 to 25 mIU/ml and are readily available to confirm the diagnosis in a patient with an acute abdomen.

Once the diagnosis of a ruptured ectopic pregnancy is made,

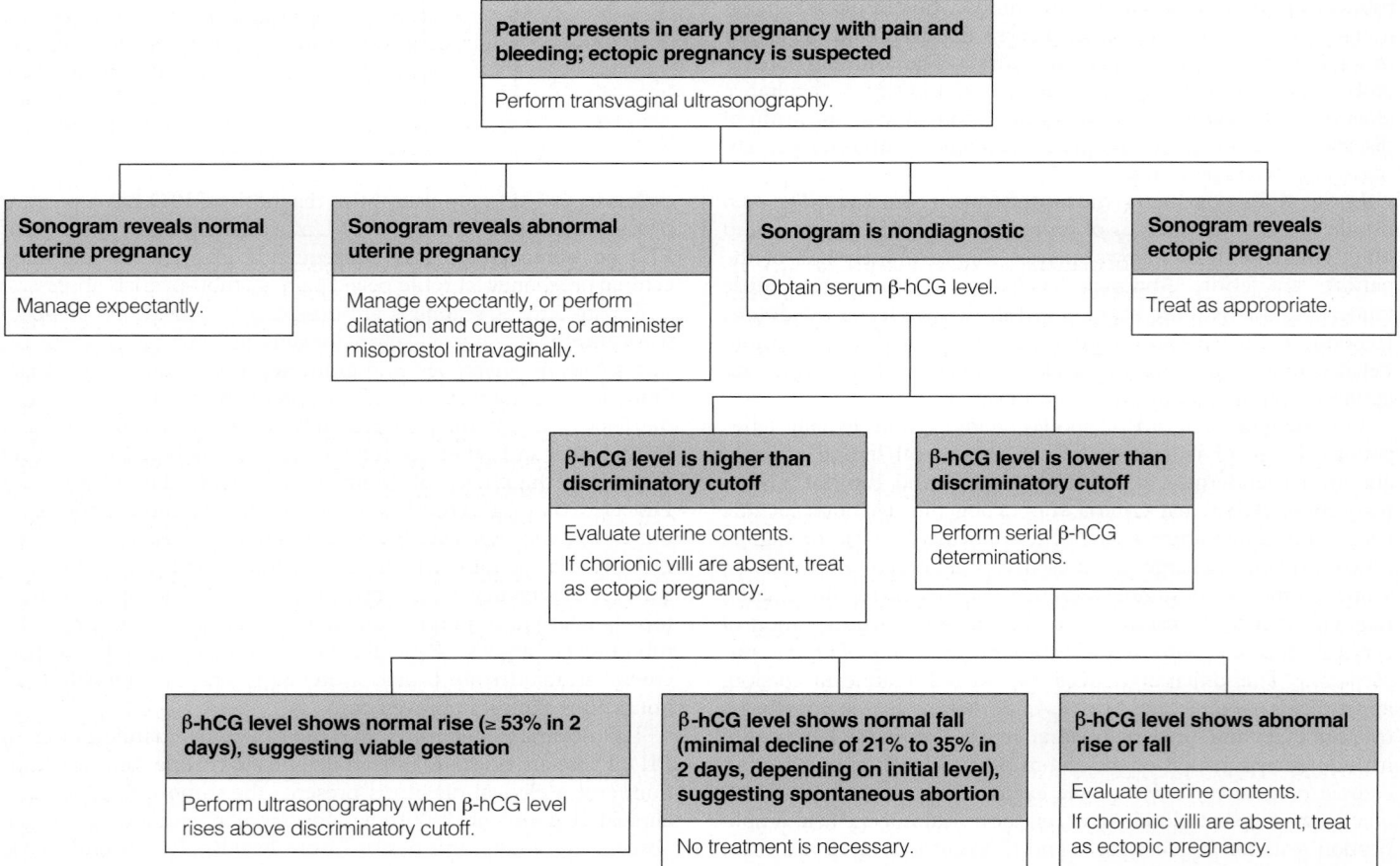

Figure 1 Algorithm illustrates evaluation of patients with suspected ectopic pregnancy.[9]

treatment consists of surgical removal of the ectopic gestation; there is no role for medical management (e.g., methotrexate) in the treatment of this condition. It should be kept in mind that not all ruptured ectopic gestations necessitate laparotomy. Hemodynamically stable patients can often be treated laparoscopically, depending on the clinical situation, the physical characteristics of the patient, and the equipment available. Diagnostic laparoscopy is an excellent tool for both diagnosis and treatment in such patients.

The patient's desire for future fertility must be considered before surgical intervention is initiated. For patients who wish to bear children in the future, conservative, tube-sparing surgery has been recommended. Linear salpingosotomy is performed by making an incision in the antimesenteric aspect of the tube overlying the bulge of the ectopic gestation. The products of conception are removed, hemostasis is achieved through electrocauterization, and the tubal defect is left open to heal by secondary intention. In cases of ectopic pregnancies at the distal or fimbrial portion of the fallopian tube, fimbrial expression with extrusion of the products of conception has also been performed. Patients undergoing conservative surgery should be followed with serial β-hCG determinations to ensure that there is no residual trophoblastic tissue. For patients who are hemodynamically unstable or who have no further desire of pregnancy, salpingectomy is the procedure of choice. Salpingectomy may also be necessary for adequate hemostasis after an unsuccessful attempt at salpingostomy.

VULVAR HEMATOMA

Vulvar hematomas are usually the result of blunt trauma (e.g., from straddle injuries, automobile accidents, or physical assault). The most important task in the management of a child with a vulvar hematoma is to determine the full extent of the problem. Management is usually conservative unless the hematoma is rapidly expanding. If the hematoma is not expanding after a minimum of 4 hours of observation, if the patient is able to void clear urine, and if the hematoma is not large enough to cause undue distress, nonsurgical treatment is indicated.[10] Administration of analgesics and application of ice packs and pressure to the affected vulva for 8 to 12 hours after the event typically yield considerable symptomatic improvement. If the hematoma is expanding, is causing considerable pain, or is obstructing the urethra, it should be incised and evacuated with the patient under anesthesia. Any actively bleeding vessels should be ligated, and the cavity should be closed in layers. If the bed of the hematoma continues to ooze, a pack can be placed to tamponade any residual bleeding.

BARTHOLIN GLAND ABSCESS

Simple incision and drainage of a Bartholin gland abscess usually achieves prompt relief of symptoms, but it may increase the risk of later recurrence. The preferred approach has been to create a fistulous tract so as to marsupialize the gland cavity. To perform a marsupialization, a small elliptical incision is made in the vestibular mucosa overlying the wall of the abscess. The elliptical piece of mucosa is removed, exposing the wall of the Bartholin abscess. The wall of the abscess is then entered, and the contents of the abscess are evacuated. A portion of the wall underlying the elliptical mucosal defect is excised, and the wall of the cyst is approximated to the edge of the mucosa with a few 3-0 absorbable sutures. Alternatively, the Bartholin abscess may be stabilized manually and entered via a stab incision. The contents are evacuated, and a Word catheter is inserted into the cavity. The balloon is then inflated and left in place for drainage of the cyst. Marsupialization is accomplished by epithelializing the catheter tract.

Outpatient Gynecologic Problems

PELVIC MASS

The differential diagnosis of a pelvic mass is determined by the viscera occupying the pelvis and their potential pathologic alterations. The most common cause of an adnexal mass is an enlarged ovary. During the reproductive years, the majority of ovarian masses are functional cysts. Such cysts range in size from a few centimeters to 8 to 10 cm in diameter and usually disappear in 1 to 3 months. A premenopausal woman with a cystic adnexal mass less than 8 cm in diameter is usually followed for at least one menstrual cycle; the majority of such masses undergo spontaneous regression. Transvaginal ultrasonography may be particularly useful for establishing the size of the mass, as well as for distinguishing a simple cyst from a complex mass. A premenopausal patient with a large (> 8–10 cm), predominantly solid, fixed, or irregular mass should be surgically evaluated. A postmenopausal patient with a simple unilocular cyst measuring less than 5 to 6 cm in diameter can be followed expectantly, provided that the CA 125 level is normal. In an autopsy study of 234 postmenopausal women who died of nongynecologic causes, 15% had ovarian cysts, and 3.8% had an ovarian cyst between 2 and 5 cm in diameter.[11] A postmenopausal patient with a large, suspicious (i.e., bilateral, irregular, fixed, solid, or accompanied by ascites), or complex mass requires surgical intervention.

Endometriosis is a benign, progressive disease defined as the presence of ectopic endometrial glands and stroma in aberrant locations in the pelvis. Hemorrhage may occur within the glandular tissue, followed by fibroblastic proliferation. The ovaries are the most common site of involvement, and ovarian involvement often results in obvious endometriotic cysts. Approximately 10% of cases may involve the rectosigmoid as well, and, depending on the degree of scarification, such involvement may be difficult to distinguish from a primary bowel neoplasm. Symptoms include pelvic pain and infertility. Medical therapy with nonsteroidal anti-inflammatory drugs (NSAIDs), combined oral contraceptives, progestins, or long-acting gonadotropin-releasing hormone (GnRH) agonists may be considered. The goals of conservative therapy are removal of gross endometriosis, lysis of adhesions, and restoration of normal anatomy. Definitive surgical treatment with hysterectomy and bilateral salpingo-oophorectomy is reserved for patients who experience intractable pain and who are no longer desirous of bearing children.

The majority of adnexal masses in women of childbearing age can be managed with cystectomy and ovarian preservation. Laparoscopic aspiration of an adnexal cyst as an isolated procedure is not recommended, because of the frequency of recurrence and the absence of any definitive pathology. Persistent cysts, cystadenomas, dermoids, and endometriomas may be managed with cystectomy, which removes the epithelial cyst lining and provides a tissue diagnosis. In a premenopasual patient with an adnexum that is not salvageable or is suspicious for malignancy, a salpingo-oophorectomy may be performed. In a postmenopausal patient with a mass, the entire ovary and tube should be removed for pathologic assessment. In carefully selected cases (e.g., patients with a negative CA 125 determination or a small, benign-appearing mass), removal of the ovary and tube can be done laparoscopically. Laparotomy is still considered the standard of care for the evaluation of potentially cancerous masses. A solid mass in a postmenopausal woman, the presence of ascites, and bilateral disease are all suggestive of malignancy. The two major concerns regarding the use of laparoscopy in the management of ovarian cancers remain the risk of tumor spillage and the delay in initiating definitive treatment.

In an open cystectomy, the ovary is immobilized, and the ovarian capsule is incised with a scalpel near the base of the cyst. Traction is placed on the incised ovarian capsule, and a Metzenbaum scissors is used to dissect the areolar tissue between the cyst wall and the capsule. After the cyst is removed, hemostasis is obtained in the bed of the cyst cavity. To reduce the risk of adhesions, the ovary usually is not sutured together. In a laparoscopic cystectomy, the utero-ovarian ligament is held so as to expose the antimesenteric aspect of the ovary. The ovarian capsule is incised with a monopolar scissors, and the cyst wall is exposed; the cyst wall is then bluntly separated from the ovarian capsule. The presence of an intact cyst wall facilitates the dissection. Eventually, the cyst is aspirated, and the remaining cyst wall is separated from the ovarian capsule by means of a 5 mm grasper. Repeated twisting of the cyst wall around the grasper (the so-called hair-curler technique) allows the cyst wall to be pulled away from the ovarian capsule. The collapsed cyst is then removed through one of the port sites and inspected for interior papillations or nodularities. The bed of the excision is inspected for hemostasis. To minimize adhesions, the edges of the ovary are not approximated with sutures.

In a postmenopausal patient with an ovarian mass, salpingo-oophorectomy is preferred, with the entire adnexum submitted for pathologic evaluation. In an open salpingo-oophorectomy, the broad ligament is entered by dividing the round ligament or by dividing the peritoneum lateral to the infundibulopelvic ligament. After the ureter is identified, the infundibulopelvic ligament is skeletonized, clamped, and ligated. The adnexum is mobilized toward the uterus, where the proximal fallopian tube and the utero-ovarian ligament are clamped, cut, and ligated. In selected postmenopausal patients with adnexal masses, salpingo-oophorectomy can be accomplished laparoscopically with bipolar electrodesiccation, suture ligation, or automatic staplers for control of the infundibulopelvic ligament.

LEIOMYOMAS

Leiomyomas, or myomas, arise as benign tumors from the myometrium and are the most common tumors of the uterus. Leiomyomas are often multiple and are grouped according to their location within the uterus; intramural, subserosal, and submucosal sites are the most common locations. Symptoms include pressure from an enlarging uterus, abnormal uterine bleeding, dysmenorrhea, and adverse pregnancy outcomes. The majority of women with myomas, however, are asymptomatic. In general, the severity of the symptoms is determined by the size and number of the fibroids, as well as by their location. The diagnosis of myomas is typically made through palpation of an irregular, enlarged uterus, though other causes of uterine enlargement or asymmetry must also be considered. Difficult cases may be resolved by employing ultrasonography or MRI to examine the uterus.

Small, asymptomatic leiomyomas may be managed with observation once a stable uterine size has been established. The need for intervention is determined on the basis of interval growth, lesion location, and patient symptoms. Rapid growth or enlargement of the uterus is another indication for surgical treatment because of the possibility of a uterine sarcoma, as well as an increased risk of operative complications. Women with symptomatic leiomyomas may be treated with myomectomy, hysterectomy, or, as is now becoming more common, uterine artery embolization. The choice between myomectomy and hysterectomy is usually determined by the patient's age, parity, and, most important, desire for future childbearing. The therapeutic effect of uterine artery embolization is thought to result from irreversible postembolic ischemia that causes necrosis and shrinkage of the myomas.

Hysterectomy is the most commonly performed major nonobstetric operation in the United States, with approximately 600,000 done each year. Although hysterectomies can be performed via a vaginal or a laparoscopic approach, more than 60% are performed abdominally, especially for the treatment of leiomyomata.[12] An abdominal hysterectomy follows a clamp, cut, and tie approach and proceeds in a lateral-to-medial direction. The round ligaments are divided early in the procedure. Access to the broad ligament is gained by dividing the infundibulopelvic ligaments and performing salpingo-oophorectomy or by dividing the proximal tube at the utero-ovarian ligament and preserving the adnexa. The vesicouterine fold is transversely divided in an area where the bladder flap appears mobile. The bladder is reflected below the level of the uterine cervix, and the uterine arteries are skeletonized. Each uterine artery pedicle is clamped adjacent to the cervix, then cut and tied, and the cardinal ligaments are serially transected. Each pedicle is clamped, divided, and ligated medial to the previous purchase of tissue. Eventually, the vagina is entered, the specimen is amputated from the vaginal apex, and the open vaginal tube is closed. Potential urinary tract morbidity includes injury to the bladder (resulting in fistulas) and ureteral damage, most often occurring with clamping of the gonadal vessels (i.e., the infundibulopelvic ligament) or clamping of the uterine arteries.

ABNORMAL UTERINE BLEEDING

Abnormal uterine bleeding is one of the most frequent complaints expressed by patients seeking gynecologic care. Such bleeding is not in itself a diagnosis but, rather, a symptom that warrants evaluation. The term abnormal uterine bleeding includes excessive uterine bleeding (menorrhagia), bleeding between menses, and any combination of the two, as well as postmenopausal bleeding. Excessive uterine bleeding has been quantitatively defined as either menses persisting for longer than 7 days or a total menstrual blood loss that exceeds 80 ml. It is better, however, to define excessive bleeding in terms of the degree to which the abnormal bleeding deviates from a particular patient's established menstrual pattern—for example, an increase of two or more in the number of sanitary pads used daily or menses that persist for 3 or more days longer than normal. The differential diagnosis includes systemic disease (e.g., coagulopathies, hypothyroidism, and cirrhosis), reproductive tract disease (e.g., complications of pregnancy, benign disorders, and malignant lesions), iatrogenic causes (e.g., an intrauterine device [IUD]), and dysfunctional uterine bleeding. Dysfunctional uterine bleeding can only be established by excluding the other causes of abnormal uterine bleeding; it usually represents noncyclic bleeding resulting from disordered hormonal interaction.

The most important function of the history and the physical examination is to determine the source and the cause of the bleeding. A thorough examination is necessary to assess the lower genital tract, the cervix, the size of the uterus, and the status of the adnexal structures. If the patient is of reproductive age, determination of the urinary or serum β-hCG level should be considered at an early stage of evaluation. Serum β-hCG levels may remain elevated for as long as 38 days after a first-trimester abortion.[13] Complications of pregnancy (e.g., threatened or incomplete abortions, ectopic pregnancies, retained placental tissue, or trophoblastic disease) are an important cause of abnormal uterine bleeding in women of childbearing age. An endometrial biopsy should be performed in women who have risk factors for endometrial cancer (e.g., obesity, chronic anovulation, or unopposed estrogen therapy), women with menorrhagia who are older than 35 to 40 years, and postmenopausal women who experience uterine bleeding. The

Table 2 Bethesda System for Reporting and Interpreting Results of Pap Smear

Section of Report	Explanation
Negative for intraepithelial lesion or malignancy	This section is where a "normal" result (the desired outcome) is reported. Abnormal findings not related to cancer risk are reported in two subcategories: (1) organisms (e.g., evidence of *Trichomonas*, fungal, herpesvirus, or some other infection) and (2) other nonneoplastic findings (e.g., evidence of injury and response to injury).
Endometrial cells present in woman 40 years of age or older	This section is to alert the physician that cells from the lining of the uterus are present when they normally should not be. It is a check on the status of the uterus and endometrium rather than the cervix.
Epithelial cell abnormalities*	This section is where abnormalities associated with the risk of developing cancer are reported. These abnormalities occur over a spectrum ranging from slight changes to definite cancer. They are initially classified into squamous cell changes and glandular cell changes. *Squamous cell abnormalities* Atypical squamous cells (ASC): cellular abnormalities that qualitatively or quantitatively fall short of definitive diagnosis of squamous epithelial lesion ASC of undetermined significance (ASC-US) ASC for which HSIL or high-grade changes cannot be excluded (ASC-H) Low-grade squamous intraepithelial lesion (LSIL): encompasses HPV infection, CIN I, and mild dysplasia High-grade squamous intraepithelial lesion (HSIL): encompasses CIN II and III, moderate dysplasia, severe dysplasia, and carcinoma in situ Squamous cell carcinoma (SCC): characterized by tumor diathesis (blood and necrotic debris), prominent macronuclei, and parachromatin clearing *Glandular cell abnormalities* Atypical glandular cells (AGC) (endocervical, endometrial, or not otherwise specified) AGC favoring neoplasia (endocervical or not otherwise specified) Endocervical adenocarcinoma in situ (AIS) Adenocarcinoma (endocervical, endometrial, extrauterine, or not otherwise specified)
Other malignancies	This section is where any malignant tumors other than primary SCC and glandular adenocarcinoma are reported.

* Patients with LSIL, HSIL, SCC, persistent ASC-US, ASC-US with high-risk HPV types, ASC-H, AGC, AIS, or adenocarcinoma undergo outpatient evaluation with colposcopy.

istration of estrogens to stabilize the endometrium and terminate bleeding; subsequently, after 24 hours of I.V. estrogen therapy, the patient is switched to an oral contraceptive. Excessive blood loss with ovulatory cycles can be managed with NSAIDs, an oral contraceptive, the levonorgestrel IUD, or surgical intervention (i.e., endometrial ablation). In one study, use of the levonorgestrel IUD resulted in an 87% reduction in menstrual blood loss after 3 months and a 95% reduction after 6 months, compared with blood loss recorded during pretreatment menses.[14]

Squamous Dysplasias and Gynecologic Malignancies

SQUAMOUS DYSPLASIAS OF LOWER GENITAL TRACT

Infection with low-risk human papillomavirus (HPV) types, such as HPV 6 and HPV 11, results in condylomas of the lower genital tract. Infection with high-risk types, such as HPV 16 and HPV 18, may result in dysplasias that have the potential to progress to invasive disease. The majority of sexually active women eventually become infected with high-risk HPV types. In most women, however, this infection proves transient: at 12 months' follow-up, 70% of HPV-infected women are HPV negative, and at 24 months' follow-up, 91% are HPV negative.[15] Those women who experience persistent infections are at highest risk for the subsequent development of significant cervical dysplasias.

The Papanicolaou (Pap) smear is a screening test used to identify women who may have cervical dysplasia (also referred to as cervical intraepithelial neoplasia [CIN]) and early invasive disease. Patients with abnormal smears as determined by the Bethesda system [*see Table 2*] undergo outpatient triage with colposcopy. This technique uses a bright light source and magnification to examine the cervix after the application of dilute acetic acid, which acts as a mucolytic agent and accentuates epithelial and vascular changes suggestive of dysplasia. Small biopsies are obtained from abnormal-appearing areas to allow mapping of potential areas of dysplasia. Expectant management is recommended for patients with mild squamous cell dysplasia (i.e., CIN I); treatment aimed at eliminating the dysplasia is usually recommended for patients with more significant lesions (i.e., CIN II or CIN III). In the past, many patients with cervical dysplasia were treated with ablative therapies, such as cryotherapy or laser vaporization. Currently, a loop electrocautery excision procedure (LEEP) is often employed to treat

Table 3 International Federation of Gynecology and Obstetrics Surgical Staging System for Endometrial Carcinoma

Stage		Description
I	IA	Tumor is limited to endometrium
	IB	Tumor invades ≤ 50% of myometrium
	IC	Tumor invades > 50% of myometrium
II	IIA	Tumor involves endocervical glands
	IIB	Tumor invades cervical stroma
III	IIIA	Tumor invades uterine serosa or adnexa, peritoneal cytology is positive, or both
	IIIB	Tumor metastasizes to vagina
	IIIC	Tumor metastasizes to pelvic or para-aortic lymph nodes
IV	IVA	Tumor invades bladder or bowel mucosa
	IVB	Tumor metastasizes to distant sites, including intra-abdominal or inguinal lymph nodes

ectocervix is cleansed with antiseptic solution, and a flexible plastic catheter containing an obturator is advanced into the uterine cavity. The obturator is withdrawn, and tissue fragments are aspirated into the plastic catheter. Patients who are unable to tolerate this procedure may be evaluated by means of transvaginal ultrasonography. An endometrial stripe thinner than 5 mm is unlikely to represent an endometrial cancer.

Treatment of abnormal uterine bleeding depends on the underlying cause. Patients with demonstrated organic pathology are managed as appropriate for the specific condition present. Excessive uterine bleeding resulting from anovulation can be managed with cyclic progestins or an oral contraceptive. Acute severe menorrhagia (often accompanied by hemodynamic instability) can initially be managed with volume support and intravenous admin-

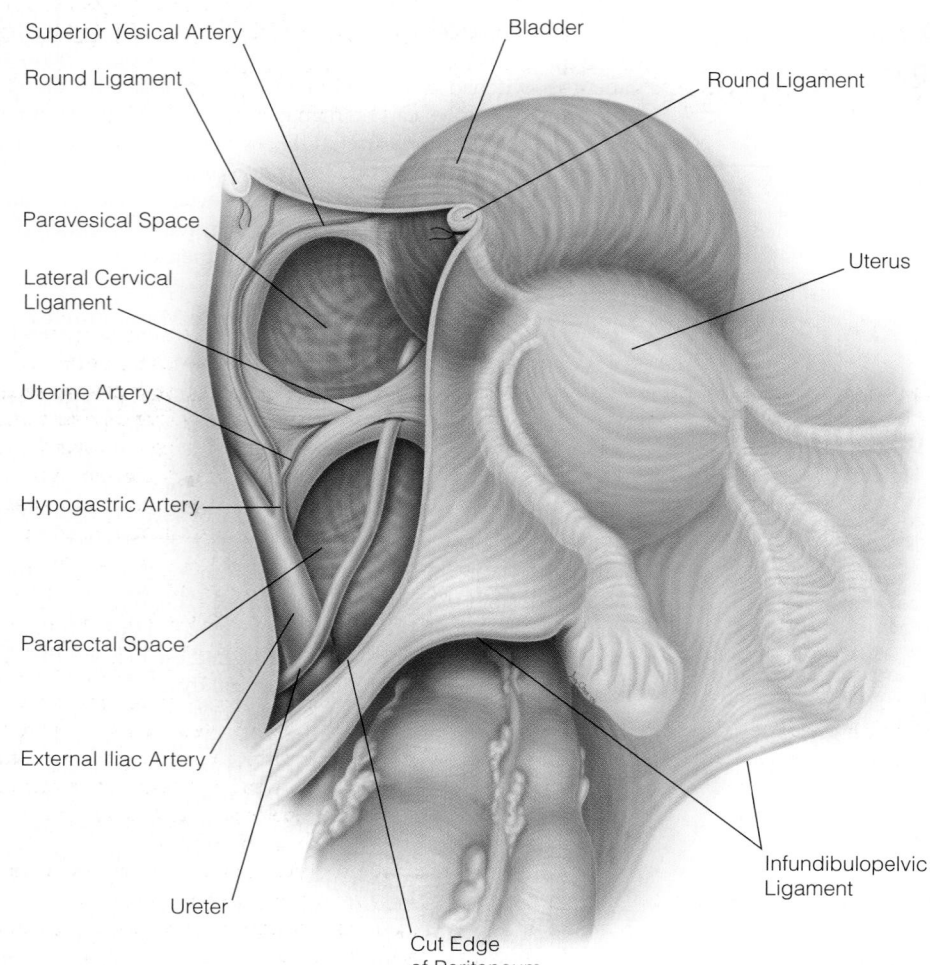

Superior Vesical Artery

Round Ligament

Paravesical Space

Lateral Cervical Ligament

Uterine Artery

Hypogastric Artery

Pararectal Space

External Iliac Artery

Ureter

Cut Edge of Peritoneum

Bladder

Round Ligament

Uterus

Infundibulopelvic Ligament

Figure 2 **Depicted are the retroperitoneal spaces of the pelvis (i.e., the pararectal and paravesical spaces). Dissection of the pararectal and paravesical spaces demonstrates the base of the cardinal ligament separating the two spaces. In this representation, the superior vesical artery has been mobilized from the lateral wall of the bladder and relocated to a lateral position.[25]**

the dysplasia, as well as to submit tissue for pathologic analysis. Cold-knife cervical conization may be performed as an alternative to LEEP; it avoids creating thermal artifacts and may be more useful in patients who have glandular dysplasias or appear to be at risk for early invasive disease.

Women who have undergone a total hysterectomy for benign disease may discontinue Pap smear screening. Women who have undergone a hysterectomy and have a history of a significant cervical dysplasia (CIN II or CIN III) should continue annual Pap smear screening until three consecutive satisfactory negative cytology results have been obtained, at which point routine cytology screening can be discontinued. Women who have had high-grade squamous dysplasias of the cervix may also experience the development of vaginal dysplasia after hysterectomy.

Vaginal dysplasia is asymptomatic and typically is detected only after an abnormal Pap smear. Initial evaluation consists of colposcopy with directed biopsies of abnormal-appearing vaginal mucosa. Significant dysplasias may be either ablated with superficial laser vaporization or excised. Excision with partial vaginectomy is definitive treatment from a pathologic perspective, but it may be associated with a higher rate of complications.

Vulvar dysplasia may be visible in the form of discrete, slightly raised (papular), often pigmented lesions. Biopsy of the lesion establishes the diagnosis and rules out obvious invasive disease. Multifocal disease involving non–hair-bearing areas (often seen in young patients) can usually be treated with superficial laser vaporization or with topical application of imiquimod, an immune

response modifier in cream form that is currently used in the treatment of condyloma. Lesions in hair-bearing areas and confluent lesions (often seen in postmenopausal women) are best treated with wide local excision. Large unifocal confluent lesions may contain occult invasive foci that are identifiable only through excision and careful pathologic evaluation. The lesion, along with a 4 to 5 mm margin of normal tissue, is incised with a scalpel and dissected away from the underlying dermis with an electrocautery. The superficial defect is closed in one layer with interrupted sutures; a rhomboid flap may be required for more sizeable defects.

ENDOMETRIAL CANCER

Endometrial carcinoma is the most common gynecologic malignancy and accounts for more than 95% of uterine cancers. Although the majority of these carcinomas occur on a sporadic basis, an endometrial cancer can also be the initial manifestation of the Lynch syndrome (hereditary nonpolyposis colorectal cancer [HNPCC]) [*see 56 Hereditary Colorectal Cancer and Polyposis Syndromes*]. The lifetime risk of endometrial cancer for women with the Lynch syndrome is 40% to 60%, which equals or exceeds their risk of colorectal cancer.[16] In the United States, approximately 40,000 new cases of endometrial cancer are diagnosed each year, of which 7,000 prove fatal. About 75% of these cases involve postmenopausal women, with the remaining 25% involving premenopausal women; only about 5% of cases involve women younger than 40 years. Endometrial cancers are adenocarcinomas and usually resemble the glands of the endometrial lining; however, approximately 10% have a nonendometrioid (i.e., papillary serous or clear cell) histology, a pattern associated with a biologically aggressive behavior. Abnormal vaginal bleeding or postmenopausal bleeding is the most common presenting complaint. Outpatient endometrial biopsy with aspiration of tissue from the uterine cavity often establishes the diagnosis. If the tissue obtained is insufficient or the patient cannot tolerate outpatient evaluation, dilatation and curettage (often with hysteroscopy) is performed with the patient under anesthesia.

Approximately 75% of patients with endometrial cancer have early disease. Therapy typically consists of hysterectomy, bilateral salpingo-oophorectomy, procurement of peritoneal specimens for cytologic examination, and staging. The regional lymph nodes are the most frequent site of occult metastatic disease. Accordingly, the surgical staging criteria [see Table 3] emphasize the pathologic status of the regional lymph nodes with selective pelvic and para-aortic lymphadenectomy. Although there are direct lymphatic channels from the uterus to the para-aortic area, it is uncommon to find positive para-aortic nodes in the absence of pelvic nodal involvement.

Selective pelvic lymphadenectomy removes the lymphatic tissue from the anterior and medial surfaces of the iliac vessels and from the obturator fossa superior to the obturator nerve. Sampling of the pelvic lymph nodes is facilitated by developing the pararectal and paravesical spaces in the retroperitoneum of the pelvis [see Figure 2]. The pararectal space is developed by means of blunt dissection between the ureter medially and the internal iliac (hypogastric) artery laterally. Dissection through the loose areolar tissue proceeds caudomedially toward the coccyx. The paravesical space is developed by sweeping the obliterated superior vesical artery and the bladder medially. The space is bordered by the pubic symphysis anteriorly and the obturator internus laterally. Development of the spaces provides the exposure necessary for skeletonizing the iliac vessels and the obturator nerve. Selective para-aortic lymphadenectomy consists of removing precaval and aortic lymphatic tissue from the level of the inferior mesenteric artery to the middle of the common iliac artery bilaterally. Sampling of the para-aortic lymph nodes is then accomplished via either a direct or a lateral approach. With a direct approach, an incision is made into the peritoneum overlying the right common iliac artery and extended over the aorta. With a lateral approach, an incision is made in the lateral paracolic gutters, with the right or left colon reflected medially. In one study, a median of 11 pelvic and three para-aortic lymph nodes were obtained at selective lymphadenectomy.[17]

OVARIAN CANCER

Of all the reproductive tract malignancies, ovarian cancer poses the greatest clinical challenge. Although ovarian cancers can arise from germ cells, sex-cord cells, or stromal cells, approximately 85% arise from the coelomic epithelium and thus are termed epithelial cancers. The peak incidence of invasive ovarian epithelial cancers is between 56 and 60 years of age. Approximately 5% to 10% of these cancers have a hereditary component; women with BRCA1/BRCA2 or Lynch syndrome (HNPCC) germline mutations are at increased risk. Prophylactic salpingo-oophorectomy in patients with BRCA1/BRCA2 mutations virtually eliminates the risk of ovarian and tubal cancer and reduces the risk of breast and primary peritoneal cancer.[18,19]

Ovarian cancer is the second most common gynecologic malignancy, but it has the highest fatality-to-case ratio of any reproductive tract cancer. Ovarian epithelial carcinomas spread primarily through exfoliation of cells, which places the entire peritoneal cavity at risk for metastases. Moreover, early recognition is difficult because the majority of patients have only vague and nonspecific complaints. Not surprisingly, 60% to 70% of patients have advanced (stage III or IV) disease at diagnosis. Detection of ovarian cancer is further hindered by the fact that there is no effective screening test. The tumor-associated antigen CA 125 is expressed by more than 80% of ovarian epithelial cancers; however, though CA 125 levels are employed in following up patients with documented disease, they are not useful for screening purposes. In a group of 1,110 women at increased risk for ovarian cancer, annual surveillance with serum CA 125 determinations and additional transvaginal ultrasonography was unable to detect tumors at an early enough stage to influence the prognosis.[20]

Surgical intervention serves three purposes in the setting of ovarian epithelial cancer: diagnosis, staging, and tumor debulking (cytoreduction). The staging of ovarian cancer is based on the pathologic findings at surgery [see Table 4]. Only a minority of women have stage I disease at diagnosis, and the decision whether to employ paclitaxel and carboplatinum chemotherapy is predicated on the surgical extent of the disease. Unfortunately, thorough intraoperative staging is not always performed. In a series of 785 women found to have ovarian cancer in 1991, lymphadenectomy was not done in 66% of the patients with presumptive stage I or II disease.[21]

In patients who appear to have early rather than advanced dis-

Table 4 International Federation of Gynecology and Obstetrics Surgical Staging System for Ovarian Cancer

Stage		Characteristics
I		Tumor growth is limited to ovaries.
	IA	Tumor is limited to one ovary; there is no ascitic fluid containing malignant cells; there is no tumor on external surface; capsule is intact
	IB	Tumor is limited to the two ovaries; there is no ascitic fluid containing malignant cells; there is no tumor on external surface; capsules are intact
	IC	Tumor is either stage IA or IB, but (a) there is tumor on surface of one or both ovaries, (b) capsule is ruptured, or (c) ascitic fluid containing malignant cells is present or peritoneal washings are positive
II		Tumor involves one or both ovaries, with pelvic extension.
	IIA	Tumor extends or metastasizes to uterus or Fallopian tubes
	IIB	Tumor extends to other pelvic tissues
	IIC	Tumor is either stage IIA or IIB, but (a) there is tumor on surface of one or both ovaries, (b) one or both capsules are ruptured, or (c) ascitic fluid containing malignant cells is present or peritoneal washings are positive
III		Tumor involves one or both ovaries, with peritoneal implants outside pelvis, positive retroperitoneal or inguinal nodes, or both. Superficial liver metastasis equals stage III. Tumor is limited to true pelvis, but with histologically proven malignant extension to small bowel or omentum.
	IIIA	Tumor is grossly limited to true pelvis, with negative nodes but with histologically confirmed microscopic seeding of abdominal peritoneal surfaces
	IIIB	Tumor involves one or both ovaries, with negative nodes but with histologically confirmed implants on abdominal peritoneal surfaces, none of which are > 2 cm in diameter
	IIIC	Abdominal implants > 2 cm in diameter are present, retroperitoneal or inguinal nodes are positive, or both
IV		Tumor involves one or both ovaries, with distant metastasis. If pleural effusion is present, cytologic test results must be obtained to assign a case to stage IV. Parenchymal liver metastasis equals stage IV.

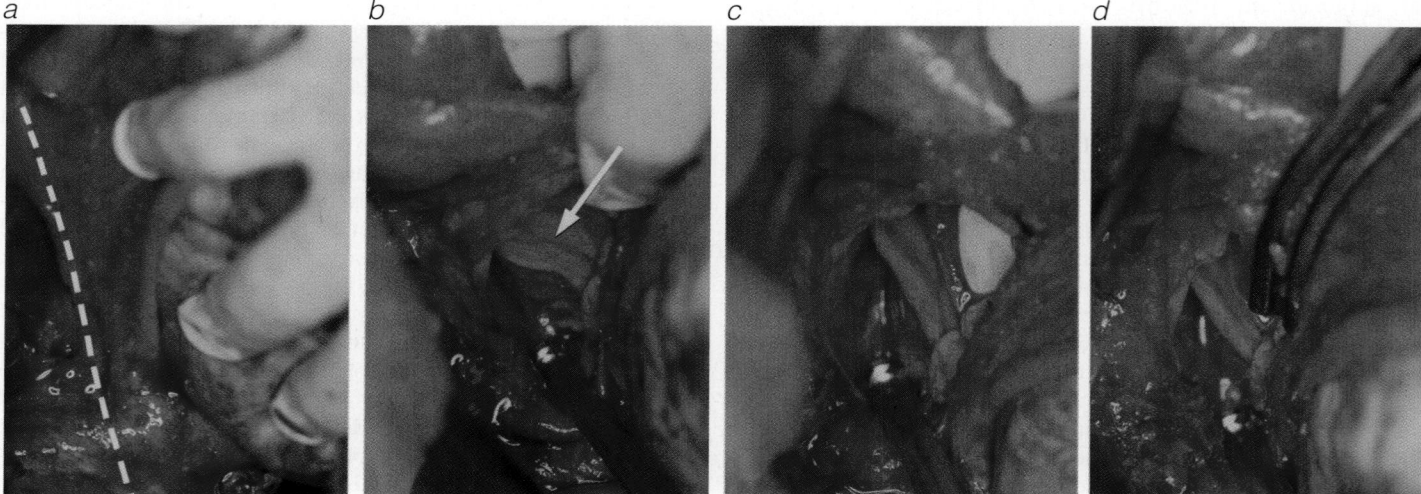

Figure 3 Shown is a retroperitoneal approach to a large, fixed ovarian mass that is adherent to adjacent structures. (*a*) The mass is drawn medially, and the peritoneum lateral to the infundibulopelvic ligament is divided (dotted line) to afford entry into the retroperitoneum of the pelvis. (*b*) The ureter (arrow) is identified on the medial leaf of the broad ligament in a location below the infundibulopelvic ligament. (*c*) An opening is made below the infundibulopelvic ligament and superior to the ureter, and the primary blood supply to the ovarian mass is thereby isolated. (*d*) The gonadal vessels are clamped, cut, and ligated. The mass is then dissected from the adjacent tissues in view of the ureter.

ease, the emphasis is on accurate staging. At least 30% of patients whose disease is seemingly confined to the pelvis show some evidence of upper abdominal or nodal spread. A midline incision is made, and upon entry into the peritoneal cavity, any free abdominal fluid is submitted for cytologic evaluation. If no abdominal fluid is present, pelvic washings are done with 50 to 100 ml of saline, and the saline is recovered and submitted for cytologic evaluation. The ovarian tumor should be removed intact (if possible) and submitted for frozen-section analysis. The intra-abdominal surfaces and the viscera are systematically inspected. Any suspicious areas or adhesions are subjected to biopsy. Random peritoneal biopsies are performed on the lateral upper and lower paracolic gutters, the bladder flap, the cul-de-sac, and the pelvic sidewalls. Sterile tongue depressors are used to obtain cytologic specimens from both infradiaphragmatic surfaces. An infracolic omentectomy is performed. The regional nodes are palpated, and any enlarged lymph nodes are removed. Finally, the pelvic and para-aortic nodes are sampled to allow detection of any occult spread.

Because the majority of patients with ovarian epithelial cancers present with advanced disease, the main goal of surgical intervention is often tumor debulking. The purpose of cytoreduction is to remove the primary cancer, as well as any metastases. If complete resection of metastases is not feasible, the aim is to reduce the bulk of the residual disease to, ideally, a diameter of 1 cm or less (so-called optimal debulking). Optimal cytoreduction enhances the response to I.V. paclitaxel and carboplatinum chemotherapy, and patients with minimal residual disease have a distinct survival advantage over those with more substantial residual disease. Furthermore, current data indicate that patients who have undergone optimal debulking may be candidates for intraperitoneal, as opposed to I.V., chemotherapy. There is evidence to suggest that the use of intraperitoneal chemotherapy may improve survival rates.[22]

The removal of pelvic disease is accomplished via a retroperitoneal approach [*see Figure 3*]. Although ovarian cancers commonly involve and distort peritoneal surfaces, they usually do not have a significant effect on the retroperitoneal anatomy. The retroperi-

toneum is entered laterally along the surface of the psoas muscle. The procedure is initiated by either dividing the round ligament or entering the peritoneum lateral to the infundibulopelvic ligament. Upon entry into the retroperitoneal space, the infundibulopelvic ligament, the ureter, and the great vessels are identified. The pararectal and paravesical spaces may be developed to facilitate the removal of locally advanced pelvic disease [*see Figure 2*]. If the disease involves the bowel, its mesentery, or both, resection and reanastomosis may be necessary, either to remove an obstruction or to achieve optimal tumor debulking. Small bowel resection may be required to achieve optimal cytoreduction in as many as 10% of patients.[23,24]

Primary peritoneal and tubal cancers are relatively rare malignancies whose presentation may include a mass, malignant ascites, or pain. These tumors are more frequent in patients with *BRCA1/BRCA2* mutations, and they bear a histologic resemblance to, as well as behave as, ovarian epithelial carcinomas. Treatment is identical to that of ovarian cancer, with initial surgical intervention establishing the diagnosis and the disease stage. After tumor debulking, paclitaxel and carboplatinum chemotherapy is administered. Patients with tubal cancers should undergo hysterectomy and bilateral salpingo-oophorectomy. If there is no evidence of gross tumor spread, a staging procedure is performed that includes sampling of the pelvic and para-aortic lymph nodes, infracolic omentectomy, and procurement of peritoneal specimens for cytologic examination through multiple peritoneal biopsies.

CERVICAL CANCER

Although cervical cancer is only the third most common gynecologic malignancy in the United States, it is the most common genital tract cancer in the world. Patients with early invasive carcinomas may present with nothing more than an abnormal Pap smear, but most complain of postcoital bleeding or a bloody vaginal discharge. With early disease, colposcopy or conizatation may be required to establish the diagnosis; however, the majority of patients have a gross cervical lesion, and punch biopsy is usually

Table 5 International Federation of Gynecology and Obstetrics Surgical Staging System for Cervical Cancer

Stage	Characteristics
I	IA Tumor is invasive carcinoma that can be diagnosed only by microscopy IA1: Tumor has measured stromal invasion of ≤ 3 mm and extension of ≤ 7 mm IA2: Tumor has measured stromal invasion of > 3 but < 5 mm and extension of ≤ 7 mm IB Tumor is clinically visible lesion limited to cervix or microscopic lesion more extensive than stage IA IB1: Tumor is clinically visible lesion with maximum diameter of ≤ 4 cm IB2: Tumor is clinically visible lesion with maximum diameter of > 4 cm
II	Tumor invades beyond uterus but does not reach pelvic wall or lower third of vagina. IIA Tumor does not obviously involve parametrium IIB Tumor obviously involves parametrium
III	Tumor extends to pelvic wall. On rectal examination, there is no cancer-free space between tumor and pelvic wall. Tumor involves lower third of vagina. All cases with hydronephrosis or a nonfunctioning kidney are included unless known to be attributable to another cause. IIIA Tumor involves lower third of vagina, with no extension to pelvic wall IIIB Tumor extends to pelvic wall, hydronephrosis is present, or kidney is nonfunctioning
IV	Tumor extends beyond true pelvis or involves mucosa of bladder or rectum (as proved by biopsy). Bullous edema per se does not permit case to be allotted to stage IV. IVA Tumor spreads to adjacent organs IVB Tumor spreads to distant organs

performed to establish the diagnosis. As a result of the necrotic debris and blood, cytology yields false negative results in as many as 50% of invasive cervical carcinomas. When a gross cervical lesion is present, biopsy and histologic evaluation are mandatory.

The staging of cervical cancer is based on the clinical findings and takes into account the results of pelvic examination, chest radiography, and intravenous pyelography (IVP) [*see Table 5*]. Stage I cervical cancer denotes disease that is limited to the cervix itself. It may be subdivided into stages IA (microscopic disease) and IB (more advanced or grossly visible disease). The assignment of a cervical cancer to stage IA requires that cervical conization be done to assess the depth and lateral extent of stromal invasion. Microinvasive carcinoma is a tumor that invades the cervical stroma to a depth of 3 mm or less, without lymphovascular space involvement. Stage II cancer denotes disease that involves the upper two thirds of the vagina or parametrial disease that has not reached the pelvic sidewall. Stage IIIB cancer denotes parametrial disease that has reached the pelvic sidewall or results in ureteral obstruction.

Treatment of cervical cancer is predicated on the patient's suitability for surgery and on the stage and bulk of the tumor. Young patients with early, genuine microinvasive carcinomas and a desire for future childbearing may be followed conservatively after conization with negative margins. For the majority of patients with microinvasive cancers, definitive treatment consists of simple abdominal or vaginal hysterectomy; the risk of pelvic nodal metastasis is lower than 1%. Patients with stage IA2, IB, and IIA disease may be treated with radical hysterectomy. This surgical procedure differs from simple abdominal hysterectomy in several respects. In

a simple hysterectomy for benign disease, the vascular pedicles are placed close to the uterus and the cervix. A radical hysterectomy dissects out the lower aspect of the ureters, allowing wider clearance of the central specimen and the adjacent adventitial tissues (e.g., cardinal ligaments and parametria). At an early point in the procedure, the pararectal and paravesical spaces are developed [*see Figure 2*]. If the disease appears to be limited to the central specimen, the uterine artery is divided at its point of origin from the superior vesical artery and mobilized over the ureter. The parametria, lying between the pararectal and paravesical spaces, are divided. The ureters are separated from the medial peritoneum of the posterior leaf of the broad ligament, then dissected out to the point where they insert into the bladder. Once the distal ureters have been mobilized, clamps are placed into the paravaginal tissues, and an extra margin of lateral tissue is removed. The rectovaginal septum is also developed to allow division of the uterosacral ligaments closer to their point of origin at the sacrum. The upper 2 cm of the vagina is removed in continuity with the rest of the specimen. A systematic pelvic lymph node dissection is then performed, with skeletonization of the common iliac artery, the external iliac artery, the external iliac vein, and the obturator nerve.

Patients who have more advanced disease (stage IIB or higher) or are unable to undergo surgery are treated with radiotherapy and chemotherapy as a radiation sensitizer. Initially, protracted, fractionated external beam radiotherapy is administered. By using a number of fields, external beam treatment distributes radiation to the central tumor and the pelvic lymph nodes in a relatively homogeneous fashion. External radiotherapy is followed by intracavitary radiotherapy, in which a radioisotope is placed into the uterus, the cervix, and the upper vagina. The radiation delivered by intracavitary radiotherapy is distributed according to the inverse square law: a substantial amount is delivered to the central tumor, but the dose falls off rapidly in adjacent tissues as the distance from the central lesion increases.

VULVAR CANCER

Vulvar cancers arise from the epidermis of the vulva and are usually of squamous histology. Approximately 30% to 40% of vulvar cancers are related to exposure to HPV, usually in younger patients and those with preexisting vulvar dysplasia. In the majority of patients, however, no clear cause can be identified. Vulvar carcinomas spread by embolization along lymphatic channels, which ter-

Table 6 Characteristics of Complete and Partial Moles

Parameter	Complete Mole	Partial Mole
Anatomy	No fetus or fetal parts present	Fetus or fetal parts present
Histology	Generalized villous swelling; diffuse trophoblastic proliferation	Focal trophoblastic proliferation and villous swelling; villous scalloping and prominent trophoblastic inclusions
Karyotype	Diploid, usually 46 XX (all genetic material is paternal)	Diandric triploidy
Presentation	Uterus large for dates; preeclampsia; hyperthyroidism; theca-lutein cysts	Missed or incomplete abortion
Natural history	20% chance of requiring chemotherapy	3% to 4% chance of requiring chemotherapy

minate at the inguinofemoral lymph nodes. Superficial and medial lymph nodes are the ones most commonly involved. The pelvic lymph nodes are rarely involved unless the ipsilateral inguinal nodes contain metastatic disease.

Treatment must take into account both the primary vulvar lesion and the possibility of inguinal node metastasis. Historically, radical vulvectomy with bilateral groin dissection was the standard of care for the treatment of vulvar cancers. Currently, the emphasis is on performing the most conservative surgical procedure that is consistent with cure of the disease. Radical local excision with surgical evaluation of the inguinal nodes has become the modern standard of care for most patients. The vulvar lesion is excised with margins of at least 1 cm. The incision is carried to the inferior fascia of the urogenital diaphragm, which is coplanar with the fascia lata of the thigh and the fascia over the pubic symphysis. If more than 1 mm of stromal invasion is noted, surgical evaluation of the inguinofemoral lymph nodes is required. Bilateral groin dissections are not necessary unless the lesion is on the clitoris, the anterior labia minora, or the perineum or lies within 1 cm of the midline. If the extent of stromal invasion is 1 mm or less, node dissection is not necessary, because the risk of groin metastasis is low.

Surgical evaluation of the inguinal nodes has also evolved over time. The current surgical options are (1) a superficial inguinal node dissection that removes the lymphatic tissue above the fascia lata and the cribriform fascia and (2) a complete inguinofemoral node dissection that removes both the superficial nodes and the deep nodes lying below the cribriform fascia and medial to the femoral vein. Advocates of the first option view the superficial inguinal nodes as the sentinel lymph nodes of the groin and consequently maintain that a more extensive dissection is generally not required.

Patients found to have positive inguinal nodes at groin dissection receive adjuvant radiotherapy. Patients with advanced, unresectable primary disease, who in the past were treated with exenteration, now are treated with radiation and chemotherapy as a radiation sensitizer. Local (perineal) recurrences are treated with wide local resection. Unfortunately, recurrences in the inguinal nodes after primary therapy usually are refractory to further therapy and often prove fatal.

GESTATIONAL TROPHOBLASTIC DISEASE

Gestational trophoblastic disease is a blanket term for a range of placenta-derived neoplasias that include hydatidiform mole, invasive mole, gestational choriocarcinoma, and placental site tumor. Of these conditions, the one most frequently encountered is hydatidiform mole, or molar gestation. In the United States, moles occur in approximately one of every 1,000 to 1,200 pregnancies. Patients present with vaginal bleeding, passage of mole tissue through the vagina, a uterus that is large for the gestational age (as determined on the basis of the last menstrual period), or medical complications deriving from the mole. The diagnosis is established through ultrasonographic examination of the uterus. Therapy consists of evacuation of the uterine contents (ideally by suction curettage) and subsequent serial serum β-hCG determinations, with adequate contraception during the follow-up period. Moles usually are complete but sometimes are partial (i.e., occur with fetal tissue or even a fetus). The distinction between complete and partial moles, though initially regarded as little more than a medical curiosity, actually reflects identifiable differences in anatomy, histology, presentation, and natural history [see Table 6].

If β-hCG levels rise or plateau or there is evidence of metastatic disease, further therapy for postmolar malignant gestational trophoblastic neoplasia is required. Before effective chemotherapy became available, it was common practice to perform hysterectomy, allowing pathologic assessment of the uterine contents (persistent mole, invasive mole, or choriocarcinoma).

Currently, most women with gestational trophoblastic disease can be successfully managed by means of chemotherapy, without risk to the reproductive organs. Patients are evaluated for metastases with various radiologic studies and are stratified according to prognostic risk factors (as assessed by criteria developed by the National Institutes of Health, the International Federation of Gynecology and Obstetrics, or the World Health Organization). Sites of metastatic disease are documented; however, to avoid the risk of a major hemorrhage, they are not subjected to biopsy. Therapy is governed by the level of risk present. Single-agent therapy (with methotrexate or actinomycin D) is given to patients with low-risk disease, and aggressive multiagent therapy is given to patients with high-risk disease.

References

1. Boberg JT, ex-sec. Surgical Operative Log Project: 1994–1995, Residency Review Committee for Surgery. Accreditation Council for Graduate Medical Education, Chicago, 1995

2. Landercasper J, Bintz M, Cogbill TH, et al: Spectrum of general surgery in rural America. Arch Surg 132:494, 1997

3. Nguyen HN, Averette HE, Hoskins W, et al: National Survery of Ovarian Carcinoma Part V. Cancer 72:3663, 1993

4. Borgfeldt C, Andolf E: Transvaginal sonographic ovarian findings in a random sample of women 25-40 years old. Ultrasound Obstet Gynecol 13:345, 1999

5. Mage G, Canis M, Manhes H, et al: Laparoscopic management of adnexal torsion: a review of 35 cases. J Reprod Med 34:520, 1989

6. Webb EM, Green GE, Scoutt LM: Adnexal mass with pelvic pain. Radiol Clin N Am 42:329, 2004

7. Oelsner G, Admon D, Bider D, et al: Long-term follow-up of the twisted ischemic adnexa managed by detorsion. Fertil Steril 60:976, 1993

8. Centers for Disease Control and Prevention:

Sexually transmitted diseases treatment guidelines, 2006. MMWR Recomm Rep 55(RR-11):1, 2006

9. Seeber BE, Barnhart KT: Suspected ectopic pregnancy. Obstet Gynecol 107:399, 2006

10. Brenner PF: Prepubertal vulvar lacerations and hematomas, labial adhesions, and prolapse of the urethra. In: Management of Common Problems in Obstetrics and Gynecology, Mishell DR, Goodwin TM, Brenner PF (eds), Blackwell Publishing, Williston, VT, 2002

11. Dorum A, Blom GP, Ekerhovd E, et al: Prevalence and histologic diagnosis of adnexal cysts in postmenopausal women: An autopsy study. Amer J Obstet Gynecol 192:48, 2005

12. Farquhar CM, Steiner CA: Hysterectomy rates in the United States 1990–1997. Obstet Gynecol 99:229, 2002

13. Marrs RP, Kletzky OA, Howard WF, et al: Disappearance of human chorionic gonadotropin and resumption of ovulation following abortion. Am J Obstet Gynecol 135:731, 1979

14. Tang GWK, Lo SST: Levonorgestrel intrauter-

ine device in the treatment of menorrhagia in Chinese women: Efficacy versus acceptability. Contraception 51:231, 1995

15. Ho GY, Bierman R, Beardsley L, et al: Natural history of cervicovaginal papillomavirus infection in young women. N Engl J Med 338:423, 1998

16. Schmeler KM, Lynch HT, Chen L, et al: Prophylactic surgery to reduce the risk of gynecologic cancers in the Lynch syndrome. N Engl J Med 354:261, 2006

17. Cragun JM, Havrilesky LJ, Calingaert B, et al: Retrospective analysis of selective lymphadenectomy in apparent early-stage endometrial cancer. J Clin Oncol 23:3668, 2005

18. Kauff ND, Satagopan JM, Robson ME, et al: Risk-reducing salpingo-oophorectomy in women with a BRCA1 or BRCA2 mutation. N Engl J Med 346:1609, 2002

19. Rebbeck TR, Lynch HT, Neuhausen SL, et al: Prophylactic oophorectomy in carriers of BRCA1 or BRCA2 mutations. N Engl J Med 346:1616, 2002

20. Stirling D, Evans GR, Pichert G, et al: Screening for familial ovarian cancer: Failure of current protocols to detect ovarian cancer at an early stage according to the International Federation of Gynecology and Obstetrics system. J Clin Oncol 23:5588, 2005

21. Munoz KA, Harlan LC, Trimble EL: Patterns of care for women with ovarian cancer in the United States. J Clin Oncol 15:3408, 1997

22. Armstrong DK, Bundy B, Wenzel L, et al: Intraperitoneal cisplatin and paclitaxel in ovarian cancer. N Engl J Med 354:34, 2006

23. Gershenson DM: Primary cytoreduction for advanced ovarian epithelial cancer. Obstet Gynecol Clin N Am 21:121, 1994

24. Walker JL, Armstrong DK, Huang HQ, et al: Intraperitoneal catheter outcomes in a phase III trial of intravenous verus intraperitoneal chemotherapy in optimal stage III ovarian and primary peritoneal cancer: A Gynecologic Oncology Group study. Gynecol Oncol 100:27, 2006

25. Knapp RC, Donahue VA, Friedman EA: Dissection of paravesical and pararectal spaces in pelvic operations. Surg Gynecol Obstet 137:758, 1973

Acknowledgment

Figure 2 Alice Y. Chen.

INDEX

Note: Page numbers followed by *t* indicate tables; numbers followed by *f* indicate figures.

S